THE UNIVERSAL REFERENCE SYSTEM

International Affairs

Volume I of the

POLITICAL SCIENCE, GOVERNMENT, AND PUBLIC POLICY SERIES

Included in this series:

Volume	I	*International Affairs (Second Edition)*
Volume	II	*Legislative Process, Representation, and Decision Making*
Volume	III	*Bibliography of Bibliographies in Political Science, Government, and Public Policy*
Volume	IV	*Administrative Management: Public and Private Bureaucracy*
Volume	V	*Current Events and Problems of Modern Society*
Volume	VI	*Public Opinion, Mass Behavior, and Political Psychology*
Volume	VII	*Law, Jurisprudence, and Judicial Process*
Volume	VIII	*Economic Regulation: Business, and Government*
Volume	IX	*Public Policy and the Management of Science*
Volume	X	*Comparative Government and Cultures*

POLITICAL SCIENCE, GOVERNMENT, & PUBLIC POLICY SERIES

Volume I

International Affairs

An annotated and intensively indexed compilation of significant books, pamphlets, and articles, selected and processed by The UNIVERSAL REFERENCE SYSTEM—a computerized information retrieval service in the social and behavioral sciences.

Prepared under the direction of

ALFRED DE GRAZIA, GENERAL EDITOR
Professor of Social Theory in Government, New York University, and Founder, *The American Behavioral Scientist*

CARL E. MARTINSON, MANAGING EDITOR

and

JOHN B. SIMEONE, CONSULTANT

Published by
PRINCETON RESEARCH PUBLISHING COMPANY
Princeton, New Jersey

For information, address:

UNIVERSAL REFERENCE SYSTEM
32 Nassau Street, Princeton, N.J. 08540

. . . and see the subscription information contained on the last page of this volume.

Standard Book No. 87635-001-5
Library of Congress Catalog Card No. 68-57819

Printed and Bound in the U.S.A. by
Kingsport Press, Inc., Kingsport, Tenn.

Contents

Advisory Committee* for the UNIVERSAL REFERENCE SYSTEM

CHAIRMAN: Alfred de Grazia, *New York University*

Kenneth J. Arrow, *Stanford University*
Peter Bock, *Brooklyn College*
Kenneth E. Boulding, *University of Michigan*
Hadley Cantril, *The Institute for International Social Research, Princeton*
Bernard C. Cohen, *The University of Wisconsin*
Richard M. Cyert, *Carnegie Institute of Technology*
Karl W. Deutsch, *Harvard University*
Ward Edwards, *University of Michigan*
Luther H. Evans, *Director of International and Legal Collections, Columbia University Law Library*
Helen Fairbanks, *Woodrow Wilson School of Public and International Affairs*
Richard F. Fenno, Jr., *University of Rochester*
William J. Gore, *Indiana University*
E. de Grolier, *International Social Science Council, Paris*
Stanley Hoffmann, *Harvard University*
Thomas Hovet, *University of Oregon*
Morton A. Kaplan, *University of Chicago*
Harold D. Lasswell, *Yale University Law School*
Wayne Leys, *University of Southern Illinois*
Charles A. McClelland, *School of International Relations, University of Southern California*
Hans J. Morgenthau, *City University of New York*
Stuart S. Nagel, *University of Illinois*
Robert C. North, *Stanford University*
A. F. K. Organski, *University of Michigan*
Robert Pages, *Chef du Laboratoire de Psychologie Sociale a la Sorbonne*
E. Raymond Platig, *Director, External Research Division, U. S. Department of State*
James A. Robinson, *Ohio State University*
Stein Rokkan, *Bergen, Norway, and Chairman, International Committee on Documentation in the Social Sciences*
James N. Rosenau, *Douglass College, Rutgers University*
Giovanni Sartori, *University of Florence*
John R. Schmidhauser, *University of Iowa*
Glendon A. Schubert, Jr., *York University*
Martin Shubik, *Yale University*
David L. Sills, *The Population Council*
Herbert A. Simon, *Carnegie Institute of Technology*
J. David Singer, *Mental Health Research Institute, University of Michigan*
Richard C. Snyder, *University of California at Irvine*
Richard N. Swift, *New York University*
Joseph Tanenhaus, *University of Iowa*
S. Sidney Ulmer, *University of Kentucky*
Quincy Wright, *University of Virginia*

*Not all members advise in all areas.

Introduction to the CODEX of International Affairs

The CODEX of *International Affairs* appears here in its second edition, following by four years its initial appearance in a substantially different form. It is enlarged by over four hundred documents in the net, from 3030 to 3460, and carries the field of international affairs up to the end of 1966. A volume for 1967 and another for 1968 are shortly to be published, and their contents will bring the total number of documents available in the UNIVERSAL REFERENCE SYSTEM on the subject to about 4,700.

By "international affairs" is meant relations among persons or organizations of different states, among nations, between nations and individuals of other nations, and between the government and people of any given state on matters concerning foreign policy. Completeness is out of the question; by the end of 1966, hundreds of thousands of published works dealt with world affairs. The present list aims at satisfying the needs of the great middle group of scholars that stands between, on the one hand, the most general public interested in any good text or a current informative essay and, on the other hand, the highly specialized scholar. The CODEX can, of course, serve both of these types also, but not ideally. It is recommended, however, that the scholar who is beginning his specialization—as, for example, on a senior paper, a thesis, an article, or a dissertation—search his topic first in this CODEX. He or she may go on afterwards into more specialized sources, using perhaps one of 880 bibliographies (BIBLIOG, BIBLIOG/A) listed in the Index below, or going to the appropriate entries in CODEX III, which is a *Bibliography of Bibliographies in Political Science, Government, and Public Policy*. Generally in the URS, except in CODEX V, on *Current Affairs*, discussions of ongoing controversies have been held to a minimum in the listings, as have been also merely descriptive or journalistic treatments.

A scrutiny of the Grazian Index will reveal certain Descriptors that have been omitted as entries to the Index and others that have been omitted both as entries and in their entirety. It will perhaps surprise a user to learn that he cannot go into the Index and find a listing of items under DIPLOM (Diplomacy). Why is this done? The reason is that two thirds of all documents on international affairs deal in one way or another with diplomacy. This is far too broad a concept and consequently too long a list for anyone to scan and use; 2,470 documents would be compiled. The whole volume, itself, is, so to speak, a single index listing under the entry, International Affairs. So, indeed, if one insists, he may read the whole catalog and two out of three listings will say something about diplomacy.

Now the scholar who wishes to search for titles on a specific topic, say "European Diplomacy before the Treaty of Versailles" can look up MOD/EUR (Modern Europe 1700-1918, including European settlement and pre-Revolutionary Russia), and among the 139 documents listed there find many treating of DIPLOM (Diplomacy). Or, if he is interested in the lives of diplomats, he can look up BIOG (Biography) and there he will find references to DIPLOM (Diplomacy) that will contain material on the lives of diplomats. Certain Unique Descriptors not in the Grazian Index because they are not general to the political and behavioral sciences will also give entree to problems of diplomacy, as, for example, the names of individual countries, treaties, and problems (e.g., BERLIN/BLO, Berlin Blockade). Hundreds of ways of finding aspects of diplomacy are thus available.

The same is true of INT/ORG (international organizations), ATTIT (attitudes, opinions, ideologies), and a few other terms. They enrich the Index details but are not entries to the Index. In addition, some Index Descriptors of the Grazian Index are suppressed entirely during the computer print-out, because they are irrelevant, unclear in context, or needed only in the technical operation of the system.

Substantial changes have been introduced into this new edition of the CODEX on *International Affairs*. We have already referred to the 400 new documents. In addition, the Catalog of the CODEX has been alphabetized. Now an author can be searched directly in the Catalog. Authors, too, in their alphabetical place, are listed in the Index along with their accession number.

Equally important was the decision (and the ensuing computer-programming) that resulted in the iteration of the author and title of a work in each of its entries in the Index.

The individual documents are still listed beneath the Index entry Descriptor according to their date of publication and beneath the date according to format—as a book, long report, or short article. The number of Unique Descriptors has been greatly enlarged, permitting more specialized entree to the Index. The situation dealing with cross-references ("See Also" and "See") has been improved by expansion of their number.

A Directory of Publishers is included, to assist in ordering listed materials. It is one of the most complete and up-to-date files of publishing organizations. The number of documents in languages other than English is relatively modest. This situation will be improved in years to come. Still, no existing political science service provides as many foreign books. It should be mentioned that the "classics" of international relations (such as the works of Machiavelli and Alberico Gentili) are included in the CODEX to permit easy access to the historical roots of the science.

Unquestionably, numerous problems of inclusion and exclusion will continue to present themselves. But the URS is a living corpus; corrections, deletions, and additions are easily made, and once made, perpetuated in subsequent printings. As was the case with the First Edition, we cordially invite users to send in comments, corrections, and materials. They will be carefully considered and gratefully employed.

How To Use This CODEX

(Hypothetical Example is Used)

1. Frame your need as specifically as possible. (Example: "I want articles written in 1968 that deal with the activities of labor leaders and small business owners in city politics in America.")
2. Scan the Dictionary of Descriptors in this Volume, page xv and following, for URS terms that match your subject. (Example: for cities you find MUNIC and LOC/G; for labor, LABOR; for small companies, SML/CO.) Find the number of titles each Descriptor carries. For rapidity select terms having few entries; for comprehensiveness, select terms having many entries.
3. Having identified terms that match your subject, enter the Index at one of them, say SML/CO, which heads a list of works on small business. For rapid identification of highly relevant titles, search the narrow right-hand column, which contains the Critical Descriptors; these index the primary facets of a work. Even if you read every title under a Descriptor, the critical column will help you identify works of high probable value. Titles are arranged by year of publication and within each year by format: books (B), long articles (L), short articles (S), and chapters (C). The designation "N" covers serials and titles lacking dates or published over several years. The Index entry carries author, title, secondary Descriptors (which index secondary facets of the work), page of the Catalog containing full citation and annotation, and Catalog accession number. Secondary Descriptors are always arranged in the order of the Topical and Methodological Index.
4. Listings of the document would be found in fourteen places in the Index, that is, under each of its numerous significant facets. One of them could be located in a search of "the small company in politics" as follows:

SAMPLE CATALOG LISTING

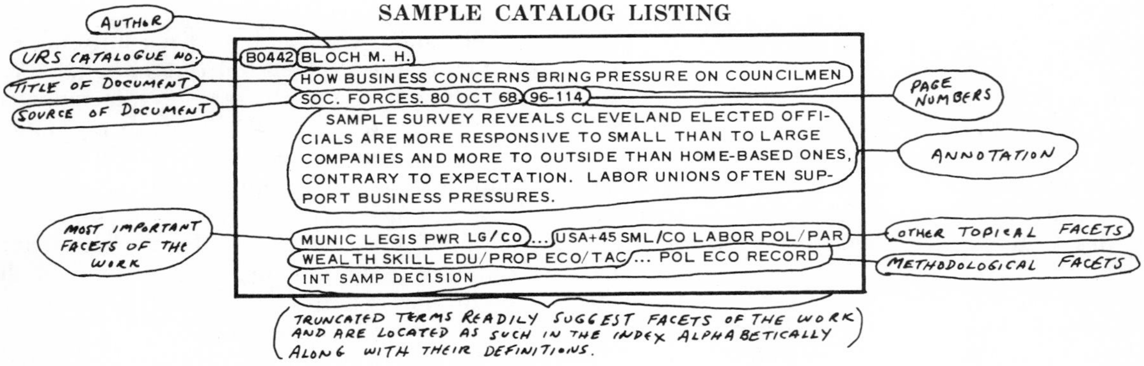

SAMPLE INDEX LISTING

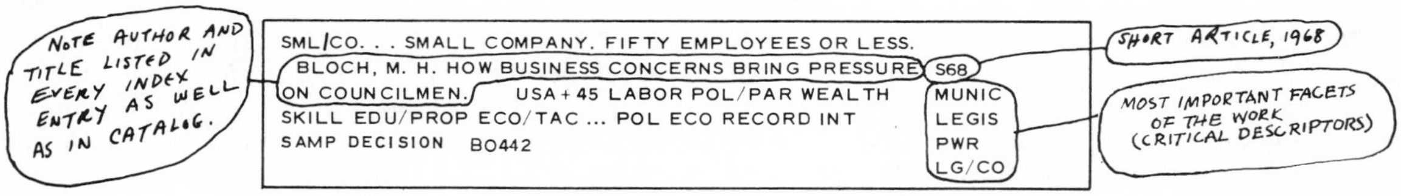

5. Jot down the page numbers and the accession numbers of items that interest you and look them up in the Catalog. There you will find the full citation and a brief annotation of each work.
6. You may locate information on methods authors employ, as well as topics they discuss. Survey the methodological Descriptors in the Grazian Index, pp. xiii-xiv, and locate the relevant Descriptors in the Index of Documents. (Example: if you wished to discover whether any studies of urban business politics had employed recorded interviews, you would look up the term INT [interviews]).
7. Read the Topical and Methodological classification of terms (Grazian Index System) once or twice to grasp the ways in which ideas and groups of related ideas are compressed. The truncated Descriptors, though obvious, are defined in the dictionary of the Index.
8. Although the Catalog is arranged alphabetically by author (except for Volumes II and III), accession numbers have been retained. The major exception to alphabetical arrangement is the group of journals and unsigned articles that begin the Catalog.
9. The Catalogs of Volumes I, IV, V, VI, VII, VIII, IX, and X do not carry Descriptors.
10. The Directory of Publishers pertains to all ten CODEXes.

Concerning the UNIVERSAL REFERENCE SYSTEM in General

The Universal Reference System is a computerized documentation and information retrieval system employing citations of material above a modest level of quality, appearing in all social and behavioral sciences, annotated. It is indexed by author and employs a set of Standard Descriptors that are arranged according to a master system of topics and methodological techniques, plus various Unique Descriptors.

The flow chart on page x, entitled "The Universal Reference System," shows the numerous steps taken to process documents which come from the intellectual community until they cycle back into the same community as delivered instruments of improved scholarship.

Background of the Work

The many fields of social sciences have suffered for a long time from inadequate searching systems and information storage. The rate of development of periodical and book literature is well known to be far beyond the capacities of the existing book-form document retrieval services. Thousands of new books appear each year, dealing with society and man. Thousands of journals pour forth articles. Hundreds of periodicals are founded each year.

Countries outside of the United States have gone into the social sciences, so that the need for making available foreign publications in intelligible form is ever greater. If there is a light year's distance between present capabilities and the best available service in the social sciences, there is an even greater distance to be traversed in bringing into use the material being published in languages other than English.

A vicious economic cycle is at work in the matter of information retrieval, too: Scholars and students give up research because there are no tools to search with, and therefore their demand for searching tools decreases because they have learned to get along without the materials. Thus, the standards of all the social sciences are lowered because of an anticipated lack of success in handling the problem of information retrieval. The economic risk, therefore, of an information retrieval service has to be taken into account: Many professionals are like the Bengal peasant who cannot aid in his own economic development because he cannot conceive of the nature of the problem and has learned to live as a victim outside of it.

A study in the June, 1964, issue of *The American Behavioral Scientist* magazine showed what the need is today, even before the full capabilities of new systems are appreciated. One-half of a sample of social and behavioral scientists reported that, due to inadequate bibliographic aids, they had discovered significant information on some research too late to use it, and that this information would have significantly affected the scope and nature of their research. In a number of cases, the problem of the researcher was reported to be inadequate access to pre-existing materials, and in other cases was said to be insufficient means of addressing oneself to current material.

So the current ways of information retrieval, or lack thereof, are deficient with respect both to retrospective searching and to current material, not to mention the alarming problem of access to prospective material, in the form of current research project activities and current news of scientific development in relevant categories.

The international scholarly associations centered mainly in Paris have endeavored, with help of UNESCO and other sources of aid, to bring out bibliographies and abstracting services. These services are not fully used, because of their format, their incompleteness, their lack of selectivity, their formulation in traditional and conventional terms of the social sciences (slighting the so-called inter-disciplinary subject matters in methodology), and the simple indexing that they employ. Continuous efforts are being made to solve such problems. Lately, such solutions have been sought via computerized systems. The American Council of Learned Societies, for example, has funded projects at New York University to which the computer is integral.

The Universal Reference System is endeavoring to take an immediately practical view of the literature-access problem, while designing the system so that it will remain open to advances and permit a number of alterations. One must contemplate projects leading to automatic reading and indexing; retrieval of information in the form of propositions, historical dates, and other factual materials; encyclopedic information-providing services; movement into other scientific fields joining social and natural science materials; automatized printing and reproduction of a large variety of materials in quantities ranging from individual to thousands of copies, and provision for televised or other rapid-fire communication services from information retrieval centers.

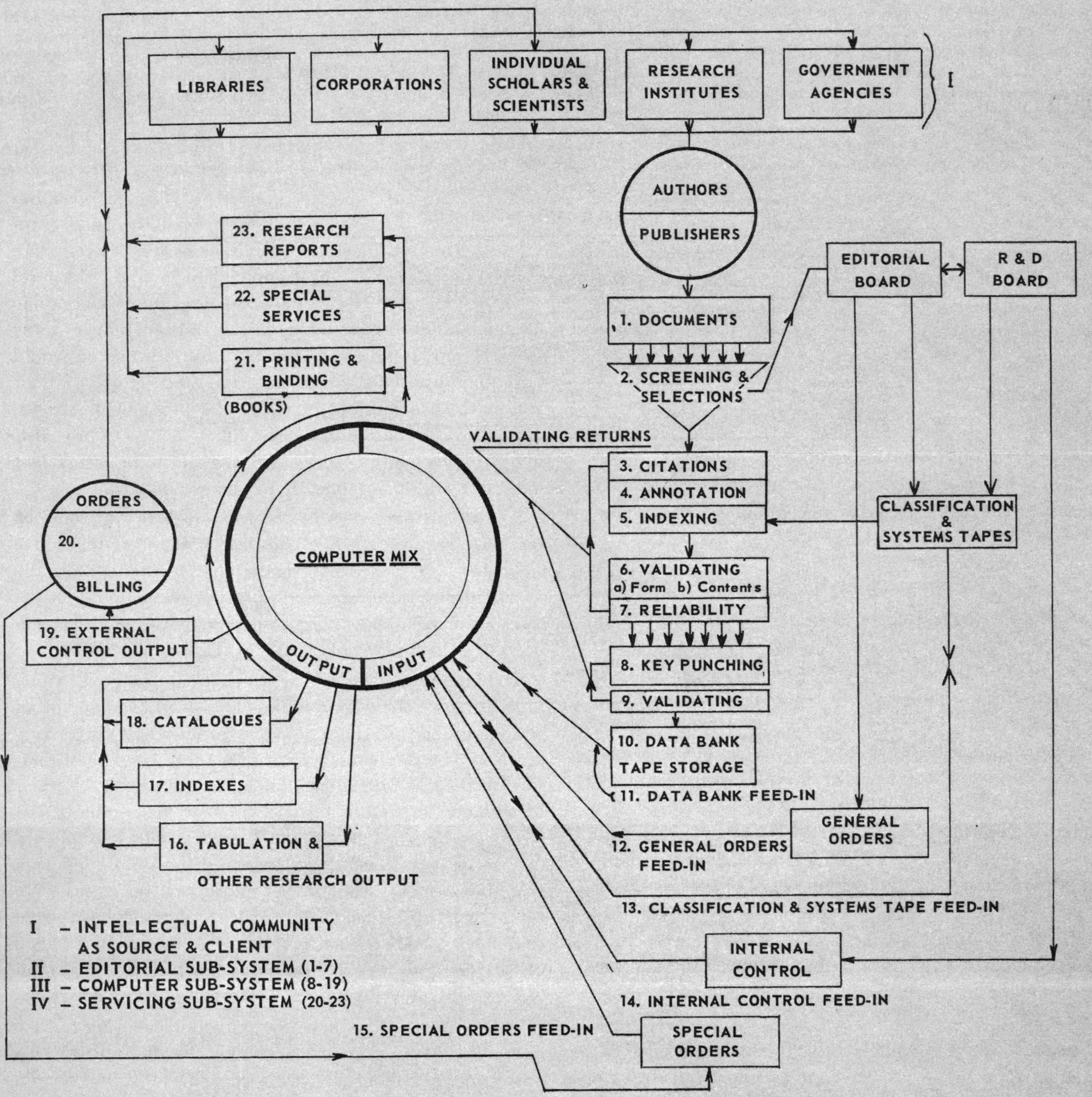

UNIVERSAL REFERENCE SYSTEM

A diagrammatic representation of the numerous steps taken to process documents which come from the intellectual community until they cycle back to the same community as pinpointed sources of information.

The Grazian Classification and Indexing System

The theory behind the URS Classification System is operational. It asks the question: "*Who* says, '*Who does what with whom, where and when, by what means, why*' and *how does he know so?*" This question leads to the general categories and subcategories of the system, which is presented in its logical form on pages **xii-xiv**, along with the truncated terms used in the computerized Index of Documents. The advantage of reading the logical classification is that one will learn in a few minutes the general meaning of the truncated terms and can usually go directly and rapidly to the proper terms in the Index.

The Grazian classification cuts across various disciplines of social science to call attention to the methodological aspects of works which would appear to be important to scholars in the behavioral, instrumental, positivistic tradition of philosophy and science.

The constant recourse to method also serves as a screening device for eliminating numerous documents that are purely evaluative, journalistic, nonempirical, or of an intuitive type. The Grazian index contains some 351 Standard Descriptor categories at the present time. To them are added Unique Descriptors as they occur. Some additional categories logically subtending from the existing ones will be added as time goes on. These will be expanded as part of the original coding as the need is shown. (Several categories may be altered, too, on the same grounds.) From two to four of the Standard and Unique Descriptors are selected as most important facets of the work and are indicated as Critical Descriptors. These are printed apart in the Index of Documents.

The possibilities of utilizing cross-categories are immediate. Cross-categories can be used (both by the searcher and by the creator of the index) to provide a more specialized bibliography. This Cross-Faceting can permit adjusting to changes in the interests of scientists. An almost infinite number of cross-categories is possible, of course. The user of the system will find it set up beyond any existing system to facilitate this. In the future, and upon request, complicated cross-category or multi-faceted searches will be performed by the Universal Reference System's machinery. The ultimate instrumental goal is Controlled Faceting—contractible or expansible according to need and logic.

In practice, the Standard Descriptors, the Unique Descriptors, the Critical Descriptors, the Multiple Faceting, and the Cross-Faceting are interlaced in the operations of documentary analysis and control. Thus, to allow for gaps in the system, to go along with conventional practice, to employ more specialized terms, and to carry important proper nouns, the indexing rules permit the documentary analyst to add Unique Descriptors to the Standard Descriptors already taken from the master list. There are 63 of these in the *Codex of Legislative Process, Representation, and Decision-Making*. The total number of descriptors finally averaged 13 per item.

Some persons have inquired whether it might be useful to print out the whole descriptor rather than a truncated term. Several reasons arbitrate against this procedure, at least for the present. In most cases there is really no single term for which the printed-out truncated descriptor is the symbol. Most Standard Descriptors stand for several synonymous words and related ideas. Printing out the full descriptor *word* would be deluding in many cases, leading searchers to believe a word has only its face meaning.

Moreover, if all truncated descriptors were spelled out, the search time (after the first few searches) would be extended greatly since the eye would have to cover much more lettering and space. Furthermore, the size of the CODEX would be at least tripled, for the space provided for permuting would have to be open enough to carry the longest, not the average, words. There are other technical difficulties.

The repetition of numerous descriptors following each entry in the Index of Documents serves the purpose of targeting the search precisely. The richness of descriptors also postpones the moment of returning to the catalogue and thus enlarges the marginal utility of the first resort to the catalogue.

The intensive indexing of each document, which ranges from 10 to 20 entries, serves a purpose. Intensive indexing permits a document to exhibit all of its important facets to the searcher. The ratio of index carriage to title carriage is here termed the "carriage ratio." The carriage ratio of the URS is much higher than that of most bibliographies. The magnitude of the difference shows the meaning of high intensity indexing. Under other systems, unlike the URS CODEX, a topic is understated in the index. And, less obviously, topics other than the one carried as a flag in the title are sunk into oblivion; thus "Relations Between France and Indochina," which may be a valuable work on questions of economic development, would probably not be indexed on that question at all.

To sum up, the URS, when used as in this CODEX, thoroughly exposes the facets of a listed document. It makes the document thoroughly *retrievable*.

Also under consideration are suggestions to eliminate (or suppress) more of the descriptors. What is the optimal number? It is difficult to say, *a priori*. Experience and experiment will tell, over time. Meanwhile, the Critical Descriptors offer a researcher the "fast search," if he pleases. The more numerous group of descriptors in the final column offers a more complete faceting.

The search time of a researcher should be an important concern of a bibliographer. Search time begins to run, of course, with the knowledge of and access to a work that probably covers a searcher's need. It runs, too, with the ingenuity of the searcher's phrasing of his need. Then it runs with the presence of the works needed in the list searched; a missing document can be translated into lost time. An index saves time, too, when the term searched is the term under which a document is indexed; the need to compromise between detailed vocabularies and generalized ones is evident: it can reasonably be argued that more time is lost in research in social science in getting on the same semantic beam than in solving substantive problems of the "real world." Finally, the structure of an index should lessen search time while permitting a rich search.

Research and experimentation are in order, and it is hoped that a by-product of the initial publications of the Universal Reference System will be an increased stimulation of research into research procedures with respect to the URS' problems and to those of other reference systems.

Topical and Methodological Index (Grazian Index System)

The truncated descriptors (left of each column) and their expanded definitions (right of each column) that follow were employed in systematically computerizing the topics and methods of the Social and Behavioral Sciences. Truncated descriptors that are underscored in the listing that follows have not been carried in the left-hand index entry column of this CODEX; several others (denoted by a double underscore) have been entirely eliminated from this CODEX. Fuller definitions are included in the Index of Documents. So are proper names, place names, organization names, and incidents.

I. TOPICS

1. TIME—SPACE—CULTURE INDEX: Cultural-temporal location of subject.

Centuries covered (e.g., -4; 14-19; 20)

PREHIST	Prehistoric.
MEDIT-7	Mediterranean and Near East, pre-Islamic.
PRE/AMER	Pre-European Americas.
CHRIST-17C	Christendom to 1700.
AFR	Sub-Sahara Africa.
ASIA	China, Japan, Korea.
S/ASIA	India, Southeast Asia, Oceania, except European settlements.
ISLAM	Islamic world.
MOD/EUR	Europe, 1700 to 1918, including European settlements.
USA-45	USA, 1700 to 1945.
WOR-45	Worldwide to 1945.
L/A+17C	Latin America since 1700.
EUR+WWI	Europe, 1918 to present, including colonies, but excluding Communist countries.
COM	Communist countries.
USA+45	USA since 1945.
WOR+45	Worldwide since 1945.
FUT	Future.
SPACE	Outer space.
UNIV	Free of historical position.
SEA	Locale of activity is aquatic.
AIR	Locale of activity is aerial.

(Nations are readily identifiable.)

2. INSTITUTIONAL INDEX: (or subject treated).

A. General

SOCIETY	Society as a whole.
CULTURE	Cultural patterns.
STRUCT	Social structure.
CONSTN	Constitution. Basic group structure.
LAW	Sanctioned practices, enforced ethics in a community.
ELITES	A power-holding group.
INTELL	Intelligentsia.
SOC/INTEG	Social integration.
STRATA	Social strata.
CLIENT	Clients.

B. Economic type

ECO/UNDEV	Developing countries.
ECO/DEV	Developed countries.

C. Economic function

AGRI	Agriculture, including hunting.
R+D	Research and development organization.
FINAN	Financial services.
INDUS	All or most industry.
COM/IND	Communications industry.
CONSTRUC	Construction and building.
DIST/IND	Distributive system: Includes transportation, warehousing.
EXTR/IND	Extractive industry.
MARKET	Marketing system.
PROC/MFG	Processing or manufacturing.
SERV/IND	Service industry.

D. Organizations

SML/CO	Small company: 50 employees or less.
LG/CO	Company of more than 50 employees.
LABOR	Labor unions.
PROF/ORG	Professional organizations, including guilds.
PUB/INST	Habitational institutions: hospitals, prisons, sanitariums, etc.
POL/PAR	Political party.
SCHOOL	School (except University).
ACADEM	Higher learning.
PERF/ART	Performing arts groupings.
SECT	Church, sect, religious group.
FAM	Family.
KIN	Kinship groups.
NEIGH	Neighborhood.
LOC/G	Local governments.
MUNIC	Cities, villages, towns.
PROVS	State or province.
NAT/G	National governments.
FACE/GP	Acquaintance group: face-to-face association.
VOL/ASSN	Voluntary association.
INT/ORG	International organizations.

3. ORGANIC OR INTERNAL STRUCTURE INDEX: Subgroupings or substructures treated.

CONSULT	Consultants.
FORCES	Armed forces and police.
DELIB/GP	Conferences, committees, boards, cabinets.
LEGIS	Legislatures.
CT/SYS	Court systems.
EX/STRUC	Formal executive establishment.
TOP/EX	Individuals holding executive positions.
CHIEF	Chief officer of a government.
WORKER	Workers and work conditions.

4. PROCESSES AND PRACTICES: Procedures or tactics used by subject or discussed as subject.

A. Creating and Sciencing

CREATE	Creative and innovative processes.
ACT/RES	Combined research and social action.
COMPUTER	Computer techniques.
INSPECT	Inspecting quality, output, legality.
OP/RES	Operations research.
PLAN	Planning.
PROB/SOLV	Problem-solving and decision-making.
TEC/DEV	Development and change of technology.

B. Economizing

ACCT	Accounting, bookkeeping.
BAL/PWR	Balance of power.
BARGAIN	Bargaining, trade.
BUDGET	Budgeting, fiscal planning.
CAP/ISM	Enterprise, entrepreneurship.
DIPLOM	Diplomacy.
ECO/TAC	Economic measures or tactics.
FOR/AID	Foreign aid.
INT/TRADE	International trade.
RATION	Rationing, official control of goods or costs.
RENT	Renting.
TARIFFS	Tariffs.
TAX	Taxation.

C. Awarding

GIVE	Giving, philanthropy.
LICENSE	Legal permit.
PAY	Paying.
RECEIVE	Receiving of welfare.
REPAR	Reparations.
TRIBUTE	Payments to dominant by minor power, racketeering.
WORSHIP	Worship, ritual.

D. Symbolizing

DOMIN	Domination.
EDU/PROP	Education or propaganda.
LEGIT	Legitimacy.
PRESS	Printed media.
RUMOR	Rumor, gossip.
TV	Television.
WRITING	Writing.

E. Evaluating

CONFER	Group consultation.
DEBATE	Organized collective arguments.

ETIQUET	Etiquette, fashion, manners.
PRICE	Pricing.
SENIOR	Seniority.

F. Determining

ADJUD	Judicial behavior and personality.
ADMIN	Behavior of non-top executive personnel (except armed forces).
AGREE	Agreements, treaties, compacts.
AUTOMAT	Automation.
COLONIAL	Colonialism.
CONTROL	Specific ability of power to determine achievement.
EXEC	Executive, regularized management.
FEEDBACK	Feedback phenomena.
GAMBLE	Speculative activity.
LEAD	Leading.
LOBBY	Lobbying.
NEUTRAL	Neutralism, neutrality.
PARL/PROC	Parliamentary procedures (legislative).
PARTIC	Participation: civic apathy or activity.
REGION	Regionalism.
RISK	Risk, uncertainty, certainty.
ROUTINE	Procedural and work systems.
SANCTION	Sanctions of law and social law.
TASK	A specific operation within a work setting.
TIME	Timing, time-factor.

G. Forcing

ARMS/CONT	Arms control and disarmament.
COERCE	Force and violence.
CRIME	Criminal behavior.
CROWD	Mass behavior.
DEATH	Death-related behavior.
DETER	Military deterrence.
GUERRILLA	Guerrilla warfare.
MURDER	Murder, assassination.
NUC/PWR	All uses of nuclear energy.
REV	Revolution.
SUICIDE	Suicide.
WAR	War.
WEAPON	Conventional military weapons.

H. Choosing

APPORT	Apportionment of assemblies.
CHOOSE	Choice, election.
REPRESENT	Representation.
SUFF	Suffrage.

I. Consuming

DREAM	Dreaming.
LEISURE	Unobligated time expenditures.
SLEEP	Sleep-related behavior.
EATING	Eating, cuisine.

5. RELATIONS INDEX: Relationship of individuals and/or group under discussion.

CIVMIL/REL	Civil-military relation.
GOV/REL	Relations between local or state governments and governmental agencies.
GP/REL	Relations among groups, except nations.
INT/REL	Relations among sovereign states.
INGP/REL	Relations within groups.
PERS/REL	Relations between persons; interpersonal communication.
RACE/REL	Race relations.

6. CONDITIONS AND MEASURES (of activities being discussed).

ADJUST	Social adjustment, socialization.
BAL/PAY	Balance of payments.
CENTRAL	Centralization.
CONSEN	Consensus.
COST	Costs.
DEMAND	In economic sense, a demand.
DISCRIM	Social differentiation in support of inequalities.
EFFICIENCY	Effectiveness, measures.
EQUILIB	Equilibrium (technical).
FEDERAL	Federalism.
HAPPINESS	Satisfaction and unhappiness.
ILLEGIT	Bastardy.
INCOME	Income distribution, shares, earnings.
ISOLAT	Isolation and community.
LITERACY	Ability to read and write.
MAJORITY	Behavior of major parts of grouping.
MARRIAGE	Legal wedlock.
NAT/LISM	Nationalism.
OPTIMAL	Optimality in its economic usages.
OWN	Ownership.
PEACE	Freedom from conflict or termination of hostilities.
PRIVIL	Privilege, parliamentary.
PRODUC	Productivity.
PROFIT	Profit in economic sense.
RATIONAL	Instrumental rationality.
STRANGE	Estrangement or outsiders.
TOTALISM	Totalitarianism.
UTIL	Utility as in economics.
UTOPIA	Envisioned general social conditions.

7. PERSONALITY INDEX: Behavior of actors to their actions.

HABITAT	Ecology.
HEREDITY	Genetic influences on personality.
DRIVE	Drive, morale, or antithesis.
PERCEPT	Perception.
PERSON	Personality and human nature.
ROLE	Role, reference group feelings, cross-pressures.
AGE	Age factors in general.
AGE/C	Infants and children.
AGE/Y	Youth, adolescence.
AGE/A	Adults.
AGE/O	Old.
SEX	Sexual behavior.
SUPEGO	Conscience, superego, and responsibility.
RIGID/FLEX	Rigidity/flexibility; exclusive/inclusive.
ATTIT	Attitudes, opinions, ideology.
DISPL	Displacement and projection.
AUTHORIT	Authoritarianism, as personal behavior.
BIO/SOC	Bio-social processes: drugs, psychosomatic phenomena, etc.
ANOMIE	Alienation, anomie, generalized personal anxiety.

8. VALUES INDEX: Basically desired (or nondesired) conditions held or believed in by subjects.

HEALTH	Well-being, bodily and psychic integrity (sickness).
KNOWL	Enlightenment (ignorance).
LOVE	Affection, friendship (hatred).
MORAL	Rectitude, morality (immorality), goodness.
PWR	Power, participation in decision-making (impotence).
RESPECT	Respect, social class attitudes (contempt, disrespect).
SKILL	Skill, practical competence (incompetence).
WEALTH	Wealth, access to goods and services (poverty).
ALL/VALS	All, or six or more of above.
ORD/FREE	Security, order, restraint (change, experience, freedom).
SOVEREIGN	Sovereignty; home-rule.

9. IDEOLOGICAL TOPIC: Ideology discussed in work.

CATHISM	Roman Catholicism.
CONSERVE	Traditionalism.
FASCISM	Fascism.
LAISSEZ	Laissez-faire-ism (old liberal).
MARXISM	Marxism.
MYSTISM	Mysticism.
NEW/LIB	New Liberalism (welfare state).
OBJECTIVE	Value-free thought.
PACIFISM	Pacifism.
PLURISM	Socio-political order of autonomous groups.
POPULISM	Majoritarianism.
RELATISM	Relativism.
SOCISM	Socialism.
TECHRACY	Socio-political order dominated by technicians.
ALL/IDEOS	Three or more of above.

II. METHODOLOGY (What techniques are dealt with by the author and what techniques the document employs or describes).

10. ETHICAL STANDARDS APPLIED BY AUTHOR

ETHIC	Personal ethics (private and professional).
LAW/ETHIC	Ethics of laws and court processes.

POLICY	Treats ethics of public policies.

11. IDEOLOGY OF AUTHOR (where clear).

ANARCH	Anarchism.
CATH	Roman Catholic.
CONVNTL	Conventional: unsystematic acceptance of values in common currency.
FASCIST	Totalitarian with nonworker, upper class, or leader cult.
MAJORIT	Majoritarian, consensual.
MARXIST	Marxist Communist in viewpoint.
MYSTIC	Otherworldly, mystical.
OLD/LIB	Old liberal, laissez-faire.
PACIFIST	Pacifist.
PLURIST	Pluralist.
REALPOL	Realpolitik, Machiavellism.
RELATIV	Relativist.
SOCIALIST	Socialist (except Communist).
TECHNIC	Technocratic.
TRADIT	Traditional or aristocratic.
WELF/ST	Welfare state advocate.

12. FIELD INDEX: Fields, discipline, or methodological approach of document.

ART/METH	Fine Arts, Graphics, Performing Arts, Aesthetics.
CRIMLGY	Criminology.
DECISION	Decision-making and gaming (game theory).
ECO	Economics and economic enterprise.
ECOMETRIC	Econometrics, mathematical economics.
EPIST	Epistemology, sociology of knowledge.
GEOG	Demography and geography.
HEAL	Health sciences.
HIST	History (including current events).
HUM	Methods of the "Humanities." Literary analysis.
INT/LAW	International law. Uses legal approach.
JURID	Uses legal approach. Concerns largely the laws.
MGT	Administrative management.
PHIL/SCI	Scientific method and Philosophy of Science.
POL	Deals with political and power process.
PSY	Psychology.
SOC	Sociology.
SOC/WK	Social services.

13. CONCEPTS: Document is noteworthy for systematic and/or basic treatment of:

CONCPT	Subject-matter abstract concepts.
METH/CNCPT	Methodological concepts.
MYTH	Treats assumptions unconsciously accepted, fictions.
NEW/IDEA	Word inventions, new concepts and ideas.

14. LOGIC, MATHEMATICS, AND LANGUAGE

LOG	Logic: syntax, semantics, pragmatics.
MATH	Mathematics.
STAT	Statistics.
AVERAGE	Mean, average behaviors.
PROBABIL	Probability, chance.
MODAL	Modal types, fashions.
CORREL	Correlations (statistical).
REGRESS	Regression analysis.
QUANT	Nature and limits of quantification.
CLASSIF	Classification, typology, set theory.
INDICATOR	Numerical indicator, index weights.
LING	Linguistics.
STYLE	The styles and terminology of scientific communications.

15. DIRECT OBSERVATION

OBS	Trained or participant observation.
SELF/OBS	Self-observation, psycho-drama.
OBS/ENVIR	Social milieu of and resistances to observation.
CONT/OBS	Controlled direct observation.
RECORD	Recording direct observations. (But not content analysis, q.v.)

16. INTERVIEWS

INT	Interviews, short or long, in general.
STAND/INT	Standardized interviews.
DEEP/INT	Depth interviews.
UNPLAN/INT	Impromptu interview.
RESIST/INT	Social resistance to interviewing.
REC/INT	Recording, systematizing, and analyzing of interviews.

17. QUESTIONNAIRES

QU	Questionnaires in general, short or long.
DEEP/QU	Depth questionnaires, including projective or probing.
QU/SEMANT	Semantic and social problems of questionnaires.
SYS/QU	Systematizing and analyzing questionnaires.

18. TESTS AND SCALES

TESTS	Theory and uses of tests and scales.
APT/TEST	Aptitude tests.
KNO/TEST	Tests for factual knowledge, beliefs, or abilities.
PERS/TEST	Personality tests.
PROJ/TEST	Projective tests.

19. UNIVERSES AND SAMPLING

CENSUS	Census.
SAMP	Sample survey in general.
SAMP/SIZ	Sizes and techniques of sampling.
NET/THEORY	Systematic group-member connections analysis.

20. ANALYSIS OF TEMPORAL SEQUENCES

BIOG	Biography, personality development, and psychoanalysis.
HIST/WRIT	Historiography.
TIME/SEQ	Chronology and genetic series of men, institutions, processes, etc.
TREND	Projection of trends, individual and social.
PREDICT	Prediction of future events.

21. COMMUNICATION CONTENT ANALYSIS

CON/ANAL	Quantitative content analysis.
DOC/ANAL	Conventional analysis of records or documents.

22. INFORMATION STORAGE AND RETRIEVAL

OLD/STOR	Conventional libraries, books, records, tape, film.
THING/STOR	Artifacts and material evidence.
COMPUT/IR	Mechanical and electronic information retrieval.

23. GRAPHICS AND AUDIO-VISUAL TECHNIQUES: Used in the research and/or in the presentation.

AUD/VIS	Film and sound, photographs.
CHARTS	Graphs, charts, diagrams, maps.
EXHIBIT	Exhibits.
PROG/TEAC	Programmed instruction.

24. COMPARATIVE ANALYSIS INDEX

METH/COMP	Of methods, approaches, styles.
IDEA/COMP	Of ideas, methods, ideologies.
PERS/COMP	Of persons.
GP/COMP	Of groups.
GOV/COMP	Of governments.
NAT/COMP	Of nations.

25. EXPERIMENTATION

LAB/EXP	Laboratory or strictly controlled groups.
SOC/EXP	"Social" experimentation.
HYPO/EXP	Hypothetical, intellectual constructs.

26. MODELS: Intellectual representations of objects or processes.

SIMUL	Scientific models.
ORG/CHARTS	Blueprints and organization charts.
STERTYP	Stereotypes, ideologies, utopias.
GAME	Game or Decision Theory models.

27. GENERAL THEORY

GEN/LAWS	Systems based on substantive relations, such as idealism, economic determinism.
GEN/METH	Systems based on methodology, such as cycles, pragmatism, sociometry.

28. SPECIAL FORMATS

ANTHOL	Anthology, symposium, collection.
BIBLIOG	Bibliography over fifty items, or of rare utility.
BIBLIOG/A	Contains bibliography over fifty items or of rare utility, annotated.
DICTIONARY	Dictionary.
INDEX	List of names or subjects.
METH	Document heavily emphasizes methodology (Part II) rather than topics (Part I).
T	Textbook.

Dictionary of Descriptors in this Volume

(Incorporating List of Frequency of Descriptors in Index)

This Dictionary contains all Descriptors employed in this volume, and thus enables you to identify in a few minutes every Descriptor that may pertain to your subject. The frequency list calls your attention to the number of works carried under each Descriptor and assists you in determining the term at which you may most advantageously begin your search in the Index. A modest system of cross-references may be found in the Dictionary that appears in the Index.

DESCRIPTOR		*FREQUENCY*	*PAGE*
ABM/DEFSYS	Anti-ballistic missile defense systems	1	171
ABRIKSSV/D	Dimitri Abrikossov	1	171
ACADEM	University, graduate school	63	171
ADENAUER/K	Konrad Adenauer	6	173
ADJUD	Judicial and adjudicative processes and behavior	218	173
ADJUST	Social adjustment, socialization	30	179
ADMIN	Behavior of non-top executive personnel in organizational structure	379	180
AEA	Atomic Energy Authority of UN	1	190
AEC	Atomic Energy Commission	2	190
AFGHANISTN	Afghanistan	5	190
AFL/CIO	American Federation of Labor, Congress of Industrial Organizations	1	190
AFR	Africa	297	190
AFR/STATES	Organization of African States	2	198
AFRICA/E	East Africa	2	198
AFRICA/SW	South-West Africa	4	198
AFRICA/W	West Africa	6	199
AGE	Age Factors	2	199
AGE/A	Adults	1	199
AGE/C	Infants and children	2	199
AGE/Y	Youth and adolescence	10	199
AGREE	Agreements, treaties, compacts	58	199
AGRI	Agriculture, including hunting	210	201
AID	U. S. Agency for International Development	18	206
AIR	Locale of activity is aerial	18	207
ALBANIA	Albania	7	208
ALGERIA	Algeria	16	208
ALL/IDEOS	Concerns three or more of the terms listed in the ideological topic index, p. xiii	51	208
ALL/VALS	Concerns six or more of the terms listed in the values index, p. xiii	174	210
ANARCH	Anarchism	3	215
ANGLO/SAX	Anglo-Saxon	1	215
ANOMIE	Alienation, anomie, generalized personal anxiety	12	215
ANTARCTICA	Antarctica	2	216
ANTHOL	Anthology, symposium	158	216
ANTI/SEMIT	Anti-semitism	1	220
APPORT	Apportionment of assemblies	1	220
AQUINAS/T	Saint Thomas Aquinas	1	220
ARABS	Arab world and culture	6	220
ARGENTINA	Argentina	5	221
ARMS/CONT	Arms control, disarmament	287	221
ART/METH	Fine and performing arts	22	229
ASA	Association of South-East Asia	1	229
ASIA	China, Japan, Korea, Bhutan, Afghanistan, Taiwan	229	229
ATLAN/ALL	Atlantic Alliance	1	236
AUD/VIS	Film and sound, photographs	19	236
AUSTRALIA	Australia	16	236
AUSTRIA	Austria	8	237
AUTHORIT	Authoritarianism, personal	11	237
AUTOMAT	Automation	7	237
BAGHDAD	Baghdad, Iraq	1	238
BAL/PAY	Balance of payments	94	238
BAL/PWR	Balance of power	413	240
BALKANS	Balkans	1	252
BALTIC	Baltic Sea and countries	1	252
BAO/DAI	Bao Dai	1	252
BARGAIN	Bargaining, trade	11	252
BELGIUM	Belgium	12	253
BENTHAM/J	Jeremy Bentham	2	253
BERLIN	Berlin	6	253
BERLIN/BLO	Berlin Blockade	5	253
BIBLIOG	Bibliography over 50 items	552	254
BIBLIOG/A	Annotated bibliography over 50 items	328	268
BIO/SOC	Bio-social processes: drugs, psychosomatic phenomena, etc.	10	277
BIOG	Biography, personality development, psychoanalysis	79	277
BIRCH/SOC	John Birch Society	1	279
BIRTH/CON	Birth control	6	279
BISMARCK/O	Otto von Bismarck	6	280
BLACK/EUG	Eugene Black	1	280
BOER/WAR	Boer War	1	280
BOLIVIA	Bolivia	3	280
BOLIVAR/S	Simon Bolivar	1	280
BOLSHEVISM	Bolshevism, Bolshevists, Bolsheviks	3	280
BORDEN/R	Sir Robert Borden	1	281
BORNEO	Borneo	1	281
BOSTON	Boston, Massachusetts	1	281
BOURGUIBA	Habib Bourguiba	1	281
BOXER/REBL	Boxer Rebellion	1	281
BRAZIL	Brazil	24	281
BRIAND/A	Aristide Briand	1	282
BUDDHISM	Buddhism	2	283
BUDGET	Budgeting, fiscal planning	83	283
BULGARIA	Bulgaria	11	285
BUNDY/M	McGeorge Bundy	1	285
BUREAUCRCY	Bureaucracy	1	285
BURGANDA	Burganda	1	286
BURMA	Burma	9	286
CAB	Civil Aeronautics Board	1	286
CALVIN/J	John Calvin	1	286
CAMBODIA	Cambodia	6	286
CAMEROON	Cameroon	3	287
CANADA	Canada	36	287
CANAL/ZONE	Panama Canal Zone	2	288
CAP/ISM	Capitalism, entrepreneurship	108	288
CARIBBEAN	Caribbean	3	291
CARRANZA/V	Venustianzo Carranza	1	291
CASEBOOK	Casebook (e.g., legal, sociological)	6	291
CASTRO/F	Fidel Castro	4	292
CATH	Roman Catholic	9	292
CATHISM	Roman Catholicism	18	292
CENSUS	Population enumeration	30	292
CENTO	Central Treaty Organization	1	293
CENTRAL	Centralization	27	293
CENTRL/AFR	Central African Republic	1	294
CEYLON	Ceylon	11	294
CHACO/WAR	Chaco War	1	295
CHAD	Chad	1	295
CHAMBRLN/J	Joseph Chamberlain	1	295
CHAMBRLN/N	Neville Chamberlain	1	295
CHIEF	Chief officer of a government	139	295
CHILE	Chile	9	299
CHINA	China in general	1	299
CHINA/COM	People's Republic of China	125	299
CHOOSE	Choice, election	104	303
CHOU/ENLAI	Chou En-lai	1	305
CHRISTIAN	Christian belief, churches	6	305
CHRIST-17C	Christendom to 1700	24	306
CHURCH/STA	Church-state relations	5	306
CHURCHLL/W	Sir Winston Churchill	4	307
CIA	Central Intelligence Agency	4	307

CATALOGUE OF DOCUMENTS

0001 AFRICANA NEWSLETTER.
STANFORD: HOOVER INSTITUTE.
QUARTERLY PUBLISHED BY HOOVER INSTITUTION; FIRST PUBLISHED OCT. 1962. EACH ISSUE CONTAINS LISTINGS OF WORKS PUBLISHED IN AND ABOUT SUB-SAHARA AFRICA AND AFRICAN-RELATED DOCUMENTS. ALSO PROVIDES INFORMATION AS TO WHERE MATERIALS LOCATED. WORKS CHIEFLY IN FRENCH AND ENGLISH. CONTAINS INFORMATION ON ACQUISITIONS, BIBLIOGRAPHIC STUDIES, AND RESEARCH PROJECTS.

0002 AMERICAN JOURNAL OF INTERNATIONAL LAW.
CHICAGO: AM SOC INTERNAT LAW.
QUARTERLY FIRST PUBLISHED IN 1907 WHICH HAS BOOK REVIEW SECTION AND LIST OF BOOKS AND ARTICLES CURRENTLY PUBLISHED. TREATS CONTEMPORARY INTERNATIONAL LAW AND RELATIONS. INCLUDES SOURCES IN ENGLISH, FRENCH, AND GERMAN.

0003 AMERICAN POLITICAL SCIENCE REVIEW.
WASHINGTON: AMER POL SCI ASSOC.
QUARTERLY JOURNAL SINCE 1906 WHICH DEALS WITH GOVERNMENT, POLITICS, LAW, AND INTERNATIONAL RELATIONS. CONTAINS EXTENSIVE BOOK REVIEW SECTION AND BIBLIOGRAPHIES OF BOOKS, SERIALS, GOVERNMENT DOCUMENTS, PAMPHLETS, AND DOCTORAL DISSERTATIONS. CLASSIFIED IN FIVE CATEGORIES: POLITICAL THEORY, AMERICAN POLITICS, COMPARATIVE PUBLIC ADMINISTRATION, COMPARATIVE GOVERNMENT, AND INTERNATIONAL POLITICS.

0004 ANNALS OF THE AMERICAN ACADEMY OF POLITICAL AND SOCIAL SCIENCE.
PHILA: AMER ACAD POL & SOC SCI.
ISSUED BIMONTHLY. INCLUDES BOOK DEPARTMENT WITH CRITICAL REVIEWS OF LATEST WORKS IN AMERICAN HISTORY AND GOVERNMENT, EUROPEAN HISTORY AND GOVERNMENT, ASIA AND AFRICA, ECONOMICS, SOCIOLOGY AND ANTHROPOLOGY. INCLUDES UNANNOTATED BIBLIOGRAPHY OF RECENT WORKS IN SOCIAL SCIENCES, LISTED ALPHABETICALLY. FIRST PUBLISHED IN 1890.

0005 INTL. STUD. Q.; JOURNAL OF INTERNATIONAL STUDIES ASSOCIATION.
LOS ANGELES: U OF S CAL INTL REL.
PUBLICATION, BEGUN IN 1962, WHICH ISSUES ANNUAL BIBLIOGRAPHY OF ABOUT 1,170 ITEMS. PUBLISHED CURRENTLY IN FIELD OF INTERNATIONAL RELATIONS. BIBLIOGRAPHY ORGANIZED TOPICALLY AND IS LIMITED TO ENGLISH-LANGUAGE PUBLICATIONS. INCLUDES SECTIONS ON POLITICAL, ECONOMIC, AND SOCIAL COMMUNITY FORMATION AND FACTORS AND RELATIONSHIPS OF PERSONALITY, CULTURE, NATIONALISM AND RACE IN ATTITUDES AND IDEOLOGIES.

0006 BULLETIN ANALYTIQUE DE DOCUMENTATION POLITIQUE, ECONOMIQUE, ET SOCIALE CONTEMPORAINE.
PARIS: PR UNIV DE FRANCE.
MONTHLY PUBLICATION SINCE 1946 LISTING PRINCIPAL ARTICLES FROM OVER 1,000 FRENCH AND FOREIGN PERIODICALS ON POLITICAL, SOCIAL, AND ECONOMIC ISSUES. TITLES TRANSLATED INTO FRENCH AND ANNOTATED. ANNUAL INDEX OF TITLES AND LIST OF PERIODICALS USED. ENTRIES DIVIDED INTO NATIONAL PROBLEMS OR INTERNATIONAL RELATIONS AND COMPARATIVE STUDIES. FIRST SECTION ARRANGED BY COUNTRY, SECOND BY FIELD OF STUDY.

0007 CANADIAN GOVERNMENT PUBLICATIONS (1955-)
OTTAWA: QUEEN'S PRINTER.
ANNUAL CATALOGUE INCORPORATING "DAILY CHECKLIST" AND "MONTHLY CATALOGUE OF GOVERNMENT PUBLICATIONS." ENTRIES SUBDIVIDED UNDER GENERAL TOPICS, PARLIAMENTARY PUBLICATIONS AND DEPARTMENTAL PUBLICATIONS. FIRST PART OF BOOK IN ENGLISH, SECOND IN FRENCH. INCLUDES SECTION OF INTERNATIONAL PUBLICATIONS.

0008 CURRENT THOUGHT ON PEACE AND WAR.
DURHAM: CURRENT THOUGHT INC.
"WORLD AFFAIRS DIGEST" OF BOOKS AND ARTICLES, UNPUBLISHED MEMORANDA, AND REPORTS, UN AND GOVERNMENTAL DOCUMENTS, AND RESEARCH AND MANUSCRIPTS IN PROGRESS ON CURRENT INTERNATIONAL ISSUES. CONTENTS ARRANGED TOPICALLY: CRISES AREAS AND ISSUES, MILITARY, INTERNATIONAL ECONOMIC FACTORS IN INTERNATIONAL RELATIONS, ETC. EXTENSIVE ANNOTATION OF ABOUT 600 ITEMS. FIRST PUBLISHED 1959. APPEARS TWICE A YEAR.

0009 INTERNATIONAL AFFAIRS.
LONDON: OXFORD U PR.
QUARTERLY WITH SECTION WHICH REVIEWS BOOKS, ARRANGED BY SUBJECT HEADINGS AND GEOGRAPHICAL AREAS. ALSO CONTAINS LIST OF CURRENT PUBLICATIONS NOT REVIEWED. CONCERNED WITH INTERNATIONAL RELATIONS, LAW, AND ECONOMICS. FIRST PUBLISHED 1922.

0010 INTERNATIONAL BOOK NEWS, 1928-1934.
BOSTON: WORLD PEACE FOUNDATION.
AN IRREGULARLY ISSUED BIBLIOGRAPHY, COVERING THE PERIOD FROM JANUARY, 1928 THROUGH MAY, 1934, PUBLISHED BY THE WORLD PEACE FOUNDATION. CATALOGS A GREAT VARIETY OF MATERIAL AVAILABLE FROM OFFICIAL AND SEMI-OFFICIAL INTERNATIONAL COOPERATIVE AGENCIES, AS WELL AS THE WORLD PEACE FOUNDATION ITSELF. DESCRIPTIVELY ANNOTATED LISTINGS ARE TOPICALLY ARRANGED AND DOCUMENT MATERIAL PUBLISHED FROM 1914 TO 1934.

0011 INTERNATIONAL REVIEW OF ADMINISTRATIVE SCIENCES.
BRUSSELS: INTL INST OF ADMIN SCI.
QUARTERLY PUBLICATION, BEGUN IN 1928. CONTAINS SECTION REVIEWING BOOKS AND SERIALS. BIBLIOGRAPHIC SECTION DIVIDED INTO ONE REVIEWING BOOKS RELATING TO PROBLEMS AND ASPECTS OF ADMINISTRATION, AND ONE CONTAINING LIST OF PERIODICAL ARTICLES CLOSELY RELATED TO INTERNATIONAL RELATIONS. LIST IS ALPHABETICAL BY AUTHOR. INCLUDES WESTERN-LANGUAGE SOURCES.

0012 INTERNATIONAL STUDIES.
NEW YORK: ASIA PUBL HOUSE, 1941.
QUARTERLY PUBLICATION BEGUN IN 1941. CONTAINS BOOK REVIEWS WHICH DEAL WITH INTERNATIONAL POLITICS, LAW, AND ECONOMICS. TREATS WORLD BUT FOCUSES ON ASIA. PROVIDES SURVEY OF SOURCE MATERIAL AND RECENT RESEARCH. ANNUAL BIBLIOGRAPHY.

0013 JOURNAL OF ASIAN STUDIES.
ANN ARBOR: ASSOC ASIAN STUD.
QUARTERLY JOURNAL WITH BOOK REVIEWS AND AN ANNUAL "BIBLIOGRAPHY OF ASIAN STUDIES" SINCE 1936. LISTS BOOKS AND PERIODICAL ARTICLES IN WESTERN LANGUAGES. ENTRIES ARRANGED BY COUNTRY AND SUBDIVIDED BY SUBJECT. EACH SUBJECT IS DIVIDED INTO BOOKS AND PERIODICALS. ALSO CONTAINS AN ALPHABETICAL LISTING BY AUTHOR.

0014 JOURNAL OF CONFLICT RESOLUTION.
ANN ARBOR: U MICH CONFL RESO.
QUARTERLY FOR RESEARCH ON WAR AND PEACE. FIRST PUBLISHED 1957. CONTAINS BOOK REVIEW SECTION WHICH TREATS INTERNATIONAL RELATIONS. EMPHASIZES RELATED ASPECTS OF THE SOCIAL AND BEHAVIORAL SCIENCES. COVERS PERIOD SINCE WWII AND REVIEWS BOOKS IN ENGLISH AND EUROPEAN LANGUAGES. LIST OF BOOKS IN ADDITION TO REVIEWS.

0015 JOURNAL OF INTERNATIONAL AFFAIRS.
NEW YORK: COLUMBIA U SCH INT AFF.
QUARTERLY PUBLICATION, BEGUN IN 1947, CONCERNED WITH CONTEMPORARY INTERNATIONAL RELATIONS. HAS BOOK REVIEW SECTION AND LIST OF BOOKS RECEIVED.

0016 JOURNAL OF MODERN HISTORY.
CHICAGO: U OF CHICAGO PRESS.
QUARTERLY, FIRST PUBLISHED IN 1929, REVIEWS BOOKS WHICH DEAL WITH POLITICAL AND DIPLOMATIC HISTORY ON A WORLDWIDE BASIS. ANNUAL AUTHOR INDEX.

0017 JOURNAL OF POLITICS.
NEW YORK: SOUTHERN POL SCI ASSN.
QUARTERLY PUBLICATION, BEGUN IN 1939, WHICH DEALS WITH POLITICS, GOVERNMENT, AND LAW PRIMARILY IN US. INCLUDES FOREIGN COUNTRIES. CONTAINS BOOK REVIEW SECTION.

0018 LITERATUR-VERZEICHNIS DER POLITISCHEN WISSENSCHAFTEN.
MUNICH: GUENTER OLZOG VERLAG.
ANNUAL PUBLICATION SINCE 1952 WHICH LISTS LITERATURE OF POLITICAL SCIENCE. LISTS BOOKS PUBLISHED IN WEST GERMANY PRIMARILY WITH SOME AUSTRIAN, EAST GERMAN, AND SWISS TITLES. CONTAINS AUTHOR AND PUBLISHER INDEXES. TOPICS INCLUDE SOCIETY AND STATE, CONSTITUTION, ECONOMICS, INTERNATIONAL RELATIONS, SCIENCE AND POLITICS, AND PUBLICATIONS.

0019 MIDDLE EAST JOURNAL.
WASHINGTON: MIDDLE EAST INST.
QUARTERLY PERIODICAL DEVOTED TO MIDDLE EAST SOCIAL SCIENCES AND HUMANITIES. HAS A BOOK REVIEW SECTION AND A BIBLIOGRAPHICAL LISTING. LISTINGS ARE IN ORIGINAL LANGUAGE - ENGLISH, FRENCH, GERMAN. ALSO CONTAINS SHORTER BOOK NOTICES, LIST OF RECENT BOOKS, LIST OF FORTHCOMING BOOKS, ANNUAL LIST OF PERIODICALS SURVEYED, AND ANNUAL LIST OF RESEARCH PROJECTS. FIRST PUBLISHED 1947.

0020 MIDWEST JOURNAL OF POLITICAL SCIENCE.
DETROIT: WAYNE STATE U PR.
QUARTERLY PUBLICATION, BEGUN IN 1957, WITH BOOK REVIEW SECTION AND BIBLIOGRAPHICAL LISTING. TREATS VARIOUS ASPECTS OF POLITICAL SCIENCE, INTERNATIONAL RELATIONS, AND FOREIGN AFFAIRS. CONCERNED WITH US PRIMARILY, SOME FOREIGN.

0021 NEUE POLITISCHE LITERATUR.
STUTTGART: RING-VERLAG.
MONTHLY JOURNAL WITH BIMONTHLY BIBLIOGRAPHY. FIRST PUBLISHED 1956. LISTS ARTICLES FROM SELECTED GERMAN, FRENCH, AND ENGLISH-LANGUAGE POLITICAL SCIENCE PERIODICALS. ENTRIES ENTERED BY SUBJECT AND INCLUDE POLITICAL THEORY, INTERNATIONAL POLITICS, ECONOMY AND SOCIETY, GERMANY, INTERNATIONAL COMMUNISM, EAST EUROPE, RUSSIA, ASIA AND AFRICA, NORTH AND SOUTH AMERICA.

0022 PEKING REVIEW.
PEKING: PEKING REVIEW.
WEEKLY PERIODICAL EXPRESSING CHINESE COMMUNIST VIEWS. WEEKLY SUMMARY OF EVENTS, NATIONAL AND INTERNATIONAL, FOLLOWED BY ENGLISH TRANSLATIONS OF GOVERNMENT DOCUMENTS, NEWSPAPER EDITORIALS, AND PERIODICAL ARTICLES. FIRST ISSUE MARCH, 1958. INDEXED BY SUBJECT IN LAST ISSUE OF YEAR.

0023 POLITICAL SCIENCE QUARTERLY.

NEW YORK: COLUMBIA U PRESS.
QUARTERLY PERIODICAL, BEGUN IN 1886, WHICH CONTAINS EXTENSIVE BOOK REVIEW SECTION AND BOOK NOTES. MAJORITY OF PUBLICATIONS REVIEWED ARE AMERICAN. JOURNAL TREATS ALL ASPECTS OF POLITICAL SCIENCE - NATIONAL GOVERNMENTS, THEORY, LABOR DISPUTES AND CONTROL, INTERNATIONAL RELATIONS, PROBLEMS OF MODERN WARFARE, ETC.

0024 REVIEW OF POLITICS.
SOUTH BEND: U OF NOTRE DAME.
QUARTERLY PUBLICATION WITH BOOK REVIEWS. FIRST PUBLISHED 1939, IT DEALS WITH POLITICS, GOVERNMENT, AND FOREIGN AFFAIRS.

0025 SOCIAL RESEARCH.
NEW YORK: NEW SCHOOL SOC RES.
FIRST PUBLISHED IN 1934, THIS QUARTERLY HAS A BOOK REVIEW SECTION WHICH DEALS WITH POLITICAL SCIENCE AND THE SOCIAL SCIENCES AND FOREIGN AFFAIRS. CONCENTRATES ON CURRENT EVENTS. REVIEWS BOOKS WRITTEN PRIMARILY IN ENGLISH, BUT SOME EUROPEAN INCLUDED.

0026 AFRICAN RESEARCH BULLETIN.
EXETER: AFRICAN RESEARCH LTD.
MONTHLY PUBLICATION FIRST PRINTED IN 1964 WHICH SYNTHESIZES PRESS ARTICLES AND NEWS BULLETINS ON CURRENT EVENTS IN AFRICA. HAS MATERIAL ON INTERNATIONAL POLITICAL DEVELOPMENTS, INTERNAL POLITICAL DEVELOPMENTS OF INDEPENDENT AND NONINDEPENDENT TERRITORIES, POLITICAL DEVELOPMENTS WITH NATIONS OVERSEAS, SOCIAL AND CULTURAL DEVELOPMENTS.

0027 ARBITRATION JOURNAL.
NEW YORK: AMER ARBITRATION ASSN.
QUARTERLY PUBLICATION OF THE AMERICAN ARBITRATION ASSOC., WHICH REVIEWS AND ANALYZES CASES, PROBLEMS, AND LEGAL PROCEDURES OF DOMESTIC AND INTERNATIONAL COMMERCIAL ARBITRATION. MOST ISSUES INCLUDE A BRIEF CRITICALLY ANNOTATED LIST OF READINGS IN ARBITRATION AND AN UNANNOTATED LIST OF NOTES AND ARTICLES ON FOREIGN TRADE ARBITRATION. ALL ISSUES CONTAIN A REVIEW OF COURT DECISIONS IN ALL TYPES OF ARBITRATION CASES.

0028 AUSTRALIAN PUBLIC AFFAIRS INFORMATION SERVICE.
SYDNEY: AUSTRALIAN PUBLIC AFF. INFO.SCE.
ISSUED MONTHLY BY NATIONAL LIBRARY OF AUSTRALIA. GUIDE TO MATERIAL ON AUSTRALIAN POLITICAL, ECONOMIC, SOCIAL, AND CULTURAL AFFAIRS. INDEXES BOOKS AND ARTICLES, BOTH DOMESTIC AND FOREIGN, DURING CURRENT OR TWO PRECEDING YEARS. INCLUDES SELECTED LIST OF AUSTRALIAN PERIODICALS. ARRANGEMENT IS ALPHABETICAL BY SUBJECT. FIRST PUBLISHED JULY, 1945.

0029 BIBLIO, CATALOGUE DES OUVRAGES PARUS EN LANGUE FRANCAISE DANS LE MONDE ENTIER.
PARIS: SERVICE BIBLIOGRAPHIQUEMESSAGERIES HACHETTE
MONTHLY CATALOGUE OF FRENCH PUBLICATIONS ON VARIOUS SUBJECTS. ITEMS CROSS-REFERENCED BY TITLE, AUTHOR, AND SUBJECT.

0030 BIBLIOGRAPHIE DER SOZIALWISSENSCHAFTEN.
DRESDEN: KRAUS, LTD, 1905.
COLLECTION OF PERIODICALS LISTING PUBLICATIONS IN THE SOCIAL SCIENCES. ARRANGED BY SUBJECT, IT COVERS ITEMS PUBLISHED IN ENCYCLOPEDIAS, BIBLIOGRAPHIES, AND COMPENDS THROUGHOUT THE WORLD ON THEORY OF POLITICAL AND SOCIAL ECONOMY, SOCIAL POLITICS, DEMOGRAPHY, LAW, ETHNOGRAPHY, ETC. CONTAINS AUTHOR, SUBJECT, AND TITLE INDEXES. PUBLISHED ANNUALLY SINCE 1905.

0031 DAILY SUMMARY OF THE JAPANESE PRESS.
WASHINGTON: US GOVERNMENT.
PUBLISHED SINCE 1964 BY US EMBASSY IN TOKYO, CONTAINS TRANSLATIONS OF ARTICLES FROM MAJOR JAPANESE NEWSPAPERS.

0032 CHINA QUARTERLY.
LONDON: INFO BULLETIN LTD.
FIRST PUBLISHED IN 1935, JOURNAL IS DEVOTED TO CHINESE DOMESTIC EVENTS AND FOREIGN RELATIONS. WITH FEW EXCEPTIONS, SCHOLARLY WORK CONCENTRATES ON 20TH-CENTURY QUARTERLY SECTION OF BOOK REVIEWS OF SIGNIFICANT CURRENT STUDIES. CONTAINS ALSO A QUARTERLY CHRONICLE AND DOCUMENTATION AND AN INDEX OF DOCUMENTS.

0033 DOCUMENTATION ECONOMIQUE: REVUE BIBLIOGRAPHIQUE DE SYNTHESE.
PARIS: PR UNIV DE FRANCE.
QUARTERLY JOURNAL FIRST PUBLISHED IN 1947 WHICH SYNTHESIZES AND CLASSIFIES BY CONTENT PRINCIPAL ECONOMIC REVIEWS AND FRENCH AND FOREIGN ECONOMIC STUDIES. CONTAINS ABSTRACTS OF WORKS IN FIELDS OF POLITICS AND ECONOMICS; DEMOGRAPHY, AND ON TYPES OF ECONOMIC ACTIVITY: FINANCES; COMMUNICATION AND TRANSPORT INDUSTRIES; SOCIAL ASPECTS OF ECONOMIC PROCESSES; AND INTERNATIONAL ECONOMIC RELATIONS.

0034 FOREIGN AFFAIRS.
NEW YORK: COUNCIL ON FOREIGN REL.
QUARTERLY, FIRST PUBLISHED 1922, CONTAINING BOOK REVIEW SECTION AND LISTS OF DOCUMENTS AND PAMPHLETS PUBLISHED BY US AND BRITISH GOVERNMENTS AND BY INTERNATIONAL ORGANIZATIONS. DEALS WITH INTERNATIONAL RELATIONS SINCE WWI. INCLUDES TITLES IN ENGLISH, GERMAN, AND FRENCH.

0035 HANDBOOK OF LATIN AMERICAN STUDIES.
GAINESVILLE: U OF FLA PR.
ANNOTATED ANNUAL GUIDE LISTING ABOUT 4,000 BOOKS AND ARTICLES ON ALL SUBJECTS. ITEMS ARRANGED BY SUBJECT AND BY COUNTRY. FIRST PUBLISHED 1935.

0036 INDIA: A REFERENCE ANNUAL.
NEW DELHI: INDIAN MIN OF INFO.
FIRST PUBLISHED IN 1953 BY PUBLICATIONS DIVISION OF THE MINISTRY OF INFORMATION AND BROADCASTING, WITH OBJECT OF PROVIDING AUTHENTIC INFORMATION ON VARIOUS ASPECTS ON NATIONAL LIFE WITHIN COUNTRY AND ABROAD. SELECT BIBLIOGRAPHY INCLUDES ADDITIONAL INFORMATION FROM GOVERNMENT REPORTS AND PUBLICATIONS, REFERENCE WORKS, AND OTHER BOOKS.

0037 LATIN AMERICA IN PERIODICAL LITERATURE.
LOS ANGELES: U CAL LAT AMER STUD.
SUMMARIES INCLUDING BIBLIOGRAPHICAL INFORMATION OF PERIODICALS ARTICLES PUBLISHED WITHIN AND OUTSIDE US. ABSTRACTIONS ARRANGED TOPICALLY: SOCIAL SCIENCES; HUMANITIES; SCIENCE AND TECHNOLOGY; MISCELLANEOUS. JOURNAL PUBLISHED ON MONTHLY BASIS SINCE 1962. PERIODICALS ABSTRACTED ARE THOSE RECEIVED AT UCLA LIBRARY IN THAT PERIOD. EACH ISSUE CONTAINS ABOUT 130 ITEMS.

0038 LONDON TIMES OFFICIAL INDEX.
LONDON: LONDON TIMES, INC.
QUARTERLY, DETAILED SUBJECT INDEX TO NEWSPAPER ARTICLES. CUMULATED ANNUALLY. FIRST PUBLISHED 1906.

0039 PUBLISHERS' CIRCULAR, THE OFFICIAL ORGAN OF THE PUBLISHERS' ASSOCIATION OF GREAT BRITAIN AND IRELAND.
SURREY: PUBL CIRCULAR LTD.
WEEKLY LISTING OF BRITISH PUBLICATIONS INCLUDING PAMPHLETS AND GOVERNMENT PUBLICATIONS. CHANGED IN 1959 TO "BRITISH BOOKS" AND ISSUED MONTHLY. FIRST PUBLISHED 1873.

0040 REVUE FRANCAISE DE SCIENCE POLITIQUE.
PARIS: PR UNIV DE FRANCE.
FRENCH QUARTERLY FIRST PUBLISHED IN 1951, CONTAINS SECTION DEVOTED TO CRITICAL REVIEWS OF RECENT IMPORTANT PUBLICATIONS IN POLITICAL SCIENCE AND SECTION LISTING RECENT PUBLICATIONS RECEIVED BY JOURNAL. CONTAINS ALSO LISTING OF BRITISH COMMONWEALTH POLITICAL SCIENCE REFERENCE WORKS AND JOURNALS.

0041 SEMINAR: THE MONTHLY SYMPOSIUM.
NEW DELHI: SEMINAR.
JOURNAL, PUBLISHED ON MONTHLY BASIS, DEVOTED TO DISCUSSIONS OF SINGLE MAJOR ISSUES DEBATED BY WRITERS OF A VARIETY OF POLITICAL PERSUASIONS. CONFINED TO PROBLEMS CRUCIAL TO INDIAN SOVEREIGNTY AND NATIONAL DEVELOPMENT. SAMPLE ISSUES: NUCLEAR WEAPONS; ROLE OF PARLIAMENT; IMPLICATIONS OF NATIONAL POLICY; LANGUAGE CONTROVERSY; ETC. EACH ISSUE CONTAINS SECTION OF SELECTED RELEVANT READINGS. APPEARED 1959.

0042 THE JAPAN SCIENCE REVIEW: LAW AND POLITICS: LIST OF BOOKS AND ARTICLES ON LAW AND POLITICS.
TOKYO: UNION JAP SOC LAWS + POL.
DESIGNED TO INTRODUCE FOREIGN SCHOLARS TO CURRENT WORKS IN JAPANESE LAW AND POLITICS. FIRST PUBLISHED IN 1956 AND PUBLISHED ANNUALLY THROUGH 1960. SECTIONS ON LEGAL HISTORY AND PHILOSOPHY; COMPARATIVE LAW; CONSTITUTION; ADMINISTRATIVE AND INTERNATIONAL LAW; CIVIL LAW; COMMERCIAL AND CRIMINAL LAW; POLITICS AND INTERNATIONAL POLITICS; SOCIOLOGY OF LAW.

0043 THE MIDDLE EAST AND NORTH AFRICA.
LONDON: EUROPA PUBLICATIONS.
SURVEY AND DIRECTORY OF 29 MIDDLE EASTERN AND NORTH AFRICAN COUNTRIES WITH GEOGRAPHICAL, HISTORICAL, AND ECONOMIC SURVEYS; CONCISE INFORMATION ABOUT POLITICAL, INDUSTRIAL, FINANCIAL, CULTURAL, AND EDUCATIONAL ORGANIZATIONS; AND A BIOGRAPHICAL SECTION OF PROMINENT PERSONALITIES OF THE REGION. BIENNIAL PUBLICATION FIRST ISSUED IN 1948.

0044 THE WORLD IN FOCUS.
CHICAGO: LIB INTERNAT REL.
A MONTHLY INDEX OF SELECTED MATERIALS ON FOREIGN AFFAIRS: BOOKS, PAMPHLETS, AND MAGAZINE ARTICLES. FIRST ISSUED IN 1945 BY LIBRARY OF INTERNATIONAL RELATIONS. CEASED PUBLICATION IN 1951 AND CONTINUED IN 1963 BY THE INTERNATIONAL INFORMATION SERVICE.

0045 THE WORLD OF LEARNING.
LONDON: EUROPA PUBLICATIONS.
ANNOTATED GUIDE TO NATIONAL AND INTERNATIONAL LEARNED SOCIETIES AND RESEARCH INSTITUTES. CONTAINS A SYSTEMATIC CLASSIFICATION FOR SUCH ORGANIZATIONS IN 156 COUNTRIES AND ON THE INTERNATIONAL LEVEL. COMPLETE INFORMATION ON ALL INSTITUTIONS OF HIGHER LEARNING IS PROVIDED FOR EACH COUNTRY. LISTS AND DESCRIBES MUSEUMS, ART GALLERIES, LIBRARIES, AND ARCHIVES. ISSUED BIENNIALLY SINCE 1934.

0046 SCHOLARLY BOOKS IN AMERICA; A QUARTERLY BIBLIOGRAPHY OF UNIVERSITY PRESS PUBLICATIONS.
NEW YORK: AMER U PR SERVICES.
EACH ISSUE CONTAINS ARTICLES AND NOTES ABOUT UNIVERSITY PRESS PUBLISHING AND ANNOTATED LISTINGS OF PUBLICATIONS ISSUED BY MEMBERS OF THE ASSOCIATION OF AMERICAN UNIVERSITY PRESSES. ENTRIES ARRANGED BY SUBJECT.

0047 AVTOREFERATY DISSERTATSII.
MOSCOW: AVTOREFERATY DISSERTATSY.
AUTHORS' ABSTRACTS OF RUSSIAN DISSERTATIONS AND THESES, ARRANGED BY SUBJECT, AT END OF EACH ISSUE OF "KNIZHNAIA LETOPIS, ORGAN GOSUDARSTVENNOI BIBLIOTEKI SSSR." WEEKLY SINCE 1907.

0048 JAHRBUCH DER DISSERTATIONEN.
BONN: BONN UNIV.
LISTING OF DISSERTATIONS IN POLITICAL SCIENCE FROM RHEINISCHE FRIEDRICH-WILHELM UNIVERSITY, BONN. SUMMARY OF EACH ENTRY. CLASSIFIED ARRANGEMENT. ISSUED PERIODICALLY SINCE 1954.

0049 INTERNATIONAL BIBLIOGRAPHY OF POLITICAL SCIENCE.
CHICAGO: ALDINE PUBLISHING CO, 1954.
ANNUAL LISTING SINCE 1954 OF ARTICLES, BOOKS, SERIALS, GOVERNMENT DOCUMENTS COVERING FIELD OF POLITICAL SCIENCE AS A WHOLE. SURVEYS OVER 1,000 JOURNALS IN ABOUT 20 LANGUAGES. TITLES TRANSLATED INTO ENGLISH. ITEMS GROUPED INTO SIX TOPICS: POLITICAL SCIENCE, POLITICAL THOUGHT, GOVERNMENT AND PUBLIC ADMINISTRATION, GOVERNMENTAL PROCESS, INTERNATIONAL RELATIONS, AND AREA STUDIES. 4,000 TO 5,000 ENTRIES.

0050 FOREIGN AFFAIRS BIBLIOGRAPHY: A SELECTED AND ANNOTATED LIST OF BOOKS ON INTERNATIONAL RELATIONS 1919-1962 (4 VOLS.)
NEW YORK: FOREIGN AFFAIRS BIBL, 1933.
EACH VOLUME INCLUDES 19,000 ANNOTATED REFERENCES TO BOOKS ON INTERNATIONAL AFFAIRS. LISTS ITEMS IN ALL IMPORTANT LANGUAGES OF WORLD, INCLUDING PRINCIPAL ASIATIC LANGUAGES. CONTAINS REFERENCES TO WORKS ON POLITICAL, SOCIAL, CULTURAL AND RELIGIOUS FACTORS IN INTERNATIONAL RELATIONS; INTERNATIONAL LAW, ORGANIZATION AND GOVERNMENT; THE TWO WORLD WARS; AND PARTICULAR ISSUES OF GEOGRAPHIC REGIONS. 1ST VOL. 1933.

0051 THE GUIDE TO CATHOLIC LITERATURE, 1888-1940.
DETROIT: WALTER **ROMING** & CO, 1940, 1239 PP.
SUBJECT-TITLE INDEX OF PUBLICATIONS IN ALL LANGUAGES ON ALL SUBJECTS BY CATHOLICS OR OF INTEREST TO CATHOLICS PUBLISHED 1888-1940. SINCE 1940 IT APPEARS ANNUALLY AS AN INTERNATIONAL, ANNOTATED BIBLIOGRAPHY WITH ENTRIES INDEXED BY AUTHOR-TITLE-SUBJECT, MORE THAN A QUARTER OF A MILLION BIOGRAPHICAL, DESCRIPTIVE, AND CRITICAL NOTES. INCLUDES INDEX OF MAGAZINES CITED IN THE GUIDE.

0052 ITALIAN LIBRARY OF INFORMATION: OUTLINE STUDIES (VOL. V)
NEW YORK: ITALIAN LIBRARY OF INFO., 1940, 670 PP.
SERIES OF NINE MONTHLY OUTLINE STUDIES PUBLISHED FROM MAY TO DECEMBER OF 1940 EMPHASIZING ITALIAN ROLE IN AFRICAN COLONIALISM. DISCUSSES ITALIAN EAST AFRICAN EMPIRE, LIBYA, AND HER POSSESSIONS IN MEDITERRANEAN.

0053 INDIA QUARTERLY, A JOURNAL OF INTERNATIONAL AFFAIRS.
BOMBAY: ASIA PUBL HOUSE, 1945.
QUARTERLY, BEGUN IN 1945, WITH BOOK REVIEW SECTION AND A BIBLIOGRAPHICAL LISTING OF CURRENT INDIAN PUBLICATIONS IN SOCIAL SCIENCES. ANNUAL INDEX OF BOOKS, AUTHORS, AND ARTICLES. JOURNAL CONCERNED WITH INTERNATIONAL RELATIONS, ECONOMICS, AND WORLD POLITICS AND GOVERNMENT.

0054 BIBLIOGRAFIIA DISSERTATSII: DOKTORSKIE DISSERTATSII ZA 1941-1944 (2 VOLS.)
MOSCOW: UDARSTVENNA BIBL LENINA, 1946.
LIST OF DISSERTATIONS IN RUSSIAN UNIVERSITIES ON ALL SUBJECTS. ARRANGED BY SUBJECT. ALSO CONTAINS AUTHOR AND INSTITUTION INDEXES.

0055 GUIDE TO THE RECORDS IN THE NATIONAL ARCHIVES.
WASHINGTON: GOVT PR OFFICE, 1948, 68 PP.
RECORDS ARRANGED BY DEPARTMENTS AND BUREAUS OF US FEDERAL GOVERNMENT. TREATS LATIN AND CENTRAL AMERICA.

0056 THE CURRENT DIGEST OF THE SOVIET PRESS.
NEW YORK: JOINT COMM SLAVIC STUD.
WEEKLY PUBLICATION CONTAINING TRANSLATIONS OF CURRENT ARTICLES IN PRAVDA AND IZVESTIA AND 60 OTHER SOVIET NEWSPAPERS AND PERIODICALS. EACH ISSUE HAS COMPLETE LISTING OF ONE WEEK'S CONTENTS OF PRAVDA AND IZVESTIA. TRANSLATIONS OCCUR ABOUT ONE MONTH AFTER PUBLICATION. A QUARTERLY SUBJECT INDEX IS ISSUED. BEGAN PUBLICATION IN 1949.

0058 CATALOGO GENERAL DE LA LIBRERIA ESPANOLA E HISPANOAMERICANA 1901-1930; AUTORES (5 VOLS., 1932-1951)
MADRID: CAMARAS OFFIC DEL LIBRO, 1951.
BIBLIOGRAPHY OF SPANISH-LANGUAGE BOOKS FROM SPAIN AND LATIN AMERICA. ENTRIES CLASSIFIED ALPHABETICALLY BY AUTHOR.

0059 "THE EMERGING COMMON MARKETS IN LATIN AMERICA."
FED. RES. BANK N.Y. MON. REV., 42 (SEPT. 60), 154-60.
DISCUSSES ECONOMIC INTEGRATION PROGRAM IN LATIN AMERICA. ANALYZES AGREEMENT TO ELIMINATE BARRIERS. APPRAISES STEPS TAKEN TO COORDINATE INDUSTRIAL DEVELOPMENT. CONSIDERS SIGNIFICANCE OF MONTEVIDEO TREATY IN DEVELOPMENT OF LATIN AMERICAN COMMON MARKET. PREDICTS INCREASE IN INVESTMENTS IN LATIN AMERICA.

0060 ARMS CONTROL.
DAEDALUS, 89 (FALL 60), 669-1075.
ESSAYS COVER PROBLEMS AND GOALS OF, AND PREREQUISITES FOR ARMS CONTROL. EXAMINE CHARACTER OF RECENT PROPOSALS AND AGREEMENTS. TREAT ARMS RACE, LIMITED WAR STRATEGY, ROLE OF SMALLER POWERS, INSPECTION TECHNIQUES, ARMS STABILIZATION, AND UNILATERAL DISARMAMENT.

0061 "CRITERIA FOR ALLOCATING INVESTMENT RESOURCES AMONG VARIOUS FIELDS OF DEVELOPMENT IN UNDERDEVELOPED ECONOMIES."
ECO. BUL. FOR ASIA & FAR EAST, 12 (JUNE 61), 30-44.
AN ANNOTATED BIBLIOGRAPHY OF 68 WORKS ON INVESTMENT CRITERIA AND TECHNIQUES FOR ALLOCATING INVESTMENT RESOURCES IN PLANNING THE DEVELOPMENT OF UNDERDEVELOPED ECONOMIES. INTRODUCTORY NOTE DESCRIBES MAIN FEATURES OF VARIOUS CRITERIA, INCLUDING THEIR EFFICIENCY, WEAKNESSES, AND RELATIONSHIPS AMONG THEM. ENTRIES SELECTED FROM SOURCES IN ENGLISH PUBLISHED BETWEEN 1946-60; TOPICALLY ARRANGED.

0062 "HIGHER EDUCATION AND ECONOMIC AND SOCIAL DEVELOPMENT IN LATIN AMERICA: A BIBLIOGRAPHY."
EDUCATION IN THE AMERICAS, 1 (1962), 1-39.
ANNOTATED SELECTION OF BOOKS AND ARTICLES. TOPICS INCLUDE SOCIO-ECONOMIC BACKGROUND OF HIGHER EDUCATION, LATIN AMERICAN UNIVERSITIES, UNIVERSITY AND ECONOMIC AND SOCIAL DEVELOPMENT, UNIVERSITY ASSOCIATIONS, INTERNATIONAL COOPERATION, DISCIPLINES OF STUDY, CONFERENCES, AND DIRECTORIES.

0063 ROUND TABLE ON EUROPE'S ROLE IN LATIN AMERICAN DEVELOPMENT.
BUENOS AIRES: INTER-AM DEV BANK, 1962, 88 PP.
TEXTS OF STATEMENTS BY PANELISTS AND EXTRACTS OF COMMENTS BY OTHER PARTICIPANTS IN THIRD MEETING OF BOARD OF GOVERNORS OF INTER-AMERICAN DEVELOPMENT BANK. ASSESSES ROLE OF EUROPE IN ECONOMIC DEVELOPMENT OF LATIN AMERICA, STIMULATING EXCHANGE OF IDEAS ON BEST WAY TO STRENGTHEN RELATIONS AND INCREASE EUROPE'S CONTRIBUTION.

0064 BRITISH AID.
LONDON: MIN OF OVERSEAS DEVEL, 1963, 260 PP.
OVERSEAS DEVELOPMENT INSTITUTE SURVEY OF BRITISH AID TO DEVELOPING COUNTRIES. COVERS BOTH GOVERNMENT AID AND PRIVATE CONTRIBUTIONS. CONTAINS SECTIONS ON FIELDS OF FINANCE, EDUCATION, AND TECHNICAL ASSISTANCE. HISTORICAL BACKGROUND ALSO OUTLINED.

0065 THE SPECIAL COMMONWEALTH AFRICAN ASSISTANCE PLAN.
LONDON: COMMONWEALTH ECO COMM, 1964, 75 PP.
REPORTS THREE YEARS' OPERATIONS OF SPECIAL COMMONWEALTH AFRICAN ASSISTANCE PLAN. NOTES BROADENING BASIS OF UK ASSISTANCE. SHOWS TREND TOWARD INCREASE OF HELP IN DEVELOPING NATIONS, PARTICULARLY IN AFRICA.

0066 AFRO ASIAN SOLIDARITY AGAINST IMPERIALISM.
PEKING: FOREIGN LANG PR, 1964, 439 PP.
DOCUMENTS, SPEECHES, AND PRESS INTERVIEWS FROM VISITS OF COMMUNIST CHINESE LEADERS TO 13 AFRICAN AND ASIAN COUNTRIES. INCLUDES PRINCIPALLY SPEECHES BY CHOU EN-LAI IN THE ARAB WORLD, EMERGING AFRICAN NATIONS, AND SOUTHEAST ASIA PERTAINING TO OVERTHROW OF "WESTERN IMPERIALISM" AND PROMOTION OF STATE SOVEREIGNTY.

0067 "FURTHER READING."
SEMINAR, (JUNE 64), 63-65.
BIBLIOGRAPHY ON KASHMIR AND "THE SUB-CONTINENTAL IMPLICATIONS OF A CRITICAL QUESTION."

0068 "FURTHER READING."
SEMINAR, (SEPT. 65), 43-46.
BIBLIOGRAPHY ON THE POLITICAL-ECONOMIC BASIS OF A GROWING ALLIANCE BETWEEN INDIA AND THE SOVIET UNION.

0069 "FURTHER READING."
SEMINAR, (MAY 65), 41-42.
BIBLIOGRAPHY "ON THE MANY FACETS OF... GOA'S CRISIS OF TRANSITION."

0070 ANALYSIS AND ASSESSMENT OF THE ECONOMIC EFFECTS: PUBLIC LAW 480 TITLE I PROGRAM TURKEY.
ANKARA: UNIV OF ANKARA, 1965, 525 PP.
EVALUATES TITLE I PROGRAM BETWEEN US AND INDIA SINCE 1954. REVIEWS TURKISH ECONOMIC POLICY FOR 40 YEARS PRIOR. TITLE I DEALS PRIMARILY WITH US LOANS TO HELP TURKS SET UP INDUSTRIAL AND AGRICULTURAL PROGRAMS, AND PROVIDES CERTAIN FOOD PRODUCTS. STUDY EMPHASIZES CONTROL AND DISTRIBUTION OF MONEY FROM US. COVERS IMPACT OF PROGRAM ON CITIES, PEOPLE, AND INTERNATIONAL SCENE.

0071 WHITE HOUSE CONFERENCE ON INTERNATIONAL COOPERATION(VOL.II)

WASHINGTON: NATL CITIZ COMN REP, 1965, 25 PP.
COMMITTEE REPORTS MADE AT 1965 WHITE HOUSE CONFERENCE. INCLUDED ARE REPORTS ON LABOR, MANPOWER, NATURAL RESOURCES, CONSERVATION AND DEVELOPMENT, ATOMIC ENERGY, PEACEKEEPING OPERATIONS, POPULATION, SCIENCE AND TECHNOLOGY, SOCIAL WELFARE, SPACE, TECHNICAL COOPERATION AND DEVELOPMENT, TRADE, TRANSPORATION, URBAN DEVELOPMENT, WOMEN, AND YOUTH ACTIVITIES.

0072 PEACE RESEARCH ABSTRACTS.
ONTARIO: CANADIAN PEACE RES INST, 1965.
MONTHLY PUBLICATION SINCE 1965, WHICH CONTAINS ABSTRACTS OF BOOKS AND ARTICLES. INCLUDES SUCH TOPICS AS DISARMAMENT, FALLOUT, AND ECONOMIC AID. APPROXIMATELY 12,000 ABSTRACTS PER YEAR.

0073 "RESEARCH WORK 1965-1966."
HIST. STUDIES OF AUSTRAL. N.Z., 12 (OCT. 66), 464-473.
AN UNANNOTATED BIBLIOGRAPHY OF THESES BEGUN AND/OR COMPLETED IN THE PERIOD 1965-66. MATERIAL IN ENGLISH-LANGUAGE. 180 ENTRIES. MATERIAL IN BIBLIOGRAPHY CONSISTS OF MA AND PHD THESES DIVIDED INTO TWO CATEGORIES RESEARCH WORK 1966 THESES COMMENCED AND RESEARCH WORK 1966, THESES COMPLETED 1965-66.

0074 "WORLD BANK CONVENTION ON INVESTMENT DISPUTES; A BIBLIOGRAPHICAL NOTE."
ARBITRATION JOURNAL, 21 (1966), 180-181.
AN UNANNOTATED BIBLIOGRAPHY OF IMPORTANT DOCUMENTS AND ARTICLES ON THE WORLD BANK. FOUR OFFICIAL DOCUMENTS LISTED INCLUDE REPORTS FROM THE EXECUTIVE DIRECTORS OF THE WORLD BANK, THE US SENATE, AND PRES. JOHNSON. NINE ARTICLES FROM AMERICAN AND FOREIGN JOURNALS LISTED ALPHABETICALLY BY AUTHOR. ENTRIES PUBLISHED IN 1965 AND 1966 IN ENGLISH, FRENCH, AND GERMAN. BRIEF EXPLANATION OF RESPONSIBILITIES OF BANK.

0075 "FURTHER READING."
SEMINAR, (APR. 64), 50-53.
BIBLIOGRAPHY "ON THE FUNDAMENTALS ON INDIA'S FOREIGN POLICY IN A CHANGED INTERNATIONAL SITUATION."

0076 BRITISH DEVELOPMENT POLICIES: 1966 (PAMPHLET)
LONDON: OVERSEAS DEVELOPMT INST, 1966, 85 PP.
FIRST OF OVERSEAS DEVELOPMENT INSTITUTE'S REVIEWS OF BRITISH POLICIES: AID, PRIVATE INVESTMENT, AND TRADE. SHOWS HOW BRITAIN'S PRESENT FINANCIAL DIFFICULTIES HAVE CAST A SHADOW OVER DEVELOPMENT OVERSEAS. PUTS FORWARD PRACTICAL STEPS THAT CAN BE TAKEN TO STRENGTHEN BRITISH CONTRIBUTIONS.

0077 SUPPLEMENTAL FOREIGN ASSISTANCE FISCAL YEAR 1966: VIETNAM.
WASHINGTON: GOVT PR OFFICE, 1966, 743 PP.
HEARINGS BEFORE COMMITTEE ON FOREIGN RELATIONS, US SENATE, IN SECOND SESSION OF 89TH CONGRESS. INCLUDES VERBATIM ACCOUNT OF SECOND SESSION, WITH FOCUS UPON US INVOLVEMENT IN VIETNAM.

0078 "CHINESE STATEMENT ON NUCLEAR PROLIFERATION."
BUL. ATOMIC SCIENTISTS, 23 (MAY 67), 53-54.
COMMUNIST CHINESE STATEMENT CONDEMNING THE PROPOSED NON-PROLIFERATION TREATY ON NUCLEAR WEAPONS. THE US AND USSR ARE SEEN AS ATTEMPTING TO KEEP A NUCLEAR MONOPOLY FOR THEIR OWN REASONS.

0079 "POLITICAL PARTIES ON FOREIGN POLICY IN THE INTER-ELECTION YEARS 1962-66."
INDIA Q., 23 (JAN.-MAR. 67), 47-75.
SUMMARIZES ATTITUDES OF VARIOUS POLITICAL PARTIES IN INDIA AS STATED IN THEIR DOCUMENTS, 1962-66, FROM TIME OF CHINESE ATTACK ON INDIA THROUGH CHINA'S DEVELOPMENT OF NUCLEAR WEAPONS.

0080 "RESTRICTIVE SOVEREIGN IMMUNITY, THE STATE DEPARTMENT, AND THE COURTS."
NORTHWESTERN U. LAW REVIEW, 62 (JULY-AUG.67), 397-427.
DISCUSSES 20TH-CENTURY APPLICATION OF DOCTRINES OF IMMUNITY. EXAMINES INTERRELATIONSHIP BETWEEN COURTS AND EXECUTIVE DEPARTMENT IN FIELD OF SOVEREIGN IMMUNITY, SHOWING EXTENT OF EXECUTIVE CONTROL OVER JUDICIARY. SEEKS TO DETERMINE WHETHER JUDICIAL DEFERENCE IS CONSONANT WITH ORIGINAL DOCTRINES, PRESENT CONCEPTS, OR RIGHTS OF AMERICANS. SUGGESTS SOVEREIGN IMMUNITY IS AN OUTDATED CONCEPT.

0081 PROLOG
DIGEST OF THE SOVIET UKRANIAN PRESS.
NEW YORK: PROLOG RES & PUB ASSN.
MONTHLY DIGEST IN ENGLISH SUMMARIZING SOVIET UKRANIAN NEWS RELEASES. FIRST PUBLISHED IN 1957, DIGEST CONTAINS EITHER FULL TEXT OF ORIGINAL OR EXCERPTS FROM ORIGINAL. PROVIDES BRIEF NOTES AT END OF EACH ISSUE AND PREFATORY COMMENTS WHEN NECESSARY. ANNUAL INDEX OF MAJOR UKRANIAN NEWSPAPERS AND PERIODICALS IS COMPILED EACH JANUARY. MATERIAL TOPICALLY ORGANIZED.

0082 ABOSCH H.
THE MENACE OF THE MIRACLE: GERMANY FROM HITLER TO ADENAUER.
LONDON: COLLET'S HOLDINGS, 1962, 277 PP.
ARGUES THAT "GERMAN PROBLEM" STILL IS NOT SOLVED, THAT ALLIES HAVE SUBSTITUTED "DESIRES FOR REALITIES," AND THAT GERMANY MOST LIKELY WILL LEAD US INTO THIRD WORLD WAR. CONDEMNS REARMAMENT OF GERMANY. OFFERS RECENT DEVELOPMENTS IN GERMAN DOMESTIC AND FOREIGN POLITICS AS CONCLUSIVE PROOF.

0083 ABSHIRE D.M. ED., ALLEN R.V. ED.
NATIONAL SECURITY: POLITICAL, MILITARY, AND ECONOMIC STRATEGIES IN THE DECADE AHEAD.
NEW YORK: PRAEGER, 1963, 1039 PP., $10.00.
A NUMBER OF SPECIALISTS IN INTERNATIONAL POLITICS AND SCIENCE ATTEMPT TO MAKE A SYSTEMATIC INQUIRY INTO CRITICAL CHOICES WHICH CONFRONT U.S. AND THE FREE WORLD IN THE NEXT TEN YEARS. COVERS SINO-SOVIET STRATEGY, POLITICAL REQUIREMENTS FOR U.S. STRATEGY, MILITARY STRATEGIES, ECONOMIC STRATEGIES, AND HOW STRATEGY REQUIREMENTS CAN BE MET WITHIN FRAMEWORK OF FREE ECONOMY. OUTLINES IN DETAIL THE RANGE OF ALTERNATIVES UPON WHICH OUR NATIONAL SECURITY MAY DEPEND.

0084 ABT J.J.
"WORLD OF SENATOR FULBRIGHT."
NEW WORLD REVIEW, 35 (JUNE 67), 9-12.
REVIEWS "THE ARROGANCE OF POWER" BY SENATOR FULBRIGHT, FROM A MARXIST-SOCIALIST STANDPOINT. STRESSES FULBRIGHT'S OPPOSITION TO VIETNAM, HIS TOLERATION OF COMMUNISM, BUT CONCLUDES THAT HE ONLY REPRESENTS ONE SEGMENT OF THE RULING CLASS WHICH IS "WILLING TO GIVE UP A CERTAIN PORTION OF THE LOOT TO PRESERVE THE REMAINDER." CALLS HIM A USEFUL ALLY IN SUPPORT OF PEACE.

0085 ACHESON D.A.
SKETCHES FROM LIFE.
NEW YORK: HARPER & ROW, 1961, 206 PP., LC#61-09701.
SKETCHES OF OUTSTANDING FIGURES IN INTERNATIONAL RELATIONS, WITH BRIEF ANALYSIS OF THEIR EFFECTS ON DIPLOMACY. INCLUDES ADENAUER, EDEN, CHURCHILL, SALAZAR.

0086 ADAMS A.E., MATLEY I.M., MCCAGG W.O.
AN ATLAS OF RUSSIAN AND EAST EUROPEAN HISTORY.
NEW YORK: FREDERICK PRAEGER, 1967, 204 PP., LC#66-18884.
COLLECTION OF MAPS GIVING BASIC GEOGRAPHIC AND DEMOGRAPHIC DATA ON EASTERN EUROPE AND RUSSIA. ALSO INCLUDES MAPS SHOWING POLITICAL AND SOCIAL CHANGES FROM THE FOURTH CENTURY UNTIL THE PRESENT.

0087 ADAMS V.
THE PEACE CORPS IN ACTION.
CHICAGO: FOLLETT PUBLISHING CO, 1964, 318 PP., LC#64-23606.
OBJECTIVE REPORT OF ORIGIN, ORGANIZATION, AND DEVELOPMENT OF PEACE CORPS. EMPHASIZES TYPE OF PEOPLE INVOLVED, THEIR GOALS, VALUES, ETC. INCLUDES CRITICISM AND NEGATIVE ASPECTS OF CORPS, BUT FEELS IT IS WORTHY TOOL OF FOREIGN POLICY.

0088 ADENAUER K.
MEMOIRS 1945-53.
CHICAGO: HENRY REGNERY CO, 1965, 478 PP., LC#65-26906.
TRANSLATION OF ADENAUER'S MEMOIRS FROM END OF WWII TO US VISIT IN 1953. EXAMINES RELATIONS WITH ALLIES AND OCCUPATION, ESTABLISHMENT OF FEDERAL REPUBLIC, FOREIGN POLICY, REARMAMENT, MEMBERSHIP IN NATO, AND FULL SOVEREIGNTY.

0089 ADENAUER K.
MEINE ERINNERUNGEN, 1945-53 (VOL. I), 1953-55 (VOL. II)
STUTTGART: DEUTSCHE VERLAGSANST, 1965, 1145 PP.
MEMOIRS OF KONRAD ADENAUER, BEGINNING WITH COLLAPSE OF GERMANY IN 1945, COVERING POSTWAR DEVELOPMENT OF GERMANY, PRIMARILY FROM PERSPECTIVES OF POLITICS AND INTERNATIONAL RELATIONS.

0090 ADIE W.A.C.
"CHINA'S 'SECOND LIBERATION'."
INTERNATIONAL AFF (UK) 43 (JULY 67), 439-454.
DESCRIBES MAOIST CULTURAL REVOLUTION AND ITS SIGNIFICANCE FOR OUTSIDE WORLD. REVEALS PARADOX AND OBSCURITY IN DOGMA AND IDEOLOGICAL STRUGGLE WITHIN PARTY. SUGGESTS THAT CHINESE SOCIETY HAS SUFFERED GREATLY FROM UPHEAVAL AND WILL NOT BE OF MUCH DANGER TO WEST ALTHOUGH LEADERS' POWERS SHOULD NOT BE UNDERESTIMATED.

0091 ADLER G.J.
BRITISH INDIA'S NORTHERN FRONTIER: 1865-95.
LONDON: LONGMANS, GREEN & CO, 1963, 392 PP.
DESCRIBES FORMATION AND EXECUTION OF BRITISH POLICY IN NORTHERN INDIA, AND REACTIONS TO THE THREAT OF ADVANCING IMPERIAL RUSSIA. TREATS EASTERN TURKISTAN, KASHMIR, AND TRIBAL TERRITORIES; UPPER OXUS FRONTIER OF AFGHANISTAN; THREE PAMIR CRISES; AND SETTLEMENT OF NORTHERN FRONTIER.

0092 ADLER M.J.
HOW TO THINK ABOUT WAR AND PEACE.
NEW YORK: SIMON SCHUSTER, 1944, 308 PP.
PRESENTS WAYS OF STIMULATING CITIZENS INTO THINKING ABOUT INTERNATIONAL PEACE-MAKING MEANS AND METHODS. ASSERTING THAT PEACE IS POSSIBLE, SUGGESTS MEANS TO SECURE PEACE. PREDICTS FUTURE TRENDS, AND CITES NEED FOR ESTABLISHMENT OF A WORLD ORGANIZATION TO PROMOTE WORLD PEACE.

0093 ADLER S.
THE ISOLATIONIST IMPULSE: ITS TWENTIETH-CENTURY REACTION.
NEW YORK: ABELARD-SCHUMAN, 1957, 538 PP., LC#57-5629.
DIPLOMATIC AND INTELLECTUAL HISTORY ANALYZES IMPACT OF ISOLATIONIST IDEAS AND ATTITUDES ON CONTEMPORARY AMERICAN FOREIGN POLICY. TRACES POST-WILSONIAN ISOLATIONIST THOUGHT. BRIEFLY EXAMINES HISTORICAL ROOTS OF ISOLATIONIST TRADITION THROUGH 1950'S.

0094 AFRICAN BIBLIOGRAPHIC CENTER
A CURRENT BIBLIOGRAPHY ON AFRICAN AFFAIRS.
WASHINGTON: AFRICAN BIBLIOG CTR.
BIMONTHLY EVALUATION AND REVIEWS OF CURRENT PUBLICATIONS FROM FOREIGN AND DOMESTIC PUBLISHING HOUSES. ALSO INCLUDES JOURNAL ARTICLES. ITEMS ARRANGED BY GENERAL SUBJECT AND BY GEOGRAPHICAL SUBJECT SECTION. AUTHOR INDEX. INCLUDES TOPICS SUCH AS AFRICAN STUDIES, BIBLIOGRAPHY, CIVILIZATION, COMMERCE, FOREIGN ECONOMIC ASSISTANCE, POLITICS AND GOVERNMENT, AND TECHNICAL ASSISTANCE.

0095 AFRICAN BIBLIOGRAPHIC CENTER
THE SCENE IS GUINEA AND THE PERSONAGE IS SEKOU TOURE: A SELECTED CURRENT READING LIST, 1959-1962 (PAMPHLET)
WASHINGTON: AFRICAN BIBLIOG CTR, 1963, 4 PP.
AN UNANNOTATED BIBLIOGRAPHY OF 59 BOOKS AND ARTICLES PUBLISHED BETWEEN 1959-62 CONCERNING GUINEA UNDER THE LEADERSHIP OF TOURE. ONE IN A SERIES OF SIX PAMPHLETS ABOUT NEW AFRICAN NATIONS ISSUED BY THE AFRICAN BIBLIOGRAPHIC CENTER. MAJORITY OF ARTICLES CITED FROM BRITISH AND AMERICAN PERIODICALS.

0096 AFRICAN BIBLIOGRAPHIC CENTER
THE SCENE IS KENYA AND THE PERSONAGE IS TOM MBOYA: A SELECTED CURRENT READING LIST FROM 1956-1962 (PAMPHLET)
WASHINGTON: AFRICAN BIBLIOG CTR, 1963, 4 PP.
AN UNANNOTATED BIBLIOGRAPHY OF 57 BOOKS, NEWSPAPER AND MAGAZINE ARTICLES PUBLISHED BETWEEN 1956-62 ABOUT KENYA UNDER THE RULE OF MBOYA. MOST SOURCES QUOTED ARE AMERICAN AND ENGLISH PERIODICALS, NOTABLY THE "ECONOMIST."

0097 AFRICAN BIBLIOGRAPHIC CENTER
"US TREATIES AND AGREEMENTS WITH COUNTRIES IN AFRICA, 1957 TO MID-1963."
AFR. BIBLIOG. CTR., SPEC. SERIES, 3 (JAN. 65), 1-13.
AN IRREGULARLY ISSUED PUBLICATION COVERING TREATIES AND AGREEMENTS PUBLISHED AND CURRENTLY IN PRINT ON AFRICA DURING PERIOD 1957-63. MULTILATERAL TREATIES EXCLUDED. BIBLIOGRAPHY CONTAINS 147 ENTRIES ARRANGED BY SUBJECT, THEN ALPHABETICALLY BY COUNTRY-TITLE, AND THEN CHRONOLOGICALLY BY DATE OF AGREEMENT. SUBJECT AND COUNTRY INDEX INCLUDED.

0098 AFRICAN BIBLIOGRAPHIC CENTER
"A CURRENT VIEW OF AFRICANA: A SELECT AND ANNOTATED BIBLIOGRAPHICAL PUBLISHING GUIDE, 1965-1966."
AFR. BIBLIOG. CTR., SPEC. SERIES, 4 (JULY 66), 1-17.
ANNOTATED BIBLIOGRAPHICAL COLLECTION INTENDED TO COLLATE A WIDE RANGE OF TITLES PUBLISHED BY US AND FOREIGN PUBLISHING HOUSES OVER TWO-YEAR PERIOD, 1965-66, IN FIELD OF AFRICAN STUDIES. COLLECTION OF 73 ENTRIES ARRANGED BY PUBLISHER, AUTHOR INDEX, TITLE, AND SUBJECT INDEX. COMPLETE BIBLIOGRAPHICAL INFORMATION PLUS DESCRIPTIVE ANNOTATIONS.

0099 AFRICAN BIBLIOGRAPHIC CENTER
"A DESCRIPTIVE STUDY OF CURRENT AFRICAN FOREIGN RELATIONS."
AFR. BIBLIOG. CTR., CUR. RDG., 4 (1966), 1-8.
UNANNOTATED BIBLIOGRAPHICAL STUDY OF BACKGROUND INFORMATION ON CURRENT ASPECTS OF FOREIGN POLICY DECISIONS BY AND BETWEEN AFRICAN NATIONS. LISTS 43 ENTRIES IN GENERAL READING SELECTIONS, AND TREATIES AND AGREEMENTS MADE DURING JANUARY AND FEBRUARY, 1966, WITH A RESUME OF EACH TREATY. GEOGRAPHICAL APPENDIX INCLUDED.

0100 AFRICAN BIBLIOGRAPHIC CENTER
"THE NEW AFRO-ASIAN STATES IN PERSPECTIVE, 1960-1963: A SELECT BIBLIOGRAPHY."
AFR. BIBLIOG. CTR., CUR. RDG., 3 (1966), 1-20.
UNANNOTATED BIBLIOGRAPHY OF RECENT BOOKS AND ARTICLES PUBLISHED BETWEEN 1960-63 ON GENERAL INFORMATION ABOUT THE NEW AFRO-ASIAN NATIONS. CONTAINS 230 ENTRIES, MOSTLY IN ENGLISH, WITH RUSSIAN TITLES TRANSLITERATED. TOPICS INCLUDE LABOR, FOREIGN INVESTMENTS, THE UN, AND SCIENTIFIC DEVELOPMENTS. AUTHOR INDEX APPENDED TO BIBLIOGRAPHY.

0101 AFRICAN BIBLIOGRAPHIC CENTER
"THE SWORD AND GOVERNMENT: A PRELIMINARY AND SELECTED BIBLIOGRAPHICAL GUIDE TO AFRICAN MILITARY AFFAIRS; PART I."
AFR. BIBLIOG. CTR., CUR. RDG., 5 (APR. 67), 1-5.
A DESCRIPTIVELY ANNOTATED BIBLIOGRAPHY OF 65 BOOKS, ARTICLES, AND PAMPHLETS RELATING TO THE AFRICAN MILITARY IN A BROAD OR SPECIFIC SCOPE. SOURCES IN FRENCH AND ENGLISH PUBLISHED BETWEEN 1962-66. TOPICALLY ORGANIZED.

0102 AHLUWALIA K.
THE LEGAL STATUS, PRIVILEGES AND IMMUNITIES OF SPECIALIZED AGENCIES OF UN AND CERTAIN OTHER INTERNATIONAL ORGANIZATIONS
THE HAGUE: MARTINUS NIJHOFF, 1964, 230 PP.
FACTUAL STUDY OF PRIVILEGES AND IMMUNITIES IN INTERNATIONAL LAW. DISCUSSES LEGAL STATUS OF ARMED FORCES IN FOREIGN COUNTRIES, PUBLIC VESSELS, AND DIPLOMATIC AGENTS. INCLUDES UN ORGANIZATIONS, OFFICIALS AND REPRESENTATIVES OF MEMBER STATES, AND RIGHTS OF HOST STATES TO EXPEL VISITING EXPERTS.

0103 AIR FORCE ACADEMY ASSEMBLY '59
INTERNATIONAL STABILITY AND PROGRESS (PAMPHLET)
COLORADO SPRINGS: USAF ACADEMY, 1959, 96 PP.
REPORT OF 1959 CONFERENCE TO DISCUSS QUESTIONS OF FOREIGN ASSISTANCE. CONCLUDES THAT MILITARY ASSISTANCE PROGRAMS HAVE HELPED CREATE AND MAINTAIN A SUBSTANTIALLY LARGER AND MORE EFFECTIVE DEFENSE POSTURE AROUND USSR THAN A SIMILAR DOLLAR INVESTMENT IN US'S OWN DEFENSE ESTABLISHMENT COULD HAVE PRODUCED. SUGGESTS EFFORTS BE MADE TO CREATE PUBLIC UNDERSTANDING OF PROGRAM.

0104 AIR FORCE ACADEMY LIBRARY
INTERNATIONAL ORGANIZATIONS AND MILITARY SECURITY SYSTEMS (PAMPHLET) (SPECIAL BIBLIOGRAPHY SERIES, NUMBER 25)
COLORADO SPRINGS: USAF ACADEMY, 1962, 28 PP.
SELECTED LIST OF ABOUT 220 ITEMS ON THIS SUBJECT HELD BY USAF ACADEMY LIBRARY. COVERS VARIOUS INTERNATIONAL ORGANIZATIONS, WITH MOST EMPHASIS GIVEN TO UN. ARRANGED BY ORGANIZATION TREATED; SUBDIVIDED INTO BOOKS, PERIODICALS, AND GOVERNMENT DOCUMENTS. ALL IN ENGLISH. INDICATES SOURCES OF ADDITIONAL INFORMATION.

0105 AIR UNIVERSITY LIBRARY
INDEX TO MILITARY PERIODICALS.
MONTGOMERY: MAXWELL AFB.
QUARTERLY SINCE 1949, SUPERSEDED BY ANNUAL AND TRIENNIAL CUMULATIVE ISSUES. INDEXES SIGNIFICANT ARTICLES, NEWS ITEMS, AND EDITORIALS APPEARING IN 70 MILITARY AND AERONAUTICAL PERIODICALS. ALL ENTRIES IN ENGLISH. ITEMS ARRANGED BY SUBJECT AND BY COUNTRY.

0106 AIR UNIVERSITY LIBRARY
LATIN AMERICA, SELECTED REFERENCES.
MONTGOMERY: AIR U, 1965, 43 PP.
ITEMS ARRANGED BY TYPE OF PUBLICATION: BOOKS, PERIODICALS, DOCUMENTS - UNDER SUBJECT HEADINGS. TREATS SOURCES ON OAS, COMMUNISM IN LATIN AMERICA, ECONOMICS, ROLE OF THE MILITARY, POLITICS, GOVERNMENT, AND EDUCATION.

0107 ALBERTINI L.
THE ORIGINS OF THE WAR OF 1914 (3 VOLS.)
LONDON: OXFORD U PR, 1952, 2111 PP.
DISCUSSES BACKGROUND, REMOTE CAUSES, AND OBVIOUS PRELUDES TO OUTBREAK OF WWI: EUROPEAN RELATIONS FROM THE CONGRESS OF BERLIN TO THE SARAJEVO MURDER. INCLUDES EXHAUSTIVE ACCOUNT OF EVENTS AT SARAJEVO AND OF RUSSIAN, AUSTRIAN, AND FRENCH MOBILIZATIONS. RECORDS VARIOUS DECLARATIONS OF WAR AND NEUTRALITY, AND MACHINATIONS OF EUROPEAN ALLIANCES.

0108 ALBONETTI A.
"IL SECONDO PROGRAMMA QUINQUENNALE 1963-67 ED IL BILANCIO RICERCHE ED INVESTIMENTI PER IL 1963 DELL'ERATOM."
DR. ECON. NUCL., 4 (NO.2, 62), 163-78.
HISTORICAL APPROACH TO QUESTION OF DEVELOPMENT OF RESEARCH INSTITUTE. DEALS WITH NEW PROGRAM PLANS AND RELATES THEM TO ITALIAN ECONOMY. POINTS OUT OTHER NATIONS' NUCLEAR POWER POLITICS.

0109 ALBRECHT-CARRIE R.
FRANCE, EUROPE AND THE TWO WORLD WARS.
GENEVA: LIBRAIRIE DROZ, 1960, 339 PP.
COVERS FRENCH AND EUROPEAN POLITICAL DEVELOPMENTS, FROM 1914 TO 1936. CONSIDERS THE RELATIONSHIP BETWEEN THE FRENCH DOMESTIC SITUATION AND THE FOREIGN POLICY OF FRANCE. EMPHASIZES THE EFFECTS OF WWI AND BETWEEN-WAR FRENCH POLICIES, AND HOW THE FRENCH PEOPLE WOULD NOT FACE THE UNPLEASANT REALITIES OF DEMOCRATIC POWER.

0110 ALBRECHT-CARRIE R.
THE MEANING OF THE FIRST WORLD WAR.
ENGLEWOOD CLIFFS: PRENTICE HALL, 1965, 181 PP., LC#65-13180.
ATTEMPTS TO EXPLAIN IN WHAT SENSE AND IN WHAT MANNER WWI CONSTITUTED A DEFINITIVE BREAK WITH THE PAST, AND THE PASSING OF THE EUROPEAN ERA. EMPHASIZES EUROPEAN SETTING OF WAR, AND INTERNATIONAL RELATIONS. FOCUSES ON THE 50-YEAR PERIOD PRIOR TO OUTBREAK OF WAR IN ORDER TO UNDERSTAND MAIN CURRENTS OF THAT PAST.

0111 ALEXANDER L.M.
WORLD POLITICAL PATTERNS.
SKOKIE: RAND MCNALLY & CO, 1957, 516 PP., LC#57-8445.
ANALYSIS OF COMPLEX PATTERNS OF POLITICAL ORGANIZATION THROUGHOUT WORLD ON CONTINENTAL, NATIONAL, AND LOCAL LEVELS. ATTEMPTS TO DETERMINE INFLUENCE OF NATIONALISM, IMPERIALISM, AND OTHER SOCIO-POLITICAL FORCES ON PATTERN OF POLITICAL CONTROL OF VARIOUS GEOGRAPHIC REGIONS. PROVIDES INTRODUCTION TO GEOGRAPHIC BASIS OF INTERNATIONAL AFFAIRS. PRIMARILY INTENDED FOR STUDENTS.

0112 ALEXANDER R.
"LATIN AMERICA AND THE COMMUNIST BLOC."
CURR. HIST., 44 (FEB. 63), 73-77.
CONCLUDES ONLY CUBA HAS MOVED OVER TO COMMUNIST CAMP. DESIRE FOR GREATER INDEPENDENCE OF MANY LATIN-AMERICAN COUNTRIES HAS LED TO RELAXING OF BONDS WHICH HAVE TIED THESE NATIONS TO USA. IN SPITE OF CUBA, LATIN AMERICA, ON THE WHOLE, MAINTAINS RELATIVELY TENUOUS CONNECTIONS WITH COMMUNIST BLOC. JACOBIN LEFT (CASTRO), HOWEVER, HAS STRENGTHENED INFLUENCE OF SOVIET UNION.

0113 ALEXANDROWICZ C.H., ED.
A BIBLIOGRAPHY OF INDIAN LAW.
LONDON: OXFORD U PR, 1958, 69 PP.
ARRANGED BY TYPE OF SOURCE AND TYPE OF LAW WITH AN ANNOTATED INTRODUCTION DESCRIBING GENERAL MATERIALS AND SECONDARY SOURCES. INDEX TO AUTHORS AND DIRECTORY OF PUBLISHERS CONCLUDE BOOK. MANY ITEMS IN ENGLISH.

0114 ALEXANDROWICZ C.H.
INTERNATIONAL ECONOMIC ORGANIZATION.
LONDON: STEVENS, 1952, 263 PP.
VIEWS PERMANENT INTERNATIONAL ORGANIZATIONS FOR THEIR NATIONAL AND INTERNATIONAL PURPOSE. STRESSES THAT INTER-CONNECTED ACTIVITIES OF PRIVATE AND PUBLIC AGENCIES REQUIRE CONSIDERATION OF BOTH LAW AND ECONOMICS.

0115 ALEXANDROWICZ C.H.
WORLD ECONOMIC AGENCIES: LAW AND PRACTICE.
LONDON: STEVENS, 1962, 310 PP.
DISCUSSES FORMATION AND OPERATION OF WORLD ECONOMIC AGENCIES AS THEY INFLUENCE INTERNATIONAL LAW. EMPHASIZES INTERNAL STRUCTURE OF ORGANIZATIONS, DISTRIBUTION OF POWER, CONSEQUENCES OF UNIVERSAL MEMBERSHIP, LAW-PROMOTING FUNCTIONS, AND SIGNIFICANCE OF ADMINISTRATIVE PROCEDURES AND JUSTICE.

0116 ALFIERI D.
DICTATORS FACE TO FACE.
NEW YORK: NEW YORK U PR, 1955, 307 PP., LC#56-5399.
PERSONAL ACCOUNT BY ITALIAN AMBASSADOR TO HITLER OF MAJOR EVENTS AND ISSUES MARKING WARTIME RELATIONSHIPS BETWEEN GERMANY AND ITALY. DESCRIBES EVENTS DURING SEVERAL MAJOR MILITARY AND DIPLOMATIC DEVELOPMENTS AND FOCUSES ON ATTITUDES AND BEHAVIOR OF HITLER, MUSSOLINI, AND HIGH-RANKING STATESMEN AND MILITARY LEADERS.

0117 ALGER C.F.
"NON-RESOLUTION CONSEQUENCES OF THE UNITED NATIONS AND THEIR EFFECT ON INTERNATIONAL CONFLICT."
J. CONFL. RESOLUT., 5 (JUNE 61), 128-46.
ANALYZES CHARACTERISTICS OF GENERAL ASSEMBLY. AIMS TO PROVIDE DIRECTION FOR RESEARCH ON THE EFFECT OF THE UN AND OTHER INTERNATIONAL ORGANIZATIONS ON INTERNATIONAL RELATIONS.

0118 ALGER C.F.
"THE EXTERNAL BUREAUCRACY IN UNITED STATES FOREIGN AFFAIRS."
ADMIN. SCI. QUART., 7 (JUNE 62), 50-78.
ANALYSIS CONCLUDES THAT BASIC FUNCTION OF BUREAUCRATS IS COMMUNICATION OF INFORMATION AND PERSPECTIVES FROM COUNTRY OF PLACEMENT TO BUREAUCRATIC CENTER AND VICE VERSA.

0119 ALGER C.F.
"HYPOTHESES ON RELATIONSHIPS BETWEEN THE ORGANIZATION OF INTERNATIONAL SOCIETY AND INTERNATIONAL ORDER."
PROC. AMER. SOC. INT. LAW, (1963), 36-46.
ATTEMPTS TO COMBINE PERSPECTIVES AND HYPOTHESES OF INTERNATIONAL LAW AND OF SOCIAL SCIENCE IN SEARCH OF THE ORIGINS AND DYNAMICS OF THE RULE OF LAW.

0120 ALGER C.F.
"UNITED NATIONS PARTICIPATION AS A LEARNING EXPERIENCE."
PUB. OPIN. QUART., 27 (FALL 63), 411-26.
INVESTIGATION OF THE IMPACT OF PARTICIPATION IN THE UN UPON NATIONAL REPRESENTATIVES WITH RESPECT TO THEIR ATTITUDES ABOUT THE OPERATION OF THE UN, ABOUT PARTICULAR ISSUES, PARTICULAR NATIONS, AND THEIR SUBSEQUENT BEHAVIOR.

0121 ALIGHIERI D.
ON WORLD GOVERNMENT.
INDIANAPOLIS: BOBBS-MERRILL, 1957, 80 PP.
SETS FORTH DOCTRINE OF WORLD POLITICS AND GOVERNMENT CONSISTING OF THREE FUNDAMENTAL THESES: FIRST, CONCEPT OF WORLD UNITY ADVOCATING POLITICAL SUBORDINATION OF ALL KINGDOMS AND REPUBLICS TO ONE SOVEREIGN RULE; SECOND, INDEPENDENCE OF HEAD OF STATE FROM CONTROL OF RELIGIOUS AUTHORITY; AND THIRD, ESSENTIAL ROMAN NATURE OF UNIVERSAL STATE BASED ON ROMAN CORPUS JURIS.

0122 ALIX C.
LE SAINT-SIEGE ET LES NATIONALISMES EN EUROPE 1870-1960.
PARIS: EDITIONS SIREY, 1962, 367 PP.
CONCERNS ATTITUDE OF CATHOLIC CHURCH TOWARD VARIOUS FORMS OF NATIONALISM. DISCUSSES GENERAL ATTITUDES, THEN SPECIFIC CASES - NATIONALISM WITH REGARD TO CHURCH IN AUSTRO-HUNGARIAN EMPIRE, IN IRELAND, IN COMMUNIST AND FASCIST COUNTRIES, ETC.

0123 ALLEN H.C.
THE ANGLO-AMERICAN PREDICAMENT: THE BRITISH COMMONWEALTH, THE UNITED STATES AND EUROPEAN UNITY.
NEW YORK: ST. MARTINS, 1960, 241 PP.
SUGGESTS THAT ONLY AN ATLANTIC UNION INCLUDING NORTH AMERICA, AUSTRALIA AND WESTERN EUROPE CAN SUSTAIN THE UNITED KINGDOM'S POSITION IN 20TH CENTURY WORLD AFFAIRS. MAINTAINS THAT ONLY SUCH A UNION WILL ENSURE WESTERN VICTORY OVER INTERNATIONAL COMMUNISM.

0124 ALLEN R.L.
"UNITED NATIONS TECHNICAL ASSISTANCE: SOVIET AND EAST-EUROPEAN PARTICIPATION."
INT. ORGAN., 11 (AUTUMN 57), 615-634.
DEALS WITH ENTRY (1953) OF SOVIET UNION INTO U.N. TECHNICAL-ASSISTANCE PROGRAM. CITES REASONS FOR PARTICIPAION AND EVALUATES USEFULNESS OF CONTRIBUTION. DEMONSTRATES CHIEF DIFFICULTY TO BE NON-CONVERTIBILITY OF RUBLES, MAKING ADMINISTRATION OF FUNDS COMPLICATED. WARNS AGAINST POLITICAL EXPLOITATION OF SOVIET 'CONTRIBUTIONS'.

0125 ALLEN R.L.
SOVIET INFLUENCE IN LATIN AMERICA.
WASHINGTON: PUBL. AFF. PR., 1959, 108 PP.
DURING THE POST-WAR PERIOD, THE INCREASED RUSSIAN-LATIN AMERICAN TRADE HAS LED TO INCREASED SOVIET INFLUENCE OVER LATIN AMERICAN NATIONS' AFFAIRS. WITHOUT EMPHASIZING THE POLITICAL ASPECTS OF THE RELATIONSHIP, GIVES A DETAILED ANALYSIS OF THE INCREASED TRADE OVER THE PAST DECADE.

0126 ALLEN R.L.
SOVIET ECONOMIC WARFARE.
WASHINGTON: PUB. AFF. PR., 1960, 293 PP., $5.00.
PRESENTS THE MAJOR FEATURES OF RUSSIAN ECONOMIC RELATIONS WITH FOREIGN COUNTRIES. GIVES A CONCEPTUAL FRAMEWORK FOR SYSTEMATIC ECONOMIC ANALYSIS OF GOVERNMENT TRADING, WITHIN THE PURVIEW OF ECONOMIC AND TECHNICAL ASSISTANCE. CONCLUDES THAT PRIVATE INVESTMENT IN FOREIGN TRADE PROMOTES HUMAN VALUES.

0127 ALLEN W.R. ED., ALLEN C.L. ED.
FOREIGN TRADE AND FINANCE.
NEW YORK: MACMILLAN, 1959, 500 PP., LC#59-7442.
ESSAYS DISCUSSING PROBLEMS IN INTERNATIONAL ECONOMIC EQUILIBRIUM AND THEIR RELATION TO GENERAL POLICY ISSUES IN TRADE AND FINANCE PROBLEMS. DISCUSS RELATIONSHIP BETWEEN DOMESTIC AND INTERNATIONAL EQUILIBRIUM AND MEANS OF ADJUSTMENT TO EQUILIBRIUM. EMPHASIZE ANALYTICAL APPROACH TO SPECIFIC PROBLEMS BUT ARE NOT TECHNICAL OR DETAILED. DIRECTED TOWARD STUDENTS AND NONSPECIALISTS.

0128 ALMEYDA M.C.
REFLEXIONES POLITICAS.
SANTIAGO: PRENSA LATINO AMER, 1958, 135 PP.
ANALYSIS OF INTERNATIONAL AND CHILEAN NATIONAL PROBLEMS. EXAMINES ECONOMY OF CHILE AND RELATION TO LATIN AMERICA AND US. DISCUSSION OF INTERNAL CONFLICT AMONG VARIOUS POLITICAL GROUPS AND OUTLOOK FOR FUTURE NATIONAL DEVELOPMENT.

0129 ALMOND G.A.
THE AMERICAN PEOPLE AND FOREIGN POLICY.
NEW YORK: HARCOURT BRACE, 1950, 269 PP.
STRUCTURAL ANALYSIS OF AMERICAN ATTITUDES TOWARD FOREIGN POLICY. DESCRIBES ENVIRONMENT IN WHICH AMERICANS MAKE FOREIGN POLICY DECISIONS, HISTORIC TRENDS OF CULTURE AND CHARACTER IN US, AND SHIFTS IN MASS ATTITUDES SINCE WWII AND THEIR DISTRIBUTION IN SOCIAL STRUCTURE. MAINTAINS THAT DEMOCRATIC IDEAL FALLS SHORT IN FOREIGN POLICY-MAKING AND STUDIES ELITE STRUCTURE THAT MAKES DECISIONS.

0130 ALPHAND H.
"FRANCE AND HER ALLIES."
ORBIS, 7 (SPRING 63), 17-31.
CLARIFIES FRENCH POLICY IN FACE OF NEW PROBLEMS OF THERMONUCLEAR AGE. NATIONAL DEFENSE POLICY RESTS ON ALLIANCE AND ECONOMIC AND POLITICAL INTERDEPENDENCE. JUSTIFIES NECESSITY OF INDEPENDENT NUCLEAR FORCE. CLARIFIES REJECTION OF BRITISH CANDIDATURE IN COMMON MARKET AS SAFEGUARD OF SPIRIT AND LETTER OF EXISTING TREATIES BRITAIN WISHED TO MODIFY.

0131 ALTHING F.A.M.
EUROPEAN ORGANIZATIONS AND FOREIGN RELATIONS OF STATES: A COMPARATIVE ANALYSIS OF DECISION-MAKING.
LEYDEN: AW SIJTHOFF, 1962, 290 PP.
STUDY OF FIVE EUROPEAN ORGANIZATIONS, DECISION-MAKING IN THESE ORGANIZATIONS, AND IMPACT ON MEMBER STATES' FOREIGN POLICY. VIEWS INTEGRATION AS PROCESS IN WHICH DECISION-MAKING STRUCTURES OF EUROPEAN BODIES ARE SUBSTITUTED FOR THOSE PROVIDED FOR IN CONSTITUTIONS OF MEMBER STATES.

0132 ALVIM J.C.
A REVOLUCAO SEM RUMO.
RIO DE JANEIRO: EDICOES DO VAL, 1964, 92 PP.
ANALYZES BRAZILIAN NEED FOR REVOLUTION TO GAIN PROGRESS

IN UNDEVELOPED NATION. EXAMINES REASONS BEHIND 1964 REVOLT AND NEED TO REFORM BRAZIL TO ACHIEVE SOCIAL AND ECONOMIC BALANCE NATIONALLY AND INTERNATIONALLY. DISCUSSES FAULTS OF NEW GOVERNMENT IN OVERLY LIMITING DEMOCRACY IN ATTEMPT TO RESTORE ORDER.

0133 ALWAN M.
ALGERIA BEFORE THE UNITED NATIONS.
NEW YORK: SPELLER, 1959, 120 PP.
PRESENTS ALGERIAN CASE FOR INDEPENDENCE FROM FRANCE WHO HAS LOOKED UPON ALGERIA AS AN INTEGRAL PART OF HER METROPOLITAN TERRITORY IN CONTRAST TO COLONY. FRENCH REFUSAL TO ABIDE BY PRINCIPLES OF UN CHARTER IN SOLVING ALGERIAN ISSUE HAS STRAINED HER RELATIONS WITH AFRO-ASIAN COUNTRIES. SUGGESTS IMMEDIATE NEGOTIATIONS BASED ON PRINCIPLE OF SELF-DETERMINATION AS ONLY REAL AND HONORABLE SOLUTION. ANALYZES BLOC VOTING IN UN ON DRAFT RESOLUTIONS.

0134 AMER COUNCIL OF LEARNED SOCIET
THE ACLS CONSTITUENT SOCIETY JOURNAL PROJECT.
NEW YORK: AMER COUN LEARNED SOC.
AMERICAN COUNCIL OF LEARNED SOCIETIES IS ESTABLISHING A BIBLIOGRAPHICAL DATA PROCESSING CENTER IN CONJUNCTION WITH NYU'S INSTITUTE FOR COMPUTER RESEARCH IN THE HUMANITIES. ONE OF FIRST PROJECTS IS COMPILATION OF ABSTRACTS FROM LEADING JOURNALS IN THE SOCIAL SCIENCES AND HUMANITIES. DATA WILL BE PROCESSED TO PRODUCE ANNUAL INDEX OF CONSTITUENT SOCIETY JOURNALS AND SPECIALIZED INDEXES.

0135 AMERICAN ASSEMBLY
THE UNITED STATES AND THE MIDDLE EAST.
ENGEWOOD CLIFFS: PRENTICE HALL, 1964, 182 PP.
TREATS RADICAL CHANGES IN ISLAMIC THINKING, EDUCATIONAL REVOLUTION, REGIONAL POLITICS AND ISRAEL'S POSITION IN THE MIDDLE EAST. TRACES DEVELOPMENT OF USA POLICY IN THAT AREA AND CURRENT POLICY PROBLEMS.

0136 AMERICAN ASSEMBLY COLUMBIA U
THE SECRETARY OF STATE.
ENGLEWOOD CLIFFS: PRENTICE HALL, 1960, 200 PP., LC#60-53378.
STUDIES ROLE OF SECRETARY, HOW THIS OFFICE HAS DEVELOPED AND CHANGED WITH NATURE OF INTERNATIONAL RELATIONS, PERSONAL AND OFFICIAL RELATIONS WITH PRESIDENT, DEALINGS WITH CONGRESS, PRESSURE GROUPS, AND PUBLIC.

0137 AMERICAN ASSEMBLY COLUMBIA U
A WORLD OF NUCLEAR POWERS?
NEW YORK: COLUMBIA U PRESS, 1966, 176 PP., LC#66-29073.
STUDY OF POSSIBLE PROLIFERATION OF NUCLEAR NATIONS IN FUTURE. NON-NUCLEAR POWERS' REPRESENTATIVES ANALYZE PROBLEMS, COSTS, TECHNOLOGICAL POSSIBILITY OF NUCLEAR POWER'S SPREADING, AND EFFECT ON INTERNATIONAL RELATIONS, SUGGESTING METHOD TO PREVENT SPREAD EVEN WITHOUT ARMS CONTROL.

0138 AMERICAN ASSEMBLY COLUMBIA U
THE UNITED STATES AND THE PHILIPPINES.
ENGLEWOOD CLIFFS: PRENTICE HALL, 1966, 179 PP., LC#66-22802.
SEVEN ESSAYS ANALYZING "SPECIAL RELATIONSHIP" EXISTING BETWEEN THE TWO NATIONS: COLONIAL RELATIONSHIP, PHILIPPINE SOCIETY IN TRANSITION, PHILIPPINE FOREIGN POLICY, MUTUAL SECURITY, ROLE OF AMERICAN INVESTMENT AND TRADE, AND THE PROBLEMS OF DECOLONIALIZATION.

0139 AMERICAN ASSOCIATION LAW LIB
INDEX TO FOREIGN LEGAL PERIODICALS.
LONDON: U LON, INST ADVAN LEG ST, 1960.
MAKES AVAILABLE CONTENTS OF MAIN LEGAL PERIODICALS DEALING WITH INTERNATIONAL LAW, COMPARATIVE, AND MUNICIPAL LAW OF ALL COUNTRIES EXCLUDING US AND UK. THREE QUARTERLY PARTS WERE ISSUED DURING 1960, FOLLOWED BY ANNUAL BOUND VOLUME. LEGAL ARTICLES ARE INDEXED IF AT LEAST FOUR PAGES IN LENGTH. LISTS 253 REVIEWS. INCLUDES 51 COUNTRIES.

0140 AMERICAN BIBLIOGRAPHIC SERVICE
INTERNATIONAL GUIDE TO INDIC STUDIES - A QUARTERLY INDEX TO PERIODICAL LITERATURE.
DARIEN, CONN: AMER BIBLIOGRAPHIC SERVICE
BIBLIOGRAPHIC INFORMATION CLASSIFIED UNDER 3 HEADINGS: CURRENT ARTICLES AND MINOR PUBLICATIONS (SOURCES PUBLICATION IDENTIFIED); SUBJECT-INDEX IN WHICH MAJOR TOPICS AND PERSONALITIES ARE INDEXED MAINLY IN ENGLISH; AND A REVIEW-INDEX IN WHICH MAJOR REVIEW ARTICLES ARE INDEXED BY AUTHOR, EDITOR OR TRANSLATOR. FIRST VOLUME PUBLISHED IN JUNE 1963. PERTINENT LANGUAGES RETAINED.

0141 AMERICAN BIBLIOGRAPHIC SERVICE
QUARTERLY CHECKLIST OF ORIENTAL STUDIES.
DARIEN, CONN: AMER BIBLIOGRAPHIC SERVICE
INTERNATIONAL SURVEY OF NEW AND RECENT PUBLICATIONS (INCLUDING PAPERBACKS, REVISED EDITIONS, REPRINTS AND TRANSLATIONS) IN ENGLISH, FRENCH, GERMAN, AND WESTERN LANGUAGES. CITES AVAILABLE BIBLIOGRAPHIC AND PURCHASING INFORMATION BUT NO ANNOTATIONS. CONTAINS INDEX OF AUTHORS, EDITORS AND TRANSLATORS. INCLUDES ABOUT 850 LISTINGS PER VOLUME. FIRST PUBLISHED 1957.

0142 AMERICAN BIBLIOGRAPHICAL CTR
LIST OF PERIODICALS: AMERICA:HISTORY AND LIFE AND HISTORICAL ABSTRACTS (BIBLIOGRAPHY AND REFERENCE SERIES NO. 3)
SANTA BARBARA: CLIO, 1967, 16 PP., LC#67-20727.
LIST OF PERIODICALS USED BY THE AMERICAN BIBLIOGRAPHICAL CENTER IN ITS TWO PUBLICATIONS, "AMERICA: HISTORY AND LIFE" AND "HISTORICAL ABSTRACTS." INCLUDES FOREIGN PERIODICALS IN MANY LANGUAGES. ENTRIES LISTED BY GEOGRAPHICAL REGION.

0143 AMERICAN DOCUMENTATION INST
DOCUMENTATION ABSTRACTS.
WASHINGTON: AMER DOCUMENT INST.
QUARTERLY, FIRST PUBLISHED MARCH 1966, CONTAINS ABSTRACTS FROM CURRENT BOOKS, PAPERS, GOVERNMENT DOCUMENTS, AND RESEARCH PERTAINING TO INFORMATION RETRIEVAL. ENTRIES ARRANGED BY SUBJECT. INCLUDES REGIONAL, NATIONAL, AND INTERNATIONAL PROGRAMS, INFORMATION SYSTEMS AND TECHNIQUES, COMPUTERS, EQUIPMENT, ETC. MAJORITY ENGLISH-LANGUAGE SOURCES; SOME EUROPEAN.

0144 AMERICAN ECONOMIC ASSOCIATION
THE JOURNAL OF ECONOMIC ABSTRACTS.
EVANSTON, ILL: AMER ECO ASSOC.
FIRST PUBLISHED IN 1963, THIS JOURNAL IS DESIGNED TO ASSIST ECONOMISTS AROUND THE WORLD IN BECOMING ACQUAINTED WITH METHOD AND CONCLUSIONS OF RECENT RESEARCH REPORTED IN GENERAL ECONOMIC JOURNALS. PUBLISHED QUARTERLY. ABSTRACTS SELECTED ON AN INTERNATIONAL SCOPE. SUMMARY CLASSIFIED TOPICALLY.

0145 AMERICAN ECONOMIC ASSOCIATION
INDEX OF ECONOMIC JOURNALS 1886-1965 (7 VOLS.)
HOMEWOOD: RICHARD IRWIN, 1965, 2200 PP.
INDEX COVERING ENGLISH-LANGUAGE ARTICLES IN MAJOR ECONOMIC JOURNALS PUBLISHED BETWEEN 1886 AND 1965. INCLUDES CLASSIFIED INDEX IN WHICH MATERIAL IS ARRANGED BY SUBJECT; CONTAINS AN AUTHOR INDEX.

0146 AMERICAN ECONOMIC REVIEW
"SIXTY-THIRD LIST OF DOCTORAL DISSERTATIONS IN POLITICAL ECONOMY IN AMERICAN UNIVERSITIES AND COLLEGES."
AMER. ECO. REVIEW, 56 (SEPT. 66), 1024-1062.
THE ANNOTATED LIST SPECIFIES DOCTORAL DEGREES CONFERRED DURING THE ACADEMIC YEAR TERMINATING JUNE, 1966. ABSTRACTS OF MANY OF THE DISSERTATIONS ARE SUPPLIED. LIST EXCLUDES THESES UNDERTAKEN IN THE SAME PERIOD.

0147 AMERICAN FOREIGN LAW ASSN
BIOGRAPHICAL NOTES ON THE LAWS AND LEGAL LITERATURE OF URUGUAY AND CURACAO.
CHICAGO: AMER FOREIGN LAW ASSOC, 1933, 42 PP.
SELECTED BIBLIOGRAPHY OF DOCUMENTS, MOST IN SPANISH. ARRANGED BY TYPE OF LAW: CIVIL, COMMERCE, CRIMINAL, ETC.

0148 AMERICAN FRIENDS OF VIETNAM
AID TO VIETNAM: AN AMERICAN SUCCESS STORY (PAMPHLET)
NEW YORK: AMER FRIENDS VIETNAM, 1959, 92 PP., LC#59-13623.
CONSTRUCTIVE DISCUSSION AND CRITICISM OF US POLICY IN VIETNAM. FEEL US IS MAKING HEADWAY AND SHOULD BE PROUD. DISCUSS PAST ERRORS AND PROGRAMS TO RECTIFY THEM IN FUTURE. CONCENTRATE ON ICA PROGRAM SINCE 1955, BUILDING STRONG NATIONAL ARMY, AND US VOLUNTARY AID.

0149 AMERICAN FRIENDS SERVICE COMM
PEACE IN VIETNAM: A NEW APPROACH IN SOUTHEAST ASIA: A REPORT.
NEW YORK: HILL AND WANG, 1966, 112 PP.
RESULTS OF STUDY BY AMERICAN FRIENDS SERVICE COMMITTEE. DISCUSSES NATIONALISM IN SOUTHEAST ASIA, NEEDS FOR SOCIO-ECONOMIC CHANGE, AND THE ROLE OF CHINA AND THE US. CONCLUDES WITH SUGGESTIONS FOR A POSSIBLE SETTLEMENT.

0150 AMERICAN HISTORICAL SOCIETY
LIST OF DOCTORAL DISSERTATIONS IN HISTORY IN PROGRESS OR COMPLETED IN COLLEGES AND UNIVERSITIES IN THE UNITED STATES.
NEW YORK: AMER HISTORICAL SOCIETY.
A BIBLIOGRAPHY OF DOCTORAL DISSERTATIONS IN HISTORY. INDICATES CHANGING TRENDS OF INTEREST IN RESEARCH PROJECTS. ISSUED ANNUALLY SINCE 1955.

0151 AMERICAN JOURNAL COMP LAW
THE AMERICAN JOURNAL OF COMPARATIVE LAW READER.
NEW YORK: OCEANA PUBLISHING, 1966, 493 PP., LC#66-11925.
PRESENTS IN ECONOMIC FORMAT CONTRIBUTIONS THAT HAVE APPEARED IN AMERICAN JOURNAL OF COMPARATIVE LAW. GROUPED IN THREE PARTS: FIRST INCLUDES MAGISTRAL REVIEW OF COMPLEX OF INSTITUTIONS CREATED TO COORDINATE NATIONAL LEGAL SYSTEMS; SECOND INCLUDES REMEDIES PROVIDED TO REVIEW REGULATIONS AND DECISIONS OF COMMUNITY INSTITUTIONS; THIRD DEALS WITH INTERNATIONAL LAW, EUROPEAN COURT OF JUSTICE, ETC.

0152 AMERICAN LAW INSTITUTE
FOREIGN RELATIONS LAW OF THE UNITED STATES: RESTATEMENT, SECOND.
NEW YORK: AMERICAN LAW INSTITUTE, 1962, 679 PP.
OFFICIAL DRAFT OF RESTATEMENT OF US FOREIGN RELATIONS

PROMULGATED BY AMERICAN LAW INSTITUTE IN 1962. INCLUDES LAWS DERIVED FROM LEGISLATIVE AND EXECUTIVE ACTION, INTERNATIONAL AGREEMENTS AND TRIBUNALS, COURTS AND PRECEDENT DECISIONS BOTH ABROAD AND IN US. DRAWS UPON INTERNATIONAL AND DOMESTIC LAW TO CLARIFY. DRAWS OPINIONS FROM GROUP ACTION IN CONSIDERING LAWS.

0153 AMES J.G.
COMPREHENSIVE INDEX TO THE PUBLICATIONS OF THE UNITED STATES GOVERNMENT , 1881-1893.
WASHINGTON: US GOVERNMENT, 1905, 1590 PP.
ONLY GENERAL BIBLIOGRAPHY FOR THESE YEARS OF GOVERNMENT PUBLICATIONS. FEW EXECUTIVE DOCUMENTS ISSUED DURING THIS PERIOD; CHIEFLY CONGRESSIONAL DOCUMENTS COVERING THE 47TH THROUGH 52ND CONGRESSES. THREE COLUMNS PER PAGE WITH KEY ARRANGEMENT BY SUBJECT IN SECOND COLUMN; THIRD COLUMN GIVES CONGRESSIONAL SESSION, SERIES AND NUMBER OF CONGRESSIONAL DOCUMENT. A PERSONAL INDEX INCLUDED IN SECOND VOLUME.

0154 AMORY J.F.
AROUND THE EDGE OF WAR: A NEW APPROACH TO THE PROBLEMS OF AMERICAN FOREIGN POLICY.
NEW YORK: CLARKSON N POTTER, 1961, 185 PP., LC#61-17877.
EXAMINES THE INSTRUMENTS OF FOREIGN POLICY FORMATION AND ENFORCEMENT IN THE US. EMPHASIZES ROLE OF FOREIGN AID. ANALYZES CONDITIONS, MEANS, CONTENT, AND OBJECTIVES OF FOREIGN POLICY THAT POLICY-MAKERS CAN CONTROL. DISCUSSES NUCLEAR WAR, ESPIONAGE, PROPAGANDA, AND THE ROLE OF LATIN AMERICA.

0155 AMRAM P.W.
"REPORT ON THE TENTH SESSION OF THE HAGUE CONFERENCE ON PRIVATE INTERNATIONAL LAW."
AMER. J. INT. LAW, 59 (JAN. 65), 87-93.
FIRST U.S. PARTICIPATION AS FULL MEMBER OF CONFERENCE. DISCUSSES CONVENTION ON INTERNATIONAL ADOPTION OF CHILDREN, SERVICE ABROAD OF JUDICIAL-AND EXTRA-JUDICIAL DOCUMENTS IN CIVIL AND COMMERCIAL MATTERS, AND 'CHOICE OF COURT.'

0156 ANAND R.P.
COMPULSORY JURISDICTION OF INTERNATIONAL COURT OF JUSTICE.
INTERNATIONAL STUDIES Q., 8 (JAN.67), 213-241.
PRESENTS HISTORICAL BACKGROUND OF INTERNATIONAL LAW, AND POINTING TO ITS INHERENT WEAKNESSES ATTEMPTS TO OUTLINE A PROGRAM FOR CREATING A MORE EFFICIENT WORLD JUDICIAL BODY. CITES PAST EXAMPLES AND TECHNIQUES CONCERNED WITH ENFORCEMENT OF JURIDICAL DECREES, AND CALLS FOR MORE POWERS FOR THE WORLD COURT.

0157 ANAND R.P.
"SOVEREIGN EQUALITY OF STATES IN INTERNATIONAL LAW."
INT. STUDIES, 8 (JAN. 67), 213-241.
TRACES ORIGINS, DEVELOPMENT, AND DISCUSSIONS OF IDEA OF SOVEREIGN EQUALITY AMONG STATES. DISCUSSION OF INTERNATIONAL ORGANIZATIONS AND PRESERVATION OF PRINCIPLE. DENIES THAT UN PRESERVES PRINCIPLE.

0158 ANDERSON N., NIJKERK K.F.
"INTERNATIONAL SEMINARS: AN ANALYSIS AND AN EVALUATION."
ADMIN SCI. QUART., 3 (SEPT. 58), 229-50.
SYSTEMATIC, SCIENTIFIC STUDY ON EFFECTIVENESS OF 24 INTERNATIONAL SEMINARS EVALUATED AND COMPARED BY SEMINAR MEMBERS AND BY DELEGATES OF LARGER REGIONAL ORGANIZATIONS.

0159 ANDREATTA L.
VIETNAM, A CHECKLIST.
NEW YORK: AMER FRIENDS VIETNAM, 1967.
BIBLIOGRAPHICAL LIST OF ENGLISH-LANGUAGE PUBLICATIONS PUBLISHED ERRATICALLY THROUGH 1962. LISTS BOOKS, MONOGRAPHS, AND ARTICLES FROM POPULAR AND SCHOLARLY SOURCES. GREATER PART DEALS EXCLUSIVELY WITH WRITINGS ON VIETNAM AND ARE SELECTED FROM NEWSPAPERS.

0160 ANDREWS D.H. ED., HILLMON T.J. ED.
LATIN AMERICA: A BIBLIOGRAPHY OF PAPERBACK BOOKS.
WASHINGTON: LIBRARY OF CONGRESS, 1964, 38 PP., LC#64-60047.
LISTS PAPERBACKS AVAILABLE IN 1963 ON LATIN AMERICA. EXCLUDES DICTIONARIES, TEXTBOOKS, JUVENILE LITERATURE, AND FOR THE MOST PART SPECIALIZED PAMPHLETS OR MONOGRAPHS PUBLISHED BY UNIVERSITIES AND AGENCIES. ENTRIES ARE ARRANGED ALPHABETICALLY BY AUTHOR; 240 ENTRIES. INCLUDES INDEX AND LIST OF PUBLISHERS.

0161 ANGELL N.
DEFENCE AND THE ENGLISH-SPEAKING ROLE.
LONDON: PALL MALL PRESS, 1958, 116 PP.
EXAMINES IMPLICATIONS OF MODERN THREAT TO PEACE BY RUSSO-CHINESE TOTALITARIAN COMMUNISM. MAINTAINS THAT NEUTRALITY IS INCOMPATIBLE WITH PEACE AND DEFENSE; THAT UN IS BEST-SUITED VEHICLE FOR INTERNATIONAL UNDERSTANDING; THAT COMMUNIST PROPAGANDA HAS USED LIBERAL SLOGANS TO UNDERMINE DEMOCRACY; AND THAT BOTH BRITAIN AND US MUST TEMPER THEIR NATIONALISM TO COOPERATE IN DEFENSE OF DEMOCRATIC IDEALS.

0162 ANGLIN D.
"UNITED STATES OPPOSITION TO CANADIAN MEMBERSHIP IN THE PAN AMERICAN UNION: A CANADIAN VIEW."
INT. ORGAN., 15 (WINTER 61), 1-20.
HISTORY OF DEBATES OVER CANADA'S ADMISSION TO THE UNION. ALSO DISCUSSED ARE CANADA'S MEMBERSHIP IN THE COMMONWEALTH, AND U.S. AND LATIN AMERICAN ATTITUDES TOWARDS CANADA'S STAND ON SOME MAJOR ISSUES. A POLICY INDEPENDENT OF BOTH LONDON AND WASHINGTON IS RECOMMENDED.

0163 ANGUILE G.
"CIVILISATION DU PLAN DANS L'EUROPE ET L'AFRIQUE DE DEMAIN."
REV. JURID. POLIT. OUTREMER, 17 (JULY-SEPT. 63), 353-364.
ILLUSTRATES INTER-AFRICAN AND AFRO-EUROPEAN PLANS FOR FUTURE DEVELOPEMENT. GIVES SCHEMATIC PRESENTATION OF CRITICAL POINTS ON THREE-YEAR ECONOMIC PLAN OF GABON.

0164 ANSPRENGER F.
POLITIK IM SCHWARZEN AFRIKA.
BONN: DEUTSCHE AFRIKA GESELLSCHAFT, 1961, 516 PP.
STUDY OF RISE OF POLITICAL INDEPENDENCE IN AFRICA, WITH SUBJECT OF FRENCH COLONIAL RULE, REFORM, AND REVOLUTIONARY MOVEMENTS IN LIGHT OF RISING AFRICAN NATIONALISM DISCUSSED IN GREAT DETAIL. APPENDED BIBLIOGRAPHY CONTAINING DOCUMENTS, MAPS, CHARTS, TIMETABLES, ETC.

0165 ANTHEM T.
"CYPRUS* WHAT NOW?"
CONTEMPORARY REV., 210 (MAY 67), 235-240.
FURTHER CRISIS OVER CYPRUS HAS BEEN FORESTALLED ONLY BY MORE SERIOUS CRISES ELSEWHERE. THIS, AS WELL AS GREAT POWER UNWILLINGNESS TO TAKE DIFFICULT DECISIONS, HAS ALSO HELD BACK ANY POSSIBLE SETTLEMENT. UNION WITH GREECE IS THE ONLY REALISTIC SOLUTION, GIVEN THE VAST MAJORITY OF THE POPULATION, WHICH IS GREEK, AND THE DISPROPORTIONATE AMOUNT OF TURKISH POWER ON THE ISLAND DOES NOT ALTER THIS.

0166 ANTWERP-INST UNIVERSITAIRE
BIBLIOGRAPHIC COMPENDIUM: DEVELOPING COUNTRIES (ANTWERP-INST UNIVERSITAIRE DES TERRITOIRES D'OUTRE-MER)
ANTWERP: ANT INST U TERR D'OUTRE, 1968, 157 PP.
APPROXIMATELY 1,000 BOOKS AND ARTICLES IN DUTCH, ENGLISH, FRENCH, GERMAN, ITALIAN, PORTUGUESE, AND SPANISH ARRANGED BY INTERNATIONAL DECIMAL SYSTEM WITH AUTHOR INDEX FROM 1955 THROUGH 1963.

0167 APTHEKER H.
AMERICAN FOREIGN POLICY AND THE COLD WAR.
NEW YORK: NEW CENTURY PUBL, 1962, 416 PP.
DISCUSSES US FOREIGN POLICY SINCE WWII WITHIN FRAMEWORK OF MARXIST-LENINIST OUTLOOK WHICH AUTHOR BELIEVES "MAKES MORE SENSE OF THE WORLD AS IT IS TODAY THAN ANY OTHER GENERALIZATION KNOWN." EMPHASIZES NEO-COLONIALIST NATURE OF US POLICIES.

0168 APEL H.
"LES NOUVEAUX ASPECTS DE LA POLITIQUE ETRANGERE ALLEMANDE."
POLITIQUE ETRANGERE, 32 (1967), 5-21.
EXAMINATION OF GERMAN FOREIGN POLICY ON QUESTIONS OF EUROPEAN UNITY, FRANCO-GERMAN RELATIONS, AND EASTERN EUROPEAN COUNTRIES. ARGUES THAT EEC CONSTITUTES BASIS FOR POLITICAL SOLIDARITY OF WESTERN EUROPE. ENVISIONS EEC AS FOUNDATION OF DETENTE BETWEEN EAST AND WEST EUROPE. DENIES THAT HALLSTEIN DOCTRINE CONTRADICTS TRADE WITH EAST BUT SAYS DIPLOMATIC RELATIONS MUST BE EXTENDED TO EAST GERMANY.

0169 APPADORAI A.
THE USE OF FORCE IN INTERNATIONAL RELATIONS.
BOMBAY: ASIA PUBL HOUSE, 1958, 124 PP.
PROPOSES THAT NATIONS GIVE UP SOVEREIGNTY AND SURRENDER RIGHT TO USE FORCE TO UN. FEELS MARXIST IDEA OF CLASS CONFLICT AND INTERVENTION MUST BE ABANDONED AND INTERNATIONAL COOPERATION IN DEVELOPMENT OF BACKWARD NATIONS UNDERTAKEN. ADMONISHES THAT PEACEFUL COEXISTENCE MUST BECOME A REALITY, OR CIVILIZATION WILL PERISH.

0170 APTER D.E.
"THE GOLD COAST IN TRANSITION."
PRINCETON: PRINCETON U PRESS, 1955.
A CASE STUDY OF POLITICAL INSTITUTIONAL TRANSFER, PLANNED AS THE FIRST OF TWO FIELD STUDIES IN BRITISH COLONIAL AFRICA ON THE DEVELOPMENT OF CONCILIAR ORGANS OF RULE AND SELF-GOVERNMENT. PROCEEDS FROM CONVICTION THAT DEVELOPMENT OF PARLIAMENTARY GOVERNMENT IN UNDERDEVELOPED AREAS REFINES TRADITIONAL CONCEPTUAL PREMISES OF POLITICAL ASPECTS OF SOCIAL CHANGE. BIBLIOGRAPHY OF BOOKS, DOCUMENTS, OFFICIAL PAPERS.

0171 APTER D.E. ED.
IDEOLOGY AND DISCONTENT.
NEW YORK: FREE PRESS, 1964, 342 PP., $9.95.
A COMPARATIVE TREATMENT OF IDEOLOGIES AS 'FRAMEWORKS OF CONSCIOUSNESS' DESIGNED TO INTERPRET THE WORLD FOR PURPOSES OF ACTING IN IT. ESSAYS ON THE STRUGGLE FOR CONSENSUS IN NEW INDEPENDENT NATIONS, JAPAN AND THE GROWTH OF WESTERN INFLUENCE, THE FOUNDATIONS OF ARAB NATIONALISM, SOCIALISM AND DEMOCRACY IN AFRICA, AND THE AMERICAN RADICAL RIGHT. BIBLIOGRAPHY INCLUDED.

0172 APTHEKER H.
DISARMAMENT AND THE AMERICAN ECONOMY: A SYMPOSIUM.
NEW YORK: NEW CENTURY, 64 PP, 1960, $.75.
COLLECTION OF ARTICLES WITH MARXIST VIEWPOINT, ATTEMPTING TO DEMONSTRATE THAT DISARMAMENT WILL NOT CREATE SEVERE ECONOMIC CRISIS. ECONOMIC, POLITICAL AND IDEOLOGICAL FACTORS ARE CONSIDERED.

0173 ARMENGALD A.
"ECONOMIE ET COEXISTENCE."
POLIT. ETRANG., 29 (64), 231-47.
ASKS IF THE CAPITALIST SYSTEM CAN SURVIVE THE INTERNATIONAL STRUGGLE OF ECONOMIES, AND QUESTIONS ITS ROLE IN THAT CONFLICT. SUGGESTS THAT TRADE BETWEEN THE SELLER'S MARKET OF THE WEST AND THE BUYERS MARKET OF THE EAST EUROPEAN NATIONS MIGHT PROVIDE AN AREA FOR FUTURE STABILIZATION OF INTERNATIONAL RELATIONS.

0174 ARMSTRONG J.A.
"THE SOVIET-AMERICAN CONFRONTATION: A NEW STAGE?"
RUSSIAN REVIEWS, 23 (APR. 64), 97-115.
EXAMINES SALIENT FEATURES OF SOVIET-AMERICAN RELATIONS. ASSESSES IMPLICATIONS OF CUBAN CRISIS, TEST-BAN AGREEMENT, AND COMMERCIAL ACTIVITIES. ADVOCATES CONTINUANCE OF MODERATE US POLICY TOWARD USSR BECAUSE THWARTING OF USSR'S EXPANSIONIST AIMS AND FAILURE TO MEET OWN INTERNAL DEMANDS WILL GRADUALLY ERODE SOVIET CONTROL.

0175 ARNOLD G.
TOWARDS PEACE AND A MULTIRACIAL COMMONWEALTH.
LONDON: CHAPMAN AND HALL, 1964, 184 PP.
DISCUSSES BRITAIN'S DECLINE AS WORLD POWER AND NEED FOR NEW POLICIES TO MEET NEW POWER CONDITIONS. EMPHASIZES NEED FOR CLOSER ECONOMIC AND POLITICAL TIES BETWEEN COMMONWEALTH NATIONS AS FORCE FOR UNITY IN MODERN WORLD SITUATION.

0176 ARNOLD G.L.
THE PATTERN OF WORLD CONFLICT.
NEW YORK: DIAL, 1955, 250 PP., LC#55-7670.
ANALYSIS OF PRESENT CONFLICT SITUATION AS RELATED TO ATLANTIC COMMUNITY. DISCUSSES EXPERIENCE OF ECONOMIC PLANNING AND STATE INTERVENTION.

0177 ARNOLD H.J.P.
AID FOR DEVELOPING COUNTRIES.
CHESTER SPRINGS: DEFOUR, 1962, 159 PP.
ANALYZES PATTERNS AND AMOUNT OF AID TO UNDERDEVELOPED NATIONS BY THE WEST, SOVIET BLOC AND INTERNATIONAL ORGANIZATIONS. SUGGESTS DESIGNING AID TO MEET SPECIFIC NEEDS OF INDIVIDUAL COUNTRIES CONSIDERING THEIR ECONOMIC NEEDS AND POLITICAL BACKGROUND.

0178 ARON R.
WAR AND INDUSTRIAL SOCIETY.
LONDON: OXFORD U. PR., 1908, 63 PP.
DETERMINES WHETHER INDUSTRIAL CIVILIZATIONS INHERENTLY PEACEFUL. TRACES DEVELOPMENT OF EUROPEAN POLITICS FROM TIME OF AUGUSTE COMTE TO PRESENT. CONCLUDES 20TH CENTURY POLITICS DEVELOPS IN ACCORDANCE WITH TRADITION.

0179 ARON R.
CENTURY OF TOTAL WAR.
NEW YORK: DOUBLEDAY, 1954, 379 PP.
DISCUSSES HISTORY OF WAR IN THE TWENTIETH CENTURY THROUGH ANALYSIS OF THE ORIGINS AND CONSEQUENCES OF WORLD WAR ONE, AND HOW THEY LAY THE GROUNDWORK FOR WORLD WAR TWO AND THE PRESENT COLD WAR SITUATION, AND THEIR IMPACT ON THE DEVELOPMENT OF POLITICAL IDEOLOGIES AND POLICIES IN TODAY'S WORLD.

0180 ARON R. ED.
FRANCE DEFEATS EDC.
NEW YORK: PRAEGER, 1957, 225 PP.
HISTORICAL DEVELOPMENT AND ANALYSIS OF DEBATE IN FRANCE REGARDING HER DECISION NOT TO PARTICIPATE IN A EUROPEAN DEFENSE COMMUNITY. PROBLEMS FACING FRANCE IN JOINING A SUPRA-NATIONAL ARMY ARE OBSERVED. PERIOD DISCUSSED IS 1950 TO 1954.

0181 ARON R. ET AL.
L'UNIFICATION ECONOMIQUE DE L'EUROPE.
NEUCHATEL: LA BACONNIERE, 1957, 162 PP.
COLLECTION OF ESSAYS WRITTEN BY OFFICIALS OF NATIONS WITHIN THE COMMON MARKET AND TWO SCHOLARS REPRESENTING GREAT BRITAIN AND SWITZERLAND. INDIVIDUAL AUTHORS PROBE ATTITUDES AND PROBLEMS OF THEIR COUNTRIES WITH REGARD TO EUROPEAN UNIFICATION. THOUGH UNITY ACHIEVED WOULD BE ECONOMIC, WRITERS RECOGNIZE POLITICAL ASPECTS OF PROBLEM.

0182 ARON R.
ON WAR: ATOMIC WEAPONS AND GLOBAL DIPLOMACY (TRANS. BY TERENCE KILMARTIN)
LONDON: SECKER AND WARBURG, 1958, 126 PP.
STATES THAT NO SINGLE WEAPON WILL SUFFICE TO CHANGE HUMAN NATURE. CLAIMING A "REALIST" ATTITUDE, AUTHOR BELIEVES THAT TREND OF INTERNATIONAL POLITICS DEPENDS AS MUCH ON MEN AND SOCIETY AS UPON WEAPONS. CLAIMS ATOMIC WEAPONS HAVE PLAYED ONLY A LATENT ROLE IN THE COURSE OF INTERNATIONAL EVENTS.

0183 ARON R.
IMPERIALISM AND COLONIALISM (PAMPHLET)
CAMBRIDGE: LEEDS U PRESS, 1959, 18 PP.
REVIEWS HISTORY OF IMPERIALISM AND COLONIALISM, TRACING POLITICAL AND ECONOMIC INTERPRETATIONS MOST COMMON IN RECENT THOUGHT. SHOWS THAT "COLONIAL PROBLEMS" EXIST ONLY IN TERRITORIES RULLED BY A FEARFUL EUROPEAN MINORITY. POINTS OUT INSIGNIFICANCE OF COLONIES AS PRESENT SOURCES OF INCOME. CALLS UPON EUROPEANS TO TREAT FORMER SUBJECTS AS EQUALS.

0184 ASAMOAH O.Y.
THE LEGAL SIGNIFICANCE OF THE DECLARATIONS OF THE GENERAL ASSEMBLY OF THE UNITED NATIONS.
THE HAGUE: MARTINUS NIJHOFF, 1966, 274 PP.
EXPLAINS DIFFERENT TYPES OF DECLARATIONS OF UN GENERAL ASSEMBLY RELATING TO DEVELOPMENT OF INTERNATIONAL LAW. STATES EXISTING INTERNATIONAL LAWS AND NEW LAWS, EXAMINES PROMOTION OF CHARTER PROGRAMS, AND INVESTIGATES SIGNIFICANCE OF DECLARATIONS FOR GOVERNMENT OF US AND MEMBER STATES.

0185 ASHER R.E.
THE UNITED NATIONS AND THE PROMOTION OF THE GENERAL WELFARE.
WASHINGTON: BROOKINGS INST., 1957, 1216 PP.
DEALS WITH NON-POLITICAL ORGANS OF UNITED NATIONS. FIRST SECTION OF VOLUME OUTLINES EVOLUTION OF THE UN AND REMAINING CHAPTERS ASSESS THE ROLES, FUNCTIONS, SUCCESSES AND FAILURES OF THE UN IN NON-POLITICAL FIELD.

0186 ASHER R.E., KOTSCHING W.M., BROWN W.A.
THE UNITED NATIONS AND ECONOMIC AND SOCIAL COOPERATION.
WASHINGTON: BROOKINGS INST, 1957, 561 PP., LC#57-9377.
CRITICAL ANALYSIS OF UN PROGRAMS IN ECONOMIC AND SOCIAL DEVELOPMENT WHICH EXAMINES STRUCTURE AND PROCEDURES OF SPECIALIZED UN AGENCIES AND EVALUATES EFFECTIVENESS OF PAST PROGRAMS. DISCUSSES LONG RANGE AID PROGRAMS ASSOCIATED WITH EXPANSION OF INTERNATIONAL TRADE AND IMPROVEMENT OF TRANSPORTATION AND COMMUNICATIONS. EMPHASIS IS ON PROBLEMS OF UNDERDEVELOPED COUNTRIES.

0187 ASHFORD D.E.
"A CASE STUDY IN THE DIPLOMACY OF SOCIAL REVOLUTION."
WORLD POLIT., 13 (APR. 61), 423-34.
SEEKS TO CLARIFY WHAT HAMPERED THE MEASURES TAKEN BY US TO ACHIEVE PEACE THROUGH ECONOMIC AID PROGRAM. CALLS FOR NEW METHODS FOR REACHING GOALS OF FOREIGN POLICY.

0188 ASHRAF S. ET AL.
"INDIA AND WORLD AFFAIRS: AN ANNUAL BIBLIOGRAPHY, 1962."
INT. STUD., 5 (JAN. 64), 313-51.
EXTENSIVE, UNANNOTATED BIBLIOGRAPHY DEALING WITH INDIA'S FOREIGN RELATIONS AND EXPRESSIONS OF INDIAN OPINION ON WORLD AFFAIRS.

0189 ASIA FOUNDATION
LIBRARY NOTES.
SAN FRANCISCO: ASIA FOUNDATION.
BIMONTHLY PUBLICATION SINCE 1951 LISTING MATERIALS PRIMARILY ON ASIA. INCLUDES BOOKS, UN DOCUMENTS AND REPORTS, SERIAL PUBLICATION, PAMPHLETS, FOREIGN AND DOMESTIC GOVERNMENT DOCUMENTS, AND ELUSIVE MATERIALS, CATEGORIZED BY COUNTRY AND SUBJECT. ALSO CONTAINS ABSTRACTS OF PERIODICAL ARTICLES. ANNUAL INDEX. MATERIALS IN ENGLISH.

0190 ASIA SOCIETY
AMERICAN INSTITUTIONS ANS ORGANIZATIONS INTERESTED IN ASIA; A REFERENCE DIRECTORY (2ND ED.)
NEW YORK: TAPLINGER PUBL CO, 1961, 581 PP., LC#61-11435.
DIRECTORY TO THE ACTIVITIES AND INTERESTS OF NONGOVERNMENTAL AMERICAN INSTITUTIONS AND NONPROFIT ORGANIZATIONS RELATING TO ASIA. DESCRIBES THE PROGRAMS OF 1,000 UNIVERSITIES, RELIGIOUS AND EDUCATIONAL ORGANIZATIONS, FOUNDATIONS, MUSEUMS, LIBRARIES, AND PROFESSIONAL SOCIETIES. ACTIVITIES INCLUDE CURRENT TEACHING AND REASEARCH PROGRAMS, TECHNICAL ASSISTANCE PROJECTS, AND STUDENT PROGRAMS.

0191 ASIAN-AFRICAN CONFERENCE
SELECTED DOCUMENTS OF THE BANDUNG CONFERENCE (PAMPHLET)
NEW YORK: INST OF PACIFIC RELNS, 1955, 35 PP.
CONTAINS SPEECHES BY SUKARNO, KOTELAWALA, ROMULO, CHOU EN-LAI, DELIVERED AT THE CONFERENCE, APRIL 18-24, 1955. ALSO CONTAINS THE FINAL COMMUNIQUE OF THE CONFERENCE.

0192 ASPREMONT-LYNDEN H.
RAPPORT SUR L'ADMINISTRATION BELGE DU RUANDA-URUNDI PENDANT L'ANNEE 1959.
BRUSSELS: IMPR VAN MUYSEWINKEL, 1960, 494 PP.
DOCUMENTS AND SUMMARIZES BELGIAN COLONIAL ADMINISTRATION OF RUANDA-URUNDI FOR 1959. INCLUDES DESCRIPTIVE DATA INDICATING GEOGRAPHY AND DEMOGRAPHY OF THE AREA; INDICATES LEGAL STATUS OF THE INHABITANTS; DESCRIBES EXTENT AND SCOPE OF COLONIAL COOPERATION WITH INTERNATIONAL AND REGIONAL

AGENCIES; STRESSES SOCIAL, ECONOMIC, AND POLITICAL PROGRESS OF THE REGION.

0193 ATLANTIC INSTITUTE
ATLANTIC STUDIES.
BOULOGNE S. SEINE: ATLANTIC INSTITUTE.
PERIODICAL, APPEARING SINCE 1964, COVERS CURRENT POLITICAL, ECONOMIC, MILITARY, SOCIAL, JUDICIAL, AND CULTURAL STUDIES AMONG ATLANTIC COUNTRIES. ONLY STUDIES PLANNED OR IN PROGRESS ARE REPORTED, NONE OF WHICH HAVE BEEN PUBLISHED PRIOR TO INCLUSION. SPECIAL SECTION INCLUDES PUBLISHED RESEARCH PREVIOUSLY ANNOTATED AS IN PROGRESS. ENGLISH AND EUROPEAN LANGUAGES. ARRANGED BY SUBJECT.

0194 ATTIA G.E.D.
"LES FORCES ARMEES DES NATIONS UNIES EN COREE ET AU MOYEN-ORIENT."
GENEVA: LIBRAIRIE DROZ, 1963.
LEGAL STUDY OF UN EFFORTS TO "MAINTAIN THE PEACE" BY SENDING INTERNATIONAL FORCES INTO THE CONFLICT AREA. THE BIBLIOGRAPHY OF OVER 600 ITEMS INCLUDES UN AND INDIVIDUAL STATE DOCUMENTS AND BOOKS AND ARTICLES, IN FRENCH AND ENGLISH, FROM 1921 TO 1958. DOCUMENTS ARRANGED BY SOURCE AND DATE, OTHER ITEMS ALPHABETICALLY BY AUTHOR.

0195 ATTWOOD W.
THE REDS AND THE BLACKS.
NEW YORK: HARPER & ROW, 1967, 341 PP., LC#67-15746.
US REACTION TO CHINESE AND SOVIET ATTEMPTS TO GAIN INFLUENCE IN AFRICA. AUTHOR REPORTS ON PERSONAL EXPERIENCES AND VIEWS OF CONDUCT OF FOREIGN AFFAIRS. INCLUDES INFORMATION ABOUT OPERATION OF US GOVERNMENT AND POLITICAL CAMPAIGN OF 1960.

0196 AUBREY H.G.
COEXISTENCE: ECONOMIC CHALLENGE AND RESPONSE.
WASHINGTON: NATL PLANNING ASSN, 1961, 323 PP., LC#61-14482.
ORGANIZES MAIN THREADS OF SEVEN RELATED STUDIES ON COMPETITVE COEXISTENCE BETWEEN EAST AND WEST AND REVIEWS ENTIRE PROBLEM. CONSIDERS NEEDS AND ASPIRATIONS OF DEVELOPING COUNTRIES AND WEIGHS ABILITY OF EAST AND WEST TO MEET SUCH NEEDS. STUDIES POLITICAL IMPACT OF INSTITUTIONS, INSTRUMENTS, TECHNIQUES OF COMPETITION; LOOKS BEYOND COMPETITION TO LONG-RANGE RESPONSIBILITY OF THE WEST.

0197 AUBREY H.G.
ATLANTIC ECONOMIC COOPERATION.
NEW YORK: FREDERICK PRAEGER, 1967, 214 PP., LC#67-13866.
EXAMINES ORGANIZATION FOR ECONOMIC COOPERATION AND DEVELOPMENT AND EVERY ASPECT OF ITS FUNCTIONS. GIVES HISTORY OF PAST ACTIONS AND PLANS FOR FUTURE ACTIVITIES. RELATES TO OEEC AND GATT. STRESSES SUBSTANCE OVER INSTITUTIONAL ASPECTS. IMPORTANCE TO INDUSTRIAL COUNTRIES EMPHASIZED.

0198 AUVADE R.
BIBLIOGRAPHIE CRITIQUE DES OEUVRES PARUES SUR L'INDOCHINE FRANCAISE: UN SIECLE D'HISTOIRE ET D'ENSEIGNEMENT.
PARIS: S P MAISONNEUVE & LAROSE, 1965, 149 PP.
BIBLIOGRAPHIC ESSAY ON DEVELOPMENT OF RESEARCH INSTITUTES AND UNIVERSITIES IN INDOCHINA. FIRST PART IS DEVOTED TO ARCHIVES AND LIBRARIES; AUTHOR ANALYZES SELECTED BIBLIOGRAPHIES ON SUBJECT. SECOND PART CONCENTRATES ON A CRITICAL BIBLIOGRAPHY OF WORKS ON SCHOLARLY ORGANIZATION OF INDOCHINA, AND ON ALL ASPECTS TOUCHING ON CULTURAL TIES BETWEEN FRANCE AND INDOCHINA.

0199 AVRAMOVIC D.
POSTWAR GROWTH IN INTERNATIONAL INDEBTEDNESS.
BALTIMORE: JOHNS HOPKINS PRESS, 1958, 228 PP., LC#58-14424.
EXAMINES INTERNATIONAL LONG-TERM CAPITAL MOVEMENTS, CHANGES IN PATTERN OF EXPORTS, AND PROBLEM OF ADJUSTMENT TO CHANGES IN BALANCE OF PAYMENTS. TABLES ON ECONOMIC GROWTH, VOLUME OF EXPORT, GROWTH IN REAL INCOME, CAPITAL FORMATION, GROWTH RATES IN IMPORTS, ETC. OF SELECTED COUNTRIES.

0200 BACON F.
"OF THE TRUE GREATNESS OF KINGDOMS AND ESTATES" (1612) IN F. BACON, ESSAYS."
NEW YORK: EP DUTTON, 1962.
PROPOSES THAT GREATNESS IN A NATION IS RESULT OF PROFESSING ARMS AS ITS PRINCIPAL HONOR, STUDY, AND OCCUPATION. SUGGESTS THAT TO INSURE GREATNESS, NATIONS HAVE LAWS WHICH PROMOTE WAGING OF JUST WARS. COMMENTS, "LET NO NATION SIT TOO LONG UPON A PROVOCATION." URGES THAT KEEPING TREATIES IS VITAL. COMMENDS WAR AS NECESSARY EXERCISE FOR HEALTHY STATES, BUT WARNS AGAINST CIVIL STRIFE.

0201 BACON F.
"OF EMPIRE" (1612) IN F. BACON, ESSAYS."
NEW YORK: EP DUTTON, 1962.
DISCUSSES PROBLEMS OF RULERSHIP AND OF MAINTAINING POWER OF KINGS. SUGGESTS THAT VIGILANCE IS MOST IMPORTANT QUALITY. COMMENDS LIBERAL APPROACH TO RULING. URGES EFFORTS FOR PROSPERITY BECAUSE IT LEADS MORE TO ACCEPTANCE AND COMPLACENCE, WHEREAS POVERTY ENGENDERS REBELLION AND VIOLENCE. SUGGESTS METHODS OF USING NOBLES TO AID IN RULING, AND NONINTERVENTION AS MOST DESIRABLE TYPE OF DIPLOMACY.

0202 BAGU S.
ARGENTINA EN EL MUNDO.
MEXICO CITY: FONDO DE CULTURA ECONOMICA,1961, 211PP.
ANALYZES POSITION OF ARGENTINA IN WORLD AFFAIRS. COVERS ROLE OF ARGENTINA IN OAS AND OTHER HEMISPHERIC RELATIONS INCLUDING ITS PRO-NAZI ATTITUDE DURING WWII. DISCUSSES POSTWAR ECONOMIC AND POLITICAL CHANGES AND INFLUENCE OF FURTHER INDUSTRIALIZATION ON NATIONAL SOCIAL CHANGE AND POLITICS.

0203 BAILEY S.D.
"THE FUTURE COMPOSITION OF THE TRUSTEESHIP COUNCIL."
INT. ORG., 13 (SUMMER 59), 412-421.
DISCUSSES THE THREAT TO WORKABILITY OF THE COUNCIL CREATED BY THE RAPID DISAPPEARANCE OF THE TRUST TERRITORIES. POINTS OUT THE PROBLEM OF HAVING MAJORITY OF COLONIAL AND FORMER COLONIAL NATIONS ON THE PERMANENT TRUSTEESHIP COUNCIL BECAUSE OF THEIR MEMBERSHIP ON THE SECURITY COUNCIL. A NUMBER OF POSSIBLE SOLUTIONS ARE SUGGESTED.

0204 BAILEY S.D.
THE GENERAL ASSEMBLY OF THE UNITED NATIONS.
NEW YORK: PRAEGER, 1960, 377 PP.
EXPLAINS FUNCTIONS AND PURPOSES OF VARIOUS ORGANS WITHIN THE UN. DESCRIBES ORGANIZATIONAL WORKINGS OF THE GENERAL ASSEMBLY SESSIONS AND BLOC VOTING PATTERNS OF ITS MEMBERS ON DIVERSE ISSUES. GIVES SOME PROJECTIONS OF FUTURE OF THE UN.

0205 BAILEY S.D.
THE SECRETARIAT OF THE UNITED NATIONS.
NEW YORK: CARNEGIE ENDOWMENT, 1962, 113 PP.
DISCUSSES EVOLUTION, ORGANIZATIONAL WORK, AND GROWING STRENGTH OF THE SECRETARIAT AND OF THE SECRETARY-GENERAL. PRESENTS MAJOR HISTORICAL EVENTS IN WHICH THE UN DECISIONS PLAYED IMPORTANT ROLE.

0206 BAILEY S.D.
"THE TROIKA AND THE FUTURE OF THE UN."
INT. CONCIL., 538 (MAY 62), 3-64.
SEES THE TROIKA AS A DEVICE WHICH WOULD CONFINE THE UN TO A DIPLOMATIC FORUM AND WOULD BRING MAJOR OPERATIONAL ACTIVITIES TO A HALT. EMPHASIZES THAT IT IS NOT MERELY AN ADMINISTRATIVE ADJUSTMENT, BUT A METHOD OF BRINGING THE VETO INTO SECRETARIAT. GENERAL AND BRIEF DISCUSSION OF UN, INTERNATIONAL CIVIL SERVICE AND SECRETARY-GENERAL.

0207 BAILEY S.D.
THE UNITED NATIONS: A SHORT POLITICAL GUIDE.
NEW YORK: FREDERICK PRAEGER, 1963, 141 PP., LC#63-18536.
INTRODUCTORY GUIDE TO UN - HOW IT DEVELOPED, HOW IT FUNCTIONS, CHALLENGES IT MUST FACE IN FUTURE. ALSO DESCRIBES STRUCTURE AND POLITICAL FUNCTIONS.

0208 BAILEY T.A.
A DIPLOMATIC HISTORY OF THE AMERICAN PEOPLE (7TH ED.)
NEW YORK: APPLETON, 1964, 973 PP., LC#64-10909.
TRACES DIPLOMATIC HISTORY OF US IN DETAIL FROM COLONIAL BACKGROUND UNTIL DIPLOMACY OF NEW FRONTIER. INCLUDES CHARTS AND MAPS. BIBLIOGRAPHY OF 600 ENTRIES IN ENGLISH, PUBLISHED WORKS AND OFFICIAL DOCUMENTS, 1950-63, LISTED TOPICALLY.

0209 BAINS J.S. ED.
STUDIES IN POLITICAL SCIENCE.
NEW YORK: ASIA PUBL HOUSE, 1961, 450 PP.
DEALS WITH INTERNATIONAL LAW AND RELATIONS INCLUDING JURISDICTION AND THEORY; POLITICAL RESEARCH AND THEORY; AND PUBLIC ADMINISTRATION. CONCENTRATES ON WORK IN INDIA AND BY INDIANS, BUT TOPICS ARE WORLD-WIDE.

0210 BALDWIN D.A.
ECONOMIC DEVELOPMENT AND AMERICAN FOREIGN POLICY.
CHICAGO: U OF CHICAGO PRESS, 1966, 291 PP., LC#66-20597.
DISCUSSES US POLICY TOWARD UNDERDEVELOPED COUNTRIES IN PROMPTING ECONOMIC GROWTH. EXAMINES FOREIGN AID PROGRAMS, LOANS (SOFT LOAN EXPERIMENT), AND OTHER FOREIGN-POLICY MEASURES INTENDED TO FURTHER ECONOMIC DEVELOPMENT ABROAD (1940-62).

0211 BALFOUR A.J.
ESSAYS SPECULATIVE AND POLITICAL.
NEW YORK: GEORGE H. DORAN, 1921, 241 PP.
INCLUDED IN SPECULATIVE ESSAYS IS "DECADENCE," AN ANALYSIS OF THE CAUSES OF THE STAGNATION AND DECAY OF SOCIETIES AND AN ATTEMPT TO DISCOVER WAYS MODERN SOCIETY CAN ESCAPE FATE OF OTHER RACES. BELIEVES IN IMPORTANCE OF SCIENTIFIC RESEARCH AND THAT, SO FAR, THERE ARE NO REGRESSIVE SYMPTOMS IN WESTERN CIVILIZATION. "ESSAYS POLITICAL" EXPRESS AUTHOR'S CHANGING VIEW OF GERMANY BEFORE AND DURING WWI.

0212 BALL M.M.
NATO AND THE EUROPEAN MOVEMENT.
NEW YORK: PRAEGER, 1959, 486 PP.
TRACES EVOLUTION OF MOVEMENT TO UNITE EUROPE AND OBSERVES DEVELOPMENT OF NATO. OUTLINES ORIGINS, AIMS, STRUCTURE,

PRINCIPAL ACTIVITIES AND PROBLEMS OF ORGANIZATIONS WITHIN EUROPEAN AND NORTH ATLANTIC AREAS. ALSO CONSIDERS INTER-ORGANIZATION RELATIONSHIPS.

0213 BALL M.M.
"ISSUES FOR THE AMERICAS: NON-INTERVENTION VS HUMAN RIGHTS AND THE PRESERVATION OF DEMOCRATIC INSTITUTIONS."
INT. ORGAN., 15 (WINTER 61), 21-37.
DEALS WITH SEVERAL CURRENT PROBLEMS OF LATIN AMERICA. QUESTIONS WHETHER OAS CAN PROTECT HUMAN RIGHTS THROUGH AN ENFORCEABLE TREATY, AND DO MORE TO ESTABLISH DEMOCRATIC INSTITUTIONS. CALLS FOR NEW HOPE TO ACHIEVE BETTER FUTURE.

0214 BALL W.M.
NATIONALISM AND COMMUNISM IN EAST ASIA.
MELBOURNE: U. PR., 1956, 220 PP.
IDENTIFIES THREE-FOLD REVOLUTION IN EAST ASIA CAUSED BY DESIRE FOR INDEPENDENCE, ASPIRATIONS OF ECONOMIC AND SOCIAL WELL-BEING, AND A RACIAL REVOLT AGAINST THE WEST. PRESCRIBES USE OF MILITARY, ECONOMIC AND PSYCHOLOGICAL EXPEDIENTS TO MEET COMMUNIST CHALLENGE IN THE REGION. RANGE OF SUBJECT MATTER INCLUDES JAPAN, CHINA, KOREA, INDO-CHINA, BURMA, THAILAND, PHILIPPINES, MALAYA, INDONESIA AND INDIA.

0215 BALOGH T.
"L'INFLUENCE DES INSTITUTIONS MONETAIRES ET COMMERCIALES SUR LA STRUCTURE ECONOMIQUE AFRICAIN."
REV. ECON., 14 (NO. 2, 63), 177-95.
TRACES HISTORY OF ECONOMIC RELATIONS AMONG VARIOUS INTRANATIONAL AND INTERNATIONAL GROUPS. ANALYZES COMPARATIVE ECONOMIC DEVELOPMENT WITHIN EUROPEAN COMMON MARKET. CONSIDERS EFFECT OF THESE DEVELOPMENTS ON AFRICAN STATES.

0216 BANFIELD J.
"FEDERATION IN EAST-AFRICA."
INT. J., 18 (SPRING 63), 181-194.
EXAMINES EAST-AFRICAN EXPERIENCE WITH FEDERATION FROM THE EARLY PERIOD OF COLONIAL RULE TO THE PRESENT WITH REFERENCE TO RECENT UPSURGE OF INTEREST BY KENYA, TANGANYIKA AND UGANDA IN FEDERATION AS A REGIONAL ALTERNATIVE TO NATIONAL DEVELOPMENT. SURVEYS ACCOMPLISHMENT AND AREAS OF CONFLICT THAT REMAIN. GREATEST OBSTACLE TO EAST-AFRICAN UNITY IS ABSENCE OF 'PRINCIPLES OF COHESION'.

0217 BARALL M.
"THE UNITED STATES GOVERNMENT RESPONDS."
ANN. AMER. ACAD. POLIT. SOC. SCI., 334 (MARCH 61), 133-142.
USA CAN HELP DEVELOP LATIN AMERICAN POTENTIAL BY LENDING FINANCIAL AID AND ADVICE PERTAINING TO CAPITAL-FORMATION AS WELL AS CONTRIBUTING TO AGRICULTURAL AND EDUCATIONAL TRAINING. BUT LATIN AMERICA MUST HELP HERSELF BY REFORMING ITS ECONOMIC STRUCTURE AND DEVELOPING PLANS BASED ON SOLID PRIORITIES. ALTHOUGH WESTERN HEMISPHERE IS INTERDEPENDENT, LATIN AMERICA CAN ACHIEVE SELF-RELIANCE.

0218 BARANSON J.
TECHNOLOGY FOR UNDERDEVELOPED AREAS: AN ANNOTATED BIBLIOGRAPHY.
NEW YORK: PERGAMON PRESS, 1967, 81 PP., LC#67-14273.
INTERDISCIPLINARY BIBLIOGRAPHY OF 319 ITEMS FROM JOURNALS AND BOOKS SELECTED FROM 2,000 EUROPEAN AND AMERICAN SOURCES. ENTRIES, ARRANGED BY SUBJECT, TREAT SOCIO-CULTURAL INFLUENCES ON TECHNOLOGY, PRODUCTS AND SYSTEMS, INSTITUTIONAL ARRANGEMENTS, AND MAJOR ASPECTS OF ECONOMIC THEORY. ITEMS ARE ANNOTATED.

0219 BARBER H.W.
FOREIGN POLICIES OF THE UNITED STATES.
NEW YORK: DRYDEN, 1953, 614 PP.
SURVEY OF AMERICAN FOREIGN POLICY CONTAINS SHORT HISTORY OF SUBJECT, EXAMINES MODERN FUNDAMENTAL CONCEPTS AND RELATES THEM TO POLICY PROCESS IN SPECIFIC GEOGRAPHIC AREAS. POSES PROBLEMS FOR FUTURE POLICY.

0220 BARGHOORN F.C.
THE SOVIET IMAGE OF THE UNITED STATES: A STUDY IN DISTORTION
NEW YORK: HARCOURT BRACE, 1950, 297 PP.
SOVIET PROPAGANDA AGAINST THE UNITED STATES IS ONE OF MAIN INSTRUMENTS OF AGGRESSIVE SOVIET FOREIGN POLICY. CONSIDERS WHAT MAY BE DONE.

0221 BARKER A.J.
SUEZ: THE SEVEN DAY WAR.
LONDON: FABER, 1964, 223 PP.
STORY OF 'SUEZ WAR' WHICH REVEALED BRITISH MILITARY UNPREPAREDNESS. EMPHASIZES MILITARY ASPECTS OF CRISIS AND CONCLUDES OPERATION MARKED END OF AN ERA.

0222 BARKUN M.
"CONFLICT RESOLUTION THROUGH IMPLICIT MEDIATION."
J. OF CONFLICT RESOLUTION, 8 (JUNE 64), 121-130.
SUGGESTS THAT SOCIETIES USING MEDIATION PROCESS OF CONFLICT RESOLUTION HAVE LEGAL SYSTEM EVEN THOUGH THEY LACK CENTRALIZED SOVEREIGN POWER. MEDIATION REQUIRES CONSENSUS AND OBEDIENCE TO BE SUCCESSFUL. MAINTAINS THAT INTERNATIONAL GOVERNMENT IS IMPROBABLE BECAUSE OF UNWILLINGNESS OF NATIONS TO BE SUBORDINATED TO CENTRAL POWER AND BECAUSE OF LACK OF CONSENSUS AND OBEDIENCE.

0223 BARMAN R.K., TANDON J.C., SINGH D.
"INDO-PAKISTANI RELATIONS 1947-1965: A SELECTED BIBLIOGRAPHY."
INT. STUDIES, 8 (JULY-OCT. 66), 177-212, 1-2.
AN UNANNOTATED BIBLIOGRAPHY OF INDO-PAKISTANI RELATIONS. CONTAINS 980 ENTRIES. DIVIDED INTO TWO PARTS: PART ONE IS BOOKS AND PAMPHLETS, PART TWO IS PERIODICAL ARTICLES. ENGLISH-LANGUAGE PUBLICATIONS.

0224 BARNES W., MORGAN J.
THE FOREIGN SERVICE OF THE UNITED STATES.
WASHINGTON: DEPT/STATE, 1961, 430 PP., $3.50.
ACCOUNT OF ORIGINS AND DEVELOPMENT OF FOREIGN SERVICE, AS WELL AS A DESCRIPTION OF ITS PRESENT STATUS.

0225 BARNET R.
WHO WANTS DISARMAMENT.
BOSTON: BEACON, 1960, 141 PP.
RELATIONSHIP OF DISARMAMENT TO AMERICAN SECURITY AND TO SOVIET GOALS IS OBSERVED. A CRITICAL EXAMINATION OF VARIOUS PROPOSALS THAT HAVE SOUGHT TO ACHIEVE 'ARMS CONTROL' IS ALSO PRESENTED.

0226 BARNET R.
"RUSSIA, CHINA, AND THE WORLD: THE SOVIET ATTITUDE ON DISARMAMENT (PART 3)."
PROBL. COMMUNISM, 10 (MAY-JUNE 61), 32-37.
RECENT DEVELOPMENTS INDICATE CHANGES IN SOVIET APPROACH TO DISARMAMENT BUT DO NOT REVEAL DEPTH OR EXTENT OF CHANGES. USSR DOES NOT SEEM TO UNDERSTAND THAT RADICAL DISARMAMENT WOULD NECESSITATE PROFOUND CHANGES IN THE WORLD, INCLUDING DRASTIC RE-ORIENTATION OF DOMESTIC AND FOREIGN POLICIES.

0227 BARR S.
CITIZENS OF THE WORLD.
GARDEN CITY: DOUBLEDAY, 1952, 285 PP.
CRITICAL ATTACK ON AMERICAN FOREIGN POLICY CALLING FOR A REVAMPING ALONG POLITICAL AS OPPOSED TO MILITARY LINES.

0228 BARROS J.
"THE GREEK-BULGARIAN INCIDENT OF 1925: THE LEAGUE OF NATIONS AND THE GREAT POWERS."
PROC. AMER. PHIL. SOC., 108 (AUG. 64), 354-85.
THE INCIDENT IS PRESENTED AS BEST EXAMPLE OF EFFECTIVE ACTION BY LEAGUE OF NATIONS TO PRESERVE THE PEACE. STRESSES GREAT POWER UNANIMITY AND FACT THAT DISPUTANTS WERE SMALL UNALLIED POWERS AS THE KEY FACTORS IN LEAGUE SUCCESS.

0229 BARROS J.F.P.
THE INTERNATIONAL POLICE: THE USE OF FORCE IN THE STRUCTURE OF PEACE (PAMPHLET)
RIO DE JANEIRO: INST BRAZIL STUD, 1944, 60 PP.
PROPOSAL FOR A "SOCIETY OF NATIONS" AS WORLD POLICE FORCE TO ENFORCE JURIDICAL DECISIONS AND KEEP STATES AUTONOMOUS. FEELS NECESSITY TO GIVE UP SOME RIGHTS AND FREEDOMS TO OBTAIN BIGGER ONES FOR ALL MANKIND. REPORTS ON BRAZIL'S PREPARATIONS AND WILLINGNESS TO JOIN WORLD PEACE GROUP - NOT A PEACE GROUP RULED BY BIG POWERS.

0230 BARTHELEMY G.
"LE NOUVEAU FRANC (CFA) ET LA BANQUE CENTRALE DES ETATS DE L'AFRIQUE DE L'OUEST."
TIERS-MONDE, 4 (NOS.13-14, 63), 275-77.
DISCUSSES STRUCTURE AND PURPOSES OF AFRICAN FINANCIAL COMMUNITY AND ADOPTION OF NEW AFRICAN FRANC. ANALYZES POSSIBLE FUTURE DEVELOPMENTS IN THE MONETARY DISTRIBUTION CENTERS. INDICATES THAT PRESENT SET-UP ENJOYS CONSIDERABLE AUTONOMY. CONSIDERS INTERRELATIONSHIP OF SIX STATES.

0231 BARTLETT R.J.
THE LEAGUE TO ENFORCE PEACE.
CHAPEL HILL: U.N.C. PR., 1944, 252 PP.
AIMS TO AVOID POSSIBLE RECURRENCE OF FAILURE OF INTERNATIONAL PEACE-KEEPING ORGANIZATION. ANALYZES USA ACTIVITIES LEADING TO ESTABLISHMENT OF LEAGUE. CONNECTS REJECTION OF LEAGUE TO POLITICAL FACTIONALISM.

0232 BASCH A.
THE FUTURE OF FOREIGN LENDING FOR DEVELOPMENT (PAMPHLET)
ANN ARBOR: CTR RES ON ECO DEVEL, 1962, 45 PP., LC#62-63218.
ANALYZES EXTERNAL ASSISTANCE IN POSTWAR PERIOD, EXPORTS FROM UNDERDEVELOPED COUNTRIES, FLOW OF EXTERNAL ASSISTANCE IN RECENT YEARS, FUTURE REQUIREMENTS, AND RESPONSIBILITIES OF DEVELOPED NATIONS. PROPOSES A MOVE FROM CONVENTIONAL LOANS TO LENIENT TERM LOANS AND GRANTS.

0233 BASSETT R.
DEMOCRACY AND FOREIGN POLICY: A CASE HISTORY, THE SINO-JAPANESE DISPUTE, 1931-1933.
LONDON: LONGMANS, GREEN & CO, 1952, 654 PP.
CASE HISTORY OF REACTION TO JAPANESE INVASION OF MANCHURIA IN 1931 OF BRITAIN, US, AND LEAGUE OF NATIONS. EMPHASIS ON BRITISH RESPONSE TO CRISIS AND ANALYSIS OFIT.

0234 BATOR V.
"ONE WAR* TWO VIETNAMS."
MILITARY REV., 47 (JUNE 67), 82-88.
STRESSES THAT THE "ESSENCE OF GENEVA" WAS TO SPLIT VIETNAM AND THAT PACIFISTS WHO USE THE GENEVA AGREEMENT ON FACE VALUE ARE DECEIVING THEMSELVES AS TO THE DIPLOMATIC UNDERTONES OF THE TREATY. DESCRIBES SOCIAL AND POLITICAL FORCES THAT MOTIVATED THE CONFERENCE, REASONS FOR PARTITION, TNE "REAL INTENIIONS" OF THE SIGNATORIES. CONCLUDES THAT VIETNAM MUST REMAIN DIVIDED INDEFINITELY.

0235 BAULIN J.
THE ARAB ROLE IN AFRICA.
BALTIMORE: PENGUIN BOOKS, 1962, 144 PP.
STUDY OF CONTEMPORARY NORTH AFRICA AND ITS RELATION TO REST OF CONTINENT. INCLUDES ISLAM IN AFRICA, EGYPTIAN ARABISM AND AFRICANISM, ALGERIAN NATIONALISM, TUNISIA UNDER BOURGUIBA, AND MOROCCAN MONARCHY.

0236 BAUMANN G.
GRUNDLAGEN UND PRAXIS DER INTERNATIONALEN PROPAGANDA.
ESSEN: ESSENER VERLAGSANSTALT, 1941, 280 PP.
CRITICAL INQUIRY INTO BASES AND METHODS OF INTERNATIONAL PROPAGANDA. EMPHASIS ON POLITICAL CAUSES OF THE HATRED FOR GERMANY, ESPECIALLY IN ENGLAND AND FRANCE. ENGLISH PROPAGANDA METHODS DURING WWI DISCUSSED IN DETAIL.

0237 BEAL J.R.
JOHN FOSTER DULLES, A BIOGRAPHY.
NEW YORK: HARPER, 1957, 331 PP.
THE STORY OF THE LIFE OF THE LATE US SECRETARY OF STATE WHICH ASSERTS HE WAS 'ONE MAN WHO WAS NEVER DECEIVED ABOUT THE NATURE OF THE SOVIET MENACE.'

0238 BEALE H.K.
THEODORE ROOSEVELT AND THE RISE OF AMERICA TO WORLD POWER.
BALTIMORE: JOHNS HOPKINS PRESS, 1956, 600 PP., LC#56-10225.
STUDY OF MOTIVES AND POLICY OF THEODORE ROOSEVELT AS THEY HAVE DETERMINED CONTEMPORARY US FOREIGN POLICY. ATTEMPTS TO UNDERSTAND POLICIES OF ROOSEVELT'S ADMINISTRATION THROUGH STUDY OF PERSONALITY OF PRESIDENT. EXAMINES IMPORTANT DIPLOMATIC ENTENTES OF PERIOD. EXTENSIVE NOTES AND BIBLIOGRAPHICAL REFERENCES.

0239 BEALES A.C.
THE HISTORY OF PEACE.
NEW YORK: DIAL, 1931, 335 PP.
A HISTORICAL PRESENTATION OF ORGANIZED EFFORTS TO CREATE WORLD PEACE FROM EARLIEST PEACE INSTITUTIONS IN 1815 TO 1925. DESCRIBES VARIOUS PEACE SOCIETIES, AND POINTS OUT THE EFFECT OF WORLD MOVEMENT ON HUMANITY.

0240 BEARD C.A.
THE DEVIL THEORY OF WAR; AN INQUIRY INTO NATURE OF HISTORY AND THE POSSIBILITY OF KEEPING OUT OF WAR.
NEW YORK: VANGUARD PRESS, 1936, 124 PP., LC#36-9792.
MAINTAINS THAT ANY ATTEMPT TO EXPLAIN WAR INVOLVES INTERPRETATION OF HUMAN HISTORY. INQUIRES INTO NATURE OF HISTORY AND FINDS THAT THEORY THAT WICKED MEN MAKE WAR IS FALSE. STATES THAT WAR IS OUTCOME OF PEACEFUL PURSUITS OF ALL MEN. DESCRIBES FOUR ACTS THAT BROUGHT US INTO WWI. PRESENTS SUGGESTIONS FOR KEEPING US OUT OF WORLD WARS: NEUTRALISM, ISOLATIONAISM, AND INTERNAL DEVELOPMENT.

0241 BEARDSLEY S.W., EDGELL A.G.
HUMAN RELATIONS IN INTERNATIONAL AFFAIRS: A GUIDE TO SIGNIFICANT INTERPRETATION AND RESEARCH.
WASHINGTON: PUBLIC AFFAIRS PRESS, 1956, 40 PP., LC#56-10389.
EXTENSIVELY ANNOTATED BIBLIOGRAPHY OF 117 PUBLICATIONS REPRESENTATIVE OF MODERN THOUGHT ON BEHAVIOR OF MEN IN THEIR SOCIAL ENVIRONMENT RELATING TO INTERNATIONAL PROBLEMS. RELEVANT ANTHROPOLOGY, PSYCHOLOGY, AND SOCIOLOGY EMPHASIZED. LIMITED TO BOOKS PUBLISHED IN ENGLISH DURING, OR SINCE, WWII. INCLUDES TOPICAL CROSS-REFERENCE GUIDE, SHORT SELECTED BIBLIOGRAPHY, AND LISTING OF PERIODICALS.

0242 BEATON L., MADDOX U.
THE SPREAD OF NUCLEAR WEAPONS.
NEW YORK: FREDERICK PRAEGER, 1962, 216 PP., LC#62-20275.
ESTIMATES HOW FAR SPREAD OF NUCLEAR WEAPONS IS LIKELY TO GO. COVERS TECHNICAL PROBLEMS OF DEVELOPING SUCH WEAPONS, COUNTRY-BY-COUNTRY APPRAISAL OF LIKELY MEMBERS OF NUCLEAR CLUB, AND PRESENT AND FUTURE PROBLEM OF SPREAD.

0243 BEAUFRE A.
NATO AND EUROPE.
NEW YORK: VINTAGE BOOKS, 1966, 170 PP., LC#66-28867.
ANALYSIS OF DEVELOPMENT OF NATO AND STATUS OF EUROPEAN UNITY. DISCUSSES STRUCTURE AND STRATEGY OF NATO DEFENSE AND RECENT CHANGES IN ATTITUDE AND ORGANIZATION.

0244 BECHHOEFER B.G.
POSTWAR NEGOTIATIONS FOR ARMS CONTROL.
WASHINGTON: BROOKINGS INST., 1961, 641 PP.
DEALS WITH ARMAMENTS CONTROL PROBLEM AS A SENIOR OFFICER IN STATE DEPT. PRESENTS ANALYTICAL REVIEW OF UNSUCCESSFUL SEARCH FOR EFFECTIVE CONTROL.

0245 BECHHOEFER B.G.
"UNITED NATIONS PROCEDURES IN CASE OF VIOLATIONS OF DISARMAMENT AGREEMENTS."
J. ARMS CONTR., 1 (JULY 63), 191-202.
DISCUSSES UN'S STRUCTURE AND PAST HISTORY IN ORDER TO ASSESS UN'S EFFECTIVENESS AND AVAILIBILITY IN MATTERS CONCERNING DISARMAMENT VIOLATIONS. UN MILITARY FORCE AND INTERNATIONAL COURT OF JUSTICE ARE REJECTED AS POTENTIAL ORGANS OF CONTROL. RECOMMENDS SECURITY COUNCIL AND GENERAL ASSEMBLY AS POTENTIAL VEHICLES FOR EFFECTING SANCTIONS.

0246 BECKEL G.
WORKSHOPS FOR THE WORLD; THE SPECIALIZED AGENCIES OF THE UN.
NEW YORK: ABELARD-SCHUMAN, 1954, 213 PP., LC#53-11284.
PURPOSE: TO BRING TOGETHER IN NARRATIVE FORM CASE STUDIES OF UN AGENCIES AT WORK. PRESENTS SIGNIFICANT CONTRIBUTIONS OF AGENCIES AND INCLUDES REFERENCE MATERIAL FOR EACH AGENCY. ALSO GIVES ROLE OF US AND FOUNDING OF AGENCIES.

0247 BEERS H.P. ED.
THE FRENCH IN NORTH AMERICA.
BATON ROUGE: LOUISIANA ST U PR, 1957, 410 PP., LC#57-11541.
ACTIVITIES OF AMERICAN AND CANADIAN INSTITUTIONS, HISTORIANS, AND OTHERS OF FRENCH NATIONALITY TRACED, AND THEIR WORK IN COMPILING RECORDS OF MAJOR OCCURRENCES RECORDED.

0248 BEERS H.P.
"THE FRENCH IN NORTH AFRICA: A BIBLIOGRAPHICAL GUIDE TO FRENCH ARCHIVES, REPRODUCTIONS, AND RESEARCH MISSIONS."
BATON ROUGE: LOUISIANA ST U PR, 1957.
HISTORY OF PRINCIPAL DEPOSITORIES IN FRANCE CONTAINING MATERIAL RELATING TO THE US AND CANADA AND DESCRIPTIONS OF THEIR HOLDINGS. TRACES ORIGINS OF EFFORTS TO OBTAIN REPRODUCTIONS OF FRENCH ARCHIVES AND THEIR DISTRIBUTION OVER US AND CANADA. BIBLIOGRAPHY LISTS SIGNIFICANT MANUSCRIPTS, PRINTED ARCHIVES, INVENTORIES, PRINTED SOURCES, AND SECONDARY PUBLICATIONS.

0249 BEGUIN B.
"ILO AND THE TRIPARTITE SYSTEM."
INT. CONCIL., 523 (MAY 59), 401-48.
EACH NATION IN ILO REPRESENTED BY SPOKESMEN FOR WORKERS, EMPLOYERS, AND GOVERNMENTS. ILO FOUNDED IN 1919 AS MEANS OF CONCILIATION BETWEEN THE THREE BODIES. TRACES DEVELOPMENT OF SYSTEM, CHANGES, AND PROBLEMS WITH FASCIST AND COMMUNIST STATES. MAJOR CURRENT PROGRAM IS SOCIAL AND ECONOMIC DEVELOPMENT OF UNDERDEVELOPED NATIONS.

0250 BEHRENDT R.F.
MODERN LATIN AMERICA IN SOCIAL SCIENCE LITERATURE.
ALBUQUERQUE: U OF N MEX PR, 1949, 122 PP.
LISTS, ANNOTATES, AND INDEXES BOOKS, PAMPHLETS, AND PERIODICALS IN ENGLISH IN THE FIELDS OF ECONOMICS, POLITICS, AND SOCIOLOGY. ARRANGED BY GENERAL TOPICS, BY REGION, AND BY INDIVIDUAL COUNTRY. INCLUDES CHECKLIST OF BIBLIOGRAPHIES AND GENERAL REFERENCE WORKS. ITEMS DATE CHIEFLY FROM 1930'S AND 1940'S.

0251 BEHRENDT R.F.
MODERN LATIN AMERICA IN SOCIAL SCIENCE LITERATURE (SUPPLEMENTS I AND II)
WASHINGTON: PAN AMERICAN UNION, 1950, 122 PP.
SPONSORED BY THE PAN AMERICAN UNION. COMPILES MATERIALS FROM OCTOBER, 1948-MAY, 1950. STRESSES SCHOLARLY AND SCIENTIFIC WORKS. INCLUDES ITEMS DEALING WITH ECONOMICS, POLITICS, AND SOCIOLOGY. IN ENGLISH AND SPANISH.

0252 BEIM D.
"THE COMMUNIST BLOC AND THE FOREIGN-AID GAME."
WEST. POLIT. QUART., 17 (DEC. 64), 784-799.
PROPOSING A MODEL OF FOREIGN AID AS A 3-PLAYER, NON-ZERO-SUM GAME, AUTHOR ASSERTS THAT SUCH A MODEL WOULD ENABLE ANALYSTS TO REVEAL NATURE OF THE INTEREST UNDERLYING A VARIETY OF GRANTS AND CREDITS AND TO DEDUCE THE MOTIVATIONS OF A COUNTRY DISPENSING SUCH ASSISTANCE LARGELY FROM ITS ACTIONS.

0253 BELGION M.
"THE CASE FOR REHABILITATING MARSHAL PETAIN."
QUARTERLY REV., (APR. 67), 205-212.
AUTHOR SUPPORTS MOVEMENT FOR REPARATION TO BE DONE TO THE REPUTATION OF MARSHAL PETAIN AND PRESENTS FACTS ABOUT HIM AND REASONS WHY HE MUST BE EXONERATED OF CHARGE OF BETRAYING FRANCE UNJUSTLY. FEELS PETAIN WAS A TRAGIC FIGURE AND SUBJECT OF FATE.

0254 BELKNAP G., CAMPBELL A.
"POLITICAL PARTY IDENTIFICATION AND ATTITUDES TOWARD FOREIGN POLICY" (BMR)"
PUBLIC OPINION QUART., 15 (WINTER 51), 601-623.
SUGGESTS MANNER IN WHICH MECHANISM OF POLITICAL PARTY IDENTIFICATION OPERATES TO INFLUENCE OPINIONS OF VOTERS ON FOREIGN POLICY ISSUES. DATA FROM POPULATION SAMPLING

SHOWS THAT FOR MANY PEOPLE DEMOCRATIC OR REPUBLICAN ATTITUDES ON FOREIGN POLICY RESULT FROM CONSCIOUS OR UNCONSCIOUS ADHERENCE TO A RECEIVED PARTY LINE, RATHER THAN FROM INFLUENCES INDEPENDENT OF PARTY IDENTIFICATION.

0255 BELL C.
NEGOTIATION FROM STRENGTH.
LONDON: CHATTO/WINDUS, 1962, 220 PP.
STUDY OF THE CIRCUMSTANCES UNDER WHICH PHRASE 'NEGOTIATION FROM STRENGTH' BECAME CURRENT AS A FORMULATION OF WESTERN COLD WAR POLICY. ALSO EXAMINES VARIOUS INTERPRETATIONS OF PHRASE.

0256 BELL C.
THE DEBATABLE ALLIANCE.
LONDON: OXFORD U PR, 1964, 130 PP.
ANALYSIS OF RELATIONSHIP BETWEEN USA AND GREAT BRITAIN, FOCUSING ON DEVELOPMENTS FOLLOWING WWII AND CONSIDERING ANGLO-AMERICAN RELATIONS AS KEY ELEMENT IN INTERNATIONAL POWER BALANCE.

0257 BELL W. ED.
THE DEMOCRATIC REVOLUTION IN THE WEST INDIES.
CAMBRIDGE: SCHENKMAN PUBL CO, 1967, 232 PP., LC#67-31921.
COLLECTION OF DESCRIPTIONS AND ANALYSES OF ENGLISH-SPEAKING CARIBBEAN NATIONS AND SELF-GOVERNING TERRITORIES. DISCUSSES PROBLEMS OF THIS UNDERDEVELOPED AREA AND ATTITUDES OF PEOPLE AND LEADERS TOWARD INDEPENDENCE, NATIONALISM, DEMOCRACY, EQUALITY, AND RACE.

0258 BELOFF M.
THOMAS JEFFERSON AND AMERICAN DEMOCRACY.
LONDON: ENGLISH U PRESS, 1948, 271 PP.
ENGLISH STUDY VIEWS JEFFERSON AS ESSENTIAL TO THE UNDERSTANDING OF THE AMERICAN MIND AND AS INTELLECTUAL PROGENITOR OF AMERICAN ISOLATIONISM. EXAMINES HIS VIEWS IN LIGHT OF CONFLICTING IDEALS AND FACTS, TENSION PRODUCERS THAT MAKE JEFFERSON VERY SIMILAR TO CONTEMPORARY MAN. COVERS PERIOD 1743-1826, INCLUDING HIS ROLE IN REVOLUTION, VIRGINIA STATESMANSHIP, AND THE PRESIDENCY.

0259 BELOFF M.
"NATIONAL GOVERNMENT AND INTERNATIONAL GOVERNMENT."
INT. ORGAN., 13 (AUTUMN 59), 538-49.
APPEALS FOR ADDITIONAL RESEARCH IN FIELD OF RELATIONSHIPS, BOTH FORMAL AND INFORMAL ONES, BETWEEN SPECIFIC GOVERNMENTS AND SPECIFIC INTERNATIONAL ORGANIZATIONS. ASSERTS THIS WOULD ALLOW ONE TO ESCAPE THE GENERAL TERMS SUCH AS SOVEREIGNTY, AND THUS FORM MORE OBJECTIVE JUDGEMENTS ON THE ACTUAL OPERATIONS OF INTERNATIONAL BODIES.

0260 BELOFF M.
NEW DIMENSIONS IN FOREIGN POLICY: A STUDY IN BRITISH ADMINISTRATION.
LONDON: ALLEN UNWIN, 1961, 208 PP.
ASSESSES PROBLEMS OF INTEGRATING NATIONAL POLITICAL SYSTEMS WITH POST-WAR INTERNATIONAL ORGANIZATIONS. PRESENT ARRANGEMENT OF WESTERN EUROPEAN AND NORTH ATLANTIC COMMUNITY POSES PROBLEMS OF CREATION, ADAPTATION, AND COORDINATION. CHOOSING BETWEEN ISOLATION AND PARTICIPATION IS QUANDARY FACING GOVERNMENT LEADERS.

0261 BELOFF M.
THE UNITED STATES AND THE UNITY OF EUROPE.
WASHINGTON: BROOKINGS INST., 1963, 124 PP.
TRACES THE DEVELOPMENT AND IMPLEMENTATION OF CONCEPT OF 'UNITED STATES OF EUROPE' AND DISCLOSES ITS INFLUENCE ON USA POLICY. EUROPEAN POST-WAR RECOVERY, DEFENSE, COMMON MARKET, ATLANTIC ALLIANCE AND ROLE OF GREAT BRITAIN ARE AMONG TOPICS DISCUSSED.

0262 BELOFF M.
"BRITAIN, EUROPE AND THE ATLANTIC COMMUNITY."
INT. ORGAN., 17 (SUMMER 63), 574-92 PP.
DISCUSSES BRITAIN'S RELATIONS WITH EUROPE IN THE DEVELOPMENT OF AN ATLANTIC COMMUNITY, AND THE PROBLEMS THAT SUCH AN ORGANIZATION WOULD POSE FOR HER OTHER INTERNATIONAL RELATIONS.

0263 BELSHAW C.
"TRAINING AND RECRUITMENT: SOME PRINCIPLES OF INTERNATIONAL AID."
INT. J., 18 (WINTER 62-63), 43-57.
'THE PROVISIONS OF EXPERTS TO SERVE IN TECHNICAL CAPACITIES ABROAD, AND OF FACILITIES TO PROVIDE HIGHER EDUCATION AND TRAINING ASSISTANCE FOR THE PEOPLES OF RAPIDLY DEVELOPING COUNTRIES CONSTITUTE' MOST DIFFICULT ELEMENTS IN INTERNATIONAL AID. DESCRIBES ACTIVITIES OF MANY NATIONAL AND INTERNATIONAL AID ORGANIZATIONS AND THEIR METHODS OF WORK.

0264 BEMIS S.F., GRIFFIN G.G.
GUIDE TO THE DIPLOMATIC HISTORY OF THE UNITED STATES, 1775-1921.
NEW YORK: HOLT RINEHART WINSTON, 1935, 979 PP., LC#35-26001.
AN EXTREMELY COMPLETE BIBLIOGRAPHIC GUIDE TO PRINTED MATERIALS AND MANUSCRIPT SOURCES. DIVIDED INTO TWO MAIN PARTS: PART 1, BIBLIOGRAPHY, LISTING 5,318 ANNOTATED ITEMS; PART 2, REMARKS ON THE SOURCES, INCLUDING MANUSCRIPT SOURCES. INDEXES OF COLLECTIONS OF PERSONAL PAPERS AND AUTHORS.

0265 BEMIS S.F.
THE LATIN AMERICAN POLICY OF THE UNITED STATES: AN HISTORICAL INTERPRETATION.
NEW YORK: HARCOURT BRACE, 1943, 470 PP.
EXAMINES US POLICY IN LATIN AMERICA AS INFLUENCED BY BELIEF IN SOVEREIGNTY OF NATIONS. BEGINS WITH TERRITORIAL PROBLEMS OF NORTH AMERICA IN 1776. STUDIES MONROE DOCTRINE, MANIFEST DESTINY, DOLLAR DIPLOMACY, WOODROW WILSON AND MEXICO, DOCTRINE OF NONINTERVENTION, GOOD NEIGHBOR POLICY, AND DIPLOMATIC RELATIONS THROUGH 1942. MAINTAINS THAT US POLICY IS BASED ON INTERESTS OF NATIONAL SECURITY.

0266 BEMIS S.F.
A SHORT HISTORY OF AMERICAN FOREIGN POLICY AND DIPLOMACY.
NEW YORK: HOLT RINEHART WINSTON, 1959, 737 PP., LC#59-5439.
STUDIES AMERICAN FOREIGN POLICY AND DIPLOMACY FROM 1763-1959, EMPHASIZING EXPANSION OF FOREIGN RELATIONS IN 20TH CENTURY. EXPLORES OBJECTIVES AND PRINCIPLES OF FOREIGN POLICY.

0267 BENES E.
INTERNATIONAL SECURITY.
CHICAGO: U. CHI. PR., 1939, 153 PP.
DISCUSSES SECURITY ASPECTS OF NEGOTIATION OF TREATIES OF MUTUAL ASSISTANCE. EXAMINES POLICY CONSISTENCIES AND INCONSISTENCIES OF GREAT POWERS. STRESSES ARBITRATION, DISARMAMENT AND SECURITY. APPRAISES ROLES OF ENGLAND AND GERMANY IN POST-WORLD WAR ONE EUROPEAN DIPLOMACY.

0268 BENNETT J.C. ED.
NUCLEAR WEAPONS AND THE CONFLICT OF CONSCIENCE.
NEW YORK: CHAS SCRIBNER'S SONS, 1962, 191 PP., LC#62-9653.
EXAMINES MORAL AND ETHICAL ISSUES INVOLVED IN USE OF NUCLEAR WEAPONS. STATES PROBLEM IN LIGHT OF HISTORY OF WARFARE, CURRENT INTERNATIONAL SITUATION, AND SCIENTIFIC ESTIMATES OF EFFECT OF NUCLEAR WAR. DISCUSSES IMPACT OF DESTRUCTIVE POWER ON MEANING OF HISTORY AND ON "FAITH IN PROVIDENCE AND HUMAN DESTINY.

0269 BENTHAM J.
A PLAN FOR AN UNIVERSAL AND PERPETUAL PEACE (1838) (PAMPHLET)
LONDON: SWEET AND MAXWELL, LTD, 1927, 44 PP.
PROPOSES REDUCTION AND FIXATION OF FORCES IN MAJOR COUNTRIES IN EUROPE, AND EMANCIPATION OF COLONIAL DEPENDENCIES OF EACH STATE. CLAIMS THAT COLONIES ARE OF LITTLE OR NO VALUE TO MOTHER COUNTRIES, BUT A CONSTANT SOURCE OF INTERNATIONAL STRIFE. URGES ESTABLISHMENT OF INTERNATIONAL COURTS TO SETTLE DISPUTES. PAYS LITTLE HEED TO ECONOMICS OF COLONIALISM; DISPUTES EXISTENCE OF REAL CONFLICTS OF INTEREST.

0270 BENTHAM J.
"PRINCIPLES OF INTERNATIONAL LAW" IN J. BOWRING, ED., THE WORKS OF JEREMY BENTHAM."
ORIGINAL PUBLISHER NOT AVAILABLE, 1843.
FOUR ESSAYS CONSIDERING OBJECTS OF INTERNATIONAL LAW, JURISDICTION, WAR, AND PEACE. AUTHOR BELIEVES THAT OBJECTS OF INTERNATIONAL LAW INCLUDE DOING NO INJURY TO OTHER NATIONS AND DOING GREATEST POSSIBLE GOOD TO OTHER NATIONS, WHILE PROTECTING WELFARE OF ONE'S OWN NATION. CONSIDERS POTENTIAL AND ACTUAL JURISDICTION, AND RIGHTFUL OR MORAL JURISDICTION. DISCUSSES CAUSES OF WAR AND PLAN FOR PEACE.

0271 BENTLEY E.
"VIETNAM: THE STATE OF OUR FEELINGS."
COLUMBIA UNIV. FORUM, 10 (SUMMER 67), 9-14.
ANALYZES AMERICAN SOCIETY, MORES, AND "FEELINGS" TODAY. FINDS THERE IS ONLY ONE JOB NOW: TO END THE WAR IN VIETNAM. FEELS THAT WAR IMPEDES PROGRESS IN CIVIL RIGHTS, POVERTY ROGRAM, AND INTERNATIONAL RELATIONS. SUGGESTS T CRITERION FOR EACH CIVIC ACTION MUST BE WHETHER IT CONTRIBUTES TO EFFORT TO END THE WAR.

0272 BERKES R.N.B.
"THE NEW FRONTIER IN THE UN."
CURR. HIST., 42 (JAN. 62), 43-48.
DEALS WITH THE NEW IMAGE OF THE USA IN THE UNITED NATIONS - THAT OF BUILDING GREATER RAPPORT WITH THE WORLD OUTSIDE THE SOVIET ORBIT. LASTED UNTIL THE CUBAN FIASCO WHEN STEVENSON BEGAN TO 'SOUND LIKE LODGE.'

0273 BERKES R.N.B.
"THE US AND WEAPONS CONTROL."
CURRENT HIST., 47 (AUG. 64), 65-116.
EIGHT ARTICLES EXPLORING UNITED STATES VIEWS ON WEAPONS CONTROL, DISARMAMENT, AND ALTERNATE PATHS TOWARD PEACE AND MILITARY SECURITY.

0274 BERLE A.A.
NATURAL SELECTION OF POLITICAL FORCES.
LAWRENCE: U. KANSAS PR., 1950, 100 PP.

POLITICS AS ORGANIZED POWER IS MOST SUCCESSFUL IF IT APPROACHES UNIVERSALITY IN FIELD OF APPLICATION AND GIVES INDIVIDUALS SENSE OF HARMONY. ATTEMPTS TO PROVE THESIS BY REFERING TO HISTORICAL FACTS. ASSERTS THAT THESE CRITERIA CONSTITUTE THE NATURAL SELECTION OF POLITICS.

0275 BERLE A.A. JR.
"THE 20TH CENTURY CAPITALIST REVOLUTION."
NEW YORK: HARCOURT BRACE, 1954.
STUDY OF THE MODERN CORPORATION FROM A QUASI-POLITICAL ANGLE. ARGUES THAT LARGE CORPORATION MANAGEMENTS HAVE REACHED A POSITION OF CONCENTRATED ECONOMIC POWER WHICH FORCES THEM TO CONSIDER AND PARTICIPATE IN POLITICAL, INTERNATIONAL, AND PHILOSOPHICAL CONSIDERATIONS. BRIEF ANNOTATED BIBLIOGRAPHY OF AMERICAN ECONOMIC WRITINGS PUBLISHED AFTER 1933.

0276 BERLE A.A.
TIDES OF CRISIS: A PRIMER OF FOREIGN RELATIONS.
NEW YORK: MACMILLAN, 1957, 328 PP.
TRIES TO CLOSE THE GAP BETWEEN PUBLIC OPINION AND 'NECESSARY' POLICY. ADVISES THAT PEACE CAN BE ACHIEVED ONLY THROUCH UNITED NATIONS AND RECOMMENDS THAT A POWERFUL UN BE UNITED NATIONS AND RECOMMENDS THAT A POWERFUL UN BE THE OBJECT OF AMERICAN FOREIGN POLICY.

0277 BERLINER J.S.
SOVIET ECONOMIC AID: THE AID AND TRADE POLICY IN UNDER-DEVELOPED COUNTRIES.
NEW YORK: PRAEGER, 1958, 232 PP., $4.25.
DENOTES PRINCIPAL OBJECTIVES OF RUSSIAN SUPPLY PROGRAMS, 1953-57. CONSIDERS COMMITMENTS AND TYPE OF ASSISTANCE RENDERED. APPRAISES BENEFITS OF TRADE AND AID PROGRAM TO DONOR AND RECIPIENTS, THE PROGRAMS' IMPACT ON SOVIET ECONOMY AND RUSSIAN ABILITY TO CONTINUE THIS UNDERTAKING.

0278 BERNHARDI F.
ON THE WAR OF TODAY.
NEW YORK: DODD MEAD, 1914, 2 VOLS., 858 PP.
DISCUSSES NECESSARY BASIS FOR ALL DOCTRINES OF WAR. DEALS WITH RELATIONSHIP OF ATTACK AND DEFENSE IN MODERN WARFARE.

0279 BERNSTEIN B.J., MATUSOW A.J.
THE TRUMAN ADMINISTRATION.
NEW YORK: HARPER & ROW, 1966, 518 PP., LC#66-13938.
ANALYSIS OF TRUMAN ADMINISTRATION WHICH ATTEMPTS TO PRESENT OBJECTIVE VIEW OF TRUMAN'S HANDLING OF MOST CRUCIAL DOMESTIC AND FOREIGN ISSUES OCCURRING DURING HIS TERM OF OFFICE. CONSIDERS A-BOMB DECISION, HANDLING OF MCCARTHY'S ATTACKS ON ADMINISTRATION, KOREAN AND COLD WAR POLICIES AND OTHER ISSUES. STRESSES SUCCESSES AND FAILURES AND STRESSES IMPOSSIBILITY OF GENERALIZATION CONCERNING ERA.

0280 BESSON W.
DIE GROSSEN MACHTE - STRUKTURFRAGEN DER GEGENWARTIGEN WELT-POLITIK.
FREIBURG: VERLAG ROMBACH + CO, 1966, 81 PP.
DISCUSSES POLITICS OF WORLD POWERS SINCE WWII AND SEEKS TO ESTABLISH A GENERAL PICTURE OF WORLD-POLITICAL TENDENCIES. INCLUDES ESSAY ON MEANING AND IMPORTANCE OF KENNEDY'S LEADERSHIP.

0281 BEST H.
"THE SOVIET STATE AND ITS INCEPTION."
NEW YORK: PHILOSOPHICAL LIB, 1951.
SOCIOLOGICAL APPRAISAL OF PRE-AND POST-REVOLUTIONARY HISTORY OF USSR AND STUDY OF SOCIAL PHILOSOPHY UNDERLYING THE SOVIET MOVEMENT. UNANNOTATED BIBLIOGRAPHY OF MATERIAL PUBLISHED IN ENGLISH INCLUDED. BOOKS ARRANGED CHRONOLOGICALLY FROM 1917 THROUGH 1950: SMALL SECTION OF PERIODICALS ARRANGED BY DATE OF FIRST PUBLICATION.

0282 BESTERMAN T.
A WORLD BIBLIOGRAPHY OF BIBLIOGRAPHIES (4TH ED.)
LAUSANNE: SOCIETAS BIBLIOGRAPH, 1966, 8425 PP.
AN ANNOTATED BIBLIOGRAPHY ARRANGED ALPHABETICALLY BY SUBJECT. UNDER EACH HEADING THE ORDER OF ENTRIES IS ARRANGED CHRONOLOGICALLY BY DATE OF PUBLICATION. SPECIAL POINTS CLARIFIED IN TEXT BY CROSS-REFERENCES TO HEADINGS. FIRST EDITION CARRIED SYSTEMATICALLY FROM 1470 TO 1935: THE FOURTH EDITION IS CARRIED THROUGH 1963, WITH MANY LATER ENTRIES. ESTIMATES ITEMS COVERED IN PUBLICATIONS LISTED. AUTHOR INDEX INCLUDED.

0283 BESTERS H., BOESCH E.E. ED.
ENTWICKLUNGSPOLITIK - HANDBUCH UND LEXIKON.
STUTTGART: KREUZ-VERLAG, 1966, 1769 PP.
DICTIONARY AND HANDBOOK DISCUSSING CENTRAL PROBLEMS OF UNDERDEVELOPED NATIONS. EXAMINES IN BRIEF ESSAYS ECONOMIC, POLITICAL, AND SOCIAL PROBLEMS OF UNDERDEVELOPED COUNTRIES WITH PARTICULAR EMPHASIS ON ECONOMIC PLANNING. INCLUDES CATEGORIES ON POLITICAL DEVELOPMENT, FOREIGN AID, AND ROLE OF CHURCH.

0284 BEVERIDGE W.
THE PRICE OF PEACE.
NEW YORK: NORTON, 1945, 160 PP.
IMPUTES FORGING OF WAR TO INTERNATIONAL ANARCHY. RELATION OF WW I TO WW 2 AND CAUSES OF BOTH ARE EXAMINED. ANALYZES FAILURES OF VERSAILLES TREATY AND LEAGUE OF NATIONS. PRICE OF PEACE IS ACCEPTANCE AND ENFORCEMENT OF IMPARTIAL ARBITRATION IN ALL DISPUTES BETWEEN NATIONS. APPENDIX INCLUDES TEXTS OF PERTINENT CHARTERS, TREATIES SUCH AS FOURTEEN POINTS, CRIMEA CONFERENCE ET AL.

0285 BIBLIOTHEQUE PALAIS DE LA PAIX
CATALOGUE OF THE PEACE PALACE LIBRARY, SUPPLEMENT 1937-1952 (7 VOLS.)
GENEVA: LEAGUE OF NATIONS, 1962.
SUPPLEMENTARY LISTING OF MATERIALS IN PEACE PALACE LIBRARY CONTAINED IN SEVEN VOLUMES. LISTS BIBLIOGRAPHIES, PERIODICALS, SERIAL WORKS, AND OTHER WORKS IN CHRONOLOGICAL ORDER. LIBRARY IS DEVOTED TO INTERNATIONAL LAW: PRIVATE, PUBLIC, AND COMMERCIAL.

0286 BIERZANECK R.
"LA NON-RECONAISSANCE ET LE DROIT INTERNATIONAL CONTEMPORAIN."
ANNU. FRANC. DR. INTER., 8 (1962), 117-37.
SURVEYS PATTERNS OF DIPLOMACY IN INTERNATIONAL RELATIONS. STUDIES INTERNATIONAL LAW AND NON-RECOGNITION OF NATIONS. EXAMINES ESTABLISHMENT AND SEVERING OF DIPLOMATIC RELATIONS. RELATES INTERNATIONAL LAW TO NATIONAL SECURITY PROBLEMS.

0287 BILLERBECK K.
SOVIET BLOC FOREIGN AID TO UNDERDEVELOPED COUNTRIES.
HAMBURG: HAMB WIRTSCHAFTS ARCHIV, 1960, 161 PP.
STUDIES PROBLEMS OF "SOVIET DEVELOPMENT AID" CONFRONTING NATIONS RECEIVING AID NOW AND THOSE THAT WILL RECEIVE IT IN FUTURE. EMPHASIZES INTRINSIC NATURE OF SOVIET AID, ITS UNIQUE METHODS AND TACTICS, AND CONSEQUENCES FOR RECEIVING NATIONS. STUDIES 1953-1960 AND PREDICTS DEVELOPMENTS THROUGH 1970. APPENDIX SUMMARIZES AID TO EACH NATION.

0288 BINANI G.D., RAMA RAO T.V.
INDIA AT A GLANCE (REV. ED.)
BOMBAY: ORIENT LONGMANS, 1954, 1756 PP.
A COMPREHENSIVE REFERENCE MANUAL ON INDIA THAT PROVIDES A CLASSIFIED SYSTEM OF INFORMATION ON 25 TOPICS OF GENERAL AND SPECIALIZED INTEREST. COORDINATES INFORMATION ON THE NATIONAL GOVERNMENT, FOREIGN POLICY, NATIONAL ECONOMY, COMMUNICATIONS, INDUSTRIAL FINANCE, PRODUCTION TRENDS, THE JUDICIAL SYSTEM, ETC. INCLUDES A GENERAL INDEX AND DETAILED TABLE OF CONTENTS.

0289 BINDER L.
THE IDEOLOGICAL REVOLUTION IN THE MIDDLE EAST.
NEW YORK: WILEY, 1964, 287 PP., $6.50.
PLACES NATIONALIST MOVEMENT IN GEOGRAPHICAL, CULTURAL AND HISTORICAL SETTING. NOTES EMERGENCE OF POLITICS FREE OF RELIGIOUS DOMINATION. ANALYZES IDEOLOGICAL CONTENT OF BAA'TH PARTY, OF RADICAL REFORM NATIONALISM, AND OF PAN-ARABISM.

0290 BIRDSALL P.
VERSAILLES TWENTY YEARS AFTER.
LONDON: ALLEN & UNWIN, 1941, 350 PP.
ANALYSIS OF DIPLOMATIC FORCES WHICH SHAPED THE TREATY: PERSONAL AND POLITICAL FORCES PULLING BETWEEN WILSONIAN PRINCIPLES OF A NEW WORLD ORDER AND PRINCIPLES OF REACTIONARY NATIONALISM. BIBLIOGRAPHY: 50 LISTINGS OF RECORDS AND PUBLISHED WORKS IN ENGLISH LISTED ALPHABETICALLY BY AUTHOR; 1920-38 PUBLICATIONS.

0291 BIRMINGHAM D.
TRADE AND CONFLICT IN ANGOLA.
LONDON: OXFORD U PR, 1966, 178 PP.
STUDIES IMPACT OF PORTUGAL ON ANGOLA IN RELATION TO NONCOLONIAL AFRICAN STATES, AND THE COMMERCIAL AND MILITARY EFFECTS ON AFRICA AND MBUNDU KINGDOM, IMPORTANT DURING FIRST THREE CENTURIES OF EUROPEAN CONTACT WITH THE AREA.

0292 BISHOP D.G.
THE ADMINISTRATION OF BRITISH FOREIGN RELATIONS.
SYRACUSE: U. PR., 1961, 410 PP.
A COMPREHENSIVE VIEW OF RELEVANT INSTITUTIONS, THEIR ORGANIZATION AND METHODS OF PROCEDURE. HISTORIC EXAMPLES OF DEVELOPMENT ARE PRESENTED. INCLUDES CRITICISM AND PROPOSALS FOR INSTITUTIONAL REFORM.

0293 BISHOP O.B. ED.
PUBLICATIONS OF THE GOVERNMENTS OF NOVA SCOTIA, PRINCE EDWARD ISLAND, NEW BRUNSWICK 1758-1952.
OTTAWA: NATL LIB OF CANADA, 1957, 237 PP.
INCLUDES ONLY THOSE PAMPHLETS OR BOOKS WHICH HAVE BEEN PRINTED "WITH THE IMPRINT OF, OR AT THE EXPENSE OF, OR BY AUTHORITY OF ANY ONE OF THE THREE GOVERNMENTS OF THE MARITIME PROVINCE." PAPERS. BROADSIDES, HANDBILLS, PROCLAMATIONS, AND MAPS HAVE BEEN OMITTED, AS HAVE WORKS DEALING WITH THE JUDICIAL AND MUNICIPAL ASPECTS OF GOVERNMENT.

0294 BISHOP O.B. ED.
PUBLICATIONS OF THE GOVERNMENT OF THE PROVINCE OF CANADA 1841-1867.

OTTAWA: NATL LIB OF CANADA, 1963.
BIBLIOGRAPHY COMPILED FROM HOLDINGS OF THE LAWSON MEMORIAL LIBRARY AT UNIVERSITY OF WESTERN ONTARIO, THE LEGISLATIVE LIBRARY FOR ONTARIO, AND THE LIBRARY OF THE PUBLIC ARCHIVES OF CANADA. HAS AN INTRODUCTION TO THE MATERIALS.

0295 BISSAINTHE M.
DICTIONNAIRE DE BIBLIOGRAPHIE HAITIENNE.
METUCHEN: SCARECROW PRESS, 1951, 1052 PP., LC#51-12164.
EXTENSIVE BIBLIOGRAPHY OF BOOKS AND PAMPHLETS PUBLISHED IN HAITI OR ABROAD BY HAITIANS 1804-1949. LISTS JOURNALISTS WITH A KEY TO THEIR NEWSPAPERS. INCLUDES LIST OF PERIODICALS PUBLISHED BETWEEN 1764-1949. ITEMS IN ENGLISH, SPANISH, AND FRENCH ARRANGED ALPHABETICALLY BY AUTHOR, INCLUDING SUBJECT AND TITLE INDEXES.

0296 BLACK C.E.
THE DYNAMICS OF MODERNIZATION: A STUDY IN COMPARATIVE HISTORY.
NEW YORK: HARPER & ROW, 1966, 207 PP., LC#66-20757.
DISCUSSES DEFINITION AND CHARACTERISTICS OF MODERNIZATION AND PRESENTS A CHRONOLOGICAL TIMETABLE FOR THE DEVELOPMENT OF MODERNIZING SOCIETIES. PRESENTS SEVEN MAIN PATTERNS OF GROWTH AND TRACES THE EXPERIENCES OF 175 CONTEMPORARY SOCIETIES WITH PREDICTIONS AS TO THEIR FUTURE. DISCUSSES PERIODS OF CONSOLIDATION OF MODERNIZING LEADERSHIP, ECONOMIC AND SOCIAL TRANSFORMATION, AND INTEGRATION OF SOCIETY.

0297 BLACK E.R.
THE DIPLOMACY OF ECONOMIC DEVELOPMENT.
CAMBRIDGE: HARVARD U. PR., 1960, 74 PP., $3.00.
INVESTIGATES THE 'REVOLUTION OF RISING EXPECTATIONS' IN UNDERDEVELOPED COUNTRIES, FOCUSING ATTENTION UPON THE IMPACT OF SCIENCE AND TECHNOLOGY AND QUALITY OF LEADERSHIP. DIPLOMACY IS VIEWED AS A CHALLENGE TO ILLUMINATE CHOICES RATHER THAN TO IMPOSE SOLUTIONS IN SHAPING ECONOMIC POLICIES.

0298 BLACK J.E. ED., THOMPSON K.W. ED.
FOREIGN POLICIES IN A WORLD OF CHANGE.
NEW YORK: HARPER ROW, 1963, 756 PP.
CHAPTERS COVERING THE FOREIGN POLICIES OF 24 NATIONS, AND, WITH THE EXCEPTION OF RED CHINA AND NIGERIA, WRITTEN BY LEADING INDIGENOUS SCHOLARS. EACH CONTRIBUTOR SUMMARIZES HISTORIC FOREIGN POLICIES, NATIONAL INTEREST, AND PRESENT FOREIGN POLICY PROBLEMS.

0299 BLACKETT P.M.S.
ATOMIC WEAPONS AND EAST-WEST RELATIONS.
NEW YORK: CAMBRIDGE U. PR., 1956, 107 PP.
DISCUSSES THE EFFECT OF THE NUCLEAR WEAPONS ON CURRENT WORLD SITUATION ANALYZES THOUGHTS AND OPINIONS ABOUT NUCLEAR WEAPONS AND ABOUT CONTROVERSY ON THEIR USE. CONCLUDES WITH SOME GENERAL OUTLINES FOR FUTURE MILITARY POLICIES.

0300 BLACKETT P.M.S.
STUDIES OF WAR: NUCLEAR AND CONVENTIONAL.
NEW YORK: HILL WANG, 1962, 242 PP., $3.95.
A CHALLENGE TO BASIC WESTERN MILITARY POLICIES AND AN ASSERTION THAT DISARMAMENT IS POSSIBLE. THE WEST HAS OVER-RELIED ON SUPERBOMBS AND HAS NOT PREPARED ADEQUATELY FOR LAND WAR.

0301 BLACKSTOCK P.W.
THE STRATEGY OF SUBVERSION.
CHICAGO: QUADRANGLE BOOKS, INC, 1964, 349 PP., LC#64-19620.
EXAMINES PROBLEMS OF MANAGEMENT AND CONTROL IN COVERT ESPIONAGE OPERATIONS. STUDIES EFFECTS UPON US STATE DEPARTMENT, MILITARY ESTABLISHMENT, AND INTELLIGENCE COMMUNITY. USES CASE STUDIES AND HISTORICAL ANALYSIS.

0302 BLACKSTOCK P.W.
AGENTS OF DECEIT: FRAUDS, FORGERIES AND POLITICAL INTRIGUES AMONG NATIONS.
CHICAGO: QUADRANGLE BOOKS, INC, 1966, 315 PP., LC#66-12134.
ANALYSIS OF HISTORICAL FORGERIES EITHER OF RUSSIAN ORIGIN OR PERPETRATED BY RUSSIANS, FROM TIME OF PETER THE GREAT TO PRESENT SOVIET REGIME. STUDIES HISTORICAL VALIDITY OF CONTROVERSIAL EVIDENCE SUPPORTING SOVIET HISTORY. APPENDIX, "THE SISSON DOCUMENTS," IS BY GEORGE KENNAN.

0303 BLAISDELL D.C.
"PRESSURE GROUPS, FOREIGN POLICIES, AND INTERNATIONAL POLITICS."
ANN. AMER. ACAD. POLIT. SOC. SCI., 319 (SEPT. 58), 542-550.
DEMONSTRATES CONFLICT AND CO-ORDINATION OF GROUPS AND NATIONAL INTERESTS, POINTING OUT DOMINATING ROLE OF MILITARY INTERESTS IN AMERICAN DIPLOMACY. EVALUATES INTERNATIONAL NON-GOVERNMENTAL ORGANIZATIONS' PARTICIPATION IN BROAD POLICY DECISIONS.

0304 BLAISDELL D.C.
"INTERNATIONAL ORGANIZATION."
NEW YORK: RONALD PRESS, 1966.
SELECTED BIBLIOGRAPHY OF BOOKS, PERIODICALS, DOCUMENTS, AND JOURNALS DEALING WITH ORGANIZATION OF THE NATION-STATES, PARTICULARLY THE UN AND ITS SPECIALIZED AGENCIES. SOURCES CATEGORIZED BY INDIVIDUAL CHAPTER. APPROXIMATELY 275 ENTRIES.

0305 BLAKE J.W.
EUROPEAN BEGINNINGS IN WEST AFRICA 1454-1578.
NEW YORK: LONGMANS, GREEN & CO, 1937, 212 PP.
"SURVEY OF 1ST CENTURY OF WHITE ENTERPRISE IN WEST AFRICA, WITH SPECIAL EMPHASIS UPON RIVALRY OF GREAT POWERS." BEGINS WITH PORTUGUESE MONOPOLY OVER TRADE WITH GUINEA IN 1450'S AND DISCUSSES CASTILIAN RIVALRY FROM 1454 TO 1480. EXAMINES STRONG MONOPOLY FROM 1480 TO 1530 AND ATTEMPTS BY FRANCE, ENGLAND, AND HOLLAND TO DESTROY IT.

0306 BLANCHARD C.H.
KOREAN WAR BIBLIOGRAPHY.
ALBANY: KOREAN CONFLICT RES FDN, 1964, 181 PP., LC#64-55065.
CONTAINS 9,000 LISTINGS OF BOOKS, ARTICLES, AND DOCUMENTS IN ENGLISH ARRANGED BY SUBJECT. PUBLICATION DATES OF ENTRIES, 1949-63. MAPS INCLUDED.

0307 BLANCHARD W.
"THAILAND."
NEW HAVEN: HUMAN REL AREA FILES, 1958.
EIGHTH VOLUME IN THE COUNTRY SERIES PUBLISHED BY THE HUMAN RELATIONS AREA FILES, PROMOTING RESEARCH AND COMPARATIVE STUDY IN SOCIAL AND BEHAVIORAL SCIENCES. THIS VOLUME EXAMINES SOCIOLOGICAL, POLITICAL, ECONOMIC ASPECTS OF THAI SOCIETY IN ORDER TO DEFINE BASIC CULTURAL AND INSTITUTIONAL PATTERNS AND TO IDENTIFY VALUES AND ATTITUDES. EXTENSIVE BIBLIOGRAPHY OF SOCIAL, POLITICAL, AND ECONOMIC SOURCES.

0308 BLANSHARD P.
COMMUNISM, DEMOCRACY AND CATHOLIC POWER.
BOSTON: BEACON, 1951, 332 PP.
ATTEMPTS TO ANALYZE RESEMBLANCES BETWEEN KREMLIN AND VATICAN. IMPLIES BOTH, USING ANTIDEMOCRATIC AND AUTHORITARIAN METHODS TO RULE OVER HUMAN MIND, ARE IN DIRECT CONFLICT.

0309 BLANSHARD P.
FREEDOM AND CATHOLIC POWER IN SPAIN AND PORTUGAL: AN AMERICAN INTERPRETATION.
BOSTON: BEACON PRESS, 1962, 300 PP., LC#62-9368.
DISCUSSES RELATIONSHIP BETWEEN CATHOLICISM AND FASCIST DICTATORSHIPS IN SPAIN AND PORTUGAL AND IMPORTANCE FOR US CATHOLICISM AND DIPLOMATIC RELATIONS. INCLUDES EFFECTS OF CATHOLIC DICTATORSHIP ON NON-CATHOLICS, EDUCATION, COMMUNICATION, CEREMONIES, ECONOMICS, AND INFLUENCE ON AMERICAN POWER IN AFRICA THROUGH RELATIONS WITH PORTUGAL.

0310 BLAUSTEIN A.P.
MANUAL ON FOREIGN LEGAL PERIODICALS AND THEIR INDEX.
NEW YORK: OCEANA PUBLISHING, 1962, 137 PP., LC#62-11757.
GUIDE TO 253 PERIODICALS LISTED IN "INDEX TO FOREIGN LEGAL PERIODICALS" DURING ITS FIRST YEAR OF PUBLICATION. PROVIDES DATA ON TOPICS COVERED BY PERIODICALS AND LANGUAGES IN WHICH PUBLISHED. ALSO INCLUDES BIBLIOGRAPHICAL DATA ON TITLES LISTED.

0311 BLOCH-MORHANGE J.
VINGT ANNEES D'HISTOIRE CONTEMPORAINE.
PARIS: LIBRAIIE PLON, 1963, 380 PP.
HISTORICAL STUDY OF INTERNATIONAL AFFAIRS FROM 1939 TO 1960 EXAMINING ALLIED ACTION DURING WWII AND POSTWAR RELATIONS OF COLD WAR. DISCUSSES PRINCIPAL NATIONAL LEADERS AND THEIR POLICIES.

0312 BLOM-COOPER L. ED.
THE LITERATURE OF THE LAW AND THE LANGUAGE OF THE LAW (2 VOLS.)
NEW YORK: MACMILLAN, 1967, 845 PP.
COLLECTION OF LEGAL DOCUMENTS AND WRITINGS BY LAWYERS AND NONLAWYERS FROM US, CANADA, ENGLAND, AUSTRALIA, IRELAND, NEW ZEALAND, AND ISRAEL. PERTAINS TO ALL ASPECTS OF LAW AND GOES BACK IN HISTORY TO TIME OF SOCRATES.

0313 BLOOMFIELD L.
THE UNITED NATIONS AND US FOREIGN POLICY.
BOSTON: LITTLE BROWN, 1967, 268 PP., LC#67-18883.
STATES US FOREIGN POLICY GOALS FOR NEXT DECADES AS PEACE, SECURITY, AND STABILITY. ANALYZES GOALS AS RELATED TO UN PROCEDURES AND ACTIONS OF THE PAST. REALISTIC EVALUATION OF POTENTIAL USEFULNESS OF UN TO FURTHER AMERICAN POLICIES.

0314 BLOOMFIELD L.M.
EGYPT, ISRAEL AND THE GULF OF AQABA: IN INTERNATIONAL LAW.
TORONTO: CARSWELL, 1957, 240 PP.
CITES HISTORICAL, GEOGRAPHICAL AND LEGAL BACKGROUND OF ARAB-ISRAELI DISPUTE OVER TRAVEL RIGHTS. LIST RESOLUTIONS AND CITES SPECIFIC SETTLEMENTS AND ACTS OF AGGRESSION RESULTING FROM BORDER DISPUTES, AND RELATES INVOLVEMENT OF OTHER NATIONAL AND INTERNATIONAL ORGANIZATIONS IN ISSUES.

0315 BLOOMFIELD L.P.

EVOLUTION OR REVOLUTION: THE UNITED NATIONS AND THE PROBLEM OF PEACEFUL TERRITORIAL CHANGE.
CAMBRIDGE: HARVARD U. PR., 1957, 220 PP.
EXAMINES RECORD OF PEACEFUL CHANGE UNDER BOTH UNITED NATIONS AND LEAGUE OF NATIONS FOCUSING ATTENTION ON ITS LEGAL ASPECTS. POINTS OUT SIGNIFICANCE OF 'CONVERSIONS' AS IT AFFECTS USA FOREIGN POLICY.

0316 BLOOMFIELD L.P.
WESTERN EUROPE AND THE UN - TRENDS AND PROSPECTS.
CAMBRIDGE: MIT CTR INTL STUDIES, 1959, 110 PP.
APPRAISAL OF ATTITUDES OF WESTERN EUROPE TOWARD UN, LISTED COUNTRY BY COUNTRY, INCLUDING UN AS IT RELATES TO EACH ONE'S NATIONAL INTERESTS, DOMESTIC POLITICS, AND SPECIAL HISTORY WITH UN.

0317 BLOOMFIELD L.P.
"THE UNITED NATIONS IN CRISIS: THE ROLE OF THE UN IN USA FOREIGN POLICY."
DAEDALUS, 91 (FALL 62), 749-765.
ASCRIBES 'CRISIS' TO POLITICAL, SOCIAL AND TECHNOLOGICAL REVOLUTIONS IN UNDERDEVELOPED COUNTRIES. ASSERTS THAT USA OBJECTIVES ARE PROMOTED BY UN ACTIONS AND RECOMMENDS FULLER PARTICIPATION BY FORMER IF WORLD BODY IS TO SURVIVE.

0318 BLOOMFIELD L.P.
"INTERNATIONAL FORCE IN A DISARMING BUT REVOLUTIONARY WORLD."
INT. ORGAN., 17 (SPRING 63), 444-464.
DEMONSTRATES IMPACT OF DISARMAMENT ON 'STRESS SITUATIONS' ARISING FROM REVOLUTIONARY TRENDS. WARNS AGAINST THE EMPLOYMENT OF INTERNATIONAL FORCE TO COUNTERCHECK DISORDER, RECOGNIZING THE LIMITATIONS INHERENT IN SUCH SOLUTIONS.

0319 BLOOMFIELD L.P.
"HEADQUARTERS-FIELD RELATIONS: SOME NOTES ON THE BEGINNING AND END OF ONUC."
INT. ORGAN., 17 (SPRING 63), 377-393.
VOICES CONCERN OVER CONTROL OF UNITED NATIONS OPERATIONS IN THE CONGO BY CIVILIAN AUTHORITIES. QUESTIONS POLITICAL CONSTRAINT OF ARMED FORCES IN THE FIELD AND RECOMMENDS RIOT POLICE BE USED INSTEAD OF INFANTRY IN FUTURE ACTION.

0320 BLOOMFIELD L.P.
INTERNATIONAL MILITARY FORCES: THE QUESTION OF PEACE-KEEPING IN AN ARMED AND DISARMING WORLD.
BOSTON: LITTLE BROWN, 1964, 296 PP., LC#64-17098.
DISCUSSES PROBLEM OF UN FORCES TODAY AND IN A DISARMING WORLD, AND ASSESSES RECPONSIBLITY OF POLICY-MAKERS AND SCHOLARS. STRESSES HIGHLY POLITICAL NATURE OF THE ISSUE. INCLUDES SEVERAL ESSAYS BY UN OFFICIALS AND SCHOLARLY OBSERVERS APPRAISING PAST EMPLOYMENT OF FORCES, LOGISTICAL PROBLEMS, AND PLAUSIBILITY OF INTERNATIONAL FORCES IN A DISARMED WORLD.

0321 BLOOMFIELD L.P., CLEMENS W.C. JR., GRIFFITHS F.
KHRUSHCHEV AND THE ARMS RACE.
CAMBRIDGE: M I T PRESS, 1966, 338 PP., LC#66-19361.
SOVIET ATTITUDES AND POLICIES TOWARD ARMS IN KHRUSHCHEV DECADE LISTED BY THREE PERIODS, TO SPUTNIK, TO CUBA, TO OUSTER OF KHRUSHCHEV. INCLUDES CONSIDERATION OF FACTORS INFLUENCING ARMS CONTROL POLICY.

0322 BLUM L.
PEACE AND DISARMAMENT (TRANS. BY A. WERTH)
LONDON: JONATHAN CAPE, 1932, 202 PP.
BELIEVES THAT NO INTERNATIONAL PEACE ORGANIZATION CAN BE EFFECTIVE IN AN ARMED EUROPE. DISARMAMENT IS A CAUSE, NOT AN EFFECT, OF SECURITY, AND IS ONE OF ITS ESSENTIAL ELEMENTS. BELIEVES NATIONS REFUSE TO DISARM BECAUSE THEY STILL FEAR EACH OTHER. SOCIALISM WILL LEAD TO PEACE THROUGH "MORAL DISARMAMENT." BY PUTTING PRESSURE ON GOVERNMENT, WORKING CLASS CAN HELP DESTROY OLD INSTINCTS AND CONTROL GOVERNMENT.

0323 BLUM L.
FOR ALL MANKIND (TRANS. BY W. PICKLES)
LONDON: VICTOR GOLLANCZ, 1946, 143 PP.
WRITTEN DURING VICHY REGIME IN FRANCE, DEFENDS DEMOCRATIC PRINCIPLES. SAYS FRANCE WAS DEFEATED IN WWII BECAUSE OF IRRESOLUTION OF BOURGEOISIE, NOT BECAUSE OF WEAKNESSES OF DEMOCRATIC GOVERNMENT. BOURGEOISIE IS CONSIDERED THE RULING CLASS. SEES NAZISM AS ENDING BOURGEOIS RULE, BUT ALSO TURNING BACK PROGRESS OF CIVILIZATION. PROPOSES SOCIALIST DEMOCRACY.

0324 BLUM Y.Z.
"INDONESIA'S RETURN TO THE UNITED NATIONS."
INT. AND COMP. LAW Q., 16 (APR. 67), 522-531.
CONSIDERS JURIDICAL MEANING OF INDONESIA'S CESSATION OF ACTIVITIES IN UN IN JANUARY, 1965, AND LEGAL CONSEQUENCES FLOWING FROM HER POSITION. CONCLUDES THAT INDONESIA'S BOND OF MEMBERSHIP WITH UN TERMINATED ON WITHDRAWAL AND THAT INDONESIA MUST NECESSARILY REAPPLY AS NONMEMBER.

0325 BODENHEIMER E.
TREATISE ON JUSTICE.
NEW YORK: PHILOSOPHICAL LIB, 1967, 314 PP., LC#67-11987.
VIEWS JUSTICE AS MATERIAL VALUE WHICH SHAPES OR AFFECTS QUALITY OF LIFE. ASSUMES PROBLEMS OF JUSTICE ARE CONNECTED WITH CERTAIN BASIC EXISTENTIAL HUMAN NEEDS ASCERTAINED BY HUMAN PHILOSOPHICAL ENDEAVOR. REJECTS VIEW OF JUSTICE AS FRATIONAL IDEAL BEYOND OBJECTIVE METHODS OF RESEARCH. CONSIDERS CONCEPTS AND GOALS OF JUSTICE AND DIVISIONS: POLITICAL, SOCIAL, PENAL, ECONOMIC, INTERNATIONAL.

0326 BODENHEIMER S.J.
"THE 'POLITICAL UNION' DEBATE IN EUROPE* A CASE STUDY IN INTERGOVERNMENTAL DIPLOMACY."
INTL. ORGANIZATION, 21 (WINTER 67), 24-54.
DISCUSSION OF THE PROBLEMS CONFRONTING THE SIX MEMBERS OF THE EEC IF POLITICAL UNION IS TO OCCUR. AUTHOR EXAMINES PAST EXPERIENCE AND FUTURE PROSPECTS OF POLITICAL COOPERATION AND RULES OUT ABSOLUTE EITHER/OR CHOICE BETWEEN DECLINE OF NATIONAL STATE STRUCTURES VS. NATIONAL SOVEREIGNTY AS THE ONLY ALTERNATIVES.

0327 BOGARDUS E.S.
"THE SOCIOLOGY OF A STRUCTURED PEACE."
SOCIOL. SOC. RES., 44 (MAY 1960), 352-357.
CONSIDERS ACHIEVEMENT OF WORLD PEACE THROUGH STRUCTURES OF THE UN, AND USE OF UN ORGANS AS BASIS FOR INTERNATIONAL LAW. ALSO SUGGESTS, AS A SOCIOLOGICAL APPROACH TO PEACE, THE DEVELOPMENT OF A POINT OF VIEW, NATIONAL PHILOSOPHY AND BEHAVIOR WHICH WOULD BE CONDUCIVE TO MUTUAL TRUST AMONG NATIONS.

0328 BOGART L.
"MEASURING THE EFFECTIVENESS OF AN OVERSEAS INFORMATION CAMPAIGN."
PUB. OPIN. QUART., 21 (WINTER 58), 475-98.
INTERVIEWS OF CROSS SECTION OF GREEK POPULATION BEFORE AND AFTER U.S. INFORMATION AGENCY CAMPAIGN ON U.S. SUPPORT FOR HUMAN RIGHTS, INDICATE THAT THE CAMPAIGN DID NOT ALTER PUBLIC OPINION. IT DID, HOWEVER, INFORM THE POPULATION AND FURNISH SUPPORTING ARGUMENTS FOR EXISTING OPINIONS.

0329 BOGGS S.W.
INTERNATIONAL BOUNDARIES.
NEW YORK: COLUMB. U. PR., 1940, 272 PP.
CRITICISM OF THE METHOD AND MOTIVE EMPLOYED BY GOVERNMENTS IN DETERMINING BOUNDARIES. ARGUES THAT LEADERS MUST TAKE INTO ACCOUNT NOT ONLY NATIONAL INTERESTS AND AMBITIONS BUT 'IDEALISM OF INTERNATIONAL RELATIONS'.

0330 BOHATTA H., HODES F.
INTERNATIONALE BIBLIOGRAPHIE.
FRANKFURT: V KLOSTERMANN, 1950, 652 PP.
A BIBLIOGRAPHY OF BIBLIOGRAPHIES LISTING NATIONAL AND INTERNATIONAL BIBLIOGRAPHICAL PUBLICATIONS ON CULTURAL AS WELL AS EXACT SCIENCES. INCLUDES BIBLIOGRAPHIES ON NEWSPAPERS, PRINTING, BOOK TRADE, ETC. IT IS ARRANGED BY SUBJECT AND COUNTRY AND PURPORTS TO LIST ALL BIBLIOGRAPHIES PUBLISHED, EXCLUDING ONLY BIBLIOGRAPHIES OF PERSONS.

0331 BOHN L.
"WHOSE NUCLEAR TEST: NON-PHYSICAL INSPECTION AND TEST BAN."
J. CONFL. RESOLUT., 7 (SEPT. 63), 379-393.
SPECULATES ON ADVANTAGES OFFERED BY CONCEALED NUCLEAR-TESTING WITH REGARD TO WEAPONS DEVELOPMENT AND THE N-TH NATION PROBLEM. INABILITY OF PHYSICAL METHODS TO DETECT MID-OCEAN OR SPACE EXPLOSIONS HAS NECESSITATED EMPLOYMENT OF NON-PHYSICAL TECHNIQUES ANALOGOUS TO CRIMINAL INVESTIGATION AND COURT SYSTEMS.

0332 BOISSIER P.
HISTORIE DU COMITE INTERNATIONAL DE LA CROIX ROUGE.
PARIS: PLON, 1963, 512 PP.
TRACES DEVELOPMENT OF THE INTERNATIONAL RED CROSS IN THE PERIOD FROM 1859 TO 1905. EMPHASIS ON ROLE OF THE SOCIETY IN FOSTERING GENERAL RULES OF 'HUMANE WARFARE.'

0333 BOKOR-SZEGO H.
"LA CONVENTION DE BELGRADE ET LE REGIME DU DANUBE."
ANNU. FRANC. DR. INTER., 8 (1962), 192-205.
OUTLINES ECONOMIC GROWTH BORDERING DANUBE RIVER AND PRINCIPAL ARRANGEMENTS FOR ITS REGULATION ARRIVED AT BY BELGRADE CONVENTION OF 1948. DESCRIBES STRUCTURE AND FUNCTION OF DANUBE COMMISSION. SHOWS CHANGES EFFECTED BY COMMUNIST REGIME.

0334 BONNEFOUS M.
EUROPE ET TIERS MONDE.
LEYDEN: SYTHOFF, 1961, 116 PP.
CONSIDERS EUROPE'S AID TO THE UNDERDEVELOPED COUNTRIES OF AFRICA AND QUESTIONS WHETHER THESE TECHNICAL CONNECTIONS WILL MORE FAVORABLY BIND THE COUNTRIES THAN THE FORMER HISTORICAL ONES.

0335 BONNET H.
THE UNITED NATIONS, WHAT THEY ARE, WHAT THEY MAY BECOME.
CHICAGO: WORLD CITIZENS ASS., 1942, 100 PP., $0.25.
REVIEWS COLLABORATION BETWEEN ALLIED FORCES ENFORCING

PRINCIPLES OF ATLANTIC CHARTER AND SPECULATES HOW MACHINERY COULD BE RETAINED FOR USE IN SETTLING POST-WAR INTERNATIONAL DISPUTES. URGES IMMEDIATE FORMATION OF INTERNATIONAL POLITICAL COUNCIL TO PROMOTE SOLIDARITY OF ALLIANCES.

0336 BORBA DE MORAES R., BERRIEN W.
MANUAL BIBLIOGRAFICO DE ESTUDOS BRASILEIROS.
RIO DE JANEIRO: GRAFICA ED SOUNA, 1949, 895 PP.
DETAILED BIBLIOGRAPHY OF BRAZILIAN RESEARCH.

0337 BORCHARD E.H., STUMBERG G.W.
GUIDE TO THE LAW AND LEGAL LITERATURE OF FRANCE.
WASHINGTON: LIBRARY OF CONGRESS, 1931, 242 PP., LC#30-26002.
BIBLIOGRAPHICAL ESSAY AND GUIDE DESIGNED TO FURNISH PRACTICAL INFORMATION ON THE LEGAL INSTITUTIONS OF FRANCE; METHODS BY WHICH IT HAS SOLVED ECONOMIC AND SOCIAL PROBLEMS FACING IT IN AN INDUSTRIAL AGE; LEGAL METHOD, DOCTRINE, AND PHILOSOPHY OF SCIENTIFIC INVESTIGATION UNDERLYING CONSTITUTIONAL INSTITUTIONS.

0338 BORCHARD E.M.
BIBLIOGRAPHY OF INTERNATIONAL LAW AND CONTINENTAL LAW.
WASHINGTON: LIBRARY OF CONGRESS, 1913, 93 PP.
DISCUSSES VARIOUS BOOKS DEALING WITH INTERNATIONAL AND CONTINENTAL LAW. INCLUDES AN INTRODUCTION AND SECTIONS DEVOTED TO SPECIFIC COUNTRIES, GENERAL AREAS SUCH AS COMMERCIAL LAW, PUBLIC LAW (CONSTITUTIONAL, COLONIAL, AND ADMINISTRATIVE), CRIMINAL LAW, CANON LAW. CONTAINS AN INDEX, COMMENTS ON EACH WORK, FOOTNOTES, ETC.

0339 BORGESE G.A. ED.
COMMON CAUSE.
NEW YORK: COMM. FRAME WORLD CONST., 1947-51, 4 VOLS.
REPORT PUBLISHED TO CLARIFY THE ISSUES SURROUNDING THE QUESTION OF WORLD GOVERNMENT BY CONTRIBUTORS FROM THE SPECIALIZED-STUDY FIELDS OF PSYCHOLOGY, SOCIOLOGY, ECONOMICS, POLITICS AND PHILOSOPHY.

0340 BORGESE G. A.
FOUNDATIONS OF THE WORLD REPUBLIC.
CHICAGO: U. CHI. PR., 1953, 328 PP.
AN EXAMINATION OF THE PREREQUISITES AND INGREDIENTS FOR FORMATION OF A WORLD REPUBLIC. DEFENDS MAJORITY RULE AND REFUTES ARGUMENTS THAT NATIONAL INTERESTS AND THE VARIETY OF CULTURES EXTANT NECESSARILY MILITATE AGAINST ITS FEASIBILITY FOR MANKIND. CONSIDERS THE WORLD AS A TOTALITY AND VIEWS OUR COLLECTIVE VALUES AS ENFORCEABLE. PRESENTS THE CHICAGO DRAFT OF 1947 AS THE BEST WORLD CONSTITUTION YET PROPOSED.

0341 BORGESE G.A.
GOLIATH: THE MARCH OF FASCISM.
NEW YORK: VIKING PRESS, 1937, 483 PP.
DESCRIBES ORIGINS AND RISE OF FASCISM IN EUROPE, FOCUSING ON ITALY. TRACES ITALIAN ROOTS BACK TO DANTE, MYTHS OF ROME, AND MACHIAVELLI. DISCUSSES EARLY CAREER OF MUSSOLINI AND HIS SUBSEQUENT ROLE IN FASCIST RISE. EXAMINES FASCIST POLICIES TOWARD CHURCH, POLITICAL PARTIES, AND LAW. FEELS EXPANSION OF ITALY IS DANGEROUS AND IMPLORES WORLD TO ACT DECISIVELY.

0342 BORKENAU F.
EUROPEAN COMMUNISM.
NEW YORK: HARPER & ROW, 1951, 564 PP.
STUDIES EUROPEAN COMMUNISM, CONCENTRATING ON EARLY COMINFORM PERIOD (1934-45). SHOWS EVOLUTION OF COMMUNIST POLICY DURING POPULAR FRONT PERIOD IN FRANCE, AND OF GENERAL COMMUNIST LINE DURING WWII. ATTEMPTS TO CLARIFY STALIN'S ATTITUDE TOWARD RISE OF HITLER, AND RUSSIAN POLICY DURING LATTER PART OF SPANISH CIVIL WAR.

0343 BORNSTEIN J., MILTON P.R.
ACTION AGAINST THE ENEMY'S MIND.
INDIANAPOLIS: BOBBS-MERRILL, 1942, 294 PP.
TWO STUDIES OF PSYCHOLOGICAL WARFARE DURING WWII DEAL SPECIFICALLY WITH NAZI APPLICATION OF IT. ENUMERATES PROGRAM IN US THAT UTILIZED ISOLATIONISM, ANTI-SEMITISM, AND FEAR OF COMMUNISM.

0344 BOUDET P., BOURGEOIS R.
BIBLIOGRAPHIE DE L'INDOCHINE FRANCAISE.
HANOI: IMPRIM D'EXTREME ORIENT, 1929, 75 PP.
TWO-VOLUME BIBLIOGRAPHY OF FRENCH MATERIALS ON FRENCH INDOCHINA. VOLUME I, PUBLISHED IN 1929, COVERS ISSUING DATES 1913-1926. VOLUME II, PUBLISHED IN 1943, COVERS PERIOD 1933-1935. MATERIAL IN FORMER VOLUME IS ARRANGED BY SUBJECT AND INCLUDES ALPHABETICAL AUTHOR INDEX. VOLUME II IS CLASSIFIED ALPHABETICALLY BY AUTHOR.

0345 BOULDING K.E.
"ECONOMIC ISSUES IN INTERNATIONAL CONFLICT."
KYLKOS, 6 (NO.2, 53), 97-118.
ASSERTS WAR IS BECOMING ENTRENCHED AS DOMINANT INSTITUTION OF SOCIETY WITH INORDINATE AMOUNT OF NATIONAL ECONOMIC RESOURCES BEING ALLOCATED FOR DEFENSE. CONTRASTS ECONOMIC APPROACHES OF WESTERN AND COMMUNIST BLOCS TOWARDS DEVELOPING NATIONS, CONCLUDING WEST SHOULD INCREASE AID TO THEM.

0346 BOULDING K.E.
"NATIONAL IMAGES AND INTERNATIONAL SYSTEMS."
J. CONFL. RESOUL., 3 (JUNE 59), 120-31.
DISCUSSES PROBLEM OF FORMATION AND INTERPRETATION OF IMAGES OF NATIONS IN THE CONDUCT OF INTERNATIONAL POLITICS AND EVALUATES THE IMPACT OF THESE IMAGES ON THEIR RELATIONS. CONCLUDES THAT PRESENT SYSTEM, BASED ON ACCEPTANCE OF UNSOPHISTICATED IMAGES, BE REPLACED BY DECISION MAKING GROUP WHICH VIEWS IMAGE OF WORLD FROM MANY VIEWPOINTS.

0347 BOULDING K.E.
CONFLICT AND DEFENSE: A GENERAL THEORY.
NEW YORK: HARPER/ROW, 1962, 491 PP.
INTERNATIONAL RELATIONS ARE SUBJECTED TO MATHEMATICS BY AN ECONOMIST TO DETERMINE IF CONFLICTS AMONG NATIONS CAN BE PREDICTED TO A USEFUL DEGREE. AN ABSTRACT SOCIAL THEORY WITH A RATIONAL METHODOLOGY. PART 1 EVOLVES A GENERAL THEORY OF WAR AND PART 2 APPLIES IT TO SPECIAL CASES, EMPHASIZING THE DIFFERENCES. EXPLORES GAME THEORY AND VIEWS OF BEHAVIORISTS.

0348 BOULDING K.E.
"THE PREVENTION OF WORLD WAR THREE."
VIRGINIA QUART. REV., 38 (WINTER 62), 1-12.
ASSERTS THAT CLOSE INTER-RELATIONS AMONG ALL GOVERNMENTS OF THE WORLD IS A DANGER THAT MUST BE ADAPTED TO AND MADE VIABLE THROUGH MUTUAL AGREEMENTS LEADING TO DISARMAMENT AND WORLD FEDERATION.

0349 BOULDING K.E.
THE IMPACT OF THE SOCIAL SCIENCES.
NEW BRUNSWICK: RUTGERS U PR, 1966, 119 PP., LC#66-64653.
AN EXPLORATION OF THE IMPACT OF THE SOCIAL SCIENCES ON THREE CENTRAL AREAS: INTERNATIONAL RELATIONS, ECONOMICS, AND FIELD OF ETHICS, RELIGION, AND LAW.

0350 BOURBON-BUSSET J.
"HOW DECISIONS ARE MADE IN FOREIGN POLITICS: PSYCHOLOGY IN INTERNATIONAL POLITICS."
REV. POLIT., 20 (OCT. 58), 591-614.
EXPANSION OF WORLD POLITICS AND DIMINISHING SIZE OF THE GLOBE, BOTH THE RESULT OF TECHNOLOGICAL ADVANCE, ARE THE SIGNIFICANT DEVELOPMENTS OF OUR TIME. LEADERSHIP HAS BECOME AN IMPORTANT CONCERN OF POLITICAL ANALYSTS AND STATESMEN. INCREASED COMMUNICATIONS ACTUATE 'NEW DOUBTS'. ASSERTS THAT CHRISTIAN PRINCIPLES MUST BE RESPECTED EVERYWHERE.

0351 BOURNE H.E.
THE WORLD WAR: A LIST OF THE MORE IMPORTANT BOOKS PUBLISHED BEFORE 1937 (PAMPHLET)
WASHINGTON: LIBRARY OF CONGRESS, 1937, 17 PP.
160 ITEMS ANNOTATED. INDEXED BY AUTHOR AND ARRANGED BY TOPIC. INCLUDES FRENCH, ENGLISH, GERMAN, ITALIAN, AND OTHER LANGUAGES. ALSO CONTAINS A 17-PAGE SUPPLEMENT PRINTED AND UPDATED IN APRIL, 1934, WHICH LISTS 152 MORE BOOKS RELEVANT TO THE MILITARY HISTORY OF WORLD WAR I.

0352 BOUSCAREN A.T.
SOVIET FOREIGN POLICY: A PATTERN OF PERSISTANCE.
NEW YORK: FORDHAM U. PR., 1962, 187 PP.
DISCUSSES IDEOLOGICAL BASIS OF SOVIET FOREIGN POLICY AND THE CLOSE RELATIONSHIP BETWEEN IT AND THE INTERNATIONAL COMMUNIST MOVEMENT.

0353 BOWETT D.W.
SELF-DEFENSE IN INTERNATIONAL LAW.
MANCHESTER: U. PR., 1958, 294 PP.
APPLYING LEGAL STANDARDS, AUTHOR ANALYZES THE RIGHT OF SELF-DEFENSE, PAYING PARTICULAR ATTENTION TO THE PROVISIONS AND EXPERIENCES UNDER THE U.N. CHARTER. DICHOTOMIZES WORK INTO TWO TECHNICAL CATEGORIES: THE SUBSTANTIVE RIGHTS FOR WHICH SELF-DEFENSE IS A PERMISSIBLE MEANS OF PROTECTION AND THE ANTITHESIS OF THE RIGHTS OF SELF-DEFENSE AND 'JUST WAR'.

0354 BOWETT D.W.
THE LAW OF INTERNATIONAL INSTITUTIONS.
NEW YORK: PRAEGER, 1965, 347 PP.
PRESENTS A DETAILED DESCRIPTION OF INTERNATIONAL INSTITUTIONS ARISING IN THE WAKE OF TWO WORLD WARS. BESIDES OUTLINING INSTITUTIONAL STRUCTURES, E.G. THE UNITED NATIONS OR THE WARSAW TREATY ORGANIZATION, FOCUSES ATTENTION ON GENERAL PROBLEMS OF INTERNATIONAL ORGANIZATIONS.

0355 BOWIE R.
"POLICY FORMATION IN AMERICAN FOREIGN POLICY."
ANN. AMER. ACAD. POLIT. SOC. SCI., 330 (JULY 60), 1-10.
DISCUSSES COMPLEXITY OF POLICY-MAKING UNDER MODERN CONDITIONS. ANALYZES INSTITUTIONS AND PROCEDURES INVOLVED IN USA FOREIGN RELATIONS.

0357 BOWIE R.R. ED., FRIEDRICH C.J. ED.
"STUDIES IN FEDERALISM."
BOSTON: LITTLE BROWN, 1954.
REPRODUCTION OF STUDIES BY EUROPEAN FEDERAL MOVEMENT ON THE FEDERAL LEGISLATURE, EXECUTIVE, JUDICIARY, DEFENSE, FOREIGN AFFAIRS QUESTIONS. CONTAINS ALSO CONTRIBUTIONS IN FIELDS OF COMMERCE, TRANSPORTATION, AND CUSTOMS, PUBLIC

FINANCE, AGRICULTURE, LABOR AND SOCIAL SECURITY, CITIZENSHIP RIGHTS, APPENDEXES CONTAINING DRAFT RESOLUTIONS AND TREATIES OF EUROPEAN COMMUNITY. EXTENSIVE BIBLIOGRAPHY.

0358 BOWLES C.
AFRICA'S CHALLENGE TO AMERICA.
BERKELEY: U OF CALIF PR, 1956, 134 PP., LC#56-10997.
DISCUSSES AMERICAN FAILURE TO ADAPT ITS FOREIGN POLICY TO ANTI-COLONIAL REVOLUTIONS IN AFRICAN COUNTRIES AFTER WWII. ARGUES THAT AMERICAN TRADITIONS OF SELF-DETERMINATION AND SELF-GOVERNMENT SHOULD BE BASIS OF ITS FOREIGN POLICY TOWARD UNDERDEVELOPED COUNTRIES. CRITICIZES AMERICAN PREOCCUPATION WITH SOVIET COLD WAR ACTIVITIES AND URGES INCREASED AMERICAN SUPPORT AND AID TO AFRICAN STRUGGLE FOR INDEPENDENCE.

0359 BOWLES C.
IDEAS, PEOPLE AND PEACE.
NEW YORK: HARPER & ROW, 1958, 151 PP., LC#57-11780.
EXAMINES NATURE OF COLD WAR AND POSTWAR CHALLENGE OF COMMUNISM, PROBLEMS OF DEVELOPING WORLD, AND SUGGESTIONS FOR CREATIVE AMERICAN RESPONSE.

0360 BOWLES C.
THE COMING POLITICAL BREAKTHROUGH.
NEW YORK: HARPER & ROW, 1959, 209 PP., LC#59-13278.
CONTENDS THAT EXISTING AMERICAN POLITICAL AND ECONOMIC POLICIES ARE NOT PROPERLY GEARED TO EMERGING PRESSURES AND PROBLEMS ON DOMESTIC AND INTERNATIONAL SCENES. URGES REASSERTION OF TRADITIONAL AMERICAN DEMOCRATIC BELIEF AND NEW DEFINITION OF NATIONAL PURPOSE IN 20TH-CENTURY TERMS. PREDICTS 1960 ELECTION TO BE MOST DECISIVE OF CENTURY WITH WINNING PARTY REMAINING DOMINANT FOR MANY YEARS.

0361 BOWLES C.
THE CONSCIENCE OF A LIBERAL.
NEW YORK: HARPER & ROW, 1962, 351 PP., LC#62-16422.
COLLECTION OF ARTICLES AND SPEECHES DISCUSSING SEVERAL PROBLEM AREAS IN AMERICAN POLICY AND DOMESTIC AFFAIRS DURING POST-WWII ERA. SOME MAJOR ISSUES DISCUSSED INCLUDE AMERICAN OBJECTIVES IN INTERNATIONAL POLITICS, ARMS RACE, CIVIL RIGHTS, AND DOMESTIC ECONOMIC STABILITY.

0362 BOYCE A.N.
EUROPE AND SOUTH AFRICA.
CAPETOWN: JUTA & CO, LTD, 1936, 440 PP.
HISTORICAL STUDY OF PARALLEL DEVELOPMENTS AND RELATED EVENTS IN EUROPE AND SOUTH AFRICA FROM 1915-39. FOCUSES ON RELATIONSHIPS BETWEEN SOUTH AFRICA AND GREAT BRITAIN BUT ALSO EMPHASIZES BROADER SOCIAL AND POLITICAL DEVELOPMENTS IN EUROPE SUCH AS RISE OF NATIONALISM AND INDUSTRIALISM AND DEMANDS FOR LIBERAL REFORM.

0363 BOYD A., BOYD F.
WESTERN UNION: A STUDY OF THE TREND TOWARD EUROPEAN UNITY.
WASHINGTON: PUBLIC AFFAIRS PRESS, 1949, 175 PP.
DISCUSSES PAST AND PRESENT TRENDS TOWARD UNITY IN EUROPE, FROM IDEAS OF ERASMUS, ROUSSEAU, AND KANT TO CHURCHILL AND SENATOR JW FULBRIGHT. FEELS THAT CREATION OF COUNCIL OF EUROPE WILL STRENGTHEN DEMOCRATIC FORCES OF CONTINENT AND IMPLEMENT MARSHALL PLAN, NORTH ATLANTIC SECURITY ALLIANCE. INCLUDES COPIES OF PERTINENT PUBLIC SPEECHES, TREATIES, AND CONVENTION ESTABLISHING OEEC.

0364 BOYD J.P.
NUMBER 7: ALEXANDER HAMILTON'S SECRET ATTEMPTS TO CONTROL AMERICAN FOREIGN POLICY.
PRINCETON: PRINCETON U PRESS, 1964, 166 PP., LC#64-8515.
THE HAMILTON-BECKWITH AFFAIR AND HAMILTON'S EFFORTS TO FORGE ANGLO-AFRICAN TIES ARE ANALYZED, ALONG WITH SOME OF THE REACTIONS OF HAMILTON'S OPPONENTS. ALMOST HALF OF THIS BOOK CONSISTS OF DOCUMENTS ON THE WAR CRISIS OF 1790.

0365 BOZZA T.
SCRITTORI POLITICI ITALIANI DAL 1550 AL 1650.
ROME: EDIZ DI STORIA E LETTERAT, 1949, 218 PP.
CHRONOLOGICAL ARRANGEMENT OF ITALIAN POLITICAL WRITINGS FROM 1550-1650. GIVES BIBLIOGRAPHICAL DESCRIPTION OF WRITING AND ANNOTATION AND BIBLIOGRAPHY OF ITS AUTHOR. INDICATES LIBRARY WHERE WRITING MAY BE OBTAINED. CONTAINS BRIEF HISTORICAL SURVEY AND GENERAL BIBLIOGRAPHICAL SECTION.

0366 BRACKETT R.D.
PATHWAYS TO PEACE.
MINNEAPOLIS: T S DENISON + CO, 1965, 387 PP., LC#65-20095.
OUTLINES AVENUES BY WHICH MOTIVATED CITIZENS CAN ASSUME PARTICIPATION IN EDUCATIONAL AND RELIGIOUS ACTIVITIES THAT LEAD TO INTERNATIONAL PEACE AND COOPERATION. CHAPTERS ARE DEVOTED TO SPECIFIC AREAS OF EDUCATIONAL EXCHANGE, IMPROVED FOREIGN LANGUAGE FACITILTY, AND VOLUNTARY ASSOCIATIONS SUCH AS THE PEACE CORPS.

0367 BRACKMAN A.C.
SOUTHEAST ASIA'S SECOND FRONT: THE POWER STRUGGLE IN THE MALAY ARCHIPELAGO.
NEW YORK: FREDERICK PRAEGER, 1966, 341 PP., LC#65-24939.
A HISTORY OF COMMUNIST AGITATION AND ATTEMPTS AT REVOLUTION IN THE MALAY PENINSULA. BELIEVES THAT THE AREA IS NOT HOMOGENEOUS AND THAT THERE IS A CONFLICT IN THE AREA BETWEEN AUTHORITARIAN AND REPRESENTATIVE SYSTEMS OF GOVERNMENT. ATTEMPTS TO PRESENT THE "STRATEGY AND TRAPS OF THE PROTAGONISTS" (COMMUNISTS). ANTI-COMMUNIST IN OUTLOOK.

0368 BRANDENBURG E.
FROM BISMARCK TO THE WORLD WAR; A HISTORY OF GERMAN FOREIGN POLICY, 1870-1914 (TRANS. BY ANNIE ELIZABETH ADAMS)
LONDON: OXFORD U PR, 1927, 542 PP., LC#27-17234.
GERMAN FACTUAL STUDY OF PERIOD PRIOR TO WWI IN GERMANY. BEGINS WITH GENERAL SITUATION IN 1871; THEN STUDIES CHAMBERLAIN'S OFFER OF ALLIANCE, ANGLO-FRENCH ENTENTE, BOSNIAN CRISIS, BALKAN WARS, AND OUTBREAK OF WWI. MAINTAINS THAT CAREFUL STUDY OF RECORDS SHOWS THAT WARLIKE AIM OF GERMAN POLICY WAS UNFOUNDED.

0369 BRECHER M.
THE NEW STATES OF ASIA.
LONDON: OXFORD U PR, 1963, 226 PP.
POLITICAL ANALYSIS OF NEW ASIAN NATIONS. TREATS COLONIALISM AND COMING OF INDEPENDENCE, SEARCH FOR POLITICAL STABILITY, STATE SYSTEM, NEUTRALISM, AND NEW STATES IN WORLD POLITICS.

0370 BREGMAN A.
"WHITHER RUSSIA?"
PROBLEMS OF COMMUNISM, 16 (MAY-JUNE 67), 50-54.
DELINEATES THE EXTENT OF INTERDEPENDENCE BETWEEN USSR AND EASTERN EUROPE AND OF POTENTIAL SOCIAL AND IDEOLOGICAL INTERACTION. ARGUES THAT THE URGE OF YOUNG LIBERAL EAST EUROPEAN MARXISTS TO REFORM VESTED BUREAUCRATIC INTERESTS AND CREATE A FREER SOCIETY MAY INFLUENCE USSR TO LIBERALIZE ITS OWN SYSTEM. CALLS THE PROCESS "EVOLUTIONARY," PERHAPS AFTER A FINNISH OR RUMANIAN MODEL.

0371 BRENNAN D.G.
"SETTING AND GOALS OF ARMS CONTROL."
DAEDALUS, 89 (WINTER 1960), 681-707.
ANALYZES THE STRATEGY ON WHICH ARMS CONTROL IS BASED, INCLUDING A REVIEW OF THE CONTEMPORARY MILITARY GOALS OF DETERRENCE, LIMITED WAR AND GENERAL WAR. ELABORATES ON EFFECTS OF THERMONUCLEAR ACTIONS IN CONFINED AREAS AND CONTENDS THEIR OCCURRENCE CAN BE AVOIDED BY ACHIEVING A WORKABLE ARMAMENT AGREEMENT WITH THE SOVIET UNION BASED ON COMMON OBJECTIVES AND ENFORCED BY INTERNATIONAL SANCTIONS.

0372 BRENNAN D.G. ED.
ARMS CONTROL, DISARMAMENT, AND NATIONAL SECURITY.
NEW YORK: GEORGE BRAZILLER, 1961, 475 PP., LC#61-12952.
EXPLORES POTENTIAL ROUTES AND OBSTACLES TO ARMS CONTROL; ILLUSTRATES MAJOR CONSIDERATIONS BEARING ON DECISIONS OF NATIONAL POLICY. BEGINS WITH GOALS AND REQUIREMENTS OF ARMS CONTROL; DISCUSSES POLICY ISSUES AND PROBLEMS, LIMITED WAR, AND ECONOMIC IMPLICATIONS. SUBSTANCE OF ARMS CONTROL, PARTICIPATION, AND TECHNIQUES ARE COVERED. ENDS WITH US POLICY AND ARMS CONTROL THROUGH WORLD LAW.

0373 BRETTON H.L.
STRESEMANN AND THE REVISION OF VERSAILLES: A FIGHT FOR REASON.
STANFORD: STANFORD U PRESS, 1953, 199 PP., LC#53-6446.
STUDIES POLITICAL AND DIPLOMATIC PHASES OF PROCESS OF REVISIONISM THROUGH WHICH TREATY OF VERSAILLES PASSED. CONCENTRATES ON PERIOD 1918-30. EXAMINES ROLE OF GUSTAV STRESEMANN IN MAKING AND CONDUCTING A REVISIONIST FOREIGN POLICY. ATTEMPTS TO DISCOVER SEQUENCE OF ATTACKS ON TREATY, AND INTERNATIONAL AND GERMAN BACKGROUND OF STRESEMANN'S STRATEGY.

0374 BRIDGMAN J., CLARKE D.E.
GERMAN AFRICA: A SELECT ANNOTATED BIBLIOGRAPHY.
STANFORD: HOOVER INSTITUTE, 1965, 120 PP., LC#64-7917.
SOME 900 NEWSPAPERS, PERIODICALS, OFFICIAL AND SEMI-OFFICIAL GERMAN DOCUMENTS, AND BRITISH CONFIDENTIAL PAPERS ON GERMAN EAST AFRICA, GERMAN SOUTHWEST AFRICA, TOGO, AND CAMEROON ARE ANNOTATED. WORKS FROM 1890-1965, MOSTLY IN GERMAN.

0375 BRIERLY J.L.
THE LAW OF NATIONS (2ND ED.)
LONDON: OXFORD U PR, 1936, 271 PP.
MAINTAINS THAT LAW OF NATIONS IS NEITHER A CHIMERA NOR A PANACEA, BUT AN INSTITUTION FOR BUILDING SANER INTERNATIONAL ORDER. EXAMINES ORIGIN AND CHARACTER OF INTERNATIONAL LAW, LEGAL ORGANIZATION, DISPUTES BETWEEN STATES, TREATIES, FORCE, WAR, ETC.

0376 BRIERLY J.L.
THE OUTLOOK FOR INTERNATIONAL LAW.
OXFORD: CLARENDON, 1961, 1944, 142 PP.
FOCUSES ON SYSTEM OF INTERNATIONAL LAW, ITS SCOPE, FUNCTIONS AND SHORTCOMINGS, AND PRESENTS HISTORY OF ITS ROLE IN FOSTERING ORDERLINESS AMONG NATIONS. SUGGESTS WIDER SUPPORT FOR ITS PRINCIPLES BY INDIVIDUAL STATES TO MAKE IT MORE EFFECTIVE IN THE SETTLEMENT OF DISPUTES.

0377 BRIERLY J.L.
THE BASIS OF OBLIGATION IN INTERNATIONAL LAW, AND OTHER PAPERS.
LONDON: OXFORD U PR, 1958, 387 PP.
COLLECTION OF JL BRIERLY'S WRITINGS ON INTERNATIONAL LAW. SELECTIONS INCLUDED ILLUSTRATE THE PROGRESSIVENESS OF HIS CONCEPTION OF LAW. TREAT MATTERS OF DOMESTIC JURISDICTION, THEORY OF IMPLIED STATE COMPLICITY IN INTERNATIONAL CLAIMS, NATURE OF DISPUTES, AND LEGISLATIVE FUNCTION IN INTERNATIONAL RELATIONS.

0378 BRIMMER B.
A GUIDE TO THE USE OF UNITED NATIONS DOCUMENTS.
NEW YORK: OCEANA PUBLISHING, 1962, 272 PP.
INCLUDES REFERENCES TO PUBLICATIONS OF ALL SPECIALIZED AGENCIES OF THE UN AND SPECIAL UN BODIES.

0379 BRITISH COMMONWEALTH REL CONF
EXTRACTS FROM THE PROCEEDINGS OF THE SIXTH UNOFFICIAL CONFERENCE (PAMPHLET)
LONDON: OXFORD U PR, 1959, 64 PP.
REPORTS AND PAPERS ON DISPUTES BETWEEN COMMONWEALTH COUNTRIES, PARLIAMENTARY SYSTEM OF GOVERNMENT, COMMON MARKET, INTERNATIONAL INVESTMENT, DEFENSE, AND STATUS OF UK IN COMMONWEALTH.

0380 BRODIE B.
THE OBSOLETE WEAPON: ATOMIC POWER AND WORLD ORDER.
NEW YORK: HARCOURT, 1946, 214 PP.
EXPLORES PROBLEM OF WAR IN ATOMIC AGE. POINTS OUT MILITARY AND POLITICAL CONSEQUENCES OF POLICIES RELATED TO NUCLEAR WEAPONS. FOCUSES ON EFFECT OF WEAPONS ON INTERNATIONAL ORGANIZATION AND ON SOVIET-AMERICAN. CONCLUDES WITH STUDY OF INTERNATIONAL CONTROL OF NUCLEAR WEAPONS.

0381 BRODIE B.
STRATEGY IN THE MISSILE AGE.
PRINCETON: U. PR., 1959, 423 PP.
POINTS OUT THE DIFFICULTIES ENCOUNTERED IN ATTEMPTING TO DEVISE EFFECTIVE STRATEGIES IN MISSILE AGE. TRACES THE DEVELOPMENT OF CERTAIN CHARACTERISITCS OF MILITARY THINKING WHICH HAVE HAD AND CONTINUE TO HAVE GREAT INFLUENCE ON SECURITY PROGRAMS. PROPOSES NEW APPROACHES TO PROBLEMS OF NUCLEAR WARFARE.

0382 BRODY H.
UN DIARY: THE SEARCH FOR PEACE.
NEW YORK: CLASSICS PRESS, 1957, 286 PP.
RECORDS PROCEEDINGS OF UN FROM JANUARY, 1956, TO JULY, 1957. INCLUDES SUEZ CRISIS AND HUNGARIAN UPRISING.

0383 BRODY R.A.
"DETERRENCE STRATEGIES: AN ANNOTATED BIBLIOGRAPHY."
J. OF CONFLICT RESOLUTION, 4 (DEC. 60), 443-457.
AN ANNOTATED BIBLIOGRAPHY ON DETERRENCE STRATEGIES. MATERIAL PUBLISHED IN ENGLISH, RANGING FROM 1955 TO 1959. CONTAINS 38 ENTRIES.

0384 BROEKMEIJER M.W.J.
DEVELOPING COUNTRIES AND NATO.
LEYDEN: AW SIJTHOFF, 1963, 208 PP.
DISCUSSES PROBLEMS OF UNDERDEVELOPED COUNTRIES, NATURE OF TECHNICAL AID FROM WEST, PRIVATE INVESTMENT, AND ORGANIZATIONAL STRUCTURE OF FOREIGN AID. MAINTAINS THAT ECONOMIC DEVELOPMENT OF UNDERDEVELOPED NATIONS CAN ONLY BE KEPT FREE FROM COMMUNIST SUBVERSION THROUGH STRENGTHENING OF NATO DETERRENT POWER.

0385 BROEKMEIJER M.W.J.
FICTION AND TRUTH ABOUT THE "DECADE OF DEVELOPMENT"
NEW YORK: HUMANITIES PRESS, 1966, 151 PP., LC#66-25082.
CRITICAL ANALYSIS OF FOREIGN AID TO DEVELOPING NATIONS. DESCRIBES CHARACTERISTICS OF DEVELOPING WORLD. URGES BETTER UNDERSTANDING OF THEIR TRADITIONAL VALUES, INCREASED INVESTMENT IN EDUCATION, AND COOPERATION OF PUBLIC AND PRIVATE AID. DISCUSSES SEVERAL AID PROJECTS THAT WERE VERY SUCCESSFUL.

0386 BROGAN D.W.
THE PRICE OF REVOLUTION.
NEW YORK: HARPER & ROW, 1951, 280 PP.
CONCERNED WITH REVOLUTIONS, USE OF POLITICAL VIOLENCE TO TREAT SOCIAL AND ECONOMIC PROBLEMS. STATES THAT COSTS OF REVOLUTION SHOULD BE CONSIDERED ALONG WITH BENEFITS. STUDIES AMERICAN, FRENCH, AND RUSSIAN REVOLUTIONS, NATIONALISM AND IMPERIALISM, AND EFFECT OF REVOLUTIONS ON CHURCHES. MAINTAINS THAT PRESENT WORLD SITUATION IS ONE OF REVOLUTION INVOLVING US AND USSR'S OPPOSING IDEOLOGIES.

0387 BROMBERGER M., BROMBERGER S.
LES SECRETS DE L'EXPEDITION D'EGYPTE.
PARIS: AYMON, 1957, 269 PP.
DISCUSSES DIPLOMATIC AND MILITARY EVENTS OF SUEZ CRISIS FROM JULY TO DECEMBER 1956 EMPHASIZING WESTERN DISUNITY AND SOVIET REACTION.

0388 BROMKE A.
"DISENGAGEMENT IN EAST EUROPE."
INT. J., 14 (SUMMER 59), 168-74.
DEPICTS ATTITUDES OF SOVIET UNION AND EAST EUROPEAN SATELLITES. INDICATES POSSIBILITIES OF SOVIET MILITARY DISENGAGEMENT. CONSIDERS STRATEGIC USELESSNESS OF SATELLITES SINCE DEVELOPMENT OF H-BOMB AND ICBMS. STRESSES THAT WITHDRAWAL OF SOVIET MILITARY AND NEUTRALIZATION OF EASTERN EUROPE HINGES ON ASSURANCE THAT EAST EUROPE WILL REMAIN FRIENDLY AND NOT REVERT TO CAPITALISM.

0389 BROMKE A. ED.
THE COMMUNIST STATES AT THE CROSSROADS BETWEEN MOSCOW AND PEKING.
NEW YORK: FREDERICK PRAEGER, 1965, 270 PP., LC#65-12191.
TWELVE ESSAYS DEALING WITH IMPACT OF SINO-SOVIET SCHISM OF EARLY 1960'S UPON COMMUNIST WORLD AND RESULTING SPREAD OF "POLYCENTRISM." DEMONSTRATES GROWING DIVERGENCES WITHIN FORMERLY SILENT SATELLITE COUNTRIES AND STATES, PROJECTING THROUGH THE 1960'S THEIR IMPACT UPON WORLD POLITICS.

0390 BROOK D.
THE UNITED NATIONS AND CHINA DILEMMA.
NEW YORK: VINTAGE, 1956, 82 PP.
BRIEF HISTORY OF CHINESE REVOLUTION AND ITS AFTERMATH. EXAMINES POLITICAL FACTORS WHICH MAKE REPRESENTATION OF COMMUNIST CHINA IN THE UN AN EXCEPTIONALLY DIFFICULT PROBLEM. RECOMMENDS FORMATION OF COMMITTEE WHOSE FINDINGS SHOULD BE BINDING ON ALL THE UN ORGANS.

0391 BROOKES E.H.
THE COMMONWEALTH TODAY.
PIETERMARITZBURG: U NATAL PR, 1959, 70 PP.
DISCUSSES NATURE OF BRITISH COMMONWEALTH AS SPIRITUAL, LEGAL, AND ECONOMIC ENTITY. EXAMINES ITS OPERATION IN AFRICA AND ITS RELATIONSHIP WITH US. DRAWS UPON EXAMPLES FROM ROMAN EMPIRE AND SPECULATES UPON EXISTENCE OF WORLD-STATE BY DRAWING UPON EXPERIENCE OF BRITISH EMPIRE.

0392 BROOKINGS INSTITUTION
MAJOR PROBLEMS OF UNITED STATES FOREIGN POLICY.
WASHINGTON: BROOKINGS INST., 1947-.
SERIES OF ANNUAL ANALYTIC SURVEYS ATTEMPTING TO PRESENT AN OVER-ALL VIEW OF THE WORLD SITUATION AND OF THE POSITION OF THE US IN WORLD AFFAIRS. TRIES TO APPROXIMATE METHOD USED BY GOVERNMENT OFFICIALS IN THE FORMULATION OF FOREIGN POLICIES, AND TO FURNISH WORKING MATERIALS TO THE READER FOR ACQUIRING A KNOWLEDGE OF THE NATURE OF THE POLICY-MAKING PROCESS. EXTENSIVE BIBLIOGRAPHIES.

0393 BROOKINGS INSTITUTION
MAJOR PROBLEMS OF UNITED STATES FOREIGN POLICY.
WASHINGTON, D.C.: BROOKINGS INSTITUTION, 1950, 416 PP.
DISCUSSES INTERESTS AND OBJECTIVES OF US BETWEEN 1949 AND 1951. EXAMINES RELATIONS WITH EUROPE AND PROBLEMS OF COUNTERACTING COMMUNISM. ALSO DISCUSSES NEAR EAST, AFRICAN, AND ASIAN "PROBLEM AREAS."

0394 BROOKINGS INSTITUTION
UNITED STATES FOREIGN POLICY: STUDY NO 9: THE FORMULATION AND ADMINISTRATION OF UNITED STATES FOREIGN POLICY.
WASHINGTON: BROOKINGS INST, 1960, 191 PP.
STUDY DONE FOR US SENATE COMMITTEE ON FOREIGN RELATIONS. APPRAISES ENDS AND MEANS OF US FOREIGN POLICY IN RELATION TO CHANGING WORLD CONDITIONS. COVERS CONGRESSIONAL AND EXECUTIVE PROCEDURE, ROLE OF MULTILATERAL ORGANIZATIONS, RELATION WITH MILITARY ESTABLISHMENT, OUR AMBASSADORIAL SETUP, PERSONNEL MANAGEMENT, AND INTELLIGENCE AND INFORMATIONAL OPERATIONS. MAKES MANY RECOMMENDATIONS.

0395 BROOKINGS INSTITUTION
BROOKINGS PAPERS ON PUBLIC POLICY.
WASHINGTON: BROOKINGS INST, 1965, 220 PP., LC#65-18919.
DISCUSSES FOREIGN POLICY, EDUCATION AND PUBLIC SERVICE, WAGE POLICY AND REGULATION OF COMPETITION, TAXATION AND FISCAL POLICY, AND CONGRESSIONAL CONTROL OF ADMINISTRATION.

0396 BROOKS S., ENGELENBURG F.V.
BRITAIN AND THE BOERS.
NEW YORK: N AMER REVIEW PUB CO, 1899, 48 PP.
A PRESENTATION OF VARIOUS VIEWS RELATED TO THE QUESTION OF LEGITIMACY AND INTERNATIONAL LAW IN THE BRITAIN-BOER WAR. DISCUSSES SOME OF THE HISTORICAL CIRCUMSTANCES THAT PRODUCED THE WAR.

0397 BROWN A.D.
PANAMA CANAL AND PANAMA CANAL ZONE: A SELECTED LIST OF REFERENCES.
WASHINGTON: LIBRARY OF CONGRESS, 1943, 57 PP.
LISTS, INDEXES, AND ANNOTATES 430 BOOKS, ARTICLES, AND PAMPHLETS PRIMARILY IN ENGLISH AND SPANISH PERTINENT TO THE POLITICS, SOCIAL CONDITIONS, ECONOMIC SITUATION, CULTURE, AND HISTORY OF THE PANAMA CANAL ZONE AS WELL AS TOLLS AND TRAFFIC, DEFENSES, AND INTERNATIONAL ASPECTS OF THE CANAL ITSELF. ITEMS DATE FROM 1920'S AND INCLUDE BIBLIOGRAPHIES.

0398 BROWN A.D.
BRITISH POSSESSIONS IN THE CARIBBEAN AREA: A SELECTED LIST OF REFERENCES.
WASHINGTON: LIBRARY OF CONGRESS, 1943, 192 PP.
LIST COMPILED AT REQUEST OF ANGLO-AMERICAN CARIBBEAN COMMISSION. ONLY LATEST AVAILABLE ISSUES OF REPORTS AND OTHER ANNUAL PUBLICATIONS NOTED. CONTAINS 1,487 ITEMS ON BIBLIOGRAPHIES; HISTORY; ECONOMIC AND SOCIAL CONDITIONS; POLITICS AND GOVERNMENT; INTERNATIONAL ASPECTS OF DEVELOPMENT; ETC. SELECTIONS REFER ALSO TO INDIVIDUAL COUNTRIES.

0399 BROWN A.D., JONES H.D., HELLMAN F.S.
GREECE: SELECTED LIST OF REFERENCES.
WASHINGTON: LIBRARY OF CONGRESS, 1943, 101 PP.
AIMS TO PRESENT ITEMS APPEARING IN THE DECADE PRIOR TO GERMAN INVASION OF GREECE IN 1940. INCLUDES 765 BOOKS, ARTICLES, PAMPHLETS, ETC., ON GEOGRAPHY, HISTORY, POLITICS, ECONOMICS, SOCIOLOGY, AND RECENT CRISES AND CONDITIONS IN GREECE. DEALS WITH GENERAL TOPICS AS WELL AS SPECIFIC AREAS (ATHENS, MACEDONIA, SALONIKA, THE ISLANDS, ETC.). ALSO INCLUDES AN AUTHOR INDEX.

0400 BROWN B.E.
"L'ONU ABANDONNE LA HONGRIE."
REV. DR. INT., 40 (NO.4, 62), 328-29.
STATES THAT UN ABANDONMENT OF HUNGARY IN '56 WAS ONE OF THE BIGGEST POLITICAL MISTAKES COMMITTED BY THE ORGANIZATION. CALLS FOR IMPROVED FUNCTIONING OF HUMAN RIGHTS COMMISSION.

0401 BROWN E.S.
MANUAL OF GOVERNMENT PUBLICATIONS.
NEW YORK: APPLETON, 1950, 121 PP.
ANNOTATED LISTING OF APPROXIMATELY 1,000 BOOKS, PERIODICALS, ARTICLES, AND PAMPHLETS PUBLISHED BY US GOVERNMENT, STATES, AND FOREIGN GOVERNMENTS. INCLUDES LAWS, CONSTITUTIONS, MUNICIPAL AND LOCAL GOVERNMENT, RECORDS OF LEGISLATURES, AND INTERNATIONAL ORGANIZATIONS.

0402 BROWN H., REAL J.
COMMUNITY OF FEAR.
NEW YORK: FUND FOR THE REPUBLIC, 1960, 40 PP.
DISCUSSES NATURE OF ARMS RACE AND POSSIBLE CONSEQUENCES OF ITS PERPETUATION. EXAMINES ADVANCES IN MILITARY TECHNOLOGY SINCE WWII, DESTRUCTIVE POWER OF NUCLEAR WEAPONS, AND SPREAD OF NUCLEAR MILITARY TECHNOLOGY. EXAMINES FEASIBILITY OF LIMITED WAR AND POSSIBLE ACCIDENTAL CAUSES OF NUCLEAR WAR.

0403 BROWN J.F. ED., HODGES C. ED. ET AL.
CONTEMPORARY WORLD POLITICS.
NEW YORK: WILEY, 1939, 703 PP.
REPORT OF SYMPOSIUM SEEKING TO DEAL PRAGMATICALLY WITH INTERNATIONAL RELATIONS. INCLUDES FIVE MAJOR SECTIONS STUDYING ELEMENTS IN WORLD CONFLUCT INCLUDING NATIONALISM, POWER POLITICS, REGIONALISM, PUBLIC OPINION AND WORLD ORGANIZATIONS. ALSO PRESENTS VIEWS OF VARIOUS RELIGIOUS AND ACADEMIC LEADERS ON ROADS TO WORLD PEACE.

0404 BROWN J.F.
THE NEW EASTERN EUROPE.
NEW YORK: FREDERICK PRAEGER, 1966, 306 PP., LC#65-24939.
COVERS IMPORTANT POLITICAL, ECONOMIC, AND CULTURAL DEVELOPMENTS WITHIN EASTERN EUROPEAN STATES EXCLUDING ALBANIA AND YUGOSLAVIA. DISCUSSES INTRABLOC RELATIONS, EAST EUROPEAN RELATIONS WITH WESTERN POWERS, AND SUMMARY OF SITUATION AT TIME OF KHRUSHCHEV'S FALL.

0405 BROWN L.C.
LATIN AMERICA, A BIBLIOGRAPHY.
KINSVILLE: TEX COL ARTS & INDUS, 1962, 80 PP.
LIST OF MATERIALS IN LIBRARY OF TEXAS A&I ON LATIN AMERICA, WITH PARTICULAR EMPHASIS ON INTERNATIONAL RELATIONS, POLITICS, AND GOVERNMENT. CONTAINS LIST OF ARTICLES ON LATIN AMERICA.

0406 BROWN L.C. ED.
STATE AND SOCIETY IN INDEPENDENT NORTH AFRICA.
WASHINGTON: MIDDLE EAST INST, 1966, 332 PP., LC#66-20316.
COMPARES ASPECTS OF FOUR NORTH AFRICAN COUNTRIES AFTER THEIR INDEPENDENCE WAS GAINED. CONSIDERS MAIN COMMON INFLUENCES TO BE GEOGRAPHY, ARAB-MUSLIM CULTURE AND COLONIAL EXPERIENCE UNDER FRENCH.

0407 BROWN S.
"AN ALTERNATIVE TO THE GRAND DESIGN."
WORLD POLIT., 17 (JAN. 65), 232-242.
CRITICIZES GRAND DESIGN FOR ATLANTIC PARTNERSHIP (POLICY TOWARD NATO, EEC AND REACTION TO FRENCH ASSERTIVENESS). PROPOSES 'NORTH ATLANTIC CONCERT WITH ITS WEB OF SPECIAL RELATIONSHIPS IN TRADE AND DEFENSE - DOMINATION AND SUBORDINATION.' DOES NOT SUGGEST ABANDONMENT OF MULTI-NATION COMMITMENTS AND ORGANIZATIONAL ARRANGEMENTS WHEN FEASIBLE. CAN ADJUST TO GLOBAL TREND OF MULTI-POLARITY.

0408 BROWN W.N.
THE UNITED STATES AND INDIA AND PAKISTAN (REV. ED.)
CAMBRIDGE: HARVARD U PR, 1963, 444 PP., LC#63-13807.
STUDY OF DEVELOPMENT OF INDIA AND PAKISTAN UNDER BRITISH RULE, DRIVE FOR INDEPENDENCE, AND ATTAINMENT OF NATIONHOOD. DISCUSSES CONFLICT BETWEEN BOTH NATIONS AND THEIR IMPORTANCE IN WORLD AFFAIRS AND RELATIONSHIP TO US.

0409 BROWNLIE I.
PRINCIPLES OF PUBLIC INTERNATIONAL LAW.
NEW YORK: OXFORD U PR, 1966, 646 PP.
EMPHASIZES TECHNICAL ASPECTS OF INTERNATIONAL LAW. COVERS TOPICS OF SOVEREIGNTY, SOURCES OF INTERNATIONAL LAW, RECOGNITION, TREATIES, JUDICIAL SETTLEMENT OF INTERNATIONAL PUTES, ETC. COMPREHENSIVE IN SCOPE. DESIGNED AS A REFERENCE FOR UNDERGRADUATE AND GRADUATE STUDENTS. EXTENSIVELY FOOTNOTED WITH CITATION TO INTERNATIONAL AND DOMESTIC CASES.

0410 BRUNER J.S. ED.
"TOWARD A COMMON GROUND-INTERNATIONAL SOCIAL SCIENCE."
J. SOC. ISSUES., 3 (WINTER 47), 1-66.
ARTICLES BY BRUNER, P. W. MARTIN, G. ALLPORT, AND G. MURPHY ON INTERNATIONAL COOPERATION, RESEARCH IN POLITICAL AND SOCIAL PSYCHOLOGY, RESEARCH ON SOCIAL ISSUES, AND THE ESTABLISHMENT OF INTERNATIONAL SCIENTIFIC RESEARCH.

0411 BRYANT A.
A CHOICE FOR DESTINY: COMMONWEALTH AND THE COMMON MARKET.
LONDON: COLLINS, 1962, 63 PP.
FOLLOWING BURKE, AUTHOR EXPRESSES CONVICTION THAT, IF BRITAIN JOINS WESTERN EUROPEAN COMMUNITY WITHOUT NATIONS OF COMMONWEALTH, ERROR OF 18TH-CENTURY FORBEAR WHO ALIENATED AND LOST AMERICAN COLONIES WILL BE REPEATED. FEELS ELECTORS OF BRITAIN AND FELLOW BRITISH NATIONS SHOULD BE CONSULTED ON ISSUE OF PERMANENT SEPARATION FROM EACH OTHER.

0412 BRYCE J.
INTERNATIONAL RELATIONS.
NEW YORK: MACMILLAN, 1922, 275 PP.
ANALYSES FORCES IN THE MIDDLE AGES, POLITICAL AND NONPOLITICAL FORCES LEADING DIRECTLY TO WORLD WAR ONE: PROBLEMS OF DIPLOMACY, RELATION OF FOREIGN POLICY TO CITIZENS, ADVANTAGES OF A CONCILIATION METHOD FOR SETTLING DISPUTES AND THE POSSIBILITY OF CREATING A WORLD STATE. THE RESPONSIBILITY FOR PEACE IS IN THE ABILITY OF PEOPLE TO USE DEMOCRACY.

0413 BRYCE J.
THE HOLY ROMAN EMPIRE.
NEW YORK: MACMILLAN, 1932, 575 PP.
BEGINNING WITH THIRD CENTURY, TRACES GROWTH AND DECLINE AS INSTITUTIONAL SYSTEM AND ENDS WITH UNIFICATION OF GERMAN EMPIRE. ELABORATES THEORY OF EMPIRE WHILE DETAILING POLITICAL HISTORY OF GERMANY AND MEDIEVAL ITALY. CONCLUDES ESSENCE OF HOLY ROMAN EMPIRE AS LOVE OF PEACE, BROTHERHOOD AND SUPREMACY OF THE SPIRITUAL LIFE.

0414 BRYNES A.
WE GIVE TO CONQUER.
NEW YORK: W W NORTON, 1966, 219 PP., LC#66-18077.
MAINTAINS THAT ALL UNILATERAL FOREIGN AID TO POORER NATIONS IS ESSENTIALLY IMPERIALISTIC AND SEEKS TO CREATE, MAINTAIN, AND DEFEND SPHERES OF INFLUENCE UNDER GUISE OF PHILANTHROPY. US AID ENCOURAGES EMERGENCE OF MIDDLE CLASS, RUSSIAN AID CREATES NEW PROLETARIAT. BECAUSE TWO NATIONS TEND TO HAVE INFLUENCE IN IDENTICAL AREAS, POLICIES CAN HAVE AS THEIR CONSEQUENCES ANOTHER WORLD WAR.

0415 BRZEZINSKI Z.K.
"SOVIET QUIESCENCE."
COLUMBIA UNIV. FORUM, 6 (FALL 63), 17-20.
CONTENDS THAT FROM THE SOVIET POINT OF VIEW THE TEST BAN AGREEMENT IS IN HARMONY WITH A NEW PHASE IN AMERICAN-SOVIET RELATIONS, A PHASE OF QUIESCENCE. ARGUES THAT THIS NEW PHASE WAS USHERED IN BY THE CUBAN INCIDENT, NOT BY THE SINO-SOVIET IDEOLOGICAL CONFLICT. OUTLINES THREE DANGERS FOR AMICABLE SOVIET-US RELATIONS: EXTREMISM IN US PUBLIC OPINION, PROBLEMS IN DEFENSE AREAS, AND US-EUROPEAN AFFAIRS.

0416 BRZEZINSKI Z.K.
"THE ORGANIZATION OF THE COMMUNIST CAMP."
WORLD POLIT., 13 (JAN. 61), 175-209.
OUTLINES INSTITUTIONAL ASPECTS OF SOVIET CAMP REGARDING MULTILATERAL ORGANIZATIONS AND BILATERAL AGREEMENTS SUCH AS MUTUAL AID TREATIES AND CULTURAL AGREEMENTS. DYNAMIC ASPECTS OF UNITY VIEWED THROUGH FREQUENCY OF HIGH LEVEL MEETINGS, PUBLICATIONS, MILITARY PREPONDERANCE OF USSR AND UNIFORM BLOC LITERATURE.

0417 BRZEZINSKI Z.K.
"PEACEFUL ENGAGEMENT IN COMMUNIST DISUNITY."
CHINA QUART., 10 (APR.-JUNE 62), 64-71.
DESCRIBES FRAGMENTATION OF SOVIET BLOC. ADVOCATES WEST NOTE AND PROMOTE PROCESS OF CHANGE IN COMMUNIST WORLD AND ACCORDINGLY VARY POLICY TOWARDS AND TREATMENT OF DIFFERING COMMUNIST STATES.

0418 BRZEZINSKI Z.K. ED.
AFRICA AND THE COMMUNIST WORLD.
STANFORD: U. PR., 1963, 272 PP., $5.00.
A COMPREHENSIVE REVIEW OF RECENT COMMUNIST POLICIES TOWARD AFRICA BY EIGHT AUTHORITIES ON COMMUNISM. CONTEMPORARY ANALYSIS OF PROGRAMS ADOPTED BY VARIOUS COMMUNIST STATES TO ESTABLISH THEIR INFLUENCE AMONG NEWLY EMERGING AFRICAN STATES.

0419 BRZEZINSKI Z.K.
IDEOLOGY AND POWER IN SOVIET POLITICS.
NEW YORK: FREDERICK PRAEGER, 1967, 291 PP., LC#66-18893.
MAKES DISTINCTION BETWEEN IDEOLOGICAL AND POWER INFLUENCE ON SOVIET FOREIGN POLICY, AND INDICATES LACK OF DISTINCTION BECAUSE OF DEPENDENCE OF LEADERS UPON DOGMATIC IDEOLOGY FOR DETERMINATION OF USAGE OF POWER. ANALYZES CONFLICTS IN SYSTEM CONSISTING OF THIS POWER-IDEOLOGY CONGLOMERATION. APPLICATION OF THEORY TO CURRENT FOREIGN AFFAIRS PROBLEMS.

0420 BRZEZINSKI Z.K.
THE SOVIET BLOC: UNITY AND CONFLICT (2ND ED., REV., ENLARGED)
CAMBRIDGE: HARVARD U PR, 1967, 599 PP., LC#67-12531.
EXAMINES HOW SOVIET BLOC HAS CHANGED OVER THE YEARS, WHAT PROBLEMS FACED AND CONTINUE TO FACE ITS LEADERS, AND HOW LEADERS GO ABOUT SOLVING THESE IN TERMS OF THEIR GENERAL IDEOLOGICAL ORIENTATION. ALSO SHOWS HOW INTERNAL CHANGES IN USSR AFFECTED POLITICAL DEVELOPMENTS WITHIN OTHER COMMUNIST STATES AND CHANGED THE PATTERN OF RELATIONS AMONG THEM.

0421 BUCHAN A.
NATO IN THE 1960'S.
NEW YORK: PRAEGER, 1960, 131 PP.
CONTENDS NATO INDISPENSABLE FOR STABILITY IN THE COLD WAR AND POINTS OUT THAT THE PRESENT PROBLEM OF DISARMAMENT MUST BE SURMOUNTED. ASSERTS THAT RETENTION OF NATIONAL SOVEREIGNTY IS COMPATIBLE WITH ALLIANCE. SUMMARIZES NATO'S PURPOSE AND ITS MEANING FOR EUROPE.

0422 BUCHAN A.
"THE MULTILATERAL FORCE."
INTERNATIONAL AFFAIRS (U.K.), 40, (OCT.64) 619-637.
DISCUSSES DEBATE OVER CONTROL OF NUCLEAR STRATEGY. OUTLINES ISSUES INVOLVED, NOTABLY USA AND EUROPEAN RESPONSIBILITIES. TRACES 3 SOLUTIONS PROPOSED: (1) MULTI-NATIONAL APPROACH, (2) DEVELOPMENT OF TRANS-ATLANTIC ECONOMIC RELATIONSHIP WITH CONTROL OF NUCLEAR FORCE UNDER EEC, (3) DEVELOPMENT OF MLF. CRITICIZES MLF AS 'EXPENSIVE AND TIME CONSUMING DETOUR'.

0423 BUCHAN A. ED.
A WORLD OF NUCLEAR POWERS?
ENGLEWOOD CLIFFS: PRENTICE HALL, 1966, 176 PP., LC#66-29073.
CHALLENGE TO INTERNATIONAL STABILITY THAT WOULD RESULT FROM INCREASE IN NUMBER OF NUCLEAR POWERS; STEPS SMALL POWERS CAN TAKE IF NO AGREEMENT IS REACHED BY BIG POWERS; KIND OF AGREEMENTS NECESSARY AS A RESULT OF PROLIFERATION ARE ALL DEALT WITH.

0424 BUCHANAN W.
"STEREOTYPES AND TENSIONS AS REVEALED BY THE UNESCO INTERNATIONAL POLL."
INT. SOC. SCI. BULL., 3 (AUTUMN 51), 515-29.
UNESCO POLL REVEALS: A)TENDENCY IN ALL COUNTRIES SURVEYED TO ASSOCIATE CERTAIN PEOPLES WITH SPECIFIC CHARACTERISTICS, AND B)TENDENCY OF ALL POPULATIONS TO DESCRIBE THE RUSSIAN IN SAME TERMS. AGREE LESS IN DESCRIBING AMERICANS.

0425 BUCHANAN W., KRUGMAN H.E., VAN WAGENEN R.W.
AN INTERNATIONAL POLICE FORCE AND PUBLIC OPINION IN THE UNITED STATES, 1939-1953.
PRINCETON: PRIN U WORLD POL INST, 1954, 39 PP.
ANALYSIS OF AMERICAN PUBLIC OPINION POLLS OVER PAST 15 YEARS CONCERNING AN INTERNATIONAL POLICE FORCE. INCLUDES STATISTICS, OPPOSING ATTITUDES, AND CONCLUDES THAT MAJORITY HAVE NOT SERIOUSLY THOUGHT OF INTERNATIONAL CONTROL AGENCY AS PROPOSAL FOR MAINTAINING PEACE.

0426 BUCHMANN J.
L'AFRIQUE NOIRE INDEPENDANTE.
PARIS: LIB GEN DROIT ET JURIS, 1962, 434 PP.
STUDY OF INDEPENDENT BLACK AFRICA REGARDING FACTORS OF POLITICAL INTEGRATION, ELEMENTS OF SOCIAL STRUCTURE, INFLUENCES OF COLONIAL POWERS, AND GROWTH OF NATIONALISM. EXPLAINS POLITICAL ORGANIZATION AND INSTITUTIONS AS WELL AS DEVELOPMENT OF POLITICAL GROUPS AND PARTICIPATION IN GOVERNING PROCESS.

0427 BUCK P.W.
CONTOL OF FOREIGN RELATIONS IN MODERN NATIONS.
NEW YORK: NORTON, 1957, 865 PP.
ANALYSIS OF INTERNAL POLICY-MAKING FACTORS OF LATIN AMERICA, USA, COMMONWEALTH COUNTRIES, FRANCE, HOLLAND, JAPAN AND RUSSIA. DEMONSTRATES THAT A NUCLEAR STALEMATE, ECONOMIC PROGRESS AND CONTINUED COOPERATION COULD LEAD TO MORE EFFECTIVE INTERNATIONAL ORGANIZATION. ADVOCATES STABLE WORLD COMPOSED OF SEVERAL POWER CENTERS.

0428 BUELL R.
INTERNATIONAL RELATIONS.
NEW YORK: HOLT, 1929, 758 PP.
A TEXTBOOK CASE STYLE STUDY, WELL-DOCUMENTED, OF THE PROBLEMS ARISING HISTORICALLY AMONG STATES. ANALYSES ARE MADE OF THE SOCIO-ECONOMIC BASES OF THESE DISPUTES AND THE SETTLEMENTS ATTEMPTED OR ATTAINED IN THE PAST.

0429 BULL H.
THE CONTROL OF THE ARMS RACE.
NEW YORK: INST. STRAT. STUDIES, 1961, 215 PP.
A STUDY OF THE ARMS RACE AND OF THE REDUCTION OF ARMS OR RESTRAINT METHODS OF CONTROL. EMPHASIS IS PLACED ON THE COMPLEXITY OF THE ISSUE RATHER THAN ON RECOMENDATIONS OF SPECIFIC CONTROL MEASURES.

0430 BULLOUGH V.L.
"THE ROMAN EMPIRE VS PERSIA, 363-502: A STUDY OF SUCCESSFUL DETERRENCE."
J. CONFL. RESOLUT., 7 (MAR. 63), 55-68.
DESCRIBES DETERRENCE FACTORS PRESENT AND DEMONSTRATES THAT A 'COLD WAR' RELATIONSHIP IS PRECARIOUS EVEN WITHOUT THE THREAT OF NEW WEAPONS OR SCIENTIFIC BREAKTHROUGHS.

0431 BUNDESMIN FUR VERTRIEBENE
ZEITTAFEL DER VORGESCHICHTE UND DES ABLAUFS DER VERTREIBUNG SOWIE DER UNTERBRINGUNG UND EINGLIEDERUNG DER (2 VOLS.)
BONN: BUNDESMIN FUR VERTRIEBENE, 1959, 454 PP.
CHRONOLOGICAL TABLE OF EVENTS RELATING TO GERMAN REFUGEE AND EXPULSION PROBLEM BETWEEN 1938-58. INCLUDES EXTENSIVE BIBLIOGRAPHY ON REFUGEE PROBLEMS, ASSIMILATION, RIGHTS OF DOMICILE, AND RIGHTS OF SELF-DETERMINATION IN GERMAN PARLIAMENT.

0432 BURDETTE F.L., WILLMORE J.N., WITHERSPOON J.V.
POLITICAL SCIENCE: A SELECTED BIBLIOGRAPHY OF BOOKS IN PRINT, WITH ANNOTATIONS (PAMPHLET)
COLLEGE PARK: U MD, BUR PUB ADM, 1961, 97 PP., LC#61-64130.
CONTAINS APPROXIMATELY 250 TITLES WITH EXTENSIVE THOUGH NONCRITICAL ANNOTATIONS IN ALL FIELDS OF POLITICAL SCIENCE: AMERICAN NATIONAL GOVERNMENT, COMPARATIVE GOVERNMENT, INTERNATIONAL POLITICS, POLITICAL PARTIES, PUBLIC OPINION AND ELECTORAL PROCESS, POLITICAL THEORY, PUBLIC ADMINISTRATION, PUBLIC LAW, AND LOCAL AND STATE GOVERNMENT. DESIGNED FOR REFERENCE USERS.

0433 BUREAU ECONOMIC RES LAT AM
THE ECONOMIC LITERATURE OF LATIN AMERICA (2 VOLS.)
CAMBRIDGE: HARVARD U PR, 1935, 663 PP., LC#35-55976.
LIST OF BOOKS AND OFFICIAL PUBLICATIONS COVERING ALL ASPECTS OF ECONOMICS, FINANCE, AND COMMERCE, INCLUDING ECONOMIC HISTORY OF REGION AND PRIMITIVE ECONOMY. FOREIGN-LANGUAGE SOURCES LISTED. ARRANGED BY COUNTRIES; INDEPENDENT SOUTH AMERICA IN VOLUME I, OTHER IN VOLUME II. GENERAL CONSIDERATIONS IN BOTH.

0434 BUREAU OF PUBLIC AFFAIRS
AMERICAN FOREIGN POLICY: CURRENT DOCUMENTS.
WASHINGTON: DEPT OF STATE, 1956, 442 PP.
A SERIES OF ANNUAL ONE-VOLUME COLLECTIONS OF PRINCIPAL MESSAGES, ADDRESSES, STATEMENTS, REPORTS, DIPLOMATIC NOTES, AND TREATIES IN A CALENDAR YEAR WHICH INDICATE THE SCOPE, GOALS, AND IMPLEMENTATION OF US FOREIGN POLICY. DOCUMENTS ARRANGED BY TOPIC IN 13 CLASSIFICATIONS FROM GENERAL POLICY THROUGH GEOGRAPHICAL AND POLITICAL AREAS TO SPECIFIC PROGRAMS.

0435 BURKE E.
THOUGHTS ON THE PROSPECT OF A REGICIDE PEACE (PAMPHLET)
ORIGINAL PUBLISHER NOT AVAILABLE, 1796, 131 PP.
CONSIDERS PROSPECT OF PEACEFUL COEXISTENCE WITH WHAT HE CALLS FRANCE'S "REPUBLIC OF REGICIDE," WARNING AGAINST IT. ALTHOUGH HE FAVORED AMERICAN INDEPENDENCE, BURKE CONSIDERS FRENCH REVOLUTION UNJUST AND ATROCIOUS. ATTACKS REGICIDE GOVERNMENT AS WILLFUL, AMBITIOUS, AND UNCONTROLLED; AND CRITICIZES REVOLUTION AS DESTRUCTIVE AND LEADING TO ANARCHY. LINKS JACOBINISM, REGICIDE, ATHEISM, AND WAR.

0436 BURKE E.
"RESOLUTIONS FOR CONCILIATION WITH AMERICA" (1775), IN E. BURKE, COLLECTED WORKS, VOL. 2."
BOSTON: LITTLE BROWN, 1883.
ARGUES THAT SINCE WAR SELDOM SUBJECTS A POPULATION PERMANENTLY, AND SINCE TRADE WITH AMERICA IS SO GREAT, A PEACEFUL SOLUTION TO THE DISPUTE WITH THE AMERICAN COLONIES SHOULD BE FOUND. PROPOSES TO ALLOW COLONIES TO GOVERN THEMSELVES ON MATTERS OF TAXATION AND DEFENSE, WHILE ENGLAND WOULD LOOSELY CONTROL MATTERS OF TRADE.

0437 BURKE F.G.
AFRICA'S QUEST FOR ORDER.
ENGLEWOOD CLIFFS: PRENTICE HALL, 1964, 177 PP., LC#64-12854.
ANALYZES MAJOR POLITICAL AND ECONOMIC EVENTS IN AFRICA IN

ORDER TO EMPHASIZE RECURRING FORCES AND THEMES IN THE AFRICAN REVOLUTION: TRIBALISM, URBANISM, YOUTH, LEADERSHIP, AND RACE. EXAMINES INTERRELATIONSHIP OF RESHAPING AND EXTENDING POLITICAL, CULTURAL, AND SOCIAL BOUNDARIES; ESTABLISHMENT OF NEW NATION STATES; AND CREATION OF NEW INTERNATIONAL RELATIONS.

0438 BURNET A.
"TOO MANY ALLIES."
POLIT. QUART., 32 (APR.-JUNE 61), 146-56.
BRIEF HISTORY OF BRITAIN'S TREATY OBLIGATIONS WHICH EXPANDED IN THE POSTWAR YEARS WHEN BRITISH GOVERNMENT BELIEVED IT COULD STILL PLAY AUTHORITATIVE AND ENERGETIC ROLE THROUGHOUT THE WORLD. CONCLUDES WITH STRUCTURAL ANALYSIS OF CENTO, NATO AND SEATO.

0439 BURNS A.
IN DEFENCE OF COLONIES; BRITISH COLONIAL TERRITORIES IN INTERNATIONAL AFFAIRS.
LONDON: ALLEN & UNWIN, 1957, 338 PP.
DEFENDS BRITISH COLONIALISM AGAINST ATTACKS BY OTHER NATIONS THAT HAVE NOT BEEN AS SUCCESSFUL IN TERRITORIAL RULE. TREATS VALIDITY OF OTHER NATIONS' CLAIMS TO CERTAIN BRITISH COLONIES. MAINTAINS THAT GOAL OF BRITISH COLONIALISM IS NOT SELF-DEVELOPMENT BUT DEVELOPMENT OF ECONOMIES AND DEMOCRATIC GOVERNMENTS IN UNDERDEVELOPED AREAS, AND EVENTUAL INDEPENDENCE.

0440 BURNS A.L.
"THE INTERNATIONAL CONSEQUENCES OF EXPECTING SURPRISE."
WORLD POL., 10 (JULY 58), 512-536.
CONCERNED WITH NATIONAL RESPONSES IN SURPRISE SITUATIONS - SUPRISE ARISING FROM TECHNOLOGICAL OR BASIC SCIENTIFIC DISCOVERY UNKNOWN TO THE OTHER SIDE. COMPETING POWERS WHEN INVOLVED IN POTENTIALLY SURPRISING SITUATIONS AND POSSESSING RESEARCH APPARATUS MAY EITHER BLINDLY COMMIT DISENGAGE OR COMBINE THEMSELVES. A DETERRENT DEPENDS UPON CERTAINTY RATHER THAN UPON INVINCIBILITY OR SUPRISE.

0441 BURNS A.L., HEATHCOTE N.
PEACE-KEEPING BY U.N.FORCES - FROM SUEZ TO THE CONGO.
NEW YORK: PRAEGER, 1963, 256 PP., $6.00.
DECLARES THAT U.N. HAS CHANGED SINCE ITS INCEPTION, FUNCTIONING SOLEY AS AN INSTITUTION THAT FORMALIZES AND MAKES LEGITIMATE INTERNATIONAL POLITICAL AFFILIATIONS. WITH REGARD TO PEACE-KEEPING OPERATIONS, SUGGESTS THAT NEUTRAL NATIONS TRAIN RIOT POLICE AND THAT AN INDEPENDENT CIVIL SERVICE BE ESTABLISHED.

0442 BURNS C.D.
INTERNATIONAL POLITICS.
LONDON: METHUEN, 1920, 189 PP.
ANALYSES GROWTH OF POWER POLITICS DURING MIDDLE AGES, CONSEQUENCES OF SOVEREIGNTY AND DIFFERENCES IN CULTURES ON NATIONS, AND THE IMPACT OF UNDERDEVELOPED NATIONS ON INTERNATIONAL TRADE IN TERMS OF CONTACTS AMONG GOVERNMENT OFFICIALS. STRESSES IMPORTANCE OF DIRECT CONTACTS AMONG PEOPLES TO PROMOTE UNDERSTANDING AND PEACE.

0443 BURNS E.B.
"TRADITIONS AND VARIATIONS IN BRAZILIAN FOREIGN POLICY."
J. INTER-AMER. STUDIES, 10 (APR. 67), 195-212.
TRACES TRADITIONAL POLICY OF CLOSE RELATIONS WITH US, LATIN AMERICAN LEADERSHIP, PAN AMERICANISM, AND CONCERN FOR INTERNATIONAL PRESTIGE. SHOWS HOW OPPOSING GROUPS HAVE EMERGED SINCE RIO BRANCO TO CHALLENGE THIS POLICY, ESPECIALLY TIES WITH US. ARGUES THAT PRESENT PERIOD IS TRANSITIONAL.

0444 BURNS E.L.M.
MEGAMURDER.
NEW YORK: PANTHEON BOOKS, 1967, 297 PP., LC#67-13323.
UNSPARING EXAMINATION OF AMERICAN MILITARY STRATEGY. POINTS OUT THAT MILITARY MEN HAVE FORGOTTEN "RAISON D'ETRE" OF MILITARY STRATEGY: PROTECTION OF CIVILIAN POPULATION, NOT FURTHER DEVELOPMENT OF WEAPONS AND STRATEGIES "PER SE."

0445 BURR R.N. ED., HUSSEY R.D. ED.
DOCUMENTS ON INTER-AMERICAN COOPERATION: VOL. I, 1810-1881; VOL. II, 1881-1948.
PHILADELPHIA: U PENNSYLVANIA PR, 1955, 214 PP., LC#55-9972.
TWO-VOLUME WORK OF OFFICIAL AND PRIVATE DOCUMENTS RELATED TO EFFORTS UNITING SPANISH AMERICAN COUNTRIES POLITICALLY OR TEMPORARILY FOR CERTAIN GOALS AMONG THESE COUNTRIES THEMSELVES. VOLUME II DEALS WITH ORGANIZATION ON MORE FORMAL LEVELS, INCLUDING NON-SPANISH AMERICAN COUNTRIES, LEADING TO FORMATION OF PAN AMERICAN UNION AND OAS.

0446 BURTON J.W.
PEACE THEORY: PRECONDITIONS OF DISARMAMENT.
NEW YORK: KNOPF, 1962, 201 PP.
ATTEMPTS TO PROVIDE BASIC THEORY FOR THE FORMULATION OF A POLICY OF INTERNATIONAL RELATIONS. DEVELOPS A 'PATTERN OF A STABLE CONDITION OF PEACE' WHICH MIGHT SERVE AS A GUIDE TO A MORE FRUITFUL APPROACH TOWARD DISARMAMENT.

0447 BURTON J.W.
"INTERNATIONAL RELATIONS: A GENERAL THEORY."
CAMBRIDGE: UNIVERSITY PRESS, 1965.
STUDY OF INTERNATIONAL RELATIONS WHICH ASSUMES THAT ORTHODOX POWER THEORY IS UNSUPPORTABLE, PARTICULARLY IN THE NUCLEAR AGE. BIBLIOGRAPHY OF ABOUT 180 ITEMS IN ENGLISH THROUGH 1964, ARRANGED ALPHABETICALLY BY AUTHOR. INCLUDES BOOKS, ARTICLES, PUBLICLY PRESENTED PAPERS.

0448 BURTON M.E.
THE ASSEMBLY OF THE LEAGUE OF NATIONS.
CHICAGO: U. CHI. PR., 1941, 441 PP.
ORIGIN, HISTORY AND CHARACTER OF ASSEMBLY. PRESENTS EARLY PROPOSALS AND DRAFTS FOR ASSEMBLY STRUCTURE. OUTLINES AND EVALUATES COMMITTEES, RULES, AND DISPUTES. CONSIDERS EFFECTS OF PUBLICITY. APPENDIX INCLUDES LEAGUE CONVENANT.

0449 BUSS C.A.
THE FAR EAST: A HISTORY OF RECENT AND CONTEMPORARY INTERNATIONAL RELATIONS IN EAST ASIA.
NEW YORK: MACMILLAN, 1955, 720 PP.
A DEVELOPMENTAL ANALYSIS OF THE POLITICAL CONDITION OF THE MODERN STATES OF EAST ASIA IN THE LIGHT OF THEIR RELATIONS AMONG THEMSELVES AND WITH THE WEST DURING THE LAST ONE HUNDRED YEARS.

0450 BUSSCHAU W.J.
GOLD AND INTERNATIONAL LIQUIDITY.
JOHANNESBURG: S AFR INST INT AFF, 1961, 102 PP.
TEXT OF LECTURES EXPLORING FLOW OF CREDIT IN RELATION TO GOLD IN INTERNATIONAL MONETARY SYSTEM. EXPLORES PRACTICAL AND THEORETICAL ASPECTS OF GOLD PROBLEM PRESENTING ARGUMENTS WITH STATISTICAL AND MONETARY BACKGROUND. EXPRESSES NEED FOR RESTORATION OF GOLD STANDARD.

0451 BUTLER G., MACOBY S.
THE DEVELOPMENT OF INTERNATIONAL LAW.
LONDON: LONGMANS/GREEN, 1928, 566 PP.
PRESENTS HISTORY OF INTERNATIONAL DIPLOMACY. ANALYZES CHANGES IN INTERNATIONAL LAW AS FUNCTION OF 'CHANGES IN THE STATE SYSTEM AND IN THE PRACTICE OF NATIONS'. DIVIDES ANALYSIS INTO THREE PERIODS: 'THE PRINCE,' 'THE JUDGE,' AND 'THE CONCERT.'

0452 BUTLER N.M.
THE INTERNATIONAL MIND.
NEW YORK: SCRIBNER, 1913, 114 PP.
URGES SETTING UP OF INDEPENDENT JUDICIARY FOR SETTLEMENT OF INTERNATIONAL DISPUTES. BELIEVES IT WILL OFFER BEST SOLUTION FOR SETTLING BUSINESS AND INTERNATIONAL RIVALRIES, AND MAY PREVENT WAR BY REMOVING CAUSAL FACTORS. POINTS OUT THAT COURT MUST HAVE FULL SUPPORT OF GOVERNMENTS INVOLVED, PUBLIC OPINION, STATESMEN, AND JOURNALISTS TO BE EFFECTIVE.

0453 BUTOW R.J.C.
JAPAN'S DECISION TO SURRENDER.
STANFORD: STANFORD U PRESS, 1954, 259 PP., LC#54-8145.
NARRATES EVENTS OF EARLY MONTHS OF JAPAN'S WWII MILITARY CONQUEST. DESCRIBES SUCCESSIVE CRISES GROWING OUT OF JAPAN'S MOUNTING DEFEATS LATER IN THE WAR. TELLS OF DEVELOPMENTS OF LAST DAYS OF JAPAN'S TRAGEDY. SHOWS HOW SMALL GROUP WITHIN RULING ELITE COMMITTED JAPANESE GOVERNMENT TO SALVAGING, THROUGH NEGOTIATION, A PART OF WHAT THE MILITARY COULD NO LONGER MAINTAIN.

0454 BUTT R.
"THE COMMON MARKET AND CONSERVATIVE POLITICS, 1961-2."
GOVERNMENT AND OPPOSITION, 12 (APR.-JULY 67), 372-386.
DISCUSSES HOW DECISION FOR BRITAIN TO SEEK ENTRY INTO EEC WAS TAKEN AND ARGUES THAT IT DID NOT ARISE FROM TRADITIONAL INFLUENCES IN CONSERVATIVE PARTY BUT OUT OF PERSONAL POLICY OF MACMILLAN. ANALYZES REACTION 6F CONSERVATIVES TO IDEA OF BRITISH MEMBERSHIP AND SIGNIFICANCE OF OPPOSITION TO IDEA IN TERMS OF EVENTUAL SUCCESS OF MEMBERSHIP ATTEMPT.

0455 BUTTINGER J.
"THE SMALLER DRAGON; A POLITICAL HISTORY OF VIETNAM."
NEW YORK: FREDERICK PRAEGER, 1958.
A HISTORY OF VIETNAMESE POLITICAL SUBMISSION AND GROWTH COVERING THE PERIOD OF CHINESE RULE THROUGH 1957. POLITICAL EVENTS SINCE 1900 TREATED IN A BRIEF CHRONOLOGICAL SUMMARY. ANNOTATED BIBLIOGRAPHY DIVIDED INTO TWO CATEGORIES, HISTORY AND CIVILIZATION. LISTS ALL IMPORTANT WORKS ON VIETNAM THROUGH 1957; CONSISTS TO A LARGE EXTENT OF CONTRIBUTIONS TO PERIODICALS AND SCHOLARLY REVIEWS. SOURCES MOSTLY IN FRENCH.

0456 BUTTINGER J.
"VIETNAM* FRAUD OF THE 'OTHER WAR'."
DISSENT, 14 (MAY-JUNE 67), 376-384.
THE "SOCIAL REVOLUTION" IN VIETNAM, PROMISED BY THE HAWAII AND GUAM CONFERENCES, IS A TOTAL FAILURE. IT HAS NOT BEEN GIVEN SERIOUS ATTENTION, AND NO STEPS AT ALL HAVE BEEN AT LAND REFORM, THE REAL KEY TO AN IMPROVEMENT FOR THE SOUTH VIETNAMESE PEOPLE. BOTH US OFFICIALS AND CITIZENS HAVE BEEN DELUDED OR ARE DELUDING THEMSELVES ABOUT THE REAL LACK OF ANY SIGNIFICANT PROGRESS. CITES DOCUMENTS.

0457 BUTTS R.F.
AMERICAN EDUCATION IN INTERNATIONAL DEVELOPMENT.
NEW YORK: HARCOURT BRACE, 1963, 138 PP., LC#63-16547.
STUDIES AMERICA'S GROWING INVOLVEMENT IN EDUCATIONAL DEVELOPMENT OF NEW NATIONS. INCLUDES INCREASING KNOWLEDGE OF OTHER PEOPLES, PROVIDING TECHNICAL ASSISTANCE TO OTHER COUNTRIES, AND SUPPLYING TEACHERS FOR EDUCATIONAL NEEDS.

0458 BUTWELL R.
SOUTHEAST ASIA TODAY - AND TOMORROW.
NEW YORK: FREDERICK PRAEGER, 1964, 182 PP., LC#64-22490.
ANALYZES SOUTHEAST ASIA FROM PRE-EUROPEAN PERIOD TO ATTAINMENT OF INDEPENDENCE AND STUDIES WESTERN INFLUENCE IN PRESENT SITUATION. EXAMINES NATIONS THAT WERE ABLE TO CHOOSE FUNCTIONAL FORM OF GOVERNMENT AND THOSE STILL SEEKING WORKING SYSTEM. ORGANIZATION AND OPERATION OF THESE GOVERNMENTS, THEIR PROBLEMS AND POLICIES IN RELATION TO OTHER NATIONS, AND COMMUNISM ARE COVERED.

0459 BUTZ O.
GERMANY: DILEMMA FOR AMERICAN POLICY.
GARDEN CITY: DOUBLEDAY, 1954, 69 PP., LC#54-8072.
ANALYSIS OF DEVELOPMENT OF AMERICAN FOREIGN POLICY IN GERMANY FROM 1941-54. STRESSES STRATEGIC IMPORTANCE OF GERMANY IN COLD WAR POLITICAL RELATIONS AND SPECIFICALLY IN POSTWAR AMERICAN-SOVIET RELATIONS. FOCUSES ON BASIC AIMS NAD MOTIVES BEHIND AMERICAN POLICY DECISIONS IN REGARD TO GERMANY AND ASSESSES EFFECTIVENESS OF THESE DECISIONS.

0460 BYNKERSHOEK C., TENNEY F. ED.
QUAESTIONUM JURIS PUBLICI LIBRI DUO.
OXFORD: CLARENDON PR., 1930, 284 PP.
A CARNEGIE ENDOWMENT TRANSLATION OF THIS GREAT EIGHTEENTH CENTURY CLASSIC ON THE NATURE, RULES, AND EFFECTS OF WAR AND ON VARIOUS RIGHTS OF SOVEREIGN STATES.

0461 BYRD E.M. JR.
TREATIES AND EXECUTIVE AGREEMENTS IN THE UNITED STATES: THEIR SEPARATE ROLES AND LIMITATIONS.
LONDON: HEINEMANN, 1960, 276 PP.
HISTORICAL AND ANALYTICAL TREATMENT OF UNITED STATES' SHIFT FROM USE OF TREATIES TO USE OF EXECUTIVE AGREEMENTS. COVERS THE FOUNDING FATHERS' WRITINGS ON FOREIGN AFFAIRS AND TREATIES THEY MADE, THE SUPREME COURT'S VIEW, TREATY POWER, JOINT CONGRESSIONAL-EXECUTIVE ACTIONS, PRESIDENTIAL ACTIONS, AND FOREIGN AFFAIRS IN A FEDERAL SYSTEM.

0462 BYRNES R.F.
BIBLIOGRAPHY OF AMERICAN PUBLICATIONS ON EAST CENTRAL EUROPE, 1945-1957 (VOL. XXII)
BLOOMINGTON: INDIANA U PR, 1957, 213 PP.
COMPILES, ANNOTATES, AND INDEXES 2,810 ITEMS PUBLISHED IN US CONCERNING EAST CENTRAL EUROPE. ARRANGED BY COUNTRY AND SUBDIVIDED TOPICALLY. DEALS WITH AREA STUDIES, HISTORY, POLITICS, LAW, AND OTHER GENERAL SUBJECTS. INCLUDES A LONG LIST OF JOURNALS SEARCHED FOR COMPILATION.

0463 CADWELL R.
COMMUNISM IN THE MODERN WORLD.
PHILADELPHIA: DORRANCE CO, 1962, 251 PP., LC#62-11054.
PORTRAYS PRESENT INTERNATIONAL SITUATION AS CONFLICT BETWEEN DEMOCRATIC AND COMMUNIST CAMPS, VIEWING COMMUNIST SYSTEM AS ENSLAVEMENT OF INDIVIDUAL AND SUBORDINATION OF ALL HUMAN RIGHTS AND VALUES TO STATE. STRESSES THREAT TO DEMOCRATIC FREEDOM POSED BY COMMUNISM AND DISCUSSES IDEOLOGY AND POLICIES OF SOVIET COMMUNISM WHICH CREATE THIS THREAT.

0464 CAHIER P.
"LE DROIT INTERNE DES ORGANISATIONS INTERNATIONALES."
REV. GEN. DR. INT. PUB., 34 (NO.3, 63), 563-602.
BRIEF HISTORY OF INTERNAL LAW OF INTERNATIONAL ORGANIZATIONS. SEEKS TO CLARIFY WHETHER INTERNATIONAL LAW APPLICABLE TO MEMBER STATES OF SUPRA-NATIONAL ORGANIZATIONS. EXPLAINS RELATIONS BETWEEN INTERNATIONAL ORGANIZATIONS AND NATIONAL GOVERNMENTS.

0465 CAHIER P.
"LE RECOURS EN CONSTATATION DE MANQUEMENTS DES ETATS MEMBRES DEVANT LA COUR DES COMMUNAUTES EUROPEENNES."
CAHIERS DU DROIT EUR., 2 (1967), 123-163.
STUDIES FORMALITIES OBSERVED IN REACHING HIGH AUTHORITY'S DECISION AND COMMISSION'S OPINION, AND PROBLEMS OF ADMISSION AND PROCEDURE IN CONTEXT OF ARTICLES 88 AND 89 OF ECSC'S CONSTITUTION. EXAMINES EFFECTS OF JUDGMENTS OF COURT AND PROBLEMS OF POSSIBLE SANCTIONS.

0466 CALDER R.
COMMON SENSE ABOUT A STARVING WORLD.
NEW YORK: MACMILLAN, 1962, 176 PP., LC#61-14371.
SURVEYS FACTS OF POPULATION EXPLOSION, ANALYZES THEM IN CONTEXT OF WESTERN ATTITUDES AND APPREHENSIONS ABOUT IMPACT OF AID TO UNDERDEVELOPED COUNTRIES UPON WESTERN STANDARD OF LIVING. DISCUSSES POLITICAL ASPECTS OF FOOD PRODUCTION AND DISTRIBUTION, URGING CONCERTED ACTION TO RAISE FOOD PRODUCTION AND CONTROL POPULATION.

0467 CALDER R.
TWO-WAY PASSAGE.
LONDON: HEINEMANN, 1964, 186 PP.
DISCUSSES VARIOUS ASPECTS OF MUTUAL AID PROGRAMS TO UNDERDEVELOPED NATIONS, POPULATION EXPLOSION, WASTE IN FOREIGN AID, AND FORMS OF IMAGINATIVE PLANNING. MAINTAINS THAT CENTRAL AIM OF FOREIGN AID SHOULD BE INVESTMENT IN HUMAN RESOURCES.

0468 CALLEO D.P.
EUROPE'S FUTURE: THE GRAND ALTERNATIVES.
NEW YORK: HORIZON PRESS, 1965, 185 PP., LC#65-26723.
EXPLAINS MAJOR WAYS OF LOOKING AT EUROPE'S FUTURE. DISCUSSES CONFLICTING CONCEPTS OF POSTWAR NATIONALISM AND FEDERALISM. DESCRIBES COMMON MARKET IDEA OF FEDERALIST EUROPE, DE GAULLE'S CONCEPT OF A NATIONALIST EUROPE, AND US IDEA OF AN ATLANTIC EUROPE. SUGGESTS THAT A STRONG UNION OF STATES, INCLUDING BRITAIN, WOULD RESULT FROM SYNTHESIS OF BEST IN EACH CONCEPT.

0469 CALVO SERER R.
LAS NUEVAS DEMOCRACIAS.
MADRID: EDICIONES RIALP, 1964, 249 PP.
STUDY OF INTERNATIONAL POLITICAL CHANGES SINCE WWII AND THEIR EFFECTS ON DEMOCRACY IN WORLD. DISCUSSES NEWLY DEMOCRATIC NATIONS AND ESTABLISHMENT OF DICTATORSHIPS AND COMMUNISM IN AFRO-ASIAN NATIONS DURING THIS PERIOD. ALSO COVERS US SYSTEM AND ITS IMPACT ON WORLD.

0470 CALVOCORESSI P.
SOUTH AFRICA AND WORLD OPINION.
LONDON: OXFORD U PR, 1961, 68 PP.
REACTION OF DIFFERENT AREAS TO POLICIES OF SOUTH AFRICA. ANALYZES THEIR DIFFERENCES, SOUTH AFRICA'S RELATIONS IN WORLD COMMUNITY; INCLUDES SPEECHES AND RESOLUTIONS RELATED TO WORLD OPINION OF SOUTH AFRICA.

0471 CALVOCORESSI P.
WORLD ORDER AND NEW STATES: PROBLEMS OF KEEPING THE PEACE.
NEW YORK: PRAEGER, 1962, 113 PP., $4.25.
DISCUSSES ROLE OF THE GREAT POWERS AS GUARDIANS OF PEACE, AND COLD WAR INTERFERENCE WITH THIS ROLE. CONSIDERS INTERNAL INSTABILITY OF NEW AFRO-ASIAN COUNTRIES. VIEWS ASSISTANCE POSSIBLE FROM DEMOCRATIC COUNTRIES. EXAMINES UN ACTION FOR PEACE AND SUGGESTS STEPS FOR INCREASED EFFECTIVENESS.

0472 CAMERON J.
THE AFRICAN REVOLUTION.
NEW YORK: RANDOM HOUSE, INC, 1961, 281 PP.
TRACES AFRICAN QUEST FOR POLITICAL LIBERATION IN SIXTIES. PAST HISTORY AS WELL AS FUTURE AND RISING PERSONALITIES IS EXAMINED. DEALS WITH PROBLEMS OF POVERTY, IGNORANCE, INEXPERIENCE, DEMAGOGUERY, AND ISOLATION, WHICH LIE DEEPER THAN INSTANT REVOLUTION AND DENUNCIATION OF COLONIAL DEMANDS. REVOLT IS AGAINST AFRICA ITSELF: ITS COLONIAL PAST, TRIBAL ISOLATION, AND DIVISIONS.

0473 CAMPAIGNE J.G.
AMERICAN MIGHT AND SOVIET MYTH.
CHICAGO: REGNERY, 1960, 218 PP., $2.00.
HOLDS THAT DESPITE EXPENDITURES AND PROGRAMS, AMERICAN FOREIGN POLICY HAS FAILED TO HALT COMMUNIST EXPANSION. SEES RELIANCE ON ALLIES AND UN AS PREVENTING EFFECTIVE INDEPENDENT ACTION, WHILE ECONOMIC AID FURTHERS INEFFICIENCY AND SOCIALISM. ALSO HOLDS THAT SOVIET ECONOMIC COMPETITION IS NO GENUINE THREAT.

0474 CAMPBELL J.C.
DEFENSE OF THE MIDDLE EAST: PROBLEMS OF AMERICAN POLICY.
NEW YORK: HARPER, 1958, 392 PP.
THE FINDINGS OF STUDY GROUPS ESTABLISHED BY THE COUNCIL ON FOREIGN RELATIONS WITH RESPECT TO A LACK OF COMPREHENSIVE MIDDLE EAST POLICY AMONG WESTERN ALLIANCE. FIRST, A SELECTIVE TREATMENT OF DEVELOPMENT OF USA ANTICOMMUNIST POLICY IN THE AREA AS INTRODUCTION TO DECISIONS AND ATTITUDES TODAY. SECOND, THE PROBLEMS TODAY. THIRD, EIGHT LONG-TERM PROPOSALS FOR AVOIDING CRISES AND KEEPING MID-EAST IN FREE WORLD.

0475 CAMPBELL J.C.
"THE MIDDLE EAST IN THE MUTED COLD WAR."
DENVER: U. PR., 1964, 33 PP.
OUTLINES MAIN EPISODES OF RECENT PAST. DEMONSTRATES DECLINE OF WESTERN INFLUENCE CONSIDERED IMPERIALIST. NOTES NASSER'S 'POSITIVE NEUTRALISM,' POLICY OF PLAYING EAST AND WEST AGAINST EACH OTHER, AND IMPROVED RELATIONS WITH WEST SINCE 1958. EXAMINES SOVIET AIMS IN AREA.

0476 CANELAS O.A.
RADIOGRAFIA DE LA ALIANZA PARA EL ATRASO.
LA PAZ: LIBRERIA ALTIPLANO, 1963, 311 PP.
DISCUSSES PRESENT LATIN AMERICA SITUATION REGARDING US POLICIES SUCH AS ALLIANCE FOR PROGRESS. EXPLAINS REASON FOR LATIN AMERICAN REVOLUTIONS TO REMOVE US POWER. COMPARES LATIN AMERICA TO AFRO-ASIAN COUNTRIES THAT BECAME INDEPENDENT FROM COLONIAL POWERS.

0477 CANFIELD L.H.
THE PRESIDENCY OF WOODROW WILSON: PRELUDE TO A WORLD IN CRISIS.
RUTHERFORD: FAIRLEIGH DICKEN PR, 1966, 299 PP., LC#66-24796.
ANALYSIS OF ALL ASPECTS OF WILSON'S PRESIDENTIAL ADMINISTRATION. PORTRAYS HIS TERM AS TRAGEDY, HIS RISE TO FAME IN HIS FIGHT FOR PEACE AND NEUTRALITY, AND HIS PHYSICAL AND MENTAL DETERIORATION AFTER HIS PEOPLE REJECTED THE LEAGUE OF NATIONS.

0478 CANNING HOUSE LIBRARY
AUTHOR AND SUBJECT CATALOGUES OF THE CANNING HOUSE LIBRARY (5 VOLS.)
BOSTON: HALL, 1966.
BIBLIOGRAPHICAL LISTING OF BOOKS IN CANNING HOUSE LIBRARY IN LONDON PERTAINING TO LATIN AMERICA. OVER 30,000 ENTRIES OF 19TH- AND 20TH-CENTURY PUBLICATIONS. FOUR VOLUMES ON SPANISH-SPEAKING LATIN AMERICAN COUNTRIES AND ONE ON BRAZIL.

0479 CARDINALL A.W.
A BIBLIOGRAPHY OF THE GOLD COAST.
ACCRA: GOVT PRINTER, 1932, 384 PP., LC#32-24984.
BIBLIOGRAPHY OF EARLY PERIOD OF BRITISH ADMINISTRATION.

0480 CARDOZA M.H.
DIPLOMATS IN INTERNATIONAL COOPERATION: STEPCHILDREN OF THE FOREIGN SERVICE.
ITHACA: CORNELL U. PR., 1962, 142 PP.
CONSIDERS IMPACT OF COOPERATIVE INTERNATIONAL ORGANIZATIONS ON THE PRACTICES OF DIPLOMACY. BRIEFLY TRACES THE DEVELOPMENT OF TRADITIONAL DIPLOMACY, AND INDICATES HOW IT DIFFERS FROM THE PRESENT-DAY DIPLOMATIC METHODS. DISCUSSES SUCH ORGANIZATIONS AS OEEC AND NATO, POINTING OUT EFFECTS THEY HAVE HAD ON DIPLOMACY.

0481 CAREW-HUNT R.C.
BOOKS ON COMMUNISM.
NY, LONDON: AMPERSAND PR INC, 1959, 333 PP.
BRIEF AND SELECTIVE CRITICAL ANNOTATIONS ON WORLDWIDE COMMUNISM IN NUMEROUS TOPICS INCLUDING THEORY AND BACKGROUND OF RUSSIAN REVOLUTION. LAST SECTION LISTS UK, COMMONWEALTH, AND US OFFICIAL DOCUMENTS AND PUBLICATIONS.

0482 CARIBBEAN COMMISSION
CURRENT CARIBBEAN BIBLIOGRAPHY.
PORT OF SPAIN, TRINDAD: KENT HSE, 1951.
VOLUME I OF THIS SERIES WAS PUBLISHED IN JUNE 1951. THE BIBLIOGRAPHY IS A CUMULATIVE WORK NOW PUBLISHED ANNUALLY. DIVIDED INTO THREE SECTIONS: (1) PERIODICALS AND NEWSPAPERS, (2) GOVERNMENT SERIALS, (3) MONOGRAPHS. A GEOGRAPHICAL INDEX AND DIRECTORY OF PUBLISHERS WITH ADDRESSES ARE APPENDED TO THE BIBLIOGRAPHY.

0483 CARIBBEAN COMMISSION
A CATALOGUE OF CARIBBEAN COMMISSION PUBLICATIONS (PAMPHLET)
PORT OF SPAIN: CARIBBEAN COMN, 1957, 25 PP.
LISTS PUBLICATIONS OF CARIBBEAN COMMISSION TO 1957. ITEMS ARRANGED BY SUBJECT.

0484 CARLETON W.G.
"AMERICAN FOREIGN POLICY: MYTHS AND REALITIES."
VIRGINIA QUART. REV., 37 (SPRING 61), 177-97.
ANALYZES MYTH OF TOLERATING LIMITED WARS TO ASSURE PEACE. REALISTIC NEW FOREIGN POLICIES SUGGEST BETTER UNDERSTANDING OF ANTI-IMPERIALIST REVOLUTIONS. EXAMINES NEW DIMENSIONS FOR US ECONOMIC AID TO UNDERDEVELOPED COUNTRIES.

0485 CARLO A.M., MANTECON J.
ENSAYO DE UNA BIBLIOGRAFIA DE BIBLIOGRAFIAS MEXICANAS.
MEXICO CITY: DIR GEN ACCION SOC, 1943, 224 PP.
A BIBLIOGRAPHY OF BIBLIOGRAPHIES PUBLISHED IN AND ABOUT MEXICO. ENTRIES CLASSIFIED BY SUBJECT. CONTAINS CATALOGUES, DIRECTORIES OF BOOKS, PERIODICALS, AND LIBRARIES.

0486 CARLSTON K.S.
"NATIONALIZATION: AN ANALYTIC APPROACH."
NORTHWEST. UNIV. LAW REV., 54 (1959), 405-33.
CONSIDERS THE DISPERSION OF POLITICAL SOVEREIGNTY THROUGHOUT THE GLOBE, AND THE JARRING EFFECTS OF THE MULTITUDE OF IDEOLOGIES AND ATTITUDES TOWARD PLANNING AND SOCIAL ORGANIZATION WHICH HAVE COME INTO CONFLICT WITH THE INCREASING CENTRALIZATION OF THE INTERNATIONAL ECONOMIC SYSTEM. THESE SAME FACTS HAVE ALSO MADE INTERNATIONAL LAW MORE DIFFICULT TO DETERMINE AND TO APPLY.

0487 CARLSTON K.S.
LAW AND ORGANIZATION IN WORLD SOCIETY.
URBANA: U. ILL. PR., 1962, 356 PP., $6.50.
A BLEND OF LEGAL DOCTRINE AND ORGANIZATION THEORY LEADING TOWARD A THEORY OF LAW AND ORDER IN WORLD SOCIETY. THEORY IS BASED ON THE SUBJECT OF NATIONALIZATION OF CONCESSION AGREEMENTS WITH FOREIGN INVESTORS.

0488 CARNEGIE ENDOWMENT
CURRENT RESEARCH IN INTERNATIONAL AFFAIRS: SELECTED BIBLIOGRAPHY OF WORK IN PROGRESS BY PRIVATE RESEARCH AGENCIES.
NEW YORK: CARNEGIE ENDOWMENT.
ANNUAL PUBLICATION FROM 1948-1952 OF CURRENT RESEARCH BY PRIVATE RESEARCH AGENCIES, AND DEPARTMENTS AND SPECIAL RESEARCH INSTITUTES OF UNIVERSITIES IN THE US, AND, TO A LIMITED EXTENT, IN UK. RESEARCH COVERS RELATIONS BETWEEN TWO OR MORE COUNTRIES; PARTICULAR PROBLEMS WITH INTERNATIONAL SIGNIFICANCE; PROBLEMS OF PARTICULARLY CRUCIAL GEOGRAPHIC AREAS. ARRANGED ALPHABETICALLY BY INSTITUTION. INDEXES.

0489 CARNEGIE ENDOWMENT INT. PEACE
PERSPECTIVES ON PEACE - 1910-1960.
NEW YORK: PRAEGER, 1960, 202 PP.
COMPILATION OF ESSAYS BY OUTSTANDING STATESMEN AND LEADERS OF PUBLIC OPINION. RANGE OF TOPICS INCLUDES: INTERNATIONAL ORGANIZATION, DIPLOMACY, INTERNATIONAL LAW, EDUCATION, REGIONALISM, COLLECTIVE SECURITY, ECONOMIC INTEGRATION AND WORLD COMMONWEALTH.

0490 CARNEGIE ENDOWMENT INT. PEACE
"POLITICAL QUESTIONS (ISSUES BEFORE THE NINETEENTH GENERAL ASSEMBLY)."
INT. CONCIL., 550 (NOV. 64), 5-62.
DISCUSSES FOLLOWING PROBLEMS WHICH WERE RAISED DURING NINETEENTH SESSION: FINANCES, PEACE KEEPING FORCES, DISARMAMENT, ARMS CONTROL, CHARTER REVISION, RED CHINA, RADIATION, PALESTINE REFUGEES, CYPRUS, AND THE PEACEFUL USES OF ATOMIC ENERGY.

0491 CARNEGIE ENDOWMENT INT. PEACE
"COLONIAL COUNTRIES AND PEOPLES (ISSUES BEFORE THE NINETEENTH GENERAL ASSEMBLY)."
INT. CONCIL. 550 (NOV. 64), 63-88.
DISCUSSES PROBLEMS ARISING IN FOLLOWING DEPENDENCIES WHICH WERE RAISED DURING NINETEENTH SESSION: SOUTHERN RHODESIA, SOUTH WEST AFRICA, THE PORTUGESE TERRITORIES, OMAN, ADAN, AND BRITISH GUIANA.

0492 CARNEGIE ENDOWMENT INT. PEACE
"HUMAN RIGHTS (ISSUES BEFORE THE NINETEENTH GENERAL ASSEMBLY)."
INT. CONCIL., 550 (NOV. 64), 88-117.
DISCUSSES ISSUE OF RACIAL DISCRIMINATION AND PROBLEM OF REFUGEES WHICH WERE RAISED DURING THE NINETEENTH SESSION.

0493 CARNEGIE ENDOWMENT INT. PEACE
"ECONOMIC AND SOCIAL QUESTION (ISSUES BEFORE THE NINETEENTH GENERAL ASSEMBLY)."
INT. CONCIL., 550 (NOV. 64), 117-87.
DISCUSSES PROBLEMS CONCERNING THE FOLLOWING WHICH WERE RAISED DURING NINETEENTH SESSION: GATT, COMMODITY TRADE, TECHNICAL COOPERATION, PATENTS, UN SPECIAL FUND, AND UN TRAINING AND RESEARCH INSTITUTE.

0494 CARNEGIE ENDOWMENT INT. PEACE
"LEGAL QUESTIONS (ISSUES BEFORE THE NINETEENTH GENERAL ASSEMBLY)."
INT. CONCIL., 550 (NOV. 64), 187-97.
DISCUSSES ISSUES OF INTERNATIONAL LAW WHICH WERE RAISED DURING NINETEENTH SESSION, INCLUDING CODIFICATION, DEVELOPMENT AND TREATIES.

0495 CARNEGIE ENDOWMENT INT. PEACE
"ADMINISTRATION AND BUDGET (ISSUES BEFORE THE NINETEENTH GENERAL ASSEMBLY)."
INT. CONCIL., 550 (NOV. 64), 197-205.
DISCUSSES MONETARY AND ADMINISTRATIVE ISSUES WHICH WERE RAISED DURING THE NINETEENTH SESSION.

0496 CARNELL F. ED.
THE POLITICS OF THE NEW STATES: A SELECT ANNOTATED BIBLIOGRAPHY WITH SPECIAL REFERENCE TO THE COMMONWEALTH.
LONDON: OXFORD U PR, 1961, 171 PP.
PARTIALLY ANNOTATED BIBLIOGRAPHY OF 1599 TITLES ON THE NEW STATES OF AFRICA AND ASIA IN FRENCH AND ENGLISH. ITEMS ARE ARRANGED BY TOPIC, CROSS-REFERENCED AND INDEXED BY AUTHOR AND GEOGRAPHICAL LOCATION. SECTION ON APPROACHES TO THE STUDY OF POLITICS INCLUDES WORKS ON WESTERN STATES. COVERS GENERAL HISTORICAL BACKGROUND ON COLONIALISM AND STUDIES OF PROBLEMS IN COLONIALISM.

0497 CARR E.H.
PROPAGANDA IN INTERNATIONAL POLITICS (PAMPHLET)
LONDON: OXFORD U PR, 1939, 32 PP.
TREATS PROPAGANDA IN MODERN POLITICS. DISCUSSES NATURE OF PROPAGANDA, ITS USE IN WAR, INTERNATIONAL AGREEMENTS TO RESTRAIN PROPAGANDA, ITS ORGANIZATION, AND TRUTH AND MORALITY IN INTERNATIONAL PROPAGANDA.

0498 CARR E.H.
THE TWENTY YEARS' CRISIS 1919-1939.
LONDON: MACMILLAN, 1940, 307 PP.
DISCUSSES TRENDS OF INTERNATIONAL POLITICS 1919-1939. EXPLAINS ORIGINS OF INTERNATIONAL SCIENCE. SHOWS CONFLICT OF UTOPIAN AND REALISTIC IDEAS. TRACES PARTS PLAYED BY POWER, LAW, MORALITY IN POLICY FORMULATION. HOPES MORALITY WILL GUIDE NEW INTERNATIONAL ORDER.

0499 CARR E.H.
NATIONALISM AND AFTER.
NEW YORK: MACMILLAN, 1945, 76 PP.
MODERN STATE, SERVING INTERESTS OF INDIVIDUALS AND GROUPS, ENCOURAGED DEVELOPMENT OF SELF-DEFEATING NATIONALISM. NEW AGE OF INTERDEPENDENCE WILL LEAD TO REGIONALISM AND SUPRANATIONAL ORGANIZATIONS.

0500 CARRINGTON C.E.
THE COMMONWEALTH IN AFRICA (PAMPHLET)
P1962 284 57 02840
REPORTS ON CONFERENCE HELD BY AFRICAN COMMONWEALTH NATIONS IN 1962. DEALS WITH COLD WAR AND AFRICA, PAN-AFRICANISM, COMMON MARKET AND BRITAIN'S DESIRE TO JOIN, ECONOMIC INDEPENDENCE, DEMOCRATIC INSTITUTIONS BEST SUITED FOR PLANNING AND DEVELOPMENT IN AFRICA, AND FUTURE OF COMMONWEALTH COOPERATION IN AFRICA.

0501 CARRINGTON C.E.
THE LIQUIDATION OF THE BRITISH EMPIRE.
LONDON: GEORGE HARRAP & CO, 1951, 96 PP.
TRACES DISINTEGRATION OF BRITISH EMPIRE SINCE WWII. DISCUSSES INDEPENDENCE MOVEMENTS IN INDIA, RHODESIA, KENYA, GHANA, AND NIGERIA. EXAMINES PROBLEM OF RACE RELATIONS, FRENCH COLONIAL SYSTEM, COMMONWEALTH TRADE, AND PRINCIPLES OF COOPERATION AMONG COMMONWEALTH COUNTRIES.

0502 CARROLL H.N.
THE HOUSE OF REPRESENTATIVES AND FOREIGN AFFAIRS.
PITTSBURGH: U. PR., 1958, 365 PP.
STUDY OF ROLE THAT HOUSE ASSUMES IN FORMULATING FOREIGN POLICY. PRESENTS A HISTORY OF THE 'LOWER BRANCH', DESCRIBES THE WORKINGS OF COMMITTEES, AND EMPHASIZES THE ACTIVITIES, BOTH OFFICIAL AND UNOFFICIAL, OF LATTER GROUP.

0503 CARROLL K.J.
"SECOND STEP TOWARD ARMS CONTROL."
MILITARY REV., 47 (MAY 67), 77-84.
AFTER SURVEYING DIFFICULTIES IN THE HISTORY OF ARMS CONTROL DURING PAST TWO DECADES, THE AUTHOR PRESENTS THE CRITERIA FOR SURE AND ACCEPTABLE INSPECTION. SHOWS HOW SUBMARINES COULD BE RESTRICTED WITH SHORELINE INSPECTION AND ON-BOARD OBSERVERS. SUGGESTS THAT USA- USSR ACCORD IN THIS AREA COULD SERVE AS PILOT EXPERIMENT FOR FUTURE DISARMAMENT.

0504 CARTER G.M.
"THE POLITICS OF INEQUALITY: SOUTH AFRICA SINCE 1948."
NEW YORK: FREDERICK PRAEGER, 1958.
POLITICAL STUDY OF SOUTH AFRICA IN PERIOD AFTER NATIONAL PARTY CAME TO OFFICE IN 1948. COMPREHENSIVE SURVEYS OF POLITICAL PARTY ORGANIZATION AND ELECTIONS, WITH EXTENSIVE INFORMATION ON 1953 GENERAL ELECTION. CONTAINS LENGTHY APPENDIXES AND PARTY DEVELOPMENTS AND ELECTION CHARTS. EXTENSIVE BIBLIOGRAPHY.

0505 CASEY R.G.
THE FUTURE OF THE COMMONWEALTH.
LONDON: FREDERICK MULLER, 1964, 187 PP.
DISCUSSES FUTURE OF BRITISH COMMONWEALTH UNDER FORCES OF NATIONALISM AND INDEPENDENCE MOVEMENTS. SUGGESTS FORMS OF ECONOMIC AND TECHNICAL AID BY ENGLAND TO COMMONWEALTH COUNTRIES. EXAMINES IMPLICATIONS OF POSSIBLE BRITISH ENTRY INTO COMMON MARKET.

0506 CASSELL F.
GOLD OR CREDIT? THE ECONOMICS AND POLITICS OF INTERNATIONAL MONEY.
NEW YORK: FREDERICK PRAEGER, 1965, 216 PP.
EXAMINES TWO ALTERNATE BASES FOR MONETARY CONTROL, GOLD STANDARD OR INTERNATIONAL CREDIT. GIVES PROBLEM WITH BOTH METHODS AND SOLUTIONS. SACRIFICES NEEDED TO FACILITATE SOLUTIONS SUCH AS END TO ECONOMIC SOVEREIGNTY, COMMON MARKETS, AND COMMON CURRENCY ARE DISCUSSED. MAINTAINS THAT SYSTEM OF INTERNATIONAL CREDIT WOULD FURTHER WORLD ECONOMIES IN MOST EFFECTIVE MANNER.

0507 CASTANEDA J.
"THE UNDERDEVELOPED NATIONS AND THE DEVELOPMENT OF INTERNATIONAL LAW."
INT. ORGAN., 15 (WINTER 61), 38-48.
CLARIFIES POSSIBILITIES AND LIMITATIONS OF PURELY DECLARATIVE CODES OF CUSTOMARY RULES ADOPTED BY GENERAL ASSEMBLY AS MEANS OF DISCHARGING THAT ORGAN'S RESPONSIBILITIES. CONCLUDES WITH EXAMINATION OF SOME OF UNDERLYING POLITICAL ASSUMPTIONS THAT FORM FOUNDATION OF THIS APPROACH.

0508 CASTLE E.W.
THE GREAT GIVEAWAY: THE REALITIES OF FOREIGN AID.
CHICAGO: HENRY REGNERY CO, 1957, 186 PP., LC#57-8243.
INVESTIGATES PROGRAMS FOR FOREIGN AID, THEIR ORGANIZATION, COSTS, FAILURES, AND RESULTS, TO STIMULATE DISCUSSION OF PROBLEM SO THAT BETTER PROGRAM CAN BE DEVISED.

0509 CBS
CONVERSATIONS WITH WALTER LIPPMANN.
BOSTON: LITTLE BROWN, 1965, 242 PP., LC#65-16875.
COLLECTION OF CONVERSATIONS WITH WALTER LIPPMANN BROADCAST OVER CBS, 1960-65, DISCUSSING WIDE RANGE OF TOPICS OF DOMESTIC AND INTERNATIONAL POLITICS.

0510 CECIL L.
ALBERT BALLIN; BUSINESS AND POLITICS IN IMPERIAL GERMANY 1888-1918.
PRINCETON: PRINCETON U PRESS, 1967, 388 PP., LC#66-21830.
STUDIES PLACE OF ALBERT BALLIN IN BUSINESS AND POLITICS OF IMPERIAL GERMANY. DISCUSSES ANGLO-GERMAN RELATIONS AND RIVALRY IN INTERNATIONAL SHIPPING AND NAVAL CONSTRUCTION AND REACTIONARY POLITICAL AND SOCIAL SYSTEMS IN INDUSTRIALIZED GERMANY. INCLUDES HYPOTHESIS THAT BUSINESS LEADERS SUCH AS BALLIN OPPOSED REFORM BECAUSE OF FEAR OF SOCIALISM AND DESIRE TO CONTROL GOVERNMENT.

0511 CENTRAL ASIAN RESEARCH CENTRE
RUSSIA LOOKS AT AFRICA (PAMPHLET)
LONDON: CENT ASIAN RES CENTRE, 1960, 21 PP.
SURVEY OF RUSSIAN WRITING ON AFRICA 1800-1960 BY TOPICS, WITH BRIEF COMMENTARIES ON AUTHORS.

0512 CENTRO PARA EL DESARROLLO
LA ALIANZA PARA EL PROGRESO Y EL DESARROLLO SOCIAL DE AMERICA LATINA.
SANTIAGO: CEN PARAEL DESARROLLO, 1963, 104 PP.
CENTER FOR ECONOMIC AND SOCIAL DEVELOPMENT OF LATIN AMERICA ANALYZES ALLIANCE FOR PROGRESS. EXAMINES NEEDS OF LATIN AMERICAN NATIONS IN DRIVE FOR SOCIAL CHANGE, COVERING METHODS AND REQUIREMENTS FOR ECONOMIC GROWTH INCLUDED IN ALLIANCE FOR PROGRESS PROPOSALS.

0513 CEPEDE M., HOUTART F., GROND L.
POPULATION AND FOOD.
NEW YORK: SHEED AND WARD, 1964, 461 PP., LC#63-8546.
EXAMINES RATES OF POPULATION GROWTH, AVERAGE LIFE EXPECTANCIES, STANDARDS OF LIVING, AID TO UNDERDEVELOPED NATIONS, USE OF SURPLUS FOODS, AND FAMILY PLANNING. ARGUES THAT POOR SOCIAL AND ECONOMIC ORGANIZATION AND MANAGEMENT ARE TO BLAME FOR THE DIFFICULTIES BROUGHT ON BY RAPIDLY GROWING POPULATION, THAT US HAS THE TECHNOLOGY TO PRODUCE MORE THAN ENOUGH FOR A WORLD POPULATION OF OVER TEN BILLION.

0514 CERAMI C.A.
ALLIANCE BORN OF DANGER.
NEW YORK: HARCOURT BRACE, 1963, 181 PP., LC#63-13686.
DISCUSSES RELATIONS OF US, COMMON MARKET, AND ATLANTIC ALLIANCE: PROBLEMS OF UNITY, PROSPECTS FOR FUTURE INTEGRATION, UK'S RELATION TO CONTINENT, AND ROLE OF AMERICA IN WESTERN EUROPE.

0515 CHAKRAVARTI P.C.
"INDIAN NON-ALIGNMENT AND UNITED STATES POLICY."
CURR. HIST., 44 (MAR. 63), 129-134.
ALTHOUGH ECONOMIC INTERDEPENDENCE COUPLED WITH GROWING VOLUME OF INTELLECTUAL AND CULTURAL COLLABORATION HAS STRENGTHENED BONDS OF AMITY AND UNDERSTANDING BETWEEN INDIA AND USA, THE PAST 15 YEARS HAVE REVEALED SERIOUS DIFFERENCES OF OPINION ON QUESTIONS OF FOREIGN POLICY.

0516 CHALUPA V.
RISE AND DEVELOPMENT OF A TOTALITARIAN STATE.
LEYDEN: H E STENFERT KROESE, 1959, 294 PP.
DISCUSSES VARIOUS CONCEPTS OF TOTALITARIANISM. EXAMINES ROLE OF COMMUNIST PARTY, SEIZURE OF POWER IN USSR, STRUCTURE OF COMMUNIST SOCIETY, AND INTERNATIONAL INTEGRATION OF COMMUNIST FORCES. ALSO STUDIES RISE OF TOTALITARIANISM IN CZECHOSLOVAKIA.

0517 CHAMBERLAIN L.H.
AMERICAN FOREIGN POLICY.
NEW YORK: RHINEHART, 1948, 825 PP.
A GENERAL INTRODUCTION TO AMERICAN FOREIGN POLICY. DISCUSSES THE CONSTITUTION AS ITS BASIS. TREATS COUNTRIES THAT HAVE BEEN EITHER VICTIMS OR BENEFICIARIES OF USA POLICIES.

0518 CHAND A.
"INDIA AND TANZANIA."
INDIAN FOREIGN REV., 4 (JUNE 67).
REVIEWS CLOSE RELATIONSHIP AND COMMON INTERESTS OF INDIA AND TANZANIA. CLAIMS THAT AN IDENTITY OF HISTORICAL DESTINY HAS FORGED STRONG LINKS BETWEEN ASIA AND AFRICA. SHOWS HOW TANZANIA, LIKE INDIA, HAS ADOPTED NATIONAL PLANNING FOR ECONOMIC PROGRESS. TANZANIA ACCEPTS ECONOMIC AID FROM ALL NATIONS BUT WILL NOT ALLOW POLITICAL DIRECTION FROM ANY QUARTER IN HER DESIRE TO REMAIN NEUTRAL.

0519 CHANDLER E.H.S.
THE HIGH TOWER OF REFUGE: THE INSPIRING STORY OF REFUGEE RELIEF THROUGHOUT THE WORLD.
NEW YORK: FREDERICK PRAEGER, 1959, 264 PP., LC#59-14997.
PICTURE OF REFUGEE SITUATIONS AND WORK AS SEEN BY DIRECTOR OF THE SERVICE TO REFUGEES OF WORLD COUNCIL OF CHURCHES. TELLS OF GREAT EFFORTS OF CHURCH ORGANIZATIONS

TO ALLEVIATE SUFFERING AND TO PLACE REFUGEES IN COUNTRIES WHERE THEY CAN CONTRIBUTE THEIR TALENT. FEELS MIGRATION KEY IS TO MOVE PEOPLE FROM OVER-CROWDED LANDS TO THOSE WHICH NEED THEM.

0520 CHANG C.J.
THE MINORITY GROUPS OF YUNN AN AND CHINESE POLITICAL EXPANSION INTO SOUTHEAST ASIA (DOCTORAL THESIS)
ANN ARBOR: U OF MICH PR, 1956, 199 PP.
STUDY OF HAN-CHINESE POLITICAL EXPANSION AMONG THE NON-HAN-CHINESE TRIBAL PEOPLES IN YUNN AN FRONTIER AREA. REVIEWS THREE PHASES OF TERRITORIAL EXPANSION: CULTURAL COLONIZATION OR SINCIZATION, COMMUNIST POLITICAL CONQUEST, AND IMPLEMENTATION OF REGIONAL AUTONOMY. CONCLUDES THAT PRESENT TECHNIQUES WILL LEAD TO DEFINITE CHINESE EXPANSION BEYOND THE BORDER.

0521 CHANG H.
WITHIN THE FOUR SEAS.
NEW YORK: TWAYNE, 1958, 254 PP., LC#58-14293.
CONSIDERS PROBLEM OF WORLD PEACE BY APPLYING THOUGHTS AND OBSERVATIONS OF CONFUCIUS TO PRESENT CONDITIONS. MAINTAINS THAT WEST MAY LEARN LESSON OF "SPIRITUAL OR CULTURAL COHESION" FROM KNOWLEDGE OF TRADITION OF EAST.

0522 CHARLESWORTH J.C.
"AMERICA AND A NEW ASIA."
ANN. AMER. ACAD. POLIT. SOC. SCI., 294 (JULY 54), 1-157.
DISCUSSION OF USA RELATIONS WITH FAR EASTERN COUNTRIES, INDIA AND THE MIDDLE EAST IN RELATION TO RECEDING COLONIALISM, ASIAN AND MIDDLE EASTERN NATIONALISM AND EXPANDING COMMUNISM.

0523 CHARLETON W.G.
"THE REVOLUTION IN AMERICAN FOREIGN POLICY."
NEW YORK: RANDOM HOUSE, INC, 1963.
ATTEMPTS TO PLACE RECENT AND CONTEMPORARY EVENTS IN HISTORICAL PERSPECTIVE IN ORDER TO TREAT THE PRESENT AS HISTORY, USING A COMBINATION OF NARRATIVE AND INTERPRETIVE TECHNIQUES. COVERS THE PERIOD FROM THE DEPARTURE FROM AMERICAN CONTINENTALISM DURING THE SPANISH-AMERICAN WAR THROUGH AMERICAN FOREIGN POLICY IN THE COLD WAR. UNANNOTATED BIBLIOGRAPHY, ORGANIZED BY RELEVANCE TO CHAPTER HEADINGS.

0524 CHASE E.P.
THE UNITED NATIONS IN ACTION.
NEW YORK: MCGRAW HILL, 1950, 464 PP.
DESCRIPTION OF UN AS SECURITY AND WELFARE ORGANIZATION. COVERS MEMBERSHIP, ORGANIZATION AND PROCEDURES OF AGENCIES, COUNCILS, THE GENERAL ASSEMBLY AND THE SECURITY COUNCIL. INCLUDES EXPLORATIONS OF PROBLEMS, DISPUTES AND RESOLUTIONS.

0525 CHEEVER D.S., HAVILAND H.F.
ORGANIZING FOR PEACE.
BOSTON: HOUGHTON, 1954, 917 PP.
OVERVIEW OF INTERNATIONAL ORGANIZATIONS AND WORLD AFFAIRS, STARTING WITH HISTORY AND PRINCIPLES OF PAST AND PRESENT ORGANIZATIONS. PARTICULAR EMPHASIS ON LEAGUE OF NATIONS AND UN. COMPARES AND CONTRASTS STRUCTURE, FUNCTION, AND ACTIVITIES OF THESE TWO ORGANIZATIONS.

0526 CHENERY H.B., STROUT A.M.
"FOREIGN ASSISTANCE AND ECONOMIC DEVELOPMENT"
AMER. ECO. REVIEW, 56 (SEPT. 66), 679-733.
OUTLINES THEORETICAL FRAMEWORK DESIGNED TO ANALYZE THE PROCESS OF DEVELOPMENT WITH EXTERNAL ASSISTANCE IN QUANTITATIVE TERMS. USES THIS FRAMEWORK TO EVALUATE CURRENT PERFORMANCE OF DEVELOPING COUNTRIES AND TO ASSESS THEIR FUTURE NEEDS FOR ASSISTANCE UNDER VARIOUS ASSUMPTIONS.

0527 CHENG C.
ECONOMIC RELATIONS BETWEEN PEKING AND MOSCOW: 1949-63.
NEW YORK: FREDERICK PRAEGER, 1964, 119 PP., LC#64-23512.
STUDY OF SINO-SOVIET ECONOMIC RELATIONS FROM 1949 THROUGH 1963 IN SOVIET AID TO CHINESE INDUSTRY, EQUIPMENT AND TECHNOLOGY, TRADE, AND FINANCIAL AID. FUTURE DEVELOPMENTS PREDICTED.

0528 CHIDZERO B.T.G.
TANGANYIKA AND INTERNATIONAL TRUSTEESHIP.
NEW YORK: OXFORD U. PR., 1961, 286 PP., $6.10.
EXAMINES CONSTITUTIONAL AND POLITICAL DEVELOPMENTS IN THE TERRITORY FROM INCEPTION OF MANDATE SYSTEM TO CURRENT UN TRUSTEESHIP. COMPARES PARALLEL OR CONTRASTING DEVELOPMENTS IN OTHER BRITISH-AFRICAN DEPENDENCIES.

0529 CHILDS J.B.
FOREIGN GOVERNMENT PUBLICATIONS (PAMPHLET)
WASHINGTON: LIBRARY OF CONGRESS, 1928, 9 PP.
SURVEY OF IMPORTANT ACCESSIONS DURING FISCAL YEAR ENDING JUNE 39, 1927. DETAILED LIST OF OFFICIAL PUBLICATIONS WHICH CONTAIN LEGISLATIVE PROCEEDINGS, STATE LAWS AND PROCLAMATIONS FROM MEXICO, OFFICIAL GAZETTES FROM BRAZIL, AND NOTEWORTHY PUBLICATIONS LISTED BY COUNTRY FROM WHICH RECEIVED.

0530 CHILDS J.R.
AMERICAN FOREIGN SERVICE.
NEW YORK: HOLT RINEHART WINSTON, 1948, 261 PP.
STUDIES EVOLUTION OF US FOREIGN SERVICE AND DISCUSSES ITS NATURE AS A CAREER. SHOWS RELATIONS BETWEEN SERVICE AND DEPARTMENT OF STATE AND OTHER GOVERNMENT AGENCIES. ANALYZES PROFESSION AND PRACTICE OF DIPLOMACY, AND PORTRAYS AN EMBASSY AND AMBASSADOR IN ACTION. DESCRIBES EMBASSY'S POLITICAL, CONSULAR, ECONOMIC, INFORMATION, AND CULTURAL RELATIONS SECTIONS.

0531 CHINA INSTITUTE OF AMERICA.
CHINA AND THE UNITED NATIONS.
NEW YORK: MANHATTAN PUBL., 1959, 285 PP.
STUDIES CHINESE PARTICIPATION IN AND ATTITUDES TOWARDS THE UN, VIEWING MEMBERSHIP AS FULFILLMENT OF HER AIM OF EQUALITY OF NATIONS. DEALS WITH POSITION OF CHINA AS ONE OF THE FOUNDERS AND ORGANIZERS OF THE WORLD ORGANIZATION, AS WELL AS HER POSITION IN IT TODAY. CONSIDERS CHINESE SUPPORT OF LEAGUE OF NATIONS, AS MEANS TOWARD COLLECTIVE SECURITY.

0532 CHIU H.
"COMMUNIST CHINA'S ATTITUDE TOWARD INTERNATIONAL LAW"
AMER. J. OF INT. LAW, 60 (JAN. 66), 245-267.
EXAMINES ATTITUDE OF COMMUNIST CHINA TOWARD BASIC PROBLEMS OF INTERNATIONAL LAW SUCH AS ROLE, DEFINITION, AND NATURE. DISCUSSES SYSTEMS AND SOURCES OF SUCH LAW, SCIENCE OF INTERNATIONAL LAW IN COMMUNIST CHINA, AND RELATION BETWEEN INTERNATIONAL AND MUNICIPAL LAW. MAINTAINS THAT CHINESE VIEW OF INTERNATIONAL LAW IS MORE MARXIST-LENINIST AND MORE PRIMITIVE THAN SOVIET VIEW.

0533 CHO S.S.
KOREA IN WORLD POLITICS 1940-1950; AN EVALUATION OF AMERICAN RESPONSIBILITY.
BERKELEY: U OF CALIF PR, 1967, 338 PP., LC#67-14968.
TREATS AMERICAN POLICY TOWARD KOREA FROM CAIRO CONFERENCE IN 1943 TO KOREAN WAR IN 1950. FOCUSES ON MAKING OF POLICIES AND REASONS FOR FAILURE. DISCUSSES TRUSTEESHIP PROJECT AND DIVISION AT 38TH PARALLEL. STUDIES US-USSR RELATIONS AND BEGINNINGS OF AMERICAN MILITARY GOVERNMENT. EXAMINES IMPACT OF CONTAINMENT AND PRESENT PERMANENCE OF KOREAN DIVISION. ANALYZES AID PROGRAM AND FINDS IT VERY INADEQUATE.

0534 CHOWDHURI R.N.
INTERNATIONAL MANDATES AND TRUSTEESHIP SYSTEMS.
GENEVA: NIJHOFF, 1955, 328 PP.
DISCUSSES HISTORY, OPERATION, AND FUNCTION OF INTERNATIONAL MANDATE SYSTEM, TRUSTEESHIP SYSTEM, AND OF AGENCIES ADMINISTERING THEM. PROVIDES EXAMPLES OF PROBLEMS FACING TRUSTEESHIP COUNCIL AND SOLUTIONS REACHED.

0535 CHRISTENSEN A.N. ED.
THE EVOLUTION OF LATIN AMERICAN GOVERNMENT: A BOOK OF READINGS.
NEW YORK: HOLT RINEHART WINSTON, 1951, 747 PP.
SELECTIONS DISCUSSING HISTORICAL FACTORS, CONSTITUTIONAL BASES, AND PRACTICAL ORGANIZATION OF LATIN AMERICAN GOVERNMENTS. EMPHASIZES DISPARITY BETWEEN CONSTITUTIONS AND ACTUAL FUNCTIONING OF GOVERNMENT. SECTIONS ON LATIN AMERICAN SOCIAL PROBLEMS AND INTERNATIONAL AFFAIRS.

0536 CHUKWUEMEKA N.
AFRICAN DEPENDENCIES: A CHALLENGE TO WESTERN DEMOCRACY.
NEW YORK: WM FREDERICK PRESS, 1950, 207 PP.
STUDY OF NIGERIA IN REGARD TO ECONOMIC DEVELOPMENT BY EXAMINATION OF RESOURCES, COMMERCE, AND INDUSTRIES. INCLUDES OPINIONS AS TO HOW DEVELOPED COUNTRIES CAN AID IN GROWTH OF COUNTRIES SUCH AS NIGERIA.

0537 CHUNG Y.S. ED.
KOREA: A SELECTED BIBLIOGRAPHY 1959-1963.
SEOUL: KOREA RESEARCHER & PUBL, 1965, 117 PP.
MOST OF THE ENTRIES IN THIS BIBLIOGRAPHY ARE FOUND IN THE KOREAN UNIT OF THE LIBRARY OF CONGRESS, AND ARE OF SOUTH KOREAN ORIGIN. THE WORKS, ON BOTH NORTH AND SOUTH KOREA REFLECT REVOLUTIONARY NATURE OF THE FOUR-YEAR PERIOD COVERED. A BROAD RANGE OF FIELDS IN THE SOCIAL SCIENCES AND HUMANITIES IS COVERED. HAS AN INTROUDCTION AND LIMITED ANNOTATIONS.

0538 CHURCHILL W.
THE GATHERING STORM.
BOSTON: HOUGHTON, 1948, 784 PP.
COVERS THE YEARS FROM THE END OF WW 1 TO THE BEGINNING OF WW 2, TERMED THE 'UNNECESSARY WAR.' PRESENTS POLITICAL AND MILITARY EVENTS FROM PERSONAL VIEWPOINT.

0539 CHURCHILL W.
TRIUMPH AND TRAGEDY.
BOSTON: HOUGHTON, 1953, 800 PP.
ACCOUNT OF WW 2 FROM PERSONAL VIEWPOINT. COVERS PERIOD FROM D-DAY TO POTSDAM, ENDING WITH OWN DEFEAT IN BRITISH ELECTION.

0540 CLAGETT H.L.

COMMUNIST CHINA: RUTHLESS ENEMY OR PAPER TIGER (PAMPHLET)
WASHINGTON: DEPT OF THE ARMY, 1962, 137 PP.
WELL ANNOTATED BASIC AND ADVANCED MATERIALS FROM 1948-62 IN ENGLISH CONCERNED PRIMARILY WITH AIMS, STRENGTHS, AND WEAKNESSES OF COMMUNIST CHINA. INCLUDES ARTICLES, BOOKS, AND DOCUMENTS OF BOTH US AND CHINESE GOVERNMENTS. MORE THAN 1000 ITEMS TOPICALLY ARRANGED.

0541 CLARK G., SOHN L.B.
WORLD PEACE THROUGH WORLD LAW; TWO ALTERNATIVE PLANS.
CAMBRIDGE: HARVARD U PR, 1966, 535 PP., LC#66-21198.
PRESENTS PLAN FOR MAINTENANCE OF WORLD PEACE IN FORM OF REVISED UN CHARTER. MAINTAINS THAT WORLD PEACE CANNOT EXIST WITHOUT ENFORCEABLE WORLD LAW FOR PREVENTION OF WAR. REVISES MEMBERSHIP, GENERAL ASSEMBLY, EXECUTIVE COUNCIL, ECONOMIC AND SOCIAL AND TRUSTEESHIP COUNCILS, DISARMAMENT PROCESS, WORLD POLICY FORCE, JUDICIAL AND REVENUE SYSTEMS, PENALTIES, PRIVILEGES, AND RATIFICATION AND AMENDMENT PLANS.

0542 CLARK S.V.O.
CENTRAL BANK COOPERATION: 1924-31.
NEW YORK: FED RESERVE BANK OF NY, 1967, 234 PP., LC#67-17650
DEALS WITH EFFORTS OF AMERICAN, BRITISH, FRENCH, AND GERMAN CENTRAL BANKERS TO RE-ESTABLISH AND MAINTAIN INTERNATIONAL FINANCIAL STABILITY IN 1924-31 AND FRUSTRATION OF EFFORTS DURING CRISIS AT END OF THAT PERIOD. SUGGESTS FAILURES OF 1929-31 CAN BE TRACED BASICALLY TO SLOWNESS OF WESTERN DEMOCRACIES TO REALIZE PROBLEMS AT HAND WERE RADICALLY DIFFERENT FROM THOSE OF 1920'S AND DEMANDED NEW TECHNIQUES.

0543 CLARK W.
"NEW FORCES IN THE UN."
INT. AFF., 36 (JULY 60), 322-30.
DEALS WITH CHANGES IN THE RELATIONSHIP BETWEEN SECURITY COUNCIL AND GENERAL ASSEMBLY. ANALYZES THE LARGE BODY OF EX-COLONIAL NATIONS AND THEIR SEARCH FOR LEADERSHIP. SUMS UP BRITISH DIPLOMATIC AFFAIRS WITHIN THE ORGANIZATION.

0544 CLAUDE I.
"THE MANAGEMENT OF POWER IN THE CHANGING UNITED NATIONS."
INT. ORGAN., 15 (SPRING 61), 219-35.
THE REAL QUESTION FOR OUR TIME IS NOT WHETHER THE UN IS LIKELY TO DEVELOP A COLLECTIVE SECURITY SYSTEM, OR TO REPLACE THE BALANCE OF POWER, BUT THE MANNER IN WHICH IT CAN AND WILL MODIFY THE OPERATION OF THE BALANCE SYSTEM AND CONTRIBUTE TO THE PREVENTION OF WAR.

0545 CLAUDE I.
"THE UNITED NATIONS AND THE USE OF FORCE."
INT. CONCIL., 532 (MAR. 61), 323-84.
'THE POTENTIAL USEFULNESS OF THE UN IN DEALING WITH THE DANGERS OF INTERNATIONAL VIOLENCE DOES NOT LIE IN THE IMPOSITION OF COERCIVE RESTRAINT, BUT IN THE POSSIBILITY TO HELP STATES TO AVOID EXACERBATION OF SITUATIONS WHICH MIGHT PRODUCE NUCLEAR WARS.'

0546 CLAUDE I.
"THE OAS, THE UN, AND THE UNITED STATES."
INT. CONCIL., 547 (7AR. 64), 3-67.
DISCUSSES FIVE CASES INVOLVING RELATIONS BETWEEN THE UN AND THE OAS. CONCLUDES THAT THE ORIGINAL CONCEPT OF REGIONAL AGENCIES OPERATING UNDER UN SUPERVISION AND CONTROL HAS BEEN EMPTIED OF CONTENT. SUGGESTS CONSEQUENCES OF THIS FOR THE PEACE-KEEPING FUNCTIONS OF THE UN.

0547 CLAUDE I.
SWORDS INTO PLOWSHARES.
NEW YORK: RANDOM, 1964, 451 PP., $9.95.
REVIEWS PROBLEMS, PROGRESS, AND PROSPECTS OF SIGNIFICANT INTERNATIONAL AGENCIES. FOCUSES ON THEIR THEORETICAL BASES, EVOLVING TRENDS, CONSTITUTIONAL PROBLEMS, AND MAJOR OPERATIONAL ISSUES. MAJOR EMPHASIS ON UN.

0548 CLAUSEWITZ C.V.
ON WAR (VOL. III)
NEW YORK: BARNES AND NOBLE, 1966, 350 PP.
ANALYZES CONDUCT AND TACTICS OF WAR, VARIOUS ATTACKS, AND OBJECTIVES. ALSO COVERS DIVERSION, INVASION, AND TOTAL PLANNING OF WARFARE, INCLUDING POLITICAL STRATEGY.

0549 CLENDENON C., COLLINS R., DUIGNAN P.
AMERICANS IN AFRICA 1865-1900.
STANFORD: HOOVER INSTITUTE, 1966, 129 PP., LC#66-14462.
THIRD VOLUME IN HOOVER INSTITUTION STUDIES INVESTIGATING US INVOLVEMENT IN AFRICA. STUDY CONCENTRATES ON AMERICAN PARTICIPATION IN AFRICAN AFFAIRS WITH SOME ON AFRICAN REACTIONS TO INVOLVEMENT IN ECONOMY, MISSION WORK, AND PHILANTHROPY. BIBLIOGRAPHY INCLUDES UNPUBLISHED PAPERS, BOOKS, PAMPHLETS, ARTICLES, AND GOVERNMENT DOCUMENTS ON US IN AFRICA AS WELL AS AFRICAN CONDITIONS RELATING TO FOREIGNERS.

0550 CLEVELAND H.
"THE FUTURE ROLE OF THE UNITED STATES IN THE UNITED NATIONS."
ANN. AMER. POLIT. SOC. SCI., 342 (JULY 62), 69-79.
REASSURES THOSE WHO VIEW UN AS THREAT TO USA INTERESTS AND DEMONSTRATES RELATIONSHIP BETWEEN UN AND COMMON FOREIGN POLICY PROBLEMS OF USA GOVERNMENT. STATES WHAT ROLE USA WILL PLAY IN THE FUTURE AND ITS ATTITUDES ON CERTAIN ISSUES SUCH AS FORMER COLONIAL AREAS, PEACEKEEPING, NATION-BUILDING AND QUESTIONS OF PROCEDURE.

0551 CLEVELAND H.
"CRISIS DIPLOMACY."
FOREIGN AFFAIRS, 41 (JULY 63), 638-649.
DISCUSSES MANAGEMENT OF A FOREIGN POLICY CRISIS. SUGGESTS FIVE "LESSONS" FOR SUCH DECISION-MAKING: KEEPING OBJECTIVES LIMITED, DECIDING LIMITS OF ACTION, SELECTING THE GENTLEST FORM OF FORCE NECESSARY, WIDENING THE COMMUNITY OF THE CONCERNED, RECOGNIZING THAT DECISION-MAKERS MUST ABIDE BY THE LAWS, AND TAKING NOTICE OF PRECEDENTS MADE.

0552 CLINGHAM T.A. JR.
"LEGISLATIVE FLOTSAM AND INTERNATIONAL ACTION IN THE 'YARMOUTH CASTLE'S' WAKE."
G. WASH. LAW REV., 35 (MAY 67), 675-697.
EVALUATES AND REVIEWS RESPONSES CREATED BY PUBLIC AND LEGISLATIVE INTEREST IN PROBLEMS OF TRANSPORTATION SAFETY. EXAMINES THREE APPROACHES OF REMEDIAL PROCESS: LEGISLATIVE PROPOSALS SEEKING DIRECT APPLICATION OF SAFETY STANDARDS ON DOMESTIC AND INTERNATIONAL SHIPPING, INDIRECT APPLICATIONS, AND THOSE SEEKING ABOVE GOAL THROUGH INTERNATIONAL ACCORD.

0553 CLUBB O.E. JR.
THE UNITED STATES AND THE SINO-SOVIET BLOC IN SOUTHEAST ASIA.
WASHINGTON: BROOKINGS INST., 1962, 173 PP.
GENERAL STATEMENT ON USA AND USSR ACTIVITIES IN SOUTHEAST ASIA. SUGGESTS ALTERNATIVE POLICY POSITIONS FOR USA.

0554 CLYDE P.H.
THE FAR EAST: A HISTORY OF THE IMPACT OF THE WEST ON EASTERN ASIA.
ENGLEWOOD CLIFFS: PRENTICE HALL, 1948, 868 PP.
ANALYSIS OF HISTORICAL CHANGE IN SINO-JAPANESE POLITICS, CULTURE, ECONOMICS, AND INTERNATIONAL RELATIONS RESULTING FROM CONTACT AND CONFLICT WITH THE WEST, 1860-1940.

0555 COCHRANE J.D.
"US ATTITUDES TOWARD CENTRAL-AMERICAN INTEGRATION."
INTERAMER. ECON. AFF., 18 (AUTUMN 64), 73-91.
EXAMINING THE UNDERLYING REASONS FOR U.S. SUPPORT OF CENTRAL-AMERICAN ECONOMIC INTEGRATION, THE AUTHOR SUGGESTS THAT U.S. APPROVAL APPEARS TO BE BASED ON THE EXPECTATION THAT THIS DEVELOPMENT WILL PROMOTE ECONOMIC AND SOCIAL GROWTH, REGIONAL UNITY, AND THE LIBERALIZATION OF INTERNATIONAL TRADE.

0556 COFFEY J.
"THE SOVIET VIEW OF A DISARMED WORLD."
J. CONFL. RESOLUT., 8 (MAR. 64), 1-6.
OUTLINES THE SOVIET VIEW OF A DISARMED WORLD WITH REGARD TO THE UN AND INTERNATIONAL PEACE-KEEPING FORCES AND ASSESSES IMPLICATIONS OF THESE VIEWS FOR U.S. NATIONAL INTERESTS.

0557 COFFIN F.M.
WITNESS FOR AID.
BOSTON: HOUGHTON MIFFLIN, 1964, 273 PP., LC#64-14522.
DISCUSSION OF ORGANIZATION OF AGENCY FOR INTERNATIONAL DEVELOPMENT, ITS RELATION TO PUBLIC AND CONGRESS; HISTORY OF AID AND FOREIGN AID PROGRAM; OBJECTIVES OF PROGRAM, THEIR CONFUSION, AND ATTEMPT TO FIND CONSENSUS; CONTRIBUTIONS OF DEVELOPING COUNTRIES, COMMUNIST COUNTRIES AND EUROPE TO AID; AND PROPOSAL TO COMBINE ORGANIZATIONS, LAWMAKERS, AND PUBLIC IN POLICY-MAKING FOR FOREIGN AID.

0558 COHEN A.
"THE NEW AFRICA AND THE UN."
INT. AFF., 36 (OCT. 60), 476-488.
DISCUSSES THE IMPACT OF RAPID EMERGENCE OF THE NEW AFRICAN NATIONS UPON THE UNITED NATIONS AND THEIR PROBABLE VOTING TRENDS, ESPECIALLY ON ISSUES OF PEACE, RACE, AND AID TO UNDERDEVELOPED COUNTRIES.

0559 COHEN B.C.
CITIZEN EDUCATION IN WORLD AFFAIRS.
PRINCETON: U. PR., 1953, 145 PP.
IMPLIES 'DUPLICATION OF EFFORT' IN MANY FOREIGN-AFFAIRS ORGANIZATIONS AND ASSERTS THAT MODERN COMMUNICATIONS-MEDIA HAVE RENDERED THEIR ORIGINAL EDUCATIONAL FUNCTIONS OBSOLETE. RECOMMENDS NEW ROLE FOR INTERNATIONAL RELATIONS ASSOCIATIONS IN POLICY-MAKING AND IN CONDUCTING RESEARCH IN POLITICAL SCIENCE AND COMMUNICATION FIELDS.

0560 COHEN M.
"BASIC PRINCIPLES OF INTERNATIONAL LAW."
CAN. BAR REV., 42 (SEPT. 64), 449-62.
REASSESSES CLASSICAL PRINCIPLES OF INTERNATIONAL LAW, PLACING SPECIAL EMPHASIS ON TRADITIONAL RELATIONS OF STATES. ANALYZES DISILLUSIONMENT WITH INTERNATIONAL LAW AFTER BOTH WORLD WARS AND PRESENTS NEW PERSPECTIVES ON NATURE OF LAW

AND LEGAL SYSTEMS IN GENERAL.

0561 COHEN M. ED.
LAW AND POLITICS IN SPACE: SPECIFIC AND URGENT PROBLEMS IN THE LAW OF OUTER SPACE.
MONTREAL: MCGILL U. PR., 1964, 221 PP.
CONFERENCE PAPERS PERTAIN TO INTERNATIONAL ARRANGEMENTS FOR SATELLITE COMMUNICATIONS, POLLUTION AND CONTAMINATION IN SPACE, ARMS CONTROL, DISARMAMENT AND OBSERVATION IN SPACE, PROSPECTS FOR AN OUTER SPACE REGIME. FIND THAT MAJOR POWERS USE LAW TO SERVE NATIONAL INTERESTS.

0562 COHEN M.L.
SELECTED BIBLIOGRAPHY OF FOREIGN AND INTERNATIONAL LAW.
PHILADELPHIA: VILLANOVA LAW SCH, 1964, 6 PP.
ANNOTATED BIBLIOGRAPHY OF REFERENCE BOOKS FOR SMALL AND MEDIUM-SIZE LIBRARIES. CONTAINS LISTINGS OF PUBLICATION SERIES OR SURVEYS IN ENGLISH ON THE LAW OF FOREIGN COUNTRIES AND SELECTED NON-DOCUMENTARY SOURCES FOR INTERNATIONAL LAW REFERENCE WORK.

0563 COHEN P.A.
"WANG T'AO AND INCIPIENT CHINESE NATIONALISM."
J. OF ASIAN STUDIES, 67 (AUG. 26), 559-574.
THROUGH STUDY OF ONE THOUGHTFUL CHINESE EDITOR WHO IN 1895 WAS SPEAKING OF NATIONALISM, AUTHOR FINDS SOME REASONS FOR CHINA'S CONSERVATISM AND BUREAUCRATIC RESISTANCE TO MODERNIZATION IN EARLY 20TH CENTURY. PERSISTENT DIVORCE BETWEEN LOCUS OF POLITICAL POWER AND LOCUS OF COMMITMENT TO INNOVATION WAS ONLY BEGINNING TO EMERGE IN WANG'S DAY.

0564 COHN K.
"CRIMES AGAINST HUMANITY."
GERMAN FOREIGN POLICY, 6 (FEB. 67), 160-169.
COMMENTARY ON 21ST SESSION OF COMMISSION FOR HUMAN RIGHTS WHOSE ASSEMBLY, ACCORDING TO AUTHOR, WAS NECESSITATED BY WEST GERMAN APPLICATION OF STATUTE OF LIMITATIONS TO CRIMES AGAINST HUMANITY. DISCUSSION OF PROSECUTION OF WAR CRIMES IN BOTH GERMANIES IN POST-WAR PERIOD WITH CONDEMNATION OF CURRENT WEST GERMAN ATTITUDE TO WAR CRIMINALS AND NAZI REGIME.

0565 COLBY C.C. ED.
GEOGRAPHICAL ASPECTS OF INTERNATIONAL RELATIONS.
CHICAGO: U. CHI. PR., 1938, 296 PP.
EVALUATES THE NEW INTERNATIONAL PATTERN IN LIGHT OF THE LACK OF VACANT LAND, STATE INTERVENTION IN ECONOMIC LIFE AND THE EFFECT OF DOMESTIC POLICIES ON THE WORLD. THE STUDY ASKS FOR A NATIONAL PLAN FOR CONTROL OF THE ENVIRONMENT BECAUSE OF THE COMPLEXITY OF THE HUMAN USE OF THE LAND AND ITS NATURAL RESOURCES.

0566 COLE A.B., TOTTEN G.O., UYEHARA C.H.
SOCIALIST PARTIES IN POSTWAR JAPAN.
NEW HAVEN: YALE U PR, 1966, 490 PP., LC#66-21511.
COMBINES HISTORICAL METHOD WITH POLITICAL DESCRIPTION AND ANALYSIS TO STUDY JAPAN'S NON-COMMUNIST SOCIAL DEMOCRATIC PARTIES FROM 1945-61. PROVIDES HISTORICAL SURVEY OF PARTY DEVELOPMENT; OUTLINES AND EVALUATES ECONOMIC POLICIES; AND CONSIDERS FOREIGN POLICIES OF SOCIALISTS. CONSIDERS PARTY ORGANIZATION AND LEADERSHIP, RELATIONS BETWEEN PARTY AND LABOR UNIONS, AND SUPPORT FROM VARIOUS SOCIAL STRATA.

0567 COLLINS H., ABRAMSKY C.
KARL MARX AND THE BRITISH LABOUR MOVEMENT; YEARS OF THE FIRST INTERNATIONAL.
NEW YORK: ST MARTIN'S PRESS, 1965, LC#65-11740.
AN ASSESSMENT OF THE FIRST INTERNATIONAL IN RELATION TO THE INDUSTRIAL AND POLITICAL MOVEMENT OF THE BRITISH WORKING CLASS. PROVIDES A NEW INTERPRETATION OF MARX'S "INAUGURAL ADDRESS," AND EVALUATES ITS SIGNIFICANCE IN THE DEVELOPMENT OF THE IDEOLOGY CONTAINED IN "DAS KAPITAL." CONTAINS A COMPREHENSIVE BIBLIOGRAPHY ON THE FIRST INTERNATIONAL: OFFICIAL STATEMENTS, MANUSCRIPTS, NEWSPAPERS, PAMPHLETS, AND BOOKS.

0568 COLLISON R.L.
BIBLIOGRAPHICAL SERVICES THROUGHOUT THE WORLD: 1950-59 (VOL. 9)
PARIS: UNESCO, 1961, 228 PP.
CUMULATIVE REPORT DESCRIBES THE ACCOMPLISHMENTS OF THE INTERNATIONAL ADVISORY COMMITTEE ON BIBLIOGRAPHY SET UP BY UNESCO IN 1953 TO SUPERVISE, ENCOURAGE, AND CO-ORDINATE NATIONAL BIBLIOGRAPHIC SERVICES THROUGHOUT THE WORLD. LISTS ACTIVITIES IN CORRESPONDING COUNTRIES, AND SECTION DESCRIBES THE EFFORTS OF VARIOUS INTERNATIONAL ORGANIZATIONS. INTRODUCTION SUMMARIZES OVER-ALL BIBLIOGRAPHIC FIELD.

0569 COLLISON R.L.
BIBLIOGRAPHIES, SUBJECT AND NATIONAL: A GUIDE TO THEIR CONTENTS, ARRANGEMENT, AND USE (2ND REV. ED.)
LONDON: CROSBY, LOCKWOOD, & SONS, 1962, 185 PP.
INFORMAL BIBLIOGRAPHY OF BIBLIOGRAPHIES ARRANGED TOPICALLY AND WITH EXTENSIVE ANNOTATIONS. LISTS BIBLIOGRAPHIES OF INDIVIDUALS AND BIBLIOGRAPHIES OF EUROPEAN-LANGUAGE LITERATURE. MAJORITY OF ITEMS WITH THIS EXCEPTION ARE IN ENGLISH. NO LIMITATION SET ON PARTICULAR TIME PERIOD.

0570 COLOMBOS C.J. ED.
THE INTERNATIONAL LAW OF THE SEA.
LONDON: LONGMANS, GREEN & CO, 1962, 754 PP.
COMPILATION OF PRESENTLY ACCEPTED INTERNATIONAL MARITIME LAW, COVERING SOURCES AND DEVELOPMENTS, TRADE, BODIES OF WATER, FISHING, NAVIGATION, WARSHIPS AND CHANGES RESULTING FROM WAR.

0571 COLUMBIA U SCHOOL OF LAW
PUBLIC INTERNATIONAL DEVELOPMENT FINANCING IN SENEGAL.
NEW YORK: COLUMBIA U PRESS, 1963, 150 PP.
STUDIES PROGRAMS AND RELATIONS OF FOREIGN INSTITUTIONS INVOLVED IN PUBLIC FINANCING OF ECONOMIC DEVELOPMENT IN SENEGAL. INCLUDES SENEGAL'S ECONOMIC AND POLITICAL STRUCTURE, INTERNAL ECONOMIC PLANNING, SURVEY OF ALL EXTERNAL ASSISTANCE RECEIVED, CASE STUDIES OF SPECIAL AID PROGRAMS. EVALUATES PROGRAMS TO DEVELOP MORE EFFICIENT MEANS OF ORGANIZING PUBLIC AID FROM FOREIGN SOURCES.

0572 COLUMBIA U SCHOOL OF LAW
PUBLIC INTERNATIONAL DEVELOPMENT FINANCING IN INDIA.
NEW YORK: COLUMBIA U LAW SCHOOL, 1964, 256 PP.
EMPHASIZES INSTITUTIONAL ASPECTS OF PUBLIC INTERNATIONAL DEVELOPMENT FINANCING FOR ECONOMIC ADVANCEMENT OF LESS DEVELOPED REGIONS. CONCENTRATES ON FUNCTIONING AND INTERRELATIONSHIPS OF INSTITUTIONS CONCERNED - NATIONAL, REGIONAL, AND MULTILATERAL. GIVES ACCOUNT OF SUCCESSES AND FAILURES; CONSIDERS FEASIBILITY OF ALTERNATIVE ARRANGEMENTS FOR MORE EFFECTIVE ORGANIZATIONAL PROCEDURES IN INDIA.

0573 COMISION DE HISTORIO
GUIA DE LOS DOCUMENTOS MICROFOTOGRAFIADOS POR LA UNIDAD MOVIL DE LA UNESCO.
INST PANAMERICANO DE GEOGRAFIA, 1963, 317 PP.
LIST OF BOOKS, DOCUMENTS, AND MATERIALS IN THE ARCHIVES OF SEVERAL LATIN AMERICAN NATIONS THAT HAVE BEEN MICROFILMED BY UNESCO.

0574 COMM. STUDY ORGAN. PEACE
"PRELIMINARY REPORT."
INT. CONCIL., 369 (APRIL 41), 195-525.
THIS WORK CONSIDERS VARIOUS PEACE-KEEPING ORGANIZATIONS THAT WERE IN EXISTENCE BEFORE THE SECOND WORLD WAR. EMPHASIS IS PLACED ON ECONOMIC AND POLITICAL ORGANIZATIONS, FUTURE GOALS FOR WORLD PEACE AND METHODS OF IMPLEMENTATION.

0575 COMM. STUDY ORGAN. PEACE
"ORGANIZATION OF PEACE."
INT. CONCIL., 369 (APR. 41), 368-527.
COLLECTION OF FIFTEEN BRIEF ESSAYS ON SOCIAL JUSTICE, ECONOMIC ORGANIZATION OF PEACE, AND INTERNATIONAL POLITICAL ORGANIZATION.

0576 COMM. STUDY ORGAN. PEACE
UNITED NATIONS GUARDS AND TECHNICAL FIELD SERVICES.
NEW YORK: 1944, 461 PP.
SUPPORTS RECOMMENDATION FOR UN POLICE FORCE IN UN UNIFORM, SEPARATE FROM FORCES OF SEVERAL NATIONS CARRYING OUT MILITARY OPERATIONS. SPECIAL FORCE WOULD ALSO PROVIDE UN FIELD SERVICES.

0577 COMM. STUDY ORGAN. PEACE
"SECURITY THROUGH THE UNITED NATIONS."
INT. CONCIL., 432 (JUNE 47), 423-448.
EMPHASIS PLACED ON NEED TO INSTIGATE ARMAMENTS CONTROL DUE TO ADVENT OF ATOMIC WARFARE. TREATIES ARE CONSIDERED NECESSARY TO REDUCE THE PRODUCTION OF WEAPONS WHICH WOULD LEAD TO DESTRUCTION OF MANKIND. LEADERS OF NATIONS SHOULD USE U.N. STRUCTURE TO EFFECT STABILITY.

0578 COMM. STUDY ORGAN. PEACE
"A TEN YEAR RECORD, 1939-1949."
NEW YORK: AMER. ASS. UN, 1949, 48 PP.
REVEALS ACTIVITIES OF COMMISSION FROM OUTBREAK OF WW 2 TO 1949 AND INCORPORATES PROSPECTS FOR UN CHARTER. EXAMINES SPECIFIC PROBLEMS OF UN AND SEEKS MEANS OF STRENGTHENING CHARTER.

0579 COMM. STUDY ORGAN. PEACE
REPORTS.
NEW YORK: 1940-55., 5VOLS.
SERIES OF PAMPHLETS REPRESENTS A COMPREHENSIVE STUDY OF THE ORGANIZATIONS NECESSARY FOR WORLD PEACE. REPORTS COVER DISARMAMENT, ECONOMIC WELFARE, SELF-DEFENSE AND HUMAN RIGHTS ON AN INTERNATIONAL LEVEL. DETAILED ANALYSIS OF COLLECTIVE SECURITY UNDER THE UNITED NATIONS.

0580 COMM. STUDY ORGAN. PEACE
STRENGTHENING THE UNITED NATIONS.
NEW YORK: HARPER, 1957, 276 PP.
RECOMMENDS CHANGES IN CHARTER, PRACTICES AND POLICIES OF U.N. AS WELL AS MODIFICATION IN USA POLICY TOWARDS THE WORLD-STRUCTURE. PROPOSES RESTRICTION OF VETO POWER, GREATER USE OF WORLD COURT, EXPANSION OF TECHNICAL ASSISTANCE AND PERMANENT POLICE-FORCE.

0581 COMM. STUDY ORGAN. PEACE
ORGANIZING PEACE IN THE NUCLEAR AGE.
NEW YORK: N.Y.U. PR., 1959, 245 PP.
PRESENTS SPECIFIC METHODS BY WHICH THE UN CAN BE STRENGTHENED SO THAT IT WILL BE ABLE TO AID MANKIND MORE FULLY. THROUGH A SYSTEM OF INTERNATIONAL LAW RATHER THAN THROUGH POLITICALLY ORIENTED ACTION FROM INDIVIDUAL MEMBERS, IT IS HOPED THAT UN WILL SUCCEED WHERE THE NATIONS HAVE FAILED.

0582 COMMONWEALTH OF WORLD CITIZENS
THE BIRTH OF A WORLD PEOPLE.
LONDON: DENNIS DOBSON, 1956, 59 PP.
DESCRIBES ORIGIN, IDEOLOGY, AND FUNCTIONS OF COMMONWEALTH OF WORLD CITIZENS AND ITS GOAL OF SERVING AS IMPARTIAL AGENCY FOR WORLD SERVICE, MEDIATION, AND MAINTENANCE OF WORLD PEACE. EXPLAINS COMMONWEALTH'S REFUSAL TO ALIGN ITSELF WITH ANY OF CONFLICTING IDEOLOGIES INVOLVED IN EAST-WEST CONFLICT. CONTAINS COMMONWEALTH'S PROVISIONAL CONSTITUTION AND PROVIDES COMMENTARY ON ITS MAJOR POINTS.

0583 CONF ON FUTURE OF COMMONWEALTH
THE FUTURE OF THE COMMONWEALTH.
LONDON: H M STATIONERY OFFICE, 1963, 51 PP.
GENERAL DISCUSSION OF ROLE OF BRITISH COMMONWEALTH IN RACE RELATIONS, MUTUAL DEFENSE, ECONOMIC PROGRESS, AND POLITICAL STABILITY. SUGGESTS TECHNICAL AID, TRAINING OF ADMINISTRATORS, COOPERATION IN AGRICULTURAL MATTERS, AND EDUCATION AS CHIEF MEASURES TO ACHIEVE ECONOMIC PROGRESS AND POLITICAL COHESION.

0584 CONFERENCE ATLANTIC COMMUNITY
AN INTRODUCTORY BIBLIOGRAPHY.
LEYDEN: SYTHOFF, 1961, 900 PP.
ANNOTATED BIBLIOGRAPHY LIMITED TO BOOKS AND ARTICLES PUBLISHED SINCE 1945 IN UK, US, FRANCE, GERMANY, AUSTRIA, AND ITALY. BASIC READING LIST FOR STUDY OF PROBLEMS OF ATLANTIC COMMUNITY. WRITINGS ORGANIZED ACCORDING TO HISTORY AND PROBLEMS OF COMMUNITY, ORGANIZATIONAL STRUCTURE OF PROGRESS, RELATIONS OF COMMUNITY TO COMMUNIST WORLD. SUBJECT INDEX AND CROSS-REFERENCING. EXTENSIVE CONTENT ANALYSIS.

0585 CONN S., FAIRCHILD B.
THE FRAMEWORK OF HEMISPHERE DEFENSE.
WASHINGTON: G.P.O., 1960, 407 PP.
STUDIES THE ESTABLISHMENT OF UNISPHERE DEFENSE FOSTERED BY THE US. DISCUSSES USA ALLIANCES WITH CANADA AND MEXICO AND THE PROTECTIVE POLICY TOWARD LATIN AMERICA WHICH WAS MADE POSSIBLE BASED ON THE TRUST ENGENDERED BY THE GOOD NEIGHBOR POLICY. FOCUSES ON THE IDEA THAT HAD HEMISPHERIC RELATIONS NOT BEEN AT THIS LEVEL, USA COULD NOT HAVE RESPONDED AS QUICKLY NOR AS STRONGLY AS WE DID TO THE JAPANESE ATTACK.

0586 CONNEL-SMITH G.
THE INTERAMERICAN SYSTEM.
LONDON: OXFORD U PR, 1966, 376 PP.
HISTORY OF OAS, 1890-1965. PROSPECTS FOR REGIONALISM, OAS AND CUBA, RELATIONS WITHIN OAS, AND OAS AS AN INTERNATIONAL ORGANIZATION ARE DISCUSSED.

0587 CONNERY R.H., DAVID P.T.
"THE MUTUAL DEFENSE ASSISTANCE PROGRAM."
AMER. POLT. SCI. REV., 45 (JUNE 51), 321-47.
DESCRIBES FORMATION OF NATO AND ITS CONCEPT OF MUTUAL DEFENSE ASSISTANCE. ANALYZES PROBLEMS CREATED AND METHODS EMPLOYED TO ACHIEVE RAPID PEACE-TIME REARMAMENT OF USA AND NATO ALLIES IN FACE OF GROWING COMMUNIST THREAT IN EUROPE AND KOREA.

0588 CONNOR W.
"SELF-DETERMINATION: THE NEW PHASE."
WORLD POLITICS, 20 (OCT. 67), 30-53.
DISCUSSES QUESTION: CAN TWO OR MORE SELF-DIFFERENTIATING CULTURE-GROUPS COEXIST WITHIN A SINGLE POLITICAL STRUCTURE? EXAMINES GROWTH OF NATIONALISM AND MULTINATIONALISM; STUDIES ISSUE OF SELF-DETERMINATION OF MINORITIES. SHOWS THAT NATIONAL OR ETHNIC CONSCIOUSNESS MAKES MULTINATIONALISM ALMOST IMPOSSIBLE.

0589 CONOVER H.F.
WORLD GOVERNMENT: A LIST OF SELECTED REFERENCES (PAMPHLET)
WASHINGTON: LIBRARY OF CONGRESS, 1947, 11 PP.
ANNOTATED BIBLIOGRAPHY OF 65 PAMPHLETS, BOOKS, NEWSPAPER AND MAGAZINE ARTICLES, PREPARED AS AN AID TO DISCUSSION ON THE TOPIC OF THE ESTABLISHMENT OF A WORLD FEDERAL GOVERNMENT, IN WHICH ALL NATIONS ARE UNITED UNDER A SINGLE LEGAL STRUCTURE. INCLUDES BIBLIOGRAPHIES, JOURNALS, BACKGROUND WORKS, AND ARGUMENTS. SOURCES ARE DESCRIPTIVELY ANNOTATED AND WERE PUBLISHED BETWEEN 1945-47.

0590 CONOVER H.F. ED.
A SELECTED LIST OF REFERENCES ON THE DIPLOMATIC & TRADE RELATIONS OF THE US WITH THE USSR, 1919-1935 (PAMPHLET)
WASHINGTON: LIBRARY OF CONGRESS, 1935, 29 PP.
AN UNANNOTATED BIBLIOGRAPHY OF 332 BOOKS, PAMPHLETS, ARTICLES, AND CONGRESSIONAL SPEECHES ON DIPLOMATIC AND TRADE RELATIONS BETWEEN US-USSR. SOURCES ARRANGED ALPHABETICALLY ACCORDING TO SUBJECT. EMPHASIS PRIMARILY ON BRITISH AND AMERICAN DOCUMENTS; SOME RUSSIAN WORKS AND TRANSLATIONS APPEAR.

0591 CONOVER H.F. ED.
A BRIEF LIST OF REFERENCES ON WESTERN HEMISPHERE DEFENSE (PAMPHLET)
WASHINGTON: LIBRARY OF CONGRESS, 1940, 15 PP.
AN UNANNOTATED BIBLIOGRAPHY OF 159 PAMPHLETS, BOOKS, AND PERIODICALS PUBLISHED BY THE LIBRARY OF CONGRESS. CONTAINS LIST OF BIBLIOGRAPHIES AS WELL AS SPECIAL FOREIGN POLICY REPORTS AND CONGRESSIONAL SPEECHES.

0592 CONOVER H.F. ED.
FOREIGN RELATIONS OF THE UNITED STATES: A LIST OF RECENT BOOKS (PAMPHLET)
WASHINGTON: LIBRARY OF CONGRESS, 1940, 55 PP.
A PARTIALLY ANNOTATED BIBLIOGRAPHY OF 388 BOOKS, PERIODICALS, AND PAMPHLETS IN ENGLISH AND FRENCH. SUPPLEMENT TO MIMEOGRAPHED LISTS RELEASED IN 1929 AND 1935. ARRANGED BY FORMAT AND SUBDIVIDED BY REGION. CONTAINS GUIDES TO BIBLIOGRAPHIES, GENERAL WORKS, HISTORIES AND PERIODICALS. INDEXED PRIMARILY BY AUTHOR AND BROAD SUBJECT CLASSES. CONCENTRATES ON AMERICAN FOREIGN POLICY.

0593 CONOVER H.F. ED.
JAPAN-ECONOMIC DEVELOPMENT AND FOREIGN POLICY, A SELECTED LIST OF REFERENCES (PAMPHLET)
WASHINGTON: LIBRARY OF CONGRESS, 1940, 34 PP.
UNANNOTATED BIBLIOGRAPHY INCLUDES JAPANESE INDUSTRIAL DEVELOPMENT, FOREIGN TRADE, AND INTERNATIONAL RELATIONS. NOTES JAPANESE ECONOMIC AND MILITARY STATUS PLUS PREWAR EXPANSION POLICIES. CONTAINS 403 LISTINGS.

0594 CONOVER H.F. ED.
FRENCH COLONIES IN AFRICA: A LIST OF REFERENCES.
WASHINGTON: LIBRARY OF CONGRESS, 1942, 89 PP.
UNANNOTATED BIBLIOGRAPHY OF PERIODICALS, REFERENCES, AND OFFICIAL PUBLICATIONS CONTAINING 1265 WORKS PUBLISHED IN FRENCH, ENGLISH, AND GERMAN. CLASSIFICATION FOR FRENCH NORTH AFRICAN COLONIES IS BY SUBJECT WITH SUBDIVISIONS FOR EACH COUNTRY. FRENCH WEST AFRICA CLASSIFIED BY PROVINCES. INDEPENDENT SECTIONS FOR THE FOUR REMAINING FRENCH COLONIES. SPECIAL EMPHASIS ON LARGE BIBLIOGRAPHIES.

0595 CONOVER H.F. ED.
NEW ZEALAND: A SELECTED LIST OF REFERENCES (PAMPHLET)
WASHINGTON: LIBRARY OF CONGRESS, 1942, 68 PP.
A DESCRIPTIVELY ANNOTATED BIBLIOGRAPHY OF 622 GOVERNMENT DOCUMENTS, BOOKS, PAMPHLETS, AND PERIODICALS IN ENGLISH. TOPICALLY ARRANGED INTO ELEVEN CATEGORIES: BIBLIOGRAPHIES, GENERAL SURVEYS, TRAVEL, HISTORY, WAR EFFORTS AND DEFENSE, ECONOMICS AND POLITICS, EDUCATION AND CULTURE, NATURAL HISTORY, THE MAORI, WESTERN SAMOA, AND NEW ZEALAND DEPENDENCIES.

0596 CONOVER H.F. ED.
THE BALKANS: A SELECTED LIST OF REFERENCES.
WASHINGTON: LIBRARY OF CONGRESS, 1943, 264 PP.
A SERIES OF UNANNOTATED BIBLIOGRAPHIES ON THE BALKAN NATIONS:ALBANIA, BULGARIA, RUMANIA, AND YUGOSLAVIA. RESTRICTED IN MOST PART TO WORKS PUBLISHED SINCE TREATY OF VERSAILLES, AND TO WRITINGS PUBLISHED IN WEST EUROPEAN LANGUAGES. WITHIN EACH NATION, IS TOPICALLY ARRANGED AND INDEXED BOTH BY AUTHOR AND SUBJECT. LISTS 2438 BOOKS, PERIODICALS, ARTICLES, AND PAMPHLETS. COMPILED FOR LIBRARY OF CONGRESS.

0597 CONOVER H.F. ED.
SOVIET RUSSIA: SELECTED LIST OF REFERENCES.
WASHINGTON: LIBRARY OF CONGRESS, 1943, 85 PP.
AN UNANNOTATED BIBLIOGRAPHY OF 811 BOOKS, PAMPHLETS, AND PERIODICALS CONCERNING THE SOVIET UNION FROM THE BEGINNING OF THE THIRD FIVE-YEAR PLAN IN 1938 TO HER WAR EFFORT. (SOME EARLIER WORKS INCLUDED AS WELL.) TOPICALLY ARRANGED, AND INDEXED ACCORDING TO AUTHOR. SOURCES ARE EITHER ENGLISH OR TRANSLATIONS FROM THE RUSSIAN INTO ENGLISH.

0598 CONOVER H.F. ED.
THE GOVERNMENTS OF THE MAJOR FOREIGN POWERS: A BIBLIOGRAPHY.
WASHINGTON: LIBRARY OF CONGRESS, 1945, 45 PP.
LISTINGS OF 428 ENGLISH WORKS AS SUPPLEMENT TO TEXTBOOK ON FOREIGN GOVERNMENTS PUBLISHED BY US MILITARY ACADEMY AT WEST POINT. CLASSIFICATIONS FOLLOW CHAPTER HEADINGS OF THAT WORK. INCLUDES ASPECTS OF POLITICAL AND MILITARY ORGANIZATION OF FRANCE, GREAT BRITAIN, ITALY, GERMANY, USSR, AND JAPAN. AUTHOR INDEX. COMPILED FOR LIBRARY OF CONGRESS.

0599 CONOVER H.F. ED.
ITALY: ECONOMICS, POLITICS AND MILITARY AFFAIRS, 1940-1945.
WASHINGTON: LIBRARY OF CONGRESS, 1945, 85 PP.
AN UNANNOTATED BIBLIOGRAPHY OF 749 BOOKS, ARTICLES, AND GOVERNMENT PAMPHLETS IN ITALIAN AND ENGLISH ON ITALIAN ECONOMY, LEGISLATION, AND MILITARY PERFORMANCE DURING WAR YEARS. SOURCES INCLUDE MATERIAL ON WHOLE ECONOMIC LIFE OF

ITALY DURING MUSSOLINI'S FINAL YEARS, COLLAPSE OF FASCIST STATE, AND PERIOD OF RECONSTRUCTION. BIBLIOGRAPHY DIVIDED INTO ECONOMIC ASPECTS AND POLITICAL-MILITARY ASPECTS.

0600 CONOVER H.F. ED.
THE NAZI STATE: WAR CRIMES AND WAR CRIMINALS.
WASHINGTON: LIBRARY OF CONGRESS, 1945, 131 PP.
BIBLIOGRAPHY COMPILED FOR US CHIEF OF COUNSEL FOR THE PERSECUTION OF AXIS CRIMINALITY. MAIN EMPHASIS ON GERMAN SOURCES BUT INCLUDES SOME FRENCH AND ENGLISH. BASIC CLASSIFICATIONS: THEORY OF WAR CRIMES; THE NATIONALIST-SOCIALIST STATE; WAR ATROCITIES. THE LAST PART IS SUBDIVIDED BY SUBJECT AND COUNTRY. INCLUDES 1,084 LISTINGS AND INDEX WITH SOME CROSS-REFERENCING.

0601 CONOVER H.F. ED.
NON-SELF-GOVERNING AREAS.
WASHINGTON: LIBRARY OF CONGRESS, 1947, 467 PP.
ANNOTATED BIBLIOGRAPHY OF 3603 BOOKS AND ARTICLES FROM ENGLISH, FRENCH, GERMAN, AND SPANISH SOURCES. ARRANGED IN THREE MAIN SECTIONS: POLICIES AND PRACTICES OF COLONIAL GOVERNMENT, MANDATES AND TRUSTEESHIPS, AND REGIONS. SOURCES SELECTED FOR STATISTICAL AND TECHNICAL INFORMATION RELATING TO ECONOMIC, SOCIAL, AND EDUCATIONAL CONDITIONS IN NON-SELF-GOVERNING AREAS THROUGHOUT THE WORLD.

0602 CONOVER H.F. ED.
A GUIDE TO BIBLIOGRAPHIC TOOLS FOR RESEARCH IN FOREIGN AFFAIRS.
WASHINGTON: LIBRARY OF CONGRESS, 1956, 145 PP., LC#56-60049.
AN ANNOTATED BIBLIOGRAPHY OF 292 MANUALS, SERIALS, JOURNALS, SURVEYS, INDEXES, BIBLIOGRAPHIES. COMPILED AS A GUIDE FOR INITIAL STEPS IN RESEARCH ON INTERNATIONAL STUDIES. SOURCES PRIMARILY IN ENGLISH ALTHOUGH MATERIALS IN SPANISH, ITALIAN, GERMAN, FRENCH INCLUDED. THREE MAIN CATEGORIES: GENERAL REFERENCE WORK, SPECIALIZED SOURCES FOR REGIONAL STUDIES, AND SOURCES FOR BIBLIOGRAPHY AND RESEARCH.

0603 CONOVER H.F. ED.
NORTH AND NORTHEAST AFRICA; A SELECTED ANNOTATED LIST OF WRITINGS.
NEW YORK: NY PUBLIC LIBRARY, 1957, 182 PP., LC#57-60062.
AN ANNOTATED BIBLIOGRAPHY OF 343 BOOKS, PERIODICALS, AND PAMPHLETS REVIEWING SOCIAL, ECONOMIC, AND POLITICAL ASPECTS OF MAJOR ISSUES IN EACH COUNTRY UNDER CONSIDERATION. CONTENT ARRANGED GEOGRAPHICALLY: ALGERIA, MOROCCO, TUNISIA, SAHARA, LIBYA, SPANISH AFRICA, EGYPT, THE SUDAN, ETHIOPIA, AND THE SOMALILANDS. SOURCES IN ENGLISH, FRENCH, ITALIAN, AND SPANISH. MAIN CONCERN IS WITH CURRENT AFFAIRS.

0604 CONOVER H.F. ED.
SERIALS FOR AFRICAN STUDIES.
WASHINGTON: LIBRARY OF CONGRESS, 1961, 163 PP., LC#61-60072.
CONTAINS 2,000 TITLES FROM WORKING CARD FILE AT AFRICANA SECTION OF LIBRARY OF CONGRESS. ANNOTATIONS CONSIST LARGELY OF BIBLIOGRAPHICAL DETAIL. INCLUDES MATERIAL IN WESTERN AND AFRICAN LANGUAGES.

0605 CONWELL-EVANS T.P.
THE LEAGUE COUNCIL IN ACTION.
LONDON: OXFORD U. PR., 1929, 291 PP.
A STUDY OF THE COUNCIL OF THE LEAGUE OF NATIONS AND ITS PEACE FUNCTIONS. STUDIES THE COUNCIL AS A REPRESENTATIVE WORLD BODY IN WHICH A JURISPRUDENCE DEVELOPS BASED ON NEW PRINCIPLES IN INTERNATIONAL LAW.

0606 COOK T., MOOS M.
POWER THROUGH PURPOSE.
BALTIMORE: JOHNS HOPKINS PR., 1954, 216 PP.
DISCUSSES BI-POLAR CONFLICT IN MODERN WORLD. CLAIMS THAT THIS CONFLICT INVOLVES FUNDAMENTAL ISSUE BETWEEN WAYS OF LIFE AND CONCEPTS OF MAN. URGES USA TO CLARIFY COMMITMENTS TO VALUES OF FREEDOM IN ORDER TO STRENGTHEN ITS POSITION.

0607 COOKSON J.
BEFORE THE AFRICAN STORM.
INDIANAPOLIS: BOBBS-MERRILL, 1954, 279 PP., LC#54-6506.
AUTHOR EXPLORES AFRICAN REVOLUTION COUNTRY BY COUNTRY. SEES 19TH-CENTURY EUROPEAN IMPERIALISM AS SOURCE OF CURRENT PROBLEMS IN AFRICA, BUT THESE HEADACHES CONCERN WORLD IN FIGHT AGAINST COMMUNISM.

0608 COOMBS P.H., BIGELOW K.W.
EDUCATION AND FOREIGN AID.
CAMBRIDGE: HARVARD U PR, 1965, 74 PP., LC#65-13840.
ANALYZES US EDUCATIONAL AID TO FOREIGN NATIONS AND SUGGESTS METHODS OF IMPROVEMENT. FEELS NEED FOR COOPERATIVE STRATEGY TO PLAN EDUCATIONAL PROJECTS AND SECURE MORE QUALIFIED PERSONNEL. ANALYZES SPECIFICALLY US POLICY IN AFRICA, ITS PROBLEMS, AND PROSPECTS FOR MORE PRACTICAL EDUCATIONAL PROGRAMS IN FUTURE.

0609 COOPER S.
BEHIND THE GOLDEN CURTAIN: A VIEW OF THE USA.
NEW YORK: CHAS SCRIBNER'S SONS, 1965, 244 PP., LC#66-23989.
EXAMINES MISUNDERSTANDINGS AND MUTUAL IGNORANCE OF US AND GREAT BRITAIN ABOUT EACH OTHER'S CULTURE. PRESENTS REASONS FOR AND CAUSES OF THIS BARRIER'S EXISTENCE AND ITS EFFECT ON AMERICAN SOCIETY AND HER IMAGE ABROAD.

0610 COORDINATING COMM DOC SOC SCI
INTERNATIONAL REPERTORY OF SOCIAL SCIENCE DOCUMENTATION CENTERS (PAMPHLET)
PARIS: UNESCO, 1952, 42 PP.
COVERS CENTERS INTENDED MAINLY FOR SPECIALISTS IN VARIOUS SOCIAL SCIENCES. ARRANGED ALPHABETICALLY BY COUNTRY WITH A SECTION ON DOCUMENTATION CENTERS OF INTERNATIONAL ORGANIZATIONS. GIVES INFORMATION ON SUBJECTS COVERED, PUBLICATIONS, DIRECTORS, SERVICES, AND ORGANIZATIONS. PREPARED BY CO-ORDINATING COMMITTEE ON DOCUMENTATION IN THE SOCIAL SCIENCES.

0611 COPLIN W.D.
THE FUNCTIONS OF INTERNATIONAL LAW.
SKOKIE: RAND MCNALLY & CO, 1966, 294 PP., LC#66-19440.
ATTEMPTS TO DEVELOP GENERAL THEORY OF ROLE OF LAW AND LEGISLATION IN INTERNATIONAL ENVIRONMENT; COVERS VARIOUS ASPECTS OF THE LAW. INCLUDES A NUMBER OF INTERNATIONAL TREATIES AS EXAMPLES. DISCUSSES SUBSTANTIVE LAW, LAW AS A MEANS OF PREVENTING VIOLENCE, LAW TO PROMOTE WELFARE, AND ATTEMPTS OF INTERNATIONAL ORGANIZATIONS TO ENFORCE IT.

0612 CORBETT P.E., SMITH A.A.
CANADA AND WORLD POLITICS.
LONDON: FABER/GWYER, 1928, 244 PP.
USING CANADA AS THE FOCAL POINT, ATTEMPTS TO EXAMINE THE GENERAL POLICIES AND PROBLEMS OF THE DOMINIONS. PROBES INTO PAST CONSTITUTIONS AND CONVENTIONS DEFINING AUTHORITY WITHIN AND AMONG THE DOMINIONS, AND SHOWS RELATIONSHIP WITH OTHER NATIONS AND INTERNATIONAL ORGANIZATIONS, I.E. LEAGUE OF NATIONS. PROPOSES IDEA OF 'PERSONAL UNION' AS BEST METHOD OF PRESERVING THE BRITISH EMPIRE'S CONSTITUTIONAL UNITY.

0613 CORBETT P.E.
POST WAR WORLDS.
NEW YORK: INSTIT. PAC. RELAT., 1942, 211 PP.
EXAMINES THE CAUSES OF THE BREAKDOWN OF INTERNATIONAL INSTITUTIONS SET UP AFTER THE LAST WAR. SUMMARIZES RECENT THOUGHT ON CREATING A MORE EFFECTIVE COMMUNITY OF STATES. OUTLINES ESSENTIAL AGENCIES NECESSARY TO A WORLD COMMONWEALTH.

0614 CORBETT P.E.
"OBJECTIVITY IN THE STUDY OF INTERNATIONAL AFFAIRS."
WORLD AFF., 4 (JULY 50), 257-63.
STATES THAT INTERNAL RELATIONS MERITS STUDY AT UNIVERSITY LEVEL. REFUTES CRITICISM THAT SUBJECT BARS OBJECTIVE STUDY.

0615 CORBETT P.E.
LAW AND SOCIETY IN THE RELATIONS OF STATES.
NEW YORK: HARCOURT BRACE, 1951, 337 PP.
BEGINS WITH STUDY OF WAY IN WHICH PRINCIPAL THEORIES OF INTERNATIONAL LAW ORIGINATED. PROCEEDS WITH INQUIRY INTO SOME FAMILIAR PATTERNS OF INTERNATIONAL PRACTICE, SHOWING EXTENT TO WHICH THEY HAVE BEEN SHAPED BY LEGAL REASONING. CONCLUDES THAT FUTURE OF INTERNATIONAL LAW IS ONE WITH THE FUTURE OF INTERNATIONAL ORGANIZATION.

0616 CORBETT P.E.
LAW IN DIPLOMACY.
PRINCETON: U. PR., 1959, 290 PP.
PROPOSES TO STUDY AND, IN SOME DEGREE, MEASURE THE INFLUENCE OF LEGAL NOTIONS ON FOREIGN POLICY WITHOUT ASSUMING OR ELABORATING UPON A SYSTEM OF INTERNATIONAL LAW. FOCUSES ATTENTION UPON THE USE OF LEGAL LANGUAGE, CATEGORIES, AND PROCEDURES IN BRITISH, AMERICAN AND SOVIET DIPOLMACY.

0617 CORDIER A.W. ED., FOOTE W. ED.
THE QUEST FOR PEACE.
NEW YORK: COLUMBIA U PRESS, 1965, 390 PP., LC#65-10357.
ARTICLES DISCUSSING MECHANICS OF PEACE-MAKING, INCLUDING APPRAISAL OF UN, KEEPING THE PEACE, DISARMAMENT, NEW ATTITUDES IN ECONOMIC RELATIONS, AND HUMAN RIGHTS IN WORLD AFFAIRS.

0618 CORDIER H.
BIBLIOTECA SINICA.
PARIS: E GUILMATO.
ANNOTATED BIBLIOGRAPHY CONTINUED FROM 1800-1922 OF WORKS ON PRE-COMMUNIST CHINA. ITEMS ARRANGED TOPICALLY AND INCLUDE A MAJORITY OF WORKS IN CHINESE LANGUAGE. WORK DIVIDED INTO ITEMS ON CHINA PROPER, FOREIGNERS IN CHINA FROM ANCIENT TIMES, FOREIGN RELATIONS, CHINESE IN FOREIGN COUNTRIES, COLONIES OF CHINA. COVERS ALL CHINESE HISTORY.

0619 CORET A.
"LE STATUT DE L'ILE CHRISTMAS DE L'OCEAN INDIEN."
ANNU. FRANC. DR. INTER., 8 (62), 208-9.
EXAMINES INTERNATIONAL AGREEMENTS BETWEEN AUSTRALIA AND NEW ZEALAND CONCERNING CHRISTMAS ISLAND. STUDIES ECONOMIC RESOURCES AND POLITICAL DIRECTION OF THE ISLAND. DESCRIBES

EFFORTS TO ACHIEVE UNIFIED NATIONAL GOVERNMENT.

0620 CORET A.
"LES PROVINCES PORTUGALLES D'OUTREMER ET L'ONU."
REV. JURID. POLIT. OUTREMER, 16 (APR.-JUNE 62), 173-221.
DEFINES POLITICAL STRUCTURE OF PORTUGESE OVERSEAS PROVINCES, FOCUSING ON RELATIONSHIP OF LOCAL GOVERNMENT AND CENTRAL ADMINISTRATIVE BODIES. POINTS OUT PROBLEMS INVOLVED IN TRANSFERRING CONTROL OF PROVINCES TO UN. REPORTS UN DEBATES AND RESOLUTIONS ON ANGOLA AND ON GOA.

0621 CORET A.
"LA DECLARATION DE L'ASSEMBLEE GENERAL DE L'ONU SUR L'OCTROI DE L'INDEPENDENCE AUX PAYS ET AUX PEUPLES." COLONIAUX.
REV. JURID. POLIT. OUTREMER, 18 (JAN.-MARCH 62), 222-34.
EXAMINES UN ASSEMBLY DECLARATION CONCEDING INDEPENDENCE TO COLONIAL PEOPLES. PRESENTS GENERAL PROBLEMS OF DECOLONIZATION. PRESENTS SUGGESTED SOLUTIONS OF USSR, NIGERIA, AND MEXICO. RELATES DECLARATION TO SPECIFIC CASES: OVERSEAS PORTUGESE PROVINCES AND WESTERN NEW GUINEA.

0622 CORET A.
"L'INDEPENDANCE DU SAMOA OCCIDENTAL."
REV. JURID. POLIT. OUTREMER, 16 (JAN.-MARCH 62), 135-172.
DISCUSSES HISTORICAL AND GEOGRAPHIC FACTORS WHICH LED TO SAMOAN NATIONAL INDEPENDENCE. OUTLINES PROBLEMS ENCOUNTERED AT CONSTITUTIONAL CONVENTION IN 1954 HELD TO CREATE POLITICAL STRUCTURE. FOCUSES ON RELATION OF JUDICIAL ORGANIZATION TO INTERNATIONAL LAW.

0623 CORFO
CHILE, A SELECTED BIBLIOGRAPHY IN ENGLISH (PAMPHLET)
NEW YORK: CHILEAN DEVEL CORP, 1964, 21 PP.
ENGLISH-LANGUAGE BIBLIOGRAPHY OF BOOKS, PERIODICALS, GOVERNMENT DOCUMENTS, PAMPHLETS. FIRST PART CONSISTS OF PUBLICATIONS SINCE 1950; SECOND PART CONTAINS MATERIAL FROM 1700-1950. PUBLISHED BY THE NEW YORK OFFICE OF CORFO (CORPORACION DE FOMENTO DE LA PRODUCCION).

0624 CORMACK M. ED.
SELECTED PAMPHLETS ON THE UNITED NATIONS AND INTERNATIONAL RELATIONS (PAMPHLET)
NEW YORK: CARNEGIE ENDOWMENT, 1951, 33 PP.
ANNOTATED GUIDE TO PAMPHLETS ON INTERNATIONAL ORGANIZATION, POLITICS, AND PROGRAMS. EMPHASIZES ORGANIZATION AND WORK OF UN AND ITS SPECIALIZED AGENCIES, AND FOREIGN POLICY OF US. 172 ITEMS WERE PUBLISHED BETWEEN 1945-1951. ITEMS LISTED DEAL WITH STRUCTURE RATHER THAN ORGANIZATIONAL OPERATIONS OF UN. LISTED ALPHABETICALLY BY TOPIC. INCLUDES LIST OF DISTRIBUTORS.

0625 CORNELL U DEPT ASIAN STUDIES
SOUTHEAST ASIA PROGRAM DATA PAPER.
ITHACA: CORNELL U, DEPT ASIAN ST, 1950.
A COLLECTION OF ARTICLES AND BIBLIOGRAPHIES PUBLISHED BY THE CORNELL UNIVERSITY SOUTHEAST ASIA PROGRAM. THE DATA PAPER HAS BEEN ISSUED IN PERIODICAL FORM SEVERAL TIMES EACH YEAR SINCE 1950. SEVERAL VOLUMES IN THE SERIES ARE DEVOTED TO COMPILING A CHECKLIST OF ALL AVAILABLE PUBLICATIONS ON INDIVIDUAL AREAS IN SOUTHEAST ASIA. COVERS INTERDISCIPLINARY STUDIES IN HUMANITIES AND SOCIAL AND NATURAL SCIENCES.

0626 CORNELL UNIVERSITY LIBRARY
SOUTHEAST ASIA ACCESSIONS LIST.
ITHACA: CORNELL U, DEPT ASIAN ST.
MONTHLY LISTING OF BOOKS, SERIALS, MONOGRAPHS, CONFERENCES, GOVERNMENT DOCUMENTS. ITEMS ARE ARRANGED BY COUNTRY. INCLUDES MATERIAL IN VARIOUS LANGUAGES FOR CAMBODIA, INDONESIA, MALAYSIA, PHILIPPINES, THAILAND, AND VIETNAM. GIVES FULL BIBLIOGRAPHIC INFORMATION.

0627 CORWIN E.S.
"THE CONSTITUTION AND WORLD ORGANIZATION."
PRINCETON: U. PR., 1944, 64 PP.
CONTENT ANALYSIS OF CONSTITUTIONAL TERMS TO DETERMINE WHETHER THEY BLOCK USA ENTRANCE INTO UN. PROBES FOLLOWING TERMS AND CONCEPTUAL BASES: NATIONAL SOVEREIGNTY, DUAL FEDERALISM, SEPARATION OF POWERS AND SENATE TREATY POWERS.

0628 CORY R.H. JR.
"FORGING A PUBLIC INFORMATION POLICY FOR THE UNITED NATIONS."
INT. ORG., 7 (MAY 53), 229-42.
ATTEMPTS TO CLARIFY WHAT ARE PROBLEMS FACING UN DELEGATES DECIDING WAY IN WHICH INTERNATIONAL SECRETARIAT SHOULD ATTEMPT TO INFLUENCE PUBLIC OPINION.

0629 COSER L., GASS H.M.
"AMERICA AND THE WORLD REVOLUTION."
COMMENTARY, 36 (OCT. 63), 278-98.
ASSAYS AMERICA'S CAPACITY TO COMPETE WITH COMMUNIST BLOC IN ECONOMIC DEVELOPMENT AND SOCIAL IMPROVEMENT OF UNDERDERVELOPED AREAS. OUTLINES PREREQUISITES FOR DEVELOPMENT AND EXPLAINS LIMITS OF EXTERNALLY IMPOSED SOLUTIONS.

0630 COSGROVE C.A.
"AGRICULTURE, FINANCE AND POLITICS IN THE EUROPEAN COMMUNITY."
INTL. RELATIONS, 3 (APR. 67), 208-225.
DISCUSSES COMMON FARM POLICY AS SYMBOL OF INTEGRATION IN EEC. INTERACTION OF NATIONAL AND EEC INTERESTS NEGOTIATING FOR COMMON FARM POLICY ILLUSTRATES POLITICAL NATURE OF INTEGRATION. ANALYZES MAY-JULY 1966 DECISIONS TO DEMONSTRATE EFFECT OF INTERPLAY OF INTERESTS ON EEC DECISION-MAKING. ALTHOUGH COMMUNITY SPIRIT OVERPOWERED NATIONAL INTEREST IN MAY-JUNE, STILL DANGER NATIONAL INTEREST WILL DESTROY EEC.

0631 COSTA RICA UNIVERSIDAD BIBL
LISTA DE TESIS DE GRADO DE LA UNIVERSIDAD DE COSTA RICA.
SAN JOSE: CIUDAD U, 1962, 131 PP.
BIBLIOGRAPHICAL LISTING OF THESES ACCEPTED AT THE UNIVERSITY OF COSTA RICA IN 1961. EACH ITEM INCLUDES AN ABSTRACT. ENTRIES ARRANGED BY DEPARTMENT.

0632 COTTRELL A.J., DOUGHERTY J.E.
THE POLITICS OF THE ATLANTIC ALLIANCE.
NEW YORK: PRAEGER, 1964, 248 PP.
ANALYZES MAJOR POLITICAL AND ECONOMIC ASPECTS OF NATO, POINTING OUT PROBLEMS OF ACHIEVING AND MAINTAINING UNITY OF THE WEST. CHALLENGES LEADERS TO SURMOUNT THE CRISES.

0633 COTTRELL L.S. JR., EBERHART S.
AMERICAN PUBLIC OPINION ON WORLD AFFAIRS IN THE ATOMIC AGE.
PRINCETON: U. PR., 1948, 152 PP.
PUBLIC OPINION SURVEY CONDUCTED BY THE COMMISSION ON THE SOCIAL ASPECTS OF ATOMIC ENERGY SHOWS THAT A SMALL MAJORITY OF AMERICANS PREFER ISOLATIONISM. CONCLUDES THAT THERE IS A GREAT NEED TO EDUCATE THE PUBLIC ON PROBLEMS OF FOREIGN RELATIONS.

0634 COTTRELL W.F.
ENERGY AND SOCIETY.
NEW YORK: MCGRAW HILL, 1955, 330 PP.
VIEWS WORLD'S ECONOMIC, SOCIAL AND POLITICAL HISTORY AND RELATIONS AS FUNCTIONS OF ENERGY AND OFFERS THESIS THAT ENERGY AVAILABLE TO MAN LIMITS WHAT HE CAN DO AND INFLUENCES WHAT HE WILL DO. SUGGESTS THAT 'BALANCE OF POWER' BETWEEN AT LEAST THREE MAJOR CENTERS OF ENERGY WILL PROVIDE FUTURE GUARANTEE AGAINST WAR.

0635 COUDENHOVE-KALERGI
AN IDEA CONQUERS THE WORLD.
NEW YORK: ROY, 1954, 310 PP.
AUTOBIOGRAPHY OF A LEADING PROPONENT OF PAN-EUROPEAN ORGANIZATION DISCUSSES BOTH HIS PERSONAL BACKGROUND AS A MEMBER OF A POLITICALLY IMPORTANT FAMILY, AND THE HISTORICAL DEVELOPMENTS OF THE TWENTIETH CENTURY THAT PROMPTED OR PREVENTED REALIZATION OF HIS MOVEMENTS' GOALS.

0636 COUDENHOVE-KALERGI
FROM WAR TO PEACE.
LONDON: CAPE, 1959, 224 PP.
PRESENTS AN HISTORICAL STUDY CONCERNING THE POSSIBILITY OF CREATING A UNIVERSAL ORDER FOR PEACE. CREATING A US-USSR ENFORCED TRUCE, HOPES TO CREATE A FEDERAL GOVERNMENT BASED ON NATO, USING ENGLISH LANGUAGE AS INTERNATIONAL TONGUE AND SLOWLY PROGRESSING TOWARDS RELIGIOUS AND RACIAL UNITY WITHIN NEXT 50 YEARS.

0637 COUNCIL BRITISH NATIONAL BIB
BRITISH NATIONAL BIBLIOGRAPHY.
LONDON: COUN BRIT NATL BIBLIOG, 1950, 700 PP.
A SUBJECT LIST OF BRITISH BOOKS PUBLISHED FROM 1950-67 BASED UPON BOOKS DEPOSITED AT THE CLASSIFIED OFFICE OF THE BRITISH MUSEUM. OVER 20,000 ENTRIES IN EACH VOLUME.

0638 COUNCIL OF EUROPE
EUROPEAN CONVENTION ON HUMAN RIGHTS - COLLECTED TEXTS (5TH ED.)
STRASBOURG: COUNCIL OF EUROPE, 1966, 125 PP.
COLLECTION OF DOCUMENTS ON RULES OF PROCEDURE, RATIFICATIONS, MEMBERS, PROTOCOLS, DECLARATIONS, AND RESERVATIONS OF EUROPEAN COMMISSION OF HUMAN RIGHTS. PRINTED IN ENGLISH AND FRENCH.

0639 COUNCIL ON FOREIGN RELATIONS
DOCUMENTS ON AMERICAN FOREIGN RELATIONS.
BOSTON: WORLD PEACE FOUNDATION, 1938, LC#39-28987.
ANNUAL PUBLICATION BEGUN IN 1938 CONTAINING SOURCE MATERIAL RELEVANT TO AMERICAN FOREIGN RELATIONS. FOUNDED BY WORLD PEACE FOUNDATION; CONTINUED AFTER 1952 BY COUNCIL ON FOREIGN RELATIONS. INCLUDES DOCUMENTS OF UN AND OAS, RELEVANT STATEMENTS ON FOREIGN POLICY, AND KEY ISSUES. ARRANGED BY TOPIC. INCLUDES INDEX AND, IN EARLIER EDITIONS, STATISTICAL TABLES IN THE APPENDIX.

0640 COUNCIL ON WORLD TENSIONS
A STUDY OF WORLD TENSIONS AND DEVELOPMENT.
NEW YORK: DODD, 1962, 217 PP.
DEALS WITH SIGNIFICANT TENSIONS WITHIN AND AMONG NATIONS

STRIVING FOR RAPID ADVANCEMENT. STRESSES NEED FOR POLITICAL, ECONOMIC AND EDUCATIONAL COOPERATION, AND SUGGESTS THAT THE PSYCHOLOGICAL GAP AMONG NATIONS IS A HINDRANCE TO DEVELOPMENT.

0641 COUNCIL ON WORLD TENSIONS
RESTLESS NATIONS.
NEW YORK: DODD, MEAD, 1962, 217 PP., LC#62-16328.
COLLECTION OF ARTICLES STUDYING WORLD TENSIONS AND DEVELOPMENT, INCLUDING FIELDS OF POLITICS, ECONOMICS, EDUCATION, AND DEVELOPMENT POLICY.

0642 COUSINS N.
WHO SPEAKS FOR MAN.
NEW YORK: MACMILLAN, 1953, 318 PP.
EVALUATES THE PROBLEMS THAT MAN FACES IN OUR PRESENT WORLD OF COMPLEXITIES AND ANXIETIES. THE AUTHOR FOCUSES ON THE HORROR OF WARFARE INCLUDING HIS PERSONAL OBSERVATIONS IN GERMANY, JAPAN, KOREA, ETC., AND SUGGESTS THE FORMATION OF A WORLD GOVERNMENT TO SOLVE THE QUESTION OF MAN'S PERSONAL SURVIVAL.

0643 COUTY P.
"L'ASSISTANCE POUR LE DEVELOPPEMENT: POINT DE VUE SCANDINAVES."
TIERS-MONDE, 4 (NOS.13-14, 63), 278-84.
STUDIES FINANCIAL SITUATION OF FINLAND AND SWEDEN. SHOWS THAT TRADITIONAL INDIFFERENCE TO PROBLEMS OF UNDERDEVELOPED COUNTRIES CHANGED TO INVOLVEMENT. RELATES THEIR NEW INTEREST TO PLANS FOR WIDER COMMERCIAL ACTIVITY.

0644 COWEN Z.
THE BRITISH COMMONWEALTH OF NATIONS IN A CHANGING WORLD.
EVANSTON: NORTHWESTERN U PRESS, 1965, 117 PP., LC#65-12096.
TRACES DEVELOPMENT OF BRITISH COMMONWEALTH AND ITS INSTITUTIONS, PARTICULARLY IN LEGAL AND STRUCTURAL PERSPECTIVE. EXAMINES RECENT CHANGES AND INQUIRES INTO POLITICS AND PROSPECTS OF CONTEMPORARY COMMONWEALTH.

0645 COX R.
PAN-AFRICANISM IN PRACTICE.
LONDON: OXFORD U PR, 1964, 95 PP.
STUDY OF DEVELOPMENT OF PAN-AFRICAN FREEDOM MOVEMENT OF EAST, CENTRAL, AND SOUTHERN AFRICA. EMPHASIZES THE ESSENTIALLY EAST AFRICAN CHARACTER AND ORIGIN OF THE MOVEMENT. TRACES DEVELOPMENT FROM JOINT LIBERATION MOVEMENT TO ECONOMIC UNION OF INDEPENDENT NATIONS WITH EVENTUAL GOAL OF POLITICAL UNION. CONCENTRATES ON ANALYSIS OF ACTIVITIES OF MOVEMENT 1958-64.

0646 COX R.H.
"LOCKE ON WAR AND PEACE."
LONDON: OXFORD U PR, 1960.
ARGUES THAT CONCEPT OF "STATE OF NATURE" HAS MEANING FOR CONTEMPORARY SOCIETY. DISCUSSES CONCEPTS OF SOVEREIGN COMMONWEALTH, STATE OF NATURE AND LAW OF NATURE, LOCKE AND CHRISTIAN TRADITION, LAW OF NATURE AS THE LAW OF NATIONS, AND ITS RELATION TO ECONOMY OF POWER. CONTAINS EXTENSIVE BIBLIOGRAPHY.

0647 COX R.H. ED.
THE STATE IN INTERNATIONAL RELATIONS.
SAN FRANCISCO: CHANDLER, 1965, 262 PP., LC#65-16764.
COLLECTION OF ESSAYS ON INDEPENDENCE, THEORY OF SOVEREIGNTY, WAR AND PEACE, CONSTITUTIONAL DEMOCRACY, FASCISM, AND FORMS OF GOVERNMENTS. EXAMINES EVILS OF SOVEREIGNTY AND METHOD OF INTEGRATION OF STATE INTO LARGER COMMUNITY OF STATES.

0648 COYLE D.C.
THE UNITED NATIONS AND HOW IT WORKS.
NEW YORK: COLUMBIA U PRESS, 1966, 256 PP., LC#55-7776.
GENERAL DISCUSSION OF ROLE AND INTERNAL OPERATION OF UN. EXAMINES ITS FUNCTION IN INTERNATIONAL DISPUTES, TRADE, EDUCATION, DISARMAMENT, TECHNICAL SERVICES, REGIONAL ARRANGEMENTS, AND CONQUEST OF SPACE.

0649 CRABB C.
BIPARTISAN FOREIGN POLICY: MYTH OR REALITY.
EVANSTON: ROW PETERSON, 1957, 279 PP.
EXAMINES CONCEPT OF BIPARTISAN FOREIGN POLICY AND ITS EMERGENCE DURING WW 2. NOTES IMPLICATIONS FOR AMERICAN POLITICO-GOVERNMENTAL SYSTEM. ATTEMPTS TO APPLY BIPARTISAN PRINCIPLE TO FIVE CASES OF FOREIGN RELATIONS.

0650 CRABBS R.F., HOLMQUIST F.W.
UNITED STATES HIGHER EDUCATION AND WORLD AFFAIRS.
NEW YORK: FREDERICK PRAEGER, 1967, 208 PP., LC#66-21775.
PARTIALLY ANNOTATED BIBLIOGRAPHY RELATING AMERICAN EDUCATION TO WORLD AFFAIRS, INCLUDING TEACHING, RESEARCH, INTERNATIONAL EXCHANGE, AND COOPERATION.

0651 CRAIG G.A. ED., GILBERT F.
THE DIPLOMATS 1919-1939.
PHILA: W B SAUNDERS CO, 1953, 700 PP., LC#53-6378.
COLLECTION OF ESSAYS ON INTER-WAR DIPLOMACY. EXAMINES DIPLOMATIC EFFORTS OF PARTICULAR OFFICIALS, PLUS FOREIGN POLICY OF MAJOR EUROPEAN POWERS.

0652 CRAIG G.A.
THE POLITICS OF THE PRUSSIAN ARMY 1640-1945.
LONDON: OXFORD U PR, 1955, 536 PP.
TRACES HISTORY OF PRUSSIAN ARMY AS POLITICAL AND SOCIAL FACTOR INFLUENCING PRUSSIAN GOVERNMENT 1640-1945. NOTES PARTICIPATION OF MILITARY LEADERS IN FORMATION OF INTERNAL AND FOREIGN POLICIES AND TRACES ARMY AS A STRATEGIC FACTOR IN PRUSSIAN INTERNATIONAL RELATIONS. DISCUSSES RELATIONS OF VARIOUS PRUSSIAN HEADS OF STATE WITH ARMY AND DESCRIBES ARMY INVOLVEMENT WITH HITLER BEFORE WWII.

0653 CRAIG G.A.
FROM BISMARCK TO ADENAUER: ASPECTS OF GERMAN STATECRAFT.
BALTIMORE: JOHNS HOPKINS PRESS, 1958, 156 PP., LC#58-59683.
LECTURES ON GERMAN NATIONAL POLICY FROM 2ND-4TH REICHS. VIEW HISTORY OF GERMAN DIPLOMACY AS A DESCENT FROM BISMARCK THROUGH WILHELMINE YEARS TO ARMY DOMINATION AND WWI. SEE POST-WWI PERIOD AS INDECISIVE AND HITLERIAN ERA AS PIT FROM WHICH EMERGED ADENAUER'S BURNISHED STATECRAFT. BELIEVE ISSUES OBSCURED BY SLOGANS, IDEOLOGIES, AND RESORTS TO FORCE.

0654 CRAIG G.A.
WAR, POLITICS, AND DIPLOMACY.
NEW YORK: FREDERICK PRAEGER, 1966, 297 PP., LC#66-26550.
DISCUSSES MILITARY PROBLEMS IN AUSTRIAN ARMY AND IN ALLIANCE AGAINST NAPOLEON, CIVIL-MILITARY RELATIONS IN PRUSSIA, IMPACT OF GERMAN MILITARY ON SOCIAL LIFE DURING WWII, AND DIPLOMATIC TACTICS OF TOTALITARIAN AND EMERGING NATIONS. INCLUDES ESSAYS ON DIPLOMACY OF BISMARCK AND DULLES, AND CONSTITUTIONAL CONFLICT IN PRUSSIA.

0655 CRANDALL S.B.
TREATIES: THEIR MAKING AND ENFORCEMENT.
NEW YORK: COLUMB. U. PR., 1904, 255 PP.
STUDIES TREATY MAKING WITH FOREIGN STATES FROM COLONIAL DAYS TO PRESENT. DETAILED COVERAGE OF SCOPE AND TYPES OF TREATIES.

0656 CRANE R.D.
"LAW AND STRATEGY IN SPACE."
ORBIS, 6 (SUMMER 62), 281-300.
USA MUST TAKE INITIATIVE IN FORMULATING SPACE LAWS WHICH WOULD SERVE TO PROMOTE SCIENTIFIC RESEARCH AND ECONOMIC PROGRESS. IN ORDER TO FACILITATE GROWTH OF A FREE AND PEACEFUL WORLD ORDER, IT'S NECESSARY TO IMPLEMENT ON A HIGHER MORAL LEVEL USA MILITARY AND POLITICAL STRATEGIES.

0657 CRANE R.D.
"SOVIET ATTITUDE TOWARD INTERNATIONAL SPACE LAW."
AMER. J. INT. LAW, 56 (JULY 62), 685-723.
SOVIET UNION FAVORS OFFENSIVE STRATEGY IN INTERNATIONAL SPACE LAW. EMPLOY DOUBLE STANDARD, PROMOTING LAWS THAT FURTHER THEIR INTERESTS. URGES USA TO TAKE INITIATIVE IN DEVELOPING INTERNATIONAL SPACE COOPERATION.

0658 CRANE R.D.
"THE CUBAN CRISIS: A STRATEGIC ANALYSIS OF AMERICAN AND SOVIET POLICY."
ORBIS, 6 (JAN. 63), 528-563.
EXAMINES REASONS BEHIND SOVIET MILITARY BUILD-UP ON CUBA: TO BALANCE NUCLEAR POWER AND TO SHOW LATIN AMERICA THAT USSR COULD AWE US. MAINTAINS THAT SOVIETS MISUNDERSTOOD US FOREIGN POLICY AND THAT US ACTED TO FORCE SOVIET COMPREHENSION. CRITICIZES POSTCRISIS US POLICY OF MODERATION, AND URGES POLICY OF MAXIMUM SECURITY WITH MORE THAN MINIMUM RISK.

0659 CRANE R.D.
"BASIC PRINCIPLES IN SOVIET SPACE LAW."
LAW CONTEMP. PROBL., 29 (AUTUMN 64), 943-55.
CONSIDERS THE THREE PRINCIPLES OF SOVIET SPACE LAW: PEACEFUL COEXISTENCE, PEACEFUL COOPERATION, AND DISARMAMENT. SUGGESTS THAT SOVIET MANIPULATION OF THEM BE UNDERSTOOD NOT AS A MEANS OF RESOLVING CONFLICT BUT RATHER AS A METHOD OF DIRECTING CONFLICT TOWARDS THE ACHIEVEMENT OF COMMUNIST WORLD DOMINATION.

0660 CRANMER-BYNG J.L.
"THE CHINESE ATTITUDE TOWARDS EXTERNAL RELATIONS."
INT. J., 21 (WINTER 66), 57-77.
HISTORY OF CHINESE RELATIONS WITH NON-CHINESE PEOPLES SINCE 1793, EMPHASIZING PRESENT ATTITUDES AND DIFFERENCES BETWEEN CONFUCIAN AND MAOIST DOCTRINES, CONTEMPORARY FOREIGN POLICY, AND RELATIVE CHINESE INEXPERIENCE WITH ALLIANCES.

0661 CRAWFORD E.T., LYONS G.M.
"FOREIGN AREA RESEARCH: A BACKGROUND STATEMENT."
AMER. BEHAVIORAL SCIENTIST, 10 (JUNE 67), 3-7.
SETS FORTH PROBLEMS STUDIED BY 1966 CONFERENCE ON GOVERNMENT PROGRAMS IN BEHAVIORAL SCIENCES. DISCUSSES STATUS AND PRIORITIES IN FOREIGN AREAS RESEARCH, CONDUCT OF

FIELD RESEARCH, AND TASK OF COORDINATION AND UTILIZATION OF RESEARCH FINDINGS. PROPOSES FURTHER STUDY OF ROLE OF SOCIAL SCIENTISTS IN POLICY-MAKING PROCESS.

0662 CREMEANS C.
THE ARABS AND THE WORLD: NASSER'S ARAB NATIONALIST POLICY.
NEW YORK: PRAEGER, 1963, 338 PP., $6.50.
STUDIES EVOLUTION, STRENGTHS, WEAKNESSES AND IMPLICATIONS OF NASSER'S ARAB NATIONALISM. FOCUSES ON NASSER'S AMBITIONS, AMBIVALENCE AND POLICY FORMULATION IN POLITICAL, ECONOMIC, AND SOCIAL MATTERS. OFFERS SUGGESTIONS FOR AMERICAN FOREIGN POLICY FOR NEAR EAST.

0663 CROAN M.
"POLYCENTRISM: COMMUNIST INTERNATIONAL RELATIONS."
SURVEY, 42 (JUNE 62), 9-19.
PRESENTS PROBLEMS CREATED BY SOVIET CONSTANT AND 'FRUITLESS' SEARCH TO RECONCILE NATIONAL AND INTERNATIONAL COMMUNIST AIMS AND BY THEIR STRUGGLE FOR COMMUNIST WORLD LEADERSHIP WITH CHINA. COMPARES COMMUNIST UNITY UNDER STRONG STALIN'S LEADERSHIP AND DISUNITY OF PRESENT PERIOD.

0664 CROWE S.E.
THE BERLIN WEST AFRICA CONFERENCE, 1884-85.
LONDON: LONGMANS, GREEN & CO, 1942, 249 PP.
STUDIES 19TH-CENTURY EUROPEAN DIPLOMACY LEADING TO PARTITIONING OF AFRICA. TREATS EUROPEAN BALANCE OF POWER AND ITS INFLUENCE ON CONFERENCE, WHICH HAD BEEN CALLED TO CREATE FREEDOM OF TRADE IN CONGO BASIN. RELATES THIS CONFERENCE TO FREE TRADE AREAS AND SPHERES OF INFLUENCE FOR EUROPEAN POWERS.

0665 CROWLEY D.W.
THE BACKGROUND TO CURRENT AFFAIRS.
LONDON: MACMILLAN, 1966, 390 PP.
ATTEMPTS TO IDENTIFY AND EXPLAIN MAIN HISTORICAL FORCES OPERATING IN CONTEMPORARY WORLD AND TO CLARIFY ASSUMPTIONS BEHIND POLICIES OF THE POWERS. EXAMINES BRITAIN'S ROLE IN WORLD AFFAIRS AND CONCLUDES IT MUST BE ONE OF INFLUENCE RATHER THAN POWER.

0666 CROZIER B.
THE MORNING AFTER; A STUDY OF INDEPENDENCE.
NEW YORK: OXFORD U PR, 1963, 299 PP.
ANALYSIS OF INDEPENDENCE IN DEVELOPING NATIONS AND PROBLEMS OF ORGANIZATION AND ADMINISTRATION IN NEW STATUS. DISCUSSES DIFFICULTIES IN CHANGING FROM COLONIAL RULE AND ROLE OF NATIONAL LEADERS IN EARLY YEARS OF NEW NATIONS AND POSITION OF THESE NATIONS IN COLD WAR.

0667 CURRIE D.P. ED.
FEDERALISM AND THE NEW NATIONS OF AFRICA.
CHICAGO: U OF CHICAGO PRESS, 1964, 440 PP., LC#64-23421.
STUDIES AFRICAN PROBLEMS IN DIFFERENT REGIONS AND SYSTEM OF FEDERALISM IN AFRICA AS REGARDS ECONOMIC GROWTH, UNITY, AND TAXATION. RELATIONS OF INDIVIDUALS AND MINORITY GROUPS TO GOVERNMENT AND INTERNATIONAL LEGAL ASPECTS OF FEDERAL SYSTEM ARE EXAMINED IN COMPARISON WITH US AND CANADIAN FEDERALISM.

0668 CURRIE L.
ACCELERATING DEVELOPMENT: THE NECESSITY AND MEANS.
NEW YORK: MCGRAW HILL, 1966, 255 PP., LC#65-21573.
ANALYZES PROBLEM AND PROPOSES PROGRAM FOR CONTINUING UNDERDEVELOPMENT. DISCUSSES NEED FOR "BREAKTHROUGH" APPROACH AND STATES PREREQUISITES NECESSARY FOR SUCCESSFUL PROGRAM. DESCRIBES GOALS, DIAGNOSIS, AND STRATEGY APPLIED TO COLOMBIA AS TESTING GROUND FOR DEVELOPMENT POLICIES OF US.

0669 CURTIS G.L.
"THE UNITED NATIONS OBSERVER GROUP IN LEBANON."
INT. ORGAN., 18 (AUTUMN 64), 738-65.
A HISTORICAL ACCOUNT OF THE SITUATION IN LEBANON WHICH RESULTED IN THE ESTABLISHMENT OF THE UN OBSERVATION GROUP, ITS SUBSEQUENT OPERATION IN LEBANON FROM JUNE TO DECEMBER 1958 AND SETBACKS SUFFERED AS A RESULT OF AMERICAN TROOP LANDINGS IN JULY.

0670 CUTLER R.
"THE DEVELOPMENT OF THE NATIONAL SECURITY COUNCIL."
FOREIGN AFFAIRS, 34 (APR. 56), 441-458
SUMMARIZES IMPORTANT ASPECTS OF NATIONAL SECURITY COUNCIL. POINTS UP COUNCIL'S DIFFERENT USE UNDER TRUMAN AND EISENHOWER. DISCUSSES PROPOSITION THAT COUNCIL INCLUDE IN ITS REGULAR MEMBERSHIP A NUMBER OF QUALIFIED CIVILIANS, AND ARGUES AGAINST SUCH A CHANGE.

0671 CZERNIN F.
VERSAILLES - 1919.
NEW YORK: PUTNAM, 1964, 437 PP.
ATTEMPTS TO SHOW BY DOCUMENTARY EVIDENCE HOW THE FIVE MAIN, AND MOST CONTROVERSIAL, CLAUSES OF THE TREATY OF VERSAILLES CAME TO BE WRITTEN THE WAY THEY WERE AND WHAT PARALLELOGRAMS OF FORCES SHAPED THEM. REVEALS IMPACT OF PERSONALITIES ON NEGOTIATIONS AND SCRUTINIZES THE TROUBLESOME QUESTIONS OF REPARATIONS, COLONIES, BORDERS AND THE COVENANT OF THE LEAGUE.

0672 D'AMATO D.
"LEGAL ASPECTS OF THE FRENCH NUCLEAR TESTS."
AMER. J. OF INT. LAW, 61 (JAN. 67).
DISCUSSES FRANCE'S RESPONSIBILITY UNDER INTERNATIONAL LAW FOR ITS 1966 NUCLEAR TESTING IN TAHITI. DISCUSSES THE COMPLEX PROBLEMS IN PROVING THE ILLEGALITY OF THE TESTS, BUT IMPLIES THAT PREVIOUS EVIDENCE OF RADIOACTIVE CONTAMINATION IN OTHER TESTS CAN BE THE BASIS FOR A STRONG CLAIM.

0673 DAENIKER G.
STRATEGIE DES KLEIN STAATS.
STUTTGART: VERL HUBER FRAUENFELD, 1966, 230 PP.
DISCUSSES THE STRATEGY OF A SMALL STATE, SWITZERLAND, IN MAINTAINING ITSELF IN THE ATOMIC AGE. ARGUES FOR NUCLEAR ARMAMENT OF SWITZERLAND, MILITARY DEFENSE, AND CONTINUED POLITICAL EXISTENCE. DESCRIBES NEW DIMENSIONS OF THREAT DERIVING FROM NUCLEAR WEAPONS. QUESTIONS EXPHASIS ON CONVENTIONAL WEAPONS IN SWITZERLAND.

0674 DAHLIN E.
FRENCH AND GERMAN PUBLIC OPINION ON DECLARED WAR AIMS 1914-1918.
STANFORD: STANFORD U PRESS, 1933, 163 PP., LC#33-14010.
DISCUSSES FRENCH AND GERMAN PUBLIC ATTITUDES IN WWI ON ANNEXATIONS, PEACE, BELGIUM AND BUFFER STATES, RUSSIAN PEACE FORMULAS, WILSON'S PROPOSALS, ETC. CONCLUDES THAT PEACE WAS NOT REACHED BECAUSE OF "IMPERIALISTIC AIMS" OF BOTH GOVERNMENTS.

0675 DALLIN A.
THE SOVIET UNION AT THE UNITED NATIONS: AN INQUIRY INTO SOVIET MOTIVES AND OBJECTIVES.
NEW YORK: PRAEGER, 1962, 246 PP.
ASSAYS TO ANALYZE SOVIET MOTIVES AND OBJECTIVES WITH REGARD TO THEIR ACTIVITIES IN THE UN AND MAKES INFERENCES ABOUT SOVIET'S VIEW OF THE UN FROM THESE ACTIVITIES.

0676 DALLIN A.
"THE SOVIET VIEW OF THE UNITED NATIONS."
INT. ORGAN., 16 (WINTER 62), 21-36.
SOVIET UNION HAS ATTEMPTED TO KEEP U.N. ALIVE BUT WEAK, SAFE-GUARDING OWN FREEDOM OF ACTION WHILE KEEPING THE WORLD-ORGANIZATION OUT OF BLOC AFFAIRS. ALTHOUGH SOVIETS HAVE GAINED POLITICAL ADVANTAGES FROM UN MEMBERSHIP AND WILL CONTINUE TO DOMINATE UN FOR ITS OWN ENDS, THE USSR WILL OPPOSE ANY 'INCREASE IN AFFIRMATIVE ROLE' FOR THE ORGANIZATION AS RECENTLY PRESCRIBED BY HAMMERSKJOLD.

0677 DALLIN A. ED., HARRIS J. ED., HODNETT G. ED.
DIVERSITY IN INTERNATIONAL COMMUNISM: A DOCUMENTARY RECORD, 1961-1963.
NEW YORK: COLUMBIA U PRESS, 1963, 867 PP., LC#62-21515.
PROVIDES MOST IMPORTANT AVAILABLE DOCUMENTATION ON CURRENT TRENDS WITHIN INTERNATIONAL COMMUNIST MOVEMENT. CONCERNED WITH ISSUES DIVIDING MOVEMENT SINCE 22ND CONGRESS OF COMMUNIST PARTY OF THE SOVIET UNION HELD IN OCTOBER, 1961. DOCUMENTS REPRODUCED IN APPENDIX CONCERN ITALIAN AND FRENCH PARTY PUBLICATIONS ON MOSCOW CONFERENCES OF EIGHTY-ONE COMMUNIST PARTIES IN NOVEMBER-DECEMBER, 1960.

0678 DALLIN A. ED.
THE SOVIET UNION, ARMS CONTROL AND DISARMAMENT.
NEW YORK: PRAEGER, 1964, 282 PP.
INVESTIGATES AND EVALUATES SOVIET INTEREST IN DISARMAMENT FROM 1957 TO 1963. ANALYZES ASPECTS OF IDEOLOGY, ECONOMICS, PUBLIC OPINION, AND MILITARY DOCTRINES AS FORCES FOR OR AGAINST DISARMAMENT. PRESENTS SOVIET PROPOSALS.

0679 DALLIN D.J.
SOVIET FOREIGN POLICY AFTER STALIN.
PHILADELPHIA: LIPPINCOTT, 1961, 543 PP.
ANALYZES STALIN'S POSTWAR FOREIGN POLICY AND ITS CONTINUANCE BY MALENKOV AND KHRUSCHEV. TRACES SOVIET RELATIONS WITH SATELLITES, WEST, MIDDLE EAST AND FAR EAST. OUTLINES ALL SOVIET TREATIES, ALLIANCES, CONFERENCES, AND AGREEMENTS.

0680 DANIELS R.V.
"THE CHINESE REVOLUTION IN RUSSIAN PERSPECTIVE."
WORLD POLIT., 13 (JAN. 61), 210-30.
CHINESE COMMUNIST HISTORY FOLLOWS PECULIAR PATTERN. COMPARISON WITH USSR SUGGESTS VARIOUS INTERPRETATIONS OF STATUS OF COMMUNISM IN FAR EAST. CONCLUDES THAT IN PRESENT-DAY COMMUNISM POLITICAL SUPERSTRUCTURE IS CREATOR OF ECONOMIC SYSTEM.

0681 DARBY W.E.
INTERNATIONAL TRIBUNALS.
LONDON: PEACE SOCIETY, 1897, 168 PP.
VARIOUS SCHEMES OF INTERNATIONAL TRIBUNALS ARE PRESENTED: FROM THE AMPHICTYONIC COUNCIL OF ANCIENT GREECE TO ANGLO-AMERICAN ARBITRATION TREATY OF 1897 AS WELL AS PROPOSALS BY BENTHAM AND KANT. AUTHOR LISTS 140 INSTANCES OF INTERNATIONAL ARBITRATION SINCE 1815 AS CONCLUSIVE PROOF OF PRACTICABILITY OF ARBITRATION AS CHIEF MEANS OF SETTLING

INTERNATIONAL DISPUTES.

0682 DARLING F.C.
"THE GEOPOLITICS OF AMERICAN FOREIGN POLITICS IN ASIA."
UNITED ASIA, 15 (MAY 63), 370-76.
TRACES STEPS OF USA AND SOVIET UNION IN ASIA SINCE 1947. HUGE POPULATION, NATURAL RESOURCES, AND STRATEGIC LOCATION VITAL TO USA INTERESTS. RELIES ON MILITARY AID TO OFFSET COMMUNIST PROPAGANDA, POLITICAL SUBVERSION, GUERRILLA WARFARE, AND ECONOMIC PENETRATION. RECOMMENDS POLICY CHANGES.

0683 DAVAR F.C.
IRAN AND INDIA THROUGH THE AGES.
BOMBAY: ASIA PUBL HOUSE, 1962, 312 PP.
HISTORY OF RELATIONS AND CULTURAL INTERCHANGE BETWEEN TWO NATIONS FROM PREHISTORIC MIGRATIONS TO PRESENT DAY. AUTHOR HOPES KNOWLEDGE OF CULTURAL AFFINITIES WILL PRODUCE MORE FRIENDLY POLITICAL RELATIONS.

0684 DAVEE R.
"POUR UN FONDS DE DEVELOPPEMENT SOCIAL."
TIERS-MONDE, 4 (NOS.13-14, 63), 181-92.
STATES THAT UN ECONOMIC AID PROGRAM PARTS REQUIRE COORDINATION. EXAMINES PROGRAM OF TECHNICAL ASSISTANCE TO VARIOUS NATIONS. EXAMINES PROBLEM OF URGENT SOCIAL REFORMS. INDICATES PATTERNS OF INTERNATIONAL COOPERATION.

0685 DAVENPORT J.
"ARMS AND THE WELFARE STATE."
YALE REV., 47 (SPR. 58), 335-346.
BELIEVES THAT US NEEDS A STRONG AND EFFECTIVE GOVERNMENT FOR NATIONAL DEFENSE, DIPLOMACY, SOUND MONEY, AND TO RESIST MONOPOLY IN BUSINESS AND LABOR, BUT THIS DOES NOT HAVE TO MEAN 'WELFARE STATE'. ARGUES FOR A NEW 'INTELLECTUAL COMMUNITY SYNTHESIS, WHICH WILL TAKE THE THREAT OF RUSSIAN DANGER SERIOUSLY, WHILE KEEPING FREE SOCIETY AT HOME. ANSWER TO TOBIN'S 'DEFENSE, DOLLARS AND DOCTINES' OF SAME ISSUE.

0686 DAVIDS J.
AMERICA AND THE WORLD OF OUR TIME: UNITED STATES DIPLOMACY IN THE TWENTIETH CENTURY.
NEW YORK: RANDOM, 1960, 597 PP., $7.50.
PRESENTS THE DIPLOMACY OF THE UNITED STATES IN THE CONTEXT OF WORLD POLITICS AND STUDIES AMERICA'S ROLE IN FOREIGN AFFAIRS. DISCUSSES THE CIRCUMSTANCES THAT CONTRIBUTED TO AMERICA'S INVOLVEMENT IN POWER POLITICS, THE CHANGES IN FOREIGN POLICY BEFORE AND AFTER WW 2 AND THE DIPLOMATIC BACKGROUND OF THE COLD WAR.

0687 DAVIDSON A.B. ED., OLDEROGGE D.A. ED., SOLODOVNIKOV V.G. ED.
RUSSIA AND AFRICA.
MOSCOW: NANKA PUBL HOUSE, 1966, 248 PP.
VOLUME CONTAINS REPORTS MADE AT CONFERENCE ON HISTORICAL RELATIONS OF PEOPLES OF SOVIET UNION AND AFRICA IN MOSCOW, MAY 19-21, 1965. VARIOUS ASPECTS OF CONTACTS BETWEEN USSR AND AFRICA DURING PAST FIFTY YEARS ARE EXAMINED AND INCLUDE MATERIAL TO OCTOBER, 1965, REVOLUTION IN AFRICA. BIBLIOGRAPHY IN RUSSIAN INCLUDES TRAVELERS' WRITINGS ON GEOGRAPHY AND PEOPLE IN AFRICA AND INVESTIGATIONS ON VARIOUS COUNTRIES.

0688 DAVIES U.P. JR.
FOREIGN AND OTHER AFFAIRS.
NEW YORK: W W NORTON, 1964, 219 PP., LC#63-09879.
CRITIZES ALLEGED UNREALISTIC APPROACH OF US FOREIGN POLICY IN 1960'S, INCLUDING GRAND DESIGN FOR UNITED EUROPE, ALLIANCE FOR PROGRESS, POLICY IN SOUTHEAST ASIA, AND FOREIGN AID.

0689 DAVIS E.P.
PERIODICALS OF INTERNATIONAL ORGANIZATIONS; PART I, THE UN AND SPECIALIZED AGENCIES; PART II, INTER-AMERICAN ORGS.
WASHINGTON: PAN AMERICAN UNION, 1950, 21 PP.
GENERAL INDEX AND ANNOTATED LISTING OF PERIODICALS OF GOVERNMENTAL AND INTERNATIONAL ORGANIZATIONS. LISTS ONLY THE MORE IMPORTANT PERIODICALS OF MAJOR ORGANIZATIONS OF INTERGOVERNMENTAL CHARACTER SUCH AS UN, OAS, ETC. THREE CATEGORIES OF ORGANIZATION: WORLDWIDE, REGIONAL, AND POSTWAR TRANSITIONAL BODIES. SPANISH, ENGLISH.

0690 DAVIS H.B.
"LENIN AND NATIONALISM: THE REDIRECTION OF THE MARXIST THEORY OF NATIONALISM."
SCIENCE AND SOCIETY, 31 (SPRING 67), 64-185.
EXAMINES THE SCOPE AND DEPTH OF LENIN'S STUDY OF NATIONALISM. STRESSES IDEOLOGICAL SIMILARITIES BETWEEN STALIN AND LENIN AND DISTINGUISHES THE PARTICULARLY LENINIST VIEW THAT NATIONALISM TO OPPOSE OPPRESSION IS JUSTIFIABLE. REVEALS LENIN'S OPINIONS OF NATURAL-CULTURAL AUTONOMY, PATRIOTISM, INTERNATIONALISM, THE DIALECTICS OF NATIONALISM, IMPERIALISM AND NATIONALISM, AND RELATED TOPICS.

0691 DAVIS H.E.
PIONEERS IN WORLD ORDER.
NEW YORK: COLUMB. U. PR., 1944, 272 PP.
COLLECTION OF ESSAYS EVALUATING THE WORK OF THE LEAGUE OF NATIONS, COVERING THE ORGANIZATIONAL, ECONOMIC, POLITICAL, AND SOCIAL ASPECTS.

0692 DAVIS V.
POSTWAR DEFENSE POLICY AND THE US NAVY, 1943-1946.
CHAPEL HILL: U OF N CAR PR, 1966, 371 PP., LC#66-15503.
WAYS IN WHICH NAVY OFFICERS IN POLICY-MAKING POSITIONS FOLLOWING WWII THOUGHT ABOUT, PLANNED, AND TRIED TO PREPARE THE NAVY FOR POSTWAR ERA AND AMERICA'S CONFRONTATION WITH USSR. DESCRIBES THEIR POLITICAL EFFORTS AT GETTING THEIR VIEWS ACCEPTED.

0693 DAVISON W.P.
INTERNATIONAL POLITICAL COMMUNICATION.
NEW YORK: FREDERICK PRAEGER, 1965, 404 PP., LC#65-24723.
SEARCHES FOR WAYS US CAN UTILIZE PUBLIC COMMUNICATION MORE EFFECTIVELY TO ADVANCE ITS FOREIGN POLICIES. ATTEMPTS REALISTICALLY TO EVALUATE POLITICAL EFFECTS OF NEWSPAPERS, RADIO, FILM, AND EXCHANGE OF PERSONS. SUGGESTS THAT CORNERSTONE OF INTERNATIONAL COMMUNICATION POLICY SHOULD BE TRADITION OF FREE PUBLIC DISCUSSION. GOVERNMENT PROGRAMS SHOULD ADHERE TO STANDARDS OF OBJECTIVITY AND TRUTHFULNESS.

0694 DAWSON K.H.
"THE UNITED NATIONS IN A DISUNITED WORLD."
WORLD POLIT., 6 (JAN. 54), 209-35.
STUDIES FAILURE OF LEAGUE OF NATIONS. CRITICIZES COMMON TENDENCY NOWADAYS TO ATTRIBUTE THIS FAILURE TO SOME DEFECT IN THE ORIGINAL MACHINERY RATHER THAN TO LACK OF ADEQUATE SUPPORT FROM ITS MEMBERS. CONCLUDES THAT UN, BY INTRODUCING SPECIFIC COOPERATIVE TECHNIQUES, IS CONTINUALLY GAINING NEW SUPPORT.

0695 DAWSON R.H.
THE DECISION TO AID RUSSIA* FOREIGN POLICY AND DOMESTIC POLITICS.
CHAPEL HILL: U OF N CAR PR, 1959, 315 PP.
DESCRIBES PROCESS OF POLICY-MAKING WHICH RESULTED IN DECISION TO EXTEND LEND-LEASE TO RUSSIA, 1941. SHOWS RLATION OF THIS SERIES OF DECISIONS CONCERNING POLICY TOWARDS SOVIET UNION TO BROADER COMPLEX OF FOREIGN POLICY PROBLEMS WHICH SIMULTANEOUSLY CONFRONTED US OFFICIALS. RELATES DECISION TO AID SOVIET UNION TO CLIMATE OF PUBLIC OPINION.

0696 DE ARECHAGA E.J.
VOTING AND THE HANDLING OF DISPUTES IN THE SECURITY COUNCIL.
NEW YORK: CARNEGIE ENDOWMENT, 1950, 182 PP.
EXAMINES EARLY SECURITY COUNCIL DECISIONS AND LATER TRENDS. DESCRIBES UN VETO VOTE, PRESENT-DAY HANDLING OF DISPUTES, METHODS OF AVOIDING OR ENDING HOSTILITIES, AND INVESTIGATORY POWERS.

0697 DE BLIJ H.J.
SYSTEMATIC POLITICAL GEOGRAPHY.
NEW YORK: JOHN WILEY, 1967, 618 PP., LC#66-28752.
PRESENTS INTRODUCTION TO FIELD OF POLITICAL GEOGRAPHY, WITH PROFESSIONAL PAPERS AND CASE STUDIES. DISCUSSES RISE OF NATION-STATE, ITS ELEMENTS, RESTRICTIONS, FUNCTIONS, AND ROLE IN GEOPOLITICAL ACTIVITY, AND ITS INTERNAL STRUCTURE. APPLIES STUDY TO COLONIALISM, SUPRA-NATIONALISM, AND EMERGENT WORLD FORCES.

0698 DE BLOCH J.
THE FUTURE OF WAR IN ITS TECHNICAL, ECONOMIC, AND POLITICAL RELATIONS (1899)
BOSTON: WORLD PEACE FOUNDATION, 1914, 380 PP.
SUMMARY FOR POPULAR USE OF ORIGINAL RUSSIAN AND FRENCH EDITIONS. THESIS IS THAT WAR IN EUROPE IS IMPOSSIBLE. THIS ASSUMPTION IS BASED ON THE FACT THAT THE INCREASED FIREPOWER AND ACCURACY OF RIFLES AND ARTILLERY WILL MEAN SUICIDE TO ANY ATTACKING ARMY. ALSO ARGUES THAT MODERN WAR WOULD BE SO COSTLY AS TO BANKRUPT ANY NATION. CONCLUDES THAT NATIONS WILL AVOID WAR.

0699 DE CALLIERES F.
THE PRACTICE OF DIPLOMACY.
LONDON: CONSTABLE, 1919, 146 PP.
OUTLINES PERSONAL QUALITIES AND RANGE OF KNOWLEDGE AUTHOR CLAIMS ARE NECESSARY FOR NEGOTIATORS IN EXECUTING INSTRUCTIONS. REGARDS DIPLOMACY AS AN 'ART.'

0700 DE CONDE A.
A HISTORY OF AMERICAN FOREIGN POLICY.
NEW YORK: CHAS SCRIBNER'S SONS, 1963, 914 PP., LC#63-7615.
INTRODUCTION TO HISTORY OF AMERICAN FOREIGN POLICY, EMBODYING LATEST SCHOLARSHIP. ANALYZES MAIN FORCES AND IDEAS SHAPING POLICY AND COURSES FOLLOWED. PRIMARY EMPHASIS IS ON BROAD POLICY. CARRIES HISTORY THROUGH EARLY SIXTIES.

0701 DE GAULLE C.
THE EDGE OF THE SWORD.
NEW YORK: CRITERION, 1960, 128 PP., LC#59-12197.
DISCUSSES POSTWAR POSITION AND DEFENSE ATTITUDES IN EUROPE AND FRANCE. FEELS INTERNATIONAL AGREEMENTS HAVE LITTLE WEIGHT UNLESS SUPPORTED BY TROOPS. HOPES MILITARY ELITE WILL ONCE MORE ASSUME ITS DUTY AND PREPARE FOR WAR.

0702 DE GAULLE C.
"FRENCH WORLD VIEW."
UNITED ASIA, 16 (MAR.-APR. 64), 107-11.
PROCLAIMS FRENCH CONTRIBUTION TO SHRINKING WORLD, MUTUAL BENEFITS OF AID TO DECOLONIZED REGIONS, REASONS FOR ESTABLISHING DIPLOMATIC RELATION WITH CHINA.

0703 DE HERRERA C.D. ED.
LISTA BIBLIOGRAFICA DE LOS TRABAJOS DE GRADUACION Y TESIS PRESENTADOS EN LA UNIVERSIDAD, 1939-1960.
PANAMA CITY: U OF PANAMA, 1960, 186 PP.
COMPILATION OF THESES PRESENTED AT THE UNIVERSITY OF PANAMA. ENTRIES ARRANGED BY FACULTY AND THE SCHOOLS WITHIN EACH.

0704 DE HUSZAR G.B. ED.
PERSISTENT INTERNATIONAL ISSUES.
NEW YORK: HARPER & ROW, 1947, 262 PP.
INDIVIDUAL ANALYSES OF EACH MAJOR PROBLEM FACING WORLD AFTER WWII OR ANY WAR. POINTS OUT FAILURES AFTER WWI. SUBJECTS INCLUDE: RELIEF, REFUGEES, HEALTH, FOOD, TRANSPORTATION, INDUSTRY, MONEY, LABOR, POLITICS, AND EDUCATION.

0705 DE KIEWIET C.W.
THE IMPERIAL FACTOR IN SOUTH AFRICA.
NEW YORK: CAMBRIDGE U PRESS, 1937, 341 PP.
STUDY OF COLONIAL HISTORY OF SOUTH AFRICA DURING 19TH CENTURY. DISCUSSES FAILURE OF BRITISH IMPERIAL POLICY AS WELL AS GENERAL CULTURAL PROBLEMS WHICH AROSE FROM CONTACT BETWEEN NATIVES AND WHITES.

0706 DE MADARIAGA S.
THE WORLD'S DESIGN.
LONDON: ALLEN UNWIN, 1938, 291 PP.
ANALYSIS OF PAST AND PRESENT IDEOLOGIES. OFFERS CRITIQUE OF LEAGUE OF NATIONS AND SUGGESTIONS FOR AN IDEOLOGY FOR FUTURE. ADVOCATES AN END TO SOVEREIGNTY. URGES WORLD-WIDE ORGANIZATION.

0707 DE MADARIAGA S.
"TOWARD THE UNITED STATES OF EUROPE."
ORBIS, 6 (OCT. 62), 422-34.
UNITY ON CONTINENTAL BASIS A NECESSITY FOR EUROPE SINCE NATIONALITY IS OUTDATED FORCE IN THE WORLD. ASSERTS THAT UNITY CAN BE ACHIEVED SUCCESSFULLY BY COUNTRIES SHARING COMMON CIVILIZATION. PROBLEMS IN UNIFICATION ARE: HOW MUCH SOVEREIGNTY SHOULD BE SURRENDERED AND HOW SHOULD IT BE ADMINISTERED.

0708 DE MARTENS G.F.
RECUEIL GENERALE DE TRAITES ET AUTRES ACTES RELATIFS AUX RAPPORTS DE DROIT INTERNATIONAL (41 VOLS.)
GREISWALD: LIBRAIRIE JULIUS ABEL.
LENGTHY SERIES FIRST BEGUN BY GEORGE MARTENS AND CONTINUED IN THE 20TH CENTURY BY HEINRICH TRIEPEL. COVERS TREATIES AND AGREEMENTS OF EUROPEAN COUNTRIES FOR PERIOD 1760-1944. ALTHOUGH PRIMARILY CONCERNED WITH EUROPEAN EVENTS RELATED TREATIES IN OTHER COUNTRIES ARE INCLUDED. IN FRENCH, ARRANGED ALPHABETICALLY AND CHRONOLOGICALLY.

0709 DE REPARAZ G.
GEOGRAFIA Y POLITICA.
BARCELONA: EDITORIAL MENTORA, 1929, 277 PP.
TWENTY-FIVE LESSONS OF NATURAL HISTORY, INCLUDING POLITICS AS A PRODUCT OF GEOGRAPHY, GEOGRA AND RUSSIAN REVOLUTION, GEOGRAPHIC ANALYSIS OF IBERIAN PENINSULA, GEOGRAPHY IN HISTRY OF CHILE.

0710 DE ROUGEMONT D.
"THE CAMPAIGN OF THE EUROPEAN CONGRESSES."
GOVERNMENT AND OPPOSITION, 22 (APR.-JULY 67), 329-349.
ARGUES THAT ERA OF CONGRESSES, 1947-49, PRECEDED A EUROPEAN REVOLUTION AND INAUGURATED COUNCIL OF EUROPE & COMMUNITY OF THE SIX. ATTEMPTS TO RECREATE PSYCHOLOGICAL AND HISTORICAL REALITY OF GREAT CONGRESSES. RECOLLECTIONS BASED ON PERSONAL JOURNAL AND LETTERS, DRAFTS, AND MINUTES OF COMMITTEES COLLECTED AT CENTRE EUROPEEN DE LA CULTURE IN GENEVA. CONCLUDES WITH CALL FOR FEDERAL EUROPE.

0711 DE RUSETT A.
STRENGTHENING THE FRAMEWORK OF PEACE.
LONDON: ROYAL INST OF INTL AFF, 1950, 225 PP.
A STUDY OF CURRENT PROPOSALS FOR AMENDING, DEVELOPING, OR REPLACING PRESENT INTERNATIONAL INSTITUTIONS FOR THE MAINTENANCE OF PEACE. PROPOSALS INCLUDE: STRENGTHENING THE UN, EMPLOYING AN INTERNATIONAL POLICE FORCE, CREATING A WORLD FEDERAL GOVERNMENT, AND UNIFYING EUROPE.

0712 DE SMITH S.A.
"CONSTITUTIONAL MONARCHY IN BURGANDA."
POLIT. QUART., 26 (JAN.-MAR. 55), 4-17.
SURVEYS POLITICAL SITUATION IN BURGANDA. PRESENTS HISTORY OF THE POLITICAL RELATIONS, THE VARIOUS REFORMS MADE, AND THE 1954 AGREEMENTS FOR INDEPENDENCE. INCLUDES DETAILED ANALYSIS OF THE DISCUSSIONS OF THE PROTECTORATE GOVERNMENT AND THE KINGDOM OF BURGANDA. CONCLUDES WITH COMMENTS ON THE PROBLEMS AND CHALLENGES OF POLITICAL INTEGRATION.

0713 DE SMITH S.A.
THE NEW COMMONWEALTH AND ITS CONSTITUTIONS.
LONDON: STEVENS, 1964, 312 PP.
SURVEYS GENERAL DEVELOPMENTS OF NEWLY SELF-GOVERNING COMMONWEALTH COUNTRIES, CONCENTRATING ON THOSE WHICH HAVE ACQUIRED NEW CONSTITUTIONS SINCE 1957. OUTLINES CONSTITUTIONAL STRUCTURE OF COMMONWEALTH ASSOCIATION AND TRANSITION OF NEW NATIONS TO SELF-GOVERNMENT. TREATS SAFEGUARDS AGAINST ABUSE OF MAJORITY POWER, BILLS OF RIGHTS AND PRESIDENTIAL REGIMES.

0714 DE VATTEL E.
THE LAW OF NATIONS.
ORIGINAL PUBLISHER NOT AVAILABLE, 1796, 563 PP.
LAW OF NATIONS IS A SCIENCE, "CONSISTING IN A JUST AND RATIONAL APPLICATION OF THE LAW OF NATURE" TO THE AFFAIRS OF MAN AND PRINCES. STUDY BASED ON CHRISTIAN WOLFF'S WORK ON SAME SUBJECT. DISAGREES WITH WOLFF THAT ESTABLISHMENT OF LAW IS VOLUNTARY. BELIEVES MEN RESORT TO LAW ONLY TO PROTECT THEMSELVES AGAINST "DEPRAVITY OF THE MULTITUDE." THERE ARE VOLUNTARY LAWS, BUT NECESSARY ONES COME FROM LAW OF NATURE.

0715 DE VICTORIA F., SCOTT G.B. ED.
DE INDIS ET DE JURE BELLI (1557) IN F. DE VICTORIA, DE INDIS ET DE JURE BELLI REFLECTIONES.
WASHINGTON: CARNEGIE ENDOWMENT, 1917, 475 PP.
WORK BY SPANISH THEOLOGIAN CONSISTS OF LECTURES ON THE RIGHTS OF THE INDIANS AND THE RIGHTS OF WAR. BELIEVES THAT CHRISTIANS MAY SERVE IN AND MAKE WAR. A WRONG COMMITTED IS THE ONLY JUST REASON FOR MAKING WAR. DISCUSSES PUNISHMENT OF WRONG-DOER. SUBJECTS DO NOT HAVE TO PARTICIPATE IF THEY BELIEVE WAR UNJUST. DISCUSSES LAWFULNESS OF KILLING, SEIZURE, ETC. RIGHTS OF INDIANS CONCERN RIGHTS TO PROPERTY.

0716 DE VISSCHER C.
THEORY AND REALITY IN PUBLIC INTERNATIONAL LAW.
PRINCETON: U. PR., 1957, 381 PP.
EXAMINES CONTENTS OF INTERNATIONAL LAW AND STUDIES POLITICAL SYSTEMS, POWER, POWER RELATIONSHIPS, IDEOLOGIES AND INTERNATIONAL INSTITUTIONS. CONCLUDES THAT DESPITE LIMITATIONS, INTERNATIONAL LAW CAN GENERATE PRINCIPLES TO GUIDE SOVEREIGNTIES TOWARDS SUPPORTING HUMAN VALUES.

0717 DEAN A.W.
"SECOND GENEVA CONFERENCE OF THE LAW OF THE SEA: THE FIGHT FOR FREEDOM OF THE SEAS."
AMER. J. INT. LAW, 54-55 (OCT.60 - JULY 61), 751-89, 675-80.
ATTEMPTS TO SETTLE CONTROVERSIES OVER WIDTH OF TERRITORIAL SEA. SHOWS DANGERS TO FREEDOM OF NAVIGATION, FREE COMMERCE, AND COMMUNICATION INHERENT IN ANY EXTENSION. STUDIES COMPROMISE BETWEEN USA PROPOSED SIX MILE LIMIT AND USSR PLAN FOR TWELVE MILE EXTENSION OF RIGHTS. ALSO RECOUNTS PREVIOUS AGREEMENTS OVER AIR SPACE AND RELATED ISSUES.

0718 DEAN V.M.
THE NATURE OF THE NON-WESTERN WORLD.
NEW YORK: MENTOR, 1957, 284 PP.
COMPARES THE WEST AND THE NON-WEST (AFRICA, ASIA, THE MIDDLE EAST, USSR, THE FAR EAST, AND LATIN AMERICA) IN THEIR HISTORICAL DEVELOPMENTS AND PRESENT-DAY CONDITIONS, CONCLUDING THAT THE BASIC DIFFERENCES ARISE FROM THE WEST'S EARLIER TECHNOLOGICAL DEVELOPMENT. SUGGESTS DIFFERENCES ARE DECREASING DUE TO CURRENT NON-WESTERN TECHNOLOGICAL PROGRESS AND THAT WEST SHOULD ASSIST IN THIS PROGRESS.

0719 DEAN V.M.
BUILDERS OF EMERGING NATIONS.
NEW YORK: HOLT RINEHART WINSTON, 1961, 277 PP., LC#61-08068.
DISCUSSES MEN AND IDEAS SHAPING EMERGING NATIONS. INCLUDES PORTRAITS OF 18 LEADERS, AND DISCUSSES AUTHORITARIANISM, ECONOMIC DEVELOPMENT, SOCIAL TRANSFORMATIONS, AND FOREIGN POLICIES.

0720 DEANE H.
THE WAR IN VIETNAM (PAMPHLET)
NEW YORK: MONTHLY REVIEW PR, 1963, 32 PP., LC#63-19862.
ANALYZES WAR IN VIETNAM SINCE 1954, SHOWING HOW US IS TRYING ONLY TO PROTECT ITS ECONOMIC INTERESTS AND RETAIN "FEUDAL REGIME" IN SOUTH. COMPARES US TACTICS TO NAZIS'. STRESSES THAT ALL US SEEKS TO DO IS STOP COMMUNISM, OR ANY FORM OF SOCIALISM THAT THREATENS CAPITALISM, AT ANY PRICE. REFERS TO AVAILABLE DOCUMENTATION.

0721 DECOTTIGNIES R., BIEVILLE MARC D.E.
LES NATIONALITES AFRICAINES.
PARIS: EDITIONS A PEDONE, 1963, 419 PP.
CONCERNS LAW IN AFRICAN STATES WHICH WERE FORMER FRENCH COLONIES. ATTEMPTS TO DISTINGUISH COMMON MANIFESTATIONS OF LAW IN STATES. STUDIES SPECIFIC LAW IN 14 STATES AND REPRODUCES ACTUAL CODES.

0722 DEENER D.R. ED.
CANADA - UNITED STATES TREATY RELATIONS.
DURHAM: DUKE U PR, 1963, 250 PP., LC#63-13312.
GENERAL AND SPECIFIC TREATMENT OF CANADA'S TREATY

RELATIONS WITH US SINCE 1782. POLITICS, STRATEGY, PROBLEMS, AND CASE STUDIES ARE INCLUDED.

0723 DEGRAS J. ED.
THE COMMUNIST INTERNATIONAL, 1919-1943: DOCUMENTS (3 VOLS.)
LONDON: OXFORD U PR, 1956.
DOCUMENTS INCLUDE PROGRAMMATIC AND THEORETICAL STATEMENT OF COMMUNIST INTERNATIONAL FORMULATING GENERAL POLICY; STATEMENTS ON CURRENT EVENTS; LETTERS TO AND RESOLUTIONS ON NATIONAL COMMUNIST PARTIES; DOCUMENTS REFERRING TO PARTY'S INTERNAL ORGANIZATION. INTRODUCTORY REMARKS GIVE BRIEFLY THE CONTEXT OF DOCUMENT. CONCLUDES WITH LIST OF SOURCES.

0724 DEHIO L.
GERMANY AND WORLD POLITICS IN THE TWENTIETH CENTURY.
NEW YORK: ALFRED KNOPF, 1959, 142 PP.
GERMAN HISTORIAN ANALYZES PART PLAYED BY GERMANY IN POLITICS OF 1900-1950 AND SUGGESTS IDEAS OF GERMANS ABOUT WHAT THAT PART SHOULD BE. RELATES RANKE AND BISMARCK TO RISE OF GERMAN IMPERIALISM AND CONSIDERS IMPACT OF THIS ON TWO WORLD WARS. CONSIDERS VERSAILLES 35 YEARS AFTER RATIFICATION AND THEORIZES ON THE PASSING OF THE EUROPEAN SYSTEM AS CENTER OF WORLD POWER.

0725 DEHIO L.
THE PRECARIOUS BALANCE: FOUR CENTURIES OF THE EUROPEAN POWER STRUGGLE.
NEW YORK: ALFRED KNOPF, 1962, 295 PP.
DISCUSSES EUROPEAN SYSTEM OF STATES FROM MIDDLE AGES TO PRESENT. EXAMINES THREATS TO UNITY PRESENTED BY SPANISH, FRENCH, AND GERMAN "BIDS FOR SUPREMACY."

0726 DEITCHMAN S.J.
LIMITED WAR AND AMERICAN DEFENSE POLICY.
CAMBRIDGE: M.I.T. PR., 1964, 273 PP., $10.00.
DEALS WITH MILITARY, POLITICAL, AND TECHNICAL ASPECTS OF EFFECTIVE STRATEGY IN LIMITED WAR. ASSESSES MILITARY SYSTEMS AND THEIR DEPLOYMENT. POINTS UP SPECIAL PROBLEMS OF UNCONVENTIONAL WARFARE.

0727 DELANEY R.F.
THE LITERATURE OF COMMUNISM IN AMERICA.
WASHINGTON: CATHOLIC U PR, 1962, 433 PP.
ANNOTATED BIBLIOGRAPHY OF BOOKS, PERIODICALS, AND GOVERNMENT PAMPHLETS COMPRISING AN INTRODUCTION TO THE MAJOR AREAS OF COMMUNIST ACTIVITY, BOTH NATIONAL AND INTERNATIONAL. CONCENTRATES ON THE DANGERS POSED BY COMMUNIST STRATEGY, TACTICS, AND OBJECTIVES TO THE "FREE WORLD." COVERS THE RISE AND DEVELOPMENT OF COMMUNISM IN THE US, TOGETHER WITH ANALYSIS OF THE UNDERLYING THEORY AND ANTECEDENT HISTORY.

0728 DELGADO J.
"EL MOMENTO POLITICO HISPANOAMERICA."
REV. INST. CIENC. SOC., (NO.3, 64), 105-20.
COMPARES POLITICAL INFLUENCE OF USA TO THAT OF CHINA AND USSR IN SOUTH AND CENTRAL AMERICA. SEES MAJOR TRENDS AS INVOLVING CHOICE OF DEMOCRACY, AUTHORITARIANISM, AND GROWTH OF HISPANIC NATIONALISM. SPECIAL REFERENCE MADE TO USA-PANAMA CRISIS.

0729 DELLA PORT G.
"PROBLEMI E PROSPETTIVE DI COESISTENZA FRA ORIENTE ED OCCIDENTE, (PART 3)."
COMUN. INT., 16 (JULY 61), 503-26.
EFFECTS OF EAST-WEST RELATIONS ON UNCOMMITTED COUNTRIES. PROBLEMS OF INTERNATIONAL PAYMENTS, PRICES, FOREIGN AID TECHNIQUES.

0730 DELZELL C.F.
MUSSOLINI'S ENEMIES - THE ITALIAN ANTI-FASCIST RESISTANCE.
PRINCETON: PRINCETON U PRESS, 1961, 620 PP., LC#61-7406.
EXAMINES UNDERGROUND OPPOSITION TO ITALIAN FASCISM FROM 1924 TO END OF WWII. DISCUSSES ROLE OF CHURCH, COMMUNISTS, AND VARIOUS PARTISAN MOVEMENTS. DESCRIBES IN DETAIL MILITARY OPERATIONS AGAINST EXISTING ORDER.

0731 DEMAS W.G.
THE ECONOMICS OF DEVELOPMENT IN SMALL COUNTRIES WITH SPECIAL REFERENCE TO THE CARIBBEAN.
MONTREAL: MCGILL U PR, 1965, 150 PP., LC#65-26563.
PROBES NATURE OF ECONOMIC GROWTH IN SMALL COUNTRIES, DISTINGUISHING ITS PROBLEMS FROM THOSE OF LARGER DEVELOPING NATIONS. COVERS SELF-SUSTAINED GROWTH IN UNDERDEVELOPED AREAS. DISCUSSES SPECIFIC SITUATION OF CARIBBEAN ECONOMIES CONCERNING THEIR SPECIAL CHARACTERISTICS AND PROBLEMS IN PLANNING.

0732 DERWINSKI E.J.
"THE COST OF THE INTERNATIONAL COFFEE AGREEMENT."
INTER. AMER. ECON. AFF., 18 (AUTUMN 64), 93-96.
CONGRESSMAN DERWINSKI ACCUSES STATE DEPARTMENT OF MANIPULATING EXPORT-QUOTAS OF THE COFFEE AGREEMENT IN ORDER TO PROVIDE IMMENSE EXPANSION IN FOREIGN AID DONATIONS. DEPARTMENT IS CRITICIZED FOR FAILURE TO FULFILL ITS PLEDGE TO CONGRESS.

0733 DESHMUKH C.D.
THE COMMONWEALTH AS INDIA SEES IT.
NEW YORK: CAMBRIDGE U PRESS, 1964, 34 PP.
BRIEFLY TRACES INDIA'S POSITION IN BRITISH COMMONWEALTH FROM 1858 TO INDEPENDENCE AFTER WWII. DISCUSSES ADVANTAGES GAINED FROM CONTINUED MEMBERSHIP IN COMMONWEALTH AND ATTITUDE OF INDIAN PUBLIC OFFICIALS TOWARD COMMONWEALTH ASSOCIATION.

0734 DETHINE P.
BIBLIOGRAPHIE DES ASPECTS ECONOMIQUES ET SOCIAUX DE L'INDUSTRIALISATION EN AFRIQUE.
BRUSSELS: CEN DOC ECO ET SOC AFR, 1961, 136 PP.
AN ANNOTATED BIBLIOGRAPHY OF 726 ENTRIES COVERING THE ECONOMIC AND SOCIAL FACTORS INVOLVED IN THE INDUSTRIALIZATION OF THE THIRD WORLD. SELECTIONS ARE INTERNATIONAL IN SCOPE AND WERE CHOSEN FROM 1940-60 PUBLICATIONS. ARRANGED IN ONE COMPREHENSIVE ALPHABETICAL LIST.

0735 DEUTSCH K.W.
"NATIONALISM AND SOCIAL COMMUNICATION: AN INQUIRY INTO THE FOUNDATIONS OF NATIONALITY."
CAMBRIDGE: M I T PRESS, 1953.
THEORY OF ORIGINS OF ETHNIC NATIONALITY BASED ON CONCEPTION OF A PEOPLE AS A COMMUNITY OF SOCIAL COMMUNICATION. SURVEYS OTHER THEORIES OF ORIGIN OF NATIONALISM; REVIEWS BASIC SOCIAL SCIENCE CONCEPTS RELEVANT TO UNDERSTANDING OF NATIONALISM. OFFERS QUANTITATIVE AND QUALITATIVE INSTITUTIONAL FACTORS RELEVANT TO DEVELOPMENT OF NATIONAL UNITY. BIBLIOGRAPHY ARRANGED BY FIELD.

0736 DEUTSCH K.W.
POLITICAL COMMUNITY AND THE NORTH ATLANTIC AREA: INTERNATIONAL ORGANIZATION IN THE LIGHT OF HISTORICAL EXPERIENCE.
PRINCETON: U. PR., 1957, 228 PP.
HISTORICAL STUDY OF PAST EXPERIENCES OF WESTERN STATES IN FINDING MEANS TO ELIMINATE WAR. TRACES THE ATTEMPTS AT POLITICAL INTEGRATION, SUGGESTING CONDITIONS WHICH ARE NECESSARY FOR SUCH A PROCESS OR FOR THE FORMATION OF A COMMUNITY SECURITY SYSTEM.

0737 DEUTSCH K.W.
"MASS COMMUNICATIONS AND THE LOSS OF FREEDOM IN NATIONAL DECISION MAKING."
J. CONFL. RESOLUT., 1 (JUNE 57), 200-11.
PROPOSED RESEARCH METHOD FOR DEVELOPING TECHNIQUES IN THREE IMPORTANT AREAS: IDENTIFICATION OF CONFLICT SITUATIONS LIKELY TO IGNITE WAR, THE EVALUATION OF PARTICULAR CONFLICT SITUATIONS, AND THEIR PROBABLE CAUSES OF DEVELOPMENT. ALSO SUGGESTS FURTHER POSSIBLE TECHNIQUES FOR CONTROLLING SUCH SITUATIONS.

0739 DEUTSCH K.W.
"TOWARD AN INVENTORY OF BASIC TRENDS AND PATTERNS IN COMPARATIVE AND INTERNATIONAL POLITICS."
AMER. POLIT. SCI. REV., 54 (MARCH 60), 34-58.
ANALYZES TYPES AND MODELS OF POLITICAL BEHAVIOR IN ORDER FIND BEHAVIOR PATTERN OF PARTICULAR STATE UNDER PARTICULAR CIRCUMSTANCES. DISCUSSES METHODS OF EVALUATING QUANTATIVE DATE WITH HELP OF NUMEROUS DATA CHARTS AND STATISTICS.

0740 DEUTSCH K.W., ECKSTEIN A.
"NATIONAL INDUSTRIALIZATION AND THE DECLINING SHARE OF THE INTERNATIONAL ECONOMIC SECTOR."
WORLD POLIT., 13 (JAN. 61), 267-99.
GIVES SOME REASONS THAT RENDER PLAUSIBLE THE THESIS THAT THE RATIO OF FOREIGN TRADE TO NATIONAL INCOME WILL CONTINUE TO DECLINE IN MANY COUNTRIES, AS WELL AS THE WORLD AS A WHOLE, FOR SOME TIME TO COME.

0741 DEUTSCH K.W.
"TOWARDS WESTERN EUROPEAN INTEGRATION: AN INTERIM ASSESSMENT."
J. INT. AFF., 16 (1962), 89-101.
TENTATIVELY ASSESSES RESULTS OF THE POLICIES OF WESTERN EUROPEAN UNIFICATION DURING THE PERIOD 1946-1961. CONSIDERS THE STEPS AND PROBLEMS ON THE PATH TO FURTHER UNIFICATION. SCRUTINIZES QUESTION OF UNIVERSAL AND SPECIFIC AS OPPOSED TO PARTICULAR AND DIFFUSE SUPRA-NATIONAL ORGANIZATIONS. ANOTHER DECADE OF EUROPEAN PLURALISM BUT MODIFYING INFLUENCES ASTIR.

0742 DEUTSCH K.W.
"ARMS CONTROL AND EUROPEAN UNITY* THE NEXT TEN YEARS."
BUL. ATOMIC SCIENTISTS, 23 (MAY 67), 21-24.
A DISCUSSION, BASED ON EXTENSIVE RESEARCH FOR A FORTHCOMING BOOK, OF EUROPEAN ATTITUDES TOWARD ARMS CONTROL, EUROPEAN UNITY AND THE ATLANTIC ALLIANCE, AND INDEPENDENT NUCLEAR FORCES. WHILE EUROPEAN INTEGRATION IS EXPECTED TO PROCEED SLOWLY, THERE IS GENERAL AGREEMENT AS TO THE DESIRABILITY OF DECREASED INTERNATIONAL TENSION AND OF ARMS CONTROL, AND THE UNDESIRABILITY OF EXPANDED NUCLEAR FORCES.

0743 DEUTSCHE BIBLIOTH FRANKF A M
DEUTSCHE BIBLIOGRAPHIE.
FRANKFURT: DEUT BIBLIOG FRANKFE.
WEEKLY REGISTER (JAN 1965-JULY 1967) LISTING BOOKS

PUBLISHED IN THE PRECEDING YEARS (1965 AND 1966). ARRANGED BY SUBJECT AND HAS SUCH CLASSIFICATIONS AS PHILOSOPHY, LAW, AND ADMINISTRATION, SOCIAL SCIENCES, POLITICS, DEFENSE, FINE ARTS, ETC. HAS A SUBJECT-AUTHOR INDEX. FOREIGN PUBLICATIONS INCLUDED.

0744 DEUTSCHE BUCHEREI
DEUTSCHE NATIONALBIBLIOGRAPHIE.
LEIPZIG: VEB VERLAG FUR BUCH-BIBL.
QUARTERLY PUBLICATION LISTING CURRENT BOOKS, PAMPHLETS, AND DISSERTATIONS NOT AVAILABLE THROUGH THE REGULAR BOOK-TRADE. ARRANGEMENT IS BY SUBJECT AND RANGES FROM CATEGORIES SUCH AS CLASSICS OF MARXISM/LENINISM TO SUCH DIVERSE ITEMS AS HISTORY, YOUTH MOVEMENTS, AND PHILOSOPHY. INCLUDES FOREIGN ITEMS IF IN GERMAN.

0745 DEUTSCHE BUCHEREI
JAHRESVERZEICHNIS DES DEUTSCHEN SCHRIFTUMS.
LEIPZIG: VEB VERLAG FUR BUCH-BIBL.
ANNUAL BIBLIOGRAPHY OF BOOKS IN GERMAN PUBLISHED DURING THE PERIOD UNDER CONSIDERATION IN GERMANY, AUSTRIA, SWITZERLAND, AND OTHER COUNTRIES. EACH VOLUME DIVIDED INTO TWO SECTIONS: WORKS ORGANIZED BY AUTHOR; WORKS INDEXED UNDER SUBJECT.

0746 DEUTSCHE BUCHEREI
DEUTSCHES BUCHERVERZEICHNIS.
LEIPZIG: VEB VERLAG FUR BUCH-BIBL.
ANNUAL LISTING OF PRIMARY PUBLICATIONS IN BOTH EAST AND WEST GERMANY. ENTRIES ARRANGE ALPHABETICALLY BY AUTHOR WITH A SUBJECT INDEX. FIRST PUBLISHED 1911.

0747 DEUTSCHE GES AUSWARTIGE POL
STRATEGIE UND ABRUSTUNGSPOLITIK DER SOWJETUNION.
ALFRED METZNER VERLAG, 1964, 346 PP.
COLLECTION OF PUBLIC ADDRESSES AND ESSAYS BY SOVIET POLITICIANS, MILITARY OFFICIALS, SCIENTISTS, AND JOURNALISTS ON QUESTIONS OF MILITARY STRATEGY AND DISARMAMENT. DISCUSSES POLITICAL AND PSYCHOLOGICAL PREPAREDNESS, MISSILE DEFENSE SYSTEMS, TECHNOLOGICAL PROBLEMS OF DISARMAMENT, CHARACTER OF MODERN WAR, ETC.

0748 DEUTSCHE GESELLS. VOELKERRECHT
DIE VOLKERRECHTLICHEN DISSERTATIONEN AN DEN WESTDEUTSCHEN UNIVERSITATEN, 1945-1957.
KARLSRUHE: DEUTSCHE GES. VOELKERRECHT, 1958, 52 PP.
BIBLIOGRAPHY OF WEST GERMAN DISSERTATIONS ON INTERNATIONAL LAW.

0749 DEUTSCHER I.
THE GREAT CONTEST: RUSSIA AND THE WEST.
NEW YORK: OXFORD U PR, 1960, 86 PP.
A LOOK AT SOVIET FOREIGN POLICY AND THE STATE OF INTERNATIONAL AFFAIRS. KEEPING IN MIND THAT FOREIGN POLICY IS GUIDED BY DOMESTIC, BRINGS INTO OPEN IMPLICATIONS OF PEACEFUL COEXISTENCE AND COMPETITION WHICH WILL DETERMINE OUTCOME OF EAST-WEST CONTEST; MAKES BLATANT PLEA FOR

0750 DEVADHAR Y.C.
"THE ROLE OF FOREIGN PRIVATE CAPITAL IN INDIA'S ECONOMIC DEVELOPMENT* ASSESSMENT OF POLICY AND PERFORMANCE."
INT. STUDIES, 8 (JAN. 67), 242-277.
ATTEMPTS BROAD EVALUATION OF OFFICIAL POLICY ON FOREIGN CAPITAL INVESTMENT IN INDIAN ECONOMY DURING PAST 15 YEARS. DISCUSSES EVOLUTION OF POLICY, PATTERNS AND MOTIVATIONS OF FOREIGN PRIVATE INVESTMENTS, BALANCE OF PAYMENTS IMPLICATIONS OF INVESTMENTS, LEGAL AND COLLABORATION PROBLEMS.

0751 DEVILLERS P.H.
"L'URSS, LA CHINE ET LES ORIGINES DE LA GUERRE DE COREE."
REV. FRANCE SCI. POLIT., 6 (DEC-64), 1179-1194.
HISTORICAL EVOLUTION OF KOREAN CONFLICT. DEPICTS WAR AS RESULT OF NORTH KOREAN INITIATIVE. MENTIONS EFFORTS OF RUSSIANS TO RESTRAIN THE NORTH KOREANS AND ALSO THE BEGINNING OF RUSSO-CHINESE CONFLICT.

0752 DEWEY J.
"ETHICS AND INTERNATIONAL RELATIONS."
FOR. AFF., 1 (MAR. 23), 85-95.
EXAMINES DEMISE OF NATURAL LAW AS APPLICABLE TO INTERNATIONAL RELATIONS. POSITS FAILURE OF BOTH HEGELIAN AND UTILITARIAN ETHICAL POSITIONS. ADVOCATES WORLD-WIDE AGREEMENT TO OUTLAW WAR AS FIRST STEP TOWARD A MODERN INTERNATIONAL ETHICS.

0753 DIA M.
THE AFRICAN NATIONS AND WORLD SOLIDARITY.
NEW YORK: PRAEGER, 1961, 145 PP., $4.85.
PRIME MINISTER OF SENEGAL ANALYZES ECONOMIC PROBLEMS OF EMERGENT AFRICAN NATIONS. ADVOCATES LEOPOLD SENGHOR'S 'AFRICAN SOLIALISM', ARGUING AGAINST USE OF SOVIET MODEL. WRITTEN BEFORE DISSOLUTION OF WEST AFRICAN FEDERATION IN 1960.

0754 DIAS R.W.M.
A BIBLIOGRAPHY OF JURISPRUDENCE (2ND ED.)
LONDON: BUTTERWORTHS, 1964, 234 PP.
AN ANNOTATED BIBLIOGRAPHY OF LEGAL BOOKS AND PERIODICALS, DESIGNED TO ACCOMPANY THE SECOND EDITION OF THE TEXTBOOK ENTITLED "JURISPRUDENCE." ENTRIES ORGANIZED INTO 20 CATEGORIES OF LEGAL, SOCIOLOGICAL, AND ECONOMIC DISCIPLINE AND SPECIALTY. COVERS WORKS PUBLISHED THROUGH 1962, BUT MOST BOOKS LISTED WERE ISSUED BETWEEN 1900-1950. ANNOTATIONS CRITICAL AS WELL AS DESCRIPTIVE. SOURCES IN ENGLISH.

0755 DIAZ J.S.
MANUAL DE BIBLIOGRAFIA DE LA LITERATURA ESPANOLA.
BARCELONA: GUSTAVO GILI, 1962, 604 PP.
BIBLIOGRAPHY OF OVER 20,000 BOOKS PUBLISHED IN LATIN AMERICA AND SPAIN FROM THE MIDDLE AGES THROUGH 20TH CENTURY. ENTRIES ARE LISTED BY CENTURY OF PUBLICATION.

0756 DICKEY J.S. ED.
THE UNITED STATES AND CANADA.
ENGLEWOOD CLIFFS: PRENTICE HALL, 1964, 184 PP., LC#64-21215.
RELATIONSHIP BETWEEN US AND CANADA. A STUDY OF PROBLEMS ARISING OUT OF THEIR CLOSE PROXIMITY. OUTLOOK FOR THE RELATIONSHIP FROM A CANADIAN AND AN AMERICAN PERSPECTIVE. A SOCIOLOGIST'S VIEW.

0757 DICKINSON E.
THE EQUALITY OF STATES IN INTERNATIONAL LAW.
CAMBRIDGE: HARVARD U. PR., 1920, 424 PP.
DISCUSSES SOURCES OF PRINCIPLE OF EQUALITY OF STATES FROM ANTIQUITY TO MODERN TIMES. EXAMINES INTERNAL AND EXTERNAL LIMITATIONS ON EQUALITY OF STATES. CONCLUDES THAT PRINCIPLE CANNOT BE APPLIED TO INTERNATIONAL ORGANIZATION AND THAT IT WAS NOT APPLIED TO THE LEAGUE OF NATIONS.

0758 DICKS H.V.
"NATIONAL LOYALTY, IDENTITY, AND THE INTERNATIONAL SOLDIER."
INT. ORGAN., 17 (SPRING 63), 425-43.
A PROVOCATIVE APPLICATION OF LESSONS LEARNED FROM MORALE PROBLEMS OF NATIONAL ARMED FORCES TO A HYPOTHETICAL INTERNATIONAL CONSTABULARY.

0759 DIEBOLD W. JR.
THE SCHUMAN PLAN: A STUDY IN ECONOMIC COOPERATION, 1950-1959.
NEW YORK: PRAEGER, 1959, 750 PP.
RECOUNTS THE ORIGINS OF THE SCHUMAN PLAN AND EVENTS WHICH LED TO FORMATION OF THE EUROPEAN COAL AND STEEL COMMUNITY. CONSIDERS THE COMMUNITY'S OPERATIONS, DEVELOPMENTS, PROSPECTS, AND IMPLICATIONS FOR AMERICAN FOREIGN POLICY. DISCUSSES ITS RELATION TO PROSPECT OF EUROPEAN INTEGRATION.

0760 DIEBOLD W. JR.
"THE NEW SITUATION OF INTERNATIONAL TRADE POLICY."
INT. J., 18 (AUTUMN 63', 425-42.
CONSIDERS TRADE RELATIONS AMONG EUROPEAN COUNTRIES. EXAMINES COMMON MARKET AND ITS CHANGING DIRECTION AND TRADE EXPANSION ACT OF THE USA. COMMENTS ON COMMERCIAL QUESTIONS AND TRANSATLANTIC RELATIONS. SUGGESTS EQUAL TREATMENT OF ALL NATIONS IS THE ANSWER TO ECONOMIC BETTERMENT OF FREE WORLD.

0761 DIHN N.Q.
"L'INTERNATIONALISATION DU MEKONG."
ANNU. FRANC. DR. INTER., 8 (1962), 91-115.
ANALYZES TREATY SIGNED BY CAMBODIA, LAOS, AND VIETNAM ON DEC. 12, 1954. CONTENDS THAT ITS ECONOMIC FUNCTION WILL DETERMINE POLITICAL PATTERNS AMONG THESE COUNTRIES.

0762 DILLA H.M. ED., MARTIN C.C. ED.
CLASSIFIED LIST OF MAGAZINE ARTICLES ON THE EUROPEAN WAR.
WASHINGTON: LIBRARY OF CONGRESS, 1917, 33 PP.
LISTING OF ABOUT 500 ARTICLES PUBLISHED IN 1917 IN US CONCERNING INVOLVEMENT OF US IN WAR AS WELL AS INTERACTION WITH NONCOMBATANT NATIONS. MINUTELY CLASSIFIED AS TO SUBJECT BY EXTENSIVELY DETAILED OUTLINE.

0763 DILLARD D.
ECONOMIC DEVELOPMENT OF THE NORTH ATLANTIC COMMUNITY.
ENGLEWOOD CLIFFS: PRENTICE HALL, 1967, 747 PP., LC#67-15169.
CHRONOLOGICALLY ANALYZES NORTH ATLANTIC ECONOMY FROM MIDDLE AGES TO PRESENT, RELATING AND COMPARING EUROPEAN AND AMERICAN DEVELOPMENT. EXAMINES POLITICAL AND ECONOMIC RELATIONS, INDUSTRIALIZATION, LABOR ORGANIZATIONS, WAR, BALANCE-OF-PAYMENTS, AND ACTIONS OF COUNTRIES ON BOTH SIDES OF ATLANTIC REGARDING BACKWARD AREAS.

0764 DILLON D.R.
LATIN AMERICA, 1935-1949; A SELECTED BIBLIOGRAPHY.
NEW YORK: UNITED NATIONS, 1952.
COMPILATION OF IMPORTANT MATERIALS ON THE LAW, HISTORY, INTERNATIONAL RELATIONS, ECONOMICS, SOCIOLOGY, AND EDUCATION OF LATIN AMERICA IN GENERAL AND INDIVIDUAL NATIONS.

0765 DIMOCK M.E.
BUSINESS AND GOVERNMENT (4TH ED.)
NEW YORK: HOLT RINEHART WINSTON, 1961, 505 PP., LC#61-7854.

ORIGINAL ANALYSIS OF WORKING RELATIONS BETWEEN ECONOMIC ORGANIZATIONS AND GOVERNMENT, SUPPLEMENTED BY CONSIDERATIONS OF NEW LABOR LEGISLATION; RECESSIONS; FOREIGN AID PROGRAMS; COMMUNIST BLOC EXPENDITURES; SPACE PROGRAM; FARM POLICIES; ANTI-TRUST ENFORCEMENT; PUBLIC UTILITY REGULATION AND PUBLIC POWER PROJECTS. SUGGESTIONS FOR SUPPLEMENTARY READINGS FOLLOW EACH CHAPTER.

0766 DINH TRAN VAN
"VIETNAM: A THIRD WAY"
NEW POLITICS, 5 (FALL 66), 5-13.
VIEWS WAR IN VIETNAM AS A CIVIL CONFLICT, A PEASANT PROBLEM, AND A PROCESS OF SELF-IDENTIFICATION OF VIETNAMESE IN 20TH CENTURY. BUDDHIST-SOCIALIST BLOC PROPOSES NON-COMMUNIST, NON-AMERICAN WAY TO SOLVE THESE PROBLEMS AND END WAR. BLOC AIMS INCLUDE UNIFIED AND NEUTRALIST VIETNAM, RECONSTRUCTION OF SOCIETY AND ECONOMIC INDEPENDENCE, FREEDOM FROM MILITARY ALLIANCES, REMOVAL OF US-BACKED MILITARY.

0767 DODD S.C.
"THE SCIENTIFIC MEASUREMENT OF FITNESS FOR SELF-GOVERNMENT."
SCI. MON., 80 (FEB. 54), 94-99.
ESTABLISHES A CRITERIA FOR MEASURING FITNESS OF DEVELOPING NATIONS FOR ACHIEVING INDEPENDENCE. USES STATISTICAL INDICES TO MEASURE FITNESS FOR SELF-GOVERNMENT. THREE CYCLES OF MEASUREMENT ARE QUALITATIVE CYCLE, QUANTITATIVE, AND THE CORRELATIVE.

0768 DOHERTY D.K. ED.
PRELIMINARY BIBLIOGRAPHY OF COLONIZATION AND SETTLEMENT IN LATIN AMERICA AND ANGLO-AMERICA.
NEW YORK: INST HUMAN REL PRESS.
ISSUED IN ENGLISH, PORTUGUESE, AND SPANISH. EMPHASIZES PERSON AND AGENCIES ATTEMPTING COLONIZATION AND DEVELOPMENT.

0769 DOLE C.F.
THE AMERICAN CITIZEN.
BOSTON: D C HEATH, 1891, 315 PP.
DISCUSSION OF BASIC PRINCIPLES OF CITIZENSHIP AND POLITICAL HABITS OF AMERICAN CITIZEN. BASIC OBJECT IS TO "ILLUSTRATE THE MORAL PRINCIPLES WHICH UNDERLIE THE LIFE OF CIVILIZED MEN." DISCUSSION RANGES FROM STRICTLY PERSONAL POLITICAL HABITS TO FUNDAMENTAL PRINCIPLES OF INTERNATIONAL LAW.

0770 DOMENACH J.M.
LA PROPAGANDE POLITIQUE.
PARIS: PR UNIV DE FRANCE, 1965, 127 PP.
ANALYZES TECHNIQUES, RULES, AND SOURCES FOR PROPAGANDA IN THE 20TH CENTURY. EXAMINES THE PROCESSES OF MYTH-MAKING, EXAGGERATION, DISTORTION, ISOLATING A COMMON ENEMY, CREATING A UNANIMOUS FRONT, ETC. DEALS WITH CONDITIONS, SOCIAL FORCES, IDEOLOGICAL SOURCES, AND TECHNICAL DEVELOPMENTS IN PUBLICITY AND PSYCHOLOGY THAT HAVE PROMOTED PROPAGANDIZING AND THE MOLDING OF PUBLIC OPINION.

0771 DONALD A.D.
JOHN F. KENNEDY AND THE NEW FRONTIER.
NEW YORK: HILL AND WANG, 1966, 264 PP., LC#66-26031.
COLLECTION OF WRITINGS EXAMINING THE NATURE OF PRESIDENT KENNEDY'S LEADERSHIP, HIS GOALS, AND HIS ACCOMPLISHMENTS.

0772 DONOUGHUE B.
BRITISH POLITICS AND THE AMERICAN REVOLUTION: THE PATH TO WAR 1773-75.
NEW YORK: ST MARTIN'S PRESS, 1964, 324 PP., LC#64-21438.
EXAMINES ACTIVITIES OF BRITISH GOVERNMENT IMMEDIATELY PRIOR TO OUTBREAK OF WAR BETWEEN BRITAIN AND AMERICAN COLONIES. TRACES FORMATION OF BRITISH POLICY TOWARD AMERICA PRECEDING THE REVOLUTION.

0773 DORE R.
"BIBLIOGRAPHIE DES 'LIVRES JAUNES' A LA DATE DU 1ER JANVIER 1922."
REVUE DE BIBLIOTHEQUES, 32 (JULY-DEC. 22), 109-136, 7-12.
AN UNANNOTATED BIBLIOGRAPHY OF 213 OFFICIAL DIPLOMATIC DOCUMENTS DATING FROM 1861-1912. ORGANIZED GEOGRAPHICALLY WITHIN EACH CONTINENT AND SEPARATED INTO CATEGORIES OF POLITICAL, ECONOMIC, AND SOCIAL AFFAIRS. VOLUME INDEXED ALPHABETICALLY BY SUBJECT AND GEOGRAPHICALLY BY COUNTRY.

0774 DOS SANTOS M.
BIBLIOGRAPHIA GERAL, A DESCRIPCAO BIBLIOGRAFICA DE LIVROS TANTO DE AUTORES PORTUGUEZES COMO BRASILEIROS...
LISBON: TYPOGRAFIA MENDONCA, 1917.
DESCRIPTIVE BIBLIOGRAPHY OF BOOKS BY BRAZILIAN AND PORTUGUESE AUTHORS PRINTED FROM 15TH TO 20TH CENTURIES; CONCERNED WITH HISTORY OF BRAZIL AND PORTUGUESE POSSESSIONS.

0775 DOSSICK J.J.
"DOCTORAL DISSERTATIONS ON RUSSIA, THE SOVIET UNION, AND EASTERN EUROPE."
SLAVIC REVIEW, 25 (DEC. 65), 710-717.
COMPILES LIST OF 123 TITLES OF DOCTORAL THESES ACCEPTED BY AMERICAN, CANADIAN, AND BRITISH UNIVERSITIES. THIRTY-FIVE UNIVERSITIES LISTED. BULK OF MATERIAL PERTAINS TO SOCIAL SCIENCES, LITERATURE, AND LANGUAGE. BIBLIOGRAPHY ARRANGED TOPICALLY WITHOUT ANNOTATION OR INDEX.

0776 DOSSICK J.J.
DOCTORAL RESEARCH ON PUERTO RICO AND PUERTO RICANS.
NEW YORK: NEW YORK U PR, 1967, 34 PP.
LIST OF 320 DOCTORAL DISSERTATIONS ACCEPTED IN AMERICAN UNIVERSITIES DURING THE PAST 68 YEARS. FIFTY PER CENT ARE BY PUERTO RICANS. INCLUDES DISSERTATIONS ON POLITICAL SCIENCE AND RELATED DISCIPLINES. MANY ARE ON THE RELATIONSHIP TO THE US.

0777 DOUGHERTY J.E.
"KEY TO SECURITY: DISARMAMENT OR ARMS STABILITY."
ORBIS, 4 (FALL 60), 261-83.
SEES PROPOSALS FOR ARMS CONTROL AS FAILING DUE TO LACK OF APPROPRIATE LEGAL BASIS AND ABUNDANCE OF TECHNICAL COMPLEXITIES. CRITICIZES NUCLEAR MORATORIUM EXPERIENCE AS LACKING IN INSPECTION SAFEGUARDS AND LIMITING NEEDED RESEARCH. ADVOCATES OPEN EXPRESSION OF STRENGTH ON BOTH SIDES AND CONCRETE REDUCTIONS, AS ONLY WAY TO EFFECTIVE PROGRAM.

0778 DOUGLAS W.O.
"SYMPOSIUM ON WORLD ORGANIZATION."
YALE LAW J., 55 (AUG. 46), 865-869.
URGES DEVELOPMENT OF EFFECTIVE SYSTEM OF INTERNATIONAL LAW. REGARDS LAW AS HISTORY OF GROWTH AND MATURITY OF PEOPLE. IF USA INTENDS TO MEET CHANGING WORLD CONDITIONS, SYSTEM OF THIS NATURE A NECESSITY.

0779 DOUGLAS W.O.
DEMOCRACY'S MANIFESTO.
GARDEN CITY: DOUBLEDAY, 1962, 48 PP., LC#62-10468.
CALL BY JUSTICE DOUGLAS FOR IDEOLOGICAL COUNTER-OFFENSIVE IN WORLD AFFAIRS WARNING THAT OUR POLICIES IN RESPONSE TO COMMUNIST CHALLENGE HAVE BEEN NEGATIVE TO DATE, CITING ALLIANCE FOR PROGRESS AS APPROPRIATE EXAMPLE.

0780 DOUMA J. ED.
BIBLIOGRAPHY ON THE INTERNATIONAL COURT INCLUDING THE PERMANENT COURT, 1918-1964.
NEW YORK: HUMANITIES PRESS, 1966, 387 PP., LC#52-4918.
ANNOTATED BIBLIOGRAPHY COVERING 1918-64, PUBLISHED AS SUPPLEMENT TO SERIES BY HAMBRO. TWO PARTS: FIRST DEALS WITH PERMANENT COURT OF INTERNATIONAL JUSTICE; SECOND CONCERNS PRESENT COURT INSTITUTED BY UN. CONTAINS 3,572 ENTRIES IN SEVERAL LANGUAGES. INCLUDES INDEXES OF SUBJECTS AND AUTHORS.

0781 DOYLE S.E.
"COMMUNICATION SATELLITES* INTERNAL ORGANIZATION FOR DEVELOPMENT AND CONTROL."
CALIF. LAW REV., 55 (MAY 67), 431-448.
ARGUES THAT PROBLEM POSED BY COMMUNICATION SATELLITES IS ORGANIZATION OF INTERNATIONAL COOPERATIVE TO DEVELOP AND EXPLOIT SYSTEM. EXAMINES COMMUNICATIONS SATELLITE COOPERATION AND INTELSAT AND EXPLORES POLICY PROBLEMS THAT BECOME DIFFICULT AS SATELLITE TECHNOLOGY ADVANCES INCLUDING QUESTIONS OF PRIVATE OWNERSHIP AND DIRECT BROADCASTING.

0782 DRACHKOVITCH M.M.
UNITED STATES AID TO YUGOSLAVIA AND POLAND.
WASHINGTON: AMER ENTERPRISE INST, 1963, 124 PP., LC#63-19993
DESCRIBES US FOREIGN AID POLICY TOWARD YUGOSLAVIA AND POLAND, INCLUDING HISTORICAL RECORD, ADMINISTRATION'S CASE FAVORING AID, CASE AGAINST SUCH ASSISTANCE, AND A CONSIDERATION OF RELATED ISSUES.

0783 DRACHKOVITCH M.M.
"THE EMERGING PATTERN OF YUGOSLAV-SOVIET RELATIONS."
ORBIS, 5 (WINTER 62), 437-52.
GENERAL EVALUATION OF TITOIST FOREIGN POLICY, PARTICULARLY IN RELATION TO USSR, SOVIET BLOC, AND EMERGING BLOC OF NON-ALIGNED COUNTRIES. COMPARES AND CONTRASTS DIFFERENT APPROACHES TAKEN BY STALIN AND KHRUSHCHEV. PROBES FUTURE OF YUGOSLAVIA WITH OR WITHOUT TITO.

0784 DRACHKOVITCH M.M. ED., LAZITCH B. ED.
THE COMINTERN HISTORICAL HIGHLIGHTS.
NEW YORK: FREDERICK PRAEGER, 1966, 430 PP., LC#66-13962.
EXAMINES THE COMINTERN'S CLAIM TO MARXIST LEGITIMACY AND CONCLUDES THAT LENIN DRASTICALLY ALTERED MARX'S VIEWS. RECOLLECTIONS OF FORMER TOP LEADERS GIVE INSIGHT INTO THE PERSONALITIES THAT SHAPED COMINTERN POLICY.

0785 DRAKE S.T.C.
"DEMOCRACY ON TRIAL IN AFRICA."
ANN. AMER. ACAD. POLIT. SOC. SCI., 354 (JULY 64), 110-21.
SUGGESTS THAT AS POLITICAL AND SOCIAL CONDITIONS BECOME MORE STABLE AND IF AND WHEN SUSTAINED ECONOMIC GROWTH TAKES PLACE, SOME OF THE DEMOCRATIC VALUES NEVER KNOWN TO THE AFRICAN MASSES, AS WELL AS OTHERS WHICH HAVE BEEN SACRIFICED TO ACHIEVE NATIONAL UNITY AND RAPID MODERNIZATION WILL EMERGE.

0786 DREIER J.C.
THE ORGANIZATION OF AMERICAN STATES AND THE

HEMISPHERE CRISIS.
NEW YORK: HARPER, 1962, 147 PP.
ASSESSES ITS ACHIEVEMENTS AND ITS SHORTCOMINGS, ITS PROBLEMS AND OPPORTUNITIES. ANALYZES MAIN ISSUES ON WHICH FUTURE OF SYSTEM DEPENDS. 'HISTORIC CHANGE IN USA POLICY EXPRESSED IN THE ACT OF BOGOTA OF 1960 AND THE ALLIANCE FOR PROGRESS SHOULD SERVE TO REASSURE THE LATIN AMERICAN PEOPLES AND CREATE A BASIS FOR BUILDING A RENEWED CONFIDENCE.'

0787 DREIER J.C.
THE ALLIANCE FOR PROGRESS.
BALTIMORE: JOHNS HOPKINS PRESS, 1962, 146 PP., LC#62-18508.
LECTURES ON ALLIANCE FOR PROGRESS: HISTORICAL BACKGROUND, ECONOMIC ASPECTS, POLITICAL GOALS, SOCIAL CHANGE, AND POSITION IN INTERNATIONAL AFFAIRS.

0788 DRUCKER P.F.
AMERICA'S NEXT TWENTY YEARS.
NEW YORK: HARPER & ROW, 1957, 114 PP., LC#57-7974.
EXAMINES LABOR SHORTAGES AND ENROLLMENT PRESSURES ON COLLEGES AND UNIVERSITIES IN US IN LIGHT OF POPULATION EXPLOSION. DISCUSSES ROLE OF AUTOMATION IN ECONOMY AND CONCLUDES WITH ANALYSIS OF FOREIGN AID ISSUES AND SOME PRESSING ISSUES IN DOMESTIC POLITICS (TRANSPORTATION, HOUSING, URBAN RENEWAL, MEDICAL CARE, ETC.).

0789 DU BOIS W.E.B.
THE WORLD AND AFRICA.
NEW YORK: INTERNATIONAL PUBLRS, 1965, 352 PP., LC#65-16392.
STUDY OF ROLE OF AFRICA IN THE DEVELOPMENT OF WORLD HISTORY. DISCUSSES CONDITION OF NEGRO IN US; FEELS NEGROES HAVE NO IDEA OF WORLD TREND TOWARD SOCIALISM, SO CONTINUE TO BE EXPLOITED UNDER CAPITALISM.

0790 DUBOIS J.
DANGER OVER PANAMA.
INDIANAPOLIS: BOBBS-MERRILL, 1964, 409 PP., LC#64-23196.
EXAMINES US RELATIONS WITH PANAMA SINCE 1846, CONCENTRATING ON PERIOD SINCE WWII. DISCUSSES POLITICAL HISTORY OF PANAMA, TREATIES WITH US ABOUT CANAL, FLAG WAR, TREATY WAR, AND COMMUNIST ROLE IN THESE REVOLTS. LOOKS AT PRESENT RELATIONS BETWEEN US AND PANAMA, AND FUTURE OF POLICY ON CANAL. SUGGESTS SUBSIDIES TO CANAL ZONE SCHOOLS TO EDUCATE PANAMANIANS AS PARTIAL SOLUTION.

0791 DUCHACEK I.D.
CONFLICT AND COOPERATION AMONG NATIONS.
NEW YORK: HOLT, 1960, 649 PP.
STUDY OF FACTORS AFFECTING COOPERATION, DOMINATION OR CONFLICT AMONG NATIONS. ENCOMPASSES THE NATURE OF INTERNATIONAL SOCIETY AND THE STRUGGLE FOR POWER AND ORDER.

0792 DUCLOS P.
L'EVOLUTION DES RAPPORTS POLITIQUES DEPUIS 1750 (LIBERTE, INTEGRATION, UNITE)
PARIS: PR UNIV DE FRANCE, 1950, 344 PP.
SURVEY OF POLITICAL CIVILIZATION, EMPHASIZING PRINCIPLE OF INTEGRATION, LIBERALISM, WORLD SOLIDARITY, AND THE CONFLICT BETWEEN INDIVIDUAL AND STATE. INCLUDES US AND EUROPE.

0793 DUCLOUX L.
FROM BLACKMAIL TO TREASON.
LONDON: ANDRE DEUTSCH, 1958, 240 PP.
STUDIES POLITICAL CRIME AND CORRUPTION IN FRANCE, 1920-40. REFUTES BELIEF, ALLEGEDLY CIRCULATED BY ROYALIST PROPAGANDISTS, THAT SURETE NATIONALE WAS INSTRUMENT OF POLITICAL COERCION AND FOREIGN POWERS BETWEEN WORLD WARS.

0794 DUDDEN A.P. ED.
WOODROW WILSON AND THE WORLD OF TODAY.
PHILA: U OF PENN PR, 1957, 96 PP., LC#57-7219.
DISCUSSIONS OF WILSON'S LEADERSHIP IN MAKING US A WORLD POWER, WWI, HIS POLITICAL SKILLS AND ROLE IN THE LEAGUE OF NATIONS, AND END OF ISOLATIONISM.

0795 DUFFY J.
"PORTUGAL IN AFRICA."
CAMBRIDGE: HARVARD U PR, 1962.
BIBLIOGRAPHY OF WORKS IN ENGLISH TOTALLY OR PARTLY CONCERNED WITH VARIOUS ASPECTS OF PORTUGUESE AFRICA. ONLY WORKS PUBLISHED IN LAST TWENTY YEARS INCLUDED. MAJORITY OF SOURCES ARE PORTUGUESE.

0796 DULLES J.
WAR, PEACE AND CHANGE.
NEW YORK: HARPER, 1939, 170 PP.
OUTLINES WORLD TENSIONS FROM 1919 TO 1939. DESCRIBES INTENTIONS OF FRANCE, ENGLAND AND THE USA AS PEACEFUL, THOSE OF ITALY, GERMANY AND JAPAN AS AGGRESSIVE. CONCLUDES THAT RELIGIOUS AND INTERNATIONAL ORGANIZATIONS WILL STRIVE FOR PEACE BY PROVIDING INFORMATION AND LEADERSHIP.

0797 DULLES J.F.
WAR OR PEACE.
NEW YORK: MACMILLAN, 1950, 274 PP.
ANALYZES DANGEROUS SITUATION OF WORLD AFTER WWII, EMPHASIZING IMPORTANCE OF RESOLUTION, STRENGTH, AND COOL JUDGMENT IN FACING RUSSIAN THREAT. TRACES COURSE OF INTERNATIONAL AFFAIRS AND US POLICY AFTER WWII. EXPLAINS CURRENT POLICIES, WEIGHING GAINS AGAINST REVERSES. FINALLY SETS FORTH CONSTRUCTIVE PROGRAM FOR STRENGTHENING UN AND DRAWING TOGETHER FREE PEOPLE BEHIND POLICIES UNITED FOR PEACE.

0798 DUMON F.
LA COMMUNAUTE FRANCO-AFRO-MALGACHE: SES ORIGINES, SES INSTITUTIONS, SON EVOLUTION.
BRUSSELS: U LIBRE DE BRUXELLES, 1960, 294 PP.
CONSIDERS EVOLUTION AND NATURE OF FRENCH "COMMUNAUTE" IN AFRICA. CONCERNS POLITICAL PARTIES, CONSTITUTIONAL REVISIONS, AND MOVEMENTS FOR CONFEDERATION AND FEDERATION BETWEEN AFRICAN COUNTRIES AND BETWEEN AFRICAN COUNTRIES AND FRANCE. HALF OF BOOK CONTAINS REPRODUCTIONS OF CONSTITUTIONS.

0799 DUNN F.
THE PRACTICE AND PROCEDURE OF INTERNATIONAL CONFERENCES.
BALTIMORE: JOHNS HOPKINS PR., 1929, 223 PP.
INTRODUCTION TO STUDY OF THE CONFERENCE AS INSTRUMENT OF INTERNATIONAL COLLECTIVE ACTION. ALSO OFFERS GENERAL HISTORICAL BACKGROUND OF CONFERENCES AND SUMMARIZES CURRENT PRACTICES.

0800 DUNN F.
"THE PRESENT COURSE OF INTERNATIONAL RELATIONS RESEARCH."
WORLD POLIT., 2 (OCT. 49), 80-95.
OBSERVES CHANGE IN FOCUS OF RESEARCH IN INTERNATIONAL RELATIONS FROM REFORM APPROACH TO A MORE REALISTIC PATH. SHOWS TREND TOWARD SPECIALIZATION AND CONCENTRATION ON SPECIFIC PROBLEMS AND AREAS. DISCUSSES ROLE OF VALUE ANALYSIS AND CITES REASONS IT HAS BEEN UNDERESTIMATED.

0801 DUNN F.S. ED.
CURRENT RESEARCH IN INTERNATIONAL AFFAIRS.
NEW YORK: CARNEGIE ENDOWMENT, 1952, 193 PP.
SURVEY OF RESEARCH CARRIED ON BY PRIVATE RESEARCH AGENCIES AND SPECIAL RESEARCH INSTITUTES OF UNIVERSITIES IN US AND UK. ARRANGED BY ORGANIZATIONS. CONTAINS 981 ITEMS ON FOREIGN POLICY, INTERNATIONAL RELATIONS, AND INTERNATIONAL LAW. ANNOTATED.

0802 DUNN F.S.
PEACE-MAKING AND THE SETTLEMENT WITH JAPAN.
PRINCETON: PRINCETON U PRESS, 1963, 204 PP., LC#63-07155.
STUDIES AMERICAN POLICY IN FAR EAST, ESPECIALLY WITH JAPAN, IN DECADE AFTER PEARL HARBOR. DISCUSSES WAR-TIME PEACE PLANS, PEACE-MAKING AND COLD WAR, SAN FRANCISCO CONFERENCE OF 1951, AND EFFECT OF TREATY ON WESTERN SECURITY IN PACIFIC.

0803 DUNNING W.A.
"HISTORY OF POLITICAL THEORIES FROM LUTHER TO MONTESQUIEU."
LONDON: MACMILLAN, 1905.
SECOND VOLUME OF "HISTORY OF POLITICAL THEORIES," COVERING THE 16TH CENTURY THROUGH THE MIDDLE OF THE 18TH CENTURY. TWELVE CHAPTERS REVIEW POLITICAL PHILOSOPHY OF REFFORMATION, ANTI-MONARCHISTS, BODIN, GROTIUS, PURITAN REVOLUTION, HOBBES, SPINOZA, BOSSUET, LOCKE, HUME, AND MONTESQUIEU. BIBLIOGRAPHY OF ORIGINAL SOURCES, HISTORICAL, CRITICAL, AND DESCRIPTIVE WORKS. EUROPEAN SOURCES.

0804 DUPUY R.E., DUPUY T.N.
"MILITARY HERITAGE OF AMERICA."
NEW YORK: MCGRAW HILL, 1956.
COMPREHENSIVE TEXT ON AMERICAN MILITARY HISTORY WHICH TOUCHES ON IMPORTANT FOREIGN MILITARY EVENTS BEFORE AND AFTER 1775. SPECIAL EMPHASIS PLACED ON MODERN WAR TACTICS AND HISTORY. STRESSES TWO THEMES OF IMMUTABILITY OF PRINCIPLES OF WAR AND CONSTANTLY CHANGING NATURE OF ACTUAL WAGING OF WAR. EXTENSIVE BIBLIOGRAPHY CONTAINS ITEMS ON THEORY, POLICY, HISTORY, AND MILITARY ANALYSIS.

0805 DURBIN E.F.M.
THE POLITICS OF DEMOCRATIC SOCIALISM; AN ESSAY ON SOCIAL POLICY.
LONDON: ROUTLEDGE & KEGAN PAUL, 1948, 384 PP.
EXAMINES REASONS FOR 20TH-CENTURY TRAGEDIES, SUCH AS TWO WORLD WARS AND ECONOMIC CRISIS. STUDIES AGGRESSIVE NATURE OF MAN, EXPLORES CAPITALISM AND SUGGESTS REFORMS, AND DISCUSSES MARXIST THEORY OF DISTRIBUTION OF ECONOMIC POWER AND SOCIAL PRIVILEGE. CONSIDERS SOCIALIST DEMOCRACY THE BEST SOLUTION. CONSTRUCTS PROGRAM FOR DEMOCRATIC SOCIALIST PARTY.

0806 DUROSELLE J.B.
LES NOUVEAUX ETATS DANS LES RELATIONS INTERNATIONALES.
PARIS: LIBRAIRIE ARMAND COLIN, 1962.
SURVEYS FOREIGN RELATIONS PROBLEMS OF NEWLY INDEPENDENT COUNTRIES. EXAMINES EXTERNAL MODELS, ESPECIALLY RUSSIA AND CHINA, THESE COUNTRIES IMITATE. ANALYZES INFLUENCE OF FORMER GOVERNING POWERS. CONSIDERS ATTITUDES TOWARDS MAJOR INTERNATIONAL PROBLEMS AND ORGANIZATIONS.

0807 DUROSELLE J.B.

HISTOIRE DIPLOMATIQUE DE 1919 A NOS JOURS (3RD ED.)
PARIS: LIBRARIE DALLOZ, 1962, 780 PP.
COMPACT AND COMPREHENSIVE DIPLOMATIC HISTORY FROM 1919-1957. INTERESTING FOR FRENCH VIEWPOINT ON HISTORICAL ISSUES. PARTIALLY ANNOTATED BIBLIOGRAPHY OF ABOUT 240 ITEMS ARRANGED BY SUBJECT.

0808 DUROSELLE J.B. ED., MEYRIAT J. ED.
LA COMMUNAUTE INTERNATIONALE FACE AUX JEUNES ETATS.
PARIS: LIBRAIRIE ARMAND COLIN, 1964, 417 PP.
PAPERS GIVEN AT FRENCH CONFERENCE IN 1962 ON PLACE OF YOUNG EMERGING NATIONS IN INTERNATIONAL AFFAIRS AND THEIR RELATIONS WITH FORMER COLONIZERS. EXAMINES RELATIONS OF NEW NATIONS WITH WEST, OF MEMBERS OF SEATO WITH NEW NATIONS OF SOUTHEAST ASIA, OF NEW NATIONS WITH COMMUNIST COUNTRIES, AND THE LIKE.

0809 DUROSELLE J.B. ED., MEYRIAT J.
POLITIQUES NATIONALES ENVERS LES JEUNES ETATS.
PARIS: LIBRAIRIE ARMAND COLIN, 1964, 347 PP.
STUDY OF RELATIONS OF FORMER COLONIAL POWERS WITH NEW NATIONS. DISCUSSES FORMER GREAT COLINIZERS SUCH AS FRANCE AND GREAT BRITAIN; US AND USSR, WHO HAVE DISAPPROVED OF COLONIALISM BUT HAVE PRACTICED OTHER FORMS OF DOMINATION; AND YUGOSLAVIA AND ISRAEL, BOTH MORE DEVELOPED THAN MOST FORMER COLONIALIZED STATES. CONSIDERS NEW PRESSURES THAT GREAT POWERS EXERT UPON NEW NATIONS.

0810 DUROSELLE J.B.
"LE CONFLIT DE TRIESTE 1943-1954: ETUDES DE CAS DE CONFLITS INTERNATIONAUX III."
BRUSSELS: INST. SOCIOLOG. DE L'UNIV. LIBRE, 1966.
FULLY DOCUMENTED STUDY OF THE ITALO-YUGOSLAV CONFLICT OVER THE TRIESTE AREA. BIBLIOGRAPHY OF APPROXIMATELY 360 ITALIAN, YUGOSLAVIAN, FRENCH, AND ENGLISH BOOKS, OFFICIAL DOCUMENTS, PERIODICALS, NONPUBLISHED SOURCES, AND INTERVIEWS FROM 1910 THROUGH 1961 ARRANGED ALPHABETICALLY BY AUTHOR UNDER GENRES AND COUNTRY OF PUBLICATION.

0811 DUROSELLE J.B.
"THE FUTURE OF THE ATLANTIC COMMUNITY."
INTERNATIONAL JOURNAL, 21 (FALL 66), 421-446.
DISCUSSES MYTHS OF UNITY AND INDEPENDENCE IN CONTEMPORARY ATLANTIC COMMUNITY, CLAIMING THAT WESTERN UNITY DOES NOT EXIST, NOR DOES WESTERN INDEPENDENCE, EITHER POLITICALLY OR ECONOMICALLY. ASSERTS THAT REASONS FOR WESTERN COOPERATION IN LATE 1940'S HAVE DISAPPEARED. LISTS SUGGESTIONS FOR RENEWED ATLANTIC COOPERATION.

0812 DUTOIT B.
LA NEUTRALITE SUISSE A L'HEURE EUROPEENNE.
PARIS: LIBR. GEN. DR. JURIS., 1962, 139 PP.
TRACES EVOLUTION OF SWISS NEUTRALITY AND DISCUSSES THE IMPACT OF THE GROWTH OF INTERNATIONAL AND REGIONAL ORGANIZATIONS ON THIS CONCEPT.

0813 DUTT R.P.
THE INTERNATIONALE.
LONDON: LAWRENCE & WISHART, 1964, 418 PP.
CHRONOLOGICAL HISTORICAL SURVEY OF DEVELOPMENT OF COMMUNISM THROUGH INTERNATIONALE SINCE INDUSTRIAL REVOLUTION. EMPHASIS ON VARIOUS IDEOLOGIES AND INEVITABLE EVOLUTION OF SOCIALISM TO COMMUNISM. INCLUDES WORLD POLITICAL EVENTS THAT RESULTED IN COMMUNIST TRIUMPH AND CAPITALIST FAILURE.

0814 DYCK H.V.
WEIMAR GERMANY AND SOVIET RUSSIA 1926-1933.
NEW YORK: COLUMBIA U PRESS, 1966, 279 PP., LC#66-14594.
STUDIES INSTABILITY OF DIPLOMATIC RELATIONS BETWEEN GERMANY AND SOVIET RUSSIA FROM 1926-1933. DISCUSSES NEUTRALITY OF TREATY OF BERLIN, INFLUENCE OF ANGLO-SOVIET BREAK ON GERMAN-SOVIET RELATIONS, AND METHODS OF POLICY FORMATION BY BOTH PARTIES.

0815 DYSON F.J.
"THE FUTURE DEVELOPMENT OF NUCLEAR WEAPONS."
FOR. AFF., 38 (APRIL 60), 457-64.
RADICALLY NEW KINDS OF NUCLEAR WEAPONS ARE TECHNICALLY POSSIBLE. MILITARY AND POLITICAL EFFECTS OF SUCH WEAPONS WOULD BE IMPORTANT. DEVELOPMENT OF WEAPONS CAN BE ARRESTED ONLY BY INTERNATIONAL CONTROL OF ALL NUCLEAR OPERATIONS. AN INTERNATIONAL DETECTIVE FORCE WITH UNRESTRICTED RIGHTS OF TRAVEL AND INSPECTION IS IMPERATIVE.

0816 EAGLETON C.
INTERNATIONAL GOVERNMENT.
NEW YORK: RONALD, 1932, 672 PP.
OUTLINES THE PRINCIPLES OF INTERNATIONAL LAW AND THE INSTITUTIONS, ORGANIZATIONS AND PROBLEMS OF INTERNATIONAL SOCIETY. INTRODUCTORY SURVEY OF INTERNATIONAL RELATIONSHIPS STRESSING GOVERNMENTAL ASPECT.

0817 EASTON S.C.
"THE RISE AND FALL OF WESTERN COLONIALISM."
NEW YORK: FREDERICK PRAEGER, 1964.
HISTORICAL STUDY OF PERIOD OF COLONIAL EXPANSION FROM ACQUISITION OF COLONIES TO DEFEAT THROUGH POSTWAR INDEPENDENCE MOVEMENTS. COVERS EXPANSION, SUBJECTION, AND PARTITION OF THE ISLAMIC WORLD, THE CARIBBEAN, AFRICA, AND THE EAST. UNANNOTATED BIBLIOGRAPHY OF GENERAL AND SPECIALIZED WORKS ON IMPERIALISM AND COLONIALISM THROUGH 1939; GENERAL WORKS ON RETREAT OF COLONIALISM; AND REGIONAL STUDIES.

0818 EAYRS J. ED.
THE COMMONWEALTH AND SUEZ: A DOCUMENTARY SURVEY.
LONDON: OXFORD U PR, 1964, 483 PP.
CONTAINS SELECTED DOCUMENTS, OFTEN ABRIDGED, PERTAINING TO THE NATIONALIZATION OF THE SUEZ CANAL, WITH COMMENTARY BY THE EDITOR. INCLUDES REACTIONS OF COMMONWEALTH NATIONS TO THE NATIONALIZATION; DOCUMENTS PRECEDING AND FOLLOWING THE INVASION OF SUEZ, 1956; DOCUMENTS ABOUT THE COMMONWEALTH AND THE UN EMERGENCY FORCE.

0819 EBENSTEIN W.
TWO WAYS OF LIFE.
NEW YORK: HOLT RINEHART WINSTON, 1962, 406 PP.
COMPARES POLITICAL AND ECONOMIC SYSTEMS OF MARXISM AND FREE MARKETING, THEIR SOCIO-CULTURAL EFFECTS, AND SUGGESTS WAYS OF COMBATING COMMUNISM. AIMS AT USE AS HIGH SCHOOL TEXT CONTAINS READINGS BY MARX, ENGELS, LENIN, LOCKE, ROUSSEAU, JEFFERSON, AND MILL.

0820 ECKHARDT A.R., ECKARDT A.L.
"SILENCE IN THE CHURCHES."
MIDSTREAM, 13 (OCT. 67), 27-32.
CHRISTIAN STUDIES SILENCE OF CHRISTIAN CHURCHES DURING RECENT MIDDLE EAST CRISIS. MAINTAINS THAT CHRISTIANS HAVE BEEN TAUGHT ANTI-SEMITISM AND SEE ISRAEL AS "PERVASIVELY SECULAR STATE" THAT DOESN'T MAKE APPROPRIATE SEPARATION OF CHURCH AND STATE. CHRISTIANS DO NOT SUPPORT ISRAEL AS RELIGIOUS STATE BECAUSE OF SEPARATION AND BECAUSE OF DESIRE TO EXONERATE SELVES FROM GUILT OF ANTI-SEMITISM.

0821 ECONOMIDES C.P.
LE POUVOIR DE DECISION DES ORGANISATIONS INTERNATIONALES EUROPEENNES.
LEYDEN: AW SIJTHOFF, 1964, 167 PP., LC#64-7605.
COMPARATIVE STUDY OF POWER OF DECISION. CONSIDERS EUROPEAN INTERNATIONAL AND INTERGOVERNMENTAL ORGANIZATIONS SUCH AS NATO, COUNCIL OF EUROPE, AND OEEC; AND SUPRANATIONAL ORGANIZATIONS SUCH AS EURATOM AND EEC. STUDIES POWER OF DECISION IN REFERENCE TO MEMBER STATES AND TO INTERNAL ORDER OF ORGANIZATIONS THEMSELVES.

0822 EDUCATION AND WORLD AFFAIRS
THE UNIVERSITY LOOKS ABROAD: APPROACHES TO WORLD AFFAIRS AT SIX AMERICAN UNIVERSITIES.
NEW YORK: WALKER, 1965, 300 PP., LC#66-12633.
STUDY OF INTEREST AND IMPORTANCE OF US UNIVERSITIES IN WORLD AFFAIRS BY EXAMINING INTERNATIONAL ASPECT OF STUDENT BODY, CURRICULA, RESEARCH, OVERSEAS PROGRAMS OF STANFORD, MICHIGAN STATE, TULANE, WISCONSIN, CORNELL, AND INDIANA.

0823 EDWARDS C.D.
TRADE REGULATIONS OVERSEAS.
NEW YORK: OCEANA PUBLISHING, 1966, 752 PP., LC#64-23357.
DISCUSSES POLICIES OF COMMON MARKET COUNTRIES, IRELAND, SOUTH AFRICA, NEW ZEALAND, AND JAPAN TOWARD MONOPOLIES, RESTRICTIVE AGREEMENTS, AND RESTRICTIVE BUSINESS PRACTICES.

0824 EFIMENCO N.M.
"CATEGORIES OF INTERNATIONAL INTEGRATION."
INDIA QUARTERLY, 16 (JULY-SEPT. 60), 259-269.
THE DISINTEGRATION OF THE SOVEREIGN STATE IS VIEWED IN RELATION TO THE RISE OF A WORLD COMMUNITY. CITING SPECIFIC MEANS OF GLOBAL INTEGRATION (IE, MUTUAL ACCOMODATION, LEGAL UNIVERSALISM, INSTITUTIONALISM, TRANSFORMATION-AS TO UTOPIAN ORDERS) ATTEMPTS TO PRESENT METHOD OF STUDYING DISINTEGRATION OF POLITICS AND OF ORGANIZING FUTURE RESEARCH AIMED AT STABILIZING WORLD POLITICS.

0825 EGBERT D.D.
"POLITICS AND ART IN COMMUNIST BULGARIA"
SLAVIC REVIEW, 26 (JUNE 67), 204-216.
ANALYZES BULGARIAN ARTISTS' SUBSERVIENCE TO SOVIET IDEOLOGICAL DOMINANCE. FINDS THAT EVEN BULGARIAN ART MAY BE AFFECTED BY WAVE OF NATIONALISM SWEEPING COMMUNIST NATIONS. THOUGH NO NONOBJECTIVE ART HAS YET BEEN PRODUCED, NEW SPIRIT IS REFLECTED IN AVANT-GARDE DISLIKE OF SOVIET "SOCIALIST REALISM" DESPITE RISK OF OFFICIAL DISFAVOR.

0826 EGYPTIAN SOCIETY OF INT LAW
THE MONROVIA CONFERENCE (PAMPHLET)
CAIRO: EGYPTIAN SOC INT LAW, 1959, 15 PP.
RESOLUTIONS OF CONFERENCE OF INDEPENDENT AFRICAN STATES ON ALGERIAN WAR, NUCLEAR TESTING IN THE SAHARA, RACIAL DISCRIMINATION, AND REMAINING FRENCH COLONIES, 1959.

0827 EHRENBURG I.
THE WAR: 1941-1945 (VOL. V OF "MEN, YEARS - LIFE," TRANS. BY TATIANA SHEBUNINA)

CLEVELAND: WORLD, 1964, 198 PP., LC#65-16679.
AUTOBIOGRAPHICAL ACCOUNT COVERS WWII FROM SOVIET VIEWPOINT. DESCRIBES HOW RUSSIA WAS TAKEN UNAWARES, ITS NEAR-DEFEAT BY HITLER'S INVADING ARMIES, AND ITS FINAL VICTORY. GIVES PERSONAL RECOLLECTIONS OF DAY-TO-DAY CRISES, REACTIONS OF GENERAL POPULATION, AND ATTITUDES OF GOVERNMENT OFFICIALS AS REPORTED IN NEWSPAPERS, OVER THE RADIO, AND FROM FIRST-HAND KNOWLEDGE.

0828 EINSTEIN A.
THE WORLD AS I SEE IT.
NEW YORK: COVICI/FRIEDE, 1939, 290 PP.
A COLLECTION OF ESSAYS AND CORRESPONDENCE PRESENTING VIEWS ON SUCH SUBJECTS AS HISTORY, SCIENCE, PACIFISM, NATIONALISM, DISARMAMENT, ETHICS, AND THE MEANING OF LIFE AND RELIGION.

0829 EINSTEIN A., NATHAN O. ED., MORDAN H. ED.
EINSTEIN ON PEACE.
NEW YORK: SIMON SCHUSTER, 1960, 704 PP.
COMPILATION OF EINSTEIN'S LETTERS AND THOUGHTS ON INTERNATIONAL RELATIONS, ATOMIC POWER, TOTALITARIANISM, CIVIL LIBERTIES AND RELATED MATTERS. ALSO INCLUDES SYMPATHETIC COMMENTARY ON HIS POSITIONS BY THE EDITORS.

0830 EINZIG P.
A DYNAMIC THEORY OF FORWARD EXCHANGE.
NEW YORK: ST. MARTINS, 1961, 573 PP.
REVISION OF 1937 BOOK RE IMPORTANCE OF FORWARD MARGINS ON FOREIGN MONETARY EXCHANGE WITH NEW EMPHASIS ON HOW MUCH THE DYNAMISM OF FORWARD EXCHANGE IS LIABLE TO INFLUENCE THE ECONOMY FOR BETTER OR WORSE. HISTORY OF FORWARD EXCHANGE, AND ITS MOVEMENT BY VARIOUS CURRENCIES. SUGGESTS MINIMAL INTERFERENCE WITH FREE MARKET.

0831 EISENDRATH C.
"THE OUTER SPACE TREATY."
FOREIGN SERVICE J., 44 (MAY 67), 27-44.
DISCUSSES EVOLUTION OF TREATY ON OUTER SPACE EXPLORATION COMPLETED THROUGH UN IN 1966. WORK ON TREATY BEGAN IN 1957, WAS FOSTERED BY NASA, UN COMMITTEE ON THE PEACEFUL USES OF OUTER SPACE, AND HAD PRECEDENT IN THE ANTARCTIC TREATY OF 1959. TREATY'S MAIN SUCCESS WAS IN CREATING DEMILITARIZED ZONE IN OUTER SPACE.

0832 EISENHOWER D.D.
PEACE WITH JUSTICE: SELECTED ADDRESSES.
NEW YORK: COLUMBIA U PRESS, 1961, 273 PP., LC#61-7096.
KEY SPEECHES OF EISENHOWER FROM 1950-60 ON PEACE IN WORLD TROUBLED BY COLD WAR AND RUSSIAN EXPANSION. STRESSES CIVIC RESPONSIBILITY AND ACTION AND PATRIOTISM THROUGH FAITH IN MAN. DEALS WITH MORALITY OF MEN IN US, FOREIGN POLICY, AND "INADEQUACIES OF SUMMIT CONFERENCES."

0833 EISENHOWER D.D.
WAGING PEACE 1956-61: THE WHITE HOUSE YEARS.
GARDEN CITY: DOUBLEDAY, 1965, 741 PP., LC#65-19046.
PERSONAL ACCOUNT OF 2ND TERM OF OFFICE FROM ELECTION THROUGH JFK. PORTRAYS SELF AS "VICAR OF PEACE" IN CRISES OF SUEZ, SPUTNIKS, CIVIL RIGHTS, BERLIN, AND GENEVA. ANALYZES REASONS FOR ACTIONS AND DECISIONS IN ALL CASES. INCLUDES SUBJECTIVE REFLECTIONS ON COLD WAR AND FUTURE OF US SOCIETY.

0834 EKIRCH A.A. JR.
IDEAS, IDEALS, AND AMERICAN DIPLOMACY.
NEW YORK: APPLETON, 1966, 205 PP., LC#66-16284.
CONSIDERS AMERICAN FOREIGN POLICY IN RELATION TO US HISTORY AND CULTURE. ANALYZES WAYS IN WHICH FOREIGN POLICY WAS AFFECTED BY ISOLATIONISM, MANIFEST DESTINY AND MISSION, NATIONALISM, IMPERIALISM, INTERNATIONALISM, PEACE, AND DEMOCRACY. DISCUSSES CONTEMPORARY CONFLICT IN IDEALS BETWEEN NATIONALISM AND INTERNATIONALISM ABOUT PRESERVING WORLD PEACE.

0835 ELAHI K.N. ED., MOID A. ED., SIDDIQUI A.H. ED.
A GUIDE TO WORKS OF REFERENCE PUBLISHED IN PAKISTAN (PAMPHLET)
KARACHI: KARACHI U LIB, PAKIS BIBLIOG, 1953, 36 PP.
SOME OF THE WORKS LISTED IN THIS GUIDE ARE ANNOTATED WHILE OTHERS ARE NOT; LOCATION IN VARIOUS PAKISTANI LIBRARIES IS GIVEN. ARRANGED UNDER SUBJECT HEADINGS.

0836 ELDER R.E.
"THE PUBLIC STUDIES DIVISION OF THE DEPARTMENT OF STATE: PUBLIC OPINION ANALYSTS IN THE FORMULATION AND CONDUCT OF." AMERICAN FOREIGN POLICY.
WEST. POLIT. QUART., 10 (DEC. 57), 783-792.
DISCUSSES ORGANIZATION AND FUNCTION OF THIS DIVISION OF THE STATE DEPARTMENT.

0837 ELIAS T.O.
GOVERNMENT AND POLITICS IN AFRICA.
NEW YORK: ASIA PUBL HOUSE, 1963, 288 PP.
WRITTEN VERSION OF SERIES OF LECTURES DELIVERED IN INDIA ON CONTEMPORARY PROBLEMS OF GOVERNMENT AND POLITICS IN AFRICA. MATERIAL TOPICALLY AND CHRONOLOGICALLY ARRANGED. COVERS PERIOD FROM ANCIENT AFRICAN CIVILIZATIONS THROUGH MOVEMENTS FOR REFORM IN CONTEMPORARY AFRICA. ORGANIZES MATERIAL GEOGRAPHICALLY WITHIN EACH CHAPTER. BRIEF LISTS OF BRITISH AND INDIAN SOURCES AT END OF EACH TOPIC.

0838 EL-NAGGAR S.
FOREIGN AID TO UNITED ARAB REPUBLIC.
CAIRO: INST OF NATIONAL PLANNING, 1963, 93 PP.
DISCUSSES AID TO UAR, TYPES AND ORGANIZATION OF PROGRAMS, AMERICAN AND SOVIET AID. PRESENTS STUDIES OF SPECIFIC AID PROGRAMS, SUCH AS SURPLUS AGRICULTURAL PRODUCTS, RURAL IMPROVEMENT, DAMS, INDUSTRIALIZATION, AND MILITARY AID. INCLUDES RESULTS AND PROBLEMS OF FOREIGN AID.

0839 ELKIN A.B.
"OEEC-ITS STRUCTURE AND POWERS."
EUROP. YRB., 4 (58), 96-149.
STUDIES POWER AND JURISDICTION OF OEEC VIS A VIS ITS MEMBER GOVERNMENTS. COUNCIL IS MAIN ORGAN WITH SUBORDINATE BODIES, SUCH AS STEERING BOARD FOR TRADE. ORIGINAL RULE OF UNANIMOUS VOTE HAS CHANGED TO MAJORITY RULE IN SUBORDINATE ORGANS.

0840 ELLENDER A.J.
A REPORT ON UNITED STATES FOREIGN OPERATIONS IN AFRICA.
WASHINGTON: GOVT PR OFFICE, 1963, 803 PP.
SENATOR FROM LOUISIANA REPORTS ON RECENT AFRICAN TOUR, GIVING SHORT HISTORICAL BACKGROUND OF AFRICA, AND HIS OBSERVATIONS ON AND ENCOUNTERS WITH US MISSION HEADS AND STAFFS IN EACH COUNTRY VISITED. APPENDIX TO REPORT FURNISHES STATISTICAL DATA IN ANSWER TO QUESTIONNAIRES COVERING ALL ASPECTS OF US FOREIGN OPERATIONS.

0841 ELLERT R.B.
NATO 'FAIR TRIAL' SAFEGUARDS: PRECURSOR TO AN INTERNATIONAL BILL OF PROCEDURAL RIGHTS.
THE HAGUE: MARTINUS NIJHOFF, 1963, 89 PP.
STUDY OF NATO AGREEMENT REGARDING CRIMINAL JURISDICTION OVER MEMBERS OF NATO MILITARY FORCES STATIONED IN MEMBER COUNTRIES. GRANTS JURISDICTION TO NATION IN WHICH LOCATED AT TIME OF ALLEGED CRIME AND LEGAL GUARANTEES OF FAIR TRIAL.

0842 ELLIOTT J.R.
THE APPEAL OF COMMUNISM IN THE UNDERDEVELOPED NATIONS.
DUBUQUE: BROWN, 1962, 156 PP.
ATTEMPTS TO EXPLAIN WHY COMMUNISM HAS SUCH GREAT APPEAL IN UNDERDEVELOPED NATIONS, ESPECIALLY IN COMPARISON TO THE IDEAS EXPORTED FROM THE US. EXAMINES THEORY AND PRACTICE OF PRIVATE ENTERPRISE, THEORY AND PRACTICE OF COMMUNISM, BOTH MARXIST AND LENINIST, AND CONSIDERS THE ECONOMIC PROBLEMS AND NEEDS OF UNDERDEVELOPED NATIONS.

0843 ELLSWORTH P.T.
"INTERNATIONAL ECONOMY."
NEW YORK: MACMILLAN, 1950.
CONTAINS 400 ENTRIES FROM BOOKS AND ARTICLES WRITTEN FROM 1900-1950 IN ENGLISH ON INTERNATIONAL ECONOMICS. ARRANGED BY CHAPTER, SELECTIVE EMPHASIS ON HISTORICAL DEVELOPMENT.

0844 ELTON G.E.
IMPERIAL COMMONWEALTH.
LONDON: COLLINS, 1945, 544 PP.
A GENERAL HISTORY OF THE BRITISH EMPIRE FROM 1485 TO THE 20TH CENTURY. AN HISTORICAL ACCOUNT OF THE GROWTH AND THE DEVELOPMENT OF THE EMPIRE THROUGH MAJOR EUROPEAN AND GLOBAL CONFLICTS. SPECIAL CHAPTERS DEVOTED TO COLONIZATION OF THE AMERICAS, INDIA, AUSTRALIA, AND AFRICA.

0845 EMBREE A.T. ED.
A GUIDE TO PAPERBACKS ON ASIA; SELECTED AND ANNOTATED (PAMPHLET)
NEW YORK: ASIA SOCIETY, 1964, 89 PP.
AN ANNOTATED COMPILATION OF PAPERBOUND BOOKS AND PAMPHLETS CURRENTLY IN PRINT. LISTS OVER 500 TITLES, ALL AMERICAN PUBLICATIONS. 1966 SUPPLEMENT CONTAINS 240 PAPERBACKS PUBLISHED FROM 1964 THROUGH 1966. ENTRIES DIVIDED INTO ASIA IN GENERAL, SOUTH ASIA, SOUTHEAST ASIA, AND EAST ASIA. INCLUDES POLITICAL, HISTORICAL, ECONOMIC, SOCIAL, AND CULTURAL TOPICS.

0846 EMBREE A.T. ED., MESKILL J. ED. ET AL.
ASIA: A GUIDE TO BASIC BOOKS (PAMPHLET)
NEW YORK: ASIA SOCIETY, 1966, 57 PP.
ANNOTATED COMPILATION OF 316 ENGLISH-LANGUAGE BOOKS. ENTRIES LISTED BY COUNTRY UNDER FOUR GENERAL TOPICS: ASIA IN GENERAL, SOUTH ASIA, SOUTHEAST ASIA, AND EAST ASIA. INCLUDES MODERN POLITICAL, SOCIAL, AND ECONOMIC DEVELOPMENT. PUBLICATION DATES RANGE FROM 1920 THROUGH 1966.

0847 EMERSON R.
FROM EMPIRE TO NATION: THE RISE TO SELF-ASSERTION OF ASIAN AND AFRICAN PEOPLES.
CAMBRIDGE: HARVARD U PR, 1960, 466 PP., LC#60-5883.
ARGUES THAT RISE OF NATIONALISM AMONG NON-EUROPEAN PEOPLES IS A CONSEQUENCE OF IMPERIAL SPREAD OF WESTERN EUROPEAN CIVILIZATION. FOCUSES ON OVERSEAS EXPANSION OF EUROPE, ITS

AFTERMATH, AND NATURE OF NEW NATIONALISM. EXTENSIVE NOTES AND BIBLIOGRAPHY.

0848 EMERSON R.
"THE ATLANTIC COMMUNITY AND THE EMERGING COUNTRIES."
INT. ORGAN., 17 (SUMMER 63), 628-649.
EXAMINES DIVERSITY OF ATTITUDES LINKING OR DIVIDING THE EMERGING NATIONS AND THOSE WITHIN THE ATLANTIC COMMUNITY. EXPLORES RELATIONSHIPS BETWEEN THE GROUPS BY DRAWING ON EXPERIENCE OF COMMON MARKET AND REACTION TO IT BY NEWLY INDEPENDENT TERRITORIES. CONCLUDES THAT CONFLICT POSSIBLE BETWEEN INTERESTS OF EMERGING NATIONS AND ATLANTIC COMMUNITY NATIONS, BUT COOPERATION ALSO POSSIBLE FOR JOINT AND SEPARATE ENDS.

0849 EMERSON R. ED., KILSON M. ED.
THE POLITICAL AWAKENING OF AFRICA.
ENGLEWOOD CLIFFS: PRENTICE HALL, 1965, 175 PP., LC#65-20605.
AFRICAN AND WESTERN REACTIONS TO COLONIALISM, GROWING AFRICAN NATIONALISM, AFRICAN POLITICAL PARTIES, AND QUESTION OF UNITY AND INTERACTION AMONG AFRICAN STATES.

0850 EMME E.M. ED.
THE IMPACT OF AIR POWER - NATIONAL SECURITY AND WORLD POLITICS.
PRINCETON: VAN NOSTRAND, 1959, 914 PP., LC#59-8554.
COLLECTION OF ESSAYS ON NATURE AND THEORIES OF AIR WARFARE. DISCUSSES AIR WARFARE IN WWII AND LESSONS DRAWN. COMPARES SOVIET AND US AIR POLICY AND EXAMINES AIR POWER IN EUROPE AND ASIA.

0851 ENGEL J.
THE SECURITY OF THE FREE WORLD.
NEW YORK: WILSON, 1960, 211 PP., $3.00.
SERIES OF READINGS ON INTERNATIONAL RESPONSES TO THE COMMUNIST CHALLENGE. INCLUDES DISCUSSION OF NATURE OF SOVIET AIMS, POSSIBILITIES AND PROBLEMS OF THE UN, NATO'S RECORD AND ITS FUTURE, RELATIONS AMONG WESTERN NATIONS, ARMS CONTROL DISPUTES AND APPROACHES TO UNDERDEVELOPED WORLD.

0852 ENGEL-JANOSI F.
OSTERREICH UND DER VATIKAN (2 VOLS)
GRAZ: VERLAG STYRIA, 1960, 743 PP.
DISCUSSES RELATIONS BETWEEN AUSTRIA AND VATICAN FROM 1903 TO END OF WWI. EXAMINES DIPLOMATIC MANEUVERS, ATTITUDE OF CHURCH TOWARD NATIONALITY PROBLEM, AND RELATIONS BETWEEN CHURCH AND AUSTRIA DURING WWI.

0853 ENGELMAN F.L.
THE PEACE OF CHRISTMAS EVE.
NEW YORK: HARCOURT BRACE, 1960, 333 PP., LC#62-10495.
HISTORY OF WAR OF 1812, EMPHASIZING PEACE TREATY THAT ENDED CONFLICT, AND PERSONALITIES OF THOSE INVOLVED. MAINTAINS WAR AND TREATY-MAKING HELPED SHAPE CHARACTER OF US IN SUBSEQUEST FOREIGN AFFAIRS.

0854 COMMITTEE ECONOMIC DEVELOPMENT
THE DOLLAR AND THE WORLD MONETARY SYSTEM: A STATEMENT ON NATIONAL POLICY (PAMPHLET)
NEW YORK: COMM FOR ECO DEV, 1966, 76 PP., LC#66-30658.
DETAILED STUDY OF POSSIBLE WAYS TO BRING US INTERNATIONAL ACCOUNTS INTO BALANCE. ANALYZES US AS WORLD BANKER AND PROBLEM ITS DEFICIT IS CREATING FOR ALL LONG-RANGE INTERNATIONAL MONETARY PLANS. SUGGESTS REDUCTION OF GOVERNMENT SPENDING, INCREASED FREEDOM FOR PRIVATE CAPITAL TRANSACTIONS, REDUCTION OF FOREIGN AID TO EUROPE, AND STRENGTHENING OF INTERNATIONAL MONETARY AGREEMENTS.

0855 EPSTEIN F.T. ED., WHITTAKER C.H. ED.
THE AMERICAN BIBLIOGRAPHY OF RUSSIAN AND EAST EUROPEAN STUDIES FOR 1964.
BLOOMINGTON: INDIANA U PR, 1966, 119 PP., LC#58-63499.
BIBLIOGRAPHICAL LISTING OF BOOKS AND ARTICLES PUBLISHED IN ENGLISH IN THE US IN 1964. ALSO INCLUDES BOOKS PUBLISHED IN ENGLISH THROUGHOUT THE WORLD WITH THE EXCEPTION OF RUSSIA AND EAST EUROPE. TRANSLATIONS NOT INCLUDED. ITEMS GROUPED BY SUBJECT AND COUNTRY. CONTAINS AUTHOR INDEX. 2,260 ENTRIES.

0856 EPSTEIN H.M. ED.
REVOLT IN THE CONGO.
NEW YORK: FACTS ON FILE, INC, 1964, 187 PP., LC#64-16075.
RECORD OF CONGOLESE REBELLION AND ATTENDANT EVENTS, DRAWN FROM NEWS REFERENCE MATERIALS, 1960-1964, SUPPLEMENTED BY A SECTION ON THE CONGO AND ITS PEOPLES.

0857 EPSTEIN L.D.
BRITAIN - UNEASY ALLY.
CHICAGO: U CHI, CTR POLICY STUDY, 1954, 279 PP.
ANALYZES BRITISH OPINION AND REACTION TO US FOREIGN POLICY, AID, AND TRADE PROGRAMS IN POSTWAR PERIOD, 1945-52. INCLUDES ATTITUDES OF CONSERVATIVE AND LABOUR PARTIES AND OF PUBLIC. DISCUSSES DIFFERENCES IN ATTITUDES OF BOTH COUNTRIES AND MEASURES TAKEN IN KOREAN CONFLICT.

0858 ERB G.F.
"THE UNITED NATIONS CONFERENCE ON TRADE AND DEVELOPMENT (UNCTAD): A SELECTED CURRENT READING LIST."
AFR. BIBLIOG. CTR., CUR. RDG., 4 (1966), 1-14.
A PARTIALLY ANNOTATED BIBLIOGRAPHY ON UNCTAD: PROCEEDINGS OF THE CONFERENCE; BACKGROUND AND CURRENT ACTIVITIES; DEVELOPMENT FINANCING; INTERNATIONAL MONETARY ISSUES AND THE DEVELOPING COUNTRIES. CONTAINS INTRODUCTION AND BRIEF DESCRIPTION OF UNCTAD. ALL SOURCES PUBLISHED IN ENGLISH, SPANISH, AND GERMAN BETWEEN 1958-65.

0859 ERDMAN P.E., BENVENISTE G., PRENTICE E.S.
COMMON MARKETS AND FREE TRADE AREAS (PAMPHLET)
MENLO PARK: STANFORD U RES INST, 1960, 37 PP.
OUTLINES WORLD-WIDE TREND TOWARD ECONOMIC REGIONAL GROUPINGS, FACTORS AND CAUSES CREATING TREND, NATURE OF PROPOSED SCHEMES, AND POTENTIAL PROBLEMS AND ISSUES THE US WILL FACE AS RESULT. FOCUSES UPON LATIN AMERICA, ASIA, AND AFRICA. ISSUES RELATE TO IMPACT OF EUROPEAN ECONOMIC COMMUNITY AND OTHER EUROPEAN ORGANIZATIONS UPON US.

0860 ERHARD L.
THE ECONOMICS OF SUCCESS.
PRINCETON: VAN NOSTRAND, 1963, 412 PP.
ANALYSIS OF WEST GERMAN ECONOMIC DEVELOPMENT BY MINISTER OF ECONOMIC AFFAIRS RESPONSIBLE FOR ECONOMIC POLICY AND PLANNING. INCLUDES VARIOUS ARTICLES AND SPEECHES ON SPECIFIC ASPECTS OF GERMAN AND INTERNATIONAL ECONOMICS.

0861 ERICKSON J. ED.
THE MILITARY-TECHNICAL REVOLUTION.
NEW YORK: FREDERICK PRAEGER, 1966, 284 PP., LC#66-13680.
COLLECTION OF PAPERS ON IMPACT OF MILITARY REVOLUTION ON STRATEGY AND FOREIGN POLICY. EXAMINES US MILITARY STRATEGY IN NUCLEAR AGE, EFFECT OF OVER-ALL STRATEGY CHANGES ON EAST-WEST FOREIGN POLICY PLANNING AND REACTION, AND ATTITUDE OF OTHER NATIONS TOWARD BOTH MAJOR POWERS.

0862 ESTEP R.
AN AIR POWER BIBLIOGRAPHY.
MONTGOMERY: AIR U, 1956, 199 PP.
COVERS PUBLICATIONS 1950-56 ON AIR POWER, EQUIPMENT, PERFORMANCE, LAW, PUBLIC RELATIONS, BUDGETING AND AREAS RELATED TO USAF; 3,250 ENTRIES.

0863 ESTHUS R.A.
FROM ENMITY TO ALLIANCE: US AUSTRALIAN RELATIONS.
SEATTLE: U OF WASHINGTON PR, 1964, 180 PP., LC#64-20486.
TRACES RISING IMPORTANCE OF AUSTRALIA IN PACIFIC AFFAIRS DURING 1930'S, NOTING OCASSIONAL BY ACRIMONIOUS US-AUSTRALIAN RELATIONS DURING THIS PERIOD. DISCUSSES ENMITY ARISING FROM TRADE AND SHIPPING COMPETITION. DESCRIBES ABRUPT CHANGES IN RELATIONS AFTER OUTBREAK OF WAR IN EUROPE AND EVENTUAL ALLIANCE IN PACIFIC WAR. ANALYZES COMMON INTERESTS REMAINING AFTER WWII AND SUBSEQUENT CHANGES IN RELATIONS.

0864 ESTHUS R.A.
THEODORE ROOSEVELT AND JAPAN.
SEATTLE: U OF WASHINGTON PR, 1966, 329 PP., LC#66-19567.
ROOSEVELT AND HIS FAR EASTERN FOREIGN POLICY EXTENSIVELY REPORTED. BIOGRAPHICAL MATERIAL ON PERSONS INVOLVED DURING THIS PERIOD, VARIOUS TREATIES AND CONFERENCES, AND POLICY EVOLUTION ARE INCLUDED. DETAILED HISTORICAL PRESENTATION OF INTERNATIONAL RELATIONS OF THIS PERIOD.

0865 ETHIOPIAN MINISTRY INFORMATION
AFRICAN SUMMIT CONFERENCE ADDIS ABABA, ETHIOPIA, 1963.
ADDIS ABABA: MIN OF INFORMATION, 1963, 111 PP.
CONTAINS TEXTS OF APPROXIMATELY 35 SPEECHES DELIVERED BY HEADS OF STATE AND GOVERMENT AT ADDIS ABABA SUMMIT CONFERENCE IN 1963. ALSO INCLUDES SOME MAJOR RESOLUTIONS ADOPTED BY CONFERENCE. SPEECHES EMPHASIZE AFRICAN BROTHERHOOD AND INDEPENDENT NATIONS' SUPPORT OF AFRICAN PEOPLES STILL UNDER COLONIAL RULE.

0866 ETIENNE G.
"'LOIS OBJECTIVES' ET PROBLEMES DE DEVELOPPEMENT DANS LE CONTEXTE CHINE-URSS."
TIERS-MONDE, 4 (NO.16, 63), 609-27.
DESCRIBES SEVERAL ASPECTS OF MOST RECENT CHINESE ECONOMIC POLICY. SEEKS TO CLARIFY CONTENT OF WHAT RUSSIANS TERM OBJECTIVE STRUCTURAL LAW. FOCUSES ON GEOGRAPHIC, DEMOGRAPHIC AND SOCIO-ECONOMIC DIFFERENCES CURRENTLY HINDERING SINO-SOVIET RELATIONS.

0867 ETSCHMANN R.
DIE WAHRUNGS- UND DEVISENPOLITIK DES OSTBLOCKS UND IHRE AUSWIRKUNGEN AUF DIE WIRTSCHAFTSBEZIEHUNGEN ZWISCHEN OST U WEST
BONN: UNIV OF BONN, 1959, 213 PP.
EXAMINES ECONOMIC AND FOREIGN TRADE POLICIES OF EASTERN COUNTRIES WITH EMPHASIS ON CURRENCY STANDARDS AND FOREIGN EXCHANGE. FOCUSES ON CZECHOSLOVAKIA, POLAND, HUNGARY, RUMANIA, BULGARIA, USSR, CHINA, AND EAST GERMANY.

0869 ETZIONI A.
"EUROPEAN UNIFICATION: A STRATEGY OF CHANGE."
WORLD POLIT., 16 (OCT. 63), 32-51.

A THOROUGH REVIEW OF STRATEGY ADOPTED IN FORMING THE EUROPEAN ECONOMIC COMMUNITY. CREDIT FOR SUCCESS OF EEC IS ATTRIBUTED NOT ONLY TO BACKGROUND CONDITIONS OF MEMBER COUNTRIES, BUT ALSO TO STRATEGY OF CHANGE EMPLOYED BY THOSE WHO INITIATED AND SUPPORTED EEC.

0870 ETZIONI A.
"EUROPEAN UNIFICATION AND PERSPECTIVES ON SOVEREIGNTY."
DAEDALUS, 92 (SUMMER 63), 498-520.
QUESTIONS WHETHER SOVEREIGNTY CAN BE POOLED. SEES ESTABLISHMENT OF EUROPEAN COMMUNITY AS FIRST DEMONSTRATION OF ITS FEASIBILITY. COMPARES THIS ORGANIZATION WITH THEORETICAL MODELS AND WITH OTHER FORMS OF INTERNATIONAL ORGANIZATION. EXAMINES QUESTION OF PACE FOR SUCH UNIFICATION. DENIES DICHOTOMY EXISTS BETWEEN NATIONAL AND SUPRANATIONAL INTERESTS. SUGGESTS ECONOMIC UNIFICATION AS GOOD STARTING-POINT.

0871 ETZIONI A.
WINNING WITHOUT WAR.
GARDEN CITY: DOUBLEDAY, 1964, 271 PP., $4.95.
REVIEWS THE CHANGING NATURE OF SOVIET FOREIGN POLICY AND THE DYNAMICS OF THE SINO-SOVIET RIFT, EXPLORES THE DIFFICULTIES OF THE WESTERN BLOC AND ANALYZES THE FUTURE ROLE OF THE NEW NATIONS AND THE EFFECT OF CHANGES IN WEAPONS TECHNOLOGY. PUTS FORWARD SPECIFIC PROPOSALS FOR U.S. POLICY REGARDING DETERRENCE, INTERVENTION IN DEVELOPING NATIONS, AND THE REVISION OF THE UN.

0872 EUBANK K.
THE SUMMIT CONFERENCES.
NORMAN: U OF OKLAHOMA PR, 1966, 225 PP., LC#66-22711.
HISTORY OF MAJOR SUMMIT CONFERENCES SINCE VERSAILLES, INCLUDING MUNICH, 1938, TEHERAN, YALTA, POTSDAM, AND GENEVA. NOTES INABILITY TO SECURE WORLD PEACE AND STABILITY.

0873 EUDIN X.J., SLUSSER R.M.
SOVIET FOREIGN POLICY 1928-34: DOCUMENTS AND MATERIALS (VOL. I)
UNIVERSITY PARK: PENN STATE U PR, 1966, 353 PP., LC#66-25465
ANALYZES POLICY KREMLIN MADE FOR COMMUNIST OFFICIALS DURING INTERWAR YEARS. INCLUDES NARRATIVE SUMMARY OF MAIN POLITICAL EVENTS OF TIME: INTERVENTION IN MANCHURIA, THREATS FROM JAPAN TENSION WITH FRANCE AND ENGLAND, AND ENTRY INTO LEAGUE OF NATIONS. CONTAINS EXCERPTS FROM MINUTES OF PARTY CONGRESS AND PLENUMS, AND COMINTERN JOURNALS THAT REVEAL POLICY.

0874 EUROPA PUBLICATIONS LIMITED
THE EUROPA YEAR BOOK.
LONDON: EUROPA PUBLICATIONS.
ANNUALLY PUBLISHED SINCE 1926 IN TWO VOLUMES. PROVIDES ESSENTIAL BIOGRAPHICAL DETAILS ABOUT CURRENT WORLD PERSONALITIES, DIRECTORY OF ESSENTIAL INFORMATION ABOUT EVERY COUNTRY INCLUDING SUBJECT MATTER AND LOCATION OF NEWSPAPERS, PERIODICALS, NEWS AGENCIES, PUBLISHERS, RADIO, AND TELEVISION. ALSO GUIDE TO EDUCATIONAL, SCIENTIFIC, CULTURAL, AND POLITICAL ORGANIZATIONS THROUGHOUT THE WORLD.

0875 EUROPA-ARCHIV
DEUTSCHES AND AUSLANDISCHES SCHRIFTTUM ZU DEN REGIONALEN SICHERHEITSVEREINBARUNGEN 1945-1956.
FRANKFURT: EUROPE-ARCHIV, 1967, 64 PP.
NUMBER 14 IN EUROPA-ARCHIV SERIES OF "TOPICAL BIBLIOGRAHIES" (AKTUELLE BIBLIOGRAPHIEN). CONCERNS GERMAN AND FOREIGN LITERATURE ON MUTUAL SECURITY ARRANGEMENTS.

0876 EVANS C. ED.
AMERICAN BIBLIOGRAPHY... (12 VOLUMES)
NEW YORK: PETERSMITH, 1941.
A CHRONOLOGICAL DICTIONARY OF ALL BOOKS, PAMPHLETS, AND PERIODICAL PUBLICATIONS PRINTED IN THE UNITED STATES OF AMERICA FROM GENESIS OF PRINTING IN 1639 DOWN TO AND INCLUDING THE YEAR 1820.

0877 EVANS M.S.
THE FRINGE ON TOP.
NEW YORK: AMER FEATURE, 1962, 223 PP.
ANALYSIS OF POLITICAL POWER AND POLICIES OF RADICAL LEFT IN AMERICAN GOVERNMENT. STRESSES DANGER OF INCREASED POWER AND INFLUENCE OF LIBERAL EXTREMISM, AND CRITICIZES KENNEDY ADMINISTRATION FOR ITS ALLEGED ENCOURAGEMENT OF THIS ELEMENT. FOCUSES ON RADICAL LEFT'S ATTEMPT TO IMPOSE POLITICAL AND ECONOMIC CENTRALIZATION ON AMERICAN SOCIETY AND ITS POLICY OF CONCILIATION TOWARD USSR.

0878 EWING B.G.
PEACE THROUGH NEGOTIATION: THE AUSTRIAN EXPERIENCE.
WASHINGTON: PUBLIC AFFAIRS PRESS, 1966, 93 PP., LC#66-28241.
BELIEVES LBJ TO BE HYPOCRITICAL IN STATING THAT US WANTS A "PEACEFUL, NEGOTIATED SETTLEMENT IN VIETNAM." AUSTRIAN PEACE OF 1955 INDICATES THAT "INTRACTABLE PROBLEMS OF EAST AND WEST CAN BE RESOLVED WITH PATIENCE AND REASON." RUSSIAN WITHDRAWAL FROM AUSTRIA SUGGESTED AS POSSIBLE PATTERN FOR US WITHDRAWAL FROM VIETNAM.

0879 EWING L.L. ED., SELLERS R.C. ED.
THE REFERENCE HANDBOOK OF THE ARMED FORCES OF THE WORLD.
WASHINGTON: R C SELLERS + ASSN, 1966, LC#66-17547.
OBJECTIVE ASSESSMENT OF THE MILITARY STRENGTH OF NATIONS OF THE WORLD. PROVIDES INFORMATION ON DEFENSE BUDGET, TOTAL POPULATION, MANPOWER IN ARMED FORCES, AND DEFENSE BUDGET AS PERCENTAGE OF GNP. LISTS INDIVIDUAL MANPOWER SOURCES FOR ARMY, AIR FORCE, AND NAVAL DIVISIONS. PROVIDES DATA ON AIRCRAFT AND NAVAL EQUIPMENT AND TYPE OF MILITARY ASSISTANCE RECEIVED FROM FOREIGN POWERS.

0880 FABAR R.
THE VISION AND THE NEED: LATE VICTORIAN IMPERIALIST AIMS.
NEW YORK: HUMANITIES PRESS, 1966, 150 PP.
EXPLORES INFLUENCE, NATURE, AND ACCURACY OF KIPLING'S VIEWS ON BRITISH EMPIRE, TOGETHER WITH THOSE OF LATE 19TH-CENTURY IMPERIALISTS. ATTEMPTS TO UNDERSTAND "LATE VICTORIAN MOOD" AND SIMULTANEOUS ELEMENTS OF EXPANSION AND WITHDRAWAL IN LATE BRITISH IMPERIALISTIC PERIOD.

0881 FABER K.
DIE NATIONALISTISCHE PUBLIZISTIK DEUTSCHLANDS VON 1866 BIS 1871 (2 VOLS.)
DUSSELDORF: DROSTE VERLAG, 1963, 680 PP.
A COLLECTION OF PERIODICALS, PAMPHLETS, AND BOOKS ON NATIONALISTIC PUBLICATIONS, ARRANGED CHRONOLOGICALLY AND BY AREA. ITEMS ARE ARRANGED UNDER SUCH SUBJECTS AS THE NON-PRUSSIAN STATES OF NORTHERN GERMANY, EFFECTS OF THE WAR ON PARTY LIFE, GERMAN-RUSSIAN RELATIONS, ETC. IT CONTAINS AN AUTHOR INDEX, AND COVERS MATERIAL PUBLISHED FROM 1866 THROUGH THE SPRING OF 1871.

0882 FABREGA J.
"ANTECEDENTES EXTRANJEROS EN LA CONSTITUCION PANAMENA."
CENTRO, 3 (FEB. 67), 25-29.
EXAMINES PANAMANIAN CONSTITUTION OF 1946 AND FOREIGN INFLUENCES UPON ITS FINAL FORM. STUDIES COLOMBIAN CONSTITUTION OF 1886, SOCIAL ASPECTS OF MEXICAN CONSTITUTION OF 1917, AND CONSTITUTIONS OF CUBA AND URUGUAY IN 1940.

0883 FAGG J.E.
CUBA, HAITI, AND THE DOMINICAN REPUBLIC.
ENGLEWOOD CLIFFS: PRENTICE HALL, 1965, 181 PP., LC#65-23298.
EXAMINATION OF THREE MAIN CARIBBEAN NATIONS, CUBA, HAITI, AND DOMINICAN REPUBLIC AS TO DEVELOPMENT AS COLONIES AND REPUBLICS. DISCUSSES REVOLUTION AGAINST COLONIAL RULERS AND INFLUENCE OF US IN HISTORY OF EACH COUNTRY.

0884 FAHS C.B.
"GOVERNMENT IN JAPAN."
NEW YORK: NYC COL, INST PAC REL, 1940.
PART OF THE DOCUMENTATION OF AN INQUIRY ORGANIZED BY THE INSTITUTE OF PACIFIC RELATIONS INTO THE PROBLEMS ARISING FROM THE CONFLICT IN THE FAR EAST. ITS PURPOSE WAS TO OFFER AN IMPARTIAL AND CONSTRUCTIVE ANALYSIS OF THE SITUATION IN FAR EAST WITH VIEW TO INDICATING MAJOR ISSUES TO BE CONSIDERED IN ADJUSTMENT OF INTERNATIONAL RELATIONS. ANALYSIS OF ECONOMIC AND POLITICAL CONDITIONS. ANNOTATED BIBLIOGRAPHY.

0885 FAIRBANK J.K. ED., BANNO M. ED.
JAPANESE STUDIES OF MODERN CHINA.
TOKYO: CHARLES E TUTTLE, 1955, 331 PP.
DESCRIBES MORE THAN 1,000 BOOKS AND ARTICLES WHICH CONSTITUTE THE MAIN PART OF JAPANESE RESEARCH ON MODERN CHINA, OR 19TH- AND 20TH-CENTURY CHINA. WORKS IN THE SOCIAL SCIENCES AND HISTORY ARE CRITICALLY EVALUATED. INDEX OF AUTHORS' NAMES INCLUDED.

0887 FALK R.A.
"THE REALITY OF INTERNATIONAL LAW."
WORLD POLIT., 14 (JAN. 62), 353-63.
REVIEWS TWO BOOKS CONCERNED WITH THE POLITICAL SIGNIFICANCE OF INTERNATIONAL LAW AND THE RELATIONSHIPS BETWEEN LAW AND THE USE OF VIOLENCE. BOTH WORKS CONSIDER RELATIONS OF LEGAL ORDER AND NUCLEAR WAR AND THE EFFECT OF NATIONAL INTEREST UPON INTERNATIONAL LEGAL ORDER.

0888 FALK R.A.
LAW, MORALITY, AND WAR IN THE CONTEMPORARY WORLD.
NEW YORK: PRAEGER, 1963, 120 PP.
ASSERTS THAT INTERNATIONAL LAW PLACED ON THE BASIS OF A UTILITARIAN ETHICS WILL BEST SERVE THE SURVIVAL OF MANKIND IN THE NUCLEAR AGE. PROPOSES TO INTERRELATE NATIONAL INTEREST TO INTERNATIONAL COOPERATION. THE UPHOLDING OF STABILITY SHOULD BE A PRIMARY OBJECTIVE. THE MORAL USE OF FORCES PRESUPPOSES BENEFICIAL EFFECTS FOR ALL HUMANITY.

0889 FALK R.A.
THE ROLE OF DOMESTIC COURTS IN THE INTERNATIONAL LEGAL ORDER.
SYRACUSE: U. PR. 1964, 184 PP., $6.50.
CENTRAL THESIS IS THAT 'RULES OF DEFERENCE APPLIED BY DOMESTIC COURTS ADVANCE THE DEVELOPMENT OF INTERNATIONAL LAW FASTER THAN DOES AN INDISCRIMINATE INSISTANCE UPON APPLYING CHALLENGED SUBSTANTIVE NORMS IN ORDER TO DETERMINE THE VALIDITY OF THE OFFICIAL ACTS OF FOREIGN STATES.'

0890 FALK R.A.
"INTERNATIONAL LEGAL ORDER."
AMER. J. INT. LAW, 59 (JAN. 65), 66-71.
CONSTRUCTIVE CRITICISM OF THE 'SPECIFIC APPROACH' TO INTERNATIONAL LAW. DAMAGE INFLICTED UPON INTERNATIONAL LEGAL ORDER BY ALLOWING NEWLY INDEPENDENT STATES OF ASIA AND AFRICA TO PARTICIPATE AS FULL-FLEDGED MEMBERS. ASSERTS THAT CERTAIN DISTINGUISHED AMERICAN JURISTS ARE 'LENDING GOOD NAMES TO AN IMAGE OF WORLD COMMUNITY THAT APPEARS TO REFLECT SOCIALIST RATHER THAN WESTERN VALUES.

0891 FALK R.A.
THE AFTERMATH OF SABBATINO: BACKGROUND PAPERS AND PROCEEDINGS OF SEVENTH HAMMARSKJOLD FORUM.
NEW YORK: OCEANA PUBLISHING, 1965, 228 PP., LC#65-19486.
DISCUSSES PROBLEMS UNDERLYING AN ASSESSMENT OF THE APPROPRIATE ROLE FOR DOMESTIC COURTS IN CASES SIMILAR TO SABBATINO CASE. CASE WAS A DISAGREEMENT ABOUT DEGREE TO WHICH US COURTS CAN AND SHOULD EXAMINE MERITS OF AN ALLEGATION THAT FOREIGN EXPROPRIATION OF ALIEN PROPERTY VIOLATES RULES OF CUSTOMARY INTERNATIONAL LAW. AUTHOR AGREES WITH JUSTICE HARLAN'S MAJORITY OPINION.

0892 FALK S.L.
"DISARMAMENT IN HISTORICAL PERSPECTIVE."
MILITARY REVIEW, 44 (DEC. 64), 36-48.
IN A REVIEW OF HISTORY OF PROPOSALS AND ATTEMPTS TO A-CHIEVE ARMS CONTROL, AUTHOR DESCRIBES FOUR GENERAL CATEGOR-IES, DISARMAMENT BY EXTERMINATION, DISARMAMENT BY IMPOSI-TION, DISARMAMENT BY NEGOTIATION, AND UNILATERAL DISARMA-MENT. AUTHOR SUGGESTS CAREFUL STUDY OF EARLIER PROPOSALS TO DETERMINE APPLICABILITY OF PREVIOUS CONCEPTS IN NUCLEAR AGE.

0893 FALKOWSKI M.
"SOCIALIST ECONOMISTS AND THE DEVELOPING COUNTRIES."
J. OF PHILOSOPHY, (MAR. 67), 16-28.
ECONOMIC GROWTH IN "THIRD WORLD" COUNTRIES DEPENDS, IN THE VIEW OF EMINENT POLISH ECONOMISTS SUCH AS LANGE AND KA-LECKI, UPON THE INDUSTRIALIZATION PROCESS. CAREFUL ANALYSIS OF THE SPECIFIC PROBLEMS OF THE INDIVIDUAL COUNTRY IS PRE-INDUSTRIALIZATION; ONLY THEN CAN THE ECONOMICALLY BACKWARD COUNTRIES ACHIEVE SOME ECONOMIC STABILITY AND FREEDOM.

0894 FALL B.B.
STREET WITHOUT JOY.
NEW YORK: STACKPOLE, 1964, 408 PP., LC#64-23038.
REVISED AND UPDATED VERSION OF A HISTORY OF THE INDOCHINA WAR FROM WWII THROUGH MID-1964. DISCUSSES TACTICS OF INSURGENCY WAR, SET-PIECE BATTLE, FRENCH AND AMERICAN STRATEGY AND PRACTICE, LOSS OF LAOS, AND FUTURE OF REVOLUTIONARY WAR. MAINTAINS THAT COMPARATIVE ANALYSES OF SIMILAR WARS SHOW THAT THE ESSENTIAL FACTOR IS POPULAR SUPPORT. A DETAILED ACCOUNT.

0895 FALL B.B.
VIET-NAM WITNESS, 1953-66.
NEW YORK: FREDERICK PRAEGER, 1966, 363 PP., LC#66-18898.
EXAMINES EVENTS IN VIETNAM FROM DEFEAT OF FRENCH TO AMERICAN POLICY OF 1966. EMPHASIZES SIGNIFICANCE OF FRANCE'S FAILURE TO CREATE REPRESENTATIVE GOVERNMENT IN VIETNAM; STRENGTH OF COMMUNIST GRASS-ROOTS GOVERNMENT IN 1953; IMPACT OF BUDDHIST SECTS' REBELLION IN 1955; AND SAIGON'S LOSS OF CONTROL OVER ITS LOCAL ADMINISTRATION IN 1957.

0896 FANI-KAYODE R.
BLACKISM (PAMPHLET)
LONDON: V COOPER & PARTNERS LTD, 1965, 99 PP.
DISCUSSION OF AUTHOR'S OPINION ON UNIFICATION OF AFRICAN PEOPLES AND SOLIDARITY OF ALL BLACK PEOPLE AROUND WORLD. EXPLAINS NEED FOR AFRICA TO CREATE THIRD FORCE IN POLITICAL SITUATION OF TODAY. CLAIMS UNIFICATION OF COLORED RACES IS ONLY WAY TO GAIN POWER AND INFLUENCE IN WORLD AFFAIRS. EXPLAINS ROLE OF UNDERDEVELOPED NATIONS IN UN AS INDICATION OF POWER POTENTIAL.

0897 FANON F.
STUDIES IN A DYING COLONIALISM.
NEW YORK: MONTHLY REVIEW PR, 1965, 181 PP., LC#65-21737.
DOCUMENTATION BY AN ALGERIAN OF STRUGGLE FOR ALGERIAN INDEPENDENCE, WRITTEN DURING THE CONFLICT WITH FRANCE. DISCUSSES ALGERIAN FAMILY, THE ROLE OF COLONIALISM IN PROVIDING FOR SUBJECT PEOPLES, AND ALGERIA'S EUROPEAN MINORITY.

0898 FOOD AND AGRICULTURE ORG.
FOOD AND AGRICULTURE ORGANIZATION AFRICAN SURVEY.
ROME: UN FAO, 1962, 168 PP.
SEEKS TO IDENTIFY AFRICAN RURAL PROBLEMS OBJECTIVELY, MARK OUT DIRECTIONS FOR INTERNATIONAL ACTION, AND POINT TO WAYS IT MAY BE MORE EFFECTIVE. REVEALS RISING STAN-DARD OF LIVING BUT NEED TO CHECK RURAL BACKWARDNESS. CALLS FOR INTEGRATED APPROACH TO SOCIAL AND ECONOMIC PROBLEMS. RE-PORT DIVIDED INTO THREE PARTS: SETTING, TECHNICAL CHANGE AND USE OF RESOURCES, PROBLEMS IN RURAL DEVELOPMENT.

0899 FARIES J.C.
THE RISE OF INTERNATIONALISM.
NEW YORK: GRAY, 1915, 207 PP.
PRESENTS PRINCIPLES OF, AND STIMULI TO INTERNATIONALISM. DISCUSSES EFFECTS OF POPULATION LEVEL, LANGUAGE, AND EDUCA-TIONAL FACILITIES ON SUBJECT. FINDS INTERNATIONAL FAIRS, DIPLOMATIC CONFERENCES, ETC., ARE EFFECTIVE MEANS TO PEACE.

0900 FARQUHAR D.M.
"CHINESE COMMUNIST ASSESSMENTS OF A FOREIGN CONQUEST DYNASTY."
CHINA Q., 30 (APR.-JUNE 67), 79-92.
ANALYZES WAY IN WHICH PARTY HAS EVALUATED CHINESE DYNAS-TIES THAT CONQUERED FOREIGN LANDS. GIVES REASONS WHY PARTY MIGHT CLASSIFY DYNASTY "GOOD" OR "BAD", DEPENDING ON ITS MOTIVES. EMPHASIZES ORIGINAL CHINESE HISTORIANS' WRITINGS ON SUBJECT, AND FINDS NOTHING WRITTEN SINCE 1949.

0901 FARWELL G.
MASK OF ASIA: THE PHILIPPINES.
NEW YORK: FREDERICK PRAEGER, 1966, 227 PP., LC#66-1808.
OBSERVATIONS ON HISTORICAL EMERGENCE OF PHILIPPINE IS-LANDS INTO WORLD POLITICS: GROWTH OF NATIONALISM, CULTURE, TRADITIONS OF ISLANDS, RELIGIOUS AND SOCIAL STRUCTURE, THE POSSIBILITIES OF DEMOCRACY IN ASIA. SHORT BIBLIOGRAPHY INCLUDED.

0902 FATEMI N.S., PHALLE T.D., KEEFE G.M.
THE DOLLAR CRISIS.
RUTHERFORD: FAIRLEIGH DICKEN PR, 1963, 317 PP., LC#63-23017.
ANALYSIS OF BALANCE OF PAYMENTS PROBLEM AND FACTORS CREATING IT. US FOREIGN PROGRAMS STUDIED WITH RECOMMENDA-TIONS DESIGNED TO PRESERVE GOOD OF PROGRAM AND REDUCE COST. ANALYSIS OF PRIVATE INVESTMENT AND STEPS TAKEN BY GOVERNMENT AND LEGISLATIVE ENACTMENT TO ENCOURAGE SUBSTITUTION OF PRIVATE INVESTMENT FOR GOVERNMENT AID.

0903 FATOUROS A.A.
GOVERNMENT GUARANTEES TO FOREIGN INVESTORS.
NEW YORK: COLUMBIA U PRESS, 1962, 411 PP., LC#62-12873.
ANALYZES VARIOUS FORMS AND MODALITIES BY WHICH STATES EN-TER INTO ARRANGEMENTS WITH FOREIGN INVESTORS. ALSO STUDIES ASPECTS SUCH AS EXCHANGE RESTRICTIONS, EMPLOYMENT OF FOREIGN PERSONNEL, LEGAL EFFECTS OF TREATY PROMISES, AND STATE CONTRACTS.

0904 FATOUROS A.A., KELSON R N.
CANADA'S OVERSEAS AID.
TORONTO: CAN INST OF INTL AFF, 1964, 123 PP.
STUDY OF CANADIAN FOREIGN AID, 1950-62, BASED UPON CONFERENCE ON CANADIAN OVERSEAS AID, 1962. STUDIES TYPES, AIMS AND MOTIVES, DISTRIBUTION, AMOUNT AND FORMS, ADMINIS-TRATION OF AID. RECOMMENDS CONTINUED AID PROGRAM.

0905 FAWCETT J.E.S.
"GIBRALTAR* THE LEGAL ISSUES."
INTER-AMERICAN ECON. AFF., 43 (APR. 67), 236-251.
EXAMINES LEGAL ISSUES INVOLVED IN CURRENT DISPUTE BETWEEN BRITAIN AND SPAIN. SURVEYS PROBLEMS OF TERRITORIAL TITLE, FRONTIER QUESTIONS, & DECOLONIZATION. DESCRIBES DISPUTE OVER GIBRALTAR AS CLAIM IN WHICH LEGAL ARGUMENTS USED NOT IN OR-DER THAT ISSUES BE PROPERLY DETERMINED, BUT IN ORDER TO FOR-TIFY POLITICAL CLAIM. CRITICIZES SPAIN FOR REFUSING TO HAVE LEGAL RIGHTS JUDICIALLY DETERMINED.

0906 FEHRENBACH T.R.
THIS KIND OF PEACE.
NEW YORK: DAVID MCKAY, 1966, 345 PP., LC#66-17238.
STUDIES ORGANIZATION AND DEVELOPMENT OF UN. EXAMINES RELATIONS OF MEMBER NATIONS TO ITS STRUCTURE AND ACTIVITIES AS A WORLD BODY ACTIVELY PARTICIPATING IN CONFLICTS AND CHANGES. DISCUSSES ATTITUDE OF WORLD LEADERS TOWARD UN POLICIES.

0907 FEILCHENFELD E.H.
THE INTERNATIONAL ECONOMIC LAW OF BELLIGERENT OCCUPATION.
WASHINGTON: CARNEGIE ENDOWMENT, 1942, 181 PP.
CITES HAGUE REGULATIONS OF 1907 REFERRING TO SECTION PERTAINING TO MILITARY AUTHORITY OVER THE TERRITORY OF THE HOSTILE STATE. BRINGS TOGETHER HISTORICAL INTERPRETATIONS AND CURRENT PRACTICES RELATING TO THE ECONOMICS OF BELLIGERENT OCCUPATION. OFFERS THESE AS AIDS TO THOSE FORMULATING USA POLICY IN WW 2 MILITARY GOVERNMENT.

0908 FEIS H.
SEEN FROM E A, THREE INTERNATIONAL EPISODES.
NEW YORK: KNOPF, 1947, 313 PP.
HISTORICAL NARRATIVE OF USA POLICY BETWEEN WORLD WARS FOR SECURING RUBBER AND OIL RESERVES USED IN NATIONAL DEFENSE. DISCUSSES FAILURE OF LEAGUE OF NATIONS TO ENFORCE EFFECTIVE SANCTIONS AGAINST ITALY.

0909 FEIS H.
THE ROAD TO PEARL HARBOR.
PRINCETON: PRINCETON U PRESS, 1950, 356 PP.
GIVES ACCOUNT OF POLICIES AND ACTIONS OF US GOVERNMENT

AND JAPANESE GOVERNMENT LEADING TO OUTBREAK OF WAR BETWEEN THEM. PROBES DIPLOMATIC AND ECONOMIC RELATIONS, SPHERE OF INTEREST CONFLICTS, NEGOTIATIONS, AND GENERAL, CHANGING INTERNATIONAL RELATIONS INFLUENCING POLICIES OF TWO GOVERNMENTS.

0910 FEIS H.
THE CHINA TANGLE.
PRINCETON: PRINCETON U PRESS, 1953, 445 PP., LC#53-10142.
TRACES AMERICAN ACTIONS CONCERNING CHINA DURING AND AFTER WWII, DEALING WITH WARTIME MILITARY AND ECONOMIC ASSISTANCE, DECISIONS, AND DIFFICULTIES; DETERMINATION OF CHINESE FUTURE IN PACIFIC; CIVIL WAR; AND EFFORTS OF US TO CONTROL COURSE OF CHINESE POLITICAL DEVELOPMENT. MUCH OF TEXT DEVOTED TO WARTIME.

0911 FEIS H.
BETWEEN WAR AND PEACE: THE POTSDAM CONFERENCE.
PRINCETON: PRINCETON U PRESS, 1960, 367 PP., LC#60-12230.
DEALS WITH POTSDAM CONFERENCE AFTER WWII; ALSO COVERS PRECEDING EVENTS FROM TIME OF GERMAN SURRENDER. INCLUDES EXTENSIVE NOTES ON ACTUAL US DEALINGS WITH GERMANS AND PLANS FOR RESTORATION, LEND-LEASE, ETC. COMPLETE RESOLUTIONS OF BERLIN CONFERENCE.

0912 FEIS H.
FOREIGN AID AND FOREIGN POLICY.
NEW YORK: ST. MARTIN'S, 1964, 245 PP., $5.00.
REGARDS FOREIGN AID AS INTEGRAL PART OF FOREIGN POLICY. STRESSES IMPORTANCE OF PROGRAMMING FOR SOCIAL REFORM AND ECONOMIC CHANGE. COVERS OBSTACLES TO COOPERATION: AMERICAN RACE AND COLOR PREJUDICES, CLIMATE, MISUSE OF RESOURCES, LAND OWNERSHIP SYSTEMS, EXCESSIVE NATIONALISM, ETC. TREATS DILEMMAS OF AID ALLOTMENT.

0913 FELD B.T.
"A PLEDGE* NO FIRST USE."
BUL. ATOMIC SCIENTISTS, 23 (MAY 67), 46-48.
AN ARGUMENT FOR THE ADOPTION OF A TREATY PLEDGING NO FIRST USE OF NUCLEAR WEAPONS AGAINST NON-NUCLEAR NATIONS. SUCH A TREATY MIGHT PROVIDE IMPETUS TO FURTHER STEPS FOR ARMS CONTROL, AS WELL AS INHIBITING NUCLEAR PROLIFERATION. SUCH A TREATY WOULD ALSO BE AN ACKNOWLEDGMENT OF THE LIMITED UTILITY OF NUCLEAR WEAPONS IN THE SOLUTION OF CONFLICT.

0914 FELDMAN H.
"AID AS IMPERIALISM?"
INTER-AMERICAN ECON. AFF., 43 (APR. 67), 219-235.
SUGGESTS THAT FOREIGN AID MAY, IN ITS RESULTS, PROVE TO BE INSTRUMENT OF A RESURGING IMPERIALISM. SKETCHES INSTANCES OF ECONOMIC INSTABILITY & INCREASING POVERTY IN NATIONS WHICH HAVE RECEIVED LARGE AMOUNTS OF FOREIGN AID. SUGGESTS 3 CAUSES FOR THIS SITUATION* POOR LEADERSHIP, CORRUPTION, AND LACK OF WILL TO IMPROVE. CONTENDS DETERIORATING ECONOMIC SITUATION MAY LEAD TO ECONOMIC CONQUEST OF ASIA BY WEST.

0915 FELKER J.L.
SOVIET ECONOMIC CONTROVERSIES.
CAMBRIDGE: M I T PRESS, 1966, 172 PP., LC#66-26017.
ANALYZES SOVIET UNION ECONOMIC SYSTEM, CONCENTRATING ON DEVELOPING MARKETING SYSTEM, POST-STALIN REFORMS, AND CHANGES IN TRADE, PRICING, AND PROFITS IN USSR. COVERS LENINIST AND STALINIST THEORY, ITS APPLICATION TO SOVIET INDUSTRIAL ORGANIZATION OVER YEARS, AND RESULTING CHANGES.

0916 FENWICK C.G.
INTERNATIONAL LAW.
NEW YORK: APPLETON, 1948, 623 PP.
DISCUSSES NATURE, SCOPE, AND STRUCTURE OF SUBJECT. RELATES INTERNATIONAL LAW TO MUNICIPAL LAW. EXAMINES ORGANIZATION OF INTERNATIONAL COMMUNITY, FOCUSING ON UN AND REGIONAL PLANS. ANALYZES CONFLICT SETTLEMENT PROCEDURES.

0917 FENWICK C.G.
"ISSUES AT PUNTA DEL ESTE: NON-INTERVENTION VS COLLECTIVE SECURITY."
AMER. J. INT. LAW, 56 (APR. 62), 469-74.
REVIEWS QUESTIONS IN INTERNATIONAL LAW RAISED AT MEETING ON INTERPRETATION OF RIO TREATY (1947) AND ITS RELATION TO CUBAN QUESTION. SUMMARIZES ACTIONS TAKEN AT PUNTA DEL ESTE.

0918 FERKISS V.C.
AFRICA'S SEARCH FOR IDENTITY.
NEW YORK: BASIC BOOKS, 1966, 346 PP., LC#65-25970.
ARGUES THAT FOUNDATION OF AFRICAN POLITICS IS SEARCH FOR ROLE IN INTERNATIONAL RELATIONS, UNIQUE POLITICAL AND CULTURAL IDENTITY. DISCUSSES ASPECTS OF THIS SEARCH FOR IDENTITY: POLITICAL INDEPENDENCE FROM OUTSIDE RULE, REDISCOVERY OF OWN PAST, AND TRULY AFRICAN ROLE IN WORLD POLITICS.

0919 FERNBACH A.P.
"SOVIET COEXISTENCE STRATEGY."
WASHINGTON: PUBL. AFF. PR., 1960, 60 PP.
DESCRIPTION OF THE IMPACT OF SOVIET PARTICIPATION IN THE INTERNATIONAL LABOR ORGANIZATION.

0920 FERRELL R.H.
PEACE IN THEIR TIME.
NEW HAVEN: YALE U PR, 1952, 286 PP., LC#52-5361.
DISCUSSES THE ORIGIN OF THE KELLOGG-BRIAND PACT OF 1928, WHICH OUTLAWED WAR. ANALYZES INTERNATIONAL ATTEMPTS TO SECURE A PERMANENT PEACE AFTER WWI. EMPHASIZES ARISTIDE BRIAND'S STRUGGLES IN THE NEGOTIATIONS. INCLUDES LEAGUE OF NATIONS'S ROLE IN POST-WWI DIPLOMACY.

0921 FERRELL R.H.
AMERICAN DIPLOMACY: A HISTORY.
NEW YORK: W W NORTON, 1959, 576 PP., LC#59-6082.
STUDIES US DIPLOMACY AND MAJOR EVENTS THAT INFLUENCED IT FROM REVOLUTION TO EISENHOWER'S SECOND ADMINISTRATION. EMPHASIZES 20TH-CENTURY, DEALING REGIONALLY WITH WORLD AND CHRONOLOGICALLY WITH WORLD WARS.

0922 FERRERO G.
PEACE AND WAR (TRANS. BY BERTHA PRITCHARD)
LONDON: MACMILLAN, 1933, 244 PP.
SERIES OF LECTURES DISCUSSES HISTORY OF WARFARE AND MAN'S OBSESSION WITH IT. GREATEST THREAT TO WESTERN CIVILIZATION IS "SUPER WAR" WAGED WITHOUT REASON. BELIEVES MAN NEEDS TO REDISCOVER HUMANISTIC AND CHRISTIAN VALUES. THERE MUST BE NO MORE WAR, BECAUSE THE MORE TERRIBLE THE WAR, THE HARDER IT IS TO ESTABLISH LASTING PEACE. THOSE WHO TOOK INITIATIVE IN ENDING MONARCHY SHOULD HELP BRING ABOUT END TO REVOLUTION.

0923 FICHTE J.G.
ADDRESSES TO THE GERMAN NATION.
LA SALLE: OPEN COURT, 1922, 269 PP.
SPEECHES GIVEN TO GERMAN PEOPLE AFTER GERMAN DEFEAT IN FRANCO-PRUSSIAN WAR. SPEECHES GLORIFY EVERYTHING GERMAN AND ARE REGARDED AS THE BEGINNING OF GERMAN NATIONALISM. IDEAS OF CLOSED COMMERIAL STATE, PRINCIPLE OF NATIONALITY, SUPERIORITY OF GERMAN CULTURE, AND DEVELOPMENT OF EDUCATION HAD PROFOUND EFFECT ON FUTURE DEVELOPMENT OF GERMANY.

0924 FIELD G.C.
POLITICAL THEORY.
LONDON: METHUEN, 1956, 297 PP.
DISCUSSES VARIOUS ASPECTS OF POLITICAL THEORY AS CONCEPT OF SOVEREIGNTY, STATE, INDIVIDUAL LIBERTY, ETC. EXAMINES IN DETAIL MACHINERY OF DEMOCRACY AND RELATIONS BETWEEN STATES. CONCLUDES WITH ESSAY ON RELATION BETWEEN POLITICS, ECONOMICS, AND ETHICS.

0925 FIFIELD R.H.
"WOODROW WILSON AND THE FAR EAST."
NEW YORK: THOMAS Y CROWELL, 1952.
DIVIDED INTO MANUSCRIPT SOURCES: OFFICIAL AND PRIVATE PAPERS; PRINTED SOURCES; OFFICIAL DOCUMENTS OF US, FRANCE, CHINA, GERMANY, GREAT BRITAIN, JAPAN, RUSSIA; AND MEMOIRS, BIOGRAPHIES, SPECIAL STUDIES, HISTORIES, ARTICLES, AND NEWSPAPERS.

0926 FIFIELD R.H.
WOODROW WILSON AND THE FAR EAST.
NEW YORK: THOMAS Y CROWELL, 1952, 383 PP., LC#52-12518.
ANALYZES SHANTUNG QUESTION AT PARIS PEACE CONFERENCE TO STUDY WILSON AS NEGOTIATOR. UTILIZES MEMORANDA PLUS CONFERENCE RECORDS TO REVEAL COMPLEXITY OF CONTROVERSY AND PROCESS OF WILSON'S FINAL COURSE OF ACTION.

0927 FIFIELD R.H.
"THE DIPLOMACY OF SOUTHEAST ASIA: 1945-1958."
NEW YORK: HARPER & ROW, 1958.
ARGUES THAT PERIOD 1945-58 WAS FORMATIVE FOR NATIONAL DEVELOPMENT AND INTERNATIONAL RECOGNITION FOR STATES OF SOUTHEAST ASIA. FOCUSES ON ASIAN RELATIONS WITH CONSIDERATIONS OF BACKGROUND OF INDEPENDENCE, REGIONALISM, AND ROLE OF UNITED NATIONS. LARGE BIBLIOGRAPHY ORGANIZED ALPHABETICALLY BY COUNTRY.

0928 FIFIELD R.H.
SOUTHEAST ASIA IN UNITED STATES POLICY.
NEW YORK: PRAEGER, 1963, 488 PP., $6.50.
IN SEEKING TO DEVELOP A RATIONALE FOR AMERICAN POLICY IN SOUTHEAST ASIA, THE AUTHOR SUGGESTS GUIDELINES FOR MAKING IT APPLICABLE THROUGH DIFFERENT INSTRUMENTALITIES NOW AND IN THE YEARS AHEAD.

0929 FIGANIERE J.C.
BIBLIOTHECA HISTORICA PORTUGUEZA.
LISBON: NA TIPOGRAFIA DO PANORAMA, 1850, 349 PP.
BIBLIOGRAPHY OF PORTUGUESE BOOKS AND DOCUMENTS ON PORTUGUESE POLITICAL, CIVIL, AND RELIGIOUS HISTORY. ALSO INCLUDES PORTUGUESE POSSESSIONS.

0930 FILENE P.G.
AMERICANS AND THE SOVIET EXPERIMENT, 1917-1933.
CAMBRIDGE: HARVARD U PR, 1967, 384 PP., LC#67-11669.
EXAMINES AMERICAN ATTITUDES TOWARD THE USSR FROM HER ESTABLISHMENT UNTIL US DIPLOMATIC RECOGNITION. TREATS VIEWS FROM ALL AREAS OF POLITICAL AND INTELLECTUAL SPECTRUM. CASE STUDIES OF FOUR US JOURNALISTS WHO WENT TO RUSSIA AS COMMUN-

ISTS, THREE OF WHOM WERE DISILLUSIONED. ALSO TREATS AMERICAN ATTITUDES TOWARD CAPITALISM, SOCIALISM, AND AMERICAN SOCIETY.

0931 FINE S.
RECENT AMERICA* CONFLICTING INTERPRETATIONS OF THE GREAT ISSUES (2ND ED.)
NEW YORK: MACMILLAN, 1967, 480 PP.
EXAMINES POLITICAL, SOCIAL, ECONOMIC, AND CULTURAL ASPECTS OF 20TH CENTURY AMERICAN HISTORY FROM T ROOSEVELT TO PRESENT. WRITINGS ARE GROUPED INTO 14 TOPICS AND COVER ITEMS SUCH AS BOMBING OF HIROSHIMA, PROHIBITION, GOLDWATERISM, EFFECTS OF KENNEDY'S RELIGION ON 1960 CAMPAIGN, NEW DEAL, THE TWO WORLD WARS, KOREA, ANE TRUMAN-MACARTHUR CONTROVERSY.

0932 FINER H.
DULLES OVER SUEZ.
CHICAGO: QUADRANGLE BOOKS, INC, 1964, 538 PP., LC#64-10924.
SCHOLARLY ANALYSIS OF THEORY AND PRACTICE OF DIPLOMACY OF JOHN FOSTER DULLES FOCUSING ON CRITICAL IMPORTANCE OF DULLES' ROLE IN 1956 SUEZ CRISIS. EMPHASIZES SEVERITY OF EVENT AND THREAT OF ATOMIC WORLD WAR WHICH IT POSED. PORTRAYS SUBORDINATION OF PRESIDENT TO STATE DEPARTMENT DURING DULLES' TERM OF OFFICE. CHIEF SOURCE OF WORK IS SERIES OF INTERVIEWS WITH OVER 30 LEADING WORLD STATESMEN.

0933 FINKELSTEIN L.S.
"THE UNITED NATIONS AND ORGANIZATIONS FOR CONTROL OF ARMAMENT."
INT. ORGAN., 16 (WINTER 62', 1-19.
DISCUSSES INDEPENDENT ROLE OF DISARMAMENT NEGOTIATIONS UNDER UN GUIDANCE. SUGGESTS THAT SUBORDINATING ARMS CONTROL TO UN MAKES TASK HARDER BECAUSE INTERESTED POWERS FAVOR AUTONOMOUS HANDLING OF PROBLEM. SUGGESTS ARMS CONTROL MIGHT BENEFIT IF THERE WERE A LIASON BETWEEN UN AND AGENCIES AND IF THE AGENCIES COULD REFER FOR SETTLEMENT BY UN CERTAIN POLITICAL QUESTIONS.

0934 FINKLE J.L., GABLE R.W.
POLITICAL DEVELOPMENT AND SOCIAL CHANGE.
NEW YORK: JOHN WILEY, 1966, 599 PP.
STUDIES POLITICS IN EMERGING NATIONS, FOCUSING ON FUNCTIONAL RELATIONSHIPS BETWEEN THE POLITICAL SYSTEM AND NONPOLITICAL ELEMENTS IN THE SOCIAL SYSTEM. TOPICS INCLUDE THE SYSTEMS APPROACH TO POLITICAL DEVELOPMENT, INDIVIDUALS AND IDEAS IN DEVELOPING POLITIES, THE MODERNIZERS, AND THE POLITICS OF DEVELOPMENT AND NATION-BUILDING.

0935 FISCHER G.
"UNE NOUVELLE ORGANIZATION REGIONALE: L'ASA."
ANNU. FRANC. DR. INTER., 8 (1962), 210-14.
NEW REGIONAL ORGANIZATION, ASA, ESTABLISHED AS SIGNIFICANT MEANS TO ECONOMIC, TECHNICAL, AND CULTURAL COOPERATION. QUESTIONS WHETHER CAN ACHIEVE GOALS. POINTS UP POLITICAL WEAKNESS OF PARTICIPATING COUNTRIES.

0936 FISCHER L.
"THE SOVIET-AMERICAN ANTAGONISM: HOW WILL IT END."
A. AMER. POLIT. SOC. SCI., 324 (JULY 59), 39-45.
STUDIES USA, USSR IDEOLOGICAL DISPUTE. REALIZES THIRD WAR UNLIKELY BUT COLD WAR AS ESSENTIAL FEATURE OF PRESENT STRUGGLE FOR POWER SUPREMACY. THINKS USA SHOULD NOT TRY TO REMAKE WORLD IN WESTERN IMAGE. DOES NOT CONSIDER RUSSIA AND CHINA CAPABLE OF CONVERTING USA INTO MARXIST BLOC. FORSEES DISENGAGEMENT AS THE ONLY COURSE FOR FUTURE.

0937 FISCHER L.
RUSSIA, AMERICA, AND THE WORLD.
NEW YORK: HARPER & ROW, 1960, 244 PP., LC#61-06193.
EXAMINES SOVIET AND AMERICAN FOREIGN POLICY TOWARD REST OF WORLD SINCE WWII. INCLUDES ROOTS OF SOVIET POLICY, POLITICAL DEVELOPMENTS IN ASIA, FUTURE OF COMMUNISN; SUGGESTS A FOREIGN POLICY FOR US.

0938 FISCHER L.
THE SOVIETS IN WORLD AFFAIRS.
NEW YORK: ALFRED KNOPF, 1960, 616 PP.
HISTORY OF SOVIET FOREIGN RELATIONS, 1917-29, INCLUDI G VERSAILLES, BOLSHEVIK ATTITUDES TOWARD POLAND, UK, JAPAN, CHINESE REVOLUTION, DISARMAMENT, AND PARTICIPATION IN INTERNAT.ONAL CONFERENCES.

0939 FISCHER-GALATI S. ED.
EASTERN EUROPE IN THE SIXTIES.
NEW YORK: FREDERICK PRAEGER, 1963, 242 PP., LC#63-18532.
ATTEMPT TO PRESENT AND INTERPRET PRINCIPAL PROBLEMS AND DEVELOPMENTS IN CONTEMPORARY EASTERN EUROPE ON "AREA BASIS." AUTHOR DISCUSSES SOVIET BLOC, ALBANIA, AND YUGOSLAVIA.

0940 FISHER R. ED.
INTERNATIONAL CONFLICT AND BEHAVIORAL SCIENCE: THE CRAIGVILLE PAPERS.
NEW YORK: BASIC, 1964, 290 PP., $6.50.
BY EXAMINING ASSUMPTIONS OR INFLUENCES AFFECTING DECISION-MAKERS IN AN INTERNATIONAL CONFLICT SITUATION THE CONTRIBUTORS SUGGEST BOTH CHANGES WHICH OUGHT TO BE MADE IN THE WAY INTERNATIONAL CONFLICT IS HANDLED AND HOW SUCH CHANGES MIGHT BE BROUGHT ABOUT. SIXTEEN ESSAYS ON TOPICS SUCH AS PERCEPTIONS OF THE COLD WAR, THE DEVELOPMENT OF INTERNATIONAL COMMUNITY, AND THE PEACE MOVEMENT.

0941 FISHER S.N. ED.
NEW HORIZONS FOR THE UNITED STATES IN WORLD AFFAIRS.
COLUMBUS: OHIO STATE U PR, 1966, 162 PP., LC#66-63003.
DISCUSSES NEW TASKS OF US IN FOREIGN AFFAIRS, EXAMINING POSSIBILITY OF INCREASING FOREIGN AID. ANALYZES CONTINUED RELATIONS WITH UN. COVERS OUTLOOK OF POLICY IN GENERAL, AND GIVES SPECIAL ATTENTION TO SPECIFIC AREAS OF NEED.

0942 FITZGERALD C.P.
THE BIRTH OF COMMUNIST CHINA (2ND ED.)
NEW YORK: FREDERICK PRAEGER, 1966, 288 PP., LC#65-27021.
ANALYZES CHINESE REVOLUTION; EXAMINES HISTORY OF THE MOVEMENT. STUDIES INTRODUCTION AND DEVELOPMENT OF COMMUNISM IN STRUGGLE FOR REPUBLIC. DEALS WITH NATIONALIST CONTROL OF OVERNMENT AND WWII UNITY LEADING TO LATER COMMUNIST VICTORY. VIEWS CHINA SINCE EARLY 1950'S AND CHINESE POLICY IN FAR EAST AND TOWARD WEST.

0943 FITZGIBBON R.H.
"DICTATORSHIP AND DEMOCRACY IN LATIN AMERICA."
INT. AFF., 37 (JAN. 60), 48-57.
HISTORICAL APPROACH SEEKING TO ACHIEVE BETTER UNDERSTANDING OF PROBLEM. DESCRIBES CURRENTS OF CHANGE DIRECTED TOWARD REFORM AND MODERNIZATION. CALLS FOR ECONOMIC AND POLITICAL INTEGRATION OF LATIN AMERICAN COUNTRIES.

0944 FITZSIMMONS T., MALOF P. ET AL.
"USSR: ITS PEOPLE, ITS SOCIETY, ITS CULTURE."
NEW HAVEN: HUMAN REL AREA FILES, 1960.
ANALYSIS DEFINING DOMINANT SOCIOLOGICAL, POLITICAL, AND ECONOMIC ASPECTS OF FUNCTIONING SOCIETY, AND IDENTIFICATION OF PATTERNS OF CHARACTERISTIC BEHAVIOR. EMPHASIS ON SOCIAL ORGANIZATION, VALUES AND PATTERNS OF LIVING; INCLUDES MATERIAL ON POLITICAL AND ECONOMIC ORGANIZATION OF SOCIETY. CONTAINS EXTENSIVE SELECTED AND SOMEWHAT SPECIALIZED BIBLIOGRAPHY.

0945 FLECHTHEIM O.K. ED.
FUNDAMENTALS OF POLITICAL SCIENCE.
LISBON: MENDONCA, 1952, 587 PP., LC#52-7604.
INTRODUCTORY TEXT DEFINES FUNDAMENTAL PRINCIPLES GOVERNING POLITICAL RELATIONSHIPS; EMPHASIZES PRINCIPLES AND PROBLEMS RATHER THAN LAWS AND INSTITUTIONS. SURVEYS AND EVALUATES FORMS OF GOVERNMENT AND POLITICAL BEHAVIOR IN POLITICAL SYSTEMS THROUGHOUT WORLD. INCLUDES GROWTH OF POLITICAL IDEAS, ELEMENTS OF NATION STATE, CONSTITUTIONAL CONCEPT, PUBLIC OPINION, POLITICAL PARTIES, ETC.

0946 FLEMING D.F.
THE COLD WAR AND ITS ORIGINS: 1950-1960 (VOL. II)
GARDEN CITY: DOUBLEDAY, 1961, 1158 PP.
CHRONOLGICAL ANALYSIS OF COLD WAR IN ASIA--CHINA, KOREA, SOUTH EAST ASIA, FORMOSA; COLD WAR IN EUROPE, 1955-60 --POLAND, HUNGARY, SUEZ, AND US ACTIONS WITH EACH. TREATS OF SPUTNIKS AND AFTERMATH OF WORLD AFFAIRS, DISCUSSING "WHY WEST LOST COLD WAR" AS WELL AS FUTURE.

0947 FLEMING D.F.
THE COLD WAR AND ITS ORIGINS: 1917-1950 (VOL. I)
GARDEN CITY: DOUBLEDAY, 1961, 540 PP.
CHRONOLOGICAL ANALYSIS OF COLD WAR FROM WWI AND BOLSHEVIK REVOLUTION THROUGH SOVIET A-BOMB TESTS, 1949-50. DISCUSSES DEVELOPMENT OF COMMUNISM AS IDEOLOGY, GERMAN-RUSSIAN RELATIONS, WWII, AND ITS AFTERMATH IN EUROPE WITH US INTERVENTION.

0948 FLEMING D.F.
"CAN PAX AMERICANA SUCCEED?"
ANN. ACAD. POL. SOC. SCI., 360 (JULY 65), 127-139.
THE DECISION TO USE FORCE IN VIETNAM HAS DONE IRREPARABLE HARM TO AMERICA'S IMAGE IN ASIA AND IS FORCING THE USSR AND CHINA TOGETHER IN SPITE OF THEIR DIFFERENCES. IT HAS ALSO INCREASED HOSTILITY TOWARD AMERICAN ECONOMIC OUTTHRUSTS IN WEST EUROPE, WHICH ENCOURAGES ECONOMIC COOPERATION BETWEEN WEST AND EAST EUROPE. THE DANGER OF AN INVOLUNTARY "FORTRESS AMERICA" LOOMS LARGE.

0949 FLEMMING D.
THE TREATY VETO OF THE AMERICAN SENATE.
NEW YORK: PUTNAM, 1930, 325 PP.
THE REJECTION OF TREATIES BY THE US SENATE IS OFTEN PART OF AN ATTEMPT TO EXTEND ITS OWN POWER OVER INTERNATIONAL RELATIONS. RESULTS ARE THE MOST SERIOUS WHEN MACHINERY FOR THE PEACEFUL SETTLEMENT OF INTERNATIONAL DISPUTES IS INVOLVED.

0950 FLEMMING D.
THE UNITED STATES AND THE LEAGUE OF NATIONS, 1918-1920.
NEW YORK: PUTNAM, 1932, 559 PP.
TRACES IDEATIONAL ORIGINS OF LEAGUE, FRAMING OF TREATY AND FATE OF TREATY IN SENATE. FOLLOWS COURSE OF DEBATE,

AMENDMENTS, COMPROMISES, AND COMMITTEE WORK. REJECTION OF TREATY SEEN AS CONTINUANCE OF PREVIOUS ANTI-PEACE TREATY POLICY. COOPERATION OF SOVEREIGN STATES ESSENTIAL TO LEAGUE. ITS ECONOMIC INTERESTS DEMAND USA MEMBERSHIP.

0951 FLEMMING D.
THE UNITED STATES AND WORLD ORGANIZATION, 1920-1933.
NEW YORK: COLUMB. U. PR., 1938, 569 PP.
OUTLINES EVENTS FOLLOWING AMERICAN REFUSAL TO JOIN LEAGUE, INCLUDING WASHINGTON PEACE CONFERENCE, DISARMAMENT TALKS, SEIZURE OF MANCHURIA, AND DOMESTIC EVENTS. OBSERVES CONTEMPORANEOUS AMERICAN FOREIGN POLICY AND JOURNALISTIC OPINIONS ON LEAGUE. CONCLUDES FUTURE PEACE REQUIRES AMERICAN PARTICIPATION IN WORLD GOVERNMENT.

0952 FLOREN LOZANO L.
BIBLIOGRAFIA DE LA BIBLIOGRAFIA DOMINICANA.
TRUJILLO: ROQUES ROMAN, 1948, 66 PP.
BIBLIOGRAPHY OF BIBLIOGRAPHIES ON DOMINICAN REPUBLIC. ENTRIES ARRANGED BY SUBJECT, AND SPANISH-LANGUAGE ITEMS ARE ANNOTATED. CONTAINS 230 ENTRIES, MAJORITY IN SPANISH LANGUAGE. INCLUDES INDEX OF AUTHORS, SUBJECTS, AND BIOGRAPHIES.

0953 FLORES E.
LAND REFORM AND THE ALLIANCE FOR PROGRESS (PAMPHLET)
PRINCETON: CTR OF INTL STUDIES, 1963, 14 PP.
DISCUSSES PROSPECTS OF ALLIANCE FOR PROGRESS, ARGUING THAT IT CAN SUCCEED ONLY IF IT ACCEPTS DRASTIC REVOLUTIONARY CHANGE IN LATIN AMERICA, EMPHASIZING IMPORTANCE OF LAND REFORM AS INTEGRAL PART OF CHANGE.

0954 FLORES R.H.
CATALOGO DE TESIS DOCTORALES DE LAS FACULTADES DE LA UNIVERSIDAD DE EL SALVADOR.
EL SALVADOR: U DE EL SALVADOR, 1960, 620 PP.
CATALOG OF DOCTORAL THESES PRESENTED FROM 1878 TO 1960 AT UNIVERSITY OF EL SALVADOR. ENTRIES ARRANGED BY FACULTY AND CLASSIFIED BY DEWEY CLASSIFICATION SYSTEM.

0955 FLORIN J., HERZ J.H.
"BOLSHEVIST AND NATIONAL SOCIALIST DOCTRINES OF INTERNATIONAL LAW."
SOC. RES., 7 (FEB. 40), 1-31.
CASE STUDY OF FUNCTION OF SOCIAL SCIENCE IN TOTALITARIAN DICTATORSHIP. ADVANCES NEW FOUNDATION OF INTERNATIONAL LAW BASED ON TOTALITARIAN IDEOLOGY. CONTENDS INTERNATIONAL LAW REFLECTS NATIONS' ATTITUDES TOWARDS INTERNATIONAL RELATIONS.

0956 FLYNN A.H. ED.
WORLD UNDERSTANDING: A SELECTED BIBLIOGRAPHY.
NEW YORK: OCEANA PUBLISHING, 1965, 263 PP., LC#65-22167.
SELECTED ANNOTATED BIBLIOGRAPHY OF BOOKS, PAMPHLETS, AND RESOURCE MATERIALS DEALING WITH THE UN AND ITS GLOBAL ACTIVITIES. BOOKS ARE LISTED TOPICALLY AND ARE GRADED ACCORDING TO RECOMMENDED AGE LEVELS FOR READERS. LEVELS RANGE FROM PRESCHOOL TO ADULT. INCLUDES PUBLISHERS AND SOURCES INDEX AND AUTHOR-TITLE INDEX.

0957 FOCSANEANU L.
"LES GRANDS TRAITES DE LA REPUBLIQUE POPULAIRE DE CHINE."
ANNU. FRANC. DR. INTER., 8 (1962), 139-77.
DEALS WITH FOREIGN POLICY PROBLEMS AND CONVENTIONS HELD BY CHINESE POPULAR REPUBLIC SINCE GOVERNMENT SET UP IN 1949. ANALYZES TREATY WITH USSR AND ITS EFFECTS ON DOMESTIC SOCIO-POLITICAL STRUCTURE. SPECIAL ATTENTION GIVEN BANDUNG CONFERENCE.

0958 FOOTMAN D. ED.
INTERNATIONAL COMMUNISM.
LONDON: CHATTO, 1960, 151 PP.
DESCRIBES THE COMINTERN IN ITS 1920-30 PERIOD WITH FOCUS ON DEVELOPMENT OF UNITED FRONT MOVEMENT IN FRANCE, GERMANY, AND CHINA. REVIEWS POST-WW 2 INTERNATIONAL COMMUNISM IN TERMS OF ITS CENTRALISTIC, POLICENTRISTIC AND REVISIONIST TENDENCIES.

0959 FORBES H.W.
THE STRATEGY OF DISARMAMENT.
WASHINGTON: PUBL. AFF. PR., 1962, 158 PP.
DISCUSSES STEPS TAKEN TOWARDS GENERAL DISARMAMENT AND CONCLUDES 'SUBSTANTIAL AGREEMENT AMONG THE GREAT POWERS ON DISARMAMENT IS IMPOSSIBLE SO LONG AS EACH OF THEM SUSPECTS OTHERS OF AGGRESSIVE INTENTIONS.'

0960 FORD A.G.
THE GOLD STANDARD 1880-1914: BRITAIN AND ARGENTINA.
LONDON: OXFORD U PR, 1962, 200 PP.
STUDIES OPERATIONS OF GOLD STANDARD IN EACH COUNTRY PRIOR TO WWI. EMPHASIZES STRUCTURE OF INTERNATIONAL ACCOUNTS AND SYSTEMS, POINTING OUT TRADE, ETC., BETWEEN THESE NATIONS AS AN EXAMPLE. THEORIZES FROM NEW APPROACH BALANCE OF PAYMENTS' PROBLEMS AND THEIR SOLUTIONS WHICH LED TO SUCCESS OF GOLD STANDARD IN ENGLAND AND ITS FAILURE IN ARGENTINA.

0961 FORD FOUNDATION
REPORT OF THE STUDY FOR THE FORD FOUNDATION ON POLICY AND PROGRAM.
DETROIT: FORD FOUND., 1949, 139 PP.
MAJOR OBJECTIVES ARE TO ARRIVE AT A CLEARER UNDERSTANDING OF THE MEANING OF HUMAN WELFARE AND TO CONSIDER THE WAYS IN WHICH IT IS MOST THWARTED AND THREATENED. PROPOSES PROGRAMS WHICH THE FOUNDATION MIGHT SPONSOR AND OUTLINES PROCEDURES.

0962 FOREIGN POLICY ASSOCIATION
"US CONCERN FOR WORLD LAW."
INTERCOM, 9 (MAY-JUNE 67), 40-47.
DISCUSSES THE CONTROVERSY OVER US ADOPTION OF THE UNIVERSAL DECLARATION OF HUMAN RIGHTS AND OVER THE CONNALLY AMMENDMENT TO THE JURISDICTION OF THE INTERNATIONAL COURT OF JUSTICE. DEMONSTRATES THE NECESSITY OF WORLD LAW FOR THE SUPERVISION OF DISARMAMENT AND THE MAINTENANCE OF PEACE.

0963 FOREIGN POLICY CLEARING HOUSE
STRATEGY FOR THE 60'S.
WASHINGTON: FOR POL CLEAR HOUSE, 1960, 155 PP., LC#60-53527.
SUMMARY AND ANALYSIS OF STUDIES PREPARED BY 13 FOREIGN POLICY RESEARCH CENTERS FOR US SENATE. DEALS PRIMARILY WITH US FOREIGN-POLICY INSTRUMENTS, AND WITH THE CHALLENGE OF EMERGING NATIONS, OF COMMUNISM, AND OF MILITARY DEFENSE.

0964 FOREIGN TRADE LIBRARY
NEW TITLES RECEIVED IN THE LIBRARY.
PHILA: FOREIGN TRADE LIBRARY.
BIMONTHLY PUBLICATION SINCE 1964. ANNOTATED, ALPHABETICAL LISTING OF BOOKS AND SERIALS. ITEMS ALSO ARRANGED IN SECOND SECTION BY GEOGRAPHIC REGION. SUBJECTS INCLUDE GENERAL DESCRIPTION AND HISTORY, COMMERCE, BUSINESS AND ECONOMIC CONDITIONS, INDUSTRIES, AND GENERAL STATISTICS.

0965 FORGAC A.A.
NEW DIPLOMACY AND THE UNITED NATIONS.
NEW YORK: PAGEANT PR, 1965, 173 PP., LC#65-24549.
TRACES EVOLUTION OF DIPLOMACY AND EXAMINES FUNCTIONS OF DIPLOMATS AND FOREIGN OFFICE. DESCRIBES CEREMONIALS, TITLES AND PRECEDENTS, AND ANALYZES DIPLOMATIC PRACTICES OF UK, GERMANY, USSR, AND FRANCE. EXAMINES IMPACT OF UN ON MODERN DIPLOMACY.

0966 FORM W.H. ED., BLUM A.A. ED.
INDUSTRIAL RELATIONS AND SOCIAL CHANGE IN LATIN AMERICA.
GAINESVILLE: U OF FLA PR, 1965, 177 PP., LC#65-18667.
ATTEMPTS TO EVOLVE THEORIES OF INDUSTRIAL RELATIONS THROUGH COMPARATIVE ANALYSIS. ESSAYS UNIFIED BY COMMON THESIS THAT THE STATE OF A NATION'S INDUSTRIAL RELATIONS IS CORRELATED TO SOCIAL CHANGES WITHIN THAT COUNTRY.

0967 FORSTMANN A.
DIE GRUNDLAGEN DER AUSSENWIRTSCHAFTSTHEORIE.
BERLIN: VERL DUNCKER AND HUM, 1956, 418 PP.
DISCUSSES THEORY AND PRINCIPLES OF FOREIGN TRADE AS DEVELOPED SINCE WWI. GOES BEYOND PRINCIPLES INHERENT IN EXCHANGE OF GOODS AND EXAMINES IN DETAIL QUESTIONS OF CURRENCY AND ECONOMIC CONDITIONS AFTER WWI AND WWII.

0968 FORTESCUE G.K. ED.
SUBJECT INDEX OF THE MODERN WORKS ADDED TO THE LIBRARY OF THE BRITISH MUSEUM IN THE YEARS 1881-1900 (3 VOLS.)
LONDON: W CLOWES & SONS, LTD, 1903.
CONTAINS ABOUT 155,000 ENTRIES REFERRING TO BOOKS FIRST PUBLISHED OR REISSUED BETWEEN JANUARY, 1881, AND DECEMBER, 1900. UNDER EACH COUNTRY ARE FOUND WORKS ON ANTIQUITIES, ARMY, COLONIES, CONSTITUTION AND GOVERNMENT, HISTORY, LAW, NAVY, POLITICS, SOCIAL LIFE, TOPOGRAPHY, TRADE, AND FINANCE.

0969 FOSTER J.G.
BRITAIN IN WESTERN EUROPE: WEU AND THE ATLANTIC ALLIANCE.
LONDON: OXFORD U. PR., 1956, 120 PP.
ANALYZES THE SIGNIFICANCE OF WESTERN EUROPEAN UNION, A MILITARY ALLIANCE INCLUDING ENGLAND, FRANCE, WEST GERMANY, AND ITALY, DESIGNED TO BRING ABOUT GERMAN REARMAMENT. EXAMINES HISTORY OF WESTERN EUROPEAN INTEGRATION MOVEMENTS SINCE 1946.

0970 FOSTER J.W.
THE PRACTICE OF DIPLOMACY AS ILLUSTRATED IN THE FOREIGN RELATIONS OF THE UNITED STATES.
BOSTON: HOUGHTON MIFFLIN, 1906, 401 PP.
ILLUSTRATES ROLE OF DIPLOMAT IN FIELD OF INTERNATIONAL RELATIONS. DESCRIBES RULES AND PROCEDURE OF DIPLOMATIC INTERCOURSE. RECORDS FAILURES AND SUCCESSES OF AMERICAN DIPLOMACY ABROAD. INCLUDES SHORT BIBLIOGRAPHY, MOSTLY RECOLLECTIONS, MEMOIRS, BIOGRAPHIES WITH SOME BOOKS ON INTERNATIONAL LAW AND FOREIGN RELATIONS.

0971 FOSTER W.C.
"ARMS CONTROL AND DISARMAMENT IN A DIVIDED WORLD."
ANN. AMER. ACAD. POLIT. SOC. SCI., 342 (JULY 62), 80-8.
DISCUSSES REVOLUTION IN NUCLEAR WEAPONS AND THE NEED FOR ARMS CONTROL DESPITE THE CLASH IN IDEOLOGIES. SUGGESTS EXPLORING POSSIBILITIES OF PEACEFUL SOLUTION ON BASIS OF NUCLEAR STRATEGIC STANDOFF, EVOLUTION OF SOVIET UNION,

ATLANTIC COMMUNITY AND THE UN, AND COMMON INTERESTS OF THE WESTERN AND COMMUNIST WORLDS. PRESENTS THE USA POSITION AND HOPE FOR THE FUTURE.

0972 FOX W.T.R.
UNITED STATES POLICY IN A TWO POWER WORLD.
NEW HAVEN: YALE U PR, 1947, 17 PP.
DISCUSSES US-SOVIET RELATIONS, DECLARING NEED FOR US TO SUPPORT NATIONS OF WESTERN EUROPE SO THAT THEY MAY FUNCTION AS BUFFER STATES. ENCOURAGES FOREIGN AID TO NEUTRALS AS SOUND ACTION, SINCE US DOES NOT NEED TO DOMINATE EUROPE TO PREVENT SOVIETS FROM DOMINATING IT. MAJOR UNCERTAINTY REVEALED IS EFFECT OF NUCLEAR WEAPONS IN INTERNATIONAL AFFAIRS.

0973 FOX W.T.R.
"INTERWAR INTERNATIONAL RELATIONS RESEARCH: THE AMERICAN EXPERIENCE."
WORLD POLIT., 2 (OCT. 49), 67-79.
FINDS RESEARCH PRIOR TO WW 2 TO BE LARGELY HISTORICAL, SUBJECTIVE AND UTOPIAN. NEW APPROACH ATTEMPTS TO BE VALUE-FREE, EMPHASIZING INTERNATIONAL POLITICS.

0974 FOX W.T.R.
"CIVIL-MILITARY RELATIONS."
WORLD POLIT., 6 (OCT. 53-JULY 54), 278-288.
IDENTIFIES VARIOUS GROUPS CONCERNED WITH CIVIL-MILITARY RESEARCH PROJECTS. ATTENTION FOCUSED ON PUBLIC-POLICY PROBLEMS POSED BY MILITARY MOBILIZATION DURING PEACE-TIME. URGES NEED FOR EFFECTIVE CO-ORDINATION OF MILITARY, DIPLOMATIC AND INDUSTRIALIZATION POLICIES.

0975 FOX W.T.R. ED.
THEORETICAL ASPECTS OF INTERNATIONAL RELATIONS.
NOTRE DAME: U. PR., 1959, 118 PP.
AN ANTHOLOGY OF SEVEN ARTICLES ON INTERNATIONAL RELATIONS. WORK OF P NITZE, H MORGENTHAU, W FOX, K WALTZ, L KINDLEBERGER, A WOLFERS AND R NIEBUHR ARE INCLUDED. ARTICLES ARE FROM A SYMPOSIUM HELD AT COLUMBIA UNIVERSITY IN 1957.

0976 FOX W.T.R.
"THE USES OF INTERNATIONAL RELATIONS THEORY.
IN (FOX, THE THEORETICAL ASPECTS OF INTERNATIONAL RELATIONS, SOUTH BEND: NOTRE DAME U. PR., 1959, 24-49).
DISCUSSES RELATIONSHIP OF INTERNATIONAL RELATIONS THEORY TO PUBLIC POLICY. THESIS THAT THEORY AIDS EFFICIENCY IN ATTAINING DESIRED ENDS AND MINIMIZES AREA OF CHOICE FOR POLICY MAKERS.

0977 FRANCK P.G.
AFGHANISTAN BETWEEN EAST AND WEST: THE ECONOMICS OF COMPETITIVE COEXISTENCE (PAMPHLET)
WASHINGTON: NATL PLANNING ASSN, 1960, 86 PP., LC#60-14091.
STUDIES NATION VITALLY DEPENDENT ON TRADE, LANDLOCKED, AT MERCY OF TRANSIT RIGHTS ACCORDED BY ADJOINING COUNTRIES, AND POLITICALLY EXPOSED TO USSR ACROSS AN INDEFENSIBLE BORDER. ANALYZES HISTORY AND STATE OF USSR AND WESTERN AID, SHOWING FIERCE COMPETITION THAT HAS ARISEN. SUGGESTS THAT INTERNATIONAL ORGANIZATION (SUCH AS UN) SHOULD ADMINISTER AID TO REDUCE TENSION AND RELIEVE PRESSURES ON AFGHANISTAN.

0978 FRANCK P.G.
AFGHANISTAN: BETWEEN EAST AND WEST.
WASHINGTON: NAT. PLAN. ASSN., 1960, 183 PP.
SIXTH STUDY IN AREA OF THE ECONOMICS OF COMPETITIVE COEXISTENCE. PRESENTS ECONOMIC, POLITICAL, SOCIAL AND GEOGRAPHIC SITUATION OF AFGHANISTAN. CONCLUDES WITH ANALYSIS OF WESTERN AND SOVIET AID PROGRAMS WITH PARTICULAR EMPHASIS ON THEIR COMPETITIVE ASPECTS.

0979 FRANK E. ED.
LAWMAKERS IN A CHANGING WORLD.
ENGLEWOOD CLIFFS: PRENTICE HALL, 1966, 186 PP., LC#66-28110.
ESSAYS IN COMPARATIVE GOVERNMENT WHICH FOCUS ON LEGISLATURE AND PEOPLE, RELATIONSHIPS, AND STRUCTURAL FRAMEWORK ENTERING LAWMAKING PROCESS. LEGISLATURE AS AN INSTITUTION IS PERCEIVED IN HUMAN TERMS.

0980 FRANK I.
"NEW PERSPECTIVES ON TRADE AND DEVELOPMENT."
FOREIGN AFFAIRS, 45 (APR. 67), 520-540.
ASSESSES EFFECT OF UNCTAD ON TRADE PROBLEMS OF LOW-INCOME COUNTRIES. ANALYZES FACTORS CONTRIBUTING TO SLOW RATE OF PROGRESS ON RECOMMENDATIONS OF FIRST UNCTAD MEETING. CONCLUDES UNCTAD HAS MADE GREAT CONTRIBUTION TO ACCOMMODATION OF UNDERDEVELOPED NATION'S NEEDS BY ADVANCED NATIONS; HOWEVER, IT IS NECESSARY TO CHANGE POLICIES IN UNDERDEVELOPED NATIONS TO RESHAPE WORLD TRADE IN THEIR INTERESTS.

0981 FRANKEL J.
THE MAKING OF FOREIGN POLICY: AN ANALYSIS OF DECISION-MAKING
LONDON: OXFORD U PR, 1963, 231 PP.
STUDY OF FOREIGN POLICY-MAKING INVOLVES INTERNATIONAL AND DOMESTIC ENVIRONMENT, RATIONALITY, DISCUSSION OF CHOICE, AND DECISIONAL STAGES, INCLUDING FOREIGN MINISTRY, SUBSIDIARY SERVICES AND AGENCIES, AND PROCESS OF POLICY FORMATION.

0982 FRANKEL M.
"THE WAR IN VIETNAM."
CURRENT, (JUNE 67), 4-18.
CONTENDS THAT THE PRINCIPAL STRUGGLE IN VIETNAM IS BETWEEN THE NLF AND THE ARVN (ARMY OF THE REPUBLIC OF SOUTH-VIETNAM) AND THAT US PARTICIPATION IS ANCILLARY. DISCUSSES HOW LONG THE WAR WILL LAST, THE FEASIBILITY OF A VIABLE COALITION, THE DIFFICULTIES OF NEGOTIATED SETTLEMENT, THE HOPES AND FEARS OF THE VIET ONG, AND THEIR CHANCES OF SUCCESS. (FROM NY TIMES MAGAZINE, APR 30, 1967.)

0983 FRANKEL S.H.
CAPITAL INVESTMENT IN AFRICA.
LONDON: OXFORD U PR, 1938, 487 PP.
1935 PICTURE OF INVESTMENT OF EUROPEAN CAPITAL IN AFRICA WHICH HAS SERVED DEVELOPMENT OF CERTAIN COUNTRIES. AUTHOR PRESENTS STATISTICAL DATA AND SEEKS TO INTERPRET EFFECT OF MODERN ECONOMIC FORCES ON STRUCTURE OF AFRICAN SOCIETY.

0984 FRANKEL S.H.
"ECONOMIC ASPECTS OF POLITICAL INDEPENDENCE IN AFRICA."
INT. AFF., 36 (OCT. 60), 440-446.
RAISES SERIOUS DOUBTS REGARDING EFFECTS OF POLITICAL INDEPENDENCE ON ECONOMY OF EMERGENT AFRICAN STATES. EXPLAINS THEORY IN ECONOMIC TERMS OF ABSOLUTE INDEPENDENCE COUPLED WITH ABSOLUTE ISOLATION. SHOWS HOW NEW AFRICA IS ESTABLISHING ECONOMIC RELATIONSHIP WITH REST OF THE WORLD, BUT FEELS PRESENT CONDITIONS IN AFRICA OFFER LITTLE INDUCEMENT FOR CAPITAL AND SKILLED ASSISTANCE FROM ABROAD.

0985 FRANKLAND N.
THE BOMBING OFFENSIVE AGAINST GERMANY.
LONDON: FABER AND FABER, 1965, 129 PP.
CONSIDERS FIVE YEARS' CAMPAIGN IN WWII AND PLACE OF AIR POWER IN HISTORY. COMPARES BOMBING OFFENSIVE TO NAVAL BLOCKADE. DISCUSSES RELATIVE EFFECTIVENESS OF OFFENSIVE BOMBING AS STRATEGIC DEVICE.

0986 FRANKLIN W.O.
"CLAUSEWITZ ON LIMITED WAR."
MILITARY REV., 47 (JUNE 67), 23-29.
SHOWS HOW GREAT 19TH-CENTURY PRUSSIAN MILITARY STRATEGIST FORESAW AND SKETCHED SOME OF THE TACTICS OF MODERN GUERRILLA INSURGENCY. DEFINES CLAUSEWITZ' TRIPARTITE STRATEGY FOR LIMITED WAR: INVASION, DESTRUCTION OF SENSITIVE AREAS, AND, ESPECIALLY, WEARING OUT THE ENEMY. CONCLUDES THAT WESTMORELAND AND THE STRATEGISTS OF WASHINGTON HAVE LEARNED MUCH FROM CLAUSEWITZ IN THEIR CONDUCT OF VIETNAM WAR.

0987 FRANZ G. ED.
TEILUNG UND WIEDERVEREINIGUNG.
GOTTINGEN: MUSTERSCHMIDT VERLAG, 1963, 299 PP.
COLLECTION OF ESSAYS ON POLITICAL PROBLEMS OF DIVISION AND REUNIFICATION IN EUROPE AND ASIA. DISCUSSES DIVISION OF NETHERLANDS, IRELAND, POLAND, ITALY, GERMANY, KOREA, AND VIETNAM.

0988 FRASER L.
PROPAGANDA.
LONDON: OXFORD U PR, 1957, 218 PP.
ANALYSIS OF CONCEPT OF PROPAGANDA AND ITS HISTORICAL POSITION, INCLUDING ITS USE IN WWI, NAZI PROPAGANDA AT HOME AND ABROAD, AND OTHER FORMS USED IN WWII. COMMUNIST USE OF PROPAGANDA AND DOUBLETALK IS EXAMINED IN VARIOUS EXAMPLES, AS WELL AS APPLICATION OF IT BY ALL GROUPS IN EDUCATION AND HISTORY.

0989 FRASER S. ED.
GOVERNMENTAL POLICY AND INTERNATIONAL EDUCATION.
NEW YORK: JOHN WILEY, 1965, 373 PP., LC#65-26845.
EXAMINES INTEREST AND INVOLVEMENT OF GOVERNMENT IN INTERNATIONAL EDUCATION, INCLUDING INSTITUTIONAL STUDIES, INTERNATIONAL EDUCATION UNDER COMMUNISM, AND AREA STUDIES.

0990 FRASER-TYTLER W.K.
AFGHANISTAN: A STUDY OF POLITICAL DEVELOPMENTS IN CENTRAL AND SOUTHERN ASIA (3RD ED.)
LONDON: OXFORD U PR, 1967, 362 PP.
STUDY OF AFGHANISTAN'S HISTORY AND PEOPLES. PICTURES THE GEOGRAPHY AND ITS ROLE IN HISTORY, AND DESCRIBES EARLY EMPIRES AND RISE OF ISLAM AND MONGOL EMPIRE. TRACES HISTORY OF COMPETING KINGS AND PROBLEM OF TRIBAL CONFLICTS. TRACES DEVELOPMENTS OF 1948-64. HOPES FOR AN END TO "BUFFER STATE POLICY" FORCED UPON AFGHANISTAN BY US, USSR, AND INDIA.

0991 FRAZIER E.F.
RACE AND CULTURE CONTACTS IN THE MODERN WORLD.
NEW YORK: KNOPF, 1957, 338 PP., $6.00.
SYSTEMATIC DISCUSSION OF WORLD RACE AND CULTURE PHENOMENA OF LAST TWO CENTURIES IN FOUR PARTS: ECOLOGICA, ECONOMIC, POLITICAL, AND SOCIAL ORGANIZATION AND RELATIONS.

0992 FREE L.A.
SIX ALLIES AND A NEUTRAL.
GLENCOE: FREE PR., 1959, 210 PP., $5.00.

DESCRIBES PSYCHOLOGICAL DYNAMICS THAT INFLUENCE THE FOREIGN POLICY OF SEVEN NATIONS: THE UNITED STATES, BRITAIN, FRANCE, WEST GERMANY, ITALY, JAPAN, AND INDIA. INVESTIGATES THE PSYCHOLOGY OF THEIR POLITICAL LEADERS AS RELATED TO INTERNATIONAL SPHERE.

0993 FREE L.A.
THE ATTITUDES, HOPES AND FEARS OF NIGERIANS.
PRINCETON: INST FOR INTL SOC RES, 1964, 81 PP.
RESEARCH BY INSTITUTE FOR ADVANCED SOCIAL RESEARCH CONSISTING OF NIGERIAN NATION-WIDE PUBLIC OPINION SURVEY, INTERVIEWING 100 MEMBERS OF NIGERIAN FEDERAL HOUSE OF REPRESENTATIVES AND UNSTRUCTURED INTERVIEWS BY WRITER PERSONALLY, IN GOVERNMENTAL, OFFICIAL, AND ELITE CIRCLES IN LAGOS AND NIGERIA.

0994 FREEMAN H.A., PAULLIN O.
COERCION OF STATES IN FEDERAL UNIONS (PAMPHLET)
PHILA: PACIFIST RESEARCH BUREAU, 1943, 67 PP.
EXAMINE HISTORICAL DEVELOPMENT OF NATIONAL FEDERATIONS, WITH RESPECT TO INFLUENCES WORKING TOWARD OR FROM UNITY, GIVING SPECIAL ATTENTION TO USE OF FORCE. GIVE PACIFIST VIEW OF FEDERALISM AND MANNER OF ACHIEVING WORLD PEACE UTILIZING IT. CONSIDER COHESIVE FORCES PRESENT IN WORLD THAT COULD CONTRIBUTE TO NONVIOLENT SOLUTION TO WWII, WHICH AT TIME OF WRITING WAS IN SECOND YEAR OF US INVOLVEMENT.

0995 FREIDEL F. ED., POLLACK N. ED.
AMERICAN ISSUES IN THE TWENTIETH CENTURY.
SKOKIE: RAND MCNALLY & CO, 1966, 526 PP., LC#66-10803.
CONSIDER BASIC NATIONAL POLICY PROBLEMS OF EVERY DECADE OF 20TH CENTURY. SPECIALISTS IN VARIOUS FIELDS DISCUSS CRUCIAL DOMESTIC AND INTERNATIONAL ISSUES THAT THREATENED US SECURITY IN EACH PERIOD. RELEVANT PHILOSOPHIES OR PROGRAMS OF PRESIDENTS TREATED.

0996 FREMANTLE H.E.S.
THE NEW NATION, A SURVEY OF THE CONDITION AND PROSPECTS OF SOUTH AFRICA.
LONDON: JOHN OUSLEY, 1909, 328 PP.
DISCUSSES EFFECTS OF COLONIALISM, EMERGING NATIONALISM, AND DIFFICULTIES OF NEW STATE. UNIFICATION OF DUTCH, ENGLISH SETTLERS, ECONOMY, TRADE, AND RELATIONS WITH OTHER COUNTRIES ARE INCLUDED.

0997 FRENCH D.S.
"DOES THE U.S. EXPLOIT THE DEVELOPING NATIONS?"
COMMONWEAL, 86 (MAY 67), 257-259.
WHILE REJECTING ANY DOCTRINAIRE APPROACH, THIS ESSAY ARGUES THAT THE US IS SYSTEMATICALLY WORKING TO PRESERVE AN INTERNATIONAL ECONOMIC ORDER WHICH IS DISADVANTAGEOUS TO THE UNDERDEVELOPED COUNTRIES. THE US HAS SHOWN ITSELF COMMITTED TO THE PRESENT SYSTEM, AS IN THE COCOA CONFERENCE, THOUGH UNDER THIS SYSTEM THE INCOME OF DEVELOPED NATIONS IS GROWING FAR MORE RAPIDLY THAN THAT OF UNDERDEVELOPED NATIONS.

0998 FREUD A.
OF HUMAN SOVEREIGNTY.
NEW YORK: PHILOSOPHICAL LIB, 1964, 341 PP., LC#65-10993.
EXAMINES NATIONALISM AS CAUSE OF INTERNATIONAL UNREST, THE ARMS RACE, NATIONAL BELLIGERENCE, AND WAR. SUGGESTS INTEGRATION AND SUPRA-NATIONAL BLOCS AS REMEDIAL TACTICS.

0999 FREUND G.
UNHOLY ALLIANCE.
NEW YORK: HARCOURT BRACE, 1957, 283 PP.
ILLUMINATES PREVIOUSLY OBSCURE ASPECTS OF GERMAN-SOVIET COLLABORATION IN POST-WWI PERIOD FROM EXTENSIVE RESEARCH INTO DOCUMENTARY MATERIAL ONLY RECENTLY AVAILABLE. COVERS RELATIONS BETWEEN TWO COUNTRIES FROM BREST-LITOVSK TO 1927. TOPICS COVERED RANGE FROM ANTI-WESTERN POLITICAL ALIGNMENT TO LITTLE-KNOWN FACETS OF MILITARY COOPERATION.

1000 FREUND L.
POLITISCHE WAFFEN.
FRANKFURT: BERNARD AND GRAEFE VERL, 1966, 180 PP.
DISCUSSES POLITICAL STRATEGIES OF DEFENSE IN GERMANY AND WESTERN EUROPE AT LARGE. EXAMINES PROPAGANDA, DIPLOMATIC MANEUVERS, AND MILITARY STRATEGY AS VEHICLE OF POLITICS OF PEACE.

1001 FREYMOND J.
WESTERN EUROPE SINCE THE WAR.
NEW YORK: FREDERICK PRAEGER, 1964, 236 PP., LC#64-13495.
HISTORICAL ESSAY ON ATLANTIC EUROPE SINCE WWII, INCLUDING APPRAISAL OF POST-WAR OUTLOOK AND STRATEGY, ECONOMIC REDEVELOPMENT, CRISES OF 1950'S, AND DEBATE OF GRAND DESIGN, USUALLY FROM FRENCH POINT OF VIEW.

1002 FRIEDMANN W.
METHODS AND POLICIES OF PRINCIPAL DONOR COUNTRIES IN PUBLIC INTERNATIONAL DEVELOPMENT FINANCING: PRELIMINARY APPRAISAL.
NEW YORK: COLUMBIA U LAW SCHOOL, 1962, 49 PP.
ANALYZES FOREIGN AID MACHINERY IN US, UK, WEST GERMANY, AND FRANCE, AS WELL AS EEC, SHOWING THERE IS AGREEMENT ON PRE-EMINENCE OF NEED FOR TECHNICAL ASSISTANCE, BUT DISAGREEMENT ON CONCEPT AND PRINCIPLES OF CAPITAL AID FOR DEVELOPING COUNTRIES. POINTS OUT NATURE OF OTHER ISSUES UPON WHICH NATIONS AGREE AND DIFFER. SUGGESTS FURTHER TASKS FOR MULTILATERAL COORDINATION.

1003 FRIEDMANN W.
AN INTRODUCTION TO WORLD POLITICS (5TH ED.)
NEW YORK: ST MARTIN'S PRESS, 1965, 497 PP., LC#62-17721.
ANALYZES ELEMENTS OF INTERNATIONAL PROBLEMS, ESPECIALLY EVOLUTION OF CONFLICT INVOLVING BALANCE OF POWER. ALSO COVERS REGIONAL ASPECTS OF WORLD POLITICS, FOCUSING ON NEAR EAST, ASIA, AFRICA, AND LATIN AMERICA. LONG-TERM PROBLEMS SUCH AS POPULATION, ECONOMIC DEVELOPMENT, AND PEACE ARE DISCUSSED. APPENDIXES INCLUDE UN MEMBERSHIP AND WORLDWIDE VITAL STATISTICS.

1004 FRIEDMANN W.G. ED., KALMANOFF G. ED.
JOINT INTERNATIONAL BUSINESS VENTURES.
NEW YORK: COLUMB. U. PR., 1961, 558 PP.
EXAMINES PROBLEMS AND PROSPECTS OF PARTNERSHIP IN BUSINESS ASSOCIATIONS BETWEEN DEVELOPED AND LESS DEVELOPED COUNTRIES. OUTLINES TYPES OF JOINT VENTURES, SURVEYS THEIR IMPORTANCE IN RELATION TO TOTAL FOREIGN INVESTMENTS, ANALYZES THEIR RESULTS IN INDIVIDUAL COUNTRIES, AND REVIEWS GOVERNMENTAL REGULATIONS AFFECTING THEM.

1005 FRIEDMANN W.G.
"THE USES OF 'GENERAL PRINCIPLES' IN THE DEVELOPMENT OF INTERNATIONAL LAW."
AMER. J. INT. LAW, 57 (APRIL 63), 279-299.
DISCUSSES THE CHANGING TRENDS IN INTERNATIONAL LAW. SINCE THERE IS GENERAL DISAGREEMENT ON MANIFEST CONTENT OF NATURAL LAW, THE 'GENERAL PRINCIPLES OF LAW RECOGNIZED BY CIVILIZED NATIONS' PLAY AN INCREASING ROLE IN INTERNATIONAL CONDUCT. PURPOSE IS TO REAFFIRM THE USE OF 'PRINCIPLES' ON A PRAGMATIC BASIS.

1006 FRIEDMANN W.G.
THE CHANGING STRUCTURE OF INTERNATIONAL LAW.
NEW YORK: COLUMB. PR., 1964, 410 PP., $8.75.
ANALYZES CHANGES IN STRUCTURE OF INTERNATIONAL RELATIONS THAT, IN TURN, HAVE AFFECTED INTERNATIONAL LAW. STRESSES DISTINCTION BETWEEN LAW OF COEXISTENCE AND LAW OF COOPERATION. DEFINES PRINCIPLES AND PROCESSES OF LEGAL CHANGE IN FIELD AND POINTS TO MANY FIELDS PREVIOUSLY CONCERN OF MUNICIPAL LAW, NOW CONCERN OF INTERNATIONAL LAW.

1007 FRIEDRICH C.J.
REVOLUTION: NOMOS VIII.
NEW YORK: ATHERTON PRESS, 1966, 246 PP., LC#65-28141.
ESSAYS DISCUSS REVOLUTION IN RELATION TO SEVERAL AREAS OF SOCIAL SCIENCES AND EMPHASIZE 20TH-CENTURY SOCIO-POLITICAL CONDITIONS. EMPHASIS IS NOT ON CONCRETE HISTORICAL ANALYSIS; INSTEAD ENTRIES ARE ARRANGED IN THREE GENERAL CONCEPTUAL CATEGORIES STRESSING GENERAL THEORY OF REVOLUTION, IDEOLOGY OF INTERNATIONAL POLITICAL ORDER, AND PROBLEMS RESULTING FROM MARXIST MODES OF REVOLUTION.

1008 FRIEDRICH-EBERT-STIFTUNG
THE SOVIET BLOC AND DEVELOPING COUNTRIES.
HANNOVER: VERLAG FUR LITERATUR, 1962, 39 PP.
DESCRIBES FOREIGN AID POLICIES OF SOVIET BLOC NATIONS AS BEING PART OF POLITICAL PROGRAM TO GAIN ALLIES AMONG UNDERDEVELOPED NATIONS IN ECONOMIC COMPETITION WITH WEST. TAKES NOTE OF ORGANIZATIONS FOR THIS PURPOSE AND FOR CULTURAL AND SCIENTIFIC COOPERATION. FOCUSES PARTICULARLY ON USSR, COMMUNIST CHINA, AND EAST GERMANY.

1009 FRIEND A.
"THE MIDDLE EAST CRISIS"
NEW POLITICS, 5 (FALL 66), 30-37.
DESCRIBES EVENTS LEADING UP TO MIDDLE EAST WAR OF 1967. EXAMINES DEVELOPMENTS IN SYRIA AND PLAN TO ESTABLISH ARAB UNITY AND DESTROY ISRAEL, AND DIVISIVE EFFECT WAR HAD ON WORLD COMMUNIST MOVEMENT. MAINTAINS THAT ARAB SOCIALIST MOVEMENT IS ONLY WAY TO FOSTER ARAB-JEWISH COOPERATION NECESSARY FOR PEACE IN MIDDLE EAST.

1010 FRISCH D.
ARMS REDUCTION: PROGRAM AND ISSUES.
NEW YORK: TWENTIETH CENTURY FUND, 1961, 162 PP.
DISCUSSES SPECIFIC PLANS FOR, AND IMPORTANT COMPONENTS OF ARMS CONTROL. AIMS TO ADVANCE INTELLECTUAL ASPECT OF POLICY FORMULATION.

1011 FRUTKIN A.W.
SPACE AND THE INTERNATIONAL COOPERATION YEAR: A NATIONAL CHALLENGE (PAMPHLET)
WASHINGTON: GOVT PR OFFICE, 1965, 19 PP.
SHORT STUDY OF PRESENT SPACE PROJECTS, ROLE OF INTERNATIONAL SCIENTIFIC COMMUNITY, EUROPEAN REGIONAL ORGANIZATIONS, AND GLOBAL COMMERCIAL COMMUNICATIONS SATELLITE SYSTEM.

1012 FRYDENSBERG P. ED.
PEACE-KEEPING: EXPERIENCE AND EVALUATION: THE OSLO

PAPERS.
OSLO: NORWEGIAN INST OF INT AFF, 1964, 339 PP.
CONTAINS REPORT OF STUDY COMMISSION SET UP BY NORWEGIAN INSTITUTE OF INTERNATIONAL AFFAIRS AND ITS STRATEGIC STUDY GROUP IN 1961. VOLUME CONTAINS SECTIONS ON POLITICAL AND PHILOSOPHICAL PROBLEMS; CENTRAL PLANNING OF OPERATIONS; REGIONAL COMMAND, EARMARKING AND TRAINING; AND LEGAL QUESTIONS INVOLVED IN UN CONFLICT MANAGEMENT.

1013 FUCHS G.
GEGEN HITLER UND HENLEIN.
MUNICH: RUETTEN UND LOENING, 1961, 334 PP.
TRACES NATURE AND DEVELOPMENT OF GERMAN-CZECHOSLOVAKIAN RELATIONS BETWEEN 1918 - 33. EXAMINES IN DETAIL ANTI-FASCIST AND ANTIIMPERIALIST MOVEMENTS AMONG WORKERS' PARTIES IN CZECHOSLOVAKIA BETWEEN 1933 - 38, WITH EMPHASIS ON COOPERATIVE EFFORTS OF CZECHS, SLOVAKIANS, AND GERMANS TO OPPOSE POLITICS OF AGGRESSION OF FASCIST GERMANY.

1014 FULBRIGHT J.W.
THE ARROGANCE OF POWER.
NEW YORK: RANDOM HOUSE, INC, 1966, 264 PP.
ARGUES THAT US HAS REACHED A HISTORICAL TURNING POINT IN WHICH SHE MUST FACE THE CONTENT AND MEANING OF HER ROLE AS A WORLD POWER. ADDS THAT THE DECLINE AND FALL OF ALL GREAT NATIONS IS RESULT OF MISUNDERSTANDING LIMITATIONS OF POWER. LENGTHY DISCUSSION OF ROLE OF AMERICA IN REVOLUTIONS OF ECONOMICALLY UNDERDEVELOPED AREAS.

1015 FULBRIGHT J.W.
PROSPECTS FOR THE WEST.
CAMBRIDGE: HARVARD U PR, 1963, 132 PP., LC#63-20765.
EVALUATION OF CURRENT POLITICAL CONDITION IN US AND FREE WORLD, FOCUSING ON BALANCE OF POWER BETWEEN EAST AND WEST, RELATIONS BETWEEN US AND ITS WESTERN ALLIES, AND DOMESTIC PROGRAMS IN EDUCATION AND UNEMPLOYMENT. ARGUES THAT FUTURE OF FREE WORLD DEPENDS ON STRENGTHENING OF FREE SOCIETIES RATHER THAN CONFLICTS WITH USSR AND COMMUNIST COUNTRIES.

1016 FULBRIGHT J.W.
OLD MYTHS AND NEW REALITIES.
NEW YORK: RANDOM HOUSE, INC, 1964, 147 PP., LC#64-22439.
ESSAYS BASED ON SPEECHES MADE BY THE SENATOR IN 1963 ON CHANGES IN NATURE OF COLD WAR, NATIONAL SECURITY, ATLANTIC PARTNERSHIP, AND US PUBLIC OPINION ON INTERNATIONAL ISSUES.

1017 FULLER C.D.
TRAINING OF SPECIALISTS IN INTERNATIONAL RELATIONS.
WASHINGTON: AMER. COUNCIL EDUC., 1957, 136 PP.
BELIEVES MORE EMPHASIS ON ECONOMIC GEOGRAPHY AND BEHAVIORAL SCIENCES MUST BE MADE. URGES DEVELOPMENT OF SPECIALIZED SKILLS, OTHER THAN RESEARCH AND ANALYSIS, SUCH AS WRITTEN AND ORAL EXPRESSION. EVALUATION OF USA GRADUATE-SCHOOL PROGRAMS IN INTERNATIONAL RELATIONS.

1018 FULLER G.F. ED.
FOREIGN RELIEF AND REHABILITATION (PAMPHLET)
WASHINGTON: LIBRARY OF CONGRESS, 1943, 28 PP.
CONTAINS 246 ENTRIES, MOST WRITTEN 1940-43, DISCUSSING PROBLEMS AND SOLUTIONS FOR THE REHABILITATION OF EUROPE AT CONCLUSION OF WWII. ALSO DEALS WITH SIMILAR SITUATIONS AFTER WWI. MANY ARTICLES REFER TO WORK OF RED CROSS AND THE QUAKERS; OTHERS DISCUSS PROBLEMS OF REHABILITATING EUROPE'S JEWS. DISCUSSES FUTURE ROLE OF UN IN SEVERAL ARTICLES. COMPILED FOR LIBRARY OF CONGRESS.

1019 FULLER G.H. ED.
A SELECTED LIST OF REFERENCES ON THE EXPANSION OF THE US NAVY, 1933-1939 (PAMPHLET)
WASHINGTON: LIBRARY OF CONGRESS, 1939, 34 PP.
CONTAINS 410 LISTINGS OF CONGRESSIONAL COMMITTEE REPORTS AND GENERAL PUBLICATION ARTICLES DISCUSSING DEVELOPMENT OF US NAVAL FORCES PRIOR TO WWII.

1020 FULLER G.H. ED.
A LIST OF BIBLIOGRAPHIES ON PROPAGANDA (PAMPHLET)
WASHINGTON: LIBRARY OF CONGRESS, 1940, 6 PP.
LISTS 41 BOOKS AND ARTICLES ON THE DEVELOPMENT OF PROPAGANDA TECHNIQUES IN THE 20TH CENTURY. ARTICLES NOT LIMITED TO POLITICAL PROPAGANDA, BUT EMPHASIS IS ON PROPAGANDA AS A MILITARY TOOL. CONTAINS LISTINGS OF OTHER BIBLIOGRAPHIES.

1021 FULLER G.H. ED.
DEFENSE FINANCING: A SUPPLEMENTARY LIST OF REFERENCES (PAMPHLET)
WASHINGTON: LIBRARY OF CONGRESS, 1942, 45 PP.
CONTAINS 451 LISTINGS OF BOOKS AND ARTICLES SUPPLEMENTING 1941 BIBLIOGRAPHY "DEFENSE FINANCING." HAS SEPARATE CLASSIFICATIONS FOR US, UK, CANADA, AUSTRALIA, AND MISCELLANEOUS. MANY LISTINGS ARE CONGRESSIONAL DISCUSSIONS AND REPORTS.

1022 FULLER G.H.
AUSTRALIA: A SELECT LIST OF REFERENCES.
WASHINGTON: LIBRARY OF CONGRESS, 1942, 101 PP.
BIBLIOGRAPHY OF 793 ITEMS ON AUSTRALIA PUBLISHED UNDER AUSPICES OF THE LIBRARY OF CONGRESS. RELEVANT ITEMS ON HISTORY, WAR EFFORTS AND DEFENSE, GOVERNMENT AND POLITICS, FOREIGN RELATIONS, ECONOMICS, AND SOCIAL LIFE AND CUSTOMS. INCLUDES AUTHOR INDEX. ARRANGEMENT IS ALPHABETICAL.

1023 FULLER G.H. ED.
MILITARY GOVERNMENT: A LIST OF REFERENCES (A PAMPHLET)
WASHINGTON: LIBRARY OF CONGRESS, 1944, 14 PP.
CONTAINS 122 ENTRIES OF ARTICLES IN FRENCH, GERMAN, AND ENGLISH CONCERNING LEGAL, ADMINISTRATIVE, AND SOCIOLOGICAL PROBLEMS INVOLVED IN MILITARY JURISDICTION IN OCCUPIED COUNTRIES. COMPILED FOR LIBRARY OF CONGRESS.

1024 FULLER G.H. ED.
TURKEY: A SELECTED LIST OF REFERENCES.
WASHINGTON: LIBRARY OF CONGRESS, 1944, 114 PP.
CONTAINS 916 LISTINGS OF BOOKS AND ARTICLES, MOST PUBLISHED 1930-44, DEALING WITH MANY ASPECTS OF MODERN AND HISTORICAL TURKEY, INCLUDING GEOGRAPHY, GEOLOGY, POLITICAL HISTORY, ECONOMIC AND SOCIAL CONDITIONS, ART AND LETTERS. INCLUDES LISTING OF MAPS AND OTHER BIBLIOGRAPHIES. MANY ENTRIES IN FRENCH AND GERMAN.

1025 FULLER J.F.C.
THE CONDUCT OF WAR, 1789-1961.
NEW BRUNSWICK: RUTGERS U PR, 1961, 352 PP., LC#61-10261.
AUTHOR BELIEVES THAT IF IMPACT ON WARFARE OF CHANGES IN CIVILIZATION HAD BEEN PROPERLY CONSIDERED, THE WORLD SITUATION WOULD BE LESS CONFUSED AND DANGEROUS. CONSIDERS EFFECT OF PRESSURES OF ECONOMIC, POLITICAL, AND SOCIAL DEVELOPMENT ON WARFARE. STUDIES EFFECTS OF FRENCH, INDUSTRIAL, AND RUSSIAN REVOLUTIONS ON WAR, AND CONSIDERS INCREASED DESTRUCTIVE CAPACITY OF MODERN WARFARE.

1026 FURNIA A.H.
THE DIPLOMACY OF APPEASEMENT: ANGLO-FRENCH RELATIONS AND THE PRELUDE TO WORLD WAR II 1931-1938.
THE UNIVERSITY PR OF WASH, DC, 1960, 454 PP., LC#60-14506.
DISCUSSES BRITISH AND FRENCH FOREIGN POLICY IN RELATION TO COLLECTIVE SECURITY AND MAINTENANCE OF STATUS QUO. TRACES IN DETAIL DIPLOMATIC MANEUVERS OF FRENCH AND ENGLISH OFFICIALS PRIOR TO WWII.

1027 FURNISS E.S.
AMERICAN MILITARY POLICY: STRATEGIC ASPECTS OF WORLD POLITICAL GEOGRAPHY.
NEW YORK: RINEHART, 1957, 494 PP., $6.50.
EXAMINES PARTICIPATION OF THE MILITARY IN AMERICAN FOREIGN POLICY WITH PRIMARY AIM OF SEEING HOW MILITARY POWER CAN CONTRIBUTE TO ATTAINING FOREIGN POLICY OBJECTIVES IN THEIR GEOGRAPHICAL CONTEXTS AND HOW THEY CAN OFFSET COMMUNIST CAPABILITIES.

1028 FURNISS E.S.
"SOME PERSPECTIVES ON AMERICAN MILITARY ASSISTANCE."
PRINCETON: CENT. INT. STUD., 1957, 39 PP.
PRESENTS SCOPE, OBJECTIVES, AND KINDS OF MILITARY AID. EVALUATES AID PROGRAM PROGRESS AND BENEFITS CLAIMED. CRITICIZES PROGRAM FOR EXASCERBATING REGIONAL TENSIONS, CAUSING ECONOMIC DISLOCATIONS, AND FOR STRAINING ECONOMIES. CONTENDS NEEDS OF STRATEGIC FAR EAST NOT PRIMARILY MILITARY.

1029 FURNIVALL J.S.
NETHERLANDS INDIA.
NEW YORK: MACMILLAN, 1939, 502 PP.
STUDIES ECONOMIC AND SOCIAL DEVELOPMENT OF NETHERLANDS INDIA WITH SPECIAL REFERENCE TO ITS NATURE AS A PLURALISTIC SOCIETY. HISTORICALLY TRACES GENERAL POLITICAL AND ECONOMIC CHANGES IN ENVIRONMENT AND RELATES THEM TO VAST DIFFERENCES IN CULTURE AND RACE OF ITS INHABITANTS. FOLLOWS RISE OF LIBERALISM AND NOTES MAJOR CHANGES IN COLONIAL POLICY.

1030 GALBRAITH J.K.
"A POSITIVE APPROACH TO ECONOMIC AID."
FOR. AFF., 39 (APRIL 61) 444-457.
PRESENTS REASONS FOR FAILURE OF FOREIGN AID: LACK OF EDUCATION, SOCIAL JUSTICE, RELIABLE GOVERNMENT AND UNDERSTANDING OF USE OF AID. ADVOCATES REALISTIC APPROACH BY AN INSTITUTE CONCERNED SOLELY WITH ELIMINATING ESSENTIAL PROBLEMS IN UNDERDEVELOPED NATIONS AND HELPING NATIONS USE AID EFFECTIVELY. AID SHOULD BE COMMENSURATE WITH RESOURCES.

1031 GALLAGHER M.P.
THE SOVIET HISTORY OF WORLD WAR II.
NEW YORK: FREDERICK PRAEGER, 1963, 206 PP.
HISTORIOGRAPHY OF WARTIME PROPAGANDA IN SOVIET RUSSIA. CONTROL OF PRESS BY MILITARY, GOVERNMENT CONTROL OF COMMUNICATIONS, EFFECT ON POPULACE OF DOCTORED NEWS ALL DEALT WITH.

1032 GALLOIS P.M.
THE BALANCE OF TERROR: STRATEGY FOR THE NUCLEAR AGE.
BOSTON: HOUGHTON, 1961, 234 PP.
ATTEMPTS A RATIONAL FORMULATION OF DIPLOMACY OF DISSUASION FOR ATOMIC AGE. ATTEMPTS TO DEVISE NUCLEAR POWER STRATEGY THAT WILL NEITHER SET OFF AN ACCIDENTAL WAR NOR LEAVE WEST IN POWERLESS STATE.

1033 GALLOWAY E. ED.
ABSTRACTS OF POSTWAR LITERATURE (VOL. IV) JAN.-JULY, 1945 NOS. 901-1074.
WASHINGTON: LIBRARY OF CONGRESS, 1945.
LAST VOLUME IN SERIES ENTITLED POSTWAR ABSTRACTS. CONTAINS ABSTRACTS OF 174 SELECTED BOOKS, PAMPHLETS, AND PERIODICALS DEALING WITH A VARIETY OF POSTWAR PROBLEMS. NATIONAL AND INTERNATIONAL.

1034 GALLOWAY G.B.
AMERICAN PAMPHLET LITERATURE OF PUBLIC AFFAIRS (PAMPHLET)
WASHINGTON: NAT ECO SOCIAL PLAN, 1937, 16 PP.
ANNOTATED BIBLIOGRAPHICAL GUIDE TO PAMPHLETS ISSUED IN THE FIELDS OF ECONOMIC AND SOCIAL PLANNING FROM 1931-36. MATERIALS RANGE IN SCOPE FROM MUNICIPAL TO INTERNATIONAL. LISTS 13 MISCELLANEOUS AND 36 PUBLIC AFFAIRS PAMPHLET SERIES.

1035 GALTUNG J.
"ON THE EFFECTS OF INTERNATIONAL ECONOMIC SANCTIONS, WITH EXAMPLES FROM THE CASE OF RHODESIA."
WORLD POLITICS, 19 (APR. 67), 378-416.
USES RHODESIA AS A SOURCE OF EXAMPLES AND ILLUSTRATIONS FOR AN EXPLORATORY STUDY OF INTERNATIONAL ECONOMIC SANCTIONS. PURPOSE IS TO GET SOME IMPRESSIONS ABOUT THE PSYCHOLOGICAL AND SOCIAL MECHANISMS OF ECONOMIC BOYCOTT WHEN THEY ARE OPERATING. DISCUSSES THE GENERAL THEORY OF SANCTIONS AND THE DEFENSE AGAINST THEM.

1036 GAMER R.E.
"URGENT SINGAPORE, PATIENT MALAYSIA."
INT. J., 21 (WINTER 66), 42-56.
INVESTIGATES OBSTACLES TO POLITICAL UNITY BETWEEN MALAYSIA AND SINGAPORE, INCLUDING DIFFERENCES OF ECONOMICAL TACTICS AND POLITICAL POLICIES, DOMESTIC AND FOREIGN.

1037 GANDILHON J.
"LA SCIENCE ET LA TECHNIQUE A L'AIDE DES REGIONS PEU DEVELOPPEES."
POLIT. ETRANG., (NO.3, 63), 221-40.
RECOMMENDS CLOSER ECONOMIC RELATIONS WITH UNDERDEVELOPED REGIONS. SCIENTIFIC AID PROGRAMS SHOULD AIM TO APPLY RESEARCH TO TECHNOLOGY. GIVES INSIGHTS INTO FRENCH SCIENTIFIC SITUATION AND UN SCIENTIFIC AID PROGRAM.

1038 GANDOLFI A.
"LES ACCORDS DE COOPERATION EN MATIERE DE POLITIQUE ETRANGERE ENTRE LA FRANCE ET LES NOUVEAUX ETATS AFRICAINS ET." MALGACHE.
REV. JURID. POLIT. OUTREMER, 17 (APR.-JUNE 63), 202-19.
REVIEWS AGREEMENTS FOR COOPERATION BETWEEN FRANCE AND AFRICAN STATES AND MADAGASCAR. OUTLINES COMMON POLICY OBJECTIVES, RELATING THEM TO AFRICAN ECONOMIC PROBLEMS. INCLUDES LISTS OF DETAILED AGREEMENTS.

1039 GANGAL S.C.
"SURVEY OF RECENT RESEARCH: INDIA AND THE COMMONWEALTH"
INT. STUDIES, 6 (JAN. 65), 333-344.
"THIS IS A SURVEY (BOOKS AND ARTICLES) OF PRIMARY AND SECONDARY SOURCES ON A DOMINANT ASPECT OF INDIA'S FOREIGN POLICY AND RELATIONS, NAMELY INDIA'S MEMBERSHIP OF, AND ROLE IN, THE COMMONWEALTH FROM 1947 UP TO DATE." WRITINGS HAVE BEEN CLASSIFIED INTO BOOKS AND ARTICLES AND ARE SURVEYED IN CHRONOLOGICAL ORDER.

1040 GANGE J.
UNIVERSITY RESEARCH ON INTERNATIONAL AFFAIRS.
WASHINGTON: AMER. COUNC. EDUC., 1958, 145 PP., $3.00.
REPORTS SURVEY OF 60 UNIVERSITIES ON STATUS, SUPPORT, ADMINISTRATION AND PROBLEMS, OF INTERNATIONAL RESEARCH AGENCIES. CONCLUDES THERE IS NEED FOR MORE OBJECTIVE MEASURES IN ORDER TO GIVE FIELD A MORE SCIENTIFIC STATUS.

1041 GANGULI B.N.
ECONOMIC INTEGRATION.
BOMBAY: ASIA PUBL HOUSE, 1961, 13 PP.
DISCUSSION OF CONCEPT AND IMPLICATIONS OF ECONOMIC INTEGRATION ON REGIONAL, NATIONAL, AND INTERNATIONAL CHANGE. FOCUSES ON ECONOMIC GROUPS UNDERGOING CHANGES IN BEHAVIOR PATTERNS DUE TO PROCESS OF ECONOMIC CHANGE.

1042 GARDINIER D.E.
CAMEROON: UNITED NATIONS CHALLENGE TO FRENCH POLICY.
LONDON: OXFORD U PR, 1963, 142 PP.
STUDY OF EFFECTS OF UN TRUSTEESHIP IN CAMEROON ON THE POLITICAL RELATIONSHIPS BETWEEN CAMEROON AND FRANCE. DISCUSSES CAMEROON'S INDEPENDENCE AS IT INFLUENCES DEVELOPMENT OF FRENCH FOREIGN POLICY AND AS IT AFFECTS CAMEROON'S RELATIONS WITH ITS AFRICAN NEIGHBORS.

1043 GARDNER L.C.
ECONOMIC ASPECTS OF NEW DEAL DIPLOMACY.
MADISON: U. WISC. PR., 1964, 409 PP., $7.50.
INDICATES THAT THE NEW DEAL'S APPROACH TO FOREIGN POLICY WAS AS MUCH SHAPED BY OLDER PRINCIPLES AND TRADITIONS AS BY ANY INITIATED BY FDR. DISCUSSES THE ECONOMIC ORIENTATION OF THE GOOD NEIGHBOR POLICY, THE ROLE OF CORDELL HULL, AND THE INFLUENCE OF SUCH FINANCIERS AS THOMAS LAMONT, NORMAN H. DAVIS, AND WILL CLAYTON.

1044 GARDNER R.N.
"NEW DIRECTIONS IN UNITED STATES FOREIGN ECONOMIC POLICY."
NEW YORK: FOR. POL. ASSN., 1959, 77 PP.
ASSERTS THAT SOVIET ECONOMIC CHALLENGE HAS GENERATED CHANGE IN USA ECONOMIC STRATEGY. SUGGESTS INCREASED EMPHASIS ON FOREIGN AID PROGRAMS TO REACH POLICY OBJECTIVES. DECLARES THAT NATIONAL SURVIVAL DEPENDENT UPON READINESS OF USA TO COMPREHEND TEMPORARILY EXPEDIENT POLITICAL FACTS.

1045 GARDNER R.N.
"COOPERATION IN OUTER SPACE."
FOR. AFF., 41 (JAN. 63), 344-59.
DEALS WITH COOPERATION IN OUTER SPACE AFFAIRS ON A BILATERAL AND WORLD-WIDE BASIS FOR ULTIMATE ATTAINMENT OF WORLD PEACE. PRESENT UN ACTIVITIES REVEAL MULTITUDE OF COOPERATIVE PROJECTS DESPITE WHAT IS FELT TO BE OBSTRUCTIVE EFFORTS BY USSR.

1046 GARDNER R.N.
"THE SOVIET UNION AND THE UNITED NATIONS."
LAW CONTEMP. PROBL., 29 (AUTUMN 64), 845-57.
DELINEATES BASIC INCOMPATIBILITIES BETWEEN COMMUNIST DOCTRINES AND PRINCIPLES OF THE UNITED NATIONS' CHARTER AS WELL AS THE ACTUAL DISAGREEMENTS BETWEEN THE SOVIET UNION AND THE WORLD ORGANIZATION.

1047 GARDNER R.N.
"GATT AND THE UNITED NATIONS CONFERENCE ON TRADE AND DEVELOPMENT."
INT. ORGAN., 18 (AUTUMN 64), 685-704.
NOTES UN'S ROLE IN HELPING TO DEFINE AND SOLVE PROBLEMS OF INTERNATIONAL TRADE BARRIERS AND SPECIFIC PROBLEMS FACING TRADE OF SMALL UNDER-DEVELOPED NATIONS. CITES AMBITIOUS GOALS OF KENNEDY ROUND ON TARIFFS, AND SHOWS GATT'S COMPLEX ROLE IN DEALING WITH THIS NEW POLICY OF ACROSS-THE-BOARD TRADE. POINTS TO NEED FOR POLICY OF SELF-DEVELOPMENT.

1048 GAREAU F.H.
"BLOC POLITICS IN WEST AFRICA."
ORBIS, 5 (WINTER 62), 470-88.
VIEWS 'GHANA-GUINEA-MALI UNION' AND BRAZZAVILLE BLOC AS THE TWO DOMINANT ELEMENTS IN WEST AFRICA. REVIEWS HISTORY OF EACH NATION IN BOTH BLOCS AND IN 'THIRD GROUP' INFLUENCING THEM. ANALYZES THEIR UN VOTING RECORD.

1049 GAMARNIKOW M.
"INFLUENCE-BUYING IN WEST AFRICA."
EAST EUROPE, 3 (JULY 64), 2-8.
ASSERTS AID FROM SOVIET BLOC COUNTRIES TO WEST AFRICAN NATIONS HAS BEEN ONLY MODERATELY SUCCESSFUL IN SECURING COMMUNIST POLITICAL GOALS. CONCLUDES NATIONALISM, RATHER THAN COMMUNISM OR SOCIALISM, APPEARS TO BE THE CONTROLLING IDEOLOGY.

1050 GARNER W.R.
THE CHACO DISPUTE; A STUDY OF PRESTIGE DIPLOMACY.
WASHINGTON: PUBLIC AFFAIRS PRESS, 1966, 151 PP., LC#66-23370
CONSIDERS CONCEPT OF PRESTIGE IN INTERNATIONAL POLITICS AND CRITICIZES CONTEMPORARY RESEARCH IN PRESTIGE THEORY. PRESENTS DIPLOMATIC HISTORY OF CHACO WAR (1928-38) TO SUGGEST THAT PEACE-MAKING PRESTIGE MAY BE NATION'S GOAL QUITE APART FROM PROTECTING MATERIAL STATUS QUO. THIS MAY BE SEEN IN US'S AND ARGENTINA'S CONFLICT FOR PRESTIGE-DOMINANCE OF LATIN AMERICA.

1051 GARNICK D.H.
"ON THE ECONOMIC FEASIBILITY OF A MIDDLE EASTERN COMMON MARKET."
MID. EAST. J., 14 (SUMMER 60), 265-276.
VIEWS PROSPECTS FOR FORMATION OF ECONOMIC UNION. ENUMERATES THREE MAJOR OBSTACLES: LACK OF (1)POLITICAL LIAISONS, (2)PARALLEL SYSTEMS OF ECONOMICS AND (3)SIMILAR LEVELS OF ECONOMIC STABILITY. EQUAL DISTRIBUTION OF RESOURCES, GROWTH POTENTIAL, REGIONAL COOPERATION AND STIMULATION OF TRADE CITED AS AIDS TO EVENTUAL ECONOMIC UNION.

1052 GARTHOFF R.L.
SOVIET STRATEGY IN THE NUCLEAR AGE.
NEW YORK: PRAEGER, 1958, 283 PP., $4.50.
PROJECTION OF FUTURE STRATEGY BASED ON ANALYSIS OF PRESENT SOVIET STRATEGY. EMPHASIZES SOVIET STRATEGICAL AIM AT STABILITY BECAUSE OF IDEOLOGICAL DESIRE TO IMPROVE AND STRENGTHEN THEIR POSITION AS WORLD POWER. GIVES SOME ESTIMATES OF THE SOVIET MILITARY LEADERSHIP POTENTIAL IN THERMONUCLEAR WAR.

1053 GATZKE H.W.
GERMANY'S DRIVE TO THE WEST.
BALTIMORE: JOHNS HOPKINS PRESS, 1950, 316 PP.
STUDY OF GERMANY'S WESTERN WAR AIMS DURING WWI. DISCUSSES ANTECEDENTS AND TACTICS EMPLOYED FOR WESTERN EXPANSION. CONSIDERS THE DISPUTE BETWEEN THE AGRICULTURALLY MINDED EASTERN

EXPANSIONISTS AND THE INDUSTRY-MINDED WESTERN EXPANSIONISTS. FOLLOWS THE COURSE OF THE WAR'S INFLUENCE ON GERMANY'S GOVERNMENT.

1054 GAULD W.A.
MAN, NATURE, AND TIME, AN INTRODUCTION TO WORLD STUDY.
LONDON: G BELL & SONS, 1946, 291 PP.
PRESENTS MAN, NATURE, AND TIME AS INTERRELATED FORCES IN DETERMINATION OF WORLD ORGANISM. CONTENDS THAT MAN RATHER THAN NATURE DETERMINES PATH OF HISTORY. TRACES EFFECTS OF INTERACTION BETWEEN MAN AND NATURE ON COURSE OF HISTORY AND DISCUSSES HUMAN ASPECTS OF WORLD ORDER, LANGUAGE, CULTURE, ECONOMIC, SOCIAL, AND POLITICAL ORDERS, AND POPULATION PATTERNS. NOTES FORCES AFFECTING WORLD INTERGROUP RELATIONS.

1055 GAVIN J.M.
WAR AND PEACE IN THE SPACE AGE.
NEW YORK: HARPER & ROW, 1958, 304 PP., LC#58-11396.
US MISSILE, SPACE, ATOMIC POWER DEVELOPMENT FOUND BEHIND USSR. SUGGESTS VITAL ALTERATIONS OF MILITARY, SCIENTIFIC, TECHNOLOGICAL GOALS, TRAINING IMPROVEMENTS, PSYCHOLOGICAL INVENTIVENESS, MOBILE WEAPONS SYSTEM, HIGH PRIORITY FOR SATELLITE PROGRAM, AND STRATEGY FOR PEACE TO MAKE WAR UNLIKELY.

1056 GEHLEN M.P.
"THE POLITICS OF COEXISTENCE: SOVIET METHODS AND MOTIVES."
BLOOMINGTON: INDIANA U PR, 1967.
LISTING OF 70 BOOKS--RUSSIAN- AND ENGLISH-LANGUAGE PUBLICATIONS--PERTAINING TO THE POLITICAL, MILITARY, ECONOMIC, AND IDEOLOGICAL ASPECTS OF RUSSIA'S COEXISTENCE POLICY WITH CAPITALIST, NEUTRAL, AND COMMUNIST COUNTRIES FROM THE DEATH OF STALIN THROUGH THE 23RD PARTY CONGRESS.

1057 GENEVEY P.
"LE DESARMEMENT APRES LE TRAITE DE VERSAILLES."
POLITIQUE ENTRANGERE, 32 (1967), 87-112.
POLITICAL AND MILITARY SKETCH OF PERIOD 1919-1927 IN GERMANY CONCLUDES THAT GERMAN DISARMAMENT WAS INEFFECTIVE BECAUSE IT FAILED TO EFFECT MILITARISTIC SPIRIT OR INDUSTRIAL CAPACITY OF NATION. ARGUES THAT LIMITED ARMS CONTROL IS POSSIBLE IF LINKED TO INTERNATIONAL SYSTEM OF INSPECTION.

1058 GENTILI A.
DE LEGATIONIBUS.
NEW YORK: OXFORD U. PR., 1924, 198 PP.
SIXTEENTH CENTURY EMBRYONIC STUDY IN INTERNATIONAL LAW QUESTIONING THE RIGHT OF LEGATION FOR EXCOMMUNICATED PERSONS. DEFINES RELIGION AS AN EXCLUSIVE PERSONAL RELATIONSHIP TO GOD AND CONCLUDES THAT THE RIGHT OF LEGATION THUS REMAINS INTACT DESPITE RELIGIOUS DIFFERENCES.

1059 GENTILI A., SCOTT J.B. ED.
DE JURE BELLI, LIBRI TRES (1612) (VOL. 2)
LONDON: OXFORD U PR, 1933, 479 PP.
DISCUSSES WAR IN GENERAL, WHO MAY MAKE IT, AND WHAT CAUSES JUSTIFY IT. TREATS LAWFUL WAY OF CONDUCTING WAR; DECLARATIONS OF WAR; ACTS FORBIDDEN AND PERMITTED; TREATMENT OF ENEMY, PRISONERS, AND HOSTAGES; AND CONCLUSION OF TRUCES. DISCUSSES CONCLUSION OF WAR, RIGHTS OF OCCUPATION, AND ESTABLISHMENT OF PEACE. ATTEMPTS TO ESTABLISH BASIS FOR LAWS ON FACT RATHER THAN ABSTRACT OR THEOLOGICAL IDEAS.

1060 GEORGE A.L., GEORGE J.L.
WOODROW WILSON AND COLONEL HOUSE.
NEW YORK: DAY, 1956, 362 PP.
ANALYSIS OF RELATIONSHIP BETWEEN THESE TWO MEN AND THEIR INFLUENCE, INDIVIDUALLY AND TOGETHER, ON AMERICAN FOREIGN POLICY AT THE TIME OF WORLD WAR ONE.

1061 GEORGE M.
THE WARPED VISION.
PITTSBURGH: U OF PITTSBURGH PR, 1965, 238 PP., LC#65-14623.
ANALYZES BRITISH APPEASEMENT FOREIGN POLICY, PERIOD 1933-1939. CONCENTRATES ON ATTITUDES OF LEADERS OF CONSERVATIVE GOVERNING GROUP, WHOM AUTHOR HOLDS PRIMARILY RESPONSIBLE FOR APPEASEMENT POLICIES.

1062 GERARD-LIBOIS J.
KATANGA SECESSION.
MADISON: U OF WISCONSIN PR, 1966, 377 PP., LC#66-22851.
ANALYZES WHERE THE IDEA FOR KATANGA'S SECESSION ORIGINATED, HOW IT WAS DEVELOPED AND PROCLAIMED, AND WHAT FACTORS CALLED A HALT TO THE SECESSION. BASES ACCOUNT ON COLLECTIONS OF PUBLIC SOURCES CURRENTLY AVAILABLE AND ON ORAL ACCOUNTS AND UNPUBLISHED DOCUMENTS; THESE PERMIT AN UNDERSTANDING OF THE SECESSION AND ITS WORKINGS, PARTICULARLY IN MATTERS INVOLVING MILITARY PERSONNEL AND ASSISTANCE.

1063 GERASSI J.
THE GREAT FEAR IN LATIN AMERICA.
NEW YORK: CROWELL COLLIER, 1965, 478 PP., LC#64-23646.
FINDS LATIN AMERICAN SOCIO-ECONOMIC STRUCTURE CORRUPT, IMMORAL, AND LARGELY UNSALVAGEABLE. ASSERTS INEVITABILITY OF REVOLUTION AND NEED FOR REALISTIC US AID PROGRAM, ANALYZING ALLIANCE FOR PROGRESS AND COOPERATION INTERNAL TO LATIN AMERICA.

1064 GERBET P.
"LA MISE EN OEUVRE DU MARCHE COMMUN AGRICOLE."
REV. FRANCAISE SCI. POL., 4 (AUG 64), 761-73.
EVOLUTION AND ANALYSIS OF THE AGRICULTURAL POLICIES OF THE EUROPEAN COMMON MARKET, EXPLAINING ROLE OF VARIOUS PRESSURE GROUPS IN THEIR FORMULATION.

1065 GERMANY FOREIGN MINISTRY
DOCUMENTS ON GERMAN FOREIGN POLICY 1918-1945, SERIES C (1933-1937) VOLS. I-V.
WASHINGTON: US GOVERNMENT, 1954, 3562 PP.
CHRONICLES RISE OF THIRD REICH IN GERMANY, CONSISTING ENTIRELY OF DOCUMENTS DESCRIBING IMMENSE RANGE OF GERMAN DIPLOMATIC ACTIVITY, INCLUDING LETTERS, TELEGRAMS, AND MEMORANDA, SENT AND RECEIVED BY GERMAN FOREIGN MINISTRY. PUBLISHED DURING 1954-66.

1066 GESELLSCHAFT RECHTSVERGLEICH
BIBLIOGRAPHIE DES DEUTSCHEN RECHTS (BIBLIOGRAPHY OF GERMAN LAW, TRANS. BY COURTLAND PETERSON)
KARLSRVHE: VERLAG CF MULLER, 1964, 584 PP.
ANALYTIC AND THOROUGHLY CATEGORIZED BIBLIOGRAPHY OF WORKS, DOCUMENTS, STUDIES, TEXTS, ETC., INVOLVING GERMAN LAW. INCLUDES A LENGTHY INTRODUCTION BY PROFESSOR FRITZ BAUR ELUCIDATING GERMAN LAW AND LEGAL PROCEDURES SINCE 1949. BILINGUAL EDITION WITH ENGLISH AND GERMAN ANNOTATION.

1067 GIBSON J.S.
IDEOLOGY AND WORLD AFFAIRS.
BOSTON: HOUGHTON MIFFLIN, 1964, 372 PP.
DISCUSSES IMPACT OF IDEOLOGIES ON MEN AND NATIONS INCLUDING NATURE AND EVOLUTION OF DEMOCRACY, DEMOCRACY AND FOREIGN POLICY, EVOLUTION OF COMMUNIST IDEOLOGY, RIGHT-WING TOTALITARIANISM, CONTEMPORARY AUTHORITARIANISM, AND FUTURE PROSPECTS.

1068 GILBERT M., GOTT R.
THE APPEASERS.
BOSTON: HOUGHTON MIFFLIN, 1963, 444 PP., LC#63-9079.
COVERS HISTORY OF BRITISH POLICY TOWARD NAZI GERMANY AND OF THOSE WHO SUPPORTED AND OPPOSED IT. DESCRIBES IN DETAIL ITS FORMATION, OPERATION, AND THE MISCONCEPTIONS ABOUT IT. EMPHASIZES COLONIAL AND ECONOMIC APPEASEMENT, ANGLO-FRENCH DISSENSION, GOVERNMENT-CABINET CONFLICT, AND WIDESPREAD FEAR OF COMMUNISM.

1069 GILBERT M.
THE EUROPEAN POWERS 1900-45.
LONDON: WEIDENFIELD & NICOLSON, 1965, 307 PP.
HISTORY OF GREAT POWERS FROM BOER WAR TO END OF WWII. COVERS TWO WORLD WARS, RUSSIAN REVOLUTION, ITALIAN FASCISM, EMPHASIZING DOMESTIC FACTORS THAT SHAPED FOREIGN POLICIES OF EACH EUROPEAN NATION.

1070 GILBERT M.
THE ROOTS OF APPEASEMENT.
NEW YORK: NEW AMERICAN LIB, 1966, 254 PP., LC#67-14724.
STUDY OF ORIGINS OF APPEASEMENT IN INTERNATIONAL RELATIONS. ANALYZES BRITISH POLICY TOWARD GERMANY, 1918-39. ARGUES THAT APPEASEMENT IS NECESSARY POLICY IN CURRENT INTERNATIONAL AFFAIRS. REVIEWS EVENTS LEADING TO AND FOLLOWING DECISIONS AT MUNICH.

1071 GILBERT R.
COMPETITIVE COEXISTENCE: THE NEW SOVIET CHALLENGE.
NEW YORK: BOOKMAILER, 1956, 182 PP.
APPRAISES MILITANT COMMUNISM AS MENACE TO FREE PEOPLES. DEALS WITH FATE OF SOVIET RUSSIA'S PROLETARIAT AND PEASANTRY. DESCRIBES DETERMINATION OF COMMUNIST LEADERS TO CONQUER ALL MAJOR WORLD POWERS THROUGH COLD WAR TACTICS. QUESTIONS POSSIBILITY OF PEACEFUL COEXISTENCE.

1072 GILBERT R., ED.
GENOCIDE IN TIBET.
NEW YORK:AMER ASIAN EDUC EXC, 1959, 103 PP., LC#59-15425.
STUDIES COMMUNIST AGGRESSION IN TIBET AND INDICATES ATTEMPTS OF CHINESE TO ERADICATE TIBETAN RACE. USES STATEMENTS OF NATIVES, TRAVELERS, AND DALAI LAMA TO SUPPORT THEORY.

1073 GILPIN R.
AMERICAN SCIENTISTS AND NUCLEAR WEAPONS POLICY.
PRINCETON: U. PR., 1962, 352 PP.
TRACES AMERICAN SCIENTIFIC THOUGHT FROM EARLY POST-HIROSHIMA POLICY (OR LACK OF SIGNIFICANT POLICY) THROUGH DEVELOPMENT OF VARIOUS IDEALISTIC THEORIES TO THE EVENTUAL EMERGENCE OF PRESENT SOCIAL MATURITY. DEPICTS SCIENTISTS AS BEING FACED WITH THE CHOICE OF WORKING FOR DISARMAMENT OR DETERRENCE IN SEEKING WORLD STABILITY, BUT AS BECOMING RESOLVED TO THE INEVITABILITY OF THE LATTER.

1074 GINSBURGS G.
"PEKING-LHASA-NEW DELHI."
POLIT. SCI. QUART., 75 (SEPT. 60), 338-354.
SURVEYS CHINESE-TIBETAN RELATIONS FROM PRE-COMMUNIST DAYS

TO PRESENT. TRACES GROWTH OF CHINESE POWER IN TIBET FROM 1950-54 PERIOD OF MODERATION, THROUGH PERIOD OF INCREASED USE OF FORCE TO '59 UPRISING AND ITS SUPPRESSION. CONCLUDES THAT TIBET, NOW FULLY CONTROLLED BY PEKING, IS BEING USED AS BASE FOR PENETRATION SOUTHWARD.

1075 GINSBURGS G.
"WARS OF NATIONAL LIBERATION - THE SOVIET THESIS."
LAW CONTEMP. PROBL., 29 (AUTUMN 64), 910-42.
SURVEYS AND REFUTES SOVIET LEGAL ARGUMENTS WHICH SUGGEST THAT PRINCIPLES OF INTERNATIONAL LAW EXIST WHICH STATE THAT ARMED HOSTILITIES IN COLONIAL AND DEPENDENT TERRITORIES ARE CLASSIFIED AS INTERNATIONAL WARS.

1076 GIRAUD A.
CIVILISATION ET PRODUCTIVITE.
PARIS: PICHON ET DURAND-AUZIAS, 1954, 202 PP.
AUTHOR BELIEVES CIVILIZATION IS IN TRANSITION BETWEEN INDUSTRIAL AGE AND PRODUCTIVE AGE. BOOK DISCUSSES PRODUCTION IN TERMS OF GENERAL EVOLUTION OF MAN. CONSIDERS PLACE OF WORK IN PRODUCTION, PRECURSORS OF CONTEMPORARY PRODUCTION, PRODUCTION IN OTHER COUNTRIES, PLACE OF MAN IN PRODUCTION, AND THE DIRECTION INTERNATIONAL RELATIONS SHOULD TAKE IN THE FACE OF PRODUCTIVE REVOLUTION.

1077 GIRAUD E.
"L'INTERDICTION DU RECOURS A LA FORCE, LA THEORIE ET LA PRATIQUE DES NATIONS UNIES."
REV. GEN. DR. INT. PUB., 34 (NO.3, 63), 501-44.
SEVERAL PAPERS DEFINE AGGRESSION ACCORDING TO INTERNATIONAL LAW AND UN CHARTER. ANALYZE UN IMPLEMENTATION OF ARTICLE 2 OF CHARTER DURING MOST FAMOUS CRISES: ALGERIA, HUNGARY, CONGO, CUBA.

1078 GJUPANOVIC H., ADAMOVITCH A.
LEGAL SOURCES AND BIBLIOGRAPHY OF YUGOSLAVIA.
NEW YORK: FREDERICK PRAEGER, 1964, 353 PP., LC#64-15520.
TOPICALLY ARRANGES, ANNOTATES, AND THOROUGHLY INDEXES BY SUBJECT AND AUTHOR 2,467 ITEMS IN EUROPEAN LANGUAGES RELATING TO THE DEVELOPMENT AND SUBSTANCE OF YUGOSLAVIAN LAW. COVERS THE FORMATION OF YUGOSLAVIA, THE KINGDOM, WORLD WAR II, AND THE PRESENT POLITICAL AND LEGAL ORDER. MATERIALS ARE VERY DIVERSIFIED: DOCUMENTS, SERIALS, MONOGRAPHS, RECORDS, COURT DECISIONS, TREATIES, PERIODICALS, ETC.

1079 GLAZER M.
THE FEDERAL GOVERNMENT AND THE UNIVERSITY.
PRINCETON: PRIN U INDUS REL CTR, 1966, 4 PP.
CONTAINS MAGAZINE AND JOURNAL ARTICLES DEALING WITH FEDERAL GOVERNMENT SUPPORT OF SOCIAL SCIENCE RESEARCH AND IMPACT OF PROJECT CAMELOT. ALL ENTRIES ARE IN ENGLISH AND WERE PUBLISHED 1960-66. ARRANGED ACCORDING TO FOLLOWING TOPICS: GOVERNMENT-UNIVERSITY RELATIONS, GOVERNMENT SUPPORT FOR SOCIAL SCIENCE RESEARCH, AND PROJECT CAMELOT.

1080 GLEASON J.H.
THE GENESIS OF RUSSOPHOBIA IN GREAT BRITAIN: A STUDY OF THE INTERACTION OF POLICY AND OPINION.
CAMBRIDGE: HARVARD U PR, 1950, 314 PP.
STUDIES THE DISRUPTION OF CORDIALITY AND THE GROWTH OF HOSTILITY BETWEEN RUSSIA AND BRITAIN BETWEEN 1815 AND 1841. AUTHOR BELIEVES ANGLO-RUSSIAN HOSTILITY WAS THE FRUIT OF COMPETITIVE IMPERIAL AMBITIONS, WHICH TRANSFORMED TWO POWERS HITHERTO REMOTE INTO NEIGHBORS IN THEIR COLONIAL SPHERES. EMPLOYS BOTH PRIMARY AND SECONDARY SOURCES.

1081 GLENN N.D., SIMMONS J.G.
"ARE REGIONAL CULTURAL DIFFERENCES DIMINISHING?"
PUBLIC OPINION QUART., 31 (1967), 176-193.
CHALLENGES ASSUMPTION THAT US IS LOSING REGIONAL CULTURAL DIFFERENCES. EXAMINES ATTITUDES OF 21-39 AND OVER 40 AGE GROUPS. DATA REVEALS DIFFERENCES HAVE INCREASED. DIVERGENCE REPORTED ON PERSONAL MORALITY, PRESTIGE OF OCCUPATIONS, RACIAL MINORITIES, INTERNATIONAL RELATIONS, AND POLITICS.

1082 GLOBERSON A.
"SOCIAL GROWTH IN THE DEVELOPING COUNTRIES."
COEXISTENCE, 4 (JAN. 67), 63-69.
OF PRIMARY IMPORTANCE IN ASSISTANCE TO DEVELOPING NATIONS ARE PROGRAMS FOR SOCIAL GROWTH, SINCE IN LONG RUN, SOCIAL GROWTH IS NECESSARY TO ECONOMIC GROWTH. IT IS INSUFFICIENT AND POSSIBLY DAMAGING MERELY TO OFFER ECONOMIC AID WHICH DEPENDS ON FOREIGN TECHNICIANS OR WHICH PROVIDES TOOLS BUT NOT SKILL. ASSISTANCE IN DEVELOPING WORK PRACTICES AND MODES OF APPROACH TO SOCIAL AND ECONOMIC AFFAIRS IS OF GREAT AID TOO.

1083 GLUBB J.B.
WAR IN THE DESERT: AN R.A.F. FRONTIER CAMPAIGN.
LONDON: HODDEN & STAUGHTON, 1960, 352 PP.
DESCRIBES ROLE OF ROYAL AIR FORCE IN THE ARABIAN DESERT CAMPAIGNS OF 1920'S. MAINTAINS THAT BRITISH INTERVENTION PROVED BENEFICIAL SINCE IT PREVENTED WARRING PEOPLES FROM DESTROYING EACH OTHER.

1085 GODET M. ED.
INDEX BIBLIOGRAPHICUS: INTERNATIONAL CATALOGUE OF SOURCES OF CURRENT BIBLIOGRAPHIC INFORMATION.
BOSTON: WORLD PEACE FOUNDATION, 1925, 233 PP.
SELECTED BIBLIOGRAPHY ARRANGED BY SUBJECT; PERIODICALS AND INSTITUTIONAL PUBLICATIONS. MOST EUROPEAN LANGUAGES INCLUDED. PUBLICATIONS DATE LARGELY FROM 1900-1925. COVERS PHILOSOPHY, RELIGION, SOCIAL SCIENCES, LAW, PHILOLOGY, NATURAL SCIENCES, MATHEMATICS. 1,000 ENTRIES.

1086 GODUNSKY Y., SELIVANOV V.
"'APOSTLES OF PEACE' IN LATIN AMERICA."
INTER-AM. ECO. AFFAIRS, 4 (APR. 67), 24-28.
ARGUES THAT PEACE CORPS SET UP BY US TO DISORGANIZE NATIONAL-LIBERATION MOVEMENT IN LATIN AMERICA AND PROMOTE US NEO-COLONIALIST POLICY.

1088 GOLAY J.F.
"THE FOUNDING OF THE FEDERAL REPUBLIC OF GERMANY."
CHICAGO: U OF CHICAGO PRESS, 1958.
DISCUSSES PROCESS IN WHICH CONSTITUTIONAL FOUNDATIONS OF THE GERMAN FEDERAL REPUBLIC ORIGINATED IN PREVIOUS GERMAN CONSTITUTIONAL AND POLITICAL DEVELOPMENT. REVIEWS PRESENT NEEDS AND INTERESTS OF WEST GERMAN PEOPLE AND INFLUENCES BROUGHT TO BEAR BY WESTERN ALLIED GOVERNMENTS. PARTIALLY ANNOTATED BIBLIOGRAPHY OF 19 GERMAN AND AMERICAN DOCUMENTS AND VARIOUS BOOKS, PERIODICALS, AND NEWSPAPERS.

1089 GOLD J.
"INTERPRETATION BY THE INTERNATIONAL MONETARY FUND OF ITS ARTICLES OF AGREEMENT."
INT. AND COMP. LAW Q., 16 (APR. 67), 287-329.
DISCUSSION OF DEVELOPMENTS IN THE CHARTER OF THE FUND IN THE LAST TWELVE YEARS. VARIETY AND EXPANSIVENESS OF INTERPRETATION OF LEGAL DOCUMENT HAVE CONTRIBUTED TO CONTINUED VITALITY OF DOCUMENTS. DISCUSSES NUMBER OF INFLUENTIAL FORCES ON EVOLUTION OF DOCUMENT.

1090 GOLDMAN M.I.
"SOVIET ECONOMIC GROWTH SINCE THE REVOLUTION."
CURRENT HISTORY, 53 (OCT. 67), 230-235.
CONSIDERS PAST 50 YEARS OF SOVIET ECONOMIC GROWTH AND SPECULATES ON WHAT MIGHT HAVE TAKEN PLACE. DISCUSSES DIFFICULTIES THAT CONTINUE TO PLAGUE SOVIET ECONOMY, SUCH AS COLLECTIVIZATION CAMPAIGN, EXCESS OF AGRICULTURAL LABOR, AND FALL OF CAPITAL PRODUCTIVITY. REFORM EFFORTS INCLUDE DOMESTIC REFORM AND INCREASE IN FOREIGN TRADE. STATES THAT USSR HAS CHANGED INTO HIGHLY INDUSTRIALIZED ECONOMY.

1091 GOLDSCHMIDT W. ED.
THE UNITED STATES AND AFRICA.
NEW YORK: FREDERICK PRAEGER, 1963, 298 PP., LC#63-20154.
ESSAYS ON SOCIAL AND POLITICAL PROBLEMS OF AFRICA, WITH PARTICULAR EMPHASIS ON CHARACTER OF US INTERESTS IN AFRICAN POLITICAL AND ECONOMIC DEVELOPMENT.

1092 GOLDWATER B.M.
WHY NOT VICTORY? A FRESH LOOK AT AMERICAN FOREIGN POLICY.
NEW YORK: MCGRAW HILL, 1962, 201 PP., LC#62-14674.
CONSERVATIVE APPRAISAL OF US ROLE IN POST-WWII INTERNATIONAL CRISES. DEALS WITH COMMUNIST MENACE, USE AND MISUSE OF AMERICA'S POWER, CUBAN CRISIS, UN, AND WORLD COURT. PRESENTS OPINION ON FOREIGN AID AND POLICY. CALLS FOR A NEW NATIONALISM TO UNITE FREE WORLD AGAINST COMMUNISM AND RETURN TO TRADITIONAL AMERICAN VALUES. VICTORY MUST BE PRIMARY GOAL.

1093 GOLDWERT M.
CONSTABULARY IN THE DOMINICAN REPUBLIC AND NICARAGUA.
GAINESVILLE: U OF FLA INTER-AMER, 1961, LC#55-62581.
STUDY OF MOTIVES OF US INTERVENTION IN LATIN AMERICAN COUNTRIES IN EARLY DECADES OF 20TH CENTURY. FOCUSES ON INTERVENTION IN DOMINICAN REPUBLIC BETWEEN 1916 AND 1924 AND IN NICARAGUA FROM 1927 TO 1932. CONTENDS THAT US WAS ATTEMPTING TO STABILIZE POLITICAL CONDITIONS THAT THREATENED US SECURITY AND SPECIFICALLY THAT GOAL OF US INTERVENTION WAS ESTABLISHMENT OF NONPARTISAN CONSTABULARY.

1094 GOLDWIN R.A. ED., LERNER R. ED., STOURZH G. ED.
READINGS IN AMERICAN FOREIGN POLICY.
NEW YORK: OXFORD U PR, 1959, 709 PP., LC#59-9819.
PRESENTS OPPOSING VIEWS ON DIFFERENT POLICIES, GROUPED UNDER HEADINGS COVERING GENERAL FOREIGN AFFAIRS; US GROWTH AND EXPANSION; US RELATIONS WITH EUROPE, LATIN AMERICA, THE FAR EAST, USSR, AND UNDERDEVELOPED COUNTRIES; AND POLICY IN THE NUCLEAR AGE.

1095 GOLDWIN R.A. ED., STOURZH G. ED.,
READINGS IN RUSSIAN FOREIGN POLICY.
NEW YORK: OXFORD U PR, 1959, 775 PP., LC#59-9820.
SELECTIONS ARRANGED TOPICALLY; INCLUDES PRIMARY AND SECONDARY SOURCE MATERIALS AND MAPS. AMONG TOPICS COVERED ARE: THE RUSSIAN PEOPLE, CZARISM AND RUSSIAN REVOLUTION, WORLD REVOLUTION AND NATIONAL INTEREST, THEORY OF COMMUNISM, RUSSIA AND THE EAST, IDEOLOGY AND BALANCE OF POWER, COLD WAR, HUNGARIAN AND YUGOSLAVIAN SOCIALISM, AND "WHAT GUIDES RUSSIAN FOREIGN POLICY?"

1096 GOLDWIN R.A. ED.
WHY FOREIGN AID? - TWO MESSAGES BY PRESIDENT KENNEDY AND ESSAYS.
SKOKIE: RAND MCNALLY & CO, 1962, 140 PP., LC#63-19359.
PRESENTS EIGHT ESSAYS TO CLARIFY QUESTION: WHY FOREIGN AID, WHILE DOUBTS AS TO ITS AIMS AND RESULTS SEEM TO PERSIST AND EVEN INCREASE. MOST AUTHORS ARGUE THAT, WHILE SUCH AID HAS BECOME A SOLID PART OF US PUBLIC POLICY SINCE WWII, PRESENT UNDERSTANDING OF BASIC TASK OF US AID TO UNDER-DEVELOPED NATIONS IS NOT CLEAR OR PROFOUND ENOUGH TO SERVE AS RELIABLE GUIDE TO POLICY.

1097 GOLDWIN R.A. ED.
FOREIGN AND MILITARY POLICY.
CHICAGO: U OF CHICAGO PRESS, 1963.
PAPERS ON CONTEMPORARY ISSUES IN FOREIGN POLICY AND MILITARY STRATEGY, INCLUDING US POLICY, WESTERN BLOC, DISARMAMENT, COMMUNIST BLOC, SOVIET POLICY, NEW STATES, AND US AND UN.

1099 GONZALEZ PEDRERO E.
ANATOMIA DE UN CONFLICTO.
MEXICO CITY: FACULTAD U VERACRUZ, 1963, 136 PP.
ANALYSIS OF WORLD AFFAIRS AND RELATIONS AMONG NATIONS IN PRESENT COLD WAR SITUATION. EXAMINES STATUS OF UNDERDEVELOPED COUNTRIES IN REGARD TO POLITICS OF LARGER MORE POWERFUL NATIONS.

1100 GOOCH G.P.
ENGLISH DEMOCRATIC IDEAS IN THE SEVENTEENTH CENTURY (2ND ED.)
NEW YORK: CAMBRIDGE U PRESS, 1927, 315 PP.
CONCERNED WITH DEMOCRATIC FEATURES OF ENGLISH MONARCHICAL GOVERNMENT. BEGINS WITH ORIGIN AND GROWTH OF DEMOCRATIC IDEAS. DISCUSSES ORIGIN OF REPUBLICANISM AND FOUNDATION OF REPUBLIC; PRESENTS VIEW OF ANTAGONISTS OF OLIGARCHY AND INCLUDES POLITICAL IDEAS OF THE ARMY, RISE OF INFLUENTIAL RELIGIOUS BODIES, AND REVOLUTION OF 1688. RELATIONS WITH US AND COMMONWEALTH AND MOVEMENT FOR LAW REFORM ARE STUDIED.

1101 GOODMAN E.
"THE CRY OF NATIONAL LIBERATION: RECENT SOVIET ATTITUDES TOWARDS NATIONAL SELF-DETERMINATION."
INT. ORGAN., 14 (WINTER 60), 92-106.
SOVIET UNION APPLIES PRINCIPLE OF SELF-DETERMINATION ONLY TO NON-SOVIET COUNTRIES. USING EXTRACTS OF UN DEBATES, SHOWS HOW TERM IS USED AS POLITICAL WEAPON.

1102 GOODRICH L.M.
THE UNITED NATIONS AND THE MAINTENANCE OF INTERNATIONAL PEACE AND SECURITY.
WASHINGTON: BROOKINGS INST., 1955, 709 PP.
SEEKS TO AID UNDERSTANDING OF PROBLEMS FACING UN BY ANALYZING AND APPRAISING FUNCTION OF UN SYSTEM. EMPHASIZES WORK OF GENERAL ASSEMBLY AND SECURITY COUNCIL IN PEACE-KEEPING AND UN PLAN FOR REGULATION OF ARMAMENTS.

1103 GOODRICH L.M.
KOREA: A STUDY OF US POLICY IN THE UNITED NATIONS.
NEW YORK: COUNCIL FOR. REL., 1956, 235 PP., $3.25.
EXPLORATION OF KOREAN QUESTION IN UN FROM VJ DAY TO CESSATION OF COLLECTIVE ACTION. DISCUSSES ROLE OF USA IN POST-WAR PROCEEDINGS, AND INTERACTION OF USA POLICIES AND UN AIMS AND ACTIVITY.

1104 GOODRICH L.M.
THE UNITED NATIONS.
NEW YORK: CROWELL, 1959, 419 PP.
EXAMINES HOW STRUCTURE, FUNCTIONS, AND PROCEDURES OF UN ARE RELATED TO ITS PRINCIPLES. RELATES CONCESSIONS MADE IN RECOGNITION OF POWER POLITICS AND NATIONAL INTEREST.

1105 GOODRICH L.M.
"GEOGRAPHICAL DISTRIBUTION OF THE STAFF OF THE UN SECRETARIAT."
INT. ORGAN., 16 (SUMMER 62), 465-82.
STUDIES PROBLEM OF SATISFYING GEOGRAPHIC REQUIREMENTS AND EMPLOYING QUALIFIED PERSONS. ORIGINAL UN STAFF COMPRISED OF AMERICANS, BRITISH, AND CANADIANS. ADMITTANCE OF TWENTY AFRICAN STATES IN 1960 LED TO DEMANDS FOR GREATER GEOGRAPHICAL BALANCE.

1106 GOODRICH L.M., HAMBRO E.
"CHARTER OF THE UNITED NATIONS: COMMENTARY AND DOCUMENTS."
BOSTON: WORLD PEACE FOUNDATION, 1946.
COMMENTARY ON CONSTITUTION INCLUDES DISCUSSION OF ITS HISTORY AND ORIGINS, ORGANIZATION OF ORIGINATING CONFERENCE, CONTENT OF CHARTER, ITS IMPLEMENTATION. HAS COMMENTARY ON ARTICLES, LIST OF DOCUMENTS AND EXTENSIVE BIBLIOGRAPHY WHICH CONTAINS REFERENCES TO MANY ORIGINAL SOURCES.

1108 GOODWIN G.L.
"THE EXPANDING UNITED NATIONS: 2- DIPLOMATIC PRESSURES AND TECHNIQUES."
INT. AFF., 37 (APR. 61), 170-80.
ANALYTIC STUDY OF COMPETETIVE COEXISTENCE AND ITS DISRUPTIVE EFFECT ON THE MECHANICAL MAJORITIES WITHIN THE ORGANIZATION. BASED ON ANY REALISTIC CALCULATION, THE RELATION OF FORCES IN THE UN HAS CLEARLY MOVED TO THE ADVANTAGE OF THE USSR.

1109 GORDENKER L.
THE UNITED NATIONS AND THE PEACEFUL UNIFICATION OF KOREA.
GENEVA: NIJHOFF, 1959, 306 PP.
DISCUSSES THE ROLE OF UN FIELD COMMISSIONS IN KOREA PRIOR TO AND DURING THE OUTBREAK OF HOSTILITIES. EXAMINES THE COMISSIONS' ACTIVITIES AND INSIGHTS THEY PROVIDED FOR UN FIELD BODIES. CONCLUDES: FIELD COMMISSIONS WERE NOT THE BEST POSSIBLE ORGAN FOR DELICATE KOREAN SITUATION BEFORE 1950.

1110 GORDON B.
"ECONOMIC IMPEDIMENTS TO REGIONALISM IN SOUTH EAST ASIA."
ASIAN SURV., 3 (MAY 63), 235-44.
ANALYZES PAST AND PRESENT ECONOMIC ASPECTS OF REGION. PRESENT CONDITIONS AND FATE OF NEW PROPOSALS AFFECTED MAINLY BY TWO TOPICS: TRADE RELATIONSHIPS AND NATURE OF INDIVIDUAL DEVELOPMENT PROGRAMS. CONSIDERS FACTORS HINDERING INTER-REGIONAL TRADE. SCORES NEGLECT OF AGRICULTURAL DEVELOPMENT.

1111 GORDON B.K.
THE DIMENSIONS OF CONFLICT IN SOUTHEAST ASIA.
ENGLEWOOD CLIFFS: PRENTICE HALL, 1966, 201 PP., LC#66-14699.
ANALYZES CERTAIN MAJOR INTRA-REGIONAL CONFLICTS IN ORDER TO EMPHASIZE SEPARATE AND DISTINCT CHARACTER OF INDIVIDUAL SOUTHEAST ASIAN NATIONS. EXAMINES INITIAL, TENTATIVE EFFORTS AMONG LEADERS IN SOUTHEAST ASIA TO ESTABLISH RELATIVELY FORMAL PATTERNS OF COLLABORATION AMONG THEIR STATES. DISCUSSES COLLABORATION AS A REGIONAL REFLECTION OF A GLOBAL TENDENCY AND AS COMPARATIVE BEHAVIORAL POLITICS.

1112 GORDON D.L., DANGERFIELD R.
THE HIDDEN WEAPON: THE STORY OF ECONOMIC WARFARE.
NEW YORK: HARPER, 1947, 238 PP.
DESCRIBES BRITISH AND AMERICAN DEVICES OF ECONOMIC WARFARE DURING WW 2, DIRECTED TOWARDS CUTTING OF AXIS POWERS FROM FOREIGN SUPPLIES OF STRATEGIC MATERIALS. CONSIDERS NEUTRALITY AND INTERNATIONAL LAW GOVERNING RELATIONS OF NON-BELLIGERENTS AND BELLIGERENTS TO BE NOW EXTINCT DUE TO NATURE OF MODERN WAR. SEES NEED FOR ENFORCEABLE LAWS WHICH WILL ELIMINATE WAR.

1113 GORDON G.N., FALK I., HODAPP W.
THE IDEA INVADERS.
NEW YORK: HASTINGS HOUSE, 1963, 256 PP., LC#63-13563.
DISCUSSES REASONS FOR AMERICA'S POOR IMAGE ABROAD. SHOWS HOW US PROPAGANDA ACTUALLY OPERATES THROUGH OFFICIAL AND UNOFFICIAL CHANNELS. EVALUATES EFFECTIVENESS OF US MOVIES, TELEVISION, RADIO, BOOKS, AND MAGAZINES. COMPARES RUSSIAN PROPAGANDA METHODS WITH THOSE OF US. SUGGESTS DEVELOPMENT OF AN "EAR OF AMERICA" PROGRAM.

1114 GORDON L.
"THE ORGANIZATION FOR EUROPEAN ECONOMIC COOPERATION."
INT. ORGAN., 10 (FEB. 56), 1-11.
CONTENDS OEEC HAS HAD INFLUENCE ON ATTITUDES AND ACTIONS OF MEMBER STATES. EXAMINES SUCCESSES IN ALLOCATION OF AID, TRADE AND PAYMENTS LIBERALIZATION, PRODUCTIVITY INCREASE, AND CURRENCY STABILIZATION. OEEC FAILED IN RECOVERY PROGRAMS, ECONOMIC INTEGRATION.

1115 GORDON L.
A NEW DEAL FOR LATIN AMERICA.
CAMBRIDGE: HARVARD U PR, 1963, 146 PP., LC#63-13812.
ADDRESSES BY US AMBASSADOR TO BRAZIL EXPLAINING PHILOSOPHY, PURPOSES, AND WORKING METHODS OF THE ALLIANCE FOR PROGRESS. ANALYZES DIFFICULTIES CONFRONTING THE PROGRAM. DISCUSSES ECONOMIC ASPECTS, DEMOCRATIC REVOLUTION, EDUCATIONAL FOUNDATIONS, AND FREE INITIATIVE.

1116 GORER G., RICKMAN J.
THE PEOPLE OF GREAT RUSSIA: A PSYCHOLOGICAL STUDY.
LONDON: CRESSET PRESS, 1949, 235 PP.
ATTEMPTS TO ISOLATE AND ANALYZE PRINCIPAL MOTIVES THAT INFORM AND UNDERLIE TYPICAL BEHAVIOR OF THE GREAT RUSSIAN PEOPLE. EXPLORES MEANS BY WHICH THESE MOTIVES ARE ELICITED AND MAINTAINED IN THE CHILDREN OF THE SOCIETY, SO THAT SOCIETY MAINTAINS ITS IDENTITY. DEVELOPS "SWADDLING HYPOTHESIS." FINDS POLICY IS FORMED BY SMALL GROUP OF LEADERS. FINDS BASIC FEAR OF FOREIGNERS PREVALENT.

1117 GOULD L.P.
THE PRICE OF SURVIVAL.
WASHINGTON: PUBLIC AFFAIRS PRESS, 1959, 96 PP., LC#59-13655.
STUDIES BASIC PROBLEM OF WESTERN CIVILIZATION EMPHASIZING HISTORICAL PRECEDENTS OF EXTINCT CULTURES AS A LESSON FOR CONTEMPORARY SOCIETY. PROPOSES CONDITIONS BASIC TO SURVIVAL, INCLUDING AWARENESS, MOTIVATION, AND RESPONSIBILITY.

1118 GOWING M.
BRITAIN AND ATOMIC ENERGY 1939-1945.
NEW YORK: ST MARTIN'S PRESS, 1964, 464 PP.
FIRST AUTHORITATIVE ACCOUNT OF ROLE PLAYED BY BRITAIN IN

DEVELOPMENT OF THE FIRST ATOMIC BOMBS. AUTHOR IS HISTORIAN AND ARCHIVIST FOR UK ATOMIC ENERGY AUTHORITY. ILLUSTRATES RELATIONSHIP BETWEEN SCIENCE AND GOVERNMENT.

1119 GRACIA-MORA M.R.
"INTERNATIONAL RESPONSIBILITY FOR SUBVERSIVE ACTIVITIES AND HOSTILE PROPAGANDA BY PRIVATE PERSONS AGAINST."
FOREIGN STATES.
INDIANA LAW J., 35 (SPRING 60), 306-35.
CHRONOLOGICAL SURVEY OF INTERNATIONAL LAW ON SUBJECT. ANALYSIS OF MANNER IN WHICH USA AND BRITAIN, EUROPE, SOUTH AMERICA, AND USSR PREVENT PRIVATE HOSTILE ACTIVITY CONSTITUTING DANGER TO FOREIGN NATIONS.

1120 GRAEBNER N.A.
THE NEW ISOLATIONISM: A STUDY IN POLITICS AND FOREIGN POLICY SINCE 1960.
NEW YORK: RONALD, 1961, 289 PP., $4.00.
INTERNAL POLITICAL FORCES AND CAMPAIGN PROMISES HAVE IMPEDED TRUMAN AND EISENHOWER ADMINISTRATIONS FROM PURSUING REALISTIC FOREIGN POLICY.

1121 GRAEBNER N.A., ED.
AN UNCERTAIN TRADITION: AMERICAN SECRETARIES OF STATE IN THE 20TH CENTURY.
NEW YORK: MCGRAW HILL, 1961, 341 PP.
ESSAYS ON FOURTEEN TWENTIETH CENTURY AMERICAN SECRETARIES OF STATE FROM HAY TO DULLES. THEIR YEARS IN OFFICE MARK THE TRANSITION IN AMERICAN FOREIGN POLICY FROM IDEALISM TO REALISM. TRACES CONSTITUTIONAL AND POLITICAL PROBLEMS FACED BY THESE MEN.

1122 GRAEBNER N.A.
COLD WAR DIPLOMACY 1945-1960.
PRINCETON: VAN NOSTRAND, 1962, 191 PP.
CAREFULLY TRACES, IN NARRATIVES AND DOCUMENTS, AMERICAN FOREIGN POLICY THROUGH THE FIFTEEN POSTWAR YEARS.

1123 GRAEBNER N.A. ED.
THE COLD WAR: IDEOLOGICAL CONFLICT OR POWER STRUGGLE?
BOSTON: D C HEATH, 1963, 105 PP., LC#63-21049.
US SCHOLARS ANALYZE REASONS FOR EXISTENCE OF COLD WAR. SEE RUSSIA AS TRADITIONALLY POWERFUL NATION SEEKING SECURITY AGAINST PROVEN ANTAGONIST. FEEL CONTAINMENT THROUGH DIPLOMACY POSSIBLE AS RUSSIA'S KEY CONCERN IS NATIONAL INTEREST. OTHERS ARGUE RUSSIA THREATENS FOUNDATIONS OF FREE WORLD AND SEEKS ONLY WORLD DOMINATION. COLD WAR IS FIGHT OF FREEDOM VS. TYRANNY TO END. BIBLIOGRAPHY FOR FURTHER READINGS.

1124 GRAHAM F.D.
PROTECTIVE TARIFFS.
NEW YORK: HARPER, 1934, 176 PP.
ANALYSIS OF ARGUMENTS FOR AND AGAINST PROTECTION IN INTERNATIONAL TRADE AND SUGGESTIONS FOR FUTURE TRADE POLICIES FOR USA.

1125 GRAHAM F.D.
THE THEORY OF INTERNATIONAL VALUES.
PRINCETON: U. PR., 1948, 349 PP.
PRESENTS A THEORY WHICH IS A COMPLETE REFUTATION OF CLASSICAL DOCTRINES, AND DISCUSSES INTERNATION ECONOMICS AND TRADE IN THE LIGHT OF THIS NEW THEORY.

1126 GRAHAM G.S.
THE POLITICS OF NAVAL SUPREMACY; STUDIES IN BRITISH MARITIME ASCENDANCY.
NEW YORK: CAMBRIDGE U PRESS, 1965, 132 PP.
EXAMINES CONSEQUENCES AND LIMITATIONS OF BRITISH NAVAL SUPREMACY WITHIN FRAMEWORK OF 19TH-CENTURY POLITICS; INCLUDES FOREIGN POLICY AND NAVAL STRATEGY. BEGINS WITH BRITAIN'S POWER ON THE ATLANTIC, THEN CONCENTRATES ON THE PACIFIC WHERE IMPERIAL ATTENTION SHIFTED IN 19TH CENTURY. CLOSES WITH MEDITERRANEAN CORRIDOR FROM GIBRALTAR TO BOMBAY AND ILLUSION OF "PAX BRITANNICA."

1127 GRAHAM I.C.C., LEIB B.S.
PUBLICATIONS OF THE SOCIAL SCIENCE DEPARTMENT, THE RAND CORPORATION, 1948-1966.
NEW YORK: THE RAND CORP, 1966, 97 PP.
UNANNOTATED LISTING OF BOOKS, PAPERS, REPORTS, MEMORANDA, AND TRANSLATIONS PUBLISHED BY OR FOR RAND CORPORATION. ONE HALF OF THE PUBLICATIONS TREAT VARIOUS FACETS OF SOVIET GOVERNMENT AND POLITICAL POLICIES. INCLUDES MATERIAL ON MOST EVERY COUNTRY AND MUCH EMPHASIS ON INTERNATIONAL RELATIONS AND PROBLEMS OF MODERN WARFARE. INDEXED BY AUTHOR.

1128 GRANDIN T.
"THE POLITICAL USE OF THE RADIO."
GENEVA STUD., 10 (AUG. 39), 116 PP.
REVIEWS PRE-WAR NATIONAL AND INTERNATIONAL POLITICAL RADIO BROADCASTS AS TO THEIR USE AND EFFECTIVENESS. EXAMINES CONTEMPORARY CONTROL MECHANISMS AND POINTS OUT NEED FOR MORE STRINGENT CONTROLS IN THE FUTURE.

1129 GRANT N.
COMMUNIST PSYCHOLOGICAL OFFENSIVE: DISTORTION IN THE TRANSLATION OF OFFICIAL DOCUMENTS (PAMPHLET)
WASHINGTON: RES INST SINO-SOV, 1961, 20 PP.
ANALYSIS OF THE STATEMENT DELIVERED BY M. A. SUSLOV AT THE EIGHTY-FIRST PARTY CONFERENCE TO THE CPSU PLENUM IN JANUARY, 1961, AND N. KHRUSHCHEV'S STATEMENT AT A PRIMARY PARTY MEETING ON JANUARY 6, 1961. AUTHOR SUGGESTS THE PREMIER'S MODERATE SPEECH WAS INTENDED FOR FOREIGN CONSUMPTION ONLY.

1130 GRASES P.
ESTUDIOS BIBLIOGRAFICOS.
CARACAS: IMPRENTA NACIONAL, 1961, 387 PP.
BIBLIOGRAPHY OF VENEZUELA.

1131 GRAUBARD S.R. ED.
"TOWARD THE YEAR 2000: WORK IN PROGRESS."
DAEDALUS, (SUMMER 67), 1-994.
PAPERS FROM AMERICAN ACADEMY OF ARTS AND SCIENCES' COMMISSION ON YEAR 2000. DESCRIBES COMMISSION AND SUGGESTS ALTERNATIVE CHOICES IN FUTURE DECISIONS OF SOCIETY. STUDIES FORECASTING, EVALUATES SOCIAL PREDICTIONS, AND EXAMINES ISSUES OF POLITICS, EDUCATION, BEHAVIOR AND PERSONALITY, CHURCHES, YOUTH, ROLES, PRIVACY, COMMUNICATION, INTERNATIONAL RELATIONS, AND PSYCHOLOGICAL PERSPECTIVES.

1132 GRAVEN J.
"LE NOUVEAU DROIT PENAL INTERNATIONAL."
REV. DR. INT., 40 (NO. 4, 62, 330-48.
ANALYZES DRAFTS OF INTERNATIONAL PENAL LAW MADE BY SEVERAL COUNTRIES. EXAMINES CAPABILITIES OF COURT OF GENEVA. POINTS OUT PROCEDURES AVAILABLE TO DEFENDENTS. BASES ANALYSIS ON RECENT COURT DECISIONS.

1133 GREAT BRITAIN CENTRAL OFF INF
CONSULTATION AND CO-OPERATION IN THE COMMONWEALTH.
LONDON: H M STATIONERY OFFICE, 1963, 56 PP.
DESCRIBES MAIN MACHINERY OF CONSULTATION AND COOPERATION IN THE COMMONWEALTH, TOGETHER WITH HISTORICAL BACKGROUND AND DISCUSSION OF SPECIFIC TOPICS OF CONCERN TO COMMONWEALTH NATIONS.

1134 GREAT BRITAIN CENTRAL OFF INF
THE COLOMBO PLAN (PAMPHLET)
LONDON: H M STATIONERY OFFICE, 1964, 79 PP.
DESCRIBES ORIGINS OF COLOMBO PLAN, ITS WORKINGS, RESOURCES OF REGION, PROGRESS IN AREAS OF EXTERNAL CAPITAL ASSISTANCE, TECHNICAL COOPERATION, AND AID FROM BRITAIN.

1135 GREAT BRITAIN CENTRAL OFF INF
CONSTITUTIONAL DEVELOPMENT IN THE COMMONWEALTH.
LONDON: H M STATIONERY OFFICE, 1964, 40 PP.
SUMMARY OF LONG-RANGE DEVELOPMENT OF CONSTITUTIONAL GOVERNMENT IN THE COMMONWEALTH AND REVIEW OF CURRENT STATUS OF CONSTITUTIONAL GOVERNMENT IN MEMBER NATIONS AND IN DEPENDENCIES WHICH ARE MOVING TOWARD INDEPENDENCE.

1136 GREAVES H.R.G.
THE LEAGUE COMMITTEES AND WORLD ORDER.
LONDON: OXFORD U. PR., 1931, 266 PP.
EXTENSIVE VIEW OF LEAGUE'S WORK. SHOWS SIGNIFICANCE OF TECHNICAL AND ADVISORY COUNCILS. FEELS INTERNATIONALISM MUST RULE DIVERSITIES.

1137 GREECE PRESBEIA U.S.
BRITISH OPINION ON CYPRUS.
WASHINGTON: ROYAL GREEK INFO, 1956, 160 PP.
COLLECTION OF BRITISH PRESS AND PARLIAMENTARY OPINION AGAINST THE GOVERNMENT'S POLICIES OF "INTRANSIGENCE AND COERCION" IN CYPRUS; CLAIMS THAT LARGE MAJORITY OF BRITONS DISAGREE VEHEMENTLY. ATTEMPTS TO PROVE THIS BY MASSIVE QUOTATION FROM PUBLICATIONS AND OFFICIAL DOCUMENTS.

1138 GREEN L.C.
"POLITICAL OFFENSES, WAR CRIMES AND EXTRADITION."
INT. COMP. LAW QUART., 11 (APRIL 62), 329-54.
DEFINES ROLE OF INTERPOL IN APPREHENSION OF WAR CRIMINALS. DISTINGUISHES BETWEEN POLITICAL OFFENSES AND WAR CRIMES. SUGGESTS THAT LATTER TRANSGRESS AGAINST LAWS OF WAR AND THAT WAR CRIMINALS SHOULD BE EXTRADITED.

1139 GREEN L.C.
"RHODESIAN OIL: BOOTLEGGERS OR PIRATES?"
INT. J., 21 (SUMMER 66), 350-353.
ANALYZES LEGAL ASPECTS OF SANCTIONS AGAINST RHODESIA, INCLUDING LEGITIMACY OF BRITISH STAND, DEFINITION OF ILLEGAL TRADE WITH RHODESIA, AND ATTITUDES IN UN AND OAU.

1140 GREENBERG S.
"JUDAISM AND WORLD JUSTICE."
WORLD JUSTICE, 5 (MAR. 64), 315-21.
ASSERTS CONCEPT OF JUSTICE IN THE JUDIAC TRADITION HOLDS THAT LOVE FOR GOD IS BEST REFLECTED AND MOST FULLY REALIZED IN ACTS OF LOVE AND CHARITY TOWARDS FELLOW MAN. HENCE A WARLESS WORLD MAKES POSSIBLE MANKIND'S NOBLEST SELF-FULFILLMENT.

1141 GREENE K.R.C.
INSTITUTIONS AND INDIVIDUALS: AN ANNOTATED LIST OF DIRECTORIES USEFUL IN INTERNATIONAL ADMINISTRATION.
CHICAGO: PUBLIC ADMIN CLEAR HSE, 1953.
GUIDE TO DIRECTORIES OF INSTITUTIONS AND INDIVIDUALS. INCLUDES 220 WORKS ALL OF WHICH WERE PUBLISHED AFTER 1945. ANNOTATIONS INDICATE EXTENT TO WHICH BOOK FULFILLS FUNCTIONS. ENTRIES ARE ARRANGED ALPHABETICALLY WITH CROSS REFERENCES. MOST ENTRIES DESCRIBE PUBLICATIONS IN FRENCH, ENGLISH, AND OTHER WEST EUROPEAN LANGUAGES.

1142 GREENSPAN M.
THE MODERN LAW OF LAND WARFARE.
BERKELEY: U. CALIF. PR., 1959, 724 PP.
COMPREHENSIVE EXAMINATION OF PRECEDENTS AND PRACTICES OF WAR LAWS. INSPECTING PREVIOUS SANCTIONS AND ENFORCEMENT PROCEDURES, AUTHOR PRESENTS ABSTRACT MODEL OF METHODS AND INSTRUMENTS OF WARFARE.

1143 GREENSPAN M.
"INTERNATIONAL LAW AND ITS PROTECTION FOR PARTICIPANTS IN UNCONVENTIONAL WARFARE."
ANN. AMER. ACAD. POLIT. SOC. SCI., 341 (MAY 62), 30-41.
GENEVA CONVENTIONS APPLY TO PARTICIPANTS IN GUERRILLA WARFARE SO LONG AS SATISFY FOLLOWING REQUIREMENTS: BELONG TO ORGANIZED MOVEMENT IN CONFLICT, HAVE COMMANDERS BEARING RESPONSIBILITY FOR SUBORDINATES, WEAR DISTINCTIVE INSIGNIA, CARRY ARMS OPENLY, AND OBEY LAWS AND CUSTOMS OF WAR.

1144 GREGORY W.
LIST OF THE SERIAL PUBLICATIONS OF FOREIGN GOVERNMENTS, 1815-1931.
WASH, DC: AMER COUNC LEARNED SOC, 1932, 720 PP.
LISTS BY COUNTRY GOVERNMENT SERIAL PUBLICATIONS. INCLUDES LAW REPORTS, DIGESTS, STATUTES, AND OFFICIAL GAZETTES.

1145 GREGORY W. ED.
INTERNATIONAL CONGRESSES AND CONFERENCES 1840-1937: A UNION LIST OF THEIR PUBLICATIONS AVAILABLE IN US AND CANADA.
NEW YORK: H W WILSON, 1938, 229 PP.
LIST OF ORGANIZATION MEETINGS AND LOCATION OF THEIR DOCUMENTS AND PUBLICATIONS IN THE LIBRARIES OF NORTH AMERICA. ARRANGED ALPHABETICALLY BY NAME OF CONFERENCE.

1146 GRENVILLE J.A.S., YOUNG G.B.
POLITICS, STRATEGY, AND AMERICAN DEMOCRACY: STUDIES IN FOREIGN POLICY, 1873-1917.
NEW HAVEN: YALE U PR, 1966, 352 PP., LC#66-12498.
ANALYZES US TRANSFORMATION FROM RURAL TO INDUSTRIAL SOCIETY IN PERIOD BETWEEN CIVIL WAR AND WWI. ESPECIALLY COVERS AMERICAN FOREIGN POLICY DEVELOPMENT IN RELATION TO POLITICS. STUDIES INVOLVEMENT IN VENEZUELA, CUBA, HAWAII, AND THE PHILIPPINES, AND IN THE WAR WITH SPAIN. EXAMINES THE SEARCH FOR A POLICY. DISCUSSES ISOLATIONISTS, EXPANSIONISTS, AND THE QUEST FOR SECURITY.

1147 GRETTON P.
MARITIME STRATEGY - A STUDY OF DEFENSE PROBLEMS.
NEW YORK: FREDERICK PRAEGER, 1965, LC#65-25485.
DISCUSSES HISTORY AND PRINCIPLES OF MARITIME STRATEGY, FACTORS AFFECTING IT (NUCLEAR WEAPONS), AND INSTRUMENTS OF MARITIME STRATEGY (SUBMARINES, AIR-CRAFT CARRIERS,ETC.). EXAMINES SIZE OF BRITISH FORCES AND THAT OF POTENTIAL ENEMIES.

1148 GRIERSON P.
BOOKS ON SOVIET RUSSIA 1917-42: A BIBLIOGRAPHY AND A GUIDE TO READING.
LONDON: METHEUN, 1943, 354 PP.
PRIMARILY LISTS BOOKS PUBLISHED IN BRITAIN. INCLUDES SOME FROM OVERSEAS WITH A FEW IN FOREIGN LANGUAGES. ARRANGED BY TOPICS IN AN INFORMAL STYLE COVERING ALL ASPECTS OF SOVIET LIFE AND MATERIAL ON SOVIET LEADERS.

1149 GRIFFIN A.P.C. ED.
LIST OF BOOKS RELATING TO THE THEORY OF COLONIZATION, GOVERNMENT OF DEPENDENCIES, PROTECTORATES, AND RELATED TOPICS.
WASHINGTON: LIBRARY OF CONGRESS, 1900, 156 PP.
CONTAINS 2,000 LISTINGS OF BOOKS AND ARTICLES ON MANY ASPECTS OF COLONIALISM. DIVIDED INTO 27 SEPARATE HEADINGS; THE LISTINGS REFER TO WORKS ON THE THEORY OF COLONIALIZATION AS WELL AS SPECIFIC REFERENCES TO THE POLICIES AND COLONIAL HISTORIES OF THE US, UK, FRANCE, GERMANY, ITALY, SPAIN, THE NETHERLANDS, AND PORTUGAL. MANY ENTRIES IN FRENCH, GERMAN, AND SPANISH. MOST ARTICLES LISTED WERE PUBLISHED 1897-1900.

1150 GRIFFIN A.P.C. ED.
LIST OF BOOKS ON SAMOA (PAMPHLET)
WASHINGTON: LIBRARY OF CONGRESS, 1901, 54 PP.
CONTAINS ABOUT 500 LISTINGS OF BOOKS AND ARTICLES ON GUAM AND SAMOA, MOST PUBLISHED IN LATE 19TH CENTURY. INCLUDES MANY GOVERNMENTAL RECORDS OF US, UK, AND GERMAN DEALINGS IN SAMOA. SOME ARTICLES IN GERMAN. COMPILED FOR LIBRARY OF CONGRESS.

1151 GRIFFIN A.P.C. ED.
SELECT LIST OF REFERENCES ON THE MONROE DOCTRINE (PAMPHLET)
WASHINGTON: LIBRARY OF CONGRESS, 1903, 10 PP.
ABOUT 50 ANNOTATED BOOKS, ARTICLES, AND DOCUMENTS ARRANGED BY AUTHOR AND EXTENDING FROM 1855 TO 1903. SOME IN SPANISH.

1152 GRIFFIN A.P.C. ED.
LISTS PUBLISHED 1902-03: ANGLO-SAXON INTERESTS (PAMPHLET)
WASHINGTON: LIBRARY OF CONGRESS, 1903, 12 PP.
APPROXIMATELY 85 ENTRIES OF BOOKS AND ARTICLES IN PERIODICALS ON ANGLO-SAXON INTERESTS IN WORLD. PUBLICATIONS FROM 1880-1903. ARRANGED ALPHABETICALLY BY AUTHORS, EXCEPT FOR ARTICLES WHICH ARE CHRONOLOGICAL FROM 1885-1903. SOME ENTRIES ARE FRENCH.

1153 GRIFFIN A.P.C. ED.
LIST OF REFERENCES ON THE US CONSULAR SERVICE (PAMPHLET)
WASHINGTON: LIBRARY OF CONGRESS, 1905, 27 PP.
CONTAINS APPROXIMATELY 200 REFERENCES TO WORKS DESCRIBING THE HISTORY AND CONSTITUTION OF THE US CONSULAR SERVICE AND PRESENTING PLANS FOR ITS REFORM. DOES NOT INCLUDE REPORTS PUBLISHED BY CONSULAR BUREAU. APPENDED GENERAL LISTING OF WORKS ON CONSULAR SYSTEM. CONTAINS FRENCH, GERMAN, AND SPANISH ARTICLES. COMPILED FOR LIBRARY OF CONGRESS.

1154 GRIFFIN A.P.C. ED.
SELECT LIST OF REFERENCES ON THE BRITISH TARIFF MOVEMENT.
WASHINGTON: LIBRARY OF CONGRESS, 1906, 60 PP.
LISTS ABOUT 280 BOOKS FULLY ANNOTATED AS TO CONTENT AND OTHER RELEVANT INFORMATION. ARRANGED ALPHABETICALLY BY AUTHOR. SOME 300 ARTICLES ARRANGED CHRONOLOGICALLY. INCLUDES AN AUTHOR INDEX AND AN INTRODUCTION DEALING WITH BOOKS ABOUT THE TARIFF QUESTION. DEALS WITH CHAMBERLAIN'S PROPOSAL TO GIVE PREFERENTIAL TREATMENT TO COLONIES IN TRADE RELATIONS. COMPILED FOR LIBRARY OF CONGRESS.

1155 GRIFFIN A.P.C.
LIST OF WORKS RELATING TO THE FRENCH ALLIANCE IN THE AMERICAN REVOLUTION.
WASHINGTON: LIBRARY OF CONGRESS, 1907, 40 PP.
ANNOTATED LISTING OF APPROXIMATELY 350 BOOKS AND ARTICLES IN FRENCH AND ENGLISH RELATING TO THE FRENCH ALLIANCE DURING THE REVOLUTIONARY WAR. ENTRIES WRITTEN PRINCIPALLY FROM LATE 1800'S THROUGH 1906. ARRANGED ACCORDING TO AUTHOR.

1156 GRIFFIN A.P.C. ED.
LIST OF REFERENCES ON INTERNATIONAL ARBITRATION.
WASHINGTON: LIBRARY OF CONGRESS, 1908, 151 PP.
LISTS APPROXIMATELY 900 ARTICLES, MANY ANNOTATED, CONCERNING INTERNATIONAL ARBITRATION; PRIMARILY CONCERNED WITH THE 1907 HAGUE CONFERENCE. ALSO CONTAINS RELATED SECTIONS ON ARMS LIMITATIONS AND FOREIGN DEBT COLLECTION, AS WELL AS DISCUSSIONS OF FRENCH OCCUPATION OF MEXICO AND COLONIAL QUESTIONS IN VENEZUELA AND SANTO DOMINGO. MANY ARTICLES IN FRENCH AND GERMAN, AND ARE DATED FROM 1886 TO 1907.

1157 GRIFFIN A.P.C. ED., MEYER H.H.B. ED.
LIST OF REFERENCES ON RECIPROCITY (2ND REV. ED.)
WASHINGTON: LIBRARY OF CONGRESS, 1910, 117 PP.
LISTS ABOUT 1,000 REFERENCES TO BOOKS AND ARTICLES ON US RECIPROCITY DEALINGS WITH CANADA, NEWFOUNDLAND, CUBA, HAWAII, AND GREAT BRITAIN, AS WELL AS THE MCKINLEY ACT OF 1890-94. DEALS PRIMARILY WITH INTERNATIONAL AGREEMENTS MADE IN 19TH CENTURY. REFERS TO SPECIFIC CONTRACTUAL DOCUMENTS AS WELL AS COMMENTARIES. CONTAINS SOME ARTICLES IN GERMAN. COMPILED FOR LIBRARY OF CONGRESS.

1158 GRIFFIN A.P.C. ED., PHILLIPS P.L.
LIST OF BOOKS RELATING TO CUBA (PAMPHLET)
WASHINGTON: LIBRARY OF CONGRESS, 1898, 61 PP.
A LISTING OF BOOKS AND PERIODICALS (MOST PUBLISHED IN 19TH CENTURY) CONCERNING CUBA IN GENERAL AND SPECIFIC CUBAN CITIES. BOOK ENTRIES ARE ANNOTATED. ALSO CONTAINS LISTING OF ALL MAPS OF CUBA IN THE LIBRARY OF CONGRESS PRIOR TO 1898. MANY OF THE PUBLICATIONS ARE IN SPANISH AND FRENCH SOURCES. CONTAINS APPROXIMATELY 600 ENTRIES.

1159 GRIFFIN G.G. ED.
A GUIDE TO MANUSCRIPTS RELATING TO AMERICAN HISTORY IN BRITISH DEPOSITORIES.
WASHINGTON: LIBRARY OF CONGRESS, 1946, 313 PP.
NOT A COMPLETE LISTING OF DOCUMENTS RELATING TO US HISTORY IN BRITISH DEPOSITORIES, BUT A GUIDE TO FACSIMILE REPRODUCTIONS OF MANUSCRIPTS AVAILABLE IN THE LIBRARY OF CONGRESS. SOURCES INCLUDE OFFICIAL ARCHIVES OF BRITAIN, CANADA, SCOTLAND, WALES, IRELAND, AND VARIOUS PRIVATE COLLECTIONS. MANUSCRIPTS ARE MOSTLY 18TH-CENTURY RECORDS COVERING MANY DIVERSE TOPICS.

1160 GRIFFITH E.S. ED.
RESEARCH IN POLITICAL SCIENCE: THE WORK OF PANELS OF RESEARCH COMMITTEE, APSA.
PRINCETON* UNIV. REF. SYSTEM, 1948, 238 PP., LC#49-63042.
ARTICLES, MANY BY LEADING MEN IN THE FIELD, DISCUSSING PROBLEMS OF POLITICAL SCIENCE RESEARCH. IN ADDITION TO STANDARD DIVISIONS, STUDY OF WAR, MILITARY OCCUPATION,

AND POLITICAL COMMUNICATIONS ARE INCLUDED. EDITOR CLOSES WITH CHAPTERS ON METHOD AND PROSPECTS. INCLUDES LIST OF SOURCES.

1161 GRIFFITH W.E.
ALBANIA AND THE SINO-SOVIET RIFT.
CAMBRIDGE: M I T PRESS, 1963, 423 PP., LC#63-10880.
DETAILED, SYSTEMATIC, DOCUMENTED EXAMINATION OF BACKGROUND, CAUSES, COURSE, AND SIGNIFICANCE OF SOVIET-ALBANIAN BREAK. INTENSIVE DECIPHERING AND ANALYSIS OF ESOTERIC COMMUNIST COMMUNICATIONS OCCUPY ONE HALF OF VOLUME. SHOWS HOW BADLY MOSCOW HAS HANDLED UPSURGE OF NATIONALISM IN A SMALL COUNTRY, AND HOW THE RESULTANT BLOW TO SOVIET PRESTIGE HAS REVEALED POSSIBILITY OF MOSCOW'S IMPOTENCE.

1162 GRIFFITH W.E. ED.
COMMUNISM IN EUROPE (2 VOLS.)
CAMBRIDGE: M I T PRESS, 1964, 406 PP., LC#64-21409.
STUDY IS INTENDED TO RELATE IN DEPTH THE INTERACTION BETWEEN DOMESTIC DEVELOPMENTS AND SINO-SOVIET RIFT DEVELOPMENTS WITHIN MAJOR EUROPEAN COMMUNIST STATES. MAJOR ATTENTION IS GIVEN TO INTERNAL DEVELOPMENTS WITHIN THE SEVERAL PARTIES AND STATES.

1163 GRIFFITH SB I.I.
THE CHINESE PEOPLE'S LIBERATION ARMY.
NEW YORK: MCGRAW HILL, 1967, 398 PP., LC#67-16302.
ANALYSIS OF HISTORY AND STRUCTURE OF PEOPLE'S LIBERATION ARMY AND ITS INTEGRATION INTO CHINESE SOCIETY. COVERS ESTABLISHMENT, AIMS, AND PRESENT CAPABILITIES. ENCOMPASSES FOREIGN AND DOMESTIC POLICIES. PORTRAIT OF RED CHINESE LEADERS AND SOLDIERS.

1164 GRIFFITHS F.
"THE POLITICAL SIDE OF 'DISARMAMENT'."
INTERNATIONAL JOURNAL, 22 (SPRING 67), 293-305.
CONTENDS THAT APPROACH TO DISARMAMENT AND ARMS CONTROL IGNORED RECENT METHODS OF POLITICAL ANALYSIS. EXPRESSES NEED FOR THEORETICAL PERSPECTIVE ON ARMS PROBLEM. POLITICAL ACTION NECESSARY FOR INTERNATIONAL CHANGE CAN COME ABOUT ONLY THROUGH DEVELOPMENT OF THEORY OF INTERNATIONAL RELATIONS. PREDICTS A POSSIBLE TRANSNATIONALIZATION OF INTERESTS IN WHICH NATIONAL SELF-DETERMINATION BECOMES OBSOLETE.

1165 GRISMER R.
A NEW BIBLIOGRAPHY OF THE LITERATURES OF SPAIN AND SPANISH AMERICA.
MINNEAPOLIS: PERRINE BOOK CO, 1941, 248 PP., LC#41-24332.
LIST OF BOOKS, PERIODICALS, DISSERTATIONS, ETC., MOSTLY IN SPANISH BUT INCLUDING OTHER LANGUAGES, ARRANGED ALPHABETICALLY. TITLES INCLUDE ANTHROPOLOGY, ARCHAEOLOGY, ART, ECONOMICS, EDUCATION, GEOGRAPHY, HISTORY, LAW, PHILOSOPHY, ETC.

1166 GRISWOLD A.W.
THE FAR EASTERN POLICY OF THE UNITED STATES.
NEW YORK: HARCOURT BRACE, 1938, 530 PP.
TRACES FAR EASTERN POLICY OF US FROM 1898-1938. EMPHASIZES COMMERCIAL AIMS OF DIPLOMACY AND OPEN DOOR POLICY. DISCUSSES ANNEXATION OF PHILIPPINES, THEODORE ROOSEVELT'S POLICY, WWI, WILSON AND JAPAN, TREATIES AFTER WWI, IMMIGRATION, LEAGUE OF NATIONS, CHINESE NATIONALISM JAPAN'S MOVEMENT INTO MANCHURIA, AND FDR'S POLICY.

1167 GROB F.
THE RELATIVITY OF WAR AND PEACE: A STUDY IN LAW, HISTORY, AND POLITICS.
TORONTO: RYERSON PRESS, 1949, 402 PP.
DISCUSSES DEFINITIONS OF PEACE AND WAR FROM POINT OF VIEW OF INTERNATIONAL AND MUNICIPAL LAW, HISTORY, AND POLITICS. REVIEWS TERMINOLOGY, TREATS CASES IN WHICH LEGAL STANDING OF WAR OR PEACE HAS NEVER BEEN DECIDED AND BATTLES FOUGHT IN PEACE TIME. STUDIES LEGAL DEBATES. MAINTAINS THAT DEFINITIONS ARE RELATIVE TO SITUATION.

1168 GROBLER J.H.
AFRICA'S DESTINY.
JOHANNESBURG: BOOK OF THE MONTH, 1958, 207 PP.
A BOER AND SUPPORTER OF SOUTH AFRICA'S NATIONAL PARTY GOVERNMENT, AUTHOR EMPHASIZES SEPARATE CONSTITUTIONAL DEVELOPMENT TO ATTAIN PEACEFUL COEXESTENCE. CONSIDERS APARTHEID AN INTERMEDIARY PHASE TOWARD SOLUTION.

1169 GRODZINS M. ED., RABINOWITCH E. ED.
THE ATOMIC AGE: FORTY-FIVE SCIENTISTS AND SCHOLARS SPEAK ON NATIONAL AND WORLD AFFAIRS.
NEW YORK: BASIC, 1963, 616 PP.
DOCUMENTS EVOLUTION OF INTERRELATIONSHIP OF WORLD OF SCIENCE AND POLITICS. TRACES FAILURE TO ACHIEVE INTERNATIONAL CONTROL OF ATOMIC ENERGY, ATTEMPTS TO PREVENT WAR, END OF USA NUCLEAR MONOPOLY, DEVELOPMENT OF ATOMIC WEAPONS AND POLICY, PROSPECTS FOR DISARMAMENT AND ARMS CONTROL.

1170 GROPP A.E.
UNION LIST OF LATIN AMERICAN NEWSPAPERS IN LIBRARIES IN THE UNITED STATES.
WASHINGTON: PAN AMERICAN UNION, 1953, 235 PP.
FULL BIBLIOGRAPHIC INFORMATION GIVEN ON EACH NEWSPAPER, INCLUDING LOCATION OF LIBRARIES CONTAINING IT. ITEMS ARRANGED BY COUNTRY AND CITY. INDEX OF TITLES OF PAPERS ON MICROFILM.

1171 GROSS F.
FOREIGN POLICY ANALYSIS.
NEW YORK: PHILOSOPHICAL LIB, 1954, 179 PP.
EXPLANATION OF MEANS AND APPROACH TO ANALYSIS OF FOREIGN POLICY. AUTHOR REGARDS FOREIGN POLICY AS RESULT OF MULTIPLE FACTORS IN PLANNING, NOT SINGLE DECISION OF ONE MAN. DEALS WITH VARIOUS FACTORS THAT INFLUENCE NATIONAL CONCEPTS AND CHOICE OF POLITICAL NATURE.

1172 GROSS F.
"THE US NATIONAL INTEREST AND THE UN."
ORBIS, 7 (SUMMER 63), 367-85.
IF THE WORLD IS TO BE MADE SAFE FOR PEACE AND DEMOCRACY, THE USA MUST DEVELOP NEW DIPLOMATIC METHODS TO PROMOTE AMERICAN INTERESTS IN A CHANGING WORLD COMMUNITY.

1173 GROSS F.
WORLD POLITICS AND TENSION AREAS.
NEW YORK: NEW YORK U PR, 1966, 377 PP., LC#65-19520.
PRESENTS A SOCIOLOGICAL AND INTERDISCIPLINARY STUDY OF TYPES OF TENSIONS, ANTAGONISMS, AND CONFLICTS WITHIN LIMITED GEOGRAPHICAL AREAS THAT DO OR DO NOT LEAD TO USE OF FORCE AND VIOLENCE. CASE STUDIES INCLUDE NEW YORK, VENEZUELA, SOMALIA, SILESIA, AND CHINA'S AMBITIONS IN ASIA. OFFERS CRITERIA FOR APPRAISING, REDUCING, AND EVENTUALLY ELIMINATING, INTERNATIONAL TENSIONS THAT MAY ERUPT INTO A MAJOR WAR.

1174 GROSS J.A.
"WHITEHALL AND THE COMMONWEALTH."
J. COMMONWEALTH POLIT. STUD., 2 (NOV. 64), 189-206.
HISTORICAL DEVELOPMENT OF THE RISE AND FALL OF THE COLONIAL OFFICE IN THE BRITISH EMPIRE STRUCTURE. ANALYZES AND EVALUATES FORTHCOMING ABSORPTION OF COLONIAL OFFICE BY THE COMMONWEALTH RELATIONS OFFICE IN LIGHT OF BRITAIN'S CHANGING ROLE IN THE WORLD TODAY.

1175 GROSS L.
"THE PEACE OF WESTPHALIA, 1648-1948."
AMER. J. OF INT. LAW, 42 (JAN. 48), 20-41.
DISCUSSES BACKGROUND AND CHARACTER OF PEACE OF WESTPHALIA AS FIRST ATTEMPT AT WORLD UNITY. IMPLICATIONS OF CHARTER INCLUDE IMPETUS TO SYSTEM OF INTERNATIONAL LAW, STIMULUS TO THEORY AND PRACTICE OF BALANCE OF POWER, AND DEVELOPMENT OF WORLD-WIDE POLITICAL SYSTEM. CHARTER ENCOURAGED INDIVIDUALISM OF NATIONAL STATES, AN UNDESIRABLE TRAIT STILL EXTANT IN INTERNATIONAL AFFAIRS.

1176 GROSS L.
"IMMUNITIES AND PRIVILEGES OF DELIGATIONS TO THE UNITED NATIONS."
INT. ORGAN., 16 (SUMMER 62), 483-520.
PRESENTS PROVISIONS ON STATUS OF DELEGATIONS. SHOWS PROBLEMS ARISING DURING STAY IN USA. SUGGESTS USA, AS HOST COUNTRY, RE-EVALUATE POSITION ON PROVISIONS OF GENERAL CONVENTION AND ON CRITERIA FOR ACCREDITATION.

1177 GROSS L.
"PROBLEMS OF INTERNATIONAL ADJUDICATION AND COMPLIANCE WITH INTERNATIONAL LAW: SOME SIMPLE SOLUTIONS."
AMER. J. INT. LAW, 59 (JAN. 65), 48-59.
'MORE AND SPEEDIER PROGRESS COULD BE MADE BY REDUCING THE QUANTITY OF LAW - LESS LAW, LESS VIOLATION OF LAW, MORE COMPLIANCE' AS USEFUL BASIS FOR LEGAL PRECEPTS. AUTHOR APPLIES 'POSITIVE PLAIN-MEANING' AND 'SURVIVAL' PRINCIPLE.

1178 GROSSER A.
"FRANCE AND GERMANY IN THE ATLANTIC COMMUNITY."
INT. ORGAN., 17 (SUMMER 63), 550-574.
ATTEMPTS TO PUT INTO PROPER PERSPECTIVE THE NATURE OF THE ATLANTIC COMMUNITY BY A DISCUSSION OF THE ROLES OF THE TWO EXTREMES IN THE GROUP - FRANCE AND GERMANY.

1179 GROSSER A.
"Y A-T-IL UN CONFLIT FRANCO-AMERICAIN."
REV. FRANC. SCI. POLIT., 2 (APR. 64), 309-16.
TRACES EVOLUTION OF FRANCO-AMERICAN CONFLICT AND DISCUSSES PROBLEMS ARISING FROM FRANCE FOLLOWING AN INDEPENDENT POLICY WHILE STILL RELYING ON US ASSISTANCE TO SAFEGUARD HER SECURITY.

1180 GROTIUS H.
DE JURE BELLI AC PACIS.
LONDON: BASSET, 1682, 571 PP.
EXAMINES NATURE OF INTERNATIONAL LAW. QUESTIONS WHETHER ANY WAR CAN BE JUST. ANALYZES JUST AND UNJUST CAUSES OF WAR. REASONS WHAT IN CONDUCT OF WAR IS LAWFUL, WHAT IS UNLAWFUL.

1181 GRUNDER G.A.
"THE PHILIPPINES AND THE UNITED STATES."
COLORADO SPRINGS* US AIR ACAD., 1951.

STUDY OF ORIGINS AND EVOLUTION OF US POLICY TOWARD PHILIPPINES SINCE SPANISH-AMERICAN WAR. SPECIAL REFERENCE TO ECONOMIC RELATIONSHIPS, EVOLUTION OF POLITICAL INSTITUTIONS, AND THE INDEPENDENCE QUESTION. BIBLIOGRAPHY IS FOR MOST PART BASED ON GOVERNMENT DOCUMENTS.

1182 GRUNDY K.W.
"RECENT CONTRIBUTIONS TO THE STUDY OF AFRICAN POLITICAL THOUGHT."
WORLD POLITICS, 18 (JULY 66), 647-689.
AN ANNOTATED BIBLIOGRAPHY ON STUDIES OF AFRICAN POLITICAL THOUGHT. ENGLISH-LANGUAGE AND SOME FRENCH. MATERIAL RANGES FROM 1956 TO 1965; 81 ENTRIES. THE AUTHOR REVIEWS SOME OF THE PRINCIPAL PUBLICATIONS DEALING WITH AFRICAN POLITICAL ATTITUDES, IDEAS, AND IDEOLOGIES.

1183 GRUNDY K.W.
"AFRICA IN THE WORLD ARENA."
CURRENT HISTORY, 52 (MAR. 67), 129-136.
SUGGESTS NECESSITY OF COMPREHENDING INTERNAL SITUATIONS OF NEW AFRICAN NATIONS IN ORDER TO UNDERSTAND FOREIGN POLICY WHICH IS USUALLY BASED ON ANTICOLONIAL STRUGGLE. COUNTRY BY COUNTRY ANALYSIS OF ALIGNMENT WITH EAST OR WEST, AND CAUSES OF SUCH ALIGNMENT. INFLUENCE OF RED CHINA IS GROWING, BUT REACTION IS SAME AS TO USA AND USSR-NO DEPENDENCE ON COLONIZING POWER.

1184 GRZYBOWSKI K.
"INTERNATIONAL ORGANIZATIONS FROM THE SOVIET POINT OF VIEW."
LAW CONTEMP. PROBL., 29 (AUTUMN 64), 882-95.
TRACES HISTORY OF SOVIET PARTICIPATION IN INTERNATIONAL AND REGIONAL ORGANIZATIONS. REVEALS THE BASIC INABILITY OF SOVIET BLOC TO COOPERATE WITH WEST ON ECONOMIC AND SOCIAL MATTERS WHEN IDEOLOGICAL DIFFERENCES ARE INVOLVED.

1185 GRZYBOWSKI K.
THE SOCIALIST COMMONWEALTH OF NATIONS: ORGANIZATIONS AND INSTITUTIONS.
NEW HAVEN: YALE U PR, 1964, 265 PP., LC#64-20919.
ANALYSIS OF LEGAL BASES AND PRACTICES OF THE SEVERAL REGIONAL ORGANIZATIONS IN EASTERN EUROPE.

1186 GUENA Y.
HISTORIQUE DE LA COMMUNAUTE.
PARIS: FAYARD, 1962, 192 PP.
DISCUSSES EVOLUTION OF FRENCH UNION AND THE DEVELOPMENT OF INDEPENDENCE IN THE 14 FORMER FRENCH SUB-SAHARAN COLONIES IN THE PERIOD FROM 1946 TO 1962.

1187 GUERRANT E.O.
ROOSEVELT'S GOOD NEIGHBOR POLICY.
ALBUQUERQUE: U OF N MEX PR, 1950, 235 PP.
ESSENTIAL FEATURES OF LATIN AMERICAN POLICY OF FRANKLIN D. ROOSEVELT ADMINISTRATION. COVERS PRINCIPALLY THE PREWAR PERIOD. INFLUENCE OF WWII ON UNITED STATES' LATIN AMERICAN POLICY.

1188 GUETZKOW H.
"THE POTENTIAL OF CASE STUDY IN ANALYZING INTERNATIONAL CONFLICT."
WORLD POLIT., 14 (APRIL 62), 548-52.
AN EVALUATION OF A BOOK 'THE SAAR CONFLICT' BY JACQUES FREYMOND ABOUT POTENTIAL INTERNATIONAL CONFLICT. IT IS AN HISTORIC AND ANALYTIC STUDY OF GERMAN-FRENCH DISPUTE OVER SAAR AND OF THE METHOD USED TO RESOLVE IT.

1189 GUIMARAES A.P.
INFLACAO E MONOPOLIO NO BRASIL.
RIO DE JANEIRO: ED CIVIL BRASIL, 1963, 181 PP.
STUDY OF INFLATION IN BRAZIL. EXAMINES THEORIES OF INFLATION, GOVERNMENT'S ROLE, WAGE SCALE, INTERNATIONAL INFLUENCES, AND RELATION OF INFLATION TO DEVELOPING ECONOMIES.

1190 GULICK C.A., OCKERT R.A., WALLACE R.J.
HISTORY AND THEORIES OF WORKING-CLASS MOVEMENTS: A SELECT BIBLIOGRAPHY.
BERKELEY: U OF CALIF PR, 1955, 364 PP.
BIBLIOGRAPHY LIMITED TO ARTICLES, NOTES, AND OCCASIONAL DOCUMENTS IN JOURNALS AND MAGAZINES IN ENGLISH. RESTRICTED TO 250 ENTRIES ON AMERICAN MOVEMENTS. CONCERNED PRIMARILY WITH BRITISH AND SECONDARILY WITH OTHER FOREIGN MOVEMENTS. ENTRIES LISTED ALPHABETICALLY BY AUTHOR UNDER HEADINGS: TRADE UNIONISM; POLITICS; COOPERATIVES; CULTURE. DESPITE SELECTIVITY AN EXTENSIVE AND IMPORTANT LIST.

1191 GULICK E.U.
"OUR BALANCE OF POWER SYSTEM IN PERSPECTIVE."
J. CONFL. RESOLUT., 14 (WINTER 63), 9-20.
VIEWS BALANCE OF POWER IN HISTORICAL PERSPECTIVE. CONCLUDES PRESENT FORM OF INTERNATIONAL ORGANIZATION UNSUITABLE FOR ATOMIC WORLD. SEES ONLY TWO POSSIBLE ROADS TO STABLE WORLD ORGANIZATION: NUCLEAR DISARMAMENT OR A NEW SYSTEM OF INTERNATIONAL RELATIONS ALLOWING FOR SURVIVAL AND COMPETITION.

1192 GULICK E.V.
EUROPE'S CLASSICAL BALANCE OF POWER: CASE HISTORY OF THEORY AND PRACTICE OF GREAT CONCEPTS OF EUROPEAN STATECRAFT.
ITHACA: CORNELL U PRESS, 1955, 337 PP.
STUDY OF THEORY OF BALANCE OF POWER, STARTING WITH EUROPEAN AND ENGLISH WRITERS OF 18TH CENTURY, WHEN IDEA WAS MOST ENTHUSIASTICALLY SUPPORTED. STUDIES APPLICATION OF THEORY IN EARLY 19TH CENTURY, SHOWING HOW NAPOLEON'S OVERBALANCING LED TO EXTENSIVE EFFORTS AT REBALANCING OF POWER.

1193 GUNTHER F. ED.
BUCHERKUNDE ZUR WELTGESCHICHTE VON UNTERGANG DES ROMISCHEN WELTREICHES BIS ZUR GEGENWART.
MUNICH: R OLDENBOURG, 1956, 544 PP.
BIBLIOGRAPHY OF WORLD HISTORY MAINLY IN GERMAN AND LISTED BY COUNTRIES AND PERIODS. COVERS FROM FALL OF ROMAN EMPIRE TO PRESENT.

1194 GUPTA S.
KASHMIR - A STUDY IN INDIA-PAKISTAN RELATIONS.
BOMBAY: ASIA PUBL HOUSE, 1966, 511 PP.
TRACES CONFLICTS BETWEEN INDIA AND PAKISTAN OVER KASHMIR FROM PARTITION OF INDIA IN 1947 TO OUTBREAK OF HOSTILITIES IN 1965. EXAMINES ROLE OF MUSLIM LEAGUE, RESOLUTIONS IN UN, DEVELOPMENT OF NEGOTIATIONS BETWEEN 1953-56, AND CONSTITUTIONAL AND POLITICAL DEVELOPMENTS IN KASHMIR.

1195 GUPTA S.C.
"INDIA AND THE SOVIET UNION."
CURR. HIST., 44 (MAR. 63), 141-146.
AS CHINESE-INDIAN RELATIONS DETERIORATED, SOVIET-INDIAN RELATIONS SHOWED UPWARD TREND DURING WHICH PERIOD USSR DECLARED VIRTUAL NEUTRALITY ON INDIAN-CHINESE BORDER CONFLICT. HOWEVER, STUDIED ATTEMPTS MADE BY USSR AND INDIA TO DEMONSTRATE CONTINUED FRIENDSHIP.

1196 GURLAND A.R.L.
POLITICAL SCIENCE IN WESTERN GERMANY: THOUGHTS AND WRITINGS, 1950-1952 (PAMPHLET)
WASHINGTON: LIBRARY OF CONGRESS, 1952, LC#52-60058.
MORE THAN 300 ANNOTATED ITEMS PUBLISHED DURING THE THREE YEAR SPAN, 1950-52. INCLUDES ARTICLES FROM JOURNALS, BOOKS, AND ESSAYS ABOUT HALF OF WHICH ARE IN GERMAN. PRECEDED BY INTRODUCTORY ESSAY AND FOLLOWED BY AUTHOR INDEX. TOPICS INCLUDE FOREIGN POLICY, IDEOLOGY, HISTORY, AND NAZIISM.

1197 GURTOO D.H.N.
INDIA'S BALANCE OF PAYMENTS (1920-1960)
PRINCETON, NJ: PRINCETON UNIV, 1961, 241 PP.
STUDIES BALANCE-OF-PAYMENTS IN INDIA OVER 40-YEAR PERIOD. ESTIMATES INTEREST AND DIVIDENDS RECEIPTS AND PAYMENTS. DISCUSSES ANNUAL MOVEMENTS OF LONG-TERM INTERNATIONAL CAPITAL. ANALYZES MECHANISM OF ADJUSTMENT IN BALANCE-OF PAYMENTS ITEMS TO ECONOMICS, FINANCIAL, AND POLITICAL INSTABILITY OCCURRING BETWEEN 1920-60.

1198 GUTTMANN A.
THE WOUND IN THE HEART: AMERICA AND THE SPANISH CIVIL WAR.
NEW YORK: FREE PRESS OF GLENCOE, 1962, 292 PP., LC#62-15342.
ANALYSIS OF ATTITUDES AND INTERPRETATIONS CONCERNING THE CONFLICT AS RELATED TO LIBERAL DEMOCRATIC TRADITION. INCLUDES PRIMITIVISM, VOLUNTEERS, THE EMBARGO, AND POPULAR FRONT.

1199 GYORGY A. ED., GIBBS H.P. ED.
PROBLEMS IN INTERNATIONAL RELATIONS.
ENGLEWOOD CLIFFS: PRENTICE HALL, 1962, 330 PP., LC#55-6993.
ESSAYS FOCUSING ON CASE STUDIES TOPICALLY GROUPED UNDER COMMUNIST CHALLENGE AND WESTERN RESPONSE, ROLE OF LESSER POWERS, IDEOLOGY, UN, AND INTERNATIONAL LAW.

1200 GYR J.
"ANALYSIS OF COMMITTEE MEMBER BEHAVIOUR IN FOUR CULTURES."
HUM. RELAT., 4 (MAY 51) 193-202.
DESCRIBES FACTORS LEADING TO FRICTION IN INTERNATIONAL COMMITTEE AND CONFERENCE SITUATIONS. ON BASIS OF SMALL SAMPLE, AUTHOR FOUND THAT REPRESENTATIVES OF DIFFERENT CULTURES DIFFERED IN THEIR ATTITUDE TOWARD ROLE OF COMMITTEE CHAIRMAN AND THE IDEA OF DELEGATION OF AUTHORITY. DIVERGED FROM ONE ANOTHER IN THE DEGREE TO WHICH THEY TRUSTED THE MOTIVES OF OTHERS AND IN EXTENT OF COOPERATION.

1201 HAAS E.B.
"THE RECONCILIATION OF CONFLICT, COLONIAL POLICY AIMS: ACCEPTANCE OF THE LEAGUE OF NATIONS MANDATE SYSTEM."
INT. ORGAN., 6 (NOV. 52), 521-36.
DESCRIBES CONFLICTING POST-WW 1 VIEWPOINTS ON ANNEXATION AND INTERNATIONAL MANDATES. ANALYZES FRENCH AND BRITISH MOTIVATIONS WHICH LED TO ACCEPTANCE OF MANDATE SYSTEM.

1202 HAAS E.B., WHITING A.S.
DYNAMICS OF INTERNATIONAL RELATIONS.
NEW YORK: MCGRAW HILL, 1956, 557 PP.
ASSUMING THAT AIMS OF FOREIGN POLICY ARE QUALITATIVELY SIMILAR TO ENDS IMPLICIT IN ANY OTHER FIELD OF POLITICS, ALL RULES AND PRINCIPLES OF POLITICAL BEHAVIOR, ELITE LEADERSHIP

AND GROUP CONFLICT CAPABLE OF IDENTIFICATION IN DOMESTIC FIELD ARE APPLICABLE TO INTERNATIONAL SPHERE AS WELL. FOCUS ON EVER-SHIFTING DEMANDS WITHIN NATIONS WHICH CONTRIBUTE TO RECURRING CONFLICT AND COMPROMISE BETWEEN THEM.

1203 HAAS E.B.
"REGIONAL INTEGRATION AND NATIONAL POLICY."
INT. CONCIL., 513 (MAY 57), 381-442.
ANALYZING THE EXISTING MULTI-PARTITE ALLIANCES, EVALUATES MILITARY PACTS AS INSTRUMENTS OF NATIONAL POLICY AND THEIR UTILITY IN STIMULATING ALLEGIANCES TO LARGER COMMUNITIES. EXAMINES THE SHIFTING OBJECTIVES PROMPTING ALLIANCES AND RELATIVE ABILITY OF RELATIONSHIPS TO ADJUST TO CHANGING CIRCUMSTANCES. CONFLICTS BETWEEN REGIONAL ASSOCIATIONS AND U.N. AIMS ARE SURVEYED.

1204 HAAS E.B.
THE UNITING OF EUROPE.
STANFORD: U. PR., 1958, 552 PP.
DEMONSTRATES PROCESSES BY WHICH POLITICAL COMMUNITIES ARE FORMED AMONG SOVEREIGN STATES. CASE-STUDY OF EUROPEAN COAL AND STEEL COMMUNITY WHICH WAS INFLUENTIAL IN DEVELOPING HABITS OF QUASI-FEDERAL CONDUCT. INDICATES THAT POLITICAL UNITY IN A PLURALISTIC SOCIETY DOES NOT NEED MAJORITY SUPPORT OR IDENTICAL AIMS.

1205 HAAS E.B.
THE COMPARATIVE STUDY OF THE UNITED NATIONS.
WORLD POLIT., 12 (JAN. 60), 298-322.
EVALUATES CARNEGIE ENDOWMENT'S SERIES OF NATIONAL STUDIES OF UNITED NATIONS AGAINST PERSPECTIVE OF PRESENT STATE OF INTERNATIONAL RELATIONS THEORY, AND MORE PARTICULARLY THE THEORY OF INTERNATIONAL INSTITUTIONS AND THEIR DEVELOPMENT.

1206 HAAS E.B.
"CONSENSUS FORMATION IN THE COUNCIL OF EUROPE."
LONDON: STEVENS, 1960, 70 PP.
ANALYZES VOTING BEHAVIOR IN COUNCIL OF EUROPE TO DISCOVER WHETHER AND HOW NATIONAL LOYALTIES DECLINE AND REGIONAL LOYALTIES GROW AMONG THE ELITE OF PARLIAMENTARIANS. DEVELOPS NEW STATISTICAL INDEX FOR OBSERVING VOTING BEHAVIOR IN INTERNATIONAL PARLIAMENTARY ASSEMBLIES.

1207 HAAS E.B.
"INTERNATIONAL INTEGRATION: THE EUROPEAN AND THE UNIVERSAL PROCESS."
INT. ORGAN., 15 (SUMMER 61), 366-92.
EXAMINATION OF VARIOUS BLOCS OPERATING ON THE WORLD SCENE: OEEC-EPU, COUNCIL OF EUROPE, NATO, ETC. 'THE GROWTH OF FEWER AND LARGER POLITICAL COMMUNITIES WILL CONTRIBUTE TO REGIONAL, BUT NOT TO UNIVERSAL PEACE.'

1208 HAAS E.B., SCHMITTER P.C.
"ECONOMICS AND DIFFERENTIAL PATTERNS OF POLITICAL INTEGRATION: PROJECTIONS ABOUT UNITY IN LATIN AMERICA."
INT. ORGAN., 18 (AUTUMN 64), 705-37.
PRESENTS THESIS THAT 'UNDER MODERN CONDITIONS THE RELATIONSHIP BETWEEN ECONOMIC AND POLITICAL UNION HAD BEST BE TREATED AS A CONTINUUM.... POLITICAL IMPLICATIONS CAN BE ASSOCIATED WITH MOST MOVEMENTS TOWARD ECONOMIC INTEGRATION EVEN WHEN THE CHIEF ACTORS THEMSELVES DO NOT ENTERTAIN SUCH NOTIONS AT THE TIME OF ADOPTING THEIR NEW CONSTUITIVE CHARTER.' CITES LAFTA AS EXAMPLE.

1209 HABERLER G.
"INTEGRATION AND GROWTH OF THE WORLD ECONOMY IN HISTORICAL PERSPECTIVE."
AMER. ECON. REV., 54 (MARCH 64), 1-22.
A BRIEF HISTORY OF CLOSER ECONOMIC RELATIONS AMONG DIFFERENT INTRANATIONAL AND INTERNATIONAL GROUPS, FOLLOWED BY DEEPER ANALYSIS OF THE COMPARATIVE RATES OF ECONOMIC GROWTH AROUND WORLD, SHOWING THAT POORER COUNTRIES HAVE BEEN IMPROVING AS RESULT OF RICHER COUNTRIES, GREATER IMPROVEMENT TRICKLING THROUGH WORLD TRADE. RECOMMENDS FREE ECONOMIC POLICIES.

1210 HADDAD J.A.
REVOLUCAO CUBANA E REVOLUCAO BRASILEIRA.
RIO DE JANEIRO: ED CIVIL BRASIL, 1961, 325 PP.
ANALYZES CUBAN REVOLUTION RELATING AND COMPARING IT TO NEEDS OF BRAZIL. DISCUSSES REFORSM IN CUBA AND ORTANCE OF AGRARIAN AND URBAN REFORMS IN ALL LATIN AMERICA. EXAMINES EXPORT OF REVOLUTION AND REFORM FROM CUBA TO WHOLE AREA AND US REACTION.

1211 HADDOW A.
"POLITICAL SCIENCE IN AMERICAN COLLEGES AND UNIVERSITIES 1636-1900."
NEW YORK: APPLETON, 1939.
SURVEY OF COLLEGE AND UNIVERSITY INSTRUCTION IN POLITICAL SCIENCE FROM THE COLONIAL PERIOD THROUGH THE 20TH CENTURY. EXAMINES BEGINNINGS AND DEVELOPMENT OF POLITICAL SCIENCE AS AN ACADEMIC DISCIPLINE IN THE US. UNANNOTATED BIBLIOGRAPHY OF 358 WORKS IN POLITICAL ECONOMY, POLITICAL PHILOSOPHY, INTERNATIONAL LAW, CONSTITUTION, AND GOVERNMENT PRACTICES; PRINTED LECTURES IN MORAL PHILOSOPHY AND LAW.

1212 HADWEN J.G., KAUFMANN J.
HOW UNITED NATIONS DECISIONS ARE MADE.
LEYDEN: SYTHOFF, 1962, 179 PP., $3.75.
DESCRIBES MACHINERY OF UN FOR CONSIDERING ECONOMIC QUESTIONS AND INDICATES DETERMINANT FORCES AND PROCEDURES. USE PERSONAL UN EXPERIENCE AS REFERENCE, ELUCIDATES UNWRITTEN PROCEDURES OF NATIONAL DELEGATIONS.

1213 HAGRAS K.M.
UNITED NATIONS CONFERENCE ON TRADE AND DEVELOPMENT: A CASE STUDY OF UN DIPLOMACY.
NEW YORK: FREDERICK PRAEGER, 1965, 171 PP., LC#65-24706.
DISCUSSES SPIRIT OF DIPLOMACY AND INTERNATIONALISM THAT EMERGED FROM 1964 CONFERENCE. EXAMINES NEEDS OF NATIONS FOR WHICH CONFERENCE WAS CALLED; MACHINERY, PROCEEDINGS, INSTITUTIONALIZATION, AND FINDINGS OF CONFERENCE.

1214 HAGUE PERMANENT CT INTL JUSTIC
WORLD COURT REPORTS: COLLECTION OF THE JUDGEMENTS ORDERS AND OPINIONS VOLUME 3 1932-35.
WASHINGTON: CARNEGIE ENDOWMENT, 1938, 549 PP., LC#34-42544.
ACTUAL COURT CASES PRESENTED JUST PRIOR TO AMENDMENTS IN STATUTE AND RULES. INCLUDES REQUESTS FOR ADVICE, CASES TERMINATED WITHOUT JUDGMENT, AND FULL CASES IN OFFICIAL ENGLISH VERSIONS OR TRANSLATIONS.

1215 HAGUE PERMANENT CT INTL JUSTIC
WORLD COURT REPORTS: COLLECTION OF THE JUDGEMENTS ORDERS AND OPINIONS VOLUME 4 1936-42.
NEW YORK: COLUMBIA U PRESS, 1943, 513 PP.
COURT'S JURISPRUDENCE JUST AFTER AMENDED STATUTES AND RULES AND PRIOR TO GAP DURING WWI. INCLUDES TEN CASES, ONLY EIGHT OF WHICH WERE DISPOSED OF BEFORE WAR. TEXT IN OFFICIAL ENGLISH AND INCLUDES AMENDED STATUTES.

1216 HAHN W.F. ED., NEFF J.C. ED.
AMERICAN STRATEGY FOR THE NUCLEAR AGE.
GARDEN CITY: DOUBLEDAY, 1960, 455 PP., LC#60-13549.
DISCUSSES FUNDAMENTAL AND LONG-RANGE PROBLEMS IN US FOREIGN POLICY. DESCRIBES NATURE OF COMMUNISM AS ENEMY OF US, SCOPE OF MILITARY CHALLENGES, ECONOMIC POLICIES TO MEET THIS CHALLENGE, AND SPECIFIC COURSES OF ACTION TOWARD WINNING STRUGGLE.

1217 HAIGHT D.E. ED., JOHNSTON L.P. ED.
THE PRESIDENT; ROLES AND POWERS.
NEW YORK: RAND MCNALLY & CO, 1965, 400 PP., LC#65-14098.
GENERAL INTRODUCTION TO PRESIDENCY. HISTORICAL DEVELOPMENTS OF OFFICE AS WELL AS PRESENT CHARACTERISTICS. DESIGNED TO BRING OUT CONTROVERSIAL QUESTIONS ABOUT PRESIDENCY, AND THEN LEAVE THEM UNRESOLVED. TREATS PRESIDENT AS PARTY LEADER AS CHIEF EXECUTIVE AND ADMINISTRATOR, AND AS COMMANDER IN CHIEF. SHOWS HIS RELATION TO HIS ADVISORS, CONGRESS, THE PUBLIC, AND FOREIGN AFFAIRS.

1218 HAILEY
THE FUTURE OF COLONIAL PEOPLES.
PRINCETON: U. PR., 1944, 62 PP.
PRESENTS BRITISH VIEW TOWARDS COLONIAL PEOPLE AND THEIR FUTURE. CONTRASTS THE COLONIAL POLICIES OF VARIOUS COUNTRIES. CONCLUDES LONG RANGE POLICY OF GREAT BRITAIN WILL ACHIEVE SELF-GOVERNMENT IN ALL HER COLONIES.

1219 HAILEY L.
THE REPUBLIC OF SOUTH AFRICA AND THE HIGH COMMISSION TERRITORIES.
LONDON: OXFORD U PR, 1963, 136 PP.
DESCRIBES RELATION OF HIGH COMMISSION TERRITORIES TO SOUTH AFRICA, ESPECIALLY SINCE LATTER LEFT COMMONWEALTH IN 1961. INCLUDES EFFORTS BY UNION TO SECURE INCORPORATION, AND PRESENT ATTITUDES TOWARD INCORPORATION.

1220 HAJDA J., KOLAJA J.
THE COLD WAR VIEWED AS A SOCIOLOGICAL PROBLEM (PAMPHLET)
CHICAGO: CZECH FORGN INST EXILE, 1955, 28 PP.
DESCRIBES COLD WAR AND THREE SIDES COMPETING FOR LOYALTY OF THOSE BEHIND IRON CURTAIN: COMMUNIST GOVERNMENT, WEST, AND POLITICAL REFUGEES AND EMIGREES. SUGGESTS MORE EFFECTIVE COLD WAR POLICY FOR WEST, ESPECIALLY EMPHASIZING ROLE OF THIRD GROUP.

1221 HALASZ DE BEKY I.L.
A BIBLIOGRAPHY OF THE HUNGARIAN REVOLUTION 1956.
TORONTO: U OF TORONTO PRESS, 1963, 179 PP.
LISTS 2137 ITEMS RELATING TO THE HUNGARIAN REVOLUTION OF 1956: 428 BOOKS AND PAMPHLETS, 12 MOTION PICTURES, 88 MONITORED BROADCASTS, AND 1608 ARTICLES. COVERS THE PERIOD FROM OCTOBER 1956 TO DECEMBER 1960. ARRANGED BY LANGUAGE AND THOROUGHLY INDEXED. 799 ENGLISH ITEMS ARE INCLUDED.

1222 HALD M.
A SELECTED BIBLIOGRAPHY ON ECONOMIC DEVELOPMENT AND FOREIGN AID.
NEW YORK: RAND CORP, 1957, 93 PP.

AN UNANNOTATED BIBLIOGRAPHY OF 1,500 WORKS RELATING TO ECONOMIC AND OTHER ASPECTS OF GROWTH AND DEVELOPMENT IN UNDERDEVELOPED AREAS AND POLICIES OF THE US AND OTHER AGENCIES IN FOSTERING DEVELOPMENT. PRIMARY EMPHASIS ON PUBLICATIONS ISSUED BETWEEN 1950-57; ONLY ENGLISH-LANGUAGE SOURCES INCLUDED. TOPICALLY CLASSIFIED AND GEOGRAPHICALLY INDEXED.

1223 HALDANE R.B.
BEFORE THE WAR.
NEW YORK: FUNK/WAGNALLS, 1920, 234 PP.
TRACES FOREIGN POLICY OF BRITISH GOVERNMENT IN PERIOD FROM JANUARY 1906 TO AUGUST 1914. PLACES BLAME FOR THE OUTBREAK OF WORLD WAR ONE ON THE GERMANS.

1224 HALDEMAN E., BASSET E.
"SERIALS OF AN INTERNATIONAL CHARACTER."
INSTITUTE OF INTERNAT. EDUCATION, 2 (MAY-JULY 21), 1-61.
AN UNANNOTATED BIBLIOGRAPHY OF PERIODICALS AND SERIALS OF AN INTERNATIONAL CHARACTER. ENGLISH-LANGUAGE AND FRENCH, GERMAN, ITALIAN, AND SPANISH MATERIALS. RANGES FROM 1815 TO 1921. SUBJECT MATTER OF BIBLIOGRAPHY IS NONSPECIFIC AND RANGES OVER MANY CATEGORIES OF KNOWLEDGE. 840 ENTRIES.

1225 HALEY A.G. ED., HEINRICH W. ED.
FIRST COLLOQUIUM ON THE LAW OF OUTER SPACE.
VIENNA: SPRINGER VERLAG, 1959.
RECORD OF PROCEEDINGS OF SPACE LAW CONFERENCE, DISCUSSING LEGAL BOUNDARIES, SCIENTIFIC SPACE STRATEGY, PROBLEMS OF SOVEREIGNTY, AND INTERNATIONALIZATION OF OUTER SPACE.

1226 HALEY A.G.
SPACE LAW AND GOVERNMENT.
NEW YORK: APPLETON, 1963, 584 PP., $15.00.
RANGES FROM THE TRADITIONAL BASES OF INTERNATIONAL LAW AND PROBLEMS OF NATIONAL SOVEREIGNTY, ACROSS TECHNOLOGICAL CAPABILITIES AND QUESTIONS OF LIABILITY AND REGULATION, TO THE ROLE OF INTERGOVERNMENTAL AND NONGOVERNMENTAL AGENCIES IN FOCUSING ATTENTION ON SCIENTIFIC AND LEGAL ASPECTS OF SPACE EXPLORATION. A COMPREHENSIVE, DEFINITIVE STUDY OF LEGAL AND SOCIOLOGICAL ISSUES OF SPACE FLIGHT.

1227 HALL M.
"GERMANY, EAST AND WEST* DANGER AT THE CROSSROADS."
NEW WORLD REVIEW, 35 (MAY 67), 12-19.
VIEWS WITH ALARM THE CURRENT REACTIONARY SHIFT OF WEST GERMANY AND SUGGESTS THAT CHANCELLOR KEISINGER'S OVERTURES TO THE EAST MAY BE HOLLOW. STRESSES THE DANGER OF NEO-NAZISM IN WEST GERMANY, ITS ARMS DEVELOPMENT, ITS RELIANCE ON US COUPLED BY A NEW NATIONALISM. CONCLUDES THAT A NEW PARTY COMPOSED OF LEFT WING, UNIONISTS, AND PROGRESSIVES WOULD SET WEST GERMANY ON THE ROAD TO PEACE AND SECURITY.

1228 HALL W.E.
A TREATISE ON INTERNATIONAL LAW.
OXFORD: CLARENDON PR., 1924, 952 PP.
EXAMINES CHANGES IN INTERNATIONAL LAW RESULTING FROM LEAGUE OF NATIONS AND PEACE TREATIES. ATTACKS OUTMODED BASES OF LAW. VIEWS IT AS BASIS FOR SOLVING DIFFERENCES BETWEEN NATIONS. URGES EXTENSION OF LAW TO GRAPPLE WITH FUNDAMENTAL RELATIONSHIPS OF STATES.

1229 HALL W.P.
EMPIRE TO COMMONWEALTH.
NEW YORK: HOLT, 1928, 526 PP.
APPRAISES 'THOSE FORCES WITHIN THE EMPIRE.... WHICH MAKE FOR CLOSER UNION AND COHESION IN COMPARISON WITH THOSE WHICH MAKE FOR DISINTEGRATION AND DECAY.' DEVOTES MUCH SPACE TO A DISCUSSION OF THE BRITISH DOMINIONS.

1230 HALLE L.J.
DREAM AND REALITY: ASPECTS OF AMERICAN FOREIGN POLICY.
NEW YORK: HARPER & ROW, 1959, 327 PP.
ANALYZES AMERICAN FOREIGN POLICY AS IT DEVELOPED THROUGH VICISSITUDES OF HISTORY, STUDYING CONFLICT BETWEEN INVOLVEMENT AND ISOLATION. TREATS POLICY FORMATION DURING COLONIAL TIMES, INFLUENCE OF THE OLD WORLD, FRENCH REVOLUTION, HEMISPHERE PROBLEMS, ENTANGLEMENT IN PHILIPPINES, ROAD TO PEARL HARBOR, AND US'S FAR EAST COMMITMENTS. RELATES FOREIGN POLICY TO HUMAN NATURE.

1231 HALLE L.J.
THE SOCIETY OF MAN.
NEW YORK: HARPER & ROW, 1965, 203 PP.
ILLUSTRATES DUALISM OF TANGIBLE AND CONCEPTUAL WORLD BY REFERENCE TO PROBLEMS OF INTERNATIONAL RELATIONS, HISTORY OF MARXISM, PECULIARITIES OF NATIONALISM, AND EVOLUTION OF MANKIND. SHOWS HOW DUALITY ACCOUNTS FOR DIFFERENCES IN PRACTICE AND TEACHING OF INTERNATIONAL RELATIONS AND HOW MEN TRY TO MAKE WORLDS COMPATIBLE. DISCUSSES CONSEQUENCES OF LARGE GAP AND SUGGESTS DIRECTION OF SOCIETY.

1232 HALLE L.J.
"DE GAULLE AND THE FUTURE OF EUROPE."
VIRGINIA QUART. REV., 43 (WINTER 67), 1-19.
THEME OF ARTICLE IS THAT DE GAULLE IS ATTEMPTING TO GO COUNTER TO THE DIRECTION OF HISTORY IN HIS DESIGNS FOR FRANCE AND EUROPE, AND THAT ALL HIS SUCCESSES IN DETAIL WILL NOT PREVENT A GENERAL FAILURE IN THE END.

1233 HALLET R.
PEOPLE AND PROGRESS IN WEST AFRICA: AN INTRODUCTION TO THE PROBLEMS OF DEVELOPMENT.
NEW YORK: PERGAMON PRESS, 1966, 161 PP., LC#65-27376.
DESCRIBES SITUATION OF WEST AFRICA TODAY: A DEVELOPING NATION FACED WITH INDUSTRIAL, ECONOMIC, AND SOCIAL PROBLEMS WHICH MUST BE SOLVED. GIVES AN OVER-ALL PICTURE OF ALMOST ALL FACETS OF LIFE AND SUGGESTS TRENDS AND POSSIBLE SOLUTIONS TO SOME OF THE PROBLEMS. EMPHASIZES ROLE DEVELOPED NATIONS MUST PLAY IN HELPING AFRICA ACHIEVE POTENTIAL. INCLUDES SUGGESTIONS FOR FURTHER READING.

1234 HALLETT D.
"THE HISTORY AND STRUCTURE OF OEEC."
EUROP. YRB., 1 (55), 62-70.
GIVES HISTORY OF 1948 CONVENTION FOUNDING OEEC. EARLY PURPOSE TO ADMINISTER MARSHALL PLAN. OUTLINES COMPOSITION AND FUNCTIONS OF AGENCIES. MAIN PRINCIPLES ARE: PROMOTION OF EUROPEAN ECONOMIC EXPANSION, CREATION OF CLOSE TIES BETWEEN US AND BRITISH COMMONWEALTH, AND COORDINATION OF NATIONAL POLICIES.

1235 HALLSTEIN W.
"THE EUROPEAN COMMUNITY AND ATLANTIC PARTNERSHIP."
INT. ORGAN., 17 (SUMMER 63)., 771-87.
ADAPTATION TO MODERN AGE MUST BE IMAGINATIVE RESPONSE TO CHANGE, COMBINING PRACTICALITY AND IDEALISM, DETERMINATION AND FLEXIBILITY. DISCUSSES EUROPEAN COMMUNITY AND ATLANTIC PARTNERSHIP IN REFERENCE TO THESE IDEAS. CONSIDERS USA AND BRITISH RESPONSES TO EEC.

1236 HALPERIN E.
NATIONALISM AND COMMUNISM.
CAMBRIDGE: M I T PRESS, 1965, 267 PP., LC#65-21569.
ASSERTS THAT MUCH CAN BE LEARNED ABOUT POWER POLITICS IN MOSCOW BY STUDYING ACTIONS AND PRONOUNCEMENTS OF COMMUNIST PARTIES IN SMALLER NATIONS; THEREFORE, STUDY IS MADE OF CHILEAN POLITICS, 1960-66. SEES SOVIET UNION AS US'S GREATEST THREAT IN LATIN AMERICA; ANALYZES MAJOR POLITICAL PARTIES AND THEIR RECORDS.

1237 HALPERIN M.H.
"NUCLEAR WEAPONS AND LIMITED WARS."
J. CONFL. RESOLUT., 51 (JUNE 61), 46-165.
QUESTION OF WHAT ROLE TACTICAL NUCLEAR WEAPONS SHOULD PLAY HAS BEEN AN IMPORTANT ONE FOR AMERICAN POLICY-MAKERS OVER THE PAST DECADE. SUPPORTS THESIS THAT IN ALMOST ANY CONCEIVABLE LIMITED WAR THE UNITED STATES SHOULD NOT INTRODUCE NUCLEAR WEAPONS.

1238 HALPERIN M.H.
LIMITED WAR IN A NUCLEAR AGE.
NEW YORK: JOHN WILEY, 1963, 191 PP., LC#63-18625.
USING A NUMBER OF RECENT CONFLICTS, SUCH AS CUBA, KOREA, AND INDOCHINA, DEVELOPS THEORY TO EXPLAIN NATIONS' USE OF LIMITED MEANS TO SETTLE DISPUTES WHEN THEY POSSESS INFINITELY GREATER MEANS OF DESTRUCTION. PREDICTS NATURE OF FUTURE CONFRONTATIONS BETWEEN US AND USSR ON LOCAL FRONTS OR IN GLOBAL WAR.

1239 HALPERIN M.H.
CHINA AND NUCLEAR PROLIFERATION (PAMPHLET)
CHICAGO: U CHI, CTR POLICY STUDY, 1966, 48 PP.
EXAMINES CHINESE ATTITUDES TOWARD NUCLEAR PROLIFERATION. FINDS THAT CHINESE POLICY HAS BEEN MARKED BY GREAT CAUTION IN DESIRE TO AVOID NUCLEAR ATTACK. FEELS THAT CHINESE DEVELOPMENT OF NUCLEAR CAPACITY MIGHT LEAD THEM TO TAKE GREATER RISKS IN CARRYING OUT COMMUNIST REVOLUTION. ALSO DISCUSSES CHINA'S LIKELY EVALUATION OF DANGERS AND OPPORTUNITIES OF FURTHER NUCLEAR EXPANSION TO INDIA, JAPAN.

1240 HALPERIN M.H.
CONTEMPORARY MILITARY STRATEGY.
BOSTON: LITTLE BROWN, 1967, 156 PP., LC#66-26715.
EXAMINES THE ROLE OF FORCE IN INTERNATIONAL POLITICS IN THE NUCLEAR AGE FROM THE PERSPECTIVE OF THE MAJOR POWERS. ASSUMES THAT FORCE CONTINUES TO PLAY A VITAL ROLE DESPITE DEVELOPMENT OF THERMONUCLEAR WEAPONS AND INTERCONTINENTAL BALLISTIC MISSILES. REVIEWS AMERICAN, SOVIET, AND CHINESE MILITARY STRATEGY AND DETERRENCE MEASURES OPERATIVE IN ASIA AND EUROPE.

1241 HALPERIN S.W.
MUSSOLINI AND ITALIAN FASCISM.
PRINCETON: VAN NOSTRAND, 1964, 191 PP.
STUDIES PROGRESS OF FASCISM 1901-43, FROM ITS ROOTS IN TURN-OF-THE-CENTURY GOVERNMENTAL FORMS, THROUGH SOCIALISM, TO ITS DOWNFALL IN WWII. DISCUSSES RELATION OF FASCISM TO NAZISM, THE CHURCH, PROPAGANDA, AND MUSSOLINI HIMSELF. ATTRIBUTES ITS SUCCESS TO HIS POWER AS A LEADER, AND ITS FAILURE TO HIS WEAKNESS AS A STATESMAN AND AN INTELLECTUAL.

1242 HALPERN J.M.

GOVERNMENT, POLITICS, AND SOCIAL STRUCTURE IN LAOS.
NEW HAVEN: YALE U, SE ASIA STUD, 1964, 197 PP., LC#64-16987.
SURVEYS THE NATIONAL AND LOCAL GOVERNMENT OF LAOS. EXAMINES SOME OF THE FUNDAMENTAL PATTERNS OF GOVERNMENTAL STRUCTURE ON BOTH LEVELS, CORRELATING THESE WITH TRADITIONAL FAMILY STRUCTURE AND WITH OBSERVATIONS ON LAOTIAN CHARACTER. DISCUSSES RELIGION, FOREIGN INFLUENCE, CHANGING VALUE SYSTEMS, INDIVIDUAL MOBILITY, AND THE CLASH AND INTERACTION OF ROYAL, WESTERN, AND COMMUNIST SYSTEMS.

1243 HALPERN M.
THE MORALITY AND POLITICS OF INTERVENTION (PAMPHLET)
NEW YORK: COUN RELIG & INTL AFF, 1963, 36 PP., LC#63-12832.
ANALYSIS OF US FOREIGN POLICY AND INTERVENTION IN FOREIGN AFFAIRS. EXAMINES ACTION IN RELATION TO MORALITY AND RELIGIOUS VALUES.

1244 HAMADY S.
TEMPERAMENT AND CHARACTER OF THE ARABS.
NEW YORK: TWAYNE, 1960, 282 PP., LC#60-09942.
STUDIES CHARACTER OF ARABS IN AN ATTEMPT TO EXPLAIN POLITICAL SYSTEMS AND BEHAVIOR. CHANGING NATURE OF INTERNATIONAL RELATIONS HAS PUT EXTREME STRESS ON THESE PEOPLE, MADE POSSIBLE BY FEATURES OF COMMON CULTURAL PERSONALITY. DISCUSSES RELATIONSHIPS, IDENTIFICATION, INTELLECT, AND OUTLOOK.

1245 HAMBRIDGE G. ED.
DYNAMICS OF DEVELOPMENT.
NEW YORK: FREDERICK PRAEGER, 1964, 401 PP., LC#64-16678.
ARTICLES FROM INTERNATIONAL DEVELOPMENT REVIEW DEALING WITH PROBLEMS OF AGRICULTURE, INDUSTRY, EDUCATION, LEADERSHIP, ADMINISTRATION OF AID, AND HEALTH IN DEVELOPING NATIONS.

1246 HAMBRO C.J.
HOW TO WIN THE PEACE.
PHILADELPHIA: LIPPINCOTT, 1942, 384 PP.
INDICATES FRAMEWORK OF FUTURE UNIVERSAL FEDERATION OF STATES: INTERNATIONAL LAW COURTS AND LAW ENFORCEMENT, SANCTION SYSTEMS, ETC. FEELS INTERNATIONALISM IS KEY TO FUTURE.

1247 HAMILTON W.B. ED., ROBINSON K. ED., GOODWIN C.D.W. ED.
A DECADE OF THE COMMONWEALTH, 1955-1964.
DURHAM: DUKE U PR, 1966, 567 PP., LC#65-28466.
DISCUSSES BRITISH COMMONWEALTH 1955-64, INCLUDING INDEPENDENCE OF SOME OF ITS MEMBERS, INTRA-COMMONWEALTH RELATIONS, INTERNATIONAL INTERCHANGE OF INSTITUTIONS AND CULTURE, AND INTERNATIONAL AND ECONOMIC RELATIONS.

1248 HAMM H.
ALBANIA - CHINA'S BEACHHEAD IN EUROPE.
NEW YORK: FREDERICK PRAEGER, 1963, 176 PP., LC#63-14679.
STUDY OF ALBANIAN POLITICS AND SOCIETY EMPHASIZES RELATIONS WITH RED CHINA AND USSR, ALBANIA'S FINAL SPLIT WITH THE SOVIET UNION AND ALLEGIANCE TO RED CHINA, AND THE DOMESTIC CONDITIONS AND IDEOLOGICAL BASIS FOR THE SHIFT, INCLUDING EVENTS OF THE TWENTY-SECOND PARTY CONGRESS.

1249 HAMRELL S. ED., WIDSTRAND C.G. ED.
THE SOVIET BLOC, CHINA, AND AFRICA.
STOCKHOLM: ALMQUIST & WIKSELL, 1964, 173 PP.
RECORD OF THE SCANDINAVIAN INSTITUTE'S INTERNATIONAL SEMINAR OF 1963 ON CONTEMPORARY AFRICAN PROBLEMS. ELUCIDATES POLICY OF THE SOVIET BLOC AND CHINA TOWARD AFRICA AGAINST BACKGROUND OF OLD CONFLICT BETWEEN PAN-AFRICANISM AND COMMUNISM. ASSESSES DEGREE OF ACTUAL AND POTENTIAL COMMUNIST INFLUENCE ON AFRICAN CONTINENT AND REPERCUSSIONS OF SINO-SOVIET DISPUTE IN THIS CONTEXT.

1250 HANCOCK W.K.
FOUR STUDIES OF WAR AND PEACE IN THIS CENTURY.
CAMBRIDGE: U. PR., 1961, 129 PP., $5.25.
DISCUSSES CONCEPT OF NON-VIOLENCE IN ORDER TO FIND SATISFACTORY PEACE SETTLEMENT. TRACES UN PEACE FUNCTIONS DURING LAST TEN YEARS IN CONNECTION WITH PROBLEMS OF BALANCE OF POWER. CALLS FOR RE-ORGANIZATION OF PURPOSES ACCORDING TO INTERNATIONAL NECESSITIES.

1251 HANDLIN O. ED.
AMERICAN PRINCIPLES AND ISSUES.
NEW YORK: HOLT RINEHART WINSTON, 1960, 576 PP., LC#61-10827.
COLLECTION OF ESSAYS ON BASIC PRINCIPLES OF US IDEALS AND HISTORICAL PURPOSE. DISCUSSES AMERICAN SENSE OF MISSION, MATERIAL WELL-BEING, ETHICS OF INDIVIDUALISM, DEDICATION TO HUMAN RIGHTS, AND CHALLENGES TO IDEALS IN RECENT YEARS.

1252 HANNA A.J.
EUROPEAN RULE IN AFRICA (PAMPHLET)
LONDON: ROUTLEDGE & KEGAN PAUL, 1961, 36 PP.
HISTORY OF EUROPEAN COLONIALISM IN AFRICA IN LAST CENTURY. TRACES EXPANSION INTO CONTINENT, BY COUNTRY, PERIOD BEFORE WWII, PERIOD OF NATIONALISM AND FOUNDATION OF STATES, 1940-60.

1253 HANSEN A.H.
ECONOMIC STABILIZATION IN AN UNBALANCED WORLD.
NEW YORK: HARCOURT, 1932, 383 PP.
WRITTEN DURING DEPRESSION, ARGUES THAT WE MAY FIND, AS TIME PROGRESSES, THAT A HIGH DEGREE OF ECONOMIC STABILITY CAN EASILY BE PURCHASED AT TOO GREAT A COST IN BOTH FREEDOM AND PROGRESS. BELIEVES THAT MUCH OF THE WORLD'S INSTABILITY DURING DEPRESSION HAD BEEN CAUSED BY 'WRONG GOVERNMENT POLICIES AND OTHER UNFORTUNATE FORMS OF SOCIAL CONTROL.'

1254 HANSEN B.
INTERNATIONAL LIQUIDITY.
STOCKHOLM: NATL INST OF ECO RES, 1964, 48 PP.
DISCUSSES PROBLEM OF DOLLAR BECOMING INTERNATIONAL TRADE STANDARD OF PAYMENT WITH CONTINUING DRAIN UPON GOLD RESERVES AND INABILITY OF GOLD PRODUCTION TO KEEP PACE WITH EXPANSION ON TRADE. PROPOSES INTERNATIONAL BANK TO OVERCOME THIS WITH ABILITY TO ISSUE CREDIT NOTES ON NONGOLD RESERVES.

1255 HANSEN G.H.
AFRO-ASIA AND NON-ALIGNMENT.
LONDON: FABER AND FABER, 1966, 432 PP.
SUBJECTIVE ACCOUNT BY INDIA OBSERVER OF AFRO-ASIAN FOREIGN POLICY. PROPOSES STUDY OF INTERNATIONAL RELATIONS AMONG NEWLY INDEPENDENT CONTRIES OF ASIA AND AFRICA SINCE WWII. DISCUSSES CERTAIN PATTERNS IMPLICIT IN PAST 20 YEARS: ROLE OF MORALITY IN POLITICS; INTERTWINING OF AFRO-ASIAN FEELING AND NON-ALIGNMENT; CONTRAST BETWEEN ILLUSION AND REALITY.

1256 HANSON J.W. ED., BREMBECK C.S. ED.
EDUCATION AND THE DEVELOPMENT OF NATIONS.
NEW YORK: HOLT RINEHART WINSTON, 1966, 529 PP., LC#66-10088.
ANTHOLOGY ON IMPACT OF EDUCATION IN FORMATION OF DEVELOPING NATIONS. DISCUSSES WORLD TASK, ETHICS, ECONOMIC FACTORS, PLANNING, AND INTERNATIONAL CONTRIBUTIONS OF EDUCATION.

1257 HARARI M.
GOVERNMENT AND POLITICS OF THE MIDDLE EAST.
ENGLEWOOD CLIFFS: PRENTICE HALL, 1962, 179 PP., LC#62-16659.
CLAIMS US POLICY IS MILITARISTIC AND THAT ECONOMIC ASSISTANCE MAY PROVE MORE USEFUL. ADVOCATES CONSISTENT MIDDLE EAST POLICY RATHER THAN THE CONTINGENCY PLANNING OF PAST. DISCUSSES ROLE OF ISLAM IN POLITICAL INSTITUTIONS AND DOMESTIC AND FOREIGN POLICIES OF INDIVIDUAL GOVERNMENTS.

1258 HARDT J.P.
THE COLD WAR ECONOMIC GAP.
NEW YORK: FREDERICK PRAEGER, 1961, 112 PP., LC#61-10509.
DISCUSSION OF US AND SOVIET ECONOMIC STRENGTH; MAINTAINS THAT GAP BETWEEN TWO COUNTRIES HAS NARROWED CONSIDERABLY. OUTLINES POLICIES INTENDED TO INCREASE US ECONOMIC POWER.

1259 HARGREAVES J.D.
PRELUDE TO THE PARTITION OF WEST AFRICA.
LONDON: MACMILLAN, 1963, 383 PP.
HISTORICAL STUDY OF WEST AFRICA FROM FIRST EUROPEAN SETTLEMENTS THROUGH 1885. ATTEMPTS TO RELATE PROBLEMS OF FRENCH AND BRITISH SETTLEMENTS TO RELATIONS OF EUROPE WITH WEST AFRICA AS A WHOLE. BOOK IS STRICTLY A NARRATIVE; DOES NOT PROPOSE ANY INTERPRETATION OR MODEL OF IMPERIALISM.

1260 HARMON R.B.
BIBLIOGRAPHY OF BIBLIOGRAPHIES IN POLITICAL SCIENCE (MIMEOGRAPHED PAPER: LIMITED EDITION)
SAN JOSE: DIBCO PRESS, 1964, 16 PP.
AN UNANNOTATED LISTING OF GENERAL, CURRENT, AND RETROSPECTIVE BIBLIOGRAPHIES DIVIDED INTO SEVEN SUBJECT AREAS. MOST ENTRIES FROM 20TH CENTURY AND A FEW FROM LATTER 19TH OR EARLIER. INCLUDES FOREIGN PUBLICATIONS THOUGH MAJORITY ARE AMERICAN. A GOOD BASIC LIST WHICH THE AUTHOR EXPANDS IN SUBSEQUENT WORKS. SUBJECT AND AUTHOR INDEXES. BOOKS ONLY. 109 ENTRIES.

1261 HARMON R.B.
POLITICAL SCIENCE: A BIBLIOGRAPHICAL GUIDE TO THE LITERATURE
METUCHEN: SCARECROW PRESS, 1965, 388 PP., LC#65-13557.
UNANNOTATED COMPILATION OF 2,500 ENGLISH-LANGUAGE BOOKS PUBLISHED 1859 THROUGH 1963. INCLUDES SEPARATE INDEXES FOR JOURNALS, GOVERNMENT DOCUMENTS, AND AUTHORS. ENTRIES DIVIDED INTO TEN GENERAL CATEGORIES AND THEN SUBDIVIDED. INCLUDES SECTION ON GENERAL REFERENCE WORKS AND BIBLIOGRAPHIES AND A SECTION ON RESEARCH AND METHODOLOGY IN POLITICAL SCIENCE. EXCELLENT AND THOROUGH COVERAGE OF POLITICAL SCIENCE.

1262 HARMON R.B.
SOURCES AND PROBLEMS OF BIBLIOGRAPHY IN POLITICAL SCIENCE (PAMPHLET)
SAN JOSE: DIBCO PRESS, 1966, 73 PP., LC#66-18521.
A REVISED AND ENLARGED EDITION OF THE AUTHOR'S "BIBLIOGRAPHY OF BIBLIOGRAPHIES IN POLITICAL SCIENCE." MOST COMPREHENSIVE LISTING OF BIBLIOGRAPHIES, CURRENT AND RETROSPECTIVE, IN POLITICAL SCIENCE. INDEXED UNDER GENERAL TOPICS. SEPARATE AUTHOR-TITLE INDEX AND SEPARATE LISTING OF BIBLIOGRAPHIC PERIODICALS. GOOD SECTION ON GENERAL BIBLIOGRAPHIES

OF VALUE TO POLITICAL SCIENCE. 244 ENTRIES.

1263 HARNETTY P.
"CANADA, SOUTH AFRICA AND THE COMMONWEALTH."
J. COMMONWEALTH POLIT. STUD., 2 (NOV. 63), 33-44.
EXAMINES CANADA'S ROLE IN THE WITHDRAWAL OF SOUTH AFRICA FROM THE COMMONWEALTH IN 1961. REGARDS CANADA'S CHANGE FROM A MODERATE POSITION TO A FIRM STAND AGAINST APARTHEID IN MAY 1960 AS ACTING IN ACCORDANCE WITH THE OTHER COMMONWEALTH NATIONS.

1264 HARPER F.
OUT OF CHINA.
HONG KONG: CURRENT SCENE, 1964, 235 PP.
COLLECTION OF INTERVIEWS WITH REFUGEES WHO HAVE FLED RED CHINA INTO MACAO AND HONG KONG, ATTEMPTING TO SHOW THEIR VIEWS OF RED CHINA, COMMUNISM, MAO, AND WHY THEY RISKED DEATH TO ESCAPE.

1265 HARPER S.N.
THE GOVERNMENT OF THE SOVIET UNION.
PRINCETON: VAN NOSTRAND, 1938, 204 PP.
DISCUSSES SOVIET INSTITUTIONS, GOVERNMENTAL STRUCTURES, AND METHODS OF GOVERNING IMMEDIATELY PRECEDING AND AFTER BOLSHEVIK RISE TO POWER. INCLUDES ECONOMIC STRUCTURES AND PLANS, PARTY POLICY, LAW-MAKING, PUBLIC ADMINISTRATION, AND PUBLIC SERVICES. ALSO TREATS ROLE OF INDIVIDUAL IN A COLLECTIVIZED STATE, INTERNATIONAL RELATIONSHIPS, GOAL OF WORLD REVOLUTION, AND 1937-38 TREASON TRIALS.

1266 HARRIMAN A.
PEACE WITH RUSSIA?
NEW YORK: SIMON AND SCHUSTER, 1959, 174 PP., LC#60-06082.
DESCRIBES CHANGES IN USSR FROM STALIN TO KHRUSHCHEV; RATIONALE OF COMPETITIVE COEXISTENCE; ATTITUDES OF RUSSIAN CITIZENRY; DOMESTIC POLICIES AND INTERNATIONAL IMPLICATIONS; AND SUGGESTIONS FOR US POLICY.

1267 HARRIS N.D.
INTERVENTION AND COLONIZATION IN AFRICA.
BOSTON: HOUGHTON MIFFLIN, 1914, 384 PP., LC#15-1468.
TRACES COLONIAL EXPANSION INTO AFRICA AT END OF 19TH CENTURY PRINCIPALLY THROUGH DETAILED ACCOUNTS OF SPECIFIC CASES, SUCH AS THE CONGO, THE SUDAN, NIGERIA, SOUTH AFRICA, AND TUNISIA.

1268 HARRIS N.D.
EUROPE AND AFRICA.
BOSTON: HOUGHTON MIFFLIN, 1927, 479 PP., LC#27-4161.
TRACES COLONIAL EXPANSION INTO AFRICA BEFORE WWI PRINCIPALLY THROUGH DETAILED ACCOUNTS OF SPECIFIC CASES, SUCH AS THE CONGO, THE SUDAN, NIGERIA, SOUTH AFRICA, AND TUNISIA.

1269 HARRIS S.E. ED.
THE DOLLAR IN CRISIS.
NEW YORK: HARCOURT BRACE, 1961, 311 PP., LC#61-11205.
COMPARES FOUR POSSIBLE MEANS TO STOP DOLLAR OUTFLOW AND LOSS OF GOLD RESERVES: RISE IN EXPORTS AND REDUCTION IN IMPORTS, REDUCTION IN NET OUTFLOW OF CAPITAL, CURTAILING US GOVERNMENT EXPENDITURES AND LOANS ABROAD, AND RISE OF INTERNATIONAL RESOURCES.

1270 HARRISON H.V.
THE ROLE OF THEORY IN INTERNATIONAL RELATIONS.
PRINCETON: VAN NOSTRAND, 1964, 118 PP., $2.95.
ESSAYS ANALYZE WHY NO INTEGRATED THEORY EXISTS IN FIELD, POSSIBLE APPROACHES FOR ITS CONSTRUCTION, METHODOLOGICAL AND SUBSTANTIVE PROBLEMS INVOLVED, USES OF THEORY IN POLITICS.

1271 HARRISON J.P.
GUIDE TO MATERIALS ON LATIN AMERICA IN THE NATIONAL ARCHIVES (2 VOLS.)
WASHINGTON: US NATL ARCH GEN SER, 1961.
CONTAINS PUBLICATIONS BY US DEPARTMENTS OF STATE, WAR, AND TREASURY ON LATIN AMERICA. ALL ENTRIES LOCATED IN THE NATIONAL ARCHIVES.

1272 HARRISON S.
INDIA AND THE UNITED STATES.
NEW YORK: MACMILLAN, 1961, 244 PP.
CONFERENCE IN 1959 OF MAJOR ADMINISTRATORS REPRESENTING BOTH COUNTRIES DEALT WITH ISSUES OF NEUTRALISM AND FOREIGN ASSISTANCE. VARIOUS PROPOSALS ADVANCED TO ALLEVIATE INDIA'S FOOD CRISES AND POPULATION-GROWTH PROBLEM.

1273 HART A.B. ED.
AMERICAN HISTORY TOLD BY CONTEMPORARIES.
NEW YORK: MACMILLAN, 1901, 653 PP.
ORIGINAL TEXTS OF WRITINGS 1689-1783, DESCRIBING WIDE VARIETY OF ASPECTS OF COLONIAL LIFE. BOOK COVERS COLONIAL, REVOLUTIONARY, AND FEDERAL PERIODS ON SUBJECTS SUCH AS WITCHCRAFT, FAMILY, CURRENCY, COURTS, COMMERCE, AND RELATIONS BOTH AMONG THE COLONIES AND WITH ENGLAND.

1274 HART B.H.L.
THE MEMOIRS OF CAPTAIN LIDDELL HART (VOL. I)
LONDON: CASSELL & CO LTD, 1965, 434 PP.
AUTOBIOGRAPHY OF CAPTAIN IN BRITISH ARMY; COVERS YEARS 1914-1937. BEGINS WITH YOUTH AND EARLY CAREER AS A MILITARY CORRESPONDENT; DISCUSSES NEW CONCEPTIONS OF MECHANIZED WARFARE, INTRODUCTION OF MECHANIZED FORCES AND AIRPOWER, MILITARY DEVELOPMENTS, FRUSTRATIONS, AND BRITAIN'S STRATEGIC POLICY. INCLUDES DISCUSSION OF LLOYD GEORGE AND T. E. LAWRENCE.

1275 HARTLEY A.
A STATE OF ENGLAND.
NEW YORK: HILLARY HOUSE PUBL, 1963, 255 PP.
STUDY OF BRITISH SOCIETY SINCE WWII AND IMPACT OF REDUCTION OF WORLD POSITION ON INTELLECTUAL COMMUNITY. INDICATES SENSE OF FRUSTRATION HAS HIT PEOPLE AS RESULT OF POOR ECONOMIC CONDITIONS AND LOSS OF WORLD PRESTIGE. EXAMINES STATUS OF WELFARE STATE, INTELLECTUAL ATTITUDE, FOREIGN AFFAIRS, AND EDUCATIONAL SYSTEM AS REMEDIES FOR NATIONAL DECLINE.

1276 HARTT J.
"ANTARCTICA: ITS IMMEDIATE PRACTICALITIES."
PROC. INST. WORLD AFF., 35 (59), 71-77.
CLAIMS U.S. MUST MEET CHALLENGE OF SOVIET UNION IN ANTARCTIC TO PREVENT MILITARY EXPLOITATION OF 12 NATION TREATY TO EXPLORE ANTARCTIC. DISCUSSES PROPOSAL FOR YEAR ROUND INTERNATIONAL AIRPORT ON MCMURDO SOUND TO LINK NATIONS OF SOUTHERN HEMISPHERE. CONCLUDES AIRPORT IS PRACTICAL AND NECESSARY.

1277 HARVARD BUREAU ECO RES LAT AM
THE ECONOMIC LITERATURE OF LATIN AMERICA: A TENTATIVE BIBLIOGRAPHY.
CAMBRIDGE: HARVARD U PR, 1936, 348 PP., LC#36-55976.
A BIBLIOGRAPHY IN SPANISH AND ENGLISH OF PRELIMINARY SURVEY OF THE ECONOMIC LITERATURE ON LATIN AMERICA CONCERNED PRIMARILY WITH WORKS FROM MEXICO, CENTRAL AMERICA, AND THE CARIBBEAN; 6,276 ITEMS INCLUDED.

1278 HARVARD LAW SCHOOL LIBRARY
ANNUAL LEGAL BIBLIOGRAPHY.
CAMBRIDGE: HARVARD LAW SCHOOL.
ANNUAL CUMULATION OF ARTICLES AND MONOGRAPHS RECEIVED BY HARVARD LAW SCHOOL LIBRARY INCLUDING ENTRIES IN "CURRENT LEGAL BIBLIOGRAPHY." FIRST PUBLISHED 1961.

1279 HARVARD LAW SCHOOL LIBRARY
CURRENT LEGAL BIBLIOGRAPHY.
CAMBRIDGE: HARVARD LAW SCHOOL, 1960.
BIBLIOGRAPHY OF MATERIAL RECEIVED BY HARVARD'S LAW SCHOOL LIBRARY PUBLISHED NINE TIMES A YEAR. INCLUDED IN "ANNUAL LEGAL BIBLIOGRAPHY."

1280 HARVARD UNIVERSITY LAW LIBRARY
CATALOG OF INTERNATIONAL LAW AND RELATIONS.
NEW YORK: OCEANA PUBLISHING.
ANNUAL LISTING OF BOOKS, MONOGRAPHIC SERIES, SERIAL PUBLICATIONS, AND DOCUMENTS OF WORLD AUTHORS FROM ALL COUNTRIES ON TOPICS OF INTERNATIONAL LAW. CATALOG BASED ON COLLECTION OF SPANISH DIPLOMAT, MARQUIS DE OLIVAT. FIRST PUBLISHED 1965.

1281 HARVARD UNIVERSITY LAW SCHOOL
INTERNATIONAL PROBLEMS OF FINANCIAL PROTECTION AGAINST NUCLEAR RISK.
NEW YORK: ATOMIC INDUS FORUM, 1959, 96 PP.
STUDIES PROBLEMS DERIVING FROM POSSIBILITY OF SERIOUS NUCLEAR INDUSTRIAL ACCIDENT AS TO LIABILITY LIMITATIONS, INSURANCE, PROCESSING OF CLAIMS, COMPUTING PREMIUMS, AND ROLE OF GOVERNMENT. ALSO CONCERNED WITH PROBLEMS OF INTERNATIONAL COOPERATION IN THESE LAWSUITS.

1282 HARVARD WIDENER LIBRARY
INDOCHINA: A SELECTED LIST OF REFERENCES.
CAMBRIDGE: HARVARD, WIDENER LIB, 1945, 108 PP.
LISTING OF MAINLY FRENCH-LANGUAGE WORKS IN THE WIDENER LIBRARY AT HARVARD. ARRANGED BY COUNTRY AND TOPIC. SOME WORKS ARE ANNOTATED.

1283 HARVEY M.F.
"THE PALESTINE REFUGEE PROBLEM: ELEMENTS OF A SOLUTION."
ORBIS, 3 (SUMMER 59), 193-207.
CONTENDS THAT THE REGULATED REPATRIATION OF ARAB REFUGEES INTO ISRAEL IS THE LOGICAL SOLUTION TO THE DIFFICULT SITUATION IN THE MIDDLE-EAST.

1284 HASAN H.S.
PAKISTAN AND THE UN.
NEW YORK: MANHATTAN, 1961, 328 PP.
ASSUMES THAT ORGANIZATIONS SIGNIFICANCE AND FUNCTIONING DEPENDS PRIMARILY UPON THE ATTITUDES AND POLICIES OF MEMBER NATIONS. DEPICTS PAKISTANI POINTS OF VIEW, AS OFFICIALLY STATED AND UNOFFICIALLY CONSIDERED, AND OBSERVES THE WORKING OF CHARTER SYSTEM PRESCRIBES MODIFICATIONS AND ASSESSES POSSIBILITY OF ACCOMPLISHING THIS.

1285 HASSE A.R.
INDEX TO UNITED STATES DOCUMENTS RELATING TO FOREIGN AFFAIRS, 1828-1861 (3 VOLS.)
WASHINGTON: CARNEGIE ENDOWMENT, 1914.
INDEX OF REFERENCE TO ENTIRE PUBLISHED RECORD OF DOCUMENTS, PAPERS, CORRESPONDENCE AND, TO A CONSIDERABLE EXTENT, LEGISLATION AND DECISIONS UPON INTERNATIONAL OR DIPLOMATIC QUESTIONS. MATERIAL IS ARRANGED ALPHABETICALLY AND CHRONOLOGICALLY UNDER AUTHOR.

1286 HASSON J.A.
THE ECONOMICS OF NUCLEAR POWER.
LONDON: LONGMANS, GREEN & CO, 1965, 160 PP.
DEVELOPMENT OF METHODOLOGICAL FRAMEWORK TO STUDY NEW INDUSTRY OF NUCLEAR POWER AND ITS EFFECT ON SOCIAL WELFARE INCLUDING NUCLEAR PROGRAMS IN US, UNITED KINGDOM, AND INDIA, AND ECONOMIC DECISIONS OF NUCLEAR DEVELOPMENT.

1287 HATCH J.
AFRICA TODAY-AND TOMORROW: AN OUTLINE OF BASIC FACTS AND MAJOR PROBLEMS.
NEW YORK: PRAEGER, 1962, 343 PP., $4.00.
GENERAL SURVEY OF HISTORICAL BACKGROUND OF AFRICAN TERRITORIES. COUNTRY BY COUNTRY EXAMINATION OF POLITICAL AND CONSTITUTIONAL DEVELOPMENTS - ECONOMIC AND SOCIAL PROBLEMS. CONCLUDES WITH OBSERVATIONS ON BROAD ISSUES: PAN-AFRICANISM, REACTIONS TO COLD WAR, ROLE IN UN, AND RACIAL PREJUDICES.

1288 HAUSER P. ED.
POPULATION AND WORLD POLITICS.
GLENCOE: FREE PR., 1958, 297 PP.
EVALUATES RELATIONS BETWEEN POPULATION AND INTERNATIONAL AFFAIRS. APPRAISES INTERACTION OF POPULATION AND RESOURCES, ECONOMIC DEVELOPMENT, AND POLITICS. STUDY OF IMPLICATIONS AND SIGNIFICANCE OF SUBSISTANCE LEVELS OF UNDERDEVELOPED NATIONS ON THE COLD WAR.

1289 HAUSER P.
WORLD POPULATION PROBLEMS (PAMPHLET)
NEW YORK: FOREIGN POLICY ASSN, 1965, 46 PP., LC#65-28770.
INCLUDES DISCUSSION OF MANY ASPECTS OF POPULATION PROBLEMS, SHOWING POPULATION GROWTH AND EXPLOSION, PROJECTIONS FOR FUTURE IN DEVELOPED AND LESS-DEVELOPED AREAS, ECONOMIC AND POLITICAL IMPLICATIONS, GAINS TO BE MADE FROM POPULATION CONTROL, AND SUGGESTION THAT US USE ITS GREAT RESOURCES TO HELP SOLVE POPULATION PROBLEMS IN UNDERDEVELOPED COUNTRIES.

1290 HAVILAND H.F.
THE POLITICAL ROLE OF THE GENERAL ASSEMBLY.
NEW YORK: CARNEGIE ENDOWMENT, 1951, 190 PP.
A DISCUSSION OF THE EXPANSION OF THE POLITICAL ROLE IN THE FACE OF POTENTIAL THREATS TO INTERNATIONAL PEACE. OUTLINES TWENTY-TWO MAJOR ISSUES INVOLVING ABOUT ONE HUNDRED AND FIVE SEPARATE RESOLUTIONS OF THE FIRST FIVE YEARS OF THE UNITED NATIONS.

1291 HAVILAND H.F.
"FOREIGN AID AND THE POLICY PROCESS: 1957."
AMER. POLIT. SCI. REV., 52 (SEPT. 58), 689-724.
FACTIONS FOR AND AGAINST THE AID PROGRAM ARE CLASSIFIED. INTERACTION BETWEEN THE EXECUTIVE AND TWO HOUSES EMPHASIZED. INEFFECTIVE RELATIONSHIP FOUND BETWEEN THE SUBSTANTIVE AND APPROPRIATION COMMITTEES OF CONGRESS.

1292 HAVILAND H.F.
"PROBLEMS OF AMERICAN FOREIGN POLICY."
WASHINGTON: BROOKINGS INST., 1960, 116 PP.
ANALYZES AND DISCUSSES: THE COMMUNIST IDEOLOGICAL AND ECONOMIC OFFENSIVES, COMMUNIST INTERNAL POLITICS, SOVIET MILITARY POTENTIAL, WESTERN MILITARY CAPABILITY, THE BERLIN QUESTION, AND ECONOMIC DEVELOPMENTS IN ASIA AND AFRICA.

1293 HAVILAND H.F.
"BUILDING A POLITICAL COMMUNITY."
INT. ORGAN., 17 (SUMMER 63), 733-53.
INDENTIFIES AND ANALYZES PRINCIPAL CONSIDERATIONS OF ATLANTIC POLITICAL COMMUNITY. MILITARY PROBLEM GENERATES STRONGEST PRESSURES FOR CLOSER POLITICAL RELATIONS. CONSIDERS MAJOR ECONOMIC PROBLEMS. PRESENTS ATTITUDES OF UNITED KINGDOM, NEUTRALS AND UNDERDEVELOPED NATIONS TOWARDS ATLANTIC COMMUNITY.

1294 HAY P.
FEDERALISM AND SUPRANATIONAL ORGANIZATIONS: PATTERNS FOR NEW LEGAL STRUCTURES.
URBANA: U OF ILLINOIS PR, 1966, 335 PP.
EXAMINES NATURE OF SUPRANATIONAL EEC LAW AND ITS RELATION TO THE DOMESTIC LAW OF MEMBER STATES. DISCUSSES PROVISIONS OF THE TREATY ESTABLISHING THE EUROPEAN ECONOMIC COMMUNITY, AND POINTS OUT "FEDERAL" CHARACTER OF EEC AND ITS LAW. REJECTS TRADITIONAL NOTION THAT SOVEREIGNTY IS AN INALIENABLE ATTRIBUTE OF STATEHOOD, AND FINDS THAT MEMBERS OF EEC HAVE ACTUALLY TRANSFERRED THEIR SOVEREIGN POWERS.

1295 HAYER T.
FRENCH AID.
LONDON: OVERSEAS DEVELOPMT INST, 1966, 230 PP.
DESCRIBES FRENCH AID IN CONTEXT BOTH OF FRANCE'S PAST COLONIAL POLICY AND FRENCH INTEREST IN THE THIRD WORLD. SIGNIFICANCE OF SIZE OF FRENCH PROGRAM IS FULLY DISCUSSED. EXAMINES CLOSENESS OF FRANCO-AFRICAN RELATIONS AND CONSIDERS ADVANTAGES AND DISADVANTAGES. STUDY IS ONE OF OVERSEAS DEVELOPMENT INSTITUTE'S.

1296 HAYTER W.
THE DIPLOMACY OF THE GREAT POWERS.
NEW YORK: MACMILLAN, 1961, 74 PP.
DISCUSSES DIPLOMACY OF US, USSR, GREAT BRITAIN, AND FRANCE. EMPHASIS IS ON DIPLOMATIC METHODS AND GOVERNMENT POLICIES THAT DETERMINE THEM. EACH COUNTRY IS DISCUSSED SEPARATELY. ORIENTATION IS BASICALLY IMPRESSIONISTIC AND APPROACH IS INFORMAL.

1297 HAYTON R.D.
"THE ANTARCTIC SETTLEMENT OF 1959."
AMER. J. INT. LAW, 54 (APR. 60), 349-71.
BRIEF HISTORY OF ANTARCTIC EXPLORATION. ACCOUNTS OF IGY AND WASHINGTON CONFERENCE ON ANTARCTICA. PRINCIPLES OF CONFERENCE EMBODIED IN TREATY ENSURING USE OF ANTARCTICA FOR EXCLUSIVELY PEACEFUL PURPOSES. INCLUDES CRITICAL ANALYSIS OF TREATY PROVISIONS AND SPECULATIONS CONCERNING FUTURE INTERNATIONAL ROLE OF AREA.

1298 HAZARD J.N.
"THE SOVIET SYSTEM OF GOVERNMENT."
CHICAGO: U OF CHICAGO PRESS, 1960.
A TEXTBOOK OF COMPARATIVE GOVERNMENT EMPHASIZING THE RELATION OF FORMAL, LEGAL INSTITUTIONS TO CONTEXTUAL ELEMENTS OF A POLITICAL SYSTEM--IDEOLOGY, SOCIAL STRUCTURE, PRESSURE GROUPS, ETC. SOVIET INSTITUTIONS ANALYZED IN TERMS OF THEIR OPERATION, FACTORS OF INFLUENCE, DEVELOPING TRENDS, AND CONTRAST TO WESTERN SYSTEMS. ANNOTATED BIBLIOGRAPHY OF DOCUMENTS, BOOKS, AND PERIODICALS PUBLISHED SINCE WORLD WAR II.

1299 HAZARD J.N.
"CODIFYING PEACEFUL COEXISTANCE."
AMER. J. INT. LAW., 55 (JAN. 61), 109-20.
BRIEF HISTORY OF ALL DRAFTS MADE TO GIVE COMPLETE DEFINITION OF COEXISTANCE. DIFFICULTY LIES IN CONSTRUCTING PRECISE DEFINITION. BASED ON STUDIES OF PRINCIPAL DOMESTIC AND INTERNATIONAL ORGANIZATIONS CONCERNED WITH SUBJECT.

1300 HAZARD J.N.
"CO-EXISTENCE LAW BOWS OUT."
AMER. J. INT. LAW, 59 (JAN. 65), 59-66.
INTERNATIONAL LAW ASSOCIATION, FOLLOWING LEAD OF UNITED NATIONS, HAS REVISED ITS THINKING IN REGARD TO PEACEFUL CO-EXISTENCE. FINDING CONCEPT OBSCURE AND IDEOLOGICALLY CONFUSING, ASSOCIATION IS NOW DEFINING ITS RESEARCH IN TERMS OF INTERNATIONAL SECURITY AND COOPERATION.

1301 HAZARD J.N.
"POST-DISARMAMENT INTERNATIONAL LAW."
AMER. J. OF INT. LAW, 61 (JAN. 67), 78-83.
DISCUSSES THE LIMITATIONS OF A PROPOSAL BY O.V. BOGDANOV (USSR) AT 1966 CONFERENCE OF INTERNATIONAL LAW ASSOCIATION, THAT COMPLETE WORLD DISARMAMENT WILL NOT ONLY ELIMINATE THE NEED FOR LARGE STANDING ARMIES, BUT ALSO CREATE A PACIFISTIC INTERNATIONAL SPIRIT WHICH WILL MAKE EVEN A UN ARMY UNNECESSARY. AUTHOR SUGGESTS THAT BOGDANOV'S REPORT GIVES VALID GOAL, BUT UNDERESTIMATES THE STEPS TO REACH IT.

1302 HAZLEWOOD A.
THE ECONOMICS OF "UNDER-DEVELOPED" AREAS.
LONDON: OXFORD U PR, 1959, 156 PP.
LIST OF 1,027 BOOKS, ARTICLES AND OFFICIAL PUBLICATIONS CONCERNED WITH ECONOMICS AND FINANCE, DEMOGRAPHY, RESOURCES, PLANNING, AND CONCEPTS OF ECONOMIC DEVELOPMENT. ARRANGED BY TOPIC WITH DETAILED TABLE OF CONTENTS.

1303 HAZLEWOOD A.
THE ECONOMICS OF DEVELOPMENT: AN ANNOTATED LIST OF BOOKS AND ARTICLES PUBLISHED 1958-1962.
LONDON: OXFORD U PR, 1964, 104 PP.
CONFINED TO ENGLISH-LANGUAGE PUBLICATIONS OF PERIOD 1958-1962. ORGANIZED BY CONTENT AND TYPE OF STUDY: THEORIES AND PROBLEMS; HISTORICAL STUDIES; AREA STUDIES; NATIONAL INCOME AND COMPONENTS; POPULATION, LABOR, AND MANAGEMENT; AGRICULTURE AND LAND; INDUSTRY; COMMERCE AND TRANSPORT; MONEY AND BANKING; GOVERNMENT; INTERNATIONAL ECONOMICS.

1304 HEADICAR B.M. ED.
CATALOGUE OF THE BOOKS, PAMPHLETS, AND OTHER DOCUMENTS IN THE EDWARD FRY LIBRARY OF INTERNATIONAL LAW...
LONDON: ST CLEMENT'S PRESS, 1923, 174 PP.
CATALOGUE ARRANGED IN TWO PARTS: FIRST PART ENTRIES ARE PRINTED ACCORDING TO LOCATION IN HISTORY LIBRARY OF LONDON SCHOOL OF ECONOMICS; IN SECOND PART CATALOGUE IS AN ALPHABETICAL INDEX TO AUTHORS, SUBJECTS AND TITLES. VERY LITTLE DESCRIPTION OF CONTENTS.

1305 HEADLAM-MORLEY
BIBLIOGRAPHY IN POLITICS FOR THE HONOUR SCHOOL OF PHILOSOPHY, POLITICS AND ECONOMICS (PAMPHLET)
LONDON: OXFORD U PR, 1949, 56 PP.
UNANNOTATED BIBLIOGRAPHY DESIGNED PRIMARILY FOR THOSE WORKING FOR THE HONOUR SCHOOL; THUS IT IS NEITHER EXHAUSTIVE NOR SELF-CONTAINED. ENTRIES ARRANGED INTO NINE TOPICAL CLASSIFICATIONS COVERING HISTORY AND THEORY OF POLITICAL INSTITUTIONS FROM HOBBES THROUGH 1948. LISTS BOTH 19TH AND 20TH CENTURY WORKS, WITH EMPHASIS ON MORE RECENT PUBLICATIONS.

1306 HEATH D.B.
"BOLIVIA UNDER BARRIENTOS."
CURRENT HISTORY, 53 (NOV. 67), 275-282, 307.
EXAMINES RECENT DEVELOPMENTS IN BOLIVIA, REVEALING THE INTRICATE INTERPLAY OF VALUES, PERSONALITIES, AND EVENTS THAT COMBINE TO SHAPE ITS CURRENT SITUATION. DISCUSSES RECENT REVOLUTIONARY MOVEMENTS AND BOLIVIA'S FOREIGN RELATIONS. NOTES THAT ALTHOUGH DOMESTIC UNREST CONTINUES TO PLAGUE THE COUNTRY, BOLIVIA'S ECONOMY IS BECOMING PROGRESSIVELY STRONGER.

1307 HEILBRONER R.L.
"DYNAMICS OF FOREIGN AID: PROBLEMS OF UNDERDEVELOPED NATIONS PLAGUE ASSISTANCE PROGRAM."
NEW LEADER, 44 (SEPT. 6), 18-21.
CAUTIONS AGAINST EXPECTATIONS OF QUICK RESULTS. ESTIMATES 20-30 YEARS FOR ACCUMULATION OF CAPITAL. FORESEES CLASS DISPLACEMENT LEADING TO SOCIAL TENSION, AND INCREASE IN ANTI-AMERICAN AND PRO-SOCIALIST SENTIMENTS.

1308 HEIMANN E.
FREEDOM AND ORDER: LESSONS FROM THE WAR.
NEW YORK: CHAS SCRIBNER'S SONS, 1947, 344 PP.
TRACES RELATIONSHIP BETWEEN PERSONAL FREEDOM AND SOCIAL ORDER. CONCRETE NONTECHNICAL ANALYSES OF STRUCTURE OF WORLD, NATIONAL AND INTERNATIONAL, INSTITUTIONAL AND SPIRITUAL.

1309 HEINDEL R.H., KALIJARVI T.V., WILCOX F.O.
"THE NORTH ATLANTIC TREATY IN THE UNITED STATES SENATE."
AMER. J. OF INT. LAW, 43 (OCT. 49), 633-665.
ANALYZES ROLE OF US SENATE IN DECISIONS IN FOREIGN POLICY AND SUMMARIZES IMPORTANT ISSUES IN DEBATE SURROUNDING NORTH ATLANTIC TREATY.

1310 HEKHUIS D.J. ED., MCCLINTOCK C.G. ED., BURNS A.L. ED.
INTERNATIONAL STABILITY: MILITARY, ECONOMIC AND POLITICAL DIMENSIONS.
NEW YORK: WILEY, 1964, 296 PP., $6.00.
ESSAYS DEFINE STABILITY, ANALYZE THREATS TO STABILITY, AND STUDY MEANS FOR ALLEVIATING INSTABILITY. STUDY MUTUAL DETERRENCE, REGIONAL DEFENSE, DISARMAMENT, ARMS CONTROL.

1311 HELMREICH E.C.
"KADAR'S HUNGARY."
CURR. HIST., 48 (MAR. 65), 142-148.
EVEN THOUGH REVOLUTION OF 1956 UNSUCCESSFUL, DEMAND FOR MORE LIBERAL POLICIES EXPRESSED BY INSURGENTS OF THAT TIME HAS BEEN FULFILLED. NO INCLINATION IN BUDAPEST TO TURN FROM MOSCOW TO PEKING OR ELSEWHERE DESPITE GROWING INDEPENDENCE.

1312 HEMLEBEN S.J.
PLANS FOR WORLD PEACE THROUGH SIX CENTURIES.
CHICAGO: U. CHI. PR., 1943, 227 PP.
AN ATTEMPT TO TRACE THE HISTORICAL BACKGROUND AND DEVELOPMENT OF IDEA OF ORGANIZATION TO SECURE PERMANENT PEACE FROM FOURTEENTH CENTURY TO LEAGUE OF NATIONS.

1313 HENDERSON W. ED.
SOUTHEAST ASIA: PROBLEMS OF UNITED STATES POLICY.
CAMBRIDGE: M.I.T. PR., 1963, 273 PP., $6.75.
THIRTEEN SPECIALISTS ON THE POLITICAL,STRATEGIC, ECONOMIC, AND SOCIO-CULTURAL ASPECTS OF SOUTHEAST ASIA EXAMINE U.S. POLICY SINCE 1945 IN LIGHT OF THE HISTORY OF THE PEOPLES, THE DEVELOPMENT AND STRENGTH OF NATIONAL STATES, AND THE RECORD AND PROBABLE INTENTIONS OF THE CHINESE. REVIEWS THE FACTORS INFLUENCING PAST AMERICAN POLICY AND OUTLINES THOSE WHICH WASHINGTON SHOULD CONSIDER IN FORMULATING FUTURE POLICIES.

1314 HENDRICKS D.
PAMPHLETS ON THE FIRST WORLD WAR: AN ANNOTATED BIBLIOGRAPHY (OCCASIONAL PAPER NO. 79)
URBANA: U OF ILL, SCHOOL LIB SCI, 1962, 33 PP.
BIBLIOGRAPHICAL LISTING WITH SOME ANNOTATION OF THE PAMPHLET COLLECTION OWNED BY MILIKIN UNIVERSITY IN DECATUR, ILLINOIS. MOST OF THE PUBLICATIONS ARE IN ENGLISH, BUT VIEWS OF VARIOUS COUNTRIES INVOLVED ARE REPRESENTED. ENTRIES ARRANGED ALPHABETICALLY BY AUTHOR WITH A SEPARATE SUBJECT INDEX PROVIDED. 500 ITEMS. MAJORITY OF ENTRIES WERE WRITTEN 1914-1919.

1315 HENKIN L.
ARMS CONTROL AND INSPECTION IN AMERICAN LAW.
NEW YORK: COLUMB. U. PR., 1958, 289 PP.
STUDIED FROM POINT OF VIEW OF LEGAL AND ADMINISTRATIVE PROBLEMS INVOLVED IN ENFORCING AN INSPECTION SYSTEM IN USA. WRITTEN PRIMARILY FOR THOSE INTERESTED IN DEVELOPMENT OF INTERNATIONAL INSTITUTIONS. CONTENDS THAT THE PROVISIONS OUTLINED MAKE NO OR FEW INROADS INTO ACCEPTED CONSTITUTIONAL LIMITATIONS.

1316 HENKIN L.
ARMS CONTROL: ISSUES FOR THE PUBLIC.
ENGLEWOOD CLIFFS: PRENTICE HALL, 1961, 207 PP.
REPORT ON THE NINETEENTH AMERICAN ASSEMBLY ON ARMS CONTROL. ESSAYS ON VARIOUS ASPECTS OF DISARMAMENT PROBLEMS OF INSPECTION AND US FOREIGN POLICY. PARTICULAR EMPHASIS FOCUSED ON QUESTION OF SOVIET NATIONAL INTEREST AND EUROPEAN VIEWS OF USA ARMS CONTROL PROJECTS.

1317 HENKYS R. ED.
DEUTSCHLAND UND DIE OSTLICHEN NACHBARN.
STUTTGART: KREUZ-VERLAG, 1966, 237 PP.
COLLECTION OF ESSAYS ON GERMAN REFUGEE PROBLEM ESPECIALLY IN RELATION TO ASSIMILATION, RIGHTS OF DOMICILE, POLISH ATTITUDE TOWARD ODER-NEISSE REGIONS, AND WEST GERMAN GOVERNMENT POSITION ON EASTERN BORDER.

1318 HERRERA F.
"EUROPEAN PARTICIPATION IN THE LATIN AMERICAN REGIONAL INTEGRATION"
CENTRO, 3 (FEB. 67), 30-36.
PRESENTS ARGUMENT FOR LATIN AMERICA'S DESIRE TO COOPERATE WITH EUROPEAN ECONOMIC COMMUNITIES ON MULTILATERAL BASIS. SEEKS SOLIDARITY THROUGH INTERDEPENDENCE AND MUTUAL PROTECTION. TRACES DEVELOPMENT OF LATIN AMERICA AS CULTURAL EXPANSION OF EUROPE, AND ENUMERATES FINANCIAL TIES WITH EUROPE.

1319 HERZ J.H.
INTERNATIONAL POLITICS IN THE ATOMIC AGE.
NEW YORK: COLUMB. U. PR., 1959, 360 PP.
PROCEEDS FROM DEFINITION OF SOVEREIGN STATE TO DISCUSSION OF ITS DEVELOPMENT. RELATES NATIONS TO EVOLUTION OF WORLD POLITICS. STUDIES IMPACT OF ATOMIC POWER, BLOC RELATIONSHIPS, DEFENSE, DETERRENCE AND PROSPECTS FOR PEACE. SEES USA AS HAVING PRIME RESPONSIBILITY TO INITIATE ACTION FOR PEACE.

1320 HERZ J.H.
"THE RELEVANCY AND IRRELEVANCY OF APPEASEMENT."
SOC. RES., 39 (FALL 64), 296-320.
EMPHASIZES MEANING AND ROLE OF APPEASEMENT IN INTERNATIONAL POLITICS AND SEEKS TO DEFINE OTHER AREAS IN WHICH IT IS SIGNIFICANT. CONSIDERS PROBLEMS OF POLITICAL PHILOSOPHY, EMPIRICAL HISTORY, CONFLICT AND VALUE THEORY.

1321 HERZ M.F.
BEGINNINGS OF THE COLD WAR.
BLOOMINGTON: INDIANA U PR, 1966, 214 PP., LC#66-10093.
SUMMARIZES AND HIGHLIGHTS THE EVENTS OF EARLY 1945 THAT ENCOMPASS THE MAJOR BEGINNINGS OF THE COLD WAR. EMPHASIZES EVENTS IN POLAND, THE UNITED NATIONS, AND THE ROLES OF CORDELL HULL, HARRY HOPKINS, CHURCHILL, FDR, AND STALIN. DISCUSSES THE DEVELOPMENT OF RUSSIAN SPHERES OF INFLUENCE IN EASTERN EUROPE.

1322 HETHERINGTON H.
SOME ASPECTS OF THE BRITISH EXPERIMENT IN DEMOCRACY.
TORONTO: RYERSON PRESS, 1962, 57 PP.
INVOLVES POLITICAL AND EDUCATIONAL ASPECTS OF DEMOCRACY IN ENGLAND AND THE COMMONWEALTH IN AFRICA. DEMOCRACY IS STILL AN EXPERIMENT WITH NO DEGREE OF LASTING SUCCESS.

1323 HEWES T.
EQUALITY OF OPPORTUNITY - THE AMERICAN IDEAL AND KEY TO WORLD PEACE.
PITTSFIELD, MASS: B FRANKLIN PR, 1959, 114 PP.
ARGUES THAT WORLD TURMOIL OF LATE 1950'S IS TRACEABLE TO THE NEGLECT OF THE AMERICAN BELIEF IN THE PRINCIPLE THAT "EQUALITY OF INDIVIDUAL AND ECONOMIC OPPORTUNITY" IS MAN'S INHERENT NATURE. PROPOSES ADOPTION OF THIS PRINCIPLE AS SUBSTANCE OF US DOMESTIC AND FOREIGN POLICY, AS THE ALTERNATIVE TO THE THREAT OF "COLLECTIVISM."

1325 HEYSE T.
PROBLEMS FONCIERS ET REGIME DES TERRES (ASPECTS ECONOMIQUES, JURIDIQUES ET SOCIAUX)
BRUSSELS: CEDESA, 1960, 163 PP.
BIBLIOGRAPHY OF 875 ITEMS COVERING PUBLISHED LITERATURE ON ECONOMIC, JUDICIAL, AND SOCIAL IMPLICATIONS OF TENURE OF LAND IN THE BELGIAN CONGO AND RUANDI-URANDI FOR PERIOD 1948-1959. EMPHASIZES PROBLEMS OF WATER AND HUNTING AND FISHING RIGHTS FOR ECONOMICALLY UNDERDEVELOPED COUNTRIES AND ROLE OF INTERNATIONAL ORGANIZATIONS IN SOLVING TERRITORIAL DISPUTES. INCLUDES AUTHOR AND SUBJECT INDEXES.

1326 HIBBERT R.A.
"THE MONGOLIAN PEOPLE'S REPUBLIC IN THE 1960'S."
WORLD TODAY, 23 (MAR. 67), 122-130.
THE MONGOLIAN PEOPLE'S REPUBLIC, CREATED IN 1921, BEGAN

TO TAKE ITS PLACE AS A FULL MEMBER OF THE INTERNATIONAL COMITY ONLY A DOZEN OR SO YEARS AGO. THE AUTHOR TRACES THE POLITICAL AND ECONOMIC DEVELOPMENT OF THE COUNTRY AND CONCLUDES THAT WHILE GROWTH HAS BEEN SLOW AT THE BEGINNING, THE OUTLOOK FOR THE MPR IS BRIGHT.

1327 HICKEY D.
"THE PHILOSOPHICAL ARGUMENT FOR WORLD GOVERNMENT."
WORLD JUSTICE, 6 (DEC. 64).
CITING PAST THEORIES AND DOCUMENTS, DISCUSSES THE MEANING AND POSSIBILITY OF A WORLD GOVERNMENT CONCLUDING THAT 'FOR THE SAKE OF PEACE AND PROSPERITY, FOR THE SAKE OF ORDER, SECURITY AND THE FREE PURSUIT OF ART, CULTURE AND EDUCATION A WORLD GOVERNMENT RULING A WORLD STATE IS A HUMAN NECESSITY.'

1328 HIGGANS B.
UNITED NATIONS AND U.S. FOREIGN ECONOMIC POLICY.
HOMEWOOD: IRWIN, 1962, 235 PP., $5.25.
CONSIDERS AMOUNT AND KINDS OF AID USA SHOULD GIVE THROUGH UN OR BILATERALLY TO MEET OBJECTIVES. REVIEWS USA AND UN AID ALLOCATION. RECOMMENDS IDEAL STRUCTURE FOR EXECUTING USA FOREIGN POLICY.

1329 HIGGINS R.
THE ADMINISTRATION OF UNITED KINGDOM FOREIGN POLICY THROUGH THE UNITED NATIONS (PAMPHLET)
SYRACUSE: SYRACUSE U PRESS, 1966, 63 PP., LC#66-18648.
STUDIES IMPACT OF UN ON ADMINISTRATION OF BRITISH FOREIGN POLICY, AND ON TRADITIONAL DIPLOMACY, INCLUDING ADJUSTMENTS WITHIN BRITISH GOVERNMENT TO CENTRAL FORUM PROVIDED BY UN.

1330 HILL M.
IMMUNITIES AND PRIVILEGES OF INTERNATIONAL OFFICIALS.
WASHINGTON: CARNEGIE ENDOWMENT, 1947, 281 PP.
DESCRIBES EXPERIENCE OF LEAGUE OF NATIONS' OFFICIALS IN SWITZERLAND, NETHERLANDS, CANADA, ET. AL. DOCUMENTS IMMUNITIES AND PRIVILEGES OF LEAGUE OF NATIONS AND UN OFFICIALS.

1331 HILL N.
INTERNATIONAL ADMINISTRATION.
NEW YORK: MCGRAW HILL, 1931, 292 PP.
AN ANALYSIS OF INTERNATIONAL ADMINISTRATIVE BODIES INCLUDING COMMISSIONS, INFORMATIONAL BUREAUS, CONVENTIONS, MANDATE SYSTEM SUPERVISED BY THE LEAGUE OF NATIONS, ETC. INCLUDES APPENDIX OF RELATED DOCUMENTS.

1332 HILL N.
CLAIMS TO TERRITORY IN INTERNATIONAL LAW AND RELATIONS.
NEW YORK: OXFORD U. PR., 1945, 248 PP.
ANALYZES TERRITORIAL DISPUTES, IN VIEW OF THEIR NATURE AND PROCEDURES AVAILABLE FOR SOLUTION. DISCUSSES BOTH LEGAL AND NON-LEGAL CLAIMS, PARTICULARLY THOSE IN EUROPE AND THE WESTERN HEMISPHERE. CATEGORIZES CLAIMS INTO STRATEGIC, GEOGRAPHIC, ECONOMIC, HISTORIC, AND ETHNIC AND DISCUSSES EACH GROUPING SEPARATELY.

1333 HILSMAN R. JR.
"INTELLIGENCE AND POLICY MAKING IN FOREIGN AFFAIRS."
WORLD POLIT., 5 (OCT. 52), 1-45.
IDENTIFIES DOCTRINES GOVERNING CIA. EXAMINES INTERNATIONAL RESEARCH INFLUENCING STATE DEPARTMENT ROLE IN FOREIGN AFFAIRS. DISCUSSES ATTITUDES AND SKILLS OF OPERATORS. SETS UP A MODEL OF INTELLIGENCE AND EVALUATES AMERICAN DOCTRINES IN THE LIGHT OF THIS MODEL.

1334 HILSMAN R. JR.
"THE NEW COMMUNIST TACTIC: PRECIS-INTERNAL WAR."
SAN DIEGO: INST. WORLD AFF., 1961.
ARGUES THAT USSR VIEWS INTERNAL (OR GUERRILLA) WARFARE AS BEST METHOD FOR COMMUNIST EXPANSION. DISCUSSES THREAT POSED BY INTERNAL WARFARE, PROBLEMS OF MILITARY SECURITY AS RELATED TO MAINTAINANCE OF FREE NATIONS, AND RE-ORGANIZATION OF USA ECONOMIC AID PROGRAM. CONSIDERS THESE ISSUES IN LIGHT OF POLITICAL FACTORS INVOLVED.

1335 HINDEN R.
EMPIRE AND AFTER.
LONDON: ESSENTIAL BOOKS, LTD, 1949, 195 PP.
STUDY OF BRITISH IMPERIAL ATTITUDES, EMPHASIZING PRESENT CENTURY AND DOMESTIC PRESSURES BEHIND POLICIES, INCLUDING DISSOLUTION OF EMPIRE. AUTHOR'S ATTITUDE ANTI-IMPERIALIST.

1336 HINDLEY D.
"FOREIGN AID TO INDONESIA AND ITS POLITICAL IMPLICATIONS."
PACIFIC AFFAIRS, 36 (SUMMER 63), 107-119.
FEELS THAT FOREIGN AID IS PRIMARILY A TOOL WITH WHICH DONOR GOVERNMENTS SEEK TO PRODUCE POLITICAL RESULTS TO BENEFIT THEMSELVES. OUTLINES SOURCES, AMOUNTS, AND UTILIZATION OF AID RECEIVED BY INDONESIAN GOVERNMENT SINCE 1949. EXAMINES SHORT-TERM AND LONGER-TERM EFFECTS OF THIS AID ON POLITICAL SITUATION WITHIN INDONESIA.

1337 HINSHAW R.
THE EUROPEAN COMMUNITY AND AMERICAN TRADE: A STUDY IN ATLANTIC ECONOMICS AND POLICY.
NEW YORK: PRAEGER, 1964, 188 PP., $4.95.
EVALUATES COMMON MARKET AND RELATED ORGANIZATIONS IN TERMS OF AMERICAN INTERESTS. SHOWS HOW UNDERDEVELOPED NATIONS AFFECTED BY EUROPEAN MOVES TOWARD INTEGRATION. EXAMINES IMPLICATIONS FOR AMERICAN TRADE POLICY.

1338 HINSLEY F.H.
POWER AND THE PURSUIT OF PEACE.
NEW YORK: CAMBRIDGE U PRESS, 1963, 416 PP.
STUDY OF WAR AND PEACE, WITH ANALYSIS OF THEORIES OF INTERNATIONAL RELATIONS. EXAMINES HISTORY OF INTERNATIONALIST THEORIES TO THE END OF THE 17TH CENTURY; THEORIES OF ROUSSEAU, KANT, AND BENTHAM; AND THOUGHT LEADING TO THE LEAGUE OF NATIONS. INCLUDES HISTORY OF THE MODERN STATES' SYSTEM TO 1900, AND INTERNATIONAL ORGANIZATIONS AND RELATIONS IN THE 20TH CENTURY.

1339 HIRSCHMAN A.O.
DEVELOPMENT PROJECTS OBSERVED.
WASHINGTON: BROOKINGS INST, 1967, 197 PP., LC#67-27683.
POLITICAL ECONOMIST STUDIES COMPARATIVE BEHAVIOR AND STRUCTURAL CHARACTERISTICS OF DEVELOPMENT PROJECTS. USES 11 WORLD BANK PROJECTS IN 11 COUNTRIES AS BASIS. BELIEVES EVEN BEST-RESEARCHED PROJECTS ARE SUBJECT TO UNFORESEEN PROBLEMS AND WINDFALLS. DISCUSSES UNCERTAINTIES IN SUPPLY OF TECHNOLOGY, ADMINISTRATION, FINANCE; AND IN DEMAND. EXAMINES PROJECT IMPLEMENTATION, DESIGN, AND APPRAISAL.

1340 HIRSHBERG H.S., MELINAT C.H.
SUBJECT GUIDE TO UNITED STATES GOVERNMENT PUBLICATIONS.
CHICAGO: AMER LIB ASSN, 1947, 228 PP.
COMPILATION OF BOOKS, PAMPHLETS, SERIALS, DIRECTORIES, BIBLIOGRAPHIES, AND HANDBOOKS.

1341 HISPANIC SOCIETY OF AMERICA
CATALOGUE (10 VOLS.)
BOSTON: HALL, 1965.
BIBLIOGRAPHY OF BOOKS ON VARIOUS FACETS OF LATIN AMERICA DURING THE COLONIAL PERIOD. INCLUDES MATERIAL ON SPAIN AND PORTUGAL.

1342 HISS D.
"UNITED STATES PARTICIPATION IN THE UNITED NATIONS."
NEW YORK: AMER. ASSN. UN, 1947, 47 PP.
A SKETCH OF PROBLEMS IN FORMULATION OF AMERICAN POLICY IMPLEMENTAION REGARDING THE UN. ARGUES THAT POLICY MUST BE MADE MORE CAREFULLY, THAT THERE SHOULD BE BETTER COORDINATION AMONG US AGENCIES INVOLVED WITH THE UN, AND THAT THE DUALISM BETWEEN PLANNING AND OPERATION IS UNTENABLE.

1343 HISTORICAL RESEARCH INSTITUTE
A SHORT BIBLIOGRAPHY OF INDO-MUSLIM HISTORY.
LAHORE, PAKISTAN: PUNJAB UNIV, 1961, 160 PP.
INTENDED TO PROVIDE GUIDANCE ON WAYS OF OBTAINING INFORMATION ON THE PERIOD 1858-1961, THE MOST IMPORTANT PERIOD IN THE HISTORY OF THE SUBCONTINENT. COVERS FIELDS SUCH AS THE NATIONAL MOVEMENT, POLITICAL PARTIES, BIBLIOGRAPHY, EDUCATION AND THE ALIGARH MOVEMENT.

1344 HISTORICUS
"LETTERS AND SOME QUESTIONS OF INTERNATIONAL LAW."
LONDON: MACMILLAN, 1863, 44 PP.
AMERICAN CIVIL WAR POSED INTERNATIONAL LAW PROBLEMS FOR BELLIGERENT AND NEUTRAL NATIONS. FOCUSES ON RIGHTS OF CAPTURE ON THE HIGH SEAS AND BLOCKADE-RUNNING. DEFINES NATURE OF CONTRABAND CARGO.

1345 HOAG M.W.
"ECONOMIC PROBLEMS OF ALLIANCE."
J. POLIT. ECON., 65 (DEC. 57), 522-34.
EVALUATES THE CUSTOMARY VIEW OF ALLIANCE AND ITS DRAWBACKS, THEN CONSIDERS ALTERNATE VIEWS IN TERMS OF RELEVANCY AND WORKABILITY. BELIEVES WE ARE LIVING IN AN AGE OF FERMENT IN MILITARY STRATEGY, AND USING NATO AS AN EXAMPLE, SHOWS THE UNDERLYING IMPORTANCE OF ECONOMICS.

1346 HOBBS C.C.
SOUTHEAST ASIA, 1935-45: A SELECTED LIST OF REFERENCE BOOKS (PAMPHLET)
WASHINGTON: LIBRARY OF CONGRESS, 1946, 85 PP.
ANNOTATED BIBLIOGRAPHY LISTS BOOKS AND SIGNIFICANT MONOGRAPHS IN FRENCH, ENGLISH, AND DUTCH PERTINENT TO SOUTHEAST ASIA. AREA DIVISIONS INCLUDE BURMA, SIAM, INDOCHINA, MALAYA, AND THE EAST INDIAN ARCHIPELAGO (INDONESIA). INCLUDES ECONOMICS, GEOGRAPHY, SOCIAL CONDITIONS, GOVERNMENTS, WWII AND RECONSTRUCTION, CULTURE, AND POLITICS. CONTAINS APPROXIMATELY 750 LISTINGS.

1347 HOBSON J.A.
TOWARDS INTERNATIONAL GOVERNMENT.
LONDON: ALLEN UNWIN, 1915 216 PP.
OUTLINES SKETCH FOR COUNCIL OF NATIONS WITH STRONG EXECUTIVE POWER TO SECURE PEACEFUL CIVILIZATION. CLAIMS THAT SOVEREIGNTY IS OBSOLETE AND NEW ERA OF INTERNATIONALISM CALLS FOR INTERNATIONAL GOVERNMENT, COUNCILS, COURTS, ETC.

1348 HOBSON J.A.
IMPERIALISM.
LONDON: ALLEN UNWIN, 1938, 386 PP.
STUDY DESIGNED TO GIVE MORE PRECISION TO A TERM WHICH HAS BECOME A POWERFUL MOVEMENT IN THE CURRENT POLITICS OF THE CIVILIZED WORLD. IN PART ONE THE ECONOMIC ORIGINS OF IMPERIALISM ARE TRACED WITH STATISTICAL METHODS AND RESULTS PROVIDED. IN PART TWO THE THEORY AND PRACTICE OF IMPERIALISM ARE INVESTIGATED AS WELL AS ITS POLITICAL AND MORAL REACTIONS UPON THE WESTERN NATION ENGAGING IN IT.

1349 HODGE G.
"THE RISE AND DEMISE OF THE UN TECHNICAL ASSISTANCE ADMINISTRATION."
CAN. PUBLIC ADMIN., 10 (MAR. 67), 1-24.
AN EXPLORATION OF THE FACTORS CONTRIBUTING TO THE DECLINE OF THE TAA OF THE UN. FACTORS STUDIED INCLUDE INTERNAL AND EXTERNAL PRESSURES, LEADERSHIP AND PERSONALITIES, MAINTENANCE OF GOALS, INTERGROUP RIVALRIES, COALITIONS, AND ITS EXPENDABILITY. CHIEF FAULT OF AN ORGANIZATION IS THAT IT IS A TOOL CREATED TO DO A SPECIFIC JOB RATHER THAN A NATURAL PRODUCT OF SOCIAL NEEDS AND PRESSURES.

1350 HODGES C.
THE BACKGROUND OF INTERNATIONAL RELATIONS.
NEW YORK: WILEY, 1931, 743 PP.
CONSIDERS INTERDEPENDENCE OF PEOPLE, SPREAD OF POPULAR GOVERNMENT, AND ECONOMIC ACTIVITY NECESSARY FOR COMPETITION AND COOPERATION AMONG NATIONS. DISCUSSES HISTORY OF MODERN STATE, GEOGRAPHIC INFLUENCES, EXPANSIONIST DRIVES, INTERNATIONAL BUSINESS, AND MASS COMMUNICATIONS. ANALYZES LEAGUE OF NATIONS FAILURE. BELIEVES NATIONAL GOVERNMENTS MUST CREATE FOUNDATIONS FOR PEACE.

1351 HODGKIN T.
NATIONALISM IN COLONIAL AFRICA.
NEW YORK: NEW YORK U PR, 1957, 216 PP., LC#57-8133.
DESCRIBES AND ACCOUNTS FOR THE POLITICAL INSTITUTIONS AND IDEAS OF AFRICAN NATIONALISM IN RELATION TO HISTORICAL DEVELOPMENT. BRIEF ACCOUNTS OF POLICIES PURSUED BY COLONIAL POWERS AS FACTORS IN EMERGING TYPES OF NATIONALISM. EXAMINES CHARACTERISTIC FEATURES OF NEW PROTO-INDUSTRIAL AFRICAN TOWNS. INCLUDES SELECTED BIBLIOGRAPHY.

1352 HOEVELER H.J. ED.
INTERNATIONALE BEKAMPFUNG DES VERBRECHENS.
HAMBURG: VERLAG DEUTSCHE POLIZEI, 1966, 264 PP.
TRACES DEVELOPMENT OF INTERNATIONAL CRIMINOLOGY WITH REFERENCE TO DRUG ADDICTION, MAFIA, PROSTITUTION, ETC. DISCUSSES RISE OF EUROPEAN INTERNATIONAL LEGAL ORDER WITH EMPHASIS ON EXTRADITION AGREEMENTS. EXAMINES BRIEFLY POLICE METHODS IN SWITZERLAND, AUSTRIA, ENGLAND (SCOTLAND YARD), AND US (FBI).

1353 HOFFMAN P.
WORLD WITHOUT WANT.
NEW YORK: HARPER, 1962, 144 PP.
ENJOINS ECONOMICALLY ADVANCED NATIONS TO USE THEIR WEALTH AND TECHNOLOGY TO ASSIST UNDERDEVELOPED COUNTRIES ACHIEVE A DECENT STANDARD OF LIVING. THIS RESPONSIBILITY MUST BE ASSUMED OR WORLD CHAOS WILL RESULT. RECOMMENDS THAT FOREIGN AID MUST BE GIVEN TOP PRIORITY.

1354 HOFFMANN P.G.
ONE HUNDRED COUNTRIES, ONE AND ONE QUARTER BILLION PEOPLE.
WASHINGTON: A D + M LASKER FDN, 1960, 62 PP.
EXAMINES GROWTH OF GOVERNMENTAL ASSISTANCE TO UNDERDEVELOPED NATIONS. DISCUSSES MANPOWER NEEDS, WORK OF UN, TRADE POLICIES, AND GENERAL PURPOSES AND METHODS OF DISTRIBUTION OF ECONOMIC AID. CHARTS.

1355 HOFFMANN S.
"IMPLEMENTATION OF INTERNATIONAL INSTRUMENTS ON HUMAN RIGHTS."
PROC. AMER. SOC. INT. LAW, (1959), 235-245.
PRESENT WORLD SITUATION NECESSITATES ORIGINATING GUARANTEES OF HUMAN RIGHTS AT THE NATIONAL RATHER THAN AT THE INTERNATIONAL LEVEL. INTERNATIONAL SYSTEM MUST PRIMARILY CONCERN ITSELF WITH BASIC ISSUES OF COLD WAR.

1356 HOFFMANN S.
"RESTRAINTS AND CHOICES IN AMERICAN FOREIGN POLICY."
DAEDALUS, 91 (FALL 62), 668-703.
CONTENDS THAT AMERICAN FOREIGN POLICY HAS NOT ADAPTED TO MEET THE CHALLENGES PRESENTED BY THE CHANGING WORLD SITUATION. SUGGESTS AMERICAN DEFENSIVE POSITION, POLICY OF 'GOING IT ALONE', LIBERALISM, CONSERVATISM AND IMPATIENCE ARE NOT APPROPRIATE TO NATION'S POSITION IN WORLD.

1357 HOFFMANN S.
"CE QU'EN PENSENT LES AMERICAINS."
REV. FRANC. SCI. POLIT., 2 (APR. 64), 317-23.
DISCUSSES US REACTION TO FRENCH CONTEMPORARY POLICY OF 'INDEPENDENCE' ON THE INTERNATIONAL SCENE AND THE RESULTING CHALLANGE TO US LEADERSHIP OF THE WESTERN ALLIANCE.

1358 HOFFMANN S.
"EUROPE'S IDENTITY CRISIS: BETWEEN THE PAST AND AMERICA."
DAEDALUS, (FALL 64), 1244-97.
A REVIEW OF A NUMBER OF THEORIES CONCERNING EUROPEAN-AMERICAN RELATIONS, CONCLUDING THAT THERE IS REASON TO BE CONTENT WITH A SEPARATION BASED UPON MUTUAL GOOD-WILL, UNDERSTANDING, AND FUNCTIONAL AND MILITARY COOPERATION.

1359 HOFFMANN S., ED.
CONTEMPORARY THEORY IN INTERNATIONAL RELATIONS.
ENGLEWOOD CLIFFS: PRENTICE HALL, 1960, 293 PP., LC#59-15939.
BOOK CALLS FOR THEORY IN INTERNATIONAL RELATIONS UNDERSTOOD AS A SET OF INTERRELATED QUESTIONS TO GUIDE EMPIRICAL AND NORMATIVE RESEARCH. CONTAINS SELECTED READINGS THAT ARE CRITICALLY COMMENTED ON BY THE EDITOR. FIRST PART ARGUES NEED FOR THEORY, SECOND PART DISCUSSES CONTEMPORARY APPROACHES, AND THIRD PART MAKES SUGGESTIONS FOR MORE SATISFACTORY EFFORT TOWARD THEORY.

1360 HOFMANN L. ED.
UNITED STATES AND CANADIAN PUBLICATIONS ON AFRICA IN 1964.
STANFORD: HOOVER INSTITUTE, 1966, 180 PP., LC#62-60021.
LISTS 1,183 ENTRIES, BY TOPICS AND BY REGIONS, COVERING SUB-SAHARAN AFRICA. SOME FOREIGN WORKS. SEEKS TO INCLUDE ALL US AND CANADIAN SOURCES FOR YEAR IN QUESTION. INCLUDES BIBLIOGRAPHIES. PART OF ANNUAL SERIES DATING TO 1962.

1361 HOGAN W.N.
INTERNATIONAL CONFLICT AND COLLECTIVE SECURITY: THE PRINCIPLE OF CONCERN IN INTERNATIONAL ORGANIZATION.
LEXINGTON: U OF KY PR, 1955, 202 PP., LC#55-7000.
DISCUSSES COLLECTIVE SECURITY THROUGH INTERNATIONAL ORGANIZATION BASED ON THE PRINCIPLE THAT UNILATERAL VIOLENCE AGAINST ANY MEMBER CONSTITUTES AN OFFENSE AGAINST ALL MEMBERS. ANALYZES RELEVANT TRENDS SINCE WORLD WAR I FROM VIEWPOINT OF STRUCTURE AND FUNCTION, ESPECIALLY AS APPLIED TO THE LEAGUE OF NATIONS AND THE UN.

1362 HOHENBERG J.
BETWEEN TWO WORLDS.
NEW YORK: FREDERICK PRAEGER, 1967, 507 PP., LC#66-21781.
STUDIES EFFECTS AND PROCESS OF NEWS AND OPINION EXCHANGE BETWEEN ASIA AND USA. MAJOR THESIS IS THAT EFFECT ON GOVERNMENTAL ACTION AND PUBLIC OPINION OF THE MATERIAL REPORTED BY VARIOUS MEDIA IS MAJOR, AND GREATER THAN NORMALLY ASSUMED. GIVES MUCH DETAILED INFORMATION ABOUT SOURCES, COVERAGE, INCIDENTS.

1363 HOLBO P.S.
"COLD WAR DRIFT IN LATIN AMERICA."
CURR. HIST., 44 (FEB. 63), 65-72.
REVIEWS LATIN-AMERICAN RELATIONS WITH USA. CUBAN CRISIS REVEALED AGAIN THE SUBORDINATE POSITION OF LATIN-AMERICAN COUNTRIES IN INTERNATIONAL AFFAIRS. CAN ONLY BE HOPED THAT MORE ENLIGHTENED STATESMEN WORKING WITH OFFICIALS OF OAS AND ALLIANCE FOR PROGRESS WILL OVERCOME NARROW INTERESTS.

1364 HOLBORN H.
THE POLITICAL COLLAPSE OF EUROPE.
NEW YORK: ALFRED KNOPF, 1951, 207 PP.
SKETCHES EVENTS OF EUROPEAN HISTORY FROM TIME OF POLISH PARTITIONS TO WWII. INTERPRETS TRANSFORMATION OF WORLD HISTORY AND OF EUROPEAN POLITICAL METHODS AND RELATIONS AS OWING TO WWI AND US PARTICIPATION. ASSERTS THAT US FOUNDED ERRONEOUS POLICY ON EXPECTATION OF EUROPEAN RETURN TO OLD ORDER AND PRE-WWI POLITICS, A RETURN NO LONGER POSSIBLE.

1365 HOLCOMBE A.N.
STRENGTHENING THE UNITED NATIONS.
NEW YORK: HARPER, 1957, 276 PP.
HAVING SURVEYED THE RECORD AND APPRAISED THE PROPOSALS FROM VARIOUS QUARTERS, ADVANCES THREE RECOMMENDATIONS IN ORDER TO REINFORCE THE WORLD ORGANIZATION. PROPOSES CHANGES IN UN CHARTER, INNOVATIVE MODIFICATION OF EXISTING PRACTICES IN UN STRUCTURE AND FUNCTION, AND ALTERATION OF POLICIES OF USA.

1366 HOLDSWORTH M. ED.
SOVIET AFRICAN STUDIES 1918-1959.
LONDON: ROYAL INST OF INTL AFF, 1961, 156 PP.
ANALYZES SOVIET WRITINGS ON AFRICA PUBLISHED FROM 1920 TO 1958; IN TWO PARTS: GENERAL FUNCTIONAL STUDIES, AND REGIONAL STUDIES. CONCENTRATES ON AFRICA SOUTH OF THE SAHARA. BRIEF ANNOTATIONS INDICATE CONTENTS OF INDIVIDUAL ENTRIES OR THE PARTICULAR AUTHOR'S LINE OF APPROACH. SHORT ACCOUNT OF SOVIET INSTITUTIONS CONCERNED WITH AFRICAN STUDIES IS GIVEN.

1367 HOLLAND T.E. ED.
STUDIES IN INTERNATIONAL LAW.
LONDON: OXFORD U. PR., 1898, 314 PP.
ESSAYS AND LECTURES ON THE LAW OF WAR WITH PARTICULAR EMPHASIS ON GENTILI'S IMPACT ON INTERNATIONAL LAW. TOPICS DISCUSSED INCLUDE: RELATION OF INTERNATIONAL LAW AND ACTS OF PARLIAMENT, TREATY RELATIONS BETWEEN RUSSIA AND TURKEY, AND

THE INTERNATIONAL POSITION OF THE SUEZ CANAL.

1368 HOLLAND T.E.
LETTERS UPON WAR AND NEUTRALITY.
NEW YORK: LONGMANS, 1909, 166 PP.
COLLECTION OF LETTERS, PUBLISHED IN 'THE TIMES', ON INTERNATIONAL LAW. DEALS WITH NON-MILITARY MEASURES FOR SETTLING DISPUTES, CODIFICATION OF WAR LAWS, WAR CONDUCT, RIGHTS AND DUTIES OF NEUTRALS, AND USES OF INTERNATIONAL COURTS FOR ADJUDICATION.

1369 HOLLERMAN L.
JAPAN'S DEPENDENCE ON THE WORLD ECONOMY.
PRINCETON: PRINCETON U PRESS, 1967, 291 PP., LC#66-26586.
STUDIES ENCOUNTER BETWEEN GOVERNMENTAL ECONOMIC PLANNING VIDUAL PREROGATIVES. IDENTIFIES STRUCTURAL DIFFICULTIES OF TIES OF JAPAN'S ECONOMY DURING LIBERALIZATION AND EVALUATES POLICIES ASSOCIATED WITH LIBERALIZATION.

1370 HOLLINS E.J. ED.
PEACE IS POSSIBLE: A READER FOR LAYMEN.
NEW YORK: GROSSMAN PUBL, 1966, 339 PP., LC#66-26537.
REPRINTS SPEECHES AND ESSAYS BY LEADING ECONOMISTS, LAWYERS, RELIGIOUS FIGURES, PSYCHIATRISTS, SCHOLARS, AND POLITICAL FIGURES (KENNAN, JOHN XXIII, G. MYRDAL). PRESENTS CURRENT SITUATION, SEEING WAR AS MAJOR PROBLEM; SUGGESTS OTHER PROBLEMS (POPULATION, POVERTY) MAY YIELD WHEN PEACE IS ESTABLISHED. SUGGESTIONS FOR CHANGE AND WORLD ORDER. EXPLORES DILEMMAS, INDICATES TRANSITIONAL STEPS.

1371 HOLMAN A.G.
SOME MEASURES AND INTERPRETATIONS OF EFFECTS OF US FOREIGN ENTERPRISES ON US BALANCE OF PAYMENTS.
MENLO PARK: STANFORD U RES INST, 1962, 65 PP.
SHOWS HOW US PRIVATE FOREIGN INVESTMENTS AFFECT DEFICIT IN BALANCE OF PAYMENTS. VARIABLES OF DIRECT EFFECTS INCLUDE METHODS OF FINANCING AND EXPANDING FOREIGN ENTERPRISES, EARNINGS TRANSFERRED OR REINVESTED, AND NET EFFECT OF TRADE. RESULTS INDICATE THAT BALANCE OF PAYMENTS WAS POSITIVELY AFFECTED BY US FOREIGN INVESTMENTS DURING 1950-59.

1372 HOLSTI K.J.
INTERNATIONAL POLITICS* A FRAMEWORK FOR ANALYSIS.
ENGLEWOOD CLIFFS: PRENTICE HALL, 1967, 505 PP., LC#67-19787.
PRESENTS AN INTEGRATED FRAMEWORK FOR ANALYZING THE BEHAVIOR OF STATES WITH EMPAHSIS ON THE SYSTEMATIC AND DOMESTIC SOURCES OF EXTERNAL POLITICAL GOALS, BARGAINING METHODS USED TO ACHIEVE AND DEFEND OBJECTIVES AND INTERESTS, RESTRAINTS ON POLICIES, AND BEHAVIOR AND PROCEDURES CONDUCIVE TO RESOLUTION OF INTERNATIONAL CONFLICTS. GOOD BIBLIOGRAPHIES AT CHAPTER ENDS.

1373 HOLSTI O.R.
"EAST-WEST CONFLICT AND SINO-SOVIET RELATIONS"
J OF APPLIED BEHAVIORAL SCIENCE, 1 (APR.-JUNE 65), 115-130.
EXAMINES THE HYPOTHESIS THAT A HIGH LEVEL OF INTERCOALITION CONFLICT TENDS TO INCREASE INTRACOALITION UNITY, WHEREAS MORE RELAXED RELATIONS BETWEEN BLOCS TEND TO MAGNIFY DIFFERENCES WITHIN THE ALLIANCE. SEVENTY-EIGHT DOCUMENTS WRITTEN BY LEADING CHINESE AND SOVIET DECISION-MAKERS BETWEEN 1959 AND 1963 WERE CONTENT-ANALYZED ON IBM 7090. HYPOTHESIS CONFIRMED FOR SINO-SOVIET RELATIONS.

1374 HOLT R.T.
RADIO FREE EUROPE.
MINNEAPOLIS: U. MINN. PR., 1958, 249 PP.
STUDY OF ORIGINS, ORGANIZATIONAL STRUCTURE, OPERATIONS AND PURPOSES OF RADIO FREE EUROPE. DISCUSSES PROPAGANDA CAMPAIGNS OF NETWORK FROM 1953 TO 1957 AND EVALUATES THEIR EFFECTIVENESS. CRITICIZES WASHINGTON FOR LACK OF OFFICIAL SUPPORT FOR THESE EFFORTS AND RELUCTANCE TO DEVELOP DEFINITE PROGRAM FOR LIBERATING SATELLITES. CONTENDS THEIR PEACEFUL EMANCIPATION POSSIBLE THROUGH EFFORTS OF NETWORK.

1375 HOLT R.T., VAN DE VELDE R.W.
STRATEGIC PSYCHOLOGICAL OPERATIONS AND AMERICAN FOREIGN POLICY.
CHICAGO: U OF CHICAGO PRESS, 1960, 237 PP., LC#60-14238.
ATTEMPTS TO DETERMINE ROLE OF PSYCHOLOGICAL INSTRUMENTS IN THE GENERAL PATTERN OF FOREIGN POLICY IMPLEMENTATION. DISCUSSES INTELLIGENCE OPERATIONS, ORGANIZATION, AND PERSONNEL. CASE STUDY OF US PSYCHOLOGICAL OPERATIONS IN ITALY DURING WWII AND US ELECTIONS IN 1948.

1376 HOLT R.T., TURNER J.E.
THE POLITICAL BASIS OF ECONOMIC DEVELOPMENT.
PRINCETON: VAN NOSTRAND, 1966, 411 PP.
ANALYZES ECONOMIC DEVELOPMENT AS A FUNCTION OF POLITICAL AND SOCIAL CHANGE, USING HISTORICAL EXAMPLES. COMPARES POLITICAL SYSTEMS AND THEIR RESPECTIVE EFFECTS ON CULTURE AND ECONOMIC GROWTH.

1377 HOLTON G. ED.
"ARMS CONTROL."
DAEDALUS, 89 (FALL 60), 674-1075.
COORDINATED GROUP OF PAPERS ON ART AND SCIENCE OF CONTROLLING WAR. COMPRISES HANDBOOK ON PROBLEMS OF ARMS CONTROL AND NATIONAL POLICY. ALSO INCLUDES SELECTED CRITICAL BIBLIOGRAPHY.

1378 HONEY P.J.
COMMUNISM IN NORTH VIETNAM: ITS ROLE IN THE SINO-SOVIET DISPUTE.
CAMBRIDGE: M I T PRESS, 1963, 207 PP., LC#63-22436.
STUDY OF FACTORS AFFECTING NORTH VIETNAM'S ERRATIC POLITICAL INCLINATIONS IN RELATION TO SINO-SOVIET CONFICT THAT INCLUDES NEUTRALITY AND VIET CONG OBJECTIVES.

1379 HONORD S.
PUBLIC RELATIONS IN ADMINISTRATION.
BRUSSELS: INTL INST OF ADMIN SCI, 1963, 83 PP.
BRIEF DESCRIPTION OF THE METHODS OF PUBLICATION AND DISTRIBUTION OF PUBLIC DOCUMENTS IN MORE THAN 30 COUNTRIES. DISCUSSES VARIOUS KINDS OF OFFICIAL PUBLICATIONS AS WELL AS PROBLEMS RELATING TO COPYRIGHT AND REPRODUCTION. APPENDED IS A LIST OF NATIONAL REPORTS AND A BIBLIOGRAPHY CITING PRIMARY SOURCES OF CURRENT BIBLIOGRAPHIES OF OFFICIAL PUBLICATIONS.

1380 HOOK S. ED.
WORLD COMMUNISM: KEY DOCUMENTARY MATERIAL.
ERI, 1962, 256 PP., LC#63-815.
PRESENTS THEORY AND HISTORICAL PRACTICE OF INTERNATIONAL COMMUNIST MOVEMENT BY MEANS OF RELEVANT DOCUMENTS, MOST FROM OFFICIAL COMMUNIST SOURCES. INCLUDES MATERIAL ON COMMUNISM IN USSR, US, AND IN OTHER SELECTED COUNTRIES. ALSO INCLUDES PERTINENT INTRODUCTORY MATERIALS AND ANALYSES OF RELATED EVENTS AND ACTIVITIES.

1381 HOOVER INSTITUTION
UNITED STATES AND CANADIAN PUBLICATIONS ON AFRICA.
STANFORD: HOOVER INSTITUTE.
UNANNOTATED ANNUAL LISTING (SINCE 1962) OF BOOKS, PAMPHLETS, AND SERIAL PUBLICATIONS DEALING WITH SOCIAL SCIENCES AND HUMANITIES OF SUB-SAHARA AFRICA. PART I ARRANGES ITEMS BY SUBJECT; PART II BY TYPE OF PUBLICATION UNDER SPECIFIC REGION. CONTAINS AUTHOR INDEX.

1382 HORECKY P.L.
"LIBRARY OF CONGRESS PUBLICATIONS IN AID OF USSR AND EAST EUROPEAN RESEARCH."
SLAVIC REVIEW, 23 (JAN. 64), 309-327.
AN ANNOTATED BIBLIOGRAPHY OF RESEARCH AIDS PUBLISHED BY THE LIBRARY OF CONGRESS TO ASSIST IN RESEARCHING USSR AND EAST EUROPEAN MATERIAL IN THE LIBRARY OF CONGRESS. CONTAINS ENTRIES IN ENGLISH, RANGING FROM 1929-1963.

1383 HORELICK A.L., RUSH M.
STRATEGIC POWER AND SOVIET FOREIGN POLICY.
CHICAGO: U OF CHICAGO PRESS, 1966, 225 PP., LC#66-13874.
ANALYSIS OF SOVIET MILITARY AND FOREIGN POLICY STRATEGY IN NUCLEAR AGE. EXAMINES IMPACT OF NUCLEAR POWER ON EXTENT AND TYPE OF INTERNATIONAL POLITICS AND REACTION. DISCUSSES CUBA AND BERLIN CRISES.

1384 HORMANN K.
PEACE AND MODERN WAR IN THE JUDGEMENT OF THE CHURCH.
BALTIMORE: NEWMAN PRESS, 1966, 162 PP., LC#66-16570.
HEAVILY-DOCUMENTED STUDY ON THE TEACHING OF THE ROMAN CATHOLIC CHURCH CONCERNING PEACE AND MODERN WAR. ANALYTIC DISCUSSION IS BASED ON CONTENTION THAT THE CHURCH, IN ACCORDANCE WITH WILL OF GOD, CONSIDERS HERSELF THE CUSTODIAN OF PEACE. EXAMINES ATTITUDE OF CHURCH TOWARD LEGAL ORGANIZATIONS OF PEACE, LAWFULNESS OF A JUST WAR, AND RIGHT OF MILITARY DEFENSE.

1385 HORN O.B.
BRITISH PUBLIC OPINION AND THE FIRST PARTITION OF POLAND.
EDINBURGH & LONDON: OLIVER& BOYD, 1945, 98 PP.
COLLECTS AND ANALYZES BRITISH SENTIMENT 1772 TO 1775 ON THE POLISH PREDICAMENT; SHOWS CONCLUSIVELY THAT PUBLIC OPINION SUPPORTED GOVERNMENT'S POLICY OF INACTION, AND THAT MANY FACTORS MADE IT DIFFICULT FOR ENGLAND TO ACT, NOTABLY THE LACK OF ALLIES ON THE CONTINENT; SHOWS DIFFERENCE BETWEEN 18TH- AND 19TH-CENTURY VIEWS OF POLAND.

1386 HORNE D.
THE LUCKY COUNTRY: AUSTRALIA TODAY.
BALTIMORE: PENGUIN BOOKS, 1964, 223 PP.
JOURNALISTIC LOOK AT AUSTRALIAN CULTURE, SOCIAL STRUCTURE, AND POLITICAL SYSTEM. DISCUSSES POWER STRUCTURE OF THE SIXTIES AND PLURALITY OF POLITICAL AND SOCIAL INSTITUTIONAL RELATIONSHIPS MODELED ON GREAT BRITAIN'S. ANALYZES KEY ISSUES OF AUSTRALIAN DOMESTIC AND FOREIGN POLICY: RACE RELATIONS AND ALLIANCES WITH WEST AND EAST.

1387 HOROWITZ D.
HEMISPHERES NORTH AND SOUTH: ECONOMIC DISPARITY AMONG NATIONS.
BALTIMORE: JOHNS HOPKINS PRESS, 1966, 118 PP., LC#66-23002.
ATTEMPTS TO CONSTRUCT BRIDGE BETWEEN NEW ECONOMICS AND REALITIES OF SITUATION IN WORLD DIVIDED BETWEEN HAVES AND

HAVE-NOTS, AND TO JOIN ECONOMIC AND POLITICAL ACTION TOWARD IMPLEMENTATION OF A POLICY OF CHANGE. PROPOSES THAT INTERESTS OF DEVELOPING NATIONS RECEIVE PRIORITY IN POLICY EVEN AT PRICE OF SLIGHT SLOWING DOWN IN EXPANSION OF RICH NATIONS.

1388 HOROWITZ I.L.
REVOLUTION IN BRAZIL.
NEW YORK: EP DUTTON, 1964, 430 PP., LC#64-13916.
EXAMINES ECONOMIC, SOCIAL, AND POLITICAL CHANGES IN BRAZIL TODAY. AUTHOR ANALYZES 20TH-CENTURY DEVELOPMENT AND INCLUDES OBSERVATIONS OF BRAZILIAN SOCIAL SCIENTISTS AND POLITICAL LEADERS ON NEED FOR CHANGES IN ECONOMIC AND POLITICAL STRUCTURE AND BRAZIL'S POSITION IN WORLD AFFAIRS.

1389 HORVATH J.
"MOSCOW'S AID PROGRAM: THE PERFORMANCE SO FAR."
EAST EUROPE, 12(NOV. 63), 8-24.
EXAMINES WHAT THE SOVIET BLOC HAS ACCOMPLISHED SO FAR IN THE EXPORT OF MACHINERY AND TECHNIQUES. CONCLUDES THAT 'THE OVERRIDING OBJECTIVE IS NOT SO MUCH TO HELP THE NEW NATIONS EMERGE FROM ECONOMIC BACK-WARDNESS AS IT IS TO SPEED THEIR TRANSITION FROM BACK-WARDNESS TO SOCIALISM.'

1390 HOSCH L.G.
"PUBLIC ADMINISTRATION ON THE INTERNATIONAL FRONTIER."
PUB. PERSON. REV., 25 (JULY 64), 165-70.
SINCE EARLY IN ITS EXISTENCE, THE UN HAS BEEN HELPING GOVERNMENTS EAGER TO IMPROVE ADMINISTRATIVE PRACTICES. EXAMINES THE WORLD-WIDE INTEREST IN THIS AREA AND WHAT INTERNATIONAL AGENCIES ARE DOING TO SPUR ITS GROWTH.

1391 HOSELITZ B.F. ED.
THE PROGRESS OF UNDERDEVELOPED AREAS.
CHICAGO: U. CHI. PR., 1952, 297 PP.
SPECIALISTS IN VARIOUS SOCIAL SCIENCES CONSIDER PROBLEMS OF RENDERING ECONOMIC AID TO UNDERDEVELOPED COUNTRIES. INDICATE THAT ECONOMIC DEVELOPMENT IS A PROBLEM AREA WITH DIMENSIONS IN SEVERAL SOCIAL SCIENCE FIELDS. STRESS HUMAN IMPLICATIONS OF TECHNOLOGICAL AND ECONOMIC CHANGE.

1392 HOSELITZ B.F. ED.
ECONOMICS AND THE IDEA OF MANKIND.
NEW YORK: COLUMB. U. PR., 1965, 277 PP., $6.95.
ESSAYS BASED ON ASSUMPTION THAT MANKIND INTERDEPENDENT. STUDY HOW MANKIND WOULD FUNCTION AS WHOLE IN PRODUCTION, DISTRIBUTION, AND CONSUMPTION OF GOODS AND WHAT WOULD CHARACTERIZE SUCH AN ECONOMY.

1393 HOSKYNS C.
"THE AFRICAN STATES AND THE UNITED NATIONS: 1958-1964."
INT. AFF., 40 (JULY 64), 466-80.
AFRICAN STATES REGARD UNITED NATIONS AS INDISPENSIBLE IN FORMULATING AND CARRYING OUT THEIR FOREIGN POLICY. ACTIVITY AND INFLUENCE OF AFRICAN GROUP HAS PASSED THROUGH FOUR STAGES. PRESENT PERIOD REVEALS INFLUENTIAL UNITED GROUP, ESPECIALLY IN PRESSING UNITED NATIONS FOR FURTHER ACTIONS AGAINST SOUTH AFRICA.

1394 HOSMAR J.K.
A SHORT HISTORY OF ANGLO-SAXON FREEDOM.
NEW YORK: CHAS SCRIBNER'S SONS, 1890, 420 PP.
CONSTITUTIONAL HISTORY FROM ROMAN TIMES TO PRESENT, INCLUDING CONQUEST OF BRITAIN, MAGNA CARTA AND RISE OF PARLIAMENT, SETTLEMENT OF AMERICA, REVOLUTION OF 1688, AMERICAN REVOLUTION, US CONSTITUTION, AND FRATERNITY OF ENGLISH-SPEAKING PEOPLES.

1395 HOUSTON J.A.
LATIN AMERICA IN THE UNITED NATIONS.
NEW YORK: CARNEGIE ENDOWMENT, 1956, 660 PP.
VIEWS PARTICIPATION OF LATIN AMERICAN REPUBLICS IN LAYING FOUNDATIONS FOR FUNCTIONING OF UNITED NATIONS. DEALS WITH THOSE AREAS OF PARTICULAR LATIN AMERICAN INTEREST, INDICAT-ING AMOUNT OF AGREEMENT OF DIVERGENCE AMONG STATES ON PAR-TICULAR ISSUES.

1396 HOVET T. JR.
BLOC POLITICS IN THE UNITED NATIONS.
CAMBRIDGE: HARVARD U PR, 1960, 197 PP., LC#60-7993.
STUDIES ALLIANCES, REGIONAL ASSOCIATIONS, COMMON MAR-KETS, AND EMERGING FEDERATIONS, AND THEIR ROLE WITHIN UN. BASED ON COMPREHENSIVE COLLECTION OF STATISTICS OF UN VOTES MAINTAINED AT NEW YORK UNIVERSITY. EXAMINES BLOCS AND GROUPS ACTING SEPARATELY AND IN COALITION. DISCUSSES POLICY IMPLICATIONS.

1397 HOVET T. JR.
AFRICA IN THE UNITED NATIONS.
EVANSTON: NORTHWEST. U. PR., 1963, 336 PP., $8.50.
DETAILED ANALYSES AND INTERPRETATION OF THE VOTING RECORDS OF THE AFRICAN MEMBERS IN THE GENERAL ASSEMBLY. PRESENTS A NUMBER OF MEASURES OF COHESION OF THE AFRICAN CAUCUSING GROUP AS A WHOLE AND OF ITS SUB-GROUPS. EXAMINES AFRICAN IMPACT ON U.N. POLICY AND ON THE POLICIES OF OTHER MEMBERS. THE 66 PERCENT AGREEMENT OF AFRICAN WITH SOVIET BLOC VOTING IS FOUND TO REFLECT SOVIET ADHERENCE TO THE AFRICAN 'LINE' RATHER THAN VICE VERSA.

1398 HOVET T. JR.
"THE ROLE OF AFRICA IN THE UNITED NATIONS."
ANN. AMER. ACAD. POLIT. SOC. SCI., 354 (JULY 64), 122-34.
THE IMPACT OF AFRICA IN THE UN HAS BEEN TO SHIFT EMPHASIS FROM EAST-WEST TO NORTH-SOUTH DIFFERENCES, WITH PARTICULAR STRESS ON MORAL-POLITICAL ISSUES, BASIC SOCIAL AND ECONOMIC PROBLEMS. OVERALL, AFRICAN STATES HAVE CONDUCTED THEMSELVES IN A POLITICALLY RESPONSIBLE MANNER AND CAN BE EXPECTED TO CONTINUE TO DO SO.

1399 HOWARD J.E.
PARLIAMENT AND FOREIGN POLICY IN FRANCE.
LONDON: CRESSET PRESS, 1948, 172 PP.
STUDY OF ORIGINS, NATURE, AND METHODS OF PARLIAMENTARY CONTROL OF FOREIGN POLICY DURING THIRD FRENCH REPUBLIC. FOCUSES ON PERIOD 1919-39. DISCUSSES LEGAL AND HISTORICAL BASIS OF CONTROL, SHOWING CONSTITUTIONAL ORIGINS. SHOWS THAT ALTHOUGH THE ELECTORATE MAINTAINED SOME VOICE IN FOREIGN POLICY, PUBLIC ATTITUDES RENDERED POSSIBLE THE INCREASING CONTROL BY THE CHAMBERS OF PARLIAMENT.

1400 HOWARD M.
"MILITARY POWER AND INTERNATIONAL ORDER."
INT. AFF., 40 (JULY 64), 397-408.
'MILITARY POWER... INTRINSIC PART OF THE STRUCTURE OF INTERNATIONAL ORDER' BUT MUST REASSESS USE IN AGE OF MASS WAR. SUPPORTS SUBORDINATION OF MILITARY TO POLITICAL ACTIVITIES AND EXPRESSES INTEREST IN CONCEPT OF LIMITED WAR.

1401 HOWARD-ELLIS C.
THE ORIGIN, STRUCTURE AND WORKING OF THE LEAGUE OF NATIONS.
LONDON: ALLEN UNWIN, 1928, 528 PP.
FOCUSES ATTENTION ON INTERNATIONAL LABOR ORGANIZATION AND COURT OF JUSTICE. ASSERTS THAT PRIMARY FUNCTION OF LEAGUE IS TO ELIMINATE WAR AND CREATE AN EFFECTIVE WORLD SOCIETY.

1402 HOYT E.C.
"UNITED STATES REACTION TO THE KOREAN ATTACK."
AMER. J. INT. LAW, 55 (JANUARY 1961), 45-76.
CASE STUDY OF LEGAL PRINCIPLES OF UNITED NATIONS CHARTER AS BOTH A RESTRAINING FORCE AND AN INCENTIVE TO ACTION IN UNITED STATES REACTION TO 1950 COMMUNIST ATTACK IN KOREA. OUTLINES PERTINENT PRINCIPLES, AND CONSIDERS BASIS OF USA ACTION AND ITS DOMESTIC AND INTERNATIONAL CONSEQUENCES. DISCUSSES LEGAL METHODS OF LIMITING CONFLICT AND SUGGESTS THEIR APPLICATION TO KOREA MIGHT HAVE REDUCED SCOPE OF WAR.

1403 HUBER G.
DIE FRANZOSISCHE PROPAGANDA IM WELTKRIEG GEGEN DEUTSCHLAND 1914 BIS 1918.
MUNICH: F A PFEIFFER VERLAG, 1928, 314 PP.
STUDY OF FRENCH PROPAGANDA DURING WWI. DISCUSSES THE GERMAN MENTALITY, GERMAN WAR AIMS,AND GERMAN NATURE AS THE SUBJECTS OF FRENCH PROPAGANDA. NEWSPAPERS, BOOKS, MAGAZINES AND LEAFLETS ARE MAIN MEDIA DISCUSSED.

1404 HUDSON G.F., LOWENTHAL R. ET AL.
THE SINO-SOVIET DISPUTE.
NEW YORK: FREDERICK PRAEGER, 1961, 227 PP., LC#61-15894.
DOCUMENTARY ANALYSIS OF SINO-SOVIET DISPUTE OVER GLOBAL POLICIES BETWEEN 1960 AND 1961. CONTAINS SPEECHES, NEWSPAPER EXTRACTS, RESOLUTIONS, ETC.

1405 HUDSON G.F.
"THE HARD AND BITTER PEACE; WORLD POLITICS SINCE 1945."
NEW YORK: FREDERICK PRAEGER, 1967.
CONTEMPORARY HISTORY OF WORLD POLITICS SINCE 1945 WHICH ATTEMPTS TO DISCERN MAIN THEMES OF THE AGE AND INTERPRET THEIR PRESENT AND FUTURE SIGNIFICANCE. ARGUES THAT AS LONG AS THERE EXISTS NO WORLD GOVERNMENT, RELATIONS BETWEEN STATES MUST OPERATE IN TERMS OF THEIR ACTUAL OR POTENTIAL CAPACITY FOR WAGING WAR. PARTIALLY ANNOTATED BIBLIOGRAPHY OF WORKS CITED IN TEXT AND FURTHER READINGS.

1406 HUDSON M.O.
"THE PERMANENT COURT OF INTERNATIONAL JUSTICE AND THE QUES-TION OF AMERICAN PARTICIPATION."
CAMBRIDGE: HARVARD U. PR., 1925, 389 PP.
A COLLECTION OF PAPERS ON ESTABLISHMENT OF THE COURT, AN-NUAL REPORTS OF ACTIVITY AND THE QUESTION OF AMERICA'S RE-LATION TO COURT. CONTAINS APPENDIX OF PERTINENT DOCUMENTS. COURT AIDS PEACE BY SETTLING DISPUTES AND BY BUILDING UP BODY OF INTERNATIONAL CASE LAW.

1407 HUDSON M.O.
BY PACIFIC MEANS.
NEW HAVEN: YALE U. PR., 1935, 200 PP.
DESCRIBES AND ENUMERATES THE PACIFIC MEANS AVAILABLE TO PARTIES IN DISPUTES: THE LEAGUE, THE PERMANENT COURT OF INTERNATIONAL JUSTICE AND TREATIES ON PACIFIC SETTLEMENT

PRIOR TO AND SINCE 1920. EXPLORES IMPLEMENTATIONS OF BRIAND-KELLOGG PACT.

1408 HUDSON M.O.
INTERNATIONAL TRIBUNALS PAST AND FUTURE.
WASHINGTON: CARNEGIE ENDOWMENT, 1944, 287 PP.
SKETCHES EVOLUTION OF INTERNATIONAL TRIBUNALS FROM 1794 TO PRESENT AND DEALS EXTENSIVELY WITH GENERAL PROBLEMS OF INTERNATIONAL TRIBUNALS CONCERNING STRUCTURE AND SCOPE OF ACTION. ALSO PRESENTS SUGGESTIONS FOR FUTURE TREATMENT OF PRESENT PROBLEMS OF ADJUDICATION. THESIS IS THAT ADMINISTRATION OF INTERNATIONAL LAW MUST BE FRAMEWORK OF INTERNATIONAL RELATIONS.

1409 HUDSON M.O. ED.
INTERNATIONAL LEGISLATION: 1929-1931.
WASHINGTON: CARNEGIE ENDOWMENT, 1936, 1180 PP.
SUBTITLED "A COLLECTION OF THE TEXTS OF MULTIPARTITE INTERNATIONAL INSTRUMENTS OF GENERAL INTEREST." UNIFORM PRESENTATION OF LEGISLATIVE INSTRUMENTS NEEDED IN INTERNATIONAL LAW; FOCUSES ON LEGISLATIVE PROCESS AS ONE OF CHIEF METHODS IN 20TH-CENTURY INTERNATIONAL LAW. INCLUDES INTERNATIONAL LABOR CONVENTIONS, PAYMENT OF REPARATIONS, MARITIME LAW, WAR, ARBITRATION, AND CONCILIATION.

1410 HUDSON R.
"WAS THIS WAR NECESSARY? THE UN AND THE MIDDLE EAST"
WAR/PEACE REPORT, 7 (JUNE 67), 3-6.
DEALS WITH EVENTS LEADING UP TO MIDDLE EAST CRISIS OF JUNE, 1967, AND WAYS IN WHICH UN MANAGED CRISIS. SUGGESTS IMPROVEMENTS IN POWER STRUCTURE OF UN, ESPECIALLY REMOVAL OF VETO POWER, THAT WOULD ALLOW MORE CONSTRUCTIVE FUNCTIONING. ADVOCATES FOUNDING OF PEACE-KEEPING MAJORITY THAT COULD CONSTITUTE BINDING DECISIONS ON PROBLEMS OF WAR.

1411 HUELIN D.
"ECONOMIC INTEGRATION IN LATIN AMERICAN: PROGRESS AND PROBLEMS."
INT. AFF., 40 (JULY 64), 430-439.
LATIN AMERICA'S ECONOMIC AND SOCIAL PROBLEMS RELATED TO FAILURE OF REGION TO MAINTAIN SHARE IN WORLD TRADE. LATIN AMERICAN FREE TRADE ASSOCIATION REALIZES FUTURE OF ECONOMIC INTEGRATION LIES IN SIGNIFICANTLY EXPANDING MARKET OF MANUFACTURED GOODS.

1412 HUGENDUBEL P.
DIE KRIEGSMACHE DER FRANZOSISCHEN PRESSE.
BERLIN: GEORG STILKE, 1936, 153 PP.
STUDY OF THE INFLUENCE OF FRENCH PRESS ON THE DEVELOPMENT AND EVENTUAL ERUPTION OF WWI. DISCUSSES POWER OF PUBLIC OPINION IN FRANCE AND CITES EVIDENCE IN SUPPORT OF FRENCH PRESS AGITATION TO CREATE AN IMAGE OF A MILITARISTIC GERMANY.

1413 HUGHES E.M.
AMERICA THE VINCIBLE.
GARDEN CITY: DOUBLEDAY, 1959, 306 PP., LC#59-9783.
EXAMINES US FOREIGN POLICY AND ATTEMPTS TO EXPLAIN TODAY'S PREDICAMENTS. SUGGESTS THAT IMPROVEMENT OF INTERNATIONAL RELATIONS ON PERSONAL LEVEL MIGHT HELP SOLVE COLD WAR PROBLEMS. FEELS US "POWER" POLICIES INCREASE TENSION.

1414 HULL E.W.S.
"THE POLITICAL OCEAN."
FOREIGN AFFAIRS, 45 (APR. 67), 492-502.
PREDICTS THAT THE OCEANS WILL ASSUME NEW DIMENSIONS AMONG INTERNATIONAL PROBLEMS. NEW USES OF SEA RESOURCES WILL PRODUCE VAST ECONOMIC, POLITICAL, TECHNOLOGICAL, AND INDUSTRIAL CHANGES. ADVOCATES INTERNATIONAL ADMINISTRATION OF LAWS TO PROTECT THE OCEANS SO THAT ALL NATIONS WILL BENEFIT FROM RESOURCES. OCEANOGRAPHY CAN SERVE AS BRIDGE FOR CONTACT AND COOPERATION IN THE FUTURE TO TRANSCEND NATIONAL INTERESTS.

1415 HUMPHREY D.D.
THE UNITED STATES AND THE COMMON MARKET.
NEW YORK: PRAEGER, 1962, 176 PP.
TRADE IS AN IMPORTANT MEANS OF SUPPORTING BASIC FOREIGN POLICY AND BUILDING INTERNATIONAL ORDER. THE COMMON MARKET HAS PRESENTED A PROBLEM TO OUR TRADE POLICY. USING AN ANALYTIC APPROACH, REFUTES U.S. PROTECTIVE ATTITUDE AND SUGGESTS TRADE EXPANSION THROUGH TARIFF REDUCTION. CONTENDS THAT, IN THIS WAY, USA WILL MAINTAIN INDUSTRIAL LEADERSHIP AND HIGH STANDARD OF LIVING.

1416 HUMPHREY H.H.
"REGIONAL ARMS CONTROL AGREEMENTS."
J. CONFL. RESOLUT., 7 (SEPT. 63), 265-71.
SEES SUBJECT OF ARMS CONTROL AS BEING CLEARLY RELATED TO THAT OF DISARMAMENT AND CRITICIZES POLICY-MAKERS FOR ATTEMPTING TO TREAT EACH ONE EXCLUSIVELY. ARGUES FOR SERIOUS ATTEMPTS AT REGIONAL ARMS CONTROL AGREEMENTS AND CONSIDERS PROSPECTS FOR DENUCLEARIZATION ZONE IN LATIN AMERICA.

1417 HUMPHREYS R.A.
LATIN AMERICAN HISTORY: A GUIDE TO THE LITERATURE IN ENGLISH.
LONDON: OXFORD U PR, 1958, 197 PP.
SELECTIVE GUIDE COVERS LITERATURE ON ANCIENT PERIODS AND CULTURE THROUGH MODERN LATIN AMERICA. HISTORY INTERPRETED HERE AS EXCLUDING ARCHAEOLOGY, ETHNOLOGY, GEOGRAPHY, AND LITERATURE. INCLUDES LIST OF PERIODICAL PUBLICATIONS, AUTHOR INDEX, AND BIOGRAPHICAL INDEX.

1418 HUNT B.I.
BIPARTISANSHIP: A CASE STUDY OF THE FOREIGN ASSISTANCE PROGRAM, 1947-56 (DOCTORAL THESIS)
AUSTIN: U OF TEXAS PR, 1958, 455 PP.
STUDY OF PERIOD IN WHICH FOREIGN ASSISTANCE POLICIES WERE FORMULATED AND CARRIED OUT ON BIPARTISAN BASIS. PARTICULAR ATTENTION GIVEN TO PROGRAMS OF AID TO GREECE AND TURKEY, THE MARSHALL PLAN, NATO, MUTUAL DEFENSE ASSISTANCE ACT OF 1951, AND MUTUAL SECURITY ACT.

1419 HUNTINGTON S.P. ED.
CHANGING PATTERNS OF MILITARY POLITICS.
NEW YORK: FREE PRESS, 1962, 272 PP.
THEORETICAL ESSAYS AND EMPIRICAL STUDIES RELATED TO EACH OTHER BY UNDERLYING CONTINUUM OF EVOLUTION OF NEW CIVIL-MILITARY RELATIONSHIP. RANGE OF SUBJECT MATTER INCLUDES REVOLUTIONARY PATTERNS OF VIOLENCE, RE-EVALUATION OF THE GARRISON STATE, ANALYSIS OF MILITARY BEHAVIOR IN INTERNATIONAL ORGANIZATIONS, COMPARISON OF CIVIL AND MILITARY TYPES, AND A CRITIQUE OF POLITICS IN THE NATIONAL GUARD.

1420 HURST C.
GREAT BRITAIN AND THE DOMINIONS.
CHICAGO: U. CHI. PR., 1928, 511 PP.
DISCUSSES INTERNATIONAL AND DOMESTIC RELATIONS OF BRITISH EMPIRE. EMPHASIS ON EMPIRE AS POLITICAL UNIT ALTHOUGH SPECIFIC NATIONAL CHARACTERISTICS ARE EXPLORED IN DEPTH.

1421 HUSS P.J., CARPOZI G.J. JR.
RED SPIES IN THE UN.
NEW YORK: COWARD MCCANN, 1965, 287 PP., LC#65-13278.
SEEKS TO CALL US ATTENTION TO ESPIONAGE INCIDENTS AND SPECIFIES CASES WHICH THREATEN CAUSE OF INTERNATIONAL PEACE. CITES DISCOVERY OF RUSSIAN SUBMARINES OFF US EASTERN COAST, KHRUSCHEV VISIT, COLD WAR ESPIONAGE TACTICS, AND CUBAN SABOTEURS.

1422 HUSSEY W.D.
THE BRITISH EMPIRE AND COMMONWEALTH 1500 TO 1961.
NEW YORK: CAMBRIDGE U PRESS, 1963, 363 PP.
HISTORY OF BRITISH EMPIRE AND COMMONWEALTH, PERIOD 1500-1961. INCLUDES FIRST SETTLEMENTS IN NORTH AMERICA; ENGLISH EAST INDIA COMPANY; OLD EMPIRE; LOSS OF AMERICAN COLONIES; SECOND BRITISH EMPIRE OF AUSTRALIA; NEW ZEALAND; SOUTHERN AFRICA; WEST INDIES; TROPICAL AFRICA; INDIA; AND PROTECTORATES.

1423 HUTCHINSON E.C.
"AMERICAN AID TO AFRICA."
ANN. AMER. ACAD. POLIT. SOC. SCI., 354 (JULY 64), 65-74.
ARBITRARY BOUNDARIES, TRIBALISM, ILLITERACY, ABSENCE OF NECESSARY ECONOMIC AND SOCIAL INSTITUTIONS, AND CONTRASTING DEVELOPMENT POTENTIALS ARE SOME OBSTACLES TO ECONOMIC DEVELOPMENT. SUGGESTS USA CONCENTRATE ON INCREASING VOLUME AND DEVELOPMENT OF INTERNAL MARKET BY IMPROVED DISTRIBUTION OF PRODUCTS AND BY BUILDING UP LOCAL INDUSTRIES.

1424 HUTTENBACH R.A.
BRITISH IMPERIAL EXPERIENCE.
NEW YORK: HARPER & ROW, 1966, 225 PP., LC#66-15671.
TRACES HISTORY OF BRITISH EMPIRE CHARTERING OF EAST INDIA COMPANY TO FOUNDATION OF COMMONWEALTH. DELINEATES TWO PERIODS OF IMPERIALISM: MERCANTILIST, ENDING ABOUT 1800, AND COMMERCIAL OR "SECOND BRITISH EMPIRE," FOUNDED ON AMBITIONS TO INCREASE FAR EASTERN TRADE. DISCUSSES HOW COURSE OF EVENTS THRUST EMPIRE INTO UNINTENTIONAL INVOLVEMENT.

1425 HUTTENBACK R.A.
BRITISH RELATIONS WITH THE SIND, 1799-1843.
BERKELEY: U OF CALIF PR, 1962, 161 PP., LC#62-9266.
ANALYZES IMPERIALISTIC POLICIES OF GREAT BRITAIN IN RELATION TO 18TH- AND 19TH-CENTURY INDIA. DISCUSSES FRENCH THREAT TO BRITISH IMPERIALISM, ESTABLISHMENT OF BRITAIN'S IMPERIAL POWER, THE ANNEXATION, AND ITS RESULTS THROUGH 1850. CONTENDS ANGLO-SIND RELATIONS VERIFY INCONSISTENCY OF GOVERNMENTAL POLICY TOWARD IMPERIAL DOMAIN.

1426 HYDE C.C.
INTERNATIONAL LAW, CHIEFLY AS INTERPRETED AND APPLIED BY THE UNITED STATES (3 VOLS., 2ND REV. ED.)
BOSTON: LITTLE BROWN, 1947, 2489 PP.
PORTRAYS US VIEWS ON INTERNATIONAL LAW UP UNTIL 1941. OBSERVES HOW STATES ACT AND MAY BE EXPECTED TO ACT UNDER CERTAIN CONDITIONS. DISCUSSES CERTAIN ASPECTS OF INTERNATIONAL LAW, CLASSIFICATION OF STATES, NORMAL RIGHTS AND DUTIES, NATIONALITY, DIPLOMATIC INTERCOURSE, WAR, ETC.

1427 HYDE D.

THE PEACEFUL ASSAULT.
CHESTER SPRINGS: DUFOUR, 1963, 127 PP., LC#63-21146.
STUDIES NEW TACTICS OF USSR TO EXPORT COMMUNISM THROUGH SUBVERSION AND ECONOMIC PENETRATION. EXAMINES RATIONALE OF PEACEFUL CO-EXISTENCE AND BURYING CAPITALISM. USES EGYPT AS A CASE STUDY.

1428 HYDE L.K.G.
THE US AND THE UN.
NEW YORK: MANHATTAN, 1960, 249 PP.
ATTEMPTS TO GIVE THE READER SOME IDEA OF ACTION TAKEN BY USA DURING THE DECADE 1945-55 TO ADVANCE AMERICAN FOREIGN POLICY OBJECTIVES IN SOCIAL AND ECONOMIC FIELDS. EXPLORES THE REFUGEE PROBLEM, AND THE EFFORTS FOR ACHIEVING A FINANCIAL AID PLAN.

1429 HYVARINEN R.
"MONISTIC AND PLURALISTIC INTERPRETATIONS IN THE STUDY OF INTERNATIONAL POLITICS."
SOCIETAS SCIENTIARUM FENNICA, 24 (1958), 5-157.
AN EXAMINATION OF SELECTED CONCEPTIONS CONCERNING INTERNATIONAL POLITICS FROM VIEWPOINT OF SIGNIFICANCE UPON THE GENERAL METHODOLOGICAL PROBLEMS ENCOUNTERED IN POLITICAL SCIENCE. CRITICAL EXAMINATION OF MONISTIC INTERPRETATIONS OF GEOGRAPHICAL THEORIES, RACE THEORIES, AND THEORIES OF IMPERIALISM; ATTENTION DEVOTED TO PLURALISTIC THEORIES AS WELL. EXTENSIVE UNANNOTATED BIBLIOGRAPHY, TOPICALLY ARRANGED.

1430 IBERO-AMERICAN INSTITUTES
IBEROAMERICANA.
STOCKHOLM: IBERO-AMER INST, 1964.
BIBLIOGRAPHIC COMPILATION OF BOOKS AND PAMPHLETS IN THE LIBRARIES OF THE IBERO-AMERICAN INSTITUTES OF STOCKHOLM AND GOTHENBURG. ITEMS ARRANGED BY AUTHOR, COUNTRY, AND SUBJECT.

1431 ICHHEISER G.
"MISUNDERSTANDING IN INTERNATIONAL RELATIONS."
AMER. SOCIOL. REV., 16 (JUNE 51), 311-16.
DISCUSSES 'DYNAMIC SYSTEMS' OF INTERRELATION BETWEEN CULTURE, EMOTIONS AND PERCEPTION, AND OF 'LIMITS OF INSIGHT' WHICH HE CONSIDERS AS BASIC TO INTERCULTURAL AND INTERNATIONAL MISUNDERSTANDING. ALSO DEALS WITH TWO TYPES OF NATIONALISM, 'CONSCIOUS' AND 'UNCONSCIOUS', WHICH FURTHER CONTRIBUTE TO CONFUSION, WITH PARTICULAR EMPHASIS ON THE LATTER, OFTEN FOUND AMONG THE 'OBJECTIVE' AND UNPREJUDICED.

1432 IKLE F.C.
"NTH COUNTRIES AND DISARMAMENT."
BULL. AT. SCI., 16 (DEC. 60), 391-94.
PRESENTS COUNTERARGUMENTS TO GENERAL PROPOSALS FOR CONTROLLING SPREAD OF NUCLEAR WEAPONS. CITES RELUCTANCE OF SMALLER POWERS TO STARTING NUCLEAR WAR FOR FEAR OF MAJOR POWERS. NOTES LIMITATIONS OF ATTEMPTS TO ENFORCE UNIVERSAL TEST BAN AND CONTENDS ENFORCEMENT MAY BE EASIER FOR INTERNATIONAL BODIES TO ACCOMPLISH AS EVEN MORE COUNTRIES ACQUIRE NUCLEAR CAPABILITIES.

1433 IKLE F.C.
HOW NATIONS NEGOTIATE.
NEW YORK: HARPER ROW, 1964, 272 PP., $5.95.
RELATES THE PROCESS OF INTERNATIONAL NEGOTIATION TO ITS POSSIBLE OUTCOMES. DESCRIBES HOW NATIONS NEGOTIATE FOR SIDE EFFECTS, HOW THEY ARE CONTROLLED BY THEIR REPUTATIONS AS BARGAINERS, HOW THEY ARE STEERED BY PRESSURE GROUPS WITHIN THEIR OWN COUNTRIES, AND HOW NEGOTIATION IS EFFECTED BY DIFFERENT PERSONALITY TYPES.

1434 IMF AND IBRD, JOINT LIBRARY
LIST OF RECENT ADDITIONS.
JOINT LIBRARY OF IMF AND IBRD.
MONTHLY PUBLICATION LISTING RECENT BOOKS, GOVERNMENT DOCUMENTS, MONOGRAPHS, AND ANNUAL REPORTS RELATING TO NATIONAL AND INTERNATIONAL BANKING AND ECONOMICS. PUBLICATIONS PRIMARILY IN ENGLISH. ENTRIES ARRANGED ALPHABETICALLY BY AUTHOR AND BY COUNTRY. FIRST PUBLISHED 1947.

1435 IMF AND IBRD, JOINT LIBRARY
LIST OF RECENT PERIODICAL ARTICLES.
JOINT LIBRARY OF IMF AND IBRD.
MONTHLY PUBLICATION, BEGUN IN 1947, LISTING RECENT PERIODICAL ARTICLES PERTAINING TO INTERNATIONAL BANKING AND ECONOMICS. ENGLISH-LANGUAGE TITLES PRIMARILY. ENTRIES ARRANGED BY TOPIC: ECONOMIC THEORY, DESCRIPTIVE ECONOMICS, AND MATERIALS ON INTERNATIONAL MONETARY FUND, INTERNATIONAL DEVELOPMENT ASSOCIATION, AND INTERNATIONAL BANK FOR RECONSTRUCTION AND DEVELOPMENT.

1436 IMLAH A.H.
ECONOMIC ELEMENTS IN THE PAX BRITANNICA.
CAMBRIDGE: HARVARD U. PR., 1958, 224 PP.
STUDIES BRITISH FOREIGN TRADE IN 19TH CENTURY AS TO LONG-RANGE ECONOMIC POLICIES. NOTES THE IMPORTANCE OF BRITISH FREE-TRADE POLICY IN PROMOTING WORLD PEACE AFTER NAPOLEONIC WARS. COMPARES 19TH CENTURY BRITISH POLICY TO POST WW 1 AMERICAN ATTITUDES. CONCENTRATES ON EXAMINATION OF ECONOMICS OF BRITAIN'S FOREIGN TRADE.

1437 INDIAN COUNCIL WORLD AFFAIRS
SELECT ARTICLES ON CURRENT AFFAIRS (BIBLIOGRAPHICAL SERIES: 7)
NEW DELHI: INDIAN SCH INTL STUD, 1956.
YEARLY PUBLICATION FIRST PUBLISHED IN 1956. CONTAINS EXTENSIVE SELECT REFERENCES TO PERIODICAL LITERATURE ON INTERNATIONAL AFFAIRS, THE UNITED NATIONS, COMMONWEALTH, COMMUNIST BLOC, WESTERN BLOC, UNDERDEVELOPED AREAS, POLITICAL IDEOLOGIES. REFERENCES ALSO TO PARTICULAR EUROPEAN, ASIAN, AFRICAN, AND MIDDLE EASTERN COUNTRIES. ARTICLES ENTIRELY IN ENGLISH.

1438 INDIAN COUNCIL WORLD AFFAIRS
DEFENCE AND SECURITY IN THE INDIAN OCEAN AREA.
NEW DELHI: IND COUNCIL WORLD AFF, 1958, 180 PP.
STUDIES COUNTRIES BORDERING INDIAN OCEAN. COVERS GEOGRAPHY, ECONOMIC BASES OF MILITARY SECURITY, PEOPLES, GROUP AND SEPARATE PROBLEMS OF COUNTRIES, ARMAMENTS AND ARMED FORCES, INTERESTS OF OUTSIDE POWERS, AND REGIONAL PROBLEMS OF SECURITY.

1439 INGHAM K.
A HISTORY OF EAST AFRICA.
LONDON: LONGMANS, GREEN & CO, 1962, 458 PP.
HISTORY OF EAST AFRICA FROM ANCIENT TIMES TO MODERN CONSTITUTIONAL DEVELOPMENT AND EMERGENCE OF AFRICAN NATIONALISM. INCLUDES CHAPTERS ON EAST AFRICA, INTERNATIONAL DIPLOMACY, COLONIAL ADMINISTRATION, THE SECOND WORLD WAR, AND POLITICS AND ADMINISTRATION FROM 1919-1939. CHARTS, MAPS, AND SELECT BIBLIOGRAPHY IN ENGLISH AND FRENCH.

1440 INGLEHART R.
"AN END TO EUROPEAN INTEGRATION."
AM. POL. SCI. REV., 61 (MAR. 67), 91-105.
REPLY TO EARLIER ARTICLE CONCLUDING THAT PROCESS OF INTEGRATION HAD STOPPED IN EUROPE. USING SAME DATA, THIS ARTICLE CLAIMS ONLY RECENTLY HAS PROCESS BECOME FULL SCALE. INTERPRETATION IS BASED ON PUBLIC OPINION POLLS AS WELL AS ACTUAL RESULTS ACHIEVED IN INTERNATIONAL RELATIONS.

1441 INGRAM D.
COMMONWEALTH FOR A COLOUR-BLIND WORLD.
NEW YORK: HUMANITIES PRESS, 1965, 224 PP.
DISCUSSES OPPORTUNITIES PROVIDED BY COMMONWEALTH FOR PEOPLE OF DIFFERENT RACES AND VARYING BACKGROUNDS TO WORK TOGETHER AS ONE GROUP. DISCUSSES PROBLEMS OF NATIONS WITH DIFFERENT RACES JOINING TOGETHER. PRESENTS SOLUTIONS AND IDEAS FOR FUTURE PLANS.

1442 INSTITUT DE DROIT INTL
TABLEAU GENERAL DES RESOLUTIONS (1873-1956)
PARIS: INST DE DROIT INTERNAT, 1957, 404 PP.
COMPILATION OF PUBLIC LAWS AND PRIVATE RIGHTS, ESPECIALLY THOSE OF FOREIGNERS. INCLUDES TERRITORIAL JURISDICTION, ARBITRATION, COMMERCE AND CONTRACTS.

1443 INSTITUT INTERMEDIAIRE INTL
REPERTOIRE GENERAL DES TRAITES ET AUTRES ACTES DIPLOMATIQUES CONCLUS DEPUIS 1895 JUSQU'EN 1920.
LEYDEN: HARLEM & CO, 1926, 516 PP.
A CHRONOLOGICALLY ARRANGED, UNANNOTATED BIBLIOGRAPHY OF 4,412 TREATIES AND DIPLOMATIC ARRANGEMENTS CONCLUDED BETWEEN 1895-1920, PRIMARILY AMONG WESTERN POWERS. PROVIDES ALPHABERICAL TABLES OF TREATIES AND LISTING OF NATIONAL COLLECTIONS OF DIPLOMATIC HISTORY. SEPARATE DIVISIONS OF BILATERAL AND MULTILATERAL TREATIES.

1444 INSTITUTE MEDITERRANEAN AFF
THE PALESTINE REFUGEE PROBLEM.
NEW YORK: INST FOR MEDIT AFF, 1958, 133 PP.
ANALYZES REFUGEE PROBLEM TO SHOW THAT IN PAST TEN YEARS NO ATTEMPT AT "INTEGRAL, JUST SOLUTION HAS BEEN TRIED OUT" DUE TO TENSION AND THREAT OF WAR BETWEEN ISRAEL AND UAR. STUDIED ALL EXISTING PLANS FOR LONG-RANGE GOALS AND EVOLVED RECONCILIATION PLAN TO "REPATRIATE AND RESETTLE REFUGEES IN CONSECUTIVE STAGES."

1445 INSTITUTE OF HISPANIC STUDIES
HISPANIC AMERICAN REPORT.
STANFORD: INST HISP AM BRAZ STUD.
MONTHLY PUBLICATION SINCE 1948 WHICH REVIEWS BOOKS ON CONTEMPORARY SOCIAL SCIENCES AND HUMANITIES IN LATIN AMERICA, SPAIN, AND PORTUGAL. EMPHASIS ON INTERNATIONAL RELATIONS, POLITICS, AND ECONOMICS. SOURCES IN ENGLISH, SPANISH, AND PORTUGUESE.

1446 INSTITUTE POLITISCHE WISSEN
POLITISCHE LITERATUR (3 VOLS.)
FRANKFURT: INST FUR POL WISS, 1955.
A COLLECTION OF PERIODICALS (1953-54) REVIEWING PUBLICATIONS ON POLITICAL LITERATURE. THE PERIODICALS APPEAR MONTHLY AND INCLUDE REVIEWS (IN GERMAN) OF FOREIGN PUBLICATIONS FOR YEARS 1952-55.

1447 INT. SOC. SCI. BULL.
"TECHNIQUES OF MEDIATION AND CONCILIATION."

INT. SOC. SCI. BULL., 10 (NO.1, 58), 507-628.
COMPILATION OF ARTICLES CONCERNING TECHNIQUES OF MEDIATION AND CONCILIATION IN FIELDS OF INTERNATIONAL LAW AND COLLECTIVE INDUSTRIAL DISPUTES. DISCUSSES THE FUNCTION OF CONCILIATION IN CIVIL PROCEDURES OF MANY EUROPEAN NATIONS AND OF USA.

1448 INTERAMERICAN CULTURAL COUN
LISTA DE LIBROS REPRESENTAVOS DE AMERICA.
WASHINGTON: PAN AMERICAN UNION, 1959, 364 PP.
ANNOTATED BIBLIOGRAPHY OF THE MOST SIGNIFICANT PUBLICATIONS IN THE SOCIAL SCIENCES. ENTRIES ARRANGED BY COUNTRY.

1449 INTERAMERICAN ECO AND SOC COUN
THE ALLIANCE FOR PROGRESS: ITS FIRST YEAR: 1961-1962.
WASHINGTON: PAN AMERICAN UNION, 1963, 198 PP.
REPORT ON PROGRESS OF ECONOMIC ANS SOCIAL DEVELOPMENT IN LATIN AMERICA FROM 1961 TO 1962 RESULTING FROM LONG-TERM DEVELOPMENT PLANS INSITUTED BY ALLIANCE FOR PROGRESS. PROVIDES OVER-ALL EVALUATION OF SOUTH AMERICAN PROGRESS AND PROSPECTS FOR FUTURE GAINS IN SOCIAL AND ECONOMIC AREAS, AND DISCUSSES SPECIFIC PROBLEMS AND ACHIEVEMENTS MADE IN EACH OF COUNTRIES INVOLVED.

1450 INTERNATIONAL BANK RECONST DEV
THE WORLD BANK IN AFRICA: SUMMARY OF ACTIVITIES.
WASHINGTON: INTL BANK REC & DEV, 1961, 61 PP.
SUMMARIZES LOANS MADE BY WORLD BANK TO AFRICAN MEMBER NATIONS CHIEFLY FOR DEVELOPMENT OF TRANSPORTATION, POWER, COMMUNICATIONS, AGRICULTURE, AND VARIOUS SEGMENTS OF INDUSTRY. DETAILS SPECIFIC PROJECTS AND NOTES EFFECTS OF WORLD BANK FINANCING ON GENERAL NATIONAL DEVELOPMENT. COVERS ENTIRE PERIOD OF EXISTENCE OF WORLD BANK.

1451 INTERNATIONAL BANK RECONST DEV
THE WORLD BANK GROUP IN ASIA.
WASHINGTON: INTL BANK REC & DEV, 1963, 90 PP.
DESCRIBES FUNCTIONS AND METHODS OF WORLD BANK AND ITS AFFILIATES. DISCUSSES IN DETAIL THEIR EFFORTS SINCE 1950 TO PROMOTE ECONOMIC DEVELOPMENT OF ASIA. LISTS NUMBER AND PURPOSE OF LOANS MADE BY BANK TO SEVERAL ASIAN COUNTRIES AND DESCRIBES PROJECTS FOR WHICH FUNDS WERE USED.

1452 INTERNATIONAL COMN JURISTS
AFRICAN CONFERENCE ON THE RULE OF LAW.
GENEVA: INTL COMN OF JURISTS, 1961, 181 PP.
PROCEEDINGS OF CONFERENCE OF INTERNATIONAL COMMISSION OF JURISTS HELD IN LAGOS, NIGERIA IN JANUARY, 1961. PURPOSE OF CONFERENCE WAS TO ASSESS LEGAL SYSTEMS AND POLITICAL SITUATIONS IN NEWLY INDEPENDENT SUB-SAHARA STATES. REVIEWS DECISIONS AND POLICIES ADOPTED BY CONFERENCE BASED ON CONCEPT OF RULE OF LAW AS DEFINED AT 1955 ATHENS CONFERENCE.

1453 INTERNATIONAL COURT OF JUSTICE
CHARTER OF THE UNITED NATIONS, STATUTE AND RULES OF COURT AND OTHER CONSTITUTIONAL DOCUMENTS.
THE HAGUE: INTL COURT OF JUSTICE, 1947, 141 PP.
CONTAINS UN CHARTER, STATUTE AND RULES OF THE ICJ, TOGETHER WITH FIVE UN RESOLUTIONS OF 1946 AS TO PRIVILEGES AND IMMUNITIES OF COURT MEMBERS, THEIR PENSIONS, ADMINISTRATION OF THE COURT, CONDITIONS UNDER WHICH THE IJC SHALL BE OPEN TO STATES NOT PARTIES TO THE STATUTE, AND CONDITIONS UNDER WHICH SWITZERLAND MAY BECOME A PARTY. IN FRENCH AND ENGLISH.

1454 INTERNATIONAL ECO POLICY ASSN
THE UNITED STATES BALANCE OF PAYMENTS.
WASHINGTON: INTL ECO POLICY ASSN, 1966, 200 PP., LC#66-23129
ANALYSIS OF US ECONOMIC STRATEGY, EMPHASIZING IMPACT OF DIRECT FOREIGN INVESTMENT AND OTHER ECONOMIC FACTORS ON US BALANCE OF PAYMENTS. ATTEMPTS TO DETERMINE CAUSE OF PERSISTENT US DEFICITS. CONSIDERS BOTH PUBLIC AND PRIVATE INTERNATIONAL TRANSACTIONS AND THEIR EFFECTS ON BALANCE OF PAYMENTS.

1455 INTERNATIONAL ECONOMIC ASSN
STABILITY AND PROGRESS IN THE WORLD ECONOMY: THE FIRST CONGRESS OF THE INTERNATIONAL ECONOMIC ASSOCIATION.
NEW YORK: ST. MARTIN'S, 1958, 266 PP.
RECORDS 1956 CONGRESS ON SUBJECT. FIVE ASPECTS COVERED: PROBLEMS OF RICHER AND POORER COUNTRIES, MONETARY FACTORS IN STABILITY, INTERNATIONAL STABILITY AND THE NATIONAL ECONOMY. CLOSING ADDRESS CONCLUDES THAT COMMONWEALTH TYPE OF DEVELOPMENT MORE FEASIBLE THAN WORLD ECONOMIC COORDINATION.

1456 INTERNATIONAL FEDN DOCUMENTTN
BIBLIOGRAPHY OF DIRECTORIES OF SOURCES OF INFORMATION (PAMPHLET)
HAGUE: INTL FEDERATION FOR DOCUM, 1960, 22 PP.
LIST OF INTERNATIONAL AND NATIONAL DIRECTORIES OF SOURCES OF SCIENTIFIC, TECHNICAL, AND ECONOMIC INFORMATION. ARRANGED FIRST BY INTERNATIONAL, THEN NATIONAL, DIRECTORIES ALPHABETICALLY.

1457 INTERNATIONAL LABOUR OFFICE
SUBJECT GUIDE TO PUBLICATIONS OF THE INTERNATIONAL LABOUR OFFICE, 1919-1964.
GENEVA: INTL LABOUR OFFICE, 1967, 478 PP.
SUBJECT GUIDE LISTS ITEMS UNDER SINGLE HEADING WITH CROSS-REFERENCES TO MORE SPECIFIC HEADINGS. INCLUDES ALPHABETICAL AUTHOR INDEX. IN ADDITION TO PRINTED SALES PUBLICATIONS, LIST INCLUDES IMPORTANT SERIES PRODUCED BY OFFSET PROCESSES.

1458 INTERNATIONAL LAW ASSOCIATION
A FORTY YEARS' CATALOGUE OF THE BOOKS, PAMPHLETS AND PAPERS IN THE LIBRARY OF THE INTERNATIONAL LAW ASSOCIATION.
LONDON: R FLINT & CO, 1915, 70 PP.
BIBLIOGRAPHICAL INDEX TO 1,500 ITEMS IN ASSOCIATION'S LIBRARY, TOPICALLY CLASSIFIED INTO FIVE MAIN CATEGORIES COVERING: INTERNATIONAL LAW, POLITICS, COMPARATIVE LAW, CONSTITUTIONAL LAW, AND MUNICIPAL LAW. MOST PUBLICATIONS DATE FROM 1875.

1459 INTERNATIONAL MONETARY FUND
COMPENSATORY FINANCING OF EXPORT FLUCTUATIONS (PAMPHLET)
WASHINGTON: INTL MONETARY FUND, 1963, 27 PP.
REPORTS WAYS IN WHICH INTERNATIONAL MONETARY FUND MIGHT PLAY INCREASED PART IN COMPENSATORY FINANCING OF EXPORT FLUCTUATIONS OF PRIMARY EXPORTING COUNTRIES. FUND BELIEVES USE OF ITS FUNDS BY NATIONS EXPERIENCING DEFICITS ARISING OUT OF EXPORT SHORTFALLS IS LEGITIMATE, SINCE IT ENABLES NATIONS TO PURSUE DEVELOPMENT PROGRAMS DESPITE BALANCE-OF-PAYMENTS PROBLEMS.

1460 INTERNATIONAL SOCIAL SCI COUN
SOCIAL SCIENCES IN THE USSR.
HAGUE: MOUTON & CO, 1965, 297 PP.
BIBLIOGRAPHICAL SURVEY PREPARED BY THE USSR ACADEMY OF SCIENCES ON UNESCO'S INITIATIVE IN ORDER TO FAMILIARIZE SCIENTISTS IN FOREIGN COUNTRIES WITH THE STATUS OF RESEARCH DONE IN THE SOCIAL SCIENCES IN THE USSR SINCE 1945. PROVIDES INFORMATION ON THE BASIC APPROACH OF SOVIET SOCIAL SCIENTISTS TO THE PROBLEMS ON WHICH THEY ARE WORKING AND RESULTS OF THEIR WORK. LISTS MAJOR WORKS THROUGH 1961.

1461 INTERNATIONAL STUDIES
"INDIA AND WORLD AFFAIRS: AN ANNUAL BIBLIOGRAPHY"
NEW YORK: ASIA PUBL HOUSE.
ANNUAL FEATURE OF PERIODICAL, "INTERNATIONAL STUDIES" IS BIBLIOGRAPHY ON INDIA. FIRST PART LISTS BOOKS, PERIODICAL ARTICLES, AND DOCUMENTS ON INDIA'S FOREIGN RELATIONS. THE SECOND PART IS CONCERNED WITH INDIAN PUBLIC OPINION ON WORLD AFFAIRS.

1462 INTL ATOMIC ENERGY AGENCY
INTERNATIONAL CONVENTIONS ON CIVIL LIABILITY FOR NUCLEAR DAMAGE.
VIENNA: INTL ATOMIC ENERGY COMN, 1966.
COMPILES FOUR INTERNATIONAL CONVENTIONS ON CIVIL LIABILITY FOR NUCLEAR DAMAGE. CONVENTIONS CHANNEL EXCLUSIVE LIABILITY TO OPERATOR OF NUCLEAR INSTALLATION AND HOLD HIM ABSOLUTELY LIABLE UPON PROOF OF CAUSATION. CONVENTIONS INCLUDE PROVISIONS CONCERNING RIGHTS OF RECOURSE, ENFORCEMENT OF FOREIGN JUDGMENTS, AND LIMITS OF LIABILITY.

1463 INTL CONF ON WORLD POLITICS-5
EASTERN EUROPE IN TRANSITION.
BALTIMORE: JOHNS HOPKINS PRESS, 1966, 364 PP., LC#66-24409.
REPORT OF FIFTH INTERNATIONAL CONFERENCE ON WORLD POLITICS HELD IN THE NETHERLANDS, 1965. STUDIES COUNTRIES OF CENTRAL, EASTERN, AND SOUTHEASTERN EUROPE, AND FACTORS UNDERLYING TRANSFORMATION OF THIS AREA. DISCUSSES GROWTH OF POLYCENTRISM UNDER THE IMPACT OF SINO-SOVIET CONFLICT, POST-1957 INTERBLOC ORGANIZATIONS, AND CHANGING IDEOLOGICAL, POLITICAL, AND SOCIAL ATTITUDES.

1464 INTL INF CTR LOCAL CREDIT
GOVERNMENT MEASURES FOR THE PROMOTION OF REGIONAL ECONOMIC DEVELOPMENT.
THE HAGUE: MARTINUS NIJHOFF, 1964, 159 PP.
ANALYSIS OF UNEQUAL SOCIAL AND CULTURAL DEVELOPMENT OF SPECIFIC REGIONS IN NATIONS SINCE WWII. STUDIES NATURE AND CAUSES OF INEQUALITY IN EACH MEMBER NATION AND EVALUATES PROGRAMS IN PROGRESS TO RECTIFY SITUATION. ESTABLISHES CRITERIA FOR SPECIAL AREAS, SUGGESTS METHODS OF IMPROVING AREA, AND OFFERS AID IN ADMINISTERING REGION.

1465 PRESS & INFO. DIV. FR. EMBASSY
FRENCH AFRICA: A DECADE OF PROGRESS 1948-1958 (PAMPHLET)
NEW YORK: PRESS & INFO. DIV. FRENCH EMBASSY, 1958, 40 PP.
STATISTICAL CHARTS ON OPERATIONS OF FRENCH INVESTMENT FUND FOR SOCIAL AND ECONOMIC DEVELOPMENT IN FRENCH WEST AFRICA AND IN FRENCH EQUATORIAL AFRICA. REPORTS PROGRESS IN AGRICULTURE, ROAD BUILDING, PUBLIC HEALTH, EDUCATION, AND MINING.

1466 IRIKURA J.K.
SOUTHEAST ASIA: SELECTED ANNOTATED BIBLIOGRAPHY OF JAPANESE PUBLICATIONS.
NEW HAVEN: HUMAN REL AREA FILES, 1956, 544 PP., LC#56-71519.
CONTAINS 965 EXTENSIVELY ANNOTATED ITEMS ON HISTORY,

GOVERNMENT, ECONOMY, FOREIGN RELATIONS, FOREIGN TRADE, HEALTH, WELFARE AND EDUCATION, AND MINORITIES OF AREA. PARTICULAR EMPHASIS ON JAPAN-SOUTHEAST ASIAN RELATIONS. WORKS ON BURMA, INDOCHINA, INDONESIA, MALAYA, PHILIPPINES, AND THAILAND.

1467 IRISH M.D. ED.
WORLD PRESSURES ON AMERICAN FOREIGN POLICY.
LONDON: PRENTICE HALL INTL, 1964, 172 PP., LC#64-11462.
STUDIES FACTORS IN THE EXTERNAL ENVIRONMENT THAT AFFECT THE CREATION AND IMPLEMENTATION OF AMERICAN FOREIGN POLICY. INCLUDES DISCUSSIONS OF THEORY, IDEOLOGY, AND FOREIGN POLICY; WESTERN EUROPE, BRITISH POLITICS, AND AMERICAN POLICIES; THE COMMUNIST BLOC, COLONIALISM, DICTATORSHIP, AND THE AMERICAN POLITICAL TRADITION; SOUTH AFRICA, LATIN AMERICA, AND ASIA IN TRANSITION.

1468 IRIYE A.
AFTER IMPERIALISM; THE SEARCH FOR A NEW ORDER IN THE FAR EAST 1921-1931.
CAMBRIDGE: HARVARD U PR, 1965, 375 PP., LC#65-22052.
DEVELOPS FRAMEWORK IN WHICH DIPLOMATIC HISTORY OF FAR EAST IN 1920'S CAN BE STUDIED. BASES STUDY ON COLLAPSE OF DIPLOMACY OF IMPERIALISM AS MECHANISM FOR POWER POLITICS AND SEARCH FOR NEW ORDER. EMPHASIZES EVENTS IN JAPAN. STUDIES ATTEMPTS BY US, USSR, JAPAN, AND CHINA TO FIND NEW BASIS FOR POWER AND REASONS FOR FAILURE OF EACH EFFORT.

1469 ISENBERG I. ED.
FRANCE UNDER DE GAULLE (THE REFERENCE SHELF VOL. 39 NO. 1)
NEW YORK: H W WILSON, 1967, 189 PP., LC#67-17464.
VARIOUS ASPECTS OF GAULLISM - WHAT IT IS, WHAT IT MEANS, WHAT IT HAS DONE-- ARE EXAMINED AND ANALYZED FROM VARYING POINTS OF VIEW. INCLUDES 29 ARTICLES EXCERPTED FROM MAGAZINES, BOOKS, AND ADDRESSES BY DE GAULLE, ILLUSTRATING HIS VIEWS ON ATLANTIC ALLIANCE, BRITAIN AND THE COMMON MARKET, USSR, AND CHINA.

1470 ISLAM R.
INTERNATIONAL ECONOMIC COOPERATION AND THE UNITED NATIONS.
NEW YORK: UNITED NATIONS, 1958, 129 PP.
DISCUSSES DEVELOPMENTS IN SEVERAL AREAS OF INTERNATIONAL ECONOMIC AID OCCURRING UNDER AUSPICES OF LEAGUE OF NATIONS AND UN. GREATER EMPHASIS IS ON UN ACTIVITIES, SPECIFICALLY ON FORMATION OF SPECIALIZED UN AGENCIES FOR MAINTAINING VARIOUS INTERNATIONAL SERVICES AND ECONOMIC PLANS. STRESSES NECESSITY OF FULL-FLEDGED ECONOMIC COOPERATION IN WORLD COMMUNITY UNDER UN REGULATION.

1471 JACK H.
"NONALIGNMENT AND A TEST BAN AGREEMENT: THE ROLE OF THE NON-ALIGNED STATES."
J. CONFL. RESOLUT., 7 (SEPT. 64), 542-52.
CHRONICLES EFFORTS OF NON-ALIGNED NATIONS, FROM 1954-62, TO BRING ABOUT A TEST BAN AGREEMENT AMONG THE NUCLEAR POWERS. ANALYZES VOTING PATTERNS IN UN ON TEST BAN RESOLUTIONS AND WARNS OF POSSIBLE SPREAD OF NUCLEAR WEAPONS TO THE NON-ALIGNED NATIONS.

1472 JACK H.A. ED.
RELIGION AND PEACE: PAPERS FROM THE NATIONAL INTER-RELIGIOUS CONFERENCE ON PEACE, WASHINGTON, 1966.
INDIANAPOLIS: BOBBS-MERRILL, 1966, 135 PP., LC#66-27885.
PAPERS CALLING FOR GREATER AWARENESS AMONG RELIGIOUS PERSONS AND ORGANIZATIONS OF INTERNATIONAL SITUATION TODAY. AMERICANS ARE ENCOURAGED TO OPEN COMMUNICATIONS AND TRADE ROUTES WITH RED CHINA, REEXAMINE RATIONALES OF US POLICY, AND URGE ADMINISTRATION TO SETTLE VIETNAM SITUATION QUICKLY AND PEACEFULLY. OTHER PAPERS DEAL GENERALLY WITH RELIGION'S RESPONSIBILITY AND POSSIBILITIES FOR PEACE IN THE WORLD.

1473 JACKSON B.W.
FIVE IDEAS THAT CHANGE THE WORLD.
NEW YORK: W W NORTON, 1959, 188 PP., LC#59-6802.
ANALYZES INEVITABILITY OF FREEDOM OF MAN FOR SELF-DESTRUCTION BY TRACING DEVELOPMENT OF FIVE IDEAS THROUGHOUT WORLD. AIMS TO INFORM UNDEVELOPED, UNCOMMITTED NATIONS OF THEIR ROLE IN DECIDING WHICH IDEOLOGY CONTROLS OR RUINS MAN. ANALYZES THESE IDEOLOGIES FULLY IN PRESENT WORLD TO GIVE BROAD VIEW OF FUTURE.

1474 JACKSON E.
MEETING OF THE MINDS: A WAY TO PEACE THROUGH MEDIATION.
NEW YORK: MCGRAW HILL, 1952, 200 PP.
STUDY IN PRACTICES AND TECHNIQUES OF MEDIATION IN BOTH LABOR AND INTERNATIONAL DISPUTES. EXPLORES PARALLELS WITHIN AREAS AND DISCUSSES PROBLEMS OF SECURING AGREEMENTS. VIEWS THE RELATIONSHIP BETWEEN MEDIATION AND THE INSTITUTION AND POWER SETTING IN WHICH IT TAKES PLACE. VIEWS MEDIATION AS ART AND EMPHASIZES PERSONAL QUALITIES OF MEDIATOR. BELIEVES EXPERIENCES IN TWO FIELDS ARE SIMILAR SO THAT UNITED NATIONS MAY PROFIT FROM MEDIATION PROCEEDINGS.

1475 JACKSON E.
"CONSTITUTIONAL DEVELOPMENTS OF THE UNITED NATIONS: THE GROWTH OF ITS EXECUTIVE CAPACITY."
PROC. AMER. SOC. INT. LAW., 55 (APR. 61), 138-49.
SURVEYS EXPERIENCE OF UN SINCE FOUNDING. SUGGESTS THAT PROCEDURE AND PRACTICE OF GENERAL ASSEMBLY NEED MODIFICATION FOR MORE EFFECTIVE PARLIAMENTARY DIPLOMACY.

1476 JACKSON E.
"THE FUTURE DEVELOPMENT OF THE UNITED NATIONS: SOME SUGGESTIONS FOR RESEARCH."
J. CONFL. RESOLUT., 5 (JUNE 61), 119-27.
SEES FUTURE OF UN CHARACTERIZED BY STRUGGLE FOR CONTROL OF THE ORGANIZATION. MAKES TWELVE PROPOSALS FOR RESEARCH ON THE SECURITY COUNCIL, FINANCIAL MANAGEMENT, AND INTERNATIONAL LAW.

1477 JACKSON M.V.
EUROPEAN POWERS AND SOUTH-EAST AFRICA: A STUDY OF INTERNATIONAL RELATIONS ON SOUTH-EAST COAST OF AFRICA, 1796-1856.
LONDON: LONGMANS, GREEN & CO, 1942, 284 PP.
STUDIES EXPLOITATION, EMPHASIZING OCEAN STRATEGY, COMMERCE, AND FOREIGN POWER STRUGGLE TO GAIN TERRITORY AND ACCESS TO VITAL TRADE ROUTES.

1478 JACKSON R.G.A.
THE CASE FOR AN INTERNATIONAL DEVELOPMENT AUTHORITY (PAMPHLET)
SYRACUSE: SYRACUSE U PRESS, 1959, 67 PP., LC#59-9104.
LECTURES IN FAVOR OF THE ESTABLISHMENT OF A COOPERATING INTERNATIONAL ORGANIZATION WHICH WOULD CHANNEL FOREIGN AID OF ALL COUNTRIES TO ALL UNDERDEVELOPED AREAS. MEMBERSHIP WOULD BE OPEN TO ALL, INCLUDING COMMUNIST COUNTRIES THOUGH THEY WOULD BE IN MINORITY, AND VOTING WOULD BE WEIGHED IN RELATION TO CONTRIBUTION. THIS BODY WOULD FACILITATE ADMINISTRATION OF FOREIGN AID AND MAKE IT MORE EQUITABLE.

1479 JACKSON R.H.
INTERNATIONAL CONFERENCE ON MILITARY TRIALS.
WASHINGTON: US GOVERNMENT, 1949, 441 PP.
A DOCUMENTARY RECORD OF NEGOTIATIONS OF THE REPRESENTATIVES OF THE US, THE PROVISIONAL GOVERNMENT OF FRANCE, GREAT BRITAIN, AND THE USSR AT THE LONDON CONFERENCE, JUNE 26-AUGUST 8, 1945. CONTAINS FORMAL STATEMENTS ON PRINCIPLES OF SUBSTANTIVE LAW AND METHODS OF PROCEDURE FOR THE PROSECUTION AND TRIAL OF MAJOR EUROPEAN WAR CRIMINALS. CULMINATES IN THE CHARTER OF THE INTERNATIONAL MILITARY TRIBUNAL.

1480 JACKSON W.G.F.
"NUCLEAR PROLIFERATION AND THE GREAT POWERS."
MILITARY REV., 47 (JUNE 67), 72-81.
BRITISH MAJOR GENERAL ANALYZES WHAT FACTORS HAVE CAUSED NUCLEAR PROLIFERATION AND HOW IT CAN BE CONTROLLED. CITES NATIONALISM AND FEAR AS CHIEF MOTIVES OF ARMS RACE. DISCUSSES VARIOUS WAYS IN WHICH NATIONS MIGHT SUBMIT TO SUPRANATIONAL AUTHORITY TO MAINTAIN PEACE. CONCLUDES THAT BRITAIN MUST BOTH SUPPORT SUCH EFFORTS AT COOPERATION AND MAINTAIN HER OWN INTERESTS.

1481 JACKSON W.V.
LIBRARY GUIDE FOR BRAZILIAN STUDIES.
PITTSBURGH: U OF PITT BOOK CTRS., 1964, 197 PP., LC#64-66279
BIBLIOGRAPHY OF RESEARCH COLLECTIONS ON BRAZIL IN 74 AMERICAN UNIVERSITIES.

1482 JACOB P.E.
"THE DISARMAMENT CONSENSUS."
INT. ORGAN., 14 (SPRING 60), 235-60.
DISCUSSES AREAS OF EAST-WEST AGREEMENT. LIST AREAS OF DISAGREEMENT SUCH AS: EXTENT OF ACCESS BY CONTROL TEAMS AND SCOPE OF THE VETO. SUSPECTS RUSSIA MORE WILLING TO COMPROMISE THAN HAS BEEN GENERALLY BELIEVED. RECOMMENDS DIVORCING POLITICAL CONDITIONS FROM DISARMAMENT PROPOSALS.

1483 JACOB P.E. ED., TOSCANO J.V. ED.
THE INTEGRATION OF POLITICAL COMMUNITIES.
PHILADELPHIA: LIPPINCOTT, 1964, 314 PP., $5.95.
INTERDISCIPLINARY SEMINAR HELD AT U. OF PENN. ASSESSES INTEGRATED POLITICAL BEHAVIOR AT THE METROPOLITAN AND INTERNATIONAL LEVELS. MODELS WERE DESIGNED TO ANALYZE QUANTITATIVE AND QUALITATIVE DATA BEARING ON THE DEVELOPMENT OF INTEGRATION AT THESE DIFFERENT POLITICAL LEVELS.

1484 JACOBSON H.K.
"THE USSR AND ILO."
INT. ORG. 14 (SUMMER 60), 402-428.
STATES THAT SOVIET UNION RE-ENTRY HAS BEEN A SHARP REVERSAL OF ITS PAST POLICIES. ANALYZES ILO POTENTIALITIES AS CONSTRUCTIVE FORCE FOR GUIDING DEVELOPMENT OF LABOR AND MANAGEMENT IN NEWLY INDEPENDENT COUNTRIES. CALLS FOR BETTER WAY OF MEETING PROBLEMS OF SOVIET PARTICIPATION.

1485 JACOBSON H.K.
AMERICAN FOREIGN POLICY.
NEW YORK: RANDOM, 1960, 755 PP.
ANTHOLOGY REFLECTING UPON: PUBLIC DEBATE, DEMOCRATIC PROCESSES, NATIONAL INTERESTS, EUROPE AND NATO, COLONIALISM, COMMUNISM AND FOREIGN TRADE.

1486 JACOBSON H.K.
"THE UNITED NATIONS AND COLONIALISM: A TENTATIVE APPRAISAL."
INT. ORGAN., 16 (WINTER 62), 137-56.
SHOWS DECREASING ROLE OF UN IN COLONIAL AFFAIRS AS MORE COLONIES ACHIEVE INDEPENDENCE. NOTES LACK OF SOVIET AFFECT ON COLONIAL AFFAIRS, BUT CITES US INVOLVEMENT IN STRUGGLE BETWEEN COLONIAL AND ANTI-COLONIAL POWERS. ASSESSES UN CONTRIBUTION TO COLONIAL REVOLUTION AS MODEST, BUT TO STABILITY AND DEVELOPMENT AS SIGNIFICANT.

1487 JACOBSON H.K.
THE USSR AND THE UN'S ECONOMIC AND SOCIAL ACTIVITIES.
NOTRE DAME: U. PR., 1963, 309 &P., $6.95.
AN ANALYSIS OF RUSSIAN POLICY WITH RESPECT TO ECONOMIC AND SOCIAL ACTIVITIES OF UN, THE REACTIONS OF OTHER STATES TO THESE POLICIES, AND THE IMPACT OF RESULTING INTERACTION ON UN'S INSTITUTIONS AND FUNCTIONS. REPRESENTS A FULL-SCALE EFFORT TO SUBJECT THE THEORY OF FUNCTIONALISM TO A PRAGMATIC SCRUTINY.

1488 JADOS S.S.
DOCUMENTS ON RUSSIAN-AMERICAN RELATIONS: WASHINGTON TO EISENHOWER.
WASHINGTON: CATHOLIC U PR, 1965, 416 PP., LC#65-12569.
COLLECTION OF DOCUMENTS THAT EMANATED FROM US AND RUSSIAN LEADERS DEALING WITH FOREIGN POLICY, 1790-1960. PRESENTED IN CHRONOLOGICAL ORDER AND SELECTED ACCORDING TO IMPORTANCE IN HISTORY OF THE TWO NATIONS. INCLUDES BIBLIOGRAPHY ENABLING QUICK REFERENCE TO SOURCES IN OTHER COLLECTIONS OF DOCUMENTS.

1489 JAECKH A.
WELTSAAT; ERLEBTES UND ERSTREBTES.
STUTTGART: DEUTSCHE VERLAGSANST, 1960, 340 PP.
AUTOBIOGRAPHY OF A GERMAN POLITICAL THINKER AND ADVISER TO GERMAN POLITICAL LEADERS FROM TIME OF KAISER THROUGH WEIMAR REPUBLIC TO KONRAD ADENAUER; ORIENTALIST MEMOIRS OF HIS VARIED LIFE, EMPHASIZING HIS POLITICAL INVOLVEMENTS IN A VARIETY OF ADVISORY AND ACADEMIC CAPACITIES IN GERMANY, ENGLAND, US.

1490 JAGAN C.
THE WEST ON TRIAL.
NEW YORK: INTERNATIONAL PUBL CO, 1967, 471 PP.
EXPLANATION OF POLITICAL SITUATION IN GUYANA AS SEEN BY JAGAN. SEES BEST HOPE IN FAST ECONOMIC AND SOCIAL REFORM. DESCRIBES PERSONAL INVOLVEMENT IN FIGHT FOR INDEPENDENCE FROM BRITAIN. CITES US SUPPRESION OF SOCIALIST MOVEMENTS AS A MAJOR REASON FOR FAILURE OF SOCIALISM SO FAR.

1491 JAIRAZBHOY R.A.
FOREIGN INFLUENCE IN ANCIENT INDIA.
BOMBAY: ASIA PUBL HOUSE, 1963, 195 PP.
ACCOUNT OF IMPACT UPON FORMATION OF INDIAN CULTURE BY FOREIGN CONQUERERS: MESOPOTAMIAN, PERSIAN, GREEK, ROMAN, PARTHO-SASSANIAN, AND MUSLIM. SHOWS PARTICULAR INFLUENCES UPON ART, LANGUAGE, RELIGION, AND EDUCATION.

1492 JAKOBSON M.
THE DIPLOMACY OF THE WINTER WAR.
CAMBRIDGE: HARVARD U PR, 1961, 281 PP., LC#61-5578.
DISCUSSES SOVIET-FINNISH CONFLICT OF 1939-40 AND PRAISES FINNS FOR THEIR DEFENSE OF DEMOCRACY AND FREEDOM AGAINST SOVIET ENCROACHMENT. DISCUSSES WAR IN RELATION TO TOTAL EUROPEAN SITUATION. TRACES DIPLOMATIC AND MILITARY COURSE OF CONFLICT UP TO 1940 FINNISH-SOVIET PEACE TREATY.

1493 JALEE P.
THE PILLAGE OF THE THIRD WORLD (TRANS. BY MARY KLOPPER)
NEW YORK: MONTHLY REVIEW PR, 1965, 115 PP., LC#68-13069.
INVESTIGATES WHETHER, DESPITE TERMINATION OF COLONIAL TIES, DEVELOPED AREAS OF THE WORLD CONTINUE TO EXPLOIT UNDERDEVELOPED NATIONS BY VIRTUE OF LONG-ESTABLISHED ECONOMIC RELATIONSHIPS. USES STATISTICS TO SHOW EXISTENCE OF EXPLOITATION, EMPHASIZING FACT OF STARVATION IN LANDS PRODUCING MUCH OF WORLD'S FOOD. ALSO SHOWS THAT MOST RAW MATERIAL DOES NOT RETURN IN FORM OF GOODS.

1494 JAMESON J.F.
THE AMERICAN REVOLUTION CONSIDERED AS A SOCIAL MOVEMENT.
BOSTON: BEACON PRESS, 1956, 105 PP.
EXAMINES THE DEMOCRATIC AND HUMANE STRIVINGS THAT ACCOMPANIED THE REVOLUTION AND DISCUSSES HOW THEY RESULTED IN WIDENING THE SUFFRAGE, REDISTRIBUTING TO SMALLER HOLDERS THE GREAT ESTATES OF TORY REFUGEES, AND LIBERALIZING TIME-HONORED INHERITANCE LAWS. ANALYZES THE EFFECTS OF THESE INFLUENCES IN HASTENING SEPARATION OF CHURCH AND STATE AND PROMOTING MOVEMENTS FOR THE RESTRICTION OF SLAVERY.

1495 JANOWITZ M.
THE MILITARY IN THE POLITICAL DEVELOPMENT OF NEW NATIONS: AN ESSAY IN COMPARATIVE ANALYSIS.
CHICAGO: U. CHI. PR., 1964, 134 PP., $4.50.
STUDY OF WHY THE ROLE OF MILITARY OFFICERS IN THE DOMESTIC LIFE OF NEW NATIONS IS GREATER THAN THE ROLE OF MILITARY OFFICERS IN THE DOMESTIC AFFAIRS OF THE WESTERN INDUSTRIALIZED NATIONS. INCLUDES A COUNTRY-BY-COUNTRY ANALYSIS OF THE PHENOMENON. CONCLUDES IN PART THAT THE CAPACITY TO ACT IN POLITICS IS NOT A CONSTANT.

1496 JAPAN MOMBUSHO DAIGAKU GAKIYUT
BIBLIOGRAPHY OF THE STUDIES ON LAW AND POLITICS (PAMPHLET)
TOKYO: JAPAN MINISTRY EDUCATION, 1955, 83 PP.
UNANNOTATED BIBLIOGRAPHY OF 918 WORKS IN FIELDS OF LAW AND POLITICS THAT APPEARED IN VARIOUS JAPANESE SCHOLARLY BOOKS, JOURNALS, BULLETINS, ETC., IN 1952. AUTHOR, TITLE, AND JOURNAL GIVEN IN BOTH ROMAN SCRIPT AND CHARACTERS. WORKS ARRANGED ALPHABETICALLY BY AUTHOR WITHIN 16 SUBJECT CLASSIFICATIONS, AND INDEXED BY AUTHOR. LIST OF ALL PERIODICALS MENTIONED IS APPENDED TO TEXT.

1497 JAPANESE ASSOCIATION INT. LAW
JAPAN AND THE UNITED NATIONS.
NEW YORK: MANHATTAN, 1958, 246 PP.
EXAMINES ORGANIZATION AND FUNCTION OF UN, DEVELOPMENT OF JAPANESE ATTITUDES TOWARD THE ORGANIZATION AND VARIOUS PROBLEMS ARISING WITHIN THE INSTITUTION. CITES JAPANESE OBJECTIONS TO JOINING UN, AND CONCLUDES WITH A DISCUSSION OF UN CONCERN WITH JAPANESE SECURITY AND FAR EASTERN SITUATIONS.

1498 JASZI O., LEWIS J.D.
AGAINST THE TYRANT.
NEW YORK: FREE PRESS OF GLENCOE, 1957, 288 PP.
HISTORICAL AND ANALYTICAL ACCOUNT OF THEORY OF TYRANNICIDE AS IT DEVELOPED UP TO 1660 AND OF ROLE THIS THEORY HAS PLAYED IN MODERN REVOLUTIONARY MOVEMENTS. ATTEMPTS TO RESTATE TRADITIONAL THEORY IN TERMS OF MODERN INSTANCES AND CONDITIONS.

1499 JAVITS B.A., KEYSERLING L.H.
THE PEACE BY INVESTMENT CORPORATION.
WASHINGTON: COMM PEACE INVESTMT, 1961, 63 PP.
DISCUSSION OF PURPOSE, AIMS, AND METHODS OF PEACE BY INVESTMENT CORPORATION WHICH STRIVES TO PROMOTE INTERNATIONAL ECONOMIC DEVELOPMENT THROUGH PEOPLE-TO-PEOPLE RELATIONS. CRITICIZES GOVERNMENT'S FAILURE TO MEET FOREIGN AND DOMESTIC ECONOMIC CHALLENGES. EXPLAINS NEW PROGRAMS SUCH AS PEACE CORPS AND FOOD FOR PEACE, WHICH USE VAST AMERICAN ECONOMIC POTENTIALS TO PROMOTE INTERNATIONAL ECONOMIC WELL-BEING.

1500 JAVITS J.K.
"POLITICAL ACTION VITAL FOR LATIN AMERICAN INTEGRATION."
CENTRO, 2 (JAN. 66), 11-15.
PROPOSES ESTABLISHMENT OF COMMITTEE FOR ECONOMIC UNION OF AMERICAS. INVITES PARTICIPATION OF POLITICAL PARTIES, TRADE UNIONS, AND PRIVATE CORPORATIONS. ASSESSES PACE OF PRESENT PLAN FOR ECONOMIC INTEGRATION AS TOO SLOW.

1501 JAVITS J.K.
"LAST CHANCE FOR A COMMON MARKET."
FOREIGN AFFAIRS, 45 (APR. 67), 449-462.
ADVOCATES SUPPORT OF ECONOMIC INTEGRATION OF LATIN AMERICA IMPLEMENTED BY A LATIN AMERICAN COMMON MARKET. THE INDIVIDUAL LATIN AMERICAN NATIONS MUST REALIZE THAT THEIR NATIONAL ECONOMIC PROBLEMS ARE NOT EXCLUSIVELY THEIR OWN, BUT PART OF A GENERAL LATIN AMERICAN ECONOMIC CRISIS. SHOWS IMMEDIATE NEED FOR JOINT ACTION AND CAPABLE LEADERSHIP TO ACHIEVE RAPID ECONOMIC RECOVERY.

1502 JEFFRIES C.
TRANSFER OF POWER: PROBLEMS OF THE PASSAGE TO SELF-GOVERNMENT.
NEW YORK: FREDERICK PRAEGER, 1960, 148 PP.
DISCUSSES PROBLEMS OF INDEPENDENCE, CONDITIONS REQUIRED TO MAKE IT EFFECTIVE, AND ROLE OF BRITISH GOVERNMENT IN ACHIEVING EFFECTIVE TRANSFER OF POWER. EXAMINES EXPERIENCE OF CEYLON, MALAYA, GOLD COAST, NIGERIA, CARIBBEAN AREA, AND CENTRAL AFRICA.

1503 JELAVICH C.
TSARIST RUSSIA AND BALKAN NATIONALISM.
BERKELEY: U OF CALIF PR, 1962, 304 PP., LC#58-12830.
A STUDY OF THE INFLUENCE OF RUSSIA IN THE INTERNAL AFFAIRS OF BULGARIA AND SERBIA, 1879-1886. SHOWS HOW RUSSIAN POLICY, CONNECTED AS IT WAS TO HER INTERESTS AS A MAJOR EUROPEAN POWER, CAME INTO CONFLICT WITH BULGARIAN NATIONALISM, BUT WAS SUPPORTED BY THE SERBIAN PEOPLE, WHO RESENTED AUSTRO-HUNGARIAN DOMINATION.

1504 JENKS C.W.
THE INTERNATIONAL PROTECTION OF TRADE UNION FREEDOM.
NEW YORK: PRAEGER, 1957, 592 PP.
STUDIES GROWTH, DEVELOPMENT AND EFFECTIVENESS OF CURRENT INTERNATIONAL LAWS GUARANTEEING FREEDOM OF ASSOCIATION TO THE WORLD'S TRADE UNIONS AND THE PROCEDURAL ARRANGEMENTS CONCERNED WITH THE LAWS. SPECULATES AS TO FUTURE EFFECTIVENESS OF LAWS IN CONNECTION WITH THE UNIONS'RIGHTS.

1505 JENKS C.W.
THE COMMON LAW OF MANKIND.
NEW YORK: PRAEGER, 1958, 456 PP.
DEALS WITH DEVELOPMENT OF LAW AFTER WW 2. GENERAL

CONCEPTION THAT CONTEMPORARY INTERNATIONAL LAW CAN NO LONGER BE PRESENTED WITHIN ITS CLASSICAL FRAMEWORK. SUGGESTS TNAT IT MUST BE REGARDED AS THE COMMON LAW OF MANKIND 'IN AN EARLY STAGE OF ITS DEVELOPMENT.'

1506 JENKS C.W.
INTERNATIONAL IMMUNITIES.
NEW YORK: OCEANA, 1961, 178 PP., $6.00.
DISCUSSES HISTORICAL DEVELOPMENT OF PRINCIPLE OF INTERNATIONAL IMMUNITY. ATTEMPTS TO POINT OUT FUTURE COURSE. CITES EXAMPLES OF BEHAVIOR OF INTERNATIONAL ORGANIZATIONS IN CONNECTION WITH IMPORTANT CASES.

1507 JENNINGS W.I.
THE COMMONWEALTH IN ASIA.
LONDON: CLARENDON PRESS, 1951, 124 PP.
ANALYSIS OF THE PROBLEMS RESULTING FROM INDEPENDENCE OF CEYLON, INDIA, AND PAKISTAN FROM UNITED KINGDOM; EXAMINES TENTATIVE SOLUTIONS. DISCUSSES DIVERSITY OF PEOPLES, COMMUNALISM, EDUCATION, CLASS DIVISIONS, RESPONSIBLE GOVERNMENT, CONSTITUTIONS OF CEYLON AND INDIA, AND RELATIONS WITH THE COMMONWEALTH.

1508 JENNINGS W.I.
PROBLEMS OF THE NEW COMMONWEALTH.
DURHAM: DUKE U PR, 1958, 114 PP., LC#58-6972.
REVISION OF THREE LECTURES DELIVERED BY AUTHOR AT COMMONWEALTH STUDIES CENTER, DUKE UNIVERSITY. FOCUS ON INFLUENCE OF INDIA, PAKISTAN, AND CEYLON ON STRUCTURE AND FUNCTION OF THE COMMONWEALTH. CONSIDER THE MANY ECONOMIC AND POLITICAL PROBLEMS FACING THE ORGANIZATION.

1509 JENNINGS R.
PROGRESS OF INTERNATIONAL LAW.
NEW YORK: CAMBRIDGE, 1960, 223 PP.
TRACES EVOLUTION AND HISTORY OF CONTEMPORARY CONCEPT OF INTERNATIONAL LAW AND EXAMINES THE POSSIBILITIES FOR ITS FUTURE DEVELOPMENT.

1510 JENNINGS W.I.
THE COMMONWEALTH IN ASIA.
NEW YORK: OXFORD U PR, 1951, 124 PP.
EXAMINES PROBLEMS IN INDIA, CEYLON, AND PAKISTAN CREATED BY INDEPENDENCE. BEGINS WITH HISTORY OF ETHNIC ORIGINS, EMPHASIZING DIVERSITY OF PEOPLE, AND EUROPEAN INFILTRATION. DISCUSSES COMMUNALISM, EDUCATION, AND CLASS DIVISIONS AS PROBLEMS. FINAL CHAPTERS DEAL WITH INDEPENDENCE, POLITICAL FORMS, AND CONCEPT OF RESPONSIBLE GOVERNMENT; INCLUDES CONSTITUTIONS OF EACH COUNTRY AND COMMONWEALTH RELATIONS.

1511 JENNINGS W.I.
PROBLEMS OF THE NEW COMMONWEALTH.
DURHAM: DUKE U PR, 1958, 114 PP., LC#58-6972.
ANALYZES ROLE OF FOUR ASIAN MEMBERS OF SECOND COMMONWEALTH, AN ORGANIZATION BASED ON COMMON ADMIRATION OF POLITICAL IDEALS INSTEAD OF TRADITIONAL BASES OF LANGUAGE, RACE, OR CULTURE. EMPHASIZES IMPORTANCE OF ASSIMILATION OF BRITISH POLITICAL IDEAS FOR CONTINUITY OF COMMONWEALTH AND SOLUTION TO PROBLEMS OF AN AREA. ALSO DISCUSSES PROBLEMS RESULTING FROM COALITION.

1512 JENNINGS W.I.
DEMOCRACY IN AFRICA.
NEW YORK: CAMBRIDGE U PRESS, 1963, 89 PP.
EXAMINES POLITICAL PROBLEMS OF EMERGING NATIONS ONCE UNDER BRITISH RULE AS THEY SET UP GOVERNMENTS. DISCUSSES RELATIONSHIP OF WESTERN CULTURE TO AFRICAN CULTURE WITH ITS NATIONALISM AND RAPIDLY CHANGING SOCIETIES. STUDIES BRITISH FORM OF DEMOCRACY AND ITS APPLICABILITY FOR AFRICA. STATES THAT PROBLEMS OF NATIONS TRYING TO BE DEMOCRACIES CAN BE SOLVED.

1513 JENSEN D.L.
DIPLOMACY AND DOGMATISM.
CAMBRIDGE: HARVARD U PR, 1964, 322 PP., LC#63-20769.
TRACES ACTIVITIES OF MENDOZA, SPANISH AMBASSADOR IN FRANCE, AND EXTENT OF CONNECTION BETWEEN SPAIN AND FRENCH CATHOLIC LEAGUE. EXAMINES ROLE THAT MENDOZA AND CATHOLIC LEAGUE PLAYED IN COUNTER REFORMATION.

1514 JESSUP P.C.
A MODERN LAW OF NATIONS.
NEW YORK: MACMILLAN, 1948, 236 PP.
EXPLORES SOME UNDERLYING BASES FOR A MODERN LAW OF NATIONS. DISCUSSES PAST ATTEMPTS AT INTERGOVERNMENTAL RELATIONSHIPS. STRESSES THAT INTERNATIONAL LAW MUST BE DIRECTLY APPLICABLE TO THE INDIVIDUAL, AND THAT THERE MUST BE DEFINITE COMMITMENT TO OBSERVANCE BY INTERNATIONAL SOCIETY.

1515 JESSUP P.C.
TRANSNATIONAL LAW.
NEW HAVEN: YALE U. PR., 1956, 113 PP.
THREE LECTURES ON THE LAW WHICH 'REGULATES ACTIONS OR EVENTS THAT TRANSCEND NATIONAL FRONTIERS', CIVIL, CRIMINAL, PUBLIC, AND PRIVATE. DEFINES THE TERMS AND DISCUSSES THE PROBLEMS OF SEEKING PROPER JURISDICTION AND CHOOSING THE CORRECT LAW.

1516 JEWELL M.E.
SENATORIAL POLITICS AND FOREIGN POLICY.
LEXINGTON: U. KENTUCKY PR., 1963, 214 PP.
STUDIES POLITICAL PROCESSES OF US SENATE THROUGH AN EXAMINATION OF ITS FOREIGN POLICY PROGRAM DURING YEARS 1947 THROUGH 1960. STRESSES INFLUENCE OF BOTH PRESIDENT AND PUBLIC OPINION UPON BODY'S LEGISLATION. CONCLUDES THAT POLITICAL PARTIES 'CAN CONTRIBUTE A GREATER MEASURE OF RATIONALITY AND RESPONSIBILITY TO THE POLICYMAKING PROCESS....'

1517 JIMENEZ E.
VOTING AND HANDLING OF DISPUTES IN THE SECURITY COUNCIL.
NEW YORK: CARNEGIE ENDOWMENT, 1950, 189 PP.
DESCRIBES EVOLUTION, LEGALITY, AND FUNCTION OF SECURITY COUNCIL VOTING PROCEDURES, SUBMISSION OF DISPUTES, METHODS OF SETTLEMENT, RESOLUTIONS, ETC. STRESSES GROWTH OF POWERS.

1518 JOHNS HOPKINS UNIVERSITY LIB
RECENT ADDITIONS.
BALTIMORE: J HOPKINS INTL STUD.
MONTHLY LISTING OF BOOKS RECEIVED IN LIBRARY OF SCHOOL OF ADVANCED INTERNATIONAL STUDIES, JOHNS HOPKINS UNIVERSITY. ENTRIES LISTED BY GEOGRAPHIC AREA. EACH ISSUE IS MIMEOGRAPHED LIST OF ABOUT 30 PAGES AND 300 ITEMS.

1519 JOHNSON A.M., SUPPLE B.E.
BOSTON CAPITALISTS AND WESTERN RAILROADS: A STUDY IN THE NINETEENTH CENTURY RAILROAD INVESTMENT PROCESS.
CAMBRIDGE: HARVARD U PR, 1967, 416 PP., LC#67-13254.
TREATS INVESTMENT DECISION-MAKING IN 19TH CENTURY THROUGH STUDY OF BOSTON FINANCIERS' DEALINGS IN WESTERN RAILROADS. BOSTONIAN EXPERIENCE IN OVERSEAS TRADE PROVIDED BOTH CAPITAL AND TECHNIQUES USEFUL IN WESTERN INVESTMENT, WITH GREAT CONSEQUENCES FOR AMERICAN ECONOMIC GROWTH. BOTH OPPORTUNIST AND DEVELOPMENTAL INVESTMENT IS DISCUSSED.

1520 JOHNSON D.G.
THE STRUGGLE AGAINST WORLD HUNGER (HEADLINE SERIES, NO. 184) (PAMPHLET)
NEW YORK: FOREIGN POLICY ASSN, 1967, 63 PP., LC#67-27423.
SUMMARIZES WORLD FOOD PROBLEM TODAY AND POSSIBLE FUTURE SITUATION. SUGGESTS IMPORTANCE OF PROGRAMS WHICH CAN EVENTUALLY MAKE DEVELOPING NATIONS AGRICULTURALLY SELF-SUFFICIENT, INSTEAD OF DEPENDENT ON US AID.

1521 JOHNSON D.H.N.
"THE SOUTH-WEST AFRICA CASES."
INTL. RELATIONS, 3 (APR. 67), 157-176.
HEAVILY DOCUMENTED ARGUMENT THAT JUDGMENT OF INTERNATIONAL COURT OF JUSTICE CONCERNING SOUTHWEST AFRICA WAS NOT, AS OTHERS CONTEND, A MISCARRIAGE OF JUSTICE. ARGUES THAT GIVEN SITUATION CREATED BY PREVIOUS JUDGMENT IN 1962, THE 1966 JUDGMENT WAS FAIR DECISION. HOWEVER, PRESENTS ALTERNATIVE SITUATIONS MORE FAVORABLE THAN ACTUAL OCCURRENCE IN 1962.

1522 JOHNSON E.A.J. ED.
THE DIMENSIONS OF DIPLOMACY.
BALTIMORE: JOHNS HOPKINS PRESS, 1964, 135 PP., LC#64-25072.
ESSAYS ON PROBLEMS IN DIPLOMACY AND FOREIGN RELATIONS BY EMINENT SCHOLARS. SOME TOPICS INCLUDED ARE TECHNIQUES OF DIPLOMACY, RELATIONSHIPS BETWEEN DIPLOMACY AND ECONOMICS, SCIENTIFIC ADVANCES, AND MILITARY POWER.

1523 JOHNSON H.G.
THE WORLD ECONOMY AT THE CROSSROADS.
LONDON: OXFORD U PR, 1965, 105 PP.
SURVEY OF CURRENT PROBLEMS OF INTERNATIONAL ECONOMIC ORGANIZATION INVOLVING FREE WORLD COUNTRIES. EMPHASIZES MONETARY, TRADE, AND ECONOMIC-DEVELOPMENT PROBLEMS ON INTERNATIONAL LEVEL. DISCUSSES FORMATION OF INTERNATIONAL ECONOMIC INSTITUTIONS UP TO POST-WWII ERA, NOTING SEVERE POLITICAL AND ECONOMIC CONFLICTS AMONG NATIONS COMPRISING THESE INSTITUTIONS.

1524 JOHNSON J.
"THE UNITED STATES AND THE LATIN AMERICAN LEFT WINGS."
YALE REV., 56 (SPRING 67), 321-335.
DISCUSSION OF LATIN AMERICAN LEFTISTS, BOTH INTELLECTUALS AND POLITICIANS, COMPARISON OF MOTIVATIONS. NON-COMMUNIST LEFTISM IS SEEN AS HAVING MOST POLITICAL PROMISE FOR LA. IT IS AN URBAN PHENOMENON, VANGUARD OF THE YOUNG WHO ARE A LARGE SEGMENT OF THE POPULATION. ORGANIZED LABOR FAVORS LEFTISTS. RADICAL REFORMISM HAS BECOME FASHIONABLE. US NEEDS TO REASSESS ITS CONSERVATIVE POSITION - A LOSING ONE.

1525 JOHNSON L.B.
MY HOPE FOR AMERICA.
NEW YORK: RANDOM HOUSE, INC, 1964, 127 PP., LC#64-8358.
PERSONAL DISCUSSION OF LBJ'S PHILOSOPHY OF GOVERNMENT, AS A DEMOCRAT LEADING "GREAT SOCIETY." COVERS HIS HOPES FOR, AND FAITH IN AMERICA'S FUTURE AND HIS PLANS AND BELIEFS FOR ADMINISTRATION'S DOMESTIC AND FOREIGN POLICIES. INCLUDES HIS VIEWS ON FUTURE ROLE OF DEMOCRATIC PARTY.

1526 JOHNSON O.H.
"THE ENGLISH TRADITION IN INTERNATIONAL LAW."
INT. COMP. LAW QUART., 11 (APR. 62), 416-45.
TRACES EXISTENCE AND COMPREHENSION OF INTERNATIONAL LAW TO MIDDLE AGES. AREA NEGLECTED SINCE END OF PRIZE COURTS. PROPOSES BROADER STUDY IN UNIVERSITIES. URGES OFFICIALS IN PERTINENT POSITIONS TO GAIN FAMILARITY WITH SUBJECT.

1527 JOHNSTON D.M.
THE INTERNATIONAL LAW OF FISHERIES: A FRAMEWORK FOR POLICY-ORIENTED INQUIRIES.
NEW HAVEN: YALE U PR, 1965, 554 PP., LC#65-22325.
SHOWS INABILITY OF CLASSIC LEGAL CONCEPTS, DOMINATED BY IDEA OF TERRITORIAL SOVEREIGNTY, TO SATISFY CONTEMPORARY NEEDS AND DEMANDS RELATING TO EXPLOITATION OF FISHERIES. CONCLUDES THAT DEVELOPMENT OF LAW DEPENDS ON FUNCTIONAL REASSESSMENT OF EXISTING LAW.

1528 JOHNSTON D.M.
"LAW, TECHNOLOGY AND THE SEA."
CALIF. LAW REV., 55 (MAY 67), 449-472.
EXPLORES CONFLICT BETWEEN INTERNATIONAL LAW AND VALUE OF EFFICIENCY INHERENT IN MODERN TECHNOLOGY AS EXPRESSED IN CHANGES TAKING PLACE IN LAW OF THE SEA. CATEGORIZES USES OF SEA SUGGESTED BY TECHNOLOGY AND FIELDS IMPLIED FOR INTERNATIONAL LEGISLATION. DISCUSSES SPECIFIC ASPECTS OF CURRENT TREATIES AND LEGISLATION. DISPUTES NOTION OF TERRITORIALITY AT SEA. RECOMMENDS NEW APPROACHES TO PROPER LEGAL FRAMEWORK.

1529 JOHNSTONE A.
UNITED STATES DIRECT INVESTMENT IN FRANCE: AN INVESTIGATION OF THE FRENCH CHARGES.
CAMBRIDGE: M I T PRESS, 1965, 109 PP., LC#65-22005.
STUDIES FRENCH CLAIMS THAT US INVESTMENT PRESENTS THREAT TO ECONOMIC SOVEREIGNTY. POINTS OUT VIEWS OF BOTH AMERICAN BUSINESS AND FRENCH SOCIAL, POLITICAL, AND ECONOMIC INTERESTS. CONCLUSIONS GENERALLY SUPPORT FRENCH OFFICIALS. INCLUDES RECOMMENDATIONS FOR BOTH US AND FRENCH GOVERNMENTS.

1530 JONES A.C. ED.
NEW FABIAN COLONIAL ESSAYS.
LONDON: HOGARTH PR, 1959, 271 PP.
ESSAYS ON ASPECTS OF MODERN COLONIALISM. RELATIONSHIPS OF SOCIALISM AND LABOR PARTY TO COLONIAL POLICY AND COLONIALISM IN WORLD POLITICS ARE DISCUSSED. PRESENTS POLITICAL, SOCIAL, AND ECONOMIC OBJECTIVES OF COLONIALISM. ADMINISTRATION AND EDUCATIONAL SYSTEM ARE EXAMINED ALONG WITH COLONIAL LIBERATION POLICY AND CHANCES FOR SOCIALIST COMMONWEALTH.

1531 JONES H.D.
UNESCO: A SELECTED LIST OF REFERENCES.
WASHINGTON: LIBRARY OF CONGRESS, 1948, 56 PP.
242 BOOKS, OFFICIAL DOCUMENTS, PAMPHLETS, ARTICLES ANNOTATED TO INDICATE CONTENT, CONNECTION OF AUTHOR TO UNESCO, AND OTHER PERTINENT INFORMATION. INDEXED BY AUTHOR AND LISTED BY SUBJECT. PURPORTS TO SELECT BASIC MATERIAL THAT COVERS THE BACKGROUND, HISTORY, PURPOSE, FUNCTION, AND PROGRAM OF UNESCO.

1532 JONES J.M.
THE FIFTEEN WEEKS (FEBRUARY 21-JUNE 5, 1947)
NEW YORK: VIKING PRESS, 1955, 296 PP., LC#55-8923.
HISTORY OF MARSHALL PLAN AND TRUMAN DOCTRINE. DETAILS SITUATION THAT LED UP TO THEIR CONCEPTION. ATTEMPTS AN INTIMATE STORY OF POLITICAL BACKGROUND IN WASHINGTON DURING FIFTEEN CRUCIAL WEEKS.

1533 JORDAN A.
"MILITARY ASSISTANCE AND NATIONAL POLICY."
ORBIS, 2 (SUMMER 58), 236-53.
PRESENTS HISTORY OF MILITARY AID AND RESULTS OF AID TO ALLIES AND 'FRIENDLY' UNDERDEVELOPED NATIONS. SUGGESTS THAT INADEQUATE AID TO CHINA RESULTED IN COMMUNIST VICTORY. MAKES RECOMMENDATIONS FOR ALTERNATIVE AID POLICY.

1534 JORDAN A.
"POLITICAL COMMUNICATION: THE THIRD DIMENSION OF STRATEGY."
ORBIS, 8(FALL 64), 670-85.
ANALYSIS OF EFFORTS TO INFLUENCE FOREIGN AUDIENCES. DISCUSSION OF PAST AMERICAN TECHNIQUES SUGGESTS THAT AN ORGANIC, AS OPPOSED TO AN INERT, SYSTEM OF COMMUNICATION BE DEVISED. SURVEYS POTENTIAL USES OF EXISTING ORGANIZATIONS AND PUBLICATIONS, BOTH GOVERNMENTAL AND PRIVATE.

1535 JORDAN A.A. JR.
FOREIGN AID AND THE DEFENSE OF SOUTHEAST ASIA.
NEW YORK: FREDERICK PRAEGER, 1962, 272 PP., LC#62-14862.
DIVIDES FOREIGN AID INTO MILITARY ASSISTANCE, STABILITY SUPPORT, AND ECONOMIC DEVELOPMENT AND DESCRIBES CLOSE INTERRELATION. PRESENTS RATIONALE BEHIND AND PLANS FOR EACH TYPE OF AID. DISCUSSES WARFARE IN SOUTHEAST ASIA, BUDGETARY AND FISCAL PROBLEMS, MILITARY DETERRENCE, AND OVERPOPULATION AS ASPECTS OF FOREIGN AID THAT MUST BE CONSIDERED IN POLICY-MAKING.

1536 JORDAN N., MCNEIL E.B., SAWYER J.
"INTERNATIONAL RELATIONS AND THE PSYCHOLOGIST."
BULL. AT. SCI., 19 (NOV. 63), 29-38.
THREE ARTICLES, INCLUDING A BITING ATTACK ON THE IRRELEVANCY OF MOST PSYCHOLOGICAL THEORY AND METHOD AS NOW APPLIED TO INTERNATIONAL RELATIONS, AN EQUALLY SHARP REJOINDER, AND AN OBJECTIVE STATEMENT OF WHAT PSYCHOLOGY CAN CONTRIBUTE TO UNDERSTANDING OF INTERNATIONAL RELATIONS AND POLICY.

1537 JOSEPH F.M. ED.
AS OTHERS SEE US: THE UNITED STATES THROUGH FOREIGN EYES.
PRINCETON: U. PR., 1959, 360 PP.
TWENTY WRITERS FROM DIFFERENT PARTS OF THE WORLD FORM A MOSAIC THAT REPRESENTS THE WORLD'S VIEW OF USA. AUTHOR BELIEVES THAT VALUE OF USA CONTRIBUTION, NOW THAT IT FINDS ITSELF IN LEADING WORLD-ROLE, DEPENDS ON RELATION BETWEEN WHAT USA THINKS ABOUT ITSELF AND WHAT OTHERS THINK ABOUT IT.

1538 JOSHI P.S.
THE TYRANNY OF COLOUR.
DURBAN, S.A.: E.P.& COMMERCIAL PRINT. CO., 2942,318 PP.
STUDIES INDIAN'S PROBLEM IN SOUTH AFRICA FROM FIRST IMMIGRATIONS OF 1860 THROUGH 1939, INCLUDING RACIAL POLICIES OF GOVERNMENT AGAINST INDIAN MINORITY, LATTER'S REACTION, AND GENERAL DISCUSSIONS OF RACE PROBLEMS IN SOUTH AFRICA.

1539 JOY C.T.
HOW COMMUNISTS NEGOTIATE.
NEW YORK: MACMILLAN, 1955, 178 PP., $3.50.
CHRONICLE OF AUTHOR'S EXPERIENCES IN COPING WITH COMMUNIST PSYCHOLOGY AND METHODS WHILE NEGOTIATING KOREAN TRUCE AGREEMENT FROM 1951 TO 1953 AS CHIEF OF UNITED NATIONS COMMAND DELEGATION TO KOREAN ARMISTICE CONFERENCE. FAR EAST POLICIES OF TRUMAN AND ACHESON ARE CRITICIZED, WITH PREFERENCE SHOWN FOR KOREAN STRATEGY RECOMMENDED BY GENERAL MAC ARTHUR.

1540 JOYCE W.
THE PROPAGANDA GAP.
NEW YORK: HARPER & ROW, 1963, 144 PP., LC#63-12055.
MAINTAINS US IS LOSING THE COLD WAR BECAUSE OF FAILURE TO USE ALL THE PROPAGANDA TECHNIQUES AT ITS DISPOSAL. SUGGESTS USE OF PRIVATE PROFESSIONAL COMMUNICATORS AND UNIVERSITY PERSONNEL IN CREATING A CABINET LEVEL PROPAGANDA AGENCY.

1541 JUAN T.L.
ECONOMIC AND SOCIAL DEVELOPMENT OF MODERN CHINA: A BIBLIOGRAPHICAL GUIDE.
NEW HAVEN: HUMAN REL AREA FILES, 1956, 87 PP.
BIBLIOGRAPHY OF MONOGRAPHS AND PAMPHLETS PUBLISHED IN ENGLISH, FRENCH, AND GERMAN FROM BEGINNING OF 20TH CENTURY THROUGH 1955. CONTAINS ITEMS ON STATISTICS, ECONOMIC HISTORY, BASIC ECONOMIC RESOURCES, AGRICULTURE, INDUSTRY, COMMERCE AND COMMUNICATION, TRANSPORTATION, MONEY AND BANKING, AND INTERNATIONAL ECONOMIC RELATIONS.

1542 JUDD P. ED.
AFRICAN INDEPENDENCE: THE EXPLODING EMERGENCE OF THE NEW AFRICAN NATIONS.
NEW YORK: DELL PUBL CO, 1963, 512 PP.
ESSAYS PRESENT BACKGROUNDS, POLITICAL STRUGGLES, AND PROBLEMS OF INDEPENDENCE AMONG EMERGENT NATIONS.

1543 JUVILER P.H.
"INTERPARLIAMENTARY CONTACTS IN SOVIET FOREIGN POLICY."
AMER. SLAV. EASTEUROPE. REV., 20 (FEB. 61), 25-39.
BRIEF HISTORY OF THE INTERNATIONAL PARLIAMENTARY UNION FROM ITS FOUNDATION IN 1889 TO THE PRESENT. DESCRIBES STRUCTURE AND PURPOSE OF THE PARLIAMENTARY GROUP RECENTLY ORIGINATED AROUND THE USSR, AND EXPECTS IT TO BECOME A USEFUL CHANNEL OF CONTACT WITH THE WEST.

1544 KADEN E.H., SPRINGER M.
DER POLITISCHE CHARAKTER DER FRANZOSISCHEN KULTURPROPAGANDA AM RHEIN.
BERLIN: FRANZ VAHLEN, 1923, 86 PP.
STUDY OF METHODS AND AIMS OF FRENCH PROPAGANDA IN EFFORT TO DECLARE RHINE RIVER THE NATURAL BORDER OF THE FRENCH NATION AND CULTURE.

1545 KAFKA G.
FREIHEIT UND ANARCHIE.
MUNICH: E REINHARDT VERLAG, 1949, 115 PP.
DEALS WITH THE FOUR FREEDOMS (FREEDOM FROM WANT, FREEDOM OF RELIGIOUS EXPRESSION, FREEDOM OF OPINION, AND FREEDOM FROM FEAR) AS EXPRESSED IN THE ATLANTIC CHARTER.

1546 KAHIN G.M. ED.
MAJOR GOVERNMENTS OF ASIA (2ND ED.)
ITHACA: CORNELL U PRESS, 1963, 719 PP., LC#63-15940.
STUDY IN COMPARATIVE GOVERNMENT DEVOTED TO CHINA, PAKISTAN, INDIA, INDONESIA, AND JAPAN. EACH GOVERNMENT IS HANDLED BY A DIFFERENT AUTHOR WHO HAS ARRANGED MATERIAL ACCORDING TO HIS OWN JUDGEMENT. ALL TREAT HISTORICAL

BACKGROUND OF PRESENT POLITICAL ORGANIZATION. INCLUDES SECTION OF SELECTED READINGS.

1547 KAHN H.
THINKING ABOUT THE UNTHINKABLE.
NEW YORK: HORIZON, 1962, 254 PP.
DISCUSSES PROBLEMS CREATED BY MODERN TECHNOLOGY AND BY CONTEMPORARY INTERNATIONAL RELATIONS. CALLS FOR A WORLD GOVERNMENT TO HANDLE THE PROBLEMS PRESENTED BY THE THERMONUCLEAR AGE.

1548 KAHN H.
ON ESCALATION; METAPHORS AND SCENARIOS.
NEW YORK: FREDERICK PRAEGER, 1965, 308 PP., LC#65-18080.
SYSTEMATIC ANALYSIS OF VARIED ISSUES THAT ARISE IN ESCALATION SITUATIONS OR CRISES. EXAMINES LONG-RUN IMPLICATIONS OF ARMS RACE. INVESTIGATES WAYS IN WHICH IMPROVEMENTS IN INTERNATIONAL ORDER MAY BE IMPLEMENTED, AND THE POLITICAL, MILITARY, SOCIAL, AND ECONOMIC CONSEQUENCES OF DIFFERENT MODES OF TRANSITION. IDENTIFIES AREAS OF OPPOSITION AND COMPATIBILITY IN NATIONAL INTEREST AND SECURITY.

1549 KAHN H., DIBBLE C.
"CRITERIA FOR LONG-RANGE NUCLEAR CONTROL POLICIES."
CALIF. LAW REV., 55 (MAY 67), 473-492.
ARGUES THAT TECHNICAL AND FINANCIAL OBSTACLES TO NUCLEAR PROLIFERATION WILL NO LONGER BE IMPORTANT IN THE FUTURE, THAT PROLIFERATION WILL BE RADICALLY DIFFERENT PROBLEM FROM TODAY. SUGGESTS CRITERIA BY WHICH NUCLEAR POLICY SHOULD BE JUDGED. INCLUDES SUGGESTIONS ON MERITS OF "LEX TALIONIS" AND REGIONAL DEFENSE SYSTEMS. ADVOCATES UNIVERSE OF SEMI-EQUAL NATIONAL POWERS.

1550 KAISER R.G.
"THE TRUMAN DOCTRINE* HOW IT ALL BEGAN."
FOREIGN SERVICE J., 44 (MAY 67), 17-18.
GIVES SOME BACKGROUND TO TRUMAN DOCTRINE. DISCUSSES RELATION OF BRITAIN TO USSR AS DOMINATING FACTOR IN DETERMINING CONGRESSIONAL APPROVAL OF BILL. SOME DISCUSSION OF INFLUENCES OF ECONOMIC SITUATION OF BRITAIN.

1551 KALDOR N.
ESSAYS ON ECONOMIC POLICY (VOL. II)
LONDON: DUCKWORTH, 1964, 320 PP.
FIRST PART OF STUDY DISCUSSES ECONOMIC POLICIES FOR MAINTAINING INTERNATIONAL STABILITY WITH SPECIFIC REFERENCE TO PROBLEMS IN INTERNATIONAL TRADE AND PAYMENTS. SECOND PART DEVOTED TO DISCUSSIONS OF VARIED TOPICS IN ECONOMIC CONDITIONS OF FIVE DIFFERENT COUNTRIES.

1552 KALIJARVI T.V.
MODERN WORLD POLITICS (3RD ED.)
NEW YORK: THOMAS Y CROWELL, 1953, 631 PP., LC#53-7883.
GENERAL DISCUSSION OF PRINCIPLES OF INTERNATIONAL RELATION AND WORLD POLITICS. EXAMINES TECHNIQUES OF POWER POLITICS (ESPIONAGE, DIPLOMACY, ECONOMIC CONFLICT) AND DISCUSSES POLITICS OF "GREAT REGIONS" (NEAR EAST, UK, USSR, US, EAST ASIA).

1553 KALUODA J.
"COMMUNIST STRATEGY IN LATIN AMERICA."
YALE REV., 50 (SEPT. 60), 32-41.
A STUDY OF TECHNIQUES EMPLOYED IN ESTABLISHING COMMUNIST SOCIETIES IN LATIN AMERICA. DEVELOPMENTS IN CUBA COMPARED TO COMMUNIST EUROPE TO INDICATE MOVEMENTS IN LATIN AMERICA. STRESSES NEED TO HELP OAS TO DESTROY THE COMMUNIST BASE OF OPERATION IN CUBA.

1554 KANDELL I.L.
UNITED STATES ACTIVITIES IN INTERNATIONAL CULTURAL RELATIONS.
NEW YORK: AMER. COUNC. EDUC., 1945, 102 PP.
SURVEY OF ACTIVITIES OF PRIVATE AND GOVERNMENTAL AGENCIES IN FIELD IN PERIOD BETWEEN THE WORLD WARS. EMPHASIZES AMERICAN SHIFT FROM CULTURAL DEBTOR TO EXPORTER.

1555 KANET R.E.
THE SOVIET UNION AND SUB-SAHARAN AFRICA: COMMUNIST POLICY TOWARD AFRICA, 1917-1965.
PRINCETON, N.J.: PRINCETON UNIVERSITY, 1966,565 PP.
STUDIES SOVIET POLICY IN AFRICA. FIRST SECTION OFFERS DETAILED HISTORICAL BACKGROUND TO CONTEMPORARY POLICY, WHILE SECOND SECTION EXAMINES SHIFT IN SOVIET THINKING IN MID-FIFTIES. ARGUES THAT SOVIET POLICY IN AFRICA IS BASICALLY PEACEFUL AND SOVIETS DO NOT WANT VIOLENT REVOLUTIONS BUT ECONOMIC AND SOCIAL PROGRESS.

1556 KANTOR H.
A BIBLIOGRAPHY OF UNPUBLISHED DOCTORAL DISSERTATIONS AND MASTERS' THESES DEALING WITH GOVTS, POL, INT REL OF LAT AM.
WASHINGTON, D.C.: INTER-AM. BIB&LIB. ASSN.,1953, 85PP.
UNANNOTATED BIBLIOGRAPHY OF UNPUBLISHED RESEARCH PAPERS COMPILED FOR THE LATIN AMERICAN AFFAIRS COMMITTEE OF THE AMERICAN POLITICAL SCIENCE ASSOCIATION. OUTLINES THE TOPICS WHICH HAVE RECEIVED MOST ATTENTION AND THOSE WHICH HAVE BEEN NEGLECTED IN AREAS OF GOVERNMENT, POLITICS, AND INTERNATIONAL RELATIONS.

1557 KAPLAN D.
THE ARAB REFUGEES: AN ABNORMAL PROBLEM.
JERUSALEM: RUBIN MASS, 1959, 230 PP.
ANALYZES PROBLEM OF ARAB REFUGEES WHO HAVE RECEIVED MORE UN AID FOR LONGER PERIOD THAN ANY GROUP. FEELS UN NOT DEALING WITH PROBLEM CORRECTLY. IT IS NOT "HUMANITARIAN PROBLEM TO BE SOLVED BY ECONOMIC MEANS, BUT POLITICAL ONE." ARAB REFUGEES ARE REFUGEES IN ARAB NATIONS WHERE LEADERS FAIL TO ACCEPT THEM AND ARE EXPLOITING UN.

1558 KAPLAN L. ED., PAINE C.S. ED.
REVIEW INDEX.
CHICAGO: FOLLETT PUBLISHING CO.
UNANNOTATED QUARTERLY GUIDE TO PROFESSIONAL REVIEWS FIRST ISSUED IN 1941. CLASSIFIED ALPHABETICALLY BY SUBJECT WITH A NAME INDEX IN EACH ISSUE. INCLUDES PUBLICATIONS IN BUSINESS, INDUSTRY, AND FINANCE; ECONOMICS; INTERNATIONAL RELATIONS AND HISTORY; LABOR; POLITICAL SCIENCE; POPULATION STUDIES; PSYCHOLOGY; RACE AND MINORITY PROBLEMS; AND SOCIOLOGY. ANNUAL CUMULATIONS ISSUED.

1559 KAPLAN M.
"BALANCE OF POWER, BIPOLARITY AND OTHER MODELS OF INTERNATIONAL SYSTEMS" (BMR)"
AM. POL. SCI. REV., 51 (SEPT. 57), 684-695.
SURVEY OF THE STATE OF INTERNATIONAL POLITICAL THEORY SINCE 1945. ARGUES FOR USE OF SYSTEMS THEORY IN UNDERSTANDING INTERNATIONAL RELATIONS. HE PRESENTS SIX ALTERNATIVE MODELS OF INTERNATIONAL SYSTEMS: "BALANCE OF POWER" SYSTEM, LOOSE BIPOLAR SYSTEM, TIGHT BIPOLAR SYSTEM, THE UNIVERSAL SYSTEM, HIERARCHICAL SYSTEM, AND THE UNIT VETO SYSTEM.

1560 KAPLAN M.A.
SYSTEM AND PROCESS OF INTERNATIONAL POLITICS.
NEW YORK: WILEY, 1957, 283 PP.
A STUDY OF THE HISTORY OF INTERNATIONAL RELATIONS IS NECESSARY IN ORDER TO DISCERN WHICH FACTORS ARE REALLY ESSENTIAL TO AN UNDERSTANDING OF THIS FIELD. AN EXAMINATION OF THE REGULATORY PROCESSES, VALUES, AND STRATEGY AS THEY APPLY TO INTERNATIONAL RELATIONS IS ALSO REQUIRED.

1561 KAPLAN M.A.
"SOME PROBLEMS IN THE STRATEGIC ANALYSIS OF INTERNATIONAL POLITICS."
PRINCETON: CENT. INT. STUD., 1959, 37 PP.
FEELS MUCH OF PRESENT-DAY INTERNATIONAL POLITICS IS A GAME TO ESTABLISH SIGNALS, I.E., TO CONTROL EXPECTATIONS. ANALYZES SPECIFIC NON-ZERO-SUM GAMES. GIVES HYPOTHETICAL EXAMPLES AND RELATES THEM TO HISTORICAL EVENTS. TREATS IN DETAIL PROBLEMS OF COORDINATION OR TACIT COOPERATION.

1562 KAPLAN M.A., BURNS A.L., QUANDT R.E.
"THEORETICAL ANALYSIS OF THE BALANCE OF POWER."
BEHAV. SCI., 5 (JULY 60), 240-52.
PROPOSES THEORY OF COMPETITIVE GAME OF INTERNATIONAL POLITICS. DEPICTS FORMATION OF ALLIANCES AND COUNTER ALLIANCES. OUTLINES PROBLEMS OF SUPRANATIONAL NATIONS. DISCUSSES THE STABILITY OF A BALANCE OF POWER SYSTEM.

1563 KAPLAN M.A., KATZENBACH N.
THE POLITICAL FOUNDATIONS OF INTERNATIONAL LAW.
NEW YORK: WILEY, 1961 372 PP.
TRADITIONAL TOPICS ASSOCIATED WITH PATTERNS OF INTERNATIONAL POLICY. ANALYZES AND EVALUATES FRAMEWORK OF VARYING ORGANIZATIONAL DOCTRINES.

1564 KAPLAN M.A.
"OLD REALITIES AND NEW MYTHS."
WORLD POLIT., 17 (JAN. 65), 334-367.
SEVERE CRITICISM OF WASHINGTON AND SENATOR FULBRIGHT. ASSERTS THAT BY MOST IMPORTANT OPERATIONAL TESTS, USA FOREIGN POLICY IS BANKRUPT. ALSO USA KNOWS ART OF WAR MUCH BETTER THAN PEACE. TOP-ECHELON ORGANIZATIONS IN STATE DEPARTMENT AND EXECUTIVE OFFICE OF PRESIDENT DO NOT FUNCTION WELL. AUTHOR DEMANDS THAT USA FOREIGN POLICY HARMONIZE WITH POSSIBILITIES, RESOURCES, IDEALS AND WILL.

1565 KARDELJE
SOCIALISM AND WAR.
BELGRADE: PUBL HOUSE JUGOSLAVIA, 1960, 210 PP.
STUDY OF COMMUNIST CHINESE CRITICISM OF YUGOSLAVIA'S POLICY OF COEXISTENCE. EXAMINES NATURE OF WAR TODAY AND ITS IMPORTANCE TO SOCIALIST WORLD.

1566 KAREFA-SMART J. ED., ADEBO S.O. ED.
AFRICA: PROGRESS THROUGH COOPERATION.
NEW YORK: DODD, MEAD, 1966, 288 PP., LC#66-12809.
SPEECHES AND PAPERS PREPARED FOR THE 1965 AFRICAN CONFERENCE ON PROGRESS THROUGH COOPERATION. STUDY WAYS IN WHICH AFRICAN NATIONS CAN HASTEN ECONOMIC AND SOCIAL DEVELOPMENT, MEET PRESSING NEEDS OF THEIR PEOPLE, RAISE THEIR STANDARDS OF LIVING, AND ESTABLISH ADVANTAGEOUS DOMESTIC AND INTERNATIONAL RELATIONS. INQUIRE INTO

PRACTICAL WAYS FOR EFFECTIVE USE OF RESOURCES AND AID.

1567 KAROL K.S.
CHINA, THE OTHER COMMUNISM (TRANS. BY TOM BAISTOW)
NEW YORK: HILL AND WANG, 1967, 474 PP., LC#66-27608.
TRACES HISTORY OF COMMUNIST CHINA, EXAMINING CHANGES IN PARTY ORGANIZATION, CONTROL, AND INTERNAL AND EXTERNAL OBJECTIVES. DISCUSSES POLITICAL ORGANIZATION AND IDEOLOGICAL INDOCTRINATION OF PEASANT POPULATION, ITS EFFECTS ON THE RURAL CULTURE, AND SPECIFIC PROLETARIAN RESPONSES. INCLUDES STRUCTURE AND FUNCTION OF NATIONAL GOVERNMENT AND DISCUSSES CHINESE INTERNATIONAL RELATIONS AND WORLD GOALS.

1568 KARPOV P.V.
"PEACEFUL COEXISTENCE AND INTERNATIONAL LAW."
LAW CONTEMP. PROBL., 29 (AUTUMN 64), 865-70.
ADVOCATES NECESSITY OF COEXISTANCE BETWEEN SOCIALISM AND CAPITALISM AND OUTLINES BASIC PRINCIPLES OF THE DOCTRINE AS THEY SHOULD BE APPLIED TO INTERNATIONAL LAW.

1569 KARUNAKARAN K.P.
INDIA IN WORLD AFFAIRS, 1952-1958 (VOL. II)
LONDON: OXFORD U PR, 1959, 400 PP.
SECOND VOLUME IN SERIES WHICH REVIEWS INDIA'S FOREIGN RELATIONS AND INTERPRETS HER FOREIGN POLICY. COVERS PERIOD 1952-58. BIBLIOGRAPHY OF BOOKS, ARTICLES, AND DOCUMENTS.

1570 KATZ R.
DEATH IN ROME.
NEW YORK: MACMILLAN, 1967, 320 PP.
EXAMINATION OF THE ARDEATINE MASSACRE OF 1944 WHEN GERMANS MURDERED 355 ITALIAN CIVILIANS IN REPRISAL FOR A PARTISAN ATTACK ON A GERMAN POLICE UNIT. AUTHOR RELATES CONSEQUENT RIGHT-WING AND LEFT-WING TURMOIL IN ITALIAN POLITICAL FACTIONS AND ROLE OF POPE PIUS XII.

1571 KATZ S.M., MCGOWEN F.
A SELECTED LIST OF US READINGS ON DEVELOPMENT.
WASHINGTON: AGENCY FOR INTL DEV, 1963, 362 PP.
LIST OF SELECTED READINGS ON APPLICATION OF SCIENCE AND TECHNOLOGY TO PROBLEMS OF LESS-DEVELOPED NATIONS. REPRESENTATIVE SAMPLE OF CURRENT AMERICAN RESEARCH PAPERS, ACADEMIC STUDIES, AND OPERATIONAL REPORTS ON MAJOR AREAS OF SCIENCE AND TECHNOLOGY. CONTAINS FAIRLY EXTENSIVE ANNOTATIONS OF 1,195 ITEMS PUBLISHED AFTER 1950. MATERIAL ORGANIZED BY SUBJECT; INCLUDES AUTHOR INDEX.

1572 KAUFMANN W.W.
THE MC NAMARA STRATEGY.
NEW YORK: HARPER & ROW, 1964, 339 PP., LC#64-12672.
DISCUSSES MC NAMARA'S POLICY AND INNOVATIONS IN DEFENSE DEPARTMENT. EXPLAINS CHANGES IN DECISION-MAKING PROCESS AND PROCEDURAL REFORMS, SUCH AS COST-EFFECTIVENESS APPROACH TO PROJECTS AND SYSTEMS. DETAILED DESCRIPTION OF SHIFT FROM CONCEPT OF MASSIVE RETALIATION TO STRATEGY OF FLEXIBLE RESPONSE AND LIMITED WARFARE. DRAWN LARGELY FROM DIRECT TESTIMONY OF THE SECRETARY AND PENTAGON OFFICIALS.

1573 KAWALKOWSKI A.
"POUR UNE EUROPE INDEPENDENTE ET REUNIFIEE."
POLIT. ETRANG., 28 (NO.3, 63), 195-221.
POINTS UP NECESSITY OF NUCLEAR AUTONOMY. FOCUSES ATTENTION ON DE GAULLE'S POLITICAL PLANS AND ECONOMIC OBJECTIVES. ANALYZES AMERICAN AND RUSSIAN ATTITUDES WITH RESPECT TO THESE AIMS.

1574 KEENAN G.F.
RUSSIA, THE ATOM AND THE WEST.
LONDON: OXFORD U. PR., 1957, 120 PP.
SERIES OF LECTURES DISCUSSING INTERNATIONAL SITUATION INCLUDING: THE SOVIET INTERNAL SITUATION, SOVIET MIND AND WORLD REALITIES, THE PROBLEM OF EASTERN AND CENTRAL EUROPE, NATO, AND ANGLO-AMERICAN RELATIONS.

1575 KEENLEYSIDE H.L.
INTERNATIONAL AID: A SUMMARY.
NEW YORK: JAMES H HEINEMAN, 1966, 343 PP., LC#66-22154.
ATTEMPTS TO REVIEW CONTEMPORARY CIRCUMSTANCES NECESSITATING AID PROGRAMS, TO PRESENT HISTORICAL SUMMARY OF INTERNATIONAL ASSISTANCE, DESCRIPTION OF CURRENT PROGRAMS, AND STEPS FOR FUTURE ACTION BASED ON PAST EXPERIENCE.

1576 KEEP J. ED., BRISBY L. ED.
CONTEMPORARY HISTORY IN THE SOVIET MIRROR.
NEW YORK: FREDERICK PRAEGER, 1964, 331 PP., LC#64-13490.
ANTHOLOGY ANALYZES SOVIET HISTORIOGRAPHER'S IMAGE OF REALITY AS COMPARED TO ACTUAL REALITY. EMPHASIZES METHOD OF SOVIET HISTORIOGRAPHY. CONTRIBUTORS STRESS INACCURACY OF SOVIET HISTORIOGRAPHY OWING TO GOVERNMENTAL CENSORSHIP AND PROPAGANDA, WHICH CREATE AN ATMOSPHERE OF NECESSARY COMPLIANCE ON THE PART OF HISTORIOGRAPHERS. EMPHASIZES TRENDS OF WRITING SINCE THE REVOLUTION.

1577 KEESING F.M.
THE SOUTH SEAS IN THE MODERN WORLD.
NEW YORK: JOHN DAY, 1941, 393 PP.
SURVEYS ISLAND REGION OF PACIFIC IN ATTEMPT TO DEFINE POLITICAL, STRATEGIC, AND ECONOMIC ROLE OF OCEANIC ISLANDS IN MODERN WORLD. CONCENTRATES ON ECONOMIC STRUCTURE OF ISLAND AND FORMS OF GOVERNMENT AS MODIFIERS OF CULTURE.

1578 KEETON G.W., SCHWARZENBERGER G.
MAKING INTERNATIONAL LAW WORK.
LONDON: STEVENS, 1946, 266 PP.
NOTHING LESS THAN WORLD GOVERNMENT CAN PROVIDE SECURE BASIS FOR INTERNATIONAL LAW. IN ABSENCE OF WORLD FEDERATION, POWERS MAY MAINTAIN AN UNEASY EQUILIBRIUM BUT THAT RULE OF LAW BETWEEN NATIONS WILL REMAIN AS PRECARIOUS AS IN THE PAST. DISCUSSES DEVELOPMENT OF INTERNATIONAL LAW AND SURVEYS EXISTING PROBLEMS.

1579 KELLY F.K.
"A PROPOSAL FOR AN ANNUAL REPORT ON THE STATE OF MANKIND."
CENTER MAGAZINE, 1 (OCT.-NOV. 67), 38-41.
PROPOSES THAT UN SECRETARY GENERAL GIVE WORLD A FULL REPORT EVERY YEAR ON STATE OF MANKIND, TO EVALUATE MAN'S DEEPEST PROBLEMS AND MAKE RECOMMENDATIONS. PURPOSE: TO START GLOBAL DIALOGUE, INVITING SUGGESTIONS FOR DEVELOPING WORLD CIVILIZATION. PRINTS LETTERS OF REACTION FROM EUGENE CARSON BLAKE, REINHOLD NIEBUHR, PAUL HOFFMAN, AND MANY OTHERS.

1580 KELSEN H.
LAW AND PEACE IN INTERNATIONAL RELATIONS.
CAMBRIDGE: HARVARD U. PR, 1942, 181 PP.
DEFINES LAW AS AN ORDER FOR THE PROMOTION OF PEACE. ANALYZES STRUCTURE OF PREVAILING SYSTEM OF NORMS LABELED INTERNATIONAL LAW TO SEE IF IT CONFORMS TO HIS CONCEPT. ADVOCATES ESTABLISHMENT OF INTERNATIONAL COURT WITH COMPULSORY JURISDICTION AS FIRST STEP IN REFORMING INTERNATIONAL RELATIONS.

1581 KELSEN H.
THE LAW OF THE UNITED NATIONS.
NEW YORK: PRAEGER, 1951, 994 PP.
A JURISTIC APPROACH TO PROBLEMS FACED BY UN. THESIS IS THAT WORDING OF LAWS PERMITS VARYING INTERPRETATIONS THAT ALLOW AFFECTED ORGANS TO DEVELOP AND EXPAND. PRESENTS ALL POSSIBLE INTERPRETATIONS OF BASIC PROBLEMS OF UN.

1582 KELSEN H.
"RECENT TRENDS IN THE LAW OF THE UNITED NATIONS."
LONDON: STEVENS, 1951, 991-94.
SUPPLEMENT TO BOOK 'THE LAW OF THE UNITED NATIONS.' VIEWS RECENT EVENTS SUCH AS NATO AND THE KOREAN WAR AS RELEVANT LEGAL PROBLEMS. REFLECTS ON GENERAL ASSEMBLY MOTION 'UNITING FOR PEACE.' THESIS IS THAT WORDING OF LAWS PERMITS VARYING INTERPRETATIONS. LAW ADAPTED TO CHANGING CIRCUMSTANCES.

1583 KELSEN H.
PRINCIPLES OF INTERNATIONAL LAW.
NEW YORK: RINEHART, 1952, 461 PP.
EXAMINATION OF NATURE OF INTERNATIONAL LAW WITH REFERENCE TO SPHERES OF VALIDITY, ESSENTIAL FUNCTIONS AND APPLICATION.

1584 KENEN P.B.
GIANT AMONG NATIONS: PROBLEMS IN UNITED STATES FOREIGN ECONOMIC POLICY.
NEW YORK: HARCOURT BRACE, 1960, 232 PP., LC#60-9395.
ANALYZES US PROGRAMS OF FOREIGN AID AND TRADE AND PROPOSES RE-EVALUATION OF BOTH. ADVOCATES TRADE ADJUSTMENT LEGISLATION, INCREASED INVESTMENT ABROAD, MORE EFFICIENT USE OF FUNDS, INTERNATIONALIZATION OF AID EFFORTS, LESS POLITICAL INFLUENCE ON AID, ESPECIALLY CONNECTIONS TO COLD WAR.

1585 KENEN P.B.
BRITISH MONETARY POLICY AND THE BALANCE OF PAYMENTS 1951-57.
CAMBRIDGE: HARVARD U PR, 1960, 325 PP., LC#60-11556.
SURVEYS BRITAIN'S DOMESTIC ECONOMIC POLICIES, ESPECIALLY HER MONETARY POLICIES, IN THE LIGHT OF HER BALANCE-OF-PAYMENTS POSITION, FOCUSING ON GOVERNMENT'S ATTITUDE AND RESPONSE TO BALANCE-OF-PAYMENTS CRISIS. CONTENDS THAT ATTEMPTS TO MAINTAIN EXTERNAL BALANCE HAVE REVOLUTIONIZED BANK OF ENGLAND POLICIES, AFFECTING VOLUME PRICE OF CREDIT RATHER THAN CONDITIONS IN DISCOUNT MARKET.

1586 KENNAN G.F.
REALITIES OF AMERICAN FOREIGN POLICY.
PRINCETON: PRINCETON U PRESS, 1954, 120 PP., LC#54-9021.
LECTURES DELIVERED IN STAFFORD LITTLE SERIES AT PRINCETON UNIVERSITY, 1954; CRITICAL OF UTOPIAN TENDENCIES IN US FOREIGN POLICY. GREATEST DANGER OF SOVIET POLICY IS ITS ATTEMPT TO PROMOTE CONFLICT WITHIN US ALLIANCE SYSTEM.

1587 KENNAN G.F.
RUSSIA, THE ATOM AND THE WEST.
NEW YORK: HARPER & ROW, 1958, 116 PP., LC#58-8078.
REFRAMES CONTAINMENT ARGUMENT AS OFFERED IN 1948. ESSAYS ANALYZE CURRENT WORLD POLITICS, EMPHASIZING CAUTION IN NATO BUILD-UP.

1588 KENNAN G.F.
THE DECISION TO INTERVENE: SOVIET-AMERICAN RELATIONS, 1917-1920 (VOL. II)
NEW YORK: ATHENEUM PUBLISHERS, 1958, 513 PP., LC#56-8382.
ILLUSTRATED STUDY OF SOVIET-AMERICAN RELATIONSHIP DURING WWI TREATS PRIMARILY THE AMERICAN COMMITMENT AND INTERVENTION. PICTURES THE IDEOLOGICAL CONFLICT, DISTRUST, AND LACK OF COMMUNICATION BETWEEN THE NEW RUSSIAN REVOLUTIONARY GOVERNMENT AND THE US.

1589 KENNAN G.F.
"PEACEFUL CO-EXISTENCE: A WESTERN VIEW."
FOREIGN AFFAIRS, 38 (JAN. 60), 171-190.
IN REPLY TO KHRUSHCHEV'S ARTICLE IN-OCTOBER 1959 ISSUE, KENNAN ASSERTS THAT SOVIET LEADER CONCEALED RUSSIAN HISTORY OF INTERNATIONAL VIOLENCE. PROBLEMS ARISING FROM SOVIET OCCUPATION OF CENTRAL EUROPE ARE REVIEWED AND THE DIVERGENT INTERPRETATIONS OF 'VALUE OF TRADE' ASSESSED.

1590 KENNAN G.F.
RUSSIA AND THE WEST.
BOSTON: LITTLE BROWN, 1960, 411 PP.
COVERS THREE DECADES OF USA-SOVIET DIPLOMATIC RELATIONS FROM 1917 TO END OF WW 2. DISCUSSES INDIVIDUAL EPISODES AND PROBLEMS, MAJOR LEADERS AS STATESMEN, IMPORTANT ENGAGEMENTS.

1591 KENNEDY J.F., NEVINS A. ED.
THE STRATEGY OF PEACE.
NEW YORK: HARPER & ROW, 1960, 233 PP., LC#60-7530.
SPEECHES AND STATEMENTS BY SENATOR JOHN F. KENNEDY ON DEFENSE, PEACE, NATIONAL SECURITY, AND RELATED DOMESTIC ISSUES. US MOVEMENT FROM CRISIS TO CRISIS RESULTS FROM LACK OF STRATEGY FOR PEACE RELEVANT TO CONTEMPORARY WORLD AND FROM US FAILURE TO PAY THE ATTENDANT PRICE OF SUCH A STRATEGY - ESPECIALLY IN SOCIAL INVENTIVENESS, MORAL STAMINA, PHYSICAL COURAGE.

1592 KENNEDY J.F.
TO TURN THE TIDE.
NEW YORK: HARPER & ROW, 1962, 235 PP., LC#61-12221.
SELECTION OF PRESIDENT KENNEDY'S SPEECHES AND WRITINGS FROM HIS ELECTION THROUGH 1961 ADJOURNMENT OF CONGRESS. GREATEST EMPHASIS IS ON IMPORTANT INTERNATIONAL ISSUES BUT ALSO INCLUDES DISCUSSION OF DOMESTIC ECONOMIC SITUATION, SPACE PROGRAM, CIVIL RIGHTS, AND OTHER INTERNAL AFFAIRS.

1593 KENNEDY J.F.
THE BURDEN AND THE GLORY.
NEW YORK: HARPER & ROW, 1964, 293 PP., LC#64-2673.
EXERPTS FROM JFK'S SPEECHES AND STATEMENTS DURING LAST TWO YEARS OF HIS ADMINISTRATION. DISCUSSES ALL HOPES AND GOALS OF HIS DOMESTIC AND FOREIGN POLICIES DURING TIMES OF CRISIS. INCLUDES SPEECH ON DEFENSE HE WAS TO MAKE IN DALLAS.

1594 KENNEDY W.P.
THE LAW AND CUSTOM OF THE SOUTH AFRICAN CONSTITUTION.
LONDON: OXFORD U PR, 1935, 640 PP.
STUDIES DEVELOPMENT AND NATURE OF SOUTH AFRICAN CONSTITUTION AND DISCUSSES ITS OPERATION THROUGH EXECUTIVE BRANCH AND PARLIAMENT. INCLUDES DISCUSSION OF ORGANS OF PROVINCIAL GOVERNMENTS, THE ADMINISTRATION OF JUSTICE, AND FOREIGN RELATIONS.

1595 KENT G.O. ED.
A CATALOG OF FILES AND MICROFILMS OF THE GERMAN FOREIGN MINISTRY ARCHIVES, 1920-1945 (3 VOLS.)
STANFORD: HOOVER INSTITUTE, 1962, 2209 PP., LC#62-19204.
IN GERMAN, LISTS TITLES OF INNUMERABLE ITEMS FOUND IN ARCHIVES. VOLUMES TWO AND THREE PUBLISHED IN 1964 AND 1966, RESPECTIVELY. DIVISION IS BY SECTIONS OF THE FOREIGN MINISTRY, AS EXPLAINED IN INTRODUCTION.

1596 KENT R.K.
FROM MADAGASCAR TO THE MALAGASY REPUBLIC.
NEW YORK: FREDERICK PRAEGER, 1962, 182 PP., LC#62-11772.
TRACES HISTORY OF MADAGASCAR FROM FRENCH COLONIAL ADMINISTRATION TO REVOLT IN 1947. ALSO DISCUSSES POLITICAL AND ECONOMIC PROBLEMS SINCE INDEPENDENCE.

1597 KENWORTHY L.S.
FREE AND INEXPENSIVE MATERIALS ON WORLD AFFAIRS (PAMPHLET)
WASHINGTON: PUBLIC AFFAIRS PRESS, 1954, 94 PP., LC#54-10983.
TOPICAL AND NATIONAL LISTING OF MAPS, PAMPHLETS, AND FILM STRIPS WITH MINIMAL ANNOTATION. MATERIALS ARE INTENDED TO BE TEACHING AIDS FOR SUBUNIVERSITY PUPILS. ADDRESSES OF PUBLISHERS FOLLOW 1300 LISTINGS. ALL IN ENGLISH-LANGUAGE SOURCES.

1598 KERNER R.J.
SLAVIC EUROPE: A SELECTED BIBLIOGRAPHY IN THE WESTERN EUROPEAN LANGUAGES.
CAMBRIDGE: HARVARD U PR, 1918, 402 PP.
LISTED BY SUBJECT WITH MORE IMPORTANT ITEMS EMPHASIZED. ALL WESTERN EUROPEAN LANGUAGES INCLUDED. EVERY VARIETY OF SOURCE WITH CONCLUDING AUTHOR INDEX. ITEMS NUMBER 4500.

1599 KERNER R.J.
NORTHEAST ASIA: A SELECTED BIBLIOGRAPHY (2 VOLS.)
BERKELEY: U OF CALIF PR, 1939, 1296 PP.
TOPICALLY ARRANGED WITHIN REGIONAL AND NATIONAL CATEGORIES. INCLUDES EVERY TYPE OF SOURCE AND SOURCES IN ALL LANGUAGES WITH TRANSLITERATED TITLES. CROSS-REFERENCED WITH CONCLUDING SUBJECT INDEX. ITEMS NUMBER 14,000 IN TWO VOLS.

1601 KERTESZ S.D. ED.
AMERICAN DIPLOMACY IN A NEW ERA.
NOTRE DAME: U OF NOTRE DAME, 1961, 601 PP., LC#61-8466.
VOLUME ENDEAVORS TO CLARIFY COURSE OF AMERICAN FOREIGN POLICY SINCE 1945, ITS MAJOR OBJECTIVES, AND PROBLEMS OF FORMULATING AND IMPLEMENTING THEM. EXAMINES MAJOR FOREIGN POLICY ISSUES TOGETHER WITH DIPLOMACY. DEALS WITH POLICY-MAKING AND ORGANIZATIONAL PROBLEMS.

1602 KETCHAM E.H.
PRELIMINARY SELECT BIBLIOGRAPHY OF INTERNATIONAL LAW (PAMPHLET)
SYRACUSE: SYRACUSE U PRESS, 1937, 69 PP.
UNANNOTATED MATERIALS ARRANGED BY SUBJECT IN ENGLISH AND FRENCH. PRIMARILY DEVOTED TO PERIODICALS IN THE DISCIPLINE. APPROXIMATELY 1400 ITEMS.

1603 KEYES J.G.
A BIBLIOGRAPHY OF WESTERN LANGUAGE PUBLICATIONS CONCERNING NORTH VIETNAM IN THE CORNELL LIBRARY.
ITHACA: CORNELL U, DEPT ASIAN ST, 1966, 292 PP.
SUPPLEMENT TO 1964 BIBLIOGRAPHY INCLUDES MAINLY MATERIALS PUBLISHED DURING THE 1960'S ABOUT NORTH VIETNAM. GROUPED BY SUBJECT AND INDEXED BY AUTHOR, OVER 1500 ITEMS ANNOTATED. ARTICLES, BOOKS, PAMPHLETS, DOCUMENTS, MICROFILMS. ITEMS FROM 1945-1964, INCLUSIVE. ALSO ANNOTATES THE US JOINT PUBLICATIONS RESEARCH SERVICE MATERIAL ON NORTH VIETNAM.

1604 KEYFITZ N.
"WESTERN PERSPECTIVES AND ASIAN PROBLEMS."
HUM. ORGAN., 1 (SPRING 60), 28-31.
CONTENDS THAT DIFFERENT BACKGROUNDS PRODUCE VARYING PERSPECTIVES OF THE SAME PROBLEM. ASIAN AND EUROPEAN ATTITUDES REGARDING TECHNICAL ASSISTANCE, WORK, CORRUPTION, POPULATION GROWTH AND FAMILY ARE CONTRASTED AND ELUCIDATED.

1605 KEYNES J.M.
THE ECONOMIC CONSEQUENCES OF THE PEACE.
NEW YORK: HARCOURT, 1919, 298 PP.
DEPICTS SOCIO-ECONOMIC EUROPEAN SITUATION AFTER WORLD WAR ONE. ASSESSES THAT PEACE OF VERSAILLES WAS BASED ON UNSTABLE PRINCIPLES. DISCUSSES PROGRAM UNDER FOLLOWING HEADS: REVISION OF THE TREATY, SETTLEMENT OF INTER-ALLY INDEBTEDNESS, INTERNATIONAL LOAN AND REFORM OF CURRENCY, POLITICAL RELATIONS OF CENTRAL EUROPE TOWARD RUSSIA.

1606 KHADDURI M.
MODERN LIBYA: A STUDY IN POLITICAL DEVELOPMENT.
BALTIMORE: JOHNS HOPKINS PR., 1963, 404 PP.
OUTLINES EXISTENCE AS ITALIAN COLONY, BRITISH-OCCUPIED COUNTRY DURING WW 2, ENTITY UNDER UN AUSPICES AND FINALLY, ITS EMERGENCE AS INDEPENDENT NATION. EVOLUTION OF ITS CONSTITUTIONAL MONARCHY AND GOVERNMENT-MACHINERY ARE DESCRIBED ALONG WITH HISTORY OF REGIMES TO 1961. FACTORS OF UNITY, COHESION AND DEVELOPMENT ARE ASSESSED. TEXT OF WHEELUS AIR-BASE AGREEMENT INCLUDED.

1607 KHAN A.W.
INDIA WINS FREEDOM: THE OTHER SIDE.
KARACHI: PAKISTAN EDUCATION PUBL, 1961, 405 PP.
EXAMINES MAULANA AZAD'S "INDIA WINS FREEDOM" AND SEEKS TO PRESENT BIRTH, PROGRESS, AND CULMINATION OF PAKISTAN MOVEMENT. DISCUSSES LEADERSHIP OF INDIAN NATIONAL CONGRESS AND RISE OF MUSLIM STRUGGLE FOR INDEPENDENCE.

1608 KHAN M.Z.
"ISLAM AND INTERNATIONAL RELATIONS."
WORLD JUSTICE, 5 (MAR. 64), 293-307.
SEES RELIGION AS A VITAL DIMENSION OPERATIVE IN SPHERE OF INTERNATIONAL RELATIONS. AIM OF ISLAM HERE IS 'AN ASSOCIATION OF STRONG AND STABLE STATES ALLIED TOGETHER IN PERSUANCE OF PEACE, FREEDOM OF CONSCIENCE, AND PROMOTION OF HUMAN WELFARE.'

1609 KHAN M.Z.
"THE PRESIDENT OF THE GENERAL ASSEMBLY."
INT. ORGAN., 18 (SPRING 64), 231-40.
CITES EVOLUTION AND DESIGNATION OF THE OFFICE UNDER UN CHARTER USING COMPARISONS WITH US AND BRITISH LEGISLATURES TO CLARIFY ROLE. AS AN EX-PRESIDENT, POINTS OUT SPECIFIC CHARACTERISTICS OF POSITION AS IT RELATES TO THE GENERAL ASSEMBLY, REGIONALISM, AND EFFECTIVENESS AND STRENGTH OF LEADER.

1610 KHOURI F.J.
"THE JORDON RIVER CONTROVERSY."
REV. POLIT., 27 (JAN. 65), 32-57.
TRACES GROWING ARAB-ISRAELI HOSTILITIES FROM EARLY 1920

ZIONIST MOVEMENTS IN PALESTINE THROUGH CREATION AND DEVELOPMENT OF MODERN-DAY ISRAEL. POINTING OUT THE GREAT IMPORTANCE OF WATER TO BOTH NATIONS, CITES THE VARIOUS DISPUTES AND ACTIONS CONCERNING THE JORDON RIVER, E.G. MAIN PLAN, ARAB PLAN, ISRAELI PLAN. FORSEES INCREASED VIOLENCE AS TWO NATIONS CONTINUE TO EXPAND AND NEED FOR WATER INCREASES.

1611 KHRUSHCHEV N.
FOR VICTORY IN PEACEFUL COMPETITION WITH CAPITALISM.
NEW YORK: DUTTON, 1960, 784 PP.
COLLECTION OF SPEECHES ATTEMPT TO SUPPORT SOVIET CLAIM THAT IT PROMOTES PEACEFUL COEXISTENCE THROUGH COOPERATION WITH THE WEST. PREDICTS ECONOMIC VICTORY FOR COMMUNISM.

1612 KHRUSHCHEV N.S.
KHRUSHCHEV IN NEW YORK.
NEW YORK: CROSSCURRENTS PR, 1960, 286 PP.
COLLECTION OF SPEECHES AND PROPOSALS TO UN MADE BY KHRUSHCHEV DURING HIS VISIT TO NEW YORK, SEPT. 19 TO OCT. 13, 1960, AND FOLLOW-UP REPORT AFTER RETURN TO MOSCOW.

1613 KHRUSHCHEV N.S.
KHRUSHCHEV IN AMERICA.
NEW YORK: CROSSCURRENTS PR, 1960, 231 PP.
REPRODUCES TEXTS OF KHRUSHCHEV'S SPEECHES MADE IN US IN 1959. TRANSLATED INTO ENGLISH WITH EDITORIAL COMMENTS BY AMERICAN NEWSPAPERS AND INTERVIEWERS. SPEECHES DEAL WITH FOREIGN RELATIONS, TRADE, SPACE, DECADENT AMERICAN SOCIETY, AND GLORIES OF COMMUNISM.

1614 KHRUSHCHEV N.S.
THE NEW CONTENT OF PEACEFUL COEXISTENCE IN THE NUCLEAR AGE.
NEW YORK: CROSSCURRENTS PR, 1963, 48 PP., LC#63-14090.
SPEECH BY KHRUSHCHEV AT 6TH CONGRESS OF SOCIALIST UNITY PARTY OF GERMANY, BERLIN, JAN. 16, 1963, SUPPORTING DEVELOPMENT OF SOCIALIST PARTY IN GERMANY.

1615 KIDDER F.E. ED., BUSHONG A.D., ED.
THESES ON PAN AMERICAN TOPICS.
WASHINGTON: PAN AMERICAN UNION, 1962, 124 PP.
UNANNOTATED LISTING OF DOCTORAL THESES FROM US AND CANADA RELATING TO THE AMERICAS. INDEXED BY AUTHOR, SCHOOL, AND TOPIC. TOPICS INCLUDE GENERAL HISTORY, POLITICS, INTERNATIONAL RELATIONS, ECONOMICS, SOCIAL CONDITIONS, CULTURE, GOVERNMENT, HEALTH, FINE ARTS, LAW, LANGUAGES, RELIGION, GEOGRAPHY, AND OTHERS. THESES PERTAIN PRINCIPALLY TO CENTRAL AND SOUTH AMERICA. CONTAINS 2,253 LISTINGS.

1616 KIERNAN V.G.
"INDIA AND THE LABOUR PARTY."
NEW LEFT REV., 42 (APR.-MAY 67), 44-55.
THE FAILURE OF THE LABOUR PARTY TO DEVELOP SOCIALISM IN INDIA REFLECTS ITS GENERAL INABILITY TO COMMUNICATE ITS IDEAL EFFECTIVELY ENOUGH TO GENERATE SUCCESSFUL REFORM. INSTEAD OF REALISTICALLY APPRAISING INDIA'S REACTION TO BRITISH CAPITALISM THE LABOUR PARTY OFFERED ONLY VAGUE IDEALISTIC ENCOURAGEMENT, LOSING ITS POTENTIAL INFLUENCE ON INDIAN SOCIALISM.

1618 KIM Y.K. ED.
PATTERNS OF COMPETITIVE COEXISTENCE: USA VS. USSR.
NEW YORK: G P PUTNAM'S SONS, 1966, 484 PP., LC#66-10471.
COLLECTION OF READINGS ON PEACEFUL COEXISTENCE AS IT HAS EMERGED IN POST-STALIN PERIOD. CONTAINS 48 SELECTIONS, DRAWN FROM BOTH EASTERN AND (PRIMARILY) WESTERN SOURCES, COVERING PEACEFUL COMPETITION BETWEEN EAST AND WEST AND DEALING, AMONG OTHERS, WITH MILITARY PRE ECONOMIC GROWTH, INTERNATIONAL ORGANIZATIONS, IDEOLOGY, TRADE AND FOREIGN AID, AND PROBLEMS OF ACCOMMODATION.

1619 KIMMINICH O.
RUSTUNG UND POLITISCHE SPANNUNG.
GUTERSLOH: C BERTELSMANN VERLAG, 1964, 296 PP.
DISCUSSES CAUSES OF WAR IN RELATION TO HUMAN NATURE, INTERNAL STRUCTURE OF STATE, AND INTERNATIONAL RELATIONS. EXAMINES ARMAMENT WITHOUT INTENTION OF WAR AND ITS IMPACT ON FOREIGN RELATIONS.

1620 KINDLEBERGER C.P.
INTERNATIONAL ECONOMICS.
HOMEWOOD: IRWIN, 1958, 636 PP.
ANALYSIS OF THE FIELD, INCLUDING TRADE AND FINANCE, AND COVERS SUBJECT OF BALANCE OF PAYMENTS, TARIFFS, CARTELS, EXCHANGE CONTROL, AND INTERGOVERNMENTAL ECONOMIC ASSISTANCE.

1621 KINDLEBERGER C.P.
"UNITED STATES ECONOMIC FOREIGN POLICY: RESEARCH REQUIREMENTS FOR 1965."
WORLD POLIT., 11 (JULY 59), 588-613.
RESEARCH PROJECTION OF FUTURE ECONOMIC PROBLEMS STATED ACCORDING TO ALLOCATION, DISTRIBUTION AND ADJUSTMENT OF RESOURCES. DESCRIBES CURRENT AND POSSIBLE FUTURE TRENDS THAT THE USA MAY ENCOUNTER IN DEALING WITH DIFFERENT ECONOMIC AND MONETARY BLOCS.

1622 KINDLEBERGER C.P.
FOREIGN TRADE AND THE NATIONAL ECONOMY.
NEW HAVEN: YALE U PR, 1962, 265 PP., LC#62-16236.
STUDY OF FOREIGN TRADE TYPE AND QUANTITY OF A NATION'S IMPORTS AND EXPORTS AND IMPACT OF SUCH TRADE ON NATIONAL ECONOMY. DISCUSSES TRANSPORTATION, RESOURCES, CAPITAL, TECHNOLOGY, AND RELATIONSHIP BETWEEN PUBLIC AND PRIVATE SECTORS IN VARIOUS NATIONS.

1623 KINDLEBERGER C.P.
EUROPE AND THE DOLLAR.
CAMBRIDGE: M I T PRESS, 1966, 297 PP., LC#66-15568.
COLLECTION OF PAPERS THAT HAVE APPEARED OUTSIDE ROUTINE SCHOLARLY CHANNELS, DEALING WITH THEMES OF INTERNATIONAL FINANCE AMONG DEVELOPED COUNTRIES --THE DOLLAR, EUROPEAN CURRENCIES, WORLD LIQUIDITY, BALANCE-OF-PAYMENTS ADJUSTMENT. SEVERAL THREADS RUN THROUGHOUT: IMPORTANCE OF SUPPLY, NEED FOR INTERNATIONAL COOPERATION, SUPERIORITY OF UNWRITTEN TO FORMAL CONSTITUTIONS IN INSTITUTIONAL MACHINERY.

1624 KING G.
THE UNITED NATIONS IN THE CONGO: A QUEST FOR PEACE.
NEW YORK: CARNEGIE ENDOWMENT, 1962, 184 PP., $1.95.
RELATES EVENTS OF CONGO CRISIS AND THE UN AS IT EVOLVED BETWEEN FIRST FATEFUL MEETING OF SECURITY COUNCIL IN 1960 AND EFFORTS DURING 1962 SUMMER TO SOLVE KATANGA PROBLEM. SEES ONUC SUCCESSFUL IN SENSE OF WARDING OF MAJOR COLD WAR CONFLICT IN CONGO.

1625 KING-HALL S.
POWER POLITICS IN THE NUCLEAR AGE: A POLICY FOR BRITAIN.
LONDON: VICTOR GOLLANCZ, 1962, 224 PP.
THEORIZES THAT ENGLAND SHOULD GIVE UP HER MILITARY NUCLEAR POWER IN ORDER TO HELP SPEED UP WORLD DISARMAMENT AND CUT DOWN ARMS RACE. FEELS THIS MOVE WOULD HELP ENGLAND REGAIN HER 19TH-CENTURY POSITION AS WORLD POWER. ANALYZES POWER POLITICS IN NUCLEAR WORLD TO SUPPORT THEORY.

1626 KINGSLEY R.E.
"THE US BUSINESS IMAGE IN LATIN AMERICA."
BUSINESS TOPICS, 15 (1967), 74-80.
EXAMINES SIX AREAS OF ANTI-US BUSINESS OPINION: SEMANTIC, HISTORICAL, PRAGMATIC, POLITICAL, IDEOLOGICAL, AND INFERENTIAL. FEELS THAT PROBLEM IS BASICALLY ONE OF POOR COMMUNICATIONS; US MUST REVISE OWN THINKING FIRST, RATHER THAN THAT OF LATIN AMERICA. MUST FRAME COMMUNICATIONS FROM VIEWPOINT OF RECIPIENT, NOT OF COMMUNICATOR.

1627 KINGSTON-MCCLOUG E.
DEFENSE; POLICY AND STRATEGY.
NEW YORK: FREDERICK PRAEGER, 1960, 272 PP., LC#60-7662.
KINGSTON-MCCLOUGHTY EXPLAINS PROBLEMS INVOLVED IN EVOLUTION OF DEFENSE POLICY AND IN DEVELOPMENT OF INTERNATIONAL FRAMEWORK OF PLANNING. EMPHASIZES INCREASED IMPORTANCE OF POLITICAL LEADER IN MAKING DEFENSE POLICY AND STRATEGIC DECISIONS. DISCUSSES VARIOUS TYPES OF DEFENSE SYSTEMS AND THEIR ORGANIZATION.

1628 KINTNER W.R.
"THE PROJECTED EUROPEAN UNION AND AMERICAN RESPONSIBILITIES."
ANN. AMER. ACAD. POLIT. SOC. SCI., 348 (JULY 63), 121-31.
FOLLOWS USA MILITARY POLICIES IN EUROPE FROM FORMATION OF NATO IN 1947 TO PRESENT. EUROPEAN DISCONTENT WITH PRESENT USA MILITARY STRATEGY MAY HAVE DIVISIVE EFFECT ON EUROPEAN UNITY. SUGGESTS SOLUTION LIES IN POLICY OF GREATER SHARING OF NUCLEAR POWER WITH OTHER NATO MEMBERS.

1629 KIPP K.
"DIE POLITISCHE BEDEUTUNG DER 'GEGENKUSTE' DARGESTELLT AM BEISPIEL DER USA IM 20. JAHRHUNDERT"
WEHRKUNDE, 16 (AUG. 67), 397-409.
DISCUSSES DEVELOPMENT OF US SEA POWER AND IMPACT OF LARGE COASTAL AREAS UPON FORMULATION OF FOREIGN POLICY. TRACES MOOD OF ISOLATIONISM, JAPANESE EXPANSION, IMPACT OF WWII ON BALANCE OF POWER, AND FORMULATION OF POLICY OF CONTAINMENT.

1630 KIRCHHEIMER O.
GEGENWARTSPROBLEME DER ASYLGEWAHRUNG.
COLOGNE: WESTDEUTSCHER VERLAG, 1959, 65 PP.
EXAMINES POLITICAL AND LEGAL IMPLICATIONS OF GRANTING ASYLUM TO POLITICAL REFUGEES. SHOWS THAT MODERN MASS MIGRATIONS RESULTING FROM POLITICAL UPHEAVAL AND PERSECUTION HAVE MADE OLDER DOCTRINES INAPPLICABLE. MAINTAINS THAT STRICT OBSERVANCE OF PRINCIPLE OF POLITICAL ASYLUM IS NECESSARY TO PREVENT 'ARBITRARY RULE AND DESTRUCTION OF FREEDOM."

1631 KIRDAR U.
THE STRUCTURE OF UNITED NATIONS ECONOMIC AID TO UNDERDEVELOPED COUNTRIES.
THE HAGUE: MARTINUS NIJHOFF, 1966, 361 PP., LC#66-54220.
DETAILED STUDY OF VARIOUS FORMS OF FINANCIAL AND TECHNICAL ASSISTANCE TO UNDERDEVELOPED COUNTRIES, EMPHASIZING AID PROGRAMS THAT ARE MEDIATED AND ADMINISTERED BY UN AND OTHER INTERNATIONAL BODIES. STRESSES INTERNATIONAL NATURE OF ECO-

NOMIC AID PROGRAMS IN RELATION TO BOTH ORGANIZATIONAL STRUCTURE AND POLITICAL IMPLICATIONS.

1632 KIRK G.
THE STUDY OF INTERNATIONAL RELATIONS.
NEW YORK: COUNCIL FOR. REL., 1947, 113 PP.
DEALS WITH TWO BASIC QUESTIONS: OBJECTIVES OF INSTRUCTION IN INTERNATIONAL RELATIONS AND HOW THEY ARE TO BE ATTAINED IN AMERICAN UNIVERSITIES. ATTEMPTS TO ESTABLISH A MEANING FOR THE STUDY OF INTERNATIONAL RELATIONS AT THE UNIVERSITY LEVEL.

1633 KIRK G.
"MATTERIALS FOR THE STUDY OF INTERNATIONAL RELATIONS."
WORLD POLIT., 1 (APR. 49', 426-430.
ATTEMPTS TO SET FORTH THEORY OF INTERNATIONAL RELATIONS VIA SYSTEMATIC EXAMINATION OF CONCEPTUAL STRUCTURE WHICH APPEARS TO BE PRESENT IN MODERN THINKING ABOUT THE SUBJECT.

1634 KIRK G.
THE CHANGING ENVIRONMENT OF INTERNATIONAL RELATIONS.
WASHINGTON: BROOKINGS INST., 1956, 158 PP.
STUDIES RELATIONSHIP OF MODERN FORCES AND AMERICAN FOREIGN POLICY. FORESEES DIVERGENT NATIONAL FORMS AND CHANGES IN POWER LOCUS. CALLS UNIVERSAL ACCEPTANCE OF MUTUAL SECURITY CONCEPT PREREQUISITE FOR WORLD ORDER.

1635 KIRK R., MCCLELLAN J.
THE POLITICAL PRINCIPLES OF ROBERT A. TAFT.
NEW YORK: FLEET PUBL CORP, 1967, 213 PP., LC#67-24073.
ANALYZES IDEAS AND INFLUENCES OF SENATOR TAFT. EXAMINES HIS CONVICTIONS OF FREEDOM, JUSTICE, LABOR POLICY, SOCIAL REFORM, FOREIGN AFFAIRS, AND RESPONSIBILITIES OF POLITICAL PARTIES. SUPPORTS TAFT'S BELIEFS IN POLITICS, ORDER, AND FREEDOM. DESCRIBES HIS SOCIAL IMPROVEMENT PROGRAMS AS GENEROUS; CLAIMS THAT HE WAS NOT AN ISOLATIONIST.

1636 KIRKWOOD K.
BRITAIN AND AFRICA.
LONDON: CHATTO AND WINDUS, 1965, 235 PP.
HISTORY OF RELATIONS BETWEEN BRITAIN AND SUB-SAHARA AFRICA BY PERIOD (TO 1914, TO 1939, TO 1964), AND BY REGION (EAST, WEST, AND SOUTH AFRICA). CONCLUDING CHAPTER ON RELATIONS WITH INDEPENDENT AFRICA EMPHASIZES BRITAIN'S CHANGING ROLE AND POLICIES.

1637 KIRPICEVA I.K.
HANDBUCH DER RUSSISCHEN UND SOWJETISCHEN BIBLIOGRAPHIEN (5 VOLS.)
LEIPZIG: VEB VERL FUR BUCH BIBL, 1962.
ANNOTATED BIBLIOGRAPHICAL SURVEY OF SOVIET AND RUSSIAN BIBLIOGRAPHIES FROM 18TH CENTURY THROUGH 1959. INFORMATION GIVEN IN TABLE FORM; RUSSIAN CHARACTERS TRANSLITERATED AND FREQUENTLY TRANSLATED INTO GERMAN. TOPICALLY CLASSIFIED AND INDEXED BY AUTHOR. INCLUDES COMPREHENSIVE AND SPECIALIZED BIBLIOGRAPHIES, WORKS WITH APPENDED SUPPLEMENTARY READING LISTS, AND PERIODICALS.

1638 KIS T.I.
LES PAYS DE L'EUROPE DE L'EST: LEURS RAPPORTS MUTUELS ET LE PROBLEME DE LEUR INTEGRATION DANS L'ORBITE DE L'USSR.
LOUVAIN: EDITORIAL NAUWELAERTS, 1964, 271 PP.
EXAMINES MUTUAL INTERESTS OF EAST EUROPEAN COUNTRIES AND THEIR INTEGRATION AS SOVIET SATELLITES SINCE WWII. STUDIES DISINTEGRATION OF RUSSIAN EMPIRE, NEW POLICY OF INTEGRATION WITH "POPULAR DEMOCRACIES" IN EUROPE, AND COMMUNIST IDEOLOGY CONCERNING THE STATE, INDIVIDUAL RIGHTS, POLITICS, AND INTERNATIONAL RELATIONS. INCLUDES BIBLIOGRAPHY OF ABOUT 280 ITEMS.

1639 KISER M.
"ORGANIZATION OF AMERICAN STATES."
WASHINGTON: PAN AMER. UNION, 1955, 74 PP.
A HANDBOOK ABOUT ORGANIZATION DESCRIBING WHAT IT IS, HOW IT IS ORGANIZED, WHAT IT DOES, AND THE INTER-AMERICAN AGENCIES.

1640 KISSINGER H.A.
NUCLEAR WEAPONS AND FOREIGN POLICY.
NEW YORK: HARPER, 1957, 455 PP.
ATTEMPTS TO MODIFY ASSUMPTIONS ABOUT NUCLEAR WAR, DIPLOMACY, NATURE OF PEACE. PROPOSES PLAN OF STRATEGY, COUNSELS GUIDED DOCTRINE INCLUDING FULLER COMMUNICATION OF INTENTIONS TO POWERS. REVIEWS FACTS ON SURVIVAL AFTER NUCLEAR ATTACK.

1641 KISSINGER H.A.
"THE SEARCH FOR STABILITY."
FOR. AFF., 37 (JULY 59), 537-60.
IDENTIFIES THE SPECIFIC PROBLEMS INVOLVED IN ESTABLISHING PEACE BETWEEN THE WEST AND THE SOVIET UNION. THE WEST MUST ESTABLISH CONVICTIONS ABOUT THE MEASURES IT PROPOSES AND STICK TO THEM. THE ROLE OF NATO AND THE UNITED STATES IN THE REUNIFICATION OF GERMANY IS DISCUSSED AT LENGTH.

1642 KISSINGER H.A.
THE NECESSITY FOR CHOICE.
NEW YORK: HARPER, 1961, 370 PP.
APPRAISAL OF MAJOR ISSUES CONFRONTING USA FOREIGN POLICY. FEELS UNITED STATES' POSITION IN WORLD HAS DETERIORATED IN PAST DECADE AND CHALLENGES POLICY MAKERS TO RESOLVE THE MANY ISSUES WHICH HAVE BEEN IGNORED SINCE 1945, PRIMARILY, DETERRENCE, LIMITED WAR PLANS, ARMS CONTROL AND THE ATLANTIC COMMUNITY.

1643 KISSINGER H.A.
"STRAINS ON THE ALLIANCE."
FOR. AFF., 41 (JAN. 63), 261-85.
DISCUSSES PROBLEMS DISRUPTING ATLANTIC ALLIANCE: USA VACILLATION ON ISSUE OF NUCLEAR RETALIATION, GERMAN DESIRE FOR RE-UNIFICATION, AND FRENCH DESIRE FOR THIRD FORCE. MAINTAINS MANY PROPOSED SOLUTIONS IGNORE PSYCHOLOGICAL CONSIDERATIONS.

1644 KISSINGER H.A.
"COALITION DIPLOMACY IN A NUCLEAR AGE."
FOR. AFF., 42 (JUL 64), 525-45.
EFFECTIVE DIPLOMACY WITHIN THE ATLANTIC ALLIANCE REQUIRES THAT MEMBERS INSPECT OBJECTIVES WHICH ARE COMMON AND THOSE WHICH ARE DIVERSE. GRANTS THAT NATIONAL PERSPECTIVES PRODUCE DIFFERING STRATEGIC VIEWS. EXAMINES SCOPE AND LIMITS OF CONSULTATION.

1645 KISTIAKOWSKY G.B.
"SCIENCE AND FOREIGN AFFAIRS."
SCIENCE, 131 (APR. 60), 1019-1024.
SCIENTIFIC LEADERSHIP DIRECTLY AFFECTS FOUR ASPECTS OF FOREIGN AFFAIRS: NATIONAL IMAGE, RELATIONS BETWEEN NATIONS, ARMS CONTROL MEASURES, AND TECHNICAL AID TO UNDERDEVELOPED NATIONS.

1646 KITCHEN H. ED.
A HANDBOOK OF AFRICAN AFFAIRS.
NEW YORK: FREDERICK PRAEGER, 1964, 311 PP., LC#64-16680.
COUNTRY-BY-COUNTRY POLITICAL GUIDE TO AFRICA. INCLUDES BRIEF HISTORCAL SUMMARY, DESCRIPTION OF ARMED FORCES OF EACH COUNTRY, AND ORGANIZATION OF AFRICAN UNITY. FOUR ARTICLES ON CONTEMPORARY AFRICAN PROSE AND POETRY.

1647 KITZINGER V.W.
THE CHALLENGE OF THE COMMON MARKET.
OXFORD: BLACKWELL, 1961, 168 PP.
EXAMINES HISTORIC AND ECONOMIC FACTORS ACTING AS STIMULUS TO COMMON MARKET ESTABLISHMENT. EXAMINES PROS AND CONS OF BRITISH CANDIDATURE. ANALYZES EFFECT OF BRITISH ENTRY ON HER INDUSTRY, WORLD POSITION AND COMMONWEALTH.

1648 KLEIMAN R.
ATLANTIC CRISIS; AMERICAN DIPLOMACY CONFRONTS A RESURGENT EUROPE.
NEW YORK: W W NORTON, 1963, 158 PP., LC#63-22748.
CONCERNED WITH KENNEDY'S "GRAND DESIGN" TO CREATE AN ATLANTIC PARTNERSHIP AND THE SETBACK IT RECEIVED BY DE GAULLE'S VETO IN 1963. SEEKS TO ANSWER WHY DE GAULLE THWARTED THIS CONCEPT AND WHY HE VOTOED BRITAIN'S ENTRY INTO COMMON MARKET. EXAMINES SHORTCOMINGS OF US AND OTHER EUROPEAN COUNTRIES; REVIEWS JOHNSON'S POSITION AND PRESENTS GOALS FOR A FUTURE ATLANTIC PARTNERSHIP AND ITS SUCCESS.

1649 KLEIN S.
"A SURVEY OF SINO-JAPANESE TRADE, 1950-1966"
CHINA MAINLAND REVIEW, 2 (DEC. 66), 185-191.
EXAMINES TRADE RELATIONS BETWEEN JAPAN AND CHINA FROM 1950 TO 1966. INCLUDES AGREEMENTS MADE AND POLITICAL ASPECTS OF TRADE. CONCLUDES THAT FRICTION IN RELATIONSHIP WILL CONTINUE TO INCREASE BECAUSE OF JAPANESE DESIRE TO REMAIN CLOSE TO US AND TAIWAN, POLITICAL PROPAGANDA OF CHINESE COMMUNISTS, AND POOR QUALITY OF CHINESE GOODS TRADED TO JAPAN.

1650 KLUCKHOHN F.L.
THE NAKED RISE OF COMMUNISM.
DERBY: MONARCH BOOKS, INC, 1962, 286 PP.
DISCUSSES GROWTH OF COMMUNISM AND ITS TAKE-OVER IN UNKNOWING COUNTRIES. INCLUDES THEORIES AND DOCTRINES; HISTORY OF COMMUNISM IN RUSSIA, BALTIC, EASTERN EUROPE, CHINA; SUCCESSES AND FAILURES; ITS LEADERS; ITS PRESENT POSITION IN WORLD AFFAIRS; AND WHAT CAN BE DONE ABOUT ITS SPREAD.

1651 KNIERIEM A.
THE NUREMBERG TRIALS.
CHICAGO: HENRY REGNERY CO, 1959, 561 PP., LC#59-8417.
WRITTEN BY GERMAN LAWYER ACQUITTED AT NUREMBERG WHO LATER TOOK UP STUDY OF LEGAL PROBLEMS OF TRIAL. ATTEMPTS TO DISCOVER, ANALYZE, AND CLARIFY LEGAL ISSUES OF COMPLEX CASES. ASSERTS THAT TRIAL WAS SUCCESSFUL IN TAMING HATRED AND REVENGE OF EUROPE AND US, BUT WAS FAILURE AS AN ATTEMPT TO ENFORCE INTERNATIONAL LAW AND ORDER FOR THE MOMENT AND FOR FUTURE.

1652 KNIGHT R.

BIBLIOGRAPHY ON INCOME AND WEALTH, 1957-1960 (VOL VIII)
NEW HAVEN: NATL ASSN RES INCOMES, 1964, 304 PP.
BIBLIOGRAPHY CONSOLIDATES AND SUPPLEMENTS ANNUAL REPORTS OF INTERNATIONAL ASSOCIATION FOR RESEARCH ON INCOME AND WEALTH IN NATIONS. INCLUDES WORKS ON CONCEPTS AND METHODS RELATING TO INCOME AND WEALTH MEASUREMENT AND ON INTERNATIONAL COMPARISONS OF NATIONAL ESTIMATES. PARTICULAR ATTENTION IS GIVEN TO UNDERDEVELOPED COUNTRIES, LONG-TERM ECONOMIC GROWTH, AND FINANCIAL ACCOUNTING. ANNOTATED.

1653 KNOLES G.H. ED.
THE RESPONSIBILITIES OF POWER, 1900-1929.
NEW YORK: MACMILLAN, 1967, 320 PP.
COLLECTION OF ESSAYS BY EMINENT LEADERS AND THINKERS OF THE PERIOD 1900-29. BEGINS WITH AMERICAN COLONIAL EXPERIENCE IN THE PHILIPPINES AND ENDS WITH "GREAT CRASH." ESSAYS COVER AMERICAN PHILOSOPHY, POVERTY, RELIGION, NATIONAL REFORM OF T ROOSEVELT, WILSON'S DEMOCRACY, WWI, HOLMES' OPINIONS, LEAGUE OF NATIONS, ECONOMICS, SOCIAL OBJECTIVES, POPULATION MAKE-UP, ETC.

1654 KNORR K.E.
RUBLE DIPLOMACY: CHALLENGE TO AMERICAN FOREIGN AID(PAMPHLET)
PRINCETON: CTR OF INTL STUDIES, 1956, 42 PP.
EXAMINES SINO-SOVIET BLOC POLICY OF TRADE, LOANS, AND TECHNICAL ASSISTANCE TO UNDERDEVELOPED COUNTRIES. USSR MAINTAINS SUCH DEALINGS ARE BUSINESSLIKE AND WITHOUT POLITICAL STRINGS IMPOSED BY IMPERIALISTIC US AID. PRESENTS FACTS OF BLOC DRIVE SINCE 1955, DESCRIBES OBJECTIVES, EVALUATES EFFECTIVENESS OF ECONOMIC DIPLOMACY, AND SUGGESTS POINTS FOR AMERICAN DIPLOMACY.

1655 KNORR K.E., VERBA S.
THE INTERNATIONAL SYSTEM.
PRINCETON: U. PR., 1961, 237 PP.
ILLUSTRATES THE USEFULNESS OF THEORY IN UNDERSTANDING INTERNATIONAL RELATIONS. THE VARIOUS GAME THEORIES, THOUGH MODELS, ARE NOT TO BE THOUGHT OF AS MERE MINIATURES OF THE REALITIES. THE MODEL BEST SERVES ITS PURPOSE WHEN IT'S PREDICTIVE OR DESCRIPTIVE WITH RESPECT TO ACTIVITY AT A HIGH LEVEL OF GENERALITY.

1656 KNORR K.E.
ON THE USES OF MILITARY POWER IN THE NUCLEAR AGE.
PRINCETON: PRINCETON U PRESS, 1966, 185 PP., LC#66-21834.
ANALYSIS OF CURRENT MILITARY POWER AND CONTROL. EXPLAINS CHANGES IN INTERNATIONAL CONFLICT SINCE ADVENT OF NUCLEAR WEAPONS AND STATUS OF NUCLEAR AND NON-NUCLEAR POWERS IN FIELD OF INTERNATIONAL RELATIONS.

1657 KNOX V.H.
PUBLIC FINANCE: INFORMATION SOURCES.
DETROIT: GALE RESEARCH CO, 1964, 142 PP., LC#64-16503.
BIBLIOGRAPHY IN FIELDS OF PUBLIC FINANCE AND TAXATION. STRESSES NEW STUDIES IN FIELDS; MOST OF THE MATERIAL COVERS PERIOD OF 1960'S. ANNOTATIONS ARE INCLUDED WHERE TITLES ARE UNCLEAR. INCLUDES ITEMS ON GENERAL FIELD AS WELL AS MATERIALS ON REVENUES, PUBLIC EXPENDITURES, PUBLIC DEBT, FISCAL POLICY AND ADMINISTRATION, AND INTERNATIONAL PUBLIC FINANCE. CONTAINS AUTHOR AND SUBJECT INDEXES; IN ENGLISH.

1658 KOENIG L.W.
THE TRUMAN ADMINISTRATION: ITS PRINCIPLES AND PRACTICE.
NEW YORK: NEW YORK U PR, 1956, 394 PP., LC#56-7425.
ANALYZES COMPLEX PROBLEMS TRUMAN FACED ASSUMING POWER IN MIDDLE OF WORLD WAR AND IN FOUR MONTHS COPING WITH PROBLEM OF DEMOBILIZING NATION GEARED FOR WAR FOR THREE YEARS. INCLUDES PROBLEM OF USING BOMB AND POLITICAL SCENE AT POTSDAM, WHICH INITIATED COLD WAR. FOLLOWS HIM THROUGH IKE'S ELECTION.

1659 KOH S.J.
STAGES OF INDUSTRIAL DEVELOPMENT IN ASIA.
PHILA: U OF PENN PR, 1966, 461 PP., LC#65-22081.
STUDY OF COMPARATIVE HISTORY OF THE COTTON INDUSTRY IN JAPAN, INDIA, CHINA, AND KOREA. DISCUSSES THREE FACTORS WHICH HAD LIMITING EFFECT ON INDUSTRIALIZATION IN THESE COUNTRIES. PRIOR ECONOMIC EXPERIENCE, SOCIAL ORGANIZATION, AND POLITICAL INSTITUTIONS. CONTAINS NUMEROUS CHARTS AND TABLES.

1660 KOHN H.
FORCE OR REASON; ISSUES OF THE TWENTIETH CENTURY.
CAMBRIDGE: HARVARD U PR, 1937, 167 PP.
ANALYZES FACTORS OF POST-WWI WORLD AND TRACES THEIR BACKGROUND. CONCERNED PRIMARILY WITH ISSUES OF CULT OF FORCE, OF DETHRONEMENT OF REASON, AND OF CRISIS OF IMPERIALISM. SEES MAJOR PROBLEM OF 20TH CENTURY AS ENLARGEMENT OF DEMOCRACY. DISCUSSES CHANGING NATURE OF WAR AND COMPARES CHANGING IDEOLOGIES. CONSIDERS FORCE AS AN END IN ITSELF, PSYCHOLOGICAL MOTIVES OF IMPERIALISM, AND TOTALITARIANISM.

1661 KOHN H.
REVOLUTIONS AND DICTATORSHIPS.
CAMBRIDGE: HARVARD U PR, 1939, 420 PP.
CRITICAL IDEOLOGICAL STUDY OF DEVELOPING REVOLUTIONS AND DICTATORSHIPS OF 1920'S AND 1930'S, SEEN AS ANTITHETICAL TO LIBERAL WESTERN NATIONALISM. VIEWED AGAINST BACKGROUND OF FRENCH REVOLUTION AND NAPOLEONIC INDIVIDUALISM, NAZISM AND FASCISM BECOME DEMENTED NATIONALISM, IRONICALLY ORIGINATING IN MESSIANISM OF ANCIENT JEWS. DISCUSSES RISE OF FASCIST AND COMMUNIST STATES AND REVOLUTIONS IN TURKISH AND ARAB WORLDS.

1662 KOHN H.
NATIONALISM: ITS MEANING AND HISTORY.
NEW YORK: MACMILLAN, 1955, 171 PP., LC#55-10910.
STUDIES HISTORICAL GROWTH OF NATIONALISM, USING WRITINGS OF MAJOR POLITICAL PHILOSOPHERS FROM MACHIAVELLI TO SUN YAT-SEN. COMPARES FORMS OF NATIONALISM IN DIFFERENT COUNTRIES, AND CONSIDERS IT A MAJOR IDEOLOGY PRESENTING REAL THREAT TO WESTERN CIVILIZATION.

1663 KOHN L.Y.
"ISRAEL AND NEW NATION STATES OF ASIA AND AFRICA."
ANN. AMER. ACAD. POLIT. SOC. SCI., 324 (JULY 59), 96-102.
EXPLORES THE GROWING RAPPORT BETWEEN ISRAEL AND NEWLY EMERGING UNDERDEVELOPED COUNTRIES. THE NEW NATIONS, INSTEAD OF RELYING ON SOVIET OR WESTERN TECHNIQUES, SEE IN ISRAEL'S METHOD OF DEVELOPMENT A GOOD ALTERNATIVE AND AN EXAMPLE FOR THEIR OWN DEVELOPMENT. DISCUSSES INCREASED TRADE, TECHNICAL AND ECONOMIC ASSISTANCE BETWEEN THESE COUNTRIES.

1664 KOHNSTAMM M.
THE EUROPEAN COMMUNITY AND ITS ROLE IN THE WORLD.
COLUMBIA: U OF MO PR, 1964, 82 PP., LC#64-20099.
THREE LECTURES DEALING WITH DEVELOPMENT OF CONTINENTAL EUROPEAN COMMUNITY, ITS RELATIONS WITH GREAT BRITAIN AND US, AND ITS PRESENT DIFFICULTIES AND FUTURE DECISIONS.

1665 KOJIMA K.
"THE PATTERN OF INTERNATIONAL TRADE AMONG ADVANCED COUNTRIES."
HITOTSUBASHI J. ECON., 5 (JUNE 64), 16-36.
ANALYZES TREND OF RAPIDLY INCREASING TRADE AMONG ADVANCED INDUSTRIAL COUNTRIES, WHICH HAS BEEN DEVELOPING SINCE WORLD WAR TWO. SEES THIS RAPID EXPANSION OF TRADE AMONG THEST COUNTRIES AS PRIMARILY IN 'HORIZONTAL TRADE', AMONG MANUFACTURERS AND SPECIFICALLY CONSIDERS INTRA-BLOC TRADE OF EEC AND TRADE AMONG USA, UK, EEC AND JAPAN IN LIGHT OF THIS.

1666 KOLARZ W.
"THE IMPACT OF COMMUNISM ON WEST AFRICA."
INT. AFF., 38 (APRIL 62), 156-69.
DESCRIBES LEFT LEANING PARTIES OF WEST AFRICA AS 'FELLOW TRAVELERS' NOT YET CERTAIN OF THEIR INTENTIONS. MAIN COMMUNIST ATTACK IS DIRECTED AT TRAINING OF YOUNG AFRICAN LEADERS, JOURNALISTS AND THROUGH WORLD FEDERATION OF TRADE UNIONS. CAPTURE OF MASS LEFT-WING PARTIES WOULD BE DONE BY INTERNAL COMMUNIST 'PUTSCH' OR BY COMPELLING NATIONALIST PARTIES TO MERGE WITH THEM. COMMUNIST HAVE ARRICAN SOUL AGAINST THEM.

1667 KOLARZ W.
BOOKS ON COMMUNISM.
NEW YORK: OXFORD U PR, 1964, 568 PP.
ARRANGED BY SUBJECT AND BY COUNTRY, INCLUDING OFFICIAL DOCUMENTS AND PUBLICATIONS. ALL 2,500 ITEMS USEFULLY ANNOTATED AND ALL IN ENGLISH. EMPHASIS ON USSR.

1668 KOLARZ W.
COMMUNISM AND COLONIALISM.
NEW YORK: ST MARTIN'S PRESS, 1964, 147 PP.
DISCUSSES SOVIET ATTITUDE TOWARD ITS OWN SUBJECT PEOPLE, AND COLONIAL AND EX-COLONIAL PEOPLE OF ASIA AND AFRICA. EXPOSES "DELIBERATE DECEPTION" OF DEVELOPING NATIONS BY POLITICAL PROPAGANDA.

1669 KOMESAR N.K. ED., MARSON C.C. ED.
"PRESIDENTIAL AMENDMENT & TERMINATION OF TREATIES* THE CASE OF THE WARSAW CONVENTION."
UNIV. CHICAGO LAW REV., 34 (SPRING 67), 580-616.
REVIEWS US COMMITMENT TO MATTERS OF INTERNATIONAL CIVIL AVIATION WITHIN FRAMEWORK OF WARSAW CONVENTION AS ALTERED BY THE "NEW PLAN." INVESTIGATES CONSTITUTIONAL QUESTIONS RAISED BY PROCEDURE THROUGH WHICH NEW ARRANGEMENT CREATED. EXAMINES LEGAL BASES FOR INDEPENDENT EXECUTIVE AUTHORITY TO TERMINATE OR MODIFY TREATIES. CONCLUDES THAT PRESIDENT EXCEEDED THE AUTHORITY OF HIS OFFICE.

1670 KORBEL J.
POLAND BETWEEN EAST AND WEST: SOVIET AND GERMAN DIPLOMACY TOWARD POLAND 1919-1933.
PRINCETON: PRINCETON U PRESS, 1963, 321 PP., LC#63-9993.
STUDY OF THE INTRIGUES AGAINST THE NEWLY INDEPENDENT POLISH STATE, BASED IN PART ON GERMAN FOREIGN OFFICE FILES. ILLUSTRATES GERMAN AND SOVIET REACTIONS TO POLISH ATTEMPTS TO RE-ESTABLISH POLAND AS A MAJOR POWER, AND TO EACH OTHERS' DIPLOMATIC MOVES. TRACES BOTH MILITARY AND DIPLOMATIC CAMPAIGNS OVER POLAND, ENDING WITH POLISH-SOVIET AND POLISH-GERMAN PACTS.

1671 KORBONSKI A.
"COMECON."

INT. CONCIL. 549 (SEPT. 64), 1-62.
TRACES BROADLY THE DEVELOPMENT OF COMECON FROM ITS ORIGIN AND SKETCHES ITS CURRENT INSTITUTIONAL FRAMEWORK AND POLICIES FROM AN ECONOMIC AND POLITICAL VIEWPOINT. CONSIDERS RAPID ADVANCE IN ECONOMIC INTEGRATION IMPROBABLE.

1672 KORBONSKI A.
"USA POLICY IN EAST EUROPE."
CURR. HIST., 48 (MAR. 65), 129-134.
WHILE CHANGE IN USA ATTITUDE TOWARD EAST EUROPE HAS BEEN RATHER STRIKING, ITS PRESENT POLICY IS ESSENTIALLY STATIC AND SHORT-RUN. MOST MOVE ON FRONTS OTHER THAN BRIDGES OF AID, TRADE AND CULTURAL EXCHANGE EVEN AT COST OF ANTAGONIZING TEMPORARILY CLOSEST ALLIES.

1673 KOTANI H.
"PEACE-KEEPING: PROBLEMS FOR SMALLER COUNTRIES."
INT. J., 19 (1964), 308-325.
NOTES THE PROBLEMS WHICH ARISE WHEN SMALLER COUNTRIES COME IN CONTACT WITH A U.N. FORCE. WORK IS INTENDED AS A PRACTICAL STUDY OF THEIR PROBLEMS AND ALSO ATTEMPTS TO EXAMINE THE WAYS IN WHICH SMALLER COUNTRIES CAN MAKE A GREATER CONTRIBUTION TO THE ORGANIZATION OF A FUTURE UNITED NATIONS FORCE.

1674 KRAFT J.
THE GRAND DESIGN.
NEW YORK: HARPER, 1962, 122 PP.
DESCRIBES GENESIS OF ATLANTIC PARTNERSHIP, AND ITS INTERNATIONAL IMPLICATIONS AS WELL AS THOSE FOR THE US.

1675 KRANNHALS H.V.
"COMMAND INTEGRATION WITHIN THE WARSAW PACT."
MIL. REV., 41 (MAY 61), 40-52.
PACT CONSIDERED FINAL STEP IN MILITARY INTEGRATION UNDER SUPREME SOVIET COMMAND. DEVELOPMENT HAD BEEN IN PROCESS OVER PRECEDING DECADE.

1676 KRAUS J.
"A MARXIST IN GHANA."
PROBLEMS OF COMMUNISM, 16 (MAY-JUNE 67), 42-49.
PORTRAYS THE RISE AND FALL OF NKRUMAH, HIS EFFORTS TO ESTABLISH SOCIALIST STATE IN GHANA, HIS ATTEMPTS TO DISSEMINATE MARXIST VIEWPOINT THROUGHOUT AFRICA, AND THE POLITTICAL AND IDEOLOGICAL FORCES BEHIND HIS IDEAS AND PROGRAMS. DESCRIBES EXTENT OF SOCIALIZATION, ITS ECONOMIC AND SOCIAL EFFECTS, ITS INTERNATIONAL REPERCUSSIONS. CONCLUDES THAT SOCIALISM HAS BEEN A "MANIPULATIVE MYTH" TO ADVANCE NKRUMAH.

1677 KRAUS O.
THEORIE DER ZWISCHENSTAATLICHEN WIRTSCHAFTSBEZIEHUNGEN.
BERLIN: VERL DUNCKER AND HUM, 1956, 308 PP.
DISCUSSES ORIGINS OF WORLD TRADE AND ECONOMIC PRINCIPLES, SUCH AS BALANCE OF PAYMENTS, ESTABLISHMENT OF COST AND PRICES, RELATION OF FOREIGN TRADE TO INTERNAL DEVELOPMENT, AND POLITICS OF GOLD CURRENCY.

1678 KRAUSE L.B. ED.
THE COMMON MARKET: PROGRESS AND CONTROVERSY.
ENGLEWOOD CLIFFS: PRENTICE HALL, 1964, 182 PP., LC#64-16427.
PROGRESS OF EEC AS DEPICTED BY STATESMEN, ECONOMISTS, AND SCHOLARS FROM BOTH EUROPE AND AMERICA. POSSIBLE CONSEQUENCES OF FRANCE'S VETO OF GREAT BRITAIN'S BID FOR MEMBERSHIP.

1679 KRAUSE W.
ECONOMIC DEVELOPMENT: THE UNDERDEVELOPED WORLD AND THE AMERICAN INTEREST.
BELMONT: WADSWORTH, 1961, 524 PP., LC#61-7374.
DISCUSSES ECONOMIC DEVELOPMENT IN UNDERDEVELOPED COUNTRIES, THEIR PROBLEMS, ATTEMPTS AT IMPROVEMENTS, AND AMERICAN INTEREST IN PROBLEMS OF DEVELOPMENT, AMERICAN SOLUTIONS, POSSIBILITIES FOR FURTHER AMERICAN AID, AND IMPLICATIONS FOR US AND WORLD OF ITS SUCCESSES AND FAILURES IN ASSISTING ECONOMICALLY UNDEVELOPED COUNTRIES.

1680 KRAVIS I.B.
DOMESTIC INTERESTS AND INTERNATIONAL OBLIGATIONS: SAFEGUARDS IN INTERNATIONAL TRADE ORGANIZATIONS.
PHILADELPHIA: U. PENN. PR., 1963, 448 PP.,$8.50.
AN EXAMINATION OF THE NATURE OF INTERNATIONAL COMMITMENTS AND OF THE MANNER IN WHICH DOMESTIC INTERESTS HAVE BEEN SAFEGUARDED IN THREE EUROPEAN ARRANGEMENTS-ORGANIZATION FOR EUROPEAN ECONOMIC COOPERATION'S CODE OF LIBERALIZATION, EUROPEAN COAL AND STEEL COMMUNITY, AND EUROPEAN ECONOMIC COMMUNITY.

1681 KRAVIS I.B., DAVENPORT M.W.S.
"THE POLITICAL ARITHMETIC OF INTERNATIONAL BURDEN-SHARING."
J. POLIT. ECON., 71 (AUG. 63), 309-30.
A COMPREHENSIVE STUDY WHICH REVIEWS OVERALL DIMENSIONS OF THE PROBLEMS CONNECTED WITH EXPENDITURES ON INTERNATIONAL ORGANIZATIONS. A SIZE-DISTRIBUTION OF INCOME FOR TEN SELECTED COUNTRIES IS CONSTRUCTED, AND TAX SCHEDULES OF DIFFERENT DEGREES OF PROGRESSIVITY ARE APPLIED TO NATIONS AND TO INDIVIDUALS IN ORDER TO DETERMINE RATIONAL SHARES IN COSTS.

1682 KREININ M.E.
"THE 'OUTER-SEVEN' AND EUROPEAN INTEGRATION."
AMER. ECON. REV., 50 (JUNE 60), 370-386.
EUROPEAN FREE-TRADE ASSOCIATION (EFTAA), A SCHEME DEVISED TO RIVAL EEC (WHICH DISCRIMINATES AGAINST NON-MEMBER NATIONS), SEEN AS TEMPORARY ARRANGEMENT TO PROVIDE SPUR TOWARDS A BROADER ALL-EUROPEAN AGREEMENT. COMPARISON DEMONSTRATES COMMON MARKET MUCH MORE LIKELY TO HAVE FAVORABLE IMPACT ON WORLD-PATTERN RESOURCE UTILIZATION. CONCLUSION THAT EFTAA'S CREATION WILL DEEPEN DIVISION IN EUROPE.

1683 KRETZSCHMAR W.W.
AUSLANDSHILFE ALS MITTEL DER AUSSENWIRTSCHAFTS- UND AUSSENPOLITIK.
MUNICH: R OLDENBOURG, 1964, 256 PP.
CRITICAL STUDY OF US FOREIGN AID POLICY. EXAMINES IMPACT OF FOREIGN AID COMMITMENTS ON AGRICULTURE AND SHIPPING. DISCUSSES EFFECTIVENESS OF US AID WITH REFERENCE TO THREE CASE STUDIES (CHINA, GERMANY, UK) AND ATTEMPTS TO ESTABLISH AIMS AND OBJECTIVES OF FOREIGN AID. INCLUDES ANALYSIS OF POLITICAL STRUCTURE OF US AND ITS IMPACT ON SHAPING OF FOREIGN AID POLICY.

1684 KRIPALANI A.J.B.
"FOR PRINCIPLED NEUTRALITY."
FOR. AFF., 38 (OCT. 59), 46-60.
INDIAN POLITICIAN VIEWS INDIAN NEUTRALITY IN FOREIGN POLICY FOUNDED ON GANDHIAN PRINCIPLES OF NONVIOLENCE AND TRUTH AS FUNDAMENTALLY CORRECT BUT WEAK AND VACILLATING IN PRACTICE. EXPRESSES INDIAN FAILURE TO SAFEGUARD HER VITAL INTERESTS. EXPOSES INDIA'S ACQUIESCENCE IN CHINA'S RAPE OF TIBET AND MISHANDLING OF KASHMIR PROBLEM. DISAGREES WITH INDIAN RELIANCE ON FOREIGN AID. SUGGESTS REALISM AND CONSISTENCY IN FOREIGN POLICY.

1685 KRISTENSEN T.
THE ECONOMIC WORLD BALANCE.
COPENHAGEN: MUNKSGAARD, 1960, 377 PP.
CURRENT BALANCE OF ECONOMIC POWER BETWEEN EAST AND WEST AND FACTORS OF CHANGE SUCH AS INCREASED CONTACTS AND TRADE VOLUME ARE CONSIDERED. EXPORT OF CAPITAL AND TECHNICAL SKILLS TO UNDERDEVELOPED COUNTRIES ADVOCATED. EVALUATES FUTURE ECONOMIC GROWTH IN VARIOUS REGIONS AND GIVES PROPOSALS FOR FURTHER STUDY.

1686 KRISTENSEN T.
"THE SOUTH AS AN INDUSTRIAL POWER."
COOPERATION AND CONFLICT, 2 (1967), 61-66.
PRESENTS PICTURE OF ECONOMIC EVOLUTION OF DEVELOPED AND DEVELOPING COUNTRIES OF FREE WORLD FROM 1960-2000. FINDS THAT ECONOMIC GAP, PER CAPITA, WILL WIDEN BETWEEN TWO GROUPS BECAUSE OF POPULATION GROWTH IN DEVELOPING COUNTRIES. FEELS ONLY SOLUTION IS INCREASED INDUSTRIAL DEVELOPMENT TO MECHANIZE AGRICULTURAL METHODS AND INCREASE PRODUCTIVITY.

1687 KROPOTKIN P.
MUTUAL AID, A FACTOR OF EVOLUTION (1902)
BOSTON: EXTENDING HORIZON BOOKS, 1955, 362 PP.
THESIS OF BOOK IS THAT "IN THE ETHICAL PROGRESS OF MAN, MUTUAL SUPPORT - NOT MUTUAL STRUGGLE - HAS HAD THE LEADING PART." BELIEVES THAT MUTUAL AID IS AND HAS BEEN VITAL TO PROGRESS OF SOCIAL INSTITUTIONS. ARGUES AGAINST DARWIN'S THEORY OF SURVIVAL OF FITTEST AND STRUGGLE FOR EXISTENCE. MEN HAVE A SENSE, PERHAPS ONLY INSTINCTUAL, OF HUMAN SOLIDARITY.

1688 KRUSCHE H.
"THE STRIVING OF THE KIESINGER-STRAUS GOVERNMENT FOR NUCLEAR WEAPONS IS A THREAT TO EUROPEAN SECURITY."
GERMAN FOREIGN POLICY, 6 (FEB. 67), 152-160.
ARGUES THAT BONN POLICIES POTENTIALLY THREATEN EUROPEAN AND WORLD PEACE. NECESSARY TO LIMIT ARMS RACE AND DANGERS OF NUCLEAR CONFLICT. WESTBGERMANY OPPOSED TO ARMS CONTROL AND THUS EVENTUAL GERMAN REUNIFICATION. ARGUES THAT WEST GERMANY CONSTITUTES MAIN SOURCE OF TENSION BETWEEN EUROPEAN STATES. SOME DOCUMENTATION.

1689 KUENNE R.E.
THE POLARIS MISSILE STRIKE* A GENERAL ECONOMIC SYSTEMS ANALYSIS.
COLUMBUS: OHIO STATE U PR, 1966, 434 PP., LC#66-10715.
STUDY OF THE POLARIS DETERRENCE SYSTEM DEALING WITH ITS EFFECTIVENESS IN PREVENTING SOVIET UNION FROM LAUNCHING A THERMONUCLEAR ATTACK. OFFERS ECONOMIC SOLUTIONS AND PRESENTS A PROBABILISTIC MODEL SUSCEPTIBLE TO USE BY COMPUTER. HYPOTHESIZES ABOUT NATIONAL SECURITY AND ARMS CONTROL.

1690 KULISCHER E.M.
EUROPE ON THE MOVE: WAR AND POPULATION CHANGES, 1917-1947.
NEW YORK: COLUMB. U. PR., 1948, 377 PP.
POPULATIONS TEND TO SHIFT WHERE THERE IS GREATEST ECONOMIC OPPORTUNITY WHICH ACTS AS FORCE TOWARDS WORLD POPULATION BALANCE. WW2 SEEN AS A RESULT OF EXCESS POPULATION FORCING EXCESS PRODUCTION THAT 'HAD TO BECOME' WAR PRODUCT-

ION. FURTHER WARS PREDICTED UNLESS GERMANY AND RUSSIA CAN EXPORT EXCESS POPULATION. POPULATION CONTROL IS REGARDED AS ULTIMATELY NECESSARY.

1691 KULSKI W.W.
PEACEFUL CO-EXISTENCE: AN ANALYSIS OF SOVIET FOREIGN POLICY.
CHICAGO: REGNERY, 1959, 662 PP.
DEFINES BASIC MOTIVATION OF SOVIET POLICY WHICH AIMS AT GLOBAL VICTORY OF SOCIALIST SYSTEM. PLACES SOVIET UNION AT THE CENTER OF IDEOLOGICAL STRUGGLE. CONSIDERS SOVIET ACCEPTANCE OF STATUS QUO ON INTERNATIONAL PROBLEMS ONLY A TEMPORARY PHASE. REVIEWS SOVIET TECHNIQUE OF SELECTING UNDERDEVELOPED AREAS AS TARGETS FOR SOCIAL, POLITICAL, AND ECONOMIC EXPLOITATION.

1692 KULSKI W.W.
"PEACEFUL COEXISTENCE."
CHICAGO: HENRY REGNERY CO, 1959.
ANALYSIS OF SOVIET FOREIGN POLICY COVERING THE PERIOD FROM THE REVOLUTION THROUGH KHRUSHCHEV AND COMMUNIST INTERNATIONAL MOVEMENT. DISCUSSES FOREIGN POLICY OF SOVIETS WITH A PARALLEL ANALYSIS OF CURRENT POLICIES IN SEVERAL EAST EUROPEAN COMMUNIST PARTIES. BELIEVES SOVIET POLICY GUIDED BY DOUBLE MOTIVATION OF STRONG NATIONALISM AND INTERNATIONALISM. BIBLIOGRAPHY OF RUSSIAN AND ENGLISH SOURCES.

1693 KULSKI W.W.
INTERNATIONAL POLITICS IN A REVOLUTIONARY AGE.
NEW YORK: J B LIPPINCOTT, 1964, 639 PP., LC#64-12758.
GENERAL STUDY OF CONTEMPORARY INTERNATIONAL RELATIONS. DISCUSSES DIPLOMACY, NATIONALISM, INTERNATIONAL LAW, IDEOLOGY, UN, NONALIGNMENT, AND WAR IN NUCLEAR ERA.

1694 KULSKI W.W.
"DEGAULLE AND THE WORLD: THE FOREIGN POLICY OF THE FIFTH FRENCH REPUBLIC."
SYRACUSE: SYRACUSE U PRESS, 1966.
STUDIES DE GAULLE'S FOREIGN POLICY, ATTRIBUTING TO IT A REALISTIC VIEW OF WORLD AFFAIRS AND A MYSTICAL VIEW OF FRANCE. BIBLIOGRAPHY OF 150 ITEMS, MOSTLY BOOKS BUT ALSO OFFICIAL SOURCES AND PERIODICALS, THROUGH 1966. WORKS CITED ARE VIRTUALLY ALL IN FRENCH.

1695 KUNZ J.
"SANCTIONS IN INTERNATIONAL LAW."
AMER. J. INT. LAW, 54 (APR. 60), 324-47.
CONTENDS THAT INTERNATIONAL LAW SANCTIONS ARE 'PRIMITIVE' INSOFAR AS THEY OPERATE IN A DE-CENTRALIZED LEGAL ORDER. SUCH A SYSTEM HAS NO CENTRAL INSTITUTION FOR MAKING OR APPLYING LEGAL RULES.

1696 KUNZ J.
"THE CHANGING SCIENCE OF INTERNATIONAL LAW."
AMER. J. INT. LAW, 56 (APRIL 64), 488-499.
INTERNATIONAL LAW SHIFTING FROM THE CLASSICAL ANGLO-AMERICAN AND CONTINENTAL METHODS. CRITICIZES THE 'NEO-REALISTS', 'WORLD-LAW' THEORISTS AND OTHER THEORETICAL IDEALISTS OUTSIDE THE OCCIDENT. LAW IS NECESSARY FOR REGULATING AFFAIRS OF MEN AND PROMOTING WORLD PEACE BUT DOESN'T BELIEVE THAT THESE 'NEW CONCEPTS' WILL FURTHER DEVELOPMENT.

1697 KUWAIT ARABIA
KUWAIT FUND FOR ARAB ECONOMIC DEVELOPMENT (PAMPHLET)
KUWAIT: GOVERNMENT PRINTING PR, 1963, 17 PP.
LAW ESTABLISHING KUWAIT FUND, THE PURPOSE OF WHICH IS TO ASSIST ARAB STATES IN DEVELOPING THEIR ECONOMIES AND PROVIDE THEM WITH LOANS NECESSARY FOR THE EXECUTION OF THEIR PROGRAMS OF DEVELOPMENT. ALSO CONTAINS KUWAIT FUND'S CHARTER OUTLINING ADMINISTRATION, OPERATIONS, AND GENERAL PROVISIONS.

1698 KYLE K.
"BACKGROUND TO THE CRISIS"
SURVIVAL, 9 (AUG. 67), 246-249.
PROGRAM BY BBC ON ARAB-ISRAELI CRISIS. STATES THAT BRITAIN'S "INTELLECTUAL INCOHERENCE" CAUSED PROBLEM AND THAT ARABS ARE COMPLETELY IN RIGHT. WEST SUPPORTS ISRAEL DESPITE THIS KNOWLEDGE OUT OF GUILT OVER JEWS. DISCUSSES ISRAEL'S RIGHT TO EXISTENCE, RUSSIAN POSITION, AND SITUATION OF BORDER RAIDS AND REPRISALS. WRITTEN BEFORE OUTBREAK OF WAR IN JUNE, 1967.

1699 KYRIAK T.E. ED.
ASIAN DEVELOPMENTS: A BIBLIOGRAPHY.
ANNAPOLIS: RES MICROFILM PUBL.
QUARTERLY PERIODICAL INDEXING ALL JOINT PUBLICATIONS RESEARCH SERVICE MATERIALS TRANSLATED IN THAT QUARTER. FOREIGN DOCUMENTS, SCHOLARLY WORKS, AND OTHER MATERIALS NOT AVAILABLE IN ENGLISH ARE INDEXED BY SUBJECT AND CROSS-REFERENCED WITH OTHER THREE AREA BIBLIOGRAPHIES IN THIS SERIES. ALL ITEMS ARE IN SOCIAL SCIENCES WITH ABOUT 110 ITEMS INCLUDED. BEGUN 1962.

1700 KYRIAK T.E. ED.
CHINA: A BIBLIOGRAPHY.
ANNAPOLIS: RES MICROFILM PUBL.
MONTHLY PERIODICAL INDEXING ALL JOINT PUBLICATIONS RESEARCH SERVICE MATERIALS TRANSLATED IN THE MONTH COVERED. FOREIGN DOCUMENTS, SCHOLARLY WORKS, AND OTHER MATERIALS NOT AVAILABLE IN ENGLISH ARE INDEXED BY SUBJECT AND CROSS-REFERENCED WITH THE OTHER THREE AREA BIBLIOGRAPHIES IN THIS SERIES. ALL ITEMS ARE IN SOCIAL SCIENCES. BEGUN 1962.

1701 KYRIAK T.E. ED.
EAST EUROPE: BIBLIOGRAPHY--INDEX TO US JPRS RESEARCH TRANSLATIONS.
ANNAPOLIS: RES MICROFILM PUBL.
A PERIODICAL PUBLISHED MONTHLY INDEXING ALL JOINT PUBLICATIONS RESEARCH SERVICE MATERIALS TRANSLATED IN THE MONTH COVERED. FOREIGN DOCUMENTS, SCHOLARLY WORKS, AND OTHER MATERIALS NOT AVAILABLE IN ENGLISH ARE INDEXED BY SUBJECT AND CROSS-REFERENCED WITH THE OTHER THREE AREA BIBLIOGRAPHIES IN THIS SERIES. MOST ITEMS ARE IN SOCIAL SCIENCES WITH ABOUT 110 ITEMS PER PERIODICAL. INCLUDES INDEX TO MICROFILM.

1702 KYRIAK T.E.
INTERNATIONAL DEVELOPMENTS: A BIBLIOGRAPHY (SERIAL)
ANNAPOLIS: RES MICROFILM PUBL.
PUBLISHED BIMONTHLY FROM 1962; ANNOTATED BIBLIOGRAPHY AND "GUIDE TO CONTENTS OF A COLLECTION OF US JOINT PUBLICATIONS RESEARCH SERVICE TRANSLATIONS IN THE SOCIAL SCIENCES EMANATING FROM AFRICA, LATIN AMERICA, NEAR EAST, AND WESTERN EUROPE." PROVIDES AN INTRODUCTION EXPLAINING HOW THIS GUIDE MAY BE USED FOR INFORMATION RETRIEVAL.

1703 KYRIAK T.E. ED.
SOVIET UNION: BIBLIOGRAPHY INDEX TO US JPRS RESEARCH TRANSLATIONS.
ANNAPOLIS: RES MICROFILM PUBL.
PERIODICAL PUBLISHED MONTHLY INDEXING ALL JOINT PUBLICATIONS RESEARCH SERVICE MATERIALS TRANSLATED IN THE MONTH COVERED. FOREIGN DOCUMENTS, SCHOLARLY WORKS, AND OTHER MATERIALS NOT AVAILABLE IN ENGLISH. INDEXED BY SUBJECT AND CROSS-REFERENCED WITH THE OTHER THREE AREA BIBLIOGRAPHIES IN THIS SERIES. MOST ITEMS ARE IN SOCIAL SCIENCES WITH ABOUT 110 ITEMS PER PERIODICAL. INCLUDES INDEX TO MICROFILM.

1704 KYRIAK T.E. ED.
INTERNATIONAL COMMUNIST DEVELOPMENTS 1957-1961: INDEX TO TRANSLATIONS FROM AFRICA, ASIA, LATIN AMERICA, WEST EUROPE.
ANNAPOLIS: RES MICROFILM PUBL, 1962, 54 PP., LC#62-20270.
GUIDE TO THE JPRS TRANSLATIONS OF COMMUNIST DOCUMENTS FROM COUNTRIES OUTSIDE SINO-SOVIET BLOC. INDEX BY COUNTRIES ON PAGES 49-54. ALL MATERIAL FROM 1957-61 MUCH IN NATURE OF PRESS RELEASES; INCLUDES MANY PARTY PLATFORMS.

1705 LA DOCUMENTATION FRANCAISE
CHRONOLOGIE INTERNATIONAL.
PARIS: PR UNIV DE FRANCE.
BI-MONTHLY SUPPLEMENT, "NOTES ET ETUDES DOCUMENTAIRES," WHICH DETAILS IMPORTANT EVENTS IN INTERNATIONAL RELATIONS CHRONOLOGICALLY. FIRST APPEARED IN 1963. CHRONOLOGICAL ARRANGEMENT WITHIN TOPIC. COVERS TREATIES, CONFERENCES, COMMUNIQUES, TRIPS, NOTES, MESSAGES, ETC. LIMITED COMMENTARY IN EVENTS. COUNTRY INDEX.

1706 LABRIOLA A.
ESSAYS ON THE MATERIALISTIC CONCEPTION OF HISTORY.
CHICAGO: CHARLES H KERR, 1908, 246 PP.
POPULARIZATION OF HISTORICAL MATERIALISM BY AN ITALIAN COMMUNIST. ATTEMPTS TO EXPLAIN ITALIAN AND INTERNATIONAL EVENTS ACCORDING TO MARXIST TOOLS OF ANALYSIS.

1707 LACOUTRE J.
VIETNAM: BETWEEN TWO TRUCES.
NEW YORK: RANDOM HOUSE, INC, 1965, 295 PP.
ANALYZES VIETNAM WAR AS PRODUCT OF LOCAL CRISES, AND THE RESULT OF PROBLEMS FACED BY DEVELOPING POLITICAL SYSTEMS OF ECONOMICALLY UNDERDEVELOPED AREAS. CONCLUDES US INVOLVEMENT IN VIETNAM IS A MISTAKE BECAUSE IT GIVES VIETNAM POLITICAL CRISIS MORE IMPORTANCE THAN IT IS DUE IN INTERNATIONAL RELATIONS.

1708 LACOUTRE J.
"HO CHI MINH."
ESPRIT, 35 (MAR. 67), 432-443.
ANALYSIS OF INTERNAL IDEOLOGICAL STRUGGLES IN NORTH VIETNAM. CONFLICT BETWEEN HO CHI MINH, PRO-RUSSIAN COMMUNIST AND PRO-CHINESE ELEMENTS OF STATE. RESULT IS POSITIVE NONALIGNMENT. ARGUES THAT NATIONALISM AND REALPOLITIK ARE MOTIVATING FORCES OF VIETNAMESE FOREIGN POLICY.

1709 LADOR-LEDERER J.J.
INTERNATIONAL NON-GOVERNMENTAL ORGANIZATIONS: A STUDY IN AUTONOMOUS ORGANIZATION AND IUS GENTIUM.
LEYDEN: AW SIJTHOFF, 1963, 403 PP.
ANALYSIS OF STATE-INDIVIDUAL RELATIONS IN INTERNATIONAL LAW THROUGH AN EXAMINATION OF INTERNATIONAL NON-GOVERNMENTAL ORGANIZATIONS. AUTHOR CLASSIFIES AND STUDIES DIFFERENT FORMS OF THIS TYPE OF ORGANIZATION IN ATTEMPT TO CLARIFY INDIVIDUAL'S POSITION

AS A DEFENDANT, AS A CLAIMANT OF ECONOMIC RIGHTS, AS A PARTY IN CONTRACTUAL AGREEMENTS.

1710 LAFAVE W.R. ED.
LAW AND SOVIET SOCIETY.
URBANA: U OF ILLINOIS PR, 1965, 297 PP., LC#65-19109.
CASE STUDIES DEMONSTRATE DEVELOPMENT OF SOVIET LAW UNDER KHRUSHCHEV IN ALL BRANCHES OF CIVIL LAW. SPECIAL TOPICS INCLUDE SPREAD OF LEGAL SYSTEM ABROAD AND RELATION OF JURISPRUDENCE TO MARXISM.

1711 LAFEBER W.
THE NEW EMPIRE: AN INTERPRETATION OF AMERICAN EXPANSION, 1860-1898.
ITHACA: CORNELL U PRESS, 1963, 444 PP.
EXAMINES INDUSTRIAL REVOLUTION IN AMERICA, DEEMING IT CRUCIAL TO FOREIGN POLICY AND TRANSITION TO MODERN EMPIRE. STUDIES THE YEARS OF PREPARATION, THE INTELLECTUAL FORMULATION, THE FOREIGN STRATEGY, THE ECONOMIC GROWTH, AND US REACTION TO WORLD PROBLEMS. ALSO CONSIDERS DEPRESSION DIPLOMACY, VENEZUELAN CRISIS, CHANGING FRIENDS AND FOES, AND APPROACH TO WAR AS A STRONG WORLD POWER.

1712 LALL A.
MODERN INTERNATIONAL NEGOTIATION: PRINCIPLES AND PRACTICE.
NEW YORK: COLUMBIA U PRESS, 1966, 404 PP., LC#66-17587.
STUDIES FIELD OF INTERNATIONAL NEGOTIATIONS, DESCRIBING VARIETY OF AVAILABLE FORMS; PROCESSES AND TACTICS; AND ROLE OF NATIONAL INTERESTS. STUDIES MAJOR ISSUES OF LAST TWENTY YEARS INVOLVING EITHER MULTILATERAL OR BILATERAL METHODS, PUBLIC OR QUIET DIPLOMACY, CONFERENCE OR PARLIAMENTARY DIPLOMACY.

1713 LAMBERG R.F.
PRAG UND DIE DRITTE WELT.
HANNOVER: VERLAG FUR LITERATUR, 1966, 291 PP.
EXAMINES POLITICAL AND ECONOMIC RELATIONS BETWEEN CZECHOSLOVAKIA AND DEVELOPING NATIONS OF ASIA, AFRICA AND LATIN AMERICA. DISCUSSES FOREIGN TRADE, TECHNOLOGICAL ASSISTANCE, AND LOAN PROGRAMS.

1714 LANDEN R.G.
OMAN SINCE 1856: DISRUPTIVE MODERNIZATION IN A TRADITIONAL ARAB SOCIETY.
PRINCETON: PRINCETON U PRESS, 1967, 488 PP.
STUDY OF EFFECTS OF ECONOMIC DEVELOPMENT IN OMAN POINTS OUT LATE 19TH CENTURY AS TIME OF IRREVOCABLE CHANGE IN CULTURE OF REGION. DESCRIBES PERSIAN GULF AREA BEFORE 19TH CENTURY AND TRACES HISTORY OF OMAN GOVERNMENT ALONG WITH ESTABLISHMENT OF BRITISH PREDOMINANCY. DISCUSSES EFFECTS OF OIL DEVELOPMENT ON CULTURLAND POLITICAL ESTABLISHMENTS.

1715 LANDHEER B., VAN ESSEN J.L.F.
FUNDAMENTALS OF PUBLIC INTERNATIONAL LAW (SELECTIVE BIBLIOGRAPHIES OF THE LIBRARY OF THE PEACE PALACE, VOL. I; PAMPH)
LEYDEN: SYTHOFF, 1953, 85 PP.
AN ANNOTATED BIBLIOGRAPHY OF MATERIALS IN THE LIBRARY OF THE PEACE PALACE THAT WERE PUBLISHED BETWEEN 1872-1952 ON BOTH GENERAL AND PARTICULAR ASPECTS OF PUBLIC INTERNATIONAL LAW. MATERIAL IS TOPICALLY ARRANGED WITHIN CATEGORIES OF GENERAL, SPECIFIC, AND SPECIAL WORKS. SOURCES IN WESTERN LANGUAGES ARE ANNOTATED IN LANGUAGE OF ORIGINAL PUBLICATION. INDEXED ALPHABETICALLY BY AUTHOR.

1716 LANDHEER B., VAN ESSEN J.L.F.
RECOGNITION IN INTERNATIONAL LAW (SELECTIVE BIBLIOGRAPHIES OF THE LIBRARY OF THE PEACE PALACE, VOL. II; PAMPHLET)
LEYDEN: SYTHOFF, 1954, 28 PP.
SYSTEMATIC, ANNOTATED BIBLIOGRAPHY OF WORKS ON RECOGNITION LAW AVAILABLE AT THE PEACE PALACE LIBRARY. CLASSIFIES MATERIAL ON RECOGNITION IN GENERAL, AS WELL AS SPECIFIC STUDIES ON LEGAL EFFECT, PRACTICE, STIMSON DOCTRINE, ETC. SOURCES INCLUDE ALL WESTERN-LANGUAGE PUBLICATIONS FROM 1899 TO 1953.

1717 LANDHEER B. ED., ROBERTSON A.H. ED.
EUROPEAN YEARBOOK, 1955.
THE HAGUE: MARTINUS NIJHOFF, 1955, 515 PP.
REPRINTS BASIC DOCUMENTS AND SUMMARIZES ORGANIZATION OF BRUSSELS TREATY ORGANIZATION, OEEC, COE, ECSC, NORTHERN COUNCIL, AND EUROPEAN CONFERENCE OF MINISTERS OF TRANSPORT, ORGANIZATION FOR NUCLEAR RESEARCH, AND CONFERENCE ON ORGANIZATION OF AGRICULTURAL MARKETS. TRACES HISTORY OF EACH AND COMMENTS ON POLITICAL, ECONOMIC, AND MILITARY GOALS AND FUNCTIONS. DESCRIBES EUROPEAN DEFENSE COMMUNITY.

1718 LANDHEER B.
ETHICAL VALUES IN INTERNATIONAL DECISION-MAKING.
THE HAGUE: MARTINUS NIJOFF, 1960, 103 PP.
EXAMINES CONDITIONS UNDER WHICH CO-OPERATION MAY OCCUR IN WORLD AFFAIRS BY MAKING ASSUMPTIONS ABOUT HUMAN NATURE AND STATE-CONDUCT. COMMON ETHICAL VALUES ARE POSSIBLE IF INDIVIDUALS DESIRE A 'NORMAL LIFE' AND IF STATES REFRAIN FROM EMPHASIZING DIFFERENCES. FOSTERS EQUITABLE DISTRIBUTION OF INCOME AND NATURAL EQUALITY OF MAN. DEFINES SOCIAL GOALS OF A STATE AND PRESENTS SEVERAL CONFERENCE PAPERS.

1719 LANDIS E.S.
"THE SOUTH WEST AFRICA CASES* REMAND TO THE UNITED NATIONS."
CORNELL LAW Q., 52 (SPRING 67), 627-671.
EXAMINATION OF PROCEEDINGS BEFORE INTERNATIONAL COURT OF JUSTICE IN SOUTH WEST AFRICA CASES. EMPHASIS GIVEN TO ARGUMENTS OF PARTIES AND DEVELOPMENT OF POSITIONS DURING COURSE OF LITIGATION. COMPARISON OF COURT'S HOLDING AND RATIONALE WITH PRIOR HOLDING IN LITIGATION. CONCLUSION CONSIDERS PROBABLE OUTCOME OF CASE. WELL DOCUMENTED THROUGHOUT.

1720 LANDSKRON W.A.
OFFICIAL SERIAL PUBLICATIONS RELATING TO ECONOMIC DEVELOPMENT IN AFRICA SOUTH OF THE SAHARA (PAMPHLET)
CAMBRIDGE: M I T PRESS, 1961, 44 PP.
LIST OF SERIAL REPORTS PUBLISHED IN ENGLISH COVERS BROAD RANGE OF SUBJECTS PERTAINING TO ECONOMIC DEVELOPMENT; ONLY REPORTS ON HEALTH AND EDUCATION HAVE BEEN EXCLUDED. INCLUDES STUDIES OF PRIVATE CORPORATIONS OPERATING UNDER GOVERNMENT APPROVAL AND OFFICIAL REPORTS ON UK'S COLONIES AND PROTECTORATES AND UN DOCUMENTS. REPORTS ARE ALL KNOWN TO BE AVAILABLE IN US. GEOGRAPHIC ARRANGEMENT.

1721 LANFALUSSY A.
"EUROPE'S PROGRESS: DUE TO COMMON MARKET."
LLOYD BANK REV., 62 (OCT. 61), 1-16.
REVIEWS DATA SHOWING THAT COMMON MARKET HAD NOT CAUSED GREAT ADVANCES. WARNS AGAINST LIMITS OF HIS FIGURES BECAUSE OF IMPONDERABLES OF MORALE AND POSSIBLE GROWING EFFECT NOT YET TOO APPARENT.

1722 LANGE O.
ECONOMIC DEVELOPMENT, PLANNING, AND INTERNATIONAL COOPERATION.
CAIRO: CENTRAL BANK OF EGYPT, 1963, 40 PP., LC#63-13434.
LECTURES DELIVERED AT THE CENTRAL BANK OF EGYPT IN 1961. EXAMINES PATTERNS OF ECONOMIC DEVELOPMENT; PLANNING ECONOMIC DEVELOPMENT; AND ASPECTS AND POSSIBILITIES FOR INTERNATIONAL COOPERATION, APPROACH IS MAINLY EMPIRICAL.

1723 LANGE O.R.
"DISARMAMENT ECONOMIC GROWTH AND INTERNATIONAL CO-OPERATION" (PAMPHLET)
LEEDS: LEEDS UNIV. PRESS, 1962, 11 PP.
SOLUTION TO TWO MAJOR WORLD PROBLEMS OF DISARMAMENT AND ECONOMIC DEVELOPMENT LIES IN INTERNATIONAL COOPERATION. DISARMAMENT LEADS TO PROBLEMS OF CONVERSION AND ALTERNATIVE USES OF RESOURCES. SOCIALIST AND CAPITALIST SYSTEMS DIFFER IN CONVERSION ABILITY ACCORDING TO AMOUNT OF CENTRAL PLANNING. AFTER SUCCESSFUL CONVERSION THE UNUSED RESOURCES WOULD BE AVAILABLE TO AID IN ECONOMIC DEVELOPMENT.

1724 LANGER W.L.
THE FRANCO-RUSSIAN ALLIANCE: 1890-1894.
CAMBRIDGE: HARVARD U PR, 1929, 455 PP.
HISTORY OF FRENCH-RUSSIAN RELATIONS AT CLOSE OF 19TH CENTURY. SHOWS HOW BISMARCKIAN POLICY WAS NULLIFIED BY HIS SUCCESSORS, THEREBY MAKING THE ALLIANCE POSSIBLE. OBJECT OF BOOK IS TO PLACE THE ALLIANCE IN ITS EUROPEAN CONTEXT AND EXPLAIN IT AS THE PRODUCT OF THE GENERAL INTERNATIONAL SITUATION. STRICTLY CHRONOLOGICAL APPROACH. POSITION AND POLICY OF ENGLAND ARE DETAILED.

1725 LANGER W.L., ARMSTRONG H.
FOREIGN AFFAIRS BIBLIOGRAPHY.
NEW YORK: COUNCIL FOR. REL., 1933, 551 PP.
PERTINENT MATERIAL RELATING TO INTERNATIONAL RELATIONS WITH PARTICULAR EMPHASIS ON WW1 AND POST WAR PERIOD.

1726 LANGER W.L.
THE DIPLOMACY OF IMPERIALISM 1890-1902.
NEW YORK: ALFRED KNOPF, 1935, 797 PP.
A CHRONOLOGICAL NARRATIVE OF THE TRIUMPH AND PROBLEMS OF IMPERIALISM IN EUROPEAN DIPLOMACY. SPECIAL STRESS LAID UPON MOVEMENT OF LATE-VICTORIAN IMPERIALISM IN ORDER TO ANALYZE THE DEPENDENCE OF WORLD POWERS ON BRITISH POLICY. COVERS ERA FROM FRANCO-RUSSIAN ENTENTE AND ALLIANCE TO ANGLO-JAPANESE ALLIANCE. EXTENSIVE ANNOTATED BIBLIOGRAPHICAL NOTES INCLUDED AT THE END OF EACH CHAPTER.

1727 LANGER W.L., GLEASON S.E.
THE UNDECLARED WAR, 1940-1941.
NEW YORK: HARPER & ROW, 1953, 963 PP., LC#53-7738.
EXTENSIVELY AND IN GREAT DETAIL DESCRIBES WORLD CRISIS AT INCEPTION OF EUROPEAN PHASE OF WWII AND DEVELOPMENT OF US POLICY IN ITS GLOBAL SETTING, ANALYZING "THE TORTURED EMERGENCE" OF US AS WORLD LEADER.

1728 LANOUE G.R. ED.
A BIBLIOGRAPHY OF DOCTORAL DISSERTATIONS ON POLITICS AND RELIGION.
NEW YORK: NATL COUNC OF CHURCHES, 1963, 49 PP., LC#63-21606.
A COMPILATION OF DOCTORAL DISSERTATIONS UNDERTAKEN IN AMERICAN AND CANADIAN UNIVERSITIES 1940-62. ENTRIES LISTED UNDER FIVE TOPICS: PHILOSOPHY AND THEORY; FOREIGN; AMERICAN NATIONAL; AMERICAN REGIONAL, STATE, AND LOCAL; AND AMERICAN

CONSTITUTIONAL AND LEGAL. SOME 649 DISSERTATIONS LISTED.

1729 LAPRADELLE ED.
ANNUAIRE DE LA VIE INTERNATIONALE: POLITIQUE, ECONOMIQUE, JURIDIQUE.
PARIS: EDITIONS INTERNATIONALES, 1928, 598 PP.
FRENCH PUBLICATION COVERING THE YEARS 1927-28, WHICH CLASSIFIES OFFICIAL PUBLICATIONS, SCHOLARLY AND CRITICAL WORKS, JOURNALS, AND PERIODICAL ARTICLES ON INTERNATIONAL RELATIONS, DIPLOMACY, AND INTERNATIONAL LAW. COMPREHENSIVE SUBJECT AND AUTHOR TABLES PROVIDE PARTIAL CROSS REFERENCES. BIBLIOGRAPHICAL INFORMATION GIVEN IN LANGUAGE OF PUBLICATION; SOURCES IN ALL WESTERN LANGUAGES.

1730 LAQUEUR W.Z.
THE SOVIET UNION AND THE MIDDLE EAST.
NEW YORK: PRAEGER, 1959, 366 PP.
FOLLOWS EVOLUTION OF SOVIET ATTITUDE SINCE 1917. ANALYZES SOVIET MOTIVES IN MIDDLE EAST. STUDIES RECENT POLICY TRENDS. CONTENDS SOVIET SEEMS TO SUPPORT NATIONAL MOVEMENTS BUT HAS LONG-RANGE AIMS FOR AREA.

1731 LAQUEUR W.Z. ED., LABEDZ L. ED.
THE FUTURE OF COMMUNIST SOCIETY.
NEW YORK: FREDERICK PRAEGER, 1962, 196 PP., LC#62-9509.
ESSAYS EXAMINE COMMUNISM IN PAST AND PRESENT TO PROJECT ITS FUTURE. BEGIN WITH THIRD CPSU PROGRAM OF 1961, STUDY ITS ECONOMIC PLANS, AND ANALYZE IDEOLOGICAL CHANGES. TREAT MARXIAN PHILOSOPHY AND PRACTICE, FUNCTION OF LAW, SOCIAL INSTITUTIONS, UTOPIAN TRADITION, AND WITHERING AWAY OF STATE. CONCLUDE WITH RUSSIA AND CHINA (TWO ROADS TO COMMUNISM), SOCIAL AND ECONOMIC POLICY, AND FUTURE GOALS.

1732 LAQUEUR W.Z. ED., LABEDZ L. ED.
POLYCENTRISM.
NEW YORK: FREDERICK PRAEGER, 1962, 259 PP., LC#62-18268.
ANALYZES DECLINE OF MONOLITHIC COMMUNISM IN RECENT YEARS, INCLUDING THE SINO-SOVIET SCHISM, REVISIONISM, AND THE IMPACT OF POLYCENTRISM ON COMMUNIST PARTIES IN EASTERN EUROPE, WESTERN EUROPE, AND THE UNDERDEVELOPED WORLD.

1733 LARSEN K.
NATIONAL BIBLIOGRAPHIC SERVICES: THEIR CREATION AND OPERATION.
PARIS: UNESCO, 1953, 146 PP.
DEFINES PURPOSE, SCOPE, AND TECHNIQUES FOR ESTABLISHING A BIBLIOGRAPHIC CENTER UNDER THE AUSPICES OF UNESCO; OUTLINES ITS FUNCTIONS, STRESSES ITS IMPORTANCE, AND SPECIFIES TECHNIQUES. DESCRIBES THE MEANS FOR PROCURING, PRODUCING, AND PROMOTING MATERIALS; DEALS WITH THE UNION CATALOGUE, DIRECTORIES, INFORMATION SERVICE, ADMINISTRATION OF THE CENTER, ETC.

1734 LARSON A.
WHEN NATIONS DISAGREE.
BATON ROUGE: LOUISIANA ST U PR, 1961, 249 PP.
CONSIDERS NATURE OF INTERNATIONAL LAW, ITS FOUNDATIONS, ENFORCEMENT, AND ORGANIZATION. DISCUSSES ITS PRESENT STATE AND MAJOR PROBLEMS THAT HAVE ARISEN WITH IT IN THE PAST. GIVES SPECIAL EMPHASIS TO RELATION OF US TO WORLD LAW AND ITS ROLE AS DEFENDER-ENFORCER. SUMMARIZES NECESSITIES OF NEAR FUTURE.

1735 LARUS J. ED.
COMPARATIVE WORLD POLITICS.
BELMONT: WADSWORTH, 1965, 274 PP., LC#64-21773.
PROVIDES READINGS INTRODUCING PRE-MODERN INTERSTATE RELATIONS OF CHINESE EMPIRE, PRE-MUSLIM INDIA, AND ISLAMIC COMMUNITY, PLUS CLASSICAL WESTERN NATION-STATE. ALSO SEEKS TO PRESENT EVIDENCE OF CONTINUITY AND DISCONTINUITY BETWEEN WESTERN NATION-STATE SYSTEM AND NON-WESTERN ANTECEDENTS.

1736 LARUS J. ED.
FROM COLLECTIVE SECURITY TO PREVENTIVE DIPLOMACY.
NEW YORK: JOHN WILEY, 1965, 556 PP., LC#65-27359.
READINGS IN INTERNATIONAL ORGANIZATION AND THE MAINTENANCE OF PEACE, ESPECIALLY ISSUES BEFORE THE LEAGUE OF NATIONS AND THE UN. DISCUSSES FUTURE PROSPECTS FOR INTERNATIONAL ORGANIZATIONS.

1737 LARY M.B.
PROBLEMS OF THE UNITED STATES AS WORLD TRADER AND BANKER.
NEW YORK: NATL BUREAU ECO RES, 1963, 175 PP., LC#63-11079.
FOCUSES ON PROBLEMS OF ASSESSING ELEMENTS OF STRENGTH AND WEAKNESS IN OUR INTERNATIONAL TRADE AND FINANCIAL POSITION OF IMPROVING ADJUSTMENT PROCESSES SO AS TO DIMINISH EXTERNAL CONSTRAINT OF DOMESTIC AND FOREIGN ECONOMIC POLICIES. ALSO DISCUSSES PROBLEM OF MAKING ADAPTATIONS IN OUR POLICIES TO PREVENT OUR INCREASED INTERNATIONAL EXPOSURE FROM HINDERING PURSUIT OF ECONOMIC STABILITY AND GROWTH.

1738 LASKY V.
THE UGLY RUSSIAN.
NEW YORK: POCKET BOOKS, 1965, 313 PP., LC#65-21060.
TRACES NATURE OF SOVIET ATTITUDE TOWARD UNDERDEVELOPED NATIONS IN ASIA, AFRICA, AND NEAR EAST. BASED ON EXTENSIVE TRAVELS IN ALL PARTS OF THE WORLD. EXAMINES IN DETAIL "BIGOTRY OF COMMUNIST OFFICIALS TOWARD DARKER PEOPLES" AND SPECIFIC SHORTCOMINGS OF RUSSIAN FOREIGN POLICY.

1739 LASSWELL H.D.
"THE GARRISON STATE" (BMR)"
AMER. J. OF SOCIOLOGY, 46 (JAN. 41), 455-468.
EXAMINES POSSIBILITY THAT WORLD IS MOVING TOWARD CONDITION OF "GARRISON STATES," IN WHICH MILITARY IS MOST POWERFUL GROUP IN SOCIETY. EXAMINES TREND AWAY FROM SUPREMACY OF BUSINESSMEN. POSTULATES METHODS BY WHICH MILITARY GROUPS WILL GAIN SUPREMACY, SUCH AS ECONOMIC TACTICS AND MANIPULATION OF PUBLIC SYMBOLS.

1740 LASSWELL H.D.
"THE SCIENTIFIC STUDY OF INTERNATIONAL RELATIONS."
YRB. WORLD AFF., 12 (58), 1-28.
SURVEY OF SCIENTIFIC CONTRIBUTIONS TO INTERNATIONAL STUDIES IN RECENT YEARS. FOCUSES ON THEORIES OF WORLD POLITICAL EQUILIBRIUM, THEORIES OF MILITARY, DIPLOMATIC, IDEOLOGICAL AND ECONOMIC STRATEGY AND METHODS OF OBTAINING AND PROCESSING DATA.

1741 LASSWELL H.D.
"UNIVERSALITY IN PERSPECTIVE."
PROC. AMER. SOC. INT. LAW, (1959), 1-9.
IT IS NECESSARY TO CREATE A STRONGER AND MORE DECISIVE SYSTEM OF INTERNATIONAL ORDER IF MAN IS TO SURVIVE. THE UNIVERSAL SYSTEM OF PUBLIC ORDER CAN BE IMPLEMENTED WITHOUT RESORTING TO TOTALITARIANISM.

1742 LATHAM E.
THE COMMUNIST CONTROVERSY IN WASHINGTON.
CAMBRIDGE: HARVARD U PR, 1966, 446 PP., LC#66-14447.
DISCUSSES NATURE AND EXTENT OF COMMUNIST INFILTRATION INTO US GOVERNMENT FROM NEW DEAL TO MCCARTHY ERA. FOCUSES ATTENTION ON CIVILIAN AGENCIES (NATIONAL LABOR RELATIONS BOARD, DEPARTMENT OF STATE, ETC.).

1743 LATIFI D.
INDIA AND UNITED STATES AID.
BOMBAY: PUBLIC AFFAIRS FORUM, 1960, 135 PP.
HISTORICALLY ANALYZES EFFECTS OF US FOREIGN AID ON INDIAN ECONOMY AND RELATIONS. COMPARES US ASSISTANCE TO BRITISH COLONIALISM AND ITS EFFECTS ON INDIAN ECONOMY. TRACES ECONOMIC GROWTH 1949-60 WITH US AID. DISCUSSES EFFECTIVENESS OF WASHINGTON'S POLICIES IN ASIA IN GENERAL.

1744 LATOURETTE K.S.
CHINA.
ENGLEWOOD CLIFFS: PRENTICE HALL, 1964, 152 PP., LC#64-23560.
EXAMINES WHY COMMUNISTS SUCCEEDED IN TAKING OVER MAINLAND, HOW SUCCESSFULLY AIMS HAVE BEEN CARRIED OUT, HOW MUCH OLD CHINA PERSISTS, AND PROSPECTS FOR CONTINUED COMMUNIST CONTROL. GIVES HISTORICAL BACKGROUND.

1745 LAUERHAUSS L.
COMMUNISM IN LATIN AMERICA: THE POST-WAR YEARS (1945 -1960) (PAPER)
LOS ANGELES: U CAL LAT AMER STUD, 1962, 78 PP.
ONE THOUSAND BOOKS, ARTICLES AND GOVERNMENT DOCUMENTS COVERING ENTIRE REGION, PERIOD 1945-60. ARRANGED BY COUNTRY OR AREA. INCLUDES WORKS ON SOCIO-ECONOMICS AND POLITICS WHICH ARE RELEVANT TO TOPIC, AND COMMUNISM IN GENERAL WHERE APPLICABLE. WRITINGS OF MAJOR LATIN COMMUNISTS ISSUED 1945-60. INCLUDES MANY FOREIGN-LANGUAGE SOURCES.

1746 LAUTERPACHT E.
"THE UNITED NATIONS EMERGENCY FORCE."
NEW YORK: PRAEGER, 1960, 48 PP.
COLLECTION OF DOCUMENTS CONCERNING ESTABLISHMENT AND OPERATION OF UNITED NATIONS EMERGENCY FORCE, WHICH BEAR UPON LEGAL ASPECTS OF ITS STATUS. CONTAINS RESOLUTIONS OF GENERAL ASSEMBLY AND LETTERS OF SECRETARY GENERAL.

1747 LAUTERPACHT E. ED.
"THE SUEZ CANAL SETTLEMENT."
NEW YORK: PRAEGER, 1960, 82 PP.
A COLLECTION OF PAPERS ON THE LEGALITY OF THE SUEZ SETTLEMENT. COVERS TIME FROM OCTOBER 1956 TO MARCH 1959.

1748 LAUTERPACHT H.
PRIVATE LAW SOURCES AND ANALOGIES OF INTERNATIONAL LAW.
LONDON: LONGMANS, 1927, 326 PP.
COMMENTARY ON ARTICLE 38 OF STATUTE OR PERMANENT COURT OF INTERNATIONAL JUSTICE WHICH RECOGNIZES GENERAL PRINCIPLES OF LAW ACCEPTED BY CIVILIZED STATES AS BINDING, THOUGH ONLY SUPPLEMENTARY SOURCES OF DECISION IN JUDICIAL SETTLEMENT OF DISPUTES. AUTHOR ACCEPTS RECOURSE TO PRIVATE LAW AND REJECTS MODERN POSITIVISM. RECOGNIZES THAT ANALOGOUS RULES OF PRIVATE LAW AID IN DEVELOPING UNIVERSAL LEGAL ORDER.

1749 LAUTERPACHT H.
THE FUNCTION OF LAW IN THE INTERNATIONAL COMMUNITY.
OXFORD: CLARENDON PR., 1933, 469 PP.

DISCUSSES, THROUGH REFERENCE TO PROBLEMS OF INTERNATIONAL JUDICIAL FUNCTION, THE PRINCIPAL ISSUES OF THE PHILOSOPHY OF INTERNATIONAL LAW.

1750 LAUTERPACHT H.
INTERNATIONAL LAW AND HUMAN RIGHTS.
NEW YORK: PRAEGER, 1950, 475 PP.
ANALYZES LEGAL EFFECTS OF PROVISIONS OF UN CHARTER ON ORGANS CHARGED WITH THEIR INTERPRETATION AND APPLICATION.

1751 LAVES W.H.C., THOMSON C.A.
UNESCO.
BLOOMINGTON: IND. U. PR., 1957, 469 PP.
HISTORY OF UNESCO CONTRASTING GOALS AND ACCOMPLISHMENTS AND CONCLUDING ORGANIZATION MOST SUCCESFUL IN ADVANCEMENT OF KNOWLEDGE THROUGH TECHNICAL ASSISTANCE AND LEAST SUCCESSFUL IN PROMOTION OF INTERNATIONAL UNDERSTANDING. URGES INCREASED EFFORTS ON THE PART OF THE MEMBER STATES.

1752 LAWSON R.
INTERNATIONAL REGIONAL ORGANIZATIONS.
NEW YORK: PRAEGER, 1962, 387 PP.
DISCUSSES POSTWAR PROLIFERATION OF REGIONAL ORGANIZATIONS UNDER UN AND MEANS DEVISED TO EFFECT FUNCTIONS. LISTS SERIES OF DOCUMENTS PRINTED BY VARIOUS REGIONAL ORGANIZATIONS.

1753 LAWYERS COMM AMER POLICY VIET
VIETNAM AND INTERNATIONAL LAW: AN ANALYSIS OF THE LEGALITY OF THE US MILITARY INVOLVEMENT.
FLANDERS: O'HARE BOOKS, 1967, LC#67-19573.
COMPREHENSIVE ANALYSIS OF LEGAL ISSUES RAISED BY VIETNAM WAR, DOCUMENTING THE CONCLUSION THAT US MILITARY INVOLVEMENT VIOLATES INTERNATIONAL LAW. ISSUES DISCUSSED INCLUDE UNPRECEDENTED CHARACTER OF INVOLVEMENT, VIOLATION OF UN CHARTER, 1954 GENEVA ACCORDS, UNLAWFUL METHODS OF WARFARE, LEGAL ASPECTS OF US COMMITMENT, AND POSSIBLE PEACEFUL SOLUTIONS FOR SETTLEMENT.

1754 LE GHAIT E.
NO CARTE BLANCHE TO CAPRICORN; THE FOLLY OF NUCLEAR WAR.
NEW YORK: BOOKFIELD HOUSE, 1960, 114 PP.
ANALYSIS OF NATO NUCLEAR STRATEGY. EXAMINES DANGERS OF INCREASED BUILD-UP OF NUCLEAR WEAPONS IN EUROPE RELATIVE TO POPULATION AND CREATION OF HOSTILITIES IN WESTERN EUROPEAN NATIONS BACAUSE OF RISKS FROM DEPLOYMENT OF SUCH WEAPONS.

1755 LEAGUE OF NATIONS
CATALOGUE OF PUBLICATIONS, 1920-1935.
BOSTON: WORLD PEACE FOUNDATION, 1935, 312 PP.
CONTAINS TITLES OF DOCUMENTS AND PERIODICAL PUBLICATIONS LISTED AS AVAILABLE UP TO 1935. HEADINGS UNDER WHICH GROUPED CORRESPOND TO SECTIONS OF SECRETARIAT FROM WHICH THEY ORIGINATE. ALL DOCUMENTS ARE PUBLISHED IN ENGLISH AND FRENCH. CONTAINS ALPHABETICAL TABLE OF CONTENTS.

1756 LEAGUE OF WOMEN VOTERS OF US
FOREIGN AID AT THE CROSSROADS.
WASHINGTON: LEAGUE WOMEN VOTERS, 1966, 78 PP.
INVESTIGATES FOREIGN AID FROM SEVERAL VIEWPOINTS. DISCUSSES PROBLEM OF POPULATION EXPLOSION, REVIEWS US AID EFFORTS PAST AND PRESENT, AND PRESENTS TOOLS FOR MORE EFFECTIVE AID. DISCUSSES ALLIANCE FOR PROGRESS AND OTHER EFFORTS AT MUTUAL AID, SUCH AS UN AND REGIONAL ORGANIZTIONS. REVEALS PROBLEMS IN GIVING AND IN RECEIVING, POLITICS OF AID, CURRENT PROBLEMS, AND NEW SOLUTIONS.

1757 LEAR J.
"PEACE: SCIENCE'S NEXT GREAT EXPLORATION."
SAT. REV., (DEC. 60), 51-52.
DISCUSSES JEROME WEISNER'S VIEWS ON ARMS CONTROL AND DISARMAMENT. MAINTAINS ARMS CONTROL SYSTEM FEASIBLE NOW. ADVOCATES PRESIDENTIAL ENDORSEMENT OF PLAN, REORGANIZATION OF SCIENCE STRUCTURE IN FEDERAL GOVERNMENT, AND FORMATION OF PEACE ORGANIZATION.

1758 LEDUC G.
"L'AIDE INTERNATIONALE AU DEVELOPPEMENT."
TIERS-MONDE, 4 (NOS.13-14, 63), 237-60.
DESCRIBES GENERAL PRINCIPLES FOR ACHIEVING PROGRAM. CONSIDERS NATIONAL AND INTERNATIONAL FINANCIAL RESOURCES. CONCLUDES WITH EXAMINATION OF DIFFERENT FORMS OF ECONOMIC AID.

1759 LEE C.
THE POLITICS OF KOREAN NATIONALISM.
BERKELEY: U OF CALIF PR, 1963, 342 PP., LC#63-19029.
ACCOUNT OF KOREANS' STRUGGLES FOR INDEPENDENCE FROM FOREIGN REGIMES. ATTEMPTS TO DISCOVER UNIFORMITIES AND RECURRING PATTERNS OF NATIONALIST POLITICAL MOVEMENTS. EXAMINES LATER HALF OF YI DYNASTY (1392-1910), CHANGES THAT CULMINATED IN JAPANESE ANNEXATION IN 1910, JAPANESE RULE FROM 1919-45, AND ACTIVITIES OF NATIONALISTS ABROAD AND WITHIN KOREA.

1760 LEE L.T.
VIENNA CONVENTION ON CONSULAR RELATIONS.
DURHAM: RULE OF LAW PRESS, 1966, 315 PP., LC#66-25083.
DESCRIBES AND ANALYZES FEATURES OF VIENNA CONVENTION ON CONSULAR RELATIONS ADOPTED AT 1963 VIENNA CONFERENCE. DISCUSSES CONSULAR RELATIONS IN GENERAL, FUNCTION OF CONSULS, PRIVILEGES AND IMMUNITIES, AND RELATIONSHIP OF CONSULS AND DIPLOMATS. MAINTAINS THAT AGREEMENT HAS FURTHERED INTERNATIONAL UNDERSTANDING AND UNITY OF LAW.

1761 LEE M.
THE UNITED NATIONS AND WORLD REALITIES.
NEW YORK: PERGAMON PRESS, 1965, 255 PP., LC#65-26895.
EXAMINES THE UN IN RELATION TO POLITICAL, SOCIAL, AND ECONOMIC PROBLEMS OF LAST TWO DECADES. TRACES ORIGINS OF UN. STUDIES PROBLEMS OF DISARMAMENT AND DECOLONIALIZATION, AND THEIR IMPACT ON THE UN. EMPHASIZES CONGO CRISES. EXAMINES NATIONAL ATTITUDES TOWARD UN AND FUTURE PROSPECTS OF ORGANIZATION.

1762 LEFEVER E.W.
ETHICS AND UNITED STATUS FOREIGN POLICY.
NEW YORK: MERIDIAN, 1957, 199 PP.
ATTEMPTS TO RELATE JUDEO-CHRISTIAN MORALITY TO THE REALITIES OF AMERICAN FOREIGN POLICY. BELIEVES THAT RELATIVE JUSTICE IS THE HEART OF BOTH ETHICS AND POLITICS. ATTACKS LEGALISM AND SELF-RIGHTEOUSNESS. FEELS THAT THEY OBSCURE THE 'MORAL AMBIGUITY' OF MAN AND OFTEN LEAD TO A DISASTROUS FOREIGN POLICY.

1763 LEFEVER E.W.
ARMS AND ARMS CONTROL.
NEW YORK: PRAEGER, 1962, 337 PP.
FOCUSES ATTENTION ON THE PRICE OF MILITARY STABILITY, TECHNOLOGY, CO-EXISTENCE OF WAR AND DISARMAMENT AND THE SOVIET ATTITUDE TOWARDS DISARMAMENT.

1764 LEFF N.H.
"EXPORT STAGNATION AND AUTARKIC DEVELOPMENT IN BRAZIL, 1947-1962."
QUART. J. OF ECO., 81 (MAY 67), 286-301.
EXAMINES STAGNATION OF BRAZILIAN EXPORTS OF PRODUCTS OTHER THAN COFFEE. CONSIDERS CAUSES OF POOR EXPORT PERFORMANCE AND EFFECTS OF IT ON GROWTH, PARTICULARLY THE RESULTANT PATTERN OF AUTARKIC DEVELOPMENT.

1765 LEGGE J.D.
INDONESIA.
ENGLEWOOD CLIFFS: PRENTICE HALL, 1964, 184 PP., LC#64-23558.
ANALYSIS OF POLITICAL DEVELOPMENT EMPHASIZING HINDU AND EUROPEAN INFLUENCE WITH DISCUSSION OF PATERNALISM, THE PLURAL SOCIETY, AND PERSONAL DICTATORSHIP.

1766 LEGISLATIVE REFERENCE SERVICE
WORLD COMMUNIST MOVEMENT: SELECTIVE CHRONOLOGY, 1818-1957 (4 VOLS.)
WASHINGTON: US GOVERNMENT, 1961.
CHRONOLOGY RELATES INTERNATIONAL COMMUNISM TO INTERNATIONAL RELATIONS. PLACES GREATEST EMPHASIS ON PERIOD AFTER 1945. CHRONOLOGY IS ELABORATED TO SOME EXTENT AND KEY TO SOURCES IS PROVIDED.

1767 LEGUM C., LEGUM M.
SOUTH AFRICA: CRISIS FOR THE WEST.
NEW YORK: FREDERICK PRAEGER, 1964, 333 PP., LC#64-22216.
SOUTH AFRICAN RACIAL CRISIS CANNOT BE RESOLVED WITHOUT INTERNATIONAL INTERVENTION. ARGUMENTS AGAINST INTERVENTION PRESENTED AND REFUTED. ORIGINS OF THE CRISIS AND RESULTS THAT WILL FOLLOW A LAISSEZ-FAIRE POLICY ARE DESCRIBED.

1768 LEHMAN R.L. ED., PRICE F.W. ED.
AFRICA SOUTH OF THE SAHARA (PAMPHLET)
NEW YORK: MISSIONARY RES LIB, 1961, 70 PP.
GEOGRAPHICAL ARRANGEMENT IS USED IN LISTING BOOKS IN THIS BIBLIOGRAPHY. AREAS DEALT WITH ARE: WEST AFRICA, EQUATORIAL AFRICA, SOUTH AFRICA, CENTRAL AFRICA, EAST AFRICA, AND MADAGASKAR. HAS SECTION ON REFERENCE AND BIBLIOGRAPHICAL WORKS AND GENERAL WORKS. A VARIETY OF FIELDS ARE COVERED. SOME WORKS ARE ANNOTATED.

1769 LEIGH M.B. ED.
CHECK LIST OF HOLDINGS ON BORNEO IN THE CORNELL UNIVERSITY LIBRARIES (PAMPHLET)
ITHACA: CORNELL U, DEPT ASIAN ST, 1966, 74 PP.
EXTENSIVE BIBLIOGRAPHICAL LISTING OF MONOGRAPHS AND SERIALS COMPILED FOR CORNELL'S SOUTHEAST ASIA PROGRAM. MANY ENTRIES IN DUTCH. PUBLICATIONS TREAT VARIOUS ASPECTS OF BORNEO; INCLUDES POLITICAL MATERIAL. MONOGRAPHS ARE SUBDIVIDED INTO BORNEO IN GENERAL, INDONESIAN BORNEO, AND EAST MALAYSIA AND BRUNEI. SERIALS SUBDIVIDED INTO INDONESIAN BORNEO AND EAST MALAYSIA AND BRUNEI.

1770 LEISS A.C. ED.
APARTHEID AND UNITED NATIONS COLLECTIVE MEASURES.
WASHINGTON: CARNEGIE ENDOWMENT, 1965, 170 PP.
ESSAYS EXAMINE SOUTH AFRICA'S POLICY OF APARTHEID AND REACTION OF REST OF WORLD, WHICH PRESENT DIFFICULTIES AND DANGERS TO UN. DISCUSS UN INVOLVEMENT IN SOUTH AFRICAN

ISSUES AND POSITIONS OF UN MEMBERS, TRENDS AND DIVERSITY OF SOUTH AFRICAN SOCIETY (FUTURE OF APARTHEID), UN DIPLOMACY, AND MILITARY AND ECONOMIC EFFORTS TO ALTER THE FUTURE.

1771 LENGYEL E.
AFRICA: PAST, PRESENT, AND FUTURE.
NEW YORK: OXFORD BOOK CO, 1966, 154 PP.
PROVIDES BASIC INFORMATION NEEDED TO UNDERSTAND AFRICA'S PRESENT DEVELOPMENTS AND FUTURE POSSIBILITIES. SURVEYS GEOGRAPHY, HISTORY, ETHNIC BACKGROUND, AND ECONOMIES. DISCUSSES PRESENT STATUS OF REGIONS AND COUNTRIES, RACE PROBLEMS IN SOUTH AFRICA, AND ECONOMIC AND POLITICAL DIFFICULTIES OF NEW STATES.

1772 LENIN V.I.
THE WAR AND THE SECOND INTERNATIONAL.
LONDON: LAWRENCE & WISHART, 1932, 68 PP.
ANALYSIS OF NATURE AND CAUSES OF DISLOYALTY OF CHIEF SOCIALIST PARTIES IN EUROPE TO FUNDAMENTAL CONVICTIONS OF PARTY. ATTRIBUTES DISLOYALTY TO OPPORTUNISM, CHAUVINISM, AND POLICY OF COMPROMISE. PROVIDES ANALYSIS OF FORCES CAUSING WAR, NATURE OF IMPERIALISM, AND SOCIAL REFORMISM.

1773 LENIN V.I.
IMPERIALISM: THE HIGHEST STAGE OF CAPITALISM.
NEW YORK: INTERNATIONAL PUBLRS, 1939, 128 PP.
PRESENTS, ON BASIS OF "BOURGEOIS STATISTICS," AGURMENT THAT WWI WAS IMPERIALIST WAR OF CAPITALISTS. STATES THAT IMPERIALISM IS ON EVE OF SOCIALIST REVOLUTION AND THAT SPLIT IN LABOR MOVEMENT IS RESULT OF IMPERIALISM. DESCRIBES PARTITION OF WORLD AND SPREAD OF RAILROADS AS CHIEF SIGN OF CAPITALISM. CRITICIZES KAUTSKYISM. STUDIES PROCESS OF DECAY OF CAPITALISM.

1774 LENS S.
THE FUTILE CRUSADE.
CHICAGO: QUADRANGLE BOOKS, INC, 1964, 256 PP., LC#64-14137.
EXAMINES AND ANALYZES FAILURE OF ANTI-COMMUNISM OBSESSION DOMINATING OUR LIVES SINCE 1945. PRESENTS ARRAY OF MATERIAL ON DEVELOPMENT OF USSR, LATIN AMERICA, AND ASIA. EXPLAINS DATED CLICHES AND POINTS OUT DISTORTED FACTS.

1775 LENSEN G.A. ED.
REVELATIONS OF A RUSSIAN DIPLOMAT: THE MEMOIRS OF DMITRII I. ABRIKOSSOV.
SEATTLE: U OF WASHINGTON PR, 1964, 329 PP., LC#64-18426.
EXPERT IN RUSSIAN FOREIGN POLICY DURING TSARIST DAYS REFLECTS ON SERVICE IN LONDON, PEKING, AND TOKYO. INCLUDES BOLSHEVIK MOVEMENT AND COMMENTS ON PRIVATE LIVES OF PROMINENT FIGURES.

1776 LENT H.B.
THE PEACE CORPS: AMBASSADORS OF GOOD WILL.
PHILADELPHIA: WESTMINSTER PR, 1966, 472 PP., LC#66-17697.
DESCRIBES AIMS OF PEACE CORPS, ITS BEGINNINGS, AND APPLICATION, SELECTION, AND TRAINING PROCESS. DISCUSSES TEN VOLUNTEERS AND THEIR PROJECTS. EXAMINES PROBLEM OF RE-ENTRY INTO AMERICAN LIFE.

1777 LENZ F.
DIE BEWEGUNGEN DER GROSSEN MACHTE.
WURTTEMBERG: ULRICH STENOR VERL, 1953, 35 PP.
EXAMINES RISE OF USSR AND US TO POSITIONS OF WORLD POWER. DISCUSSES CONCEPT OF BALANCE OF POWER, WRITINGS OF FAMOUS HISTORIANS ON WORLD HISTORY AND TRENDS, AND PRINCIPLES OF NATIONAL GROWTH AND HISTORICAL EVOLUTION.

1778 LEONARD L.L.
INTERNATIONAL ORGANIZATION.
NEW YORK: MCGRAW HILL, 1951, 600 PP.
TRACES HISTORY AND CHARACTERISTICS OF INTERNATIONAL OR- GANIZATIONS AND DELINEATES BEGINNINGS OF LEAGUE OF NATIONS, UN. COMPARES PROCESSES OF DECISION-MAKING AND IMPLEMENTA- TION WITH THOSE OF SOVEREIGN STATES. EXAMINES POLITICAL, ECONOMIC,D SOCIAL, AND COLONIAL ACTIVITIES OF THE LEAGUE AND UN. DISCUSSES ORGANIZATION AND FUNCTION OF SEPARATE UN ORGANS AND RECOUNTS PAST ACTIONS OF UN AND LEAGUE.

1779 LEONARD L.L.
"INTERNATIONAL ORGANIZATION (1ST ED.)"
NEW YORK: MCGRAW HILL, 1951.
APPROXIMATELY 500 ENGLISH AND FRENCH BOOKS, PERIODICALS, AND OFFICIAL PUBLICATIONS FROM 1911 THROUGH 1950 . ARRANGED ALPHABETICALLY BY AUTHOR UNDER RESPECTIVE CHAPTERS AND GENRES.

1780 LEOPOLD R.W.
THE GROWTH OF AMERICAN FOREIGN POLICY: A HISTORY.
NEW YORK: ALFRED KNOPF, 1962, 848 PP.
BEGINS WITH ANALYSIS OF THE FORMATIVE YEARS 1775-1889, DESCRIBING THE PRINCIPLES AND PRACTICES OF AMERICA. STUDY INCLUDES US EMERGENCE AS WORLD POWER, THE FIRST TEST, THE INTERWAR COMPROMISE, THE SECOND STRUGGLE FOR SURVIVAL, AND THE YEARS OF "NEITHER PEACE NOR WAR." CONCLUDES THAT STRONG, COMPETENT GOVERNMENT IS NEEDED TO FORM FLEXIBLE, CREATIVE, AND INTELLIGENT FOREIGN POLICY FOR FUTURE.

1781 LERCHE C.O. JR.
FOREIGN POLICY OF THE AMERICAN PEOPLE (REV. ED.)
ENGLEWOOD CLIFFS: PRENTICE HALL, 1961, 524 PP., LC#61-11093.
EXPLAINS FOREIGN POLICY AS CONCEPT AND SETS FORTH OBJEC- TIVES OF US POLICY. SETS IT IN HISTORICAL AND CONTEMPORARY PERSPECTIVE. MOVES ON TO SITUATIONAL CASES SINCE 1945: IMPACT OF COMMUNISM, COLD WAR, ASIA. CONCLUDES WITH REQUIRE- MENTS OF FUTURE AMERICAN POLICY.

1782 LERCHE C.O. JR., SAID A.A.
CONCEPTS OF INTERNATIONAL POLITICS.
ENGLEWOOD CLIFFS: PRENTICE-HALL, 1963, 314 PP., $4.95.
SYSTEMATIC DEVELOPMENT OF THE CONCEPTS OF THE STATE AND FOREIGN POLICY, THE NOTION OF POLITICS AS THE CRUCIAL FORM OF INTERSTATE RELATIONSHIPS, AND SUBSTANTIVE PROBLEMS OF INTERNATIONAL POLITICS SUCH AS WAR, IDEOLOGY, TECHNOLOGY, TRADE, AND COMMUNICATION.

1783 LERCHE C.O. JR.
AMERICA IN WORLD AFFAIRS.
NEW YORK: MCGRAW HILL, 1963, 114 PP., LC#63-13144.
ELEMENTARY GUIDE TO SOME FUNDAMENTAL CONSIDERATIONS INVOLVED IN AMERICAN FOREIGN POLICY. FIRST, ATTEMPTS TO ANALYZE WORLD ARENA IN WHICH US MOVES. THEN DEALS WITH HISTORY OF US FOREIGN POLICY AND GOVERNMENTAL MECHANISMS FOR FORMULATION AND EXECUTION OF POLICY. FINAL FOCUS IS ON US ACTION IN STRUGGLE WITH USSR AND RELATED ISSUES.

1784 LERCHE C.O. JR.
THE COLD WAR AND AFTER.
ENGLEWOOD CLIFFS: PRENTICE HALL, 1965, 147 PP., LC#65-14997.
ANALYZES SOVIET FOREIGN POLICY 1945-60, COMPARING IT TO AMERICAN. DISCUSSES COLD WAR, BALANCE OF POWER, ATTEMPTS AT EXPANSION. ATTEMPTS PREDICTION OF FUTURE SOVIET-AMERICAN RELATIONS.

1785 LERNER A.P.
THE ECONOMICS OF CONTROL.
NEW YORK: MACMILLAN, 1960, 428 PP.
STATES THAT PRINCIPAL PROBLEMS OF A CONTROLLED ECONOMY ARE EMPLOYMENT, MONOPOLY, AND DISTRIBUTION OF INCOME. ANA- LYZES BENEFITS OF BOTH CAPITALISTIC AND COLLECTIVIST ECONO- MIES, AND WARNS AGAINST RIGHTIST OR LEFTIST POLITICAL DOGMA- TISM.

1786 LERNER D., KRAMER M.N.
"FRENCH ELITE PERSPECTIVES ON THE UNITED NATIONS."
INT. ORGAN., 17 (WINTER 63), 54-74.
ATTEMPTS TO QUALIFY CONVENTIONAL STEREOTYPES BY DIF- FERENTIATING FRENCH ELITE OPINIONS REGARDING THE UN AND CHARACTERIZING THEM IN TERMS OF MOTIVATION, CONTENT, AND OUTCOME.

1787 LERNER M.
THE AGE OF OVERKILL: A PREFACE TO WORLD POLITICS.
NEW YORK: SIMON AND SCHUSTER, 1962, 329 PP., LC#62-19077.
ANALYSIS OF PAST AND FUTURE OF WORLD POLITICS IN AGE WHEN TWO NATIONS CAN DESTROY ALL CIVILIZATION. CONSIDERS PRESENT LINE-UP OF POWER CENTERS AND CLUSTERS; DESCRIBES GRAND DESIGN OF COMMUNISM AS POLITICAL RELIGION IN THIS AGE. ANALYZES PSYCHOLOGY, IDEAS, AND FORCE OF EMERGING NATIONS; LOOKS AT LEADERSHIP OF VARIOUS NATIONS; TELLS WHAT CAN AND MUST BE DONE BY ALL PERSONS NOW.

1788 LERNER W.
"THE HISTORICAL ORIGINS OF THE SOVIET DOCTRINE OF PEACEFUL COEXISTENCE."
LAW CONTEMP. PROBL., 29 (AUTUMN 64), 865-70.
REVIEWS SOVIET POLICIES, SHOWING THAT DOCTRINE OF PEACE- FUL COEXISTENCE HAS ALTERNATED WITH THAT OF WORLD REVOLU- TION. CONCLUDES THAT COEXISTENCE IS DOCTRINE OF CONVENIENCE, NOT CONVICTION.

1789 LESSING P.
AFRICA'S RED HARVEST.
NEW YORK: JOHN DAY, 1962, 207 PP., LC#62-21016.
PRESENTS AN OUTLINE FOR THE PATTERN OF COMMUNIST BLOC ACTIVITIES IN AFRICA. TRACES THE DEVELOPMENT OF CHINESE AND RUSSIAN COMMUNIST INFLUENCE IN AFRICAN AFFAIRS. CONTENDS THAT THE WEST MUST DEVELOP A FOOTHOLD OF INFLUENCE IN THOSE NATIONS WHICH STILL MAY BE RECEPTIVE TO A NON-COMMUNIST POWER AS A PREVENTATIVE MEASURE TO INCREASING TENSION IN THE COLD WAR.

1790 LETHBRIDGE H.J.
CHINA'S URBAN COMMUNES.
HONG KONG: DRAGONFLY BOOKS, 1961, 74 PP.
ANALYZES STRUCTURE OF THESE COMMUNES WHICH PROVIDE SOCIAL ORGANIZATION FOR ONE FOURTH OF WORLD'S PEOPLE. SEES SIGNIF- ICANCE OF THESE COMMUNES FOR REST OF WORLD SINCE CHINA FEELS US WILL BE ORGANIZED THIS WAY "WHEN WORKERS AND PEASANTS SEIZE POWER." COVERS ORIGIN OF COMMUNAL IDEA, ITS PLACE IN CHINESE IDEOLOGY, AND REASONS FOR ITS RAPID GROWTH SINCE 1960.

1791 LEVENSTEIN A.

FREEDOM'S ADVOCATE - A TWENTY-FIVE YEAR CHRONICLE.
NEW YORK: VIKING PRESS, 1965, 304 PP., LC#65-15220.
PRESENTS RECORD OF FREEDOM HOUSE, A GROUP OF PEOPLE DEDICATED TO CAUSE OF FREEDOM SINCE WWII. EXAMINES GROUP'S INVOLVEMENT IN MAJOR CRISES US HAS FACED SINCE WWII, AND ANALYZES THEIR PHILOSOPHY OF FREEDOM.

1792 LEVI M.
"LES DIFFICULTES ECONOMIQUES DE LA GRANDE-BRETAGNE."
POLITIQUE ENTRANGERE, 32 (1967), 48-67.
EXAMINATION OF PRINCIPAL CAUSES RELATED TO FOREIGN AFFAIRS OF ECONOMIC PROBLEMS OF GREAT BRITAIN. SPECIAL EMPHASIS ON LOW PRODUCTIVITY AND FOREIGN TRADE PATTERNS, I.E. DESIRE TO PLAY DOMINANT ROLE AMONG NATIONS WHICH WISHED TO ASSERT EMERGING AUTONOMY. DISCUSSES REASONS FOR EEC'S REJECTION OF BRITISH ENTRANCE INTO ORGANIZATION.

1793 LEVI W.
FUNDAMENTALS OF WORLD ORGANIZATION.
MINNEAPOLIS: U OF MINN PR, 1950, 225 PP.
EMPHASIZING HUMAN PROBLEMS, ATTEMPTS TO CONSTRUCT VIABLE FRAMEWORK FOR WORLD ORGANIZATION THAT WILL AVOID MANY OF PROBLEMS FACED BY LEAGUE OF NATIONS AND UN. DISCUSSES POLITICAL, ECONOMIC, WELFARE, AND CULTURAL PROBLEMS, AND THE TYPE OF ORGANIZATION BEST SUITED FOR EACH.

1794 LEVI W.
"CHINA AND THE UNITED NATIONS."
CURR. HIST., 47 (SEPT. 64), 149-155.
CHINA WILL MAKE CONCESSIONS IN ORDER TO JOIN THE U.N. AUTHOR POINTS OUT THAT ALL NATIONS USE THE U.N. AS AN INSTRUMENT IN PURSUIT OF THEIR NATIONAL INTERESTS.

1795 LEVIN J.V.
THE EXPORT ECONOMIES: THEIR PATTERN OF DEVELOPMENT IN HISTORICAL PERSPECTIVE.
CAMBRIDGE: HARVARD U PR, 1960, 347 PP., LC#60-13291.
ANALYSIS OF CHANGES IN COUNTRIES WHICH BASE ECONOMY ON EXPORT. SPECIFICALLY EXAMINES PERU'S GUANO EXPORTS AND RICE IN CASE OF BURMA.

1796 LEVINE R.A. ED.
"THE ANTHROPOLOGY OF CONFLICT."
J. CONFL. RESOLUT., 5 (MAR. 61), 3-108.
CROSS-CULTURAL STUDY OF INTRAFAMILY, INTRA COMMUNITY, INTERCOMMUNITY STRUCTURAL LEVELS. EVALUATION OF CULTURAL PATTERNS, SOURCES, AND FUNCTIONS OF CONFLICT BASED ON SPECIALIZED LITERATURE.

1797 LEVONTIN A.V.
THE MYTH OF INTERNATIONAL SECURITY: A JURIDICAL AND CRITICAL ANALYSIS.
JERUSALEM: MAGNES, 1957, 346 PP.
CONTENTION THAT INTERNATIONAL LAW PROVIDES SECURITY IS CRITICALLY ANALYZED AND FOUND INADEQUATE. THE BELIEF THAT STATES CAN BE SOVEREIGN AND INDEPENDENT YET ABLE TO ESTABLISH INTERNATIONAL SECURITY SYSTEMS IS GROUNDLESS. ADVISES SOVEREIGN WORLD GOVERNMENT TO REPLACE SOVEREIGN STATE SYSTEM.

1798 LEVY H.V.
LIBERDADE E JUSTICA SOCIAL (2ND ED.)
SAO PAULO: LIVRARIA MARTINS EDITORA, 1962, 203 PP.
DISCUSSION OF SOCIAL JUSTICE AND LIBERTY UNDER MARXISM, SOVIET SYSTEM, AND US CAPITALISM IN AUSTRIA, ENGLAND, AND BRAZIL. INCLUDES STUDY OF RELATED DOCUMENTS OF 20TH COMMUNIST PARTY CONGRESS OF USSR, UN, NEW CLASS BY DJILAS, AND BRAZILIAN DELEGATION TO 48TH WORLD INTER-PARLIAMENTARY CONFERENCE IN WARSAW.

1799 LEWIN E. ED.
RECENT PUBLICATIONS IN THE LIBRARY OF THE ROYAL COLONIAL INSTITUTE (PAMPHLET)
LONDON: ROYAL COLONIAL INST, 1926, 30 PP.
ILLUSTRATIONS OF RELATIONS BETWEEN PARTS OF THE BRITISH EMPIRE, THEIR EFFECT ON GOVERNMENT, PARLIAMENTARY PROCESS, AND CONSTITUTIONALISM.

1800 LEWIN E.
ROYAL EMPIRE SOCIETY BIBLIOGRAPHIES NO. 9: SUB-SAHARA AFRICA.
LONDON: ROYAL COMMONWEALTH SOC, 1945, 104 PP.
INTENDED TO DEAL SPECIFICALLY WITH SOUTH AFRICA, DIVIDES SOURCES INTO FOUR CATEGORIES: ADMINISTRATIVE, POLITICAL, ECONOMIC, AND SOCIOLOGICAL.

1801 LEWIS J.P.
QUIET CRISIS IN INDIA.
WASHINGTON: BROOKINGS INST., 1962, 350 PP.
STUDY OF INDIA'S ECONOMIC EXPERIMENT IN AGRICULTURE AND RURAL INDUSTRY, INCLUDING DEVELOPMENT STRATEGY IN THESE TWO AREAS. CONSIDERS ROLE PLAYED BY US IN INDIA'S ECONOMIC PROBLEMS AND INFLUENCE OF US FOREIGN AID. SPECULATES OUTLOOK FOR PRIVATE ENTERPRISE AND EXPORT PROBLEMS IN INDIA.

1802 LEWIS P.R.
LITERATURE OF THE SOCIAL SCIENCES: AN INTRODUCTORY SURVEY AND GUIDE.
LONDON: LIBRARY ASSOC, 1960, 222 PP.
LISTS AND DISCUSSES MATERIALS PERTINENT TO SOCIAL SCIENCES DATING FROM THE 1800'S FOR THE INTEREST OF THE BRITISH READER. SURVEYS ECONOMIC THEORY AND HISTORY, ESPECIALLY IN THE UK; STATISTICS; COMMERCE AND INDUSTRY; POLITICAL SCIENCE, ADMINISTRATION, AND THEORY; LAW; INTERNATIONAL RELATIONS; AND SOCIOLOGY. INCLUDES AN INDEX AND SUGGESTIONS FOR MAKING USE OF RESEARCH SOURCES.

1803 LEWIS S.
TOWARDS INTERNATIONAL CO-OPERATION (1ST ED.)
NEW YORK: PERGAMON PRESS, 1966, 327 PP., LC#66-17789.
TEXTBOOK DEALING WITH AREAS OF CHANGE AND PROBLEMS IN INTERNATIONAL COOPERATION THAT MUST BE RESOLVED IN ORDER TO UNITE THE DIVERSE PEOPLES OF WORLD. DISCUSSES HISTORY OF INTERNATIONAL COOPERATION AND POSSIBLITIES FOR FUTURE WORLD GOVERNMENT.

1804 LEWIS W.A.
POLITICS IN WEST AFRICA.
LONDON: ALLEN & UNWIN, 1965, 90 PP.
ANALYSIS OF PRESENT-DAY POLITICS IN WEST AFRICA. STUDIES ORIGIN AND BASIS OF POLITICAL PARTIES, ISSUES OF ECONOMIC POLICY, INTERNATIONAL RELATIONS, FEDERALISM, SINGLE PARTY SYSTEM, AND FORM OF REPRESENTATION AND PROSEPCT FOR CHANGE.

1805 LEWY G.
"SUPERIOR ORDERS, NUCLEAR WARFARE AND THE DICTATES OF CONSCIENCE: THE DILEMMA OF MILITARY OBEDIENCE IN THE ATOMIC." AGE.
AMER. POLIT. SCI. REV., 55 (MARCH 61), 3-23.
DISCUSSES 3 ASPECTS OF INTERNATIONAL LAW: VALIDITY OF THE PLEA OF SUPERIOR ORDERS AS A DEFENSE IN WAR CRIME TRIALS, LEGALITY OF USE OF NUCLEAR WEAPONS, PRESENT AND FUTURE OF THE LAW OF WAR.

1806 LEYPOLOT F. ED., BOWKER R.R. ED., APPLETON A.I. ED.
AMERICAN CATALOGUE OF BOOKS, 1876-1910 (19 VOLS.)
NEW YORK: PUBLISHER'S WEEKLY INC.
AN AMERICAN NATIONAL TRADE BIBLIOGRAPHY. VOLUME ONE LISTS BOOKS IN PRINT IN 1876 AND IS THEREFORE GUIDE TO BOOKS PUBLISHED PRIOR TO THAT DATE. IT IS SUPPLEMENTED BY "ANNUAL AMERICAN CATALOG" AND "PUBLISHERS' WEEKLY." INCLUDED IN VOLUMES ARE SOCIETY PROCEEDINGS AND A SECTION ON GOVERNMENT DOCUMENTS. AFTER 1905, CONTAINS RECORDS UNDER AUTHOR, TITLE, SUBJECT, AND SERIES OF BOOKS PUBLISHED IN US FROM 1905-10.

1807 LIBRARY HUNGARIAN ACADEMY SCI
HUNGARIAN PUBLICATIONS ON ASIA AND AFRICA, 1950-1962: A SELECTED BIBLIOGRAPHY (PAMPHLET)
BUDAPEST: HUNG ACAD SCI PUBL, 1963, 106 PP.
MATERIALS ON AFRICA AND ASIA WRITTEN ONLY BY HUNGARIAN AUTHORS. ARRANGED BY CONTINENT AND SUBDIVIDED BY COUNTRY. MOST OF 800 ITEMS IN HUNGARIAN, BUT SOME IN FRENCH. HUNGARIAN TITLES TRANSLATED. MOST WORKS ARE SCHOLARLY IN NATURE WITH CONCLUDING AUTHOR INDEX.

1808 LIBRARY INTERNATIONAL REL
INTERNATIONAL INFORMATION SERVICE.
NEW YORK: INTL CHAMBER COMMERCE, 1963.
QUARTERLY PUBLICATION WITH ANNOTATIONS OF BOOKS, MONOGRAPHS, GOVERNMENT DOCUMENTS, AND PAMPHLETS ON CONTEMPORARY POLITICAL, ECONOMIC AND SOCIAL DEVELOPMENTS IN ALL PARTS OF THE WORLD. BEGUN IN 1963, ENTRIES ARRANGED BY SUBJECT AND TYPE OF PUBLICATION. INCLUDES HISTORY, POLITICS, LAW, INTERNATIONAL ECONOMICS AND SOCIOLOGY, ETC.

1809 LICHTHEIM G.
THE NEW EUROPE: TODAY AND TOMORROW.
NEW YORK: FREDERICK PRAEGER, 1963, 232 PP., LC#63-11152.
ARGUMENTS UNDERLYING CURRENT DEBATE OVER WESTERN EUROPE'S FUTURE ROLE WITHIN THE EMERGING ATLANTIC COMMUNITY. TECHNICAL QUESTIONS REGARDING ECONOMICS OF EUROPEAN INTEGRATION. MOSTLY POLITICAL BUT PARTLY DEVOTED TO ANALYSIS OF FACTS AND FIGURES RELATING TO ECONOMICS.

1810 LIEFMANN-KEIL E.
OKONOMISCHE THEORIE DER SOZIALPOLITIK.
GOTTINGEN: SPRINGER VERLAG, 1961, 424 PP.
EXAMINES ECONOMIC BASIS OF SOCIAL POLITICS AND SEEKS TO ESTABLISH RELEVANCE OF ECONOMIC JUDGMENTS ABOUT REALIZED POLITICAL DEMANDS. DISCUSSES DISTRIBUTION OF INCOME, PUBLIC EXPENDITURES, WORKING CONDITIONS AND MINIMUM WAGES, AND CONCLUDES WITH EXAMINATION OF INTERNATIONAL SOCIAL POLITICS THROUGH INTERNATIONAL ORGANIZATIONS.

1811 LIEUWEN E.
ARMS AND POLITICS IN LATIN AMERICA.
NEW YORK: PRAEGER, 1960, 296 PP., $4.75.
ANALYZES INTERPLAY OF POLITICAL FORCES IN LATIN AMERICA AGAINST BACKGROUND OF DYNAMIC PROCESS OF GROWTH AND SOCIAL CHANGE. ALSO EXAMINES U.S. POLICIES TOWARD LATIN AMERICA, PARTICULARLY MILITARY POLICY AND CONCLUDES THAT BA-

SIC AIM OF U.S. MUST BE A PROSPEROUS AND STABLE LATIN AMERICA THAT WILL ADVANCE SECURITY OF HEMISPHERE.

1812 LIEUWEN E.
U.S. POLICY IN LATIN AMERICA: A SHORT HISTORY.
NEW YORK: FREDERICK PRAEGER, 1965, 149 PP., LC#65-24724.
DISCUSSES SALIENT FEATURES OF US POLICIES IN LATIN AMERICA. INCLUDES MONROE DOCTRINE, IMPERIALISM AND PAN-AMERICANISM, GOOD NEIGHBOR POLICY, COLD WAR 1945-65, AND ALLIANCE FOR PROGRESS.

1813 LIEUWEN E.
GENERALS VS PRESIDENTS: NEOMILITARISM IN LATIN AMERICA.
NEW YORK: FREDERICK PRAEGER, 1964, 160 PP., LC#64-22492.
AN EXAMINATION OF THE CHANGES MADE BY PRESIDENT KENNEDY IN THE TRADITIONAL US POLICY TOWARD THE LATIN AMERICAN MILITARY. EMPHASIZES PRESENT-DAY MILITARISM AND THE RELATION BETWEEN ARMED FORCES AND THE SOCIO-POLITICAL CRISIS IN MOST LATIN AMERICAN COUNTRIES. ARGUMENT RESTS UPON BASIC ASSUMPTION THAT LATIN AMERICAN IS PRESENTLY IN THE MIDST OF AN ACUTE SOCIAL, ECONOMIC, AND POLITICAL CRISIS.

1814 LIGOT M.
"LA COOPERATION MILITAIRE DANS LES ACCORDS, PASSES ENTRE LA FRANCE ET LES ETATS AFRICAINS ET MALGACHE D'EXPRESSION." FRANCAISE.
REV. JURID. POLIT. OUTREMER, 17 (OCT.-DEV. 63), 517-32.
EXAMINES MILITARY AGREEMENTS OF FRANCE AND FRENCH SPEAKING AFRICAN COUNTRIES. BECAUSE OF STRATEGIC POSITION OF AFRICAN COUNTRIES, FRANCE CONTINUES POLICY OF DEFENDING FORMER COLONIES. GIVES LARGE AMOUNTS OF TECHNICAL AID.

1815 LILIENTHAL D.E.
CHANGE, HOPE, AND THE BOMB.
PRINCETON: U. PR., 1963, 168 PP.
THINKS THAT THE PRESENT DISARMAMENT NEGOTIATIONS ARE DECEPTIVELY DANGEROUS, THAT OUR VIEW OF THE PLACE OF THE ATOM IN THE MODERN WORLD HAS BEEN MAINLY WRONG AND THAT WE HAVE ALLOWED OUR SCIENTIFIC LEADERS TOO MUCH INFLUENCE IN NON-SCIENTIFIC AREAS OF PUBLIC POLICY.

1816 LILLICH R.B.
INTERNATIONAL CLAIMS: THEIR ADJUDICATION BY NATIONAL COMMISSIONS.
SYRACUSE: U. PR., 1962, 139 PP.
TRACES HISTORY, ORGANIZATION AND JURISPRUDENCE OF NATIONAL COMMISSIONS AS A PROCEDURAL DEVICE FOR THE SETTLEMENT OF INTERNATIONAL CLAIMS. DISCUSSES SPECIFIC PARTNERSHIP AND CORPORATE PROBLEMS, REQUIREMENTS FOR INDIVIDUAL CLAIMANTS AND PRECEDENT-VALUE OF DECISIONS BY COMMISSIONS.

1817 LILLICH R.B.
"INTERNATIONAL CLAIMS: THEIR ADJUDICATION BY NATIONAL COMMISSIONS."
SYRACUSE: SYRACUSE U PRESS, 1962.
LISTS OF BOOKS, ARTICLES, INTERNATIONAL AGREEMENTS, AND STATUTES DEALING WITH INTERNATIONAL LAW APPLICATIONS IN STATE RESPONSIBILITY TO INDIVIDUALS AFFECTED BY GOVERNMENTAL ACTION. ABOUT 250 ENTRIES ARE LISTED BY TYPE OF MATERIAL; RANGE FROM 1794 TO 1961 BUT CONCENTRATED IN LAST FEW DECADES OF PERIOD. BOOK GIVES HISTORY, ORGANIZATION, JURISPRUDENCE, AND EVALUATION OF NATIONAL CLAIMS COMMISSIONS.

1818 LINCOLN G.
ECONOMICS OF NATIONAL SECURITY.
NEW YORK: PRENTICE-HALL, 1950, 567 PP.
ANALYZES ECONOMIC REQUIREMENTS OF NATIONAL SECURITY AND EXAMINES PRESENT READINESS OF THE U.S. ECONOMY TO ACHIEVE RAPID AND EFFICIENT MOBILIZATION AGAINST COMMUNIST THREAT, INDICATING STRENGTHS AND WEAKNESSES AND POSSIBLE REMEDIES ALONG THE LINES OF INCREASED GOVERNMENTAL CONTROL AND DIRECTION OF THE NATIONAL ECONOMY.

1819 LINCOLN G.
"FACTORS DETERMINING ARMS AID."
PROC. ACAD. POLIT. SCI., 25 (MAY 53) 263-72.
THE MAIN FACTOR DETERMINING QUANTITY AND DIRECTION OF FUTURE ARMS AID IS SOVIET TANGIBLE REACTION TO AMERICAN PROPOSED POINTS FOR ACHIEVING PEACE. BY SEEKING NATIONAL SECURITY THROUGH COLLECTIVE ACTION USA MUST PROVIDE AID, ACCORDING TO NEEDS OF EACH PARTICULAR ALLY AT THE PARTICULAR TIME, ADEQUATE FOR PURPOSE OF HALTING COMMUNIST EXPANSION IN THE AREA.

1820 LINDBERG L.
POLITICAL DYNAMICS OF EUROPEAN ECONOMIC INTEGRATION.
STANFORD: U. PR., 1963, 295 PP.
ATTEMPTS TO EXAMINE THE EEC AS AN INSTITUTIONAL SYSTEM AND ASSESS ITS IMPACT ON DECISION-MAKING PATTERNS OF THE COMMON MARKET COUNTRIES. RELATES THIS TO PROBLEM OF EUROPEAN INTEGRATION.

1821 LINDBLOM C.E.
THE INTELLIGENCE OF DEMOCRACY; DECISION MAKING THROUGH MUTUAL ADJUSTMENT.
NEW YORK: FREE PRESS, 1965, 352 PP., LC#65-16269.
ELABORATES ON IDEA THAT PEOPLE AND GOVERNMENTS CAN COORDINATE WITHOUT EXTERNAL FORCE OR CONTROL AND WITHOUT A COMMON PURPOSE. COMPARES COORDINATION BY MUTUAL ADJUSTMENT TO THAT BY A CENTRAL COORDINATOR; COMMENTS ON CONFLICTING VIEWS. DISCUSSES ELEMENTS AND PARTICIPANTS IN PROCESS, GOVERNMENTAL PROCESS, PROBLEM-SOLVING STRATEGY, AND POLICY-MAKING METHODS.

1822 LINDHOLM R.W.
"ACCELERATED DEVELOPMENT WITH A MINIMUM OF FOREIGN AID AND ECONOMIC CONTROLS."
SOC. ECON. STUD., 9 (MAR. 60), 57-67.
A POLICY PROPOSAL WHOSE MAIN POINTS ARE: A MONEY SUPPLY INCREASING LESS RAPIDLY THAN PRODUCTIVITY, GOVERNMENT INVESTMENT IN POWER, TRANSPORTATION, AND EDUCATION, EMPHASIS ON LAND AND GROSS RECEIPTS TAXES TO REDUCE IMPACT ON PRICES, AND SIPHONING OFF OF PROFITS.

1823 LINDSAY K.
EUROPEAN ASSEMBLIES: THE EXPERIMENTAL PERIOD 1949-1959.
NEW YORK: PRAEGER, 1960, 267 PP.
EXAMINES EXPERIMENTIAL BEGINNINGS OF EUROPEAN ASSEMBLIES. OUTLINES RELATIONS WITH NATIONAL BODIES, INHERENT PROBLEMS AND POSSIBILITIES FOR FUTURE EVOLUTION.

1824 LINEBARGER P.
PSYCHOLOGICAL WARFARE.
WASHINGTON, DC: COMBAT FORCES PR, 1948, 259 PP.
DEFINES CONCEPT OF PSYCHOLOGICAL WARFARE AND ITS INHERENT LIMITS. DESCRIBES ITS USE IN BOTH WWI AND WWII AND STUDIES ACTUAL PROCEDURES IN PLANNING AND OPERATION.

1825 LING D.L.
"TUNISIA: FROM PROTECTORATE TO REPUBLIC."
BLOOMINGTON: INDIANA U PR, 1967.
BOOK IN GENERAL TRACES DEVELOPMENT OF TUNISIA FROM A FRENCH PROTECTORATE THROUGH ITS FIGHT FOR INDEPENDENCE INTO A MODERN NATION. GOOD BIBLIOGRAPHIC LISTING OF TUNISIAN GOVERNMENT PUBLICATIONS, FRENCH, BRITISH, AND AMERICAN PUBLICATIONS, DIPLOMATIC DOCUMENTS AND CORRESPONDENCE, PERIODICALS, AND NEWSPAPERS. 200 ENTRIES.

1826 LINK R.G.
ENGLISH THEORIES OF ECONOMIC FLUCTUATIONS: 1815-1848.
NEW YORK: COLUMBIA U PRESS, 1959, 226 PP., LC#58-11901.
STUDY IN HISTORY OF ECONOMIC THOUGHT FROM END OF NAPOLEONIC WARS THROUGH 1848. WORKS OF SIX ECONOMISTS ARE EXAMINED: MALTHUS, TOOKE, MILL, ATTWOOD, JOPLIN, AND JAMES WILSON. USES TO WHICH THEORIES WERE PUT IN ANALYZING CONTEMPORARY ECONOMIC FLUCTUATIONS ALSO DESCRIBED.

1827 LIPPMANN W.
US FOREIGN POLICY: SHIELD OF THE REPUBLIC.
NEW YORK: LITTLE BROWN, 1943, 177 PP.
ASSERTS US FOREIGN POLICY HAS REMAINED UNADJUSTED TO CONTEMPORARY CONDITIONS, AND THUS HAS BEEN UNPREPARED TO WAGE WAR OR MAKE PEACE IN A MANNER BEST SUITED TO THE ACHIEVEMENT OF GOALS IN THIS AREA.

1828 LIPPMANN W.
US WAR AIMS.
BOSTON: LITTLE/BROWN, 1944, 235 PP.
FEELS WAR AIMS SHAPE AND STRUCTURE POSTWAR AIMS. ADVOCATES FORMATION OF A UNIVERSAL SOCIETY, A VOLUNTARY ASSOCIATION OF SOVEREIGN STATES. CLAIMS U.S. HAS HISTORIC ROLE TO FULFILL IN NEW MORAL ORDER.

1829 LIPPMANN W.
ISOLATION AND ALLIANCES: AN AMERICAN SPEAKS TO THE BRITISH.
BOSTON: LITTLE BROWN, 1952, 56 PP., LC#52-1196.
DISCUSSES US PUBLIC OPINION ON FOREIGN RELATIONS UNTIL 1945 AND MAINTAINS THAT ISOLATIONISM HAS BEEN DOMINANT THEME OF US ATTITUDE. EXAMINES REALITIES OF WORLD SITUATION SINCE WWII AND THE CHALLENGE TO TRADITIONAL US POLICIES.

1830 LIPPMANN W.
THE COMING TESTS WITH RUSSIA.
BOSTON: LITTLE BROWN, 1961, 37 PP., LC#61-14950.
DISCUSSES THE FUTURE OF DISARMAMENT, BERLIN, AND THE UNCOMMITTED NATIONS WITH REFERENCE TO COMMUNIST GOALS. CENTERS ON THE FUTURE OF GERMANY. MENTIONS KHRUSHCHEV'S VIEWS ON LAOS, CUBA, AND THE UN. GIVES A SHORT ACCOUNT OF USSR'S FOREIGN POLICY UNDER KHRUSHCHEV. BASED ON LIPPMANN'S INTERVIEW WITH KHRUSHCHEV.

1831 LIPPMANN W.
WESTERN UNITY AND THE COMMON MARKET.
BOSTON: LITTLE BROWN, 1962, 51 PP., LC#62-18624.
PRESENTS AUTHOR'S VIEWS CONCERNING THE WESTERN ALLIANCE: THE COMMON MARKET, ENLARGED BY THE ADMISSION OF GREAT BRITAIN AND JOINED WITH THE US IN A WIDE FREE-TRADING AREA. DISCUSSES THE RELATIONSHIP BETWEEN THE WESTERN ECONOMIC COMMUNITY AND THE NUCLEAR STALEMATE, THE SUCCESS OF THE COMMON MARKET, THE LACK OF ANY KNOWN AND CLEAR SUCCESSION IN FRANCE AND GERMANY, AND THE FADING US ECONOMIC PRE-EMINENCE.

1832 LIPSHART A.
"THE ANALYSIS OF BLOC VOTING IN THE GENERAL ASSEMBLY."
AM. POL. SCI. REV., 57 (DEC. 63), 902-917.
REVIEWS AND EVALUATES TECHNIQUES USED IN IDENTIFICATION OF BLOC VOTING IN GENERAL ASSEMBLY AS WELL AS COHESIVENESS OF BLOC. PROPOSES AN ALTERNATIVE METHOD AS ANALYSIS OF BLOC VOTING ON BASIS OF PREDETERMINED GROUPS IS UNRELIABLE. CITES RICE BEYLE METHOD AS SUPERIOR TECHNIQUE IN BLOC IDENTIFICATION AND VOTING ANALYSIS.

1833 LIPSON L.
"AN ARGUMENT ON THE LEGALITY OF RECONNAISSANCE STATELLITES."
PROC. AMER. SOC. INT. LAW, 55(APR. 61), 174-176.
DEALS WITH LEGAL PROBLEM TO WHICH MUCH ATTENTION HAS BEEN DEVOTED. ATTEMPTS TO SHOW WHAT WERE THE RELEVANT DIFFERENCES BETWEEN THE FLIGHTS OF GAGARIN AND POWERS FROM THE STANDPOINT OF INTERNATIONAL LAW.

1834 LIPSON L.
"PEACEFUL COEXISTENCE."
LAW CONTEMP. PROBL., 29 (AUTUMN 64), 871-81.
PRESENTS A LEGALISTIC INQUIRY INTO WHETHER OR NOT THIS DOCTRINE IS IN REALITY THE BASIS FOR CONTEMPORARY INTERNATIONAL LAW. ALSO EXAMINES SOVIET ATTITUDES TOWARDS THIS DOCTRINE.

1835 LISKA G.
THE GREATER MAGHREB: FROM INDEPENDENCE TO UNITY? (PAMPHLET)
WASHINGTON: CENTER FOR POL RES, 1963, 75 PP.
ANALYSIS OF NORTH AFRICAN UNITY OF ALGERIA, MOROCCO, AND TUNISIA. DISCUSSES PRACTICAL DRIVE FOR UNIFICATION OF POLITICAL AUTHORITY AND ECONOMIC CONDITIONS, AND PROSPECTS FOR NORTH AFRICA AS A UNIT AND IN ITS RELATIONS WITH OTHER AREAS.

1836 LISKA G.
INTERNATIONAL EQUILIBRIUM.
CAMBRIDGE: HARVARD U. PR., 1957, 223 PP.
LIMITATION OF POWER IN NATION-STATE AND IN REGIONAL ORGANIZATIONS HELPS MAINTAIN POWER EQUILIBRIUM IN INTERNAT&ONAL RELATIONS.

1837 LISKA G.
THE NEW STATECRAFT.
CHICAGO: U. CHI. PR., 1960, 246 PP., $5.00.
FOREIGN AID IS AN INTEGRAL PART OF FOREIGN POLICY. DEBUNKS IDEA THAT IT'S A SELF-SUFFICIENT ENTERPRISE IN ITSELF. AID IS VIEWED FROM SUCH VANTAGE POINTS AS ITS PLACE IN THE COLD WAR, ROLE IN INTERNATIONAL SECURITY, AND ITS INFLUENCE ON RECIPIENT COUNTRY. WITH REGARD TO INDIVIDUAL RECIPIENTS, DEMANDS THAT FOREIGN AID BE CONSISTENT IF DONOR IS TO SECURE 'INTERNALLY COHERENT' FOREIGN POLICY.

1838 LISKA G.
EUROPE ASCENDANT.
BALTIMORE: JOHNS HOPKINS PRESS, 1964, 182 PP., LC#64-16189.
STUDIES CONDITIONS NECESSARY FOR A UNIFIED EUROPE. SUGGESTS STRATEGY OF REGIONAL ECONOMIC COOPERATION THAT WILL EVENTUALLY INCLUDE A COMMUNIST CENTRAL EUROPE.

1839 LISSITZYN O.J.
"THE INTERNATIONAL COURT OF JUSTICE."
NEW YORK: CARNEGIE ENDOWMENT, 1951, 118 PP.
AN APPRAISAL OF THE COURT AS INSTRUMENT OF INTERNATIONAL PEACE, ITS PAST RECORD AND FUTURE POTENTIALITIES. FEELS GREATEST CONDITION IS DEVELOPMENT OF INTERNATIONAL LAW.

1840 LISSITZYN O.J.
"SOME LEGAL IMPLICATIONS OF THE U-2 AND RB-47 INCIDENTS."
AMER. J. INT. LAW, 56 (JAN. 62), 135-142.
SINCE THE LAUNCHING OF SPUTNIK I, SOVIET EXPERTS IN INTERNATIONAL LAW HAVE SUGGESTED AN 'UPPER LIMIT TO AIR SOVEREIGNTY' ABOVE WHICH, LAW SIMILAR TO THE LAW OF THE HIGH SEAS, WOULD APPLY. THE U-2 CONSIDERED AN INTRUDER. NO 'UPPER LIMIT' HAS BEEN AGREED UPON. THE RECONNAISSANCE-SATELLITE DEVELOPMENT REDUCES LIKELIHOOD OF ANY SPACE-LAW AGREEMENT.

1841 LISSITZYN O.J.
"INTERNATIONAL LAW IN A DIVIDED WORLD."
INT. CONCIL., 542 (MAR. 63), 60 PP.
DEALS WITH SOME OF THE MAJOR PROBLEMS PRESENTED BY THE RESURGENCE OF INTEREST IN THE FIELD. SEES A SLOW EROSION OF THE EXTREME HOSTILITY TO OTHER SYSTEMS OF PUBLIC ORDER IMPLICIT IN COMMUNIST IDEOLOGY, AND A CONCOMITANT INCREASE IN THE ROLE OF LAW IN RELATIONS BETWEEN THE WEST AND COMMUNIST STATES. NEWER AND LESS DEVELOPED NATIONS APPEAR TO BE NEITHER AS MONOLITHIC IN THEIR APPROACH NOR AS ADAMANT IN THEIR OPPOSITION TO TRADITIONAL NORMS AS ONE MIGHT FIRST BELIEVE.

1842 LISSITZYN O.J.
"TREATIES AND CHANGED CIRCUMSTANCES (REBUS SIC STANTIBUS)"
AMER. J. OF INT. LAW, 61 (OCT. 67), 895-922.
MAINTAINS THAT PROBLEM OF EFFECT OF CHANGE IN CIRCUMSTANCES ON TREATY RELATIONSHIPS IS ONE OF INTERPRETATION OF INTENTIONS AND EXPECTATIONS. PRESENTS SEVERAL OPINIONS ON EFFECT ON CHANGE OF CIRCUMSTANCES AND DISCUSSES SEVERAL INSTANCES. EXAMINES RELEVANT PROVISIONS OF DRAFT ARTILLES ON LAW OF TREATIES BY INTERNATIONAL LAW COMMISSION IN 1966.

1843 LISTER L.
EUROPE'S COAL AND STEEL COMMUNITY.
NEW YORK: TWENTIETH CENTURY FUND, 1960, 495 PP.
TRACES THE DEVELOPMENT OF THE ECSC DURING ITS FIRST SIX YEARS OF EXISTENCE. TREATS ECSC AS A STEP TOWARDS EUROPEAN INTEGRATION. VIEWING ITS PROBLEMS IN ECONOMIC TERMS, OFFERS SUGGESTIONS FOR IMPROVING EFFICIENCY THROUGH GREATER INTERNATIONAL SPECIALIZATION.

1844 LITTLE I.M.D.
AID TO AFRICA.
NEW YORK: MACMILLAN, 1964, 76 PP., LC#64-22219.
STUDIES AID TO UNDERDEVELOPED COUNTRIES WITH PARTICULAR REFERENCE TO BRITISH AID POLICY, ESPECIALLY THOSE IN SUB-SAHARAN AFRICA, EXCLUDING REPUBLIC OF SOUTH AFRICA. CONSIDERS REASONS FOR GIVING AID, PROBLEM OF ADMINISTERING IT, ROLE OF PRIVATE CAPITAL, AND IMPORTANCE OF TECHNICAL DEVELOPMENT IN ASSISTING THESE COUNTRIES.

1845 LIU K.C.
AMERICANS AND CHINESE: A HISTORICAL ESSAY AND BIBLIOGRAPHY.
CAMBRIDGE: HARVARD U PR, 1963, 211 PP., LC#63-19141.
ARRANGED BY TYPE OF SOURCE AND INCLUDING MANUSCRIPTS, ARCHIVES, NEWSPAPERS, PERIODICALS, AND FIRST PERSON WORKS MOSTLY IN ENGLISH. TYPES SUBDIVIDED BY TOPIC AND DATE. APPROXIMATELY 1,800 ENTRIES. SOME ANNOTATION.

1846 LIVNEH E.
ISRAEL LEGAL BIBLIOGRAPHY IN EUROPEAN LANGUAGES.
JERUSALEM: HEBREW U PR, 1963, 85 PP.
BRIEF INTRODUCTION TO LEGAL HISTORY OF MODERN PALESTINE AND LIST OF 311 BASIC ENTRIES DIVIDED INTO THREE SECTIONS: LEGISLATION, LAW REPORTS, BOOKS AND ARTICLES. THIRD SECION SUBDIVIDED BY PUBLIC, CIVIL, AND CRIMINAL TOPICS. PUBLICATIONS LARGELY 1948-63.

1847 LIVNEH E.
"A NEW BEGINNING."
MIDSTREAM, 13 (OCT. 67), 18-26.
DISCUSSES EVENTS BEFORE AND AFTER SIX DAY WAR OF JUNE, 1967. URGES APPRECIATION OF ISRAELI PSYCHOLOGY TO COMPREHEND EVENTS. SUGGESTS THAT WAR SEPARATED POWER AND EVIL IN JEWISH MIND. EXAMINES GLOBAL EFFECTS OF ISRAEL BECOMING MAJOR FORCE IN MIDDLE EAST, ESPECIALLY ON US-USSR RELATIONS. PRESENTS THREE PLANS FOR DEALING WITH NEW TERRITORY AND STATES NEED FOR INCREASED IMMIGRATION FOR SUCCESS OF ISRAEL.

1848 LLOYD W.B.
"PEACE REQUIRES PEACEMAKERS."
SANTA BARBARA: CENTER STUDY DEMOC. INSTIT., 1964, 49 PP.
PROPOSAL, FOLLOWED BY ROUND-TABLE DISCUSSION, ADVOCATES ACTIVE MEDIATION ROLE FOR NON-ALIGNED NATIONS: SWITZERLAND, INDIA, AFRO-ASIAN STATES. POINTS TO MEDIATION SUCCESSES OF CANTONS IN SWISS CONFEDERATION.

1849 LOCKHART W.B., KAMISAR Y., CHOPER J.H.
CASES AND MATERIALS ON CONSTITUTIONAL RIGHTS AND LIBERTIES.
MINNEAPOLIS: WEST PUBL CO, 1964, 864 PP.
EXAMINATION OF CIVIL LIBERTIES EMPHASIZING NATURE OF DUE PROCESS, LIMITATIONS ON GOVERNMENTAL POWER, RIGHTS OF THE ACCUSED, FREEDOM OF SPEECH AND ASSOCIATION, CONCEPT OF STATE ACTION, AND FRANCHISE AND APPORTIONMENT.

1850 LODGE H.C. ED.
THE HISTORY OF NATIONS (25 VOLS.)
NEW YORK: COLLIERS, 1928.
COLLECTION OF ESSAYS ON WORLD HISTORY BY LEADING AUTHORITIES. INCLUDES BIBLIOGRAPHY AND INDEXES.

1851 LOEWENHEIM F.L. ED.
PEACE OR APPEASEMENT? HITLER, CHAMBERLAIN AND THE MUNICH CRISIS.
BOSTON: HOUGHTON MIFFLIN, 1965, 204 PP.
COLLECTS LETTERS, NOTES, SPEECHES, AND OTHER MATERIAL PRECEDING MUNICH CONFERENCE, ESPECIALLY CORRESPONDENCE BETWEEN CHAMBERLAIN AND HITLER. GIVES COMPARISON OF ATTITUDES OF OUTSIDERS THEN AND NOW.

1852 LOFTUS M.L.
"INTERNATIONAL MONETARY FUND, 1962-1965: A SELECTED BIBLIOGRAPHY."
INTL. MONETARY FUND STAFF BUL., 12 (NOV. 65), 470-524.
AN UNANNOTATED BIBLIOGRAPHY OF MATERIALS WHICH DESCRIBE THE FUNCTIONS, ORGANIZATION, AND ACTIVITIES OF INTERNATIONAL MONETARY FUND. MATERIAL RANGES FROM 1962-65 IN ENGLISH, FRENCH, GERMAN, SPANISH, NORWEGIAN, AND RUSSIAN LANGUAGES. 648 ENTRIES.

1853 LOGAN R.W.
THE AFRICAN MANDATES IN WORLD POLITICS.
WASHINGTON: PUBLIC AFFAIRS PRESS, 1948, 220 PP.

DISCUSSES INFLUENCE OF MANDATE COLONIES TAKEN FROM GERMANY IN WWI IN WORLD POLITICS BETWEEN WARS. TRACES GERMAN POLICY REGARDING RECOVERY OF COLONIES AFTER WWI, AND THEIR IMPORTANCE AS A POINT OF NEGOTIATION WITH HITLER BEFORE WWII. NOTES ROLE OF COLONIES IN POST-WWII INTERNATIONAL AFFAIRS PARTICULARLY CITING EFFECTS ON TRUSTEE NATIONS.

1854 LONDON K. ED.
"SINO-SOVIET RELATIONS IN THE CONTEXT OF THE 'WORLD SOCIALIST SYSTEM'."
IN (LONDON K, UNITY AND CONTRADICTION, NEW YORK: PRAEGER, 1962, 409-421).
'THE COHESION OF THE COMMUNIST BLOC, WHILE BASED ON THE PRINCIPLES OF MARXISM-LENINISM, IS ACHIEVED BY INTERNATIONAL COMMUNIST ORGANIZATION... WRITER IS RELUCTANT TO BELIEVE THAT THE COMMUNISTS WOULD SACRIFICE, FOR WHATEVER CAUSE, THEIR GREATEST ASSET - UNITY OF THE SOCIALIST CAMP.'

1855 LONDON K. ED.
EASTERN EUROPE IN TRANSITION.
BALTIMORE: JOHNS HOPKINS PRESS, 1966, 364 PP., LC#66-24409.
STUDIES POLITICAL, SOCIAL, AND ECONOMIC CHANGES IN EASTERN EUROPE SINCE KHRUSHCHEV ERA. EXAMINES TRANSITION FROM SYSTEM OF RIGID CONTROL BY USSR TO ONE OF LOOSELY CONNECTED SEMI-INDEPENDENT NATIONS. COVERS NATURE OF NATIONALISM AND EFFECT OF SINO-SOVIET SPLIT.

1856 LONDON INSTITUTE WORLD AFFAIRS
THE YEAR BOOK OF WORLD AFFAIRS.
LONDON: LONDON INST WORLD AFFAIR.
ANNUAL COLLECTION OF ARTICLES AND REPORTS WRITTEN PRIMARILY BY BRITISH SCHOLARS. FIRST PUBLISHED IN 1946, THE YEARBOOK CONTAINS ABOUT TEN ANALYTICAL ESSAYS ON MAJOR PROBLEMS OF INTERNATIONAL RELATIONS. REPORTS ON WORLD AFFAIRS ARE PROVIDED ALSO, INDICATING THE ECONOMIC, SOCIOLOGICAL, PSYCHOLOGICAL, AND LEGAL ASPECTS OF VARIOUS ISSUES. EXTENSIVE BIBLIOGRAPHICAL LISTINGS APPEAR IN EACH VOLUME.

1857 LONDON LIBRARY ASSOCIATION
ATHENAEUM SUBJECT INDEX. 1915-1918.
LONDON: LONDON LIB ASSOC.
AN ANNUAL SUBJECT INDEX TO PERIODICALS PUBLISHED BETWEEN 1915 AND 1918. INCLUDES SUBJECT ENTRIES, WITH AUTHOR INDEXES COVERING THE YEARS 1915-16 AND 1917-19. CONCENTRATES ON GENERAL SOCIAL SCIENCE PERIODICALS.

1858 LONDON SCHOOL ECONOMICS-POL
ANNUAL DIGEST OF PUBLIC INTERNATIONAL LAW CASES.
LONDON: BUTTERWORTHS, 1919.
AN ANNUAL DIGEST OF DECISIONS WHICH ARE CONCERNED WITH THE INTERPRETATION OF MUNICIPAL STATUTES ON MATTERS BEARING UPON INTERNATIONAL LAW, IN PARTICULAR, QUESTIONS OF JURISDICTION, NATIONALITY, AND EXTRADITION. SINCE 1932, 28 VOLUMES HAVE BEEN PUBLISHED COVERING PERIOD 1919-63. EACH VOLUME CONTAINS ALPHABETICAL AND GEOGRAPHICAL LISTS OF CASES, TABLE OF TREATIES, AND BETWEEN 140-390 SUMMARIZED ENTRIES.

1859 LONG B.
THE WAR DIARY OF BRECKINRIDGE LONG: SELECTIONS FROM THE YEARS 1939-1944.
LINCOLN: U OF NEB PR, 1966, 410 PP., LC#65-19693.
DIARY OF ASSISTANT SECRETARY OF STATE DURING WWII, GIVING A PERSONAL GLIMPSE INTO MACHINATIONS OF WARTIME DIPLOMACY. LONG WAS POLICY-MAKER AND HAD BROAD EXPERIENCE IN MANY AREAS OF STATE DEPARTMENT ACTIVITY, INCLUDING FORMULATION OF POSTWAR POLICY PLANS.

1860 LOOMIE A.J.
THE SPANISH ELIZABETHANS: THE ENGLISH EXILES AT THE COURT OF PHILIP II.
NEW YORK: FORDHAM U PR, 1963, 280 PP., LC#63-14407.
ANALYZES CHIEF WAYS IN WHICH SPAIN AIDED EXILES DURING ANGLO-SPANISH WAR. COVERS BASIC RELATIONSHIP BETWEEN SPAIN AND ENGLISH CATHOLICS AND PROBLEMS THAT SPAIN'S POLICY CREATED. ANALYZES FIVE LEADING REFUGEES, USING THEIR CASES TO ILLUSTRATE BASIC TRENDS AND DIFFICULTIES IN SPANISH POLICY.

1861 LOPEZ M.M. ED.
CATALOGOS DE PUBLICACIONES PERIODICAS MEXICANAS.
MEXICO CITY: EDIT STYLO DURANG, 1959.
BIBLIOGRAPHY OF MEXICAN PERIODICALS EXCLUDING DAILY AND ART REPRODUCTION PUBLICATIONS. CLARIFIES CONTENT OF PERIODICAL WHERE TITLE IS NOT CLEAR. INDICATES PAGE NUMBER, PUBLISHER, ILLUSTRATIONS, COSTS, PLACE PUBLISHED, ADVERTISEMENTS, DATES OF PUBLICATION AND OTHER PERTINENT INFORMATION. LISTED ALPHABETICALLY BY STATE OR DISTRICT. BASED ON PUBLICATIONS CURRENT IN 1928.

1862 LOPEZIBOR J.
"L'EUROPE, FORME DE VIE."
TABLE RONDE, 181 (FEB. 63), 162-75.
EUROPEAN WAY OF LIFE IS PRESENTED IN LIGHT OF PARTICULAR HISTORIC ATTITUDES THAT PERMITTED BIRTH AND DEVELOPMENT OF EUROPEAN NATIONS. STUDIES ITS CULTURAL PATTERNS AND RELATES THEM TO CHRISTIAN CONSCIENCE WHICH IS SEEN AS FIRST COMMON BASIS FOR EUROPEAN UNITY.

1863 LORIMER J.
THE INSTITUTES OF THE LAW OF NATIONS.
EDINBURGH: BLACKWOOD, 1880, 572 PP.
DISCUSSES NATURE AND CHARACTERISTICS OF INTERNATIONAL LAW AND EXPLAINS IN DETAIL ITS SOURCES. ALSO SURVEYS THE ENTIRE FIELD OF INTERNATIONAL RELATIONS AND THE ROLE OF THE LAW OF NATURE IN THIS FIELD.

1864 LOSMAN D.L.
"FOREIGN AID, SOCIALISM AND THE EMERGING COUNTRIES"
DUQUESNE REVIEW, 12 (SPRING 67), 47-65.
EXPLAINS CAUSES OF EXPANSION OF GOVERNMENT POWERS AND PROGRAMS IN UNDERDEVELOPED COUNTRIES ASSISTED BY US FOREIGN AID. CONTENDS THAT SOCIAL, POLITICAL, AND ECONOMIC FACTORS EXISTING TODAY IN UNDERDEVELOPED COUNTRIES HAVE FORCED GOVERNMENTS TO ASSUME MORE POWERS, AND SUCH INCREASED GOVERNMENT ACTIVITIES WILL SPEED THE LONG-DELAYED DEVELOPMENT.

1865 LOVEDAY A.
REFLECTIONS ON INTERNATIONAL ADMINISTRATION.
LONDON: OXFORD U. PR., 1956, 334 PP., $7.20.
A DETAILED ANALYSIS OF THE ORGANIZATION AND OPERATION OF INTERNATIONAL AGENCIES. DISCUSSION OF PERSONNEL POLICY IN TERMS OF NATURE OF WORK, STANDARDS, MORALE AND RECRUITMENT, AND ADMINISTRATION FUNCTION IN RELATION TO PROBLEMS OF RESEARCH, BUDGET, FINANCE CONTROL, AND COORDINATION IN ANY DEALINGS WITH POLITICAL ORGANIZATIONS OF AN INTERNATIONAL INSTITUTION.

1866 LOVELL R.I.
THE STRUGGLE FOR SOUTH AFRICA, 1875-1899.
NEW YORK: MACMILLAN, 1934, 438 PP.
ANALYSIS OF SOUTH AFRICA AS SEEN IN DIPLOMATIC RELATIONS AND WAR IN THIS AREA. DEALS WITH EUROPEAN EXPANSION AND IN DETAIL WITH ANGLO-GERMAN RELATIONS, THE TWO MOST IMPORTANT POWERS ACTIVE IN SOUTH AFRICA. DISCUSSES POLICIES OF CECIL RHODES AND CONQUEST OF SOUTHERN RHODESIA.

1867 LOWELL A.L.
GOVERNMENTS AND PARTIES IN CONTINENTAL EUROPE, VOL. II.
BOSTON: HOUGHTON MIFFLIN, 1896, 455 PP.
DISCUSSES VARIOUS ASPECTS OF THE INTERNAL POLITICS OF GERMANY, AUSTRIA-HUNGARY, AND SWITZERLAND, INCLUDING DYNAMICS OF POLITICAL POWER WITHIN EACH NATION, HISTORY OF POLITICAL PARTIES, AND INSTITUTIONS PECULIAR TO EACH.

1868 LOWENSTEIN A.K.
BRUTAL MANDATE: A JOURNEY TO SOUTH WEST AFRICA.
NEW YORK: MACMILLAN, 1962, 257 PP., LC#62-14204.
WORKINGS OF UN IN REPUBLIC OF SOUTH AFRICA. AN APPRAISAL OF US GOVERNMENT POLICY AND AN INDICATION OF WHAT CONCERNED INDIVIDUALS COULD DO.

1869 LOWENSTEIN R.
POLITICAL RECONSTRUCTION.
NEW YORK: MACMILLAN, 1946, 498 PP.
AN ATTACK ON INTERNAL SELF-DETERMINATION. THESIS IS THAT NATIONS' RIGHT TO CHOOSE FORM OF GOVERNMENT THEY DESIRE WILL LEAD TO WW3. FEELS INTERNAL SOVEREIGNTY MUST BE DESTROYED TO ATTAIN STABLE WORLD ORDER.

1870 LUARD E.
THE COLD WAR: A RE-APPRAISAL.
NEW YORK: FREDERICK PRAEGER, 1964, 347 PP., LC#64-25786.
SURVEYS HISTORY OF COLD WAR (1945-PRESENT). DISCUSSES RISE OF COMMUNISM IN FAR EAST, PARTITION OF EUROPE, POLARIZATION OF COMMUNIST WORLD, POLYCENTRISM IN WEST, CONDITIONS OF COEXISTENCE, ETC. EXPRESSES THOUGHTS ON FUTURE DEVELOPMENTS.

1871 LUARD E. ED.
THE EVOLUTION OF INTERNATIONAL ORGANIZATIONS.
LONDON: THAMES AND HUDSON, LTD, 1966, 342 PP.
SERIES OF CASE STUDIES UNDERTAKEN BY EXPERTS IN EACH FIELD. DESIGNED TO CONSIDER CHANGES THAT HAVE OCCURRED IN IMPORTANT INTERNATIONAL ORGANIZATIONS, AND TO ASSESS ON BASIS OF HISTORY, FACTORS INFLUENCING OR INHIBITING CHANGE DURING THEIR EVOLUTION. LEAGUE OF NATIONS, WORLD BANK, INTERNATIONAL MONETARY FUND AMONG ORGANIZATIONS TREATED.

1872 LUKACS J.
A HISTORY OF THE COLD WAR.
GARDEN CITY: DOUBLEDAY, 1961, 288 PP.
SURVEYS HISTORICAL ORIGINS, MOVEMENTS AND PERSONALITIES OF COLD WAR, FOCUSING ON 1956 AS CRUCIAL YEAR. SEES CONTEST AS IDEOLOGICAL AND SPIRITUAL. NOTES SPREAD OF DEMOCRACY, MIGRATIONS OF PEOPLE, RIGHTIST TREND OF 20TH CENTURY. HOLDS RELATIONSHIP OF USA AND USSR TO EUROPE IS OF KEY IMPORTANCE.

1873 LUNDBERG F.
THE COMING WORLD TRANSFORMATION.
GARDEN CITY: DOUBLEDAY, 1963, 387 PP., LC#62-15908.
ATTEMPTS TO PREDICT, ON A SYSTEMATIC AND THEORETICALLY JUSTIFIABLE BASIS, FUTURE DEVELOPMENTS OF BASIC AND GENERAL

IMPORTANCE. USING HISTORICAL BASES, EXAMINES PREVIOUS 150-YEAR SPANS AND POSTULATES CHANGES IN RATE OF DEVELOPMENT AND TYPE OF DEVELOPMENT. CONSIDERS TECHNICAL DEVELOPMENTS OF PRESENT AND PROJECTS THEIR EFFECTS ON FUTURE SOCIETY, GOVERNMENT, AND ECONOMICS.

1874 LUTHULI A., KAUNDA K., MBOYA T.
AFRICA'S FREEDOM.
NEW YORK: BARNES AND NOBLE, 1964, 94 PP.
ESSAYS BY LEADING AFRICAN STATESMEN ON ECONOMIC, POLITICAL, AND SOCIAL PROBLEMS; TREAT COLONIALISM AND PAN-AFRICANISM IN DETAIL. DISCUSS ROLES OF PRESS, LABOR UNIONS, YOUTH GROUPS, ETC., IN CONTEXT OF MODERNIZATION.

1875 LUTZ F.A.
GELD UND WAHRUNG.
TUBINGEN: J C B MOHR, 1962, 267 PP.
EXAMINES CURRENCY PROBLEMS AND POLICIES IN RELATION TO ECONOMIC GROWTH, INFLATION, AND INTERNATIONAL ECONOMIC BALANCE. DISCUSSES GOLD STANDARD, EUROPEAN CURRENCY PROBLEMS BETWEEN 1946-50, AND IMPORTANCE OF INVESTMENTS TO ECONOMIC DEVELOPMENT.

1876 LUTZ F.A.
THE PROBLEM OF INTERNATIONAL ECONOMIC EQUILIBRIUM.
AMSTERDAM: NORTH HOLLAND PUBL CO, 1962, 75 PP.
LECTURES EXPLORING COMPLEX PROBLEMS MONETARY AUTHORITIES ARE FACING IN INTERNATIONAL FIELD. INVESTIGATES CAUSES OF BALANCE-OF-PAYMENTS DISEQUILIBRIUM, PURCHASING-POWER-PARITY THEORY, INFLATION, PRODUCTIVITY, INTERNATIONAL CAPITAL MOVEMENTS, AND PROBLEMS OF INTERNATIONAL LIQUIDITY.

1877 LYND S., HAYDEN T.
THE OTHER SIDE.
NEW YORK: NEW AMERICAN LIB, 1966, 238 PP., LC#67-15194.
ACCOUNT OF TRIP TO NORTH VIETNAM MADE BY THREE AMERICANS IN 1965 IN DEFIANCE OF STATE DEPARTMENT BAN ON TRAVEL TO NORTH VIETNAM. EMPHASIZES ILLEGALITY OF AMERICAN INTERFERENCE IN VIETNAMESE INTERNAL AFFAIRS AND IMPORTANCE OF AMERICAN WITHDRAWAL TO ENABLE NEGOTIATIONS AND END FIGHTING.

1878 LYON P.
"NEUTRALITY AND THE EMERGENCE OF THE CONCEPT OF NEUTRALISM."
REV. POLIT., 22 (APR. 60), 255-68.
CONTRASTS NEUTRALISM - A POLITAL TERM, AND NEUTRALITY - A LEGAL-POLITICAL CONCEPT. POSES DIFFICULTY OF DISTINGUISHING BETWEEN THESE TERMS IN RELATION TO MODERN CONCEPTS OF WAR AND PEACE IN THE COLD WAR. TRACES HISTORICAL DEVELOPMENT OF BOTH CONCEPTS AND THEIR SIGNIFICANCE TO THE UN SYSTEM AND WORLD PEACE.

1879 LYON P.
NEUTRALISM.
LONDON: LEICESTER UNIV PRESS, 1963, 215 PP.
SEES NEUTRALISM AS AN IDEOLOGY. COMPARATIVE APPROACH TO NEUTRALIST REGIMES INCLUDING SIX PROTOTYPES. NOTES AND CASE STUDIES ON FAILURE OF BELGRADE CONFERENCE. SEES NEUTRALISM AS NECESSARY "BUFFER FORCE" IN INTERNATIONAL POLITICS.

1880 LYONS F.S.L.
INTERNATIONALISM IN EUROPE 1815-1914.
LEYDEN: AW SIJTHOFF, 1963, 412 PP., LC#63-16252.
PRESENTS HISTORY OF INTERNATIONALISM IN EUROPE FROM 1815-1914. STUDIES MACHINERY OF INTERNATIONAL COOPERATION AND DISCUSSES SEVERAL AREAS OF COOPERATION. THESE INCLUDE ECONOMIC, LABOR, COMMUNICATION, LEGAL, RELIGIOUS, AND HUMANITARIAN COOPERATION. ALSO INVESTIGATES ATTEMPTS TO ESTABLISH PEACEFUL EXISTENCE.

1881 LYONS G.M. ED.
AMERICA: PURPOSE AND POWER.
CHICAGO: QUADRANGLE BOOKS, INC, 1965, 384 PP., LC#65-18243.
ESSAYS PUBLISHED BY PUBLIC AFFAIRS CENTER AT DARTMOUTH COLLEGE. DEALS WITH RELATIONSHIP OF POWER AND PURPOSE IN DESCRIBING DEVELOPMENT OF US SOCIETY AND ANALYZING MILITARY DEFENSE, ECONOMIC AID, URBANIZATION, WORLD TRADE, TECHNOLOGICAL INNOVATION, AND CIVIL RIGHTS.

1882 ROBINSON R.D.
INTERNATIONAL MANAGEMENT.
NEW YORK: HOLT RINEHART WINSTON, 1967, 178 PP., LC#67-11817.
DESIGNED FOR BASIC MANAGEMENT COURSES, TO PROVIDE THEORETICAL STRUCTURE, RELEVANT DETAILS, AND CASE MATERIAL FOR FIELD OF INTERNATIONAL MANAGEMENT. CONCERNS STRATEGY AND INTERRELATIONSHIPS OF MARKETING, SUPPLY LABOR, MANAGEMENT, OWNERSHIP, FINANCE, LAW, AND CONTROL.

1883 MAC CHESNEY B.
"SOME COMMENTS ON THE 'QUARANTINE' OF CUBA."
AMER. J. INT. LAW., 57 (JULY 63), 592-97.
DISCUSSES LEGAL QUESTIONS RAISED BY THE CUBAN CRISIS, ASSERTING THAT INTERNATIONAL LAW MUST BE RE-INTERPRETED WITHIN THE CONTEXT OF THE MID-TWENTIETH CENTURY'S POLITICS. FEELS USA FOLLOWED DOCTRINE OF SELF-DEFENSE.

1884 MAC MILLAN W.M.
THE ROAD TO SELF-RULE.
NEW YORK: FREDERICK PRAEGER, 1959, 296 PP.
BASICALLY HISTORICAL STUDY OF COLONIAL EVOLUTION OF AFRICAN PEOPLE UNDER BRITISH RULE. DESCRIBES SOCIAL AND CULTURAL BACKGROUNDS AND EXTENT TO WHICH BRITISH COLONIAL RULE HAS ALTERED OLD WAY OF LIFE. DISCUSSES PROGRESS TOWARD INDEPENDENCE BEING MADE BY AFRICANS UNDER BRITISH CONTROL.

1885 MACARTHUR D.
REVITALIZING A NATION.
CHICAGO: HERITAGE FOUNDATION, 1952, 141 PP.
STATES BELIEFS AND OPINIONS OF MACARTHUR AND THE POLICY THEY EMBODY, GLEANED FROM PUBLIC PRONOUNCEMENTS ON SUCH SUBJECTS AS: JAPAN'S ROLE IN THE FUTURE OF ASIA, PROBLEMS OF KOREA AND COMMUNISM, AID TO EUROPE, TAXES, AND POSSIBILITIES FOR WWIII.

1886 MACDONALD D.F.
THE AGE OF TRANSITION: BRITAIN IN THE NINETEENTH & TWENTIETH CENTURIES.
NEW YORK: ST MARTIN'S PRESS, 1967, 249 PP., LC#67-11555.
DISCUSSES 150 YEARS OF BRITISH HISTORY; HER RISE TO POWER AND EMPIRE, THEN HER DRAMATIC DECLINE WITH LOSS OF COMMERCIAL ADVANTAGE AND EMPIRE. DISCUSSES INTERNAL ECONOMIC DEVELOPMENT, REFORM, AND CONSTITUTIONAL CHANGE.

1887 MACDONALD R.S.J.
"THE RESORT TO ECONOMIC COERCION BY INTERNATIONAL POLITICAL ORGANIZATIONS."
U. TORONTO LAW J., 17 (1967), 85-169.
SURVEYS FOUR SPECIFIC ETHIOPIAN CASES OF 1935, DOMINICAN CASE OF 1960, AND THE CURRENT SOUTH AFRICAN AND CUBAN CASES - WHICH HAVE BEEN HANDLED BY THREE PRINCIPAL INTERNATIONAL ORGANIZATIONS, AND REVIEWS VARIETIES OF ECONOMIC MEASURES EMPLOYED TO MAKE THESE STATES CONFORM TO THE ORGANIZATIONS' POLICIES.

1888 MACDONALD R.W.
THE LEAGUE OF ARAB STATES: A STUDY IN THE DYNAMICS OF REGIONAL ORGANIZATION.
PRINCETON: PRINCETON U PRESS, 1965, 407 PP., LC#65-10832.
ANALYZES STRUCTURAL AND OPERATIONAL ASPECTS OF ARAB LEAGUE INCLUDING TREATIES, BALANCE OF POWER, AND AMERICAN INVOLVEMENT. INCLUDES BIBLIOGRAPHY CITING DOCUMENTS, BOOKS, ARTICLES, PERIODICALS, AND NEWSPAPERS CONTAINING MATERIAL ON SUBJECT. ARRANGED BY NATURE OF SOURCE AND ALPHABETICALLY. INCLUDES FOREIGN-LANGUAGE MATERIAL.

1889 MACHOWSKI K.
"SELECTED PROBLEMS OF NATIONAL SOVEREIGNTY WITH REFERENCE TO THE LAW OF OUTER SPACE."
PROC. AMER. SOC. INT. LAW, 55 (APR. 61), 169-74.
WARNS AGAINST POSSIBILITY OF USING OUTER SPACE FOR MILITARY PURPOSES. ASSERTS THAT ANY LEGAL SETTLEMENT ON MAN'S ACTIVITY MUST BE BASED ON THE SAME PREMISES, NAMELY THE PRESERVATION OF SECURITY OF STATES.

1890 MACIVER R.M.
TOWARDS AN ABIDING PEACE.
NEW YORK: MACMILLAN, 1944, 195 PP.
FEELS COUNTRIES NEED TO SET ASIDE SELF-INTERESTED IDEOLOGIES TO BUILD SECURE PEACE ON FRAMEWORK OF INTERNATIONAL LAW. PROPOSES NEW INTERNATIONAL ORGANIZATION TO MITIGATE ECONOMIC INSTABILITY OF NATIONS. CALLS TO USA TO TAKE LEAD IN ECONOMIC REGENERATION OF EUROPEAN COMMUNITY.

1891 MACIVER R.M. ED.
GREAT EXPRESSIONS OF HUMAN RIGHTS.
NEW YORK: HARPER, 1950, 321 PP.
SURVEYS MAGNA CHARTA, THE AMERICAN BILL OF RIGHTS, NATURAL LAWS, THE DECLARATION OF THE RIGHTS OF MAN AND CITIZEN. STUDIES LINCOLN'S POLITICAL ACTION. DISCUSSES THE FUNERAL ORATION OF PERICLES. RELATES INDIVIDUAL FREEDOM TO SOCIAL DETERMINISM.

1892 MACIVER R.M.
THE NATIONS AND THE UN.
NEW YORK: MANHATTAN, 1959, 186 PP.
INSIGHTS PROVIDED ON SUCH TOPICS AS: HOW NATIONAL INTEREST IS SERVED, STATE POLICIES ARE AFFECTED AND THE FUTURE OF WORLD ORGANIZATIONS. AUTHOR FEELS THE UNITED NATIONS IS A NEW FORM OF DIPLOMACY AND ACTS AS THE GUARDIAN OF DEVELOPING COUNTRIES.

1893 MACK R.T.
RAISING THE WORLDS STANDARD OF LIVING.
NEW YORK: CITADEL, 1953, 285 PP.
DEALS WITH FOREIGN AID PROGRAMS OF POST-WAR PERIOD. DETAILS SEVERAL AID PROGRAMS SUCH AS POINT FOUR AND TECHNICAL ASSISTANCE CONFERENCE OF THE UN. CITES IRAN AS EXAMPLE.

1894 MACKENTOSH J.M.
STRATEGY AND TACTICS OF SOVIET FOREIGN POLICY.
LONDON: OXFORD U. PR., 1962, 332 PP.
TRACES HISTORICAL DEVELOPMENT OF SUBJECT. MAINLY CONCERNED WITH THE SOVIET POST-WAR POLICY, PARTICULARLY WITH

RESPECT TO MAINLAND CHINA AND THE WEST IN GENERAL.

1895 MACKESY P.
THE WAR FOR AMERICA, 1775-1783.
CAMBRIDGE: HARVARD U PR, 1964, 565 PP.
HISTORY OF ENGLISH-AMERICAN CONFLICT WHICH PROPOSES TO EXAMINE THE MAKING AND EXECUTION OF STRATEGY IN ONE OF ENGLAND'S GREAT 18TH-CENTURY WARS, AND CREATES A DETAILED MODEL OF THE MACHINE AT WORK. ATTEMPTS TO JUDGE WAR MINISTRY IN LIGHT OF CIRCUMSTANCES RATHER THAN RESULTS. STUDY OF BRITISH STRATEGY AND LEADERSHIP IN LAST WAR AGAINST BOURBONS.

1896 MACLAURIN J.
THE UNITED NATIONS AND POWER POLITICS.
LONDON: ALLEN UNWIN, 1951, 468 PP.
ATTEMPT TO DESCRIBE MACHINERY AND ORGANIC STRUCTURE OF UNITED NATIONS AND ITS RELATIONS WITH NATIONAL GOVERNMENTS. TRACES SPECIFIC WORLD PROBLEMS ON THEIR COURSE THROUGH THE UN, PRESENTING ONLY SAMPLE CASES. VIEWS UN IN FRAMEWORK OF COLD WAR.

1897 MACLES L.M.
LES SOURCES DU TRAVAIL BIBLIOGRAPHIQUE (3 VOLS.)
GENEVA: LIBRAIRIE DROZ, 1958.
FRENCH GUIDE TO BIBLIOGRAPHIC MATERIALS. COVERS GENERAL BIBLIOGRAPHIES, HUMANITIES AND SOCIAL SCIENCES, AND SOURCES IN NATURAL AND APPLIED SCIENCES. MATERIALS CITED PUBLISHED THROUGHOUT WORLD.

1898 MACLURE M. ED., ANGLIN D. ED.
AFRICA: THE POLITICAL PATTERN.
TORONTO: TORONTO UNIV PRESS, 1961, 124 PP.
ESSAYS DISCUSSING GENERAL PROBLEMS IN POLITICAL DEVELOPMENT AND CULTURAL AFFAIRS IN SUB-SAHARA AFRICA. EACH ESSAY DEVOTED TO PROBLEMS OF SEPARATE COUNTRY OR REGION.

1899 MACMAHON A.W.
ADMINISTRATION IN FOREIGN AFFAIRS.
UNIVERSITY, ALA: U. PR., 1953, 275 PP.
DISCUSSES ADMINISTRATIVE PROCESS EMPLOYED BY US GOVERNMENT IN THE FORMULATION AND EXECUTION OF ITS FOREIGN POLICY. ARGUES THAT ADMINISTRATION'S GOALS DETERMINE ITS STRUCTURE. DEMONSTRATES THIS BY SHOWING POST-WAR STRUCTURAL CHANGES IN THE STATE DEPARTMENT TO BE RELATED TO NEW FOREIGN POLICY PROGRAM AIMS.

1900 MACMAHON A.W. ED.
FEDERALISM: MATURE AND EMERGENT.
GARDEN CITY: DOUBLEDAY, 1955, 557 PP.
REVIEWS NATURE AND ROLE OF FEDERALISM IN THE MODERN ERA. EXAMINES THE MECHANISMS PROVIDING FOR CONTROLS AND BALANCES IN FEDERALIST SYSTEMS. PROBES THE COMPLEX INTERACTION AMONG GOVERNMENTAL LEVELS IN TREATING NATIONAL PROBLEMS WITHIN FEDERAL FRAMEWORK. NOTES THE APPLICABILITY OF FEDERALIST PRINCIPLES TO FORMATIONS IN THE POLITICAL COMMUNITY OF WESTERN EUROPE.

1901 MACMINN N. ED., HAINDS J.R. ED. ET AL.
BIBLIOGRAPHY OF THE PUBLISHED WRITINGS OF JOHN STUART MILL.
EVANSTON: NORTHWESTERN U PRESS, 1945, 101 PP.
MATERIALS CHRONOLOGICALLY ARRANGED, INCLUDING LETTERS, REVIEWS, OBSERVATIONS, ARTICLES, ESSAYS, AND NOTES, ALL ANNOTATED. NO INDEX FOR THE APPROXIMATELY 800 ITEMS.

1902 MACRIDIS R.C. ED.
FOREIGN POLICY IN WORLD POLITICS (3RD ED.)
ENGLEWOOD CLIFFS: PRENTICE HALL, 1967, 401 PP., LC#67-12251.
COMPARES FOREIGN POLICIES OF MAJOR NATIONS, ANALYZING PARTICULAR GOVERNMENTAL STRUCTURES, NATIONAL WORLD-VIEWS, CHARACTERISTICS OF HISTORICAL AND GEOGRAPHICAL POSITION TO ELUCIDATE THEIR DIRECTION, EFFICACY, AND EFFECT ON FUTURE POLICY-MAKING.

1903 MACWHINNEY E.
"LES CONCEPT SOVIETIQUE DE 'COEXISTENCE PACIFIQUE' ET LES RAPPORTS JURIDIQUES ENTRE L'URSS ET LES ETATS OCIDENTAUX."
REV. GEN. DR. INT. PUB., 34 (NO., 63), 545-62.
DEALS WITH SOVIET INTERPRETATION OF 'PEACEFUL COEXISTENCE) AND ITS APPLICATION TO INTERNATIONAL LAW. STUDIES INFLUENCE OF LAW ON TRANSFORMATION OF SOCIETIES. DISCUSSES JURIDICAL RELATIONS BETWEEN EAST AND WEST AS VIEWED THROUGH SOVIET DOCTRINE AND TACTICS USED TO ACHIEVE SOVIET GOALS.

1904 MAGATHAN W.
"SOME BASES OF WEST GERMAN MILITARY POLICY."
J. CONFL. RESOLUT., 4 (MAR. 60), 123-37.
FOCUSES ON WEST GERMAN CONCERN ABOUT ITS SECURITY POLICY, EMPHASIZING ITS DEVELOPMENT IN TERMS OF STRUCTURE, ECONOMICS AND DEMOGRAPHY. OUTLINES BOTH MILITARY POLICY AND ARMED FORCES DEPLOYMENT.

1905 MAGGS P.B.
"SOVIET VIEWPOINT ON NUCLEAR WEAPONS IN INTERNATIONAL LAW."
LAW CONTEMP. PROBL., 29 (AUTUMN 64), 956-70.
EXPLAINS SOVIET APPROACH TO LEGAL PROBLEMS CONNECTED WITH THE MILITARY USE OF NUCLEAR WEAPONS AS WELL AS THE TESTING, CONSTRUCTION, POSSESSION, STATIONING AND TRANSFER OF SUCH WEAPONS.

1906 MAHAR J.M.
INDIA: A CRITICAL BIBLIOGRAPHY.
TUCSON: U OF ARIZONA PR, 1964, 119 PP., LC#64-17992.
LIST OF 2023 TITLES, MOSTLY BOOKS WITH FEW FOREIGN-LANGUAGE SOURCES. ARRANGED BY TOPIC IN DETAIL; PUBLICATIONS SINCE 1940 GIVEN GREATEST ATTENTION.

1907 MAIER J. ED., WEATHERHEAD R.W. ED.
POLITICS OF CHANGE IN LATIN AMERICA.
NEW YORK: FREDERICK PRAEGER, 1964, 258 PP., LC#64-13382.
COLLECTION OF ESSAYS BY LATIN AMERICAN SPECIALISTS. ANALYZES CHANGES IN POLITICS AND SOCIAL STRUCTURE IN CONTEMPORARY LATIN AMERICA, NOTING BRAZIL AS ESPECIALLY DIFFERENT IN BACKGROUND AND DEVELOPMENT. EXAMINES INTERACTION OF ALL WESTERN HEMISHPERE NATIONS, ALSO CONCEPT OF ALLIANCE FOR PROGRESS.

1908 MAINE H.S.
INTERNATIONAL LAW.
LONDON: MURRAY, 1894, 234 PP.
DEALS WITH ORIGINS, SOURCES AND AUTHORITY OF INTERNATIONAL LAW. CONSIDERS THE PROBLEM OF SANCTION. STUDIES STATE SOVEREIGNITY AND TERRITORIAL RIGHTS. SURVEYS THE DECLARATION OF PARIS. GIVES PROPOSAL FOR ELIMINATING WAR.

1909 MAIR L.P.
THE PROTECTION OF MINORITIES.
LONDON: CHRISTOPHERS, 1928, 232 PP.
POINTS OUT EXAMPLES OF PAST CONSIDERATION OF PROBLEM, FOCUSING ON MINORITIES TREATIES. DESCRIBES CONDITIONS FOR MINORITIES IN ALMOST ALL EUROPEAN COUNTRIES. CONCLUDES WITH CASE STUDIES RELATED TO NATIONALITY.

1910 MAISEL A.Q.
AFRICA: FACTS AND FORECASTS.
NEW YORK: DUELL, SLOAN & PEARCE, 1943, 307 PP.
DISCUSSES SIGNIFICANT SOCIAL AND ECONOMIC CHANGES OCCURRING IN AFRICA DUE TO ATLANTIC CHARTER AND TO AFRICA'S IMPORTANT ROLE IN WWII. LOOKS AHEAD TO POSTWAR ERA AND EMPHASIZES IMPORTANCE OF WORLD LEADERS ADAPTING THEIR FOREIGN POLICIES TO CHANGING NEEDS OF AFRICAN PEOPLES. SEPARATE DISCUSSIONS OF ALL MAJOR COUNTRIES AND POSSESSIONS.

1911 MALCLES L.N.
BIBLIOGRAPHICAL SERVICES THROUGHOUT THE WORLD (VOL. 4)
PARIS: UNESCO, 1955, 353 PP.
AIMS TO "PRESENT AN ACCOUNT OF BIBLIOGRAPHIC ACTIVITIES IN VARIOUS COUNTRIES DURING THE PERIOD SEPTEMBER 1951-AUGUST 1952, AND TO FORMULATE: DEFINITE VIEWS ON THE PRESENT SITUATION; SUGGESTIONS FOR THE FUTURE." PROVIDES LISTS OF BOOKS ON BIBLIOGRAPHIES, ANALYTICAL TABLES, INDEXES BY SUBJECT AND COUNTRY. SUGGESTS MEANS FOR DEVELOPING, EXPANDING, AND COORDINATING NATIONAL BIBLIOGRAPHIC SERVICES.

1912 MALIK C.
MAN IN THE STRUGGLE FOR PEACE.
NEW YORK: HARPER & ROW, 1963, 242 PP., LC#63-8007.
ANALYSIS OF "INTERNATIONAL PROBLEM OF COMMUNISM" (BY PAST PRESIDENT OF UN GENERAL ASSEMBLY) AS NEED FOR WEST TO PROMOTE A REVOLUTION OR A PEACEFUL PROMISE TO THE WORLD AS COMMUNISM DOES. WEST "IS ONLY PREPARED TO FIGHT WAR, WHILE COMMUNISM CAN FIGHT PEACE AND WAR AND DOES."

1913 MALINOWSKI W.R.
"CENTRALIZATION AND DE-CENTRALIZATION IN THE UNITED NATIONS' ECONOMIC AND SOCIAL ACTIVITIES."
INT. ORGAN., 16 (SUMMER 62), 521-541.
ALTHOUGH U.N. ORGANIZED AS CENTRALIZED UNIT, THE JOINING TO THE PARENT GROUP OF REGIONAL SYSTEMS DEVOID OF RESPONSIBILITY, SOON BROKE THIS DOWN. REGIONAL STAFFS OFTEN ACT INDEPENDENTLY OF SECRETARY-GENERAL IN SPECIALIZED AREAS WITH WHICH THEY ARE MOST FAMILIAR THEREBY CRIPPLING UTILITY.

1914 MALLIN J.
FORTRESS CUBA; RUSSIA'S AMERICAN BASE.
CHICAGO: HENRY REGNERY CO, 1965, 192 PP., LC#65-19165.
DESCRIBES CASTRO'S TAKEOVER OF CUBA AND HIS ROLE IN WORLD COMMUNISM. DISCUSSES CHE GUEVERA'S PLAN FOR CONQUEST OF OTHER LATIN AMERICAN NATIONS THROUGH GUERRILLA WARFARE. ADVOCATES US TRAINING OF CUBAN EXILES AND THEIR RETURN TO CUBA TO FIGHT CASTRO WITHOUT DIRECT US INTERVENTION.

1915 MALLORY W.H.
POLITICAL HANDBOOK AND ATLAS OF THE WORLD: PARLIAMENTS, PARTIES AND PRESS AS OF JANUARY 1, 1966.
NEW YORK: HARPER & ROW, 1966, 360 PP., LC#28-12165.
DESIGNED TO FURNISH NECESSARY FACTUAL BACKGROUND FOR UNDERSTANDING POLITICAL EVENTS IN ALL INDEPENDENT GOVERNMENTS UP TO 1966. MATERIAL LISTED BY COUNTRY.

1916 MANDER J.
BERLIN: HOSTAGE FOR THE WEST.

BALTIMORE: PENGUIN BOOKS, 1962, 124 PP.
EXAMINES STATUS OF BERLIN SINCE WWII AND ITS RELATION TO EAST AND WEST. DEALS WITH SIGNIFICANCE OF BERLIN TO GERMAN FUTURE, PRESENT POLITICS, AND WESTERN COMMITMENTS TO AID AND DEFEND WEST BERLIN.

1917 MANDER L.
FOUNDATIONS OF MODERN WORLD SOCIETY.
STANFORD: U. PR., 1947, 928 PP.
CONSIDERS ASPECTS OF INTERNATIONAL AFFAIRS AND HANDLING OF THEM BY INTERNATIONAL AGENCIES. THESIS IS THAT POLITICAL ORGAN MUST ADAPT TO NEW DEMANDS OF CONTEMPORARY CIVILIZATION RELYING MORE ON INTERNATIONAL RELATIONS.

1918 MANGER W. ED.
THE ALLIANCE FOR PROGRESS: A CRITICAL APPRAISAL.
WASHINGTON: PUBLIC AFFAIRS PRESS, 1963, 131 PP.
ARTICLES DISCUSSING OBJECTIVES, PROBLEMS, AND FUTURE OF ALLIANCE FOR PROGRESS, INCLUDING ECONOMIC ASPECTS, RELATION TO CULTURAL VALUES, ROLE OF EDUCATION, POLITICAL IMPLICATIONS, AND RELATION TO OAS.

1919 MANGIN G.
"LES ACCORDS DE COOPERATION EN MATIERE DE JUSTICE ENTRE LA FRANCE ET LES ETATS AFRICAINS ET MALGACHE."
REV. JURID. POLIT. OUTREMER, 16 (JULY-SEPT. 62), 339-64.
IDENTIFIES AGREEMENTS BETWEEN FRANCE AND AFRICAN STATES ON PROBLEMS OF JUSTICE, TRANSITIONAL DISPOSITION OF JUDICIAL PERSONNEL. TREATS FRENCH EFFECT ON AFRICAN EVOLUTION. INCLUDES LIST OF ARTICLES DEALING WITH CIVIL AND CRIMINAL LAW.

1920 MANGONE G.
"THE IDEA AND PRACTICE OF WORLD GOVERNMENT."
NEW YORK: COLUMB. U. PR., 1951, 278 PP.
ENUMERATES VARIOUS FORMS PREFERABLE FOR WORLD GOVERNMENT. DESCRIBES PROBABLE SUBSEQUENT ECONOMIC AND SPIRITUAL PROGRESS. DENOTES PLACE OF JUSTICE AND INTERNATIONAL LAW IN NEW WORLD ORGANIZATION.

1921 MANGONE G.
A SHORT HISTORY OF INTERNATIONAL ORGANIZATION.
NEW YORK: MCGRAW-HILL, 1954, 326 PP.
HISTORICALLY TRACES DEVELOPMENT OF INTERNATIONAL ORGANIZATIONS FROM NAPOLEONIC ERA TO THE UN. DISCUSSES INCEPTION AND GROWTH OF INTERNATIONAL LAW.

1922 MANGONE G.
"THE UNITED NATIONS AND UNITED STATES FOREIGN POLICY."
TEXAS QUART., 6 (SPRING 63), 11-18.
CRITICIZES CHANGING CHARACTER OF UN. SAYS UN HAS EXCEEDED ORIGINAL POWERS AND HAS SPENT EXCESSIVE AMOUNTS. USA DEFENSE POLICY AND ECONOMIC ASSISTANCE PROGRAMS ARE INDEPENDENT OF UN. REFUTES CHARGES OF UN IRRESPONSIBILITY. HOLDS UN NOT COUNTER TO VITAL USA INTERESTS.

1923 MANN F.A.
"THE BRETTON WOODS AGREEMENT IN THE ENGLISH COURTS."
INT. AND COMP. LAW Q., 16 (APR. 67), 539-542.
DISCUSSION OF SHARIF V. AZAD AND CLARIFICATION OF TROUBLESOME INTERNATIONAL TEXT. ARGUES THAT MATTERS RELATING TO PERFORMANCE, SUCH AS SUPERVENIENT ILLEGALITY OR IMPOSSIBILITY, ARE NOT CAUGHT BY ARTICLE VIII (2) (B) AND THEREFORE REMAIN SUBJECT TO GENERAL LAW.

1924 MANNING C.A.W.
"THE PRETENTIONS OF INTERNATIONAL RELATIONS."
UNIVERSITIES QUART., 7 (AUG. 53), 361-71.
CONCERNED WITH THE TEACHING OF INTERNATIONAL RELATIONS AT BRITISH UNIVERSITIES. DISCUSSES SCOPE OF SUBJECT AND EMPHASIZES THE TRAINED LOGICAL 'HABIT OF MIND' THAT SHOULD BE IMPARTED TO THE STUDENT.

1925 MANNING C.A.W.
THE UNIVERSITY TEACHING OF SOCIAL SCIENCES: INTERNATIONAL RELATIONS.
PARIS: UNESCO, 1954, 100 PP.
TREATS UNIVERSAL PROBLEM OF THE TEACHING OF SOCIAL SCIENCES WITH SPECIAL REFERENCE TO STUDY OF INTERNATIONAL RELATIONS AT THE UNIVERSITY LEVEL. EXAMINES METHODOLOGICAL TECHNIQUES, NATURE AND AFFINITIES OF INTERNATIONAL RELATIONS AS DISTINCT DISCIPLINE AND MAKE-UP OF INTERNATIONAL RELATIONS AS AN INTER-DISCIPLINARY FIELD.

1926 MANNING C.A.W.
THE NATURE OF INTERNATIONAL SOCIETY.
NEW YORK: WILEY, 1962, 220 PP.
A METHODOLOGICAL LOOK AT WORLD SOCIETY AND DIPLOMACY WITH HYPOTHESES ON IMPROVING ORDER THROUGH MORE EFFECTIVE RAPPORT AND PLANS BETWEEN GOVERMENTS. SAYS THERE IS A PLURAL POLITICAL SYSTEM AND A SINGLE DIPLOMATIC ONE OF SOVEREIGN STATES. FEELS ANALYSIS OF GOVERMENTS SHOULD BE TOTAL, NOT SEGMENTED. DISTINGUISHES THE NATION FROM THE STATE AS A NOTION FROM A FACT. SEES MYTH AS A SINE QUA NON TO WORLD POLITICAL LIFE.

1927 MANOLIU F.
"PERSPECTIVES D'UNE INTEGRATION ECONOMIQUE LATINOAMERICAINE."
TIERS-MONDE, 4 (NOS.13-14, 63), 29-64.
SUGGESTS THAT CONCEPT OF INTEGRATION IS FRAMEWORK FOR TREATIES OF MONTEVIDEO, ALIENZA PARA EL PROGRESO, AND DECLARATION OF PUNTA DEL ESTE. ANALYZES INFLUENCE OF INTERAMERICAN BANK. DISCUSSES CEPAL DOCTRINE BASED ON PERIPHERIC REGIONS BEHAVIOR.

1928 MANSERGH N.
THE COMING OF THE FIRST WORLD WAR: A STUDY IN EUROPEAN BALANCE, 1878-1914.
LONDON: LONGMANS, GREEN & CO, 1949, 257 PP.
REINTERPRETS EVENTS PRECEDING WWI IN LIGHT OF EVENTS BEFORE, DURING, AND AFTER WWII. DISCUSSES PATH THAT LED FROM GERMAN PREDOMINANCE IN EUROPE THROUGH FORMATION OF TWO RIVAL ALLIANCE SYSTEMS WHICH DIVIDED CONTINENT BETWEEN THEM TO OUTBREAK OF WAR IN 1914. CONCERNED PRIMARILY WITH RELATIONS BETWEEN GREAT POWERS AND PARALLEL CHANGES IN CONCEPT OF INTERNATIONAL RELATIONS.

1929 MANSERGH N. ED.
DOCUMENTS AND SPEECHES ON BRITISH COMMONWEALTH AFFAIRS 1931-1952.
LONDON: OXFORD U PR, 1953, 604 PP.
COLLECTION OF DOCUMENTS AND SPEECHES ON LEGAL DEVELOPMENT, ECONOMIC POLICIES, FOREIGN POLICY, DEFENSE, ABDICATION OF EDWARD VIII, INDIAN CONSTITUTIONAL REFORMS, IRISH RELATIONS WITH UK, WWII, INDIAN INDEPENDENCE, AND INTERNATIONAL SECURITY BETWEEN 1931 AND 1952.

1930 MANSERGH N., WILSON R.R. ET AL.
COMMONWEALTH PERSPECTIVES.
DURHAM: DUKE U PR, 1958, 214 PP., LC#58-11381.
ESSAYS BY ECONOMISTS, HISTORIANS, AND POLITICAL SCIENTISTS ON STRUCTURE OF BRITISH COMMONWEALTH AND FORCES PULLING FOR UNITY AND SEPARATENESS. INCLUDES TOPICS OF MEMBERSHIP, FOREIGN POLICY FROM 1945-56, LAWS AFFECTING MEMBER NATIONS, DEMOGRAPHY AND ITS PULL TO UNITY AND DISUNITY, EMERGENCE OF GHANA, HEALTH AND WELFARE PROGRAMS IN AUSTRALIA, AND EVOLUTION OF STERLING AREA.

1931 MANSERGH N.
SURVEY OF BRITISH COMMONWEALTH AFFAIRS: PROBLEMS OF WARTIME CO-OPERATION AND POST-WAR CHANGE 1939-1952.
LONDON: OXFORD U PR, 1958, 469 PP.
ANALYZES IMPORTANT PROBLEMS OF COMMONWEALTH DURING THREE CRITICAL TIMES: NEED FOR UNITY DURING WWII; ADAPTABILITY OF ORGANIZATION TO NON-EUROPEAN MEMBERS AFTER WAR; PRESERVATION OF COHESION DURING CHANGE IN BALANCE OF POWER AND OTHER DOMESTIC AND EXTERNAL CHANGES IN MID-CENTURY.

1932 MANSERGH N. ED.
DOCUMENTS AND SPEECHES ON COMMONWEALTH AFFAIRS 1952-1962.
LONDON: OXFORD U PR, 1963, 775 PP.
LIST OF DOCUMENTS AND SPEECHES ON BRITISH COMMONWEALTH CONSTITUTIONAL STRUCTURE, INDEPENDENCE MOVEMENTS, FOREIGN AFFAIRS, DEFENSE, TRADE, MIDDLE EAST CRISIS, EUROPEAN COMMON MARKET, EDUCATION, AND MIGRATION BETWEEN 1952 AND 1962.

1933 MANSERGH N.
"THE PARTITION OF INDIA IN RETROSPECT."
INTERNATIONAL JOURNAL, 21 (WINTER 66), 1-19.
DISCUSSES PROBLEMS CREATED BY CREATION OF INDEPENDENT INDIA AND PAKISTAN, AND DIFFERENT INTERPRETATIONS GIVEN TO PARTITION: SUCCESSION OR SECESSION. INCLUDES HISTORICAL BACKGROUND.

1934 MANSFIELD P.
NASSER'S EGYPT.
BALTIMORE: PENGUIN BOOKS, 1965, 222 PP.
HISTORY OF EGYPT SINCE REVOLUTION OF 1952 EXAMINES PRESIDENT NASSER'S POLICIES, INCLUDING EGYPTIAN RELATIONS WITH ARAB WORLD, EAST AND WEST, AND AFRICA, AS WELL AS DOMESTIC POLICIES.

1935 MANTOUX E.
THE CARTHAGINIAN PEACE.
NEW YORK: SCRIBNER, 1952, 203 PP.
EVALUATES AND CRITICIZES KEYNES'S 'THE ECONOMIC CONSEQUENCES OF PEACE' IN LIGHT OF SUBSEQUENT EVENTS. SHOWS THAT HITLER, IN REARMING GERMANY BEFORE WAR, WAS ABLE TO PUT ASIDE SUMS GREATER THAN THOSE KEYNES HAD DEEMED POSSIBLE.

1936 MANZER R.A.
"THE UNITED NATIONS SPECIAL FUND."
INT. ORGAN., 18 (AUTUMN 64), 766-89.
HISTORICAL ACCOUNT OF THE UN SPECIAL FUND INCLUDING DISCUSSIONS OF ITS GOVERNING COUNCIL, THE FUND'S SECRETARIAT EXECUTIVE AGENCIES AND NATIONAL DIRECTORATES, CRITERIA AND PRIORITIES FOR FUND PROJECTS, THE IMPLEMENTATION AND EXECUTION OF PROJECTS, AND FINANCIAL POLICY.

1937 MARCUS W.
US PRIVATE INVESTMENT AND ECONOMIC AID IN UNDERDEVELOPED COUNTRIES (PAMPHLET)
WASHINGTON: PUBLIC AFFAIRS PRESS, 1959, 42 PP.

DISCUSSES PRESENT INVESTMENT AND FOREIGN AID PROGRAMS AND NEED FOR NEW ONES. SHOWS ROLES OF PRIVATE AND PUBLIC EFFORTS TO MOBILIZE CAPITAL, NEED FOR EDUCATED PUBLIC TO PUSH BETTER POLICY INTO ACTION. CONCLUSIONS ARE THAT PRIVATE INVESTMENT MUST BE INCREASED, AIDED BY LIBERAL GOVERNMENT LOAN POLICY, AND THAT PRIVATE AND PUBLIC ACTIONS SHOULD BE CONSOLIDATED UNDER REVOLUTIONARY PLAN.

1938 MARIAS J.
"A PROGRAM FOR EUROPE."
J. INT. AFF., 16 (NO.1, 62), 7-17.
EUROPE MUST UNITE THROUGH A PROCESS OF INCORPORATION. SEEKS TO DISCOVER WHY THE UNDERTAKING OF UNITY HAS NOT BEEN STRONG. SUGGESTS SYSTEM OF INTERNAL PROGRAMS, EACH DESIGNED FOR AN INDIVIDUAL COUNTRY, BUT ALL INTER-RELATED TO ACCOMPLISH THIS AIM.

1939 MARITAIN J.
HUMAN RIGHTS: COMMENTS AND INTERPRETATIONS.
NEW YORK: COLUMB. U. PR., 1949, 288 PP.
ESSAYS DEALING WITH THE GENERAL PROBLEMS OF HUMAN RIGHTS. ANALYZES IN DETAIL SUCH SUBJECTS AS: THE RESPECT OF CULTURAL DIVERSITY, THE SOCIAL IMPLICATION OF SCIENCE, THE VALUE OF OBJECTIVE INFORMATION, THE RIGHT TO EDUCATION, AND THE SPECIAL POSITION OF PRIMITIVE PEOPLES.

1940 MARITAIN J.
L'HOMME ET L'ETAT.
PARIS: PR UNIV DE FRANCE, 1953, 204 PP.
DISCUSSES CENTRAL CONCEPTS OF POLITICAL PHILOSOPHY, SUCH AS SOVEREIGNTY, MEANS OF CONTROL, NATURAL LAW AND HUMAN LAW, PROBLEM OF AUTHORITY, AND RELATION BETWEEN CHURCH AND STATE. CONCLUDES WITH PLEA FOR NECESSITY OF POLITICAL UNIFICATION OF MANKIND.

1941 MARITANO N., OBAID A.H.
AN ALLIANCE FOR PROGRESS.
MINNEAPOLIS: T S DENISON + CO, 1963, 205 PP., LC#63-21948.
DISCUSSES ALLIANCE FOR PROGRESS: HISTORICAL BACKGROUND, NUMBER AND NATURE OF OBSTACLES CONFRONTING IT, INCLUDING COLTURAL AND PSVCHOLOGICAL OBSTACLES, CONDITIONS FOR ECONOMIC GROWTH AND SOCIAL PROGRESS, DIRECTION OF FOREIGN AID, AND FUTURE PROSPECTS.

1942 MARK M.
"BEYOND SOVEREIGNTY."
WASHINGTON: PUBLIC AFFAIRS PRESS, 1965.
AN ESSAY ON THE "POST-NATION-STATE ERA" AND THE TRANSITION TO TRANSNATIONALISM, WARNING AGAINST A US NEO-ISOLATIONISM. BIBLIOGRAPHY OF ABOUT 150 ITEMS IN ENGLISH TO 1964, LIMITED TO WORKS ON VARIOUS ASPECTS OF CONTEMPORARY INTERNATIONAL POLITICS SUCH AS NATIONALISM, INTERNATIONAL ECONOMY, UNDERDEVELOPED NATIONS, POWER BLOCS, AND MILITARY MATTERS. ARRANGED BY SUBJECT AND AUTHOR.

1943 MARKHAM J.W. ET AL.
THE COMMON MARKET: FRIEND OR COMPETITOR.
NEW YORK: N.Y.U. PR., 1964, 123 PP., $3.00.
THREE ESSAYS ADDRESSED TO 1) WHY THE EEC HAS ENCOURAGED A SYSTEM OF PRIVATE ENTERPRISE THAT HAS NOT REQUIRED THE TRANSFER OF NATIONAL POLITICAL PREROGATIVES FROM MEMBER GOVERNMENTS, 2) THE ROLE OF DIRECT AMERICAN INVESTMENT IN EUROPE, AND 3) EFFECTS ON AMERICAN EXPORTS AND IMPORTS OF EEC TARIFFS.

1944 MARRARO H.R.
"AMERICAN OPINION ON THE UNIFICATION OF ITALY."
NEW YORK: COLUMBIA U PRESS, 1932.
AMONG BIBLIOGRAPHICAL ENTRIES ARE NEWSPAPERS, BOOKS DATING BACK TO 1850 (SEVERAL IN ITALIAN), MAGAZINE ARTICLES AND PAMPHLETS, AND GOVERNMENT DOCUMENTS.

1945 MARRIOTT J.A.
COMMONWEALTH OR ANARCHY: A SURVEY OF PROJECTS OF PEACE.
NEW YORK: COLUMB. U. PR., 1939, 223 PP.
SETS FORTH IMPORTANT PEACE PROJECTS OF 16TH TO 20TH CENTURIES AGAINST RESPECTIVE HISTORICAL BACKGROUNDS. FEELS WORLD SHOULD FOLLOW BRITISH EMPIRE AS MODEL FOR NEW TYPE OF INTERNATIONAL GOVERNMENT. LOOKS TO SYSTEM OF TRUSTEESHIPS.

1946 MARRIOTT J.A.
DICTATORSHIP AND DEMOCRACY.
LONDON: OXFORD U PR, 1935, 217 PP.
SUPPORTS PLURALISM IN WORLD GOVERNMENT, STATING THAT, ALTHOUGH POPULISM IS BEST FOR ENGLAND, PERHAPS THERE ARE COUNTRIES WHERE DICTATORSHIPS ARE BETTER. ATTEMPTS TO APOLOGIZE FOR CONCESSIONS BEING MADE TO HITLER AT THAT TIME, BY DISCUSSING PREVIOUS DICTATORSHIPS THROUGHOUT EUROPE'S HISTORY AND CLAIMING THAT WHATEVER SYSTEM MAINTAINS PEACE IS OF VALUE.

1947 MARTELLI G.
"PORTUGAL AND THE UNITED NATIONS."
INT. AFF., 40 (JULY 64), 453-65.
PORTUGAL'S DEFIANCE OF UN WITH RESPECT TO HER COLONIES RESULTS FROM BOTH SELF-INTEREST AND CONVICTION THAT MOTHER COUNTRY HAS MISSION IN AFRICA.

1948 MARTHELOT P.
"PROGRES DE LA REFORME AGRAIRE."
TIERS-MONDE, 4 (NOS.13-14, 63), 261-64.
CRITICIZES THIRD PUBLIC REPORT MADE BY UN COUNCIL OF ECONOMY AND SOCIOLOGY ON APRIL 5, 1962 ON SUBJECT OF AGRARIAN REFORM. EMPHASIZES ITS LACK OF CLARITY AND ITS TREATMENT OF THE QUESTION OF PRODUCTIVITY.

1949 MARTIN E.M.
"NEW TRENDS IN UNITED STATES ECONOMIC FOREIGN POLICY."
ANN. AMER. ACAD. POLIT. SOC. SCI., 330 (JULY 60).
POINTS OUT DIFFICULTY OF REACHING TOTAL ACCORD ON ANY FOREIGN POLICY DECISION DUE TO THE VAST ECONOMIC INTERESTS OF AMERICAN BUSINESS. IN SPITE OF THIS FACTOR, MANY DECISIONS ON FOREIGN AID, FOREIGN TRADE AND GENERAL FOREIGN POLICY ARE REACHED. DISCUSSES THE BACKGROUND OF SOME OF THESE DECISIONS.

1950 MARTIN J.J.
AMERICAN LIBERALISM AND WORLD POLITICS, 1931-41 (2 VOLS.)
NEW YORK: DEVIN ADAIR, 1964, 1337 PP., LC#62-13471.
STUDY OF LIBERAL OPINION, AND SHIFTS IN IT, BETWEEN 1931 AND 1941. SEEKS TO DETERMINE WHETHER EARLY PACIFISM AND FLEXIBILITY OR LATER RIGIDITY TOWARD OTHER SYSTEMS WAS GREATER ERROR. ACCUSES LIBERALS OF IRRATIONALITY AND OF ENABLING COMMUNISTS TO UNDERMINE THEM SUCCESSFULLY.

1951 MARTIN L.J.
INTERNATIONAL PROPAGANDA: ITS LEGAL AND DIPLOMATIC CONTROL.
MINNEAPOLIS: U OF MINN PR, 1958, 284 PP., LC#58-7928.
DISCUSSES OPERATION OF PROPAGANDA AGENCIES IN VARIOUS COUNTRIES AND ATTEMPTS MADE TO CONTROL DISSEMINATION OF PROPAGANDA THROUGH MUNICIPAL LAW AND INTERNATIONAL AGREEMENTS. INCLUDES A BRIEF HISTORICAL INTRODUCTION. CONCLUDES THAT "INTERNATIONAL PROPAGANDA HAS LITTLE CHANCE OF BEING CONTROLLED AT THE INTERNATIONAL LEVEL."

1952 MARTIN L.W. ED.
NEUTRALISM AND NONALIGNMENT.
NEW YORK: FREDERICK PRAEGER, 1962, 249 PP., LC#62-18584.
COLLECTION OF PAPERS ON POSTWAR POLITICS OF NONALIGNMENT OF NEW STATES AND RELATION TO US FOREIGN POLICY. EXAMINES ATTITUDE OF DEVELOPING NATIONS TO MAJOR POWERS AND INTERNATIONAL RELATIONS IN UN.

1953 MARTIN L.W.
DIPLOMACY IN MODERN EUROPEAN HISTORY.
NEW YORK: MACMILLAN, 1966, 138 PP., LC#66-17387.
ESSAYS DISCUSSING CENTRAL IMPORTANCE OF DIPLOMACY IN WESTERN EUROPEAN POLITICAL RELATIONS FROM TIME OF ITS ORIGIN IN 15TH-CENTURY ITALY TO ITS MODIFICATIONS AND REFINEMENTS IN COLD WAR ERA. TOPICS ARE BROAD IN SCOPE AND ORIENTATION IS SCHOLARLY AND TECHNICAL. EMPHASIS IS ON SOCIAL, HISTORICAL, AND POLITICAL FACTORS.

1954 MAS LATRIE L.
RELATIONS ET COMMERCE DE L'AFRIQUE SEPTENTRIONALE OU MAGREB AVEC LES NATIONS CHRETIENNES AU MOYEN AGE.
PARIS: LIBRAIRIE FIRMIN DIDOT ET CIE, 1886, 550 PP
SURVEY OF NORTH AFRICA OR THE MAGREB DURING THE MIDDLE AGES, EMPHASIZING CONFLICTING CHRISTIAN AND ARAB CIVILIZATION, FOREIGN INVASION, AND COMMERCE. EXAMINES CUSTOMS, DYNASTIES, AND PIRACY.

1955 MASON E.S.
THE DIPLOMACY OF ECONOMIC ASSISTANCE (PAMPHLET)
MIDDLEBURY: MIDDLEBURY COLLEGE, 1966, 26 PP.
EXAMINES EXTENT TO WHICH IT IS DESIRABLE FOR US TO ATTACH CONDITIONS TO FOREIGN AID, PARTICULARLY IN RELATION TO SOUTHERN ASIA (INDIA, PAKISTAN). CONCLUDES THAT "POLITICAL STRINGS" ARE LIKELY TO BE INEFFECTIVE BUT THAT ECONOMIC CONDITIONS ARE OFTEN WARRANTED AS EXPRESSION OF INTIMATE INVOLVEMENT IN ECONOMIC DEVELOPMENT OF AID-RECEIVING COUNTRIES.

1956 MASON E.S.
FOREIGN AID AND FOREIGN POLICY.
NEW YORK: HARPER, 1964, 118 PP.
AID FROM LARGE COUNTRIES IS PREDOMINANTLY BILATERAL. GEOGRAPHICAL DISTRIBUTION OF AID SUGGESTS PRIMARY INTEREST IN MUTUAL SECURITY. 'AS AN INSTRUMENT OF FOREIGN POLICY... AID IS A USELESS TOOL UNLESS IT CAN BE ASSUMED THAT THERE IS A STRONG OCMMUNITY OF INTEREST BETWEEN AID-GIVING AND AID-RECEIVING COUNTRIES.'

1957 MASON H.L.
TOYNBEE'S APPROACH TO WORLD POLITICS.
NEW ORLEANS: TULANE U PR, 1958, 151 PP.
EXPLICATES TOYNBEE'S THEORY OF HISTORY AND ANALYZES PROPOSALS HE MAKES FOR CONSIDERING PRESENT WORLD RELATIONS. EMPHASIZES HIS RELIGIOUS SOLUTION FOR WORLD PROBLEMS.

1958 MASON J.B. ED., PARISH H.C. ED.
THAILAND BIBLIOGRAPHY.

GAINESVILLE: U OF FLORIDA LIB, 1958, 245 PP.
CONTAINS MORE THAN 2,300 ENTRIES, MANY ANNOTATED, TO BOOKS, ARTICLES, AND DOCUMENTS IN NINE WESTERN LANGUAGES. WORKS ON HISTORY, GOVERNMENT, INTERNATIONAL RELATIONS, PUBLIC ADMINISTRATION, ECONOMICS, ARCHEOLOGY, GEOGRAPHY, SOCIOLOGY, EDUCATION, ART, LANGUAGE STUDY, AND THE NATURAL SCIENCES. HAS A LIST OF BIBLIOGRAPHIES.

1959 MASSEY V.
CANADIANS AND THEIR COMMONWEALTH: THE ROMANES LECTURE DELIVERED IN THE SHELDONIAN THEATRE JUNE 1, 1961 (PAMPHLET)
LONDON: OXFORD U PR, 1961, 20 PP.
ADDRESS TO AN ENGLISH AUDIENCE ASKING THAT CANADA BE JUDGED BY WHAT SHE DOES WITH HER VAST RESOURCES. DISCUSSES CANADA'S PLURALISM, HER ROLE AS INTERPRETER BETWEEN US AND GREAT BRITAIN, AND ATTITUDE TOWARD COMMONWEALTH TODAY. BRIEFLY SURVEYS PROBLEMS OF COMMONWEALTH WITH WHICH CANADIANS ARE CONCERNED.

1960 MASTERS D. ED.
"ONE WORLD OR NONE."
NEW YORK: MCGRAW HILL, 1946, 79 PP., $1.00.
REPORT TO PUBLIC ON FULL MEANING OF ATOMIC BOMB. ANALYSIS OF BASIC PROBLEMS INVOLVED VIA ARTICLES BY LEADERS IN ATOMIC ENGINEERING. STRESSES APPROACHES TO AVERTING INEVITABLE HORROR IMPLIED IN ATOMIC DISASTER.

1961 MASTERS R.D.
INTERNATIONAL LAW IN INTERNATIONAL COURTS.
NEW YORK: COLUMBIA U. PR., 1932, 245 PP.
'DEALS WITH THE ENFORCEMENT OF PARTICULAR AND UNIVERSAL, CUSTOMARY AND CONVENTIONAL INTERNATIONAL LAW IN THE COURTS OF GERMANY, SWITZERLAND, FRANCE, AND BELGIUM.'

1962 MASTERS R.D.
"RUSSIA AND THE UNITED NATIONS."
YALE REV., 52 (WINTER 63), 176-87.
CONTENDS THAT THE GENERAL ASSEMBLY AND THE SECRETARIAT HAVE TOO MUCH POWER WHICH COULD BE USED AGAINST THE USA. RECOMMENDS ADOPTION OF SOVIET TROIKA PLAN OR SIMULTANEOUS ABANDONMENT OF TROIKA PROPOSAL BY USSR AND OF THE UNITING FOR PEACE RESOLUTION BY USA.

1963 MASTERS R.D.
"A MULTI-BLOC MODEL OF THE INTERNATIONAL SYSTEM."
AMER. POLIT. SCI. REV., 55 (DEC. 61), 780-98.
RECOMMENDS ANALYSIS OF WORLD ORDER IN TERMS OF A SYSTEM OF COMPETING BLOCS, EACH LIMITING BUT NOT DESTROYING THE OTHERS, WITH FREEDOM OF MOVEMENT IN AND OUT OF THEM. SUGGESTS THIS IS PREFERABLE TO AN OVER-CONTAINMENT POLICY OR 'GO IT ALONE.'

1964 MATECKI B.
ESTABLISHMENT OF THE INTERNATIONAL FINANCE CORPORATION AND UNITED STATES POLICY.
NEW YORK: PRAEGER, 1957, 194 PP., $5.00.
DISCUSSES INFLUENCE OF INTERNATIONAL ORGANIZATIONS ON NATIONAL POLICY. EXAMINES RELATIONSHIP OF INTERNATIONAL INSTITUTIONS TO USA FOREIGN ECONOMIC POLICY THROUGH STUDY OF INTERNATIONAL FINANCE CORPORATION. FINDS THAT INTERNATIONAL INSTITUTIONS PROVIDE NEW IDEAS FOR AND HAVE DIRECT INFLUENCE ON NATIONAL POLICY.

1965 MATHISEN T.
METHODOLOGY IN THE STUDY OF INTERNATIONAL RELATIONS.
NEW YORK: MACMILLAN, 1959, 265 PP.
STRESSES THE NEED FOR THE CONCEPT OF A WORLD SOCIETY. BY UNDERSTANDING THIS PERCEPTUAL FRAMEWORK, SUBGROUPS CAN BE STUDIED BY THEIR INTERACTION SYSTEMS AND TRENDS AND CHANGES CAN BE MORE EASILY EXAMINED. PRESENTS AND ANALYZES PREVIOUS STUDIES AND INDICATES SOME OF THE PROBLEMS.

1966 MATHUR P.N.
"GAINS IN ECONOMIC GROWTH FROM INTERNATIONAL TRADE."
KYKLOS, 16 (FALL 63), 609-23.
INTERNATIONAL TRADE OPERATES TO CHANGE STRUCTURE OF PRODUCTION WITHIN A COUNTRY. EFFECTS A REDUCTION IN AVERAGE CAPITAL OUT-PUT RATIO BY IMPORTATION OF HIGH-COST MATERIALS AND GOODS.

1967 MATLOFF M., SNELL E.M.
STRATEGIC PLANNING FOR COALITION WARFARE.
WASHINGTON: DEPT OF THE ARMY, 1953, 430 PP.
STUDIES EVOLUTION OF AMERICAN STRATEGY BEFORE AND DURING FIRST YEAR OF PARTICIPATION IN WWII, EMPHASIZING PROBLEMS OF COORDINATION OF EFFORTS BETWEEN ARMED FORCES, AND BRITISH AND AMERICAN STRATEGIES.

1968 MATTHEWS D.G. ED.
A CURRENT VIEW OF AFRICANA (PAMPHLET)
WASHINGTON: AFRICAN BIBLIOG CTR, 1964, 32 PP.
SELECTED AND ANNOTATED BIBLIOGRAPHY ON AFRICAN AFFAIRS.

1969 MATTHEWS D.G.
"A CURRENT BIBLIOGRAPHY ON ETHIOPIAN AFFAIRS: A SELECT BIBLIOGRAPHY FROM 1950-1964."
AFR. BIBLIOG. CTR., SPEC. SERIES, 3 (MAR. 65), 1-46.
A PARTIALLY ANNOTATED BIBLIOGRAPHY OF 594 BOOKS, ARTICLES, AND OFFICIAL DOCUMENTS PUBLISHED BETWEEN 1950-64 ON ETHOPIA. EMPHASIS PLACED ON ENGLISH-LANGUAGE PUBLICATIONS, BUT SOME SOURCES IN FRENCH, RUSSIAN, ITALIAN, AND GERMAN. BRIEF DESCRIPTIVE ANNOTATIONS SUPPLIED WHEN TITLE INSUFFICIENTLY CLEAR TO EXPLAIN CONTENTS OF A GIVEN PUBLICATION. A SYSTEMATIC GUIDE FOR RESEARCH OR GENERAL USE.

1970 MATTHEWS D.G. ED.
"A CURRENT BIBLIOGRAPHY ON SUDANESE AFFAIRS; A SELECT BIBLIOGRAPHY FROM 1960-1964."
AFR. BIBLIOG. CTR., SPEC. SERIES, 3 (JULY 65), 1-28.
COMPREHENSIVE LISTING OF 378 UNANNOTATED BOOKS, OFFICIAL DOCUMENTS, AND PERIODICAL ENTRIES, WHICH COVER SUBJECTS OF GOVERNMENT AND RELIGION. EMPHASIS ON ENGLISH-LANGUAGE PUBLICATIONS ISSUED BETWEEN 1960-65. RUSSIAN ENTRIES TRANSLITERATED; GERMAN, FRENCH, AND ITALIAN SOURCES INCLUDED.

1971 MATTHEWS D.G. ED.
"LE TIERS MONDE: A SELECT AND PRELIMINARY BIBLIOGRAPHIC SURVEY OF MANPOWER IN DEVELOPING COUNTRIES, 1960-1964."
AFR. BIBLIOG. CTR., SPEC. SERIES, 3 (JULY 65), 1-30.
A PARTIALLY ANNOTATED BIBLIOGRAPHY DESIGNED TO PRESENT A LISTING OF 306 MATERIALS CONCERNING MANPOWER, PUBLISHED FROM 1960-64 WITH A FEW ENTRIES FROM EARLY 1965. BULK OF MATERIAL DEVOTED TO AFRICA, ALTHOUGH ENTRIES FOR OTHER GEOGRAPHIC AREAS ARE INCLUDED. AUTHOR INDEX APPENDED.

1972 MATTHEWS D.G. ED.
"ETHIOPIAN OUTLINE: A BIBLIOGRAPHIC RESEARCH GUIDE."
AFR. BIBLIOG. CTR., SPEC. SERIES, 4 (FEB. 66), 1-17.
SUPPLEMENT TO "A CURRENT BIBLIOGRAPHY ON ETHIOPIAN AFFAIRS." PREPARED FOR INTERNATIONAL CONFERENCE OF ETHIOPIAN STUDIES HELD APRIL 2-8, 1966. CONTAINS CHRONOLOGICAL AND RESEARCH DATA LISTING NEW ETHIOPIAN CABINET AS OF APRIL 11, 1966. SUBJECT BIBLIOGRAPHY OF 93 UNANNOTATED ENTRIES PUBLISHED BETWEEN 1960-65; AUTHOR INDEX.

1973 MATTHEWS M.A.
THE AMERICAN INSTITUTE OF INTERNATIONAL LAW AND THE CODIFICATION OF INTERNATIONAL LAW (PAMPHLET)
NEW YORK: CARNEGIE ENDOWMENT, 1933, 17 PP.
LIST OF OFFICIAL PUBLICATIONS OF THIS PAN AMERICAN ORGANIZATION FROM 1913-32 FOLLOWED BY UNOFFICIAL REPORTS AND ARTICLES FROM SAME PERIOD. ENTRIES IN ALL HEMISPHERIC LANGUAGES WITH SOME EUROPEAN COMMENTS ON INTERNATIONAL LAW IN AMERICAS. ARRANGED BY AUTHOR. LIST OF UNOFFICIAL PUBLICATIONS IS ANNOTATED.

1974 MATTHEWS M.A.
DIPLOMACY: SELECT LIST ON DIPLOMACY, DIPLOMATIC AND CONSULAR PRACTICE, AND FOREIGN OFFICE ORGANIZATION (PAMPHLET)
NEW YORK: CARNEGIE ENDOWMENT, 1936, 7 PP.
OVER 70 TITLES PUBLISHED OVER BROAD TIME SPAN, ARRANGED BY AUTHOR. MOSTLY BOOKS, WITH FEW GOVERNMENT DOCUMENTS.

1975 MATTHEWS M.A.
INTERNATIONAL LAW: SELECT LIST OF WORKS IN ENGLISH ON PUBLIC INTERNATIONAL LAW: WITH COLLECTIONS OF CASES AND OPINIONS.
NEW YORK: CARNEGIE ENDOWMENT, 1936, 21 PP.
INCLUDES BOOKS AND TREATISES PRIMARILY. SEPARATED INTO GENERAL WORKS (NUMBERING 200) AND 21 TITLES AT END DEALING WITH CASES AND OPINIONS. ARRANGED BY AUTHOR; BRIEF ANNOTATIONS. PUBLICATIONS COVER BROAD TIME SPAN, MOSTLY 20TH CENTURY. (PAMPHLET)

1976 MATTHEWS M.A.
FEDERALISM: SELECT LIST OF REFERENCES ON FEDERAL GOVERNMENT REGIONALISM...EXAMPLES OF FEDERATIONS (PAMPHLET)
NEW YORK: CARNEGIE ENDOWMENT, 1938, 11 PP.
BRIEF LIST OF BOOKS WITH FEW PAMPHLETS AND GOVERNMENT DOCUMENTS, INCLUDING SOME FOREIGN LANGUAGE SOURCES. THREE PAGES OF GENERAL WORKS, SEVEN ON SPECIFIC FEDERATIONS, ONE PAGE RELATING TO LEAGUE OF NATIONS, ETC. PUBLISHED IN 19TH AND 20TH CENTURIES.

1977 MATTHEWS M.A.
INTERNATIONAL POLICE (PAMPHLET)
WASHINGTON: CARNEGIE ENDOWMENT, 1944, 18 PP.
UNANNOTATED BIBLIOGRAPHY OF PROPOSALS FOR COOPERATIVE DEFENSE THROUGH THE USE OF INTERNATIONAL ARMIES, NAVIES, AND AIR FORCES. SOURCES ARE INTERNATIONAL IN SCOPE AND DATE FROM 1930.

1978 MATTHEWS T.
WAR IN ALGERIA.
NEW YORK: FORDHAM U PR, 1961, 147 PP., LC#62-10305.
DISCUSSES REASONS FOR OUTBREAK OF REVOLUTION IN ALGERIA AND MAJOR POLITICAL AND MILITARY EVENTS MARKING EIGHT YEARS OF REVOLUTION. STRESSES IMPORTANCE OF GRANTING ALGERIAN INDEPENDENCE IN ORDER TO END WAR AND NECESSITY OF FRENCH AND ALGERIAN COOPERATION TO SUSTAIN INDEPENDENCE.

1979 MAUD J.
AID FOR DEVELOPING COUNTRIES.

LONDON: U OF LONDON PRESS, 1964, 23 PP.
DISCUSSES IMPORTANCE OF FOREIGN AID TO POLITICAL SECURITY AND OBLIGATION OF DEVELOPED NATIONS TO UNDEVELOPED. GIVES ANALYSIS OF BRITAIN'S SPENDING COMPARED TO REST OF FREE WORLD AND COMMUNIST BLOC.

1980 MAW B.
BREAKTHROUGH IN BURMA: MEMOIRS OF A REVOLUTION, 1939-1946.
NEW HAVEN: YALE U PR, 1967, 512 PP., LC#67-24504.
MEMOIRS OF LEADER IN STRUGGLE FOR BURMESE INDEPENDENCE. TRACES RISE OF BURMESE NATIONALISM, DESCRIBING EVENTS AND MEN OF THOSE YEARS: EMPORER OF JAPAN; PREMIER TOJO; GENERAL IIDA, CONQUEROR OF BURMA; AND OTHER SOUTHEAST ASIAN LEADERS. REVEALS BURMESE FRUSTRATIONS UNDER COLONIALISM, AND THEIR DESPERATE ACCEPTANCE OF ASSISTANCE FROM ANY ALLY. AUTHOR IS INFLUENTIAL CRITIC OF PRESENT MILITARY REGIME.

1981 MAXWELL B.W.
INTERNATIONAL RELATIONS.
NEW YORK: CROWELL, 1939, 663 PP.
A GENERAL DISCUSSION ON THE PROBLEMS AND PROSPECTS OF INTERNATIONAL RELATIONS. ATTEMPTS TO RECORD THE MOST IMPORTANT DEVELOPMENTS IN INTERNATIONAL AFFAIRS SINCE THE FIRST WORLD WAR. A HISTORICAL AS WELL AS AN ANALYTICAL STUDY OF THE VARIOUS INTERNATIONAL AND NATIONAL EVENTS THAT HAVE MOLDED THE PRESENT STRUCTURE OF INTERNATIONAL RELATIONS.

1982 MAY E.R. ED.
ANXIETY AND AFFLUENCE: 1945-1965.
BUENOS AIRES: LIBERIA PANAMER, 1966, 404 PP., LC#66-14810.
DISCUSSES ATTEMPTS FROM 1946-65 TO DEAL WITH ASPECTS OF LIVING IN AFFLUENT SOCIETY UNDER CONSTANT THREAT OF NUCLEAR WAR. INCLUDES BARUCH PLAN, MARSHALL PLAN, NATO, AND CAMP DAVID MEETINGS. CRISES STUDIED ARE BERLIN BLOCKADE, CHINA, KOREA, CUBA, RED SCARE, MC CARTHYISM, AND CIVIL RIGHTS.

1983 MAYER A.J.
POLITICAL ORIGINS OF THE NEW DIPLOMACY, 1917-1918.
NEW HAVEN: YALE U PR, 1959, 393 PP., LC#59-6799.
SEEKS TO EXPLICATE POLITICAL DYNAMICS OF EMERGENCE OF NEW DIPLOMACY. EXAMINES POLITICS OF WAR AIMS IN WWI. ANALYZES INTERACTION BETWEEN DOMESTIC AND INTERNATIONAL POLITICS.

1984 MAYER P. ED.
THE PACIFIST CONSCIENCE.
CHICAGO: HENRY REGNERY CO, 1966, 478 PP., LC#65-15053.
ANTHOLOGY DOCUMENTS VARIOUS ASPECTS OF PACIFISM, INTERNATIONAL RELATIONS, CONSCIENTIOUS OBJECTION, RACE RELATIONS, AND CHRISTIAN ETHICS. AMONG THOSE WHOSE WRITINGS ARE REPRESENTED ARE THE EARLY PHILOSOPHERS, LAO-TZU, AND ERASMUS; THE QUAKERS AND CONSCIENTIOUS OBJECTORS; THOREAU; AND TWENTIETH-CENTURY FIGURES SUCH AS FREUD AND MARTIN LUTHER KING.

1985 MAYNE R.
THE COMMUNITY OF EUROPE.
LONDON: GOLLANCZ, 1963, 192 PP.
BRIEF HISTORY OF EVOLVING ENTITY OF THE EUROPEAN COMMUNITY, INCLUDING POLITICAL AND ECONOMIC BACKGROUND, POST-WAR DEBATES, BRITISH 'DILEMMA,' AND EUROPE'S RELATION TO REST OF WORLD. ALSO DISCUSSES VARIOUS EUROPEAN REGIONAL ORGANIZATIONS.

1986 MAZRUI A.A.
"ON THE CONCEPT 'WE ARE ALL AFRICANS'."
AMER. POLIT. SCI. REV., 57 (MARCH 63), 88-97.
A THOROUGH REVIEW OF THE VARIOUS ASPECTS OF AFRICAN SELF-CONSCIOUSNESS. A CLEAR DISTINCTION IS MADE BETWEEN NARROWER TERRITORIAL OR TRIBAL NATIONALISMS AND THE WIDE CONTINENTALISTIC BRAND.

1987 MAZRUI A.A.
"THE UNITED NATIONS AND SOME AFRICAN POLITICAL ATTITUDES."
INT. ORGAN., 18 (SUMMER 64), 499-520.
FOLLOWING AN ANALYSIS OF AFRICAN CONCEPTION OF SOVEREIGNTY, OUTLINES ALTERNATIVE ROLES OF UNITED NATIONS IN AN AFRICA THAT IS PRESENTLY DIVIDED.

1988 MAZRUI A.A.
TOWARDS A PAX AFRICANA.
CHICAGO: U OF CHICAGO PRESS, 1967, 287 PP., LC#67-12232.
DISCUSSION OF PEACE-KEEPING IN AFRICA. SECTIONS ON IDEOLOGY, IDENTITY, FREEDOM FROM COLONIALISM, PAN-AFRICANISM, NEUTRALISM. CONCERN IS WITH ALL POLITICAL IDEAS BEING EXPRESSED IN MODERN AFRICA. SPECIFIC REFERENCES TO VARIOUS DISTURBANCES AND THEIR CAUSES.

1989 MBOYA T.
FREEDOM AND AFTER.
BOSTON: LITTLE BROWN, 1963, 288 PP., LC#63-20102.
AFRICAN LEADER EXPLAINS OWN SITUATION IN DEVELOPING AFRICA, AND PROBLEMS FACING NEW NATIONS. DISCUSSES NATIONALISM, PAN-AFRICANISM, SOCIALISM, COLONIAL INFLUENCE, AND USE OF VIOLENCE IN ACHIEVING DESIRED GOALS.

1990 MC CLELLAN G.S. ED.
INDIA.
NEW YORK: H W WILSON, 1960, 164 PP., LC#60-8238.
ESSAYS ON SOCIO-ECONOMIC AND POLITICAL PROBLEMS, DISCUSSING NEUTRALITY, TIBET, KASHMIR, AND RELATIONS WITH THE US. GANDHI AND NEHRU ARE ALSO CONSIDERED.

1991 MCCLELLAND C.A.
THEORY AND THE INTERNATIONAL SYSTEM.
NEW YORK: MACMILLAN, 1966, 138 PP.
DISCUSSES RELATIONSHIP BETWEEN THEORY AND INTERNATIONAL RELATIONS. FOCUSES ON INTERNATIONAL SYSTEM, SYSTEM ANALYSIS, AND INTERNATIONAL COMMUNICATIONS AND COMMUNICATIONS THEORY.

1992 MC DOWELL R.B.
IRISH PUBLIC OPINION, 1750-1800.
LONDON: FABER AND FABER, 1943, 306 PP.
STUDY OF ATTITUDES CONCERNING SOCIO-POLITICAL PROBLEMS EMPHASIZING REFORM, RADICALISM AND THE UNION. DISCUSSION INCLUDES THE HOUSE OF COMMONS, CONTROVERSIALISTS, THE TITHE DISPUTE, REGENCY CRISIS, AND VOLUNTEERS.

1993 MC GOVERN G.S.
WAR AGAINST WANT.
NEW YORK: WALKER, 1964, 148 PP., LC#64-23992.
STUDY OF DEVELOPMENT OF OFFICE OF FOOD FOR PEACE UNDER KENNEDY ADMINISTRATION AND ITS PRESENT STATUS AND IMPORTANCE IN US FOREIGN AID POLICY.

1994 MC LELLAN D.S.
THE COLD WAR IN TRANSITION.
NEW YORK: MACMILLAN, 1966, 149 PP., LC#66-15371.
CHRONOLOGICAL VIEW OF COLD WAR AND US AND SOVIET ACTION. DISCUSSES BI-POLAR FORMATION OF POSTWAR WORLD. EXAMINES ALLIANCES AND MILITARY IMPORTANCE OF POLICY-MAKING AND EVOLUTION OF "THIRD WORLD" BESIDES US AND USSR.

1995 MCBRIDE J.H.
THE TEST BAN TREATY: MILITARY, TECHNOLOGICAL, AND POLITICAL IMPLICATIONS.
WASHINGTON: US GOVERNMENT, 1967, 197 PP., LC#67-14660.
TRACES BACKGROUND OF TREATY, INCLUDING RELATIVE LEVELS OF NUCLEAR DEVELOPMENT IN US AND USSR. NOTES OPPOSITE CONCLUSIONS REACHED BY TWO SENATE COMMITTEES INVESTIGATING TREATY INDEPENDENTLY. ANALYZES MILITARY AND TECHNOLOGICAL ADVANTAGES AND DISADVANTAGES FOR US. DISCUSSES TESTING AND SAFEGUARDS DEMANDED BY JOINT CHIEFS. ANALYZES POLITICAL ADVANTAGES CLAIMED, NOTING ONLY ONE AS PERSUASIVE.

1996 MCCAMY J.
THE ADMINISTRATION OF AMERICAN FOREIGN AFFAIRS.
NEW YORK: KNOPF, 1950, 364 PP.
DEALS WITH FOREIGN POLICIES IN TERMS OF ORGANIZATION OF GOVERNMENT. CONSIDERS THE OBJECTS OF ADMINISTRATION, THEIR COSTS AND EFFECTS IN POLITICAL ECONOMY. INCLUDES STUDIES OF THE DEPARTMENT OF STATE, PRESSURE GROUPS AND CONGRESS.

1997 MCCLELLAND C.A.
"THE FUNCTION OF THEORY IN INTERNATIONAL RELATIONS."
J. CONFL. RESOLUT., 4 (JULY 60), 303-36.
ASSERTS THEORY SHOULD BE A MEANS TOWARDS DEMONSTRABLE KNOWLEDGE OF THE REGULARITIES IN INTERNATIONAL RELATIONS. SHOULD HAVE WITHIN IT, A MEANS OF DECIPHERING THE SPECIAL FIELD OF INTERNATIONAL RELATIONS FROM THE MILIEU OF THE TOTAL SOCIAL REALITY.

1998 MCCLELLAND C.A. ED.
NUCLEAR WEAPONS, MISSILES, AND FUTURE WAR: PROBLEM FOR THE SIXTIES.
SAN FRANCISCO: CHANDLER, 1960, 235 PP., LC#60-8430.
EXAMINES PROBLEMS RELATING TO NUCLEAR WEAPONS AND THE THREAT OF WAR. STUDIES ARE ORGANIZED AROUND THEMES OF DEFINING THE INTERNATIONAL SITUATION; IMPLICATIONS, HOPES, AND FEARS; PROPOSALS AND DESCRIPTIONS.

1999 MCCLINTOCK R.
THE MEANING OF LIMITED WAR.
BOSTON: HOUGHTON MIFFLIN, 1967, 239 PP., LC#67-10558.
EMPHASIS OF STUDY IS ON OBJECTIVES OF 20TH-CENTURY LIMITED WARFARE. STUDIES MANNER IN WHICH CONFLICTS OF THE PAST 2 DECADES HAVE BEEN SETTLED. SPECIFIC WARS STUDIED INCLUDE GREEK CIVIL WAR, KOREAN WAR, ARAB-ISERAELI WARS OF 1946-49 AND 1956, "WARS OF NATIONAL LIBERATION" IN VIETNAM, AND CHINESE ATTACK ON HIMALAYAN FRONTIERS OF INDIA. INCLUDES EXAMINATION OF US DEFENSE POLICY.

2000 MCCLURE W.
INTERNATIONAL EXECUTIVE AGREEMENTS.
NEW YORK: COLUMB. U. PR., 1941, 449 PP.
DEMONSTRATES INCREASED UTILIZATION OF DEMOCRATIC METHOD. COMPREHENSIVE REVIEW OF EXECUTIVE AGREEMENTS SHOWS EXTENSIVE USE OF METHOD.

2001 MCCOLL G.D.
THE AUSTRALIAN BALANCE OF PAYMENTS.
MELBOURNE: MELBOURNE UNIV PRESS, 1965, 180 PP., LC#65-21859.
DISCUSSES HOME AND INTERNATIONAL ASPECTS OF AUSTRALIAN

BALANCE OF PAYMENTS. TREATS IMPORTS AND EXPORTS OF GOODS AND SERVICES, CAPITAL FLOW AND SERVICING COSTS, DIRECTION OF TRADE AND PAYMENTS, EXTERNAL IMBALANCE, AND OFFICIAL POLICY.

2002 MCCORD W.
"ARMIES AND POLITICS; A PROBLEM IN THE THIRD WORLD."
DISSENT, 14 (JULY-AUG. 67), 440-452.
EXAMINES MILITARY GOVERNMENTS IN COUNTRIES OF AFRICA AND NEAR EAST. DISCUSSES POSSIBILITIES OF LIBERAL OR SOCIAL DEMOCRACY AND OF ECONOMIC DEVELOPMENT AND SOCIAL REFORM UNDER MILITARY RULE. CONCLUDES THAT MILITARY RULE SELDOM AIDS GROWTH OF DEMOCRACY AND PARALYZES ECONOMY. QUESTIONS AMERICAN MILITARY ASSISTANCE AND FOREIGN AID POLICY.

2003 MCCREARY E.A.
"THOSE AMERICAN MANAGERS DON'T IMPRESS EUROPE."
FORTUNE, 6 (DEC. 64).
CONDENSATION OF BOOK, 'THE AMERICANIZATION OF EUROPE', REVEALING THE ATTITUDES OF EUROPEAN MANAGERS TOWARD INFLUX OF AMERICAN PERSONNEL WHO DIRECT OVERSEAS OPERATIONS OF U.S. COMPANIES. THEY FEEL THAT TOP MEN STAY HOME AND SEND LESS CAPABLE MEN ABROAD. STATES DIFFERENCES IN STAFF-ORGANIZATION AND MARKETING TECHNIQUES.

2004 MCDOUGAL M.S., LIPSON L.
"PERSPECTIVES FOR A LAW OF OUTER SPACE."
AMER. J. INT. LAW, 2 (JULY, 58), 407-31.
DUE TO INTERDEPENDENCE OF SCIENTIFIC, MILITARY, AND COMMERCIAL OBJECTIVES, AND ACTIVITIES IN OUTER SPACE AN INTERNATIONAL CONVENTION FOR OUTER SPACE LAW IS NOT NOW POSSIBLE. FORECAST LAUNCHING OF SATELLITES FOR AND REGISTRATION BY U.N. AND UNILATERAL DISARMAMENT AS FIRST STEPS IN FUTURE CODE OF LAWS.

2005 MCDOUGAL M.S., LASSWELL H.D.
"THE IDENTIFICATION AND APPRAISAL OF DIVERSE SYSTEMS OF PUBLIC ORDER (BMR)"
AMER. J. OF INT. LAW, 53 (1959), 1-29.
DISCUSSES ROLE OF SCHOLAR IN RESEARCHING SYSTEMS OF GOVERNMENT AND MODERNIZING INTERNATIONAL LAW TO MAKE IT EFFECTIVE IN TODAY'S POLITICAL SITUATION. EXAMINES PROBLEMS OF RECONCILING DIFFERENT IDEOLOGIES TO PEACEFUL COEXISTENCE.

2006 MCDOUGAL M.S., FELICIANO F.P.
LAW AND MINIMUM WORLD PUBLIC ORDER.
NEW HAVEN: YALE U. PR., 1961, 872 PP.
STUDYING JURIDICAL PROCEDURES IN INTERNATIONAL RELATIONS, OUTLINES EXISTANT METHODS OF COERCION AND FUTURE TRENDS IN FIELD OF INTERNATIONAL CONTROL. PROCEEDS TO STUDY PROBLEM AS RELATED TO INTERPRETATION OF LAW, STATE PARTICIPATION, SANCTIONS, OPEN WARFARE (LOCAL LEVEL), AND ACTUAL MILITARY OCCUPATION.

2007 MCDOUGAL M.S., BURKE W.T.
THE PUBLIC ORDER OF THE OCEANS.
NEW HAVEN: YALE U. PR., 1962, 1226 PP.
CLARIFICATION OF 'COMMON INTEREST' IN CONTINUED MAINTENANCE OF AN INTERNATIONAL LAW OF THE SEA WHICH REJECTS ALL CLAIMS OF SPECIAL INTEREST AND UPHOLDS EVERY DECISION IN FAVOR OF INCLUSIVE RATHER THAN EXCLUSIVE INTERESTS. SURVEYS THE ARBITRAMENT PROCESSES BY WHICH GENERAL WORLD COMMUNITY ALLOCATES ACCESS TO, AND AUTHORITY OVER, THE OCEANS DURING TIMES OF RELATIVE PEACE.

2008 MCDOUGAL M.S.
"THE SOVIET-CUBAN QUARANTINE AND SELF-DEFENSE."
AMER. J. INT. LAW, 57 (JULY 63), 597-604.
ALTHOUGH USSR DID NOT EXECUTE ARMED ATTACK AGAINST USA, THE MEANS IT APPLIED INDICATED THE DANGER THAT COULD EMANATE FROM CUBAN TERRITORY. ARTICLE 51 OF THE U.N. CHARTER JUSTIFIES AMERICAN 'QUARANTINE' OF 1962.

2009 MCDOUGAL M.S., LASSWELL H.D., VLASIC I.A.
LAW AND PUBLIC ORDER IN SPACE.
NEW HAVEN: YALE U PR, 1963, 1147 PP., LC#63-13968.
ANALYSIS OF PRESENT STATUS AND LAW, AND NATIONAL POLICY RELATED TO OUTER SPACE. EXAMINES MAJOR PROBLEMS IN DECISION-MAKING REGARDING EARTH-SPACE ACTIVITY AND INTERNATIONAL RELATIONS AS MAN MORE DEEPLY EXPLORES SPACE.

2010 MCDOUGAL M.S., GOODMAN R.M.
"CHINESE PARTICIPATION IN THE UNITED NATIONS: THE LEGAL IMPERATIVES OF A NEGOTIATED SOLUTION"
AMER. J. OF INT. LAW, 60 (OCT. 66), 671-727.
EXAMINES ADMISSION OF CHINA TO UN. COMPARES SOLUTIONS OF BASING ADMISSION ON MEMBERSHIP, CREDENTIALS, OR REPRESENTATION. PROVIDES HISTORY AND FACTUAL CONTEXT OF DECISION OF ADMISSION AND PARTICIPATION. RECOMMENDS APPLICATION OF PRINCIPLES OF UNIVERSALITY OF MEMBERSHIP AND RESPONSIBILITY IN DECISION-MAKING AS BASES FOR ADMISSION POLICY.

2011 MCGHEE G.C.
"EAST-WEST RELATIONS TODAY."
DEPT OF STATE BULLETIN, 50 (MAR. 64), 488-496.
PRESENTS ARGUMENTS FOR AND AGAINST TWO DIFFERENT APPROACHES TO CURRENT PROBLEMS IN EAST-WEST RELATIONS. ONE IS TO SEARCH PATIENTLY FOR SMALL AREAS OF AGREEMENT. SECOND IS TO REFUSE SMALL CONCESSIONS WITHOUT PROGRESS TOWARD SOLUTIONS OF MAJOR PROBLEMS. ADVOCATES COOPERATION OF ALL WESTERN COUNTRIES IN FORMULATING POLICY OF AGREEMENT WHENEVER POSSIBLE.

2012 MCINTYRE W.D.
COLONIES INTO COMMONWEALTH.
LONDON: BLANFORD PRESS, 1966, 391 PP.
TRACES HISTORICAL DEVELOPMENT OF BRITISH COMMONWEALTH FROM AMERICAN REVOLUTION THROUGH COLONIALISM AND ACQUISITION OF DOMINIONS OF CANADA, NEW ZEALAND, AUSTRALIA, SOUTH AFRICA, INDIA. DOCTRINES OF EMPIRE AND TRUSTEESHIP, NEW COMMONWEALTH OF ASIAN AND CARIBBEAN NATIONS, AFRICAN ADDITIONS, AND GRADUAL INDEPENDENCE OF SOME OF THESE AREAS ARE COVERED.

2013 MCKAY V. ED.
AFRICAN DIPLOMACY STUDIES IN THE DETERMINANTS OF FOREIGN POLICY.
NEW YORK: FREDERICK PRAEGER, 1966, 210 PP., LC#66-13669.
COMPARATIVE STUDY OF ECONOMIC, CULTURAL, MILITARY, AND POLITICAL DETERMINANTS OF AFRICAN DIPLOMACY. DISCUSSES THE ASPIRATIONS AND INHERENT RACISM OF AFRICA'S POLITICS IN ATTEMPT TO DETERMINE WHY ITS STATES ACT AS THEY DO AND WHAT ATTITUDE THE US SHOULD TAKE TOWARD THEM.

2014 MCKENNA J.
DIPLOMATIC PROTEST IN FOREIGN POLICY: ANALYSIS AND CASE STUDIES.
CHICAGO: LOYOLA U. PR., 1962, 222 PP.
ASSAYS CIRCUMSTANCES FAVORABLE TO USE OF DIPLOMATIC PROTEST AS AN INSTRUMENT OF FOREIGN POLICY. USES USA CASE STUDIES TO EXEMPLIFY INCIDENTS WHERE METHOD IS APPLICABLE.

2015 MCKEON R. ED.
DEMOCRACY IN A WORLD OF TENSION.
CHICAGO: U. CHI. PR, 1951, 540 PP.
EFFORT TO UNCOVER THE TRADITIONS OF THOUGHT AND THE BASIC ASSUMPTIONS OF THEORY WHICH INFLUENCE DISCUSSIONS AND NEGOTIATIONS IN WHICH DEMOCRACY IS INVOLVED. INQUIRY IS THEN DIRECTED TO RELATIONS AND OPPOSITIONS OF IDEAS, PRECONCEPTIONS AND PREFERENCES.

2016 MCKINNEY R.
REVIEW OF THE INTERNATIONAL ATOMIC POLICIES AND PROGRAMS OF THE UNITED STATES (5 VOLS.)
WASHINGTON: US GOVERNMENT, 1960, 2079 PP.
STUDIES INTERNATIONAL PROGRAMS AND POLICIES OF THE US CONCERNING PEACEFUL USES OF ATOMIC ENERGY. APPRAISES AND EVALUATES THESE POLICIES IN RELATION TO ORIGINAL PREMISES AND PURPOSES. EXPLORES ALTERNATIVE COURSES OF ACTION. COVERS US RELATIONSHIPS WITH DEVELOPED AND LESS-DEVELOPED COUNTRIES, ALLIES, AND COMMUNIST NATIONS.

2017 MCMAHON A.H.
"INTERNATIONAL BOUNDARIES."
J. ROYAL SOC. ARTS, 84 (NOV. 25), 2-13.
ACCOUNT OF AUTHOR'S BOUNDARY-MAKING EXPERIENCES. REFERS DISTINCTION BETWEEN DELIMITATION AND DEMARCATION. FORMER SIGNIFY AGREEMENTS, LATTER SIGNIFY PHYSICAL MARKERS. FEELS DEMARCATION NECESSARY TO LESSEN CHANCES OF CONFLICT.

2018 MCNAIR A.D.
THE LAW OF TREATIES: BRITISH PRACTICE AND OPINIONS.
NEW YORK: COLUMBIA U PRESS, 1938, 578 PP.
PRESENTS BRITISH PRACTICE IN THE CONCLUSION, TERMINATION, INTERPRETATION, SCOPE, AND MODIFICATION OF TREATIES. STATES LAWS WHICH ARE RELEVANT TO PRECEDING TOPICS. LEGAL SOURCES WITH WHICH IT DEALS ARE PRECEDENTS OF BRITISH GOVERNMENT AND DECISIONS OF BRITISH COURTS. AUTHOR EMPHASIZES THAT WORK IS NOT AN OFFICIAL GOVERNMENT ONE AND THAT IT IS NOT A TREATISE ON THE INTERNATIONAL LAW OF TREATIES.

2019 MCNAIR A.D.
THE LEGAL EFFECTS OF WAR.
NEW YORK: CAMBRIDGE U PRESS, 1966, 469 PP.
EXAMINES IMPACT OF WAR ON LEGAL POSITION OF PRIVATE PERSONS, WITH EMPHASIS ON ENGLISH LAW AND EFFECTS WHICH OCCUR WHEN BRITAIN IS BELLIGERENT OR NEUTRAL. DISCUSSES IMPACT ON TRADE, EMPLOYMENT, CONTRACTS, BILLS OF EXCHANGE, ETC.

2020 MCNEAL R.H.
"THE LEGACY OF THE COMINTERN."
INT. J., 21 (SPRING 66), 199-204.
ANALYZES ROLE OF COMINTERN IN COMMUNIST RELATIONS, INCLUDING STALIN'S DECISION TO ABOLISH THIRD INTERNATIONAL IN 1943, AND CONTEMPORARY PROBLEMS OF INTERNATIONAL COMMUNIST UNITY.

2021 MCNEILL W.H.
AMERICA, BRITAIN, AND RUSSIA; THEIR COOPERATION AND CONFLICT
LONDON: OXFORD U PR, 1953, 819 PP.
SURVEYS INTERNATIONAL RELATIONS AMONG THESE COUNTRIES, 1941-46, RECORDING ALL IMPORTANT INTERNATIONAL TRANSACTIONS.

BREAKING DOWN WAR CHRONOLOGICALLY, EXAMINES EACH VIEWPOINT IN SUCCESSION. DETAILED IN-DEPTH STUDY OF INTERACTIONS.

2022 MCNEILL W.H.
GREECE: AMERICAN AID IN ACTION.
NEW YORK: TWENTIETH CENT FUND, 1957, 239 PP., LC#57-12382.
DESCRIBES IMPACT OF US FOREIGN AID IN GREECE, ITS CULTURE, ECONOMY, AND SOCIAL SYSTEMS, RECORDING AMOUNT OF AID, BALANCE OF PAYMENTS, CURRENCY EXCHANGE RATE, AND COST OF LIVING. ALSO DISCUSSES DIFFERENCES IN US AND UK ADMINISTRATIONS.

2023 MCNELLY T. ED.
SOURCES IN MODERN EAST ASIAN HISTORY AND POLITICS.
NEW YORK: APPLETON, 1967, 422 PP., LC#67-18502.
PROVIDES SUPPLEMENTARY READING FOR COURSES IN HISTORY, POLITICS, AND IDEOLOGIES OF MODERN CHINA, JAPAN, KOREA, AND VIETNAM. EDITORIAL NOTES SUMMARIZE RECENT POLITICAL HISTORY OF EAST ASIA AND SUGGEST SIGNIFICANCE AND INTERRELATIONS OF SELECTIONS. DOCUMENTS COVER REFORM AND REVOLUTION IN CHINA, EMERGENCE OF JAPANESE EMPIRE WWI AND WWII IN FAR EAST, COMMUNIST RULE IN CHINA, AND WAR IN VIETNAM.

2024 MCSHERRY J.E.
RUSSIA AND THE UNITED STATES UNDER EISENHOWER, KHRUSHCHEV, AND KENNEDY.
UNIVERSITY PARK: PENN STATE U PR, 1965, 227 PP.
INTERPRETIVE ANALYSIS OF OFFICIAL AND UNOFFICIAL SOVIET STATEMENTS MADE WHILE SIX INTERNATIONAL CRISES INVOLVING US ANS USSR WERE IN PROGRESS. MUCH OF ANALYSIS BASED ON STATEMENT BY KHRUSHCHEV. DESCRIBES INTRIGUES AND WORKINGS IN SOVIET POLITICS DURING THESE CRISES.

2025 MCSPADDEN J.W. ED.
THE AMERICAN STATESMAN'S YEARBOOK.
NEW YORK: MCBRIDE, NAST & CO.
AN ANNOTATED ANNUAL REFERENCE VOLUME SUMMARIZING THE LATEST GOVERNMENTAL REPORTS FROM OFFICIAL SOURCES IN WASHINGTON, THE STATE CAPITALS, AND MOST FOREIGN COUNTRIES. DIVIDED INTO THREE MAIN PARTS: INDIVIDUAL STATES AND THE US AS A WHOLE, FOREIGN COUNTRIES IN ALPHABETICAL ORDER, RECORDS AND STATISTICS. BIBLIOGRAPHIES FREQUENTLY APPENDED TO CHAPTERS. INDEXED BY TOPIC AND COUNTRY. PUBLISHED ANNUALLY SINCE 1912.

2026 MCWHINNEY E.
"CO-EXISTENCE, THE CUBA CRISIS, AND COLD WAR-INTERNATIONAL WAR."
INT. J., 18 (WINTER 62), 67-74.
APPRAISES THE IMMEDIATE AFTERMATH OF CUBAN MISSILE CRISIS AND INFERS THAT CONCEPT OF CO-EXISTENCE IS SOUND. FURTHER APPLICATION OF INTERNATIONAL LAW WILL DEPEND ON THE BALANCE OF POWER IN THE COLD WAR ENVIRONMENT.

2027 MCWHINNEY E.
"PEACEFUL COEXISTENCE" AND SOVIET-WESTERN INTERNATIONAL LAW.
LEYDEN: AW SIJTHOFF, 1964, 135 PP., LC#64-22593.
COMPARES SOVIET THEORY AND PRACTICE OF "PEACEFUL COEXISTENCE" AS DEFINED IN LAW TO POSITIONS TAKEN BY SOVIET LEADERS IN INTERNATIONAL AFFAIRS. RELATES CURRENT SOVIET CAMPAIGN TO SOVIET POSITION ON INTERNATIONAL LAW AND EXAMINES WESTERN RESPONSES TO CAMPAIGN.

2028 MEADE J.E., WELLS S.J., LIESNER H.H.
CASE STUDIES IN EUROPEAN ECONOMIC UNION.
LONDON: OXFORD U. PR., 1962, 424 PP.
CONSIDER ECONOMIC MECHANISMS AND ARRANGEMENTS NECESSARY TO EFFECTIVE ECONOMIC UNION. BASE ANALYSIS ON STUDY OF BELGIUM-LUXEMBOURG UNION, BENELUX, AND EUROPEAN COAL AND STEEL COMMUNITY.

2029 MEAGHER R.F.
PUBLIC INTERNATIONAL DEVELOPMENT FINANCING IN SUDAN.
NEW YORK: COLUMBIA U LAW SCHOOL, 1965, 127 PP.
STUDIES PROGRAMS AND RELATIONS OF FOREIGN INSTITUTIONS INVOLVED IN PUBLIC FINANCING OF ECONOMIC DEVELOPMENT IN SUDAN. INCLUDES SUDAN'S ECONOMIC AND POLITICAL STRUCTURE, TEN YEAR PLAN, PUBLIC FINANCIAL INSTITUTIONS; NEED FOR EXTERNAL ASSISTANCE, ITS SOURCES AND AMOUNT; CASE STUDIES OF IMPORTANT AID IN TRANSPORTATION, IRRIGATION, AND INDUSTRY.

2030 MECHAM J.L.
THE UNITED STATES AND INTER-AMERICAN SECURITY, 1889-1960.
AUSTIN: U OF TEXAS PR, 1961, 514 PP., LC#61-1-426.
DESCRIBES POSITION OF US IN OAS. EXAMINES STRUCTURE OF INTER-AMERICAN ALLIANCE AND CHANGES IN RELATIONS THROUGH TWO WORLD WARS. STUDIES DEVELOPMENT OF OAS AND INTEGRATION OF INTER-AMERICAN SYSTEM INTO UN.

2031 MEDIVA J.T.
LA IMPRENTA EN MEXICO, 1539-1821 (8 VOLS.)
SANTIAGO: IMPRESO CASA DEL AUTOR, 1965.
BIBLIOGRAPHY OF 12,412 ITEMS: ALL WORKS PUBLISHED IN MEXICO BETWEEN 1539 AND 1821. LITTLE BIBLIOGRAPHICAL INFORMATION GIVEN. TITLES CONSIDERED SELF-EXPLANATORY. MATERIAL CONTAINED IN EIGHT VOLUMES. ARRANGEMENT IS CHRONOLOGICAL. INCLUDES AUTHOR INDEX.

2032 MEERHAEGHE M.
INTERNATIONAL ECONOMIC INSTITUTIONS.
LONDON: LONGMANS, GREEN & CO, 1966, 404 PP.
PART I PRESENTS THEORY OF INTERNATIONAL ECONOMIC RELATIONS, INCLUDING TRADE, BALANCE-OF-PAYMENTS EQUILIBRIUM, AND POLICY. PART II DESCRIBES AND APPRAISES WORLD ORGANIZATIONS: INTERNATIONAL MONETARY FUND, INTERNATIONAL BANK FOR RECONSTRUCTION AND DEVELOPMENT, GATT, COMMODITY AGREEMENTS. PART III FOCUSES ON EUROPEAN ORGANIZATIONS: BENELUX, ORGANIZATION FOR ECONOMIC CO-OPERATION AND DEVELOPMENT.

2033 MEHDI M.T.
PEACE IN THE MIDDLE EAST.
NEW YORK: NEW WORLD PRESS, 1967, 108 PP., LC#67-20933.
CONTENDS THAT HITLER'S PERSECUTION OF JEWS IN WWII WHICH LED TO RISE OF ZIONISM MUST BE CALLED FUNDAMENTAL MOTIVE FOR ESTABLISHMENT OF ISRAEL IN 1948. DISCUSSES NATURE OF WORLDWIDE ANTI-SEMITISM AND OF BASIC CONFLICTS WHICH EXIST BETWEEN ISRAEL AND ARAB NATIONS. PROPOSES SOLUTION BASED ON GRADUAL DISSOLUTION OF ISRAEL BY MIGRATIONS OF JEWS TO THEIR NATIVE COUNTRIES, AUSTRALIA, OR NORTH AMERICA.

2034 MEHROTRA S.R.
INDIA AND THE COMMONWEALTH 1885-1929.
LONDON: ALLEN & UNWIN, 1965, 287 PP.
STUDIES TRANSFORMATION OF BRITISH EMPIRE INTO COMMONWEALTH. EMPHASIZES ROLE INDIANS PLAYED IN MAKING IT MULTIRACIAL. ANALYZES THREE MAJOR POLITICAL PARTIES IN INDIA AND THEIR ATTITUDES TO BRITAIN IN THIS PERIOD. REVEALS INTERNATIONAL POLITICAL SCIENCE THAT LED TO COMMONWEALTH'S PRESENT STATUS. BIBLIOGRAPHY OF FURTHER READINGS ON SUBJECT OR ON EACH COUNTRY AT TIME.

2035 MELMAN S.
INSPECTION FOR DISARMAMENT.
NEW YORK: COLUMB. U. PR., 1958, 291 PP., $6.00.
REVIEW WORKABLE SYSTEMS OF INSPECTION TO ENSURE COMPLIANCE WITH INTERNATIONAL DISARMAMENT AGREEMENTS. INSPECTION METHODS INCLUDE AERIAL INSPECTION, REVIEW OF BUDGETS, DETECTION OF RADIATION HAZARDS, CONTROL OF FISSIONABLE MATERIALS PRODUCTION, AND INSPECTION OF SAMPLING. TECHNIQUES OF CLANDESTINE PRODUCTION AND PSYCHOLOGICAL ASPECTS OF EVASION ARE EXPLORED IN DETAIL.

2036 MENDE T.
WORLD POWER IN THE BALANCE.
NEW YORK: NOONDAY, 1953, 188 PP.
PROBES POWER SHIFT FROM EUROPE TO AMERICA SINCE 1900. ADVOCATES REVIVAL OF WESTERN UTOPIANISM ON HUMANISTIC BASIS. DEFINES POWER AS BEING NON-PERMANENT AND AS CONSISTING OF MATERIAL AND IMMATERIAL ELEMENTS. FORSEES FUTURE CONFLICTS BETWEEN WEST AND NEW WORLD POWERS LIKE RUSSIA, BUT FEELS COMPROMISE CAN PRODUCE IDEAL WORLD.

2037 MENDEL D.H. JR.
THE JAPANESE PEOPLE AND FOREIGN POLICY.
BERKELEY: U OF CALIF PR, 1961, 269 PP., LC#61-14533.
STUDY OF PUBLIC OPINION IN JAPAN AFTER TREATY OF 1952. INCLUDES RELATIONS WITH NEIGHBORING COUNTRIES, DEFENSE POLICY, US BASES, AND JAPAN IN WORLD POLITICS GENERALLY.

2038 MENDELSSOHN S.
SOUTH AFRICAN BIBLIOGRAPHY (2 VOLS.)
LONDON: KEGAN, PAUL& CO, 1910.
A COMPREHENSIVE BIBLIOGRAPHY OF LITERATURE RELATING TO SOUTH AFRICA FROM THE EARLIEST PERIOD TO 1910. ENTRIES ARE CRITICALLY AND DESCRIPTIVELY ANNOTATED, AND CATALOGUED ALPHABETICALLY BY AUTHOR. MOST WORKS PUBLISHED BETWEEN 1880-1910. AUTHOR'S INTRODUCTION PROVIDES LENGTHLY SUMMARY OF SOUTH AFRICAN HISTORY.

2039 MENDES C.
NACIONALISMO E DESENVOLVIMENTO.
RIO DE JANEIRO: INST ESTUD AFRO, 1963, 398 PP.
STUDY OF NATIONALISM AND DEVELOPMENT IN UNDERDEVELOPED NATIONS OF AFRICA, ASIA, AND LATIN AMERICA. DISCUSSES RELATIONSHIP OF THESE AREAS TO DEVELOPED COUNTRIES AND COLONIAL POWERS.

2040 MENEZES A.J.
O BRASIL E O MUNDO ASIO-AFRICANO (REV. ED.)
RIO DE JANEIRO: EDICIONES GRD, 1960, 363 PP.
STUDY OF WORLD ROLE OF BRAZIL AND ITS RELATION TO NEW NATIONS OF AFRICA AND ASIA. DEALS WITH HISTORICAL ASSOCIATIONS WITH AFRO-ASIAN AREA AND IMPORTANCE OF STRONGER INDEPENDENT FOREIGN POLICY SO THAT BRAZIL ATTAINS WORLD LEADERSHIP.

2041 MENEZES A.J.
SUBDESENVOLVIMENTO E POLITICA INTERNACIONAL.
RIO DE JANEIRO: EDICIONES GRD, 1963, 223 PP.
STUDY OF UNDERDEVELOPED WORLD IN FIELD OF INTERNATIONAL POLITICS. DISCUSSES NATIONALISM AND WORLD WIDE POLITICAL AND ECONOMIC COMPETITION AMONG NATIONS. DEALS WITH POSITION OF BRAZIL AND ITS PLANS FOR INDEPENDENT GROWTH IN POWER AND INFLUENCE.

2042 MENON K.P.S.
MANY WORLDS.
LONDON: OXFORD U PR, 1965, 324 PP.
INDIAN STATEMENTS RECALLING COLONIAL INDIA AND STRUGGLE FOR INDEPENDENCE, RISE OF COLD WAR AND STRUGGLE OF TWO WORLDS, AND EMERGENCE OF NEW NATIONS AND ITS EFFECT ON INTERNATIONAL RELATIONS AND POWER.

2043 MERKL P.H.
GERMANY: YESTERDAY AND TOMORROW.
NEW YORK: OXFORD U PR, 1965, 362 PP., LC#65-22799.
ANALYZES PROMINENT ISSUES OF GERMAN HISTORY. DESCRIBES POST-WAR POLITICS AND ECONOMICS AND QUESTIONS FUTURE DIRECTIONS OF GERMAN DEMOCRACY.

2044 MERRITT R.L.
"WOODROW WILSON AND THE 'GREAT AND SOLEMN REFERENDUM,' 1920."
REV. POLIT., 27 (JAN. 65), 78-104.
PRESENTS A STUDY OF THE MAN AND HIS IDEOLOGY. REVIEWING WILSON'S PAST HISTORY, EXAMINES HIS CONCEPTION OF THE REFERENDUM AND HIS EFFORTS TO BRING US INTO THE LEAGUE OF NATIONS. SHOWS THE PERSONALITY DEFECTS WHICH BROUGHT ABOUT HIS PERSONAL DEFEAT, AND THE DEFEAT OF THE REFERENDUM.

2045 MERRITT R.L.
"SELECTED ARTICLES AND DOCUMENTS ON INTERNATIONAL LAW AND RELATIONS."
AM. POL. SCI. REV., 59 (SEPT. 65), 764-770.
AN UNANNOTATED BIBLIOGRAPHY OF ARTICLES AND DOCUMENTS ON INTERNATIONAL LAW AND RELATIONS. INCLUDES ENGLISH-LANGUAGE, SOME FRENCH, GERMAN, RUSSIAN, AND SPANISH ARTICLES. GROUPED UNDER 20 HEADINGS. MATERIAL PUBLISHED FROM 1963-65. CONTAINS 270 ENTRIES.

2046 MERRITT R.L.
"SELECTED ARTICLES AND DOCUMENTS ON COMPARATIVE GOVERNMENT AND CROSS-NATIONAL RESEARCH."
AM. POL. SCI. REV., 60 (SEPT. 66), 747-752.
AN UNANNOTATED BIBLIOGRAPHY OF COMPARATIVE GOVERNMENT AND CROSS-NATIONAL RESEARCH. ENGLISH-LANGUAGE AND SOME FRENCH, GERMAN, AND ITALIAN. MATERIAL RANGES FROM 1965-66. CONTAINS 160 ENTRIES.

2047 METZ I.
DIE DEUTSCHE FLOTTE IN DER ENGLISCHEN PRESSE, DER NAVY SCARE VOM WINTER 1904/05.
BERLIN: EMIL EBERING, 1936, 27 PP.
DISCUSSES IMPACT OF BRITISH PRESS PUBLICATIONS ABOUT GERMAN FLEET UPON FOREIGN OFFICE AND PUBLIC OPINION. MAINTAINS THAT SCARE PRODUCED BY "PRESS POLITICIANS" ABOUT SIZE OF GERMAN NAVY WAS IMPORTANT FACTOR IN BRINGING ABOUT WWI.

2048 MEYER F.S. ED.
WHAT IS CONSERVATISM?
NEW YORK: HOLT RINEHART WINSTON, 1964, 242 PP., LC#64-11014.
COLLECTION OF ESSAYS ON CONSERVATIVE POLITICAL AND ECONOMIC PHILOSOPHY. DISCUSSES ROLE OF TRADITION, EDUCATION, AND REASON IN CONSERVATIVE THOUGHT.

2049 MEYER H.H.B. ED.
LIST OF REFERENCES ON EMBARGOES (PAMPHLET)
WASHINGTON: LIBRARY OF CONGRESS, 1917, 44 PP., LC#16-26004.
LIST MAKES SPECIAL REFERENCE TO LITERATURE DEALING WITH EARLY ATTEMPTS TO PLACE EMBARGO ON EXPORTATION OF FOODSTUFFS AND MUNITIONS OF WAR, ESPECIALLY DURING PERIODS 1807-1808 AND 1812-13. INTERNATIONAL ASPECTS OF QUESTION DISCUSSED IN BOOKS AND ARTICLES LISTED UNDER HEADING INTERNATIONAL AL LAW." DISCUSSIONS AND LITERATURE ON SUBJECT ARE ARRANGED TOPICALLY. CONTAINS AUTHOR INDEX.

2050 MEYER H.H.B.
THE UNITED STATES AT WAR, ORGANIZATIONS AND LITERATURE.
WASHINGTON: US GOVERNMENT, 1917, 115 PP.
DESCRIBES 157 US GOVERNMENT AGENCIES AND OTHER INSTITUTIONS CALLED INTO EXISTENCE BY WWI. GIVES ANNOTATED LISTING OF THEIR PUBLICATIONS PRINCIPALLY CONCERNING INDUSTRIAL AND FARM PRODUCTION, FOREIGN TRADE, AND DOMESTIC PROBLEMS. SUBJECT AND NAME INDEX.

2051 MEYER H.H.B. ED.
SELECT LIST OF REFERENCES ON ECONOMIC RECONSTRUCTION: INCLUDING REPORTS OF THE BRITISH MINISTRY OF RECONSTRUCTION.
WASHINGTON: LIBRARY OF CONGRESS, 1919, 47 PP., LC#19-41919.
ANNOTATED LIST OF 158 ENTRIES FROM 1914-19 CONCERNED WITH PROBLEMS OF SOCIO-ECONOMIC RECOVERY. INCLUDES BOOKS, PAMPHLETS AND PARTICULARLY GOVERNMENT REPORTS. BOTH EUROPE AND US INCLUDED. ESPECIALLY A BROAD RANGE OF BRITISH REPORTS. ARRANGED BY AUTHOR. LIBRARY OF CONGRESS COMPILATION.

2052 MEYER H.H.B. ED.
LIST OF REFERENCES ON THE TREATY-MAKING POWER.
WASHINGTON: LIBRARY OF CONGRESS, 1920, 213 PP., LC#20-26005.
LIST OF REFERENCES TO DISCUSSIONS OF CONSTITUTIONAL ARRANGEMENTS FOR TREATY-MAKING. CONTAINS GENERAL DISCUSSIONS ON TREATY-MAKING AS FOUND LARGELY IN TREATISES ON INTERNATIONAL LAW AND DISCUSSIONS OF PRACTICE IN OTHER COUNTRIES. DISCUSSION ON US CONSTITUTIONAL PROVISIONS IS LARGELY HISTORICAL: TREATY-MAKING UNDER CONFEDERATION, ETC. ITEMS ON SPECIAL TREATIES GROUPED CHRONOLOGICALLY. SOME 1,010 ITEMS.

2053 MEYER J.
"CUBA S'ENFERME DANS SA REVOLUTION."
ESPRIT, 35 (MAR. 67), 548-559.
ANALYZES AND COMPARES CONFLICT BETWEEN GUEVERA AND CASTRO TO THAT BETWEEN TROTSKY AND STALIN: INTERNATIONAL AND NATIONAL COMMUNISM. TRACES DEVELOPMENT OF SINO-CUBAN AND RUSSIAN-CUBAN RELATIONS. CUBAN ROLE IN LATIN AMERICAN AFFAIRS TAKEN AS MODEL. STUDIES CASTRO AS CHARISMATIC LEADER, ORGANIZER, AND ADMINISTRATOR.

2054 MEYERHOFF A.E.
THE STRATEGY OF PERSUASION: THE USE OF ADVERTISING SKILLS IN FIGHTING THE COLD WAR.
NEW YORK: COWARD MCCANN, 1965, 190 PP., LC#64-25768.
MAINTAINS THAT US, ALTHOUGH PERSUASION TECHNIQUES ARE HIGHLY DEVELOPED, HAS NEVER USED THEM IN INTERNATIONAL RELATIONS. PROPOSES THAT ADVERTISING SKILLS BE EMPLOYED TO "SELL" AMERICAN IDEAS. COMPARES PRESENT US PROPAGANDA TO MORE EFFECTIVE SOVIET SYSTEM AND DISCUSSES METHODS OF APPLYING ADVERTISING TECHNIQUES TO PROPAGANDA.

2055 MEYNAUD J., BEY A.S.
TRADE UNIONISM IN AFRICA; A STUDY OF ITS GROWTH AND ORIENTATION (TRANS. BY ANGELA BRENCH)
LONDON: METHUEN, 1967, 242 PP.
PRESENTS SOCIO-ECONOMIC AND EXTERNAL FACTORS RESPONSIBLE FOR FORMATION OF AFRICAN TRADE UNIONS AND DIRECTION OF THEIR DEVELOPMENT. EMPHASIZES EMERGENCE OF POLITICAL FACTORS, ESPECIALLY NATIONALISM, DURING AND AFTER DEMANDS FOR INDEPENDENCE. DISCUSSES PROBLEMS CONFRONTING UNIONS IN INDEPENDENT NATIONS AND PAN-AFRICAN FORCE URGING INTERNATIONAL RECOGNITION.

2056 MEYRIAT J. ED.
ETUDES DES BIBLIOGRAPHIES COURANTES DES PUBLICATIONS OFFICIELLES NATIONALES.
PARIS: UNESCO, 1958, 260 PP.
PROVIDES A SUMMARY GUIDE DESCRIBING DIFFERENT TYPES OF OFFICIAL PUBLICATIONS, STATE GAZETTES, ETC.,AS WELL AS MEANS OF IMPROVING PUBLICATION OF ADMINISTRATIVE DOCUMENTS, FACILITATING IDENTIFICATION OF OFFICIAL PUBLICATIONS, AND IMPROVING THEIR BIBLIOGRAPHICAL CONTROL. ALSO INCLUDES AN INVENTORY OF COUNTRIES, INDEXES, AND ANNEXES WITH SUPPLEMENTARY BIBLIOGRAPHIC MATERIAL.

2057 MEYRIAT J. ED.
LA SCIENCE POLITIQUE EN FRANCE, 1945-1958; BIBLIOGRAPHIES FRANCAISES DE SCIENCES SOCIALES (VOL. I)
PARIS: FDN NAT DES SCIENCES POL, 1960, 134 PP.
ANNOTATED BIBLIOGRAPHY OF 603 ENTRIES REPRESENTING FRENCH POLITICAL SCIENCE PUBLICATIONS SINCE 1945, WITH EMPHASIS ON PERIOD OF 1950-58. MATERIAL SEPARATED INTO NINE CATEGORIES REPRESENTING METHODOLOGICAL, HISTORICAL, THEORETICAL, INSTITUTIONAL, INTERNATIONAL, AND NATIONAL STUDIES. SPECIAL INDEXES TO SCHOLARLY PERIODICALS, AUTHORS, AND EDITORS.

2058 MEYROWITZ H.
"LES JURISTES DEVANT L'ARME NUCLAIRE."
REV. GEN. DR. INT. PUB., 67 (63), 820-73.
SEVERAL PAPERS ON NUCLEAR WEAPONS AND LAW RELATED TO WAR. STUDIES RESPONSIBILITIES OF INTERNATIONAL BODIES TO SAFEGUARD POSITIVE RIGHTS. EXAMINES ALTERNATIVE DECISIONS ON NUCLEAR ARMS UPON WHICH JURISTS MAY BASE AND DEVELOP A CASE THEORY.

2059 MEZERIK A.G. ED.
ATOM TESTS AND RADIATION HAZARDS (PAMPHLET)
NEW YORK: INTL REVIEW SERVICE, 1961, 59 PP.
EXAMINES POSTWAR PROBLEMS OF NUCLEAR ARMS CONTROL IN REGARD TO HEALTH DANGERS, AND UN ACTIVITIES TO LIMIT USE AND SPREAD OF NUCLEAR WEAPONS. DISCUSSES TEST BAN TREATY AND CONFERENCES ON TOPIC.

2060 MEZERIK A.G. ED.
U-2 AND OPEN SKIES (PAMPHLET)
NEW YORK: INTL REVIEW SERVICE, 1960, 46 PP.
DISCUSSION OF U-2 INCIDENT OF MAY 1, 1960, IN CHRONOLOGY OF EVENTS, USSR'S INITIAL REACTION, UN DEBATES AND DISCUSSION, OPEN SKIES PROPOSAL, AND EFFECT ON GENEVA CONFERENCE ON DISARMAMENT.

2061 MEZERIK A.G. ED.
COLONIALISM AND THE UNITED NATIONS (PAMPHLET)
NEW YORK: INTL REVIEW SERVICE, 1964, 105 PP.
CONCERNED WITH ANTI-COLONIALIST PROVISIONS OF UN CHARTER; ATTEMPTS TO RECONCILE THIS WITH FACT THAT UN SEEMS TO FAVOR GREAT POWERS. DISCUSSES ROLE OF GENERAL ASSEMBLY, RISE OF ASIAN-AFRICAN INFLUENCE, AND EXPANSION OF SECURITY COUNCIL. REFERS TO COLONIAL CRISES IN ALGERIA AND CYPRUS, 1955-62, AND TO OTHER AREAS. INCLUDES POLICIES OF NATIONS, NEO-

COLONIALISM, AND CHARTER REVISION; PROVISIONS APPENDED.

2062 MEZERIK A.G.
ECONOMIC DEVELOPMENT AIDS FOR UNDERDEVELOPED COUNTRIES.
NEW YORK: INTL REVIEW SERVICE, 1961, 108 PP., LC#61-2436.
SUMMARY OF POST-WWII ECONOMIC AID TO UNDERDEVELOPED COUNTRIES DERIVED PRIMARILY FROM UN SOURCES AND CONSISTING OF FINANCIAL AND TECHNICAL ASSISTANCE.

2063 MEZERIK A.G.
OUTER SPACE: UN, US, USSR (PAMPHLET)
NEW YORK: INTL REVIEW SERVICE, 1960, 52 PP.
SHORT OUTLINE OF RECENT ACTIVITIES OF US AND USSR IN AND CONCERNING SPACE EXPLORATION. SURVEYS ROLE OF UN IN ATTEMPTS AT TREATY-MAKING AND REVIEWS VARIOUS THEORIES OF SOVEREIGNTY IN SPACE, COMMITTEES AND ORGANIZATIONS CONCERNED, AND PRACTICAL AND LEGAL PROBLEMS INVOLVED.

2064 MEZERIK A.G.ED.
FINANCIAL ASSISTANCE FOR ECONOMIC DEVELOPMENT.
NEW YORK: INTL REVIEW SERVICE, 1959, 71 PP.
REVIEW OF EXCHANGES OF WORLD-WIDE FINANCIAL ASSISTANCE SINCE 1950. CHRONOLOGY OF UNRRA'S ACTIVITIES 1943-59. INCLUDES ANALYSES OF POLICIES AND DEVELOPMENTS IN INTERNATIONAL FINANCIAL RELATIONS.

2065 MICAUD C.A.
THE FRENCH RIGHT AND NAZI GERMANY 1933-1939: A STUDY OF PUBLIC OPINION.
DURHAM: DUKE U PR, 1943, 255 PP.
FOLLOWS THE EVOLUTION OF FOREIGN POLICY OF THE FRENCH RIGHT WITH RELATION TO NAZI GERMANY. EXPLAINS THE REVERSAL OF THE RIGHT'S POSITION FROM AN ANTI-GERMAN POLICY OF INTEGRAL DEFENSE OF THE STATUS QUO OF THE PEACE TREATIES TO THE ACCEPTANCE OF GERMAN EXPANSION IN CENTRAL AND EASTERN EUROPE.

2066 MICHAEL D.N.
PROPOSED STUDIES ON THE IMPLICATIONS OF PEACEFUL SPACE ACTIVITIES FOR HUMAN AFFAIRS.
WASHINGTON: GOVT PR OFFICE, 1961, 272 PP.
DESIGNATES SEVERAL AREAS OF STUDY AND SUGGESTS RESEARCH PROGRAMS FOR FUTURE EXAMINATION OF PROBLEMS AND CONSEQUENCES OF SPACE ACTIVITY AS RELATED TO SOCIAL INSTITUTIONS AND VARIOUS AREAS OF SOCIAL ENDEAVOR. PROVIDES DETAILED ANALYSES OF PROSPECTIVE PLANS FOR STUDYING IMPLICATIONS FOR INDUSTRY, COMMUNICATIONS, NATIONAL GOALS, AND OTHER IMPORTANT TOPICS AND ISSUES IN DEVELOPMENT OF US SPACE PROGRAM.

2067 MIDDLEBUSH F., HILL C.
ELEMENTS OF INTERNATIONAL RELATIONS.
NEW YORK: MCGRAW HILL, 1940, 458 PP.
AN HISTORICAL AND ANALYTICAL INTRODUCTION TO THE BASIC CONCEPTS AND PROCEDURES OF FIELD OF INTERNATIONAL RELATIONS, ORGANIZED SO AS TO LEAD STUDENT GRADUALLY INTO THE MORE DIFFICULT ASPECTS OF SUBJECT.

2068 MIDDLETON D.
CRISIS IN THE WEST.
LONDON: SECKER AND WARBURG, 1965, 286 PP.
NOTES WITH DISMAY DECLINE OF COOPERATION IN ATLANTIC ALLIANCE AND STRENGTH OF OPPOSITION TO EUROPEAN UNITY, INCLUDING REVIVAL OF NATIONALISM, DISCUSSION OF POLITICAL SITUATION WITHIN MAJOR WEST EUROPEAN STATES, PROGRESS OF ECONOMIC UNITY, AND CONTINUING SOVIET CHALLENGE.

2069 MIKESELL R.F.
"AMERICA'S ECONOMIC RESPONSIBILITY AS A GREAT POWER."
AMER. ECON. REV., 50 (MAY 60), 258-71.
STATES ONLY USA HAS ECONOMIC AND MILITARY CAPABILITY TO OPPOSE COMMUNISM. CHALLENGE COMPLICATED BY RAPID CHANGES IN RELATIVE POWER POSITION. DEFINES OBSTACLES IN LESS DEVELOPED AREAS. COUNSELS MEANINGFUL DOMESTIC ECONOMIC GROWTH.

2070 MIKESELL R.F.
PUBLIC INTERNATIONAL LENDING FOR DEVELOPMENT.
NEW YORK: RANDOM HOUSE, INC, 1966, 244 PP., LC#66-10538.
EXPLORES POLICIES AND PROBLEMS OF PUBLIC INTERNATIONAL LENDING AGENCIES AIDING SOCIAL AND ECONOMIC PROGRESS IN DEVELOPING NATIONS. EMPHASIZES PROBLEMS OF RELATIONSHIP OF THEORIES OF ECONOMIC DEVELOPMENT AND APPROACHES OF LENDING AGENCIES. ALSO TRACES DEVELOPMENT OF INTERNATIONAL LENDING AGENCIES, TYPES OF LOANS AND INVESTMENT, AND INTERNATIONAL MEETINGS TO FOUND ORGANIZATIONS.

2071 MIKSCHE F.O.
"DEFENSE ORGANIZATION FOR WESTERN EUROPE."
MIL. REV., 41 (JAN. 1961), 52-61.
A EUROPEAN VIEW OF THE COMBAT ORGANIZATION OF NATO. WARNS AGAINST OVEREMPHASIS ON NUCLEAR ARMAMENT, AND SUGGESTS THE WEST REBUILD ITS MILITARY SYSTEM, WITH MORE DEPENDENCE ON A NUMERICALLY STRONG INFANTRY. CONTENDS THAT NUCLEAR WAR IS UNLIKELY.

2072 MILLAR T.B.
"THE COMMONWEALTH AND THE UNITED NATIONS."
INT. ORGAN., 16 (AUTUMN 62), 436-57.
ELABORATES ON THE FACT THAT ONE SIXTH OF UN MEMBERS ARE ALSO COMMONWEALTH MEMBERS. STUDIES VOTING PATTERNS, RELATIONSHIPS BETWEEN MEMBERS AND IMPLIES THAT UN ACTS AS A SAFETY VALUE FOR TENSIONS OF COMMONWEALTH MEMBERS.

2073 MILLARD E.L.
FREEDOM IN A FEDERAL WORLD.
NEW YORK: OCEANA, 1959, 206 PP.
PRESENTS THE VIEW THAT A WORLD LEVEL FEDERAL GOVERNMENT IS NECESSARY TO INSURE BOTH PEACE AND FREEDOM IN THE FUTURE. EXPLAINS WORLD LAW AND THE METHOD USED TO CREATE IT.

2074 MILLER D.H.
THE DRAFTING OF THE COVENANT.
NEW YORK: PUTNAM, 1928, 1142 PP.
COMPRENSIVE HISTORY OF LEAGUE OF NATIONS COVENANT. ASSEMBLES ALL OFFICIAL DOCUMENTS LEADING UP TO FINAL DRAFT. PRESENTS COVENANT AS RESULT OF COLLECTIVE EFFORTS IN SEVERAL COUNTRIES.

2075 MILLER E.
THE NEUROSES OF WAR.
NEW YORK: MACMILLAN, 1940, 250 PP.
SURVEYS LITERATURE ON SUBJECT. DISCUSSES EFFECT OF MODERN WARFARE ON CIVILIAN POPULATION. PRESENTS CLINICAL CASE STUDIES OF WAR-NEUROSES, INCLUDING PSYCHOSOMATIC DISORDERS. EVALUATES USE OF SUGGESTION AND HYPNOSIS IN TREATMENT OF NEUROSES. EXPLORES PUBLIC MORALE AND REACTION TO 'WAR OF NERVES.'

2076 MILLER E.
"LEGAL ASPECTS OF UN ACTION IN THE CONGO."
AMER. J. INT. LAW, 55 (JAN. 61), 1-28.
ATTEMPTS TO DEMONSTRATE THAT CONSIDERATIONS OF LAW AND PRINCIPLE CAN PLAY A ROLE IN INTERNATIONAL ACTION, IN SPITE OF POLITICAL CONFLICT AND TENSION.

2077 MILLER J.D.B.
THE COMMONWEALTH IN THE WORLD (3RD ED.)
CAMBRIDGE: HARVARD U PR, 1965, 304 PP.
STUDIES COMMONWEALTH, ITS GROWTH AND STATUS AS INTERNATIONAL ENTITY. EXAMINES INTERESTS AND POLICIES OF INDIVIDUAL MEMBERS TOWARD ONE ANOTHER NON-MEMBER NATIONS, AND PRESENT SYSTEM OF FUNCTIONING.

2078 MILLER J.D.B.
THE POLITICS OF THE THIRD WORLD.
NEW YORK: OXFORD U PR, 1967, 126 PP.
STUDY OF INTERNATIONAL RELATIONS OF THIRD WORLD NATIONS OF AFRO-ASIAN NEUTRALIST BLOC. SUBJECTS ARE COMMON INTERESTS, UN ACTIONS, OTHER INTERNATIONAL ORGANIZATIONS SUCH AS ARAB LEAGUE, BANDUNG CONFERENCE. CITES LACK OF UNITY EXCEPT ON SYMBOLIC ISSUES AS VITAL CHARACTERISTIC.

2079 MILLER R.I.
DAG HAMMARSKJOLD AND CRISES DIPLOMACY.
NEW YORK: OCEANA PUBLISHING, 1961, 344 PP., LC#61-14005.
STORY OF HAMMARSKJOLD'S DRAMATIC RISE IN STATURE AND INFLUENCE. TOLD THROUGH A SERIES OF CASE STUDIES IN CRISES DIPLOMACY. FOUR FACTORS CONSIDERED IN DESCRIPTION AND ANALYSIS INCLUDE: BACKGROUND OF ISSUE; NATIONS INVOLVED, THEIR RESPECTIVE INTERESTS AND ACTIONS; THE UN; AND MR. HAMMARSKJOLD HIMSELF. SPECIAL ATTENTION GIVEN TO HIS ROLE AS SECRETARY-GENERAL.

2080 MILLER W.J., ROBERTS H.L., SHULMAN M.D.
THE MEANING OF COMMUNISM.
MORRISTOWN, NJ: SILVER BURDETT, 1963, 192 PP., LC#63-10162.
INTRODUCTION TO COMMUNIST THEORY AND PRACTICE FROM CONSERVATIVE VIEW. BEGINS WITH MARXIST THEORY; DISCUSSES LENIN AND HIS ROLE IN COMMUNIST PARTY, POLITICAL STRUCTURE, AND HARDENING OF COMMUNIST DICTATORSHIP UNDER STALIN; AND INCLUDES USSR IN WWII, LIFE IN USSR IN 1960'S, FOREIGN POLICY, INTERNATIONAL COMMUNISM, AND INTERNATIONAL RELATIONS.

2081 MILLIKAN M.F., ROSTOW W.W.
A PROPOSAL: KEY TO AN EFFECTIVE FOREIGN POLICY.
NEW YORK: HARPER & ROW, 1957, 170 PP., LC#56-12227.
PROPOSES NEW PROGRAM OF AMERICAN FOREIGN POLICY THAT CALLS FOR INCREASE IN FOREIGN AID SPENDING FOR ECONOMIC DEVELOPMENT OF UNDERDEVELOPED AREAS TO ACHIEVE GREATER AWARENESS THAT AMERICA'S GOAL IS THAT OF ALL COUNTRIES: DEVELOPMENT OF VIABLE DEMOCRATIC SOCIETIES AND THEREFORE A MORE SECURE WORLD. CRITICIZES PREVIOUS FOREIGN AID PROGRAMS.

2082 MILLIKAW M.F. ED., BLACKMER D.L.M. ED.
THE EMERGING NATIONS: THEIR GROWTH AND UNITED STATES POLICY.
BOSTON: LITTLE BROWN, 1961, 168 PP., LC#61-12119.
ANALYSIS OF PROCESS OF TRANSITION FROM "TRADITIONAL TO MODERN SOCIETY," POINTING OUT FACTORS THAT WILL BE DETERMINED BY US ACTIONS IN THESE NATIONS. IT IS ESSENTIAL TO FREE WORLD THAT US PERCEIVE THESE FACTORS AND INFLUENCE THESE NATIONS TO BE INDEPENDENT, DEMOCRATIC, AND PEACE-

LOVING.

2083 MILLIKEN M.
"NEW AND OLD CRITERIA FOR AID."
PROC. ACAD. POLIT. SCI., 27 (JAN 62), 112-24.
DISCUSSES CRITERIA FOR USA AID PROGRAMS. ANALYZES INFLUENCE OF USA ON ECONOMIC SITUATIONS IN OTHER COUNTRIES. SETS FORTH CONDITIONS FOR SUCCESSFUL UTILIZATION OF USA RESOURCES OF INFLUENCE.

2084 MILLIS W., MURRAY J.C.
FOREIGN POLICY AND THE FREE SOCIETY.
NEW YORK: OCEANA PUBLISHING, 1958, 116 PP., LC#58-12355.
DISCUSSES FOREIGN AND MILITARY POLICIES OF US IN THEIR RELATION TO CHARACTER, STANDARDS, AND GOALS OF FREE SOCIETY, INCLUDING ABRIDGED PANEL DISCUSSION OF CONSULTANTS ON THE BASIC ISSUES TO THE FUND FOR THE REPUBLIC.

2085 MILLIS W.
"THE DEMILITARIZED WORLD."
SANTA BARBARA: CENTER STUDY DEMOC. INSTIT., 1964, 61 PP.
SEES STABILIZATION OF USA-SOVIET COLD WAR SINCE 1954, AND TREND TO NON-VIOLENT REGULATION OF POWER STRUGGLES. FORESEES CONSTITUTION FOR DEMILITARIZED WORLD BASED ON ASSUMPTION THAT MAJOR WARS OBSOLETE. OUTLINES SUPRA-NATIONAL AUTHORITY.

2086 MINIFIE J.M.
PEACEMAKER OR POWDER-MONKEY.
LONDON: MCCLELLAND AND STEWART, 1960, 181 PP.
DISCUSSES CANADA'S ROLE IN REVOLUTIONARY, UNSTABLE WORLD SITUATION AND ITS POTENTIAL TO BECOME LEADER OF "MIDDLE NATIONS." DISCUSSES IMPORTANCE OF CANADA'S MAINTENANCE OF NEUTRALITY AND SIGNIFICANT ROLE IT CAN ASSUME BY AVOIDING TOTALLY SUBORDINATE ROLE TO US IN MATTERS OF MILITARY AND FOREIGN POLICY.

2087 MINISTERE DE L'EDUC NATIONALE
CATALOGUE DES THESES DE DOCTORAT SOUTENUES DEVANT LES UNIVERSITAIRES FRANCAISES.
PARIS: MIN DE L'EDUCATION NAT.
ANNUAL PUBLICATION SINCE 1884 LISTING DOCTORAL THESES IN FRENCH UNIVERSITIES. ITEMS ARRANGED BY UNIVERSITY AND FACULTY, THEN ALPHABETICALLY BY AUTHOR.

2088 MINISTERE FINANCES ET ECO
BULLETIN BIBLIOGRAPHIQUE.
PARIS: MIN FIN ET AFFAIRS ECO.
PUBLISHED FIVE TIMES A YEAR SINCE 1948, THIS PERIODICAL CONTAINS ABSTRACTS FROM BOOKS AND ARTICLES PERTAINING TO CURRENT ECONOMIC LIFE. EMPHASIS PRIMARILY ON FRENCH COLONIES AND FORMER COLONIES. SOURCES PRIMARILY FRENCH; SOME ENGLISH. TOPICS INCLUDE POLITICAL INSTITUTIONS, ECONOMIC ORGANIZATIONS, PRODUCTION, EXCHANGES. GEOGRAPHICAL INDEX.

2089 GT. BRIT MIN OVERSEAS DEV, LIB
TECHNICAL CO-OPERATION -- A BIBLIOGRAPHY.
LONDON: MIN OF OVERSEAS DEVEL.
MONTHLY LISTING, FIRST PUBLISHED 1964, OF CURRENT OFFICIAL PUBLICATIONS OF THE COMMONWEALTH, DOCUMENTS, PROCESSED AND UNPUBLISHED MATERIALS, AND OTHER REPORTS AND BULLETINS FROM FOREIGN INSTITUTIONS. ENTRIES PERTAIN TO ECONOMIC, SOCIAL, LEGAL, AND STATISTICAL ASPECTS OF TECHNICAL DEVELOPMENT.

2090 MITCHELL P.
AFRICAN AFTERTHOUGHTS.
LONDON: HUTCHINSON & CO, 1954, 288 PP.
NARRATES AUTHOR'S CAREER AS GOVERNOR OF PROTECTORATE OF UGANDA AND AS DISTRICT OFFICER BEFORE THAT. EXAMINES HISTORY OF COLONIALISM, KAISER'S WAR, INDIRECT RULE, LAND TENURE, AND SITUATION FROM 1935-40. DISCUSSES EFFECTS OF WWII, ACTIONS OF MAU MAU, AND SITUATION IN 1954.

2091 MITRANY D.
A WORKING PEACE SYSTEM.
LONDON: NATIONAL PEACE COUNCIL, 1946, 64 PP.
MODERN TREND SHOULD BE TOWARD UNITY THROUGH FUNCTIONAL EVOLUTION. PREFERS TO BRING NATIONS ACTIVELY TOGETHER WITH EXECUTIVE AGENCIES RETAINING SOVEREIGNTY OF EACH NATION.

2092 MOBERG E.
"THE EFFECT OF SECURITY POLICY MEASURES: DISCUSSION RELATED TO SWEDEN'S SECURITY POLICY."
COOPERATION AND CONFLICT, 2 (1967), 67-81.
ANALYZES MORAL AND PRACTICAL PROBLEMS INVOLVED IN DECIDING TOTAL AMOUNG OF RESOURCES TO BE SPENT ON SWEDEN'S SECURITY, AND WHERE RESOURCES SHOUD BE ALLOCATED. PROVIDES "ANALYTICAL SCHEME" TO VIEW RELATIONSHIP BETWEEN SECURITY POLICY MEASURE AND GOAL ATTAINMENT, AND APPLIES SCHEME TO SOME OF SWEDEN'S PROBLEMS.

2093 MOCH J.
HUMAN FOLLY: DISARM OR PERISH.
LONDON: GOLLANCZ, 1955, 220 PP.
DEVELOPES THE DISARMAMENT QUESTION THROUGH FIRST STUDYING THE MILITARY-TECHNICAL SITUATION AS IT DEVELOPED SINCE CREATION OF ATOMIC BOMB, AND THEN REVIEWING USA'S ATTEMPTS TO REACH A PEACEFUL SOLUTION. FORSEES INEVIBILITY OF CONFLICT UNLESS PROGRESS MADE IN FIELD OF DISARMAMENT.

2094 MOCKFORD J.
SOUTH-WEST AFRICA AND THE INTERNATIONAL COURT (PAMPHLET)
LONDON: DIPLOMATIC PRESS, 1950, 16 PP.
DISCUSSES STATUS OF SOUTH-WEST AFRICA AND ITS PEOPLE AS GERMAN COLONY, UNDER BRITISH RULE, AND UNDER CONTROL OF SOUTH AFRICA. DEALS WITH SOVEREIGNTY OF SOUTH-WEST AFRICA AND INTERNATIONAL ATTEMPTS TO SEPARATE IT FROM SOUTH AFRICAN DOMINATION.

2095 MOCKLER-FERRYMAN A.
BRITISH WEST AFRICA.
LONDON: SWAN SONNENSCHEIN, 1900, 512 PP.
COMPREHENSIVE STUDY OF BRITISH POSSESSIONS IN WEST AFRICA WHICH ALSO TRACES HISTORY OF EUROPEAN COLONIALISM IN AFRICA, STRESSING ITS SIGNIFICANCE IN INTERNATIONAL POLITICS. EXAMINES EACH BRITISH WEST AFRICAN POSSESSION IN DETAIL, DISCUSSING PROBLEMS OF GOVERNMENT AND TRADE; EXPLORATIONS AND MILITARY CONFLICTS; AND DIFFICULTIES ARISING FROM CULTURAL DIFFERENCES OF BRITISH AND AFRICANS.

2096 MODELSKI G.
ATOMIC ENERGY IN THE COMMUNIST BLOC.
NEW YORK: CAMBRIDGE, 1959, 221 PP.
THE COMMUNIST BLOC'S INCREASED KNOWLEDGE IN THE ATOMIC ENERGY FIELD DURING THE PAST DECADE IS SPECTACULAR NOT ONLY IN ITS GROWTH, BUT ALSO IN ITS DIVERSIFICATION AND DISSEMINATION OF ACQUIRED KNOWLEDGE. THIS SPREAD OF KNOWLEDGE AMONG THE NATIONS WILL HAVE DEFINITE REPERCUSSIONS IN THE QUEST FOR INTERNATIONAL CONTROL OF ATOMIC ENERGY.

2097 MODELSKI G.
"AUSTRALIA AND SEATO."
INT. ORG., (SUMMER 60), 429-37.
DESCRIBES AUSTRALIAN INFLUENCE IN SOUTH EAST ASIA. DISCUSSES VALUABLE ROLE IT HAS COME TO PLAY WITHIN THE TREATY. DESCRIBES SEATO'S POLITICAL AND MILITARY FUNCTIONS. ANALYZES AMERICAN INTEREST IN AUSTRALIA.

2098 MODELSKI G. ED.
SEATO-SIX STUDIES.
VANCOUVER: PUB. REL. CENTER, U. BRIT. COLUMB., 1962, 287 PP.
CONCERNED WITH FUNCTIONS OF SEATO, PLACE OF SMALL NATIONS WITHIN SEATO, ROLE OF TWO LARGE MEMBER STATES, COMMUNIST CHINA AND INDIA, AND THEIR RELATIONS TO MEMBER STATES. ALSO COVERS ROLE OF GREAT POWERS IN ASIAN TRADE RELATIONSHIPS.

2099 MODELSKI G.
"STUDY OF ALLIANCES."
J. CONFL. RESOLUT., 7 (DEC. 63), 769-76.
REVIEWS RECENT BOOKS ON ALLIANCES. FAVORS FINER DISTINCTIONS BETWEEN TERMS.

2100 MOLLAU G.
INTERNATIONAL COMMUNISM AND WORLD REVOLUTION: HISTORY AND METHODS.
NEW YORK: PRAEGER, 1961, 357 PP.
TRACES INTERNATIONAL COMMUNIST MOVEMENT FROM 1848 TO PRESENT. INCLUDES DISCUSSION OF THE RUSSIAN REVOLUTION, THE SOVIET UNION, THE COMINTERN, THE COMINFORM AND THE METHODS USED TO ACHIEVE SOVIET GOALS.

2101 MOLNAR T.
AFRICA: A POLITICAL TRAVELOGUE.
NEW YORK: FLEET PUBL CORP, 1965, 303 PP., LC#65-16312.
AN EDUCATED TOUR THROUGH THE POLITICS AND STRUCTURE OF AFRICAN SOCIETY. BRINGS OUT THAT NATIONAL INDEPENDENCE CAME NOT SO MUCH AS A RESULT OF AFRICANS' EFFORTS BUT RATHER WAS CAUSED BY SITUATION IN EUROPE AT THE TIME. STUDIES COMMUNIST OUTREACH TODAY.

2103 MONCONDUIT F.
LA COMMISSION EUROPEENNE DES DROITS DE L'HOMME.
LEYDEN, NETHERLANDS: AW SIJTHOFF, 1965, 559 PP.
WORK UNDERTAKEN UNDER AUSPICES OF COUNCIL OF EUROPE ON EUROPEAN COMMISSION FOR HUMAN RIGHTS, THE JUDICIAL BODY OF THE COUNCIL. PRESENTS GENERAL THEORY ON RIGHT TO JUDGE AND ON POWERS OF COMMISSION, SPECIFIES TERMS AND IMPORT OF TREATY WHICH CREATED IT, AND STUDIES ITS JUDICIAL ACTIONS.

2104 MONCRIEFF A. ED.
THE STRATEGY OF SURVIVAL.
LONDON: BRITISH BROADCAST CORP, 1962, 57 PP.
DISCUSSIONS ON BBC CONCERNING EAST-WEST RELATIONS. EXAMINATION OF MILITARY STRATEGY AND FOREIGN POLICY OF BRITAIN.

2105 MONCRIEFF A. ED.
SECOND THOUGHTS ON AID.
LONDON: BRITISH BROADCAST CORP, 1965, 138 PP.
BEGINS WITH ESSENTIAL BROAD POLITICAL AND PHILOSOPHICAL ISSUES FROM POINTS OF VIEW OF DONORS AND RECIPIENTS. ARGUES URGENCY OF ECONOMIC PROBLEM AND EXAMINES PRACTICES OF PRIVATE INVESTMENT AND INTERNATIONAL INSTITUTIONS. USING

FACTS ABOUT AGRICULTURE, TECHNICAL ASSISTANCE, AND EDUCATION STATES THAT ROLE OF ECONOMICS MAY BE LIMITED. CONSIDERS POSSIBLE CONTRIBUTION FROM OTHER SOCIAL SCIENCE DISCIPLINES.

2106 MONGER G.W.
THE END OF ISOLATION.
NEW YORK: THOMAS NELSON AND SONS, 1963, 343 PP.
DISCUSSES BRITISH FOREIGN POLICY 1900-1907 AND DECLINE OF HER EMPIRE AND PAX BRITANNICA WHICH MADE ISOLATIONISM AND A LACK OF ALLIES AN IMPRACTICAL FOREIGN POLICY. CONSIDERS CRITICAL EVENTS PRIOR TO WWI: RISE OF GERMANY AND JAPAN; RUSSO-JAPANESE WAR; RUSSIAN ENTENTE, AND MOROCCAN CRISIS. EXAMINES ESPECIALLY BRITAIN'S RELATIONS WITH FRANCE AND GERMANY.

2107 MONNIER J.P.
"LA SUCCESSION D'ETATS EN MATIERE DE RESPONSABILITE INTERNATIONALE."
ANNU. FRANC. DR. INTER., 8 (1962), 65-90.
DISCUSSES QUESTION OF LEGAL OBLIGATIONS OF MANY STATES THAT HAVE ALTERED CONSTITUTIONAL STRUCTURE. SHOWS THAT RECENT JURIDICAL DECISIONS HAS LEFT PROBLEM UNRESOLVED. CONCLUDES ALTERED STATE HAS RETROACTIVE RESPONSIBILITY.

2108 MONPIED E., ROUSCOS G., ZALESKI E.
BIBLIOGRAPHIE FEDERALISTE: ARTICLES ET DOCUMENTS PUBLIES DANS LES PERIODIQUES PARUS EN FRANCE NOV. 1945-OCT. 1950.
PARIS: UNION FEDER INTER-UNIV, 1950, 162 PP.
LISTS, ANNOTATES, AND INDEXES 1,227 ARTICLES APPEARING IN FRENCH PERIODICALS FROM 1945 TO 1950. DEALS WITH THEORIES AND DOCTRINES OR FEDERALISM; EUROPEAN FEDERATIONS; WORLD FEDERAL GOVERNMENT; FEDERALIST ACTIVITIES THROUGHOUT THE WORLD. COUNTRY-BY-COUNTRY GUIDE TO FEDERALISM WITH AN INTRODUCTION STATING FEDERALIST PRINCIPLES AND POLICIES.

2109 MONPIED E., ZALESKI E. ET AL.
BIBLIOGRAPHIE FEDERALISTE: OUVRAGES CHOISIS (VOL. I, MIMEOGRAPHED PAPER)
PARIS: UNION FEDER INTER-UNIV, 1950, 87 PP.
LISTS AND ANNOTATES 640 ITEMS PUBLISHED PRIOR TO, DURING, AND SINCE WORLD WAR I DEALING WITH FEDERALISM, EUROPEAN FEDERATION, OR WORLD GOVERNMENT. ARRANGED TOPICALLY AND CHRONOLOGICALLY.

2110 MONPIED E., ROUSSOS G., ZALESKI E.
FEDERALIST BIBLIOGRAPHY: ARTICLES AND DOCUMENTS PUBLISHED IN BRITISH PERIODICALS 1945-1951 (MIMEOGRAPHED)
LONDON: FED TRUST FOR ED & RES, 1951, 137 PP.
COMPILES, ANNOTATES, AND INDEXES 1,354 ARTICLES DEALING WITH WORLD FEDERALISM, EUROPEAN UNITY, ETC. RESTRICTED TO THOSE PUBLISHED IN UK BETWEEN 1945 AND 1951.

2111 MONTALVA E.F.
"THE ALLIANCE THAT LOST ITS WAY."
FOREIGN AFFAIRS, 45 (APR. 67), 437-448.
ANALYZES ECONOMIC AND POLITICAL PROBLEMS RESULTING FROM FAILURE OF ALLIANCE FOR PROGRESS TO PROMOTE INTEGRATION OF LATIN AMERICA. DECLARES SALVATION OF ALLIANCE DEPENDS ON THREE FACTORS: SUPPORT OF INTEGRATION OF LA NATIONS, DISCOURAGEMENT OF ARMAMENTS RACE, AND PLANNING COOPERATIVE SOLUTION FOR ECONOMIC TRADE PROBLEMS. BELIEVES IMMEDIATE GOAL SHOULD BE COMPLETE INTER-AMERICAN COOPERATION.

2112 MONTER W.
THE GOVERNMENT OF GENEVA, 1536-1605 (DOCTORAL THESIS)
PRINCETON: PRIN U, DEPT OF HIST, 1963, 299 PP.
CONCENTRATING ON POLITICS IN NARROW SENSE AND OMITTING ECCLESIASTICAL DEVELOPMENTS, AUTHOR PROVIDES GENERAL REINTERPRETATION OF GENEVA'S POLITICAL HISTORY 1536-1605. ATTEMPTS TO SHED LIGHT ON ASPECTS OF CALVIN'S ROME. RELATES HISTORY OF GENEVAN PUBLIC FINANCE DURING FIRST 70 YEARS OF NDEPENDENCE. ALSO EXPLAINS ASPECTS OF ADMINISTRATION, EVOLUTION OF RULING CLASS; ASSESSES CALVIN'S POLITICAL ROLE.

2113 MONTGOMERY B.L.
AN APPROACH TO SANITY; A STUDY OF EAST-WEST RELATIONS.
CLEVELAND: WORLD, 1960, 94 PP., LC#60-6684.
COLLECTION OF LECTURES AND ARTICLES BY VISCOUNT MONTGOMERY ON EAST-WEST CONFLICT. DISCUSSES STRUCTURE AND CHANGES IN NATO ALLIANCE, TALKS WITH KHRUSHCHEV, AND CHRONOLOGICAL ANALYSIS OF INTERNATIONAL RELATIONS FROM WWII TO 1960'S.

2114 MONTGOMERY H., CAMBRAY P.G.
"A DICTIONARY OF POLITICAL PHRASES AND ILLUSIONS WITH A SHORT BIBLIOGRAPHY."
NEW YORK: EP DUTTON, 1906.
BIBLIOGRAPHY INCLUDES WORKS ON POLITICAL SUBJECTS RELEVANT TO ENGLISH DOMESTIC AND FOREIGN POLICY. PARTICULARLY EMPHASIZES COLONIAL ISSUE. INDEX OF NAMES. DICTIONARY GIVES HISTORY AND EVOLUTION OF COMMONLY USED POLITICAL TERMS.

2115 MONTGOMERY J.D.
THE POLITICS OF FOREIGN AID: AMERICAN EXPERIENCE IN SOUTHEAST ASIA.
NEW YORK: FREDERICK PRAEGER, 1962, 336 PP., LC#62-16827.
INTERNATIONAL PURPOSES AND ACHIEVEMENTS OF FOREIGN AID, PROBLEMS OF MUTUALITY IN FOREIGN AID, ORGANIZING FOREIGN AID, AMERICAN POLITICS AND FOREIGN AID ARE DISCUSSED.

2116 MONTGOMERY J.D. ED., SIFFIN W.J. ED.
APPROACHES TO DEVELOPMENT: POLITICS, ADMINISTRATION AND CHANGE.
NEW YORK: MCGRAW HILL, 1966, 299 PP., LC#66-14536.
EXAMINES RELATIONSHIP BETWEEN ADMINISTRATIVE CONCEPTS AND THEIR SOCIO-POLITICAL CONTEXT. INCLUDES STUDIES OF POLITICAL DEVELOPMENT; POLITICS OF DEVELOPMENT ADMINISTRATION; RURAL GOVERNMENT AND STRATEGY OF AGRICULTURAL DEVELOPMENT; STRATEGY AND TACTICS OF PUBLIC ADMINISTRATION; TECHNICAL ASSISTANCE.

2117 MOODY M. ED.
CATALOG OF INTERNATIONAL LAW AND RELATIONS (20 VOLS.)
NEW YORK: OCEANA PUBLISHING, 1965, 64-0000 PP.
BOOK CATALOG OF INTERNATIONAL RELATIONS. TWENTY VOLUMES ARRANGED ALPHABETICALLY. AUTHOR, SUBJECT AND TITLE ARRANGED IN SINGLE ALPHABETICAL FILE. CONTAINS SOME 360,000 ITEMS IN ALL LANGUAGES.

2118 MOOMAW I.W.
THE CHALLENGE OF HUNGER.
NEW YORK: FREDERICK PRAEGER, 1966, 222 PP., LC#66-13670.
DESCRIBES NEED FOR INCREASES IN FOREIGN AID AND PROGRAM TO ACCOMPLISH IT. DISCUSSES PAST WASTEFULNESS IN PROGRAM AND IMPORTANCE OF FOREIGN AID TO NATIONAL INTEREST AND POSSIBLE ROLE OF PRIVATE INDUSTRY IN HELPING.

2119 MOON P.
DIVIDE AND QUIT.
BERKELEY: U OF CALIF PR, 1962, 302 PP.
DISCUSSES CAUSES OF DISTURBANCES IN PUNJAB IN 1947 AND POLITICAL EVENTS PRECEEDING UPHEAVAL. ALSO GIVES DETAILED DESCRIPTION OF EVENTS IN STATE OF BAHAWALPUR FROM AUGUST, 1947 ONWARD AS OBSERVED BY THE AUTHOR.

2120 MOON P.T.
"SYLLABUS ON INTERNATIONAL RELATIONS."
LONDON: MACMILLAN, 1925.
COMPREHENSIVE SURVEY OF ECONOMIC, GEOGRAPHIC, SOCIOLOGICAL ASPECTS OF INTERNATIONAL RELATIONS FOR UNDERGRADUATE USE. CITATION OF SOURCE MATERIAL GENERALLY CONFINED TO THAT LEVEL. GENERAL BIBLIOGRAPHY AT END AND BIBLIOGRAPHICAL REFERENCES FOR EACH CHAPTER INCLUDED. TRACES HISTORY OF INTERNATIONAL RELATIONS UP TO 1920'S.

2121 MOOR C.C.
HOW TO USE UNITED NATIONS DOCUMENTS (PAPER)
NEW YORK: NEW YORK U PR, 1952, 26 PP.
PREPARED FOR USE BY RESEARCH SCHOLARS AND LIBRARIANS. DISCUSSES METHODS AND PROBLEMS OF RESEARCH, BASIC TOOLS AND GUIDES OF BOTH THE UN AND ITS ORGANS, AND ALSO INCLUDES A BASIC SUBJECT GUIDE AS WELL AS APPENDIXES. CONTAINS A LIST OF 18 BOOKS PERTINENT TO INTERNATIONAL DOCUMENTATION.

2122 MOORE B.T.
NATO AND THE FUTURE OF EUROPE.
NEW YORK: HARPER, 1958, 263 PP.
CONCERNED WITH EFFECT ON NATO OF NUCLEAR WEAPONS AND THE CHANGING POLITICAL AND ECONOMIC STRUCTURE OF WESTERN EUROPE. CONSIDERS ORGANIZATIONS UNITING WESTERN EUROPE AND CONTRASTS WITH 'LOOSER ELEMENTS' IN NATO ASSOCIATION. CONCLUDES THAT WESTERN EUROPE AND NORTH AMERICA CANNOT CONTINUE TO SEPARATE THEIR STRATEGIC ALLIANCES FROM ECONOMIC UNITS.

2123 MOORE N.
"THE LAWFULNESS OF MILITARY ASSISTANCE TO THE REPUBLIC OF VIET NAM."
AMER. J. OF INT. LAW, 61 (JAN. 67), 1-34.
ARGUES THAT US MILITARY INTERVENTION IN VIET NAM IS LAWFUL BY UN STANDARDS BECAUSE (1) THE CONFLICT IS NOT A CIVIL WAR, BUT INVASION OF ONE COUNTRY BY ANOTHER, AND (2) US IS ACTING TO RESTORE AND MAINTAIN THE INTERNATIONAL BALANCE EXISTING PRIOR TO THIS INVASION. SUGGESTS THAT US INTERESTS BE CLARIFIED IN THAT THE US HAS NO INTENTION OF ALTERING THE TERRITORIAL INTEGRITY OF THE DEMOCRATIC VIETNAMESE REPUBLIC.

2124 MOORE R.J.
SIR CHARLES WOOD'S INDIAN POLICY: 1853-66.
MANCHESTER: MANCHESTER UNIV PR, 1966, 284 PP.
HISTORICAL ANALYSIS OF POLICY OF PRESIDENT OF BOARD OF CONTROL FOR INDIA IN LORD ABERDEEN'S GOVERNMENT. DESCRIBES PROBLEMS OF ADMINISTRATIVE DISARRAY FACED AND HIS EFFICIENT SOLUTIONS; AUTHOR INCLUDES FAVORABLE EVALUATION OF "WHIG IMPERIALIST."

2125 MOORE W.E.
"PREDICTING DISCONTINUITIES IN SOCIAL CHANGE."
AMER. SOC. REV., 29 (JUNE 64), 331-38.
DISCUSSES REVOLUTIONS AND THEIR CAUSES, INTERMINGLED WITH THEORY OF CHANGE IN RELATION TO TECHNOLOGY, TIME AND CYCLES.

2126 MORA J.A.

"THE ORGANIZATION OF AMERICAN STATES."
INT. ORGAN., 14 (FALL 60), 514-523.
OUTLINES PRINCIPLES, RULES AND ORGANS THROUGH WHICH MEMBER STATES SEEK TO ATTAIN SYSTEM'S OBJECTIVES. DISCUSSION OF MAJOR ISSUE (ECONOMIC CO-OPERATION BETWEEN MEMBERS) AND EXPRESSION OF ENCOURAGEMENT AT 'CURRENT VISION OF MEMBERS.'

2127 MORAES F.
THE REVOLT IN TIBET.
NEW YORK: MACMILLAN, 1960, 223 PP., LC#60-6644.
DESCRIBES COMMUNIST CHINESE INVASION OF TIBET WHICH BEGAN IN 1950 AND DOCUMENTS AIMS AND BACKGROUND OF INVASION. DESCRIBES ECONOMIC EXPLOITATION AND RELIGIOUS AND SOCIAL REPRESSION OF TIBETANS BY CHINESE; ANALYZES TIBET'S ROLE IN CURRENT RELATIONS BETWEEN INDIA AND RED CHINA.

2128 MORALES C.J.
"TRADE AND ECONOMIC INTEGRATION IN LATIN AMERICA."
SOC. SCI., 35 (OCT. 60), 231-37.
ILLUSTRATES ARRANGEMENTS FOR ECONOMIC INTEGRATION BY LATIN AMERICAN COUNTRIES, BUT CONSIDERS ECONOMIC FOUNDATIONS NOT FAVORABLE FOR SUCH PLANS AND INDUSTRIAL DEVELOPMENT NOT SUFFICIENTLY ADVANCED. PROPOSES A TRADE FREE ZONE AS AN ALTERNATIVE SCHEME. LAFTA COUNTRIES' PLANS TO ELIMINATE TARIFFS AND OTHER TRADE BARRIERS MAY PROMOTE INTRA-REGIONAL TRADE.

2129 MOREL E.D.
AFFAIRS OF WEST AFRICA.
LONDON: HEINEMANN, 1902, 381 PP.
CONSIDERS THE RACIAL, POLITICAL, AND COMMERCIAL PROBLEMS, AND THEIR YEARLY INCREASE IN MAGNITUDE, CONNECTED WITH THE ADMINISTRATION OF WEST AFRICA BY GREAT BRITAIN AND OTHER POWERS OF WESTERN EUROPE THAT PARTICIPATED IN THE SCRAMBLE FOR AFRICAN TERRITORY. INCLUDES STUDIES OF TRIBES, PLANTATIONS, TRADE, FINANCE, AND GOVERNMENT. HAS MANY INTERESTING OLD PHOTOGRAPHS.

2130 MOREL E.D.
THE BRITISH CASE IN FRENCH CONGO.
LONDON: HEINEMANN, 1903, 215 PP.
CRITICISM OF DRASTIC MEASURES TAKEN BY FRENCH GOVERNMENT IN FRENCH CONGO TO INTERFERE WITH BRITISH TRADE AND ABUSE RIGHTS OF BRITISH MERCHANTS. ARGUES THAT CONCESSIONS DECREE OF 1899 , WHICH AUTHORIZED MEASURES, VIOLATED BERLIN ACT OF 1885 THAT ESTABLISHED RIGHT OF FREE TRADE FOR ALL NATIONS IN CONGO BASIN. ASSESSES DAMAGE DONE TO FRENCH AND BRITISH INTERESTS BY ACTIONS OF THE CONCESSIONNAIRE REGIME.

2131 MORGAN T. ED.
GOLDWATER EITHER/OR; A SELF-PORTRAIT BASED UPON HIS OWN WORDS.
WASHINGTON: PUBLIC AFFAIRS PRESS, 1964, 72 PP., LC#64-8212.
COLLECTION OF PUBLIC STATEMENTS BY BARRY GOLDWATER ON HIS VIEWS OF ELECTION ISSUES DURING PRESIDENTIAL COMPAIGN OF 1964. TOPICS COVER EXTREMISM, AGRICULTURE, CIVIL RIGHTS, ECONOMICS, EDUCATION, LABOR, POVERTY, NATURAL RESOURCES, SOCIAL REFORM, DEFENSE, FOREIGN POLICY, AND ROLE OF CONSTITUTION. INCLUDES PRESS COMMENTS ON HIS STATEMENTS.

2132 MORGENSTERN O.
THE COMMAND AND CONTROL STRUCTURE (PAMPHLET)
PRINCETON: PRIN U ECONOMET RES, 1962, 25 PP.
ADDRESS TO NINTH MILITARY OPERATIONS RESEARCH SYMPOSIUM. SEES URGENT NEED TO PROVIDE SATISFACTORY COMMAND-CONTROL SYSTEM. IF US NEGLECTS TO, IT HAS NO FOUNDATION FOR POLITICAL ACTIONS INVOLVING THE VERY EXISTENCE OF NATION AND THE PRESERVATION OF PEACE.

2133 MORGENSTERN O.
"GOAL: AN ARMED, INSPECTED, OPEN WORLD."
FORTUNE, 62 (JULY 60), 93-95, 219-27.
SEES INTERNATIONAL ARMAMENT STABILIZATION SUCCESS AS DEPENDENT UPON ASSURED MUTUAL DETERRENCE, EFFECTIVE ARMS CONTROL, AND FREE MOVEMENT OF SCIENTIFIC DATA. BELIEVES ARMS LIMITATIONS BY EQUAL REDUCTIONS OR FREEZING STOCKPILES ACTUALLY MAINTAINS INEQUALITIES. HOLDS THAT INSPECTIONS SYSTEM MUST COVER FUTURE PRODUCTION AND THAT RESEARCH IN ALLIED FIELDS BEST ACHIEVED UNDER OPEN WORLD ATMOSPHERE.

2134 MORGENSTERN O.
STRATEGIE - HEUTE (2ND ED.)
STUTTGART: FISCHER VERLAG, 1962, 320 PP.
DISCUSSES PROBLEMS OF MILITARY STRATEGY RESULTING FROM US-USSR CONFRONTATION. EXAMINES TECHNOLOGICAL ADVANCES, ECONOMIC STRENGTH, PROBLEMS OF MILITARY SECURITY, PROLIFERATION OF NUCLEAR WEAPONS, AND FEASIBILITY OF LIMITED WAR. CENTERS ON COMPARISON BETWEEN US AND USSR.

2135 MORGENTHAU H.J.
POLITICS AMONG NATIONS: THE STRUGGLE FOR POWER AND PEACE.
NEW YORK: ALFRED KNOPF, 1948, 489 PP.
ATTEMPTS TO DETECT AND UNDERSTAND FORCES THAT DETERMINE POLITICAL RELATIONS AMONG NATIONS, AND TO COMPREHEND WAYS THOSE FORCES ACT UPON EACH OTHER. SEEKS TO UNDERSTAND MID-20TH CENTURY POLITICS. SHOWS THAT PEACE CAN BE MAINTAINED ONLY BY BALANCE OF POWER, INTERNATIONAL LAW AND MORALITY, AND WORLD PUBLIC OPINION.

2136 MORGENTHAU H.J.
MORGENTHAU DIARY (CHINA) (2 VOLS.)
WASHINGTON: US GOVERNMENT, 1965, 1699 PP.
RECORD OF SECRETARY OF TREASURY MORGENTHAU'S ACTIVITIES RELATING TO CHINA, FROM JANUARY, 1934 TO JULY, 1945. PREPARED BY SUBCOMMITTEE TO INVESTIGATE ADMINISTRATION OF INTERNAL SECURITY ACT AND OTHER SECURITY LAWS OF SENATE COMMITTEE ON THE JUDICIARY.

2137 MORGENTHAU H.J.
"THE TWILIGHT OF INTERNATIONAL MORALITY" (BMR)"
ETHICS, 58 (JAN. 48), 79-99.
DISCUSSES ETHICAL LIMITATIONS ON INTERNATIONAL POLICIES AND DIFFERENCES IN MORAL RESTRAINTS IN TIMES OF PEACE AND WAR. DISCUSSES ETHIC OF PROTECTING HUMAN LIFE, HOW THIS IS MAINTAINED, AND HOW THIS IS DISREGARDED. EXAMINES UNIVERSAL ETHICS VERSUS NATIONALISTIC UNIVERSALISM. FINDS MORALITY HAS DISAPPEARED IN MODERN WORLD AS EACH NATION SEEKS TO IMPOSE ITS SYSTEM ON REST OF WORLD.

2138 MORGENTHAU H.J.
POLITICS IN THE TWENTIETH CENTURY: IMPASSE OF AMERICAN FOREIGN POLICY.
CHICAGO: U. CHI. PR., 1962, 305 PP.
EXAMINES AMERICAN FOREIGN POLICY WEAKNESSES, POSITIVE AND NEGATIVE EFFECTS. DISCUSSES POST-WAR TACTICS, MISCONCEPTIONS AND INTERESTS.

2139 MORGENTHAU H.J.
POLITICS IN THE 20TH CENTURY: RESTORATION OF AMERICAN POLITICS.
CHICAGO: U. CHI. PR., 1962, 384 PP.
SELECTION OF REPRESENTATIVE ESSAYS ON POLITICAL PHILOSOPHY. COVER USA DOMESTIC POLICIES, INTERNATIONAL RELATIONS, AND CONTEMPORARY CONCERNS OF UN, SUCH AS REGIONALISM. SEES 20TH POLITICS AS US-CENTERED.

2140 MORGENTHAU H.J.
"A POLITICAL THEORY OF FOREIGN AID."
AMER. POLIT. SCI. REV., 56 (JUNE 62), 301-309.
SEES NEED TO DEVELOPE INTELLIGIBLE THEORY OF FOREIGN AID, SO TO PROVIDE STANDARDS FOR DISCUSSION. CLASSIFIES AID INTO 6 TYPES AND PARTICULARY DISCUSSES THE ASPECTS AND SUCCESSES OF AID 'FOR ECONOMIC DEVELOPMENT.' CONCLUDES THAT US MUST LEARN TO CHOOSE QUANTITY AND QUALITY OF AID APPROPRIATE TO SITUATION, TO ATTUNE DIFFERENT TYPES OF AID TO EACH OTHER, AND TREAT FOREIGN AID AS INTEGRAL PART OF POLITICAL POLICY.

2141 MORGENTHAU H.J.
"THE POLITICAL CONDITIONS FOR AN INTERNATIONAL POLICE FORCE."
INT. ORGAN., 17 (SPRING 63), 393-403.
EFFECTIVENESS AND RELIABILITY OF INTERNATIONAL POLICE FORCE DEPEND ON LEGAL ORDER AND MAINTENANCE OF POLITICAL STATUS QUO. WOULD FUNCTION BEST IN TOTALLY DISARMED WORLD.

2142 MORISON E.E.
TURMOIL AND TRADITION: A STUDY OF THE LIFE AND TIMES OF HENRY L. STIMSON.
BOSTON: HOUGHTON MIFFLIN, 1960, 565 PP.
BIOGRAPHY OF THE STATESMAN FROM 1867-1950. COVERS MOST ASPECTS OF HIS PUBLIC LIFE, INCLUDING HIS SERVICE AS UNITED STATES DISTRICT ATTORNEY, SECRETARY OF WAR UNDER PRESIDENT TAFT, SECRETARY OF STATE UNDER PRESIDENT HOOVER, AND SECRETARY OF WAR UNDER PRESIDENT FRANKLIN ROOSEVELT.

2143 MORLEY F.
THE SOCIETY OF NATIONS.
WASHINGTON: BROOKINGS INST., 1932, 678 PP.
UNDERTAKES EXAMINATION OF CONSTITUTIONAL DEVELOPMENTS OF THE LEAGUE OF NATIONS AND OF ITS GROWTH FROM FIRST PAPER PLANS TO THE COMPLICATED INTERNATIONAL MACHINERY ESTABLISHED AT GENEVA.

2144 MORLEY L., MORLEY F.
THE PATCHWORK HISTORY OF FOREIGN AID.
WASHINGTON: AMER ENTERPRISE INST, 1961, 55 PP., LC#61-11619.
DISCUSSION OF AMERICAN FOREIGN AID DEVELOPMENT AND HISTORICAL SETTING AFTER WWII: AID FOR RELIEF AND RECONSTRUCTION; MARSHALL PLAN AND ECONOMIC COOPERATION ACT OF 1948; AID FOR MILITARY ALLIANCES WITH KOREA, NATIONALIST CHINA, ASIA; AID FOR ECONOMIC DEVELOPMENT; AND RIVALRY BETWEEN US AND USSR.

2145 MORRAY J.P.
FROM YALTA TO DISARMAMENT: COLD WAR DEBATE.
NEW YORK: MONTHLY REVIEW PR, 1961, 368 PP., LC#61-1405.
ORIGIN OF COLD WAR SEEN IN CHURCHILL'S FULTON, MISSOURI, SPEECH. EMPHASIS ON DISARMAMENT NEGOTIATIONS; HIGHLY CRITICAL OF US POLICY.

2146 MORRAY J.P.
THE SECOND REVOLUTION IN CUBA.

NEW YORK: MONTHLY REVIEW PR, 1962, 173 PP.
SYMPATHETIC ACCOUNT OF THE CUBAN REVOLUTION. ATTEMPTS TO SEE THE EVENTS IN CUBA AS A REPLICATION OF THE 1917 OCTOBER REVOLUTION IN RUSSIA. HIGHLY CRITICAL OF US POLICY TOWARD CUBA; MARXIST EXPLANATION OF THE FUTURE COURSE OF THE REVOLUTION.

2147 MORRIS B.S.
INTERNATIONAL COMMUNISM AND AMERICAN POLICY.
NEW YORK: ATHERTON PRESS, 1966, 179 PP., LC#66-20834.
ATTEMPTS TO PLACE SINO-SOVIET SPLIT IN HISTORICAL PERSPECTIVE AND TO DEFINE AMERICAN POSITION IN RELATION TO FRAGMENTATION OF INTERNATIONAL COMMUNISM.

2148 MORRIS H.C.
THE HISTORY OF COLONIZATION.
NEW YORK: MACMILLAN, 1900, 842 PP.
DISCUSSES ORIGINS, METHODS AND OBJECTIVES OF COLONIZATION, AND CITES ADVANTAGES AND DISADVANTAGES OF SUCH A POLICY. STUDIES THE CAUSES WHICH LEAD TO THE EVENTUAL SEVERANCE OF COLONIAL TIES AND THE ESTABLISHMENT OF INDEPENDENT STATES.

2149 MORRIS R.B.
THE PEACEMAKERS; THE GREAT POWERS AND AMERICAN INDEPENDENCE.
NEW YORK: HARPER & ROW, 1965, 572 PP., LC#65-20435.
ANALYSIS OF DIPLOMATIC NEGOTIATIONS INVOLVED IN OBTAINING PEACE AND INDEPENDENCE IN REVOLUTIONARY WAR. DEALS WITH ACTIVITIES OF REVOLUTIONARY LEADERS AND EUROPEAN POWERS TO END CONFLICT IN 1782-83 PEACE NEGOTIATIONS.

2150 MORTON L.
STRATEGY AND COMMAND: THE FIRST TWO YEARS.
WASHINGTON: US GOVERNMENT, 1962, 761 PP., LC#61-60001.
OFFICIAL HISTORY OF US ARMY IN PACIFIC IN WWII, THIS VOLUME COVERS FIRST TWO YEARS. INCLUDES ROAD TO WAR, PEARL HARBOR TO MIDWAY, SEIZING INITIATIVE, AND EMERGING PATTERNS, PLUS OFFICIAL DOCUMENTS AND MAPS.

2151 MOSELY P.E.
THE KREMLIN AND WORLD POLITICS.
NEW YORK: VINTAGE BOOKS, 1960, 560 PP., LC#60-09146.
DISCUSSES SOVIET POLICY 1940-1960 AND ITS EFFECT ON INTERNATIONAL RELATIONS. EXAMINES NEGOTIATION TECHNIQUES, RUSSIAN EXPANSIONISM, AND OBJECTIVES OF FOREIGN POLICY. APPLIES THESE TO ANALYSIS OF POSTWAR ACTIONS IN GERMANY, EASTERN EUROPE, THE COLD WAR, SOVIET POLICY IN TWO-POWER WORLD, AND CHANGES AFTER STALIN'S DEATH.

2152 MOSELY P.E. ED.
THE SOVIET UNION, 1922-1962: A FOREIGN AFFAIRS READER.
NEW YORK: FREDERICK PRAEGER, 1963, 497 PP., LC#63-10826.
STUDIES POLITICAL HISTORY EMPHASIZING THE STALIN ERA. DISCUSSES REVOLUTIONARY RUSSIA, STRATEGY, AND PEACEFUL COEXISTENCE.

2153 MOSELY P.E.
"EASTERN EUROPE IN WORLD POWER POLITICS: WHERE DE-STALINIZATION HAS LED."
MODERN AGE, 11 (SPRING 67), 19-130.
ALTHOUGH EASTERN EUROPEAN SATELLITE COUNTRIES CAN BOAST A DEFINITE NATIONAL IDENTITY AND INCREASED ECONOMIC OPPORTUNITIES, THE NECESSARY PRE-CONDITION FOR THIS FREEDOM REMAINS ALLEGIANCE TO THE BASIC TENETS OF MARXISM-LENINISM. AN ATTEMPT IS MADE TO ASSESS THE EFFECT OF KHRUSHCHEV'S DE-STALINIZATION POLICY ON MAOIST CHINA.

2154 MOSKOWITZ H., ROBERTS J.
US SECURITY, ARMS CONTROL, AND DISARMAMENT 1961-1965.
WASHINGTON: DEPT OF THE ARMY, 1965, 140 PP.
CONTAINS 1400 LISTINGS IN ENGLISH FROM BOOKS, ARTICLES, AND DOCUMENTS. ARRANGED BY SUBJECT; PUBLICATION DATES OF ENTRIES OCTOBER, 1961-JANUARY, 1965. EXCERPTS FROM LISTINGS IN ANNOTATIONS.

2155 MOSTECKY V. ED., BUTLER W.E. ED.
SOVIET LEGAL BIBLIOGRAPHY.
CAMBRIDGE: HARVARD LAW SCHOOL, 1965, 288 PP.
INCLUDES MATERIALS PUBLISHED IN USSR SINCE 1917 AS ACQUIRED BY HARVARD LAW SCHOOL LIBRARY THROUGH JANUARY 1965. 4,068 ITEMS DIVIDED BY TYPE OF MATERIAL: LEGISLATION, COURT REPORTS, ETC., AND SUBDIVIDED BY SUBJECT. CONSTITUTIONS, ETC.; ARRANGED CHRONOLOGICALLY. SHORT ANNOTATIONS INDICATE SCOPE OF BOOK. CONCLUDES WITH AUTHOR INDEX.

2156 MOUSKHELY M. ED.
L'URSS ET LES PAYS DE L'EST.
STRASBOURG: CENTRE RECHERCHES URRS, 1960.
ANNUAL PUBLICATION WHICH SYSTEMATICALLY LISTS AND CRITICALLY ANALYZES ARTICLES ON SOVIET-ASIAN RELATIONS FROM PRINCIPAL MAGAZINES AND REVIEWS. EMPHASIZES ECONOMIC, POLITICAL, IDEOLOGICAL, AND CULTURAL TIES BETWEEN COUNTRIES. CRITICAL ANALYSES ARE WRITTEN BY SPECIALISTS FROM THE CENTRE DE RECHERCHES SUR L'URSS ET LES PAYS DE L'EST. FIRST PUBLISHED IN 1960.

2157 MOUSKHELY M.
"LA NAISSANCE DES ETATS EN DROIT INTERNATIONAL PUBLIC."
REV. GEN. DR. INT. PUB., 66 (NO.3, 62), 469-85.
FORMATION OF NEW STATES RAISES SEVERAL PROBLEMS. ANALYZES RELATION OF CONSEQUENCES TO DOMESTIC AND INTERNATIONAL. STUDIES DIRECTION OF DEVELOPMENT OF STIMSON DOCTRINE AND SUPRA-NATIONAL ORGANIZATIONS.

2158 MOUSKHELY M.
"LE BLOC COMMUNISTE ET LA COMMUNAUTE ECONOMIQUE EUROPEENNE."
REV. ECON. POLIT., 73 (NO.3, 63), 406-38.
EXAMINES SOURCES OF USSR HOSTILITY TOWARD EEC. EXPOSES SOVIET BLOC ECONOMIC MYTHS AND EUROPEAN REALITIES. RELATES QUESTION TO LABOR PROBLEMS AND TO ECONOMIES OF AFRICAN UNDERDEVELOPED COUNTRIES.

2159 MOUSSA P.
THE UNDERPRIVILEGED NATIONS.
LONDON: SIDGWICK + JACKSON, 1962, 198 PP.
ANALYSIS OF INTERNATIONAL IMPLICATIONS OF POLITICAL AND ECONOMIC GROWTH OF UNDERDEVELOPED COUNTRIES THROUGHOUT WORLD. VIEWS PROBLEMS OF UNDERDEVELOPED COUNTRIES ON COMPARATIVE BASIS WITH CONDITIONS OF INDUSTRIALIZED, PROSPEROUS COUNTRIES. STRESSES IMPORTANCE OF POLICIES OF WORLD POWERS TOWARD POORER NATIONS IN MAINTAINING INTERNATIONAL POLITICAL STABILITY.

2160 MOWER A.G.
"THE OFFICIAL PRESSURE GROUP OF THE COUNCIL OF EUROPE'S CONSULATIVE ASSEMBLY."
INT. ORGAN., 18 (SPRING 64), 292-306.
'THE UNIVERSAL AND REGIONAL INTERNATIONAL ORGANIZATIONS ...CONFRONT ONE BASIC QUESTION: HOW TO MOVE SUCCESSFULLY FROM INTERNATIONAL RECOMMENDATION TO NATIONAL ACTION.' SHOWS THE DEVELOPMENT OF THE COUNCIL OF EUROPE AND THE CONCEPTION, DEVELOPMENT, STRUCTURE AND PROCEDURES OF THE WORKING PARTY, AND ITS USE AS A PRESSURE GROUP ON THE NATIONAL LEVEL. CITES ITS PROPAGANDISTIC FUNCTIONS AND CAPABILITIES.

2161 MOWRY G.E.
THE URBAN NATION 1920-1960.
NEW YORK: HILL AND WANG, 1965, 278 PP., LC#65-17423.
INTERPRETS FOUR DECADES OF US HISTORY. EXPLORES TRANSFORMATION OF SOCIETY THROUGH URBANIZATION AND MASS-PRODUCTION-CONSUMPTION ECONOMY. SHOWS HOW THESE FORCES HAVE WEAKENED LOCAL AND STATE GOVERNMENTS TO AGGRANDIZEMENT OF NATIONAL AUTHORITY, AND TURNED US FOREIGN POLICY FROM ISOLATIONISM WORLDWIDE INVOLVEMENT IN AFFAIRS OF OTHER NATIONS.

2162 MOYER K.E.
FROM IRAN TO MORROCCO; FROM TURKEY TO THE SUDAN: A SELECTED AND ANNOTATED BIBLIOGRAPHY OF NORTH AFRICA AND NEAR EAST...
NEW YORK: MISSIONARY RES LIB, 1957, 51 PP.
BIBLIOGRAPHICAL SELECTION ON NORTH AFRICA AND NEAR AND MIDDLE EAST AREA DRAWN OUT OF CONTENTS OF MISSIONARY RESEARCH LIBRARY AT UNION THEOLOGICAL SEMINARY. VOLUME CONTAINS APPROXIMATELY 650 ENTRIES WITH BRIEF DESCRIPTIVE NOTES. MATERIAL IS CLASSIFIED GEOGRAPHICALLY AND TOPICALLY. DOES NOT CONTAIN INDEXES. REFERENCES TO ECONOMICS, POLITICS, FOREIGN RELATIONS, AND GOVERNMENT.

2163 MUDGE G.A.
"DOMESTIC POLICIES AND UN ACTIVITIES* THE CASE OF RHODESIA AND THE REPUBLIC OF SOUTH AFRICA."
INTL. ORGANIZATION, 21 (WINTER 67), 55-78.
A STUDY OF THE EFFECTIVENESS AND EFFECT OF UN CENSORSHIP ON THE NATIONAL GOVERNMENTS AND POLITICAL DYNAMICS OF COUNTRIES CRITICIZED. RHODESIA AND SOUTH AFRICA ARE EXAMINED SPECIFICALLY TO DETERMINE THE IMPACT OF THE UN. REACTIONS WITHIN THE PARLIAMENTS OF THE TWO GOVERNMENTS AND THE IMPORTANT CONSEQUENCES IN ELECTIONS ARE COVERED.

2164 MUGRIDGE D.H.
AMERICAN HISTORY AND CIVILIZATION: LIST OF GUIDES AND ANNOTATED OR SELECTIVE BIBLIOGRAPHIES.
WASHINGTON: LIBRARY OF CONGRESS, 1950, 18 PP.
DRAWS UPON WIDE RANGE OF BIBLIOGRAPHIC MATERIAL TO PRESENT A WORKING GUIDE OF USEFUL AND COMPREHENSIVE BIBLIOGRAPHIES ON US HISTORY AND CIVILIZATION. INCLUDES 107 ITEMS ARRANGED TOPICALLY UNDER SUCH HEADS AS GOVERNMENT, POLITICS, MUSIC, REGIONS, SCIENCE, HISTORY, ETC.

2165 MUGRIDGE D.H., MCCRUM B.P.
A GUIDE TO THE STUDY OF THE UNITED STATES OF AMERICA: REPRESENTATIVE BOOKS REFLECTING THE DEVELOPMENT OF AMERICAN LIFE.
WASHINGTON: LIBRARY OF CONGRESS, 1960, 1193 PP.
WIDELY ANNOTATED GUIDE TO LITERATURE REFLECTING OR STUDYING AMERICAN CIVILIZATION. CONTAINS 6,487 ITEMS ON SUBJECTS VARYING FROM SCIENTIFIC AND SOCIAL QUESTIONS TO THE ARTS AND POLITICS. SPECIFIC AREAS COVERED IN SOCIAL SCIENCES ARE: PERIODICALS AND JOURNALISM; GEOGRAPHY; GENERAL AND DIPLOMATIC HISTORY; MILITARY HISTORY AND FORCES; POPULATION; CONSTITUTION, GOVERNMENT AND POLITICS, ETC.

2166 MULLENBACH P.

CIVILIAN NUCLEAR POWER: ECONOMIC ISSUES AND POLICY FORMATION.
NEW YORK: TWENTIETH CENT. FUND, 1963, 406 PP., $8.50.
CONCERNED WITH THE EXTENT TO WHICH THE U.S. CAN MAINTAIN WORLD LEADERSHIP IN PEACETIME DEVELOPMENT OF NUCLEAR ENERGY. EVALUATES POLICY FORMATION, BASED ON ECONOMIC ANALYSIS OF THE ISSUES UNDERLYING POWER REACTOR DEVELOPMENT DURING THE PERIOD 1953-1961.

2167 MULLER C.F.J. ED., VAN JAARSVELD F.A. ED., VAN WIJK T. ED.
A SELECT BIBLIOGRAPHY OF SOUTH AFRICAN HISTORY; A GUIDE FOR HISTORICAL RESEARCH.
PRETORIA: U OF SOUTH AFRICA, 1966, 215 PP.
LISTS BOOKS AND SOME UNPUBLISHED THESES ON VARIOUS SOUTH AFRICAN HISTORICAL SUBJECTS. MAJORITY OF ENTRIES DUTCH PUBLICATIONS; MANY ENGLISH-LANGUAGE SOURCES AND SOME EUROPEAN INCLUDED. ALL TITLES TRANSLATED INTO ENGLISH. ITEMS ARRANGED ALPHABETICALLY BY AUTHOR UNDER SUBJECT AND PERIOD; 2,521 ENTRIES PUBLISHED IN 20TH CENTURY. AUTHOR INDEX.

2168 MULLEY F.W.
THE POLITICS OF WESTERN DEFENSE.
NEW YORK: PRAEGER, 1962, 282 PP., $6.75.
DISCUSSES DEFENSE APPARATUS OF NATO. URGES DEVELOPMENT OF SYSTEM OF JOINT POLITICAL CONTROL OVER USE AND DEPLOYMENT OF TACTICAL AND STRATEGIC NUCLEAR WEAPONS IN ORDER TO STRENGTHEN ALLIANCE. ASSERTING THAT NATO IS PURELY A DEFENSIVE MILITARY ALLIANCE, PLEADS FOR POLITICAL CONSULTATIONS AMONG ITS MEMBER STATES IN AN EFFORT TO COORDINATE INDIVIDUAL NATIONAL POLICIES.

2169 MULLEY F.W.
"NUCLEAR WEAPONS: CHALLENGE TO NATIONAL SOVEREIGNTY."
ORBIS, 7 (SPRING 63), 32-40.
EXPLORES NEGATIVE FRENCH REACTION TO ANGLO-AMERICAN NASSAU AGREEMENT AND ABANDONMENT OF SKYBOLT PROJECT. POINTS OUT EUROPEAN NATIONS WANT PARTNERSHIP, NOT USA PATRONAGE. EXPLORES DE GAULLE'S AMBITIONS FOR INDEPENDENT EUROPE AND HOW PLAN WOULD AFFECT NATO. SUGGESTS USA PRESIDENT SURRENDER EXCLUSIVE DECISION-MAKING RIGHTS OVER NATO NUCLEAR FORCES.

2170 MUNGER E.S.
NOTES ON THE FORMATION OF SOUTH AFRICAN FOREIGN POLICY.
LONDON: THE BODLEY HEAD, 1965, 102 PP.
STUDY OF DEVELOPING POLITICAL ATTITUDES AND CONTRIBUTING FACTORS DISCUSSING PROVINCIALISM, THE FOREIGN SERVICE, FEED-BACK INSTITUTIONS AND PROGRAMS, AND OBSERVATIONS ABOUT LACK OF CONTACT AMONG FOREIGN OFFICIALS.

2171 MUNKMAN C.A.
AMERICAN AID TO GREECE.
NEW YORK: FREDERICK PRAEGER, 1958, 306 PP., LC#58-9694.
FIRST TWO CHAPTERS EXPLAIN POSTWAR AID PROGRAMS. SUCCEEDING PART FOLLOWS PARTICULAR PROGRAM: GREECE, FROM PLANNING STAGE TO PRESENT. FINAL CHAPTERS REVEAL PROBLEMS IN LIGHT OF LESSONS OBSERVED IN CASE STUDY.

2172 MUNRO L.
UNITED NATIONS, HOPE FOR A DIVIDED WORLD.
NEW YORK: HOLT, 1960, 185 PP.
OUTLINES UN SYSTEM AS TO ORGANIZATION AND FUNCTION. EXAMINING POSSIBILITY OF WORLD PEACE THROUGH INTERNATIONAL CO-OPERATION, ASSESSES UN'S INFLUENCE ON WORLD SITUATIONS.

2173 MUNRO L.
"CAN THE UNITED NATIONS ENFORCE PEACE."
FOR. AFF., 38 (JAN. 60), 209-18.
STRESSES NEED FOR THE ESTABLISHMENT OF AN EFFECTIVE UNITED NATIONS FORCE READILY AVAILABLE IN ANY EMERGENCY. CITES THE POSSIBILITY OF A STRONGER 'PEACE OBSERVATION COMMISSION' AND SCRUTINIZES HAMMARSKJOLD'S OBJECTIONS TO A PERMANENT FORCE.

2174 MURACCIOLE L.
"LA LOI FONDAMENTALE DE LA REPUBLIQUE DU CONGO."
REV. JURID. POLIT. OUTREMER, 16 (APR.-JUNE 62), 279-311.
ANALYZES FUNDAMENTAL LAW OF CONGO REPUBLIC ENACTED ON MAY 19, 1960. LAW DEALS WITH POLITICAL ORGANIZATION. TRACES LAW'S EVOLUTION. COMMENTS ON ITS GENERAL CHARACTERISTICS. OUTLINES CENTRAL CONGOLEGE INSTITUTIONS. RELATES CONGO TO SUB-SAHARAN POLITICAL SITUATIONS.

2175 MURACCIOLE L.
"LA BANQUE CENTRALE DES ETATS DE L'AFRIQUE DE L'OUEST."
REV. JURID. POLIT. OUTREMER, 16 (JULY-SEPT. 62), 375-424.
COMPREHENSIVE ANALYSIS OF ACTIVITIES OF CENTRAL BANK OF WESTERN AFRICAN STATES DURING 1961 AND ITS RECENT EVOLUTION. RELATES ACTIVITIES TO INTERNATIONAL ECONOMIC RELATIONS. DISCUSSES MAJOR SOURCES OF COMMERCE AND PRODUCTION. CONCLUDES WITH ANALYSIS OF MONETARY AND FINANCIAL INSTITUTIONS.

2176 MURPHY G.
IN THE MINDS OF MEN: THE STUDY OF HUMAN BEHAVIOR AND SOCIAL TENSIONS IN INDIA.
NEW YORK: BASIC, 1953, 292 PP.
REPORTS CONSTRUCTIVE FORCES FOSTERING NATIONAL UNITY, AND CAUSES OF SOCIAL TENSION SUCH AS HINDU-MOSLEM CONFLICTS AND CONFLICTS AMONG CASTES. DEMONSTRATES UNESCO'S FUNCTION AS AMELIORATIVE FORCE IN SOCIAL CONTEXT.

2177 MURPHY G.G.
SOVIET MONGOLIA: A STUDY OF THE OLDEST POLITICAL SATELLITE.
BERKELEY: U OF CALIF PR, 1966, 224 PP., LC#66-22455.
DISCUSSES RELATIONSHIP BETWEEN OUTER MONGOLIA AND USSR FROM 1921-1960. EXAMINES SOCIAL, POLITICAL, AND ECONOMIC CONDITIONS AND TRANSITION TO PLANNED ECONOMY. DISCUSSES COSTS AND BENEFITS OF SATELLITESHIP.

2178 MURPHY J.C.
"SOME IMPLICATIONS OF EUROPE'S COMMON MARKET.
IN (COOK P, ECONOMIC DEVELOPMENT AND INTERNATIONAL TRADE,."
DALLAS: SOUTHERN METHODIST U. PR., 1959, P. 33-49).
RAISES TWO QUESTIONS: 1)WILL GEOGRAPHIC DISTRIBUTION OF PRODUCTION AND PATTERN OF TRADE BENEFIT EUROPE AND FREE WORLD, AND 2)WILL COMMON MARKET LEAD TO LARGER SCALE ECONOMIC PRODUCTION. SUPPORTS AFFIRMATIVE ANSWER TO BOTH QUESTIONS.

2179 MURPHY J.C.
"INTERNATIONAL INVESTMENT AND THE NATIONAL INTEREST."
S. ECON. J., 22 (JULY 60), 11-17.
SINCE NATIONAL AND PRIVATE INTERESTS DIVERGE IN MATTER OF FOREIGN INVESTMENT, QUESTIONS THESIS THAT NATIONAL ECONOMIC INTEREST JUSTIFIES STIMULATING PRIVATE FOREIGN INVESTMENT. CONCLUDES THAT PRIVATE COMPARISON OF RATE OF RETURN ON INVESTMENT AT HOME AND ABROAD INADEQUATE GUIDE TO INVESTING IN THE NATIONAL INTEREST.

2180 MURRA R.O.
POST-WAR PROBLEMS: A CURRENT LIST OF UNITED STATES GOVERNMENT PUBLICATIONS (PAMPHLET)
WASHINGTON: LIBRARY OF CONGRESS, 1944.
FIRST PUBLISHED IN 1944 WITH SUPPLEMENTS IN 1944 AND 1945 AND CONTAINS IN ALL PARTS SOME 3,000 ANNOTATED AND LOCATED ARTICLES, SPEECHES, PAMPHLETS, GOVERNMENT DEPARTMENTAL REPORTS, AND MATERIALS IN NEAR-PRINT FORMS. PUBLICATIONS DATE FROM 1944-45 AND ARE ARRANGED TOPICALLY WITH CONCLUDING CROSS-REFERENCED SUBJECT AND AUTHOR INDEX.

2181 MURRAY J.N.
THE UNITED NATIONS TRUSTEESHIP SYSTEM.
URBANA: ILL. U. PR., 1957, 283 PP.
DESCRIBES ORIGIN OF TRUSTEESHIP SYSTEM AND FUNCTIONING OF TRUSTEESHIP COUNCIL. DETAILS COUNCIL STRUCTURE. DEMONSTRATES ACTION IN CASE OF FORMER ITALIAN SOMALILAND.

2182 MURRAY J.N.
"UNITED NATIONS PEACE-KEEPING AND PROBLEMS OF POLITICAL CONTROL."
INT. J., 18 (AUTUMN 63), 442-457.
OVER THE YEARS, THE DEVELOPMENT OF U.N. PEACE-KEEPING ROLE HAS BEEN INFLUENCED BY POLITICAL ATTITUDES AND CIRCUMSTANCES WHICH SHIFTED THE POWER TO ORIGINATE PEACE-KEEPING MACHINERY FROM SECURITY COUNCIL TO THE SECRETARY-GENERAL VIA THE GENERAL ASSEMBLY. U.N. PEACE-KEEPING FORCE IS NECESSARY FOR A PEACEFUL WORLD.

2183 MURTY B.S.
PROPAGANDA AND WORLD PUBLIC ORDER.
NEW HAVEN: YALE U PR, 1967, 320 PP., LC#68-24505.
EMPLOYS A POLICY-ORIENTED JURISPRUDENTIAL APPROACH TO SEEK SOLUTIONS TO PROBLEMS OF REGULATION OF PROPAGANDA. SUGGESTS THAT NEW POLICIES MUST AIM AT PROMOTING FREEDOM OF INFORMATION AND MAINTAINING WORLD PUBLIC ORDER. EMPHASIZES PRESENT AND POTENTIAL ROLE OF UN IN REGULATING USE OF PROPAGANDA.

2184 MURUMBI J., NEWMAN P.K. ET AL.
PROBLEMS OF ECONOMIC DEVELOPMENT IN EAST AFRICA.
NAIROBI: EAST AFRICA PUBL HOUSE, 1965, 107 PP.
INCLUDES TEN PAPERS ON ECONOMIC PLANNING, MANPOWER UTILIZATION, AND REGIONAL DEVELOPMENT. PUBLISHED AS SECOND IN SERIES BY EAST AFRICAN INSTITUTE OF SOCIAL AND CULTURAL AFFAIRS. ECONOMIC PROBLEMS, TRENDS, SOCIALISM, AGRICULTURAL DEVELOPMENT, INDUSTRIAL LOCATION, TAX STRUCTURE, ROLE OF CENTRAL BANK, WAGES, AND EMPLOYMENT ARE TOPICS TREATED.

2185 MUSSO AMBROSI L.A. ED.
BIBLIOGRAFIA DE BIBLIOGRAFIAS URUGUAYAS.
MONTEVIDEO: AGRUPACION BIB, 1964, 102 PP.
URUGUAYAN BIBLIOGRAPHY OF BIBLIOGRAPHIES INCLUDING BOOKS, PERIODICALS, PAMPHLETS, AND NEWSPAPER ARTICLES. OVER 200 ENTRIES ARE URUGUAYAN BIBLIOGRAPHIC PERIODICALS. ABOUT 650 MATERIALS LISTED.

2186 MYERS D.P.
MANUAL OF COLLECTIONS OF TREATIES AND OF COLLECTIONS RELATING TO TREATIES.
CAMBRIDGE: HARVARD U PR, 1922, 685 PP.
CONTAINS CONTRACTUAL AND CONVENTIONAL MATERIAL OF INTERNATIONAL RELATIONS TO OUTBREAK OF WWI. ARRANGEMENT

OF MATERIALS DETERMINED BY CONTENT; WITHIN SUBJECT HEADINGS ARRANGEMENT IS CHRONOLOGICAL. APPENDIX INCLUDES NOTES ON HISTORY OF DOCUMENTS. PRINTED IN FRENCH AND ENGLISH. CONTAINS 3,468 ITEMS.

2187 MYINT H.
THE ECONOMICS OF THE DEVELOPING COUNTRIES.
LONDON: HUTCHINSON & CO, 1964, 192 PP.
ANALYZES POST-WAR ECONOMIC STATUS OF DEVELOPING NATIONS. EXAMINES EXPORTS, MONETARY SYSTEM, MINING, AGRICULTURE, POPULATION GROWTH, ECONOMIC PROGRAMS, AND PATTERNS OF DEVELOPMENT POLICY.

2188 MYRDAL A.R., ALTMEYER A.J., RUSK D.
AMERICA'S ROLE IN INTERNATIONATIONAL SOCIAL WELFARE.
NEW YORK: COLUMB. U. PR., 1955, 109 PP.
STUDY OF PROBLEMS AND MAIN DEVELOPMENTAL RISK OF INTERNATIONAL SOCIAL WELFARE, WITH SCHEMA OF STEPS FOR BALANCED DEVELOPMENT. OFFERS PROGRAM TO MEET NEED FOR MORE KNOWLEDGE IN FIELD. STUDIES USA TRAINING OF SOCIAL WORKERS. NOTES PROBLEMS OF SOCIAL WORK EDUCATION.

2189 MYRDAL G.
CHALLENGE TO AFFLUENCE.
LONDON: VICTOR GOLLANCZ, 1963, 172 PP., LC#63-19684.
AUTHOR FEELS THAT AMERICAN ECONOMIC STAGNATION IS PRINCIPAL WORLD PROBLEM. DESCRIBES THE DYNAMICS OF THAT STAGNATION AND ITS INTERNATIONAL IMPLICATIONS, ESPECIALLY REGARDING THE SOVIET BLOC AND WESTERN EUROPE.

2190 NADLER E.B.
"SOME ECONOMIC DISADVANTAGES OF THE ARMS RACE."
J. CONFL. RESOLUT., 7 (SEPT. 63), 503-09.
STUDIES WAYS IN WHICH GROWTH OF MILITARY-INDUSTRIAL COMPLEX PREVENTS EFFECTIVE CONTROL OF AMERICAN ECONOMY. PROBLEM CONTRIBUTES TO BUSINESS STAGNATION AND UNEMPLOYMENT. OFFERS SOLUTIONS.

2191 NAFZIGER R.O.
INTERNATIONAL NEWS AND THE PRESS: COMMUNICATIONS, ORGANIZATION OF NEWS-GATHERING INTERNATIONAL AFFAIRS AND FOREIGN...
NEW YORK: H W WILSON, 1940, 193 PP.
ANNOTATED BIBLIOGRAPHY OF ABOUT 5,500 ENTRIES; DOCUMENTS, BOOKS, PAMPHLETS, MAGAZINE ARTICLES, AND STUDIES DEALING WITH INTERNATIONAL NEWS COMMUNICATIONS AND FOREIGN PRESS. ITEMS REFER TO PROBLEMS AND ISSUES OF NEWS-GATHERING ORGANIZATION; WASHINGTON CORRESPONDENCE; FOREIGN CORRESPONDENCE; CENSORSHIP, PRESS LAWS, AND PROPAGANDA; PRESS AND PUBLIC OPINION IN WORLD AFFAIRS; WAR AND THE PRESS.

2192 NAHM A.C.
JAPANESE PENETRATION OF KOREA, 1894-1910.
STANFORD: STANFORD BOOKSTORE, 1959, 103 PP.
BIBLIOGRAPHY OF 100,000 PAGES FROM ARCHIVES AND DOCUMENTS SECTION OF THE JAPANESE GENERAL IN SEOUL, COVERING PERIOD FROM SINO-JAPANESE WAR OF 1894 TO JAPANESE ANNEXATION OF KOREA IN 1910. UNIQUE DOCUMENTS ARE PRESERVED ON MICROFILM AT HOOVER INSTITUTE. INCLUDES SELECTIVE DESCRIPTIVE ANNOTATIONS. EMPHASIS PLACED ON KOREAN FOREIGN RELATIONS AND JAPANESE-ASIAN POLICIES. CONTAINS CHRONOLOGY WITH ITEMS.

2193 NAMIER L.B.
DIPLOMATIC PRELUDE 1938-1939.
LONDON: MACMILLAN, 1948, 500 PP.
STUDIES EUROPEAN DIPLOMATIC ACTIVITIES, 1938-39. DISCUSSE PRE-MUNICH GERMAN WHITE BOOK AND POLISH WHITE BOOK. SHOWS EVENTS WHICH LED FROM MUNICH TO PRAGUE, AND REALIGNMENTS AFTER HITLER'S FIRST CONQUESTS. DESCRIBES ANGLO-RUSSIAN NEGOTIATIONS, SUMMER 1939, GERMAN-POLISH RELATIONS OF THE SAME PERIOD, AND EVENTS OF AND REACTIONS TO HITLER'S MOVE IN AUGUST.

2194 NANES A., EFRON R.
"THE EUROPEAN COMMUNITY AND THE UNITED STATES: EVOLVING RELATIONS."
REV. POLIT., 22 (APR. 60), 175-86.
TRACES DEVELOPMENT OF EUROPEAN ECONOMIC INTEGRATION, FOCUSING ON COMMON MARKET AND EURATOM. REVIEW USA POSITIONS ON UNILATERAL INSPECTION AND DISCUSS 1960 DILLON PROPOSALS FOR ECONOMIC REORGANIZATION AND AID TO UNDERDEVELOPED COUNTRIES.

2195 NANES A.
"DISARMAMENT: THE LAST SEVEN YEARS."
CURR. HIST., 42 (MAY 62), 267-274.
SUMMARIZING NEGOTIATIONS SINCE 1955, AUTHOR CALLS ATTENTION TO 'CRUCIAL POINT THAT HAS NEVER BEEN RESOLVED... USA INSISTENCE ON EFFECTIVE INTERNATIONAL INSPECTION AND SOVIET SUSPICION OF SAME AS COVER FOR ESPIONAGE.' ESSENTIALLY, DISARMAMENT TALKS HAVE FAILED: PROSPECTS FOR A TEST-BAN ARE CURRENTLY DIM. ONE REASON FOR HOPE IS GROWING PUBLIC CONSCIOUSNESS OF DESTRUCTIVE NATURE OF MODERN WEAPONS.

2196 NANTWI E.K.
THE ENFORCEMENT OF INTERNATIONAL JUDICIAL DECISIONS AND ARBITAL AWARDS IN PUBLIC INTERNATIONAL LAW.
LEYDEN: AW SIJTHOFF, 1966, 209 PP., LC#66-18228.
NOTES MAJOR CASES IN HISTORY OF INTERNATIONAL ADJUDICATION. DISCUSSES CONFLICT OF NATIONAL SOVEREIGNTY WITH SUBMISSION TO ADJUDICATION; ALSO OBLIGATIONS INDUCING STATES TO COMPLY WITH JUDGMENTS. EXAMINES MEASURES OF ENFORCEMENT BY SINGLE NATIONS AND THOSE OF INTERNATIONAL ORGANIZATIONS. INCLUDES VARIOUS ORGANIZATIONS CONCERNED WITH INTERNATIONAL DISPUTES AND THEIR RESPECTIVE FUNCTIONS; ALSO EXAMPLE CASES.

2197 NASA
PROCEEDINGS OF CONFERENCE ON THE LAW OF SPACE AND OF SATELLITE COMMUNICATIONS: CHICAGO 1963.
WASHINGTON: US GOVERNMENT, 1964, 205 PP.
SURVEYS LEGAL PROBLEMS OF SPACE AGE AND FORMULATES TENTATIVE LEGAL VIEWS ON SPACE. TREATS PROBLEMS OF LAW AND FOREIGN DIPLOMACY THAT ARE EXPECTED IN HANDLING COMMUNICATIONS SATELLITE, BECAUSE IT IS A "YANKEE INVENTION COMMITTED TO FREE ENTERPRISE." INCLUDES TEXT OF SATELLITE ACT OF 1962.

2198 NATION ASSOCIATES
SECURITY AND THE MIDDLE EAST - THE PROBLEM AND ITS SOLUTION.
NEW YORK: THE NATION ASSOCIATES, 1954, 159 PP.
DISCUSSES CURRENT DEVELOPMENTS IN ARAB-ISRAELI RELATIONS. EXAMINES SOCIAL, POLITICAL, AND ECONOMIC CONDITIONS IN BOTH COUNTRIES, ROLE OF COMMUNISM, AND POTENTIALS FOR DEVELOPMENT IN NEAR EAST.

2199 NATIONAL ACADEMY OF SCIENCES
THE GROWTH OF WORLD POPULATION: ANALYSIS OF THE PROBLEMS AND RECOMMENDATIONS FOR RESEARCH AND TRAINING (PAMPHLET)
WASHINGTON: NATL ACADEMY OF SCI, 1963, 38 PP., LC#63-60059.
FEELS WORLD TASK IS TO "ACHIEVE ACCEPTANCE OF DESIRABILITY OF CONTROLLING FAMILIES," SINCE GOAL OF NATIONS IS TO ACHIEVE HIGHEST POSSIBLE STANDARD OF LIVING FOR PEOPLE. ADVISES INTENSE TRAINING IN BIO-MEDICAL PLUS SOCIAL ASPECTS ON AN INTERNATIONAL LEVEL, LED BY US.

2200 NATIONAL BANK OF LIBYA
INFLATION IN LIBYA (PAMPHLET)
TRIPOLI: NATIONAL BANK OF LIBYA, 1961, 86 PP.
DEFINES INFLATION IN GENERAL, AND ANALYZES WIDELY RECOGNIZED TENDENCY IN LIBYAN ECONOMY FOR THE GENERAL PRICE LEVEL TO RISE. ATTEMPTS TO FIND OUT MOST EFFECTIVE AND PRACTICAL WAYS TO COPE WITH INFLATION WITHOUT ADVERSELY AFFECTING ECONOMIC DEVELOPMENT.

2201 NATIONAL BOOK CENTRE PAKISTAN
BOOKS ON PAKISTAN: A BIBLIOGRAPHY.
KARACHI: STERLING PRINTING & PUB, 1965, 71 PP.
EMPHASIZES CULTURAL ASPECTS; INCLUDES BOOKS ON PAKISTAN PUBLISHED OUTSIDE THE COUNTRY. SECTIONS ON HISTORY, IDEOLOGY, AND POLITICS; CONSTITUTIONAL STUDIES; ADMINISTRATION AND BASIC DEMOCRACY; SOCIOLOGY, CUSTOM AND FOLKLORE. ALL PUBLICATIONS ARE IN ENGLISH. CONTAINS INDEXES OF PUBLISHERS AND TITLES.

2202 NATIONAL CENTRAL LIBRARY
LATIN AMERICAN ECONOMIC AND SOCIAL SERIALS.
LONDON: NATIONAL CENTRAL LIBRARY, 1965.
LIST OF SERIALS IN LIBRARIES OF LONDON PERTAINING TO LATIN AMERICAN SOCIAL AND ECONOMIC DEVELOPMENT.

2203 NATIONAL COUN APPLIED ECO RES
DEVELOPMENT WITHOUT AID.
NEW DELHI: NATL COUN APPL ECO RES, 1966, 95 PP.
DISCUSSES PROBLEMS FOR INDIA RESULTING FROM LITTLE OR NO ECONOMIC AID. PROPOSES INCREASED FOREIGN AID AND USE OF OPPORTUNITIES FOR SELF-RELIANCE. AID SHOULD BE PLANNED TOWARD GRADUAL REDUCTION AS ECONOMY BECOMES MORE SELF-SUSTAINING. DEPENDS ON SAVINGS, EXPORTS, EFFECTIVE UTILIZATION OF AID, IMPORT SUBSTITUTES, AND TECHNOLOGICAL DEVELOPMENT.

2204 NATIONAL PLANNING ASSOCIATION
1970 WITHOUT ARMS CONTROL (PAMPHLET)
WASHINGTON: NATL PLANNING ASSN, 1958, 72 PP., LC#58-11014.
STUDIES EXTENT TO WHICH TECHNOLOGY OF MODERN WEAPONS SYSTEMS CAN ASSURE NATIONAL SECURITY, FACTORS OF SECURITY PROGRAM THAT WILL MOTIVATE STABLE WORLD SECURITY BALANCE, FEASIBILITY OF INTERNATIONAL REGULATION OF ARMAMENTS, AND METHODS OF LIMITING INTERNATIONAL VIOLENCE THROUGH ARMS CONTROL. EXAMINES PRESENT AND FUTURE WEAPONS SYSTEMS.

2205 NAVILLE A.
LIBERTE, EGALITE, SOLIDARITE: ESSAIS D'ANALYSE.
PARIS: LIBRAIRIE PAYOT, 1924, 124 PP.
ANALYSIS OF LIBERTY, EQUALITY, AND SOLIDARITY EMPHASIZING FREE WILL, CIVIL AND NATURAL FREEDOM, COMMERCIAL AND SOCIAL JUSTICE INCLUDING POLITICAL HARMONY, INTEREST CONFLICT, DEPENDENCE, COLLABORATION, AND THE SOCIETY OF NATIONS.

2206 NEAL F.W.
TITOISM IN ACTION.
BERKELEY: U OF CALIF PR, 1958, 331 PP., LC#58-10291.
TRACES DEVELOPMENT OF NEW THEORIES OF COMMUNISM IN YUGOSLAVIA. EXAMINES EVOLUTION OF NEW POLITICAL STRUCTURE AND

ECONOMIC SYSTEM. ANALYZES THEORIES BEHIND NEW REFORMS, AND EXPLAINS AND EVALUATES THEIR SIGNIFICANCE. WORK BASED ON YUGOSLAV LAW, GOVERNMENT DOCUMENTS, AND JOURNALS.

2207 NEAL F.W.
US FOREIGN POLICY AND THE SOVIET UNION.
SANTA BARBARA: CTR DEMO INST, 1961, 60 PP.
PLEA FOR THOROUGHGOING RE-EVALUATION OF OUR FOREIGN POLICY. LIFE OF NATIONS DEPENDS ON SUCH A DISPASSIONATE RE-STUDY AND RE-THINKING IN TERMS OF REALITIES OF THERMO-NUCLEARAGE. PARTICULARLY PERTINENT TO US-USSR RELATIONS.

2208 NEAL F.W.
WAR AND PEACE AND GERMANY.
NEW YORK: NORTON, 1962, 166 PP.
ANALYZES AMERICAN POLICY ON BERLIN AND GERMANY SINCE WORLD WAR TWO, RELATING IT TO RUSSIAN POLICY AND ACTIONS. PRESENTS HISTORICAL AND COMPREHENSIVE ACCOUNT OF BERLIN, THE CRISIS AND THE WEST GERMAN STATE. OFFERS SUGGESTIONS FOR FUTURE AMERICAN POLICY.

2209 NEALE A.D.
THE FLOW OF RESOURCES FROM RICH TO POOR.
CAMBRIDGE: HARV CTR INTL AFFAIRS, 1960, 83 PP.
DISCUSSES PROBLEMS ENCOUNTERED BY HEALTHY NATIONS IN MOBILIZING AND TRANSFERRING RESOURCES TO POORER NATIONS. ADVOCATES INCREASE IN SPEED AND AMOUNT OF FLOW OF RESOURCES FROM RICH TO POOR NATIONS AND ATTRIBUTES LIMITATIONS OF VOLUME OF AID TO POOR NATIONS TO POLITICAL RATHER THAN ECONOMIC FACTORS.

2210 NEARING S.
"A WARLESS WORLD."
NEW YORK: VANGUARD, 1939, 31 PP.
DISCUSSES POSSIBILITIES OF A WORLD FREE FROM THE THREATS OF WAR, AND DESCRIBES THE STRUCTURE OF JUST SUCH A WORLD. ALSO ANALYZES CONCEPTS IN FIELD OF MARX, LENIN AND BLOCH.

2211 NEHEMKIS P.
LATIN AMERICA: MYTH AND REALITY.
NEW YORK: ALFRED KNOPF, 1964, 286 PP.
ATTEMPTS TO EXPOSE IMMENSITY OF FALSE INFORMATION CONCERNING LATIN AMERICA WHICH PREVENTS MUTUAL UNDERSTANDING BETWEEN LATIN AND NORTH AMERICANS CONCERNING THEIR RESPECTIVE POLITICAL AND CULTURAL HERITAGES. EMPHASIS IS ON LATIN AMERICAN POLITICAL DISORDERS AND ECONOMIC PROBLEMS.

2212 NEHRU J.
MILITARY ALLIANCE (PAMPHLET)
NEW DELHI: LOK SABHA SECRETARIAT,1957, 14 PP.
EXCERPTS FROM NEHRU'S SPEECHES IN PARLIAMENT, INCLUDING DISCUSSION OF SEATO, ALLIANCES IN NUCLEAR AGE, FUTILITY OF MILITARY ALLIANCES, AND THEIR RELATION TO US CHARTER.

2213 NEHRU J.
SPEECHES.
NEW DELHI: PUBL DIV GOVT INDIA, 1958, 1200 PP.
OVER 300 SPEECHES DELIVERED BY NEHRU, 1946-57 IN THREE VOLUMES. FOREIGN AFFAIRS, ECONOMIC DEVELOPMENT, INDIAN HISTORY.

2214 NEIDLE A.F.
"PEACE KEEPING AND DISARMAMENT."
AMER. J. INT. LAW, 57 (JAN. 63), 46-72.
REPORT ON CONFERENCE DISCUSSIONS OF EIGHTEEN-NATION COMMITTEE ON DISARMAMENT. POINTS OUT CONCEPTUAL DIFFERENCES OF WEST AND SOVIET UNION ON RELATIONSHIP BETWEEN PEACEKEEPING AND DISARMAMENT.

2215 NEISSER H., MODIGLIANI
NATIONAL INCOMES AND INTERNATIONAL TRADE.
URBANA: U OF ILLINOIS PR, 1953, 396 PP., LC#52-12404.
STUDY AIMS TO ESTABLISH IN QUANTITATIVE TERMS THE RELATION BETWEEN FOREIGN TRADE AND LEVEL OF DOMESTIC ECONOMIC ACTIVITIES OF VARIOUS COUNTRIES PARTICIPATING IN INTERNATIONAL EXCHANGE. PERIOD COVERED IS ROUGHLY YEARS BETWEEN WWI AND WWII.

2216 NEISSER H.
"THE EXTERNAL EQUILIBRIUM OF THE UNITED STATES ECONOMY."
SOC. RES., 31 (SUMMER 64), 214-233.
DISCUSSION OF AMERICAN BALANCE OF PAYMENTS PROBLEM. FAVORS SOME LIMITATION OF OVERSEAS CAPITAL INVESTMENT. FEELS A HIGHER DOMESTIC INTEREST RATE WOULD HELP WITHOUT RETARDING INDUSTRIAL INVESTMENT. SEES FAVORABLE OUTLOOK FOR IMPROVEMENT OF UNITED STATES POSITION IN THE LATE SIXTIES.

2217 NELSON M.F.
"KOREA AND THE OLD ORDERS IN EASTERN ASIA."
BATON ROUGE: LOUISIANA ST U PR, 1945.
FRENCH AND ENGLISH MANUSCRIPTS, OCCIDENTAL DOCUMENTS, TRANSLATIONS FROM THE ORIENT, BOOKS, AND PERIODICALS ARRANGED ALPHABETICALLY IN GENRES BY AUTHOR AND PUBLISHED 1736 THROUGH 1942; APPROXIMATELY 250 ENTRIES.

2218 NELSON M.F.
KOREA AND THE OLD ORDERS IN EASTERN ASIA.
BATON ROUGE: LOUISIANA ST U PR, 1945, 326 PP.
PRIMARILY STUDIES INTERNATIONAL POLITICAL STATUS, WITH EMPHASIS ON THE CONFUCIAN FAMILISM AND MONARCHIES, MONGOLS, WESTERN CONTACTS, AND LOSS OF INTERNATIONAL PERSONALITY.

2219 NEUBURGER O.
GUIDE TO OFFICIAL PUBLICATIONS OF THE OTHER AMERICAN REPUBLICS: VENEZUELA (VOL. XIX)
WASHINGTON: LIBRARY OF CONGRESS, 1948, 59 PP.
COMPILES ALL STATE PUBLICATIONS PUBLISHED BY VENEZUELA SINCE ITS INDEPENDENCE IN 1811 AND AVAILABLE IN THE LIBRARY OF CONGRESS. PART OF A PROJECT UNDER THE AUSPICES OF THE STATE DEPARTMENT'S INTERDEPARTMENTAL COMMITTEE ON SCIENTIFIC AND CULTURAL COOPERATION. INCLUDES SERIALS, MONOGRAPHS, AND BOOKS. ARRANGED BY AGENCY OR DEPARTMENT OF ISSUANCE. PROVIDES AN INDEX TO TITLES.

2220 NEUCHTERLEIN D.E.
"THAILAND* ANOTHER VIETNAM?"
MILITARY REV., 47 (JUNE 67), 59-63.
NOTES INCREASE OF COMMUNIST INSURGENCY IN NORTHEASTERN AREA OF THAILAND AND GIVES BACKGROUND OF INFILTRATION. SURVEYS ADVANTAGES WHICH THAILAND HAS OVER VIETNAM: PROSPERITY, STABILITY, NATIONAL UNITY, EFFICIENT GOVERNMENT. DESCRIBES US FACILITIES AND POLICY. CONCLUDES THAT THE THAIS WITH THEIR LONG HISTORY OF NATIONHOOD CAN TAKE CARE OF THEMSELVES.

2221 NEUMANN F.
THE DEMOCRATIC AND THE AUTHORITARIAN STATE: ESSAYS IN POLITICAL AND LEGAL THEORY.
NEW YORK: FREE PRESS OF GLENCOE, 1957, 303 PP., LC#56-6878.
VOLUME OF PAPERS COLLECTED AND PREPARED BY FRANZ NEUMANN WITH A FEW ADDED BY EDITOR HERBERT MARCUSE, ALL DEALING WITH POLITICAL THEORY AND LEGAL THEORY. MAIN ATTENTION ON THE CHANGE IN FUNCTION OF LAW IN MODERN SOCIETY AND POLITICAL FREEDOM. INCLUDES WRITINGS OF FRANZ NEUMANN: A SELECTED CHRONOLOGICAL BIBLIOGRAPHY.

2222 NEUMANN R.G.
THE GOVERNMENT OF THE GERMAN FEDERAL REPUBLIC.
NEW YORK: HARPER & ROW, 1966, 192 PP., LC#66-22517.
HISTORICAL INTRODUCTION TO GERMANY'S GOVERNMENTAL STRUCTURE, THE CONTROVERSIAL ISSUE OF REUNIFICATION AND ITS POLITICAL SIGNIFICANCE; GERMANY'S PLACE IN EUROPEAN AND ATLANTIC WORLDS. DISCUSSES REASONS FOR HER POLITICAL STABILITY AND INSTABILITY, AND POINTS OF COOPERATION AND FRICTION BETWEEN GERMANY AND HER NEIGHBORS. CONSIDERS WHICH ASPECTS OF ADENAUER REGIME WILL HAVE LASTING SIGNIFICANCE.

2223 NEWBURY C.W.
THE WEST AFRICAN COMMONWEALTH.
DURHAM: DUKE U PR, 1964, 106 PP.
LECTURES ON THE PROBLEMS OF SELF-GOVERNMENT IN WEST AFRICA AND THE SIGNIFICANCE OF VOLUNTARY ASSOCIATION WITH THE COMMONWEALTH, THE TENSIONS BETWEEN THIS ASSOCIATION AND TENDENCIES TOWARD PAN-AFRICANISM, AND THE ROLE AND PROBLEMS OF EDUCATED ELITES AND TRADITIONAL CHIEFS IN TRANSFER OF POWER.

2224 NEWBURY C.W.
BRITISH POLICY TOWARDS WEST AFRICA: SELECT DOCUMENTS 1786-1874.
LONDON: OXFORD U PR, 1965, 656 PP.
VOLUME PROVIDES MATERIALS FOR HISTORY OF EUROPEAN RELATIONS WITH WEST AFRICA FOR THE PERIOD FROM THE TERMINATION OF SLAVE TRADE UNTIL SOME TEN YEARS BEFORE INTERNATIONAL PARTITION. MOST OF MATERIAL IS COLLECTED FROM STATE PAPERS PUBLISHED FOR THE FIRST TIME IN THIS REFERENCE.

2225 NEWCOMER H.A.
INTERNATIONAL AIDS TO OVERSEAS INVESTMENTS AND TRADE.
KENT: KENT ST U BUR ECO BUS RES, 1964, 67 PP.
TREATISE WHICH COLLATES FACTUAL INFORMATION CONCERNING DEVELOPMENT OF INTERNATIONAL PRIVATE INVESTMENT AND TRADE. EXAMINES INVESTMENT PROCEDURE AND DISCUSSES COOPERATIVE TREATIES AND CONVENTIONS BETWEEN AGENCIES OF THE UN AND NATIONAL GOVERNMENTS. CONTAINS BRIEF UNANNOTATED BIBLIOGRAPHIES FOR EACH CHAPTER. EMPHASIZES ROLE OF UN INTERNATIONAL AGENCIES IN WORLD ECONOMIC DEVELOPMENT AND RECONSTRUCTION.

2226 NEWMAN R.P.
RECOGNITION OF COMMUNIST CHINA? A STUDY IN ARGUMENT.
NEW YORK: MACMILLAN, 1961, 318 PP., LC#61-15184.
DISCUSSES "SHOULD US EXTEND DIPLOMATIC RECOGNITION TO COMMUNIST CHINA?" ATTEMPTS TO DEVELOP LOGICAL ARGUMENTS FOR VIABLE ALTERNATIVES, ASSUMING THE MORAL, POLITICAL, AND LEGAL ISSUES. CONCLUDES THAT SOME SORT OF MODIFICATION IS CALLED FOR.

2227 NICE R.W. ED.
TREASURY OF LAW.
NEW YORK: PHILOSOPHICAL LIB, 1964, 553 PP., LC#64-20425.
DOCUMENTS FROM ANCIENT THROUGH MODERN TIMES ON MAN'S DETERMINATION TO GOVERN INTERPERSONAL AND INTERNATIONAL

CONDUCT THROUGH LAW. MOST REFLECT REGULATION OF PRACTICE, DEALING WITH SPECIFIC ISSUES OF THEIR TIMES; MANY SHOW INFLUENCE OF RELIGIOUS AND MORAL NORMS; OTHER ARE BASED ON THE "PURE" LAW TRADITION.

2228 NICHOLAS H.G.
THE UNITED NATIONS AS A POLITICAL INSTITUTION.
LONDON: OXFORD U. PR., 1962, 232 PP., $1.75.
EXPLORES ORIGIN AND TRACES HISTORICAL EVOLUTION OF UN. ANALYZES ITS CHARACTER IN TERMS OF INTERNATIONAL POLITICS.

2229 NICHOLAS H.G.
"UN PEACE FORCES AND THE CHANGING GLOBE: THE LESSONS OF SUEZ AND CONGO."
INT. ORGAN., 17 (SPRING 63), 321-337.
ANALYZING THE OPERATIONS OF UNEF AND UNOC, AUTHOR WARNS THAT SIMILAR SITUATIONS WILL OCCUR AND THAT THESE DIFFICULIES MUST BE OVERCOME BY ACTIONS OF SECURITY COUNCIL, GENERAL ASSEMBLY AND SECRETARIAT. NO INTERNATIONAL FORCE IS EXEMPT FROM THE AXIOM OF 'HE WHO WILLS THE END MUST WILL THE MEANS AS WELL'.

2230 NICOL D.
AFRICA - A SUBJECTIVE VIEW.
NEW YORK: HUMANITIES PRESS, 1964, 88 PP.
FIVE LECTURES GIVEN AT UNIVERSITY OF GHANA IN 1963. STRESSES PRAGMATIC ADJUSTMENT OF IDEALS TO AFRICAN MILIEU, IMPORTANCE OF UNEMOTIONAL REACTION TO WESTERN VIEWS AND CRITICISMS, AND USE OF SUCH CRITICISMS AS MAY BE HELPFUL. DISCUSSES POLITICS, PAN-AFRICANISM, LEADERS, UNIVERSITIES, CIVIL SERVICE, WRITERS ON AND OF AFRICA. SUGGESTS WHAT IS GOOD AND WHAT MUST BE DONE TO IMPROVE CONDITIONS.

2231 NICOLSON H.G.
CURZON: THE LAST PHASE, 1919-1925.
NEW YORK: HARCOURT BRACE, 1939, 416 PP.
TRACES CAREER OF LORD CURZON AS FOREIGN SECRETARY FROM 1918-24. USES PAPERS, TELEGRAMS, DISPATCHES, MINUTES, AND RECORDS OF INTERVIEWS FOR DETAILED EXAMINATION OF HIS ACTIVITIES AND PROBLEMS OF BRITISH FOREIGN POLICY.

2232 NICOLSON H.G.
DIPLOMACY (3RD ED.)
LONDON: OXFORD U PR, 1963, 268 PP.
DISCUSSES ORIGINS AND EVOLUTION OF DIPLOMATIC PRACTICE, RECENT CHANGES IN METHOD, ITS RELATION TO COMMERCE, AND ADMINISTRATION OF THE FOREIGN SERVICE. ALSO EXAMINES ROLE OF LEAGUE OF NATIONS AS INSTRUMENT OF DIPLOMACY. RESTRICTED TO DISCUSSION OF "MANAGEMENT OF INTERNATIONAL RELATIONS BY NEGOTIATIONS."

2233 NICOLSON H.G.
THE OLD DIPLOMACY AND THE NEW.
LONDON: DAVIES MEM INST POL STUD, 1961, 10 PP.
BRIEF DISCUSSION OF NEW "DEMOCRATIC" DIPLOMACY WHICH CONSIDERS ADJUSTMENT OF MODERN DIPLOMATIC CONCEPTS AND METHODS TO MORE "CAUTIOUS" SYSTEM THAT WAS PRACTICED PRIOR TO WWI. EMPHASIS IS ON BRITISH DIPLOMACY BUT DISCUSSION EXTENDS TO ISSUES OF INTERNATIONAL IMPORTANCE.

2234 NIEBUHR R.
CHRISTIANITY AND POWER POLITICS.
NEW YORK: CHAS SCRIBNER'S SONS, 1940, 226 PP.
OCCASIONAL ESSAYS UNITED BY THESIS THAT MODERN CHRISTIAN AND SECULAR PERFECTIONISM, WHICH PLACES A PREMIUM UPON NON-PARTICIPATION IN CONFLICT, IS A VERY SENTIMENTALIZED VERSION OF CHRISTIAN FAITH AND IS AT VARIANCE WITH PROFOUNDEST INSIGHTS OF CHRISTIANITY. FEELS LIBERALISM DISTILLS MORAL PERVERSITY OUT OF ITS MORAL ABSOLUTES. ILLUMINATES MODERN EVENTS WHEREIN PEACEFUL EFFORTS HAVE SURRENDERED TO EVIL.

2235 NIEBUHR R.
THE CHILDREN OF LIGHT AND THE CHILDREN OF DARKNESS: A VINDICATION OF DEMOCRACY AND CRITIQUE OF TRADITIONAL DEFENSE
NEW YORK: CHAS SCRIBNER'S SONS, 1947, 190 PP.
PRESENTS A POLITICAL PHILOSOPHY, BASED UPON RELIGIOUS AND THEOLOGICAL CONVICTIONS, OF MAN, COMMUNITY, AND PROPERTY. DISCUSSES MARXIST ILLUSIONS ABOUT NATURE OF PROPERTY, AND DEMOCRATIC TRADITIONS OF PLURALISM. ANALYZES VARIOUS IDEAS OF UNIVERSALISM AND PROPOSES A WORLD COMMUNITY TO BRING PEACE AND DEMOCRATIC INSTITUTIONS TO ALL MEN.

2236 NIEBUHR R.
"THE MORAL IMPLICATIONS OF LOYALTY TO THE UNITED NATIONS."
NEW HAVEN: HAZEN FOUND., 1952, 14 PP.
REFLECTS ON MORAL AND SPIRITUAL MEANING OF UNESCO AND THE U.N. TO AVOID WAR AND THE SPREAD OF COMMUNISM, SUBSTANCE MUST BE GIVEN THE ORIGINAL CHARTER THROUGH LOYALTY, FIDELITY AND RESOLUTENESS. TO INTEGRATE THE FREE WORLD AND TO ENGENDER MUTUAL TRUST, TECHNICAL HELP IS MORE EFFECTIVE THAN ABSTRACT COMMITMENTS.

2237 NIEBUHR R.
NATIONS AND EMPIRES.
LONDON: FABER AND FABER, 1959, 306 PP.
STUDY OF PERENNIAL PATTERNS, RECURRING PROBLEMS, AND SIMILAR STRUCTURES OF POLITICAL ORDER. EMPHASIS ON CURRENT PROBLEMS, SUCH AS COLD WAR, NUCLEAR STALEMATE, DEMOCRACY AND AUTHORITY, AND CHRISTIANITY'S ROLE IN CURRENT HISTORY.

2238 NIEBUHR R.
"THE SOCIAL MYTHS IN THE COLD WAR."
J. INT. AFFAIRS, 21 (1967), 40-56.
SOCIAL MYTH IS SEEN AS BASIS FOR NATIONAL PRIDE AND JUSTIFICATION. DISTORTION OF INTENT, ACTIONS, IDEOLOGIES BY OVERSIMPLIFICATION OR OTHERWISE IS GIVEN AS A MAJOR CAUSE OF INTERNATIONAL STRESS. MORAL JUSTIFICATION OF ACTIONS HAS BECOME IMMEDIATE METHOD OF US, AND ALSO ADOPTED BY OTHERS. RELATION TO WAR IN VIETNAM.

2239 NIEDERGANG M.
LA REVOLUTION DE SAINT-DOMINGUE.
PARIS: LIBRAIIE PLON, 1966, 230 PP.
ANALYZES DOMINICAN REPUBLIC REVOLUTION OF APRIL, 1965 CAUSING US AND INTER-AMERICAN TROOPS TO OCCUPY NATION. DISCUSSES EVENTS FROM DEALTH OF TRUJILLO TO INTERVENTION DEALING WITH DOMINICAN POLITICS AND US INFLUENCE IN ITS AFFAIRS. EXAMINES EXTENT OF COMMUNITST CONTROL AND POWER IN REVOLUTIONARY GROUPS.

2240 NIEMEYER G.
LAW WITHOUT FORCE: THE FUNCTION OF POLITICS IN INTERNATIONAL LAW.
PRINCETON: PRINCETON U PRESS, 1941, 408 PP.
A STUDY OF THE NATURE OF LAW AND INTERNATIONAL RELATIONS. COMPARES LEGAL THEORY AND POLITICAL REALITY. ARGUES THAT LAW AND SOCIAL ORDER ARE CONCERNED WITH RELATIONSHIPS AND NOT WITH SEPARATE INDIVIDUALS AND GROUPS; THEREFORE, THE STANDARDS OF LEGAL ORDER SHOULD BE DERIVED FROM THE IDEA OF INTERRELATED ACTIVITIES AND NOT FROM INDIVIDUALS AND GROUPS. CONCEPT IS RELATED TO OUTBREAK OF WWII.

2241 NIJHOFF M.
ANNUAIRE EUROPEEN (VOL. XII)
THE HAGUE: MARTINUS NIJHOFF, 1966, 887 PP.
PROVIDES A GUIDE AND SUMMARY TO THE REPORTS AND ACTIVITIES OF VARIOUS INTRA-EUROPEAN ORGANIZATIONS: CUSTOMS CO-OPERATION COUNCIL, EUROPEAN COMMUNITIES EEC, EURATOM, ECSC, ETC.), EUROPEAN FREE TRADE ASSOCIATION, AND OTHERS. PROVIDES A LENGTHY BIBLIOGRAPHY OF REPORTS ISSUED BY THESE VARIOUS INTRA-EUROPEAN AGENCIES.

2242 NIZARD L.
"CUBAN QUESTION AND SECURITY COUNCIL."
REV. GEN. DR. INT. PUB., 66(NO.3, 62), 486-545.
CASTRO'S ACTION IN CUBA IS VIEWED AS AN IMPORTANT THREAT TO AMERICAN INTERESTS AND SECURITY. COMPLAINTS TO SECURITY COUNCIL, MADE BY INVOLVED PARTIES, ARE PRESENTED. DEMONSTRATES HOW CONCEPTS OF THE UN CHARTER WERE APPLIED FOR PROPOSING CONSTRUCTIVE SOLUTIONS.

2243 NKRUMAH K.
NEO-COLONIALISM: THE LAST STAGE OF IMPERIALISM.
LONDON: THOMAS NELSON & SONS, 1965, 280 PP.
NKRUMAH'S NOTED ATTACK ON THE "WORST FORM OF IMPERIALISM" SHOWS HOW FOREIGN INVESTMENTS IN AN UNDERDEVELOPED COUNTRY LEAD TO DANGEROUS CONTROL BY CAPITALIST POWER AND TO TOTAL SUBJUGATION AND PUPPET GOVERNMENTS.

2244 NOBECOURT R.G.
LES SECRETS DE LA PROPAGANDE EN FRANCE OCCUPEE.
PARIS: LIB ARTHEME FAYARD, 1962, 530 PP.
ANALYSIS OF PROPAGANDA EMPLOYED IN OCCUPIED FRANCE DURING WWII AND METHODS USED. EXAMINES ORGANIZATION AND OPERATION OF VICHY GOVERNMENT IN RELATION TO ITS PROPAGANDA ACTIVITIES IN FRANCE. ALSO STUDIES GERMAN AND ALLIED PROPAGANDA REGARDING WAR. DETAILS APPROACH USED AFTER OPENING OF SECOND FRONT IN EAST AND THIS CHANGE ON INFORMATION AND DISTRIBUTION.

2245 NOEL-BAKER D.
THE ARMS RACE.
NEW YORK: OCEANA, 1958, 603 PP.
ASSESSMENT OF DANGER OF THE ARMS RACE AND IMPORTANCE OF DISARMAMENT IN NATIONAL AND INTERNATIONAL POLICY. LISTS TECHNICAL AND POLITICAL PROBLEMS THAT ARISE WHEN GOVERNMENTS CONSIDER DISARMAMENT. OUTLINES HISTORY OF 'NUCLEAR NEGOTIATIONS' AND ADVOCATES TOTAL AND COMPLETE DISARMAMENT.

2246 NOGEE J.L.
"THE DIPLOMACY OF DISARMAMENT."
INT. CONCIL., 526 (JAN. 60), 233-303.
TRACES CHANGES IN THE IDEAS AND METHODS OF DISARMAMENT NEGOTIATION, AND THE MAIN IMPEDIMENTS TO A FINAL SETTLEMENT, ASSERTING CONTROL IS THE MAIN OBSTACLE. MAIN STIMULANTS INCLUDE PUBLIC OPINION, FEAR OF NUCLEAR PROLIFERATION AND ECONOMIC PRESSURES.

2247 NOGEE J.L.
SOVIET POLICY TOWARD INTERNATIONAL CONTROL OF ATOMIC ENERGY.
SOUTH BEND: NOTRE DAME PR., 1961, 306 PP., $6.50.
ANALYZES SOVIET ATTITUDES TOWARD INTERNATIONALIZATION OF

THE ATOM. OBSERVES THAT IMMODERATE SELF-INTEREST IS BASIS OF USSR POLICY. CLAIMS THAT USSR IS ABLE TO DEDICATE ITSELF TO ANY GIVEN TASK BUT IS WEAK IN ITS ABILITY TO WITHSTAND EXPOSURE TO AN ATMOSPHERE OF FREEDOM. CONCLUDES THAT SOVIET UNION CAN ONLY VIEW THE OUTSIDE WORLD WITH SUSPICION.

2248 NOGEE J.L.
"PROPOGANDA AND NEGOTIATION: THE CASE OF THE TEN NATION DISARMAMENT COMMITTEE."
J. CONFL. RESOLUT., 7 (SEPT. 63), 510-521.
DEALS WITH THE ROLE, USE AND FUNCTION OF PROPOGANDA DURING DISARMAMENT NEGOTIATIONS AND OFFERS THE TEN NATION DISARMAMENT COMMITTEE AS A CASE STUDY. DISTINGUISHES BETWEEN PROPOSALS,STATEMENTS AND NEGOTIATING POSTURES THAT ARE PRIMARILY PROPOGANDISTIC IN NATURE AND THOSE DESIGNED TO REACH AN AGREEMENT ON OR ABOUT SOME PHASE OF DISARMAMENT.

2249 NOLLAU G.
INTERNATIONAL COMMUNISM AND WORLD REVOLUTION; HISTORY AND METHODS (TRANS. BY VICTOR ANDERSEN)
LONDON: HOLLIS AND CARTER, 1961, 357 PP.
EXPLORES ORIGINS AND FEATURES OF COLLABORATION OF PARTIES OF WORKING CLASS, NATIONALLY AND INTERNATIONALLY. DISCUSSES CONCEPT OF "PROLETARIAN INTERNATIONALISM," ORIGINS OF INTERNATIONAL MOVEMENT, DEVELOPMENT OF WORLD CONGRESS, AND ORGANIZATION OF GROUPS. STUDIES COMINTERN AND COMINFORM AND INTERNATIONALISM AFTER DEATH OF STALIN.

2250 NORMAN E.H.
"JAPAN'S EMERGENCE AS A MODERN STATE: POLITICAL AND ECONOMIC PROBLEMS OF THE MEIJI PERIOD."
NEW YORK: INTL SECR INST PAC REL, 1940.
SELECTS AND ANALYZES PECULIARITIES OF THE MEIJI SETTLEMENT WHICH HAVE CONDITIONED MODERN JAPANESE ECONOMY, POLITICAL LIFE, AND FOREIGN POLICY. TRACES THEM FROM FEUDALISM TO CONSOLIDATION OF STATE POWER UNDER NEW CONSTITUTION AT END OF 19TH CENTURY. CENTRAL ISSUE IS RAPID CREATION OF CENTRALIZED ABSOLUTE STATE AFTER 1868 AND GROWTH OF INDUSTRIAL ECONOMY. SELECT BIBLIOGRAPHY IN WESTERN LANGUAGES.

2251 NORTH R.C.
"DECISION MAKING IN CRISIS: AN INTRODUCTION."
J. CONFL. RESOLUT., 6 (SEPT. 62), 197-200.
INTRODUCTION TO CONTEMPORARY STUDY OF INTERNATIONAL CRISES. FOCUSES ON CLARIFYING THE RELATIONSHIP BETWEEN CONFLICT AND INTEGRATION AND TESTS A SERIES OF GENERAL HYPOTHESES ABOUT THE BEHAVIOR OF STATES.

2252 NORTH R.C. ET AL.
CONTENT ANALYSIS: A HANDBOOK WITH APPLICATIONS FOR THE STUDY OF INTERNATIONAL CRISIS.
EVANSTON: NORTHWESTERN U. PR., 1963, 182 PP., $2.95.
A VALUABLE INTRODUCTION TO A USEFUL RESEARCH TECHNIQUE. INCLUDES CONCRETE ILLUSTRATIONS PLUS GUIDES 'FOR DECIDING WHETHER, WHEN, AND WHAT FORM OF CONTENT ANALYSIS SHOULD BE USED.' THE EXAMPLES COME FROM RESEARCH ON THE ORIGINS OF WORLD WAR I AND ON CONTEMPORARY SINO-SOVIET RELATIONS. SPECIAL FORMS DISCUSSED INCLUDE: THE CONVENTIONAL FREQUENCY COUNT AND QUALITATIVE IDENTIFICATIONS, Q-SORTS, PAIR COMPARISONS, AND EVALUATIVE ASSERTION ANALYSIS.

2253 NORTH R.C., EUDIN X.J.
M. N. ROY'S MISSION TO CHINA: THE COMMUNIST-KUOMINTANG SPLIT OF 1927.
BERKELEY: U OF CALIF PR, 1963, 399 PP., LC#62-21387.
DOCUMENTED STUDY OF CHINESE-RUSSIAN COMMUNIST RELATIONS. PROVIDES DOCUMENTS RECONSTRUCTING PROCEEDINGS OF FIFTH CONGRESS OF THE CHINESE COMMUNIST PARTY AND PERTINENT DISCUSSIONS AND CONTROVERSIES IMMEDIATELY PRECEDING AND FOLLOWING ITS SESSION. SIX CHAPTERS OF COMMENTARY ON WRITINGS OF M. N. ROY PROVIDING MINIMAL HISTORICAL CONTEXT.

2254 NORTH R.C.
"COMMUNICATION AS AN APPROACH TO POLITICS."
AMER. BEHAVIORAL SCIENTIST, (APR. 67), 12-23.
AUTHOR UTILIZES, IN HIS PROJECT, STUDIES IN INTERNATIONAL CONFLICT AND INTEGRATION, CONCEPTS OF COMMUNICATION WHICH HAVE RECENTLY BROUGHT A BEHAVIORAL VIEWPOINT TO POLITICAL STUDIES. SHOWS HOW METHODS CAN BE USED WHICH POINT UP RELATIONSHIPS OF VARIOUS INTERACTING INDIVIDUALS AND ORGANIZATIONS IN WAYS ANALOGOUS TO COMMUNICATION THEORY.

2255 NORTHROP F.S.C.
THE TAMING OF THE NATIONS.
NEW YORK: MACMILLAN, 1952, 362 PP.
TREATS GENERAL PRINCIPLES AND SPECIFIC CONTEMPORARY PROBLEMS OF FOREIGN POLICY. ANALYZES SPIRITUAL FOUNDATIONS OF WESTERN CIVILIZATION. EXPLORES THEORY AND PRACTISE OF SOVIET COMMUNISM. DISCUSSES HIROSHIMA AND KOREAN WAR. OFFERS PROPOSAL FOR AN EFFECTIVE WORLD LAW.

2256 NORTHROP F.S.C.
EUROPEAN UNION AND UNITED STATES FOREIGN POLICY: A STUDY IN SOCIOLOGICAL JURISPRUDENCE.
NEW YORK: MACMILLAN, 1954, 230 PP.
HISTORICAL ACCOUNT OF RELATION BETWEEN EUROPEAN UNION AND UNITED STATES FOREIGN POLICY, BEGINNING WITH HAGUE CONGRESS IN 1948. VIEWS EUROPEAN UNION AS EXPERIMENT IN SOCIOLOGICAL JURISPRUDENCE IN ITS ATTEMPT AT IMPOSING SUPRANATIONAL 'POSITIVE LAW' UPON 14 DIVERSE LIVING ASSOCIATIONS.

2257 NOVE A.
COMMUNIST ECONOMIC STRATEGY: SOVIET GROWTH AND CAPABILITIES.
WASHINGTON: NATL PLANNING ASSN, 1959, 82 PP., LC#59-15078.
DISCUSSES RESOURCES AND INTERNAL ECONOMIC ORGANIZATION OF USSR IN RELATION TO "COMPETITIVE COEXISTENCE." EXAMINES MANPOWER, SCIENTIFIC PROGRESS, MATERIAL RESOURCES, PLANNING EFFICIENCY, AGRICULTURE, AND GENERAL COMMUNIST BLOC GROWTH. MAINTAINS THAT WEST "WILL CONTINUE TO BE THE PRINCIPAL TRADING PARTNER" OF "UNCOMMITTED COUNTRIES."

2258 NOVE A.
"THE SOVIET MODEL AND UNDERDEVELOPED COUNTRIES."
INT. AFF., 37 (JAN. 61), 29-38.
ANALYZES FACTORS WEAKENING GROWTH OF ECONOMIC ACTIVITY RELATING TO PARTICULAR COUNTRIES. COMPARES COMMUNIST AND WESTERN PROPAGANDA METHODS, AND THEIR PURPOSE OF MOBILIZING PEOPLE TO CARRY OUT DIFFICULT TASKS. WARNS THAT WEST'S ALTERNATIVE SUGGESTIONS ARE NOT ALWAYS ATTUNED TO GOALS.

2259 NOVE A.
COMMUNISM AT THE CROSSROADS.
CAMBRIDGE: LEEDS U PRESS, 1964, 31 PP.
ANALYSIS OF PRESENT STATE OF COMMUNIST DEVELOPMENT IN WORLD. EXAMINES BASIS OF MARXISM AS APPLIED TO SOVIET UNION AND INTERNATIONAL COMMUNISM.

2260 NUMELIN R.
"THE BEGINNINGS OF DIPLOMACY."
NEW YORK: PHILOSOPHICAL LIB, 1950.
SOCIOLOGICAL ESSAY BASED ON ETHNOLOGICAL FIELD RESEARCHES OF TECHNIQUES OF DIPLOMACY OF NONLITERATE PEOPLES. EXTENSIVE BIBLIOGRAPHY IS COMPOSED OF HISTORICAL AND PHILOSOPHICAL LITERATURE, LITERATURE OF INTERNATIONAL LAW AND SOCIOLOGY, ETHNOLOGICAL, ETHNO-SOCIOLOGICAL, AND GEOGRAPHICAL LITERATURE IN EUROPEAN LANGUAGES.

2261 NUNEZ JIMENEZ A.
LA LIBERACION DE LAS ISLAS.
HAVANA: EDITORIAL LEX, 1959, 623 PP.
DESCRIBES FIRST YEAR OF FIDEL CASTRO'S POWER IN CUBA. EXPLAINS LAWS AND PROGRAMS BEGUN BY REVOLUTIONARY GOVERNMENT AND DIPLOMATIC MISSIONS TO EUROPE AND US IN SEARCH OF AID AND SUPPORT FOR NEW REGIME. DEVOTES LARGE SECTION TO PLAN AND PROCESS OF AGRARIAN REFORM AND LAWS OF ENACTMENT.

2262 NURTY K.S., BOUQUET A.C.
STUDIES IN PROBLEMS OF PEACE.
BOMBAY: ASIA PUBL., 375 PP.
INTENSIVE STUDY OF VARIOUS ASPECTS OF QUEST FOR PEACE. INCLUDES AN HISTORICAL ACCOUNT OF PEACE MOVEMENTS. CONSIDERS THEORETICAL ASPECTS OF MOVEMENTS, EMPHASIZING HINDU PHILOSOPHY.

2263 NUSSBAUM D.
A CONCISE HISTORY OF THE LAW OF NATIONS.
NEW YORK: MACMILLAN, 1954, 378 PP.
BRIEF HISTORY OF INTERNATIONAL LAW SINCE FIRST GREEK AND ROMAN EFFORTS FOR A COMPLETE DEFINITION. DEPICTS JURIDICAL SCIENCE IN THE MIDDLE AGES AND IN MODERN TIMES. INCLUDES HISTORIOGRAPHY OF INTERNATIONAL RELATIONS.

2264 NYE J.S. JR.
"EAST AFRICAN ECONOMIC INTEGRATION."
J. MOD. AFRICAN STUD., 1 (DEC. 63), 475-502.
EVALUATES A LONG-TERM EXPERIMENT IN ECONOMIC AND ADMINISTRATIVE UNION AMONG KENYA, TANGANYIKA, UGANDA. ECONOMIC INTEGRATION IS EXTENSIVE BUT THERE IS NO GOOD PROSPECT OF CONTINUED STABILITY WITHOUT POLITICAL UNION--AND ECONOMIC INTEGRATION HAS YET TO PRODUCE ANY FORCES LEADING AUTOMATICALLY IN THIS DIRECTION.

2265 NYERERE J.K.
FREEDOM AND UNITY/UHURU NA UMOJA: A SELECTION FROM WRITINGS AND SPEECHES, 1952-65.
NEW YORK: OXFORD U PR, 1967, 366 PP.
WORKS BY NYERERE, ILLUSTRATING HIS CONTRIBUTION TO POLITICAL THOUGHT AND DEVELOPMENT IN AFRICA. EMPHASIZES DEMOCRATIC CHANGE IN AFRICA FROM WITHIN AND OPPOSITION TO CHANGE FROM WITHOUT BY FORCES OVER WHICH AFRICANS HAVE NO CONTROL.

2266 O'BRIEN W.
"THE ROLE OF FORCE IN THE INTERNATIONAL JURIDICAL ORDER."
CATH. LAWYER, 6 (WINTER 60), 22-32.
CONTENDS THAT FORCE IS IMPORTANT TO THE CONCEPT OF INTERNATIONAL JURIDICAL ORDER. POSTULATES ON THE IMPORTANCE OF FORCE AS A REALITY, AS A LEGAL NECESSITY, AND AS A MORAL MEANS OF ATTAINING WORLD PEACE. ADHERES TO SCHOLASTIC VIEW OF JUST AND UNJUST WARS, AND CONCLUDES WITH A PLEA FOR MORE SERIOUS STUDY OF THE LAWS OF WAR IN ORDER TO LIMIT AND REGULATE IT.

2267 O'BRIEN W.V.
"EVENTS AND TRENDS: PATTERNS OF AFRICAN INTERNATIONAL POLITICAL BEHAVIOR."
WOLRD JUSTICE, 8 (DEC. 66), 194-210.
AN ANNOTATED BIBLIOGRAPHY OF PATTERN OF AFRICAN INTERNATIONAL POLITICAL BEHAVIOR. MATERIAL IN ENGLISH-LANGUAGE AND SOME FRENCH AND GERMAN. 34 ENTRIES. MATERIAL RANGES FROM 1957-66.

2268 O'CONNELL M.R.
IRISH POLITICS AND SOCIAL CONFLICT IN THE AGE OF THE AMERICAN REVOLUTION.
PHILA: U OF PENN PR, 1965, 444 PP., LC#64-24494.
ILLUSTRATED STUDY RELATING SOCIAL AND POLITICAL DEVELOPMENT INCLUDING CLASS CONFLICTS AND PRESSURES OF RADICALISM AND REFORM. EMPHASIZES FORMATION AND ACTIVITIES OF VOLUNTEERS.

2269 O'CONNOR A.M.
AN ECONOMIC GEOGRAPHY OF EAST AFRICA.
NEW YORK: FREDERICK PRAEGER, 1966, 292 PP., LC#66-22358.
CONCERNED WITH ECONOMIC ACTIVITIES IN EAST AFRICA, INDICATING MAIN FACTORS AFFECTING BOTH EXISTENCE AND DISTRIBUTION OF ACTIVITIES. BACKGROUND PICTURE OF GEOGRAPHY AND ECONOMY OF REGION.

2270 O'LEARY M.K.
THE POLITICS OF AMERICAN FOREIGN AID.
NEW YORK: ATHERTON, 1967, 172 PP., LC#67-18274.
EXAMINES PROCESS OF ALLOCATION OF US BUDGET FOR FOREIGN AID. DISCUSSES PRESIDENTIAL AND CONGRESSIONAL ACTIONS AND OPINION OF PUBLIC AND POLITICAL PARTIES ON VALUE OF AID.

2271 OAKES J.B.
THE EDGE OF FREEDOM.
NEW YORK: HARPER & ROW, 1961, 129 PP., LC#61-06438.
EXAMINES CLASH OF US AND USSR IN UNDEVELOPED COUNTRIES. VIEWS NEUTRALISM AS POLITICAL IDEOLOGY. STUDIES CASES IN AFRICA AND EUROPE. STUDIES EFFECTS OF TERMINATING COLONIALISM, AND NEW GOVERNMENTS' PRECIPITATION OF IDEOLOGICAL STRUGGLES.

2272 OAS
DOCUMENTOS OFICIALES DE LA ORGANIZACION DE LOS ESTADOS AMERICANOS.
RIO DE JANEIRO: ORG AMER STATES.
PERIODICAL LISTING OF OAS DOCUMENTS AND PUBLICATIONS TITLES IN ENGLISH AND SPANISH.

2273 OBERMANN E.
VERTEIDIGUNG PER FREIHEIT.
STUTTGART: STUTTG VERL KANTOR, 1966, 614 PP.
DISCUSSES WAR AND DEFENSE OF FREEDOM IN EUROPEAN CONSCIOUSNESS, COMMUNIST TEACHING ON WAR AND PEACE, WESTERN AND EASTERN MILITARY ALLIANCES, AND GERMAN CONTRIBUTION TO EUROPEAN DEFENSE.

2274 OCHENG D.
"ECONOMIC FORCES AND UGANDA'S FOREIGN POLICY."
TRANSACTIONS, 2 (OCT. 62), 27-29.
EXAMINES NEED FOR DIPLOMATIC UNITY OF UGANDA WITH TANGANYIKA AND KENYA TO DEAL WITH THEIR ECONOMIC PROBLEMS. WEIGHS BENEFITS OF JOINING EEC AND PROPOSES ESTABLISHMENT OF OVERSEAS MISSIONS IN THE NAME OF ALL THREE RATHER THAN SEPARATELY.

2275 OCHENG D.
"AN ECONOMIST LOOKS AT UGANDA'S FUTURE."
TRANSACTIONS, 1 (NOV. 61), 17-20.
EXPLORES UGANDA'S POSSIBLE SOURCES OF INCOME AFTER INDEPENDENCE WITH A BRIEF EXPLANATION OF PRESENT SYSTEM OF ECONOMY. PROPOSES POSSIBLE SOURCES AND MEANS OF OBTAINING CAPITAL FOR DEVELOPMENT.

2276 ODA S.
"THE NORMALIZATION OF RELATIONS BETWEEN JAPAN AND THE REPUBLIC OF KOREA."
AMER. J. OF INT. LAW, 61 (JAN. 67), 35-56.
STUDIES THE EFFECTS OF THE 1965 TREATY BETWEEN JAPAN AND ROK RECOGNIZING ROK AS THE OFFICIAL GOVERNMENT OF KOREA, RATIFYING ITS INDEPENDENCE FROM JAPANESE COLONIALISM, AND DETAILING CLAIMS SETTLEMENTS, FISHING RIGHTS, CULTURAL COOPERATION AND LEGALITY OF KOREAN RESIDENTS IN JAPAN. CONCLUDES IN CAUTIOUS HOPE THAT JAPANESE RECOGNITION OF ROK WILL NOT HEIGHTEN TENSION BETWEEN NORTH AND SOUTH KOREA.

2277 OECD
MARSHALL PLAN IN TURKEY.
PARIS: ORG FOR ECO COOP AND DEV, 1955, 40 PP.
REPORT ON OPERATION OF MARSHALL PLAN IN TURKISH ECONOMY. COLLECTION OF STATISTICAL DATA ON EXPENDITURES IN AGRICULTURE, NATIONAL DEFENSE, PUBLIC WORKS, COMMUNICATIONS, AND INDUSTRY.

2278 OECD
STATISTICS OF BALANCE OF PAYMENTS 1950-61.
PARIS: ORG FOR ECO COOP AND DEV, 1961, 134 PP.
PRESENTS AND COMPARES STATISTICS FOR NATIONS IN OECD EACH YEAR REGARDING THEIR BALANCE OF PAYMENTS. INCLUDES SEPARATE LISTS FOR EACH MEMBER NATION IN ALPHABETICAL ORDER.

2279 OECD
SCIENCE AND THE POLICIES OF GOVERNMENTS: THE IMPLICATIONS OF SCIENCE AND TECHNOLOGY FOR NATL AND INTL AFFAIRS.
PARIS: ORG FOR ECO COOP AND DEV, 1963, 55 PP.
EXPLORES NEED FOR NATIONAL AND INTERNATIONAL POLICIES TO STRENGTHEN SCIENCE AND TECHNOLOGY. EXAMINES MUTUAL EFFECTS AND IMPLICATIONS OF SCIENCE AND OF POLICIES GOVERNING NATIONAL AND INTERNATIONAL AFFAIRS GENERALLY. SUGGESTS WAYS TO MEET PARTICULAR NEEDS WITHIN AND AMONG NATIONS. FOCUSES ON POLICY IMPLICATIONS OF NATURAL SCIENCES. STRESSES CLOSE RELATION BETWEEN SCIENCE POLICY AND EDUCATIONAL POLICY.

2280 OECD
DEVELOPMENT ASSISTANCE EFFORTS - POLICIES OF THE MEMBERS.
PARIS: ORG FOR ECO COOP AND DEV, 1964, 114 PP.
REPORT BY DEVELOPMENT ASSISTANCE COMMITTEE OF OECD ON VOLUME OF AID, GEOGRAPHIC DISTRIBUTION, CONDITIONS FOR ASSISTANCE, COORDINATION EFFORTS, TECHNICAL AID, AND PROPOSALS ON STRENGTHENING ASSISTANCE EFFORTS OF OECD.

2281 OECD
THE FLOW OF FINANCIAL RESOURCES TO LESS DEVELOPED COUNTRIES 1956-1963.
PARIS: ORG FOR ECO COOP AND DEV, 1964, 165 PP.
PROVIDES FACTUAL INFORMATION ON FLOW OF FINANCIAL RESOURCES AS REPORTED BY INDIVIDUAL DONOR COUNTRIES TO LESS DEVELOPED NATIONS BETWEEN 1956-63. INCLUDES CONTRIBUTIONS OF MULTILATERAL AGENCIES AND FOCUSES ON SIZE OF AID, FEATURES OF POLICIES OF COUNTRY EXTENDING AID, AND INSTITUTIONAL METHODS BY WHICH FINANCIAL AID IS GRANTED.

2282 OEEC
LIBERALISATION OF CURRENT INVISIBLES AND CAPITAL MOVEMENTS BY THE OEEC (PAMPHLET)
PARIS: ORG FOR ECO COOP AND DEV, 1961, 47 PP.
ANALYZES OPERATIONS OF OEEC IN AREA OF "CURRENT INVISIBLES" OR PAPER RECORDED PAYMENTS MADE BY MEMBER NATIONS. CONCENTRATES ON EFFORTS TO "FREE INTERNATIONAL MOVEMENTS OF CAPITAL" BETWEEN MEMBER NATIONS, SIMILAR TO ACCOMPLISHMENTS IN TRADE. AIM IS TO RESTORE FREEDOM PRIOR TO WWII. PROVIDES GENERAL SURVEY OF OPERATIONS OF OEEC.

2283 OGBURN W.
TECHNOLOGY AND INTERNATIONAL RELATIONS.
CHICAGO: U. CHI. PR., 1949, 201 PP., $4.00.
EXAMINES POSTWAR LEGACY OF INVENTIONS AND SCIENTIFIC DISCOVERIES AND RELATES THEM TO THEIR AFFECTS UPON INTERNATIONAL RELATIONS. FOCUSES UPON INFLUENCES OF STEAM, STEEL, ATOM BOMB, AVIATION AND MASS COMMUNICATIONS UPON THE RANKING OF POWERS, SPHERES OF INFLUENCE, FEDERATION OF NATIONS, AND SOCIAL INSTITUTIONS.

2284 OGILVY-WEBB M.
THE GOVERNMENT EXPLAINS: A STUDY OF THE INFORMATION SERVICES
MYSTIC, CONN: VERRY LAWRENCE, 1965, 229 PP.
STUDIES BRITAIN'S GOVERNMENT INFORMATION SERVICES: THEIR DEVELOPMENT FROM TENTATIVE BEGINNINGS TO PRESENT DAY; WAY IN WHICH THEY ARE ORGANIZED AND FUNCTION; PROBLEMS OF STAFFING. ATTEMPTS TO ASSESS THEIR PERFORMANCE AND THE JOB THEY DO ON THE HOME FRONT.

2285 OHLIN B.
INTERREGIONAL AND INTERNATIONAL TRADE.
CAMBRIDGE: HARVARD U. PR., 1933, 617 PP.
INQUIRES INTO CONSTRUCTING A THEORY OF INTERNATIONAL TRADE IN HARMONY WITH THE MUTUAL-INTERDEPENDENCE THEORY OF PRICING AND THUS INDEPENDENT OF THE CLASSICAL LABOR THEORY OF VALUE. CALLS FOR COLLABORATION BETWEEN ECONOMISTS AND ECONOMIC GEOGRAPHERS.

2286 OHLIN G.
FOREIGN AID POLICIES RECONSIDERED.
PARIS: ORG FOR ECO COOP AND DEV, 1966, 120 PP.
STUDY AND EVALUATION OF AID PROGRAMS IN DEVELOPED COUNTRIES. EXAMINES EVOLUTION OF AID DOCTRINE, PUBLIC OPINION ON FOREIGN AID, VOLUME OF AID AND ITS MEASUREMENT, FORMS OF FINANCIAL AID, AND IDEAS ON FORMULATION OF CODE FOR DEVELOPMENT ASSISTANCE. CONCLUDES THAT KEY TO AID EFFECTIVENESS IS UNDERSTANDING RELATIONSHIP BETWEEN NATION GIVING AND PEOPLE RECEIVING THE AID.

2287 OKINSHEVICH L.A., GOROKHOFF C.J.
LATIN AMERICA IN SOVIET WRITINGS, 1945-1958: A BIBLIOGRAPHY.
WASHINGTON: LIBRARY OF CONGRESS, 1959, 257 PP., LC#59-64248.
LISTS 2385 ITEMS ORIGINALLY WRITTEN BY RUSSIANS AND RUSSIAN TRANSLATIONS OF WORKS RELATING TO LATIN AMERICA BY WRITERS OF ALL NATIONALITIES PUBLISHED IN USSR BETWEEN 1945 AND 1958. ENTRIES ARRANGED BY SUBJECT-MATTER: GENERAL REFERENCE WORKS, ANTHROPOLOGY, EDUCATION, GEOGRAPHY, GOVERNMENT AND POLITICS, HISTORY, INTERNATIONAL RELATIONS, LABOR, LAW, SOCIAL CONDITIONS, ETC.

2288 OLIVIER G.
"ASPECTS JURIDIQUES DE L'ADOPTION DU TRAITE CECA A LA CRISE CHARBONNIERE (SUITE ET FIN)"
CAHIERS DU DROIT EUR., 2 (1967), 163-177.
DISCUSSION OF USE OF ARTICLE 95, AL. 1 & 2 OF ECSC CHARTER DURING COAL CRISES. ARGUES THAT FUNDAMENTAL CHANGES IN EUROPEAN FUEL SITUATION NECESSITATE CHANGES IN ECSC TREATY. ARGUES THAT GREATER ATTENTION SHOULD BE PAID TO PROBLEMS OF FIXING QUOTAS IN CRISES THAN TO QUESTIONS OF ORGANIZATION OF INTERNATIONAL TREATY.

2289 OLSON L.
JAPAN TODAY AND TOMORROW (PAMPHLET) (HEADLINE SERIES, NO. 181)
NEW YORK: FOREIGN POLICY ASSN, 1967, 63 PP.
BRIEFLY SUGGESTS THE POSITION AND PROBLEMS OF JAPAN, UNIQUE PHENOMENON IN ASIA DUE TO ADVANCED INDUSTRIAL SOCIETY, WESTERNIZATION, HERITAGE OF AMERICAN OCCUPATION OVERLAID ON ORIENTAL TRADITION. COVERS DOMESTIC AND FOREIGN POLITICS.

2290 OLSON W.C., SONDERMANN F.A.
THE THEORY AND PRACTICE OF INTERNATIONAL RELATIONS (2ND ED.)
ENGLEWOOD CLIFFS: PRENTICE HALL, 1966, 478 PP., LC#66-19880.
EXAMINES THEORY AND PRACTICE OF INTERNATIONAL RELATIONS. ANALYZES STATE SYSTEM AND FACTORS WHICH DETERMINE A STATE'S ABILITY TO ACHIEVE ITS GOALS. STUDIES VARIOUS DIMENSIONS OF POLICY, AND DEGREE TO WHICH NATIONS HAVE ARRIVED AT AN ORGANIZATIONAL AND LEGAL BASIS FOR WORKING TOGETHER. STRESSES RESPONSIBILITY OF NATIONAL LEADERSHIP IN FOREIGN POLICY.

2291 OMAN C.
A HISTORY OF THE ART OF WAR: THE MIDDLE AGES FROM THE FOURTH TO THE FOURTEENTH CENTURY.
LONDON: METHUEN, 1898, 667 PP.
DEALS WITH THE CHARACTERISTIC TACTICS, STRATEGY AND MILITARY ORGANIZATION OF THE ART OF WAR FROM THE DOWNFALL OF ROMAN EMPIRE TO THE FOURTEENTH CENTURY, AND ILLUSTRATES THEM BY DETAILED ACCOUNTS OF TYPICAL CAMPAIGNS AND BATTLES.

2292 OPLER M.E.
"SOCIAL ASPECTS OF TECHNICAL ASSISTANCE IN OPERATION."
PARIS: UNESCO, 1954, 79 PP.
REPORT OF JOINT CONFERENCE OF U.N. AGENCIES ON PROBLEMS OF ADMINISTRATION OF TECHNICAL ASSISTANCE. DEALS WITH SOCIAL, CULTURAL, ECONOMIC, AND POLITICAL IMPEDIMENTS TO EXECUTION OF TECHNICAL ASSISTANCE MISSIONS AND POSSIBLE SOLUTIONS.

2293 OPPENHEIM L.
THE FUTURE OF INTERNATIONAL LAW.
NEW YORK: CARNEGIE ENDOWMENT, 1921, 68 PP.
SEEKS TO DEFINE ORGANIZATION OF STATES. ANALYZES PROBLEMS TREATED IN INTERNATIONAL LEGISLATION. OFFERS PROPOSALS THAT WOULD AID INTERPRETATION. STUDIES INTERNATIONAL ADMINISTRATION OF JUSTICE.

2294 OPPENHEIM L., LAUTERPACHT H. ED.
INTERNATIONAL LAW: A TREATISE (7TH ED., 2 VOLS.)
LONDON: LONGMANS, GREEN & CO, 1953, 1891 PP.
THIS EDITION EXPANDS SECTIONS ON UN, TRUSTEESHIP SYSTEM, AND ILO. SECTIONS ON LEAGUE OF NATIONS AND MANDATES SYSTEM ARE REDUCED, BIBLIOGRAPHIES UPDATED. OTHER SUBJECTS COVERED INCLUDE FOUNDATION, DEVELOPMENT, SUBJECTS, AND OBJECTS OF LAW OF NATIONS; ORGANS OF THE STATES FOR INTERNATIONAL RELATIONS; INTERNATIONAL TRANSACTIONS; SETTLEMENT OF DIFFERENCES; WAR; AND NEUTRALITY.

2295 ORBAN M.
"L'EUROPE EN FORMATION ET SES PROBLEMES."
MEM. PUB. SOC. SCI. ARTS LETT. HAINAUT, 72(NO.2,62), 161-90.
DEALS WITH GOVERNMENTAL POLICIES PROPOSED IN ORDER TO ACHIEVE UNIFICATION. DESCRIBES ECONOMIC AND POLITICAL FACTORS OBSTRUCTING THIS ACHIEVEMENT.

2296 ORFIELD L.B.
THE GROWTH OF SCANDINAVIAN LAW.
PHILA: U OF PENN PR, 1953, 363 PP.
DEVELOPMENT OF LAW AND LEGAL INSTITUTIONS IN DENMARK, ICELAND, NORWAY, AND SWEDEN. CHAPTERS LISTED BY COUNTRY, WITH HISTORICAL AND POLITICAL BACKGROUND.

2297 ORGANSKI A.F.K.
WORLD POLITICS.
NEW YORK: KNOPF, 1958, 461 PP.
PRESENTS A METHODOLOGICAL APPROACH TO THE STUDY OF INTERNATIONAL RELATIONS. EXAMINES CONCEPT AND CHARACTERISTICS OF NATIONS. DESCRIBES INTERNATIONAL RELATIONSHIPS INCLUDING, COLONIALISM, PRESENT-DAY ECONOMIC AND POWER INTERACTIONS, SIGNIFICANCE AND MANIPULATION OF WORLD POWER. REVIEWS FORM, PURPOSE AND PROBLEMS OF INTERNATIONAL ORGANIZATIONS. SUGGESTS FUTURE DEVELOPMENT OF SIGNIFICANT PATTERNS.

2298 ORVIK N.
"NATO: THE ROLE OF THE SMALL MEMBERS."
INT. J., 21 (SPRING 66), 173-185.
STUDIES ROLE PLAYED BY LESS POWERFUL MEMBERS OF NATO. INCLUDES WIDELY DIFFERENT PROBLEMS FACED BY EACH TODAY, CONTRIBUTION TO ALLIANCE, WHAT THEY HAVE TO OFFER, AND EFFECT ON FUTURE OF NATO.

2299 OSGOOD C.E.
"COGNITIVE DYNAMICS IN THE CONDUCT OF HUMAN AFFAIRS."
PUB. OPIN. QUART., 24 (SUMMER 60), 340-65.
SURVEYS RESEARCH ON SUBJECT IN ORDER TO INDICATE ESSENTIAL SIMILARITIES OF THEORIES PROPOSED AND TO POINT OUT SIGNIFICANCE OF SUBJECT FOR CONTEMPORARY HUMAN AFFAIRS.

2300 OSGOOD C.E.
AN ALTERNATIVE TO WAR OR SURRENDER.
URBANA: U. ILL. PR., 1962, 183 PP., $1.45.
PRESENTS MODEL OF SOCIAL-PSYCHOLOGICAL LOGIC AND KNOWLEDGE APPLIED TO WORLD PEACE. DESCRIBES A PROGRAM FOR ORGANIZATION CALLED GRADUATED RECIPROCATION IN TENSION-REDUCTION. ARGUES THAT UNDERLYING SOCIAL DYNAMICS OF INTERNATIONAL RELATIONS WILL BRING INEVITABLE MUTUAL DISASTER AND FOIL PROCESS OF TENSION-REDUCTION.

2301 OSGOOD R.E.
NATO: THE ENTANGLING ALLIANCE.
CHICAGO: U. CHI. PR., 1962, 416 PP., $7.50.
EXAMINES ROLE OF NATO IN INTEGRATED EUROPEAN COMMUNITY. DISCUSSES NATURE OF SECURITY DILEMMA FACING NATO, PROBLEMS OF STRATEGY, CONTROL AND DIFFUSION OF NUCLEAR WEAPONS. CONCLUDES THAT NATO MUST DEPEND LESS ON NUCLEAR CAPABILITY AND THAT EUROPEAN MEMBERS MUST SHOULDER MORE RESPONSIBILITY IN SUPPORT OF NATO.

2302 OVERSTREET H., OVERSTREET B.
THE WAR CALLED PEACE.
NEW YORK: W W NORTON, 1961, 368 PP., LC#61-5612.
DISCUSSES IMPACT OF KHRUSHCHEV'S POLICIES ON COMMUNIST-FREE WORLD RELATIONS. ANALYZES INTENSIFICATION OF IDEOLOGICAL CONFLICT AND GENERAL FEELINGS OF FEAR AND SUSPICION BETWEEN "FREE MAN" "COMMUNIST MAN" RESULTING FROM KRUSHCHEV'S DIPLOMATIC ACTIONS AND POLICIES.

2303 OWEN C.F.
"US AND SOVIET RELATIONS WITH UNDERDEVELOPED COUNTRIES: LATIN AMERICA-A CASE STUDY."
INTER-AMER. ECON. AFF., 14 (WINTER 60), 85-116.
ILLUSTRATES COMPATIBILITY OF NATIONAL ASPIRATIONS WITH ECONOMIC INTERNATIONALISM. AS OUTSTANDING EXAMPLE, CITES CASE OF ARGENTINA, WHERE STATE OIL MONOPOLY, YPF, SUCCESSFULLY NEGOTIATED WITH USA OIL INTERESTS. CONSIDERS NATIONALISM AS FORCE DRIVING LATIN AMERICAN AND AFRICAN COUNTRIES TO TRADE WITH SOVIET UNION.

2304 OWEN W.
STRATEGY FOR MOBILITY.
WASHINGTON: BROOKINGS INST., 1964, 249 PP., $5.00.
SHOWS HOW, IN SOME INSTANCES, THE FAILURE TO PROVIDE ADEQUATE TRANSPORT HAS BEEN THE MAJOR MISSING ELEMENT IMPEDING ECONOMIC PROGRESS, AND IN OTHERS HOW TRANSPORT FACILITIES HAVE FAILED TO MAKE AN EFFECTIVE CONTRIBUTION BECAUSE THEY WERE POORLY CONCEIVED OR INEFFECTIVELY LINKED WITH BROADER DEVELOPMENT OBJECTIVES. PROPOSES A BETTER TRANSPORT STRATEGY FOR THE DEVELOPING NATIONS.

2305 VON BORCH H.
FRIEDE TROTZ KRIEG.
MUNICH: R PIPER AND CO VERLAG, 1966, 375 PP.
DISCUSSES INTERNATIONAL TENSIONS SINCE 1950. EXAMINES ESCALATION IN ARMAMENT, GERMAN UNIFICATION PROBLEM, DEVELOPMENT OF NEW COLD WAR POLITICS, AND "WORLD ANXIETY" PRODUCED BY THREAT OF NUCLEAR WAR.

2306 HEUSS E.
WIRTSCHAFTSSYSTEME UND INTERNATIONALER HANDEL.
ZURICH: POLYGRAPHISCHER VERLAG, 1955, 224 PP.
DISCUSSES PRINCIPLES OF INTERNATIONAL TRADE IN RELATION TO MARKET 2ECONOMY, MARKET ECONOMY WITH AUTONOMOUS CURRENCY POLICY, MONOPOLIZED MARKET ECONOMY, AND SOCIALIST ECONOMIC SYSTEMS. CONCLUDES WITH CONTRAST BETWEEN PLANNED AND MARKET ECONOMIES.

2307 PACHTER H.M.
COLLISION COURSE; THE CUBAN MISSILE CRISIS AND COEXISTENCE.
NEW YORK: FREDERICK PRAEGER, 1963, 261 PP., LC#63-18528.
CURRENT HISTORY OF EVENTS INVOLVED IN THE CUBAN MISSILE CRISIS OF OCTOBER, 1962. DISCUSSES PRINCIPAL PERSONS INVOLVED - KHRUSHCHEV, CASTRO, KENNEDY, U THANT. POINTS OUT FORCES WHICH MOTIVATED THEIR ACTIONS. ANALYZES AND FORMULATES GENERAL CONCLUSIONS ABOUT POWER CONFLICTS IN NUCLEAR AGE; PRESENTS PRINCIPLES OF COEXISTENCE WHICH MAY PREVENT COLD WAR FROM BEING ACTIVATED.

2308 PADELFORD N.J.
"REGIONAL COOPERATION IN THE SOUTH PACIFIC: THE SOUTH PACIFIC COMMISSION."
INT. ORG., 13 (SUMMER 59), 380-393.

TRACES HISTORIC DEVELOPMENT, NATURE AND PURPOSE OF THE COMMISSION. DESCRIBES ESTABLISHMENT OF THE RESEARCH COUNCIL WHOSE OBJECTIVE IS AIDING AND BETTERING LIFE OF INHABITANTS AND PREPARING THEM FOR EVENTUAL SELF-DETERMINATION.

2309 PADELFORD N.J.
"POLITICS AND CHANGE IN THE SECURITY COUNCIL."
INT. ORGAN., 14 (SUMMER 60), 381-401.
EXAMINES EFFECT OF CHANGES IN WORLD POLITICAL SITUATION AND THE GREAT INCREASE IN UN MEMBERSHIP ON SECURITY COUNCIL. NOTES GREAT IMBALANCE IN COUNCIL REPRESENTATION, MAINLY AS CONCERNS AFRO-ASIAN BLOC. CONSIDERS PROPOSALS AND THEIR CONSEQUENCES FOR ENLARGING MEMBERSHIP AND CHANGING STRUCTURE OF SECURITY COUNCIL. URGES CREATION OF TWO ADDITIONAL ELECTIVE SEATS.

2310 PADELFORD N.J.
"POLITICS AND THE FUTURE OF ECOSOC."
INT. ORGAN., 15 (AUTUMN 61), 564-80.
CONCERNED WITH PRESSURES TO INCREASE SIZE AND SCOPE OF ECOSOC. CONSIDERS AMENDMENTS ALLOWING INCREASED REPRESENTATION OF AFRO-ASIAN STATES AND EFFECT OF CHANGES. EXAMINES FINANCIAL STRAIN ON UN AND US FROM DEMANDS FOR INCREASED FUNDS FOR ECONOMIC AND TECHNICAL ASSISTANCE.

2311 PADELFORD N.J.
"FINANCIAL CRISIS AND THE UNITED NATIONS."
WORLD POLIT., 15 (JULY 63), 531-568.
DETAILED ANALYSIS OF UNITED NATIONS' ASSESSMENTS. FINANCIAL CRISIS DUE TO MEMBERS WHO, FOR POLITICAL NOT ECONOMIC REASONS, DO NOT PAY THEIR BILLS. IF UN IS TO SURVIVE, ADEQUATE MEANS OF FINANCING MUST BE FOUND.

2312 PADELFORD N.J. ED., EMERSON R. ED.
AFRICA AND WORLD ORDER.
NEW YORK: FREDERICK PRAEGER, 1963, 152 PP., LC#63-10264.
ON CONTEMPORARY AFRICA, INCLUDING ITS BEHAVIOR IN UN, ITS UNIFICATION MOVEMENTS, PAN-AFRICANISM, AND IMPACT ON COMMONWEALTH.

2313 PADELFORD N.J.
"THE ORGANIZATION OF AFRICAN UNITY."
INT. ORGAN., 18 (SUMMER 64), 521-42.
CONSIDERS MAJOR PROBLEMS OF FUNCTIONAL COOPERATION AND GRADUALISM AS OPPOSED TO UNITY AND CENTRALIZATION IN THE HISTORICAL DEVELOPMENT OF AFRICAN UNITY. EXAMINES PRINCIPLE ORGANS ESTABLISHED BY THE ORGANIZATION'S CHARTER AND THE RESOLUTIONS THUS FAR ADOPTED.

2314 PADELFORD N.J., LINCOLN G.A.
THE DYNAMICS OF INTERNATIONAL POLITICS (2ND ED.)
NEW YORK: MACMILLAN, 1967, 640 PP.
DESCRIBES BACKGROUND OF INTERNATIONAL POLITICS AND DISCUSSES MAJOR FACTORS. EMPHASIS IS PLACED ON DECISION-MAKING PROCESS. INCLUDES INSTRUMENTS AND PATTERNS OF FOREIGN POLICY, ORGANIZATION OF INTERNATIONAL COMMUNITY, ECONOMIC AND POLITICAL PRINCIPLES, IMPACT OF TECHNOLOGICAL CHANGE, GROWING POPULATION, AND SHIFTING RELATIONSHIPS WITHIN POWER BLOCS. TEXTS TO IMPORTANT TREATIES INCLUDED.

2315 PAENSON I. ED.
SYSTEMATIC GLOSSARY ENGLISH, FRENCH, SPANISH, RUSSIAN OF SELECTED ECONOMIC AND SOCIAL TERMS.
NEW YORK: PERGAMON PRESS, 1963, 414 PP., LC#63-10029.
DICTIONARY OF TERMS FROM ECONOMICS AND SOCIAL SCIENCES IN ENGLISH, FRENCH, SPANISH AND RUSSIAN, ARRANGED ACCORDING TO SUBJECT. TRANSLATIONS ARE CAREFUL AND COMPLETE.

2316 PAGAN B.
HISTORIA DE LOS PARTIDOS POLITICOS PUERTORRIQUENOS 1898-1956
SAN JUAN: LIBERIA CAMPOS, 1959, 342 PP.
HISTORICAL SURVEY OF POLITICAL PARTIES IN PUERTO RICO FROM 1898-1956. DEALS WITH US INVASION AND MILITARY GOVERNMENT AND FORMATION OF EARLY POLITICAL PARTIES. EXPLAINS BASIS OF PARTY ORGANIZATION, ELECTORAL ACTIVITIES AND ACTION OF PARTIES IN OFFICE.

2317 PAGINSKY P.
GERMAN WORKS RELATING TO AMERICA, 1493-1800; A LIST COMPILED FROM THE COLLECTIONS OF THE NEW YORK PUBLIC LIBRARY.
NEW YORK: NY PUBLIC LIBRARY, 1942, 217 PP.
ANNOTATED BIBLIOGRAPHY OF WORKS IN GERMAN, ARRANGED CHRONOLOGICALLY WITH ANNOTATIONS IN ENGLISH.

2318 PAKISTAN MINISTRY OF FINANCE
FOREIGN ECONOMIC AID: A REVIEW OF FOREIGN ECONOMIC AID TO PAKISTAN.
RAWALPINDI: PAKISTAN MIN FINANCE, 1962, 118 PP.
DETAILED REPORT PRESENTING IN RETROSPECT THE POSITION OF ECONOMIC ASSISTANCE TO PAKISTAN BY FRIENDLY COUNTRIES AND AGENCIES. STUDY GROUPED UNDER HEADINGS OF US AID; AID RECEIVED UNDER COLOMBO PLAN FROM COMMONWEALTH COUNTRIES AND JAPAN; AID FROM UN, FORD FOUNDATION, AND EUROPEAN COUNTRIES; AND FOREIGN LOANS AND CREDITS FROM EIGHT COUNTRIES.

2319 PALMER E.E. ED.
AMERICAN FOREIGN POLICY.
SYRACUSE: SYR U, MAXWELL SCHOOL, 1958, 100 PP.
PRESENTS ARTICLES DEALING WITH MORE PERMANENT ASPECTS OF FOREIGN POLICY. OUTLINES GENERAL AREAS OF AMERICAN POLICY. DEBATES ITS ETHICAL FOUNDATIONS, AND DISCUSSES WHETHER ECONOMIC POLICY SHOULD BE DETERMINED ON THE BASIS OF DOMESTIC EFFECTS ALONE OR INTERNATIONAL CONSEQUENCES, AS WELL. DEALS ALSO WITH GOVERNMENTAL INSTITUTIONS INVOLVED AND EFFECTS OF CULTURAL MORES UPON THEM.

2320 PALMER E.E. ED.
THE COMMUNIST CHALLENGE.
SYRACUSE: SYR U, MAXWELL SCHOOL, 1958, 125 PP.
PRESENTS BASIC STRUCTURE OF IDEAS OF WORLD COMMUNISM, AS THEY HAVE DEVELOPED SINCE THE PUBLICATION OF THE COMMUNIST MANIFESTO IN 1848. REVIEWS GENERAL PROBLEMS OF DEALING WITH UNCOMMITTED NATIONS AND BASIC CONCEPTS AND PROGRAMS OF US FOREIGN POLICY. OFFERS SUGGESTIONS FOR PREVENTING SPREAD OF COMMUNISM AND FACILITATING PEACE.

2321 PALMER N.D., PERKINS H.C.
INTERNATIONAL RELATIONS.
BOSTON: HOUGHTON MIFFLIN, 1957, 860 PP.
STUDIES PATTERN OF INTERNATIONAL RELATIONS FIRST FROM THEORETICAL VIEWPOINT. CONSIDERS BASIC INSTRUMENTS FOR PROMOTION OF NATIONAL INTEREST: DIPLOMACY, PROPAGANDA, ECONOMICS, WAR, AND IMPERIALISM. TREATS CONTROLS OF INTERSTATE RELATIONS, SUCH AS BALANCE OF POWER, INTERNATIONAL LAW, TREATIES, AND INTERNATIONAL ORGANIZATIONS. DISCUSSES MAJOR CHANGES AFTER WWII.

2322 PALMER N.D.
THE INDIAN POLITICAL SYSTEM.
BOSTON: HOUGHTON MIFFLIN, 1961, 277 PP.
COMPREHENSIVE VIEW OF EVOLVING INDIAN POLITICAL SYSTEM IN RELATION TO HER CULTURE, SOCIETY, AND HISTORY. DISCUSSES THE NATIONALIST MOVEMENT, INDIAN STATE, CENTRAL GOVERNMENT, POLITICAL PARTIES, AND FOREIGN RELATIONS AS BASIC THEMES.

2323 PALMER N.D.
"INDIA AS A FACTOR IN UNITED STATES FOREIGN POLICY."
INT. STUDIES, 6 (JULY 64), 49-68.
FACTORS INFLUENCING THE VARYING INTENSITY OF RELATIONS WITH INDIA ARE ENUMERATED AND INQUIRY MADE INTO THE DONOR-RECIPIENT RELATIONSHIP. CONCLUDES THAT A NEW ERA OF MATURE, CLOSE RELATIONS HAS BEGUN.

2324 PALYI M.
MANAGED MONEY AT THE CROSSROADS: THE EUROPEAN EXPERIENCE.
NOTRE DAME: U OF NOTRE DAME, 1958, 196 PP., LC#57-11375.
SURVEY OF FINANCIAL CENTERS OF EUROPE. ANALYZES METHODS OF MANAGING AND CONVERTING MONEY SINCE 1900'S. COVERS POSTWAR RECOVERY METHODS, INFLATIONARY CONTROLS, AND DEVALUATION TACTICS. BIBLIOGRAPHY OF SELECTED READINGS ON SUBJECT.

2325 PAN S., LYONS D.
VIETNAM CRISIS.
NEW YORK: TWIN CIRCLE PUBL CO, 1966, 334 PP., LC#66-23533.
HISTORY OF VIETNAM FROM ITS BEGINNINGS TO PRESENT TIME, BASED ON LONG ASSOCIATIONS WITH VIETNAMESE. FOCUSES ON PERIOD FROM WWII TO 1966. DISCUSSES PRESENT POSITIONS OF NORTH AND SOUTH VIETNAMESE GOVERNMENTS AND PEOPLE, AND US AND FRENCH POLICIES, HOPES THAT SPREAD OF COMMUNIST CHINA WILL BE CHECKED BY VIETNAM WAR.

2326 PAN AMERICAN UNION
REPERTORIO DE PUBLICACIONES PERIODICAS ACTUALES LATINO-AMERICANAS.
PARIS: UNESCO, 1958.
DIRECTORY OF LATIN AMERICAN PERIODICALS ARRANGED BY DEWEY DECIMAL SYSTEM.

2327 PAN AMERICAN UNION
FIFTH MEETING OF CONSULTATION OF MINISTERS OF FOREIGN AFFAIRS OF AMERICAN STATES.
WASHINGTON: PAN AMERICAN UNION, 1960, 23 PP.
PROVIDES SUMMARY ACCOUNT OF PROCEEDINGS OF MEETING OF MINISTERS OF 21 REPUBLICS FORMING OAS IN SANTIAGO, CHILE, IN 1959. TOPICS DISCUSSED INCLUDE STUDIES ON INTER-AMERICAN JURIDICAL RELATIONSHIPS, PROGRAMS FOR ECONOMIC DEVELOPMENT, AND OAS'S POLICIES OF NONINTERVENTION AND NONAGGRESSION.

2328 PAN AMERICAN UNION
PUBLICATIONS: PAU AND OFFICIAL RECORDS OF THE OAS, IN ENGLISH, SPANISH, PORTUGUESE, AND FRENCH, 1958-59.
WASHINGTON: PAN AMERICAN UNION, 1959, 32 PP.
"LISTS PUBLICATIONS AVAILABLE FOR SALE AND ISSUED BY PAN AMERICAN UNION...REPORTS AND STUDIES OF ACTIVITIES IN THE AMERICAN REPUBLICS...MONOGRAPHS...PERIODICALS...OFFICIAL RECORDS OF THE OAS." ITEMS CLASSIFIED BY SUBJECT.

2329 PAN AMERICAN UNION
DOCUMENTOS OFICIALES DE LA ORGANIZACION DE LOS ESTADOS AMERICANOS, INDICE Y LISTA (VOL. III, 1962)

WASHINGTON: PAN AMERICAN UNION, 1963, 501 PP.
OFFICIAL OAS DOCUMENTS FOR 1962, ARRANGED BY SERIES, WITH FULL ALPHABETICAL INDEX INDICATING PROPER SERIES AND DOCUMENT NUMBER. VOLUMES I AND II APPEARED AS "INDICE Y LISTA GENERAL DE LOS DOCUMENTOS OFICIALES."

2330 PANHUYS H.F.
THE ROLE OF NATIONALITY IN INTERNATIONAL LAW.
LEYDEN: AW SIJTHOFF, 1959, 251 PP.
TRACES CHANGING EFFECTS OF NATIONALITY ON LEGAL RIGHTS OF ALIENS IN INTERNATIONAL LAW AND IN TIME OF WAR, GIVING DIGEST OF TRADITIONAL FUNCTIONS OF NATIONALITY AND PRESENT ARRANGEMENTS.

2331 PANIKKAR K.M. ED., PERSHAD A. ED.
THE VOICE OF FREEDOM: SELECTED SPEECHES OF PANDIT MOTILAL NEHRU.
NEW YORK: ASIA PUBL HOUSE, 1961, 563 PP.
SELF-EXPLAINED AND FULLY ANNOTATED SPEECHES BY PANDIT MOTILAL NEHRU. CONGRESSIONAL SPEECHES STRESS RESPONSIBLE SELF-GOVERNMENT AND INDEPENDENCE; UNITED PROVINCE COUNCIL SPEECHES CONCERN MONTAGU-CHELMSFORD REFORMS; LEGISLATIVE ASSEMBLY SPEECHES COVER VARIOUS LAWS AND BILLS.

2332 PANIKKAR K.M.
REVOLUTION IN AFRICA.
BOMBAY: ASIA PUBL HOUSE, 1961, 202 PP.
STUDIES EMERGENCE OF AFRICA: NATIONALISM; RISE OF NATION STATES; POLITICAL PARTIES AND LEADERS; PAN-AFRICANISM; POLITICS IN UNDER-DEVELOPED COUNTRIES; CASE STUDY OF GUINEA.

2333 PANJAB U EXTENSION LIBRARY
INDIAN NEWS INDEX.
LUDHIANA, PUNJAB: PANJAB U LIB, 1965.
QUARTERLY CROSS-REFERENCES SUBJECT GUIDE TO SELECTED ENGLISH NEWSPAPERS OF INDIA; FIRST ISSUED IN 1965. INDEXES EIGHT CALCUTTA, BOMBAY, MADRAS, AMBALA, AND NEW DELHI NEWSPAPERS. INDEX IS TOPICAL AND ARRANGEMENT OF SUBJECTS IS ALPHABETICAL. NAME INDEX CATEGORIZES INDIVIDUAL CONTRIBUTIONS SUCH AS ARTICLES, LETTERS TO THE EDITOR, OPINIONS, AND STATEMENTS.

2334 PANT Y.P.
PLANNING IN UNDERDEVELOPED ECONOMIES.
ALLAHABAD: INDIAN PRESS, LTD, 1955, 160 PP.
DESCRIPTION OF PLANNING IN INDIA UNDER VARIOUS FOREIGN RULERS. EXPLAINS ECONOMIC PLANNING AT PRESENT, DESCRIBING FIRST FIVE YEAR PLAN, AND MAKES SUGGESTIONS FOR NEPAL.

2335 PARMELEE M.
GEO-ECONOMIC REGIONAL AND WORLD FEDERATION.
NEW YORK: EXPOSITION, 1949, 137 PP., $2.50.
ATTEMPT AT DELINEATION OF REGIONS ACCORDING TO GEOGRAPHIC AND ECONOMIC PRINCIPLES. REGIONALISM AS BASIS FOR WORLD FEDERATION ANALYZED IN TERMS OF THE FORCES FOR AND AGAINST IT, ITS NATURE, BASES, AND FUNCTIONS. GEOGRAPHIC, ECONOMIC, AND GEO-ECONOMIC REGIONS ARE DISCUSSED AND RELATED. CLASSIFICATIONS ARE PROPOSED.

2336 PARRINGTON V.L.
MAIN CURRENTS IN AMERICAN THOUGHT (VOL.I)
NEW YORK: HARCOURT BRACE, 1927, 413 PP.
DISCUSSION OF INFLUENCES OF EUROPEAN POLITICAL AND RELIGIOUS THOUGHT ON COLONIAL AMERICA. TRACES CONFLICTS BETWEEN LIBERAL POLITICAL PHILOSOPHY AND REACTIONARY THEOLOGY. CONCLUDES THAT AMERICAN POLITICAL THOUGHT EMERGED IN THIS PERIOD AS A NEW BRAND OF LIBERALISM. BIOGRAPHICAL ACCOUNTS OF ROGER WILLIAMS, BENJAMIN FRANKLIN, AND THOMAS JEFFERSON.

2337 PASSIN H. ED.
THE UNITED STATES AND JAPAN.
ENGLEWOOD CLIFFS: PRENTICE HALL, 1966, 174 PP., LC#66-14703.
COLLECTION OF ESSAYS DISCUSSING POLITICAL AND ECONOMIC RELATIONS BETWEEN US AND JAPAN. MAINTAINS THAT INTERNAL POLITICAL STRIFE IN JAPAN REFLECTS IN LARGE MEASURE THE MEMORY OF DEFEAT AND OCCUPATION BY US. DISCUSSES ECONOMIC RELATIONS IN LIGHT OF COMMON OBJECTIVES AND CONCLUDES WITH PROJECTION OF FUTURE TRENDS.

2338 PASTUHOV V.D.
A GUIDE TO THE PRACTICE OF INTERNATIONAL CONFERENCES.
WASHINGTON: CARNEGIE ENDOWMENT, 1945, 275 PP.
DEALS WITH PLANNING, STAFFING, BUDGETING, ORGANIZING, DIRECTING AND ACTUAL HOLDING OF INTERNATIONAL CONFERENCES AND COMMITTEE MEETINGS, DEVOTING SPECIAL ATTENTION TO FOLLOW-UP WORK. LINKS TECHNICAL PROCESSES WITH THEORY AND REPRESENTATIVE LITERATURE IN THIS FIELD.

2339 PATAI R.
CULTURES IN CONFLICT; AN INQUIRY INTO THE SOCIO-CULTURAL PROBLEMS OF ISRAEL AND HER NEIGHBORS (2ND REV. ED.)
NEW YORK: HERZL PRESS, 1961, 80 PP.
LOOKS AT TRADITIONAL SOCIAL STRUCTURE, VALUES, AND ATTITUDES OF ARAB STATES. PORTRAYS MODERN, WESTERN CULTURE OF ISRAEL AND VALUES OF EUROPEAN JEWS IN ISRAEL; COMPARES CULTURE OF EUROPEAN AND ORIENTAL JEWS. ANALYZES TRANSITION FROM TRADITIONAL TO MODERN SOCIETY IN ISRAEL AND ARAB STATES, AND CONSIDERS POSSIBILITY OF CULTURAL UNDERSTANDING BETWEEN ISRAEL AND HER NEIGHBORS. TREATS WADI SALIB EVENTS.

2340 PATEL H.M.
THE DEFENCE OF INDIA (PAMPHLET)
NEW YORK: ASIA PUBL HOUSE, 1963, 32 PP.
ANALYSIS OF INDIAN DEFENCE POLICY AND MILITARY ORGANIZATION, EXAMINING FRONTIER, NEIGHBORING COUNTRIES, POTENTIAL ENEMY ACTIONS, AND ABILITY OF NATION TO DEFEND ITSELF. SPECIFICALLY CONCERNS CONFLICT WITH CHINA AND PAKISTAN.

2341 PATRA A.C.
THE ADMINISTRATION OF JUSTICE UNDER THE EAST INDIA COMPANY IN BENGAL, BIHAR AND ORISSA.
NEW YORK: ASIA PUBL HOUSE, 1963, 233 PP.
APPRAISAL OF DISPENSATION OF JUSTICE BY PRINCIPAL JUDICIAL INSTITUTIONS OPERATING UNDER EAST INDIA COMPANY IN BENGAL. FOCUSES ON AREA OF LEGAL ADMINISTRATION.

2342 PAUKER G.J.
"TOWARD A NEW ORDER IN INDONESIA."
FOREIGN AFFAIRS, 45 (APR. 67), 503-519.
ANALYZES INDONESIAN SHIFT FROM OLD ORDER OF SUKARNO TO NEW ORDER ESTABLISHED BY THE MILITARY. COMMENTS ON SUKARNO'S REMOVAL AS MOST URGENT STEP NECESSARY FOR POLITICAL AND ECONOMIC STABILITY. PREDICTS CONSOLIDATION OF NEW ORDER WILL SIGNIFY IMPROVEMENT OF US-INDONESIAN RELATIONS, AND A POWERFUL FUTURE FOR INDONESIA IN THE COMMUNITY OF NATIONS.

2343 PEARSON L.B.
DIPLOMACY IN THE NUCLEAR AGE.
CAMBRIDGE: HARVARD U PR, 1959, 114 PP., LC#59-11514.
TEXT OF 1958 CLAYTON LECTURES CONCERNING EFFECTS OF NUCLEAR ENERGY UPON POWER, FOREIGN POLICY, AND DIPLOMACY. EXAMINES TRANSITIONS IN DIPLOMATIC METHODS, COLLECTIVE ACTION POLICIES, NEGOTIATION, RELATION OF POWER AND POLICY, AND CONCLUDES WITH "THE FOUR FACES OF PEACE."

2344 PEASLEE A.J.
INTERNATIONAL GOVERNMENT ORGANIZATIONS, CONSTITUTIONAL DOCUMENTS.
GENEVA: NIJHOFF, 1961, 2 VOLS.
REFERENCE WORK ON SUBJECT DESCRIBES FUNCTIONS, PROTOCOL ARRANGEMENTS, AND CONSTITUTIONAL OF SEVERAL HUNDRED ORGANIZATIONS.

2345 PEASLEE A.J.
INTERNATIONAL GOVERNMENTAL ORGANIZATIONS (2 VOLS.)
THE HAGUE: MARTINUS NIJHOFF, 1961.
CONTAINS AMENDMENTS AND DOCUMENTS FOR 38 ORGANIZATIONS AND ENTRIES FOR 35 ORGANIZATIONS. LISTING IS ALPHABETICAL AND ONLY MULTILATERAL BODIES ARE INCLUDED. GENERALLY, THE CONSTITUTIONAL DOCUMENTS OF ONLY THE PRINCIPAL ORGANIZATION ARE INCLUDED, NOT THE DOCUMENTS OF SUBORDINATE AGENCIES. BRIEF DESCRIPTIONS OF THE ORGANIZATIONS ARE GIVEN.

2346 PECKERT J.
DIE GROSSEN UND DIE KLEINEN MAECHTE.
STUTTGART: DEUTSCHE VERLAGSANST, 1961, 193 PP.
THEORETICAL PRESENTATION OF CHANGES IN THE NATIONAL INTEREST OF VARIOUS MODERN STATES AND RELATION OF THESE CHANGES TO THREE IMPORTANT CONTEMPORARY PROBLEM AREAS: THE POLITICS OF ALLIANCES, POLITICS VIS-A-VIS DEVELOPING NATIONS, AND THE POLITICS OF EUROPE.

2347 PECQUET P.
THE DIPLOMACY OF THE CONFEDERATE CABINET OF RICHMOND AND ITS AGENTS ABROAD (LIMITED ED.)
TUSCALOOSA: CONFEDERATE PUBL CO, 1963, 130 PP.
MEMORANDUM NOTES CONDEMNING SOUTHERN POSITION DURING CIVIL WAR AND CONFEDERACY'S DIPLOMATIC RELATIONS WITH EUROPE. WRITTEN BY OBSERVER.

2348 PELCOVITS N.A.
OLD CHINA HANDS AND THE FOREIGN OFFICE.
NEW YORK: KINGS CROWN PR, 1948, 347 PP.
STUDY OF THE OPINIONS AND ATTITUDES ON ANGLO-CHINESE RELATIONS HELD BY BRITISH MERCHANTS ENGAGED IN THE CHINA TRADE, AND OF THEIR RELEVANCE TO THE FORMATION, IN THE 19TH CENTURY OF BRITISH FOREIGN POLICY TOWARD CHINA. DISCUSSES THE EVENTS THAT CAUSED THE BRITISH GOVERNMENT TO DECIDE AGAINST MAKING CHINA A "SECOND INDIA."

2349 PENICK J.L. JR. ED., PURSELL C.W. JR. ED. ET AL.
THE POLITICS OF AMERICAN SCIENCE, 1939 TO THE PRESENT.
SKOKIE: RAND MCNALLY & CO, 1965, 287 PP., LC#65-14099.
READINGS ON ISSUES OF PRESENT DAY (WELFARE STATE, COLD WAR, INTERNATIONALISM, ETC.) THAT HAVE INFLUENCED AND HELPED MOLD STRUCTURE OF US SCIENTIFIC COMMUNITY. ATTEMPTS TO ILLUMINATE QUESTIONS OF POLICY AND ADMINISTRATION RATHER THAN TECHNICAL PROBLEMS OF SCIENCE.

2350 PENNOCK J.R. ED.
SELF-GOVERNMENT IN MODERNIZING NATIONS.

ENGLEWOOD CLIFFS: PRENTICE HALL, 1964, 118 PP., LC#64-23554.
DISCUSSES PROBLEMS OF EMERGING NATIONS IN MODERNIZING THEIR WORKINGS. TREATS DIFFICULTIES IN SOCIAL, POLITICAL, AND ECONOMIC DEVELOPMENT FROM BOTH INTERNAL AND EXTERNAL VIEWPOINTS. COVERS INSTABILITY, CRISIS MANAGEMENT, ONE-PARTY SYSTEM, COMMUNISM, AND US POLICY TOWARD EMERGING NATIONS.

2351 PENTONY D.E. ED.
THE UNDERDEVELOPED LANDS.
SAN FRANCISCO: CHANDLER, 1960, 196 PP, $1.50.
STUDIES PROBLEMS OF UNDERDEVELOPMENT IN ASIA, AFRICA AND LATIN AMERICA, 'STRIPPED OF SOME OF ITS COLD-WAR OVERTONES'. INCLUDES DISCUSSION OF: RUBLE DIPLOMACY, TRADE AND AID, OBSTACLES TO ECONOMIC DEVELOPMENT, GANDHI'S VIEWS ON MACHINES AND TECHNOLOGY, AND ECONOMIC COOPERATION UNDER UN AUSPICES.

2352 PENTONY D.E. ED.
UNITED STATES FOREIGN AID.
SAN FRANCISCO: CHANDLER, 1960, 147 PP., LC#60-07597.
DISCUSSES OBJECTIVES OF US FOREIGN AID, MILITARY, ECONOMIC, AND HUMANITARIAN. GIVES BACKGROUND OF FOREIGN AID PROGRAM AND EXAMINES VARYING METHODS OF AID IN ITS ADMINISTRATION. USES TWO CASE STUDIES OF AID TO ANALYZE ITS EFFECTIVENESS.

2353 PERAZA SARAUSA F.
BIBLIOGRAFIAS CUBANAS.
WASHINGTON: GOVT PR OFFICE, 1945, 58 PP.
ANNOTATED BIBLIOGRAPHY OF BIBLIOGRAPHIES ON CUBA. ENTRIES DATE FROM 1861 THROUGH 1944. OFFERS BRIEF OUTLINE OF CUBA'S BIBLIOGRAPHICAL HISTORY. FIRST SECTION IS GENERAL BIBLIOGRAPHIES, SECOND IS BIBLIOGRAPHIES ACCORDING TO SUBJECT, THIRD IS PERSONAL BIBLIOGRAPHIES. 485 ENTRIES WITH ANNOTATIONS IN SPANISH. INCLUDES INDEX.

2354 PEREZ ORTIZ R. ED.
ANUARIO BIBLIOGRAFICO COLOMBIANO, 1961.
BOGOTA: INST CARO Y CUERVO, 1963, 178 PP.
COLOMBIAN BIBLIOGRAPHICAL ANNUAL FOR 1961 COVERING GENERAL PUBLICATIONS FOR THAT YEAR.

2355 PERHAM M.
AFRICANS AND BRITISH RULE.
LONDON: OXFORD U PR, 1941, 98 PP.
STUDIES GROWTH OF BRITAIN'S POLICIES TOWARD HER COLONIES IN AFRICA. DESCRIBES CONTINENT AS IT WAS BEFORE EUROPEAN OCCUPATION AND TRACES PROCESS BY WHICH BRITISH AFRICA WAS GAINED AND HOW IT HAS BEEN GOVERNED. EXAMINES POLITICAL AND ECONOMIC USES AND ABUSES OF IMPERIALISM. DESCRIBES HOW BRITAIN RULES INDIRECTLY THROUGH AFRICAN SELF-GOVERNMENT. CALLS FOR INCREASED EFFORTS TOWARD MUTUAL UNDERSTANDING.

2356 PERHAM M.
COLONIAL GOVERNMENT: ANNOTATED READING LIST ON BRITISH COLONIAL GOVERNMENT.
LONDON: OXFORD U PR, 1950, 80 PP.
SELECTED LIST OF PAMPHLETS, LEGISLATION, BIBLIOGRAPHIES, CONFIDENTIAL MATERIAL, AND JOURNALS FOR STUDENTS OF BRITISH COLONIALISM. NOT OVERLY SPECIALIZED; CONCENTRATES ON LARGER COLONIES. MAINLY PRIMARY SOURCE MATERIAL FROM PUBLICATIONS CIRCA 1950. INCLUDES A FEW PUBLICATIONS FROM OUTSIDE UNITED KINGDOM.

2357 PERKINS B.
THE FIRST RAPPROCHEMENTS: ENGLAND AND THE UNITED STATES, 1795-1805.
PHILA: U OF PENN PR, 1955, 257 PP., LC#55-9468.
CRITICAL ANALYSIS OF LIMITATIONS IN CONVENTIONAL VIEW OF RELATIONS BETWEEN ENGLAND AND US FOLLOWING JAY TREATY. PRIMARILY CONCERNED WITH NEGLECTED DEVELOPMENTS IN CHAIN OF EVENTS CULMINATING IN MADISON'S WAR MESSAGE OF 1812. CONTENDS HISTORIANS HAVE IGNORED PROBLEMS OF ENGLISH AS OPPOSED TO AMERICAN OPINION, FORMULATION OF CONSTRUCTIVE BRITISH POLICY, AND UNSATISFACTORY RELATIONS.

2358 PERKINS B.
PROLOGUE TO THE WAR: ENGLAND AND THE UNITED STATES, 1805-1812.
BERKELEY: U OF CALIF PR, 1963, 457 PP., LC#61-14018.
SURVEYS DEVELOPMENT OF BRITISH POLICY AND AMERICAN REACTION LEADING TO WAR OF 1812, EMPHASIZING AMERICAN SEARCH FOR NATIONAL RESPECTABILITY AND INDEPENDENCE FROM EUROPE.

2359 PERKINS D.
THE UNITED STATES AND THE CARIBBEAN.
CAMBRIDGE: HARVARD U PR, 1947, 253 PP.
PRE-CASTRO DISCUSSION OF US POLICY TOWARD CUBA, DOMINICAN REPUBLIC, HAITI, AND CENTRAL AMERICAN COUNTRIES. FAVORS SELF-RESTRAINT OF POWERFUL US, ADVOCATING MODERATE USE OF ITS PHYSICAL POWER AND MAINTENANCE OF LONG-TERM VIEW OF NATIONAL INTERESTS. EVALUATES ECONOMIC, POLITICAL, AND SOCIAL BACKGROUND OF CARIBBEAN NATIONS AT THAT PERIOD. DISCUSSES ASPECTS OF GOOD-NEIGHBOR POLICY.

2360 PERKINS D.
THE UNITED STATES AND LATIN AMERICA.
BATON ROUGE: LOUISIANA ST U PR, 1961, 124 PP., LC#61-7544.
DISCUSSES POLITICAL AND ECONOMIC RELATIONS BETWEEN US AND LATIN AMERICA FROM MONROE DOCTRINE TO PRESENT. EXAMINES HISTORY IN TERMS OF HEMISPHERIC INTEGRITY AND NATIONAL SECURITY.

2361 PERKINS D.
AMERICA'S QUEST FOR PEACE.
BLOOMINGTON: INDIANA U PR, 1962, 122 PP., LC#61-13718.
ANALYSIS OF US ATTITUDE AND PROPOSALS FOR WORLD PEACE. DISCUSSES INTERNATIONAL LAWS AND TREATIES, ORGANIZATION OF NATIONS, AND DISARMAMENT PROPOSALS.

2362 PERKINS D., VAN DEUSEN G.G.
THE AMERICAN DEMOCRACY: ITS RISE TO POWER.
NEW YORK: MACMILLAN, 1964, 687 PP., LC#64-14963.
TRACES HISTORICAL DEVELOPMENT FROM THE NEW WORLD TO A WORLD POWER AND INVOLVEMENT WITH EUROPEAN AND LATIN AMERICAN POLITICS.

2363 PERLO V.
EL IMPERIALISMO NORTHEAMERICANO.
BUENOS AIRES: EDITORIAL PLATINA, 1961, 338 PP.
ANALYSIS OF US ECONOMIC POLICY AND INTERNATIONAL TRADE JUDGED AD ECONOMIC IMPERIALISM. EXTREMELY SOCIALISTIC OUTLOOK OF US INVESTMENT AND EXPORT PROGRAMS AROUND WORLD. DISCUSSES RACIAL DISCRIMINATION AND MILITARY POLICY BESIDES INTERNATIONAL ECONOMIC RELATIONS.

2364 PERLO V.
"NEW DIMENSIONS IN EAST-WEST TRADE."
NEW WORLD REVIEW, 35 (MAY 67), 22-26.
DISCUSSES THE EXPANSION OF LONG-TERM TRADE COMMITMENTS BETWEEN USSR AND US AND WESTERN EUROPE AS A FORCE FOR PEACE. CRITICIZES US FOR THE "CONFIDENCE GAP" HINDERING FURTHER TRADE BY MAINTAINING A COLD WAR ECONOMY FOR SO LONG.

2365 PERRE J.
LES MUTATIONS DE LA GUERRE MODERNE: DE LA REVOLUTION FRANCAISE A LA REVOLUTION NUCLEAIRE.
PARIS: PAYOT, 1962, 419 PP.
HISTORY OF NATIONAL WARS, WORLD WARS, AND POST WAR CONDITIONS FROM 1792 TO 1962. TRACES CAUSES, GOALS, EXTENTS, MURDEROUS EFFECTS, FORMS, AND CONSEQUENCES. AUTHOR OFFERS HISTORICAL PROJECTIONS. BELIEVES ANOTHER WORLD WAR IS NOT INEVITABLE, BUT ROAD TO PEACE IS NARROW, UPHILL, UNEVEN, ARDUOUS, EXHAUSTING.

2366 PESELT B.M.
"COMMUNIST ECONOMIC OFFENSIVE."
LAW CONTEMP. PROBL., 29 (AUTUMN 64), 983-99.
TRACES EVOLUTION OF SOVIET VIEW TOWARDS POLICY AND PROBLEMS OF FOREIGN AID TO UNDERDEVELOPED NATIONS. MOTIVES AND AIMS OF SUCH AID IS ASSESSED AND THE FORMS OF SOVIET BILATERAL AGREEMENTS IS ANALYZED.

2367 PETERSON E.N.
"HISTORICAL SCHOLARSHIP AND WORLD UNITY."
SOC. RES., 20 (WINTER 60), 439-50.
DEPICTS NEW TRAINING PLAN FOR STUDYING WORLD-WIDE HISTORICAL PROBLEMS. SUGGESTS DIRECTIONS IN ORDER TO ACHIEVE DEVELOPMENT GOALS. DEPICTS PAST STEREOTYPED ASPECTS RELATED TO NATIONALIST POLICIES.

2368 PETERSON H.C., FITE G.C.
OPPONENTS OF WAR 1917-1918.
MADISON: U OF WISCONSIN PR, 1957, 399 PP., LC#57-5239.
DISCUSSES PEOPLE AND ORGANIZATIONS THAT OPPOSED WWI. PRESENTS PICTURE OF INTOLERANCE AND HYSTERIA AMONG SUCH MAJOR GROUPS AS ANARCHISTS, SOCIALISTS, AND IWW'S AND SEEKS TO RELATE PRESSURE OF PUBLIC OPINION TO VALUE OF FREEDOM.

2369 PETKOFF D.K.
"RECOGNITION AND NON-RECOGNITION OF STATES AND GOVERNMENTS IN INTERNATIONAL LAW."
ASSEN. CAPT. EUROP. NAT. SECRETARIAT, 5 (MAR. 62), 25-52.
DISCUSSES DECLARATIVE AND CONSTITUTIVE THEORIES ON NATURE OF RECOGNITION UNDER INTERNATIONAL LAW. APPLIES THEORIES TO CURRENT POLITICAL SITUATION. ANALYZES ISSUE OF RECOGNITION IN REGARD TO EAST-WEST RELATIONS. MAKES POLICY RECOMMENDATIONS FOR INTERNATIONAL DIPLOMACY.

2370 PETTEE G.S.
THE PROCESS OF REVOLUTION.
NEW YORK: HARPER, 1938, 167 PP.
BELIEVES SOCIOLOGY OFFERS MOST ILLUMINATING AND COMPREHENSIVE DEFINITION OF REVOLUTION. THEORY IS BASED UPON THREE GREAT REVOLUTIONS: FRENCH, RUSSIAN, AND SPANISH. SURVEYS FASCIST MOVEMENT AND NOTES POSSIBLE DEMOCRATIC ALTERNATIVE.

2371 PEUKERT W.
"WEST GERMANY'S 'RED TRADE'."
GERMAN FOREIGN POLICY, 6 (FEB. 67).
ANALYZES REASONS FOR FAILURE OF WEST GERMAN POLICY OF ECONOMIC SANCTIONS ON SOCIALIST COUNTRIES. AFTER SEVENTEEN

YEARS OF ECONOMIC SANCTIONS IN WHICH TRADE WAS CONTINUOUSLY OBSTRUCTED, THE RESULT WAS ONLY TO HANDICAP WEST GERMAN TRADE. URGES SUPPORT OF RED TRADE BY NONSOCIALIST COUNTRIES. DOCUMENTATION.

2372 PHADINIS U. ED., MOORTHY S.D. ED.
DOCUMENTS ON ASIAN AFFAIRS: A SELECT BIBLIOGRAPHY.
NEW DELHI: INDIAN COUNCIL, 1959, 153 PP.
LIMITED TO DOCUMENTS AVAILABLE IN THE ENGLISH LANGUAGE AND ABOUT ASIAN COUNTRIES. INDICATES WHERE TEXTS OF THE DOCUMENTS CAN BE FOUND. DEALS WITH POLITICAL, ECONOMIC, AND SOCIAL AFFAIRS.

2373 PHELPS J.
"STUDIES IN DETERRENCE VIII: MILITARY STABILITY AND ARMS CONTROL: A CRITICAL SURVEY."
CHINA LAKE: U.S.N.O.T.S., 1963, 22 PP., (NOTS TP 3173).
EXAMINES THE TRENDS TOWARD MILITARY STABILITY IN ORDER TO DRAW FORTH IMPLICATIONS FOR SEABORNE DETERRENCE FORCES AND NAVY PLANNING. ANALYZES THE DEPENDENCE OF STRATEGIC STABILITY ON WEAPONS. PROPOUNDS SOME RESEARCH PROBLEMS ASSOCIATED WITH EXTENDING THE TIME PERIOD FOR A STABLE MILITARY ENVIRONMENT. QUESTIONS THE USEFULNESS OF STABILITY AS AN ANALYTIC TOOL IN CONSIDERING AND EVALUATING MEASURES TO INCREASE MILITARY SECURITY.

2374 PHELPS J.
"INFORMATION AND ARMS CONTROL."
J. ARMS CONTR., 1 (APR. 63), 44-55.
FUNDAMENTAL DIFFICULTY IN NEGOTIATING DISARMAMENT HAS BEEN GREAT DIFFERENCE IN VIEWS ON DISSEMINATION OF ARMS INFORMATION, AND ON INSPECTION.

2375 PHILIPPINE STUDIES PROGRAM
SELECTED BIBLIOGRAPHY ON THE PHILIPPINES, TOPICALLY ARRANGED AND ANNOTATED.
NEW HAVEN: HUMAN REL AREA FILES, 1956, 138 PP.
GENERAL PHILIPPINE BIBLIOGRAPHY WITH ANNOTATED REFERENCES TO IMPORTANT HISTORICAL, ECONOMIC, ANTHROPOLOGICAL, GOVERNMENTAL, AND RELIGIOUS WORKS ON THE PHILIPPINES.

2376 PHILLIPS J.F.V.
KWAME NKRUMAH AND THE FUTURE OF AFRICA.
NEW YORK: FREDERICK PRAEGER, 1960, 270 PP., LC#61-05235.
STUDIES ROLE OF NKRUMAH IN DEVELOPING NATIONS; POLITICAL AND PHILOSOPHICAL IMPACT, ACCOMPLISHMENTS IN GHANA, AND INFLUENCE IN ALL OF AFRICA; PROJECTIONS OF INDEPENDENCE AND ITS EFFECT ON THEM.

2377 PHILLIPSON C.
THE INTERNATIONAL LAW AND CUSTOM OF ANCIENT GREECE AND ROME.
LONDON: MACMILLAN, 1911, 830 PP.
OFFERS A COMPREHENSIVE AND SYSTEMATIC ACCOUNT OF THE SUBJECT. TRIES TO REVEAL THE EXISTENCE OF A SYSTEM OF INTERNATIONAL LAW IN THE ANCIENT WORLD. WORK IS BASED ON GREEK AND ROMAN BASIC SOCIAL INSTITUTIONS.

2378 PIKE F.B.
CHILE AND THE UNITED STATES 1880-1962: THE EMERGENCE OF CHILE'S CRISIS AND THE CHALLENGE TO US DIPLOMACY.
NOTRE DAME: U OF NOTRE DAME, 1963, 466 PP., LC#63-9097.
DISCUSSES US-CHILEAN RELATIONS IN REGARD TO HIATUS BETWEEN RULERS AND RULED IN CHILE, US CONTRIBUTIONS TO CHILE'S PRESENT SOCIAL UNREST, AND CHILEAN DISTRUST OF US.

2379 PIKE F.B. ED.
FREEDOM AND REFORM IN LATIN AMERICA.
SOUTH BEND: U OF NOTRE DAME, 1967, 308 PP., LC#59-10417.
EXAMINES CHANGES SHAPING TRENDS IN LATIN AMERICA: DESIRE FOR INDIVIDUAL FREEDOM, SOCIAL AND ECONOMIC REFORM, AND RISE OF ARTICULATE MIDDLE CLASS. POINTS UP NECESSITY FOR FASTER ECONOMIC PROGRESS WITHIN FRAMEWORK OF TRADITIONAL WESTERN VALUES. DEFENDS FIGHTERS FOR FREEDOM. COVERS POPULATION PROBLEM AND ROLES OF CATHOLIC CHURCH AND US IN LATIN AMERICAN FREEDOMS AND REFORMS.

2380 PINCUS J.
"THE COST OF FOREIGN AID."
REV. ECON. STAT., 23 (NOV. 63), 360-68.
DISCUSSION OF DEFINITIONS OF DONOR NATIONS FOR VALUING ECONOMIC AID AND HOW MORE APPROPRIATE CRITERIA MIGHT BE ESTABLISHED. ON THE BASIS OF THESE CRITERIA, COMPUTES THE REAL COST OF U.S. BILATERAL AID TO UNDERDEVELOPED CONTRIES IN 1961, CONCLUDING THAT REAL COST WAS MUCH LESS THAN OFFICIAL TOTALS IMPLY.

2381 PIPER D.C.
THE INTERNATIONAL LAW OF THE GREAT LAKES.
DURHAM: DUKE U PR, 1967, 165 PP., LC#67-29860.
EXTRACTS FROM CONVENTIONAL RULES AND CUSTOMARY PRACTICES OF INTERNATIONAL LAW GOVERNING CANADIAN-AMERICAN RELATIONS WITH REGARD TO GREAT LAKES. TOPICS ARE INTERNATIONAL BOUNDARY, CRIMINAL AND ADMIRALITY JURISDICTION FOR WHICH LAKES ARE CONSIDERED HIGH SEAS, USE OF WATER RESOURCES, FISHING INDUSTRY, NAVIGATION RIGHTS, NAVAL ARMAMENTS, MUNICIPAL PROBLEMS. APPENDIX OF TREATIES.

2382 PIQUEMAL M.
"LES PROBLEMES DES UNIONS D'ETATS EN AFRIQUE NOIRE."
REV. JURID. POLIT. OUTREMER, 16 (JAN.-MARCH 62), 21-58.
EXPLORES PROBLEMS FACING DEVELOPING AFRICAN COUNTRIES. MAJOR DILEMMA IS WHETHER OR NOT TO ADOPT FEDERALIST SYSTEM. SHOWS SOCIAL STRATIFICATION OF OLD COLONIAL SYSTEMS. PRESENTS POLITICAL IDEOLOGIES OF AFRICAN LEADERS. DISCUSSES POSSIBILITIES FOR ECONOMIC UNION, AND ANALYZES FRANCE'S ROLE IN THIS PROJECT.

2383 PIQUEMAL M.
"LA COOPERATION FINANCIERE ENTRE LA FRANCE ET LES ETATS AFRICAINS ET MALGACHE."
REV. JURID. POLIT. OUTREMER, 16 (OCT.-DEC. 62), 437-54.
DESCRIBES GENERAL POLITICAL CHARACTERISTICS OF FINANCIAL COOPERATION BETWEEN FRANCE AND AFRICAN STATES. FOCUSES ON PROBLEMS OF PUBLIC FINANCE AND BUDGET CONTROL. DISCUSSES METHODS OF MINTING CURRENCY. REVEALS INSTITUTIONAL RULES OF MULTILATERAL AFRICAN COOPERATION.

2384 PIQUET H.S.
THE US BALANCE OF PAYMENTS AND INTERNATIONAL MONETARY RESERVES.
WASHINGTON: AMER ENTERPRISE INST, 1966, 98 PP., LC#66-17531.
ANALYZES US PROBLEM OF INTERNATIONAL PAYMENTS WHICH HAVE BEEN INCURRING DEFICITS SINCE 1950. FEELS THIS IS NO CRISIS, FOR AMOUNT OF DEFICIT IS DECREASING ANNUALLY. EMPHASIZES PROBLEM IN RELATION TO WORLD, AS US IS CENTRAL BANKER FOR WORLD. FEELS CRITICISM OF US FAILURE TO CHECK OUTFLOW OF GOLD IN EXCHANGE FOR DOLLAR IS NOT JUSTIFIED.

2385 PITTMAN J., PITTMAN M.
PEACEFUL COEXISTENCE.
NEW YORK: INTERNATIONAL PUBLRS, 1964, 156 PP., LC#64-8445.
DISCUSSES PEACEFUL COEXISTENCE IN THEORY AND PRACTICE IN SOVIET UNION WITH EMPHASIS ON ITS BEARING ON FOREIGN POLICY, MILITARY DOCTRINE, AND ATTITUDE OF RUSSIAN PEOPLE TOWARD US. CONSIDERS EFFECTS ON SINO-SOVIET RIFT ON COEXISTENCE ASPIRATIONS OF RUSSIA AND US.

2386 PLAMENATZ J.
ON ALIEN RULE AND SELF-GOVERNMENT.
NEW YORK: LONGMANS, 1960, 224 PP.
ATTEMPTS TO ANALYZE AND CLARIFY CONTROVERSY ABOUT SELF-GOVERNMENT AND RELATIONSHIP BETWEEN FORMER IMPERIAL POWERS AND NEW NATIONS. SUGGESTS THAT CONSTITUTIONALISM AND DEMOCRACY, ALTHOUGH WESTERN IN ORIGIN, CAN DEVELOP IN EMERGING NATIONS, BUT WARNS THEM THAT DEVELOPMENT OF CONSTITUTIONAL GOVERNMENT AND DEMOCRACY WILL BE STEMMED UNLESS THE FORMER IS CLOSELY FOLLOWED BY THE LATTER.

2387 PLAYFAIR R.L. ED.
"A BIBLIOGRAPHY OF MOROCCO."
LONDON: JOHN MURRAY, 1893.
ANNOTATED BIBLIOGRAPHY OF WORKS IN VARIOUS LANGUAGES REGARDING MOROCCO FROM EARLIEST TIMES THROUGH THE END OF 1891. INCLUDES ROMAN AND GREEK WRITINGS AND EARLY EXPLORERS' ACCOUNTS OF GEOGRAPHY, THE PEOPLE, AND THEIR CULTURE. LATER WORKS INCLUDE HISTORY OF THE COUNTRY, ECONOMICS, SOCIAL CONDITIONS, RELIGION, LEADERS, MILITARY SUBJECTS, INTERNATIONAL RELATIONS, ETC.

2388 PLAYNE C.E.
THE PRE-WAR MIND IN BRITAIN.
LONDON: ALLEN & UNWIN, 1928, 444 PP.
EXAMINES ATTITUDES, NEUROSES, AND PSYCHOLOGICAL CONDITIONING IMMEDIATE TO WORLD WAR I. INCLUDES COMMERCIALISM, MILITARISM, AND ANGLO-GERMAN CONFLICT OF INTEREST.

2389 PLAZA G.
"FOR A REGIONAL MARKET IN LATIN AMERICA."
FOR. AFF., 34 (JULY 59), 607-16.
EVALUATES NEEDS OF GROWING MIDDLE CLASS AND EXPECTATIONS OF MASSES IN LATIN AMERICAN SOCIAL REVOLUTION NOW BEGINNING. SUGGESTS THAT ONLY ECONOMIC INTEGRATION WILL ALLOW EFFICIENT USE OF ECONOMIC AND POLITICAL RESOURCES.

2390 PLISCHKE E.
AMERICAN FOREIGN RELATIONS: A BIBLIOGRAPHY OF OFFICIAL SOURCES.
COLLEGE PARK: U MD, BUR GOVT RES, 1955, 71 PP.
INCLUSIVE AND ACCESSIBLE LISTING OF OFFICIAL SOURCES IN AMERICAN FOREIGN RELATIONS. INCLUDES ONLY MATERIALS PUBLISHED IN ENGLISH WITH EMPHASIS ON RECENT MATERIALS. GUIDE TO PUBLISHED SOURCE MATERIALS CONTAINS REFERENCES TO VARIOUS SPECIFIC COLLECTIONS, COMPILATIONS, SERIES, AND SPECIAL REPORTS. CONCENTRATES ON OFFICIAL SOURCES; UNOFFICIAL DOCUMENTS OF INTEREST CONTAINED IN APPENDIX.

2391 PLISCHKE E.
SYSTEMS OF INTEGRATING THE INTERNATIONAL COMMUNITY.
PRINCETON: VAN NOSTRAND, 1964, 198 PP.
OVERVIEW OF MAIN CONTEMPORARY TYPES OF INTERSTATE INTEGRATION: CONFEDERATION, SUPRANATIONAL ASSOCIATION, FEDERA-

TION, AND POLITICAL ASSOCIATION FOUND WITHIN COMMUNIST BLOC.

2392 PLISCHKE E.
"INTEGRATING BERLIN AND THE FEDERAL REPUBLIC OF GERMANY."
J. OF POLITICS, 27 (FEB. 65), 35-65.
ANALYZES IN DETAIL WEST BERLIN RELATION WITH WEST GERMANY IN LEGAL, POLITICAL, ADMINISTRATIVE, AND FINANCIAL TERMS. ASSERTS THAT INTEGRATION REQUIRES EFFECTIVE GOVERNMENT AND VIABLE ECONOMY IN ORDER TO THWART EAST GERMAN PRESSURES AND CLAIMS ON IT.

2393 POGANY A.H., POGANY H.L.
POLITICAL SCIENCE AND INTERNATIONAL RELATIONS, BOOKS RECOMMENDED FOR AMERICAN CATHOLIC COLLEGE LIBRARIES.
METUCHEN: SCARECROW PRESS, 1967, 387 PP., LC#67-10196.
UNANNOTATED LISTING OF 5,800 BOOKS PERTINENT TO POLITICAL SCIENCE AND INTERNATIONAL RELATIONS. ORGANIZED AROUND HISTORY OF WORLD POLITICAL THEORY, POLITICAL AND CONSTITUTIONAL HISTORY OF WORLD, GOVERNMENT ADMINISTRATION, POLITICAL ECONOMY, INTERNATIONAL LAW, AND INTERNATIONAL RELATIONS. ENTRIES PRINCIPALLY TAKEN FROM 1955-66 PERIOD. AUTHOR AND SUBJECT INDEX.

2394 POLLACK R.S.
THE INDIVIDUAL'S RIGHTS AND INTERNATIONAL ORGANIZATION.
NORTHAMPTON: SMITH COLLEGE, 1966, 122 PP., LC#65-28710.
DISCUSSES STATUS OF INDIVIDUAL IN PUBLIC INTERNATIONAL LAW. EXAMINES TREATIES, CONVENTIONS, COVENANTS, EUROPEAN CONVENTION ON HUMAN RIGHTS, AND CONCLUDES WITH REFLECTIONS ON WORLD LEGAL ORDER.

2395 POOLE D.C.
THE CONDUCT OF FOREIGN RELATIONS UNDER MODERN DEMOCRATIC CONDITIONS.
NEW HAVEN: YALE U. PR., 1924, 197 PP.
CONSIDERS THE INSTRUMENTS AND PROCESSES OF FOREIGN POLICY AND THE EFFECT OF NATIONAL AND INTERNATIONAL ORGANIZATION ON IT. RELATES THE PROBLEMS OF OPEN DIPLOMACY AND THE METHODS OF INFORMATION DISSEMINATION. CONCLUDES RESPONSIBILITY IN WORLD AFFAIRS WILL GROW AS KNOWLEDGIBLE POPULAR JUDGEMENT IS EXPRESSED.

2396 POOLE W.F., FLETCHER W.I.
INDEX TO PERIODICAL LITERATURE.
BOSTON: JAMES R OSGOOD & CO, 1882, 1442 PP.
UNANNOTATED CROSS-REFERENCED INDEX OF ARTICLES PUBLISHED BEFORE 1881 IN ENGLISH LANGUAGE. ALL SUBJECTS INCLUDED WITH INITIAL SUBJECT INDEX. INCLUSIVE DATES 1800 TO 1881; INCLUDES BRITISH PERIODICALS.

2397 POSTON R.W.
DEMOCRACY SPEAKS MANY TONGUES.
NEW YORK: HARPER & ROW, 1962, 206 PP., LC#62-14591.
COMPARES METHODS OF ADMINISTERING FOREIGN AID IN LATIN AMERICAN COUNTRIES TO PREVENT SPREAD OF COMMUNISM. DISCUSSES PRIVATE VS. PUBLIC AID AND SPECIAL FORM OF AID, COMMUNITY DEVELOPMENT, WORKING WITH EACH COMMUNITY AS SEPARATE PROBLEM, AND ENLISTING AID OF LOCAL ADMINISTRATORS.

2398 POTTER P.B.
AN INTRODUCTION TO THE STUDY OF INTERNATIONAL ORGANIZATION.
NEW YORK: CENTURY, 1922, 647 PP.
SHOWS HOW THE STANDING SYSTEM OF INTERNATIONAL ORGANIZATTION HAS EXPANDED AND DEVELOPED. BY DISCLOSING THE CAUSES, DESCRIBING BASIC INSTITUTIONS AND ANALYZING THE PRINCIPLES UNDERLYING THEM. ATTEMPTS TO MAKE SOME SUGGESTIONS REGARDING STEPS WHICH MIGHT PROFITABLY BE TAKEN IN THE IMPROVEMENT AND DEVELOPMENT OF THE EXISTING INSTITUTIONS OF INTERNATIONAL GOVERNMENT.

2399 POTTER P.B.
"NEUTRALITY, 1955."
AMER. J. OF INT. LAW, 50 (JAN. 56), 101-102.
EDITORIAL COMMENT REVIEWS BRIEFLY EVOLUTION OF CONCEPT OF NEUTRALITY AND TRACES CHANGE IN ATTITUDES. RIGHT OF NATION TO REMAIN NEUTRAL REMAINED UNCHALLENGED UNTIL 20TH CENTURY, WHEN DOUBTS AROSE AS TO ITS JUSTIFIABILITY. LEAGUE OF NATIONS DISCREDITED IT FURTHER; UN OUTLAWED IT. FINDS IT HAS NOW BEEN REPLACED BY NEUTRALISM, I.E., RIGHT TO REFUSE TO TAKE SIDES IN COLD WAR.

2400 POTTER P.B.
"OBSTACLES AND ALTERNATIVES TO INTERNATIONAL LAW."
AMER. J. INT. LAW, 3 (JULY 59), 647-651.
THE PAST 45 YEARS HAS SEEN THE REPLACEMENT OF INTERNATIONAL LAW BY A SYSTEM OF INTERNATIONAL LEGISLATION AND ADMINISTRATION. EFFORTS MUST NOW BE MADE TO INSTITUTE THESE NEW SYSTEMS.

2401 POTTER P.B.
"RELATIVE VALUES OF INTERNATIONAL RELATIONS, LAW, AND ORGANIZATIONS."
AMER. J. INT. LAW, 54 (APR. 60), 379-82.
VIEWS PHENOMENA OF RISE IN NUMBER OF INDEPENDENT STATES AND ESTABLISHMENT OF INTERNATIONAL ORGANIZATIONS. STATES THAT EFFORTS SHOULD BE MADE TO ALTER THE CURRENT USAGE OF DIPLOMACY IN FAVOR OF INTERNATIONAL LEGISLATIVE SYSTEM.

2402 POUNDS N.J.G. ET AL.
"THE POLITICS OF PARTITION."
J. INT. AFF., 18 (NO.2, 64), 161-252.
WHOLE ISSUE DEVOTED TO A THEORETICAL AND COMPARATIVE ANALYSIS OF THE SOCIO-POLITICAL CONCEPT OF PARTITION. PARTITION IS SEEN AS PROVIDING A KEY TO CURRENT CRISES AS WELL AS TO AREAS OF POTENTIAL STRIFE. DEALS WITH THE CAMEROONS, INDIA, JERUSALEM, KOREA, VIETNAM, PAKISTAN AND UNION OF SOUTH AFRICA.

2403 COLUMBIA BUR. OF APPLIED SOC. R.
ATTITUDES OF PROMINENT AMERICANS TOWARD "WORLD PEACE THROUGH WORLD LAW" (SUPRA-NATL ORGANIZATION FOR WAR PREVENTION)
NEW YORK: COLUMBIA U APP SOC RES, 1959.
ANALYZES OPINION OF PERSONS LISTED IN "WHO'S WHO IN AMERICA" CONCERNING TWO PLANS FOR AN INTERNATIONAL AGENCY TO SETTLE NATIONAL DISPUTES IN WORLD LAW COURTS. OPINION ANALYSIS IS BASED ON ATTITUDINAL CHARACTERISTICS AND SOCIAL VARIABLES; EXTENSIVE USE OF TABLES AND STATISTICS.

2404 PRABHAKAR P.
"SURVEY OF RESEARCH AND SOURCE MATERIALS; THE SINO-INDIAN BORDER DISPUTE."
INT. STUDIES, 7 (JULY 65), 120-127.
ENTRIES DEAL WITH LEGAL CLAIMS OF THE DISPUTE, CHINESE GOALS IN THE AREA, AND THE IMPACT OF THE DISPUTE ON WORLD POLITICS. TREATS FOREIGN POLICY OF INDIA.

2405 PRAKASH B.
INDIA AND THE WORLD.
HOSHIARPUR: DEVA DALTA SHASTRI, 1964, 292 PP.
DISCUSSES MAIN TRENDS OF INDIA'S POLICIES, CONTACTS, AND RELATIONSHIPS WITH THE WORLD. MAINTAINS THAT INDIA'S TRADITION OF FRIENDSHIP, GOOD WILL, AND COOPERATION TOWARD OTHER COUNTRIES MAY ENABLE US TO LOOK AT WORLD PROBLEMS "FROM NEW ANGLES OF VISION."

2406 PRASAD B.
"SURVEY OF RECENT RESEARCH: STUDIES ON INDIA'S FOREIGN POLIC AND RELATIONS."
INT. STUDIES, 5 (APR. 64), 35-449.
SURVEY OF THE MAIN BOOKS ON SUBJECT OF INDIA'S FOREIGN POLICY AND RELATIONS WHICH HAVE APPEARED IN YEARS SINCE INDEPENDENCE. DEALS WITH SUCH TOPICS AS ORIGINS AND HISTORICAL BACKGROUND, ROLE IN THE UNITED NATIONS, INDIA AND PAKISTAN, INDIA AND THE COMMONWEALTH, ETC.

2407 PRATT I.A.
MODERN EGYPT: A LIST OF REFERENCES TO MATERIAL IN THE NEW YORK PUBLIC LIBRARY.
NEW YORK: NY PUBLIC LIBRARY, 1929, 320 PP.
EXTENSIVE LIST OF WORKS DEALING WITH ASPECTS OF MODERN EGYPT. INCLUDES SECTIONS ON ANTHROPOLOGY AND ETHNOLOGY, GEOGRAPHY, HISTORY, GOVERNMENT, LAW, FOREIGN RELATIONS, ECONOMIC HISTORY, ETC. MATERIAL IS ARRANGED TOPICALLY BUT INCLUDES AUTHOR INDEX.

2408 PRATT R.C.
"AFRICAN REACTIONS TO THE RHODESIAN CRISIS."
INT. J., 21 (SPRING 66), 186-198.
RESPONSE OF SUB-SAHARA AFRICA TO UNILATERAL DECLARATION OF INDEPENDENCE, TRACING EUROPEAN MINORITY'S MOVE TO RIGHT, AFRICAN RELATIONS WITH BRITAIN, AND A REVIEW OF FUTURE ALTERNATIVES.

2409 PRESTON W. JR.
ALIENS AND DISSENTERS: FEDERAL SUPPRESSION OF RADICALS 1903-1933.
CAMBRIDGE: HARVARD U PR, 1963, 352 PP., LC#63-10873.
STUDY OF PERIOD IN AMERICAN HISTORY WHEN MEN PREFERRED TO BLAME HERETICS AND ALIENS FOR DIFFICULTIES CONFRONTING SOCIETY. TRACES ORIGINS AND EXAMINES CONSEQUENCES OF RESTRAINTS ON LIBERTY THAT RESULTED FROM PRECEDENTS ESTABLISHED IN TREATMENT OF HELPLESS ALIENS IN 1890'S. SHOWS HOW OUR SOCIETY TODAY REFLECTS BOTH THIS INTOLERANCE AND BRAVE RESISTANCE TO DOMINANT TREND MAINTAINED BY MANY AMERICANS.

2410 PRICE D.K.
THE SECRETARY OF STATE.
ENGLEWOOD CLIFFS: PRENTICE HALL, 1960, 200 PP.
ESSAYS CONCERNED WITH DIFFERENT FUNCTIONS OF SECRETARY OF STATE: POLICY FORMULATION, POLICY EXECUTION, MANAGEMENT OF STATE DEPARTMENT, LINK OF PRESIDENT AND CONGRESS.

2411 PRICE D.K.
THE NEW DIMENSIONS OF DIPLOMACY: THE ORGANIZATION OF THE US GOVERNMENT FOR ITS NEW ROLE IN WORLD AFFAIRS (PAMPHLET)
NEW YORK: WOODROW WILSON FDN, 1951, 29 PP.
TO PLAY STEADY AND CONSISTENT ROLE IN WORLD AFFAIRS, US MUST NOT MERELY SEEK ADEQUATE GOVERNMENTAL INSTRUMENTS, BUT MUST ALSO WORK FOR CONTINUOUS IMPROVEMENT OF COORDINATION OF NATIONAL POLICIES THAT ARE PURSUED IN AN INTERDEPENDENT WORLD FRAMEWORK. OTHERWISE INTERNAL CONFLICT MAY PARALYZE

NATIONAL PURPOSE, AUTHOR WARNS.

2412 PRINCETON UNIV. CONFERENCE
CURRENT PROBLEMS IN NORTH AFRICA.
PRINCETON: PRINCETON U PRESS, 1960, 76 PP.
DEALS WITH CONTEMPORARY NORTH AFRICA IN EFFORT TO HELP ELIMINATE AMERICANS' GENERAL IGNORANCE OF AREA. INCLUDES TRANSITIONAL POLITICS IN MOROCCO AND TUNISIA, AMERICAN POLICY IN ALGERIA, AND IMPLICATIONS OF NORTH AFRICAN OIL.

2413 PRINCETON UNIV. CONFERENCE
"ARAB DEVELOPMENT IN THE EMERGING INTERNATIONAL ECONOMY."
PRINCETON: HASKINS, 1963, 57 PP.
PAPERS ON THE DEVELOPMENT OF REGIONAL AND INTERNATIONAL TRADE AND PROMOTION OF ARAB ECONOMIC COOPERATION. ALSO EXAMINES U. S. AID POLICY AND HOW IT IS LIKELY TO AFFECT ECONOMIC DEVELOPMENTS IN THE ARAB STATES.

2414 PRITTIE T.
GERMANY DIVIDED: THE LEGACY OF THE NAZI ERA.
BOSTON: LITTLE BROWN, 1960, 381 PP., LC#60-11642.
SUGGESTS THAT THE GERMAN CHARACTER HAS CHANGED NOW THAT GERMANS ARE BEING GIVEN A CHANCE TO DISCOVER THEIR OWN SOUL; IT SHOULD BE THE JOB OF OTHER FREE NATIONS TO HELP THEM IN THE STRESSES AND STRAINS THAT WILL TEST THEM STERNLY. PRIMARY CONCERN MUST BE TO REUNITE TWO GERMANIES.

2415 OAU PROVISIONS SECTION
ORGANIZATION OF AFRICAN UNITY: BASIC DOCUMENTS AND RESOLUTIONS (PAMPHLET)
ADDIS ABABA: ORG OF AFRICAN UNITY, 1964, 79 PP.
CHARTER AND RESOLUTIONS CONCERNING PURPOSE, MEMBERSHIP, STRUCTURE, AND PROCEDURES OF THIS ORGANIZATION FOR PROMOTING EMERGING STATES OF AFRICA. RESOLUTIONS INCLUDE NUCLEAR TESTING, EDUCATION, ECONOMIC MEASURES, AND RELATIONSHIP TO UN AND OTHER NATIONS.

2416 PUFENDORF S.
LAW OF NATURE AND OF NATIONS (ABRIDGED)
ORIGINAL PUBLISHER NOT AVAILABLE, 1716, 339 PP.
"MORAL ENTITIES" WERE DESIGNED BY GOD FOR THE REGULATION OF HUMAN LIFE. THEY EXIST IN THE STATE, WHICH IS THAT CONDITION IN WHICH MEN ARE SETTLED FOR EXERCISE OF ACTIONS. POWER IS "THAT BY WHICH A MAN IS QUALIFIED TO DO A THING LAWFULLY AND WITH A MORAL EFFECT." DISCUSSES MORAL KNOWLEDGE AND ACTION, STATE OF NATURE, LAW OF NATURE, DUTY OF MAN TOWARD HIMSELF AND GOD, SELF-DEFENSE, TREATIES, AND SO ON.

2417 PUGWASH CONFERENCE
"ON BIOLOGICAL AND CHEMICAL WARFARE."
BULL. ATOM. SCI., 15 (OCT. 59), 337-39.
ASSESSMENT OF POTENTIALITIES OF CHEMICAL AND BIOLOGICAL AGENTS AS WEAPONS AND EXPLORATION OF MEANS TO PREVENT PRODUCTION FOR USE IN WAR. EVALUATES POSSIBILITY OF INTERNATIONAL CONTROL BUT ENCOUNTERS DIFFICULTIES IN EXERCISING CONTROLS. FEELS PROPER INSPECTION BY UN SCIENTIFIC COMMISSION TO DISPEL INTERNATIONAL SUSPICION AND TENSION.

2418 PUTTKAMMER E.W.
WAR AND THE LAW.
CHICAGO: U. CHI. PR., 1944, 205.
ANALYZES WARTIME CIVIL LIBERTIES, THE RELATION BETWEEN THE ARMED FORCES AND THE CIVILIAN POPULATION, THE EFFECT ON LABOR, THE WORKING OF INTERNATIONAL CARTELS AND THE ECONOMICS OF WARTIME PRICE CONTROL. CONCLUDES WITH STUDY OF MILITARY JUSTICE.

2419 PYE L.W.
"SOVIET AND AMERICAN STYLES IN FOREIGN AID."
ORBIS, 4 (JULY 60), 159-73.
SOVIETS CONSIDER ECONOMIC AID TO BE MORE BLUNT AND LIMITED INSTRUMENT OF FOREIGN POLICY THAN WE DO. SOVIETS THROUGH LOGIC OF POLITICS ARE ABLE TO RECONCILE GOALS AMD TECHNIQUES, WHILE USA, IN DENYING USE OF POLITICS, IS WITHOUT AN EXPLICIT METHOD FOR DEALING WITH RELATIONSHIP BETWEEN GOALS AND TECHNIQUES OF FOREIGN AID. PRESENTS EIGHT MOST IMPORTANT DIFFERENCES OF VIEW ABOUT FOREIGN AID BETWEEN USA AND USSR.

2420 PYE L.W.
"THE POLITICAL IMPULSES AND FANTASIES BEHIND FOREIGN AID."
PROC. ACAD. POLIT. SCI., 27 (JAN. 62), 92-111.
ILLUSIONS THAT USA AID IS NON-POLITICAL, THAT UNDERDEVELOPED COUNTRIES ARE ALL MORAL AND THE BELIEFS IN CULTURAL RELATIVISM AND MISSIONARY ZEAL HAVE ADVERSE EFFECTS ON FOREIGN-AID PROGRAMS. FOREGOING FACTORS LEAD TO AMBIVALENCE. RELATION BETWEEN AID AND EVOLUTION OF WORLD ORDER IS PRESENTED AND SUGGESTIONS MADE TO FACILITATE CHANGE FROM A COLONIAL INTERNATIONAL SYSTEM TO A NEW WORLD ORDER.

2421 PYRAH G.B.
IMPERIAL POLICY AND SOUTH AFRICA 1902-1910.
LONDON: OXFORD U PR, 1955, 272 PP.
DISCUSSES BRITISH IMPERIAL POLICY IN SOUTH AFRICA AFTER BOER WAR AND GRANTING RESPONSIBLE GOVERNMENT TO EX-BOER REPUBLICS AS LINK BETWEEN GLADSTONIAN IMPERIAL POLICY AND EMERGENCE OF COMMONWEALTH IDEA IN 1917.

2422 QUADE Q.L.
"THE TRUMAN ADMINISTRATION AND THE SEPARATION OF POWERS: THE CASE OF THE MARSHALL PLAN."
REV. POLIT., 27 (JAN. 65), 58-77.
GIVES INSIGHT INTO THE POLICY-MAKING PROCEDURES LEADING TO THE FORMATION OF AMERICAN FOREIGN POLICY - USES MARSHALL PLAN AS CASE STUDY BECAUSE OF ITS SIGNIFICANCE TO POST-WAR ECONOMIC AND POLITICAL DEVELOPMENT AND THE CHANGE IN US FOREIGN POLICY. GIVES INSIGHT INTO DESIGN AND STRUCTURE OF MARSHALL PLAN AND ITS INCEPTION.

2423 QUAISON-SACKEY A.
AFRICA UNBOUND: REFLECTIONS OF AN AFRICAN STATESMAN.
NEW YORK: PRAEGER, 1963, 174 PP., $4.95.
GHANA'S REPRESENTATIVE TO THE U.N. DISCUSSES THE AFRICAN INDEPENDENCE MOVEMENT, THE AFRICAN PERSONALITY, UNITY, NEUTRALISM AND NON-ALIGNMENT, AND AFRICA AND THE U.N. MAIN OBJECTIVE IS TO CORRECT THE IMAGE OF AFRICA AS A DARK CONTINENT INHABITED SOLELY BY SAVAGES.

2424 QUAN K.L. ED.
INTRODUCTION TO ASIA: A SELECTIVE GUIDE TO BACKGROUND READING.
WASHINGTON: LIBRARY OF CONGRESS, 1955, 214 PP., LC#54-60018.
BIBLIOGRAPHY "INTENDED TO HELP THE PUBLIC UNDERSTAND THE PROBLEMS AND ASPIRATIONS OF ASIA, THEIR CAUSES, THEIR HISTORICAL GROWTH, THEIR CULTURAL BACKGROUND, AND THEIR RELATIONS TO THE WEST." STANDARD AND AUTHORITATIVE WORKS ON ALL COUNTRIES IN ASIA ARE INCLUDED. LIMITED MOSTLY TO ENGLISH-LANGUAGE SOURCES; ANNOTATED.

2425 QUBAIN F.I.
INSIDE THE ARAB MIND: A BIBLIOGRAPHIC SURVEY OF LITERATURE IN ARABIC ON ARAB NATIONALISM AND UNITY.
ARLINGTON: MIDDLE EAST RES ASSN, 1960, 100 PP.
BIBLIOGRAPHY OF 96 ARABIC TITLES, ALL BOOKS AND PAMPHLETS, AND A SUPPLEMENTARY LISTING OF 145 ENGLISH TITLES MOST OF WHICH ARE ARTICLES. ENGLISH SECTION CONTAINS SECTION ON ARAB NATIONALISM AND NASSERISM NOT FOUND IN ARABIC PART. ARAB TITLES ARE EXTENSIVELY ANNOTATED. INCLUDES AUTHOR AND SUBJECT INDEXES.

2426 QUIGG P.W. ED.
AFRICA: A FOREIGN AFFAIRS READER.
NEW YORK: FREDERICK PRAEGER, 1964, 346 PP., LC#64-12589.
PROBLEMS OF EMERGING AFRICA, PAST AND PRESENT, EFFECTS OF COLONIALISM, EMERGING NATIONALISM, AND VIEWS OF NEW AFRICAN LEADERS ARE COVERED.

2427 QUIGLEY H.S.
"TOWARD REAPPRAISAL OF OUR CHINA POLICY."
VIRGINIA QUART. REV., 37 (SUMMER 59), 466-80.
BUILDS A STRONG CASE IN FAVOR OF ADMISSION OF RED CHINA TO UN BASED ON LOGIC AND REALITY. RECOMMENDS REAPPRAISAL OF CHINA POLICY SINCE NONRECOGNITION HAS MADE LITTLE IMPACT ON COMMUNIST POLICY. SUPPORTS CHANGE OF ATTITUDE TOWARD CHINA WITH REGARD TO INCREASED CULTURAL AND COMMERCIAL INTERCOURSE WITH PEKING THUS LESSENING CHANCES OF WAR. PASSES QUESTION OF STATUS OF TAIWAN TO INTERNATIONAL COURT OF JUSTICE.

2428 QUIRK R.E.
AN AFFAIR OF HONOR: WOODROW WILSON AND THE OCCUPATION OF VERACRUZ.
LEXINGTON: U OF KY PR, 1962, 184 PP., LC#62-13972.
TRACES THE VERACRUZ OCCUPATION IN 1914 FROM THE TAMPICO INCIDENT ON APRIL 9, 1914, TO THE END OF OCCUPATION SEVEN MONTHS LATER. CLAIMS THAT WILSON'S MOTIVE WAS TO TEACH THE MEXICANS AND ALL OF LATIN AMERICA A LESSON. BUT MORE SPECIFICALLY, HE SOUGHT TO TOPPLE THE REGIME OF PRESIDENT HUERTA. FINDS THIS ATTITUDE OF TRYING TO IMPOSE US WILL ON OTHER NATIONS THE CAUSE OF ITS TROUBLES WITH THEM.

2429 QURESHI I.H.
THE STRUGGLE FOR PAKISTAN.
KARACHI: U OF KARACHI PRESS, 1965, 394 PP.
SURVEYS HISTORY OF MUSLIM-HINDU RELATIONS FROM 1857 TO SEPARATION AFTER WWII AND ESTABLISHMENT OF SEPARATE MUSLIM STATE.

2430 RABIER J.-.R.
"THE EUROPEAN IDEA AND NATIONAL PUBLIC OPINIONS."
LEX ET SCIENTIA, 12 (APR.-JULY 67), 443-454.
ANALYSIS OF PUBLIC OPINION'S REACTION TO CONCEPTION OF FEDERAL EUROPE. FIND THAT POLLS PRESENT CONTRADICTIONS. MORE SPECIAL QUESTIONS ON UNION RECEIVED NEGATIVE REACTION AND THOSE IN FAVOR BASE OPINIONS ON NEBULOUS KNOWLEDGE. MOTIVATIONS FOR ATTITUDE IN FAVOR ARE VAGUE AND SUPERFICIAL. URGES ESTABLISHMENT OF WORKING MODEL OF PROCESS OF INTEGRATION.

2431 RADVANYI L.
"PROBLEMS OF INTERNATIONAL OPINION SURVEYS."
INT. J. OPIN. ATTIT. RES., 1 (JUNE 47), 30-51.
ASSERTS INTERNATIONAL PUBLIC OPINION POOLS COULD

PLAY A VITAL ROLE IN INTERNATIONAL AFFAIRS. SOCIAL SCIENCES SHOULD STUDY PROBLEMS OF PHRASEOLOGY, POPULAR ATTITUDES TOWARD POLLS, METHODS OF SAMPLING, AND THE NATURE OF INTERVIEWERS TO MAKE THE RESULTS OF SUCH SURVEYS MORE VALID.

2432 RAGATZ L.J.
LITERATURE OF EUROPEAN IMPERIALISM.
WASHINGTON: P PEARLMAN, 1944, 153 PP.
BIBLIOGRAPHY OF SELECTED WORKS IN VARIOUS LANGUAGES DEALING WITH EUROPEAN IMPERIALISM SINCE 1815. OFFERS SOURCES FOR STUDY OF BACKGROUND CAUSES AND PRESENT RESULTS. TWO PARTS: OUTLYING POSSESSIONS AND INTERNATIONAL RIVALRIES. NO INDEXES.

2433 RAGHAVAN M.D.
INDIA IN CEYLONESE HISTORY, SOCIETY AND CULTURE.
BOMBAY: ASIA PUBL HOUSE, 1964, 190 PP.
ANALYSIS OF SOCIAL AND CULTURAL RELATIONS BETWEEN INDIA AND CEYLON. DISCUSSES STRUCTURE OF CEYLONESE SOCIETY AND INFLUENCE OF INDIA ON RELIGION, LANGUAGE, ART, LAW, AND CUSTOMS.

2434 RAJAN M.S.
"UNITED NATIONS AND DOMESTIC JURISDICTION."
LONDON: LONGMANS, GREEN & CO, 1958.
ABOUT 350 REFERENCES TO 20TH CENTURY MATERIAL CONCERNING LEGAL ASPECTS OF INTERNATIONAL RELATIONS ALMOST EXCLUSIVELY IN ENGLISH. INCLUDES DOCUMENTS OF THE UN AND ITS VARIOUS AGENCIES. MAJORITY OF WORKS ARE POST-WWII.

2435 RALEIGH J.S.
"THE MIDDLE EAST IN 1960: A POLITICAL SURVEY."
MID. EAST. AFF., 12 (FEB. 61), 34-55.
STUDIES VARIOUS FACTORS INFLUENCING POLITICAL BASIS OF PRIVATE, GOVERNMENTAL AND INTERNATIONAL ORGANIZATIONS. EXAMINES STRUCTURE AND FUNCTION OF ARAB LEAGUE AND INDICATES SOME FUTURE TRENDS.

2436 RALSTON D.B.
THE ARMY OF THE REPUBLIC; THE PLACE OF THE MILITARY IN THE POLITICAL EVOLUTION OF FRANCE 1871-1914.
CAMBRIDGE: M I T PRESS, 1967, 395 PP., LC#67-16494.
EXAMINES ROLE OF ARMY IN FRENCH THIRD REPUBLIC AFTER FRANCO-PRUSSIAN WAR. DISCUSSES INCOMPATIBILITY OF HIGH COMMAND WITH CIVIL GOVERNMENT AND NECESSITY FOR LARGE STANDING ARMY TO ENSURE NATIONAL SECURITY. ANALYZES MILITARY LEGISLATION AND COMMENTS ON MILITARY INFLUENCE IN FORMATION OF PUBLIC POLICY. NOTES DREYFUS AFFAIR, 1897-1900, AND VARIOUS SPECIFIC PROBLEMS OF MILITARY ADMINISTRATION.

2437 RAMAZANI R.K.
THE MIDDLE EAST AND THE EUROPEAN COMMON MARKET.
CHARLOTTESVILLE: U. VA. PR., 1964, 152 PP., $3.75.
STUDIES ADVERSE EFFECT OF EEC ON MAJOR MIDDLE EASTERN EXPORTS: PETROLEUM, GRAINS, FRUIT, ETC. ALSO EXPLORES POSITIVE AND NEGATIVE REACTIONS TOWARD EEC: ATTEMPTS AT COOPERATION BY NON-ARAB COUNTRIES, OPPOSITION BY ARAB COUNTRIES.

2438 RAMERIE L.
"TENSION AU SEIN DU COMECON: LE CAS ROUMAIN."
POLIT. ENTRANG., 28 (NO. 3, 63), 249-57.
NOTES TENSION WITHIN COMECON. SINCE COMECON FAVORS RUSSIAN ECONOMY, SOME COUNTRIES IN COMMUNIST BLOC MUST TURN TO WESTERN GOVERNMENTS TO ACHIEVE ECONOMIC GOALS. RUSSIAN SUPPLIES ARE OF UNSATISFACTORY QUANTITY AND QUALITY.

2439 RAMSEY J.A.
"THE STATUS OF INTERNATIONAL COPYRIGHTS."
LEX ET SCIENTIA, 4 (JAN.-MAR. 67), 1-9.
DISCUSSION OF INTERNATIONAL COPYRIGHT AGREEMENTS FROM BERNE UNION TO UNIVERSAL COPYRIGHT CONVENTION, THE SUPPLEMENTARY NETWORK OF BILATERAL ARRANGEMENTS BETWEEN VARIOUS STATES, AND INTERNATIONAL AGREEMENTS ON NEW MEDIA. TREATS RELATIONS OF COMMUNIST COUNTRIES TO TRADITIONAL TREATIES AND NON-COMMUNIST COUNTRIES RE COMMUNICATIONS COPYRIGHTS.

2440 RAND SCHOOL OF SOCIAL SCIENCE
INDEX TO LABOR ARTICLES.
LONDON: MEYER LONDON MEM LIB.
MONTHLY UNANNOTATED GUIDE TO ARTICLES CURRENTLY APPEARING IN SELECTED PERIODICALS. COVERS BUSINESS AND LABOR CONDITIONS, TRADE UNIONISM, LABOR LEGISLATION, DISPUTES AND ARBITRATION, AND INTERNATIONAL ORGANIZATIONS. FIRST ISSUED IN 1926.

2441 RANIS G. ED.
THE UNITED STATES AND THE DEVELOPING ECONOMIES.
NEW YORK: W W NORTON, 1964, 174 PP., LC#63-21712.
DISCUSSES VALUE AND ROLE OF US FOREIGN AID IN CONTRIBUTING TO ECONOMIC ADVANCE OF BACKWARD NATIONS, IMPORTANCE TO TRADE DEVELOPMENT, AND USE AS TOOL TO PREVENT COMMUNIST DOMINATION. ANALYZES INSTRUMENTS OF FOREIGN AID AND EFFECT ON INTERNAL ECONOMY OF DONOR NATION.

2442 RANSHOFFEN-WERTHEIMER EF
THE INTERNATIONAL SECRETARIAT: A GREAT EXPERIMENT IN INTERNATIONAL ADMINISTRATION.
WASHINGTON: CARNEGIE ENDOWMENT, 1945, 500 PP.
ANALYZES EXPERIENCE OF LEAGUE OF NATIONS' SECRETARIAT IN INTERNATIONAL ADMINISTRATION. DISCUSSES HISTORY OF SECRETARIAT: STRUCTURAL DEVELOPMENT, LEADERSHIP, AND PERSONNEL PROBLEMS.

2443 RANSOM H.H. ED.
AN AMERICAN FOREIGN POLICY READER.
NEW YORK: THOMAS Y CROWELL, 1965, 690 PP., LC#65-16871.
ASSEMBLES VARIED MATERIAL THAT ILLUSTRATES THE ISSUES AND CHOICES FACED BY AMERICAN FOREIGN POLICY MAKERS PRINCIPALLY SINCE WWII. ASSUMES THAT IMPLICIT AND EXPLICIT POWER OF US FOREIGN POLICY CAN BE ANALYZED IN TERMS OF ITS INSTRUMENTAL MEANS, APPLIED AT VARIOUS DEGREES IN CONCRETE SITUATIONS. THESE INSTRUMENTS ARE MILITARY, ECONOMIC, PROPAGANDISTIC, AND DIPLOMATIC; ESSAYS CENTER ON THEM.

2444 RAO V.K.R.
INTERNATIONAL AID FOR ECONOMIC DEVELOPMENT - POSSIBILITIES AND LIMITATIONS.
CAMBRIDGE: LEEDS U PRESS, 1960, 29 PP.
DETAILED CRITICAL ANALYSIS OF INTERNATIONAL ECONOMIC AID PROGRAMS EMPHASIZING OBLIGATIONS AND VITAL IMPORTANCE OF INCREASED AID FROM DEVELOPED NATIONS. STRESSES LIMITATIONS IMPOSED ON VOLUME AND EFFECTIVENESS OF ECONOMIC AID BY NUMEROUS POLITICAL AND SOCIAL AS WELL AS ECONOMIC FACTORS IN DEVELOPED AND UNDERDEVELOPED COUNTRIES. EXAMINES ACTIVITIES OF UN AGENCIES AND OTHER INTERNATIONAL ECONOMIC BODIES.

2445 RAO V.K.R., NARAIN D.
FOREIGN AID AND INDIA'S ECONOMIC DEVELOPMENT.
NEW YORK: ASIA PUBL HOUSE, 1963, 111 PP.
DEALS WITH CHARACTER, MAGNITUDE, AND ORGANIZATION OF FOREIGN AID, CONDITIONS ON WHICH INDIA HAS RECEIVED IT, IMPACT IT HAS MADE ON ECONOMY, AND PROBLEMS THAT HAVE ARISEN. ALSO TOUCHES UPON WHAT INFLUENCE AID HAS HAD ON RELATIONS BETWEEN INDIA AND AID-GIVING COUNTRIES. MAKES SUGGESTIONS REGARDING GIVING AND RECEIVING OF FOREIGN AID IN FUTURE IN THE LIGHT OF INDIA'S EXPERIENCE.

2446 RAPPAPORT A.
THE BRITISH PRESS AND WILSONIAN NEUTRALITY.
STANFORD: STANFORD U PRESS, 1951, 162 PP.
EXAMINATION OF 37 MAJOR NEWSPAPERS AND PERIODICALS OF ENGLAND AND SCOTLAND FROM 1914-1917. PRESENTS SYSTEMATIC RECORD OF BRITISH VIEWS TOWARD US NEUTRALITY POLICIES. INCLUDES PAPERS REPRESENTING ALL GEOGRAPHICAL AREAS AND POLITICAL GROUPS. REVEALS GREAT HOSTILITY TO US POLICY CONTRIBUTING TO STRAINED ANGLO-AMERICAN RELATIONS OF PERIOD.

2447 RAPPAPORT A. ED.
ISSUES IN AMERICAN DIPLOMACY: WORLD POWER AND LEADERSHIP SINCE 1895 (VOL. II)
NEW YORK: MACMILLAN, 1965, 412 PP.
OPPOSING ARGUMENTS ON MAJOR POLITICAL DECISIONS. EMPHASIS ON WILSON, ROOSEVELT, AND UNITED STATES' INFLUENCE ON LATIN AMERICAN AND EUROPEAN AFFAIRS.

2448 RAPPAPORT P. ED.
SOCIAL SCIENCE SERIALS IN SPECIAL LIBRARIES IN THE NEW YORK AREA; A SELECTED LIST.
NEW YORK: SPECIAL LIBRARIES ASSN, 1961, 82 PP.
BIBLIOGRAPHIC CHECKLIST TO HOLDINGS IN NEW YORK'S SPECIALIZED LIBRARIES. FORMAT OF ENTRIES CLOSELY FOLLOWS STYLE OF THE "UNION LIST OF PERIODICALS." ALL PERIODICALS LISTED UNDER THEIR LATEST TITLES WITH APPROPRIATE CROSS REFERENCES FROM OLDER TITLES. SELECTED FROM THE LISTINGS IN TECHNOLOGY, BUSINESS, EDUCATION, INDUSTRIAL ARTS, INTERNATIONAL, PUBLIC AFFAIRS, AND PSYCHOLOGY PERIODICAL INDEXES.

2449 RAPPARD W.E.
THE CRISIS OF DEMOCRACY.
CHICAGO: U. CHI. PR., 1938, 287 PP.
FOCUSES ON CHANGES WHICH HAVE COME OVER MEN'S MINDS IN ALL COUNTRIES SINCE THE WORLD WAR WITH RESPECT TO THE INSTITUTIONS AND IDEALS OF POPULAR GOVERNMENTS.

2450 RAPPARD W.E.
THE QUEST FOR PEACE.
CAMBRIDGE: HARVARD U. PR., 1940, 510 PP.
DESCRIBES GROWTH AND DESTINY OF THE IDEA THAT LASTING PEACE SHOULD RESULT FROM THE WORLD WAR. EXAMINES GENERAL POST-WAR SITUATION IN EUROPE, THE PROBLEM OF COLLECTIVE SECURITY, AND THE STRUGGLE FOR DISARMAMENT.

2451 RAVENS J.P.
STAAT UND KATHOLISCHE KIRCHE IN PREUSSENS POLNISCHEN TEILUNGSGEBIETEN.
WIESBADEN: OTTO HARRASSOWITZ, 1963, 181 PP.
EXAMINES DISPUTES BETWEEN PRUSSIA AND CATHOLIC CHURCH IN AREAS FORMERLY BELONGING TO POLAND BUT JOINED WITH PRUSSIA IN POLISH DIVISIONS OF 1772, 1793, AND 1795. DISCUSSES IN DETAIL POLITICAL, LEGAL, AND SOCIAL ACTIVITIES OF CATHOLIC CHURCH.

2452 RAY H.
"THE POLICY OF RUSSIA TOWARDS SINO-INDIAN CONFLICT."
POLIT. QUART., 36 (JAN. 65), 92-104.
CHRONOLOGY OF THE FLUCTUATING SOVIET ATTITUDE TOWARDS THE SINO-INDIAN CONFLICT RANGING FROM NEUTRALISM TO SUPPORT OF CHINA, BACK TO NEUTRALISM, AND THEN TO SUPPORT OF INDIA. PRESENTED AGAINST THE BACKGROUND OF THE WIDENING SINO-SOVIET SPLIT. IT IS CONCLUDED THAT THE MAJOR PREOCCUPATION OF THE SOVIETS WAS THE MAINTENANCE OF THE NON-ALIGNMENT POLICY OF INDIA.

2453 RAY J.
"THE EUROPEAN FREE-TRADE ASSOCIATION AND ITS IMPACT ON INDIA'S TRADE."
INT. STUDIES, 3 (JULY 61), 25-44.
TRACES EVENTS LEADING UP TO THE FORMATION OF THE EUROPEAN FREE TRADE AREA. HISTORY OF INDIA'S TRADE WITH COUNTRIES OF THE PACT IS ANALYZED WITH STRESS ON HER EXPORTS TO ENGLAND. SURVEYS EFFECTS ON INDIA'S FUTURE TRADE WITH THESE NATIONS FROM POINT OF VIEW OF TARIFF, INCREASED PRODUCTIVITY AND INCOME OF THE MEMBER NATIONS.

2454 RAZAFIMBAHINY J.
"L'ORGANISATION AFRICAINE ET MALGACHE DE COOPERATION ECONOMIQUE."
REV. JURID. POLIT., 17 (APR.-JUNE 1962), 177-201.
STUDIES STRUCTURE OF ORGANIZATION OF AFRICAN STATES AND MADAGASCAR FOR ECONOMIC COOPERATION. STUDIES ITS METHODS OF ACHIEVING ECONOMIC, TECHNICAL, SCIENTIFIC AND CULTURAL CO-OPERATION BETWEEN DEVELOPING AFRICAN COUNTRIES. EVALUATES CURRENT PROGRAMS AND ACHIEVEMENTS TO DATE.

2455 REES D.
KOREA: THE LIMITED WAR.
NEW YORK: ST MARTIN'S PRESS, 1964, 511 PP.
STUDIES KOREAN WAR IN LIGHT OF TRUMAN ADMINISTRATION'S CONTAINMENT POLICY. ANALYZES POLICY AS BASIS FOR LIMITING SCOPE OF THE WAR. DETAILS MILITARY CAMPAIGNS. DISCUSSES TRUMAN-MAC ARTHUR CONTROVERSY, AND ROLE OF UN.

2456 REGALA R.
WORLD PEACE THROUGH DIPLOMACY AND LAW.
MANILA, PHIL: CENTRAL LAW BOOK, 1964, 270 PP.
DISCUSSES ROLE OF DIPLOMACY, INTERNATIONAL LAW, AND INTERNATIONAL ORGANIZATIONS IN THEORY AND PRACTICE OF MAINTAINING WORLD PEACE.

2457 REID H.D.
RECUEIL DES COURS; TOME 45: LES SERVITUDES INTERNATIONALES III.
PARIS: RECUEIL SIREY, 1933, 798 PP.
ESSAYS STUDY INTERNATIONAL RIGHTS WHICH EMPHASIZE INTERNATIONAL CONSTITUTIONAL LAW, INCLUDING COMMUNICATIONS, STRAITS, INDIVIDUAL MORALITY, AND MORALITY IN GENERAL.

2458 REIDY J.W.
"LATIN AMERICA AND THE ATLANTIC TRIANGLE."
ORBIS, 8 (SPRING 64), 52-65.
DECLARES THAT THE ESSENCE OF A U.S. STRATEGY FOR THE AMERICAS IS TO BRING LATIN AMERICA FULLY WITHIN THE MODERN WEST.

2459 REIFF H.
THE UNITED STATES AND THE TREATY LAW OF THE SEA.
MINNEAPOLIS: U. MINN. PR., 1959, 451 PP.
MULTI-PARTITE AGREEMENTS BETWEEN USA AND OTHER NATIONS REGARDING THE USE OF THE SEA ARE PAINSTAKINGLY DISCUSSED. FOCUSES ON THE HISTORICAL AS WELL AS THE ETHICAL ASPECTS OF 'SEA-USAGE' AND CONCLUDES WITH OPTIMISTIC NOTE THAT THE SEA SHOULD ONE DAY BE APPLIED AS A FORCE WHICH WILL FOREVER UNIFY THE COMMUNITY OF NATIONS.

2460 REINSCH P.
SECRET DIPLOMACY: HOW FAR CAN IT BE ELIMINATED.
NEW YORK: HARCOURT, 1922, 231 PP.
WRITING IN WILSON'S TIME, AUTHOR TRACES THE HISTORICAL DEVELOPMENT OF SECRET DIPLOMACY AND MAKES BOTH A PRACTICAL AND MORAL EVALUATION OF ITS RESULTS. CONCLUDES THAT THE PRACTICE OF SECRET DIPLOMACY IS INCOMPATIBLE WITH DEMOCRATIC THEORY AND THAT IT ESTABLISHES A FATAL CYCLE OF SUSPICION, ARMAMENTS AND WAR. BELIEVES IT FORCES THE WORLD TO LIVE IN FEAR AND EXPRESSES HOPE FOR OPEN DIPLOMACY.

2461 REINTANZ G.
"THE SPACE TREATY."
GERMAN FOREIGN POLICY, 6 (FEB. 67), 147-152.
ANALYSIS OF 1966 UN SPACE TREATY. SOME DISCUSSION OF ITS EVOLUTION. EMPHASIZES EFFECTS OF "ALL-STATES" PROVISIONS CLAUSE, I.E. THE PRINCIPLE OF UNIVERSALITY APPLIED FOR THE FIRST TIME TO INTERNATIONAL TREATY. ANALYZES WEST GERMAN REACTION TO TREATY RE HER RELATIONS TO EAST GERMANY. AUTHOR IS EAST GERMAN AND ANTI-AMERICAN.

2462 REISCHAUER R.
"JAPAN'S GOVERNMENT--POLITICS."
LONDON: THOMAS NELSON & SONS, 1939.
EXAMINES FUNDAMENTALS OF JAPANESE POLITICAL THEORY AND EVOLUTION OF STATE FROM PRIMITIVE TRIBAL FORM TO STRONGLY CENTRALIZED GOVERNMENT OF 20TH CENTURY. ANALYZES POLITICAL AND CULTURAL SIGNIFICANCE OF POLICY OF "THE IMPERIAL WAY." LENGTHY DISCUSSION OF ORGANIZATION OF JAPANESE GOVERNMENT IN 1939. SHORT SELECT BIBLIOGRAPHY IN ENGLISH.

2463 REISS J.
GEORGE KENNANS POLITIK DER EINDAMMUNG.
BERLIN: COLLOQUIUM VERLAG, 1957, 100 PP.
EXAMINES BASIC CONTENT OF KENNAN'S FORMULATION OF POLICY OF CONTAINMENT. DISCUSSES RISE OF POLICY AND ITS APPLICATION IN TRUMAN DOCTRINE, MARSHALL PLAN, NATO, RIO PACT, ETC. STUDIES CHARACTER OF SOVIET SYSTEM, AIMS AND TACTICS OF BOLSHEVISM, AND BRIEFLY DISCUSSES POLICY OF LIBERATION.

2464 REITZEL W., KAPLAN M.A., COBLENZ C.
UNITED STATES FOREIGN POLICY, 1945-1955.
WASHINGTON: BROOKINGS INST., 1956, 536 PP., $2.00.
ANALYZES THE 'OFFICIAL PURPOSES AND ACTIONS OF THE US IN ITS FOREIGN POLICIES AND RELATIONS DURING THE TEN YEARS SINCE THE WAR IN ORDER TO TRY TO RECAPTURE THE KEY DECISIONS THAT WERE MADE AND THE GROUNDS ON WHICH ONE COURSE OF ACTION RATHER THAN ANOTHER WAS CHOSEN.'

2465 REMAK J.
THE GENTLE CRITIC: THEODOR FONTANE AND GERMAN POLITICS, 1848-1898.
SYRACUSE: SYRACUSE U PRESS, 1964, 104 PP., LC#64-16920.
ANALYZES GERMAN SOCIETY AND POLITICAL THOUGHT IN SECOND HALF OF 19TH CENTURY ACCORDING TO FONTANE, GERMAN NOVELIST OF PERIOD. COVERS FONTANE'S LIFE AND POLITICAL DEALINGS BEFORE STUDYING PEOPLE IN THEIR ROLES IN SOCIETY - JUNKERS, VICARS, ETC. ANALYZES BISMARCK IN DETAIL AND RELATIONSHIP BETWEEN PRUSSIA AND HIS EMPIRE. UNLIKE MOST GERMAN CRITICS, FONTANE GIVES FAVORABLE VIEW OF THIS PERIOD.

2466 REQUA E.G., STATHAM J.
THE DEVELOPING NATIONS: A GUIDE TO INFORMATION SOURCES CONCERNING THEIR ECON, POLIT, TECHNICAL, AND SOCIAL PROBLEMS.
DETROIT: GALE RESEARCH CO, 1965, 339 PP., LC#65-17576.
A COMPREHENSIVE ANNOTATED BIBLIOGRAPHY OF SOURCES ON ECONOMIC DEVELOPMENT, FOREIGN AID, AND RESULTING SOCIAL PROBLEMS IN UNDERDEVELOPED COUNTRIES. ENTRIES ARE FROM ENGLISH-LANGUAGE JOURNALS, SCHOLARLY BOOKS, GOVERNMENT DOCUMENTS, AND PUBLICATIONS OF INTERNATIONAL AGENCIES. SEPARATE SECTION LISTING AGENCIES ADMINISTERING AID, PERIODICALS; DIRECTORY AND BIBLIOGRAPHY OF BIBLIOGRAPHIES. AUTHOR AND TITLE INDEX.

2467 REUBENS E.D.
"THE BASIS FOR REORIENATION OF AMERICAN FOREIGN AID POLICY."
SOC. SCI., 34 (OCT. 59), 218-22.
ANALYZES MAJOR FOREIGN AID PROBLEMS FACED BY UNITED STATES. ASSISTANCE TO UNDERDEVELOPED COUNTRIES BECOMES A MORAL RESPONSIBILITY RATHER THAN ECONOMIC NECESSITY SINCE AMERICAN ECONOMY IS INDEPENDENT OF TRADE WITH UNDERDEVELOPED NATIONS. COMPARES RELATIVE ADVANTAGES ENJOYED BY USSR IN FOREIGN AID PROGRAM. STRESSES NEED FOR INTERNATIONAL ADMINISTRATION OF ECONOMIC AID FOR DEVELOPMENT.

2468 REUSS H.S.
THE CRITICAL DECADE - AN ECONOMIC POLICY FOR AMERICA AND THE FREE WORLD.
NEW YORK: MCGRAW HILL, 1964, 227 PP., LC#63-23048.
EXAMINES US TRADE AND FOREIGN AID POLICIES, PROBLEMS OF UNEMPLOYMENT, BALANCE OF PAYMENTS, ROLE OF CONGRESS IN SHAPING EFFECTIVE AID PROGRAMS, FOREIGN TRADE POLICIES, AND INTERNAL ECONOMIC STABILITY.

2469 REUTER P.
INTERNATIONAL INSTITUTIONS.
LONDON: ALLEN UNWIN, 1958, 316 PP., $5.50.
ATTEMPT IS MADE TO DEFINE THE ELEMENTS OF INTERNATIONAL SOCIETY IN TERMS OF THE PRINCIPLES OF GROUP PSYCHOLOGY. ALSO HISTORICAL AND ANALYTIC APPROACH TO ORIGINS, FOUNDATIONS AND STRUCTURAL INTERACTION OF STATES AND INTERNATIONAL ORGANIZATIONS.

2470 REYNOLDS P.A.
BRITISH FOREIGN POLICY IN THE INTER-WAR YEARS.
LONDON: LONGMANS, GREEN & CO, 1954, 182 PP.
TRACES COURSE OF POLICY DEVELOPMENT, 1919-39, DISCUSSING CHANGES BY RELATING THEM TO POLITICAL PRESSURES, ECONOMIC INFLUENCES, PUBLIC OPINION, AND NEGOTIATIONS. ALSO DISCUSSES RELATIONS WITH US AND EFFECT ON BRITISH POLICY.

2471 RHYNE C.S.
"LAW AS AN INSTRUMENT FOR PEACE."
BOSTON U. LAW REV., 40 (SPRING 60), 187-196.
BELIEVES THAT LAW IS THE ONLY DEVELOPED STRUCTURE WHICH CAN REGULATE THE USE OF NEW INSTRUMENTS OF POWER SO AS TO MAKE IT A PEACEFUL RATHER THAN A DESTRUCTIVE FORCE. RECOMMENDS A WORLD LEGAL ORDER WHICH CAN BE ACHIEVED BY TAKING THE LOGIC OF SUCH A WORLD-ORDER TO THE PEOPLE ON A

WORLD-WIDE BASIS. DISCUSSES THE WEAKNESSES OF THE PRESENT WORLD COURT.

2472 RICE E.A.
THE DIPLOMATIC RELATIONS BETWEEN THE UNITED STATES AND MEXICO 1925-1929.
WASHINGTON: CATHOLIC U PR, 1959, 224 PP.
DISCUSSES US ATTEMPTS TO INFLUENCE MEXICO TO GIVE UP ITS STATE RELIGION WHICH IT FELT CONTRIBUTED TO INSTABILITY OF GOVERNMENT, CONCENTRATES ON ROLE OF MORROW, AMERICAN AMBASSADOR.

2473 RICE G.W.
THE SOVIET POSITION ON DEPENDENT TERRITORIES IN THE UNITED NATIONS (THESIS, OHIO STATE UNIVERSITY)
COLUMBUS: OHIO STATE UNIV, 1961, 337 PP.
EXAMINES SOVIET ATTITUDE TOWARD COLONIAL POWERS AND ASKS IF SOVIET POLICIES MAY NOT BE TO HASTEN THE WEAKENING OF THE WEST. CHALLENGES THE SOVIET CLAIM THAT IT IS SINCERELY INTERESTED IN FURTHERING THE RIGHTS OF DEPENDENT PEOPLES. CONCLUDES THAT SOVIET COLONIAL POLICY IS MERELY AN ARM OF ITS TOTAL FOREIGN POLICY, WHOSE GOAL IS THE WEAKENING OF THE WEST.

2474 RICHARDSON I.L.
BIBLIOGRAFIA BRASILEIRA DE ADMINISTRACAO PUBLICA E ASSUNTOS CORRELATOS.
RIO DE JAN: FUND GETULIO VARGAS, 1964, 840 PP.
BIBLIOGRAPHY OF 7,300 ITEMS ON BRAZILIAN DEVELOPMENT IN FIELD OF PUBLIC ADMINISTRATION. COVERS PERIOD 1940-61. CONTAINS REFERENCES TO CONSTITUTIONAL RIGHTS; POLITICAL THEORY; CENTRAL GOVERNMENT ORGANIZATION; INTERNATIONAL RELATIONS, LAWS, AND ORGANIZATIONS; STATE, LOCAL, AND TERRI-ORIAL GOVERNMENTS; POLITICAL PARTIES AND ELECTIONS; ADMINIS-TRATIVE LAW; PLANNING, ETC.

2475 RICHTER J.H.
"TOWARDS AN INTERNATIONAL POLICY ON AGRICULTURAL TRADE."
KYKLOS, 16 (NO.2, 60), 203-27.
DISCUSSES PROBLEMS OF 'TRADE IN AGRICULTURAL PRODUCTS OF TEMPERATE ZONE.' ANALYZES PROBLEM OF MAINTAINING INTERNA-TIONAL TRADE AND NEED FOR 'PROGRAMS OF AGRICULTURAL SUPPORT IN BOTH IMPORTING AND EXPORTING COUNTRIES.' MAKES RECOM-MENDATIONS FOR RECONCILING THESE ISSUES.

2476 RIENOW R.
CONTEMPORARY INTERNATIONAL POLITICS.
NEW YORK: THOMAS Y CROWELL, 1961, 431 PP., LC#61-10668.
DISCUSSES FACTORS SHAPING CURRENT INTERNATIONAL POLITICS, INCLUDING CONTEMPORARY SITUATION, INSTRUMENTS OF POWER, CON-TROL OF POWER, PROBLEMS OF INTERNATIONAL LIFE, AND POWER AND PEACE.

2477 RIESELBACH L.N.
THE ROOTS OF ISOLATIONISM* CONGRESSIONAL VOTING AND PRESI-DENTIAL LEADERSHIP IN FOREIGN POLICY.
INDIANAPOLIS: BOBBS-MERRILL, 1966, 240 PP., LC#67-18661.
GIVES BRIEF HISTORY OF ISOLATIONISM TO ILLUSTRATE NATURE OF THE PROBLEM AND THEN EXAMINES CONTENT AND EVOLUTION OF CONGRESSIONAL ISOLATIONISM. ALSO EXAMINES POLITICAL CHARAC-TERISTICS AND SOCIAL BACKGROUND OF ISOLATIONIST CONGRESSMAN AND CONSTITUENCY CHARACTERISTICS. INCLUDES IDEOLOGICAL ORI-ENTATION, IDEOLOGY AND FOREIGN POLICY VOTING, LEGISTATIVE SYSTEM, AND PRESIDENTIAL LEADERSHIP.

2478 RIESELBACH L.N.
"QUANTITATIVE TECHNIQUES FOR STUDYING VOTING BEHAVIOR IN THE UNITED NATIONS GENERAL ASSEMBLY."
INT. ORGAN., 14 (1960), 291-306.
DEALS WITH POSSIBLE MEANS OF SOLVING THE QUESTIONS REGARDING BLOC-VOTING PATTERNS. DATA PRESENTED TO GIVE OPPOSITION-VIEWER OPPORTUNITY TO REWORK THE FIGURES TO SUIT HIS OWN STANDARDS.

2479 RIGGS F.W.
FORMOSA UNDER CHINESE NATIONALIST RULE.
NEW YORK: MACMILLAN, 1952, 195 PP.
DESCRIBES MILITARY, POLITICAL, ECONOMIC AND SOCIAL CON-DITIONS ON FORMOSA UNDER NATIONALIST RULE, ASSESSING ITS STRENGTH AND WEAKNESS FOR PURPOSE OF CLARIFYING SOME OF THE ISSUES WHICH MUST BE TAKEN INTO ACCOUNT IN FORMULATING US POLICY TOWARD COMMUNIST AND NATIONALIST CHINA.

2480 RIGGS R.
POLITICS IN THE UNITED NATIONS: A STUDY OF UNITED STATES INFLUENCE IN THE GENERAL ASSEMBLY.
URBANA: U. ILL. PR., 1958, 208 PP.
ATTEMPTS TO DETERMINE TO WHAT EXTENT USA POLICY INFLUEN-CES THE GENERAL ASSEMBLY. USA MOST SUCCESSFUL ON POLITICAL QUESTIONS INVOLVING SECURITY BUT ON SLIPPERY FOOTING WITH REGARD TO COLONIALISM. ENUMERATES METHODS USED BY USA TO EXERT AUTHORITY.

2481 RIGGS R.
"OVER-SELLING THE U.N. CHARTER, FACT AND MYTH."
INT. ORGAN., 14 (SPRING 60), 39-60.
DISCUSSES AMERICAN PUBLIC OPINION AND ITS EXPECTATIONS FOR A UNITED NATIONS IN THE 1940'S. SURVEYS IMPORTANCE OF BIG-POWER CONCORD AND STATE DEPARTMENT PRESENTATION OF U.N. TO USA PUBLIC. OFFICIAL USA ATTITUDE IS SCRUTINIZED, REVEAL-ING FALSE ASSUMPTIONS AND IMPRESSIONS. MYTHS CREATED BY THE PRESS OR PRIVATE SEGMENTS OF AMERICAN SOCIETY ARE EXPLAINED IN LIGHT OF THE FACTS OF THE WORLD-STRUCTURE.

2482 RIMALOV V.V.
ECONOMIC COOPERATION BETWEEN USSR AND UNDERDEVELOPED COUNTRIES.
MOSCOW: FOREIGN LANG PUBL HOUSE, 1962, 162 PP.
EXPLAINS SOVIET POLICY OF SUPPORT FOR NATIONAL-LIBERATION MOVEMENT, AIMS AND CHARACTER OF SOVIET ECONOMIC AID, AND PROGRAMS IN VARIOUS AREAS OF WORLD.

2483 RIPLEY R.B.
"INTERAGENCY COMMITTEES AND INCREMENTALISM: THE CASE OF AID TO INDIA."
MIDWEST J. POLIT. SCI., 8 (MAY 64), 143-165.
STUDY OF THE AMERICAN AID PROGRAM TO INDIA FROM 1951-1962 AS A METHOD OF ANALYZING THE FUNCTIONING OF INTERAGENCY COM-MITTEES. HYPOTHESES ARE EXAMINED THAT (1) THESE COMMITTEES TEND TO REMAIN STABLE AND INERT, AND (2) THEY PRODUCE AN IN-CREMENTAL SITUATION. AFFIRMATIVE CONCLUSIONS ARE DRAWN BUT INCREMENTALISM IS DECLARED NOT INEVITABLE.

2484 RISTIC D.N.
YUGOSLAVIA'S REVOLUTION OF 1941.
UNIVERSITY PARK: PENN STATE U PR, 1966, 175 PP., LC#66-18191
STUDY OF YUGOSLAVIAN COUP D'ETAT OF MARCH, 1941, WRITTEN BY AN EYEWITNESS. DISCUSSES FACTORS WHICH SHAPED YUGOSLAV PUBLIC OPINION: TRADITIONAL ANTI-GERMANISM, SYMPATHY WITH HEROISM OF US AND ENGLAND, AND DESIRE TO AVOID FATE OF POLAND AND FRANCE. SHOWS HOW MANY YUGOSLAVIANS RESISTED AXIS PRESSURE TO SIGN TRIPARTITE PACT. RECORDS MAJOR PERSONALITIES AND ISSUES OF THE COUP.

2485 RITNER P.
THE DEATH OF AFRICA.
NEW YORK: MACMILLAN, 1960, 312 PP.
CONTENDS THAT BLACK AFRICA IS CAUGHT IN SOCIAL AND ECONOMIC SNARE LEADING TO CHAOS, THAT AFRICA CANNOT SOLVE ITS PROBLEMS ALONE, AND THAT US MUST STEP IN TO AVOID HOSTILE AFRICA OF FUTURE.

2486 RIUKIN A.
THE AFRICAN PRESENCE IN WORLD AFFAIRS.
NEW YORK: FREE PRESS OF GLENCOE, 1963, 304 PP., LC#63-13542.
STUDY OF EMERGING AFRICA, INCLUDING PROBLEMS OF GROWTH AND STABILITY, GROWTH MODELS, AGRICULTURAL MODERNIZATION, EDUCATION, POLITICAL SYSTEMS, NATIONALISM AND NEUTRALISM, AND AFRICAN IMPACT ON WORLD BALANCE OF POWER.

2487 RIVKIN A.
"AFRICAN ECONOMIC DEVELOPMENT: ADVANCED TECHNOLOGY AND THE STAGES OF GROWTH."
J. HUM. REL., 8 (SUMMER 60), 617-645.
CONCERNED WITH BASIC PROBLEM AREAS OF AFRICAN ECONOMIC DEVELOPMENT (INCLUDING AGRICULTURE, MINING, TRANSPORTATION, AND LABOR), AND ROLE ADVANCED FREE WORLD TECHNOLOGY CAN PLAY IN ENSURING FREEDOM AND INDEPENDENCE OF AFRICAN STATES. POINTS OUT DANGERS OF EXCESSIVE RAPIDITY IN GROWTH, AND IN-CORPORATING TECHNOLOGY INTO CULTURAL PROCESSES OF AFRICA.

2488 RIVKIN A.
AFRICA AND THE WEST.
NEW YORK: PRAEGER, 1962, 241 PP., $5.00.
ANALYZES AFRICAN POLITICAL AND ECONOMIC DEVELOPMENT, PARTICULARLY IN RELATION TO WESTERN EUROPE, EEC, USA AND ISRAEL. ALSO DEALS WITH ROLE OF U.N. IN CONGO AND TRUST TERRITORIES. PROPOSES A NEW MULTI-LATERAL AID ORGANIZATION TO ENSURE PEACEFUL DEVELOPMENT OF AFRICAN STATES AND AN EMBARGO ON ARMS TO THE LATTER.

2489 RIVKIN A.
THE AFRICAN PRESENCE IN WORLD AFFAIRS.
NEW YORK: MACMILLAN, 1963, 304 PP., LC#63-13542.
DISCUSSES MAJOR IDEOLOGICAL ASPECTS OF POLITICAL REVOLUTION IN AFRICAN STATES SOUTH OF SAHARA IN 1950'S. EMPHASIZES PROBLEMS OF POLITICAL GROWTH AND ECONOMIC CHANGE AND THEIR INFLUENCE ON STATES' INTERNATIONAL ROLES. POINTS OUT IMPORTANCE OF CLOSE AMERICAN ATTENTION TO INTERNAL DYNAMICS OF STATES' ECONOMIC AND POLITICAL STRUGGLES TO ENSURE THEIR ALIGNMENT WITH FREE WORLD.

2490 RIVKIN A.
AFRICA AND THE EUROPEAN COMMON MARKET (PAMPHLET)
DENVER: U OF DENVER, 1964, 61 PP.
ANALYSIS OF RELATION TO EUROPEAN COMMON MARKET OF AFRICAN STATES. INCLUDES AFRICAN NATIONS ACCEPTED AS ASSOCIATE MEMBERS BY 1963 CONVENTION OF ASSOCIATION AND THOSE NOT PART OF CONVENTION. EXAMINES DEVELOPMENT OF AFRICAN COMMON MARKET AS ADDITION OR ALTERNATIVE TO EEC.

2491 ROACH J.R. ED.

THE UNITED STATES AND THE ATLANTIC COMMUNITY; ISSUES AND PROSPECTS.
AUSTIN: U OF TEXAS PR, 1967, 87 PP., LC#67-27782.
STUDIES PRESENT PLACE OF NATO AS PEACE-KEEPING FORCE. ADVOCATES REVISION OF POLICIES AND FUNCTIONS OF NATO TO MEET CHANGES IN WORLD SITUATION PARTIALLY CAUSED BY NATO ITSELF. CONSIDERS IMPLICATIONS OF ECONOMIC RECOVERY OF EUROPE, END OF COLONIALISM, LESSENING OF SOVIET THREAT, ADVANTAGES IN MODERN TECHNOLOGY, AND UNIFICATION OF EUROPE FOR US POSITION IN NATO AND FOREIGN POLICY.

2492 ROBBINS L.
ECONOMIC PLANNING AND INTERNATIONAL ORDER.
NEW YORK: MACMILLAN, 1937, 330 PP.
VIEWS VARIOUS TYPES OF PLANNING: INDEPENDENT NATIONAL PLANNING, PARTIAL INTERNATION AND COMPLETE INTERNATIONAL PLANNING. POINTS OUT CHARACTERISTICS OF EACH TYPE. CONCLUDES WITH ANALYSIS OF KEYNESIAN DOCTRINE.

2493 ROBBINS L.
ECONOMIC CAUSES OF WAR.
LONDON: CAPE, 1939, 124 PP.
ATTEMPTS TO CONTRIBUTE TO THE DISCOVERY OF THE CAUSES OF WAR 'BY INQUIRING TO WHAT EXTENT WAR CAN BE REGARDED AS BEING DUE TO ECONOMIC CAUSES.'

2494 ROBERTS H.L.
RUSSIA AND AMERICA.
NEW YORK: NEW AMERICAN LIB, 1956, 251 PP., LC#55-11968.
BASED UPON DISCUSSIONS OF STUDY GROUP AT COUNSEL ON FOREIGN RELATIONS, 1953-55. REPORT RESTS UPON FAITH IN DEMOCRATIC PROCESS AS MEANS OF MEETING COMPLEX PROBLEMS CONFRONTING THE US IN THIS CENTURY. DISCUSSED ARE THE COMMUNIST THREAT, VARIOUS ASPECTS OF US FOREIGN POLICY, AND AREAS OF CONFLICT: GERMANY, EASTERN EUROPE, AND SOUTHEAST ASIA.

2495 ROBERTS H.L.
FOREIGN AFFAIRS BIBLIOGRAPHY, 1952-1962.
NEW YORK: RR BOWKER, 1964, 752 PP., LC#33-7094.
A SELECTED AND ANNOTATED CUMULATIVE BIBLIOGRAPHY OF BOOKS ON INTERNATIONAL RELATIONS BASED LARGELY UPON NOTES APPEARING QUARTERLY IN "FOREIGN AFFAIRS." RETAINS SCHEMATIC CLASSIFICATION OF EARLIER VOLUMES: GENERAL INTERNATIONAL RELATIONS, THE WORLD SINCE 1914, AND THE WORLD BY REGIONS, EMPHASIZING ANALYTICAL, CHRONOLOGICAL, AND REGIONAL TREATMENTS RESPECTIVELY. LIMITED TO WORKS PUBLISHED FROM 1953-62.

2496 ROBERTSON A.H.
EUROPEAN INSTITUTIONS: COOPERATION, INTEGRATION, UNIFICATION
NEW YORK: FREDERICK PRAEGER, 1959, 371 PP., LC#59-8407.
DISCUSSES PROBLEMS OF EUROPEAN POLITICAL AND ECONOMIC UNIFICATION, FROM FORMATIVE PERIOD (1947-49) TO DEVELOPMENT OF EUROPEAN ECONOMIC COMMUNITY AND EURATOM. INCLUDES DOCUMENTARY APPENDIX.

2497 ROBERTSON A.H.
THE LAW OF INTERNATIONAL INSTITUTIONS IN EUROPE.
NEW YORK: OCEANA, 1961, 140 PP.
DISCUSSES THE 'EUROPEAN IDEA' (ITS POLITICAL SIGNIFICANCE AND IDEOLOGICAL CONNOTATION) AND TRACES HISTORICAL DEVELOPMENT OF THIS CONCEPT THROUGH MAJOR TREATIES, CONFERENCES AND COOPERATIVE ORGANIZATIONS. ASSIGNS SPECIAL PLACE FOR HUMAN RIGHTS IN COUNCIL OF EUROPE PHILOSOPHY.

2498 ROBERTSON A.H.
HUMAN RIGHTS IN EUROPE.
MANCHESTER: U. PR., 1963, 280 PP.
ANALYZES EUROPEAN CONVENTION TEN YEARS AFTER ITS CONCEPTION, FOCUSING ON THE APPLICATION OF THE IDEALS SET FORTH IN THE CHARTER. STUDIES THE VARIOUS BODIES CREATED TO CARRY OUT THE DOCTRINES, AND, USING CASE STUDIES, DRAWS CONCLUSIONS AS TO THE EFFICASY OF THE ORGANIZATION AS A GUARANTOR OF HUMAN RIGHTS.

2499 ROBERTSON B.C.
REGIONAL DEVELOPMENT IN THE EUROPEAN ECONOMIC COMMUNITY.
LONDON: ALLEN & UNWIN, 1962, 95 PP.
CONSIDERS PRINCIPLES BASIC TO REGIONAL PLANNING IN GENERAL; ANALYZES DEVELOPMENT SCHEMES OF SOUTHERN ITALY AND SOUTHWEST FRANCE AND ASSESSES THEIR SUCCESS IN BRINGING PROSPERITY. GIVES AN ACCOUNT OF WAYS IN WHICH EEC IS CONCERNED WITH REGIONAL DEVELOPMENT THROUGH READAPTATION PROVISIONS OF COAL AND STEEL COMMUNITY. SUMS UP ACHIEVEMENTS AND INDICATES FUTURE OF REGIONAL POLICIES OF EEC.

2500 ROBERTSON D.J. ED.
THE BRITISH BALANCE OF PAYMENTS.
LONDON: OLIVER & BOYD, 1966, 187 PP.
SYMPOSIUM CONSIDERING PERFORMANCE OF EXPORTS AND BURDEN OF IMPORT, WITH SPECIAL ATTENTION ON EUROPEAN PROSPECTS AND INVISABLE EARNINGS. EXAMINES MONETARY ASPECTS OF BALANCE OF PAYMENTS IN TERMS OF CAPITAL MOVEMENTS, AND IN RELATION TO MULTIPLE FUNCTIONS OF STERLING AND ROLE OF FISCAL POLICY.

2501 ROBINS D.B.
EVOLVING UNITED STATES POLICIES TOWARD THE EMERGING NATIONS OF ASIA AND AFRICA (PAMPHLET)
WASH, DC: AMER ASSN UNIV WOMEN, 1961, 40 PP.
A SYLLABUS PREPARED TO ASSIST STUDY GROUPS TO ASSESS US POLICY TOWARD THE EMERGING NATIONS OF ASIA AND AFRICA. CURRENT BIBLIOGRAPHIES GIVEN ON WORLD AFFAIRS IN GENERAL; BLACK AFRICA; NORTH AFRICA AND THE MIDDLE EAST; PAKISTAN, INDIA, AND SOUTHEAST ASIA. WORKSHOP TOPICS SUGGESTED. BRIEF COMMENTS OFFERED ON STATE OF CURRENT WORLD AFFAIRS AND US FOREIGN POLICY.

2502 ROBINSON A.D.
DUTCH ORGANIZED AGRICULTURE IN INTERNATIONAL POLITICS, 1945-1960.
THE HAGUE: NIJHOFF, 1962, 192 PP.
AN ANALYSIS OF THE NATURE AND PARTICIPATION OF PRESSURE GROUPS IN SEVERAL FOREIGN ISSUES OF EUROPEAN UNITY.

2503 ROBINSON H.
DEVELOPMENT OF THE BRITISH EMPIRE.
BOSTON: HOUGHTON, 1936, 475 PP.
PRESENTS PROBLEMS OF COLONIAL GOVERNMENT, COLONIZATION OF AMERICA AND REVOLUTION ON ATLANTIC SEABORD, CANADIAN INDEPENDENCE, ASIAN AND AFRICAN COLONIZATION, AND FINALLY MANDATED TERRITORIES HELD UNDER CONTRACT WITH THE LEAGUE OF NATIONS. THE ECONOMICS OF EMPIRE, WITH ITS CONFLICTING AND DIVERSE INTERESTS AND GROWING NATIONALISM AMONG COLONIES IS DISCUSSED.

2504 ROBINSON J.A.
THE MONRONEY RESOULUTION: CONGRESSIONAL INITIATIVE IN FOREIGN POLICY MAKING.
NEW YORK: HOLT RINEHART WINSTON, 1959, 16 PP., LC#59-12380.
ACCOUNT OF ENACTMENT OF SENATE RESOULUTION URGING EXECUTIVE TO CONSIDER AN INTERNATIONAL DEVELOPMENT ASSOCIATION AS AN AFFILIATE OF WORLD BANK; CASE STUDY SUGGESTS AREAS IN WHICH CONGRESS CAN TAKE INITIATIVE IN FOREIGN POLICY.

2505 ROBINSON J.A.
"CONGRESS AND FOREIGN POLICY-MAKING: A STUDY IN LEGISLATIVE INFLUENCE AND INITIATIVE."
HOMEWOOD: DORSEY, 1962.
ARGUES CONGRESS'S INFLUENCE IN FOREIGN POLICY IS PRIMARILY ONE OF LEGITIMATING AND AMENDING POLICIES INITIATED BY EXECUTIVE TO DEAL WITH PROBLEMS USUALLY IDENTIFIED BY EXECUTIVE; AND THAT REASON FOR THIS DEVELOPMENT LIES IN CHANGING CHARACTER OF INFORMATION OR INTELLIGENCE NEEDS IN MODERN POLICY-MAKING. CONTAINS EXTENSIVE BIBLIOGRAPHY AND NOTES ON AVAILABILITY OF UNPUBLISHED SOURCES.

2506 ROBINSON M.E.
EDUCATION FOR SOCIAL CHANGE: ESTABLISHING INSTITUTES OF PUBLIC AND BUSINESS ADMINISTRATION ABROAD (PAMPHLET)
WASHINGTON: BROOKINGS INST, 1961, 90 PP.
REPORT ON CONFERENCE OF REPRESENTATIVES OF AMERICAN UNIVERSITIES THAT HAVE HELPED TO ESTABLISH PUBLIC AND BUSINESS ADMINISTRATION INSTITUTES ABROAD. AIMS OF CONFERENCE WERE TO REVIEW PROGRESS AND STUDY PROCESS OF FOUNDING SUCH INSTITUTIONS AND THEIR EFFECT ON SOCIAL CHANGE.

2507 ROBOCK S.H.
OVERVIEW OF TOTAL BRAZILIAN SETTING, NEWER REGIONAL PATTERNS NING AND FOREIGN AID.
WASHINGTON: BROOKINGS INST, 1963, 213 PP., LC#63-20977.
STATEMENT OF AUTHOR'S GENERAL CONCEPT OF DEVELOPMENT AND VERVIEW OF TOTAL BRAZILIAM SETTING, RECENT REGIONAL PATTERNS OF BRAZILIAN DEVELOPMENT, STRUCTURE AND TRENDS OF NORTHEAST ECONOMY. TRACES HISTORY OF INDIGENOUS DEVELOPMENT EFFORTS, LEADING TO TODAY'S ECONOMIC DEVELOPMENT PROGRAMS NOW ESTABLISHED AS NATIONAL POLICY. VIEWS FUTURE PROSPECTS FOR FOREIGN AID WHICH EMERGED FROM NORTHEAST EXPERIENCE.

2508 ROBOCK S.H. ED., SOLOMON L.M. ED.
INTERNATIONAL DEVELOPMENT 1965.
NEW YORK: OCEANA PUBLISHING, 1966, 197 PP., LC#64-8541.
PRESENTATIONS AND DISCUSSIONS BY MEMBERS OF SOCIETY FOR INTERNATIONAL DEVELOPMENT ON FOREIGN AID, POPULATION GROWTH, ADULT LITERACY, PUBLIC AND PRIVATE PLANNING, RELATION OF ECONOMIC GROWTH TO LEGAL ORDER, PEACE CORPS EFFORTS, PUBLIC HEALTH, AND AGRICULTURAL AID.

2509 ROCK V.P.
A STRATEGY OF INTERDEPENDENCE.
NEW YORK: CHAS SCRIBNER'S SONS, 1964, 399 PP., LC#64-12837.
PRESENTS PROGRAM FOR CONTROLLING CONFLICT BETWEEN USA AND USSR AND BY WHICH NUCLEAR WAR WOULD BE AVERTED. PROGRAM VIEWS INTERNATIONAL SOCIETY AS SINGLE COMMUNITY WHICH MUST CONTROL CONFLICTS BY CROSS-NATIONAL DIFFUSION OF POWER. DISCUSSES THEORETICAL BASIS AND POLITICAL FEASIBILITY OF ESTABLISHING INTERNATIONAL ORDER BASED ON STRATEGY OF INTERDEPENDENCE.

2510 ROCKE J.R.M.
"THE BRITISH EXPORT BATTLE FOR THE CARIBBEAN"
BOARD OF TRADE JOURNAL, (SEPT. 67), 507-513.
AFTER INDEPENDENCE CARIBBEAN TRADE WAS NO LONGER LIMITED

TO ENGLAND. SITUATION OF COMPETITION FORCED ENGLAND TO CHANGE TRADE POLICIES AND METHODS. DESCRIBES AREAS IN WHICH ENGLAND SHOULD INCREASE ACTIVITIES INCLUDING PERSONAL VISITS, DESIGN AND STYLING, AND MARKET RESEARCH. EMPHASIZES NEED FOR INCREASED COOPERATION BETWEEN BRITISH GOVERNMENT POSTS AND MANUFACTURERS.

2511 ROCKEFELLER BROTHERS FUND, INC.
INTERNATIONAL SECURITY - THE MILITARY ASPECT.
GARDEN CITY: DOUBLEDAY, 1958, 63 PP.
REPORT ON STRATEGIC PROBLEMS, DEFENSE ORGANIZATION, NUCLEAR WEAPON SYSTEMS, ALLIANCES, CIVIL DEFENSE, DISARMAMENT, AND BUDGETS FOR NATIONAL SECURITY. MAINTAINS THAT RETALIATORY FORCE OF US IS INADEQUATELY DISPERSED AND PROTECTED.

2512 RODNEY W.
"THE ENTENTE STATES OF WEST AFRICA."
INT. J., 21 (1965), 78-92.
DISCUSSES FRENCH-SPEAKING AFRICA AND HER CHANGING POLICIES TOWARD CLOSER TIES WITH US AND AWAY FROM DEPENDENCE ON FRANCE. REVIEWS PROSPECTS FOR ECONOMIC AND EDUCATIONAL DEVELOPMENT.

2513 RODRIGUES J.H.
BRAZIL AND AFRICA.
BERKELEY: U OF CALIF PR, 1965, 382 PP., LC#65-23155.
REVIEW OF AFRO-BRAZILIAN RELATIONS, MUTUAL CONTRIBUTIONS, AND ANALYSIS OF RACIAL DEMOCRACY; INCLUDES MISCEGENATION, THE COMMON MARKET, SLAVE TRADE, AND THE CONGO.

2514 ROGERS W.C.
INTERNATIONAL ADMINISTRATION: A BIBLIOGRAPHY (PUBLICATION NO 92; A PAMPHLET)
CHICAGO: PUBLIC ADMIN SERVICE, 1945, 32 PP.
ENGLISH-LANGUAGE BIBLIOGRAPHY OF WORKS PUBLISHED BOTH PRIOR TO 1939 AND IN PERIOD 1939-1945. INCLUDES BOOKS, PAMPHLETS, AND PERIODICALS RELATED TO ADMINISTRATION OR MANAGEMENT OF VARIED ACTIVITIES UNDERTAKEN BY PUBLIC AUTHORITIES ON CENTRAL, LOCAL, AND SPECIAL LEVELS INTERNATIONALLY. EACH ITEM RECEIVES ANNOTATION OF SEVERAL LINES.

2515 ROGERS W.C., STUHLER B. ET AL.
"A COMPARISON OF INFORMED AND GENERAL PUBLIC OPINION ON US FOREIGN POLICY."
PUBLIC OPINION QUART., 31 (1967), 242-252.
COMPARES VIEWS OF GENERAL PUBLIC WITH THOSE OF EXPERTS IN EDUCATION, BUSINESS, POLITICS, ETC., ON US FOREIGN POLICY. SHOWS LARGE GAP PERSISTED BETWEEN GROUPS, AND THAT RESPONSE OF EXPERTS WAS "SPECIFIC, MANY-SIDED, ANALYTICAL, AND FLEXIBLE." RESPONSES OF PUBLIC (INCLUDING COLLEGE-EDUCATED) WERE "VAGUE AND SPORADIC."

2516 ROGGER H.
"EAST GERMANY: STABLE OR IMMOBILE."
CURR. HIST., 48 (MAR. 65), 135-141.
ULBRICHT'S REGIME, FOR REASONS OF ITS OWN, HAS HAD TO RESIST THE NEW WAVE OF DE-STALINIZATION SET OFF BY SOVIET PARTY CONGRESS OF 1961. THE NEGOTIATIONS, AGREEMENTS, AND GUARANTEES NEEDED TO BRING ABOUT GERMAN RE-UNIFICATION WOULD REQUIRE VASTLY GREATER CHANGES IN SOVIET SPHERE. NOT LIKELY TO TAKE PLACE WHILE ULBRICHT REMAINS IN CHARGE.

2517 ROLFE S.E.
GOLD AND WORLD POWER.
NEW YORK: HARPER & ROW, 1965, 276 PP., LC#66-10658.
EXAMINES DATA CONSTITUTING BALANCE-OF-PAYMENTS STATISTICS. INVESTIGATES VARIOUS POSSIBLE TYPES OF EQUILIBRATING ADJUSTMENTS IN ORDER TO PROVIDE ANALYTIC FRAMEWORK OF PROTOTYPES OF ADJUSTMENT MECHANISMS AVAILABLE TO FREE NATIONS. TREATS ROOTS OF CURRENT SYSTEM.

2518 ROMANOVSKY S.
"MISUSE OF CULTURAL COOPERATION."
INTERNATIONAL AFFAIRS (USSR), 4 (APR. 67), 56-61.
DISCUSSION OF PROPAGANDIZING CULTURAL EXCHANGE AND ECONOMIC DEVELOPMENT PROGRAMS OF US GOVERNMENT. CITES PEACE CORPS AS A SEMI-AUTONOMOUS AGENCY WITHIN STATE DEPARTMENT AND PENETRATION OF UNIVERSITIES BY CIA. CLAIMS CULTURAL CONTACTS HAVE BECOME MEANS OF IDEOLOGICAL SUBVERSION BY AMERICAN IMPERIALISM. EMPHASIZES DIFFERENCE IN LENIN'S AND MARX'S CONCEPTION OF CULTURAL CONTACT.

2519 ROMEIN J.
THE ASIAN CENTURY.
BERKELEY: U OF CALIF PR, 1965, 448 PP.
DISCUSSES HISTORY OF NATIONAL MOVEMENTS IN ASIA AND RELATION OF TRADITION TO NEWLY EMERGING SOCIAL PATTERNS. DESCRIBES HISTORICAL DEVELOPMENT OF ASIA IN THREE ASPECTS: ITS EXTENT, ITS SHORTNESS COMPARED TO ITS SIGNIFICANCE, AND ITS RESULTS.

2520 ROOSEVELT J. ED.
THE LIBERAL PAPERS.
GARDEN CITY: DOUBLEDAY, 1962, 354 PP., LC#62-10458.
ESSAYS ON VARIED TOPICS OF WORLD AFFAIRS BY MEMBERS OF LIBERAL PROJECT, A GROUP OF CONGRESSMEN, INTELLECTUALS, SCIENTISTS, AND SCHOLARS WHOSE PURPOSE IS TO BRIDGE GAP BETWEEN REALMS OF FREE STUDY AND POLITICAL ACTION. STRESS THEMES OF FOREIGN POLICY AND AMERICAN DEFENSE, AND SUGGEST "LIBERAL" APPROACHES.

2521 ROOT E.
ADDRESSES ON INTERNATIONAL SUBJECTS.
CAMBRIDGE: HARVARD U. PR., 1916, 463 PP.
DEALS WITH THE NEED OF POPULAR UNDERSTANDING OF INTERNATIONAL LAW. FOCUSES ON POLITICAL QUESTION RAISED UNDER JAPANESE TREATY AND SAN FRANCISCO SCHOOL BOARD RESOLUTION. EXPLAINS THE RELATIONS BETWEEN INTERNATIONAL TRIBUNALS OF ARBITRATION AND THE JURISDICTION OF NATIONAL COURTS.

2522 ROOT E.
THE MILITARY AND COLONIAL POLICY OF THE US.
CAMBRIDGE: HARVARD U. PR., 1916, 502 PP.
COLLECTION OF ADDRESSES AND SPEECHES COVERING THE PERIOD OF ROOT'S SERVICE AS SECRETARY OF WAR, SECRETARY OF STATE, AND SENATOR OF THE US. DEALS WITH THE CHARACTER OF THE AMERICAN ARMY, STUDIES THE PRINCIPLES OF COLONIAL POLICY, AND EXPLORES MILITARY EDUCATION WITHIN THE ARMY WAR COLLEGE. CONCLUDES WITH SURVEY OF THE NEW MILITIA SYSTEM.

2523 ROOT E.
"THE EFFECT OF DEMOCRACY ON INTERNATIONAL LAW."
PROC. AMER. SOC. INT. LAW, (1917', 2-11.
TRIES TO ESTIMATE FUTURE POSSIBILITIES OF INTERNATIONAL LAW AND TO FORM USEFUL OPINION ABOUT METHODS BY WHICH LAW CAN BE MADE MORE BINDING UPON INTERNATIONAL CONDUCT.

2524 ROPKE W.
INTERNATIONAL ORDER AND ECONOMIC INTEGRATION.
DORDRECHT: D REIDEL PUBL CO, 1959, 280 PP.
EVALUATES RELATION BETWEEN ECONOMICS AND PEACE. TRACES HISTORY OF IDEOLOGICAL CONFLICTS IN EUROPE AND OTHER AREAS. PROPOSES IDEAS FOR ECONOMIC UNIFICATION AS A MEANS FOR ACHIEVING STABILITY IN INTERNATIONAL RELATIONS.

2525 ROPKE W.
A HUMANE ECONOMY.
CHICAGO: HENRY REGNERY CO, 1960, 312 PP., LC#60-09661.
ATTEMPTS TO SHOW NECESSITY FOR CHANGE IN ECONOMIC SYSTEMS OF TODAY BY HISTORICAL EXAMPLES, NEED FOR INTERNATIONAL ORGANIZATION TO STABILIZE WORLD, AND SOCIAL CHANGES POSSIBLE IN UNIFIED ECONOMIC ASSOCIATIONS. COMPARES ECONOMIC IDEAS.

2526 ROSAMOND R.
CRUSADE FOR PEACE: EISENHOWER'S PRESIDENTIAL LEGACY WITH THE PROGRAM FOR ACTION.
NEW YORK: LEXINGTON PUBL CO, 1962, 243 PP., LC#62-13149.
ANALYSIS OF PERTINENT EXCERPTS FROM EISENHOWER'S KEY SPEECHES AND STATEMENTS WHILE PRESIDENT. ORGANIZED TO FORM A "LEGACY OF NEW PUBLIC PHILOSOPHY; DEMOCRACY'S ANSWER TO COMMUNISM, TYRANNY, AND GLOBAL POVERTY."

2527 ROSCIO J.G.
OBRAS.
CARACAS: LA DECIM CONF INTERAMER, 1953, 489 PP.
WRITINGS OF A PHILOSOPHICAL LEADER OF SOUTH AMERICAN LIBERATION MOVEMENTS. INCLUDES "THE TRIUMPH OF LIBERTY OVER DESPOTISM."

2528 ROSE S.
"ASIAN NATIONALISM* THE SECOND STAGE."
INTER-AMERICAN ECON. AFF., 43 (APR. 67), 282-292.
TRACES TRANSITION IN OBJECTIVES OF ASIAN NATIONALISM FROM STRUGGLE FOR INDEPENDENCE TO ONE OF SURVIVAL. CONTENDS THIS CONCERN FOR SURVIVAL RESULTS IN MORE PRAGMATIC, LESS DOGMATIC POLICIES. POLICY ATTENDS TO REGIONAL & BORDER DISPUTES, NOT TO GLOBAL CONCERNS. SUGGESTS NO NECESSITY FOR CHOICE BETWEEN WESTERN AND COMMUNIST SYSTEMS EXISTS IN ASIA, ONLY CONCERN FOR INDEPENDENCE AND NATIONAL UNITY.

2529 ROSECRANCE R.N.
ACTION AND REACTION IN WORLD POLITICS.
BOSTON: LITTLE BROWN, 1963, 314 PP., $6.00.
INTERPRETS CURRENT INTERNATIONAL RELATIONS THROUGH THE PERSPECTIVE OF THE PAST. REVIEWS NINE DISTINCT INTERNATIONAL SYSTEMS WHICH HAVE FUNCTIONED SINCE 18TH CENTURY, SUCH AS CONCERT OF EUROPE, LEAGUE OF NATIONS, AND UNITED NATIONS. OBJECTIVE IS TO ILLUMINATE ELEMENTS OF VARIOUS INTERNATIONAL SYSTEMS AND TO EXAMINE THEIR INTERRELATIONS.

2530 ROSECRANCE R.N. ED.
THE DISPERSION OF NUCLEAR WEAPONS: STRATEGY AND POLITICS.
NEW YORK: COLUMB. U. PR., 1964, 343 PP., $7.50.
DISCUSSES THE EXPERIENCE OF BRITAIN AND FRANCE IN THEIR ATTEMPT TO ACQUIRE DETERRENT CAPABILITIES COMPARABLE TO THAT OF THE U.S. AND THE SOVIET UNION. EVALUATES THE EFFECT ON RED CHINA'S POSITIONS IN SOUTHEAST ASIA WHEN SHE ACHIEVES NUCLEAR STATUS, AND CONSIDERS THE QUESTION OF WHETHER THE SPREAD OF NUCLEAR WEAPONS WILL JEOPARDIZE INTERNATIONAL PEACE.

2531 ROSENAU J.N. ED.
INTERNATIONAL POLITICS AND FOREIGN POLICY: A READER IN RESEARCH AND THEORY.
NEW YORK: FREE PRESS OF GLENCOE, 1961, 511 PP., LC#61-14106.
ANTHOLOGY OF 55 ARTICLES ON THEORETICAL MODELS OF INTERNATIONAL POLITICS OR POLICY; INQUIRES INTO MEANING OF BASIC CONCEPTS IN FIELD; CASE STUDIES ILLUSTRATING OPERATION OF KEY PROCESSES IN DECISION-MAKING IN WESTERN AND NON-WESTERN SOCIETIES. EACH STUDY IS FOLLOWED BY SERIES OF NOTES WITH BIBLIOGRAPHICAL REFERENCES.

2532 ROSENAU J.N.
PUBLIC OPINION AND FOREIGN POLICY; AN OPERATIONAL FORMULA.
NEW YORK: RANDOM HOUSE, INC, 1961, 118 PP., LC#61-15287.
EMPIRICAL INVESTIGATION OF THE CIRCULATION OF FOREIGN POLICY IDEAS IN US AND THE CONTRIBUTION THAT NATIONAL LEADERS MAKE TO THIS PROCESS. PROVIDES A CRITIQUE OF THE STATE OF THE FIELD, DISCUSSING CONFUSION OF CONCEPTS AND LACK OF PRECISE TERMINOLOGY. EXAMINES FLOW OF INFLUENCE VERSUS FLOW OF OPINION, WITH SPECIAL EMPHASIS ON GOVERNMENTAL, INSTITUTIONAL, AND ASSOCIATIONAL OPINION-MAKERS.

2533 ROSENAU J.N. ED.
INTERNATIONAL ASPECTS OF CIVIL STRIFE.
PRINCETON: PRINCETON U PRESS, 1964, 322 PP., LC#64-16727.
COLLECTED ESSAYS RELATE DOMESTIC CONFLICT TO INTERNATIONAL POLITICS, EMPHASIZING INTERVENTION, INTERNATIONAL SETTLEMENT, AND INTERNATIONAL COALITIONS.

2534 ROSENAU J.N. ED.
DOMESTIC SOURCES OF FOREIGN POLICY.
NEW YORK: MACMILLAN, 1967, 352 PP.
MULTIDISCIPLINARY APPROACH TO STUDY OF INFLUENCE OF DOMESTIC FACTORS IN THE FORMULATION AND CONDUCT OF FOREIGN POLICY. EXCERPTS FROM SEVERAL DISCIPLINES - POLITICAL SCIENCE, SOCIOLOGY, AND PSYCHOLOGY - DISCUSS SUCH TOPICS AS VOTING AND FOREIGN POLICY, MASS COMMUNICATIONS AND FOREIGN POLICY AND THE SIGNIFICANCE OF VARIOUS INTEREST GROUPS.

2535 ROSENBERG A.
DEMOCRACY AND SOCIALISM.
BOSTON: BEACON, 1965, 364 PP., $2.45.
DEFINES AND EXPLORES DEMOCRACY BEFORE 1845, FOCUSING ON OUTSTANDING FIGURES AND MOVEMENTS. STUDIES CONTRIBUTIONS OF MARX AND ENGELS TO POLITICAL MOVEMENT, ANALYZES DEFEAT OF DEMOCRACY IN FRANCE, 1848, AND SUBSEQUENT GROWTH OF SOCIALIST MOVEMENT.

2536 ROSENHAUPT H.W.
HOW TO WAGE PEACE.
NEW YORK: DAY, 1949, 249 PP.
ASSESSES THE NECESSITY OF CREATIVE COMMON ACTION IN ORDER TO ACHIEVE POSITIVE RESULTS. ANALYZES INTRANATIONAL GROUPS INTERESTED IN PROBLEM OF MAINTAINING PEACE. DISCUSSES RELEVANT POLITICAL MOVEMENTS WITHIN THE CONGRESS. EXPLORES CERTAIN RESEARCH INSTITUTES.

2537 ROSENNE S.
THE INTERNATIONAL COURT OF JUSTICE.
LEIDEN: SIJTHOFF, 1957, 592 PP.
ANALYSIS OF POSITION OF THIS BODY WITHIN THE UNITED NATIONS SYSTEM. FOCUSES ON THE INTERPLAY OF ITS POLITICAL AND LEGAL FACTORS AND INCLUDES A COMPREHENSIVE REVIEW, WITH FREQUENT EVALUATIONS, OF THE ORGANIZATION, PRACTICE AND PROCEDURE OF THE COURT.

2538 ROSENNE S.
THE WORLD COURT: WHAT IT IS AND HOW IT WORKS.
DOBBS FERRY: OCEANA, 1962, 230 PP.
TRACES HISTORY OF WORLD COURT AND DISCUSSES THE EXTENT OF ITS JURISDICTION, ITS PROCESSES AND APPROXIMATELY THREE DOZEN MAJOR CASES WHICH HAVE BEEN DECIDED BY THIS BODY.

2539 ROSNER G.
THE UNITED NATIONS EMERGENCY FORCE.
NEW YORK: COLUMB. U. PR., 1963, 292 PP.
COMPREHENSIVE ACCOUNT OF CREATION, ORGANIZATION, FUNCTIONS, STATUS AND OPERATION OF THE UNITED NATIONS EMERGENCY FORCE, ANALYZING IT FROM BOTH ITS PRACTICAL AND LEGAL ASPECTS. SEES FORCE AS SYMBOL OF GROWING COMMUNITY INTEREST IN PEACEFUL AND SETTLED WORLD.

2540 ROSS A.
CONSTITUTION OF THE UNITED NATIONS.
NEW YORK: RINEHART, 1950, 236 PP.
EXAMINES ORIGIN, GROWTH, ORGANIZATIONAL STRUCTURE, AND AIMS OF UN. DISCUSSES PRINCIPLES OF PROCEDURE AND SCOPE OF POWERS IN MAINTENANCE OF INTERNATIONAL PEACE.

2541 ROSS H. ED.
THE COLD WAR: CONTAINMENT AND ITS CRITICSS.
SKOKIE: RAND MCNALLY & CO, 1963, 53 PP., LC#63-8257.
SCHOLARS' PROS AND CONS ON US POLICIES OF: CONTAINMENT, BEGINNING WITH TRUMAN DOCTRINE. LIBERATION POLICIES OF DULLES AND EISENHOWER; MASSIVE RETALIATION, DEMOCRATS VS. REPUBLICANS; AND DISENGAGEMENT. INCLUDES QUESTIONS ON EACH POLICY.

2542 ROSSI M.
THE THIRD WORLD.
NEW YORK: FUNK AND WAGNALLS, 1963, 209 PP., LC#63-10474.
DISCUSSES UNALIGNED COUNTRIES IN REVOLUTIONARY WORLD, INCLUDING NATURE OF CHANGES, ANTICOLONIALISM, COEXISTENCE, NEUTRALISM, COLD WAR, RELATIONS BETWEEN THIRD WORLD AND WEST AND COMMUNIST BLOC, UN, AND CLOSING GAP BETWEEN THREE WORLDS.

2543 ROSTOW W.W.
"RUSSIA AND CHINA UNDER COMMUNISM."
WORLD POLIT., 7 (JULY 55), 513-31.
SEEKS TO SET FORTH CERTAIN MAJOR SIMILARITIES AND DIFFERENCES BETWEEN THESE COUNTRIES. EXAMINES (1) ROLE OF INTELLECTUALS (2) LEADERSHIP (3) PROBLEM OF EXTERNAL EXPANSION FOR INTERNATIONAL COMMUNISM. CONCLUDES WITH DIRECTION TOWARD A FOREIGN AMERICAN POLICY.

2544 ROSTOW W.W.
"THE FUTURE OF FOREIGN AID."
FOR. SERV. J., 38 (JUNE 61), 30-35.
DRAWS LESSONS FROM PAST EXPERIENCES IN FOREIGN AID, AND RECOMMENDS SEVERAL FUTURE CHANGES IN THE AMERICAN PROGRAM. SHOWS THE ROLE OF ASSISTANCE IN THE WORLD IDEOLOGICAL STRUGGLE, AND THE PARTS TO BE PLAYED BY PUBLIC AND PRIVATE AUTHORITIES IN UNDERDEVELOPED AREAS.

2545 ROTBERG I.
A POLITICAL HISTORY OF TROPICAL AFRICA.
NEW YORK: HARCOURT BRACE, 1965, 429 PP., LC#65-21072.
COMPREHENSIVE DEVELOPMENT OF GOVERNMENT IN SOUTHERN AFRICA. EARLY EMPIRES, INTERNATIONAL SLAVE TRADE, COLONIALISM, WESTERN INFLUENCES, AND INDEPENDENCE EXAMINED.

2546 ROTBERG I.
"COLONIALISM AND AFTER: THE POLITICAL LITERATURE OF CENTRAL AFRICA - A BIBLIOGRAPHIC ESSAY."
AFRICAN FORUM, 2 (WINTER 67), 66-73.
SELECTIVE SURVEY OF ABOUT 80 BOOKS AND ARTICLES IN ENGLISH ON VARIOUS ASPECTS OF POLITICS IN ZAMBIA, MALAWI, AND RHODESIA. EXCLUDES GOVERNMENT DOCUMENTS.

2547 ROTHCHILD D.
"EAST AFRICAN FEDERATION."
TRANSACTIONS, 3 (JAN. 64), 39-42.
REPORTS ON NAIROBI CONFERENCE WHICH DISCUSSED FEDERATION OF KENYA, UGANDA, AND TANGANYIKA, CONCENTRATING ON ECONOMIC ADVANTAGES OF UNITY.

2548 ROTHFELS H.
"THE GERMAN RESISTANCE IN ITS INTERNATIONAL ASPECTS" (BMR)"
INTERNATIONAL AFFAIRS (U.K.) 34 (OCT. 58), 477-489.
CONTENDS THAT SINCE HITLER WAS A DOMESTIC RATHER THAN A FOREIGN OPPRESSOR, GERMAN OPPOSITION TO HIM DID NOT DEPEND ON NATIONAL OR CLASS LOYALTIES. THUS THE GERMAN RESISTANCE HAD A MORE UNIVERSAL AND INTERNATIONAL ETHICAL BASIS THAN ANY OTHER RESISTANCE. EXAMINES POTENTIAL FOR CONSTRUCTIVE POLICY BY RESISTANCE.

2549 ROUGEMONT D.
"LES NOUVELLES CHANCES DE L'EUROPE."
TABLE RONDE, 18 (FEB. 63), 149-61.
EXAMINES THREE SIGNIFICANT FACTORS SHAPING SITUATION OF MODERN EUROPE: 1)EFFORTS FOR UNIFICATION OF EUROPEAN COMMUNITY 2)POLITICAL WITHDRAWAL OF EUROPE FROM FORMER COLONIES, COINCIDENT WITH ADOPTION BY THIRD WORLD OF EUROPEAN CIVILIZATION, AND 3)UNREGULARIZED SPREAD OF EUROPEAN ADMINISTRATIVE TECHNIQUES.

2550 ROUSSEAU J.J.
A LASTING PEACE.
ORIGINAL PUBLISHER NOT AVAILABLE, 1819, 128 PP.
CRITICIZES SAINT-PIERRE'S PLAN FOR EUROPEAN PEACE-KEEPING FEDERATION. SAINT-PIERRE'S ASSUMPTION THAT PRINCES WILL RECOGNIZE ADVANTAGES OF HIS PLAN IS DISPUTED BY ROUSSEAU, WHO ARGUES THAT RULERS DO NOT RECONGNIZE THEIR OWN SELF-INTEREST. OF WAR GENERALLY, ROUSSEAU SAYS ONLY SELF-DEFENSE CAN JUSTIFY SUCH OUTRAGEOUS ACTION.

2551 ROWAN C.T.
"NEW FRONTIERS IN RACE RELATIONS."
COLORADO QUARTERLY, 16 (FALL 67), 127-140.
DISCUSSES CORROSIVE FORCE OF RACIALISM IN FOREIGN AFFAIRS, AMERICAN EDUCATION AND URBAN ADMINISTRATION. MAINTAINS THAT CENTRAL PROBLEM IS LACK OF COMMUNICATION AMONG GROUPS THAT COULD ACT TOGETHER TO REDUCE RACIALISM, SUCH AS FEDERAL GOVERNMENT, SOCIAL ORGANIZATIONS, SCHOOLS, AND WELFARE GROUPS.

2552 ROWAN R.W.
"THE STORY OF THE SECRET SERVICE."
GARDEN CITY: DOUBLEDAY, 1937.
HISTORY OF SPYS AND ESPIONAGE THROUGH 33 CENTURIES. NOTES CONTAIN SOME REFERENCES TO BIBLIOGRAPHICAL MATERIAL,

BOTH ORIGINAL SOURCES AND OTHER HISTORIES. GREATER PORTION OF WORK DEVOTED TO ANECDOTAL ACCOUNTS OF SPYS AND SPY RINGS.

2553 ROWE C.
VOLTAIRE AND THE STATE.
NEW YORK: COLUMBIA U PRESS, 1955, 254 PP., LC#55-09097.
DISCUSSES VOLTAIRE'S THEORY OF NATION AND OF INTERNATIONAL RELATIONS, EXAMINING HIS PERSONAL PATRIOTISM AND VALUE HE ASSIGNED LOVE OF COUNTRY.

2554 ROY P.A.
SOUTH WIND RED.
CHICAGO: HENRY REGNERY CO, 1962, 242 PP., LC#62-17968.
STUDY OF LATIN AMERICAN SOCIETIES BASED UPON INTERVIEWS WITH LATIN AMERICAN LEADERS AT VARIOUS LEVELS, IN VARIOUS ORGANIZATIONS, OF VARIOUS PERSUASIONS, ASKING WHETHER A PARTICULAR SOCIETY HAS SUFFICIENT STRENGTH AND JUSTICE TO WITHSTAND COMMUNISM, AND, IF NOT, WHAT US SHOULD DO ABOUT IT. INVESTIGATES ECONOMIC, IDEOLOGICAL, EDUCATIONAL, POPULATIONAL FACTORS. STRESSES ENLIGHTENED PRIVATE ENTERPRISE.

2555 ROYAL GEOGRAPHICAL SOCIETY
BIBLIOGRAPHY OF BARBARY STATES (4 SUPPLEMENTARY PAPERS)
LONDON: SWEET AND MAXWELL, LTD, 1893, LC#10-17941.
FOUR-VOLUME BIBLIOGRAPHY ON TRIPOLI AND CYRENAICA, TUNISIA FROM EARLIEST TIMES TO 1889, ALGERIA FROM EXPEDITIONS OF CHARLES V IN 1541 TO 1887, AND MOROCCO FROM EARLIEST TIMES TO 1891.

2556 ROYAL INSTITUTE INTL AFFAIRS
THE COLONIAL PROBLEM.
LONDON: OXFORD U. PR., 1937, 448 PP.
SEVERAL PAPERS COVERING THE INTERNATIONAL ASPECT OF THE COLONIAL QUESTION, THE DIFFERENT FORMS OF COLONIAL ADMINISTRATION AND SUCH SPECIAL PROBLEMS AS COLONIAL INVESTMENT, TRADE, FINANCE AND SETTLEMENT.

2557 ROYAL INSTITUTE INTL AFFAIRS
SURVEY OF INTERNATIONAL AFFAIRS.
LONDON: OXFORD U PR, 1967.
ANNUAL SURVEY OF INTERNATIONAL POLITICAL AND ECONOMIC AFFAIRS FIRST ISSUED IN 1937. RECENT ISSUES ARE ORGANIZED TOPICALLY RATHER THAN CHRONOLOGICALLY AND CONTAIN A COMPREHENSIVE SUBJECT-PERSON INDEX. ARTICLES ARE HEAVILY DOCUMENTED AND WRITTEN BY INDIVIDUAL MEMBERS OF THE ROYAL INSTITUTE OF INTERNATIONAL AFFAIRS.

2558 RUBIN A.P.
"UNITED STATES CONTEMPORARY PRACTICE RELATING TO INTERNATIONAL LAW."
AMER. J. INT. LAW, 59 (JAN. 65), 103-30.
LISTS AND BRIEFLY EXAMINES RECENT USA COURT DECISIONS IN LIGHT OF IMPACT ON INTERNATIONAL LAW - BOUNDARY CLAIMS, DIPLOMACY AND EXTRADITION. ALSO PUBLISHES EXECUTIVE DEPARTMENT VIEWS ON SUBJECTS RELATING TO INTERNATIONAL LAW.

2559 RUBIN J.A.
YOUR HUNDRED BILLION DOLLARS.
NEW YORK: CHILTON BOOKS, 1964, 299 PP., LC#64-16528.
EXPLORES US FOREIGN AID: NATURE, AMOUNT, PURPOSE, ADMINISTRATION, DISTRIBUTION, AND EFFECT. REPORTS CHANGES 1948-64 IN RELATIVE AND ABSOLUTE SIZES OF MILITARY AND ECONOMIC AID, USE OF PEACE CORPS AND ALLIANCE FOR PROGRESS. EXAMINES RUSSIA'S ENTRY INTO FOREIGN AID AND HER COMPARATIVE SUCCESS.

2560 RUBIN R.
"THE UN CORRESPONDENT."
WEST. POLIT. QUART., 17 (DEC. 64), 615-31.
SEEKING TO DEMONSTRATE THE IMPORTANCE OF CORRESPONDENTS TO THE POLITICAL PROCESS OF THE UN, EXPLORES HOW UN CORRESPONDENTS GATHER NEWS: THEIR SOURCES OF INFORMATION, THE TECHNIQUES OF THEIR PROFESSION, AND THE IMPACT OF THEIR PRESENCE ON UN DIPLOMACY. THE ROLE OF THE CORRESPONDENT AS AN INSTRUMENT FOR PUBLIC UNDERSTANDING OF THE ACTIVITIES OF THE UN IS ALSO EXAMINED.

2561 RUBINSTEIN A.Z., THUMM G.W.
THE CHALLENGE OF POLITICS: IDEAS AND ISSUES.
ENGLEWOOD CLIFFS: PRENTICE HALL, 1965, 475 PP., LC#65-12155.
READINGS ON GREAT ISSUES OF POLITIAL BEHAVIOR, ORGANIZATION, AND PROCESSES. SELECTIONS ON ECONOMIC ROLE OF GOVERNMENT, SOURCES OF AUTHORITY, CONCEPTS OF FREEDOM, INTERNATIONAL STRUGGLE FOR POWER, AND ORGANIZATION OF PEACE AND SECURITY.

2562 RUBINSTEIN A.Z.
"RUSSIA AND THE UNCOMMITTED NATIONS."
CURR. HIST., 43 (OCT. 62), 218-223.
CREDITS THE POST-STALINIST RISE IN SOVIET PRESTIGE AND INFLUENCE AMONG UNCOMMITTED NATIONS TO WESTERN DIPLOMATIC INEPTNESS IN DEALING WITH NEUTRALISM AND SHREWD SOVIET SUPPORT AT TIMELY MOMENTS. USA MUST THRUST ITSELF INTO AFFAIRS WHICH SEEM FAR REMOVED FROM DEMANDS OF NATIONAL SECURITY. AS USSR SEEKS TO TRANSLATE GOOD-WILL INTO POLITICAL INFLUENCE, COMMUNISM WILL ENCOUNTER OPPOSITION.

2563 RUBINSTEIN A.Z.
THE SOVIETS IN INTERNATIONAL ORGANIZATIONS: CHANGING POLICY TOWARD DEVELOPING COUNTRIES, 1953-1963.
PRINCETON: U. PR., 1964, 380 PP., $7.50.
A DETAILED CASE STUDY DEALING WITH CHANGING POST-STALINIST POLICIES AND BEHAVIOR IN THE SPECIALIZED AGENCIES AND REGIONAL ECONOMIC COMMISSIONS OF THE U.N. BASED ON MATERIAL GATHERED NOT ONLY FROM THE RECORDS AND DOCUMENTS OF THE INTERNATIONAL ORGANIZATIONS BUT FROM SOVIET WRITINGS ON THESE ORGANIZATIONS.

2564 RUBINSTEIN A.Z.
"THE SOVIET IMAGE OF WESTERN EUROPE."
CURR. HIST., 47 (NOV. 64), 280-285.
GREATER DEGREE OF REALISM IN SOVIET ATTITUDES TOWARD THE WEST THAT HAS DISPELLED SOME MYTHS AND ILLUSIONS. HOWEVER, CONTINUITY OF SOVIET POLICY OBJECTIVES INDICATED WITH REFERENCE TO: OPPOSITION TO NATO, USA BASES IN EUROPE, RE-MILITARIZATION OF WEST GERMANY AND ANY/ALL MOVES TO ADVANCE WESTERN EUROPEAN UNITY.

2565 RUBINSTEIN A.Z. ED., THUMM G.W. ED.
THE CHALLENGE OF POLITICS: IDEAS AND ISSUES (2ND ED.)
ENGLEWOOD CLIFFS: PRENTICE HALL, 1965, 475 PP., LC#65-12155.
COLLECTION OF WRITINGS ON POLITICS DEALING WITH RELATION OF MAN TO SOCIETY, POLITICAL EQUALITY, GOVERNMENTAL POWER, FREEDOM VERSUS AUTHORITY, GOVERNMENTAL STRUCTURE, AND RELATIONS AMONG STATES.

2566 RUDIN H.R.
ARMISTICE 1918.
NEW HAVEN: YALE U PR, 1944, 442 PP.
STORY OF THE ARMISTICE SIGNED BY THE ENTENTE POWERS AND GERMANY. SEEKS TO TELL WHY THE GERMANS WANTED AN ARMISTICE, HOW THE ALLIES DRAFTED THE TREATY, AND HOW THE TWO DELEGATIONS CAME TO FINAL AGREEMENT. AUTHOR BELIEVES THAT THE APPOINTMENT OF THE ARMISTICE COMMISSION WAS A CIVILIAN AFFAIR; THAT THE GERMANS IN POWER IN 1918 SINCERELY DESIRED PEACE; AND THAT WILSON'S PROGRAM SPEEDED THE END OF THE WAR.

2567 RUEFF J.
BALANCE OF PAYMENTS.
NEW YORK: MACMILLAN, 1967, 256 PP.
PRESENTATION OF VARIOUS PROPOSALS FOR SOLVING BALANCE-OF-PAYMENTS DILEMMA AS IT AFFECTS INTERNATIONAL FINANCE AND COMMERCE AND THE STANDARD OF LIVING IN EVERY CURRENCY AREA. DISCUSSION INCLUDES US BALANCE-OF-PAYMENTS DEFICITS IN THE 1960'S, THEORY OF TRANSFERS WITH KEYNES' VIEWS, ELEMENTS FOR A DISCOUNT THEORY, ETC. THROUGHOUT TEXT AUTHOR TAKES INTO ACCOUNT POLITICAL FACTORS AS WELL AS ECONOMIC.

2568 RUMEU DE ARMAS A. ED.
ESPANA EEN EL AFRICA ATLANTICA.
MADRID: INST ESTUD AFRICANOS, 1957.
DOCUMENTS CHRONICLING SPANISH EXPERIENCE IN WEST AFRICA FROM 1344 TO 1549, INCLUDING LETTERS, ROYAL DECREES, INTERNATIONAL AGREEMENTS, AND SECRET INSTRUCTIONS.

2569 RUSK D.
THE WINDS OF FREEDOM.
BOSTON: BEACON PRESS, 1963, 363 PP., LC#63-10139.
SELECTIONS FROM SPEECHES AND STATEMENTS OF SECRETARY OF STATE DEAN RUSK BETWEEN JANUARY, 1961 AND AUGUST, 1962. COVERS WIDE RANGE OF SUBJECTS, INCLUDING MAKING OF FOREIGN POLICY, TRADE, FOREIGN AID, ALLIANCE FOR PROGRESS, SOUTHEAST ASIA, DISARMAMENT, UN, ETC.

2570 RUSK D.
"THE MAKING OF FOREIGN POLICY"
DEPT OF STATE BULLETIN, 50 (FEB. 64), 164-176.
TRANSCRIPT OF TELEVISION INTERVIEW BETWEEN DEAN RUSK AND ERIC GOLDMAN. DISCUSSES DECISION-MAKING PROCESS, RELATION OF DOMESTIC POLITICS TO FOREIGN POLICY, AND METHODS OF IMPROVING ADMINISTRATION PROCEDURES. EXPLORES STAFFING PROBLEMS, EXTENT OF AUTHORITY OF DEPARTMENT OF STATE, AND RELATION OF FOREIGN POLICY TO PUBLIC OPINION.

2571 RUSSEL F.M.
THEORIES OF INTERNATIONAL RELATIONS.
LONDON: APPLETON, 1936, 651 PP.
SURVEY OF DEVELOPMENT OF IDEAS OF MAN WITH REGARD TO RELATIONSHIP BETWEEN INDEPENDENT POLITICAL COMMUNITIES. IT IS DESIGNED TO DO FOR THE FIELD OF INTERNATIONAL RELATIONS WHAT HISTORICAL SURVEYS OF POLITICAL THEORY HAVE DONE FOR THE ENTIRE FIELD OF POLITICAL THOUGHT.

2572 RUSSEL R.W.
"ROLES FOR PSYCHOLOGISTS IN THE MAINTENANCE OF PEACE."
AMER. PSYCHOL., 15 (1960), 95-109.
CONSIDERATION OF APPROPRIATE PROGRAM ARISES FROM CONCERN WITH GROWING COMPLEXITY OF CONTEMPORARY AFFAIRS (COLD WAR).

2573 RUSSELL B.
UNARMED VICTORY.
NEW YORK: SIMON AND SCHUSTER, 1963, 155 PP., LC#63-16994.
PERSONAL ANALYSIS OF CUBAN CRISIS AND SINO-INDIAN CON-

FLICT. INCLUDES CORRESPONDENCE WITH KENNEDY, U THANT, AND NEHRU THAT ILLUSTRATES HIS BELIEF IN PEACE BY COMPROMISE.

2574 RUSSELL B.
WAR CRIMES IN VIETNAM.
LONDON: ALLEN & UNWIN, 1967, 178 PP., LC#67-23969.
BERTRAND RUSSELL APPEALS TO AMERICAN CONSCIENCE TO STOP WAR CRIMES IN VIETNAM. TELLS OF NAPALM, "LAZY BOMBS," CHEMICALS THAT NOT ONLY DEFOLIATE BUT POISON AND KILL, AND OF CONCENTRATION CAMPS POLITELY CALLED "RELOCATION CENTERS." FEELS RACISM IN US HAS CREATED CLIMATE IN WHICH IT IS DIFFICULT FOR AMERICANS TO UNDERSTAND WAR.

2575 RUSSELL R.B., MUTHER J.E.
A HISTORY OF THE UNITED NATIONS CHARTER: THE ROLE OF THE UNITED STATES.
WASHINGTON: BROOKINGS INSTIT., 1958, 1140 PP.
OUTLINES FOUNDATION AND DEVELOPMENT OF UN CHARTER DURING PERIOD OF WW 2 WITHIN FRAMEWORK OF U.S. POLICY. POINTS OUT PRINCIPLE IDEAS AND PROPOSALS INITIATED BY U.S. GOVERNMENT WHILE ESTABLISHING ITS SPECIFIC PROVISIONS FOR THE CHARTER.

2576 RUSSELL R.B.
UNITED NATIONS EXPERIENCE WITH MILITARY FORCES: POLITICAL AND LEGAL ASPECTS.
WASHINGTON: BROOKINGS INST, 1964, 174 PP.
ANALYSIS OF UN'S INTERNATIONAL POLICE FORCE AND PEACE-KEEPING MISSIONS. INCLUDES UNEF, UNOGIL, ONUC, AND UNSF, WITH DISCUSSION OF AVAILABILITY OF FORCES, CHARTER PROVISIONS CONCERNING ENFORCEMENT AND SANCTION, AND THE NATURE OF AN INTERNATIONAL FORCE.

2577 RUSSETT B.M.
WORLD HANDBOOK OF POLITICAL AND SOCIAL INDICATORS.
NEW HAVEN: YALE U PR, 1964, 373 PP., LC#64-20933.
PRESENTS DATA SIGNIFICANT TO THE DEVELOPMENT OF THE SCIENCE OF COMPARATIVE AND INTERNATIONAL POLITICS; ILLUSTRATES A VARIETY OF MEANS FOR ANALYZING THIS DATA. COMPARES NATIONS ON VARIOUS POLITICALLY RELEVANT INDEXES AND EXAMINES INTER-RELATIONSHIPS OF DIFFERENT POLITICAL, ECONOMIC, SOCIAL, AND CULTURAL DEVELOPMENTS. DATA SERIES SELECTED ACCORDING TO THE CRITERIA OF ACCURACY AND AVAILABILITY.

2578 RUSSETT B.M.
"CAUSE, SURPRISE, AND NO ESCAPE."
J. POLIT., 24 (FEB. 62), 3-22.
ANALYZES THE CAUSES OF WAR THROUGH CASE STUDY OF WORLD WAR ONE, WHICH WAS MORE ACCIDENTAL THAN RESULT OF DELIBERATE AGGRESSORS' PLOT. EXAMINING VARIOUS CAUSES SUCH AS REMOTE CAUSE, MEDIATE CAUSE, SURPRISE, KEY EVENT, DIRECT CAUSE, AND INEVITABLITY, AUTHOR EMPHASIZES THAT MAJOR POWERS SHOULD TRY HARDER FOR UNDERSTANDING OTHER NATIONS IN ORDER TO PREVENT ACCIDENTAL WAR.

2579 RUSSETT B.M.
"TOWARD A MODEL OF COMPETITIVE INTERNATIONAL POLITICS."
J. POLIT., 25 (MAY 63), 226-247.
GENERAL COMPARISON BETWEEN THE TWO-BLOC POLITICS OF THE UNITED NATIONS SYSTEM AND THE TWO-PARTY NATIONAL GOVERNMENT, PRESENTING VARIOUS HYPOTHESES AS TO FORCES UNDERLYING USA POLITICS BELIEVED USEFUL IN STUDYING WORLD POLITICS.

2580 SAAB H.
"THE ARAB SEARCH FOR A FEDERAL UNION."
WORLD JUSTICE, 6 (DEC. 64), 147-71.
PRESENTS HISTORICAL ANALYSIS OF ARABIC QUEST FOR A PAN-ARAB FEDERATION, TRACING THE VARIOUS ATTEMPTS AND FAILURES DURING PAST QUARTER CENTURY. CITES CHANGING GOALS FROM INDEPENDECE TO INTER-DEPENDENCE. PRESENTS THE VARIOUS IDEOLOGIES OF ARAB SOCIALISM AND BAATHIST PARTY, AND POINTS OUT THE REVOLUTIONARY NATURE OF ARAB NATIONALISM. FEELS NEED TO LOOK TOWARDS A LOOSER ORGANIZATION OF A CONFEDERAL NATURE.

2581 SABIN J.
BIBLIOTHECA AMERICANA: A DICTIONARY OF BOOKS RELATING TO AMERICA, FROM ITS DISCOVERY TO THE PRESENT TIME(29 VOLS.)
NEW YORK: BIB SOCIETY OF AMER, 1867.
A BIBLIOGRAPHY OF PUBLICATIONS PUBLISHED IN AND ABOUT AMERICA. ARRANGED BY AUTHOR AND GIVES LOCATIONS OF LIBRARIES CONTAINING ENTRIES. BOOKS IN ENGLISH, SPANISH, DUTCH, FRENCH, AND PORTUGUESE.

2582 SABLE M.H.
MASTER DIRECTORY FOR LATIN AMERICA.
LOS ANGELES: U CAL LAT AMER STUD, 1965, 438 PP.
CONTAINS TEN DICTIONARIES WITH NAMES AND ADDRESSES OF ORGANIZATIONS, ETC., CONNECTED WITH LATIN AMERICA BOTH IN THE REGION AND THE US. INCLUDES GOVERNMENTAL ESTABLISHMENTS AND POLITICAL PARTIES AS WELL AS OTHERS CONCERNED WITH AGRICULTURE, BUSINESS FINANCE, COMMUNICATIONS, EDUCATION AND RESEARCH, LABOR COOPERATIVES, RELIGION, AND INTERNATIONAL COOPERATION.

2583 SABLE M.H.
PERIODICALS FOR LATIN AMERICAN ECONOMIC DEVELOPMENT, TRADE, AND FINANCE: AN ANNOTATED BIBLIOGRAPHY (A PAMPHLET)
LOS ANGELES: U CAL LAT AM CTR, 1965, 72 PP.
LIST OF ENGLISH AND FOREIGN LANGUAGE PERIODICALS DEALING WITH FIELDS OF ECONOMICS AS RELATED TO LATIN AMERICA IN GENERAL AND INDIVIDUAL LATIN AMERICAN NATIONS. INCLUDES TITLE, SUBJECT, AND GEOGRAPHIC INDEXES. CONTAINS 220 PERIODICALS ANNOTATED.

2584 SABLE M.H.
A GUIDE TO LATIN AMERICAN STUDIES (2 VOLS)
LOS ANGELES: U CAL LAT AM CTR, 1967, 783 PP., LC#67-63021.
AN ANNOTATED BIBLIOGRAPHY OF 5,000 BOOKS, MONOGRAPHS, PERIODICALS, PAMPHLETS, AND GOVERNMENT DOCUMENTS ON LATIN AMERICAN CIVILIZATION. PUBLICATIONS ENGLISH AND SPANISH PRIMARILY, BUT INCLUDES SOME FRENCH, GERMAN, AND PORTUGUESE SOURCES. LARGE SECTION ON POLITICAL SCIENCE AND MANY ENTRIES ON RELATED FIELDS. INDEXED BY SUBJECT AND COUNTRY.

2585 SACHS M.Y.
THE WORLDMARK ENCYCLOPEDIA OF THE NATIONS (5 VOLS.)
NEW YORK: WORLDMARK PR., 1967
A COMPENDIUM OF BASIC FACTUAL DATA ON THE NATIONS AND INTERNATIONAL ORGANIZATIONS IN THE MODERN WORLD. THE STATISTICS INCLUDE GEOGRAPHIC, HISTORIC, POLITICAL, SOCIAL, AND ECONOMIC FACTORS AFFECTING THE STATE OF THE VARIOUS POLITICAL DIVISIONS OF OUR TIME.

2586 SAGER P.
MOSKAUS HAND IN INDIEN.
BERNE: SWISS EASTERN INST, 1966, 232 PP.
A STUDY OF RUSSIAN PROPAGANDA EFFORTS IN INDIA. CENTRAL THEME IS THE INFLUENCE OF THE SOVIET PRESS IN INDIA. INCLUDES A DETAILED STUDY OF SOVIET PROPAGANDA METHODS, AND A DISCUSSION OF THE ACTIVITIES OF THE COMMUNIST PARTY OF INDIA.

2587 SAINT-PIERRE C.I.
SCHEME FOR LASTING PEACE (TRANS. BY H. BELLOT)
ORIGINAL PUBLISHER NOT AVAILABLE, 1738, 140 PP.
PROPOSES AN OBLIGATORY AND PERMANENT SYSTEM OF INTERNATIONAL ARBITRATION, ACCEPTED BY EACH COUNTRY IN EUROPE AND IMPOSED ON RECALCITRANTS; AN INTERNATIONAL TRIBUNAL, FOR ARBITRATION OF DISPUTES; AND AN INTERNATIONAL ARMED FORCE TO COMPEL ACCEPTANCE OF ITS DECISIONS. CLAIMS THIS WILL ALSO LEAD TO RISE IN COMMERCE AND PRODUCTION BY CONTRIBUTING TO PEACE AND FREE TRADE.

2588 SAKAI R.K.
STUDIES ON ASIA, 1964.
LINCOLN: U OF NEB PR, 1964, 186 PP., LC#60-15432.
ASIAN HISTORY AND POLITICAL FORCES SHAPING CONTEMPORARY ASIA, EMPHASIZING CHINA AND JAPAN. INCLUDES SINO-SOVIET-BRITISH RESPONSES TO INDIAN NATIONALISM; POSTWAR JAPAN-KOREA RELATIONS; AND POLITICAL IDEOLOGY IN MALAYSIA.

2589 SALANT W.S. ET AL.
THE UNITED STATES BALANCE OF PAYMENTS IN 1968.
WASHINGTON: BROOKINGS INST, 1963, 298 PP., LC#63-21038.
REVISED VERSION OF REPORT SUBMITTED TO COUNCIL OF ECONOMIC ADVISERS, INCLUDING FINAL CHARTER ON POLICY RECOMMENDATIONS. CITES US WORLD PAYMENTS, PROBABLE CHANGES IN DEMAND AND OUTPUT, US BALANCE OF PAYMENTS, EEC, PRIVATE FOREIGN INVESTMENT, DEFENSE TRANSACTIONS, AND FOREIGN ECONOMIC ASSISTANCE.

2590 SALETORE B.A.
INDIA'S DIPLOMATIC RELATIONS WITH THE WEST.
BOMBAY: POPULAR BOOK DEPOT, 1958, 430 PP., LC#58-11844.
DISCUSSES ORIGIN OF SCIENCE OF DIPLOMACY AND DIPLOMATIC THEORY IN INDIA FROM EARLIEST TIMES UNTIL 185 B.C. EXAMINES RELATIONS BETWEEN INDIA AND PERSIA; GREECE, AND ROMAN EMPIRE; AND DIPLOMATIC ETIQUETTE AND PRACTICE IN ROMAN EMPIRE.

2591 SALETORE B.A.
INDIA'S DIPLOMATIC RELATIONS WITH THE EAST.
BOMBAY: POPULAR BOOK DEPOT, 1960, 524 PP.
DISCUSSES DIPLOMATIC MISSIONS EXCHANGED BETWEEN INDIA, CHINA, PERSIA, CENTRAL ASIA, TIBET, NEPAL, CEYLON, AND CAMBODIA, WITH EMPHASIS ON RELATIONS BETWEEN INDIA AND CHINA FROM 600 A.D. TO 1300.

2592 SALISBURY H.E.
BEHIND THE LINES - HANOI.
NEW YORK: HARPER & ROW, 1967, 243 PP., LC#67-21219.
EXTENSIVE ANSWERS TO MANY QUESTIONS ABOUT NORTH VIETNAM, ITS PEOPLE, LEADERS, POLICIES. CONSIDERS EFFECTS OF US ACTIONS, POSSIBILITIES FOR PEACE, PHILOSOPHICAL DIFFERENCES.

2593 SALISBURY H.E.
ORBIT OF CHINA.
NEW YORK: HARPER & ROW, 1967, 204 PP., LC#67-11331.
EXAMINATION OF PEOPLES REPUBLIC OF CHINA MADE BY AMERICAN JOURNALIST WITH MAIN EMPHASIS ON SINO-AMERICAN RELATIONS AND SINO-INDIAN POWER STRUGGLE FOR ASIATIC DOMINANCE. IMPACT OF SINO-SOVIET DISPUTE IS ALSO CENTRAL PART OF BOOK.

2594 SALKEVER L.R., FLYNN H.M.
SUB-SAHARA AFRICA (PAMPHLET)
GLENVIEW, ILL: SCOTT, FORESMAN, 1963, 72 PP.
EXAMINES HISTORIC PAST AND NEW PATTERNS OF AFRICAN TRADE, TECHNOLOGY, EDUCATION, AND GOVERNMENT. FOCUSES UPON CURRENT PROBLEMS OF ECONOMIC DEVELOPMENT, PATHWAYS TO ECONOMIC GROWTH, AND INTERNATIONAL RELATIONS.

2595 SALTER L.M.
RESOLUTION OF INTERNATIONAL CONFLICT.
NEW YORK: VINTAGE BOOKS, 1966, 142 PP., LC#66-22335.
STUDY OF US FOREIGN POLICY IN LIGHT OF TENUOUS EAST-WEST RELATIONS. EXAMINES ROOTS OF CONTENTION. DISCUSSES PEACE EFFORTS OF ORGANIZATIONS FROM LOCAL TO INTERNATIONAL LEVEL. QUESTIONS ETHICS AND EFFICIENCY OF US FOREIGN POLICY. DESCRIBES ROLE OF LAWYER IN WORLD PEACE EFFORTS.

2596 SALVADORI M.
"EL CAPITALISMO EN LA EUROPA DE LA POSGUERRA."
REV. INST. CIENC. SOC., (NO.3, 64), 211-30.
ANALYZES DEVELOPMENT OF THEORY AND PRACTICE OF CAPITALISM IN WESTERN EUROPE AFTER WW 2 AND ITS RELATION TO INDIVIDUALISM, RATIONALISM, AND MATERIALISM. DISCUSSES STATE CAPITALISM AND LIBERAL PRIVATE CAPITALISM IN RELATION TO ECONOMIC REBIRTH OF WESTERN EUROPE.

2597 SALVEMINI G.
PRELUDE TO WORLD WAR II.
GARDEN CITY: DOUBLEDAY, 1954, 519 PP., LC#53-13510.
BEGINS WITH ITALY'S RISE TO POWER AND MUSSOLINI'S CONTROL OF POWER. TRACES MUSSOLINI-HITLER RELATIONSHIP. TREATS AT LENGTH ITALO-ETHIOPIAN WAR. SHOWS MUSSOLINI TO BE INCOMPETENT AND NOT THE GREAT STATESMAN MANY HAVE BELIEVED HIM TO BE.

2598 SAND P.T., LYON J.T., PRATT G.N.
"AN HISTORICAL SURVEY OF INTERNATIONAL AIR LAW SINCE 1944."
MCGILL LAW J., 7 (1961), 125-60.
INDICATES THE EXTENT TO WHICH AVIATION IMPINGES UPON MANY BRANCHES OF A STATE'S LEGAL SYSTEM. FIRST SECTION EXAMINES INTERNATIONAL CIVIL AVIATION AND PUBLIC INTERNATIONAL LAW. SECOND SECTION DEALS WITH CONFLICTS OF LAW. INCLUDES ANALYSIS OF ROME CONVENTION 1952 AND HAGUE PROTOCOL 1955.

2599 SANDERS R.E.
SPAIN AND THE UNITED NATIONS 1945-1950.
NEW YORK: VANTAGE, 1966, 114 PP.
STUDIES WARTIME POLICY OF SPAIN WHICH CAUSED HER TO BE CONSIDERED INELIGIBLE FOR MEMBERSHIP IN UN. DISCUSSES UN RESOLUTIONS OSTRACIZING HER, CHANGES IN UN ATTITUDES TOWARD FRANCO THAT RESULTED IN HER "RECOGNITION" IN 1950, AND HER ADMISSION TO UN IN 1955.

2600 SANDERSON G.N.
ENGLAND, EUROPE, AND THE UPPER NILE 1882-1899.
EDINBURGH: EDINBURGH U PR, 1965, 456 PP.
DESCRIBES COMPETITION AMONG EUROPEAN POWERS FOR TERRITORY IN UPPER NILE. ALSO SHOWS INTRICATE WORKINGS OF BLACKS, EITHER FOR OR AGAINST EUROPEAN INTERESTS. PICTURES HOW AREA HAD BECOME PART OF MAINSTREAM OF GREAT POWER DIPLOMACY BY 1894.

2601 SANNWALD R.E., STOHLER J.
ECONOMIC INTEGRATION: THEORETICAL ASSUMPTIONS AND CONSEQUENCES OF EUROPEAN UNIFICATION.
PRINCETON: U. PR., 1959, 260 PP.
DISCUSSES THE COMMON MARKET'S ECONOMIC INTEGRATION. PUTS SPECIAL EMPHASIS ON THE METHOD OF INTEGRATION, CURRENCY SYSTEM, ENONOMIC STABILIZATION POLICY, FISCAL POLICY, AND FACTOR MOBILITY.

2602 SAPIN B.M., SNYDER R.C.
THE ROLE OF THE MILITARY IN AMERICAN FOREIGN POLICY.
GARDEN CITY: DOUBLEDAY, 1954, 84 PP.
EXPLORES INFLUENCE OF MILITARY ON FORMATION OF FOREIGN POLICY, INCLUDING ITS EXPANDED ROLE, ITS ORGANIZATION FOR FOREIGN POLICY-MAKING, ITS PARTICIPATION, AND PROBLEM OF APPROPRIATE ROLE.

2603 SAPIN B.M.
THE MAKING OF UNITED STATES FOREIGN POLICY.
WASHINGTON: BROOKINGS INST, 1966, 415 PP., LC#66-13626.
FOCUSES ON FORMULATION AND ADMINISTRATION OF US FOREIGN POLICY, PARTICULARLY MAJOR POLICY DECISION-MAKING WITHIN EXECUTIVE BRANCH AND IMPORTANT OVERSEAS PROGRAMS. CAREFULLY EXAMINES NATIONAL SECURITY MACHINERY AT PRESIDENTIAL LEVEL, PRESENT ORGANIZATIONAL ARRANGEMENTS, AND THEIR RECENT ANTECEDENTS.

2604 SAPP B.B.
"TRIBAL CULTURES AND COMMUNISM."
MILITARY REV., 47 (JUNE 67), 64-71.
DRAWS PARALLELS BETWEEN THE THEORY OF COMMUNISM AND THE PRIMITIVE TRIBAL COMMUNALISM OF 90 PER CENT OF AFRICANS, BUT ALSO NOTES THEIR RESISTANCE TO CHANGE AND CASTE SYSTEM. INDICATES THAT MANY EMERGING NATIONS FEEL THE NEED FOR AUTHORITARIAN STATE. CONCLUDES THAT DANGER OF COMMUNIST TAKEOVER OF MANY AFRICAN STATES IS GREAT. REITERATES STATE DEPARTMENT POLICY AND NEED FOR MUTUAL UNDERSTANDING.

2605 SARBADHIKARI P.
"A NOTE ON THE DOMESTIC CRISIS OF NON-ALIGNMENT."
COEXISTENCE, 4 (JAN. 67), 37-38.
DOMESTIC PROBLEMS THREATEN THE GOVERNMENTS OF MANY SELF-PROCLAIMED NONALIGNED STATES, AND THEREBY THREATEN THE BALANCE OF CO-EXISTENCE. THE PROBLEMS ARE THE LACK OF ADEQUATE ECONOMIC PROGRESS, THE GAP BETWEEN EXTERNAL DECLARATIONS OF NONALIGNMENT AND INDEPENDENCE AND INTERNAL POLITICAL MILITARY OLIGARCHIES, AND THE IDEOLOGICALLY MORE POLARIZED POSITION AGAINST DOMESTIC OPPOSITION IN MANY STATES.

2606 SARROS P.P.
CONGRESS AND THE NEW DIPLOMACY: THE FORMULATION OF MUTUAL SECURITY POLICY: 1953-60 (THESIS)
PRINCETON: PRIN U, DEPT OF POL, 1964, 425 PP.
EVALUATES ROLE OF CONGRESS IN FORMULATION OF MUTUAL SECURITY POLICY 1953-60 AND ANALYZES EFFECTS OF PARTY AFFILIATION, REGIONALISM, AND COMMITTEE WORK ON ACTIONS, USING TABULATIONS BASED ON VOTING RECORDS OF CONGRESSMEN.

2607 SATOW E.
A GUIDE TO DIPLOMATIC PRACTICE.
LONDON: LONGMANS, 1917, 407 PP.
DEALING WITH THE PRAGMATIC AND LEGAL ASPECTS OF DIPLOMACY, TREATISE IS OF VALUE TO STUDENTS OF INTERNATIONAL RELATIONS AS WELL AS LAWYERS.

2608 SAVORD R.
AMERICAN AGENCIES INTERESTED IN INTERNATIONAL AFFAIRS.
NEW YORK: COUNCIL FOR. REL., 1942, 200 PP.
INCLUDES PERTINENT DATA ON ORGANIZATIONS ENGAGED IN RESEARCH AND OTHER ACTIVITIES. LISTS BOTH OFFICERS AND STAFF MEMBERS AND CLASSIFIES THEM ACCORDING TO PRIMARY AND SECONDARY INTERESTS.

2609 SAYEED K.B.
THE POLITICAL SYSTEM OF PAKISTAN.
BOSTON: HOUGHTON MIFFLIN, 1967, 321 PP.
DELINEATES ORIGINS AND GROWTH OF MOVEMENT WHICH CULMITED IN CREATION OF PAKISTAN. EXPLAINS POLITICAL PROCESS THAT OPERATED UNDER THE BRITISH WITH CONGRESS AND MUSLIM LEAGUE AS THE TWO CONTESTANTS FOR POLITICAL POWER. OUTLINES IN DETAIL EXISTING POLITICAL SYSTEM, EMPHASIZING CAPABILITIES OF GOVERNMENT IN COPING WITH POLITICAL AND SOCIAL CHANGE.

2610 SAYEGH F.
"ARAB NATIONALISM AND SOVIET-AMERICAN RELATIONS."
A. AMER. POLIT. SOC. SCI., 324 (JULY 59), 103-110.
INDICTS WESTERN NATIONS OF SHOWING LACK OF AWARENESS AND RESPECT FOR ARAB NATIONALISM. SHOWS RESULTING ARAB REACTION IN TERMS OF POLICY TRENDS IN COLD WAR CONFLICT. POLICY SHIFT FROM UNCONCERN AND INDIFFERENCE TO ACTIVE AND POSITIVE NEUTRALITY IS CONSEQUENTIAL. CONSIDERS FAVORABLE CHANGE COULD BE BROUGHT ABOUT IF WEST TAKES INITIATIVE TO CORRECT SITUATION AND MOBILIZE ARAB NATIONALISM AGAINST COMMUNIST ADVANCE IN ARAB WORLD.

2611 SCAMMEL W.M.
INTERNATIONAL MONETARY POLICY.
NEW YORK: MACMILLAN, 1961, 417 PP.
SURVEY ON POLICY SINCE 1915 FOCUSES ON EXPERIMENTS IN INTERNATIONAL MONETARY COOPERATION OF LAST 20 YEARS. ONE SUCH EXPERIMENT DISCUSSED IS UN MONETARY AND FINANCE CONFERENCE AT BRETTON WOODS THAT PLANNED ADJUSTMENTS OF DEFICITS AND SURPLUSES IN BALANCE OF PAYMENTS.

2612 SCANLON D.G. ED.
INTERNATIONAL EDUCATION: A DOCUMENTARY HISTORY.
NY: COLUMBIA U TEACHERS COLLEGE, 1960, 196 PP., LC#60-14305.
HISTORY OF DEVELOPMENTS IN FIELD AND STUDY OF INTERNATIONAL EDUCATION. COLLECTION OF ESSAYS INCLUDES BIOGRAPHIES OF PIONEERS IN FIELD, STUDIES OF INTERNATIONAL ORGANIZATION, CROSS-CULTURAL EXCHANGES, EDUCATIONAL PRACTICES, AND INTERNATIONAL COMMUNICATION.

2613 SCANLON H.L.
INTERNATIONAL LAW: A SELECTIVE LIST OF WORKS IN ENGLISH ON PUBLIC INTERNATIONAL LAW (A PAMPHLET)
WASHINGTON: CARNEGIE ENDOWMENT, 1946, 20 PP.
INCLUDES BOOKS AND TREATISES PRIMARILY, SEPARATED INTO GENERAL TREATISES AND COLLECTIONS, AND PARTICULAR TREATMENTS WITH SOME REFERENCE TO CASES AT THE END. PUBLICATIONS OVER BROAD TIME SPAN, MOSTLY 20TH CENTURY; 250 TITLES. THIS LIST IS REVISION OF 1936 WORK. ARRANGED BY AUTHOR WITHIN DIVISIONS, BRIEF ANNOTATIONS. INCLUDES JOURNAL INDEX.

2614 SCHAAF R.W.
DOCUMENTS OF INTERNATIONAL MEETINGS.
WASHINGTON: LIBRARY OF CONGRESS, 1953, 210 PP., LC#59-60030.
ANNOTATED BIBLIOGRAPHY OF DOCUMENTS EMANATING FROM MEETINGS OF INTERNATIONAL NONGOVERNMENTAL ORGANIZATIONS DURING

1953. DOCUMENTS INCLUDE OFFICIAL REORDS AND OTHER PUBLICATIONS ISSUED BY THE ORGANIZATIONS IN VARIOUS FIELDS: ECONOMIC DEVELOPMENT, INTERNATIONAL RELATIONS, SOCIAL SCIENCE, HEALTH AND MEDICAL SCIENCE, TRANSPORTATION, AGRICULTURE, EDUCATION, LABOR, AND OTHERS.

2615 SCHACHTER O.
"THE ENFORCEMENT OF INTERNATIONAL JUDICIAL AND ARBITRAL DECISIONS."
AMER. J. INT. LAW, 54, (JAN. 60), 1-24.
DISCUSSING DIFFICULTIES FOUND IN ENFORCEMENT OF WORLD COURT DECISIONS, ANALYZES PROBLEMS AND PROCEDURES CONNECTED WITH SUCCESSFUL PARTIES CLAIMS. OUTLINES POSSIBLE REMEDIES AVAILABLE THROUGH INTERNATIONAL ORGANIZATIONS.

2616 SCHACHTER O.
"DAG HAMMARSKJOLD AND THE RELATION OF LAW TO POLITICS."
AMER. J. INT. LAW, 56 (JAN. 62), 1-8.
DISCUSSION DIVIDED INTO FOUR CATEGORIES: LAW AS A SOURCE AND BASIS OF POLICY, PRINCIPLES AND FLEXIBILITY, RELATION BETWEEN LAW AND DIPLOMACY, AND POWER AND ACTION. SEES NEED FOR PRACTICAL ACTION WHICH WOULD IMPART A NEW DIMENSION TO EFFORTS TO GIVE VIGOR AND EFFICACY TO A NORMATIVE STRUCTURE BASED ON THE COMMON INTERESTS OF 'THE MANY'.

2617 SCHACHTER O.
"SCIENTIFIC ADVANCES AND INTERNATIONAL LAWMAKING."
CALIF. LAW REV., 55 (MAY 67), 423-430.
ARGUES THAT GROWTH OF INTERNATIONAL INSTITUTIONS HAS BEEN CHARACTERISTIC RESPONSE OF GOVERNMENTS AND SCIENTIFIC BODIES TO SCIENTIFIC AND TECHNOLOGICAL ADVANCES. DISCUSSES TYPES OF INTERNATIONAL ORGANIZATIONS AND POLICY ALTERNATIVES WHICH ARE ARTICULATED IN LAW. ASSUMES THAT CONSCIOUS LAWMAKING MUST BE SOUGHT THROUGH MULTILATERAL TREATIES, AND STATISTIC RETRIEVAL HAS BECOME CRUCIAL TO POLICY-MAKING.

2618 SCHAPIRO J.S.
THE WORLD IN CRISES: POLITICAL AND SOCIAL MOVEMENTS IN THE TWENTIETH CENTURY.
NEW YORK: MCGRAW HILL, 1950.
ANALYZES POLITICAL, SOCIAL, AND ECONOMIC MOVEMENTS OF FIRST HALF OF 20TH CENTURY IN ATTEMPT TO UNDERSTAND TENDENCIES LEADING TO WORLD WAR AND REVOLUTION. EXPLANATION OF DEVELOPMENTS OF SOCIAL DEMOCRACY, COFLICT OF NATIONALISM AND INTERNATIONAL ECONOMIC ORDER, FAILURES OF COLONIAL IMPERIALISM AND LAISSEZ-FAIRE ECONOMY. ANALYZES BACKGROUND OF TOTALITARIANISM. EXTENSIVE BIBLIOGRAPHY INCLUDED.

2619 SCHATTEN F.
COMMUNISM IN AFRICA.
NEW YORK: FREDERICK PRAEGER, 1966, 352 PP., LC#65-14187.
CONSIDERS INTERACTIONS AND CHARACTERISTICS OF AFRICAN NATIONALISM, COMMUNIST ACTIVITIES, AND POSITION OF THE WEST. STATES THAT END OF WESTERN COLONIALISM WAS DUE TO EAST-WEST CONFLICT RATHER THAN ENLIGHTENED POLICY OF WEST. DISCUSSES COMMUNIST GOALS, SUCCESSES, AND FAILURES IN AFRICA. CONCLUDES THAT WEST MUST TRY TO RECOVER MORAL INITIATIVE, AND HELP AFRICA TO ATTAIN INDEPENDENT EXISTENCE.

2620 SCHECHTER A.H.
INTERPRETATION OF AMBIGUOUS DOCUMENTS BY INTERNATIONAL ADMINISTRATIVE TRIBUNALS.
NEW YORK: FREDERICK PRAEGER, 1964, 183 PP.
ANALYSIS OF INTERNATIONAL LEGAL DEVELOPMENTS SINCE WWII. EXAMINES ACTIONS OF UN ADMINISTRATIVE TRIBUNAL, ILO ADMINISTRATIVE TRIBUNAL, AND EUROPEAN COURT OF JUSTICE IN INTERPRETATIONS OF INTERNATIONAL RULES AND REGULATIONS.

2621 SCHEINGOLD S.A.
"THE RULE OF LAW IN EUROPEAN INTEGRATION: THE PATH OF THE SCHUMAN PLAN."
NEW HAVEN: YALE U PR, 1965.
STUDY OF RECIPROCAL RELATIONSHIP BETWEEN LEGAL AND POLITICAL ASPECTS OF EUROPEAN INTEGRATION. SELECTIVE BIBLIOGRAPHY OF ABOUT 150 BOOKS, DOCUMENTS, AND ARTICLES IN FRENCH AND ENGLISH, TO 1964. REFERENCE GIVEN TO MORE COMPLETE BIBLIOGRAPHICAL SOURCES.

2622 SCHELLING T.C.
"BARGAINING COMMUNICATION, AND LIMITED WAR."
J. CONFL. RESOLUT., 1 (MAR. 57), 19-36.
EXAMINES PRINCIPLES AND BEHAVIOR WHICH UNDERLIE TACIT BARGAINING. DESCRIBES ANALOGOUS SITUATION IN LIMITED WAR. POINTS OUT THAT SAME PRINCIPLES CAN BE FOUND IN EXPLICIT BARGAINING WITH FULL COMMUNICATION.

2623 SCHELLING T.C., MORTON H.H.
STRATEGY AND ARMS CONTROL.
NEW YORK: TWENTIETH CENTURY FUND, 1961, 148 PP., $2.50.
ARMS CONTROL AGREEMENT HAS TO BE AIMED AT REDUCING THE LIKELIHOOD OF CRISES AND LOCAL WARS. POSSIBILITY OF GENERAL WAR EVOLVING FROM LIMITED WARFARE IS DEMONSTRATED.

2624 SCHELLING T.C.
"STRATEGIC PROBLEMS OF AN INTERNATIONAL ARMED FORCE."
INT. ORGAN., 7 (SPRING 63), 465-486.
THE ORGANIZATION AND MAINTENANCE OF AN INTERNATIONAL MILITARY AUTHORITY OPERATING IN A DISARMED WORLD IS CONSIDERED. CONCLUDES THAT SUCH A FORCE WOULD NOT BE CAPABLE OF PREVENTING RE-ARMAMENT OF A MAJOR INDUSTRIAL POWER AND COULD ITSELF BECOME A THREAT TO FREEDOM AND INDEPENDENCE OF NATIONS. PROBLEM IS TO MAINTAIN SUFFICIENT DETERRENCE SO AS TO PERMIT COUNTRIES TO TAKE STEPS FOR THEIR OWN PROTECTION.

2625 SCHIEDER T. ED.
DOCUMENTS ON THE EXPULSION OF THE GERMANS FROM EASTERN-CENTRAL-EUROPE (VOL. II/III)
BONN: FED MIN REFUG& WAR VICTIM, 1961, 569 PP.
REPORTS ON THE FATE OF ETHNIC GERMANS IN HUNGARY AND RUMANIA PRIOR TO, DURING, AND AFTER WWII. DETAILS TRANSFERS AND EXPULSION OF POPULATION BY SS AND USSR. CONTAINS DOCUMENTS, LAWS, AND DECREES. ALSO CONTAINS INFORMATION ON LIVING CONDITIONS IN POST-WAR YEARS.

2626 SCHIFFER W.
THE LEGAL COMMUNITY OF MANKIND.
NEW YORK: COLUMB. U. PR., 1954, 367 PP.
PRESENTS CRITICAL EXAMINATION OF HISTORIC BASES OF CONCEPT OF WORLD ORGANIZATION. ANALYZES CONCEPT OF NATURAL LAW AND GROWTH OF SCIENCE OF INTERNATIONAL LAW, CONCEPT OF COMMUNITY OF MANKIND, AND THEORY OF NATURAL INTERESTS OF MEN. SCRUTINIZES ATTEMPTS AT WORLD POLITY MADE BY LEAGUE OF NATIONS.

2627 SCHILLING W.R.
"SCIENTISTS, FOREIGN POLICY AND POLITICS."
AMER. POLIT. SCI. REV., 56 (JUNE 62), 287-300.
ASSERTS THE TECHNOLOGICAL ADVANCES OF THE TWENTIETH CENTURY NECESSITATE A CLOSE RELATIONSHIP BETWEEN SCIENCE AND GOVERNMENT. CONCLUDES STATESMEN WILL DETERMINE TO WHAT EXTENT SCIENCE WILL BE PUT TO FUTURE USE.

2628 SCHLESINGER J.R.
THE POLITICAL ECONOMY OF NATIONAL SECURITY.
NEW YORK: PRAEGER, 1960, 292 PP.
EMPHASIZES THE CORRELATION BETWEEN GROSS NATIONAL PRODUCT AND BUDGET ALLOCATIONS FOR DEFENSE. THE IMPORTANCE OF BUDGETARY PLANNING AND STRATEGIC IMPLICATIONS OF INTERNATIONAL TRADE ARE CITED. CRITICIZES THE 'COMPARTMENTALIZED' APPROACH TO ASSESSMENT OF ECONOMIC FACTORS BEARING ON NATIONAL SECURITY. OUTLINES THE SOVIET ECONOMY AND THE ECONOMIC PROGRAMS OF UNDERDEVELOPED COUNTRIES.

2629 SCHMELTZ G.W.
LA POLITIQUE MONDIALE CONTEMPORAINE.
PARIS: LA COLOMBE, 1963, 613 PP., 30 FRS.
ATTEMPTS TO ANALYZE POST-WAR POLITICAL DEVELOPMENT THROUGH A STUDY OF THE GROWTH AND FUNCTION OF INTERNATIONAL ORGANIZATIONS, DEVELOPMENT OF EAST-WEST POLITICO-MILITARY CONFLICT (USING SPECIFIC INTER-NATION STUDIES), AND THE DECOLONIZATION PROCESS OF WEST EUROPEAN NATIONS. CITES TREATIES, MEETINGS, ORGANIZATIONS AND SPECIFIC EXAMPLES TO SUPPORT THEORIES.

2630 SCHMIDT H.
VERTEIDIGUNG ODER VERGELTUNG.
MUNICH: SEEWALD VERLAG, 1961, 290 PP.
A GERMAN CONTRIBUTION TO THE STRATEGIC PROBLEM OF NATO. BOOK LARGELY LIMITED TO ASPECTS OF MILITARY STRATEGY. REVIEWS VARIOUS PROBLEMS: KOREA, CUBA, DETERRENCE, SOVIET STRATEGY, US POLICY AND THE STRATEGIC VACUUM, THE ABILITY OF NATO TO DEFEND GERMANY, AND THE QUESTION OF STABILITY.

2631 SCHMIDT W.E.
"THE CASE AGAINST COMMODITY AGREEMENTS."
LAW CONTEMP. PROBL., 28 (SPRING 63), 313-327.
ECONOMIST TAKES ISSUE WITH SUPPORTERS OF INTERNATIONAL COMMODITY AGREEMENTS AS MEASURE TO ACCELERATE DEVELOPMENT IN LATIN AMERICA AND OTHER UNDERDEVELOPED COUNTRIES. USING CHARTER OF PUNTA DEL ESTE AS EXAMPLE OF OPPOSING VIEW, DISCUSSION CENTERS ABOUT DESIRABILITY OF STABILIZATION, THE ALTERING OF SECULAR TRENDS, AND COMPENSATION FOR FLUCTUATING EXPORT PROCEEDS.

2632 SCHMIDT-VOLKMAR E.
DER KULTURKAMPF IN DEUTSCHLAND 1871-1890.
GOTTINGEN: MUSTERSCHMIDT VERLAG, 1962, 387 PP.
EXAMINES CHURCH-STATE RELATIONS IN GERMANY UNDER BISMARCK. TRACES DISPUTES OF PRUSSIA WITH CATHOLIC CHURCH AND ITS IMPACT ON PARTY LIFE, OTHER GERMAN STATES, AND EUROPE IN GENERAL.

2633 SCHMITT B.E.
THE COMING OF THE WAR, 1914 (2 VOLS.)
NEW YORK: CHAS SCRIBNER'S SONS, 1930, 1053 PP.
EXHAUSTIVE ANALYSIS OF DIPLOMATIC DOCUMENTS ASSEMBLED AFTER WWI. NARRATES COURSE OF EVENTS IMMEDIATELY LEADING TO WAR AND CRISIS OF JULY, 1914. DEALS WITH THE INTERNATIONAL SITUATION IN GENERAL, PROBING EVENTS AND EXCHANGES THAT RESHAPED IT, ULTIMATELY, INTO WAR.

2634 SCHMITT H.A.

THE PATH TO EUROPEAN UNITY.
BATON ROUGE: LOUISIANA ST U PR, 1962, 272 PP., LC#62-18669.
ANALYSIS OF EUROPEAN PLAN FOR UNION FROM POSTWAR DRIVE OF MARSHALL PLAN TO FORMATION OF COMMON MARKET. STUDIES US AID AND POLICY REGARDING EUROPEAN UNION AND STRUCTURE AND OPERATION OF EUROPEAN COAL AND STEEL COMMUNITY'S ECONOMIC AND POLITICAL EFFECTS TOWARD UNITY.

2635 SCHMITT K.M., BURKS D.D.
"EVOLUTION OR CHAOS: DYNAMICS OF LATIN AMERICAN GOVERNMENT AND POLITICS."
NEW YORK: FREDERICK PRAEGER, 1963.
SURVEYS BROADLY BASIC IDEAS AND ATTITUDES OF LATIN AMERICANS TOWARD INTERNAL CONDITIONS AND INTERNATIONAL RELATIONS. DISCUSSES SOCIAL CONDITIONS AND INSTITUTIONS AND OUTLINES ECONOMIC FACTORS DIRECTLY IMPINGING ON POLITICS. EMPHASIS ON DETAILED INVESTIGATION OF INTEREST GROUPS, POLITICAL PARTIES, AND INTERACTION OF POLITICAL FORCES. BRIEFLY STUDIES INDIVIDUAL COUNTRIES. CONTAINS EXTENSIVE BIBLIOGRAPHY.

2636 SCHNAPPER B.
LA POLITIQUE ET LE COMMERCE FRANCAIS DANS LE GOLFE DE GUINEE DE 1838 A 1871.
HAGUE: MOUTON & CO, 1961, 286 PP.
STUDY OF FRENCH POLITICAL AND COMMERCIAL IMPERIALISM ON THE GULF OF GUINEA, EMPHASIZING FORTIFIED COMMERCIAL INSTALLATIONS, COLONIZATION, AND TRADE PRODUCTS.

2637 SCHNEIDER G.
HANDBUCH DER BIBLIOGRAPHIE.
LEIPZIG: HEIRSEMANN, 1930, 674 PP.
BIBLIOGRAPHY OF BIBLIOGRAPHIES IN ALL SUBJECTS WITH SOME ANNOTATIONS. PUBLISHED IN ENGLISH IN 1934.

2638 SCHNEIDER H.W.
"MAKING THE FASCIST STATE."
LONDON: OXFORD U PR, 1928.
INVESTIGATES CONSTRUCTION OF FASCIST THEORIES INTERMS OF VARYING PRACTICAL SITUATIONS INTO WHICH THE MOVEMENT WAS FORCED BY CIRCUMSTANCES. EMPHASIZES INTERACTION BETWEEN FACT AND PHILOSOPHIC FICTION, PRACTICAL EXIGENCIES AND SOCIAL THEORIES. EXTENSIVE BIBLIOGRPAHY DEALS WITH GENERAL POLITICAL THEORY AND HISTORY OF FASCISM RATHER THAN WITH TECHNICAL DETAILS. MAJORITY OF WORKS ARE IN ITALIAN.

2639 SCHNEIDER J.
TREATY-MAKING POWER OF INTERNATIONAL ORGANIZATIONS.
GENEVA: DROZ, 1959, 150 PP.
USING THE METHODOLOGY OF LAW, ANALYZES HISTORICAL AS WELL AS CONTEMPORARY PRACTICES OF INTERNATIONAL ORGANIZATIONS IN REGARD TO TREATY-MAKING POWERS. IN ESSENCE, A STUDY OF THE CHARACTER OF AGREEMENTS MADE BY WORLD-STRUCTURES SINCE WW 2.

2640 SCHNEIDER R.M.
"THE US IN LATIN AMERICA."
CURR. HIST., 48 (JAN. 65), 1-8.
USA UNDERSTANDING OF 'LIMITS OF INFLUENCE' MORE ADVANCED. ALTHOUGH APPEAL OF RADICAL LEFT HAS DIMINISHED, LATIN AMERICA NOT YET CONVINCED THAT DEMOCRACY, USA AND ALLIANCE FOR PROGRESS HAVE MUCH TO OFFER. MUST CONVINCE EMERGING MASSES THAT A BETTER LIFE CAN BE ATTAINED THROUGH REPRESENTATIVE POLITICAL PROCESSES.

2641 SCHOEDER P.W.
THE AXIS ALLIANCE AND JAPANESE-AMERICAN RELATIONS 1941.
ITHACA: CORNELL U PRESS, 1958, 243 PP.
CONCENTRATES ON ASPECT OF TRIPARTITE ALLIANCE, AS IT AFFECTED JAPANESE-AMERICAN NEGOTIATIONS PRECEDING WWII. TRIES TO GIVE AN INTERPRETATION DIFFERENT FROM ONE CURRENTLY PREVAILING, CONCENTRATING ON ANALYSIS MORE THAN NARRATION.

2642 SCHOFLING J.A.
"EFTA: THE OTHER EUROPE."
J. COMMONWEALTH POLIT. STUD., 40 (OCT. 64), 674-684.
EXAMINES HISTORICAL BACKGROUND OF DEVELOPMENT OF EUROPEAN FREE TRADE ASSOCIATION, GIVING ATTENTION TO ITS PRESENT POLITICAL SIGNIFICANCE, ITS INTERNAL ORGANIZATION, AND ITS EXTERNAL RELATIONS. GIVES SPECIAL CONSIDERATION TO ITS RELATIONS WITH EEC.

2643 SCHONBRUNN G.
WELTKRIEGE UND REVOLUTIONEN 1914-1945.
MUNICH: BAYERISCHER SCHULB VERLAG, 1961, 616 PP.
DISCUSSES WWI, REVOLUTIONS IN RUSSIA AND GERMANY, RISE OF TOTALITARIANISM, ECONOMIC CRISIS, RISE OF NAZISM, AND WWII.

2644 SCHRADER R.
SCIENCE AND POLICY.
NEW YORK: PERGAMON PRESS, 1963, 81 PP., LC#63-11117.
DISCUSSES INTERACTION OF SCIENTIFIC AND POLITICAL AFFAIRS. TREATS IMPACT OF SCIENCE AND TECHNOLOGY ON POLICY PROBLEMS, MILITARY AFFAIRS, ADMINISTRATION, INTERNATIONAL RELATIONS, AND UNDERDEVELOPED WORLD, PROPOSING NEW GOVERNMENTAL POLICIES.

2645 SCHRAMM W.
"MASS MEDIA AND NATIONAL DEVELOPMENT: THE ROLE OF INFORMATION IN DEVELOPING COUNTRIES."
STANFORD: STANFORD U PRESS, 1964.
STUDY CONDUCTED UNDER AUSPICES OF UNESCO DESIGNED TO EXAMINE CONTRIBUTION OF EFFECTIVE COMMUNICATION TO SOCIAL AND EXONOMIC DEVELOPMENT. ANALYZES COMMUNICATIONS RESEARCH AS FACET OF ECONOMIC AND SOCIAL DEVELOPMENT; HOW IT MAY EFFECT SOCIAL CHANGE; DISTRIBUTION OF MASS MEDIA THROUGHOUT WORLD; DEVELOPMENT OF MASS MEDIA. INCLUDES EXTENSIVE NOTES AND LARGE SELECT BIBLIOGRAPHY.

2646 SCHREIBER H.
TEUTON AND SLAV - THE STRUGGLE FOR CENTRAL EUROPE (TRANS. BY J. CLEUGH)
NEW YORK: ALFRED KNOPF, 1965, 392 PP.
TRACES EARLY SLAVONIC MOVEMENTS ACROSS EUROPE AND ENSUING CONFLICT WITH TEUTONIC PEOPLES. DISCUSSES STRUGGLE OVER BALTIC LANDS FROM EARLY COLONIZATION TO WWII.

2647 SCHRODER P.M.
METTERNICH'S DIPLOMACY AT ITS ZENITH, 1820-1823.
AUSTIN: U. TEXAS PR., 1962, 292 PP., $5.00.
PRESENTS A HISTORICAL-BIOGRAPHICAL DISSERTATION ON THE MAN AND HIS POLITICAL INFLUENCE ON POST-NAPOLEONIC ERA.

2648 SCHUMAN F.L.
"INTERNATIONAL IDEALS AND THE NATIONAL INTEREST."
ANN. AMER. ACAD. POLIT. SOC. SCI., 280 (MARCH 52), 27-36.
APPRAISES RESULTS OF A MORAL CODE WITHIN THE FRAMEWORK OF INTERNATIONAL POLITICS, EXPLAINING HOW ETHICAL ABSTRACTIONS CAN MISDIRECT MEN INTO WARS. BELIEVES THAT FOR THE INTERESTS OF MANKIND, EACH SOVEREIGN STATE SHOULD NOT ACT AS A MORAL AGENT BUT ACCORDING TO OWN NATIONAL INTEREST.

2649 SCHUMAN F.L.
THE COMMONWEALTH OF MAN.
NEW YORK: KNOPF, 1952, 494 PP.
TRACES POLITICAL PHILOSOPHIES OF SOCIAL SCIENTISTS AND APPLIES FINDINGS TO ANARCHY AND ORDER IN WORLD COMMUNITY. DISCUSSES PATHOLOGY OF POWER POLITICS AND WARNS AGAINST WORLD GOVERNMENT BY CONQUEST. FAVORS A VOLUNTARY EXTENSION OF THE PRINCIPLES OF FEDERALISM AS OPPOSED TO FUNCTIONALIST PLANNING OR COLLECTIVE SECURITY.

2650 SCHUMAN F.L.
INTERNATIONAL POLITICS.
NEW YORK: MCGRAW HILL, 1958, 745 PP.
'MEN HAVE WILLS AND ARE NOT MERE PLAYTHINGS OF CHANCE. IF THEY WILL GO ON IN THEIR ANCIENT WAYS IN AN EPOCH IN WHICH THE NEW POWERS AT THEIR DISPOSAL RENDER THESE WAYS A RECIPE FOR ANARCHY, VIOLENCE OR DEATH, THEY CANNOT REASONABLY EXPECT THE GREAT SOCIETY TO SURVIVE THE EFFECTS OF THEIR FOLLY... OR IT MIGHT BE MORE MUDDLING THROUGH AND THE DAWN OF A NEW ERA OF LIFE.'

2651 SCHUMAN F.L.
THE COLD WAR: RETROSPECT AND PROSPECT.
BATON ROUGE: LOUISIANA ST U PR, 1962, 104 PP., LC#62-16466.
PERSONAL COMMENTARIES ON RELATIONS OF US AND RUSSIA SINCE WWII. DISCUSSES PROBLEM OF BOTH SIDES PREPARING FOR MILITARY WAR IN NUCLEAR AGE AND DELUSION THAT COMMUNISM IS MILITARY THREAT. DISCUSSES COMMUNISM AS SOCIAL ORDER OR "CULT" NEEDING TO BE UNDERSTOOD TO BE FOUGHT, AND PROSPECTS OF COLD WAR IN FUTURE BASED ON PAST ACTIONS OF "POWER POLITICS." INCLUDES SMALL BIBLIOGRAPHY OF MORE SPECIFIC WORKS IN FIELD.

2652 SCHUMANN H.
"IMPERIALISMUS-KRITIK UND KOLONIALISMUS-FORSCHUNG."
NEUE POLITISCHE LITERATUR, 12 (1967), 186-199.
CRITICAL REVIEW OF MAJOR WORKS ON PROBLEMS OF COLONIALISM AND IMPERIALISM. DISCUSSES WORKS PUBLISHED IN MANY DIFFERENT COUNTRIES, BUT CENTERS ON EXAMINATION OF EAST-GERMAN PUBLICATIONS.

2653 SCHURZ W.L.
AMERICAN FOREIGN AFFAIRS: A GUIDE TO INTERNATIONAL AFFAIRS.
NEW YORK: DUTTON, 1959, 265 PP.
POINTS OUT BASIC ISSUES IN INTERNATIONAL AFFAIRS AS AN INTRODUCTION TO THE FIELD OF POLICY MAKING, EMPHASIZING THE IMPORTANCE OF PUBLIC OPINION, DISCUSSES THE INFLUENCE OF VARIOUS ELEMENTS UPON US FOREIGN POLICY, E.G. INTERNATIONAL OPINION, MASS MEDIA, CREATION OF NEW STATES AND POLITICS.

2654 SCHUSTER E.
GUIDE TO LAW AND LEGAL LITERATURE OF CENTRAL AMERICAN REPUBLICS.
CHICAGO: AMER FOREIGN LAW ASSOC, 1937, 152 PP.
ENTRIES INCLUDE SEVERAL TYPES OF LEGAL PUBLICATIONS DATING FROM LATE 1800'S TO 1936. COUNTRIES COVERED INCLUDE COSTA RICA, GUATEMALA, HONDURAS, NICARAGUA, PANAMA, AND SALVADOR. PUBLICATIONS LISTED IN SPANISH; ANNOTATIONS CONTAIN COMPARATIVE ANALYSIS OF RELATIONSHIPS BETWEEN LEGAL SYSTEMS OF THE SIX COUNTRIES AND ARE IN ENGLISH. APPROXIMATELY 700 ENTRIES.

2655 SCHWARTZ H.
THE RED PHOENIX: RUSSIA SINCE WORLD WAR II.
NEW YORK: FREDERICK PRAEGER, 1961, 417 PP., LC#61-11062.
TRACES INTERNAL POLITICAL DEVELOPMENT, ECONOMIC GROWTH, SCIENTIFIC ADVANCES, AND FOREIGN RELATIONS OF USSR SINCE WWII. DISCUSSES US-SOVIET RELATIONS AND COMPETITION AS WELL AS RELATIONS WITH RED CHINA.

2656 SCHWARTZ L.E.
INTERNATIONAL ORGANIZATIONS AND SPACE COOPERATION.
DURHAM: DUKE U PR, 1962, 108 PP.
COLLECTS BASIC DATA ON PUBLIC AND PRIVATE INTERNATIONAL ORGANIZATIONS INVOLVED IN SPACE PROGRAMS. STUDIES ORIGINS, HISTORY, AIMS, STRUCTURE, PAST ACHIEVEMENTS, AND PLANS OF ALL BODIES WITH ROLES IN SPACE COORDINATION, INCLUDING INTERNATIONAL COUNCIL OF SCIENTIFIC UNIONS, INTERNATIONAL GEOPHYSICAL YEAR, COMMITTEE ON SPACE RESEARCH, UN AND ITS COMMITTEES, AND INTERNATIONAL CIVIL AVIATION ORGANIZATION.

2657 SCHWARTZ M.A.
PUBLIC OPINION AND CANADIAN IDENTITY.
BERKELEY: U OF CALIF PR, 1967, 300 PP.
COMPILATION AND INTERPRETATION OF GALLUP POLL MATERIALS ON CANADIAN PUBLIC OPINION. DESCRIBES HOW CANADIANS VIEW THEIR NATION AND ROLE OF POLITICAL PARTIES IN SHAPING A MORE INTEGRATED NATIONAL IDENTITY. EXAMINES EXTENT OF REGIONAL AND ETHNIC DIVISION. ILLUSTRATES USEFULNESS OF SURVEY DATA IN ANALYZING LARGE-SCALE SOCIAL SYSTEMS.

2658 SCHWARTZ M.D. ED.
CONFERENCE ON SPACE SCIENCE AND SPACE LAW.
S HACKENSACK: FRED B ROTHMAN CO, 1964, 176 PP.
ARTICLES IN LAW AND SCIENCE ON FUTURE OF MAN IN SPACE, INCLUDING PEACEFUL USES, MILITARY STRATEGY, INTERNATIONAL COOPERATION, SPACE AND NATIONAL ECONOMY, AND LEGAL PROBLEMS.

2659 SCHWARZ U.
AMERICAN STRATEGY: A NEW PERSPECTIVE.
GARDEN CITY: DOUBLEDAY, 1966, 178 PP., LC#66-15443.
STUDIES GROWTH OF STRATEGIC THINKING IN US, INCLUDING THOUGHTS AND EXPERIENCES OF BOTH WORLD WARS, EFFECTS OF TECHNOLOGICAL DEVELOPMENT, CURRENT PROBLEMS AND STRATEGIES, AND AMERICAN SECURITY LEADERSHIP OF ATLANTIC ALLIANCE.

2660 SCHWARZENBERGER G.
POWER POLITICS: AN INTRODUCTION TO THE STUDY OF INTERNATIONAL RELATIONS AND POST-WAR PLANNING.
LONDON: JONATHAN CAPE, 1941, 448 PP.
STUDY OF INTERNATIONAL RELATIONS BASED ON HISTORICAL ANALYSIS AND EMPHASIZING CONCEPTUAL IDEAS AS WELL AS WORK PROCESSES AND FUNCTIONS. DISCUSSES ROLE OF LAW AND POWER IN THE FORMULATION OF FOREIGN POLICY. LENGTHY EXAMINATION OF UTOPIAN SCHEMES OF INTERNATIONAL ORGANIZATIONS AND FEDERALIST MOVEMENTS. CONTAINS LISTS OF SUGGESTED READINGS FOLLOWING EACH CHAPTER.

2661 SCHWARZENBERGER G.
THE FRONTIERS OF INTERNATIONAL LAW.
LONDON: STEVENS, 1962, 320 PP.
ATTEMPTS TO DETERMINE MODERN TEMPORAL, FUNCTIONAL, AND ANALYTICAL FRONTIERS OF INTERNATIONAL LAW. EXPLORES SOCIAL FACTORS UNDERLYING GROWTH OF UNIVERSAL LEGAL SYSTEM, EMPHASIZES POLITICAL AND SOCIAL ENDS SERVED BY INTERNATIONAL LAW, AND ARGUES EAST-WEST RIFT HAS FOSTERED CLOSER LEGAL INTEGRATION ON BIPOLAR LEVEL SINCE SOCIAL AND ECONOMIC INTERDEPENDENCE ARE EXPANDING WITHIN BLOC SYSTEM AND REGIONALLY.

2662 SCHWEBEL M. ED.
"BEHAVIORAL SCIENCE AND HUMAN SURVIVAL."
NEW YORK: TRIDENT PR, 1965.
ANTHOLOGY OF PAPERS PRESENTED AT AMERICAN ORTHOPSYCHIATRIC ASSOCIATION MEETING IN 1963. SAMPLING OF GENERAL PAPERS ON OVER-ALL TOPIC OF SURVIVAL, THOSE SPECIFICALLY THEORETICAL, THOSE DRAWING ON EMPIRICAL DATA, AND SELECTION OF PAPERS ON CURRENT REPORTS ON PEACE RESEARCH ACTIVITIES. CONTAINS INDIVIDUAL REFERENCES AND CONCLUDING ANNOTATED BIBLIOGRAPHY OF PUBLISHED LITERATURE ON PEACE.

2663 SCHWEBEL S.M.
"THE SECRETARY-GENERAL OF THE UN."
CAMBRIDGE: HARVARD U. PR., 1952, 299 PP.
CONSIDERS THE MOST SIGNIFICANT ASPECTS OF THE POSITION, ITS POLITICAL POWERS AND PRACTICE. ANALYZES ITS RELATION WITH THE GENERAL ASSEMBLY, WITH GOVERNMENT, WITH NON-POLITICAL ORGANS AND OUTLINES FUTURE TRENDS.

2664 SCHWELB E.
"INTERNATIONAL CONVENTIONS ON HUMAN RIGHTS."
INT. LAW COMP. QUART., 9 (OCT. 60).
STUDY OF MEANS TO IMPLEMENT HUMAN RIGHTS. PROVISIONS OF UN CHARTER TRACE VARIOUS CONVENTIONS IN THE PAST WITH REGARD TO GENOCIDE, PROTECTION OF WAR VICTIMS, CULTURAL PROPERTY, STATE-LESS PERSONS ET AL. PRAGMATIC VIEW OF INTERNATIONAL COMMUNITY AS IT EXISTS TODAY AND ITS CHANCES OF RESOLVING PRACTICAL DIFFERENCES, STRESSES OPINION THAT 'ENFORCEMENT OF HUMAN RIGHTS' IS POLITICAL-MORAL MATTER, NOT A LEGAL ISSUE.

2665 SCHWELB E.
"OPERATION OF THE EUROPEAN CONVENTION ON HUMAN RIGHTS."
INT. ORGAN., 18 (SUMMER 64), 558-85.
EFFECTIVENESS OF EUROPEAN COMMISSION OF HUMAN RIGHTS IS ILLUSTRATED BY SELECTED CASES WHICH DEMONSTRATE HOW THE COMMISSION ENSURED OBSERVANCE OF OBLIGATIONS BETWEEN VARIOUS PARTIES. CONCLUDES WORK OF COMMISSION IS SIGNIFICANT ADVANCE IN INTERNATIONAL PROTECTION OF HUMAN RIGHTS.

2666 SCHWELB E.
HUMAN RIGHTS AND THE INTERNATIONAL COMMUNITY.
CHICAGO: QUADRANGLE BOOKS, INC, 1964, 95 PP., LC#64-16781.
TRACES HISTORICAL EVENTS LEADING TO UN UNIVERSAL DECLARATION OF HUMAN RIGHTS IN 1948. EXAMINES DECLARATION AS STANDARD FOR THE MEASUREMENT OF INTERNATIONAL RECOGNITION OF HUMAN RIGHTS. DISCUSSES PENETRATION OF DECLARATION INTO INTERNATIONAL LAW AND ITS EFFECTS ON INDIVIDUAL NATIONS' HUMAN RIGHTS POLICY. REVIEWS LATER UN RESOLUTIONS REGARDING COLONIALISM AND VARIOUS AREAS OF INTERNATIONAL COOPERATION.

2667 SCHWERIN K.
"LAW LIBRARIES AND FOREIGN LAW COLLECTION IN THE USA."
INT. AND COMP. LAW Q., 11 (APR. 62), 537-567.
STUDIES BOTH US LAW LIBRARIES IN GENERAL AND THEIR FOREIGN LAW COLLECTIONS. REVIEWS SOME MAJOR LAW LIBRARIES AND LIBRARY FACILITIES AND SYSTEMS. SURVEYS MAJOR COLLECTIONS OF FOREIGN LAW, AND METHODS OF DEVELOPING THESE COLLECTIONS.

2668 SCITOUSKY T.
ECONOMIC THEORY AND WESTERN EUROPEAN INTEGRATION.
STANFORD: U. PR., 1958, 154 PP.
RANGE OF SUBJECT MATTER INCLUDES: THE CURRENCY UNION, COAL AND STEEL COMMUNITY, EMPLOYMENT, PRODUCTIVITY AND THE BALANCE OF PAYMENTS PROBLEM. REJECTS THE TRADITIONAL FREE-TRADE ARGUMENT AND POINTS OUT THAT INCREASED COMPETITION WOULD ONLY RESULT IN INDIRECT BENEFITS TO UNION.

2669 SCOTT A.M., WALLACE E.
POLITICS, USA; CASES ON THE AMERICAN DEMOCRATIC PROCESS.
NEW YORK: MACMILLAN, 1961, 571 PP., LC#61-6164.
COLLECTION OF CASES ON TOPICS OF STATES' RIGHTS, COURT SYSTEM, CIVIL LIBERTIES, LOYALTY, ELECTIONS, PUBLIC RELATIONS, PRESSURE GROUPS, CONGRESS, EXECUTIVE BRANCH, WELFARE AND ECONOMY, FOREIGN POLICY, STATE AND LOCAL GOVERNMENT, AND PREJUDICE. SERVES AS DIFFERENT APPROACH TO INTRODUCTORY GOVERNMENT TEXTBOOK.

2670 SCOTT A.M.
THE REVOLUTION IN STATECRAFT: INFORMAL PENETRATION.
NEW YORK: RANDOM HOUSE, INC, 1965, 194 PP., LC#65-23340.
COMPREHENSIVE ANALYSIS OF A DEVELOPMENT THAT HAS REVOLUTIONIZED MODERN STATECRAFT: ADVENT OF INFORMAL RELATIONS BETWEEN NATIONS. DISCUSSES EVOLUTION OF INFORMAL ACCESS TECHNIQUES, INCLUDING ECONOMIC AID, INFORMATION PROGRAMS, POLITICAL WARFARE, MILITARY TRAINING OPERATIONS, AND CULTURAL EXCHANGE PROGRAMS.

2671 SCOTT A.M.
THE FUNCTIONING OF THE INTERNATIONAL POLITICAL SYSTEM.
NEW YORK: MACMILLAN, 1967, 244 PP., LC#67-15541.
APPLIES SYSTEMS ANALYSIS TO INTERNATIONAL POLITICS. DEMONSTRATES INHERENT CAPACITIES OF THIS APPROACH AND OFFERS SET OF ASSUMPTIONS ABOUT INTERNATIONAL POLITICS, FOCUSING UPON ACTORS' INTERACTION PATTERNS, THEREBY AVOIDING THE TRADITIONAL EQUILIBRIUM ANALYSIS. REFLECTS AUTHOR'S INTEREST IN COMMUNICATIONS THEORY AND CONCERN WITH PROBLEMS OF PERCEPTION.

2672 SCOTT J.B.
"LAW, THESTATE, AND THE INTERNATIONAL COMMUNITY (2 VOLS.)"
NEW YORK: COLUMBIA U PRESS, 1939.
A WORK IN TWO VOLUMES: VOLUME I IS A SURVEY AND COMMENTARY ON THE DEVELOPMENT OF LEGAL, POLITICAL, AND INTERNATIONAL IDEALS; VOLUME II IS A COLLECTION OF EXTRAS ILLUSTRATING THE GROWTH OF THEORIES AND PRINCIPLES OF JURISPRUDENCE, GOVERNMENT, AND THE LAW OF NATIONS. VOLUME II CONTAINS A GENERAL UNANNOTATED BIBLIOGRAPHY AND A BIBLIOGRAPHY OF SOURCE MATERIALS FROM WHICH QUOTATIONS HAVE BEEN TAKEN.

2673 SCOTT J.B.
"ANGLO-SOVIET TRADE AND ITS EFFECTS ON THE COMMONWEALTH."
ROYAL CENT. ASIAN J., 49 (JAN. 62), 40-46.
DISCUSSES PROBLEMS CREATED BY SOVIET SHIFT IN TRADE AND PURCHASE PRACTICES FROM LONDON COMMONWEALTH TRADE OFFICES TO DIRECT AND BILATERAL TRADE WITH COMMONWEALTH COUNTRIES. WARNS THAT INCREASED SOVIET EXPORTS MAY ENDANGER ALREADY DIFFICULT BRITISH TRADE SITUATION.

2674 SCOTT W.A., WITHEY S.B.
THE UNITED STATES AND THE UNITED NATIONS: THE PUBLIC VIEW 1945-1955.
NEW YORK: MANHATTAN PUBL CO, 1958, 314 PP.
EXAMINES ATTITUDES OF AMERICAN PUBLIC TOWARD OPERATIONS OF UN FROM 1945-55. BASED ON RESEARCH MATERIAL PROVIDED BY PRIVATE OPINION RESEARCH COMPANIES, CONSIDERS LEVEL OF INFORMATION, EXPECTATIONS, OPINIONS ON UN OPERATIONS, AND

INTEREST IN FOREIGN AFFAIRS OF AMERICAN PEOPLE.

2675 SCOTT W.E.
ALLIANCE AGAINST HITLER.
DURHAM: DUKE U PR, 1962, 296 PP., LC#62-20214.
HISTORY OF ORIGIN OF FRANCO-SOVIET PACT OF 1935 CAUSED BY RISE, AND COMMON FEAR, OF HITLER. INCLUDES HISTORICAL BAKCGROUND AND CONTEMPORARY DOMESTIC AND INTERNATIONAL POLITICAL SITUATIONS.

2676 SEABURY P.
THE WANING OF SOUTHERN "INTERNATIONALISM" (PAMPHLET)
PRINCETON: PRINCETON U PRESS, 1957, 30 PP.
EXAMINES ROOTS OF SOUTHERN "INTERNATIONALISM." SUGGESTS THAT INTERNAL CONDITIONS WHICH MADE SOUTH, AS A REGION, RESPONSIVE TO "INTERNATIONALISM" OF FIRST HALF OF 20TH CENTURY WERE TRANSITORY, LIKE CONDITIONS WHICH MADE THE MIDWEST ISOLATIONIST. THESE CONDITIONS DID NOT MAKE SOUTH EQUALLY RECEPTIVE TO "INTERNATIONALISM" OF LATER PERIOD. SOUTH MAY REAR AN ISOLATIONIST HEAD IN FUTURE YEARS.

2677 SEABURY P.
BALANCE OF POWER.
SAN FRANCISCO: CHANDLER, 1965, 219 PP., LC#65-15418.
ESSAYS BY LEADING STATESMEN, PHILOSOPHERS, HISTORIANS, AND POLITICIANS ON IDEA OF BALANCE OF POWER IN EUROPEAN AND WORLD POLITICS. SELECTIONS FROM ARISTOTLE, HUME, HITLER, WILSON, KENNEDY, ETC.

2678 SEARA M.V.
"COSMIC INTERNATIONAL LAW."
DETROIT: WAYNE STATE U PR, 1965.
A GENERAL STUDY OF PROBLEMS IN INTERNATIONAL LAW AND SPACE, MODIFIED FROM SPANISH EDITION. BIBLIOGRAPHY OF ABOUT 400 BOOKS AND PERIODICALS IN ALL MAJOR LANGUAGES, UP TO 1963. ARRANGED BY AREA, INCLUDING GENERAL AND SPECIAL PROBLEMS OF INTERNATIONAL LAW, AIR LAW, OUTER SPACE, AND TECHNICAL WORKS.

2679 SEELEY J.R.
THE EXPANSION OF ENGLAND.
LONDON: MACMILLAN, 1902, 309 PP.
BRIEF HISTORY OF ENGLAND IN THE EIGHTEENTH CENTURY-ANALYZES THE OLD COLONIAL SYSTEM, THE EFFECT OF THE NEW WORLD ON THE OLD AND THE EXPANSION OF COMMERCE. SURVEYS CONQUEST OF INDIA AND ITS INFLUENCE ON ENGLAND.

2680 SEGAL A.
"THE INTEGRATION OF DEVELOPING COUNTRIES: SOME THOUGHTS ON EAST AFRICA AND CENTRAL AMERICA."
J. COMMON MARKET STUDIES, 5 (MAR. 67), 252-283.
NOTES THE CONSISTENT DESIRE OF EMERGING COUNTRIES FOR REGIONAL ALLIANCES WITH EACH OTHER DESPITE RECORD OF FAILURE. COMPARES THE SUCCESS OF THE CENTRAL AMERICAN COMMON MARKET WITH THE GROWING DISINTEGRATION OF THE EAST AFRICAN ECONOMIC UNION. CONCLUDES THAT THE LACK OF A POLITICAL THREAT IN THE CACM GAVE IT THE SUPPORT OF DEVELOPED NATIONS. SUGGESTS THAT POLITICAL UNITY MAY COST ECONOMIC INTEGRATION.

2681 SEGAL R.
SANCTIONS AGAINST SOUTH AFRICA.
BALTIMORE: PENGUIN BOOKS, 1964, 272 PP.
TWENTY-TWO ARTICLES FROM INTERNATIONAL CONFERENCE ON ECONOMIC SANCTIONS AGAINST SOUTH AFRICA OF 1964, DESCRIBING ECONOMIC, RACIAL, POLITICAL, LEGAL, AND STRATEGIC ASPECTS OF SANCTIONS.

2682 SEGUNDO-SANCHEZ M.
OBRAS (2 VOLS.)
CARACAS: BANCO CENTRAL VENEZ, 1964.
VOLUME I IS SUBTITLED (IN SPANISH) "CONTRIBUTION TO THE KNOWLEDGE OF THE FOREIGN BOOKS CONCERNING VENEZUELA AND ITS GREAT MEN, PUBLISHED OR REPRINTED, SINCE THE NINETEENTH CENTURY." VOLUME II CONTAINS BIBLIOGRAPHIC AND HISTORICAL STUDIES. A SEPARATE ANALYTICAL AUTHOR-TITLE INDEX IS PROVIDED.

2683 SELOSOEMARDJAN O.
SOCIAL CHANGES IN JOGJAKARTA.
ITHACA: CORNELL U PRESS, 1962, 447 PP., LC#62-14114.
VIEWS SOCIAL, ECONOMIC, POLITICAL CHANGE IN INDONESIA, RESULT OF 1958 REVOLUTION. EFFECT OF DUTCH AND JAPANESE OCCUPATIONS ON JAVANESE CULTURE AND THE ROLE OF JAVA AS A LEADER IN ECONOMIC AND SOCIAL PROGRESS IN THE AREA ARE CONSIDERED.

2684 SEMJONOW J.M.
DIE FASCHISTISCHE GEOPOLITIK IM DIENSTE DES AMERIKANISCHEN IMPERIALISMUS.
BERLIN: DIETZ VERLAG, 1955, 211 PP.
MAINTAINS MAIN TREND OF MODERN HISTORY IS THE PROGRESSIVE WEAKENING OF CAPITALISM AND IMPERIALISM AND STRENGTHENING OF CAMP OF FREEDOM, DEMOCRACY, AND SOCIALISM. TRACES HISTORY OF US EXPANSION AND INTERNATIONAL INVOLVEMENT AND CONSIDERS FOREIGN POLICY SINCE WWII EXTENSION OF FASCISTIC, MONOPOLISTIC, AND AGGRESSIVE PRACTICES.

2685 SENCOURT R.
"FOREIGN POLICY* AN HISTORIC RECTIFICATION."
QUARTERLY REV., (APR. 67), 213-226.
REVIEWS HISTORY OF CONSERVATIVE POLICY SINCE WWI. AUTHOR CONCLUDES THAT CONSERVATIVES MUST RID THEMSELVES OF ILLUSIONS ABOUT THE TWO WARS IF THEY ARE TO DECIDE WHAT THEIR PARTY STANDS FOR AND EVENTUALLY REGAIN THE GOVERNMENT FROM LABOUR.

2686 SERENI A.P.
THE ITALIAN CONCEPTION OF INTERNATIONAL LAW.
NEW YORK: COLUMB. U. PR., 1943, 353 PP.
MAJOR PURPOSE IS TO SHOW THAT THE FASCISM OF THE PRE-WAR ERA WAS A DEVIATION FROM THE NORMAL COURSE OF ITALIAN JUSTICE AND FREEDOM.

2687 SETHE P.
SCHICKSALSSTUNDEN DER WELTGESCHICHTE (6TH ED.)
FRANKFURT: VERL HEINR SCHEFFLER, 1960, 328 PP.
GENERAL HISTORY OF FOREIGN POLICY OF GREAT POWERS FROM CHARLES V TO CHURCHILL. DISCUSSES WARS AND STRUGGLES FOR NATIONALY UNITY.

2688 SETON-WATSON H.
NEITHER WAR NOR PEACE.
NEW YORK: PRAEGER, 1960, 473 PP.
ANALYZES MAJOR FORCES AND CONFLICTS IN INTERNATIONAL RELATIONS SINCE 1945. FOCUSES ON EXPANSION OF TOTALITARIANISM IN RUSSIA AND ASIA AND THE GROWTH OF ANTI-EUROPEAN NATIONALISM AMONG AFRO-ASIA NATIONS. EXAMINES CHALLENGES TO EXISTING WESTERN POLICIES, LEADERSHIP. VIEWS EVENTUAL CHALLENGE TO WESTERN DEMOCRATIC INFLUENCE IN WORLD POLITICS.

2689 SEYID MUHAMMAD V.A.
THE LEGAL FRAMEWORK OF WORLD TRADE.
NEW YORK: FREDERICK PRAEGER, 1958, 348 PP., LC#58-8538.
DEALS WITH LEGAL ASPECTS OF INTERNATIONAL TRADE, EMPHASIZING GENERAL AGREEMENT ON TARIFFS AND TRADE OF 1947. INCLUDES RELATION OF GENERAL AGREEMENT TO INTERNATIONAL LAW AND OTHER INTERNATIONAL ORGANIZATIONS; ORGANIZATION OF GENERAL AGREEMENT GROUP; RULES AND PROCEDURE ON TARIFF NEGOTIATIONS AND OTHER ASPECTS OF WORLD TRADE; AND APPRAISAL OF GENERAL AGREEMENT.

2690 SEYLER W.C.
"DOCTORAL DISSERTATIONS IN POLITICAL SCIENCE IN UNIVERSITIES OF THE UNITED STATES AND CANADA."
AM. POL. SCI. REV., 60 (SEPT. 66), 778-803.
AN UNANNOTATED BIBLIOGRAPHY OF DOCTORAL DISSERTATIONS IN POLITICAL SCIENCE. MATERIAL IS FROM LATE 1965 TO 1966. ENGLISH LANGUAGE. CONTAINS 1,150 ENTRIES.

2691 SHAFFER H.G.
THE COMMUNIST WORLD: MARXIST AND NON-MARXIST VIEWS.
NEW YORK: APPLETON, 1967, 558 PP., LC#67-21993.
INTRODUCES GENERAL PHILOSOPHY OF COMMUNIST WORLD, POINTING OUT ASPECTS OF HOMOGENEITY AND HETEROGENEITY. GROUPS INDIVIDUAL COMMUNIST NATIONS BY GEORGRAPHICAL AREAS, PRESENTING NATIVE AND FOREIGN VIEWS OF MARXIST IDEOLOGY. MOST MARXIST VIEWS REFLECT OFFICIAL EXPRESSIONS FROM COMMUNIST NATIONS.

2692 SHANNON D.A.
THE DECLINE OF AMERICAN COMMUNISM; A HISTORY OF THE COMMUNIST PARTY OF THE UNITED STATES SINCE 1945.
NEW YORK: HARCOURT BRACE, 1959, 425 PP., LC#59-11170.
STUDY OF COMMUNIST INFLUENCE IN US. EXAMINES PARTY IN RELATION TO SEGMENTS OF AMERICAN SOCIETY, PARTY ORGANIZATION AND STRENGTH, AND OPPOSITION FROM STRONG ANTI-COMMUNIST FACTIONS. TREATS YEARS OF SUSPICION, SMITH ACT CASES, PROGRESSIVE PARTY, AND CIO EXPULSIONS. ANALYZES KHRUSHCHEV ERA AND EFFECT ON PARTY OF THAW IN COLD WAR, DECLINE OF STALIN AS HERO, AND DECLINE OF PARTY IN US.

2693 SHAPIRO D.
A SELECT BIBLIOGRAPHY OF WORKS IN ENGLISH ON RUSSIAN HISTORY, 1801-1917.
OXFORD: BLACKWELL, 1962, 106 PP.
BIBLIOGRAPHY OF 1,070 BOOKS AND ARTICLES IN ENGLISH. INCLUDES CROSS REFERENCES. ITEMS ARRANGED BY SUBJECT: GENERAL HISTORY, FOREIGN RELATIONS, EXPANSION, ADMINISTRATION AND LAW, ARMED FORCES AND CAMPAIGNS, SOCIETY AND INTELLIGENTSIA, ECONOMIC HISTORY, LAND AND PEASANTS, REVOLUTIONARY MOVEMENTS, NATIONALITIES AND BORDERLANDS, SOCIAL THOUGHT AND PHILOSOPHY.

2694 SHAPP W.R.
FIELD ADMINISTRATION IN THE UNITED NATIONS SYSTEM.
NEW YORK: FREDERICK PRAEGER, 1961, 570 PP.
SURVEYS UN FIELD ORGANIZATION, ITS RELATION TO CENTRAL CONTROL, AND WAY AID PROGRAMMES ARE MANAGED. FOCUSES ON METHODS OF IMPROVING EFFICIENCY IN OPERATIONS AND IN AID GATHERING. PRESENTS DATA FROM MANY INTERVIEWS WITH WORLD-WIDE PERSONNEL. CONSIDERS HAMPERING FACTORS TO BE INTERNAL INSTITUTIONAL RELATIONSHIPS AND NATIONAL AND BLOC POLITICS.

2695 SHARMA J.S.
MAHATMA GANDHI: A DESCRIPTIVE BIBLIOGRAPHY.
NEW DELHI: S CHAND AND CO, 1954, 565 PP.
BIBLIOGRAPHY OF 3,671 ITEMS IN TEN OTHER LANGUAGES THAN INDIAN. CONTAINS SECTIONS ON HIS LIFE AND PERSONALITY AND ITEMS ON HIS VIEWS ON POLITICS, INDIAN PROBLEMS, FOREIGN RELATIONS, ETC. WORK IS ARRANGED SO AS TO PRESENT CHRONOLOGY OF GANDHI'S LIFE AND STRUGGLE FOR INDIAN INDEPENDENCE. VOLUME IS BOTH COMPREHENSIVE AND ANNOTATED. MAJORITY OF REFERENCES ARE IN ENGLISH.

2696 SHARP G.
"THE NEED OF A FUNCTIONAL SUBSTITUTE FOR WAR."
INTL. RELATIONS, 3 (APR. 67), 187-207.
ATTEMPT TO RE-EXAMINE PROBLEM OF WAR IN CONTEXT OF GENERAL VIOLENT SOCIAL AND POLITICAL CONFLICT. ADVOCATES RESEARCH ON THREE TASKS AS POSSIBLE CONTRIBUTIONS TO ABOLI-ON OF WAR: ESTABLISH VALIDITY OF FUNCTIONAL ANALYSIS OF WAR, EXAMINE NATURE OF SUBSTITUTE TECHNIQUES TO REPLACE VIOLENT CONFLICT, DEVELOP DETAILED SUBSTITUTE FOR WAR TO REPLACE SPECIFIC CONFLICT SITUATIONS.

2697 SHARP W.R.
FIELD ADMINISTRATION IN THE UNITED NATION SYSTEM: THE CONDUCT OF INTERNATIONAL ECONOMIC AND SOCIAL PROGRAMS.
NEW YORK: PRAEGER, 1961, 570 PP.
CLASSIFIES AND DESCRIBES THE VARIOUS FORMS OF FIELD ORGANIZATIONS WITHIN THE U.N., AND ANALYZES THEIR ADMINISTRATIVE AND PLANNING PROBLEMS. ALSO DISCUSSES THE FUTURE DEVELOPMENT OF THESE ORGANIZATIONS.

2698 SHAW C. ED.
LEGAL PROBLEMS IN INTERNATIONAL TRADE AND INVESTMENT.
NEW HAVEN: YALE U PR, 1962, 265 PP.
DESCRIBES WAYS PUBLIC AND PRIVATE INTERNATIONAL BUSINESS TRANSACTIONS ARE CONDUCTED. INCLUDES LAWYER'S ROLE IN TRANSACTIONS; PROBLEMS OF INTERNATIONAL TRADE AND INVESTMENT BETWEEN DEVELOPED NATIONS AND UNDEVELOPED ONES OF AFRICA, ASIA, AND SOUTH AMERICA; ANTI-TRUST PROBLEMS; REGIONAL MARKETING AND TAX PROBLEMS.

2699 SHELBY C. ED.
LATIN AMERICAN PERIODICALS CURRENTLY RECEIVED IN THE LIBRARY OF CONGRESS AND IN LIBRARY OF DEPARTMENT OF AGRICULTURE.
WASHINGTON: LIBRARY OF CONGRESS, 1944, 249 PP.
ANNOTATED LISTING BY TITLE OF 1,600 CURRENTLY RECEIVED PERIODICALS, EXCLUDING NEWSPAPERS, TECHNICAL JOURNALS, OR YEARBOOKS. MOST IN SPANISH OR PORTUGUESE WITH SOME ENGLISH. CRITERIA FOR INCLUSION IS PERIODICAL'S CHIEF CONCERN WITH LATIN AMERICA. INDEX BY COUNTRY OF PUBLICATION AND SUBJECT.

2700 SHERMAN M.
"GUARANTEES AND NUCLEAR SPREAD."
INT. J., 21 (FALL 66), 484-490.
DISCUSSES POLICY OF SECURITY ALLIANCE TO CONTAIN SPREAD OF NUCLEAR WEAPONS, EMPHASIZING US STRATEGY IN RELATION TO NATO ALLIES, AND DETERRENT STRENGTH OF GUARANTEE POLICY.

2701 SHERSHNEV Y.
"THE KENNEDY ROUND* PLANS AND REALITY."
INTERNATIONAL AFFAIRS (USSR) (APR.67), 29-34.
GIVES HISTORY OF KENNEDY ROUND EMPHASIZING CHANGES IN RELATIONSHIP OF US TO COMMON MARKET. INEFFECTUALITY OF DISCUSSION EMPHASIZES CHANGES IN BALANCE OF FORCES IN WORLD CAPITALIST MARKET. EUROPE WANTS GREATER TRADE AND POLITICAL CONCESSIONS FROM US. KENNEDY ROUND ILLUSTRATES EVOLUTION OF INTER-IMPERIALIST CONTRADICTIONS. PREDICTS US POSTWAR HEGEMONY IN WESTERN EUROPE ENDED.

2702 SHIRATO I.
JAPANESE SOURCES ON THE HISTORY OF THE CHINESE COMMUNIST MOVEMENT (PAMPHLET)
NY: COLUMBIA U, EAST ASIAN INST, 1953, 69 PP., LC#53-12343.
ANNOTATED BIBLIOGRAPHY OF SELECTED MATERIALS IN JAPANESE DEALING WITH THE HISTORY OF THE CHINESE COMMUNIST MOVEMENT. MATERIALS ARE FROM THE EAST ASIATIC LIBRARY OF COLUMBIA UNIVERSITY AND A DIVISION OF THE LIBRARY OF CONGRESS. LISTS ONLY BOOKS OR PARTS THEREOF, MONOGRAPHS, PAMPHLETS, AND SIGNIFICANT PERIODICAL ARTICLES.

2703 SHOEMAKER R.L.
"JAPANESE ARMY AND THE WEST."
MILITARY REV., 47 (MAY 67), 10-17.
SURVEYS ORIGIN AND DEVELOPMENT OF JAPANESE MILITARY FROM THE RISE OF SHOGUNS AND SAMURAI TO ITS WESTERNIZATION AT TURN OF CENTURY. POSES QUESTION OF WHY JAPAN DELAYED ITS MILITARY DEVELOPMENT FOR TWO AND A HALF CENTURIES AFTER EXPOSURE TO THE WEST, HOW IT DEVELOPED SO QUICKLY, AND WHY IT CHOSE FRANCE AS MILITARY EXEMPLAR FOR REFORM. CONCLUDES, AND SHOWS, THAT INTERNAL AND EXTERNAL FACTORS WERE IDEAL.

2704 SHONFIELD A.
THE ATTACK ON WORLD POVERTY.
NEW YORK: RANDOM, 1960, 269 PP.
NEED AID YIELDING MAXIMUM RESULTS. MOST ATTEMPTS POORLY ORGANIZED, MAKE LITTLE USE OF NATURAL RESOURCES. EXAMINES PART TO BE PLAYED BY INTERNATIONAL ORGANIZATIONS, SUCH AS THE WORLD BANK.

2705 SHONFIELD A.
"AFTER BRUSSELS."
FOR. AFF., 41 (JULY 63), 721-731.
DISCUSSES EUROPEAN ECONOMIC COMMUNITY AND FREE-TRADE AREA, FOCUSING ATTENTION ON BRITAIN'S UNSUCCESSFUL ATTEMPT TO ENTER EEC IN 1962. ALSO EXAMINES PROSPECT OF GREATER COHESION AND INTEGRATION IN COMMON MARKET. BELIEVES BRITAIN WILL TRY TO USE EFTA TO GET COMPENSATORY TRADE ADVANTAGES FOR INCREASED DISCRIMINATION THAT IS EXPECTED TO BE EXERCISED AGAINST HER BY EEC.

2706 SHOTWELL J.
ON THE RIM OF THE ABYSS.
NEW YORK: MACMILLAN, 1936, 400 PP.
ANALYZES PATTERNS OF NATIONAL POLICY. SURVEYS ALTERNATIVES TO NEUTRAL POSITIONS. DEPICTS POLITICAL SITUATION IN EUROPE SINCE WW 1. EXAMINES LEAGUE OF NATIONS STRUCTURE.

2707 SHOTWELL J.
"AFTER THE WAR."
INT. CONCIL., 376 (JAN. 42), 31-35.
PROPOSES USE OF INTERNATIONAL ORGANIZATIONS TO MEET FUTURE WORLD PROBLEMS IN HEALTH AND ECONOMICS. THE WORK ADVOCATES AN INTERNATIONAL BILL OF RIGHTS TO SECURE PERSONAL LIBERTIES FOR ALL PEOPLES.

2708 SHOTWELL J.
"LESSON OF THE LAST WORLD WAR."
NEW YORK: AMER. INST. CONSULTING ENGINEERS, 1942, 46 PP.
'WITHOUT PROVIDING FOR CONTINUING PROBLEMS OF FUTURE IN INTERNATIONAL WORLD, WE WILL LOSE RESULTS OF VICTORY AS WE LOST IT AFTER WW 1... TREATY CONCLUDING PRESENT WAR CAN'T FOLLOW TRADITIONAL PRECEDENT NOR USE METHODS OF 25 YEARS AGO... NOT OVERPOWERING BELLIGERENTS OR ESTABLISH TERRITORIAL BOUNDARIES... MUST MEET ECONOMIC CONDITIONS.'

2709 SHUKRI A.
THE CONCEPT OF SELF-DETERMINATION IN THE UNITED NATIONS.
CAIRO: AL JADIDAH PRESS, 1965, 374 PP., LC#NE-3607.
TRACES THE DEVELOPMENT OR THE CONCEPT OF SELF-DETERMINATION PRIOR TO, IN, AND SINCE THE UN CHARTER. STRESSES THE RELATION BETWEEN SELF-DETERMINATION AND COLONIALISM. LOOKS AT THE ISSUE FROM THE ECONOMIC, LEGAL, AND HUMAN ANGLE. ALSO PROVIDES A BIBLIOGRAPHY OF DOCUMENTS, ARTICLES, AND BOOKS RELEVANT TO THE QUESTION OF SELF-DETERMINATION.

2710 SHULIM J.I.
THE OLD DOMINION AND NAPOLEON BONAPARTE.
NEW YORK: COLUMBIA U PRESS, 1952, 332 PP.
DISCUSSES PUBLIC OPINION IN VIRGINIA ON NAPOLEON, FRENCH DOMESTIC DEVELOPMENTS, FRANCO-EUROPEAN AND FRANCE-AMERICAN RELATIONS BETWEEN 1789-1809. INCLUDES ANALYSIS OF ATTITUDES TOWARD FRENCH REVOLUTION.

2711 SHULMAN M.D.
"'EUROPE' VERSUS 'DETENTE'."
FOREIGN AFFAIRS, 45 (APR. 67), 389-402.
HOLDS THAT THERE IS NO CONTRADICTION IN AMERICAN EFFORTS TO STRENGTHEN US-EUROPEAN ALLIANCE WHILE IMPROVING US-USSR RELATIONS. MAINTAINS SOVIET THREAT MORE POLITICAL-ECONOMIC THAN MILITARY, THEREFORE US-EUROPEAN ALLIANCE IS NOW UNITED BY SHARED VALUES AND GOALS RATHER THAN BY MILITARY THREAT FROM SOVIETS. ADVOCATES A LIMITED DETENTE BETWEEN US-USSR TO SOLVE EUROPEAN PROBLEMS AND AVOID NUCLEAR WAR.

2712 SHWADRAN B.
"MIDDLE EAST OIL, 1962."
MID. EAST AFF., 14 (OCT. 63), 226-235.
VOICES CONCERN OVER SOVIET OIL ENTERING NON-COMMUNIST COUNTRIES. INVESTIGATED FROM VIEW-POINT OF COMMON MARKET, THE MIDDLE EAST AND WESTERN OIL COMPANIES.

2713 SIDGWICK H.
THE ELEMENTS OF POLITICS.
LONDON: MACMILLAN, 1891, 623 PP.
A COMPREHENSIVE STUDY OF POLITICAL THEORY AND PRACTICE IN RELATION TO 19TH-CENTURY SOCIETY. THE SCOPE, CONCEPTION AND PRINCIPLES OF POLITICS ARE BASED ON WRITINGS OF J.S. MILL AND BENTHAM. MAJOR AREAS DISCUSSED INCLUDE JURISPRUDENCE, INTERNATIONAL LAW, MAINTENANCE AND STRUCTURE OF GOVERNMENT, RELATION OF JUDICIARY TO LEGISLATURE AND EXECUTIVE, LOCAL AND FEDERAL GOVERNMENTS, AND SOVEREIGNTY AND ORDER.

2714 SIEGFRIED A.
AMERICA COMES OF AGE: A FRENCH ANALYSIS (TRANS. BY H.H. HEMMING AND DORIS HEMMING)
NEW YORK: HARCOURT BRACE, 1927, 358 PP.
AN EXAMINATION OF US SOCIETY AND CULTURE IN THE EARLY 20TH CENTURY. DISCUSSES ORIGINS OF THE POPULATION AND MAJOR RELIGIOUS AND RACIAL TRENDS. DESCRIBES EFFECTS OF INDUSTRIALIZATION ON STANDARD OF LIVING AND WORLD TRADE. EXPLAINS NATURE OF US POLITICAL SYSTEM AND AMERICA'S EMERGENCE AS A WORLD POWER, WITH SPECIAL ATTENTION TO

RELATIONS WITH BRITAIN AND FRANCE.

2715 SILBERNER E.
"THE PROBLEM OF WAR IN NINETEENTH CENTURY ECONOMIC THOUGHT."
PRINCETON: U. PR., 1946, 333 PP.
ANALYZES IDEAS OF 19TH CENTURY ECONOMISTS ON RELATIONSHIP BETWEEN WAR AND ECONOMICS, THE PART WAR PLAYED IN ECONOMIC EVOLUTION, THE EFFECT OF DISARMAMENT ON THE NATIONAL ECONOMY, AND SOCIAL REFORM AS MEANS TO WORLD PEACE.

2716 SILVA SOLAR J., CHONCHOL J.
EL DESARROLLO DE LA NUEVA SOCIEDAD EN AMERICA.
SANTIAGO: EDITORIAL U SANTIAGO, 1965, 160 PP.
ANALYZES LATIN AMERICAN SOCIETY AND ITS DEVELOPMENT, AS WELL AS BASIS OF LAND OWNERSHIP RELATED TO SOCIAL STRUCTURE. LAND DISCUSSED AS TO IMPORTANCE IN CONCEPT OF SOCIAL CHANGE SINCE SMALL GROUP CONTROLS LARGEST AMOUNT OF LAND. IN SAME APPROACH TO CHANGE, AUTHOR EXAMINES UNDERDEVELOPMENT OF LATIN AMERICA AND NEED FOR REFORM AND INTEGRATION OF AREA.

2717 SIMOES DOS REIS A.
BIBLIOGRAFIA DAS BIBLIOGRAFIAS BRASILEIRAS.
RIO DE JANEIRO: INST.NACIONAL DO LIVRO, 1942,186 PP.
BIBLIOGRAPHY OF BRAZILIAN BIBLIOGRAPHIES. INCLUDES BOOKS AND PERIODICALS. ENTRIES ARE ARRANGED ALPHABETICALLY BY AUTHOR.

2718 SIMONDS F.H., EMENY B.
THE GREAT POWERS IN WORLD POLITICS.
NEW YORK: AMERICAN BOOK, 1935, 640 PP.
STUDIES INTERNATIONAL RELATIONS BY EXAMINING NATIONAL POLICIES OF MAJOR WORLD POWERS. ATTEMPTS TO RESOLVE PRESENT RELATIONSHIPS INTO THEIR ESSENTIAL ELEMENTS. EMPHASIZES ECONOMIC ISSUES IN 1930'S AS FOUNDATIONS OF POLICY AT THAT TIME. CONCERNED WITH TRANSITION FROM WWI TO DEPRESSION OF 1929. CONSIDERS NAZISM AND FASCISM CHARACTERISTIC OF GREAT PEOPLES IN REVOLT AGAINST POVERTY.

2719 SIMONS H.
"WORLD-WIDE CAPABILITIES FOR PRODUCTION AND CONTROL OF NUCLEAR WEAPONS."
DAEDALUS, 88 (SUMMER 59), 385-409.
REPORT DEALS WITH SIGNIFICANT PROBLEMS OF NUCLEAR DISSEMINATION. DISCUSSES COUNTRY'S REQUIREMENTS, CAPABILITY, ACCESS TO FISSIONABLE MATERIALS, AND TECHNICAL PROBLEMS ARISING FROM THE NUCLEAR REACTOR INSTALLATIONS. OFFERS SOLUTIONS TO LIMIT ATOMIC ENERGY TO PEACEFUL USES.

2720 SIMPSON J.L., FOX H.
INTERNATIONAL ARBITRATION: LAW AND PRACTICE.
NEW YORK: FREDERICK PRAEGER, 1959, 330 PP., LC#59-7392.
SURVEY OF SETTLEMENT BY JUDICIAL MEANS OF DISPUTES BETWEEN NATIONS. CONCENTRATES ON PERIOD AFTER WWII, HAGUE COURT, GERMAN TRIALS, ETC. COVERS INFORMAL ARBITRATION AND FORMAL TRIBUNALS, BOTH PROCESSES AND RELATION TO EACH OTHER. EMPHASIS ON ACTUAL PRACTICE OF COURTS. INCLUDES ALPHABETICAL TABLE OF CASES AND APPENDIX OF MODEL RULES ON ARBITRAL PROCEDURE.

2721 SINEY M.C.
THE ALLIED BLOCKADE OF GERMANY: 1914-1916.
ANN ARBOR: U OF MICH PR, 1957, 339 PP., LC#57-5143.
ANALYSIS OF MEASURES TAKEN BY ALLIES DURING WWI TO INTERFERE WITH AND STOP GERMAN TRADE. CONSIDERS BLOCKADE MEASURES ESSENTIALLY AS INSTRUMENTS OF ECONOMIC WARFARE. ALSO EXAMINES LEGAL ASPECTS OF BLOCKADE AND OF TRADE RESTRICTIONS PLACED ON NEUTRAL STATES. CONCENTRATES LARGELY ON BRITISH NEGOTIATIONS WITH SCANDIANAVIAN COUNTRIES.

2722 SINGER D. ED.
QUANTITATIVE INTERNATIONAL POLITICS* INSIGHTS AND EVIDENCE.
NEW YORK: MACMILLAN, 1967, 352 PP.
PRESENTATION OF DATA-BASED STUDIES TOUCHING ON ALL AREAS OF INTERNATIONAL POLITICS, FROM THE PSYCHOLOGY OF INDIVIDUAL DECISION-MAKERS TO THE BEHAVIOR OF ENTIRE NATIONS AND ALLIANCE SYSTEMS. DEMONSTRATES HOW THE RIGOROUS METHODOLOGY OF THE BEHAVIORAL SCIENCES CAN BE BROUGHT TO BEAR ON THE RAW INFORMATION OF WORLD POLITICS TO SORT OUT USEFUL DATA, TEST HYPOTHESES, AND SUPPORT MEANINGFUL GENERALIZATIONS.

2723 SINGER H.W.
INTERNATIONAL DEVELOPMENT: GROWTH AND CHANGE.
NEW YORK: MCGRAW HILL, 1964, 295 PP., $7.50.
ANALYZES TRENDS IN ECONOMIC THEORY ON UNDERDEVELOPED ECONOMIES. STRESSES NEED FOR PREINVESTMENT WORK AND FOR PLANS UTILIZING TOTAL RESOURCES OF COUNTRIES. RELATES EDUCATION AND POPULATION TO ECONOMIC DEVELOPMENTS. TREATS OBSTACLES TO AFRICAN AND BRAZILIAN GROWTH.

2724 SINGER J.D.
"THREAT PERCEPTION AND THE ARMAMENT TENSION DILEMMA."
J. CONFL. RESOLUT., 2 (MAR. 58), 90-105.
EXPOSES RISKS IMPLICIT IN PERPETUATION OF ARMS RACE. DESCRIBES VARIOUS APPROACHES TO DISARMAMENT. CRITICIZES THREE MAIN APPROACHES FOR AVOIDING ISSUE OF THREAT TO NATIONAL SECURITY PERCEIVED BY DECISION MAKERS. OFFERS SUGGESTIONS ON INTERNATIONAL ARMS CONTROL.

2725 SINGER J.D.
"THE LEVEL OF ANALYSIS: PROBLEMS IN INTERNATIONAL RELATIONS."
WORLD POLIT., 14 (OCT. 61), 77-92.
THERE EXISTS A SYSTEMIC LEVEL OF ANALYSIS WHICH IMPELS THE OBSERVER TOWARD MORE DETERMINISTIC INTERPRETATIONS, AND A NATIONAL LEVEL WHICH PERMITS GREATER DIFFERENTIATIONS AMONG NATIONAL BEHAVIOR PATTERNS.

2726 SINGER J.D.
FINANCING INTERNATIONAL ORGANIZATION: THE UNITED NATIONS BUDGET PROCESS.
GENEVA: NIJHOFF, 1961, 185 PP.
TRACES IN DETAIL SIX MAJOR EVOLUTIONARY PHASES OF FINANCIAL SYSTEM. PUTS BUDGET PLANNING PROCESS IN SETTING OF INTERNATIONAL RELATIONS. EMPHASIZES CYCLICAL DYNAMICS OF UN BUDGET PROCESS.

2727 SINGER J.D.
DETERRENCE, ARMS CONTROL AND DISARMAMENT: TOWARD A SYNTHESIS IN NATIONAL SECURITY POLICY.
COLUMBUS: OHIO STATE U. PR., 1962, 279 PP.
THOUGH DETERRENCE, ARMS CONTROL AND DISARMAMENT ARE VIEWED AS REPRESENTING THREE DIFFERENT SETS OF PROBLEMS, AUTHOR MAINTAINS THAT THEY MUST BE DEALT WITH IN TERMS OF A SINGLE CONTEXT. ALL FACETS OF A SINGLE PROBLEM: NATIONAL SECURITY IN THE NUCLEAR-MISSILE ERA.

2728 SINGER J.D.
"STABLE DETERRENCE AND ITS LIMITS."
WEST. POLIT. QUART., 44 (SEPT. 62), 449-64.
DISCUSSES WAYS FOR STABILIZING BALANCE OF TERROR. ANALYZES LIMITS TO STABILITY. CONSIDERS IT ONLY A WAY-STATION TOWARD COMPREHENSIVE DISARMAMENT UNDER SUPERNATURAL CONTROL.

2729 SINGER J.D. ED.
"WEAPONS MANAGEMENT IN WORLD POLITICS: PROCEEDINGS OF THE INTERNATIONAL ARMS CONTROL SYMPOSIUM, DECEMBER, 1962."
J. CONFL. RESOLUT., 7 (MAR. 63), 185-652/J. ARMS CONTR., 1 (NO.4, 63), 279-746.
SOME 43 ESSAYS AND RESEARCH REPORTS BY MEN SUCH AS KARL DEUTSCH, QUINCY WRIGHT, HUBERT HUMPHREY. DISCUSSES IN DETAIL, AMONG OTHER THINGS, HOW TO MANAGE WEAPONS, DISARM NATIONS, AND NEGOTIATE DISARMAMENT. SEEKS 'PRIMARILY A MIX OF INNOCENCE AND REALISM, FRESHNESS AND SOPHISTICATION, SO THAT THE HARD-SOFT DICHOTOMY WOULD BE BLURRED IN A PROBLEM-ORIENTED--AS OPPOSED TO A POLICY-ORIENTED--CONTEXT.'

2730 SINGER K.
THE IDEA OF CONFLICT.
MELBOURNE: U. PR., 1949, 181 PP.
TRACES IDEA OF CONFLICT BY ANALYZING PAST STRIFE AND SHOWING HOW EMBODIED IN PRESENT WORLD CONFLICTS. DENOTES INTERPLAY OF FORCES AND VARIETY OF ORDINARY OCCASIONS FROM WHICH CONFLICTS ARISE.

2731 SINGER L.
ALLE LITTEN AN GROSSENWAHN: VON WOODROW WILSON BIS MAO TSE-TUNG.
STUTTGART: SEEWALD VERLAG, 1966, 309 PP.
DISCUSSES HISTORICAL EVENTS OF 20TH CENTURY IN FRAMEWORK OF DIPLOMACY OF DICTATORS. MAINTAINS THAT TRAGEDIES OF CENTURY MUST BE EXPLAINED AS RESULT OF "MEGALOMANIA" OF LEADING PUBLIC OFFICIALS, INCLUDING WILSON, CHURCHILL, ROOSEVELT, STALIN, HITLER, ETC.

2732 SINGER M.R., SENSENIG B.
"ELECTIONS WITHIN THE UNITED NATIONS: AN EXPERIMENTAL STUDY UTILIZING STATISTICAL ANALYSIS."
INT. ORGAN., 17 (AUTUMN 63), 901-25.
CONCLUDES THAT THE MAJOR DETERMINING FACTORS IN ELECTION TO UN OFFICES ARE POWER, PRO-U.S. ALIGNMENT IN THE COLD WAR, AND ECONOMIC TIES WITH THE U.S.

2733 SINGH L.P.
THE POLITICS OF ECONOMIC COOPERATION IN ASIA; A STUDY OF ASIAN INTERNATIONAL ORGANIZATIONS.
COLUMBIA: U OF MO PR, 1966, 271 PP., LC#66-17956.
STUDIES ASIAN ECONOMIC ORGANIZATIONS AND THE POLITICS OF AND INITIATIVES FOR ECONOMIC COOPERATION AND INTEGRATION IN ASIA. CONSIDERS ECONOMIC AND NONECONOMIC FACTORS AFFECTING REGIONAL ECONOMIC COOPERATION; ASSESSES EFFORTS TOWARD INTEGRATION. STUDIES UN'S ECONOMIC COMMISSION FOR ASIA AND THE FAR EAST, COLOMBO PLAN, SEATO, AND COOPERATION OUTSIDE OF INTERNATIONAL ORGANIZATIONS.

2734 SINGH N., NAWAS M.K.
"THE CONTEMPORARY PRACTICE OF INDIA IN THE FIELD OF INTERNATIONAL LAW."
INT. STUDIES, 6 (JULY 64), 69-86.
TRACES EVOLUTION OF INTERNATIONAL LAW AS IT RELATES TO PRACTICES AND ACTIONS OF INDIA IN THE INTERNATIONAL DOMAIN FOR 1962. CONCEPTS OF RECOGNITION, JURISDICTION AND TERRITORY WERE SCRUTINIZED. LEGAL IMPLICATIONS OF COMMUNIST

CHINESE OCCUPATION OF LADAKH PROVINCE EXPLORED.

2735 SINGH N.
THE DEFENCE MECHANISM OF THE MODERN STATE.
BOMBAY: ASIA PUBL HOUSE, 1964, 479 PP.
DISCUSSES POLITICAL AND MILITARY FUNCTIONS OF CHIEFS OF STAFF COMMITTEES IN COMMONWEALTH COUNTRIES. NOTES DEFENSE STRUCTURE OF US AND POSITION OF MILITARY LEADERS IN WWII TOTALITARIAN STATES AND COMMUNIST BLOC. EXAMINES COLLECTIVE DEFENSE ORGANIZATIONS AND CONSTITUTIONAL POSITION OF MILITARY IN WESTERN NATIONS; NOTES ROLE IN FORMING DEFENSE POLICIES.

2736 SIPKOV I.
LEGAL SOURCES AND BIBLIOGRAPHY OF BULGARIA.
NEW YORK: FREDERICK PRAEGER, 1956, 199 PP., LC#57-13220.
ONE OF THE SERIES OF BIBLIOGRAPHIES PREPARED BY THE MID-EUROPEAN LAW PROJECT AND PUBLISHED BY THE MID-EUROPEAN STUDIES CENTER: COVERS NEW LEGAL COLLECTIONS, NEW WRITINGS, AND NEW PERIODICALS WHICH HAVE APPEARED SINCE THE ESTABLISHMENT OF COMMUNIST GOVERNMENT IN BULGARIA. SURVEYS LEGAL SOURCES, ROOTS OF THE NATIONAL LEGISLATIVE SYSTEM, AND TRANSITION TO PRESENT SYSTEM. PRIMARILY RECENT PUBLICATIONS.

2737 SKALWEIT S.
FRANKREICH UND FRIEDRICH DER GROSSE.
BONN: LUDWIG ROHRSCHEID VERLAG, 1952, 201 PP.
ANALYZES PUBLIC OPINION IN FRANCE OF 18TH CENTURY TOWARD PRUSSIA AND PARTICULARLY THE REIGN OF FREDERICK THE GREAT. ATTEMPTS TO DISCOVER BASIC MOTIVES AND RELATE THEM TO SOCIAL AND POLITICAL ORIGINS. BASED ON MEMOIRS, DIARIES, CORRESPONDENCE, AND POLITICAL PAMPHLETS.

2738 SKILLING H.G.
THE GOVERNMENTS OF COMMUNIST EAST EUROPE.
NEW YORK: THOMAS Y CROWELL, 1966, 256 PP., LC#66-14616.
COMPARATIVE STUDY OF GOVERNMENTS, BRINGING OUT HISTORY OF RISE OF EASTERN EUROPEAN REGIMES. ANALYZES CONSTITUTIONAL FORMS AND PARTY STRUCTURE, THE EXECUTIVES OF STATES, PLUS INNER COUNCILS AND CENTRAL COMMITTEES OF POWER ELITE. SHOWS HOW VARIOUS INTEREST GROUPS AFFECT DECISION-MAKING AND EXECUTION OF POLICY; DEMONSTRATES THAT TOTALITARIANISM IS IN GREAT TRANSITION IN EASTERN EUROPE.

2739 SKILLING H.G.
"THE RUMANIAN NATIONAL COURSE."
INT. J., 21 (FALL 66), 470-483.
DESCRIBES RESURGENT NATIONALISM IN RUMANIA AND RESULTING INDEPENDENT POLICY WITHIN COMMUNIST BLOC. ALSO CONSIDERS REPERCUSSIONS IN NON-COMMUNIST WORLD RESULTING FROM SUCH INDEPENDENCE.

2740 SKUBISZEWSKI K.
"FORMS OF PARTICIPATION OF INTERNATIONAL ORGANIZATION IN THE LAW MAKING PROCESS."
INT. ORGAN., 18 (AUTUMN 64), 790-805.
'THIS ARTICLE SEEKS TO LIST AND BRIEFLY ANALYZE THE DIFFERENT WAYS AND FORMS WHEREBY CONTEMPORARY INTERNATIONAL ORGANIZATIONS PARTICIPATE IN THE MAKING OF NEW RULES OF PUBLIC INTERNATIONAL LAW.' TREATIES, RESOLUTIONS BEARING ON INTERNATIONAL LAW, ENACTMENT OF INTERNAL LAW OF INTERNATIONAL ORGANIZATION, AND LAW MAKINGS ARE DISCUSSED.

2741 SLESSOR J.
WHAT PRICE COEXISTENCE?
NEW YORK: FREDERICK PRAEGER, 1961, 153 PP., LC#61-13864.
SURVEY OF MAJOR ISSUES IN CURRENT INTERNATIONAL POLITICAL AFFAIRS AND FOREIGN POLICY STRATEGIES NOW BEING FOLLOWED BY WESTERN POWERS. EMPHASIS IS ON COLD WAR DEVELOPMENTS PRINCIPALLY INVOLVING MEMBERS OF NATO ALLIANCE. FOCUSES ON ARMS CONTROL, POSSIBILITIES OF FUTURE NUCLEAR WARFARE, AND OTHER ASPECTS OF MILITARY POLICY.

2742 SLICK T.
PERMANENT PEACE: A CHECK AND BALANCE PLAN.
ENGLEWOOD CLIFFS: PRENTICE HALL, 1958, 182 PP.
SEES NECESSITY OF BRINGING ALL NATIONS UNDER A RULE OF LAW IF WE ARE TO ARRIVE AT A WORLD SYSTEM WITH PERMANENT PEACE. BELIEVES MOST IMPORTANT STEP IS TO TRANSFER PORTION OF NATIONAL SOVEREIGNTY TO INTERNATIONAL AUTHORITY AND THAT IT IS TO THIS FACT THAT THERE IS MOST PUBIC RESISTANCE.

2743 SMITH A.
LECTURES ON JUSTICE, POLICE, REVENUE AND ARMS (1763)
LONDON: OXFORD U PR, 1896, 293 PP.
DISCUSSES THEORIES OF JURISPRUDENCE FROM LAISSEZ-FAIRE STANDPOINT. CONSIDERS JUSTICE TO BE SECURITY FROM INJURY; PRICE CEILINGS AN OBJECTIVE OF LAW ENFORCEMENT; AND PREFERRED MEANS OF TAXATION TO BE THAT WHICH IS LEAST DISCOMFITING. CONCENTRATES ON ENGLISH JUDICIAL SYSTEM FOR EXAMPLES. ALSO EXAMINES POSSIBILITY OF EXISTENCE OF NATURAL LAW'S AFFECTING INTERNATIONAL RELATIONS.

2744 SMITH A.L. JR.
THE DEUTSCHTUM OF NAZI GERMANY AND THE UNITED STATES.
THE HAGUE: MARTINUS NIJHOFF, 1965, 172 PP.
STUDIES RELATIONSHIP BETWEEN GERMAN EMIGRANTS TO US, AND GERMANY AFTER WWI. WITH NAZISM CAME BELIEF THAT ALL GERMAN COLONIES ABROAD MUST MAINTAIN THEIR NATIONAL AND RACIAL IDENTITY AND BECOME "MISSIONARIES" OF NATIONAL SOCIALISM FOR FURTHER EXPANSION OF GERMANY. INCLUDES DISCUSSION OF AGENCIES ESTABLISHED FOR THIS PURPOSE, THEIR ACTIVITIES, AND EFFECTS OF PLAN ON ESTABLISHED GERMAN-AMERICANS.

2745 SMITH C.M., WINOGRAD B., JWAIDEH A.R.
INTERNATIONAL COMMUNICATION AND POLITICAL WARFARE: AN ANNOTATED BIBLIOGRAPHY (A PAPER)
NEW YORK: RAND CORP, 1952, 508 PP.
ARRANGED INTO SIX TOPICS CONTAINING 1,659 ENTRIES INCLUDING FOREIGN LANGUAGES. DEALS WITH PROPAGANDA OF VARIOUS KINDS, RESEARCH AND INTELLIGENCE, AND A BIBLIOGRAPHY OF JOURNALS. CONTAINS DETAILED TABLE OF CONTENTS, EACH MAJOR SECTION PRECEDED BY YELLOW PAGE EXPLAINING ITS SCOPE AND CONTENT.

2746 SMITH D.M.
AMERICAN INTERVENTION, 1917.
BOSTON: HOUGHTON MIFFLIN, 1966, 260 PP.
ASKS WHETHER US INVOLVEMENT IN WWI WAS DUE TO SENTIMENT, SELF-INTEREST, OR IDEALS. INCLUDES DOCUMENTS AND SECONDARY READINGS DEALING WITH US SHIFT FROM NEUTRALITY IN WWI. DISCUSSES ROLE OF PROPAGANDA, US ATTITUDES TOWARD THE WAR, ROLE OF INTERNATIONAL TRADE, EFFECT OF THE SINKING OF THE LUSITANIA, AND USE OF SUBMARINE WARFARE. ATTEMPTS TO ASCERTAIN CAUSES FOR WWI.

2747 SMITH J.E.
THE DEFENSE OF BERLIN.
BALTIMORE: JOHNS HOPKINS PRESS, 1963, 431 PP., LC#63-17670.
ANALYSIS OF BERLIN AS FACTOR OF INTERNATIONAL RELATIONS SINCE WWII. EXAMINES ALLIED WARTIME PLANS REGARDING OCCUPATION OF BERLIN AND POSTWAR STATUS AND PROTECTION. DEALS WITH DIVISION OF CITY, BLOCKADE BY USSR, AND THE BERLIN WALL.

2748 SMUTS J.C.
AFRICA AND SOME WORLD PROBLEMS.
LONDON: OXFORD U PR, 1930, 184 PP.
GENERAL SMUTS' 1929 LECTURES IN ENGLAND ON SEVERAL AFRICAN TOPICS: DAVID LIVINGSTONE, CECIL RHODES, THE DISCOVERY AND SETTLEMENT OF THE CONTINENT, AND THE QUESTION OF NATIVE POLICY IN SOUTH AFRICA. SMUTS STOUTLY DEFENDS RHODES'S NEW GLEN GREY LEGISLATION WHEREBY WHITES AND BLACKS ARE GUARANTEED SEPARATE AND PARALLEL RIGHTS AND DEVELOPMENT. INCLUDES DISCUSSION OF LEAGUE AND WORLD PEACE.

2749 SNELL J.L. ED.
THE MEANING OF YALTA: BIG THREE DIPLOMACY AND THE NEW BALANCE OF POWER.
BATON ROUGE: LOUISIANA ST U PR, 1956, 239 PP., LC#56-7960.
ILLUSTRATED STUDY OF CONFERENCE EMPHASIZING NATIONAL INTEREST, POLITICAL COMMITMENTS, AND INITIAL OPTIMISM OF NATIONAL PEACEMAKING.

2750 SNOW J.H.
GOVERNMENT BY TREASON.
NEW CANAAN: LONG HOUSE, 1962, 79 PP., LC#62-19462.
EXAMINES AMERICA'S USE OF TAX MONEY AND GENERAL FISCAL POLICY, ESPECIALLY THAT OF FOREIGN AID. MAINTAINS THAT AMERICAN PEOPLE ARE BEING MISLED ABOUT DANGERS OF COMMUNISM, FOREIGN POLICY, AND USE OF TAX REVENUE. AMERICA SHOULD USE HER WEALTH TO ADVANCE DOMESTICALLY AND PEOPLE SHOULD RETAKE TAXING POWER FROM CONGRESS TO PREVENT MISUSE.

2751 SNYDER L.L.D. ED.
THE IMPERIALISM READER.
PRINCETON: VAN NOSTRAND, 1962, 619 PP.
DOCUMENTS AND READINGS ON MODERN EXPANSIONISM, TRACING THE MEANING, ORIGINS AND DEVELOPMENT OF IMPERIALISM.

2752 SNYDER R.C., FURNISS E.S.
AMERICAN FOREIGN POLICY.
NEW YORK: RINEHART, 1955, 846 PP.
STUDIES OF SUBJECT AND ITS FORMULATION, PRINCIPLES, AND PROGRAMS. INCLUDES HISTORICAL BACKGROUND, THE DECISION-MAKING PROCESS, ORGANIZATION AND FUNCTIONS OF STATE DEPARTMENT, AND POSTWAR INTERNATIONAL ENVIRONMENT.

2753 SNYDER R.N., PAIGE G.D.
"THE UNITED STATES DECISION TO RESIST AGGRESSION IN KOREA."
ITHACA: CORNELL U. PR., 1958, 37 PP.
CONCERNED WITH DEVISING A MORE ADEQUATE THEORY FOR THE DESCRIPTION AND EXPLANATION OF INTERNATIONAL RELATIONS. BASED ON CASE-STUDY OF A MAJOR FOREIGN-POLICY DECISION ANALYZED IN TERMS OF A GENERALIZED CONCEPTUAL SCHEME. SYSTEMATICAL ANALYSIS OF DOCUMENTS, MEMOIRS AND HEARINGS.

2754 SOBEL L.A. ED.
SOUTH VIETNAM: US-COMMUNIST CONFRONTATION IN SOUTHEAST ASIA 1961-65.
NEW YORK: FACTS ON FILE, INC, 1966, 238 PP., LC#66-23943.
REFERENCE BOOK IN JOURNALISTIC STYLE ON SPECIFIC EVENTS IN VIETNAM FROM 1961-65. PRESENTS GEOGRAPHIC ASPECTS OF

STRUGGLE, US AID TO DIEM, GROWING US INTERVENTION IN 1962, OVERTHROW OF DIEM AND CIVIL WAR OF 1963, EXPANSION OF WAR TO NORTH VIETNAM IN 1964, AIR WAR, PEACE ATTEMPTS, US BUILD-UP IN SOUTH, AND DOMESTIC PROBLEMS IN US IN 1965.

2755 SOBEL R.
THE ORIGINS OF INTERVENTIONISM: THE UNITED STATES AND THE RUSSO-FINNISH WAR.
NEW YORK: BOOKMAN ASSOCIATES, 1960, 204 PP., LC#60-14918.
STUDIES EFFECT OF RUSSO-FINNISH WAR ON US ATTITUDES TOWARD FOREIGN AFFAIRS. DEALS WITH IMPACT OF THE WAR UPON US ISOLATIONISM. REVIEWS OPINIONS OF PUBLIC AND PRESS. ANALYZES CONGRESSIONAL ACTION INVOLVED. DISCUSSES INTERVENTIONISM AS PART OF US FOREIGN POLICY.

2756 SOC OF COMP LEGIS AND INT LAW
THE LAW OF THE SEA... (PAMPHLET)
LONDON: SOC COMPAR LEGISLATION, 1958, 42 PP.
CONCERNED WITH UN CONFERENCE ON LAW OF THE SEA HELD IN GENEVA IN 1958. CONSIDERS CLAIMS TO JURISDICTION OVER TERRITORIAL SEA, CONTIGUOUS ZONE, AND THE CONTINENTAL SHELF. INCLUDES RESOLUTIONS ON NUCLEAR TESTS ON HIGH SEAS, HUMANE KILLING OF MARINE LIFE, FISHERY CONSERVATION CONVENTIONS, POLLUTION OF HIGH SEAS BY RADIOACTIVE MATERIALS, AND OPTIONAL PROTOCOL OF SIGNATURE ON SETTLEMENT OF DISPUTES.

2757 SOCIAL SCIENCE RESEARCH COUN
PUBLIC REACTION TO THE ATOMIC BOMB AND WORLD AFFAIRS.
ITHACA: CORNELL U PRESS, 1947, 310 PP.
RESULTS OF SURVEYS TAKEN BEFORE AND AFTER NAVAL ATOMIC BOMB PROJECT AT BIKINI, USING BOTH EXTENSIVE SURVEY TECHNIQUES AND INTENSIVE INTERVIEWS. PRESENTS RELATIONSHIP BETWEEN OPINIONS AND SOCIAL BACKGROUND AND INTERRELATIONS OF SELECTED ATTITUDES. FINDS THAT PUBLIC FELT US SHOULD CONTINUE TO DEVELOP BOMBS AND THAT US COULD CONTROL THEM.

2758 SOCIAL SCIENCE RESEARCH COUN
BIBLIOGRAPHY OF RESEARCH IN THE SOCIAL SCIENCES IN AUSTRALIA 1957-1960.
SYDNEY: SOC SCI RES COUN AUSTRAL, 1961, 102 PP.
COVERS UNIVERSITY-SPONSORED, GOVERNMENTAL AND NONUNIVERSITY AGENCY PUBLICATIONS ISSUED FROM 1957-1960.

2759 SOCIETE DES NATIONS
TRAITES INTERNATIONAUX ET ACTES LEGISLATIFS.
PARIS: CONSEIL D'ETAT.
PUBLISHED ANNUALLY DURING 1930-40. LISTS INTERNATIONAL TREATIES AND LEGISLATIVE ACTS OF VARIOUS COUNTRIES PERTAINING TO TREATY-MAKING. EACH ISSUE CONTAINS ABOUT 1,500 ITEMS.

2760 SOHN L.B.
CASES AND OTHER MATERIALS ON WORLD LAW.
BROOKLYN: FOUNDATION PR., 1950, 1363 PP.
OUTGROWTH OF COURSE ON WORLD ORGANIZATION AT HARVARD LAW SCHOOL. CONTAINS CONSTITUTIONAL TEXTS, JUDICIAL DECISIONS, AND OFFICIAL DOCUMENTS SERVING AS AN INTERPRETATION AND APPLICATION OF THE UN CHARTER AND CONSTITUTIONS OF OTHER INTERNATIONAL AGENCIES. SECTION ON INTERNATIONAL COURTS INCLUDES REPRESENTATIVE CASES IN RE ARBITRATION AND CONCILIATION. DRAFT OF WORLD CONSTITUTION.

2761 SOHN L.B.
BASIC DOCUMENTS OF THE UNITED NATIONS.
BROOKLYN: FOUND. PR., 1956, 307 PP.
COMPILATION OF DOCUMENTS INTENDED TO SERVE AS A REFERENCE VOLUME. REPRODUCTION OF UN CHARTER ACCOMPANIED BY THIRTY-EIGHT SUPPLEMENTARY RECORDS AND FIFTEEN EXPLANATORY NOTES.

2762 SOHN L.B.
"THE DEFINITION OF AGGRESSION."
VIRGINIA LAW REV., 45 (JUNE 59), 697-701.
DEMANDS THAT THE INTERNATIONAL COURTS BE STRENGTHENED, SO THAT AGGRESSIVE NATIONS WILL BE PROSECUTED. FEELS THAT A CLEARER UNDERSTANDING OF THE LAW IS NECESSARY IN ORDER TO DO THIS.

2763 SOKOL A.E.
SEAPOWER IN THE NUCLEAR AGE.
WASHINGTON: PUBLIC AFFAIRS PRESS, 1961, 268 PP., LC#59-15850
INVESTIGATES SEA POWER AS MAJOR ASPECT OF NATIONAL POWER AND MILITARY FORCE. SEA POWER CONTRIBUTES GREATLY TO INTERNATIONAL TRADE AND IS ONE MILITARY AREA IN WHICH US IS CONSIDERABLY MORE ADVANCED THAN USSR. SUGGESTS RECONSIDERATION OF SEA POWER POLICY IN LIGHT OF NUCLEAR AGE.

2764 SOLDATI A.
"EOCNOMIC DISINTEGRATION IN EUROPE."
FOR. AFF., 38 (OCT. 59), 715-83.
RECOMMENDS ECONOMIC TIES AMONG ALL EUROPEAN COUNTRIES. DELINEATES DEVELOPMENTS NECESSARY TO ACHIEVE COMMON AGREEMENT.

2765 SOMMER T.
DEUTSCHLAND UND JAPAN ZWISCHEN DEN MACHTEN.
TUBINGEN: J C B MOHR, 1962, 540 PP.
DISCUSSES DIPLOMATIC RELATIONS BETWEEN GERMANY AND JAPAN FROM ALLIANCE IN 1935 TO 1940. SEEKS TO DESTROY POPULAR NOTION THAT CLOSE COLLABORATION EXISTED BETWEEN THE TWO POWERS. SHEDS LIGHT ON STRUCTURE AND FUNCTION OF TOTALITARIAN DIPLOMACY.

2766 SOMMER T.
"BONN CHANGES COURSE."
FOREIGN AFFAIRS, 45 (APR. 67), 477-491.
DISCUSSES GENERAL DIRECTION OF GERMANY'S FUTURE FOREIGN POLICY UNDER KIESINGER-BRANDT COALITION. PREDICTS FOREIGN POLICY CHANGES IN THREE AREAS: IN GERMANY'S RELATIONS WITH ITS WESTERN ALLIES, WITH THE COMMUNIST NATIONS, AND WITH EAST GERMANY. APPRAISES COALITION GOVERNMENT AS REALISTIC AND PRACTICAL IN ITS DOCTRINE OF DETENTE TOWARD EAST GERMANY AND ITS CONCEPT OF COOPERATIVE PARTITION WITH HER.

2767 SONDERMANN F.A.
"SOCIOLOGY AND INTERNATIONAL RELATIONS."
SOCIOL. SOC. RES., 42 (MARCH-APRIL 58), 249-255.
REVEALS THE EXISTING AND POTENTIAL RELATIONSHIP BETWEEN THE TWO FIELDS AND CITES NEED FOR A NEW APPROACH TO INTERNATIONAL RELATIONS UTILIZING THIS CONCEPT. DISCLOSES WEAKNESS OR ABSENCE OF FACTORS WHICH CONTRIBUTE TO PEACEFUL RESOLUTION OF CONFLICTS.

2768 SONNENFELDT H.
"FOREIGN POLICY FROM MALENKOV TO KHRUSHCHEV."
PROBL. COMMUNISM, 12 (MARCH-APRIL 63), 9-18.
SOVIET PRESTIGE, AFTER STALIN'S DEATH, IS EVALUATED AND CONSIDERATION GIVEN TO STEPS TAKEN TO IMPROVE IT. STALEMATE IN EUROPE HAS FOCUSED COMMUNIST ATTENTION ON EMERGING NATIONS. DEMONSTRATES SOVIET ATTEMPTS TO 'USE' ECONOMIC AID AND MILITARY DISPLAY TO ATTAIN POLITICAL OBJECTIVES.

2769 SOPER T.
EVOLVING COMMONWEALTH.
NEW YORK: PERGAMON PRESS, 1965, 141 PP., LC#65-27362.
ESSAY ON HISTORY AND DEVELOPMENT OF BRITISH EMPIRE AND COMMONWEALTH FROM COLONIALISM TO PRESENT DAY. DISCUSSES INDEPENDENCE OF SOME NATIONS, ADDITION OF OTHERS TO COMMONWEALTH; STRUCTURE OF ORGANIZATION; LAWS REGULATING GROUP RELATIONS; AND ROLE OF COMMONWEALTH IN SUCH AREAS AS COMMON MARKET.

2770 SPAAK P.H.
"THE SEARCH FOR CONSENSUS: A NEW EFFORT TO BUILD EUROPE."
FOR. AFF., 43 (JAN. 62), 199-209.
ANALYZES PROBLEMS OF COMMON MARKET AND ATLANTIC ALLIANCE, SEEING THEM AS CLOSELY INTERRELATED. CONSIDERS NATIONALISM AND ITS RECENT UPSURGE TO BE 'INTEGRATED', EUROPE'S BASIC PROBLEM AND STUDIES POSITION OF FRANCE AND GERMANY IN THIS LIGHT.

2771 SPANIER J.W., NOGEE J.L.
THE POLITICS OF DISARMAMENT.
NEW YORK: PRAEGER, 1962, 226 PP., $1.95 PP.
STUDIES ROLE PLAYED BY AMERICAN-SOVIET DISARMAMENT NEGOTIATIONS IN DIPLOMACY OF COLD WAR. ANALYZES POLITICAL OBJECTIVES SOUGHT BY BOTH NATIONS DURING THEIR NEGOTIATIONS AND TACTICS EMPLOYED TO ACHIEVE OBJECTIVES.

2772 SPANIER J.W.
"WORLD POLITICS IN AN AGE OF REVOLUTION."
NEW YORK: FREDERICK PRAEGER, 1967.
ANALYSIS OF REVOLUTION IN MILITARY TECHNOLOGY, NATIONAIST AND SOCIAL REVOLUTION THROUGHOUT UNDERDEVELOPED AREAS; AND "PERMANENT" REVOLUTION OF COMMUNISM AS HAVING PROFOUNDLY TRANSFORMED NATURE OF INTERNATIONAL POLITICS SINCE WWII. IMPACT OF THREE REVOLUTIONS UPON PRESENT STATE SYSTEM ASSESSED. ARGUES FOR IMPACT OF DOMESTIC AFFAIRS OVER INTERNATIONAL EVENTS IN CREATING POLICY. SELECTIVE BIBLIOGRAPHY.

2773 SPEARS E.L.
TWO MEN WHO SAVED FRANCE: PETAIN AND DE GAULLE.
LONDON: EYRE AND SPOTTISWOODE, 1966, 222 PP.
DESCRIBES AUTHOR'S PERSONAL EXPERIENCES WITH GENERAL PETAIN DURING WWI, SHOWING HIS GREAT LEADERSHIP ABILITY AND IMPORTANT ROLE IN VICTORY IN WWII. INCLUDES TRANSLATION OF PETAIN'S ACCOUNTS OF MUTINIES IN FRENCH ARMY IN 1917. DISCUSSES GENERAL DE GAULLE'S PERSONALITY AND ROLE IN MAKING FRANCE THE STRONG NATION SHE IS TODAY.

2774 SPECTOR I.
"SOVIET POLICY IN ASIA: A REAPPRAISAL."
CURR. HIST., 43 (NOV. 62), 257-262.
REAPPRAISAL OF SOVIET POLICY IN ORIENT DURING 1960-1962, WITH OBJECT BEING COMPLETE DE-WESTERNIZATION OF ASIA AND REORIENTATION TOWARD USSR. CONSIDERS SINO-SOVIET CONTROVERSEY AND RUSSIAN ACTIVITIES IN INDONESIA, INDIA, AND JAPAN.

2775 SPECTOR S.D.
A CHECKLIST OF PAPERBOUND BOOKS ON RUSSIA.
ALBANY: STATE U OF NY AT ALBANY, 1964, 63 PP.
AN UNANNOTATED BIBLIOGRAPHY OF PAPERBOUND BOOKS ON RUSSIA COVERING ART, GOVERNMENT, SCIENCES, LITERATURE, MEDICINE. MATERIAL IS IN ENGLISH LANGUAGE. CONTAINS 1,080 ENTRIES.

2776 SPEECKAERT G.P.
INTERNATIONAL INSTITUTIONS AND INTERNATIONAL ORGANIZATIONS.
PARIS: UNESCO, 1956, 116 PP.
AN UNANNOTATED BIBLIOGRAPHY ON INTERNATIONAL INSTITUTIONS AND INTERNATIONAL ORGANIZATIONS. MATERIAL IN ENGLISH LANGUAGE AND SOME FRENCH, GERMAN, AND ITALIAN. PUBLICATION OF MATERIAL RANGES FROM 1894 TO 1955. CONTAINS 783 ENTRIES.

2777 SPEECKAERT G.P.
SELECT BIBLIOGRAPHY ON INTERNATIONAL ORGANIZATION, 1885-1964
BRUSSELS: UNION OF INTL ASSN, 1965, 148 PP.
SOME 350 TITLES ARE LISTED ALPHABETICALLY BY AUTHOR FOR WORKS DEALING WITH INTERNATIONAL ORGANIZATION IN GENERAL. SOME 730 TITLES ARE LISTED RELATING TO 214 SPECIFIC ORGANIZATIONS; HERE THE DIVISION IS FRENCH ALPHABETIZATION OF ORGANIZATIONAL TITLES, THEN SUBDIVIDED CHRONOLOGICALLY TO PROVIDE "HISTORY AT A GLANCE." NOT ANNOTATED.

2778 SPEER J.P.
FOR WHAT PURPOSE?
WASHINGTON: PUBLIC AFFAIRS PRESS, 1960, 87 PP., LC#59-15846.
MEDITATIONS, ELABORATIONS, AND EXHORTATIONS BASED ON BIBLICAL TEXTS RELEVANT TO THEMONUCLEAR AGE. TO FIND ALTERNATIVES TO WAR FOR SETTLING DISPUTES IS IMPERATIVE. AMERICA HAS CREATED THERMONUCLEAR WARFARE AND AS A CHRISTIAN NATION MUST NOW DO SOMETHING TO CURB IT.

2779 SPEIER H. ED., KAHLER A. ED.
WAR IN OUR TIME.
NEW YORK: W W NORTON, 1939, 362 PP.
CONCERNS NATURE OF TOTAL WARFARE IN 20TH CENTURY UP TO WWII, REFERRING TO EARLIER HISTORICAL DEVELOPMENTS. TREATS POWER POLITICS, PEACE PLANS, NATIONAL SOVEREIGNTY, AND DOMESTIC POLICY VERSUS FOREIGN RELATION. ECONOMIC ASPECTS INCLUDE PRODUCTION OF RAW MATERIALS AND FOODSTUFFS, COSTS, FINANCES, AND LABOR PROBLEMS. PROBLEM OF MAINTAINING MORALE AND VALUE OF PROPAGANDA ARE EVALUATED.

2780 SPEIER H.
GERMAN REARMAMENT AND ATOMIC WAR: THE VIEWS OF GERMAN MILITARY AND POLITICAL LEADERS.
EVANSTON: ROW PETERSON, 1957, 272 PP.
DISCLOSES THAT GERMAN MILITARY EXPERTS DO NOT EXPECT ANY FUTURE USE OF NUCLEAR WEAPONS AND WILL RELY MAINLY ON LARGE HOME FORCES TO MEET THREAT OF WAR.

2781 SPEIER H.
"SOVIET ATOMIC BLACKMAIL AND THE NORTH ATLANTIC ALLIANCE."
WORLD POLIT., 9 (57), 307-328.
ANALYZES ATOMIC THREATS IN TERMS OF THEIR NATURE, CONDITIONS AND TERMS OF COMPLIANCE. THERMONUCLEAR PARITY REDUCES THREAT-VALUE OF WEAPONS. NATO DEPENDS ON AMERICAN NUCLEAR POWER RATHER THAN EQUAL DISTRIBUTION OF WEAPONS.

2782 SPEIER H.
DIVIDED BERLIN: THE ANATOMY OF SOVIET POLITICAL BLACKMAIL.
NEW YORK: PRAEGER, 1960, 201 PP.
ANALYSIS BASED ON VIEW THAT, AFTER HITLER'S DOWNFALL, WW 2 VICTORS UNABLE TO AGREE ON RESTORATION OF FORMER POLITICAL SYSTEM. TRACES HISTORY OF COLD WAR, FOCUSING ON PSYCHOLOGICAL AND POLITICAL PROBLEMS. CONCLUDES WITH U-2 INCIDENT AND PARIS CONFERENCE.

2783 SPENCE J.E.
REPUBLIC UNDER PRESSURE: A STUDY OF SOUTH AFRICAN FOREIGN POLICY.
LONDON: OXFORD U PR, 1965, 132 PP.
STRESSES LINK BETWEEN DOMESTIC AND FOREIGN POLICY AND DISCUSSES PROBABLE EFFECT OF EXTERNAL PRESSURES ON SOUTH AFRICAN GOVERNMENT; EXAMINES ITS ROLE IN INTERNATIONAL ORGANIZATIONS, ITS ECONOMIC POSITION, ITS VULNERABILITY TO CONCERTED UN ECONOMIC ACTION, AND ITS PROSPECTS FOR PEACEFUL CO-EXISTENCE WITH NEIGHBORS. OFFERS TENTATIVE CONCLUSIONS ON ABILITY TO KEEP PRESENT COURSE IN INTERNATIONAL AFFAIRS.

2784 SPENCER F.A.
WAR AND POSTWAR GREECE: AN ANALYSIS BASED ON GREEK WRITINGS.
WASHINGTON: LIBRARY OF CONGRESS, 1952, 175 PP.
SURVEYS POLITICAL AND SOCIAL EVENTS IN POSTWAR GREECE USING GREEK SOURCES PUBLISHED 1944-52: BOOKS, NEWSPAPERS, AND PERIODICALS. DISCUSSES SOURCES DEALING WITH AXIS INVASION AND OCCUPATION, GREEK RESISTANCE FORCES, LIBERATION, THE CIVIL WAR, THE LULL (1945-1946), COMMUNIST AGRESSION, RECONSTRUCTION. ALSO LISTS BOOKS ON SOCIAL AND CULTURAL PATTERNS. GENERAL INTRODUCTION TO SOURCES. UNINDEXED.

2785 SPENCER R.
"GERMANY AFTER THE AUTUMN CRISIS."
INTERNATIONAL JOURNAL, 22 (SPRING 67), 231-252.
REPORT ON POLITICAL EVENTS OF LATE 1966 AND DEVELOPMENTS RESULTING FROM NOVEMBER CRISIS. DETAILED ELECTORAL REPORT OF PARTY FORTUNES. DISCUSSION OF "TURN TO THE EAST" OF THE KIESINGER-BRANDT GOVERNMENT. EXAMINATION OF NPD RISE OF RECENT DAYS.

2786 SPENSER J.H.
"AFRICA AT THE UNITED NATIONS: SOME OBSERVATIONS."
INT. ORGAN., 16 (SPRING 62), 375-386.
DISCUSSES IMPACT OF TWENTY-EIGHT AFRICAN MEMBERS ON THE ORGANIZATION. COVERS FOLLOWING SUBJECTS: FORMATION OF THE AFRICAN CAUCUS, AFRICAN STAND ON CERTAIN IMPORTANT ISSUES BEFORE THE GENERAL ASSEMBLY, THE ISSUE OF SELF-DETERMINATION, AND THE CONCERN FOR 'STATUS QUO' AND TERRITORIAL INTEGRITY.

2787 SPICER K.
A SAMARITAN STATE?
TORONTO: TORONTO UNIV PRESS, 1966, 272 PP.
DETAILED RECORDS OF CANADA'S AID PROGRAM IN PAST SIX FORMATIVE YEARS. PREFACED BY FIRST CHAPTER WHICH POSES MAJOR ISSUES OF POLICY FOR CANADIANS, THEN MOVES INTO HISTORY OF CANADIAN AID.

2788 SPINELLI A.
"IL TRATTATO DI MOSCA E I PROBLEMI DELLA COESISTENZA PACIFICA."
MULINO, 12 (NO. 131, 63), 823-28.
SEEKS TO DEFINE MORAL REASONS SUPPORTING NECESSITY OF WORLD WITHOUT WAR. SEPARATES MYTHS FROM REALITIES. CRITICIZES FRANCE AND CHINA FOR PERPETUATING MYTHS. ANALYZES OVERRIDING INTERESTS OF NUCLEAR POWERS. REVIEWS APPROACHES TO DISARMAMENT PROBLEM BY THESE NATIONS.

2789 SPINELLI A.
THE EUROCRATS; CONFLICT AND CRISIS IN THE EUROPEAN COMMUNITY (TRANS. BY C. GROVE HAINES)
BALTIMORE: JOHNS HOPKINS PRESS, 1966, 229 PP., LC#66-14379.
DESCRIBES CENTERS OF UNITED EUROPEAN ACTION, SHOWING WAY THEY ARE INTERCONNECTED AND THEIR LIMITATIONS AND POSSIBILITIES. PRESENTS ORIGINS OF EUROPEAN COMMUNITY IDEA; GROUPS FORMED, SUCH AS EURATOM COMMISSION AND COMMON MARKET; RELATIONSHIP OF NATIONAL BUREAUCRACIES; STRENGTH OF INTEREST GROUPS; AND POLITICAL ORGANIZATION OF EUROPEAN COMMUNITY.

2790 SPIRO H.J.
POLITICS IN AFRICA: PROSPECTS SOUTH OF THE SAHARA.
ENGLEWOOD CLIFFS: PRENTICE HALL, 1962, 183 PP., LC#62-9313.
LOOKS AT POLITICAL SYSTEMS IN AFRICA AND JUDGES THEM FOR WHAT THEY ARE, RATHER THAN BY THEIR APPROXIMATION TO WESTERN SYSTEMS. BELIEVES AFRICA MAY MAKE POSITIVE CONTRIBUTION TO CONSTITUTIONAL DEVELOPMENT OF MANKIND BECAUSE HER GOVERNMENTS WERE BORN, UNLIKE WESTERN ONES, WITHOUT EMPHASIS ON BORDERS, MILITARY FORCE, OR CULTURAL HOMOGENEITY, AND THUS WILL NOT HAVE PROBLEMS CAUSED BY THOSE ISSUES.

2791 SPRINGER H.W.
"FEDERATION IN THE CARIBBEAN: AN ATTEMPT THAT FAILED."
INT. ORGAN., 16 (AUG. 62), 758-75.
TRACES EVOLUTION OF PLANS FOR CARIBBEAN FEDERATION AND DISCUSSES THE FORCES WHICH WORKED FOR AND AGAINST ITS ESTABLISHMENT.

2792 SPROUT H., SPROUT M.
MAN-MILIEU RELATIONSHIP HYPOTHESES IN THE CONTEXT OF INTERNATIONAL POLITICS.
PRINCETON: CTR OF INTL STUDIES, 1956, 101 PP.
EXAMINES THEORIES CONCERNING BEHAVIOR OF MAN IN ENVIRONMENT AS ANALYTICAL TOOL TOWARD UNDERSTANDING POLITICAL PHENOMENA. INCLUDES DETERMINISM, POSSIBILISM, PROBABILISM, AND COGNITIVE BEHAVIORALISM.

2793 SPULBER N.
THE STATE AND ECONOMIC DEVELOPMENT IN EASTERN EUROPE.
NEW YORK: RANDOM HOUSE, INC, 1966, 179 PP., LC#66-14883.
EXAMINES ROLE OF STATE IN ECONOMIC DEVELOPMENT OF SOVIET TYPE OF COUNTRY. STUDIES HISTORY OF STATE WITH RESPECT TO INDUSTRIALIZATION, CITING THE BALKAN COUNTRIES 1860-1960 IN THEIR CHANGE OF ECONOMIC STRUCTURE - CHANGE ACCOMPANIED BY EXPANSION OF STATE OWNERSHIP AND ECONOMIC ACTIVITY. COMPARES CAPITALISM TO STRUCTURED DEVELOPMENT WITH ITS CONCOMITANT DISCRIMINATION AND SELF-STYLED SUCCESS.

2794 SQUIRES J.D.
BRITISH PROPAGANDA AT HOME AND IN THE UNITED STATES FROM 1914 TO 1917.
CAMBRIDGE: HARVARD U PR, 1953, 113 PP.
ANALYSIS OF BRITISH PROPAGANDA DISTRIBUTED IN USA DURING WWI. REGARDS AMERICAN ENTRANCE INTO WAR AS ACHIEVEMENT OF MAJOR BRITISH PROPAGANDA GOAL. CONTENDS THAT EFFECTIVENESS OF BRITISH PROPAGANDA PROGRAM DURING WAR DEMONSTRATES NECESSITY AND POTENTIAL OF PROPAGANDA AS INSTRUMENT OF MODERN WARFARE.

2795 TENG SSU-YU, KENJI M., HIROMITSU K.
JAPANESE STUDIES ON JAPAN AND THE FAR EAST: A SHORT BIOGRAPHICAL AND BIBLIOGRAPHICAL INTRODUCTION.
HONG KONG: HONG KONG UNIV PR, 1961, 485 PP.
COMPILATION 760 SCHOLARS LISTING 5,000 WORKS SELECTED BY THEM AS HAVING PARTICULAR IMPORTANCE. UNDER EACH SUBJECT AUTHORS ARRANGED ALPHABETICALLY. CONTAINS ITEMS ON FAR EASTERN LEGAL INSTITUTIONS, POLITICS AND GOVERNMENT; ECON-

OMICS AND ECONOMIC DEVELOPMENT; SOCIOLOGY; INTERNATIONAL REALTIONS; HISTORY; AND CULTURE. ITEMS IN JAPANESE.

2796 ST LEGER A.
SELECTION OF WORKS FOR AN UNDERSTANDING OF WORLD AFFAIRS SINCE 1914.
WASHINGTON: LIBRARY OF CONGRESS, 1943, 87 PP.
PROVIDES A SELECTIVE LIST OF 875 ITEMS INCLUDING BOOKS, PAMPHLETS, ARTICLES, HISTORICAL STUDIES, DOCUMENTS, AND PERSONAL MEMOIRS. ARRANGED TOPICALLY AND BY COUNTRY. DESIGNED TO SERVE AS A POINT OF DEPARTURE FOR STUDY OF WORLD CONDITIONS BETWEEN WORLD WARS.

2797 STAAR R.F.
"ELECTIONS IN COMMUNIST POLAND."
MIDWEST. J. POLIT. SCI., 2 (MAY 58), 57-75.
BRIEF HISTORY OF POSTWAR POLAND'S ELECTIONS AND REFERENDUMS. EMPHASIZES EARLY COMMUNIST TECHNIQUES OF INTIMIDATION, COERCION AND FRAUD TO WIN ELECTIONS. CONCLUDES WITH ANALYSIS OF MORE RECENT DEMOCRATIC MACHINERY BEING USED NOW.

2798 STADLER K.R.
THE BIRTH OF THE AUSTRIAN REPUBLIC, 1918-1921.
LEYDEN: AW SIJTHOFF, 1966, 207 PP., LC#66-16271.
ACCOUNT OF EVENTS AND NEGOTIATIONS THAT LED TO FORMATION OF FIRST AUSTRIAN REPUBLIC AFTER WWI. DISCUSSION CENTERS ON PROBLEMS INVOLVING POLITICAL ISSUES, QUESTIONS OF TERRITORIAL SETTLEMENT, AND ECONOMIC ISSUES.

2799 STALEY E.
WAR AND THE PRIVATE INVESTOR.
CHICAGO: U. CHI. PR., 1935, 562 PP.
DOCUMENTED STUDY OF RELATIONSHIP BETWEEN PRIVATE INVESTMENTS AND INTERNATIONAL POLITICS, PARTICULARLY AS THEY BEAR ON INTERNATIONAL POLITICAL TENSIONS. OBSERVES TYPES OF COMFLICT THAT MAY ARISE BETWEEN COUNTRIES WITH TRADE RELATIONS.

2800 STALEY E.
WORLD ECONOMY IN TRANSITION.
NEW YORK: COUNCIL FOR. REL., 1939, 333 PP.
EXPLORES HOW CONFLICTING TENDENCIES OF TECHNOLOGY AND POLITICS AFFECT HUMAN WELFARE. NOTES CONSEQUENCES OF CHANGES IN STRUCTURE OF ECONOMIC ORGANIZATION ON INTERNATIONAL ECONOMIC RELATIONS AND POLICIES.

2801 STALEY E.
THE FUTURE OF UNDERDEVELOPED COUNTRIES: POLITICAL IMPLICATIONS OF ECONOMIC DEVELOPMENT.
NEW YORK: HARPER, 1954, 410 PP., $5.00.
DEFINES SUCCESSFUL DEVELOPMENT AND CONTRASTS COMMUNIST METHODS FOR ACHIEVING IT WITH THOSE OF THE WESTERN WORLD. CRITICAL ESTIMATE OF PROPAGANDA, AGRARIAN REFORM AND VARIOUS PROBLEMS ACCOMPANYING INDUSTRIALIZATION. ALTHOUGH A PREREQUISITE TO POLITICAL STABILITY, ECONOMIC DEVELOPMENT MAY NOT SUFFICE AND 'DOES NOT NECESSARILY MAKE NICE PEOPLE.'

2802 STANFORD RESEARCH INSTITUTE
POSSIBLE NONMILITARY SCIENTIFIC DEVELOPMENTS AND THEIR POTENTIAL IMPACT ON FOREIGN POLICY PROBLEMS OF THE UNITED. STATES.
WASHINGTON: G.P.O., 1959, 100 PP.
THEORIZING THAT INCREASED SCIENTIFIC KNOWLEDGE PRODUCES INCREASED WORLD TENSION, THE INITIATION OF A DEFINITE NONMILITARY SCIENTIFIC RESEARCH PROGRAM IS DESIRABLE. THIS WOULD COVER USE OF RESEARCH AND DEVELOPMENT IN FIELDS OF FOREIGN POLICY, WEATHER CONTROL OR WHEREVER NECESSARY.

2803 STANGER R.J. ED.
ESSAYS ON INTERVENTION.
COLUMBUS: OHIO STATE U PR, 1964, 125 PP., LC#64-17107.
FOUR VARIED APPROACHES TO IDEA THAT INTERNATIONAL LAW IS "AMBIGUOUS, OUTDATED, AND INADEQUATE." ALL AGREE THAT LINE BETWEEN INTERNAL STRIFE AND INTERNATIONAL CONFLICT THREATENING WORLD PEACE MUST BE DISTINCTLY DEFINED. ALL SEE NEED TO UTILIZE UN MORE OFTEN AND TO GIVE IT MORE POWERS, AS SUGGESTED.

2804 STANKIEWICZ W.J. ED.
POLITICAL THOUGHT SINCE WORLD WAR II.
NEW YORK: FREE PRESS OF GLENCOE, 1964, 462 PP., LC#63-16745.
CONTAINS THIRTY ESSAYS ON NATURE OF DEMOCRATIC AND TOTALITARIAN IDEOLOGIES. SELECTIONS ARE EXCERPTS FROM BOOKS OR ARTICLES. EMPHASIS ON IDEOLOGICAL CONFLICT AND THE RELATIONSHIP BETWEEN IDEOLOGY AND POLITICAL BEHAVIOR.

2805 STANLEY T.W.
"DECENTRALIZING NUCLEAR CONTROL IN NATO."
ORBIS, 7 (SPRING 63), 41-48.
PROPOSES SEVERAL SEPARATE COMMAND AND CONTROL SYSTEMS FOR NATO'S NUCLEAR FORCES. USA WOULD MAINTAIN CONTROL OVER MAJOR NUCLEAR FORCES FOR COUNTERFORCE AND MEDIUM-RANGE MISSILES AND TACTICAL AIRCRAFT IN EUROPE. OUTLINES HYPOTHETICAL CASES PROVING VALUE AND FEASIBILITY OF PROPOSALS.

2806 STANTON A.H. ED., PERRY S.E. ED.
PERSONALITY AND POLITICAL CRISIS.
NEW YORK: FREE PRESS OF GLENCOE, 1951, 260 PP.
ESSAYS BY HAROLD LASSWELL, TALCOTT PARSONS, DAVID RIESMAN, ET AL., ON NEW PERSPECTIVES DRAWN FROM SOCIAL SCIENCE AND PSYCHIATRY FOR THE STUDY OF WAR AND POLITICS. MAJOR TOPICS OF DISCUSSION INCLUDE PROPAGANDA AND MASS INSECURITY, PSYCHIATRIC ASPECTS OF MORALE, PERSONALITY AND SOCIAL STRUCTURE, AND THE CONCEPT OF NATIONAL CHARACTER.

2807 STARK H.
SOCIAL AND ECONOMIC FRONTIERS IN LATIN AMERICA (2ND ED.)
DUBUQUE: WC BROWN, 1961, 427 PP., LC#61-13707.
TEXTBOOK COVERING SOCIAL, ECONOMIC, AND POLITICAL CONDITIONS IN LATIN AMERICA. DISCUSSES CONTINENT AS A WHOLE: LANDS AND PEOPLES, POLITICO-MILITARY ORGANIZATION, COMMUNISM, ANTI-YANKEEISM, ECONOMIC PROGRAMS, PRODUCTION ACTIVITIES, AND INTERNATIONAL RELATIONSHIPS. OFFERS PREDICTIONS FOR FUTURE DEVELOPMENT AND ROLE OF LATIN AMERICA.

2808 STARR R.E.
POLAND 1944-1962: THE SOVIETIZATION OF A CAPTIVE PEOPLE.
BATON ROUGE: LOUISIANA ST U PR, 1962, 300 PP., LC#62-15027.
ATTEMPTS TO COMPARE SOME FEATURES OF SO-CALLED POLISH PEOPLE'S DEMOCRACY WITH THEIR COUNTERPARTS IN USSR AND OTHER EAST EUROPEAN SATELLITE COUNTRIES. EXAMINES GOVERNMENTAL DYNAMICS, INCLUDING ANALYSES OF LEGISLATIVE FOUNDATIONS AND ELECTIONS. STUDIES DOMESTIC, FOREIGN, AND DEFENSE POLICIES, DOMINANT POLITICAL PARTY, AND PRESSURE GROUPS AND QUASI-POLITICAL ORGANIZATIONS.

2809 STEEL R.
THE END OF THE ALLIANCE.
NEW YORK: VIKING PRESS, 1962, 148 PP., LC#64-15056.
DISCUSSES AMERICA AND FUTURE OF EUROPE IN LIGHT OF COLLAPSE OF OLD ALLIANCES AND NEW RESISTANCE TO US. TWO GERMANIES AND AMERICAN-RUSSIAN RELATIONS ARE CASES IN POINT.

2810 STEEL R.
"WHAT CAN THE UN DO?"
COMMENTARY, 43 (MAY 67), 84-89.
WITHIN THE FRAMEWORK OF A REVIEW OF SEVERAL BOOKS, A DISCUSSION OF THE FAILURES, SUCCESSES, AND PROBLEMS OF THE UN. THE UN, THOUGH FORCED TO BECOME SUBSERVIENT TO THE GREAT POWERS, IS USEFUL AS A SOUNDING BOARD FOR SMALL NATIONS, FOR ITS TOO-LITTLE RECOGNIZED SOCIAL AND ECONOMIC ACHIEVEMENTS, AND FOR OTHER REASONS. BUT THE ANTI-RHODESIA SANCTIONS SET A DANGEROUS PRECEDENT IN INTERFERING IN A DOMESTIC MATTER.

2811 STEEL R.
"BEYOND THE POWER BLOCS."
DISSENT, 14 (MAY-JUNE 67), 345-357.
AN ATTEMPT TO SET OUT THE PROBLEMS AND POSSIBILITIES IN INTERNATIONAL AFFAIRS IN VIEW OF THE DISINTEGRATION OF THE TWO GREAT POWER BLOCS, WITH SPECIAL REFERENCE TO THE US. THE IDEOLOGICAL ASPECT OF THE COLD WAR IS ENDED, AND THE MAIN CONTENTION NOW IS FOR POWER AND INFLUENCE. IN PLACE OF GREAT POWER CONFLICTS WILL BE STRUGGLES BETWEEN HAVES AND HAVENOTS. US MUST RECOGNIZE ITS REAL INTERESTS AND LIMITS.

2812 STEELE R.
"A TASTE FOR INTERVENTION."
NEW LEADER, 50 (JUNE 67), 13-17.
ARGUES THAT THE MAJOR INTERVENTIONIST POWER IN THE WORLD TODAY IS THE US. DISTINGUISHES POLICY FROM REALITIES, COLD WAR RHETORIC FROM GLOBAL FACTS, NATIONAL IDEALS FROM NATIONAL INTEREST, FOREIGN AID FROM FOREIGN MEDDLING. CONCLUDES THAT THE US FACES A DILEMMA OF POWER AND THAT ITS SOLUTION INVOLVES NOT ONLY AMERICA'S ROLE IN THE WORLD, BUT ALSO THE VERY BASIS OF AMERICAN DEMOCRACY.

2813 STEGER H.S., SCHRADER A., GRABENER J.
"RESEARCH ON LATIN AMERICA IN THE FEDERAL REPUBLIC OF GERMANY AND WEST BERLIN."
LATIN AMER. RESEARCH REV., 2 (SUMMER 67), 99-118.
SURVEYS RESEARCH SINCE 19TH CENTURY. DISCUSSES DISPERSION OF STUDIES TO SEVERAL UNIVERSITIES AFTER WWII AND ATTEMPTS AT UNIFICATION INTO ONE INSTITUTE, ASSOCIATION OF THEGERMAN LATIN AMERICAN INSTITUTES. DESCRIBES CURRENT RESEARCH PROJECTS AND AREAS IN WHICH RESEARCH HAS BEEN DONE, SUCH AS ATTITUDES, SOCIAL MOVEMENTS, URBANIZATION, EDUCATION, FOREIGN TRADE, AND ECONOMIC HISTORY.

2814 STEIN E. ED., NICHOLSON T.L. ED.
AMERICAN ENTERPRISE IN THE EUROPEAN COMMON MARKET: A LEGAL PROFILE.
ANN ARBOR: U. MICH. PR., 1960 2 VOLS., 1242 PP.
PROFESSORS AND INTERNATIONAL CIVIL SERVANTS IN USA AND EUROPE CONTRIBUTE TO TREATISE ON THE SUBJECT. DOCUMENTED EXTENSIVELY BY GOVERNING TREATIES AND INTERNATIONAL LAWS. FIRST VOLUME SURVEYS EUROPEAN INTEGRATION AND SECOND VOLUME PRESENTS VARIOUS LEGAL FORMS AVAILABLE TO AN ENTERPRISE IN BUSINESS OPERATIONS.

2815 STEIN E.
"MR HAMMARSKJOLD, THE CHARTER LAW AND THE FUTURE ROLE OF

THE UNITED NATIONS SECRETARY-GENERAL."
AMER. J. INT. LAW., 56 (JAN. 62), 9-32.
PROVIDES AN ACCOUNT OF HAMMARSKJOLD'S CONCEPT OF LEGAL-CONSTITUTIONAL FRAMEWORK WITHIN WHICH HE PERFORMED HIS HIGH OFFICE. IT WOULD BE UNWISE FOR MEMBER-NATIONS AND FOR UN POLITICAL ORGANS TO PLACE THE BURDEN OF THEIR RESPONSIBILITIES UPON SHOULDERS OF SECRETARY-GENERAL AND TO CHARGE HIM WITH POLITICAL TASKS WITHOUT PROPER GUIDANCE.

2816 STEIN E.
"TOWARD SUPREMACY OF TREATY-CONSTITUTION BY JUDICIAL FIAT: ON THE MARGIN OF THE COSTA CASE."
MICH. LAW REV., 63 (JAN. 65), 491-518.
STUDY OF THE RELATIONSHIP OF NATIONAL AND INTERNATIONAL LEGAL ORDERS ACCOMPLISHED BY ANALYSIS OF JUDGEMENTS HANDED DOWN ON THE SAME CASE BY AN ITALIAN COURT AND THE COURT OF THE EUROPEAN COMMUNITY. INQUIRY INTO THE CONSIDERATION OF TREATIES AS CONSTITUTIONAL IN NATURE AND AS TAKING PRECEDENCE OVER NATIONAL LAW.

2817 STEPHENS O.
FACTS TO A CANDID WORLD.
STANFORD: STANFORD U PRESS, 1955, 164 PP., LC#55-11262.
INVESTIGATES AMERICAN PROPAGANDA OVERSEAS - ITS PUBLIC OPINION, ORGANIZATION, AND OPERATION - THEN EVALUATES ITS EFFECTIVENESS.

2818 STERNBERG F.
THE MILITARY AND INDUSTRIAL REVOLUTION OF OUR TIME.
NEW YORK: FREDERICK PRAEGER, 1959, 359 PP., LC#59-7948.
ANALYSIS OF MAJOR CHANGES AND DEVELOPMENTS IN MILITARY AND INDUSTRIAL TECHNIQUES IN POSTWAR WORLD. EXAMINES US AND SOVIET MILITARY STRENGTH, NUCLEAR WEAPONS, AND RELATIONSHIP BETWEEN MILITARY AND INDUSTRY IN NEW INDUSTRIAL REVOLUTION.

2819 STETTINIUS E.R.
ROOSEVELT AND THE RUSSIANS: THE YALTA CONFERENCE.
NEW YORK: DOUBLEDAY, 1949, 324 PP.
REFUTATION OF IDEA THAT VITAL INTERESTS OF USA SACRIFICED AT YALTA TO APPEASE SOVIET UNION. AUTHOR, ROOSEVELT'S SECRETARY OF STATE AT THE CONFERENCE, STATES THAT DIFFICULTY DEVELOPED FROM FAILURE OF RUSSIANS TO HONOR AGREEMENTS. SEES CONFERENCE AS WISE, COURAGEOUS ATTEMPT BY FDR AND CHURCHILL TO STEER WORLD TOWARDS LASTING PEACE.

2820 STEUBER F.A.
THE CONTRIBUTION OF SWITZERLAND TO THE ECONOMIC AND SOCIAL DEVELOPMENT OF LOW-INCOME COUNTRIES (PAMPHLET)
WINTERTHUR: P G KELLER, 1961, 62 PP.
DISCUSSES SWITZERLAND'S ROLE IN ECONOMIC AID TO LOW-INCOME COUNTRIES, INCLUDING MOTIVES FOR AID, TRADE, INVESTMENT, LOANS, CONTRIBUTIONS OF FEDERAL AND VOLUNTARY ORGANIZATIONS, EXPANSION OF PROGRAM, AND BILATERAL APPROACH TO AID.

2821 STEVENS R.P.
LESOTHO, BATSWANA, AND SWAZILAND* THE FORMER HIGH COMMISSION TERRITORIES IN SOUTHERN AFRICA.
NEW YORK: FREDERICK PRAEGER, 1967.
STUDY OF THREE FORMER HIGH COMMISSION SOUTH AFRICAN TERRITORIES. DIVIDED INTO THREE PARTS BY TERRITORY, GIVING GENERAL INTRODUCTION AND FUTURE PROSPECTS. COVERS PRECOLONIAL AND COLONIAL ERAS, TRIBALISM AND CHIEFTAINCY, CONSTITUTIONAL AND POLITICAL DEVELOPMENTS, EMERGENCE OF POLITICAL PARTIES, AND PROGRESS TOWARD INDEPENDENCE. ECONOMIES ALSO COVERED.

2822 STEVENSON A.E.
PUTTING FIRST THINGS FIRST.
NEW YORK: RANDOM HOUSE, INC, 1960, 115 PP., LC#60-10097.
COLLECTION OF SPEECHES BY ADLAI STEVENSON IN 1959. DISCUSSES INTERNATIONAL AFFAIRS, ECONOMIC DEVELOPMENT, PUBLIC RESPONSIBILITY, EDUCATION, URBAN DEVELOPMENT, AND INDIVIDUAL RIGHTS AND RESPONSIBILITIES TO SOCIETY.

2823 STEVENSON A.E.
LOOKING OUTWARD: YEARS OF CRISIS AT THE UNITED NATIONS.
NEW YORK: HARPER, 1963, 295 PP.
SPEECHES AND WRITINGS RELATING TO THE UN SINCE APPOINTMENT AS PERMANENT USA REPRESENTATIVE. 'IN A WORLD MADE ONE BY SCIENCE AND THREATENED BY UNIVERSAL DESTRUCTION, SOME PERSONAL RIGHTS - ABOVE ALL THE RIGHT TO LIFE AND SECURITY - CAN NO LONGER BE SAFEGUARDED BY THE INDIVIDUAL NATIONAL GOVERNMENT. WORLD SOCIETY HAS TO ACHIEVE THE MINIMUM INSTITUTIONS OF ORDER.'

2824 STEWART C.F., SIMMONS G.B.
A BIBLIOGRAPHY OF INTERNATIONAL BUSINESS.
NEW YORK: COLUMBIA U PRESS, 1964, 603 PP., LC#64-19445.
UNANNOTATED BIBLIOGRAPHY CONTAINING 8,000 ENTRIES FROM BOOKS AND ARTICLES PUBLISHED IN ENGLISH AFTER 1950. COVERS MATERIALS ON COMPARATIVE BUSINESS SYSTEMS, GOVERNMENT AND INTERNATIONAL OPERATIONS, THE FIRM IN INTERNATIONAL OPERATIONS, AND INDIVIDUAL NATIONAL AND REGIONAL STUDIES. PROVIDES EXTENSIVE CROSS-REFERENCING.

2825 STEWART I.G. ED., ORD H.W. ED.
AFRICAN PRIMARY PRODUCTS AND INTERNATIONAL TRADE.
EDINBURGH: EDINBURGH U PR, 1965, 218 PP.
A COLLECTION OF ESSAYS DISCUSSING THE RELATION OF INTERNATIONAL TRADE TO "STRUCTURAL CHANGE AND GROWTH IN TROPICAL AFRICA." LARGELY A STUDY OF TRANSFORMATIONS IN TRADING SYSTEMS AND THE EXPORT OF PRIMARY GOODS AS MEANS TO ACHIEVING ECONOMIC STABILITY.

2826 STILLMAN C.W. ED.
AFRICA IN THE MODERN WORLD.
CHICAGO: U OF CHICAGO PRESS, 1955, 342 PP., LC#55-5147.
COLLECTION OF BACKGROUND INFORMATION ON AFRICA CONCERNING ITS HISTORY, RESOURCES, ECONOMIC DEVELOPMENT, AND ITS RELATIONS WITH WESTERN NATIONS. ANALYZES STATUS OF REGIONS OF AFRICA, THEIR IMPACT IN WORLD, AND RELATION TO US.

2827 STILLMAN E.O., PFAFF W.
THE NEW POLITICS: AMERICA AND THE END OF THE POSTWAR WORLD.
NEW YORK: COWARD-MCCANN, 1961, 191 PP.
CRITICIZES UNITED STATES FOREIGN POLICY SINCE WORLD WAR TWO AND CONTENDS ONE OF ITS MAIN FLAWS IS AN OVER-EMPHASIS ON OUTMODED MORALITY. CONCENTRATES ON RELATIONS WITH USSR, CHINA AND THE DEVELOPING NATIONS AND SUGGESTS MORE MUST BE DONE TO RECONCILE OUR POLICY WITH THE REALITIES OF THE INTERNATIONAL SITUATION.

2828 STILLMAN E.O., PFAFF W.
THE POLITICS OF HYSTERIA: THE SOURCES OF TWENTIETH-CENTURY CONFLICT.
NEW YORK: HARPER & ROW, 1964, 273 PP., LC#62-20118.
DISCUSSES INFLUENCE OF WESTERN CULTURE ON WORLD IN POLITICS, ECONOMICS, COLONIALIZATION; EMPHASIZES EXPLOSIVENESS OF PRESENT SITUATION OF WORLD HAVING TO DEAL WITH "DESTRUCTIVE IMPULSES OF MODERN POLITICAL AND INDUSTRIAL LIFE" THAT WESTERN CULTURE HAS CREATED.

2829 STOESSINGER J.G.
"THE INTERNATIONAL ATOMIC ENERGY AGENCY: THE FIRST PHASE."
INT. ORG., 13 (SUMMER 59), 394-411.
DESCRIBES AGENCY'S POLICY MAKING PROCESS, ADMINISTRATION, RESEARCH PROBLEMS, COORDINATION WITH OTHER INTERNATIONAL AGENCIES, AND ITS STRUGGLE TO MAINTAIN PEACE. EXAMINES RELATIONSHIPS BETWEEN ATOMIC AND NON-ATOMIC NATIONS. POINTS OUT WEAKNESS OF BILATERAL AGREEMENTS ON MATTERS OF ATOMIC AID AND FAVORS AGREEMENTS ARRANGED THROUGH THE AGENCY.

2830 STOESSINGER J.G. ET AL.
FINANCING THE UNITED NATIONS SYSTEM.
WASHINGTON: BROOKINGS INST., 1964, 348 PP., $6.75.
COMPLETE SURVEY OF THE FINANCIAL HISTORY AND BACKGROUND OF THE UN AND OTHER PAST AND PRESENT INTERNATIONAL BODIES MEMBERSHIP COSTS BUDGETARY AND ASSESSMENT PROCEDURES AND POSSIBLE SOURCES OF FUTURE REVENUES. ALL ASPECTS SET WITHIN THE POLITICAL CONTEXT OF THE UN.

2831 STOETZER O.C.
THE ORGANIZATION OF AMERICAN STATES.
NEW YORK: FREDERICK PRAEGER, 1965, 215 PP., LC#65-21109.
ANALYSIS OF BACKGROUND LEADING TO FORMATION OF OAS AND ITS PRESENT ORGANIZATION. DESCRIBES STRUCTURE, INCLUDING POLICY-MAKING BODIES, EXECUTIVE ORGANS, AND SPECIALIZED ORGANIZATION IN OAS.

2832 STOLPER W.F.
GERMANY BETWEEN EAST AND WEST: THE ECONOMICS OF COMPETITIVE COEXISTENCE.
WASHINGTON: NATL PLANNING ASSN, 1960, 80 PP., LC#60-15350.
COMPARISON OF ECONOMIC DEVELOPMENT AND POLITICAL SITUATIONS IN EAST AND WEST GERMANY SINCE WWII. ANALYZES "ECONOMIC PROSPECTS OF EAST AND WEST GERMANY IN NEXT 15 YEARS." STUDIES RELATION BETWEEN ECONOMIC MOVES AND POLITICAL ROLE OF WEST GERMANY IN THE COLD WAR STRUGGLE FOR CONTROL OF UNDEVELOPED NATIONS.

2833 STONE J.
THE PROVINCE AND FUNCTION OF LAW.
CAMBRIDGE: HARVARD U. PR., 1950, 918 PP.
CITES CURRENT DIVISIONS IN FIELD OF JURISPRUDENCE. EXPLORES RELATIONS BETWEEN LAW AND LOGIC AND LAW AND JUSTICE. DEPICTS THE NEO-HEGELIAN THEORY OF JUSTICE. FOCUSES ON CORRELATION OF LEGAL AND SOCIAL CHANGE IN MODERN TIMES. SURVEYS LAW IN PRESENT-DAY DEMOCRATIC SOCIETIES, AND THE SOCIAL, ECONOMIC, AND PSYCHOLOGICAL FACTORS IN LEGAL STABILITY AND FLUX.

2834 STONE J.
LEGAL CONTROLS OF INTERNATIONAL CONFLICT: A TREATISE ON THE DYNAMICS OF DISPUTES AND WAR LAW.
LONDON: STEVENS, 1954, 850 PP.
PRESENTS THE GENERALLY ESTABLISHED BODY OF INTERNATIONAL LAW AND ITS INSTITUTIONS, AND COMMENTS ON PHILOSOPHIC WRITINGS AND POLITICAL ACTIONS AND ATTITUDES RELATING TO IT.

2835 STONE J.

AGGRESSION AND WORLD ORDER: A CRITIQUE OF UNITED NATIONS THEORIES OF AGGRESSION.
BERKELEY: U OF CALIF PR, 1958, 226 PP.
EXAMINATION OF THE FOUNDATIONS AND ROLE OF THE UN IN THE MAINTENANCE OF INTERNATIONAL PEACE. DISCUSSES PROBLEMS OF DEFINING AGGRESSION, EXPERIENCE OF LEAGUE OF NATIONS, THE UN CHARTER AND ROLE OF THE GENERAL ASSEMBLY, AND APPLICATIONS OF PRINCIPLES TO THE 1956 SUEZ CRISIS. ANALYZES CONCEPT OF AGGRESSION WITH RELATION TO POWER POLITICS, INTERNATIONAL MORALITY, AND INDIVIDUAL CRIMINALITY.

2836 STONE J.
QUEST FOR SURVIVAL.
CAMBRIDGE: HARVARD U. PR., 1961, 104 PP.
EVALUATES FEASIBILITY OF RULE OF LAW IN ARBITRATION OF INTERNATIONAL DISPUTES, OUTLINING OBSTACLES TO THIRD-PARTY SETTLEMENT. SURVEYS SCOPE AND ENFORCEMENT OF INTERNATIONAL LAW. DEMONSTRATES FALLACIES OF CURRENT THOUGHT ON WORLD PROBLEMS.

2837 STOUT H.M.
BRITISH GOVERNMENT.
NEW YORK: OXFORD U PR, 1953, 433 PP., LC#52-14156.
DESCRIPTION OF THE PRESENT-DAY STRUCTURE AND PRACTICE OF BRITISH GOVERNMENT, INTENDED FOR AMERICAN STUDENTS. EXAMINES THE GOVERNMENT IN LIGHT OF POSTWAR DEVELOPMENTS - NEW ELECTIONS, EXPANSION OF GOVERNMENTAL FUNCTIONS UNDER THE WELFARE STATE CONCEPT, NEW COMMONWEALTH RELATIONS, ETC. DISCUSSES THE CONSTITUTION AND CONSTITUTIONAL RIGHTS, STRUCTURE OF THE PRINCIPAL INSTITUTIONS, AND POLICY FORMATION.

2838 STOVEL J.A.
CANADA IN THE WORLD ECONOMY.
CAMBRIDGE: HARVARD U PR, 1959, 364 PP., LC#59-7663.
DISCUSSES CANADIAN BALANCE OF TRADE, THEORIES OF BALANCE-OF-PAYMENTS, AND ECONOMIC DEVELOPMENTS PRIOR TO WWI. INCLUDES ANALYTICAL CRITIQUE OF VINER'S ANALYSIS OF ECONOMIC EVENTS FROM 1900-13. ALSO STUDIES ECONOMIC DEVELOPMENT, COMMERCIAL POLICY, BALANCE-OF-PAYMENTS, AND PROBLEMS OF ADJUSTMENT DURING INTERWAR PERIOD.

2839 STOWELL E.C.
INTERNATIONAL LAW.
NEW YORK: HOLT, 1931, 1558 PP.
ANALYZES VARIOUS GROUNDS UPON WHICH INTERNATIONAL INTERVENTION MAY JUSTLY BE UNDERTAKEN TO DEFEND INTERNATIONAL LAW RIGHTS, EITHER BY WAY OF INTERPOSITION OR BY INTERNATIONAL POLICE ACTIONS.

2840 STRACHEY A.
THE UNCONSCIOUS MOTIVES OF WAR; A PSYCHO-ANALYTICAL CONTRIBUTION.
NEW YORK: INTL UNIVERSITIES PR, 1957, 283 PP.
EXAMINES MOTIVES THAT CAUSE INDIVIDUALS AND NATIONS TO BE VIOLENT TOWARD EACH OTHER. BEGINS WITH UNCONSCIOUS FACTORS IN INDIVIDUAL MINDS AND SHOWS HOW THEY INFLUENCE CONSCIOUS IDEAS AND ATTITUDES. DISCUSSES HOW THEIR INFLUENCE IS ALTERED BY SOCIAL AND PUBLIC LIFE IN SUCH A WAY AS TO LEAD TO WAR. CLOSES WITH SUGGESTIONS AS TO HOW PSYCHOANALYTIC METHOD CAN OBVIATE WAR.

2841 STRACHEY J.
THE END OF EMPIRE.
NEW YORK: FREDERICK PRAEGER, 1960, 351 PP., LC#60-5459.
STUDY OF UK RELATION TO WORLD AS EMPIRE DISSOLVES AND COMMONWEALTH EMERGES. COMPARES MEANING OF EMPIRE TO MOTHER NATION, I.E., UK, AND TO COLONIES. ECONOMIC, SOCIAL, AND POLITICAL PROSPECTS OPEN TO POST-IMPERIAL NATIONS. ATTEMPTS TO DEVELOP AN EVOLVING THEORY OF IMPERIALISM.

2842 STRACHEY J.
ON THE PREVENTION OF WAR.
LONDON: MACMILLAN, 1962, 334 PP.
ANALYZES POLITICAL ATTITUDES, NUCLEAR DOCTRINES, AND THE DEFENSE AND DISARMAMENT POLICIES OF EAST AND WEST. CONCLUDES THERE ARE POSSIBILITIES OF PREVENTION OF WAR THROUGH THE STRENGTHENING OF THE UN AND THROUGH INCREASING THE EXCHANGE OF IDEAS AND GOODS BETWEEN COUNTRIES.

2843 STRACHEY J.
"COMMUNIST INTENTIONS."
PARTISAN REV., 29 (SPRING 62), 215-37.
TRACES EVOLUTION OF USSR FROM INTERNATIONALIST MOVEMENT TO RUSSIAN 'NATION-STATE-WITH-A-MISSION.' DISCUSSES ATTITUDE OF COMMUNISTS TOWARD WAR AND AGGRESSION IN GENERAL, PRESENTS FALLACIES OF ORIGINAL COMMUNIST PROGNOSIS, ANALYZES SINO-SOVIET CONTROVERSEY, PARTICULARLY WITH RESPECT TO NUCLEAR WAR. BELIEVES THERE IS NEW SOVIET ATTITUDE DUE TO APPARITION OF NEW WEAPONS AND DIVERGENCIES FROM ORIGINAL DOGMA.

2844 STRAUSS L.L.
MEN AND DECISIONS.
GARDEN CITY: DOUBLEDAY, 1962, 468 PP., LC#62-11304.
RECOLLECTIONS OF FORMER PRIVATE SECRETARY TO PRESIDENT HOOVER ABOUT IMPORTANT DECISIONS AND THEIR HISTORICAL CIRCUMSTANCES. BEGINS WITH HOOVER'S DECISION TO AID HUNGRY AND HOMELESS IN BELGIUM AND FRANCE, DISCUSSES EVENTS LEADING TO DROPPING OF ATOM BOMB IN 1945, AND CONCLUDES WITH RUSSIAN-AMERICAN EFFORTS TO AGREE ON SUPERVISION OF NUCLEAR TESTS.

2845 STRAUSZ-HUPE R.
THE BALANCE OF TOMORROW: POWER AND FOREIGN POLICY IN THE UNITED STATES.
NEW YORK: G P PUTNAM'S SONS, 1945, 302 PP.
CONCERNS FUTURE POSSIBILITIES OF WAR AND PEACE AND WHAT AMERICA'S LONG-RANGE FOREIGN POLICIES SHOULD BE. AUTHOR DISCUSSES POWER AS KEY FACTOR IN AMERICAN POLICY. BELIEVES MILITARY POWER AND ALLIANCES WITH OTHER WESTERN COUNTRIES ARE VITAL. ALSO BELIEVES THAT US SHOULD ENCOURAGE A WEST EUROPEAN FEDERATION.

2846 STRAUSZ-HUPE R., POSSONY S.T.
INTERNATIONAL RELATIONS IN THE AGE OF THE CONFLICT BETWEEN DEMOCRACY AND DICTATORSHIP (2ND ED.)
NEW YORK: MCGRAW HILL, 1954, 826 PP., LC#54-6730.
INTRODUCTORY TEXT IN THEORY AND PRACTICE OF INTERNATIONAL RELATIONS. AUTHORS BELIEVE THAT DICTATORIAL GOVERNMENT HAS BEEN ALLOWED TO FLOURISH AND PROGRESS THROUGH APATHY AND LACK OF INITIATIVE OF DEMOCRATIC GOVERNMENTS. THEREFORE, THEY ATTEMPT TO OFFER AS THOROUGH A CRITIQUE OF DEMOCRATIC FOREIGN POLICY AS OF DICTATORIAL POLICY. TEXT ATTEMPTS TO BE "EXPOSITORY" IN NATURE.

2847 STRAUSZ-HUPE R., KINTNER W.R. ET AL.
PROTRACTED CONFLICT.
NEW YORK: HARPER, 1959, 203 PP.
ASSESSMENT OF COLD WAR STRATEGY CONDUCTED BY COMMUNISTS IN LINE WITH THEIR DOCTRINE OF PROTRACTED CONFLICT. DISALLOWS GENERAL DECISIVE ENCOUNTER WITH FREE WORLD UNTIL CAPABILITY FOR TOTAL VICTORY IS ACHIEVED. BERATES SOVIET UNION FOR USING KOREA AND CHINA AS PAWNS IN THE IDEOLOGICAL CONFLICT ENABLING HERSELF TO DISCLAIM ANY LEGAL RESPONSIBILITY FOR COMMUNIST ACTIONS.

2848 STRAUSZ-HUPE R., KINTNER W.R., POSSONY S.T.
A FORWARD STRATEGY FOR AMERICA.
NEW YORK: HARPER, 1961, 451 PP.
ASSERTS TO COUNTERACT COMMUNIST THREAT, FREE WORLD MUST STRENGTHEN ITS MILITARY, ECONOMIC AND MORAL FORCES, REORGANIZE THE WESTERN INTERNATIONAL COMMUNITY, REAPPRAISE NATIONAL SOVEREIGNTY, AND PROVIDE FOR VIGOROUS LEADERSHIP. AMERICA SHOULD TAKE AN ACTIVE ROLE IN THE ACHIEVEMENT OF THESE REFORMS.

2849 STREIT C.K.
UNION NOW.
NEW YORK: HARPER, 1949, 324 PP.
DEALS WITH ESSENCE OF POLITICAL PROCESSES AND DYNAMICS OF INTERNATIONAL RELATIONS. POINTS OUT ORGANIZATIONAL PROBLEM IN DEMOCRATIC COUNTRIES IN LIGHT OF MORAL TASKS. CONSIDERS SOCIAL FACTORS OF ISOLATIONISM.

2850 STREIT C.K.
FREEDOM AGAINST ITSELF.
NEW YORK: HARPER & ROW, 1954, 316 PP., LC#54-06031.
EFFECTS OF FREEDOM ON INVENTIVENESS, POLITICS, AND IDEOLOGICAL CONFLICTS RESULTING FROM SAME. IS FREEDOM SELF-DESTRUCTIVE, AND WHAT ARE POSSIBLE MEANS TO PRESERVE IT, SPECIFICALLY THE ROLE IN INTERNATIONAL ORGANIZATIONS OF FREE STATES?

2851 STROMBERG R.N.
COLLECTIVE SECURITY AND AMERICAN FOREIGN POLICY FROM THE LEAGUE OF NATIONS TO NATO.
NEW YORK: PRAEGER, 1963, 301 PP.
TRACES 'INCEPTION, GROWTH, AND APPARENT DECLINE OF THE IDEA OF COLLECTIVE SECURITY IN MODERN INTERNATIONAL RELATIONS.' IMPUTES FAILURE TO RELUCTANCE OF NATIONS TO COMMIT SELVES TO ACTION UNDER COLLECTIVE SECURITY SYSTEM, AND TO FAILURE OF UN AS WORLD GOVERNMENT. SEES TREND TO CONSERVATIVE REALISM.

2852 STUART G.H.
FRENCH FOREIGN POLICY.
NEW YORK: CENTURY, 1921, 392 PP.
TRACES POLICY OF FRENCH FOREIGN OFFICE FROM CRISIS OF FASHODA - 1898 - TO THE CRIME OF SARAJEVO - 1914. INCLUDES DISCUSSION OF THE ENTENTE CORDIALE, THE MOROCCAN CRISIS, AND THE AGADIR AFFAIR.

2853 STUART G.H.
LATIN AMERICA AND THE UNITED STATES.
NEW YORK: CENTURY, 1928, 465 PP.
SURVEYS DIPLOMATIC AND COMMERCIAL RELATIONS BETWEEN USA AND LATIN AMERICA FROM MONROE DOCTRINE ON.

2854 STUART G.H.
THE INTERNATIONAL CITY OF TANGIER.
STANFORD: U. PR., 1931, 316 PP.
STUDIES PROBLEM PRESENTED BY TANGIER: 'PERHAPS THE OLDEST AND MOST DIFFICULT PROBLEM OF INTERNATIONAL ADMINISTRATION.'

2855 STUART G.H.
"AMERICAN DIPLOMATIC AND CONSULAR PRACTICE (2ND ED.)"
NEW YORK: APPLETON, 1952.
REVISED EDITION OF STUART'S TEXT ON THE ORGANIZATION AND FUNCTIONING OF US CONSULAR AND DIPLOMATIC MACHINERY. EDITION BASED LARGELY UPON MATERIAL OBTAINED IN WASHINGTON AND ABROAD SINCE WWII. UNANNOTATED BIBLIOGRAPHY OF BOOKS IN ENGLISH AND FRENCH PUBLISHED IN THE 19TH-20TH CENTURIES. EMPHASIS ON POST-WWI MATERIALS.

2856 STUART G.H.
LATIN AMERICA AND THE UNITED STATES (5TH ED.)
NEW YORK: APPLETON, 1955, 493 PP., LC#55-05020.
STUDIES RELATION BETWEEN US AND LATIN AMERICA SINCE MONROE DOCTRINE; TREATS INDIVIDUAL COUNTRIES. INCLUDES CHAPTERS ON GOOD NEIGHBOR POLICY AND PERIOD FOLLOWING.

2857 STURZO D.L.
NATIONALISM AND INTERNATIONALISM.
NEW YORK: ROY PUBLISHING, 1946, 308 PP.
HISTORICAL EVALUATION OF NATIONAL AND INTERNATIONAL POLITICS, CULTURAL AND SOCIAL INFLUENCE ON POLITICS, AND WAR AND PEACE; EMPHASIZING INFLUENCE OF MORALITY ON POLITICS. BEGINS WITH DEFINITION AND THEORIES OF NATIONALISM; STUDIES NATIONALISM BEFORE AND AFTER MUSSOLINI, ROLE OF UNIONS AND POLITICAL PARTIES, AND CHARACTER OF MODERN WARS. CLOSES WITH LEAGUE OF NATIONS AND UN.

2858 STURZO L.
THE INTERNATIONAL COMMUNITY AND THE RIGHT OF WAR (TRANS. BY BARBARA BARCLAY CARTER)
NEW YORK: RICHARD R SMITH, 1929, 293 PP.
STUDY OF THE SOCIOLOGICAL AND HISTORICAL ASPECTS OF WAR AND THE FORMATION OF INTERNATIONAL STRUCTURES TOWARD THE CONTROL AND/OR JUSTIFICATION OF WAR. ARGUES THAT THE THREE THEORIES ADVANCED TO EXPLAIN THE RIGHT OF WAR ARE INCOMPLETE AND CAN BE SUPPLANTED BY A FOURTH PROPOUNDING THAT WAR, LIKE SLAVERY AND DUELS, IS NOT A NECESSARY HUMAN CONDITION AND CAN BE ELIMINATED THROUGH CIVILIZED INTERNATIONAL LAW.

2859 SUAREZ F.
"ON WAR" (1621) IN SELECTIONS FROM THREE WORKS, VOL. I."
LONDON: OXFORD U PR, 1944.
DENIES THAT WAR IS INTRINSICALLY EVIL, CLAIMING THAT ANY SOVEREIGN PRINCE HAS POWER TO INITIATE IT IF HE FEELS THAT IT IS NECESSARY TO PREVENT GREATER EVIL. EVEN AGGRESSIVE WAR IS ALLOWABLE UNDER CERTAIN CIRCUMSTANCES. STATES THAT CHRISTIAN PRINCES HAVE RECOURSE TO POPE AS A HIGHER AUTHORITY, BUT IF HE DOES NOT INTERVENE THEY MAY ACT AS FREE AGENTS. SEDITION IS JUSTIFIED AGAINST TYRANTS.

2860 SUINN R.M.
"THE DISARMAMENT FANTASY* PSYCHOLOGICAL FACTORS THAT MAY PRODUCE WARFARE."
J. HUMAN RELATIONS, 15 (1967), 36-42.
REPORTS ON A WAR-GAME EXPERIMENT IN WHICH PSYCHOLOGICAL FACTORS OF FEAR, MISTRUST, AND COMPETITIVENESS LED THE PARTICIPANTS TO STOCKPILE COUNTERS (WEAPONS) AND TO "PUSH THE BUTTON" (START NUCLEAR WAR) DESPITE INTENTIONS OF GOOD WILL. CONCLUDES THAT SUCH FACTORS MAY MAKE DISARMAMENT SOLUTIONS MORE FANTASY THAN PROBABILITY.

2861 SULLIVAN G.
THE STORY OF THE PEACE CORPS.
NEW YORK: FLEET, 1964, 156 PP.
DISCUSSES HISTORY AND ORGANIZATION OF PEACE CORPS, WITH EMPHASIS ON PROJECTS AND PROGRAMS.

2862 SULZBACH W.
NATIONAL CONSCIOUSNESS.
WASHINGTON: AMER COUNC PUB AFF, 1943, 168 PP.
CONCERNS DEVELOPMENT OF NATIONALISM IN 19TH AND 20TH CENTURIES, WITH EMPHASIS ON 20TH CENTURY AND WORLD WARS. AFTER TRACING HISTORICAL BACKGROUND, EXAMINES NATIONAL CHARACTER, RACE, AND STRUGGLE FOR UNITY WITHIN NATION. EVALUSTES FIGHTING IMPULSE, NATIONAL HONOR, AND IMPERIALISM. SEES NATIONALISM AS A SECULAR RELIGION WHICH CAN AND MUST BE DE-POLITICIZED, AS WAS CHRISTIANITY.

2863 SULZBERGER C.L.
UNFINISHED REVOLUTION.
NEW YORK: ATHENEUM PUBLISHERS, 1965, 304 PP., LC#65-15916.
DISCUSSES RELATIONS BETWEEN US AND NON-COMMUNIST DEVELOPING COUNTRIES IN CONTEXT OF POLITICAL, IDEOLOGICAL, AND TECHNICAL REVOLUTIONS SINCE WWI, EMPHASIZING REVOLUTION OF SELF-DETERMINATION.

2864 SUMNER W.G.
WAR AND OTHER ESSAYS.
NEW HAVEN: YALE U PR, 1919, 381 PP.
SERIES OF ESSAYS IN WHICH AUTHOR ARGUES FOR FREE TRADE, AN END TO AMERICAN IMPERIALISM, AND AGAINST WAR. HE ARGUES FROM A SOCIOLOGICAL VIEWPOINT AND FEELS THAT IF MEN COULD FREELY TRADE WITH ONE ANOTHER THEY WOULD FIND PACIFIC MEANS FOR SETTLING THEIR DISPUTES. ALSO FEELS THAT THE PRINCIPLES OF AMERICAN DEMOCRACY DEMAND NOT ONLY FREEDOM AND EQUALITY BUT THE WILL TO LET OTHER NATIONS DETERMINE THEIR PATHS.

2865 SURANYI-UNGER T.
COMPARATIVE ECONOMIC SYSTEMS.
NEW YORK: MCGRAW HILL, 1952, 628 PP., LC#52-7446.
STRESSES INTERMEDIATE ECONOMIC SYSTEMS AND TRANSITIONS AMONG THEM RATHER THAN EXTREME CASES. EXAMINES RELATION OF WESTERN FREEDOM TO EASTERN PLANNING AND COORDINATION OF FREEDOM AND PLANNING; DISCUSSES APPROACHES TO STUDY OF ECONOMIC SYSTEMS, THE SOCIAL PREMISES OF ECONOMIC SYSTEMS. CONCLUDES WITH ANALYSIS OF ECONOMIC CONCEPTS AND FUNCTIONS. SUGGESTED READINGS FOLLOW EACH CHAPTER.

2866 SUTHERLAND G.
CONSTITUTIONAL POWER AND WORLD AFFAIRS.
NEW YORK: COLUMBIA U. PR., 1919, 202 PP.
DEALS WITH WORLD WAR ONE AND ITS EFFECTS ON AMERICAN FOREIGN RELATIONS. DEPICTS NATURE OF INTERNAL AND EXTERNAL POWERS OF THE NATIONAL GOVERNMENT. SURVEYS THE POLITICAL DIVISION BETWEEN PRESIDENT AND CONGRESS. CALLS FOR A LIBERAL CONSTITUTIONAL CONSTRUCTION IN EXTERNAL AFFAIRS.

2867 SUTTON F.X.
"REPRESENTATION AND THE NATURE OF POLITICAL SYSTEMS."
COMP. STUD. SOC. HIST., 2 (OCT. 59), 1-10.
TRACES DEVELOPMENT OF POLITICAL REPRESENTATION FROM PRIMITIVE SOCIETY TO MODERN INDUSTRIAL SOCIETY. ALSO DIFFERENTIATES BETWEEN THAT WHICH IS REPRESENTATIVE ACTION AND THAT WHICH IS AUTONOMOUS ACTIVITY OF INDIVIDUALS IN COLLECTIVITY.

2868 SVARLIEN O.
AN INTRODUCTION TO THE LAW OF NATIONS.
NEW YORK: MCGRAW HILL, 1955, 478 PP., LC#56-6173.
INTRODUCTORY TEXT IN INTERNATIONAL LAW. TREATS EACH TOPIC IN LIGHT OF ITS HISTORY, OF ITS LAW, AND IN TERMS OF TRENDS AND DEVELOPMENT. INCLUDES STUDY OF THE INTERNATIONAL COMMUNITY, THE FUNCTION OF STATES IN INTERNATIONAL LAW, TERRITORIAL PROBLEMS, DIPLOMATIC RELATIONS, HOSTILE RELATIONS BETWEEN NATIONS, AND THE INDIVIDUAL IN INTERNATIONAL LAW. BIBLIOGRAPHY OF ABOUT 200 ITEMS.

2869 SWEARER H.R., LONGAKER R.P.
CONTEMPORARY COMMUNISM: THEORY AND PRACTICE.
BELMONT: WADSWORTH, 1963, 405 PP., LC#63-18331.
PRIMARY SOURCE MATERIALS, FACTUAL DATA, AND INTERPRETIVE ESSAYS ON MAJOR ISSUES WITHIN COMMUNIST SPHERE. EARLY CHAPTERS DEAL WITH MARXIST-LENINIST THEORY; ROLE AND APPEAL OF COMMUNIST IDEOLOGY; POLITICAL, ECONOMIC, AND SOCIAL STRUCTURE OF USSR; AND CHANGING NATURE OF SOVIET SYSTEM. LAST HALF OF BOOK TREATS GOALS AND TECHNIQUES OF FOREIGN POLICY AND VARIETIES OF COMMUNISM IN WORLD.

2870 SWIFT R.N.
"THE UNITED NATIONS AND ITS PUBLIC."
INT. ORGAN., 14 (WINTER 60), 60-91.
CRITICIZES UN TECHNICAL ADVISORY COMMITTEE ON INFORMATION AND OFFICE OF PUBLIC INFORMATION. PRESENTS A COMMITTEE APPRAISAL OF OPI EFFICIENCY, ITS IMPACT ON WORLD OPINION, ITS FINANCIAL ARRANGEMENTS.

2871 SWIFT R.N.
WORLD AFFAIRS AND THE COLLEGE CURRICULUM.
WASHINGTON: AMER COUNCIL ON EDUC, 1959, 194 PP., LC#59-13499
CONTENDS THAT AMERICAN UNIVERSITIES MUST SOLVE INHERENT EDUCATIONAL PROBLEMS TO DEAL WELL WITH AREA OF WORLD AFFAIRS. DISCUSSES PROBLEM OF DEFINITION OF "WORLD AFFAIRS" IN PLANNING CURRICULA. DISCUSSES APPROACHES TO FIELD THROUGH HUMANITIES, HISTORY, AND SOCIAL AND NATURAL SCIENCES. EXAMINES WORLD AFFAIRS COURSES, MAJORS, AND SUPPLEMENTARY PROGRAMS. DEMANDS TRULY LIBERAL SPIRIT IN TREATMENT OF FIELD.

2872 SWISHER C.B.
THE THEORY AND PRACTICE OF AMERICAN NATIONAL GOVERNMENT.
BOSTON: HOUGHTON MIFFLIN, 1951, 949 PP.
EXAMINES AMERICAN POLITICS, LAW, AND ADMINISTRATION IN ACTION, AS WELL AS THE MACHINERY AND THE THEORY OF GOVERNMENT. SURVEYS FEDERAL AND STATE PROCESSES, AND FOREIGN RELATIONS IN WAR AND IN PEACE. CONCLUDES WITH QUESTIONS OF LIBERTY AND WORLD PEACE IN A WORLD WITH CONFLICTING CULTURES; UPHOLDS THE BASIC PRINCIPLES OF AMERICAN DEMOCRACY.

2873 SYATAUW J.J.G.
SOME NEWLY ESTABLISHED ASIAN STATES AND THE DEVELOPMENT OF INTERNATIONAL LAW.
THE HAGUE: MARTINUS NIJHOFF, 1961, 349 PP.
STUDIES SIGNIFICANCE OF WORLD DEVELOPMENTS FOR INTERNATIONAL LAW, FROM VIEWPOINT OF SOME NEWLY ESTABLISHED ASIAN STATES - INDIA, INDONESIA, BURMA, AND CEYLON. EXAMINES CHANGES IN BIPOLARIZATION, PROGRESS, INTERDEPENDENCE, AND EXPANSIONISM. DISCUSSES CONTRIBUTIONS OF NEW ASIAN STATES TO DEFINITIONS OF COLONIALISM, SELF-DETERMINATION, PEACEFUL COEXISTENCE, AND NEUTRALITY IN INTERNATIONAL LAW.

2874 SYMONDS R.

"REFLECTIONS IN LOCALISATION."
J. COMMONWEALTH POLIT. STUD., 2 (NOV. 64), 219-234.
STUDIES THE TRANSFER OF ADMINISTRATIVE POWER IN FORMER BRITISH COLONIES BY WHICH NATIONALS REPLACED EXPATRIATES. BRITISH POLICY IS COMPARED IN EACH COLONY AS TO DEGREE OF EDUCATION, POLITICAL AWARENESS AND ADMINISTRATIVE TRAINING ACHIEVED.

2875 SYRKIN M., CARMICHAEL J., ABEL L.
"I.F. STONE RECONSIDERS ISRAEL."
MIDSTREAM, 13 (OCT. 67), 3-17.
DISCUSSES I. F. STONE'S REVIEW OF SARTRE'S "LE CONFLIT ISRAELO-ARABE." CRITICIZES STONE FOR HIS PRO-ARAB VIEWPOINT AND FINDS FAULT WITH SEVERAL OF HIS STATEMENTS THAT CONFLICT IS BETWEEN TWO SIDES, BOTH RIGHT. STUDIES REFUGEE PROBLEM IN PARTICULAR AND QUESTION OF ROLE OF ZIONISM IN THE WAR.

2876 SZASZY E.
"L'EVOLUTION DES PRINCIPES GENERAUX DU DROIT INTERNATIONAL PRIVE DANS LES PAYS DE DEMOCRATIE POPULAIRE."
REV. CRIT. DR. INT. PRIV., 52 (NO.1, 63), 1-42.
SHOWS HOW GENERAL PRINCIPLES OF PRIVATE INTERNATIONAL LAW IN PEOPLE'S DEMOCRACY ARE DETERMINED ACCORDING TO REQUIREMENTS OF THEIR FOREIGN POLICY. POINTS OUT POSSIBLE INTERESTS COMMON TO BOTH SOCIALIST SYSTEM AND PRIVATE ENTERPRISE. PRESENTS INSIGHT INTO SOCIO-ECONOMIC BEHAVIOR OF SOVIET BLOC COUNTRIES.

2877 SZLADITS C.
BIBLIOGRAPHY ON FOREIGN AND COMPARATIVE LAW: BOOKS AND ARTICLES IN ENGLISH (SUPPLEMENT 1962)
NEW YORK: OCEANA PUBLISHING, 1964, 134 PP., LC#55-11076.
ANNOTATES AND LISTS 3,431 ITEMS ARRANGED TOPICALLY; BOOKS, ARTICLES, PAMPHLETS, SERIALS, DOCUMENTS, ETC., PERTINENT TO COMPARATIVE LAW, PUBLIC LAW, INTERNATIONAL LAW, COMMERCIAL LAW, CRIMINAL LAW, AND PRIVATE LAW. INCLUDES BIBLIOGRAPHIES, REFERENCES, LISTS OF INSTITUTIONS OF COMPARATIVE LAW, ETC.

2878 SZLADITS C.
A BIBLIOGRAPHY ON FOREIGN AND COMPARATIVE LAW (SUPPLEMENT 1964)
NEW YORK: OCEANA PUBLISHING, 1966, 119 PP., LC#55-11076.
ANNOTATED BIBLIOGRAPHY ON BOOKS AND ARTICLES IN ENGLISH FROM 1960-66. SOURCES ON COMPARATIVE LAW, GENERAL WORKS, PRIVATE LAW, COMMERCIAL LAW, LABOR LAW, LAW OF PROCEDURE, CRIMINAL LAW, CRIMINAL PROCEDURE, PUBLIC LAW, AND PRIVATE INTERNATIONAL LAW. PUBLISHED FOR PARKER SCHOOL OF FOREIGN AND COMPARATIVE LAW, COLUMBIA UNIVERSITY.

2879 SZTARAY Z.
BIBLIOGRAPHY ON HUNGARY.
NEW YORK: KOSSUTH FDN, 1960, 100 PP., LC#60-14411.
UNANNOTATED BIBLIOGRAPHY OF WRITINGS ON HUNGARY IN NON-HUNGARIAN LANGUAGES, PRINCIPALLY ENGLISH, FRENCH, GERMAN, AND SPANISH. COVERS GEOGRAPHY, HISTORY INCLUDING HUNGARIAN REVOLUTION, POLITICAL AND SOCIAL LIFE, FOREIGN AFFAIRS, ECONOMICS, RELIGION, LANGUAGE, CULTURE, AND FINE ARTS. CONTAINS APPROXIMATELY 1,500 LISTINGS.

2880 SZULC T.
THE WINDS OF REVOLUTION; LATIN AMERICA TODAY - AND TOMORROW.
NEW YORK: FREDERICK PRAEGER, 1963, 308 PP., LC#63-20969.
REPORT FROM A CORRESPONDENT OF THE NEW YORK TIMES ON REVOLUTIONARY TRENDS IN 20 LATIN AMERICAN NATIONS. CONTENDS THAT THE COMMON THEME AMONG THESE COUNTRIES TAKES THE FORM OF A DEMAND FOR BETTER MATERIAL LIFE TOGETHER WITH PROFOUND POLITICAL AND PSYCHOLOGICAL CHANGES. UNDERSCORES LATIN AMERICAN EMPHASIS ON CHANGE, EXPERIMENTATION, AND NON-TRADITIONAL PATTERNS.

2881 TABORN P., PUTIGNANO A.
RECORDS OF THE HEADQUARTERS, UNITED NATIONS COMMAND (PRELIMINARY INVENTORIES; PAPER)
WASHINGTON: US GOVERNMENT, 1960, 7 PP.
AN INVENTORY OF RECORDS OF THE UNITED NATIONS COMMAND AND SUBORDINATE AGENCIES BETWEEN 1950-57 WHICH ARE PART OF THE RECORDS OF INTERNATIONAL AGENCIES. THE RECORDS ARE SECURITY-CLASSIFIED AND CONSIST CHIEFLY OF CORRESPONDENCE, REPORTS, TRANSCRIPTS OF MEETINGS, AGREEMENTS, PUBLICATIONS, AND JOURNALS.

2882 TACKABERRY R.B.
"ORGANIZING AND TRAINING PEACE-KEEPING FORCES* THE CANADIAN VIEW."
INTERNATIONAL JOURNAL, 22 (SPRING 67), 195-209.
OUTLINES MILITARY TRAINING PROCEDURE OF CANADIAN ARMED FORCES WHICH HAVE CONTRIBUTED TO THEIR SUCCESS IN PEACE-KEEPING OPERATIONS. ADVOCATES SIMILAR ORGANIZING AND TRAINING OF UN FORCES. CALLS FOR UN COMMITTEE TO PLAN AND ESTABLISH PERMANENT PEACE-KEEPING FORCES.

2883 TAGGART F.J.
ROME AND CHINA.
BERKELEY: U. CALIF. PR., 1939, 283 PP.
INDICATES THAT WARS, UNDERTAKEN BY CHINA AND ROME IN NATIONAL INTEREST, LED INEVITABLY TO CONFLICTS AMONG NORTHERN EUROPEAN PEOPLES AND TO INVASION OF ROMAN EMPIRE.

2884 TALLON D.
"L'ETUDE DU DROIT COMPARE COMME MOYEN DE RECHERCHER LES MATIERES SUSCEPTIBLES D'UNIFICATION INTERNATIONALE."
TRAV. RECH. INST. DR. COMP. UNIV. PARIS, 22 (1963), 149-53.
CONSIDERS STUDY OF COMPARATIVE LAW MOST ADAPTIVE DISCIPLINE TO ACHIEVE COORDINATION OF JURIDIC PATTERNS. STUDY BASED ON JURISPRUDENCE RESEARCH.

2885 TAN C.C.
THE BOXER CATASTROPHE.
NEW YORK: COLUMBIA U PRESS, 1955, 276 PP., LC#55-7834.
ANALYZES BOXER REBELLION. DISCUSSES INFLUENCE OF POLICIES OF VICEROYS AND GOVERNORS ON NATIONAL POLICY. ALSO STUDIES MANCHURIAN CRISIS CREATED BY RUSSIAN OCCUPATION AFTER BOXER REBELLION. VIEWS REBELLION AS STRUGGLE OF THE CHINESE PEOPLE AGAINST FOREIGN IMPERIALISM.

2886 TANG P.S.H.
"COMMUNIST CHINA TODAY: DOMESTIC AND FOREIGN POLICIES."
NEW YORK: FREDERICK PRAEGER, 1957.
ANALYSIS OF INTERNATIONAL COMMUNISM AND ITS MANIFESTATIONS AND OPERATIONS ON THE CHINESE MAINLAND. INTERPRETATION OF COMMUNISM IN ACTION IN CHINA AND PEKING'S ROLE IN THE MOSCOW-PEKING AXIS AND ITS IMPACT ON FREE WORLD. CHARTS AND TABLES INCLUDED TO CLARIFY ORGANIZATIONAL COMPLEXITIES OF PARTY AND STATE STRUCTURE. VOLUME II IS A DOCUMENTARY AND CHRONOLOGICAL INDEX. SELECT BIBLIOGRAPHY OF BOOKS.

2887 TANNENBAUM F.
THE AMERICAN TRADITION IN FOREIGN POLICY.
NORMAN: U. OKLA. PR., 1955, 178 PP., $3.50.
TRACES DEVELOPMENT OF THEORY OF COORDINATE STATES IN INTERNAL AFFAIRS FROM CONTINENTAL CONGRESS TO PRESENT DAY CONSTITUTIONAL LAW. SCORES REALPOLITIK AND FAVORS INTERNATIONAL ORDER ANALAGOUS TO USA FEDERALIST SYSTEM AS MEANS TO SECURITY WITHOUT PERMANENT MILITARIZATION.

2888 TANNENBAUM F.
"THE UNITED STATES AND LATIN AMERICA."
POLIT. SCI. QUART., 76 (JUNE 61), 161-80.
DISCUSSES MAJOR DIMENSIONS OF USA RELATIONS WITH LATIN AMERICA WHICH RESULT FROM PERSONAL BEHAVIOR AND SOCIAL ATTITUDES. AS LATIN-AMERICAN GOVERNMENTS ARE UNSTABLE ANY ACTION ON PART OF US IS SUSPECT. CALLS FOR NEW ECONOMIC AID PLAN TO GENERATE NEW ACTIVITIES AND INTERESTS.

2889 TARDIFF G.
LA LIBERTAD; LA LIBERTAD DE EXPRESION, IDEALES Y REALIDADES AMERICANAS.
MEXICO CITY: TALLARES GRAFICAS M. CASAS, 1959, 379 PP.
DISCUSSION OF CONCEPT OF FREEDOM AND ITS PLACE IN CULTURES OF EUROPE AND MIDDLE EAST AND IN FRAMEWORKS OF THE CATHOLIC CHURCH AND THE UN. SECOND PART DEALS WITH WESTERN HEMISPHERE AND RELATIONS AMONG AMERICAN COUNTRIES AND NEED FOR FREEDOM OF EXPRESSION FOR ALL THESE COUNTRIES TO IMPROVE SITUATION OF REGION AND PEOPLE.

2890 TARLING N.
"A CONCISE HISTORY OF SOUTHEAST ASIA."
NEW YORK: FREDERICK PRAEGER, 1966.
A HISTORY OF SOUTHEAST ASIA FROM VIEWPOINT OF AUSTRALASIAN HISTORIAN. ATTEMPTS TO PROVIDE FRAMEWORK FOR APPRAISING INTERACTION OF EXTERNAL INFLUENCES AND GIVEN CONDITIONS OF SOUTHEAST ASIAN FRONTIER AREA. TRACES HISTORY OF AREA FROM 13TH CENTURY TO 1965; EMPHASIS ON INDIVIDUAL COUNTRIES SINCE 1942. BIBLIOGRAPHICAL APPENDIX OF WORKS IN ENGLISH PUBLISHED SINCE 1922; CONCENTRATION ON RECENT WORKS.

2891 TATOMIR N.
"ORGANIZATIA INTERNATIONALA A MUNCII: ASPECTE NOI ALE PROBLEMEI IMBUNATATIRII MECANISMULUI EI."
ANNU. STIINT. UNIV. IASI, STIINT. SOC., 8 (62), 133-43.
OUTLINES HISTORY OF OIT AND EXAMINES ITS STRUCTURE. INDICATES AREAS NEEDING REFORMS. STATES THAT COMPOSITION OF ITS ORGANS BEARS NO RELATION TO REALITIES OF CONTEMPORARY WORLD.

2892 TAUBENFELD H.J.
"OUTER SPACE--PAST POLITICS AND FUTURE POLICY."
PROC. AMER. SOC. INT. LAW., 55 (APR. 61), 176-89.
OUTLINES THE INHERENT DANGER OF NUCLEAR POWERS USING SPACE AS A HIGHWAY FOR DESTRUCTIVE MECHANISMS. SPECULATES THAT LIMITED CONFLICTS ARISING IN THE FUTURE IN OUTER SPACE MAY BE EXTENDED. ADVOCATES ATTAINMENT OF SPECIFIC REGULATIONS WITHIN LEGISLATIVE AND ENFORCEMENT FRAMEWORK OF AN INTERNATIONAL COSMIC SURVEILLANCE AUTHORITY.

2893 TAUBENFELD H.J.
"A TREATY FOR ANTARCTICA."
INT. COUNCIL., 531 (JAN. 61), 243-322.
APPRAISES SPECIAL FACTORS WHICH MADE POSSIBLE THE 1957 TWELVE-NATION AGREEMENT ON SCIENTIFIC RESEARCH. CONSIDERS ITS POTENTIAL RELEVANCE TO POLITICAL ISSUES.

2894 TAUBENFELD H.J.
"A REGIME FOR OUTER SPACE."
NORTHWEST. U. LAW REV., 56 (MAR.-APR. 61), 129-67.
EXPLORES LEGAL CONCEPTS WHICH COULD GOVERN OUTER SPACE TO PREVENT IT FROM BECOMING A SOURCE OF OR THEATER FOR CONFLICT. DISCUSSES INADEQUACY OF SEA AIR ANALOGIES, SCIENTIFIC DELINEATION, AND GEOCENTRIC POLITICS. PROPOSES A NEW APPROACH, RECOGNIZING THAT PROBLEM CANNOT BE COMPLETELY SOLVED AS IT IS A PROJECTION OF COLD WAR.

2895 TAUBENFELD H.J. ED.
SPACE AND SOCIETY.
NEW YORK: OCEANA PUBLISHING, 1964, 172 PP., LC#64-21185.
PAPERS FROM SEMINAR ON PROBLEMS OF OUTER SPACE SPONSORED BY CARNEGIE ENDOWMENT FOR INTERNATIONAL PEACE, CONCERNING IMPACT OF MAN IN SPACE ON MAN'S SOCIETY ON EARTH. COVERS TOPICS OF LAW, POLITICS, SPACE SCIENCE, VALUES AND GOALS OF SPACE EXPLORATION, SPACE COMMUNICATION, CLAIMS TO USE OF SPACE, MILITARY USE, AND FUTURE PROSPECTS OF SPACE EXPLORATION.

2896 TAUBENFELD R.K., TAUBENFELD H.J.
"INDEPENDENT REVENUE FOR THE UNITED NATIONS."
INT. ORGAN., 18 (SPRING 64), 241-67.
OUTLINES POSSIBLE WAYS OF RAISING MONEY FOR UN WITHOUT BEING RELIANT UPON THE PRESENT SOURCES OF INCOME WHICH ARE SUBJECT TO NATIONAL POLITICS AND OTHER UN-CONTROLABLE VARIABLES. MENTIONS SPECIFIC ALTERNATIVES, E.G. ANTARCTICS, OUTER-SPACE, OCEAN RESOURCES. EXPLAINS VARIOUS ARGUMENTS BOTH FOR AND AGAINST THESE SOURCES AND FUTURE PROSPECTS.

2897 TAYLOR A.J.P.
THE STRUGGLE FOR MASTERY IN EUROPE 1848-1918.
LONDON: OXFORD U PR, 1954, 638 PP., LC#54-13436.
STATES THAT RELATIONS BETWEEN GREAT POWERS HAVE DETERMINED HISTORY OF EUROPE. EACH POWER HAS NEVER RECOGNIZED ANY MORAL CODE OTHER THAN THAT ACCEPTED BY OWN CONSCIENCE. PEACE HAS EXISTED ONLY THROUGH BALANCE OF POWER. ANALYZES 70-YEAR PERIOD PRIOR TO WWI IN LIGHT OF STRUGGLE BETWEEN GREAT POWERS FOR CONTROL OF CONTINENT.

2898 TAYLOR D.M.
THE BRITISH IN AFRICA.
CHESTER SPRINGS: DUFOUR, 1962, 185 PP., LC#64-22679.
TRACES BRITISH COLONIALISM IN AFRICA FROM INCEPTION. SLAVERY, DOMINATION, "WHITE MAN'S BURDEN," ADMINISTRATION, ECONOMIC POLICIES, AND PREPARATION FOR SOVEREIGNTY EXAMINED. VIEWS LASTING EFFECT OF BRITAIN UPON POLITICAL, ECONOMIC, AND CULTURAL PRACTICES.

2899 TAYLOR E.
RICHER BY ASIA.
BOSTON: HOUGHTON, 1964, 420 PP.
'IN HEARTS AND MINDS OF MEN LIES SOLUTION OF WORLD'S DISEASE AND NOT IN PACTS AND ARMAMENTS... BUILDING BRIDGES BETWEEN EAST AND WEST ONLY HOPE OF AVOIDING FINAL WORLD WAR OR PREPARING MEN FOR WORLD GOVERNMENT.' ENJOINS WORLD-CITIZENRY TO APPRECIATE PRINCIPLES THAT GOVERN 'ORIENTALS.'

2900 TAYLOR M.D.
THE UNCERTAIN TRUMPET.
NEW YORK: HARPER, 1960, 203 PP.
ASSERTS THE 'DEFENSE OF THE US IS PRESENTLY CONTROLLED LARGELY BY NONMILITARY FACTORS OR BY MILITARY FACTORS WHICH HAVE BECOME OUTMODED' AND SEEKS A REAPPRAISAL OF OUR DEFENSE POSTURE.

2901 TAYLOR T.G.
CANADA'S ROLE IN GEOPOLITICS (PAMPHLET)
TORONTO: RYERSON PRESS, 1942, 28 PP.
DESCRIBES CANADA'S GEOGRAPHIC POSITION IN RELATION TO OTHER NATIONS, ITS CLIMATE, ITS RESOURCES, AND THE PROSPECT FOR FUTURE SETTLEMENT AND EXPLOITATION. ALSO EXAMINES HER SPECIAL RELATIONSHIP WITH USSR.

2902 TEITELBAUM L.M.
WOODROW WILSON AND THE MEXICAN REVOLUTION 1913-1916: A HISTORY OF UNITED STATES-MEXICAN RELATIONS.
NEW YORK: EXPOSITION PRESS, 1967, 435 PP.
STUDY OF MEXICAN-AMERICAN RELATIONS DURING EARLY YEARS OF MEXICAN REVOLUTION, FROM DEPOSAL OF MADERO TO WILSON'S SUBSEQUENT INVOLVEMENT IN MEXICAN POLITICS. COVERS ROLES PLAYED BY VILLA AND CARRANZA. GIVES CRITICAL EVALUATION OF WILSON'S ACTS. INCLUDES 100 PAGES OF FOOTNOTES.

2903 TEPASKE J.J. ED., FISHER S.N. ED.
EXPLOSIVE FORCES IN LATIN AMERICA.
COLUMBUS: OHIO STATE U. PR., 1964, 196 PP., $4.75.
EIGHT PAPERS COVER SOVIET POLICY AND CUBA, ROLE OF INTELLECTUAL IN PROMOTING CHANGE, FORCES OF CHURCH AND MILITARY IN LATIN AMERICAN LIFE. EXAMINES IMPACT OF LAND REFORM AND PROBLEMS OF POPULATION EXPLOSION AND OF POVERTY. LASTLY, PRESENTS OBSERVATIONS ON ALLIANCE FOR PROGRESS.

2904 TERRILL R.
"THE SIEGE MENTALITY."
PROBLEMS OF COMMUNISM, 16 (MAR.-APR. 67), 1-10.
THE CHINESE CULTURAL REVOLUTION SHOULD BE VIEWED AS A RESULT OF THE COMMUNIST CHINESE "SIEGE MENTALITY," THEIR SENSE THAT THE REVOLUTION IS UNDER CONSTANT ATTACK BY A REVISIONIST-IMPERIALIST COALITION. THE VIETNAM WAR IS PART OF THE US SIEGE OF CHINA, LIKE KOREA, AND THE CULTURAL REVOLUTION IS INTENDED TO STIR UP A CORPORATE SPIRIT AND IDEOLOGICAL UNITY IN PREPARATION FOR AN ANTICIPATED ATTACK.

2905 TETENS T.H.
THE NEW GERMANY AND THE OLD NAZIS.
NEW YORK: MARZANI & MUNSELL, 1961, 286 PP., LC#61-7240.
ANALYSIS OF POLITICAL SITUATION IN GERMANY CIRCA 1960; AUTHOR (AN EX-GERMAN, NOW US CITIZEN) CALLS FOR CLOSER LOOK BY US AT POLICY TOWARD GERMANY. SENSES THAT "OLD SOLDIERS NEVER DIE" AND THAT THERE IS INCIPIENT NAZISM IN GERMANY - BEHIND THE "ADENAUER FACADE." ONE MUST NOT TRUST GERMANY OR GIVE HER RESOURCES TO RISE AGAIN.

2906 THANT U.
THE UNITED NATIONS' DEVELOPMENT DECADE: PROPOSALS FOR ACTION.
NEW YORK: UNITED NATIONS, 1962, 125 PP., $1.25.
PROPOSES UN SPONSORED WORLD WIDE PROMOTION OF SOCIAL AND ECONOMIC GROWTH AMONG MEMBER NATIONS. THE ROLE OF FINANCIAL AND TECHNOLOGICAL ASSISTANCE ARE DISCUSSED AS KEY FACTORS IN THE PROGRAM.

2907 THANT U.
TOWARD WORLD PEACE.
NEW YORK: THOMAS YOSELOFF, 1964, 404 PP., LC#64-21343.
COLLECTION OF MAJOR PUBLIC ADDRESSES OF U THANT SINCE 1961. SPEECHES ON PURPOSE OF UN, MIDDLE EAST CRISIS, EDUCATION, SMALL NATIONS AND UN, SCIENCE, ETC.

2908 THAYER F.C. JR.
AIR TRANSPORT POLICY AND NATIONAL SECURITY: A POLITICAL, ECONOMIC, AND MILITARY ANALYSIS.
CHAPEL HILL: U OF N CAR PR, 1965, 352 PP., LC#65-25600.
HISTORICAL ACCOUNT OF NATURE AND DEVELOPMENT OF MILITARY AND COMMERCIAL LONG-HAUL AIRLIFT SYSTEMS. DISCUSSES NATIONAL AND INTERNATIONAL POLICY BEFORE WORLD WAR II TO PRESENT, AND RELATIONS BETWEEN MILITARY AND PRIVATE USE FROM ECONOMIC AND DEFENSE VIEWPOINTS. SUGGESTS VARIOUS REVISIONS TO AIRLINE REGULATORY PROCESS AND REFINEMENTS OF ECONOMIC THEORY. COMMENTS ON SPECIFIC MILITARY STRATEGIES FOR 1960'S.

2909 THAYER P.W.
SOUTHEAST ASIA IN THE COMING WORLD.
BALTIMORE: JOHNS HOPKINS PR., 1953, 306 PP.
CONFERENCE PAPERS COVER USA POLICY TOWARDS REGION, ECONOMIC AND IDEOLOGICAL PROBLEMS OF AREA, MUNICIPAL AND INTERNATIONAL LAW, AND ACTIVITIES OF USA BUSINESSES AND UNIVERSITIES IN ASIA.

2910 THE AFRICA 1960 COMMITTEE
MANDATE IN TRUST; THE PROBLEM OF SOUTH WEST AFRICA.
LONDON: AFRICA 1960 COMMITTEE, 1960, 31 PP.
DISCUSSION OF MANDATE OF SOUTH AFRICA OVER SOUTH WEST AFRICA. COVERS BACKGROUND OF SOUTH WEST AFRICA AS GERMAN COLONY MADE MANDATE IN 1918 AND STATUS OF AREA IN INTERNATIONAL AFFAIRS AND DOMESTIC SITUATIONS. OPPOSES PRESENT SITUATION OF SOUTH AFRICAN CONTROL OVER TERRITORY AND SEEKS CHANGE IN STATUS.

2911 THE ECONOMIST (LONDON)
THE COMMONWEALTH AND EUROPE.
LONDON: ECONOMIST INTELLIG UNIT, 1960, 606 PP.
COLLECTION AND ANALYSIS OF FACTS RELEVANT TO PATTERNS OF TRADE IN COMMONWEALTH AND EEC. INCLUDES CHAPTERS ON PRODUCTION AND TRADE OF FOODSTUFFS, RAW MATERIALS, MANUFACTURES. ANALYZES TRADE SYSTEMS IN "OLDER DOMINIONS" OF THE COMMONWEALTH, ASIAN MEMBERS, TROPICAL AFRICA, AND WEST INDIES.

2912 THEOBALD R.
THE RICH AND THE POOR: A STUDY OF THE ECONOMICS OF RISING EXPECTATIONS.
NEW YORK: POTTER, 1960, 196 PP.
EXAMINES DIFFERENT PROBLEMS ENCOUNTERED IN RAISING LIVING STANDARDS AND HOW THESE PROBLEMS COMPLICATE WORLD TRADE. ANALYZES ECONOMIC SYSTEMS OF MODERN WORLD AND THEIR THEORETICAL BASES.

2913 THEOBALD R.
THE CHALLENGE OF ABUNDANCE.
NEW YORK: CLARKSON N POTTER, 1961, 235 PP., LC#61-11426.
SETS OUT IMPLICATIONS OF CONTINUING ECONOMIC AND SOCIAL REVOLUTIONS AND SUGGESTS NECESSARY CHANGES IN POLICY. THE US AS DEVELOPED NATION MUST RECOGNIZE NEEDS OF POOR COUNTRIES. RECOGNIZES NECESSITY OF WORLD CITIZENSHIP.

2914 THEOBALD R.
NATIONAL DEVELOPMENT EFFORTS (PAMPHLET)
NEW YORK: UNITED NATIONS, 1962, 67 PP.
EXAMINES PLANS AND ACTIONS OF UNDERDEVELOPED NATIONS TO

IMPROVE THEIR ECONOMIC CONDITIONS. DISCUSSES PLANNING, EDUCATION, INDUSTRY, AGRICULTURE, INFLATION, BALANCE-OF-PAYMENTS, INVESTMENT, AND TAXATION.

2915 THEOBALD R.
FREE MEN AND FREE MARKETS.
NEW YORK: CLARKSON N POTTER, 1963, 207 PP., LC#63-18879.
RELATES DEVELOPMENT OF FREE MARKETING TO PERSONAL FREEDOM IN AFFLUENT AMERICA AND PREDICTS FUTURE OF FREE MARKETING IN EVER-INCREASING INTERACTION OF WORLD ECONOMIES. TRACES PROGRESS AND ANALYZES BEGINNINGS OF ECONOMIC CONTROL IN US.

2916 THEOBALD R. ED.
THE NEW NATIONS OF WEST AFRICA.
NEW YORK: H W WILSON, 1960, 175 PP., LC#60-08240.
EXAMINES PROBLEMS OF NEW NATIONS, ECONOMIC AND POLITICAL. ANALYZES MAJOR PROBLEMS OF SPECIFIC COUNTRIES. VIEWS RELATIONSHIP WITH EX-COLONIAL POWERS AND EFFECTS OF COLONIALISM ON ECONOMIC AND POLITICAL PRACTICES.

2917 THIEN T.T.
INDIA AND SOUTHEAST ASIA 1947-1960.
GENEVA: LIBRAIRIE DROZ, 1963, 384 PP.
STUDY OF INDIA'S POLICY TOWARDS SOUTHEAST ASIAN COUNTRIES IN PERIOD 1947-60. ATTEMPTS TO DESCRIBE INDIA'S AIMS AND OBJECTIVES, UNCOVER HER MOTIVES, AND EXAMINE DIPLOMATIC STRATEGY AND TACTICS ADOPTED TO ACHIEVE HER NATIONAL ENDS. EMPHASIS ON QUESTIONS OF MOTIVATION AND DIPLOMATIC ACTION.

2918 THIEN T.T.
"VIETNAM: A CASE OF SOCIAL ALIENATION."
INTERNATIONAL AFFAIRS (U.K.), 43 (JULY 67),455-467.
TRACES POLITICAL HISTORY OF VIETNAM SINCE UNIFICATION IN 1802 TO ILLUSTRATE GROWTH OF ALIENATION OF AGRICULTURAL PEASANTS FROM RULING ELITES. WITH INFLUX OF US MONEY THIS GAP IS INCREASING. MAINTAINS THAT SOLUTIONS NECESSITATE IDENTIFICATION OF OFFICIALS WITH PEASANTS AND PEASANT REPRESENTATION IN GOVERNMENT. US MUST DIRECT AID AWAY FROM OFFICIALS AND VIETNAMESE MUST REFORM ARMY AND CIVIL SERVICE.

2919 THOM J.M.
GUIDE TO RESEARCH MATERIAL IN POLITICAL SCIENCE (PAMPHLET)
WASHINGTON: WASHINGTON U LIBS, 1952, 34 PP.
AN ANNOTATED BIBLIOGRAPHY IN POLITICAL SCIENCE MATERIAL. 233 ENTRIES. MATERIAL IN ENGLISH AND SOME FRENCH, GERMAN, ITALIAN AND RUSSIAN.

2920 THOMAS A.V., THOMAS A.J. JR.
NONINTERVENTION: THE LAW AND ITS IMPORT IN THE AMERICAS.
DALLAS: SOUTHERN METHODIST U PR, 1965, 476 PP., LC#56-9845.
STUDIES INTERNATIONAL NONINTERVENTION LAW IN LIGHT OF GENERAL INTERNATIONAL LAW. MAINTAINS THAT LAWS REGARDING NONINTERVENTION MUST BE ADHERED TO BY ACCEPTANCE OF VALUE OF LAW, NOT POWER. INCLUDES EVOLUTION OF DOCTRINE OF NONINTERVENTION AND WAYS IN WHICH LAW DEFINES LEGALITY OR ILLEGALITY OF INTERVENTION.

2921 THOMAS D.H.
GUIDE TO THE DIPLOMATIC ARCHIVES OF WESTERN EUROPE.
PHILA: U OF PENN PR, 1959, 389 PP., LC#57-9123.
AN UNANNOTATED BIBLIOGRAPHY OF THE DIPLOMATIC ARCHIVES OF THE COUNTRIES OF WESTERN EUROPE. MATERIAL IN THE FOLLOWING LANGUAGES: ENGLISH, GERMAN, FRENCH, DUTCH, ITALIAN, DANISH, NORWEGIAN, PORTUGUESE, SPANISH, SWEDISH, SWISS. 400 ENTRIES.

2922 THOMAS J.A.
THE HOUSE OF COMMONS, 1832-1901; A STUDY OF ITS ECONOMIC AND FUNCTIONAL CHARACTER.
CARDIFF: U OF WALES PRESS, 1939, 176 PP.
ANALYZES FUNCTIONS OF HOUSE OF COMMONS, ITS STRUCTURE, AND COMPOSITION. DISCUSSES ITS LAW-MAKING POWER, DOMESTIC AND INTERNATIONAL POLICY, LEADERSHIP, AND SEGMENTS OF SOCIETY IT REPRESENTS. EXAMINES THEORY AND BEHAVIOR OF ITS MEMBERS, SIGNIFICANT LEGISLATION, AND ECONOMIC POLICY AND POWERS. CONCENTRATES ON MEASURES TO INCREASE STATE CONTROL OVER INDIVIDUALS AND PROPERTY.

2923 THOMAS J.R.T.
"SOVIET BEHAVIOR IN THE QUEMOY CRISES OF 1958."
ORBIS, 6 (SPRING 62), 38-64.
EXAMINES THE FIRMNESS OF THE SINO-SOVIET ALLIANCE. THIS IS APPROACH BY RE-EXAMINATION OF THE WORKINGS OF THE ALLIANCE IN CRISIS AFFECTING THE VITAL INTEREST OF ONE OF THE MEMBERS SUCH AS THE 1955 AND 1958 QUEMOY CRISIS. SOVIET RELUCTANCE TO BACK FUTURE CPR IS SEEN AS LIKELY TO INCREASE EVEN MORE.

2924 THOMAS N.
THE PREREQUISITES FOR PEACE.
NEW YORK: NORTON, 1959, 189 PP., $2.95.
ADVOCATES PROGRAM OF DISENGAGEMENT AT POINTS OF WORLD TENSION, A STRENTHENING OF UN BY LAW AND ENFORCEMENT POWER, AND GENERAL DISARMAMENT. ANALYZES CAUSES AND DIRECTION OF CONFLICT BETWEEN EAST AND WEST AND SUMMARIZES SPECIFIC CONFLICTS IN MIDDLE EAST, ASIA, AND EUROPE.

2925 THOMPSON D., MARSH N.S.
"THE UNITED KINGDOM AND THE TREATY OF ROME."
INT. COMP. LAW QUART., 11 (JAN. 62), 73-88.
ASSESSES LEGAL ARGUMENTS REGARDING THE ENTRY OF UNITED KINGDOM INTO THE COMMON MARKET UNDER THE TREATY OF ROME PROVISIONS. OUTLINES ADMINISTRATIVE AND JUDICIAL ASPECTS OF THE SYSTEM AND INDICATES WHAT ACTION PARLIAMENT MIGHT TAKE (IN VIEW OF ENGLISH COMMON LAW) WITH REGARD TO LABOR UNIONS. FORESEES A HARMONIZATION OF LAWS.

2926 THOMPSON J.H. ED., REISCHAUER R.D. ED.
MODERNIZATION OF THE ARAB WORLD.
PRINCETON: VAN NOSTRAND, 1966, 249 PP.
DIVERSE OPINIONS ON AND APPROACHES TO STUDY OF MODERN ARAB WORLD. EXAMINES INTERACTIONS OF TRADITIONAL PAST, CURRENT REALITIES, AND FUTURE EXPECTATIONS. EXPLORES IMPEDING AND POSITIVE ELEMENTS OF PAST, PROBLEMS OF ECONOMIC GROWTH, INTRA-ARAB AND ARAB-ISRAELI RELATIONS, POPULATION, AND SOCIAL INSTABILITY. COMPARES PROCESS OF MODERNIZATION IN ARAB COUNTRIES AND GIVES REASONS FOR DIFFERENCES.

2927 THOMPSON J.W., PADOVER S.K.
SECRET DIPLOMACY: A RECORD OF ESPIONAGE AND DOUBLE-DEALING: 1500-1815.
LONDON: JARROLDS PUBLISHERS, LTD, 1937, 286 PP.
ATTEMPTS TO SHOW THAT UNDERCOVER OPERATIONS HAVE BEEN UNIVERSALLY EMPLOYED, AND THAT SPYING AND BRIBERY HAVE PLAYED A LARGER ROLE IN DIPLOMATIC HISTORY THAN HERETOFORE BELIEVED. BOOK BASED ON OFFICIAL DOCUMENTS, MEMOIRS, MEMORANDA OF MINISTERS, POLICE REPORTS, LETTERS, AND INFORMATION OF SPIES. EXTENSIVE BIBLIOGRAPHY ARRANGED ACCORDING TO CHAPTER SUBJECTS.

2928 THOMPSON K.W.
"THE STUDY OF INTERNATIONAL POLITICS: A SURVEY OF TRENDS AND DEVELOPMENTS."
REV. POLIT., 14 (OCT. 52), 433-67.
CONSIDERS FOUR GENERAL STAGES THROUGH WHICH STUDY OF INTERNATIONAL RELATIONS HAS PASSED. STUDIES NORMATIVE ASPECT FORMULATIONS OF METHODOLOGY IN INTERNATIONAL POLITICS. CONCLUDES WITH ANALYSIS OF DILEMMAS OF RESEARCH AND THEIR NEW PERSPECTIVES.

2929 THOMPSON K.W.
"NATIONAL SECURITY IN A NUCLEAR AGE."
SOC. RES., 25 (WINTER 58), 439-448.
EXAMINATION OF FALLACIES OF A THERMONUCLEAR BALANCE OF POWER SYSTEM TO MAINTAIN PEACE. PROPOSES THAT DIPLOMATS TAKE THE INITIATIVE IN ARRIVING AT NEW AND SANER POLICIES.

2930 THOMPSON K.W.
"MORAL PURPOSE IN FOREIGN POLICY: REALITIES AND ILLUSIONS."
SOC. RES., 27 (AUTUMN 60), 261-276.
RAISES QUESTION OF POLITICS AND ETHICS. ANALYZES GOALS AND PURPOSES OF BROADER INTERNATIONAL COMMUNITY IN THE FACE OF HARSH REALITIES OF INTERNATIONAL POLITICS. CONSIDERS LEGAL AND MORAL IMPLICATIONS REGARDING DELICATE SITUATIONS LIKE U2. DISUSSES FUNDAMENTAL PROBLEMS OF POLICY COORDINATION AND DECISION-MAKING IN FOREIGN AFFAIRS. QUESTIONS ROLE OF PRIVATE CITIZEN IN VAST AND SPRAWLING POLITICAL SYSTEM.

2931 THOMPSON K.W.
POLITICAL REALISM AND THE CRISIS IN WORLD POLITICS.
PRINCETON: U. PR., 1960, 261 PP.
DISCUSSES APPROACH TO INTERNATIONAL RELATIONS AND USA FOREIGN POLICY OF AMERICAN POLITICAL REALIST THINKERS. REALIST PRINCIPLES APPLIED TO PROBLEMS, SUCH AS INTERNATIONAL MORALITY, COLLECTIVE SECURITY AND ARMAMENTS, DIPLOMACY, AND COLONIALISM.

2932 THOMPSON K.W.
"THE EMPIRICAL, NORMATIVE, AND THEORETICAL FOUNDATIONS OF INTERNATIONAL STUDIES."
REV. OF POLITICS, 29 (APR. 67), 147-159.
EXAMINES THE UNITY OF INTERNATIONAL STUDIES & ITS INEVITABLE FRAGMENTATION OF SCHOLARLY APPROACH. ARGUES THAT NO SINGLE PERSPECTIVE HOLDS MONOPOLY ON WISDOM. EXAMINES EMPIRICAL, NORMATIVE, & THEORETICAL FOUNDATIONS IN LIGHT OF THEIR CONTRIBUTIONS TO INTERNATIONAL STUDIES. ADVOCATES RESTORATION OF UNITY OF KNOWLEDGE TO HELP INTERNATIONAL STUDIES REDISCOVER THAT BOUNDARIES ARE NOT LIMITED BY DISCIPLINES.

2933 THOMPSON V., ADLOFF R.
MINORITY PROBLEMS IN SOUTHEAST ASIA.
STANFORD: STANFORD U PRESS, 1955, 295 PP., LC#55-6688.
ANALYZES THE PROBLEMS THAT SOUTHEAST ASIAN MINORITIES HAVE WITH EACH OTHER AND THE PROBLEMS THAT SOUTHEAST ASIAN STATES FACE IN THEIR RELATIONS WITH ONE ANOTHER AND WITH THE WORLD AT LARGE. DISCUSSES THE CHINESE, INDIAN, AND CHRISTIAN MINORITIES. INCLUDES BUDDHIST MAJORITY'S PROBLEMS WITH CHRISTIANS IN CAMBODIA AND LAOS, AND THE IMPACT OF THESE PROBLEMS ON ASIAN-WESTERN RELATIONS.

2934 THOMSON G.P.
NUCLEAR ENERGY IN BRITAIN DURING THE LAST WAR: THE CHERWELL SIMON LECTURE (MONOGRAPH)

LONDON: CLARENDON PRESS, 1962, 16 PP.
DISCUSSES INTERNATIONAL SCIENTIFIC RESEARCH IN ATOMIC THEORY IN US AND EUROPE THAT LED TO THE UK'S PROJECT MAUD (MILITARY APPLICATIONS OF URANIUM DETONATION) IN 1940. EXPLAINS PROBLEM OF ISOTOPE SEPARATION WHICH FINALLY LED TO CREATION OF INSTRUMENT CAPABLE OF RELEASING LARGE AMOUNTS OF RADIOACTIVE SUBSTANCE. TELLS OF COLLABORATION WITH US AND CONTRIBUTIONS OF PARTICIPATING SCIENTISTS.

2935 THORELLI H.B., GRAVES R.L., HOWELLS L.T.
INTOP: INTERNATIONAL OPERATIONS SIMULATION: PLAYER'S MANUAL.
NEW YORK: FREE PRESS OF GLENCOE, 1963, 58 PP., LC#63-13249.
PLAYER'S MANUAL FOR ONE OF THE FIRST MAJOR BUSINESS SIMULATION EXERCISES ORIENTED TOWARD SPECIFIC PROBLEM OF INTERNATIONAL AND OVERSEAS OPERATIONS; DESIGNED TO INCREASE UNDERSTANDING OF PROBLEMS OF MULTINATIONAL CORPORATIONS AND TO YIELD SUBSTANTIAL PAYOFF IN GENERAL MANAGEMENT TRAINING.

2936 THORNE C.
THE APPROACH OF WAR, 1938-1939.
NEW YORK: ST MARTIN'S PRESS, 1967, 232 PP., LC#67-10649.
ANALYZES DIPLOMATIC MANEUVERS AT BEGINNING OF WWII FROM 1938-39. DESCRIBES EUROPEAN SITUATION AND HITLER'S ALTERNATIVES; EXAMINES MEANING AND MOTIVES OF WESTERN POLICY OF APPEASEMENT; REASSESSES HITLER'S INTENTIONS, METHODS, AND RESPONSIBILITY FOR WAR. TRACES EVENTS FROM SEIZURE OF AUSTRIA TO OUTBREAK OF WAR. CRITICIZES HANDLING OF EVENTS BY WESTERN DIPLOMATS.

2937 THORNTON A.P.
THE IMPERIAL IDEA AND ITS ENEMIES.
NEW YORK: ST MARTIN'S PRESS, 1966, 372 PP.
DISCUSSES AND ANALYZES CHANGES IN ATTITUDE TOWARD THE BRITISH EMPIRE ADOPTED BY MEN IN POWER, BY MEN OUT OF IT, AND BY PUBLIC OPINION IN GENERAL DURING PERIOD 1860-1957. ASSESSES THE IMPACT THESE ATTITUDES HAVE MADE AT DIFFERENT TIMES ON THE ROLE PLAYED BY THE UK IN WORLD AFFAIRS.

2938 THUCYDIDES
THE PELOPONESIAN WARS.
NEW YORK: TWAYNE, 1963, 335 PP.
DESCRIBES STRUGGLE BETWEEN ATHENS AND SPARTA FOR SUPREMACY IN GREECE. SEES WAR AS CONFLICT OF TWO IDEAS: ATHENIAN IMPERIALISM AND GREEK PASSION FOR AUTONOMY. SEES WAR ALSO AS CONFLICT BETWEEN TWO WAYS OF LIFE: ATHENIAN DEMOCRACY AND SPARTAN DISCIPLINED CONSERVATISM.

2939 THWAITE D.
THE SEETHING AFRICAN POT: A STUDY OF BLACK NATIONALISM 1882-1935.
LONDON: CONSTABLE & CO, 1936, 250 PP.
ETHIOPIAN NATIONALISM AND ITS ACTIVITIES IN AFRICA, SECRET SOCIETIES, GUERRILLA TACTICS, POLITICAL ALIGNMENT WITH AXIS, AND ANTI-WHITE FEELING AS A UNIFYING FACTOR ARE ALL TREATED.

2940 TILLION G.
ALGERIA: THE REALITIES.
NEW YORK: ALFRED KNOPF, 1958, 115 PP., LC#58-10980.
BASED ON AUTHOR'S FIELD WORK IN ALGERIA, DESCRIBES OVERPOPULATED CONDITIONS, ECONOMIC DEGRADATION, AND SOCIAL DECAY OF THE COUNTRY. DISCUSSES COMPARATIVE PROBLEMS OF OVERPOPULATION, COLONIALISM, AND CONSERVATION. PROPOSES A FRANCO-ALGERIAN UNION IN ORDER TO SOLVE ECONOMIC PROBLEMS.

2941 TINBERGEN J.
INTERNATIONAL ECONOMIC INTEGRATION.
AMSTERDAM: ELSEVIER, 1954, 191 PP.
DISCUSSES PRESENT ECONOMIC RELATIONS OF GOVERNMENTS OF DIFFERING ECONOMIC STATUS. ADVOCATES INTERNATIONAL AGENCIES AIDING ECONOMIC INTEGRATION BY REGULATING PUBLIC FINANCE, EMPLOYMENT, RAW MATERIAL MARKETS, TRADE RESTRICTIONS, ETC.

2943 TINGSTERN H.
PEACE AND SECURITY AFTER WW II.
UPSALA: SWED. INST. INT. AFF., 1945, 191 PP.
DENOTES AIMS AND STRUCTURE OF LEAGUE OF NATIONS. DISCUSSES PROCEDURES OF CONCILIATION AND MEDIATION. EXAMINES PERMANENT COURT OF INTERNATIONAL JUSTICE AND SPECIALIZED ECONOMIC AND SOCIAL AGENCIES.

2944 TINKER H.
"POLITICS IN SOUTHEAST ASIA."
POLIT. STUD., 12 (OCT. 64), 385-388.
SURVEY OF SOME BIBLIOGRAPHICAL RESOURCES AND PRESENTATION OF MAJOR THESES OF TEN DIFFERENT TEXTS. CONCLUDES THAT SAMPLE ILLUSTRATES KINDS OF PROBLEMS WHICH MUST BE TACKLED BY THE STUDENT SEEKING TO UNDERSTAND THE NATURE OF GOVERNMENT IN THE NEW STATES.

2945 TINKER H.
SOUTH ASIA.
NEW YORK: FREDERICK PRAEGER, 1966, 287 PP.
SEEKS TO UNDERSTAND ASIAN REVOLUTIONS OF TODAY AGAINST INTERACTION OF EAST AND WEST IN FORMER YEARS. TREATS UNIQUE ASIAN QUALITIES IN LIGHT OF CONTINUING TRADITION. DISCUSSES HISTORICAL BACKGROUND, PATTERN OF GOVERNMENT, SOCIAL ORDER, RELIGION, ENTRY OF WEST, ECONOMIC AND SOCIAL CHANGE, BRITISH POLICY, GREAT SOCIAL AND RELIGIOUS MOVEMENTS, AND STRUGGLE FOR INDEPENDENCE.

2946 TIPTON J.B.
"PARTICIPATION OF THE UNITED STATES IN THE INTERNATIONAL LABOR ORGANIZATION."
URBANA: INST. LABOR INDUS. REL./U. ILL., 1959, 150 PP.
ENVISAGES CONSTRUCTIVE ROLE FOR USA IN ILO. RAPID INDUSTRIAL DEVELOPMENT IN EMERGING NATIONS PRESENTS NEW PROBLEMS TO WHICH THE US CAN CONTRIBUTE TO THE SOLUTION FROM HER OWN EXPERIENCE. TREATS SUBJECT OF AUTOMATION AND ITS IMPACT ON LABOR RELATIONS.

2947 TOLMAN E.C.
DRIVES TOWARD WAR.
NEW YORK: APPLETON, 1942, 118 PP.
EXAMINES MAN'S BASIC BIOLOGICAL DRIVES AND LEARNED SOCIAL TECHNIQUES AND RELATES THEM TO SUBCONSCIOUS ATTITUDES THAT MAY BE EXPRESSED IN COLLECTIVE AGGRESSION. CONCLUDES THAT, TO ELIMINATE WAR, BIOLOGICAL NEEDS MUST BE SATISFIED THROUGH ECONOMIC ORDER, EDUCATIONAL SYSTEMS ESTABLISHED TO ENCOURAGE IDENTIFICATION WITH ACCEPTABLE AUTHORITY, AND GROUP LOYALTY TRANSFERRED TO A SUPRANATIONAL STATE.

2948 TOMASIC D.A.
NATIONAL COMMUNISM AND SOVIET STRATEGY.
WASHINGTON: PUBLIC AFFAIRS PRESS, 1957, 225 PP., LC#57-6901.
CONCERNED WITH TITOISM IN TERMS OF SOVIET STRATEGY. GIVES ORIGINS AND DEVELOPMENTS OF TITOISM, AND DESCRIBES ITS FORMS AS THEY HAVE DEVELOPED IN OTHER STATES. DISCUSSES YUGOSLAVIA'S CIVIL WAR, BRITISH-RUSSIAN RIVALRY IN EASTERN EUROPE, AND COMMUNIST WORLD CONSPIRACY. EMPHASIZES THE SIGNIFICANCE OF TITO'S INDEPENDENT ROAD TO COMMUNISM.

2949 TONG T.
UNITED STATES DIPLOMACY IN CHINA, 1844-1860.
SEATTLE: U OF WASHINGTON PR, 1964, 332 PP., LC#64-11051.
ANALYSIS OF DIPLOMATIC RELATIONS BETWEEN CHINA AND US IN SPECIFIC PERIOD BEGINNING WITH TREATY OF WANGHIA. DEALS WITH IMPERIALISM IN CHINA AND US ACTIVITIES IN POLITICAL AND TRADE EVENTS DURING PERIOD.

2950 TORRE M.
"PSYCHIATRIC OBSERVATIONS OF INTERNATIONAL CONFERENCES."
INT. J. SOC. PSYCHIAT., 1(NO.3, 55), 48-53.
BELIEVES A COMBINATION OF ALL SKILLS IS ESSENTIAL FOR THE UNDERSTANDING AND OPERATION OF INTERNATIONAL CONFERENCES AND THIS COMBINED SOCIAL SCIENCE APPROACH OFFERS GREATEST PROMISE FOR DEVELOPMENT OF THE CONFERENCE IN FURTHERING INTERNATIONAL COLLABORATION.

2951 TOSCANO M.
THE HISTORY OF TREATIES AND INTERNATIONAL POLITICS (REV. ED.)
BALTIMORE: JOHNS HOPKINS PRESS, 1966, 685 PP., LC#66-15525.
SOURCE BOOK FOR HISTORY OF TREATIES AND DIPLOMACY, ENUMERATING MAJOR COLLECTIONS OF TREATIES, DOCUMENTS RELATING TO DIPLOMACY IN WWI AND WWII, AND SOURCES OF MEMOIRS ABOUT THESE WARS AND THEIR ORIGINS. COVERS SOURCES FROM ALL PARTS OF WORLD AND NOT ONLY EUROPE AND US.

2952 TOTOK W., WEITZEL R.
HANDBUCH DER BIBLIOGRAPHISCHEN NACHSCHLAGEWERKE.
FRANKFURT: V KLOSTERMANN, 1954, 258 PP.
BIBLIOGRAPHY OF GERMAN BIBLIOGRAPHIES IN GENERAL AND SPECIFIC SUBJECTS.

2953 TOURE S.
THE INTERNATIONAL POLICY OF THE DEMOCRATIC PARTY OF GUINEA (VOL. VII)
GUINEA: DEMOCRATIC PARTY, 1962, 241 PP.
DELINEATES INTERNATIONAL POLICY OF DEMOCRATIC PARTY OF GUINEA ON SUCH ISSUES AS AFRICAN UNITY, AFRO-ASIAN UNITY, GUINEA'S POSITION ON WAR IN ALGERIA, GHANA-GUINEA-MALI UNION, ECONOMIC CONFERENCE OF CASABLANCA POWERS, INDEPENDENCE OF CONGO AND OF GHANA, AND WORLD PEACE. INCLUDES STUDY OF POLITICAL PRINCIPLES OF DEMOCRATIC PARTY OF GUINEA.

2954 TOUVAL S.
"THE SOMALI REPUBLIC."
CURR. HIST., 46 (MARCH 64), 156-162.
PROGRESS TOWARD ECONOMIC DEVELOPMENT AND IMPROVEMENT IN LIVING CONDITIONS EXPECTED TO CONTINUE. HOWEVER CONTINUED INTERNAL INSTABILITY PROMISES UNVARYING ATTENTION OF EAST, WEST AND OTHER INTERESTED PARTIES.

2955 TOWLE L.W.
INTERNATIONAL TRADE AND COMMERCIAL POLICY.
NEW YORK: HARPER, 1947, 780 PP.
STUDIES ECONOMIC BASES OF INTERNATIONAL RELATIONS AND EFFECT ON NATIONAL INCOMES AND NATIONAL PROSPERITY. PRESENTS MAJOR ISSUES OF INTERNATIONAL ECONOMICS AND EXAMINES THEIR EFFECTS ON POLITICS. DISCUSSES METHODOLOGY OF ECONOMIC

ANALYSIS.

2956 TOWSTER J.
"THE USSR AND THE USA: CHALLENGE AND RESPONSE."
CURR. HIST., 42 (JAN. 62), 1-7.
DISCUSSES BACKGROUND OF EAST-WEST CONFLICT AND CRITICAL AREAS FOR KENNEDY ADMINISTRATION. USA HAS FAILED TO MEET OVER-ALL CHALLENGE OF USSR DUE TO INADEQUATE UNDERSTANDING OF NATURE AND SCOPE OF COMMUNISM. RECOMMENDS APPROACH BASED ON 3 ASSUMPTIONS: USSR WON'T ENGAGE IN ALL-OUT WAR AS LONG AS WEST IS MILITARY MATCH, USSR WILL EXPLOIT DIFFICULTIES IN UNDERDEVELOPED AREAS AND CONTINUE TO BELIEVE IN SPLIT-WEST.

2957 TOYNBEE A. ED., TOYNBEE V.M. ED.
THE WAR AND THE NEUTRALS.
LONDON: OXFORD U PR, 1956, 378 PP.
STUDIES ECONOMIC WARFARE OF BRITAIN AND US AGAINST GERMANY DURING WWII AND SUCCESS OF BLOCKADE. EXAMINES POSITION OF LATIN AMERICA DURING WWII, PAN-AMERICANISM, RIO DE JANEIRO CONFERENCE OF 1942, AND THEIR POLITICAL EFFECTS. DESCRIBES POLICIES OF NEUTRAL AND NONBELLIGERENT ALLIED NATIONS, INCLUDING SWEDEN, SWITZERLAND, SPAIN, PORTUGAL, AND TURKEY.

2958 TRAGER F.N.
"A SELECTED AND ANNOTATED BIBLIOGRAPHY ON ECONOMIC DEVELOPMENT, 1953-1957."
ECO. DEV. AND CULTURAL CHANGE, 6 (JULY 58), 257-329.
AN ANNOTATED BIBLIOGRAPHY OF ECONOMIC DEVELOPMENT. MATERIAL IN ENGLISH-LANGUAGE; RANGING FROM 1953 TO 1957. 409 ENTRIES. BIBLIOGRAPHY DIVIDED INTO SEVEN CLASSES: COUNTRY AND AREA STUDIES, CHARACTERISTICS AND INSTITUTIONAL ORGANIZATION OF UNDERDEVELOPED COUNTRIES, MEASUREMENT AND THEORY OF ECONOMIC GROWTH, POPULATION, LABOR AND URBANIZATION, CAPITAL ACCUMULATION, INVESTMENT, AND PRODUCTIVITY.

2959 TRAMPE G.
"DIE FORM DER DIPLOMATIC ALS POLITSCHE WAFFE."
POLITISCHE STUDIEN, 12 (SEPT 61), 607-610.
ANALYZES HISTORICAL ORIGINS AND NATURE OF DIPLOMACY AS A METHOD OF POLITICAL WARFARE.

2960 TREADGOLD D.W. ED.
THE DEVELOPMENT OF THE USSR.
SEATTLE: U OF WASHINGTON PR, 1964, 399 PP., LC#64-17390.
CONTAINS SERIES OF EXCHANGES OF DIFFERING VIEWS AMONG SOME OF THE WEST'S FOREMOST SPECIALISTS ON RUSSIA. CERTAIN FUNDAMENTAL ISSUES SINGLED OUT FOR EXAMINATION, RANGING FROM THE ORGANIZATION OF THE POLITICAL SYSTEM AND ECONOMY OF USSR AND THE DEVELOPMENT OF RUSSIAN LITERATURE, TO VARIOUS HISTORICAL STAGES THROUGH WHICH RUSSIA, THE UKRAINE, AND BELORUSSIA HAVE PASSED.

2961 TREFOUSSE H.L. ED.
THE COLD WAR: A BOOK OF DOCUMENTS.
NEW YORK: G P PUTNAM'S SONS, 1965, 296 PP., LC#65-13298.
COLLECTION OF ACTUAL KEY DOCUMENTS IN DIPLOMATIC HISTORY OF COLD WAR, WITH INTEGRATING ANALYSES. BEGINS WITH ALLIED ALIGNMENT, 1942, AND COVERS WWII, FAILURE OF PEACE TALKS AS ORIGIN OF COLD WAR, COLD WAR IN EUROPE, IN ASIA, IN LATIN AMERICA, AND IN EISENHOWER AND KENNEDY ADMINISTRATIONS. BIBLIOGRAPHY OF US, UN, AND RUSSIAN DOCUMENTS.

2962 TRIFFIN R.
EUROPE AND THE MONEY MUDDLE.
NEW HAVEN: YALE U. PR., 1957, 351 PP.
ANALYZES THREE ASPECTS OF EUROPEAN MONETARY RECOVERY AFTER WORLD WAR TWO: EXISTING PROBLEMS, THE EUROPEAN PAYMENTS UNION, AND PROSPECTS OF CONVERTIBILITY. FAVORS CLOSE REGIONAL COOPERATION.

2963 TRIFFIN R.
GOLD AND THE DOLLAR CRISIS: THE FUTURE OF CONVERTIBILITY.
NEW HAVEN: YALE U PR, 1961, 181 PP., LC#61-11398.
ANALYZES SUCCESS OF 19TH-CENTURY SYSTEM OF "INTERNATIONAL CONVERTIBILITY" AND FAILURE OF SAME SYSTEM IN 1920'S. POINTS OUT REASONS WHY 20TH CENTURY CANNOT REVERT TO 19TH-CENTURY SYSTEM WITHOUT CERTAIN RADICAL INSTITUTIONAL REFORMS.

2964 TRIFFIN R.
THE WORLD MONEY MAZE.
NEW HAVEN: YALE U PR, 1966, 585 PP., LC#66-12516.
ANALYZES INTERNATIONAL MONEY PROBLEMS 1938-64, DOLLAR SHORTAGE, FAILURE OF INTERNATIONAL MONETARY ORGANIZATIONS, AND RECURRENT CRISES IN KEY CURRENCIES: STERLING AND DOLLAR. CRITICIZES MAINTENANCE OF GOLD EXCHANGE STANDARD AND ADVOCATES SYSTEM OF GOVERNMENT CONTROL SUCH AS OEEC, EPU, AND EEC.

2965 TRIFFIN R.
THE BALANCE OF PAYMENTS AND THE FOREIGN INVESTMENT POSITION OF THE UNITED STATES.
PRINCETON: PRINCETON U PRESS, 1966, 34 PP., LC#66-28512.
ANALYZES PROBLEM OF LIQUIDITY IN FOREIGN EXCHANGE ASSETS, ROLE OF DOLLAR AS INTERMEDIARY IN EUROPEAN EXCHANGE, AND METHOD OF DEALING WITH PROBLEM THROUGH INTERNATIONAL ORGANIZATION. DUE TO GOLD STANDARD IN FOREIGN EXCHANGE AND INABILITY OF GOLD PRODUCTION TO KEEP PACE, IT BECOMES NECESSARY TO FIND CREDIT BASE SUCH AS PROPOSED.

2966 TRISKA J.F., SLUSSER R.M.
THE THEORY, LAW, AND POLICY OF SOVIET TREATIES.
STANFORD: U. PR., 1962, 593 PP.
ATTEMPT AT A SYSTEMATIC INVESTIGATION AND ANALYSIS OF SOVIET INTERNATIONAL LEGAL ARRANGEMENTS, COVERING CHIEFLY THE PERIOD FROM 1917 - 1957.

2967 TRISKA J.F.
"SOVIET TREATY LAW: A QUANTITATIVE ANALYSIS."
LAW CONTEMP. PROBL., 29 (AUTUMN 64), 896-909.
STUDY OF SOVIET TREATY DATA SHOWING RECENT DEVELOPMENTS AND TRENDS WHICH CHARACTERIZE THE SOVIET LAW OF TREATIES. IMPLICATIONS REGARDING FURTHER GROWTH AND CHANGES IN ATTITUDES ARE ASSESSED.

2968 TROTIER A.H. ED., HARMAN M. ED.
DOCTORAL DISSERTATIONS ACCEPTED BY AMERICAN UNIVERSITIES 1954-55.
NEW YORK: H W WILSON, 1955, 298 PP., LC#34-40898.
UNANNOTATED LISTING OF DOCTORAL DISSERTATIONS ACCEPTED IN US IN 1954-55. INCLUDES STATISTICS ON DOCTORAL DEGREES GRANTED IN ALL FIELDS FROM 1945-46 THROUGH 1954-55. INCLUDES PHILOSOPHY, RELIGION, GEOGRAPHY, PUBLIC HEALTH, ECONOMICS, EDUCATION, INTERNATIONAL LAW AND RELATIONS, SOCIOLOGY, ART, ARCHEOLOGY, LANGUAGES AND LITERATURE, POLITICS, HISTORY, AND OTHERS.

2969 TROTSKY L.
PROBLEMS OF THE CHINESE REVOLUTION (3RD ED. TRANS. BY MAX SCHACTMAN)
ANN ARBOR: U OF MICH PR, 1967, 432 PP.
NEW EDITION OF 1932 WORK PRESENTING TROTSKY'S INDICTMENT OF STALINIST POLICY TOWARD CHINESE REVOLUTION AND HIS PROPOSALS FOR ALTERNATIVE POLICIES. DISCUSSES BACKGROUND, MOTIVES, AND EVENTS OF CHINESE STRUGGLE, AS WELL AS SOVIET REACTIONS TO IT. CONTAINS ARTICLES AND SPEECHES BY OTHER CONTEMPORARY CRITICS OF STALIN'S CHINA POLICY. INCLUDES GLOSSARY OF NAMES AND TERMS.

2970 TRUMAN D.
"THE DOMESTIC POLITICS OF FOREIGN AID."
PROC. ACAD. POLIT. SCI., 27 (JAN. 62), 86-91.
EXAMINES EFFECT OF FOREIGN AID POLICY ON DOMESTIC POLITICS. STUDIES VOTING PATTERNS IN HOUSE OF REPRESENTATVES ON FOREIGN AID. AID PROGRAM TARGET OF MOST CRITICISM, BUT GENERALLY CONCEDED TO BE NESCESSARY AND BILLS ARE PASSED BY CONGRESS.

2971 TUCKER R.C.
"TOWARDS A COMPARATIVE POLITICS OF MOVEMENT-REGIMES" (BMR)"
AM. POL. SCI. REV., 55 (JUNE 61), 281-297.
CONSIDERS NEW APPROACH TO THEORETICAL STUDY OF SOVIET POLITICAL HISTORY AND INSTITUTIONS. SUGGESTS PROBLEM SHOULD BE STUDIED AS PHENOMENON OF METAMORPHOSIS OF MOVEMENT-REGIMES. ANALYZES POLITICS IN USSR, SHOWING CONTINUITY OF BOLSHEVIK MOVEMENT-REGIME, 1917-53. STATES THAT RISE OF STALINISM WAS METAMORPHOSIS OF ORIGINAL BOLSHEVIK MOVEMENT-REGIME INTO A NEW MOVEMENT-REGIME OF THE FUHRER TYPE.

2972 TUCKER R.C.
THE SOVIET POLITICAL MIND.
NEW YORK: PRAEGER, 1963, 238 PP.
STUDY OF STALINISM AND OF POST-STALINIST CHANGES IN THE USSR INCLUDING: THE POLITICS OF DE-STALINIZATION, STALIN AND THE USES OF PSYCHOLOGY, AND STALINISM AND THE COLD WAR.

2973 TUCKER R.C.
"THE DERADICALIZATION OF MARXIST MOVEMENTS."
AM. POL. SCI. REV., 61 (JUNE 67), 343-358.
INTERPRETATION OF POST-STALIN SOVIET IDEOLOGICAL CHANGES AS THEY APPLY TO THEORY OF WORLD REVOLUTION AND TO GENERALIZATIONS WHICH ACCOMMODATE ALL RADICAL POLITICAL MOVEMENTS.

2974 TUCKER R.W.
"PROFESSOR MORGENTHAU'S THEORY OF POLITICAL 'REALISM'."
AM. POL. SCI. REV., 46 (1952), 214-224.
TESTS HANS MORGENTHAU'S CONCEPTION OF THE NATURE OF INTERNATIONAL POLITICS. ATTEMPTS TO DISCOVER WHETHER HIS ANALYSIS IS UNAMBIGUOUS AND NONCONTRADICTORY AND WHETHER ITS APPLICATION IS CHARACTERIZED BY VAGUENESS. EXAMINES HIS MORAL ARGUMENT DEALING WITH THE "MORAL DIGNITY OF THE NATIONAL INTEREST." STATES THAT HE HAS NOT ALWAYS SEPARATED SCIENTIFIC ANALYSIS FROM POLITICAL JUDGMENTS.

2975 TUCKER R.W.
"PEACE AND WAR."
WORLD POLIT., 17 (JAN. 65), 310-333.
INDICATES THAT ARON'S OUTLOOK 'INSISTS ON THE IMPERFECTION OF ALL SOCIAL IDEAS, ALLOWS IMPOSSIBILITY OF KNOWING THE FUTURE AND CONDEMNS THE VAIN PRETENSION OF DRAFTING THE BLUE-PRINT FOR AN IDEAL SOCIETY.'

2976 TULLY A., BRITTEN M.
WHERE DID YOUR MONEY GO.
NEW YORK: SIMON AND SCHUSTER, 1964, 223 PP., LC#64-15351.
EXAMINES WASTE IN FOREIGN AID PROGRAM, FAILURES IN ADMINISTRATION, PLANNING, AND CONTROL. ANALYZES US FOREIGN AID BY COUNTRY, REGION, CATEGORY AND EFFECTIVENESS. COMPARES US AND SOVIET FOREIGN AID PROGRAMS AND THEIR RELATIVE EFFECTIVENESS.

2977 TUNSTALL W.C.B.
THE COMMONWEALTH AND REGIONAL DEFENCE (PAMPHLET)
LONDON: ATHLONE PRESS, 1959, 68 PP.
DISCUSSES ORGANIZATIONS AND SYSTEMS FOR DEFENSE OF BRITISH COMMONWEALTH FROM 1930'S THROUGH WWII. AGREEMENTS INCLUDE WHITE PAPER OF 1946, NATO, ANZUS, SECURITY PACT OF 1951, BAGHDAD PACT OF 1954-55, ANGLO-SOUTH AFRICAN AGREEMENT OF 1955, AND REGIONAL DEFENSE OF INDIAN OCEAN.

2978 TUPPER E.
"JAPAN IN AMERICAN PUBLIC OPINION."
LONDON: MACMILLAN, 1937.
APPROXIMATELY 100 BOOKS RELATING TO HISTORY OF DIPLOMATIC RELATIONS BETWEEN US AND JAPAN 1905-36; MUCH BACKGROUND MATERIAL ON AMERICAN PUBLIC OPINION, POLICIES AND POLITICS OF THE TIMES, AND EVENTS IN FAR EAST. MOST ITEMS IN ENGLISH, AND PUBLISHED 1900-36.

2979 TUPPER E.
JAPAN IN AMERICAN PUBLIC OPINION.
NEW YORK: MACMILLAN, 1937, 465 PP.
HISTORY OF DIPLOMATIC RELATIONS BETWEEN US AND JAPAN 1905-36, WITH INTERPRETATION OF EVENTS IN LIGHT OF AMERICAN PUBLIC OPINION; RELIES MOSTLY ON NEWSPAPERS; SHOWS THAT OPINION TOWARD JAPAN HAS BEEN CONSISTENT WITH ATTITUDES TOWARD OTHER STATES AND THAT SOMETIMES OPINION IS GROUP-BASED, INFUENCED BY NATIONALISTIC, ECONOMIC, PACIFISTIC, OR IDEALISTIC CONSIDERATIONS.

2980 TURNER F.C.
"THE IMPLICATIONS OF DEMOGRAPHIC CHANGE FOR NATIONALISM AND INTERNATIONALISM."
J. OF POLITICS, 27 (FEB. 65), 87-108.
SHOWS THAT NATIONALISM CONSISTS IN WIDE "COMPLIMENTARITY" OF SOCIAL COMMUNICATION AND BECOMES SUPRA-NATIONALISM WHEN DIVERSE CITIZENRIES BECOME SO LINKED. DESCRIBES LINKING EFFECTS OF PERSONAL COMMUNICATION IN IMMIGRATION, AGE, SEX, AND POPULATION PRESSURE.

2981 TURNER F.J.
"AMERICAN SECTIONALISM AND WORLD ORGANIZATION."
AMER. HIST. REV., 47 (APR. 42), 545-51.
PROPOSES SEVERAL SUGGESTIONS UPON THE BEARING OF AMERICAN EXPERIENCE ON PROBLEMS OF THE LEAGUE OF NATIONS. CALLS FOR LEGISLATIVE BODY WITH SUBSTANTIAL FUNCTIONS AS A COURT OR A COUNCIL OF NATIONS.

2982 TURNER G.B. ED., CHALLENER R.D. ED.
NATIONAL SECURITY IN THE NUCLEAR AGE.
NEW YORK: FREDERICK PRAEGER, 1960, 293 PP., LC#60-06998.
ARTICLES DISCUSSING AMERICAN DEFENSE POLICY IN COLD WAR, INCLUDING HISTORICAL BASIS FOR LIMITED CONFLICT, WEAPONS AND STRATEGY, INTERNATIONAL ASPECTS OF MILITARY POWER, RESOURCES AND ORGANIZATION, AND MILITARY INSTRUMENTS OF SECURITY.

2983 TURNER M.C. ED.
LIBROS EN VENTA EN HISPANOAMERICA Y ESPANA.
NEW YORK: RR BOWKER, 1964, 1891 PP.
EXTENSIVE LIST OF SPANISH-LANGUAGE BOOKS IN PRINT. DIVIDED INTO AUTHOR AND SUBJECT INDEXES.

2984 TURNER R.K.
BIBLIOGRAPHY ON WORLD ORGANIZATION.
NEW YORK: W WILSON MEM LIB.
ANNOTATED BIBLIOGRAPHY OF MATERIAL ON WORLD ORGANIZATION REPRINTED FROM THE QUARTERLY JOURNAL "INTERNATIONAL ORGANIZATION," PUBLISHED BY THE WORLD PEACE FOUNDATION. FIRST ISSUED IN SEPTEMBER 1947, THE BIBLIOGRAPHY LISTS DOCUMENTS, BOOKS, PAMPHLETS, AND PERIODICAL ARTICLES ON REGIONAL ORGANIZATIONS, WAR AND TRANSITIONAL AGENCIES, AND OTHER FUNCTIONAL ORGANIZATIONS.

2985 TYSON G.
NEHRU: THE YEARS OF POWER.
NEW YORK: FREDERICK PRAEGER, 1966, 206 PP.
ATTEMPTS TO ASSESS NEHRU'S YEARS OF POWER. TRACES HIS RISE TO POWER, INDIA AS A NATION, MALTHUSIAN DEMANDS, FOREIGN POLICY, INTERNATIONAL RELATIONS, LANGUAGE QUESTION, AND ESTABLISHMENT OF DEMOCRACY.

2986 U OF MICH SURVEY RESEARCH CTR
AMERICA'S ROLE IN WORLD AFFAIRS.
ANN ARBOR: U MICH SURVEY RES CTR, 1952, 170 PP.
SURVEY OF PUBLIC OPINION ON ROLE OF US IN INTERNATIONAL AFFAIRS SPECIFICALLY CONCERNING FOREIGN POLICY TOWARD EUROPE. INCLUDES DEFENSE, AID, AND IMPORTANCE OF EUROPE TO US. DEALS WITH DEVELOPMENT OF ASIA AND ATTITUDE TOWARD INTERNATIONAL CONFLICT, ESPECIALLY WITH USSR.

2987 CAIRO: DAR AL-KUTUB AL-MISRIYAH
A BIBLIOGRAPHICAL LIST OF AL MAGHRIB.
OTTAWA: NATL LIB PRESS, 1961, 66 PP.
AN UNANNOTATED AND UNCLASSIFIED LIST OF BOOKS AND ARTICLES IN WESTERN LANGUAGES HOUSED IN THE NATIONAL LIBRARY AT CAIRO. COVERS GEOGRAPHICAL, POLITICAL, AND HISTORICAL MATERIAL FROM THE 19TH-20TH CENTURIES. MOST SELECTIONS POSTDATE 1930. CONTAINS A TITLE INDEX AND SEPARATE ENGLISH- AND ARABIC-LANGUAGE LISTINGS.

2988 CAIRO: DAR AL-KUTUB AL-MISRIYAH
A BIBLIOGRAPHICAL LIST OF LIBYA.
OTTAWA: NATL LIB PRESS, 1961, 30 PP.
AN UNANNOTATED AND UNCLASSIFIED BIBLIOGRAPHY OF PUBLICATIONS IN WESTERN LANGUAGES HOUSED IN THE NATIONAL LIBRARY AT CAIRO. COVERS HISTORICAL, POLITICAL, RELIGIOUS, AND GEOGRAPHICAL STUDIES FROM 19TH-20TH CENTURIES. MOST ENTRIES POSTDATE 1920. PROVIDES COMPLETE BIBLIOGRAPHICAL DATA, EGYPTIAN NATIONAL LIBRARY CALL NUMBERS; AND A TITLE INDEX. ISSUED IN A BILINGUAL ENGLISH-ARABIC EDITION.

2989 CAIRO: DAR AL-KUTUB AL-MISRIYAH
A BIBLIOGRAPHICAL LIST OF TUNISIA.
OTTAWA: NATL LIB PRESS, 1961, 42 PP.
AN UNANNOTATED AND UNCLASSIFIED LIST OF BOOKS, PERIODICALS, AND PAMPHLETS IN WESTERN LANGUAGES HOUSED IN THE NATIONAL LIBRARY AT CAIRO. PROVIDES COMPLETE BIBLIOGRAPHICAL DATA ON 19TH-AND 20TH-CENTURY PUBLICATIONS PLUS THE EGYPTIAN NATIONAL LIBRARY CALL NUMBERS. INCLUDES TITLE INDEX AND SEPARATE DIVISIONS FOR ENGLISH- AND ARABIC-LANGUAGE ENTRIES. SELECTIONS ARE OF HISTORICAL, POLITICAL, OR RELIGIOUS VALUE.

2990 CAIRO: DAR AL-KUTUB AL-MISRIYAH
A BIBLIOGRAPHICAL LIST OF ARABIAN PENINSULA.
CAIRO: EGYPTIAN LIBRARY PRESS, 1963.
AN UNANNOTATED BILINGUAL BIBLIOGRAPHY OF BOOKS AND PERIODICALS HOUSED IN THE NATIONAL LIBRARY AT CAIRO. THE ENGLISH-ARAB BIBLIOGRAPHY IS UNCLASSIFIED BUT COMPREHENSIVE. COVERS 19TH-AND 20TH-CENTURY PUBLICATIONS IN WESTERN LANGUAGES WITH EMPHASIS ON CURRENT MATERIALS. ARRANGED BY SUBJECT, TITLE, AND GEOGRAPHIC AREA.

2991 UAR NATIONAL LIBRARY
A BIBLIOGRAPHICAL LIST OF WORKS ABOUT PALESTINE AND JORDAN (2ND ED.)
CAIRO: NATL LIBRARY PRESS, 1964, 338 PP.
BIBLIOGRAPHY PUBLISHED IN ARABIC AND ENGLISH UNDER AUSPICES OF MINISTRY OF CULTURE AND NATIONAL GUIDANCE. MATERIAL IS CLASSIFIED TOPICALLY WITH EMPHASIS ON SOCIAL SCIENCES. INCLUDES AUTHOR, TITLE, AND SUBJECT INDEXES. INCLUDES BOOKS, PERIODICALS, AND OTHER PUBLICATIONS DEALING WITH ARAB WORLD IN THE NATIONAL LIBRARY, CAIRO.

2992 ULAM A.B.
"THE COMIMFORM AND THE PEOPLE'S DEMOCRACIES."
WORLD POLIT., 3 (JAN. 51), 200-17.
EVALUATES CREATION OF COMINFORM AS AN IMPORTANT STAGE IN THE DEVELOPMENT OF EUROPEAN COMMUNISM. DISCUSSES SOCIO-POLITICAL FACTORS FACING SOVIET BLOC SATELLITES. OUTLINES RUSSIAN GAINS IN EASTERN EUROPE AS ENORMOUS ACCESSION OF STRENGTH BOTH ECONOMICALLY AND POLITICALLY.

2993 ULAM A.B.
TITOISM AND THE COMINFORM.
CAMBRIDGE: HARVARD U. PR., 1952, 243 PP.
ANALYZES YUGOSLAV COMMUNIST PARTY IN COMPARISON WITH OTHER COMMUNIST GOVERNMENTS. EVALUATES SOVIET-YUGOSLAV DISPUTE. DISCUSSES COMINFORM AND 'PEOPLE'S DEMOCRACIES'.

2994 ULYSSES
"THE INTERNATIONAL AIMS AND POLICIES OF THE SOVIET UNION: THE NEW CONCEPTS AND STRATEGY OF KHRUSHCHEV."
REV. POLIT., 24 (APRIL 62), 183-211.
DEALS WITH THE IMAGE OF KHRUSHCHEV IN THE NON-COMMUNIST WORLD. THE IMAGE IS GENERALLY DESCRIBED AS PEACEFUL-COEXISTENCE. AUTHOR BELIEVES THAT THIS IS A COMPLETE MISREPRESENTATION OF THE REALITY.

2995 UN
SPACE ACTIVITIES AND RESOURCES: REVIEW OF UNITED NATION'S NATIONAL AND INTERNATIONAL PROGRAMS.
NEW YORK: UNITED NATIONS, 1965, 172 PP.
OVER-ALL VIEW OF DEVELOPMENTS IN USE OF SPACE FOR PEACE AND BENEFIT OF MAN. COVERS ACTIVITIES OF SPECIAL AGENCIES AND INTERNATIONAL GROUPS AIDING UN. GIVES BREAKDOWN OF SPACE ACTIVITIES IN 37 SEPARATE NATIONS. EXPLANATIONS AND EVALUATIONS BY SECRETARY-GENERAL.

2996 UN DEPARTMENT PUBLIC INF
SELECTED BIBLIOGRAPHY OF THE SPECIALIZED AGENCIES RELATED TO THE UNITED NATIONS (PAMPHLET)
NEW YORK: UNITED NATIONS, 1949, 28 PP.
INCLUDES OFFICIAL DOCUMENTS OF UN, SPECIALIZED AGENCIES,

PUBLICATIONS OF MEMBER GOVERNMENTS, AS WELL AS BOOKS, PAMPHLETS, AND MAGAZINE ARTICLES. BASIC DOCUMENTS COVER STRUCTURE, HISTORY OF ACTIVITIES, FUNCTIONS, AND PROGRAMS OF SPECIALIZED AGENCIES TOGETHER WITH OFFICIAL RECORDS, PERIODICALS, AND SERIAL PUBLICATIONS ISSUED BY THEM. PERIOD REPRESENTED IS 1945-JANUARY, 1949.

2997 UN DEPARTMENT SOCIAL AFFAIRS
SOCIAL WELFARE INFORMATION SERIES: CURRENT LITERATURE AND NATIONAL CONFERENCES.
NEW YORK: UNITED NATIONS.
A HALF-YEARLY REFERENCE SOURCE PUBLICATION CLASSIFYING PUBLICATIONS ISSUED AND CONFERENCES HELD IN VARIOUS COUNTRIES ON ALL IMPORTANT SOCIAL WELFARE MATTERS, PARTICULARLY THOSE COVERED BY THE SOCIAL COMMISSION OF THE ECONOMIC AND SOCIAL COUNCIL. PUBLICATION OF SERIES BEGAN JANUARY 1948; CUMULATIVE INDEX UP TO PRESENT DATE GIVEN ON LAST PAGE OF EACH REPORT. PUBLISHED IN ORIGINAL LANGUAGE OF DOCUMENT.

2998 UN DEPT. SOC. AFF.
PRELIMINARY REPORT ON THE WORLD SOCIAL SITUATION.
NEW YORK: UNITED NATIONS, 1952, 198 PP.
PRESENTS BACKGROUND FACTS ON WORLD POPULATION AND POPULATION TRENDS. FOCUSES ON PROBLEMS OF HEALTH CONDITIONS, FOOD AND NUTRITION, HOUSING AND EDUCATION. SURVEYS SPECIFIC CIRCUMSTANCES AFFECTING LIVING STANDARDS. CONCLUDES WITH STUDY OF SOCIAL CONDITIONS IN LATIN AMERICA AND MIDDLE EAST.

2999 UN ECAFE
ADMINISTRATIVE ASPECTS OF FAMILY PLANNING PROGRAMMES (PAMPHLET)
NEW YORK: UNITED NATIONS, 1966, 64 PP.
REPORT OF MEETING OF ECAFE IN 1966 AIMED AT DISCUSSING EXPERIENCES AND PROBLEMS IN ADMINISTERING POPULATION CONTROL PROGRAMS. REPRESENTATIVES FROM 23 NATIONS TRIED TO COLLABORATE ON REGIONAL PROGRAMS, GOVERNMENT ACTION, AND NEED FOR INTERNATIONAL AID.

3000 UN ECONOMIC AND SOCIAL COUNCIL
BIBLIOGRAPHY OF PUBLICATIONS OF THE UN AND SPECIALIZED AGENCIES IN THE SOCIAL WELFARE FIELD, 1946-1952.
NEW YORK: UNITED NATIONS, 1955, 270 PP.
SPECIAL ISSUE OF THE "SOCIAL WELFARE INFORMATION SERIES," DESIGNED FOR THOSE CONCERNED WITH SPECIFIC BRANCHES OF SOCIAL WELFARE. CLASSIFIES 704 ANNOTATED ENTRIES CONCERNING INTERNATIONAL PROGRAMS, BIBLIOGRAPHIES, AND DIRECTORIES OF ORGANIZATIONS DEALING WITH THE HANDICAPPED; FAMILY, YOUTH, AND CHILD WELFARE; TRAINING FOR SOCIAL WORK, ETC. CONTAINS A SUBJECT CLASSIFICATION OUTLINE AND A CUMULATIVE INDEX.

3001 UN HEADQUARTERS LIBRARY
BIBLIOQRAPHIE DE LA CHARTE DES NATIONS UNIES.
NEW YORK: UNITED NATIONS, 1955, 128 PP.
COMPILES, ANNOTATES, AND INDEXES 2,059 ITEMS (BOOKS, DOCUMENTS, ARTICLES, PAMPHLETS, ETC.) DEALING WITH, OR DEVOTED TO, THE HISTORY, PRINCIPLES, PURPOSES, ORGANS, MEMBERSHIP, AND ORGANIZATION OF THE UN, AS DEFINED BY ITS CHARTER AND THE PROPOSALS, CONFERENCES, AND COMMITTEES PRECEDING ITS DRAFTING. ARRANGED ACCORDING TO CHARTER PROVISIONS. IN FRENCH.

3002 UN HEADQUARTERS LIBRARY
BIBLIOGRAPHY OF INDUSTRIALIZATION IN UNDERDEVELOPED COUNTRIES (BIBLIOGRAPHICAL SERIES NO. 6)
NEW YORK: UNITED NATIONS, 1956, 216 PP.
LISTS PUBLICATIONS OF UN AND SPECIALIZED AGENCIES ON SUBJECT OF INDUSTRIALIZATION AND INFORMATION ON PERTINENT RESEARCH PROJECTS BEING CARRIED OUT BY GOVERNMENTS, UNIVERSITIES, AND SCIENTIFIC INSTITUTIONS. RECORDS ALSO RELEVANT PUBLICATIONS AND UNPUBLISHED RESEARCH. ITEMS ARRANGED BY GEOGRAPHY. WRITTEN IN SPANISH, ENGLISH, AND FRENCH. ITEMS IN ALL RELEVANT LANGUAGES, INCLUDING ORIENTAL.

3003 UN INTL CONF ON PEACEFUL USE ATOM
PROGRESS IN ATOMIC ENERGY (VOL. I)
GENEVA: UN INTL CONF PEACEFUL ATOM, 1958, 525 PP.
PAPERS PRESENTED AT SECOND UN INTERNATIONAL CONFERENCE ON PEACEFUL USES OF ATOMIC ENERGY. TREATS FUTURE OF NUCLEAR POWER DEVELOPMENTS AND PROGRAMS ALL OVER WORLD. DISCUSSES SUPPLY AND TRAINING OF TECHNICAL PERSONNEL. EXAMINES DEVELOPMENT OF INTERNATIONAL COLLABORATION IN RESEARCH, FOUNDATION OF NUCLEAR CENTER IN BAGHDAD, AND INTERNATIONAL ASPECTS OF CONTAMINATION.

3004 UN PUB. INFORM. ORGAN.
EVERY MAN'S UNITED NATIONS.
NEW YORK: UN, 1964, 593 PP.
COMPREHENSIVE ANALYSIS OF FUNCTIONS AND ACTIVITIES OF UN. DESCRIBES THEIR PRINCIPAL ORGANS SUCH AS GENERAL ASSEMBLY, SECURITY COUNCIL, AND INTERNATIONAL COURT OF JUSTICE. FOCUSES ON QUESTIONS RELATED TO PROBLEMS OF INTERNATIONAL SECURITY. INCLUDES LIST OF INTER-GOVERNMENTAL AGENCIES CONNECTED WITH UN ORGANIZATION.

3005 UN SECRETARY GENERAL
PLANNING FOR ECONOMIC DEVELOPMENT.
NEW YORK: UNITED NATIONS, 1963, 156 PP.
REPORTS ON ECONOMIC PLANNING AND TECHNIQUES USED IN SEVERAL COUNTRIES. EXAMINES ORGANIZATION AND MANAGEMENT OF PLANS, AS WELL AS NATIONAL AND INTERNATIONAL POLICIES.

3006 UNCIO CONFERENCE LIBRARY
SHORT TITLE CLASSIFIED CATALOG.
NEW YORK: UNITED NATIONS, 1945, 65 PP.
UNANNOTATED BIBLIOGRAPHICAL COLLECTION OF PUBLICATIONS FROM 1900-44 ON INTERNATIONAL AND NATIONAL POLITICAL, ECONOMIC, AND SOCIAL PROBLEMS. CLASSIFIED BIOGRAPHICAL DICTIONARIES, STATISTICAL YEARBOOKS, ENCYCLOPEDIAS, AND DICTIONARIES. INCLUDES DOCUMENTS FROM LEAGUE OF NATIONS AND THE HAGUE, TOGETHER WITH TREATIES AND RELEVANT NEWSPAPER, PERIODICAL, AND JOURNAL INDEXES. SOURCES IN WESTERN LANGUAGES.

3007 UNDERHILL F.H.
THE BRITISH COMMONWEALTH: AN EXPERIMENT IN CO-OPERATION AMONG NATIONS.
DURHAM: DUKE U PR, 1956, 127 PP., LC#56-9166.
INTRODUCTORY HISTORY OF RISE OF BRITISH COMMONWEALTH. ANALYSIS EXTENDS FROM VICTORIAN LIBERAL EMPIRE THROUGH THE FIRST COMMONWEALTH AFTER WWI AND SECOND COMMONWEALTH, POST-WWII. ILLUMINATES BENEFITS DERIVED FROM UNION.

3008 UNECA LIBRARY
BOOKS ON AFRICA IN THE UNECA LIBRARY.
NEW YORK: UNITED NATIONS, 1962, 318 PP.
SELECTED LIST OF MONOGRAPHS CONCERNING ECONOMIC AND SOCIAL CONDITIONS OF AFRICA AND AFRICAN COUNTRIES. MAJORITY OF TITLES ARE GOVERNMENTAL PUBLICATIONS. TITLES ARE DIVIDED FIRST BY REGION, THEN BY GROUP OF COUNTRIES SPEAKING SAME LANGUAGE. CONTAINS AUTHOR, TITLE, AND SUBJECT INDEXES. INCLUDES 2,031 ENTRIES

3009 UNECA LIBRARY
NEW ACQUISITIONS IN THE UNECA LIBRARY.
NEW YORK: UNITED NATIONS, 1962.
PERIODICAL LISTING OF RECENT BOOKS, MONOGRAPHS, SERIAL PUBLICATIONS AND PERIODICALS COVERING CURRENT SOCIAL, ECONOMIC, CULTURAL, AND TECHNICAL PROBLEMS OF WORLD WITH SPECIAL ATTENTION TO AFRICA AND DEVELOPING NATIONS. FIRST PUBLISHED 1962. ITEMS, IN ALL LANGUAGES, ARRANGED BY SUBJECT.

3010 UNESCO
INTERNATIONAL BIBLIOGRAPHY OF POLITICAL SCIENCE (VOLUMES 1-8)
PARIS: UNESCO.
AN ANNUAL PUBLICATION IN THE SERIES OF THE GENERAL PROGRAM FOR SOCIAL SCIENCE DOCUMENTATION. AN INTERNATIONAL CURRENT BIBLIOGRAPHY CONTAINING BOOKS AND PERIODICAL ARTICLES ARRANGED IN A CLASSIFIED SCHEME WITH INDEXES BY AUTHOR AND SUBJECT. ALSO INCLUDES RELEVANT GOVERNMENT DOCUMENTS. UNANNOTATED. BEGINNING WITH VOLUME 9, 1960, PUBLISHED IN LONDON BY STEVENS & SONS AND IN CHICAGO BY ALDINE PUBLISHING CO.

3011 UNESCO
"SOME SUGGESTIONS ON TEACHING ABOUT THE UN AND ITS SPECIALIZED AGENCIES."
IN (TOWARDS WORLD UNDERSTANDING, VOL 1, NOV. 49, 26 PP.).
SUGGESTS TWO APPROACHES IN ORDER TO ACHIEVE EDUCATION FOR INTERNATIONAL UNDERSTANDING. CALLS FOR DISSEMINATION OF INFORMATION ON: OTHER LANDS AND PEOPLES, THE CONTRIBUTION OF ALL RACES, RELIGIONS AND NATIONS TO THE WORLD'S CULTURE, AND THE HISTORY OF INTERNATIONAL CONFLICTS AND THEIR CAUSES.

3012 UNESCO
"MEETING ON UNIVERSITY TEACHING OF INTERNATIONAL RELATIONS."
INT. SOC. SCI. BULL., 2 (SUMMER 50), 235-36.
REPORT OF CONFERENCE, INCLUDING LIST OF PARTICIPANTS. MEMBERS CONCLUDED THAT 'THE STUDY OF INTERNATIONAL RELATIONS HAS AMONG THE SOCIAL SCIENCES A PLACE THE IMPORTANCE OF WHICH HAS NOT YET RECEIVED DUE RECOGNITION.'

3013 UNESCO
FREEDOM AND CULTURE.
LONDON: WINGATE, 1951, 270 PP.
SERIES OF ESSAYS ON THE UN'S UNIVERSAL DECLARATION OF HUMAN RIGHTS. EXAMINES RIGHTS OF THE INDIVIDUAL TO EDUCATION AND INDEPENDENT CULTURAL DEVELOPMENT, AND TO FREEDOM IN SCIENTIFIC RESEARCH AND THE CREATIVE ARTS.

3014 UNESCO
CURRENT SOCIOLOGY (2 VOLS.)
PARIS: UNESCO, 1952, 1238 PP.
AN INTERNATIONAL BIBLIOGRAPHY OF SOCIOLOGY PREPARED BY UNESCO. INTRODUCTION IN ENGLISH AND FRENCH. TITLES IN ENGLISH OR FRENCH. STEP TOWARD THE ESTABLISHMENT OF REGULAR CHANNELS FOR THE EXCHANGE OF INFORMATION BETWEEN THE SOCIOLOGISTS OF THE WORLD.

3015 UNESCO
THESES DE SCIENCES SOCIALES: CATALOGUE ANALYTIQUE INTERNATIONAL DE THESES INEDITES DE DOCTORAT, 1940-1950.
PARIS: UNESCO, 1952, 236 PP.
3,215 ITEMS DESCRIBING DOCTORAL THESES IN THE SOCIAL

SCIENCES FROM 23 MEMBERS PARTICIPATING IN PROGRAM ORGANIZED BY UNESCO. BILINGUAL CATALOGUE, WITH TITLES EITHER IN FRENCH OR ENGLISH. CLASSIFICATION ACCORDING TO MAJOR DISCIPLINE AS PRESCRIBED BY UNIVERSAL DECIMAL SYSTEM. CONTAINS SUBJECT, AUTHOR, AND GEOGRAPHICAL INDEXES AND TABLE OF LANGUAGES.

3016 UNESCO
"THE TECHNIQUE OF INTERNATIONAL CONFERENCES."
INT. SOC. SCI. BULL., 5 (NO. 2, 53), 241-339.
COLLECTION OF ARTICLES ON METHODS OF CONDUCTING RESEARCH ON INTERNATIONAL CONFERENCES. SPECIAL TECHNIQUES AND PROCEDURES SUGGESTED. FINDINGS OF PREVIOUS UNESCO STUDIES ON INTERNATIONAL CONFERENCES REVIEWED.

3017 UNESCO
GUIDE DES CENTRES NATIONAUX D'INFORMATION BIBLIOGRAPHIQUE (VOL. III)
PARIS: UNESCO, 1953, 68 PP.
THE INTERNATIONAL ADVISORY COMMITTEE ON BIBLIOGRAPHY PREPARED THIS GUIDE TO NATIONAL BIBLIOGRAPHIC SERVICES IN ORDER TO "PROVIDE A MEANS OF CONTACT BETWEEN VARIOUS NATIONAL INFORMATION SERVICES ALREADY EXISTING." ARRANGED AND INDEXED BY COUNTRY. CONTAINS A DESCRIPTION OF EACH COUNTRY'S BIBLIOGRAPHIC RESOURCES, TECHNIQUES, ETC. INCLUDES A LIST OF BIBLIOGRAPHIES.

3018 UNESCO
BIBLIOGRAPHIC SERVICES THROUGHOUT THE WORLD (VOLS. I AND II)
PARIS: UNESCO, 1955, 352 PP.
CONTAINS TWO REPORTS RELATING TO BIBLIOGRAPHIC SERVICES THROUGHOUT THE WORLD. SPONSORED BY THE UNESCO INTERNATIONAL ADVISORY COMMITTEE ON BIBLIOGRAPHY. EACH REPORT SURVEYS PARTICULAR COUNTRIES SEPARATELY AS WELL AS INTERNATIONAL SERVICES ENGAGED IN PROMOTING INTERNATIONAL BIBLIOGRAPHIC COORDINATION AND COOPERATION. INDEXED BY SUBJECT AND TITLE. TRANSLATED FROM THE FRENCH.

3019 UNESCO
A REGISTER OF LEGAL DOCUMENTATION IN THE WORLD (2ND ED.)
PARIS: UNESCO, 1957, 423 PP.
A CATALOGUE OF DOCUMENTATION ON FOREIGN LEGAL SYSTEMS, ARRANGED ALPHABETICALLY BY COUNTRY. PROVIDES INFORMATION ON CONSTITUTIONAL LAW, LAW CODES, PERIODICALS, AND JUDICIAL CENTERS OF ACTIVITY. AT END OF EACH TERRITORIAL UNIT, A BIBLIOGRAPHY LISTS THE MAIN BIBLIOGRAPHICAL PUBLICATIONS DOCUMENTING THE LEGAL SYSTEM OF THAT AREA.

3020 UNESCO
WORLD LIST OF SOCIAL SCIENCE PERIODICALS (2ND ED.)
PARIS: UNESCO, 1957, 161 PP.
LISTS SOCIAL SCIENCE PERIODICALS BY COUNTRY IN LANGUAGE OF PUBLICATION.

3021 UNESCO
REPERTORIO DE PUBLICACIONES PERIODICAS ACTUALES LATINO AMERICANAS (VOL. VIII)
PARIS: UNESCO, 1958, 266 PP.
ANNOTATED AND INDEXED BY TOPIC AND COUNTRY OF PUBLICATION. HAS 3,376 ITEMS IN SPANISH AND PORTUGUESE. EMPLOYS UNIVERSAL DECIMAL CLASSIFICATION NUMBER. PREPARED UNDER UNESCO AUSPICES AND DRAWN FROM THE COLUMBUS MEMORIAL LIBRARY, LIBRARY OF CONGRESS, NATIONAL LIBRARY OF MEDICINE, LIBRARY OF PAN AMERICAN SANITARY BUREAU, AND FROM LIBRARIES IN FIVE LATIN AMERICAN COUNTRIES.

3022 UNESCO
GENERAL CATALOGUE OF UNESCO PUBLICATIONS AND UNESCO SPONSORED PUBLICATIONS, 1946-1959.
PARIS: UNESCO, 1962, 217 PP.
A BIBLIOGRAPHY OF ALL UNESCO PUBLICATIONS FROM 1946-59 CONTAINING 2,681 ITEMS IN BOTH FRENCH AND ENGLISH.

3023 UNESCO
WORLD COMMUNICATIONS: PRESS, RADIO, TELEVISION, FILM (4TH ED.)
PARIS: UNESCO, 1964.
AN AUTHORITATIVE REFERENCE WORK FOR MASS COMMUNICATIONS STUDIES AND MASS MEDIA ENTERPRISES. ASSESSES INTERNATIONAL MASS COMMUNICATIONS FACILITIES AND THEIR EFFECTIVE USE IN ACCELERATING ECONOMIC AND SOCIAL PROGRESS. BASED ON INFORMATION CONTAINED IN GOVERNMENTAL COMMUNICATIONS, OFFICIAL PUBLICATIONS, AND TECHNICAL JOURNALS, PROVIDES A COUNTRY-BY-COUNTRY ANALYSIS OF TECHNICAL FACILITIES.

3024 UNESCO
INTERNATIONAL ORGANIZATIONS IN THE SOCIAL SCIENCES(REV. ED.)
PARIS: UNESCO, 1965, 147 PP.
SUMMARY DESCRIPTION OF THE STRUCTURE AND ACTIVITIES OF NONGOVERNMENTAL ORGANIZATIONS SPECIALIZING IN SOCIAL SCIENCES AND IN CONSULTATIVE RELATIONSHIP WITH UNESCO. THIS BILINGUAL EDITION COMPRISES 14 INTERNATIONAL SOCIAL SCIENCE ORGANIZATIONS HAVING CONSULTATIVE AND ASSOCIATE OR INFORMATION AND CONSULTATIVE RELATIONS WITH UNESCO. LISTS THEIR GEOGRAPHICAL EXTENSION, AFFILIATED BODIES, STRUCTURE, ETC.

3025 UNESCO
HANDBOOK OF INTERNATIONAL EXCHANGES.
PARIS: UNESCO, 1965.
REFERENCE SUPPLIES INFORMATION ON AIMS, PROGRAMS, AND ACTIVITIES OF NATIONAL AND INTERNATIONAL ORGANIZATIONS; AND ON INTERNATIONAL AGREEMENTS CONCERNING INTERNATIONAL RELATIONS AND EXCHANGES IN THE FIELDS OF EDUCATION, SCIENCE, CULTURE, AND MASS COMMUNICATION. CONTAINS DATA ON THE ACTIVITIES OF 272 INTERNATIONAL AND 5,000 GOVERNMENTAL AGENCIES; LISTS 4,200 AGREEMENTS.

3026 UNESCO
PRINCIPLES AND PROBLEMS OF NATIONAL SCIENCE POLICIES.
NEW YORK: UNITED NATIONS, 1967, 99 PP.
REPORT OF MEETING OF COORDINATORS OF SCIENCE POLICY STUDIES OF UN. TWELVE NATIONS STATED THEIR GOVERNMENTS' POLICIES, PLANS FOR SCIENTIFIC RESEARCH, AND PROBLEMS. AIM IS TO DEFINE COMMON FEATURES OF SCIENTIFIC POLICY AND DETERMINE DATA NEEDED TO PREPARE SCIENTIFIC POLICIES FOR NATIONS AT DIFFERENT DEVELOPING STAGES.

3027 UNION OF INTERNATIONAL ASSNS
DIRECTORY OF PERIODICALS PUBLISHED BY INTERNATIONAL ORGANIZATIONS (2ND ED.)
PARIS: UNESCO, 1959, 241 PP.
DESCRIBES PERIODICALS OF INTER-GOVERNMENTAL ORGANIZATIONS AND INTERNATIONAL NONGOVERNMENTAL ORGANIZATIONS. DESCRIBES TOTAL OF 1,340 ITEMS. CONTAINS INDEX COMPRISING NAMES OF ORGANIZATIONS IN ENGLISH AND FRENCH, AND TITLES OF PERIODICALS IN THEIR DIFFERENT EDITIONS AND A GEOGRAPHICAL INDEX. MATERIALS LISTED BY SUBJECT.

3028 UNION OF SOUTH AFRICA
REPORT CONCERNING ADMINISTRATION OF SOUTH WEST AFRICA (6 VOLS.)
PRETORIA: U OF SOUTH AFRICA, 1937, 3000 PP.
YEARLY REPORTS, 1922-37, BY GOVERNMENT OF UNION OF SOUTH AFRICA TO COUNCIL OF LEAGUE OF NATIONS CONCERNING ADMINISTRATION OF SOUTH WEST AFRICA. COVERS TOPICS OF LEGISLATION, INTERNATIONAL RELATIONS, CONSTITUTION, COURT SYSTEM, PRISONS, ARMS AND POLICE, DEMOGRAPHY, FINANCE AND TAXES, INDUSTRY, AGRICULTURE, NATIVE AFFAIRS, HEALTH, TRADE, MISSIONS, AND ECONOMY.

3029 UNITED ARAB REPUBLIC
THE PROBLEM OF THE PALESTINIAN REFUGEES (PAMPHLET)
CAIRO: UAR INFORMATION DEPT, 1962, 95 PP.
EXAMINES PROBLEM OF PALESTINIAN REFUGEES FROM A POLITICAL VIEWPOINT. DISCUSSES ORIGINS OF PROBLEM, CONFERENCES AND POLITICAL DECISIONS; EFFECTS OF REFUGEES ON MIDDLE EAST AND INTERNATIONAL RELATIONS; PROBLEMS THAT RESULTED SUCH AS HOUSING, EDUCATION, FOOD SUPPLIES, HEALTH; SOLUTIONS TO PROBLEMS THROUGH UN, ISRAEL'S SOLUTIONS, AND ARAB RECOMMENDATIONS.

3030 UNITED ARAB REPUBLIC
TOWARDS THE SECOND AFRICAN SUMMIT ASSEMBLY.
CAIRO: UAR INFORMATION DEPT, 1964, 85 PP.
DISCUSSES AFRICAN SUMMIT ASSEMBLY OF JULY 17, 1964. PROVIDES HIGHLIGHTS OF FIRST ASSEMBLY, TEXT OF NASSER'S SPEECH TO 1SY ASSEMBLY, CHARTS OF ORGANIZATION OF AFRICAN STATES, AIMS AND SUGGESTIONS OF SEVERAL OTHER AFRICAN CONFERENCES, AND DESCRIPTION OF 34 COUNTRIES THAT WERE TO PARTICIPATE IN ASSEMBLY.

3031 UNITED NATIONS
OFFICIAL RECORDS OF THE ECONOMIC AND SOCIAL COUNCIL OF THE UNITED NATIONS.
NEW YORK: UNITED NATIONS.
OFFICIAL UN ECONOMIC AND SOCIAL COUNCIL RECORDS INCLUDE SUMMARIES OF PLENARY MEETINGS, ANNEXED ESSENTIAL DOCUMENTS, AND SUPPLEMENTS CONSISTING OF RESOLUTIONS AND COMMISSION REPORTS. ANNUAL PUBLICATION.

3032 UNITED NATIONS
OFFICIAL RECORDS OF THE UNITED NATIONS' ATOMIC ENERGY COMMISSION - DISARMAMENT COMMISSION.
NEW YORK: UNITED NATIONS.
OFFICIAL RECORDS OF THE UN ATOMIC ENERGY COMMISSION DISARMAMENT COMMISSION. CONSIST OF VERBATIM RECORDS OF ALL PLENARY MEETINGS, ANNEXED ESSENTIAL DOCUMENTS, AND SPECIAL SUPPLEMENTS COMPRISING THE REPORT TO THE SECURITY COUNCIL. PUBLISHED ANNUALLY.

3033 UNITED NATIONS
OFFICIAL RECORDS OF THE UNITED NATIONS' GENERAL ASSEMBLY.
NEW YORK: UNITED NATIONS.
OFFICIAL RECORDS OF GENERAL ASSEMBLY CONSIST OF SUMMARY OR VERBATIM REPORTS OF PLENARY MEETINGS OF THE GENERAL COMMITTEE, THE SIX MAIN COMMITTEES, AND SESSIONAL COMMITTEES; ANNEXES OF MOST SIGNIFICANT AND PERTINENT DOCUMENTS; SUPPLEMENTS INCLUDING RESOLUTIONS ADOPTED BY THE SESSION, ANNUAL REPORT AND BUDGET BY THE SECRETARY-GENERAL, COUNCIL REPORTS, COMMITTEE REPORTS, ETC. ANNUAL PUBLICATIONS.

3034 UNITED NATIONS

UNITED NATIONS PUBLICATIONS.
NEW YORK: UNITED NATIONS.
ANNUAL PUBLICATION, FIRST PUBLISHED 1945, LISTING ALL MATERIALS PUBLISHED DURING YEAR BY ALL UN DEPARTMENTS AND AGENCIES.

3035 UNITED NATIONS
YEARBOOK OF THE INTERNATIONAL LAW COMMISSION.
NEW YORK: UNITED NATIONS.
ANNUAL PUBLICATION COVERING SUMMARY RECORDS AND DOCUMENTS OF SESSIONS, INCLUDING REPORTS TO COMMISSION TO THE GENERAL ASSEMBLY, FOR PERIOD 1949-PRESENT. CUMULATIVE PUBLICATION FIRST APPEARED IN 1956. STUDIES, SPECIAL REPORTS, PRINCIPAL DRAFT RESOLUTIONS, AND AMENDMENTS PRESENTED TO COMMISSION ARE PRINTED IN ORIGINAL LANGUAGES. SUMMARY RECORDS APPEAR IN ENGLISH.

3036 UNITED NATIONS
BIBLIOGRAPHY ON INDUSTRIALIZATION IN UNDER-DEVELOPED COUNTRIES.
NEW YORK: UNITED NATIONS, 1956, 216 PP.
A BIBLIOGRAPHY IN ENGLISH, FRENCH, AND SPANISH COVERING PUBLICATIONS OF THE UNITED NATIONS, OTHER PUBLICATIONS, AND UNPUBLISHED RESEARCH. BESIDES GENERAL WORKS, IT INCLUDES MATERIAL ON AFRICA, THE MIDDLE EAST, ASIA AND THE FAR EAST, EUROPE, AND LATIN AMERICA AND THE CARIBBEAN. HAS INDEXES OF PERSONAL AND GENERAL NAMES.

3037 UNITED NATIONS
INTERNATIONAL SPACE BIBLIOGRAPHY.
NEW YORK: UNITED NATIONS, 1966, 166 PP.
LISTS ABOUT 3,000 BOOKS, REPORTS, BULLETINS, GOVERNMENT DOCUMENTS, AND PERIODICALS PUBLISHED IN 1960'S IN 34 MAJOR COUNTRIES OF THE WORLD. PREPARED TO ASSIST COMMITTEE ON PEACEFUL PURPOSES OF OUTER SPACE. ENTRIES ARRANGED BY TYPE OF MATERIAL UNDER COUNTRY; SUBDIVIDED BY SUBJECT.

3038 UNITED STATES
REPORT TO THE INTER-AMERICAN ECONOMIC AND SOCIAL COUNCIL.
WASHINGTON: GOVT PR OFFICE, 1963, 184 PP.
REPORT ON US PARTICIPATION IN ALLIANCE FOR PROGRESS, SEPTEMBER, 1963. US TECHNICAL ASSISTANCE, GRANTS-IN-AID, FEASIBILITY STUDIES ARE INCLUDED.

3039 UNITED WORLD FEDERALISTS
UNITED WORLD FEDERALISTS; PANORAMA OF RECENT BOOKS, FILMS, AND JOURNALS ON WORLD FEDERATION, THE UN, AND WORLD PEACE.
BOSTON: UNITED WORLD FEDERALISTS, 1960, 26 PP.
AN ANNOTATED BIBLIOGRAPHY OF 65 RECENT BOOKS, 14 FILMS, AND 27 JOURNALS ON WORLD FEDERATION, THE UN, AND WORLD PEACE. MOST BOOKS PUBLISHED SINCE 1955; WITH EXCEPTION OF "THE FEDERALIST," ALL BOOKS DATE FROM 1945. ENTRIES ORGANIZED TOPICALLY WITHIN NINE SUBJECT CATEGORIES AND ANNOTATED WITH EXCERPTS FROM PUBLISHED CRITIQUES OF THE WORK.

3040 UNIV KARACHI INST PUB BUS ADM
PUBLICATIONS OF THE GOVERNMENT OF PAKISTAN 1947-1957.
KARACHI: UNIV INST BUS PUB ADMIN, 1958, 187 PP.
INDEXES ALL OFFICIAL PUBLICATIONS OF THE GOVERNMENT OF PAKISTAN ISSUED FROM INDEPENDENCE DAY, AUGUST 14, 1947. WHERE THE PUBLICATION IS FOR SALE, IT IS NOTED.

3041 UNIVERSAL REFERENCE SYSTEM
INTERNATIONAL AFFAIRS: VOLUME I IN THE POLITICAL SCIENCE, GOVERNMENT, AND PUBLIC POLICY SERIES.
PRINCETON: UNIVERSAL REF SYSTEM, 1965, 1205 PP., LC#65-19793
COMPUTERIZED INFORMATION RETRIEVAL SYSTEM FOR THE SOCIAL AND BEHAVIORAL SCIENCES; ANNOTATED AND INTENSIVELY INDEXED UTILYZING THE "TOPICAL-METHODOLOGICAL INDEX" DEVELOPED BY PROFESSOR ALFRED DE GRAZIA. VOLUME CARRIES 3,000 REFERENCES IN INTERNATIONAL AFFAIRS. QUARTERLY GAZETTES BEGAN IN AUGUST, 1967.

3042 UNIVERSAL REFERENCE SYSTEM
BIBLIOGRAPHY OF BIBLIOGRAPHIES IN POLITICAL SCIENCE, GOVERNMENT, AND PUBLIC POLICY (VOLUME III)
PRINCETON* UNIV. REF. SYSTEM, 1967, 1200 PP.
COMPUTERIZED INFORMATION RETRIEVAL SYSTEM FOR THE SOCIAL AND BEHAVIORAL SCIENCES. ANNOTATED AND EXTENSIVELY INDEXED, UTILIZING "TOPICAL-METHODOLOGICAL INDEX" DEVELOPED BY PROFESSOR ALFRED DE GRAZIA. APPROXIMATELY 3,000 CITATIONS FROM SCHOLARLY JOURNALS, BOOKS, GOVERNMENT DOCUMENTS IN ENGLISH AND EUROPEAN LANGUAGES. INCLUDES CLASSICAL SOURCES THROUGH 1967. TO BE PUBLISHED EARLY 1968 WITH QUARTERLY GAZETTES.

3043 UNIVERSAL REFERENCE SYSTEM
ECONOMIC REGULATION, BUSINESS, AND GOVERNMENT (VOLUME VIII)
PRINCETON* UNIV. REF. SYSTEM, 1967, 1200 PP.
COMPUTERIZED INFORMATION RETRIEVAL SYSTEM DEALING WITH VARIOUS FACETS OF INTERNAL GOVERNANCE OF BUSINESS ACTIVITIES AND THEIR RELATION TO POLITICS. ABOUT 3000 ANNOTATIONS FROM ALL TYPES OF PUBLICATIONS IN ENGLISH AND EUROPEAN LANGUAGES. SOURCES RANGE FROM CLASSICS WITH EMPHASIS ON MATERIALS OF 1960'S. TO BE PUBLISHED EARLY 1968. QUARTERLY GAZETTES BEGAN AUG., 1967.

3044 UNIVERSAL REFERENCE SYSTEM
LAW, JURISPRUDENCE, AND JUDICIAL PROCESS (VOLUME VII)
PRINCETON: UNIVERSAL REF SYSTEM, 1967, 1200 PP.
COMPUTERIZED INFORMATION RETRIEVAL SYSTEM. TREATS SCIENCE OF STUDY OF LAW AND ITS METHODOLOGY. ANNOTATED AND EXTENSIVELY INDEXED USING PROFESSOR ALFRED DE GRAZIA'S "TOPICAL-METHODOLOGICAL INDEX." APPROXIMATELY 3,000 CITATIONS FROM ENGLISH AND EUROPEAN-LANGUAGE BOOKS, JOURNALS, DOCUMENTS RANGING FROM CLASSICS TO PRESENT. TO BE PUBLISHED EARLY 1968. QUARTERLY GAZETTES BEGAN JUNE, 1967.

3045 UNIVERSITY MICROFILMS INC
DISSERTATION ABSTRACTS: ABSTRACTS OF DISSERTATIONS AND MONOGRAPHS IN MICROFILM.
ANN ARBOR: U MICROFILMS, INC.
MONTHLY COMPILATION OF ABSTRACTS OF DOCTORAL DISSERTATIONS SUBMITTED TO UNIVERSITY MICROFILMS, INC. ARRANGEMENT IS ALPHABETICAL UNDER SUBJECT HEADING. ALPHABETICAL AUTHOR INDEX INCLUDED FOLLOWING ABSTRACTS. FIRST PUBLISHED 1938. CONFINED TO AMERICAN AND CANADIAN INSTITUTIONS.

3046 UNIVERSITY OF CALIFORNIA
STATISTICAL ABSTRACT OF LATIN AMERICA.
LOS ANGELES: U CAL LAT AMER STUD, 1955.
ANNUAL OF STATISTICS ON LATIN AMERICA NATIONS AND TERRITORIES LISTED BY SUBJECT WITH SOURCES. PUBLISHED ANNUALLY SINCE 1955.

3047 UNIVERSITY OF FLORIDA LIBRARY
DOORS TO LATIN AMERICA; RECENT BOOKS AND PAMPHLETS.
GAINESVILLE: INTERAMER BIBLIOG, 1954.
QUARTERLY INTER-AMERICAN BIBLIOGRAPHY FIRST PUBLISHED 1954. DEALS WITH SOCIAL SCIENCES AND THE HUMANITIES. ANNOTATES MATERIALS PUBLISHED IN US ON LATIN AMERICA.

3048 UNIVERSITY OF TENNESSEE
GOVERNMENT AND WORLD CRISIS.
KNOXVILLE: U OF TENN PR, 1962, 85 PP., LC#62-21409.
EXAMINES US EXPERIENCE IN DEMOCRATIC GOVERNMENT. DEALS WITH RELATION OF UN TO ECONOMIC DEVELOPMENT; DISCUSSES AIMS OF ALLIANCE FOR PROGRESS AND ROLE OF US IN BUILDING WORLD COMMUNITY.

3049 UPTON E.
THE MILITARY POLICY OF THE US.
WASHINGTON: G.P.O., 1917, 495 PP.
'THE OBJECT OF THIS WORK IS TO TREAT HISTORICALLY AND STATISTICALLY, OUR MILITARY POLICY UP TO THE PRESENT TIME, AND TO SHOW THE ENORMOUS AND UNNECESSARY SACRIFICE OF LIFE AND TREASURE, WHICH HAS ATTENDED ALL OUR ARMED STRUGGLES.'

3050 US AGENCY INTERNATIONAL DEV
US FOREIGN ASSISTANCE AND ASSISTANCE FROM INTERNATIONAL ORGANIZATIONS.
WASHINGTON: AGENCY FOR INTL DEV, 1963, 145 PP.
COLLECTION OF CHARTS AND STATISTICS ON US MILITARY AND ECONOMIC ASSISTANCE THROUGHOUT WORLD SINCE 1945. ARRANGED BY REGION AND COUNTRY LISTS LOANS, GRANTS, AND CONTRIBUTIONS TO INTERNATIONAL ORGANIZATIONS.

3051 US AGENCY INTERNATIONAL DEV
PRINCIPLES OF FOREIGN ECONOMIC ASSISTANCE (PAMPHLET)
WASHINGTON: AGENCY FOR INTL DEV, 1963, 49 PP.
SUMMARIZES PRINCIPLES THAT GUIDE US ECONOMIC ASSISTANCE PROGRAMS. DISCUSSES PROCESS OF PROGRAMMING ASSISTANCE; AVAILABLE RESOURCES SUCH AS LOANS, FOOD SURPLUS, LOCAL CURRENCY, AND PRIVATE ENTERPRISE; INTERNAL DEVELOPMENT PROGRAMS AND SELF-HELP; AID AS SOURCE OF FOREIGN EXCHANGE; AND COORDINATION OF VARIOUS AID PROGRAMS.

3052 US AGENCY INTERNATIONAL DEV
REPORT TO CONGRESS ON THE FOREIGN ASSISTANCE PROGRAM.
WASHINGTON: AGENCY FOR INTL DEV, 1964, 124 PP.
REPORT BY AID ON US FOREIGN AID PROGRAM FOR FISCAL 1964. DESCRIBES MILITARY ASSISTANCE PROGRAMS, ROLE OF PRIVATE ENTERPRISE, OTHER FREE WORLD ASSISTANCE, ADMINISTRATION OF AID, AND OPERATION OF DEVELOPMENT LOANS AND TECHNICAL COOPERATION PROGRAMS IN INDIVIDUAL COUNTRIES.

3053 US AGENCY INTERNATIONAL DEV
PROPOSED FOREIGN AID PROGRAM FOR 1968: SUMMARY PRESENTATION TO THE CONGRESS.
WASHINGTON: US GOVERNMENT, 1967, 297 PP.
FOREIGN AID BUDGET REQUESTS CITE AGRICULTURE, HEALTH, AND EDUCATION AS MAIN NEEDS. STRESSES SELF-HELP AND DEVELOPMENT AND USE OF PRIVATE RESOURCES. PROPOSES AID LARGELY IN FORM OF COMMODITIES AND SERVICES. SPECIFIES THAT 90 PER CENT OF BUDGET BE SPENT IN US TO MAINTAIN BALANCE OF PAYMENTS. GIVES FIRST PRIORITY TO PROGRAMS FOSTERING COOPERATION AMONG NEIGHBORING NATIONS WITH COMMON DEVELOPMENT PROBLEMS.

3054 US AIR FORCE ACADEMY
"AMERICAN DEFENSE POLICY."
BALTIMORE: JOHNS HOPKINS PRESS, 1965.
ANTHOLOGY OF STUDIES ON PROVISIONS FOR US MILITARY SECURITY. DEALS WITH PRINCIPAL ISSUES OF STRATEGY AND INSTITU-

TIONS AND PROCESSES THROUGH WHICH STRATEGY IS FORMULATED. BIBLIOGRAPHICAL ESSAY IS SELECTIVE AND CONSISTS OF PRELIMINARY SURVEYS OF EACH TOPIC, IDENTIFIED BY CHAPTER. STUDIES NOT CONFINED TO ANALYSIS OF US POLICY BUT INCLUDE EXAMINATIONS OF COMMUNIST AND CHINESE STRATEGIC DOCTRINES.

3055 US AIR FORCE ACADEMY ASSEMBLY
OUTER SPACE: FINAL REPORT APRIL 1-4, 1964.
NEW YORK: AMERICAN ASSEMBLY, 1964, 94 PP.
SPEECHES GIVEN AT ACADEMY BY EXPERTS ON PROBLEMS OF CONTROLLING OUTER SPACE. COVERS BOTH PEACEFUL AND HARMFUL POSSIBILITIES FOR WORLD. EVALUATES US PROGRESS, REASONS FOR PROJECTS, AND FUTURE PLANS.

3056 US BUREAU EDUC CULTURAL AFF
RESOURCES SURVEY FOR LATIN AMERICAN COUNTRIES.
WASHINGTON: DEPT OF STATE, 1965, 640 PP.
RECORD OF US PUBLIC AND PRIVATE EFFORTS TO DEVELOP HUMAN RESOURCES ESSENTIAL TO EDUCATION, CULTURE, ECONOMY, AND SOCIETY OF LATIN AMERICA. MENTIONS MORE THAN 1,200 PRIVATE ORGANIZATIONS INVOLVED IN PROJECT ALONG WITH US GOVERNMENT.

3057 US BUREAU OF THE BUDGET
THE BALANCE OF PAYMENTS STATISTICS OF THE UNITED STATES: A REVIEW AND APPRAISAL.
WASHINGTON: US GOVERNMENT, 1965, 194 PP.
REVIEWS IN DETAIL THE PURPOSES FOR WHICH BALANCE-OF-PAYMENTS STATISTICS ARE NEEDED. EXAMINES SCOPE AND QUALITY OF STATISTICS AND WAYS IN WHICH THEY ARE COLLECTED, PROCESSED, AND PRESENTED TO PUBLIC. CONSIDERS CONCEPTUAL PROBLEM OF DEFINING A BALANCE-OF-PAYMENTS DEFICIT WHICH AFFECTS BOTH PRESENTATION AND INTERPRETATION OF STATISTICS.

3058 US BUREAU OF THE CENSUS
BIBLIOGRAPHY OF SOCIAL SCIENCE PERIODICALS AND MONOGRAPH SERIES.
WASHINGTON: GOVT PR OFFICE.
ISSUED IRREGULARLY SINCE 1962. ANNOTATED, LISTING AREA STUDIES. INCLUDES MATERIALS IN NON-WESTERN LANGUAGES AND TRANSLATED INTO ENGLISH. ENTRIES CLASSIFIED BY SUBJECT AND AGENCY. COVERS WORLD FROM 1950 TO PRESENT. TOPICS INCLUDE: GENERAL SOCIAL SCIENCES, CULTURAL ANTHROPOLOGY, ECONOMICS, EDUCATION, HISTORY, LAW, POLITICAL SCIENCE, PUBLIC HEALTH, SOCIOLOGY, AND BIBLIOGRAPHIES.

3059 US COMM STRENG SEC FREE WORLD
THE SCOPE AND DISTRIBUTION OF UNITED STATES MILITARY AND ECONOMIC ASSISTANCE PROGRAMS (PAMPHLET)
WASHINGTON: DEPT OF STATE, 1963, 25 PP.
ANALYSIS OF US AID PROGRAMS TO ADVISE AND RECOMMEND NECESSARY CHANGES FOR US SECURITY. SUGGEST REDUCTION OF US MILITARY RATHER THAN ANY FOREIGN-SUPPORTED ONES. FAVORS CONTINUED ECONOMIC AID TO ASIA AND LIMITED AMOUNT TO AFRICA. GIVES GENERAL VIEWS ON US POLICY, NOT SPECIFIC PROGRAMS. DOES NOT COVER BANKING POLICIES.

3060 US COMMISSION GOVT SECURITY
RECOMMENDATIONS; AREA: IMMIGRANT PROGRAM.
WASHINGTON: US GOVERNMENT, 1957, 300 PP.
CONSIDERS MEASURES TO BE TAKEN TO PREVENT ENTRY INTO US OF SUBVERSIVE ALIENS. SETS STANDARDS OF BEHAVIOR AND SPECIFIES WHAT ACTION IS TO BE CONSIDERED AS SUBVERSIVE. ALSO GIVES DEFINITION OF UNDESIRABLE, SPECIFIED BY ATTORNEY GENERAL.

3061 US CONG INTERNAL REV TAX JT COMM
LEGISLATIVE HISTORY OF UNITED STATES TAX CONVENTIONS(VOL. 1)
WASHINGTON: GOVT PR OFFICE, 1962, 1501 PP.
COMPILATION OF LEGISLATIVE HISTORY MATERIALS RELATING TO INCOME TAX CONVENTIONS, INCLUDING INFORMATION ABOUT CONVENTIONS AND VERBATIM TEXT OF AGREEMENTS WITH SEVERAL COUNTRIES.

3062 US CONGRESS
COMMUNICATIONS SATELLITE LEGISLATION: HEARINGS BEFORE COMM ON AERON AND SPACE SCIENCES ON BILLS S2550 AND 2814.
WASHINGTON: US GOVERNMENT, 1962, 485 PP.
TESTIMONIES BY GOVERNMENT OFFICIALS CONCERNING CREATION OF WORLDWIDE COMMUNICATIONS SYSTEM, AS AMENDMENT TO NSA ACT OF 1958. INCLUDES EVIDENCE BY REPRESENTATIVES OF PRIVATE INDUSTRY, DISCUSSION OF PARTICIPANTS ON NEED FOR INTERNATIONAL COOPERATION, AND SPECIFIC TESTIMONY ON OWNERSHIP, OPERATION, AND CONTROL OF SUCH SYSTEM.

3063 US CONGRESS JOINT ECO COMM
INTERNATIONAL PAYMENTS IMBALANCES AND NEED FOR STRENGTHENING INTERNATIONAL FINANCIAL ARRANGEMENTS.
WASHINGTON: US GOVERNMENT, 1961, 340 PP.
HEARINGS BEFORE SUBCOMMITTEE ON INTERNATIONAL EXCHANGE AND PAYMENTS OF JOINT ECONOMIC COMMITTEE HEADED BY HENRY S. REUSS ON INTERNATIONAL FINANCIAL ARRANGEMENTS THAT WOULD REDUCE PROBLEM OF BALANCE OF PAYMENTS. INCLUDES TESTIMONY BY DR. REINHARD KAMITZ, PRESIDENT OF AUSTRIAN NATIONAL BANK, AND OTHER PROMINENT PEOPLE IN WORLD ECONOMIC AFFAIRS.

3064 US CONGRESS JOINT ECO COMM
FACTORS AFFECTING THE UNITED STATES BALANCE OF PAYMENTS.
WASHINGTON: US GOVERNMENT, 1962, 561 PP.
COLLECTION OF STUDIES PREPARED FOR SUBCOMMITTEE ON INTERNATIONAL EXCHANGE AND PAYMENTS OF JOINT ECONOMIC COMMITTEE HEADED BY HENRY S. REUSS ON COMPETITIVE POSITION OF US; COMMON MARKET'S EFFECT ON US EXPORTS; INTERNATIONAL MONETARY SYSTEM; EXCHANGE RATE; NEW US BALANCE OF PAYMENTS POLICY; US CAPITAL INVESTMENT IN FOREIGN COUNTRIES; AND PROBLEMS OF "KEY CURRENCY."

3065 US CONGRESS JOINT ECO COMM
ECONOMIC DEVELOPMENTS IN SOUTH AMERICA.
WASHINGTON: GOVT PR OFFICE, 1962, 151 PP.
HEARINGS BEFORE SUBCOMMITTEE ON INTER-AMERICAN ECONOMIC RELATIONSHIPS OF JOINT ECONOMIC COMMITTEE OF CONGRESS. CONSIDER HOW INTER-AMERICAN POLICIES CAN BE IMPROVED AND ALLIANCE FOR PROGRESS MADE MORE EFFECTIVE. SEEK TO IDENTIFY CHIEF DETERRENTS TO PRIVATE INVESTMENT, FIND HOPE FOR DIVERSIFIED PRODUCTION, SPECIFY TYPES OF AID, AND ASCERTAIN WILLINGNESS OF LATIN AMERICA TO BRING ABOUT PROGRESS.

3066 US CONGRESS JOINT ECO COMM
DISCRIMINATORY OCEAN FREIGHT RATES AND BALANCE OF PAYMENTS.
WASHINGTON: US GOVERNMENT, 1963, 1273 PP.
HEARINGS BEFORE JOINT ECONOMIC COMMITTEE HEADED BY PAUL H. DOUGLAS ON OCEAN FREIGHT RATES AND EFFECT ON BALANCE OF PAYMENTS. TESTIMONY BY MEMBERS OF FEDERAL MARITIME COMMISSION ON FREIGHT RATES ON US EXPORTS OF STEEL PRODUCTS, WHICH ARE HIGHER THAN THOSE OF OTHER EXPORTERS. COMMITTEE SUGGESTS THAT HIGHER RATES ARE DETRIMENTAL TO BALANCE OF PAYMENTS AND GENERAL ECONOMIC SITUATION.

3067 US CONGRESS JOINT ECO COMM
THE UNITED STATES BALANCE OF PAYMENTS.
WASHINGTON: US GOVERNMENT, 1963, 406 PP.
HEARINGS BEFORE JOINT ECONOMIC COMMITTEE HEADED BY PAUL H. DOUGLAS ON OUTLOOK FOR US BALANCE OF PAYMENTS, AND FUNCTION AND REFORM OF INTERNATIONAL MONETARY SYSTEM. INCLUDES DISCUSSIONS ON GOLD EXCHANGE STANDARD, INTERNATIONAL LIQUIDITY, FOREIGN INVESTMENT, AND TRADE.

3068 US CONGRESS JOINT ECO COMM
THE UNITED STATES BALANCE OF PAYMENTS.
WASHINGTON: US GOVERNMENT, 1963, 587 PP.
"STATEMENTS BY ECONOMISTS, BANKERS AND OTHERS ON BROOKINGS INSTITUTION STUDY OF US BALANCE OF PAYMENTS IN 1968." SUBMITTED TO JOINT ECONOMIC COMMITTEE. INCLUDES ASSUMPTIONS, METHODS, INFERENCES, AND FINDINGS OF STUDY; PROBLEMS IT PRESENTS; AND POSSIBILITY OF PREDICTION OF MORE FAVORABLE BALANCE OF PAYMENTS IN 1968 BEING REALIZED.

3069 US CONGRESS JOINT ECO COMM
GUIDELINES FOR INTERNATIONAL MONETARY REFORM.
WASHINGTON: US GOVERNMENT, 1965, 601 PP.
HEARINGS BEFORE SUBCOMMITTEE ON INTERNATIONAL EXCHANGE AND PAYMENTS OF JOINT ECONOMIC COMMITTEE HEADED BY HENRY S. REUSS ON DEVELOPMENT OF GUIDELINES FOR INTERNATIONAL MONETARY REFORM AND PARTICULAR CHARACTERISTICS OF FUTURE SYSTEM. DISCUSSES QUESTION OF EXPANDED ROLE OF INTERNATIONAL MONETARY FUND.

3070 US CONGRESS JOINT ECO COMM
NEW APPROACH TO UNITED STATES INTERNATIONAL ECONOMIC POLICY.
WASHINGTON: US GOVERNMENT, 1966, 44 PP.
HEARING BEFORE SUBCOMMITTEE ON INTERNATIONAL EXCHANGE AND PAYMENTS OF JOINT ECONOMIC COMMITTEE HEADED BY HENRY S. REUSS ON POSSIBILITY OF INTERNATIONAL CONFERENCE FOR HEADS OF STATE TO FURTHER POLITICAL MECHANISMS OF SOLUTIONS TO WORLD ECONOMIC PROBLEMS NOW THAT TECHNICAL MECHANISMS HAVE BEEN OBTAINED. DISCUSSES BALANCE OF PAYMENTS AND INTERNATIONAL MONETARY REFORM.

3071 US CONGRESS JT ATOM ENRGY COMM
ATOMIC ENERGY LEGISLATION THROUGH 89TH CONGRESS, 1ST SESSION
WASHINGTON: GOVT PR OFFICE, 1965, 328 PP.
COLLECTION OF STATUTES AND MATERIAL PERTAINING TO ATOMIC ENERGY. INCLUDES ATOMIC ENERGY ACT OF 1954 AS AMENDED, AEC AUTHORIZATION ACTS, EURATOM COOPERATION ACT, AND INTERNATIONAL ATOMIC ENERGY PARTICIPATION ACT OF 1957. LISTS APPROPRIATIONS FOR ATOMIC ENERGY PROGRAM, 1947-66.

3072 US CONGRESS SENATE
SURVEY OF THE ALLIANCE FOR PROGRESS; INFLATION IN LATIN AMERICA (PAMPHLET)
WASHINGTON: US GOVERNMENT, 1967, 46 PP.
STUDY FOR SUBCOMMITTEE ON AMERICAN REPUBLICS AFFAIRS OF COMMITTEE ON FOREIGN RELATIONS TREATING INFLATION IN LATIN AMERICA AND QUESTIONS IT RAISES FOR US FOREIGN AID POLICY. DESCRIBES CAUSES AND CONSEQUENCES OF INFLATION, MEASURES FOR AVOIDING OR ELIMINATING IT, AND ROLE OF US IN LIMITING INFLATION. SUBCOMMITTEE WAS HEADED BY WAYNE MORSE.

3073 US CONSOLATE GENERAL HONG KONG
REVIEW OF THE HONG KONG CHINESE PRESS.
WASHINGTON: US GOVERNMENT.
TRANSLATIONS OF MAJOR ARTICLES IN HONG KONG NEWSPAPERS.

QUARTERLY INDEX.

3074 US CONSULATE GENERAL HONG KONG
CURRENT BACKGROUND.
WASHINGTON: US GOVERNMENT.
FIRST PUBLISHED 1950. EACH ISSUE FOCUSES ON A PARTICULAR SUBJECT AND CONTAINS TRANSLATIONS FROM VARIOUS CHINESE COMMUNIST NEWSPAPERS AND PERIODICALS PERTAINING TO THAT SUBJECT. QUARTERLY INDEX.

3075 US CONSULATE GENERAL HONG KONG
SURVEY OF CHINA MAINLAND PRESS.
WASHINGTON: US GOVERNMENT.
FIRST PUBLISHED 1950, CONTAINS TRANSLATIONS AND SUMMARIES FROM NEW CHINA NEWS AGENCY AND MAJOR COMMUNIST NEWSPAPERS AND PERIODICALS. QUARTERLY INDEX.

3076 US CONSULATE GENERAL HONG KONG
US CONSULATE GENERAL, HONG KONG, PRESS SUMMARIES.
WASHINGTON: US GOVERNMENT.
AN EXTENSIVE PROGRAM TRANSLATING CHINESE COMMUNIST NEWSPAPERS AND PERIODICALS. FOUR SEPARATE SERIES PUBLICATIONS, EACH CONTAINING A QUARTERLY CLASSIFIED INDEX.

3077 US DEPARTMENT OF DEFENSE
US SECURITY ARMS CONTROL, AND DISARMAMENT 1961-1965 (PAMPHLET)
WASHINGTON: US GOVERNMENT, 1965, 140 PP.
CONTAINS 750 PAPERS DEALING WITH THE PROBLEMS OF ARMS CONTROL AND DISARMAMENT AND PUBLISHED FROM OCTOBER, 1961, TO JANUARY, 1965. MATERIALS ON POLICIES, STRATEGIES, CONCEPTS, NEGOTIATIONS, NUCLEAR WEAPONRY, AND SPACE AS THE NEW DIMENSION OF POLITICO-MILITARY CONFLICT ARE INCLUDED.

3078 US DEPARTMENT OF STATE
ABSTRACTS OF COMPLETED DOCTORAL DISSERTATIONS FOR THE ACADEMIC YEAR 1950-1951.
WASHINGTON: DEPT OF STATE.
YEARLY PERIODICAL FIRST PUBLISHED IN 1952 CONTAINING ABOUT 150 ABSTRACTS IN SOCIAL SCIENCES ON FOREIGN AREAS IN EACH VOLUME. ABSTRACTS ARRANGED BY COUNTRY UNDER SUCH HEADINGS AS WORLD AFFAIRS, AMERICAN AFFAIRS, EUROPEAN AFFAIRS, FAR EASTERN AFFAIRS. MATERIALS FROM 1949-1951 BUT MOST DISSERTATIONS CONCERN POST-1875 TOPICS.

3079 US DEPARTMENT OF STATE
BIBLIOGRAPHY (PAMPHLETS)
WASHINGTON: DEPT OF STATE.
SERIES OF 75 BIBLIOGRAPHIES BETWEEN 1949 AND 1953 CONTAINING FROM EIGHT TO 127 PAGES ON TOPICS OF ECONOMIC, POLITICAL, AND SOCIAL INTEREST. EMPHASIS ON INTERNATIONAL ORGANIZATIONS, FOREIGN AID AND DEVELOPMENT, AND SUCH SPECIAL TOPICS AS PSYCHOLOGICAL WARFARE. LITTLE ANNOTATION AND MOST WORKS ORIGINATE AFTER 1920, AND INCLUDE PRIMARILY ARTICLES, BOOKS, AND GOVERNMENT DOCUMENTS. INDEX IN PAMPHLET 75.

3080 US DEPARTMENT OF STATE
A TENTATIVE LIST OF TREATY COLLECTIONS.
WASHINGTON: DEPT OF STATE, 1919, 103 PP.
BOOK CONTAINS A LIST OF TREATIES. MATERIALS IN ENGLISH-LANGUAGE, AND SOME FRENCH, SPANISH, GERMAN AND RUSSIAN. CONTAINS 960 ENTRIES. ENTRIES 1900-1919.

3081 US DEPARTMENT OF STATE
NATIONAL SOCIALISM; BASIC PRINCIPLES, THEIR APPLICATION BY THE NAZI PARTY'S FOREIGN ORGANIZATION...
WASHINGTON: DEPT OF STATE, 1943, 510 PP.
TREATISE PROVIDING THE STUDY OF NAZI IDEOLOGY AND THE GENERAL PRECEPTS OF NATIONAL SOCIALISM, PARTICULARLY THE NAZI VIEWPOINT TOWARD CITIZENSHIP, LOYALTY, INDIVIDUAL RIGHTS, AND THEIR RELATION TO THE STATE. PREPARED FROM STUDIES OF GERMAN LITERATURE AND PHILOSOPHY, OFFICIAL GERMAN RECORDS, AUTHORITATIVE WRITINGS AND STATEMENTS OF GERMAN LEADERS, ETC. INDEX OF PERSONS AND ORGANIZATIONS.

3082 US DEPARTMENT OF STATE
PUBLICATIONS OF THE DEPARTMENT OF STATE: A LIST CUMULATIVE FROM OCTOBER 1, 1929 (PAMPHLET)
WASHINGTON: DEPT OF STATE, 1945, 35 PP.
LISTING BY DATE AND TITLE OF SERIAL PUBLICATIONS, WHICH INCLUDE AREA, MAP, TREATY, PASSPORT, CONFERENCE, COMMERCIAL POLICY, EXECUTIVE AGREEMENT, ARBITRATION, AND FEDERAL LAW SERIES. DATES FROM 1929-45 AND IS FOLLOWED BY LISTING OF NONSERIAL PUBLICATIONS BY DATE. SOME 2,400 PUBLICATIONS INCLUDED.

3083 US DEPARTMENT OF STATE
FOREIGN AFFAIRS HIGHLIGHTS (NEWSLETTER)
WASHINGTON: US GOVERNMENT, 1948.
NEWSLETTERS PUBLISHED MONTHLY BY STATE DEPARTMENT WITH CAPSULE SUMMARIES OF CONTEMPORARY INTERNATIONAL AFFAIRS, EMPHASIZING US POLICIES AND ACTIVITIES AND CONTAINING LIST OF RECENT DEPARTMENTAL PUBLICATIONS.

3084 US DEPARTMENT OF STATE
SOVIET BIBLIOGRAPHY (PAMPHLET)
WASHINGTON: DEPT OF STATE, 1949.
SERIES OF SOME 110 SEPARATE BIBLIOGRAPHIES PUBLISHED FROM 1949 TO 1953, AVERAGING ABOUT 18 PAGES EACH, AND CONTAINING MORE THAN 10,000 ITEMS. PUBLISHED BIMONTHLY AND INCLUDES ONLY ENGLISH-LANGUAGE WORKS SELECTED FROM SCHOLARLY JOURNALS, SPEECHES, GOVERNMENT DOCUMENTS, AND BOOKS. ARRANGED TOPICALLY AND ANNOTATED. ALL MATERIALS ARE CURRENT TO DATE OF BIBLIOGRAPHY. SUBJECT INDEX.

3085 US DEPARTMENT OF STATE
POINT FOUR: COOPERATIVE PROGRAM FOR AID IN THE DEVELOPMENT OF ECONOMICALLY UNDERDEVELOPED AREAS.
WASHINGTON: GOVT PR OFFICE, 1950, 167 PP.
EXPLAINS NATURE, PURPOSE, SCOPE, AND OPERATING ARRANGEMENTS OF POINT FOUR PROGRAM AND ITS RELATION TO UN PROGRAM OF ECONOMIC ASSISTANCE. DISCUSSES PROMOTION OF PEACE AND ECONOMIC PROGRESS, US INTEREST, AGRICULTURE, EDUCATION, AND HOUSING. STUDIES DEVELOPMENT OF INDUSTRY, NEED FOR ASSISTANCE, FINANCING OF PROGRAM THROUGH CAPITAL INVESTMENT AND TECHNICAL COOPERATION, AND LIVING STANDARDS.

3086 US DEPARTMENT OF STATE
LIVRES AMERICAINS TRADUITS EN FRANCAIS ET LIVRES FRANCAIS SUR LES ETATS-UNIS D'AMERIQUE (2ND ED.)
WASHINGTON: DEPT OF STATE, 1951, 123 PP.
SELECT BIBLIOGRAPHY LISTING AMERICAN BOOKS TRANSLATED INTO FRENCH AND FRENCH BOOKS ON THE US; ITEMS UPDATED TO MAY 1, 1951. INCLUDES 1,498 BOOKS, A PUBLISHERS' LIST, A SUBJECT AND AUTHOR INDEX, AND IS ARRANGED SO AS TO BE USEFUL FOR BOTH FRENCH AND AMERICAN READERS. INCLUDES SUMMARY ANNOTATION. TOPICS TREATED ARE EXTREMELY DIVERSIFIED.

3087 US DEPARTMENT OF STATE
POINT FOUR, NEAR EAST AND AFRICA, A SELECTED BIBLIOGRAPHY OF STUDIES ON ECONOMICALLY UNDERDEVELOPED COUNTRIES.
WASHINGTON: DEPT OF STATE, 1951, 136 PP.
ANNOTATED BIBLIOGRAPHY INCLUDES WORKS IN FRENCH AND ENGLISH DEALING PRIMARILY WITH ECONOMIC STUDIES OF VARIOUS COUNTRIES AND REGIONS OF THE NEAR EAST, SOUTH ASIA, AND AFRICA MOSTLY WRITTEN IN THE PERIOD 1940-50. COMPILED AS REFERENCE GUIDE FOR PRESIDENT'S POINT FOUR PROGRAM. CONTAINS APPROXIMATELY 1,500 LISTINGS.

3088 US DEPARTMENT OF STATE
RESEARCH ON EASTERN EUROPE (EXCLUDING USSR)
WASHINGTON: DEPT OF STATE, 1952.
LISTING OF COMPLETED AND IN PROGRESS RESEARCH PROJECTS REPORTED BY SCHOLARS TO EXTERNAL RESEARCH STAFF. PUBLISHED ERRATICALLY FROM 1952-58. PUBLISHED LARGELY TO INDICATE COMPLETION AND AVAILABILITY OF NEW RESEARCH. RESEARCH IS LISTED BY COUNTRY WITH WHICH IT IS CONCERNED. INCLUDES SOME PROJECTS BEGUN AS EARLY AS 1941 BUT BELIEVED NOT TO HAVE BEEN PUBLISHED. PUBLISHED IN 10 PARTS.

3089 US DEPARTMENT OF STATE
PUBLICATIONS OF THE DEPARTMENT OF STATE, OCTOBER 1,1929 TO JANUARY 1, 1953.
WASHINGTON: DEPT OF STATE, 1954, 207 PP.
COMPLETE LIST OF NUMBERED DEPARTMENT OF STATE PUBLICATIONS, ARRANGED ALPHABETICALLY AND WITH CROSS REFERENCES. SEPARATE INDEX FOR SERIES PUBLICATIONS.

3090 US DEPARTMENT OF STATE
ECONOMIC PROBLEMS OF UNDERDEVELOPED AREAS (PAMPHLET)
WASHINGTON: US GOVERNMENT, 1956, 59 PP.
SHOWS CURRENT STATUS OF RESEARCH ON PROBLEMS OF ECONOMIC CHANGE AND DEVELOPMENT IN UNDERDEVELOPED AREAS UNDERTAKEN BY UNIVERSITIES AND RESEARCH INSTITUTES. PROJECTS ARE LISTED BY COUNTRY WITH WHICH CONCERNED. DESIGNED TO INDICATE STATUS AND AVAILABILITY OF RESEARCH REPORTED.

3091 US DEPARTMENT OF STATE
THE SUEZ CANAL PROBLEM; JULY 26-SEPTEMBER 22, 1956.
WASHINGTON: DEPT OF STATE, 1956, 370 PP.
PROCEEDINGS OF LONDON CONFERENCE CONCERNING USE AND OPERATION OF SUEZ CANAL BY 22 NATIONS, USED AS BASIS OF NEGOTIATION WITH EGYPTIAN GOVERNMENT AFTER ITS NATIONALIZATION OF CANAL. INCLUDES US POST-CONFERENCE POLICY.

3092 US DEPARTMENT OF STATE
PUBLICATIONS OF THE DEPARTMENT OF STATE, JANUARY 1,1953 TO DECEMBER 31, 1957.
WASHINGTON: DEPT OF STATE, 1958, 230 PP.
COMPLETE LIST OF NUMBERED STATE DEPARTMENT PUBLICATIONS, ARRANGED ALPHABETICALLY AND WITH CROSS REFERENCES. SEPARATE INDEX BY SERIES FOR SERIES PUBLICATIONS.

3093 US DEPARTMENT OF STATE
POLITICAL BEHAVIOR--A LIST OF CURRENT STUDIES.
WASHINGTON: DEPT OF STATE, 1963.
ANNUAL PUBLICATION SINCE 1963 OF STATE DEPARTMENT'S EXTERNAL RESEARCH STAFF WHICH CONTAINS UNPUBLISHED MATERIALS, BOOKS, AND ARTICLES OF BEHAVIORAL SCIENCE RESEARCH ON POLITICAL PROCESSES AND INTERNATIONAL RELATIONS. LISTS WORKS COMPLETED OR IN PROGRESS. AUTHOR INDEX, GEOGRAPHIC INDEX, AND ORGANIZATION INDEX. SOURCES CITED ARE AMERICAN.

3094 US DEPARTMENT OF STATE
RESEARCH ON AFRICA (EXTERNAL RESEARCH LIST NO 5-25)
WASHINGTON: DEPT OF STATE, 1966, 55 PP.
LIST OF SOCIAL SCIENCE RESEARCH SUBMITTED BY PRIVATE US SCHOLARS AND RESEARCH CENTERS TO DEPT. OF STATE CURRENTLY IN PROGRESS OR COMPLETED BUT UNPUBLISHED FOR THE PERIOD AUGUST 1965 THROUGH FEBRUARY 1966. MAJORITY OF ENTRIES ANNOTATED ITEMS TREAT ASIA IN GENERAL AND THEN INDIVIDUAL COUNTRIES. PUBLISHED ANNUALLY SINCE 1965.

3095 US DEPARTMENT OF STATE
RESEARCH ON THE AMERICAN REPUBLICS (EXTERNAL RESEARCH LIST NO 6-25)
WASHINGTON: DEPT OF STATE, 1966, 108 PP.
LIST OF SOCIAL SCIENCE RESEARCH SUBMITTED BY PRIVATE US SCHOLARS AND RESEARCH CENTERS TO DEPT. OF STATE ON LATIN AND SOUTH AMERICA CURRENTLY IN PROGRESS OR COMPLETED DURING AUGUST 1965 THROUGH FEBRUARY 1966 BUT UNPUBLISHED AS OF LATTER DATE. MAJORITY OF ENTRIES ANNOTATED. TREATS AREA IN GENERAL, THEN DIVIDED INTO CARIBBEAN, MIDDLE AMERICA, AND SOUTH AMERICA. PUBLISHED ANNUALLY SINCE 1965.

3096 US DEPARTMENT OF STATE
RESEARCH ON THE MIDDLE EAST (EXTERNAL RESEARCH LIST NO 4-25)
WASHINGTON: DEPT OF STATE, 1966, 28 PP.
LIST OF SOCIAL SCIENCE RESEARCH SUBMITTED BY PRIVATE US SCHOLARS AND RESEARCH CENTERS TO DEPT OF STATE ON MIDDLE EAST CURRENTLY "IN PROGRESS" OR "COMPLETED" DURING AUGUST 1965-FEBRUARY 1966 BUT UNPUBLISHED AS OF LATTER DATE. MAJORITY OF ENTRIES ANNOTATED. TREATS MIDDLE EAST AS WHOLE, THEN INDIVIDUAL COUNTRIES. PUBLISHED ANNUALLY SINCE 1965.

3097 US DEPARTMENT OF STATE
RESEARCH ON THE USSR AND EASTERN EUROPE (EXTERNAL RESEARCH LIST NO 1-25)
WASHINGTON: DEPT OF STATE, 1966, 63 PP.
LIST OF SOCIAL SCIENCE RESEARCH SUBMITTED BY PRIVATE US SCHOLARS AND RESEARCH CENTERS TO DEPT OF STATE ON COMMUNIST COUNTRIES OF EASTERN EUROPE CURRENTLY "IN PROGRESS" OR "COMPLETED" BUT UNPUBLISHED AS OF LATTER DATE FOR PERIOD AUGUST 1965 THROUGH FEBRUARY 1966. MAJORITY OF ENTRIES ANNOTATED. ANNUAL PUBLICATION SINCE 1965.

3098 US DEPARTMENT OF STATE
RESEARCH ON WESTERN EUROPE, GREAT BRITAIN, AND CANADA (EXTERNAL RESEARCH LIST NO 3-25)
WASHINGTON: DEPT OF STATE, 1966, 120 PP.
SERIAL PUBLICATION OF DEPT OF STATE RECORDING SOCIAL SCIENCE RESEARCH SUBMITTED BY SCHOLARS IN US FOR PERIOD AUGUST 1965 THROUGH FEBRUARY 1966. ENTRIES ARRANGED BY SUBJECT AND CLASSIFIED AS "IN PROGRESS" OR "COMPLETED." APPEARS ANNUALLY SINCE 1965. MAJORITY OF ENTRIES ANNOTATED.

3099 US DEPARTMENT OF STATE
THE COUNTRY TEAM - AN ILLUSTRATED PROFILE OF OUR AMERICAN MISSIONS ABROAD.
WASHINGTON: US GOVERNMENT, 1967, 80 PP.
PROVIDES A COMPREHENSIVE PICTURE OF THE WORK OF PRESENT-DAY US DIPLOMATIC AND CONSULAR MISSION. INCLUDES THE ACTIVITIES OF THE AGENCY FOR INTERNATIONAL DEVELOPMENT, THE US INFORMATION SERVICE, THE DEPARTMENT OF DEFENSE , AND OTHER AGENCIES WITH OVERSEAS PROGRAMS. INDIVIDUAL CHAPTERS DESCRIBE WORK OF POLITICAL, ECONOMIC, CONSULAR, ADMINISTRATIVE, MILITARY, AND OTHER ELEMENTS OF OVERSEAS POSTS.

3100 US DEPARTMENT OF STATE
FOREIGN AFFAIRS RESEARCH (PAMPHLET)
WASHINGTON: DEPT OF STATE, 1967, 83 PP., LC#67-61715.
DESCRIPTIVE LISTINGS OF US GOVERNMENT RESOURCES AVAILABLE FOR SOCIAL AND BEHAVIORAL SCIENCE RESEARCH ON FOREIGN AREAS AND INTERNATIONAL AFFAIRS. SOURCES LISTED ALPHABETICALLY BY AGENCY AND DEFINE TYPE OF RESEARCH IN WHICH EACH IS ENGAGED. INCLUDES BIBLIOGRAPHY.

3101 US DEPARTMENT OF STATE
TREATIES IN FORCE.
WASHINGTON: US GOVERNMENT, 1967, 336 PP.
LIST OF TREATIES AND OTHER INTERNATIONAL AGREEMENTS TO WHICH US HAS BECOME A PARTY THAT WERE IN FORCE AS OF JANUARY 1, 1967. LIST ARRANGED IN TWO PARTS, FOLLOWED BY AN APPENDIX. PART I INCLUDES BILATERAL TREATIES LISTED BY COUNTRY, WITH SUBJECT HEADINGS UNDER EACH COUNTRY. PART TWO INCLUDES MULTILATERAL TREATIES, ARRANGED BY SUBJECT HEADINGS, WITH A LIST OF PARTICIPATING STATES.

3102 US DEPARTMENT OF STATE
CATALOGUE OF WORKS RELATING TO THE LAW OF NATIONS AND DIPLOMACY IN THE LIBRARY OF THE DEPARTMENT OF STATE (PAMPHLET)
WASHINGTON: GOVT PR OFFICE, 1897, 110 PP.
ANNOTATED AND ARRANGED BY AUTHOR WITH MANY ITEMS IN OTHER THAN ENGLISH. INCLUDES ABOUT 1,000 BOOKS, ARTICLES, AND PERIODICALS. LISTS AUTHORS ONLY THROUGH THE LETTER B. ITEMS FROM 1840 TO 1897.

3103 US DEPARTMENT OF THE ARMY
DISARMAMENT: A BIBLIOGRAPHIC RECORD: 1916-1960.
WASHINGTON: US GOVERNMENT, 1960, 122 PP.
CONTAINS 1,000 ENTRIES IN ENGLISH, FRENCH, AND RUSSIAN ARRANGED BY SUBJECT. PUBLICATION DATES OF LISTINGS RANGE FROM 1900-1961. ENTRIES ARE FROM BOOKS, ARTICLES, DOCUMENTS, AND DISSERTATIONS. EXCERPTS FROM LISTINGS IN ANNOTATION; INCLUDES CHRONOLOGY ON DISARMAMENT.

3104 US DEPARTMENT OF THE ARMY
AFRICA: ITS PROBLEMS AND PROSPECTS.
WASHINGTON: US GOVERNMENT, 1962, 194 PP.
ANALYTICAL SURVEY OF MATERIAL ON EMERGING AFRICAN STATES, REFLECTING STRATEGIC, POLITICAL, AND ECONOMIC FACTORS INVOLVED IN QUEST FOR INDEPENDENCE AND SOVEREIGNTY. CONTAINS 500 ORIGINAL TITLES, MOST OF WHICH ARE AVAILABLE IN ARMY LIBRARY. WORKS ARE ORGANIZED TOPICALLY AND THEN BY COUNTRY AND TERRITORY. SOME MATERIAL ON EGYPT BUT CONCENTRATES PRIMARILY ON AFRICA SOUTH OF THE SAHARA.

3105 US DEPARTMENT OF THE ARMY
GUIDE TO JAPANESE MONOGRAPHS AND JAPANESE STUDIES ON MANCHURIA: 1945-1960.
WASHINGTON: DEPT OF THE ARMY, 1962, 182 PP.
SOME 210 WELL- ANNOTATED MONOGRAPHS WRITTEN AFTER WORLD WAR II AND EMPHASIZING MILITARY OPERATIONS IN THE PACIFIC AND MANCHURIA (PRIOR TO WWII). MONOGRAPHS ARE VARIOUSLY INDEXED BY OPERATIONAL LISTINGS, TOPIC, AND UNIT. ALL IN ENGLISH AND WRITTEN BY FORMER OFFICERS OF JAPANESE ARMY AND NAVY UPON DIRECTION OF US GOVERNMENT.

3106 US DEPARTMENT OF THE ARMY
SOVIET RUSSIA: STRATEGIC SURVEY (PAMPHLET)
WASHINGTON: DEPT OF THE ARMY, 1963, 223 PP.
MORE THAN 1,000 SHORT ABSTRACTS OF SCHOLARLY AND POPULAR ARTICLES AND BOOKS MOSTLY IN ENGLISH. TONE OF BIBLIOGRAPHY IS ADMITTEDLY HOSTILE TO RUSSIA AND PORTRAYS "SOVIET UNION AS A WORLD POWER INTENT ON EXTENDING ITS INFLUENCE BEYOND ITS NATIONAL BORDERS AND DOMINATING THE WORLD. " WORKS FROM 1960-63. TOPICALLY ARRANGED WITH CONCLUDING SECTION OF CONGRESSIONAL DOCUMENTS.

3107 US DEPARTMENT OF THE ARMY
US OVERSEAS BASES: PRESENT STATUS AND FUTURE PROSPECTS (PAMPHLET)
WASHINGTON: DEPT OF THE ARMY, 1963, 133 PP.
ABOUT 400 ARTICLES, BOOKS, GOVERNMENT DOCUMENTS, AND SPEECHES HAVING OVER-ALL FAVORABLE OPINION OF EFFICACY OF US BASES ALTHOUGH SOME SOVIET OPINIONS ARE INCLUDED. MANY OF THE HEAVILY ANNOTATED SOURCES DO NOT DEVOTE ENTIRE CONTENT TO BASES. ITEMS TOPICALLY ARRANGED; PUBLISHED FROM 1955-63.

3108 US DEPARTMENT OF THE ARMY
NUCLEAR WEAPONS AND THE ATLANTIC ALLIANCE: A BIBLIOGRAPHIC SURVEY.
WASHINGTON: DEPT OF THE ARMY, 1965, 179 PP.
WIDE RANGING ANNOTATED BIBLIOGRAPHY ABSTRACTING OVER 750 UNCLASSIFIED ITEMS ON THE ATLANTIC ALLIANCE IN GENERAL AND THE IMPACT OF NUCLEAR WEAPONS POLICIES ON IT IN PARTICULAR. SUPPLEMENT ON "RED CHINA'S A-BOMB."

3109 US DEPARTMENT OF THE ARMY
COMMUNIST CHINA: A STRATEGIC SURVEY: A BIBLIOGRAPHY (PAMPHLET NO. 20-67)
WASHINGTON: DEPT OF THE ARMY, 1966, 143 PP.
BIBLIOGRAPHIC PROBE INTO THE ECONOMIC, SOCIOLOGICAL, MILITARY, AND POLITICAL MAKE-UP OF COMMUNIST CHINA. FOCUSES ON EMERGENCE AS STRATEGIC THREAT. ABSTRACTS FROM OVER 650 PERIODICAL ARTICLES, BOOKS, AND STUDIES IN ENGLISH. INCLUDES CHINA'S POLICY TO SOUTH ASIA AS A WHOLE AND TO INDIVIDUAL COUNTRIES. MAPS, CHARTS, AND DATA APPENDED.

3110 US DEPARTMENT OF THE ARMY
SOUTH ASIA: A STRATEGIC SURVEY (PAMPHLET NO. 550-3)
WASHINGTON: DEPT OF THE ARMY, 1966, 175 PP.
750 PERIODICAL ARTICLES, GOVERNMENT PUBLICATIONS, AND BOOKS PERTAINING TO MILITARY, POLITICAL, AND ECONOMIC FACETS OF SOUTH ASIAN COUNTRIES ARE ANNOTATED. ALL SOURCES CITED ARE ENGLISH-LANGUAGE PUBLICATIONS OF 1960'S THROUGH 1966. ENTRIES ARRANGED BY COUNTRY AND SUBJECT. INCLUDES SECTION OF GENERAL MATERIALS FOR RESEARCH AND REFERENCE.

3111 US DEPARTMENT OF THE ARMY
CIVILIAN IN PEACE, SOLDIER IN WAR: A BIBLIOGRAPHIC SURVEY OF THE ARMY AND AIR NATIONAL GUARD (PAMPHLET, NOS. 130-2)
WASHINGTON: DEPT OF THE ARMY, 1967, 192 PP.
ANNOTATED BIBLIOGRAPHY OF PERIODICAL ARTICLES, BOOKS, UNPUBLISHED MATERIALS, AND GOVERNMENT PUBLICATIONS PERTAINING TO THE ROLE AND FUNCTIONS OF THE MILITARY IN THE US. SOURCES CITED PUBLISHED 1938 THROUGH 1966. OVER 800 ITEMS ARRANGED BY SUBJECT. INCLUDES SECTION ON MILITIAS OF FOREIGN COUNTRIES AND ONE ON STATE MILITIAS. MAJORITY OF ENTRIES ARE GOVERNMENT PUBLICATIONS.

3112 US DEPT OF STATE
FOREIGN RELATIONS OF THE UNITED STATES; DIPLOMATIC PAPERS.
WASHINGTON: DEPT OF STATE.
MAJOR SOURCE FOR STUDY OF US FOREIGN RELATIONS. SERIES

PUBLICATION WHICH BEGAN IN 1861 AND NOW HAS OVER 180 VOLUMES. CONTAINS DIPLOMATIC COMMUNICATIONS, NOTES AND MEMORANDA, AND REPORTS. GENERAL INDEX THROUGH 1918, WITH INDEXES IN EACH VOLUME AFTER 1918.

3113 US ECON SURVEY TEAM INDONESIA
INDONESIA - PERSPECTIVE AND PROPOSALS FOR UNITED STATES ECONOMIC AID.
NEW HAVEN: YALE U, SE ASIA STUD, 1963, 205 PP.
EXAMINES ECONOMIC CONDITION, OPERATION OF LONG-TERM ECONOMIC PLANNING, PROGRESS OF ECONOMY IN AGRICULTURE, INDUSTRY, AND INTERNATIONAL TRADE, AND OBJECTIVES OF US AID IN INDONESIA. MAKES RECOMMENDATIONS FOR NEW AID PROGRAMS IN EDUCATION, INDUSTRY, AND TECHNOLOGICAL RESEARCH.

3114 US GENERAL ACCOUNTING OFFICE
EXAM OF ECONOMIC AND TECHNICAL ASSISTANCE PROGRAM FOR INDIA INT'NAT'L COOP ADMIN REPORT TO CONGRESS 1955-1958.
WASHINGTON: US GOVERNMENT, 1959, 93 PP.
REVIEWS USE OF US CAPITAL AND GOODS GIVEN INDIA TO AID HER FIVE-YEAR ECONOMIC PLAN. EMPHASIS ON ADEQUACY OF FINANCIAL AND ADMINISTRATIVE PROCEDURES. REVIEWED ALL PROGRAMS AND FOUND PROJECTS UNDERSTAFFED, "OVER PROGRAMMED," AND LACKING IN CONTROL OF DISTRIBUTION OF SUPPLIES AND CAPITAL. RECOMMENDATIONS ARE GIVEN TO SPEED UP EACH PROJECT.

3115 US GENERAL ACCOUNTING OFFICE
EXAMINATION OF ECONOMIC AND TECHNICAL ASSISTANCE PROGRAM FOR IRAN.
WASHINGTON: US GOVERNMENT, 1961, 80 PP.
REPORTS ON ADMINISTRATION OF FOREIGN AID TO IRAN, BREAKING DOWN NATURE AND AMOUNT OF AID, SPENDING PRACTICES, WASTAGE, AND PROBLEMS OF CONTROL. CASE STUDIES GIVE SPECIFIC ILLUSTRATIONS OF USAGE AND EFFECT OF US AID.

3116 UNITED STATES
REPORT TO INTER-AMERICAN ECONOMIC AND SOCIAL COUNCIL AT SECOND ANNUAL MEETING.
WASHINGTON: US GOVERNMENT, 1963, 183 PP.
REVIEW OF US ROLE AND RESPONSIBILITY IN ALLIANCE FOR PROGRESS. STUDIES ECONOMIES OF US AND LA SEPARATELY AND REVIEWS AND EVALUATES ALL US PROGRAMS FOR ECONOMIC AND FINANCIAL AID. LA RECIEVES MORE US AID THAN ANY NATION. NOTES INCREASE IN LONG-TERM LOW INTEREST LOANS. SUGGESTS WAYS TO IMPROVE PROGRAMS FOR FUTURE.

3117 US DEPARTMENT OF STATE
TREATIES IN FORCE.
WASHINGTON: US GOVERNMENT, 1967, 336 PP.
CONTAINS LIST OF TREATIES AND OTHER INTERNATIONAL AGREEMENTS TO WHICH THE US HAS BECOME A PARTY AND WHICH ARE CARRIED ON THE RECORDS OF THE DEPT. OF STATE AS BEING IN FORCE ON JAN. 1, 1967. IT INCLUDES THOSE TREATIES AND OTHER AGREEMENTS WHICH ON THAT DATE HAD NOT EXPIRED BY THEIR TERMS OR HAD NOT BEEN DENOUNCED BY THE PARTIES, REPLACED BY OTHER AGREEMENTS OR OTHERWISE DEFINITELY TERMINATED.

3118 US HOUSE COMM APPROPRIATIONS
MUTUAL SECURITY PROGRAM APPROPRIATIONS FOR 1952: HEARINGS BEFORE A SUBCOMMITTEE OF THE COMMITTEE ON APPROPRIATIONS.
WASHINGTON: US GOVERNMENT, 1951, 798 PP.
HEARINGS BEFORE SUBCOMMITTEE ON ECONOMIC COOPERATION ADMINISTRATION. TESTIMONY COVERS PROGRAMS FOR MILITARY ASSISTANCE TO NORTH ATLANTIC TREATY AREA OF WESTERN EUROPE, MIDDLE EAST (GREECE, TURKEY, IRAN), SOUTHEASTERN ASIA, AND LATIN AMERICA. TOTAL REQUEST OF SIX BILLION WEIGHED AGAINST COMMUNIST THREAT IN GENERAL AND KOREAN CONFLICT IN PARTICULAR.

3119 US HOUSE COMM APPROPRIATIONS
INTER-AMERICAN PROGRAMS FOR 1961: DENIAL OF 1962 BUDGET INFORMATION.
WASHINGTON: GOVT PR OFFICE, 1961, 354 PP.
HEARINGS BEFORE HOUSE SUBCOMMITTEE ON APPROPRIATIONS CONSIDERING APPROPRIATIONS FOR LATIN AMERICA AND CHILE. ACTING SECRETARY OF STATE CHESTER BOWLES OUTLINED PRESIDENT KENNEDY'S ALLIANCE FOR PROGRESS. ALSO TESTIFYING WERE DOUGLAS DILLON AND ADOLF BERLE. SOME REPRESENTATIVES QUESTIONED EFFICIENCY OF APPROPRIATIONS AND RECEIVED DETAILS OF NATURE AND DIRECTION OF FUNDS.

3120 US HOUSE COMM APPROPRIATIONS
HEARINGS ON FOREIGN OPERATIONS AND RELATED AGENCIES APPROPRIATIONS.
WASHINGTON: GOVT PR OFFICE, 1966, 826 PP.
STATEMENTS AND TESTIMONIES ON OPERATIONS OF ASIAN DEVELOPMENT BANK, CUBAN REFUGEE PROGRAM, EXPORT-IMPORT BANK, INTER-AMERICAN DEVELOPMENT BANK, PEACE CORPS, ETC. EXAMINES BUDGET REQUESTS OF ABOVE AGENCIES FOR FISCAL 1967.

3121 US HOUSE COMM BANKING-CURR
RECENT CHANGES IN MONETARY POLICY AND BALANCE OF PAYMENTS PROBLEMS.
WASHINGTON: US GOVERNMENT, 1963, 412 PP.
HEARINGS BEFORE HOUSE COMMITTEE ON BANKING AND CURRENCY HEADED BY WRIGHT PATMAN ON POLICY ACTIONS OTHER THAN RAISING SHORT-TERM INTEREST RATES THAT WOULD POSITIVELY AFFECT BALANCE OF PAYMENTS. ALSO INCLUDES INVESTIGATION OF EFFECTS THIS MOVE HAS HAD ON EUROPEAN CENTRAL BANKS.

3122 US HOUSE COMM FOREIGN AFFAIRS
SURVEY OF ACTIVITIES OF THE COMMITTEE ON FOREIGN AFFAIRS HOUSE OF REPRESENTATIVES: 84TH THROUGH 86TH CONGRESS.
WASHINGTON: US GOVERNMENT, 1956, 107 PP.
RECORD OF COMMITTEE OF CONGRESS RESPONSIBLE FOR ALL LEGISLATION AFFECTING US FOREIGN POLICY. CONTAINS ALL PUBLIC DOCUMENTS, STATUTES, DEBATES, ETC. ON LEGISLATION CONSIDERED, AND TEXTS OF NEW LAWS. COVERS 84TH CONGRESS, 85TH FIRST SESSION ONLY, AND 86TH.

3123 US HOUSE COMM FOREIGN AFFAIRS
HEARINGS ON DRAFT LEGISLATION TO AMEND FURTHER THE MUTUAL SECURITY ACT OF 1954 (PAMPHLET)
WASHINGTON: GOVT PR OFFICE, 1958, 350 PP.
STATEMENTS, TESTIMONY, AND MEMORANDA SUPPLIED BY GOVERNMENT OFFICIALS ON DESIRABILITY OF AMENDING MUTUAL SECURITY ACT OF 1954, PLUS COST OF US TROOPS IN EUROPE, MISSILE SYSTEMS, IMPORTATION OF ARMS, ETC. INCLUDES PROPOSALS FOR LEGISLATION.

3124 US HOUSE COMM FOREIGN AFFAIRS
HEARINGS ON THE FAR EAST AND THE PACIFIC (PAMPHLET)
WASHINGTON: GOVT PR OFFICE, 1958, 78 PP.
STATEMENTS AND DISCUSSIONS OF MUTUAL SECURITY PROGRAM IN LAOS. INCLUDES OFFICIAL STATEMENTS BY ASSISTANT TO COMPTROLLER GENERAL AND ASSOCIATE DIRECTOR OF CIVIL ACCOUNTING AND AUDITING DIVISION. CENTERS ON DISCUSSION OF ECONOMIC AND MILITARY AID.

3125 US HOUSE COMM FOREIGN AFFAIRS
HEARINGS ON REVIEW OF THE MUTUAL SECURITY PROGRAMS; EXAMINATION OF SELECTED PROJECTS IN FORMOSA AND PAKISTAN (PAMPHLET)
WASHINGTON: GOVT PR OFFICE, 1958, 284 PP.
STATEMENTS, TESTIMONIES, AND MEMORANDA BY GOVERNMENT OFFICIALS AND CORPORATION OR INTERNATIONAL AGENCY OFFICIALS, ON OPERATION OF US PROJECTS IN FORMOSA AND PAKISTAN. EXAMINES IRRIGATION, GRAIN STORAGE, AND SAWMILL PROJECTS.

3126 US HOUSE COMM FOREIGN AFFAIRS
HEARINGS ON DRAFT LEGISLATION TO AMEND FURTHER THE MUTUAL SECURITY ACT OF 1954 (PAMPHLET)
WASHINGTON: GOVT PR OFFICE, 1959, 490 PP.
STATEMENTS, TESTIMONIES, AND MEMORANDA SUPPLIED BY GOVERNMENT OFFICIALS ON DESIRABILITY OF AMENDING MUTUAL SECURITY ACT OF 1954. INCLUDES STATEMENTS ON TRADE, EXPORT OF SURPLUS COMMODITIES, LOAN FUNDS, EXTENT OF USSR AID TO AFRICA, AND SO ON.

3127 US HOUSE COMM FOREIGN AFFAIRS
HEARINGS ON A BILL TO AMEND FURTHER THE MUTUAL SECURITY ACT OF 1954.
WASHINGTON: GOVT PR OFFICE, 1960, 1110 PP.
STATEMENTS, TESTIMONIES, AND MEMORANDA SUPPLIED BY GOVERNMENT OFFICIALS ON AMENDMENT OF MUTUAL SECURITY ACT OF 1954. STATEMENTS ON EXTENT OF US DEFENSE SUPPORT IN EUROPE, UN EMERGENCY FORCE, DEFENSE EXPENDITURES OF NON-NATO ALLIES, DEVELOPMENT LOAN FUND, USSR AID TO AFRICA, UN OPERATIONS, ETC. INCLUDES CHARTS AND TABLES.

3128 US HOUSE COMM FOREIGN AFFAIRS
THE INTERNATIONAL DEVELOPMENT AND SECURITY ACT: HEARINGS BEFORE COMMITTEE ON FOREIGN AFFAIRS, HOUSE OF REP: HR7372.
WASHINGTON: GOVT PR OFFICE, 1961, 892 PP.
JUNE 7-23,1961 HEARINGS ON BILL TO PROMOTE FOREIGN POLICY, SECURITY, AND GENERAL WELFARE OF US BY ASSISTING PEOPLES OF WORLD IN THEIR EFFORTS TOWARD ECONOMIC AND SOCIAL DEVELOPMENT AND INTERNAL AND EXTERNAL SECURITY, AND LIKE PURPOSES. AMONG THOSE TESTIFYING WERE: RUSK, MCNAMARA, LEMNITZER, W.M. BUNDY, NORSTAD, DILLON, G.W. BALL.

3129 US HOUSE COMM FOREIGN AFFAIRS
HEARINGS ON H.R. 5490 TO AMEND FURTHER THE FOREIGN ASSISTANCE ACT OF 1961.
WASHINGTON: GOVT PR OFFICE, 1963, 700 PP.
STATEMENTS, MEMORANDA, AND TESTIMONY ON INTERNAL SECURITY, COST OF US DIVISIONS IN EUROPE, MILITARY ASSISTANCE PROGRAMS, FINANCING OF UN PEACEKEEPING OPERATIONS, YUGOSLAV MILITARY SALES TO INDIA, SHIPMENT OF ARMS TO CUBA, USES OF CONTINGENCY FUNDS, ETC.

3130 US HOUSE COMM FOREIGN AFFAIRS
HEARINGS ON H.R. 10502 TO AMEND FURTHER THE FOREIGN ASSISTANCE ACT OF 1961.
WASHINGTON: GOVT PR OFFICE, 1964, 840 PP.
STATEMENTS, MEMORANDA, AND TESTIMONIES BY PUBLIC AND PRIVATE OFFICIALS AND AGENCY FOR INTERNATIONAL DEVELOPMENT ON CONTINGENCY FUND PROGRAMS, SUPPORT TO EDUCATION, MILITARY SECURITY, DEVELOPMENT LOANS, ETC. AND NUMEROUS OTHER AID PROGRAMS IN ASIA, AFRICA, AND LATIN AMERICA.

3131 US HOUSE COMM FOREIGN AFFAIRS
HEARINGS ON DRAFT BILL TO AMEND FURTHER THE FOREIGN ASSIS-

TANCE ACT OF 1961.
WASHINGTON: GOVT PR OFFICE, 1965, 990 PP.
TESTIMONIES AND STATEMENTS BY PUBLIC OFFICIALS ON ECONOMIC AND MILITARY ASSISTANCE TO ASIA, AFRICA, AND LATIN AMERICA. INCLUDES MEMORANDA SUPPLIED BY AGENCY FOR INTERNATIONAL DEVELOPMENT ON COMMUNIST AID, VIETNAM COUNTERINSURGENCY, POLITICAL SITUATION IN INDIA, TUBERCULOSIS IN CHILE, DISTRIBUTION OF FERTILIZER IN VIETNAM, ETC.

3132 US HOUSE COMM FOREIGN AFFAIRS
HEARINGS ON HR 12449 A BILL TO AMEND FURTHER THE FOREIGN ASSISTANCE ACT OF 1961.
WASHINGTON: GOVT PR OFFICE, 1966, 1092 PP.
TESTIMONIES AND STATEMENTS BY PUBLIC OFFICIALS ON US FOREIGN AID PROGRAMS WITH EMPHASIS ON ACTIVITIES OF AGENCY FOR INTERNATIONAL DEVELOPMENT. INCLUDES AID MEMORANDA ON CONTINGENCY FUNDS, AID PERSONNEL REQUIREMENTS IN VIETNAM, BRAZILIAN PURCHASE OF EAST GERMAN LOCOMOTIVES, ANTI-AMERICAN STUDENT DEMONSTRATIONS, AFRICAN ATTITUDE TOWARDS US AID, ETC.

3133 US HOUSE COMM FOREIGN AFFAIRS
UNITED STATES POLICY TOWARD ASIA (PAMPHLET)
WASHINGTON: US GOVERNMENT, 1966, 12 PP.
REPORT OF SUBCOMMITTEE ON FAR EAST AND PACIFIC ON HEARINGS HELD JANUARY-MARCH, 1966. ASSESSES COMMUNIST CHINA'S CHARACTERISTICS: POWER; POLICY; RELATIONS WITH US, UN, USSR, AND VIETNAM.

3134 US HOUSE COMM FOREIGN AFFAIRS
UNITED STATES - SOUTH AFRICAN RELATIONS.
WASHINGTON: US GOVERNMENT, 1966, 391 PP.
HEARINGS BEFORE HOUSE COMMITTEE ON FOREIGN AFFAIRS ON US-SOUTH AFRICAN RELATIONS, INCLUDING TESTIMONY OF WITNESSES, AND STATEMENTS, TABLES, AND MEMORANDA SUBMITTED FOR THE RECORD. COMMITTEE CONSIDERING MEASURES AGAINST SOUTH AFRICA.

3135 US HOUSE COMM GOVT OPERATIONS
HEARINGS BEFORE A SUBCOMMITTEE OF THE COMMITTEE ON GOVERNMENT OPERATIONS.
WASHINGTON: GOVT PR OFFICE, 1958, 1301 PP.
STATEMENTS AND TESTIMONIES BY PUBLIC AND PRIVATE OFFICIALS ON FOREIGN AID CONSTRUCTION PROJECTS IN CAMBODIA AND PHILIPPINES. EXAMINES DEFENSE SUPPORT, ECONOMIC AID, AND TECHNICAL ASSISTANCE IN BROAD PERSPECTIVE. INVESTIGATES OPERATIONAL EFFICIENCY IN ROAD PROJECTS.

3136 US HOUSE COMM GOVT OPERATIONS
UNITED STATES AID OPERATIONS IN LAOS.
WASHINGTON: US GOVERNMENT, 1959, 983 PP.
HEARINGS ON US AID TO LAOS. INVESTIGATES EFFECT OF MILITARY AID ON ECONOMIC AND POLITICAL STABILITY AND METHODS OF IMPROVING ADMINISTRATION OF PROGRAM TO FURTHER POLITICAL OBJECTIVES.

3137 US HOUSE COMM GOVT OPERATIONS
OPERATIONS OF THE DEVELOPMENT LOAN FUND: HEARINGS (COMMITTEE ON GOVERNMENT OPERATIONS)
WASHINGTON: GOVT PR OFFICE, 1960, 636 PP.
INQUIRY INTO OPERATIONS AND ADMINISTRATION OF FUND. REPORT IN DIALOGUE FORM ONLY. QUESTIONS MEN HANDLING RECORDS AND MEN DISPERSING MONEY TO NATIONS. FEELS MONEY IS BEING WASTED OR NOT USED FOR WELFARE AND SECURITY OF US. RECOMMENDS CENTRALIZING FUND AND CONTROLLING PROJECTS AS WELL AS GIVING FAIR LOAN TERMS, ETC. FEELS NEED FOR OFFICIAL POLICY STATEMENT OF RULES.

3138 US HOUSE COMM GOVT OPERATIONS
US OWNED FOREIGN CURRENCIES: HEARINGS (COMMITTEE ON GOVERNMENT OPERATIONS)
WASHINGTON: GOVT PR OFFICE, 1964, 260 PP.
REVIEW OF EIGHT FOREIGN NATIONS WHERE US HAS EXCESS AMOUNTS OF FOREIGN CURRENCY FOR FUTURE NEEDS. EMPHASIS ON INDIA WHERE US HAS 20-YEAR SUPPLY OF RUPEES. SUGGESTIONS MADE TO HELP AID PROJECTS UTILIZE THIS EXCESS IN PLACE OF APPROPRIATED US DOLLARS OR TO USE EXCESS TO PAY OFF FOREIGN DEBTS.

3139 US HOUSE COMM GOVT OPERATIONS
AN INVESTIGATION OF THE US ECONOMIC AND MILITARY ASSISTANCE PROGRAMS IN VIETNAM.
WASHINGTON: US GOVERNMENT, 1966, 130 PP.
REPORTS ON US AID PROGRAM IN VIETNAM. MAINTAINS THAT INCREASED ECONOMIC AID IS NECESSARY IF POLITICAL AND MILITARY VICTORIES ARE TO BE ACHIEVED. EXAMINES IMPORT PROGRAM, CONTROL OF MONEY, AUDITS AND INSPECTIONS, AID MANAGEMENT, PORT SITUATION, CIVILIAN MEDICAL PROGRAM, PACIFICATION, MILITARY CONSTRUCTION, AND ILLICIT PRACTICES AFFECTING US AID.

3140 US HOUSE COMM ON JUDICIARY
IMMIGRATION HEARINGS.
WASHINGTON: US GOVERNMENT, 1964, 1030 PP.
REPORTS DEBATE BEFORE COMMITTEE ON JUDICIARY, ON PROPOSED CHANGE OF IMMIGRATION ACT TO ABOLISH NATIONALITY QUOTAS FOR IMMIGRANTS. INCLUDES STATEMENTS BY 60 REPRESENTATIVES.

3141 US HOUSE COMM. SCI. ASTRONAUT.
OCEAN SCIENCES AND NATIONAL SECURITY.
WASHINGTON: G.P.O., 1960, 180 PP.
AN INVESTIGATION INTO THE EXTENT TO WHICH RESEARCH IS DESIRABLE AND EXAMINES OCEONOGRAPHIC CAPABILITIES, PROPOSED PROGRAMS AND IMMEDIATE AND EMERGING ISSUES BEFORE CONGRESS. MAIN GOALS ARE ECONOMIC AND MILITARY. RESEARCH RATHER THAN DEVELOPMENT IS THE MOST CRUCIAL NEED. THE POSSIBILITY OF GAINING FOOD FROM THE OCEAN FOR POPULATION EXPLOSIAN AND ANTISUBMARINE WARFARE ARE SPECIAL CONCERNS.

3142 US LIBRARY OF CONGRESS
ACCESSIONS LIST - INDIA.
WASHINGTON: LIBRARY OF CONGRESS.
MONTHLY PUBLICATION SINCE 1962 LISTING BOOKS, SERIALS, MONOGRAPHS, AND GOVERNMENT DOCUMENTS WITH INDIAN IMPRINT. SOURCES PRIMARILY IN ASIAN LANGUAGES; SOME ENGLISH. MATERIALS ARRANGED BY LANGUAGE WITH AUTHOR INDEX. ANNUAL CUMULATIVE AUTHORS AND SERIALS INDEXES. TITLES TRANSLATED INTO ENGLISH.

3143 US LIBRARY OF CONGRESS
ACCESSIONS LIST -- ISRAEL.
WASHINGTON: LIBRARY OF CONGRESS.
MONTHLY LISTING, FIRST ISSUED 1964, OF BBOKS, SERIALS, GOVERNMENT DOCUMENTS, AND MONOGRAPHS PUBLISHED IN ISRAEL. MATERIALS IN HEBREW AND ENGLISH. ARRANGED BY AUTHOR AND SUBJECT. ANNUAL AUTOHOR AND SERIALS INDEXES.

3144 US LIBRARY OF CONGRESS
EAST EUROPEAN ACCESSIONS INDEX.
WASHINGTON: LIBRARY OF CONGRESS.
MONTHLY LIST OF PUBLICATIONS RECEIVED FROM IRON CURTAIN COUNTRIES. ENTRIES ARE ARRANGED MONTHLY BY COUNTRY AND GROUPED UNDER 17 SUBJECTS LISTED IN CONTENTS. ABOUT 15,000 ENTRIES ARE RECEIVED MONTHLY IN ALL EASTERN LANGUAGES PLUS ENGLISH.

3145 US LIBRARY OF CONGRESS
LIST OF REFERENCES ON A LEAGUE OF NATIONS.
WASHINGTON: LIBRARY OF CONGRESS, 1918, 59 PP.
COMPILATION OF BOOKS, ARTICLES, DOCUMENTS, AND SPEECHES. ARRANGED ALPHABETICALLY BY AUTHOR. PUBLICATION DATES RANGE FROM 1915 THROUH 1930; 800 ENTRIES.

3146 US LIBRARY OF CONGRESS
ECONOMICS OF WAR (APRIL 1941-MARCH 1942)
WASHINGTON: LIBRARY OF CONGRESS, 1942, 120 PP.
ANNOTATED BIBLIOGRAPHY ON ECONOMIC PROBLEMS AND POLICIES IN WARTIME INCLUDES 913 ITEMS ARRANGED BY SUBJECT AND INDEXED BY AUTHOR. LISTS REFERENCES ON GENERAL ECONOMIC CONDITIONS; INCOME, CONSUMPTION, AND EXPENDITURE; PRICES, WAGES, COST OF LIVING; INTERNATIONAL TRADE; BANKING; STATE AND MUNICIPAL FINANCE; ETC. ALSO LISTS ITEMS RELATING TO WARTIME FINANCE, POLICIES, RATIONING, LEND-LEASE ETC.

3147 US LIBRARY OF CONGRESS
POSTWAR PLANNING AND RECONSTRUCTION: APRIL-DECEMBER 1942 (SUPPLEMENT 1)
WASHINGTON: LIBRARY OF CONGRESS, 1942, 202 PP.
ANNOTATED BIBLIOGRAPHY ON POSTWAR PLANS AND PROBLEMS. CONTAINS 1316 ITEMS (INCLUDING BOOKS, ARTICLES, AND PAMPHLETS) AND COVERS THE PERIOD FROM APRIL-DECEMBER 1942. ARRANGED BY SUBJECT TREATING OF THE POLITICAL, SOCIAL, AND ECONOMIC EXCRESCENCES OF WORLD WAR II. INCLUDES A LIST OF REFERENCE AND BIBLIOGRAPHICAL MATERIALS.

3148 US LIBRARY OF CONGRESS
POLITICAL DEVELOPMENTS AND THE WAR: APRIL-DECEMBER 1942 (SUPPLEMENT 1)
WASHINGTON: LIBRARY OF CONGRESS, 1943, 337 PP.
PART OF LIBRARY OF CONGRESS SERIES CALLED "BIBLIOGRAPHIES OF THE WORLD AT WAR." INCLUDES 2506 ITEMS ARRANGED TOPICALLY AND INDEXED BY AUTHOR. LISTS BOOKS, ARTICLES, PAMPHLETS, BIBLIOGRAPHIES, REFERENCES, ETC., DEALING WITH WORLD POLITICS UNDER THE IMPACT OF WORLD WAR II.

3149 US LIBRARY OF CONGRESS
POSTWAR PLANNING AND RECONSTRUCTION: JANUARY-MARCH 1943.
WASHINGTON: LIBRARY OF CONGRESS, 1947, 135 PP.
ANNOTATED BIBLIOGRAPHY ON POSTWAR PLANS AND PROBLEMS. CONTAINS 862 ITEMS (INCLUDING BOOKS, ARTICLES, AND PAMPHLETS) AND COVERS JANUARY-DECEMBER, 1943. ARRANGED BY SUBJECT; TREATS POLITICAL, SOCIAL, ECONOMIC ASPECTS OF WORLD WAR II. LISTS BIBLIOGRAPHIC AND REFERENCE MATERIALS. PART OF LIBRARY OF CONGRESS SERIES OF "BIBLIOGRAPHIES OF THE WORLD AT WAR."

3150 US LIBRARY OF CONGRESS
THE UNITED STATES AND EUROPE: BIBLIOGRAPHY OF THOUGHT EXPRESSED IN AMERICAN PUBLICATIONS DURING 1950.
WASHINGTON: LIBRARY OF CONGRESS, 1950, 209 PP.
COMPILES, DIGESTS, INDEXES, AND TOPICALLY ARRANGES 470 ITEMS DEALING WITH US THOUGHT ON EUROPEAN PROBLEMS. DISCUSSES POLITICAL, SOCIAL, AND ECONOMIC CONDITIONS; THE CLASH OF IDEOLOGIES; SOVIET IMPERIALISM; INTERNATIONAL

COOPERATION; FOREIGN AID. INCLUDES A POSTSCRIPT ON ASIA.

3151 US LIBRARY OF CONGRESS
PUBLIC AFFAIRS ABSTRACTS.
WASHINGTON: LIBRARY OF CONGRESS, 1951, 650 PP.
SUMMARIZES BOOKS, PAMPHLETS, DOCUMENTS, AND PERIODICALS DEALING WITH PUBLIC AFFAIRS AND ESPECIALLY THOSE TOPICS CONSIDERED OF INTEREST TO MEMBERS OF CONGRESS. ITEMS ARE ALL IN ENGLISH AND ALL CURRENT WITH VOLUME IN WHICH INCLUDED. EACH MONTHLY VOLUME ABSTRACTS ABOUT 35 ITEMS WITH INDEXES BY AUTHOR AND SUBJECT. PUBLISHED 1946-1951.

3152 US LIBRARY OF CONGRESS
EAST EUROPEAN ACCESSIONS LIST (VOL. I)
WASHINGTON: LIBRARY OF CONGRESS, 1951, 1500 PP., LC#51-60032
RECORD OF EASTERN EUROPEAN MONOGRAPHS AND PERIODICALS SINCE 1939 IN ENGLISH AND LANGUAGE OF ORIGINAL COUNTRY; ARRANGED BY COUNTRY AND DIVIDED INTO PERIODICALS AND MONOGRAPHS WHICH ARE FURTHER DIVIDED INTO SUBJECTS.

3153 US LIBRARY OF CONGRESS
EGYPT AND THE ANGLO-EGYPTIAN SUDAN: A SELECTIVE GUIDE TO BACKGROUND READING (PAMPHLET)
WASHINGTON: UNIVERSITY PR WASH, 1952, 27 PP., LC#52-60008.
LIST OF BASIC WORKS WITH LENGTHY ANNOTATIONS. ARRANGED UNDER GENERAL, HISTORICAL, AND CONTEMPORARY ISSUES.

3154 US LIBRARY OF CONGRESS
UNITED STATES DIRECT ECONOMIC AID TO FOREIGN COUNTRIES: A COLLECTION OF EXCERPTS AND A BIBLIOGRAPHY (PAMPHLET)
WASHINGTON: LIBRARY OF CONGRESS, 1956, 60 PP.
PROVIDES BACKGROUND TO DEBATE ON FOREIGN AID AND SAMPLING OF VIEWS ON CONTINUANCE OF FOREIGN ECONOMIC ASSISTANCE. BIBLIOGRAPHY APPENDED AS GUIDE TO EXTENSIVE PUBLISHED MATERIAL ON SUBJECT. SHORT BIBLIOGRAPHY IS ANNOTATED.

3155 US LIBRARY OF CONGRESS
WORLD COMMUNIST MOVEMENT.
WASHINGTON: LIBRARY OF CONGRESS, 1961, 1001 PP.
A FOUR-VOLUME CHRONOLOGY PREPARED BY THE LEGISLATIVE REFERENCE SERVICE FOR USE BY THE COMMITTEE ON UN-AMERICAN ACTIVITIES COVERS 1818-1955, CHIEFLY AFTER WORLD WAR II. PURPORTS TO SHOW THAT "THE COMMUNIST MOVEMENT IS A GLOBAL MOVEMENT WITH THE SOVIET UNION AS ITS LEADER" AND HAS AN "UNMITIGATING, UNRELENTING DRIVE FOR WORLD CONQUEST." ARRANGES CHRONOLOGY TO SUPPORT THIS THESIS.

3156 US LIBRARY OF CONGRESS
UNITED STATES AND CANADIAN PUBLICATIONS ON AFRICA IN 1960.
WASHINGTON: LIBRARY OF CONGRESS, 1962, 98 PP., LC#62-60021.
INDEXES AND ANNOTATES 1,111 ITEMS DEALING WITH SUB-SAHARA AFRICA. ITEMS ARRANGED TOPICALLY IN THE GENERAL SECTIONS AND BY COUNTRY WHEN THE ITEM RESTRICTS ITSELF TO A SPECIFIC REGION. AN EFFORT WAS MADE TO SURVEY ITEMS OF CONTINUING INTEREST. INCLUDES A LIST OF BIBLIOGRAPHIES AND REFERENCES.

3157 US LIBRARY OF CONGRESS
A LIST OF AMERICAN DOCTORAL DISSERTATIONS ON AFRICA.
WASHINGTON: LIBRARY OF CONGRESS, 1962, 69 PP., LC#62-60088.
700 THESES, ON SUBJECTS RELATING TO AFRICA, WHICH HAVE BEEN ACCEPTED BY US AND CANADIAN UNIVERSITIES FROM LATE 19TH CENTURY TO 1961. ARRANGED ALPHABETICALLY BY AUTHOR.

3158 US LIBRARY OF CONGRESS
RARE BOOKS DIVISION: GUIDE TO ITS COLLECTION AND SERVICES.
WASHINGTON: LIBRARY OF CONGRESS, 1965, 51 PP., LC#64-60071.
DESCRIBES THE HOLDINGS IN ITS VARIOUS RARE BOOKS COLLECTIONS: JEFFERSON AND PETER FORCE LIBRARIES, THE VOLLBEHR COLLECTION OF INCUNABULA AND THE GUTENBERG BIBLE; COLLECTIONS OF EARLY AMERICAN IMPRINTS, WESTERN AMERICANA, CONFEDERATE STATES IMPRINTS, ETC. ALSO INDICATES PROCEDURES FOR UTILIZING THE FACILITIES OF VARIOUS COLLECTIONS AND EXHIBITS.

3159 US LIBRARY OF CONGRESS
A DIRECTORY OF INFORMATION RESOURCES IN THE UNITED STATES: SOCIAL SCIENCES.
WASHINGTON: LIBRARY OF CONGRESS, 1965, 218 PP., LC#65-62583.
PROVIDES A DIRECTORY OF ORGANIZATIONS, BOTH PRIVATE AND GOVERNMENTAL, WHICH CAN PROVIDE INFORMATION FOR RESEARCHERS IN THE SOCIAL SCIENCES. PERTINENT INFORMATION ABOUT EACH ORGANIZATION INCLUDES LOCATION, DESCRIPTION OF COLLECTIONS, AND PUBLICATIONS. ARRANGES ORGANIZATIONS BY NAME AND BY SUBJECTS WITH WHICH THEY WORK. APPROXIMATELY 1,000 ORGANIZATIONS ARE LISTED.

3160 US LIBRARY OF CONGRESS
NIGERIA: A GUIDE TO OFFICIAL PUBLICATIONS.
WASHINGTON: LIBRARY OF CONGRESS, 1966, 166 PP., LC#66-61703.
REVISION OF A SIMILAR GUIDE PUBLISHED IN 1959 WHICH COVERS PUBLICATIONS ISSUED BY NIGERIAN GOVERNMENTS FROM THE ESTABLISHMENT OF BRITISH ADMINISTRATION IN NIGERIA IN 1861 TO 1865. ALSO LISTS SELECTION OF DOCUMENTS RELEVANT TO NIGERIA AND THE BRITISH CAMEROONS ISSUED BY VARIOUS BRITISH GOVERNMENT OFFICES AND BY THE LEAGUE OF NATIONS AND UN.

3161 US MUTUAL SECURITY AGENCY
U. S. TECHNICAL AND ECONOMIC ASSISTANCE IN THE FAR EAST (PAMPHLET)
WASHINGTON: MUTUAL SECUR AGENCY, 1952, 36 PP.
CHARTS, STATISTICAL DATA, AND STATEMENTS ON PROGRAM OBJECTIVES FOR TECHNICAL AND ECONOMIC AID TO FORMOSA, STATES OF INDOCHINA, PHILIPPINES, BURMA, INDONESIA, AND THAILAND.

3162 US OPERATIONS MISSION TO VIET
BUILDING ECONOMIC STRENGTH (PAMPHLET)
WASHINGTON: US OPER MISS VIET, 1958, 80 PP.
REPORT ON US ECONOMIC AID OPERATIONS IN SOUTH VIETNAM FOR FISCAL 1958. GIVES STATISTICAL DATA ON FOOD PRODUCTION, EDUCATION, HEALTH SERVICES, INDUSTRIAL GROWTH, PUBLIC ADMINISTRATION, AND TRAINING FOR PUBLIC SERVICE ABROAD.

3163 US PRES CITIZEN ADVISERS
REPORT TO THE PRESIDENT ON THE MUTUAL SECURITY PROGRAM.
WASHINGTON: US GOVERNMENT, 1957, 36 PP.
BRIEF ANALYSIS OF COLLECTIVE SECURITY PROGRAM OF US AND RECOMMENDATIONS. URGES LONG-TERM CONTINUATION OF BOTH MILITARY AND ECONOMIC PROGRAMS, LEGALLY, FINANCIALLY, AND ADMINISTRATIVELY SEPARATED, BUT AS PART OF ONE COLLECTIVE SECURITY PROGRAM. RECOMMENDS VARIOUS PUBLIC AND PRIVATE METHODS FOR ACHIEVING COLLECTIVE SECURITY AGAINST COMMUNISM.

3164 US PRES COMM STUDY MIL ASSIST
COMPOSITE REPORT.
WASHINGTON: U.S. PRES. COMM. STUDY MIL ASSIST, 1959, 600 PP.
REPORTS ON ORGANIZATION OF US MILITARY ASSISTANCE PROGRAM AND ORGANIZATIONAL ASPECTS OF ECONOMIC AID PROGRAM. EMPHASIZES NEED FOR EFFECTIVE ADMINISTRATION AND LONG-RANGE PLANNING. TABLES, CHARTS, FIGURES.

3165 U.S. SENATE COMM. AERO. SPACE SCI.
DOCUMENTS ON INTERNATIONAL ASPECTS OF EXPLORATION AND USE OF OUTER SPACE, 1954-62: STAFF REPORT FOR COMM AERON SPACE SCI.
WASHINGTON: US GOVERNMENT, 1963, 407 PP.
EXERPTS OF OFFICIAL DOCUMENTS CONCERNING POLICY VIEWS OF US AND RUSSIA ON SPACE MATTERS. CONTAINS ANALYSIS BY US OFFICIALS. COVERS HISTORICAL EVENTS OF BOTH NATIONS, STATEMENTS BY THEIR LEADERS, AND ALL LEGISLATION CONCERNING OUTER SPACE LAWS AND PROJECTS.

3166 U.S. SENATE COMM. AERO. SPACE SCI.
US INTERNATIONAL SPACE PROGRAMS, 1959-65: STAFF REPORT FOR COMM ON AERONAUTICAL AND SPACE SCIENCES.
WASHINGTON: US GOVERNMENT, 1965, 575 PP.
COMPILATION OF EXECUIVEE AGREEMENTS, LETTERS, MEMORANDA OF UNDERSTANDING, AND ALL INTERNATIONAL ARRANGEMENTS CONCERNING OUTER SPACE, FROM 1959-65. AIMS TO REVEAL SCOPE OF US SPACE EFFORTS AND METHODS OF ACHIEVING INTERNATIONAL COOPERATION DOCUMENTS ARE ARRANGED ALPHABETICALLY BY COUNTRY OF ORIGIN.

3167 US SENATE COMM AERO SPACE SCI
INTERNATIONAL COOPERATION AND ORGANIZATION FOR OUTER SPACE.
WASHINGTON: US GOVERNMENT, 1965, 580 PP.
STAFF REPORT PREPARED FOR SENATE COMMITTEE ON AERONAUTICAL AND SPACE SCIENCES. SURVEYS ORGANIZATIONS WITH SPACE AND SPACE-RELATED PRGRAMS AND THEIR INTERRELATIONSHIPS. ANALYZES IMPACT OF FRONTIER OF OUTER SPACE UPON US FOREIGN RELATIONS, RELATIONS AMONG OTHER NATIONS, QUESTION OF ARMS CONTROL. DISCUSSES INTERNATIONAL ECONOMIC AND TECHNICAL DEVELOPMENTS, PROGRAMS, AND POLICIES OF UN AND ITS AGENCIES.

3168 US SENATE COMM AERO SPACE SCI
SOVIET SPACE PROGRAMS, 1962-65; GOALS AND PURPOSES, ACHIEVEMENTS, PLANS, AND INTERNATIONAL IMPLICATIONS.
WASHINGTON: US GOVERNMENT, 1966, 920 PP.
STAFF REPORT PREPARED FOR SENATE COMMITTEE ON AERONAUTICAL AND SPACE SCIENCES. SUMMARIZES SOVIET SPACE PROGRAMS, AND ANALYZES INTERNATIONAL, POLITICAL, AND LEGAL IMPLICATIONS. DISCUSSES SOVIET GOALS, WESTERN PROJECTIONS OF FUTURE SOVIET SPACE PLANS AND CAPABILITIES, AND SOVIET ATTITUDE TOWARD INTERNATIONAL SPACE COOPERATION.

3169 US SENATE COMM AERO SPACE SCI
TREATY ON PRINCIPLES GOVERNING ACTIVITIES OF STATES IN EXPLORATION AND USE OF OUTER SPACE, INCLUDING...BODIES.
WASHINGTON: US GOVERNMENT, 1967, 84 PP.
REPORT ON "TREATY ON OUTER SPACE," INCLUDING NEGOTIATION OF TREATY PROVISIONS, TEXT AND ANALYSIS OF TREATY, AND BACKGROUND DOCUMENTS (UN AND US RESOLUTIONS, ANTARCTIC TREATY, NUCLEAR TEST BAN TREATY). ALSO INCLUDES US AND USSR MOON EXPLORATION RECORDS. PREPARED FOR USE OF COMMITTEE ON AERONAUTICAL AND SPACE SCIENCES.

3170 US SENATE COMM APPROPRIATIONS
PERSONNEL ADMINISTRATION AND OPERATIONS OF AGENCY FOR INTERNATIONAL DEVELOPMENT: SPECIAL HEARING.
WASHINGTON: GOVT PR OFFICE, 1963, 404 PP.
ANALYSIS OF PEOPLE WHO ARE APPOINTED TO AID AGENCY TO ADMINISTER FOREIGN AID FUNDS AND PROGRAMS. FEELS PEOPLE ARE

INEFFICIENT AND UNDESERVING, AND WASTE US MONEY. SUGGESTS AGENCY PEOPLE HAVE CIVIL SERVICE STATUS AND BE OF TOP QUALITY. INVESTIGATES CERTAIN NATIONS, THEIR PROGRAMS, AND LEADERS.

3171 US SENATE COMM BANKING CURR
BALANCE OF PAYMENTS - 1965.
WASHINGTON: US GOVERNMENT, 1965, 785 PP.
DISCUSSES PROBLEMS OF CONTINUING DEFICITS IN US BALANCE OF PAYMENTS AND RESULTING OUTFLOW OF GOLD. WITNESSES DESCRIBE SOURCES OF IMBALANCE AND BREAKDOWN OF TRADE AREAS IN WHICH DOLLAR OUTFLOW IS MOST SERIOUS. OUTLINES MAJOR TRADE DEFICIENCIES AND EFFECT ON US ECONOMY.

3172 US SENATE COMM GOVT OPERATIONS
ORGANIZING FOR NATIONAL SECURITY.
WASHINGTON: US GOVERNMENT, 1961, 1338 PP.
VOLUME TWO OF THREE- VOLUME PUBLICATION OF SUBCOMMITTEE ON NATIONAL POLICY MACHINERY. CONTAINS STUDIES AND BACKGROUND MATERIALS ON THE DEVELOPMENT, COORDINATION AND EXECUTION OF FOREIGN AND DEFENSE POLICY. VOLUMES ONE AND THREE CONTAIN HEARINGS AND FINDINGS AND RECOMMENDATIONS.

3173 US SENATE COMM GOVT OPERATIONS
ADMINISTRATION OF NATIONAL SECURITY.
WASHINGTON: GOVT PR OFFICE, 1962, 201 PP.
DESCRIBES ADMINISTRATION OF SECURITY PROGRAMS UNDER KENNEDY AND EFFECT OF THIS ON FOREIGN POLICY DEVELOPMENT IN THAT PERIOD. INCLUDES TEXTS OF RELEVANT OFFICIAL STATEMENTS BY JFK, RUSK, MCNAMARA, AND BUNDY. ALSO GIVES RECENT COMMENTS BY ACHESON, NEUSTADT, AND HERTER.

3174 US SENATE COMM GOVT OPERATIONS
REPORT OF A STUDY OF US FOREIGN AID IN TEN MIDDLE EASTERN AND AFRICAN COUNTRIES.
WASHINGTON: GOVT PR OFFICE, 1963, 472 PP.
REVIEW OF US MILITARY AND ECONOMIC PROGRAMS, AND AGREEMENTS FOR THEM IN THESE NATIONS. FINDS NEED FOR RE-EVALUATION OF ESTABLISHED MEANS OF DISPERSING AND ACCOUNTING FOR MONEY SPENT ON PROJECTS, AND METHOD OF SELECTING NATIONS TO RECEIVE AID. GIVES RECOMMENDATIONS AND CRITICISMS OF ALL PROJECTS STUDIED.

3175 US SENATE COMM GOVT OPERATIONS
THE SECRETARY OF STATE AND THE AMBASSADOR.
NEW YORK: FREDERICK PRAEGER, 1964, 203 PP., LC#64-8342.
ANTHOLOGY OF SUBCOMMITTEE'S PAPERS ON THE CONDUCT OF US FOREIGN POLICY. DISCUSSES ROLES OF STATE DEPARTMENT, THE PRESIDENT, AND THE AMERICAN AMBASSADOR IN FOREIGN POLICY OPERATIONS. INCLUDES OBSERVATIONS BY DEAN RUSK ON THE NATIONAL SECURITY POLICY PROCESS.

3176 US SENATE COMM GOVT OPERATIONS
ADMINISTRATION OF NATIONAL SECURITY.
WASHINGTON: US GOVERNMENT, 1964, 190 PP.
REPRODUCES OFFICIAL DOCUMENTS AND STATEMENTS ON STAFFING AND MANAGEMENT OF FOREIGN AFFAIRS AND DEFENSE, AND RECENT COMMENTS BY FORMER OFFICIALS AND STUDENTS OF THE POLICY-MAKING PROCESS. DOCUMENTS COVER PERIOD FROM 1960-64, WITH STATEMENTS BY JFK, MCNAMARA, KENNAN, AND ACHESON.

3177 US SENATE COMM GOVT OPERATIONS
ADMINISTRATION OF NATIONAL SECURITY.
WASHINGTON: GOVT PR OFFICE, 1965, 600 PP.
STAFF REPORTS AND HEARINGS SUBMITTED TO COMMITTEE ON GOVERNMENT OPERATIONS BY ITS SUBCOMMITTEE ON NATIONAL SECURITY STAFFING AND OPERATIONS. INVESTIGATES ROLE OF SECRETARY OF STATE AND HIS DEPARTMENT IN POLICY OF NATIONAL SECURITY, AND ROLE OF US AMBASSADORS IN CONDUCT OF US FOREIGN RELATIONS.

3178 US SENATE COMM GOVT OPERATIONS
POPULATION CRISIS.
WASHINGTON: GOVT PR OFFICE, 1966, 545 PP.
HEARINGS HELD BEFORE SENATE SUBCOMMITTEE ON FOREIGN AID EXPENDITURES OF COMMITTEE ON GOVERNMENT OPERATIONS JANUARY-MARCH, 1966, ON BILL (S. 1676) TO REORGANIZE DEPARTMENT OF STATE AND DEPARTMENT OF HEALTH, EDUCATION, AND WELFARE TO ENABLE BETTER POPULATION CONTROL. AMONG WITNESSES WERE BIOLOGISTS, PHYSICIANS, AND LEADERS OF ORGANIZATIONS CONCERNED WITH VARIOUS ASPECTS OF POPULATION CONTROL.

3179 US SENATE COMM ON FOREIGN REL
A DECADE OF AMERICAN FOREIGN POLICY; BASIC DOCUMENTS, 1941-49.
WASHINGTON: US GOVERNMENT, 1949.
COLLECTION OF MORE IMPORTANT INTERNATIONAL INSTRUMENTS AND OFFICIAL STATEMENTS PERTAINING TO US FOREIGN POLICY. PROVIDES SOURCE FOR DIPLOMATIC PAPERS.

3180 US SENATE COMM ON FOREIGN REL
REVIEW OF THE UNITED NATIONS CHARTER: A COLLECTION OF DOCUMENTS.
WASHINGTON: US GOVERNMENT, 1954, 895 PP.
DOCUMENTS USED BY SENATE SUBCOMMITTEE ON THE UNITED NATIONS CHARTER IN CONSIDERATION OF CONDITIONS OF ITS RENEWAL. INCLUDES TEXT OF BASIC INTERNATIONAL INSTRUMENTS RELATED TO ADOPTION OF CHARTER; DOCUMENTARY HISTORY OF LEGISLATION SINCE 1943 WHICH RELATES TO CHARTER; ILLUSTRATIVE SELECTION OF OFFICIAL STUDIES, ACTS, ETC., RELATED TO RENEWAL AND UN MEMBERS' VIEWS ON CHARTER REVIEW.

3181 US SENATE COMM ON FOREIGN REL
SITUATION IN VIETNAM (2 VOLS.)
WASHINGTON: US GOVERNMENT, 1960, 369 PP.
HEARINGS ON FOREIGN AID PROGRAMS IN VIETNAM BEFORE SUBCOMMITTEE ON STATE DEPARTMENT ORGANIZATION AND PUBLIC AFFAIRS. INVESTIGATES RESULTS OF AID IN TERMS OF BENEFITS FOR US AND FOR VIETNAMESE AND EVALUATES TOTAL VIETNAM AID PROGRAM.

3182 US SENATE COMM ON FOREIGN REL
HEARINGS ON S 1276 A BILL TO AMEND FURTHER THE FOREIGN ASSISTANCE ACT OF 1961.
WASHINGTON: GOVT PR OFFICE, 1963, 764 PP.
STATEMENTS AND MEMORANDA ON PRESIDENT'S FOREIGN AID PROPOSALS FOR FISCAL 1964. DISCUSSES DEVELOPMENT LOANS, CONTRIBUTIONS OF FOREIGN AID BY OTHER COUNTRIES, ROLE OF PRIVATE ENTERPRISE, COST OF FOREIGN AID TO TAXPAYERS, CHARGES OF CORRUPTION IN ADMINISTRATION, ETC.

3183 US SENATE COMM ON FOREIGN REL
HEARINGS ON THE FOREIGN ASSISTANCE PROGRAM.
WASHINGTON: GOVT PR OFFICE, 1965, 772 PP.
STATEMENTS AND MEMORANDA BY SECRETARY OF STATE, ADMINISTRATOR OF AGENCY FOR INTERNATIONAL DEVELOPMENT, AND OTHER PUBLIC OFFICIALS ON DEVELOPMENT FUNDS, US OBJECTIVES, WORK OF INTERNATIONAL ORGANIZATIONS, SELF-HELP PROJECTS, AND OTHER ASPECTS OF US FOREIGN AID PROGRAM IN ASIA, AFRICA, AND LATIN AMERICA.

3184 US SENATE COMM ON FOREIGN REL
UNITED STATES POLICY TOWARD EUROPE (AND RELATED MATTERS)
WASHINGTON: GOVT PR OFFICE, 1966, 524 PP.
RECORD OF EIGHT DAYS OF HEARINGS HELD IN JUNE, 1966, BY SENATE COMMITTEE ON FOREIGN RELATIONS ON US POLICY TOWARD EUROPE. SOME MAJOR ISSUES DISCUSSED INCLUDE EFFECTS OF DE GAULLE'S POLICIES ON RELATIONS BETWEEN NATO NATIONS, QUESTION OF EUROPEAN UNITY, AND US POLICY TOWARD SHARING NUCLEAR POWER WITH NATO NATIONS. EMPHASIS THROUGHOUT HEARINGS IS ON ADAPTATION OF POLICY TO MEET CURRENT NEEDS.

3185 US SENATE COMM ON FOREIGN REL
HEARINGS ON S 2859 AND S 2861.
WASHINGTON: GOVT PR OFFICE, 1966, 752 PP.
STATEMENTS BY PUBLIC AND PRIVATE OFFICIALS ON MILITARY AND ECONOMIC AID, NATURE AND EXTENT OF SOVIET AID, DEVELOPMENT LOANS, ROLE OF PRIVATE ENTERPRISE, VALUE OF MILITARY ASSISTANCE, AND GENERAL ASPECTS OF INTERNATIONAL SECURITY.

3186 US SENATE COMM ON FOREIGN REL
ASIAN DEVELOPMENT BANK ACT.
WASHINGTON: US GOVERNMENT, 1966, 138 PP.
HEARINGS BEFORE COMMITTEE ON FOREIGN RELATIONS ON ASIAN DEVELOPMENT BANK ACT. INCLUDES TESTIMONY BY EUGENE BLACK, PRESIDENTIAL ADVISER ON SOUTHEASTERN ASIAN ECONOMIC AND SOCIAL DEVELOPMENT.

3187 US SENATE COMM ON FOREIGN REL
ARMS SALES AND FOREIGN POLICY (PAMPHLET)
WASHINGTON: US GOVERNMENT, 1967, 13 PP.
STAFF STUDY OF COMMITTEE ON FOREIGN POLICY. CONCLUDES THAT SALE OF ARMS HAS REPLACED GIVING ARMS AS PREDOMINANT FORM OF US MILITARY ASSISTANCE. BELIEVES THAT US MUST REAPPRAISE ADEQUACY OF PRESENT MACHINERY OF POLICY CONTROL AND LEGISLATIVE OVERSIGHT GOVERNING SALE OF ARMS. MAKES SPECIFIC RECOMMENDATIONS FOR IMPROVEMENT.

3188 US SENATE COMM ON FOREIGN REL
BACKGROUND INFORMATION RELATING TO SOUTHEAST ASIA AND VIETNAM (3RD REV. ED.)
WASHINGTON: US GOVERNMENT, 1967, 308 PP.
CONTAINS SUMMARY OF EVENTS IN SOUTHEAST ASIA, 1948-67, DOCUMENTS ON US-VIETNAM RELATIONS SINCE 1950, FIGURES ON US FOREIGN AID TO SOUTH VIETNAM AND ON US CASUALTIES THERE, AND DOCUMENTS PERTAINING TO PROPOSALS OF NORTH VIETNAM, NLF, SOUTH VIETNAM, AND SECRETARY GENERAL OF UN.
TIME/SEQ S/ASIA DIPLOM PEACE

3189 US SENATE COMM ON FOREIGN REL
HUMAN RIGHTS CONVENTIONS.
WASHINGTON: US GOVERNMENT, 1967, 227 PP.
SUBCOMMITTEE HEARINGS OF COMMITTEE ON FOREIGN RELATIONS HELD FEBRUARY AND MARCH, 1967, J.W. FULLBRIGHT PRESIDING. TESTIMONY DEALS WITH CONVENTION ON THE POLITICAL RIGHTS OF WOMEN, CONVENTION CONCERNING THE ABOLITION OF FORCED LABOR, AND A SUPPLEMENTARY SLAVERY CONVENTION. RECOMMENDING SENATE RATIFICATION ARE AJ. GOLDBERG, BAR ASSOCIATION REPRESENTATIVES, AND AFL-CIO MEMBERS.

3190 US SENATE COMM ON FOREIGN REL
UNITED STATES ARMAMENT AND DISARMAMENT PROBLEMS.

WASHINGTON: US GOVERNMENT, 1967, 181 PP.
HEARINGS BEFORE SUBCOMMITTEE ON DISARMAMENT OF COMMITTEE ON FOREIGN RELATIONS HEADED BY ALBERT GORE. INCLUDES DISCUSSION OF STATUS OF DEVELOPMENT OF BALLISTIC AND ANTI-BALLISTIC SYSTEMS IN US AND BRIEFING ON NONPROLIFERATION TREATY, DEPLOYMENT OF NIKE X ANTI-BALLISTIC MISSLE SYSTEM, ARMS SALES, AND OTHER DISARMAMENT AND ARMANENT PROBLEMS.

3191 US SENATE COMM ON FOREIGN REL
INTERNATIONAL DEVELOPMENT AND SECURITY: HEARINGS ON BILL (2 VOLS.)
WASHINGTON: GOVT PR OFFICE, 1961, 1221 PP.
REQUEST TO INCLUDE AS PART OF US FOREIGN AID PROGRAM A FLEXIBLE MILITARY STRATEGY TO PREVENT AGGRESSION AND PROVIDE SECURITY FOR DEVELOPING NATIONS. INCLUDES STATEMENTS OF OPINION, PRO AND CON, AND PROPOSED METHOD FOR SETTING UP SPECIAL POLICY FORCES, ETC., AND GIVING PRESIDENT SPECIAL POWERS.

3192 US SENATE COMM ON JUDICIARY
HEARING BEFORE SUBCOMMITTEE ON COMMITTEE OF JUDICIARY, UNITED STATES SENATE: S. J. RES. 3.
WASHINGTON: GOVT PR OFFICE, 1957, 480 PP.
JUNE 25, 1957 HEARINGS ON PROPOSED AMENDMENT TO CONSTITUTION RELATING TO LEGAL EFFECT OF CERTAIN TREATIES AND OTHER INTERNATIONAL AGREEMENTS. PRESENT WERE SENATORS KEFAUVER, HENNINGS, DIRKSEN.

3193 US SENATE COMM ON JUDICIARY
CONSTITUTIONAL RIGHTS OF MILITARY PERSONNEL.
WASHINGTON: US GOVERNMENT, 1962, 967 PP.
COLLECTION OF STATEMENTS MADE BY PUBLIC OFFICIALS BEFORE SUBCOMMITTEE ON CONSTITUTIONAL RIGHTS ON MILITARY JUSTICE. HEARINGS WERE INITIATED BECAUSE OF INCREASE IN "UNDESIRABLE DISCHARGES" THROUGH ADMINISTRATIVE PROCESS, RAISING QUESTION OF LEGAL SAFEGUARDS.

3194 US SENATE COMM ON JUDICIARY
REFUGEE PROBLEMS IN SOUTH VIETNAM AND LAOS: HEARINGS BEFORE SUBCOMMITTEE TO INVESTIGATE PROBLEMS OF REFUGEES, ESCAPEES.
WASHINGTON: US GOVERNMENT, 1965, 408 PP.
ANALYZES PROBLEM OF REFUGEES IN SOUTH VIETNAM FROM HUMANITARIAN POINT OF VIEW. INVESTIGATES CONDITIONS IN COMMUNIST RULED AREAS, CAUSES AND NATURE OF REFUGEE FLOW, ITS POLITICAL-MILITARY SIGNIFICANCE, COMMUNIST ACTIVITIES, AND ADEQUACY AND EFFECTIVENESS OF US AID. FAVORS ALL POSSIBLE ASSISTANCE TO REFUGEES AS PART OF EFFORT TO SAFEGUARD FREEDOM IN SOUTH VIETNAM.

3195 US SENATE COMM ON JUDICIARY
ANTITRUST EXEMPTIONS FOR AGREEMENTS RELATING TO BALANCE OF PAYMENTS.
WASHINGTON: US GOVERNMENT, 1965, 248 PP.
REPORT OF HEARINGS ON H RES 40, AN ACT TO PROVIDE FOR EXEMPTIONS FROM ANTITRUST LAWS FOR COMPANIES IN INTERNATIONAL TRADING TO ASSIST US IN MAINTAINING FAVORABLE BALANCE OF PAYMENTS. DEBATES WHETHER ANTI-MONOPOLY LAWS OR INTERNATIONAL MONETARY POSITION IS MORE INPORTANT.

3196 US SENATE COMM. GOVT. OPER.
"REVISION OF THE UN CHARTER."
WASHINGTON: G.P.O., 1950, 64 PP.
DEALS WITH EAST-WEST TENSION AND PRESSURE FOR ACTION, AND THE UN IN RELATION TO US FOREIGN POLICY. GIVES INSIGHT INTO SENATE CONCURRENT RESOLUTIONS. CONCLUDES WITH STUDY OF RESPONSIBILITIES OF THE EXECUTIVE AND CONGRESS.

3197 US SENATE SPEC COMM FOR AID
COMPILATION OF STUDIES AND SURVEYS.
WASHINGTON: GOVT PR OFFICE, 1957, 1581 PP.
PRESENTS RESULTS OF STUDIES AND SURVEYS OF US FOREIGN AID PROGRAM. DISCUSSES ROLE OF PRIVATE ORGANIZATIONS, AGRICULTURAL SURPLUS DISPOSAL, AID TECHNIQUES OF COMMUNIST BLOC, AND OPERATION OF US AID PROGRAMS IN ASIA, AFRICA, AND LATIN AMERICA.

3198 US SENATE SPEC COMM FOR AID
HEARINGS BEFORE THE SPECIAL COMMITTEE TO STUDY THE FOREIGN AID PROGRAM.
WASHINGTON: GOVT PR OFFICE, 1957, 745 PP.
STATEMENTS BY PUBLIC AND PRIVATE OFFICIALS ON US FOREIGN AID POLICIES AND OBJECTIVES. EXAMINES COSTS, NEED FOR SEPARATION OF MILITARY AND ECONOMIC AID, ATTITUDE OF US PEOPLE, SOVIET AID, ROLE OF INTERNATIONAL AGENCIES, COMPARISON OF SOVIET AND US AID TECHNIQUES, TECHNICAL ASSISTANCE PROGRAMS, RESPONSIBILITIES OF PRIVATE ENTERPRISE, ETC.

3199 US SENATE SPECIAL COMM FOR AFF
REPORT OF THE SPECIAL COMMITTEE TO STUDY THE FOREIGN AID PROGRAM (PAMPHLET)
WASHINGTON: GOVT PR OFFICE, 1957, 38 PP.
DISCUSSES OBJECTIVES OF FOREIGN AID PROGRAMS IN LIGHT OF NATIONAL SELF-INTEREST SINCE WWII. EXAMINES SHORTCOMINGS IN LEGISLATION AND ADMINISTRATION AND MAKES RECOMMENDATIONS FOR CHANGES AND CLARIFICATION OF OBJECTIVES.

3200 US SUPERINTENDENT OF DOCUMENTS
CATALOGUE OF PUBLIC DOCUMENTS OF CONGRESS AND OF ALL DEPARTMENTS OF THE GOVERNMENT OF THE UNITED STATES.
WASHINGTON: US GOVERNMENT.
COMPREHENSIVE INDEX COVERS PERIOD 1893-1945. INTENDED AS "DICTIONARY" CATALOGUE. ARRANGEMENT IS ALPHABETICAL WITH NUMBER OF DOCUMENT, SESSION TO WHICH IT BELONGS, AND VOLUME IN WHICH BOUND GIVEN IN PARENTHETICAL CLAUSE FOLLOWING EACH ENTRY.

3201 US SUPERINTENDENT OF DOCUMENTS
FOREIGN RELATIONS OF THE UNITED STATES; PUBLICATIONS RELATING TO FOREIGN COUNTRIES (PRICE LIST 65)
WASHINGTON: GOVT PR OFFICE.
SERIALS PUBLICATION OF US GOVERNMENT LISTING GOVERNMENT PUBLICATIONS CURRENTLY AVAILABLE FOR SALE. 42 EDITIONS TO DATE. LATEST EDITION CONTAINS PUBLICATIONS FROM 1955 THROUGH 1966. ENTRIES, GROUPED BY SUBJECT, INCLUDE SEPARATE LISTINGS FOR INDIVIDUAL COUNTRIES. ALSO INCLUDES SOURCES ON AIR LAWS AND TREATIES, FOREIGN ASSISTANCE ACT, COMMUNISM, STATE DEPARTMENT, TREATIES AND CONVENTIONS, ETC.

3202 US SUPERINTENDENT OF DOCUMENTS
GOVERNMENT PERIODICALS AND SUBSCRIPTION SERVICES (PRICE LIST 36)
WASHINGTON: GOVT PR OFFICE.
SERIAL PUBLICATION LISTING US GOVERNMENT PERIODICALS CURRENTLY AVAILABLE FOR SALE. ITEMS LISTED ALPHABETICALLY BY TITLE. SECTION I - LIST OF REGULARLY ISSUED PERIODICALS; SECTION II - MANUALS AND SIMILAR MATERIALS SOLD ON A SUBSCRIPTION BASIS. 126 EDITIONS TO DATE. LATEST EDITION MAY, 1967.

3203 US SUPERINTENDENT OF DOCUMENTS
MONTHLY CATALOG OF UNITED STATES GOVERNMENT PUBLICATIONS.
WASHINGTON: GOVT PR OFFICE.
PUBLISHED MONTHLY SINCE 1895, THIS BASIC INDEX TO FEDERAL PUBLICATIONS LISTS GOVERNMENT DOCUMENTS RECEIVED IN US DOCUMENTS OFFICE THE PREVIOUS MONTH. DOCUMENTS ARE LISTED UNDER GOVERNMENT AGENCIES AND DEPARTMENTS RESPONSIBLE. SUBJECT INDEX APPEARS WITH EACH ISSUE AND CUMULATED INTO ANNUAL INDEX IN DECEMBER ISSUE. INCLUDES US GOVERNMENT PERIODICALS AND SUBSCRIPTIONS.

3204 US SUPERINTENDENT OF DOCUMENTS
TARIFF AND TAXATION (PRICE LIST 37)
WASHINGTON: GOVT PR OFFICE.
SERIES PUBLICATION OF US GOVERNMENT PUBLICATIONS CURRENTLY AVAILABLE FOR SALE LISTING ITEMS BY SUBJECT. TOPICS INCLUDE US CUSTOMS COURT REPORTS, REPORT OF CASES ADJUDGED BEFORE CUSTOMS AND PATENT APPEALS COURT, INTERNAL REVENUE BUREAU, TARIFF AND TRADE, TAX COURT, TARIFF COMMISSION, PROPERTY TAX, ETC. 46 EDITIONS TO DATE. LATEST ISSUE COVERS MATERIALS PUBLISHED FROM 1951 THROUGH 1966.

3205 US SUPERINTENDENT OF DOCUMENTS
LIBRARY OF CONGRESS (PRICE LIST 83)
WASHINGTON: GOVT PR OFFICE.
SERIAL PUBLICATION LISTING US GOVERNMENT PUBLICATIONS CURRENTLY AVAILABLE FOR SALE. MAJORITY OF ITEMS ANNOTATED. INCLUDES BIBLIOGRAPHICAL PUBLICATIONS, 13 EDITIONS TO DATE, CONTAINING PUBLICATIONS FROM 1957 THROUGH 1966. ITEMS ARRANGED BY SUBJECT, INCLUDE MATERIALS ON AFRICA, COPYRIGHTS, CIVIL WAR, EUROPE, SOVIET UNION, INTERNATIONAL MEETINGS AND SCIENTIFIC ORGANIZATIONS, KENNEDY, AND PRESIDENTS OF US.

3206 US SUPERINTENDENT OF DOCUMENTS
SPACE: MISSILES, THE MOON, NASA, AND SATELLITES (PRICE LIST 79A)
WASHINGTON: GOVT PR OFFICE, 1967, 21 PP.
FIRST EDITION OF US GOVERNMENT SERIES LISTING GOVERNMENT MATERIALS CURRENTLY AVAILABLE FOR SALE. MAJORITY OF SOURCES ANNOTATED; ENTRIES PUBLISHED 1959 THROUGH 1966. TOPICS INCLUDE SPACE EDUCATION, EXPLORATION, RESEARCH TECHNOLOGY, NASA CONGRESSIONAL REPORTS, PROJECT APOLLO AND GEMINI, COMMUNICATIONS SATELLITES, INSPECTION, INTERNATIONAL COOPERATION, ETC.

3207 US TARIFF COMMISSION
LIST OF PUBLICATIONS OF THE TARIFF COMMISSION (PAMPHLET)
WASHINGTON: US GOVERNMENT, 1951, 29 PP.
A TABULATED, UNANNOTATED LIST OF PUBLICATIONS RELEASED BY THE TARIFF COMMISSION BETWEEN 1940-51. LISTED ALPHABETICALLY BY SUBJECT AND REPORT DESIGNATION.

3208 US TARIFF COMMISSION
THE TARIFF; A BIBLIOGRAPHY: A SELECT LIST OF REFERENCES.
WASHINGTON: US GOVERNMENT, 1934, 980 PP.
ALPHABETICAL LISTING OF 6,500 ITEMS, BOOKS, PAMPHLETS, AND PERIODICALS AVAILABLE IN US. INCLUDES REFERENCE TO HISTORY, STATE, FEDERAL, AND INTERNATIONAL; THEORY AND POLICY; PRACTICE; TREATIES, ADMINISTRATION; AND ECONOMIC IMPLICATIONS OF TARIFF LAWS. CONTAINS AUTHOR AND SUBJECT INDEXES. INCLUDES ANNOTATIONS WHERE WORK IS NOTABLE OR TITLE OBSCURE.

3209 VAGTS A.
"DEFENSE AND DIPLOMACY: THE SOLDIER AND THE CONDUCT OF FOREIGN RELATIONS."
NEW YORK: COL U, INST WAR-PEACE, 1956.
ATTEMPTS TO REBALANCE DIPLOMATIC AND MILITARY HISTORIOGRAPHY BY PROVIDING, IN HISTORICAL OUTLINE, DESCRIPTION OF TIES BETWEEN DIPLOMACY AND STRATEGY. HISTORICAL ANALYSIS BEGINS WITH EUROPEAN ABSOLUTISM AND CONTINUES THROUGH COLD WAR. WORK CONTAINS EXTENSIVE NOTES AND BIBLIOGRAPHY IN EUROPEAN LANGUAGES.

3210 VAN DEN BERGHE P.L. ED.
AFRICA: SOCIAL PROBLEMS OF CHANGE AND CONFLICT.
SAN FRANCISCO: CHANDLER, 1965, 549 PP., LC#65-15417.
GENERAL READINGS ON AFRICAN CULTURE, SOCIETY, POLITICAL ASPECTS OF SOCIAL CHANGE, URBANIZATION, ECONOMIC DEVELOPMENTS, AND RACIAL CONFLICTS AS RESULT OF SOCIAL CHANGE.

3211 VAN DUSEN H.P.
"HAMMARSKOLD IN THE WORLD'S SERVICE."
UNIVERSITY, 33 (SUMMER 67), 16-17.
THE ARTICLE DEALS WITH THE POLITICAL PHILOSOPHY OF DAG HAMMARSKOLD AND HIS INTEGRITY AS "WORLD SERVANT." IT INCLUDES EXCERPTS FROM ADDRESSES AND LECTURES OF HIS IN WHICH HE EXPOUNDS THE DUTY OF NEUTRALITY IN ACTION TO ONE WHO WOULD SERVE ALL THE INTERESTS OF A COMMUNITY OR WORLD AND NOT JUST PERSONAL OR VESTED INTERESTS OF A FEW.

3212 VAN DYKE V.
INTERNATIONAL POLITICS.
NEW YORK: APPLETON, 1966, 483 PP., LC#57-6219.
DESCRIBES AND EXPLAINS BEHAVIOR OF STATES IN THEIR RELATIONS WITH EACH OTHER. BASED ON ASSUMPTION THAT PROBLEM OF WAR IS MAJOR PROBLEM FACED IN INTERNATIONAL POLITICS. DISCUSSES INTERNATIONAL POLITICS WITHIN FRAMEWORK OF AN ANALOGY WITH DOMESTIC POLITICS.

3213 VAN HOOGSTRATE D.J.
AMERICAN FOREIGN POLICY: REALISTS AND IDEALISTS: A CATHOLIC INTERPRETATION.
ST LOUIS: HERDER BOOK CO, 1960, 332 PP., LC#60-9130.
TREATS PHILOSOPHICAL TOPICS OF NATURE OF MAN, NATURAL LAW, ORIGINAL SIN, ETC., PLUS COLONIALISM AND WAR, FROM VIEW OF REALIST, IDEALIST, AND CATHOLIC. REVIEWS THEORIES OF FAMED MEN ON SUBJECT. APPLIES CATHOLIC DOCTRINES AS BEST SOLUTIONS TO US FOREIGN POLICY PROBLEMS.

3214 VAN SLYCK P.
PEACE: THE CONTROL OF NATIONAL POWER.
BOSTON: BEACON PRESS, 1963, 186 PP., LC#63-21565.
SUBTITLED "A GUIDE FOR THE CONCERNED CITIZEN ON PROBLEMS OF DISARMAMENT AND STRENGTHENING OF THE UNITED NATIONS." ANALYZES MAJOR ISSUES IN WORLD AFFAIRS AND PROPOSALS FOR RESTRUCTURING PRESENT WORLD. ISSUES INCLUDE CUBAN MISSILE CRISIS, INTERNATIONAL LAW AND CONTROL OF FORCE, FINANCING PEACE, PROBLEMS OF WORLD AUTHORITY, ROLE OF UN, AND PROBLEMS OF AND PROSPECTS FOR ARMS CONTROL.

3215 VAN VALKENBURG S.
"ELEMENTS OF POLITICAL GEOGRAPHY."
ENGLEWOOD CLIFFS: PRENTICE HALL, 1944.
TREATS ELEMENTS THROUGH MODERN REGIONAL EXAMPLES. CONTAINS GENERAL DISCUSSION OF PROBLEMS OF POLITICAL GEOGRAPHY. "LEITMOTIV" OF WORK IS THEORY OF CYCLE TREND IN THE DEVELOPMENT OF NATIONS. EXAMINES PHYSICAL, ECONOMIC, AND HUMAN FACTORS IN POLITICAL-GEOGRAPHICAL EVALUATION OF STATE WITH SPECIAL REFERENCE TO FRANCE. TREATS SUBJECT OF COLONIAL EXPANSION IN CONCLUSION. INCLUDES ENGLISH BIBLIOGRAPHY.

3216 VAN WAGENEN R.W.
SOME VIEWS OF AMERICAN DEFENSE OFFICIALS ABOUT THE UNITED NATIONS (PAPER)
CAMBRIDGE: MIT CTR INTL STUDIES, 1959, 47 PP.
ANALYZES OPINIONS TOWARD UN AND ITS ROLE IN PROMOTING US NATIONAL OBJECTIVES; BASED ON INTERVIEWS WITH 25 DEPARTMENT OF DEFENSE OFFICIALS. PRIMARILY CONCERNED WITH THREE ISSUES: ABILITY OF US TO SURVIVE NUCLEAR WAR IN NEAR FUTURE, POSSIBILITY THAT WORLD PEACE CAN EVER BE ACHIEVED AND UN AS VEHICLE TO CARRY OUT US POLICY OR AS MECHANISM TO NARROW GAP BETWEEN EAST AND WEST.

3217 VANCE H.L., CLAGETT H.L.
GUIDE TO THE LAW AND LEGAL LITERATURE OF MEXICO.
WASHINGTON: LIBRARY OF CONGRESS, 1945, 269 PP.
PART OF SERIES SPONSORED BY LAW LIBRARY OF CONGRESS. SURVEY OF DEVELOPMENT OF LEGAL THEORY AND PRACTICE AND LITERATURE OF LAW. REVIEWS BIBLIOGRAPHIC ADVANCES, COLLECTIONS, PERIODICALS, DICTIONARIES. SECTIONS ON PHILOSOPHY OF LAW, COMMERCIAL, CRIMINAL AND INTERNATIONAL LAW, JUDICIAL SYSTEM, CIVIL AND CRIMINAL PROCEDURE. INDEX OF AUTHORS INCLUDED.

3218 VANDENBOSCH A., HOGAN W.N.
THE UN: BACKGROUND, ORGANIZATION, FUNCTIONS, ACTIVITIES.
NEW YORK: MCGRAW HILL, 1952, 456 PP.
OUTLINES COMPLEX OF FACTORS INVOLVED IN UN PROCEDURES AND PRACTISES. EMPHASIZES THAT FIRST PURPOSE OF UN SYSTEM IS COLLECTIVE SECURITY. TRACES DEVELOPMENT OF INTERNATIONAL COOPERATION TO PRESERVE HUMAN RIGHTS AND FUNDAMENTAL FREEDOMS.

3219 VANDENBOSCH A.
"THE SMALL STATES IN INTERNATIONAL POLITICS AND ORGANIZATION."
J. POLIT., 26 (MAY 64), 293-312.
TRACES THE HISTORY OF SMALL STATES IN INTERNATIONAL POLITICS SINCE THE CONGRESS OF VIENNA AND THE INCREASING IMPORTANCE OF SMALL STATES ON THE WORLD STAGE SINCE THE ADVENT OF THE UN.

3220 VANDERPOL A.
LA DOCTRINE SCOLASTIQUE DU DROIT DE GUERRE.
PARIS: LIBRAIRIE A. PEDONE ,1919, 434 PP.
BELIEVES THAT THERE WAS A DOCTRINE OF WAR, FOUNDED ON CHRISTIAN TRADITION, WHICH BEGAN IN MIDDLE AGES AND LASTED UNTIL SEVENTEENTH CENTURY. WAR WAS CONSIDERED AN ACT OF JUSTICE AND A PUNISHMENT OF FOREIGN EVIL-DOERS. DOCUMENTS THEORY FROM NUMEROUS SOURCES, AND INDICATES SOURCES THAT CONTRADICT IT. REPRODUCES IMPORTANT CHAPTERS OF AQUINAS, VICTORIA, AND SUAREZ ON RIGHT OF WAR.

3221 VARG P.A.
MISSIONARIES, CHINESE, AND DIPLOMATS: THE AMERICAN PROTESTANT MISSIONARY MOVEMENT IN CHINA, 1890-1952.
PRINCETON: PRINCETON U PRESS, 1958, 335 PP., LC#58-7134.
SEES HISTORY OF PROTESTANT MISSIONS IN CHINA AS A PROBLEM IN RELATIONSHIP BETWEEN TWO BASICALLY DIFFERENT CULTURES: WEST AND EAST. INTEREST CENTERS ON DIFFICULTIES IN ATTEMPTING TO EXPORT THE AMERICAN IDEOLOGIES OF CHRISTIANITY, DEMOCRACY, OR CAPITALISM. SHEDS LIGHT ON CONTEMPORARY PROPAGANDA PROBLEMS.

3222 VARLEY D.H.
A BIBLIOGRAPHY OF ITALIAN COLONISATION IN AFRICA WITH A SECTION ON ABYSSINIA.
LONDON: ROYAL INST OF INTL AFF, 1936, 92 PP.
UNANNOTATED LIST OF THE MORE IMPORTANT PUBLICATIONS ON ITALIAN COLONIZATION, ARRANGED CHRONOLOGICALLY BEGINNING WITH THOSE OF LATEST DATE. PRIMARILY ITALIAN AND ENGLISH MATERIALS FROM 1910 ON SPECIAL SECTION ON ETHIOPIA.

3223 VASAK K.
"DE LA CONVENTION EUROPEENNE A LA CONVENTION AFRICAINE DES DROITS DE L'HOMME."
REV. JURID. POLIT. OUTREMER, 16 (JAN.-MARCH 62), 59-76.
POINTS OUT INFLUENCE OF EUROPEAN CONVENTION ON HUMAN RIGHTS ON POLICIES OF DEVELOPING AFRICAN COUNTRIES. ANALYZES PATTERNS OF POLITICAL EVENTS IN CONGO AND KENYA. CONCLUDES WITH PERSPECTIVES ON AFRICAN ECONOMIC AND POLITICAL UNION.

3224 VEBLEN T.B.
AN INQUIRY INTO THE NATURE OF PEACE AND THE TERMS OF ITS PERPETUATION.
NEW YORK: MACMILLAN, 1917, 367 PP.
CONCERNS TERMS UPON WHICH PEACE CAN BE INSTITUTED AND PERPETUATED, CONDITIONS IN WORLD SITUATION WHICH WOULD MAKE PEACE POSSIBLE, AND EFFECTS OF ESTABLISHING PEACE. BELIEVES PEACE WILL BE OBTAINED IN SPITE OF THE STATE, RATHER THAN THROUGH IT. APPEALS TO PATRIOTISM HAVE BEEN USED TO DETRIMENT OF ESTABLISHING PEACE. SUGGESTS NEUTRALIZATION OF CITIZENSHIP AND ABOLITION OF FINANCIAL COMPETITION.

3225 VECCHIO G.D.
L'ETAT ET LE DROIT.
PARIS: DALLOZ, 1964, 184 PP.
DISCUSSES BASIC ELEMENTS OF STATE (TERRITORY, PEOPLE, SOVEREIGNTY), HISTORICAL EVOLUTION, EXECUTIVE, LEGISLATIVE, AND JUDICIAL FUNCTIONS, INTERNATIONAL LEGAL COMMUNITY WITH PARTICULAR REFERENCE TO UN, AND CONCLUDES WITH DISCUSSION OF AIM OF STATE. INCLUDES BRIEF ANALYSIS OF FUNCTION OF ITALIAN LEGISLATURE UNDER CONSTITUTION.

3226 VELIKONJA J.
"ITALIAN IMMIGRANTS IN THE UNITED STATES IN THE MID-SIXTIES"
INTERNATIONAL MIGRATION REVIEW, 1 (SUMMER 67), 25-37.
MIGRATORY MOVEMENT OF ITALIANS IS BEING REDUCED TO A FEW SELECTED FLOWS. EXHIBITS MINIMUM OF DISPERSAL TO RURAL AREAS AND DISTINCT PREFERENCE FOR LARGEST METROPOLITAN AREAS DUE TO EXISTING ITALIAN CLUSTERS. LITTLE CHANGE IN GEOGRAPHIC PATTERNS OF MIGRANTS SINCE 1900, BUT CHANGE IN ECONOMIC OPPORTUNITIES EVIDENCED IN REDUCED FLOWS TO MINING TOWNS.

3227 VELYAMINOV G.
AFRICA AND THE COMMON MARKET (PAMPHLET)
NEW YORK: G VELYAMINOV, 1964, 20 PP.
MAINTAINS THAT CHANGE FROM COLONIAL TO NATIONAL ECONOMY IS NECESSARY FOR ECONOMIC PROGRESS IN AFRICA. TRADE IS KEY FACTOR IN GROWTH. QUESTIONS EQUALITY AND BENEFITS OF AFFILIATION WITH EUROPEAN COMMON MARKET, STATING THAT IT IS MORE LIKE SITUATION OF NEO-COLONIALISM. ADVOCATES AFRICA'S SEPARATION FROM COMMON MARKET AND CLOSER ALLIANCES WITH SOCIALIST COUNTRIES.

3228 VERBA S., BRODY R.A., PARKER E.B.

"PUBLIC OPINION AND THE WAR IN VIETNAM."
AM. POL. SCI. REV., 61 (JUNE 67), 317-333.
RESULTS OF SURVEY OF AMERICAN ATTITUDES ON VIETNAM WAR TO DETERMINE ROLE OF PUBLIC OPINION IN INFLUENCING FOREIGN POLICY ON LIMITED WARS AND TO EXAMINE RELATIONSHIP OF PUBLIC OPINION POLLS TO ACTUAL POLICY-MAKING.

3229 VERNON R.
"A TRADE POLICY FOR THE 1960'S."
FOR. AFF., 39 (APR. 61), 458-70.
BELIEVES PRINCIPAL CONTRIBUTION OF AN APPROPIATE US TRADE POLICY IN THE NEXT DECADE IS POLITICAL RATHER THAN ECONOMIC, AND THAT GOVERNMENT ENCOURAGEMENT OF INCREASED INTERNATIONAL TRADE IS THE NECESSARY FIRST OBJECTIVE.

3230 VEROFF J.
"AFRICAN STUDENTS IN THE UNITED STATES."
J. SOC. ISSUES, 19 (JULY 63), 48-60.
THROUGH THE USE OF QUESTIONNAIRES, AUTHOR ASSESSES THE ATTITUDE OF AFRICAN STUDENTS TOWARD THE USA. DIFFERENTIATES BETWEEN STUDENTS WHO HAVE BEEN IN U.S. FOR A PERIOD OF TIME AND THOSE NEWLY ARRIVED SCHOLARS, ATTEMPTING TO DEMONSTRATE HOW ATTITUDES HAVE CHANGED IN THE INTERIM.

3231 VIEN N.C.
SEEKING THE TRUTH.
NEW YORK: VANTAGE, 1966, 195 PP.
NARRATION BY MEMBER OF DAI'S CABINET ON SITUATION IN VIETNAM AFTER FRENCH DEFEAT. TELLS STORY OF FRENCH ATTACK ON ONE VILLAGE AND EFFECT ON PEOPLE. EMPHASIZES ACTIONS, EFFORTS, AND FINAL RESIGNATION OF QUY, MINISTER OF AGRICULTURE.

3232 VIET J.
INTERNATIONAL COOPERATION AND PROGRAMMES OF ECONOMIC AND SOCIAL DEVELOPMENT.
PARIS: UNESCO, 1962, 107 PP.
ANNOTATED BIBLIOGRAPHY OF 1,141 BOOKS, ARTICLES, AND PAPERS CONCERNED WITH QUESTIONS OF INTERNATIONAL COOPERATION PROGRAMS RELATING TO THEIR DEFINITION, FORMULATION, AND EXECUTION. ENTRIES ORGANIZED BY THEIR CLASSIFICATION INTO BILATERAL, MULTILATERAL, AND REGIONAL ASSISTANCE PROGRAMS. TITLES OF DOCUMENTS PUBLISHED BY UN QUOTED IN FRENCH AND ENGLISH. COVERS MATERIAL ISSUED FROM 1944 THROUGH 1960.

3233 VIGNES D.
"L'AUTORITE DES TRAITES INTERNATIONAUX EN DROIT INTERNE."
ETUD. DR. COMP., 23 (1962), 475-85.
EMPLOYES QUANTITATIVE ANALYSIS TO ASCERTAIN FACTORS NECESSARY TO INSURE APPLICABILITY OF AN INTERNATIONAL TREATY TO NATIONAL LAW. INCLUDES ANALYSIS OF ARTICLE 55 OF 1958 FRENCH CONSTITUTION.

3234 VIGON J.
TEORIA DEL MILITARISMO.
MADRID: EDICIONES RIALP, 1955, 324 PP.
REFLECTION ON MILITARISM IN WESTERN WORLD, INCLUDING ITS RELATION TO NATIONALISM, IMPERIALISM, PACIFISM, ANTIMILITARISM, MILITARY INTERVENTION, AS WELL AS POLITICAL IMPLICATIONS OF MILITARISM.

3235 VINACKE H.M.
A HISTORY OF THE FAR EAST IN MODERN TIMES (6TH ED.)
NEW YORK: APPLETON, 1959, 877 PP., LC#59-7077.
A HISTORY OF CHINA, JAPAN, KOREA, AND EASTERN RUSSIA SINCE THE TIME OF THE MOVEMENT TO BRING CHINA INTO AN ENLARGED CONTACT WITH THE WORLD. FOCUSES ON THE POLITICAL, ECONOMIC, AND SOCIAL STRUCTURES OF ASIAN COUNTRIES, AND THE WESTERN IMPACT ON THESE INSTITUTIONS.

3236 VINER J.
STUDIES IN THE THEORY OF INTERNATIONAL TRADE.
NEW YORK: HARPER, 1937, 650 PP.
TRACES EVOLUTION OF THE MODERN THEORY OF INTERNATIONAL TRADE FROM ITS BEGINNINGS IN THE 17TH AND 18TH CENTURIES. ALSO EXAMINES VARIOUS CONTEMPORARY THEORIES ON SUBJECT.

3237 VINER J.
TRADE RELATIONS BETWEEN FREE-MARKET AND CONTROLLED ECONOMIES
NEW YORK: COLUMBIA U. PRESS, 1943, 92 PP.
DEALS WITH PROBLEMS OF COMMERCIAL POLICY WHICH ARISE FOR ANY PARTICULAR COUNTRY WHICH DOES NOT WISH TO SUBJECT ITS FOREIGN TRADE TO DIRECT REGULATION, WHEN OTHER COUNTRIES IT TRADEW WITH DO. EXAMINES REASONS FOR EXCHANGE CONTROL, ITS USE AS AN INSTRUMENT OF MONOPOLISTIC TRADING AND ECONOMIC DEVELOPMENT, IMPORT QUOTAS, AND GOVERNMENTS AS FOREIGN TRADERS.

3238 VINER J.
INTERNATIONAL ECONOMICS.
GLENCOE: FREE PR., 1951, 381 PP.
COLLECTION OF PAPERS REFER TO MAJOR POLICY ISSUES. PROVIDE THEIR HISTORICAL BACKGROUND AND PRESENT METHODS OF ANALYZING THEM. COVER INTERNATIONAL TRADE, FINANCE, DIPLOMACY, ECONOMIC COOPERATION, AND AMERICAN FOREIGN POLICY.

3239 VINER J.
"ECONOMIC FOREIGN POLICY ON THE NEW FRONTIER."
FOR. AFF., 39 (JULY 61), 560-77.
SCORES KENNEDY ON PROTECTIONIST COMMERCIAL POLICY TO PROMOTE TARIFF REDUCTION AND FOR CONTINUING ILLOGICAL FARM PROGRAM. COMMENDS KENNEDY ON PROPOSALS REORGANIZING FOREIGN AID PROGRAM. ANALYZES REMEDIES TO BALANCE-OF-PAYMENT DEFICIT.

3240 VINER J.
"REPORT OF THE CLAY COMMITTEE ON FOREIGN AID: A SYMPOSIUM."
POLIT. SCI. QUART., 78 (SEPT. 63), 321-61.
REPORT ON FOREIGN AID. STATES THAT THERE ARE REASONS FOR CONCERN WITH BOTH THE OBJECTIVES OF THE CURRENT PROGRAM OF FOREIGN AID AND WITH ITS ADMINISTRATION. ALMOST UNANIMOUS RECOMMENDATION OF DECREASE OR ABOLITION OF AID IN A NUMBER OF COUNTRIES.

3241 VINOGRADOFF P.
OUTLINES OF HISTORICAL JURISPRUDENCE (2 VOLS.)
LONDON: OXFORD U PR, 1920, 673 PP.
ANALYSIS OF METHODS AND SCHOOLS OF JURISPRUDENCE, RELATION OF LAW TO LOGIC, PSYCHOLOGY, SOCIAL SCIENCE, AND POLITICAL THEORY. DISCUSSION OF ORIGINS OF JURISPRUDENCE IN PRIMITIVE SOCIETY, FAMILY, CLAN AND TRIBE, PARTICULAR ASPECTS OF ARYAN CULTURE. SECOND VOLUME BASED ON ANALYSIS OF GREEK JURISPRUDENCE IN AGE OF DEMOCRACY. BIBLIOGRAPHY INCLUDED. ITEMS IN GERMAN, FRENCH, LATIN, ETC.

3242 VINSON J.C.
THE PARCHMENT PEACE: THE UNITED STATES SENATE AND THE WASHINGTON CONFERENCE, 1921-1922.
ATHENS: U OF GEORGIA PRESS, 1955, 259 PP., LC#55-6913.
EXAMINES ROLE OF US SENATE IN SHAPING AMERICAN FOREIGN POLICY IN CRITICAL POST-WWI PERIOD. DISCUSSES SHIFT IN GOVERNMENTAL AUTHORITY FROM PRESIDENT TOWARD CONGRESS. DESCRIBES MOVEMENT TOWARD ISOLATIONISM BUILT ON BELIEF IN UNIMPAIRED SOVEREIGNTY, IN SOLVING INTERNATIONAL PROBLEMS BY CONFERENCES, IN ACCEPTANCE OF MORAL LAW, AND IN MAINTENANCE OF PEACE VIA DISARMAMENT.

3243 VIRALLY M.
"VERS UNE REFORME DU SECRETARIAT DES NATIONS UNIES."
INT. ORGAN., 15 (SPRING 61), 236-55.
EXAMINES ROLE OF UN SECRETARY GENERAL. ASSUMES THAT AUTHORITY HE HAS ACQUIRED HAS BECOME KEYSTONE OF UN DIPLOMACY. STATES THAT SOVIET PROPOSAL WOULD DESTROY INTERNATIONAL CHARACTER OF THE SECRETARIAT.

3244 VISSON A.
AS OTHERS SEE US.
NEW YORK: DOUBLEDAY, 1948, 252 PP.
DISCUSSES EUROPEAN MISCONCEPTIONS ABOUT USA. ATTRIBUTES THEIR VIEWS TO DIFFERENCE IN VALUES.

3245 VLASIC I.A.
"THE SPACE TREATY* A PRELIMINARY EVALUATION."
CALIF. LAW REV., 55 (MAY 67), 507-519.
GIVES BACKGROUND OF SPACE TREATY AND DISCUSSES CONDITIONS WHICH INFLUENCED ITS FORMULATION. ANALYSIS OF PRINCIPAL FEATURES AND DEFICIENCIES OF TREATY. DISCUSSES EMERGENCE OF GENERAL ASSEMBLY AS PRINCIPAL WORLD COMMUNITY ORGAN FOR SETTING STANDARDS OF CONDUCT IN SPACE AGE AND THE DAMAGE DONE TO PRESTIGE BY CONCLUSION OF SPACE TREATY.

3246 VOELKMANN K.
HERRSCHER VON MORGEN?
VIENNA: ECON VERLAG, 1964, 412 PP.
STUDIES "THIRD WORLD," WHICH MAY RULE TOMARROW'S WORLD. WHILE EUROPE HAS DECLINED IN IMPORTANCE THE DEVELOPING NATIONS HAVE MOVED FROM PERIPHERY OF WORLD POLITICS TOWARD CENTER. STUDIES NATIONS THROUGHOUT WORLD AND TRENDS THAT DETERMINE THEIR CONDUCT VIS-A-VIS THE GREAT POWERS.

3247 VOGT W.
PEOPLE: CHALLENGE TO SURVIVAL.
NY: WILLIAM SLOAN ASSOCIATES, 1960, 257 PP., LC#60-13347.
PICTURE OF POPULATION PROBLEMS ALL OVER THE WORLD AS SEEN BY A TRAVELER WHO TELLS INTIMATE STORIES OF SITUATIONS IN OVERPOPULATED AREAS. SHOWS TRAGEDIES THAT MAY OCCUR IF NOTHING IS DONE, BOTH ABROAD AND IN US. REVIEWS EFFORTS OF VARIOUS ORGANIZATIONS AND GOVERNMENTS TO COMBAT POPULATION EXPLOSION, BUT PLEADS THAT ACTION BE TAKEN FASTER AND ON A GREATER SCALE.

3248 VOLPICELLI Z.
RUSSIA ON THE PACIFIC AND THE SIBERIAN RAILWAY.
LONDON: MARSTON, 1899, 373 PP.
BRIEF HISTORY OF RUSSIAN EXPANSION TO THE URAL AND SUBSEQUENT CONQUEST OF SIBERIA. ANALYZES POLITICAL CAUSES OF THE ANNEXATION OF AMUR REGION, DEPICTS TRENDS OF RUSSIAN EXPANSION.

3249 VON BECKERATH E., BRINKMANN C. ET AL.
HANDWORTERBUCH DER SOCIALWISSENSCHAFTEN (II VOLS.)
STUTTGART: FISCHER VERLAG, 1956.

A HANDBOOK OF SOCIAL SCIENCE ARRANGED TOPICALLY AND ALPHABETICALLY. DISCUSSES SUCH CULTURAL ASPECTS AS UNEMPLOYMENT, FOREIGN TRADE, BANKSPACE SYSTEMS, VOTING RIGHTS AND APPENDS TO EACH A BIBLIOGRAPHY OF THE LITERATURE. INCLUDED ARE FOREIGN MATERIALS, THOUGH MAJORITY ARE IN GERMAN.

3250 VON GLAHN G.
LAW AMONG NATIONS: AN INTRODUCTION TO PUBLIC INTERNATIONAL LAW.
NEW YORK: MACMILLAN, 1965, 293 PP., LC#65-10402.
TEXT FOR UNDERGRADUATE INTERNATIONAL LAW COURSES. MOST OF THE 34 CHAPTERS ARE FOLLOWED BY LISTS OF FROM FIVE TO TEN SUGGESTED READINGS IN OTHER SOURCES. SOME ALSO LIST CASES. INCLUDES BOOKS AND PERIODICALS, ALL IN ENGLISH. EXTENSIVE FOOTNOTES WITH REFERENCE TO OTHER MATERIAL. SUGGESTED READINGS KEPT TO MATERIAL GENERALLY AVAILABLE IN UNDERGRADUATE LIBRARIES.

3251 VON HALLER A.
DIE LETZTEN WOLLEN DIE ERSTEN SEIN.
DUSSELDORF: ECON VERLAG, 1963, 297 PP.
DISCUSSES ROLE OF WEST IN SUPPORTING DEVELOPING COUNTRIES OF AFRICA AND PREVENTING SUBVERSION OF THEIR NATIONAL INTEGRITY BY COMMUNISM. ALSO DISCUSSES WESTERN RESPONSIBILITY TOWARD UNDERDEVELOPED COUNTRIES IN ASIA.

3252 VON HARPE W.
DIE SOWJETUNION FINNLAND UND SKANDANAVIEN, 1945-1955.
TUBINGEN: BOHLAU VERLAG, 1956, 67 PP.
TWO REPORTS ABOUT POSTWAR INTERNATIONAL RELATIONSHIPS, CONCENTRATING ON USSR'S RELATIONSHIPS WITH FINLAND AND SCANDINAVIA. TREATS FINNISH PARTICIPATION IN WWII, RUSSIAN-FINNISH MUTUAL ASSISTANCE PACT, FINLAND'S SPECIAL POSITION IN SOVIET SPHERE OF INFLUENCE, POST-STALIN RELATIONSHIPS, RETURN OF PORKKALA; POSTWAR NORTHERN EUROPE, SCANDINAVIA BETWEEN ATLANTIC PACT AND EASTERN BLOC.

3253 VON GLAHN G.
LAW AMONG NATIONS: AN INTRODUCTION TO PUBLIC INTERNATIONAL LAW.
NEW YORK: MACMILLAN, 1965, 768 PP., $9.95.
PRESENTS ISSUES OF FOLLOWING TOPICS: LAW OF NATIONS, INTERNATIONAL LAW, LAW AND THE INDIVIDUAL, TERRITORIAL QUESTIONS, INTERNATIONAL TRANSACTIONS, AND WAR. GIVES FACTS, DECISIONS, AND REASONING OF SIGNIFICANT CASES.

3254 VORSPAN A., LIPMAN E.J.
JUSTICE AND JUDAISM.
NEW YORK: UN AM HEB CONGREG, 1959, 271 PP.
COMPREHENSIVELY APPLIES JUDAISM TO ALL PHASES OF MODERN LIFE, CONSIDERING EACH IN CONTEXT OF JEWISH PHILOSOPHY. GIVES RESULTING ATTITUDES ABOUT OTHER RELIGIONS, INTERNATIONAL RELATIONS, ECONOMICS ETC. CONSIDERS CULTURAL IMPLICATIONS OF PERVASIVE RELIGIOUS ORIENTATION.

3255 VOSS E.H.
NUCLEAR AMBUSH: THE TEST-BAN TRAP.
CHICAGO: REGNERY, 1963, 612 PP., $6.50.
A COMPREHENSIVE, CAREFULLY DOCUMENTED REVIEW OF NUCLEAR DEVELOPMENT AND THE HISTORY OF THE TEST-BAN NEGOTIATIONS.

3256 VYAS R.
DAWNING ON THE CAPITOL: US CONGRESS AND INDIA.
CALCUTTA: MASCAT PUBLNS LTD, 1966, 117 PP.
RECOGNIZING IMPORTANCE OF US CONGRESS IN FORMULATION OF US FOREIGN POLICY, STUDIES ATTITUDES OF CONGRESS TOWARD INDIA AS THEY MAY BE SEEN IN "CONGRESSIONAL RECORD" AND OTHER CONGRESSIONAL DOCUMENTS.

3257 WABEKE B.H. ED.
A GUIDE TO DUTCH BIBLIOGRAPHIES.
WASHINGTON: LIBRARY OF CONGRESS, 1951, 193 PP., LC#51-60014.
A PARTIALLY ANNOTATED BIBLIOGRAPHY OF 756 BOOKS, PAMPHLETS, AND PERIODICALS, ALL DUTCH PUBLICATIONS THAT SERVE A BIBLIOGRAPHICAL PURPOSE. INTENDED TO FACILITATE THE STUDY OF THE NETHERLANDS, INDONESIA, SURINAM, CURACAO, AS WELL AS FLEMISH LITERATURE AND HISTORY. TOPICALLY ARRANGED, AND INDEXED BY AUTHOR, TITLE, AND SUBJECT.

3258 WADSWORTH J.J.
THE PRICE OF PEACE.
NEW YORK: FREDERICK PRAEGER, 1962, 127 PP., LC#62-13748.
ANALYSIS OF QUESTION OF DISARMAMENT AND INTERNATIONAL PEACE. DISCUSSES PAST NEGOTIATIONS AND MILITARY AND POLITICAL FACTORS INVOLVED IN TREATY NEGOTIATIONS AND ARMS CONTROL.

3259 WAELDER R.
PROGRESS AND REVOLUTION* A STUDY OF THE ISSUES OF OUR AGE.
NEW YORK: INTERNATIONAL U PR, 1967, 372 PP., LC#66-28501.
BASIC OUTLINE OF MODERN HISTORY WITH FOCUS ON LAST 2 CENTURIES. EXAMINES TECHNOLOGICAL AND MORAL PROGRESS AND ANALYZES POWER, STRUCTURE OF GOVERNMENTS, REVOLUTIONS, AND IDEOLOGIES. ALSO REVIEWS CRISES OF MID-20TH CENTURY RESULTING FROM CONFRONTATION OF WEST, COMMUNIST WORLD, AND THE "THIRD WORLD."

3260 WAINHOUSE D.W.
REMNANTS OF EMPIRE: THE UNITED NATIONS AND THE END OF COLONIALISM.
NEW YORK: HARPER ROW, 1964, 153 PP.
CONSIDERS BALANCE SHEET OF WESTERN COLONIALISM AND RELATIONSHIPS BEING DEVELOPED IN PROCESS OF LIQUIDATING LAST VESTIGES OF EMPIRE. DISCUSSES TERRITORIES RANGING FROM LARGE DEPENDENCIES TO TINY ISLANDS, IN FRAMEWORK OF PRESSING ISSUES AND METROPOLES INVOLVED.

3261 WAINHOUSE D.W.
INTERNATIONAL PEACE OBSERVATION: A HISTORY AND FORECAST.
BALTIMORE: JOHNS HOPKINS PRESS, 1966, 663 PP., LC#66-14376.
CONCERNED WITH THE METHODS AND PROCEDURES THAT HAVE BEEN TRIED SINCE 1920 TO PREVENT WAR OR LIMIT CONFLICTS. DEALS IN PARTICULAR WITH THE USE OF THIRD-PARTY ARBITRATION. EMPHASIZES WORK OF THE LEAGUE OF NATIONS, THE UN, AND THE OAS. EVALUATES AND ANALYZES PAST PRECEDENTS AND MAKES RECOMMENDATIONS FOR THE FUTURE.

3262 WALKER A.A. ED.
OFFICIAL PUBLICATIONS OF SIERRA LEONE AND GAMBIA.
WASHINGTON: LIBRARY OF CONGRESS, 1963, 92 PP., LC#63-60090.
BIBLIOGRAPHY OF DOCUMENTS PUBLISHED SINCE ESTABLISHMENT OF CENTRAL GOVERNMENT AND PERTINENT PUBLICATIONS OF BRITISH GOVERNMENT RELATED TO ITS COLONIAL ADMINISTRATION. ARRANGED BY COUNTRY AND SUBDIVIDED ALPHABETICALLY BY AUTHOR AND TITLE UNDER PUBLISHER. CENSUS AND DEVELOPMENT PLANNING UNDER SEPARATE TOPIC. AUTHOR AND SUBJECT INDEX INCLUDED. CONTAINS 730 ITEMS IN ENGLISH.

3263 WALKER A.A. ED.
THE RHODESIAS AND NYASALAND: A GUIDE TO OFFICIAL PUBLICATIONS.
WASHINGTON: LIBRARY OF CONGRESS, 1965, 285 PP., LC#65-60089.
COMPREHENSIVE BIBLIOGRAPHY OF 1,889 ITEMS ON PUBLISHED RECORDS OF FORMER FEDERATION OF RHODESIA AND NYASALAND, FROM 1889-1963. INCLUDES PUBLICATIONS OF BRITISH COLONIAL GOVERNMENT. ARRANGED GEOGRAPHICALLY, BY GOVERNMENTAL DEPARTMENTS AND AUTHORS. INCLUDES INDEX.

3264 WALKER E.A.
BRITAIN AND SOUTH AFRICA.
LONDON: LONGMANS, GREEN & CO, 1943, 64 PP.
BRIEF HISTORY OF CAPE COLONY, BRITISH COLONIAL POLICY, BOER WAR, AND RISE OF UNION IN 1910. CONCLUDES WITH DISCUSSION OF SOUTH AFRICA'S ATTITUDE TOWARD RISE OF NAZISM AND HER ENTRY INTO WAR ON ALLIED SIDE.

3265 WALKER H.
"THE INTERNATIONAL LAW OF COMMODITY AGREEMENTS."
LAW CONTEMP. PROBL., 28 (SPRING 63), 392-415.
DISCUSSES GATT PROVISIONS, OBLIGATIONS TOWARD NON-MEMBERS, PRIMARY COMMODITY AND COTTON TEXTILE AGREEMENTS, AND THE HAVANA CHARTER. SUGGESTS THAT GENERAL AGREEMENTS ARE FRAMED TO PROMOTE INTERNATIONAL TRADE AND EFFICIENT DISTRIBUTION OF PRODUCTION BY REMOVING ARTIFICIAL BARRIERS THAT PREVENT MARKET DETERMINATION OF FREE TRADE.

3266 WALKER R.L.
"THE WEST AND THE 'NEW ASIA'."
MODERN AGE, 11 (SPRING 67),153-161.
CONTRASTS ANTI-COLONIALIST ATTITUDES OF ASIA IN 1950'S WITH DEPENDENCE ON FORMER EUROPEAN COLONIAL POWERS FOR TRADE IN 1960'S. GENERAL REJECTION BY ASIA OF MAO'S METHODS. DIFFICULTIES REMAINING ARE: US PRESENCE, DIVIDED COUNTRIES, AND THREAT OF COMMUNISM. YET TREND IS TOWARD ECONOMIC EFFICIENCY: ASIAN DEVELOPMENT BANK,ASPAC. POLITICAL CHANGES MAY RESULT FROM CHINESE TRADE WITH NON-COMMUNIST NATIONS.

3267 WALLBANK T.W. ED.
DOCUMENTS ON MODERN AFRICA.
PRINCETON: VAN NOSTRAND, 1964, 191 PP.
SELECTED READINGS TO CHARACTERIZE THE DISTINCT PERIODS OF HISTORY IN SUB-SAHARAN AFRICA IN THE LAST CENTURY. EMPHASIS IS ON RECENT PERIOD OF INDEPENDENCE.

3268 WALLERSTEIN I.M.
AFRICA* THE POLITICS OF UNITY.
NEW YORK: RANDOM HOUSE, INC, 1967, 263 PP.
EXAMINES PAN-AFRICANISM - A MOVEMENT AUTHOR BELIEVES REPRESENTED THE STRONGEST INDIGENOUS POLITICAL FORCE IN AFRICA DURING THE PERIOD 1957-65. TRACES MOVEMENT BACK TO ITS PSYCHOLOGICAL AND HISTORICAL BEGINNINGS AT THE TURN OF THE 20TH CENTURY. DIVIDES MOVEMENT INTO A "CORE" AND A "PERIPHERY."

3269 WALLERSTEIN I.M.
AFRICA; THE POLITICS OF INDEPENDENCE.
NEW YORK: RANDOM HOUSE, INC, 1961, 173 PP., LC#61-16964.
ANALYSIS OF POLITICAL DEVELOPMENT IN MODERN AFRICA: SOCIAL STRUCTURE AND SOCIAL CONFLICT AND COHESION INHERENT IN NATIONS. DISCUSSES COLONIAL SYSTEM AND ITS INFLUENCE ON INDEPENDENT STATES.

3270 WALSH E. ED.
THE HISTORY AND NATURE OF INTERNATIONAL RELATIONS.
NEW YORK: MACMILLAN, 1922, 299 PP.
COLLECTION OF LECTURES SURVEYING PRINCIPAL PHASES OF INTERNATIONAL RELATIONS FROM EARLIEST ANTIQUITY TO WORLD WAR ONE. INCLUDED ARE AREA STUDIES OF DIPLOMATIC HISTORY IN EUROPE, USA, FAR EAST, AND LATIN AMERICA.

3271 WALTERS F.P.
A HISTORY OF THE LEAGUE OF NATIONS.
LONDON: OXFORD U. PR., 1952.
TRACES THE RISE AND DECLINE OF LEAGUE IN 20-YEAR EXISTENCE. ANALYZES POLITICAL DISPUTES, INTERNAL DISSENSION, AND ECONOMIC DIFFICULTIES. EXPLORES DIFFICULTY OF PROTECTING MINORITIES AND PROBLEMS CREATED BY UPSURGE OF NATIONALISM.

3272 WAMBAUCH S.
PLEBISCITES SINCE THE WORLD WAR: WITH A COLLECTION OF OFFICIAL DOCUMENTS.
WASHINGTON: CARNEGIE ENDOWMENT, 1933, 614 PP.
EXAMINES PLEBISCITES FROM 1914 TO 1933. INCLUDES LOCAL AND INTERNATIONAL BACKGROUNDS THAT LED TO AND WERE ABLE TO ESTABLISH THE PLEBISCITE. STUDIES THE ATTEMPTED PLEBISCITES AND THE FORCES INVOLVED, AND DRAWS COMPARISONS BETWEEN THESE POST-WWI ELECTIONS. BOOK ANALYZES THE DEMOCRATIC PROCESS IN ORDER TO PROMOTE INTERNATIONAL PEACE.

3273 WANDERSCHECK H.
FRANKREICHS PROPAGANDA GEGEN DEUTSCHLAND.
BERLIN: JUNKER & DUNNHAUPT VERL, 1940, 62 PP.
DISCUSSION OF THE HISTORY OF FRENCH ANTI-GERMAN PROPAGANDA. MAINTAINS THAT AIM OF FRENCH PROPAGANDA HAS ALWAYS BEEN THE POLITICAL DISINTEGRATION OF GERMANY, WITH THE AID OF "ENGLISH-JEWISH WAR MONGERS."

3274 WARBEY W.
VIETNAM: THE TRUTH.
LONDON: MERLIN PRESS LTD, 1965, 176 PP.
ANTI-AMERICAN ACCOUNT OF THE VIETNAMESE SITUATION FROM 1945-65. INCLUDES ANALYSES OF THE INTENTIONS OF THE US, THE SOUTH VIETNAMESE NATIONAL FRONT FOR LIBERATION, AND THE GOVERNMENTS OF THE TWO VIETNAMS. EMPHASIS IS LAID ON AMERICAN VIOLATIONS OF THE 1954 GENEVA SETTLEMENT. CONSIDERS VIETNAM CONFLICT A CIVIL WAR.

3275 WARBURG J.P.
AGENDA FOR ACTION.
NEW YORK: ACADEMY PUBLISHERS, 1957, 211 PP., LC#57-12236.
STUDY OF INTERNATIONAL POLITICS IN MIDDLE EAST AND EUROPE AND IMPACT ON US FOREIGN POLICY. DISCUSSES US POSITION AND PROBLEMS OF MIDDLE EASTERN CONFLICT, INCLUDING ARAB-ISRAELI CONFRONTATION.

3276 WARBURG J.P.
"THE CENTRAL EUROPEAN CRISIS: A PROPOSAL FOR WESTERN INITIATIVE."
ANN. AMER. POLIT. SOC. SCI., 324 (JULY 59) 17-25.
APPEAL TO BRING ISSUE OF INTERFERENCE WITH WESTERN ACCESS TO WEST BERLIN BEFORE UN. URGES MILITARY AND POLITICAL DISENGAGEMENT IN BERLIN AND NEUTRALIZATION OF BOTH SECTORS. ESTIMATES THAT DISENGAGEMENT WILL BRING GRADUAL LIBERATION OF EASTERN EUROPE.

3277 WARBURG J.P.
THE UNITED STATES IN THE POSTWAR WORLD.
NEW YORK: ATHENEUM PUBLISHERS, 1966, 327 PP., LC#66-23577.
REVIEWS ORIGINS OF US POSTWAR FOREIGN POLICY AND EXAMINES ITS EFFECTS; DESCRIBES WHAT HAS BEEN DONE AND WHAT IS LEFT TO DO. ANALYZES HOW AND BY WHOM FOREIGN POLICY HAS BEEN SHAPED, AND EXAMINES CRITICISM OF US POLICY FROM OTHER COUNTRIES.

3278 WARD B.
5 IDEAS THAT CHANGE THE WORLD.
NEW YORK: NORTON, 1959, 188 PP.
TRACES HISTORY OF THEORY AND PRACTICE OF NATIONALISM AND SHOWS HOW IT CHANGES AND IS CHANGED BY FOUR OTHER BASIC IDEAS: INDUSTRIALISM, COLONIALISM, COMMUNISM AND INTERNATIONALISM.

3279 WARD B.J.
INDIA AND THE WEST.
NEW YORK: W W NORTON, 1961, 256 PP., LC#61-5713.
INDIA'S EXPERIMENTS IN ECONOMIC DEVELOPMENT HAVE CREATED IN HER SOCIETY AN AMBIVALENCE WHICH MAY OPEN A DOOR FOR COMMUNISTS TO STEP INTO. GIVES GENERAL HISTORICAL BACKGROUND OF INDIAN PLANS, AND STRONGLY SUGGESTS THAT TIME HAS COME FOR US TO RESTORE MARSHALL APPROACH TO FOREIGN POLICY. US SHOULD SAVE STARVING MASSES AND HELP INDIA REALIZE HER POTENTIAL BY INSURING SUCCESS OF INDIA'S THIRD PLAN.

3280 WARD C.
"THE 'NEW MYTHS' AND 'OLD REALITIES' OF NUCLEAR WAR."
ORBIS, 7 (SUMMER 64), 255-91.
SEES THE 'NUCLEAR STALEMATE' THEORY AS A NEW MYTH WHICH IS ACCEPTED BY PERSONS IN THE SCIENTIFIC COMMUNITY COGNIZANT OF DEFENSE MATTERS. ASSERTS THAT THE REALITIES ARE SUCH THAT THE USA MUST CONTINUE TO EMPLOY TRADITIONAL SAFEGUARDS BEFORE ACCEPTING BELIEF IN A SOVIET DETENTE.

3281 WARD P.W.
"SOVEREIGNTY: A STUDY OF A CONTEMPORARY POLITICAL NOTION."
LONDON: G ROUTLEDGE & SONS, 1928.
DISTINGUISHES AND SURVEYS THREE PERIODS IN THE DEVELOPMENT OF CONCEPT: ITS EMERGENCE FROM ANCIENT TRADITION AND LATE MEDIEVAL USAGE; ENUNCIATION AND APPLICATION BY ABSOLUTE MONARCHS; REINTERPRETATION SINCE 1688 AND HISTORICAL RISE OF RESPONSIBLE GOVERNMENT. SHORT BIBLIOGRAPHY REFERS TO CLASSIC STUDIES OF POLITICS OF NATIONALISM.

3282 WARD R.E., WATANABE H.
JAPANESE POLITICAL SCIENCE: A GUIDE TO JAPANESE REFERENCE AND RESEARCH MATERIALS (2ND ED.)
ANN ARBOR: U OF MICH PR, 1961, 210 PP.
A BRIEFLY ANNOTATED BIBLIOGRAPHY OF 1,759 ITEMS, LARGELY LIMITED TO JAPANESE TITLES WHICH TREAT POLITICAL SCIENCE SUBJECTS AND DEVELOPMENTS IN JAPAN SINCE THE MEIJI RESTORATION (1868). FOCUSES UPON RESULTS OF POST-1945 SCHOLARSHIP WHICH APPEAR IN BOOK RATHER THAN ARTICLE FORM. ARRANGED INTO 27 TOPICAL HEADINGS, AND INDEXED BY AUTHOR AND EDITOR. ANNOTATIONS EVALUATE UTILITY OF ITEM FOR REFERENCE PURPOSES.

3283 WARE E.E.
THE STUDY OF INTERNATIONAL RELATIONS IN THE UNITED STATES.
NEW YORK: COLUMB. U. PR., 1938, 540 PP.
A COMPILATION OF ORGANIZATIONS PROMOTING STUDY OF SUBJECT AREA, OF CHANNELS FOR INFORMATION ABOUT FOREIGN COUNTRIES, AND OF GOVERNMENT, BUSINESS, COMMERCIAL, UNIVERSITY AND GENERAL EDUCATIONAL ORGANIZATIONS INVOLVED IN OR ENCOURAGING FOREIGN POLICY RESEARCH. DESCRIBES ORGANIZATIONAL METHODS, AREAS OF INTEREST AND PURPOSES.

3284 WARNER D.
HURRICANE FROM CHINA.
NEW YORK: MACMILLAN, 1961, 210 PP.
'BY 1980 CHINA WILL HAVE SPREAD ITS INFLUENCE FAR BEYOND ASIA. TRIUMPHANT IN ITS NEW POWER, GOADED BY POVERTY RESULTING FROM OVERPOPULATION AND STARVATION, IT WILL BE THE GREATEST THREAT THE WESTERN WORLD HAS EVER KNOWN... TO MAO TSE-TUNG THE WORLD IS A GREAT GUERRILLA BATTLEFIELD IN WHICH THE PRINCIPLES... MAY BE APPLIED IN ASIA, AFRICA AND LATIN AMERICA FOR ISOLATION AND DESTRUCTION OF USA AND ALLIES.'

3285 WARREN S., FLORINSKY M.T. ET AL.
"FOREIGN AID AND FOREIGN POLICY."
CURR. HIST., 33 (SEPT. 57), 129-170.
DURING PAST 16 YEARS MORE THAN 100 BILLION DOLLARS SPENT ON FOREIGN AID. OBJECTIVE STUDY ANSWERS SUCH QUESTIONS AS: HOW SUCCESSFUL IS PROGRAM, IS IT A TOOL OF MILITARY POLICY, SHOULD IT BE REGARDED AS 'CALCULATED RISK-TAKING OF WELL-CONSIDERED BANKING OPERATION' AND CAN IT BE 'FOUND TO SERVE AS MORAL EQUIVALENT TO WAR.' IMPACT OF FOREIGN-AID ON 'EFFECTIVENESS OF COMMON DEFENSE' IS CONSIDERED.

3286 WARREN S.
THE PRESIDENT AS WORLD LEADER.
PHILADELPHIA: LIPPINCOTT, 1964, 480 PP., $6.95.
DESCRIBES AND ANALYZES USE OF EXECUTIVE POWER, FROM T. ROOSEVELT TO KENNEDY, IN FOREIGN POLICY, IN INTERNATIONAL CRISES OR IN COLD WAR DIPLOMACY. USE OF POWER REFLECTS CONCEPTION OF OFFICE.

3287 WASHBURN A.M.
"NUCLEAR PROLIFERATION IN A REVOLUTIONARY INTERNATIONAL SYSTEM."
PUBLIC & INTL AFF., 5 (SPRING 67), 111-133.
DANGER OF NOT RECOGNIZING NUCLEAR PROLIFERATION AS A CONTINUING PROBLEM AND REASONS FOR THIS DECREASING CONCERN. NUCLEAR PROLIFERATION IS SUBJECT TO ANALYSIS ON TWO LEVELS, THAT OF THE INTERNATIONAL SYSTEM AND THAT OF THE NATION-STATE. IMPLICATIONS OF THESE APPROACHES AND THEIR RELEVANCE TO SPRING, 1967, EIGHTEEN NATION DISARMAMENT CONFERENCES ARE DISCUSSED.

3288 WASKOW A.I.
"NEW ROADS TO A WORLD WITHOUT WAR."
YALE REV., 54 (64), 88-111.
RESEARCH ON SOCIAL AND INTERNATIONAL TENSION FINDS CONFLICT BETWEEN NATIONS TO BE INEVITABLE. THE SEARCH, THEREFORE, IS FOR RULES OF ANTICIPATION OF CONFLICT ORIGINS AND TECHNIQUES THAT SEEK TO CONTAIN CONFLICT IN SUCH A WAY THAT IT DOES NOT BREAK OUT IN ORGANIZED VIOLENCE. EXPLORES A VARIETY OF PROPOSALS FOR TENSION MANAGEMENT IN INTERNATIONAL AFFAIRS.

3289 WASKOW A.I.
KEEPING THE WORLD DISARMED.
SANTA BARBARA: CTR DEMO INST, 1965, 88 PP.
EXAMINES POSSIBILITIES FOR DEMILITARIZED WORLD ORDER SUCH AS GRADUATED DETERRENTS, NON-LETHAL EQUIVALENTS OF WAR, AND HYPOTHETICAL POLICE MISSIONS.

3290 WASSENBERGH H.A.
POST-WAR INTERNATIONAL CIVIL AVIATION POLICY AND THE LAW OF THE AIR.
THE HAGUE: NIJHOFF, 1957, 180 PP.
EXAMINES FACTORS GOVERNING DEVELOPMENT OF CIVIL AVIATION, ESPECIALLY SINCE END OF WORLD WAR 2. ANALYZES PROBLEMS ARISING IN FIELD OF FORCE BETWEEN POLITICS AND LAW IN CONNECTION WITH REGULATION OF CIVIL AVIATION THROUGHOUT THE WORLD.

3291 WATERS M.
THE UNITED NATIONS* INTERNATIONAL ORGANIZATION AND ADMINISTRATION.
NEW YORK: MACMILLAN, 1967, 512 PP.
A COLLECTION OF READINGS, SPEECHES, AND DOCUMENTS ON EVERY PHASE OF UN ORGANIZATION AND OPERATION. TRACES HISTORICAL DEVELOPMENT OF INTERNATIONAL ORGANIZATION, UN AS A CONSTITUTIONAL AND POLITICAL SYSTEM, INTERNAL AND EXTERNAL ASPECTS OF ORGANIZATION, UN AND ROLE OF LAW, ETC. EVERY AGENCY OF THE UN IS COVERED AS IS GENERAL ASSEMBLY AND SECRETARIAT.

3292 WATKINS J.T., ROBINSON W.J.
GENERAL INTERNATIONAL ORGANIZATION: A SOURCE BOOK.
PRINCETON: VAN NOSTRAND, 1956, 248 PP., LC#56-9730.
SOURCE BOOK FOR INTRODUCTORY COURSES IN INTERNATIONAL RELATIONS. CONTAINS DOCUMENTS OF THE 19TH CENTURY, DOCUMENTS ON THE LEAGUE OF NATIONS, AND THE UN, INCLUDING BOTH WRITINGS OF AND WRITINGS ABOUT THESE INTERNATIONAL ORGANIZATIONS.

3293 WATKINS K.W.
BRITAIN DIVIDED; THE EFFECT OF THE SPANISH CIVIL WAR ON BRITISH POLITICAL OPINION.
LONDON: THOMAS NELSON & SONS, 1963, 270 PP.
STUDY OF IMPACT OF SPANISH CIVIL WAR ON POLICY AND PUBLIC OPINION IN BRITAIN. EXAMINES BRITISH INTERESTS REGARDING SPAIN DURING 1930'S, IMPRESSION OF IMPORTANCE OF CIVIL WAR FOR FUTURE, ATTITUDE OF BRITISH LEFT AND RIGHT, AND FOR SPAIN IN WWII.

3294 WATT D.C.
BRITAIN AND THE SUEZ CANAL.
LONDON: ROYAL INST OF INTL AFF, 1956, 51 PP.
DOCUMENTARY ANALYSIS OF THE EXTENT OF BRITISH INTEREST IN THE NATURE AND EFFICIENCY OF MANAGEMENT OF THE SUEZ CANAL. INCLUDES SEVEN DOCUMENTS VITAL TO THE ISSUE: TEXT OF EGYPTIAN DECREE NATIONALIZING THE CANAL; TEXT OF 1888 CONVENTION OF FREE NAVIGATION OF THE SUEZ; ANGLO-EGYPTIAN TREATY OF 1936; SUEZ CANAL BASE AGREEMENT OF 1954; EXTRACTS FROM VARIOUS SUEZ COMPANY CONCESSIONS; AND SEVERAL TABLES.

3295 WEAVER J.H.
THE INTERNATIONAL DEVELOPMENT ASSOCIATION: A NEW APPROACH TO FOREIGN AID.
NEW YORK: FREDERICK PRAEGER, 1965, 286 PP., LC#65-19792.
TRACES HISTORY OF INTERNATIONAL DEVELOPMENT ASSOCIATION BY EXAMINING THREE ISSUES: SOFT LOANS, LOCAL CURRENCY, AND BILATERAL VS MULTILATERAL AID. OUTLINES ORGANIZATION OF THE ASSOCIATION, ITS RELATIONSHIP WITH INTERNATIONAL BANK, AND PROBLEMS OF ALLOCATION IN DISBURSING THE FUNDS. CONTAINS BIBLIOGRAPHY OF PUBLISHED AND UNPUBLISHED MATERIAL WRITTEN IN ENGLISH SINCE 1949.

3296 WECHSLER H.
PRINCIPLES, POLITICS AND FUNDAMENTAL LAW: SELECTED ESSAYS.
CAMBRIDGE: HARVARD U. PR., 1961.
FOUR ESSAYS ON NATIONAL EFFORTS TO GOVERN USA BY FUNDAMENTAL LAW. FOCUSES ON SUPREME COURT AS INTERPRETER OF CONSTITUTION, CONSTITUTIONAL CONTROVERSIES, PHASES OF CONSTITUTIONALISM THAT STRUCTURE GOVERNMENT AND POLICIES, AND A DEFENSE OF THE NUREMBERG TRIALS.

3297 WEIDNER E.W.
THE WORLD ROLE OF UNIVERSITIES.
NEW YORK: MCGRAW HILL, 1962, 366 PP., LC#61-18733.
EXAMINES AMERICAN INTERNATIONAL EXCHANGE AND STUDENT ABROAD PROGRAMS, EMPHASIZING FOREIGN ACADEMIC CONDITIONS AND STRUCTURE, FORMATION, AND ACHIEVEMENTS OF TECHNICAL ASSISTANCE ABROAD.

3298 WEIGERT H.W.
COMPASS OF THE WORLD, A SYMPOSIUM ON POLITICAL GEOGRAPHY.
NEW YORK: MACMILLAN, 1944, 460 PP.
STRESSES FACT THAT CERTAIN REGIONS OF WORLD HAVE ACHIEVED A PIVOTAL IMPORTANCE PARTLY BECAUSE OF THEIR GEOGRAPHICAL ADVANTAGE.

3299 WEIL G.L. ED.
A HANDBOOK ON THE EUROPEAN ECONOMIC COMMUNITY.
NEW YORK: FREDERICK PRAEGER, 1965, 480 PP., LC#65-25594.
COMPILATION OF BASIC DOCUMENTS ON HISTORY AND DEVELOPMENT OF THE EEC. INCLUDES BACKGROUND DATA ON ITS INSTITUTIONS, ASSOCIATION WITH EUROPEAN STATES, EXTERNAL RELATIONS, AND ECONOMIC AND FINANCIAL AFFAIRS. CONSIDERS THE INTERNAL MARKET, LABOR REGULATIONS, FAIR COMPETITION, AGRICULTURE, TRANSPORT, AND OVERSEAS TRADE. SUMS UP PAST PROGRESS AND LOOKS AT FUTURE GOALS.

3300 WEIL G.L.
"THE MERGER OF THE INSTITUTIONS OF THE EUROPEAN COMMUNITIES"
AMER. J. OF INT. LAW, 61 (JAN. 67), 57-65.
REPORTS ON NATURE AND SIGNIFICANCE OF MERGER TREATY OF 1965 WHICH REPLACED EEC, EURATOM, AND ECSC WITH A SINGLE COUNCIL AND COMMISSION. THIS SINGLE COMMISSION DEALING WITH EUROPEAN NATURAL POWER CONTROL IS CONSIDERED AS A MAJOR CONSTITUTIONAL DEVELOPMENT IN PROGRESS TOWARD EUROPEAN UNITY.

3301 WEIL G.L.
"THE EUROPEAN COMMUNITY* WHAT LIES BEYOND THE POINT OF NO RETURN?"
REV. OF POLITICS, 29 (APR. 67), 160-179.
DISCUSSES ESSENTIAL CHARACTERISTICS OF EEC. REVIEWS NATURE AND PROCESS OF DECISION-MAKING TO ILLUSTRATE DEVELOPMENT OF "COMMUNITY SPIRIT." EXAMINES DECLINE OF EUROPEAN POLITICAL INTEGRATION. INVESTIGATES POSSIBLE COURSES FOR FUTURE DEVELOPMENT, EITHER TO EXIST OR EXPAND. TO EXPAND EEC MUST HAVE NEW POLITICAL STIMULUS WHICH IS PROBABLY DEPENDENT ON A PUSH FROM A POWER OUTSIDE ORGANIZATION OF EEC.

3302 WEILER J.
L'ECONOMIE INTERNATIONALE DEPUIS 1950.
PARIS: PR UNIV DE FRANCE, 1965, 250 PP.
STUDY OF INTERNATIONAL ECONOMICS SINCE 1950. EXAMINES RECONSTRUCTION OF WAR TORN ECONOMIES BY MARSHALL PLAN AND DEVELOPMENT OF EUROPEAN COMMUNITY. COVERS INTERNATIONAL ECONOMIC NEGOTIATIONS ON TARIFFS AND MONETARY SYSTEMS.

3303 WEILLER J.
"UNIONS MONETAIRES ET RAPPORTS DE COOPERATION INTERNATIONALE DANS UN MONDE EN TRANSITION: L'EXAMPLE."
DE L'UNION MONETAIRE QU'EST AFRICAINE.
REV. ECON., 14 (NO. 2, 63), 196-215.
ANALYZES EFFORTS OF NEW AFRICAN COUNTRIES TO ACHIEVE A MONETARY UNION. COMPARES DEVELOPMENT TO INTERNATIONAL EXCHANGE PLAN. DISCUSSES NEW PAYMENT SYSTEM.

3304 WEINBERG A., WEINBERG L.
INSTEAD OF VIOLENCE: WRITINGS BY THE GREAT ADVOCATES OF PEACE AND NONVIOLENCE THROUGHOUT HISTORY.
NEW YORK: GROSSMAN PUBL, 1963, 486 PP., LC#63-22226.
COLLECTS WRITINGS OF PERSONS THROUGHOUT HISTORY WHO HAVE BELIEVED THAT HUMAN AFFAIRS ON PERSONAL, NATIONAL, AND INTERNATIONAL LEVELS CAN BE SETTLED BY NONVIOLENT MEANS - BY ARBITRATION, MEDIATION, OR CONCILIATION. WORKS ARE BY POLITICAL, ECONOMIC, SOCIAL, AND RELIGIOUS LEADERS FROM LAO-TSE TO POPE JOHN XXIII.

3305 WEINBERG A.K.
MANIFEST DESTINY: A STUDY OF NATIONALIST EXPANSIONISM IN AMERICAN HISTORY.
BALTIMORE: JOHNS HOPKINS PRESS, 1935, 559 PP.
DISCUSSES NATURE AND RISE OF IDEA OF MANIFEST DESTINY IN US FROM EARLY CONCEPT OF "GEOGRAPHICAL PREDESTINATION" TO EMERGENCE AS INTERNATIONAL POLICE POWER.

3306 WEINSTEIN F.B.
VIETNAM'S UNHELD ELECTIONS: THE FAILURE TO CARRY OUT THE 1956 REUNIFICATION ELECTIONS... (MONOGRAPH)
ITHACA: CORNELL U, DEPT ASIAN ST, 1966, 65 PP.
DESCRIBES EVENTS SURROUNDING HANOI'S ATTEMPTS TO BRING ABOUT REUNIFICATION OF VIETNAM THROUGH ELECTIONS PRESCRIBED BY GENEVA AGREEMENTS OF 1956. INDICATES THAT NORTH VIETNAM'S LEADERS BELIEVE US ENCOURAGED SAIGON TO REJECT GENEVA PLAN. CONCLUDES THAT ANY REALISTIC APPROACH TO NEGOTIATIONS IN THE PRESENT (1966) CONFLICT MUST RECOGNIZE HANOI'S EFFORTS TO IMPLEMENT ELECTIONS AND THE REASONS FOR FAILURE.

3307 WEINTAL E., BARTLETT C.
FACING THE BRINK* AN INTIMATE STUDY OF CRISIS DIPLOMACY.
NEW YORK: CHAS SCRIBNER'S SONS, 1967, 248 PP., LC#67-15494.
A DETAILED DISCUSSION OF PERSONALITIES AND INSTITUTIONS SHAPING FOREIGN POLICY. PARTICULAR EMPHASIS GIVEN TO FIVE INTERNATIONAL CRISES* CYPRUS, YEMEN, CUBA, VIETNAM, AND DE GAULLE AND NATO. GIVES VIEW OF HOW KENNEDY AND JOHNSON HAVE CONDUCTED FOREIGN AFFAIRS, AND CHAPTER ON SECRETARY OF STATE PROVIDES DEFINITIVE EVALUATION OF RUSK.

3308 WEINTRAUB S.
THE WAR IN THE WARDS.
GARDEN CITY: DOUBLEDAY, 1964, 179 PP., LC#64-19322.
STUDY OF KOREAN PRISONER OF WAR HOSPITAL AND RELATION OF RIOTS AND DEMONSTRATION OF NORTH KOREAN AND CHINESE INMATES TO POLICY OF US ADMINISTRATORS OF CAMP DURING PEACE NEGOTIATIONS.

3309 WEIS P.
NATIONALITY AND STATELESSNESS IN INTERNATIONAL LAW.
LONDON: STEVENS, 1956, 260 PP.
TREATISE ON VARIOUS ASPECTS OF INTERNATIONAL LAW AND BRITISH NATIONALITY LAW, CONCERNING HOW CERTAIN PRACTISES

HAVE HISTORICALLY AFFECTED AND PRESENTLY AFFECT INDIVIDUALS. EXAMINES TREATIES, STATUTES AND CASES AS COURCES OF IMFORMATION.

3310 WEISNER J.B.
WHERE SCIENCE AND POLITICS MEET.
NEW YORK: MCGRAW HILL, 1965, 302 PP., LC#65-16157.
MIRRORS BROAD RANGE OF SCIENTIFIC AND TECHNICAL ISSUES THAT CONFRONT MODERN PRESIDENT. INCLUDES DOMESTIC ISSUES OF BASIC RESEARCH AND SCIENCE, AS STIMULANTS TO ECONOMIC GROWTH, INTERNATIONAL ISSUES OF NATIONAL DEFENSE, MILITARY RESEARCH PROJECTS, TECHNOLOGY IN FOREIGN AID, AND THE LIKE. AUTHOR SERVED AS SCIENTIFIC ADVISER TO PRESIDENTS KENNEDY AND JOHNSON.

3311 WEISSBERG G.
"MAPS AS EVIDENCE IN INTERNATIONAL BOUNDARY DISPUTES: A REAPPRAISAL."
AMER. J. INT. LAW, 57 (OCT. 63), 781-803.
DISCUSSES NEW EMPHASIS ON MAPS AS IMPORTANT EVIDENCE IN BOUNDARY DISPUTES. GIVES 3 EXAMPLES FROM CASES IN INTERNATIONAL COURT OF JUSTICE. DISCUSSES INDIA-CHINA BOUNDARY CONFLICT.

3312 WELCH C.E.
DREAM OF UNITY; PAN-AFRICANISM AND POLITICAL UNIFICATION IN WEST AFRICA.
ITHACA: CORNELL U PRESS, 1966, 396 PP., LC#66-16290.
ANALYSIS OF CONCEPT OF AFRICAN REGIONAL UNITY AND PLANS AND ACTIONS TAKEN TO OBTAIN. DISCUSSES NATURE OF AFRICAN STATES AND PROSPECTS FOR INTERACTION IN WEST AFRICA.

3313 WELCH R.H.W.
THE NEW AMERICANISM, AND OTHER SPEECHES AND ESSAYS.
BELMONT: AMER OPINION, 1966, 209 PP., LC#66-26864.
SELECTIONS FROM 1957-65 FOCUS PRIMARILY ON THREAT OF COMMUNISM TO US. CLAIMS CIVIL RIGHTS MOVEMENT IS THE VEHICLE THROUGH WHICH COMMUNISTS MAY TAKE OVER US.

3314 WELLEQUET J.
LE CONGO BELGE ET LA WELTPOLITIK (1894-1914.
BRUSSELS: PR UNIV DE BRUXELLES, 1962, 499 PP.
WORK ON WHAT GERMANY THOUGHT OF CONGO BETWEEN 1894-1914 WHEN GERMANY WAS FOLLOWING ITS "WELTPOLITIK." EXTENSIVELY DOCUMENTS ANTI-CONGOLESE CAMPAIGN AND GERMAN CONQUERING AMBITIONS.

3315 WELLES S.
SEVEN DECISIONS THAT SHAPED HISTORY.
NEW YORK: HARPER, 1951, 236 PP.
CONSIDERS REASONS WHICH BROUGHT ABOUT DECISION TO RECOGNIZE THE VICHY GOVERNMENT. SURVEYS FAR-EASTERN POLICY FROM PEARL HARBOUR TO HIROSHIMA. ANALYZES UN CHARTER. GIVES OUTLINE OF POSSIBLE FUTURE ACTION.

3316 WELLESLEY COLLEGE
SYMPOSIUM ON LATIN AMERICA.
WELLESLEY: WELLESLEY COLLEGE, 1963, 223 PP.
PROCEEDINGS DISCUSS LATIN AMERICAN UNIFORMITY AND DIVERSITY; PROSPECTS FOR DEMOCRACY; PROBLEMS OF ECONOMIC AND SOCIAL DEVELOPMENT; ALLIANCE FOR PROGRESS AND ITS CULTURAL CONTRIBUTIONS; AND RELATIONS WITH US.

3317 WELLS H.
"THE OAS AND THE DOMINICAN ELECTIONS."
OBIS, 7 (SPRING 63), 150-63.
EXPLORES FACTORS CONTRIBUTING POSITIVELY TO FIRST FREE ELECTION IN DOMINICAN REPUBLIC. DETAILS OAS ROLE: PROVIDED TECHNICAL ASSISTANCE FOR SETTING UP DEMOCRATIC ELECTORAL PROCEDURES, AND OUTSIDE OBSERVERS AT CAMPAIGN END AND ON ELECTION DAY. GIVES CHRONOLOGICAL EVENTS, MAY '61-DEC. '62.

3318 WENGLER W.
"LES CONFLITS DE LOIS ET LE PRINCIPE D'EGALITE."
REV. CRIT. DR. INT. PRIV., 52 (NO. 3, 63), 503-27.
STUDIES EXISTENCE OF PRIVATE LAW IN INTERNATIONAL RELATIONS. FINDS PUBLIC ORDER EXPRESSION OF IDEA OF EQUALITY. SHOWS CONFLICTS OF LAWS AND PRINCIPLE OF EQUALITY.

3319 WENTHOLT W.
SOME COMMENTS ON THE LIQUIDATION OF THE EUROPEAN PAYMENT UNION AND RELATED PROBLEMS (PAMPHLET)
AMSTERDAM: AMST STOCK EX REPORT, 1959, 23 PP.
DISCUSSES EACH NATION'S DEBTS AND FOREIGN EXCHANGE OR GOLD RESERVES LEFT AS RESULT OF LIQUIDATION. STUDIES CREDIT TERMS, ETC., IN NEW EUROPEAN MONETARY AGREEMENT, SET UP TO SETTLE LEFT-OVER DEBTS. LIQUIDATION OF EPU SPRANG FROM CONFLICT BETWEEN FRANCE AND ENGLAND WHEN US REFUSED TO MAKE DOLLAR CONVERTIBLE TO GOLD.

3320 WEST F.J.
"THE NEW GUINEA QUESTION: AN AUSTRALIAN VIEW."
FOR. AFF., 39 (APR. 61), 504-11.
AUSTRALIA HAS PLENARY POWER TO ADMINISTER TERRITORIES TOGETHER AND TO OFFER A COMMON POLITICAL FUTURE. PRESENT AUSTRALIAN GOVERNMENT FAVORS INDEPENDENCE BECAUSE OF POLITICAL CONSEQUENCES WHICH WOULD ARISE IF IT DID NOT.

3321 WEST R.
CONSCIENCE AND SOCIETY: A STUDY OF THE PSYCHOLOGICAL PREREQUISITES OF LAW AND ORDER.
NEW YORK: EMERSON BOOKS, 1945, 261 PP.
STUDIES HUMAN NATURE IN ITS SOCIAL RELATIONSHIP, FOCUSING ON SIGNIFICANCE OF AGGRESSIVENESS. DISCUSSES CONTROL OF HUMAN NATURE BY LAW, SHOWING HOW LAW MAINTAINS ASCENDENCY OF MAN'S SOCIAL INSTINCT OVER HIS SELF-ASSERTIVE INSTINCT. STATES THAT INTERNATIONAL LAW HAS NOT SUCCEEDED IN CONTROLLING MAN'S AGGRESSIVENESS. FORECASTS ESSENTIAL STRUCTURE OF THE FUTURE WORLD ORDER THAT MANKIND SEEKS.

3322 WESTERFIELD H.
THE INSTRUMENTS OF AMERICA'S FOREIGN POLICY.
NEW YORK: CROWELL, 1963, 538 PP., $10.00.
AN ANALYSIS OF THE WAY IN WHICH AMERICAN FOREIGN POLICY FUNCTIONS TO SECURE AMERICA'S SURVIVAL IN THE CONFLICT OF COMPETITIVE CO-EXISTENCE WITH THE WORLD'S COMMUNIST POWERS. THE POLICY OF CONTAINMENT IS THOROUGHLY EXAMINED, BUT NO PRECISE PRESCRIPTIONS FOR THE CONDUCT OF FUTURE POLICY ARE DISCLOSED.

3323 WESTIN A.F. ED.
VIEWS OF AMERICA.
NEW YORK: HARCOURT BRACE, 1966, 375 PP., LC#66-17351.
COMMENTARIES FROM COMMUNIST BLOC AND DEVELOPING NATIONS ON AMERICAN LIFE, COUNTERPOINTED BY AMERICAN RESPONSES. ANALYZES SOURCES OF FOREIGN ATTITUDES. ARTICLES DISCUSS AMERICAN IDEOLOGY, POLITICS, SOCIETY, ECONOMY, AND FOREIGN POLICY.

3324 WESTWOOD A.F.
FOREIGN AID IN A FOREIGN POLICY FRAMEWORK.
WASHINGTON: BROOKINGS INST, 1966, 115 PP., LC#66-21956.
STUDIES EVOLUTION OF US FOREIGN AID PROGRAMS, INCLUDING "POINT FOUR," MILITARY ASSISTANCE, AND FOREIGN AID "STRINGS" WITH REFERENCE TO ECONOMIC DEVELOPMENT, LONG TERM PLANS, AND THE ALLIANCE FOR PROGRESS.

3325 WHEARE K.C.
THE CONSTITUTIONAL STRUCTURE OF THE COMMONWEALTH.
LONDON: OXFORD U PR, 1960, 201 PP.
DESCRIBES CONSTITUTIONAL STRUCTURE OF COMMONWEALTH AS OF MARCH, 1960; PRESENTS CONCEPTS AND CASES OF AUTONOMY, AUTOCHTHONY, EQUALITY, AND COOPERATION AMONG MEMBER STATES. DETAILS PSYCHOLOGY AND PRACTICE OF LOYALTY TO QUEEN, AND OTHER SYMBOLIC EXPRESSIONS OF UNITY.

3326 WHEELER-BENNETT J.W.
THE FORGOTTEN PEACE: BREST-LITOVSK.
NEW YORK: WILLIAM MORROW, 1939, 478 PP.
DEPICTS IN DETAIL COURSE OF NEGOTIATIONS BETWEEN RUSSIA AND GERMANY AND CENTRAL POWERS IN 1917-18, SPECIFICALLY THOSE CULMINATING IN TREATY OF BREST-LITOVSK. EXAMINES IMPLICATIONS OF GERMAN RAPACITY, ALSO INCIPIENT SOVIET TECHNIQUE OF "PARALLEL DIPLOMACY" AND THIRD INTERNATIONAL. CONTAINS MANY DOCUMENTS FROM TREATY.

3327 WHEELER-BENNETT J.W.
MUNICH: PROLOGUE TO TRAGEDY.
NEW YORK: DUELL, SLOAN & PEARCE, 1948, 507 PP.
EXAMINES INTENTIONS AND RESULTS OF MUNICH CONFERENCES, CONSIDERS APPEASEMENT AS FOUNDATION OF POLICY, AND DEMONSTRATES RESULTS AS BEING ADVERSE TO IDEOLOGICAL VIEW.

3328 WHELAN J.G.
"KHRUSHCHEV AND THE BALANCE OF WORLD POWER."
REV. POLIT., 23 (APR. 61), 131-54.
RECENT CALCULATIONS OF SOVIET FOREIGN POLICY ASSUME TIME IS RIPE TO MOUNT A GLOBAL POLITICAL OFFENSIVE AGAINST CAPITALIST WORLD. SINCE COMMUNIST IDEOLOGY IS INDISSOLUBLY WEDDED TO PRACTICE, SHOWS HOW THESE FACTORS AND THEIR IMPLICATIONS CONSTITUTE SERIOUS DANGER FOR FREE WORLD.

3329 WHITAKER A.P.
THE UNITED STATES AND THE INDEPENDENCE OF LATIN AMERICA, 1800-1830.
BALTIMORE: JOHNS HOPKINS PRESS, 1941, 632 PP.
DETAILED ANALYSIS OF POLICY DEVELOPMENT AND HISTORICAL EVENTS OF US-LATIN AMERICAN RELATIONS. THE YEARS 1800-1830, IN WHICH THE AMERICAN COLONIES OF SPAIN AND PORTUGAL ESTABLISHED INDEPENDENCE, WERE CRITICAL FOR AMERICAN FOREIGN POLICY. AUTHOR SUGGESTS ADMINISTRATIONS OF MADISON, MONROE, ADAMS FACED WORLD CRISIS MUCH LIKE THAT OF 1940.

3330 WHITAKER A.P.
"DEVELOPMENT OF AMERICAN REGIONALISM: THE ORGANIZATION OF AMERICAN STATES."
INT. CONCIL., 469, (MAR. 51), 123-164.
SHOWS VARIOUS STAGES OF DEVELOPMENT OF THE INTER-AMERICAN AGENCY. POINTS OUT THE FACT THAT THE OAS WAS CREATED IN ORDER TO PROMOTE COLLECTIVE SECURITY, AND RESULTED FROM A LACK OF FAITH AMONG THE AMERICAN NATIONS.

3331 WHITAKER A.P.
THE WESTERN HEMISPHERE IDEA.
ITHACA: CORNELL U. PR., 1954, 194 PP.
TRACES THE DEVELOPMENT OF IDEA THAT A PECULIAR RELATIONSHIP (GEOGRAPHICAL, POLITICAL AS WELL AS PHILOSOPHICAL) EXISTS BETWEEN PEOPLES OF WESTERN HEMISPHERE WHICH SETS THEM APART FROM REST OF WORLD, NOTABLY EUROPE. VARYING POLITICAL EXPRESSIONS OF THIS CONCEPT INCLUDE: MONROE DOCTRINE, DRAGO DOCTRINE AND PAN-AMERICANISM.

3332 WHITAKER A.P.
ARGENTINE UPHEAVAL.
NEW YORK: FREDERICK PRAEGER, 1956, 179 PP., LC#55-12018.
DISCUSSES FALL OF PERON AND RISE OF NEW REGIME IN ARGENTINA. EXAMINES SOCIAL STRUCTURE OF COUNTRY, POLITICAL PARTIES, AND FOREIGN POLICY UNDER BOTH REGIMES. CONCLUDES WITH PROBLEMS FACING US IN ITS ARGENTINE RELATIONS.

3333 WHITAKER A.P., JORDAN D.C.
NATIONALISM IN CONTEMPORARY LATIN AMERICA.
NEW YORK: FREE PRESS OF GLENCOE, 1966, 228 PP., LC#66-12891.
TRACES DEVELOPMENT OF LATIN AMERICAN "MULTIFORM NATIONALISM" FROM 1930'S TO PRESENT. EMPHASIZES BASIC POLITICAL, HISTORICAL, AND CULTURAL DIVERSITIES OF NATIONALISM IN EACH LATIN AMERICAN COUNTRY, BUT IDENTIFIES CONCERN WITH MATERIAL WELL-BEING AND SOCIAL JUSTICE AS MAJOR CHARACTERISTICS OF ENTIRE LATIN AMERICAN NATIONALIST GROWTH. DISCUSSES TEN COUNTRIES INDIVIDUALLY.

3334 WHITE G.M.
THE USE OF EXPERTS BY INTERNATIONAL TRIBUNALS.
SYRACUSE: SYRACUSE U PRESS, 1965, 258 PP., LC#65-15853.
DISCUSSES NATURE OF INTERNATIONAL LEGAL PROCEEDINGS AND ROLE OF VARIOUS EXPERTS. TRACES USE OF EXPERTS BY COURT SYSTEMS IN VARIOUS NATIONS AND NOTES IMPLIED RIGHT OF WORLD TRIBUNALS TO CALL ON EXPERTS. EXAMINES INSTANCES IN WHICH EXPERTS ARE USED MOST OFTEN, AS IN SUPPLYING IMPARTIAL OBSERVATION OR ACTING AS ARBITRATOR. NOTES PRIVILEGES AND IMMUNITIES OF EXPERTS, AND COMMENTS ON FEES AND EXPENSES.

3335 WHITE J.
GERMAN AID.
LONDON: MIN OF OVERSEAS DEVEL, 1965, 217 PP.
SURVEYS SOURCES, POLICY, AND STRUCTURE OF GERMAN AID AND ATTITUDE OF GERMAN PEOPLE TOWARD IT. DISCUSSES THEORETICAL RESULTS OF FOREIGN AID, ROLE OF TECHNICAL DEVELOPMENT, AND ITS IMPORTANCE TO TRADE FOR DONOR AND RECEIVER.

3336 WHITE J.A.
THE DIPLOMACY OF THE RUSSO-JAPANESE WAR.
PRINCETON: PRINCETON U PRESS, 1964, 410PP. LC#61-15751
STUDY CONCERNED WITH COSMOPOLITAN RATHER THAN NATIONAL SIGNIFICANCE OF RUSSO-JAPANESE WAR. PREWAR DIPLOMACY IN RUSSIA AND CHINA EXAMINED. DIPLOMACY DURING WAR AND POSTWAR CONFERENCES CONSIDERED WITH PARTICULAR ATTENTION TO PORTSMOUTH CONFERENCE AND NEW BALANCE OF POWER.

3337 WHITE L.C.
INTERNATIONAL NON-GOVERNMENTAL ORGANIZATIONS.
NEW BRUNSWICK: RUTGERS U. PR., 1951, 314 PP.
SURVEY OF MORE THAN 1000 NON-PROFIT ORGANIZATIONS THAT PLAY A PART IN WORLD AFFAIRS. GEARED TOWARDS APPRAISING AND DESCRIBING THE FUNCTIONS OF THESE 'INSTITUTIONS OF PEACE' THAT DEAL WITH EVERY PHASE OF HUMAN INTEREST FROM THEOLOGY TO SPORTS.

3338 WHITING A.S.
CHINA CROSSES THE YALU: THE DECISION TO ENTER THE KOREAN WAR.
NEW YORK: MACMILLAN, 1960, 219 PP.
ATTEMPTS TO DETERMINE EXTENT OF CHINESE COMMUNIST RESPONSIBILITY FOR POLICIES IN KOREAN WAR. DISCUSSES DEVELOPMENTS THAT DEMONSTRATE FULL IMPACT OF LIMITED WARFARE. ANALYZES SITUATION FROM PERSPECTIVE OF PEKING DECISION-MAKERS.

3339 WHITNEY T.P. ED.
KHRUSHCHEV SPEAKS.
ANN ARBOR: U OF MICH PR, 1963, 466 PP., LC#63-8075.
SELECTION OF FORMER SOVIET PREMIER KHRUSHCHEV'S SPEECHES, ARTICLES, AND PRESS CONFERENCES, PERIOD 1949-61. MAJOR EVENTS INCLUDED ARE THE REORGANIZATION OF AGRICULTURE, DE-STALINIZATION, KHRUSHCHEV'S AMERICAN TOUR, AND THE U-2 INCIDENT. AN OFFICIAL SOVIET BIOGRAPHY OF KHRUSHCHEV IS INCLUDED.

3340 WHITTON J.B.
THE SECOND CHANCE: AMERICA AND THE PEACE.
PRINCETON: U. PR., 1944, 235 PP.
ANALYZES HISTORY OF AMERICAN FOREIGN POLICY. SURVEYS PROBLEMS OF PEACETIME ECONOMICS. OUTLINES MINIMAL CONDITIONS NECESSARY FOR PEACE. EXAMINES POLITICAL RELATIONS WITHIN THE TREATY-MAKING AUTHORITY. POINTS OUT BASES OF FOREIGN POLICY.

3341 WHITTON J.B.
PROPAGANDA AND THE COLD WAR.
WASHINGTON: PUBLIC AFFAIRS PRESS, 1963, 119 PP., LC#63-15329
THIRTEEN ARTICLES ANALYZING ROLE OF AMERICAN INFORMATION IN COLD WAR, ITS POTENTIAL AND LIMITATIONS, SUGGESTIONS FOR IMPROVEMENT, AND ROLES OF RADIO FREE EUROPE, AMERICAN INDUSTRY, AND BOOKS.

3342 WIGGINS J.W. ED., SCHOECK H. ED.
FOREIGN AID REEXAMINED: A CRITICAL APPRAISAL.
WASHINGTON: PUBLIC AFFAIRS PRESS, 1958, 245 PP., LC#58-11888
ESSAYS ON IDEOLOGY, POLITICS, AND ECONOMICS OF US FOREIGN AID. EXAMINES PROBLEMS ASSOCIATED WITH POLITICAL INTERVENTION, POPULATION INCREASES, AND NATIONAL SOVEREIGNTY. DISCUSSES REGIONAL CONFLICTS AND PRESENTS CASE STUDY OF FAILURE OF FOREIGN AID TO CHINA.

3343 WILBUR C.M. ED., HOW J.L. ED.
DOCUMENTS ON COMMUNISM, NATIONALISM, AND SOVIET ADVISERS IN CHINA, 1918-1927.
NEW YORK: COLUMBIA U PRESS, 1956, 617 PP., LC#56-6813.
A COLLECTION OF DOCUMENTS SEIZED IN THE 1927 PEKING RAID WHICH PROVIDES INFORMATION ON COMMUNIST PHASE OF THE REVOLUTIONARY MOVEMENT IN CHINA. DIVIDED INTO SEVEN CHAPTERS COVERING THE HISTORY AND ORGANIZATION POLICIES OF THE CHINESE COMMUNIST PARTY FROM 1920-27. INCLUDES GLOSSARY OF SPECIAL TERMS, NAMES OF ORGANIZATIONS, PARTY ORGANS, AND CHINESE NAMES AND ALIASES. EXTENSIVE BIBLIOGRAPHY.

3344 WILCOX F.O., MARCY C.M.
PROPOSALS FOR CHANGES IN THE UNITED NATIONS.
WASHINGTON: BROOKINGS INST., 1955, 537 PP.
DESCRIBES AND ANALYZES PRINCIPAL PROPOSALS ADVANCED BY GOVERNMENTS, PRIVATE GROUPS, AND INDIVIDUALS. INCLUDES REVIEW OF MAJOR PROPOSALS FOR AND AGAINST PROPOSALS AND IMPACT OF PROPOSALS ON UN.

3345 WILCOX F.O.
"THE UN AND THE NON-ALIGNED NATIONS."
NEW YORK: FOR. POL. ASSN., 155 (SEPT-OCT. 62), 54 PP.
CONSIDERS AFRO-ASIAN 'CONCEPT OF THEIR ROLE IN THE UN', AND REVIEWS THEIR VARIOUS CONTRIBUTIONS TO THE WORLD-ORGANIZATION. THROUGH ANALYSIS OF THE VOTING RECORD IN THE GENERAL ASSEMBLY OF THESE NON-ALIGNED NATIONS, AUTHOR EVALUATES SIGNIFICANCE OF TRENDS WITH REGARD TO USA AND UN.

3346 WILCOX F.O. ED., HAVILAND H.F.
"THE ATLANTIC COMMUNITY: PROGRESS AND PROSPECTS."
INT. ORGAN., 17 (SUMMER 63), 521-829.
EXAMINES THE QUESTION OF WHETHER COOPERATIVE RELATIONSHIPS AMONG THE ATLANTIC NATIONS SHOULD BE DEVELOPED FURTHER, AND IF SO, FOR WHAT ENDS AND BY WHAT MEANS. INCLUDES ARTICLES BY STANLEY HOFFMAN, 'DISCORD AND COMMUNITY: THE NORTH ATLANTIC AREA AS A PARTIAL INTERNATIONAL SYSTEM', RUPERT EMERSON, 'THE ATLANTIC COMMUNITY AND WESTERN INTEGRATION', AND H. F. HAVILAND, JR., 'BUILDING A POLITICAL COMMUNITY.'

3347 WILCOX J.K., ED.
BIBLIOGRAPHY OF NEW GUIDES AND AIDS TO PUBLIC DOCUMENTS USE, 1953-1956 (PAMPHLET)
NEW YORK: SPECIAL LIBRARIES ASSN, 1957, 16 PP., LC#57-9153.
BIBLIOGRAPHY OF BIBLIOGRAPHIES THAT COVERS PUBLICATIONS ON FEDERAL, STATE, MUNICIPAL, FOREIGN, AND INTERNATIONAL LEVELS. CONTAINS 70 ANNOTATED ITEMS. INDEX OF TITLES AND PUBLISHERS.

3348 WILCOX W.A.
PAKISTAN; THE CONSOLIDATION OF A NATION.
NEW YORK: COLUMBIA U PRESS, 1963, 276 PP., LC#63-9873.
STUDY OF DEVELOPMENT OF PAKISTAN UNDER PRINCELY STATES, LEADING TO INDEPENDENCE. EXAMINES PROBLEMS OF GOVERNING AND UNIFIYING PAKISTAN AS MODERN STATE AND PROGRAMS UNDERTAKEN BY NATIONAL GOVERNMENT. EXPLAINS RELATIONSHIP OF PAKISTAN TO INDIA.

3349 WILDING N., LAUNDY P.
"AN ENCYCLOPEDIA OF PARLIAMENT."
LONDON: CASSELL & CO LTD, 1958.
COLLECTION OF INFORMATION RELATING TO PARLIAMENT AND ITS ASSOCIATED SUBJECTS. HEADINGS ARE ARRANGED IN ONE ALPHABETICAL SEQUENCE. ENTRIES CHOSEN FOR THEIR RELEVANCE TO THE CREATION AND GROWTH OF POWERS, PRIVILEGES, AND PRECEDENTS OF PARLIAMENT, OR FOR THEIR INFLUENCE ON ITS CUSTOMS AND PROCEDURES. UNANNOTATED BIBLIOGRAPHY OF POLITICAL BIOGRAPHIES AND WORKS CONCERNING THE PARLIAMENTS OF UK.

3350 WILGUS A.C.
HISTORIES AND HISTORIANS OF HISPANIC AMERICA (REPRINT ED.)
NEW YORK: COOPER SQUARE PUBL, 1965, 144 PP., LC#65-21912.
ANNOTATED BIBLIOGRAPHY OF LATIN AMERICAN HISTORICAL MATERIALS FROM THE 16TH-20TH CENTURIES. ARRANGED INTO GENERAL OR REGIONAL STUDIES WITHIN CHRONOLOGICAL PERIODS. SELECTED LIST OF BIBLIOGRAPHICAL AND BIOGRAPHICAL AIDS APPENDED TO TEXT. SOURCES IN LANGUAGES OTHER THAN SPANISH ARE INCLUDED.

3351 WILLIAMS B.H.

"FREEDOM AS A SLOGAN IN INTERNATIONAL CONFLICT."
SOCIAL SCIENCE, 42 (JAN. 67), 3-9.
AS USED BY GREAT POWERS IN EXPLAINING THEIR MILITARY OPERATION ABROAD, SLOGAN "FREEDOM," HAS SOMETIMES COVERED THE BEGINNINGS OF CONQUEST. IN THE VIETNAM CONFLICT THIS SLOGAN IS USED BY ALL FACTIONS.

3352 WILLIAMS P.
AID IN UGANDA - EDUCATION.
LONDON: MIN OF OVERSEAS DEVEL, 1966, 152 PP.
EXAMINES ROLE OF EXTERNAL AID IN PROMOTING DEVELOPMENT OF UGANDA'S EDUCATIONAL SYSTEM AND SUGGESTS WAYS IN WHICH CONTRIBUTION, PARTICULARLY THAT OF BRITAIN, MIGHT BE MADE MORE FRUITFUL. CLOSELY EXAMINES STRUCTURE AND DEVELOPMENT OF UGANDA'S EDUCATION SYSTEM AND DISCUSSES SOME OF THE DIFFICULT CHOICES FACING PLANNERS.

3353 WILLIAMS S.P. ED.
TOWARD A GENUINE WORLD SECURITY SYSTEM (PAMPHLET)
BOSTON: UNITED WORLD FEDERALISTS, 1964, 65 PP., LC#64-20453.
ANNOTATED BIBLIOGRAPHY OF SOURCES FOR AREAS OF WORLD LAW, ORDER, AND PEACE. INCLUDES INTRODUCTORY BOOKS AND SYMPOSIA FOR THE BEGINNER, TOPICAL FOCUS ON DETAILED AREAS, INDEX OF AUTHORS, EDITORS, PERIODICALS. CONTAINS 355 ENTRIES, MAJORITY DATED 1962-1963.

3354 WILLIAMS W.A.
THE UNITED STATES, CUBA, AND CASTRO: AN ESSAY ON THE DYNAMICS OF REVOLUTION AND THE DISSOLUTION OF EMPIRE.
NEW YORK: MONTHLY REVIEW PR, 1962, 179 PP., LC#62-22081.
CRITICAL STUDY OF AMERICAN INVOLVEMENT IN CUBA, ITS GOVERNMENT, AND CASTRO'S TACTICS TO CONTROL THE ISLAND. INCLUDES POLITICAL MORALITY ON EXPANSION AND INTERVENTION.

3355 WILLIAMSON J.A.
GREAT BRITAIN AND THE COMMONWEALTH.
LONDON: ADAMS & CHARLES BLACK, 1965, 214 PP.
HISTORY OF FORMATION, DEVELOPMENT, AND RELATIONS OF BRITISH EMPIRE AND COMMONWEALTH. TREATS TRANSFORMATION OF EMPIRE TO COMMONWEALTH IN DETAIL BY COVERING POLITICAL FIGURES AND WORLD EVENTS DURING PERIOD. DISCUSSES PROS AND CONS OF BRITISH POLICY TOWARD SUBJECTS.

3356 WILLIS F.R. ED.
DE GAULLE: ANACHRONISM, REALIST, OR PROPHET?
NEW YORK: HOLT RINEHART WINSTON, 1967, 122 PP., LC#67-10598.
SELECTED READINGS DEALING WITH FOUR PHASES OF DEGAULLE'S CAREER: THEORIST OF TANK WARFARE (1932-39), HEAD OF FREE FRENCH AND PREMIER OF LIBERATED FRANCE, LEADER OF THE UNSUCCESSFUL RALLY OF THE FRENCH PEOPLE, AND PREMIER OF THE FOURTH AND PRESIDENT OF THE FIFTH REPUBLIC. INCLUDES WRITINGS BY ADMIRERS (FRENCH AND FOREIGN), PASSIONATELY INVOLVED CRITICS, AND PROFESSIONALOBSERVERS.

3357 WILLOUGHBY W.R.
THE ST LAWRENCE WATERWAY: A STUDY IN POLITICS AND DIPLOMACY.
MADISON: U. WISCONSIN PR., 1961, 381 PP.
EMPHASIZES THE BEHIND-THE-SCENES POLITICAL DEVELOPMENTS (POLITICAL ECONOMICS, PRESSURE GROUPS, LEGISLATION) WHICH LED UP TO THE CREATION OF THE MODERN WATERWAY SYSTEM.

3358 WILPERT C.
"A LOOK IN THE MIRROR AND OVER THE WALL."
COMMONWEAL, 86 (MAY 67), 224-225.
RESULTS OF A RECENT SURVEY SHOW ATTITUDES IN WEST GERMANY CHANGING TOWARD REUNIFICATION WITH EAST GERMANY. MOST GERMANS FAVOR A PRAGMATIC POLICY, WITH SOME PROGRESS TOWARD REUNIFICATION. THERE IS A DECLINE IN THOSE WHO ARE STRONGLY COMMITTED TO REUNIFICATION, AND FEW ARE WILLING TO SEE REUNIFICATION AT THE COST OF BASIC CHANGES IN THE FEDERAL REPUBLIC.

3359 WILSON G.G.
HANDBOOK OF INTERNATIONAL LAW.
ST. PAUL: WEST, 1939, 567 PP.
SETS FORTH HISTORICAL DEVELOPMENT OF BASIC PRINCIPLES OF INTERNATIONAL LAW. EXAMINES PROBLEMS OF EXISTENCE, INDEPENDENCE AND EQUALITY. ANALYZES DOMAIN PROCESS. SURVEYS DIPLOMATIC AND CONSULAR RELATIONSHIPS. CONCLUDES WITH STUDY OF NATURE AND CONTEMPLATES CAUSES OF WAR.

3360 WILSON H.A.
THE IMPERIAL POLICY OF SIR ROBERT BORDEN.
GAINESVILLE: U OF FLA PR, 1966, 76 PP., LC#66-63921.
STUDIES POLITICAL CAREER OF SIR ROBERT BORDEN, PRIME MINISTER OF CANADA FROM 1911 1920. COVERS CANADIAN-BRITISH RELATIONSHIP, AND MAJOR CHANGES IN CONSTITUTIONAL STRUCTURE OF COMMONWEALTH AT THAT TIME, INCLUDING STATUS OF DOMINION.

3361 WILSON P. ED.
GOVERNMENT AND POLITICS OF INDIA AND PAKISTAN: 1885-1955; A BIBLIOGRAPHY OF WORKS IN WESTERN LANGUAGES.
BERKELEY: U CAL INST ASIA STUD, 1956, 357 PP., LC#56-63303.
BIBLIOGRAPHY INCLUDES BOOKS, PAMPHLETS, AND NONSERIAL GOVERNMENT PUBLICATIONS. WORKS ARRANGED UNDER BROAD SUBJECT DIVISIONS AND CHRONOLOGICALLY BY DATE OF PUBLICATION. WORKS INDEXED BY AUTHOR, TITLE, BY SERIES, AND PUBLISHER. INCLUDES 5,294 ITEMS ON GENERAL HISTORY, POLITICS, CONSTITUTIONAL HISTORY, GOVERNMENT AND ADMINISTRATION, AND INTERNATIONAL RELATIONS.

3362 WILSON P.
SOUTH ASIA; A SELECTED BIBLIOGRAPHY ON INDIA, PAKISTAN, CEYLON (PAMPHLET)
NEW YORK: AMER INST PACIFIC REL, 1957, 43 PP.
UNANNOTATED BIBLIOGRAPHY OF INTRODUCTORY LITERATURE, INCLUDING BIBLIOGRAPHIES, REFERENCE WORKS, AND PRIMARY SOURCE MATERIAL, STRESSING RECENT WORKS CONCERNING INDIA, PAKISTAN, AND CEYLON. CLASSIFIED WITHIN GEOGRAPHICAL DIVISIONS BY CHRONOLOGICAL SUBJECT OR FORMAT OF WORK.

3363 WING D. ED.
SHORT-TITLE CATALOGUE OF BOOKS PRINTED IN THE BRITISH ISLES, AND OF ENGLISH BOOKS PRINTED OVERSEAS; 1641-1700 (3 VOLS.)
NEW YORK: INDEX SOCIETY, 1945, 1603 PP.
LIST OF BOOKS PUBLISHED DURING THE PERIOD, ARRANGED BY AUTHOR. INCLUDES FOREIGN-LANGUAGE BOOKS PUBLISHED IN BRITISH ISLES AND BRITISH AMERICA.

3364 WINT G.
COMMUNIST CHINA'S CRUSADE: MAO'S ROAD TO POWER AND THE NEW CAMPAIGN FOR WORLD REVOLUTION.
NEW YORK: FREDERICK PRAEGER, 1965, 136 PP., LC#64-22934.
DESCRIBES COMMUNIST TAKEOVER IN CHINA AND SINO-SOVIET RELATIONS, EMPHASIZING THE IMPACT OF CHINA'S REVOLUTION UPON ASIA.

3365 WINT G. ED.
ASIA: A HANDBOOK.
NEW YORK: FREDERICK PRAEGER, 1965, 856 PP., LC#65-13263.
ARTICLES ABOUT RELATIONS BETWEEN THE ASIAN STATES AND THE REST OF THE WORLD, FOCUSING ON THE GROWTH IN WORLD POWER EXERCISED BY THESE COUNTRIES. GIVE BASIC COUNTRY-BY-COUNTRY INFORMATION AND SURVEYS, EMPHASIZING POLITICAL, SOCIAL, ECONOMIC, CULTURAL, AND RELIGIOUS ASPECTS OF ASIA, WITH MAPS AND EXTRACTS FROM TREATIES AND AGREEMENTS SIGNED SINCE WWII.

3366 WINT G. ED.
"ASIA: A HANDBOOK."
NEW YORK: FREDERICK PRAEGER, 1966.
COMPREHENSIVE REFERENCE WORK ON ASIA CONTAINING ESSAYS ON POLITICAL, SOCIAL, ECONOMIC, CULTURAL, AND RELIGIOUS ASPECTS OF ASIA; MAPS; EXTRACTS FROM TREATIES AND AGREEMENTS SIGNED SINCE 1945; AND BASIC INFORMATION AND SURVEYS ON EACH NATION. UNANNOTATED BIBLIOGRAPHY OF AMERICAN PUBLICATIONS RELEASED SINCE 1952, WITH EMPHASIS ON POST-1960 WORKS.

3367 WINTER R.C.
BLUEPRINTS FOR INDEPENDENCE.
AMSTERDAM: DJAMBATAN, 1961, 351 PP.
DISCUSSES NEW STATES AND THEIR ORGANIZATION, CITING EMERGENCE OF FORMER COLONIES, PROTECTORATES, MANDATES, AND OTHER TERRITORIES. INCLUDES DOCUMENTS OF INDEPENDENCE LISTED BY COUNTRY.

3368 WINTHROP H.
"CONTEMPORARY ECONOMIC DEHUMANIZATION* SOME DIFFICULTIES SURROUNDING ITS REDUCTION."
SOCIAL SCIENCE, 42 (APR. 67), 80-85.
CONSIDERS THE DEHUMANIZING EFFECTS OF A WORLD ECONOMY IN WHICH THE US, WITH 10 PER CENT OF WORLD POPULATION, CONSUMES 80 PER CENT OF RAW MATERIAL. CONCLUDES THAT ECONOMIC HUMANIZATION NEEDS SPECIFIC PROGRAMS OF ACTION WHICH FACE THE COMPLEX REALITIES OF ANY SUCH REFORM, INCLUDING THE POSSIBLE LOWERING OF LIVING STANDARDS IN TECHNOLOGICALLY DEVELOPED NATIONS AND THE CONTROL OF POPULATION GROWTH.

3369 WIONCZEK M.
"LATIN AMERICA FREE TRADE ASSOCIATION."
INT. CONCIL., 551 (JAN. 65), 80 PP.
CRITIQUE OF LATIN AMERICAN NATIONALISM AS A STRUCTURE ON TRADE AND ECONOMIC DEVELOPMENT IN THAT AREA. CITES UTILITY OF LAFTA IN REGIONAL COOPERATION.

3370 WITHERELL J.W.
OFFICIAL PUBLICATIONS OF FRENCH EQUATORIAL AFRICA, FRENCH CAMEROONS, AND TOGO, 1946-1958 (PAMPHLET)
WASHINGTON: LIBRARY OF CONGRESS, 1964, 78 PP., LC#64-60029.
AN ANNOTATED BIBLIOGRAPHY OF 405 PUBLICATIONS CONCERNED WITH AFRIQUE EQUATORIALE FRANCAISE AND THE TRUST TERRITORIES WHICH WERE ISSUED DURING THE TERM OF THE FOURTH REPUBLIC. COVERS PUBLICATIONS OF GOVERNMENT GENERAL OF FRENCH EQUATORIAL AFRICA, GOVERNMENTS OF FOUR TERRITORIES WHICH COMPRISED AEF, AND THE ADMINISTRATIONS IN THE CAMEROONS AND TOGO FROM 1946-58. SOURCES IN FRENCH AND ENGLISH.

3371 WITHERELL J.W. ED.
MADAGASCAR AND ADJACENT ISLANDS; A GUIDE TO OFFICIAL

PUBLICATIONS (PAMPHLET)
WASHINGTON: LIBRARY OF CONGRESS, 1965, 58 PP., LC#65-61703.
BIBLIOGRAPHY OF 927 ITEMS DATING FROM ESTABLISHMENTS OF FRENCH ADMINISTRATIONS IN MADAGASCAR, COMORO ISLANDS, AND REUNION, AND BRITISH ADMINISTRATIONS IN MAURITIUS AND SEYCHELLES. TERMINAL DATE FOR MADAGASCAR IS 1958. OTHERS CONTINUE TO PRESENT. INCLUDES PUBLICATIONS OF COLONIAL AND LOCAL GOVERNMENT. ARRANGED ALPHABETICALLY BY AUTHOR AND TITLE UNDER LOCALE. AUTHOR AND SUBJECT INDEXES INCLUDED.

3372 WITHERS W.
THE ECONOMIC CRISIS IN LATIN AMERICA.
NEW YORK: FREE PRESS OF GLENCOE, 1964, 307 PP., LC#64-21208.
SURVEYS ECONOMIC CONDITIONS AND PROBLEMS IN LATIN AMERICA, AS A WHOLE AND IN SPECIFIC COUNTRIES. BELIEVES RESISTANCE TO COMMUNISM DEPENDS ON MIDDLE CLASSES' RETENTION OF POLITICAL POWER. URGES GREATER AWARENESS BY US OF BASIC PROBLEM OF ECONOMIC DEVELOPMENT IN FORM OF SOCIALIZED CAPITALISM AS FORMULATED UNDER LEADERSHIP OF MEXICO.

3373 WITTFOGEL K.A.
"RUSSIA AND ASIA: PROBLEMS OF CONTEMPORARY AREA STUDIES AND INTERNATIONAL RELATIONS."
WORLD POLIT., 2 (JULY 50), 445-462.
MUST UNDERSTAND THE INFLUENCE OF ASIAN DESPOTISM ON RUSSIAN SOCIETY. SOVIET GOVERNMENTAL MANAGEMENT OF AGRICULTURE AND THE CONTINUED BUREAUCRATIC CONTROL OF THE ECONOMY DESPITE INDUSTRIALIZATION REFLECT THE ORIENTAL INFLUENCE. BROAD KNOWLEDGE OF FOREIGN COUNTRIES CALLED FOR IN ORDER TO MAKE USA FOREIGN-AID AN EFFECTIVE WEAPON.

3374 WODDIS J.
AFRICA: THE ROOTS OF REVOLT.
LONDON: LAWRENCE & WISHART, 1960, 285 PP.
DISCUSSES IMPACT OF IMPERIALISM ON AFRICA, SOCIAL AND ECONOMIC CHANGES CAUSING REVOLT, AND METHODS EMPLOYED TO ELIMINATE MISERY AND OPPRESSION. ATTEMPTS TO SEE PROBLEMS OF AFRICA THROUGH EYES OF AFRICANS IN POLITICS AND ECONOMY.

3375 WOETZEL R.K.
THE INTERNATIONAL CONTROL OF AIRSPACE AND OUTERSPACE.
BAD-GOPESBERG: ASGARD, 1960, 97 PP.
ANALYZES LEGAL ASPECTS OF SPACE PENETRATION. PROBES INTO THE MANY UNSOLVED PROBLEMS OF SOVEREIGNTY AND SOVEREIGN RIGHTS. CONSIDERS LEGAL CHARACTER OF SPACE IN TERMS OF INTERNATIONAL LAW. CONCLUDES THAT AIR SPACE BE LIMITED TO SIXTY MILES BASED ON THE LIMITING FACTOR OF CONVENTIONAL AIRCRAFTS IMPOSED BY CONDITIONS OF NATURE. SUGGESTS SPACE ABOVE SIXTY MILES BE CONSIDERED AS RES COMMUNIS UNDER SOME INTERNATIONAL CONTROL.

3376 WOETZEL R.K.
THE NURENBERG TRIALS IN INTERNATIONAL LAW.
NEW YORK: PRAEGER, 1962, 287 PP.
ATTEMPTS TO SHOW JURIDICAL BASIS FOR INTERNATIONAL MILITARY TRIBUNAL, WHETHER INDIVIDUAL LIABILITY ACTUALLY EXISTED FOR DENOTED CRIMES, I.E. WAR CRIMES, CRIMES AGAINST PEACE AND HUMANITY, AND WHETHER THESE CRIMES CAN ACTUALLY BE CONSIDERED INTERNATIONAL IN SCOPE.

3377 WOHL R.
FRENCH COMMUNISM IN THE MAKING 1914-1924.
STANFORD: STANFORD U PRESS, 1966, 530 PP., LC#66-15303.
STUDIES COMMUNIST MOVEMENT IN FRANCE BEGINNING WITH WORKING-CLASS MOVEMENTS BEFORE 1914 AND FOLLOWING IT TO WWI WHEN ITS PREDECESSORS FELL AND IT SURVIVED. INCLUDES DISCUSSION OF WHY WORKING-CLASS MOVEMENTS WERE SUSCEPTIBLE TO COMMUNIST CONTROL AND WHAT MADE FRENCH COMMUNISM DIFFERENT FROM THAT OF OTHER EUROPEAN COUNTRIES. EXAMINES RELATIONSHIP TO RUSSIAN REVOLUTION AND SOVIET REGIME.

3378 WOLF C.
FOREIGN AID: THEORY AND PRACTICE IN SOUTHERN ASIA.
PRINCETON: U. PR., 1960, 442 PP., $7.50.
ATTEMPTS TO CO-ORDINATE THEORY AND PRACTICE IN THE DISPOSITION OF FOREIGN-AID THROUGH A CONSIDERATION OF ALTERNATIVE METHODS OF DERIVING AN EFFECTIVE ALLOCATION FORMULA. THROUGHOUT BOOK, ATTEMPTS ARE MADE TO QUANTIFY PROXIMATE OBJECTIVES OF FOREIGN-AID AND TO SUBJECT THE RESULTING HYPOTHESES TO EMPIRICAL VERIFICATION.

3379 WOLF C.
"SOME ASPECTS OF THE 'VALUE' OF LESS-DEVELOPED COUNTRIES TO THE UNITED STATES."
WORLD POLIT., 15 (JULY 63), 623-635.
DISTINGUISHES BETWEEN 'DIRECT AND INDIRECT VALUE' OF A PARTICULAR COUNTRY TO USA, USSR AND COMMUNIST CHINA WITH REGARD TO LOCAL WARS AND 'CENTRAL-WAR CONTINGENCIES'. EXAMINES CONCEPT IN TERMS OF ITS MILITARY, ECONOMIC, POLITICAL AND PSYCHOLOGICAL ASPECTS.

3380 WOLFERS A.
BRITAIN AND FRANCE BETWEEN TWO WORLD WARS.
NEW YORK: HARCOURT BRACE, 1940, 446 PP.
DISCUSSES FOREIGN POLICIES OF BRITAIN AND FRANCE DURING INTERIM PERIOD, 1918-38. RELATES TREATY OF VERSAILLES, ECONOMIC TACTICS, AND POLITICAL ISOLATION TO ONSET OF WWII. IMPLICATES US IN POLICY ERRORS OF THESE TWO COUNTRIES.

3381 WOLFERS A.
"COLLECTIVE SECURITY AND THE WAR IN KOREA."
YALE REV., 43 (JUNE 54), 487-496.
DEFINES COLLECTIVE SECURITY TO DETERMINE WHETHER THE UN ACTION IN KOREA JUSTIFIES BEING HERALDED AS FIRST EXPERIMENT IN COLLECTIVE SECURITY. CONCLUDES THAT ACTION IN KOREA IS EXAMPLE OF COLLECTIVE MILITARY DEFENSE BASED ON TRADITIONAL POWER POLITICS.

3382 WOLFERS A. ED.
THE ANGLO-AMERICAN TRADITION IN FOREIGN AFFAIRS.
NEW HAVEN: YALE U. PR., 1956, 286 PP.
SERIES OF READINGS SHOW GROWTH OF CONCEPT OF INTERNATIONAL RELATIONS. CLASSICAL INTERNATIONAL THEORISTS DISCUSS MOTIVES OF COMMUNITY AND CONFLICT. BRITISH AND AMERICAN WRITERS ASSESS NATIONAL SECURITY MOTIVE AND MORAL DEFENSE INTERESTS.

3383 WOLFERS A.
"ACTORS IN INTERNATIONAL POLITICS.
IN (FOX,WTR. THEORETICAL ASPECTS OF INTERNATIONAL."
RELATIONS, NOTRE DAME: U. PR., 1959, CHAPTER 6, 83-1061.
AUTHOR REMINDS US TO APPROACH INTERNATIONAL POLITICS, NOT FROM USUAL IMPERSONAL MANNER, BUT BY REGARDING STATES AS MAJOR ACTORS. BEHAVIOR OF STATES AS ORGANIZED BODIES OF MEN AND HUMAN PSYCHOLOGICAL REACTIONS MUST BE SIMULTANEOUSLY STUDIED.

3384 WOLFERS A.
ALLIANCE POLICY IN THE COLD WAR.
BALTIMORE: JOHNS HOPKINS PRESS, 1959, 319 PP., LC#59-10764.
ESSAYS BY MEMBERS OF RESEARCH STAFF OF WASHINGTON CENTER OF FOREIGN POLICY RESEARCH, ON PROBLEMS OF INTER-ALLIED RELATIONS.

3385 WOLFERS A.
DISCORD AND COLLABORATION: ESSAYS ON INTERNATIONAL POLITICS.
BALTIMORE: JOHNS HOPKINS PR., 1962, 283 PP.
PROBE UNDERLYING THEORETICAL PROPOSITIONS AND PRINCIPLES OF PRESENT-DAY INTERNATIONAL RELATIONS. QUESTIONS MEANING AND PURSUIT OF 'NATIONAL SECURITY'. EVALUATES APPLICABILITY OF TRADITIONAL POLITICAL THEORY TO INTERNATIONAL RELATIONS.

3386 WOLFERS A.
"INTEGRATION IN THE WEST: THE CONFLICT OF PERSPECTIVES."
INT. ORGAN., 17 (SUMMER 63), 753-771.
BELIEVES USA MUST TURN TO THE ECONOMIC FIELD TO APPRECIATE THE SUCCESS OF EUROPEAN MOVEMENT AND TO DISCOVER (FROM THE PERSPECTIVE OF EUROPEAN NATIONS) CHIEF PREREQUISITES OF CONTINUED PROGRESS TOWARD GOAL OF COMPLETE INTEGRATION.

3387 WOLFF C.
JUS GENTIUM METHODO SCIENTIFICA PERTRACTATUM.
OXFORD: CLARENDON, 1934, 541 PP.
ANALYZES OBLIGATIONS OF NATIONS. PRESENTS THEORY OF NATIONAL OWNERSHIP, TREATIES AND OTHER AGREEMENTS. EXPLORES INTERNATIONAL LAW OF WAR. DISCUSSES PEACE AND PEACE TREATIES.

3388 WOLFF R.L.
THE BALKANS IN OUR TIME.
CAMBRIDGE: HARVARD U PR, 1956, 618 PP., LC#56-6529.
INTRODUCTORY STUDY OF BALKAN COUNTRIES - YUGOSLAVIA, RUMANIA, BULGARIA, AND ALBANIA. DESCRIBES COUNTRIES AND PEOPLE, GIVING HISTORY FROM FOURTH CENTURY TO WWII. ANALYZES BALKAN ECONOMY SINCE WWII. STUDIES WAR YEARS, COMMUNIST TAKE-OVER, SOVIET-YUGOSLAV DISPUTE, YUGOSLAVIA SINCE BREAK WITH COMINFORM, POLITICAL LIFE IN BALKANS SINCE 1948, BALKAN ECONOMIES SINCE 1948, BALKAN RELIGION, EDUCATION, CULTURE.

3389 WOOD B.
THE MAKING OF THE GOOD NEIGHBOR POLICY.
NEW YORK: COLUMBIA U PRESS, 1961, 438 PP., LC#61-15470.
ANALYZES POLICY FROM 1926 TO 1943 IN TERMS OF VARIOUS DIPLOMATIC CRISES WITH LATIN AMERICA. EACH CRISIS IS EXAMINED CLOSELY AND ITS PEACEFUL RESOLUTION IS SHOWN TO BE A BUILDING BLOCK OF THE POLICY. MAINTAINS THAT ABOLITION OF FORCE FROM US-LATIN AMERICAN DIPLOMACY CREATED A NEW FRAMEWORK WHICH THE US DID NOT WHOLLY UNDERSTAND.

3390 WOOD H.B.
"STRETCHING YOUR FOREIGN-AID DOLLAR."
PUB. ADMIN. REV., 24 (DEC. 64), 244-249.
URGING THAT PRODUCTIVITY STUDIES OF THE ECONOMIC DEVELOPMENT DOLLAR IN FOREIGN COUNTRIES MIGHT PROVIDE USEFUL INFORMATION FOR CONGRESS. THE AUTHOR CONTENDS THAT THE PRODUCTIVITY OF ECONOMIC AID CAN BE INCREASED THROUGH A MORE EXTENSIVE USE OF CONTRACTS AND A CORRESPONDING REDUCTION OF 'DIRECT-HIRE' PERSONNEL.

3391 WOODHOUSE C.M.
THE NEW CONCERT OF NATIONS.

LONDON: THE BODLEY HEAD, 1964, 103 PP.
DISCUSSES EVOLUTION OF INTERNATIONAL RELATIONS AND CALLS FOR END TO COLONIALISM AND FOREIGN AID TO UNDERDEVELOPED COUNTRIES, NOTES SOURCE OF PRESENT DISEQUILIBRIUM, OLD AND NEW NATIONALISMS, AND EMERGING CONCERT OF NATIONS.

3392 WOODWARD E.L. ED., BUTLER R. ED.
DOCUMENTS ON BRITISH FOREIGN POLICY 1919-39 (9 VOLS.)
LONDON: GT BRIT FOREIGN OFFICE, 1955.
SELECTED COLLECTION OF FOREIGN OFFICE DOCUMENTS AND COMMUNICATIONS FROM PERIOD, IN NINE VOLUMES PUBLISHED 1947-55. ARRANGED BY TOPICAL CHAPTERS WITHIN EACH YEAR OF PERIOD AND THEN CHRONOLOGICALLY. INCLUDES MATERIALS IN FRENCH AND MAPS.

3393 WOOLBERT R.G.
FOREIGN AFFAIRS BIBLIOGRAPHY, 1932-1942.
NEW YORK: HARPER & ROW, 1945, 705 PP., LC#33-7094.
A SELECTED AND ANNOTATED LIST OF 10,000 BOOKS ON INTERNATIONAL RELATIONS COVERING THE DECADE FROM MID-1932 TO MID-1942. INCLUDES BOOKS IN ALL WESTERN LANGUAGES AS WELL AS TURKISH, HEBREW, ARABIC, CHINESE, AND JAPANESE. BOOKS CLASSIFIED INTO ANALYTICAL, CHRONOLOGICAL, AND REGIONAL TREATMENTS, AND INDEXED BY AUTHOR.

3394 WOOLF L.
EMPIRE AND COMMERCE IN AFRICA.
NEW YORK: MACMILLAN, 1920, 374 PP.
DENOTES STATE'S AUTHORITY OVER ECONOMIC AFFAIRS OF COLONY. ANALYZES PSYCHOLOGICAL FACTORS MOTIVATING EUROPEAN COUNTRIES TO ENTER COLONIAL WARS. EXTENSIVE COVERAGE OF EFFECTS OF IMPERIALISM ON AFRICA. POINTS OUT POSSIBILITIES FOR AFRICAN ECONOMIC FUTURE.

3395 WOOLLEY H.B.
MEASURING TRANSACTIONS BETWEEN WORLD AREAS.
NEW YORK: NATL BUREAU ECO RES, 1966, 157 PP., LC#65-24368.
BRINGS TOGETHER PAYMENTS ACCOUNTS OF ALL COUNTRIES AND FITS THEM INTO A PLAN SHOWING WORLD TRADE AND PAYMENTS BY TRANSACTION MATRIXES. COVERS MERCHANDISE AND SERVICE TRANSACTIONS, UNILATERAL TRANSFERS, CAPITAL AND GOLD MOVEMENTS, AND MULTILATERAL SETTLEMENTS. DESCRIBES STATISTICAL RESEARCH METHODS, LIMITS OF DATA, AND IMPORTANCE OF RESULTS FOR MEASUREMENT OF MULTILATERAL SETTLEMENTS.

3396 WORLD PEACE FOUNDATION
DOCUMENTS OF INTERNATIONAL ORGANIZATIONS: A SELECTED BIBLIOGRAPHY.
BOSTON: WORLD PEACE FOUNDATION.
QUARTERLY BIBLIOGRAPHY, FIRST PUBLISHED IN 1947, IS LIMITED TO OFFICIAL DOCUMENTATION OF UN, ITS SPECIALIZED AGENCIES, LEAGUE OF NATIONS, REGIONAL ORGANIZATIONS, WAR AND TRANSITIONAL ORGANIZATIONS AND OTHER FUNCTIONAL ORGANIZATIONS. MATERIALS GROUPED BY ORGANIZATION AND TOPIC. ANNOTATIONS USED SPARINGLY. PUBLICATION CONTINUED FOR 3 YEARS. LIMITED TO MATERIALS IN LIBRARY OF WORLD PIECE FOUNDATION.

3397 WORLD PEACE FOUNDATION
"INTERNATIONAL ORGANIZATIONS: SUMMARY OF ACTIVITIES."
INT. ORGAN., 18 (SPRING 64), 302-485.
GIVES COMPLETE BREAK-DOWN OF UN'S ORGANIZATION AND FUNCTIONS THROUGH A STUDY OF MEMBERS, GENERAL ASSEMBLY, SECURITY COUNCIL AND SPECIFIC EXAMPLES OF PAST POLICIES AND PROCEDURES, E.G. INDIA-PAKISTAN DISPUTE, CYPRUS-TURKISH QUESTION.

3398 WRESZIN M.
OSWALD GARRISON VILLARD: PACIFIST AT WAR.
BLOOMINGTON: INDIANA U PR, 1965, 333 PP., LC#65-11795.
FOCUSES ON VILLARD AS EDITOR OF THE NATION FROM 1918 TO 1933, AND HIS INFLUENCE ON LIBERAL MOVEMENTS. EXAMINES HIS VIEWS ON PEACE, NEUTRALITY, THE LEAGUE, NEGRO RIGHTS, WOMAN SUFFRAGE, THE TARIFF, CIVIL LIBERTIES, NATZISM, AND THE NEW DEAL.

3399 WRIGGINS W.H.
"CEYLON: DILEMMAS OF A NEW NATION."
PRINCETON: PRINCETON U PRESS, 1960.
ANALYSIS OF THE COMPLEXITIES OF CEYLON'S POLITICAL SYSTEM AND AN EXAMINATION OF FUNDAMENTAL PROBLEMS THAT HAVE DOMINATED PUBLIC AFFAIRS SINCE INDEPENDENCE. SUGGESTS DEVELOPMENTS IN CEYLON MAY PROGNOSTICATE POSSIBILITIES FOR THE FUTURE OF OTHER NEWLY INDEPENDENT COUNTRIES IN ASIA. UNANNOTATED BIBLIOGRAPHY OF PUBLIC DOCUMENTS, BOOKS, PAMPHLETS, AND PERIODICALS. MOST SOURCES POST-1950 AND IN ENGLISH.

3400 WRIGHT P.Q., ED.
PUBLIC OPINION AND WORLD POLITICS.
CHICAGO: U OF CHICAGO PRESS, 1933, 237 PP.
EXAMINES PUBLIC OPINION AND EFFECTS OF PROPAGANDA. DISCUSSES PUBLIC OPINION AS A FACTOR IN GOVERNMENT AND STRATEGIES OF OPINION-MOLDERS. STUDIES METHODS, SLOGANS, SYMBOLS, AND HISTORY OF POLITICAL PROPAGANDA. FOCUSES ON STRATEGY OF REVOLUTIONARY AND WAR PROPAGANDA.

3401 WRIGHT Q.
"THE ENFORCEMENT OF INTERNATIONAL LAW THROUGH MUNICIPAL LAW IN THE US."
IN (U. ILL. STUD. SOC. SCI., VOL. 5, 1916, 1-264).
REFERRING TO THEORETICAL RELATIONSHIP BETWEEN MUNICIPAL AND INTERNATIONAL LAW, ATTEMPTS TO DEFINE STATUS OF INTERNATIONAL LAW ENFORCEMENT IN USA. ENUMERATES LEGAL OBLIGATIONS OF BELLIGERENT TO ENEMIES.

3402 WRIGHT Q.
THE CONTROL OF AMERICAN FOREIGN RELATIONS.
NEW YORK: MACMILLAN, 1922, 412 PP.
DRAWS PARTICULAR ATTENTION TO DIFFICULTY IN CONTROL OF FOREIGN RELATIONS FOUND IN EVERY GOVERNMENT, PARTICULARLY IN THOSE WHERE ORGANS CONDUCTING FOREIGN RELATIONS HAVE RESPONSIBILITIES DEFINED BY INTERNATIONAL LAW AND POWERS DEFINED BY CONSTITUTIONAL LAW. PRESENTS ANALYTIC ACCOUNT OF LACK OF COORDINATION BETWEEN RESPONSIBILITIES AND POWERS. PRESENTS BOTH INTERNATIONAL AND CONSTITUTIONAL VIEWPOINT.

3403 WRIGHT Q.
MANDATES UNDER THE LEAGUE OF NATIONS.
CHICAGO: U. CHI. PR., 1930, 726 PP.
TRACES ORIGINS AND DEVELOPMENT OF MANDATE SYSTEM. DESCRIBES STRUCTURE OF SYSTEM AND ACTIVITIES OF PARTICIPATING PARTIES. SEEKS PLACE FOR SYSTEM WITHIN FRAMEWORK OF INTERNATIONAL LAW.

3404 WRIGHT Q. ED.
GOLD AND MONETARY STABILIZATION.
CHICAGO: U. CHI. PR., 1932, 174 PP.
SERIES OF LECTURES COVERS INTERNATIONAL ASPECTS OF THE GOLD STANDARD, MONEY AND BUSINESS CYCLE, FEDERAL RESERVE POLICY IN DEPRESSION, THE FUTURE OF GOLD STANDARD, AND MONETARY STABILITY AND THE GOLD STANDARD.

3405 WRIGHT Q.
"FUNDAMENTAL PROBLEMS OF INTERNATIONAL ORGANIZATION."
INT. CONCIL., 369 (APR. 41), 468-492.
CONSIDERS PROBLEMS OF INTERNATIONAL ORGANIZATION IN LIGHT OF: ORDER AND ANARCHY, SCOPE OF ORGANIZATIONS, REGIONAL AND UNIVERSAL ORGANIZATIONS, CHANGE AND STABILITY, EVOLUTION AND REVOLUTION, SANCTIONS, AND AUTHORITY AND CONSENT. SEES PROBLEM OF INTERNATIONAL ORGANIZATION AS RECOGNIZING LIMITATIONS ON NATIONAL SOVEREIGNTY AND PROVIDING FOR EXERCISE OF ORGANIZATIONS POWER WHILE CREATING WORLD CITIZENSHIP SENTIMENT.

3406 WRIGHT Q.
"CONSTITUTIONAL PROCEDURES OF THE US FOR CARRYING OUT OBLIGATIONS FOR MILITARY SANCTIONS."
AMER. J. INT. LAW, 138(1944), 678-684.
CALLS FOR A CONGRESSIONAL RESOLUTION AUTHORIZING THE PRESIDENT TO USE ARMED FORCES IN COLLABORATION WITH OTHER COUNTRIES TO SUPPRESS ACTS FOUND TO CONSTITUTE AGGRESSION AND ARE CONTRARY TO INTERNATIONAL LAW.

3407 WRIGHT Q.
"THE US AND INTERNATIONAL AGREEMENTS."
AMER. J. INT. LAW., 38 (1944), 341-355.
DEALS WITH EFFORTS CONCERNING CONCLUSION OF WAR AND THE ESTABLISHMENT OF INSTITUTIONS FOR PERPETUATING PEACE. CITES PRESIDENT'S LEGAL POWERS TO NEGOTIATE ON THESE SUBJECTS AND INTERRELATIONS BETWEEN HIM AND BOTH HOUSES OF CONGRESS.

3408 WRIGHT Q.
"CONGRESS AND THE TREATY-MAKING POWER."
PROC. AMER. SOC. INT. LAW, 1952, 43-69.
DEALS WITH STATEMENT CONCERNING CONSTITUTIONAL POWERS OF THE PRESIDENT AND THE CONGRESS, INDICATING POSSIBLIITY OR PROBABILITY OF FREQUENT CONFLICTS. PRESENTS DIRECTIONS FOR CONSTITUTIONAL AMENDMENTS TO IMPROVE CONDUCT OF FOREIGN RELATIONS.

3409 WRIGHT Q.
PROBLEMS OF STABILITY AND PROGRESS IN INTERNATIONAL RELATIONSHIPS.
BERKELEY: U. CALIF. PR., 1954, 378 PP.
DISCUSSES POSSIBILITY OF USING SCIENCE, EDUCATION, ORGANIZATION, LAW AND POLITICS TO CREATE GREATER HARMONY IN FIELD OF INTERNATIONAL RELATIONS. FAVORS CENTRALIZATION OF INSTITUTIONS THROUGH UN FRAMEWORK. STUDIES GROUP BEHAVIOR.

3410 WRIGHT Q.
THE STUDY OF INTERNATIONAL RELATIONS.
NEW YORK: APPLETON, 1955, 584 PP.
ATTEMPTS TO PROVIDE A COMPREHENSIVE TEXTBOOK ON INTERNATIONAL RELATIONS. PROBES CHARACTERISTICS, SCOPE, AND LIMITS OF STUDY OF INTERNATIONAL POLITICS. DISTINGUISHES BETWEEN INTERNATIONAL RELATIONS AS A CONDITION AND AS A DISCIPLINE.

3411 WRIGHT Q.
"THE PEACEFUL ADJUSTMENT OF INTERNATIONAL RELATIONS: PROBLEMS AND RESEARCH APPROACHES."
J. SOC. ISSUES, 11 (1955), 3-12.
SEES PROBLEM SOLUTION FOR PEACEFUL WORLD AS VARIED, AND THEREFORE TYPES OF RESEARCH RELEVANT TO EACH CLASS OF PROBLEMS AS VARIED ALSO. DEVISES SCHEME OF CLASSIFICATION OF

PROBLEMS IN INTERNATIONAL RELATIONS INTO 4 TYPES, AS WELL AS CLASSIFICATION OF 4 TYPES OF RESEARCH.

3412 WRIGHT Q.
"THE VALUE OF CONFLICT RESOLUTION OF A GENERAL DISCIPLINE OF INTERNATIONAL RELATIONS."
J. CONFL. RESOLUT., 1 (MAR. 57), 4-8.
EXAMINES FORMS, NATURE AND CAUSES OF SOCIAL CONFLICT. STUDIES FEASIBILITY OF UNIFIED DISCIPLINE OF ALL ASPECTS OF INTERNATIONAL RELATIONSHIPS. MENTIONS VARIOUS METHODS FOR SETTLING INTERNATIONAL CONFLICTS. INDICATES HOW DISCIPLINE DISCUSSED WOULD AID SETTLEMENT.

3413 WRIGHT Q.
"LEGAL ASPECTS OF THE U-2 INCIDENT."
AMER. J. INT. LAW, 54 (OCT. 60), 836-54.
CONCERNED OVER US AUTHORIZATION OF U-2 FLIGHT AND VIOLATION OF INTERNATIONAL LAW - BUT DOES NOT CONSIDER U-2 AS ACT OF AGGRESSION. ASSERTS THAT FLIGHTS WERE MORALLY (NOT LEGALLY) RIGHT ACCORDING TO RULES OF SELF-PRESERVATION AND SOVIET ESPIONAGE ACTIVITIES ALTHOUGH CESSATION OF FLIGHTS AND APOLOGY WOULD HAVE BEEN APPROPRIATE. CONSIDERS USSR ACTION CORRECT. CITES DECISION-MAKING FLAWS OF USA GOVERNMENT.

3414 WRIGHT Q.
THE ROLE OF INTERNATIONAL LAW IN THE ELIMINATION OF WAR.
NEW YORK: OCEANA, 1961, 119 PP.
SURVEYS SCOPE OF INTERNATIONAL LAW, AND DISCUSSES ITS HISTORY, FUNCTIONS, CONTEMPORARY CONDITIONS, RULES OF ORDER AND FUTURE PROSPECTS.

3415 WRIGHT Q.
"STUDIES IN DETERRENCE: LIMITED WARS AND THE ROLE OF SEA-BORNE WEAPONS SYSTEMS."
CHINA LAKE: U.S.N.O.T.S., 1961.
ANALYZES GROWTH WAR TECHNIQUES AS FUNCTION OF INTERNATIONAL RELATIONS AND INCREASING SKILL. RECOMMENDS USA RE-EVALUATE ITS FOREIGN POLICY FROM WORLD VIEWPOINT. MAKES SPECIFIC SUGGESTIONS IN REGARD TO TACTICAL PROCEDURE.

3416 WRIGHT Q. ED.
PREVENTING WORLD WAR THREE.
NEW YORK: SIMON SCHUSTER, 1962, 450 PP.
ESSAYS ON PROBLEMS OF WAR AND PEACE WHICH HAVE BEEN DIVIDED INTO THREE PARTS: PROBLEMS CAUSED BY THE ARMS RACE, PROPOSALS REDUCING INTERNATIONAL TENSIONS CREATING A CLIMATE IN WHICH FRUITFUL NEGOTIATIONS MIGHT BE POSSIBLE AND STEPS THAT MUST BE TAKEN IF PROBLEMS DISCUSSED IN PARTS ONE AND TWO ARE NOT TO RECUR. ADVOCATES CHANGES IN THINKING AND SOCIAL ORGANIZATION OF HUMAN BEINGS.

3417 WRIGHT Q.
"PROJECTED EUROPEAN UNION AND AMERICAN INTERNATIONAL PRESTIGE."
ANN. AMER. ACAD. POLIT. SOC. SCI., 348 (JULY 63), 132-140.
ALTHOUGH USA ADVOCATED BRITAIN'S ENTRY INTO THE COMMON MARKET, NO LOSS OF PRESTIGE OCCURRED. ASSERTS THAT USA INFLUENCE WOULD INCREASE BY ACCOMMODATION TO OPINIONS OF DE GAULLE WITH REGARD TO HIS CONCEPT OF EUROPEAN UNION. SUGGESTS THAT REGIONAL ARRANGEMENTS SHOULD BE KEPT SMALL AND UNDER CLOSE SUPERVISION BY THE UNITED NATIONS.

3418 WRIGHT Q.
"DECLINE OF CLASSIC DIPLOMACY."
J. INT. AFF., 17 (NO.1, 63), 18-28.
HISTORICAL VIEW OF DIPLOMACY WITH ATTENTION TO UNDERLYING ASSUMPTIONS AND CONCEPTS. THE IMPACT OF DEMOCRACY, NATIONALISM, TECHNOLOGY AND UNIVERSAL IDEOLOGIES HAS UNDERMINED BASIS OF 'CLASSIC DIPLOMACY' AND THE 'BALANCE OF POWER'. NEW SOLUTIONS REQUIRED FOR CRISIS-SITUATIONS.

3419 WRIGHT Q.
A STUDY OF WAR.
CHICAGO: U OF CHICAGO PRESS, 1964, 451 PP.
STUDIES PHENOMENON OF WAR, ITS HISTORY, CAUSES, AND CONTROL. ATTEMPTS TO EXPLAIN WHY MILITARY BUDGETS RISE WHEN WAR IS CONSIDERED "OBSOLETE." MAINTAINS THAT SOLUTION TO PREVENTION OF WAR IS "ADAPTIVE STABILITY WITHIN WORLD-COMMUNITY," BUT THAT TECHNICAL AND SOCIAL DEVELOPMENTS ARE ACCENTUATING CONFLICT. INCLUDES EFFECTS OF WAR ON PEOPLE, LEGAL ASPECTS, AND STRUGGLE FOR POWER.

3420 WRIGHT T.P. JR.
AMERICAN SUPPORT OF FREE ELECTIONS ABROAD.
WASHINGTON: PUBLIC AFFAIRS PRESS, 1964, 184 PP., LC#64-19118
EXAMINES EIGHT CASE STUDIES OF US ELECTORAL INTERVENTION IN LATIN AMERICA FROM 1898-1933. NARRATES AND APPRAISES REVIVAL OF POLICY DURING COLD WAR. DISCUSSES POLICY BEHIND SUPPORT OF FREE ELECTIONS, LEADERS, METHODS, DEFINITIONS OF FREE ELECTIONS, AND ACHIEVEMENTS. MAINTAINS THAT US ENTERED DOMESTIC POLICY IN LATIN AMERICA RELUCTANTLY AND THAT OFTEN NEUTRALITY, NOT DEMOCRACY, RESULTED.

3421 WRINCH P.
THE MILITARY STRATEGY OF WINSTON CHURCHILL.
BOSTON: BOSTON U PR, 1961, 164 PP.
ANALYZES CHURCHILL'S BACKGROUND, MILITARY EDUCATION, AND CAREER CONCENTRATING ON HIS INTEREST IN "GRAND MILITARY STRATEGY." PROPOSES THEORY THAT HIS STRATEGY WAS SAME IN BOTH WORLD WARS. BOTH TIMES HE CONCENTRATED ON ACQUIRING ALLIES, AND HIS MILITARY STRATEGY THEREFORE BECAME ENMESHED IN HIS FOREIGN POLICY. FEELS STRATEGY DEVELOPED BECAUSE HE FELT ENGLAND TO BE A WEAK LAND POWER.

3422 WU E.
LEADERS OF TWENTIETH-CENTURY CHINA; AN ANNOTATED BIBLIOGRAPHY OF SELECTED CHINESE BIOGRAPHICAL WORKS IN HOOVER LIBRARY
STANFORD: HOOVER INSTITUTE, 1956, 106 PP.
ANNOTATED BIBLIOGRAPHICAL GUIDE IN CHINESE, ENGLISH, AND TRANSLITERATED CHINESE TO THE CHIEF CHINESE BIOGRAPHICAL COMPENDIA RESOURCES IN THE HOOVER LIBRARY. LISTS 500 ITEMS PUBLISHED SINCE 1900, ARRANGED ALPHABETICALLY BY AUTHOR, IN BOTH ROMANIZATION AND CHARACTERS. DESCRIPTIVE ANNOTATIONS IN ENGLISH.

3423 WUORINEN J.H.
"SCANDINAVIA."
ENGLEWOOD CLIFFS: PRENTICE HALL, 1965.
BIBLIOGRAPHICAL ESSAY OF ENGLISH BOOKS AND PERIODICALS FROM 1929-1964. ARRANGED BY GROUP TOPICS INCLUDING GENERAL HISTORIES, OFFICIAL PUBLICATIONS, ECONOMIC AND SOCIAL DEVELOPMENTS, FOREIGN POLICY AND AFFAIRS, AND SCANDINAVIAN COOPERATION. APPROXIMATELY 200 ENTRIES.

3424 WURFEL D.
"FOREIGN AID AND SOCIAL REFORM IN POLITICAL DEVELOPMENT" (BMR)
AM. POL. SCI. REV., 53 (JUNE 59), 456-482.
PRESENTS SOME GENERAL CONSIDERATIONS IN SUPPORT OF A PROPOSAL THAT US ATTEMPT TO STIMULATE SOCIAL CHANGE WITHIN CONTEXT OF A FOREIGN AID PROGRAM. DESCRIBES NATURE AND TECHNIQUES OF REFORM THROUGH ECONOMIC AID. REPORTS A PHILIPPINE PROGRAM AS CASE STUDY TO ILLUSTRATE EFFECTIVENESS OF SUCH AN AID ARRANGEMENT.

3425 WYTHE G.
THE UNITED STATES AND INTER-AMERICAN RELATIONS: A CONTEMPORARY APPRAISAL.
GANESVILLE: U. FLORIDA PR., 1964, 251 PP.
PINPOINTS SOURCES OF MISUNDERSTANDING AND TRACES EVOLUTION OF ANTI-AMERICANISM. TREATS COOPERATION IN OAS AND LATIN AMERICAN ATTITUDES TOWARD GLOBAL AND REGIONAL ORGANIZATIONS. EXAMINES CHARACTERISTICS AND PROBLEMS OF ECONOMIC STRUCTURES AND COVERS ASPECTS OF DOLLAR DIPLOMACY.

3426 WYZNER E.
"NIEKTORE ASPEKTY PRAWNE FINANSOWANIA OPERACJI ONZ W KONGO I NA BEIZKIM WSCHODZIE."
PAN. PRAVO, 18 (NO.7, 63), 41-50.
DISCUSSES CERTAIN ASPECTS OF FINANCING UN OPERATIONS IN CONGO. DOUBTS ASSEMBLY'S COMPETENCE CONCERNING EMPLOYMENT OF ARMED FORCES. STATES THAT ONLY SECURITY COUNCIL HAS THIS RIGHT.

3427 YALEM R.J.
REGIONALISM AND WORLD ORDER.
INT. AFF., 38 (OCT. 62), 460-471.
EXAMINES THE REASONS FOR THE GROWTH OF CONTEMPORARY REGIONALISM, TRACING THE LINES OF COMPATABILITY AND CONFLICT BETWEEN REGIONAL AND UNIVERSAL FORMS OF INTERNATIONAL ORGANIZATION. DISTINGUISHES BETWEEN REGIONALISM AND THE CONCEPT OF WORLD ORDER.

3428 YAMADA H.
ANNALS OF THE SOCIAL SCIENCES.
TOKYO: DOBUNKEN CO, LTD, 1957, 560 PP.
ANNOTATED BIBLIOGRAPHY WHICH TRACES THE GENERAL TRENDS OF THE SOCIAL SCIENCES THROUGH A CHRONOLOGICAL AND INTERNATIONAL SURVEY OF LITERATURE. COVERS MATERIAL SURVEYING HISTORICAL DEVELOPMENT OF THE SOCIAL SCIENCES FROM 15TH CENTURY TO WESTERN EUROPE THROUGH CONTEMPORARY INTERNATIONAL LITERATURE. SOURCES PRIMARILY IN ENGLISH, FRENCH, GERMAN, RUSSIAN, JAPANESE, AND ITALIAN.

3429 YAMAMURA K.
ECONOMIC POLICY IN POSTWAR JAPAN.
BERKELEY: U OF CALIF PR, 1967, 320 PP.
EXAMINES TWO POSTWAR ECONOMIC POLICIES - DEMOCRATIZATION IMPOSED BY "ALLIED POWERS" AND SUBSEQUENT REACTION OF DE-DEMOCRATIZATION PURSUED AND FORMULATED BY THE INDEPENDENT GOVERNMENT. CONSIDERS BOTH POLICIES IN TERMS OF WHAT, WHY, AND HOW. INCLUDES EXAMINATION OF JAPANESE ECONOMIC INSTITUTIONS AND POSTWAR GROWTH.

3430 YANAGA C.
"JAPAN SINCE PERRY."
NEW YORK: MCGRAW HILL, 1949.
COMPREHENSIVE SURVEY OF HISTORY OF JAPAN'S TRANSFORMATION INTO A MODERN POWER AND A STRONG STATE CAPABLE OF COPING WITH 19TH-CENTURY NATIONALISM AND EXPANSIONISM. COVERS PERIOD OF JAPANESE WESTERNIZATION FROM 1853 THROUGH OCCUPATION AND RECONSTRUCTION. EMPHASIS ON POLITICAL AND MILITARY IN-

STITUTIONS AS WELL AS CULTURAL AND ECONOMIC ASPECTS OF NATIONAL DEVELOPMENT. BIBLIOGRAPHY IN WESTERN LANGUAGES.

3431 YDIT M.
INTERNATIONALISED TERRITORIES.
LEYDEN: SYTHOFF, 1961, 323 PP.
TRACES HISTORY OF CONCEPT OF 'INTERNATIONALISED TERRITORIES' FROM ITS EARLY STAGES IN 19TH CENTURY TO ITS BEST KNOWN CONTEMPORARY EXAMPLE: WEST BERLIN. INCLUDES DISCUSSION OF CRACOW, SHANGHAI, TANGIER, MT. ATHOS, THE SAAR, AND JERUSALEM.

3432 YEAGER L.B.
INTERNATIONAL MONETARY RELATIONS: THEORY, HISTORY, AND POLICY.
NEW YORK: HARPER & ROW, 1966, 504 PP., LC#66-10055.
INVESTIGATES THEORY OF HOW THE SEVERAL ALTERNATIVE SYSTEMS OF INTERNATIONAL MONETARY RELATIONS OPERATE, INCLUDING SOME ABSTRACT ANALYSIS OF POLICY MEASURES. SURVEYS POLICIES PURSUED BY WORLD GOVERNMENTS OVER PAST THREE CENTURIES, AND DISCUSSES SOME PRESENT-DAY PROPOSALS FOR INTERNATIONAL MONETARY POLICY CHANGES.

3433 YEFROMOV A.
"THE TRUE FACE OF THE WEST GERMAN NATIONAL-DEMOCRATS."
INTER-AM. ECO. AFFAIRS, 4 (APR. 67), 69-73.
ASSOCIATES EMERGENCE OF NEO-NAZI PARTIES WITH WESTERN OCCUPATION AUTHORITIES AND GFR GOVERNMENT ANALYSIS OF NCD, ITS CONSTITUENCY AND LEADERS, THE EXTENT OF ITS INFLUENCE, ITS FOREIGN POLICY AND AMBIGUOUS DOMESTIC PROGRAMS. ARGUES THAT IMPORTANT FACTOR IN RESTRAINING REVIVAL OF NAZISM IS INFLUENCE OF SOVIET UNION.

3434 YOUNG A.N.
CHINA AND THE HELPING HAND.
CAMBRIDGE: HARVARD U PR, 1963, 502 PP., LC#63-20774.
DISCUSSES ROLE OF US FOREIGN AID IN CHINA, 1937-45, AND ITS CONTRIBUTION TO CHINA'S WAR EFFORT. TRACES CHANGES IN FOREIGN POLICY FROM SELF-HELP CONCEPT TO LEND-LEASE AND FINALLY GIVING. ANALYZES CURRENCY PROBLEMS DURING WWII AND CONSEQUENCE OF INFLATION'S DELAYING WAR EFFORT.

3435 YOUNG G.
FEDERALISM AND FREEDOM.
LONDON: OXFORD U. PR., 1941, 204 PP.
BRIEF HISTORY OF POLITICAL TRENDS OF EUROPEAN COUNTRIES. EVALUATES GROWTH OF GERMAN INDUSTRIAL STRENGTH, THE WORKING OF AMERICAN FEDERATION AND THE RUSSIAN PROBLEM. SURVEYS RELATIONSHIP BETWEEN ETHICS AND ECONOMICS. CONCLUDES WITH DIAGNOSIS OF ECONOMIC DISORDERS.

3436 YOUNG J.
CHECKLIST OF MICROFILM REPRODUCTIONS OF SELECTED ARCHIVES OF THE JAPANESE ARMY, NAVY, AND OTHER GOVT AGENCIES, 1868-1945.
WASHINGTON: GEORGETOWN U PRESS, 1959, 144 PP., LC#59-11156.
A GUIDE TO MICROFILM REPRODUCTIONS OF 400,000 PAGES OF HISTORICAL MATERIAL SELECTED FROM ARCHIVES OF THE JAPANESE ARMY AND NAVY MINISTRIES AND THE HOME MINISTRY. THE DOCUMENTS, IN JAPANESE, DEAL MOSTLY WITH EVENTS THAT TOOK PLACE IN EASTERN ASIA BETWEEN 1900 AND 1945. THE 1,556 UNANNOTATED ENTRIES ARE TOPICALLY ARRANGED AND APPEAR IN TRANSLITERATED JAPANESE AS WELL AS ENGLISH.

3437 YOUNG K.T.
"UNITED STATES POLICY AND VIETNAMESE POLITICAL VIABILITY 1954-1967."
ASIAN SURVEY, 7 (AUG. 67), 507-514.
EXAMINES EFFECTIVENESS OF US INVOLVEMENT IN SOUTH VIETNAMESE POLITICAL LEADERSHIP, ADMINISTRATIVE DEVELOPMENT, AND FORMATION OF POLITICAL GROUPS RESPONSIVE TO NEEDS OF VIETNAMESE PEOPLE. SUGGESTS THAT "URBAN REALIGNMENT," BROUGHT ABOUT BY RELOCATIONS, BE GIVEN A HIGHER POLITICAL PRIORITY.

3438 YOUNG T.C. ED.
NEAR EASTERN CULTURE AND SOCIETY.
PRINCETON: PRINCETON U PRESS, 1951, 250 PP.
COLLECTION OF PAPERS ON BACKGROUND OF ISLAMIC CULTURE AND PEOPLE. DISCUSSES INTERACTION OF ISLAMIC AND WESTERN THOUGHT AND INTERNATIONAL RELATIONS AMONG ISLAMIC NATIONS AND ATTITUDE TOWARD WEST.

3439 YRARRAZAVAL E.
AMERICA LATINE EN LA GUERRA FRIA.
SANTIAGO: EDITORIAL NASCIMENTO, 1959, 295 PP.
ANALYSIS OF POSITION OF LATIN AMERICA IN COLD WAR. DISCUSSES REGIONAL ECONOMIC DEVELOPMENT AND RELATIONS WITH US, EUROPE, AND USSR IN ECONOMIC AND POLITICAL MATTERS.

3440 YUAN TUNG-LI
CHINA IN WESTERN LITERATURE.
NEW HAVEN: YALE U PR, 1958, 802 PP., LC#58-59833.
BIBLIOGRAPHY OF WORKS ON CHINA PUBLISHED BETWEEN 1921 TO 1957 IN ENGLISH, FRENCH, AND GERMAN. DESCRIBES 18,000 WORKS BUT DOES NOT INCLUDE PERIODICAL ARTICLES UNLESS PUBLISHED SUBSEQUENTLY AS INDEPENDENT MONOGRAPHS. AUTHORS NAMES IN ROMAN AND CHINESE CHARACTERS. WORKS ARRANGED ACCORDING TO SUBJECT. TWO APPENDICES AND INDEX OF NAMES. PORTUGUESE WRITINGS ON MACAO INCLUDED.

3441 YUAN TUNG-LI
A GUIDE TO DOCTORAL DISSERTATIONS BY CHINESE STUDENTS IN AMERICA, 1905-1960.
WASHINGTON: SINO-AMER CULTUR SOC, 1961, 248 PP., LC#61-16700
PROVIDES A COMPLETE RECORD OF 2,789 DISSERTATIONS SUBMITTED BY CHINESE STUDENTS AND ACCEPTED BY AMERICAN UNIVERSITIES BETWEEN YEARS 1905-60. ARRANGED UNDER TWO BROAD CLASSES: HUMANITIES, SOCIAL, AND BEHAVIORAL SCIENCES; PHYSICAL, BIOLOGICAL, AND ENGINEERING SCIENCES. WITHIN EACH CLASS, ENTRIES ARRANGED ALPHABETICALLY BY AUTHOR. APPENDIX CONTAINS STATISTICAL TABLES OF DISCIPLINES AND INSTITUTIONS.

3442 ZABLOCKI C.J. ED.
SINO-SOVIET RIVALRY.
NEW YORK: FREDERICK PRAEGER, 1966, 242 PP., LC#66-26555.
DISCUSSES IMPLICATIONS FOR US POLICY OF THE SINO-SOVIET CONFLICT. ANTHOLOGY INCLUDES ARTICLES ON THE ORIGINS OF THE RIVALRY AND ITS IMPACT ON EUROPE, ASIA, AFRICA, LATIN AMERICA, AND THE US. DISCUSSES WHETHER USSR PLANNED TO INVADE CHINA IN 1963 TO STOP CHINESE NUCLEAR TESTS, AND WHETHER US HAS MORE TO FEAR FROM USSR OR CHINA.

3443 ZAGORIA D.S.
"SINO-SOVIET FRICTION IN UNDERDEVELOPED AREAS."
PROBL. COMMUNISM, 10 (MAR.-APR. 61), 1-13.
DESCRIBES STRUGGLE FOR POLITICAL AND ECONOMIC LEADERSHIP SHAKING COMMUNIST WORLD. RELATES SINO-SOVIET POLICIES TO DOMESTIC AND INTERNATIONAL PROBLEMS. INDICATES COMMON BACKGROUND OF IDEOLOGY AND ACTION.

3444 ZAGORIA D.S.
"THE FUTURE OF SINO-SOVIET RELATIONS."
ASIAN SURV., 1 (APR. 61), 3-14.
MAO'S STRATEGY, PROMISING A FASTER ROAD TO POWER, IS MORE APPEALING THAN KHRUSHCHEV'S WHICH INVOLVES A GAMBLE THAT WILL BE WON ONLY IF USSR WINS ITS ECONOMIC RACE WITH THE WEST.

3445 ZARTMAN I.W.
"THE SAHARA--BRIDGE OR BARRIER."
INT. CONCIL. 541 (JAN. 63), 62 PP.
ASSAYS THE STRENGTHS AND WEAKNESSES OF PAN-AFRICANISM, THE NOW DEFUNCT COMMON ORGANIZATION OF THE SAHARAN REGIONS, THE ARAB MAGHRED (NORTH AFRICAN UNITY), 'MOROCCO IRREDENTA', AND THE CASABLANCA GROUP.

3446 ZARTMAN I.W.
"LES RELATIONS ENTRE LA FRANCE ET L'ALGERIA DEPUIS LES ACCORDS D'EVIAN."
REV. FRANCAISE SCI. POL., 6 (DEC. 64), 1087-1113.
TRACES FRANCO-ALGERIAN ECONOMIC, POLITICAL AND CULTURAL RELATIONS IN PERIOD FROM 1962 TO 1964.

3447 ZARTMAN I.W.
"AFRICA AS A SUBORDINATE STATE SYSTEM IN INTERNATIONAL RELATIONS."
INTL. ORGANIZATION, 21 (SUMMER 67), 545-564.
DESCRIBES ACTIONS TAKEN TO PERPETUATE AFRICA AS A SUBORDINATE STATE SYSTEM IN WORLD POLITICS. DISCUSSES CHARACTERISTICS: GEOGRAPHIC REGION, INTERNATIONAL ORGANIZATION, AND AUTONOMY. STUDIES CONFIGURATION AND BASIS OF SYSTEM'S POWER, PATTERN OF RELATIONS AND NORMS OF SYSTEM. BELIEVES THAT CHANGE IN NATURE OF SUBORDINATE STATE SYSTEM IS NECESSARY.

3448 ZAUBERMAN A.
"SOVIET BLOC ECONOMIC INTEGRATION."
PROBL. COMMUNISM, 8 (JULY-AUG. 59) 23-29.
ASSERTS THAT BLOCK ECONOMIC INTEGRATION HAS FAR-REACHING POLITICAL IMPLICATIONS. INDICATES THAT IT MAY COMMEND ITSELF TO SOVIET POLICY-MAKERS AS MEANS OF STRENGTHENING INTRA-BLOC TIES AND THEREBY CONSOLIDATING SOVIET POLITICAL HEGEMONY OVER EASTERN EUROPE.

3449 ZAWODNY J.K.
"GUIDE TO THE STUDY OF INTERNATIONAL RELATIONS."
SAN FRANCISCO: CHANDLER, 1966.
AN ARRANGEMENT OF SELECTED SOURCES IN ENGLISH, CROSS-INDEXING 500 ENTRIES WHICH ARE CLASSIFIED UNDER SUBJECT HEADINGS, AND WHICH, EXCEPT FOR THE JOURNALS, HAVE BEEN ANNOTATED. INCLUDES CHAPTER ON BIBLIOGRAPHIES CONTAINING 55 LISTINGS OF BIBLIOGRAPHIES OF BIBLIOGRAPHIES, NATIONAL AND SUBJECT BIBLIOGRAPHIES, AND NATIONAL LIBRARY COLLECTIONS, PUBLISHED BETWEEN 1940-1965.

3450 ZEBOT C.A.
THE ECONOMICS OF COMPETITIVE COEXISTENCE.
NEW YORK: FREDERICK PRAEGER, 1964, 262 PP., LC#64-16695.
PRESENTS COMPARATIVE STUDY OF ROOT PROBLEMS OF ECONOMIC GROWTH IN EACH OF THREE SUBDIVISIONS IN CONTEMPORARY WORLD: NEWLY DEVELOPING COUNTRIES, SOVIET COUNTRIES, AND THE WEST. DEALS WITH UNRESOLVED PROBLEMS OF INTERDEPENDENCE AND INTER-

PLAY BETWEEN ECONOMIC DEVELOPMENT AND GROWTH AND VARIOUS SOCIAL SYSTEMS OF ORGANIZATION.

3451 ZEINE Z.N.
THE EMERGENCE OF ARAB NATIONALISM (REV. ED.)
BEIRUT: KHAYAT'S, 1966, 205 PP.
DISCUSSES ARAB NATIONALISM AS IT ROSE FROM THE OTTOMAN AND BRITISH DOMINATIONS TO ASSERTION OF INDEPENDENCE; SHOWS HOW YOUNG TURKS PROMOTED REDISCOVERY OF ARAB IDENTITY BEFORE AND DURING WAR YEARS UP TO 1918. PRIMARILY TREATS TURKISH-ARAB RELATIONS DURING THIS TIME. PORTRAYS EFFECTS OF IMPACT OF WEST IN WAKE OF OTTOMAN RULE AND EFFECT OF ISLAM ON TURKISH-ARAB RESPONSE.

3452 ZIMMERMAN I.
A GUIDE TO CURRENT LATIN AMERICAN PERIODICALS: HUMANITIES AND SOCIAL SCIENCES.
GAINESVILLE, FLA.: KALLMAN PUB. CO.,1961,367 PP., LC#61-15751.
ANNOTATED BIBLIOGRAPHY OF PERIODICALS PUBLISHED IN LATIN AMERICA OR THE US THAT ARE DESIGNED PRIMARILY FOR CIRCULATION WITHIN SOUTH AMERICA, CENTRAL AMERICA, MEXICO, OR THE WEST INDIES. YEAR 1958 SET AS BOUNDARY OF INCLUSION. ANNOTATIONS PROVIDE ADEQUATE CRITICAL AND DESCRIPTIVE INFORMATION. EXTRA BIBLIOGRAPHICAL DATA FOUND IN TITLE LIST AND CHRONOLOGICAL LIST.

3453 ZIMMERN A.
THE LEAGUE OF NATIONS AND THE RULE OF LAW.
LONDON: MACMILLAN, 1939, 542 PP.
IGNORING CONTEMPORARY POLITICS, EXPLORES THE ABILITY OF THE LEAGUE OF NATIONS IN DEVELOPING INTER-STATE RELATIONS. PRESENTS HISTORICAL BACKGROUND OF LEAGUE TILL 1936, AND TRACES AFFECTS ON PREVIOUS DIPLOMATIC METHODS.

3454 ZIMMERN A. ED.
MODERN POLITICAL DOCTRINE.
LONDON: OXFORD U. PR., 1939, 306 PP.
ELABORATES ON GOVERNMENTS' ECONOMIC PROBLEMS OF PROCESSES AND METHODS AND POINTS OUT POLITICAL DIFFICULTIES ENCOUNTERED IN THEIR ATTEMPT TO MAINTAIN WORLD ECONOMIC INTERDEPENDENCE.

3455 ZIMMERN A.
THE AMERICAN ROAD TO PEACE.
NEW YORK: DUTTON, 1953, 287 PP.
TRACES HISTORY OF AMERICAN FOREIGN POLICY FROM WORLD WAR ONE THROUGH THE ESTABLISHMENT OF THE UNITED NATIONS. CONSIDERS THE ROLE AMERICA MUST PLAY AS LEADER OF THE FREE WORLD, AND PO&NTS OUT PAST MISTAKES.

3456 ZISCHKA A.
WAR ES EIN WUNDER?
HAMBURG: MOSAIK VERLAG, 1966, 607 PP.
DISCUSSES GERMAN ECONOMIC RECOVERY AFTER WWII. EXAMINES LIMITATIONS PLACED ON INDUSTRIAL EXPANSION BY ALLIED POWERS, IMPACT OF MARSHALL PLAN, RISE OF AUTO INDUSTRY AND EXPORTS, AND CONCLUDES WITH DISCUSSION OF BEGINNINGS OF REPUBLIC AND REARMAMENT.

3457 ZLOTNICK M.
WEAPONS IN SPACE (PAMPHLET)
HARMON-ON-HUDSON: HUDSON INST, 1963, 67 PP.
ANALYSIS OF OPERATIONAL POSSIBILITIES OF WAGING WAR IN SPACE TO SAVE EARTH. INCLUDES STUDY OF PRACTICAL TACTICAL PROBLEMS OF WAR AND PSYCHOLOGICAL EFFECTS ON PEOPLE. CONSIDERS TECHNIQUES OF INSPECTION AND NEGOTIATIONS WITH SPACE WEAPONS.

3458 ZOOK P.D. ED.
FOREIGN TRADE AND HUMAN CAPITAL.
DALLAS: SOUTHERN METHODIST U PR, 1962, 103 PP., LC#62-13276.
RELATION OF ECONOMIC DEVELOPMENT, INTERNATIONAL RELATIONS, FOREIGN AID, AND PRODUCTIVITY EXAMINED. US FOREIGN AID PROGRAM EVALUATED, ESPECIALLY IN SOUTH AMERICA, AND RESULTANT EFFECTS ON BALANCE OF PAYMENTS AND ECONOMIC DEVELOPMENT APPRAISED.

3459 ZUCKERMAN S.
SCIENTISTS AND WAR.
NEW YORK: HARPER & ROW, 1967, 177 PP., LC#67-11333.
RELATION OF SCIENCE TO MILITARY AND POLITICAL DECISIONS IS DISCUSSED. ADVOCATES INTERNATIONAL COOPERATION IN RESEARCH AND DEVELOPMENT, IN INDUSTRY AND SCIENCE. DISMISSES CONCEPT OF NUCLEAR POWER AS TACTICAL FORCE, AND PREDICTS GREATER SEPARATION OF DEVELOPED AND UNDEVELOPED NATIONS. ASKS FOR SCIENTISTS' ROLE IN DECISION-MAKING. STRESSES SOCIAL FUNCTION OF SCIENCE.

A

ABA....AMERICAN BAR ASSOCIATION

ABEL L. A2875

ABILITY TESTS....SEE KNO/TEST

ABM/DEFSYS....ANTI-BALLISTIC MISSILE DEFENSE SYSTEMS

B64
DEUTSCHE GES AUSWARTIGE POL,STRATEGIE UND ABRUSTUNGSPOLITIK DER SOWJETUNION. USSR TEC/DEV DIPLOM COERCE DETER WEAPON...POLICY PSY 20 ABM/DEFSYS. PAGE 37 A0747 — NUC/PWR WAR FORCES ARMS/CONT

ABORIGINES....ABORIGINES (AUSTRALIA)

ABORTION....ABORTION

ABOSCH H. A0082

ABRAMSKY C. A0567

ABRIKOSSOV, DIMITRI....SEE ABRIKSSV/D

ABRIKSSV/D....DIMITRI ABRIKOSSOV

B64
LENSEN G.A.,REVELATIONS OF A RUSSIAN DIPLOMAT: THE MEMOIRS OF DMITRII I. ABRIKOSSOV. ASIA MOD/EUR RUSSIA USA-45 ELITES ACADEM CHIEF FORCES REV WAR PWR CONSERVE MARXISM 19/20 ABRIKSSV/D CHINJAP BOLSHEVISM. PAGE 87 A1775 — DIPLOM POLICY OBS

ABSHIRE D.M. A0083

ABT J.J. A0084

ACAD/ASST....ACADEMIC ASSISTANCE COUNCIL (U.K.)

ACADEM....UNIVERSITY, COLLEGE, GRADUATE SCHOOL, HIGHER EDUCATION

N
AFRICANA NEWSLETTER. ECO/UNDEV ACADEM SECT DIPLOM PRESS COLONIAL NAT/LISM 20. PAGE 1 A0001 — BIBLIOG/A AFR NAT/G

N
CHINA QUARTERLY. COM AGRI INDUS ACADEM POL/PAR INT/TRADE CONFER GOV/REL...TIME/SEQ CON/ANAL INDEX 20. PAGE 2 A0032 — BIBLIOG/A ASIA DIPLOM POLICY

N
THE WORLD OF LEARNING. INTELL ACT/RES EDU/PROP 20 UNESCO. PAGE 2 A0045 — BIBLIOG/A ACADEM R+D INT/ORG

N
AVTOREFERATY DISSERTATSII. USSR INTELL ACADEM NAT/G DIPLOM GOV/REL KNOWL CONCPT. PAGE 3 A0047 — BIBLIOG MARXISM MARXIST COM

N
JAHRBUCH DER DISSERTATIONEN. GERMANY/W WOR+45 ...TREND 20. PAGE 3 A0048 — BIBLIOG/A NAT/G ACADEM DIPLOM

N
AMERICAN HISTORICAL SOCIETY,LIST OF DOCTORAL DISSERTATIONS IN HISTORY IN PROGRESS OR COMPLETED IN COLLEGES AND UNIVERSITIES IN THE UNITED STATES. WOR+45 WOR-45 CULTURE SOCIETY NAT/G DIPLOM LEAD TREND. PAGE 7 A0150 — BIBLIOG ACADEM INTELL

N
MINISTERE DE L'EDUC NATIONALE,CATALOGUE DES THESES DE DOCTORAT SOUTENNES DEVANT LES UNIVERSITAIRES FRANCAISES. FRANCE LAW DIPLOM ADMIN...HUM SOC 20. PAGE 102 A2087 — BIBLIOG ACADEM KNOWL NAT/G

N
UNIVERSITY MICROFILMS INC,DISSERTATION ABSTRACTS: ABSTRACTS OF DISSERTATIONS AND MONOGRAPHS IN MICROFILM. CANADA DIPLOM ADMIN...INDEX 20. PAGE 149 A3045 — BIBLIOG/A ACADEM PRESS WRITING

N
US DEPARTMENT OF STATE,ABSTRACTS OF COMPLETED DOCTORAL DISSERTATIONS FOR THE ACADEMIC YEAR 1950-1951. WOR+45 WOR-45 ACADEM POL/PAR ECO/TAC ...POLICY SOC 19/20. PAGE 151 A3078 — BIBLIOG/A DIPLOM INT/ORG NAT/G

N/R
FULBRIGHT J.W.,THE ARROGANCE OF POWER. USA+45 WOR+45 ECO/UNDEV ACADEM LEGIS ECO/TAC FOR/AID PEACE ROLE ORD/FREE PWR 20 COLD/WAR CONGRESS. PAGE 50 A1014 — DIPLOM POLICY REV

BLI
MOOR C.C.,HOW TO USE UNITED NATIONS DOCUMENTS (PAPER). WOR+45 ACADEM CONTROL 20 UN. PAGE 103 A2121 — BIBLIOG METH INT/ORG

C39
HADDOW A.,"POLITICAL SCIENCE IN AMERICAN COLLEGES AND UNIVERSITIES 1636-1900." CONSTN MORAL...POLICY INT/LAW CON/ANAL BIBLIOG T 17/20. PAGE 59 A1211 — USA-45 LAW ACADEM KNOWL

B45
HARVARD WIDENER LIBRARY,INDOCHINA: A SELECTED LIST OF REFERENCES. CAMBODIA FRANCE S/ASIA VIETNAM COLONIAL...POLICY 19/20. PAGE 62 A1282 — BIBLIOG/A ACADEM DIPLOM NAT/G

B46
BIBLIOGRAFIIA DISSERTATSII: DOKTORSKIE DISSERTATSII ZA 19411944 (2 VOLS.). COM USSR LAW POL/PAR DIPLOM ADMIN LEAD...PHIL/SCI SOC 20. PAGE 3 A0054 — BIBLIOG ACADEM KNOWL MARXIST

B47
KIRK G.,THE STUDY OF INTERNATIONAL RELATIONS. FUT USA-45 R+D ACADEM INT/ORG CONSULT DELIB/GP INT/TRADE EDU/PROP PEACE RIGID/FLEX KNOWL VAL/FREE 20. PAGE 80 A1632 — USA+45 DIPLOM

B52
UNESCO,THESES DE SCIENCES SOCIALES: CATALOGUE ANALYTIQUE INTERNATIONAL DE THESES INEDITES DE DOCTORAT, 1940-1950. INT/ORG DIPLOM EDU/PROP...GEOG INT/LAW MGT PSY SOC 20. PAGE 147 A3015 — BIBLIOG ACADEM WRITING

B53
KANTOR H.,A BIBLIOGRAPHY OF UNPUBLISHED DOCTORAL DISSERTATIONS AND MASTERS' THESES DEALING WITH GOVTS, POL, INT REL OF LAT AM. L/A+17C INT/ORG POL/PAR ACT/RES OP/RES CONFER ATTIT...INT/LAW PHIL/SCI 20. PAGE 76 A1556 — BIBLIOG ACADEM DIPLOM NAT/G

B53
SCHAAF R.W.,DOCUMENTS OF INTERNATIONAL MEETINGS. AGRI INDUS ACADEM DIPLOM NUC/PWR RACE/REL AGE/Y HEALTH...SOC 20. PAGE 127 A2614 — BIBLIOG/A DELIB/GP INT/ORG POLICY

B54
MANNING C.A.W.,THE UNIVERSITY TEACHING OF SOCIAL SCIENCES: INTERNATIONAL RELATIONS. WOR+45 INTELL STRATA R+D ACADEM INT/ORG NAT/G CONSULT DELIB/GP ACT/RES EDU/PROP NAT/LISM ATTIT...POLICY CONT/OBS HYPO/EXP VAL/FREE LEAGUE/NAT UNESCO 20. PAGE 94 A1925 — KNOWL PHIL/SCI DIPLOM

B55
TROTIER A.H.,DOCTORAL DISSERTATIONS ACCEPTED BY AMERICAN UNIVERSITIES 1954-55. SECT DIPLOM HEALTH ...ART/METH GEOG INT/LAW SOC LING CHARTS 20. PAGE 145 A2968 — BIBLIOG ACADEM USA+45 WRITING

B56
UN HEADQUARTERS LIBRARY,BIBLIOGRAPHY OF INDUSTRIALIZATION IN UNDERDEVELOPED COUNTRIES (BIBLIOGRAPHICAL SERIES NO. 6). WOR+45 R+D ACADEM INT/ORG NAT/G. PAGE 147 A3002 — BIBLIOG ECO/UNDEV TEC/DEV

B57
DRUCKER P.F.,AMERICA'S NEXT TWENTY YEARS. USA+45 DIST/IND ACADEM MUNIC SCHOOL DIPLOM ECO/TAC AUTOMAT HABITAT HEALTH...SOC/WK TREND 20 URBAN/RNWL PUB/TRANS. PAGE 39 A0788 — WORKER FOR/AID CENSUS GEOG

B58
DEUTSCHE GESCHAFT VOLKERRECHT,DIE VOLKERRECHTLICHEN DISSERTATIONEN AN DEN WESTDEUTSCHEN UNIVERSITATEN, 1945-1957. GERMANY/W NAT/G DIPLOM ADJUD CT/SYS ...POLICY 20. PAGE 37 A0748 — BIBLIOG INT/LAW ACADEM JURID

B58
GANGE J.,UNIVERSITY RESEARCH ON INTERNATIONAL AFFAIRS. USA+45 ACADEM INT/ORG CONSULT CREATE EXEC ROUTINE...QUANT STAT INT STERTYP GEN/METH TOT/POP VAL/FREE 20. PAGE 51 A1040 — R+D MGT DIPLOM

B59
SWIFT R.W.,WORLD AFFAIRS AND THE COLLEGE CURRICULUM. USA+45 PLAN EFFICIENCY PERCEPT...HUM METH/CNCPT. PAGE 140 A2871 — ACADEM DIPLOM METH/COMP EDU/PROP

B60
DE HERRERA C.D.,LISTA BIBLIOGRAFICA DE LOS TRABAJOS DE GRADUACION Y TESIS PRESENTADOS EN LA UNIVERSIDAD, 1939-1960. PANAMA DIPLOM LEAD...SOC 20. PAGE 35 A0703 — BIBLIOG L/A+17C NAT/G ACADEM

B60
FLORES R.H.,CATALOGO DE TESIS DOCTORALES DE LAS FACULTADES DE LA UNIVERSIDAD DE EL SALVADOR. EL/SALVADR LAW DIPLOM ADMIN LEAD GOV/REL...SOC 19/20. PAGE 47 A0954 — BIBLIOG ACADEM L/A+17C NAT/G

B61
ASIA SOCIETY,AMERICAN INSTITUTIONS ANS ORGANIZATIONS INTERESTED IN ASIA; A REFERENCE DIRECTORY (2ND ED.). ASIA USA+45 CULTURE SECT DIPLOM EDU/PROP...INDEX 20. PAGE 9 A0190 — VOL/ASSN ACADEM PROF/ORG

B61
HOLDSWORTH M.,SOVIET AFRICAN STUDIES 1918-1959. USSR ACADEM NAT/G DIPLOM REGION KNOWL 20. PAGE 66 A1366 — BIBLIOG/A AFR HABITAT NAT/COMP

B61
SOCIAL SCIENCE SERIALS IN SPECIAL LIBRARIES IN THE NEW YORK AREA; A SELECTED LIST. R+D ACADEM EDU/PROP WRITING...PSY 20. PAGE 119 A2448 — BIBLIOG DIPLOM SOC

B61
ROBINSON M.E.,EDUCATION FOR SOCIAL CHANGE: ESTABLISHING INSTITUTES OF PUBLIC AND BUSINESS ADMINISTRATION ABROAD (PAMPHLET). WOR+45 SOCIETY ACADEM CONFER INGP/REL ROLE...SOC CHARTS BIBLIOG 20 ICA. PAGE 122 A2506 — FOR/AID EDU/PROP MGT ADJUST

B61
YUAN TUNG-LI,A GUIDE TO DOCTORAL DISSERTATIONS BY CHINESE STUDENTS IN AMERICA, 1905-1960. ASIA CULTURE SOCIETY ECO/UNDEV NAT/G PROB/SOLV DIPLOM LEAD ATTIT...HUM SOC STAT 20. PAGE 169 A3441 — BIBLIOG ACADEM ACT/RES OP/RES

B62
US LIBRARY OF CONGRESS,A LIST OF AMERICAN DOCTORAL DISSERTATIONS ON AFRICA. SOCIETY SECT DIPLOM EDU/PROP ADMIN...GEOG 19/20. PAGE 155 A3157 — BIBLIOG AFR ACADEM CULTURE

B62
WEIDNER E.W.,THE WORLD ROLE OF UNIVERSITIES. USA+45 WOR+45 SECT ACT/RES PROB/SOLV GIVE EFFICIENCY KNOWL ...LING CHARTS BIBLIOG 20. PAGE 162 A3297 — ACADEM EDU/PROP DIPLOM POLICY

L62
"HIGHER EDUCATION AND ECONOMIC AND SOCIAL DEVELOPMENT IN LATIN AMERICA: A BIBLIOGRAPHY." L/A+17C SOCIETY ECO/UNDEV PROF/ORG DIPLOM CONFER ...SOC 20. PAGE 3 A0062 — BIBLIOG/A ACADEM INTELL EDU/PROP

L62
SCHWERIN K.,"LAW LIBRARIES AND FOREIGN LAW COLLECTION IN THE USA." USA+45 USA-45...INT/LAW STAT 20. PAGE 130 A2667 — BIBLIOG LAW ACADEM ADMIN

B63
BUTTS R.F.,AMERICAN EDUCATION IN INTERNATIONAL DEVELOPMENT. USA+45 WOR+45 INTELL SCHOOL DIPLOM EDU/PROP...BIBLIOG 20. PAGE 23 A0457 — ACADEM FOR/AID CONSULT ECO/UNDEV

B63
HARTLEY A.,A STATE OF ENGLAND. UK ELITES SOCIETY ACADEM NAT/G SCHOOL INGP/REL CONSEN ORD/FREE NEW/LIB...POLICY 20. PAGE 62 A1275 — DIPLOM ATTIT INTELL ECO/DEV

B63
JOYCE W.,THE PROPAGANDA GAP. USA+45 COM/IND ACADEM DOMIN FEEDBACK REV CIVMIL/REL...REALPOL COLD/WAR. PAGE 75 A1540 — EDU/PROP PERCEPT BAL/PWR DIPLOM

B63
MANGER W.,THE ALLIANCE FOR PROGRESS: A CRITICAL APPRAISAL. FUT L/A+17C USA+45 CULTURE ECO/UNDEV ACADEM NAT/G SCHOOL PLAN FOR/AID...POLICY OAS. PAGE 94 A1918 — DIPLOM INT/ORG ECO/TAC REGION

B64
BLOOMFIELD L.P.,INTERNATIONAL MILITARY FORCES: THE QUESTION OF PEACE-KEEPING IN AN ARMED AND DISARMING WORLD. WOR+45 ACADEM ARMS/CONT REV PEACE 20 UN. PAGE 16 A0320 — INT/ORG FORCES FUT DIPLOM

B64
FREE L.A.,THE ATTITUDES, HOPES AND FEARS OF NIGERIANS. AFR NIGERIA ECO/UNDEV AGRI ACADEM PLAN TASK...GEOG CHARTS METH 20. PAGE 49 A0993 — NAT/LISM SYS/QU DIPLOM

B64
LENSEN G.A.,REVELATIONS OF A RUSSIAN DIPLOMAT: THE MEMOIRS OF DMITRII I. ABRIKOSSOV. ASIA MOD/EUR RUSSIA USA-45 ELITES ACADEM CHIEF FORCES REV WAR PWR CONSERVE MARXISM 19/20 ABRIKSSV/D CHINJAP BOLSHEVISM. PAGE 87 A1775 — DIPLOM POLICY OBS

B64
NICOL D.,AFRICA - A SUBJECTIVE VIEW. AFR INT/ORG PLAN ADMIN COLONIAL PARL/PROC PARTIC REGION GOV/REL LITERACY ATTIT...BIBLIOG 20 CIVIL/SERV. PAGE 109 A2230 — NAT/G LEAD CULTURE ACADEM

B65
AUVADE R.,BIBLIOGRAPHIE CRITIQUE DES OEUVRES PARUES SUR L'INDOCHINE FRANCAISE: UN SIECLE D'HISTOIRE ET D'ENSEIGNEMENT. VIETNAM DIPLOM...SOC 20. PAGE 10 A0198 — BIBLIOG/A R+D ACADEM COLONIAL

B65
EDUCATION AND WORLD AFFAIRS,THE UNIVERSITY LOOKS ABROAD: APPROACHES TO WORLD AFFAIRS AT SIX AMERICAN UNIVERSITIES. USA+45 CREATE EDU/PROP CONFER LEAD KNOWL 20 CORNELL/U MICH/STA/U STANFORD/U TULANE/U WISCONSN/U. PAGE 40 A0822 — ACADEM DIPLOM ATTIT GP/COMP

B65
MUNGER E.S.,NOTES ON THE FORMATION OF SOUTH AFRICAN FOREIGN POLICY. ACADEM POL/PAR SECT CHIEF DELIB/GP FORCES LEGIS PRESS ATTIT...TREND 20 NEGRO. PAGE 106 A2170 — AFR DOMIN POLICY DIPLOM

B65
SABLE M.H.,MASTER DIRECTORY FOR LATIN AMERICA. AGRI COM/IND FINAN R+D ACADEM LABOR NAT/G POL/PAR VOL/ASSN INT/TRADE EDU/PROP 20. PAGE 126 A2582 — INDEX L/A+17C INT/ORG DIPLOM

B65
UNESCO,HANDBOOK OF INTERNATIONAL EXCHANGES. COM/IND R+D ACADEM PROF/ORG VOL/ASSN CREATE TEC/DEV EDU/PROP AGREE 20 TREATY. PAGE 148 A3025 — INDEX INT/ORG DIPLOM PRESS

B65
US LIBRARY OF CONGRESS,A DIRECTORY OF INFORMATION RESOURCES IN THE UNITED STATES: SOCIAL SCIENCES. USA+45 ACADEM INT/ORG LABOR PROF/ORG PUB/INST SCHOOL SECT 20. PAGE 155 A3159 — BIBLIOG R+D COMPUT/IR

B65
VON GLAHN G.,LAW AMONG NATIONS: AN INTRODUCTION TO PUBLIC INTERNATIONAL LAW. WOR+45 WOR-45 INT/ORG NAT/G CREATE ADJUD WAR...GEOG CLASSIF TREND BIBLIOG. PAGE 160 A3250 — ACADEM INT/LAW GEN/LAWS LAW

S65
DOSSICK J.J.,"DOCTORAL DISSERTATIONS ON RUSSIA, THE SOVIET UNION, AND EASTERN EUROPE." USSR ACADEM DIPLOM EDU/PROP MARXISM 19/20 COLD/WAR. PAGE 38 A0775 — BIBLIOG HUM SOC

C65
SEARA M.V.,"COSMIC INTERNATIONAL LAW." LAW ACADEM ACT/RES DIPLOM COLONIAL CONTROL NUC/PWR SOVEREIGN ...GEN/LAWS BIBLIOG UN. PAGE 131 A2678 — SPACE INT/LAW IDEA/COMP INT/ORG

B66
GLAZER M.,THE FEDERAL GOVERNMENT AND THE UNIVERSITY. CHILE PROB/SOLV DIPLOM GIVE ADMIN WAR ...POLICY SOC 20. PAGE 53 A1079 — BIBLIOG/A NAT/G PLAN ACADEM

B66
TINKER H.,SOUTH ASIA. UK LAW ECO/UNDEV AGRI ACADEM SECT DIPLOM EDU/PROP REV WEALTH ALL/IDEOS...CHARTS BIBLIOG GANDHI/M NEHRU/J. PAGE 144 A2945 — S/ASIA COLONIAL TREND

B66
WELCH R.H.W.,THE NEW AMERICANISM, AND OTHER SPEECHES AND ESSAYS. USA+45 ACADEM POL/PAR SCHOOL VOL/ASSN FORCES CAP/ISM TAX REV DISCRIM 20 CIV/RIGHTS COLD/WAR BIRCH/SOC. PAGE 163 A3313 — DIPLOM FASCISM MARXISM RACE/REL

B66
WILLIAMS P.,AID IN UGANDA - EDUCATION. UGANDA UK FINAN ACADEM INT/ORG SCHOOL PROB/SOLV ECO/TAC UTIL ...STAT CHARTS 20. PAGE 165 A3352 — PLAN EDU/PROP FOR/AID ECO/UNDEV

L66
AMERICAN ECONOMIC REVIEW,"SIXTY-THIRD LIST OF DOCTORAL DISSERTATIONS IN POLITICAL ECONOMY IN AMERICAN UNIVERSITIES AND COLLEGES." ECO/DEV AGRI FINAN LABOR WORKER PLAN BUDGET INT/TRADE ADMIN DEMAND...MGT STAT 20. PAGE 7 A0146 — BIBLIOG/A CONCPT ACADEM

S66
"RESEARCH WORK 1965-1966." NEW/ZEALND ELITES ACADEM LOC/G MUNIC POL/PAR PROVS DIPLOM COLONIAL...SOC 20 AUSTRAL. PAGE 4 A0073 — BIBLIOG NAT/G CULTURE S/ASIA

B67
CRABBS R.F.,UNITED STATES HIGHER EDUCATION AND WORLD AFFAIRS. WOR+45 R+D ACADEM...POLICY 20. PAGE 32 A0650 — BIBLIOG/A NAT/G EDU/PROP DIPLOM

B67
US DEPARTMENT OF STATE,FOREIGN AFFAIRS RESEARCH (PAMPHLET). USA+45 WOR+45 ACADEM NAT/G...PSY SOC CHARTS 20. PAGE 152 A3100 — BIBLIOG INDEX R+D DIPLOM

L67
GRAUBARD S.R.,"TOWARD THE YEAR 2000: WORK IN PROGRESS." FUT ACADEM SECT DELIB/GP DIPLOM EDU/PROP AGE/Y PERSON ROLE...PSY ANTHOL. PAGE 55 A1131 — PREDICT PROB/SOLV SOCIETY CULTURE

S67
STEGER H.S.,"RESEARCH ON LATIN AMERICA IN THE FEDERAL REPUBLIC OF GERMANY AND WEST BERLIN." FINAN DIPLOM INT/TRADE EDU/PROP...GEOG JURID CHARTS 19/20. PAGE 137 A2813 — SOCIETY ECO/UNDEV ACADEM L/A+17C

ACADEM/SCI....ACADEMY OF SCIENCES (U.S.S.R.)

ACADEMY OF SCIENCES (U.S.S.R.)....SEE ACADEM/SCI

ACBC....ACTION COUNCIL FOR BETTER CITIES

ACCT....ACCOUNTING, BOOKKEEPING

ACCULTURATION....SEE CULTURE

ACD....UNITED STATES ARMS CONTROL AND DISARMAMENT AGENCY

ACHESON D. A0085

ACHESON/D....DEAN ACHESON

ACLU....AMERICAN CIVIL LIBERTIES UNION

ACQUAINTANCE GROUP....SEE FACE/GP

ACT/RES....RESEARCH FACILITATING SOCIAL ACTION

ACTION....ALLEGHENY COUNCIL TO IMPROVE OUR NEIGHBORHOODS

ACTON/LORD....LORD ACTON

ADA....AMERICANS FOR DEMOCRATIC ACTION

ADAMOVITCH A. A1078

ADAMS A.E. A0086

ADAMS V. A0087

ADAMS/J....PRESIDENT JOHN ADAMS

ADAMS/JQ....PRESIDENT JOHN QUINCY ADAMS

ADAMS/SAM....SAMUEL ADAMS

ADDICTION....ADDICTION

ADEBO S.O. A1566

ADENAUER K. A0088,A0089

ADENAUER/K....KONRAD ADENAUER

B58
CRAIG G.A.,FROM BISMARCK TO ADENAUER: ASPECTS OF GERMAN STATECRAFT. GERMANY INTELL FORCES ECO/TAC CONFER COERCE WAR GP/REL ORD/FREE PWR CONSERVE 19/20 BISMARCK/O ADENAUER/K. PAGE 32 A0653
DIPLOM LEAD NAT/G

B61
ACHESON D.,SKETCHES FROM LIFE. WOR+45 20 CHURCHLL/W EDEN/A ADENAUER/K SALAZAR/A. PAGE 4 A0085
BIOG LEAD CHIEF DIPLOM

B61
TETENS T.H.,THE NEW GERMANY AND THE OLD NAZIS. EUR+WWI GERMANY/W USA+45 NAT/G CRIME CHOOSE RACE/REL TOTALISM AGE/Y ATTIT 20 JEWS NAZI ADENAUER/K. PAGE 142 A2905
FASCISM DIPLOM FOR/AID POL/PAR

B62
ABOSCH H.,THE MENACE OF THE MIRACLE: GERMANY FROM HITLER TO ADENAUER. EUR+WWI GERMANY/W CULTURE FORCES PRESS NUC/PWR WAR CHOOSE 20 HITLER/A ADENAUER/K. PAGE 4 A0082
DIPLOM PEACE POLICY

B65
ADENAUER K.,MEMOIRS 1945-53. EUR+WWI GERMANY/W ECO/DEV CHIEF FORCES ECO/TAC WAR GOV/REL PWR SOVEREIGN 20 NATO ADENAUER/K. PAGE 4 A0088
BIOG DIPLOM NAT/G PERS/REL

B66
NEUMANN R.G.,THE GOVERNMENT OF THE GERMAN FEDERAL REPUBLIC. EUR+WWI GERMANY/W LOC/G EX/STRUC LEGIS CT/SYS INGP/REL PWR...BIBLIOG 20 ADENAUER/K. PAGE 108 A2222
NAT/G POL/PAR DIPLOM CONSTN

ADIE W.A.C. A0090

ADJUD....JUDICIAL AND ADJUDICATIVE PROCESSES

N
AMERICAN JOURNAL OF INTERNATIONAL LAW. WOR+45 WOR-45 CONSTN INT/ORG NAT/G CT/SYS ARMS/CONT WAR ...DECISION JURID NAT/COMP 20. PAGE 1 A0002
BIBLIOG/A INT/LAW DIPLOM ADJUD

N
INTERNATIONAL BOOK NEWS, 1928-1934. ECO/UNDEV FINAN INDUS LABOR INT/TRADE CONFER ADJUD COLONIAL...HEAL SOC/WK CHARTS 20 LEAGUE/NAT. PAGE 1 A0010
BIBLIOG/A DIPLOM INT/LAW INT/ORG

N
ARBITRATION JOURNAL. WOR+45 LAW INDUS JUDGE DIPLOM CT/SYS INGP/REL 20. PAGE 2 A0027
BIBLIOG MGT LABOR ADJUD

N
HARVARD LAW SCHOOL LIBRARY,ANNUAL LEGAL BIBLIOGRAPHY. USA+45 CONSTN LEGIS ADJUD CT/SYS ...POLICY 20. PAGE 62 A1278
BIBLIOG JURID LAW INT/LAW

N
HARVARD UNIVERSITY LAW LIBRARY,CATALOG OF INTERNATIONAL LAW AND RELATIONS. WOR+45 WOR-45 INT/ORG NAT/G JUDGE DIPLOM INT/TRADE ADJUD CT/SYS 19/20. PAGE 62 A1280
BIBLIOG INT/LAW JURID

N
RAND SCHOOL OF SOCIAL SCIENCE,INDEX TO LABOR ARTICLES. ECO/DEV INT/ORG LEGIS DIPLOM GP/REL ...NAT/COMP 20. PAGE 119 A2440
BIBLIOG LABOR MGT ADJUD

N
SOCIETE DES NATIONS,TRAITES INTERNATIONAUX ET ACTES LEGISLATIFS. WOR-45 INT/ORG NAT/G...INT/LAW JURID 20 LEAGUE/NAT TREATY. PAGE 135 A2759
BIBLIOG DIPLOM LEGIS ADJUD

N
US SUPERINTENDENT OF DOCUMENTS,TARIFF AND TAXATION (PRICE LIST 37). USA+45 LAW INT/TRADE ADJUD ADMIN CT/SYS INCOME OWN...DECISION GATT. PAGE 157 A3204
BIBLIOG/A TAX TARIFFS NAT/G

B00
DARBY W.E.,INTERNATIONAL TRIBUNALS. WOR-45 NAT/G ECO/TAC DOMIN LEGIT CT/SYS COERCE ORD/FREE PWR SOVEREIGN JURID. PAGE 33 A0681
INT/ORG ADJUD PEACE INT/LAW

B13
BUTLER N.M.,THE INTERNATIONAL MIND. WOR-45 INT/ORG LEGIT PWR...JURID CONCPT 20. PAGE 22 A0452
ADJUD ORD/FREE INT/LAW

B15
HOBSON J.A.,TOWARDS INTERNATIONAL GOVERNMENT. MOD/EUR STRUCT ECO/TAC EDU/PROP ADJUD ALL/VALS ...SOCIALIST CONCPT GEN/LAWS TOT/POP 20. PAGE 65 A1347
FUT INT/ORG CENTRAL

B15
INTERNATIONAL LAW ASSOCIATION,A FORTY YEARS' CATALOGUE OF THE BOOKS, PAMPHLETS AND PAPERS IN THE LIBRARY OF THE INTERNATIONAL LAW ASSOCIATION. INT/ORG DIPLOM ADJUD NEUTRAL...IDEA/COMP 19/20. PAGE 71 A1458
BIBLIOG LAW INT/LAW

B19
LONDON SCHOOL ECONOMICS-POL,ANNUAL DIGEST OF PUBLIC INTERNATIONAL LAW CASES. INT/ORG MUNIC NAT/G PROVS ADMIN NEUTRAL WAR GOV/REL PRIVIL 20. PAGE 91 A1858
BIBLIOG/A INT/LAW ADJUD DIPLOM

N19
UNITED ARAB REPUBLIC,THE PROBLEM OF THE PALESTINIAN REFUGEES (PAMPHLET). ISRAEL UAR LAW PROB/SOLV EDU/PROP CONFER ADJUD CONTROL NAT/LISM HEALTH 20 JEWS UN MIGRATION. PAGE 148 A3029
STRANGE GP/REL INGP/REL DIPLOM

B21
STUART G.H.,FRENCH FOREIGN POLICY. CONSTN INT/ORG NAT/G POL/PAR EX/STRUC FORCES PLAN ECO/TAC DOMIN EDU/PROP ADJUD COERCE ATTIT DRIVE RIGID/FLEX ALL/VALS...POLICY OBS RECORD BIOG TIME/SEQ TREND. PAGE 139 A2852
MOD/EUR DIPLOM FRANCE

L25
HUDSON M.,"THE PERMANENT COURT OF INTERNATIONAL JUSTICE AND THE QUESTION OF AMERICAN PARTICIPATION." WOR-45 LEGIT CT/SYS ORD/FREE ...JURID CONCPT TIME/SEQ GEN/LAWS VAL/FREE 20 ICJ. PAGE 68 A1406
INT/ORG ADJUD DIPLOM INT/LAW

B27
LAUTERPACHT H.,PRIVATE LAW SOURCES AND ANALOGIES OF INTERNATIONAL LAW. WOR-45 NAT/G DELIB/GP LEGIT COERCE ATTIT ORD/FREE PWR SOVEREIGN...JURID CONCPT HIST/WRIT TIME/SEQ GEN/METH LEAGUE/NAT 20. PAGE 85 A1748
INT/ORG ADJUD PEACE INT/LAW

B28
HOWARD-ELLIS C.,THE ORIGIN, STRUCTURE AND WORKING OF THE LEAGUE OF NATIONS. EUR+WWI MOD/EUR USA-45 CONSTN FORCES LEGIS ECO/TAC LEGIT COERCE ORD/FREE ...JURID SOC CONCPT LEAGUE/NAT 20 ILO ICJ. PAGE 68 A1401
INT/ORG ADJUD

B29
STURZO L.,THE INTERNATIONAL COMMUNITY AND THE RIGHT OF WAR (TRANS. BY BARBARA BARCLAY CARTER). CULTURE CREATE PROB/SOLV DIPLOM ADJUD CONTROL PEACE PERSON ORD/FREE...INT/LAW IDEA/COMP PACIFIST 20 LEAGUE/NAT. PAGE 140 A2858
INT/ORG PLAN WAR CONCPT

B32
EAGLETON C.,INTERNATIONAL GOVERNMENT. BRAZIL FRANCE GERMANY ITALY UK USSR WOR-45 DELIB/GP TOP/EX PLAN ECO/TAC EDU/PROP LEGIT ADJUD REGION ARMS/CONT COERCE ATTIT PWR...GEOG MGT VAL/FREE LEAGUE/NAT 20. PAGE 40 A0816
INT/ORG JURID DIPLOM INT/LAW

B32
GREGORY W.,LIST OF THE SERIAL PUBLICATIONS OF FOREIGN GOVERNMENTS, 1815-1931. WOR-45 DIPLOM ADJUD ...POLICY 20. PAGE 56 A1144
BIBLIOG NAT/G LAW JURID

B33
AMERICAN FOREIGN LAW ASSN,BIOGRAPHICAL NOTES ON THE LAWS AND LEGAL LITERATURE OF URUGUAY AND CURACAO. URUGUAY CONSTN FINAN SECT FORCES JUDGE DIPLOM INT/TRADE ADJUD CT/SYS CRIME 20. PAGE 7 A0147
BIBLIOG/A LAW JURID ADMIN

B33
MATTHEWS M.A.,THE AMERICAN INSTITUTE OF INTERNATIONAL LAW AND THE CODIFICATION OF INTERNATIONAL LAW (PAMPHLET). USA-45 CONSTN ADJUD CT/SYS...JURID 20. PAGE 96 A1973
BIBLIOG/A INT/LAW L/A+17C DIPLOM

B35
BEMIS S.F.,GUIDE TO THE DIPLOMATIC HISTORY OF THE
BIBLIOG/A

UNITED STATES, 17751921. NAT/G LEGIS TOP/EX PROB/SOLV CAP/ISM INT/TRADE TARIFFS ADJUD ...CON/ANAL 18/20. PAGE 13 A0264
DIPLOM USA-45

B35
KENNEDY W.P.,THE LAW AND CUSTOM OF THE SOUTH AFRICAN CONSTITUTION. AFR SOUTH/AFR KIN LOC/G PROVS DIPLOM ADJUD ADMIN EXEC 20. PAGE 78 A1594
CT/SYS CONSTN JURID PARL/PROC

B35
LANGER W.L.,THE DIPLOMACY OF IMPERIALISM 1890-1902. FRANCE GERMANY ITALY UK WOR-45 BAL/PWR INT/TRADE LEGIT ADJUD CONTROL WAR PWR SOVEREIGN...CHARTS BIBLIOG/A 19/20. PAGE 84 A1726
DIPLOM COLONIAL DOMIN

B36
HUDSON M.O.,INTERNATIONAL LEGISLATION: 1929-1931. WOR-45 SEA AIR AGRI FINAN LABOR DIPLOM ECO/TAC REPAR CT/SYS ARMS/CONT WAR WEAPON...JURID 20 TREATY LEAGUE/NAT. PAGE 69 A1409
INT/LAW PARL/PROC ADJUD LAW

B36
MATTHEWS M.A.,INTERNATIONAL LAW: SELECT LIST OF WORKS IN ENGLISH ON PUBLIC INTERNATIONAL LAW: WITH COLLECTIONS OF CASES AND OPINIONS. CHRIST-17C EUR+WWI MOD/EUR WOR-45 CONSTN ADJUD JURID. PAGE 96 A1975
BIBLIOG/A INT/LAW ATTIT DIPLOM

B37
KETCHAM E.H.,PRELIMINARY SELECT BIBLIOGRAPHY OF INTERNATIONAL LAW (PAMPHLET). WOR-45 LAW INT/ORG NAT/G PROB/SOLV CT/SYS NEUTRAL WAR 19/20. PAGE 78 A1602
BIBLIOG DIPLOM ADJUD INT/LAW

B37
SCHUSTER E.,GUIDE TO LAW AND LEGAL LITERATURE OF CENTRAL AMERICAN REPUBLICS. L/A+17C INT/ORG ADJUD SANCTION CRIME...JURID 19/20. PAGE 129 A2654
BIBLIOG/A REGION CT/SYS LAW

B37
UNION OF SOUTH AFRICA,REPORT CONCERNING ADMINISTRATION OF SOUTH WEST AFRICA (6 VOLS.). SOUTH/AFR INDUS PUB/INST FORCES LEGIS BUDGET DIPLOM EDU/PROP ADJUD CT/SYS...GEOG CHARTS 20 AFRICA/SW LEAGUE/NAT. PAGE 148 A3028
NAT/G ADMIN COLONIAL CONSTN

B38
HAGUE PERMANENT CT INTL JUSTIC,WORLD COURT REPORTS: COLLECTION OF THE JUDGEMENTS ORDERS AND OPINIONS VOLUME 3 1932-35. WOR-45 LAW DELIB/GP CONFER WAR PEACE ATTIT...DECISION ANTHOL 20 WORLD/CT CASEBOOK. PAGE 59 A1214
INT/ORG CT/SYS DIPLOM ADJUD

B38
MCNAIR A.D.,THE LAW OF TREATIES: BRITISH PRACTICE AND OPINIONS. UK CREATE DIPLOM LEGIT WRITING ADJUD WAR...INT/LAW JURID TREATY. PAGE 98 A2018
AGREE LAW CT/SYS NAT/G

B39
MAXWELL B.W.,INTERNATIONAL RELATIONS. EUR+WWI WOR-45 NAT/G CONSULT DIPLOM LEGIT ADJUD NAT/LISM ATTIT ORD/FREE SOVEREIGN...JURID LEAGUE/NAT TOT/POP VAL/FREE 20. PAGE 97 A1981
INT/ORG

B41
MCCLURE W.,INTERNATIONAL EXECUTIVE AGREEMENTS. USA-45 WOR-45 INT/ORG NAT/G DELIB/GP ADJUD ROUTINE ORD/FREE PWR...TIME/SEQ TREND CON/ANAL. PAGE 97 A2000
TOP/EX DIPLOM

B41
NIEMEYER G.,LAW WITHOUT FORCE: THE FUNCTION OF POLITICS IN INTERNATIONAL LAW. PLAN INSPECT DIPLOM REPAR LEGIT ADJUD WAR ORD/FREE...IDEA/COMP METH/COMP GEN/LAWS 20. PAGE 109 A2240
COERCE LAW PWR INT/LAW

L41
COMM. STUDY ORGAN. PEACE,"ORGANIZATION OF PEACE." USA-45 WOR-45 STRATA NAT/G ACT/RES DIPLOM ECO/TAC EDU/PROP ADJUD ATTIT ORD/FREE PWR...SOC CONCPT ANTHOL LEAGUE/NAT 20. PAGE 28 A0575
INT/ORG PLAN PEACE

B42
FEILCHENFELD E.H.,THE INTERNATIONAL ECONOMIC LAW OF BELLIGERENT OCCUPATION. EUR+WWI MOD/EUR USA-45 INT/ORG DIPLOM ADJUD ARMS/CONT LEAGUE/NAT 20. PAGE 44 A0907
ECO/TAC INT/LAW WAR

B42
FULLER G.H.,DEFENSE FINANCING: A SUPPLEMENTARY LIST OF REFERENCES (PAMPHLET). CANADA UK USA-45 ECO/DEV NAT/G DELIB/GP BUDGET ADJUD ARMS/CONT WEAPON COST PEACE PWR 20 AUSTRAL CHINJAP CONGRESS. PAGE 50 A1021
BIBLIOG/A FINAN FORCES DIPLOM

B42
HAMBRO C.J.,HOW TO WIN THE PEACE. ECO/TAC EDU/PROP ADJUD PERSON ALL/VALS...SOCIALIST TREND GEN/LAWS 20. PAGE 61 A1246
FUT INT/ORG PEACE

B42
KELSEN H.,LAW AND PEACE IN INTERNATIONAL RELATIONS. FUT WOR-45 NAT/G DELIB/GP DIPLOM LEGIT RIGID/FLEX ORD/FREE SOVEREIGN...JURID CONCPT TREND STERTYP GEN/LAWS LEAGUE/NAT 20. PAGE 77 A1580
INT/ORG ADJUD PEACE INT/LAW

B43
CONOVER H.F.,THE BALKANS: A SELECTED LIST OF REFERENCES. ALBANIA BULGARIA ROMANIA YUGOSLAVIA INT/ORG PROB/SOLV DIPLOM LEGIT CONFER ADJUD WAR NAT/LISM PEACE PWR 20 LEAGUE/NAT. PAGE 29 A0596
BIBLIOG EUR+WWI

B43
HAGUE PERMANENT CT INTL JUSTIC,WORLD COURT REPORTS: COLLECTION OF THE JUDGEMENTS ORDERS AND OPINIONS VOLUME 4 1936-42. WOR-45 CONFER PEACE ATTIT ...DECISION JURID ANTHOL 20 WORLD/CT CASEBOOK. PAGE 59 A1215
INT/ORG CT/SYS DIPLOM ADJUD

B44
DAVIS H.E.,PIONEERS IN WORLD ORDER. WOR-45 CONSTN ECO/TAC DOMIN EDU/PROP LEGIT ADJUD ADMIN ARMS/CONT CHOOSE KNOWL ORD/FREE...POLICY JURID SOC STAT OBS CENSUS TIME/SEQ ANTHOL LEAGUE/NAT 20. PAGE 34 A0691
INT/ORG ROUTINE

B44
HUDSON M.,INTERNATIONAL TRIBUNALS PAST AND FUTURE. FUT WOR-45 LAW EDU/PROP ADJUD ORD/FREE...CONCPT TIME/SEQ TREND GEN/LAWS TOT/POP VAL/FREE 18/20. PAGE 69 A1408
INT/ORG STRUCT INT/LAW

B45
HILL N.,CLAIMS TO TERRITORY IN INTERNATIONAL LAW AND RELATIONS. WOR-45 NAT/G DOMIN EDU/PROP LEGIT REGION ROUTINE ORD/FREE PWR WEALTH...GEOG INT/LAW JURID 20. PAGE 65 A1332
INT/ORG ADJUD SOVEREIGN

B45
US DEPARTMENT OF STATE,PUBLICATIONS OF THE DEPARTMENT OF STATE: A LIST CUMULATIVE FROM OCTOBER 1, 1929 (PAMPHLET). ASIA EUR+WWI ISLAM L/A+17C USA-45 ADJUD...INT/LAW 20. PAGE 151 A3082
BIBLIOG DIPLOM INT/TRADE

B45
VANCE H.L.,GUIDE TO THE LAW AND LEGAL LITERATURE OF MEXICO. LAW CONSTN FINAN LABOR FORCES ADJUD ADMIN ...CRIMLGY PHIL/SCI CON/ANAL 20 MEXIC/AMER. PAGE 158 A3217
BIBLIOG/A INT/LAW JURID CT/SYS

B46
KEETON G.W.,MAKING INTERNATIONAL LAW WORK. FUT WOR-45 NAT/G DELIB/GP FORCES LEGIT COERCE PEACE ATTIT RIGID/FLEX ORD/FREE PWR...JURID CONCPT HIST/WRIT GEN/METH LEAGUE/NAT 20. PAGE 77 A1578
INT/ORG ADJUD INT/LAW

B46
SCANLON H.L.,INTERNATIONAL LAW: A SELECTIVE LIST OF WORKS IN ENGLISH ON PUBLIC INTERNATIONAL LAW (A PAMPHLET). CHRIST-17C EUR+WWI MOD/EUR WOR-45 CT/SYS ...JURID 20. PAGE 127 A2613
BIBLIOG/A INT/LAW ADJUD DIPLOM

B47
INTERNATIONAL COURT OF JUSTICE,CHARTER OF THE UNITED NATIONS, STATUTE AND RULES OF COURT AND OTHER CONSTITUTIONAL DOCUMENTS. SWITZERLND LAW ADJUD INGP/REL...JURID 20 ICJ UN. PAGE 71 A1453
INT/LAW INT/ORG CT/SYS DIPLOM

B48
JESSUP P.C.,A MODERN LAW OF NATIONS. FUT WOR+45 WOR-45 SOCIETY NAT/G DELIB/GP LEGIS BAL/PWR EDU/PROP LEGIT PWR...INT/LAW JURID TIME/SEQ LEAGUE/NAT 20. PAGE 74 A1514
INT/ORG ADJUD

B49
JACKSON R.H.,INTERNATIONAL CONFERENCE ON MILITARY TRIALS. FRANCE GERMANY UK USA+45 USSR VOL/ASSN DELIB/GP REPAR ADJUD CT/SYS CRIME WAR 20 WAR/TRIAL. PAGE 72 A1479
DIPLOM INT/ORG INT/LAW CIVMIL/REL

B50
DE RUSETT A.,STRENGTHENING THE FRAMEWORK OF PEACE. WOR+45 VOL/ASSN FORCES CREATE INSPECT ADJUD CONTROL WAR EQUILIB FEDERAL ORD/FREE 20 UN EUROPE. PAGE 35 A0711
INT/ORG DIPLOM PEACE METH/COMP

B50
MCCAMY J.,THE ADMINISTRATION OF AMERICAN FOREIGN AFFAIRS. USA+45 SOCIETY INT/ORG NAT/G ACT/RES PLAN INT/TRADE EDU/PROP ADJUD ALL/VALS...METH/CNCPT TIME/SEQ CONGRESS 20. PAGE 97 A1996
EXEC STRUCT DIPLOM

B51
KELSEN H.,THE LAW OF THE UNITED NATIONS. WOR+45 STRUCT RIGID/FLEX ORD/FREE...INT/LAW JURID CONCPT CON/ANAL GEN/METH UN TOT/POP VAL/FREE 20. PAGE 77 A1581
INT/ORG ADJUD

B51
MACLAURIN J.,THE UNITED NATIONS AND POWER POLITICS. WOR+45 CONSULT EDU/PROP LEGIT ADJUD EXEC MORAL ORD/FREE...HUM JURID CONCPT RECORD TIME/SEQ UN COLD/WAR 20. PAGE 93 A1896
INT/ORG ROUTINE

B51
SWISHER C.B.,THE THEORY AND PRACTICE OF AMERICAN NATIONAL GOVERNMENT. CULTURE LEGIS DIPLOM ADJUD ADMIN WAR PEACE ORD/FREE...MAJORIT 17/20. PAGE 140 A2872
CONSTN NAT/G GOV/REL GEN/LAWS

L51
LISSITZYN O.J.,"THE INTERNATIONAL COURT OF JUSTICE." WOR+45 INT/ORG LEGIT ORD/FREE...CONCPT TIME/SEQ TREND GEN/LAWS VAL/FREE 20 ICJ. PAGE 90 A1839
ADJUD JURID INT/LAW

B52
FLECHTHEIM O.K.,FUNDAMENTALS OF POLITICAL SCIENCE. WOR+45 WOR-45 LAW POL/PAR EX/STRUC LEGIS ADJUD ATTIT PWR...INT/LAW. PAGE 46 A0945
NAT/G DIPLOM IDEA/COMP CONSTN

B52
KELSEN H.,PRINCIPLES OF INTERNATIONAL LAW. WOR+45 WOR-45 INT/ORG ORD/FREE...JURID GEN/LAWS TOT/POP 20. PAGE 77 A1583
ADJUD CONSTN INT/LAW

B52
THOM J.M.,GUIDE TO RESEARCH MATERIAL IN POLITICAL SCIENCE (PAMPHLET). ELITES LOC/G MUNIC NAT/G LEGIS DIPLOM ADJUD CIVMIL/REL GOV/REL PWR MGT. PAGE 143 A2919 BIBLIOG/A KNOWL

C52
STUART G.H.,"AMERICAN DIPLOMATIC AND CONSULAR PRACTICE (2ND ED.)" EUR+WWI MOD/EUR USA-45 DELIB/GP INT/TRADE ADJUD...BIBLIOG 20. PAGE 140 A2855 DIPLOM ADMIN INT/ORG

B53
OPPENHEIM L.,INTERNATIONAL LAW: A TREATISE (7TH ED., 2 VOLS.). LAW CONSTN PROB/SOLV INT/TRADE ADJUD AGREE NEUTRAL WAR ORD/FREE SOVEREIGN...BIBLIOG 20 LEAGUE/NAT UN ILO. PAGE 112 A2294 INT/LAW INT/ORG DIPLOM

B54
MILLARD E.L.,FREEDOM IN A FEDERAL WORLD. FUT WOR+45 VOL/ASSN TOP/EX LEGIT ROUTINE FEDERAL PEACE ATTIT DISPL ORD/FREE PWR...MAJORIT INT/LAW JURID TREND COLD/WAR 20. PAGE 101 A2073 INT/ORG CREATE ADJUD BAL/PWR

B54
MITCHELL P.,AFRICAN AFTERTHOUGHTS. UGANDA CONSTN NAT/G ADJUD COERCE WAR 20 WWI MAU/MAU. PAGE 102 A2090 BIOG CHIEF COLONIAL DOMIN

B54
WRIGHT Q.,PROBLEMS OF STABILITY AND PROGRESS IN INTERNATIONAL RELATIONSHIPS. FUT WOR+45 WOR-45 SOCIETY LEGIS CREATE TEC/DEV ECO/TAC EDU/PROP ADJUD WAR PEACE ORD/FREE PWR...KNO/TEST TREND GEN/LAWS 20. PAGE 167 A3409 INT/ORG CONCPT DIPLOM

B55
CHOWDHURI R.N.,INTERNATIONAL MANDATES AND TRUSTEESHIP SYSTEMS. WOR+45 STRUCT ECO/UNDEV INT/ORG LEGIS DOMIN EDU/PROP LEGIT ADJUD EXEC PWR ...CONCPT TIME/SEQ UN 20. PAGE 26 A0534 DELIB/GP PLAN SOVEREIGN

B55
HOGAN W.N.,INTERNATIONAL CONFLICT AND COLLECTIVE SECURITY: THE PRINCIPLE OF CONCERN IN INTERNATIONAL ORGANIZATION. CONSTN EX/STRUC BAL/PWR DIPLOM ADJUD CONTROL CENTRAL CONSEN PEACE...INT/LAW CONCPT METH/COMP 20 UN LEAGUE/NAT. PAGE 66 A1361 INT/ORG WAR ORD/FREE FORCES

S55
WRIGHT Q.,"THE PEACEFUL ADJUSTMENT OF INTERNATIONAL RELATIONS: PROBLEMS AND RESEARCH APPROACHES." UNIV INTELL EDU/PROP ADJUD ROUTINE KNOWL SKILL...INT/LAW JURID PHIL/SCI CLASSIF 20. PAGE 167 A3411 R+D METH/CNCPT PEACE

B56
JESSUP P.C.,TRANSNATIONAL LAW. FUT WOR+45 JUDGE CREATE ADJUD ORD/FREE...CONCPT VAL/FREE 20. PAGE 74 A1515 LAW JURID INT/LAW

B56
SIPKOV I.,LEGAL SOURCES AND BIBLIOGRAPHY OF BULGARIA. BULGARIA COM LEGIS WRITING ADJUD CT/SYS ...INT/LAW TREATY 20. PAGE 134 A2736 BIBLIOG LAW TOTALISM MARXISM

B56
US HOUSE COMM FOREIGN AFFAIRS,SURVEY OF ACTIVITIES OF THE COMMITTEE ON FOREIGN AFFAIRS HOUSE OF REPRESENTATIVES: 84TH THROUGH 86TH CONGRESS. USA+45 LAW ADJUD...POLICY STAT CHARTS 20 CONGRESS HOUSE/REP. PAGE 153 A3122 LEGIS DELIB/GP NAT/G DIPLOM

B57
ALIGHIERI D.,ON WORLD GOVERNMENT. ROMAN/EMP LAW SOCIETY INT/ORG NAT/G POL/PAR ADJUD WAR GP/REL PEACE WORSHIP 15 WORLDUNITY DANTE. PAGE 6 A0121 POLICY CONCPT DIPLOM SECT

B57
CONOVER H.F.,NORTH AND NORTHEAST AFRICA; A SELECTED ANNOTATED LIST OF WRITINGS. ALGERIA MOROCCO SUDAN UAR CULTURE INT/ORG PROB/SOLV ADJUD NAT/LISM PWR WEALTH...SOC 20 UN. PAGE 30 A0603 BIBLIOG/A DIPLOM AFR ECO/UNDEV

B57
INSTITUT DE DROIT INTL,TABLEAU GENERAL DES RESOLUTIONS (1873-1956). LAW NEUTRAL CRIME WAR MARRIAGE PEACE...JURID 19/20. PAGE 70 A1442 INT/LAW DIPLOM ORD/FREE ADJUD

B57
US SENATE COMM ON JUDICIARY,HEARING BEFORE SUBCOMMITTEE ON COMMITTEE OF JUDICIARY, UNITED STATES SENATE: S. J. RES. 3. USA+45 NAT/G CONSULT DELIB/GP DIPLOM ADJUD LOBBY REPRESENT 20 CONGRESS TREATY. PAGE 157 A3192 LEGIS CONSTN CONFER AGREE

B58
ALEXANDROWICZ,A BIBLIOGRAPHY OF INDIAN LAW. INDIA S/ASIA CONSTN CT/SYS...INT/LAW 19/20. PAGE 6 A0113 BIBLIOG LAW ADJUD JURID

B58
BOWETT D.W.,SELF-DEFENSE IN INTERNATIONAL LAW. EUR+WWI MOD/EUR WOR+45 WOR-45 SOCIETY INT/ORG CONSULT DIPLOM LEGIT COERCE ATTIT ORD/FREE...JURID 20 UN. PAGE 17 A0353 ADJUD CONCPT WAR INT/LAW

B58
DEUTSCHE GESCHAFT VOLKERRECHT,DIE VOLKERRECHTLICHEN DISSERTATIONEN AN DEN WESTDEUTSCHEN UNIVERSITATEN, 1945-1957. GERMANY/W NAT/G DIPLOM ADJUD CT/SYS ...POLICY 20. PAGE 37 A0748 BIBLIOG INT/LAW ACADEM JURID

B58
SLICK T.,PERMANENT PEACE: A CHECK AND BALANCE PLAN. FUT WOR+45 NAT/G FORCES CREATE PLAN EDU/PROP LEGIT ADJUD COERCE NAT/LISM RIGID/FLEX MORAL...HUM CONCPT METH/CNCPT NEW/IDEA TREND CHARTS TOT/POP 20. PAGE 134 A2742 INT/ORG ORD/FREE PEACE ARMS/CONT

B58
SOC OF COMP LEGIS AND INT LAW,THE LAW OF THE SEA... (PAMPHLET). WOR+45 NAT/G INT/TRADE ADJUD CONTROL NUC/PWR WAR PEACE ATTIT ORD/FREE...JURID CHARTS 20 UN TREATY RESOURCE/N. PAGE 135 A2756 INT/LAW INT/ORG DIPLOM SEA

B58
STONE J.,AGGRESSION AND WORLD ORDER: A CRITIQUE OF UNITED NATIONS THEORIES OF AGGRESSION. LAW CONSTN DELIB/GP PROB/SOLV BAL/PWR DIPLOM DEBATE ADJUD CRIME PWR...POLICY IDEA/COMP 20 UN SUEZ LEAGUE/NAT. PAGE 138 A2835 ORD/FREE INT/ORG WAR CONCPT

S58
STAAR R.F.,"ELECTIONS IN COMMUNIST POLAND." EUR+WWI SOCIETY INT/ORG NAT/G POL/PAR LEGIS ACT/RES ECO/TAC EDU/PROP ADJUD ADMIN ROUTINE COERCE TOTALISM ATTIT ORD/FREE PWR 20. PAGE 137 A2797 COM CHOOSE POLAND

B59
COMM. STUDY ORGAN. PEACE,ORGANIZING PEACE IN THE NUCLEAR AGE. FUT CONSULT DELIB/GP DOMIN ADJUD ROUTINE COERCE ORD/FREE...TECHNIC INT/LAW JURID NEW/IDEA UN COLD/WAR 20. PAGE 29 A0581 INT/ORG ACT/RES NUC/PWR

B59
CORBETT P.E.,LAW IN DIPLOMACY. UK USA+45 USSR CONSTN SOCIETY INT/ORG JUDGE LEGIT ATTIT ORD/FREE TOT/POP LEAGUE/NAT 20. PAGE 30 A0616 NAT/G ADJUD JURID DIPLOM

B59
GORDENKER L.,THE UNITED NATIONS AND THE PEACEFUL UNIFICATION OF KOREA. ASIA LAW LOC/G CONSULT ACT/RES DIPLOM DOMIN LEGIT ADJUD ADMIN ORD/FREE SOVEREIGN...INT GEN/METH UN COLD/WAR 20. PAGE 54 A1109 DELIB/GP KOREA INT/ORG

B59
GREENSPAN M.,THE MODERN LAW OF LAND WARFARE. WOR+45 INT/ORG NAT/G DELIB/GP FORCES ATTIT...POLICY HYPO/EXP STERTYP 20. PAGE 56 A1142 ADJUD PWR WAR

B59
HARVARD UNIVERSITY LAW SCHOOL,INTERNATIONAL PROBLEMS OF FINANCIAL PROTECTION AGAINST NUCLEAR RISK. WOR+45 NAT/G DELIB/GP PROB/SOLV DIPLOM CONTROL ATTIT...POLICY INT/LAW MATH 20. PAGE 62 A1281 NUC/PWR ADJUD INDUS FINAN

B59
KARUNAKARAN K.P.,INDIA IN WORLD AFFAIRS, 1952-1958 (VOL. II). INDIA ECO/UNDEV SECT FOR/AID INT/TRADE ADJUD NEUTRAL REV WAR DISCRIM ORD/FREE MARXISM ...BIBLIOG 20. PAGE 77 A1569 DIPLOM INT/ORG S/ASIA COLONIAL

B59
MACIVER R.M.,THE NATIONS AND THE UN. WOR+45 NAT/G CONSULT ADJUD ADMIN ALL/VALS...CONCPT DEEP/QU UN TOT/POP UNESCO 20. PAGE 92 A1892 INT/ORG ATTIT DIPLOM

B59
PANHUYS H.F.,THE ROLE OF NATIONALITY IN INTERNATIONAL LAW. ADJUD CRIME WAR STRANGE...JURID TREND. PAGE 114 A2330 INT/LAW NAT/LISM INGP/REL

B59
REIFF H.,THE UNITED STATES AND THE TREATY LAW OF THE SEA. USA+45 USA-45 SEA SOCIETY INT/ORG CONSULT DELIB/GP LEGIS DIPLOM LEGIT ATTIT ORD/FREE PWR WEALTH...GEOG JURID TOT/POP 20 TREATY. PAGE 120 A2459 ADJUD INT/LAW

B59
SIMPSON J.L.,INTERNATIONAL ARBITRATION: LAW AND PRACTICE. WOR+45 WOR-45 INT/ORG DELIB/GP ADJUD PEACE MORAL ORD/FREE...METH 18/20. PAGE 133 A2720 INT/LAW DIPLOM CT/SYS CONSULT

S59
CARLSTON K.S.,"NATIONALIZATION: AN ANALYTIC APPROACH." WOR+45 INT/ORG ECO/TAC DOMIN LEGIT ADJUD COERCE ORD/FREE PWR WEALTH SOCISM...JURID CONCPT TREND STERTYP TOT/POP VAL/FREE 20. PAGE 24 A0486 INDUS NAT/G NAT/LISM SOVEREIGN

S59
LASSWELL H.D.,"UNIVERSALITY IN PERSPECTIVE." FUT UNIV SOCIETY CONSULT TOP/EX PLAN EDU/PROP ADJUD ROUTINE ARMS/CONT COERCE PEACE ATTIT PERSON ALL/VALS. PAGE 85 A1741 INT/ORG JURID TOTALISM

S59
PUGWASH CONFERENCE,"ON BIOLOGICAL AND CHEMICAL WARFARE." WOR+45 SOCIETY PROC/MFG INT/ORG FORCES EDU/PROP ADJUD RIGID/FLEX ORD/FREE PWR...DECISION PSY NEW/IDEA MATH VAL/FREE 20. PAGE 118 A2417 ACT/RES BIO/SOC WAR WEAPON

S59
SOHN L.B.,"THE DEFINITION OF AGGRESSION." FUT LAW FORCES LEGIT ADJUD ROUTINE COERCE ORD/FREE PWR ...MAJORIT JURID QUANT COLD/WAR 20. PAGE 135 A2762 INT/ORG CT/SYS DETER SOVEREIGN

B60
ENGEL J.,THE SECURITY OF THE FREE WORLD. USSR WOR+45 STRATA STRUCT ECO/DEV ECO/UNDEV INT/ORG COM TREND

DELIB/GP FORCES DOMIN LEGIT ADJUD EXEC ARMS/CONT COERCE...POLICY CONCPT NEW/IDEA TIME/SEQ GEN/LAWS COLD/WAR WORK UN 20 NATO. PAGE 42 A0851 DIPLOM

B60
HARVARD LAW SCHOOL LIBRARY,CURRENT LEGAL BIBLIOGRAPHY. USA+45 CONSTN LEGIS ADJUD CT/SYS POLICY. PAGE 62 A1279 BIBLIOG JURID LAW INT/LAW

B60
PAN AMERICAN UNION,FIFTH MEETING OF CONSULTATION OF MINISTERS OF FOREIGN AFFAIRS OF AMERICAN STATES. L/A+17C FORCES PLAN PROB/SOLV ADJUD PEACE...POLICY INT/LAW 20 OAS. PAGE 113 A2327 INT/ORG DIPLOM DELIB/GP ECO/UNDEV

B60
STEIN E.,AMERICAN ENTERPRISE IN THE EUROPEAN COMMON MARKET: A LEGAL PROFILE. EUR+WWI FUT USA+45 SOCIETY STRUCT ECO/DEV NAT/G VOL/ASSN CONSULT PLAN TEC/DEV ECO/TAC INT/TRADE ADMIN ATTIT RIGID/FLEX PWR...MGT NEW/IDEA STAT TREND COMPUT/IR SIMUL EEC 20. PAGE 137 A2814 MARKET ADJUD INT/LAW

B60
WOETZEL R.K.,THE INTERNATIONAL CONTROL OF AIRSPACE AND OUTERSPACE. FUT WOR+45 AIR CONSTN STRUCT CONSULT PLAN TEC/DEV ADJUD RIGID/FLEX KNOWL ORD/FREE PWR...TECHNIC GEOG MGT NEW/IDEA TREND COMPUT/IR VAL/FREE 20 TREATY. PAGE 166 A3375 INT/ORG JURID SPACE INT/LAW

L60
DEAN A.W.,"SECOND GENEVA CONFERENCE OF THE LAW OF THE SEA: THE FIGHT FOR FREEDOM OF THE SEAS." FUT USA+45 USSR WOR+45 WOR-45 SEA CONSTN STRUCT PLAN INT/TRADE ADJUD ADMIN ORD/FREE...DECISION RECORD TREND GEN/LAWS 20 TREATY. PAGE 35 A0717 INT/ORG JURID INT/LAW

L60
KUNZ J.,"SANCTIONS IN INTERNATIONAL LAW." WOR+45 WOR-45 LEGIT ARMS/CONT COERCE PEACE ATTIT ...METH/CNCPT TIME/SEQ TREND 20. PAGE 83 A1695 INT/ORG ADJUD INT/LAW

S60
BOGARDUS E.S.,"THE SOCIOLOGY OF A STRUCTURED PEACE." FUT SOCIETY CREATE DIPLOM EDU/PROP ADJUD ROUTINE ATTIT RIGID/FLEX KNOWL ORD/FREE RESPECT ...POLICY INT/LAW JURID NEW/IDEA SELF/OBS TOT/POP 20 UN. PAGE 16 A0327 INT/ORG SOC NAT/LISM PEACE

S60
GRACIA-MORA M.R.,"INTERNATIONAL RESPONSIBILITY FOR SUBVERSIVE ACTIVITIES AND HOSTILE PROPAGANDA BY PRIVATE PERSONS AGAINST." COM EUR+WWI L/A+17C UK USA+45 USSR WOR-45 CONSTN NAT/G LEGIT ADJUD REV PEACE TOTALISM ORD/FREE...INT/LAW 20. PAGE 55 A1119 INT/ORG JURID SOVEREIGN

S60
O'BRIEN W.,"THE ROLE OF FORCE IN THE INTERNATIONAL JURIDICAL ORDER." WOR+45 NAT/G FORCES DOMIN ADJUD ARMS/CONT DETER NUC/PWR WAR ATTIT PWR...CATH INT/LAW JURID CONCPT TREND STERTYP GEN/LAWS 20. PAGE 110 A2266 INT/ORG COERCE

S60
POTTER P.B.,"RELATIVE VALUES OF INTERNATIONAL RELATIONS, LAW, AND ORGANIZATIONS." WOR+45 NAT/G LEGIT ADJUD ORD/FREE...CONCPT TOT/POP COLD/WAR 20. PAGE 117 A2401 INT/ORG LEGIS DIPLOM INT/LAW

S60
RHYNE C.S.,"LAW AS AN INSTRUMENT FOR PEACE." FUT WOR+45 PLAN LEGIT ROUTINE ARMS/CONT NUC/PWR ATTIT ORD/FREE...JURID METH/CNCPT TREND CON/ANAL HYPO/EXP COLD/WAR 20. PAGE 120 A2471 ADJUD EDU/PROP INT/LAW PEACE

S60
SCHACHTER O.,"THE ENFORCEMENT OF INTERNATIONAL JUDICIAL AND ARBITRAL DECISIONS." WOR+45 NAT/G ECO/TAC DOMIN LEGIT ROUTINE COERCE ATTIT DRIVE ALL/VALS PWR...METH/CNCPT TREND TOT/POP 20 UN. PAGE 128 A2615 INT/ORG ADJUD INT/LAW

S60
SCHWELB E.,"INTERNATIONAL CONVENTIONS ON HUMAN RIGHTS." FUT WOR+45 LAW CONSTN CULTURE SOCIETY STRUCT VOL/ASSN DELIB/GP PLAN ADJUD SUPEGO LOVE MORAL...SOC CONCPT STAT RECORD HIST/WRIT TREND 20 UN. PAGE 130 A2664 INT/ORG HUM

S60
THOMPSON K.W.,"MORAL PURPOSE IN FOREIGN POLICY: REALITIES AND ILLUSIONS." WOR+45 WOR-45 LAW CULTURE SOCIETY INT/ORG PLAN ADJUD ADMIN COERCE RIGID/FLEX SUPEGO KNOWL ORD/FREE PWR...SOC TREND SOC/EXP TOT/POP 20. PAGE 143 A2930 MORAL JURID DIPLOM

S60
WRIGHT Q.,"LEGAL ASPECTS OF THE U-2 INCIDENT." COM USA+45 USSR STRUCT NAT/G FORCES PLAN TEC/DEV ADJUD RIGID/FLEX MORAL ORD/FREE...DECISION INT/LAW JURID PSY TREND GEN/LAWS COLD/WAR VAL/FREE 20 U-2. PAGE 168 A3413 PWR POLICY SPACE

B61
ANAND R.P.,COMPULSORY JURISDICTION OF INTERNATIONAL COURT OF JUSTICE. FUT WOR+45 SOCIETY PLAN LEGIT ADJUD ATTIT DRIVE PERSON ORD/FREE...JURID CONCPT TREND 20 ICJ. PAGE 8 A0156 INT/ORG COERCE INT/LAW

B61
BAINS J.S.,STUDIES IN POLITICAL SCIENCE. INDIA WOR+45 WOR-45 CONSTN BAL/PWR ADJUD ADMIN PARL/PROC SOVEREIGN...SOC METH/COMP ANTHOL 17/20 UN. PAGE 10 A0209 DIPLOM INT/LAW NAT/G

B61
CARNELL F.,THE POLITICS OF THE NEW STATES: A SELECT ANNOTATED BIBLIOGRAPHY WITH SPECIAL REFERENCE TO THE COMMONWEALTH. CONSTN ELITES LABOR NAT/G POL/PAR EX/STRUC DIPLOM ADJUD ADMIN...GOV/COMP 20 COMMONWLTH. PAGE 24 A0496 BIBLIOG/A AFR ASIA COLONIAL

B61
LARSON A.,WHEN NATIONS DISAGREE. USA+45 WOR+45 INT/ORG ADJUD COERCE CRIME OWN SOVEREIGN...POLICY JURID 20. PAGE 85 A1734 INT/LAW DIPLOM WAR

B61
MCDOUGAL M.S.,LAW AND MINIMUM WORLD PUBLIC ORDER. WOR+45 SOCIETY NAT/G DELIB/GP EDU/PROP LEGIT ADJUD COERCE ATTIT PERSON...JURID CONCPT RECORD TREND TOT/POP 20. PAGE 98 A2006 INT/ORG ORD/FREE INT/LAW

B61
STONE J.,QUEST FOR SURVIVAL. WOR+45 NAT/G VOL/ASSN LEGIT ADMIN ARMS/CONT COERCE DISPL ORD/FREE PWR ...POLICY INT/LAW JURID COLD/WAR 20. PAGE 139 A2836 INT/ORG ADJUD SOVEREIGN

B61
US HOUSE COMM APPROPRIATIONS,INTER-AMERICAN PROGRAMS FOR 1961: DENIAL OF 1962 BUDGET INFORMATION. CHILE L/A+17C USA+45 FINAN CONSULT BUDGET ADJUD COST EFFICIENCY WEALTH...POLICY CHARTS 20 CONGRESS. PAGE 153 A3119 LEGIS FOR/AID DELIB/GP ECO/UNDEV

B61
WRIGHT Q.,THE ROLE OF INTERNATIONAL LAW IN THE ELIMINATION OF WAR. FUT WOR+45 WOR-45 NAT/G BAL/PWR DIPLOM DOMIN LEGIT PWR...POLICY INT/LAW JURID CONCPT TIME/SEQ TREND GEN/LAWS COLD/WAR 20. PAGE 168 A3414 INT/ORG ADJUD ARMS/CONT

L61
TAUBENFELD H.J.,"A REGIME FOR OUTER SPACE." FUT UNIV R+D ACT/RES PLAN BAL/PWR LEGIT ARMS/CONT ORD/FREE...POLICY JURID TREND UN TOT/POP 20 COLD/WAR. PAGE 142 A2894 INT/ORG ADJUD SPACE

B62
ALEXANDROWICZ C.H.,WORLD ECONOMIC AGENCIES: LAW AND PRACTICE. WOR+45 DIST/IND FINAN LABOR CONSULT INT/TRADE TARIFFS REPRESENT HEALTH...JURID 20 UN GATT EEC OAS ECSC. PAGE 6 A0115 INT/LAW INT/ORG DIPLOM ADJUD

B62
AMERICAN LAW INSTITUTE,FOREIGN RELATIONS LAW OF THE UNITED STATES: RESTATEMENT, SECOND. USA+45 NAT/G LEGIS ADJUD EXEC ROUTINE GOV/REL...INT/LAW JURID CONCPT 20 TREATY. PAGE 7 A0152 PROF/ORG LAW DIPLOM ORD/FREE

B62
BIBLIOTHEQUE PALAIS DE LA PAIX,CATALOGUE OF THE PEACE PALACE LIBRARY, SUPPLEMENT 1937-1952 (7 VOLS.). WOR+45 WOR-45 INT/ORG NAT/G ADJUD WAR PEACE ...JURID 20. PAGE 14 A0285 BIBLIOG INT/LAW DIPLOM

B62
COLOMBOS C.J.,THE INTERNATIONAL LAW OF THE SEA. WOR+45 EXTR/IND DIPLOM INT/TRADE TARIFFS AGREE WAR ...TIME/SEQ 20 TREATY. PAGE 28 A0570 INT/LAW SEA JURID ADJUD

B62
FATOUROS A.A.,GOVERNMENT GUARANTEES TO FOREIGN INVESTORS. WOR+45 ECO/UNDEV INDUS WORKER ADJUD ...NAT/COMP BIBLIOG TREATY. PAGE 44 A0903 NAT/G FINAN INT/TRADE ECO/DEV

B62
LILLICH R.B.,INTERNATIONAL CLAIMS: THEIR ADJUDICATION BY NATIONAL COMMISSIONS. WOR+45 WOR-45 INT/ORG LEGIT CT/SYS TOT/POP 20. PAGE 89 A1816 ADJUD JURID INT/LAW

B62
MCDOUGAL M.S.,THE PUBLIC ORDER OF THE OCEANS. WOR+45 WOR-45 SEA INT/ORG NAT/G CONSULT DELIB/GP DIPLOM LEGIT PEACE RIGID/FLEX...GEOG INT/LAW JURID RECORD TOT/POP 20 TREATY. PAGE 98 A2007 ADJUD ORD/FREE

B62
ROSENNE S.,THE WORLD COURT: WHAT IT IS AND HOW IT WORKS. WOR+45 WOR-45 LAW CONSTN JUDGE EDU/PROP LEGIT ROUTINE CHOOSE PEACE ORD/FREE...JURID OBS TIME/SEQ CHARTS UN TOT/POP VAL/FREE 20. PAGE 124 A2538 INT/ORG ADJUD INT/LAW

B62
US CONGRESS,COMMUNICATIONS SATELLITE LEGISLATION: HEARINGS BEFORE COMM ON AERON AND SPACE SCIENCES ON BILLS S2550 AND 2814. WOR+45 LAW VOL/ASSN PLAN DIPLOM CONTROL OWN PEACE...NEW/IDEA CONGRESS NASA. PAGE 150 A3062 SPACE COM/IND ADJUD GOV/REL

B62
WOETZEL R.K.,THE NURENBERG TRIALS IN INTERNATIONAL LAW. CHRIST-17C MOD/EUR WOR+45 SOCIETY NAT/G DELIB/GP DOMIN LEGIT ROUTINE ATTIT DRIVE PERSON SUPEGO MORAL ORD/FREE...POLICY MAJORIT JURID PSY SOC SELF/OBS RECORD NAZI TOT/POP. PAGE 166 A3376 INT/ORG ADJUD WAR

L62
MURACCIOLE L.,"LA LOI FONDAMENTALE DE LA REPUBLIQUE DU CONGO." WOR+45 SOCIETY ECO/UNDEV INT/ORG NAT/G LEGIS PLAN LEGIT ADJUD COLONIAL ROUTINE ATTIT SOVEREIGN 20 CONGO. PAGE 106 A2174 AFR CONSTN

S62
FALK R.A.,"THE REALITY OF INTERNATIONAL LAW." WOR+45 NAT/G LEGIT COERCE DETER WAR MORAL ORD/FREE PWR SOVEREIGN...JURID CONCPT VAL/FREE COLD/WAR 20. PAGE 43 A0887
INT/ORG ADJUD NUC/PWR INT/LAW

S62
FENWICK C.G.,"ISSUES AT PUNTA DEL ESTE: NON-INTERVENTION VS COLLECTIVE SECURITY." L/A+17C USA+45 VOL/ASSN DELIB/GP ECO/TAC LEGIT ADJUD REGION ORD/FREE OAS COLD/WAR 20. PAGE 45 A0917
INT/ORG CUBA

S62
FINKELSTEIN L.S.,"THE UNITED NATIONS AND ORGANIZATIONS FOR CONTROL OF ARMAMENT." FUT WOR+45 VOL/ASSN DELIB/GP TOP/EX CREATE EDU/PROP LEGIT ADJUD NUC/PWR ATTIT RIGID/FLEX ORD/FREE...POLICY DECISION CONCPT OBS TREND GEN/LAWS TOT/POP COLD/WAR. PAGE 46 A0933
INT/ORG PWR ARMS/CONT

S62
MONNIER J.P.,"LA SUCCESSION D'ETATS EN MATIERE DE RESPONSABILITE INTERNATIONALE." UNIV CONSTN INTELL SOCIETY ADJUD ROUTINE PERCEPT SUPEGO...GEN/LAWS TOT/POP 20. PAGE 103 A2107
NAT/G JURID INT/LAW

S62
SCHACHTER O.,"DAG HAMMARSKJOLD AND THE RELATION OF LAW TO POLITICS." FUT WOR+45 INT/ORG CONSULT PLAN TEC/DEV BAL/PWR DIPLOM LEGIT ATTIT PERCEPT ORD/FREE ...POLICY JURID CONCPT OBS TESTS STERTYP GEN/LAWS 20 HAMMARSK/D. PAGE 128 A2616
ACT/RES ADJUD

S62
THOMPSON D.,"THE UNITED KINGDOM AND THE TREATY OF ROME." EUR+WWI INT/ORG NAT/G DELIB/GP LEGIS INT/TRADE RIGID/FLEX...CONCPT EEC PARLIAMENT CMN/WLTH 20. PAGE 143 A2925
ADJUD JURID

C62
LILLICH R.B.,"INTERNATIONAL CLAIMS: THEIR ADJUDICATION BY NATIONAL COMMISSIONS." WOR+45 WOR-45 NAT/G ADJUD...JURID BIBLIOG 18/20. PAGE 89 A1817
INT/LAW DIPLOM PROB/SOLV

B63
BOWETT D.W.,THE LAW OF INTERNATIONAL INSTITUTIONS. WOR+45 WOR-45 CONSTN DELIB/GP EX/STRUC JUDGE EDU/PROP LEGIT CT/SYS EXEC ROUTINE RIGID/FLEX ORD/FREE PWR...JURID CONCPT ORG/CHARTS GEN/METH LEAGUE/NAT OAS OEEC 20 UN. PAGE 17 A0354
INT/ORG ADJUD DIPLOM

B63
FALK R.A.,LAW, MORALITY, AND WAR IN THE CONTEMPORARY WORLD. WOR+45 LAW INT/ORG EX/STRUC FORCES EDU/PROP LEGIT DETER NUC/PWR MORAL ORD/FREE ...JURID TOT/POP 20. PAGE 43 A0888
ADJUD ARMS/CONT PEACE INT/LAW

B63
MCDOUGAL M.S.,LAW AND PUBLIC ORDER IN SPACE. FUT USA+45 ACT/RES TEC/DEV ADJUD...POLICY INT/LAW JURID 20. PAGE 98 A2009
SPACE ORD/FREE DIPLOM DECISION

B63
PATRA A.C.,THE ADMINISTRATION OF JUSTICE UNDER THE EAST INDIA COMPANY IN BENGAL, BIHAR AND ORISSA. INDIA UK LG/CO CAP/ISM INT/TRADE ADJUD COLONIAL CONTROL CT/SYS...POLICY 20. PAGE 114 A2341
ADMIN JURID CONCPT

B63
PRESTON W. JR.,ALIENS AND DISSENTERS: FEDERAL SUPPRESSION OF RADICALS 1903-1933. USA-45 DIPLOM ADJUD REPRESENT RACE/REL MAJORITY...BIBLIOG/A 19/20. PAGE 117 A2409
DISCRIM GP/REL INGP/REL ATTIT

B63
ROBERTSON A.H.,HUMAN RIGHTS IN EUROPE. CONSTN SOCIETY INT/ORG NAT/G VOL/ASSN DELIB/GP ACT/RES PLAN ADJUD REGION ROUTINE ATTIT LOVE ORD/FREE RESPECT...JURID SOC CONCPT SOC/EXP UN 20. PAGE 122 A2498
EUR+WWI PERSON

L63
LISSITZYN O.J.,"INTERNATIONAL LAW IN A DIVIDED WORLD." FUT WOR+45 CONSTN CULTURE ECO/DEV ECO/UNDEV DIST/IND NAT/G FORCES ECO/TAC LEGIT ADJUD ADMIN COERCE ATTIT HEALTH MORAL ORD/FREE PWR RESPECT WEALTH VAL/FREE. PAGE 90 A1841
INT/ORG LAW

S63
BOHN L.,"WHOSE NUCLEAR TEST: NON-PHYSICAL INSPECTION AND TEST BAN." WOR+45 R+D INT/ORG VOL/ASSN ORD/FREE...GEN/LAWS GEN/METH COLD/WAR 20. PAGE 16 A0331
ADJUD ARMS/CONT TEC/DEV NUC/PWR

S63
GIRAUD E.,"L'INTERDICTION DU RECOURS A LA FORCE, LA THEORIE ET LA PRATIQUE DES NATIONS UNIES." ALGERIA COM CUBA HUNGARY WOR+45 ADJUD TOTALISM ATTIT RIGID/FLEX PWR...POLICY JURID CONCPT UN 20 CONGO. PAGE 53 A1077
INT/ORG FORCES DIPLOM

S63
MEYROWITZ H.,"LES JURISTES DEVANT L'ARME NUCLAIRE." FUT WOR+45 INTELL SOCIETY BAL/PWR DETER WAR...JURID CONCPT 20. PAGE 100 A2058
ACT/RES ADJUD INT/LAW NUC/PWR

B64
DIAS R.W.M.,A BIBLIOGRAPHY OF JURISPRUDENCE (2ND ED.). VOL/ASSN LEGIS ADJUD CT/SYS OWN...INT/LAW 18/20. PAGE 37 A0754
BIBLIOG/A JURID LAW

CONCPT

B64
FRIEDMANN W.G.,THE CHANGING STRUCTURE OF INTERNATIONAL LAW. WOR+45 INT/ORG NAT/G PROVS LEGIT ORD/FREE PWR...JURID CONCPT GEN/LAWS TOT/POP UN 20. PAGE 49 A1006
ADJUD TREND INT/LAW

B64
GJUPANOVIC H.,LEGAL SOURCES AND BIBLIOGRAPHY OF YUGOSLAVIA. COM YUGOSLAVIA LAW LEGIS DIPLOM ADMIN PARL/PROC REGION CRIME CENTRAL 20. PAGE 53 A1078
BIBLIOG/A JURID CONSTN ADJUD

B64
GRZYBOWSKI K.,THE SOCIALIST COMMONWEALTH OF NATIONS: ORGANIZATIONS AND INSTITUTIONS. FORCES DIPLOM INT/TRADE ADJUD ADMIN LEAD WAR MARXISM SOCISM...BIBLIOG 20 COMECON WARSAW/P. PAGE 58 A1185
INT/LAW COM REGION INT/ORG

B64
IKLE F.C.,HOW NATIONS NEGOTIATE. COM EUR+WWI USA+45 INTELL INT/ORG VOL/ASSN DELIB/GP ACT/RES CREATE DOMIN EDU/PROP ADJUD ROUTINE ATTIT PERSON ORD/FREE RESPECT SKILL...PSY SOC OBS VAL/FREE. PAGE 70 A1433
NAT/G PWR POLICY

B64
NASA,PROCEEDINGS OF CONFERENCE ON THE LAW OF SPACE AND OF SATELLITE COMMUNICATIONS: CHICAGO 1963. FUT WOR+45 DELIB/GP PROB/SOLV TEC/DEV CONFER ADJUD NUC/PWR...POLICY IDEA/COMP 20 NASA. PAGE 107 A2197
SPACE COM/IND LAW DIPLOM

B64
NICE R.W.,TREASURY OF LAW. WOR+45 WOR-45 SECT ADJUD MORAL ORD/FREE...INT/LAW JURID PHIL/SCI ANTHOL. PAGE 108 A2227
LAW WRITING PERS/REL DIPLOM

B64
REGALA R.,WORLD PEACE THROUGH DIPLOMACY AND LAW. S/ASIA WOR+45 ECO/UNDEV INT/ORG FORCES PLAN PROB/SOLV FOR/AID NUC/PWR WAR...POLICY INT/LAW 20. PAGE 120 A2456
DIPLOM PEACE ADJUD

B64
SCHECHTER A.H.,INTERPRETATION OF AMBIGUOUS DOCUMENTS BY INTERNATIONAL ADMINISTRATIVE TRIBUNALS. WOR+45 EX/STRUC INT/TRADE CT/SYS SOVEREIGN 20 UN ILO EURCT/JUST. PAGE 128 A2620
INT/LAW DIPLOM INT/ORG ADJUD

B64
STANGER R.J.,ESSAYS ON INTERVENTION. PLAN PROB/SOLV BAL/PWR ADJUD COERCE WAR ROLE PWR...INT/LAW CONCPT 20 UN INTERVENT. PAGE 137 A2803
SOVEREIGN DIPLOM POLICY LEGIT

B64
SZLADITS C.,BIBLIOGRAPHY ON FOREIGN AND COMPARATIVE LAW: BOOKS AND ARTICLES IN ENGLISH (SUPPLEMENT 1962). FINAN INDUS JUDGE LICENSE ADMIN CT/SYS PARL/PROC OWN...INT/LAW CLASSIF METH/COMP NAT/COMP 20. PAGE 141 A2877
BIBLIOG/A JURID ADJUD LAW

B64
TAUBENFELD H.J.,SPACE AND SOCIETY. USA+45 LAW FORCES CREATE TEC/DEV ADJUD CONTROL COST PEACE ...PREDICT ANTHOL 20. PAGE 142 A2895
SPACE SOCIETY ADJUST DIPLOM

S64
CARNEGIE ENDOWMENT INT. PEACE,"LEGAL QUESTIONS (ISSUES BEFORE THE NINETEENTH GENERAL ASSEMBLY)." WOR+45 CONSTN NAT/G DELIB/GP ADJUD PEACE MORAL ORD/FREE...RECORD UN 20 TREATY. PAGE 24 A0494
INT/ORG LAW INT/LAW

S64
COHEN M.,"BASIC PRINCIPLES OF INTERNATIONAL LAW." UNIV WOR+45 WOR-45 BAL/PWR LEGIT ADJUD WAR ATTIT MORAL ORD/FREE PWR...JURID CONCPT MYTH TOT/POP 20. PAGE 27 A0560
INT/ORG INT/LAW

S64
GARDNER R.N.,"THE SOVIET UNION AND THE UNITED NATIONS." WOR+45 FINAN POL/PAR VOL/ASSN FORCES ECO/TAC DOMIN EDU/PROP LEGIT ADJUD ADMIN ARMS/CONT COERCE ATTIT ALL/VALS...POLICY MAJORIT CONCPT OBS TIME/SEQ TREND STERTYP UN. PAGE 51 A1046
COM INT/ORG USSR

S64
HICKEY D.,"THE PHILOSOPHICAL ARGUMENT FOR WORLD GOVERNMENT." WOR+45 SOCIETY ACT/RES PLAN LEGIT ADJUD PEACE PERCEPT PERSON ORD/FREE...HUM JURID PHIL/SCI METH/CNCPT CON/ANAL STERTYP GEN/LAWS TOT/POP 20. PAGE 65 A1327
FUT INT/ORG

S64
KARPOV P.V.,"PEACEFUL COEXISTENCE AND INTERNATIONAL LAW." WOR+45 LAW SOCIETY INT/ORG VOL/ASSN FORCES CREATE CAP/ISM DIPLOM ADJUD NUC/PWR PEACE MORAL ORD/FREE PWR MARXISM...MARXIST JURID CONCPT OBS TREND COLD/WAR MARX/KARL 20. PAGE 77 A1568
COM ATTIT INT/LAW USSR

S64
KUNZ J.,"THE CHANGING SCIENCE OF INTERNATIONAL LAW." FUT WOR+45 WOR-45 INT/ORG LEGIT ORD/FREE ...JURID TIME/SEQ GEN/LAWS 20. PAGE 83 A1696
ADJUD CONCPT INT/LAW

S64
LIPSON L.,"PEACEFUL COEXISTENCE." COM USSR WOR+45 LAW INT/ORG DIPLOM LEGIT ADJUD ORD/FREE...CONCPT OBS TREND GEN/LAWS VAL/FREE COLD/WAR 20. PAGE 90 A1834
ATTIT JURID INT/LAW PEACE

S64
MCGHEE G.C.,"EAST-WEST RELATIONS TODAY." WOR+45
IDEA/COMP

PROB/SOLV BAL/PWR PEACE 20 COLD/WAR. PAGE 98 A2011 DIPLOM ADJUD

S64

SCHWELB E.,"OPERATION OF THE EUROPEAN CONVENTION ON HUMAN RIGHTS." EUR+WWI LAW SOCIETY CREATE EDU/PROP ADJUD ADMIN PEACE ATTIT ORD/FREE PWR...POLICY INT/LAW CONCPT OBS GEN/LAWS UN VAL/FREE ILO 20 ECHR. PAGE 130 A2665 INT/ORG MORAL

B65

FALK R.A.,THE AFTERMATH OF SABBATINO: BACKGROUND PAPERS AND PROCEEDINGS OF SEVENTH HAMMARSKJOLD FORUM. USA+45 LAW ACT/RES ADJUD ROLE...BIBLIOG 20 EXPROPRIAT SABBATINO HARLAN/JM. PAGE 44 A0891 SOVEREIGN CT/SYS INT/LAW OWN

B65

LAFAVE W.R.,LAW AND SOVIET SOCIETY. EX/STRUC DIPLOM DOMIN EDU/PROP PRESS ADMIN CRIME OWN MARXISM 20 KHRUSH/N. PAGE 84 A1710 JURID CT/SYS ADJUD GOV/REL

B65

MONCONDUIT F.,LA COMMISSION EUROPEENNE DES DROITS DE L'HOMME. DIPLOM AGREE GP/REL ORD/FREE PWR ...BIBLIOG 20 TREATY. PAGE 102 A2103 INT/LAW INT/ORG ADJUD JURID

B65

MOODY M.,CATALOG OF INTERNATIONAL LAW AND RELATIONS (20 VOLS.). WOR+45 INT/ORG NAT/G ADJUD ADMIN CT/SYS POLICY. PAGE 103 A2117 BIBLIOG INT/LAW DIPLOM

B65

MOSTECKY V.,SOVIET LEGAL BIBLIOGRAPHY. USSR LEGIS PRESS WRITING CONFER ADJUD CT/SYS REV MARXISM ...INT/LAW JURID DICTIONARY 20. PAGE 105 A2155 BIBLIOG/A LAW COM CONSTN

B65

PANJAB U EXTENSION LIBRARY,INDIAN NEWS INDEX. INDIA ECO/UNDEV INDUS INT/ORG SCHOOL FORCES ADJUD WAR ATTIT WEALTH 20. PAGE 114 A2333 BIBLIOG PRESS WRITING DIPLOM

B65

THOMAS A.V.,NONINTERVENTION: THE LAW AND ITS IMPORT IN THE AMERICAS. L/A+17C USA+45 USA-45 WOR+45 DIPLOM ADJUD...JURID IDEA/COMP 20 UN INTERVENT. PAGE 143 A2920 INT/LAW PWR COERCE

B65

US SENATE COMM ON JUDICIARY,ANTITRUST EXEMPTIONS FOR AGREEMENTS RELATING TO BALANCE OF PAYMENTS. FINAN ECO/TAC CONTROL WEALTH...POLICY 20 CONGRESS. PAGE 157 A3195 BAL/PAY ADJUD MARKET INT/TRADE

B65

VON GLAHN G.,LAW AMONG NATIONS: AN INTRODUCTION TO PUBLIC INTERNATIONAL LAW. WOR+45 WOR-45 INT/ORG NAT/G CREATE ADJUD WAR...GEOG CLASSIF TREND BIBLIOG. PAGE 160 A3250 ACADEM INT/LAW GEN/LAWS LAW

B65

WHITE G.M.,THE USE OF EXPERTS BY INTERNATIONAL TRIBUNALS. WOR+45 WOR-45 INT/ORG NAT/G PAY ADJUD COST...OBS BIBLIOG 20. PAGE 164 A3334 INT/LAW ROUTINE CONSULT CT/SYS

S65

AMRAM P.W.,"REPORT ON THE TENTH SESSION OF THE HAGUE CONFERENCE ON PRIVATE INTERNATIONAL LAW." USA+45 WOR+45 INT/ORG CREATE LEGIT ADJUD ALL/VALS ...JURID CONCPT METH/CNCPT OBS GEN/METH 20. PAGE 8 A0155 VOL/ASSN DELIB/GP INT/LAW

S65

GROSS L.,"PROBLEMS OF INTERNATIONAL ADJUDICATION AND COMPLIANCE WITH INTERNATIONAL LAW: SOME SIMPLE SOLUTIONS." WOR+45 SOCIETY NAT/G DOMIN LEGIT ADJUD CT/SYS RIGID/FLEX HEALTH PWR...JURID NEW/IDEA COLD/WAR 20. PAGE 57 A1177 LAW METH/CNCPT INT/LAW

S65

HAZARD J.N.,"CO-EXISTENCE LAW BOWS OUT." WOR+45 R+D INT/ORG VOL/ASSN CONSULT DELIB/GP ACT/RES CREATE PEACE KNOWL...JURID CONCPT COLD/WAR VAL/FREE 20. PAGE 63 A1300 PROF/ORG ADJUD

S65

STEIN E.,"TOWARD SUPREMACY OF TREATY-CONSTITUTION BY JUDICIAL FIAT: ON THE MARGIN OF THE COSTA CASE." EUR+WWI ITALY WOR+45 INT/ORG NAT/G LEGIT REGION NAT/LISM PWR...JURID CONCPT TREND TOT/POP VAL/FREE 20. PAGE 138 A2816 ADJUD CONSTN SOVEREIGN INT/LAW

C65

SCHEINGOLD S.A.,"THE RULE OF LAW IN EUROPEAN INTEGRATION: THE PATH OF THE SCHUMAN PLAN." EUR+WWI JUDGE ADJUD FEDERAL ATTIT PWR...RECORD INT BIBLIOG EEC ECSC. PAGE 128 A2621 INT/LAW CT/SYS REGION CENTRAL

B66

CANFIELD L.H.,THE PRESIDENCY OF WOODROW WILSON: PRELUDE TO A WORLD IN CRISIS. USA-45 ADJUD NEUTRAL WAR CHOOSE INGP/REL PEACE ORD/FREE 20 WILSON/W PRESIDENT TREATY LEAGUE/NAT. PAGE 24 A0477 PERSON POLICY DIPLOM GOV/REL

B66

CLARK G.,WORLD PEACE THROUGH WORLD LAW; TWO ALTERNATIVE PLANS. WOR+45 DELIB/GP FORCES TAX CONFER ADJUD SANCTION ARMS/CONT WAR CHOOSE PRIVIL 20 UN COLD/WAR. PAGE 27 A0541 INT/LAW PEACE PLAN INT/ORG

B66

COPLIN W.D.,THE FUNCTIONS OF INTERNATIONAL LAW. WOR+45 ECO/DEV ECO/UNDEV ADJUD COLONIAL WAR OWN SOVEREIGN...POLICY GEN/LAWS 20. PAGE 30 A0611 INT/LAW DIPLOM INT/ORG

B66

COUNCIL OF EUROPE,EUROPEAN CONVENTION ON HUMAN RIGHTS - COLLECTED TEXTS (5TH ED.). EUR+WWI DIPLOM ADJUD CT/SYS...INT/LAW 20 ECHR. PAGE 31 A0638 ORD/FREE DELIB/GP INT/ORG JURID

B66

GORDON B.K.,THE DIMENSIONS OF CONFLICT IN SOUTHEAST ASIA. S/ASIA FORCES ADJUD REGION...CHARTS 20. PAGE 54 A1111 DIPLOM NAT/COMP INT/ORG VOL/ASSN

B66

INTL ATOMIC ENERGY AGENCY,INTERNATIONAL CONVENTIONS ON CIVIL LIABILITY FOR NUCLEAR DAMAGE. FUT WOR+45 ADJUD WAR COST PEACE SOVEREIGN...JURID 20. PAGE 71 A1462 DIPLOM INT/ORG DELIB/GP NUC/PWR

B66

NANTWI E.K.,THE ENFORCEMENT OF INTERNATIONAL JUDICIAL DECISIONS AND ARBITAL AWARDS IN PUBLIC INTERNATIONAL LAW. WOR+45 WOR-45 JUDGE PROB/SOLV DIPLOM CT/SYS SUPEGO MORAL PWR RESPECT...METH/CNCPT 18/20 CASEBOOK. PAGE 107 A2196 INT/LAW ADJUD SOVEREIGN INT/ORG

B66

US SENATE COMM AERO SPACE SCI,SOVIET SPACE PROGRAMS, 1962-65; GOALS AND PURPOSES, ACHIEVEMENTS, PLANS, AND INTERNATIONAL IMPLICATIONS. USA+45 USSR R+D FORCES PLAN EDU/PROP PRESS ADJUD ARMS/CONT ATTIT MARXISM. PAGE 155 A3168 CONSULT SPACE FUT DIPLOM

B66

WEINSTEIN F.B.,VIETNAM'S UNHELD ELECTIONS: THE FAILURE TO CARRY OUT THE 1956 REUNIFICATION ELECTIONS... (MONOGRAPH). VIETNAM/S VIETNAM/N LEGIT CONFER ADJUD WAR PEACE 20 TREATY GENEVA/CON UNIFICA. PAGE 162 A3306 AGREE NAT/G CHOOSE DIPLOM

S66

"WORLD BANK CONVENTION ON INVESTMENT DISPUTES; A BIBLIOGRAPH ICAL NOTE." VOL/ASSN CONSULT CAP/ISM DIPLOM INT/TRADE 20 SENATE PRESIDENT. PAGE 4 A0074 BIBLIOG ADJUD FINAN INT/ORG

B67

BLOM-COOPER L.,THE LITERATURE OF THE LAW AND THE LANGUAGE OF THE LAW (2 VOLS.). CANADA ISRAEL UK WOR+45 WOR-45 JUDGE CT/SYS ATTIT...CRIMLGY JURID ANTHOL CMN/WLTH. PAGE 15 A0312 BIBLIOG LAW INT/LAW ADJUD

B67

KIRK R.,THE POLITICAL PRINCIPLES OF ROBERT A. TAFT. USA+45 LABOR DIPLOM ADJUD ADJUST ORD/FREE TAFT/RA. PAGE 80 A1635 POL/PAR LEAD LEGIS ATTIT

B67

LAWYERS COMM AMER POLICY VIET,VIETNAM AND INTERNATIONAL LAW: AN ANALYSIS OF THE LEGALITY OF THE US MILITARY INVOLVEMENT. VIETNAM LAW INT/ORG COERCE WEAPON PEACE ORD/FREE 20 UN SEATO TREATY. PAGE 86 A1753 INT/LAW DIPLOM ADJUD WAR

B67

UNIVERSAL REFERENCE SYSTEM,LAW, JURISPRUDENCE, AND JUDICIAL PROCESS (VOLUME VII). WOR+45 WOR-45 CONSTN NAT/G LEGIS JUDGE CT/SYS...INT/LAW COMPUT/IR GEN/METH METH. PAGE 149 A3044 BIBLIOG/A LAW JURID ADJUD

B67

US SENATE COMM ON FOREIGN REL,HUMAN RIGHTS CONVENTIONS. USA+45 LABOR VOL/ASSN DELIB/GP DOMIN ADJUD REPRESENT...INT/LAW MGT CONGRESS. PAGE 156 A3189 LEGIS ORD/FREE WORKER LOBBY

B67

WATERS M.,THE UNITED NATIONS* INTERNATIONAL ORGANIZATION AND ADMINISTRATION. WOR+45 EX/STRUC FORCES DIPLOM LEAD REGION ARMS/CONT REPRESENT INGP/REL ROLE...METH/COMP ANTHOL 20 UN LEAGUE/NAT. PAGE 162 A3291 CONSTN INT/ORG ADMIN ADJUD

L67

"RESTRICTIVE SOVEREIGN IMMUNITY, THE STATE DEPARTMENT, AND THE COURTS." USA+45 USA-45 EX/STRUC DIPLOM ADJUD CONTROL GOV/REL 19/20 DEPT/STATE SUPREME/CT. PAGE 4 A0080 SOVEREIGN ORD/FREE PRIVIL CT/SYS

L67

CAHIERS P.,"LE RECOURS EN CONSTATATION DE MANQUEMENTS DES ETATS MEMBRES DEVANT LA COUR DES COMMUNAUTES EUROPEENNES." LAW PROB/SOLV DIPLOM ADMIN CT/SYS SANCTION ATTIT...POLICY DECISION JURID ECSC EEC. PAGE 23 A0465 INT/ORG CONSTN ROUTINE ADJUD

L67

GOLD J.,"INTERPRETATION BY THE INTERNATIONAL MONETARY FUND OF ITS ARTICLES OF AGREEMENT." INT/TRADE ADJUD ATTIT...POLICY JURID. PAGE 53 A1089 CONSTN INT/ORG LAW DIPLOM

L67

LANDIS E.S.,"THE SOUTH WEST AFRICA CASES* REMAND TO THE UNITED NATIONS." ETHIOPIA LIBERIA SOUTH/AFR BAL/PWR 20 UN. PAGE 84 A1719 INT/LAW INT/ORG DIPLOM ADJUD

ANTHEM T.,"CYPRUS* WHAT NOW?" CYPRUS GREECE TURKEY NAT/G BUDGET MAJORITY 20 NATO. PAGE 8 A0165 — S67 — DIPLOM COERCE INT/TRADE ADJUD

BLUM Y.Z.,"INDONESIA'S RETURN TO THE UNITED NATIONS." INDONESIA ADJUD SANCTION REPRESENT ...JURID 20 UN. PAGE 16 A0324 — S67 — CONSTN LAW DIPLOM INT/ORG

COHN K.,"CRIMES AGAINST HUMANITY." GERMANY INT/ORG SANCTION ATTIT ORD/FREE...MARXIST CRIMLGY 20 UN. PAGE 28 A0564 — S67 — WAR INT/LAW CRIME ADJUD

D'AMATO D.,"LEGAL ASPECTS OF THE FRENCH NUCLEAR TESTS." FRANCE WOR+45 ACT/RES COLONIAL RISK GOV/REL EQUILIB ORD/FREE PWR DECISION. PAGE 33 A0672 — S67 — INT/LAW DIPLOM NUC/PWR ADJUD

FAWCETT J.E.S.,"GIBRALTAR* THE LEGAL ISSUES." SPAIN UK INT/ORG BAL/PWR LICENSE CONFER SANCTION PRIVIL ...JURID CHARTS 20. PAGE 44 A0905 — S67 — INT/LAW DIPLOM COLONIAL ADJUD

JOHNSON D.H.N.,"THE SOUTH-WEST AFRICA CASES." AFR ETHIOPIA LIBERIA SOUTH/AFR CONSULT JUDGE BAL/PWR 20. PAGE 74 A1521 — S67 — INT/LAW DIPLOM INT/ORG ADJUD

JOHNSTON D.M.,"LAW, TECHNOLOGY AND THE SEA." WOR+45 PLAN PROB/SOLV TEC/DEV CONFER ADJUD ORD/FREE ...POLICY JURID. PAGE 75 A1528 — S67 — INT/LAW INT/ORG DIPLOM NEUTRAL

MANN F.A.,"THE BRETTON WOODS AGREEMENT IN THE ENGLISH COURTS." UK JUDGE ADJUD CT/SYS...JURID PREDICT CON/ANAL 20. PAGE 94 A1923 — S67 — LAW INT/LAW CONSTN

TACKABERRY R.B.,"ORGANIZING AND TRAINING PEACE-KEEPING FORCES* THE CANADIAN VIEW." CANADA PLAN DIPLOM CONFER ADJUD ADMIN CIVMIL/REL 20 UN. PAGE 141 A2882 — S67 — PEACE FORCES INT/ORG CONSULT

SIDGWICK H.,THE ELEMENTS OF POLITICS. LOC/G NAT/G LEGIS DIPLOM ADJUD CONTROL EXEC PARL/PROC REPRESENT GOV/REL SOVEREIGN ALL/IDEOS 19 MILL/JS BENTHAM/J. PAGE 132 A2713 — B91 — POLICY LAW CONCPT

US DEPARTMENT OF STATE,CATALOGUE OF WORKS RELATING TO THE LAW OF NATIONS AND DIPLOMACY IN THE LIBRARY OF THE DEPARTMENT OF STATE (PAMPHLET). WOR-45 NAT/G ADJUD CT/SYS...INT/LAW JURID 19. PAGE 152 A3102 — B97 — BIBLIOG/A DIPLOM LAW

ADJUST....SOCIAL ADJUSTMENT, SOCIALIZATION. SEE ALSO INGP/REL

MURRA R.O.,POST-WAR PROBLEMS: A CURRENT LIST OF UNITED STATES GOVERNMENT PUBLICATIONS (PAMPHLET). WOR+45 SOCIETY FINAN INT/ORG SCHOOL WORKER TEC/DEV ECO/TAC...SOC 20. PAGE 106 A2180 — N — BIBLIOG/A ADJUST AGRI INDUS

SIEGFRIED A.,AMERICA COMES OF AGE: A FRENCH ANALYSIS (TRANS. BY H.H. HEMMING AND DORIS HEMMING). FRANCE UK POL/PAR WORKER TEC/DEV DIPLOM REGION RACE/REL ADJUST PRODUC HEREDITY...TIME/SEQ GP/COMP SOC/INTEG 20 DEMOCRAT REPUBLICAN KKK. PAGE 132 A2714 — B27 — USA-45 CULTURE ECO/DEV SOC

TOLMAN E.C.,DRIVES TOWARD WAR. UNIV PLAN DIPLOM ECO/TAC COERCE PERS/REL ADJUST HAPPINESS BIO/SOC HEREDITY HEALTH KNOWL. PAGE 144 A2947 — B42 — PSY WAR UTOPIA DRIVE

FULLER G.F.,FOREIGN RELIEF AND REHABILITATION (PAMPHLET). FUT GERMANY UK USA-45 INT/ORG PROB/SOLV DIPLOM FOR/AID ADMIN ADJUST PEACE ALL/VALS...SOC/WK 20 UN JEWS. PAGE 50 A1018 — B43 — BIBLIOG/A PLAN GIVE WAR

ST LEGER A.,SELECTION OF WORKS FOR AN UNDERSTANDING OF WORLD AFFAIRS SINCE 1914. WOR-45 INT/ORG CREATE BAL/PWR REV ADJUST 20. PAGE 137 A2796 — B43 — BIBLIOG/A WAR SOCIETY DIPLOM

KROPOTKIN P.,MUTUAL AID, A FACTOR OF EVOLUTION (1902). UNIV ADJUST ATTIT HEREDITY PERSON LOVE DARWIN/C. PAGE 82 A1687 — B55 — INGP/REL SOCIETY GEN/LAWS BIO/SOC

DE SMITH S.A.,"CONSTITUTIONAL MONARCHY IN BURGANDA." AFR UGANDA UK STRUCT CHIEF REGION INGP/REL ADJUST NAT/LISM SOVEREIGN CONSERVE ...POLICY 19/20 BURGANDA. PAGE 35 A0712 — S55 — NAT/G DIPLOM CONSTN COLONIAL

STRACHEY A.,THE UNCONSCIOUS MOTIVES OF WAR; A PSYCHO-ANALYTICAL CONTRIBUTION. UNIV SOCIETY DIPLOM DREAM GP/REL ADJUST ATTIT DISPL PERCEPT PERSON KNOWL MORAL. PAGE 139 A2840 — B57 — WAR DRIVE LOVE PSY

MANSERGH N.,SURVEY OF BRITISH COMMONWEALTH AFFAIRS: PROBLEMS OF WARTIME CO-OPERATION AND POST-WAR CHANGE 1939-1952. INDIA IRELAND S/ASIA CONSTN INT/ORG BAL/PWR COLONIAL NEUTRAL WAR ADJUST PEACE ROLE ORD/FREE...CHARTS 20 CMN/WLTH NATO UN. PAGE 94 A1931 — B58 — VOL/ASSN CONSEN PROB/SOLV INGP/REL

KAPLAN D.,THE ARAB REFUGEES: AN ABNORMAL PROBLEM. UAR WOR+45 PROB/SOLV DIPLOM GOV/REL ADJUST EFFICIENCY...POLICY GEOG INT/LAW 20 UN JEWS MIGRATION. PAGE 76 A1557 — B59 — STRANGE HABITAT GP/REL INGP/REL

STRACHEY J.,THE END OF EMPIRE. UK WOR+45 WOR-45 DIPLOM INT/TRADE DOMIN ADJUST ORD/FREE WEALTH ...SOCIALIST GOV/COMP TIME COMMONWLTH. PAGE 139 A2841 — B60 — COLONIAL ECO/DEV BAL/PWR LAISSEZ

ROBINSON M.E.,EDUCATION FOR SOCIAL CHANGE: ESTABLISHING INSTITUTES OF PUBLIC AND BUSINESS ADMINISTRATION ABROAD (PAMPHLET). WOR+45 SOCIETY ACADEM CONFER INGP/REL ROLE...SOC CHARTS BIBLIOG 20 ICA. PAGE 122 A2506 — B61 — FOR/AID EDU/PROP MGT ADJUST

SYATAUW J.J.G.,SOME NEWLY ESTABLISHED ASIAN STATES AND THE DEVELOPMENT OF INTERNATIONAL LAW. BURMA CEYLON INDIA INDONESIA ECO/UNDEV COLONIAL NEUTRAL WAR PEACE SOVEREIGN...CHARTS 19/20. PAGE 140 A2873 — B61 — INT/LAW ADJUST SOCIETY S/ASIA

JENNINGS W.I.,DEMOCRACY IN AFRICA. UK CULTURE STRUCT ECO/UNDEV DIPLOM COLONIAL GP/REL ADJUST NAT/LISM ORD/FREE...GOV/COMP 20 THIRD/WRLD. PAGE 74 A1512 — B63 — PROB/SOLV AFR CONSTN POPULISM

ANDREWS D.H.,LATIN AMERICA: A BIBLIOGRAPHY OF PAPERBACK BOOKS. SECT INT/TRADE EDU/PROP WAR GOV/REL ADJUST NAT/LISM ATTIT...ART/METH LING BIOG 20. PAGE 8 A0160 — B64 — BIBLIOG L/A+17C CULTURE NAT/G

STANKIEWICZ W.J.,POLITICAL THOUGHT SINCE WORLD WAR II. WOR+45 CAP/ISM DIPLOM COLONIAL COERCE REV REPRESENT ADJUST ANOMIE ALL/IDEOS 20. PAGE 137 A2804 — B64 — IDEA/COMP DOMIN ORD/FREE AUTHORIT

TAUBENFELD H.J.,SPACE AND SOCIETY. USA+45 LAW FORCES CREATE TEC/DEV ADJUD CONTROL COST PEACE ...PREDICT ANTHOL 20. PAGE 142 A2895 — B64 — SPACE SOCIETY ADJUST DIPLOM

LINDBLOM C.E.,THE INTELLIGENCE OF DEMOCRACY; DECISION MAKING THROUGH MUTUAL ADJUSTMENT. WOR+45 SOCIETY NAT/G PROB/SOLV DOMIN PARTIC GP/REL ORD/FREE...POLICY IDEA/COMP BIBLIOG 20. PAGE 89 A1821 — B65 — PLURISM DECISION ADJUST DIPLOM

BURTON J.W.,"INTERNATIONAL RELATIONS: A GENERAL THEORY." WOR+45 NAT/G CREATE BAL/PWR NEUTRAL COERCE DETER ADJUST...TREND IDEA/COMP GEN/METH BIBLIOG. PAGE 22 A0447 — C65 — DIPLOM GEN/LAWS ACT/RES ORD/FREE

HANSON J.W.,EDUCATION AND THE DEVELOPMENT OF NATIONS. DIPLOM TASK ADJUST EFFICIENCY...POLICY ANTHOL 20. PAGE 61 A1256 — B66 — ECO/UNDEV EDU/PROP NAT/G PLAN

ROBERTSON D.J.,THE BRITISH BALANCE OF PAYMENTS. UK WOR+45 INDUS BUDGET TAX ADJUST...CHARTS ANTHOL 20. PAGE 122 A2500 — B66 — FINAN BAL/PAY ECO/DEV INT/TRADE

THOMPSON J.H.,MODERNIZATION OF THE ARAB WORLD. FUT ISRAEL STRUCT ECO/UNDEV DIPLOM INGP/REL ATTIT ...CENSUS ANTHOL 20 ARABS. PAGE 143 A2926 — B66 — ADJUST ISLAM PROB/SOLV NAT/COMP

DUROSELLE J.B.,"LE CONFLIT DE TRIESTE 1943-1954: ETUDES DE CAS DE CONFLITS INTERNATIONAUX III." ITALY USA+45 YUGOSLAVIA ELITES DELIB/GP PLAN ADJUST ...POLICY GEOG CHARTS IDEA/COMP TIME 20 TREATY UN COLD/WAR. PAGE 40 A0810 — C66 — BIBLIOG WAR DIPLOM GEN/LAWS

CECIL L.,ALBERT BALLIN; BUSINESS AND POLITICS IN IMPERIAL GERMANY 1888-1918. GERMANY UK INT/TRADE LEAD WAR PERS/REL ADJUST PWR WEALTH...MGT BIBLIOG 19/20. PAGE 25 A0510 — B67 — DIPLOM CONSTN ECO/DEV TOP/EX

CLARK S.V.O.,CENTRAL BANK COOPERATION: 1924-31. WOR-45 PROB/SOLV ECO/TAC ADJUST BAL/PAY...TREND CHARTS METH/COMP 20. PAGE 27 A0542 — B67 — FINAN EQUILIB DIPLOM POLICY

KIRK R.,THE POLITICAL PRINCIPLES OF ROBERT A. TAFT. USA+45 LABOR DIPLOM ADJUD ADJUST ORD/FREE TAFT/RA. — B67 — POL/PAR LEAD

PAGE 80 A1635 — LEGIS ATTIT

B67
ROACH J.R.,THE UNITED STATES AND THE ATLANTIC COMMUNITY: ISSUES AND PROSPECTS. WOR+45 TEC/DEV ECO/TAC COLONIAL REGION PEACE ROLE...ANTHOL NATO COLD/WAR EEC. PAGE 121 A2491 — INT/ORG POLICY ADJUST DIPLOM

L67
GALTUNG J.,"ON THE EFFECTS OF INTERNATIONAL ECONOMIC SANCTIONS, WITH EXAMPLES FROM THE CASE OF RHODESIA." NAT/G DIPLOM EDU/PROP ADJUST EFFICIENCY ATTIT MORAL...OBS CHARTS 20. PAGE 51 A1035 — SANCTION ECO/TAC INT/TRADE ECO/UNDEV

S67
TUCKER R.C.,"THE DERADICALIZATION OF MARXIST MOVEMENTS." USSR SOCIETY DIPLOM 20. PAGE 145 A2973 — MARXISM ADJUST ATTIT REV

S67
VELIKONJA J.,"ITALIAN IMMIGRANTS IN THE UNITED STATES IN THE MID-SIXTIES" ITALY USA+45 KIN MUNIC NAT/G WORKER DIPLOM REGION GP/REL ADJUST...GEOG CHARTS SOC/INTEG 20. PAGE 158 A3226 — HABITAT ORD/FREE TREND STAT

ADJUSTMENT, SOCIAL....SEE ADJUST

ADLER G.J. A0091

ADLER M.J. A0092

ADLER S. A0093

ADLER/A....ALFRED ADLER

ADLOFF R. A2933

ADMIN....ORGANIZATIONAL BEHAVIOR, NONEXECUTIVE

N
MONPIED E.,BIBLIOGRAPHIE FEDERALISTE: ARTICLES ET DOCUMENTS PUBLIES DANS LES PERIODIQUES PARUS EN FRANCE NOV. 1945-OCT. 1950. EUR+WWI WOR+45 ADMIN REGION ATTIT MARXISM PACIFISM 20 EEC. PAGE 103 A2108 — BIBLIOG/A FEDERAL CENTRAL INT/ORG

B
DEUTSCHE BIBLIOTH FRANKF A M,DEUTSCHE BIBLIOGRAPHIE. EUR+WWI GERMANY ECO/DEV FORCES DIPLOM LEAD...POLICY PHIL/SCI SOC 20. PAGE 36 A0743 — BIBLIOG LAW ADMIN NAT/G

B
UN DEPARTMENT SOCIAL AFFAIRS,SOCIAL WELFARE INFORMATION SERIES: CURRENT LITERATURE AND NATIONAL CONFERENCES. WOR+45 INDUS SERV/IND INT/ORG CONSULT ACT/RES WEALTH...HEAL UN. PAGE 147 A2997 — BIBLIOG/A SOC/WK DIPLOM ADMIN

N
AMERICAN POLITICAL SCIENCE REVIEW. USA+45 USA-45 WOR+45 WOR-45 INT/ORG ADMIN...INT/LAW PHIL/SCI CONCPT METH 20 UN. PAGE 1 A0003 — BIBLIOG/A DIPLOM NAT/G GOV/COMP

N
INTERNATIONAL REVIEW OF ADMINISTRATIVE SCIENCES. WOR+45 WOR-45 STRATA ECO/DEV ECO/UNDEV CREATE PLAN PROB/SOLV DIPLOM CONTROL REPRESENT...MGT 20. PAGE 1 A0011 — BIBLIOG/A ADMIN INT/ORG NAT/G

N
REVIEW OF POLITICS. WOR+45 WOR-45 CONSTN LEGIS PROB/SOLV ADMIN LEAD ALL/IDEOS...PHIL/SCI 20. PAGE 2 A0024 — BIBLIOG/A DIPLOM INT/ORG NAT/G

N
BIBLIO, CATALOGUE DES OUVRAGES PARUS EN LANGUE FRANCAISE DANS LE MONDE ENTIER. FRANCE WOR+45 ADMIN LEAD PERSON...SOC 20. PAGE 2 A0029 — BIBLIOG NAT/G DIPLOM ECO/DEV

N
HANDBOOK OF LATIN AMERICAN STUDIES. LAW CULTURE ECO/UNDEV POL/PAR ADMIN LEAD...SOC 20. PAGE 2 A0035 — BIBLIOG/A L/A+17C NAT/G DIPLOM

N
THE JAPAN SCIENCE REVIEW: LAW AND POLITICS: LIST OF BOOKS AND ARTICLES ON LAW AND POLITICS. CONSTN AGRI INDUS LABOR DIPLOM TAX ADMIN CRIME...INT/LAW SOC 20 CHINJAP. PAGE 2 A0042 — BIBLIOG LAW S/ASIA PHIL/SCI

N
DEUTSCHE BUCHEREI,JAHRESVERZEICHNIS DES DEUTSCHEN SCHRIFTUMS. AUSTRIA EUR+WWI GERMANY SWITZERLND LAW LOC/G DIPLOM ADMIN...MGT SOC 19/20. PAGE 37 A0745 — BIBLIOG WRITING NAT/G

N
DEUTSCHE BUCHEREI,DEUTSCHES BUCHERVERZEICHNIS. GERMANY LAW CULTURE POL/PAR ADMIN LEAD ATTIT PERSON ...SOC 20. PAGE 37 A0746 — BIBLIOG NAT/G DIPLOM ECO/DEV

N
DOHERTY D.K.,PRELIMINARY BIBLIOGRAPHY OF COLONIZATION AND SETTLEMENT IN LATIN AMERICA AND ANGLO-AMERICA. L/A+17C PRE/AMER USA-45 ECO/UNDEV NAT/G 15/20. PAGE 38 A0768 — BIBLIOG COLONIAL ADMIN DIPLOM

N
MCSPADDEN J.W.,THE AMERICAN STATESMAN'S YEARBOOK. WOR-45 LAW CONSTN AGRI FINAN DEBATE ADMIN PARL/PROC ...CHARTS BIBLIOG/A 20. PAGE 99 A2025 — DIPLOM NAT/G PROVS LEGIS

N
MINISTERE DE L'EDUC NATIONALE,CATALOGUE DES THESES DE DOCTORAT SOUTENNES DEVANT LES UNIVERSITAIRES FRANCAISES. FRANCE LAW DIPLOM ADMIN...HUM SOC 20. PAGE 102 A2087 — BIBLIOG ACADEM KNOWL NAT/G

N
UNESCO,INTERNATIONAL BIBLIOGRAPHY OF POLITICAL SCIENCE (VOLUMES 1-8). WOR+45 LAW NAT/G EX/STRUC LEGIS PROB/SOLV DIPLOM ADMIN GOV/REL 20 UNESCO. PAGE 147 A3010 — BIBLIOG CONCPT IDEA/COMP

N
UNITED NATIONS,OFFICIAL RECORDS OF THE UNITED NATIONS' GENERAL ASSEMBLY. WOR+45 BUDGET DIPLOM ADMIN 20 UN. PAGE 148 A3033 — INT/ORG DELIB/GP INT/LAW WRITING

N
UNITED NATIONS,UNITED NATIONS PUBLICATIONS. WOR+45 ECO/UNDEV AGRI FINAN FORCES ADMIN LEAD WAR PEACE ...POLICY INT/LAW 20 UN. PAGE 148 A3034 — BIBLIOG INT/ORG DIPLOM

N
UNIVERSITY MICROFILMS INC,DISSERTATION ABSTRACTS: ABSTRACTS OF DISSERTATIONS AND MONOGRAPHS IN MICROFILM. CANADA DIPLOM ADMIN...INDEX 20. PAGE 149 A3045 — BIBLIOG/A ACADEM PRESS WRITING

N
US SUPERINTENDENT OF DOCUMENTS,TARIFF AND TAXATION (PRICE LIST 37). USA+45 LAW INT/TRADE ADJUD ADMIN CT/SYS INCOME OWN...DECISION GATT. PAGE 157 A3204 — BIBLIOG/A TAX TARIFFS NAT/G

N
WORLD PEACE FOUNDATION,DOCUMENTS OF INTERNATIONAL ORGANIZATIONS: A SELECTED BIBLIOGRAPHY. WOR+45 WOR-45 AGRI FINAN ACT/RES OP/RES INT/TRADE ADMIN ...CON/ANAL 20 UN UNESCO LEAGUE/NAT. PAGE 167 A3396 — BIBLIOG DIPLOM INT/ORG REGION

B00
GRIFFIN A.P.C.,LIST OF BOOKS RELATING TO THE THEORY OF COLONIZATION, GOVERNMENT OF DEPENDENCIES, PROTECTORATES, AND RELATED TOPICS. FRANCE GERMANY ITALY SPAIN UK USA-45 WOR-45 ECO/TAC ADMIN CONTROL REGION NAT/LISM ALL/VALS PWR...INT/LAW SOC 16/19. PAGE 56 A1149 — BIBLIOG/A COLONIAL GOV/REL DOMIN

B02
MOREL E.D.,AFFAIRS OF WEST AFRICA. UK FINAN INDUS FAM KIN SECT CHIEF WORKER DIPLOM RACE/REL LITERACY HEALTH...CHARTS 18/20 AFRICA/W NEGRO. PAGE 104 A2129 — COLONIAL ADMIN AFR

B05
GRIFFIN A.P.C.,LIST OF REFERENCES ON THE US CONSULAR SERVICE (PAMPHLET). FRANCE GERMANY SPAIN UK USA-45 WOR-45 OP/RES DOMIN ADMIN FEEDBACK ROUTINE GOV/REL...DECISION 19. PAGE 56 A1153 — BIBLIOG/A NAT/G DIPLOM CONSULT

B06
FOSTER J.W.,THE PRACTICE OF DIPLOMACY AS ILLUSTRATED IN THE FOREIGN RELATIONS OF THE UNITED STATES. MOD/EUR USA-45 NAT/G EX/STRUC ADMIN ...POLICY INT/LAW BIBLIOG 19/20. PAGE 47 A0970 — DIPLOM ROUTINE PHIL/SCI

B18
US LIBRARY OF CONGRESS,LIST OF REFERENCES ON A LEAGUE OF NATIONS. DIPLOM WAR PEACE 20 LEAGUE/NAT. PAGE 154 A3145 — BIBLIOG INT/ORG ADMIN EX/STRUC

B19
LONDON SCHOOL ECONOMICS-POL,ANNUAL DIGEST OF PUBLIC INTERNATIONAL LAW CASES. INT/ORG MUNIC NAT/G PROVS ADMIN NEUTRAL WAR GOV/REL PRIVIL 20. PAGE 91 A1858 — BIBLIOG/A INT/LAW ADJUD DIPLOM

N19
BENTHAM J.,A PLAN FOR AN UNIVERSAL AND PERPETUAL PEACE (1838) (PAMPHLET). NAT/G FORCES BAL/PWR INT/TRADE ADMIN AGREE CT/SYS ARMS/CONT SOVEREIGN WEALTH GEN/LAWS. PAGE 13 A0269 — INT/ORG INT/LAW PEACE COLONIAL

N19
HIGGINS R.,THE ADMINISTRATION OF UNITED KINGDOM FOREIGN POLICY THROUGH THE UNITED NATIONS (PAMPHLET). UK NAT/G ADMIN GOV/REL...CHARTS 20 UN PARLIAMENT. PAGE 65 A1329 — DIPLOM POLICY INT/ORG

N19
JACKSON R.G.A.,THE CASE FOR AN INTERNATIONAL DEVELOPMENT AUTHORITY (PAMPHLET). WOR+45 ECO/DEV DIPLOM GIVE CONTROL GP/REL EFFICIENCY NAT/LISM SOVEREIGN 20. PAGE 72 A1478 — FOR/AID INT/ORG ECO/UNDEV ADMIN

N19
KUWAIT ARABIA,KUWAIT FUND FOR ARAB ECONOMIC DEVELOPMENT (PAMPHLET). ISLAM KUWAIT UAR ECO/UNDEV LEGIS ECO/TAC WEALTH 20. PAGE 83 A1697 — FOR/AID DIPLOM FINAN ADMIN

N19
MEZERIK A.G.,COLONIALISM AND THE UNITED NATIONS (PAMPHLET). WOR+45 NAT/G ADMIN LEAD WAR CHOOSE EFFICIENCY PEACE ATTIT ORD/FREE...POLICY CHARTS UN — COLONIAL DIPLOM BAL/PWR

COLD/WAR. PAGE 100 A2061 — INT/ORG

B20
HALDANE R.B.,BEFORE THE WAR. MOD/EUR SOCIETY INT/ORG NAT/G DELIB/GP PLAN DOMIN EDU/PROP LEGIT ADMIN COERCE ATTIT DRIVE MORAL ORD/FREE PWR...SOC CONCPT SELF/OBS RECORD BIOG TIME/SEQ. PAGE 60 A1223 — POLICY DIPLOM UK

B22
MYERS D.P.,MANUAL OF COLLECTIONS OF TREATIES AND OF COLLECTIONS RELATING TO TREATIES. MOD/EUR INT/ORG LEGIS WRITING ADMIN SOVEREIGN...INT/LAW 19/20. PAGE 106 A2186 — BIBLIOG/A DIPLOM CONFER

B24
POOLE D.C.,THE CONDUCT OF FOREIGN RELATIONS UNDER MODERN DEMOCRATIC CONDITIONS. EUR+WWI USA-45 INT/ORG PLAN LEGIT ADMIN KNOWL PWR...MAJORIT OBS/ENVIR HIST/WRIT GEN/LAWS 20. PAGE 117 A2395 — NAT/G EDU/PROP DIPLOM

B26
INTERNATIONAL BIBLIOGRAPHY OF POLITICAL SCIENCE. WOR+45 NAT/G POL/PAR EX/STRUC LEGIS CT/SYS LEAD CHOOSE GOV/REL ATTIT...PHIL/SCI 20. PAGE 3 A0049 — BIBLIOG DIPLOM CONCPT ADMIN

S26
COHEN P.A.,"WANG T'AO AND INCIPIENT CHINESE NATIONALISM." ASIA ADMIN ATTIT 19/20 BUREAUCRCY. PAGE 28 A0563 — NAT/LISM ISOLAT CONSERVE DIPLOM

B28
HALL W.P.,EMPIRE TO COMMONWEALTH. FUT WOR-45 CONSTN ECO/DEV ECO/UNDEV INT/ORG PROVS PLAN DIPLOM EDU/PROP ADMIN COLONIAL PEACE PERSON ALL/VALS ...POLICY GEOG SOC OBS RECORD TREND CMN/WLTH PARLIAMENT 19/20. PAGE 60 A1229 — VOL/ASSN NAT/G UK

B29
BOUDET P.,BIBLIOGRAPHIE DE L'INDOCHINE FRANCAISE. S/ASIA VIETNAM SECT...GEOG LING 20. PAGE 17 A0344 — BIBLIOG ADMIN COLONIAL DIPLOM

B31
BORCHARD E.H.,GUIDE TO THE LAW AND LEGAL LITERATURE OF FRANCE. FRANCE FINAN INDUS LABOR SECT LEGIS ADMIN COLONIAL CRIME OWN...INT/LAW 20. PAGE 17 A0337 — BIBLIOG/A LAW CONSTN METH

B31
HILL N.,INTERNATIONAL ADMINISTRATION. WOR-45 DELIB/GP DIPLOM EDU/PROP ALL/VALS...MGT TIME/SEQ LEAGUE/NAT TOT/POP VAL/FREE 20. PAGE 65 A1331 — INT/ORG ADMIN

B32
CARDINALL AW,A BIBLIOGRAPHY OF THE GOLD COAST. AFR UK NAT/G EX/STRUC ATTIT...POLICY 19/20. PAGE 24 A0479 — BIBLIOG ADMIN COLONIAL DIPLOM

B32
WRIGHT Q.,GOLD AND MONETARY STABILIZATION. FUT USA-45 WOR-45 INTELL ECO/DEV INT/ORG NAT/G CONSULT PLAN ECO/TAC ADMIN ATTIT WEALTH...CONCPT TREND 20. PAGE 167 A3404 — FINAN POLICY

B33
AMERICAN FOREIGN LAW ASSN,BIOGRAPHICAL NOTES ON THE LAWS AND LEGAL LITERATURE OF URUGUAY AND CURACAO. URUGUAY CONSTN FINAN SECT FORCES JUDGE DIPLOM INT/TRADE ADJUD CT/SYS CRIME 20. PAGE 7 A0147 — BIBLIOG/A LAW JURID ADMIN

B34
US TARIFF COMMISSION,THE TARIFF; A BIBLIOGRAPHY: A SELECT LIST OF REFERENCES. USA-45 LAW DIPLOM TAX ADMIN...POLICY TREATY 20. PAGE 157 A3208 — BIBLIOG/A TARIFFS ECO/TAC

B35
KENNEDY W.P.,THE LAW AND CUSTOM OF THE SOUTH AFRICAN CONSTITUTION. AFR SOUTH/AFR KIN LOC/G PROVS DIPLOM ADJUD ADMIN EXEC 20. PAGE 78 A1594 — CT/SYS CONSTN JURID PARL/PROC

B36
ROBINSON H.,DEVELOPMENT OF THE BRITISH EMPIRE. WOR-45 CULTURE SOCIETY STRUCT ECO/DEV ECO/UNDEV INT/ORG VOL/ASSN FORCES CREATE PLAN DOMIN EDU/PROP ADMIN COLONIAL PWR WEALTH...POLICY GEOG CHARTS CMN/WLTH 16/20. PAGE 122 A2503 — NAT/G HIST/WRIT UK

B36
VARLEY D.H.,A BIBLIOGRAPHY OF ITALIAN COLONISATION IN AFRICA WITH A SECTION ON ABYSSINIA. AFR ETHIOPIA ITALY LIBYA SOMALIA AGRI FINAN LABOR TEC/DEV DIPLOM INT/TRADE RACE/REL DISCRIM 19/20. PAGE 158 A3222 — BIBLIOG COLONIAL ADMIN LAW

B37
GALLOWAY G.B.,AMERICAN PAMPHLET LITERATURE OF PUBLIC AFFAIRS (PAMPHLET). USA-45 ECO/DEV LABOR ADMIN...MGT 20. PAGE 51 A1034 — BIBLIOG/A PLAN DIPLOM NAT/G

B37
ROYAL INST. INT. AFF.,THE COLONIAL PROBLEM. WOR-45 LAW ECO/DEV ECO/UNDEV NAT/G PLAN ECO/TAC EDU/PROP ADMIN ATTIT ALL/VALS...CONCPT 20. PAGE 125 A2556 — INT/ORG ACT/RES SOVEREIGN COLONIAL

B37
UNION OF SOUTH AFRICA,REPORT CONCERNING ADMINISTRATION OF SOUTH WEST AFRICA (6 VOLS.). SOUTH/AFR INDUS PUB/INST FORCES LEGIS BUDGET DIPLOM EDU/PROP ADJUD CT/SYS...GEOG CHARTS 20 AFRICA/SW LEAGUE/NAT. PAGE 148 A3028 — NAT/G ADMIN COLONIAL CONSTN

B38
HARPER S.N.,THE GOVERNMENT OF THE SOVIET UNION. COM USSR LAW CONSTN ECO/DEV PLAN TEC/DEV DIPLOM INT/TRADE ADMIN REV NAT/LISM...POLICY 20. PAGE 62 A1265 — MARXISM NAT/G LEAD POL/PAR

B39
FURNIVALL J.S.,NETHERLANDS INDIA. INDIA NETHERLAND CULTURE INDUS NAT/G DIPLOM ADMIN WEALTH...POLICY CHARTS 17/20. PAGE 50 A1029 — COLONIAL ECO/UNDEV SOVEREIGN PLURISM

C39
REISCHAUER R.,"JAPAN'S GOVERNMENT--POLITICS." CONSTN STRATA POL/PAR FORCES LEGIS DIPLOM ADMIN EXEC CENTRAL...POLICY BIBLIOG 20 CHINJAP. PAGE 120 A2462 — NAT/G S/ASIA CONCPT ROUTINE

C40
FAHS C.B.,"GOVERNMENT IN JAPAN." FINAN FORCES LEGIS TOP/EX BUDGET INT/TRADE EDU/PROP SOVEREIGN ...CON/ANAL BIBLIOG/A 20 CHINJAP. PAGE 43 A0884 — ASIA DIPLOM NAT/G ADMIN

B41
EVANS C.,AMERICAN BIBLIOGRAPHY... (12 VOLUMES). USA-45 LAW DIPLOM ADMIN PERSON...HUM SOC 17/18. PAGE 43 A0876 — BIBLIOG NAT/G ALL/VALS ALL/IDEOS

B41
PERHAM M.,AFRICANS AND BRITISH RULE. AFR UK ECO/TAC CONTROL GP/REL ATTIT 20. PAGE 115 A2355 — DIPLOM COLONIAL ADMIN ECO/UNDEV

B42
SIMOES DOS REIS A.,BIBLIOGRAFIA DAS BIBLIOGRAFIAS BRASILEIRAS. BRAZIL ADMIN COLONIAL 20. PAGE 133 A2717 — BIBLIOG NAT/G DIPLOM L/A+17C

B43
CARLO A.M.,ENSAYO DE UNA BIBLIOGRAFIA DE BIBLIOGRAFIAS MEXICANAS. ECO/UNDEV LOC/G ADMIN LEAD 20 MEXIC/AMER. PAGE 24 A0485 — BIBLIOG L/A+17C NAT/G DIPLOM

B43
FULLER G.F.,FOREIGN RELIEF AND REHABILITATION (PAMPHLET). FUT GERMANY UK USA-45 INT/ORG PROB/SOLV DIPLOM FOR/AID ADMIN ADJUST PEACE ALL/VALS...SOC/WK 20 UN JEWS. PAGE 50 A1018 — BIBLIOG/A PLAN GIVE WAR

B43
LEWIN E.,ROYAL EMPIRE SOCIETY BIBLIOGRAPHIES NO. 9: SUB-SAHARA AFRICA. ECO/UNDEV TEC/DEV DIPLOM ADMIN COLONIAL LEAD 20. PAGE 88 A1800 — BIBLIOG AFR NAT/G SOCIETY

B44
BARTLETT R.J.,THE LEAGUE TO ENFORCE PEACE. FUT USA-45 NAT/G POL/PAR CREATE EDU/PROP ADMIN RIGID/FLEX PWR...CONCPT TREND GEN/METH LEAGUE/NAT 20. PAGE 11 A0231 — INT/ORG ORD/FREE DIPLOM

B44
DAVIS H.E.,PIONEERS IN WORLD ORDER. WOR-45 CONSTN ECO/TAC DOMIN EDU/PROP LEGIT ADJUD ADMIN ARMS/CONT CHOOSE KNOWL ORD/FREE...POLICY JURID SOC STAT OBS CENSUS TIME/SEQ ANTHOL LEAGUE/NAT 20. PAGE 34 A0691 — INT/ORG ROUTINE

B44
FULLER G.H.,MILITARY GOVERNMENT: A LIST OF REFERENCES (A PAMPHLET). ITALY UK USA-45 WOR-45 LAW FORCES DOMIN ADMIN ARMS/CONT ORD/FREE PWR ...DECISION 20 CHINJAP. PAGE 50 A1023 — BIBLIOG DIPLOM CIVMIL/REL SOVEREIGN

L44
HAILEY,"THE FUTURE OF COLONIAL PEOPLES." WOR-45 CONSTN CULTURE ECO/UNDEV AGRI MARKET INT/ORG NAT/G SECT CONSULT ECO/TAC LEGIT ADMIN NAT/LISM ALL/VALS ...SOC OBS TREND STERTYP CMN/WLTH LEAGUE/NAT PARLIAMENT 20. PAGE 59 A1218 — PLAN CONCPT DIPLOM UK

B45
CONOVER H.F.,THE GOVERNMENTS OF THE MAJOR FOREIGN POWERS: A BIBLIOGRAPHY. FRANCE GERMANY ITALY UK USSR CONSTN LOC/G POL/PAR EX/STRUC FORCES ADMIN CT/SYS CIVMIL/REL TOTALISM...POLICY 19/20. PAGE 29 A0598 — BIBLIOG NAT/G DIPLOM

B45
GALLOWAY E.,ABSTRACTS OF POSTWAR LITERATURE (VOL. IV) JAN.-JULY, 1945 NOS. 901-1074. POLAND USA+45 USSR WOR+45 INDUS LABOR PLAN ECO/TAC INT/TRADE TAX EDU/PROP ADMIN COLONIAL INT/LAW. PAGE 51 A1033 — BIBLIOG/A NUC/PWR NAT/G DIPLOM

B45
RANSHOFFEN-WERTHEIMER EF,THE INTERNATIONAL SECRETARIAT: A GREAT EXPERIMENT IN INTERNATIONAL ADMINISTRATION. EUR+WWI FUT CONSTN FACE/GP CONSULT DELIB/GP ACT/RES ADMIN ROUTINE PEACE ORD/FREE...MGT RECORD ORG/CHARTS LEAGUE/NAT WORK 20. PAGE 119 A2442 — INT/ORG EXEC

B45
ROGERS W.C.,INTERNATIONAL ADMINISTRATION: A BIBLIOGRAPHY (PUBLICATION NO 92; A PAMPHLET). WOR-45 INT/ORG LOC/G NAT/G CENTRAL 20. PAGE 123 A2514 — BIBLIOG/A ADMIN MGT DIPLOM

B45
VANCE H.L.,GUIDE TO THE LAW AND LEGAL LITERATURE OF MEXICO. LAW CONSTN FINAN LABOR FORCES ADJUD ADMIN ...CRIMLGY PHIL/SCI CON/ANAL 20 MEXIC/AMER. PAGE 158 A3217
BIBLIOG/A INT/LAW JURID CT/SYS

B45
WING D.,SHORT-TITLE CATALOGUE OF BOOKS PRINTED IN THE BRITISH ISLES, AND OF ENGLISH BOOKS PRINTED OVERSEAS: 1641-1700 (3 VOLS.). UK USA-45 LAW DIPLOM ADMIN COLONIAL LEAD ATTIT 17. PAGE 165 A3363
BIBLIOG MOD/EUR NAT/G

B46
BIBLIOGRAFIIA DISSERTATSII: DOKTORSKIE DISSERTATSII ZA 19411944 (2 VOLS.). COM USSR LAW POL/PAR DIPLOM ADMIN LEAD...PHIL/SCI SOC 20. PAGE 3 A0054
BIBLIOG ACADEM KNOWL MARXIST

B46
GRIFFIN G.G.,A GUIDE TO MANUSCRIPTS RELATING TO AMERICAN HISTORY IN BRITISH DEPOSITORIES. CANADA IRELAND MOD/EUR UK USA-45 LAW DIPLOM ADMIN COLONIAL WAR NAT/LISM SOVEREIGN...GEOG INT/LAW 15/19 CMN/WLTH. PAGE 56 A1159
BIBLIOG/A ALL/VALS NAT/G

C46
GOODRICH L.M.,"CHARTER OF THE UNITED NATIONS: COMMENTARY AND DOCUMENTS." EX/STRUC ADMIN...INT/LAW CON/ANAL BIBLIOG 20 UN. PAGE 54 A1106
CONSTN INT/ORG DIPLOM

B47
BORGESE G.,COMMON CAUSE. LAW CONSTN SOCIETY STRATA ECO/DEV INT/ORG POL/PAR FORCES LEGIS TOP/EX CAP/ISM DIPLOM ADMIN EXEC ATTIT PWR 20. PAGE 17 A0339
WOR+45 NAT/G SOVEREIGN REGION

B47
CONOVER H.F.,NON-SELF-GOVERNING AREAS. BELGIUM FRANCE ITALY UK WOR+45 CULTURE ECO/UNDEV INT/ORG LOC/G NAT/G ECO/TAC INT/TRADE ADMIN HEALTH...SOC UN. PAGE 30 A0601
BIBLIOG/A COLONIAL DIPLOM

B47
HILL M.,IMMUNITIES AND PRIVILEGES OF INTERNATIONAL OFFICIALS. CANADA EUR+WWI NETHERLAND SWITZERLND LAW LEGIS DIPLOM LEGIT RESPECT...TIME/SEQ LEAGUE/NAT UN VAL/FREE 20. PAGE 65 A1330
INT/ORG ADMIN

B47
HIRSHBERG H.S.,SUBJECT GUIDE TO UNITED STATES GOVERNMENT PUBLICATIONS. USA+45 USA-45 LAW ADMIN ...SOC 20. PAGE 65 A1340
BIBLIOG NAT/G DIPLOM LOC/G

B47
PERKINS D.,THE UNITED STATES AND THE CARIBBEAN. CUBA DOMIN/REP GUATEMALA HAITI PANAMA CULTURE ECO/UNDEV FOR/AID ADMIN COERCE HABITAT...POLICY 19/20. PAGE 115 A2359
DIPLOM L/A+17C USA-45

B48
GUIDE TO THE RECORDS IN THE NATIONAL ARCHIVES. ECO/UNDEV ADMIN COLONIAL 16/20. PAGE 3 A0055
BIBLIOG NAT/G L/A+17C DIPLOM

B48
CHILDS J.R.,AMERICAN FOREIGN SERVICE. USA+45 SOCIETY NAT/G ROUTINE GOV/REL 20 DEPT/STATE CIVIL/SERV. PAGE 26 A0530
DIPLOM ADMIN GP/REL

B48
HOWARD J.E.,PARLIAMENT AND FOREIGN POLICY IN FRANCE. FRANCE CONSTN DELIB/GP BUDGET ADMIN PARL/PROC CHOOSE...BIBLIOG/A 20 PARLIAMENT. PAGE 68 A1399
LEGIS CONTROL DIPLOM ATTIT

B48
MINISTERE FINANCES ET ECO,BULLETIN BIBLIOGRAPHIQUE. AFR EUR+WWI FRANCE CULTURE STRUCT FINAN NAT/G ACT/RES INT/TRADE ADMIN REGION PRODUC STAT. PAGE 102 A2088
BIBLIOG/A ECO/UNDEV TEC/DEV COLONIAL

B49
BORBA DE MORAES R.,MANUAL BIBLIOGRAFICO DE ESTUDOS BRASILEIROS. BRAZIL DIPLOM ADMIN LEAD...SOC 20. PAGE 17 A0336
BIBLIOG L/A+17C NAT/G ECO/UNDEV

B49
FORD FOUNDATION,REPORT OF THE STUDY FOR THE FORD FOUNDATION ON POLICY AND PROGRAM. SOCIETY R+D ACT/RES CAP/ISM FOR/AID EDU/PROP ADMIN KNOWL ...POLICY PSY SOC 20. PAGE 47 A0961
WEALTH GEN/LAWS

B49
HEADLAM-MORLEY,BIBLIOGRAPHY IN POLITICS FOR THE HONOUR SCHOOL OF PHILOSOPHY, POLITICS AND ECONOMICS (PAMPHLET). UK CONSTN LABOR MUNIC DIPLOM ADMIN 19/20. PAGE 64 A1305
BIBLIOG NAT/G PHIL/SCI GOV/REL

B49
ROSENHAUPT H.W.,HOW TO WAGE PEACE. USA+45 SOCIETY STRATA STRUCT R+D INT/ORG POL/PAR LEGIS ACT/RES CREATE PLAN EDU/PROP ADMIN EXEC ATTIT ALL/VALS ...TIME/SEQ TREND COLD/WAR 20. PAGE 124 A2536
INTELL CONCPT DIPLOM

N49
UN DEPARTMENT PUBLIC INF,SELECTED BIBLIOGRAPHY OF THE SPECIALIZED AGENCIES RELATED TO THE UNITED NATIONS (PAMPHLET). USA+45 ROLE 20 UN. PAGE 146 A2996
BIBLIOG INT/ORG EX/STRUC ADMIN

B50
FIGANIERE J.C.,BIBLIOTHECA HISTORICA PORTUGUEZA. BRAZIL PORTUGAL SECT ADMIN. PAGE 45 A0929
BIBLIOG NAT/G DIPLOM COLONIAL

B50
MONPIED E.,BIBLIOGRAPHIE FEDERALISTE: OUVRAGES CHOISIS (VOL. I, MIMEOGRAPHED PAPER). EUR+WWI DIPLOM ADMIN REGION ATTIT PACIFISM SOCISM...INT/LAW 19/20. PAGE 103 A2109
BIBLIOG/A FEDERAL CENTRAL INT/ORG

B50
PERHAM M.,COLONIAL GOVERNMENT: ANNOTATED READING LIST ON BRITISH COLONIAL GOVERNMENT. UK WOR+45 WOR-45 ECO/UNDEV INT/ORG LEGIS FOR/AID INT/TRADE DOMIN ADMIN REV 20. PAGE 115 A2356
BIBLIOG/A COLONIAL GOV/REL NAT/G

B50
US DEPARTMENT OF STATE,POINT FOUR: COOPERATIVE PROGRAM FOR AID IN THE DEVELOPMENT OF ECONOMICALLY UNDERDEVELOPED AREAS. WOR+45 AGRI INDUS INT/ORG PLAN TEC/DEV DIPLOM EDU/PROP ADMIN PEACE PRODUC WEALTH 20 CONGRESS UN. PAGE 151 A3085
ECO/UNDEV FOR/AID FINAN INT/TRADE

S50
WITTFOGEL K.A.,"RUSSIA AND ASIA: PROBLEMS OF CONTEMPORARY AREA STUDIES AND INTERNATIONAL RELATIONS." ASIA COM USA+45 SOCIETY NAT/G DIPLOM ECO/TAC FOR/AID EDU/PROP KNOWL...HIST/WRIT TOT/POP 20. PAGE 166 A3373
ECO/DEV ADMIN RUSSIA USSR

B51
SWISHER C.B.,THE THEORY AND PRACTICE OF AMERICAN NATIONAL GOVERNMENT. CULTURE LEGIS DIPLOM ADJUD ADMIN WAR PEACE ORD/FREE...MAJORIT 17/20. PAGE 140 A2872
CONSTN NAT/G GOV/REL GEN/LAWS

B51
US LIBRARY OF CONGRESS,EAST EUROPEAN ACCESSIONS LIST (VOL. I). POL/PAR DIPLOM ADMIN LEAD 20. PAGE 155 A3152
BIBLIOG/A COM SOCIETY NAT/G

B51
US TARIFF COMMISSION,LIST OF PUBLICATIONS OF THE TARIFF COMMISSION (PAMPHLET). USA+45 USA-45 AGRI EXTR/IND INDUS INT/TRADE...STAT 20. PAGE 157 A3207
BIBLIOG TARIFFS NAT/G ADMIN

C51
GRUNDER G.A.,"THE PHILIPPINES AND THE UNITED STATES." PHILIPPINE S/ASIA USA-45 NAT/G POL/PAR ADMIN SOVEREIGN...TIME/SEQ BIBLIOG 20. PAGE 57 A1181
COLONIAL POLICY DIPLOM ECO/TAC

B52
UN DEPT. SOC. AFF.,PRELIMINARY REPORT ON THE WORLD SOCIAL SITUATION. ISLAM L/A+17C WOR+45 STRATA AGRI EXTR/IND INDUS INT/ORG SCHOOL ADMIN...GEOG SOC TREND UNESCO WORK FAO 20. PAGE 147 A2998
R+D HEALTH FOR/AID

B52
US DEPARTMENT OF STATE,RESEARCH ON EASTERN EUROPE (EXCLUDING USSR). EUR+WWI LAW ECO/DEV NAT/G PROB/SOLV DIPLOM ADMIN LEAD MARXISM...TREND 19/20. PAGE 151 A3088
BIBLIOG R+D ACT/RES COM

B52
US MUTUAL SECURITY AGENCY,U. S. TECHNICAL AND ECONOMIC ASSISTANCE IN THE FAR EAST (PAMPHLET). ASIA BURMA INDONESIA PHILIPPINE TAIWAN THAILAND USA+45 AGRI INDUS PLAN EDU/PROP ADMIN HEALTH. PAGE 155 A3161
FOR/AID TEC/DEV ECO/UNDEV BUDGET

S52
MASTERS R.D.,"RUSSIA AND THE UNITED NATIONS." FUT USA+45 USSR WOR+45 CONSTN VOL/ASSN DELIB/GP TOP/EX CREATE DIPLOM ADMIN...TREND STERTYP UN 20. PAGE 96 A1962
INT/ORG PWR

S52
SCHWEBEL S.M.,"THE SECRETARY-GENERAL OF THE UN." FUT INTELL CONSULT DELIB/GP ADMIN PEACE ATTIT ...JURID MGT CONCPT TREND UN CONGRESS 20. PAGE 130 A2663
INT/ORG TOP/EX

C52
STUART G.H.,"AMERICAN DIPLOMATIC AND CONSULAR PRACTICE (2ND ED.)" EUR+WWI MOD/EUR USA-45 DELIB/GP INT/TRADE ADJUD...BIBLIOG 20. PAGE 140 A2855
DIPLOM ADMIN INT/ORG

B53
GREENE K.R.C.,INSTITUTIONS AND INDIVIDUALS: AN ANNOTATED LIST OF DIRECTORIES USEFUL IN INTERNATIONAL ADMINISTRATION. USA+45 NAT/G VOL/ASSN ...INDEX 20. PAGE 56 A1141
BIBLIOG INT/ORG ADMIN DIPLOM

B53
LARSEN K.,NATIONAL BIBLIOGRAPHIC SERVICES: THEIR CREATION AND OPERATION. WOR+45 COM/IND CREATE PLAN DIPLOM PRESS ADMIN ROUTINE...MGT UNESCO. PAGE 85 A1733
BIBLIOG/A INT/ORG WRITING

B53
MACMAHON A.W.,ADMINISTRATION IN FOREIGN AFFAIRS. NAT/G CONSULT DELIB/GP LEGIS ACT/RES CREATE ADMIN EXEC RIGID/FLEX PWR...METH/CNCPT TIME/SEQ TOT/POP VAL/FREE 20. PAGE 93 A1899
USA+45 ROUTINE FOR/AID DIPLOM

B53
MCNEILL W.H.,AMERICA, BRITAIN, AND RUSSIA; THEIR COOPERATION AND CONFLICT. UK USA-45 USSR ECO/DEV ECO/UNDEV FORCES PLAN ADMIN AGREE PERS/REL ...DECISION 20 TREATY. PAGE 98 A2021
WAR DIPLOM DOMIN

B53
STOUT H.M.,BRITISH GOVERNMENT. UK FINAN LOC/G POL/PAR DELIB/GP DIPLOM ADMIN COLONIAL CHOOSE ORD/FREE...JURID BIBLIOG 20 COMMONWLTH. PAGE 139 A2837
NAT/G PARL/PROC CONSTN NEW/LIB

S53
CORY R.H. JR.,"FORGING A PUBLIC INFORMATION POLICY FOR THE UNITED NATIONS." FUT WOR+45 SOCIETY ADMIN PEACE ATTIT PERSON SKILL...CONCPT 20 UN. PAGE 31 A0628
INT/ORG EDU/PROP BAL/PWR

B54
BINANI G.D.,INDIA AT A GLANCE (REV. ED.). INDIA COM/IND FINAN INDUS LABOR PROVS SCHOOL PLAN DIPLOM INT/TRADE ADMIN...JURID 20. PAGE 14 A0288
INDEX CON/ANAL NAT/G ECO/UNDEV

B54
STRAUSZ-HUPE R.,INTERNATIONAL RELATIONS IN THE AGE OF THE CONFLICT BETWEEN DEMOCRACY AND DICTATORSHIP (2ND ED.). INT/ORG BAL/PWR EDU/PROP ADMIN WAR PEACE PWR...CONCPT CHARTS BIBLIOG 20 COLD/WAR UN LEAGUE/NAT. PAGE 139 A2846
DIPLOM POPULISM MARXISM

B54
TOTOK W.,HANDBUCH DER BIBLIOGRAPHISCHEN NACHSCHLAGEWERKE. GERMANY LAW CULTURE ADMIN...SOC 20. PAGE 144 A2952
BIBLIOG/A NAT/G DIPLOM POLICY

B54
US SENATE COMM ON FOREIGN REL,REVIEW OF THE UNITED NATIONS CHARTER: A COLLECTION OF DOCUMENTS. LEGIS DIPLOM ADMIN ARMS/CONT WAR REPRESENT SOVEREIGN ...INT/LAW 20 UN. PAGE 156 A3180
BIBLIOG CONSTN INT/ORG DEBATE

B55
CRAIG G.A.,THE POLITICS OF THE PRUSSIAN ARMY 1640-1945. CHRIST-17C EUR+WWI MOD/EUR PRUSSIA STRUCT DIPLOM ADMIN REV WAR...SOC BIBLIOG 17/20. PAGE 32 A0652
FORCES NAT/G ROLE CHIEF

B55
GULICK C.A.,HISTORY AND THEORIES OF WORKING-CLASS MOVEMENTS: A SELECT BIBLIOGRAPHY. EUR+WWI MOD/EUR UK USA-45 INT/ORG. PAGE 58 A1190
BIBLIOG WORKER LABOR ADMIN

B55
JAPAN MOMBUSHO DAIGAKU GAKIYUT,BIBLIOGRAPHY OF THE STUDIES ON LAW AND POLITICS (PAMPHLET). CONSTN INDUS LABOR DIPLOM TAX ADMIN...CRIMLGY INT/LAW 20 CHINJAP. PAGE 73 A1496
BIBLIOG LAW PHIL/SCI

B55
SVARLIEN O.,AN INTRODUCTION TO THE LAW OF NATIONS. SEA AIR INT/ORG NAT/G CHIEF ADMIN AGREE WAR PRIVIL ORD/FREE SOVEREIGN...BIBLIOG 16/20. PAGE 140 A2868
INT/LAW DIPLOM

B55
TAN C.C.,THE BOXER CATASTROPHE. ASIA UK USSR ELITES POL/PAR VOL/ASSN FORCES PROB/SOLV DIPLOM ADMIN COLONIAL NAT/LISM PEACE TREATY 19/20 BOXER/REBL. PAGE 141 A2885
REV NAT/G WAR

B55
UN ECONOMIC AND SOCIAL COUNCIL,BIBLIOGRAPHY OF PUBLICATIONS OF THE UN AND SPECIALIZED AGENCIES IN THE SOCIAL WELFARE FIELD, 1946-1952. WOR+45 FAM INT/ORG MUNIC ACT/RES PLAN PROB/SOLV EDU/PROP AGE/C AGE/Y HABITAT...HEAL UN. PAGE 147 A3000
BIBLIOG/A SOC/WK ADMIN WEALTH

B55
UN HEADQUARTERS LIBRARY,BIBLIOQRAPHIE DE LA CHARTE DES NATIONS UNIES. CHINA/COM KOREA WOR+45 VOL/ASSN CONFER ADMIN COERCE PEACE ATTIT ORD/FREE SOVEREIGN ...INT/LAW 20 UNESCO UN. PAGE 147 A3001
BIBLIOG/A INT/ORG DIPLOM

L55
KISER M.,"ORGANIZATION OF AMERICAN STATES." L/A+17C USA+45 ECO/UNDEV INT/ORG NAT/G PLAN TEC/DEV DIPLOM ECO/TAC INT/TRADE EDU/PROP ADMIN ALL/VALS...POLICY MGT RECORD ORG/CHARTS OAS 20. PAGE 80 A1639
VOL/ASSN ECO/DEV REGION

L55
ROSTOW W.W.,"RUSSIA AND CHINA UNDER COMMUNISM." CHINA/COM USSR INTELL STRUCT INT/ORG NAT/G POL/PAR TOP/EX ACT/RES PLAN ADMIN ATTIT ALL/VALS MARXISM ...CONCPT OBS TIME/SEQ TREND GOV/COMP VAL/FREE 20. PAGE 124 A2543
COM ASIA

B56
IRIKURA J.K.,SOUTHEAST ASIA: SELECTED ANNOTATED BIBLIOGRAPHY OF JAPANESE PUBLICATIONS. CULTURE ADMIN RACE/REL 20 CHINJAP. PAGE 71 A1466
BIBLIOG/A S/ASIA DIPLOM

B56
KOENIG L.W.,THE TRUMAN ADMINISTRATION: ITS PRINCIPLES AND PRACTICE. USA+45 POL/PAR CHIEF LEGIS DIPLOM DEATH NUC/PWR WAR CIVMIL/REL PEACE ...DECISION 20 TRUMAN/HS PRESIDENT TREATY. PAGE 81 A1658
ADMIN POLICY EX/STRUC GOV/REL

B56
LOVEDAY A.,REFLECTIONS ON INTERNATIONAL ADMINISTRATION. WOR+45 WOR-45 DELIB/GP ACT/RES ADMIN EXEC ROUTINE DRIVE...METH/CNCPT TIME/SEQ CON/ANAL SIMUL TOT/POP 20. PAGE 91 A1865
INT/ORG MGT

B56
UNITED NATIONS,BIBLIOGRAPHY ON INDUSTRIALIZATION IN UNDER-DEVELOPED COUNTRIES. WOR+45 R+D INT/ORG NAT/G FOR/AID ADMIN LEAD 20 UN. PAGE 149 A3036
BIBLIOG ECO/UNDEV INDUS TEC/DEV

B56
WILSON P.,GOVERNMENT AND POLITICS OF INDIA AND PAKISTAN: 1885-1955; A BIBLIOGRAPHY OF WORKS IN WESTERN LANGUAGES. INDIA PAKISTAN CONSTN LOC/G POL/PAR FORCES DIPLOM ADMIN WAR CHOOSE...BIOG CON/ANAL 19/20. PAGE 165 A3361
BIBLIOG COLONIAL NAT/G S/ASIA

B56
WU E.,LEADERS OF TWENTIETH-CENTURY CHINA; AN ANNOTATED BIBLIOGRAPHY OF SELECTED CHINESE BIOGRAPHICAL WORKS IN HOOVER LIBRARY. ASIA INDUS POL/PAR DIPLOM ADMIN REV WAR...HUM MGT 20. PAGE 168 A3422
BIBLIOG/A BIOG INTELL CHIEF

B57
ARON R.,FRANCE DEFEATS EDC. EUR+WWI GERMANY LEGIS DIPLOM DOMIN EDU/PROP ADMIN...HIST/WRIT 20. PAGE 9 A0180
INT/ORG FORCES DETER FRANCE

B57
BEAL J.R.,JOHN FOSTER DULLES, A BIOGRAPHY. USA+45 USSR WOR+45 CONSTN INT/ORG NAT/G EX/STRUC LEGIT ADMIN NUC/PWR DISPL PERSON ORD/FREE PWR SKILL ...POLICY PSY OBS RECORD COLD/WAR UN 20 DULLES/JF. PAGE 12 A0237
BIOG DIPLOM

B57
BISHOP O.B.,PUBLICATIONS OF THE GOVERNMENTS OF NOVA SCOTIA, PRINCE EDWARD ISLAND, NEW BRUNSWICK 1758-1952. CANADA UK ADMIN COLONIAL LEAD...POLICY 18/20. PAGE 14 A0293
BIBLIOG NAT/G DIPLOM

B57
KAPLAN M.A.,SYSTEM AND PROCESS OF INTERNATIONAL POLITICS. FUT WOR+45 WOR-45 SOCIETY PLAN BAL/PWR ADMIN ATTIT PERSON RIGID/FLEX PWR SOVEREIGN ...DECISION TREND VAL/FREE. PAGE 76 A1560
INT/ORG DIPLOM

B57
US COMMISSION GOVT SECURITY,RECOMMENDATIONS; AREA: IMMIGRANT PROGRAM. USA+45 LAW WORKER DIPLOM EDU/PROP WRITING ADMIN PEACE ATTIT...CONCPT ANTHOL 20 MIGRATION SUBVERT. PAGE 150 A3060
POLICY CONTROL PLAN NAT/G

S57
ELDER R.E.,"THE PUBLIC STUDIES DIVISION OF THE DEPARTMENT OF STATE: PUBLIC OPINION ANALYSTS IN THE FORMULATION AND CONDUCT OF." INT/ORG CONSULT DOMIN EDU/PROP ADMIN ATTIT PWR...CONCPT OBS TIME/SEQ VAL/FREE 20. PAGE 41 A0836
USA+45 NAT/G DIPLOM

C57
TANG P.S.H.,"COMMUNIST CHINA TODAY: DOMESTIC AND FOREIGN POLICIES." CHINA/COM COM S/ASIA USSR STRATA FORCES DIPLOM EDU/PROP COERCE GOV/REL...POLICY MAJORIT BIBLIOG 20. PAGE 141 A2886
POL/PAR LEAD ADMIN CONSTN

B58
ISLAM R.,INTERNATIONAL ECONOMIC COOPERATION AND THE UNITED NATIONS. FINAN PLAN EXEC TASK WAR PEACE ...SOC METH/CNCPT 20 UN LEAGUE/NAT. PAGE 72 A1470
INT/ORG DIPLOM ADMIN

B58
MASON J.B.,THAILAND BIBLIOGRAPHY. S/ASIA THAILAND CULTURE EDU/PROP ADMIN...GEOG SOC LING 20. PAGE 95 A1958
BIBLIOG/A ECO/UNDEV DIPLOM NAT/G

B58
NEAL F.W.,TITOISM IN ACTION. COM YUGOSLAVIA AGRI LOC/G DIPLOM TOTALISM...BIBLIOG 20 TITO/MARSH. PAGE 107 A2206
MARXISM POL/PAR CHIEF ADMIN

B58
PAN AMERICAN UNION,REPERTORIO DE PUBLICACIONES PERIODICAS ACTUALES LATINO-AMERICANAS. CULTURE ECO/UNDEV ADMIN LEAD GOV/REL 20 OAS. PAGE 113 A2326
BIBLIOG L/A+17C NAT/G DIPLOM

B58
US HOUSE COMM GOVT OPERATIONS,HEARINGS BEFORE A SUBCOMMITTEE OF THE COMMITTEE ON GOVERNMENT OPERATIONS. CAMBODIA PHILIPPINE USA+45 CONSTRUC TEC/DEV ADMIN CONTROL WEAPON EFFICIENCY HOUSE/REP. PAGE 154 A3135
FOR/AID DIPLOM ORD/FREE ECO/UNDEV

B58
US OPERATIONS MISSION TO VIET,BUILDING ECONOMIC STRENGTH (PAMPHLET). USA+45 VIETNAM/S INDUS TEC/DEV BUDGET ADMIN EATING HEALTH...STAT 20. PAGE 155 A3162
FOR/AID ECO/UNDEV AGRI EDU/PROP

S58
BLAISDELL D.C.,"PRESSURE GROUPS, FOREIGN POLICIES, AND INTERNATIONAL POLITICS." USA+45 WOR+45 INT/ORG PLAN DOMIN EDU/PROP LEGIT ADMIN ROUTINE CHOOSE ...DECISION MGT METH/CNCPT CON/ANAL 20. PAGE 15 A0303
PROF/ORG PWR

S58
DAVENPORT J.,"ARMS AND THE WELFARE STATE." INTELL STRUCT FORCES CREATE ECO/TAC FOR/AID DOMIN LEGIT ADMIN WAR ORD/FREE PWR...POLICY SOC CONCPT MYTH OBS TREND COLD/WAR TOT/POP 20. PAGE 34 A0685
USA+45 NAT/G USSR

S58
STAAR R.F.,"ELECTIONS IN COMMUNIST POLAND." EUR+WWI SOCIETY INT/ORG NAT/G POL/PAR LEGIS ACT/RES ECO/TAC EDU/PROP ADJUD ADMIN ROUTINE COERCE TOTALISM ATTIT ORD/FREE PWR 20. PAGE 137 A2797
COM CHOOSE POLAND

C58
GOLAY J.F.,"THE FOUNDING OF THE FEDERAL REPUBLIC OF GERMANY." GERMANY/W CONSTN EX/STRUC DIPLOM ADMIN CHOOSE...DECISION BIBLIOG 20. PAGE 53 A1088
FEDERAL NAT/G PARL/PROC POL/PAR

C58
WILDING N.,"AN ENCYCLOPEDIA OF PARLIAMENT." UK LAW CONSTN CHIEF PROB/SOLV DIPLOM DEBATE WAR INGP/REL PRIVIL...BIBLIOG DICTIONARY 13/20 CMN/WLTH PARLIAMENT. PAGE 164 A3349
PARL/PROC POL/PAR NAT/G ADMIN

B59
AIR FORCE ACADEMY ASSEMBLY '59,INTERNATIONAL STABILITY AND PROGRESS (PAMPHLET). USA+45 USSR ECO/UNDEV PROB/SOLV BUDGET DIPLOM ADMIN DETER COST ATTIT...TREND 20. PAGE 5 A0103
FOR/AID FORCES WAR PLAN

B59
ALWAN M.,ALGERIA BEFORE THE UNITED NATIONS. AFR ASIA FRANCE ISLAM S/ASIA CONSTN SOCIETY STRUCT INT/ORG NAT/G ECO/TAC ADMIN COLONIAL NAT/LISM ATTIT PWR...DECISION TREND 420 UN. PAGE 7 A0133
PLAN RIGID/FLEX DIPLOM ALGERIA

B59
CHINA INSTITUTE OF AMERICA.,CHINA AND THE UNITED NATIONS. CHINA/COM FUT STRUCT EDU/PROP LEGIT ADMIN ATTIT KNOWL ORD/FREE PWR...OBS RECORD STAND/INT TIME/SEQ UN LEAGUE/NAT UNESCO 20. PAGE 26 A0531
ASIA INT/ORG

B59
GORDENKER L.,THE UNITED NATIONS AND THE PEACEFUL UNIFICATION OF KOREA. ASIA LAW LOC/G CONSULT ACT/RES DIPLOM DOMIN LEGIT ADJUD ADMIN ORD/FREE SOVEREIGN...INT GEN/METH UN COLD/WAR 20. PAGE 54 A1109
DELIB/GP KOREA INT/ORG

B59
INTERAMERICAN CULTURAL COUN,LISTA DE LIBROS REPRESENTAVOS DE AMERICA. CULTURE DIPLOM ADMIN 20. PAGE 71 A1448
BIBLIOG/A NAT/G L/A+17C SOC

B59
JONES A.C.,NEW FABIAN COLONIAL ESSAYS. UK SOCIETY POL/PAR EDU/PROP ADMIN ORD/FREE SOVEREIGN SOCISM ...ANTHOL 20 CMN/WLTH LABOR/PAR. PAGE 75 A1530
COLONIAL INT/ORG INGP/REL DOMIN

B59
MACIVER R.M.,THE NATIONS AND THE UN. WOR+45 NAT/G CONSULT ADJUD ADMIN ALL/VALS...CONCPT DEEP/QU UN TOT/POP UNESCO 20. PAGE 92 A1892
INT/ORG ATTIT DIPLOM

B59
SCHURZ W.L.,AMERICAN FOREIGN AFFAIRS: A GUIDE TO INTERNATIONAL AFFAIRS. USA+45 WOR+45 WOR-45 NAT/G FORCES LEGIS TOP/EX PLAN EDU/PROP LEGIT ADMIN ROUTINE ATTIT ORD/FREE PWR...SOC CONCPT STAT SAMP/SIZ CHARTS STERTYP 20. PAGE 129 A2653
INT/ORG SOCIETY DIPLOM

B59
US HOUSE COMM GOVT OPERATIONS,UNITED STATES AID OPERATIONS IN LAOS. LAOS USA+45 PLAN INSPECT HOUSE/REP. PAGE 154 A3136
FOR/AID ADMIN FORCES ECO/UNDEV

S59
BAILEY S.D.,"THE FUTURE COMPOSITION OF THE TRUSTEESHIP COUNCIL." FUT WOR+45 CONSTN VOL/ASSN ADMIN ATTIT PWR...OBS TREND CON/ANAL VAL/FREE UN 20. PAGE 10 A0203
INT/ORG NAT/LISM SOVEREIGN

S59
PADELFORD N.J.,"REGIONAL COOPERATION IN THE SOUTH PACIFIC: THE SOUTH PACIFIC COMMISSION." FUT NEW/ZEALND UK WOR+45 CULTURE ECO/UNDEV LOC/G VOL/ASSN...OBS CON/ANAL UNESCO VAL/FREE AUSTRAL 20. PAGE 112 A2308
INT/ORG ADMIN

S59
REUBENS E.D.,"THE BASIS FOR REORIENATION OF AMERICAN FOREIGN AID POLICY." USA+45 USSR STRUCT INT/ORG CONSULT ECO/TAC ADMIN DRIVE MORAL ORD/FREE PWR WEALTH...RELATIV MATH STAT TREND GEN/LAWS VAL/FREE 20. PAGE 120 A2467
ECO/UNDEV PLAN FOR/AID DIPLOM

S59
STOESSINGER J.G.,"THE INTERNATIONAL ATOMIC ENERGY AGENCY: THE FIRST PHASE." FUT WOR+45 NAT/G VOL/ASSN DELIB/GP BAL/PWR LEGIT ADMIN ROUTINE PWR...OBS CON/ANAL GEN/LAWS VAL/FREE 20 IAEA. PAGE 138 A2829
INT/ORG ECO/DEV FOR/AID NUC/PWR

S59
TIPTON J.B.,"PARTICIPATION OF THE UNITED STATES IN THE INTERNATIONAL LABOR ORGANIZATION." USA+45 LAW STRUCT ECO/DEV ECO/UNDEV INDUS TEC/DEV ECO/TAC ADMIN PERCEPT ORD/FREE SKILL...STAT HIST/WRIT GEN/METH ILO WORK 20. PAGE 144 A2946
LABOR INT/ORG

B60
AMERICAN ASSEMBLY COLUMBIA U,THE SECRETARY OF STATE. USA+45 ELITES NAT/G PLAN ADMIN GOV/REL CENTRAL ATTIT...POLICY MGT 20 SEC/STATE CONGRESS PRESIDENT. PAGE 7 A0136
DELIB/GP EX/STRUC GP/REL DIPLOM

B60
ASPREMONT-LYNDEN H.,RAPPORT SUR L'ADMINISTRATION BELGE DU RUANDA-URUNDI PENDANT L'ANNEE 1959. BELGIUM RWANDA AGRI INDUS DIPLOM ECO/TAC INT/TRADE DOMIN ADMIN RACE/REL...GEOG CENSUS 20 UN. PAGE 9 A0192
AFR COLONIAL ECO/UNDEV INT/ORG

B60
BAILEY S.D.,THE GENERAL ASSEMBLY OF THE UNITED NATIONS. FUT WOR+45 STRUCT LEGIS ACT/RES PLAN EDU/PROP LEGIT ADMIN EXEC PEACE ATTIT HEALTH PWR ...CONCPT TREND CHARTS GEN/LAWS UN TOT/POP VAL/FREE COLD/WAR 20. PAGE 10 A0204
INT/ORG DELIB/GP DIPLOM

B60
DUMON F.,LA COMMUNAUTE FRANCO-AFRO-MALGACHE: SES ORIGINES, SES INSTITUTIONS, SON EVOLUTION. FRANCE MADAGASCAR POL/PAR DIPLOM ADMIN ATTIT...TREND T 20. PAGE 39 A0798
JURID INT/ORG AFR CONSTN

B60
FLORES R.H.,CATALOGO DE TESIS DOCTORALES DE LAS FACULTADES DE LA UNIVERSIDAD DE EL SALVADOR. EL/SALVADR LAW DIPLOM ADMIN LEAD GOV/REL...SOC 19/20. PAGE 47 A0954
BIBLIOG ACADEM L/A+17C NAT/G

B60
FRANCK P.G.,AFGHANISTAN: BETWEEN EAST AND WEST. AFGHANISTN USA+45 USSR ECO/UNDEV PLAN ADMIN ROUTINE ATTIT PWR...STAT OBS CHARTS TOT/POP COLD/WAR 20. PAGE 48 A0978
ECO/TAC TREND FOR/AID

B60
HOLT R.T.,STRATEGIC PSYCHOLOGICAL OPERATIONS AND AMERICAN FOREIGN POLICY. ITALY USA+45 FOR/AID DOMIN RUMOR ADMIN TASK WAR CHOOSE ATTIT ALL/IDEOS...PSY COLD/WAR. PAGE 67 A1375
EDU/PROP ACT/RES DIPLOM POLICY

B60
HYDE L.K.G.,THE US AND THE UN. WOR+45 STRUCT ECO/DEV ECO/UNDEV NAT/G ACT/RES PLAN DIPLOM EDU/PROP ADMIN ALL/VALS...CONCPT TIME/SEQ GEN/LAWS UN VAL/FREE 20. PAGE 70 A1428
USA+45 INT/ORG FOR/AID

B60
KINGSTON-MCCLOUG E.,DEFENSE; POLICY AND STRATEGY. UK SEA AIR TEC/DEV DIPLOM ADMIN LEAD WAR ORD/FREE ...CHARTS 20. PAGE 79 A1627
FORCES PLAN POLICY DECISION

B60
LEWIS P.R.,LITERATURE OF THE SOCIAL SCIENCES: AN INTRODUCTORY SURVEY AND GUIDE. UK LAW INDUS DIPLOM INT/TRADE ADMIN...MGT 19/20. PAGE 88 A1802
BIBLIOG/A SOC

B60
LISKA G.,THE NEW STATECRAFT. WOR+45 WOR-45 LEGIS DIPLOM ADMIN ATTIT PWR WEALTH...HIST/WRIT TREND COLD/WAR 20. PAGE 90 A1837
ECO/TAC CONCPT FOR/AID

B60
MCKINNEY R.,REVIEW OF THE INTERNATIONAL ATOMIC POLICIES AND PROGRAMS OF THE UNITED STATES (5 VOLS.). COM FUT USA+45 ECO/DEV ECO/UNDEV INT/ORG DELIB/GP PLAN ADMIN 20 THIRD/WRLD. PAGE 98 A2016
NUC/PWR PEACE DIPLOM POLICY

B60
MEYRIAT J.,LA SCIENCE POLITIQUE EN FRANCE, 1945-1958; BIBLIOGRAPHIES FRANCAISES DE SCIENCES SOCIALES (VOL. I). EUR+WWI FRANCE POL/PAR DIPLOM ADMIN CHOOSE ATTIT...IDEA/COMP METH/COMP NAT/COMP 20. PAGE 100 A2057
BIBLIOG/A NAT/G CONCPT PHIL/SCI

B60
PENTONY D.E.,UNITED STATES FOREIGN AID. INDIA LAOS USA+45 ECO/UNDEV INT/TRADE ADMIN PEACE ATTIT ...POLICY METH/COMP ANTHOL 20. PAGE 115 A2352
FOR/AID DIPLOM ECO/TAC

B60
RAO V.K.R.,INTERNATIONAL AID FOR ECONOMIC DEVELOPMENT - POSSIBILITIES AND LIMITATIONS. FINAN PLAN TEC/DEV ADMIN TASK EFFICIENCY...POLICY SOC METH/CNCPT CHARTS 20 UN. PAGE 119 A2444
FOR/AID DIPLOM INT/ORG ECO/UNDEV

B60
SCANLON D.G.,INTERNATIONAL EDUCATION: A DOCUMENTARY HISTORY. ADMIN CONTROL ATTIT PERCEPT...BIOG ANTHOL METH 20. PAGE 127 A2612
EDU/PROP INT/ORG NAT/COMP DIPLOM

B60
STEIN E.,AMERICAN ENTERPRISE IN THE EUROPEAN COMMON MARKET: A LEGAL PROFILE. EUR+WWI FUT USA+45 SOCIETY STRUCT ECO/DEV NAT/G VOL/ASSN CONSULT PLAN TEC/DEV ECO/TAC INT/TRADE ADMIN ATTIT RIGID/FLEX PWR...MGT NEW/IDEA STAT TREND COMPUT/IR SIMUL EEC 20. PAGE 137 A2814
MARKET ADJUD INT/LAW

B60
WHEARE K.C.,THE CONSTITUTIONAL STRUCTURE OF THE COMMONWEALTH. UK EX/STRUC DIPLOM DOMIN ADMIN COLONIAL CONTROL LEAD INGP/REL SUPEGO 20 CMN/WLTH. PAGE 163 A3325
CONSTN INT/ORG VOL/ASSN SOVEREIGN

L60
DEAN A.W.,"SECOND GENEVA CONFERENCE OF THE LAW OF THE SEA: THE FIGHT FOR FREEDOM OF THE SEAS." FUT USA+45 USSR WOR+45 WOR-45 SEA CONSTN STRUCT PLAN INT/TRADE ADJUD ADMIN ORD/FREE...DECISION RECORD TREND GEN/LAWS 20 TREATY. PAGE 35 A0717
INT/ORG JURID INT/LAW

L60
JACOB P.E.,"THE DISARMAMENT CONSENSUS." USA+45 USSR WOR+45 INT/ORG NAT/G ACT/RES TEC/DEV BAL/PWR EDU/PROP ADMIN COERCE DETER NUC/PWR CONSEN RIGID/FLEX PWR...CONCPT RECORD CHARTS COLD/WAR 20. PAGE 72 A1482
DELIB/GP ATTIT ARMS/CONT

S60
"THE EMERGING COMMON MARKETS IN LATIN AMERICA." FUT L/A+17C STRATA DIST/IND INDUS LABOR NAT/G LEGIS
FINAN ECO/UNDEV

ECO/TAC ADMIN RIGID/FLEX HEALTH...NEW/IDEA TIME/SEQ INT/TRADE OAS 20. PAGE 3 A0059

S60
FRANKEL S.H.,"ECONOMIC ASPECTS OF POLITICAL INDEPENDENCE IN AFRICA." AFR FUT SOCIETY ECO/UNDEV COM/IND FINAN LEGIS PLAN TEC/DEV CAP/ISM ECO/TAC INT/TRADE ADMIN ATTIT DRIVE RIGID/FLEX PWR WEALTH ...MGT NEW/IDEA MATH TIME/SEQ VAL/FREE 20. PAGE 48 A0984
NAT/G FOR/AID

S60
GARNICK D.H.,"ON THE ECONOMIC FEASIBILITY OF A MIDDLE EASTERN COMMON MARKET." AFR ISLAM CULTURE INDUS NAT/G PLAN TEC/DEV ECO/TAC ADMIN ATTIT DRIVE RIGID/FLEX...PLURIST STAT TREND GEN/LAWS 20. PAGE 51 A1051
MARKET INT/TRADE

S60
GINSBURGS G.,"PEKING-LHASA-NEW DELHI." CHINA/COM FUT INDIA S/ASIA KIN NAT/G PROVS SECT FORCES BAL/PWR ECO/TAC DOMIN EDU/PROP LEGIT ADMIN REGION GUERRILLA PWR...TREND TIBET 20. PAGE 52 A1074
ASIA COERCE DIPLOM

S60
MODELSKI G.,"AUSTRALIA AND SEATO." S/ASIA USA+45 CULTURE INTELL ECO/DEV NAT/G PLAN DIPLOM ADMIN ROUTINE ATTIT SKILL...MGT TIME/SEQ AUSTRAL 20 SEATO. PAGE 102 A2097
INT/ORG ACT/RES

S60
MORA J.A.,"THE ORGANIZATION OF AMERICAN STATES." USA+45 LAW ECO/UNDEV VOL/ASSN DELIB/GP PLAN BAL/PWR EDU/PROP ADMIN DRIVE RIGID/FLEX ORD/FREE WEALTH ...TIME/SEQ GEN/LAWS OAS 20. PAGE 103 A2126
L/A+17C INT/ORG REGION

S60
MORALES C.J.,"TRADE AND ECONOMIC INTEGRATION IN LATIN AMERICA." FUT L/A+17C LAW STRATA ECO/UNDEV DIST/IND INDUS LABOR NAT/G LEGIS ECO/TAC ADMIN RIGID/FLEX WEALTH...CONCPT NEW/IDEA CONT/OBS TIME/SEQ WORK 20. PAGE 104 A2128
FINAN INT/TRADE REGION

S60
RIESELBACH Z.N.,"QUANTITATIVE TECHNIQUES FOR STUDYING VOTING BEHAVIOR IN THE UNITED NATIONS GENERAL ASSEMBLY." FUT S/ASIA USA+45 INT/ORG BAL/PWR DIPLOM ECO/TAC FOR/AID ADMIN PWR...POLICY METH/CNCPT METH UN 20. PAGE 121 A2478
QUANT CHOOSE

S60
SWIFT R.,"THE UNITED NATIONS AND ITS PUBLIC." WOR+45 CONSTN FINAN CONSULT DELIB/GP ACT/RES ADMIN ROUTINE RIGID/FLEX SKILL UN 20. PAGE 140 A2870
INT/ORG EDU/PROP

S60
THOMPSON K.W.,"MORAL PURPOSE IN FOREIGN POLICY: REALITIES AND ILLUSIONS." WOR+45 WOR-45 LAW CULTURE SOCIETY INT/ORG PLAN ADJUD ADMIN COERCE RIGID/FLEX SUPEGO KNOWL ORD/FREE PWR...SOC TREND SOC/EXP TOT/POP 20. PAGE 143 A2930
MORAL JURID DIPLOM

C60
FITZSIMMONS T.,"USSR: ITS PEOPLE, ITS SOCIETY, ITS CULTURE." USSR FAM SECT DIPLOM EDU/PROP ADMIN RACE/REL ATTIT...POLICY CHARTS BIBLIOG 20. PAGE 46 A0944
CULTURE STRUCT SOCIETY COM

C60
HAZARD J.N.,"THE SOVIET SYSTEM OF GOVERNMENT." USSR SOCIETY INDUS NAT/G POL/PAR DIPLOM CT/SYS...JURID CHARTS BIBLIOG/A 20. PAGE 63 A1298
COM NAT/COMP STRUCT ADMIN

B61
BAINS J.S.,STUDIES IN POLITICAL SCIENCE. INDIA WOR+45 WOR-45 CONSTN BAL/PWR ADJUD ADMIN PARL/PROC SOVEREIGN...SOC METH/COMP ANTHOL 17/20 UN. PAGE 10 A0209
DIPLOM INT/LAW NAT/G

B61
BECHHOEFER B.G.,POSTWAR NEGOTIATIONS FOR ARMS CONTROL. COM EUR+WWI USSR INT/ORG NAT/G ACT/RES BAL/PWR DIPLOM ECO/TAC EDU/PROP ADMIN REGION DETER NUC/PWR WAR WEAPON PEACE ATTIT PWR...POLICY TIME/SEQ COLD/WAR CONGRESS 20. PAGE 12 A0244
USA+45 ARMS/CONT

B61
BISHOP D.G.,THE ADMINISTRATION OF BRITISH FOREIGN RELATIONS. EUR+WWI MOD/EUR INT/ORG NAT/G POL/PAR DELIB/GP LEGIS TOP/EX ECO/TAC DOMIN EDU/PROP ADMIN COERCE 20. PAGE 14 A0292
ROUTINE PWR DIPLOM UK

B61
CARNELL F.,THE POLITICS OF THE NEW STATES: A SELECT ANNOTATED BIBLIOGRAPHY WITH SPECIAL REFERENCE TO THE COMMONWEALTH. CONSTN ELITES LABOR NAT/G POL/PAR EX/STRUC DIPLOM ADJUD ADMIN...GOV/COMP 20 COMMONWLTH. PAGE 24 A0496
BIBLIOG/A AFR ASIA COLONIAL

B61
COLLISON R.L.,BIBLIOGRAPHICAL SERVICES THROUGHOUT THE WORLD: 1950-59 (VOL. 9). WOR+45 INT/ORG EDU/PROP PRESS WRITING ADMIN CENTRAL 20 UNESCO. PAGE 28 A0568
BIBLIOG COM/IND DIPLOM

B61
FRIEDMANN W.G.,JOINT INTERNATIONAL BUSINESS VENTURES. ASIA ISLAM L/A+17C ECO/DEV DIST/IND FINAN PROC/MFG FACE/GP LG/CO NAT/G VOL/ASSN CONSULT EX/STRUC PLAN ADMIN ROUTINE WEALTH...OLD/LIB WORK 20. PAGE 49 A1004
ECO/UNDEV INT/TRADE

B61
GRAEBNER N.,AN UNCERTAIN TRADITION: AMERICAN SECRETARIES OF STATE IN THE 20TH CENTURY. USA+45 CONSTN INT/ORG NAT/G DELIB/GP TOP/EX BAL/PWR DOMIN LEGIT ADMIN ARMS/CONT ATTIT DRIVE PERSON SUPEGO ORD/FREE PWR...GEN/LAWS VAL/FREE CONGRESS. PAGE 55 A1121
USA-45 BIOG DIPLOM

B61
HASAN H.S.,PAKISTAN AND THE UN. ISLAM WOR+45 ECO/DEV ECO/UNDEV NAT/G TOP/EX ECO/TAC FOR/AID EDU/PROP ADMIN DRIVE PERCEPT...OBS TIME/SEQ UN 20. PAGE 62 A1284
INT/ORG ATTIT PAKISTAN

B61
JENKS C.W.,INTERNATIONAL IMMUNITIES. PLAN EDU/PROP ADMIN PERCEPT...OLD/LIB JURID CONCPT TREND TOT/POP. PAGE 74 A1506
INT/ORG DIPLOM

B61
KERTESZ S.D.,AMERICAN DIPLOMACY IN A NEW ERA. COM S/ASIA UK USA+45 FORCES PROB/SOLV BAL/PWR ECO/TAC ADMIN COLONIAL WAR PEACE ORD/FREE 20 NATO CONGRESS UN COLD/WAR. PAGE 78 A1601
ANTHOL DIPLOM TREND

B61
SCHNAPPER B.,LA POLITIQUE ET LE COMMERCE FRANCAIS DANS LE GOLFE DE GUINEE DE 1838 A 1871. FRANCE GUINEA UK SEA EXTR/IND NAT/G DELIB/GP LEGIS ADMIN ORD/FREE...POLICY GEOG CENSUS CHARTS BIBLIOG 19. PAGE 129 A2636
COLONIAL INT/TRADE DOMIN AFR

B61
SHAPP W.R.,FIELD ADMINISTRATION IN THE UNITED NATIONS SYSTEM. FINAN PROB/SOLV INSPECT DIPLOM EXEC REGION ROUTINE EFFICIENCY ROLE...INT CHARTS 20 UN. PAGE 131 A2694
INT/ORG ADMIN GP/REL FOR/AID

B61
SINGER J.D.,FINANCING INTERNATIONAL ORGANIZATION: THE UNITED NATIONS BUDGET PROCESS. WOR+45 FINAN ACT/RES CREATE PLAN BUDGET ECO/TAC ADMIN ROUTINE ATTIT KNOWL...DECISION METH/CNCPT TIME/SEQ UN 20. PAGE 133 A2726
INT/ORG MGT

B61
STONE J.,QUEST FOR SURVIVAL. WOR+45 NAT/G VOL/ASSN LEGIT ADMIN ARMS/CONT COERCE DISPL ORD/FREE PWR ...POLICY INT/LAW JURID COLD/WAR 20. PAGE 139 A2836
INT/ORG ADJUD SOVEREIGN

B61
US GENERAL ACCOUNTING OFFICE,EXAMINATION OF ECONOMIC AND TECHNICAL ASSISTANCE PROGRAM FOR IRAN. IRAN USA+45 AGRI INDUS DIPLOM CONTROL COST 20. PAGE 153 A3115
FOR/AID ADMIN TEC/DEV ECO/UNDEV

B61
WARD R.E.,JAPANESE POLITICAL SCIENCE: A GUIDE TO JAPANESE REFERENCE AND RESEARCH MATERIALS (2ND ED.). LAW CONSTN STRATA NAT/G POL/PAR DELIB/GP LEGIS ADMIN CHOOSE GP/REL...INT/LAW 19/20 CHINJAP. PAGE 161 A3282
BIBLIOG/A PHIL/SCI

L61
CLAUDE I.,"THE UNITED NATIONS AND THE USE OF FORCE." FUT WOR+45 SOCIETY DIPLOM EDU/PROP LEGIT ADMIN ROUTINE COERCE WAR PEACE ORD/FREE...CONCPT TREND UN 20. PAGE 27 A0545
INT/ORG FORCES

S61
JUVILER P.H.,"INTERPARLIAMENTARY CONTACTS IN SOVIET FOREIGN POLICY." COM FUT WOR+45 WOR-45 SOCIETY CONSULT ACT/RES DIPLOM ADMIN PEACE ATTIT RIGID/FLEX WEALTH...WELF/ST SOC TOT/POP CONGRESS 19/20. PAGE 75 A1543
INT/ORG DELIB/GP USSR

S61
LEWY G.,"SUPERIOR ORDERS, NUCLEAR WARFARE AND THE DICTATES OF CONSCIENCE: THE DILEMMA OF MILITARY OBEDIENCE IN THE ATOMIC." FUT UNIV WOR+45 INTELL SOCIETY FORCES TOP/EX ACT/RES ADMIN ROUTINE NUC/PWR PERCEPT RIGID/FLEX ALL/VALS...POLICY CONCPT 20. PAGE 88 A1805
DETER INT/ORG LAW INT/LAW

S61
MILLER E.,"LEGAL ASPECTS OF UN ACTION IN THE CONGO." AFR CULTURE ADMIN PEACE DRIVE RIGID/FLEX ORD/FREE...WELF/ST JURID OBS UN CONGO 20. PAGE 101 A2076
INT/ORG LEGIT

S61
NOVE A.,"THE SOVIET MODEL AND UNDERDEVELOPED COUNTRIES." COM FUT USSR WOR+45 CULTURE ECO/DEV POL/PAR FOR/AID EDU/PROP ADMIN MORAL WEALTH ...POLICY RECORD HIST/WRIT 20. PAGE 110 A2258
ECO/UNDEV PLAN

S61
TAUBENFELD H.J.,"OUTER SPACE--PAST POLITICS AND FUTURE POLICY." FUT USA+45 USA-45 WOR+45 AIR INTELL STRUCT ECO/DEV NAT/G TOP/EX ACT/RES ADMIN ROUTINE NUC/PWR ATTIT DRIVE...CONCPT TIME/SEQ TREND TOT/POP 20. PAGE 141 A2892
PLAN SPACE INT/ORG

S61
VINER J.,"ECONOMIC FOREIGN POLICY ON THE NEW FRONTIER." USA+45 ECO/UNDEV AGRI FINAN INDUS MARKET INT/ORG NAT/G FOR/AID INT/TRADE ADMIN ATTIT PWR 20 KENNEDY/JF. PAGE 159 A3239
TOP/EX ECO/TAC BAL/PAY TARIFFS

S61
VIRALLY M.,"VERS UNE REFORME DU SECRETARIAT DES NATIONS UNIES." FUT WOR+45 CONSTN ECO/DEV TOP/EX BAL/PWR ADMIN ALL/VALS...CONCPT BIOG UN VAL/FREE
INT/ORG INTELL DIPLOM

20. PAGE 159 A3243

B62
BAILEY S.D.,THE SECRETARIAT OF THE UNITED NATIONS. FUT WOR+45 DELIB/GP PLAN BAL/PWR DOMIN EDU/PROP ADMIN PEACE ATTIT PWR...DECISION CONCPT TREND CON/ANAL CHARTS UN VAL/FREE COLD/WAR 20. PAGE 10 A0205
INT/ORG EXEC DIPLOM

B62
COSTA RICA UNIVERSIDAD BIBL,LISTA DE TESIS DE GRADO DE LA UNIVERSIDAD DE COSTA RICA. COSTA/RICA LAW LOC/G ADMIN LEAD...SOC 20. PAGE 31 A0631
BIBLIOG/A NAT/G DIPLOM ECO/UNDEV

B62
FORD A.G.,THE GOLD STANDARD 1880-1914: BRITAIN AND ARGENTINA. UK ECO/UNDEV INT/TRADE ADMIN GOV/REL DEMAND EFFICIENCY...STAT CHARTS 19/20 ARGEN GOLD/STAND. PAGE 47 A0960
FINAN ECO/TAC BUDGET BAL/PAY

B62
FRIEDMANN W.,METHODS AND POLICIES OF PRINCIPAL DONOR COUNTRIES IN PUBLIC INTERNATIONAL DEVELOPMENT FINANCING: PRELIMINARY APPRAISAL. FRANCE GERMANY/W UK USA+45 USSR WOR+45 FINAN TEC/DEV CAP/ISM DIPLOM ECO/TAC ATTIT 20 EEC. PAGE 49 A1002
INT/ORG FOR/AID NAT/COMP ADMIN

B62
HADWEN J.G.,HOW UNITED NATIONS DECISIONS ARE MADE. WOR+45 LAW EDU/PROP LEGIT ADMIN PWR...DECISION SELF/OBS GEN/LAWS UN 20. PAGE 59 A1212
INT/ORG ROUTINE

B62
HARARI M.,GOVERNMENT AND POLITICS OF THE MIDDLE EAST. ISLAM USA+45 NAT/G SECT CHIEF ADMIN ORD/FREE 20. PAGE 61 A1257
DIPLOM ECO/UNDEV TEC/DEV POLICY

B62
INGHAM K.,A HISTORY OF EAST AFRICA. NAT/G DIPLOM ADMIN WAR NAT/LISM...SOC BIOG BIBLIOG. PAGE 70 A1439
AFR CONSTN COLONIAL

B62
KENNEDY J.F.,TO TURN THE TIDE. SPACE AGRI INT/ORG FORCES TEC/DEV ADMIN NUC/PWR PEACE WEALTH...ANTHOL 20 KENNEDY/JF CIV/RIGHTS. PAGE 78 A1592
DIPLOM CHIEF POLICY NAT/G

B62
LAWSON R.,INTERNATIONAL REGIONAL ORGANIZATIONS. WOR+45 NAT/G VOL/ASSN CONSULT LEGIS EDU/PROP LEGIT ADMIN EXEC ROUTINE HEALTH PWR WEALTH...JURID EEC COLD/WAR 20 UN. PAGE 86 A1752
INT/ORG DELIB/GP REGION

B62
POSTON R.W.,DEMOCRACY SPEAKS MANY TONGUES. L/A+17C USA+45 ECO/UNDEV ACT/RES ECO/TAC ADMIN ORD/FREE ...METH/COMP 20. PAGE 117 A2397
FOR/AID DIPLOM CAP/ISM MARXISM

B62
SELOSOEMARDJAN O.,SOCIAL CHANGES IN JOGJAKARTA. INDONESIA NETHERLAND ELITES STRATA STRUCT FAM POL/PAR CREATE DIPLOM INT/TRADE EDU/PROP ADMIN GOV/REL...SOC 20 JAVA CHINJAP. PAGE 131 A2683
ECO/UNDEV CULTURE REV COLONIAL

B62
SHAPIRO D.,A SELECT BIBLIOGRAPHY OF WORKS IN ENGLISH ON RUSSIAN HISTORY, 1801-1917. COM USSR STRATA FORCES EDU/PROP ADMIN REV RACE/REL ATTIT 19/20. PAGE 131 A2693
BIBLIOG DIPLOM COLONIAL

B62
TAYLOR D.,THE BRITISH IN AFRICA. UK CULTURE ECO/UNDEV INDUS DIPLOM INT/TRADE ADMIN WAR RACE/REL ORD/FREE SOVEREIGN...POLICY BIBLIOG 15/20 CMN/WLTH. PAGE 142 A2898
AFR COLONIAL DOMIN

B62
THANT U.,THE UNITED NATIONS' DEVELOPMENT DECADE: PROPOSALS FOR ACTION. WOR+45 SOCIETY ECO/UNDEV AGRI COM/IND FINAN R+D MUNIC SCHOOL VOL/ASSN CONSULT PLAN TEC/DEV ECO/TAC EDU/PROP ADMIN ROUTINE RIGID/FLEX...MGT SOC CONCPT UNESCO UN TOT/POP VAL/FREE. PAGE 142 A2906
INT/ORG ALL/VALS

B62
UNECA LIBRARY,NEW ACQUISITIONS IN THE UNECA LIBRARY. LAW NAT/G PLAN PROB/SOLV TEC/DEV ADMIN REGION...GEOG SOC 20 UN. PAGE 147 A3009
BIBLIOG AFR ECO/UNDEV INT/ORG

B62
US LIBRARY OF CONGRESS,A LIST OF AMERICAN DOCTORAL DISSERTATIONS ON AFRICA. SOCIETY SECT DIPLOM EDU/PROP ADMIN...GEOG 19/20. PAGE 155 A3157
BIBLIOG AFR ACADEM CULTURE

B62
US SENATE COMM GOVT OPERATIONS,ADMINISTRATION OF NATIONAL SECURITY. USA+45 CHIEF PLAN PROB/SOLV TEC/DEV DIPLOM ATTIT...POLICY DECISION 20 KENNEDY/JF RUSK/D MCNAMARA/R BUNDY/M HERTER/C. PAGE 156 A3173
ORD/FREE ADMIN NAT/G CONTROL

B62
WELLEQUET J.,LE CONGO BELGE ET LA WELTPOLITIK (1894-1914. GERMANY DOMIN EDU/PROP WAR ATTIT ...BIBLIOG T CONGO/LEOP. PAGE 163 A3314
ADMIN DIPLOM GP/REL COLONIAL

B62
WRIGHT Q.,PREVENTING WORLD WAR THREE. FUT WOR+45 CULTURE INT/ORG NAT/G CONSULT FORCES ADMIN ARMS/CONT DRIVE RIGID/FLEX ORD/FREE SOVEREIGN ...POLICY CONCPT TREND STERTYP COLD/WAR 20. PAGE 168 A3416
CREATE ATTIT

L62
MALINOWSKI W.R.,"CENTRALIZATION AND DE-CENTRALIZATION IN THE UNITED NATIONS' ECONOMIC AND SOCIAL ACTIVITIES." WOR+45 CONSTN ECO/UNDEV INT/ORG VOL/ASSN DELIB/GP ECO/TAC EDU/PROP ADMIN RIGID/FLEX ...OBS CHARTS UNESCO UN EEC OAS OEEC 20. PAGE 93 A1913
CREATE GEN/LAWS

L62
SCHWERIN K.,"LAW LIBRARIES AND FOREIGN LAW COLLECTION IN THE USA." USA+45 USA-45...INT/LAW STAT 20. PAGE 130 A2667
BIBLIOG LAW ACADEM ADMIN

S62
ALGER C.F.,"THE EXTERNAL BUREAUCRACY IN UNITED STATES FOREIGN AFFAIRS." USA+45 WOR+45 SOCIETY COM/IND INT/ORG NAT/G CONSULT EX/STRUC ACT/RES ...MGT SOC CONCPT TREND 20. PAGE 6 A0118
ADMIN ATTIT DIPLOM

S62
JACOBSON H.K.,"THE UNITED NATIONS AND COLONIALISM: A TENTATIVE APPRAISAL." AFR FUT S/ASIA USA+45 USSR WOR+45 NAT/G DELIB/GP PLAN DIPLOM ECO/TAC DOMIN ADMIN ROUTINE COERCE ATTIT RIGID/FLEX ORD/FREE PWR ...OBS STERTYP UN 20. PAGE 73 A1486
INT/ORG CONCPT COLONIAL

S62
PIQUEMAL M.,"LES PROBLEMES DES UNIONS D'ETATS EN AFRIQUE NOIRE." FRANCE SOCIETY INT/ORG NAT/G DELIB/GP PLAN LEGIT ADMIN COLONIAL ROUTINE ATTIT ORD/FREE PWR...GEOG METH/CNCPT 20. PAGE 116 A2382
AFR ECO/UNDEV REGION

S62
SCHILLING W.R.,"SCIENTISTS, FOREIGN POLICY AND POLITICS." WOR+45 WOR-45 INTELL INT/ORG CONSULT TOP/EX ACT/RES PLAN ADMIN KNOWL...CONCPT OBS TREND LEAGUE/NAT 20. PAGE 128 A2627
NAT/G TEC/DEV DIPLOM NUC/PWR

S62
SPRINGER H.W.,"FEDERATION IN THE CARIBBEAN: AN ATTEMPT THAT FAILED." L/A+17C ECO/UNDEV INT/ORG POL/PAR PROVS LEGIS CREATE PLAN LEGIT ADMIN FEDERAL ATTIT DRIVE PERSON ORD/FREE PWR...POLICY GEOG PSY CONCPT OBS CARIBBEAN CMN/WLTH 20. PAGE 136 A2791
VOL/ASSN NAT/G REGION

S62
TATOMIR N.,"ORGANIZATIA INTERNATIONALA A MUNCII: ASPECTE NOI ALE PROBLEMEI IMBUNATATIRII MECANISMULUI EI." EUR+WWI ECO/DEV VOL/ASSN ADMIN ...METH/CNCPT WORK ILO 20. PAGE 141 A2891
INT/ORG INT/TRADE

S62
TRUMAN D.,"THE DOMESTIC POLITICS OF FOREIGN AID." USA+45 WOR+45 NAT/G POL/PAR LEGIS DIPLOM ECO/TAC EDU/PROP ADMIN CHOOSE ATTIT PWR CONGRESS 20 CONGRESS. PAGE 145 A2970
ROUTINE FOR/AID

C62
BACON F.,"OF EMPIRE" (1612) IN F. BACON, ESSAYS." ELITES NAT/G PROB/SOLV DIPLOM ADMIN CONTROL WEALTH 16/17 KING. PAGE 10 A0201
PWR CHIEF DOMIN GEN/LAWS

B63
BOISSIER P.,HISTORIE DU COMITE INTERNATIONAL DE LA CROIX ROUGE. MOD/EUR WOR-45 CONSULT FORCES PLAN DIPLOM EDU/PROP ADMIN MORAL ORD/FREE...SOC CONCPT RECORD TIME/SEQ GEN/LAWS TOT/POP VAL/FREE 19/20. PAGE 16 A0332
INT/ORG HEALTH ARMS/CONT WAR

B63
COMISION DE HISTORIO,GUIA DE LOS DOCUMENTOS MICROFOTOGRAFIADOS POR LA UNIDAD MOVIL DE LA UNESCO. SOCIETY ECO/UNDEV INT/ORG ADMIN...SOC 20 UNESCO. PAGE 28 A0573
BIBLIOG NAT/G L/A+17C DIPLOM

B63
CONF ON FUTURE OF COMMONWEALTH,THE FUTURE OF THE COMMONWEALTH. UK ECO/UNDEV AGRI EDU/PROP ADMIN SOC/INTEG 20 COMMONWLTH. PAGE 29 A0583
DIPLOM RACE/REL ORD/FREE TEC/DEV

B63
FIFIELD R.H.,SOUTHEAST ASIA IN UNITED STATES POLICY. S/ASIA USA+45 ECO/UNDEV NAT/G DIPLOM ECO/TAC ADMIN COERCE ORD/FREE...POLICY MAJORIT 20. PAGE 45 A0928
INT/ORG PWR

B63
INTERAMERICAN ECO AND SOC COUN,THE ALLIANCE FOR PROGRESS: ITS FIRST YEAR: 1961-1962. AGRI SCHOOL PLAN TEC/DEV INT/TRADE TAX GIVE ADMIN WEALTH...SOC 20 SOUTH/AMER. PAGE 71 A1449
INT/ORG PROB/SOLV ECO/TAC L/A+17C

B63
LINDBERG L.,POLITICAL DYNAMICS OF EUROPEAN ECONOMIC INTEGRATION. EUR+WWI ECO/DEV INT/ORG VOL/ASSN DELIB/GP ADMIN WEALTH...DECISION EEC 20. PAGE 89 A1820
MARKET ECO/TAC

B63
MAYNE R.,THE COMMUNITY OF EUROPE. UK CONSTN NAT/G CONSULT DELIB/GP CREATE PLAN ECO/TAC LEGIT ADMIN ROUTINE ORD/FREE PWR WEALTH...CONCPT TIME/SEQ EEC EURATOM 20. PAGE 97 A1985
EUR+WWI INT/ORG REGION

B63
MILLER W.J.,THE MEANING OF COMMUNISM. USSR SOCIETY
MARXISM

ECO/DEV EX/STRUC WORKER TEC/DEV ADMIN TOTALISM ...POLICY CONCPT CHARTS BIBLIOG T 20 COLD/WAR LENIN/VI STALIN/J. PAGE 101 A2080 — TRADIT DIPLOM NAT/G

B63
MONTER W.,THE GOVERNMENT OF GENEVA, 1536-1605 (DOCTORAL THESIS). SWITZERLND DIPLOM LEAD ORD/FREE SOVEREIGN 16/17 CALVIN/J ROME. PAGE 103 A2112 — SECT FINAN LOC/G ADMIN

B63
PATRA A.C.,THE ADMINISTRATION OF JUSTICE UNDER THE EAST INDIA COMPANY IN BENGAL, BIHAR AND ORISSA. INDIA UK LG/CO CAP/ISM INT/TRADE ADJUD COLONIAL CONTROL CT/SYS...POLICY 20. PAGE 114 A2341 — ADMIN JURID CONCPT

B63
SCHRADER R.,SCIENCE AND POLICY. WOR+45 ECO/DEV ECO/UNDEV R+D FORCES PLAN DIPLOM GOV/REL TECHRACY BIBLIOG. PAGE 129 A2644 — TEC/DEV NAT/G POLICY ADMIN

B63
SMITH J.E.,THE DEFENSE OF BERLIN. COM GUATEMALA WOR+45 ECO/TAC ADMIN NEUTRAL ATTIT ORD/FREE SOVEREIGN...DECISION 20 DEPT/STATE. PAGE 134 A2747 — DIPLOM FORCES BAL/PWR PLAN

B63
SWEARER H.R.,CONTEMPORARY COMMUNISM: THEORY AND PRACTICE. COM USSR SOCIETY ECO/DEV POL/PAR FORCES PLAN ADMIN LEAD NAT/LISM...POLICY ANTHOL 20 LENIN/VI COM/PARTY. PAGE 140 A2869 — MARXISM CONCPT DIPLOM NAT/G

B63
THORELLI H.B.,INTOP: INTERNATIONAL OPERATIONS SIMULATION: PLAYER'S MANUAL. BRAZIL FINAN OP/RES ADMIN GP/REL INGP/REL PRODUC PERCEPT...DECISION MGT EEC. PAGE 144 A2935 — GAME INT/TRADE EDU/PROP LG/CO

B63
TUCKER R.C.,THE SOVIET POLITICAL MIND. WOR+45 ELITES INT/ORG NAT/G POL/PAR PLAN DIPLOM ECO/TAC DOMIN ADMIN NUC/PWR REV DRIVE PERSON SUPEGO PWR WEALTH...POLICY MGT PSY CONCPT OBS BIOG TREND COLD/WAR MARX/KARL 20. PAGE 145 A2972 — COM TOP/EX USSR

B63
UN SECRETARY GENERAL,PLANNING FOR ECONOMIC DEVELOPMENT. ECO/UNDEV FINAN BUDGET INT/TRADE TARIFFS TAX ADMIN 20 UN. PAGE 147 A3005 — PLAN ECO/TAC MGT NAT/COMP

B63
US SENATE COMM APPROPRIATIONS,PERSONNEL ADMINISTRATION AND OPERATIONS OF AGENCY FOR INTERNATIONAL DEVELOPMENT: SPECIAL HEARING. FINAN LEAD COST UTIL SKILL...CHARTS 20 CONGRESS AID CIVIL/SERV. PAGE 155 A3170 — ADMIN FOR/AID EFFICIENCY DIPLOM

B63
VAN SLYCK P.,PEACE: THE CONTROL OF NATIONAL POWER. CUBA WOR+45 FINAN NAT/G FORCES PROB/SOLV TEC/DEV BAL/PWR ADMIN CONTROL ORD/FREE...POLICY INT/LAW UN COLD/WAR TREATY. PAGE 158 A3214 — ARMS/CONT PEACE INT/ORG DIPLOM

B63
WALKER A.A.,OFFICIAL PUBLICATIONS OF SIERRA LEONE AND GAMBIA. GAMBIA SIER/LEONE UK LAW CONSTN LEGIS PLAN BUDGET DIPLOM...SOC SAMP CON/ANAL 20. PAGE 160 A3262 — BIBLIOG NAT/G COLONIAL ADMIN

L63
LISSITZYN O.J.,"INTERNATIONAL LAW IN A DIVIDED WORLD." FUT WOR+45 CONSTN CULTURE ECO/DEV ECO/UNDEV DIST/IND NAT/G FORCES ECO/TAC LEGIT ADJUD ADMIN COERCE ATTIT HEALTH MORAL ORD/FREE PWR RESPECT WEALTH VAL/FREE. PAGE 90 A1841 — INT/ORG LAW

S63
MARTHELOT P.,"PROGRES DE LA REFORME AGRAIRE." INTELL ECO/DEV R+D FOR/AID ADMIN KNOWL...OBS VAL/FREE UN 20. PAGE 95 A1948 — AGRI INT/ORG

S63
MODELSKI G.,"STUDY OF ALLIANCES." WOR+45 WOR-45 INT/ORG NAT/G FORCES LEGIT ADMIN CHOOSE ALL/VALS PWR SKILL...INT/LAW CONCPT GEN/LAWS 20 TREATY. PAGE 102 A2099 — VOL/ASSN CON/ANAL DIPLOM

S63
MORGENTHAU H.J.,"THE POLITICAL CONDITIONS FOR AN INTERNATIONAL POLICE FORCE." FUT WOR+45 CREATE LEGIT ADMIN PEACE ORD/FREE 20. PAGE 104 A2141 — INT/ORG FORCES ARMS/CONT DETER

S63
NYE J.S. JR.,"EAST AFRICAN ECONOMIC INTEGRATION." AFR UGANDA PROVS DELIB/GP PLAN ECO/TAC INT/TRADE ADMIN ROUTINE ORD/FREE PWR WEALTH...OBS TIME/SEQ VAL/FREE 20. PAGE 110 A2264 — ECO/UNDEV INT/ORG

S63
ROUGEMONT D.,"LES NOUVELLES CHANCES DE L'EUROPE." EUR+WWI FUT ECO/DEV INT/ORG NAT/G ACT/RES PLAN TEC/DEV EDU/PROP ADMIN COLONIAL FEDERAL ATTIT PWR SKILL...TREND 20. PAGE 124 A2549 — ECO/UNDEV PERCEPT

B64
THE SPECIAL COMMONWEALTH AFRICAN ASSISTANCE PLAN. AFR CANADA INDIA NIGERIA UK FINAN SCHOOL...CHARTS 20 COMMONWLTH. PAGE 3 A0065 — ECO/UNDEV TREND FOR/AID ADMIN

B64
BLACKSTOCK P.W.,THE STRATEGY OF SUBVERSION. USA+45 FORCES EDU/PROP ADMIN COERCE GOV/REL...DECISION MGT 20 DEPT/DEFEN CIA DEPT/STATE. PAGE 15 A0301 — ORD/FREE DIPLOM CONTROL

B64
COLUMBIA U SCHOOL OF LAW,PUBLIC INTERNATIONAL DEVELOPMENT FINANCING IN INDIA. GERMANY/W INDIA UK USA+45 INDUS PLAN TEC/DEV DIPLOM ECO/TAC GIVE ADMIN UTIL ATTIT 20. PAGE 28 A0572 — ECO/UNDEV FINAN FOR/AID INT/ORG

B64
DUROSELLE J.B.,POLITIQUES NATIONALES ENVERS LES JEUNES ETATS. FRANCE ISRAEL ITALY UK USA+45 USSR YUGOSLAVIA ECO/DEV FINAN ECO/TAC INT/TRADE ADMIN PWR 20. PAGE 40 A0809 — DIPLOM ECO/UNDEV COLONIAL DOMIN

B64
FATOUROS A.A.,CANADA'S OVERSEAS AID. CANADA WOR+45 ECO/DEV FINAN NAT/G BUDGET ECO/TAC CONFER ADMIN 20. PAGE 44 A0904 — FOR/AID DIPLOM ECO/UNDEV POLICY

B64
GESELLSCHAFT RECHTSVERGLEICH,BIBLIOGRAPHIE DES DEUTSCHEN RECHTS (BIBLIOGRAPHY OF GERMAN LAW, TRANS. BY COURTLAND PETERSON). GERMANY FINAN INDUS LABOR SECT FORCES CT/SYS PARL/PROC CRIME...INT/LAW SOC NAT/COMP 20. PAGE 52 A1066 — BIBLIOG/A JURID CONSTN ADMIN

B64
GJUPANOVIC H.,LEGAL SOURCES AND BIBLIOGRAPHY OF YUGOSLAVIA. COM YUGOSLAVIA LAW LEGIS DIPLOM ADMIN PARL/PROC REGION CRIME CENTRAL 20. PAGE 53 A1078 — BIBLIOG/A JURID CONSTN ADJUD

B64
GRZYBOWSKI K.,THE SOCIALIST COMMONWEALTH OF NATIONS: ORGANIZATIONS AND INSTITUTIONS. FORCES DIPLOM INT/TRADE ADJUD ADMIN LEAD WAR MARXISM SOCISM...BIBLIOG 20 COMECON WARSAW/P. PAGE 58 A1185 — INT/LAW COM REGION INT/ORG

B64
HAMBRIDGE G.,DYNAMICS OF DEVELOPMENT. AGRI FINAN INDUS LABOR INT/TRADE EDU/PROP ADMIN LEAD OWN HEALTH...ANTHOL BIBLIOG 20. PAGE 61 A1245 — ECO/UNDEV ECO/TAC OP/RES ACT/RES

B64
IBERO-AMERICAN INSTITUTES,IBEROAMERICANA. STRUCT ADMIN SOC. PAGE 70 A1430 — BIBLIOG L/A+17C NAT/G DIPLOM

B64
JACKSON W.V.,LIBRARY GUIDE FOR BRAZILIAN STUDIES. BRAZIL USA+45 STRUCT DIPLOM ADMIN...SOC 20. PAGE 72 A1481 — BIBLIOG L/A+17C NAT/G LOC/G

B64
KENNEDY J.F.,THE BURDEN AND THE GLORY. FUT USA+45 TEC/DEV ECO/TAC EDU/PROP ARMS/CONT MURDER RACE/REL PEACE...ANTHOL 20 KENNEDY/JF COLD/WAR NATO PRESIDENT. PAGE 78 A1593 — ADMIN POLICY GOV/REL DIPLOM

B64
KNOX V.H.,PUBLIC FINANCE: INFORMATION SOURCES. USA+45 DIPLOM ADMIN GOV/REL COST...POLICY 20. PAGE 81 A1657 — BIBLIOG/A FINAN TAX BUDGET

B64
LITTLE I.M.D.,AID TO AFRICA. AFR UK TEC/DEV DIPLOM ECO/TAC INCOME WEALTH 20. PAGE 90 A1844 — FOR/AID ECO/UNDEV ADMIN POLICY

B64
MAHAR J.M.,INDIA: A CRITICAL BIBLIOGRAPHY. INDIA PAKISTAN CULTURE ECO/UNDEV LOC/G POL/PAR SECT PROB/SOLV DIPLOM ADMIN COLONIAL PARL/PROC ATTIT 20. PAGE 93 A1906 — BIBLIOG/A S/ASIA NAT/G LEAD

B64
MUSSO AMBROSI L.A.,BIBLIOGRAFIA DE BIBLIOGRAFIAS URUGUAYAS. URUGUAY DIPLOM ADMIN ATTIT...SOC 20. PAGE 106 A2185 — BIBLIOG NAT/G L/A+17C PRESS

B64
NICOL D.,AFRICA - A SUBJECTIVE VIEW. AFR INT/ORG PLAN ADMIN COLONIAL PARL/PROC PARTIC REGION GOV/REL LITERACY ATTIT...BIBLIOG 20 CIVIL/SERV. PAGE 109 A2230 — NAT/G LEAD CULTURE ACADEM

B64
RICHARDSON I.L.,BIBLIOGRAFIA BRASILEIRA DE ADMINISTRACAO PUBLICA E ASSUNTOS CORRELATOS. BRAZIL CONSTN FINAN LOC/G NAT/G POL/PAR PLAN DIPLOM RECEIVE ATTIT...METH 20. PAGE 121 A2474 — BIBLIOG MGT ADMIN LAW

B64
RUBINSTEIN A.Z.,THE SOVIETS IN INTERNATIONAL ORGANIZATIONS: CHANGING POLICY TOWARD DEVELOPING COUNTRIES, 1953-1963. COM DELIB/GP ACT/RES ECO/TAC EDU/PROP ADMIN ATTIT ORD/FREE PWR...INT VAL/FREE UN 20. PAGE 125 A2563 — ECO/UNDEV INT/ORG USSR

B64
RUSSELL R.B.,UNITED NATIONS EXPERIENCE WITH MILITARY FORCES: POLITICAL AND LEGAL ASPECTS. AFR KOREA WOR+45 LEGIS PROB/SOLV ADMIN CONTROL EFFICIENCY PEACE...POLICY INT/LAW BIBLIOG UN. — FORCES DIPLOM SANCTION ORD/FREE

PAGE 126 A2576

B64
RUSSET B.M.,WORLD HANDBOOK OF POLITICAL AND SOCIAL INDICATORS. WOR+45 COM/IND ADMIN WEALTH...GEOG 20. PAGE 126 A2577 DIPLOM STAT NAT/G NAT/COMP

B64
SEGUNDO-SANCHEZ M.,OBRAS (2 VOLS.). VENEZUELA EX/STRUC DIPLOM ADMIN 19/20. PAGE 131 A2682 BIBLIOG LEAD NAT/G L/A+17C

B64
SULLIVAN G.,THE STORY OF THE PEACE CORPS. USA+45 WOR+45 INTELL FACE/GP NAT/G SCHOOL VOL/ASSN CONSULT EX/STRUC PLAN EDU/PROP ADMIN ATTIT DRIVE ALL/VALS ...POLICY HEAL SOC CONCPT INT QU BIOG TREND SOC/EXP WORK. PAGE 140 A2861 INT/ORG ECO/UNDEV FOR/AID PEACE

B64
SZLADITS C.,BIBLIOGRAPHY ON FOREIGN AND COMPARATIVE LAW: BOOKS AND ARTICLES IN ENGLISH (SUPPLEMENT 1962). FINAN INDUS JUDGE LICENSE ADMIN CT/SYS PARL/PROC OWN...INT/LAW CLASSIF METH/COMP NAT/COMP 20. PAGE 141 A2877 BIBLIOG/A JURID ADJUD LAW

B64
TULLY A.,WHERE DID YOUR MONEY GO. USA+45 USSR ECO/UNDEV ADMIN EFFICIENCY WEALTH...METH/COMP 20. PAGE 146 A2976 FOR/AID DIPLOM CONTROL

B64
TURNER M.C.,LIBROS EN VENTA EN HISPANOAMERICA Y ESPANA. SPAIN LAW CONSTN CULTURE ADMIN LEAD...HUM SOC 20. PAGE 146 A2983 BIBLIOG L/A+17C NAT/G DIPLOM

B64
US AGENCY INTERNATIONAL DEV,REPORT TO CONGRESS ON THE FOREIGN ASSISTANCE PROGRAM. AFR ASIA L/A+17C USA+45 INT/ORG VOL/ASSN FORCES CAP/ISM ADMIN WEAPON. PAGE 149 A3052 FOR/AID ECO/UNDEV TEC/DEV BUDGET

B64
US SENATE COMM GOVT OPERATIONS,THE SECRETARY OF STATE AND THE AMBASSADOR. USA+45 CHIEF CONSULT EX/STRUC FORCES PLAN ADMIN EXEC INGP/REL ROLE ...ANTHOL 20 PRESIDENT DEPT/STATE. PAGE 156 A3175 DIPLOM DELIB/GP NAT/G

B64
US SENATE COMM GOVT OPERATIONS,ADMINISTRATION OF NATIONAL SECURITY. USA+45 CHIEF TOP/EX PLAN DIPLOM CONTROL PEACE...POLICY DECISION 20 PRESIDENT CONGRESS. PAGE 156 A3176 ADMIN FORCES ORD/FREE NAT/G

B64
WAINHOUSE D.W.,REMNANTS OF EMPIRE: THE UNITED NATIONS AND THE END OF COLONIALISM. FUT PORTUGAL WOR+45 NAT/G CONSULT DOMIN LEGIT ADMIN ROUTINE ATTIT ORD/FREE...POLICY JURID RECORD INT TIME/SEQ UN CMN/WLTH 20. PAGE 160 A3260 INT/ORG TREND COLONIAL

B64
WITHERELL J.W.,OFFICIAL PUBLICATIONS OF FRENCH EQUATORIAL AFRICA, FRENCH CAMEROONS, AND TOGO, 1946-1958 (PAMPHLET). CAMEROON CHAD FRANCE GABON TOGO LAW ECO/UNDEV EXTR/IND INT/TRADE...GEOG HEAL 20. PAGE 165 A3370 BIBLIOG/A AFR NAT/G ADMIN

L64
SYMONDS R.,"REFLECTIONS IN LOCALISATION." AFR S/ASIA UK STRATA INT/ORG NAT/G SCHOOL EDU/PROP LEGIT KNOWL ORD/FREE PWR RESPECT CMN/WLTH 20. PAGE 140 A2874 ADMIN MGT COLONIAL

S64
CARNEGIE ENDOWMENT INT. PEACE,"ADMINISTRATION AND BUDGET (ISSUES BEFORE THE NINETEENTH GENERAL ASSEMBLY)." WOR+45 FINAN BUDGET ECO/TAC ROUTINE COST...STAT RECORD UN. PAGE 24 A0495 INT/ORG ADMIN

S64
GARDNER R.N.,"THE SOVIET UNION AND THE UNITED NATIONS." WOR+45 FINAN POL/PAR VOL/ASSN FORCES ECO/TAC DOMIN EDU/PROP LEGIT ADJUD ADMIN ARMS/CONT COERCE ATTIT ALL/VALS...POLICY MAJORIT CONCPT OBS TIME/SEQ TREND STERTYP UN. PAGE 51 A1046 COM INT/ORG USSR

S64
GROSS J.A.,"WHITEHALL AND THE COMMONWEALTH." EUR+WWI MOD/EUR INT/ORG NAT/G CONSULT DELIB/GP LEGIS DOMIN ADMIN COLONIAL ROUTINE PWR CMN/WLTH 19/20. PAGE 57 A1174 EX/STRUC ATTIT TREND

S64
HORECKY P.L.,"LIBRARY OF CONGRESS PUBLICATIONS IN AID OF USSR AND EAST EUROPEAN RESEARCH." BULGARIA CZECHOSLVK POLAND USSR YUGOSLAVIA NAT/G POL/PAR DIPLOM ADMIN GOV/REL...CLASSIF 20. PAGE 67 A1382 BIBLIOG/A COM MARXISM

S64
MOWER A.G.,"THE OFFICIAL PRESSURE GROUP OF THE COUNCIL OF EUROPE'S CONSULATIVE ASSEMBLY." EUR+WWI SOCIETY STRUCT FINAN CONSULT ECO/TAC ADMIN ROUTINE ATTIT PWR WEALTH...STAT CHARTS 20 COUNCL/EUR. PAGE 105 A2160 INT/ORG EDU/PROP

S64
RUSK D.,"THE MAKING OF FOREIGN POLICY" USA+45 CHIEF DELIB/GP WORKER PROB/SOLV ADMIN ATTIT PWR ...DECISION 20 DEPT/STATE RUSK/D GOLDMAN/E. PAGE 125 A2570 DIPLOM INT POLICY

S64
SCHWELB E.,"OPERATION OF THE EUROPEAN CONVENTION ON HUMAN RIGHTS." EUR+WWI LAW SOCIETY CREATE EDU/PROP ADJUD ADMIN PEACE ATTIT ORD/FREE PWR...POLICY INT/LAW CONCPT OBS GEN/LAWS UN VAL/FREE ILO 20 ECHR. PAGE 130 A2665 INT/ORG MORAL

B65
AMERICAN ECONOMIC ASSOCIATION,INDEX OF ECONOMIC JOURNALS 1886-1965 (7 VOLS.). UK USA+45 USA-45 AGRI FINAN PLAN ECO/TAC INT/TRADE ADMIN...STAT CENSUS 19/20. PAGE 7 A0145 BIBLIOG WRITING INDUS

B65
DAVISON W.P.,INTERNATIONAL POLITICAL COMMUNICATION. COM USA+45 WOR+45 CULTURE ECO/UNDEV NAT/G PROB/SOLV PRESS TV ADMIN 20 FILM. PAGE 34 A0693 EDU/PROP DIPLOM PERS/REL COM/IND

B65
HAGRAS K.M.,UNITED NATIONS CONFERENCE ON TRADE AND DEVELOPMENT: A CASE STUDY OF UN DIPLOMACY. CONSULT ACT/RES TEC/DEV FOR/AID INT/TRADE...BIBLIOG 20 UN LEAGUE/NAT UNCTAD. PAGE 59 A1213 INT/ORG ADMIN DELIB/GP DIPLOM

B65
HARMON R.B.,POLITICAL SCIENCE: A BIBLIOGRAPHICAL GUIDE TO THE LITERATURE. WOR+45 WOR-45 R+D INT/ORG LOC/G NAT/G DIPLOM ADMIN...CONCPT METH. PAGE 61 A1261 BIBLIOG POL/PAR LAW GOV/COMP

B65
HART B.H.L.,THE MEMOIRS OF CAPTAIN LIDDELL HART (VOL. I). UK NAT/G PLAN TEC/DEV DIPLOM ADMIN WEAPON GOV/REL PERS/REL ATTIT PWR FASCISM...POLICY 20. PAGE 62 A1274 FORCES BIOG LEAD WAR

B65
HISPANIC SOCIETY OF AMERICA,CATALOGUE (10 VOLS.). PORTUGAL PRE/AMER SPAIN NAT/G ADMIN...POLICY SOC 15/20. PAGE 65 A1341 BIBLIOG L/A+17C COLONIAL DIPLOM

B65
LAFAVE W.R.,LAW AND SOVIET SOCIETY. EX/STRUC DIPLOM DOMIN EDU/PROP PRESS ADMIN CRIME OWN MARXISM 20 KHRUSH/N. PAGE 84 A1710 JURID CT/SYS ADJUD GOV/REL

B65
MACDONALD R.W.,THE LEAGUE OF ARAB STATES: A STUDY IN THE DYNAMICS OF REGIONAL ORGANIZATION. ISRAEL UAR USSR FINAN INT/ORG DELIB/GP ECO/TAC AGREE NEUTRAL ORD/FREE PWR...DECISION BIBLIOG 20 TREATY UN. PAGE 92 A1888 ISLAM REGION DIPLOM ADMIN

B65
MOODY M.,CATALOG OF INTERNATIONAL LAW AND RELATIONS (20 VOLS.). WOR+45 INT/ORG NAT/G ADJUD ADMIN CT/SYS POLICY. PAGE 103 A2117 BIBLIOG INT/LAW DIPLOM

B65
MORGENTHAU H.,MORGENTHAU DIARY (CHINA) (2 VOLS.). ASIA USA+45 USA-45 LAW DELIB/GP EX/STRUC PLAN FOR/AID INT/TRADE CONFER WAR MARXISM 20 CHINJAP. PAGE 104 A2136 DIPLOM ADMIN

B65
NATIONAL BOOK CENTRE PAKISTAN,BOOKS ON PAKISTAN: A BIBLIOGRAPHY. PAKISTAN CULTURE DIPLOM ADMIN ATTIT ...MAJORIT SOC CONCPT 20. PAGE 107 A2201 BIBLIOG CONSTN S/ASIA NAT/G

B65
NEWBURY C.W.,BRITISH POLICY TOWARDS WEST AFRICA: SELECT DOCUMENTS 1786-1874. AFR UK INT/TRADE DOMIN ADMIN COLONIAL CT/SYS COERCE ORD/FREE...BIBLIOG/A 18/19. PAGE 108 A2224 DIPLOM POLICY NAT/G WRITING

B65
OGILVY-WEBB M.,THE GOVERNMENT EXPLAINS: A STUDY OF THE INFORMATION SERVICES. UK DELIB/GP LEGIS WORKER BUDGET DIPLOM 20. PAGE 111 A2284 EDU/PROP ATTIT NAT/G ADMIN

B65
PENNICK JL J.R.,THE POLITICS OF AMERICAN SCIENCE, 1939 TO THE PRESENT. USA+45 USA-45 INTELL TEC/DEV DIPLOM NEW/LIB...ANTHOL 20 COLD/WAR. PAGE 114 A2349 POLICY ADMIN PHIL/SCI NAT/G

B65
ROTBERG R.I.,A POLITICAL HISTORY OF TROPICAL AFRICA. EX/STRUC DIPLOM INT/TRADE DOMIN ADMIN RACE/REL NAT/LISM PWR SOVEREIGN...GEOG TIME/SEQ BIBLIOG 1/20. PAGE 124 A2545 AFR CULTURE COLONIAL

B65
SPEECKAERT G.P.,SELECT BIBLIOGRAPHY ON INTERNATIONAL ORGANIZATION, 1885-1964. WOR+45 WOR-45 EX/STRUC DIPLOM ADMIN REGION 19/20 UN. PAGE 136 A2777 BIBLIOG INT/ORG GEN/LAWS STRATA

B65
SPENCE J.E.,REPUBLIC UNDER PRESSURE: A STUDY OF SOUTH AFRICAN FOREIGN POLICY. SOUTH/AFR ADMIN COLONIAL GOV/REL RACE/REL DISCRIM NAT/LISM ATTIT ROLE...TREND 20 NEGRO. PAGE 136 A2783 DIPLOM POLICY AFR

B65
UNESCO,INTERNATIONAL ORGANIZATIONS IN THE SOCIAL SCIENCES(REV. ED.). LAW ADMIN ATTIT...CRIMLGY GEOG INT/LAW PSY SOC STAT 20 UNESCO. PAGE 148 A3024 INT/ORG R+D PROF/ORG ACT/RES

B65
US SENATE COMM GOVT OPERATIONS,ADMINISTRATION OF NATIONAL SECURITY. USA+45 DELIB/GP ADMIN ROLE ...POLICY CHARTS SENATE. PAGE 156 A3177
NAT/G ORD/FREE DIPLOM PROB/SOLV

B65
WHITE J.,GERMAN AID. GERMANY/W FINAN PLAN TEC/DEV INT/TRADE ADMIN ATTIT...POLICY 20. PAGE 164 A3335
FOR/AID ECO/UNDEV DIPLOM ECO/TAC

B65
WITHERELL J.W.,MADAGASCAR AND ADJACENT ISLANDS; A GUIDE TO OFFICIAL PUBLICATIONS (PAMPHLET). FRANCE MADAGASCAR S/ASIA UK LAW OP/RES PLAN DIPLOM ...POLICY CON/ANAL 19/20. PAGE 165 A3371
BIBLIOG COLONIAL LOC/G ADMIN

L65
MATTHEWS D.G.,"A CURRENT BIBLIOGRAPHY ON ETHIOPIAN AFFAIRS: A SELECT BIBLIOGRAPHY FROM 1950-1964." ETHIOPIA LAW CULTURE ECO/UNDEV INDUS LABOR SECT FORCES DIPLOM CIVMIL/REL RACE/REL...LING STAT 20. PAGE 96 A1969
BIBLIOG/A ADMIN POL/PAR NAT/G

S65
"FURTHER READING." INDIA ADMIN COLONIAL WAR GOV/REL ATTIT 20. PAGE 3 A0069
BIBLIOG DIPLOM NAT/G POLICY

B66
BEAUFRE A.,NATO AND EUROPE. WOR+45 PLAN CONFER EXEC NUC/PWR ATTIT...POLICY 20 NATO EUROPE. PAGE 12 A0243
INT/ORG DETER DIPLOM ADMIN

B66
BESTERMAN T.,A WORLD BIBLIOGRAPHY OF BIBLIOGRAPHIES (4TH ED.). WOR+45 WOR-45 LAW INT/ORG ADMIN CON/ANAL. PAGE 14 A0282
BIBLIOG/A DIPLOM

B66
EPSTEIN F.T.,THE AMERICAN BIBLIOGRAPHY OF RUSSIAN AND EAST EUROPEAN STUDIES FOR 1964. USSR LOC/G NAT/G POL/PAR FORCES ADMIN ARMS/CONT...JURID CONCPT 20 UN. PAGE 42 A0855
BIBLIOG COM MARXISM DIPLOM

B66
FABAR R.,THE VISION AND THE NEED: LATE VICTORIAN IMPERIALIST AIMS. MOD/EUR UK WOR-45 CULTURE NAT/G DIPLOM...TIME/SEQ METH/COMP 19 KIPLING/R COMMONWLTH. PAGE 43 A0880
COLONIAL CONCPT ADMIN ATTIT

B66
GERARD-LIBOIS J.,KATANGA SECESSION. INT/ORG FORCES DIPLOM ADMIN CONTROL WAR CHOOSE PWR...CHARTS 20 KATANGA TSHOMBE/M UN. PAGE 52 A1062
NAT/G REGION ORD/FREE REV

B66
GLAZER M.,THE FEDERAL GOVERNMENT AND THE UNIVERSITY. CHILE PROB/SOLV DIPLOM GIVE ADMIN WAR ...POLICY SOC 20. PAGE 53 A1079
BIBLIOG/A NAT/G PLAN ACADEM

B66
HARMON R.B.,SOURCES AND PROBLEMS OF BIBLIOGRAPHY IN POLITICAL SCIENCE (PAMPHLET). INT/ORG LOC/G MUNIC POL/PAR ADMIN GOV/REL ALL/IDEOS...JURID MGT CONCPT 19/20. PAGE 61 A1262
BIBLIOG DIPLOM INT/LAW NAT/G

B66
HAYER T.,FRENCH AID. AFR FRANCE AGRI FINAN BUDGET ADMIN WAR PRODUC...CHARTS 18/20 THIRD/WRLD OVRSEA/DEV. PAGE 63 A1295
TEC/DEV COLONIAL FOR/AID ECO/UNDEV

B66
HOLT R.T.,THE POLITICAL BASIS OF ECONOMIC DEVELOPMENT. STRATA STRUCT NAT/G DIPLOM ADMIN...SOC NAT/COMP BIBLIOG 20. PAGE 67 A1376
ECO/TAC GOV/COMP CONSTN EX/STRUC

B66
KEENLEYSIDE H.L.,INTERNATIONAL AID: A SUMMARY. AFR INDIA S/ASIA UK STRATA EXTR/IND TEC/DEV ADMIN RACE/REL DEMAND NAT/LISM WEALTH...TREND CHINJAP. PAGE 77 A1575
ECO/UNDEV FOR/AID DIPLOM TASK

B66
KIRDAR U.,THE STRUCTURE OF UNITED NATIONS ECONOMIC AID TO UNDERDEVELOPED COUNTRIES. AGRI FINAN INDUS NAT/G EX/STRUC PLAN GIVE TASK...POLICY 20 UN. PAGE 79 A1631
INT/ORG FOR/AID ECO/UNDEV ADMIN

B66
KNORR K.E.,ON THE USES OF MILITARY POWER IN THE NUCLEAR AGE. WOR+45 INT/ORG TEC/DEV ADMIN CONTROL WAR COST 20. PAGE 81 A1656
FORCES DIPLOM DETER NUC/PWR

B66
LEE L.T.,VIENNA CONVENTION ON CONSULAR RELATIONS. WOR+45 LAW INT/ORG CONFER GP/REL PRIVIL...INT/LAW 20 TREATY VIENNA/CNV. PAGE 86 A1760
AGREE DIPLOM ADMIN

B66
MONTGOMERY J.D.,APPROACHES TO DEVELOPMENT: POLITICS, ADMINISTRATION AND CHANGE. USA+45 AGRI FOR/AID ORD/FREE...CONCPT IDEA/COMP METH/COMP ANTHOL. PAGE 103 A2116
ECO/UNDEV ADMIN POLICY ECO/TAC

B66
MOOMAW I.W.,THE CHALLENGE OF HUNGER. USA+45 PLAN ADMIN EATING 20. PAGE 103 A2118
FOR/AID DIPLOM ECO/UNDEV ECO/TAC

B66
MOORE R.J.,SIR CHARLES WOOD'S INDIAN POLICY: 1853-66. INDIA POL/PAR CHIEF DELIB/GP DIPLOM CONTROL LEAD WOOD/CHAS. PAGE 103 A2124
COLONIAL ADMIN CONSULT DECISION

B66
SPICER K.,A SAMARITAN STATE? AFR CANADA INDIA PAKISTAN UK USA+45 FINAN INDUS PRODUC...CHARTS 20 NATO. PAGE 136 A2787
DIPLOM FOR/AID ECO/DEV ADMIN

B66
SPINELLI A.,THE EUROCRATS; CONFLICT AND CRISIS IN THE EUROPEAN COMMUNITY (TRANS. BY C. GROVE HAINES). EUR+WWI MARKET POL/PAR ECO/TAC PARL/PROC EEC OEEC ECSC EURATOM. PAGE 136 A2789
INT/ORG INGP/REL CONSTN ADMIN

B66
SZLADITS C.,A BIBLIOGRAPHY ON FOREIGN AND COMPARATIVE LAW (SUPPLEMENT 1964). FINAN FAM LABOR LG/CO LEGIS JUDGE ADMIN CRIME...CRIMLGY 20. PAGE 141 A2878
BIBLIOG/A CT/SYS INT/LAW

B66
UN ECAFE,ADMINISTRATIVE ASPECTS OF FAMILY PLANNING PROGRAMMES (PAMPHLET). ASIA THAILAND WOR+45 VOL/ASSN PROB/SOLV BUDGET FOR/AID EDU/PROP CONFER CONTROL GOV/REL TIME 20 UN BIRTH/CON. PAGE 147 A2999
PLAN CENSUS FAM ADMIN

B66
US LIBRARY OF CONGRESS,NIGERIA: A GUIDE TO OFFICIAL PUBLICATIONS. CAMEROON NIGERIA UK DIPLOM...POLICY 19/20 UN LEAGUE/NAT. PAGE 155 A3160
BIBLIOG ADMIN NAT/G COLONIAL

B66
US SENATE COMM ON FOREIGN REL,HEARINGS ON S 2859 AND S 2861. USA+45 WOR+45 FORCES BUDGET CAP/ISM ADMIN DETER WEAPON TOTALISM...NAT/COMP 20 UN CONGRESS. PAGE 156 A3185
FOR/AID DIPLOM ORD/FREE ECO/UNDEV

B66
VIEN N.C.,SEEKING THE TRUTH. FRANCE VIETNAM AGRI ADMIN WAR...BIOG 20 BAO/DAI INTERVENT. PAGE 159 A3231
NAT/G CONSULT CONSTN

B66
WARBURG J.P.,THE UNITED STATES IN THE POSTWAR WORLD. USA+45 ECO/TAC...POLICY 20 COLD/WAR. PAGE 161 A3277
FOR/AID DIPLOM PLAN ADMIN

L66
AMERICAN ECONOMIC REVIEW,"SIXTY-THIRD LIST OF DOCTORAL DISSERTATIONS IN POLITICAL ECONOMY IN AMERICAN UNIVERSITIES AND COLLEGES." ECO/DEV AGRI FINAN LABOR WORKER PLAN BUDGET INT/TRADE ADMIN DEMAND...MGT STAT 20. PAGE 7 A0146
BIBLIOG/A CONCPT ACADEM

L66
SEYLER W.C.,"DOCTORAL DISSERTATIONS IN POLITICAL SCIENCE IN UNIVERSITIES OF THE UNITED STATES AND CANADA." INT/ORG LOC/G ADMIN...INT/LAW MGT GOV/COMP. PAGE 131 A2690
BIBLIOG LAW NAT/G

S66
AFRICAN BIBLIOGRAPHIC CENTER,"A CURRENT VIEW OF AFRICANA: A SELECT AND ANNOTATED BIBLIOGRAPHICAL PUBLISHING GUIDE, 1965-1966." AFR CULTURE INDUS LABOR SECT FOR/AID ADMIN COLONIAL REV RACE/REL SOCISM...LING 20. PAGE 5 A0098
BIBLIOG/A NAT/G TEC/DEV POL/PAR

S66
MATTHEWS D.G.,"ETHIOPIAN OUTLINE: A BIBLIOGRAPHIC RESEARCH GUIDE." ETHIOPIA LAW STRUCT ECO/UNDEV AGRI LABOR SECT CHIEF DELIB/GP EX/STRUC ADMIN...LING ORG/CHARTS 20. PAGE 96 A1972
BIBLIOG NAT/G DIPLOM POL/PAR

C66
TARLING N.,"A CONCISE HISTORY OF SOUTHEAST ASIA." BURMA CAMBODIA LAOS S/ASIA THAILAND VIETNAM ECO/UNDEV POL/PAR FORCES ADMIN REV WAR CIVMIL/REL ORD/FREE MARXISM SOCISM 13/20. PAGE 141 A2890
COLONIAL DOMIN INT/TRADE NAT/LISM

B67
DE BLIJ H.J.,SYSTEMATIC POLITICAL GEOGRAPHY. WOR+45 STRUCT INT/ORG NAT/G EDU/PROP ADMIN COLONIAL ROUTINE ORD/FREE PWR...IDEA/COMP T 20. PAGE 34 A0697
GEOG CONCPT METH

B67
DOSSICK J.J.,DOCTORAL RESEARCH ON PUERTO RICO AND PUERTO RICANS. PUERT/RICO USA+45 USA-45 ADMIN 20. PAGE 38 A0776
BIBLIOG CONSTN POL/PAR DIPLOM

B67
RALSTON D.B.,THE ARMY OF THE REPUBLIC; THE PLACE OF THE MILITARY IN THE POLITICAL EVOLUTION OF FRANCE 1871-1914. FRANCE MOD/EUR EX/STRUC LEGIS TOP/EX DIPLOM ADMIN WAR GP/REL ROLE...BIBLIOG 19/20. PAGE 119 A2436
FORCES NAT/G CIVMIL/REL POLICY

B67
SABLE M.H.,A GUIDE TO LATIN AMERICAN STUDIES (2 VOLS). CONSTN FINAN INT/ORG LABOR MUNIC POL/PAR FORCES CAP/ISM FOR/AID ADMIN MARXISM SOCISM OAS. PAGE 126 A2584
BIBLIOG/A L/A+17C DIPLOM NAT/LISM

B67
SCHWARTZ M.A.,PUBLIC OPINION AND CANADIAN IDENTITY. CANADA SOCIETY LOC/G DIPLOM ADMIN LEAD REGION GP/REL SAMP. PAGE 130 A2657 — ATTIT NAT/G NAT/LISM POL/PAR

B67
UNIVERSAL REFERENCE SYSTEM,BIBLIOGRAPHY OF BIBLIOGRAPHIES IN POLITICAL SCIENCE, GOVERNMENT, AND PUBLIC POLICY (VOLUME III). WOR+45 WOR-45 LAW ADMIN...SOC CON/ANAL COMPUT/IR GEN/METH. PAGE 149 A3042 — BIBLIOG/A NAT/G DIPLOM POLICY

B67
US DEPARTMENT OF THE ARMY,CIVILIAN IN PEACE, SOLDIER IN WAR: A BIBLIOGRAPHIC SURVEY OF THE ARMY AND AIR NATIONAL GUARD (PAMPHLET, NOS. 130-2). USA+45 USA-45 LOC/G NAT/G PROVS LEGIS PLAN ADMIN ATTIT ORD/FREE...POLICY 19/20. PAGE 152 A3111 — BIBLIOG/A FORCES ROLE DIPLOM

B67
WATERS M.,THE UNITED NATIONS* INTERNATIONAL ORGANIZATION AND ADMINISTRATION. WOR+45 EX/STRUC FORCES DIPLOM LEAD REGION ARMS/CONT REPRESENT INGP/REL ROLE...METH/COMP ANTHOL 20 UN LEAGUE/NAT. PAGE 162 A3291 — CONSTN INT/ORG ADMIN ADJUD

L67
CAHIERS P.,"LE RECOURS EN CONSTATATION DE MANQUEMENTS DES ETATS MEMBRES DEVANT LA COUR DES COMMUNAUTES EUROPEENNES." LAW PROB/SOLV DIPLOM ADMIN CT/SYS SANCTION ATTIT...POLICY DECISION JURID ECSC EEC. PAGE 23 A0465 — INT/ORG CONSTN ROUTINE ADJUD

S67
HODGE G.,"THE RISE AND DEMISE OF THE UN TECHNICAL ASSISTANCE ADMINISTRATION." RISK TASK INGP/REL CONSEN EFFICIENCY 20 UN. PAGE 66 A1349 — ADMIN TEC/DEV EX/STRUC INT/ORG

S67
LOSMAN D.L.,"FOREIGN AID, SOCIALISM AND THE EMERGING COUNTRIES" WOR+45 ADMIN CONTROL PWR 20. PAGE 91 A1864 — ECO/UNDEV FOR/AID SOC

S67
NEUCHTERLEIN D.E.,"THAILAND* ANOTHER VIETNAM?" THAILAND ECO/UNDEV DIPLOM ADMIN REGION CENTRAL NAT/LISM...POLICY 20. PAGE 108 A2220 — WAR GUERRILLA S/ASIA NAT/G

S67
OLIVIER G.,"ASPECTS JURIDIQUES DE L'ADOPTION DU TRAITE CECA A LA CRISE CHARBONNIERE (SUITE ET FIN)" LAW DIST/IND PLAN DIPLOM RATION PRICE ADMIN COST DEMAND...POLICY CON/ANAL ECSC TREATY. PAGE 112 A2288 — INT/TRADE INT/ORG EXTR/IND CONSTN

S67
TACKABERRY R.B.,"ORGANIZING AND TRAINING PEACE-KEEPING FORCES* THE CANADIAN VIEW." CANADA PLAN DIPLOM CONFER ADJUD ADMIN CIVMIL/REL 20 UN. PAGE 141 A2882 — PEACE FORCES INT/ORG CONSULT

S67
THIEN T.T.,"VIETNAM: A CASE OF SOCIAL ALIENATION." VIETNAM AGRI FORCES FOR/AID ADMIN REPRESENT INGP/REL PWR 19/20. PAGE 143 A2918 — NAT/G ELITES WORKER STRANGE

S67
YOUNG K.T.,"UNITED STATES POLICY AND VIETNAMESE POLITICAL VIABILITY 1954-1967." VIETNAM/S LOC/G MUNIC FOR/AID ORD/FREE...POLICY 20. PAGE 169 A3437 — LEAD ADMIN GP/REL EFFICIENCY

N67
US SUPERINTENDENT OF DOCUMENTS,SPACE: MISSILES, THE MOON, NASA, AND SATELLITES (PRICE LIST 79A). USA+45 COM/IND R+D NAT/G DIPLOM EDU/PROP ADMIN CONTROL HEALTH...POLICY SIMUL NASA CONGRESS. PAGE 157 A3206 — BIBLIOG/A SPACE TEC/DEV PEACE

N67
US SENATE COMM ON FOREIGN REL,ARMS SALES AND FOREIGN POLICY (PAMPHLET). FINAN FOR/AID CONTROL 20. PAGE 156 A3187 — ARMS/CONT ADMIN OP/RES DIPLOM

B82
POOLE W.F.,INDEX TO PERIODICAL LITERATURE. LOC/G NAT/G DIPLOM ADMIN...HUM PHIL/SCI SOC 19. PAGE 117 A2396 — BIBLIOG USA-45 ALL/VALS SOCIETY

ADMINISTRATIVE MANAGEMENT....SEE MGT

ADOLESCENCE....SEE AGE/Y

ADVERT/ADV....ADVERTISING ADVISORY COMMISSION

ADVERTISING....SEE SERV/IND+EDU/PROP; SEE ALSO TV, PRESS

AEA....ATOMIC ENERGY AUTHORITY OF UN; SEE ALSO NUC/PWR

B64
GOWING M.,BRITAIN AND ATOMIC ENERGY 1939-1945. FRANCE UK USA+45 USA-45 NAT/G CREATE...PHIL/SCI 20 AEA. PAGE 54 A1118 — NUC/PWR DIPLOM TEC/DEV

AEC....ATOMIC ENERGY COMMISSION; SEE ALSO NUC/PWR

B63
LILIENTHAL D.E.,CHANGE, HOPE, AND THE BOMB. USA+45 WOR+45 R+D INT/ORG NAT/G DELIB/GP FORCES ACT/RES DETER RIGID/FLEX ORD/FREE...POLICY CONCPT OBS AEC 20. PAGE 89 A1815 — ATTIT MYTH ARMS/CONT NUC/PWR

B65
US CONGRESS JT ATOM ENRGY COMM,ATOMIC ENERGY LEGISLATION THROUGH 89TH CONGRESS, 1ST SESSION. USA+45 LAW INT/ORG DELIB/GP BUDGET DIPLOM 20 AEC CONGRESS CASEBOOK EURATOM IAEA. PAGE 150 A3071 — NUC/PWR FORCES PEACE LEGIS

AFGHANISTN....SEE ALSO ISLAM, ASIA

N19
FRANCK P.G.,AFGHANISTAN BETWEEN EAST AND WEST: THE ECONOMICS OF COMPETITIVE COEXISTENCE (PAMPHLET). AFGHANISTN USA+45 USA-45 USSR INDUS ECO/TAC INT/TRADE CONTROL NEUTRAL ORD/FREE MARXISM...GEOG 20 UN. PAGE 48 A0977 — FOR/AID PLAN DIPLOM ECO/UNDEV

B60
FRANCK P.G.,AFGHANISTAN: BETWEEN EAST AND WEST. AFGHANISTN USA+45 USSR ECO/UNDEV PLAN ADMIN ROUTINE ATTIT PWR...STAT OBS CHARTS TOT/POP COLD/WAR 20. PAGE 48 A0978 — ECO/TAC TREND FOR/AID

B63
ADLER G.J.,BRITISH INDIA'S NORTHERN FRONTIER: 1865-95. AFGHANISTN RUSSIA UK PROVS COLONIAL COERCE PEACE...GEOG CHARTS BIBLIOG 19 TREATY. PAGE 4 A0091 — S/ASIA FORCES DIPLOM POLICY

B66
US DEPARTMENT OF THE ARMY,SOUTH ASIA: A STRATEGIC SURVEY (PAMPHLET NO. 550-3). AFGHANISTN INDIA NEPAL PAKISTAN ECO/UNDEV INT/ORG POL/PAR FORCES FOR/AID INT/TRADE LEAD WAR...POLICY SOC TREND 20. PAGE 152 A3110 — BIBLIOG/A S/ASIA DIPLOM NAT/G

B67
FRASER-TYTLER W.K.,AFGHANISTAN: A STUDY OF POLITICAL DEVELOPMENTS IN CENTRAL AND SOUTHERN ASIA (3RD ED.). AFGHANISTN INDIA KIN FOR/AID PWR ...BIBLIOG. PAGE 48 A0990 — DIPLOM NAT/G CONSTN GEOG

AFL/CIO....AMERICAN FEDERATION OF LABOR, CONGRESS OF INDUSTRIAL ORGANIZATIONS

B59
SHANNON D.A.,THE DECLINE OF AMERICAN COMMUNISM; A HISTORY OF THE COMMUNIST PARTY OF THE UNITED STATES SINCE 1945. USA+45 LAW SOCIETY LABOR NAT/G WORKER DIPLOM EDU/PROP LEAD...POLICY BIBLIOG 20 KHRUSH/N NEGRO AFL/CIO COLD/WAR COM/PARTY. PAGE 131 A2692 — MARXISM POL/PAR ATTIT POPULISM

AFLAK/M....MICHEL AFLAK

AFR....AFRICA

N
INDIAN COUNCIL WORLD AFFAIRS,SELECT ARTICLES ON CURRENT AFFAIRS (BIBLIOGRAPHICAL SERIES: 7). AFR ASIA COM EUR+WWI S/ASIA UK COLONIAL NUC/PWR PEACE ATTIT...INT/LAW SOC 20. PAGE 70 A1437 — BIBLIOG DIPLOM INT/ORG ECO/UNDEV

N
INTERNATIONAL COMN JURISTS,AFRICAN CONFERENCE ON THE RULE OF LAW. AFR INT/ORG LEGIS DIPLOM CONFER COLONIAL ORD/FREE...CONCPT METH/COMP 20. PAGE 71 A1452 — CT/SYS JURID DELIB/GP

N
AFRICANA NEWSLETTER. ECO/UNDEV ACADEM SECT DIPLOM PRESS COLONIAL NAT/LISM 20. PAGE 1 A0001 — BIBLIOG/A AFR NAT/G

N
ANNALS OF THE AMERICAN ACADEMY OF POLITICAL AND SOCIAL SCIENCE. AFR ASIA S/ASIA WOR+45 POL/PAR DIPLOM CRIME REV...SOC BIOG 20. PAGE 1 A0004 — BIBLIOG/A NAT/G CULTURE ATTIT

N
NEUE POLITISCHE LITERATUR. AFR ASIA EUR+WWI GERMANY RUSSIA SOCIETY ECO/DEV ECO/UNDEV PLAN PROB/SOLV LEAD MARXISM...PHIL/SCI CONCPT 20. PAGE 1 A0021 — BIBLIOG DIPLOM COM NAT/G

N
AFRICAN RESEARCH BULLETIN. AFR CULTURE NAT/G COLONIAL...SOC 20. PAGE 2 A0026 — BIBLIOG/A DIPLOM PRESS

N
THE MIDDLE EAST AND NORTH AFRICA. AFR ISLAM CULTURE ECO/UNDEV AGRI NAT/G TEC/DEV FOR/AID INT/TRADE EDU/PROP...CHARTS 20. PAGE 2 A0043 — INDEX INDUS FINAN STAT

N
AFRICAN BIBLIOGRAPHIC CENTER,A CURRENT BIBLIOGRAPHY ON AFRICAN AFFAIRS. LAW CULTURE ECO/UNDEV LABOR SECT DIPLOM FOR/AID COLONIAL NAT/LISM...LING 20. — BIBLIOG/A AFR NAT/G

PAGE 5 A0094 REGION

N

HOOVER INSTITUTION,UNITED STATES AND CANADIAN PUBLICATIONS ON AFRICA. CULTURE ECO/UNDEV AGRI TEC/DEV EDU/PROP COLONIAL RAÇE/REL NAT/LISM ATTIT HEALTH...SOC SOC/WK 20. PAGE 67 A1381 BIBLIOG DIPLOM NAT/G AFR

NCO

CARRINGTON C.E.,THE COMMONWEALTH IN AFRICA (PAMPHLET). UK STRUCT NAT/G COLONIAL REPRESENT GOV/REL RACE/REL NAT/LISM...MAJORIT 20 EEC NEGRO COLD/WAR. PAGE 25 A0500 ECO/UNDEV AFR DIPLOM PLAN

B00

MOCKLER-FERRYMAN A.,BRITISH WEST AFRICA. FRANCE GERMANY NIGER SIER/LEONE UK CULTURE DIPLOM WAR RACE/REL PRODUC PROFIT WEALTH...POLICY PREDICT 19. PAGE 102 A2095 AFR COLONIAL INT/TRADE CAP/ISM

B02

MOREL E.D.,AFFAIRS OF WEST AFRICA. UK FINAN INDUS FAM KIN SECT CHIEF WORKER DIPLOM RACE/REL LITERACY HEALTH...CHARTS 18/20 AFRICA/W NEGRO. PAGE 104 A2129 COLONIAL ADMIN AFR

B03

MOREL E.D.,THE BRITISH CASE IN FRENCH CONGO. CONGO/BRAZ FRANCE UK COERCE MORAL WEALTH...POLICY INT/LAW 20 CONGO/LEOP. PAGE 104 A2130 DIPLOM INT/TRADE COLONIAL AFR

B10

MENDELSSOHN S.,SOUTH AFRICAN BIBLIOGRAPHY (2 VOLS.). SOUTH/AFR EXTR/IND LABOR SECT DIPLOM INT/TRADE COLONIAL RACE/REL DISCRIM...GEOG 20. PAGE 99 A2038 BIBLIOG/A AFR NAT/G NAT/LISM

B14

HARRIS N.D.,INTERVENTION AND COLONIZATION IN AFRICA. BELGIUM FRANCE GERMANY MOD/EUR PORTUGAL UK ECO/UNDEV BAL/PWR DOMIN CONTROL PWR...GEOG 19/20. PAGE 62 A1267 AFR COLONIAL DIPLOM

N19

FANI-KAYODE R.,BLACKISM (PAMPHLET). AFR WOR+45 INT/ORG BAL/PWR CONTROL CENTRAL...DECISION 20 UN. PAGE 44 A0896 RACE/REL ECO/UNDEV REGION DIPLOM

N19

HANNA A.J.,EUROPEAN RULE IN AFRICA (PAMPHLET). BELGIUM FRANCE MOD/EUR UK WOR+45 WOR-45 ECO/UNDEV NAT/G PARTIC SOVEREIGN...NAT/COMP 19/20. PAGE 61 A1252 DIPLOM COLONIAL AFR NAT/LISM

N19

PROVISIONS SECTION OAU,ORGANIZATION OF AFRICAN UNITY: BASIC DOCUMENTS AND RESOLUTIONS (PAMPHLET). AFR CULTURE ECO/UNDEV DIPLOM ECO/TAC EDU/PROP COLONIAL ARMS/CONT NUC/PWR RACE/REL DISCRIM NAT/LISM 20 UN OAU. PAGE 118 A2415 CONSTN EX/STRUC SOVEREIGN INT/ORG

N19

SALKEVER L.R.,SUB-SAHARA AFRICA (PAMPHLET). AFR USSR EXTR/IND NAT/G SCHOOL DIPLOM COLONIAL WEALTH ...GEOG CHARTS 16/20. PAGE 127 A2594 ECO/UNDEV TEC/DEV TASK INT/TRADE

N19

VELYAMINOV G.,AFRICA AND THE COMMON MARKET (PAMPHLET). AFR MARKET VOL/ASSN ECO/TAC COLONIAL ORD/FREE...SOCIALIST 20 THIRD/WRLD. PAGE 158 A3227 INT/ORG INT/TRADE SOVEREIGN ECO/UNDEV

B20

WOOLF L.,EMPIRE AND COMMERCE IN AFRICA. EUR+WWI MOD/EUR FINAN INDUS MARKET INT/ORG PLAN COERCE ATTIT DRIVE PWR WEALTH...CONCPT TIME/SEQ TREND CHARTS 20. PAGE 167 A3394 AFR DOMIN COLONIAL SOVEREIGN

B27

HARRIS N.D.,EUROPE AND AFRICA. BELGIUM FRANCE GERMANY MOD/EUR PORTUGAL UK ECO/UNDEV BAL/PWR PWR ...GEOG 19/20. PAGE 62 A1268 AFR COLONIAL DIPLOM

B30

SMUTS J.C.,AFRICA AND SOME WORLD PROBLEMS. RHODESIA SOUTH/AFR CULTURE ECO/UNDEV INDUS INT/ORG SECT PROB/SOLV REGION GOV/REL DISCRIM ATTIT 19/20 LEAGUE/NAT LIVNGSTN/D NEGRO. PAGE 134 A2748 LEGIS AFR COLONIAL RACE/REL

B31

STUART G.H.,THE INTERNATIONAL CITY OF TANGIER. AFR EUR+WWI MOD/EUR MOROCCO CONSTN PROVS CREATE PLAN LEGIT PEACE ORD/FREE PWR...INT/LAW OBS TIME/SEQ CON/ANAL 20 TANGIER. PAGE 139 A2854 LOC/G INT/ORG DIPLOM SOVEREIGN

B32

CARDINALL AW,A BIBLIOGRAPHY OF THE GOLD COAST. AFR UK NAT/G EX/STRUC ATTIT...POLICY 19/20. PAGE 24 A0479 BIBLIOG ADMIN COLONIAL DIPLOM

B35

KENNEDY W.P.,THE LAW AND CUSTOM OF THE SOUTH AFRICAN CONSTITUTION. AFR SOUTH/AFR KIN LOC/G PROVS DIPLOM ADJUD ADMIN EXEC 20. PAGE 78 A1594 CT/SYS CONSTN JURID PARL/PROC

B36

THWAITE D.,THE SEETHING AFRICAN POT: A STUDY OF BLACK NATIONALISM 1882-1935. ETHIOPIA SECT VOL/ASSN COERCE GUERRILLA MURDER DISCRIM MARXISM...PSY TIME/SEQ 18/20 NEGRO. PAGE 144 A2939 NAT/LISM AFR RACE/REL DIPLOM

B36

VARLEY D.H.,A BIBLIOGRAPHY OF ITALIAN COLONISATION IN AFRICA WITH A SECTION ON ABYSSINIA. AFR ETHIOPIA ITALY LIBYA SOMALIA AGRI FINAN LABOR TEC/DEV DIPLOM INT/TRADE RACE/REL DISCRIM 19/20. PAGE 158 A3222 BIBLIOG COLONIAL ADMIN LAW

B37

DE KIEWIET C.W.,THE IMPERIAL FACTOR IN SOUTH AFRICA. AFR SOUTH/AFR UK WAR...POLICY SOC 19. PAGE 35 A0705 DIPLOM COLONIAL CULTURE

B38

FRANKEL S.H.,CAPITAL INVESTMENT IN AFRICA. AFR EUR+WWI RHODESIA SOUTH/AFR UK FINAN FOR/AID COLONIAL DEMAND UTIL WEALTH...METH/CNCPT CHARTS 20 CONGO/LEOP. PAGE 48 A0983 ECO/UNDEV EXTR/IND DIPLOM PRODUC

B41

PERHAM M.,AFRICANS AND BRITISH RULE. AFR UK ECO/TAC CONTROL GP/REL ATTIT 20. PAGE 115 A2355 DIPLOM COLONIAL ADMIN ECO/UNDEV

B42

CONOVER H.F.,FRENCH COLONIES IN AFRICA: A LIST OF REFERENCES. ALGERIA FRANCE MOROCCO SOMALIA SUDAN CULTURE AGRI LOC/G SECT FORCES DIPLOM INT/TRADE NAT/LISM HEALTH...CON/ANAL 20. PAGE 29 A0594 BIBLIOG AFR ECO/UNDEV COLONIAL

B42

CROWE S.E.,THE BERLIN WEST AFRICA CONFERENCE, 1884-85. GERMANY ELITES MARKET INT/ORG DELIB/GP FORCES PROB/SOLV BAL/PWR CAP/ISM DOMIN COLONIAL ...INT/LAW 19. PAGE 33 A0664 AFR CONFER INT/TRADE DIPLOM

B42

JACKSON M.V.,EUROPEAN POWERS AND SOUTH-EAST AFRICA: A STUDY OF INTERNATIONAL RELATIONS ON SOUTH-EAST COAST OF AFRICA, 1796-1856. AFR FRANCE PORTUGAL SOUTH/AFR UK USA-45 FORCES INT/TRADE PWR...CHARTS BIBLIOG 18/19 TREATY. PAGE 72 A1477 DOMIN POLICY ORD/FREE DIPLOM

B43

LEWIN E.,ROYAL EMPIRE SOCIETY BIBLIOGRAPHIES NO. 9: SUB-SAHARA AFRICA. ECO/UNDEV TEC/DEV DIPLOM ADMIN COLONIAL LEAD 20. PAGE 88 A1800 BIBLIOG AFR NAT/G SOCIETY

B43

MAISEL A.Q.,AFRICA: FACTS AND FORECASTS. WOR+45 INT/ORG CONTROL RACE/REL SOVEREIGN...PREDICT CHARTS 20. PAGE 93 A1910 AFR WAR DIPLOM COLONIAL

B48

LOGAN R.W.,THE AFRICAN MANDATES IN WORLD POLITICS. EUR+WWI GERMANY ISLAM INT/ORG BARGAIN...POLICY INT/LAW 20. PAGE 90 A1853 WAR COLONIAL AFR DIPLOM

B48

MINISTERE FINANCES ET ECO,BULLETIN BIBLIOGRAPHIQUE. AFR EUR+WWI FRANCE CULTURE STRUCT FINAN NAT/G ACT/RES INT/TRADE ADMIN REGION PRODUC STAT. PAGE 102 A2088 BIBLIOG/A ECO/UNDEV TEC/DEV COLONIAL

B50

CHUKWUEMEKA N.,AFRICAN DEPENDENCIES: A CHALLENGE TO WESTERN DEMOCRACY. NIGERIA ECO/DEV INDUS FOR/AID INT/TRADE DOMIN 20. PAGE 26 A0536 DIPLOM ECO/UNDEV COLONIAL AFR

B50

MOCKFORD J.,SOUTH-WEST AFRICA AND THE INTERNATIONAL COURT (PAMPHLET). AFR GERMANY SOUTH/AFR UK ECO/UNDEV DIPLOM CONTROL DISCRIM...DECISION JURID 20 AFRICA/SW. PAGE 102 A2094 COLONIAL SOVEREIGN INT/LAW DOMIN

B51

CARRINGTON C.E.,THE LIQUIDATION OF THE BRITISH EMPIRE. AFR NAT/G INT/TRADE COLONIAL RACE/REL ATTIT ORD/FREE...POLICY NAT/COMP 20 CMN/WLTH. PAGE 25 A0501 SOVEREIGN NAT/LISM DIPLOM GP/REL

B51

US DEPARTMENT OF STATE,POINT FOUR, NEAR EAST AND AFRICA, A SELECTED BIBLIOGRAPHY OF STUDIES ON ECONOMICALLY UNDERDEVELOPED COUNTRIES. AGRI COM/IND FINAN INDUS PLAN INT/TRADE...SOC TREND 20. PAGE 151 A3087 BIBLIOG/A AFR S/ASIA ISLAM

B51

WHITE L.C.,INTERNATIONAL NON-GOVERNMENTAL ORGANIZATIONS. AFR ASIA COM EUR+WWI USA+45 WOR+45 INT/ORG DIPLOM INT/TRADE ALL/VALS...HUM FAO ILO EEC 20. PAGE 164 A3337 VOL/ASSN CONSULT

B53

KALIJARVI T.V.,MODERN WORLD POLITICS (3RD ED.). AFR L/A+17C MOD/EUR S/ASIA UK USSR WOR+45 INT/ORG BAL/PWR WAR PWR 20. PAGE 76 A1552 DIPLOM INT/LAW PEACE

B55

STILLMAN C.W.,AFRICA IN THE MODERN WORLD. AFR USA+45 WOR+45 INT/TRADE COLONIAL PARTIC REGION GOV/REL RACE/REL 20. PAGE 138 A2826 ECO/UNDEV DIPLOM POLICY STRUCT

S55

DE SMITH S.A.,"CONSTITUTIONAL MONARCHY IN BURGANDA." AFR UGANDA UK STRUCT CHIEF REGION INGP/REL ADJUST NAT/LISM SOVEREIGN CONSERVE ...POLICY 19/20 BURGANDA. PAGE 35 A0712 NAT/G DIPLOM CONSTN COLONIAL

C55
APTER D.E.,"THE GOLD COAST IN TRANSITION." AFR CONSTN LOC/G LEGIS DIPLOM COLONIAL CONTROL GOV/REL ...CHARTS BIBLIOG 20 CMN/WLTH. PAGE 8 A0170
ORD/FREE REPRESENT PARL/PROC NAT/G

B56
CONOVER H.F.,A GUIDE TO BIBLIOGRAPHIC TOOLS FOR RESEARCH IN FOREIGN AFFAIRS. AFR ASIA COM EUR+WWI WOR+45 BAL/PWR CON/ANAL. PAGE 30 A0602
BIBLIOG/A R+D DIPLOM INT/ORG

B56
US DEPARTMENT OF STATE,ECONOMIC PROBLEMS OF UNDERDEVELOPED AREAS (PAMPHLET). AFR ASIA ISLAM L/A+17C AGRI FINAN INDUS INT/ORG LABOR INT/TRADE ...PSY SOC 20. PAGE 151 A3090
BIBLIOG ECO/UNDEV TEC/DEV R+D

B57
CONOVER H.F.,NORTH AND NORTHEAST AFRICA; A SELECTED ANNOTATED LIST OF WRITINGS. ALGERIA MOROCCO SUDAN UAR CULTURE INT/ORG PROB/SOLV ADJUD NAT/LISM PWR WEALTH...SOC 20 UN. PAGE 30 A0603
BIBLIOG/A DIPLOM AFR ECO/UNDEV

B57
DEAN V.M.,THE NATURE OF THE NON-WESTERN WORLD. AFR ASIA L/A+17C S/ASIA CULTURE SOCIETY STRATA ECO/DEV DIPLOM ECO/TAC FOR/AID ATTIT DRIVE ALL/VALS ...RELATIV SOC CONCPT TIME/SEQ TREND TOT/POP 20. PAGE 35 A0718
ECO/UNDEV STERTYP NAT/LISM

B57
HODGKIN T.,NATIONALISM IN COLONIAL AFRICA. STRATA STRUCT MUNIC NAT/G POL/PAR LEGIS ATTIT SOVEREIGN ...POLICY TREND BIBLIOG 20. PAGE 66 A1351
AFR COLONIAL NAT/LISM DIPLOM

B57
MURRAY J.N.,THE UNITED NATIONS TRUSTEESHIP SYSTEM. AFR WOR+45 CONSTN CONSULT LEGIS EDU/PROP LEGIT EXEC ROUTINE...INT TIME/SEQ SOMALI UN 20. PAGE 106 A2181
INT/ORG DELIB/GP

B57
RUMEU DE ARMAS A.,ESPANA EEN EL AFRICA ATLANTICA. AFR CHRIST-17C PORTUGAL SPAIN DIPLOM ECO/TAC CONTROL 14/16 AFRICA/W. PAGE 125 A2568
NAT/G COLONIAL CHIEF PWR

B57
US SENATE SPEC COMM FOR AID,COMPILATION OF STUDIES AND SURVEYS. AFR ASIA L/A+17C USA+45 ECO/UNDEV AGRI INT/ORG CONSULT TEC/DEV CONFER TOTALISM...NAT/COMP 20 CONGRESS. PAGE 157 A3197
FOR/AID DIPLOM ORD/FREE DELIB/GP

C57
BEERS H.P.,"THE FRENCH IN NORTH AFRICA: A BIBLIOGRAPHICAL GUIDE TO FRENCH ARCHIVES, REPRODUCTIONS, AND RESEARCH MISSIONS." AFR CANADA FRANCE USA-45 NAT/LISM ATTIT 20. PAGE 12 A0248
BIBLIOG DIPLOM COLONIAL

B58
BERLINER J.S.,SOVIET ECONOMIC AID: THE AID AND TRADE POLICY IN UNDERDEVELOPED COUNTRIES. AFR COM ISLAM L/A+17C S/ASIA USSR ECO/DEV DIST/IND FINAN MARKET INT/ORG ACT/RES PLAN BAL/PWR WEAPON PWR WEALTH...CHARTS 20. PAGE 14 A0277
ECO/UNDEV ECO/TAC FOR/AID

B58
GROBLER J.H.,AFRICA'S DESTINY. AFR EUR+WWI SOUTH/AFR UK USA+45 ELITES KIN LOC/G DIPLOM DISCRIM ATTIT CONSERVE MARXISM 20 ROOSEVLT/T NEGRO. PAGE 57 A1168
POLICY ORD/FREE COLONIAL CONSTN

B58
MASON H.L.,TOYNBEE'S APPROACH TO WORLD POLITICS. AFR USA+45 USSR LAW WAR NAT/LISM ALL/IDEOS...HUM BIBLIOG. PAGE 95 A1957
DIPLOM CONCPT PHIL/SCI SECT

N58
INVESTMENT FUND ECO SOC DEV,FRENCH AFRICA: A DECADE OF PROGRESS 1948-1958 (PAMPHLET). AFR FRANCE EXTR/IND INDUS EDU/PROP HEALTH 20. PAGE 71 A1465
FOR/AID DIPLOM ECO/UNDEV AGRI

B59
ALWAN M.,ALGERIA BEFORE THE UNITED NATIONS. AFR ASIA FRANCE ISLAM S/ASIA CONSTN SOCIETY STRUCT INT/ORG NAT/G ECO/TAC ADMIN COLONIAL NAT/LISM ATTIT PWR...DECISION TREND 420 UN. PAGE 7 A0133
PLAN RIGID/FLEX DIPLOM ALGERIA

B59
EGYPTIAN SOCIETY OF INT LAW,THE MONROVIA CONFERENCE (PAMPHLET). AFR ALGERIA FRANCE UAR CONFER REGION NUC/PWR WAR DISCRIM 20 SAHARA AFR/STATES. PAGE 40 A0826
COLONIAL SOVEREIGN RACE/REL DIPLOM

B59
JOSEPH F.M.,AS OTHERS SEE US: THE UNITED STATES THROUGH FOREIGN EYES. AFR EUR+WWI ISLAM L/A+17C S/ASIA USA+45 CULTURE SOCIETY ECO/DEV ECO/UNDEV INT/ORG NAT/G DIPLOM ECO/TAC REV ATTIT RIGID/FLEX HEALTH ORD/FREE WEALTH 20. PAGE 75 A1537
RESPECT DOMIN NAT/LISM SOVEREIGN

B59
MAC MILLAN W.M.,THE ROAD TO SELF-RULE. SOUTH/AFR UK CULTURE SOCIETY AGRI LABOR NAT/G INT/TRADE CONTROL GP/REL...SOC 19/20. PAGE 92 A1884
AFR COLONIAL SOVEREIGN POLICY

S59
KOHN L.Y.,"ISRAEL AND NEW NATION STATES OF ASIA AND AFRICA." AFR ASIA FUT S/ASIA VOL/ASSN TEC/DEV NAT/LISM RIGID/FLEX SKILL WEALTH...RELATIV OBS TREND CON/ANAL 20. PAGE 81 A1663
ECO/UNDEV ECO/TAC FOR/AID ISRAEL

B60
ASPREMONT-LYNDEN H.,RAPPORT SUR L'ADMINISTRATION BELGE DU RUANDA-URUNDI PENDANT L'ANNEE 1959. BELGIUM RWANDA AGRI INDUS DIPLOM ECO/TAC INT/TRADE DOMIN ADMIN RACE/REL...GEOG CENSUS 20 UN. PAGE 9 A0192
AFR COLONIAL ECO/UNDEV INT/ORG

B60
CENTRAL ASIAN RESEARCH CENTRE,RUSSIA LOOKS AT AFRICA (PAMPHLET). AFR USSR COLONIAL RACE/REL...HUM 19/20 STALIN/J. PAGE 25 A0511
BIBLIOG MARXISM TREND DIPLOM

B60
DUMON F.,LA COMMUNAUTE FRANCO-AFRO-MALGACHE: SES ORIGINES, SES INSTITUTIONS, SON EVOLUTION. FRANCE MADAGASCAR POL/PAR DIPLOM ADMIN ATTIT...TREND T 20. PAGE 39 A0798
JURID INT/ORG AFR CONSTN

B60
EMERSON R.,FROM EMPIRE TO NATION: THE RISE TO SELF-ASSERTION OF ASIAN AND AFRICAN PEOPLES. S/ASIA CULTURE NAT/G SECT DIPLOM ATTIT SOVEREIGN MARXISM ...POLICY BIBLIOG 19/20. PAGE 41 A0847
NAT/LISM COLONIAL AFR ASIA

B60
HEYSE T.,PROBLEMS FONCIERS ET REGIME DES TERRES (ASPECTS ECONOMIQUES, JURIDIQUES ET SOCIAUX). AFR CONGO/BRAZ INT/ORG DIPLOM SOVEREIGN...GEOG TREATY 20. PAGE 64 A1325
BIBLIOG AGRI ECO/UNDEV LEGIS

B60
MENEZES A.J.,O BRASIL E O MUNDO ASIO-AFRICANO (REV. ED.). AFR ASIA BRAZIL WOR+45 INT/TRADE ORD/FREE PWR SOVEREIGN...POLICY 20. PAGE 99 A2040
DIPLOM BAL/PWR LEAD ECO/UNDEV

B60
PHILLIPS J.F.V.,KWAME NKRUMAH AND THE FUTURE OF AFRICA. FUT GHANA ISLAM ECO/UNDEV CHIEF DIPLOM COLONIAL RACE/REL NAT/LISM...TREND IDEA/COMP BIBLIOG 20 NKRUMAH/K. PAGE 116 A2376
BIOG LEAD SOVEREIGN AFR

B60
PLAMENATZ J.,ON ALIEN RULE AND SELF-GOVERNMENT. AFR FUT S/ASIA WOR+45 CULTURE SOCIETY ECO/UNDEV INT/ORG DOMIN EDU/PROP ATTIT RIGID/FLEX ALL/VALS...POLICY CONCPT OBS TREND CON/ANAL GEN/LAWS TOT/POP VAL/FREE. PAGE 116 A2386
NAT/G CONSTN NAT/LISM SOVEREIGN

B60
RITNER P.,THE DEATH OF AFRICA. USA+45 ECO/UNDEV DIPLOM ECO/TAC REGION RACE/REL NAT/LISM ORD/FREE ...POLICY 20 NEGRO. PAGE 121 A2485
AFR SOCIETY FUT TASK

B60
THEOBOLD R.,THE NEW NATIONS OF WEST AFRICA. GHANA NIGERIA CULTURE INT/ORG ECO/TAC FOR/AID COLONIAL RACE/REL POPULISM...ANTHOL BIBLIOG 20 UN. PAGE 143 A2916
AFR SOVEREIGN ECO/UNDEV DIPLOM

S60
COHEN A.,"THE NEW AFRICA AND THE UN." FUT ECO/UNDEV NAT/G ECO/TAC INT/TRADE CHOOSE ATTIT ORD/FREE PWR ...POLICY METH/CNCPT OBS TREND CON/ANAL GEN/LAWS TOT/POP VAL/FREE UN 20. PAGE 27 A0558
AFR INT/ORG BAL/PWR FOR/AID

S60
FRANKEL S.H.,"ECONOMIC ASPECTS OF POLITICAL INDEPENDENCE IN AFRICA." AFR FUT SOCIETY ECO/UNDEV COM/IND FINAN LEGIS PLAN TEC/DEV CAP/ISM ECO/TAC INT/TRADE ADMIN ATTIT DRIVE RIGID/FLEX PWR WEALTH ...MGT NEW/IDEA MATH TIME/SEQ VAL/FREE 20. PAGE 48 A0984
NAT/G FOR/AID

S60
GARNICK D.H.,"ON THE ECONOMIC FEASIBILITY OF A MIDDLE EASTERN COMMON MARKET." AFR ISLAM CULTURE INDUS NAT/G PLAN TEC/DEV ECO/TAC ADMIN ATTIT DRIVE RIGID/FLEX...PLURIST STAT TREND GEN/LAWS 20. PAGE 51 A1051
MARKET INT/TRADE

S60
OWEN C.F.,"US AND SOVIET RELATIONS WITH UNDERDEVELOPED COUNTRIES: LATIN AMERICA-A CASE STUDY." AFR COM L/A+17C USA+45 USSR EXTR/IND MARKET TEC/DEV DIPLOM ECO/TAC NAT/LISM ORD/FREE PWR ...TREND WORK 20. PAGE 112 A2303
ECO/UNDEV DRIVE INT/TRADE

S60
RIVKIN A.,"AFRICAN ECONOMIC DEVELOPMENT: ADVANCED TECHNOLOGY AND THE STAGES OF GROWTH." CULTURE ECO/UNDEV AGRI COM/IND EXTR/IND PLAN ECO/TAC ATTIT DRIVE RIGID/FLEX SKILL WEALTH...MGT SOC GEN/LAWS WORK TOT/POP 20. PAGE 121 A2487
AFR TEC/DEV FOR/AID

B61
ANSPRENGER F.,POLITIK IM SCHWARZEN AFRIKA. FRANCE NAT/G DIPLOM REGION REV NAT/LISM...CHARTS BIBLIOG 19/20. PAGE 8 A0164
AFR COLONIAL SOVEREIGN

B61
BONNEFOUS M.,EUROPE ET TIERS MONDE. EUR+WWI SOCIETY INT/ORG NAT/G VOL/ASSN ACT/RES TEC/DEV CAP/ISM ECO/TAC ATTIT ORD/FREE SOVEREIGN...POLICY CONCPT TREND 20. PAGE 16 A0334
AFR ECO/UNDEV FOR/AID INT/TRADE

B61
CAMERON J.,THE AFRICAN REVOLUTION. AFR UK ECO/UNDEV POL/PAR REGION RACE/REL DISCRIM PWR CONSERVE ...CONCPT SOC/INTEG 20 NEGRO. PAGE 23 A0472
REV COLONIAL ORD/FREE

DIPLOM

B61
CARNELL F.,THE POLITICS OF THE NEW STATES: A SELECT ANNOTATED BIBLIOGRAPHY WITH SPECIAL REFERENCE TO THE COMMONWEALTH. CONSTN ELITES LABOR NAT/G POL/PAR EX/STRUC DIPLOM ADJUD ADMIN...GOV/COMP 20 COMMONWLTH. PAGE 24 A0496 BIBLIOG/A AFR ASIA COLONIAL

B61
CHIDZERO B.T.G.,TANGANYIKA AND INTERNATIONAL TRUSTEESHIP. AFR WOR+45 WOR-45 ECO/DEV INT/ORG ECO/TAC DOMIN COLONIAL...RECORD CHARTS 20 TANGANYIKA CMN/WLTH. PAGE 26 A0528 ECO/UNDEV CONSTN

B61
CONOVER H.F.,SERIALS FOR AFRICAN STUDIES. ECO/UNDEV DIPLOM LEAD NAT/LISM ATTIT...SOC 20. PAGE 30 A0604 BIBLIOG AFR NAT/G

B61
DETHINE P.,BIBLIOGRAPHIE DES ASPECTS ECONOMIQUES ET SOCIAUX DE L'INDUSTRIALISATION EN AFRIQUE. AFR FINAN LABOR FOR/AID...SOC 20. PAGE 36 A0734 BIBLIOG/A ECO/UNDEV INDUS TEC/DEV

B61
DIA M.,THE AFRICAN NATIONS AND WORLD SOLIDARITY. ISLAM CULTURE ELITES ECO/DEV ECO/UNDEV INT/ORG NAT/G PLAN ECO/TAC INT/TRADE EDU/PROP NAT/LISM ATTIT DRIVE ORD/FREE WEALTH...SOCIALIST CONCPT CON/ANAL GEN/LAWS TOT/POP 20. PAGE 37 A0753 AFR REGION SOCISM

B61
HOLDSWORTH M.,SOVIET AFRICAN STUDIES 1918-1959. USSR ACADEM NAT/G DIPLOM REGION KNOWL 20. PAGE 66 A1366 BIBLIOG/A AFR HABITAT NAT/COMP

B61
INTERNATIONAL BANK RECONST DEV,THE WORLD BANK IN AFRICA: SUMMARY OF ACTIVITIES. AGRI COM/IND DIST/IND EXTR/IND INDUS TAX COST...CHARTS 20. PAGE 71 A1450 FINAN ECO/UNDEV INT/ORG AFR

B61
LANDSKROY W.A.,OFFICIAL SERIAL PUBLICATIONS RELATING TO ECONOMIC DEVELOPMENT IN AFRICA SOUTH OF THE SAHARA (PAMPHLET). AFR UK R+D ACT/RES 20 UN. PAGE 84 A1720 BIBLIOG ECO/UNDEV COLONIAL INT/ORG

B61
LEHMAN R.L.,AFRICA SOUTH OF THE SAHARA (PAMPHLET). DIPLOM COLONIAL NAT/LISM. PAGE 86 A1768 BIBLIOG/A AFR CULTURE NAT/G

B61
MACLURE M.,AFRICA: THE POLITICAL PATTERN. SOUTH/AFR CULTURE LEGIS DIPLOM COLONIAL RACE/REL 20. PAGE 93 A1898 AFR POLICY NAT/G

B61
OAKES J.B.,THE EDGE OF FREEDOM. EUR+WWI USA+45 USSR ECO/UNDEV BAL/PWR DIPLOM DOMIN COLONIAL PWR MARXISM POPULISM...IDEA/COMP 20 COLD/WAR. PAGE 111 A2271 AFR ORD/FREE SOVEREIGN NEUTRAL

B61
PANIKKAR K.M.,REVOLUTION IN AFRICA. AFR GUINEA ECO/UNDEV POL/PAR DIPLOM COLONIAL EXEC LEAD SOVEREIGN...CHARTS 20. PAGE 114 A2332 NAT/LISM NAT/G CHIEF

B61
ROBINS D.B.,EVOLVING UNITED STATES POLICIES TOWARD THE EMERGING NATIONS OF ASIA AND AFRICA (PAMPHLET). ISLAM ECO/UNDEV INT/ORG CONSULT CREATE PLAN TEC/DEV FOR/AID CONFER ALL/VALS 20 KENNEDY/JF EISNHWR/DD UN AID. PAGE 122 A2501 AFR S/ASIA DIPLOM BIBLIOG

B61
SCHNAPPER B.,LA POLITIQUE ET LE COMMERCE FRANCAIS DANS LE GOLFE DE GUINEE DE 1838 A 1871. FRANCE GUINEA UK SEA EXTR/IND NAT/G DELIB/GP LEGIS ADMIN ORD/FREE...POLICY GEOG CENSUS CHARTS BIBLIOG 19. PAGE 129 A2636 COLONIAL INT/TRADE DOMIN AFR

B61
WALLERSTEIN I.M.,AFRICA; THE POLITICS OF INDEPENDENCE. AFR SOCIETY STRUCT LEAD PARL/PROC PARTIC GP/REL...POLICY 20. PAGE 160 A3269 ECO/UNDEV DIPLOM COLONIAL ORD/FREE

S61
MILLER E.,"LEGAL ASPECTS OF UN ACTION IN THE CONGO." AFR CULTURE ADMIN PEACE DRIVE RIGID/FLEX ORD/FREE...WELF/ST JURID OBS UN CONGO 20. PAGE 101 A2076 INT/ORG LEGIT

S61
OCHENG D.,"ECONOMIC FORCES AND UGANDA'S FOREIGN POLICY." AFR UGANDA INT/TRADE TARIFFS INCOME SOVEREIGN WEALTH 20 EACM EEC TANGANYIKA. PAGE 111 A2274 ECO/TAC DIPLOM ECO/UNDEV INT/ORG

S61
PADELFORD N.J.,"POLITICS AND THE FUTURE OF ECOSOC." AFR S/ASIA ECO/UNDEV INDUS NAT/G DELIB/GP ACT/RES ORD/FREE WEALTH...CONCPT CHARTS UN 20 ECOSOC. PAGE 113 A2310 INT/ORG TEC/DEV

B62
BAULIN J.,THE ARAB ROLE IN AFRICA. AFR ALGERIA FUT ISLAM MOROCCO UAR COLONIAL NEUTRAL REV...SOC 20 TUNIS BOURGUIBA. PAGE 12 A0235 NAT/LISM DIPLOM NAT/G

SECT

B62
BLANSHARD P.,FREEDOM AND CATHOLIC POWER IN SPAIN AND PORTUGAL: AN AMERICAN INTERPRETATION. AFR PORTUGAL SPAIN USA+45 LAW LABOR DIPLOM EDU/PROP DISCRIM ISOLAT TOTALISM 20 CHURCH/STA. PAGE 15 A0309 GP/REL FASCISM CATHISM PWR

B62
CALVOCORESSI P.,WORLD ORDER AND NEW STATES: PROBLEMS OF KEEPING THE PEACE. AFR EUR+WWI S/ASIA ELITES NAT/G ECO/TAC FOR/AID EDU/PROP COERCE ATTIT DRIVE ALL/VALS...GEN/LAWS COLD/WAR 20 UN. PAGE 23 A0471 INT/ORG PEACE

B62
DUROSELLE J.B.,LES NOUVEAUX ETATS DANS LES RELATIONS INTERNATIONALES. AFR CHINA/COM FRANCE MOROCCO S/ASIA USSR ECO/UNDEV INT/ORG PLAN ECO/TAC EDU/PROP ATTIT DRIVE...TREND TOT/POP TUNIS 20. PAGE 39 A0806 NAT/G CONSTN DIPLOM

B62
FAO,FOOD AND AGRICULTURE ORGANIZATION AFRICAN SURVEY. AFR CONGO/BRAZ GHANA STRATA AGRI INT/ORG TEC/DEV FOR/AID INT/TRADE RACE/REL DEMAND EFFICIENCY PRODUC...GEOG 20 UN CONGO/LEOP. PAGE 44 A0898 ECO/TAC WEALTH EXTR/IND ECO/UNDEV

B62
GUENA Y.,HISTORIQUE DE LA COMMUNAUTE. FUT ECO/UNDEV NAT/G PLAN EDU/PROP COLONIAL REGION NAT/LISM ALL/VALS SOVEREIGN...CONCPT OBS CHARTS 20. PAGE 58 A1186 AFR VOL/ASSN FOR/AID FRANCE

B62
HATCH J.,AFRICA TODAY-AND TOMORROW: AN OUTLINE OF BASIC FACTS AND MAJOR PROBLEMS. AFR FUT ISLAM STRATA ECO/UNDEV INT/ORG NAT/G POL/PAR DELIB/GP TOP/EX EDU/PROP LEGIT CHOOSE ATTIT...TIME/SEQ TOT/POP COLD/WAR 20. PAGE 63 A1287 PLAN CONSTN NAT/LISM

B62
HETHERINGTON H.,SOME ASPECTS OF THE BRITISH EXPERIMENT IN DEMOCRACY. UK DIPLOM COLONIAL ...CONCPT 20 CMN/WLTH. PAGE 64 A1322 EDU/PROP AFR POPULISM SOC/EXP

B62
INGHAM K.,A HISTORY OF EAST AFRICA. NAT/G DIPLOM ADMIN WAR NAT/LISM...SOC BIOG BIBLIOG. PAGE 70 A1439 AFR CONSTN COLONIAL

B62
KING G.,THE UNITED NATIONS IN THE CONGO: A QUEST FOR PEACE. WOR+45 NAT/G CONSULT FORCES LEGIT COERCE WAR ORD/FREE...JURID METH/CNCPT OBS INT HIST/WRIT TIME/SEQ CONGO UN 20 COLD/WAR. PAGE 79 A1624 AFR INT/ORG

B62
LESSING P.,AFRICA'S RED HARVEST. AFR CHINA/COM COM USSR ECO/UNDEV BAL/PWR DIPLOM CONTROL PWR 20 COLD/WAR INTERVENT. PAGE 87 A1789 NAT/LISM MARXISM FOR/AID EDU/PROP

B62
LOWENSTEIN A.K.,BRUTAL MANDATE: A JOURNEY TO SOUTH WEST AFRICA. CULTURE INT/ORG NAT/G DIPLOM...GEOG 20 UN AFRICA/SW. PAGE 91 A1868 AFR POLICY RACE/REL PROB/SOLV

B62
RIVKIN A.,AFRICA AND THE WEST. AFR EUR+WWI FUT ISLAM ISRAEL USA+45 SOCIETY INT/ORG FORCES CREATE PLAN FOR/AID EDU/PROP ATTIT...CONCPT TREND EEC 20 CONGRESS UN. PAGE 121 A2488 ECO/UNDEV ECO/TAC

B62
SNYDER L.L.D.,THE IMPERIALISM READER. AFR ASIA CHINA/COM COM EUR+WWI FUT MOD/EUR USA+45 WOR+45 WOR-45 INT/ORG COLONIAL SOVEREIGN CMN/WLTH OAS 20. PAGE 134 A2751 DOMIN PWR DIPLOM

B62
SPIRO H.J.,POLITICS IN AFRICA: PROSPECTS SOUTH OF THE SAHARA. INT/ORG KIN FORCES LEGIS PROB/SOLV COERCE RACE/REL FEDERAL...TREND CHARTS BIBLIOG 20. PAGE 136 A2790 AFR NAT/LISM DIPLOM

B62
TAYLOR D.,THE BRITISH IN AFRICA. UK CULTURE ECO/UNDEV INDUS DIPLOM INT/TRADE ADMIN WAR RACE/REL ORD/FREE SOVEREIGN...POLICY BIBLIOG 15/20 CMN/WLTH. PAGE 142 A2898 AFR COLONIAL DOMIN

B62
TOURE S.,THE INTERNATIONAL POLICY OF THE DEMOCRATIC PARTY OF GUINEA (VOL. VII). AFR ALGERIA GHANA GUINEA MALI CONSTN VOL/ASSN CHIEF WAR PEACE ATTIT ...WELF/ST 20 DEMOCRAT. PAGE 144 A2953 DIPLOM POLICY POL/PAR NEW/LIB

B62
UNECA LIBRARY,BOOKS ON AFRICA IN THE UNECA LIBRARY. WOR+45 AGRI INT/ORG NAT/G PLAN WRITING REGION...SOC STAT UN. PAGE 147 A3008 BIBLIOG AFR ECO/UNDEV TEC/DEV

B62
UNECA LIBRARY,NEW ACQUISITIONS IN THE UNECA LIBRARY. LAW NAT/G PLAN PROB/SOLV TEC/DEV ADMIN REGION...GEOG SOC 20 UN. PAGE 147 A3009 BIBLIOG AFR ECO/UNDEV INT/ORG

B62
US DEPARTMENT OF THE ARMY,AFRICA: ITS PROBLEMS AND PROSPECTS. CHINA/COM USSR INT/ORG FOR/AID COLONIAL LEAD FEDERAL DRIVE SOVEREIGN MARXISM...GEOG 20 COLD/WAR. PAGE 152 A3104
BIBLIOG/A AFR NAT/LISM DIPLOM

B62
US LIBRARY OF CONGRESS,UNITED STATES AND CANADIAN PUBLICATIONS ON AFRICA IN 1960. CANADA USA+45 CULTURE TEC/DEV DIPLOM FOR/AID RACE/REL...GEOG HUM SOC SOC/WK LING 20. PAGE 155 A3156
BIBLIOG/A AFR

B62
US LIBRARY OF CONGRESS,A LIST OF AMERICAN DOCTORAL DISSERTATIONS ON AFRICA. SOCIETY SECT DIPLOM EDU/PROP ADMIN...GEOG 19/20. PAGE 155 A3157
BIBLIOG AFR ACADEM CULTURE

L62
CORET A.,"LES PROVINCES PORTUGALLES D'OUTREMER ET L'ONU." AFR PORTUGAL S/ASIA WOR+45 LOC/G NAT/G DOMIN...CONCPT TIME/SEQ UN 20 GOA. PAGE 31 A0620
INT/ORG SOVEREIGN COLONIAL

L62
MURACCIOLE L.,"LA LOI FONDAMENTALE DE LA REPUBLIQUE DU CONGO." WOR+45 SOCIETY ECO/UNDEV INT/ORG NAT/G LEGIS PLAN LEGIT ADJUD COLONIAL ROUTINE ATTIT SOVEREIGN 20 CONGO. PAGE 106 A2174
AFR CONSTN

L62
MURACCIOLE L.,"LA BANQUE CENTRALE DES ETATS DE L'AFRIQUE DE L'OUEST." AFR LAW ECO/UNDEV INT/ORG NAT/G CONSULT ECO/TAC ROUTINE...CHARTS 20. PAGE 106 A2175
ISLAM FINAN INT/TRADE

L62
WILCOX F.O.,"THE UN AND THE NON-ALIGNED NATIONS." AFR S/ASIA USA+45 ECO/UNDEV INT/ORG TEC/DEV EDU/PROP RIGID/FLEX ORD/FREE PWR...POLICY HUM CONCPT STAT OBS TIME/SEQ STERTYP GEN/METH UN 20. PAGE 164 A3345
ATTIT TREND

S62
CORET A.,"LA DECLARATION DE L'ASSEMBLEE GENERAL DE L'ONU SUR L'OCTROI DE L'INDEPENDENCE AUX PAYS ET AUX PEUPLES." AFR ASIA ISLAM NIGERIA S/ASIA USSR WOR+45 ECO/UNDEV NAT/G DELIB/GP COLONIAL ALL/VALS ...CONCPT TIME/SEQ TREND UN TOT/POP 20 MEXIC/AMER. PAGE 31 A0621
INT/ORG STRUCT SOVEREIGN

S62
GAREAU F.H.,"BLOC POLITICS IN WEST AFRICA." AFR CONGO/BRAZ GHANA GUINEA MALI WOR+45 STRUCT ECO/UNDEV INT/ORG VOL/ASSN CHOOSE ORD/FREE PWR UN 20. PAGE 51 A1048
NAT/G NAT/LISM

S62
JACOBSON H.K.,"THE UNITED NATIONS AND COLONIALISM: A TENTATIVE APPRAISAL." AFR FUT S/ASIA USA+45 USSR WOR+45 NAT/G DELIB/GP PLAN DIPLOM ECO/TAC DOMIN ADMIN ROUTINE COERCE ATTIT RIGID/FLEX ORD/FREE PWR ...OBS STERTYP UN 20. PAGE 73 A1486
INT/ORG CONCPT COLONIAL

S62
KOLARZ W.,"THE IMPACT OF COMMUNISM ON WEST AFRICA." AFR FUT SOCIETY INT/ORG NAT/G CREATE PLAN DOMIN EDU/PROP COERCE NAT/LISM ATTIT RIGID/FLEX SOCISM ...POLICY CONCPT TREND MARX/KARL 20. PAGE 81 A1666
COM POL/PAR COLONIAL

S62
MANGIN G.,"LES ACCORDS DE COOPERATION EN MATIERE DE JUSTICE ENTRE LA FRANCE ET LES ETATS AFRICAINS ET MALGACHE." AFR ISLAM WOR+45 STRUCT ECO/UNDEV NAT/G DELIB/GP PERCEPT ALL/VALS...JURID MGT TIME/SEQ 20. PAGE 94 A1919
INT/ORG LAW FRANCE

S62
PIQUEMAL M.,"LES PROBLEMES DES UNIONS D'ETATS EN AFRIQUE NOIRE." FRANCE SOCIETY INT/ORG NAT/G DELIB/GP PLAN LEGIT ADMIN COLONIAL ROUTINE ATTIT ORD/FREE PWR...GEOG METH/CNCPT 20. PAGE 116 A2382
AFR ECO/UNDEV REGION

S62
PIQUEMAL M.,"LA COOPERATION FINANCIERE ENTRE LA FRANCE ET LES ETATS AFRICAINS ET MALGACHE." ISLAM INT/ORG TOP/EX ECO/TAC...JURID CHARTS 20. PAGE 116 A2383
AFR FINAN FRANCE MADAGASCAR

S62
RAZAFIMBAHINY J.,"L'ORGANISATION AFRICAINE ET MALGACHE DE COOPERATION ECONOMIQUE." AFR ISLAM MADAGASCAR NAT/G ACT/RES ECO/TAC ALL/VALS ...TIME/SEQ 20. PAGE 120 A2454
INT/ORG ECO/UNDEV

S62
RUBINSTEIN A.Z.,"RUSSIA AND THE UNCOMMITTED NATIONS." AFR INDIA ISLAM L/A+17C LAOS S/ASIA ELITES ECO/UNDEV INT/ORG KIN CREATE PLAN TEC/DEV NAT/LISM RIGID/FLEX PWR WEALTH...METH/CNCPT TIME/SEQ GEN/LAWS WORK. PAGE 125 A2562
ECO/TAC TREND COLONIAL USSR

S62
SPENSER J.H.,"AFRICA AT THE UNITED NATIONS: SOME OBSERVATIONS." FUT ECO/UNDEV NAT/G CONSULT DELIB/GP PLAN BAL/PWR ECO/TAC EDU/PROP ATTIT RIGID/FLEX HEALTH ORD/FREE PWR WEALTH...POLICY CONCPT OBS TREND STERTYP GEN/METH UN VAL/FREE. PAGE 136 A2786
AFR INT/ORG REGION

S62
VASAK K.,"DE LA CONVENTION EUROPEENNE A LA CONVENTION AFRICAINE DES DROITS DE L'HOMME." AFR ISLAM WOR+45 LAW CONSTN ECO/UNDEV INT/ORG PERCEPT ALL/VALS 20. PAGE 158 A3223
DELIB/GP CONCPT COLONIAL

B63
AFRICAN BIBLIOGRAPHIC CENTER,THE SCENE IS GUINEA AND THE PERSONAGE IS SEKOU TOURE: A SELECTED CURRENT READING LIST, 1959-1962 (PAMPHLET). GUINEA ECO/UNDEV CHIEF FOR/AID COLONIAL...BIOG 20. PAGE 5 A0095
BIBLIOG AFR POL/PAR COM

B63
AFRICAN BIBLIOGRAPHIC CENTER,THE SCENE IS KENYA AND THE PERSONAGE IS TOM MBOYA: A SELECTED CURRENT READING LIST FROM 1956-1962 (PAMPHLET). ECO/UNDEV LABOR POL/PAR CHIEF COLONIAL CHOOSE NAT/LISM ORD/FREE 20. PAGE 5 A0096
BIBLIOG DIPLOM AFR NAT/G

B63
BURNS A.L.,PEACE-KEEPING BY U.N.FORCES - FROM SUEZ TO THE CONGO. AFR FUT ISLAM ISRAEL USSR WOR+45 NAT/G DELIB/GP BAL/PWR DOMIN LEGIT EXEC COERCE PEACE ATTIT PWR RESPECT SOVEREIGN...CONCPT UN 20. PAGE 22 A0441
INT/ORG FORCES ORD/FREE

B63
DECOTTIGNIES R.,LES NATIONALITES AFRICAINES. AFR NAT/G PROB/SOLV DIPLOM COLONIAL ORD/FREE...CHARTS GOV/COMP 20. PAGE 35 A0721
NAT/LISM JURID LEGIS LAW

B63
ELIAS T.O.,GOVERNMENT AND POLITICS IN AFRICA. CONSTN CULTURE SOCIETY NAT/G POL/PAR DIPLOM REPRESENT PERSON...SOC TREND BIBLIOG 4/20. PAGE 41 A0837
AFR NAT/LISM COLONIAL LAW

B63
ETHIOPIAN MINISTRY INFORMATION,AFRICAN SUMMIT CONFERENCE ADDIS ABABA, ETHIOPIA, 1963. ETHIOPIA DELIB/GP COLONIAL NAT/LISM...POLICY DECISION 20. PAGE 42 A0865
AFR CONFER REGION DIPLOM

B63
GARDINIER D.E.,CAMEROON: UNITED NATIONS CHALLENGE TO FRENCH POLICY. AFR CAMEROON FRANCE NAT/G LEGIS CONTROL SOVEREIGN 20 UN. PAGE 51 A1042
DIPLOM POLICY INT/ORG COLONIAL

B63
GOLDSCHMIDT W.,THE UNITED STATES AND AFRICA. USA+45 CULTURE ECO/TAC INT/TRADE GOV/REL...SOC ANTHOL 20 INTERVENT. PAGE 53 A1091
AFR ECO/UNDEV DIPLOM

B63
HAILEY L.,THE REPUBLIC OF SOUTH AFRICA AND THE HIGH COMMISSION TERRITORIES. AFR SOUTH/AFR UK INT/ORG NAT/G PROVS RACE/REL SOVEREIGN...CHARTS 19/20 COMMONWLTH. PAGE 59 A1219
COLONIAL DIPLOM ATTIT

B63
HARGREAVES J.D.,PRELUDE TO THE PARTITION OF WEST AFRICA. AFR. PAGE 61 A1259
COLONIAL DIPLOM POLICY

B63
HOVET T. JR.,AFRICA IN THE UNITED NATIONS. AFR DELIB/GP EDU/PROP LOBBY CHOOSE ORD/FREE PWR RESPECT SKILL...STAT TIME/SEQ CON/ANAL CHARTS STERTYP VAL/FREE 20 UN. PAGE 68 A1397
INT/ORG USSR

B63
JENNINGS W.I.,DEMOCRACY IN AFRICA. UK CULTURE STRUCT ECO/UNDEV DIPLOM COLONIAL GP/REL ADJUST NAT/LISM ORD/FREE...GOV/COMP 20 THIRD/WRLD. PAGE 74 A1512
PROB/SOLV AFR CONSTN POPULISM

B63
JUDD P.,AFRICAN INDEPENDENCE: THE EXPLODING EMERGENCE OF THE NEW AFRICAN NATIONS. AFR UK LAW CONSTN CULTURE KIN DIPLOM ATTIT...CHARTS BIBLIOG 20 UN DEGAULLE/C NEGRO THIRD/WRLD. PAGE 75 A1542
ORD/FREE POLICY DOMIN LOC/G

B63
MBOYA T.,FREEDOM AND AFTER. AFR LABOR POL/PAR DIPLOM EDU/PROP COERCE SOCISM 20. PAGE 97 A1989
COLONIAL ECO/UNDEV NAT/LISM INT/ORG

B63
MENDES C.,NACIONALISMO E DESENVOLVIMENTO. AFR ASIA L/A+17C STRATA INT/TRADE COLONIAL. PAGE 99 A2039
NAT/LISM ECO/UNDEV DIPLOM REV

B63
PADELFORD N.J.,AFRICA AND WORLD ORDER. AFR COLONIAL SOVEREIGN...ANTHOL BIBLIOG 20 UN UNIFICA COMMONWLTH. PAGE 113 A2312
DIPLOM NAT/G ORD/FREE

B63
QUAISON-SACKEY A.,AFRICA UNBOUND: REFLECTIONS OF AN AFRICAN STATESMAN. ISLAM CULTURE INTELL INT/ORG POL/PAR TOP/EX DOMIN EDU/PROP LEGIT ATTIT PERSON ...CONCPT OBS TIME/SEQ CHARTS STERTYP 20 UN. PAGE 118 A2423
AFR BIOG

B63
RIUKIN A.,THE AFRICAN PRESENCE IN WORLD AFFAIRS. AFR WOR+45 ECO/UNDEV AGRI INT/ORG BAL/PWR ECO/TAC COLONIAL NEUTRAL NAT/LISM PEACE SOVEREIGN 20 UN. PAGE 121 A2486
DIPLOM NAT/G POLICY PWR

B63
RIVKIN A.,THE AFRICAN PRESENCE IN WORLD AFFAIRS. ECO/UNDEV AGRI INT/ORG LOC/G NAT/LISM...OBS PREDICT GOV/COMP 20. PAGE 121 A2489
AFR NAT/G DIPLOM BAL/PWR

B63
US SENATE COMM GOVT OPERATIONS,REPORT OF A STUDY OF US FOREIGN AID IN TEN MIDDLE EASTERN AND AFRICAN COUNTRIES. AFR ISLAM USA+45 FORCES PLAN BUDGET DIPLOM TAX DETER WEALTH...STAT CHARTS 20 CONGRESS AID MID/EAST. PAGE 156 A3174
FOR/AID EFFICIENCY ECO/TAC FINAN

B63
VON HALLER A.,DIE LETZTEN WOLLEN DIE ERSTEN SEIN. AFR S/ASIA INT/TRADE REV ORD/FREE SOVEREIGN 20. PAGE 160 A3251
FOR/AID ECO/UNDEV MARXISM CAP/ISM

L63
MOUSKHELY M.,"LE BLOC COMMUNISTE ET LA COMMUNAUTE ECONOMIQUE EUROPEENNE." AFR COM EUR+WWI FUT USSR WOR+45 INTELL ECO/UNDEV LABOR POL/PAR NUC/PWR RIGID/FLEX...TIME/SEQ ORG/CHARTS EEC TOT/POP 20. PAGE 105 A2158
INT/ORG ECO/DEV

S63
ANGUILE G.,"CIVILISATION DU PLAN DANS L'EUROPE ET L'AFRIQUE DE DEMAIN." AFR EUR+WWI GABON ECO/DEV FINAN MARKET DELIB/GP ECO/TAC WEALTH...TREND 20. PAGE 8 A0163
ECO/UNDEV PLAN INT/TRADE

S63
BALOGH T.,"L'INFLUENCE DES INSTITUTIONS MONETAIRES ET COMMERCIALES SUR LA STRUCTURE ECONOMIQUE AFRICAIN." AFR EUR+WWI FUT USA+45 USA-45 WOR+45 SERV/IND INT/ORG NAT/G TOP/EX ROUTINE...INDEX EEC 20. PAGE 11 A0215
FINAN

S63
BANFIELD J.,"FEDERATION IN EAST-AFRICA." AFR UGANDA ELITES INT/ORG NAT/G VOL/ASSN LEGIS ECO/TAC FEDERAL ATTIT SOVEREIGN TOT/POP 20 TANGANYIKA. PAGE 11 A0216
EX/STRUC PWR REGION

S63
BARTHELEMY G.,"LE NOUVEAU FRANC (CFA) ET LA BANQUE CENTRALE DES ETATS DE L'AFRIQUE DE L'OUEST." FUT STRUCT INT/ORG PLAN ATTIT ALL/VALS 20. PAGE 11 A0230
AFR FINAN

S63
BLOOMFIELD L.P.,"HEADQUARTERS-FIELD RELATIONS: SOME NOTES ON THE BEGINNING AND END OF ONUC." AFR INT/ORG ROUTINE COERCE WAR WEAPON UN CONGO 20. PAGE 16 A0319
FORCES ORD/FREE

S63
GANDOLFI A.,"LES ACCORDS DE COOPERATION EN MATIERE DE POLITIQUE ETRANGERE ENTRE LA FRANCE ET LES NOUVEAUX ETATS AFRICAINS ET." AFR ISLAM MADAGASCAR WOR+45 ECO/DEV INT/ORG NAT/G DELIB/GP ECO/TAC ALL/VALS...CON/ANAL 20. PAGE 51 A1038
VOL/ASSN ECO/UNDEV DIPLOM FRANCE

S63
HARNETTY P.,"CANADA, SOUTH AFRICA AND THE COMMONWEALTH." CANADA SOUTH/AFR LAW INT/ORG VOL/ASSN DELIB/GP LEGIS TOP/EX ECO/TAC LEGIT DRIVE MORAL...CONCPT CMN/WLTH 20. PAGE 62 A1263
AFR ATTIT

S63
LIGOT M.,"LA COOPERATION MILITAIRE DANS LES ACCORDS, PASSES ENTRE LA FRANCE ET LES ETATS AFRICAINS ET MALGACHE D'EXPRESSION." ECO/UNDEV INT/ORG NAT/G VOL/ASSN...CONCPT TIME/SEQ 20. PAGE 89 A1814
AFR FORCES FOR/AID FRANCE

S63
MAZRUI A.A.,"ON THE CONCEPT 'WE ARE ALL AFRICANS'." AFR CULTURE KIN LOC/G NAT/G DOMIN EDU/PROP LEGIT ATTIT PERCEPT PERSON KNOWL ORD/FREE...TIME/SEQ TOT/POP 20. PAGE 97 A1986
PROVS INT/ORG NAT/LISM

S63
NYE J.S. JR.,"EAST AFRICAN ECONOMIC INTEGRATION." AFR UGANDA PROVS DELIB/GP PLAN ECO/TAC INT/TRADE ADMIN ROUTINE ORD/FREE PWR WEALTH...OBS TIME/SEQ VAL/FREE 20. PAGE 110 A2264
ECO/UNDEV INT/ORG

S63
VEROFF J.,"AFRICAN STUDENTS IN THE UNITED STATES." AFR USA+45 CULTURE ACT/RES FOR/AID PEACE ATTIT KNOWL...SOC RECORD DEEP/QU SYS/QU CHARTS STERTYP TOT/POP 20. PAGE 159 A3230
PERCEPT RIGID/FLEX RACE/REL

S63
WEILLER J.,"UNIONS MONETAIRES ET RAPPORTS DE COOPERATION INTERNATIONALE DANS UN MONDE EN TRANSITION: L'EXAMPLE." AFR FUT UNIV WOR+45 SOCIETY ECO/UNDEV MARKET R+D NAT/G FOR/AID PERCEPT RIGID/FLEX...NEW/IDEA 20. PAGE 162 A3303
FINAN INT/ORG

N63
LIBRARY HUNGARIAN ACADEMY SCI,HUNGARIAN PUBLICATIONS ON ASIA AND AFRICA, 1950-1962: A SELECTED BIBLIOGRAPHY (PAMPHLET). AFR ASIA HUNGARY S/ASIA ECO/UNDEV NAT/G EDU/PROP ATTIT 20 UNESCO. PAGE 88 A1807
BIBLIOG REGION DIPLOM WRITING

B64
THE SPECIAL COMMONWEALTH AFRICAN ASSISTANCE PLAN. AFR CANADA INDIA NIGERIA UK FINAN SCHOOL...CHARTS 20 COMMONWLTH. PAGE 3 A0065
ECO/UNDEV TREND FOR/AID ADMIN

B64
AFRO ASIAN SOLIDARITY AGAINST IMPERIALISM. AFR ISLAM S/ASIA ECO/UNDEV NAT/G POL/PAR TOP/EX PRESS ...INT ANTHOL 20 CHOU/ENLAI. PAGE 3 A0066
MARXISM DIPLOM EDU/PROP

CHIEF

B64
BOYD J.P.,NUMBER 7: ALEXANDER HAMILTON'S SECRET ATTEMPTS TO CONTROL AMERICAN FOREIGN POLICY. AFR UK DIPLOM WAR RESPECT WEALTH...POLICY HIST/WRIT 18 HAMILTON/A. PAGE 18 A0364
USA-45 NAT/G TOP/EX PWR

B64
BURKE F.G.,AFRICA'S QUEST FOR ORDER. AFR CULTURE KIN MUNIC NAT/G DIPLOM COLONIAL REV DISCRIM NAT/LISM AGE/Y 20. PAGE 21 A0437
ORD/FREE CONSEN RACE/REL LEAD

B64
CALVO SERER R.,LAS NUEVAS DEMOCRACIAS. AFR ASIA ISLAM USA+45 WOR+45 BAL/PWR DOMIN PARTIC INGP/REL AUTHORIT POPULISM...CONCPT 20 COM/PARTY. PAGE 23 A0469
ORD/FREE MARXISM DIPLOM POLICY

B64
COX R.,PAN-AFRICANISM IN PRACTICE. AFR DIPLOM CONFER RACE/REL ROLE SOVEREIGN...POLICY 20 PANAF/FREE. PAGE 32 A0645
ORD/FREE COLONIAL REGION NAT/LISM

B64
CURRIE D.P.,FEDERALISM AND THE NEW NATIONS OF AFRICA. CANADA USA+45 INT/TRADE TAX GP/REL ...NAT/COMP SOC/INTEG 20. PAGE 33 A0667
FEDERAL AFR ECO/UNDEV INT/LAW

B64
DE SMITH S.A.,THE NEW COMMONWEALTH AND ITS CONSTITUTIONS. AFR CYPRUS PAKISTAN S/ASIA INT/ORG NAT/G LEGIS LEGIT RIGID/FLEX PWR...CONCPT TIME/SEQ CMN/WLTH 20. PAGE 35 A0713
EX/STRUC CONSTN SOVEREIGN

B64
EPSTEIN H.M.,REVOLT IN THE CONGO. AFR CONGO/BRAZ WOR+45 NAT/G FORCES DOMIN WAR CIVMIL/REL INGP/REL MARXISM...RECORD GP/COMP 20 CONGO/LEOP UN. PAGE 42 A0856
REV COLONIAL NAT/LISM DIPLOM

B64
FREE L.A.,THE ATTITUDES, HOPES AND FEARS OF NIGERIANS. AFR NIGERIA ECO/UNDEV AGRI ACADEM PLAN TASK...GEOG CHARTS METH 20. PAGE 49 A0993
NAT/LISM SYS/QU DIPLOM

B64
HAMRELL S.,THE SOVIET BLOC, CHINA, AND AFRICA. AFR CHINA/COM COM USSR ECO/UNDEV EDU/PROP 20. PAGE 61 A1249
MARXISM DIPLOM CONTROL FOR/AID

B64
JANOWITZ M.,THE MILITARY IN THE POLITICAL DEVELOPMENT OF NEW NATIONS: AN ESSAY IN COMPARATIVE ANALYSIS. AFR ASIA ISLAM L/A+17C S/ASIA USA+45 ECO/UNDEV INT/ORG NAT/G POL/PAR DELIB/GP PLAN ECO/TAC DOMIN LEGIT COERCE ATTIT DRIVE RESPECT ...SOC CONCPT CENSUS VAL/FREE. PAGE 73 A1495
FORCES PWR

B64
KITCHEN H.,A HANDBOOK OF AFRICAN AFFAIRS. ECO/UNDEV CREATE DIPLOM COLONIAL RACE/REL...ART/METH GEOG CHARTS 20. PAGE 80 A1646
AFR NAT/G INT/ORG FORCES

B64
KOLARZ W.,COMMUNISM AND COLONIALISM. AFR ASIA USSR DISCRIM ATTIT ORD/FREE SOVEREIGN SOC/INTEG 20. PAGE 81 A1668
EDU/PROP DIPLOM TOTALISM COLONIAL

B64
LITTLE I.M.D.,AID TO AFRICA. AFR UK TEC/DEV DIPLOM ECO/TAC INCOME WEALTH 20. PAGE 90 A1844
FOR/AID ECO/UNDEV ADMIN POLICY

B64
LUTHULI A.,AFRICA'S FREEDOM. KIN LABOR POL/PAR SCHOOL DIPLOM NEUTRAL REGION REV NAT/LISM PWR WEALTH SOCISM SOC/INTEG 20. PAGE 92 A1874
AFR ECO/UNDEV COLONIAL

B64
MATTHEWS D.G.,A CURRENT VIEW OF AFRICANA (PAMPHLET). CULTURE ECO/UNDEV DIPLOM RACE/REL ATTIT 20. PAGE 96 A1968
BIBLIOG/A AFR NAT/G NAT/LISM

B64
NEWBURY C.W.,THE WEST AFRICAN COMMONWEALTH. CONSTN INTELL ECO/UNDEV VOL/ASSN CHIEF DELIB/GP LEGIS INT/TRADE COLONIAL FEDERAL ATTIT 20 COMMONWLTH AFRICA/W. PAGE 108 A2223
INT/ORG SOVEREIGN GOV/REL AFR

B64
NICOL D.,AFRICA - A SUBJECTIVE VIEW. AFR INT/ORG PLAN ADMIN COLONIAL PARL/PROC PARTIC REGION GOV/REL LITERACY ATTIT...BIBLIOG 20 CIVIL/SERV. PAGE 109 A2230
NAT/G LEAD CULTURE ACADEM

B64
PENNOCK J.R.,SELF-GOVERNMENT IN MODERNIZING NATIONS. AFR COM USA+45 ECO/DEV POL/PAR PROB/SOLV DIPLOM ECO/TAC COLONIAL REV POPULISM SOCISM 20. PAGE 114 A2350
ECO/UNDEV POLICY SOVEREIGN NAT/G

B64
QUIGG P.W.,AFRICA: A FOREIGN AFFAIRS READER. AFR FRANCE PORTUGAL UK DIPLOM LEAD PARL/PROC MARXISM ...MAJORIT METH/CNCPT GOV/COMP IDEA/COMP ANTHOL 19/20. PAGE 118 A2426
COLONIAL SOVEREIGN NAT/LISM RACE/REL

B64
RIVKIN A.,AFRICA AND THE EUROPEAN COMMON MARKET (PAMPHLET). AFR MOD/EUR WOR+45 TEC/DEV FOR/AID TARIFFS BAL/PAY...POLICY 20 EEC. PAGE 121 A2490
INT/ORG INT/TRADE ECO/TAC ECO/UNDEV

B64
RUSSELL R.B.,UNITED NATIONS EXPERIENCE WITH MILITARY FORCES: POLITICAL AND LEGAL ASPECTS. AFR KOREA WOR+45 LEGIS PROB/SOLV ADMIN CONTROL EFFICIENCY PEACE...POLICY INT/LAW BIBLIOG UN. PAGE 126 A2576
FORCES DIPLOM SANCTION ORD/FREE

B64
SEGAL R.,SANCTIONS AGAINST SOUTH AFRICA. AFR SOUTH/AFR NAT/G INT/TRADE RACE/REL PEACE PWR ...INT/LAW ANTHOL 20 UN. PAGE 131 A2681
SANCTION DISCRIM ECO/TAC POLICY

B64
SINGER H.W.,INTERNATIONAL DEVELOPMENT: GROWTH AND CHANGE. AFR BRAZIL L/A+17C WOR+45 CULTURE AGRI INDUS NAT/G ACT/RES ECO/TAC EDU/PROP WEALTH...GEOG CONCPT METH/CNCPT STAT HYPO/EXP WORK TOT/POP 20. PAGE 133 A2723
FINAN ECO/UNDEV FOR/AID INT/TRADE

B64
UNITED ARAB REPUBLIC,TOWARDS THE SECOND AFRICAN SUMMIT ASSEMBLY. AFR UAR CONSTN VOL/ASSN CHIEF PLAN DIPLOM AGREE 20 NASSER/G AFR/STATES. PAGE 148 A3030
CONFER DELIB/GP INT/ORG POLICY

B64
US AGENCY INTERNATIONAL DEV,REPORT TO CONGRESS ON THE FOREIGN ASSISTANCE PROGRAM. AFR ASIA L/A+17C USA+45 INT/ORG VOL/ASSN FORCES CAP/ISM ADMIN WEAPON. PAGE 149 A3052
FOR/AID ECO/UNDEV TEC/DEV BUDGET

B64
US HOUSE COMM FOREIGN AFFAIRS,HEARINGS ON H.R. 10502 TO AMEND FURTHER THE FOREIGN ASSISTANCE ACT OF 1961. AFR ASIA L/A+17C INT/ORG CONSULT DELIB/GP TEC/DEV ECO/TAC EDU/PROP CONFER 20 UN NATO CONGRESS AID. PAGE 153 A3130
FOR/AID DIPLOM ORD/FREE ECO/UNDEV

B64
WALLBANK T.W.,DOCUMENTS ON MODERN AFRICA. NAT/G COLONIAL GP/REL ATTIT PWR...BIBLIOG 19/20. PAGE 160 A3267
AFR NAT/LISM ECO/UNDEV DIPLOM

B64
WITHERELL J.W.,OFFICIAL PUBLICATIONS OF FRENCH EQUATORIAL AFRICA, FRENCH CAMEROONS, AND TOGO, 1946-1958 (PAMPHLET). CAMEROON CHAD FRANCE GABON TOGO LAW ECO/UNDEV EXTR/IND INT/TRADE...GEOG HEAL 20. PAGE 165 A3370
BIBLIOG/A AFR NAT/G ADMIN

L64
LLOYD W.B.,"PEACE REQUIRES PEACEMAKERS." AFR INDIA S/ASIA SWITZERLND WOR+45 INT/ORG VOL/ASSN PLAN PERSON PWR 20. PAGE 90 A1848
CONSULT PEACE

L64
POUNDS N.J.G.,"THE POLITICS OF PARTITION." AFR ASIA COM EUR+WWI FUT ISLAM S/ASIA USA-45 LAW ECO/DEV ECO/UNDEV AGRI INDUS INT/ORG POL/PAR PROVS SECT FORCES TOP/EX EDU/PROP LEGIT ATTIT MORAL ORD/FREE PWR RESPECT WEALTH. PAGE 117 A2402
NAT/G NAT/LISM

L64
SYMONDS R.,"REFLECTIONS IN LOCALISATION." AFR S/ASIA UK STRATA INT/ORG NAT/G SCHOOL EDU/PROP LEGIT KNOWL ORD/FREE PWR RESPECT CMN/WLTH 20. PAGE 140 A2874
ADMIN MGT COLONIAL

S64
CARNEGIE ENDOWMENT INT. PEACE,"COLONIAL COUNTRIES AND PEOPLES (ISSUES BEFORE THE NINETEENTH GENERAL ASSEMBLY)." AFR ISLAM L/A+17C WOR+45 DELIB/GP LEGIS ECO/TAC EDU/PROP NAT/LISM PEACE ALL/VALS...RECORD UN CMN/WLTH 20. PAGE 24 A0491
INT/ORG ECO/UNDEV COLONIAL

S64
CARNEGIE ENDOWMENT INT. PEACE,"HUMAN RIGHTS (ISSUES BEFORE THE NINETEENTH GENERAL ASSEMBLY)." AFR WOR+45 LAW CONSTN NAT/G EDU/PROP GP/REL DISCRIM PEACE ATTIT MORAL ORD/FREE...INT/LAW PSY CONCPT RECORD UN 20. PAGE 24 A0492
INT/ORG PERSON RACE/REL

S64
DE GAULLE C.,"FRENCH WORLD VIEW." AFR ASIA CHINA/COM EUR+WWI ISLAM ECO/UNDEV INT/ORG NAT/G VOL/ASSN ACT/RES DIPLOM ECO/TAC EDU/PROP ATTIT DRIVE WEALTH 20. PAGE 35 A0702
TOP/EX PWR FOR/AID FRANCE

S64
DRAKE S.T.C.,"DEMOCRACY ON TRIAL IN AFRICA." EUR+WWI FUT USA+45 ECO/UNDEV INT/ORG NAT/G POL/PAR TOP/EX EDU/PROP LEGIT ATTIT ALL/VALS...POLICY TREND GEN/LAWS VAL/FREE 20. PAGE 38 A0785
AFR STERTYP

S64
GARMARNIKOW M.,"INFLUENCE-BUYING IN WEST AFRICA." COM FUT USSR INTELL NAT/G PLAN TEC/DEV ECO/TAC DOMIN EDU/PROP REGION NAT/LISM ATTIT DRIVE ALL/VALS SOVEREIGN...POLICY PSY SOC CONCPT TREND STERTYP WORK COLD/WAR 20. PAGE 51 A1049
AFR ECO/UNDEV FOR/AID SOCISM

S64
HOSKYNS C.,"THE AFRICAN STATES AND THE UNITED NATIONS: 1958-1964." SOUTH/AFR NAT/G VOL/ASSN CONSULT BAL/PWR EDU/PROP MORAL ORD/FREE PWR ...CONCPT TREND UN 20. PAGE 68 A1393
AFR INT/ORG DIPLOM

S64
HOVET T. JR.,"THE ROLE OF AFRICA IN THE UNITED NATIONS." FUT WOR+45 NAT/G DELIB/GP DOMIN EDU/PROP LEGIT ORD/FREE PWR RESPECT SKILL...OBS TIME/SEQ TREND VAL/FREE UN 20. PAGE 68 A1398
AFR INT/ORG DIPLOM

S64
HUTCHINSON E.C.,"AMERICAN AID TO AFRICA." FUT USA+45 MARKET INT/ORG LOC/G NAT/G PUB/INST PLAN ECO/TAC ATTIT RIGID/FLEX...POLICY CONCPT TREND 20. PAGE 69 A1423
AFR ECO/UNDEV FOR/AID

S64
MARTELLI G.,"PORTUGAL AND THE UNITED NATIONS." AFR EUR+WWI ELITES INT/ORG NAT/G PROVS PLAN DIPLOM ECO/TAC DOMIN COLONIAL RIGID/FLEX MORAL ORD/FREE PWR WEALTH...MYTH UN 20. PAGE 95 A1947
ATTIT PORTUGAL

S64
MAZRUI A.A.,"THE UNITED NATIONS AND SOME AFRICAN POLITICAL ATTITUDES." ECO/TAC FOR/AID DOMIN ROUTINE CHOOSE ATTIT DRIVE MORAL PWR RESPECT WEALTH...PSY CONCPT OBS TREND UN VAL/FREE 20. PAGE 97 A1987
AFR INT/ORG SOVEREIGN

S64
PADELFORD N.J.,"THE ORGANIZATION OF AFRICAN UNITY." ECO/UNDEV INT/ORG PLAN BAL/PWR DIPLOM ECO/TAC NAT/LISM ORD/FREE PWR WEALTH...CONCPT TREND STERTYP VAL/FREE COLD/WAR 20. PAGE 113 A2313
AFR VOL/ASSN REGION

S64
ROTHCHILD D.,"EAST AFRICAN FEDERATION." AFR TANZANIA UGANDA INDUS REGION 20. PAGE 124 A2547
INT/ORG DIPLOM ECO/UNDEV ECO/TAC

S64
TOUVAL S.,"THE SOMALI REPUBLIC." AFR ISLAM SOMALIA FAM KIN NAT/G CREATE FOR/AID LEGIT ATTIT ALL/VALS ...RECORD TREND 20. PAGE 144 A2954
ECO/UNDEV RIGID/FLEX

C64
EASTON S.C.,"THE RISE AND FALL OF WESTERN COLONIALISM." AFR ISLAM L/A+17C ECO/UNDEV REV NAT/LISM...CHARTS BIBLIOG 15/20. PAGE 40 A0817
COLONIAL DIPLOM ORD/FREE WAR

B65
BRIDGMAN J.,GERMAN AFRICA: A SELECT ANNOTATED BIBLIOGRAPHY. AFR AGRI DIPLOM REPAR WAR FASCISM 20. PAGE 18 A0374
BIBLIOG/A COLONIAL NAT/G EDU/PROP

B65
COOMBS P.H.,EDUCATION AND FOREIGN AID. AFR USA+45 DIPLOM EFFICIENCY KNOWL ORD/FREE...ANTHOL 20 AID. PAGE 30 A0608
EDU/PROP FOR/AID SCHOOL ECO/UNDEV

B65
DU BOIS W.E.B.,THE WORLD AND AFRICA. USA+45 CAP/ISM DISCRIM STRANGE SOCISM...TIME/SEQ TREND IDEA/COMP 19/20 NEGRO. PAGE 39 A0789
AFR DIPLOM COLONIAL CULTURE

B65
EMERSON R.,THE POLITICAL AWAKENING OF AFRICA. ECO/UNDEV INT/ORG COLONIAL RACE/REL ORD/FREE MARXISM...TREND ANTHOL 20. PAGE 42 A0849
AFR NAT/LISM DIPLOM POL/PAR

B65
INGRAM D.,COMMONWEALTH FOR A COLOUR-BLIND WORLD. AFR INDIA UK STRATA ECO/UNDEV VOL/ASSN CREATE PLAN CONFER COLONIAL ORD/FREE SOC/INTEG 20 COMMONWLTH. PAGE 70 A1441
RACE/REL INT/ORG INGP/REL PROB/SOLV

B65
KIRKWOOD K.,BRITAIN AND AFRICA. AFR UK ECO/UNDEV ECO/TAC WAR NAT/LISM SOVEREIGN 19/20. PAGE 80 A1636
NAT/G DIPLOM POLICY COLONIAL

B65
LASKY V.,THE UGLY RUSSIAN. AFR ASIA USSR ECO/UNDEV NAT/LISM TOTALISM PERSON 20. PAGE 85 A1738
FOR/AID ATTIT DIPLOM

B65
LERCHE C.O.,THE COLD WAR AND AFTER. AFR COM S/ASIA USA+45 USSR NUC/PWR SOVEREIGN MARXISM...TIME/SEQ TREND BIBLIOG 20 COLD/WAR. PAGE 87 A1784
DIPLOM BAL/PWR IDEA/COMP

B65
LEWIS W.A.,POLITICS IN WEST AFRICA. AFR BAL/PWR DIPLOM REPRESENT...POLICY 20. PAGE 88 A1804
POL/PAR ELITES NAT/G ECO/UNDEV

B65
MANSFIELD P.,NASSER'S EGYPT. AFR ISLAM UAR ECO/UNDEV AGRI COLONIAL SOVEREIGN...CHARTS 20 NASSER/G MID/EAST. PAGE 94 A1934
CHIEF ECO/TAC DIPLOM POLICY

B65
MOLNAR T.,AFRICA: A POLITICAL TRAVELOGUE. STRUCT ECO/UNDEV DIPLOM EDU/PROP LEAD RACE/REL MARXISM 20 INTERVENT EUROPE. PAGE 102 A2101
COLONIAL AFR ORD/FREE

B65
MUNGER E.S.,NOTES ON THE FORMATION OF SOUTH AFRICAN FOREIGN POLICY. ACADEM POL/PAR SECT CHIEF DELIB/GP FORCES LEGIS PRESS ATTIT...TREND 20 NEGRO. PAGE 106
AFR DOMIN POLICY

A2170 DIPLOM

B65
NEWBURY C.W.,BRITISH POLICY TOWARDS WEST AFRICA: SELECT DOCUMENTS 1786-1874. AFR UK INT/TRADE DOMIN ADMIN COLONIAL CT/SYS COERCE ORD/FREE...BIBLIOG/A 18/19. PAGE 108 A2224
DIPLOM POLICY NAT/G WRITING

B65
NKRUMAH K.,NEO-COLONIALISM: THE LAST STAGE OF IMPERIALISM. AFR INT/ORG WORKER FOR/AID INT/TRADE EDU/PROP GOV/REL NAT/LISM SOVEREIGN POPULISM SOCISM ...SOCIALIST 20 THIRD/WRLD INTRVN/ECO. PAGE 109 A2243
COLONIAL DIPLOM ECO/UNDEV ECO/TAC

B65
REQUA E.G.,THE DEVELOPING NATIONS: A GUIDE TO INFORMATION SOURCES CONCERNING THEIR ECON, POLIT, TECHNICAL, AND SOCIAL PROBLEMS. AFR ASIA ISLAM L/A+17C INDUS INT/ORG CONSULT PLAN PROB/SOLV...SOC 20 UN. PAGE 120 A2466
BIBLIOG/A ECO/UNDEV FOR/AID TEC/DEV

B65
RODRIGUES J.H.,BRAZIL AND AFRICA. AFR BRAZIL PORTUGAL UK USA+45 USA-45 CULTURE ECO/UNDEV INT/ORG INT/TRADE RACE/REL ORD/FREE 15/20 UN MISCEGEN. PAGE 123 A2513
DIPLOM COLONIAL POLICY ATTIT

B65
ROTBERG R.I.,A POLITICAL HISTORY OF TROPICAL AFRICA. EX/STRUC DIPLOM INT/TRADE DOMIN ADMIN RACE/REL NAT/LISM PWR SOVEREIGN...GEOG TIME/SEQ BIBLIOG 1/20. PAGE 124 A2545
AFR CULTURE COLONIAL

B65
SANDERSON G.N.,ENGLAND, EUROPE, AND THE UPPER NILE 1882-1899. ISLAM MOD/EUR UAR UK CHIEF...POLICY CHARTS BIBLIOG/A 19 ARABS NEGRO. PAGE 127 A2600
AFR DIPLOM COLONIAL

B65
SOPER T.,EVOLVING COMMONWEALTH. AFR CANADA INDIA IRELAND UK LAW CONSTN POL/PAR DOMIN CONTROL WAR PWR ...AUD/VIS 18/20 COMMONWLTH OEEC. PAGE 135 A2769
INT/ORG COLONIAL VOL/ASSN

B65
SPENCE J.E.,REPUBLIC UNDER PRESSURE: A STUDY OF SOUTH AFRICAN FOREIGN POLICY. SOUTH/AFR ADMIN COLONIAL GOV/REL RACE/REL DISCRIM NAT/LISM ATTIT ROLE...TREND 20 NEGRO. PAGE 136 A2783
DIPLOM POLICY AFR

B65
STEWART I.G.,AFRICAN PRIMARY PRODUCTS AND INTERNATIONAL TRADE. ECO/UNDEV AGRI FINAN DIPLOM CONTROL 20. PAGE 138 A2825
AFR INT/TRADE INT/ORG

B65
US HOUSE COMM FOREIGN AFFAIRS,HEARINGS ON DRAFT BILL TO AMEND FURTHER THE FOREIGN ASSISTANCE ACT OF 1961. AFR ASIA L/A+17C USA+45 INT/ORG DELIB/GP TEC/DEV ECO/TAC CONFER TOTALISM 20 CONGRESS AID. PAGE 153 A3131
FOR/AID ECO/UNDEV DIPLOM ORD/FREE

B65
US SENATE COMM ON FOREIGN REL,HEARINGS ON THE FOREIGN ASSISTANCE PROGRAM. AFR ASIA L/A+17C USA+45 WOR+45 FORCES TEC/DEV BUDGET CONTROL WEAPON ORD/FREE 20 UN CONGRESS SEC/STATE. PAGE 156 A3183
FOR/AID DIPLOM INT/ORG ECO/UNDEV

B65
VAN DEN BERGHE P.L.,AFRICA: SOCIAL PROBLEMS OF CHANGE AND CONFLICT. ELITES STRATA ECO/UNDEV KIN MUNIC DIPLOM GP/REL RACE/REL NAT/LISM...ANTHOL BIBLIOG 20. PAGE 158 A3210
SOC CULTURE AFR STRUCT

B65
WALKER A.A.,THE RHODESIAS AND NYASALAND: A GUIDE TO OFFICIAL PUBLICATIONS. RHODESIA UK OP/RES PLAN PROB/SOLV DIPLOM...POLICY SOC CON/ANAL 19/20 NYASALAND. PAGE 160 A3263
BIBLIOG NAT/G COLONIAL AFR

B65
WASKOW A.I.,KEEPING THE WORLD DISARMED. AFR GERMANY/E DIPLOM CONTROL WAR 20 UN. PAGE 161 A3289
ARMS/CONT PEACE FORCES PROB/SOLV

L65
MATTHEWS D.G.,"LE TIERS MONDE: A SELECT AND PRELIMINARY BIBLIOGRAPHIC SURVEY OF MANPOWER IN DEVELOPING COUNTRIES, 1960-1964." AFR ISLAM L/A+17C INDUS PLAN PROB/SOLV TEC/DEV INT/TRADE EFFICIENCY WEALTH...STAT 20. PAGE 96 A1971
BIBLIOG/A ECO/UNDEV LABOR WORKER

S65
AFRICAN BIBLIOGRAPHIC CENTER,"US TREATIES AND AGREEMENTS WITH COUNTRIES IN AFRICA, 1957 TO MID-1963." AFR USA+45 AGRI FINAN FORCES TEC/DEV CAP/ISM FOR/AID 20. PAGE 5 A0097
BIBLIOG DIPLOM INT/ORG INT/TRADE

S65
RODNEY W.,"THE ENTENTE STATES OF WEST AFRICA." AFR FRANCE USA+45 POL/PAR SCHOOL FORCES ECO/TAC COLONIAL PWR 20 AFRICA/W. PAGE 123 A2512
DIPLOM POLICY NAT/G ECO/UNDEV

B66
CLENDENON C.,AMERICANS IN AFRICA 1865-1900. AFR USA-45 ECO/UNDEV SECT REV RACE/REL CONSERVE ...TRADIT GEOG BIBLIOG 16/18. PAGE 27 A0549
DIPLOM COLONIAL INT/TRADE

B66
FERKISS V.C.,AFRICA'S SEARCH FOR IDENTITY. AFR USA+45 CULTURE ECO/UNDEV INT/ORG NAT/G COLONIAL MARXISM 20. PAGE 45 A0918
NAT/LISM SOVEREIGN DIPLOM ROLE

B66
HALLET R.,PEOPLE AND PROGRESS IN WEST AFRICA: AN INTRODUCTION TO THE PROBLEMS OF DEVELOPMENT. COM/IND INDUS KIN DIPLOM FOR/AID INT/TRADE HEALTH ...GEOG TREND CHARTS BIBLIOG/A 20 AFRICA/W. PAGE 60 A1233
AFR SOCIETY ECO/UNDEV ECO/TAC

B66
HANSEN G.H.,AFRO-ASIA AND NON-ALIGNMENT. AFR ASIA S/ASIA NEUTRAL MORAL 20. PAGE 61 A1255
DIPLOM CONFER POLICY NAT/LISM

B66
HAYER T.,FRENCH AID. AFR FRANCE AGRI FINAN BUDGET ADMIN WAR PRODUC...CHARTS 18/20 THIRD/WRLD OVRSEA/DEV. PAGE 63 A1295
TEC/DEV COLONIAL FOR/AID ECO/UNDEV

B66
HOFMANN L.,UNITED STATES AND CANADIAN PUBLICATIONS ON AFRICA IN 1964. LAW AGRI INDUS SCHOOL...HUM SOC 20. PAGE 66 A1360
BIBLIOG AFR DIPLOM

B66
KANET R.E.,THE SOVIET UNION AND SUB-SAHARAN AFRICA: COMMUNIST POLICY TOWARD AFRICA, 1917-1965. AFR USSR ECO/UNDEV TEC/DEV EDU/PROP TASK DISCRIM PEACE WEALTH ALL/IDEOS...CHARTS BIBLIOG SOC/INTEG 19/20 NEGRO UN INTERVENT. PAGE 76 A1555
DIPLOM ECO/TAC MARXISM

B66
KAREFA-SMART J.,AFRICA: PROGRESS THROUGH COOPERATION. AFR FINAN TEC/DEV DIPLOM FOR/AID EDU/PROP CONFER REGION GP/REL WEALTH...HEAL SOC/INTEG 20. PAGE 76 A1566
ORD/FREE ECO/UNDEV VOL/ASSN PLAN

B66
KEENLEYSIDE H.L.,INTERNATIONAL AID: A SUMMARY. AFR INDIA S/ASIA UK STRATA EXTR/IND TEC/DEV ADMIN RACE/REL DEMAND NAT/LISM WEALTH...TREND CHINJAP. PAGE 77 A1575
ECO/UNDEV FOR/AID DIPLOM TASK

B66
LAMBERG R.F.,PRAG UND DIE DRITTE WELT. AFR ASIA CZECHOSLVK L/A+17C MARKET TEC/DEV ECO/TAC REV ATTIT 20 TREATY. PAGE 84 A1713
DIPLOM ECO/UNDEV INT/TRADE FOR/AID

B66
LENGYEL E.,AFRICA: PAST, PRESENT, AND FUTURE. FUT SOUTH/AFR COLONIAL RACE/REL SOVEREIGN...GEOG AUD/VIS CHARTS T 20 CONGO/LEOP NEGRO. PAGE 87 A1771
AFR CONSTN ECO/UNDEV

B66
MCKAY V.,AFRICAN DIPLOMACY STUDIES IN THE DETERMINANTS OF FOREIGN POLICY. AFR SOUTH/AFR CULTURE NEUTRAL REGION SOVEREIGN...INT/LAW GOV/COMP ANTHOL 20. PAGE 98 A2013
ECO/UNDEV RACE/REL CIVMIL/REL DIPLOM

B66
MULLER C.F.J.,A SELECT BIBLIOGRAPHY OF SOUTH AFRICAN HISTORY; A GUIDE FOR HISTORICAL RESEARCH. SOUTH/AFR UK LAW CONSTN SOCIETY STRUCT AGRI SECT DIPLOM COLONIAL LEAD RACE/REL...POLICY 17/20 NEGRO. PAGE 106 A2167
BIBLIOG AFR NAT/G

B66
O'CONNER A.M.,AN ECONOMIC GEOGRAPHY OF EAST AFRICA. AFR TANZANIA UGANDA AGRI WORKER INT/TRADE COLONIAL GOV/REL...CHARTS METH/COMP 20 AFRICA/E. PAGE 111 A2269
ECO/UNDEV EXTR/IND GEOG HABITAT

B66
SCHATTEN F.,COMMUNISM IN AFRICA. AFR GHANA GUINEA MALI CULTURE ECO/UNDEV LABOR SECT ECO/TAC EDU/PROP REV 20. PAGE 128 A2619
COLONIAL NAT/LISM MARXISM DIPLOM

B66
SPICER K.,A SAMARITAN STATE? AFR CANADA INDIA PAKISTAN UK USA+45 FINAN INDUS PRODUC...CHARTS 20 NATO. PAGE 136 A2787
DIPLOM FOR/AID ECO/DEV ADMIN

B66
US HOUSE COMM FOREIGN AFFAIRS,HEARINGS ON HR 12449 A BILL TO AMEND FURTHER THE FOREIGN ASSISTANCE ACT OF 1961. AFR ASIA L/A+17C USA+45 VIETNAM INT/ORG TEC/DEV INT/TRADE ATTIT ORD/FREE 20 UN NATO CONGRESS AID. PAGE 154 A3132
FOR/AID ECO/TAC ECO/UNDEV DIPLOM

B66
WELCH C.E.,DREAM OF UNITY; PAN-AFRICANISM AND POLITICAL UNIFICATION IN WEST AFRICA. AFR ECO/UNDEV CONFER COLONIAL LEAD...INT/LAW 20. PAGE 163 A3312
INT/ORG REGION NAT/LISM DIPLOM

B66
WESTWOOD A.F.,FOREIGN AID IN A FOREIGN POLICY FRAMEWORK. AFR ASIA INDIA IRAN L/A+17C USA+45 USSR ECO/UNDEV AGRI FORCES LEGIS PLAN PROB/SOLV ...DECISION 20 COLD/WAR. PAGE 163 A3324
FOR/AID DIPLOM POLICY ECO/TAC

B66
ZABLOCKI C.J.,SINO-SOVIET RIVALRY. AFR ASIA CHINA/COM CUBA EUR+WWI L/A+17C USA+45 USSR WOR+45 POL/PAR FORCES COERCE NUC/PWR...GOV/COMP IDEA/COMP 20 MAO KHRUSH/N. PAGE 169 A3442
DIPLOM MARXISM COM

S66
AFRICAN BIBLIOGRAPHIC CENTER,"A CURRENT VIEW OF AFRICANA: A SELECT AND ANNOTATED BIBLIOGRAPHICAL PUBLISHING GUIDE, 1965-1966." AFR CULTURE INDUS
BIBLIOG/A NAT/G TEC/DEV

LABOR SECT FOR/AID ADMIN COLONIAL REV RACE/REL SOCISM...LING 20. PAGE 5 A0098 — POL/PAR

S66
AFRICAN BIBLIOGRAPHIC CENTER,"A DESCRIPTIVE STUDY OF CURRENT AFRICAN FOREIGN RELATIONS." COM CULTURE INT/ORG SECT RACE/REL DISCRIM ATTIT 20. PAGE 5 A0099 — BIBLIOG DIPLOM AFR

S66
AFRICAN BIBLIOGRAPHIC CENTER,"THE NEW AFRO-ASIAN STATES IN PERSPECTIVE, 1960-1963: A SELECT BIBLIOGRAPHY." AFR ASIA CULTURE SOCIETY INT/ORG LABOR TEC/DEV LITERACY 20 UN. PAGE 5 A0100 — BIBLIOG DIPLOM FOR/AID INT/TRADE

S66
GREEN L.C.,"RHODESIAN OIL: BOOTLEGGERS OR PIRATES?" AFR RHODESIA UK WOR+45 INT/ORG NAT/G DIPLOM LEGIT COLONIAL SOVEREIGN 20 UN OAU. PAGE 55 A1139 — INT/TRADE SANCTION INT/LAW POLICY

S66
GRUNDY K.W.,"RECENT CONTRIBUTIONS TO THE STUDY OF AFRICAN POLITICAL THOUGHT." DIPLOM NAT/LISM ALL/IDEOS...NEW/IDEA GOV/COMP 20. PAGE 58 A1182 — BIBLIOG/A AFR ATTIT IDEA/COMP

S66
MERRITT R.L.,"SELECTED ARTICLES AND DOCUMENTS ON COMPARATIVE GOVERNMENT AND CROSS-NATIONAL RESEARCH." AFR ASIA EUR+WWI L/A+17C MOD/EUR ELITES R+D ACT/RES DIPLOM PWR...SOC CONCPT 18/20. PAGE 100 A2046 — BIBLIOG GOV/COMP NAT/G GOV/REL

S66
O'BRIEN W.V.,"EVENTS AND TRENDS: PATTERNS OF AFRICAN INTERNATIONAL POLITICAL BEHAVIOR." CULTURE SOCIETY NAT/G NAT/LISM SOCISM. PAGE 111 A2267 — BIBLIOG/A AFR TREND DIPLOM

S66
PRATT R.C.,"AFRICAN REACTIONS TO THE RHODESIAN CRISIS." RHODESIA UK LAW DIPLOM...POLICY 20. PAGE 117 A2408 — ATTIT AFR COLONIAL RACE/REL

B67
ATTWOOD W.,THE REDS AND THE BLACKS. AFR POL/PAR CHOOSE GOV/REL RACE/REL NAT/LISM...BIOG 20. PAGE 10 A0195 — DIPLOM PWR MARXISM

B67
MAZRUI A.A.,TOWARDS A PAX AFRICANA. AFR STRUCT ECO/UNDEV NAT/G DIPLOM COLONIAL REGION WAR ATTIT 20. PAGE 97 A1988 — PEACE FORCES PROB/SOLV SOVEREIGN

B67
MEYNAUD J.,TRADE UNIONISM IN AFRICA; A STUDY OF ITS GROWTH AND ORIENTATION (TRANS. BY ANGELA BRENCH). INT/ORG PROB/SOLV COLONIAL PWR...TIME/SEQ TREND ILO. PAGE 100 A2055 — LABOR AFR NAT/LISM ORD/FREE

B67
MILLER J.D.B.,THE POLITICS OF THE THIRD WORLD. AFR S/ASIA 20 UN. PAGE 101 A2078 — INT/ORG DIPLOM COLONIAL SOVEREIGN

B67
NYERERE J.K.,FREEDOM AND UNITY/UHURU NA UMOJA: A SELECTION FROM WRITINGS AND SPEECHES, 1952-65. TANZANIA ELITES ECO/UNDEV INT/ORG NAT/G CREATE DIPLOM COLONIAL REGION RACE/REL...ANTHOL 20. PAGE 110 A2265 — SOVEREIGN AFR TREND ORD/FREE

B67
US AGENCY INTERNATIONAL DEV,PROPOSED FOREIGN AID PROGRAM FOR 1968: SUMMARY PRESENTATION TO THE CONGRESS. AFR S/ASIA USA+45 AGRI TEC/DEV DIPLOM ECO/TAC BAL/PAY COST HEALTH KNOWL SKILL 20 AID CONGRESS. PAGE 149 A3053 — ECO/UNDEV BUDGET FOR/AID STAT

B67
US SUPERINTENDENT OF DOCUMENTS,LIBRARY OF CONGRESS (PRICE LIST 83). AFR ASIA EUR+WWI USA-45 USSR NAT/G DIPLOM CONFER CT/SYS WAR...DECISION PHIL/SCI CLASSIF 19/20 CONGRESS PRESIDENT. PAGE 157 A3205 — BIBLIOG/A USA+45 AUTOMAT LAW

B67
WALLERSTEIN I.,AFRICA* THE POLITICS OF UNITY. AFR INT/ORG REV SOVEREIGN...HIST/WRIT 20. PAGE 160 A3268 — TREND DIPLOM ATTIT

L67
SEGAL A.,"THE INTEGRATION OF DEVELOPING COUNTRIES: SOME THOUGHTS ON EAST AFRICA AND CENTRAL AMERICA." AFR L/A+17C INT/ORG NAT/G VOL/ASSN FOR/AID INT/TRADE EQUILIB NAT/LISM PWR 20. PAGE 131 A2680 — ECO/UNDEV DIPLOM REGION

S67
AFRICAN BIBLIOGRAPHIC CENTER,"THE SWORD AND GOVERNMENT: A PRELIMINARY AND SELECTED BIBLIOGRAPHICAL GUIDE TO AFRICAN MILITARY AFFAIRS; PART I." AFR USA+45 USSR INT/ORG POL/PAR FOR/AID COLONIAL ARMS/CONT PWR 20 UN. PAGE 5 A0101 — BIBLIOG/A FORCES CIVMIL/REL DIPLOM

S67
GRUNDY K.W.,"AFRICA IN THE WORLD ARENA." ECO/UNDEV BAL/PWR FOR/AID NEUTRAL REV NAT/LISM GOV/COMP. PAGE 58 A1183 — AFR DIPLOM INT/ORG COLONIAL

S67
JOHNSON D.H.N.,"THE SOUTH-WEST AFRICA CASES." AFR ETHIOPIA LIBERIA SOUTH/AFR CONSULT JUDGE BAL/PWR 20. PAGE 74 A1521 — INT/LAW DIPLOM INT/ORG ADJUD

S67
MCCORD W.,"ARMIES AND POLITICS; A PROBLEM IN THE THIRD WORLD." AFR ISLAM USA+45 ECO/UNDEV TOTALISM 20. PAGE 98 A2002 — FOR/AID POLICY NAT/G FORCES

S67
MUDGE G.A.,"DOMESTIC POLICIES AND UN ACTIVITIES* THE CASE OF RHODESIA AND THE REPUBLIC OF SOUTH AFRICA." RHODESIA SOUTH/AFR POL/PAR LEAD SANCTION CHOOSE RACE/REL CONSEN DISCRIM ATTIT...INT/LAW UN PARLIAMENT 20. PAGE 105 A2163 — AFR NAT/G POLICY

S67
ROTBERG R.I.,"COLONIALISM AND AFTER: THE POLITICAL LITERATURE OF CENTRAL AFRICA - A BIBLIOGRAPHIC ESSAY." AFR CHIEF EX/STRUC REV INGP/REL RACE/REL SOVEREIGN 20. PAGE 124 A2546 — BIBLIOG/A COLONIAL DIPLOM NAT/G

S67
SAPP B.B.,"TRIBAL CULTURES AND COMMUNISM." AFR USA+45 STRATA DIPLOM FOR/AID REGION CENTRAL ATTIT AUTHORIT RIGID/FLEX KNOWL. PAGE 127 A2604 — KIN MARXISM ECO/UNDEV STRUCT

S67
ZARTMAN I.W.,"AFRICA AS A SUBORDINATE STATE SYSTEM IN INTERNATIONAL RELATIONS." LAW BAL/PWR REGION CENTRAL...GEOG 20. PAGE 169 A3447 — DIPLOM INT/ORG CONSTN AFR

C67
LING D.L.,"TUNISIA: FROM PROTECTORATE TO REPUBLIC." CULTURE NAT/G POL/PAR CHIEF DIPLOM COERCE WAR PWR ...BIBLIOG 19/20 TUNIS. PAGE 89 A1825 — AFR NAT/LISM COLONIAL PROB/SOLV

B68
ANTWERP-INST UNIVERSITAIRE,BIBLIOGRAPHIC COMPENDIUM: DEVELOPING COUNTRIES (ANTWERP-INST UNIVERSITAIRE DES TERRITOIRES D'OUTRE-MER). AFR EUR+WWI SOCIETY AGRI FINAN NEIGH VOL/ASSN PROB/SOLV TEC/DEV FOR/AID INT/TRADE 20. PAGE 8 A0166 — BIBLIOG ECO/UNDEV DIPLOM PLAN

B99
BROOKS S.,BRITAIN AND THE BOERS. AFR SOUTH/AFR UK CULTURE INSPECT LEGIT...INT/LAW 19/20 BOER/WAR. PAGE 19 A0396 — WAR DIPLOM NAT/G

AFR/STATES....ORGANIZATION OF AFRICAN STATES

B59
EGYPTIAN SOCIETY OF INT LAW,THE MONROVIA CONFERENCE (PAMPHLET). AFR ALGERIA FRANCE UAR CONFER REGION NUC/PWR WAR DISCRIM 20 SAHARA AFR/STATES. PAGE 40 A0826 — COLONIAL SOVEREIGN RACE/REL DIPLOM

B64
UNITED ARAB REPUBLIC,TOWARDS THE SECOND AFRICAN SUMMIT ASSEMBLY. AFR UAR CONSTN VOL/ASSN CHIEF PLAN DIPLOM AGREE 20 NASSER/G AFR/STATES. PAGE 148 A3030 — CONFER DELIB/GP INT/ORG POLICY

AFRICA/CEN....CENTRAL AFRICA

AFRICA/E....EAST AFRICA

B65
MURUMBI J.,PROBLEMS OF ECONOMIC DEVELOPMENT IN EAST AFRICA. FINAN INDUS WORKER TEC/DEV INT/TRADE TAX DEMAND EFFICIENCY PRODUC SOCISM...TREND CHARTS 20 AFRICA/E. PAGE 106 A2184 — AGRI ECO/TAC ECO/UNDEV PROC/MFG

B66
O'CONNER A.M.,AN ECONOMIC GEOGRAPHY OF EAST AFRICA. AFR TANZANIA UGANDA AGRI WORKER INT/TRADE COLONIAL GOV/REL...CHARTS METH/COMP 20 AFRICA/E. PAGE 111 A2269 — ECO/UNDEV EXTR/IND GEOG HABITAT

AFRICA/N....NORTH AFRICA

AFRICA/SW....SOUTH WEST AFRICA

B37
UNION OF SOUTH AFRICA,REPORT CONCERNING ADMINISTRATION OF SOUTH WEST AFRICA (6 VOLS.). SOUTH/AFR INDUS PUB/INST FORCES LEGIS BUDGET DIPLOM EDU/PROP ADJUD CT/SYS...GEOG CHARTS 20 AFRICA/SW LEAGUE/NAT. PAGE 148 A3028 — NAT/G ADMIN COLONIAL CONSTN

B50
MOCKFORD J.,SOUTH-WEST AFRICA AND THE INTERNATIONAL COURT (PAMPHLET). AFR GERMANY SOUTH/AFR UK ECO/UNDEV DIPLOM CONTROL DISCRIM...DECISION JURID 20 AFRICA/SW. PAGE 102 A2094 — COLONIAL SOVEREIGN INT/LAW DOMIN

B60
THE AFRICA 1960 COMMITTEE,MANDATE IN TRUST; THE PROBLEM OF SOUTH WEST AFRICA. GERMANY STRUCT REGION SANCTION CHOOSE DISCRIM...INT/LAW 20 AFRICA/SW UN LEAGUE/NAT TRUST/TERR. PAGE 142 A2910 — NAT/G DIPLOM COLONIAL RACE/REL

B62
LOWENSTEIN A.K.,BRUTAL MANDATE: A JOURNEY TO SOUTH WEST AFRICA. CULTURE INT/ORG NAT/G DIPLOM...GEOG 20 — AFR POLICY

UN AFRICA/SW. PAGE 91 A1868 RACE/REL PROB/SOLV

AFRICA/W....WEST AFRICA

B02
MOREL E.D.,AFFAIRS OF WEST AFRICA. UK FINAN INDUS FAM KIN SECT CHIEF WORKER DIPLOM RACE/REL LITERACY HEALTH...CHARTS 18/20 AFRICA/W NEGRO. PAGE 104 A2129 COLONIAL ADMIN AFR

B37
BLAKE J.W.,EUROPEAN BEGINNINGS IN WEST AFRICA 1454-1578. FRANCE GUINEA PORTUGAL UK PWR WEALTH 16/16 AFRICA/W. PAGE 15 A0305 DIPLOM COLONIAL INT/TRADE DOMIN

B57
RUMEU DE ARMAS A.,ESPANA EEN EL AFRICA ATLANTICA. AFR CHRIST-17C PORTUGAL SPAIN DIPLOM ECO/TAC CONTROL 14/16 AFRICA/W. PAGE 125 A2568 NAT/G COLONIAL CHIEF PWR

B64
NEWBURY C.W.,THE WEST AFRICAN COMMONWEALTH. CONSTN INTELL ECO/UNDEV VOL/ASSN CHIEF DELIB/GP LEGIS INT/TRADE COLONIAL FEDERAL ATTIT 20 COMMONWLTH AFRICA/W. PAGE 108 A2223 INT/ORG SOVEREIGN GOV/REL AFR

S65
RODNEY W.,"THE ENTENTE STATES OF WEST AFRICA." AFR FRANCE USA+45 POL/PAR SCHOOL FORCES ECO/TAC COLONIAL PWR 20 AFRICA/W. PAGE 123 A2512 DIPLOM POLICY NAT/G ECO/UNDEV

B66
HALLET R.,PEOPLE AND PROGRESS IN WEST AFRICA: AN INTRODUCTION TO THE PROBLEMS OF DEVELOPMENT. COM/IND INDUS KIN DIPLOM FOR/AID INT/TRADE HEALTH ...GEOG TREND CHARTS BIBLIOG/A 20 AFRICA/W. PAGE 60 A1233 AFR SOCIETY ECO/UNDEV ECO/TAC

AFRICAN BIBLIOGRAPHIC CENTER A0094,A0095,A0096,A0097,A0098 , A0099,A0100,A0101

AFTA....ATLANTIC FREE TRADE AREA

AGE....AGE FACTORS

N19
NATIONAL ACADEMY OF SCIENCES,THE GROWTH OF WORLD POPULATION: ANALYSIS OF THE PROBLEMS AND RECOMMENDATIONS FOR RESEARCH AND TRAINING (PAMPHLET). WOR+45 CULTURE ECO/UNDEV EDU/PROP MARRIAGE AGE HEALTH...ANTHOL 20 BIRTH/CON. PAGE 107 A2199 CENSUS PLAN FAM INT/ORG

S65
TURNER F.C.,"THE IMPLICATIONS OF DEMOGRAPHIC CHANGE FOR NATIONALISM AND INTERNATIONALISM." FUT WOR+45 NAT/LISM AGE SEX CONCPT. PAGE 146 A2980 SOCIETY EDU/PROP DIPLOM ORD/FREE

AGE/A....ADULTS

S67
GLENN N.D.,"ARE REGIONAL CULTURAL DIFFERENCES DIMINISHING?" USA+45 DIPLOM RACE/REL AGE/Y AGE/A PERSON MORAL...GP/COMP 20. PAGE 53 A1081 SAMP ATTIT REGION CULTURE

AGE/C....INFANTS AND CHILDREN

B49
GORER G.,THE PEOPLE OF GREAT RUSSIA: A PSYCHOLOGICAL STUDY. RUSSIA USSR NAT/G DIPLOM LEAD AGE/C ANOMIE ATTIT DRIVE...POLICY 20. PAGE 54 A1116 ISOLAT PERSON PSY SOCIETY

B55
UN ECONOMIC AND SOCIAL COUNCIL,BIBLIOGRAPHY OF PUBLICATIONS OF THE UN AND SPECIALIZED AGENCIES IN THE SOCIAL WELFARE FIELD, 1946-1952. WOR+45 FAM INT/ORG MUNIC ACT/RES PLAN PROB/SOLV EDU/PROP AGE/C AGE/Y HABITAT...HEAL UN. PAGE 147 A3000 BIBLIOG/A SOC/WK ADMIN WEALTH

AGE/O....OLD PEOPLE

AGE/Y....YOUTH AND ADOLESCENCE

N
DEUTSCHE BUCHEREI,DEUTSCHE NATIONALBIBLIOGRAPHIE. GERMANY ECO/DEV DIPLOM AGE/Y ATTIT...PHIL/SCI SOC 20. PAGE 37 A0744 BIBLIOG NAT/G LEAD POLICY

B53
SCHAAF R.W.,DOCUMENTS OF INTERNATIONAL MEETINGS. AGRI INDUS ACADEM DIPLOM NUC/PWR RACE/REL AGE/Y HEALTH...SOC 20. PAGE 127 A2614 BIBLIOG/A DELIB/GP INT/ORG POLICY

B55
UN ECONOMIC AND SOCIAL COUNCIL,BIBLIOGRAPHY OF PUBLICATIONS OF THE UN AND SPECIALIZED AGENCIES IN THE SOCIAL WELFARE FIELD, 1946-1952. WOR+45 FAM INT/ORG MUNIC ACT/RES PLAN PROB/SOLV EDU/PROP AGE/C AGE/Y HABITAT...HEAL UN. PAGE 147 A3000 BIBLIOG/A SOC/WK ADMIN WEALTH

B61
TETENS T.H.,THE NEW GERMANY AND THE OLD NAZIS. EUR+WWI GERMANY/W USA+45 NAT/G CRIME CHOOSE RACE/REL TOTALISM AGE/Y ATTIT 20 JEWS NAZI ADENAUER/K. PAGE 142 A2905 FASCISM DIPLOM FOR/AID POL/PAR

B64
BURKE F.G.,AFRICA'S QUEST FOR ORDER. AFR CULTURE KIN MUNIC NAT/G DIPLOM COLONIAL REV DISCRIM NAT/LISM AGE/Y 20. PAGE 21 A0437 ORD/FREE CONSEN RACE/REL LEAD

B65
WHITE HOUSE CONFERENCE ON INTERNATIONAL COOPERATION(VOL.II). SPACE WOR+45 EXTR/IND INT/ORG LABOR WORKER NUC/PWR PEACE AGE/Y...CENSUS ANTHOL 20 RESOURCE/N URBAN/RNWL PUB/TRANS. PAGE 3 A0071 R+D CONFER TEC/DEV DIPLOM

B66
HOLLINS E.J.,PEACE IS POSSIBLE: A READER FOR LAYMEN. WOR+45 CULTURE PLAN RISK AGE/Y ALL/VALS SOVEREIGN...PSY CONCPT TREND 20 UN JOHN/XXIII KENNAN/G MYRDAL/G. PAGE 67 A1370 PEACE DIPLOM INT/ORG NUC/PWR

B66
ZEINE Z.N.,THE EMERGENCE OF ARAB NATIONALISM (REV. ED.). TURKEY UK NAT/G SECT TEC/DEV LEAD REV WAR AGE/Y ROLE ORD/FREE...TRADIT CHARTS BIBLIOG 20 ARABS OTTOMAN. PAGE 170 A3451 ISLAM NAT/LISM DIPLOM

L67
GRAUBARD S.R.,"TOWARD THE YEAR 2000: WORK IN PROGRESS." FUT ACADEM SECT DELIB/GP DIPLOM EDU/PROP AGE/Y PERSON ROLE...PSY ANTHOL. PAGE 55 A1131 PREDICT PROB/SOLV SOCIETY CULTURE

S67
GLENN N.D.,"ARE REGIONAL CULTURAL DIFFERENCES DIMINISHING?" USA+45 DIPLOM RACE/REL AGE/Y AGE/A PERSON MORAL...GP/COMP 20. PAGE 53 A1081 SAMP ATTIT REGION CULTURE

AGENCY FOR INTERNATIONAL DEVELOPMENT....SEE AID

AGGRESSION....SEE WAR, COERCE

AGGRESSION, PHYSICAL....SEE COERCE, DRIVE

AGREE....AGREEMENTS, CONTRACTS, TREATIES, CONCORDATS, INTERSTATE COMPACTS

N
TOSCANO M.,THE HISTORY OF TREATIES AND INTERNATIONAL POLITICS (REV. ED.). WOR-45 AGREE WAR ...BIOG 19/20 TREATY WWI. PAGE 144 A2951 DIPLOM INT/ORG

B16
PUFENDORF S.,LAW OF NATURE AND OF NATIONS (ABRIDGED). UNIV LAW NAT/G DIPLOM AGREE WAR PERSON ALL/VALS PWR...POLICY 18 DEITY NATURL/LAW. PAGE 118 A2416 CONCPT INT/LAW SECT MORAL

N19
BENTHAM J.,A PLAN FOR AN UNIVERSAL AND PERPETUAL PEACE (1838) (PAMPHLET). NAT/G FORCES BAL/PWR INT/TRADE ADMIN AGREE CT/SYS ARMS/CONT SOVEREIGN WEALTH GEN/LAWS. PAGE 13 A0269 INT/ORG INT/LAW PEACE COLONIAL

B27
BRANDENBURG E.,FROM BISMARCK TO THE WORLD WAR; A HISTORY OF GERMAN FOREIGN POLICY, 1870-1914 (TRANS. BY ANNIE ELIZABETH ADAMS). GERMANY MOD/EUR FORCES AGREE PWR 19/20 TREATY CHAMBRLN/J WWI BISMARCK/O. PAGE 18 A0368 DIPLOM POLICY WAR

B29
LANGER W.L.,THE FRANCO-RUSSIAN ALLIANCE: 1890-1894. FRANCE MOD/EUR UK USSR NAT/G CHIEF FORCES BAL/PWR AGREE WAR PEACE PWR...TIME/SEQ TREATY 19 BISMARCK/O. PAGE 84 A1724 DIPLOM

B32
BLUM L.,PEACE AND DISARMAMENT (TRANS. BY A. WERTH). NAT/G FORCES WORKER DIPLOM AGREE WAR ATTIT AUTHORIT ORD/FREE. PAGE 16 A0322 SOCIALIST PEACE INT/ORG ARMS/CONT

B33
GENTILI A.,DE JURE BELLI, LIBRI TRES (1612) (VOL. 2). FORCES DIPLOM AGREE PEACE SOVEREIGN. PAGE 52 A1059 WAR INT/LAW MORAL SUPEGO

B36
BRIERLY J.L.,THE LAW OF NATIONS (2ND ED.). WOR+45 WOR-45 INT/ORG AGREE CONTROL COERCE WAR NAT/LISM PEACE PWR 16/20 TREATY LEAGUE/NAT. PAGE 18 A0375 DIPLOM INT/LAW NAT/G

B38
MCNAIR A.D.,THE LAW OF TREATIES: BRITISH PRACTICE AND OPINIONS. UK CREATE DIPLOM LEGIT WRITING ADJUD WAR...INT/LAW JURID TREATY. PAGE 98 A2018 AGREE LAW CT/SYS NAT/G

B38
SAINT-PIERRE C.I.,SCHEME FOR LASTING PEACE (TRANS. BY H. BELLOT). INDUS NAT/G CHIEF FORCES INT/TRADE CT/SYS WAR PWR SOVEREIGN WEALTH...POLICY 18. PAGE 126 A2587 INT/ORG PEACE AGREE INT/LAW

B39
CARR E.H.,PROPAGANDA IN INTERNATIONAL POLITICS (PAMPHLET). EUR+WWI GERMANY MOD/EUR NAT/G AGREE WAR MORAL...POLICY 20 TREATY. PAGE 24 A0497 DIPLOM EDU/PROP CONTROL ATTIT

B39
WHEELER-BENNET J.W.,THE FORGOTTEN PEACE: BREST-LITOVSK. COM GERMANY USSR TOP/EX AGREE WAR PWR ...BIBLIOG 20 TREATY LENIN/VI UKRAINE. PAGE 163 A3326 PEACE DIPLOM CONFER

B40
WOLFERS A.,BRITAIN AND FRANCE BETWEEN TWO WORLD WARS. FRANCE UK INT/ORG NAT/G PLAN BARGAIN ECO/TAC AGREE ISOLAT ALL/IDEOS...DECISION GEOG 20 TREATY VERSAILLES INTERVENT. PAGE 166 A3380 DIPLOM WAR POLICY

B43
BEMIS S.F.,THE LATIN AMERICAN POLICY OF THE UNITED STATES: AN HISTORICAL INTERPRETATION. INT/ORG AGREE COLONIAL WAR PEACE ATTIT ORD/FREE...POLICY INT/LAW CHARTS 18/20 MEXIC/AMER WILSON/W MONROE/DOC. PAGE 13 A0265 DIPLOM SOVEREIGN USA-45 L/A+17C

B43
MICAUD C.A.,THE FRENCH RIGHT AND NAZI GERMANY 1933-1939: A STUDY OF PUBLIC OPINION. GERMANY UK USSR POL/PAR ARMS/CONT COERCE DETER PEACE RIGID/FLEX PWR MARXISM...FASCIST TREND 20 LEAGUE/NAT TREATY. PAGE 101 A2065 DIPLOM AGREE

B44
RUDIN H.R.,ARMISTICE 1918. FRANCE GERMANY MOD/EUR UK USA-45 NAT/G CHIEF DELIB/GP FORCES BAL/PWR REPAR ARMS/CONT 20 WILSON/W TREATY. PAGE 125 A2566 AGREE WAR PEACE DIPLOM

N47
FOX W.T.R.,UNITED STATES POLICY IN A TWO POWER WORLD. COM USA+45 USSR FORCES DOMIN AGREE NEUTRAL NUC/PWR ORD/FREE SOVEREIGN 20 COLD/WAR TREATY EUROPE/W INTERVENT. PAGE 48 A0972 DIPLOM FOR/AID POLICY

S48
GROSS L.,"THE PEACE OF WESTPHALIA, 1648-1948." WOR+45 WOR-45 CONSTN BAL/PWR FEDERAL 17/20 TREATY WESTPHALIA. PAGE 57 A1175 INT/LAW AGREE CONCPT DIPLOM

B49
BOYD A.,WESTERN UNION: A STUDY OF THE TREND TOWARD EUROPEAN UNITY. FUT REGION NAT/LISM...POLICY IDEA/COMP BIBLIOG 14/20 OEEC ERASMUS/D COUNCL/EUR FULBRGHT/J NATO. PAGE 18 A0363 DIPLOM AGREE TREND INT/ORG

B50
GATZKE H.W.,GERMANY'S DRIVE TO THE WEST. BELGIUM GERMANY MOD/EUR AGRI INDUS POL/PAR FORCES DOMIN AGREE CONTROL REGION COERCE 20 TREATY WWI. PAGE 51 A1053 WAR POLICY NAT/G DIPLOM

B50
GLEASON J.H.,THE GENESIS OF RUSSOPHOBIA IN GREAT BRITAIN: A STUDY OF THE INTERACTION OF POLICY AND OPINION. ASIA RUSSIA UK NAT/G AGREE CONTROL REV WAR LOVE PWR TREATY 19. PAGE 53 A1080 DIPLOM POLICY DOMIN COLONIAL

B52
FERRELL R.H.,PEACE IN THEIR TIME. FRANCE UK USA-45 INT/ORG NAT/G FORCES CREATE AGREE ARMS/CONT COERCE WAR TREATY 20 WILSON/W LEAGUE/NAT BRIAND/A. PAGE 45 A0920 PEACE DIPLOM

B52
LIPPMANN W.,ISOLATION AND ALLIANCES: AN AMERICAN SPEAKS TO THE BRITISH. USA+45 USA-45 INT/ORG AGREE COERCE DETER WAR PEACE MORAL 20 TREATY INTERVENT. PAGE 89 A1829 DIPLOM SOVEREIGN COLONIAL ATTIT

B53
MCNEILL W.H.,AMERICA, BRITAIN, AND RUSSIA; THEIR COOPERATION AND CONFLICT. UK USA-45 USSR ECO/DEV ECO/UNDEV FORCES PLAN ADMIN AGREE PERS/REL ...DECISION 20 TREATY. PAGE 98 A2021 WAR DIPLOM DOMIN

B53
OPPENHEIM L.,INTERNATIONAL LAW: A TREATISE (7TH ED., 2 VOLS.). LAW CONSTN PROB/SOLV INT/TRADE ADJUD AGREE NEUTRAL WAR ORD/FREE SOVEREIGN...BIBLIOG 20 LEAGUE/NAT UN ILO. PAGE 112 A2294 INT/LAW INT/ORG DIPLOM

B55
SVARLIEN O.,AN INTRODUCTION TO THE LAW OF NATIONS. SEA AIR INT/ORG NAT/G CHIEF ADMIN AGREE WAR PRIVIL ORD/FREE SOVEREIGN...BIBLIOG 16/20. PAGE 140 A2868 INT/LAW DIPLOM

B57
US SENATE COMM ON JUDICIARY,HEARING BEFORE SUBCOMMITTEE ON COMMITTEE OF JUDICIARY, UNITED STATES SENATE: S. J. RES. 3. USA+45 NAT/G CONSULT DELIB/GP DIPLOM ADJUD LOBBY REPRESENT 20 CONGRESS TREATY. PAGE 157 A3192 LEGIS CONSTN CONFER AGREE

B58
SCHOEDER P.W.,THE AXIS ALLIANCE AND JAPANESE-AMERICAN RELATIONS 1941. ASIA GERMANY UK USA-45 PEACE ATTIT...POLICY BIBLIOG 20 CHINJAP TREATY. PAGE 129 A2641 AGREE DIPLOM WAR

B59
TUNSTALL W.C.B.,THE COMMONWEALTH AND REGIONAL DEFENCE (PAMPHLET). UK LAW VOL/ASSN PLAN AGREE REGION WAR ORD/FREE 20 CMN/WLTH NATO SEATO TREATY. PAGE 146 A2977 INT/ORG FORCES DIPLOM

B61
AMORY J.F.,AROUND THE EDGE OF WAR: A NEW APPROACH TO THE PROBLEMS OF AMERICAN FOREIGN POLICY. COM L/A+17C USA+45 USSR FOR/AID EDU/PROP AGREE CONTROL ARMS/CONT NUC/PWR WAR PWR...IDEA/COMP 20 TREATY ESPIONAGE. PAGE 8 A0154 NAT/G DIPLOM POLICY

B61
FULLER J.F.C.,THE CONDUCT OF WAR, 1789-1961. FRANCE RUSSIA SOCIETY NAT/G FORCES PROB/SOLV AGREE NUC/PWR WEAPON PEACE...SOC 18/20 TREATY COLD/WAR. PAGE 50 A1025 WAR POLICY REV ROLE

B62
COLOMBOS C.J.,THE INTERNATIONAL LAW OF THE SEA. WOR+45 EXTR/IND DIPLOM INT/TRADE TARIFFS AGREE WAR ...TIME/SEQ 20 TREATY. PAGE 28 A0570 INT/LAW SEA JURID ADJUD

B62
LIPPMANN W.,WESTERN UNITY AND THE COMMON MARKET. EUR+WWI FRANCE GERMANY/W UK USA+45 ECO/DEV AGRI FINAN MARKET INT/ORG NAT/G FOR/AID AGREE WEALTH 20 EEC. PAGE 89 A1831 DIPLOM INT/TRADE VOL/ASSN

B62
SOMMER T.,DEUTSCHLAND UND JAPAN ZWISCHEN DEN MACHTEN. GERMANY DELIB/GP BAL/PWR AGREE COERCE TOTALISM PWR 20 CHINJAP TREATY. PAGE 135 A2765 DIPLOM WAR ATTIT

B63
DEENER D.R.,CANADA - UNITED STATES TREATY RELATIONS. CANADA USA+45 USA-45 NAT/G FORCES PLAN PROB/SOLV AGREE NUC/PWR...TREND 18/20 TREATY. PAGE 35 A0722 DIPLOM INT/LAW POLICY

B63
KORBEL J.,POLAND BETWEEN EAST AND WEST: SOVIET AND GERMAN DIPLOMACY TOWARD POLAND 1919-1933. EUR+WWI GERMANY POLAND USSR FORCES AGREE WAR SOVEREIGN ...BIBLIOG 20 TREATY. PAGE 81 A1670 BAL/PWR DIPLOM DOMIN NAT/LISM

S63
BRZEZINSKI Z.,"SOVIET QUIESCENCE." EUR+WWI USA+45 USSR FORCES CREATE PLAN COERCE DETER WAR ATTIT 20 TREATY EUROPE. PAGE 20 A0415 DIPLOM ARMS/CONT NUC/PWR AGREE

B64
KEEP J.,CONTEMPORARY HISTORY IN THE SOVIET MIRROR. COM USSR POL/PAR CREATE DIPLOM AGREE WAR ATTIT ...MYTH TREND ANTHOL 20 COLD/WAR STALIN/J MARX/KARL LENIN/VI. PAGE 77 A1576 HIST/WRIT METH MARXISM IDEA/COMP

B64
UNITED ARAB REPUBLIC,TOWARDS THE SECOND AFRICAN SUMMIT ASSEMBLY. AFR UAR CONSTN VOL/ASSN CHIEF PLAN DIPLOM AGREE 20 NASSER/G AFR/STATES. PAGE 148 A3030 CONFER DELIB/GP INT/ORG POLICY

B65
IRIYE A.,AFTER IMPERIALISM; THE SEARCH FOR A NEW ORDER IN THE FAR EAST 1921-1931. USA+45 USSR DOMIN AGREE COLONIAL REV PWR...BIBLIOG DICTIONARY 20 CHINJAP. PAGE 72 A1468 DIPLOM ASIA SOVEREIGN

B65
LARUS J.,FROM COLLECTIVE SECURITY TO PREVENTIVE DIPLOMACY. FUT FORCES PROB/SOLV DEBATE AGREE COERCE WAR PWR...ANTHOL 20 LEAGUE/NAT UN. PAGE 85 A1736 INT/ORG PEACE DIPLOM ORD/FREE

B65
MACDONALD R.W.,THE LEAGUE OF ARAB STATES: A STUDY IN THE DYNAMICS OF REGIONAL ORGANIZATION. ISRAEL UAR USSR FINAN INT/ORG DELIB/GP ECO/TAC AGREE NEUTRAL ORD/FREE PWR...DECISION BIBLIOG 20 TREATY UN. PAGE 92 A1888 ISLAM REGION DIPLOM ADMIN

B65
MONCONDUIT F.,LA COMMISSION EUROPEENNE DES DROITS DE L'HOMME. DIPLOM AGREE GP/REL ORD/FREE PWR ...BIBLIOG 20 TREATY. PAGE 102 A2103 INT/LAW INT/ORG ADJUD JURID

B65
UNESCO,HANDBOOK OF INTERNATIONAL EXCHANGES. COM/IND R+D ACADEM PROF/ORG VOL/ASSN CREATE TEC/DEV EDU/PROP AGREE 20 TREATY. PAGE 148 A3025 INDEX INT/ORG DIPLOM PRESS

B65
WARBEY W.,VIETNAM: THE TRUTH. FRANCE S/ASIA USA+45 VIETNAM CULTURE INT/ORG NAT/G DIPLOM FOR/AID EDU/PROP ARMS/CONT PEACE 20 TREATY NLF UN. PAGE 161 A3274 WAR AGREE

B66
COLE A.B.,SOCIALIST PARTIES IN POSTWAR JAPAN. STRATA AGRI LABOR PLAN DIPLOM ECO/TAC AGREE LEAD CHOOSE ATTIT...CHARTS 20 CHINJAP SOC/DEMPAR. PAGE 28 A0566 POL/PAR POLICY SOCISM NAT/G

B66
GARNER W.R.,THE CHACO DISPUTE; A STUDY OF PRESTIGE DIPLOMACY. L/A+17C PARAGUAY USA-45 INT/ORG AGREE PEACE...TIME/SEQ 20 BOLIV LEAGUE/NAT ARGEN CHACO/WAR. PAGE 51 A1050 WAR DIPLOM CONCPT PWR

B66
HERZ M.F.,BEGINNINGS OF THE COLD WAR. COM POLAND USA+45 USSR INT/ORG NAT/G CHIEF FOR/AID DOMIN CONFER AGREE WAR PEACE 20 STALIN/J COLD/WAR UN. DIPLOM

PAGE 64 A1321

LEE L.T.,VIENNA CONVENTION ON CONSULAR RELATIONS. WOR+45 LAW INT/ORG CONFER GP/REL PRIVIL...INT/LAW 20 TREATY VIENNA/CNV. PAGE 86 A1760 — B66 — AGREE DIPLOM ADMIN

PAN S.,VIETNAM CRISIS. ASIA FRANCE USA+45 USA-45 VIETNAM CULTURE SOCIETY INT/ORG ECO/TAC AGREE CONTROL WAR MARXISM 20. PAGE 113 A2325 — B66 — ECO/UNDEV POLICY DIPLOM NAT/COMP

VAN DYKE V.,INTERNATIONAL POLITICS. WOR+45 ECO/DEV ECO/UNDEV INT/ORG BAL/PWR AGREE ARMS/CONT NAT/LISM PEACE PWR...INT/LAW 20 TREATY UN. PAGE 158 A3212 — B66 — DIPLOM NAT/G WAR SOVEREIGN

WAINHOUSE D.W.,INTERNATIONAL PEACE OBSERVATION: A HISTORY AND FORECAST. INT/ORG PROB/SOLV BAL/PWR AGREE ARMS/CONT COERCE NUC/PWR...PREDICT METH/COMP 20 UN LEAGUE/NAT OAS TREATY. PAGE 160 A3261 — B66 — PEACE DIPLOM

WEINSTEIN F.B.,VIETNAM'S UNHELD ELECTIONS: THE FAILURE TO CARRY OUT THE 1956 REUNIFICATION ELECTIONS... (MONOGRAPH). VIETNAM/S VIETNAM/N LEGIT CONFER ADJUD WAR PEACE 20 TREATY GENEVA/CON UNIFICA. PAGE 162 A3306 — B66 — AGREE NAT/G CHOOSE DIPLOM

US DEPARTMENT OF STATE,TREATIES IN FORCE. USA+45 WOR+45 AGREE WAR PEACE 20 TREATY. PAGE 152 A3101 — B67 — BIBLIOG DIPLOM INT/ORG DETER

LISSITZYN O.J.,"TREATIES AND CHANGED CIRCUMSTANCES (REBUS SIC STANTIBUS)" WOR+45 CONSEN...JURID 20. PAGE 90 A1842 — L67 — AGREE DIPLOM INT/LAW

DE VATTEL E.,THE LAW OF NATIONS. AGRI FINAN CHIEF DIPLOM INT/TRADE AGREE OWN ALL/VALS MORAL ORD/FREE SOVEREIGN...GEN/LAWS 18 NATURL/LAW WOLFF/C. PAGE 35 A0714 — B96 — LAW CONCPT NAT/G INT/LAW

LOWELL A.L.,GOVERNMENTS AND PARTIES IN CONTINENTAL EUROPE, VOL. II. AUSTRIA GERMANY HUNGARY MOD/EUR SWITZERLND SOCIETY EX/STRUC LEGIS DIPLOM AGREE LEAD PARL/PROC PWR...POLICY 19. PAGE 91 A1867 — B96 — POL/PAR NAT/G GOV/REL ELITES

SMITH A.,LECTURES ON JUSTICE, POLICE, REVENUE AND ARMS (1763). UK LAW FAM FORCES TARIFFS AGREE COERCE INCOME OWN WEALTH LAISSEZ...GEN/LAWS 17/18. PAGE 134 A2743 — B96 — DIPLOM JURID OLD/LIB TAX

AGRI....AGRICULTURE (INCLUDING HUNTING AND GATHERING)

CANADIAN GOVERNMENT PUBLICATIONS (1955-). CANADA AGRI FINAN LABOR FORCES INT/TRADE HEALTH...JURID 20 PARLIAMENT. PAGE 1 A0007 — N — BIBLIOG/A NAT/G DIPLOM INT/ORG

PEKING REVIEW. CHINA/COM CULTURE AGRI INDUS DIPLOM EDU/PROP GUERRILLA ATTIT MARXISM...BIBLIOG 20. PAGE 1 A0022 — N — MARXIST NAT/G POL/PAR PRESS

CHINA QUARTERLY. COM AGRI INDUS ACADEM POL/PAR INT/TRADE CONFER GOV/REL...TIME/SEQ CON/ANAL INDEX 20. PAGE 2 A0032 — N — BIBLIOG/A ASIA DIPLOM POLICY

THE JAPAN SCIENCE REVIEW: LAW AND POLITICS: LIST OF BOOKS AND ARTICLES ON LAW AND POLITICS. CONSTN AGRI INDUS LABOR DIPLOM TAX ADMIN CRIME...INT/LAW SOC 20 CHINJAP. PAGE 2 A0042 — N — BIBLIOG LAW S/ASIA PHIL/SCI

THE MIDDLE EAST AND NORTH AFRICA. AFR ISLAM CULTURE ECO/UNDEV AGRI NAT/G TEC/DEV FOR/AID INT/TRADE EDU/PROP...CHARTS 20. PAGE 2 A0043 — N — INDEX INDUS FINAN STAT

SCHOLARLY BOOKS IN AMERICA; A QUARTERLY BIBLIOGRAPHY OF UNIVERSITY PRESS PUBLICATIONS. WOR+45 AGRI COM/IND NAT/G HEALTH...GEOG PHIL/SCI PSY SOC LING 20. PAGE 3 A0046 — N — BIBLIOG/A LAW MUNIC DIPLOM

"PROLOG",DIGEST OF THE SOVIET UKRANIAN PRESS. USSR LAW AGRI INDUS PROVS SCHOOL DIPLOM GOV/REL ATTIT ...HUM LING 20. PAGE 4 A0081 — N — BIBLIOG/A NAT/G PRESS COM

HOOVER INSTITUTION,UNITED STATES AND CANADIAN PUBLICATIONS ON AFRICA. CULTURE ECO/UNDEV AGRI TEC/DEV EDU/PROP COLONIAL RACE/REL NAT/LISM ATTIT HEALTH...SOC SOC/WK 20. PAGE 67 A1381 — N — BIBLIOG DIPLOM NAT/G AFR

KYRIAK T.E.,CHINA: A BIBLIOGRAPHY. ASIA CHINA/COM AGRI FINAN INDUS NAT/G INT/TRADE PRESS...SOC 20. PAGE 83 A1700 — N — BIBLIOG/A MARXISM TOP/EX POL/PAR

KYRIAK T.E.,EAST EUROPE: BIBLIOGRAPHY--INDEX TO US JPRS RESEARCH TRANSLATIONS. ALBANIA BULGARIA COM CZECHOSLVK HUNGARY POLAND ROMANIA AGRI EXTR/IND FINAN SERV/IND INT/TRADE WEAPON...GEOG MGT SOC 20. PAGE 83 A1701 — N — BIBLIOG/A PRESS MARXISM INDUS

KYRIAK T.E.,SOVIET UNION: BIBLIOGRAPHY INDEX TO US JPRS RESEARCH TRANSLATIONS. USSR ECO/DEV AGRI COM/IND CONSTRUC DIST/IND EXTR/IND PROC/MFG R+D INT/TRADE...SOC 20. PAGE 83 A1703 — N — BIBLIOG/A INDUS MARXISM PRESS

MCSPADDEN J.W.,THE AMERICAN STATESMAN'S YEARBOOK. WOR-45 LAW CONSTN AGRI FINAN DEBATE ADMIN PARL/PROC ...CHARTS BIBLIOG/A 20. PAGE 99 A2025 — N — DIPLOM NAT/G PROVS LEGIS

MURRA R.O.,POST-WAR PROBLEMS: A CURRENT LIST OF UNITED STATES GOVERNMENT PUBLICATIONS (PAMPHLET). WOR+45 SOCIETY FINAN INT/ORG SCHOOL WORKER TEC/DEV ECO/TAC...SOC 20. PAGE 106 A2180 — N — BIBLIOG/A ADJUST AGRI INDUS

UNITED NATIONS,UNITED NATIONS PUBLICATIONS. WOR+45 ECO/UNDEV AGRI FINAN FORCES ADMIN LEAD WAR PEACE ...POLICY INT/LAW 20 UN. PAGE 148 A3034 — N — BIBLIOG INT/ORG DIPLOM

US DEPARTMENT OF STATE,BIBLIOGRAPHY (PAMPHLETS). AGRI INDUS INT/ORG FOR/AID EDU/PROP WAR MARXISM ...SOC GOV/COMP METH/COMP 20. PAGE 151 A3079 — N — BIBLIOG DIPLOM ECO/DEV NAT/G

US LIBRARY OF CONGRESS,ACCESSIONS LIST - INDIA. INDIA CULTURE AGRI LOC/G POL/PAR PLAN PROB/SOLV TEC/DEV DIPLOM EDU/PROP LEAD GP/REL ATTIT 20. PAGE 154 A3142 — N — BIBLIOG S/ASIA ECO/UNDEV NAT/G

US SUPERINTENDENT OF DOCUMENTS,MONTHLY CATALOG OF UNITED STATES GOVERNMENT PUBLICATIONS. USA+45 USA-45 AGRI LABOR FORCES INT/TRADE TARIFFS TAX EDU/PROP CT/SYS ARMS/CONT RACE/REL 19/20 CONGRESS PRESIDENT. PAGE 157 A3203 — N — BIBLIOG NAT/G VOL/ASSN POLICY

WORLD PEACE FOUNDATION,DOCUMENTS OF INTERNATIONAL ORGANIZATIONS: A SELECTED BIBLIOGRAPHY. WOR+45 WOR-45 AGRI FINAN ACT/RES OP/RES INT/TRADE ADMIN ...CON/ANAL 20 UN UNESCO LEAGUE/NAT. PAGE 167 A3396 — N — BIBLIOG DIPLOM INT/ORG REGION

MONTGOMERY H.,"A DICTIONARY OF POLITICAL PHRASES AND ILLUSIONS WITH A SHORT BIBLIOGRAPHY." EUR+WWI MOD/EUR UK AGRI LABOR LOC/G NAT/G COLONIAL CHOOSE RACE/REL. PAGE 103 A2114 — C06 — BIBLIOG DICTIONARY POLICY DIPLOM

MEYER H.H.B.,LIST OF REFERENCES ON EMBARGOES (PAMPHLET). USA-45 AGRI DIPLOM WRITING DEBATE WEAPON...INT/LAW 18/20 CONGRESS. PAGE 100 A2049 — B17 — BIBLIOG DIST/IND ECO/TAC INT/TRADE

MEYER H.H.B.,THE UNITED STATES AT WAR, ORGANIZATIONS AND LITERATURE. USA-45 AGRI FINAN INDUS CHIEF FORCES DIPLOM FOR/AID INT/TRADE...SOC 20 PRESIDENT. PAGE 100 A2050 — B17 — BIBLIOG/A WAR NAT/G VOL/ASSN

PARRINGTON V.L.,MAIN CURRENTS IN AMERICAN THOUGHT (VOL.I). USA-45 AGRI POL/PAR DIPLOM TAX REGION REV 17/18 FRANKLIN/B JEFFERSN/T. PAGE 114 A2336 — B27 — COLONIAL SECT FEEDBACK ALL/IDEOS

HANSEN A.H.,ECONOMIC STABILIZATION IN AN UNBALANCED WORLD. COM EUR+WWI USA-45 WOR-45 AGRI FINAN INDUS MARKET INT/ORG LABOR VOL/ASSN EDU/PROP ATTIT HEALTH KNOWL WEALTH...HIST/WRIT TREND VAL/FREE 20. PAGE 61 A1253 — B32 — NAT/G ECO/DEV CAP/ISM SOCISM

BUREAU ECONOMIC RES LAT AM,THE ECONOMIC LITERATURE OF LATIN AMERICA (2 VOLS.). CHRIST-17C AGRI DIST/IND EXTR/IND INDUS WORKER INT/TRADE...GEOG 16/20. PAGE 21 A0433 — B35 — BIBLIOG L/A+17C ECO/UNDEV FINAN

HUDSON M.O.,INTERNATIONAL LEGISLATION: 1929-1931. WOR-45 SEA AIR AGRI FINAN LABOR DIPLOM ECO/TAC REPAR CT/SYS ARMS/CONT WAR WEAPON...JURID 20 TREATY LEAGUE/NAT. PAGE 69 A1409 — B36 — INT/LAW PARL/PROC ADJUD LAW

VARLEY D.H.,A BIBLIOGRAPHY OF ITALIAN COLONISATION IN AFRICA WITH A SECTION ON ABYSSINIA. AFR ETHIOPIA ITALY LIBYA SOMALIA AGRI FINAN LABOR TEC/DEV DIPLOM INT/TRADE RACE/REL DISCRIM 19/20. PAGE 158 A3222 — B36 — BIBLIOG COLONIAL ADMIN LAW

VINER J.,STUDIES IN THE THEORY OF INTERNATIONAL TRADE. WOR-45 CONSTN ECO/DEV AGRI INDUS MARKET INT/ORG LABOR NAT/G ECO/TAC TARIFFS COLONIAL ATTIT WEALTH...POLICY CONCPT MATH STAT OBS SAMP TREND GEN/LAWS MARX/KARL 20. PAGE 159 A3236 — B37 — CAP/ISM INT/TRADE

B38
COLBY C.C.,GEOGRAPHICAL ASPECTS OF INTERNATIONAL RELATIONS. WOR-45 ECO/DEV ECO/UNDEV AGRI EXTR/IND INDUS MARKET R+D INT/ORG NAT/G TEC/DEV ECO/TAC INT/TRADE NAT/LISM WEALTH...METH/CNCPT CHARTS GEN/LAWS 20. PAGE 28 A0565 — PLAN GEOG DIPLOM

B39
SPEIER H.,WAR IN OUR TIME. WOR-45 AGRI FINAN FORCES TEC/DEV BAL/PWR EDU/PROP WEAPON PEACE PWR...ANTHOL 20. PAGE 136 A2779 — FASCISM WAR DIPLOM NAT/G

C40
NORMAN E.H.,"JAPAN'S EMERGENCE AS A MODERN STATE: POLITICAL AND ECONOMIC PROBLEMS OF THE MEIJI PERIOD." CONSTN STRATA AGRI INDUS POL/PAR TEC/DEV CAP/ISM CIVMIL/REL...BIBLIOG 19/20 CHINJAP. PAGE 110 A2250 — CENTRAL DIPLOM POLICY NAT/LISM

B42
CONOVER H.F.,FRENCH COLONIES IN AFRICA: A LIST OF REFERENCES. ALGERIA FRANCE MOROCCO SOMALIA SUDAN CULTURE AGRI LOC/G SECT FORCES DIPLOM INT/TRADE NAT/LISM HEALTH...CON/ANAL 20. PAGE 29 A0594 — BIBLIOG AFR ECO/UNDEV COLONIAL

B42
CONOVER H.F.,NEW ZEALAND: A SELECTED LIST OF REFERENCES (PAMPHLET). NEW/ZEALND ECO/UNDEV AGRI INDUS LABOR NAT/G SCHOOL FORCES DIPLOM COLONIAL WAR ...HUM 20. PAGE 29 A0595 — BIBLIOG/A S/ASIA CULTURE

B43
BROWN A.D.,GREECE: SELECTED LIST OF REFERENCES. GREECE ECO/UNDEV AGRI FINAN INDUS LABOR SECT TEC/DEV INT/TRADE LEAD...SOC 20. PAGE 20 A0399 — BIBLIOG/A WAR DIPLOM NAT/G

B44
FULLER G.H.,TURKEY: A SELECTED LIST OF REFERENCES. ISLAM TURKEY CULTURE ECO/UNDEV AGRI DIPLOM NAT/LISM CONSERVE...GEOG HUM INT/LAW SOC 7/20 MAPS. PAGE 50 A1024 — BIBLIOG/A ALL/VALS

B44
SHELBY C.,LATIN AMERICAN PERIODICALS CURRENTLY RECEIVED IN THE LIBRARY OF CONGRESS AND IN LIBRARY OF DEPARTMENT OF AGRICULTURE. SOCIETY AGRI INDUS LABOR POL/PAR INT/TRADE...GEOG SOC 20. PAGE 132 A2699 — BIBLIOG ECO/UNDEV CULTURE L/A+17C

B44
WEIGERT H.W.,COMPASS OF THE WORLD, A SYMPOSIUM ON POLITICAL GEOGRAPHY. EUR+WWI FUT MOD/EUR S/ASIA USA-45 WOR-45 SOCIETY AGRI INDUS MARKET ECO/TAC INT/TRADE PERSON 20. PAGE 162 A3298 — TEC/DEV CAP/ISM RUSSIA GEOG

L44
HAILEY,"THE FUTURE OF COLONIAL PEOPLES." WOR-45 CONSTN CULTURE ECO/UNDEV AGRI MARKET INT/ORG NAT/G SECT CONSULT ECO/TAC LEGIT ADMIN NAT/LISM ALL/VALS ...SOC OBS TREND STERTYP CMN/WLTH LEAGUE/NAT PARLIAMENT 20. PAGE 59 A1218 — PLAN CONCPT DIPLOM UK

B45
CLAGETT H.L.,COMMUNIST CHINA: RUTHLESS ENEMY OR PAPER TIGER (PAMPHLET). CHINA/COM ECO/UNDEV AGRI INDUS NAT/G POL/PAR ECO/TAC INT/TRADE GUERRILLA ATTIT...CHARTS NAT/COMP ORG/CHARTS 20. PAGE 26 A0540 — BIBLIOG/A MARXISM DIPLOM COERCE

B45
PERAZA SARAUSA F.,BIBLIOGRAFIAS CUBANAS. CUBA CULTURE ECO/UNDEV AGRI EDU/PROP PRESS CIVMIL/REL ...POLICY GEOG PHIL/SCI BIOG 19/20. PAGE 115 A2353 — BIBLIOG/A L/A+17C NAT/G DIPLOM

N46
HOBBS C.C.,SOUTHEAST ASIA, 1935-45: A SELECTED LIST OF REFERENCE BOOKS (PAMPHLET). S/ASIA AGRI INDUS NAT/G SECT DIPLOM WAR...ART/METH GEOG SOC LING 20. PAGE 65 A1346 — BIBLIOG/A CULTURE HABITAT

B47
DE HUSZAR G.B.,PERSISTENT INTERNATIONAL ISSUES. WOR+45 WOR-45 AGRI INDUS INT/ORG PROB/SOLV EFFICIENCY WEALTH...CON/ANAL ANTHOL UN. PAGE 35 A0704 — DIPLOM PEACE ECO/TAC FOR/AID

B47
FEIS H.,SEEN FROM E A, THREE INTERNATIONAL EPISODES. EUR+WWI ITALY USA-45 WOR-45 AGRI INT/ORG NAT/G INT/TRADE LEGIT EXEC ATTIT ORD/FREE...POLICY LEAGUE/NAT TOT/POP 20 OIL. PAGE 44 A0908 — EXTR/IND ECO/TAC DIPLOM

B49
US DEPARTMENT OF STATE,SOVIET BIBLIOGRAPHY (PAMPHLET). CHINA/COM COM USSR LAW AGRI INT/ORG ECO/TAC EDU/PROP...POLICY GEOG 20. PAGE 151 A3084 — BIBLIOG/A MARXISM CULTURE DIPLOM

B50
COUNCIL BRITISH NATIONAL BIB,BRITISH NATIONAL BIBLIOGRAPHY. UK AGRI CONSTRUC PERF/ART POL/PAR SECT CREATE INT/TRADE LEAD...HUM JURID PHIL/SCI 20. PAGE 31 A0637 — BIBLIOG/A NAT/G TEC/DEV DIPLOM

B50
DAVIS E.P.,PERIODICALS OF INTERNATIONAL ORGANIZATIONS; PART I, THE UN AND SPECIALIZED AGENCIES; PART II, INTER-AMERICAN ORGS. CULTURE AGRI FINAN INDUS LABOR INT/TRADE...GEOG HEAL STAT 20 UN OAS UNESCO. PAGE 34 A0689 — BIBLIOG/A INT/ORG DIPLOM L/A+17C

B50
GATZKE H.W.,GERMANY'S DRIVE TO THE WEST. BELGIUM GERMANY MOD/EUR AGRI INDUS POL/PAR FORCES DOMIN AGREE CONTROL REGION COERCE 20 TREATY WWI. PAGE 51 A1053 — WAR POLICY NAT/G DIPLOM

B50
US DEPARTMENT OF STATE,POINT FOUR: COOPERATIVE PROGRAM FOR AID IN THE DEVELOPMENT OF ECONOMICALLY UNDERDEVELOPED AREAS. WOR+45 AGRI INDUS INT/ORG PLAN TEC/DEV DIPLOM EDU/PROP ADMIN PEACE PRODUC WEALTH 20 CONGRESS UN. PAGE 151 A3085 — ECO/UNDEV FOR/AID FINAN INT/TRADE

B51
BISSAINTHE M.,DICTIONNAIRE DE BIBLIOGRAPHIE HAITIENNE. HAITI ELITES AGRI LEGIS DIPLOM INT/TRADE WRITING ORD/FREE CATHISM...ART/METH GEOG 19/20 NEGRO TREATY. PAGE 15 A0295 — BIBLIOG L/A+17C SOCIETY NAT/G

B51
US DEPARTMENT OF STATE,POINT FOUR, NEAR EAST AND AFRICA, A SELECTED BIBLIOGRAPHY OF STUDIES ON ECONOMICALLY UNDERDEVELOPED COUNTRIES. AGRI COM/IND FINAN INDUS PLAN INT/TRADE...SOC TREND 20. PAGE 151 A3087 — BIBLIOG/A AFR S/ASIA ISLAM

B51
US TARIFF COMMISSION,LIST OF PUBLICATIONS OF THE TARIFF COMMISSION (PAMPHLET). USA+45 USA-45 AGRI EXTR/IND INDUS INT/TRADE...STAT 20. PAGE 157 A3207 — BIBLIOG TARIFFS NAT/G ADMIN

B52
RIGGS F.W.,FORMOSA UNDER CHINESE NATIONALIST RULE. CHINA/COM USA+45 CONSTN AGRI FINAN LABOR LOC/G NAT/G POL/PAR FORCES HEALTH KNOWL...STAT WORK VAL/FREE 20. PAGE 121 A2479 — ASIA FOR/AID DIPLOM

B52
UN DEPT. SOC. AFF.,PRELIMINARY REPORT ON THE WORLD SOCIAL SITUATION. ISLAM L/A+17C WOR+45 STRATA AGRI EXTR/IND INDUS INT/ORG SCHOOL ADMIN...GEOG SOC TREND UNESCO WORK FAO 20. PAGE 147 A2998 — R+D HEALTH FOR/AID

B52
US MUTUAL SECURITY AGENCY,U. S. TECHNICAL AND ECONOMIC ASSISTANCE IN THE FAR EAST (PAMPHLET). ASIA BURMA INDONESIA PHILIPPINE TAIWAN THAILAND USA+45 AGRI INDUS PLAN EDU/PROP ADMIN HEALTH. PAGE 155 A3161 — FOR/AID TEC/DEV ECO/UNDEV BUDGET

B53
SCHAAF R.W.,DOCUMENTS OF INTERNATIONAL MEETINGS. AGRI INDUS ACADEM DIPLOM NUC/PWR RACE/REL AGE/Y HEALTH...SOC 20. PAGE 127 A2614 — BIBLIOG/A DELIB/GP INT/ORG POLICY

B54
BECKEL G.,WORKSHOPS FOR THE WORLD; THE SPECIALIZED AGENCIES OF THE UN. WOR+45 AGRI DIST/IND CREATE TEC/DEV BUDGET CONTROL TASK WEALTH...CHARTS ORG/CHARTS 20 UN CASEBOOK. PAGE 12 A0246 — INT/ORG DIPLOM PEACE CON/ANAL

B54
US DEPARTMENT OF STATE,PUBLICATIONS OF THE DEPARTMENT OF STATE, OCTOBER 1,1929 TO JANUARY 1, 1953. AGRI INT/ORG FORCES FOR/AID EDU/PROP ARMS/CONT NUC/PWR ATTIT 20 DEPT/STATE OAS UN NATO. PAGE 151 A3089 — BIBLIOG DIPLOM

C54
BOWIE R.R.,"STUDIES IN FEDERALISM." AGRI FINAN LABOR EX/STRUC FORCES LEGIS DIPLOM INT/TRADE ADJUD ...BIBLIOG 20 EEC. PAGE 17 A0357 — FEDERAL EUR+WWI INT/ORG CONSTN

B55
OECD,MARSHALL PLAN IN TURKEY. TURKEY USA+45 COM/IND CONSTRUC SERV/IND FORCES BUDGET...STAT 20 MARSHL/PLN. PAGE 111 A2277 — FOR/AID ECO/UNDEV AGRI INDUS

B56
JAMESON J.F.,THE AMERICAN REVOLUTION CONSIDERED AS A SOCIAL MOVEMENT. USA-45 AGRI FINAN SECT INT/TRADE REPRESENT SUFF INGP/REL RACE/REL DISCRIM...MAJORIT 18/19 CHURCH/STA. PAGE 73 A1494 — ORD/FREE REV FEDERAL CONSTN

B56
JUAN T.L.,ECONOMIC AND SOCIAL DEVELOPMENT OF MODERN CHINA: A BIBLIOGRAPHICAL GUIDE. ASIA AGRI COM/IND DIST/IND FINAN INDUS DIPLOM...STAT 20. PAGE 75 A1541 — BIBLIOG SOC

B56
US DEPARTMENT OF STATE,ECONOMIC PROBLEMS OF UNDERDEVELOPED AREAS (PAMPHLET). AFR ASIA ISLAM L/A+17C AGRI FINAN INDUS INT/ORG LABOR INT/TRADE ...PSY SOC 20. PAGE 151 A3090 — BIBLIOG ECO/UNDEV TEC/DEV R+D

B57
FRAZIER E.F.,RACE AND CULTURE CONTACTS IN THE MODERN WORLD. WOR+45 WOR-45 SOCIETY ECO/DEV AGRI INDUS INT/ORG LABOR NAT/G PERSON RIGID/FLEX ALL/VALS...SOC TIME/SEQ WORK 19/20. PAGE 48 A0991 — CULTURE RACE/REL

B57
MILLIKAN M.F.,A PROPOSAL: KEY TO AN EFFECTIVE FOREIGN POLICY. USA+45 AGRI FINAN DELIB/GP DIPLOM REPRESENT MAJORITY...NEW/IDEA CHARTS. PAGE 101 A2081 — FOR/AID GIVE ECO/UNDEV PLAN

B57
US SENATE SPEC COMM FOR AID,COMPILATION OF STUDIES — FOR/AID

AND SURVEYS. AFR ASIA L/A+17C USA+45 ECO/UNDEV AGRI INT/ORG CONSULT TEC/DEV CONFER TOTALISM...NAT/COMP 20 CONGRESS. PAGE 157 A3197
DIPLOM ORD/FREE DELIB/GP

S57
ALLEN R.L.,"UNITED NATIONS TECHNICAL ASSISTANCE: SOVIET AND EAST-EUROPEAN PARTICIPATION." COM WOR+45 AGRI INDUS INT/ORG NAT/G FOR/AID SKILL UN 20. PAGE 6 A0124
ECO/UNDEV TEC/DEV USSR

B58
AVRAMOVIC D.,POSTWAR GROWTH IN INTERNATIONAL INDEBTEDNESS. WOR+45 AGRI INDUS CAP/ISM PRICE INCOME...NAT/COMP 20 GOLD/STAND SILVER. PAGE 10 A0199
INT/TRADE FINAN COST BAL/PAY

B58
HAUSER P.H.,POPULATION AND WORLD POLITICS. FUT WOR+45 WOR-45 AGRI DIST/IND INDUS INT/ORG PLAN ECO/TAC DISPL HEALTH COLD/WAR 20. PAGE 63 A1288
NAT/G ECO/UNDEV FOR/AID

B58
MUNKMAN C.A.,AMERICAN AID TO GREECE. GREECE USA+45 AGRI FINAN PROB/SOLV WAR PWR...CHARTS 20 UN. PAGE 106 A2171
FOR/AID PLAN ECO/DEV INT/TRADE

B58
NEAL F.W.,TITOISM IN ACTION. COM YUGOSLAVIA AGRI LOC/G DIPLOM TOTALISM...BIBLIOG 20 TITO/MARSH. PAGE 107 A2206
MARXISM POL/PAR CHIEF ADMIN

B58
NEHRU J.,SPEECHES. INDIA ECO/UNDEV AGRI INDUS INT/ORG POL/PAR DIPLOM FOR/AID NAT/LISM...ANTHOL 20. PAGE 108 A2213
PLAN CHIEF COLONIAL NEUTRAL

B58
US DEPARTMENT OF STATE,PUBLICATIONS OF THE DEPARTMENT OF STATE, JANUARY 1,1953 TO DECEMBER 31, 1957. AGRI INT/ORG FORCES FOR/AID EDU/PROP ARMS/CONT NUC/PWR ATTIT 20 DEPT/STATE OAS UN NATO. PAGE 151 A3092
BIBLIOG DIPLOM

B58
US OPERATIONS MISSION TO VIET,BUILDING ECONOMIC STRENGTH (PAMPHLET). USA+45 VIETNAM/S INDUS TEC/DEV BUDGET ADMIN EATING HEALTH...STAT 20. PAGE 155 A3162
FOR/AID ECO/UNDEV AGRI EDU/PROP

L58
TRAGER F.N.,"A SELECTED AND ANNOTATED BIBLIOGRAPHY ON ECONOMIC DEVELOPMENT, 1953-1957." WOR+45 AGRI FINAN INDUS MARKET LABOR MUNIC WORKER PLAN INT/TRADE PRODUC CENSUS. PAGE 145 A2958
BIBLIOG/A ECO/UNDEV ECO/DEV

C58
BLANCHARD W.,"THAILAND." THAILAND CULTURE AGRI FINAN INDUS FAM LABOR INT/TRADE ATTIT...GEOG HEAL SOC BIBLIOG 20. PAGE 15 A0307
NAT/G DIPLOM ECO/UNDEV S/ASIA

N58
INVESTMENT FUND ECO SOC DEV,FRENCH AFRICA: A DECADE OF PROGRESS 1948-1958 (PAMPHLET). AFR FRANCE EXTR/IND INDUS EDU/PROP HEALTH 20. PAGE 71 A1465
FOR/AID DIPLOM ECO/UNDEV AGRI

B59
HAZLEWOOD A.,THE ECONOMICS OF "UNDER-DEVELOPED" AREAS. WOR+45 DIST/IND EXTR/IND FINAN INDUS MARKET PLAN FOR/AID...GEOG 20. PAGE 63 A1302
BIBLIOG/A ECO/UNDEV AGRI INT/TRADE

B59
LINK R.G.,ENGLISH THEORIES OF ECONOMIC FLUCTUATIONS: 1815-1848. FRANCE UK AGRI WORKER DIPLOM PRICE TASK WAR DEMAND PRODUC...POLICY BIBLIOG 18 MALTHUS MILL/JS WILSON/J. PAGE 89 A1826
IDEA/COMP ECO/DEV WEALTH EQUILIB

B59
MAC MILLAN W.M.,THE ROAD TO SELF-RULE. SOUTH/AFR UK CULTURE SOCIETY AGRI LABOR NAT/G INT/TRADE CONTROL GP/REL...SOC 19/20. PAGE 92 A1884
AFR COLONIAL SOVEREIGN POLICY

B59
NOVE A.,COMMUNIST ECONOMIC STRATEGY: SOVIET GROWTH AND CAPABILITIES. USSR AGRI LABOR PLAN TEC/DEV CAP/ISM INT/TRADE EFFICIENCY MARXISM 20 THIRD/WRLD. PAGE 110 A2257
FOR/AID ECO/TAC DIPLOM INDUS

B59
NUNEZ JIMENEZ A.,LA LIBERACION DE LAS ISLAS. CUBA L/A+17C USA+45 LAW CHIEF PLAN DIPLOM FOR/AID OWN WEALTH 20 CASTRO/F. PAGE 110 A2261
AGRI REV ECO/UNDEV NAT/G

B59
ROPKE W.,INTERNATIONAL ORDER AND ECONOMIC INTEGRATION. ECO/DEV ECO/UNDEV AGRI FINAN INDUS INT/ORG WAR PEACE ORD/FREE...SOC METH/COMP 20 EEC. PAGE 123 A2524
INT/TRADE DIPLOM BAL/PAY ALL/IDEOS

B59
WARD B.,5 IDEAS THAT CHANGE THE WORLD. WOR+45 WOR-45 SOCIETY STRUCT AGRI INDUS INT/ORG NAT/G FORCES ACT/RES ARMS/CONT TOTALISM ATTIT DRIVE GEN/LAWS. PAGE 161 A3278
ECO/UNDEV ALL/VALS NAT/LISM COLONIAL

B60
ASPREMONT-LYNDEN H.,RAPPORT SUR L'ADMINISTRATION BELGE DU RUANDA-URUNDI PENDANT L'ANNEE 1959. BELGIUM RWANDA AGRI INDUS DIPLOM ECO/TAC INT/TRADE DOMIN ADMIN RACE/REL...GEOG CENSUS 20 UN. PAGE 9 A0192
AFR COLONIAL ECO/UNDEV INT/ORG

B60
HEYSE T.,PROBLEMS FONCIERS ET REGIME DES TERRES (ASPECTS ECONOMIQUES, JURIDIQUES ET SOCIAUX). AFR CONGO/BRAZ INT/ORG DIPLOM SOVEREIGN...GEOG TREATY 20. PAGE 64 A1325
BIBLIOG AGRI ECO/UNDEV LEGIS

B60
LATIFI D.,INDIA AND UNITED STATES AID. ASIA INDIA UK USA+45 AGRI FINAN INDUS COLONIAL ORD/FREE SOVEREIGN WEALTH...METH/COMP 20. PAGE 85 A1743
FOR/AID DIPLOM ECO/UNDEV

B60
LEVIN J.V.,THE EXPORT ECONOMIES: THEIR PATTERN OF DEVELOPMENT IN HISTORICAL PERSPECTIVE. BURMA PERU AGRI WORKER COLONIAL COST DEMAND INCOME 20. PAGE 88 A1795
INT/TRADE ECO/UNDEV BAL/PAY EXTR/IND

B60
MC CLELLAN G.S.,INDIA. CHINA/COM INDIA CONSTN ELITES STRATA AGRI POL/PAR FOR/AID ARMS/CONT REV MARXISM...CENSUS BIBLIOG 20 COLD/WAR GANDHI/M NEHRU/J. PAGE 97 A1990
DIPLOM NAT/G SOCIETY ECO/UNDEV

B60
PENTONY D.E.,THE UNDERDEVELOPED LANDS. FUT WOR+45 CULTURE AGRI FINAN INDUS MARKET INT/ORG LABOR NAT/G VOL/ASSN CONSULT TEC/DEV ECO/TAC EDU/PROP COLONIAL ATTIT WEALTH...OBS RECORD SAMP TREND GEN/METH WORK UN 20. PAGE 115 A2351
ECO/UNDEV POLICY FOR/AID INT/TRADE

B60
THE ECONOMIST (LONDON),THE COMMONWEALTH AND EUROPE. EUR+WWI WOR+45 AGRI FINAN INCOME...STAT CENSUS CHARTS CMN/WLTH EEC. PAGE 142 A2911
INT/TRADE INDUS INT/ORG NAT/COMP

S60
RICHTER J.H.,"TOWARDS AN INTERNATIONAL POLICY ON AGRICULTURAL TRADE." EUR+WWI USA+45 ECO/DEV NAT/G PLAN ECO/TAC ATTIT PWR WEALTH...CONCPT GEN/LAWS 20. PAGE 121 A2475
AGRI INT/ORG

S60
RIVKIN A.,"AFRICAN ECONOMIC DEVELOPMENT: ADVANCED TECHNOLOGY AND THE STAGES OF GROWTH." CULTURE ECO/UNDEV AGRI COM/IND EXTR/IND PLAN ECO/TAC ATTIT DRIVE RIGID/FLEX SKILL WEALTH...MGT SOC GEN/LAWS WORK TOT/POP 20. PAGE 121 A2487
AFR TEC/DEV FOR/AID

B61
DIMOCK M.E.,BUSINESS AND GOVERNMENT (4TH ED.). AGRI FINAN OP/RES PLAN BUDGET DIPLOM LOBBY NUC/PWR NEW/LIB SOCISM...POLICY BIBLIOG 20. PAGE 37 A0765
NAT/G INDUS LABOR ECO/TAC

B61
HADDAD J.A.,REVOLUCAO CUBANA E REVOLUCAO BRASILEIRA. BRAZIL CUBA L/A+17C STRATA AGRI WORKER EDU/PROP REGION...POLICY NAT/COMP 20. PAGE 59 A1210
REV ORD/FREE DIPLOM ECO/UNDEV

B61
HARRISON S.,INDIA AND THE UNITED STATES. FUT S/ASIA USA+45 WOR+45 INTELL ECO/DEV ECO/UNDEV AGRI INDUS INT/ORG NAT/G CONSULT EX/STRUC TOP/EX PLAN ECO/TAC NEUTRAL ALL/VALS...MGT TOT/POP 20. PAGE 62 A1272
DELIB/GP ACT/RES FOR/AID INDIA

B61
INTERNATIONAL BANK RECONST DEV,THE WORLD BANK IN AFRICA: SUMMARY OF ACTIVITIES. AGRI COM/IND DIST/IND EXTR/IND INDUS TAX COST...CHARTS 20. PAGE 71 A1450
FINAN ECO/UNDEV INT/ORG AFR

B61
STARK H.,SOCIAL AND ECONOMIC FRONTIERS IN LATIN AMERICA (2ND ED.). CUBA FUT CULTURE AGRI INDUS ECO/TAC PRODUC ATTIT MARXISM...NAT/COMP BIBLIOG T 20. PAGE 137 A2807
L/A+17C SOCIETY DIPLOM ECO/UNDEV

B61
US GENERAL ACCOUNTING OFFICE,EXAMINATION OF ECONOMIC AND TECHNICAL ASSISTANCE PROGRAM FOR IRAN. IRAN USA+45 AGRI INDUS DIPLOM CONTROL COST 20. PAGE 153 A3115
FOR/AID ADMIN TEC/DEV ECO/UNDEV

B61
US HOUSE COMM FOREIGN AFFAIRS,THE INTERNATIONAL DEVELOPMENT AND SECURITY ACT: HEARINGS BEFORE COMMITTEE ON FOREIGN AFFAIRS, HOUSE OF REP: HR7372. USA+45 AGRI INT/ORG NAT/G CONSULT DELIB/GP DIPLOM ECO/TAC INT/TRADE LOBBY REPRESENT 20 MCNAMARA/R DILLON/D RUSK/D CONGRESS. PAGE 153 A3128
FOR/AID CONFER LEGIS ECO/UNDEV

S61
"CRITERIA FOR ALLOCATING INVESTMENT RESOURCES AMONG VARIOUS FIELDS OF DEVELOPMENT IN UNDERDEVELOPED ECONOMIES." ASIA AGRI INT/ORG CAP/ISM BAL/PAY EFFICIENCY PROFIT WEALTH...STAT 20 UN. PAGE 3 A0061
BIBLIOG/A ECO/UNDEV PLAN TEC/DEV

S61
OCHENG D.,"AN ECONOMIST LOOKS AT UGANDA'S FUTURE." FUT UGANDA AGRI INDUS PLAN PROB/SOLV INT/TRADE SOVEREIGN 20. PAGE 111 A2275
ECO/UNDEV INCOME ECO/TAC OWN

S61
VINER J.,"ECONOMIC FOREIGN POLICY ON THE NEW FRONTIER." USA+45 ECO/UNDEV AGRI FINAN INDUS MARKET INT/ORG NAT/G FOR/AID INT/TRADE ADMIN ATTIT PWR 20 KENNEDY/JF. PAGE 159 A3239
TOP/EX ECO/TAC BAL/PAY TARIFFS

B62
BRIMMER B.,A GUIDE TO THE USE OF UNITED NATIONS DOCUMENTS. WOR+45 ECO/UNDEV AGRI EX/STRUC FORCES PROB/SOLV ADMIN WAR PEACE WEALTH...POLICY UN. PAGE 19 A0378
BIBLIOG/A INT/ORG DIPLOM

B62
CADWELL R.,COMMUNISM IN THE MODERN WORLD. USSR WOR+45 SOCIETY AGRI INDUS INT/ORG SECT EDU/PROP COLONIAL PEACE...SOC 20. PAGE 23 A0463
COM DIPLOM POLICY CONCPT

B62
CALDER R.,COMMON SENSE ABOUT A STARVING WORLD. WOR+45 STRATA ECO/DEV PLAN GP/REL BIO/SOC HABITAT ...POLICY GEOG STAT RECORD 20 UN BIRTH/CON. PAGE 23 A0466
FOR/AID CENSUS ECO/UNDEV AGRI

B62
FAO,FOOD AND AGRICULTURE ORGANIZATION AFRICAN SURVEY. AFR CONGO/BRAZ GHANA STRATA AGRI INT/ORG TEC/DEV FOR/AID INT/TRADE RACE/REL DEMAND EFFICIENCY PRODUC...GEOG 20 UN CONGO/LEOP. PAGE 44 A0898
ECO/TAC WEALTH EXTR/IND ECO/UNDEV

B62
KENNEDY J.F.,TO TURN THE TIDE. SPACE AGRI INT/ORG FORCES TEC/DEV ADMIN NUC/PWR PEACE WEALTH...ANTHOL 20 KENNEDY/JF CIV/RIGHTS. PAGE 78 A1592
DIPLOM CHIEF POLICY NAT/G

B62
KRAFT J.,THE GRAND DESIGN. EUR+WWI USA+45 AGRI FINAN INDUS MARKET INT/ORG NAT/G PLAN ECO/TAC TARIFFS REGION DRIVE ORD/FREE WEALTH...POLICY OBS TREND EEC 20. PAGE 82 A1674
VOL/ASSN ECO/DEV INT/TRADE

B62
LAUERHAUSS L.,COMMUNISM IN LATIN AMERICA: THE POST-WAR YEARS (1945 -1960) (PAPER). INTELL STRATA ECO/UNDEV AGRI WORKER FOR/AID INT/TRADE COLONIAL GUERRILLA 20. PAGE 85 A1745
BIBLIOG L/A+17C MARXISM REV

B62
LEWIS J.P.,QUIET CRISIS IN INDIA. INDIA USA+45 CULTURE ECO/UNDEV AGRI INDUS PROC/MFG NAT/G PLAN TEC/DEV DRIVE PWR SKILL WEALTH...MYTH 20. PAGE 88 A1801
S/ASIA ECO/TAC FOR/AID

B62
LIPPMANN W.,WESTERN UNITY AND THE COMMON MARKET. EUR+WWI FRANCE GERMANY/W UK USA+45 ECO/DEV AGRI FINAN MARKET INT/ORG NAT/G FOR/AID AGREE WEALTH 20 EEC. PAGE 89 A1831
DIPLOM INT/TRADE VOL/ASSN

B62
MORRAY J.P.,THE SECOND REVOLUTION IN CUBA. CUBA AGRI LABOR POL/PAR DIPLOM FOR/AID GUERRILLA TOTALISM MARXISM 20. PAGE 104 A2146
REV MARXIST ECO/TAC NAT/LISM

B62
ROBINSON A.D.,DUTCH ORGANIZED AGRICULTURE IN INTERNATIONAL POLITICS, 1945-1960. EUR+WWI NETHERLAND STRUCT ECO/DEV NAT/G VOL/ASSN CONSULT DELIB/GP PLAN TEC/DEV INT/TRADE EDU/PROP ATTIT RIGID/FLEX ALL/VALS...NEW/IDEA TREND EEC 20. PAGE 122 A2502
AGRI INT/ORG

B62
THANT U.,THE UNITED NATIONS' DEVELOPMENT DECADE: PROPOSALS FOR ACTION. WOR+45 SOCIETY ECO/UNDEV AGRI COM/IND FINAN R+D MUNIC SCHOOL VOL/ASSN CONSULT PLAN TEC/DEV ECO/TAC EDU/PROP ADMIN ROUTINE RIGID/FLEX...MGT SOC CONCPT UNESCO UN TOT/POP VAL/FREE. PAGE 142 A2906
INT/ORG ALL/VALS

B62
THEOBALD R.,NATIONAL DEVELOPMENT EFFORTS (PAMPHLET). WOR+45 AGRI BUDGET FOR/AID INT/TRADE TAX 20. PAGE 142 A2914
ECO/UNDEV PLAN BAL/PAY WEALTH

B62
UNECA LIBRARY,BOOKS ON AFRICA IN THE UNECA LIBRARY. WOR+45 AGRI INT/ORG NAT/G PLAN WRITING REGION...SOC STAT UN. PAGE 147 A3008
BIBLIOG AFR ECO/UNDEV TEC/DEV

B62
WILLIAMS W.A.,THE UNITED STATES, CUBA, AND CASTRO: AN ESSAY ON THE DYNAMICS OF REVOLUTION AND THE DISSOLUTION OF EMPIRE. CUBA USA+45 AGRI VOL/ASSN DIPLOM ECO/TAC DOMIN COERCE...POLICY 20 EISNHWR/DD CIA KENNEDY/JF CASTRO/F. PAGE 165 A3354
REV CONSTN COM LEAD

B63
BRITISH AID. UK AGRI DIST/IND INDUS SCHOOL TEC/DEV INT/TRADE COLONIAL DEMAND...TREND CHARTS 20. PAGE 3 A0064
FOR/AID ECO/UNDEV NAT/G FINAN

B63
CONF ON FUTURE OF COMMONWEALTH,THE FUTURE OF THE COMMONWEALTH. UK ECO/UNDEV AGRI EDU/PROP ADMIN SOC/INTEG 20 COMMONWLTH. PAGE 29 A0583
DIPLOM RACE/REL ORD/FREE TEC/DEV

B63
EL-NAGGAR S.,FOREIGN AID TO UNITED ARAB REPUBLIC. UAR USA+45 USSR AGRI FINAN INDUS FORCES EATING DEMAND...CHARTS METH/COMP 20 RESOURCE/N AID. PAGE 41 A0838
FOR/AID ECO/UNDEV RECEIVE PLAN

B63
FISCHER-GALATI S.,EASTERN EUROPE IN THE SIXTIES. ALBANIA USSR YUGOSLAVIA ECO/UNDEV AGRI MARKET LABOR WORKER DIPLOM INT/TRADE EDU/PROP GOV/REL PRODUC UTOPIA SOCISM 20. PAGE 46 A0939
MARXISM TEC/DEV BAL/PWR ECO/TAC

B63
FLORES E.,LAND REFORM AND THE ALLIANCE FOR PROGRESS (PAMPHLET). L/A+17C USA+45 STRUCT ECO/UNDEV NAT/G WORKER CREATE PLAN ECO/TAC COERCE REV 20. PAGE 47 A0953
AGRI INT/ORG DIPLOM POLICY

B63
HONEY P.J.,COMMUNISM IN NORTH VIETNAM: ITS ROLE IN THE SINO-SOVIET DISPUTE. CHINA/COM INDIA USSR VIETNAM/N AGRI POL/PAR LEGIS ECO/TAC WAR PEACE ATTIT...GEOG IDEA/COMP 20. PAGE 67 A1378
POLICY MARXISM CHIEF DIPLOM

B63
INTERAMERICAN ECO AND SOC COUN,THE ALLIANCE FOR PROGRESS: ITS FIRST YEAR: 1961-1962. AGRI SCHOOL PLAN TEC/DEV INT/TRADE TAX GIVE ADMIN WEALTH...SOC 20 SOUTH/AMER. PAGE 71 A1449
INT/ORG PROB/SOLV ECO/TAC L/A+17C

B63
KATZ S.M.,A SELECTED LIST OF US READINGS ON DEVELOPMENT. AGRI COM/IND DIST/IND INDUS LABOR PLAN FOR/AID EDU/PROP HEALTH...POLICY SOC/WK 20. PAGE 77 A1571
BIBLIOG/A ECO/UNDEV TEC/DEV ACT/RES

B63
KLEIMAN R.,ATLANTIC CRISIS; AMERICAN DIPLOMACY CONFRONTS A RESURGENT EUROPE. EUR+WWI USA+45 ECO/DEV AGRI NAT/G CHIEF FORCES PLAN LEAD ATTIT ...CONCPT 20 NATO KENNEDY/JF DEGAULLE/C EEC JOHNSON/LB. PAGE 80 A1648
DIPLOM REGION POLICY

B63
LYONS F.S.L.,INTERNATIONALISM IN EUROPE 1815-1914. LAW AGRI COM/IND DIST/IND LABOR SECT INT/TRADE TARIFFS...BIBLIOG 19/20. PAGE 92 A1880
DIPLOM MOD/EUR INT/ORG

B63
MOSELY P.E.,THE SOVIET UNION, 1922-1962: A FOREIGN AFFAIRS READER. ASIA POLAND USSR CULTURE INTELL AGRI POL/PAR WORKER INT/TRADE DOMIN WAR NAT/LISM MARXISM SOCISM 20 KHRUSH/N. PAGE 105 A2152
PWR POLICY DIPLOM

B63
PEREZ ORTIZ R.,ANUARIO BIBLIOGRAFICO COLOMBIANO, 1961. AGRI...INT/LAW JURID SOC LING 20 COLOMB. PAGE 115 A2354
BIBLIOG L/A+17C NAT/G

B63
RIUKIN A.,THE AFRICAN PRESENCE IN WORLD AFFAIRS. AFR WOR+45 ECO/UNDEV AGRI INT/ORG BAL/PWR ECO/TAC COLONIAL NEUTRAL NAT/LISM PEACE SOVEREIGN 20 UN. PAGE 121 A2486
DIPLOM NAT/G POLICY PWR

B63
RIVKIN A.,THE AFRICAN PRESENCE IN WORLD AFFAIRS. ECO/UNDEV AGRI INT/ORG LOC/G NAT/LISM...OBS PREDICT GOV/COMP 20. PAGE 121 A2489
AFR NAT/G DIPLOM BAL/PWR

B63
ROBOCK S.H.,OVERVIEW OF TOTAL BRAZILIAN SETTING, NEWER REGIONAL PATTERNS NING AND FOREIGN AID. BRAZIL ECO/UNDEV AGRI FINAN INDUS INT/ORG INCOME UTIL...CHARTS 20. PAGE 122 A2507
ECO/TAC REGION PLAN FOR/AID

B63
SALENT W.S.,THE UNITED STATES BALANCE OF PAYMENTS IN 1968. EUR+WWI UK USA+45 AGRI R+D LABOR FORCES PRODUC...GEOG CONCPT CHARTS 20 CHINJAP EEC. PAGE 126 A2589
BAL/PAY DEMAND FINAN INT/TRADE

B63
US AGENCY INTERNATIONAL DEV,US FOREIGN ASSISTANCE AND ASSISTANCE FROM INTERNATIONAL ORGANIZATIONS. USA+45 ECO/UNDEV AGRI WORKER NAT/G TEC/DEV BUDGET. PAGE 149 A3050
FOR/AID INT/ORG CHARTS STAT

B63
US ECON SURVEY TEAM INDONESIA,INDONESIA - PERSPECTIVE AND PROPOSALS FOR UNITED STATES ECONOMIC AID. INDONESIA AGRI MARKET TEC/DEV DIPLOM INT/TRADE EDU/PROP 20. PAGE 153 A3113
FOR/AID ECO/UNDEV PLAN INDUS

B63
WHITNEY T.P.,KHRUSHCHEV SPEAKS. USSR AGRI LEAD ...BIOG ANTHOL 20 KHRUSH/N STALIN/J ESPIONAGE. PAGE 164 A3339
DIPLOM MARXISM CHIEF

S63
GORDON B.,"ECONOMIC IMPEDIMENTS TO REGIONALISM IN SOUTH EAST ASIA." BURMA FUT S/ASIA THAILAND USA+45 AGRI INDUS R+D NAT/G PLAN ECO/TAC WEALTH...STAT CONT/OBS 20. PAGE 54 A1110
VOL/ASSN ECO/UNDEV INT/TRADE REGION

S63
MARTHELOT P.,"PROGRES DE LA REFORME AGRAIRE." INTELL ECO/DEV R+D FOR/AID ADMIN KNOWL...OBS VAL/FREE UN 20. PAGE 95 A1948
AGRI INT/ORG

C63
SCHMITT K.M.,"EVOLUTION OR CHAOS: DYNAMICS OF LATIN AMERICAN GOVERNMENT AND POLITICS." L/A+17C AGRI FINAN CAP/ISM EXEC LEAD BAL/PAY TOTALISM ATTIT ...TREND BIBLIOG 20. PAGE 129 A2635
DIPLOM POLICY POL/PAR LOBBY

B64
CEPEDE M.,POPULATION AND FOOD. USA+45 STRUCT ECO/UNDEV FAM PLAN TEC/DEV FOR/AID CONTROL...CATH SOC TREND 19/20. PAGE 25 A0513
FUT GEOG AGRI

CENSUS

B64
FREE L.A.,THE ATTITUDES, HOPES AND FEARS OF NIGERIANS. AFR NIGERIA ECO/UNDEV AGRI ACADEM PLAN TASK...GEOG CHARTS METH 20. PAGE 49 A0993
NAT/LISM SYS/QU DIPLOM

B64
HAMBRIDGE G.,DYNAMICS OF DEVELOPMENT. AGRI FINAN INDUS LABOR INT/TRADE EDU/PROP ADMIN LEAD OWN HEALTH...ANTHOL BIBLIOG 20. PAGE 61 A1245
ECO/UNDEV ECO/TAC OP/RES ACT/RES

B64
HAZLEWOOD A.,THE ECONOMICS OF DEVELOPMENT: AN ANNOTATED LIST OF BOOKS AND ARTICLES PUBLISHED 1958-1962. AGRI FINAN INDUS LABOR NAT/G DIPLOM INT/TRADE INCOME...MGT 20. PAGE 63 A1303
BIBLIOG/A ECO/UNDEV TEC/DEV

B64
HINSHAW R.,THE EUROPEAN COMMUNITY AND AMERICAN TRADE: A STUDY IN ATLANTIC ECONOMICS AND POLICY. EUR+WWI UK USA+45 ECO/DEV ECO/UNDEV AGRI INDUS INT/ORG NAT/G ECO/TAC TARIFFS REGION...STAT CHARTS EEC 20. PAGE 65 A1337
MARKET TREND INT/TRADE

B64
KRETZSCHMAR W.W.,AUSLANDSHILFE ALS MITTEL DER AUSSENWIRTSCHAFTS- UND AUSSENPOLITIK. ASIA GERMANY/W UK USA+45 SOCIETY STRUCT ECO/UNDEV LOBBY EFFICIENCY 20. PAGE 82 A1683
FOR/AID DIPLOM AGRI DIST/IND

B64
MASON E.S.,FOREIGN AID AND FOREIGN POLICY. USA+45 AGRI INDUS NAT/G EX/STRUC ACT/RES RIGID/FLEX ALL/VALS...POLICY GEN/LAWS MARSHL/PLN CONGRESS 20. PAGE 95 A1956
ECO/UNDEV ECO/TAC FOR/AID DIPLOM

B64
MC GOVERN G.S.,WAR AGAINST WANT. USA+45 AGRI DIPLOM INT/TRADE GIVE RECEIVE DEMAND HEALTH 20 KENNEDY/JF FOOD/PEACE. PAGE 97 A1993
FOR/AID ECO/DEV POLICY EATING

B64
MORGAN T.,GOLDWATER EITHER/OR; A SELF-PORTRAIT BASED UPON HIS OWN WORDS. USA+45 CONSTN AGRI LABOR DIPLOM RACE/REL WEALTH POPULISM...POLICY MAJORIT 20 GOLDWATR/B REPUBLICAN. PAGE 104 A2131
LEAD POL/PAR CHOOSE ATTIT

B64
MYINT H.,THE ECONOMICS OF THE DEVELOPING COUNTRIES. WOR+45 AGRI PLAN COST...POLICY GEOG 20 MONEY. PAGE 107 A2187
ECO/UNDEV INT/TRADE EXTR/IND FINAN

B64
OECD,DEVELOPMENT ASSISTANCE EFFORTS - POLICIES OF THE MEMBERS. AGRI INDUS BUDGET...GEOG NAT/COMP 20 OECD. PAGE 111 A2280
INT/ORG FOR/AID ECO/UNDEV TEC/DEV

B64
RANIS G.,THE UNITED STATES AND THE DEVELOPING ECONOMIES. COM USA+45 AGRI FINAN TEC/DEV CAP/ISM ECO/TAC INT/TRADE...POLICY METH/COMP ANTHOL 20 AID. PAGE 119 A2441
ECO/UNDEV DIPLOM FOR/AID

B64
SINGER H.W.,INTERNATIONAL DEVELOPMENT: GROWTH AND CHANGE. AFR BRAZIL L/A+17C WOR+45 CULTURE AGRI INDUS NAT/G ACT/RES ECO/TAC EDU/PROP WEALTH...GEOG CONCPT METH/CNCPT STAT HYPO/EXP WORK TOT/POP 20. PAGE 133 A2723
FINAN ECO/UNDEV FOR/AID INT/TRADE

B64
WITHERS W.,THE ECONOMIC CRISIS IN LATIN AMERICA. BRAZIL CHILE STRATA AGRI DIPLOM FOR/AID PWR SOCISM ...POLICY 20 MEXIC/AMER ARGEN. PAGE 166 A3372
L/A+17C ECO/UNDEV CAP/ISM ALL/IDEOS

L64
POUNDS N.J.G.,"THE POLITICS OF PARTITION." AFR ASIA COM EUR+WWI FUT ISLAM S/ASIA USA-45 LAW ECO/DEV ECO/UNDEV AGRI INDUS INT/ORG POL/PAR PROVS SECT FORCES TOP/EX EDU/PROP LEGIT ATTIT MORAL ORD/FREE PWR RESPECT WEALTH. PAGE 117 A2402
NAT/G NAT/LISM

S64
GERBET P.,"LA MISE EN OEUVRE DU MARCHE COMMUN AGRICOLE." ECO/DEV MARKET INT/ORG NAT/G PLAN EDU/PROP NAT/LISM WEALTH...OBS EEC VAL/FREE 20. PAGE 52 A1064
EUR+WWI AGRI REGION

S64
HUELIN D.,"ECONOMIC INTEGRATION IN LATIN AMERICAN: PROGRESS AND PROBLEMS." L/A+17C ECO/DEV AGRI DIST/IND FINAN INDUS NAT/G VOL/ASSN CONSULT DELIB/GP EX/STRUC ACT/RES PLAN TEC/DEV ECO/TAC ROUTINE BAL/PAY WEALTH WORK 20. PAGE 69 A1411
MARKET ECO/UNDEV INT/TRADE

S64
TRISKA J.F.,"SOVIET TREATY LAW: A QUANTITATIVE ANALYSIS." WOR+45 LAW ECO/UNDEV AGRI COM/IND INDUS CREATE TEC/DEV DIPLOM ATTIT PWR WEALTH...JURID SAMP TIME/SEQ TREND CHARTS VAL/FREE 20 TREATY. PAGE 145 A2967
COM ECO/TAC INT/LAW USSR

S64
ZARTMAN I.W.,"LES RELATIONS ENTRE LA FRANCE ET L'ALGERIA DEPUIS LES ACCORDS D'EVIAN." EUR+WWI FUT ISLAM CULTURE AGRI EXTR/IND FINAN INDUS POL/PAR DIPLOM ECO/TAC FOR/AID PEACE ATTIT DRIVE ALL/VALS ...TIME/SEQ VAL/FREE 20. PAGE 169 A3446
ECO/UNDEV ALGERIA FRANCE

B65
ANALYSIS AND ASSESSMENT OF THE ECONOMIC EFFECTS: PUBLIC LAW 480 TITLE I PROGRAM TURKEY. INDIA TURKEY USA+45 AGRI NAT/G PLAN BUDGET DIPLOM COST EFFICIENCY...CHARTS 20. PAGE 3 A0070
ECO/TAC FOR/AID FINAN ECO/UNDEV

B65
AMERICAN ECONOMIC ASSOCIATION,INDEX OF ECONOMIC JOURNALS 1886-1965 (7 VOLS.). UK USA+45 USA-45 AGRI FINAN PLAN ECO/TAC INT/TRADE ADMIN...STAT CENSUS 19/20. PAGE 7 A0145
BIBLIOG WRITING INDUS

B65
BRIDGMAN J.,GERMAN AFRICA: A SELECT ANNOTATED BIBLIOGRAPHY. AFR AGRI DIPLOM REPAR WAR FASCISM 20. PAGE 18 A0374
BIBLIOG/A COLONIAL NAT/G EDU/PROP

B65
FORM W.H.,INDUSTRIAL RELATIONS AND SOCIAL CHANGE IN LATIN AMERICA. L/A+17C AGRI LABOR NAT/G PLAN PROB/SOLV DIPLOM...MGT SOC ANTHOL BIBLIOG/A METH 20. PAGE 47 A0966
INDUS GP/REL NAT/COMP ECO/UNDEV

B65
INTERNATIONAL SOCIAL SCI COUN,SOCIAL SCIENCES IN THE USSR. USSR ECO/DEV AGRI FINAN INDUS PLAN CAP/ISM...INT/LAW PHIL/SCI PSY SOC 20. PAGE 71 A1460
BIBLIOG/A ACT/RES MARXISM JURID

B65
JALEE P.,THE PILLAGE OF THE THIRD WORLD (TRANS. BY MARY KLOPPER). WOR+45 AGRI INDUS ECO/TAC FOR/AID COLONIAL CONTROL PRODUC PWR WEALTH...STAT CHARTS 20 RESOURCE/N. PAGE 73 A1493
ECO/UNDEV DOMIN INT/TRADE DIPLOM

B65
JOHNSON H.G.,THE WORLD ECONOMY AT THE CROSSROADS. COM WOR-45 ECO/DEV AGRI INDUS INT/TRADE REGION NAT/LISM 20. PAGE 74 A1523
FINAN DIPLOM INT/ORG ECO/UNDEV

B65
KRAUSE W.,ECONOMIC DEVELOPMENT: THE UNDERDEVELOPED WORLD AND THE AMERICAN INTEREST. USA+45 AGRI PLAN MARXISM...CHARTS 20. PAGE 82 A1679
FOR/AID ECO/UNDEV FINAN PROB/SOLV

B65
MANSFIELD P.,NASSER'S EGYPT. AFR ISLAM UAR ECO/UNDEV AGRI COLONIAL SOVEREIGN...CHARTS 20 NASSER/G MID/EAST. PAGE 94 A1934
CHIEF ECO/TAC DIPLOM POLICY

B65
MCCOLL G.D.,THE AUSTRALIAN BALANCE OF PAYMENTS. UK USA+45 AGRI WORKER DIPLOM EQUILIB PRODUC...STAT TREND CHARTS BIBLIOG/A 20 AUSTRAL. PAGE 97 A2001
ECO/DEV BAL/PAY INT/TRADE COST

B65
MONCRIEFF A.,SECOND THOUGHTS ON AID. WOR+45 ECO/UNDEV AGRI FINAN VOL/ASSN PLAN TEC/DEV GIVE EDU/PROP ROLE WEALTH 20. PAGE 102 A2105
FOR/AID ECO/TAC INT/ORG IDEA/COMP

B65
MURUMBI J.,PROBLEMS OF ECONOMIC DEVELOPMENT IN EAST AFRICA. FINAN INDUS WORKER TEC/DEV INT/TRADE TAX DEMAND EFFICIENCY PRODUC SOCISM...TREND CHARTS 20 AFRICA/E. PAGE 106 A2184
AGRI ECO/TAC ECO/UNDEV PROC/MFG

B65
SABLE M.H.,MASTER DIRECTORY FOR LATIN AMERICA. AGRI COM/IND FINAN R+D ACADEM LABOR NAT/G POL/PAR VOL/ASSN INT/TRADE EDU/PROP 20. PAGE 126 A2582
INDEX L/A+17C INT/ORG DIPLOM

B65
SILVA SOLAR J.,EL DESARROLLO DE LA NUEVA SOCIEDAD EN AMERICA. L/A+17C SOCIETY AGRI PROB/SOLV DIPLOM PARTIC GP/REL OWN...POLICY SOC 20 REFORMERS. PAGE 133 A2716
STRUCT ECO/UNDEV REGION CONTROL

B65
STEWART I.G.,AFRICAN PRIMARY PRODUCTS AND INTERNATIONAL TRADE. ECO/UNDEV AGRI FINAN DIPLOM CONTROL 20. PAGE 138 A2825
AFR INT/TRADE INT/ORG

L65
MATTHEWS D.G.,"A CURRENT BIBLIOGRAPHY ON SUDANESE AFFAIRS; A SELECT BIBLIOGRAPHY FROM 1960-1964." SUDAN LAW CULTURE AGRI FINAN INDUS LABOR POL/PAR TEC/DEV FOR/AID RACE/REL LITERACY...LING 20. PAGE 96 A1970
BIBLIOG ECO/UNDEV NAT/G DIPLOM

L65
WIONCZEK M.,"LATIN AMERICA FREE TRADE ASSOCIATION." AGRI DIST/IND FINAN INDUS INT/ORG LABOR NAT/G TEC/DEV ECO/TAC HEALTH SKILL WEALTH...POLICY RELATIV MGT LAFTA 20. PAGE 165 A3369
L/A+17C MARKET REGION

S65
AFRICAN BIBLIOGRAPHIC CENTER,"US TREATIES AND AGREEMENTS WITH COUNTRIES IN AFRICA, 1957 TO MID-1963." AFR USA+45 AGRI FINAN FORCES TEC/DEV CAP/ISM FOR/AID 20. PAGE 5 A0097
BIBLIOG DIPLOM INT/ORG INT/TRADE

S65
HELMREICH E.C.,"KADAR'S HUNGARY." COM EUR+WWI HUNGARY USSR INTELL ECO/DEV AGRI INT/ORG TOP/EX DOMIN ALL/VALS WORK COLD/WAR 20. PAGE 64 A1311
NAT/G RIGID/FLEX TOTALISM

S65
KHOURI F.J.,"THE JORDON RIVER CONTROVERSY." LAW
ISLAM

SOCIETY ECO/UNDEV AGRI FINAN INDUS SECT FORCES INT/ORG
ACT/RES PLAN TEC/DEV ECO/TAC EDU/PROP COERCE ATTIT ISRAEL
DRIVE PERCEPT RIGID/FLEX ALL/VALS...GEOG SOC MYTH JORDAN
WORK. PAGE 78 A1610

C65
WUORINEN J.H.,"SCANDINAVIA." DENMARK FINLAND BIBLIOG
ICELAND NORWAY SWEDEN SOCIETY AGRI POL/PAR DELIB/GP NAT/G
DIPLOM INT/TRADE NEUTRAL WAR...CHARTS TREATY 20. POLICY
PAGE 168 A3423

B66
BROEKMEIJER M.W.J.,FICTION AND TRUTH ABOUT THE FOR/AID
"DECADE OF DEVELOPMENT" WOR+45 AGRI FINAN INDUS POLICY
NAT/G TEC/DEV DIPLOM EDU/PROP LEAD SKILL 20 ECO/UNDEV
THIRD/WRLD. PAGE 19 A0385 PLAN

B66
BROWN J.F.,THE NEW EASTERN EUROPE. ALBANIA BULGARIA DIPLOM
HUNGARY POLAND ROMANIA CULTURE AGRI POL/PAR WAR COM
NAT/LISM MARXISM...CHARTS BIBLIOG 20. PAGE 20 A0404 NAT/G
ECO/UNDEV

B66
BROWN L.C.,STATE AND SOCIETY IN INDEPENDENT NORTH NAT/G
AFRICA. ALGERIA LIBYA MOROCCO AGRI INDUS INT/ORG SOCIETY
POL/PAR SECT PLAN DIPLOM COLONIAL...LING NAT/COMP CULTURE
ANTHOL BIBLIOG 20 TUNIS MUSLIM. PAGE 20 A0406 ECO/UNDEV

B66
COLE A.B.,SOCIALIST PARTIES IN POSTWAR JAPAN. POL/PAR
STRATA AGRI LABOR PLAN DIPLOM ECO/TAC AGREE LEAD POLICY
CHOOSE ATTIT...CHARTS 20 CHINJAP SOC/DEMPAR. SOCISM
PAGE 28 A0566 NAT/G

B66
DAVIDSON A.B.,RUSSIA AND AFRICA. USSR AGRI MARXISM
INT/TRADE...GEOG BIBLIOG/A 18/20. PAGE 34 A0687 COLONIAL
RACE/REL
DIPLOM

B66
HAYER T.,FRENCH AID. AFR FRANCE AGRI FINAN BUDGET TEC/DEV
ADMIN WAR PRODUC...CHARTS 18/20 THIRD/WRLD COLONIAL
OVRSEA/DEV. PAGE 63 A1295 FOR/AID
ECO/UNDEV

B66
HOFMANN L.,UNITED STATES AND CANADIAN PUBLICATIONS BIBLIOG
ON AFRICA IN 1964. LAW AGRI INDUS SCHOOL...HUM SOC AFR
20. PAGE 66 A1360 DIPLOM

B66
KIRDAR U.,THE STRUCTURE OF UNITED NATIONS ECONOMIC INT/ORG
AID TO UNDERDEVELOPED COUNTRIES. AGRI FINAN INDUS FOR/AID
NAT/G EX/STRUC PLAN GIVE TASK...POLICY 20 UN. ECO/UNDEV
PAGE 79 A1631 ADMIN

B66
LEWIS S.,TOWARDS INTERNATIONAL CO-OPERATION (1ST DIPLOM
ED.). WOR+45 AGRI INDUS EDU/PROP RACE/REL ISOLAT ANOMIE
NAT/LISM ATTIT HEALTH WEALTH...CHARTS WORSHIP 20 PROB/SOLV
UN. PAGE 88 A1803 INT/ORG

B66
MONTGOMERY J.D.,APPROACHES TO DEVELOPMENT: ECO/UNDEV
POLITICS, ADMINISTRATION AND CHANGE. USA+45 AGRI ADMIN
FOR/AID ORD/FREE...CONCPT IDEA/COMP METH/COMP POLICY
ANTHOL. PAGE 103 A2116 ECO/TAC

B66
MULLER C.F.J.,A SELECT BIBLIOGRAPHY OF SOUTH BIBLIOG
AFRICAN HISTORY; A GUIDE FOR HISTORICAL RESEARCH. AFR
SOUTH/AFR UK LAW CONSTN SOCIETY STRUCT AGRI SECT NAT/G
DIPLOM COLONIAL LEAD RACE/REL...POLICY 17/20 NEGRO.
PAGE 106 A2167

B66
O'CONNER A.M.,AN ECONOMIC GEOGRAPHY OF EAST AFRICA. ECO/UNDEV
AFR TANZANIA UGANDA AGRI WORKER INT/TRADE COLONIAL EXTR/IND
GOV/REL...CHARTS METH/COMP 20 AFRICA/E. PAGE 111 GEOG
A2269 HABITAT

B66
ROBOCK S.H.,INTERNATIONAL DEVELOPMENT 1965. AGRI FOR/AID
INDUS VOL/ASSN PLAN TEC/DEV EDU/PROP HEALTH...JURID INT/ORG
20 UN PEACE/CORP. PAGE 122 A2508 GEOG
ECO/UNDEV

B66
TINKER H.,SOUTH ASIA. UK LAW ECO/UNDEV AGRI ACADEM S/ASIA
SECT DIPLOM EDU/PROP REV WEALTH ALL/IDEOS...CHARTS COLONIAL
BIBLIOG GANDHI/M NEHRU/J. PAGE 144 A2945 TREND

B66
US SENATE COMM GOVT OPERATIONS,POPULATION CRISIS. CENSUS
USA+45 ECO/DEV ECO/UNDEV AGRI SECT DELIB/GP CONTROL
PROB/SOLV FOR/AID REPRESENT ATTIT...GEOG CHARTS 20 LEGIS
CONGRESS DEPT/STATE DEPT/HEW BIRTH/CON. PAGE 156 CONSULT
A3178

B66
VIEN N.C.,SEEKING THE TRUTH. FRANCE VIETNAM AGRI NAT/G
ADMIN WAR...BIOG 20 BAO/DAI INTERVENT. PAGE 159 CONSULT
A3231 CONSTN

B66
WESTWOOD A.F.,FOREIGN AID IN A FOREIGN POLICY FOR/AID
FRAMEWORK. AFR ASIA INDIA IRAN L/A+17C USA+45 USSR DIPLOM
ECO/UNDEV AGRI FORCES LEGIS PLAN PROB/SOLV POLICY
...DECISION 20 COLD/WAR. PAGE 163 A3324 ECO/TAC

B66
WHITAKER A.P.,NATIONALISM IN CONTEMPORARY LATIN NAT/LISM
AMERICA. AGRI NAT/G WEALTH...POLICY SOC CONCPT OBS L/A+17C
TREND 20. PAGE 164 A3333 DIPLOM
ECO/UNDEV

L66
AMERICAN ECONOMIC REVIEW,"SIXTY-THIRD LIST OF BIBLIOG/A
DOCTORAL DISSERTATIONS IN POLITICAL ECONOMY IN CONCPT
AMERICAN UNIVERSITIES AND COLLEGES." ECO/DEV AGRI ACADEM
FINAN LABOR WORKER PLAN BUDGET INT/TRADE ADMIN
DEMAND...MGT STAT 20. PAGE 7 A0146

S66
MATTHEWS D.G.,"ETHIOPIAN OUTLINE: A BIBLIOGRAPHIC BIBLIOG
RESEARCH GUIDE." ETHIOPIA LAW STRUCT ECO/UNDEV AGRI NAT/G
LABOR SECT CHIEF DELIB/GP EX/STRUC ADMIN...LING DIPLOM
ORG/CHARTS 20. PAGE 96 A1972 POL/PAR

N66
BRITISH DEVELOPMENT POLICIES: 1966 (PAMPHLET). UK WEALTH
AGRI TARIFFS BAL/PAY...TREND CHARTS 20 OVRSEA/DEV. DIPLOM
PAGE 4 A0076 INT/TRADE
FOR/AID

B67
JOHNSON D.G.,THE STRUGGLE AGAINST WORLD HUNGER AGRI
(HEADLINE SERIES, NO. 184) (PAMPHLET). PLAN TEC/DEV PROB/SOLV
FOR/AID...CHARTS 20 FAO MEXIC/AMER. PAGE 74 A1520 ECO/UNDEV
HEALTH

B67
SACHS M.Y.,THE WORLDMARK ENCYCLOPEDIA OF THE WOR+45
NATIONS (5 VOLS.). ELITES SOCIETY STRATA ECO/DEV INT/ORG
ECO/UNDEV AGRI EXTR/IND FINAN LABOR LOC/G NAT/G BAL/PWR
POL/PAR SECT INT/TRADE SOVEREIGN...SOC 20. PAGE 126
A2585

B67
US AGENCY INTERNATIONAL DEV,PROPOSED FOREIGN AID ECO/UNDEV
PROGRAM FOR 1968: SUMMARY PRESENTATION TO THE BUDGET
CONGRESS. AFR S/ASIA USA+45 AGRI TEC/DEV DIPLOM FOR/AID
ECO/TAC BAL/PAY COST HEALTH KNOWL SKILL 20 AID STAT
CONGRESS. PAGE 149 A3053

S67
BUTTINGER J.,"VIETNAM* FRAUD OF THE 'OTHER WAR'." PLAN
VIETNAM/S ELITES STRUCT AGRI NAT/G FOR/AID RENT WEALTH
TREND. PAGE 22 A0456 REV
ECO/UNDEV

S67
COSGROVE C.A.,"AGRICULTURE, FINANCE AND POLITICS IN ECO/DEV
THE EUROPEAN COMMUNITY." EUR+WWI DIST/IND MARKET DIPLOM
INT/ORG VOL/ASSN DELIB/GP TEC/DEV BAL/PWR BARGAIN AGRI
ECO/TAC RATION CONFER 20 EEC. PAGE 31 A0630 INT/TRADE

S67
GOLDMAN M.I.,"SOVIET ECONOMIC GROWTH SINCE THE ECO/DEV
REVOLUTION." USSR WORKER INT/TRADE PRODUC MARXISM AGRI
...POLICY TIME/SEQ 20. PAGE 53 A1090 ECO/TAC
INDUS

S67
KRISTENSEN T.,"THE SOUTH AS AN INDUSTRIAL POWER." DIPLOM
FUT WOR+45 ECO/DEV AGRI INDUS TEC/DEV...CENSUS ECO/UNDEV
TREND CHARTS 20. PAGE 82 A1686 PREDICT
PRODUC

S67
THIEN T.T.,"VIETNAM: A CASE OF SOCIAL ALIENATION." NAT/G
VIETNAM AGRI FORCES FOR/AID ADMIN REPRESENT ELITES
INGP/REL PWR 19/20. PAGE 143 A2918 WORKER
STRANGE

B68
ANTWERP-INST UNIVERSITAIRE,BIBLIOGRAPHIC BIBLIOG
COMPENDIUM: DEVELOPING COUNTRIES (ANTWERP-INST ECO/UNDEV
UNIVERSITAIRE DES TERRITOIRES D'OUTRE-MER). AFR DIPLOM
EUR+WWI SOCIETY AGRI FINAN NEIGH VOL/ASSN PROB/SOLV PLAN
TEC/DEV FOR/AID INT/TRADE 20. PAGE 8 A0166

C93
PLAYFAIR R.L.,"A BIBLIOGRAPHY OF MOROCCO." MOROCCO BIBLIOG
CULTURE AGRI FORCES DIPLOM WAR HEALTH...GEOG JURID ISLAM
SOC CHARTS. PAGE 116 A2387 MEDIT-7

B96
DE VATTEL E.,THE LAW OF NATIONS. AGRI FINAN CHIEF LAW
DIPLOM INT/TRADE AGREE OWN ALL/VALS MORAL ORD/FREE CONCPT
SOVEREIGN...GEN/LAWS 18 NATURL/LAW WOLFF/C. PAGE 35 NAT/G
A0714 INT/LAW

AGRICULTURE....SEE AGRI

AHLUWALIA K. A0102

AHRCO....ALLEGHENY HOUSING REHABILITATION CORPORATION

AID.... US AGENCY FOR INTERNATIONAL DEVELOPEMENT

B59
US GENERAL ACCOUNTING OFFICE,EXAM OF ECONOMIC AND FOR/AID
TECHNICAL ASSISTANCE PROGRAM FOR INDIA INT'NAT'L EFFICIENCY
COOP ADMIN REPORT TO CONGRESS 1955-1958. INDIA ECO/TAC
USA+45 ECO/UNDEV FINAN PLAN DIPLOM COST UTIL WEALTH TEC/DEV
...CHARTS 20 CONGRESS AID. PAGE 153 A3114

B60
US HOUSE COMM GOVT OPERATIONS,OPERATIONS OF THE FINAN
DEVELOPMENT LOAN FUND: HEARINGS (COMMITTEE ON FOR/AID
GOVERNMENT OPERATIONS). USA+45 PLAN BUDGET DIPLOM ECO/TAC
GOV/REL COST...CHARTS 20 CONGRESS DEPT/STATE AID. EFFICIENCY
PAGE 154 A3137

B61
ROBINS D.B.,EVOLVING UNITED STATES POLICIES TOWARD THE EMERGING NATIONS OF ASIA AND AFRICA (PAMPHLET). ISLAM ECO/UNDEV INT/ORG CONSULT CREATE PLAN TEC/DEV FOR/AID CONFER ALL/VALS 20 KENNEDY/JF EISNHWR/DD UN AID. PAGE 122 A2501
AFR S/ASIA DIPLOM BIBLIOG

B61
US SENATE COMM ON FOREIGN RELS,INTERNATIONAL DEVELOPMENT AND SECURITY: HEARINGS ON BILL (2 VOLS.). ECO/UNDEV FINAN FORCES REV COST WEALTH ...CHARTS 20 AID PRESIDENT. PAGE 157 A3191
FOR/AID CIVMIL/REL ORD/FREE ECO/TAC

B63
EL-NAGGAR S.,FOREIGN AID TO UNITED ARAB REPUBLIC. UAR USA+45 USSR AGRI FINAN INDUS FORCES EATING DEMAND...CHARTS METH/COMP 20 RESOURCE/N AID. PAGE 41 A0838
FOR/AID ECO/UNDEV RECEIVE PLAN

B63
US GOVERNMENT,REPORT TO INTER-AMERICAN ECONOMIC AND SOCIAL COUNCIL AT SECOND ANNUAL MEETING. L/A+17C USA+45 VOL/ASSN TEC/DEV DIPLOM TAX EATING EFFICIENCY HEALTH...STAT CHARTS 20 AID. PAGE 153 A3116
ECO/TAC FOR/AID FINAN PLAN

B63
US SENATE COMM APPROPRIATIONS,PERSONNEL ADMINISTRATION AND OPERATIONS OF AGENCY FOR INTERNATIONAL DEVELOPMENT: SPECIAL HEARING. FINAN LEAD COST UTIL SKILL...CHARTS 20 CONGRESS AID CIVIL/SERV. PAGE 155 A3170
ADMIN FOR/AID EFFICIENCY DIPLOM

B63
US SENATE COMM GOVT OPERATIONS,REPORT OF A STUDY OF US FOREIGN AID IN TEN MIDDLE EASTERN AND AFRICAN COUNTRIES. AFR ISLAM USA+45 FORCES PLAN BUDGET DIPLOM TAX DETER WEALTH...STAT CHARTS 20 CONGRESS AID MID/EAST. PAGE 156 A3174
FOR/AID EFFICIENCY ECO/TAC FINAN

N63
US AGENCY INTERNATIONAL DEV,PRINCIPLES OF FOREIGN ECONOMIC ASSISTANCE (PAMPHLET). USA+45 FINAN GP/REL BAL/PAY EFFICIENCY 20 AID. PAGE 149 A3051
FOR/AID PLAN ECO/UNDEV ATTIT

B64
COFFIN F.M.,WITNESS FOR AID. COM EUR+WWI USA+45 DIPLOM GP/REL CONSEN ORD/FREE MARXISM...NEW/IDEA 20 CONGRESS AID. PAGE 27 A0557
FOR/AID ECO/UNDEV DELIB/GP PLAN

B64
RANIS G.,THE UNITED STATES AND THE DEVELOPING ECONOMIES. COM USA+45 AGRI FINAN TEC/DEV CAP/ISM ECO/TAC INT/TRADE...POLICY METH/COMP ANTHOL 20 AID. PAGE 119 A2441
ECO/UNDEV DIPLOM FOR/AID

B64
US HOUSE COMM FOREIGN AFFAIRS,HEARINGS ON H.R. 10502 TO AMEND FURTHER THE FOREIGN ASSISTANCE ACT OF 1961. AFR ASIA L/A+17C INT/ORG CONSULT DELIB/GP TEC/DEV ECO/TAC EDU/PROP CONFER 20 UN NATO CONGRESS AID. PAGE 153 A3130
FOR/AID DIPLOM ORD/FREE ECO/UNDEV

B64
US HOUSE COMM GOVT OPERATIONS,US OWNED FOREIGN CURRENCIES: HEARINGS (COMMITTEE ON GOVERNMENT OPERATIONS). INDIA ECO/DEV PLAN BUDGET TAX DEMAND EFFICIENCY 20 AID CONGRESS. PAGE 154 A3138
FINAN ECO/TAC FOR/AID OWN

B65
COOMBS P.H.,EDUCATION AND FOREIGN AID. AFR USA+45 DIPLOM EFFICIENCY KNOWL ORD/FREE...ANTHOL 20 AID. PAGE 30 A0608
EDU/PROP FOR/AID SCHOOL ECO/UNDEV

B65
US HOUSE COMM FOREIGN AFFAIRS,HEARINGS ON DRAFT BILL TO AMEND FURTHER THE FOREIGN ASSISTANCE ACT OF 1961. AFR ASIA L/A+17C USA+45 INT/ORG DELIB/GP TEC/DEV ECO/TAC CONFER TOTALISM 20 CONGRESS AID. PAGE 153 A3131
FOR/AID ECO/UNDEV DIPLOM ORD/FREE

B66
US HOUSE COMM FOREIGN AFFAIRS,HEARINGS ON HR 12449 A BILL TO AMEND FURTHER THE FOREIGN ASSISTANCE ACT OF 1961. AFR ASIA L/A+17C USA+45 VIETNAM INT/ORG TEC/DEV INT/TRADE ATTIT ORD/FREE 20 UN NATO CONGRESS AID. PAGE 154 A3132
FOR/AID ECO/TAC ECO/UNDEV DIPLOM

B66
US HOUSE COMM GOVT OPERATIONS,AN INVESTIGATION OF THE US ECONOMIC AND MILITARY ASSISTANCE PROGRAMS IN VIETNAM. USA+45 VIETNAM/S SOCIETY CONSTRUC FINAN FORCES BUDGET INT/TRADE PEACE HEALTH...MGT HOUSE/REP AID. PAGE 154 A3139
FOR/AID ECO/UNDEV WAR INSPECT

B67
US AGENCY INTERNATIONAL DEV,PROPOSED FOREIGN AID PROGRAM FOR 1968: SUMMARY PRESENTATION TO THE CONGRESS. AFR S/ASIA USA+45 AGRI TEC/DEV DIPLOM ECO/TAC BAL/PAY COST HEALTH KNOWL SKILL 20 AID CONGRESS. PAGE 149 A3053
ECO/UNDEV BUDGET FOR/AID STAT

AIR....LOCALE OF SUBJECT ACTIVITY IS AERIAL

B36
HUDSON M.O.,INTERNATIONAL LEGISLATION: 1929-1931. WOR-45 SEA AIR AGRI FINAN LABOR DIPLOM ECO/TAC REPAR CT/SYS ARMS/CONT WAR WEAPON...JURID 20 TREATY LEAGUE/NAT. PAGE 69 A1409
INT/LAW PARL/PROC ADJUD LAW

B53
LANGER W.L.,THE UNDECLARED WAR, 1940-1941. EUR+WWI GERMANY USA-45 USSR AIR FORCES TEC/DEV CONFER CONTROL COERCE PERCEPT ORD/FREE PWR 20 CHINJAP EUROPE. PAGE 84 A1727
WAR POLICY DIPLOM

B55
SVARLIEN O.,AN INTRODUCTION TO THE LAW OF NATIONS. SEA AIR INT/ORG NAT/G CHIEF ADMIN AGREE WAR PRIVIL ORD/FREE SOVEREIGN...BIBLIOG 16/20. PAGE 140 A2868
INT/LAW DIPLOM

B57
WASSENBERGH H.A.,POST-WAR INTERNATIONAL CIVIL AVIATION POLICY AND THE LAW OF THE AIR. WOR+45 AIR INT/ORG DOMIN LEGIT PEACE ORD/FREE...POLICY JURID NEW/IDEA OBS TIME/SEQ TREND CHARTS 20 TREATY. PAGE 162 A3290
COM/IND NAT/G INT/LAW

S58
MCDOUGAL M.S.,"PERSPECTIVES FOR A LAW OF OUTER SPACE." FUT WOR+45 AIR CONSULT DELIB/GP TEC/DEV CT/SYS ORD/FREE...POLICY JURID 20 UN. PAGE 98 A2004
INT/ORG SPACE INT/LAW

B59
EMME E.M.,THE IMPACT OF AIR POWER - NATIONAL SECURITY AND WORLD POLITICS. USA+45 USSR FORCES DIPLOM WEAPON PEACE TOTALISM...POLICY NAT/COMP 20 EUROPE. PAGE 42 A0850
DETER AIR WAR ORD/FREE

B60
KINGSTON-MCCLOUG E.,DEFENSE; POLICY AND STRATEGY. UK SEA AIR TEC/DEV DIPLOM ADMIN LEAD WAR ORD/FREE ...CHARTS 20. PAGE 79 A1627
FORCES PLAN POLICY DECISION

B60
WOETZEL R.K.,THE INTERNATIONAL CONTROL OF AIRSPACE AND OUTERSPACE. FUT WOR+45 AIR CONSTN STRUCT CONSULT PLAN TEC/DEV ADJUD RIGID/FLEX KNOWL ORD/FREE PWR...TECHNIC GEOG MGT NEW/IDEA TREND COMPUT/IR VAL/FREE 20 TREATY. PAGE 166 A3375
INT/ORG JURID SPACE INT/LAW

S61
LIPSON L.,"AN ARGUMENT ON THE LEGALITY OF RECONNAISSANCE STATELLITES." COM USA+45 USSR WOR+45 AIR INTELL NAT/G CONSULT PLAN DIPLOM LEGIT ROUTINE ATTIT...INT/LAW JURID CONCPT METH/CNCPT TREND COLD/WAR 20. PAGE 90 A1833
INT/ORG LAW SPACE

S61
MACHOWSKI K.,"SELECTED PROBLEMS OF NATIONAL SOVEREIGNTY WITH REFERENCE TO THE LAW OF OUTER SPACE." FUT WOR+45 AIR LAW INTELL SOCIETY ECO/DEV PLAN EDU/PROP DETER DRIVE PERCEPT SOVEREIGN ...POLICY INT/LAW OBS TREND TOT/POP 20. PAGE 92 A1889
UNIV ACT/RES NUC/PWR SPACE

S61
TAUBENFELD H.J.,"OUTER SPACE--PAST POLITICS AND FUTURE POLICY." FUT USA+45 USA-45 WOR+45 AIR INTELL STRUCT ECO/DEV NAT/G TOP/EX ACT/RES ADMIN ROUTINE NUC/PWR ATTIT DRIVE...CONCPT TIME/SEQ TREND TOT/POP 20. PAGE 141 A2892
PLAN SPACE INT/ORG

S62
CRANE R.D.,"LAW AND STRATEGY IN SPACE." FUT USA+45 WOR+45 AIR LAW INT/ORG NAT/G FORCES ACT/RES PLAN BAL/PWR LEGIT ARMS/CONT COERCE ORD/FREE...POLICY INT/LAW JURID SOC/EXP 20 TREATY. PAGE 32 A0656
CONCPT SPACE

S62
CRANE R.D.,"SOVIET ATTITUDE TOWARD INTERNATIONAL SPACE LAW." COM FUT USA+45 USSR AIR CONSTN DELIB/GP DOMIN PWR...JURID TREND TOT/POP 20. PAGE 32 A0657
LAW ATTIT INT/LAW SPACE

S62
LISSITZYN O.J.,"SOME LEGAL IMPLICATIONS OF THE U-2 AND RB-47 INCIDENTS." FUT USA+45 USSR WOR+45 AIR NAT/G DIPLOM LEGIT MORAL ORD/FREE SOVEREIGN...JURID GEN/LAWS GEN/METH COLD/WAR 20 U-2. PAGE 90 A1840
LAW CONCPT SPACE INT/LAW

S63
GARDNER R.N.,"COOPERATION IN OUTER SPACE." FUT USSR WOR+45 AIR LAW COM/IND CONSULT DELIB/GP CREATE KNOWL 20 TREATY. PAGE 51 A1045
INT/ORG ACT/RES PEACE SPACE

S64
CRANE R.D.,"BASIC PRINCIPLES IN SOVIET SPACE LAW." FUT WOR+45 AIR INT/ORG DIPLOM DOMIN ARMS/CONT COERCE NUC/PWR PEACE ATTIT DRIVE PWR...INT/LAW METH/CNCPT NEW/IDEA OBS TREND GEN/LAWS VAL/FREE MARX/KARL 20. PAGE 32 A0659
COM LAW USSR SPACE

B65
THAYER F.C. JR.,AIR TRANSPORT POLICY AND NATIONAL SECURITY: A POLITICAL, ECONOMIC, AND MILITARY ANALYSIS. DIST/IND OP/RES PLAN TEC/DEV DIPLOM DETER WAR COST EFFICIENCY...POLICY BIBLIOG 20 DEPT/DEFEN FAA CAB. PAGE 142 A2908
AIR FORCES CIVMIL/REL ORD/FREE

B67
US SENATE COMM ON FOREIGN REL,UNITED STATES ARMAMENT AND DISARMAMENT PROBLEMS. USA+45 AIR BAL/PWR DIPLOM FOR/AID NUC/PWR ORD/FREE SENATE TREATY. PAGE 156 A3190
ARMS/CONT WEAPON FORCES PROB/SOLV

AIR FORCE ACADEMY ASSEMBLY '59 A0103

AIR FORCE ACADEMY LIBRARY A0104

AIR UNIVERSITY LIBRARY A0105,A0106

AJAO/A....ADEROGBA AJAO

ALABAMA....ALABAMA

ALASKA....ALASKA

ALBANIA....SEE ALSO COM

N
KYRIAK T.E.,EAST EUROPE: BIBLIOGRAPHY--INDEX TO US JPRS RESEARCH TRANSLATIONS. ALBANIA BULGARIA COM CZECHOSLVK HUNGARY POLAND ROMANIA AGRI EXTR/IND FINAN SERV/IND INT/TRADE WEAPON...GEOG MGT SOC 20. PAGE 83 A1701
BIBLIOG/A PRESS MARXISM INDUS

B43
CONOVER H.F.,THE BALKANS: A SELECTED LIST OF REFERENCES. ALBANIA BULGARIA ROMANIA YUGOSLAVIA INT/ORG PROB/SOLV DIPLOM LEGIT CONFER ADJUD WAR NAT/LISM PEACE PWR 20 LEAGUE/NAT. PAGE 29 A0596
BIBLIOG EUR+WWI

B56
WOLFF R.L.,THE BALKANS IN OUR TIME. ALBANIA FUT MOD/EUR USSR YUGOSLAVIA CULTURE INT/ORG SECT DIPLOM EDU/PROP COERCE WAR ORD/FREE...CHARTS 4/20 BALKANS COMINFORM. PAGE 166 A3388
GEOG COM

B63
FISCHER-GALATI S.,EASTERN EUROPE IN THE SIXTIES. ALBANIA USSR YUGOSLAVIA ECO/UNDEV AGRI MARKET LABOR WORKER DIPLOM INT/TRADE EDU/PROP GOV/REL PRODUC UTOPIA SOCISM 20. PAGE 46 A0939
MARXISM TEC/DEV BAL/PWR ECO/TAC

B63
GRIFFITH W.E.,ALBANIA AND THE SINO-SOVIET RIFT. ALBANIA CHINA/COM USSR POL/PAR CHIEF LEGIS DIPLOM DOMIN ATTIT PWR...POLICY 20 KHRUSH/N MAO. PAGE 57 A1161
EDU/PROP MARXISM NAT/LISM GOV/REL

B63
HAMM H.,ALBANIA - CHINA'S BEACHHEAD IN EUROPE. ALBANIA CHINA/COM USSR YUGOSLAVIA ELITES SOCIETY POL/PAR DELIB/GP FORCES ECO/TAC COERCE ISOLAT PEACE MARXISM...IDEA/COMP 20 MAO. PAGE 61 A1248
DIPLOM REV NAT/G POLICY

B66
BROWN J.F.,THE NEW EASTERN EUROPE. ALBANIA BULGARIA HUNGARY POLAND ROMANIA CULTURE AGRI POL/PAR WAR NAT/LISM MARXISM...CHARTS BIBLIOG 20. PAGE 20 A0404
DIPLOM COM NAT/G ECO/UNDEV

ALBERTA....ALBERTA

ALBERTINI L. A0107

ALBONETTI A. A0108

ALBRECHT-CARRIE R. A0109,A0110

ALCOHOLISM....SEE BIO/SOC

ALEMBERT/J....JEAN LE ROND D'ALEMBERT

ALEXANDER L.M. A0111

ALEXANDER R. A0112

ALEXANDROWICZ C.H. A0113, A0114, A0115

ALFIERI D. A0116

ALGER C.F. A0117,A0118,A0119,A0120

ALGERIA....SEE ALSO ISLAM

N19
LISKA G.,THE GREATER MAGHREB: FROM INDEPENDENCE TO UNITY? (PAMPHLET). ALGERIA ISLAM MOROCCO PROB/SOLV BAL/PWR CONFER COLONIAL REPRESENT NAT/LISM 20 TUNIS. PAGE 90 A1835
ECO/UNDEV REGION DIPLOM DOMIN

B42
CONOVER H.F.,FRENCH COLONIES IN AFRICA: A LIST OF REFERENCES. ALGERIA FRANCE MOROCCO SOMALIA SUDAN CULTURE AGRI LOC/G SECT FORCES DIPLOM INT/TRADE NAT/LISM HEALTH...CON/ANAL 20. PAGE 29 A0594
BIBLIOG AFR ECO/UNDEV COLONIAL

B57
CONOVER H.F.,NORTH AND NORTHEAST AFRICA; A SELECTED ANNOTATED LIST OF WRITINGS. ALGERIA MOROCCO SUDAN UAR CULTURE INT/ORG PROB/SOLV ADJUD NAT/LISM PWR WEALTH...SOC 20 UN. PAGE 30 A0603
BIBLIOG/A DIPLOM AFR ECO/UNDEV

B58
TILLION G.,ALGERIA: THE REALITIES. ALGERIA FRANCE ISLAM CULTURE STRATA PROB/SOLV DOMIN REV NAT/LISM WEALTH MARXISM...GEOG 20. PAGE 144 A2940
ECO/UNDEV SOC COLONIAL DIPLOM

B59
ALWAN M.,ALGERIA BEFORE THE UNITED NATIONS. AFR ASIA FRANCE ISLAM S/ASIA CONSTN SOCIETY STRUCT INT/ORG NAT/G ECO/TAC ADMIN COLONIAL NAT/LISM ATTIT PWR...DECISION TREND 420 UN. PAGE 7 A0133
PLAN RIGID/FLEX DIPLOM ALGERIA

B59
EGYPTIAN SOCIETY OF INT LAW,THE MONROVIA CONFERENCE (PAMPHLET). AFR ALGERIA FRANCE UAR CONFER REGION NUC/PWR WAR DISCRIM 20 SAHARA AFR/STATES. PAGE 40 A0826
COLONIAL SOVEREIGN RACE/REL DIPLOM

B60
PRINCETON U CONFERENCE,CURRENT PROBLEMS IN NORTH AFRICA. ALGERIA LIBYA MOROCCO USA+45 EXTR/IND POL/PAR PROB/SOLV DIPLOM ECO/TAC WAR...ANTHOL 20 TUNIS. PAGE 118 A2412
POLICY ECO/UNDEV NAT/G

B61
MATTHEWS T.,WAR IN ALGERIA. ALGERIA FRANCE CONTROL ATTIT SOVEREIGN 20. PAGE 96 A1978
REV COLONIAL DIPLOM WAR

B61
UAR MINISTRY OF CULTURE,A BIBLIOGRAPHICAL LIST OF AL MAGHRIB. ALGERIA ISLAM MOROCCO UAR SECT INT/TRADE COLONIAL 19/20 TUNIS. PAGE 146 A2987
BIBLIOG DIPLOM GEOG

B62
BAULIN J.,THE ARAB ROLE IN AFRICA. AFR ALGERIA FUT ISLAM MOROCCO UAR COLONIAL NEUTRAL REV...SOC 20 TUNIS BOURGUIBA. PAGE 12 A0235
NAT/LISM DIPLOM NAT/G SECT

B62
TOURE S.,THE INTERNATIONAL POLICY OF THE DEMOCRATIC PARTY OF GUINEA (VOL. VII). AFR ALGERIA GHANA GUINEA MALI CONSTN VOL/ASSN CHIEF WAR PEACE ATTIT ...WELF/ST 20 DEMOCRAT. PAGE 144 A2953
DIPLOM POLICY POL/PAR NEW/LIB

S63
GIRAUD E.,"L'INTERDICTION DU RECOURS A LA FORCE, LA THEORIE ET LA PRATIQUE DES NATIONS UNIES." ALGERIA COM CUBA HUNGARY WOR+45 ADJUD TOTALISM ATTIT RIGID/FLEX PWR...POLICY JURID CONCPT UN 20 CONGO. PAGE 53 A1077
INT/ORG FORCES DIPLOM

S64
ZARTMAN I.W.,"LES RELATIONS ENTRE LA FRANCE ET L'ALGERIA DEPUIS LES ACCORDS D'EVIAN." EUR+WWI FUT ISLAM CULTURE AGRI EXTR/IND FINAN INDUS POL/PAR DIPLOM ECO/TAC FOR/AID PEACE ATTIT DRIVE ALL/VALS ...TIME/SEQ VAL/FREE 20. PAGE 169 A3446
ECO/UNDEV ALGERIA FRANCE

B65
FANON F.,STUDIES IN A DYING COLONIALISM. ALGERIA FRANCE STRATA FAM DIPLOM DOMIN WAR RACE/REL DISCRIM HEALTH 20. PAGE 44 A0897
NAT/LISM COLONIAL REV SOVEREIGN

B66
BROWN L.C.,STATE AND SOCIETY IN INDEPENDENT NORTH AFRICA. ALGERIA LIBYA MOROCCO AGRI INDUS INT/ORG POL/PAR SECT PLAN DIPLOM COLONIAL...LING NAT/COMP ANTHOL BIBLIOG 20 TUNIS MUSLIM. PAGE 20 A0406
NAT/G SOCIETY CULTURE ECO/UNDEV

B93
ROYAL GEOGRAPHIC SOCIETY,BIBLIOGRAPHY OF BARBARY STATES (4 SUPPLEMENTARY PAPERS). ALGERIA LIBYA MOROCCO SOCIETY STRUCT DIPLOM LEAD 14/19 TUNIS. PAGE 125 A2555
BIBLIOG ISLAM NAT/G COLONIAL

ALGIER/CHR....CHARTER OF ALGIERS

ALIENATION....SEE STRANGE

ALIGHIERI D. A0121

ALIX C. A0122

ALL/IDEOS....CONCERNS THREE OR MORE OF THE TERMS LISTED IN THE IDEOLOGICAL TOPIC INDEX, P. XIII

N
JOURNAL OF INTERNATIONAL AFFAIRS. WOR+45 ECO/UNDEV POL/PAR ECO/TAC WAR PEACE PERSON ALL/IDEOS ...INT/LAW TREND. PAGE 1 A0015
BIBLIOG DIPLOM INT/ORG NAT/G

N
REVIEW OF POLITICS. WOR+45 WOR-45 CONSTN LEGIS PROB/SOLV ADMIN LEAD ALL/IDEOS...PHIL/SCI 20. PAGE 2 A0024
BIBLIOG/A DIPLOM INT/ORG NAT/G

N
JOHNS HOPKINS UNIVERSITY LIB,RECENT ADDITIONS. WOR+45 ECO/UNDEV NAT/G POL/PAR FOR/AID INT/TRADE LEAD REGION ATTIT ALL/IDEOS TREND. PAGE 74 A1518
BIBLIOG DIPLOM INT/LAW INT/ORG

N
KYRIAK T.E.,ASIAN DEVELOPMENTS: A BIBLIOGRAPHY. INDONESIA KOREA/N VIETNAM/N CULTURE SOCIETY ECO/UNDEV NAT/G DIPLOM...SOC TREND 20 MONGOLIA. PAGE 83 A1699
BIBLIOG/A ALL/IDEOS S/ASIA ASIA

B01
GRIFFIN A.P.C.,LIST OF BOOKS ON SAMOA (PAMPHLET). GERMANY S/ASIA UK USA-45 WOR-45 ECO/UNDEV REGION ALL/VALS ORD/FREE ALL/IDEOS...GEOG INT/LAW 19 SAMOA GUAM. PAGE 56 A1150
BIBLIOG/A COLONIAL DIPLOM

B27
PARRINGTON V.L.,MAIN CURRENTS IN AMERICAN THOUGHT (VOL.I). USA-45 AGRI POL/PAR DIPLOM TAX REGION REV 17/18 FRANKLIN/B JEFFERSN/T. PAGE 114 A2336
COLONIAL SECT FEEDBACK ALL/IDEOS

B37
KOHN H.,FORCE OR REASON; ISSUES OF THE TWENTIETH CENTURY. WOR+45 NAT/G DIPLOM WAR DRIVE ORD/FREE ALL/IDEOS FASCISM PLURISM...POLICY IDEA/COMP 20. PAGE 81 A1660
COERCE DOMIN RATIONAL COLONIAL

B40
NIEBUHR R.,CHRISTIANITY AND POWER POLITICS. WOR-45 SECT DIPLOM GP/REL SUPEGO ALL/IDEOS WORSHIP 20 CHRISTIAN. PAGE 109 A2234
PARTIC PEACE MORAL

B40
WOLFERS A.,BRITAIN AND FRANCE BETWEEN TWO WORLD WARS. FRANCE UK INT/ORG NAT/G PLAN BARGAIN ECO/TAC AGREE ISOLAT ALL/IDEOS...DECISION GEOG 20 TREATY VERSAILLES INTERVENT. PAGE 166 A3380
DIPLOM WAR POLICY

B41
EVANS C.,AMERICAN BIBLIOGRAPHY... (12 VOLUMES). USA-45 LAW DIPLOM ADMIN PERSON...HUM SOC 17/18. PAGE 43 A0876
BIBLIOG NAT/G ALL/VALS ALL/IDEOS

B47
HEIMANN E.,FREEDOM AND ORDER: LESSONS FROM THE WAR. WOR-45 CONSTN FORCES CHOOSE CIVMIL/REL PERSON ALL/IDEOS SOCISM...SOC IDEA/COMP WORSHIP 20. PAGE 64 A1308
NAT/G SOCIETY ORD/FREE DIPLOM

B52
SMITH C.M.,INTERNATIONAL COMMUNICATION AND POLITICAL WARFARE: AN ANNOTATED BIBLIOGRAPHY (A PAPER). WOR+45 INTELL R+D NAT/G FORCES ACT/RES DIPLOM COERCE ALL/IDEOS. PAGE 134 A2745
BIBLIOG/A EDU/PROP WAR COM/IND

B54
STREIT C.K.,FREEDOM AGAINST ITSELF. LAW SOCIETY DIPLOM UTOPIA PWR SOVEREIGN ALL/IDEOS 17/20 NATO UN. PAGE 139 A2850
ORD/FREE CREATE INT/ORG CONCPT

B55
PANT Y.P.,PLANNING IN UNDERDEVELOPED ECONOMIES. INDIA NEPAL INT/TRADE COLONIAL SOVEREIGN ALL/IDEOS ...TIME/SEQ METH/COMP 20. PAGE 114 A2334
ECO/UNDEV PLAN ECO/TAC DIPLOM

B55
VIGON J.,TEORIA DEL MILITARISMO. NAT/G DIPLOM COLONIAL COERCE GUERRILLA CIVMIL/REL NAT/LISM MORAL ALL/IDEOS PACIFISM 18/20. PAGE 159 A3234
FORCES PHIL/SCI WAR POLICY

B56
BUREAU OF PUBLIC AFFAIRS,AMERICAN FOREIGN POLICY: CURRENT DOCUMENTS. COM USA+45 USSR WOR+45 DELIB/GP FOR/AID INT/TRADE ARMS/CONT NUC/PWR ALL/VALS ALL/IDEOS...DECISION 20 NATO. PAGE 21 A0434
BIBLIOG/A DIPLOM POLICY

B56
ROBERTS H.L.,RUSSIA AND AMERICA. CHINA/COM S/ASIA USSR FORCES TEC/DEV FOR/AID NUC/PWR ALL/IDEOS ...MAJORIT TREND NAT/COMP 20 COLD/WAR UN NATO. PAGE 122 A2494
DIPLOM INT/ORG BAL/PWR TOTALISM

B57
NEUMANN F.,THE DEMOCRATIC AND THE AUTHORITARIAN STATE: ESSAYS IN POLITICAL AND LEGAL THEORY. USA+45 USA-45 CONTROL REV GOV/REL PEACE ALL/IDEOS ...INT/LAW CONCPT GEN/LAWS BIBLIOG 20. PAGE 108 A2221
DOMIN NAT/G ORD/FREE POLICY

B58
MASON H.L.,TOYNBEE'S APPROACH TO WORLD POLITICS. AFR USA+45 USSR LAW WAR NAT/LISM ALL/IDEOS...HUM BIBLIOG. PAGE 95 A1957
DIPLOM CONCPT PHIL/SCI SECT

B59
HEWES T.,EQUALITY OF OPPORTUNITY - THE AMERICAN IDEAL AND KEY TO WORLD PEACE. USA+45 NAT/G OWN WEALTH ALL/IDEOS SOCISM...CONCPT 20. PAGE 64 A1323
POLICY PEACE ECO/TAC DIPLOM

B59
ROPKE W.,INTERNATIONAL ORDER AND ECONOMIC INTEGRATION. ECO/DEV ECO/UNDEV AGRI FINAN INDUS INT/ORG WAR PEACE ORD/FREE...SOC METH/COMP 20 EEC. PAGE 123 A2524
INT/TRADE DIPLOM BAL/PAY ALL/IDEOS

L59
MCDOUGAL M.S.,"THE IDENTIFICATION AND APPRAISAL OF DIVERSE SYSTEMS OF PUBLIC ORDER (BMR)" WOR+45 NAT/G CONSULT EDU/PROP POLICY. PAGE 98 A2005
INT/LAW DIPLOM ALL/IDEOS

B60
HOLT R.T.,STRATEGIC PSYCHOLOGICAL OPERATIONS AND AMERICAN FOREIGN POLICY. ITALY USA+45 FOR/AID DOMIN RUMOR ADMIN TASK WAR CHOOSE ATTIT ALL/IDEOS...PSY COLD/WAR. PAGE 67 A1375
EDU/PROP ACT/RES DIPLOM POLICY

B60
SPEER J.P.,FOR WHAT PURPOSE? CHINA/COM USSR CONSTN PROB/SOLV DIPLOM CONTROL TASK WAR NAT/LISM WORSHIP 20 UN. PAGE 136 A2778
PEACE SECT SUPEGO ALL/IDEOS

B61
PALMER N.D.,THE INDIAN POLITICAL SYSTEM. INDIA ECO/UNDEV SECT CHIEF COLONIAL CHOOSE ALL/IDEOS SOCISM...CHARTS BIBLIOG/A 20. PAGE 113 A2322
NAT/LISM POL/PAR NAT/G DIPLOM

B62
GUTTMAN A.,THE WOUND IN THE HEART: AMERICA AND THE SPANISH CIVIL WAR. SPAIN USA-45 POL/PAR LEGIS ECO/TAC CHOOSE ANOMIE ATTIT MARXISM...POLICY ANARCH BIBLIOG 20 ROOSEVLT/F. PAGE 58 A1198
ALL/IDEOS WAR DIPLOM CATHISM

B62
GYORGY A.,PROBLEMS IN INTERNATIONAL RELATIONS. COM CT/SYS NUC/PWR ALL/IDEOS 20 UN EEC ECSC. PAGE 58 A1199
DIPLOM NEUTRAL BAL/PWR REV

B62
HENDRICKS D.,PAMPHLETS ON THE FIRST WORLD WAR: AN ANNOTATED BIBLIOGRAPHY (OCCASIONAL PAPER NO. 79). GERMANY WOR-45 EDU/PROP NAT/LISM ATTIT PWR ALL/IDEOS 20. PAGE 64 A1314
BIBLIOG/A WAR DIPLOM NAT/G

B62
LERNER M.,THE AGE OF OVERKILL: A PREFACE TO WORLD POLITICS. USA+45 USSR WOR+45 SOCIETY ECO/UNDEV BAL/PWR NEUTRAL PARTIC REV ALL/IDEOS MARXISM ...BIBLIOG/A 20. PAGE 87 A1787
DIPLOM NUC/PWR PWR DEATH

B63
HINSLEY F.H.,POWER AND THE PURSUIT OF PEACE. WOR+45 WOR-45 PLAN RIGID/FLEX ALL/VALS ALL/IDEOS...POLICY DECISION INT/LAW 12/20 ROUSSEAU/J KANT/I BENTHAM/J LEAGUE/NAT. PAGE 65 A1338
DIPLOM CONSTN PEACE COERCE

B63
LYON P.,NEUTRALISM. ECO/UNDEV EDU/PROP COLONIAL ALL/IDEOS...IDEA/COMP 20 COLD/WAR UN. PAGE 92 A1879
NAT/COMP NAT/LISM DIPLOM NEUTRAL

B64
DUTT R.P.,THE INTERNATIONALE. COM WOR+45 WOR-45 WORKER CAP/ISM WAR ATTIT...TREND GEN/LAWS 18/20 COM/PARTY. PAGE 40 A0813
ALL/IDEOS INT/ORG MARXIST ORD/FREE

B64
GIBSON J.S.,IDEOLOGY AND WORLD AFFAIRS. FUT WOR+45 ECO/UNDEV NAT/G CAP/ISM TOTALISM ORD/FREE FASCISM MARXISM 20. PAGE 52 A1067
ALL/IDEOS DIPLOM POLICY IDEA/COMP

B64
HARMON R.B.,BIBLIOGRAPHY OF BIBLIOGRAPHIES IN POLITICAL SCIENCE (MIMEOGRAPHED PAPER: LIMITED EDITION). WOR+45 WOR-45 INT/ORG POL/PAR GOV/REL ALL/IDEOS...INT/LAW JURID MGT 19/20. PAGE 61 A1260
BIBLIOG NAT/G DIPLOM LOC/G

B64
STANKIEWICZ W.J.,POLITICAL THOUGHT SINCE WORLD WAR II. WOR+45 CAP/ISM DIPLOM COLONIAL COERCE REV REPRESENT ADJUST ANOMIE ALL/IDEOS 20. PAGE 137 A2804
IDEA/COMP DOMIN ORD/FREE AUTHORIT

B64
WITHERS W.,THE ECONOMIC CRISIS IN LATIN AMERICA. BRAZIL CHILE STRATA AGRI DIPLOM FOR/AID PWR SOCISM ...POLICY 20 MEXIC/AMER ARGEN. PAGE 166 A3372
L/A+17C ECO/UNDEV CAP/ISM ALL/IDEOS

B64
WOODHOUSE C.M.,THE NEW CONCERT OF NATIONS. WOR+45 ECO/DEV ECO/UNDEV NAT/G BAL/PWR ECO/TAC NAT/LISM PWR SOVEREIGN ALL/IDEOS 20 UN COLD/WAR. PAGE 166 A3391
DIPLOM MORAL FOR/AID COLONIAL

B64
ZEBOT C.A.,THE ECONOMICS OF COMPETITIVE COEXISTENCE. CHINA/COM USSR WOR+45 FINAN MARKET FOR/AID PRICE DEMAND EQUILIB WEALTH ALL/IDEOS 20. PAGE 169 A3450
TEC/DEV DIPLOM METH/COMP

B65
CBS,CONVERSATIONS WITH WALTER LIPPMANN. USA+45 INT/ORG NAT/G POL/PAR PLAN DIPLOM PWR ALL/IDEOS ...POLICY 20 LIPPMANN/W. PAGE 25 A0509
TV ATTIT INT

B65
GILBERT M.,THE EUROPEAN POWERS 1900-45. EUR+WWI ITALY MOD/EUR USSR REV WAR PWR ALL/IDEOS FASCISM ...AUD/VIS CHARTS BIBLIOG 20. PAGE 52 A1069
DIPLOM NAT/G POLICY BAL/PWR

B66
EMBREE A.T.,ASIA: A GUIDE TO BASIC BOOKS (PAMPHLET). ECO/UNDEV SECT FORCES DIPLOM ALL/IDEOS ...SOC 20. PAGE 41 A0846
BIBLIOG/A ASIA S/ASIA NAT/G

B66
FRANK E.,LAWMAKERS IN A CHANGING WORLD. FRANCE UK USSR WOR+45 PARTIC EFFICIENCY ROLE ALL/IDEOS ...CHARTS ANTHOL PARLIAMENT 20 UN COLD/WAR. PAGE 48 A0979
GOV/COMP LEGIS NAT/G DIPLOM

B66
HARMON R.B.,SOURCES AND PROBLEMS OF BIBLIOGRAPHY IN POLITICAL SCIENCE (PAMPHLET). INT/ORG LOC/G MUNIC POL/PAR ADMIN GOV/REL ALL/IDEOS...JURID MGT CONCPT
BIBLIOG DIPLOM INT/LAW

19/20. PAGE 61 A1262 NAT/G

B66
KANET R.E.,THE SOVIET UNION AND SUB-SAHARAN AFRICA: COMMUNIST POLICY TOWARD AFRICA, 1917-1965. AFR USSR ECO/UNDEV TEC/DEV EDU/PROP TASK DISCRIM PEACE WEALTH ALL/IDEOS...CHARTS BIBLIOG SOC/INTEG 19/20 NEGRO UN INTERVENT. PAGE 76 A1555 DIPLOM ECO/TAC MARXISM

B66
TINKER H.,SOUTH ASIA. UK LAW ECO/UNDEV AGRI ACADEM SECT DIPLOM EDU/PROP REV WEALTH ALL/IDEOS...CHARTS BIBLIOG GANDHI/M NEHRU/J. PAGE 144 A2945 S/ASIA COLONIAL TREND

S66
GRUNDY K.W.,"RECENT CONTRIBUTIONS TO THE STUDY OF AFRICAN POLITICAL THOUGHT." DIPLOM NAT/LISM ALL/IDEOS...NEW/IDEA GOV/COMP 20. PAGE 58 A1182 BIBLIOG/A AFR ATTIT IDEA/COMP

B67
MCNELLY T.,SOURCES IN MODERN EAST ASIAN HISTORY AND POLITICS. KOREA VIETNAM CULTURE DIPLOM COLONIAL REV WAR PWR ALL/IDEOS MARXISM...ANTHOL 20 CHINJAP. PAGE 99 A2023 NAT/COMP ASIA S/ASIA SOCIETY

B67
PADELFORD N.J.,THE DYNAMICS OF INTERNATIONAL POLITICS (2ND ED.). WOR+45 LAW INT/ORG FORCES TEC/DEV REGION NAT/LISM PEACE ATTIT PWR ALL/IDEOS UN COLD/WAR NATO TREATY. PAGE 113 A2314 DIPLOM NAT/G POLICY DECISION

B67
WAELDER R.,PROGRESS AND REVOLUTION* A STUDY OF THE ISSUES OF OUR AGE. WOR+45 WOR-45 BAL/PWR DIPLOM COERCE ROLE MORAL ALL/IDEOS...IDEA/COMP NAT/COMP 19/20. PAGE 160 A3259 PWR NAT/G REV TEC/DEV

S67
NIEBUHR R.,"THE SOCIAL MYTHS IN THE COLD WAR." USA+45 USSR VIETNAM PROB/SOLV BAL/PWR ARMS/CONT NAT/LISM PWR ALL/IDEOS CONCPT. PAGE 109 A2238 MYTH DIPLOM GOV/COMP

B91
SIDGWICK H.,THE ELEMENTS OF POLITICS. LOC/G NAT/G LEGIS DIPLOM ADJUD CONTROL EXEC PARL/PROC REPRESENT GOV/REL SOVEREIGN ALL/IDEOS 19 MILL/JS BENTHAM/J. PAGE 132 A2713 POLICY LAW CONCPT

ALL/PROG....ALLIANCE FOR PROGRESS

ALL/VALS....CONCERNS SIX OR MORE OF THE TERMS LISTED IN THE VALUES INDEX, P. XIII

B00
GRIFFIN A.P.C.,LIST OF BOOKS RELATING TO THE THEORY OF COLONIZATION, GOVERNMENT OF DEPENDENCIES, PROTECTORATES, AND RELATED TOPICS. FRANCE GERMANY ITALY SPAIN UK USA-45 WOR-45 ECO/TAC ADMIN CONTROL REGION NAT/LISM ALL/VALS PWR...INT/LAW SOC 16/19. PAGE 56 A1149 BIBLIOG/A COLONIAL GOV/REL DOMIN

B00
MAINE H.S.,INTERNATIONAL LAW. MOD/EUR UNIV SOCIETY STRUCT ACT/RES EXEC WAR ATTIT PERSON ALL/VALS ...POLICY JURID CONCPT OBS TIME/SEQ TOT/POP. PAGE 93 A1908 INT/ORG LAW PEACE INT/LAW

B00
MORRIS H.C.,THE HISTORY OF COLONIZATION. WOR+45 WOR-45 ECO/DEV ECO/UNDEV INT/ORG ACT/RES PLAN ECO/TAC LEGIT ROUTINE COERCE ATTIT DRIVE ALL/VALS ...GEOG TREND 19. PAGE 105 A2148 DOMIN SOVEREIGN COLONIAL

B00
VOLPICELLI Z.,RUSSIA ON THE PACIFIC AND THE SIBERIAN RAILWAY. MOD/EUR ECO/UNDEV INT/ORG FORCES PLAN DOMIN COLONIAL ROUTINE ATTIT ALL/VALS...OBS HIST/WRIT TIME/SEQ TREND CON/ANAL AUD/VIS CHARTS 18/19. PAGE 159 A3248 NAT/G ACT/RES RUSSIA

B01
GRIFFIN A.P.C.,LIST OF BOOKS ON SAMOA (PAMPHLET). GERMANY S/ASIA UK USA-45 WOR-45 ECO/UNDEV REGION ALL/VALS ORD/FREE ALL/IDEOS...GEOG INT/LAW 19 SAMOA GUAM. PAGE 56 A1150 BIBLIOG/A COLONIAL DIPLOM

B02
SEELEY J.R.,THE EXPANSION OF ENGLAND. MOD/EUR S/ASIA UK CULTURE NAT/G FORCES PLAN DOMIN EDU/PROP COLONIAL ROUTINE ATTIT ALL/VALS SOVEREIGN...CONCPT HIST/WRIT PARLIAMENT 18 CMN/WLTH. PAGE 131 A2679 INT/ORG ACT/RES CAP/ISM INDIA

B10
GRIFFIN A.P.C.,LIST OF REFERENCES ON RECIPROCITY (2ND REV. ED.). CANADA CUBA UK USA-45 WOR-45 NAT/G TARIFFS CONFER COLONIAL CONTROL SANCTION CONSEN ALL/VALS...DECISION 19/20. PAGE 56 A1157 BIBLIOG/A VOL/ASSN DIPLOM REPAR

B15
HOBSON J.A.,TOWARDS INTERNATIONAL GOVERNMENT. MOD/EUR STRUCT ECO/TAC EDU/PROP ADJUD ALL/VALS ...SOCIALIST CONCPT GEN/LAWS TOT/POP 20. PAGE 65 A1347 FUT INT/ORG CENTRAL

B16
PUFENDORF S.,LAW OF NATURE AND OF NATIONS (ABRIDGED). UNIV LAW NAT/G DIPLOM AGREE WAR PERSON ALL/VALS PWR...POLICY 18 DEITY NATURL/LAW. PAGE 118 A2416 CONCPT INT/LAW SECT MORAL

B16
ROOT E.,ADDRESSES ON INTERNATIONAL SUBJECTS. MOD/EUR UNIV USA-45 LAW SOCIETY EXEC ATTIT ALL/VALS ...POLICY JURID CONCPT 20 CHINJAP. PAGE 123 A2521 INT/ORG ACT/RES PEACE INT/LAW

B16
ROOT E.,THE MILITARY AND COLONIAL POLICY OF THE US. L/A+17C USA-45 LAW SOCIETY STRATA STRUCT INT/ORG NAT/G SCHOOL FORCES EDU/PROP ALL/VALS...OBS VAL/FREE 19/20. PAGE 123 A2522 ACT/RES PLAN DIPLOM WAR

L16
WRIGHT Q.,"THE ENFORCEMENT OF INTERNATIONAL LAW THROUGH MUNICIPAL LAW IN THE US." USA-45 LOC/G NAT/G PUB/INST FORCES LEGIT CT/SYS PERCEPT ALL/VALS ...JURID 20. PAGE 167 A3401 INT/ORG LAW INT/LAW WAR

B19
KEYNES J.M.,THE ECONOMIC CONSEQUENCES OF THE PEACE. FUT GERMANY MOD/EUR RUSSIA UK USA-45 CULTURE ECO/DEV FINAN INDUS INT/ORG TOP/EX ECO/TAC ROUTINE WAR ATTIT PERCEPT ALL/VALS...OLD/LIB MYTH OBS TIME/SEQ TREND 20 TREATY. PAGE 78 A1605 EUR+WWI SOCIETY PEACE

B19
SUTHERLAND G.,CONSTITUTIONAL POWER AND WORLD AFFAIRS. CONSTN STRUCT INT/ORG NAT/G CHIEF LEGIS ACT/RES PLAN GOV/REL ALL/VALS...OBS TIME/SEQ CONGRESS VAL/FREE 20 PRESIDENT. PAGE 140 A2866 USA-45 EXEC DIPLOM

B20
BURNS C.D.,INTERNATIONAL POLITICS. WOR-45 CULTURE SOCIETY ECO/UNDEV NAT/G VOL/ASSN DELIB/GP ACT/RES CREATE DOMIN EDU/PROP LEGIT ATTIT DRIVE RIGID/FLEX ALL/VALS...PLURIST PSY CONCPT TREND. PAGE 22 A0442 INT/ORG PEACE SOVEREIGN

B20
DICKINSON E.,THE EQUALITY OF STATES IN INTERNATIONAL LAW. WOR-45 INT/ORG NAT/G DIPLOM EDU/PROP LEGIT PEACE ATTIT ALL/VALS...JURID TIME/SEQ LEAGUE/NAT. PAGE 37 A0757 LAW CONCPT SOVEREIGN

B21
STUART G.H.,FRENCH FOREIGN POLICY. CONSTN INT/ORG NAT/G POL/PAR EX/STRUC FORCES PLAN ECO/TAC DOMIN EDU/PROP ADJUD COERCE ATTIT DRIVE RIGID/FLEX ALL/VALS...POLICY OBS RECORD BIOG TIME/SEQ TREND. PAGE 139 A2852 MOD/EUR DIPLOM FRANCE

B22
BRYCE J.,INTERNATIONAL RELATIONS. CHRIST-17C EUR+WWI MOD/EUR CULTURE INTELL NAT/G DELIB/GP CREATE BAL/PWR DIPLOM ATTIT DRIVE RIGID/FLEX ALL/VALS...PLURIST JURID CONCPT TIME/SEQ GEN/LAWS TOT/POP. PAGE 20 A0412 INT/ORG POLICY

B28
HALL W.P.,EMPIRE TO COMMONWEALTH. FUT WOR-45 CONSTN ECO/DEV ECO/UNDEV INT/ORG PROVS PLAN DIPLOM EDU/PROP ADMIN COLONIAL PEACE PERSON ALL/VALS ...POLICY GEOG SOC OBS RECORD TREND CMN/WLTH PARLIAMENT 19/20. PAGE 60 A1229 VOL/ASSN NAT/G UK

B28
STUART G.H.,LATIN AMERICA AND THE UNITED STATES. USA-45 ECO/UNDEV INT/ORG NAT/G POL/PAR PLAN DOMIN EDU/PROP COLONIAL REGION COERCE ATTIT ALL/VALS ...POLICY GEOG TREND 19/20. PAGE 139 A2853 L/A+17C DIPLOM

B30
WRIGHT Q.,MANDATES UNDER THE LEAGUE OF NATIONS. WOR-45 CONSTN ECO/DEV ECO/UNDEV NAT/G DELIB/GP TOP/EX LEGIT ALL/VALS...JURID CONCPT LEAGUE/NAT 20. PAGE 167 A3403 INT/ORG LAW INT/LAW

B31
GREAVES H.R.G.,THE LEAGUE COMMITTEES AND WORLD ORDER. WOR-45 DELIB/GP EX/STRUC EDU/PROP ALL/VALS LEAGUE/NAT VAL/FREE 20. PAGE 55 A1136 INT/ORG DIPLOM ROUTINE

B31
HILL N.,INTERNATIONAL ADMINISTRATION. WOR-45 DELIB/GP DIPLOM EDU/PROP ALL/VALS...MGT TIME/SEQ LEAGUE/NAT TOT/POP VAL/FREE 20. PAGE 65 A1331 INT/ORG ADMIN

B31
HODGES C.,THE BACKGROUND OF INTERNATIONAL RELATIONS. WOR-45 SOCIETY ECO/DEV ECO/UNDEV INT/ORG DIPLOM DOMIN EDU/PROP LEGIT WAR ATTIT DRIVE PERSON ALL/VALS...CONCPT METH/CNCPT TIME/SEQ CHARTS WORK LEAGUE/NAT 19/20. PAGE 66 A1350 NAT/G BAL/PWR

B32
BRYCE J.,THE HOLY ROMAN EMPIRE. GERMANY ITALY MOD/EUR CULTURE SOCIETY STRUCT INT/ORG NAT/G SECT DIPLOM DOMIN WAR SUPEGO ALL/VALS SOVEREIGN...GEOG SOC TIME/SEQ CHARTS STERTYP. PAGE 20 A0413 CHRIST-17C NAT/LISM

B32
MASTERS R.D.,INTERNATIONAL LAW IN INTERNATIONAL COURTS. BELGIUM EUR+WWI FRANCE GERMANY MOD/EUR SWITZERLND WOR-45 SOCIETY STRATA STRUCT LEGIT EXEC ALL/VALS...JURID HIST/WRIT TIME/SEQ TREND GEN/LAWS 20. PAGE 96 A1961 INT/ORG LAW INT/LAW

B34
EINSTEIN A.,THE WORLD AS I SEE IT. WOR-45 INTELL R+D INT/ORG NAT/G SECT VOL/ASSN FORCES CREATE EDU/PROP LEGIT ARMS/CONT WAR WEAPON NAT/LISM ALL/VALS...POLICY CONCPT 20. PAGE 41 A0828 SOCIETY PHIL/SCI DIPLOM PACIFISM

B35
STALEY E.,WAR AND THE PRIVATE INVESTOR. UNIV WOR-45 INTELL SOCIETY INT/ORG NAT/G TOP/EX CAP/ISM ECO/TAC WAR ATTIT ALL/VALS...INT TIME/SEQ TREND CON/ANAL FINAN INT/TRADE DIPLOM

WORK TOT/POP 20. PAGE 137 A2799

B36
SHOTWELL J.,ON THE RIM OF THE ABYSS. EUR+WWI USA-45 STRUCT INT/ORG ACT/RES PLAN EDU/PROP EXEC ATTIT ALL/VALS...TIME/SEQ LEAGUE/NAT TOT/POP 20. PAGE 132 A2706 — NAT/G BAL/PWR

B37
ROYAL INST. INT. AFF.,THE COLONIAL PROBLEM. WOR-45 LAW ECO/DEV ECO/UNDEV NAT/G PLAN ECO/TAC EDU/PROP ADMIN ATTIT ALL/VALS...CONCPT 20. PAGE 125 A2556 — INT/ORG ACT/RES SOVEREIGN COLONIAL

B38
DE MADARIAGA S.,THE WORLD'S DESIGN. WOR-45 SOCIETY STRUCT EDU/PROP PEACE ATTIT PERSON ALL/VALS ...SOCIALIST CONCPT TIME/SEQ TREND GEN/LAWS LEAGUE/NAT. PAGE 35 A0706 — FUT INT/ORG DIPLOM

B38
RAPPARD W.E.,THE CRISIS OF DEMOCRACY. EUR+WWI UNIV WOR-45 CULTURE SOCIETY ECO/DEV INT/ORG POL/PAR ACT/RES EDU/PROP EXEC CHOOSE ATTIT ALL/VALS...SOC OBS HIST/WRIT TIME/SEQ LEAGUE/NAT NAZI TOT/POP 20. PAGE 119 A2449 — NAT/G CONCPT

B39
WILSON G.G.,HANDBOOK OF INTERNATIONAL LAW. FUT UNIV USA-45 WOR-45 SOCIETY LEGIT ATTIT DISPL DRIVE ALL/VALS...INT/LAW TIME/SEQ TREND. PAGE 165 A3359 — INT/ORG LAW CONCPT WAR

B40
THE GUIDE TO CATHOLIC LITERATURE, 1888-1940. ALL/VALS...POLICY MYSTIC HUM PHIL/SCI 19/20. PAGE 3 A0051 — BIBLIOG/A CATHISM DIPLOM CULTURE

B40
CARR E.H.,THE TWENTY YEARS' CRISIS 1919-1939. FUT WOR-45 BAL/PWR ECO/TAC LEGIT TOTALISM ATTIT ALL/VALS...POLICY JURID CONCPT TIME/SEQ TREND GEN/LAWS TOT/POP 20. PAGE 24 A0498 — INT/ORG DIPLOM PEACE

B40
RAPPARD W.E.,THE QUEST FOR PEACE. UNIV USA-45 WOR-45 SOCIETY INT/ORG NAT/G PLAN EXEC ROUTINE WAR ATTIT DRIVE ALL/VALS...POLICY CONCPT OBS TIME/SEQ LEAGUE/NAT TOT/POP 20. PAGE 119 A2450 — EUR+WWI ACT/RES PEACE

B41
EVANS C.,AMERICAN BIBLIOGRAPHY... (12 VOLUMES). USA-45 LAW DIPLOM ADMIN PERSON...HUM SOC 17/18. PAGE 43 A0876 — BIBLIOG NAT/G ALL/VALS ALL/IDEOS

B41
YOUNG G.,FEDERALISM AND FREEDOM. EUR+WWI MOD/EUR RUSSIA USA-45 WOR-45 SOCIETY STRUCT ECO/DEV INT/ORG EXEC FEDERAL ATTIT PERSON ALL/VALS...OLD/LIB CONCPT OBS TREND LEAGUE/NAT TOT/POP. PAGE 169 A3435 — NAT/G WAR

B42
HAMBRO C.J.,HOW TO WIN THE PEACE. ECO/TAC EDU/PROP ADJUD PERSON ALL/VALS...SOCIALIST TREND GEN/LAWS 20. PAGE 61 A1246 — FUT INT/ORG PEACE

L42
SHOTWELL J.,"LESSON OF THE LAST WORLD WAR." EUR+WWI MOD/EUR USA-45 SOCIETY ECO/UNDEV INDUS VOL/ASSN CONSULT ACT/RES CREATE CAP/ISM INT/TRADE DRIVE ALL/VALS...CONCPT NEW/IDEA SELF/OBS GEN/LAWS LEAGUE/NAT NAZI 20. PAGE 132 A2708 — INT/ORG ORD/FREE

S42
TURNER F.J.,"AMERICAN SECTIONALISM AND WORLD ORGANIZATION." EUR+WWI UNIV USA-45 WOR-45 INTELL ECO/DEV TOP/EX ACT/RES PLAN EDU/PROP LEGIT ALL/VALS ...CONCPT NEW/IDEA OBS TREND LEAGUE/NAT TOT/POP 20. PAGE 146 A2981 — INT/ORG DRIVE BAL/PWR

B43
FULLER G.F.,FOREIGN RELIEF AND REHABILITATION (PAMPHLET). FUT GERMANY UK USA-45 INT/ORG PROB/SOLV DIPLOM FOR/AID ADMIN ADJUST PEACE ALL/VALS...SOC/WK 20 UN JEWS. PAGE 50 A1018 — BIBLIOG/A PLAN GIVE WAR

B44
FULLER G.H.,TURKEY: A SELECTED LIST OF REFERENCES. ISLAM TURKEY CULTURE ECO/UNDEV AGRI DIPLOM NAT/LISM CONSERVE...GEOG HUM INT/LAW SOC 7/20 MAPS. PAGE 50 A1024 — BIBLIOG/A ALL/VALS

B44
PUTTKAMMER E.W.,WAR AND THE LAW. UNIV USA-45 CONSTN CULTURE SOCIETY NAT/G POL/PAR ROUTINE ALL/VALS ...JURID CONCPT OBS WORK VAL/FREE 20. PAGE 118 A2418 — INT/ORG LAW WAR INT/LAW

B44
WHITTON J.B.,THE SECOND CHANCE: AMERICA AND THE PEACE. EUR+WWI USA-45 SOCIETY STRUCT INT/ORG NAT/G LEGIT EXEC WAR ALL/VALS...SOC CONCPT TIME/SEQ TREND CONGRESS 20. PAGE 164 A3340 — LEGIS PEACE

L44
HAILEY,"THE FUTURE OF COLONIAL PEOPLES." WOR-45 CONSTN CULTURE ECO/UNDEV AGRI MARKET INT/ORG NAT/G SECT CONSULT ECO/TAC LEGIT ADMIN NAT/LISM ALL/VALS ...SOC OBS TREND STERTYP CMN/WLTH LEAGUE/NAT PARLIAMENT 20. PAGE 59 A1218 — PLAN CONCPT DIPLOM UK

B46
GRIFFIN G.G.,A GUIDE TO MANUSCRIPTS RELATING TO AMERICAN HISTORY IN BRITISH DEPOSITORIES. CANADA IRELAND MOD/EUR UK USA-45 LAW DIPLOM ADMIN COLONIAL WAR NAT/LISM SOVEREIGN...GEOG INT/LAW 15/19 CMN/WLTH. PAGE 56 A1159 — BIBLIOG/A ALL/VALS NAT/G

B47
MANDER L.,FOUNDATIONS OF MODERN WORLD SOCIETY. WOR+45 DELIB/GP ECO/TAC INT/TRADE EDU/PROP ALL/VALS ...TIME/SEQ GEN/LAWS TOT/POP VAL/FREE ILO 20. PAGE 94 A1917 — INT/ORG EX/STRUC DIPLOM

B49
MARITAIN J.,HUMAN RIGHTS: COMMENTS AND INTERPRETATIONS. COM UNIV WOR+45 LAW CONSTN CULTURE SOCIETY ECO/DEV ECO/UNDEV SCHOOL DELIB/GP EDU/PROP ATTIT PERCEPT ALL/VALS...HUM SOC TREND UNESCO 20. PAGE 95 A1939 — INT/ORG CONCPT

B49
ROSENHAUPT H.W.,HOW TO WAGE PEACE. USA+45 SOCIETY STRATA STRUCT R+D INT/ORG POL/PAR LEGIS ACT/RES CREATE PLAN EDU/PROP ADMIN EXEC ATTIT ALL/VALS ...TIME/SEQ TREND COLD/WAR 20. PAGE 124 A2536 — INTELL CONCPT DIPLOM

B49
SINGER K.,THE IDEA OF CONFLICT. UNIV INTELL INT/ORG NAT/G PLAN ROUTINE ATTIT DRIVE ALL/VALS...POLICY CONCPT TIME/SEQ. PAGE 133 A2730 — ACT/RES SOC

L49
UNESCO,"SOME SUGGESTIONS ON TEACHING ABOUT THE UN AND ITS SPECIALIZED AGENCIES." UNIV WOR+45 SOCIETY STRATA SCHOOL WAR ALL/VALS KNOWL...SOC CONCPT UNESCO 20 UN. PAGE 147 A3011 — INT/ORG EDU/PROP

B50
LAUTERPACHT H.,INTERNATIONAL LAW AND HUMAN RIGHTS. USA+45 CONSTN STRUCT INT/ORG ACT/RES EDU/PROP PEACE PERSON ALL/VALS...CONCPT CON/ANAL GEN/LAWS UN 20. PAGE 86 A1750 — DELIB/GP LAW INT/LAW

B50
MCCAMY J.,THE ADMINISTRATION OF AMERICAN FOREIGN AFFAIRS. USA+45 SOCIETY INT/ORG NAT/G ACT/RES PLAN INT/TRADE EDU/PROP ADJUD ALL/VALS...METH/CNCPT TIME/SEQ CONGRESS 20. PAGE 97 A1996 — EXEC STRUCT DIPLOM

B50
NORTHROP F.S.C.,THE TAMING OF THE NATIONS. KOREA USA+45 USSR WOR+45 STRUCT ECO/UNDEV INT/ORG NAT/G TOP/EX NUC/PWR ATTIT ALL/VALS...TIME/SEQ 20 HIROSHIMA. PAGE 110 A2255 — CONCPT BAL/PWR

L50
US SENATE COMM. GOVT. OPER.,"REVISION OF THE UN CHARTER." FUT USA+45 WOR+45 CONSTN ECO/DEV ECO/UNDEV NAT/G DELIB/GP ACT/RES CREATE PLAN EXEC ROUTINE CHOOSE ALL/VALS...POLICY CONCPT CONGRESS UN TOT/POP 20 COLD/WAR. PAGE 157 A3196 — INT/ORG LEGIS PEACE

B51
MCKEON R.,DEMOCRACY IN A WORLD OF TENSION. UNIV LAW INTELL STRUCT R+D INT/ORG SCHOOL EDU/PROP LEGIT ATTIT DRIVE PERCEPT PERSON...POLICY JURID PSY SOC CONCPT METH/CNCPT OBS UNESCO TOT/POP VAL/FREE. PAGE 98 A2015 — SOCIETY ALL/VALS ORD/FREE

B51
UNESCO,FREEDOM AND CULTURE. FUT WOR+45 CONSTN CULTURE PERF/ART VOL/ASSN EDU/PROP PEACE ATTIT ALL/VALS SOVEREIGN...POLICY MAJORIT CONCPT TREND STERTYP GEN/LAWS UN TOT/POP 20. PAGE 147 A3013 — INT/ORG SOCIETY

B51
VINER J.,INTERNATIONAL ECONOMICS. USA-45 WOR-45 ECO/DEV INDUS NAT/G ECO/TAC ALL/VALS...TIME/SEQ 20. PAGE 159 A3238 — FINAN INT/ORG WAR INT/TRADE

B51
WHITE L.C.,INTERNATIONAL NON-GOVERNMENTAL ORGANIZATIONS. AFR ASIA COM EUR+WWI USA+45 WOR+45 INT/ORG DIPLOM INT/TRADE ALL/VALS...HUM FAO ILO EEC 20. PAGE 164 A3337 — VOL/ASSN CONSULT

L51
ULAM A.B.,"THE COMIMFORM AND THE PEOPLE'S DEMOCRACIES." EUR+WWI WOR+45 STRUCT NAT/G POL/PAR TOP/EX ACT/RES PLAN ECO/TAC DOMIN ATTIT ALL/VALS ...HIST/WRIT TIME/SEQ 20 COMINFORM. PAGE 146 A2992 — COM INT/ORG USSR TOTALISM

L51
WHITAKER A.P.,"DEVELOPMENT OF AMERICAN REGIONALISM: THE ORGANIZATION OF AMERICAN STATES." L/A+17C USA+45 VOL/ASSN DELIB/GP FORCES TOP/EX ACT/RES ECO/TAC CT/SYS REGION PEACE ALL/VALS OAS 20. PAGE 163 A3330 — INT/ORG TIME/SEQ DETER

B52
ULAM A.B.,TITOISM AND THE COMINFORM. USSR WOR+45 STRUCT INT/ORG NAT/G ACT/RES PLAN EXEC ATTIT DRIVE ALL/VALS...CONCPT OBS VAL/FREE 20 COMINTERN TITO/MARSH. PAGE 146 A2993 — COM POL/PAR TOTALISM YUGOSLAVIA

B52
VANDENBOSCH A.,THE UN: BACKGROUND, ORGANIZATION, FUNCTIONS, ACTIVITIES. WOR+45 LAW CONSTN STRUCT INT/ORG CONSULT BAL/PWR EDU/PROP EXEC ALL/VALS ...POLICY CONCPT UN 20. PAGE 158 A3218 — DELIB/GP TIME/SEQ PEACE

B53
MURPHY G.,IN THE MINDS OF MEN: THE STUDY OF HUMAN BEHAVIOR AND SOCIAL TENSIONS IN INDIA. FUT S/ASIA FAM INT/ORG NAT/G DIPLOM EDU/PROP GP/REL ATTIT — SECT STRATA INDIA

RIGID/FLEX ALL/VALS...SOC QU UNESCO 20. PAGE 106
A2176

B53
THAYER P.W.,SOUTHEAST ASIA IN THE COMING WORLD. ECO/UNDEV
ASIA S/ASIA USA+45 USA-45 SOCIETY INT/ORG ACT/RES ATTIT
ECO/TAC EDU/PROP COERCE TOTALISM ALL/VALS...JURID FOR/AID
20. PAGE 142 A2909 DIPLOM

B54
CHEEVER D.S.,ORGANIZING FOR PEACE. FUT WOR+45 INT/ORG
WOR-45 STRATA STRUCT NAT/G CREATE DIPLOM LEGIT
REGION COERCE DETER PEACE ATTIT DRIVE ALL/VALS
...TIME/SEQ TREND UN LEAGUE/NAT. PAGE 26 A0525

B54
NUSSBAUM D.,A CONCISE HISTORY OF THE LAW OF INT/ORG
NATIONS. ASIA CHRIST-17C EUR+WWI ISLAM MEDIT-7 LAW
MOD/EUR S/ASIA UNIV WOR+45 WOR-45 SOCIETY STRUCT PEACE
EXEC ATTIT ALL/VALS...CONCPT HIST/WRIT TIME/SEQ. INT/LAW
PAGE 110 A2263

L54
CHARLESWORTH J.C.,"AMERICA AND A NEW ASIA." ASIA ECO/TAC
INDIA ISLAM S/ASIA USA+45 USA-45 ECO/UNDEV NAT/G DIPLOM
POL/PAR FORCES FOR/AID DOMIN EDU/PROP COERCE DRIVE NAT/LISM
ALL/VALS MARXISM SOCISM TOT/POP 20. PAGE 26 A0522

L54
OPLER M.E.,"SOCIAL ASPECTS OF TECHNICAL ASSISTANCE INT/ORG
IN OPERATION." WOR+45 VOL/ASSN CREATE PLAN TEC/DEV CONSULT
EDU/PROP ALL/VALS...METH/CNCPT OBS RECORD TREND UN FOR/AID
20. PAGE 112 A2292

B55
WRIGHT Q.,THE STUDY OF INTERNATIONAL RELATIONS. INT/ORG
WOR+45 WOR-45 SOCIETY ECO/TAC INT/TRADE EDU/PROP DIPLOM
ALL/VALS...CONCPT GEN/METH 20. PAGE 167 A3410

L55
KISER M.,"ORGANIZATION OF AMERICAN STATES." L/A+17C VOL/ASSN
USA+45 ECO/UNDEV INT/ORG NAT/G PLAN TEC/DEV DIPLOM ECO/DEV
ECO/TAC INT/TRADE EDU/PROP ADMIN ALL/VALS...POLICY REGION
MGT RECORD ORG/CHARTS OAS 20. PAGE 80 A1639

L55
ROSTOW W.W.,"RUSSIA AND CHINA UNDER COMMUNISM." COM
CHINA/COM USSR INTELL STRUCT INT/ORG NAT/G POL/PAR ASIA
TOP/EX ACT/RES PLAN ADMIN ATTIT ALL/VALS MARXISM
...CONCPT OBS TIME/SEQ TREND GOV/COMP VAL/FREE 20.
PAGE 124 A2543

B56
BUREAU OF PUBLIC AFFAIRS,AMERICAN FOREIGN POLICY: BIBLIOG/A
CURRENT DOCUMENTS. COM USA+45 USSR WOR+45 DELIB/GP DIPLOM
FOR/AID INT/TRADE ARMS/CONT NUC/PWR ALL/VALS POLICY
ALL/IDEOS...DECISION 20 NATO. PAGE 21 A0434

B57
DEAN V.M.,THE NATURE OF THE NON-WESTERN WORLD. AFR ECO/UNDEV
ASIA L/A+17C S/ASIA CULTURE SOCIETY STRATA ECO/DEV STERTYP
DIPLOM ECO/TAC FOR/AID ATTIT DRIVE ALL/VALS NAT/LISM
...RELATIV SOC CONCPT TIME/SEQ TREND TOT/POP 20.
PAGE 35 A0718

B57
FRAZIER E.F.,RACE AND CULTURE CONTACTS IN THE CULTURE
MODERN WORLD. WOR+45 WOR-45 SOCIETY ECO/DEV AGRI RACE/REL
INDUS INT/ORG LABOR NAT/G PERSON RIGID/FLEX
ALL/VALS...SOC TIME/SEQ WORK 19/20. PAGE 48 A0991

L57
WARREN S.,"FOREIGN AID AND FOREIGN POLICY." USA+45 ECO/UNDEV
WOR+45 WOR-45 DIST/IND INDUS MARKET CONSULT CREATE ALL/VALS
DIPLOM EDU/PROP LEGIT ATTIT RIGID/FLEX...TIME/SEQ ECO/TAC
GEN/LAWS WORK 20. PAGE 161 A3285 FOR/AID

S57
SCHELLING T.C.,"BARGAINING COMMUNICATION, AND ROUTINE
LIMITED WAR." UNIV WOR+45 FACE/GP INT/ORG NAT/G DECISION
FORCES ACT/RES WAR PERCEPT ALL/VALS...PSY OBS
PROJ/TEST CHARTS HYPO/EXP GEN/LAWS TOT/POP 20.
PAGE 128 A2622

B59
ALLEN R.L.,SOVIET INFLUENCE IN LATIN AMERICA. L/A+17C
ECO/UNDEV FINAN PROC/MFG NAT/G TEC/DEV EDU/PROP ECO/TAC
EXEC ROUTINE ATTIT DRIVE PERSON ALL/VALS PWR...STAT INT/TRADE
CHARTS WORK 20. PAGE 6 A0125 USSR

B59
FREE L.A.,SIX ALLIES AND A NEUTRAL. ASIA COM PSY
EUR+WWI FRANCE GERMANY/W INDIA S/ASIA UK USA+45 DIPLOM
INT/ORG NAT/G NUC/PWR PEACE ATTIT PERCEPT
RIGID/FLEX ALL/VALS...STAT REC/INT COLD/WAR 20
CHINJAP. PAGE 48 A0992

B59
HUGHES E.M.,AMERICA THE VINCIBLE. USA+45 FOR/AID ORD/FREE
ARMS/CONT NUC/PWR PERS/REL RATIONAL ATTIT ALL/VALS DIPLOM
20 COLD/WAR. PAGE 69 A1413 WAR

B59
MACIVER R.M.,THE NATIONS AND THE UN. WOR+45 NAT/G INT/ORG
CONSULT ADJUD ADMIN ALL/VALS...CONCPT DEEP/QU UN ATTIT
TOT/POP UNESCO 20. PAGE 92 A1892 DIPLOM

B59
WARD B.,5 IDEAS THAT CHANGE THE WORLD. WOR+45 ECO/UNDEV
WOR-45 SOCIETY STRUCT AGRI INDUS INT/ORG NAT/G ALL/VALS
FORCES ACT/RES ARMS/CONT TOTALISM ATTIT DRIVE NAT/LISM
GEN/LAWS. PAGE 161 A3278 COLONIAL

S59
LASSWELL H.D.,"UNIVERSALITY IN PERSPECTIVE." FUT INT/ORG
UNIV SOCIETY CONSULT TOP/EX PLAN EDU/PROP ADJUD JURID
ROUTINE ARMS/CONT COERCE PEACE ATTIT PERSON TOTALISM
ALL/VALS. PAGE 85 A1741

B60
HYDE L.K.G.,THE US AND THE UN. WOR+45 STRUCT USA+45
ECO/DEV ECO/UNDEV NAT/G ACT/RES PLAN DIPLOM INT/ORG
EDU/PROP ADMIN ALL/VALS...CONCPT TIME/SEQ GEN/LAWS FOR/AID
UN VAL/FREE 20. PAGE 70 A1428

B60
LIEUWEN E.,ARMS AND POLITICS IN LATIN AMERICA. FUT L/A+17C
USA+45 USA-45 ECO/UNDEV INT/ORG NAT/G FORCES DIPLOM FOR/AID
COERCE ATTIT ALL/VALS VAL/FREE OAS 20. PAGE 88
A1811

B60
NURTY K.S.,STUDIES IN PROBLEMS OF PEACE. CHRIST-17C POLICY
MOD/EUR S/ASIA WOR+45 WOR-45 INT/ORG NAT/G SECT PEACE
COERCE REV NAT/LISM ALL/VALS...CONCPT MYTH PACIFISM
TIME/SEQ. PAGE 110 A2262 ORD/FREE

B60
PLAMENATZ J.,ON ALIEN RULE AND SELF-GOVERNMENT. AFR NAT/G
FUT S/ASIA WOR+45 CULTURE SOCIETY ECO/UNDEV INT/ORG CONSTN
DOMIN EDU/PROP ATTIT RIGID/FLEX ALL/VALS...POLICY NAT/LISM
CONCPT OBS TREND CON/ANAL GEN/LAWS TOT/POP SOVEREIGN
VAL/FREE. PAGE 116 A2386

B60
SPEIER H.,DIVIDED BERLIN: THE ANATOMY OF SOVIET INT/ORG
POLITICAL BLACKMAIL. COM GERMANY USA+45 USSR WOR+45 ACT/RES
NAT/G TOP/EX DOMIN EDU/PROP ALL/VALS...POLICY DIPLOM
CONCPT COLD/WAR 20 U-2. PAGE 136 A2782

S60
BOWIE R.,"POLICY FORMATION IN AMERICAN FOREIGN PLAN
POLICY." FUT USA+45 WOR+45 STRUCT ECO/DEV INT/ORG DRIVE
POL/PAR LEGIS ACT/RES EXEC ALL/VALS...POLICY OBS DIPLOM
VAL/FREE 20. PAGE 17 A0355

S60
FITZGIBBON R.H.,"DICTATORSHIP AND DEMOCRACY IN L/A+17C
LATIN AMERICA." FUT ECO/DEV ECO/UNDEV INT/ORG LOC/G ACT/RES
NAT/G TOP/EX PLAN TEC/DEV ECO/TAC CHOOSE ATTIT INT/TRADE
DRIVE PERSON ALL/VALS OAS TOT/POP 20. PAGE 46 A0943

S60
KAPLAN M.A.,"THEORETICAL ANALYSIS OF THE BALANCE OF CREATE
POWER." FUT USA+45 WOR+45 INTELL ECO/DEV INT/ORG NEW/IDEA
NAT/G CONSULT TOP/EX ACT/RES PLAN TEC/DEV ATTIT DIPLOM
ALL/VALS...METH/CNCPT TOT/POP 20. PAGE 76 A1562 NUC/PWR

S60
SCHACHTER O.,"THE ENFORCEMENT OF INTERNATIONAL INT/ORG
JUDICIAL AND ARBITRAL DECISIONS." WOR+45 NAT/G ADJUD
ECO/TAC DOMIN LEGIT ROUTINE COERCE ATTIT DRIVE INT/LAW
ALL/VALS PWR...METH/CNCPT TREND TOT/POP 20 UN.
PAGE 128 A2615

B61
HARRISON S.,INDIA AND THE UNITED STATES. FUT S/ASIA DELIB/GP
USA+45 WOR+45 INTELL ECO/DEV ECO/UNDEV AGRI INDUS ACT/RES
INT/ORG NAT/G CONSULT EX/STRUC TOP/EX PLAN ECO/TAC FOR/AID
NEUTRAL ALL/VALS...MGT TOT/POP 20. PAGE 62 A1272 INDIA

B61
PATAI R.,CULTURES IN CONFLICT; AN INQUIRY INTO THE NAT/COMP
SOCIO-CULTURAL PROBLEMS OF ISRAEL AND HER NEIGHBORS CULTURE
(2ND REV. ED.). ISLAM ISRAEL SOCIETY STRUCT DIPLOM GP/COMP
GP/REL ALL/VALS...SOC 20 JEWS ARABS. PAGE 114 A2339 ATTIT

B61
ROBINS D.B.,EVOLVING UNITED STATES POLICIES TOWARD AFR
THE EMERGING NATIONS OF ASIA AND AFRICA (PAMPHLET). S/ASIA
ISLAM ECO/UNDEV INT/ORG CONSULT CREATE PLAN TEC/DEV DIPLOM
FOR/AID CONFER ALL/VALS 20 KENNEDY/JF EISNHWR/DD UN BIBLIOG
AID. PAGE 122 A2501

L61
HILSMAN R. JR.,"THE NEW COMMUNIST TACTIC: PRECIS- FORCES
INTERNAL WAR." COM FUT USA+45 ECO/UNDEV POL/PAR COERCE
FOR/AID RIGID/FLEX ALL/VALS...TREND COLD/WAR 20. USSR
PAGE 65 A1334 GUERRILLA

S61
ALGER C.F.,"NON-RESOLUTION CONSEQUENCES OF THE INT/ORG
UNITED NATIONS AND THEIR EFFECT ON INTERNATIONAL DRIVE
CONFLICT." WOR+45 CONSTN ECO/DEV NAT/G CONSULT BAL/PWR
DELIB/GP TOP/EX ACT/RES PLAN DIPLOM EDU/PROP
ROUTINE ATTIT ALL/VALS...INT/LAW TOT/POP UN 20.
PAGE 6 A0117

S61
ASHFORD D.E.,"A CASE STUDY IN THE DIPLOMACY OF ECO/UNDEV
SOCIAL REVOLUTION." USA+45 WOR+45 DIPLOM ECO/TAC PLAN
FOR/AID REV ALL/VALS VAL/FREE 20. PAGE 9 A0187

S61
JACKSON E.,"CONSTITUTIONAL DEVELOPMENTS OF THE INT/ORG
UNITED NATIONS: THE GROWTH OF ITS EXECUTIVE EXEC
CAPACITY." FUT WOR+45 CONSTN STRUCT ACT/RES PLAN
ALL/VALS...NEW/IDEA OBS COLD/WAR UN 20. PAGE 72
A1475

S61
LEWY G.,"SUPERIOR ORDERS, NUCLEAR WARFARE AND THE DETER
DICTATES OF CONSCIENCE: THE DILEMMA OF MILITARY INT/ORG
OBEDIENCE IN THE ATOMIC." FUT UNIV WOR+45 INTELL LAW
SOCIETY FORCES TOP/EX ACT/RES ADMIN ROUTINE NUC/PWR INT/LAW
PERCEPT RIGID/FLEX ALL/VALS...POLICY CONCPT 20.
PAGE 88 A1805

S61
ROSTOW W.W.,"THE FUTURE OF FOREIGN AID." COM FUT WOR+45 ECO/DEV INDUS INT/ORG NAT/G CONSULT ACT/RES PLAN DOMIN LEGIT CHOOSE RIGID/FLEX ALL/VALS ...MAJORIT CONCPT TREND TOT/POP 20. PAGE 124 A2544 ECO/UNDEV ECO/TAC FOR/AID

S61
TANNENBAUM F.,"THE UNITED STATES AND LATIN AMERICA." FUT USA+45 NAT/G FOR/AID CHOOSE ATTIT ALL/VALS VAL/FREE 20. PAGE 141 A2888 L/A+17C ECO/DEV DIPLOM

S61
VIRALLY M.,"VERS UNE REFORME DU SECRETARIAT DES NATIONS UNIES." FUT WOR+45 CONSTN ECO/DEV TOP/EX BAL/PWR ADMIN ALL/VALS...CONCPT BIOG UN VAL/FREE 20. PAGE 159 A3243 INT/ORG INTELL DIPLOM

B62
BOULDING K.E.,CONFLICT AND DEFENSE: A GENERAL THEORY. FUT SOCIETY INT/ORG NAT/G CREATE BAL/PWR COERCE NAT/LISM DRIVE ALL/VALS...PLURIST DECISION CONCPT METH/CNCPT TREND HYPO/EXP TOT/POP 20. PAGE 17 A0347 MATH SIMUL PEACE WAR

B62
CALVOCORESSI P.,WORLD ORDER AND NEW STATES: PROBLEMS OF KEEPING THE PEACE. AFR EUR+WWI S/ASIA ELITES NAT/G ECO/TAC FOR/AID EDU/PROP COERCE ATTIT DRIVE ALL/VALS...GEN/LAWS COLD/WAR 20 UN. PAGE 23 A0471 INT/ORG PEACE

B62
DREIER J.C.,THE ORGANIZATION OF AMERICAN STATES AND THE HEMISPHERE CRISIS. CUBA USA+45 CULTURE STRATA NAT/G VOL/ASSN CONSULT FORCES ACT/RES CREATE DIPLOM ECO/TAC FOR/AID ALL/VALS...POLICY OBS OAS 20. PAGE 38 A0786 L/A+17C CONCPT

B62
GUENA Y.,HISTORIQUE DE LA COMMUNAUTE. FUT ECO/UNDEV NAT/G PLAN EDU/PROP COLONIAL REGION NAT/LISM ALL/VALS SOVEREIGN...CONCPT OBS CHARTS 20. PAGE 58 A1186 AFR VOL/ASSN FOR/AID FRANCE

B62
MANNING C.A.W.,THE NATURE OF INTERNATIONAL SOCIETY. FUT LAW NAT/G TOP/EX NAT/LISM PEACE PERCEPT PERSON ALL/VALS PLURISM...METH/CNCPT MYTH HYPO/EXP TOT/POP 20. PAGE 94 A1926 INT/ORG SOCIETY SIMUL DIPLOM

B62
ROBINSON A.D.,DUTCH ORGANIZED AGRICULTURE IN INTERNATIONAL POLITICS, 1945-1960. EUR+WWI NETHERLAND STRUCT ECO/DEV NAT/G VOL/ASSN CONSULT DELIB/GP PLAN TEC/DEV INT/TRADE EDU/PROP ATTIT RIGID/FLEX ALL/VALS...NEW/IDEA TREND EEC 20. PAGE 122 A2502 AGRI INT/ORG

B62
THANT U.,THE UNITED NATIONS' DEVELOPMENT DECADE: PROPOSALS FOR ACTION. WOR+45 SOCIETY ECO/UNDEV AGRI COM/IND FINAN R+D MUNIC SCHOOL VOL/ASSN CONSULT PLAN TEC/DEV ECO/TAC EDU/PROP ADMIN ROUTINE RIGID/FLEX...MGT SOC CONCPT UNESCO UN TOT/POP VAL/FREE. PAGE 142 A2906 INT/ORG ALL/VALS

L62
CORET A.,"L'INDEPENDANCE DU SAMOA OCCIDENTAL." S/ASIA LAW INT/ORG EXEC ALL/VALS SAMOA UN 20. PAGE 31 A0622 NAT/G STRUCT SOVEREIGN

S62
CORET A.,"LA DECLARATION DE L'ASSEMBLEE GENERAL DE L'ONU SUR L'OCTROI DE L'INDEPENDENCE AUX PAYS ET AUX PEUPLES." AFR ASIA ISLAM NIGERIA S/ASIA USSR WOR+45 ECO/UNDEV NAT/G DELIB/GP COLONIAL ALL/VALS ...CONCPT TIME/SEQ TREND UN TOT/POP 20 MEXIC/AMER. PAGE 31 A0621 INT/ORG STRUCT SOVEREIGN

S62
MANGIN G.,"LES ACCORDS DE COOPERATION EN MATIERE DE JUSTICE ENTRE LA FRANCE ET LES ETATS AFRICAINS ET MALGACHE." AFR ISLAM WOR+45 STRUCT ECO/UNDEV NAT/G DELIB/GP PERCEPT ALL/VALS...JURID MGT TIME/SEQ 20. PAGE 94 A1919 INT/ORG LAW FRANCE

S62
RAZAFIMBAHINY J.,"L'ORGANISATION AFRICAINE ET MALGACHE DE COOPERATION ECONOMIQUE." AFR ISLAM MADAGASCAR NAT/G ACT/RES ECO/TAC ALL/VALS ...TIME/SEQ 20. PAGE 120 A2454 INT/ORG ECO/UNDEV

S62
VASAK K.,"DE LA CONVENTION EUROPEENNE A LA CONVENTION AFRICAINE DES DROITS DE L'HOMME." AFR ISLAM WOR+45 LAW CONSTN ECO/UNDEV INT/ORG PERCEPT ALL/VALS 20. PAGE 158 A3223 DELIB/GP CONCPT COLONIAL

S62
VIGNES D.,"L'AUTORITE DES TRAITES INTERNATIONAUX EN DROIT INTERNE." EUR+WWI UNIV LAW CONSTN INTELL NAT/G POL/PAR DIPLOM ATTIT PERCEPT ALL/VALS ...POLICY INT/LAW JURID CONCPT TIME/SEQ 20 TREATY. PAGE 159 A3233 STRUCT LEGIT FRANCE

B63
BLACK J.E.,FOREIGN POLICIES IN A WORLD OF CHANGE. FUT INT/ORG ALL/VALS...POLICY MAJORIT MARXIST SOCIALIST TRADIT TIME/SEQ TREND ANTHOL 20. PAGE 15 A0298 WOR+45 NAT/G DIPLOM

B63
CREMEANS C.,THE ARABS AND THE WORLD: NASSER'S ARAB NATIONALIST POLICY. FUT ISLAM UAR USA+45 SOCIETY STRATA NAT/G POL/PAR PLAN DIPLOM EDU/PROP LEGIT DRIVE ALL/VALS...INT TIME/SEQ CHARTS 20 NASSER/G. PAGE 33 A0662 TOP/EX ATTIT REGION NAT/LISM

B63
FRANKEL J.,THE MAKING OF FOREIGN POLICY: AN ANALYSIS OF DECISION-MAKING. CHINA/COM EUR+WWI USA+45 ELITES INTELL FORCES LEGIS PLAN ATTIT ALL/VALS MORAL CONSERVE...GOV/COMP 20 PRESIDENT UN TREATY. PAGE 48 A0981 POLICY DECISION PROB/SOLV DIPLOM

B63
HENDERSON W.,SOUTHEAST ASIA: PROBLEMS OF UNITED STATES POLICY. COM S/ASIA CULTURE STRATA ECO/UNDEV INT/ORG DELIB/GP ACT/RES ECO/TAC DOMIN EDU/PROP LEGIT COERCE ATTIT ALL/VALS...STAT TIME/SEQ ANTHOL VAL/FREE 20. PAGE 64 A1313 ASIA USA+45 DIPLOM

B63
HINSLEY F.H.,POWER AND THE PURSUIT OF PEACE. WOR+45 WOR-45 PLAN RIGID/FLEX ALL/VALS ALL/IDEOS...POLICY DECISION INT/LAW 12/20 ROUSSEAU/J KANT/I BENTHAM/J LEAGUE/NAT. PAGE 65 A1338 DIPLOM CONSTN PEACE COERCE

B63
NORTH R.C.,CONTENT ANALYSIS: A HANDBOOK WITH APPLICATIONS FOR THE STUDY OF INTERNATIONAL CRISIS. ASIA COM EUR+WWI MOD/EUR INT/ORG TEC/DEV DOMIN EDU/PROP ROUTINE COERCE PERCEPT RIGID/FLEX ALL/VALS ...QUANT TESTS CON/ANAL SIMUL GEN/LAWS VAL/FREE. PAGE 110 A2252 METH/CNCPT COMPUT/IR USSR

B63
STEVENSON A.E.,LOOKING OUTWARD: YEARS OF CRISIS AT THE UNITED NATIONS. COM CUBA USA+45 WOR+45 SOCIETY NAT/G EX/STRUC ACT/RES LEGIT COLONIAL ATTIT PERSON SUPEGO ALL/VALS...POLICY HUM UN COLD/WAR CONGO 20. PAGE 138 A2823 INT/ORG CONCPT ARMS/CONT

L63
SZASZY E.,"L'EVOLUTION DES PRINCIPES GENERAUX DU DROIT INTERNATIONAL PRIVE DANS LES PAYS DE DEMOCRATIE POPULAIRE." COM FUT WOR+45 LAW ECO/DEV PERF/ART POL/PAR PROF/ORG ECO/TAC INT/TRADE EDU/PROP ATTIT RIGID/FLEX ALL/VALS SOCISM...JURID TREND GEN/LAWS WORK 20. PAGE 141 A2876 DIPLOM TOTALISM INT/LAW INT/ORG

L63
WILCOX F.O.,"THE ATLANTIC COMMUNITY: PROGRESS AND PROSPECTS." EUR+WWI FUT USA+45 WOR+45 SOCIETY CREATE ECO/TAC EDU/PROP LEGIT REGION ATTIT ALL/VALS ...POLICY ANTHOL VAL/FREE 20. PAGE 164 A3346 INT/ORG ACT/RES

S63
BARTHELEMY G.,"LE NOUVEAU FRANC (CFA) ET LA BANQUE CENTRALE DES ETATS DE L'AFRIQUE DE L'OUEST." FUT STRUCT INT/ORG PLAN ATTIT ALL/VALS 20. PAGE 11 A0230 AFR FINAN

S63
CHAKRAVARTI P.C.,"INDIAN NON-ALIGNMENT AND UNITED STATES POLICY." ASIA INDIA S/ASIA USA+45 CULTURE ECO/UNDEV NAT/G VOL/ASSN DELIB/GP TOP/EX FOR/AID NEUTRAL...POLICY HUM CONCPT RECORD GEN/LAWS 20. PAGE 25 A0515 ATTIT ALL/VALS COLONIAL DIPLOM

S63
COSER L.,"AMERICA AND THE WORLD REVOLUTION." COM FUT USA+45 WOR+45 INTELL SOCIETY NAT/G ECO/TAC EDU/PROP ALL/VALS SOCISM...PSY GEN/LAWS TOT/POP 20 COLD/WAR. PAGE 31 A0629 ECO/UNDEV PLAN FOR/AID DIPLOM

S63
DICKS H.V.,"NATIONAL LOYALTY, IDENTITY, AND THE INTERNATIONAL SOLDIER." FUT NAT/G COERCE ATTIT DRIVE PERCEPT PERSON RIGID/FLEX SUPEGO ALL/VALS ...PSY VAL/FREE. PAGE 37 A0758 INT/ORG FORCES

S63
GANDOLFI A.,"LES ACCORDS DE COOPERATION EN MATIERE DE POLITIQUE ETRANGERE ENTRE LA FRANCE ET LES NOUVEAUX ETATS AFRICAINS ET." AFR ISLAM MADAGASCAR WOR+45 ECO/DEV INT/ORG NAT/G DELIB/GP ECO/TAC ALL/VALS...CON/ANAL 20. PAGE 51 A1038 VOL/ASSN ECO/UNDEV DIPLOM FRANCE

S63
HOLBO P.S.,"COLD WAR DRIFT IN LATIN AMERICA." CUBA L/A+17C USA+45 USA-45 INT/ORG NAT/G NEIGH VOL/ASSN ACT/RES PLAN ECO/TAC ATTIT RIGID/FLEX ALL/VALS ...RECORD TIME/SEQ OAS LAFTA 20 COLD/WAR. PAGE 66 A1363 DELIB/GP CREATE FOR/AID

S63
LEDUC G.,"L'AIDE INTERNATIONALE AU DEVELOPPEMENT." FUT WOR+45 ECO/DEV ECO/UNDEV R+D PROF/ORG TEC/DEV ECO/TAC ROUTINE ATTIT ALL/VALS...MGT TIME/SEQ TOT/POP 20. PAGE 86 A1758 FINAN PLAN FOR/AID

S63
LOPEZIBOR J.,"L'EUROPE, FORME DE VIE." CHRIST-17C EUR+WWI FUT MOD/EUR SOCIETY SECT EDU/PROP ATTIT RIGID/FLEX ALL/VALS...POLICY HUM SOC TIME/SEQ TREND GEN/LAWS. PAGE 91 A1862 NAT/G CULTURE

S63
MODELSKI G.,"STUDY OF ALLIANCES." WOR+45 WOR-45 INT/ORG NAT/G FORCES LEGIT ADMIN CHOOSE ALL/VALS PWR SKILL...INT/LAW CONCPT GEN/LAWS 20 TREATY. PAGE 102 A2099 VOL/ASSN CON/ANAL DIPLOM

B64
APTER D.E.,IDEOLOGY AND DISCONTENT. FUT WOR+45 ACT/RES

CONSTN CULTURE INTELL SOCIETY STRUCT INT/ORG NAT/G ATTIT
DELIB/GP LEGIS CREATE PLAN TEC/DEV EDU/PROP EXEC
PERCEPT PERSON RIGID/FLEX ALL/VALS...POLICY
TOT/POP. PAGE 8 A0171

B64
JACOB P.E.,THE INTEGRATION OF POLITICAL COMMUNITIES. USA+45 WOR+45 CULTURE LOC/G MUNIC NAT/G CREATE PLAN LEGIT REGION COERCE ALL/VALS ...POLICY GEOG PSY SOC TREND HYPO/EXP GEN/LAWS VAL/FREE 20. PAGE 72 A1483
INT/ORG METH/CNCPT SIMUL STAT

B64
MASON E.S.,FOREIGN AID AND FOREIGN POLICY. USA+45 AGRI INDUS NAT/G EX/STRUC ACT/RES RIGID/FLEX ALL/VALS...POLICY GEN/LAWS MARSHL/PLN CONGRESS 20. PAGE 95 A1956
ECO/UNDEV ECO/TAC FOR/AID DIPLOM

B64
SULLIVAN G.,THE STORY OF THE PEACE CORPS. USA+45 WOR+45 INTELL FACE/GP NAT/G SCHOOL VOL/ASSN CONSULT EX/STRUC PLAN EDU/PROP ADMIN ATTIT DRIVE ALL/VALS ...POLICY HEAL SOC CONCPT INT QU BIOG TREND SOC/EXP WORK. PAGE 140 A2861
INT/ORG ECO/UNDEV FOR/AID PEACE

B64
TAYLOR E.,RICHER BY ASIA. S/ASIA CULTURE VOL/ASSN ACT/RES ATTIT DISPL PERSON ALL/VALS...INT/LAW MYTH SELF/OBS 20. PAGE 142 A2899
SOCIETY RIGID/FLEX INDIA

B64
UN PUB. INFORM. ORGAN.,EVERY MAN'S UNITED NATIONS. UNIV WOR+45 CONSTN CULTURE SOCIETY ECO/DEV ECO/UNDEV NAT/G ACT/RES PLAN ECO/TAC INT/TRADE EDU/PROP LEGIT PEACE ATTIT ALL/VALS...POLICY HUM INT/LAW CONCPT CHARTS UN TOT/POP 20. PAGE 147 A3004
INT/ORG ROUTINE

B64
VOELKMANN K.,HERRSCHER VON MORGEN? BAL/PWR COLONIAL NEUTRAL REGION RACE/REL ALL/VALS SOVEREIGN...RECORD 20 COLD/WAR THIRD/WRLD. PAGE 159 A3246
DIPLOM ECO/UNDEV CONTROL NAT/COMP

L64
ARMENGALD A.,"ECONOMIE ET COEXISTENCE." COM EUR+WWI FUT USA+45 WOR+45 ECO/DEV ECO/UNDEV FINAN INT/ORG NAT/G EXEC CHOOSE ATTIT ALL/VALS...POLICY RELATIV DECISION TREND SOC/EXP COLD/WAR WORK 20. PAGE 9 A0173
MARKET ECO/TAC CAP/ISM

L64
BERKS R.N.,"THE US AND WEAPONS CONTROL." WOR+45 LAW INT/ORG NAT/G LEGIS EXEC COERCE PEACE ATTIT RIGID/FLEX ALL/VALS PWR...POLICY TOT/POP 20. PAGE 13 A0273
USA+45 PLAN ARMS/CONT

L64
CARNEGIE ENDOWMENT INT. PEACE,"POLITICAL QUESTIONS (ISSUES BEFORE THE NINETEENTH GENERAL ASSEMBLY)." SPACE WOR+45 CONSTN FINAN NAT/G CONSULT DELIB/GP FORCES LEGIS TEC/DEV EDU/PROP LEGIT ARMS/CONT COERCE NUC/PWR ATTIT ALL/VALS...CONCPT OBS UN COLD/WAR 20. PAGE 24 A0490
INT/ORG PEACE

L64
HOFFMANN S.,"EUROPE'S IDENTITY CRISIS: BETWEEN THE PAST AND AMERICA." EUR+WWI FUT USA+45 INT/ORG NAT/G LEGIT RIGID/FLEX ALL/VALS...RELATIV TOT/POP 20. PAGE 66 A1358
COERCE POLICY

L64
WARD C.,"THE 'NEW MYTHS' AND 'OLD REALITIES' OF NUCLEAR WAR." COM FUT USA+45 USSR WOR+45 INT/ORG NAT/G DOMIN LEGIT EXEC ATTIT PERCEPT ALL/VALS ...POLICY RELATIV PSY MYTH TREND 20. PAGE 161 A3280
FORCES COERCE ARMS/CONT NUC/PWR

S64
CARNEGIE ENDOWMENT INT. PEACE,"COLONIAL COUNTRIES AND PEOPLES (ISSUES BEFORE THE NINETEENTH GENERAL ASSEMBLY)." AFR ISLAM L/A+17C WOR+45 DELIB/GP LEGIS ECO/TAC EDU/PROP NAT/LISM PEACE ALL/VALS...RECORD UN CMN/WLTH 20. PAGE 24 A0491
INT/ORG ECO/UNDEV COLONIAL

S64
DELGADO J.,"EL MOMENTO POLITICO HISPANOAMERICA." CHINA/COM FUT PANAMA USA+45 USSR INT/ORG NAT/G POL/PAR FORCES DOMIN REGION COERCE ATTIT ALL/VALS ...TRADIT CONCPT COLD/WAR 20. PAGE 36 A0728
L/A+17C EDU/PROP NAT/LISM

S64
DRAKE S.T.C.,"DEMOCRACY ON TRIAL IN AFRICA." EUR+WWI FUT USA+45 ECO/UNDEV INT/ORG NAT/G POL/PAR TOP/EX EDU/PROP LEGIT ATTIT ALL/VALS...POLICY TREND GEN/LAWS VAL/FREE 20. PAGE 38 A0785
AFR STERTYP

S64
GARDNER R.N.,"THE SOVIET UNION AND THE UNITED NATIONS." WOR+45 FINAN POL/PAR VOL/ASSN FORCES ECO/TAC DOMIN EDU/PROP LEGIT ADJUD ADMIN ARMS/CONT COERCE ATTIT ALL/VALS...POLICY MAJORIT CONCPT OBS TIME/SEQ TREND STERTYP UN. PAGE 51 A1046
COM INT/ORG USSR

S64
GARMARNIKOW M.,"INFLUENCE-BUYING IN WEST AFRICA." COM FUT USSR INTELL NAT/G PLAN TEC/DEV ECO/TAC DOMIN EDU/PROP REGION NAT/LISM ATTIT DRIVE ALL/VALS SOVEREIGN...POLICY PSY SOC CONCPT TREND STERTYP WORK COLD/WAR 20. PAGE 51 A1049
AFR ECO/UNDEV FOR/AID SOCISM

S64
GREENBERG S.,"JUDAISM AND WORLD JUSTICE." MEDIT-7 WOR+45 LAW CULTURE SOCIETY INT/ORG NAT/G FORCES EDU/PROP ATTIT DRIVE PERSON SUPEGO ALL/VALS ...POLICY PSY CONCPT GEN/LAWS JEWS. PAGE 55 A1140
SECT JURID PEACE

S64
JORDAN A.,"POLITICAL COMMUNICATION: THE THIRD DIMENSION OF STRATEGY." USA+45 WOR+45 INT/ORG NAT/G CONSULT FORCES PLAN LEGIT EXEC PERCEPT ALL/VALS ...POLICY RELATIV PSY NEW/IDEA AUD/VIS EXHIBIT TOT/POP 20. PAGE 75 A1534
EDU/PROP RIGID/FLEX ATTIT

S64
KHAN M.Z.,"ISLAM AND INTERNATIONAL RELATIONS." FUT WOR+45 LAW CULTURE SOCIETY NAT/G SECT DELIB/GP FORCES EDU/PROP ATTIT PERSON SUPEGO ALL/VALS ...POLICY PSY CONCPT MYTH HIST/WRIT GEN/LAWS. PAGE 78 A1608
ISLAM INT/ORG DIPLOM

S64
KISSINGER H.A.,"COALITION DIPLOMACY IN A NUCLEAR AGE." COM EUR+WWI USA+45 WOR+45 INT/ORG NAT/G FORCES ACT/RES DOMIN LEGIT COERCE PERCEPT ALL/VALS ...POLICY TOT/POP 20. PAGE 80 A1644
CONSULT ATTIT DIPLOM NUC/PWR

S64
KOTANI H.,"PEACE-KEEPING: PROBLEMS FOR SMALLER COUNTRIES." FUT WOR+45 NAT/G ACT/RES PLAN DOMIN EDU/PROP COERCE ALL/VALS...POLICY UN TOT/POP 20. PAGE 82 A1673
INT/ORG FORCES

S64
MOORE W.E.,"PREDICTING DISCONTINUITIES IN SOCIAL CHANGE." UNIV WOR+45 ECO/DEV ECO/UNDEV INT/ORG NAT/G COERCE ALL/VALS...METH/CNCPT TIME/SEQ TREND TOT/POP VAL/FREE 20. PAGE 103 A2125
SOCIETY GEN/LAWS REV

S64
SAAB H.,"THE ARAB SEARCH FOR A FEDERAL UNION." SOCIETY INT/ORG NAT/G DELIB/GP FORCES ACT/RES TEC/DEV ECO/TAC DOMIN LEGIT REGION ROUTINE ATTIT DRIVE RIGID/FLEX ALL/VALS...SOC CONCPT NEW/IDEA TIME/SEQ TREND. PAGE 126 A2580
ISLAM PLAN

S64
TOUVAL S.,"THE SOMALI REPUBLIC." AFR ISLAM SOMALIA FAM KIN NAT/G CREATE FOR/AID LEGIT ATTIT ALL/VALS ...RECORD TREND 20. PAGE 144 A2954
ECO/UNDEV RIGID/FLEX

S64
WASKOW A.I.,"NEW ROADS TO A WORLD WITHOUT WAR." FUT WOR+45 CULTURE INTELL SOCIETY NAT/G DOMIN LEGIT EXEC COERCE PEACE ATTIT DISPL PERCEPT RIGID/FLEX ALL/VALS...POLICY RELATIV SOC NEW/IDEA 20. PAGE 161 A3288
INT/ORG FORCES

S64
ZARTMAN I.W.,"LES RELATIONS ENTRE LA FRANCE ET L'ALGERIA DEPUIS LES ACCORDS D'EVIAN." EUR+WWI FUT ISLAM CULTURE AGRI EXTR/IND FINAN INDUS POL/PAR DIPLOM ECO/TAC FOR/AID PEACE ATTIT DRIVE ALL/VALS ...TIME/SEQ VAL/FREE 20. PAGE 169 A3446
ECO/UNDFV ALGERIA FRANCE

B65
US DEPARTMENT OF DEFENSE,US SECURITY ARMS CONTROL, AND DISARMAMENT 1961-1965 (PAMPHLET). CHINA/COM COM GERMANY/W ISRAEL SPACE USA+45 USSR WOR+45 FORCES EDU/PROP DETER EQUILIB PEACE ALL/VALS...GOV/COMP 20 NATO. PAGE 151 A3077
BIBLIOG/A ARMS/CONT NUC/PWR DIPLOM

L65
KAPLAN M.A.,"OLD REALITIES AND NEW MYTHS." USA+45 WOR+45 INT/ORG NAT/G TOP/EX ACT/RES BAL/PWR ECO/TAC EDU/PROP LEGIT RIGID/FLEX ALL/VALS...RECORD COLD/WAR 20. PAGE 76 A1564
ATTIT MYTH DIPLOM

S65
AMRAM P.W.,"REPORT ON THE TENTH SESSION OF THE HAGUE CONFERENCE ON PRIVATE INTERNATIONAL LAW." USA+45 WOR+45 INT/ORG CREATE LEGIT ADJUD ALL/VALS ...JURID CONCPT METH/CNCPT OBS GEN/METH 20. PAGE 8 A0155
VOL/ASSN DELIB/GP INT/LAW

S65
HELMREICH E.C.,"KADAR'S HUNGARY." COM EUR+WWI HUNGARY USSR INTELL ECO/DEV AGRI INT/ORG TOP/EX DOMIN ALL/VALS WORK COLD/WAR 20. PAGE 64 A1311
NAT/G RIGID/FLEX TOTALISM

S65
KHOURI F.J.,"THE JORDON RIVER CONTROVERSY." LAW SOCIETY ECO/UNDEV AGRI FINAN INDUS SECT FORCES ACT/RES PLAN TEC/DEV ECO/TAC EDU/PROP COERCE ATTIT DRIVE PERCEPT RIGID/FLEX ALL/VALS...GEOG SOC MYTH WORK. PAGE 78 A1610
ISLAM INT/ORG ISRAEL JORDAN

S65
SCHNEIDER R.M.,"THE US IN LATIN AMERICA." L/A+17C USA+45 NAT/G POL/PAR PLAN RIGID/FLEX ALL/VALS OAS 20. PAGE 129 A2640
VOL/ASSN ECO/UNDEV FOR/AID

B66
HOLLINS E.J.,PEACE IS POSSIBLE: A READER FOR LAYMEN. WOR+45 CULTURE PLAN RISK AGE/Y ALL/VALS SOVEREIGN...PSY CONCPT TREND 20 UN JOHN/XXIII KENNAN/G MYRDAL/G. PAGE 67 A1370
PEACE DIPLOM INT/ORG NUC/PWR

B67
BODENHEIMER E.,TREATISE ON JUSTICE. INT/ORG NAT/G PUB/INST ACT/RES RISK CRIME INGP/REL DISCRIM DRIVE LAISSEZ 20. PAGE 16 A0325
ALL/VALS STRUCT JURID CONCPT

B67
PIKE F.B.,FREEDOM AND REFORM IN LATIN AMERICA. BRAZIL URUGUAY CONSTN CULTURE SECT DIPLOM EDU/PROP PARTIC DRIVE ALL/VALS CATHISM...GEOG ANTHOL BIBLIOG REFORMERS BOLIV. PAGE 116 A2379
L/A+17C ORD/FREE ECO/UNDFV REV

EDU/PROP CRIME RACE/REL MARRIAGE ANOMIE ATTIT ORD/FREE...POLICY 20 UN. PAGE 160 A3254 CULTURE ACT/RES GP/REL

B62
GUTTMAN A.,THE WOUND IN THE HEART: AMERICA AND THE SPANISH CIVIL WAR. SPAIN USA-45 POL/PAR LEGIS ECO/TAC CHOOSE ANOMIE ATTIT MARXISM...POLICY ANARCH BIBLIOG 20 ROOSEVLT/F. PAGE 58 A1198 ALL/IDEOS WAR DIPLOM CATHISM

B64
EHRENBURG I.,THE WAR: 1941-1945 (VOL. V OF "MEN, YEARS - LIFE," TRANS. BY TATIANA SHEBUNINA). GERMANY USSR PRESS WRITING PERS/REL PEACE ANOMIE ATTIT PERSON...CONCPT RECORD BIOG 20 STALIN/J HITLER/A. PAGE 40 A0827 WAR DIPLOM COM MARXIST

B64
LENS S.,THE FUTILE CRUSADE. ASIA CHINA/COM L/A+17C USA+45 USSR WOR+45 ECO/DEV BAL/PWR DIPLOM NUC/PWR WAR NAT/LISM PEACE 20 COLD/WAR PRESIDENT CIA. PAGE 87 A1774 ORD/FREE ANOMIE COM MARXISM

B64
STANKIEWICZ W.J.,POLITICAL THOUGHT SINCE WORLD WAR II. WOR+45 CAP/ISM DIPLOM COLONIAL COERCE REV REPRESENT ADJUST ANOMIE ALL/IDEOS 20. PAGE 137 A2804 IDEA/COMP DOMIN ORD/FREE AUTHORIT

B66
LEWIS S.,TOWARDS INTERNATIONAL CO-OPERATION (1ST ED.). WOR+45 AGRI INDUS EDU/PROP RACE/REL ISOLAT NAT/LISM ATTIT HEALTH WEALTH...CHARTS WORSHIP 20 UN. PAGE 88 A1803 DIPLOM ANOMIE PROB/SOLV INT/ORG

B66
MAY E.R.,ANXIETY AND AFFLUENCE: 1945-1965. USA+45 DIPLOM FOR/AID ARMS/CONT RACE/REL CONSEN...ANTHOL 20 COLD/WAR KENNEDY/JF EISNHWR/DD TRUMAN/HS BERLIN/BLO. PAGE 97 A1982 ANOMIE ECO/DEV NUC/PWR WEALTH

B66
VON BORCH H.,FRIEDE TROTZ KRIEG. GERMANY USSR WOR+45 PEACE ANOMIE ATTIT 20. PAGE 112 A2305 DIPLOM NUC/PWR WAR COERCE

B67
CHO S.S.,KOREA IN WORLD POLITICS 1940-1950; AN EVALUATION OF AMERICAN RESPONSIBILITY. KOREA USA+45 USSR CONSTN INT/ORG NAT/G FORCES FOR/AID ANOMIE SUPEGO MARXISM...DECISION BIBLIOG 20. PAGE 26 A0533 POLICY DIPLOM PROB/SOLV WAR

S67
ADIE W.A.C.,"CHINA'S 'SECOND LIBERATION'." CHINA/COM SOCIETY WORKER DIPLOM TASK 20 MAO. PAGE 4 A0090 MARXISM REV INGP/REL ANOMIE

S67
SUINN R.M.,"THE DISARMAMENT FANTASY* PSYCHOLOGICAL FACTORS THAT MAY PRODUCE WARFARE." DIPLOM RISK ARMS/CONT DETER ANOMIE PERSON GAME. PAGE 140 A2860 DECISION NUC/PWR WAR PSY

ANSPRENGER F. A0164

ANTARCTICA

S59
HARTT J.,"ANTARCTICA: ITS IMMEDIATE PRACTICALITIES." FUT USA+45 USSR WOR+45 INT/ORG NAT/G CREATE TEC/DEV REGION KNOWL WEALTH...GEOG 20 ANTARTICA. PAGE 62 A1276 VOL/ASSN ORD/FREE DIPLOM

L61
TAUBENFELD H.J.,"A TREATY FOR ANTARCTICA." FUT USA+45 INTELL INT/ORG LABOR 20 TREATY ANTARCTICA. PAGE 141 A2893 R+D ACT/RES DIPLOM

ANTHEM T. A0165

ANTHOL....ANTHOLOGY, SYMPOSIUM, PANEL OF WRITERS

B01
HART A.B.,AMERICAN HISTORY TOLD BY CONTEMPORARIES. UK CULTURE FINAN SECT FORCES DIPLOM TAX RUMOR CT/SYS REV GOV/REL GP/REL...ANTHOL 17/18 PRE/US/AM FEDERALIST. PAGE 62 A1273 USA-45 COLONIAL SOVEREIGN

B19
US DEPARTMENT OF STATE,A TENTATIVE LIST OF TREATY COLLECTIONS. WOR-45 BAL/PWR INT/TRADE TARIFFS WAR PEACE ORD/FREE 20. PAGE 151 A3080 ANTHOL DIPLOM DELIB/GP

N19
NATIONAL ACADEMY OF SCIENCES,THE GROWTH OF WORLD POPULATION: ANALYSIS OF THE PROBLEMS AND RECOMMENDATIONS FOR RESEARCH AND TRAINING (PAMPHLET). WOR+45 CULTURE ECO/UNDEV EDU/PROP MARRIAGE AGE HEALTH...ANTHOL 20 BIRTH/CON. PAGE 107 A2199 CENSUS PLAN FAM INT/ORG

B21
BALFOUR A.J.,ESSAYS SPECULATIVE AND POLITICAL. SEA CULTURE CREATE WAR NAT/LISM PEACE LOVE...ART/METH INT/LAW CONCPT ANTHOL 20 JEWS. PAGE 10 A0211 PHIL/SCI SOCIETY DIPLOM

B28
LODGE H.C.,THE HISTORY OF NATIONS (25 VOLS.). UNIV LEAD...ANTHOL BIBLIOG INDEX. PAGE 90 A1850 DIPLOM SOCIETY NAT/G

B33
PUBLIC OPINION AND WORLD POLITICS. UNIV LAW CULTURE NAT/G PRESS REV GP/REL...MAJORIT METH/COMP ANTHOL 20. PAGE 167 A3400 DIPLOM EDU/PROP ATTIT MAJORITY

B37
THOMPSON J.W.,SECRET DIPLOMACY: A RECORD OF ESPIONAGE AND DOUBLE-DEALING: 1500-1815. CHRIST-17C MOD/EUR NAT/G WRITING RISK MORAL...ANTHOL BIBLIOG 16/19 ESPIONAGE. PAGE 143 A2927 DIPLOM CRIME

B38
HAGUE PERMANENT CT INTL JUSTIC,WORLD COURT REPORTS: COLLECTION OF THE JUDGEMENTS ORDERS AND OPINIONS VOLUME 3 1932-35. WOR-45 LAW DELIB/GP CONFER WAR PEACE ATTIT...DECISION ANTHOL 20 WORLD/CT CASEBOOK. PAGE 59 A1214 INT/ORG CT/SYS DIPLOM ADJUD

B39
SPEIER H.,WAR IN OUR TIME. WOR-45 AGRI FINAN FORCES TEC/DEV BAL/PWR EDU/PROP WEAPON PEACE PWR...ANTHOL 20. PAGE 136 A2779 FASCISM WAR DIPLOM NAT/G

L41
COMM. STUDY ORGAN. PEACE,"ORGANIZATION OF PEACE." USA-45 WOR-45 STRATA NAT/G ACT/RES DIPLOM ECO/TAC EDU/PROP ADJUD ATTIT ORD/FREE PWR...SOC CONCPT ANTHOL LEAGUE/NAT 20. PAGE 28 A0575 INT/ORG PLAN PEACE

B43
HAGUE PERMANENT CT INTL JUSTIC,WORLD COURT REPORTS: COLLECTION OF THE JUDGEMENTS ORDERS AND OPINIONS VOLUME 4 1936-42. WOR-45 CONFER PEACE ATTIT ...DECISION JURID ANTHOL 20 WORLD/CT CASEBOOK. PAGE 59 A1215 INT/ORG CT/SYS DIPLOM ADJUD

B44
DAVIS H.E.,PIONEERS IN WORLD ORDER. WOR-45 CONSTN ECO/TAC DOMIN EDU/PROP LEGIT ADJUD ADMIN ARMS/CONT CHOOSE KNOWL ORD/FREE...POLICY JURID SOC STAT OBS CENSUS TIME/SEQ ANTHOL LEAGUE/NAT 20. PAGE 34 A0691 INT/ORG ROUTINE

B47
DE HUSZAR G.B.,PERSISTENT INTERNATIONAL ISSUES. WOR+45 WOR-45 AGRI INDUS INT/ORG PROB/SOLV EFFICIENCY WEALTH...CON/ANAL ANTHOL UN. PAGE 35 A0704 DIPLOM PEACE ECO/TAC FOR/AID

L47
BRUNER J.S.,"TOWARD A COMMON GROUND-INTERNATIONAL SOCIAL SCIENCE." FUT WOR+45 INTELL R+D NAT/G VOL/ASSN CONSULT DELIB/GP ACT/RES CREATE PLAN TEC/DEV ATTIT ORD/FREE...PSY SOC CONCPT ANTHOL UNESCO 20. PAGE 20 A0410 INT/ORG KNOWL

B48
GRIFFITH E.S.,RESEARCH IN POLITICAL SCIENCE: THE WORK OF PANELS OF RESEARCH COMMITTEE, APSA. WOR+45 WOR-45 COM/IND R+D FORCES ACT/RES WAR...GOV/COMP ANTHOL 20. PAGE 56 A1160 BIBLIOG PHIL/SCI DIPLOM JURID

B51
STANTON A.H.,PERSONALITY AND POLITICAL CRISIS. WOR+45 WOR-45 STRUCT DIPLOM INGP/REL TOTALISM MORAL ...ANTHOL 20 LASSWELL/H PARSONS/T RIESMAN/D. PAGE 137 A2806 EDU/PROP WAR PERSON PSY

B54
GERMANY FOREIGN MINISTRY,DOCUMENTS ON GERMAN FOREIGN POLICY 1918-1945, SERIES C (1933-1937) VOLS. I-V. GERMANY MOD/EUR FORCES PLAN ECO/TAC ...FASCIST CHARTS ANTHOL 20. PAGE 52 A1065 NAT/G DIPLOM POLICY

B56
DEGRAS J.,THE COMMUNIST INTERNATIONAL, 1919-1943: DOCUMENTS (3 VOLS.). EX/STRUC...ANTHOL BIBLIOG 20. PAGE 36 A0723 COM DIPLOM POLICY POL/PAR

B56
SOHN L.B.,BASIC DOCUMENTS OF THE UNITED NATIONS. WOR+45 LAW INT/ORG LEGIT EXEC ROUTINE CHOOSE PWR ...JURID CONCPT GEN/LAWS ANTHOL UN TOT/POP OAS FAO ILO 20. PAGE 135 A2761 DELIB/GP CONSTN

B56
US LIBRARY OF CONGRESS,UNITED STATES DIRECT ECONOMIC AID TO FOREIGN COUNTRIES: A COLLECTION OF EXCERPTS AND A BIBLIOGRAPHY (PAMPHLET). USA+45 PRESS DEBATE...ANTHOL BIBLIOG/A CONGRESS. PAGE 155 A3154 FOR/AID POLICY DIPLOM ECO/UNDEV

B57
DUDDEN A.P.,WOODROW WILSON AND THE WORLD OF TODAY. USA-45 NAT/G PROVS CONTROL PARTIC WAR ISOLAT PWR SKILL...PERS/COMP ANTHOL 19/20 WILSON/W UN LEAGUE/NAT WWI. PAGE 39 A0794 CHIEF DIPLOM POL/PAR LEAD

B57
NEHRU J.,MILITARY ALLIANCE (PAMPHLET). INDIA WOR+45 NAT/G PLAN DETER NUC/PWR WAR...POLICY ANTHOL NEHRU/J SEATO UN. PAGE 108 A2212 INT/ORG DIPLOM FORCES PEACE

B57
US COMMISSION GOVT SECURITY,RECOMMENDATIONS; AREA: IMMIGRANT PROGRAM. USA+45 LAW WORKER DIPLOM POLICY CONTROL

EDU/PROP WRITING ADMIN PEACE ATTIT...CONCPT ANTHOL 20 MIGRATION SUBVERT. PAGE 150 A3060
PLAN NAT/G

B58
BRIERLY J.L.,THE BASIS OF OBLIGATION IN INTERNATIONAL LAW, AND OTHER PAPERS. WOR+45 WOR-45 LEGIS...JURID CONCPT NAT/COMP ANTHOL 20. PAGE 19 A0377
INT/LAW DIPLOM ADJUD SOVEREIGN

B58
MANSERGH N.,COMMONWEALTH PERSPECTIVES. GHANA UK LAW VOL/ASSN CONFER HEALTH SOVEREIGN...GEOG CHARTS ANTHOL 20 CMN/WLTH AUSTRAL. PAGE 94 A1930
DIPLOM COLONIAL INT/ORG INGP/REL

B58
NEHRU J.,SPEECHES. INDIA ECO/UNDEV AGRI INDUS INT/ORG POL/PAR DIPLOM FOR/AID NAT/LISM...ANTHOL 20. PAGE 108 A2213
PLAN CHIEF COLONIAL NEUTRAL

B58
PALMER E.E.,AMERICAN FOREIGN POLICY. USA+45 CULTURE ECO/UNDEV NAT/G PLAN GIVE BAL/PAY ORD/FREE WEALTH POPULISM...DECISION ANTHOL 20. PAGE 113 A2319
DIPLOM ECO/TAC POLICY

B58
PALMER E.E.,THE COMMUNIST CHALLENGE. COM USA+45 USA-45 ECO/DEV ECO/UNDEV NEUTRAL ORD/FREE POPULISM ...CONCPT NAT/COMP ANTHOL 19/20 LENIN/VI STALIN/J MAO MARX/KARL COM/PARTY. PAGE 113 A2320
MARXISM DIPLOM IDEA/COMP POLICY

B58
UN INTL CONF ON PEACEFUL USE,PROGRESS IN ATOMIC ENERGY (VOL. I). WOR+45 R+D PLAN TEC/DEV CONFER CONTROL PEACE SKILL...CHARTS ANTHOL 20 UN BAGHDAD. PAGE 147 A3003
NUC/PWR DIPLOM WORKER EDU/PROP

B59
ALLEN W.R.,FOREIGN TRADE AND FINANCE. ECO/DEV DIPLOM BAL/PAY...POLICY CONCPT ANTHOL 20. PAGE 6 A0127
INT/TRADE EQUILIB FINAN

B59
AMERICAN FRIENDS OF VIETNAM,AID TO VIETNAM: AN AMERICAN SUCCESS STORY (PAMPHLET). ASIA FUT USA+45 VIETNAM ECO/UNDEV WAR CIVMIL/REL GOV/REL...ANTHOL 20. PAGE 7 A0148
DIPLOM NAT/G FOR/AID FORCES

B59
FOX W.T.R.,THEORETICAL ASPECTS OF INTERNATIONAL RELATIONS. WOR+45 INT/ORG NAT/G POL/PAR CONSULT PLAN ECO/TAC DOMIN EDU/PROP LEGIT EXEC COERCE PWR WEALTH...RELATIV CONCPT 20. PAGE 48 A0975
DELIB/GP ANTHOL

B59
GOLDWIN R.A.,READINGS IN AMERICAN FOREIGN POLICY. USA+45 USA-45 ARMS/CONT NUC/PWR...INT/LAW 18/20. PAGE 53 A1094
ANTHOL DIPLOM INT/ORG ECO/UNDEV

B59
HALEY A.G.,FIRST COLLOQUIUM ON THE LAW OF OUTER SPACE. WOR+45 INT/ORG ACT/RES PLAN BAL/PWR CONFER ATTIT PWR...POLICY JURID CHARTS ANTHOL 20. PAGE 60 A1225
SPACE LAW SOVEREIGN CONTROL

B59
JONES A.C.,NEW FABIAN COLONIAL ESSAYS. UK SOCIETY POL/PAR EDU/PROP ADMIN ORD/FREE SOVEREIGN SOCISM ...ANTHOL 20 CMN/WLTH LABOR/PAR. PAGE 75 A1530
COLONIAL INT/ORG INGP/REL DOMIN

B60
HAHN W.F.,AMERICAN STRATEGY FOR THE NUCLEAR AGE. USA+45 NAT/G TEC/DEV ECO/TAC FOR/AID ARMS/CONT NUC/PWR ORD/FREE MARXISM...ANTHOL 20. PAGE 59 A1216
DIPLOM PLAN PEACE

B60
HOFFMANN S.H.,CONTEMPORARY THEORY IN INTERNATIONAL RELATIONS. RATIONAL...SOC METH/CNCPT METH/COMP SIMUL ANTHOL 20. PAGE 66 A1359
DIPLOM METH PHIL/SCI DECISION

B60
KHRUSHCHEV N.S.,KHRUSHCHEV IN NEW YORK. USA+45 USSR ATTIT...ANTHOL 20 UN KHRUSH/N. PAGE 79 A1612
DIPLOM PEACE ARMS/CONT

B60
MCCLELLAND C.A.,NUCLEAR WEAPONS, MISSILES, AND FUTURE WAR: PROBLEM FOR THE SIXTIES. WOR+45 FORCES ARMS/CONT DETER MARXISM...POLICY ANTHOL COLD/WAR. PAGE 97 A1998
DIPLOM NUC/PWR WAR WEAPON

B60
PENTONY D.E.,UNITED STATES FOREIGN AID. INDIA LAOS USA+45 ECO/UNDEV INT/TRADE ADMIN PEACE ATTIT ...POLICY METH/COMP ANTHOL 20. PAGE 115 A2352
FOR/AID DIPLOM ECO/TAC

B60
PRINCETON U CONFERENCE,CURRENT PROBLEMS IN NORTH AFRICA. ALGERIA LIBYA MOROCCO USA+45 EXTR/IND POL/PAR PROB/SOLV DIPLOM ECO/TAC WAR...ANTHOL 20 TUNIS. PAGE 118 A2412
POLICY ECO/UNDEV NAT/G

B60
SCANLON D.G.,INTERNATIONAL EDUCATION: A DOCUMENTARY HISTORY. ADMIN CONTROL ATTIT PERCEPT...BIOG ANTHOL METH 20. PAGE 127 A2612
EDU/PROP INT/ORG NAT/COMP DIPLOM

B60
STEVENSON A.E.,PUTTING FIRST THINGS FIRST. USA+45 INT/ORG NEIGH FOR/AID DISCRIM...ANTHOL 20. PAGE 138 A2822
DIPLOM ECO/UNDEV ORD/FREE

EDU/PROP

B60
THEOBOLD R.,THE NEW NATIONS OF WEST AFRICA. GHANA NIGERIA CULTURE INT/ORG ECO/TAC FOR/AID COLONIAL RACE/REL POPULISM...ANTHOL BIBLIOG 20 UN. PAGE 143 A2916
AFR SOVEREIGN ECO/UNDEV DIPLOM

L60
LAUTERPACHT E.,"THE SUEZ CANAL SETTLEMENT." FRANCE ISLAM ISRAEL UAR UK BAL/PWR DIPLOM LEGIT...JURID GEN/LAWS ANTHOL SUEZ VAL/FREE 20. PAGE 85 A1747
INT/ORG LAW

B61
BAINS J.S.,STUDIES IN POLITICAL SCIENCE. INDIA WOR+45 WOR-45 CONSTN BAL/PWR ADJUD ADMIN PARL/PROC SOVEREIGN...SOC METH/COMP ANTHOL 17/20 UN. PAGE 10 A0209
DIPLOM INT/LAW NAT/G

B61
BRENNAN D.G.,ARMS CONTROL, DISARMAMENT, AND NATIONAL SECURITY. WOR+45 NAT/G FORCES CREATE PROB/SOLV PARTIC WAR PEACE...DECISION INT/LAW ANTHOL BIBLIOG 20. PAGE 18 A0372
ARMS/CONT ORD/FREE DIPLOM POLICY

B61
EISENHOWER D.D.,PEACE WITH JUSTICE: SELECTED ADDRESSES. USSR PARTIC ARMS/CONT MORAL...TRADIT CONCPT GEN/LAWS ANTHOL 20 PRESIDENT COLD/WAR. PAGE 41 A0832
PEACE DIPLOM EDU/PROP POLICY

B61
HANCOCK W.K.,FOUR STUDIES OF WAR AND PEACE IN THIS CENTURY. FUT WOR+45 WOR-45 ACT/RES LEGIT DETER HEALTH...TREND ANTHOL TOT/POP VAL/FREE UN 20. PAGE 61 A1250
INT/ORG POLICY ARMS/CONT

B61
HARRIS S.E.,THE DOLLAR IN CRISIS. USA+45 MARKET INT/ORG ECO/TAC PRICE CONTROL WEALTH...METH/COMP ANTHOL 20 GOLD/STAND. PAGE 62 A1269
BAL/PAY DIPLOM FINAN INT/TRADE

B61
KERTESZ S.D.,AMERICAN DIPLOMACY IN A NEW ERA. COM S/ASIA UK USA+45 FORCES PROB/SOLV BAL/PWR ECO/TAC ADMIN COLONIAL WAR PEACE ORD/FREE 20 NATO CONGRESS UN COLD/WAR. PAGE 78 A1601
ANTHOL DIPLOM TREND

B61
PANIKKAR K.M.,THE VOICE OF FREEDOM: SELECTED SPEECHES OF PANDIT MOTILAL NEHRU. INDIA UK CONSTN FINAN FORCES LEGIS DIPLOM TAX COLONIAL...POLICY MAJORIT ANTHOL 20 NEHRU/PM. PAGE 114 A2331
NAT/LISM ORD/FREE CHIEF NAT/G

B61
ROSENAU J.N.,INTERNATIONAL POLITICS AND FOREIGN POLICY: A READER IN RESEARCH AND THEORY. ELITES ATTIT SOVEREIGN...DECISION CHARTS HYPO/EXP GAME SIMUL ANTHOL BIBLIOG METH 20. PAGE 124 A2531
ACT/RES DIPLOM CONCPT POLICY

B61
SCOTT A.M.,POLITICS, USA; CASES ON THE AMERICAN DEMOCRATIC PROCESS. USA+45 CHIEF FORCES DIPLOM LOBBY CHOOSE RACE/REL FEDERAL ATTIT...JURID ANTHOL T 20 PRESIDENT CONGRESS CIVIL/LIB. PAGE 130 A2669
CT/SYS CONSTN NAT/G PLAN

B62
ROUND TABLE ON EUROPE'S ROLE IN LATIN AMERICAN DEVELOPMENT. EUR+WWI L/A+17C PLAN BAL/PAY UTIL ROLE WEALTH...CHARTS ANTHOL 20 UN INT/AM/DEV. PAGE 3 A0063
ECO/UNDEV FINAN TEC/DEV FOR/AID

B62
BENNETT J.C.,NUCLEAR WEAPONS AND THE CONFLICT OF CONSCIENCE. WOR+45 PROB/SOLV DIPLOM WEAPON SUPEGO MORAL...ANTHOL WORSHIP 20. PAGE 13 A0268
POLICY NUC/PWR WAR

B62
COUNCIL ON WORLD TENSIONS,RESTLESS NATIONS. WOR+45 STRUCT INT/ORG NAT/G PLAN ECO/TAC...NAT/COMP ANTHOL 20. PAGE 32 A0641
ECO/UNDEV POLICY DIPLOM TASK

B62
HOOK S.,WORLD COMMUNISM: KEY DOCUMENTARY MATERIAL. CHINA/COM L/A+17C USA+45 USSR POL/PAR DIPLOM COLONIAL REV WAR...ANTHOL 20 MARX/KARL LENIN/VI COM/PARTY. PAGE 67 A1380
MARXISM COM GEN/LAWS NAT/G

B62
HUNTINGTON S.P.,CHANGING PATTERNS OF MILITARY POLITICS. EUR+WWI L/A+17C S/ASIA USA+45 WOR+45 CULTURE INT/ORG NAT/G CONSULT PLAN DOMIN EDU/PROP LEGIT DETER WAR ATTIT PERSON PWR...DECISION CONCPT SIMUL GEN/LAWS ANTHOL COLD/WAR 20. PAGE 69 A1419
FORCES RIGID/FLEX

B62
KENNEDY J.F.,TO TURN THE TIDE. SPACE AGRI INT/ORG FORCES TEC/DEV ADMIN NUC/PWR PEACE WEALTH...ANTHOL 20 KENNEDY/JF CIV/RIGHTS. PAGE 78 A1592
DIPLOM CHIEF POLICY NAT/G

B62
LAQUEUR W.,THE FUTURE OF COMMUNIST SOCIETY. CHINA/COM USSR LAW ECO/DEV NAT/G POL/PAR PLAN PROB/SOLV DIPLOM LEAD...POLICY CONCPT IDEA/COMP ANTHOL 20. PAGE 85 A1731
MARXISM COM FUT SOCIETY

B62
LAQUEUR W.,POLYCENTRISM. CHINA/COM COM USSR WOR+45 INT/ORG NAT/G ECO/TAC DOMIN LEAD ATTIT PWR SOVEREIGN...ANTHOL 20. PAGE 85 A1732
MARXISM DIPLOM BAL/PWR POLICY

B62
MARTIN L.W.,NEUTRALISM AND NONALIGNMENT. WOR+45 ATTIT PWR...POLICY ANTHOL 20 UN. PAGE 95 A1952 — DIPLOM NEUTRAL BAL/PWR INT/ORG

B62
MONCRIEFF A.,THE STRATEGY OF SURVIVAL. UK FORCES BAL/PWR CONFER DETER WAR...ANTHOL 20 COLD/WAR. PAGE 102 A2104 — PLAN DECISION DIPLOM ARMS/CONT

B62
ROOSEVELT J.,THE LIBERAL PAPERS. USA+45 WOR+45 ECO/DEV INT/ORG DELIB/GP ACT/RES PROB/SOLV DETER ATTIT...TREND IDEA/COMP ANTHOL. PAGE 123 A2520 — DIPLOM NEW/LIB POLICY FORCES

B62
ROSAMOND R.,CRUSADE FOR PEACE: EISENHOWER'S PRESIDENTIAL LEGACY WITH THE PROGRAM FOR ACTION. USA+45 PARTIC ARMS/CONT MORAL MARXISM...TRADIT CONCPT CHARTS GEN/LAWS ANTHOL 20 PRESIDENT EISNHWR/DD. PAGE 123 A2526 — PEACE DIPLOM EDU/PROP POLICY

B62
SCHUMAN F.L.,THE COLD WAR: RETROSPECT AND PROSPECT. FUT USA+45 USSR WOR+45 BAL/PWR EDU/PROP ARMS/CONT ATTIT...MAJORIT IDEA/COMP ANTHOL BIBLIOG 20 COLD/WAR. PAGE 129 A2651 — MARXISM TEC/DEV DIPLOM NUC/PWR

B62
SHAW C.,LEGAL PROBLEMS IN INTERNATIONAL TRADE AND INVESTMENT. WOR+45 ECO/DEV ECO/UNDEV MARKET DIPLOM TAX INCOME ROLE...ANTHOL BIBLIOG 20 TREATY UN IMF GATT. PAGE 132 A2698 — INT/LAW INT/TRADE FINAN ECO/TAC

B62
UNIVERSITY OF TENNESSEE,GOVERNMENT AND WORLD CRISIS. USA+45 FOR/AID ORD/FREE...ANTHOL 20 UN. PAGE 149 A3048 — ECO/DEV DIPLOM NAT/G INT/ORG

B63
ABSHIRE D.M.,NATIONAL SECURITY: POLITICAL, MILITARY, AND ECONOMIC STRATEGIES IN THE DECADE AHEAD. ASIA COM USA+45 WOR+45 ECO/DEV ECO/UNDEV INT/ORG DELIB/GP FORCES ECO/TAC COERCE ATTIT RIGID/FLEX HEALTH ORD/FREE PWR WEALTH...POLICY STAT CHARTS ANTHOL COLD/WAR VAL/FREE. PAGE 4 A0083 — FUT ACT/RES BAL/PWR

B63
BLACK J.E.,FOREIGN POLICIES IN A WORLD OF CHANGE. FUT INT/ORG ALL/VALS...POLICY MAJORIT MARXIST SOCIALIST TRADIT TIME/SEQ TREND ANTHOL 20. PAGE 15 A0298 — WOR+45 NAT/G DIPLOM

B63
COLUMBIA U SCHOOL OF LAW,PUBLIC INTERNATIONAL DEVELOPMENT FINANCING IN SENEGAL. SENEGAL FINAN DELIB/GP GIVE EFFICIENCY...CHARTS GOV/COMP ANTHOL 20. PAGE 28 A0571 — FOR/AID PLAN RECEIVE ECO/UNDEV

B63
DALLIN A.,DIVERSITY IN INTERNATIONAL COMMUNISM: A DOCUMENTARY RECORD, 1961-1963. CHINA/COM CHIEF PRESS WRITING DEBATE LEAD...POLICY ANTHOL 20. PAGE 33 A0677 — COM DIPLOM POL/PAR CONFER

B63
ERHARD L.,THE ECONOMICS OF SUCCESS. GERMANY/W WOR+45 LABOR CHIEF TAX REGION COST DEMAND ANTHOL. PAGE 42 A0860 — ECO/DEV INT/TRADE PLAN DIPLOM

B63
GOLDSCHMIDT W.,THE UNITED STATES AND AFRICA. USA+45 CULTURE ECO/TAC INT/TRADE GOV/REL...SOC ANTHOL 20 INTERVENT. PAGE 53 A1091 — AFR ECO/UNDEV DIPLOM

B63
GRAEBNER N.A.,THE COLD WAR: IDEOLOGICAL CONFLICT OR POWER STRUGGLE? USSR WOR+45 WOR-45 PROB/SOLV EDU/PROP ARMS/CONT REV NAT/LISM PEACE ORD/FREE ...IDEA/COMP ANTHOL BIBLIOG/A 20 COLD/WAR. PAGE 55 A1123 — DIPLOM BAL/PWR MARXISM

B63
HENDERSON W.,SOUTHEAST ASIA: PROBLEMS OF UNITED STATES POLICY. COM S/ASIA CULTURE STRATA ECO/UNDEV INT/ORG DELIB/GP ACT/RES ECO/TAC DOMIN EDU/PROP LEGIT COERCE ATTIT ALL/VALS...STAT TIME/SEQ ANTHOL VAL/FREE 20. PAGE 64 A1313 — ASIA USA+45 DIPLOM

B63
PADELFORD N.J.,AFRICA AND WORLD ORDER. AFR COLONIAL SOVEREIGN...ANTHOL BIBLIOG 20 UN UNIFICA COMMONWLTH. PAGE 113 A2312 — DIPLOM NAT/G ORD/FREE

B63
ROSS H.,THE COLD WAR: CONTAINMENT AND ITS CRITICSS. WOR+45 POL/PAR BAL/PWR ECO/TAC PEACE ORD/FREE ...POLICY IDEA/COMP ANTHOL T 20 COLD/WAR DULLES/JF TRUMAN/HS EISNHWR/DD. PAGE 124 A2541 — MARXISM ARMS/CONT DIPLOM

B63
SWEARER H.R.,CONTEMPORARY COMMUNISM: THEORY AND PRACTICE. COM USSR SOCIETY ECO/DEV POL/PAR FORCES PLAN ADMIN LEAD NAT/LISM...POLICY ANTHOL 20 LENIN/VI COM/PARTY. PAGE 140 A2869 — MARXISM CONCPT DIPLOM NAT/G

B63
US SENATE,DOCUMENTS ON INTERNATIONAL AS"ECTS OF EXPLORATION AND USE OF OUTER SPACE, 1954-62: STAFF REPORT FOR COMM AERON SPACE SCI. USA+45 USSR LEGIS LEAD CIVMIL/REL PEACE...POLICY INT/LAW ANTHOL 20 CONGRESS NASA KHRUSH/N. PAGE 155 A3165 — SPACE UTIL GOV/REL DIPLOM

B63
WEINBERG A.,INSTEAD OF VIOLENCE: WRITINGS BY THE GREAT ADVOCATES OF PEACE AND NONVIOLENCE THROUGHOUT HISTORY. WOR+45 WOR-45 SOCIETY SECT PROB/SOLV DIPLOM GP/REL PERS/REL PEACE...ANTHOL PACIFIST. PAGE 162 A3304 — PACIFISM WAR IDEA/COMP

B63
WELLESLEY COLLEGE,SYMPOSIUM ON LATIN AMERICA. FUT L/A+17C USA+45 INT/ORG ECO/TAC PARL/PROC REGION ANTHOL. PAGE 163 A3316 — ECO/UNDEV CULTURE ORD/FREE DIPLOM

B63
WHITNEY T.P.,KHRUSHCHEV SPEAKS. USSR AGRI LEAD ...BIOG ANTHOL 20 KHRUSH/N STALIN/J ESPIONAGE. PAGE 164 A3339 — DIPLOM MARXISM CHIEF

L63
SINGER J.D.,"WEAPONS MANAGEMENT IN WORLD POLITICS: PROCEEDINGS OF THE INTERNATIONAL ARMS CONTROL SYMPOSIUM, DECEMBER, 1962." FUT WOR+45 SOCIETY ECO/DEV INDUS INT/ORG DELIB/GP FORCES ACT/RES ECO/TAC EDU/PROP ARMS/CONT SUPEGO HEALTH ORD/FREE PWR SKILL...POLICY CHARTS SIMUL ANTHOL VAL/FREE 20. PAGE 133 A2729 — CONSULT ATTIT DIPLOM NUC/PWR

L63
WILCOX F.O.,"THE ATLANTIC COMMUNITY: PROGRESS AND PROSPECTS." EUR+WWI FUT USA+45 WOR+45 SOCIETY CREATE ECO/TAC EDU/PROP LEGIT REGION ATTIT ALL/VALS ...POLICY ANTHOL VAL/FREE 20. PAGE 164 A3346 — INT/ORG ACT/RES

B64
AFRO ASIAN SOLIDARITY AGAINST IMPERIALISM. AFR ISLAM S/ASIA ECO/UNDEV NAT/G POL/PAR TOP/EX PRESS ...INT ANTHOL 20 CHOU/ENLAI. PAGE 3 A0066 — MARXISM DIPLOM EDU/PROP CHIEF

B64
DUROSELLE J.B.,LA COMMUNAUTE INTERNATIONALE FACE AUX JEUNES ETATS. CHINA/COM COM S/ASIA USSR INT/ORG ROLE...ANTHOL 20 UN SEATO THIRD/WRLD. PAGE 40 A0808 — DIPLOM COLONIAL ECO/UNDEV SOVEREIGN

B64
GRIFFITH W.E.,COMMUNISM IN EUROPE (2 VOLS.). CZECHOSLVK USSR WOR+45 WOR-45 YUGOSLAVIA INGP/REL MARXISM SOCISM...ANTHOL 20 EUROPE/E. PAGE 57 A1162 — COM POL/PAR DIPLOM GOV/COMP

B64
HAMBRIDGE G.,DYNAMICS OF DEVELOPMENT. AGRI FINAN INDUS LABOR INT/TRADE EDU/PROP ADMIN LEAD OWN HEALTH...ANTHOL BIBLIOG 20. PAGE 61 A1245 — ECO/UNDEV ECO/TAC OP/RES ACT/RES

B64
IRISH M.D.,WORLD PRESSURES ON AMERICAN FOREIGN POLICY. ASIA COM L/A+17C SOUTH/AFR UK WOR+45 ECO/DEV ECO/UNDEV COLONIAL SANCTION COERCE REV TOTALISM...ANTHOL 20 COLD/WAR EUROPE/W INTERVENT. PAGE 72 A1467 — DIPLOM POLICY

B64
JOHNSON E.A.J.,THE DIMENSIONS OF DIPLOMACY. INT/ORG FORCES TEC/DEV WAR PEACE PWR...SOC ANTHOL 20. PAGE 74 A1522 — DIPLOM POLICY METH

B64
KEEP J.,CONTEMPORARY HISTORY IN THE SOVIET MIRROR. COM USSR POL/PAR CREATE DIPLOM AGREE WAR ATTIT ...MYTH TREND ANTHOL 20 COLD/WAR STALIN/J MARX/KARL LENIN/VI. PAGE 77 A1576 — HIST/WRIT METH MARXISM IDEA/COMP

B64
KENNEDY J.F.,THE BURDEN AND THE GLORY. FUT USA+45 TEC/DEV ECO/TAC EDU/PROP ARMS/CONT MURDER RACE/REL PEACE...ANTHOL 20 KENNEDY/JF COLD/WAR NATO PRESIDENT. PAGE 78 A1593 — ADMIN POLICY GOV/REL DIPLOM

B64
KRAUSE L.B.,THE COMMON MARKET: PROGRESS AND CONTROVERSY. EUR+WWI UK ECO/DEV REGION...ANTHOL NATO EEC. PAGE 82 A1678 — DIPLOM MARKET INT/TRADE INT/ORG

B64
NICE R.W.,TREASURY OF LAW. WOR+45 WOR-45 SECT ADJUD MORAL ORD/FREE...INT/LAW JURID PHIL/SCI ANTHOL. PAGE 108 A2227 — LAW WRITING PERS/REL DIPLOM

B64
PLISCHKE E.,SYSTEMS OF INTEGRATING THE INTERNATIONAL COMMUNITY. WOR+45 NAT/G VOL/ASSN ECO/TAC LEGIT PWR WEALTH...TIME/SEQ ANTHOL UN TOT/POP 20. PAGE 116 A2391 — INT/ORG EX/STRUC REGION

B64
QUIGG P.W.,AFRICA: A FOREIGN AFFAIRS READER. AFR FRANCE PORTUGAL UK DIPLOM LEAD PARL/PROC MARXISM ...MAJORIT METH/CNCPT GOV/COMP IDEA/COMP ANTHOL 19/20. PAGE 118 A2426 — COLONIAL SOVEREIGN NAT/LISM RACE/REL

B64
RANIS G.,THE UNITED STATES AND THE DEVELOPING ECONOMIES. COM USA+45 AGRI FINAN TEC/DEV CAP/ISM ECO/TAC INT/TRADE...POLICY METH/COMP ANTHOL 20 AID. PAGE 119 A2441 — ECO/UNDEV DIPLOM FOR/AID

B64
SCHWARTZ M.D.,CONFERENCE ON SPACE SCIENCE AND SPACE LAW. FUT COM/IND NAT/G FORCES ACT/RES PLAN BUDGET DIPLOM NUC/PWR WEAPON...POLICY ANTHOL 20. PAGE 130 A2658
SPACE LAW PEACE TEC/DEV

B64
SEGAL R.,SANCTIONS AGAINST SOUTH AFRICA. AFR SOUTH/AFR NAT/G INT/TRADE RACE/REL PEACE PWR ...INT/LAW ANTHOL 20 UN. PAGE 131 A2681
SANCTION DISCRIM ECO/TAC POLICY

B64
TAUBENFELD H.J.,SPACE AND SOCIETY. USA+45 LAW FORCES CREATE TEC/DEV ADJUD CONTROL COST PEACE ...PREDICT ANTHOL 20. PAGE 142 A2895
SPACE SOCIETY ADJUST DIPLOM

B64
TREADGOLD D.W.,THE DEVELOPMENT OF THE USSR. COM USSR ECO/DEV CREATE BAL/PWR DEBATE COLONIAL TOTALISM...HUM ANTHOL BIBLIOG 19/20. PAGE 145 A2960
MARXISM CONSERVE DIPLOM DOMIN

B64
US AIR FORCE ACADEMY ASSEMBLY,OUTER SPACE: FINAL REPORT APRIL 1-4, 1964. FUT USA+45 WOR+45 LAW DELIB/GP CONFER ARMS/CONT WAR PEACE ATTIT MORAL ...ANTHOL 20 NASA. PAGE 150 A3055
SPACE CIVMIL/REL NUC/PWR DIPLOM

B64
US SENATE COMM GOVT OPERATIONS,THE SECRETARY OF STATE AND THE AMBASSADOR. USA+45 CHIEF CONSULT EX/STRUC FORCES PLAN ADMIN EXEC INGP/REL ROLE ...ANTHOL 20 PRESIDENT DEPT/STATE. PAGE 156 A3175
DIPLOM DELIB/GP NAT/G

B65
WHITE HOUSE CONFERENCE ON INTERNATIONAL COOPERATION(VOL.II). SPACE WOR+45 EXTR/IND INT/ORG LABOR WORKER NUC/PWR PEACE AGE/Y...CENSUS ANTHOL 20 RESOURCE/N URBAN/RNWL PUB/TRANS. PAGE 3 A0071
R+D CONFER TEC/DEV DIPLOM

B65
COOMBS P.H.,EDUCATION AND FOREIGN AID. AFR USA+45 DIPLOM EFFICIENCY KNOWL ORD/FREE...ANTHOL 20 AID. PAGE 30 A0608
EDU/PROP FOR/AID SCHOOL ECO/UNDEV

B65
CORDIER A.W.,THE QUEST FOR PEACE. WOR+45 NAT/G PLAN BAL/PWR ECO/TAC ARMS/CONT NUC/PWR PWR...ANTHOL UN COLD/WAR. PAGE 30 A0617
PEACE DIPLOM POLICY INT/ORG

B65
EMERSON R.,THE POLITICAL AWAKENING OF AFRICA. ECO/UNDEV INT/ORG COLONIAL RACE/REL ORD/FREE MARXISM...TREND ANTHOL 20. PAGE 42 A0849
AFR NAT/LISM DIPLOM POL/PAR

B65
FORM W.H.,INDUSTRIAL RELATIONS AND SOCIAL CHANGE IN LATIN AMERICA. L/A+17C AGRI LABOR NAT/G PLAN PROB/SOLV DIPLOM...MGT SOC ANTHOL BIBLIOG/A METH 20. PAGE 47 A0966
INDUS GP/REL NAT/COMP ECO/UNDEV

B65
FRASER S.,GOVERNMENTAL POLICY AND INTERNATIONAL EDUCATION. CHINA/COM COM USA+45 WOR+45 CONTROL MARXISM...ANTHOL BIBLIOG/A 20 UN. PAGE 48 A0989
EDU/PROP DIPLOM POLICY NAT/G

B65
JADOS S.S.,DOCUMENTS ON RUSSIAN-AMERICAN RELATIONS: WASHINGTON TO EISENHOWER. USA+45 USA-45 USSR INT/ORG LEGIS INT/TRADE WAR PEACE...ANTHOL BIBLIOG 18/20 PRESIDENT. PAGE 73 A1488
DIPLOM CHIEF CONTROL

B65
LARUS J.,FROM COLLECTIVE SECURITY TO PREVENTIVE DIPLOMACY. FUT FORCES PROB/SOLV DEBATE AGREE COERCE WAR PWR...ANTHOL 20 LEAGUE/NAT UN. PAGE 85 A1736
INT/ORG PEACE DIPLOM ORD/FREE

B65
LOEWENHEIM F.L.,PEACE OR APPEASEMENT? HITLER, CHAMBERLAIN AND THE MUNICH CRISIS. MUNIC DELIB/GP WAR TOTALISM ATTIT SOVEREIGN...TIME/SEQ ANTHOL BIBLIOG 20 HITLER/A CHAMBRLN/N. PAGE 90 A1851
DIPLOM LEAD PEACE

B65
PENNICK JL J.R.,THE POLITICS OF AMERICAN SCIENCE, 1939 TO THE PRESENT. USA+45 USA-45 INTELL TEC/DEV DIPLOM NEW/LIB...ANTHOL 20 COLD/WAR. PAGE 114 A2349
POLICY ADMIN PHIL/SCI NAT/G

B65
RUBINSTEIN A.Z.,THE CHALLENGE OF POLITICS: IDEAS AND ISSUES (2ND ED.). UNIV ELITES SOCIETY EX/STRUC BAL/PWR PARL/PROC AUTHORIT...DECISION ANTHOL 20. PAGE 125 A2565
NAT/G DIPLOM GP/REL ORD/FREE

B65
TREFOUSSE H.L.,THE COLD WAR: A BOOK OF DOCUMENTS. ASIA L/A+17C USSR WOR+45 WOR-45 ECO/TAC FOR/AID ARMS/CONT NUC/PWR PEACE ORD/FREE...ANTHOL 20 COLD/WAR KENNEDY/JF EISNHWR/DD. PAGE 145 A2961
BAL/PWR DIPLOM MARXISM

B65
VAN DEN BERGHE P.L.,AFRICA: SOCIAL PROBLEMS OF CHANGE AND CONFLICT. ELITES STRATA ECO/UNDEV KIN MUNIC DIPLOM GP/REL RACE/REL NAT/LISM...ANTHOL BIBLIOG 20. PAGE 158 A3210
SOC CULTURE AFR STRUCT

C65
SCHWEBEL M.,"BEHAVIORAL SCIENCE AND HUMAN SURVIVAL." FORCES ARMS/CONT COERCE NUC/PWR WAR GP/REL NAT/LISM PERCEPT...POLICY PSY ANTHOL BIBLIOG/A 20 COLD/WAR. PAGE 130 A2662
PEACE ACT/RES DIPLOM HEAL

C65
US AIR FORCE ACADEMY,"AMERICAN DEFENSE POLICY." COM INT/ORG TEC/DEV FOR/AID ARMS/CONT DETER NUC/PWR ...POLICY DECISION CONCPT ANTHOL BIBLIOG/A 20 COLD/WAR NATO. PAGE 149 A3054
PLAN FORCES WAR COERCE

B66
AMERICAN ASSEMBLY COLUMBIA U,A WORLD OF NUCLEAR POWERS? FUT WOR+45 ECO/DEV BAL/PWR ECO/TAC CONTROL RISK EFFICIENCY ATTIT PWR...METH/COMP ANTHOL 20. PAGE 7 A0137
NUC/PWR DIPLOM TEC/DEV ARMS/CONT

B66
AMERICAN JOURNAL COMP LAW,THE AMERICAN JOURNAL OF COMPARATIVE LAW READER. EUR+WWI USA+45 USA-45 LAW CONSTN LOC/G MUNIC NAT/G DIPLOM...ANTHOL 20 SUPREME/CT EURCT/JUST. PAGE 7 A0151
IDEA/COMP JURID INT/LAW CT/SYS

B66
BROWN L.C.,STATE AND SOCIETY IN INDEPENDENT NORTH AFRICA. ALGERIA LIBYA MOROCCO AGRI INDUS INT/ORG POL/PAR SECT PLAN DIPLOM COLONIAL...LING NAT/COMP ANTHOL BIBLIOG 20 TUNIS MUSLIM. PAGE 20 A0406
NAT/G SOCIETY CULTURE ECO/UNDEV

B66
BUCHAN A.,A WORLD OF NUCLEAR POWERS? PEACE...ANTHOL 20. PAGE 21 A0423
NUC/PWR BAL/PWR PROB/SOLV DIPLOM

B66
DRACHOVITCH M.M.,THE COMINTERN HISTORICAL HIGHLIGHTS. USSR INT/ORG EX/STRUC LEGIT LEAD GUERRILLA...ANTHOL 20 COMINTERN LENIN/VI. PAGE 38 A0784
DIPLOM REV MARXISM PERSON

B66
ERICKSON J.,THE MILITARY-TECHNICAL REVOLUTION. USA+45 WOR+45 INT/ORG PLAN ATTIT...DECISION ANTHOL 20. PAGE 42 A0861
DIPLOM DETER POLICY NUC/PWR

B66
EUDIN X.J.,SOVIET FOREIGN POLICY 1928-34: DOCUMENTS AND MATERIALS (VOL. I). ASIA USSR WOR-45 INT/ORG POL/PAR WORKER WAR PEACE...ANTHOL 20 TREATY LEAGUE/NAT INTERVENT. PAGE 43 A0873
DIPLOM POLICY GOV/REL MARXISM

B66
FINKLE J.L.,POLITICAL DEVELOPMENT AND SOCIAL CHANGE. WOR+45 CULTURE NAT/G OP/RES PROB/SOLV DIPLOM ECO/TAC INGP/REL...METH/COMP ANTHOL 20. PAGE 46 A0934
ECO/UNDEV SOCIETY CREATE

B66
FISHER S.N.,NEW HORIZONS FOR THE UNITED STATES IN WORLD AFFAIRS. USA+45 FOR/AID...ANTHOL 20 UN. PAGE 46 A0941
DIPLOM PLAN INT/ORG

B66
FRANK E.,LAWMAKERS IN A CHANGING WORLD. FRANCE UK USSR WOR+45 PARTIC EFFICIENCY ROLE ALL/IDEOS ...CHARTS ANTHOL PARLIAMENT 20 UN COLD/WAR. PAGE 48 A0979
GOV/COMP LEGIS NAT/G DIPLOM

B66
FREIDEL F.,AMERICAN ISSUES IN THE TWENTIETH CENTURY. SOCIETY FINAN ECO/TAC FOR/AID CONTROL NUC/PWR WAR RACE/REL PEACE ATTIT...ANTHOL T 20 WILSON/W ROOSEVLT/F KENNEDY/JF TRUMAN/HS. PAGE 49 A0995
DIPLOM POLICY NAT/G ORD/FREE

B66
FRIEDRICH C.J.,REVOLUTION: NOMOS VIII. NAT/G SOCISM ...OBS TREND IDEA/COMP ANTHOL 18/20. PAGE 49 A1007
REV MARXISM CONCPT DIPLOM

B66
HAMILTON W.B.,A DECADE OF THE COMMONWEALTH, 1955-1964. UK LAW ELITES FINAN FOR/AID CONFER COLONIAL PWR...GEOG CHARTS ANTHOL 20 CMN/WLTH UN. PAGE 61 A1247
INT/ORG INGP/REL DIPLOM NAT/G

B66
HANSON J.W.,EDUCATION AND THE DEVELOPMENT OF NATIONS. DIPLOM TASK ADJUST EFFICIENCY...POLICY ANTHOL 20. PAGE 61 A1256
ECO/UNDEV EDU/PROP NAT/G PLAN

B66
INTL CONF ON WORLD POLITICS-5,EASTERN EUROPE IN TRANSITION. EUR+WWI USSR ECO/TAC NAT/LISM ATTIT SOVEREIGN...CHARTS ANTHOL 20 TREATY WARSAW/P. PAGE 71 A1463
COM NAT/COMP MARXISM DIPLOM

B66
KINDLEBERGER C.P.,EUROPE AND THE DOLLAR. EUR+WWI FRANCE GERMANY/W USA+45 CONSTN INT/ORG DIPLOM INT/TRADE...ANTHOL 20 GOLD/STAND. PAGE 79 A1623
BAL/PAY BUDGET FINAN ECO/DEV

B66
LONDON K.,EASTERN EUROPE IN TRANSITION. CHINA/COM USSR DOMIN COLONIAL CENTRAL RIGID/FLEX PWR...SOC ANTHOL 20. PAGE 91 A1855
SOVEREIGN COM NAT/LISM DIPLOM

B66
MAY E.R.,ANXIETY AND AFFLUENCE: 1945-1965. USA+45 DIPLOM FOR/AID ARMS/CONT RACE/REL CONSEN...ANTHOL 20 COLD/WAR KENNEDY/JF EISNHWR/DD TRUMAN/HS BERLIN/BLO. PAGE 97 A1982
ANOMIE ECO/DEV NUC/PWR WEALTH

B66
MAYER P.,THE PACIFIST CONSCIENCE. SECT CREATE ARMS/CONT WAR RACE/REL ATTIT LOVE...ANTHOL PACIFIST WORSHIP FREUD/S GANDHI/M LAO/TZU KING/MAR/L CONSCN/OBJ. PAGE 97 A1984
DIPLOM PACIFISM SUPEGO

B66
MCKAY V.,AFRICAN DIPLOMACY STUDIES IN THE DETERMINANTS OF FOREIGN POLICY. AFR SOUTH/AFR CULTURE NEUTRAL REGION SOVEREIGN...INT/LAW GOV/COMP ANTHOL 20. PAGE 98 A2013
ECO/UNDEV RACE/REL CIVMIL/REL DIPLOM

B66
MONTGOMERY J.D.,APPROACHES TO DEVELOPMENT: POLITICS, ADMINISTRATION AND CHANGE. USA+45 AGRI FOR/AID ORD/FREE...CONCPT IDEA/COMP METH/COMP ANTHOL. PAGE 103 A2116
ECO/UNDEV ADMIN POLICY ECO/TAC

B66
NATIONAL COUN APPLIED ECO RES,DEVELOPMENT WITHOUT AID. INDIA FINAN TEC/DEV EFFICIENCY...ANTHOL 20. PAGE 107 A2203
FOR/AID PLAN SOVEREIGN ECO/UNDEV

B66
ROBERTSON D.J.,THE BRITISH BALANCE OF PAYMENTS. UK WOR+45 INDUS BUDGET TAX ADJUST...CHARTS ANTHOL 20. PAGE 122 A2500
FINAN BAL/PAY ECO/DEV INT/TRADE

B66
THOMPSON J.H.,MODERNIZATION OF THE ARAB WORLD. FUT ISRAEL STRUCT ECO/UNDEV DIPLOM INGP/REL ATTIT ...CENSUS ANTHOL 20 ARABS. PAGE 143 A2926
ADJUST ISLAM PROB/SOLV NAT/COMP

B67
BELL W.,THE DEMOCRATIC REVOLUTION IN THE WEST INDIES. WEST/IND WOR+45 DIPLOM RACE/REL NAT/LISM ...INT QU ANTHOL 20. PAGE 13 A0257
REGION ATTIT ORD/FREE ECO/UNDEV

B67
BLOM-COOPER L.,THE LITERATURE OF THE LAW AND THE LANGUAGE OF THE LAW (2 VOLS.). CANADA ISRAEL UK WOR+45 WOR-45 JUDGE CT/SYS ATTIT...CRIMLGY JURID ANTHOL CMN/WLTH. PAGE 15 A0312
BIBLIOG LAW INT/LAW ADJUD

B67
FINE S.,RECENT AMERICA* CONFLICTING INTERPRETATIONS OF THE GREAT ISSUES (2ND ED.). USA+45 USA-45 POL/PAR SECT CONFER NUC/PWR WAR ATTIT...POLICY TREND ANTHOL PRESIDENT 20. PAGE 46 A0931
IDEA/COMP DIPLOM NAT/G

B67
KNOLES G.H.,THE RESPONSIBILITIES OF POWER, 1900-1929. USA-45 SOCIETY SECT JUDGE COLONIAL REPRESENT WEALTH POPULISM...IDEA/COMP ANTHOL PRESIDENT 20 LEAGUE/NAT. PAGE 81 A1653
PWR DIPLOM NAT/LISM WAR

B67
MACRIDIS R.C.,FOREIGN POLICY IN WORLD POLITICS (3RD ED.). EX/STRUC BAL/PWR COLONIAL NAT/LISM SKILL SOVEREIGN WEALTH...CONCPT TIME/SEQ ANTHOL 20 COLD/WAR. PAGE 93 A1902
DIPLOM POLICY NAT/G IDEA/COMP

B67
MCNELLY T.,SOURCES IN MODERN EAST ASIAN HISTORY AND POLITICS. KOREA VIETNAM CULTURE DIPLOM COLONIAL REV WAR PWR ALL/IDEOS MARXISM...ANTHOL 20 CHINJAP. PAGE 99 A2023
NAT/COMP ASIA S/ASIA SOCIETY

B67
NYERERE J.K.,FREEDOM AND UNITY/UHURU NA UMOJA: A SELECTION FROM WRITINGS AND SPEECHES, 1952-65. TANZANIA ELITES ECO/UNDEV INT/ORG NAT/G CREATE DIPLOM COLONIAL REGION RACE/REL...ANTHOL 20. PAGE 110 A2265
SOVEREIGN AFR TREND ORD/FREE

B67
PIKE F.B.,FREEDOM AND REFORM IN LATIN AMERICA. BRAZIL URUGUAY CONSTN CULTURE SECT DIPLOM EDU/PROP PARTIC DRIVE ALL/VALS CATHISM...GEOG ANTHOL BIBLIOG REFORMERS BOLIV. PAGE 116 A2379
L/A+17C ORD/FREE ECO/UNDEV REV

B67
ROACH J.R.,THE UNITED STATES AND THE ATLANTIC COMMUNITY; ISSUES AND PROSPECTS. WOR+45 TEC/DEV ECO/TAC COLONIAL REGION PEACE ROLE...ANTHOL NATO COLD/WAR EEC. PAGE 121 A2491
INT/ORG POLICY ADJUST DIPLOM

B67
SHAFFER H.G.,THE COMMUNIST WORLD: MARXIST AND NON-MARXIST VIEWS. WOR+45 SOCIETY DIPLOM ECO/TAC CONTROL SOCISM...MARXIST ANTHOL BIBLIOG/A 20. PAGE 131 A2691
MARXISM NAT/COMP IDEA/COMP COM

B67
TROTSKY L.,PROBLEMS OF THE CHINESE REVOLUTION (3RD ED. TRANS. BY MAX SCHACTMAN). ASIA USSR DIPLOM MARXISM SOCISM...IDEA/COMP ANTHOL DICTIONARY 20 STALIN/J. PAGE 145 A2969
MARXIST REV

B67
WATERS M.,THE UNITED NATIONS* INTERNATIONAL ORGANIZATION AND ADMINISTRATION. WOR+45 EX/STRUC FORCES DIPLOM LEAD REGION ARMS/CONT REPRESENT INGP/REL ROLE...METH/COMP ANTHOL 20 UN LEAGUE/NAT. PAGE 162 A3291
CONSTN INT/ORG ADMIN ADJUD

B67
WILLIS F.R.,DE GAULLE: ANACHRONISM, REALIST, OR PROPHET? FRANCE POL/PAR FORCES DIPLOM WAR PEACE ROLE ORD/FREE...POLICY IDEA/COMP ANTHOL 20 DEGAULLE/C. PAGE 165 A3356
BIOG PERSON CHIEF LEAD

L67
GRAUBARD S.R.,"TOWARD THE YEAR 2000: WORK IN PROGRESS." FUT ACADEM SECT DELIB/GP DIPLOM EDU/PROP AGE/Y PERSON ROLE...PSY ANTHOL. PAGE 55 A1131
PREDICT PROB/SOLV SOCIETY CULTURE

ANTHROPOLOGY, CULTURAL....SEE SOC

ANTHROPOLOGY, PSYCHOLOGICAL....SEE PSY

ANTI/SEMIT....ANTI-SEMITISM; SEE ALSO JEWS, GP/REL

B42
BORNSTEIN J.,ACTION AGAINST THE ENEMY'S MIND. EUR+WWI GERMANY USA-45 DIPLOM DOMIN PRESS LEAD GP/REL DISCRIM PERCEPT FASCISM MARXISM 20 JEWS NAZI ANTI/SEMIT. PAGE 17 A0343
EDU/PROP PSY WAR CONTROL

ANTIBALLISTIC MISSILE DEFENSE SYSTEMS....SEE ABM/DEFSYS

ANTI-SEMITISM....SEE JEWS, GP/REL, ANTI/SEMIT

ANTI-TRUST ACTIONS....SEE MONOPOLY, INDUS, CONTROL

ANTWERP-INST UNIVERSITAIRE A0166

ANXIETY....SEE ANOMIE

APACHE....APACHE INDIANS

APARTHEID....APARTHEID

APEL H. A0168

APPADORAI A. A0169

APPALACHIA

APPELLATE COURT SYSTEM....SEE CT/APPEALS, CT/SYS

APPLETON A.I. A1806

APPORT....DELINEATION OF LEGISLATIVE DISTRICTS

B65
BROOKINGS INSTITUTION,BROOKINGS PAPERS ON PUBLIC POLICY. USA+45 ECO/UNDEV LEGIS CAP/ISM ECO/TAC TAX EDU/PROP CONTROL APPORT 20. PAGE 19 A0395
DIPLOM FOR/AID POLICY FINAN

APRA....ALIANZA POPULAR REVOLUCIONARIA AMERICANA, A PERUVIAN POLITICAL PARTY

APSA....AMERICAN POLITICAL SCIENCE ASSOCIATION

APT/TEST....APTITUDE TESTS

APTER D.E. A0170,A0171

APTHEKER H. A0167,A0172

APTITUDE TESTS....SEE APT/TEST

AQUINAS/T....SAINT THOMAS AQUINAS

B19
VANDERPOL A.,LA DOCTRINE SCOLASTIQUE DU DROIT DE GUERRE. CHRIST-17C FORCES DIPLOM LEGIT SUPEGO MORAL ...BIOG AQUINAS/T SUAREZ/F CHRISTIAN. PAGE 158 A3220
WAR SECT INT/LAW

ARA....AREA REDEVELOPMENT ACT

ARABIA/SOU....SOUTH ARABIA

ARABS....ARAB WORLD, INCLUDING ITS CULTURE

B57
WARBURG J.P.,AGENDA FOR ACTION. ISLAM ISRAEL USA+45 FOR/AID INT/TRADE WAR NAT/LISM 20 MID/EAST EUROPE ARABS. PAGE 161 A3275
DIPLOM POLICY INT/ORG BAL/PWR

B60
HAMADY S.,TEMPERAMENT AND CHARACTER OF THE ARABS. FAM NAT/G SECT DIPLOM NAT/LISM...POLICY 20 ARABS. PAGE 61 A1244
NAT/COMP PERSON CULTURE ISLAM

PATAI R.,CULTURES IN CONFLICT; AN INQUIRY INTO THE SOCIO-CULTURAL PROBLEMS OF ISRAEL AND HER NEIGHBORS (2ND REV. ED.). ISLAM ISRAEL SOCIETY STRUCT DIPLOM GP/REL ALL/VALS...SOC 20 JEWS ARABS. PAGE 114 A2339 — B61 — NAT/COMP CULTURE GP/COMP ATTIT

SANDERSON G.N.,ENGLAND, EUROPE, AND THE UPPER NILE 1882-1899. ISLAM MOD/EUR UAR UK CHIEF...POLICY CHARTS BIBLIOG/A 19 ARABS NEGRO. PAGE 127 A2600 — B65 — AFR DIPLOM COLONIAL

THOMPSON J.H.,MODERNIZATION OF THE ARAB WORLD. FUT ISRAEL STRUCT ECO/UNDEV DIPLOM INGP/REL ATTIT ...CENSUS ANTHOL 20 ARABS. PAGE 143 A2926 — B66 — ADJUST ISLAM PROB/SOLV NAT/COMP

ZEINE Z.N.,THE EMERGENCE OF ARAB NATIONALISM (REV. ED.). TURKEY UK NAT/G SECT TEC/DEV LEAD REV WAR AGE/Y ROLE ORD/FREE...TRADIT CHARTS BIBLIOG 20 ARABS OTTOMAN. PAGE 170 A3451 — B66 — ISLAM NAT/LISM DIPLOM

ARBITRATION....SEE DELIB/GP, CONSULT, AND FUNCTIONAL GROUP CONCERNED (E.G., LABOR)

AREA STUDIES....SEE NAT/COMP

ARGENTINA....SEE ALSO L/A&17C

WHITAKER A.P.,ARGENTINE UPHEAVAL. STRUCT FORCES DIPLOM COERCE PWR 20 ARGEN. PAGE 164 A3332 — B56 — REV POL/PAR STRATA NAT/G

BAGU S.,ARGENTINA EN EL MUNDO. L/A+17C INDUS INT/TRADE WAR ATTIT ROLE...TREND 19/20 ARGEN OAS. PAGE 10 A0202 — B61 — DIPLOM INT/ORG REGION ECO/UNDEV

FORD A.G.,THE GOLD STANDARD 1880-1914: BRITAIN AND ARGENTINA. UK ECO/UNDEV INT/TRADE ADMIN GOV/REL DEMAND EFFICIENCY...STAT CHARTS 19/20 ARGEN GOLD/STAND. PAGE 47 A0960 — B62 — FINAN ECO/TAC BUDGET BAL/PAY

WITHERS W.,THE ECONOMIC CRISIS IN LATIN AMERICA. BRAZIL CHILE STRATA AGRI DIPLOM FOR/AID PWR SOCISM ...POLICY 20 MEXIC/AMER ARGEN. PAGE 166 A3372 — B64 — L/A+17C ECO/UNDEV CAP/ISM ALL/IDEOS

GARNER W.R.,THE CHACO DISPUTE; A STUDY OF PRESTIGE DIPLOMACY. L/A+17C PARAGUAY USA-45 INT/ORG AGREE PEACE...TIME/SEQ 20 BOLIV LEAGUE/NAT ARGEN CHACO/WAR. PAGE 51 A1050 — B66 — WAR DIPLOM CONCPT PWR

ARISTOCRATIC....SEE TRADIT, STRATA, ELITES

ARISTOTLE....ARISTOTLE

ARIZONA....ARIZONA

ARKANSAS....ARKANSAS

ARMED FORCES....SEE FORCES

ARMENGALD A. A0173

ARMS CONTROL....SEE ARMS/CONT, ACD

ARMS CONTROL AND DISARMAMENT AGENCY (U.S.)....SEE ACD

ARMS/CONT....ARMS CONTROL, DISARMAMENT

CONOVER H.F.,WORLD GOVERNMENT: A LIST OF SELECTED REFERENCES (PAMPHLET). WOR+45 PROB/SOLV ARMS/CONT WAR PEACE 20 UN. PAGE 29 A0589 — N — BIBLIOG/A NUC/PWR INT/ORG DIPLOM

LONDON INSTITUTE WORLD AFFAIRS,THE YEAR BOOK OF WORLD AFFAIRS. FINAN BAL/PWR ARMS/CONT WAR ...INT/LAW BIBLIOG 20. PAGE 91 A1856 — N — DIPLOM FOR/AID INT/ORG

AMERICAN JOURNAL OF INTERNATIONAL LAW. WOR+45 WOR-45 CONSTN INT/ORG NAT/G CT/SYS ARMS/CONT WAR ...DECISION JURID NAT/COMP 20. PAGE 1 A0002 — N — BIBLIOG/A INT/LAW DIPLOM ADJUD

JOURNAL OF CONFLICT RESOLUTION. FUT WOR+45 INT/ORG NAT/G FORCES CREATE PROB/SOLV ARMS/CONT NUC/PWR WEAPON SOC. PAGE 1 A0014 — N — BIBLIOG/A DIPLOM WAR

FOREIGN AFFAIRS. SPACE WOR+45 WOR-45 CULTURE ECO/UNDEV FINAN NAT/G TEC/DEV INT/TRADE ARMS/CONT NUC/PWR...POLICY 20 UN EURATOM ECSC EEC. PAGE 2 A0034 — N — BIBLIOG DIPLOM INT/ORG INT/LAW

AIR UNIVERSITY LIBRARY,INDEX TO MILITARY PERIODICALS. FUT SPACE WOR+45 REGION ARMS/CONT NUC/PWR WAR PEACE INT/LAW. PAGE 5 A0105 — N — BIBLIOG/A FORCES NAT/G DIPLOM

ATLANTIC INSTITUTE,ATLANTIC STUDIES. COM EUR+WWI USA+45 CULTURE STRUCT ECO/DEV FORCES LEAD ARMS/CONT ...INT/LAW JURID SOC. PAGE 10 A0193 — N — BIBLIOG/A DIPLOM POLICY GOV/REL

TURNER R.K.,BIBLIOGRAPHY ON WORLD ORGANIZATION. INT/TRADE CT/SYS ARMS/CONT WEALTH...INT/LAW 20. PAGE 146 A2984 — N — BIBLIOG/A INT/ORG PEACE WAR

UNITED NATIONS,OFFICIAL RECORDS OF THE UNITED NATIONS' ATOMIC ENERGY COMMISSION - DISARMAMENT COMMISSION. WOR+45 TEC/DEV DIPLOM WRITING NUC/PWR 20 UN. PAGE 148 A3032 — N — ARMS/CONT INT/ORG DELIB/GP CONFER

US SUPERINTENDENT OF DOCUMENTS,FOREIGN RELATIONS OF THE UNITED STATES; PUBLICATIONS RELATING TO FOREIGN COUNTRIES (PRICE LIST 65). UAR USA+45 VIETNAM ECO/UNDEV VOL/ASSN FOR/AID EDU/PROP ARMS/CONT HEALTH MARXISM...POLICY INT/LAW UN NATO. PAGE 157 A3201 — N — BIBLIOG/A DIPLOM INT/ORG NAT/G

US SUPERINTENDENT OF DOCUMENTS,MONTHLY CATALOG OF UNITED STATES GOVERNMENT PUBLICATIONS. USA+45 USA-45 AGRI LABOR FORCES INT/TRADE TARIFFS TAX EDU/PROP CT/SYS ARMS/CONT RACE/REL 19/20 CONGRESS PRESIDENT. PAGE 157 A3203 — N — BIBLIOG NAT/G VOL/ASSN POLICY

GRIFFIN A.P.C.,LIST OF REFERENCES ON INTERNATIONAL ARBITRATION. FRANCE L/A+17C USA-45 WOR-45 DIPLOM CONFER COLONIAL ARMS/CONT BAL/PAY EQUILIB SOVEREIGN ...DECISION 19/20 MEXIC/AMER. PAGE 56 A1156 — B08 — BIBLIOG/A INT/ORG INT/LAW DELIB/GP

FARIES J.C.,THE RISE OF INTERNATIONALISM. ASIA MOD/EUR NAT/G VOL/ASSN DELIB/GP BAL/PWR EDU/PROP ARMS/CONT RIGID/FLEX TREND. PAGE 44 A0899 — B15 — INT/ORG DIPLOM PEACE

BENTHAM J.,A PLAN FOR AN UNIVERSAL AND PERPETUAL PEACE (1838) (PAMPHLET). NAT/G FORCES BAL/PWR INT/TRADE ADMIN AGREE CT/SYS ARMS/CONT SOVEREIGN WEALTH GEN/LAWS. PAGE 13 A0269 — N19 — INT/ORG INT/LAW PEACE COLONIAL

LANGE O.R.,"DISARMAMENT ECONOMIC GROWTH AND INTERNATIONAL CO-OPERATION" (PAMPHLET). WOR+45 DIST/IND PLAN INT/TRADE GIVE TASK DETER WEALTH SOCISM 18/19 BOLIVAR/S. PAGE 84 A1723 — N19 — ARMS/CONT DIPLOM ECO/DEV ECO/UNDEV

MEZERIK A.G.,ATOM TESTS AND RADIATION HAZARDS (PAMPHLET). WOR+45 INT/ORG DIPLOM DETER 20 UN TREATY. PAGE 100 A2059 — N19 — NUC/PWR ARMS/CONT CONFER HEALTH

MEZERIK A.G.,U-2 AND OPEN SKIES (PAMPHLET). USA+45 USSR INT/ORG CHIEF FORCES PLAN EDU/PROP CONTROL SANCTION ARMS/CONT 20 UN EISNHWR/DD. PAGE 100 A2060 — N19 — DIPLOM RISK DEBATE

PROVISIONS SECTION OAU,ORGANIZATION OF AFRICAN UNITY: BASIC DOCUMENTS AND RESOLUTIONS (PAMPHLET). AFR CULTURE ECO/UNDEV DIPLOM ECO/TAC EDU/PROP COLONIAL ARMS/CONT NUC/PWR RACE/REL DISCRIM NAT/LISM 20 UN OAU. PAGE 118 A2415 — N19 — CONSTN EX/STRUC SOVEREIGN INT/ORG

ZLOTNICK M.,WEAPONS IN SPACE (PAMPHLET). FUT WOR+45 TEC/DEV DIPLOM ARMS/CONT CIVMIL/REL PEACE HABITAT ...CONCPT NEW/IDEA CHARTS. PAGE 170 A3457 — N19 — SPACE WEAPON NUC/PWR WAR

LAPRADELLE,ANNUAIRE DE LA VIE INTERNATIONALE: POLITIQUE, ECONOMIQUE, JURIDIQUE. INT/ORG CONFER ARMS/CONT 20. PAGE 85 A1729 — B28 — BIBLIOG DIPLOM INT/LAW

CONWELL-EVANS T.P.,THE LEAGUE COUNCIL IN ACTION. EUR+WWI TURKEY UK USSR WOR-45 INT/ORG FORCES JUDGE ECO/TAC EDU/PROP LEGIT ROUTINE ARMS/CONT COERCE ATTIT PWR...MAJORIT GEOG JURID CONCPT LEAGUE/NAT TOT/POP VAL/FREE TUNIS 20. PAGE 30 A0605 — B29 — DELIB/GP INT/LAW

BEALES A.C.,THE HISTORY OF PEACE. WOR-45 VOL/ASSN DELIB/GP CREATE PLAN EDU/PROP ATTIT MORAL ...TIME/SEQ VAL/FREE 19/20. PAGE 12 A0239 — B31 — INT/ORG ARMS/CONT PEACE

BLUM L.,PEACE AND DISARMAMENT (TRANS. BY A. WERTH). NAT/G FORCES WORKER DIPLOM AGREE WAR ATTIT AUTHORIT ORD/FREE. PAGE 16 A0322 — B32 — SOCIALIST PEACE INT/ORG ARMS/CONT

EAGLETON C.,INTERNATIONAL GOVERNMENT. BRAZIL FRANCE GERMANY ITALY UK USSR WOR-45 DELIB/GP TOP/EX PLAN ECO/TAC EDU/PROP LEGIT ADJUD REGION ARMS/CONT COERCE ATTIT PWR...GEOG MGT VAL/FREE LEAGUE/NAT 20. — B32 — INT/ORG JURID DIPLOM INT/LAW

PAGE 40 A0816

B34

EINSTEIN A.,THE WORLD AS I SEE IT. WOR-45 INTELL R+D INT/ORG NAT/G SECT VOL/ASSN FORCES CREATE EDU/PROP LEGIT ARMS/CONT WAR,WEAPON NAT/LISM ALL/VALS...POLICY CONCPT 20. PAGE 41 A0828
SOCIETY PHIL/SCI DIPLOM PACIFISM

B35

FOREIGN AFFAIRS BIBLIOGRAPHY: A SELECTED AND ANNOTATED LIST OF BOOKS ON INTERNATIONAL RELATIONS 1919-1962 (4 VOLS.). CONSTN FORCES COLONIAL ARMS/CONT WAR NAT/LISM PEACE ATTIT DRIVE...POLICY INT/LAW 20. PAGE 3 A0050
BIBLIOG/A DIPLOM INT/ORG

B35

SIMONDS F.H.,THE GREAT POWERS IN WORLD POLITICS. FRANCE GERMANY UK WOR-45 INT/ORG NAT/G ARMS/CONT PEACE FASCISM...POLICY GEOG 20 DEPRESSION NAZI. PAGE 133 A2718
DIPLOM WEALTH WAR

B36

HUDSON M.O.,INTERNATIONAL LEGISLATION: 1929-1931. WOR-45 SEA AIR AGRI FINAN LABOR DIPLOM ECO/TAC REPAR CT/SYS ARMS/CONT WAR WEAPON...JURID 20 TREATY LEAGUE/NAT. PAGE 69 A1409
INT/LAW PARL/PROC ADJUD LAW

B38

WARE E.E.,THE STUDY OF INTERNATIONAL RELATIONS IN THE UNITED STATES. USA+45 USA-45 WOR-45 INTELL SERV/IND INT/ORG NAT/G PROF/ORG SECT CONSULT INT/TRADE EDU/PROP ARMS/CONT...CONCPT 20. PAGE 161 A3283
KNOWL DIPLOM

B39

DULLES J.,WAR, PEACE AND CHANGE. FRANCE ITALY UK USA-45 WOR-45 LAW INT/ORG NAT/G SECT VOL/ASSN FORCES TOP/EX DOMIN ARMS/CONT COERCE ATTIT PERSON RIGID/FLEX MORAL PWR...JURID STERTYP TOT/POP LEAGUE/NAT 20. PAGE 39 A0796
EDU/PROP TOTALISM WAR

B39

FULLER G.H.,A SELECTED LIST OF REFERENCES ON THE EXPANSION OF THE US NAVY, 1933-1939 (PAMPHLET). MOD/EUR USA-45 NAT/G PLAN DIPLOM DOMIN RISK ARMS/CONT EQUILIB PWR 20 NAVY. PAGE 50 A1019
BIBLIOG FORCES WEAPON WAR

B42

FEILCHENFELD E.H.,THE INTERNATIONAL ECONOMIC LAW OF BELLIGERENT OCCUPATION. EUR+WWI MOD/EUR USA-45 INT/ORG DIPLOM ADJUD ARMS/CONT LEAGUE/NAT 20. PAGE 44 A0907
ECO/TAC INT/LAW WAR

B42

FULLER G.H.,DEFENSE FINANCING: A SUPPLEMENTARY LIST OF REFERENCES (PAMPHLET). CANADA UK USA-45 ECO/DEV NAT/G DELIB/GP BUDGET ADJUD ARMS/CONT WEAPON COST PEACE PWR 20 AUSTRAL CHINJAP CONGRESS. PAGE 50 A1021
BIBLIOG/A FINAN FORCES DIPLOM

S42

SHOTWELL J.,"AFTER THE WAR." COM EUR+WWI USA+45 USA-45 NAT/G DIPLOM INT/TRADE ARMS/CONT SOVEREIGN ...CONCPT LEAGUE/NAT TOT/POP FAO 20. PAGE 132 A2707
FUT INT/ORG PEACE

B43

MICAUD C.A.,THE FRENCH RIGHT AND NAZI GERMANY 1933-1939: A STUDY OF PUBLIC OPINION. GERMANY UK USSR POL/PAR ARMS/CONT COERCE DETER PEACE RIGID/FLEX PWR MARXISM...FASCIST TREND 20 LEAGUE/NAT TREATY. PAGE 101 A2065
DIPLOM AGREE

B43

US DEPARTMENT OF STATE,NATIONAL SOCIALISM; BASIC PRINCIPLES, THEIR APPLICATION BY THE NAZI PARTY'S FOREIGN ORGANIZATION... GERMANY WOR-45 ECO/DEV LOC/G POL/PAR FORCES DIPLOM DOMIN COLONIAL ARMS/CONT COERCE NAT/LISM PWR 20 NAZI. PAGE 151 A3081
FASCISM SOCISM NAT/G TOTALISM

B44

ADLER M.J.,HOW TO THINK ABOUT WAR AND PEACE. WOR-45 LAW SOCIETY EX/STRUC DIPLOM KNOWL ORD/FREE...POLICY TREND GEN/LAWS 20. PAGE 4 A0092
INT/ORG CREATE ARMS/CONT PEACE

B44

DAVIS H.E.,PIONEERS IN WORLD ORDER. WOR-45 CONSTN ECO/TAC DOMIN EDU/PROP LEGIT ADJUD ADMIN ARMS/CONT CHOOSE KNOWL ORD/FREE...POLICY JURID SOC STAT OBS CENSUS TIME/SEQ ANTHOL LEAGUE/NAT 20. PAGE 34 A0691
INT/ORG ROUTINE

B44

FULLER G.H.,MILITARY GOVERNMENT: A LIST OF REFERENCES (A PAMPHLET). ITALY UK USA-45 WOR-45 LAW FORCES DOMIN ADMIN ARMS/CONT ORD/FREE PWR ...DECISION 20 CHINJAP. PAGE 50 A1023
BIBLIOG DIPLOM CIVMIL/REL SOVEREIGN

B44

MATTHEWS M.A.,INTERNATIONAL POLICE (PAMPHLET). WOR-45 DIPLOM ARMS/CONT WAR 20. PAGE 96 A1977
BIBLIOG INT/ORG FORCES PEACE

B44

RUDIN H.R.,ARMISTICE 1918. FRANCE GERMANY MOD/EUR UK USA-45 NAT/G CHIEF DELIB/GP FORCES BAL/PWR REPAR ARMS/CONT 20 WILSON/W TREATY. PAGE 125 A2566
AGREE WAR PEACE DIPLOM

B46

BRODIE B.,THE OBSOLETE WEAPON: ATOMIC POWER AND WORLD ORDER. COM USA+45 USSR WOR+45 DELIB/GP PLAN ORD/FREE PWR...CONCPT TIME/SEQ TREND UN 20. PAGE 19 A0380
INT/ORG TEC/DEV ARMS/CONT NUC/PWR

L46

MASTERS D.,"ONE WORLD OR NONE." FUT WOR+45 INTELL INT/ORG ACT/RES EDU/PROP DETER ATTIT RIGID/FLEX SUPEGO KNOWL...STAT TREND ORG/CHARTS 20. PAGE 96 A1960
POLICY PHIL/SCI ARMS/CONT NUC/PWR

B47

SOCIAL SCIENCE RESEARCH COUN,PUBLIC REACTION TO THE ATOMIC BOMB AND WORLD AFFAIRS. SOCIETY CONFER ARMS/CONT...STAT QU SAMP CHARTS 20. PAGE 135 A2757
ATTIT NUC/PWR DIPLOM WAR

L47

COMM. STUDY ORGAN. PEACE,"SECURITY THROUGH THE UNITED NATIONS." COM FUT WOR+45 TOP/EX ACT/RES BAL/PWR ARMS/CONT NUC/PWR...CONCPT GEN/LAWS UN TOT/POP COLD/WAR 20. PAGE 28 A0577
INT/ORG ORD/FREE PEACE

B48

COTTRELL L.S. JR.,AMERICAN PUBLIC OPINION ON WORLD AFFAIRS IN THE ATOMIC AGE. USA+45 CULTURE INT/ORG NAT/G DIPLOM EDU/PROP PEACE RIGID/FLEX ORD/FREE ...POLICY SOC CONCPT STAND/INT TOT/POP 20. PAGE 31 A0633
SOCIETY ATTIT ARMS/CONT NUC/PWR

B50

CHASE E.P.,THE UNITED NATIONS IN ACTION. WOR+45 CONSTN DELIB/GP LEGIT ROUTINE COERCE PEACE ORD/FREE PWR...CON/ANAL GEN/LAWS UN 20. PAGE 26 A0524
INT/ORG STRUCT ARMS/CONT

B51

LEONARD L.L.,INTERNATIONAL ORGANIZATION. WOR+45 WOR-45 EX/STRUC FORCES LEGIS ECO/TAC INT/TRADE COLONIAL ARMS/CONT...SOC/WK GOV/COMP BIBLIOG. PAGE 87 A1778
NAT/G DIPLOM INT/ORG DELIB/GP

B51

US LIBRARY OF CONGRESS,PUBLIC AFFAIRS ABSTRACTS. USA+45 INT/ORG INT/TRADE ARMS/CONT...NAT/COMP 20 CONGRESS. PAGE 155 A3151
BIBLIOG/A DIPLOM POLICY

B52

FERRELL R.H.,PEACE IN THEIR TIME. FRANCE UK USA-45 INT/ORG NAT/G FORCES CREATE AGREE ARMS/CONT COERCE WAR TREATY 20 WILSON/W LEAGUE/NAT BRIAND/A. PAGE 45 A0920
PEACE DIPLOM

B52

FIFIELD R.H.,WOODROW WILSON AND THE FAR EAST. ASIA CHIEF BAL/PWR CONFER COLONIAL ARMS/CONT WAR ...TIME/SEQ NAT/COMP BIBLIOG 19/20 WILSON/W LEAGUE/NAT PRESIDENT. PAGE 45 A0926
DIPLOM DELIB/GP INT/ORG

C52

FIFIELD R.H.,"WOODROW WILSON AND THE FAR EAST." ASIA CHIEF DELIB/GP BAL/PWR CONFER COLONIAL ARMS/CONT WAR...TIME/SEQ NAT/COMP 19/20 WILSON/W LEAGUE/NAT. PAGE 45 A0925
BIBLIOG DIPLOM INT/ORG

B53

BRETTON H.L.,STRESEMANN AND THE REVISION OF VERSAILLES: A FIGHT FOR REASON. EUR+WWI GERMANY FORCES BUDGET ARMS/CONT WAR SUPEGO...BIBLIOG 20 TREATY VERSAILLES STRESEMN/G. PAGE 18 A0373
POLICY DIPLOM BIOG

B54

KENWORTHY L.S.,FREE AND INEXPENSIVE MATERIALS ON WORLD AFFAIRS (PAMPHLET). WOR+45 CULTURE ECO/UNDEV INT/TRADE ARMS/CONT NUC/PWR UN. PAGE 78 A1597
BIBLIOG/A NAT/G INT/ORG DIPLOM

B54

REYNOLDS P.A.,BRITISH FOREIGN POLICY IN THE INTER-WAR YEARS. CZECHOSLVK GERMANY POLAND UK USA-45 POL/PAR FORCES ECO/TAC ARMS/CONT WAR ATTIT 20. PAGE 120 A2470
DIPLOM POLICY NAT/G

B54

US DEPARTMENT OF STATE,PUBLICATIONS OF THE DEPARTMENT OF STATE, OCTOBER 1,1929 TO JANUARY 1, 1953. AGRI INT/ORG FORCES FOR/AID EDU/PROP ARMS/CONT NUC/PWR ATTIT 20 DEPT/STATE OAS UN NATO. PAGE 151 A3089
BIBLIOG DIPLOM

B54

US SENATE COMM ON FOREIGN REL,REVIEW OF THE UNITED NATIONS CHARTER: A COLLECTION OF DOCUMENTS. LEGIS DIPLOM ADMIN ARMS/CONT WAR REPRESENT SOVEREIGN ...INT/LAW 20 UN. PAGE 156 A3180
BIBLIOG CONSTN INT/ORG DEBATE

B55

COMM. STUDY ORGAN. PEACE,REPORTS. WOR-45 ECO/DEV ECO/UNDEV VOL/ASSN CONSULT FORCES PLAN TEC/DEV DOMIN EDU/PROP NUC/PWR ATTIT PWR WEALTH...JURID STERTYP FAO ILO 20 UN. PAGE 28 A0579
WOR+45 INT/ORG ARMS/CONT

B55

GOODRICH L.,THE UNITED NATIONS AND THE MAINTENANCE OF INTERNATIONAL PEACE AND SECURITY. WOR+45 CONSTN ACT/RES CREATE PLAN PERCEPT PWR...ORG/CHARTS GEN/LAWS UN 20. PAGE 54 A1102
INT/ORG ORD/FREE ARMS/CONT PEACE

B55

MOCH J.,HUMAN FOLLY: DISARM OR PERISH. USA+45 WOR+45 SOCIETY INT/ORG NAT/G ACT/RES EDU/PROP ATTIT PERSON KNOWL ORD/FREE PWR...MAJORIT TOT/POP COLD/WAR 20. PAGE 102 A2093
FUT DELIB/GP ARMS/CONT NUC/PWR

B55

VINSON J.C.,THE PARCHMENT PEACE: THE UNITED STATES SENATE AND THE WASHINGTON CONFERENCE, 1921-1922. USA-45 INT/ORG DELIB/GP PLAN ARMS/CONT GOV/REL ISOLAT PEACE ATTIT SOVEREIGN...INT/LAW BIBLIOG 20
POLICY DIPLOM NAT/G LEGIS

SENATE PRESIDENT CONGRESS LEAGUE/NAT CHINJAP. PAGE 159 A3242

B56

BLACKETT P.M.S.,ATOMIC WEAPONS AND EAST-WEST RELATIONS. FUT WOR+45 INT/ORG DELIB/GP COERCE ATTIT RIGID/FLEX KNOWL...RELATIV HIST/WRIT TREND GEN/METH COLD/WAR 20. PAGE 15 A0299

FORCES PWR ARMS/CONT NUC/PWR

B56

BUREAU OF PUBLIC AFFAIRS,AMERICAN FOREIGN POLICY: CURRENT DOCUMENTS. COM USA+45 USSR WOR+45 DELIB/GP FOR/AID INT/TRADE ARMS/CONT NUC/PWR ALL/VALS ALL/IDEOS...DECISION 20 NATO. PAGE 21 A0434

BIBLIOG/A DIPLOM POLICY

B57

FURNISS E.S.,AMERICAN MILITARY POLICY: STRATEGIC ASPECTS OF WORLD POLITICAL GEOGRAPHY. COM EUR+WWI ISLAM L/A+17C USA+45 WOR+45 INT/ORG ACT/RES ARMS/CONT COERCE NUC/PWR ATTIT PWR...GEOG NEW/IDEA VAL/FREE COLD/WAR 20. PAGE 50 A1027

FORCES DIPLOM

B57

KISSINGER H.A.,NUCLEAR WEAPONS AND FOREIGN POLICY. FUT USA+45 WOR+45 INT/ORG FORCES ACT/RES TEC/DEV DIPLOM ARMS/CONT COERCE ATTIT KNOWL PWR...DECISION GEOG CHARTS 20. PAGE 80 A1640

PLAN DETER NUC/PWR

B58

APPADORAI A.,THE USE OF FORCE IN INTERNATIONAL RELATIONS. WOR+45 CULTURE ECO/UNDEV CAP/ISM ARMS/CONT REV WAR ATTIT PERSON SOVEREIGN MARXISM ...INT/LAW PACIFIST 20 UN INTERVENT THIRD/WRLD COLD/WAR. PAGE 8 A0169

PEACE FEDERAL INT/ORG

B58

ARON R.,ON WAR: ATOMIC WEAPONS AND GLOBAL DIPLOMACY (TRANS. BY TERENCE KILMARTIN). WOR+45 SOCIETY FORCES BAL/PWR WAR WEAPON PERSON...SOC 20. PAGE 9 A0182

ARMS/CONT NUC/PWR COERCE DIPLOM

B58

GAVIN J.M.,WAR AND PEACE IN THE SPACE AGE. SPACE USA+45 USSR FORCES PLAN TEC/DEV BAL/PWR DIPLOM ARMS/CONT WEAPON CIVMIL/REL...CHARTS GP/COMP 20 NATO COLD/WAR. PAGE 52 A1055

WAR DETER NUC/PWR PEACE

B58

HENKIN L.,ARMS CONTROL AND INSPECTION IN AMERICAN LAW. LAW CONSTN INT/ORG LOC/G MUNIC NAT/G PROVS EDU/PROP LEGIT EXEC NUC/PWR KNOWL ORD/FREE...OBS TOT/POP CONGRESS 20. PAGE 64 A1315

USA+45 JURID ARMS/CONT

B58

JENKS C.W.,THE COMMON LAW OF MANKIND. EUR+WWI MOD/EUR SPACE WOR+45 INT/ORG BAL/PWR ARMS/CONT COERCE SUPEGO MORAL...TREND 20. PAGE 73 A1505

JURID SOVEREIGN

B58

KENNAN G.F.,RUSSIA, THE ATOM AND THE WEST. USA+45 USSR INT/ORG ARMS/CONT MARXISM 20 NATO. PAGE 77 A1587

BAL/PWR NUC/PWR CONTROL DIPLOM

B58

MELMAN S.,INSPECTION FOR DISARMAMENT. USA+45 WOR+45 SOCIETY INT/ORG NAT/G CONSULT ACT/RES PLAN EDU/PROP CONTROL DETER PEACE ATTIT PERSON KNOWL...PSY STAT OBS CHARTS TOT/POP VAL/FREE 20. PAGE 99 A2035

FUT ORD/FREE ARMS/CONT NUC/PWR

B58

NATIONAL PLANNING ASSOCIATION,1970 WITHOUT ARMS CONTROL (PAMPHLET). WOR+45 PROB/SOLV TEC/DEV DIPLOM CONFER DETER NUC/PWR WAR...CHARTS 20 COLD/WAR. PAGE 107 A2204

ARMS/CONT ORD/FREE WEAPON PREDICT

B58

NOEL-BAKER D.,THE ARMS RACE. WOR+45 NAT/G DELIB/GP ACT/RES TEC/DEV EDU/PROP NUC/PWR ATTIT KNOWL PWR ...CONCPT OBS LEAGUE/NAT 20 COLD/WAR. PAGE 109 A2245

FUT INT/ORG ARMS/CONT PEACE

B58

ROCKEFELLER BROTH FUND INC,INTERNATIONAL SECURITY - THE MILITARY ASPECT. USA+45 INT/ORG NAT/G BUDGET ARMS/CONT WAR WEAPON PEACE ORD/FREE 20 NATO. PAGE 123 A2511

NUC/PWR DETER FORCES DIPLOM

B58

SLICK T.,PERMANENT PEACE: A CHECK AND BALANCE PLAN. FUT WOR+45 NAT/G FORCES CREATE PLAN EDU/PROP LEGIT ADJUD COERCE NAT/LISM RIGID/FLEX MORAL...HUM CONCPT METH/CNCPT NEW/IDEA TREND CHARTS TOT/POP 20. PAGE 134 A2742

INT/ORG ORD/FREE PEACE ARMS/CONT

B58

US DEPARTMENT OF STATE,PUBLICATIONS OF THE DEPARTMENT OF STATE, JANUARY 1,1953 TO DECEMBER 31, 1957. AGRI INT/ORG FORCES FOR/AID EDU/PROP ARMS/CONT NUC/PWR ATTIT 20 DEPT/STATE OAS UN NATO. PAGE 151 A3092

BIBLIOG DIPLOM

S58

SINGER J.D.,"THREAT PERCEPTION AND THE ARMAMENT TENSION DILEMMA." WOR+45 WOR-45 ELITES INT/ORG NAT/G DELIB/GP PLAN LEGIT COERCE DETER ATTIT RIGID/FLEX PWR...DECISION PSY 20. PAGE 133 A2724

PERCEPT ARMS/CONT BAL/PWR

S58

THOMPSON K.W.,"NATIONAL SECURITY IN A NUCLEAR AGE." USA+45 WOR+45 SOCIETY INT/ORG NAT/G TOP/EX DIPLOM DOMIN EDU/PROP LEGIT ARMS/CONT COERCE ORD/FREE ...TREND STERTYP TOT/POP VAL/FREE COLD/WAR 20. PAGE 143 A2929

FORCES PWR BAL/PWR

B59

BRODIE B.,STRATEGY IN THE MISSILE AGE. FUT WOR+45 CONSULT PLAN COERCE DETER RIGID/FLEX PWR...CONCPT TIME/SEQ TREND 20. PAGE 19 A0381

ACT/RES FORCES ARMS/CONT NUC/PWR

B59

GOLDWIN R.A.,READINGS IN AMERICAN FOREIGN POLICY. USA+45 USA-45 ARMS/CONT NUC/PWR...INT/LAW 18/20. PAGE 53 A1094

ANTHOL DIPLOM INT/ORG ECO/UNDEV

B59

HERZ J.H.,INTERNATIONAL POLITICS IN THE ATOMIC AGE. FUT USA+45 WOR+45 WOR-45 SOCIETY NAT/G FORCES PLAN COERCE DETER ATTIT DRIVE ORD/FREE PWR...TREND COLD/WAR 20. PAGE 64 A1319

INT/ORG ARMS/CONT NUC/PWR

B59

HUGHES E.M.,AMERICA THE VINCIBLE. USA+45 FOR/AID ARMS/CONT NUC/PWR PERS/REL RATIONAL ATTIT ALL/VALS 20 COLD/WAR. PAGE 69 A1413

ORD/FREE DIPLOM WAR

B59

THOMAS N.,THE PREREQUISITES FOR PEACE. ASIA EUR+WWI FUT ISLAM S/ASIA WOR+45 FORCES PLAN BAL/PWR EDU/PROP LEGIT ATTIT PWR...SOCIALIST CONCPT COLD/WAR 20 UN. PAGE 143 A2924

INT/ORG ORD/FREE ARMS/CONT PEACE

B59

WARD B.,5 IDEAS THAT CHANGE THE WORLD. WOR+45 WOR-45 SOCIETY STRUCT AGRI INDUS INT/ORG NAT/G FORCES ACT/RES ARMS/CONT TOTALISM ATTIT DRIVE GEN/LAWS. PAGE 161 A3278

ECO/UNDEV ALL/VALS NAT/LISM COLONIAL

S59

KISSINGER H.A.,"THE SEARCH FOR STABILITY." COM GERMANY MOD/EUR USA+45 USA-45 USSR INT/ORG ARMS/CONT NUC/PWR ORD/FREE PWR COLD/WAR 20 NATO. PAGE 80 A1641

FUT ATTIT BAL/PWR

S59

LASSWELL H.D.,"UNIVERSALITY IN PERSPECTIVE." FUT UNIV SOCIETY CONSULT TOP/EX PLAN EDU/PROP ADJUD ROUTINE ARMS/CONT COERCE PEACE ATTIT PERSON ALL/VALS. PAGE 85 A1741

INT/ORG JURID TOTALISM

S59

SIMONS H.,"WORLD-WIDE CAPABILITIES FOR PRODUCTION AND CONTROL OF NUCLEAR WEAPONS." FUT WOR+45 INDUS INT/ORG NAT/G ECO/TAC ATTIT PWR SKILL...TREND CHARTS VAL/FREE 20. PAGE 133 A2719

TEC/DEV ARMS/CONT NUC/PWR

B60

ARMS CONTROL. FUT UNIV WOR+45 INTELL R+D INT/ORG NAT/G VOL/ASSN CONSULT CREATE EDU/PROP PEACE...HUM GEN/LAWS TOT/POP 20. PAGE 3 A0060

DELIB/GP ORD/FREE ARMS/CONT NUC/PWR

B60

ALBRECHT-CARRIE R.,FRANCE, EUROPE AND THE TWO WORLD WARS. EUR+WWI FRANCE GERMANY MOD/EUR UK ECO/DEV NAT/G FORCES BAL/PWR DOMIN ARMS/CONT PEACE PWR 20 TREATY EUROPE. PAGE 5 A0109

DIPLOM WAR

B60

APTHEKER H.,DISARMAMENT AND THE AMERICAN ECONOMY: A SYMPOSIUM. FUT USA+45 ECO/DEV DIST/IND FINAN INDUS PROC/MFG LABOR NAT/G POL/PAR CONSULT PLAN CAP/ISM INT/TRADE PEACE ATTIT MORAL WEALTH...TREND GEN/LAWS TOT/POP 20. PAGE 9 A0172

MARXIST ARMS/CONT

B60

BARNET R.,WHO WANTS DISARMAMENT. COM EUR+WWI USA+45 USSR INT/ORG NAT/G BAL/PWR DIPLOM EDU/PROP COERCE DETER NUC/PWR WAR WEAPON ATTIT PWR...TIME/SEQ COLD/WAR CONGRESS 20. PAGE 11 A0225

PLAN FORCES ARMS/CONT

B60

BROWN H.,COMMUNITY OF FEAR. FORCES TEC/DEV ARMS/CONT COERCE PEACE 20. PAGE 20 A0402

NUC/PWR WAR DIPLOM DETER

B60

BUCHAN A.,NATO IN THE 1960'S. EUR+WWI USA+45 WOR+45 INT/ORG ACT/RES PLAN LEGIT COERCE DETER ATTIT DRIVE RIGID/FLEX ORD/FREE...METH/CNCPT TIME/SEQ TREND GEN/LAWS COLD/WAR 20 NATO. PAGE 21 A0421

VOL/ASSN FORCES ARMS/CONT SOVEREIGN

B60

CARNEGIE ENDOWMENT INT. PEACE,PERSPECTIVES ON PEACE - 1910-1960. WOR+45 WOR-45 INTELL INT/ORG CONSULT ACT/RES EDU/PROP ATTIT KNOWL ORD/FREE...TIME/SEQ TREND EEC OAS UNESCO NAZI 20. PAGE 24 A0489

FUT CONCPT ARMS/CONT PEACE

B60

DEUTSCHER I.,THE GREAT CONTEST: RUSSIA AND THE WEST. USA+45 USSR SOCIETY INDUS ARMS/CONT ATTIT ...CONCPT IDEA/COMP 20 COLD/WAR. PAGE 37 A0749

PEACE DIPLOM PWR

B60

EINSTEIN A.,EINSTEIN ON PEACE. FUT WOR+45 WOR-45 SOCIETY NAT/G PLAN BAL/PWR CAP/ISM DIPLOM ARMS/CONT DETER NAT/LISM...POLICY RELATIV HUM PHIL/SCI CONCPT BIOG COLD/WAR LEAGUE/NAT NAZI. PAGE 41 A0829

INT/ORG ATTIT NUC/PWR PEACE

B60

ENGEL J.,THE SECURITY OF THE FREE WORLD. USSR WOR+45 STRATA STRUCT ECO/DEV ECO/UNDEV INT/ORG DELIB/GP FORCES DOMIN LEGIT ADJUD EXEC ARMS/CONT COERCE...POLICY CONCPT NEW/IDEA TIME/SEQ GEN/LAWS COLD/WAR WORK UN 20 NATO. PAGE 42 A0851

COM TREND DIPLOM

B60
FISCHER L.,THE SOVIETS IN WORLD AFFAIRS. CHINA/COM COM EUR+WWI USSR INT/ORG CONFER LEAD ARMS/CONT REV PWR...CHARTS 20 TREATY VERSAILLES. PAGE 46 A0938 DIPLOM NAT/G POLICY MARXISM

B60
FOREIGN POLICY CLEARING HOUSE,STRATEGY FOR THE 60'S. FUT USA+45 WOR+45 ECO/UNDEV FORCES BAL/PWR TASK ARMS/CONT DETER PWR MARXISM 20 SENATE. PAGE 47 A0963 DIPLOM NAT/G POLICY ACT/RES

B60
HAHN W.F.,AMERICAN STRATEGY FOR THE NUCLEAR AGE. USA+45 NAT/G TEC/DEV ECO/TAC FOR/AID ARMS/CONT NUC/PWR ORD/FREE MARXISM...ANTHOL 20. PAGE 59 A1216 DIPLOM PLAN PEACE

B60
KHRUSHCHEV N.S.,KHRUSHCHEV IN NEW YORK. USA+45 USSR ATTIT...ANTHOL 20 UN KHRUSH/N. PAGE 79 A1612 DIPLOM PEACE ARMS/CONT

B60
MC CLELLAN G.S.,INDIA. CHINA/COM INDIA CONSTN ELITES STRATA AGRI POL/PAR FOR/AID ARMS/CONT REV MARXISM...CENSUS BIBLIOG 20 COLD/WAR GANDHI/M NEHRU/J. PAGE 97 A1990 DIPLOM NAT/G SOCIETY ECO/UNDEV

B60
MCCLELLAND C.A.,NUCLEAR WEAPONS, MISSILES, AND FUTURE WAR: PROBLEM FOR THE SIXTIES. WOR+45 FORCES ARMS/CONT DETER MARXISM...POLICY ANTHOL COLD/WAR. PAGE 97 A1998 DIPLOM NUC/PWR WAR WEAPON

B60
MORISON E.E.,TURMOIL AND TRADITION: A STUDY OF THE LIFE AND TIMES OF HENRY L. STIMSON. USA+45 USA-45 POL/PAR CHIEF DELIB/GP FORCES BAL/PWR DIPLOM ARMS/CONT WAR PEACE 19/20 STIMSON/HL ROOSEVLT/F TAFT/WH HOOVER/H REPUBLICAN. PAGE 104 A2142 BIOG NAT/G EX/STRUC

B60
TABORN P.,RECORDS OF THE HEADQUARTERS, UNITED NATIONS COMMAND (PRELIMINARY INVENTORIES; PAPER). WOR+45 DIPLOM CONFER PEACE ATTIT...POLICY UN. PAGE 141 A2881 BIBLIOG/A WAR ARMS/CONT INT/ORG

B60
TURNER G.B.,NATIONAL SECURITY IN THE NUCLEAR AGE. KOREA USA+45 PLAN DIPLOM ARMS/CONT DETER WAR WEAPON ...BIBLIOG 20 COLD/WAR NATO. PAGE 146 A2982 NAT/G POLICY FORCES NUC/PWR

B60
UNITED WORLD FEDERALISTS,UNITED WORLD FEDERALISTS; PANORAMA OF RECENT BOOKS, FILMS, AND JOURNALS ON WORLD FEDERATION, THE UN, AND WORLD PEACE. CULTURE ECO/UNDEV PROB/SOLV FOR/AID ARMS/CONT NUC/PWR ...INT/LAW PHIL/SCI 20 UN. PAGE 149 A3039 BIBLIOG/A DIPLOM INT/ORG PEACE

B60
US DEPARTMENT OF THE ARMY,DISARMAMENT: A BIBLIOGRAPHIC RECORD: 1916-1960. DETER WAR WEAPON PEACE 20 UN LEAGUE/NAT COLD/WAR NATO. PAGE 152 A3103 BIBLIOG/A ARMS/CONT NUC/PWR DIPLOM

B60
VAN HOOGSTRATE D.J.,AMERICAN FOREIGN POLICY: REALISTS AND IDEALISTS: A CATHOLIC INTERPRETATION. BAL/PWR FOR/AID ARMS/CONT GOV/REL PEACE LOVE MORAL SOVEREIGN CATHISM...BIBLIOG 20. PAGE 158 A3213 CATH DIPLOM POLICY IDEA/COMP

L60
BRENNAN D.G.,"SETTING AND GOALS OF ARMS CONTROL." FUT USA+45 USSR WOR+45 INTELL INT/ORG NAT/G VOL/ASSN CONSULT PLAN DIPLOM ECO/TAC ADMIN KNOWL PWR...POLICY CONCPT TREND COLD/WAR 20. PAGE 18 A0371 FORCES COERCE ARMS/CONT DETER

L60
HOLTON G.,"ARMS CONTROL." FUT WOR+45 CULTURE INT/ORG NAT/G FORCES TOP/EX PLAN EDU/PROP COERCE ATTIT RIGID/FLEX ORD/FREE...POLICY PHIL/SCI SOC TREND COLD/WAR. PAGE 67 A1377 ACT/RES CONSULT ARMS/CONT NUC/PWR

L60
JACOB P.E.,"THE DISARMAMENT CONSENSUS." USA+45 USSR WOR+45 INT/ORG NAT/G ACT/RES TEC/DEV BAL/PWR EDU/PROP ADMIN COERCE DETER NUC/PWR CONSEN RIGID/FLEX PWR...CONCPT RECORD CHARTS COLD/WAR 20. PAGE 72 A1482 DELIB/GP ATTIT ARMS/CONT

L60
KUNZ J.,"SANCTIONS IN INTERNATIONAL LAW." WOR+45 WOR-45 LEGIT ARMS/CONT COERCE PEACE ATTIT ...METH/CNCPT TIME/SEQ TREND 20. PAGE 83 A1695 INT/ORG ADJUD INT/LAW

L60
NOGEE J.L.,"THE DIPLOMACY OF DISARMAMENT." WOR+45 INT/ORG NAT/G CONSULT DELIB/GP TOP/EX BAL/PWR DIPLOM EDU/PROP COERCE DETER WEAPON PEACE ATTIT ...RECORD TIME/SEQ TOT/POP VAL/FREE COLD/WAR 20. PAGE 109 A2246 PWR ORD/FREE ARMS/CONT NUC/PWR

S60
BRODY R.A.,"DETERRENCE STRATEGIES: AN ANNOTATED BIBLIOGRAPHY." WOR+45 PLAN ARMS/CONT NUC/PWR WAR WEAPON DECISION. PAGE 19 A0383 BIBLIOG/A FORCES DETER DIPLOM

S60
DOUGHERTY J.E.,"KEY TO SECURITY: DISARMAMENT OR ARMS STABILITY." COM USA+45 USSR INT/ORG NAT/G CREATE EDU/PROP COERCE DETER ATTIT PWR...DECISION CONCPT MYTH NEW/IDEA TREND 20 COLD/WAR. PAGE 38 A0777 FORCES ORD/FREE ARMS/CONT NUC/PWR

S60
DYSON F.J.,"THE FUTURE DEVELOPMENT OF NUCLEAR WEAPONS." FUT WOR+45 DELIB/GP ACT/RES PLAN DETER WEAPON ATTIT PWR...POLICY 20. PAGE 40 A0815 INT/ORG ARMS/CONT NUC/PWR

S60
GULICK E.U.,"OUR BALANCE OF POWER SYSTEM IN PERSPECTIVE." FUT WOR+45 WOR-45 ECO/DEV DOMIN ROUTINE NUC/PWR PEACE PWR WEALTH...PLURIST CONCPT HIST/WRIT GEN/METH TOT/POP 20. PAGE 58 A1191 INT/ORG TREND ARMS/CONT BAL/PWR

S60
IKLE F.C.,"NTH COUNTRIES AND DISARMAMENT." WOR+45 DELIB/GP ECO/TAC DOMIN EDU/PROP LEGIT ROUTINE COERCE RIGID/FLEX ORD/FREE...MARXIST TREND 20. PAGE 70 A1432 FUT INT/ORG ARMS/CONT NUC/PWR

S60
LEAR J.,"PEACE: SCIENCE'S NEXT GREAT EXPLORATION." USA+45 INT/ORG TOP/EX TEC/DEV EDU/PROP ROUTINE PEACE KNOWL SKILL 20. PAGE 86 A1757 EX/STRUC ARMS/CONT NUC/PWR

S60
MORGENSTERN O.,"GOAL: AN ARMED, INSPECTED, OPEN WORLD." COM EUR+WWI USA+45 R+D INT/ORG NAT/G TEC/DEV BAL/PWR COERCE NUC/PWR ORD/FREE PWR...TREND 20. PAGE 104 A2133 FORCES CONCPT ARMS/CONT DETER

S60
MUNRO L.,"CAN THE UNITED NATIONS ENFORCE PEACE." WOR+45 LAW INT/ORG VOL/ASSN BAL/PWR LEGIT ARMS/CONT COERCE DETER PEACE PWR...CONCPT REC/INT TREND UN 20 HAMMARSK/D. PAGE 106 A2173 FORCES ORD/FREE

S60
O'BRIEN W.,"THE ROLE OF FORCE IN THE INTERNATIONAL JURIDICAL ORDER." WOR+45 NAT/G FORCES DOMIN ADJUD ARMS/CONT DETER NUC/PWR WAR ATTIT PWR...CATH INT/LAW JURID CONCPT TREND STERTYP GEN/LAWS 20. PAGE 110 A2266 INT/ORG COERCE

S60
RHYNE C.S.,"LAW AS AN INSTRUMENT FOR PEACE." FUT WOR+45 PLAN LEGIT ROUTINE ARMS/CONT NUC/PWR ATTIT ORD/FREE...JURID METH/CNCPT TREND CON/ANAL HYPO/EXP COLD/WAR 20. PAGE 120 A2471 ADJUD EDU/PROP INT/LAW PEACE

B61
AMORY J.F.,AROUND THE EDGE OF WAR: A NEW APPROACH TO THE PROBLEMS OF AMERICAN FOREIGN POLICY. COM L/A+17C USA+45 USSR FOR/AID EDU/PROP AGREE CONTROL ARMS/CONT NUC/PWR WAR PWR...IDEA/COMP 20 TREATY ESPIONAGE. PAGE 8 A0154 NAT/G DIPLOM POLICY

B61
BECHHOEFER B.G.,POSTWAR NEGOTIATIONS FOR ARMS CONTROL. COM EUR+WWI USSR INT/ORG NAT/G ACT/RES BAL/PWR DIPLOM ECO/TAC EDU/PROP ADMIN REGION DETER NUC/PWR WAR WEAPON PEACE ATTIT PWR...POLICY TIME/SEQ COLD/WAR CONGRESS 20. PAGE 12 A0244 USA+45 ARMS/CONT

B61
BRENNAN D.G.,ARMS CONTROL, DISARMAMENT, AND NATIONAL SECURITY. WOR+45 NAT/G FORCES CREATE PROB/SOLV PARTIC WAR PEACE...DECISION INT/LAW ANTHOL BIBLIOG 20. PAGE 18 A0372 ARMS/CONT ORD/FREE DIPLOM POLICY

B61
BULL H.,THE CONTROL OF THE ARMS RACE. COM USA+45 INT/ORG NAT/G PLAN TEC/DEV DIPLOM ATTIT...RELATIV DECISION CONCPT SELF/OBS TREND CON/ANAL GEN/METH 20 COLD/WAR. PAGE 21 A0429 FORCES PWR ARMS/CONT NUC/PWR

B61
EISENHOWER D.D.,PEACE WITH JUSTICE: SELECTED ADDRESSES. USSR PARTIC ARMS/CONT MORAL...TRADIT CONCPT GEN/LAWS ANTHOL 20 PRESIDENT COLD/WAR. PAGE 41 A0832 PEACE DIPLOM EDU/PROP POLICY

B61
FRISCH D.,ARMS REDUCTION: PROGRAM AND ISSUES. USA+45 INT/ORG NAT/G ACT/RES REGION NUC/PWR ATTIT PWR...POLICY 20. PAGE 49 A1010 PLAN FORCES ARMS/CONT DIPLOM

B61
GRAEBNER N.,AN UNCERTAIN TRADITION: AMERICAN SECRETARIES OF STATE IN THE 20TH CENTURY. USA+45 CONSTN INT/ORG NAT/G DELIB/GP TOP/EX BAL/PWR DOMIN LEGIT ADMIN ARMS/CONT ATTIT DRIVE PERSON SUPEGO ORD/FREE PWR...GEN/LAWS VAL/FREE CONGRESS. PAGE 55 A1121 USA-45 BIOG DIPLOM

B61
HANCOCK W.K.,FOUR STUDIES OF WAR AND PEACE IN THIS CENTURY. FUT WOR+45 WOR-45 ACT/RES LEGIT DETER HEALTH...TREND ANTHOL TOT/POP VAL/FREE UN 20. PAGE 61 A1250 INT/ORG POLICY ARMS/CONT

B61
HENKIN L.,ARMS CONTROL: ISSUES FOR THE PUBLIC. EUR+WWI FUT USA+45 USSR INT/ORG NAT/G DIPLOM EDU/PROP DETER NUC/PWR ATTIT PWR...CONCPT RECORD HIST/WRIT TIME/SEQ TOT/POP COLD/WAR 20. PAGE 64 A1316 WOR+45 DELIB/GP ARMS/CONT

B61
KISSINGER H.A.,THE NECESSITY FOR CHOICE. FUT USA+45 ECO/UNDEV NAT/G PLAN BAL/PWR ECO/TAC ARMS/CONT DETER NUC/PWR ATTIT...POLICY CONCPT RECORD GEN/LAWS COLD/WAR 20. PAGE 80 A1642 TOP/EX TREND DIPLOM

B61
LIPPMANN W.,THE COMING TESTS WITH RUSSIA. COM CUBA GERMANY USSR FORCES CONTROL NEUTRAL COERCE NUC/PWR REV WAR PWR...INT 20 KHRUSH/N BERLIN. PAGE 89 A1830
BAL/PWR DIPLOM MARXISM ARMS/CONT

B61
MORRAY J.P.,FROM YALTA TO DISARMAMENT: COLD WAR DEBATE. USA+45 CAP/ISM FOR/AID CONTROL NUC/PWR 20 UN COLD/WAR CHURCHLL/W. PAGE 104 A2145
MARXIST ARMS/CONT DIPLOM BAL/PWR

B61
NEAL F.W.,US FOREIGN POLICY AND THE SOVIET UNION. USA+45 USSR INT/ORG ECO/TAC ARMS/CONT MAJORITY NAT/LISM ATTIT RESPECT MARXISM 20. PAGE 108 A2207
DIPLOM POLICY PEACE

B61
NOGEE J.L.,SOVIET POLICY TOWARD INTERNATIONAL CONTROL OF ATOMIC ENERGY. COM USA+45 WOR+45 INTELL NAT/G ACT/RES DIPLOM EDU/PROP NUC/PWR TOTALISM PERCEPT KNOWL PWR...TIME/SEQ COLD/WAR 20. PAGE 109 A2247
INT/ORG ATTIT ARMS/CONT USSR

B61
SCHELLING T.C.,STRATEGY AND ARMS CONTROL. FUT UNIV WOR+45 INT/ORG PLAN TEC/DEV BAL/PWR LEGIT PERCEPT HEALTH...CONCPT VAL/FREE 20. PAGE 128 A2623
ROUTINE POLICY ARMS/CONT

B61
SCHMIDT H.,VERTEIDIGUNG ODER VERGELTUNG. COM CUBA GERMANY/W USSR FORCES DIPLOM ARMS/CONT DETER NUC/PWR...POLICY CHARTS HYPO/EXP SIMUL BIBLIOG 20 NATO COLD/WAR. PAGE 128 A2630
PLAN WAR BAL/PWR ORD/FREE

B61
SLESSOR J.,WHAT PRICE COEXISTENCE? COM INT/ORG NAT/G FORCES COLONIAL ARMS/CONT WAR...POLICY TREND 20 NATO COLD/WAR. PAGE 134 A2741
DIPLOM PEACE WOR+45 NUC/PWR

B61
STONE J.,QUEST FOR SURVIVAL. WOR+45 NAT/G VOL/ASSN LEGIT ADMIN ARMS/CONT COERCE DISPL ORD/FREE PWR ...POLICY INT/LAW JURID COLD/WAR 20. PAGE 139 A2836
INT/ORG ADJUD SOVEREIGN

B61
WRIGHT Q.,THE ROLE OF INTERNATIONAL LAW IN THE ELIMINATION OF WAR. FUT WOR+45 WOR-45 NAT/G BAL/PWR DIPLOM DOMIN LEGIT PWR...POLICY INT/LAW JURID CONCPT TIME/SEQ TREND GEN/LAWS COLD/WAR 20. PAGE 168 A3414
INT/ORG ADJUD ARMS/CONT

L61
TAUBENFELD H.J.,"A REGIME FOR OUTER SPACE." FUT UNIV R+D ACT/RES PLAN BAL/PWR LEGIT ARMS/CONT ORD/FREE...POLICY JURID TREND UN TOT/POP 20 COLD/WAR. PAGE 142 A2894
INT/ORG ADJUD SPACE

S61
BARNET R.,"RUSSIA, CHINA, AND THE WORLD: THE SOVIET ATTITUDE ON DISARMAMENT (PART 3)." ASIA CHINA/COM FUT INT/ORG NAT/G POL/PAR VOL/ASSN ARMS/CONT ATTIT ...POLICY CONCPT TIME/SEQ TREND TOT/POP VAL/FREE 20. PAGE 11 A0226
COM PLAN TOTALISM USSR

S61
CARLETON W.G.,"AMERICAN FOREIGN POLICY: MYTHS AND REALITIES." FUT USA+45 WOR+45 ECO/UNDEV INT/ORG EX/STRUC ARMS/CONT NUC/PWR WAR ATTIT...POLICY CONCPT CONT/OBS GEN/METH COLD/WAR TOT/POP 20. PAGE 24 A0484
PLAN MYTH DIPLOM

B62
BEATON L.,THE SPREAD OF NUCLEAR WEAPONS. WOR+45 NAT/G PLAN PROB/SOLV DIPLOM ECO/TAC DETER...POLICY 20 COLD/WAR. PAGE 12 A0242
ARMS/CONT NUC/PWR TEC/DEV FUT

B62
BLACKETT P.M.S.,STUDIES OF WAR: NUCLEAR AND CONVENTIONAL. EUR+WWI USA+45 DELIB/GP ACT/RES CREATE PLAN TEC/DEV LEGIT COERCE WAR ORD/FREE PWR ...POLICY TECHNIC TIME/SEQ 20. PAGE 15 A0300
INT/ORG FORCES ARMS/CONT NUC/PWR

B62
BURTON J.W.,PEACE THEORY: PRECONDITIONS OF DISARMAMENT. COM EUR+WWI USA+45 NAT/G FORCES BAL/PWR DIPLOM ECO/TAC EDU/PROP REGION COERCE DETER PEACE ATTIT PWR TOT/POP COLD/WAR 20. PAGE 22 A0446
INT/ORG PLAN ARMS/CONT

B62
DUROSELLE J.B.,HISTOIRE DIPLOMATIQUE DE 1919 A NOS JOURS (3RD ED.). FRANCE INT/ORG CHIEF FORCES CONFER ARMS/CONT WAR PEACE ORD/FREE...T TREATY 20 COLD/WAR. PAGE 39 A0807
DIPLOM WOR+45 WOR-45

B62
FORBES H.W.,THE STRATEGY OF DISARMAMENT. FUT WOR+45 INT/ORG VOL/ASSN CONSULT ARMS/CONT COERCE NUC/PWR WAR DRIVE RIGID/FLEX ORD/FREE PWR...POLICY CONCPT OBS TREND STERTYP 20. PAGE 47 A0959
PLAN FORCES DIPLOM

B62
GILPIN R.,AMERICAN SCIENTISTS AND NUCLEAR WEAPONS POLICY. COM FUT USA+45 WOR+45 INT/ORG NAT/G PROF/ORG CONSULT FORCES CREATE TEC/DEV BAL/PWR EDU/PROP ARMS/CONT WAR PERCEPT KNOWL MORAL PWR ...PHIL/SCI SOC CONCPT GEN/LAWS 20. PAGE 52 A1073
INTELL ATTIT DETER NUC/PWR

B62
GOLDWATER B.M.,WHY NOT VICTORY? A FRESH LOOK AT AMERICAN FOREIGN POLICY. USA+45 WOR+45 FOR/AID LEAD ARMS/CONT WAR PEACE ATTIT ORD/FREE PWR MARXISM ...INT/LAW 20 TREATY ECHR COUNCL/EUR. PAGE 53 A1092
DIPLOM POLICY CONSERVE NAT/LISM

B62
KAHN H.,THINKING ABOUT THE UNTHINKABLE. FUT USA+45 LAW NAT/G CONSULT FORCES ACT/RES CREATE PLAN TEC/DEV BAL/PWR DIPLOM EDU/PROP ARMS/CONT DETER ATTIT...CONCPT OBS TREND COLD/WAR 20. PAGE 76 A1547
INT/ORG ORD/FREE NUC/PWR PEACE

B62
KING-HALL S.,POWER POLITICS IN THE NUCLEAR AGE: A POLICY FOR BRITAIN. UK WOR+45 PLAN ECO/TAC CONTROL RISK ARMS/CONT MORAL PWR RESPECT...OLD/LIB 20. PAGE 79 A1625
BAL/PWR NUC/PWR POLICY DIPLOM

B62
LEFEVER E.W.,ARMS AND ARMS CONTROL. COM USA+45 INT/ORG TEC/DEV DIPLOM ORD/FREE 20. PAGE 86 A1763
ATTIT PWR ARMS/CONT BAL/PWR

B62
MONCRIEFF A.,THE STRATEGY OF SURVIVAL. UK FORCES BAL/PWR CONFER DETER WAR...ANTHOL 20 COLD/WAR. PAGE 102 A2104
PLAN DECISION DIPLOM ARMS/CONT

B62
OSGOOD R.E.,NATO: THE ENTANGLING ALLIANCE. USA+45 WOR+45 VOL/ASSN FORCES TOP/EX PLAN DETER WEAPON DRIVE RIGID/FLEX ORD/FREE PWR...TREND 20 NATO. PAGE 112 A2301
INT/ORG ARMS/CONT PEACE

B62
PERKINS D.,AMERICA'S QUEST FOR PEACE. USA+45 WOR+45 DIPLOM CONFER NAT/LISM ATTIT 20 UN TREATY. PAGE 115 A2361
INT/LAW INT/ORG ARMS/CONT PEACE

B62
PERRE J.,LES MUTATIONS DE LA GUERRE MODERNE: DE LA REVOLUTION FRANCAISE A LA REVOLUTION NUCLEAIRE. DIPLOM ARMS/CONT DEATH REV WEAPON GP/REL PEACE ATTIT...STAT PREDICT BIBLIOG 18/20 WWI. PAGE 115 A2365
WAR FORCES NUC/PWR

B62
ROSAMOND R.,CRUSADE FOR PEACE: EISENHOWER'S PRESIDENTIAL LEGACY WITH THE PROGRAM FOR ACTION. USA+45 PARTIC ARMS/CONT MORAL MARXISM...TRADIT CONCPT CHARTS GEN/LAWS ANTHOL 20 PRESIDENT EISNHWR/DD. PAGE 123 A2526
PEACE DIPLOM EDU/PROP POLICY

B62
SCHUMAN F.L.,THE COLD WAR: RETROSPECT AND PROSPECT. FUT USA+45 USSR WOR+45 BAL/PWR EDU/PROP ARMS/CONT ATTIT...MAJORIT IDEA/COMP ANTHOL BIBLIOG 20 COLD/WAR. PAGE 129 A2651
MARXISM TEC/DEV DIPLOM NUC/PWR

B62
SINGER J.D.,DETERRENCE, ARMS CONTROL AND DISARMAMENT: TOWARD A SYNTHESIS IN NATIONAL SECURITY POLICY. COM USA+45 INT/ORG BAL/PWR DETER ORD/FREE...POLICY COLD/WAR 20. PAGE 133 A2727
FUT ACT/RES ARMS/CONT

B62
SPANIER J.W.,THE POLITICS OF DISARMAMENT. COM USA+45 USSR EDU/PROP ATTIT ORD/FREE PWR RESPECT ...MYTH RECORD 20 COLD/WAR. PAGE 135 A2771
INT/ORG DELIB/GP ARMS/CONT

B62
STRACHEY J.,ON THE PREVENTION OF WAR. FUT WOR+45 INT/ORG NAT/G ACT/RES PLAN BAL/PWR DOMIN EDU/PROP PEACE ATTIT...POLICY TREND TOT/POP COLD/WAR 20 UN. PAGE 139 A2842
FORCES ORD/FREE ARMS/CONT NUC/PWR

B62
WADSWORTH J.J.,THE PRICE OF PEACE. WOR+45 TEC/DEV CONTROL NUC/PWR PEACE ATTIT TREATY 20. PAGE 160 A3258
DIPLOM INT/ORG ARMS/CONT POLICY

B62
WRIGHT Q.,PREVENTING WORLD WAR THREE. FUT WOR+45 CULTURE INT/ORG NAT/G CONSULT FORCES ADMIN ARMS/CONT DRIVE RIGID/FLEX ORD/FREE SOVEREIGN ...POLICY CONCPT TREND STERTYP COLD/WAR 20. PAGE 168 A3416
CREATE ATTIT

B62
YALEN R.,REGIONALISM AND WORLD ORDER. EUR+WWI WOR+45 WOR-45 INT/ORG VOL/ASSN DELIB/GP FORCES TOP/EX BAL/PWR DIPLOM DOMIN REGION ARMS/CONT PWR ...JURID HYPO/EXP COLD/WAR 20. PAGE 168 A3427
ORD/FREE POLICY

S62
BOULDING K.E.,"THE PREVENTION OF WORLD WAR THREE." FUT WOR+45 INT/ORG PLAN BAL/PWR PEACE ORD/FREE PWR ...NEW/IDEA TREND TOT/POP COLD/WAR 20. PAGE 17 A0348
VOL/ASSN NAT/G ARMS/CONT DIPLOM

S62
CRANE R.D.,"LAW AND STRATEGY IN SPACE." FUT USA+45 WOR+45 AIR LAW INT/ORG NAT/G FORCES ACT/RES PLAN BAL/PWR LEGIT ARMS/CONT COERCE ORD/FREE...POLICY INT/LAW JURID SOC/EXP 20 TREATY. PAGE 32 A0656
CONCPT SPACE

S62
FINKELSTEIN L.S.,"THE UNITED NATIONS AND ORGANIZATIONS FOR CONTROL OF ARMAMENT." FUT WOR+45 VOL/ASSN DELIB/GP TOP/EX CREATE EDU/PROP LEGIT ADJUD NUC/PWR ATTIT RIGID/FLEX ORD/FREE...POLICY DECISION CONCPT OBS TREND GEN/LAWS TOT/POP COLD/WAR. PAGE 46 A0933
INT/ORG PWR ARMS/CONT

S62
FOSTER W.C.,"ARMS CONTROL AND DISARMAMENT IN A DIVIDED WORLD." COM FUT USA+45 USSR WOR+45 INTELL INT/ORG NAT/G VOL/ASSN CONSULT CREATE PLAN TEC/DEV EDU/PROP LEGIT NUC/PWR ATTIT RIGID/FLEX...CONCPT TREND TOT/POP 20 UN. PAGE 47 A0971
DELIB/GP POLICY ARMS/CONT DIPLOM

S62
HOFFMANN S.,"RESTRAINTS AND CHOICES IN AMERICAN FOREIGN POLICY." USA-45 INT/ORG NAT/G PLAN ARMS/CONT ATTIT...POLICY CONCPT OBS TREND GEN/METH COLD/WAR 20. PAGE 66 A1356
USA+45 ORD/FREE DIPLOM

S62
NANES A.,"DISARMAMENT: THE LAST SEVEN YEARS." COM EUR+WWI USA+45 USSR INT/ORG FORCES TOP/EX CREATE LEGIT NUC/PWR DISPL ORD/FREE...CONCPT TIME/SEQ CON/ANAL 20. PAGE 107 A2195
DELIB/GP RIGID/FLEX ARMS/CONT

S62
RUSSETT B.M.,"CAUSE, SURPRISE, AND NO ESCAPE." FUT WOR-45 CULTURE SOCIETY INT/ORG FORCES TEC/DEV BAL/PWR EDU/PROP ARMS/CONT NUC/PWR WAR WEAPON PEACE KNOWL ORD/FREE PWR...POLICY CONCPT RECORD TIME/SEQ TREND GEN/LAWS 20 WWI. PAGE 126 A2578
COERCE DIPLOM

S62
SINGER J.D.,"STABLE DETERRENCE AND ITS LIMITS." FUT WOR+45 R+D INT/ORG CONSULT ACT/RES TEC/DEV ARMS/CONT COERCE DRIVE PERCEPT RIGID/FLEX ORD/FREE PWR...MYTH SIMUL TOT/POP 20. PAGE 133 A2728
NAT/G FORCES DETER NUC/PWR

B63
BOISSIER P.,HISTORIE DU COMITE INTERNATIONAL DE LA CROIX ROUGE. MOD/EUR WOR-45 CONSULT FORCES PLAN DIPLOM EDU/PROP ADMIN MORAL ORD/FREE...SOC CONCPT RECORD TIME/SEQ GEN/LAWS TOT/POP VAL/FREE 19/20. PAGE 16 A0332
INT/ORG HEALTH ARMS/CONT WAR

B63
FALK R.A.,LAW, MORALITY, AND WAR IN THE CONTEMPORARY WORLD. WOR+45 LAW INT/ORG EX/STRUC FORCES EDU/PROP LEGIT DETER NUC/PWR MORAL ORD/FREE ...JURID TOT/POP 20. PAGE 43 A0888
ADJUD ARMS/CONT PEACE INT/LAW

B63
GOLDWIN R.A.,FOREIGN AND MILITARY POLICY. COM USSR WOR+45 ECO/DEV INT/ORG FORCES PLAN ECO/TAC REGION ARMS/CONT MARXISM 20 UN. PAGE 54 A1097
DIPLOM POLICY PWR NAT/G

B63
GONZALEZ PEDRERO E.,ANATOMIA DE UN CONFLICTO. WOR+45 ECO/DEV ECO/UNDEV ECO/TAC FOR/AID CONTROL ARMS/CONT GOV/REL...NAT/COMP 20 COLD/WAR. PAGE 54 A1099
DIPLOM DETER BAL/PWR

B63
GRAEBNER N.A.,THE COLD WAR: IDEOLOGICAL CONFLICT OR POWER STRUGGLE? USSR WOR+45 WOR-45 PROB/SOLV EDU/PROP ARMS/CONT REV NAT/LISM PEACE ORD/FREE ...IDEA/COMP ANTHOL BIBLIOG/A 20 COLD/WAR. PAGE 55 A1123
DIPLOM BAL/PWR MARXISM

B63
LILIENTHAL D.E.,CHANGE, HOPE, AND THE BOMB. USA+45 WOR+45 R+D INT/ORG NAT/G DELIB/GP FORCES ACT/RES DETER RIGID/FLEX ORD/FREE...POLICY CONCPT OBS AEC 20. PAGE 89 A1815
ATTIT MYTH ARMS/CONT NUC/PWR

B63
PACHTER H.M.,COLLISION COURSE; THE CUBAN MISSILE CRISIS AND COEXISTENCE. CUBA USA+45 DIPLOM ARMS/CONT PEACE MARXISM...DECISION INT/LAW 20 COLD/WAR KHRUSH/N KENNEDY/JF CASTRO/F. PAGE 112 A2307
WAR BAL/PWR NUC/PWR DETER

B63
ROSS H.,THE COLD WAR: CONTAINMENT AND ITS CRITICSS. WOR+45 POL/PAR BAL/PWR ECO/TAC PEACE ORD/FREE ...POLICY IDEA/COMP ANTHOL T 20 COLD/WAR DULLES/JF TRUMAN/HS EISNHWR/DD. PAGE 124 A2541
MARXISM ARMS/CONT DIPLOM

B63
STEVENSON A.E.,LOOKING OUTWARD: YEARS OF CRISIS AT THE UNITED NATIONS. COM CUBA USA+45 WOR+45 SOCIETY NAT/G EX/STRUC ACT/RES LEGIT COLONIAL ATTIT PERSON SUPEGO ALL/VALS...POLICY HUM UN COLD/WAR CONGO 20. PAGE 138 A2823
INT/ORG CONCPT ARMS/CONT

B63
US DEPARTMENT OF THE ARMY,SOVIET RUSSIA: STRATEGIC SURVEY (PAMPHLET). USSR POL/PAR PLAN DOMIN EDU/PROP ARMS/CONT GUERRILLA WAR WEAPON...TREND CHARTS ORG/CHARTS 20. PAGE 152 A3106
BIBLIOG/A MARXISM DIPLOM COERCE

B63
VAN SLYCK P.,PEACE: THE CONTROL OF NATIONAL POWER. CUBA WOR+45 FINAN NAT/G FORCES PROB/SOLV TEC/DEV BAL/PWR ADMIN CONTROL ORD/FREE...POLICY INT/LAW UN COLD/WAR TREATY. PAGE 158 A3214
ARMS/CONT PEACE INT/ORG DIPLOM

B63
VOSS E.H.,NUCLEAR AMBUSH: THE TEST-BAN TRAP. WOR+45 COM/IND INT/ORG NAT/G DELIB/GP FORCES LEGIS TOP/EX ACT/RES DOMIN EDU/PROP LEGIT ROUTINE COERCE ATTIT PERCEPT RIGID/FLEX HEALTH MORAL ORD/FREE PWR. PAGE 160 A3255
TEC/DEV HIST/WRIT ARMS/CONT NUC/PWR

L63
PHELPS J.,"STUDIES IN DETERRENCE VIII: MILITARY STABILITARY AND ARMS CONTROL: A CRITICAL SURVEY." FUT WOR+45 INT/ORG ACT/RES EDU/PROP COERCE NUC/PWR WAR HEALTH PWR...POLICY TECHNIC TREND SIMUL TOT/POP 20. PAGE 116 A2373
FORCES ORD/FREE ARMS/CONT DETER

L63
SCHELLING T.C.,"STRATEGIC PROBLEMS OF AN INTERNATIONAL ARMED FORCE." WOR+45 ECO/DEV INT/ORG NAT/G PLAN BAL/PWR LEGIT ARMS/CONT COERCE DETER ORD/FREE PWR...POLICY CONCPT COLD/WAR 20. PAGE 128 A2624
CREATE FORCES

L63
SINGER J.D.,"WEAPONS MANAGEMENT IN WORLD POLITICS: PROCEEDINGS OF THE INTERNATIONAL ARMS CONTROL SYMPOSIUM, DECEMBER, 1962." FUT WOR+45 SOCIETY ECO/DEV INDUS INT/ORG DELIB/GP FORCES ACT/RES ECO/TAC EDU/PROP ARMS/CONT SUPEGO HEALTH ORD/FREE PWR SKILL...POLICY CHARTS SIMUL ANTHOL VAL/FREE 20. PAGE 133 A2729
CONSULT ATTIT DIPLOM NUC/PWR

S63
BECHHOEFER B.G.,"UNITED NATIONS PROCEDURES IN CASE OF VIOLATIONS OF DISARMAMENT AGREEMENTS." COM USA+45 USSR LAW CONSTN NAT/G EX/STRUC FORCES LEGIS BAL/PWR EDU/PROP CT/SYS ARMS/CONT ORD/FREE PWR ...POLICY STERTYP UN VAL/FREE 20. PAGE 12 A0245
INT/ORG DELIB/GP

S63
BLOOMFIELD L.P.,"INTERNATIONAL FORCE IN A DISARMING BUT REVOLUTIONARY WORLD." INT/ORG COERCE REV DRIVE PWR...CONCPT STERTYP GEN/LAWS 20. PAGE 16 A0318
FORCES ORD/FREE ARMS/CONT GUERRILLA

S63
BOHN L.,"WHOSE NUCLEAR TEST: NON-PHYSICAL INSPECTION AND TEST BAN." WOR+45 R+D INT/ORG VOL/ASSN ORD/FREE...GEN/LAWS GEN/METH COLD/WAR 20. PAGE 16 A0331
ADJUD ARMS/CONT TEC/DEV NUC/PWR

S63
BRZEZINSKI Z.,"SOVIET QUIESCENCE." EUR+WWI USA+45 USSR FORCES CREATE PLAN COERCE DETER WAR ATTIT 20 TREATY EUROPE. PAGE 20 A0415
DIPLOM ARMS/CONT NUC/PWR AGREE

S63
HALLSTEIN W.,"THE EUROPEAN COMMUNITY AND ATLANTIC PARTNERSHIP." EUR+WWI USA+45 MARKET NAT/G VOL/ASSN DELIB/GP ARMS/CONT NUC/PWR ATTIT PWR...CONCPT STAT TIME/SEQ TREND OEEC 20 EEC. PAGE 60 A1235
INT/ORG ECO/TAC UK

S63
HUMPHREY H.H.,"REGIONAL ARMS CONTROL AGREEMENTS." WOR+45 FORCES PLAN LEGIT COERCE ATTIT HEALTH ORD/FREE...HUM METH/CNCPT MYTH OBS INT TREND TOT/POP 20. PAGE 69 A1416
L/A+17C INT/ORG ARMS/CONT REGION

S63
MORGENTHAU H.J.,"THE POLITICAL CONDITIONS FOR AN INTERNATIONAL POLICE FORCE." FUT WOR+45 CREATE LEGIT ADMIN PEACE ORD/FREE 20. PAGE 104 A2141
INT/ORG FORCES ARMS/CONT DETER

S63
NEIDLE A.F.,"PEACE KEEPING AND DISARMAMENT." COM USA+45 USSR WOR+45 INT/ORG NAT/G BAL/PWR EDU/PROP LEGIT ATTIT PWR 20. PAGE 108 A2214
DELIB/GP ACT/RES ARMS/CONT PEACE

S63
NOGEE J.L.,"PROPOGANDA AND NEGOTIATION: THE CASE OF THE TEN NATION DISARMAMENT COMMITTEE." COM EUR+WWI USA+45 VOL/ASSN DELIB/GP FORCES DIPLOM DOMIN LEGIT PWR...METH/CNCPT STERTYP COLD/WAR VAL/FREE 20. PAGE 110 A2248
INT/ORG EDU/PROP ARMS/CONT

S63
PHELPS J.,"INFORMATION AND ARMS CONTROL." COM SPACE USA+45 USSR WOR+45 R+D INT/ORG NAT/G DELIB/GP DIPLOM ORD/FREE...CONCPT 20. PAGE 116 A2374
KNOWL ARMS/CONT NUC/PWR

S63
SPINELLI A.,"IL TRATTATO DI MOSCA E I PROBLEMI DELLA COESISTENZA PACIFICA." CHINA/COM COM FRANCE FUT WOR+45 INT/ORG VOL/ASSN PEACE...POLICY MYTH 20. PAGE 136 A2788
ATTIT ARMS/CONT TOTALISM

B64
BLOOMFIELD L.P.,INTERNATIONAL MILITARY FORCES: THE QUESTION OF PEACE-KEEPING IN AN ARMED AND DISARMING WORLD. WOR+45 ACADEM ARMS/CONT REV PEACE 20 UN. PAGE 16 A0320
INT/ORG FORCES FUT DIPLOM

B64
DALLIN A.,THE SOVIET UNION, ARMS CONTROL AND DISARMAMENT. COM INT/ORG VOL/ASSN EX/STRUC DIPLOM NUC/PWR ATTIT PWR TOT/POP COLD/WAR 20. PAGE 33 A0678
ORD/FREE ARMS/CONT USSR

B64
DEUTSCHE GES AUSWARTIGE POL,STRATEGIE UND ABRUSTUNGSPOLITIK DER SOWJETUNION. USSR TEC/DEV DIPLOM COERCE DETER WEAPON...POLICY PSY 20 ABM/DEFSYS. PAGE 37 A0747
NUC/PWR WAR FORCES ARMS/CONT

B64
GRODZINS M.,THE ATOMIC AGE: FORTY-FIVE SCIENTISTS AND SCHOLARS SPEAK ON NATIONAL AND WORLD AFFAIRS. FUT USA+45 WOR+45 R+D INT/ORG NAT/G CONSULT TEC/DEV EDU/PROP ATTIT PERSON ORD/FREE...HUM CONCPT TIME/SEQ CON/ANAL. PAGE 57 A1169
INTELL ARMS/CONT NUC/PWR

B64
KENNEDY J.F.,THE BURDEN AND THE GLORY. FUT USA+45 TEC/DEV ECO/TAC EDU/PROP ARMS/CONT MURDER RACE/REL
ADMIN POLICY

PEACE...ANTHOL 20 KENNEDY/JF COLD/WAR NATO PRESIDENT. PAGE 78 A1593
GOV/REL DIPLOM

B64
KIMMINICH O.,RUSTUNG UND POLITISCHE SPANNUNG. INDUS ARMS/CONT COERCE NAT/LISM PEACE PERSON ORD/FREE ...POLICY GEOG 20. PAGE 79 A1619
DIPLOM FORCES WEAPON WAR

B64
ROBERTS HL,FOREIGN AFFAIRS BIBLIOGRAPHY, 1952-1962. ECO/DEV SECT PLAN FOR/AID INT/TRADE ARMS/CONT NAT/LISM ATTIT...INT/LAW GOV/COMP IDEA/COMP 20. PAGE 122 A2495
BIBLIOG/A DIPLOM INT/ORG WAR

B64
US AIR FORCE ACADEMY ASSEMBLY,OUTER SPACE: FINAL REPORT APRIL 1-4, 1964. FUT USA+45 WOR+45 LAW DELIB/GP CONFER ARMS/CONT WAR PEACE ATTIT MORAL ...ANTHOL 20 NASA. PAGE 150 A3055
SPACE CIVMIL/REL NUC/PWR DIPLOM

B64
WILLIAMS S.P.,TOWARD A GENUINE WORLD SECURITY SYSTEM (PAMPHLET). WOR+45 INT/ORG FORCES PLAN NUC/PWR ORD/FREE...INT/LAW CONCPT UN PRESIDENT. PAGE 165 A3353
BIBLIOG/A ARMS/CONT DIPLOM PEACE

L64
BERKS R.N.,"THE US AND WEAPONS CONTROL." WOR+45 LAW INT/ORG NAT/G LEGIS EXEC COERCE PEACE ATTIT RIGID/FLEX ALL/VALS PWR...POLICY TOT/POP 20. PAGE 13 A0273
USA+45 PLAN ARMS/CONT

L64
CARNEGIE ENDOWMENT INT. PEACE,"POLITICAL QUESTIONS (ISSUES BEFORE THE NINETEENTH GENERAL ASSEMBLY)." SPACE WOR+45 CONSTN FINAN NAT/G CONSULT DELIB/GP FORCES LEGIS TEC/DEV EDU/PROP LEGIT ARMS/CONT COERCE NUC/PWR ATTIT ALL/VALS...CONCPT OBS UN COLD/WAR 20. PAGE 24 A0490
INT/ORG PEACE

L64
WARD C.,"THE 'NEW MYTHS' AND 'OLD REALITIES' OF NUCLEAR WAR." COM FUT USA+45 USSR WOR+45 INT/ORG NAT/G DOMIN LEGIT EXEC ATTIT PERCEPT ALL/VALS ...POLICY RELATIV PSY MYTH TREND 20. PAGE 161 A3280
FORCES COERCE ARMS/CONT NUC/PWR

S64
ARMSTRONG J.A.,"THE SOVIET-AMERICAN CONFRONTATION: A NEW STAGE?" CUBA USA+45 USSR PLAN PROB/SOLV INT/TRADE CONTROL ARMS/CONT NUC/PWR MARXISM 20 COLD/WAR INTERVENT. PAGE 9 A0174
DIPLOM POLICY INSPECT

S64
COFFEY J.,"THE SOVIET VIEW OF A DISARMED WORLD." COM USA+45 INT/ORG NAT/G EX/STRUC EDU/PROP COERCE PERCEPT ORD/FREE PWR...TREND STERTYP VAL/FREE 20 UN. PAGE 27 A0556
FORCES ATTIT ARMS/CONT USSR

S64
CRANE R.D.,"BASIC PRINCIPLES IN SOVIET SPACE LAW." FUT WOR+45 AIR INT/ORG DIPLOM DOMIN ARMS/CONT COERCE NUC/PWR PEACE ATTIT DRIVE PWR...INT/LAW METH/CNCPT NEW/IDEA OBS TREND GEN/LAWS VAL/FREE MARX/KARL 20. PAGE 32 A0659
COM LAW USSR SPACE

S64
FALK S.L.,"DISARMAMENT IN HISTORICAL PERSPECTIVE." WOR-45 NAT/G PLAN NUC/PWR PEACE ORD/FREE PWR ...TIME/SEQ AUD/VIS VAL/FREE LEAGUE/NAT 20. PAGE 44 A0892
INT/ORG COERCE ARMS/CONT

S64
GARDNER R.N.,"THE SOVIET UNION AND THE UNITED NATIONS." WOR+45 FINAN POL/PAR VOL/ASSN FORCES ECO/TAC DOMIN EDU/PROP LEGIT ADJUD ADMIN ARMS/CONT COERCE ATTIT ALL/VALS...POLICY MAJORIT CONCPT OBS TIME/SEQ TREND STERTYP UN. PAGE 51 A1046
COM INT/ORG USSR

S64
HOFFMANN S.,"CE QU'EN PENSENT LES AMERICAINS." EUR+WWI INT/ORG VOL/ASSN PLAN BAL/PWR DIPLOM DOMIN EDU/PROP REGION ARMS/CONT DRIVE ORD/FREE PWR ...POLICY CONCPT OBS TREND STERTYP COLD/WAR VAL/FREE 20. PAGE 66 A1357
USA+45 ATTIT FRANCE

S64
MAGGS P.B.,"SOVIET VIEWPOINT ON NUCLEAR WEAPONS IN INTERNATIONAL LAW." USSR WOR+45 INT/ORG FORCES DIPLOM ARMS/CONT ATTIT ORD/FREE PWR...POLICY JURID CONCPT OBS TREND CON/ANAL GEN/LAWS VAL/FREE 20. PAGE 93 A1905
COM LAW INT/LAW NUC/PWR

B65
PEACE RESEARCH ABSTRACTS. FUT WOR+45 R+D INT/ORG NAT/G PLAN TEC/DEV BAL/PWR DIPLOM FOR/AID NUC/PWR HEALTH. PAGE 4 A0072
BIBLIOG/A PEACE ARMS/CONT WAR

B65
ADENAUER K.,MEINE ERINNERUNGEN, 1945-53 (VOL. I), 1953-55 (VOL. II). EUR+WWI GERMANY CHIEF FORCES PROB/SOLV DIPLOM ARMS/CONT INGP/REL PEACE SOVEREIGN ...OBS/ENVIR RECORD 20. PAGE 4 A0089
NAT/G BIOG SELF/OBS

B65
CORDIER A.W.,THE QUEST FOR PEACE. WOR+45 NAT/G PLAN BAL/PWR ECO/TAC ARMS/CONT NUC/PWR PWR...ANTHOL UN COLD/WAR. PAGE 30 A0617
PEACE DIPLOM POLICY INT/ORG

B65
KAHN H.,ON ESCALATION; METAPHORS AND SCENARIOS. FORCES DIPLOM ARMS/CONT WAR CIVMIL/REL...INT/LAW 20. PAGE 76 A1548
NUC/PWR ACT/RES INT/ORG ORD/FREE

B65
LEE M.,THE UNITED NATIONS AND WORLD REALITIES. ECO/UNDEV FORCES WAR PEACE ATTIT ROLE WEALTH 20 UN. PAGE 86 A1761
INT/ORG COLONIAL ARMS/CONT DIPLOM

B65
MOSKOWITZ H.,US SECURITY, ARMS CONTROL, AND DISARMAMENT 1961-1965. FORCES DIPLOM DETER WAR WEAPON...CHARTS 20 UN COLD/WAR NATO. PAGE 105 A2154
BIBLIOG/A ARMS/CONT NUC/PWR PEACE

B65
TREFOUSSE H.L.,THE COLD WAR: A BOOK OF DOCUMENTS. ASIA L/A+17C USSR WOR+45 WOR-45 ECO/TAC FOR/AID ARMS/CONT NUC/PWR PEACE ORD/FREE...ANTHOL 20 COLD/WAR KENNEDY/JF EISNHWR/DD. PAGE 145 A2961
BAL/PWR DIPLOM MARXISM

B65
US DEPARTMENT OF DEFENSE,US SECURITY ARMS CONTROL, AND DISARMAMENT 1961-1965 (PAMPHLET). CHINA/COM COM GERMANY/W ISRAEL SPACE USA+45 USSR WOR+45 FORCES EDU/PROP DETER EQUILIB PEACE ALL/VALS...GOV/COMP 20 NATO. PAGE 151 A3077
BIBLIOG/A ARMS/CONT NUC/PWR DIPLOM

B65
US DEPARTMENT OF THE ARMY,NUCLEAR WEAPONS AND THE ATLANTIC ALLIANCE: A BIBLIOGRAPHIC SURVEY. ASIA COM EUR+WWI USA+45 FORCES DIPLOM WEAPON...STAT 20 NATO. PAGE 152 A3108
BIBLIOG/A ARMS/CONT NUC/PWR BAL/PWR

B65
US SENATE COMM AERO SPACE SCI,INTERNATIONAL COOPERATION AND ORGANIZATION FOR OUTER SPACE. FUT USA+45 WOR+45 PROF/ORG VOL/ASSN CONSULT DELIB/GP PLAN TEC/DEV ARMS/CONT GP/REL PEACE 20 UN NASA. PAGE 155 A3167
DIPLOM SPACE R+D NAT/G

B65
WARBEY W.,VIETNAM: THE TRUTH. FRANCE S/ASIA USA+45 VIETNAM CULTURE INT/ORG NAT/G DIPLOM FOR/AID EDU/PROP ARMS/CONT PEACE 20 TREATY NLF UN. PAGE 161 A3274
WAR AGREE

B65
WASKOW A.I.,KEEPING THE WORLD DISARMED. AFR GERMANY/E DIPLOM CONTROL WAR 20 UN. PAGE 161 A3289
ARMS/CONT PEACE FORCES PROB/SOLV

L65
TUCKER R.W.,"PEACE AND WAR." UNIV CULTURE SOCIETY INT/ORG NAT/G ACT/RES DOMIN DETER WAR ATTIT DISPL ...POLICY CONCPT MYTH GEN/LAWS 20. PAGE 145 A2975
PWR COERCE ARMS/CONT PEACE

C65
SCHWEBEL M.,"BEHAVIORAL SCIENCE AND HUMAN SURVIVAL." FORCES ARMS/CONT COERCE NUC/PWR WAR GP/REL NAT/LISM PERCEPT...POLICY PSY ANTHOL BIBLIOG/A 20 COLD/WAR. PAGE 130 A2662
PEACE ACT/RES DIPLOM HEAL

C65
US AIR FORCE ACADEMY,"AMERICAN DEFENSE POLICY." COM INT/ORG TEC/DEV FOR/AID ARMS/CONT DETER NUC/PWR ...POLICY DECISION CONCPT ANTHOL BIBLIOG/A 20 COLD/WAR NATO. PAGE 149 A3054
PLAN FORCES WAR COERCE

B66
AMERICAN ASSEMBLY COLUMBIA U,A WORLD OF NUCLEAR POWERS? FUT WOR+45 ECO/DEV BAL/PWR ECO/TAC CONTROL RISK EFFICIENCY ATTIT PWR...METH/COMP ANTHOL 20. PAGE 7 A0137
NUC/PWR DIPLOM TEC/DEV ARMS/CONT

B66
BLOOMFIELD L.P.,KHRUSHCHEV AND THE ARMS RACE. USA+45 USSR ECO/DEV BAL/PWR EDU/PROP CONFER NUC/PWR ATTIT...CHARTS 20 KHRUSH/N. PAGE 16 A0321
ARMS/CONT COM POLICY DIPLOM

B66
CLARK G.,WORLD PEACE THROUGH WORLD LAW; TWO ALTERNATIVE PLANS. WOR+45 DELIB/GP FORCES TAX CONFER ADJUD SANCTION ARMS/CONT WAR CHOOSE PRIVIL 20 UN COLD/WAR. PAGE 27 A0541
INT/LAW PEACE PLAN INT/ORG

B66
COYLE D.C.,THE UNITED NATIONS AND HOW IT WORKS. ECO/UNDEV DELIB/GP BAL/PWR EDU/PROP ARMS/CONT NUC/PWR WAR 20 UN. PAGE 32 A0648
INT/ORG PEACE DIPLOM INT/TRADE

B66
EKIRCH A.A. JR.,IDEAS, IDEALS, AND AMERICAN DIPLOMACY. USA+45 USA-45 INT/ORG DOMIN COLONIAL ARMS/CONT DETER ISOLAT NAT/LISM...MAJORIT BIBLIOG 19/20 COLD/WAR. PAGE 41 A0834
DIPLOM LEAD PEACE

B66
EPSTEIN F.T.,THE AMERICAN BIBLIOGRAPHY OF RUSSIAN AND EAST EUROPEAN STUDIES FOR 1964. USSR LOC/G NAT/G POL/PAR FORCES ADMIN ARMS/CONT...JURID CONCPT 20 UN. PAGE 42 A0855
BIBLIOG COM MARXISM DIPLOM

B66
GRAHAM I.C.C.,PUBLICATIONS OF THE SOCIAL SCIENCE DEPARTMENT, THE RAND CORPORATION, 1948-1966. USSR WOR+45 NAT/G ARMS/CONT DETER WAR NAT/LISM...SOC GOV/COMP. PAGE 55 A1127
BIBLIOG DIPLOM NUC/PWR FORCES

B66
HALPERIN M.H.,CHINA AND NUCLEAR PROLIFERATION
NUC/PWR

(PAMPHLET). CHINA/COM FUT INDIA USA+45 USSR ARMS/CONT WAR 20 CHINJAP. PAGE 60 A1239 FORCES POLICY DIPLOM

B66
KIM Y.K.,PATTERNS OF COMPETITIVE COEXISTENCE: USA VS. USSR. USA+45 USSR ECO/DEV ECO/UNDEV INT/ORG FOR/AID INT/TRADE ARMS/CONT...BIBLIOG 20 COLD/WAR. PAGE 79 A1618 DIPLOM PEACE BAL/PWR DETER

B66
KUENNE R.E.,THE POLARIS MISSILE STRIKE* A GENERAL ECONOMIC SYSTEMS ANALYSIS. USA+45 USSR NAT/G BAL/PWR ARMS/CONT WAR...MATH PROBABIL COMPUT/IR CHARTS HYPO/EXP SIMUL. PAGE 82 A1689 NUC/PWR FORCES DETER DIPLOM

B66
MAY E.R.,ANXIETY AND AFFLUENCE: 1945-1965. USA+45 DIPLOM FOR/AID ARMS/CONT RACE/REL CONSEN...ANTHOL 20 COLD/WAR KENNEDY/JF EISNHWR/DD TRUMAN/HS BERLIN/BLO. PAGE 97 A1982 ANOMIE ECO/DEV NUC/PWR WEALTH

B66
MAYER P.,THE PACIFIST CONSCIENCE. SECT CREATE ARMS/CONT WAR RACE/REL ATTIT LOVE...ANTHOL PACIFIST WORSHIP FREUD/S GANDHI/M LAO/TZU KING/MAR/L CONSCN/OBJ. PAGE 97 A1984 DIPLOM PACIFISM SUPEGO

B66
SCHWARZ U.,AMERICAN STRATEGY: A NEW PERSPECTIVE. USA+45 USA-45 INT/ORG TEC/DEV BAL/PWR DIPLOM LEAD ARMS/CONT DETER NUC/PWR WAR 20 NATO. PAGE 130 A2659 NAT/G POLICY FORCES PWR

B66
UNITED NATIONS,INTERNATIONAL SPACE BIBLIOGRAPHY. FUT INT/ORG TEC/DEV DIPLOM ARMS/CONT NUC/PWR ...JURID SOC UN. PAGE 149 A3037 BIBLIOG SPACE PEACE R+D

B66
US SENATE COMM AERO SPACE SCI,SOVIET SPACE PROGRAMS, 1962-65; GOALS AND PURPOSES, ACHIEVEMENTS, PLANS, AND INTERNATIONAL IMPLICATIONS. USA+45 USSR R+D FORCES PLAN EDU/PROP PRESS ADJUD ARMS/CONT ATTIT MARXISM. PAGE 155 A3168 CONSULT SPACE FUT DIPLOM

B66
VAN DYKE V.,INTERNATIONAL POLITICS. WOR+45 ECO/DEV ECO/UNDEV INT/ORG BAL/PWR AGREE ARMS/CONT NAT/LISM PEACE PWR...INT/LAW 20 TREATY UN. PAGE 158 A3212 DIPLOM NAT/G WAR SOVEREIGN

B66
WAINHOUSE D.W.,INTERNATIONAL PEACE OBSERVATION: A HISTORY AND FORECAST. INT/ORG PROB/SOLV BAL/PWR AGREE ARMS/CONT COERCE NUC/PWR...PREDICT METH/COMP 20 UN LEAGUE/NAT OAS TREATY. PAGE 160 A3261 PEACE DIPLOM

S66
ORVIK N.,"NATO: THE ROLE OF THE SMALL MEMBERS." EUR+WWI FUT USA+45 CONSULT FORCES PROB/SOLV ARMS/CONT DETER NUC/PWR PWR 20 NATO. PAGE 112 A2298 NAT/G DIPLOM INT/ORG POLICY

C66
BLAISDELL D.C.,"INTERNATIONAL ORGANIZATION." FUT WOR+45 ECO/DEV DELIB/GP FORCES EFFICIENCY PEACE ORD/FREE...INT/LAW 20 UN LEAGUE/NAT NATO. PAGE 15 A0304 BIBLIOG INT/ORG DIPLOM ARMS/CONT

B67
BLOOMFIELD L.,THE UNITED NATIONS AND US FOREIGN POLICY. USA+45 DIPLOM LEAD ARMS/CONT DETER PWR 20 UN. PAGE 15 A0313 INT/ORG PLAN CONFER IDEA/COMP

B67
HALPERIN M.H.,CONTEMPORARY MILITARY STRATEGY. ASIA CHINA/COM USA+45 USSR INT/ORG FORCES ACT/RES PLAN TEC/DEV BAL/PWR COERCE WAR...METH/COMP BIBLIOG 20 NATO. PAGE 60 A1240 DIPLOM NUC/PWR DETER ARMS/CONT

B67
MCBRIDE J.H.,THE TEST BAN TREATY: MILITARY, TECHNOLOGICAL, AND POLITICAL IMPLICATIONS. USA+45 USSR DELIB/GP FORCES LEGIS TEC/DEV BAL/PWR TREATY. PAGE 97 A1995 ARMS/CONT DIPLOM NUC/PWR

B67
PIPER D.C.,THE INTERNATIONAL LAW OF THE GREAT LAKES. CANADA EXTR/IND MUNIC LICENSE ARMS/CONT CRIME...GEOG 19/20. PAGE 116 A2381 CONCPT DIPLOM INT/LAW

B67
SALISBURY H.E.,ORBIT OF CHINA. ASIA CHINA/COM DIPLOM PEACE PWR 20. PAGE 126 A2593 EDU/PROP OBS INT ARMS/CONT

B67
US SENATE COMM ON FOREIGN REL,UNITED STATES ARMAMENT AND DISARMAMENT PROBLEMS. USA+45 AIR BAL/PWR DIPLOM FOR/AID NUC/PWR ORD/FREE SENATE TREATY. PAGE 156 A3190 ARMS/CONT WEAPON FORCES PROB/SOLV

B67
WATERS M.,THE UNITED NATIONS* INTERNATIONAL ORGANIZATION AND ADMINISTRATION. WOR+45 EX/STRUC FORCES DIPLOM LEAD REGION ARMS/CONT REPRESENT INGP/REL ROLE...METH/COMP ANTHOL 20 UN LEAGUE/NAT. PAGE 162 A3291 CONSTN INT/ORG ADMIN ADJUD

L67
GENEVEY P.,"LE DESARMEMENT APRES LE TRAITE DE VERSAILLES." EUR+WWI GERMANY INT/ORG PROB/SOLV CONFER WAR...POLICY PREDICT 20. PAGE 52 A1057 ARMS/CONT PEACE DIPLOM FORCES

S67
"CHINESE STATEMENT ON NUCLEAR PROLIFERATION." CHINA/COM USA+45 USSR DOMIN COLONIAL PWR. PAGE 4 A0078 NUC/PWR BAL/PWR ARMS/CONT DIPLOM

S67
AFRICAN BIBLIOGRAPHIC CENTER,"THE SWORD AND GOVERNMENT: A PRELIMINARY AND SELECTED BIBLIOGRAPHICAL GUIDE TO AFRICAN MILITARY AFFAIRS; PART I." AFR USA+45 USSR INT/ORG POL/PAR FOR/AID COLONIAL ARMS/CONT PWR 20 UN. PAGE 5 A0101 BIBLIOG/A FORCES CIVMIL/REL DIPLOM

S67
CARROLL K.J.,"SECOND STEP TOWARD ARMS CONTROL." WOR+45 INT/ORG VOL/ASSN FORCES PROB/SOLV RISK WEAPON 20 COLD/WAR. PAGE 25 A0503 ARMS/CONT DIPLOM PLAN NUC/PWR

S67
DEUTSCH K.W.,"ARMS CONTROL AND EUROPEAN UNITY* THE NEXT TEN YEARS." USA+45 ELITES NAT/G BAL/PWR DIPLOM NUC/PWR...INT KNO/TEST NATO EEC. PAGE 36 A0742 ARMS/CONT PEACE REGION PLAN

S67
EISENDRATH C.,"THE OUTER SPACE TREATY." CHINA/COM COM USA+45 DIPLOM CONTROL NUC/PWR...INT/LAW 20 UN COLD/WAR TREATY. PAGE 41 A0831 SPACE INT/ORG PEACE ARMS/CONT

S67
FELD B.T.,"A PLEDGE* NO FIRST USE." DELIB/GP BAL/PWR DOMIN DETER. PAGE 45 A0913 ARMS/CONT NUC/PWR DIPLOM PEACE

S67
FOREIGN POLICY ASSOCIATION,"US CONCERN FOR WORLD LAW." USA+45 WOR+45 DELIB/GP JUDGE BAL/PWR CONFER PEACE ORD/FREE 20 UN. PAGE 47 A0962 INT/LAW INT/ORG DIPLOM ARMS/CONT

S67
GRIFFITHS F.,"THE POLITICAL SIDE OF 'DISARMAMENT'." FUT WOR+45 NUC/PWR NAT/LISM PEACE...NEW/IDEA PREDICT METH/COMP GEN/LAWS 20. PAGE 57 A1164 ARMS/CONT DIPLOM

S67
HALL M.,"GERMANY, EAST AND WEST* DANGER AT THE CROSSROADS." GERMANY ELITES CHIEF FORCES DIPLOM ECO/TAC REPAR ARMS/CONT...SOCIALIST 20. PAGE 60 A1227 NAT/LISM ATTIT FASCISM WEAPON

S67
HAZARD J.N.,"POST-DISARMAMENT INTERNATIONAL LAW." FUT USSR WOR+45 INT/ORG DELIB/GP FORCES DETER EQUILIB SOVEREIGN MARXISM 20 UN. PAGE 63 A1301 INT/LAW ARMS/CONT PWR PLAN

S67
JACKSON W.G.F.,"NUCLEAR PROLIFERATION AND THE GREAT POWERS." FUT UK WOR+45 INT/ORG DOMIN ARMS/CONT DETER ORD/FREE PACIFIST. PAGE 72 A1480 NUC/PWR ATTIT BAL/PWR NAT/LISM

S67
KAHN H.,"CRITERIA FOR LONG-RANGE NUCLEAR CONTROL POLICIES." WOR+45 INT/ORG TEC/DEV DOMIN DETER WAR WEAPON ISOLAT ORD/FREE POLICY. PAGE 76 A1549 NUC/PWR ARMS/CONT BAL/PWR DIPLOM

S67
KRUSCHE H.,"THE STRIVING OF THE KIESINGER-STRAUS GOVERNMENT FOR NUCLEAR WEAPONS IS A THREAT TO EUROPEAN SECURITY." EUR+WWI GERMANY BAL/PWR SANCTION WEAPON PEACE ORD/FREE...MARXIST 20 NATO COLD/WAR. PAGE 82 A1688 ARMS/CONT INT/ORG NUC/PWR DIPLOM

S67
NIEBUHR R.,"THE SOCIAL MYTHS IN THE COLD WAR." USA+45 USSR VIETNAM PROB/SOLV BAL/PWR ARMS/CONT NAT/LISM PWR ALL/IDEOS CONCPT. PAGE 109 A2238 MYTH DIPLOM GOV/COMP

S67
REINTANZ G.,"THE SPACE TREATY." WOR+45 DIPLOM CONTROL ARMS/CONT NUC/PWR WAR...MARXIST 20 COLD/WAR UN TREATY. PAGE 120 A2461 SPACE INT/LAW INT/ORG PEACE

S67
SHARP G.,"THE NEED OF A FUNCTIONAL SUBSTITUTE FOR WAR." FUT UNIV WOR+45 CULTURE SOCIETY INT/ORG CONSULT DELIB/GP ACT/RES CREATE BAL/PWR CONFER ARMS/CONT NUC/PWR 20. PAGE 132 A2696 PEACE WAR DIPLOM PROB/SOLV

S67
SHULMAN M.D.,"'EUROPE' VERSUS 'DETENTE'." USA+45 USSR INT/ORG CONTROL ARMS/CONT DETER 20. PAGE 132 A2711 DIPLOM BAL/PWR NUC/PWR

S67
SUINN R.M.,"THE DISARMAMENT FANTASY* PSYCHOLOGICAL FACTORS THAT MAY PRODUCE WARFARE." DIPLOM RISK ARMS/CONT DETER ANOMIE PERSON GAME. PAGE 140 A2860 DECISION NUC/PWR WAR PSY

S67
VLASCIC I.A.,"THE SPACE TREATY* A PRELIMINARY EVALUATION." FUT USSR WOR+45 R+D ACT/RES TEC/DEV DIPLOM CONFER ARMS/CONT PEACE...PREDICT UN TREATY. SPACE INT/LAW INT/ORG

PAGE 159 A3245 NEUTRAL

S67
WASHBURN A.M.,"NUCLEAR PROLIFERATION IN A REVOLUTIONARY INTERNATIONAL SYSTEM." WOR+45 NAT/G DELIB/GP PLAN TEC/DEV...POLICY 20. PAGE 161 A3287
ARMS/CONT NUC/PWR DIPLOM CONFER

C67
GEHLEN M.P.,"THE POLITICS OF COEXISTENCE: SOVIET METHODS AND MOTIVES." COM USSR NAT/G INT/TRADE EDU/PROP ARMS/CONT DETER KNOWL...CHARTS IDEA/COMP 20 COLD/WAR. PAGE 52 A1056
BIBLIOG PEACE DIPLOM MARXISM

C67
HUDSON G.F.,"THE HARD AND BITTER PEACE; WORLD POLITICS SINCE 1945." ASIA COM S/ASIA USSR WOR+45 COLONIAL WAR...TREND BIBLIOG/A 20 COLD/WAR UN. PAGE 68 A1405
DIPLOM INT/ORG ARMS/CONT BAL/PWR

N67
US SENATE COMM ON FOREIGN REL,ARMS SALES AND FOREIGN POLICY (PAMPHLET). FINAN FOR/AID CONTROL 20. PAGE 156 A3187
ARMS/CONT ADMIN OP/RES DIPLOM

ARMSTRONG H. A1725

ARMSTRONG J.A. A0174

ARMY....ARMY (ALL NATIONS)

ARNOLD G. A0175

ARNOLD G.L. A0176

ARNOLD H.J.P. A0177

ARNOLD/M....MATTHEW ARNOLD

ARON R. A0178,A0179,A0180,A0181,A0182,A0183

ART/METH....FINE AND PERFORMING ARTS

B21
BALFOUR A.J.,ESSAYS SPECULATIVE AND POLITICAL. SEA CULTURE CREATE WAR NAT/LISM PEACE LOVE...ART/METH INT/LAW CONCPT ANTHOL 20 JEWS. PAGE 10 A0211
PHIL/SCI SOCIETY DIPLOM

L21
HALDEMAN E.,"SERIALS OF AN INTERNATIONAL CHARACTER." WOR-45 DIPLOM...ART/METH GEOG HEAL HUM INT/LAW JURID PSY SOC. PAGE 60 A1224
BIBLIOG PHIL/SCI

B22
FICHTE J.G.,ADDRESSES TO THE GERMAN NATION. GERMANY PRUSSIA ELITES NAT/G SECT CREATE INT/TRADE HEREDITY ...ART/METH LING 19 FRANK/PARL. PAGE 45 A0923
NAT/LISM CULTURE EDU/PROP REGION

B41
GRISMER R.,A NEW BIBLIOGRAPHY OF THE LITERATURES OF SPAIN AND SPANISH AMERICA. CHRIST-17C MOD/EUR PRE/AMER SPAIN CULTURE DIPLOM EDU/PROP...ART/METH GEOG HUM PHIL/SCI 20. PAGE 57 A1165
BIBLIOG LAW NAT/G ECO/UNDEV

N46
HOBBS C.C.,SOUTHEAST ASIA, 1935-45: A SELECTED LIST OF REFERENCE BOOKS (PAMPHLET). S/ASIA AGRI INDUS NAT/G SECT DIPLOM WAR...ART/METH GEOG SOC LING 20. PAGE 65 A1346
BIBLIOG/A CULTURE HABITAT

B48
FLOREN LOZANO L.,BIBLIOGRAFIA DE LA BIBLIOGRAFIA DOMINICANA. DOMIN/REP NAT/G DIPLOM EDU/PROP CIVMIL/REL...POLICY ART/METH GEOG PHIL/SCI HIST/WRIT 20. PAGE 47 A0952
BIBLIOG/A BIOG L/A+17C CULTURE

B50
MUGRIDGE D.H.,AMERICAN HISTORY AND CIVILIZATION: LIST OF GUIDES AND ANNOTATED OR SELECTIVE BIBLIOGRAPHIES. NAT/G SECT DIPLOM RACE/REL DISCRIM ATTIT...ART/METH SOC 18/20. PAGE 105 A2164
BIBLIOG/A USA-45 SOCIETY

B51
BISSAINTHE M.,DICTIONNAIRE DE BIBLIOGRAPHIE HAITIENNE. HAITI ELITES AGRI LEGIS DIPLOM INT/TRADE WRITING ORD/FREE CATHISM...ART/METH GEOG 19/20 NEGRO TREATY. PAGE 15 A0295
BIBLIOG L/A+17C SOCIETY NAT/G

B51
US DEPARTMENT OF STATE,LIVRES AMERICAINS TRADUITS EN FRANCAIS ET LIVRES FRANCAIS SUR LES ETATS-UNIS D'AMERIQUE (2ND ED.). FRANCE USA+45 SECT DIPLOM EDU/PROP LEISURE...ART/METH GEOG HUM 20. PAGE 151 A3086
BIBLIOG/A SOC

B51
WABEKE B.H.,A GUIDE TO DUTCH BIBLIOGRAPHIES. BELGIUM INDONESIA NETHERLAND DIPLOM INT/TRADE WAR NAT/LISM KNOWL...ART/METH HUM JURID CON/ANAL 14/20. PAGE 160 A3257
BIBLIOG/A NAT/G CULTURE COLONIAL

B55
TROTIER A.H.,DOCTORAL DISSERTATIONS ACCEPTED BY AMERICAN UNIVERSITIES 1954-55. SECT DIPLOM HEALTH ...ART/METH GEOG INT/LAW SOC LING CHARTS 20. PAGE 145 A2968
BIBLIOG ACADEM USA+45 WRITING

B57
BYRNES R.F.,BIBLIOGRAPHY OF AMERICAN PUBLICATIONS ON EAST CENTRAL EUROPE, 1945-1957 (VOL. XXII). SECT DIPLOM EDU/PROP RACE/REL...ART/METH GEOG JURID SOC LING 20 JEWS. PAGE 23 A0462
BIBLIOG/A COM MARXISM NAT/G

B58
YUAN TUNG-LI,CHINA IN WESTERN LITERATURE. SECT DIPLOM...ART/METH GEOG JURID SOC BIOG CON/ANAL. PAGE 169 A3440
BIBLIOG ASIA CULTURE HUM

B60
SZTARAY Z.,BIBLIOGRAPHY ON HUNGARY. HUNGARY MOD/EUR CULTURE INDUS SECT DIPLOM REV...ART/METH SOC LING 18/20. PAGE 141 A2879
BIBLIOG NAT/G COM MARXISM

B62
COLLISON R.L.,BIBLIOGRAPHIES, SUBJECT AND NATIONAL: A GUIDE TO THEIR CONTENTS, ARRANGEMENT, AND USE (2ND REV. ED.). SECT DIPLOM...ART/METH GEOG HUM PHIL/SCI SOC MATH BIOG 20. PAGE 28 A0569
BIBLIOG/A CON/ANAL BIBLIOG

B62
KIDDER F.E.,THESES ON PAN AMERICAN TOPICS. LAW CULTURE NAT/G SECT DIPLOM HEALTH...ART/METH GEOG SOC 13/20. PAGE 79 A1615
BIBLIOG CHRIST-17C L/A+17C SOCIETY

B62
UNESCO,GENERAL CATALOGUE OF UNESCO PUBLICATIONS AND UNESCO SPONSORED PUBLICATIONS, 1946-1959. WOR+45 ...POLICY ART/METH HUM PHIL/SCI UN. PAGE 148 A3022
BIBLIOG INT/ORG ECO/UNDEV SOC

B63
JAIRAZBHOY R.A.,FOREIGN INFLUENCE IN ANCIENT INDIA. INDIA ELITES SECT DIPLOM EDU/PROP COLONIAL REGION GP/REL...ART/METH LING WORSHIP +/14 GRECO/ROMN MESOPOTAM PERSIA PARTH/SASS. PAGE 73 A1491
CULTURE SOCIETY COERCE DOMIN

B64
ANDREWS D.H.,LATIN AMERICA: A BIBLIOGRAPHY OF PAPERBACK BOOKS. SECT INT/TRADE EDU/PROP WAR GOV/REL ADJUST NAT/LISM ATTIT...ART/METH LING BIOG 20. PAGE 8 A0160
BIBLIOG L/A+17C CULTURE NAT/G

B64
KITCHEN H.,A HANDBOOK OF AFRICAN AFFAIRS. ECO/UNDEV CREATE DIPLOM COLONIAL RACE/REL...ART/METH GEOG CHARTS 20. PAGE 80 A1646
AFR NAT/G INT/ORG FORCES

B64
RAGHAVAN M.D.,INDIA IN CEYLONESE HISTORY, SOCIETY AND CULTURE. CEYLON INDIA S/ASIA LAW SOCIETY INT/TRADE ATTIT...ART/METH JURID SOC LING 20. PAGE 119 A2433
DIPLOM CULTURE SECT STRUCT

S67
EGBERT D.D.,"POLITICS AND ART IN COMMUNIST BULGARIA" BULGARIA COM USSR CULTURE DIPLOM INGP/REL TOTALISM...TREND 20. PAGE 40 A0825
CREATE ART/METH CONTROL MARXISM

ARTHUR/CA....PRESIDENT CHESTER ALAN ARTHUR

ARTIFACTS....SEE THING/STOR

ARTISTIC ACHIEVEMENT....SEE CREATE

ASA ....ASSOCIATION OF SOUTH-EAST ASIA

S62
FISCHER G.,"UNE NOUVELLE ORGANIZATION REGIONALE: L'ASA." S/ASIA WOR+45 ECO/UNDEV VOL/ASSN PERCEPT RIGID/FLEX...TIME/SEQ 20 ASA. PAGE 46 A0935
INT/ORG DRIVE REGION

ASAMOAH O.Y. A0184

ASHER R.E. A0185,A0186

ASHFORD D.E. A0187

ASHRAF S. A0188

ASIA....SEE ALSO APPROPRIATE TIME/SPACE/CULTURE INDEX

N
INDIAN COUNCIL WORLD AFFAIRS,SELECT ARTICLES ON CURRENT AFFAIRS (BIBLIOGRAPHICAL SERIES: 7). AFR ASIA COM EUR+WWI S/ASIA UK COLONIAL NUC/PWR PEACE ATTIT...INT/LAW SOC 20. PAGE 70 A1437
BIBLIOG DIPLOM INT/ORG ECO/UNDEV

N
ANNALS OF THE AMERICAN ACADEMY OF POLITICAL AND SOCIAL SCIENCE. AFR ASIA S/ASIA WOR+45 POL/PAR DIPLOM CRIME REV...SOC BIOG 20. PAGE 1 A0004
BIBLIOG/A NAT/G CULTURE ATTIT

N
INTERNATIONAL STUDIES. ASIA S/ASIA WOR+45 ECO/UNDEV INT/ORG NAT/G LEAD ATTIT WEALTH...SOC 20. PAGE 1 A0012
BIBLIOG/A DIPLOM INT/LAW INT/TRADE

N
JOURNAL OF ASIAN STUDIES. CULTURE ECO/DEV SECT DIPLOM EDU/PROP WAR NAT/LISM...PHIL/SCI SOC 20. PAGE 1 A0013
BIBLIOG ASIA S/ASIA

NAT/G

N

NEUE POLITISCHE LITERATUR. AFR ASIA EUR+WWI GERMANY RUSSIA SOCIETY ECO/DEV ECO/UNDEV PLAN PROB/SOLV LEAD MARXISM...PHIL/SCI CONCPT 20. PAGE 1 A0021 — BIBLIOG DIPLOM COM NAT/G

N

DAILY SUMMARY OF THE JAPANESE PRESS. NAT/G DIPLOM LEAD 20 CHINJAP. PAGE 2 A0031 — BIBLIOG PRESS ASIA ATTIT

N

CHINA QUARTERLY. COM AGRI INDUS ACADEM POL/PAR INT/TRADE CONFER GOV/REL...TIME/SEQ CON/ANAL INDEX 20. PAGE 2 A0032 — BIBLIOG/A ASIA DIPLOM POLICY

N

AMERICAN BIBLIOGRAPHIC SERVICE,QUARTERLY CHECKLIST OF ORIENTAL STUDIES. CULTURE LOC/G NAT/G DIPLOM ...HIST/WRIT CON/ANAL 20. PAGE 7 A0141 — BIBLIOG S/ASIA ASIA

N

ASIA FOUNDATION,LIBRARY NOTES. LAW CONSTN CULTURE SOCIETY ECO/UNDEV INT/ORG NAT/G COLONIAL LEAD REGION NAT/LISM ATTIT 20 UN. PAGE 9 A0189 — BIBLIOG/A ASIA S/ASIA DIPLOM

N

CORDIER H.,BIBLIOTECA SINICA. SOCIETY STRUCT SECT DIPLOM COLONIAL...GEOG SOC CON/ANAL. PAGE 30 A0618 — BIBLIOG/A NAT/G CULTURE ASIA

N

KYRIAK T.E.,ASIAN DEVELOPMENTS: A BIBLIOGRAPHY. INDONESIA KOREA/N VIETNAM/N CULTURE SOCIETY ECO/UNDEV NAT/G DIPLOM...SOC TREND 20 MONGOLIA. PAGE 83 A1699 — BIBLIOG/A ALL/IDEOS S/ASIA ASIA

N

KYRIAK T.E.,CHINA: A BIBLIOGRAPHY. ASIA CHINA/COM AGRI FINAN INDUS NAT/G INT/TRADE PRESS...SOC 20. PAGE 83 A1700 — BIBLIOG/A MARXISM TOP/EX POL/PAR

N

US CONSOLATE GENERAL HONG KONG,REVIEW OF THE HONG KONG CHINESE PRESS. ECO/UNDEV LOC/G NAT/G PLAN DIPLOM EDU/PROP LEAD GP/REL MARXISM...POLICY INDEX 20. PAGE 150 A3073 — BIBLIOG/A ASIA PRESS ATTIT

N

US CONSULATE GENERAL HONG KONG,CURRENT BACKGROUND. CHINA/COM ECO/UNDEV LOC/G NAT/G PLAN DIPLOM EDU/PROP LEAD REV ATTIT...POLICY INDEX 20. PAGE 151 A3074 — BIBLIOG/A MARXIST ASIA PRESS

N

US CONSULATE GENERAL HONG KONG,SURVEY OF CHINA MAINLAND PRESS. CHINA/COM ECO/UNDEV LOC/G NAT/G PLAN DIPLOM EDU/PROP LEAD REV ATTIT...POLICY INDEX 20. PAGE 151 A3075 — BIBLIOG/A MARXIST ASIA PRESS

N

US CONSULATE GENERAL HONG KONG,US CONSULATE GENERAL, HONG KONG, PRESS SUMMARIES. CHINA/COM ECO/UNDEV LOC/G NAT/G PLAN DIPLOM EDU/PROP LEAD REV ATTIT...POLICY INDEX 20. PAGE 151 A3076 — BIBLIOG/A MARXIST ASIA PRESS

NLO

WHITE J.A.,THE DIPLOMACY OF THE RUSSO-JAPANESE WAR. ASIA KOREA RUSSIA FORCES CONFER CONTROL PEACE ...BIBLIOG 19 CHINJAP. PAGE 164 A3336 — DIPLOM WAR BAL/PWR

B15

FARIES J.C.,THE RISE OF INTERNATIONALISM. ASIA MOD/EUR NAT/G VOL/ASSN DELIB/GP BAL/PWR EDU/PROP ARMS/CONT RIGID/FLEX TREND. PAGE 44 A0899 — INT/ORG DIPLOM PEACE

B22

WALSH E.,THE HISTORY AND NATURE OF INTERNATIONAL RELATIONS. ASIA L/A+17C MOD/EUR USA-45 WOR-45 NAT/G FORCES TOP/EX BAL/PWR REGION ATTIT ORD/FREE RESPECT ...CONCPT HIST/WRIT TREND. PAGE 161 A3270 — INT/ORG TIME/SEQ DIPLOM

S26

COHEN P.A.,"WANG T'AO AND INCIPIENT CHINESE NATIONALISM." ASIA ADMIN ATTIT 19/20 BUREAUCRCY. PAGE 28 A0563 — NAT/LISM ISOLAT CONSERVE DIPLOM

B38

FLEMMING D.,THE UNITED STATES AND WORLD ORGANIZATION, 1920-1933. ASIA FUT WOR-45 NAT/G TOP/EX DIPLOM ECO/TAC EDU/PROP LEGIT COERCE WAR ...TIME/SEQ LEAGUE/NAT 20 CHINJAP. PAGE 47 A0951 — USA-45 INT/ORG PEACE

B38

GRISWOLD A.W.,THE FAR EASTERN POLICY OF THE UNITED STATES. ASIA S/ASIA USA-45 INT/ORG INT/TRADE WAR NAT/LISM...BIBLIOG 19/20 LEAGUE/NAT ROOSEVLT/T ROOSEVLT/F WILSON/W TREATY. PAGE 57 A1166 — DIPLOM POLICY CHIEF

B39

KERNER R.J.,NORTHEAST ASIA: A SELECTED BIBLIOGRAPHY (2 VOLS.). KOREA RUSSIA NAT/G DIPLOM...GEOG 19/20 CHINJAP. PAGE 78 A1599 — BIBLIOG ASIA SOCIETY CULTURE

B39

TAGGART F.J.,ROME AND CHINA. MEDIT-7 INT/ORG NAT/G FORCES LEGIS TOP/EX PLAN PWR SOVEREIGN...CHARTS TOT/POP ROM/EMP. PAGE 141 A2883 — ASIA WAR

B40

CONOVER H.F.,FOREIGN RELATIONS OF THE UNITED STATES: A LIST OF RECENT BOOKS (PAMPHLET). ASIA CANADA L/A+17C UK INT/ORG INT/TRADE TARIFFS NEUTRAL WAR PEACE...INT/LAW CON/ANAL 20 CHINJAP. PAGE 29 A0592 — BIBLIOG/A USA-45 DIPLOM

B40

CONOVER H.F.,JAPAN-ECONOMIC DEVELOPMENT AND FOREIGN POLICY, A SELECTED LIST OF REFERENCES (PAMPHLET). CULTURE FINAN INDUS NAT/G FORCES INT/TRADE WAR ...SOC TREND 20 CHINJAP. PAGE 29 A0593 — BIBLIOG ASIA ECO/DEV DIPLOM

C40

FAHS C.B.,"GOVERNMENT IN JAPAN." FINAN FORCES LEGIS TOP/EX BUDGET INT/TRADE EDU/PROP SOVEREIGN ...CON/ANAL BIBLIOG/A 20 CHINJAP. PAGE 43 A0884 — ASIA DIPLOM NAT/G ADMIN

B42

CORBETT P.E.,POST WAR WORLDS. ASIA EUR+WWI FUT S/ASIA USA-45 ECO/DEV ECO/UNDEV NAT/G DELIB/GP FORCES PLAN ROUTINE ATTIT PWR 20. PAGE 30 A0613 — WOR-45 INT/ORG

B45

NELSON M.F.,KOREA AND THE OLD ORDERS IN EASTERN ASIA. ASIA FRANCE KOREA RUSSIA DELIB/GP INT/TRADE DOMIN CONTROL WAR ORD/FREE...POLICY BIBLIOG. PAGE 108 A2218 — DIPLOM BAL/PWR ATTIT CONSERVE

B45

US DEPARTMENT OF STATE,PUBLICATIONS OF THE DEPARTMENT OF STATE: A LIST CUMULATIVE FROM OCTOBER 1, 1929 (PAMPHLET). ASIA EUR+WWI ISLAM L/A+17C USA-45 ADJUD...INT/LAW 20. PAGE 151 A3082 — BIBLIOG DIPLOM INT/TRADE

C45

NELSON M.F.,"KOREA AND THE OLD ORDERS IN EASTERN ASIA." KOREA WOR-45 DELIB/GP INT/TRADE DOMIN CONTROL WAR ATTIT ORD/FREE CONSERVE...POLICY TREATY. PAGE 108 A2217 — BIBLIOG DIPLOM BAL/PWR ASIA

B48

CLYDE P.H.,THE FAR EAST: A HISTORY OF THE IMPACT OF THE WEST ON EASTERN ASIA. CHINA/COM CULTURE INT/TRADE DOMIN COLONIAL WAR PWR...CHARTS BIBLIOG 19/20 CHINJAP. PAGE 27 A0554 — DIPLOM ASIA

B48

PELCOVITS N.A.,OLD CHINA HANDS AND THE FOREIGN OFFICE. ASIA BURMA UK ECO/UNDEV NAT/G ECO/TAC FOR/AID TARIFFS DOMIN COLONIAL GOV/REL SOVEREIGN 19 HONG/KONG TREATY. PAGE 114 A2348 — INT/TRADE ATTIT DIPLOM

B50

BROOKINGS INSTITUTION,MAJOR PROBLEMS OF UNITED STATES FOREIGN POLICY. AFR ASIA INDIA UK USA+45 USSR BAL/PWR FOR/AID WAR PEACE TOTALISM MARXISM SOCISM 20 CHINJAP COLD/WAR. PAGE 19 A0393 — DIPLOM POLICY ORD/FREE

B50

GLEASON J.H.,THE GENESIS OF RUSSOPHOBIA IN GREAT BRITAIN: A STUDY OF THE INTERACTION OF POLICY AND OPINION. ASIA RUSSIA UK NAT/G AGREE CONTROL REV WAR LOVE PWR TREATY 19. PAGE 53 A1080 — DIPLOM POLICY DOMIN COLONIAL

S50

WITTFOGEL K.A.,"RUSSIA AND ASIA: PROBLEMS OF CONTEMPORARY AREA STUDIES AND INTERNATIONAL RELATIONS." ASIA COM USA+45 SOCIETY NAT/G DIPLOM ECO/TAC FOR/AID EDU/PROP KNOWL...HIST/WRIT TOT/POP 20. PAGE 166 A3373 — ECO/DEV ADMIN RUSSIA USSR

B51

WELLES S.,SEVEN DECISIONS THAT SHAPED HISTORY. ASIA FRANCE FUT USA+45 WOR+45 WOR-45 CONSTN STRUCT INT/ORG NAT/G ACT/RES EDU/PROP DRIVE...POLICY CONCPT TIME/SEQ TREND TOT/POP UN 20 CHINJAP. PAGE 163 A3315 — USA-45 DIPLOM WAR

B51

WHITE L.C.,INTERNATIONAL NON-GOVERNMENTAL ORGANIZATIONS. AFR ASIA COM EUR+WWI USA+45 WOR+45 INT/ORG DIPLOM INT/TRADE ALL/VALS...HUM FAO ILO EEC 20. PAGE 164 A3337 — VOL/ASSN CONSULT

S51

GYR J.,"ANALYSIS OF COMMITTEE MEMBER BEHAVIOUR IN FOUR CULTURES." ASIA ISLAM L/A+17C USA+45 INT/ORG VOL/ASSN LEGIT ATTIT...INT DEEP/QU SAMP CHARTS 20. PAGE 58 A1200 — DELIB/GP CULTURE

B52

BASSETT R.,DEMOCRACY AND FOREIGN POLICY: A CASE HISTORY, THE SINOJAPANESE DISPUTE, 1931-1933. ASIA UK 20 CHINJAP. PAGE 11 A0233 — DIPLOM WAR INT/ORG SANCTION

B52

FIFIELD R.H.,WOODROW WILSON AND THE FAR EAST. ASIA CHIEF BAL/PWR CONFER COLONIAL ARMS/CONT WAR ...TIME/SEQ NAT/COMP BIBLIOG 19/20 WILSON/W LEAGUE/NAT PRESIDENT. PAGE 45 A0926 — DIPLOM DELIB/GP INT/ORG

B52

MACARTHUR D.,REVITALIZING A NATION. ASIA COM FUT KOREA WOR+45 NAT/G FOR/AID TAX GIVE WAR ATTIT SOCISM 20 CHINJAP EUROPE. PAGE 92 A1885 — LEAD FORCES TOP/EX POLICY

B52

RIGGS F.W.,FORMOSA UNDER CHINESE NATIONALIST RULE. CHINA/COM USA+45 CONSTN AGRI FINAN LABOR LOC/G — ASIA FOR/AID

NAT/G POL/PAR FORCES HEALTH KNOWL...STAT WORK VAL/FREE 20. PAGE 121 A2479
DIPLOM

B52
U OF MICH SURVEY RESEARCH CTR,AMERICA'S ROLE IN WORLD AFFAIRS. ASIA COM EUR+WWI USA+45 USSR FOR/AID WAR AUTHORIT ORD/FREE...DEEP/QU 20. PAGE 146 A2986
DIPLOM NAT/G ROLE POLICY

B52
US MUTUAL SECURITY AGENCY,U. S. TECHNICAL AND ECONOMIC ASSISTANCE IN THE FAR EAST (PAMPHLET). ASIA BURMA INDONESIA PHILIPPINE TAIWAN THAILAND USA+45 AGRI INDUS PLAN EDU/PROP ADMIN HEALTH. PAGE 155 A3161
FOR/AID TEC/DEV ECO/UNDEV BUDGET

C52
FIFIELD R.H.,"WOODROW WILSON AND THE FAR EAST." ASIA CHIEF DELIB/GP BAL/PWR CONFER COLONIAL ARMS/CONT WAR...TIME/SEQ NAT/COMP 19/20 WILSON/W LEAGUE/NAT. PAGE 45 A0925
BIBLIOG DIPLOM INT/ORG

B53
FEIS H.,THE CHINA TANGLE. ASIA COM USA+45 USA-45 FORCES ECO/TAC REV ATTIT 20 INTERVENT. PAGE 45 A0910
POLICY DIPLOM WAR FOR/AID

B53
THAYER P.W.,SOUTHEAST ASIA IN THE COMING WORLD. ASIA S/ASIA USA+45 USA-45 SOCIETY INT/ORG ACT/RES ECO/TAC EDU/PROP COERCE TOTALISM ALL/VALS...JURID 20. PAGE 142 A2909
ECO/UNDEV ATTIT FOR/AID DIPLOM

B54
NUSSBAUM D.,A CONCISE HISTORY OF THE LAW OF NATIONS. ASIA CHRIST-17C EUR+WWI ISLAM MEDIT-7 MOD/EUR S/ASIA UNIV WOR+45 WOR-45 SOCIETY STRUCT EXEC ATTIT ALL/VALS...CONCPT HIST/WRIT TIME/SEQ. PAGE 110 A2263
INT/ORG LAW PEACE INT/LAW

L54
CHARLESWORTH J.C.,"AMERICA AND A NEW ASIA." ASIA INDIA ISLAM S/ASIA USA+45 USA-45 ECO/UNDEV NAT/G POL/PAR FORCES FOR/AID DOMIN EDU/PROP COERCE DRIVE ALL/VALS MARXISM SOCISM TOT/POP 20. PAGE 26 A0522
ECO/TAC DIPLOM NAT/LISM

S54
WOLFERS A.,"COLLECTIVE SECURITY AND THE WAR IN KOREA." ASIA KOREA USA+45 INT/ORG DIPLOM ROUTINE ...GEN/LAWS UN COLD/WAR 20. PAGE 166 A3381
ACT/RES LEGIT

B55
BUSS C.,THE FAR EAST: A HISTORY OF RECENT AND CONTEMPORARY INTERNATIONAL RELATIONS IN EAST ASIA. WOR+45 WOR-45 CONSTN INT/ORG NAT/G BAL/PWR ATTIT PWR SOVEREIGN...GEOG JURID SOC CONCPT METH/CNCPT 19/20. PAGE 22 A0449
ASIA DIPLOM

B55
JAPANESE STUDIES OF MODERN CHINA. ASIA DIPLOM LEAD REV MARXISM 19/20 CHINJAP. PAGE 43 A0885
BIBLIOG/A SOC

B55
JOY C.T.,HOW COMMUNISTS NEGOTIATE. COM USA+45 CONSTN CULTURE ECO/UNDEV NAT/G CONSULT DELIB/GP FORCES PLAN ECO/TAC DOMIN EDU/PROP LEGIT EXEC ROUTINE COERCE WAR CHOOSE PEACE ATTIT RIGID/FLEX ORD/FREE PWR...POLICY 20. PAGE 75 A1539
ASIA INT/ORG DIPLOM

B55
QUAN K.L.,INTRODUCTION TO ASIA: A SELECTIVE GUIDE TO BACKGROUND READING. ECO/UNDEV NAT/G PROB/SOLV DIPLOM ATTIT 20. PAGE 118 A2424
BIBLIOG/A S/ASIA CULTURE ASIA

B55
TAN C.C.,THE BOXER CATASTROPHE. ASIA UK USSR ELITES POL/PAR VOL/ASSN FORCES PROB/SOLV DIPLOM ADMIN COLONIAL NAT/LISM PEACE TREATY 19/20 BOXER/REBL. PAGE 141 A2885
REV NAT/G WAR

L55
ROSTOW W.W.,"RUSSIA AND CHINA UNDER COMMUNISM." CHINA/COM USSR INTELL STRUCT INT/ORG NAT/G POL/PAR TOP/EX ACT/RES PLAN ADMIN ATTIT ALL/VALS MARXISM ...CONCPT OBS TIME/SEQ TREND GOV/COMP VAL/FREE 20. PAGE 124 A2543
COM ASIA

B56
BALL W.M.,NATIONALISM AND COMMUNISM IN EAST ASIA. ASIA BURMA EUR+WWI KOREA USA+45 ECO/UNDEV NAT/G POL/PAR DIPLOM ECO/TAC FOR/AID EDU/PROP COERCE RACE/REL NAT/LISM DRIVE SOVEREIGN...TREND 20 CHINJAP. PAGE 11 A0214
S/ASIA ATTIT

B56
BROOK D.,THE UNITED NATIONS AND CHINA DILEMMA. CHINA/COM FUT WOR+45 ECO/UNDEV NAT/G DELIB/GP ACT/RES DIPLOM ROUTINE NAT/LISM TOTALISM ATTIT DRIVE...CONCPT OBS TIME/SEQ UN TOT/POP TIME UN 20. PAGE 19 A0390
ASIA INT/ORG BAL/PWR

B56
CHANG C.J.,THE MINORITY GROUPS OF YUNN AN AND CHINESE POLITICAL EXPANSION INTO SOUTHEAST ASIA (DOCTORAL THESIS). ASIA CHINA/COM S/ASIA FORCES TEC/DEV DIPLOM EDU/PROP...GEOG BIBLIOG 20. PAGE 26 A0520
GP/REL REGION DOMIN MARXISM

B56
CONOVER H.F.,A GUIDE TO BIBLIOGRAPHIC TOOLS FOR RESEARCH IN FOREIGN AFFAIRS. AFR ASIA COM EUR+WWI WOR+45 BAL/PWR CON/ANAL. PAGE 30 A0602
BIBLIOG/A R+D DIPLOM INT/ORG

B56
GOODRICH L.,KOREA: A STUDY OF US POLICY IN THE UNITED NATIONS. ASIA USA+45 STRUCT CONSULT DELIB/GP ATTIT DRIVE PWR...JURID GEN/LAWS COLD/WAR 20 UN. PAGE 54 A1103
INT/ORG DIPLOM KOREA

B56
JUAN T.L.,ECONOMIC AND SOCIAL DEVELOPMENT OF MODERN CHINA: A BIBLIOGRAPHICAL GUIDE. ASIA AGRI COM/IND DIST/IND FINAN INDUS DIPLOM...STAT 20. PAGE 75 A1541
BIBLIOG SOC

B56
KIRK G.,THE CHANGING ENVIRONMENT OF INTERNATIONAL RELATIONS. ASIA S/ASIA USA+45 WOR+45 ECO/UNDEV INT/ORG NAT/G FOR/AID EDU/PROP PEACE KNOWL ...PLURIST COLD/WAR TOT/POP 20. PAGE 80 A1634
FUT EXEC DIPLOM

B56
US DEPARTMENT OF STATE,ECONOMIC PROBLEMS OF UNDERDEVELOPED AREAS (PAMPHLET). AFR ASIA ISLAM L/A+17C AGRI FINAN INDUS INT/ORG LABOR INT/TRADE ...PSY SOC 20. PAGE 151 A3090
BIBLIOG ECO/UNDEV TEC/DEV R+D

B56
WU E.,LEADERS OF TWENTIETH-CENTURY CHINA; AN ANNOTATED BIBLIOGRAPHY OF SELECTED CHINESE BIOGRAPHICAL WORKS IN HOOVER LIBRARY. ASIA INDUS POL/PAR DIPLOM ADMIN REV WAR...HUM MGT 20. PAGE 168 A3422
BIBLIOG/A BIOG INTELL CHIEF

B57
CRABB C.,BIPARTISAN FOREIGN POLICY: MYTH OR REALITY. ASIA COM EUR+WWI ISLAM USA+45 USA-45 INT/ORG NAT/G LEGIS TOP/EX PWR CONGRESS 20. PAGE 32 A0649
POL/PAR ATTIT DIPLOM

B57
DEAN V.M.,THE NATURE OF THE NON-WESTERN WORLD. AFR ASIA L/A+17C S/ASIA CULTURE SOCIETY STRATA ECO/DEV DIPLOM ECO/TAC FOR/AID ATTIT DRIVE ALL/VALS ...RELATIV SOC CONCPT TIME/SEQ TREND TOT/POP 20. PAGE 35 A0718
ECO/UNDEV STERTYP NAT/LISM

B57
US SENATE SPEC COMM FOR AID,COMPILATION OF STUDIES AND SURVEYS. AFR ASIA L/A+17C USA+45 ECO/UNDEV AGRI INT/ORG CONSULT TEC/DEV CONFER TOTALISM...NAT/COMP 20 CONGRESS. PAGE 157 A3197
FOR/AID DIPLOM ORD/FREE DELIB/GP

B58
BOWLES C.,IDEAS, PEOPLE AND PEACE. ASIA CHINA/COM FUT INDIA USA+45 USSR ECO/UNDEV INT/ORG LEAD TASK MARXISM 20 NATO UN COLD/WAR. PAGE 18 A0359
PEACE POLICY NAT/G DIPLOM

B58
CHANG H.,WITHIN THE FOUR SEAS. ASIA WAR MORAL MARXISM...IDEA/COMP NAT/COMP 20 CONFUCIUS. PAGE 26 A0521
PEACE DIPLOM KNOWL CULTURE

B58
JAPANESE ASSOCIATION INT. LAW,JAPAN AND THE UNITED NATIONS. SOCIETY ROUTINE ATTIT DRIVE PERCEPT RIGID/FLEX ORD/FREE...METH/CNCPT CON/ANAL CHINJAP UN. PAGE 73 A1497
ASIA INT/ORG

B58
SCHOEDER P.W.,THE AXIS ALLIANCE AND JAPANESE-AMERICAN RELATIONS 1941. ASIA GERMANY UK USA-45 PEACE ATTIT...POLICY BIBLIOG 20 CHINJAP TREATY. PAGE 129 A2641
AGREE DIPLOM WAR

B58
VARG P.A.,MISSIONARIES, CHINESE, AND DIPLOMATS: THE AMERICAN PROTESTANT MISSIONARY MOVEMENT IN CHINA, 1890-1952. ASIA ECO/UNDEV NAT/G PROB/SOLV CAP/ISM EDU/PROP COLONIAL NAT/LISM ATTIT MARXISM...NAT/COMP STERTYP 20 CHINJAP PROTESTANT MISSION. PAGE 158 A3221
CULTURE DIPLOM SECT

B58
YUAN TUNG-LI,CHINA IN WESTERN LITERATURE. SECT DIPLOM...ART/METH GEOG JURID SOC BIOG CON/ANAL. PAGE 169 A3440
BIBLIOG ASIA CULTURE HUM

L58
SNYDER R.N.,"THE UNITED STATES DECISION TO RESIST AGGRESSION IN KOREA." ASIA KOREA S/ASIA USA+45 USA-45 WOR+45 INT/ORG DELIB/GP BAL/PWR COERCE PWR ...CONCPT REC/INT RESIST/INT COLD/WAR 20. PAGE 134 A2753
QUANT METH/CNCPT DIPLOM

S58
JORDAN A.,"MILITARY ASSISTANCE AND NATIONAL POLICY." ASIA FUT USA+45 WOR+45 ECO/DEV ECO/UNDEV INT/ORG NAT/G PLAN ECO/TAC ROUTINE WEAPON ATTIT RIGID/FLEX PWR...CONCPT TREND 20. PAGE 75 A1533
FORCES POLICY FOR/AID DIPLOM

N58
US HOUSE COMM FOREIGN AFFAIRS,HEARINGS ON REVIEW OF THE MUTUAL SECURITY PROGRAMS; EXAMINATION OF SELECTED PROJECTS IN FORMOSA AND PAKISTAN (PAMPHLET). ASIA PAKISTAN TAIWAN INDUS CONSULT DELIB/GP LEGIS BUDGET CONFER DEBATE 20. PAGE 153 A3125
FOR/AID ECO/UNDEV DIPLOM ECO/TAC

B59
ALWAN M.,ALGERIA BEFORE THE UNITED NATIONS. AFR ASIA FRANCE ISLAM S/ASIA CONSTN SOCIETY STRUCT
PLAN RIGID/FLEX

INT/ORG NAT/G ECO/TAC ADMIN COLONIAL NAT/LISM ATTIT PWR...DECISION TREND 420 UN. PAGE 7 A0133 — DIPLOM ALGERIA — B59

AMERICAN FRIENDS OF VIETNAM,AID TO VIETNAM: AN AMERICAN SUCCESS STORY (PAMPHLET). ASIA FUT USA+45 VIETNAM ECO/UNDEV WAR CIVMIL/REL GOV/REL...ANTHOL 20. PAGE 7 A0148 — DIPLOM NAT/G FOR/AID FORCES — B59

CAREW-HUNT R.C.,BOOKS ON COMMUNISM. NAT/G POL/PAR DIPLOM REV...BIOG 19/20. PAGE 24 A0481 — BIBLIOG/A MARXISM COM ASIA — B59

CHINA INSTITUTE OF AMERICA.,CHINA AND THE UNITED NATIONS. CHINA/COM FUT STRUCT EDU/PROP LEGIT ADMIN ATTIT KNOWL ORD/FREE PWR...OBS RECORD STAND/INT TIME/SEQ UN LEAGUE/NAT UNESCO 20. PAGE 26 A0531 — ASIA INT/ORG — B59

FREE L.A.,SIX ALLIES AND A NEUTRAL. ASIA COM EUR+WWI FRANCE GERMANY/W INDIA S/ASIA UK USA+45 INT/ORG NAT/G NUC/PWR PEACE ATTIT PERCEPT RIGID/FLEX ALL/VALS...STAT REC/INT COLD/WAR 20 CHINJAP. PAGE 48 A0992 — PSY DIPLOM — B59

GILBERT R.,GENOCIDE IN TIBET. ASIA SECT CHIEF DIPLOM 20. PAGE 52 A1072 — MARXISM MURDER WAR GP/REL — B59

GORDENKER L.,THE UNITED NATIONS AND THE PEACEFUL UNIFICATION OF KOREA. ASIA LAW LOC/G CONSULT ACT/RES DIPLOM DOMIN LEGIT ADJUD ADMIN ORD/FREE SOVEREIGN...INT GEN/METH UN COLD/WAR 20. PAGE 54 A1109 — DELIB/GP KOREA INT/ORG — B59

NAHM A.C.,JAPANESE PENETRATION OF KOREA, 1894-1910. ASIA KOREA NAT/G...POLICY 20 CHINJAP. PAGE 107 A2192 — BIBLIOG/A DIPLOM WAR COLONIAL — B59

PHADINIS U.,DOCUMENTS ON ASIAN AFFAIRS: A SELECT BIBLIOGRAPHY. ASIA...SOC 20. PAGE 116 A2372 — BIBLIOG NAT/G DIPLOM — B59

THOMAS N.,THE PREREQUISITES FOR PEACE. ASIA EUR+WWI FUT ISLAM S/ASIA WOR+45 FORCES PLAN BAL/PWR EDU/PROP LEGIT ATTIT PWR...SOCIALIST CONCPT COLD/WAR 20 UN. PAGE 143 A2924 — INT/ORG ORD/FREE ARMS/CONT PEACE — B59

VINACKE H.M.,A HISTORY OF THE FAR EAST IN MODERN TIMES (6TH ED.). KOREA S/ASIA USSR CONSTN CULTURE STRATA ECO/UNDEV NAT/G CHIEF FOR/AID INT/TRADE GP/REL...SOC NAT/COMP 19/20 CHINJAP. PAGE 159 A3235 — STRUCT ASIA — B59

YOUNG J.,CHECKLIST OF MICROFILM REPRODUCTIONS OF SELECTED ARCHIVES OF THE JAPANESE ARMY, NAVY, AND OTHER GOVT AGENCIES, 1868-1945. DELIB/GP LEGIS DIPLOM EDU/PROP CIVMIL/REL 19/20 CHINJAP. PAGE 169 A3436 — BIBLIOG ASIA FORCES WAR — S59

KOHN L.Y.,"ISRAEL AND NEW NATION STATES OF ASIA AND AFRICA." AFR ASIA FUT S/ASIA VOL/ASSN TEC/DEV NAT/LISM RIGID/FLEX SKILL WEALTH...RELATIV OBS TREND CON/ANAL 20. PAGE 81 A1663 — ECO/UNDEV ECO/TAC FOR/AID ISRAEL — S59

QUIGLEY H.S.,"TOWARD REAPPRAISAL OF OUR CHINA POLICY." CHINA/COM USA+45 INT/ORG PLAN ECO/TAC PERCEPT ORD/FREE...DECISION PSY CON/ANAL GEN/METH VAL/FREE 20. PAGE 118 A2427 — ASIA KNOWL DIPLOM — B60

EMERSON R.,FROM EMPIRE TO NATION: THE RISE TO SELF-ASSERTION OF ASIAN AND AFRICAN PEOPLES. S/ASIA CULTURE NAT/G SECT DIPLOM ATTIT SOVEREIGN MARXISM ...POLICY BIBLIOG 19/20. PAGE 41 A0847 — NAT/LISM COLONIAL AFR ASIA — B60

FOOTMAN D.,INTERNATIONAL COMMUNISM. ASIA EUR+WWI FRANCE FUT GERMANY MOD/EUR S/ASIA USA-45 WOR+45 WOR-45 INTELL LABOR TOTALISM MARXISM WORK 20. PAGE 47 A0958 — COM INT/ORG STRUCT REV — B60

KENNAN G.F.,RUSSIA AND THE WEST. ASIA COM EUR+WWI GERMANY UK USA+45 USA-45 USSR INT/ORG NAT/G VOL/ASSN DOMIN REV WAR PWR...TIME/SEQ 20. PAGE 78 A1590 — EXEC DIPLOM — B60

LATIFI D.,INDIA AND UNITED STATES AID. ASIA INDIA UK USA+45 AGRI FINAN INDUS COLONIAL ORD/FREE SOVEREIGN WEALTH...METH/COMP 20. PAGE 85 A1743 — FOR/AID DIPLOM ECO/UNDEV — B60

MENEZES A.J.,O BRASIL E O MUNDO ASIO-AFRICANO (REV. ED.). AFR ASIA BRAZIL WOR+45 INT/TRADE ORD/FREE PWR SOVEREIGN...POLICY 20. PAGE 99 A2040 — DIPLOM BAL/PWR LEAD ECO/UNDEV — B60

MORAES F.,THE REVOLT IN TIBET. ASIA CHINA/COM INDIA CULTURE CONTROL COERCE WAR TOTALISM...POLICY SOC WORSHIP 20 TIBET INTERVENT. PAGE 104 A2127 — COLONIAL FORCES DIPLOM ORD/FREE — B60

MOUSKHELY M.,L'URSS ET LES PAYS DE L'EST. ASIA COM S/ASIA USSR PRESS...SOC 20. PAGE 105 A2156 — BIBLIOG/A DIPLOM ATTIT — B60

SALETORE B.A.,INDIA'S DIPLOMATIC RELATIONS WITH THE EAST. ASIA CEYLON INDIA NEPAL S/ASIA CULTURE 7/14 PERSIA. PAGE 126 A2591 — DIPLOM NAT/COMP ETIQUET — B60

SETON-WATSON H.,NEITHER WAR NOR PEACE. ASIA USSR WOR+45 ELITES INT/ORG NAT/G EX/STRUC FORCES BAL/PWR ECO/TAC EDU/PROP COERCE NAT/LISM ORD/FREE WEALTH TOT/POP 20. PAGE 131 A2688 — ATTIT PWR DIPLOM TOTALISM — B60

WHITING A.S.,CHINA CROSSES THE YALU: THE DECISION TO ENTER THE KOREAN WAR. ASIA CHINA/COM KOREA ECO/UNDEV R+D INT/ORG TOP/EX ACT/RES BAL/PWR ATTIT PWR...GEN/METH 20. PAGE 164 A3338 — PLAN COERCE WAR — S60

GINSBURGS G.,"PEKING-LHASA-NEW DELHI." CHINA/COM FUT INDIA S/ASIA KIN NAT/G PROVS SECT FORCES BAL/PWR ECO/TAC DOMIN EDU/PROP LEGIT ADMIN REGION GUERRILLA PWR...TREND TIBET 20. PAGE 52 A1074 — ASIA COERCE DIPLOM — S60

HAVILAND H.F.,"PROBLEMS OF AMERICAN FOREIGN POLICY." ASIA COM USA+45 WOR+45 INT/ORG NAT/G CONSULT ECO/TAC FOR/AID DOMIN COERCE NUC/PWR ATTIT DRIVE ORD/FREE PWR RESPECT SKILL...POLICY GEOG OBS SAMP TREND GEN/METH METH COLD/WAR UN 20. PAGE 63 A1292 — ECO/UNDEV FORCES DIPLOM — S60

KEYFITZ N.,"WESTERN PERSPECTIVES AND ASIAN PROBLEMS." ASIA EUR+WWI S/ASIA SOCIETY FOR/AID ...POLICY SOC CONCPT STERTYP WORK TOT/POP 20. PAGE 78 A1604 — CULTURE ATTIT — C60

WRIGGINS W.H.,"CEYLON: DILEMMAS OF A NEW NATION." ASIA CEYLON CONSTN STRUCT POL/PAR SECT FORCES DIPLOM GOV/REL NAT/LISM...CHARTS BIBLIOG 20. PAGE 167 A3399 — PROB/SOLV NAT/G ECO/UNDEV — B61

ASIA SOCIETY,AMERICAN INSTITUTIONS ANS ORGANIZATIONS INTERESTED IN ASIA; A REFERENCE DIRECTORY (2ND ED.). ASIA USA+45 CULTURE SECT DIPLOM EDU/PROP...INDEX 20. PAGE 9 A0190 — VOL/ASSN ACADEM PROF/ORG — B61

CARNELL F.,THE POLITICS OF THE NEW STATES: A SELECT ANNOTATED BIBLIOGRAPHY WITH SPECIAL REFERENCE TO THE COMMONWEALTH. CONSTN ELITES LABOR NAT/G POL/PAR EX/STRUC DIPLOM ADJUD ADMIN...GOV/COMP 20 COMMONWLTH. PAGE 24 A0496 — BIBLIOG/A AFR ASIA COLONIAL — B61

DALLIN D.J.,SOVIET FOREIGN POLICY AFTER STALIN. ASIA CHINA/COM EUR+WWI GERMANY IRAN UK YUGOSLAVIA INT/ORG NAT/G VOL/ASSN FORCES TOP/EX BAL/PWR DOMIN EDU/PROP COERCE ATTIT PWR 20. PAGE 33 A0679 — COM DIPLOM USSR — B61

FLEMING D.F.,THE COLD WAR AND ITS ORIGINS: 1950-1960 (VOL. II). ASIA FUT HUNGARY POLAND WOR+45 TEC/DEV DOMIN NUC/PWR REV PEACE...T 20 COLD/WAR EISNHWR/DD SUEZ. PAGE 46 A0946 — MARXISM DIPLOM BAL/PWR — B61

FLEMING D.F.,THE COLD WAR AND ITS ORIGINS: 1917-1950 (VOL. I). ASIA USSR WOR+45 WOR-45 TEC/DEV FOR/AID NUC/PWR REV WAR PEACE FASCISM...T 20 COLD/WAR NATO BERLIN/BLO. PAGE 46 A0947 — DIPLOM MARXISM BAL/PWR — B61

FRIEDMANN W.G.,JOINT INTERNATIONAL BUSINESS VENTURES. ASIA ISLAM L/A+17C ECO/DEV DIST/IND FINAN PROC/MFG FACE/GP LG/CO NAT/G VOL/ASSN CONSULT EX/STRUC PLAN ADMIN ROUTINE WEALTH...OLD/LIB WORK 20. PAGE 49 A1004 — ECO/UNDEV INT/TRADE — B61

LUKACS J.,A HISTORY OF THE COLD WAR. ASIA COM EUR+WWI USA+45 USA-45 INT/ORG NAT/G DELIB/GP ACT/RES BAL/PWR DIPLOM DOMIN EDU/PROP LEGIT DRIVE ORD/FREE...TREND COLD/WAR 20. PAGE 91 A1872 — PWR TIME/SEQ USSR — B61

SSU-YU T.,JAPANESE STUDIES ON JAPAN AND THE FAR EAST: A SHORT BIOGRAPHICAL AND BIBLIOGRAPHICAL INTRODUCTION. ASIA CULTURE ECO/UNDEV NAT/G DIPLOM 20 CHINJAP. PAGE 136 A2795 — BIBLIOG SOC — B61

WARNER D.,HURRICANE FROM CHINA. ASIA CHINA/COM FUT L/A+17C USA+45 CULTURE NAT/G FORCES TOP/EX FOR/AID DRIVE PWR...CONCPT TIME/SEQ SEATO WORK 20. PAGE 161 A3284 — ATTIT TREND REV — B61

YUAN TUNG-LI,A GUIDE TO DOCTORAL DISSERTATIONS BY CHINESE STUDENTS IN AMERICA, 1905-1960. ASIA CULTURE SOCIETY ECO/UNDEV NAT/G PROB/SOLV DIPLOM LEAD ATTIT...HUM SOC STAT 20. PAGE 169 A3441 — BIBLIOG ACADEM ACT/RES OP/RES — L61

HOYT E.C.,"UNITED STATES REACTION TO THE KOREAN — ASIA

ATTACK." COM KOREA USA+45 CONSTN DELIB/GP FORCES PLAN ECO/TAC DOMIN EDU/PROP LEGIT ROUTINE COERCE WAR ATTIT DISPL RIGID/FLEX ORD/FREE PWR...POLICY INT/LAW TREND UN 20. PAGE 68 A1402
INT/ORG BAL/PWR DIPLOM

S61
"CRITERIA FOR ALLOCATING INVESTMENT RESOURCES AMONG VARIOUS FIELDS OF DEVELOPMENT IN UNDERDEVELOPED ECONOMIES." ASIA AGRI INT/ORG CAP/ISM BAL/PAY EFFICIENCY PROFIT WEALTH...STAT 20 UN. PAGE 3 A0061
BIBLIOG/A ECO/UNDEV PLAN TEC/DEV

S61
BARNET R.,"RUSSIA, CHINA, AND THE WORLD: THE SOVIET ATTITUDE ON DISARMAMENT (PART 3)." ASIA CHINA/COM FUT INT/ORG NAT/G POL/PAR VOL/ASSN ARMS/CONT ATTIT ...POLICY CONCPT TIME/SEQ TREND TOT/POP VAL/FREE 20. PAGE 11 A0226
COM PLAN TOTALISM USSR

S61
DANIELS R.V.,"THE CHINESE REVOLUTION IN RUSSIAN PERSPECTIVE." ASIA CHINA/COM COM USSR INTELL INT/ORG TOP/EX REV TOTALISM PWR...POLICY WORK VAL/FREE 20. PAGE 33 A0680
POL/PAR PLAN

S61
ZAGORIA D.S.,"SINO-SOVIET FRICTION IN UNDERDEVELOPED AREAS." ASIA CHINA/COM COM ACT/RES PLAN ATTIT ORD/FREE PWR COLD/WAR 20. PAGE 169 A3443
ECO/UNDEV ECO/TAC INT/TRADE USSR

S61
ZAGORIA D.S.,"THE FUTURE OF SINO-SOVIET RELATIONS." CHINA/COM INT/ORG NAT/G POL/PAR VOL/ASSN ACT/RES PLAN PERSON...METH/CNCPT TIME/SEQ TOT/POP VAL/FREE 20 MAO KHRUSH/N. PAGE 169 A3444
ASIA COM TOTALISM USSR

B62
CLUBB O.E. JR.,THE UNITED STATES AND THE SINO-SOVIET BLOC IN SOUTHEAST ASIA. ASIA CHINA/COM COM USA+45 USSR ECO/UNDEV INT/ORG NAT/G FORCES TOP/EX PLAN ECO/TAC DOMIN COERCE GUERRILLA ATTIT RIGID/FLEX...POLICY OBS TREND 20. PAGE 27 A0553
S/ASIA PWR BAL/PWR DIPLOM

B62
MODELSKI G.,SEATO-SIX STUDIES. ASIA CHINA/COM INDIA S/ASIA INT/ORG NAT/G ECO/TAC DETER ATTIT ORD/FREE PWR...TIME/SEQ COLD/WAR TOT/POP 20 SEATO. PAGE 102 A2098
MARKET ECO/UNDEV INT/TRADE

B62
MORGENTHAU H.J.,POLITICS IN THE 20TH CENTURY: RESTORATION OF AMERICAN POLITICS. ASIA GERMANY USA+45 USSR WOR+45 NAT/G PLAN EDU/PROP LEGIT NUC/PWR ATTIT PWR SKILL...CONCPT TREND COLD/WAR 20. PAGE 104 A2139
INT/ORG DIPLOM

B62
SNYDER L.L.D.,THE IMPERIALISM READER. AFR ASIA CHINA/COM COM EUR+WWI FUT MOD/EUR USA+45 WOR+45 WOR-45 INT/ORG COLONIAL SOVEREIGN CMN/WLTH OAS 20. PAGE 134 A2751
DOMIN PWR DIPLOM

B62
US DEPARTMENT OF THE ARMY,GUIDE TO JAPANESE MONOGRAPHS AND JAPANESE STUDIES ON MANCHURIA: 1945-1960. CHINA/COM NAT/G DIPLOM LEAD COERCE WAR ...CHARTS 19/20 CHINJAP. PAGE 152 A3105
BIBLIOG/A FORCES ASIA S/ASIA

L62
PETKOFF D.K.,"RECOGNITION AND NON-RECOGNITION OF STATES AND GOVERNMENTS IN INTERNATIONAL LAW." ASIA COM USA+45 WOR+45 NAT/G ACT/RES DIPLOM DOMIN LEGIT COERCE ORD/FREE PWR...CONCPT GEN/LAWS 20. PAGE 115 A2369
INT/ORG LAW INT/LAW

S62
BRZEZINSKI Z.K.,"PEACEFUL ENGAGEMENT IN COMMUNIST DISUNITY." ASIA CHINA/COM USA+45 USSR NAT/G TOP/EX CREATE ECO/TAC FOR/AID DOMIN ATTIT PERCEPT RIGID/FLEX PWR...PSY 20. PAGE 20 A0417
COM DIPLOM TOTALISM

S62
CORET A.,"LA DECLARATION DE L'ASSEMBLEE GENERAL DE L'ONU SUR L'OCTROI DE L'INDEPENDENCE AUX PAYS ET AUX PEUPLES." AFR ASIA ISLAM NIGERIA S/ASIA USSR WOR+45 ECO/UNDEV NAT/G DELIB/GP COLONIAL ALL/VALS ...CONCPT TIME/SEQ TREND UN TOT/POP 20 MEXIC/AMER. PAGE 31 A0621
INT/ORG STRUCT SOVEREIGN

S62
CROAN M.,"POLYCENTRISM: COMMUNIST INTERNATIONAL RELATIONS." ASIA STRUCT INT/ORG NAT/G POL/PAR CONSULT PLAN DOMIN EDU/PROP COERCE ATTIT RIGID/FLEX SOCISM...POLICY CONCPT TREND CON/ANAL GEN/LAWS MARX/KARL. PAGE 33 A0663
COM CREATE DIPLOM NAT/LISM

S62
FOCSANEANU L.,"LES GRANDS TRAITES DE LA REPUBLIQUE POPULAIRE DE CHINE." ASIA CHINA/COM COM USSR WOR+45 INT/ORG NAT/G POL/PAR ACT/RES PLAN DIPLOM EDU/PROP ...CONCPT TIME/SEQ 20 TREATY. PAGE 47 A0957
VOL/ASSN TOTALISM

S62
LONDON K.,"SINO-SOVIET RELATIONS IN THE CONTEXT OF THE 'WORLD SOCIALIST SYSTEM'." ASIA CHINA/COM COM USSR INT/ORG NAT/G TOP/EX BAL/PWR DIPLOM DOMIN ATTIT PERCEPT RIGID/FLEX PWR MARXISM...METH/CNCPT TREND 20. PAGE 91 A1854
DELIB/GP CONCPT SOCISM

S62
SPECTOR I.,"SOVIET POLICY IN ASIA: A REAPPRAISAL." ASIA CHINA/COM COM INDIA INDONESIA ECO/UNDEV INT/ORG DOMIN EDU/PROP REGION RESPECT...CONCPT TREND TOT/POP COLD/WAR 20 CHINJAP. PAGE 135 A2774
S/ASIA PWR FOR/AID USSR

S62
STRACHEY J.,"COMMUNIST INTENTIONS." ASIA USSR YUGOSLAVIA INT/ORG NAT/G FORCES DOMIN EDU/PROP COERCE NUC/PWR NAT/LISM PEACE RIGID/FLEX PWR MARXISM...CONCPT MYTH OBS TIME/SEQ TREND COLD/WAR TOT/POP 20. PAGE 139 A2843
COM ATTIT WAR

B63
ABSHIRE D.M.,NATIONAL SECURITY: POLITICAL, MILITARY, AND ECONOMIC STRATEGIES IN THE DECADE AHEAD. ASIA COM USA+45 WOR+45 ECO/DEV ECO/UNDEV INT/ORG DELIB/GP FORCES ECO/TAC COERCE ATTIT RIGID/FLEX HEALTH ORD/FREE PWR WEALTH...POLICY STAT CHARTS ANTHOL COLD/WAR VAL/FREE. PAGE 4 A0083
FUT ACT/RES BAL/PWR

B63
BRECHER M.,THE NEW STATES OF ASIA. ASIA S/ASIA INT/ORG BAL/PWR COLONIAL NEUTRAL ORD/FREE PWR 20 UN. PAGE 18 A0369
NAT/G ECO/UNDEV DIPLOM POLICY

B63
BRZEZINSKI Z.K.,AFRICA AND THE COMMUNIST WORLD. AFR ASIA COM CULTURE SOCIETY INT/ORG DELIB/GP ACT/RES ECO/TAC COERCE ORD/FREE PWR WEALTH...STAT TOT/POP VAL/FREE 20. PAGE 21 A0418
ATTIT EDU/PROP DIPLOM USSR

B63
DUNN F.S.,PEACE-MAKING AND THE SETTLEMENT WITH JAPAN. ASIA USA+45 USA-45 FORCES BAL/PWR ECO/TAC CONFER WAR PWR SOVEREIGN 20 CHINJAP COLD/WAR TREATY. PAGE 39 A0802
POLICY PEACE PLAN DIPLOM

B63
HENDERSON W.,SOUTHEAST ASIA: PROBLEMS OF UNITED STATES POLICY. COM S/ASIA CULTURE STRATA ECO/UNDEV INT/ORG DELIB/GP ACT/RES ECO/TAC DOMIN EDU/PROP LEGIT COERCE ATTIT ALL/VALS...STAT TIME/SEQ ANTHOL VAL/FREE 20. PAGE 64 A1313
ASIA USA+45 DIPLOM

B63
INTERNATIONAL BANK RECONST DEV,THE WORLD BANK GROUP IN ASIA. ASIA S/ASIA INDUS TEC/DEV ECO/TAC...RECORD 20 IBRD WORLD/BANK. PAGE 71 A1451
INT/ORG DIPLOM ECO/UNDEV FINAN

B63
KAHIN G.M.,MAJOR GOVERNMENTS OF ASIA (2ND ED.). ASIA INDIA INDONESIA PAKISTAN S/ASIA DIPLOM...SOC 20 CHINJAP. PAGE 75 A1546
GOV/COMP POL/PAR ELITES

B63
LIU K.C.,AMERICANS AND CHINESE: A HISTORICAL ESSAY AND BIBLIOGRAPHY. ASIA USA+45 USA-45 SOCIETY SECT 18/20. PAGE 90 A1845
BIBLIOG/A GP/REL DIPLOM ATTIT

B63
MENDES C.,NACIONALISMO E DESENVOLVIMENTO. AFR ASIA L/A+17C STRATA INT/TRADE COLONIAL. PAGE 99 A2039
NAT/LISM ECO/UNDEV DIPLOM REV

B63
MOSELY P.E.,THE SOVIET UNION, 1922-1962: A FOREIGN AFFAIRS READER. ASIA POLAND USSR CULTURE INTELL AGRI POL/PAR WORKER INT/TRADE DOMIN WAR NAT/LISM MARXISM SOCISM 20 KHRUSH/N. PAGE 105 A2152
PWR POLICY DIPLOM

B63
NORTH R.C.,CONTENT ANALYSIS: A HANDBOOK WITH APPLICATIONS FOR THE STUDY OF INTERNATIONAL CRISIS. ASIA COM EUR+WWI MOD/EUR INT/ORG TEC/DEV DOMIN EDU/PROP ROUTINE COERCE PERCEPT RIGID/FLEX ALL/VALS ...QUANT TESTS CON/ANAL SIMUL GEN/LAWS VAL/FREE. PAGE 110 A2252
METH/CNCPT COMPUT/IR USSR

B63
NORTH R.C.,M. N. ROY'S MISSION TO CHINA: THE COMMUNIST-KUOMINTANG SPLIT OF 1927. ASIA USSR STRATA LEGIS WORKER LEAD REV ATTIT ROLE SOCISM 20 ROY/MN COM/PARTY. PAGE 110 A2253
POL/PAR MARXISM DIPLOM

B63
YOUNG A.N.,CHINA AND THE HELPING HAND. ASIA USA+45 FINAN INDUS ECO/TAC GIVE WEALTH...METH/COMP 20 LEND/LEASE GOLD/STAND. PAGE 169 A3434
FOR/AID DIPLOM WAR

S63
ALEXANDER R.,"LATIN AMERICA AND THE COMMUNIST BLOC." ASIA COM CUBA L/A+17C USA+45 USSR NAT/G VOL/ASSN TEC/DEV FOR/AID LEGIT PWR WEALTH COLD/WAR 20. PAGE 6 A0112
ECO/UNDEV RECORD

S63
CHAKRAVARTI P.C.,"INDIAN NON-ALIGNMENT AND UNITED STATES POLICY." ASIA INDIA S/ASIA USA+45 CULTURE ECO/UNDEV NAT/G VOL/ASSN DELIB/GP TOP/EX FOR/AID NEUTRAL...POLICY HUM CONCPT RECORD GEN/LAWS 20. PAGE 25 A0515
ATTIT ALL/VALS COLONIAL DIPLOM

S63
ETIENNE G.,"'LOIS OBJECTIVES' ET PROBLEMES DE DEVELOPPEMENT DANS LE CONTEXTE CHINE-URSS." ASIA CHINA/COM COM FUT STRUCT INT/ORG VOL/ASSN TOP/EX TEC/DEV ECO/TAC ATTIT RIGID/FLEX...GEOG MGT TIME/SEQ TOT/POP 20. PAGE 42 A0866
TOTALISM USSR

S63
WOLF C.,"SOME ASPECTS OF THE 'VALUE' OF LESS-DEVELOPED COUNTRIES TO THE UNITED STATES." ASIA CHINA/COM COM USA+45 USSR ECO/UNDEV BAL/PWR ECO/TAC
CONCPT GEN/LAWS DIPLOM

FOR/AID DOMIN EDU/PROP ATTIT PWR...POLICY METH/CNCPT CONT/OBS TREND CHARTS 20. PAGE 166 A3379

N63
LIBRARY HUNGARIAN ACADEMY SCI,HUNGARIAN PUBLICATIONS ON ASIA AND AFRICA, 1950-1962: A SELECTED BIBLIOGRAPHY (PAMPHLET). AFR ASIA HUNGARY S/ASIA ECO/UNDEV NAT/G EDU/PROP ATTIT 20 UNESCO. PAGE 88 A1807 — BIBLIOG REGION DIPLOM WRITING

B64
CALVO SERER R.,LAS NUEVAS DEMOCRACIAS. AFR ASIA ISLAM USA+45 WOR+45 BAL/PWR DOMIN PARTIC INGP/REL AUTHORIT POPULISM...CONCPT 20 COM/PARTY. PAGE 23 A0469 — ORD/FREE MARXISM DIPLOM POLICY

B64
CHENG C.,ECONOMIC RELATIONS BETWEEN PEKING AND MOSCOW: 1949-63. ASIA CHINA/COM COM USSR FINAN INDUS CONSULT TEC/DEV INT/TRADE...PREDICT CHARTS BIBLIOG 20. PAGE 26 A0527 — DIPLOM FOR/AID MARXISM

B64
EMBREE A.T.,A GUIDE TO PAPERBACKS ON ASIA; SELECTED AND ANNOTATED (PAMPHLET). CULTURE SOCIETY ECO/UNDEV SECT DIPLOM COLONIAL MARXISM...SOC 20. PAGE 41 A0845 — BIBLIOG/A ASIA S/ASIA NAT/G

B64
IRISH M.D.,WORLD PRESSURES ON AMERICAN FOREIGN POLICY. ASIA COM L/A+17C SOUTH/AFR UK WOR+45 ECO/DEV ECO/UNDEV COLONIAL SANCTION COERCE REV TOTALISM...ANTHOL 20 COLD/WAR EUROPE/W INTERVENT. PAGE 72 A1467 — DIPLOM POLICY

B64
JANOWITZ M.,THE MILITARY IN THE POLITICAL DEVELOPMENT OF NEW NATIONS: AN ESSAY IN COMPARATIVE ANALYSIS. AFR ASIA ISLAM L/A+17C S/ASIA USA+45 ECO/UNDEV INT/ORG NAT/G POL/PAR DELIB/GP PLAN ECO/TAC DOMIN LEGIT COERCE ATTIT DRIVE RESPECT ...SOC CONCPT CENSUS VAL/FREE. PAGE 73 A1495 — FORCES PWR

B64
KOLARZ W.,COMMUNISM AND COLONIALISM. AFR ASIA USSR DISCRIM ATTIT ORD/FREE SOVEREIGN SOC/INTEG 20. PAGE 81 A1668 — EDU/PROP DIPLOM TOTALISM COLONIAL

B64
KRETZSCHMAR W.W.,AUSLANDSHILFE ALS MITTEL DER AUSSENWIRTSCHAFTS- UND AUSSENPOLITIK. ASIA GERMANY/W UK USA+45 SOCIETY STRUCT ECO/UNDEV LOBBY EFFICIENCY 20. PAGE 82 A1683 — FOR/AID DIPLOM AGRI DIST/IND

B64
LATOURETTE K.S.,CHINA. ASIA CHINA/COM FUT USSR ECO/UNDEV ECO/TAC WAR 19/20. PAGE 85 A1744 — MARXISM NAT/G POLICY DIPLOM

B64
LENS S.,THE FUTILE CRUSADE. ASIA CHINA/COM L/A+17C USA+45 USSR WOR+45 ECO/DEV BAL/PWR DIPLOM NUC/PWR WAR NAT/LISM PEACE 20 COLD/WAR PRESIDENT CIA. PAGE 87 A1774 — ORD/FREE ANOMIE COM MARXISM

B64
LENSEN G.A.,REVELATIONS OF A RUSSIAN DIPLOMAT: THE MEMOIRS OF DMITRII I. ABRIKOSSOV. ASIA MOD/EUR RUSSIA USA-45 ELITES ACADEM CHIEF FORCES REV WAR PWR CONSERVE MARXISM 19/20 ABRIKSSV/D CHINJAP BOLSHEVISM. PAGE 87 A1775 — DIPLOM POLICY OBS

B64
PERKINS D.,THE AMERICAN DEMOCRACY: ITS RISE TO POWER. ASIA USSR LAW CULTURE FINAN EDU/PROP COLONIAL CHOOSE...POLICY CHARTS BIBLIOG WORSHIP PRESIDENT 15/20 NEGRO. PAGE 115 A2362 — LOC/G ECO/TAC WAR DIPLOM

B64
REES D.,KOREA: THE LIMITED WAR. ASIA KOREA WOR+45 NAT/G CIVMIL/REL PERS/REL PERSON...POLICY CHARTS 20 UN TRUMAN/HS MACARTHR/D. PAGE 120 A2455 — DIPLOM WAR INT/ORG FORCES

B64
ROSECRANCE R.N.,THE DISPERSION OF NUCLEAR WEAPONS: STRATEGY AND POLITICS. ASIA COM FUT S/ASIA USA+45 INT/ORG NAT/G DELIB/GP FORCES ACT/RES TEC/DEV BAL/PWR COERCE DETER ATTIT RIGID/FLEX ORD/FREE ...POLICY CHARTS VAL/FREE. PAGE 123 A2530 — EUR+WWI PWR PEACE

B64
SAKAI R.K.,STUDIES ON ASIA, 1964. ASIA CHINA/COM ISRAEL MALAYSIA S/ASIA USA+45 USSR ECO/UNDEV FAM POL/PAR SECT CONSULT NAT/LISM...POLICY SOC 20 CHINJAP. PAGE 126 A2588 — PWR DIPLOM

B64
TONG T.,UNITED STATES DIPLOMACY IN CHINA, 1844-1860. ASIA USA-45 ECO/UNDEV ECO/TAC COERCE GP/REL...INT/LAW 19 TREATY. PAGE 144 A2949 — DIPLOM INT/TRADE COLONIAL

B64
US AGENCY INTERNATIONAL DEV,REPORT TO CONGRESS ON THE FOREIGN ASSISTANCE PROGRAM. AFR ASIA L/A+17C USA+45 INT/ORG VOL/ASSN FORCES CAP/ISM ADMIN WEAPON. PAGE 149 A3052 — FOR/AID ECO/UNDEV TEC/DEV BUDGET

B64
US HOUSE COMM FOREIGN AFFAIRS,HEARINGS ON H.R. 10502 TO AMEND FURTHER THE FOREIGN ASSISTANCE ACT OF 1961. AFR ASIA L/A+17C INT/ORG CONSULT DELIB/GP TEC/DEV ECO/TAC EDU/PROP CONFER 20 UN NATO CONGRESS AID. PAGE 153 A3130 — FOR/AID DIPLOM ORD/FREE ECO/UNDEV

L64
KORBONSKI A.,"COMECON." ASIA ECO/DEV ECO/UNDEV ECO/TAC BAL/PAY NAT/LISM 20 COMECON. PAGE 81 A1671 — COM INT/ORG INT/TRADE

L64
POUNDS N.J.G.,"THE POLITICS OF PARTITION." AFR ASIA COM EUR+WWI FUT ISLAM S/ASIA USA-45 LAW ECO/DEV ECO/UNDEV AGRI INDUS INT/ORG POL/PAR PROVS SECT FORCES TOP/EX EDU/PROP LEGIT ATTIT MORAL ORD/FREE PWR RESPECT WEALTH. PAGE 117 A2402 — NAT/G NAT/LISM

S64
DE GAULLE C.,"FRENCH WORLD VIEW." AFR ASIA CHINA/COM EUR+WWI ISLAM ECO/UNDEV INT/ORG NAT/G VOL/ASSN ACT/RES DIPLOM ECO/TAC EDU/PROP ATTIT DRIVE WEALTH 20. PAGE 35 A0702 — TOP/EX PWR FOR/AID FRANCE

S64
DEVILLERS P.H.,"L'URSS, LA CHINE ET LES ORIGINES DE LA GUERRE DE COREE." ASIA CHINA/COM USSR INT/ORG ECO/TAC EDU/PROP ATTIT RIGID/FLEX PWR...STAND/INT HIST/WRIT COLD/WAR 20. PAGE 37 A0751 — WOR+45 KOREA

S64
LEVI W.,"CHINA AND THE UNITED NATIONS." ASIA CHINA CHINA/COM WOR+45 WOR-45 CONSTN NAT/G DELIB/GP EX/STRUC FORCES ACT/RES EDU/PROP PWR...POLICY RECORD TIME/SEQ GEN/LAWS UN COLD/WAR 20. PAGE 88 A1794 — INT/ORG ATTIT NAT/LISM

S64
PRASAD B.,"SURVEY OF RECENT RESEARCH: STUDIES ON INDIA'S FOREIGN POLIC AND RELATIONS." ASIA INDIA PAKISTAN USA+45 NAT/G INT/TRADE GOV/REL 20 UN CMN/WLTH. PAGE 117 A2406 — BIBLIOG DIPLOM ROLE POLICY

N64
GREAT BRITAIN CENTRAL OFF INF,THE COLOMBO PLAN (PAMPHLET). ASIA S/ASIA USA+45 VOL/ASSN...CHARTS 20 COMMONWLTH RESOURCE/N. PAGE 55 A1134 — FOR/AID PLAN INT/ORG ECO/UNDEV

B65
CHUNG Y.S.,KOREA: A SELECTED BIBLIOGRAPHY 1959-1963. ASIA KOREA NAT/G DIPLOM 20. PAGE 26 A0537 — BIBLIOG/A SOC

B65
GRETTON P.,MARITIME STRATEGY - A STUDY OF DEFENSE PROBLEMS. ASIA UK USSR DIPLOM COERCE DETER NUC/PWR WEAPON...CONCPT NAT/COMP 20. PAGE 56 A1147 — FORCES PLAN WAR SEA

B65
IRIYE A.,AFTER IMPERIALISM; THE SEARCH FOR A NEW ORDER IN THE FAR EAST 1921-1931. USA-45 USSR DOMIN AGREE COLONIAL REV PWR...BIBLIOG DICTIONARY 20 CHINJAP. PAGE 72 A1468 — DIPLOM ASIA SOVEREIGN

B65
LARUS J.,COMPARATIVE WORLD POLITICS. ASIA INDIA WOR+45 WOR-45 BAL/PWR WAR PEACE RATIONAL MORAL PWR ...REALPOL INT/LAW MUSLIM. PAGE 85 A1735 — GOV/COMP IDEA/COMP DIPLOM NAT/COMP

B65
LASKY V.,THE UGLY RUSSIAN. AFR ASIA USSR ECO/UNDEV NAT/LISM TOTALISM PERSON 20. PAGE 85 A1738 — FOR/AID ATTIT DIPLOM

B65
MORGENTHAU H.,MORGENTHAU DIARY (CHINA) (2 VOLS.). ASIA USA+45 USA-45 LAW DELIB/GP EX/STRUC PLAN FOR/AID INT/TRADE CONFER WAR MARXISM 20 CHINJAP. PAGE 104 A2136 — DIPLOM ADMIN

B65
REQUA E.G.,THE DEVELOPING NATIONS: A GUIDE TO INFORMATION SOURCES CONCERNING THEIR ECON, POLIT, TECHNICAL, AND SOCIAL PROBLEMS. AFR ASIA ISLAM L/A+17C INDUS INT/ORG CONSULT PLAN PROB/SOLV...SOC 20 UN. PAGE 120 A2466 — BIBLIOG/A ECO/UNDEV FOR/AID TEC/DEV

B65
ROMEIN J.,THE ASIAN CENTURY. ASIA COM S/ASIA DIPLOM COLONIAL TIME 20. PAGE 123 A2519 — REV NAT/LISM CULTURE MARXISM

B65
TREFOUSSE H.L.,THE COLD WAR: A BOOK OF DOCUMENTS. ASIA L/A+17C USSR WOR+45 WOR-45 ECO/TAC FOR/AID ARMS/CONT NUC/PWR PEACE ORD/FREE...ANTHOL 20 COLD/WAR KENNEDY/JF EISNHWR/DD. PAGE 145 A2961 — BAL/PWR DIPLOM MARXISM

B65
US DEPARTMENT OF THE ARMY,NUCLEAR WEAPONS AND THE ATLANTIC ALLIANCE: A BIBLIOGRAPHIC SURVEY. ASIA COM EUR+WWI USA+45 FORCES DIPLOM WEAPON...STAT 20 NATO. PAGE 152 A3108 — BIBLIOG/A ARMS/CONT NUC/PWR BAL/PWR

B65
US HOUSE COMM FOREIGN AFFAIRS,HEARINGS ON DRAFT BILL TO AMEND FURTHER THE FOREIGN ASSISTANCE ACT OF 1961. AFR ASIA L/A+17C USA+45 INT/ORG DELIB/GP TEC/DEV ECO/TAC CONFER TOTALISM 20 CONGRESS AID. PAGE 153 A3131 — FOR/AID ECO/UNDEV DIPLOM ORD/FREE

B65
US SENATE COMM ON FOREIGN REL,HEARINGS ON THE FOREIGN ASSISTANCE PROGRAM. AFR ASIA L/A+17C USA+45 — FOR/AID DIPLOM

WOR+45 FORCES TEC/DEV BUDGET CONTROL WEAPON ORD/FREE 20 UN CONGRESS SEC/STATE. PAGE 156 A3183 — INT/ORG ECO/UNDEV

B65
WINT G.,COMMUNIST CHINA'S CRUSADE: MAO'S ROAD TO POWER AND THE NEW CAMPAIGN FOR WORLD REVOLUTION. ASIA CHINA/COM USA+45 USSR NAT/G POL/PAR DOMIN COERCE WAR PWR...POLICY CHARTS IDEA/COMP BIBLIOG 20 MAO. PAGE 165 A3364 — DIPLOM MARXISM REV COLONIAL

B65
WINT G.,ASIA: A HANDBOOK. ASIA COM INDIA USSR CULTURE INTELL NAT/G...GEOG STAT CENSUS NAT/COMP WORSHIP 20 TREATY CHINJAP. PAGE 165 A3365 — DIPLOM SOC

S65
FLEMING D.F.,"CAN PAX AMERICANA SUCCEED?" ASIA CHINA/COM EUR+WWI USSR VIETNAM BAL/PWR DIPLOM DOMIN COERCE GOV/REL 20. PAGE 46 A0948 — DECISION ATTIT ECO/TAC

S65
PRABHAKAR P.,"SURVEY OF RESEARCH AND SOURCE MATERIALS; THE SINO-INDIAN BORDER DISPUTE." CHINA/COM INDIA LAW NAT/G PLAN BAL/PWR WAR...POLICY 20 COLD/WAR. PAGE 117 A2404 — BIBLIOG ASIA S/ASIA DIPLOM

S65
RAY H.,"THE POLICY OF RUSSIA TOWARDS SINO-INDIAN CONFLICT." ASIA CHINA/COM COM INDIA USSR NAT/G TOP/EX FOR/AID EDU/PROP NEUTRAL COERCE PEACE RIGID/FLEX PWR...METH/CNCPT TIME/SEQ VAL/FREE 20. PAGE 120 A2452 — S/ASIA ATTIT DIPLOM WAR

B66
AMERICAN FRIENDS SERVICE COMM,PEACE IN VIETNAM: A NEW APPROACH IN SOUTHEAST ASIA: A REPORT. ASIA S/ASIA USA+45 VIETNAM ORD/FREE 20 TREATY. PAGE 7 A0149 — PEACE WAR NAT/LISM DIPLOM

B66
BESSON W.,DIE GROSSEN MACHTE - STRUKTURFRAGEN DER GEGENWARTIGEN WELTPOLITIK. ASIA USSR WOR+45 ATTIT ...IDEA/COMP 20 KENNEDY/JF. PAGE 14 A0280 — NAT/COMP DIPLOM STRUCT

B66
EMBREE A.T.,ASIA: A GUIDE TO BASIC BOOKS (PAMPHLET). ECO/UNDEV SECT FORCES DIPLOM ALL/IDEOS ...SOC 20. PAGE 41 A0846 — BIBLIOG/A ASIA S/ASIA NAT/G

B66
ESTHUS R.A.,THEODORE ROOSEVELT AND JAPAN. ASIA USA-45 FORCES CONFER WAR SOVEREIGN...BIBLIOG 20 CHINJAP. PAGE 42 A0864 — DIPLOM DELIB/GP

B66
EUDIN X.J.,SOVIET FOREIGN POLICY 1928-34: DOCUMENTS AND MATERIALS (VOL. I). ASIA USSR WOR-45 INT/ORG POL/PAR WORKER WAR PEACE...ANTHOL 20 TREATY LEAGUE/NAT INTERVENT. PAGE 43 A0873 — DIPLOM POLICY GOV/REL MARXISM

B66
FITZGERALD C.P.,THE BIRTH OF COMMUNIST CHINA (2ND ED.). ASIA CHINA/COM STRUCT BAL/PWR DIPLOM ECO/TAC INT/TRADE WEALTH 20. PAGE 46 A0942 — REV MARXISM ECO/UNDEV

B66
HANSEN G.H.,AFRO-ASIA AND NON-ALIGNMENT. AFR ASIA S/ASIA NEUTRAL MORAL 20. PAGE 61 A1255 — DIPLOM CONFER POLICY NAT/LISM

B66
KOH S.J.,STAGES OF INDUSTRIAL DEVELOPMENT IN ASIA. ASIA INDIA KOREA STRATA STRUCT NAT/G INT/TRADE ...CHARTS 19/20 CHINJAP. PAGE 81 A1659 — INDUS ECO/UNDEV ECO/DEV LABOR

B66
LAMBERG R.F.,PRAG UND DIE DRITTE WELT. AFR ASIA CZECHOSLVK L/A+17C MARKET TEC/DEV ECO/TAC REV ATTIT 20 TREATY. PAGE 84 A1713 — DIPLOM ECO/UNDEV INT/TRADE FOR/AID

B66
PAN S.,VIETNAM CRISIS. ASIA FRANCE USA+45 USA-45 VIETNAM CULTURE SOCIETY INT/ORG ECO/TAC AGREE CONTROL WAR MARXISM 20. PAGE 113 A2325 — ECO/UNDEV POLICY DIPLOM NAT/COMP

B66
SINGER L.,ALLE LITTEN AN GROSSENWAHN: VON WOODROW WILSON BIS MAO TSE-TUNG. ASIA UK USSR INT/ORG DELIB/GP BAL/PWR DOMIN ATTIT PERSON 20 WILSON/W ROOSEVLT/F. PAGE 133 A2731 — DIPLOM TOTALISM WAR CHIEF

B66
SINGH L.P.,THE POLITICS OF ECONOMIC COOPERATION IN ASIA; A STUDY OF ASIAN INTERNATIONAL ORGANIZATIONS. ASIA INT/ORG ACT/RES PLAN GP/REL...POLICY GP/COMP BIBLIOG 20 UN SEATO. PAGE 133 A2733 — ECO/UNDEV ECO/TAC REGION DIPLOM

B66
UN ECAFE,ADMINISTRATIVE ASPECTS OF FAMILY PLANNING PROGRAMMES (PAMPHLET). ASIA THAILAND WOR+45 VOL/ASSN PROB/SOLV BUDGET FOR/AID EDU/PROP CONFER CONTROL GOV/REL TIME 20 UN BIRTH/CON. PAGE 147 A2999 — PLAN CENSUS FAM ADMIN

B66
US DEPARTMENT OF STATE,RESEARCH ON AFRICA (EXTERNAL RESEARCH LIST NO 5-25). LAW CULTURE ECO/UNDEV POL/PAR DIPLOM EDU/PROP LEAD REGION MARXISM...GEOG LING WORSHIP 20. PAGE 152 A3094 — BIBLIOG/A ASIA S/ASIA NAT/G

B66
US HOUSE COMM FOREIGN AFFAIRS,HEARINGS ON HR 12449 A BILL TO AMEND FURTHER THE FOREIGN ASSISTANCE ACT OF 1961. AFR ASIA L/A+17C USA+45 VIETNAM INT/ORG TEC/DEV INT/TRADE ATTIT ORD/FREE 20 UN NATO CONGRESS AID. PAGE 154 A3132 — FOR/AID ECO/TAC ECO/UNDEV DIPLOM

B66
WESTWOOD A.F.,FOREIGN AID IN A FOREIGN POLICY FRAMEWORK. AFR ASIA INDIA IRAN L/A+17C USA+45 USSR ECO/UNDEV AGRI FORCES LEGIS PLAN PROB/SOLV ...DECISION 20 COLD/WAR. PAGE 163 A3324 — FOR/AID DIPLOM POLICY ECO/TAC

B66
ZABLOCKI C.J.,SINO-SOVIET RIVALRY. AFR ASIA CHINA/COM CUBA EUR+WWI L/A+17C USA+45 USSR WOR+45 POL/PAR FORCES COERCE NUC/PWR...GOV/COMP IDEA/COMP 20 MAO KHRUSH/N. PAGE 169 A3442 — DIPLOM MARXISM COM

S66
AFRICAN BIBLIOGRAPHIC CENTER,"THE NEW AFRO-ASIAN STATES IN PERSPECTIVE, 1960-1963: A SELECT BIBLIOGRAPHY." AFR ASIA CULTURE SOCIETY INT/ORG LABOR TEC/DEV LITERACY 20 UN. PAGE 5 A0100 — BIBLIOG DIPLOM FOR/AID INT/TRADE

S66
CRANMER-BYNG J.L.,"THE CHINESE ATTITUDE TOWARDS EXTERNAL RELATIONS." ASIA CHINA/COM EXEC NAT/LISM MARXISM...POLICY 20. PAGE 32 A0660 — ATTIT DIPLOM NAT/G

S66
MERRITT R.L.,"SELECTED ARTICLES AND DOCUMENTS ON COMPARATIVE GOVERNMENT AND CROSS-NATIONAL RESEARCH." AFR ASIA EUR+WWI L/A+17C MOD/EUR ELITES R+D ACT/RES DIPLOM PWR...SOC CONCPT 18/20. PAGE 100 A2046 — BIBLIOG GOV/COMP NAT/G GOV/REL

C66
WINT G.,"ASIA: A HANDBOOK." ASIA S/ASIA INDUS LABOR SECT PRESS RACE/REL MARXISM...STAT CHARTS BIBLIOG 20. PAGE 165 A3366 — ECO/UNDEV DIPLOM NAT/G SOCIETY

N66
US HOUSE COMM FOREIGN AFFAIRS,UNITED STATES POLICY TOWARD ASIA (PAMPHLET). CHINA/COM USA+45 USSR VIETNAM INT/ORG NAT/G PWR MARXISM 20 UN. PAGE 154 A3133 — POLICY ASIA DIPLOM PLAN

B67
HALPERIN M.H.,CONTEMPORARY MILITARY STRATEGY. ASIA CHINA/COM USA+45 USSR INT/ORG FORCES ACT/RES PLAN TEC/DEV BAL/PWR COERCE WAR...METH/COMP BIBLIOG 20 NATO. PAGE 60 A1240 — DIPLOM NUC/PWR DETER ARMS/CONT

B67
HOHENBERG J.,BETWEEN TWO WORLDS. ASIA S/ASIA USA+45 PRESS TV PERS/REL ISOLAT...INT CHARTS METH/COMP 20. PAGE 66 A1362 — COM/IND DIPLOM EFFICIENCY KNOWL

B67
MCNELLY T.,SOURCES IN MODERN EAST ASIAN HISTORY AND POLITICS. KOREA VIETNAM CULTURE DIPLOM COLONIAL REV WAR PWR ALL/IDEOS MARXISM...ANTHOL 20 CHINJAP. PAGE 99 A2023 — NAT/COMP ASIA S/ASIA SOCIETY

B67
SALISBURY H.E.,ORBIT OF CHINA. ASIA CHINA/COM DIPLOM PEACE PWR 20. PAGE 126 A2593 — EDU/PROP OBS INT ARMS/CONT

B67
TROTSKY L.,PROBLEMS OF THE CHINESE REVOLUTION (3RD ED. TRANS. BY MAX SCHACTMAN). ASIA USSR DIPLOM MARXISM SOCISM...IDEA/COMP ANTHOL DICTIONARY 20 STALIN/J. PAGE 145 A2969 — MARXIST REV

B67
US SUPERINTENDENT OF DOCUMENTS,LIBRARY OF CONGRESS (PRICE LIST 83). AFR ASIA EUR+WWI USA-45 USSR NAT/G DIPLOM CONFER CT/SYS WAR...DECISION PHIL/SCI CLASSIF 19/20 CONGRESS PRESIDENT. PAGE 157 A3205 — BIBLIOG/A USA+45 AUTOMAT LAW

B67
YAMAMURA K.,ECONOMIC POLICY IN POSTWAR JAPAN. ASIA FINAN POL/PAR DIPLOM LEAD NAT/LISM ATTIT NEW/LIB POPULISM 20 CHINJAP. PAGE 168 A3429 — ECO/DEV POLICY NAT/G TEC/DEV

L67
"POLITICAL PARTIES ON FOREIGN POLICY IN THE INTER-ELECTION YEARS 1962-66." ASIA COM INDIA USA+45 PLAN ATTIT...DECISION 20. PAGE 4 A0079 — POL/PAR DIPLOM POLICY

S67
HIBBERT R.A.,"THE MONGOLIAN PEOPLE'S REPUBLIC IN THE 1960'S." INT/ORG PLAN FOR/AID 20. PAGE 64 A1326 — ASIA ECO/UNDEV PROB/SOLV DIPLOM

S67
ROSE S.,"ASIAN NATIONALISM* THE SECOND STAGE." ASIA COM ECO/UNDEV NAT/G PROB/SOLV DIPLOM FOR/AID DOMIN NEUTRAL REGION TASK...METH/COMP 20. PAGE 123 A2528 — NAT/LISM S/ASIA BAL/PWR COLONIAL

S67
SHOEMAKER R.L.,"JAPANESE ARMY AND THE WEST." ASIA ELITES EX/STRUC DIPLOM DOMIN EDU/PROP COERCE ATTIT AUTHORIT PWR 1/20 CHINJAP. PAGE 132 A2703 — FORCES TEC/DEV WAR TOTALISM

S67
WALKER R.L.,"THE WEST AND THE 'NEW ASIA'." CHINA/COM ECO/UNDEV DIPLOM...PREDICT 20. PAGE 160 A3266 — ASIA INT/TRADE COLONIAL REGION

C67
HUDSON G.F.,"THE HARD AND BITTER PEACE; WORLD POLITICS SINCE 1945." ASIA COM S/ASIA USSR WOR+45 COLONIAL WAR...TREND BIBLIOG/A 20 COLD/WAR UN. PAGE 68 A1405 — DIPLOM INT/ORG ARMS/CONT BAL/PWR

ASIA FOUNDATION A0189

ASIA SOCIETY A0190

ASIAN-AFRICAN CONFERENCE A0191

ASIANS....ASIANS, ASIAN MINORITIES

ASPREMONT-LYNDEN H. A0192

ASQUITH/HH....HERBERT HENRY ASQUITH

ASSASSINATION....SEE MURDER

ASSIMILATION....SEE GP/REL+INGP/REL

ASSOCIATIONS....SEE VOL/ASSN

AT+T....AMERICAN TELEPHONE AND TELEGRAPH

ATATURK/MK....MUSTAFA KEMAL ATATURK

ATHENS....ATHENS, GREECE

ATLAN/ALL....ATLANTIC ALLIANCE

B63
CERAMI C.A.,ALLIANCE BORN OF DANGER. EUR+WWI USA+45 USSR ECO/DEV INDUS VOL/ASSN ECO/TAC REGION ATTIT MARXISM ATLAN/ALL 20 NATO EEC. PAGE 25 A0514 — DIPLOM INT/ORG NAT/G POLICY

ATLANTA....ATLANTA, GEORGIA

ATLANTIC ALLIANCE....SEE ATLAN/ALL

ATLANTIC INSTITUTE A0193

ATLASES....SEE MAPS

ATOM BOMB....SEE NUC/PWR

ATOMIC ENERGY AUTHORITY OF UN....SEE AEA

ATOMIC ENERGY COMMISSION....SEE AEC + COUNTRY'S NAME

ATTENTION....SEE PERCEPT

ATTIA G.E.O. A0194

ATTIT....ATTITUDES, OPINIONS, IDEOLOGY

ATTLEE/C....CLEMENT ATLEE

ATTRNY/GEN....ATTORNEY GENERAL

ATTWOOD W. A0195

AUBREY H.G. A0196,A0197

AUD/VIS....FILM AND SOUND (INCLUDING PHOTOGRAPHY)

N
KYRIAK T.E.,INTERNATIONAL DEVELOPMENTS: A BIBLIOGRAPHY (SERIAL). WOR+45...COMPUT/IR AUD/VIS CHARTS. PAGE 83 A1702 — BIBLIOG NAT/G DIPLOM

B00
VOLPICELLI Z.,RUSSIA ON THE PACIFIC AND THE SIBERIAN RAILWAY. MOD/EUR ECO/UNDEV INT/ORG FORCES PLAN DOMIN COLONIAL ROUTINE ATTIT ALL/VALS...OBS HIST/WRIT TIME/SEQ TREND CON/ANAL AUD/VIS CHARTS 18/19. PAGE 159 A3248 — NAT/G ACT/RES RUSSIA

B49
STETTINIUS E.R.,ROOSEVELT AND THE RUSSIANS: THE YALTA CONFERENCE. UK USSR WOR+45 WOR-45 INT/ORG VOL/ASSN TOP/EX ACT/RES EDU/PROP PEACE ATTIT DRIVE PERSON SUPEGO PWR...POLICY CONCPT MYTH OBS TIME/SEQ AUD/VIS COLD/WAR 20 CHURCHLL/W YALTA ROOSEVLT/F. PAGE 138 A2819 — DIPLOM DELIB/GP BIOG

B57
BRODY H.,UN DIARY: THE SEARCH FOR PEACE. HUNGARY WOR+45 DELIB/GP ROUTINE REV WAR ORD/FREE...AUD/VIS 20 UN SUEZ. PAGE 19 A0382 — INT/ORG PEACE DIPLOM POLICY

B60
ENGELMAN F.L.,THE PEACE OF CHRISTMAS EVE. UK USA-45 NAT/G FORCES CONFER PERS/REL...AUD/VIS BIBLIOG 19 TREATY. PAGE 42 A0853 — WAR PEACE DIPLOM PERSON

B60
PRITTIE T.,GERMANY DIVIDED: THE LEGACY OF THE NAZI ERA. EUR+WWI GERMANY RACE/REL SUPEGO...PSY AUD/VIS BIBLIOG/A 20 NAZI. PAGE 118 A2414 — STERTYP PERSON ATTIT DIPLOM

B61
DEAN V.M.,BUILDERS OF EMERGING NATIONS. WOR+45 ECO/UNDEV ECO/TAC NEUTRAL TOTALISM ORD/FREE PWR ...BIOG AUD/VIS IDEA/COMP BIBLIOG 20 COLD/WAR. PAGE 35 A0719 — NAT/G CHIEF POLICY DIPLOM

S61
KRANNHALS H.V.,"COMMAND INTEGRATION WITHIN THE WARSAW PACT." COM USSR WOR+45 DELIB/GP EDU/PROP ...CONCPT AUD/VIS CHARTS COLD/WAR TOT/POP VAL/FREE 20 TREATY WARSAW/P. PAGE 82 A1675 — INT/ORG FORCES TOTALISM

B62
MORTON L.,STRATEGY AND COMMAND: THE FIRST TWO YEARS. USA-45 NAT/G CONTROL EXEC LEAD WEAPON CIVMIL/REL PWR...POLICY AUD/VIS CHARTS 20 CHINJAP. PAGE 105 A2150 — WAR FORCES PLAN DIPLOM

B62
RIMALOV V.V.,ECONOMIC COOPERATION BETWEEN USSR AND UNDERDEVELOPED COUNTRIES. USSR FINAN TEC/DEV INT/TRADE DOMIN EDU/PROP COLONIAL NAT/LISM DRIVE SOVEREIGN...AUD/VIS 20. PAGE 121 A2482 — FOR/AID PLAN ECO/UNDEV DIPLOM

B63
HALASZ DE BEKY I.L.,A BIBLIOGRAPHY OF THE HUNGARIAN REVOLUTION 1956. COM HUNGARY USSR DIPLOM COERCE MARXISM...POLICY AUD/VIS 20 UN COLD/WAR. PAGE 59 A1221 — BIBLIOG REV FORCES ATTIT

B64
LOCKHART W.B.,CASES AND MATERIALS ON CONSTITUTIONAL RIGHTS AND LIBERTIES. USA+45 FORCES LEGIS DIPLOM PRESS CONTROL CRIME WAR PWR...AUD/VIS T WORSHIP 20 NEGRO. PAGE 90 A1849 — ORD/FREE CONSTN NAT/G

S64
FALK S.L.,"DISARMAMENT IN HISTORICAL PERSPECTIVE." WOR-45 NAT/G PLAN NUC/PWR PEACE ORD/FREE PWR ...TIME/SEQ AUD/VIS VAL/FREE LEAGUE/NAT 20. PAGE 44 A0892 — INT/ORG COERCE ARMS/CONT

S64
JORDAN A.,"POLITICAL COMMUNICATION: THE THIRD DIMENSION OF STRATEGY." USA+45 WOR+45 INT/ORG NAT/G CONSULT FORCES PLAN LEGIT EXEC PERCEPT ALL/VALS ...POLICY RELATIV PSY NEW/IDEA AUD/VIS EXHIBIT TOT/POP 20. PAGE 75 A1534 — EDU/PROP RIGID/FLEX ATTIT

B65
GILBERT M.,THE EUROPEAN POWERS 1900-45. EUR+WWI ITALY MOD/EUR USSR REV WAR PWR ALL/IDEOS FASCISM ...AUD/VIS CHARTS BIBLIOG 20. PAGE 52 A1069 — DIPLOM NAT/G POLICY BAL/PWR

B65
SOPER T.,EVOLVING COMMONWEALTH. AFR CANADA INDIA IRELAND UK LAW CONSTN POL/PAR DOMIN CONTROL WAR PWR ...AUD/VIS 18/20 COMMONWLTH OEEC. PAGE 135 A2769 — INT/ORG COLONIAL VOL/ASSN

B66
EUBANK K.,THE SUMMIT CONFERENCES. EUR+WWI USA+45 USA-45 MUNIC BAL/PWR WAR PEACE PWR...POLICY AUD/VIS 20 GENEVA/CON TEHERAN YALTA POTSDAM. PAGE 43 A0872 — CONFER NAT/G CHIEF DIPLOM

B66
LENGYEL E.,AFRICA: PAST, PRESENT, AND FUTURE. FUT SOUTH/AFR COLONIAL RACE/REL SOVEREIGN...GEOG AUD/VIS CHARTS T 20 CONGO/LEOP NEGRO. PAGE 87 A1771 — AFR CONSTN ECO/UNDEV

B66
LENT H.B.,THE PEACE CORPS: AMBASSADORS OF GOOD WILL. USA+45 ECO/UNDEV...INT TESTS BIOG AUD/VIS SOC/INTEG 20 PEACE/CORP. PAGE 87 A1776 — VOL/ASSN FOR/AID DIPLOM CONSULT

AUGUSTINE....SAINT AUGUSTINE

AUST/HUNG....AUSTRIA-HUNGARY

AUSTRALIA....SEE ALSO S/ASIA, COMMONWLTH

N
AUSTRALIAN PUBLIC AFFAIRS INFORMATION SERVICE. LAW — BIBLIOG

...HEAL HUM MGT SOC CON/ANAL 20 AUSTRAL. PAGE 2 A0028
NAT/G CULTURE DIPLOM

B42
FULLER G.H.,DEFENSE FINANCING: A SUPPLEMENTARY LIST OF REFERENCES (PAMPHLET). CANADA UK USA-45 ECO/DEV NAT/G DELIB/GP BUDGET ADJUD ARMS/CONT WEAPON COST PEACE PWR 20 AUSTRAL CHINJAP CONGRESS. PAGE 50 A1021
BIBLIOG/A FINAN FORCES DIPLOM

B42
FULLER G.H.,AUSTRALIA: A SELECT LIST OF REFERENCES. FORCES DIPLOM WAR 20 AUSTRAL. PAGE 50 A1022
BIBLIOG SOC

B45
ELTON G.E.,IMPERIAL COMMONWEALTH. INDIA UK DIPLOM DOMIN WAR NAT/LISM SOVEREIGN...TRADIT CHARTS T 15/20 CMN/WLTH AUSTRAL PRE/US/AM. PAGE 41 A0844
REGION CONCPT COLONIAL

B58
MANSERGH N.,COMMONWEALTH PERSPECTIVES. GHANA UK LAW VOL/ASSN CONFER HEALTH SOVEREIGN...GEOG CHARTS ANTHOL 20 CMN/WLTH AUSTRAL. PAGE 94 A1930
DIPLOM COLONIAL INT/ORG INGP/REL

S59
PADELFORD N.J.,"REGIONAL COOPERATION IN THE SOUTH PACIFIC: THE SOUTH PACIFIC COMMISSION." FUT NEW/ZEALND UK WOR+45 CULTURE ECO/UNDEV LOC/G VOL/ASSN...OBS CON/ANAL UNESCO VAL/FREE AUSTRAL 20. PAGE 112 A2308
INT/ORG ADMIN

S60
MODELSKI G.,"AUSTRALIA AND SEATO." S/ASIA USA+45 CULTURE INTELL ECO/DEV NAT/G PLAN DIPLOM ADMIN ROUTINE ATTIT SKILL...MGT TIME/SEQ AUSTRAL 20 SEATO. PAGE 102 A2097
INT/ORG ACT/RES

S61
WEST F.J.,"THE NEW GUINEA QUESTION: AN AUSTRALIAN VIEW." WOR+45 INT/ORG VOL/ASSN LEGIT PERCEPT ...POLICY TIME/SEQ AUSTRAL VAL/FREE 20 CMN/WLTH. PAGE 163 A3320
S/ASIA ECO/UNDEV

S62
CORET A.,"LE STATUT DE L'ILE CHRISTMAS DE L'OCEAN INDIEN." FUT S/ASIA ECO/DEV ECO/UNDEV VOL/ASSN DELIB/GP PLAN...RELATIV OBS TIME/SEQ TREND AUSTRAL 20. PAGE 30 A0619
NAT/G INT/ORG NEW/ZEALND

B63
MANSERGH N.,DOCUMENTS AND SPEECHES ON COMMONWEALTH AFFAIRS 1952-1962. CANADA INDIA PAKISTAN UK CONSTN FORCES ECO/TAC EDU/PROP COLONIAL DETER WAR ORD/FREE SOVEREIGN...POLICY 20 AUSTRAL. PAGE 94 A1932
BIBLIOG/A FEDERAL INT/TRADE DIPLOM

B64
CASEY R.G.,THE FUTURE OF THE COMMONWEALTH. INDIA PAKISTAN UK ECO/UNDEV INT/ORG TEC/DEV COLONIAL SUPEGO 20 EEC AUSTRAL. PAGE 25 A0505
DIPLOM SOVEREIGN NAT/LISM FOR/AID

B64
ESTHUS R.A.,FROM ENMITY TO ALLIANCE: US AUSTRALIAN RELATIONS. S/ASIA DIST/IND VOL/ASSN FORCES ATTIT 20 AUSTRAL TREATY CMN/WLTH. PAGE 42 A0863
DIPLOM WAR INT/TRADE FOR/AID

B64
HORNE D.,THE LUCKY COUNTRY: AUSTRALIA TODAY. UK CULTURE STRATA ATTIT PWR PLURISM...GOV/COMP 20 AUSTRAL. PAGE 67 A1386
RACE/REL DIPLOM NAT/G STRUCT

B65
MCCOLL G.D.,THE AUSTRALIAN BALANCE OF PAYMENTS. UK USA+45 AGRI WORKER DIPLOM EQUILIB PRODUC...STAT TREND CHARTS BIBLIOG/A 20 AUSTRAL. PAGE 97 A2001
ECO/DEV BAL/PAY INT/TRADE COST

B66
SOCIAL SCIENCE RESEARCH COUN,BIBLIOGRAPHY OF RESEARCH IN THE SOCIAL SCIENCES IN AUSTRALIA 1957-1960. LAW R+D DIPLOM 20 AUSTRAL. PAGE 135 A2758
BIBLIOG SOC PSY

S66
"RESEARCH WORK 1965-1966." NEW/ZEALND ELITES ACADEM LOC/G MUNIC POL/PAR PROVS DIPLOM COLONIAL...SOC 20 AUSTRAL. PAGE 4 A0073
BIBLIOG NAT/G CULTURE S/ASIA

AUSTRIA....SEE ALSO APPROPRIATE TIME/SPACE/CULTURE INDEX

N
DEUTSCHE BUCHEREI,JAHRESVERZEICHNIS DES DEUTSCHEN SCHRIFTUMS. AUSTRIA EUR+WWI GERMANY SWITZERLND LAW LOC/G DIPLOM ADMIN...MGT SOC 19/20. PAGE 37 A0745
BIBLIOG WRITING NAT/G

B30
SCHMITT B.E.,THE COMING OF THE WAR, 1914 (2 VOLS.). AUSTRIA FRANCE GERMANY MOD/EUR RUSSIA UK PLAN ROUTINE ORD/FREE. PAGE 128 A2633
WAR DIPLOM

B52
ALBERTINI L.,THE ORIGINS OF THE WAR OF 1914 (3 VOLS.). AUSTRIA FRANCE GERMANY MOD/EUR RUSSIA UK PROB/SOLV NEUTRAL PWR...BIBLIOG 19/20. PAGE 5 A0107
WAR DIPLOM FORCES BAL/PWR

B60
ENGEL-JANOSI F.,OSTERREICH UND DER VATIKAN (2 VOLS). AUSTRIA VATICAN NAT/LISM PEACE PERSON CATHISM 20. PAGE 42 A0852
DIPLOM ATTIT WAR

B66
EWING B.G.,PEACE THROUGH NEGOTIATION: THE AUSTRIAN EXPERIENCE. AUSTRIA USSR VIETNAM CONFER CONTROL DETER WAR ATTIT HEALTH PWR...POLICY 20. PAGE 43 A0878
PEACE DIPLOM MARXISM

B66
HOEVELER H.J.,INTERNATIONALE BEKAMPFUNG DES VERBRECHENS. AUSTRIA SWITZERLND WOR+45 INT/ORG CONTROL BIO/SOC...METH/COMP NAT/COMP 20 MAFIA SCOT/YARD FBI. PAGE 66 A1352
CRIMLGY CRIME DIPLOM INT/LAW

B66
STADLER K.R.,THE BIRTH OF THE AUSTRIAN REPUBLIC, 1918-1921. AUSTRIA PLAN TASK PEACE...POLICY DECISION 20. PAGE 137 A2798
NAT/G DIPLOM WAR DELIB/GP

B96
LOWELL A.L.,GOVERNMENTS AND PARTIES IN CONTINENTAL EUROPE, VOL. II. AUSTRIA GERMANY HUNGARY MOD/EUR SWITZERLND SOCIETY EX/STRUC LEGIS DIPLOM AGREE LEAD PARL/PROC PWR...POLICY 19. PAGE 91 A1867
POL/PAR NAT/G GOV/REL ELITES

AUTHORIT....AUTHORITARIANISM, PERSONAL; SEE ALSO DOMIN

B27
GOOCH G.P.,ENGLISH DEMOCRATIC IDEAS IN THE SEVENTEENTH CENTURY (2ND ED.). UK LAW SECT FORCES DIPLOM LEAD PARL/PROC REV ATTIT AUTHORIT...ANARCH CONCPT 17 PARLIAMENT CMN/WLTH REFORMERS. PAGE 54 A1100
IDEA/COMP MAJORIT EX/STRUC CONSERVE

B32
BLUM L.,PEACE AND DISARMAMENT (TRANS. BY A. WERTH). NAT/G FORCES WORKER DIPLOM AGREE WAR ATTIT AUTHORIT ORD/FREE. PAGE 16 A0322
SOCIALIST PEACE INT/ORG ARMS/CONT

B52
U OF MICH SURVEY RESEARCH CTR,AMERICA'S ROLE IN WORLD AFFAIRS. ASIA COM EUR+WWI USA+45 USSR FOR/AID WAR AUTHORIT ORD/FREE...DEEP/QU 20. PAGE 146 A2986
DIPLOM NAT/G ROLE POLICY

B64
CALVO SERER R.,LAS NUEVAS DEMOCRACIAS. AFR ASIA ISLAM USA+45 WOR+45 BAL/PWR DOMIN PARTIC INGP/REL AUTHORIT POPULISM...CONCPT 20 COM/PARTY. PAGE 23 A0469
ORD/FREE MARXISM DIPLOM POLICY

B64
STANKIEWICZ W.J.,POLITICAL THOUGHT SINCE WORLD WAR II. WOR+45 CAP/ISM DIPLOM COLONIAL COERCE REV REPRESENT ADJUST ANOMIE ALL/IDEOS 20. PAGE 137 A2804
IDEA/COMP DOMIN ORD/FREE AUTHORIT

B65
FAGG J.E.,CUBA, HAITI, AND THE DOMINICAN REPUBLIC. CUBA DOMIN/REP HAITI L/A+17C NAT/G DIPLOM ECO/TAC DOMIN CHOOSE AUTHORIT ROLE SOVEREIGN POPULISM 17/20. PAGE 43 A0883
COLONIAL ECO/UNDEV REV GOV/COMP

B65
RUBINSTEIN A.Z.,THE CHALLENGE OF POLITICS: IDEAS AND ISSUES (2ND ED.). UNIV ELITES SOCIETY EX/STRUC BAL/PWR PARL/PROC AUTHORIT...DECISION ANTHOL 20. PAGE 125 A2565
NAT/G DIPLOM GP/REL ORD/FREE

B66
BRACKMAN A.C.,SOUTHEAST ASIA'S SECOND FRONT: THE POWER STRUGGLE IN THE MALAY ARCHIPELAGO. CHINA/COM INDONESIA MALAYSIA ECO/UNDEV INT/ORG NAT/G FORCES DIPLOM EDU/PROP REGION COERCE GUERRILLA AUTHORIT POPULISM...MAJORIT 20 KENNEDY/JF SEATO. PAGE 18 A0367
S/ASIA MARXISM REV

S67
PAUKER G.J.,"TOWARD A NEW ORDER IN INDONESIA." COM INDONESIA S/ASIA ECO/UNDEV POL/PAR EX/STRUC TOP/EX BAL/PWR ECO/TAC FOR/AID DOMIN NAT/LISM AUTHORIT ORD/FREE PWR 20. PAGE 114 A2342
REV NAT/G DIPLOM CIVMIL/REL

S67
SAPP B.B.,"TRIBAL CULTURES AND COMMUNISM." AFR USA+45 STRATA DIPLOM FOR/AID REGION CENTRAL ATTIT AUTHORIT RIGID/FLEX KNOWL. PAGE 127 A2604
KIN MARXISM ECO/UNDEV STRUCT

S67
SHOEMAKER R.L.,"JAPANESE ARMY AND THE WEST." ASIA ELITES EX/STRUC DIPLOM DOMIN EDU/PROP COERCE ATTIT AUTHORIT PWR 1/20 CHINJAP. PAGE 132 A2703
FORCES TEC/DEV WAR TOTALISM

AUTHORITY....SEE DOMIN

AUTOMAT....AUTOMATION; SEE ALSO COMPUTER, PLAN

N
AMERICAN DOCUMENTATION INST,DOCUMENTATION ABSTRACTS. WOR+45 NAT/G COMPUTER CREATE TEC/DEV DIPLOM EDU/PROP REGION KNOWL...PHIL/SCI CLASSIF
BIBLIOG/A AUTOMAT COMPUT/IR

LING. PAGE 7 A0143 R+D

B57
DRUCKER P.F.,AMERICA'S NEXT TWENTY YEARS. USA+45 DIST/IND ACADEM MUNIC SCHOOL DIPLOM ECO/TAC AUTOMAT HABITAT HEALTH...SOC/WK TREND 20 URBAN/RNWL PUB/TRANS. PAGE 39 A0788
WORKER FOR/AID CENSUS GEOG

B63
OECD,SCIENCE AND THE POLICIES OF GOVERNMENTS: THE IMPLICATIONS OF SCIENCE AND TECHNOLOGY FOR NATL AND INTL AFFAIRS. WOR+45 INT/ORG EDU/PROP AUTOMAT ...POLICY PHIL/SCI 20. PAGE 111 A2279
CREATE TEC/DEV DIPLOM NAT/G

B65
LYONS G.M.,AMERICA: PURPOSE AND POWER. UK USA+45 FINAN INDUS MARKET WORKER TEC/DEV DIPLOM AUTOMAT NUC/PWR WAR RACE/REL ORD/FREE 20 EEC CONGRESS SUPREME/CT CIV/RIGHTS. PAGE 92 A1881
PWR PROB/SOLV ECO/DEV TASK

B65
MOWRY G.E.,THE URBAN NATION 1920-1960. USA+45 USA-45 SOCIETY ECO/DEV MUNIC FOR/AID INT/TRADE AUTOMAT...BIBLIOG/A 20. PAGE 105 A2161
TEC/DEV NAT/G TOTALISM DIPLOM

B67
BARANSON J.,TECHNOLOGY FOR UNDERDEVELOPED AREAS: AN ANNOTATED BIBLIOGRAPHY. FUT WOR+45 CULTURE INDUS INT/ORG CREATE PROB/SOLV INT/TRADE EDU/PROP AUTOMAT ...CONCPT METH. PAGE 11 A0218
BIBLIOG/A ECO/UNDEV TEC/DEV R+D

B67
US SUPERINTENDENT OF DOCUMENTS,LIBRARY OF CONGRESS (PRICE LIST 83). AFR ASIA EUR+WWI USA-45 USSR NAT/G DIPLOM CONFER CT/SYS WAR...DECISION PHIL/SCI CLASSIF 19/20 CONGRESS PRESIDENT. PAGE 157 A3205
BIBLIOG/A USA+45 AUTOMAT LAW

AUTOMOBILE....AUTOMOBILE

AUVADE R. A0198

AVERAGE....MEAN, AVERAGE BEHAVIORS

AVRAMOVIC D. A0199

AZERBAIJAN....AZERBAIJAN, IRAN

B

BA/MBUTI....BA MBUTI - THE FOREST PEOPLE (CONGO)

BABIES....SEE AGE/C

BACKUS/I....ISAAC BACKUS

BACON F. A0200,A0201

BACON/F....FRANCIS BACON

BADEN....BADEN

BAGHDAD....BAGHDAD, IRAQ

B58
UN INTL CONF ON PEACEFUL USE,PROGRESS IN ATOMIC ENERGY (VOL. I). WOR+45 R+D PLAN TEC/DEV CONFER CONTROL PEACE SKILL...CHARTS ANTHOL 20 UN BAGHDAD. PAGE 147 A3003
NUC/PWR DIPLOM WORKER EDU/PROP

BAGU S. A0202

BAHAWALPUR....BAHAWALPUR, PAKISTAN

BAHIA....BAHIA

BAIL....BAIL

BAILEY S.D. A0203,A0204,A0205,A0206,A0207

BAILEY T.A. A0208

BAILEY/JM....JOHN MORAN BAILEY

BAILEY/S....S. BAILEY

BAILEY/T....THOMAS BAILEY

BAINS J.S. A0209

BAKUBA....BAKUBA TRIBE

BAL/PAY....BALANCE OF PAYMENTS

B08
GRIFFIN A.P.C.,LIST OF REFERENCES ON INTERNATIONAL ARBITRATION. FRANCE L/A+17C USA-45 WOR-45 DIPLOM CONFER COLONIAL ARMS/CONT BAL/PAY EQUILIB SOVEREIGN ...DECISION 19/20 MEXIC/AMER. PAGE 56 A1156
BIBLIOG/A INT/ORG INT/LAW DELIB/GP

B48
GRAHAM F.D.,THE THEORY OF INTERNATIONAL VALUES. FUT WOR+45 WOR-45 ECO/DEV FINAN INT/ORG PLAN TEC/DEV CAP/ISM DIPLOM ECO/TAC TARIFFS ROUTINE BAL/PAY DRIVE PWR WEALTH SOCISM...POLICY STAT HYPO/EXP GEN/LAWS 20. PAGE 55 A1125
NEW/IDEA INT/TRADE

C50
ELLSWORTH P.T.,"INTERNATIONAL ECONOMY." ECO/DEV ECO/UNDEV FINAN LABOR DIPLOM FOR/AID TARIFFS BAL/PAY EQUILIB NAT/LISM OPTIMAL...INT/LAW 20 ILO GATT. PAGE 41 A0843
BIBLIOG INT/TRADE ECO/TAC INT/ORG

B53
NEISSER H.,NATIONAL INCOMES AND INTERNATIONAL TRADE. FRANCE GERMANY SWEDEN UK USA-45 EXTR/IND FINAN INDUS TEC/DEV PRICE BAL/PAY EQUILIB INCOME WEALTH...CHARTS METH 19 CHINJAP. PAGE 108 A2215
INT/TRADE PRODUC MARKET CON/ANAL

B54
TINBERGEN J.,INTERNATIONAL ECONOMIC INTEGRATION. WOR+45 WOR-45 ECO/UNDEV NAT/G ECO/TAC BAL/PAY ...METH/CNCPT STAT TIME/SEQ GEN/METH OEEC 20. PAGE 144 A2941
INT/ORG ECO/DEV INT/TRADE

B56
KRAUS O.,THEORIE DER ZWISCHENSTAATLICHEN WIRTSCHAFTSBEZIEHUNGEN. TARIFFS WAR COST 20. PAGE 82 A1677
INT/TRADE DIPLOM BAL/PAY ECO/TAC

B57
MCNEILL W.H.,GREECE: AMERICAN AID IN ACTION. GREECE UK USA+45 FINAN CAP/ISM INT/TRADE BAL/PAY PRODUC WEALTH...POLICY METH/COMP 20. PAGE 99 A2022
FOR/AID DIPLOM ECO/UNDEV

B57
TRIFFIN R.,EUROPE AND THE MONEY MUDDLE. USA+45 INT/ORG NAT/G CONSULT PLAN ECO/TAC EXEC ROUTINE BAL/PAY WEALTH...METH/CNCPT OBS TREND CHARTS STERTYP GEN/METH EEC VAL/FREE ECSC. PAGE 145 A2962
EUR+WWI ECO/DEV REGION

B58
AVRAMOVIC D.,POSTWAR GROWTH IN INTERNATIONAL INDEBTEDNESS. WOR+45 AGRI INDUS CAP/ISM PRICE INCOME...NAT/COMP 20 GOLD/STAND SILVER. PAGE 10 A0199
INT/TRADE FINAN COST BAL/PAY

B58
PALMER E.E.,AMERICAN FOREIGN POLICY. USA+45 CULTURE ECO/UNDEV NAT/G PLAN GIVE BAL/PAY ORD/FREE WEALTH POPULISM...DECISION ANTHOL 20. PAGE 113 A2319
DIPLOM ECO/TAC POLICY

B58
SCITOUSKY T.,ECONOMIC THEORY AND WESTERN EUROPEAN INTEGRATION. EUR+WWI INT/ORG ACT/RES INT/TRADE REGION BAL/PAY WEALTH...METH/CNCPT STAT CHARTS GEN/METH ECSC TOT/POP EEC OEEC 20. PAGE 130 A2668
ECO/TAC

B59
ALLEN W.R.,FOREIGN TRADE AND FINANCE. ECO/DEV DIPLOM BAL/PAY...POLICY CONCPT ANTHOL 20. PAGE 6 A0127
INT/TRADE EQUILIB FINAN

B59
ROPKE W.,INTERNATIONAL ORDER AND ECONOMIC INTEGRATION. ECO/DEV ECO/UNDEV AGRI FINAN INDUS INT/ORG WAR PEACE ORD/FREE...SOC METH/COMP 20 EEC. PAGE 123 A2524
INT/TRADE DIPLOM BAL/PAY ALL/IDEOS

B59
STOVEL J.A.,CANADA IN THE WORLD ECONOMY. CANADA PRICE DEMAND...STAT CHARTS BIBLIOG 20 VINER/J. PAGE 139 A2838
INT/TRADE BAL/PAY FINAN ECO/TAC

B60
KENEN P.B.,GIANT AMONG NATIONS: PROBLEMS IN UNITED STATES FOREIGN ECONOMIC POLICY. USA+45 FINAN DIPLOM TARIFFS BAL/PAY WEALTH 20 COLD/WAR. PAGE 77 A1584
FOR/AID ECO/UNDEV INT/TRADE PLAN

B60
KENEN P.B.,BRITISH MONETARY POLICY AND THE BALANCE OF PAYMENTS 1951-57. UK PLAN BUDGET ECO/TAC INT/TRADE PAY PRICE COST ATTIT 20. PAGE 77 A1585
BAL/PAY PROB/SOLV FINAN NAT/G

B60
LEVIN J.V.,THE EXPORT ECONOMIES: THEIR PATTERN OF DEVELOPMENT IN HISTORICAL PERSPECTIVE. BURMA PERU AGRI WORKER COLONIAL COST DEMAND INCOME 20. PAGE 88 A1795
INT/TRADE ECO/UNDEV BAL/PAY EXTR/IND

B60
THEOBALD R.,THE RICH AND THE POOR: A STUDY OF THE ECONOMICS OF RISING EXPECTATIONS. WOR+45 CONSTN ECO/DEV ECO/UNDEV INT/ORG NAT/G PLAN FOR/AID ROUTINE BAL/PAY ORD/FREE PWR WEALTH...GEOG TREND WORK 20. PAGE 142 A2912
ECO/TAC INT/TRADE

S60
MARTIN E.M.,"NEW TRENDS IN UNITED STATES ECONOMIC FOREIGN POLICY." USA+45 INTELL DELIB/GP FOR/AID INT/TRADE ROUTINE BAL/PAY...RELATIV 20. PAGE 95 A1949
NAT/G PLAN DIPLOM

B61
EINZIG P.,A DYNAMIC THEORY OF FORWARD EXCHANGE. FUT WOR+45 WOR-45 INT/TRADE BAL/PAY WEALTH...OLD/LIB NEW/IDEA OBS TREND 20. PAGE 41 A0830
FINAN ECO/TAC

B61
GURTOO D.H.N.,INDIA'S BALANCE OF PAYMENTS (1920-1960). INDIA FINAN DIPLOM FOR/AID INT/TRADE PRICE COLONIAL...CHARTS BIBLIOG 20. PAGE 58 A1197
BAL/PAY STAT ECO/TAC ECO/UNDEV

B61
HARRIS S.E.,THE DOLLAR IN CRISIS. USA+45 MARKET INT/ORG ECO/TAC PRICE CONTROL WEALTH...METH/COMP
BAL/PAY DIPLOM

ANTHOL 20 GOLD/STAND. PAGE 62 A1269
FINAN INT/TRADE

B61
OECD,STATISTICS OF BALANCE OF PAYMENTS 1950-61. WOR+45 FINAN ECO/TAC INT/TRADE DEMAND WEALTH...STAT NAT/COMP 20 OEEC OECD. PAGE 111 A2278
BAL/PAY ECO/DEV INT/ORG CHARTS

B61
OEEC,LIBERALISATION OF CURRENT INVISIBLES AND CAPITAL MOVEMENTS BY THE OEEC (PAMPHLET). WOR+45 ECO/DEV BUDGET ECO/TAC ORD/FREE 20. PAGE 111 A2282
FINAN INT/ORG INT/TRADE BAL/PAY

B61
SCAMMEL W.M.,INTERNATIONAL MONETARY POLICY. WOR+45 WOR-45 ACT/RES ECO/TAC LEGIT WEALTH...GEN/METH UN 20. PAGE 127 A2611
INT/ORG FINAN BAL/PAY

B61
TRIFFIN R.,GOLD AND THE DOLLAR CRISIS: THE FUTURE OF CONVERTIBILITY. USA+45 USA-45 INT/ORG PROB/SOLV BUDGET INT/TRADE PRICE...STAT CHARTS 19/20 GOLD/STAND. PAGE 145 A2963
FINAN ECO/DEV ECO/TAC BAL/PAY

B61
US CONGRESS JOINT ECO COMM,INTERNATIONAL PAYMENTS IMBALANCES AND NEED FOR STRENGTHENING INTERNATIONAL FINANCIAL ARRANGEMENTS. USA+45 WOR+45 DELIB/GP DIPLOM INT/TRADE...CHARTS 20 CONGRESS OEEC. PAGE 150 A3063
BAL/PAY INT/ORG FINAN PROB/SOLV

S61
"CRITERIA FOR ALLOCATING INVESTMENT RESOURCES AMONG VARIOUS FIELDS OF DEVELOPMENT IN UNDERDEVELOPED ECONOMIES." ASIA AGRI INT/ORG CAP/ISM BAL/PAY EFFICIENCY PROFIT WEALTH...STAT 20 UN. PAGE 3 A0061
BIBLIOG/A ECO/UNDEV PLAN TEC/DEV

S61
DELLA PORT G.,"PROBLEMI E PROSPETTIVE DI COESISTENZA FRA ORIENTE ED OCCIDENTE, (PART 3)." COM FUT WOR+45 NAT/G BAL/PWR FOR/AID BAL/PAY PWR WEALTH...SOC CONCPT GEN/LAWS COLD/WAR 20. PAGE 36 A0729
INT/TRADE

S61
VINER J.,"ECONOMIC FOREIGN POLICY ON THE NEW FRONTIER." USA+45 ECO/UNDEV AGRI FINAN INDUS MARKET INT/ORG NAT/G FOR/AID INT/TRADE ADMIN ATTIT PWR 20 KENNEDY/JF. PAGE 159 A3239
TOP/EX ECO/TAC BAL/PAY TARIFFS

B62
ROUND TABLE ON EUROPE'S ROLE IN LATIN AMERICAN DEVELOPMENT. EUR+WWI L/A+17C PLAN BAL/PAY UTIL ROLE WEALTH...CHARTS ANTHOL 20 UN INT/AM/DEV. PAGE 3 A0063
ECO/UNDEV FINAN TEC/DEV FOR/AID

B62
FORD A.G.,THE GOLD STANDARD 1880-1914: BRITAIN AND ARGENTINA. UK ECO/UNDEV INT/TRADE ADMIN GOV/REL DEMAND EFFICIENCY...STAT CHARTS 19/20 ARGEN GOLD/STAND. PAGE 47 A0960
FINAN ECO/TAC BUDGET BAL/PAY

B62
HOLMAN A.G.,SOME MEASURES AND INTERPRETATIONS OF EFFECTS OF US FOREIGN ENTERPRISES ON US BALANCE OF PAYMENTS. USA+45 COST INCOME WEALTH...MATH CHARTS 20. PAGE 67 A1371
BAL/PAY INT/TRADE FINAN ECO/TAC

B62
HUMPHREY D.D.,THE UNITED STATES AND THE COMMON MARKET. USA+45 INDUS MARKET INT/ORG PLAN EDU/PROP BAL/PAY DRIVE PWR WEALTH...TREND STERTYP EEC 20. PAGE 69 A1415
ATTIT ECO/TAC

B62
KINDLEBERGER C.P.,FOREIGN TRADE AND THE NATIONAL ECONOMY. WOR+45 ECO/DEV ECO/UNDEV ECO/TAC COST DEMAND 20. PAGE 79 A1622
INT/TRADE GOV/COMP BAL/PAY POLICY

B62
LUTZ F.A.,THE PROBLEM OF INTERNATIONAL ECONOMIC EQUILIBRIUM. FINAN PRODUC WEALTH 20 MONEY. PAGE 92 A1876
DIPLOM EQUILIB BAL/PAY PROB/SOLV

B62
THEOBALD R.,NATIONAL DEVELOPMENT EFFORTS (PAMPHLET). WOR+45 AGRI BUDGET FOR/AID INT/TRADE TAX 20. PAGE 142 A2914
ECO/UNDEV PLAN BAL/PAY WEALTH

B62
US CONGRESS JOINT ECO COMM,FACTORS AFFECTING THE UNITED STATES BALANCE OF PAYMENTS. USA+45 DELIB/GP PLAN DIPLOM FOR/AID PRODUC WEALTH...CHARTS 20 CONGRESS OEEC. PAGE 150 A3064
BAL/PAY INT/TRADE ECO/TAC FINAN

B62
ZOOK P.D.,FOREIGN TRADE AND HUMAN CAPITAL. L/A+17C USA+45 FINAN DIPLOM ECO/TAC PRODUC...POLICY 20. PAGE 170 A3458
INT/TRADE ECO/UNDEV FOR/AID BAL/PAY

B63
FATEMI N.S.,THE DOLLAR CRISIS. USA+45 INDUS NAT/G LEGIS BUDGET TAX COST...CHARTS METH/COMP 20 EEC. PAGE 44 A0902
PROB/SOLV BAL/PAY FOR/AID PLAN

B63
GUIMARAES A.P.,INFLACAO E MONOPOLIO NO BRASIL. BRAZIL FINAN NAT/G PLAN PAY...METH/COMP 20. PAGE 58 A1189
ECO/UNDEV PRICE INT/TRADE BAL/PAY

B63
INTERNATIONAL MONETARY FUND,COMPENSATORY FINANCING OF EXPORT FLUCTUATIONS (PAMPHLET). WOR+45 ECO/DEV ECO/UNDEV INT/ORG WEALTH...TREND 20 IMF MONEY. PAGE 71 A1459
BAL/PAY FINAN BUDGET INT/TRADE

B63
LARY M.B.,PROBLEMS OF THE UNITED STATES AS WORLD TRADER AND BANKER. USA+45 NAT/G PLAN DIPLOM FOR/AID ...TREND CHARTS. PAGE 85 A1737
ECO/DEV FINAN BAL/PAY INT/TRADE

B63
MYRDAL G.,CHALLENGE TO AFFLUENCE. USA+45 WOR+45 FINAN INT/ORG NAT/G PLAN ECO/TAC INT/TRADE BAL/PAY ORD/FREE 20 EUROPE/W. PAGE 107 A2189
ECO/DEV WEALTH DIPLOM PRODUC

B63
SALENT W.S.,THE UNITED STATES BALANCE OF PAYMENTS IN 1968. EUR+WWI UK USA+45 AGRI R+D LABOR FORCES PRODUC...GEOG CONCPT CHARTS 20 CHINJAP EEC. PAGE 126 A2589
BAL/PAY DEMAND FINAN INT/TRADE

B63
US CONGRESS JOINT ECO COMM,DISCRIMINATORY OCEAN FREIGHT RATES AND BALANCE OF PAYMENTS. USA+45 SEA DELIB/GP DISCRIM...CHARTS 20 CONGRESS. PAGE 150 A3066
BAL/PAY DIST/IND PRICE INT/TRADE

B63
US CONGRESS JOINT ECO COMM,THE UNITED STATES BALANCE OF PAYMENTS. USA+45 DELIB/GP BUDGET PRICE PRODUC 20 CONGRESS GOLD/STAND MONEY. PAGE 150 A3067
BAL/PAY INT/TRADE FINAN ECO/TAC

B63
US CONGRESS JOINT ECO COMM,THE UNITED STATES BALANCE OF PAYMENTS. USA+45 DELIB/GP CONFER...MATH PREDICT CHARTS 20 CONGRESS. PAGE 150 A3068
BAL/PAY ECO/TAC INT/TRADE CONSULT

B63
US HOUSE COMM BANKING-CURR,RECENT CHANGES IN MONETARY POLICY AND BALANCE OF PAYMENTS PROBLEMS. USA+45 DELIB/GP PLAN DIPLOM...CHARTS 20 CONGRESS. PAGE 153 A3121
BAL/PAY FINAN ECO/TAC POLICY

S63
NADLER E.B.,"SOME ECONOMIC DISADVANTAGES OF THE ARMS RACE." USA+45 INDUS R+D FORCES PLAN TEC/DEV ECO/TAC FOR/AID EDU/PROP PWR WEALTH...TREND COLD/WAR 20. PAGE 107 A2190
ECO/DEV MGT BAL/PAY

C63
SCHMITT K.M.,"EVOLUTION OR CHAOS: DYNAMICS OF LATIN AMERICAN GOVERNMENT AND POLITICS." L/A+17C AGRI FINAN CAP/ISM EXEC LEAD BAL/PAY TOTALISM ATTIT ...TREND BIBLIOG 20. PAGE 129 A2635
DIPLOM POLICY POL/PAR LOBBY

N63
US AGENCY INTERNATIONAL DEV,PRINCIPLES OF FOREIGN ECONOMIC ASSISTANCE (PAMPHLET). USA+45 FINAN GP/REL BAL/PAY EFFICIENCY 20 AID. PAGE 149 A3051
FOR/AID PLAN ECO/UNDEV ATTIT

B64
HANSEN B.,INTERNATIONAL LIQUIDITY. USA+45 INT/ORG ECO/TAC PRICE CONTROL WEALTH...POLICY 20. PAGE 61 A1254
BAL/PAY INT/TRADE DIPLOM FINAN

B64
KALDOR N.,ESSAYS ON ECONOMIC POLICY (VOL. II). CHILE GERMANY INDIA FINAN...GOV/COMP METH/COMP 20 KEYNES/JM. PAGE 76 A1551
BAL/PAY INT/TRADE METH/CNCPT ECO/UNDEV

B64
REUSS H.S.,THE CRITICAL DECADE - AN ECONOMIC POLICY FOR AMERICA AND THE FREE WORLD. USA+45 FINAN POL/PAR WORKER PLAN DIPLOM ECO/TAC TARIFFS BAL/PAY ...POLICY 20 CONGRESS GOLD/STAND. PAGE 120 A2468
FOR/AID INT/TRADE LABOR LEGIS

B64
RIVKIN A.,AFRICA AND THE EUROPEAN COMMON MARKET (PAMPHLET). AFR MOD/EUR WOR+45 TEC/DEV FOR/AID TARIFFS BAL/PAY...POLICY 20 EEC. PAGE 121 A2490
INT/ORG INT/TRADE ECO/TAC ECO/UNDEV

L64
CARNEGIE ENDOWMENT INT. PEACE,"ECONOMIC AND SOCIAL QUESTION (ISSUES BEFORE THE NINETEENTH GENERAL ASSEMBLY)." WOR+45 ECO/DEV ECO/UNDEV INDUS R+D DELIB/GP CREATE PLAN TEC/DEV ECO/TAC FOR/AID BAL/PAY...RECORD UN 20. PAGE 24 A0493
INT/ORG INT/TRADE

L64
KORBONSKI A.,"COMECON." ASIA ECO/DEV ECO/UNDEV ECO/TAC BAL/PAY NAT/LISM 20 COMECON. PAGE 81 A1671
COM INT/ORG INT/TRADE

S64
HJELIN D.,"ECONOMIC INTEGRATION IN LATIN AMERICAN: PROGRESS AND PROBLEMS." L/A+17C ECO/DEV AGRI DIST/IND FINAN INDUS NAT/G VOL/ASSN CONSULT DELIB/GP EX/STRUC ACT/RES PLAN TEC/DEV ECO/TAC ROUTINE BAL/PAY WEALTH WORK 20. PAGE 69 A1411
MARKET ECO/UNDEV INT/TRADE

S64
MCCREARY E.A.,"THOSE AMERICAN MANAGERS DON'T IMPRESS EUROPE." EUR+WWI USA+45 CULTURE STRATA
MARKET ACT/RES

ECO/DEV TOP/EX INT/TRADE ATTIT DRIVE PERSON RIGID/FLEX...CONCPT 20. PAGE 98 A2003 — BAL/PAY CAP/ISM

S64

NEISSER H.,"THE EXTERNAL EQUILIBRIUM OF THE UNITED STATES ECONOMY." FUT USA+45 NAT/G ACT/RES PLAN ECO/TAC ATTIT WEALTH...METH/CNCPT GEN/METH VAL/FREE 20. PAGE 108 A2216 — FINAN ECO/DEV BAL/PAY INT/TRADE

B65

CASSELL F.,GOLD OR CREDIT? THE ECONOMICS AND POLITICS OF INTERNATIONAL MONEY. WOR+45 PLAN PROB/SOLV BAL/PAY SOVEREIGN WEALTH 20 OEEC GOLD/STAND. PAGE 25 A0506 — FINAN INT/ORG DIPLOM ECO/TAC

B65

DEMAS W.G.,THE ECONOMICS OF DEVELOPMENT IN SMALL COUNTRIES WITH SPECIAL REFERENCE TO THE CARIBBEAN. WOR+45 BAL/PAY DEMAND EFFICIENCY PRODUC...GEOG CARIBBEAN. PAGE 36 A0731 — ECO/UNDEV PLAN WEALTH INT/TRADE

B65

MCCOLL G.D.,THE AUSTRALIAN BALANCE OF PAYMENTS. UK USA+45 AGRI WORKER DIPLOM EQUILIB PRODUC...STAT TREND CHARTS BIBLIOG/A 20 AUSTRAL. PAGE 97 A2001 — ECO/DEV BAL/PAY INT/TRADE COST

B65

ROLFE S.E.,GOLD AND WORLD POWER. UK USA+45 WOR-45 INDUS WORKER INT/TRADE DEMAND...MGT CHARTS 20 GOLD/STAND. PAGE 123 A2517 — BAL/PAY EQUILIB ECO/TAC DIPLOM

B65

US BUREAU OF THE BUDGET,THE BALANCE OF PAYMENTS STATISTICS OF THE UNITED STATES: A REVIEW AND APPRAISAL. USA+45 FINAN NAT/G PROB/SOLV DIPLOM. PAGE 150 A3057 — BAL/PAY STAT METH/COMP BUDGET

B65

US CONGRESS JOINT ECO COMM,GUIDELINES FOR INTERNATIONAL MONETARY REFORM. USA+45 WOR+45 DELIB/GP BAL/PAY 20 CONGRESS IMF MONEY. PAGE 150 A3069 — DIPLOM FINAN PLAN INT/ORG

B65

US SENATE COMM BANKING CURR,BALANCE OF PAYMENTS - 1965. USA+45 ECO/TAC PRICE WEALTH...CHARTS 20 CONGRESS GOLD/STAND. PAGE 156 A3171 — BAL/PAY FINAN DIPLOM INT/TRADE

B65

US SENATE COMM ON JUDICIARY,ANTITRUST EXEMPTIONS FOR AGREEMENTS RELATING TO BALANCE OF PAYMENTS. FINAN ECO/TAC CONTROL WEALTH...POLICY 20 CONGRESS. PAGE 157 A3195 — BAL/PAY ADJUD MARKET INT/TRADE

B66

INTERNATIONAL ECO POLICY ASSN,THE UNITED STATES BALANCE OF PAYMENTS. INT/ORG NAT/G PROB/SOLV BUDGET DIPLOM INT/TRADE WEALTH 20. PAGE 71 A1454 — BAL/PAY ECO/TAC POLICY FINAN

B66

INTERNATIONAL ECONOMIC ASSN,STABILITY AND PROGRESS IN THE WORLD ECONOMY: THE FIRST CONGRESS OF THE INTERNATIONAL ECONOMIC ASSOCIATION. WOR+45 ECO/DEV ECO/UNDEV DELIB/GP FOR/AID BAL/PAY...TREND CMN/WLTH 20. PAGE 71 A1455 — INT/TRADE

B66

KINDLEBERGER C.P.,EUROPE AND THE DOLLAR. EUR+WWI FRANCE GERMANY/W USA+45 CONSTN INT/ORG DIPLOM INT/TRADE...ANTHOL 20 GOLD/STAND. PAGE 79 A1623 — BAL/PAY BUDGET FINAN ECO/DEV

B66

LEAGUE OF WOMEN VOTERS OF US,FOREIGN AID AT THE CROSSROADS. USA+45 WOR+45 DELIB/GP PROB/SOLV DIPLOM INT/TRADE RECEIVE BAL/PAY...CHARTS 20 UN. PAGE 86 A1756 — FOR/AID GIVE ECO/UNDEV PLAN

B66

LUARD E.,THE EVOLUTION OF INTERNATIONAL ORGANIZATIONS. UK WOR+45 BUDGET INT/TRADE WAR BAL/PAY PEACE ORD/FREE...POLICY 19/20 EEC ILO LEAGUE/NAT UN. PAGE 91 A1871 — INT/ORG EFFICIENCY CREATE TREND

B66

MEERHAEGHE M.,INTERNATIONAL ECONOMIC INSTITUTIONS. EUR+WWI FINAN INDUS MARKET PLAN TARIFFS BAL/PAY EQUILIB...POLICY BIBLIOG/A 20 GATT OEEC EEC IBRD EURCOALSTL. PAGE 99 A2032 — ECO/TAC ECO/DEV INT/TRADE INT/ORG

B66

PIQUET H.S.,THE US BALANCE OF PAYMENTS AND INTERNATIONAL MONETARY RESERVES. USA+45 PROB/SOLV INT/TRADE GOV/REL EQUILIB...POLICY STAT CHARTS 20 GOLD/STAND. PAGE 116 A2384 — BAL/PAY DIPLOM FINAN ECO/TAC

B66

ROBERTSON D.J.,THE BRITISH BALANCE OF PAYMENTS. UK WOR+45 INDUS BUDGET TAX ADJUST...CHARTS ANTHOL 20. PAGE 122 A2500 — FINAN BAL/PAY ECO/DEV INT/TRADE

B66

TRIFFIN R.,THE WORLD MONEY MAZE. INT/ORG ECO/TAC PRICE OPTIMAL WEALTH...METH/COMP 20 EEC OEEC GOLD/STAND SILVER. PAGE 145 A2964 — BAL/PAY FINAN INT/TRADE DIPLOM

B66

TRIFFIN R.,THE BALANCE OF PAYMENTS AND THE FOREIGN INVESTMENT POSITION OF THE UNITED STATES. USA+45 INT/ORG INT/TRADE PRICE CONTROL...POLICY 20 GOLD/STAND. PAGE 145 A2965 — BAL/PAY DIPLOM FINAN ECO/TAC

B66

US CONGRESS JOINT ECO COMM,NEW APPROACH TO UNITED STATES INTERNATIONAL ECONOMIC POLICY. USA+45 WOR+45 CHIEF DELIB/GP CONFER...CHARTS 20 CONGRESS MONEY. PAGE 150 A3070 — DIPLOM ECO/TAC BAL/PAY FINAN

B66

WOOLLEY H.B.,MEASURING TRANSACTIONS BETWEEN WORLD AREAS. WOR+45 FINAN...STAT NET/THEORY CHARTS DICTIONARY 20 GOLD/STAND. PAGE 167 A3395 — INT/TRADE BAL/PAY DIPLOM ECOMETRIC

B66

YEAGER L.B.,INTERNATIONAL MONETARY RELATIONS: THEORY, HISTORY, AND POLICY. WOR+45 WOR-45 INT/TRADE BAL/PAY...NAT/COMP 18/20 MONEY. PAGE 169 A3432 — FINAN DIPLOM ECO/TAC IDEA/COMP

N66

BRITISH DEVELOPMENT POLICIES: 1966 (PAMPHLET). UK AGRI TARIFFS BAL/PAY...TREND CHARTS 20 OVRSEA/DEV. PAGE 4 A0076 — WEALTH DIPLOM INT/TRADE FOR/AID

N66

EOMMITTEE ECONOMIC DEVELOPMENT,THE DOLLAR AND THE WORLD MONETARY SYSTEM: A STATEMENT ON NATIONAL POLICY (PAMPHLET). USA+45 NAT/G PLAN PROB/SOLV BUDGET ECO/TAC FOR/AID INCOME...POLICY 20 GOLD/STAND EUROPE. PAGE 42 A0854 — FINAN BAL/PAY DIPLOM ECO/DEV

B67

CLARK S.V.O.,CENTRAL BANK COOPERATION: 1924-31. WOR-45 PROB/SOLV ECO/TAC ADJUST BAL/PAY...TREND CHARTS METH/COMP 20. PAGE 27 A0542 — FINAN EQUILIB DIPLOM POLICY

B67

DILLARD D.,ECONOMIC DEVELOPMENT OF THE NORTH ATLANTIC COMMUNITY. EUR+WWI MOD/EUR USA+45 USA-45 ECO/UNDEV LABOR CAP/ISM WAR BAL/PAY...NAT/COMP 15/20. PAGE 37 A0763 — ECO/DEV INT/TRADE INDUS DIPLOM

B67

RUEFF J.,BALANCE OF PAYMENTS. WOR+45 FINAN TEC/DEV DIPLOM TARIFFS PRICE CONTROL...POLICY CONCPT IDEA/COMP. PAGE 125 A2567 — INT/TRADE BAL/PAY ECO/TAC NAT/COMP

B67

US AGENCY INTERNATIONAL DEV,PROPOSED FOREIGN AID PROGRAM FOR 1968: SUMMARY PRESENTATION TO THE CONGRESS. AFR S/ASIA USA+45 AGRI TEC/DEV DIPLOM ECO/TAC BAL/PAY COST HEALTH KNOWL SKILL 20 AID CONGRESS. PAGE 149 A3053 — ECO/UNDEV BUDGET FOR/AID STAT

B67

US CONGRESS SENATE,SURVEY OF THE ALLIANCE FOR PROGRESS: INFLATION IN LATIN AMERICA (PAMPHLET). USA+45 MARKET INT/ORG DIPLOM INT/TRADE BAL/PAY SENATE. PAGE 150 A3072 — L/A+17C FINAN POLICY FOR/AID

L67

DEVADHAR Y.C.,"THE ROLE OF FOREIGN PRIVATE CAPITAL IN INDIA'S ECONOMIC DEVELOPMENT* ASSESSMENT OF POLICY AND PERFORMANCE." INDIA INDUS PLAN TEC/DEV BUDGET DIPLOM ECO/TAC BAL/PAY PRODUC WEALTH ...CHARTS 20. PAGE 37 A0750 — CAP/ISM FOR/AID POLICY ACT/RES

S67

FELDMAN H.,"AID AS IMPERIALISM?" INDIA PAKISTAN UK USA+45 BAL/PWR CAP/ISM DIPLOM ECO/TAC DOMIN BAL/PAY WEALTH...POLICY 20. PAGE 45 A0914 — COLONIAL FOR/AID S/ASIA ECO/UNDEV

S67

FRENCH D.S.,"DOES THE U.S. EXPLOIT THE DEVELOPING NATIONS?" INT/ORG NAT/G CAP/ISM BAL/PAY WEALTH POLICY. PAGE 49 A0997 — ECO/UNDEV INT/TRADE ECO/TAC COLONIAL

S67

LEFF N.H.,"EXPORT STAGNATION AND AUTARKIC DEVELOPMENT IN BRAZIL, 19471962." BRAZIL ECO/TAC TARIFFS 20. PAGE 86 A1764 — BAL/PAY INT/TRADE WEALTH DIPLOM

S67

LEVI M.,"LES DIFFICULTES ECONOMIQUES DE LA GRANDE-BRETAGNE." UK INT/ORG TEC/DEV BARGAIN DIPLOM DOMIN REPRESENT DEMAND WEALTH...POLICY 20 EEC. PAGE 88 A1792 — BAL/PAY INT/TRADE PRODUC

BAL/PWR....BALANCE OF POWER

N

LONDON INSTITUTE WORLD AFFAIRS,THE YEAR BOOK OF WORLD AFFAIRS. FINAN BAL/PWR ARMS/CONT WAR ...INT/LAW BIBLIOG 20. PAGE 91 A1856 — DIPLOM FOR/AID INT/ORG

N

LA DOCUMENTATION FRANCAISE,CHRONOLOGIE INTERNATIONAL. FRANCE WOR+45 CHIEF PROB/SOLV BAL/PWR CONFER LEAD...POLICY CON/ANAL 20. PAGE 83 A1705 — BIBLIOG/A DIPLOM TIME/SEQ

NLO

WHITE J.A.,THE DIPLOMACY OF THE RUSSO-JAPANESE WAR. ASIA KOREA RUSSIA FORCES CONFER CONTROL PEACE ...BIBLIOG 19 CHINJAP. PAGE 164 A3336 — DIPLOM WAR BAL/PWR

B06
GRIFFIN A.P.C.,SELECT LIST OF REFERENCES ON THE BRITISH TARIFF MOVEMENT. MOD/EUR UK BAL/PWR BARGAIN ECO/TAC LAISSEZ 20. PAGE 56 A1154
BIBLIOG/A INT/TRADE TARIFFS COLONIAL

B14
DE BLOCH J.,THE FUTURE OF WAR IN ITS TECHNICAL, ECONOMIC, AND POLITICAL RELATIONS (1899). MOD/EUR TEC/DEV BUDGET INT/TRADE DETER GUERRILLA WEAPON COST PEACE 20. PAGE 34 A0698
WAR BAL/PWR PREDICT FORCES

B14
HARRIS N.D.,INTERVENTION AND COLONIZATION IN AFRICA. BELGIUM FRANCE GERMANY MOD/EUR PORTUGAL UK ECO/UNDEV BAL/PWR DOMIN CONTROL PWR...GEOG 19/20. PAGE 62 A1267
AFR COLONIAL DIPLOM

B15
FARIES J.C.,THE RISE OF INTERNATIONALISM. ASIA MOD/EUR NAT/G VOL/ASSN DELIB/GP BAL/PWR EDU/PROP ARMS/CONT RIGID/FLEX TREND. PAGE 44 A0899
INT/ORG DIPLOM PEACE

B17
SATOW E.,A GUIDE TO DIPLOMATIC PRACTICE. MOD/EUR INT/ORG BAL/PWR LEGIT ORD/FREE PWR SOVEREIGN ...POLICY GEN/METH 20. PAGE 127 A2607
GEN/LAWS DIPLOM

B19
US DEPARTMENT OF STATE,A TENTATIVE LIST OF TREATY COLLECTIONS. WOR-45 BAL/PWR INT/TRADE TARIFFS WAR PEACE ORD/FREE 20. PAGE 151 A3080
ANTHOL DIPLOM DELIB/GP

N19
BARROS J.F.P.,THE INTERNATIONAL POLICE: THE USE OF FORCE IN THE STRUCTURE OF PEACE (PAMPHLET). BRAZIL WOR+45 WOR-45 FORCES DISCRIM NAT/LISM ORD/FREE SOVEREIGN...POLICY NEW/IDEA WORSHIP 20. PAGE 11 A0229
PEACE INT/ORG COERCE BAL/PWR

N19
BENTHAM J.,A PLAN FOR AN UNIVERSAL AND PERPETUAL PEACE (1838) (PAMPHLET). NAT/G FORCES BAL/PWR INT/TRADE ADMIN AGREE CT/SYS ARMS/CONT SOVEREIGN WEALTH GEN/LAWS. PAGE 13 A0269
INT/ORG INT/LAW PEACE COLONIAL

N19
DEANE H.,THE WAR IN VIETNAM (PAMPHLET). CHINA/COM VIETNAM BAL/PWR DIPLOM ECO/TAC SOCISM INTERVENT COLD/WAR INTERVENT COLD/WAR. PAGE 35 A0720
WAR SOCIALIST MORAL CAP/ISM

N19
FANI-KAYODE R.,BLACKISM (PAMPHLET). AFR WOR+45 INT/ORG BAL/PWR CONTROL CENTRAL...DECISION 20 UN. PAGE 44 A0896
RACE/REL ECO/UNDEV REGION DIPLOM

N19
LISKA G.,THE GREATER MAGHREB: FROM INDEPENDENCE TO UNITY? (PAMPHLET). ALGERIA ISLAM MOROCCO PROB/SOLV BAL/PWR CONFER COLONIAL REPRESENT NAT/LISM 20 TUNIS. PAGE 90 A1835
ECO/UNDEV REGION DIPLOM DOMIN

N19
MEZERIK A.G.,COLONIALISM AND THE UNITED NATIONS (PAMPHLET). WOR+45 NAT/G ADMIN LEAD WAR CHOOSE EFFICIENCY PEACE ATTIT ORD/FREE...POLICY CHARTS UN COLD/WAR. PAGE 100 A2061
COLONIAL DIPLOM BAL/PWR INT/ORG

B22
BRYCE J.,INTERNATIONAL RELATIONS. CHRIST-17C EUR+WWI MOD/EUR CULTURE INTELL NAT/G DELIB/GP CREATE BAL/PWR DIPLOM ATTIT DRIVE RIGID/FLEX ALL/VALS...PLURIST JURID CONCPT TIME/SEQ GEN/LAWS TOT/POP. PAGE 20 A0412
INT/ORG POLICY

B22
WALSH E.,THE HISTORY AND NATURE OF INTERNATIONAL RELATIONS. ASIA L/A+17C MOD/EUR USA-45 WOR-45 NAT/G FORCES TOP/EX BAL/PWR REGION ATTIT ORD/FREE RESPECT ...CONCPT HIST/WRIT TREND. PAGE 161 A3270
INT/ORG TIME/SEQ DIPLOM

B27
HARRIS N.D.,EUROPE AND AFRICA. BELGIUM FRANCE GERMANY MOD/EUR PORTUGAL UK ECO/UNDEV BAL/PWR PWR ...GEOG 19/20. PAGE 62 A1268
AFR COLONIAL DIPLOM

B29
BUELL R.,INTERNATIONAL RELATIONS. WOR+45 WOR-45 CONSTN STRATA FORCES TOP/EX ADMIN ATTIT DRIVE SUPEGO MORAL ORD/FREE PWR SOVEREIGN...JURID SOC CONCPT 20. PAGE 21 A0428
INT/ORG BAL/PWR DIPLOM

B29
DUNN F.,THE PRACTICE AND PROCEDURE OF INTERNATIONAL CONFERENCES. WOR-45 NAT/G DELIB/GP BAL/PWR LEGIT EXEC ROUTINE PEACE ORD/FREE RESPECT...JURID CONCPT METH/CNCPT OBS RECORD TIME/SEQ 20. PAGE 39 A0799
INT/ORG DIPLOM

B29
LANGER W.L.,THE FRANCO-RUSSIAN ALLIANCE: 1890-1894. FRANCE MOD/EUR UK USSR NAT/G CHIEF FORCES BAL/PWR AGREE WAR PEACE PWR...TIME/SEQ TREATY 19 BISMARCK/O. PAGE 84 A1724
DIPLOM

B30
BYNKERSHOEK C.,QUAESTIONUM JURIS PUBLICI LIBRI DUO. CHRIST-17C MOD/EUR CONSTN ELITES SOCIETY NAT/G PROVS EX/STRUC FORCES TOP/EX BAL/PWR DIPLOM ATTIT MORAL...TRADIT CONCPT. PAGE 23 A0460
INT/ORG LAW NAT/LISM INT/LAW

B31
HODGES C.,THE BACKGROUND OF INTERNATIONAL RELATIONS. WOR-45 SOCIETY ECO/DEV ECO/UNDEV INT/ORG DIPLOM DOMIN EDU/PROP LEGIT WAR ATTIT DRIVE PERSON ALL/VALS...CONCPT METH/CNCPT TIME/SEQ CHARTS WORK LEAGUE/NAT 19/20. PAGE 66 A1350
NAT/G BAL/PWR

B35
CONOVER H.F.,A SELECTED LIST OF REFERENCES ON THE DIPLOMATIC & TRADE RELATIONS OF THE US WITH THE USSR, 1919-1935 (PAMPHLET). USA-45 USSR DELIB/GP LEGIS OP/RES PROB/SOLV BAL/PWR BARGAIN 20. PAGE 29 A0590
BIBLIOG DIPLOM INT/TRADE

B35
LANGER W.L.,THE DIPLOMACY OF IMPERIALISM 1890-1902. FRANCE GERMANY ITALY UK WOR-45 BAL/PWR INT/TRADE LEGIT ADJUD CONTROL WAR PWR SOVEREIGN...CHARTS BIBLIOG/A 19/20. PAGE 84 A1726
DIPLOM COLONIAL DOMIN

B36
RUSSEL F.M.,THEORIES OF INTERNATIONAL RELATIONS. EUR+WWI FUT MOD/EUR USA-45 INT/ORG DIPLOM...JURID CONCPT. PAGE 125 A2571
PWR POLICY BAL/PWR SOVEREIGN

B36
SHOTWELL J.,ON THE RIM OF THE ABYSS. EUR+WWI USA-45 STRUCT INT/ORG ACT/RES PLAN EDU/PROP EXEC ATTIT ALL/VALS...TIME/SEQ LEAGUE/NAT TOT/POP 20. PAGE 132 A2706
NAT/G BAL/PWR

B38
HOBSON J.A.,IMPERIALISM. MOD/EUR UK WOR-45 CULTURE ECO/UNDEV NAT/G VOL/ASSN PLAN EDU/PROP LEGIT REGION COERCE ATTIT PWR...POLICY PLURIST TIME/SEQ GEN/LAWS 19/20. PAGE 66 A1348
DOMIN ECO/TAC BAL/PWR COLONIAL

B39
BENES E.,INTERNATIONAL SECURITY. GERMANY UK NAT/G DELIB/GP PLAN BAL/PWR ATTIT ORD/FREE PWR LEAGUE/NAT 20 TREATY. PAGE 13 A0267
EUR+WWI INT/ORG WAR

B39
BROWN J.F.,CONTEMPORARY WORLD POLITICS. WOR-45 NAT/G PLAN BAL/PWR EDU/PROP LEGIT REGION NAT/LISM ORD/FREE PWR SOVEREIGN...POLICY CONCPT HIST/WRIT TIME/SEQ GEN/LAWS LEAGUE/NAT. PAGE 20 A0403
INT/ORG DIPLOM PEACE

B39
SPEIER H.,WAR IN OUR TIME. WOR-45 AGRI FINAN FORCES TEC/DEV BAL/PWR EDU/PROP WEAPON PEACE PWR...ANTHOL 20. PAGE 136 A2779
FASCISM WAR DIPLOM NAT/G

B39
ZIMMERN A.,THE LEAGUE OF NATIONS AND THE RULE OF LAW. WOR-45 STRUCT NAT/G DELIB/GP EX/STRUC BAL/PWR DOMIN LEGIT COERCE ORD/FREE PWR...POLICY RECORD LEAGUE/NAT TOT/POP VAL/FREE 20 LEAGUE/NAT. PAGE 170 A3453
INT/ORG LAW DIPLOM

B39
ZIMMERN A.,MODERN POLITICAL DOCTRINE. WOR-45 CULTURE SOCIETY ECO/UNDEV DELIB/GP EX/STRUC CREATE DOMIN COERCE NAT/LISM ATTIT RIGID/FLEX ORD/FREE PWR WEALTH...POLICY CONCPT OBS TIME/SEQ TREND TOT/POP LEAGUE/NAT 20. PAGE 170 A3454
NAT/G ECO/TAC BAL/PWR INT/TRADE

B40
CARR E.H.,THE TWENTY YEARS' CRISIS 1919-1939. FUT WOR-45 BAL/PWR ECO/TAC LEGIT TOTALISM ATTIT ALL/VALS...POLICY JURID CONCPT TIME/SEQ TREND GEN/LAWS TOT/POP 20. PAGE 24 A0498
INT/ORG DIPLOM PEACE

B40
CONOVER H.F.,A BRIEF LIST OF REFERENCES ON WESTERN HEMISPHERE DEFENSE (PAMPHLET). USA-45 NAT/G CONSULT DELIB/GP FORCES BAL/PWR CONFER DETER...PREDICT CON/ANAL 20. PAGE 29 A0591
BIBLIOG DIPLOM PLAN INT/ORG

B42
BONNET H.,THE UNITED NATIONS, WHAT THEY ARE, WHAT THEY MAY BECOME. FUT WOR-45 CREATE BAL/PWR ECO/TAC PWR...TREND GEN/LAWS 20. PAGE 16 A0335
INT/ORG ORD/FREE

B42
CROWE S.E.,THE BERLIN WEST AFRICA CONFERENCE, 1884-85. GERMANY ELITES MARKET INT/ORG DELIB/GP FORCES PROB/SOLV BAL/PWR CAP/ISM DOMIN COLONIAL ...INT/LAW 19. PAGE 33 A0664
AFR CONFER INT/TRADE DIPLOM

S42
TURNER F.J.,"AMERICAN SECTIONALISM AND WORLD ORGANIZATION." EUR+WWI UNIV USA-45 WOR-45 INTELL ECO/DEV TOP/EX ACT/RES PLAN EDU/PROP LEGIT ALL/VALS ...CONCPT NEW/IDEA OBS TREND LEAGUE/NAT TOT/POP 20. PAGE 146 A2981
INT/ORG DRIVE BAL/PWR

B43
LIPPMANN W.,US FOREIGN POLICY: SHIELD OF THE REPUBLIC. USA-45 WOR-45 CULTURE INT/ORG POL/PAR CREATE BAL/PWR DOMIN EDU/PROP WAR ORD/FREE PWR ...PLURIST CONCPT TREND CON/ANAL 20. PAGE 89 A1827
NAT/G DIPLOM PEACE

B43
ST LEGER A.,SELECTION OF WORKS FOR AN UNDERSTANDING OF WORLD AFFAIRS SINCE 1914. WOR-45 INT/ORG CREATE BAL/PWR REV ADJUST 20. PAGE 137 A2796
BIBLIOG/A WAR SOCIETY DIPLOM

B44
RUDIN H.R.,ARMISTICE 1918. FRANCE GERMANY MOD/EUR UK USA-45 NAT/G CHIEF DELIB/GP FORCES BAL/PWR REPAR ARMS/CONT 20 WILSON/W TREATY. PAGE 125 A2566
AGREE WAR PEACE DIPLOM

B45
NELSON M.F.,KOREA AND THE OLD ORDERS IN EASTERN ASIA. ASIA FRANCE KOREA RUSSIA DELIB/GP INT/TRADE DOMIN CONTROL WAR ORD/FREE...POLICY BIBLIOG. PAGE 108 A2218
DIPLOM BAL/PWR ATTIT CONSERVE

B45
STRAUSZ-HUPE R.,THE BALANCE OF TOMORROW: POWER AND FOREIGN POLICY IN THE UNITED STATES. FUT USA+45 ECO/DEV EXTR/IND INT/ORG FORCES BAL/PWR REGION NUC/PWR...GEOG CHARTS 20 COLD/WAR EUROPE/W. PAGE 139 A2845
DIPLOM PWR POLICY WAR

C45
NELSON M.F.,"KOREA AND THE OLD ORDERS IN EASTERN ASIA." KOREA WOR-45 DELIB/GP INT/TRADE DOMIN CONTROL WAR ATTIT ORD/FREE CONSERVE...POLICY TREATY. PAGE 108 A2217
BIBLIOG DIPLOM BAL/PWR ASIA

L47
COMM. STUDY ORGAN. PEACE,"SECURITY THROUGH THE UNITED NATIONS." COM FUT WOR+45 TOP/EX ACT/RES BAL/PWR ARMS/CONT NUC/PWR...CONCPT GEN/LAWS UN TOT/POP COLD/WAR 20. PAGE 28 A0577
INT/ORG ORD/FREE PEACE

B48
JESSUP P.C.,A MODERN LAW OF NATIONS. FUT WOR+45 WOR-45 SOCIETY NAT/G DELIB/GP LEGIS BAL/PWR EDU/PROP LEGIT PWR...INT/LAW JURID TIME/SEQ LEAGUE/NAT 20. PAGE 74 A1514
INT/ORG ADJUD

B48
MORGENTHAL H.J.,POLITICS AMONG NATIONS: THE STRUGGLE FOR POWER AND PEACE. FUT WOR+45 INT/ORG OP/RES PROB/SOLV BAL/PWR CONTROL ATTIT MORAL ...INT/LAW BIBLIOG 20 COLD/WAR. PAGE 104 A2135
DIPLOM PEACE PWR POLICY

B48
US DEPARTMENT OF STATE,FOREIGN AFFAIRS HIGHLIGHTS (NEWSLETTER). COM USA+45 INT/ORG PLAN BAL/PWR WAR PWR...BIBLIOG 20 COLD/WAR NATO UN DEPT/STATE. PAGE 151 A3083
DIPLOM NAT/G POLICY

S48
GROSS L.,"THE PEACE OF WESTPHALIA, 1648-1948." WOR+45 WOR-45 CONSTN BAL/PWR FEDERAL 17/20 TREATY WESTPHALIA. PAGE 57 A1175
INT/LAW AGREE CONCPT DIPLOM

S48
MORGENTHAU H.J.,"THE TWILIGHT OF INTERNATIONAL MORALITY" (BMR)" WOR+45 WOR-45 BAL/PWR WAR NAT/LISM PEACE...POLICY INT/LAW IDEA/COMP 15/20 TREATY INTERVENT. PAGE 104 A2137
MORAL DIPLOM NAT/G

B49
HINDEN R.,EMPIRE AND AFTER. UK POL/PAR BAL/PWR DIPLOM INT/TRADE WAR NAT/LISM PWR 17/20. PAGE 65 A1335
NAT/G COLONIAL ATTIT POLICY

B49
MANSERGH N.,THE COMING OF THE FIRST WORLD WAR: A STUDY IN EUROPEAN BALANCE, 1878-1914. GERMANY MOD/EUR VOL/ASSN COLONIAL CONTROL PWR 19/20 TREATY. PAGE 94 A1928
DIPLOM WAR BAL/PWR

B50
BERLE A.A.,NATURAL SELECTION OF POLITICAL FORCES. FUT WOR+45 WOR-45 CULTURE SOCIETY INT/ORG NAT/G FORCES EDU/PROP LEGIT COERCE...CONCPT HIST/WRIT TREND 20. PAGE 13 A0274
POL/PAR BAL/PWR DIPLOM

B50
BROOKINGS INSTITUTION,MAJOR PROBLEMS OF UNITED STATES FOREIGN POLICY. AFR ASIA INDIA UK USA+45 USSR BAL/PWR FOR/AID WAR PEACE TOTALISM MARXISM SOCISM 20 CHINJAP COLD/WAR. PAGE 19 A0393
DIPLOM POLICY ORD/FREE

B50
NORTHROP F.S.C.,THE TAMING OF THE NATIONS. KOREA USA+45 USSR WOR+45 STRUCT ECO/UNDEV INT/ORG NAT/G TOP/EX NUC/PWR ATTIT ALL/VALS...TIME/SEQ 20 HIROSHIMA. PAGE 110 A2255
CONCPT BAL/PWR

B51
HOLBORN H.,THE POLITICAL COLLAPSE OF EUROPE. EUR+WWI MOD/EUR USA-45 BAL/PWR PEACE POLICY. PAGE 66 A1364
DIPLOM ORD/FREE WAR

B51
US HOUSE COMM APPROPRIATIONS,MUTUAL SECURITY PROGRAM APPROPRIATIONS FOR 1952: HEARINGS BEFORE A SUBCOMMITTEE OF THE COMMITTEE ON APPROPRIATIONS. KOREA L/A+17C ECO/DEV ECO/UNDEV INT/ORG INSPECT BAL/PWR DIPLOM DEBATE WAR...POLICY STAT ASIA/S 20 CONGRESS NATO COLD/WAR MID/EAST. PAGE 153 A3118
LEGIS FORCES BUDGET FOR/AID

S51
CONNERY R.H.,"THE MUTUAL DEFENSE ASSISTANCE PROGRAM." COM EUR+WWI KOREA USA+45 NAT/G VOL/ASSN CREATE PLAN BAL/PWR EDU/PROP PERCEPT...POLICY DECISION CONCPT NATO 20. PAGE 29 A0587
INT/ORG FORCES FOR/AID

B52
ALBERTINI L.,THE ORIGINS OF THE WAR OF 1914 (3 VOLS.). AUSTRIA FRANCE GERMANY MOD/EUR RUSSIA UK PROB/SOLV NEUTRAL PWR...BIBLIOG 19/20. PAGE 5 A0107
WAR DIPLOM FORCES BAL/PWR

B52
BARR S.,CITIZENS OF THE WORLD. USA+45 WOR+45 CULTURE FORCES LEGIS ACT/RES BAL/PWR LEGIT PEACE ATTIT ORD/FREE PWR...PLURIST CONCPT OBS TIME/SEQ COLD/WAR 20. PAGE 11 A0227
NAT/G INT/ORG DIPLOM

B52
FIFIELD R.H.,WOODROW WILSON AND THE FAR EAST. ASIA CHIEF BAL/PWR CONFER COLONIAL ARMS/CONT WAR ...TIME/SEQ NAT/COMP BIBLIOG 19/20 WILSON/W LEAGUE/NAT PRESIDENT. PAGE 45 A0926
DIPLOM DELIB/GP INT/ORG

B52
SCHUMAN F.,THE COMMONWEALTH OF MAN. WOR+45 WOR-45 LAW CULTURE ELITES SOCIETY FAM INT/ORG NAT/G VOL/ASSN TOP/EX PLAN BAL/PWR LEGIT ATTIT DISPL DRIVE...POLICY MYTH TREND TOT/POP ILO OEEC 20. PAGE 129 A2649
CONCPT GEN/LAWS

B52
VANDENBOSCH A.,THE UN: BACKGROUND, ORGANIZATION, FUNCTIONS, ACTIVITIES. WOR+45 LAW CONSTN STRUCT INT/ORG CONSULT BAL/PWR EDU/PROP EXEC ALL/VALS ...POLICY CONCPT UN 20. PAGE 158 A3218
DELIB/GP TIME/SEQ PEACE

L52
THOMPSON K.W.,"THE STUDY OF INTERNATIONAL POLITICS: A SURVEY OF TRENDS AND DEVELOPMENTS." UNIV USA+45 WOR+45 WOR-45 SOCIETY ECO/DEV R+D ACT/RES PLAN ROUTINE ATTIT DRIVE PERCEPT PERSON...CONCPT OBS TREND GEN/LAWS TOT/POP. PAGE 143 A2928
INT/ORG BAL/PWR DIPLOM

S52
SCHUMAN F.,"INTERNATIONAL IDEALS AND THE NATIONAL INTEREST." WOR+45 WOR-45 INT/ORG VOL/ASSN DELIB/GP CREATE BAL/PWR DOMIN PEACE PERSON MORAL PWR SOVEREIGN...POLICY GEN/LAWS TOT/POP LEAGUE/NAT 20. PAGE 129 A2648
ATTIT CONCPT

C52
FIFIELD R.H.,"WOODROW WILSON AND THE FAR EAST." ASIA CHIEF DELIB/GP BAL/PWR CONFER COLONIAL ARMS/CONT WAR...TIME/SEQ NAT/COMP 19/20 WILSON/W LEAGUE/NAT. PAGE 45 A0925
BIBLIOG DIPLOM INT/ORG

B53
KALIJARVI T.V.,MODERN WORLD POLITICS (3RD ED.). AFR L/A+17C MOD/EUR S/ASIA UK USSR WOR+45 INT/ORG BAL/PWR WAR PWR 20. PAGE 76 A1552
DIPLOM INT/LAW PEACE

B53
LENZ F.,DIE BEWEGUNGEN DER GROSSEN MACHTE. USA+45 USA-45 USSR SOCIETY STRATA STRUCT NAT/G PERSON MARXISM...CONCPT IDEA/COMP NAT/COMP 18/20. PAGE 87 A1777
BAL/PWR TREND DIPLOM HIST/WRIT

B53
MENDE T.,WORLD POWER IN THE BALANCE. FUT USA+45 USSR WOR-45 ECO/DEV ECO/TAC INT/TRADE EDU/PROP UTOPIA ATTIT...HUM CONCPT TREND COLD/WAR TOT/POP 20. PAGE 99 A2036
WOR+45 PWR BAL/PWR

S53
CORY R.H. JR.,"FORGING A PUBLIC INFORMATION POLICY FOR THE UNITED NATIONS." FUT WOR+45 SOCIETY ADMIN PEACE ATTIT PERSON SKILL...CONCPT 20 UN. PAGE 31 A0628
INT/ORG EDU/PROP BAL/PWR

S53
LINCOLN G.,"FACTORS DETERMINING ARMS AID." COM FUT USA+45 USSR WOR+45 ECO/DEV NAT/G CONSULT PLAN TEC/DEV DIPLOM DOMIN EDU/PROP PERCEPT PWR ...DECISION CONCPT TREND MARX/KARL 20. PAGE 89 A1819
FORCES POLICY BAL/PWR FOR/AID

B54
ARON R.,CENTURY OF TOTAL WAR. FUT WOR+45 WOR-45 SOCIETY INT/ORG NAT/G FORCES TOP/EX CREATE BAL/PWR DOMIN EDU/PROP COERCE DETER PEACE TOTALISM PWR ...TIME/SEQ TREND COLD/WAR TOT/POP VAL/FREE LEAGUE/NAT 20. PAGE 9 A0179
ATTIT WAR

B54
COOK T.,POWER THROUGH PURPOSE. USA+45 WOR+45 WOR-45 INT/ORG VOL/ASSN BAL/PWR DIPLOM EDU/PROP LEGIT PERSON...GEN/LAWS LEAGUE/NAT 20. PAGE 30 A0606
ATTIT CONCPT

B54
COOKSON J.,BEFORE THE AFRICAN STORM. BELGIUM CENTRL/AFR FRANCE UK ECO/UNDEV POL/PAR CREATE BAL/PWR RACE/REL NAT/LISM ORD/FREE CONSERVE MARXISM SOC/INTEG 20 CONGO/LEOP. PAGE 30 A0607
COLONIAL REV DISCRIM DIPLOM

B54
KENNAN G.F.,REALITIES OF AMERICAN FOREIGN POLICY. USA+45 INT/ORG NUC/PWR TOTALISM 20 COLD/WAR. PAGE 77 A1586
DIPLOM BAL/PWR DECISION DETER

B54
MILLARD E.L.,FREEDOM IN A FEDERAL WORLD. FUT WOR+45 VOL/ASSN TOP/EX LEGIT ROUTINE FEDERAL PEACE ATTIT DISPL ORD/FREE PWR...MAJORIT INT/LAW JURID TREND COLD/WAR 20. PAGE 101 A2073
INT/ORG CREATE ADJUD BAL/PWR

B54
SALVEMINI G.,PRELUDE TO WORLD WAR II. ITALY MOD/EUR INT/ORG BAL/PWR EDU/PROP CONTROL TOTALISM...TREND NAT/COMP BIBLIOG 19 HITLER/A LEAGUE/NAT MUSSOLIN/B. PAGE 127 A2597
WAR FASCISM LEAD PWR

B54
STRAUSZ-HUPE R.,INTERNATIONAL RELATIONS IN THE AGE OF THE CONFLICT BETWEEN DEMOCRACY AND DICTATORSHIP (2ND ED.). INT/ORG BAL/PWR EDU/PROP ADMIN WAR PEACE PWR...CONCPT CHARTS BIBLIOG 20 COLD/WAR UN LEAGUE/NAT. PAGE 139 A2846
DIPLOM POPULISM MARXISM

B54
TAYLOR A.J.P.,THE STRUGGLE FOR MASTERY IN EUROPE 1848-1918. MOD/EUR VOL/ASSN FORCES BAL/PWR DOMIN CONTROL PEACE MORAL 19/20 TREATY EUROPE WWI. PAGE 142 A2897
DIPLOM WAR PWR

B55
ARNOLD G.L.,THE PATTERN OF WORLD CONFLICT. USA+45 INT/ORG ECO/TAC INT/TRADE PEACE 20 EUROPE. PAGE 9 A0176
DIPLOM BAL/PWR NAT/LISM PLAN

B55
BURR R.N.,DOCUMENTS ON INTER-AMERICAN COOPERATION: VOL. I, 1810-1881; VOL. II, 1881-1948. DELIB/GP BAL/PWR INT/TRADE REPRESENT NAT/LISM PEACE HABITAT ORD/FREE PWR SOVEREIGN...INT/LAW 20 OAS. PAGE 22 A0445
BIBLIOG DIPLOM INT/ORG L/A+17C

B55
BUSS C.,THE FAR EAST: A HISTORY OF RECENT AND CONTEMPORARY INTERNATIONAL RELATIONS IN EAST ASIA. WOR+45 WOR-45 CONSTN INT/ORG NAT/G BAL/PWR ATTIT PWR SOVEREIGN...GEOG JURID SOC CONCPT METH/CNCPT 19/20. PAGE 22 A0449
ASIA DIPLOM

B55
COTTRELL W.F.,ENERGY AND SOCIETY. FUT WOR+45 WOR-45 ECO/DEV ECO/UNDEV INT/ORG NAT/G DETER ORD/FREE PWR SKILL WEALTH...SOC TIME/SEQ TOT/POP VAL/FREE 20. PAGE 31 A0634
TEC/DEV BAL/PWR PEACE

B55
GULICK E.V.,EUROPE'S CLASSICAL BALANCE OF POWER: CASE HISTORY OF THEORY AND PRACTICE OF GREAT CONCEPTS OF EUROPEAN STATECRAFT. MOD/EUR INT/ORG VOL/ASSN FORCES ORD/FREE 18/19 TREATY. PAGE 58 A1192
IDEA/COMP BAL/PWR PWR DIPLOM

B55
HOGAN W.N.,INTERNATIONAL CONFLICT AND COLLECTIVE SECURITY: THE PRINCIPLE OF CONCERN IN INTERNATIONAL ORGANIZATION. CONSTN EX/STRUC BAL/PWR DIPLOM ADJUD CONTROL CENTRAL CONSEN PEACE...INT/LAW CONCPT METH/COMP 20 UN LEAGUE/NAT. PAGE 66 A1361
INT/ORG WAR ORD/FREE FORCES

B55
JONES J.M.,THE FIFTEEN WEEKS (FEBRUARY 21-JUNE 5, 1947). EUR+WWI USA+45 PROB/SOLV BAL/PWR...POLICY TIME/SEQ 20 COLD/WAR MARSHL/PLN TRUMAN/HS WASHING/DC. PAGE 75 A1532
DIPLOM ECO/TAC FOR/AID

B55
ROWE C.,VOLTAIRE AND THE STATE. FRANCE MOD/EUR BAL/PWR CONTROL TASK SUPEGO ORD/FREE PWR...CONCPT 18 VOLTAIRE. PAGE 125 A2553
NAT/G DIPLOM NAT/LISM ATTIT

B56
BEALE H.K.,THEODORE ROOSEVELT AND THE RISE OF AMERICA TO WORLD POWER. USA-45 BAL/PWR COLONIAL DRIVE PERSON PWR...POLICY BIBLIOG 20 ROOSEVLT/T PRESIDENT. PAGE 12 A0238
DIPLOM CHIEF BIOG

B56
BROOK D.,THE UNITED NATIONS AND CHINA DILEMMA. CHINA/COM FUT WOR+45 ECO/UNDEV NAT/G DELIB/GP ACT/RES DIPLOM ROUTINE NAT/LISM TOTALISM ATTIT DRIVE...CONCPT OBS TIME/SEQ UN TOT/POP TIME UN 20. PAGE 19 A0390
ASIA INT/ORG BAL/PWR

B56
CONOVER H.F.,A GUIDE TO BIBLIOGRAPHIC TOOLS FOR RESEARCH IN FOREIGN AFFAIRS. AFR ASIA COM EUR+WWI WOR+45 BAL/PWR CON/ANAL. PAGE 30 A0602
BIBLIOG/A R+D DIPLOM INT/ORG

B56
ROBERTS H.L.,RUSSIA AND AMERICA. CHINA/COM S/ASIA USSR FORCES TEC/DEV FOR/AID NUC/PWR ALL/IDEOS ...MAJORIT TREND NAT/COMP 20 COLD/WAR UN NATO. PAGE 122 A2494
DIPLOM INT/ORG BAL/PWR TOTALISM

B56
SNELL J.L.,THE MEANING OF YALTA: BIG THREE DIPLOMACY AND THE NEW BALANCE OF POWER. EUR+WWI GERMANY USA-45 USSR FORCES PLAN BAL/PWR DIPLOM WAR CHOOSE PEACE...CHARTS BIBLIOG 20 UN CHINJAP ROOSEVLT/F. PAGE 134 A2749
CONFER CHIEF POLICY PROB/SOLV

B56
US DEPARTMENT OF STATE,THE SUEZ CANAL PROBLEM; JULY 26-SEPTEMBER 22, 1956. UAR WOR+45 BAL/PWR COERCE NAT/LISM ATTIT ORD/FREE SOVEREIGN 20 SUEZ. PAGE 151 A3091
DIPLOM CONFER INT/TRADE

B56
VON HARPE W.,DIE SOWJETUNION FINNLAND UND SKANDANAVIEN, 1945-1955. EUR+WWI FINLAND GERMANY USSR WAR INGP/REL ORD/FREE SOVEREIGN MARXISM ...POLICY GOV/COMP BIBLIOG 20 STALIN/J. PAGE 160 A3252
DIPLOM COM NEUTRAL BAL/PWR

B56
WOLFERS A.,THE ANGLO-AMERICAN TRADITION IN FOREIGN AFFAIRS. UK USA+45 WOR-45 CULTURE SOCIETY ECO/DEV INT/ORG NAT/G CREATE PLAN BAL/PWR ECO/TAC EDU/PROP PEACE DISPL DRIVE...TREND GEN/LAWS 20. PAGE 166 A3382
ATTIT CONCPT DIPLOM

B57
BROMBERGER M.,LES SECRETS DE L'EXPEDITION D'EGYPTE. FRANCE ISLAM UAR UK USA+45 USSR WOR+45 INT/ORG NAT/G FORCES BAL/PWR ECO/TAC DOMIN WAR NAT/LISM ATTIT PWR SOVEREIGN...MAJORIT TIME/SEQ CHARTS SUEZ COLD/WAR 20. PAGE 19 A0387
COERCE DIPLOM

B57
BUCK P.W.,CONTOL OF FOREIGN RELATIONS IN MODERN NATIONS. FRANCE L/A+17C NETHERLAND USSR WOR+45 INT/ORG TOP/EX BAL/PWR DOMIN EDU/PROP COERCE PEACE ATTIT...CONCPT TREND 20 CMN/WLTH. PAGE 21 A0427
NAT/G PWR DIPLOM

B57
KAPLAN M.A.,SYSTEM AND PROCESS OF INTERNATIONAL POLITICS. FUT WOR+45 WOR-45 SOCIETY PLAN BAL/PWR ADMIN ATTIT PERSON RIGID/FLEX PWR SOVEREIGN ...DECISION TREND VAL/FREE. PAGE 76 A1560
INT/ORG DIPLOM

B57
LEVONTIN A.V.,THE MYTH OF INTERNATIONAL SECURITY: A JURIDICAL AND CRITICAL ANALYSIS. FUT WOR+45 WOR-45 LAW NAT/G VOL/ASSN ACT/RES BAL/PWR ATTIT ORD/FREE ...JURID METH/CNCPT TIME/SEQ TREND STERTYP 20. PAGE 88 A1797
INT/ORG INT/LAW SOVEREIGN MYTH

B57
LISKA G.,INTERNATIONAL EQUILIBRIUM. WOR+45 WOR-45 SOCIETY INT/ORG FORCES DETER ATTIT ORD/FREE PWR ...GEN/LAWS 19/20. PAGE 90 A1836
NAT/G BAL/PWR REGION DIPLOM

B57
PALMER N.D.,INTERNATIONAL RELATIONS. WOR+45 INT/ORG NAT/G ECO/TAC EDU/PROP COLONIAL WAR PWR SOVEREIGN ...POLICY T 20 TREATY. PAGE 113 A2321
DIPLOM BAL/PWR NAT/COMP

B57
US PRES CITIZEN ADVISERS,REPORT TO THE PRESIDENT ON THE MUTUAL SECURITY PROGRAM. COM USA+45 WOR+45 FINAN INDUS PLAN BUDGET CAP/ISM DIPLOM FOR/AID INT/TRADE REGION 20 SECUR/PROG. PAGE 155 A3163
BAL/PWR FORCES INT/ORG ECO/TAC

B57
WARBURG J.P.,AGENDA FOR ACTION. ISLAM ISRAEL USA+45 FOR/AID INT/TRADE WAR NAT/LISM 20 MID/EAST EUROPE ARABS. PAGE 161 A3275
DIPLOM POLICY INT/ORG BAL/PWR

S57
KAPLAN M.,"BALANCE OF POWER, BIPOLARITY AND OTHER MODELS OF INTERNATIONAL SYSTEMS" (BMR)" ACT/RES BAL/PWR...PHIL/SCI METH 20. PAGE 76 A1559
DIPLOM GAME METH/CNCPT SIMUL

B58
ARON R.,ON WAR: ATOMIC WEAPONS AND GLOBAL DIPLOMACY (TRANS. BY TERENCE KILMARTIN). WOR+45 SOCIETY FORCES BAL/PWR WAR WEAPON PERSON...SOC 20. PAGE 9 A0182
ARMS/CONT NUC/PWR COERCE DIPLOM

B58
BERLINER J.S.,SOVIET ECONOMIC AID: THE AID AND TRADE POLICY IN UNDERDEVELOPED COUNTRIES. AFR COM ISLAM L/A+17C S/ASIA USSR ECO/DEV DIST/IND FINAN MARKET INT/ORG ACT/RES PLAN BAL/PWR WEAPON PWR WEALTH...CHARTS 20. PAGE 14 A0277
ECO/UNDEV ECO/TAC FOR/AID

B58
GARTHOFF R.L.,SOVIET STRATEGY IN THE NUCLEAR AGE. FUT USSR R+D INT/ORG NAT/G ACT/RES TEC/DEV DOMIN DETER WAR ATTIT PWR...RELATIV METH/CNCPT SELF/OBS TREND CON/ANAL STERTYP GEN/LAWS 20. PAGE 51 A1052
COM FORCES BAL/PWR NUC/PWR

B58
GAVIN J.M.,WAR AND PEACE IN THE SPACE AGE. SPACE USA+45 USSR FORCES PLAN TEC/DEV BAL/PWR DIPLOM ARMS/CONT WEAPON CIVMIL/REL...CHARTS GP/COMP 20 NATO COLD/WAR. PAGE 52 A1055
WAR DETER NUC/PWR PEACE

B58
IMLAH A.H.,ECONOMIC ELEMENTS IN THE PAX BRITANNICA. MOD/EUR USA+45 USA-45 ECO/DEV INT/ORG NAT/G BAL/PWR ECO/TAC PEACE ATTIT PWR WEALTH...STAT CHARTS VAL/FREE 19. PAGE 70 A1436
MARKET UK

B58
JENKS C.W.,THE COMMON LAW OF MANKIND. EUR+WWI MOD/EUR SPACE WOR+45 INT/ORG BAL/PWR ARMS/CONT COERCE SUPEGO MORAL...TREND 20. PAGE 73 A1505
JURID SOVEREIGN

B58
KENNAN G.F.,RUSSIA, THE ATOM AND THE WEST. USA+45 USSR INT/ORG ARMS/CONT MARXISM 20 NATO. PAGE 77 A1587
BAL/PWR NUC/PWR CONTROL DIPLOM

B58
KINDLEBERGER C.P.,INTERNATIONAL ECONOMICS. WOR+45 WOR-45 ECO/DEV ECO/UNDEV FINAN VOL/ASSN ACT/RES DIPLOM ECO/TAC LEGIT REGION ATTIT DRIVE ORD/FREE WEALTH...POLICY STAT TREND GEN/LAWS EEC ECSC OEEC 20. PAGE 79 A1620
INT/ORG BAL/PWR TARIFFS

B58
MANSERGH N.,SURVEY OF BRITISH COMMONWEALTH AFFAIRS: PROBLEMS OF WARTIME CO-OPERATION AND POST-WAR CHANGE 1939-1952. INDIA IRELAND S/ASIA CONSTN INT/ORG BAL/PWR COLONIAL NEUTRAL WAR ADJUST PEACE ROLE ORD/FREE...CHARTS 20 CMN/WLTH NATO UN. PAGE 94 A1931
VOL/ASSN CONSEN PROB/SOLV INGP/REL

B58
MILLIS W.,FOREIGN POLICY AND THE FREE SOCIETY. USA+45 WOR+45 SOCIETY NAT/G FORCES BAL/PWR FOR/AID EDU/PROP DETER ATTIT PWR 20 COLD/WAR. PAGE 102 A2084
DIPLOM POLICY ORD/FREE CONSULT

B58
ORGANSKI A.F.K.,WORLD POLITICS. FUT WOR+45 SOCIETY INT/ORG
STRUCT NAT/G BAL/PWR ECO/TAC DOMIN NAT/LISM ATTIT DIPLOM
KNOWL ORD/FREE PWR...CONCPT METH/CNCPT TREND
STERTYP GEN/LAWS TOT/POP 20. PAGE 112 A2297

B58
RIGGS R.,POLITICS IN THE UNITED NATIONS: A STUDY OF INT/ORG
UNITED STATES INFLUENCE IN THE GENERAL ASSEMBLY.
USA+45 WOR+45 LEGIS TOP/EX CREATE BAL/PWR DIPLOM
DOMIN EDU/PROP COLONIAL ROUTINE ATTIT RIGID/FLEX
PWR...CONCPT OBS HIST/WRIT CHARTS STERTYP GEN/LAWS
UN COLD/WAR 20. PAGE 121 A2480

B58
STONE J.,AGGRESSION AND WORLD ORDER: A CRITIQUE OF ORD/FREE
UNITED NATIONS THEORIES OF AGGRESSION. LAW CONSTN INT/ORG
DELIB/GP PROB/SOLV BAL/PWR DIPLOM DEBATE ADJUD WAR
CRIME PWR...POLICY IDEA/COMP 20 UN SUEZ LEAGUE/NAT. CONCPT
PAGE 138 A2835

L58
SNYDER R.N.,"THE UNITED STATES DECISION TO RESIST QUANT
AGGRESSION IN KOREA." ASIA KOREA S/ASIA USA+45 METH/CNCPT
USA-45 WOR+45 INT/ORG DELIB/GP BAL/PWR COERCE PWR DIPLOM
...CONCPT REC/INT RESIST/INT COLD/WAR 20. PAGE 134
A2753

S58
SINGER J.D.,"THREAT PERCEPTION AND THE ARMAMENT PERCEPT
TENSION DILEMMA." WOR+45 WOR-45 ELITES INT/ORG ARMS/CONT
NAT/G DELIB/GP PLAN LEGIT COERCE DETER ATTIT BAL/PWR
RIGID/FLEX PWR...DECISION PSY 20. PAGE 133 A2724

S58
THOMPSON K.W.,"NATIONAL SECURITY IN A NUCLEAR AGE." FORCES
USA+45 WOR+45 SOCIETY INT/ORG NAT/G TOP/EX DIPLOM PWR
DOMIN EDU/PROP LEGIT ARMS/CONT COERCE ORD/FREE BAL/PWR
...TREND STERTYP TOT/POP VAL/FREE COLD/WAR 20.
PAGE 143 A2929

B59
BALL M.M.,NATO AND THE EUROPEAN MOVEMENT. EUR+WWI DELIB/GP
USA+45 INT/ORG FORCES BAL/PWR EDU/PROP LEGIT REGION STRUCT
ATTIT ORD/FREE PWR...STAT OBS TIME/SEQ TREND CHARTS
ORG/CHARTS STERTYP COLD/WAR EEC OEEC 20 NATO.
PAGE 10 A0212

B59
BLOOMFIELD L.P.,WESTERN EUROPE AND THE UN - TRENDS INT/ORG
AND PROSPECTS. EUR+WWI BAL/PWR DIPLOM ECO/TAC TREND
COLONIAL ATTIT PWR...POLICY 20 UN EUROPE/W. PAGE 16 FUT
A0316 NAT/G

B59
DEHIO L.,GERMANY AND WORLD POLITICS IN THE DIPLOM
TWENTIETH CENTURY. EUR+WWI FRANCE GERMANY MOD/EUR WAR
UK USSR NAT/G CHIEF BAL/PWR DOMIN COLONIAL CONTROL NAT/LISM
LEAD...IDEA/COMP 20 VERSAILLES. PAGE 36 A0724 SOVEREIGN

B59
HALEY A.G.,FIRST COLLOQUIUM ON THE LAW OF OUTER SPACE
SPACE. WOR+45 INT/ORG ACT/RES PLAN BAL/PWR CONFER LAW
ATTIT PWR...POLICY JURID CHARTS ANTHOL 20. PAGE 60 SOVEREIGN
A1225 CONTROL

B59
THOMAS D.H.,GUIDE TO THE DIPLOMATIC ARCHIVES OF BIBLIOG
WESTERN EUROPE. EUR+WWI ELITES INT/ORG NAT/G DIPLOM
BAL/PWR INT/TRADE PEACE. PAGE 143 A2921 CONFER

B59
THOMAS N.,THE PREREQUISITES FOR PEACE. ASIA EUR+WWI INT/ORG
FUT ISLAM S/ASIA WOR+45 FORCES PLAN BAL/PWR ORD/FREE
EDU/PROP LEGIT ATTIT PWR...SOCIALIST CONCPT ARMS/CONT
COLD/WAR 20 UN. PAGE 143 A2924 PEACE

B59
WOLFERS A.,ALLIANCE POLICY IN THE COLD WAR. COM DIPLOM
INT/ORG FORCES COLONIAL CONTROL NUC/PWR 20 NATO UN DETER
COLD/WAR. PAGE 166 A3384 BAL/PWR

L59
KAPLAN M.A.,"SOME PROBLEMS IN THE STRATEGIC DECISION
ANALYSIS OF INTERNATIONAL POLITICS." UNIV R+D BAL/PWR
INT/ORG CREATE PLAN DIPLOM EDU/PROP COERCE DISPL
PWR...METH/CNCPT NEW/IDEA HYPO/EXP TOT/POP 20.
PAGE 76 A1561

S59
BROMKE A.,"DISENGAGEMENT IN EAST EUROPE." COM USSR BAL/PWR
INT/ORG DIPLOM EDU/PROP NEUTRAL NUC/PWR DRIVE
RIGID/FLEX PWR...PSY CONCPT CON/ANAL GEN/METH
VAL/FREE 20. PAGE 19 A0388

S59
KISSINGER H.A.,"THE SEARCH FOR STABILITY." COM FUT
GERMANY MOD/EUR USA+45 USA-45 USSR INT/ORG ATTIT
ARMS/CONT NUC/PWR ORD/FREE PWR COLD/WAR 20 NATO. BAL/PWR
PAGE 80 A1641

S59
POTTER P.B.,"OBSTACLES AND ALTERNATIVES TO INT/ORG
INTERNATIONAL LAW." WOR+45 NAT/G VOL/ASSN DELIB/GP LAW
BAL/PWR DOMIN ROUTINE...JURID VAL/FREE 20. PAGE 117 DIPLOM
A2400 INT/LAW

S59
STOESSINGER J.G.,"THE INTERNATIONAL ATOMIC ENERGY INT/ORG
AGENCY: THE FIRST PHASE." FUT WOR+45 NAT/G VOL/ASSN ECO/DEV
DELIB/GP BAL/PWR LEGIT ADMIN ROUTINE PWR...OBS FOR/AID
CON/ANAL GEN/LAWS VAL/FREE 20 IAEA. PAGE 138 A2829 NUC/PWR

B60
ALBRECHT-CARRIE R.,FRANCE, EUROPE AND THE TWO WORLD DIPLOM
WARS. EUR+WWI FRANCE GERMANY MOD/EUR UK ECO/DEV WAR
NAT/G FORCES BAL/PWR DOMIN ARMS/CONT PEACE PWR 20
TREATY EUROPE. PAGE 5 A0109

B60
ALLEN H.C.,THE ANGLO-AMERICAN PREDICAMENT: THE INT/ORG
BRITISH COMMONWEALTH, THE UNITED STATES AND PWR
EUROPEAN UNITY. EUR+WWI FUT UK USA+45 WOR+45 BAL/PWR
ECO/DEV NAT/G PLAN DETER...CONCPT OBS TIME/SEQ
TREND COLD/WAR VAL/FREE CMN/WLTH 20. PAGE 6 A0123

B60
BARNET R.,WHO WANTS DISARMAMENT. COM EUR+WWI USA+45 PLAN
USSR INT/ORG NAT/G BAL/PWR DIPLOM EDU/PROP COERCE FORCES
DETER NUC/PWR WAR WEAPON ATTIT PWR...TIME/SEQ ARMS/CONT
COLD/WAR CONGRESS 20. PAGE 11 A0225

B60
BROOKINGS INSTITUTION,UNITED STATES FOREIGN POLICY: DIPLOM
STUDY NO 9: THE FORMULATION AND ADMINISTRATION OF INT/ORG
UNITED STATES FOREIGN POLICY. USA+45 WOR+45 CREATE
EX/STRUC LEGIS BAL/PWR FOR/AID EDU/PROP CIVMIL/REL
GOV/REL...INT COLD/WAR. PAGE 19 A0394

B60
CONN S.,THE FRAMEWORK OF HEMISPHERE DEFENSE. CANADA USA+45
L/A+17C USA-45 NAT/G FORCES BAL/PWR DOMIN WAR PEACE INT/ORG
DISPL PWR RESPECT...PLURIST CONCPT HIST/WRIT DIPLOM
HYPO/EXP MEXIC/AMER 20 ROOSEVLT/F. PAGE 29 A0585

B60
DUCHACEK I.D.,CONFLICT AND COOPERATION AMONG INT/ORG
NATIONS. WOR+45 WOR-45 SOCIETY NAT/G DOMIN DETER BAL/PWR
PWR SKILL COLD/WAR 20. PAGE 39 A0791 DIPLOM

B60
EINSTEIN A.,EINSTEIN ON PEACE. FUT WOR+45 WOR-45 INT/ORG
SOCIETY NAT/G PLAN BAL/PWR CAP/ISM DIPLOM ARMS/CONT ATTIT
DETER NAT/LISM...POLICY RELATIV HUM PHIL/SCI CONCPT NUC/PWR
BIOG COLD/WAR LEAGUE/NAT NAZI. PAGE 41 A0829 PEACE

B60
FEIS H.,BETWEEN WAR AND PEACE: THE POTSDAM DIPLOM
CONFERENCE. EUR+WWI NAT/G DELIB/GP PROB/SOLV REPAR CONFER
WAR CIVMIL/REL...BIBLIOG 20. PAGE 45 A0911 BAL/PWR

B60
FISCHER L.,RUSSIA, AMERICA, AND THE WORLD. FUT DIPLOM
USA+45 USSR WOR+45 FORCES PLAN BAL/PWR ECO/TAC POLICY
FOR/AID NEUTRAL TASK NUC/PWR PWR 20 COLD/WAR. MARXISM
PAGE 46 A0937 ECO/UNDEV

B60
FOREIGN POLICY CLEARING HOUSE,STRATEGY FOR THE DIPLOM
60'S. FUT USA+45 WOR+45 ECO/UNDEV FORCES BAL/PWR NAT/G
TASK ARMS/CONT DETER PWR MARXISM 20 SENATE. PAGE 47 POLICY
A0963 ACT/RES

B60
FURNIA A.H.,THE DIPLOMACY OF APPEASEMENT: ANGLO- DIPLOM
FRENCH RELATIONS AND THE PRELUDE TO WORLD WAR II BAL/PWR
1931-1938. FRANCE GERMANY UK ELITES NAT/G DELIB/GP COERCE
FORCES WAR PEACE RIGID/FLEX 20. PAGE 50 A1026

B60
KARDELJE,SOCIALISM AND WAR. CHINA/COM WOR+45 MARXIST
YUGOSLAVIA DIPLOM EDU/PROP ATTIT...POLICY CONCPT WAR
IDEA/COMP COLD/WAR. PAGE 76 A1565 MARXISM
BAL/PWR

B60
KENNEDY J.F.,THE STRATEGY OF PEACE. USA+45 WOR+45 PEACE
BAL/PWR DIPLOM INGP/REL ORD/FREE...GOV/COMP PLAN
NAT/COMP 20. PAGE 78 A1591 POLICY
NAT/G

B60
KHRUSHCHEV N.,FOR VICTORY IN PEACEFUL COMPETITION TOP/EX
WITH CAPITALISM. COM FUT USSR WOR+45 CONSTN SOCIETY PWR
INDUS INT/ORG DELIB/GP PLAN BAL/PWR DIPLOM PERSON CAP/ISM
MARXISM...MARXIST WORK 20 COLD/WAR. PAGE 79 A1611 SOCISM

B60
KRISTENSEN T.,THE ECONOMIC WORLD BALANCE. FUT ECO/UNDEV
WOR+45 CULTURE ECO/DEV BAL/PWR INT/TRADE REGION PWR ECO/TAC
WEALTH...STAT TREND CHARTS 20. PAGE 82 A1685 FOR/AID

B60
LE GHAIT E.,NO CARTE BLANCHE TO CAPRICORN; THE DETER
FOLLY OF NUCLEAR WAR. WOR+45 INT/ORG BAL/PWR DIPLOM NUC/PWR
RISK COERCE...CENSUS 20 NATO. PAGE 86 A1754 PLAN
DECISION

B60
MENEZES A.J.,O BRASIL E O MUNDO ASIO-AFRICANO (REV. DIPLOM
ED.). AFR ASIA BRAZIL WOR+45 INT/TRADE ORD/FREE PWR BAL/PWR
SOVEREIGN...POLICY 20. PAGE 99 A2040 LEAD
ECO/UNDEV

B60
MONTGOMERY B.L.,AN APPROACH TO SANITY; A STUDY OF DIPLOM
EAST-WEST RELATIONS. CONFER WAR EFFICIENCY ATTIT INT/ORG
...POLICY 20 NATO COLD/WAR KHRUSH/N. PAGE 103 A2113 BAL/PWR
DETER

B60
MORISON E.E.,TURMOIL AND TRADITION: A STUDY OF THE BIOG
LIFE AND TIMES OF HENRY L. STIMSON. USA+45 USA-45 NAT/G
POL/PAR CHIEF DELIB/GP FORCES BAL/PWR DIPLOM EX/STRUC
ARMS/CONT WAR PEACE 19/20 STIMSON/HL ROOSEVLT/F
TAFT/WH HOOVER/H REPUBLICAN. PAGE 104 A2142

B60
MOSELY P.E.,THE KREMLIN AND WORLD POLITICS. EUR+WWI GERMANY USA+45 USSR CHIEF TOP/EX BAL/PWR DOMIN PEACE PWR...METH 20 COLD/WAR STALIN/J EUROPE/E. PAGE 105 A2151
COM DIPLOM POLICY WAR

B60
SCHLESINGER J.R.,THE POLITICAL ECONOMY OF NATIONAL SECURITY. USA+45 USSR WOR+45 ECO/DEV ECO/UNDEV NAT/G DELIB/GP TOP/EX BAL/PWR DIPLOM INT/TRADE ATTIT PWR...STERTYP TOT/POP 20. PAGE 128 A2628
PLAN ECO/TAC

B60
SETHE P.,SCHICKSALSSTUNDEN DER WELTGESCHICHTE (6TH ED.). NAT/G BAL/PWR DOMIN REV PWR...NAT/COMP 16/20. PAGE 131 A2687
DIPLOM WAR PEACE

B60
SETON-WATSON H.,NEITHER WAR NOR PEACE. ASIA USSR WOR+45 ELITES INT/ORG NAT/G EX/STRUC FORCES BAL/PWR ECO/TAC EDU/PROP COERCE NAT/LISM ORD/FREE WEALTH TOT/POP 20. PAGE 131 A2688
ATTIT PWR DIPLOM TOTALISM

B60
STOLPER W.F.,GERMANY BETWEEN EAST AND WEST: THE ECONOMICS OF COMPETITIVE COEXISTENCE. FUT GERMANY/E GERMANY/W WOR+45 FINAN POL/PAR BUDGET ECO/TAC FOR/AID INT/TRADE...STAT CHARTS METH/COMP 20 COLD/WAR. PAGE 138 A2832
ECO/DEV DIPLOM GOV/COMP BAL/PWR

B60
STRACHEY J.,THE END OF EMPIRE. UK WOR+45 WOR-45 DIPLOM INT/TRADE DOMIN ADJUST ORD/FREE WEALTH ...SOCIALIST GOV/COMP TIME COMMONWLTH. PAGE 139 A2841
COLONIAL ECO/DEV BAL/PWR LAISSEZ

B60
THOMPSON K.W.,POLITICAL REALISM AND THE CRISIS IN WORLD POLITICS. USA+45 USA-45 SOCIETY INT/ORG NAT/G LEGIS TOP/EX LEGIT DETER ATTIT ORD/FREE PWR ...GEN/LAWS TOT/POP 20. PAGE 143 A2931
PLAN HUM BAL/PWR DIPLOM

B60
VAN HOOGSTRATE D.J.,AMERICAN FOREIGN POLICY: REALISTS AND IDEALISTS: A CATHOLIC INTERPRETATION. BAL/PWR FOR/AID ARMS/CONT GOV/REL PEACE LOVE MORAL SOVEREIGN CATHISM...BIBLIOG 20. PAGE 158 A3213
CATH DIPLOM POLICY IDEA/COMP

B60
WHITING A.S.,CHINA CROSSES THE YALU: THE DECISION TO ENTER THE KOREAN WAR. ASIA CHINA/COM KOREA ECO/UNDEV R+D INT/ORG TOP/EX ACT/RES BAL/PWR ATTIT PWR...GEN/METH 20. PAGE 164 A3338
PLAN COERCE WAR

L60
JACOB P.E.,"THE DISARMAMENT CONSENSUS." USA+45 USSR WOR+45 INT/ORG NAT/G ACT/RES TEC/DEV BAL/PWR EDU/PROP ADMIN COERCE DETER NUC/PWR CONSEN RIGID/FLEX PWR...CONCPT RECORD CHARTS COLD/WAR 20. PAGE 72 A1482
DELIB/GP ATTIT ARMS/CONT

L60
LAUTERPACHT E.,"THE SUEZ CANAL SETTLEMENT." FRANCE ISLAM ISRAEL UAR UK BAL/PWR DIPLOM LEGIT...JURID GEN/LAWS ANTHOL SUEZ VAL/FREE 20. PAGE 85 A1747
INT/ORG LAW

L60
NOGEE J.L.,"THE DIPLOMACY OF DISARMAMENT." WOR+45 INT/ORG NAT/G CONSULT DELIB/GP TOP/EX BAL/PWR DIPLOM EDU/PROP COERCE DETER WEAPON PEACE ATTIT ...RECORD TIME/SEQ TOT/POP VAL/FREE COLD/WAR 20. PAGE 109 A2246
PWR ORD/FREE ARMS/CONT NUC/PWR

S60
CLARK W.,"NEW FORCES IN THE UN." FUT UK WOR+45 CONSTN BAL/PWR DIPLOM DRIVE PWR SKILL...CONCPT TREND UN TOT/POP 20. PAGE 27 A0543
INT/ORG ECO/UNDEV SOVEREIGN

S60
COHEN A.,"THE NEW AFRICA AND THE UN." FUT ECO/UNDEV NAT/G ECO/TAC INT/TRADE CHOOSE ATTIT ORD/FREE PWR ...POLICY METH/CNCPT OBS TREND CON/ANAL GEN/LAWS TOT/POP VAL/FREE UN 20. PAGE 27 A0558
AFR INT/ORG BAL/PWR FOR/AID

S60
EFIMENCO N.M.,"CATEGORIES OF INTERNATIONAL INTEGRATION." UNIV WOR+45 INT/ORG NAT/G ACT/RES CREATE PEACE...CONCPT TREND 20. PAGE 40 A0824
PLAN BAL/PWR SOVEREIGN

S60
GINSBURGS G.,"PEKING-LHASA-NEW DELHI." CHINA/COM FUT INDIA S/ASIA KIN NAT/G PROVS SECT FORCES BAL/PWR ECO/TAC DOMIN EDU/PROP LEGIT ADMIN REGION GUERRILLA PWR...TREND TIBET 20. PAGE 52 A1074
ASIA COERCE DIPLOM

S60
GOODRICH L.,"GEOGRAPHICAL DISTRIBUTION OF THE STAFF OF THE UN SECRETARIAT." FUT WOR+45 CONSTN BAL/PWR DIPLOM EDU/PROP LEGIT ROUTINE RIGID/FLEX...CHARTS UN 20. PAGE 54 A1105
INT/ORG EX/STRUC

S60
GULICK E.V.,"OUR BALANCE OF POWER SYSTEM IN PERSPECTIVE." FUT WOR+45 WOR-45 ECO/DEV DOMIN ROUTINE NUC/PWR PEACE PWR WEALTH...PLURIST CONCPT HIST/WRIT GEN/METH TOT/POP 20. PAGE 58 A1191
INT/ORG TREND ARMS/CONT BAL/PWR

S60
KENNAN G.F.,"PEACEFUL CO-EXISTENCE: A WESTERN VIEW." COM EUR+WWI USA+45 USSR WOR+45 PLAN BAL/PWR DIPLOM INT/TRADE PWR...POLICY CONCPT OBS HIST/WRIT TREND GEN/LAWS COLD/WAR 20 KHRUSH/N. PAGE 78 A1589
ATTIT COERCE

S60
LYON P.,"NEUTRALITY AND THE EMERGENCE OF THE CONCEPT OF NEUTRALISM." WOR+45 WOR-45 INT/ORG NAT/G BAL/PWR NEUTRAL ATTIT PWR...POLICY TIME/SEQ TREND COLD/WAR TOT/POP VAL/FREE 20 UN. PAGE 92 A1878
CONCPT

S60
MIKESELL R.F.,"AMERICA'S ECONOMIC RESPONSIBILITY AS A GREAT POWER." COM FUT USA+45 USSR WOR+45 INT/ORG PLAN ECO/TAC FOR/AID EDU/PROP CHOOSE WEALTH ...POLICY 20. PAGE 101 A2069
ECO/UNDEV BAL/PWR CAP/ISM

S60
MORA J.A.,"THE ORGANIZATION OF AMERICAN STATES." USA+45 LAW ECO/UNDEV VOL/ASSN DELIB/GP PLAN BAL/PWR EDU/PROP ADMIN DRIVE RIGID/FLEX ORD/FREE WEALTH ...TIME/SEQ GEN/LAWS OAS 20. PAGE 103 A2126
L/A+17C INT/ORG REGION

S60
MORGENSTERN O.,"GOAL: AN ARMED, INSPECTED, OPEN WORLD." COM EUR+WWI USA+45 R+D INT/ORG NAT/G TEC/DEV BAL/PWR COERCE NUC/PWR ORD/FREE PWR...TREND 20. PAGE 104 A2133
FORCES CONCPT ARMS/CONT DETER

S60
MUNRO L.,"CAN THE UNITED NATIONS ENFORCE PEACE." WOR+45 LAW INT/ORG VOL/ASSN BAL/PWR LEGIT ARMS/CONT COERCE DETER PEACE PWR...CONCPT REC/INT TREND UN 20 HAMMARSK/D. PAGE 106 A2173
FORCES ORD/FREE

S60
RIESELBACH Z.N.,"QUANTITATIVE TECHNIQUES FOR STUDYING VOTING BEHAVIOR IN THE UNITED NATIONS GENERAL ASSEMBLY." FUT S/ASIA USA+45 INT/ORG BAL/PWR DIPLOM ECO/TAC FOR/AID ADMIN PWR...POLICY METH/CNCPT METH UN 20. PAGE 121 A2478
QUANT CHOOSE

B61
AUBREY H.G.,COEXISTENCE: ECONOMIC CHALLENGE AND RESPONSE. USSR WOR+45 ACT/RES BAL/PWR CAP/ISM DIPLOM ECO/TAC FOR/AID INT/TRADE PEACE SOCISM ...METH/COMP NAT/COMP COLD/WAR. PAGE 10 A0196
POLICY ECO/UNDEV PLAN COM

B61
BAINS J.S.,STUDIES IN POLITICAL SCIENCE. INDIA WOR+45 WOR-45 CONSTN BAL/PWR ADJUD ADMIN PARL/PROC SOVEREIGN...SOC METH/COMP ANTHOL 17/20 UN. PAGE 10 A0209
DIPLOM INT/LAW NAT/G

B61
BECHHOEFER B.G.,POSTWAR NEGOTIATIONS FOR ARMS CONTROL. COM EUR+WWI USSR INT/ORG NAT/G ACT/RES BAL/PWR DIPLOM ECO/TAC EDU/PROP ADMIN REGION DETER NUC/PWR WAR WEAPON PEACE ATTIT PWR...POLICY TIME/SEQ COLD/WAR CONGRESS 20. PAGE 12 A0244
USA+45 ARMS/CONT

B61
DALLIN D.J.,SOVIET FOREIGN POLICY AFTER STALIN. ASIA CHINA/COM EUR+WWI GERMANY IRAN UK YUGOSLAVIA INT/ORG NAT/G VOL/ASSN FORCES TOP/EX BAL/PWR DOMIN EDU/PROP COERCE ATTIT PWR 20. PAGE 33 A0679
COM DIPLOM USSR

B61
FLEMING D.F.,THE COLD WAR AND ITS ORIGINS: 1950-1960 (VOL. II). ASIA FUT HUNGARY POLAND WOR+45 TEC/DEV DOMIN NUC/PWR REV PEACE...T 20 COLD/WAR EISNHWR/DD SUEZ. PAGE 46 A0946
MARXISM DIPLOM BAL/PWR

B61
FLEMING D.F.,THE COLD WAR AND ITS ORIGINS: 1917-1950 (VOL. I). ASIA USSR WOR+45 WOR-45 TEC/DEV FOR/AID NUC/PWR REV WAR PEACE FASCISM...T 20 COLD/WAR NATO BERLIN/BLO. PAGE 46 A0947
DIPLOM MARXISM BAL/PWR

B61
GRAEBNER N.,THE NEW ISOLATIONISM: A STUDY IN POLITICS AND FOREIGN POLICY SINCE 1960. USA+45 INT/ORG LOC/G NAT/G POL/PAR LEGIS BAL/PWR EDU/PROP CHOOSE ATTIT PERSON ORD/FREE 20 TRUMAN/HS EISNHWR/DD. PAGE 55 A1120
EXEC PWR DIPLOM

B61
GRAEBNER N.,AN UNCERTAIN TRADITION: AMERICAN SECRETARIES OF STATE IN THE 20TH CENTURY. USA+45 CONSTN INT/ORG NAT/G DELIB/GP TOP/EX BAL/PWR DOMIN LEGIT ADMIN ARMS/CONT ATTIT DRIVE PERSON SUPEGO ORD/FREE PWR...GEN/LAWS VAL/FREE CONGRESS. PAGE 55 A1121
USA-45 BIOG DIPLOM

B61
KERTESZ S.D.,AMERICAN DIPLOMACY IN A NEW ERA. COM S/ASIA UK USA+45 FORCES PROB/SOLV BAL/PWR ECO/TAC ADMIN COLONIAL WAR PEACE ORD/FREE 20 NATO CONGRESS UN COLD/WAR. PAGE 78 A1601
ANTHOL DIPLOM TREND

B61
KISSINGER H.A.,THE NECESSITY FOR CHOICE. FUT USA+45 ECO/UNDEV NAT/G PLAN BAL/PWR ECO/TAC ARMS/CONT DETER NUC/PWR ATTIT...POLICY CONCPT RECORD GEN/LAWS COLD/WAR 20. PAGE 80 A1642
TOP/EX TREND DIPLOM

B61
KNORR K.E.,THE INTERNATIONAL SYSTEM. FUT SOCIETY INT/ORG NAT/G PLAN BAL/PWR DIPLOM WAR PWR ...DECISION METH/CNCPT CONT/OBS GAME METH UN 20. PAGE 81 A1655
ACT/RES SIMUL ECO/UNDEV

B61
LIPPMANN W.,THE COMING TESTS WITH RUSSIA. COM CUBA GERMANY USSR FORCES CONTROL NEUTRAL COERCE NUC/PWR REV WAR PWR...INT 20 KHRUSH/N BERLIN. PAGE 89 A1830
BAL/PWR DIPLOM MARXISM ARMS/CONT

B61
LUKACS J.,A HISTORY OF THE COLD WAR. ASIA COM EUR+WWI USA+45 USA-45 INT/ORG NAT/G DELIB/GP
PWR TIME/SEQ

ACT/RES BAL/PWR DIPLOM DOMIN EDU/PROP LEGIT DRIVE ORD/FREE...TREND COLD/WAR 20. PAGE 91 A1872 — USSR

B61
MILLIKAW M.F.,THE EMERGING NATIONS: THEIR GROWTH AND UNITED STATES POLICY. FUT USA+45 WOR+45 WOR-45 NAT/G PLAN TEC/DEV BAL/PWR GOV/REL PEACE ORD/FREE 20. PAGE 101 A2082 — ECO/UNDEV POLICY DIPLOM FOR/AID

B61
NOLLAU G.,INTERNATIONAL COMMUNISM AND WORLD REVOLUTION: HISTORY AND METHODS. RUSSIA USSR INT/ORG NAT/G POL/PAR VOL/ASSN FORCES BAL/PWR DIPLOM EXEC REGION WAR ATTIT PWR MARXISM...CONCPT TIME/SEQ COLD/WAR 19/20. PAGE 102 A2100 — COM REV

B61
MORLEY L.,THE PATCHWORK HISTORY OF FOREIGN AID. KOREA/S USA+45 USSR LAW FINAN INT/ORG TEC/DEV BAL/PWR GIVE 20 COLD/WAR NATO. PAGE 104 A2144 — FOR/AID ECO/UNDEV FORCES DIPLOM

B61
MORRAY J.P.,FROM YALTA TO DISARMAMENT: COLD WAR DEBATE. USA+45 CAP/ISM FOR/AID CONTROL NUC/PWR 20 UN COLD/WAR CHURCHLL/W. PAGE 104 A2145 — MARXIST ARMS/CONT DIPLOM BAL/PWR

B61
OAKES J.B.,THE EDGE OF FREEDOM. EUR+WWI USA+45 USSR ECO/UNDEV BAL/PWR DIPLOM DOMIN COLONIAL PWR MARXISM POPULISM...IDEA/COMP 20 COLD/WAR. PAGE 111 A2271 — AFR ORD/FREE SOVEREIGN NEUTRAL

B61
OVERSTREET H.,THE WAR CALLED PEACE. USSR WOR+45 COM/IND INT/ORG POL/PAR BAL/PWR EDU/PROP PEACE ATTIT...CONCPT 20 KHRUSH/N. PAGE 112 A2302 — DIPLOM COM POLICY LEAD

B61
PECKERT J.,DIE GROSSEN UND DIE KLEINEN MAECHTE. COM GERMANY/W ECO/DEV ECO/UNDEV NAT/G WAR RACE/REL PEACE...POLICY GP/COMP GOV/COMP 20 COLD/WAR. PAGE 114 A2346 — DIPLOM ECO/TAC BAL/PWR

B61
RIENOW R.,CONTEMPORARY INTERNATIONAL POLITICS. WOR+45 INT/ORG BAL/PWR EDU/PROP COLONIAL NEUTRAL REGION WAR PEACE...INT/LAW 20 COLD/WAR UN. PAGE 121 A2476 — DIPLOM PWR POLICY NAT/G

B61
SCHELLING T.C.,STRATEGY AND ARMS CONTROL. FUT UNIV WOR+45 INT/ORG PLAN TEC/DEV BAL/PWR LEGIT PERCEPT HEALTH...CONCPT VAL/FREE 20. PAGE 128 A2623 — ROUTINE POLICY ARMS/CONT

B61
SCHMIDT H.,VERTEIDIGUNG ODER VERGELTUNG. COM CUBA GERMANY/W USSR FORCES DIPLOM ARMS/CONT DETER NUC/PWR...POLICY CHARTS HYPO/EXP SIMUL BIBLIOG 20 NATO COLD/WAR. PAGE 128 A2630 — PLAN WAR BAL/PWR ORD/FREE

B61
WRIGHT Q.,THE ROLE OF INTERNATIONAL LAW IN THE ELIMINATION OF WAR. FUT WOR+45 WOR-45 NAT/G BAL/PWR DIPLOM DOMIN LEGIT PWR...POLICY INT/LAW JURID CONCPT TIME/SEQ TREND GEN/LAWS COLD/WAR 20. PAGE 168 A3414 — INT/ORG ADJUD ARMS/CONT

B61
WRINCH P.,THE MILITARY STRATEGY OF WINSTON CHURCHILL. UK WOR-45 SEA VOL/ASSN TEC/DEV BAL/PWR LEAD WAR PEACE ATTIT...POLICY 20 CHURCHLL/W. PAGE 168 A3421 — CIVMIL/REL FORCES PLAN DIPLOM

L61
HOYT E.C.,"UNITED STATES REACTION TO THE KOREAN ATTACK." COM KOREA USA+45 CONSTN DELIB/GP FORCES PLAN ECO/TAC DOMIN EDU/PROP LEGIT ROUTINE COERCE WAR ATTIT DISPL RIGID/FLEX ORD/FREE PWR...POLICY INT/LAW TREND UN 20. PAGE 68 A1402 — ASIA INT/ORG BAL/PWR DIPLOM

L61
TAUBENFELD H.J.,"A REGIME FOR OUTER SPACE." FUT UNIV R+D ACT/RES PLAN BAL/PWR LEGIT ARMS/CONT ORD/FREE...POLICY JURID TREND UN TOT/POP 20 COLD/WAR. PAGE 142 A2894 — INT/ORG ADJUD SPACE

L61
WRIGHT Q.,"STUDIES IN DETERRENCE: LIMITED WARS AND THE ROLE OF SEABORNE WEAPONS SYSTEMS." FUT USA+45 WOR+45 SEA INT/ORG NAT/G FORCES ACT/RES WAR WEAPON ORD/FREE TOT/POP 20. PAGE 168 A3415 — TEC/DEV SKILL BAL/PWR DETER

S61
ALGER C.F.,"NON-RESOLUTION CONSEQUENCES OF THE UNITED NATIONS AND THEIR EFFECT ON INTERNATIONAL CONFLICT." WOR+45 CONSTN ECO/DEV NAT/G CONSULT DELIB/GP TOP/EX ACT/RES PLAN DIPLOM EDU/PROP ROUTINE ATTIT ALL/VALS...INT/LAW TOT/POP UN 20. PAGE 6 A0117 — INT/ORG DRIVE BAL/PWR

S61
CLAUDE I.,"THE MANAGEMENT OF POWER IN THE CHANGING UNITED NATIONS." WOR+45 PERCEPT UN TOT/POP VAL/FREE 20. PAGE 27 A0544 — INT/ORG DELIB/GP BAL/PWR

S61
DELLA PORT G.,"PROBLEMI E PROSPETTIVE DI COESISTENZA FRA ORIENTE ED OCCIDENTE, (PART 3)." COM FUT WOR+45 NAT/G BAL/PWR FOR/AID BAL/PAY PWR WEALTH...SOC CONCPT GEN/LAWS COLD/WAR 20. PAGE 36 A0729 — INT/TRADE

S61
GOODWIN G.L.,"THE EXPANDING UNITED NATIONS: 2-DIPLOMATIC PRESSURES AND TECHNIQUES." COM ECO/UNDEV TOP/EX BAL/PWR DIPLOM DOMIN...POLICY CONCPT UN COLD/WAR 20. PAGE 54 A1108 — INT/ORG PWR

S61
RALEIGH J.S.,"THE MIDDLE EAST IN 1960: A POLITICAL SURVEY." FUT ISLAM INTELL KIN BAL/PWR EDU/PROP NAT/LISM...TREND VAL/FREE 20. PAGE 119 A2435 — INT/ORG EX/STRUC

S61
VIRALLY M.,"VERS UNE REFORME DU SECRETARIAT DES NATIONS UNIES." FUT WOR+45 CONSTN ECO/DEV TOP/EX BAL/PWR ADMIN ALL/VALS...CONCPT BIOG UN VAL/FREE 20. PAGE 159 A3243 — INT/ORG INTELL DIPLOM

S61
WHELAN J.G.,"KHRUSHCHEV AND THE BALANCE OF WORLD POWER." FUT WOR+45 INT/ORG VOL/ASSN CAP/ISM DIPLOM SKILL...POLICY COLD/WAR 20 KHRUSH/N. PAGE 163 A3328 — COM PWR BAL/PWR USSR

B62
ALTHING F.A.M.,EUROPEAN ORGANIZATIONS AND FOREIGN RELATIONS OF STATES: A COMPARATIVE ANALYSIS OF DECISION-MAKING. EUR+WWI CONSTN ELITES BAL/PWR INT/TRADE SOVEREIGN TREATY. PAGE 6 A0131 — DELIB/GP INT/ORG DECISION DIPLOM

B62
BAILEY S.D.,THE SECRETARIAT OF THE UNITED NATIONS. FUT WOR+45 DELIB/GP PLAN BAL/PWR DOMIN EDU/PROP ADMIN PEACE ATTIT PWR...DECISION CONCPT TREND CON/ANAL CHARTS UN VAL/FREE COLD/WAR 20. PAGE 10 A0205 — INT/ORG EXEC DIPLOM

B62
BOULDING K.E.,CONFLICT AND DEFENSE: A GENERAL THEORY. FUT SOCIETY INT/ORG NAT/G CREATE BAL/PWR COERCE NAT/LISM DRIVE ALL/VALS...PLURIST DECISION CONCPT METH/CNCPT TREND HYPO/EXP TOT/POP 20. PAGE 17 A0347 — MATH SIMUL PEACE WAR

B62
BURTON J.W.,PEACE THEORY: PRECONDITIONS OF DISARMAMENT. COM EUR+WWI USA+45 NAT/G FORCES BAL/PWR DIPLOM ECO/TAC EDU/PROP REGION COERCE DETER PEACE ATTIT PWR TOT/POP COLD/WAR 20. PAGE 22 A0446 — INT/ORG PLAN ARMS/CONT

B62
CLUBB O.E. JR.,THE UNITED STATES AND THE SINO-SOVIET BLOC IN SOUTHEAST ASIA. ASIA CHINA/COM COM USA+45 USSR ECO/UNDEV INT/ORG NAT/G FORCES TOP/EX PLAN ECO/TAC DOMIN COERCE GUERRILLA ATTIT RIGID/FLEX...POLICY OBS TREND 20. PAGE 27 A0553 — S/ASIA PWR BAL/PWR DIPLOM

B62
DEHIO L.,THE PRECARIOUS BALANCE: FOUR CENTURIES OF THE EUROPEAN POWER STRUGGLE. FRANCE GERMANY SPAIN NAT/G DOMIN PWR...GOV/COMP 8/20. PAGE 36 A0725 — BAL/PWR WAR DIPLOM COERCE

B62
DUTOIT B.,LA NEUTRALITE SUISSE A L'HEURE EUROPEENNE. EUR+WWI MOD/EUR INT/ORG NAT/G VOL/ASSN PLAN BAL/PWR LEGIT NEUTRAL REGION PEACE ORD/FREE SOVEREIGN...CONCPT OBS TIME/SEQ TREND STERTYP VAL/FREE LEAGUE/NAT UN 20. PAGE 40 A0812 — ATTIT DIPLOM SWITZERLND

B62
GILPIN R.,AMERICAN SCIENTISTS AND NUCLEAR WEAPONS POLICY. COM FUT USA+45 WOR+45 INT/ORG NAT/G PROF/ORG CONSULT FORCES CREATE TEC/DEV BAL/PWR EDU/PROP ARMS/CONT WAR PERCEPT KNOWL MORAL PWR ...PHIL/SCI SOC CONCPT GEN/LAWS 20. PAGE 52 A1073 — INTELL ATTIT DETER NUC/PWR

B62
GYORGY A.,PROBLEMS IN INTERNATIONAL RELATIONS. COM CT/SYS NUC/PWR ALL/IDEOS 20 UN EEC ECSC. PAGE 58 A1199 — DIPLOM NEUTRAL BAL/PWR REV

B62
KAHN H.,THINKING ABOUT THE UNTHINKABLE. FUT USA+45 LAW NAT/G CONSULT FORCES ACT/RES CREATE PLAN TEC/DEV BAL/PWR DIPLOM EDU/PROP ARMS/CONT DETER ATTIT...CONCPT OBS TREND COLD/WAR 20. PAGE 76 A1547 — INT/ORG ORD/FREE NUC/PWR PEACE

B62
KING-HALL S.,POWER POLITICS IN THE NUCLEAR AGE: A POLICY FOR BRITAIN. UK WOR+45 PLAN ECO/TAC CONTROL RISK ARMS/CONT MORAL PWR RESPECT...OLD/LIB 20. PAGE 79 A1625 — BAL/PWR NUC/PWR POLICY DIPLOM

B62
LAQUEUR W.,POLYCENTRISM. CHINA/COM COM USSR WOR+45 INT/ORG NAT/G ECO/TAC DOMIN LEAD ATTIT PWR SOVEREIGN...ANTHOL 20. PAGE 85 A1732 — MARXISM DIPLOM BAL/PWR POLICY

B62
LEFEVER E.W.,ARMS AND ARMS CONTROL. COM USA+45 INT/ORG TEC/DEV DIPLOM ORD/FREE 20. PAGE 86 A1763 — ATTIT PWR ARMS/CONT BAL/PWR

B62
LERNER M.,THE AGE OF OVERKILL: A PREFACE TO WORLD POLITICS. USA+45 USSR WOR+45 SOCIETY ECO/UNDEV BAL/PWR NEUTRAL PARTIC REV ALL/IDEOS MARXISM ...BIBLIOG/A 20. PAGE 87 A1787 — DIPLOM NUC/PWR PWR DEATH

B62
LESSING P.,AFRICA'S RED HARVEST. AFR CHINA/COM COM — NAT/LISM

USSR ECO/UNDEV BAL/PWR DIPLOM CONTROL PWR 20 COLD/WAR INTERVENT. PAGE 87 A1789
MARXISM FOR/AID EDU/PROP

B62
MANDER J.,BERLIN: HOSTAGE FOR THE WEST. FUT GERMANY WOR+45 FOR/AID RISK ATTIT ORD/FREE 20 BERLIN COLD/WAR. PAGE 93 A1916
DIPLOM BAL/PWR DOMIN DETER

B62
MARTIN L.W.,NEUTRALISM AND NONALIGNMENT. WOR+45 ATTIT PWR...POLICY ANTHOL 20 UN. PAGE 95 A1952
DIPLOM NEUTRAL BAL/PWR INT/ORG

B62
MONCRIEFF A.,THE STRATEGY OF SURVIVAL. UK FORCES BAL/PWR CONFER DETER WAR...ANTHOL 20 COLD/WAR. PAGE 102 A2104
PLAN DECISION DIPLOM ARMS/CONT

B62
SCHRODER P.M.,METTERNICH'S DIPLOMACY AT ITS ZENITH, 1820-1823. MOD/EUR ELITES INT/ORG VOL/ASSN DELIB/GP ECO/TAC EDU/PROP DISPL PWR SOVEREIGN...POLICY CONCPT GEN/LAWS 19 METTRNCH/K. PAGE 129 A2647
ORD/FREE BIOG BAL/PWR DIPLOM

B62
SCHUMAN F.L.,THE COLD WAR: RETROSPECT AND PROSPECT. FUT USA+45 USSR WOR+45 BAL/PWR EDU/PROP ARMS/CONT ATTIT...MAJORIT IDEA/COMP ANTHOL BIBLIOG 20 COLD/WAR. PAGE 129 A2651
MARXISM TEC/DEV DIPLOM NUC/PWR

B62
SCOTT W.E.,ALLIANCE AGAINST HITLER. EUR+WWI FRANCE GERMANY USSR BAL/PWR LEAD TOTALISM PWR FASCISM MARXISM...POLICY BIBLIOG 20 HITLER/A. PAGE 131 A2675
WAR DIPLOM FORCES

B62
SINGER J.D.,DETERRENCE, ARMS CONTROL AND DISARMAMENT: TOWARD A SYNTHESIS IN NATIONAL SECURITY POLICY. COM USA+45 INT/ORG BAL/PWR DETER ORD/FREE...POLICY COLD/WAR 20. PAGE 133 A2727
FUT ACT/RES ARMS/CONT

B62
SOMMER T.,DEUTSCHLAND UND JAPAN ZWISCHEN DEN MACHTEN. GERMANY DELIB/GP BAL/PWR AGREE COERCE TOTALISM PWR 20 CHINJAP TREATY. PAGE 135 A2765
DIPLOM WAR ATTIT

B62
STRACHEY J.,ON THE PREVENTION OF WAR. FUT WOR+45 INT/ORG NAT/G ACT/RES PLAN BAL/PWR DOMIN EDU/PROP PEACE ATTIT...POLICY TREND TOT/POP COLD/WAR 20 UN. PAGE 139 A2842
FORCES ORD/FREE ARMS/CONT NUC/PWR

B62
WOLFERS A.,DISCORD AND COLLABORATION: ESSAYS ON INTERNATIONAL POLITICS. WOR+45 CULTURE SOCIETY INT/ORG NAT/G BAL/PWR DIPLOM DOMIN NAT/LISM PEACE PWR...POLICY CONCPT STYLE RECORD TREND GEN/LAWS 20. PAGE 166 A3385
ATTIT ORD/FREE

B62
YALEN R.,REGIONALISM AND WORLD ORDER. EUR+WWI WOR+45 WOR-45 INT/ORG VOL/ASSN DELIB/GP FORCES TOP/EX BAL/PWR DIPLOM DOMIN REGION ARMS/CONT PWR ...JURID HYPO/EXP COLD/WAR 20. PAGE 168 A3427
ORD/FREE POLICY

L62
STEIN E.,"MR HAMMARSKJOLD, THE CHARTER LAW AND THE FUTURE ROLE OF THE UNITED NATIONS SECRETARY-GENERAL." WOR+45 CONSTN INT/ORG DELIB/GP FORCES TOP/EX BAL/PWR LEGIT ROUTINE RIGID/FLEX PWR ...POLICY JURID OBS STERTYP UN COLD/WAR 20 HAMMARSK/D. PAGE 137 A2815
CONCPT BIOG

L62
ULYSSES,"THE INTERNATIONAL AIMS AND POLICIES OF THE SOVIET UNION: THE NEW CONCEPTS AND STRATEGY OF KHRUSHCHEV." FUT USSR WOR+45 SOCIETY INT/ORG NAT/G POL/PAR FORCES TOP/EX PLAN DOMIN EDU/PROP COERCE ATTIT PERSON PWR...TREND COLD/WAR 20 KHRUSH/N. PAGE 146 A2994
COM POLICY BAL/PWR DIPLOM

S62
BOULDING K.E.,"THE PREVENTION OF WORLD WAR THREE." FUT WOR+45 INT/ORG PLAN BAL/PWR PEACE ORD/FREE PWR ...NEW/IDEA TREND TOT/POP COLD/WAR 20. PAGE 17 A0348
VOL/ASSN NAT/G ARMS/CONT DIPLOM

S62
CRANE R.D.,"LAW AND STRATEGY IN SPACE." FUT USA+45 WOR+45 AIR LAW INT/ORG NAT/G FORCES ACT/RES PLAN BAL/PWR LEGIT ARMS/CONT COERCE ORD/FREE...POLICY INT/LAW JURID SOC/EXP 20 TREATY. PAGE 32 A0656
CONCPT SPACE

S62
LONDON K.,"SINO-SOVIET RELATIONS IN THE CONTEXT OF THE 'WORLD SOCIALIST SYSTEM'." ASIA CHINA/COM COM USSR INT/ORG NAT/G TOP/EX BAL/PWR DIPLOM DOMIN ATTIT PERCEPT RIGID/FLEX PWR MARXISM...METH/CNCPT TREND 20. PAGE 91 A1854
DELIB/GP CONCPT SOCISM

S62
MCWHINNEY E.,"CO-EXISTENCE, THE CUBA CRISIS, AND COLD WAR-INTERNATIONAL WAR." CUBA USA+45 USSR WOR+45 NAT/G TOP/EX BAL/PWR DIPLOM DOMIN LEGIT PEACE RIGID/FLEX ORD/FREE...STERTYP COLD/WAR 20. PAGE 99 A2026
CONCPT INT/LAW

S62
RUSSETT B.M.,"CAUSE, SURPRISE, AND NO ESCAPE." FUT WOR-45 CULTURE SOCIETY INT/ORG FORCES TEC/DEV BAL/PWR EDU/PROP ARMS/CONT NUC/PWR WAR WEAPON PEACE KNOWL ORD/FREE PWR...POLICY CONCPT RECORD TIME/SEQ TREND GEN/LAWS 20 WWI. PAGE 126 A2578
COERCE DIPLOM

S62
SCHACHTER O.,"DAG HAMMARSKJOLD AND THE RELATION OF LAW TO POLITICS." FUT WOR+45 INT/ORG CONSULT PLAN TEC/DEV BAL/PWR DIPLOM LEGIT ATTIT PERCEPT ORD/FREE ...POLICY JURID CONCPT OBS TESTS STERTYP GEN/LAWS 20 HAMMARSK/D. PAGE 128 A2616
ACT/RES ADJUD

S62
SPENSER J.H.,"AFRICA AT THE UNITED NATIONS: SOME OBSERVATIONS." FUT ECO/UNDEV NAT/G CONSULT DELIB/GP PLAN BAL/PWR ECO/TAC EDU/PROP ATTIT RIGID/FLEX HEALTH ORD/FREE PWR WEALTH...POLICY CONCPT OBS TREND STERTYP GEN/METH UN VAL/FREE. PAGE 136 A2786
AFR INT/ORG REGION

S62
THOMAS J.R.T.,"SOVIET BEHAVIOR IN THE QUEMOY CRISES OF 1958." CHINA/COM FUT USSR WOR+45 INT/ORG VOL/ASSN FORCES PLAN BAL/PWR DOMIN COERCE NUC/PWR REV WAR ATTIT DRIVE ORD/FREE...POLICY OBS RECORD COLD/WAR FOR/POL 20. PAGE 143 A2923
COM PWR

B63
ABSHIRE D.M.,NATIONAL SECURITY: POLITICAL, MILITARY, AND ECONOMIC STRATEGIES IN THE DECADE AHEAD. ASIA COM USA+45 WOR+45 ECO/DEV ECO/UNDEV INT/ORG DELIB/GP FORCES ECO/TAC COERCE ATTIT RIGID/FLEX HEALTH ORD/FREE PWR WEALTH...POLICY STAT CHARTS ANTHOL COLD/WAR VAL/FREE. PAGE 4 A0083
FUT ACT/RES BAL/PWR

B63
BRECHER M.,THE NEW STATES OF ASIA. ASIA S/ASIA INT/ORG BAL/PWR COLONIAL NEUTRAL ORD/FREE PWR 20 UN. PAGE 18 A0369
NAT/G ECO/UNDEV DIPLOM POLICY

B63
BURNS A.L.,PEACE-KEEPING BY U.N.FORCES - FROM SUEZ TO THE CONGO. AFR FUT ISLAM ISRAEL USSR WOR+45 NAT/G DELIB/GP BAL/PWR DOMIN LEGIT EXEC COERCE PEACE ATTIT PWR RESPECT SOVEREIGN...CONCPT UN 20. PAGE 22 A0441
INT/ORG FORCES ORD/FREE

B63
CROZIER B.,THE MORNING AFTER; A STUDY OF INDEPENDENCE. WOR+45 EX/STRUC PLAN BAL/PWR COLONIAL GP/REL 20 COLD/WAR. PAGE 33 A0666
SOVEREIGN NAT/LISM NAT/G DIPLOM

B63
DUNN F.S.,PEACE-MAKING AND THE SETTLEMENT WITH JAPAN. ASIA USA+45 USA-45 FORCES BAL/PWR ECO/TAC CONFER WAR PWR SOVEREIGN 20 CHINJAP COLD/WAR TREATY. PAGE 39 A0802
POLICY PEACE PLAN DIPLOM

B63
FISCHER-GALATI S.,EASTERN EUROPE IN THE SIXTIES. ALBANIA USSR YUGOSLAVIA ECO/UNDEV AGRI MARKET LABOR WORKER DIPLOM INT/TRADE EDU/PROP GOV/REL PRODUC UTOPIA SOCISM 20. PAGE 46 A0939
MARXISM TEC/DEV BAL/PWR ECO/TAC

B63
FRANZ G.,TEILUNG UND WIEDERVEREINIGUNG. GERMANY IRELAND ITALY NETHERLAND POLAND CULTURE BAL/PWR CHOOSE NAT/LISM ORD/FREE SOVEREIGN 19/20. PAGE 48 A0987
DIPLOM WAR NAT/COMP ATTIT

B63
FULBRIGHT J.W.,PROSPECTS FOR THE WEST. COM USA+45 USSR INT/ORG NAT/G SCHOOL PROB/SOLV NUC/PWR WAR PEACE ORD/FREE...PREDICT METH/COMP 20 DEGAULLE/C. PAGE 50 A1015
DIPLOM BAL/PWR CONCPT POLICY

B63
GONZALEZ PEDRERO E.,ANATOMIA DE UN CONFLICTO. WOR+45 ECO/DEV ECO/UNDEV ECO/TAC FOR/AID CONTROL ARMS/CONT GOV/REL...NAT/COMP 20 COLD/WAR. PAGE 54 A1099
DIPLOM DETER BAL/PWR

B63
GRAEBNER N.A.,THE COLD WAR: IDEOLOGICAL CONFLICT OR POWER STRUGGLE? USSR WOR+45 WOR-45 PROB/SOLV EDU/PROP ARMS/CONT REV NAT/LISM PEACE ORD/FREE ...IDEA/COMP ANTHOL BIBLIOG/A 20 COLD/WAR. PAGE 55 A1123
DIPLOM BAL/PWR MARXISM

B63
JOYCE W.,THE PROPAGANDA GAP. USA+45 COM/IND ACADEM DOMIN FEEDBACK REV CIVMIL/REL...REALPOL COLD/WAR. PAGE 75 A1540
EDU/PROP PERCEPT BAL/PWR DIPLOM

B63
KORBEL J.,POLAND BETWEEN EAST AND WEST: SOVIET AND GERMAN DIPLOMACY TOWARD POLAND 1919-1933. EUR+WWI GERMANY POLAND USSR FORCES AGREE WAR SOVEREIGN ...BIBLIOG 20 TREATY. PAGE 81 A1670
BAL/PWR DIPLOM DOMIN NAT/LISM

B63
MENEZES A.J.,SUBDESENVOLVIMENTO E POLITICA INTERNACIONAL. BRAZIL WOR+45 PLAN CONTROL LEAD NAT/LISM ORD/FREE 20 THIRD/WRLD. PAGE 99 A2041
ECO/UNDEV DIPLOM POLICY BAL/PWR

B63
PACHTER H.M.,COLLISION COURSE; THE CUBAN MISSILE CRISIS AND COEXISTENCE. CUBA USA+45 DIPLOM ARMS/CONT PEACE MARXISM...DECISION INT/LAW 20 COLD/WAR KHRUSH/N KENNEDY/JF CASTRO/F. PAGE 112
WAR BAL/PWR NUC/PWR DETER

A2307

B63
RIUKIN A.,THE AFRICAN PRESENCE IN WORLD AFFAIRS. AFR WOR+45 ECO/UNDEV AGRI INT/ORG BAL/PWR ECO/TAC COLONIAL NEUTRAL NAT/LISM PEACE SOVEREIGN 20 UN. PAGE 121 A2486 DIPLOM NAT/G POLICY PWR

B63
RIVKIN A.,THE AFRICAN PRESENCE IN WORLD AFFAIRS. ECO/UNDEV AGRI INT/ORG LOC/G NAT/LISM...OBS PREDICT GOV/COMP 20. PAGE 121 A2489 AFR NAT/G DIPLOM BAL/PWR

B63
ROSECRANCE R.N.,ACTION AND REACTION IN WORLD POLITICS. FUT WOR-45 SOCIETY DELIB/GP ACT/RES CREATE DIPLOM ECO/TAC DOMIN EDU/PROP COERCE ATTIT PERSON SUPEGO ORD/FREE PWR...CHARTS SIMUL LEAGUE/NAT VAL/FREE UN 19/20. PAGE 123 A2529 WOR+45 INT/ORG BAL/PWR

B63
ROSS H.,THE COLD WAR: CONTAINMENT AND ITS CRITICSS. WOR+45 POL/PAR BAL/PWR ECO/TAC PEACE ORD/FREE ...POLICY IDEA/COMP ANTHOL T 20 COLD/WAR DULLES/JF TRUMAN/HS EISNHWR/DD. PAGE 124 A2541 MARXISM ARMS/CONT DIPLOM

B63
ROSSI M.,THE THIRD WORLD. FUT WOR+45 INT/ORG NAT/G CAP/ISM COLONIAL PEACE PWR MARXISM 20 UN THIRD/WRLD. PAGE 124 A2542 ECO/UNDEV DIPLOM BAL/PWR NEUTRAL

B63
SMITH J.E.,THE DEFENSE OF BERLIN. COM GUATEMALA WOR+45 ECO/TAC ADMIN NEUTRAL ATTIT ORD/FREE SOVEREIGN...DECISION 20 DEPT/STATE. PAGE 134 A2747 DIPLOM FORCES BAL/PWR PLAN

B63
US DEPARTMENT OF THE ARMY,US OVERSEAS BASES: PRESENT STATUS AND FUTURE PROSPECTS (PAMPHLET). USA+45 DIPLOM NUC/PWR ATTIT ORD/FREE...POLICY CHARTS 20. PAGE 152 A3107 BIBLIOG/A WAR BAL/PWR DETER

B63
VAN SLYCK P.,PEACE: THE CONTROL OF NATIONAL POWER. CUBA WOR+45 FINAN NAT/G FORCES PROB/SOLV TEC/DEV BAL/PWR ADMIN CONTROL ORD/FREE...POLICY INT/LAW UN COLD/WAR TREATY. PAGE 158 A3214 ARMS/CONT PEACE INT/ORG DIPLOM

B63
WATKINS K.W.,BRITAIN DIVIDED; THE EFFECT OF THE SPANISH CIVIL WAR ON BRITISH POLITICAL OPINION. SPAIN UK POL/PAR BAL/PWR LOBBY NEUTRAL 20. PAGE 162 A3293 EDU/PROP WAR POLICY DIPLOM

B63
WESTERFIELD H.,THE INSTRUMENTS OF AMERICA'S FOREIGN POLICY. WOR+45 ECO/DEV NAT/G CONSULT EX/STRUC LEGIS BAL/PWR FOR/AID INT/TRADE DOMIN EDU/PROP LEGIT ATTIT KNOWL ORD/FREE PWR WEALTH...OBS COLD/WAR TOT/POP VAL/FREE. PAGE 163 A3322 USA+45 INT/ORG DIPLOM

L63
CRANE R.D.,"THE CUBAN CRISIS: A STRATEGIC ANALYSIS OF AMERICAN AND SOVIET POLICY." CUBA USA+45 USSR BAL/PWR RISK DETER NUC/PWR PERCEPT ORD/FREE 20. PAGE 32 A0658 DIPLOM POLICY FORCES

L63
RUSSETT B.M.,"TOWARD A MODEL OF COMPETITIVE INTERNATIONAL POLITICS." USA+45 WOR+45 INT/ORG NAT/G POL/PAR VOL/ASSN LEGIS BAL/PWR DIPLOM LEGIT PWR...CONCPT CONT/OBS STERTYP GEN/LAWS TOT/POP COLD/WAR 20 UN. PAGE 126 A2579 ATTIT EDU/PROP

L63
SCHELLING T.C.,"STRATEGIC PROBLEMS OF AN INTERNATIONAL ARMED FORCE." WOR+45 ECO/DEV INT/ORG NAT/G PLAN BAL/PWR LEGIT ARMS/CONT COERCE DETER ORD/FREE PWR...POLICY CONCPT COLD/WAR 20. PAGE 128 A2624 CREATE FORCES

S63
BECHHOEFER B.G.,"UNITED NATIONS PROCEDURES IN CASE OF VIOLATIONS OF DISARMAMENT AGREEMENTS." COM USA+45 USSR LAW CONSTN NAT/G EX/STRUC FORCES LEGIS BAL/PWR EDU/PROP CT/SYS ARMS/CONT ORD/FREE PWR ...POLICY STERTYP UN VAL/FREE 20. PAGE 12 A0245 INT/ORG DELIB/GP

S63
EMERSON R.,"THE ATLANTIC COMMUNITY AND THE EMERGING COUNTRIES." FUT WOR+45 ECO/DEV ECO/UNDEV R+D NAT/G DELIB/GP BAL/PWR ECO/TAC EDU/PROP ROUTINE ORD/FREE PWR WEALTH...POLICY CONCPT TREND GEN/METH EEC 20 NATO. PAGE 42 A0848 ATTIT INT/TRADE

S63
HAVILAND H.F.,"BUILDING A POLITICAL COMMUNITY." EUR+WWI FUT UK USA+45 ECO/DEV ECO/UNDEV INT/ORG NAT/G DELIB/GP BAL/PWR ECO/TAC NEUTRAL ROUTINE ATTIT PWR WEALTH...CONCPT COLD/WAR TOT/POP 20. PAGE 63 A1293 VOL/ASSN DIPLOM

S63
MACWHINNEY E.,"LES CONCEPT SOVIETIQUE DE 'COEXISTENCE PACIFIQUE' ET LES RAPPORTS JURIDIQUES ENTRE L'URSS ET LES ETATS OCIDENTAUX." COM FUT WOR+45 LAW CULTURE INTELL POL/PAR ACT/RES BAL/PWR ...INT/LAW 20. PAGE 93 A1903 NAT/G CONCPT DIPLOM USSR

S63
MCDOUGAL M.S.,"THE SOVIET-CUBAN QUARANTINE AND SELF-DEFENSE." CUBA USA+45 USSR WOR+45 INT/ORG NAT/G BAL/PWR NUC/PWR ATTIT...JURID CONCPT. PAGE 98 A2008 ORD/FREE LEGIT SOVEREIGN

S63
MEYROWITZ H.,"LES JURISTES DEVANT L'ARME NUCLAIRE." FUT WOR+45 INTELL SOCIETY BAL/PWR DETER WAR...JURID CONCPT 20. PAGE 100 A2058 ACT/RES ADJUD INT/LAW NUC/PWR

S63
NEIDLE A.F.,"PEACE KEEPING AND DISARMAMENT." COM USA+45 USSR WOR+45 INT/ORG NAT/G BAL/PWR EDU/PROP LEGIT ATTIT PWR 20. PAGE 108 A2214 DELIB/GP ACT/RES ARMS/CONT PEACE

S63
SHWADRAN B.,"MIDDLE EAST OIL, 1962." ISLAM USSR ECO/DEV DIST/IND INDUS PLAN BAL/PWR DISPL DRIVE ...POLICY STAT TREND GEN/LAWS EEC OEEC 20 OIL. PAGE 132 A2712 MARKET ECO/TAC INT/TRADE

S63
SONNENFELDT H.,"FOREIGN POLICY FROM MALENKOV TO KHRUSHCHEV." WOR+45 NAT/G FORCES BAL/PWR DIPLOM ECO/TAC COERCE ATTIT PWR...CONCPT HIST/WRIT COLD/WAR 20. PAGE 135 A2768 COM DOMIN FOR/AID USSR

S63
VINER J.,"REPORT OF THE CLAY COMMITTEE ON FOREIGN AID: A SYMPOSIUM." USA+45 WOR+45 NAT/G CONSULT PLAN BAL/PWR ATTIT WEALTH...MGT CONCPT TOT/POP 20. PAGE 159 A3240 ACT/RES ECO/TAC FOR/AID

S63
WOLF C.,"SOME ASPECTS OF THE 'VALUE' OF LESS-DEVELOPED COUNTRIES TO THE UNITED STATES." ASIA CHINA/COM COM USA+45 USSR ECO/UNDEV BAL/PWR ECO/TAC FOR/AID DOMIN EDU/PROP ATTIT PWR...POLICY METH/CNCPT CONT/OBS TREND CHARTS 20. PAGE 166 A3379 CONCPT GEN/LAWS DIPLOM

S63
WRIGHT Q.,"DECLINE OF CLASSIC DIPLOMACY." CHRIST-17C EUR+WWI MOD/EUR WOR+45 WOR-45 INT/ORG NAT/G DELIB/GP BAL/PWR ATTIT PWR...HIST/WRIT LEAGUE/NAT. PAGE 168 A3418 TEC/DEV CONCPT DIPLOM

C63
CHARLETON W.G.,"THE REVOLUTION IN AMERICAN FOREIGN POLICY." COM PROB/SOLV FOR/AID DOMIN COLONIAL NEUTRAL DETER WAR ISOLAT NAT/LISM...BIBLIOG 19/20 UN COLD/WAR NATO. PAGE 26 A0523 DIPLOM INT/ORG BAL/PWR

N63
PATEL H.M.,THE DEFENCE OF INDIA (PAMPHLET). CHINA/COM INDIA PAKISTAN WOR+45 TEC/DEV BAL/PWR DIPLOM CONTROL WAR. PAGE 114 A2340 FORCES POLICY SOVEREIGN DETER

N63
US COMM STRENG SEC FREE WORLD,THE SCOPE AND DISTRIBUTION OF UNITED STATES MILITARY AND ECONOMIC ASSISTANCE PROGRAMS (PAMPHLET). USA+45 PLAN BAL/PWR BUDGET DIPLOM CONTROL CIVMIL/REL ATTIT. PAGE 150 A3059 DELIB/GP POLICY FOR/AID ORD/FREE

B64
ALVIM J.C.,A REVOLUCAO SEM RUMO. BRAZIL NAT/G BAL/PWR DIPLOM INT/TRADE PARTIC WEALTH...POLICY SOC SOC/INTEG 20. PAGE 6 A0132 REV CIVMIL/REL ECO/UNDEV ORD/FREE

B64
ARNOLD G.,TOWARDS PEACE AND A MULTIRACIAL COMMONWEALTH. UK TEC/DEV BAL/PWR COLONIAL GP/REL NAT/LISM PEACE SOVEREIGN...POLICY SOC/INTEG 20 CMN/WLTH. PAGE 9 A0175 DIPLOM INT/TRADE FOR/AID ORD/FREE

B64
BELL C.,THE DEBATABLE ALLIANCE. COM UK USA+45 NAT/G FORCES PLAN BAL/PWR NUC/PWR WAR ATTIT...GOV/COMP 20. PAGE 13 A0256 DIPLOM PWR PEACE POLICY

B64
BLANCHARD C.H.,KOREAN WAR BIBLIOGRAPHY. KOREA FAM BAL/PWR RATION MURDER WEAPON MARXISM...CHARTS 20. PAGE 15 A0306 BIBLIOG/A WAR DIPLOM FORCES

B64
CALVO SERER R.,LAS NUEVAS DEMOCRACIAS. AFR ASIA ISLAM USA+45 WOR+45 BAL/PWR DOMIN PARTIC INGP/REL AUTHORIT POPULISM...CONCPT 20 COM/PARTY. PAGE 23 A0469 ORD/FREE MARXISM DIPLOM POLICY

B64
COTTRELL A.J.,THE POLITICS OF THE ATLANTIC ALLIANCE. EUR+WWI USA+45 INT/ORG NAT/G DELIB/GP EX/STRUC BAL/PWR DIPLOM REGION DETER ATTIT ORD/FREE ...CONCPT RECORD GEN/LAWS GEN/METH NATO 20. PAGE 31 A0632 VOL/ASSN FORCES

B64
CZERNIN F.,VERSAILLES - 1919. EUR+WWI USA-45 FACE/GP POL/PAR VOL/ASSN DELIB/GP TOP/EX CREATE BAL/PWR DIPLOM LEGIT NAT/LISM PEACE ATTIT RIGID/FLEX ORD/FREE PWR...CON/ANAL LEAGUE/NAT 20 VERSAILLES. PAGE 33 A0671 INT/ORG STRUCT

B64
HEKHUIS D.J.,INTERNATIONAL STABILITY: MILITARY, ECONOMIC AND POLITICAL DIMENSIONS. FUT WOR+45 LAW ECO/UNDEV INT/ORG NAT/G VOL/ASSN FORCES ACT/RES TEC/DEV DETER REGION

BAL/PWR PWR WEALTH...STAT UN 20. PAGE 64 A1310

B64
HOROWITZ I.L.,REVOLUTION IN BRAZIL. BRAZIL L/A+17C ELITES STRATA NAT/G BAL/PWR PARTIC ATTIT 20. PAGE 68 A1388
ECO/UNDEV DIPLOM POLICY ORD/FREE

B64
KAUFMANN W.W.,THE MC NAMARA STRATEGY. TOP/EX INSPECT BAL/PWR DIPLOM CONTROL DETER GUERRILLA NUC/PWR WEAPON COST PWR...METH/COMP 20 MCNAMARA/R KENNEDY/JF JOHNSON/LB NATO DEPT/DEFEN. PAGE 77 A1572
FORCES WAR PLAN PROB/SOLV

B64
LENS S.,THE FUTILE CRUSADE. ASIA CHINA/COM L/A+17C USA+45 USSR WOR+45 ECO/DEV BAL/PWR DIPLOM NUC/PWR WAR NAT/LISM PEACE 20 COLD/WAR PRESIDENT CIA. PAGE 87 A1774
ORD/FREE ANOMIE COM MARXISM

B64
LISKA G.,EUROPE ASCENDANT. EUR+WWI ECO/DEV FORCES INT/TRADE MARXISM 20 EEC. PAGE 90 A1838
DIPLOM BAL/PWR TARIFFS CENTRAL

B64
NOVE A.,COMMUNISM AT THE CROSSROADS. USSR INT/ORG POL/PAR TOTALISM...POLICY CONCPT 20. PAGE 110 A2259
DIPLOM BAL/PWR MARXISM ORD/FREE

B64
REMAK J.,THE GENTLE CRITIC: THEODOR FONTANE AND GERMAN POLITICS, 1848-1898. GERMANY PRUSSIA CULTURE ELITES BAL/PWR DIPLOM WRITING GOV/REL...HUM BIOG 19 BISMARCK/O JUNKER FONTANE/T. PAGE 120 A2465
PERSON SOCIETY WORKER CHIEF

B64
ROSECRANCE R.N.,THE DISPERSION OF NUCLEAR WEAPONS: STRATEGY AND POLITICS. ASIA COM FUT S/ASIA USA+45 INT/ORG NAT/G DELIB/GP FORCES ACT/RES TEC/DEV BAL/PWR COERCE DETER ATTIT RIGID/FLEX ORD/FREE ...POLICY CHARTS VAL/FREE. PAGE 123 A2530
EUR+WWI PWR PEACE

B64
ROSENAU J.N.,INTERNATIONAL ASPECTS OF CIVIL STRIFE. CHINA/COM CUBA EUR+WWI USA+45 USSR BAL/PWR EDU/PROP NEUTRAL COERCE MORAL...NAT/COMP 20 COLD/WAR UN. PAGE 124 A2533
POLICY DIPLOM REV WAR

B64
STANGER R.J.,ESSAYS ON INTERVENTION. PLAN PROB/SOLV BAL/PWR ADJUD COERCE WAR ROLE PWR...INT/LAW CONCPT 20 UN INTERVENT. PAGE 137 A2803
SOVEREIGN DIPLOM POLICY LEGIT

B64
TREADGOLD D.W.,THE DEVELOPMENT OF THE USSR. COM USSR ECO/DEV CREATE BAL/PWR DEBATE COLONIAL TOTALISM...HUM ANTHOL BIBLIOG 19/20. PAGE 145 A2960
MARXISM CONSERVE DIPLOM DOMIN

B64
VOELKMANN K.,HERRSCHER VON MORGEN? BAL/PWR COLONIAL NEUTRAL REGION RACE/REL ALL/VALS SOVEREIGN...RECORD 20 COLD/WAR THIRD/WRLD. PAGE 159 A3246
DIPLOM ECO/UNDEV CONTROL NAT/COMP

B64
WOODHOUSE C.M.,THE NEW CONCERT OF NATIONS. WOR+45 ECO/DEV ECO/UNDEV NAT/G BAL/PWR ECO/TAC NAT/LISM PWR SOVEREIGN ALL/IDEOS 20 UN COLD/WAR. PAGE 166 A3391
DIPLOM MORAL FOR/AID COLONIAL

B64
WRIGHT Q.,A STUDY OF WAR. LAW NAT/G PROB/SOLV BAL/PWR NAT/LISM PEACE ATTIT SOVEREIGN...CENSUS SOC/INTEG. PAGE 168 A3419
WAR CONCPT DIPLOM CONTROL

L64
CURTIS G.L.,"THE UNITED NATIONS OBSERVER GROUP IN LEBANON." ISLAM USA+45 NAT/G CONSULT ACT/RES PLAN BAL/PWR LEGIT ATTIT KNOWL...HIST/WRIT UN 20 UN. PAGE 33 A0669
INT/ORG FORCES DIPLOM LEBANON

L64
MILLIS W.,"THE DEMILITARIZED WORLD." COM USA+45 USSR WOR+45 CONSTN NAT/G EX/STRUC PLAN LEGIT ATTIT DRIVE...CONCPT TIME/SEQ STERTYP TOT/POP COLD/WAR 20. PAGE 102 A2085
FUT INT/ORG BAL/PWR PEACE

S64
COHEN M.,"BASIC PRINCIPLES OF INTERNATIONAL LAW." UNIV WOR+45 WOR-45 BAL/PWR LEGIT ADJUD WAR ATTIT MORAL ORD/FREE PWR...JURID CONCPT MYTH TOT/POP 20. PAGE 27 A0560
INT/ORG INT/LAW

S64
GROSSER A.,"Y A-T-IL UN CONFLIT FRANCO-AMERICAIN." EUR+WWI USA+45 INT/ORG NAT/G PLAN BAL/PWR DIPLOM EDU/PROP NUC/PWR ATTIT DRIVE ORD/FREE PWR...CONCPT OBS TIME/SEQ TREND STERTYP VAL/FREE COLD/WAR. PAGE 57 A1179
VOL/ASSN NAT/LISM FRANCE

S64
HOFFMANN S.,"CE QU'EN PENSENT LES AMERICAINS." EUR+WWI INT/ORG VOL/ASSN PLAN BAL/PWR DIPLOM DOMIN EDU/PROP REGION ARMS/CONT DRIVE ORD/FREE PWR ...POLICY CONCPT OBS TREND STERTYP COLD/WAR VAL/FREE 20. PAGE 66 A1357
USA+45 ATTIT FRANCE

S64
HOSKYNS C.,"THE AFRICAN STATES AND THE UNITED NATIONS: 1958-1964." SOUTH/AFR NAT/G VOL/ASSN CONSULT BAL/PWR EDU/PROP MORAL ORD/FREE PWR ...CONCPT TREND UN 20. PAGE 68 A1393
AFR INT/ORG DIPLOM

S64
HOWARD M.,"MILITARY POWER AND INTERNATIONAL ORDER." WOR+45 SOCIETY INT/ORG NAT/G BAL/PWR DOMIN COERCE NUC/PWR WEAPON PWR...NEW/IDEA 20. PAGE 68 A1400
FORCES ATTIT WAR

S64
MCGHEE G.C.,"EAST-WEST RELATIONS TODAY." WOR+45 PROB/SOLV BAL/PWR PEACE 20 COLD/WAR. PAGE 98 A2011
IDEA/COMP DIPLOM ADJUD

S64
PADELFORD N.J.,"THE ORGANIZATION OF AFRICAN UNITY." ECO/UNDEV INT/ORG PLAN BAL/PWR DIPLOM ECO/TAC NAT/LISM ORD/FREE PWR WEALTH...CONCPT TREND STERTYP VAL/FREE COLD/WAR 20. PAGE 113 A2313
AFR VOL/ASSN REGION

S64
RUBINSTEIN A.Z.,"THE SOVIET IMAGE OF WESTERN EUROPE." COM EUR+WWI FRANCE GERMANY GERMANY/W USA+45 USSR INT/ORG NAT/G VOL/ASSN FORCES TOP/EX BAL/PWR EDU/PROP ORD/FREE PWR...MYTH RECORD NATO EEC 20. PAGE 125 A2564
RIGID/FLEX ATTIT

B65
PEACE RESEARCH ABSTRACTS. FUT WOR+45 R+D INT/ORG NAT/G PLAN TEC/DEV BAL/PWR DIPLOM FOR/AID NUC/PWR HEALTH. PAGE 4 A0072
BIBLIOG/A PEACE ARMS/CONT WAR

B65
ALBRECHT-CARRIE R.,THE MEANING OF THE FIRST WORLD WAR. MOD/EUR USA-45 INT/ORG BAL/PWR PEACE ATTIT LAISSEZ MARXISM...CONCPT BIBLIOG 19/20 LEAGUE/NAT WWI. PAGE 5 A0110
DIPLOM WAR

B65
CORDIER A.W.,THE QUEST FOR PEACE. WOR+45 NAT/G PLAN BAL/PWR ECO/TAC ARMS/CONT NUC/PWR PWR...ANTHOL UN COLD/WAR. PAGE 30 A0617
PEACE DIPLOM POLICY INT/ORG

B65
FLYNN A.H.,WORLD UNDERSTANDING: A SELECTED BIBLIOGRAPHY. WOR+45 PROB/SOLV BAL/PWR DIPLOM EFFICIENCY PEACE UN. PAGE 47 A0956
BIBLIOG/A INT/ORG EDU/PROP ROUTINE

B65
FRIEDMANN W.,AN INTRODUCTION TO WORLD POLITICS (5TH ED.). WOR+45 ECO/UNDEV BAL/PWR FOR/AID INT/TRADE PEACE...STAT CENSUS CHARTS BIBLIOG T 20 COLD/WAR UN THIRD/WRLD. PAGE 49 A1003
DIPLOM INT/ORG PROB/SOLV

B65
GILBERT M.,THE EUROPEAN POWERS 1900-45. EUR+WWI ITALY MOD/EUR USSR REV WAR PWR ALL/IDEOS FASCISM ...AUD/VIS CHARTS BIBLIOG 20. PAGE 52 A1069
DIPLOM NAT/G POLICY BAL/PWR

B65
GRAHAM G.S.,THE POLITICS OF NAVAL SUPREMACY; STUDIES IN BRITISH MARITIME ASCENDANCY. UK SEA NAT/G BAL/PWR LEAD WAR WEAPON PEACE...POLICY 18/19 COMMONWLTH. PAGE 55 A1126
FORCES PWR COLONIAL DIPLOM

B65
HUSS P.J.,RED SPIES IN THE UN. CZECHOSLVK USA+45 USSR COM/IND FORCES EDU/PROP NUC/PWR MARXISM 20 UN COLD/WAR. PAGE 69 A1421
PEACE INT/ORG BAL/PWR DIPLOM

B65
LARUS J.,COMPARATIVE WORLD POLITICS. ASIA INDIA WOR+45 WOR-45 BAL/PWR WAR PEACE RATIONAL MORAL PWR ...REALPOL INT/LAW MUSLIM. PAGE 85 A1735
GOV/COMP IDEA/COMP DIPLOM NAT/COMP

B65
LERCHE C.O.,THE COLD WAR AND AFTER. AFR COM S/ASIA USA+45 USSR NUC/PWR SOVEREIGN MARXISM...TIME/SEQ TREND BIBLIOG 20 COLD/WAR. PAGE 87 A1784
DIPLOM BAL/PWR IDEA/COMP

B65
LEWIS W.A.,POLITICS IN WEST AFRICA. AFR BAL/PWR DIPLOM REPRESENT...POLICY 20. PAGE 88 A1804
POL/PAR ELITES NAT/G ECO/UNDEV

B65
MENON K.P.S.,MANY WORLDS. INDIA BAL/PWR CAP/ISM COLONIAL REV ORD/FREE PWR MARXISM...POLICY 20 COLD/WAR. PAGE 100 A2042
BIOG DIPLOM NAT/G

B65
MORRIS R.B.,THE PEACEMAKERS; THE GREAT POWERS AND AMERICAN INDEPENDENCE. BAL/PWR CONFER COLONIAL NEUTRAL PEACE ORD/FREE TREATY 18 PRE/US/AM. PAGE 105 A2149
SOVEREIGN REV DIPLOM

B65
RUBINSTEIN A.,THE CHALLENGE OF POLITICS: IDEAS AND ISSUES. BAL/PWR COLONIAL WAR TOTALISM ORD/FREE PWR MARXISM SOCISM...INT/LAW 20. PAGE 125 A2561
NAT/G SOVEREIGN DIPLOM NAT/LISM

B65
RUBINSTEIN A.Z.,THE CHALLENGE OF POLITICS: IDEAS AND ISSUES (2ND ED.). UNIV ELITES SOCIETY EX/STRUC BAL/PWR PARL/PROC AUTHORIT...DECISION ANTHOL 20.
NAT/G DIPLOM GP/REL

PAGE 125 A2565 ORD/FREE

B65
SEABURY P.,BALANCE OF POWER. INT/ORG DETER PEACE ATTIT...INT/LAW. PAGE 131 A2677 BAL/PWR DIPLOM WAR

B65
STOETZER O.C.,THE ORGANIZATION OF AMERICAN STATES. L/A+17C EX/STRUC FOR/AID CONFER PARL/PROC ORD/FREE SOVEREIGN...POLICY INT/LAW 20 OAS. PAGE 138 A2831 INT/ORG REGION DIPLOM BAL/PWR

B65
SULZBERGER C.L.,UNFINISHED REVOLUTION. USA+45 WOR+45 INT/ORG TEC/DEV BAL/PWR FOR/AID COLONIAL NEUTRAL PWR SOVEREIGN MARXISM 20. PAGE 140 A2863 DIPLOM ECO/UNDEV POLICY NAT/G

B65
TREFOUSSE H.L.,THE COLD WAR: A BOOK OF DOCUMENTS. ASIA L/A+17C USSR WOR+45 WOR-45 ECO/TAC FOR/AID ARMS/CONT NUC/PWR PEACE ORD/FREE...ANTHOL 20 COLD/WAR KENNEDY/JF EISNHWR/DD. PAGE 145 A2961 BAL/PWR DIPLOM MARXISM

B65
US DEPARTMENT OF THE ARMY,NUCLEAR WEAPONS AND THE ATLANTIC ALLIANCE: A BIBLIOGRAPHIC SURVEY. ASIA COM EUR+WWI USA+45 FORCES DIPLOM WEAPON...STAT 20 NATO. PAGE 152 A3108 BIBLIOG/A ARMS/CONT NUC/PWR BAL/PWR

L65
KAPLAN M.A.,"OLD REALITIES AND NEW MYTHS." USA+45 WOR+45 INT/ORG NAT/G TOP/EX ACT/RES BAL/PWR ECO/TAC EDU/PROP LEGIT RIGID/FLEX ALL/VALS...RECORD COLD/WAR 20. PAGE 76 A1564 ATTIT MYTH DIPLOM

S65
BROWN S.,"AN ALTERNATIVE TO THE GRAND DESIGN." EUR+WWI FUT USA+45 INT/ORG NAT/G EX/STRUC FORCES CREATE BAL/PWR DOMIN RIGID/FLEX ORD/FREE PWR ...NEW/IDEA RECORD EEC NATO 20. PAGE 20 A0407 VOL/ASSN CONCPT DIPLOM

S65
FLEMING D.F.,"CAN PAX AMERICANA SUCCEED?" ASIA CHINA/COM EUR+WWI USSR VIETNAM BAL/PWR DIPLOM DOMIN COERCE GOV/REL 20. PAGE 46 A0948 DECISION ATTIT ECO/TAC

S65
MAC CHESNEY B.,"SOME COMMENTS ON THE 'QUARANTINE' OF CUBA." USA+45 WOR+45 NAT/G BAL/PWR DIPLOM LEGIT ROUTINE ATTIT ORD/FREE...JURID METH/CNCPT 20. PAGE 92 A1883 INT/ORG LAW CUBA USSR

S65
PRABHAKAR P.,"SURVEY OF RESEARCH AND SOURCE MATERIALS; THE SINO-INDIAN BORDER DISPUTE." CHINA/COM INDIA LAW NAT/G PLAN BAL/PWR WAR...POLICY 20 COLD/WAR. PAGE 117 A2404 BIBLIOG ASIA S/ASIA DIPLOM

C65
BURTON J.W.,"INTERNATIONAL RELATIONS: A GENERAL THEORY." WOR+45 NAT/G CREATE BAL/PWR NEUTRAL COERCE DETER ADJUST...TREND IDEA/COMP GEN/METH BIBLIOG. PAGE 22 A0447 DIPLOM GEN/LAWS ACT/RES ORD/FREE

C65
MARK M.,"BEYOND SOVEREIGNTY." WOR+45 WOR-45 ECO/UNDEV BAL/PWR INT/TRADE NUC/PWR REV WAR MARXISM NEW/LIB BIBLIOG. PAGE 95 A1942 NAT/LISM NAT/G DIPLOM INTELL

B66
AMERICAN ASSEMBLY COLUMBIA U,A WORLD OF NUCLEAR POWERS? FUT WOR+45 ECO/DEV BAL/PWR ECO/TAC CONTROL RISK EFFICIENCY ATTIT PWR...METH/COMP ANTHOL 20. PAGE 7 A0137 NUC/PWR DIPLOM TEC/DEV ARMS/CONT

B66
BLOOMFIELD L.P.,KHRUSHCHEV AND THE ARMS RACE. USA+45 USSR ECO/DEV BAL/PWR EDU/PROP CONFER NUC/PWR ATTIT...CHARTS 20 KHRUSH/N. PAGE 16 A0321 ARMS/CONT COM POLICY DIPLOM

B66
BUCHAN A.,A WORLD OF NUCLEAR POWERS? PEACE...ANTHOL 20. PAGE 21 A0423 NUC/PWR BAL/PWR PROB/SOLV DIPLOM

B66
COYLE D.C.,THE UNITED NATIONS AND HOW IT WORKS. ECO/UNDEV DELIB/GP BAL/PWR EDU/PROP ARMS/CONT NUC/PWR WAR 20 UN. PAGE 32 A0648 INT/ORG PEACE DIPLOM INT/TRADE

B66
CRAIG G.A.,WAR, POLITICS, AND DIPLOMACY. PRUSSIA CONSTN FORCES CIVMIL/REL TOTALISM PWR 19/20 BISMARCK/O DULLES/JF NAPOLEON/B. PAGE 32 A0654 WAR DIPLOM BAL/PWR

B66
CROWLEY D.W.,THE BACKGROUND TO CURRENT AFFAIRS. UK WOR+45 INT/ORG BAL/PWR NUC/PWR ATTIT ROLE 20 COLD/WAR. PAGE 33 A0665 DIPLOM PWR POLICY

B66
EUBANK K.,THE SUMMIT CONFERENCES. EUR+WWI USA+45 USA-45 MUNIC BAL/PWR WAR PEACE PWR...POLICY AUD/VIS 20 GENEVA/CON TEHERAN YALTA POTSDAM. PAGE 43 A0872 CONFER NAT/G CHIEF DIPLOM

B66
FEHRENBACH T.R.,THIS KIND OF PEACE. WOR+45 LEAD PARTIC WAR EFFICIENCY ATTIT UN. PAGE 44 A0906 PEACE DIPLOM INT/ORG

BAL/PWR

B66
FITZGERALD C.P.,THE BIRTH OF COMMUNIST CHINA (2ND ED.). ASIA CHINA/COM STRUCT BAL/PWR DIPLOM ECO/TAC INT/TRADE WEALTH 20. PAGE 46 A0942 REV MARXISM ECO/UNDEV

B66
GILBERT M.,THE ROOTS OF APPEASEMENT. EUR+WWI GERMANY UK MUNIC BAL/PWR FASCISM...NEW/IDEA 20. PAGE 52 A1070 DIPLOM REPAR PROB/SOLV POLICY

B66
HORELICK A.L.,STRATEGIC POWER AND SOVIET FOREIGN POLICY. CUBA USSR FORCES PLAN CIVMIL/REL...POLICY DECISION 20 COLD/WAR. PAGE 67 A1383 DIPLOM BAL/PWR DETER NUC/PWR

B66
KIM Y.K.,PATTERNS OF COMPETITIVE COEXISTENCE: USA VS. USSR. USA+45 USSR ECO/DEV ECO/UNDEV INT/ORG FOR/AID INT/TRADE ARMS/CONT...BIBLIOG 20 COLD/WAR. PAGE 79 A1618 DIPLOM PEACE BAL/PWR DETER

B66
KUENNE R.E.,THE POLARIS MISSILE STRIKE* A GENERAL ECONOMIC SYSTEMS ANALYSIS. USA+45 USSR NAT/G BAL/PWR ARMS/CONT WAR...MATH PROBABIL COMPUT/IR CHARTS HYPO/EXP SIMUL. PAGE 82 A1689 NUC/PWR FORCES DETER DIPLOM

B66
MC LELLAN D.S.,THE COLD WAR IN TRANSITION. USSR WOR+45 CONTROL LEAD NUC/PWR NAT/LISM SOVEREIGN 20 COLD/WAR THIRD/WRLD. PAGE 97 A1994 BAL/PWR DETER DIPLOM POLICY

B66
SCHWARZ U.,AMERICAN STRATEGY: A NEW PERSPECTIVE. USA+45 USA-45 INT/ORG TEC/DEV BAL/PWR DIPLOM LEAD ARMS/CONT DETER NUC/PWR WAR 20 NATO. PAGE 130 A2659 NAT/G POLICY FORCES PWR

B66
SINGER L.,ALLE LITTEN AN GROSSENWAHN: VON WOODROW WILSON BIS MAO TSE-TUNG. ASIA UK USSR INT/ORG DELIB/GP BAL/PWR DOMIN ATTIT PERSON 20 WILSON/W ROOSEVLT/F. PAGE 133 A2731 DIPLOM TOTALISM WAR CHIEF

B66
VAN DYKE V.,INTERNATIONAL POLITICS. WOR+45 ECO/DEV ECO/UNDEV INT/ORG BAL/PWR AGREE ARMS/CONT NAT/LISM PEACE PWR...INT/LAW 20 TREATY UN. PAGE 158 A3212 DIPLOM NAT/G WAR SOVEREIGN

B66
WAINHOUSE D.W.,INTERNATIONAL PEACE OBSERVATION: A HISTORY AND FORECAST. INT/ORG PROB/SOLV BAL/PWR AGREE ARMS/CONT COERCE NUC/PWR...PREDICT METH/COMP 20 UN LEAGUE/NAT OAS TREATY. PAGE 160 A3261 PEACE DIPLOM

C66
KULSKI W.W.,"DEGAULLE AND THE WORLD: THE FOREIGN POLICY OF THE FIFTH FRENCH REPUBLIC." FRANCE ECO/UNDEV POL/PAR BAL/PWR DETER NUC/PWR ATTIT PWR ...RECORD BIBLIOG DEGAULLE NATO EEC. PAGE 83 A1694 POLICY SOVEREIGN PERSON DIPLOM

B67
BURNS E.L.M.,MEGAMURDER. WOR+45 LAW INT/ORG NAT/G BAL/PWR DIPLOM DETER MURDER WEAPON CIVMIL/REL PEACE ...INT/LAW TREND 20. PAGE 22 A0444 FORCES PLAN WAR NUC/PWR

B67
EUROPA-ARCHIV,DEUTSCHES AND AUSLANDISCHES SCHRIFTTUM ZU DEN REGIONALEN SICHERHEITSVEREINBARUNGEN 1945-1956. WOR+45 FORCES BAL/PWR REGION. PAGE 43 A0875 BIBLIOG INT/ORG PEACE DETER

B67
HALPERIN M.H.,CONTEMPORARY MILITARY STRATEGY. ASIA CHINA/COM USA+45 USSR INT/ORG FORCES ACT/RES PLAN TEC/DEV BAL/PWR COERCE WAR...METH/COMP BIBLIOG 20 NATO. PAGE 60 A1240 DIPLOM NUC/PWR DETER ARMS/CONT

B67
MACRIDIS R.C.,FOREIGN POLICY IN WORLD POLITICS (3RD ED.). EX/STRUC BAL/PWR COLONIAL NAT/LISM SKILL SOVEREIGN WEALTH...CONCPT TIME/SEQ ANTHOL 20 COLD/WAR. PAGE 93 A1902 DIPLOM POLICY NAT/G IDEA/COMP

B67
MCBRIDE J.H.,THE TEST BAN TREATY: MILITARY, TECHNOLOGICAL, AND POLITICAL IMPLICATIONS. USA+45 USSR DELIB/GP FORCES LEGIS TEC/DEV BAL/PWR TREATY. PAGE 97 A1995 ARMS/CONT DIPLOM NUC/PWR

B67
MCCLINTOCK R.,THE MEANING OF LIMITED WAR. FUT WOR+45 NAT/G FORCES GUERRILLA REV...POLICY SAMP/SIZ TREND NAT/COMP 45 COLD/WAR. PAGE 97 A1999 WAR NUC/PWR BAL/PWR DIPLOM

B67
POGANY A.H.,POLITICAL SCIENCE AND INTERNATIONAL RELATIONS, BOOKS RECOMMENDED FOR AMERICAN CATHOLIC COLLEGE LIBRARIES. INT/ORG LOC/G NAT/G FORCES BAL/PWR ECO/TAC NUC/PWR...CATH INT/LAW TREATY 20. PAGE 117 A2393 BIBLIOG DIPLOM

B67
ROYAL INSTITUTE INTL AFFAIRS,SURVEY OF INTERNATIONAL AFFAIRS. WOR+45 WOR-45 FINAN INT/TRADE PWR...CHARTS 20. PAGE 125 A2557 DIPLOM BAL/PWR INT/ORG

B67
SACHS M.Y.,THE WORLDMARK ENCYCLOPEDIA OF THE NATIONS (5 VOLS.). ELITES SOCIETY STRATA ECO/DEV ECO/UNDEV AGRI EXTR/IND FINAN LABOR LOC/G NAT/G POL/PAR SECT INT/TRADE SOVEREIGN...SOC 20. PAGE 126 A2585 WOR+45 INT/ORG BAL/PWR

B67
SCOTT A.M.,THE FUNCTIONING OF THE INTERNATIONAL POLITICAL SYSTEM. INT/ORG OP/RES PROB/SOLV COERCE WAR EQUILIB...METH/CNCPT BIBLIOG. PAGE 130 A2671 DIPLOM DECISION BAL/PWR

B67
US SENATE COMM ON FOREIGN REL,UNITED STATES ARMAMENT AND DISARMAMENT PROBLEMS. USA+45 AIR BAL/PWR DIPLOM FOR/AID NUC/PWR ORD/FREE SENATE TREATY. PAGE 156 A3190 ARMS/CONT WEAPON FORCES PROB/SOLV

B67
WAELDER R.,PROGRESS AND REVOLUTION* A STUDY OF THE ISSUES OF OUR AGE. WOR+45 WOR-45 BAL/PWR DIPLOM COERCE ROLE MORAL ALL/IDEOS...IDEA/COMP NAT/COMP 19/20. PAGE 160 A3259 PWR NAT/G REV TEC/DEV

L67
LANDIS E.S.,"THE SOUTH WEST AFRICA CASES* REMAND TO THE UNITED NATIONS." ETHIOPIA LIBERIA SOUTH/AFR BAL/PWR 20 UN. PAGE 84 A1719 INT/LAW INT/ORG DIPLOM ADJUD

S67
"CHINESE STATEMENT ON NUCLEAR PROLIFERATION." CHINA/COM USA+45 USSR DOMIN COLONIAL PWR. PAGE 4 A0078 NUC/PWR BAL/PWR ARMS/CONT DIPLOM

S67
APEL H.,"LES NOUVEAUX ASPECTS DE LA POLITIQUE ETRANGERE ALLEMANDE." EUR+WWI GERMANY POL/PAR BAL/PWR ECO/TAC INT/TRADE NUC/PWR NAT/LISM PEACE ...POLICY 20 EEC COLD/WAR. PAGE 8 A0168 DIPLOM INT/ORG FEDERAL

S67
BATOR V.,"ONE WAR* TWO VIETNAMS." S/ASIA VIETNAM DIPLOM SUFF ATTIT ORD/FREE 20. PAGE 12 A0234 WAR BAL/PWR NAT/G STRUCT

S67
COSGROVE C.A.,"AGRICULTURE, FINANCE AND POLITICS IN THE EUROPEAN COMMUNITY." EUR+WWI DIST/IND MARKET INT/ORG VOL/ASSN DELIB/GP TEC/DEV BAL/PWR BARGAIN ECO/TAC RATION CONFER 20 EEC. PAGE 31 A0630 ECO/DEV DIPLOM AGRI INT/TRADE

S67
DEUTSCH K.W.,"ARMS CONTROL AND EUROPEAN UNITY* THE NEXT TEN YEARS." USA+45 ELITES NAT/G BAL/PWR DIPLOM NUC/PWR...INT KNO/TEST NATO EEC. PAGE 36 A0742 ARMS/CONT PEACE REGION PLAN

S67
FAWCETT J.E.S.,"GIBRALTAR* THE LEGAL ISSUES." SPAIN UK INT/ORG BAL/PWR LICENSE CONFER SANCTION PRIVIL ...JURID CHARTS 20. PAGE 44 A0905 INT/LAW DIPLOM COLONIAL ADJUD

S67
FELD B.T.,"A PLEDGE* NO FIRST USE." DELIB/GP BAL/PWR DOMIN DETER. PAGE 45 A0913 ARMS/CONT NUC/PWR DIPLOM PEACE

S67
FELDMAN H.,"AID AS IMPERIALISM?" INDIA PAKISTAN UK USA+45 BAL/PWR CAP/ISM DIPLOM ECO/TAC DOMIN BAL/PAY WEALTH...POLICY 20. PAGE 45 A0914 COLONIAL FOR/AID S/ASIA ECO/UNDEV

S67
FOREIGN POLICY ASSOCIATION,"US CONCERN FOR WORLD LAW." USA+45 WOR+45 DELIB/GP JUDGE BAL/PWR CONFER PEACE ORD/FREE 20 UN. PAGE 47 A0962 INT/LAW INT/ORG DIPLOM ARMS/CONT

S67
GODUNSKY Y.,"'APOSTLES OF PEACE' IN LATIN AMERICA." L/A+17C USA+45 BAL/PWR DIPLOM FOR/AID DOMIN COLONIAL CIVMIL/REL MARXIST. PAGE 53 A1086 ECO/UNDEV REV VOL/ASSN EDU/PROP

S67
GRUNDY K.W.,"AFRICA IN THE WORLD ARENA." ECO/UNDEV BAL/PWR FOR/AID NEUTRAL REV NAT/LISM GOV/COMP. PAGE 58 A1183 AFR DIPLOM INT/ORG COLONIAL

S67
HULL E.W.S.,"THE POLITICAL OCEAN." FUT UNIV WOR+45 EXTR/IND R+D VOL/ASSN PLAN BAL/PWR ECO/TAC PEACE WEALTH 20 UN. PAGE 69 A1414 DIPLOM ECO/UNDEV INT/ORG INT/LAW

S67
INGLEHART R.,"AN END TO EUROPEAN INTEGRATION." PROB/SOLV BAL/PWR NAT/LISM...PSY SOC INT CHARTS GP/COMP 20. PAGE 70 A1440 DIPLOM EUR+WWI REGION ATTIT

S67
JACKSON W.G.F.,"NUCLEAR PROLIFERATION AND THE GREAT POWERS." FUT UK WOR+45 INT/ORG DOMIN ARMS/CONT DETER ORD/FREE PACIFIST. PAGE 72 A1480 NUC/PWR ATTIT BAL/PWR NAT/LISM

S67
JOHNSON D.H.N.,"THE SOUTH-WEST AFRICA CASES." AFR ETHIOPIA LIBERIA SOUTH/AFR CONSULT JUDGE BAL/PWR 20. PAGE 74 A1521 INT/LAW DIPLOM INT/ORG ADJUD

S67
KAHN H.,"CRITERIA FOR LONG-RANGE NUCLEAR CONTROL POLICIES." WOR+45 INT/ORG TEC/DEV DOMIN DETER WAR WEAPON ISOLAT ORD/FREE POLICY. PAGE 76 A1549 NUC/PWR ARMS/CONT BAL/PWR DIPLOM

S67
KAISER R.G.,"THE TRUMAN DOCTRINE* HOW IT ALL BEGAN." COM EUR+WWI USA+45 R+D INT/ORG BAL/PWR ECO/TAC PEACE TRUMAN/DOC. PAGE 76 A1550 DIPLOM ECO/UNDEV FOR/AID

S67
KRUSCHE H.,"THE STRIVING OF THE KIESINGER-STRAUS GOVERNMENT FOR NUCLEAR WEAPONS IS A THREAT TO EUROPEAN SECURITY." EUR+WWI GERMANY BAL/PWR SANCTION WEAPON PEACE ORD/FREE...MARXIST 20 NATO COLD/WAR. PAGE 82 A1688 ARMS/CONT INT/ORG NUC/PWR DIPLOM

S67
MONTALVA E.F.,"THE ALLIANCE THAT LOST ITS WAY." L/A+17C USA+45 R+D BAL/PWR INT/TRADE RECEIVE REV PEACE...POLICY 20. PAGE 103 A2111 ECO/UNDEV DIPLOM FOR/AID INT/ORG

S67
NIEBUHR R.,"THE SOCIAL MYTHS IN THE COLD WAR." USA+45 USSR VIETNAM PROB/SOLV BAL/PWR ARMS/CONT NAT/LISM PWR ALL/IDEOS CONCPT. PAGE 109 A2238 MYTH DIPLOM GOV/COMP

S67
ODA S.,"THE NORMALIZATION OF RELATIONS BETWEEN JAPAN AND THE REPUBLIC OF KOREA." NAT/G BAL/PWR REPAR INT/LAW. PAGE 111 A2276 DIPLOM LEGIS DECISION

S67
PAUKER G.J.,"TOWARD A NEW ORDER IN INDONESIA." COM INDONESIA S/ASIA ECO/UNDEV POL/PAR EX/STRUC TOP/EX BAL/PWR ECO/TAC FOR/AID DOMIN NAT/LISM AUTHORIT ORD/FREE PWR 20. PAGE 114 A2342 REV NAT/G DIPLOM CIVMIL/REL

S67
PERLO V.,"NEW DIMENSIONS IN EAST-WEST TRADE." UK USA+45 USSR WOR+45 ECO/DEV NAT/G CAP/ISM PEACE WEALTH LAISSEZ...SOCIALIST MGT 20. PAGE 115 A2364 BAL/PWR ECO/TAC INT/TRADE

S67
ROSE S.,"ASIAN NATIONALISM* THE SECOND STAGE." ASIA COM ECO/UNDEV NAT/G PROB/SOLV DIPLOM FOR/AID DOMIN NEUTRAL REGION TASK...METH/COMP 20. PAGE 123 A2528 NAT/LISM S/ASIA BAL/PWR COLONIAL

S67
SARBADHIKARI P.,"A NOTE ON THE DOMESTIC CRISIS OF NON-ALIGNMENT." ELITES INTELL ECO/UNDEV FOR/AID DOMIN. PAGE 127 A2605 NEUTRAL WEALTH TOTALISM BAL/PWR

S67
SHARP G.,"THE NEED OF A FUNCTIONAL SUBSTITUTE FOR WAR." FUT UNIV WOR+45 CULTURE SOCIETY INT/ORG CONSULT DELIB/GP ACT/RES CREATE BAL/PWR CONFER ARMS/CONT NUC/PWR 20. PAGE 132 A2696 PEACE WAR DIPLOM PROB/SOLV

S67
SHERSHNEV Y.,"THE KENNEDY ROUND* PLANS AND REALITY." EUR+WWI USA+45 INT/ORG DIPLOM TARIFFS DOMIN CONFER PWR...MARXIST PREDICT. PAGE 132 A2701 ECO/TAC ECO/DEV INT/TRADE BAL/PWR

S67
SHULMAN M.D.,"'EUROPE' VERSUS 'DETENTE'." USA+45 USSR INT/ORG CONTROL ARMS/CONT DETER 20. PAGE 132 A2711 DIPLOM BAL/PWR NUC/PWR

S67
SOMMER T.,"BONN CHANGES COURSE." GERMANY/W NAT/G POL/PAR PROB/SOLV NAT/LISM 20 NATO BERLIN/BLO. PAGE 135 A2766 DIPLOM BAL/PWR INT/ORG

S67
STEEL R.,"WHAT CAN THE UN DO?" RHODESIA ECO/UNDEV DIPLOM ECO/TAC SANCTION...INT/LAW UN. PAGE 137 A2810 INT/ORG BAL/PWR PEACE FOR/AID

S67
STEEL R.,"BEYOND THE POWER BLOCS." USA+45 USSR ECO/UNDEV NEUTRAL NUC/PWR NAT/LISM ATTIT...GEOG NATO WARSAW/P COLD/WAR. PAGE 137 A2811 DIPLOM TREND BAL/PWR PLAN

S67
ZARTMAN I.W.,"AFRICA AS A SUBORDINATE STATE SYSTEM IN INTERNATIONAL RELATIONS." LAW BAL/PWR REGION CENTRAL...GEOG 20. PAGE 169 A3447 DIPLOM INT/ORG CONSTN AFR

C67
HUDSON G.F.,"THE HARD AND BITTER PEACE; WORLD POLITICS SINCE 1945." ASIA COM S/ASIA USSR WOR+45 COLONIAL WAR...TREND BIBLIOG/A 20 COLD/WAR UN. PAGE 68 A1405 DIPLOM INT/ORG ARMS/CONT BAL/PWR

N67
US GOVERNMENT,TREATIES IN FORCE. NAT/G ECO/TAC FOR/AID INT/TRADE NUC/PWR 20. PAGE 153 A3117 DIPLOM INT/ORG BAL/PWR

BALANCE OF PAYMENTS....SEE BAL/PAY

BALANCE OF POWER....SEE BAL/PWR

BALDWIN D.A. A0210

BALDWIN/J....JAMES BALDWIN

BALFOUR A.J. A0211

BALKANS....BALKANS

B56
WOLFF R.L.,THE BALKANS IN OUR TIME. ALBANIA FUT MOD/EUR USSR YUGOSLAVIA CULTURE INT/ORG SECT DIPLOM EDU/PROP COERCE WAR ORD/FREE...CHARTS 4/20 BALKANS COMINFORM. PAGE 166 A3388
GEOG
COM

BALL M.M. A0212,A0213

BALL W.M. A0214

BALOGH T. A0215

BALTIC

B65
SCHREIBER H.,TEUTON AND SLAV - THE STRUGGLE FOR CENTRAL EUROPE (TRANS. BY J. CLEUGH). GERMANY POLAND PRUSSIA USSR SOCIETY STRUCT SECT DIPLOM BALTIC. PAGE 129 A2646
GP/REL
WAR
RACE/REL
NAT/LISM

BALTIMORE....BALTIMORE, MD.

BANDA/HK....H.K. BANDA, PRIME MINISTER OF MALAWI

BANFIELD J. A0216

BANK/ENGL....THE BANK OF ENGLAND

BANKING....SEE FINAN

BANKRUPTCY....BANKRUPTCY

BANNO M. A0885

BANTU....BANTU NATION AND CULTURE

BANTUSTANS....BANTUSTANS, REPUBLIC OF SOUTH AFRICA

BAO/DAI....BAO DAI

B66
VIEN N.C.,SEEKING THE TRUTH. FRANCE VIETNAM AGRI ADMIN WAR...BIOG 20 BAO/DAI INTERVENT. PAGE 159 A3231
NAT/G
CONSULT
CONSTN

BARALL M. A0217

BARANSON J. A0218

BARBARIAN....BARBARIAN

BARBER H.W. A0219

BARGAIN....BARGAINING; SEE ALSO ECO/TAC, MARKET, DIPLOM

B06
GRIFFIN A.P.C.,SELECT LIST OF REFERENCES ON THE BRITISH TARIFF MOVEMENT. MOD/EUR UK BAL/PWR BARGAIN ECO/TAC LAISSEZ 20. PAGE 56 A1154
BIBLIOG/A
INT/TRADE
TARIFFS
COLONIAL

B35
CONOVER H.F.,A SELECTED LIST OF REFERENCES ON THE DIPLOMATIC & TRADE RELATIONS OF THE US WITH THE USSR, 1919-1935 (PAMPHLET). USA-45 USSR DELIB/GP LEGIS OP/RES PROB/SOLV BAL/PWR BARGAIN 20. PAGE 29 A0590
BIBLIOG
DIPLOM
INT/TRADE

B40
WOLFERS A.,BRITAIN AND FRANCE BETWEEN TWO WORLD WARS. FRANCE UK INT/ORG NAT/G PLAN BARGAIN ECO/TAC AGREE ISOLAT ALL/IDEOS...DECISION GEOG 20 TREATY VERSAILLES INTERVENT. PAGE 166 A3380
DIPLOM
WAR
POLICY

B48
LOGAN R.W.,THE AFRICAN MANDATES IN WORLD POLITICS. EUR+WWI GERMANY ISLAM INT/ORG BARGAIN...POLICY INT/LAW 20. PAGE 90 A1853
WAR
COLONIAL
AFR
DIPLOM

S64
BARKUN M.,"CONFLICT RESOLUTION THROUGH IMPLICIT MEDIATION." UNIV BARGAIN CONSEN FEDERAL JURID. PAGE 11 A0222
CONSULT
CENTRAL
INT/LAW
IDEA/COMP

B66
ZISCHKA A.,WAR ES EIN WUNDER? GERMANY/W ECO/DEV FINAN LG/CO BARGAIN CAP/ISM FOR/AID RATION 20 MARSHL/PLN. PAGE 170 A3456
ECO/TAC
INT/TRADE
INDUS
WAR

B67
HOLSTI K.J.,INTERNATIONAL POLITICS* A FRAMEWORK FOR ANALYSIS. WOR+45 WOR-45 NAT/G EDU/PROP DETER WAR WEAPON PWR BIBLIOG. PAGE 67 A1372
DIPLOM
BARGAIN
POLICY
INT/LAW

B67
JOHNSON A.M.,BOSTON CAPITALISTS AND WESTERN RAILROADS: A STUDY IN THE NINETEENTH CENTURY RAILROAD INVESTMENT PROCESS. CREATE BARGAIN INT/TRADE GAMBLE KNOWL 19 BOSTON. PAGE 74 A1519
FINAN
DIST/IND
CAP/ISM
ECO/UNDEV

S67
COSGROVE C.A.,"AGRICULTURE, FINANCE AND POLITICS IN THE EUROPEAN COMMUNITY." EUR+WWI DIST/IND MARKET INT/ORG VOL/ASSN DELIB/GP TEC/DEV BAL/PWR BARGAIN ECO/TAC RATION CONFER 20 EEC. PAGE 31 A0630
ECO/DEV
DIPLOM
AGRI
INT/TRADE

S67
FRANK I.,"NEW PERSPECTIVES ON TRADE AND DEVELOPMENT." PROB/SOLV BARGAIN DIPLOM FOR/AID CONFER GP/REL WEALTH 20 UN GATT. PAGE 48 A0980
ECO/UNDEV
INT/ORG
INT/TRADE
ECO/TAC

S67
LEVI M.,"LES DIFFICULTES ECONOMIQUES DE LA GRANDE-BRETAGNE." UK INT/ORG TEC/DEV BARGAIN DIPLOM DOMIN REPRESENT DEMAND WEALTH...POLICY 20 EEC. PAGE 88 A1792
BAL/PAY
INT/TRADE
PRODUC

BARGHOORN F.C. A0220

BARKER A.J. A0221

BARKUN M. A0222

BARMAN R.K. A0223

BARNES W. A0224

BARNET R. A0225,A0226

BARNETT/R....ROSS BARNETT

BAROTSE....BAROTSE TRIBE OF RHODESIA

BARR S. A0227

BARROS J. A0228

BARROS J.F.P. A0229

BARTHELEMY G. A0230

BARTLETT C. A3307

BARTLETT R.J. A0231

BASCH A. A0232

BASHILELE....BASHILELE TRIBE

BASSET E. A1224

BASSETT R. A0233

BATAK....BATAK TRIBE, PHILIPPINES

BATISTA/J....JUAN BATISTA

BATOR V. A0234

BAULIN J. A0235

BAUMANN G. A0236

BAVARIA....BAVARIA

BAWONGO....BAWONGO TRIBE

BAYESIAN INFLUENCE....SEE SIMUL

BEAL J.R. A0237

BEALE H.K. A0238

BEALES A.C. A0239

BEARD C.A. A0240

BEARD/CA....CHARLES A. BEARD

BEARDSLEY S.W. A0241

BEATON L. A0242

BEAUFRE A. A0243

BECCARIA/C....CAESARE BONESARA BECCARIA

BECHHOEFER B.G. A0244,A0245

BECKEL G. A0246

BECKER/E....ERNEST BECKER

BEERS H.P. A0247,A0248

BEGUIN B. A0249

BEHAV/SCI....BEHAVIORAL SCIENCES

BEHAVIOR TESTS....SEE PERS/TEST

BEHAVIORSM....BEHAVIORISM

BEHRENDT R.F. A0250,A0251

BEIM D. A0252

BELGION M. A0253

BELGIUM....BELGIUM

B14
HARRIS N.D.,INTERVENTION AND COLONIZATION IN AFRICA. BELGIUM FRANCE GERMANY MOD/EUR PORTUGAL UK ECO/UNDEV BAL/PWR DOMIN CONTROL PWR...GEOG 19/20. PAGE 62 A1267 — AFR COLONIAL DIPLOM

N19
HANNA A.J.,EUROPEAN RULE IN AFRICA (PAMPHLET). BELGIUM FRANCE MOD/EUR UK WOR+45 WOR-45 ECO/UNDEV NAT/G PARTIC SOVEREIGN...NAT/COMP 19/20. PAGE 61 A1252 — DIPLOM COLONIAL AFR NAT/LISM

B27
HARRIS N.D.,EUROPE AND AFRICA. BELGIUM FRANCE GERMANY MOD/EUR PORTUGAL UK ECO/UNDEV BAL/PWR PWR ...GEOG 19/20. PAGE 62 A1268 — AFR COLONIAL DIPLOM

B32
MASTERS R.D.,INTERNATIONAL LAW IN INTERNATIONAL COURTS. BELGIUM EUR+WWI FRANCE GERMANY MOD/EUR SWITZERLND WOR-45 SOCIETY STRATA STRUCT LEGIT EXEC ALL/VALS...JURID HIST/WRIT TIME/SEQ TREND GEN/LAWS 20. PAGE 96 A1961 — INT/ORG LAW INT/LAW

B33
DAHLIN E.,FRENCH AND GERMAN PUBLIC OPINION ON DECLARED WAR AIMS 1914-1918. BELGIUM FRANCE GERMANY NAT/G POL/PAR DIPLOM COERCE REV WAR PEACE 20 WWI WILSON/W. PAGE 33 A0674 — ATTIT EDU/PROP DOMIN NAT/COMP

B47
CONOVER H.F.,NON-SELF-GOVERNING AREAS. BELGIUM FRANCE ITALY UK WOR+45 CULTURE ECO/UNDEV INT/ORG LOC/G NAT/G ECO/TAC INT/TRADE ADMIN HEALTH...SOC UN. PAGE 30 A0601 — BIBLIOG/A COLONIAL DIPLOM

B50
GATZKE H.W.,GERMANY'S DRIVE TO THE WEST. BELGIUM GERMANY MOD/EUR AGRI INDUS POL/PAR FORCES DOMIN AGREE CONTROL REGION COERCE 20 TREATY WWI. PAGE 51 A1053 — WAR POLICY NAT/G DIPLOM

B51
WABEKE B.H.,A GUIDE TO DUTCH BIBLIOGRAPHIES. BELGIUM INDONESIA NETHERLAND DIPLOM INT/TRADE WAR NAT/LISM KNOWL...ART/METH HUM JURID CON/ANAL 14/20. PAGE 160 A3257 — BIBLIOG/A NAT/G CULTURE COLONIAL

B54
COOKSON J.,BEFORE THE AFRICAN STORM. BELGIUM CENTRL/AFR FRANCE UK ECO/UNDEV POL/PAR CREATE BAL/PWR RACE/REL NAT/LISM ORD/FREE CONSERVE MARXISM SOC/INTEG 20 CONGO/LEOP. PAGE 30 A0607 — COLONIAL REV DISCRIM DIPLOM

B60
ASPREMONT-LYNDEN H.,RAPPORT SUR L'ADMINISTRATION BELGE DU RUANDA-URUNDI PENDANT L'ANNEE 1959. BELGIUM RWANDA AGRI INDUS DIPLOM ECO/TAC INT/TRADE DOMIN ADMIN RACE/REL...GEOG CENSUS 20 UN. PAGE 9 A0192 — AFR COLONIAL ECO/UNDEV INT/ORG

B62
MEADE J.E.,CASE STUDIES IN EUROPEAN ECONOMIC UNION. BELGIUM EUR+WWI LUXEMBOURG NAT/G INT/TRADE REGION ROUTINE WEALTH...METH/CNCPT STAT CHARTS ECSC TOT/POP OEEC EEC 20. PAGE 99 A2028 — INT/ORG ECO/TAC

B65
WEIL G.L.,A HANDBOOK ON THE EUROPEAN ECONOMIC COMMUNITY. BELGIUM EUR+WWI FRANCE GERMANY/W ITALY CONSTN ECO/DEV CREATE PARTIC GP/REL...DECISION MGT CHARTS 20 EEC. PAGE 162 A3299 — INT/TRADE INT/ORG TEC/DEV INT/LAW

BELIEF....SEE SECT, ATTIT

BELKNAP G. A0254

BELL C. A0255,A0256

BELL W. A0257

BELLAS/HES....NATIONAL BELLAS HESS

BELOFF M. A0258,A0259,A0260,A0261,A0262

BELSHAW C. A0263

BEMIS S.F. A0264,A0265,A0266

BEN/BELLA....AHMED BEN BELLA

BENES E. A0267

BENESE....BENES

BENGAL....BENGAL + BENGALIS

BENIN....BENIN - DISTRICT IN NIGERIA

BENNETT J.C. A0268

BENTHAM J. A0269,A0270

BENTHAM/J....JEREMY BENTHAM

B63
HINSLEY F.H.,POWER AND THE PURSUIT OF PEACE. WOR+45 WOR-45 PLAN RIGID/FLEX ALL/VALS ALL/IDEOS...POLICY DECISION INT/LAW 12/20 ROUSSEAU/J KANT/I BENTHAM/J LEAGUE/NAT. PAGE 65 A1338 — DIPLOM CONSTN PEACE COERCE

B91
SIDGWICK H.,THE ELEMENTS OF POLITICS. LOC/G NAT/G LEGIS DIPLOM ADJUD CONTROL EXEC PARL/PROC REPRESENT GOV/REL SOVEREIGN ALL/IDEOS 19 MILL/JS BENTHAM/J. PAGE 132 A2713 — POLICY LAW CONCPT

BENTLEY E. A0271

BENTLEY/AF....ARTHUR F. BENTLEY

BENVENISTE G. A0859

BERGSON/H....HENRI BERGSON

BERGSON/WJ....W. JAMES BERGSON

BERKELEY....BERKELEY, CALIFORNIA

BERKES R.N.B. A0272, A0273

BERLE A.A. A0274,A0275,A0276

BERLIN....BERLIN

B61
LIPPMANN W.,THE COMING TESTS WITH RUSSIA. COM CUBA GERMANY USSR FORCES CONTROL NEUTRAL COERCE NUC/PWR REV WAR PWR...INT 20 KHRUSH/N BERLIN. PAGE 89 A1830 — BAL/PWR DIPLOM MARXISM ARMS/CONT

B61
YDIT M.,INTERNATIONALISED TERRITORIES. FUT WOR+45 WOR-45 CONSTN VOL/ASSN CREATE PLAN LEGIT PEACE ORD/FREE...GEOG INT/LAW JURID SOC NEW/IDEA OBS RECORD SAMP TIME/SEQ TREND 19/20 BERLIN. PAGE 169 A3431 — LOC/G INT/ORG DIPLOM SOVEREIGN

B62
MANDER J.,BERLIN: HOSTAGE FOR THE WEST. FUT GERMANY WOR+45 FOR/AID RISK ATTIT ORD/FREE 20 BERLIN COLD/WAR. PAGE 93 A1916 — DIPLOM BAL/PWR DOMIN DETER

B62
NEAL F.W.,WAR AND PEACE AND GERMANY. EUR+WWI USSR STRUCT INT/ORG NAT/G FORCES DOMIN EDU/PROP LEGIT EXEC COERCE ORD/FREE...HUM SOC NEW/IDEA OBS TIME/SEQ TOT/POP COLD/WAR 20 BERLIN. PAGE 108 A2208 — USA+45 POLICY DIPLOM GERMANY

B65
EISENHOWER D.D.,WAGING PEACE 1956-61: THE WHITE HOUSE YEARS. USA+45 DIPLOM LEAD INGP/REL RACE/REL PEACE ATTIT...TRADIT TIME/SEQ 20 EISNHWR/DD PRESIDENT COLD/WAR CIV/RIGHTS BERLIN. PAGE 41 A0833 — TOP/EX BIOG ORD/FREE POLICY

S65
PLISCHKE E.,"INTEGRATING BERLIN AND THE FEDERAL REPUBLIC OF GERMANY." EUR+WWI GERMANY/W LEGIS TEC/DEV DOMIN ORD/FREE PWR...JURID 20 BERLIN. PAGE 117 A2392 — DIPLOM NAT/G MUNIC

BERLIN/BLO....BERLIN BLOCKADE

B50
US LIBRARY OF CONGRESS,THE UNITED STATES AND EUROPE: BIBLIOGRAPHY OF THOUGHT EXPRESSED IN AMERICAN PUBLICATIONS DURING 1950. EUR+WWI GERMANY USA+45 USSR INT/ORG DIPLOM COLONIAL SOVEREIGN — BIBLIOG/A SOC ATTIT

...POLICY 20 COLD/WAR UN BERLIN/BLO. PAGE 154 A3150

S59
WARBURG J.P.,"THE CENTRAL EUROPEAN CRISIS: A PROPOSAL FOR WESTERN INITIATIVE." EUR+WWI INT/ORG NAT/G LEGIT DETER WAR...CONCPT BER/BLOC UN 20. PAGE 161 A3276 — PLAN GERMANY

B61
FLEMING D.F.,THE COLD WAR AND ITS ORIGINS: 1917-1950 (VOL. I). ASIA USSR WOR+45 WOR-45 TEC/DEV FOR/AID NUC/PWR REV WAR PEACE FASCISM...T 20 COLD/WAR NATO BERLIN/BLO. PAGE 46 A0947 — DIPLOM MARXISM BAL/PWR

B66
MAY E.R.,ANXIETY AND AFFLUENCE: 1945-1965. USA+45 DIPLOM FOR/AID ARMS/CONT RACE/REL CONSEN...ANTHOL 20 COLD/WAR KENNEDY/JF EISNHWR/DD TRUMAN/HS BERLIN/BLO. PAGE 97 A1982 — ANOMIE ECO/DEV NUC/PWR WEALTH

S67
SOMMER T.,"BONN CHANGES COURSE." GERMANY/W NAT/G POL/PAR PROB/SOLV NAT/LISM 20 NATO BERLIN/BLO. PAGE 135 A2766 — DIPLOM BAL/PWR INT/ORG

BERLINER J.S. A0277

BERNAYS/EL....EDWARD L. BERNAYS

BERNHARDI F. A0278

BERNSTEIN B.J. A0279

BERRIEN W. A0336

BESSARABIA....BESSARABIA; SEE ALSO USSR

BESSON W. A0280

BEST H. A0281

BESTERMAN T. A0282

BEVERIDGE W. A0284

BEY A.S. A2055

BHUMIBOL/A....BHUMIBOL ADULYADEJ

BHUTAN....SEE ALSO ASIA

BIAFRA....BIAFRA

BIBLE....BIBLE: OLD AND NEW TESTAMENTS

BIBLIOG....BIBLIOGRAPHY OVER 50 ITEMS

N
INDIAN COUNCIL WORLD AFFAIRS,SELECT ARTICLES ON CURRENT AFFAIRS (BIBLIOGRAPHICAL SERIES: 7). AFR ASIA COM EUR+WWI S/ASIA UK COLONIAL NUC/PWR PEACE ATTIT...INT/LAW SOC 20. PAGE 70 A1437 — BIBLIOG DIPLOM INT/ORG ECO/UNDEV

N
LONDON INSTITUTE WORLD AFFAIRS,THE YEAR BOOK OF WORLD AFFAIRS. FINAN BAL/PWR ARMS/CONT WAR ...INT/LAW BIBLIOG 20. PAGE 91 A1856 — DIPLOM FOR/AID INT/ORG

N
SABIN J.,BIBLIOTHECA AMERICANA: A DICTIONARY OF BOOKS RELATING TO AMERICA, FROM ITS DISCOVERY TO THE PRESENT TIME(29 VOLS.). CONSTN CULTURE SOCIETY ECO/DEV LOC/G EDU/PROP NAT/LISM...POLICY GEOG SOC 19. PAGE 126 A2581 — BIBLIOG L/A+17C DIPLOM NAT/G

N
US DEPT OF STATE,FOREIGN RELATIONS OF THE UNITED STATES; DIPLOMATIC PAPERS. USA-45 NAT/G WAR PEACE ATTIT 19/20. PAGE 152 A3112 — BIBLIOG DIPLOM POLICY

B
DEUTSCHE BIBLIOTH FRANKF A M,DEUTSCHE BIBLIOGRAPHIE. EUR+WWI GERMANY ECO/DEV FORCES DIPLOM LEAD...POLICY PHIL/SCI SOC 20. PAGE 36 A0743 — BIBLIOG LAW ADMIN NAT/G

N
BACKGROUND; JOURNAL OF INTERNATIONAL STUDIES ASSOCIATION. INT/ORG FORCES ACT/RES EDU/PROP COERCE NAT/LISM PEACE ATTIT...INT/LAW CONCPT 20. PAGE 1 A0005 — BIBLIOG DIPLOM POLICY

N
JOURNAL OF ASIAN STUDIES. CULTURE ECO/DEV SECT DIPLOM EDU/PROP WAR NAT/LISM...PHIL/SCI SOC 20. PAGE 1 A0013 — BIBLIOG ASIA S/ASIA NAT/G

N
JOURNAL OF INTERNATIONAL AFFAIRS. WOR+45 ECO/UNDEV POL/PAR ECO/TAC WAR PEACE PERSON ALL/IDEOS ...INT/LAW TREND. PAGE 1 A0015 — BIBLIOG DIPLOM INT/ORG NAT/G

N
LITERATUR-VERZEICHNIS DER POLITISCHEN WISSENSCHAFTEN. GERMANY/W WOR+45 CONSTN SOCIETY ECO/DEV INT/ORG POL/PAR LEAD REPRESENT GOV/REL GP/REL...POLICY PHIL/SCI. PAGE 1 A0018 — BIBLIOG EUR+WWI DIPLOM NAT/G

N
MIDDLE EAST JOURNAL. CULTURE SECT DIPLOM LEAD GOV/REL ATTIT...POLICY PHIL/SCI SOC LING BIOG 20. PAGE 1 A0019 — BIBLIOG ISLAM NAT/G ECO/UNDEV

N
NEUE POLITISCHE LITERATUR. AFR ASIA EUR+WWI GERMANY RUSSIA SOCIETY ECO/DEV ECO/UNDEV PLAN PROB/SOLV LEAD MARXISM...PHIL/SCI CONCPT 20. PAGE 1 A0021 — BIBLIOG DIPLOM COM NAT/G

N
PEKING REVIEW. CHINA/COM CULTURE AGRI INDUS DIPLOM EDU/PROP GUERRILLA ATTIT MARXISM...BIBLIOG 20. PAGE 1 A0022 — MARXIST NAT/G POL/PAR PRESS

N
ARBITRATION JOURNAL. WOR+45 LAW INDUS JUDGE DIPLOM CT/SYS INGP/REL 20. PAGE 2 A0027 — BIBLIOG MGT LABOR ADJUD

N
AUSTRALIAN PUBLIC AFFAIRS INFORMATION SERVICE. LAW ...HEAL HUM MGT SOC CON/ANAL 20 AUSTRAL. PAGE 2 A0028 — BIBLIOG NAT/G CULTURE DIPLOM

N
BIBLIO, CATALOGUE DES OUVRAGES PARUS EN LANGUE FRANCAISE DANS LE MONDE ENTIER. FRANCE WOR+45 ADMIN LEAD PERSON...SOC 20. PAGE 2 A0029 — BIBLIOG NAT/G DIPLOM ECO/DEV

N
BIBLIOGRAPHIE DER SOZIALWISSENSCHAFTEN. WOR-45 CONSTN SOCIETY ECO/DEV ECO/UNDEV DIPLOM LEAD WAR PEACE...PHIL/SCI SOC 19/20. PAGE 2 A0030 — BIBLIOG LAW CONCPT NAT/G

N
DAILY SUMMARY OF THE JAPANESE PRESS. NAT/G DIPLOM LEAD 20 CHINJAP. PAGE 2 A0031 — BIBLIOG PRESS ASIA ATTIT

N
FOREIGN AFFAIRS. SPACE WOR+45 WOR-45 CULTURE ECO/UNDEV FINAN NAT/G TEC/DEV INT/TRADE ARMS/CONT NUC/PWR...POLICY 20 UN EURATOM ECSC EEC. PAGE 2 A0034 — BIBLIOG DIPLOM INT/ORG INT/LAW

N
INDIA: A REFERENCE ANNUAL. INDIA CULTURE COM/IND R+D FORCES PLAN RECEIVE EDU/PROP HEALTH...STAT CHARTS BIBLIOG 20. PAGE 2 A0036 — CONSTN LABOR INT/ORG

N
LONDON TIMES OFFICIAL INDEX. UK LAW ECO/DEV NAT/G DIPLOM LEAD ATTIT 20. PAGE 2 A0038 — BIBLIOG INDEX PRESS WRITING

N
PUBLISHERS' CIRCULAR, THE OFFICIAL ORGAN OF THE PUBLISHERS' ASSOCIATION OF GREAT BRITAIN AND IRELAND. EUR+WWI MOD/EUR UK LAW PROB/SOLV DIPLOM COLONIAL ATTIT...HUM 19/20 CMN/WLTH. PAGE 2 A0039 — BIBLIOG NAT/G WRITING LEAD

N
SEMINAR: THE MONTHLY SYMPOSIUM. INDIA ACT/RES TEC/DEV DIPLOM ATTIT...BIBLIOG 20. PAGE 2 A0041 — NAT/G ECO/UNDEV SOVEREIGN POLICY

N
THE JAPAN SCIENCE REVIEW: LAW AND POLITICS: LIST OF BOOKS AND ARTICLES ON LAW AND POLITICS. CONSTN AGRI INDUS LABOR DIPLOM TAX ADMIN CRIME...INT/LAW SOC 20 CHINJAP. PAGE 2 A0042 — BIBLIOG LAW S/ASIA PHIL/SCI

N
THE WORLD IN FOCUS. WOR+45 LEAD ATTIT...POLICY TREND. PAGE 2 A0044 — BIBLIOG INT/ORG INT/LAW DIPLOM

N
AVTOREFERATY DISSERTATSII. USSR INTELL ACADEM NAT/G DIPLOM GOV/REL KNOWL CONCPT. PAGE 3 A0047 — BIBLIOG MARXISM MARXIST COM

N
AMERICAN BIBLIOGRAPHIC SERVICE,INTERNATIONAL GUIDE TO INDIC STUDIES - A QUARTERLY INDEX TO PERIODICAL LITERATURE. INDIA CULTURE NAT/G DIPLOM...EPIST SOC BIOG 20. PAGE 7 A0140 — BIBLIOG S/ASIA CON/ANAL

N
AMERICAN BIBLIOGRAPHIC SERVICE,QUARTERLY CHECKLIST OF ORIENTAL STUDIES. CULTURE LOC/G NAT/G DIPLOM ...HIST/WRIT CON/ANAL 20. PAGE 7 A0141 — BIBLIOG S/ASIA ASIA

N
AMERICAN HISTORICAL SOCIETY,LIST OF DOCTORAL DISSERTATIONS IN HISTORY IN PROGRESS OR COMPLETED IN COLLEGES AND UNIVERSITIES IN THE UNITED STATES. WOR+45 WOR-45 CULTURE SOCIETY NAT/G DIPLOM LEAD TREND. PAGE 7 A0150 — BIBLIOG ACADEM INTELL

N
CARIBBEAN COMMISSION,CURRENT CARIBBEAN BIBLIOGRAPHY. FRANCE NETHERLAND UK CULTURE ECO/UNDEV PRESS LEAD ATTIT...GEOG SOC 20. PAGE 24 A0482
BIBLIOG NAT/G L/A+17C DIPLOM

N
CORNELL UNIVERSITY LIBRARY,SOUTHEAST ASIA ACCESSIONS LIST. LAW SOCIETY STRUCT ECO/UNDEV POL/PAR TEC/DEV DIPLOM LEAD REGION. PAGE 31 A0626
BIBLIOG S/ASIA NAT/G CULTURE

N
COUNCIL ON FOREIGN RELATIONS,DOCUMENTS ON AMERICAN FOREIGN RELATIONS. INT/ORG ECO/TAC NUC/PWR WAR WEAPON...POLICY CON/ANAL CHARTS 20 OAS UN. PAGE 31 A0639
BIBLIOG USA+45 USA-45 DIPLOM

N
DE MARTENS G.F.,RECUEIL GENERALE DE TRAITES ET AUTRES ACTES RELATIFS AUX RAPPORTS DE DROIT INTERNATIONAL (41 VOLS.). EUR+WWI MOD/EUR USA-45 ...INDEX TREATY 18/20. PAGE 35 A0708
BIBLIOG INT/LAW DIPLOM

N
DEUTSCHE BUCHEREI,DEUTSCHE NATIONALBIBLIOGRAPHIE. GERMANY ECO/DEV DIPLOM AGE/Y ATTIT...PHIL/SCI SOC 20. PAGE 37 A0744
BIBLIOG NAT/G LEAD POLICY

N
DEUTSCHE BUCHEREI,JAHRESVERZEICHNIS DES DEUTSCHEN SCHRIFTUMS. AUSTRIA EUR+WWI GERMANY SWITZERLND LAW LOC/G DIPLOM ADMIN...MGT SOC 19/20. PAGE 37 A0745
BIBLIOG WRITING NAT/G

N
DEUTSCHE BUCHEREI,DEUTSCHES BUCHERVERZEICHNIS. GERMANY LAW CULTURE POL/PAR ADMIN LEAD ATTIT PERSON ...SOC 20. PAGE 37 A0746
NAT/G DIPLOM ECO/DEV

N
DOHERTY D.K.,PRELIMINARY BIBLIOGRAPHY OF COLONIZATION AND SETTLEMENT IN LATIN AMERICA AND ANGLO-AMERICA. L/A+17C PRE/AMER USA-45 ECO/UNDEV NAT/G 15/20. PAGE 38 A0768
BIBLIOG COLONIAL ADMIN DIPLOM

N
EUROPA PUBLICATIONS LIMITED,THE EUROPA YEAR BOOK. CONSTN FINAN INDUS POL/PAR DIPLOM TV CT/SYS...STAT BIOG CHARTS WORSHIP 20. PAGE 43 A0874
BIBLIOG NAT/G PRESS INT/ORG

N
HARVARD LAW SCHOOL LIBRARY,ANNUAL LEGAL BIBLIOGRAPHY. USA+45 CONSTN LEGIS ADJUD CT/SYS ...POLICY 20. PAGE 62 A1278
BIBLIOG JURID LAW INT/LAW

N
HARVARD UNIVERSITY LAW LIBRARY,CATALOG OF INTERNATIONAL LAW AND RELATIONS. WOR+45 WOR-45 INT/ORG NAT/G JUDGE DIPLOM INT/TRADE ADJUD CT/SYS 19/20. PAGE 62 A1280
BIBLIOG INT/LAW JURID

N
HOOVER INSTITUTION,UNITED STATES AND CANADIAN PUBLICATIONS ON AFRICA. CULTURE ECO/UNDEV AGRI TEC/DEV EDU/PROP COLONIAL RACE/REL NAT/LISM ATTIT HEALTH...SOC SOC/WK 20. PAGE 67 A1381
BIBLIOG DIPLOM NAT/G AFR

N
IMF AND IBRD, JOINT LIBRARY,LIST OF RECENT ADDITIONS. WOR+45 ECO/DEV ECO/UNDEV BUDGET FOR/AID RATION...CONCPT IDEA/COMP. PAGE 70 A1434
BIBLIOG INT/ORG INT/TRADE FINAN

N
IMF AND IBRD, JOINT LIBRARY,LIST OF RECENT PERIODICAL ARTICLES. WOR+45 ECO/DEV ECO/UNDEV BUDGET FOR/AID RATION...CONCPT IDEA/COMP. PAGE 70 A1435
BIBLIOG INT/ORG INT/TRADE FINAN

N
INTERNATIONAL STUDIES,"INDIA AND WORLD AFFAIRS: AN ANNUAL BIBLIOGRAPHY" INDIA INT/TRADE PARTIC GOV/REL 20. PAGE 71 A1461
BIBLIOG POLICY DIPLOM ATTIT

N
JOHNS HOPKINS UNIVERSITY LIB,RECENT ADDITIONS. WOR+45 ECO/UNDEV NAT/G POL/PAR FOR/AID INT/TRADE LEAD REGION ATTIT ALL/IDEOS TREND. PAGE 74 A1518
BIBLIOG DIPLOM INT/LAW INT/ORG

N
KAPLAN L.,REVIEW INDEX. USA+45 USA-45 FINAN INDUS LABOR RACE/REL...GEOG PSY SOC 20. PAGE 76 A1558
BIBLIOG PROF/ORG ECO/DEV DIPLOM

N
KYRIAK T.E.,INTERNATIONAL DEVELOPMENTS: A BIBLIOGRAPHY (SERIAL). WOR+45...COMPUT/IR AUD/VIS CHARTS. PAGE 83 A1702
BIBLIOG NAT/G DIPLOM

N
LEYPOLOT F.,AMERICAN CATALOGUE OF BOOKS, 1876-1910 (19 VOLS.). NAT/G DIPLOM...CON/ANAL 19/20. PAGE 88 A1806
BIBLIOG USA-45 PROF/ORG PROC/MFG

N
LONDON LIBRARY ASSOCIATION,ATHENAEUM SUBJECT INDEX. 1915-1918. NAT/G DIPLOM NAT/LISM 20. PAGE 91 A1857
BIBLIOG CON/ANAL

SOC

N
MINISTERE DE L'EDUC NATIONALE,CATALOGUE DES THESES DE DOCTORAT SOUTENNES DEVANT LES UNIVERSITAIRES FRANCAISES. FRANCE LAW DIPLOM ADMIN...HUM SOC 20. PAGE 102 A2087
BIBLIOG ACADEM KNOWL NAT/G

N
MINISTRY OF OVERSEAS DEVELOPME,TECHNICAL CO-OPERATION -- A BIBLIOGRAPHY. UK LAW SOCIETY DIPLOM ECO/TAC FOR/AID...STAT 20 CMN/WLTH. PAGE 102 A2089
BIBLIOG TEC/DEV ECO/DEV NAT/G

N
OAS,DOCUMENTOS OFICIALES DE LA ORGANIZACION DE LOS ESTADOS AMERICANOS. L/A+17C ATTIT 20 OAS. PAGE 111 A2272
BIBLIOG INT/ORG DIPLOM POLICY

N
RAND SCHOOL OF SOCIAL SCIENCE,INDEX TO LABOR ARTICLES. ECO/DEV INT/ORG LEGIS DIPLOM GP/REL ...NAT/COMP 20. PAGE 119 A2440
BIBLIOG LABOR MGT ADJUD

N
SOCIETE DES NATIONS,TRAITES INTERNATIONAUX ET ACTES LEGISLATIFS. WOR-45 INT/ORG NAT/G...INT/LAW JURID 20 LEAGUE/NAT TREATY. PAGE 135 A2759
BIBLIOG DIPLOM LEGIS ADJUD

N
UNESCO,INTERNATIONAL BIBLIOGRAPHY OF POLITICAL SCIENCE (VOLUMES 1-8). WOR+45 LAW NAT/G EX/STRUC LEGIS PROB/SOLV DIPLOM ADMIN GOV/REL 20 UNESCO. PAGE 147 A3010
BIBLIOG CONCPT IDEA/COMP

N
UNITED NATIONS,UNITED NATIONS PUBLICATIONS. WOR+45 ECO/UNDEV AGRI FINAN FORCES ADMIN LEAD WAR PEACE ...POLICY INT/LAW 20 UN. PAGE 148 A3034
BIBLIOG INT/ORG DIPLOM

N
UNITED NATIONS,YEARBOOK OF THE INTERNATIONAL LAW COMMISSION....CON/ANAL 20 UN. PAGE 149 A3035
BIBLIOG INT/ORG INT/LAW DELIB/GP

N
UNIVERSITY OF CALIFORNIA,STATISTICAL ABSTRACT OF LATIN AMERICA. L/A+17C DIPLOM 20. PAGE 149 A3046
BIBLIOG NAT/G ECO/UNDEV STAT

N
US DEPARTMENT OF STATE,BIBLIOGRAPHY (PAMPHLETS). AGRI INDUS INT/ORG FOR/AID EDU/PROP WAR MARXISM ...SOC GOV/COMP METH/COMP 20. PAGE 151 A3079
BIBLIOG DIPLOM ECO/DEV NAT/G

N
US LIBRARY OF CONGRESS,ACCESSIONS LIST - INDIA. INDIA CULTURE AGRI LOC/G POL/PAR PLAN PROB/SOLV TEC/DEV DIPLOM EDU/PROP LEAD GP/REL ATTIT 20. PAGE 154 A3142
BIBLIOG S/ASIA ECO/UNDEV NAT/G

N
US LIBRARY OF CONGRESS,ACCESSIONS LIST -- ISRAEL. ISRAEL CULTURE ECO/UNDEV POL/PAR PLAN PROB/SOLV TEC/DEV DIPLOM EDU/PROP LEAD WAR ATTIT 20 JEWS. PAGE 154 A3143
BIBLIOG ISLAM NAT/G GP/REL

N
US LIBRARY OF CONGRESS,EAST EUROPEAN ACCESSIONS INDEX. NAT/G ISOLAT ATTIT KNOWL...POLICY 20. PAGE 154 A3144
BIBLIOG COM MARXIST DIPLOM

N
US SUPERINTENDENT OF DOCUMENTS,CATALOGUE OF PUBLIC DOCUMENTS OF CONGRESS AND OF ALL DEPARTMENTS OF THE GOVERNMENT OF THE UNITED STATES. DIPLOM ATTIT ...POLICY DICTIONARY 20 CONGRESS. PAGE 157 A3200
BIBLIOG NAT/G WRITING USA-45

N
US SUPERINTENDENT OF DOCUMENTS,MONTHLY CATALOG OF UNITED STATES GOVERNMENT PUBLICATIONS. USA+45 USA-45 AGRI LABOR FORCES INT/TRADE TARIFFS TAX EDU/PROP CT/SYS ARMS/CONT RACE/REL 19/20 CONGRESS PRESIDENT. PAGE 157 A3203
BIBLIOG NAT/G VOL/ASSN POLICY

N
WORLD PEACE FOUNDATION,DOCUMENTS OF INTERNATIONAL ORGANIZATIONS: A SELECTED BIBLIOGRAPHY. WOR+45 WOR-45 AGRI FINAN ACT/RES OP/RES INT/TRADE ADMIN ...CON/ANAL 20 UN UNESCO LEAGUE/NAT. PAGE 167 A3396
BIBLIOG DIPLOM INT/ORG REGION

BLI
MOOR C.C.,HOW TO USE UNITED NATIONS DOCUMENTS (PAPER). WOR+45 ACADEM CONTROL 20 UN. PAGE 103 A2121
BIBLIOG METH INT/ORG

NLO
WHITE J.A.,THE DIPLOMACY OF THE RUSSO-JAPANESE WAR. ASIA KOREA RUSSIA FORCES CONFER CONTROL PEACE ...BIBLIOG 19 CHINJAP. PAGE 164 A3336
DIPLOM WAR BAL/PWR

B03
FORTESCUE G.K.,SUBJECT INDEX OF THE MODERN WORKS ADDED TO THE LIBRARY OF THE BRITISH MUSEUM IN THE YEARS 1881-1900 (3 VOLS.). UK LAW CONSTN FINAN NAT/G FORCES INT/TRADE COLONIAL 19. PAGE 47 A0968
BIBLIOG INDEX WRITING

B03
GRIFFIN A.P.C.,SELECT LIST OF REFERENCES ON THE
BIBLIOG

MONROE DOCTRINE (PAMPHLET). L/A+17C NAT/G TOP/EX 19/20. PAGE 56 A1151
DIPLOM COLONIAL

B03
GRIFFIN A.P.C.,LISTS PUBLISHED 1902-03: ANGLO-SAXON INTERESTS (PAMPHLET). UK USA-45 ELITES SOCIETY DIPLOM ISOLAT 19/20. PAGE 56 A1152
BIBLIOG COLONIAL RACE/REL DOMIN

C05
DUNNING W.A.,"HISTORY OF POLITICAL THEORIES FROM LUTHER TO MONTESQUIEU." LAW NAT/G SECT DIPLOM REV WAR ORD/FREE SOVEREIGN CONSERVE...TRADIT BIBLIOG 16/18. PAGE 39 A0803
PHIL/SCI CONCPT GEN/LAWS

B06
FOSTER J.W.,THE PRACTICE OF DIPLOMACY AS ILLUSTRATED IN THE FOREIGN RELATIONS OF THE UNITED STATES. MOD/EUR USA-45 NAT/G EX/STRUC ADMIN ...POLICY INT/LAW BIBLIOG 19/20. PAGE 47 A0970
DIPLOM ROUTINE PHIL/SCI

C06
MONTGOMERY H.,"A DICTIONARY OF POLITICAL PHRASES AND ILLUSIONS WITH A SHORT BIBLIOGRAPHY." EUR+WWI MOD/EUR UK AGRI LABOR LOC/G NAT/G COLONIAL CHOOSE RACE/REL. PAGE 103 A2114
BIBLIOG DICTIONARY POLICY DIPLOM

B13
BORCHARD E.M.,BIBLIOGRAPHY OF INTERNATIONAL LAW AND CONTINENTAL LAW. EUR+WWI MOD/EUR UK LAW INT/TRADE WAR PEACE...GOV/COMP NAT/COMP 19/20. PAGE 17 A0338
BIBLIOG INT/LAW JURID DIPLOM

B15
INTERNATIONAL LAW ASSOCIATION,A FORTY YEARS' CATALOGUE OF THE BOOKS, PAMPHLETS AND PAPERS IN THE LIBRARY OF THE INTERNATIONAL LAW ASSOCIATION. INT/ORG DIPLOM ADJUD NEUTRAL...IDEA/COMP 19/20. PAGE 71 A1458
BIBLIOG LAW INT/LAW

B17
DILLA H.M.,CLASSIFIED LIST OF MAGAZINE ARTICLES ON THE EUROPEAN WAR. MOD/EUR USA-45 WOR-45 PEACE ATTIT 20. PAGE 37 A0762
BIBLIOG WAR DIPLOM POLICY

B17
MEYER H.H.B.,LIST OF REFERENCES ON EMBARGOES (PAMPHLET). USA-45 AGRI DIPLOM WRITING DEBATE WEAPON...INT/LAW 18/20 CONGRESS. PAGE 100 A2049
BIBLIOG DIST/IND ECO/TAC INT/TRADE

B18
KERNER R.J.,SLAVIC EUROPE: A SELECTED BIBLIOGRAPHY IN THE WESTERN EUROPEAN LANGUAGES. BULGARIA CZECHOSLVK GERMANY/E POLAND RUSSIA YUGOSLAVIA NAT/G DIPLOM MARXISM...LING 19/20. PAGE 78 A1598
BIBLIOG SOCIETY CULTURE COM

B18
US LIBRARY OF CONGRESS,LIST OF REFERENCES ON A LEAGUE OF NATIONS. DIPLOM WAR PEACE 20 LEAGUE/NAT. PAGE 154 A3145
BIBLIOG INT/ORG ADMIN EX/STRUC

B20
MEYER H.H.B.,LIST OF REFERENCES ON THE TREATY-MAKING POWER. USA-45 CONTROL PWR...INT/LAW TIME/SEQ 18/20 TREATY. PAGE 100 A2052
BIBLIOG DIPLOM CONSTN

B20
VINOGRADOFF P.,OUTLINES OF HISTORICAL JURISPRUDENCE (2 VOLS.). GREECE MEDIT-7 LAW CONSTN FACE/GP FAM KIN MUNIC CRIME OWN...INT/LAW IDEA/COMP BIBLIOG. PAGE 159 A3241
JURID METH

L21
HALDEMAN E.,"SERIALS OF AN INTERNATIONAL CHARACTER." WOR-45 DIPLOM...ART/METH GEOG HEAL HUM INT/LAW JURID PSY SOC. PAGE 60 A1224
BIBLIOG PHIL/SCI

L22
DORE R.,"BIBLIOGRAPHIE DES 'LIVRES JAUNES' A LA DATE DU 1ER JANVIER 1922." FRANCE CONFER 19/20. PAGE 38 A0773
BIBLIOG DIPLOM INT/ORG

B23
HEADICAR B.M.,CATALOGUE OF THE BOOKS, PAMPHLETS, AND OTHER DOCUMENTS IN THE EDWARD FRY LIBRARY OF INTERNATIONAL LAW... UK INT/ORG 20. PAGE 63 A1304
BIBLIOG INT/LAW DIPLOM

C25
MOON P.T.,"SYLLABUS ON INTERNATIONAL RELATIONS." EUR+WWI MOD/EUR USA-45 FORCES COLONIAL WAR WEAPON NAT/LISM...POLICY BIBLIOG T 19/20. PAGE 103 A2120
INT/ORG DIPLOM NAT/G

B26
INTERNATIONAL BIBLIOGRAPHY OF POLITICAL SCIENCE. WOR+45 NAT/G POL/PAR EX/STRUC LEGIS CT/SYS LEAD CHOOSE GOV/REL ATTIT...PHIL/SCI 20. PAGE 3 A0049
BIBLIOG DIPLOM CONCPT ADMIN

B26
INSTITUT INTERMEDIAIRE INTL,REPERTOIRE GENERAL DES TRAITES ET AUTRES ACTES DIPLOMATIQUES CONCLUS DEPUIS 1895 JUSQU'EN 1920. MOD/EUR WOR-45 INT/ORG VOL/ASSN DELIB/GP INT/TRADE WAR TREATY 19/20. PAGE 70 A1443
BIBLIOG DIPLOM

B26
LEWIN E.,RECENT PUBLICATIONS IN THE LIBRARY OF THE ROYAL COLONIAL INSTITUTE (PAMPHLET). CANADA UK EX/STRUC PARL/PROC NAT/LISM SOVEREIGN 20 CMN/WLTH PARLIAMENT. PAGE 88 A1799
BIBLIOG COLONIAL CONSTN DIPLOM

B28
CHILDS J.B.,FOREIGN GOVERNMENT PUBLICATIONS (PAMPHLET). LEGIS DIPLOM 19/20. PAGE 26 A0529
BIBLIOG PRESS NAT/G

B28
LAPRADELLE,ANNUAIRE DE LA VIE INTERNATIONALE: POLITIQUE, ECONOMIQUE, JURIDIQUE. INT/ORG CONFER ARMS/CONT 20. PAGE 85 A1729
BIBLIOG DIPLOM INT/LAW

B28
LODGE H.C.,THE HISTORY OF NATIONS (25 VOLS.). UNIV LEAD...ANTHOL BIBLIOG INDEX. PAGE 90 A1850
DIPLOM SOCIETY NAT/G

C28
SCHNEIDER H.W.,"MAKING THE FASCIST STATE." ITALY CULTURE LABOR DIPLOM REV WAR NAT/LISM TOTALISM ATTIT DRIVE SOCISM...BIBLIOG PARLIAMENT 20. PAGE 129 A2638
FASCISM POLICY POL/PAR

C28
WARD P.W.,"SOVEREIGNTY: A STUDY OF A CONTEMPORARY POLITICAL NOTION." CONSTN NAT/G DIPLOM REPRESENT PLURISM...IDEA/COMP BIBLIOG. PAGE 161 A3281
SOVEREIGN CONCPT NAT/LISM

B29
BOUDET P.,BIBLIOGRAPHIE DE L'INDOCHINE FRANCAISE. S/ASIA VIETNAM SECT...GEOG LING 20. PAGE 17 A0344
BIBLIOG ADMIN COLONIAL DIPLOM

B29
PRATT I.A.,MODERN EGYPT: A LIST OF REFERENCES TO MATERIAL IN THE NEW YORK PUBLIC LIBRARY. UAR ECO/UNDEV...GEOG JURID SOC LING 20. PAGE 117 A2407
BIBLIOG ISLAM DIPLOM NAT/G

B32
CARDINALL AW,A BIBLIOGRAPHY OF THE GOLD COAST. AFR UK NAT/G EX/STRUC ATTIT...POLICY 19/20. PAGE 24 A0479
BIBLIOG ADMIN COLONIAL DIPLOM

B32
GREGORY W.,LIST OF THE SERIAL PUBLICATIONS OF FOREIGN GOVERNMENTS, 1815-1931. WOR-45 DIPLOM ADJUD ...POLICY 20. PAGE 56 A1144
BIBLIOG NAT/G LAW JURID

B33
WAMBAUCH S.,PLEBISCITES SINCE THE WORLD WAR: WITH A COLLECTION OF OFFICIAL DOCUMENTS. WOR-45 COLONIAL SANCTION...MAJORIT DECISION CHARTS BIBLIOG 19/20 WWI. PAGE 161 A3272
DIPLOM CONSTN NAT/G CHOOSE

B35
BUREAU ECONOMIC RES LAT AM,THE ECONOMIC LITERATURE OF LATIN AMERICA (2 VOLS.). CHRIST-17C AGRI DIST/IND EXTR/IND INDUS WORKER INT/TRADE...GEOG 16/20. PAGE 21 A0433
BIBLIOG L/A+17C ECO/UNDEV FINAN

B35
CONOVER H.F.,A SELECTED LIST OF REFERENCES ON THE DIPLOMATIC & TRADE RELATIONS OF THE US WITH THE USSR, 1919-1935 (PAMPHLET). USA-45 USSR DELIB/GP LEGIS OP/RES PROB/SOLV BAL/PWR BARGAIN 20. PAGE 29 A0590
BIBLIOG DIPLOM INT/TRADE

B35
LEAGUE OF NATIONS,CATALOGUE OF PUBLICATIONS, 1920-1935. GOV/REL 20 LEAGUE/NAT. PAGE 86 A1755
BIBLIOG INT/ORG DIPLOM

B36
HARVARD BUREAU ECO RES LAT AM,THE ECONOMIC LITERATURE OF LATIN AMERICA: A TENTATIVE BIBLIOGRAPHY. NAT/G TARIFFS CENTRAL COST DEMAND 20. PAGE 62 A1277
BIBLIOG ECO/UNDEV L/A+17C INT/TRADE

B36
VARLEY D.H.,A BIBLIOGRAPHY OF ITALIAN COLONISATION IN AFRICA WITH A SECTION ON ABYSSINIA. AFR ETHIOPIA ITALY LIBYA SOMALIA AGRI FINAN LABOR TEC/DEV DIPLOM INT/TRADE RACE/REL DISCRIM 19/20. PAGE 158 A3222
BIBLIOG COLONIAL ADMIN LAW

B37
KETCHAM E.H.,PRELIMINARY SELECT BIBLIOGRAPHY OF INTERNATIONAL LAW (PAMPHLET). WOR-45 LAW INT/ORG NAT/G PROB/SOLV CT/SYS NEUTRAL WAR 19/20. PAGE 78 A1602
BIBLIOG DIPLOM ADJUD INT/LAW

B37
THOMPSON J.W.,SECRET DIPLOMACY: A RECORD OF ESPIONAGE AND DOUBLE-DEALING: 1500-1815. CHRIST-17C MOD/EUR NAT/G WRITING RISK MORAL...ANTHOL BIBLIOG 16/19 ESPIONAGE. PAGE 143 A2927
DIPLOM CRIME

B37
TUPPER E.,JAPAN IN AMERICAN PUBLIC OPINION. USA-45 POL/PAR VOL/ASSN INT/TRADE DISCRIM...BIBLIOG 20 CHINJAP TREATY. PAGE 146 A2979
ATTIT IDEA/COMP DIPLOM PRESS

C37
ROWAN R.W.,"THE STORY OF THE SECRET SERVICE." WOR-45 REV...BIOG BIBLIOG. PAGE 124 A2552
WAR COERCE DIPLOM

C37
TUPPER E.,"JAPAN IN AMERICAN PUBLIC OPINION." USA+45 POL/PAR VOL/ASSN INT/TRADE DISCRIM ...IDEA/COMP 20 CHINJAP. PAGE 146 A2978
BIBLIOG ATTIT DIPLOM PRESS

B38
GREGORY W.,INTERNATIONAL CONGRESSES AND CONFERENCES 1840-1937: A UNION LIST OF THEIR PUBLICATIONS
BIBLIOG INT/ORG

AVAILABLE IN US AND CANADA. WOR-45 LEGIS ATTIT ...POLICY 19/20. PAGE 56 A1145
CONFER

B38
GRISWOLD A.W.,THE FAR EASTERN POLICY OF THE UNITED STATES. ASIA S/ASIA USA-45 INT/ORG INT/TRADE WAR NAT/LISM...BIBLIOG 19/20 LEAGUE/NAT ROOSEVLT/T ROOSEVLT/F WILSON/W TREATY. PAGE 57 A1166
DIPLOM POLICY CHIEF

B39
FULLER G.H.,A SELECTED LIST OF REFERENCES ON THE EXPANSION OF THE US NAVY, 1933-1939 (PAMPHLET). MOD/EUR USA-45 NAT/G PLAN DIPLOM DOMIN RISK ARMS/CONT EQUILIB PWR 20 NAVY. PAGE 50 A1019
BIBLIOG FORCES WEAPON WAR

B39
KERNER R.J.,NORTHEAST ASIA: A SELECTED BIBLIOGRAPHY (2 VOLS.). KOREA RUSSIA NAT/G DIPLOM...GEOG 19/20 CHINJAP. PAGE 78 A1599
BIBLIOG ASIA SOCIETY CULTURE

B39
THOMAS J.A.,THE HOUSE OF COMMONS, 1832-1901; A STUDY OF ITS ECONOMIC AND FUNCTIONAL CHARACTER. UK LAW STRATA FINAN DIPLOM CONTROL LEAD LOBBY REPRESENT WEALTH...POLICY STAT BIBLIOG 19/20 PARLIAMENT. PAGE 143 A2922
PARL/PROC LEGIS POL/PAR ECO/DEV

B39
WHEELER-BENNET J.W.,THE FORGOTTEN PEACE: BREST-LITOVSK. COM GERMANY USSR TOP/EX AGREE WAR PWR ...BIBLIOG 20 TREATY LENIN/VI UKRAINE. PAGE 163 A3326
PEACE DIPLOM CONFER

C39
HADDOW A.,"POLITICAL SCIENCE IN AMERICAN COLLEGES AND UNIVERSITIES 1636-1900." CONSTN MORAL...POLICY INT/LAW CON/ANAL BIBLIOG T 17/20. PAGE 59 A1211
USA-45 LAW ACADEM KNOWL

C39
REISCHAUER R.,"JAPAN'S GOVERNMENT--POLITICS." CONSTN STRATA POL/PAR FORCES LEGIS DIPLOM ADMIN EXEC CENTRAL...POLICY BIBLIOG 20 CHINJAP. PAGE 120 A2462
NAT/G S/ASIA CONCPT ROUTINE

C39
SCOTT J.B.,"LAW, THESTATE, AND THE INTERNATIONAL COMMUNITY (2 VOLS.)" INTELL INT/ORG NAT/G SECT INT/TRADE WAR...INT/LAW GEN/LAWS BIBLIOG. PAGE 130 A2672
LAW PHIL/SCI DIPLOM CONCPT

B40
CONOVER H.F.,A BRIEF LIST OF REFERENCES ON WESTERN HEMISPHERE DEFENSE (PAMPHLET). USA-45 NAT/G CONSULT DELIB/GP FORCES BAL/PWR CONFER DETER...PREDICT CON/ANAL 20. PAGE 29 A0591
BIBLIOG DIPLOM PLAN INT/ORG

B40
CONOVER H.F.,JAPAN-ECONOMIC DEVELOPMENT AND FOREIGN POLICY, A SELECTED LIST OF REFERENCES (PAMPHLET). CULTURE FINAN INDUS NAT/G FORCES INT/TRADE WAR ...SOC TREND 20 CHINJAP. PAGE 29 A0593
BIBLIOG ASIA ECO/DEV DIPLOM

C40
NORMAN E.H.,"JAPAN'S EMERGENCE AS A MODERN STATE: POLITICAL AND ECONOMIC PROBLEMS OF THE MEIJI PERIOD." CONSTN STRATA AGRI INDUS POL/PAR TEC/DEV CAP/ISM CIVMIL/REL...BIBLIOG 19/20 CHINJAP. PAGE 110 A2250
CENTRAL DIPLOM POLICY NAT/LISM

B41
BIRDSALL P.,VERSAILLES TWENTY YEARS AFTER. MOD/EUR POL/PAR CHIEF CONSULT FORCES LEGIS REPAR PEACE ORD/FREE...BIBLIOG 20 PRESIDENT TREATY. PAGE 14 A0290
DIPLOM NAT/LISM WAR

B41
EVANS C.,AMERICAN BIBLIOGRAPHY... (12 VOLUMES). USA-45 LAW DIPLOM ADMIN PERSON...HUM SOC 17/18. PAGE 43 A0876
BIBLIOG NAT/G ALL/VALS ALL/IDEOS

B41
GRISMER R.,A NEW BIBLIOGRAPHY OF THE LITERATURES OF SPAIN AND SPANISH AMERICA. CHRIST-17C MOD/EUR PRE/AMER SPAIN CULTURE DIPLOM EDU/PROP...ART/METH GEOG HUM PHIL/SCI 20. PAGE 57 A1165
BIBLIOG LAW NAT/G ECO/UNDEV

B41
SCHWARZENBERGER G.,POWER POLITICS: AN INTRODUCTION TO THE STUDY OF INTERNATIONAL RELATIONS AND POST-WAR PLANNING. INT/ORG FORCES COERCE WAR FEDERAL PEACE MORAL...POLICY CONCPT CON/ANAL BIBLIOG 20. PAGE 130 A2660
DIPLOM UTOPIA PWR

B42
CONOVER H.F.,FRENCH COLONIES IN AFRICA: A LIST OF REFERENCES. ALGERIA FRANCE MOROCCO SOMALIA SUDAN CULTURE AGRI LOC/G SECT FORCES DIPLOM INT/TRADE NAT/LISM HEALTH...CON/ANAL 20. PAGE 29 A0594
BIBLIOG AFR ECO/UNDEV COLONIAL

B42
FULLER G.H.,AUSTRALIA: A SELECT LIST OF REFERENCES. FORCES DIPLOM WAR 20 AUSTRAL. PAGE 50 A1022
BIBLIOG SOC

B42
JACKSON M.V.,EUROPEAN POWERS AND SOUTH-EAST AFRICA: A STUDY OF INTERNATIONAL RELATIONS ON SOUTH-EAST COAST OF AFRICA, 1796-1856. AFR FRANCE PORTUGAL SOUTH/AFR UK USA-45 FORCES INT/TRADE PWR...CHARTS BIBLIOG 18/19 TREATY. PAGE 72 A1477
DOMIN POLICY ORD/FREE DIPLOM

B42
SIMOES DOS REIS A.,BIBLIOGRAFIA DAS BIBLIOGRAFIAS BRASILEIRAS. BRAZIL ADMIN COLONIAL 20. PAGE 133 A2717
BIBLIOG NAT/G DIPLOM L/A+17C

B43
BROWN A.D.,BRITISH POSSESSIONS IN THE CARIBBEAN AREA: A SELECTED LIST OF REFERENCES. UK NAT/G DIPLOM...GEOG 20 CARIBBEAN. PAGE 20 A0398
BIBLIOG COLONIAL ECO/UNDEV L/A+17C

B43
CARLO A.M.,ENSAYO DE UNA BIBLIOGRAFIA DE BIBLIOGRAFIAS MEXICANAS. ECO/UNDEV LOC/G ADMIN LEAD 20 MEXIC/AMER. PAGE 24 A0485
BIBLIOG L/A+17C NAT/G DIPLOM

B43
CONOVER H.F.,THE BALKANS: A SELECTED LIST OF REFERENCES. ALBANIA BULGARIA ROMANIA YUGOSLAVIA INT/ORG PROB/SOLV DIPLOM LEGIT CONFER ADJUD WAR NAT/LISM PEACE PWR 20 LEAGUE/NAT. PAGE 29 A0596
BIBLIOG EUR+WWI

B43
CONOVER H.F.,SOVIET RUSSIA: SELECTED LIST OF REFERENCES. USSR CULTURE INDUS NAT/G TOP/EX TEC/DEV BUDGET WAR CIVMIL/REL EFFICIENCY MARXISM 20. PAGE 29 A0597
BIBLIOG ECO/DEV COM DIPLOM

B43
LEWIN E.,ROYAL EMPIRE SOCIETY BIBLIOGRAPHIES NO. 9: SUB-SAHARA AFRICA. ECO/UNDEV TEC/DEV DIPLOM ADMIN COLONIAL LEAD 20. PAGE 88 A1800
BIBLIOG AFR NAT/G SOCIETY

B43
MC DOWELL R.B.,IRISH PUBLIC OPINION, 1750-1800. IRELAND CONSTN VOL/ASSN WORKER ORD/FREE CATHISM CONSERVE...POLICY IDEA/COMP BIBLIOG 18/ PARLIAMENT. PAGE 97 A1992
ATTIT NAT/G DIPLOM REV

B44
FULLER G.H.,MILITARY GOVERNMENT: A LIST OF REFERENCES (A PAMPHLET). ITALY UK USA-45 WOR-45 LAW FORCES DOMIN ADMIN ARMS/CONT ORD/FREE PWR ...DECISION 20 CHINJAP. PAGE 50 A1023
BIBLIOG DIPLOM CIVMIL/REL SOVEREIGN

B44
MATTHEWS M.A.,INTERNATIONAL POLICE (PAMPHLET). WOR-45 DIPLOM ARMS/CONT WAR 20. PAGE 96 A1977
BIBLIOG INT/ORG FORCES PEACE

B44
RAGATZ L.J.,LITERATURE OF EUROPEAN IMPERIALISM. ECO/TAC INT/TRADE DOMIN GOV/REL DEMAND NAT/LISM PWR WEALTH 19/20. PAGE 119 A2432
BIBLIOG COLONIAL INT/ORG ECO/UNDEV

B44
SHELBY C.,LATIN AMERICAN PERIODICALS CURRENTLY RECEIVED IN THE LIBRARY OF CONGRESS AND IN LIBRARY OF DEPARTMENT OF AGRICULTURE. SOCIETY AGRI INDUS LABOR POL/PAR INT/TRADE...GEOG SOC 20. PAGE 132 A2699
BIBLIOG ECO/UNDEV CULTURE L/A+17C

C44
VAN VALKENBURG S.,"ELEMENTS OF POLITICAL GEOGRAPHY." FRANCE COM/IND INDUS NAT/G SECT RACE/REL...LING TREND GEN/LAWS BIBLIOG 20. PAGE 158 A3215
GEOG DIPLOM COLONIAL

B45
CONOVER H.F.,THE GOVERNMENTS OF THE MAJOR FOREIGN POWERS: A BIBLIOGRAPHY. FRANCE GERMANY ITALY UK USSR CONSTN LOC/G POL/PAR EX/STRUC FORCES ADMIN CT/SYS CIVMIL/REL TOTALISM...POLICY 19/20. PAGE 29 A0598
BIBLIOG NAT/G DIPLOM

B45
CONOVER H.F.,ITALY: ECONOMICS, POLITICS AND MILITARY AFFAIRS, 1940-1945. ITALY ELITES NAT/G POL/PAR EX/STRUC TOP/EX DIPLOM DOMIN CONTROL COERCE WAR CIVMIL/REL EFFICIENCY 20. PAGE 29 A0599
BIBLIOG TOTALISM FORCES

B45
CONOVER H.F.,THE NAZI STATE: WAR CRIMES AND WAR CRIMINALS. GERMANY CULTURE NAT/G SECT FORCES DIPLOM INT/TRADE EDU/PROP...INT/LAW BIOG HIST/WRIT TIME/SEQ 20. PAGE 30 A0600
BIBLIOG WAR CRIME

B45
NELSON M.F.,KOREA AND THE OLD ORDERS IN EASTERN ASIA. ASIA FRANCE KOREA RUSSIA DELIB/GP INT/TRADE DOMIN CONTROL WAR ORD/FREE...POLICY BIBLIOG. PAGE 108 A2218
DIPLOM BAL/PWR ATTIT CONSERVE

B45
UNCIO CONFERENCE LIBRARY,SHORT TITLE CLASSIFIED CATALOG. WOR-45 DOMIN COLONIAL WAR...SOC/WK 20 LEAGUE/NAT UN. PAGE 147 A3006
BIBLIOG DIPLOM INT/ORG INT/LAW

B45
US DEPARTMENT OF STATE,PUBLICATIONS OF THE DEPARTMENT OF STATE: A LIST CUMULATIVE FROM OCTOBER 1, 1929 (PAMPHLET). ASIA EUR+WWI ISLAM L/A+17C USA-45 ADJUD...INT/LAW 20. PAGE 151 A3082
BIBLIOG DIPLOM INT/TRADE

B45
WING D.,SHORT-TITLE CATALOGUE OF BOOKS PRINTED IN THE BRITISH ISLES, AND OF ENGLISH BOOKS PRINTED OVERSEAS; 1641-1700 (3 VOLS.). UK USA-45 LAW DIPLOM ADMIN COLONIAL LEAD ATTIT 17. PAGE 165 A3363
BIBLIOG MOD/EUR NAT/G

C45
NELSON M.F.,"KOREA AND THE OLD ORDERS IN EASTERN ASIA." KOREA WOR-45 DELIB/GP INT/TRADE DOMIN CONTROL WAR ATTIT ORD/FREE CONSERVE...POLICY TREATY. PAGE 108 A2217
BIBLIOG DIPLOM BAL/PWR ASIA

B46
BIBLIOGRAFIIA DISSERTATSII: DOKTORSKIE DISSERTATSII ZA 19411944 (2 VOLS.). COM USSR LAW POL/PAR DIPLOM ADMIN LEAD...PHIL/SCI SOC 20. PAGE 3 A0054
BIBLIOG ACADEM KNOWL MARXIST

C46
GOODRICH L.M.,"CHARTER OF THE UNITED NATIONS: COMMENTARY AND DOCUMENTS." EX/STRUC ADMIN...INT/LAW CON/ANAL BIBLIOG 20 UN. PAGE 54 A1106
CONSTN INT/ORG DIPLOM

B47
HIRSHBERG H.S.,SUBJECT GUIDE TO UNITED STATES GOVERNMENT PUBLICATIONS. USA+45 USA-45 LAW ADMIN ...SOC 20. PAGE 65 A1340
BIBLIOG NAT/G DIPLOM LOC/G

B48
GUIDE TO THE RECORDS IN THE NATIONAL ARCHIVES. ECO/UNDEV ADMIN COLONIAL 16/20. PAGE 3 A0055
BIBLIOG NAT/G L/A+17C DIPLOM

B48
CLYDE P.H.,THE FAR EAST: A HISTORY OF THE IMPACT OF THE WEST ON EASTERN ASIA. CHINA/COM CULTURE INT/TRADE DOMIN COLONIAL WAR PWR...CHARTS BIBLIOG 19/20 CHINJAP. PAGE 27 A0554
DIPLOM ASIA

B48
GRIFFITH E.S.,RESEARCH IN POLITICAL SCIENCE: THE WORK OF PANELS OF RESEARCH COMMITTEE, APSA. WOR+45 WOR-45 COM/IND R+D FORCES ACT/RES WAR...GOV/COMP ANTHOL 20. PAGE 56 A1160
BIBLIOG PHIL/SCI DIPLOM JURID

B48
MORGENTHAL H.J.,POLITICS AMONG NATIONS: THE STRUGGLE FOR POWER AND PEACE. FUT WOR+45 INT/ORG OP/RES PROB/SOLV BAL/PWR CONTROL ATTIT MORAL ...INT/LAW BIBLIOG 20 COLD/WAR. PAGE 104 A2135
DIPLOM PEACE PWR POLICY

B48
US DEPARTMENT OF STATE,FOREIGN AFFAIRS HIGHLIGHTS (NEWSLETTER). COM USA+45 INT/ORG PLAN BAL/PWR WAR PWR...BIBLIOG 20 COLD/WAR NATO UN DEPT/STATE. PAGE 151 A3083
DIPLOM NAT/G POLICY

B49
BORBA DE MORAES R.,MANUAL BIBLIOGRAFICO DE ESTUDOS BRASILEIROS. BRAZIL DIPLOM ADMIN LEAD...SOC 20. PAGE 17 A0336
BIBLIOG L/A+17C NAT/G ECO/UNDEV

B49
BOYD A.,WESTERN UNION: A STUDY OF THE TREND TOWARD EUROPEAN UNITY. FUT REGION NAT/LISM...POLICY IDEA/COMP BIBLIOG 14/20 OEEC ERASMUS/D COUNCL/EUR FULBRGHT/J NATO. PAGE 18 A0363
DIPLOM AGREE TREND INT/ORG

B49
GROB F.,THE RELATIVITY OF WAR AND PEACE: A STUDY IN LAW, HISTORY, AND POLLTICS. WOR+45 WOR-45 LAW DIPLOM DEBATE...CONCPT LING IDEA/COMP BIBLIOG 18/20. PAGE 57 A1167
WAR PEACE INT/LAW STYLE

B49
HEADLAM-MORLEY,BIBLIOGRAPHY IN POLITICS FOR THE HONOUR SCHOOL OF PHILOSOPHY, POLITICS AND ECONOMICS (PAMPHLET). UK CONSTN LABOR MUNIC DIPLOM ADMIN 19/20. PAGE 64 A1305
BIBLIOG NAT/G PHIL/SCI GOV/REL

B49
US SENATE COMM ON FOREIGN REL,A DECADE OF AMERICAN FOREIGN POLICY; BASIC DOCUMENTS, 1941-49. USA+45 USA-45 NAT/G 20 CONGRESS. PAGE 156 A3179
BIBLIOG DIPLOM POLICY

N49
UN DEPARTMENT PUBLIC INF,SELECTED BIBLIOGRAPHY OF THE SPECIALIZED AGENCIES RELATED TO THE UNITED NATIONS (PAMPHLET). USA+45 ROLE 20 UN. PAGE 146 A2996
BIBLIOG INT/ORG EX/STRUC ADMIN

B50
BOHATTA H.,INTERNATIONALE BIBLIOGRAPHIE. WOR+45 LAW CULTURE PRESS. PAGE 16 A0330
BIBLIOG DIPLOM NAT/G WRITING

B50
DUCLOS P.,L'EVOLUTION DES RAPPORTS POLITIQUES DEPUIS 1750 (LIBERTE, INTEGRATION, UNITE). LAW INT/ORG FEDERAL TOTALISM ATTIT PWR...MAJORIT BIBLIOG 18/20 PARLIAMENT EUROPE. PAGE 39 A0792
ORD/FREE DIPLOM NAT/G GOV/COMP

B50
FIGANIERE J.C.,BIBLIOTHECA HISTORICA PORTUGUEZA. BRAZIL PORTUGAL SECT ADMIN. PAGE 45 A0929
BIBLIOG NAT/G DIPLOM COLONIAL

C50
ELLSWORTH P.T.,"INTERNATIONAL ECONOMY." ECO/DEV ECO/UNDEV FINAN LABOR DIPLOM FOR/AID TARIFFS BAL/PAY EQUILIB NAT/LISM OPTIMAL...INT/LAW 20 ILO GATT. PAGE 41 A0843
BIBLIOG INT/TRADE ECO/TAC INT/ORG

C50
NUMELIN R.,"THE BEGINNINGS OF DIPLOMACY." INT/TRADE WAR GP/REL PEACE STRANGE ATTIT...INT/LAW CONCPT BIBLIOG. PAGE 110 A2260
DIPLOM KIN CULTURE LAW

N50
SCHAPIRO J.S.,THE WORLD IN CRISES: POLITICAL AND SOCIAL MOVEMENTS IN THE TWENTIETH CENTURY. USA+45 INT/ORG LABOR PLAN CAP/ISM DIPLOM COLONIAL PEACE TOTALISM ATTIT LAISSEZ...BIBLIOG 20 COLD/WAR. PAGE 128 A2618
NAT/LISM TEC/DEV REV WAR

B51
CATALOGO GENERAL DE LA LIBRERIA ESPANOLA E HISPANOAMERICANA 1901-1930; AUTORES (5 VOLS., 1932-1951). SPAIN COLONIAL GOV/REL...SOC 20. PAGE 3 A0058
BIBLIOG L/A+17C DIPLOM NAT/G

B51
BISSAINTHE M.,DICTIONNAIRE DE BIBLIOGRAPHIE HAITIENNE. HAITI ELITES AGRI LEGIS DIPLOM INT/TRADE WRITING ORD/FREE CATHISM...ART/METH GEOG 19/20 NEGRO TREATY. PAGE 15 A0295
BIBLIOG L/A+17C SOCIETY NAT/G

B51
LEONARD L.L.,INTERNATIONAL ORGANIZATION. WOR+45 WOR-45 EX/STRUC FORCES LEGIS ECO/TAC INT/TRADE COLONIAL ARMS/CONT...SOC/WK GOV/COMP BIBLIOG. PAGE 87 A1778
NAT/G DIPLOM INT/ORG DELIB/GP

B51
US TARIFF COMMISSION,LIST OF PUBLICATIONS OF THE TARIFF COMMISSION (PAMPHLET). USA+45 USA-45 AGRI EXTR/IND INDUS INT/TRADE...STAT 20. PAGE 157 A3207
BIBLIOG TARIFFS NAT/G ADMIN

C51
BEST H.,"THE SOVIET STATE AND ITS INCEPTION." USSR CULTURE INDUS DIPLOM WEALTH...GEOG SOC BIBLIOG 20. PAGE 14 A0281
COM GEN/METH REV MARXISM

C51
GRUNDER G.A.,"THE PHILIPPINES AND THE UNITED STATES." PHILIPPINE S/ASIA USA-45 NAT/G POL/PAR ADMIN SOVEREIGN...TIME/SEQ BIBLIOG 20. PAGE 57 A1181
COLONIAL POLICY DIPLOM ECO/TAC

C51
LEONARD L.L.,"INTERNATIONAL ORGANIZATION (1ST ED.)" WOR+45 FINAN DELIB/GP ECO/TAC GIVE DOMIN SANCTION PEACE BIO/SOC ORD/FREE...INT/LAW 20 UN LEAGUE/NAT. PAGE 87 A1779
BIBLIOG POLICY DIPLOM INT/ORG

B52
ALBERTINI L.,THE ORIGINS OF THE WAR OF 1914 (3 VOLS.). AUSTRIA FRANCE GERMANY MOD/EUR RUSSIA UK PROB/SOLV NEUTRAL PWR...BIBLIOG 19/20. PAGE 5 A0107
WAR DIPLOM FORCES BAL/PWR

B52
DILLON D.R.,LATIN AMERICA, 1935-1949; A SELECTED BIBLIOGRAPHY. LAW EDU/PROP...SOC 20. PAGE 37 A0764
BIBLIOG L/A+17C NAT/G DIPLOM

B52
FIFIELD R.H.,WOODROW WILSON AND THE FAR EAST. ASIA CHIEF BAL/PWR CONFER COLONIAL ARMS/CONT WAR ...TIME/SEQ NAT/COMP BIBLIOG 19/20 WILSON/W LEAGUE/NAT PRESIDENT. PAGE 45 A0926
DIPLOM DELIB/GP INT/ORG

B52
SURANYI-UNGER T.,COMPARATIVE ECONOMIC SYSTEMS. FINAN MARKET DIPLOM PRICE WEALTH...GEOG SOC BIBLIOG METH T 20. PAGE 140 A2865
LAISSEZ PLAN ECO/DEV IDEA/COMP

B52
UNESCO,CURRENT SOCIOLOGY (2 VOLS.). SOCIETY STRATA R+D GP/REL ATTIT PERSON 20 UN. PAGE 147 A3014
BIBLIOG SOC INT/ORG CULTURE

B52
UNESCO,THESES DE SCIENCES SOCIALES: CATALOGUE ANALYTIQUE INTERNATIONAL DE THESES INEDITES DE DOCTORAT, 1940-1950. INT/ORG DIPLOM EDU/PROP...GEOG INT/LAW MGT PSY SOC 20. PAGE 147 A3015
BIBLIOG ACADEM WRITING

B52
US DEPARTMENT OF STATE,RESEARCH ON EASTERN EUROPE (EXCLUDING USSR). EUR+WWI LAW ECO/DEV NAT/G PROB/SOLV DIPLOM ADMIN LEAD MARXISM...TREND 19/20. PAGE 151 A3088
BIBLIOG R+D ACT/RES COM

C52
FIFIELD R.H.,"WOODROW WILSON AND THE FAR EAST." ASIA CHIEF DELIB/GP BAL/PWR CONFER COLONIAL ARMS/CONT WAR...TIME/SEQ NAT/COMP 19/20 WILSON/W LEAGUE/NAT. PAGE 45 A0925
BIBLIOG DIPLOM INT/ORG

C52
STUART G.H.,"AMERICAN DIPLOMATIC AND CONSULAR PRACTICE (2ND ED.)" EUR+WWI MOD/EUR USA-45 DELIB/GP INT/TRADE ADJUD...BIBLIOG 20. PAGE 140 A2855
DIPLOM ADMIN INT/ORG

B53
BRETTON H.L.,STRESEMANN AND THE REVISION OF VERSAILLES: A FIGHT FOR REASON. EUR+WWI GERMANY FORCES BUDGET ARMS/CONT WAR SUPEGO...BIBLIOG 20 TREATY VERSAILLES STRESEMN/G. PAGE 18 A0373
POLICY DIPLOM BIOG

B53
ELAHI K.N.,A GUIDE TO WORKS OF REFERENCE PUBLISHED IN PAKISTAN (PAMPHLET). PAKISTAN DIPLOM COLONIAL LEAD. PAGE 41 A0835
BIBLIOG S/ASIA NAT/G

B53
GREENE K.R.C.,INSTITUTIONS AND INDIVIDUALS: AN ANNOTATED LIST OF DIRECTORIES USEFUL IN INTERNATIONAL ADMINISTRATION. USA+45 NAT/G VOL/ASSN ...INDEX 20. PAGE 56 A1141
BIBLIOG INT/ORG ADMIN DIPLOM

B53
GROPP A.E.,UNION LIST OF LATIN AMERICAN NEWSPAPERS IN LIBRARIES IN THE UNITED STATES. USA+45 DIPLOM ATTIT 20. PAGE 57 A1170
BIBLIOG PRESS L/A+17C NAT/G

B53
KANTOR H.,A BIBLIOGRAPHY OF UNPUBLISHED DOCTORAL DISSERTATIONS AND MASTERS' THESES DEALING WITH GOVTS, POL, INT REL OF LAT AM. L/A+17C INT/ORG POL/PAR ACT/RES OP/RES CONFER ATTIT...INT/LAW PHIL/SCI 20. PAGE 76 A1556
BIBLIOG ACADEM DIPLOM NAT/G

B53
OPPENHEIM L.,INTERNATIONAL LAW: A TREATISE (7TH ED., 2 VOLS.). LAW CONSTN PROB/SOLV INT/TRADE ADJUD AGREE NEUTRAL WAR ORD/FREE SOVEREIGN...BIBLIOG 20 LEAGUE/NAT UN ILO. PAGE 112 A2294
INT/LAW INT/ORG DIPLOM

B53
ORFIELD L.B.,THE GROWTH OF SCANDINAVIAN LAW. DENMARK ICELAND NORWAY SWEDEN LAW DIPLOM...BIBLIOG 9/20. PAGE 112 A2296
JURID CT/SYS NAT/G

B53
STOUT H.M.,BRITISH GOVERNMENT. UK FINAN LOC/G POL/PAR DELIB/GP DIPLOM ADMIN COLONIAL CHOOSE ORD/FREE...JURID BIBLIOG 20 COMMONWLTH. PAGE 139 A2837
NAT/G PARL/PROC CONSTN NEW/LIB

C53
DEUTSCH K.W.,"NATIONALISM AND SOCIAL COMMUNICATION: AN INQUIRY INTO THE FOUNDATIONS OF NATIONALITY." CULTURE STRUCT DIPLOM DOMIN ATTIT ORD/FREE SOVEREIGN...SOC STAT CHARTS IDEA/COMP BIBLIOG. PAGE 36 A0735
NAT/LISM CONCPT PERCEPT STRATA

B54
BUTOW R.J.C.,JAPAN'S DECISION TO SURRENDER. USA-45 USSR CHIEF FORCES DOMIN NUC/PWR...BIBLIOG 20 TREATY CHINJAP. PAGE 22 A0453
ELITES DIPLOM WAR PEACE

B54
SALVEMINI G.,PRELUDE TO WORLD WAR II. ITALY MOD/EUR INT/ORG BAL/PWR EDU/PROP CONTROL TOTALISM...TREND NAT/COMP BIBLIOG 19 HITLER/A LEAGUE/NAT MUSSOLIN/B. PAGE 127 A2597
WAR FASCISM LEAD PWR

B54
SAPIN B.M.,THE ROLE OF THE MILITARY IN AMERICAN FOREIGN POLICY. USA+45 INT/ORG PROB/SOLV DETER NUC/PWR ATTIT PWR...BIBLIOG 20 NATO. PAGE 127 A2602
DIPLOM POLICY CIVMIL/REL NAT/G

B54
STRAUSZ-HUPE R.,INTERNATIONAL RELATIONS IN THE AGE OF THE CONFLICT BETWEEN DEMOCRACY AND DICTATORSHIP (2ND ED.). INT/ORG BAL/PWR EDU/PROP ADMIN WAR PEACE PWR...CONCPT CHARTS BIBLIOG 20 COLD/WAR UN LEAGUE/NAT. PAGE 139 A2846
DIPLOM POPULISM MARXISM

B54
US DEPARTMENT OF STATE,PUBLICATIONS OF THE DEPARTMENT OF STATE, OCTOBER 1,1929 TO JANUARY 1, 1953. AGRI INT/ORG FORCES FOR/AID EDU/PROP ARMS/CONT NUC/PWR ATTIT 20 DEPT/STATE OAS UN NATO. PAGE 151 A3089
BIBLIOG DIPLOM

B54
US SENATE COMM ON FOREIGN REL,REVIEW OF THE UNITED NATIONS CHARTER: A COLLECTION OF DOCUMENTS. LEGIS DIPLOM ADMIN ARMS/CONT WAR REPRESENT SOVEREIGN ...INT/LAW 20 UN. PAGE 156 A3180
BIBLIOG CONSTN INT/ORG DEBATE

C54
BOWIE R.R.,"STUDIES IN FEDERALISM." AGRI FINAN LABOR EX/STRUC FORCES LEGIS DIPLOM INT/TRADE ADJUD ...BIBLIOG 20 EEC. PAGE 17 A0357
FEDERAL EUR+WWI INT/ORG CONSTN

B55
BURR R.N.,DOCUMENTS ON INTER-AMERICAN COOPERATION: VOL. I, 1810-1881; VOL. II, 1881-1948. DELIB/GP BAL/PWR INT/TRADE REPRESENT NAT/LISM PEACE HABITAT ORD/FREE PWR SOVEREIGN...INT/LAW 20 OAS. PAGE 22 A0445
BIBLIOG DIPLOM INT/ORG L/A+17C

B55
CRAIG G.A.,THE POLITICS OF THE PRUSSIAN ARMY 1640-1945. CHRIST-17C EUR+WWI MOD/EUR PRUSSIA STRUCT DIPLOM ADMIN REV WAR...SOC BIBLIOG 17/20. PAGE 32 A0652
FORCES NAT/G ROLE CHIEF

B55
GULICK C.A.,HISTORY AND THEORIES OF WORKING-CLASS MOVEMENTS: A SELECT BIBLIOGRAPHY. EUR+WWI MOD/EUR UK USA-45 INT/ORG. PAGE 58 A1190
BIBLIOG WORKER LABOR ADMIN

B55
JAPAN MOMBUSHO DAIGAKU GAKIYUT,BIBLIOGRAPHY OF THE STUDIES ON LAW AND POLITICS (PAMPHLET). CONSTN INDUS LABOR DIPLOM TAX ADMIN...CRIMLGY INT/LAW 20 CHINJAP. PAGE 73 A1496
BIBLIOG LAW PHIL/SCI

B55
LANDHEER B.,EUROPEAN YEARBOOK, 1955. CONSTN ECO/DEV DIST/IND FINAN DELIB/GP ECO/TAC DETER NUC/PWR ...BIBLIOG 20 EEC. PAGE 84 A1717
EUR+WWI INT/ORG GOV/REL INT/TRADE

B55
MALCLES L.N.,BIBLIOGRAPHICAL SERVICES THROUGHOUT THE WORLD (VOL. 4). WOR+45 INT/ORG VOL/ASSN DIPLOM PRESS WRITING 20 UNESCO. PAGE 93 A1911
BIBLIOG ROUTINE COM/IND

B55
PERKINS B.,THE FIRST RAPPROCHEMENTS: ENGLAND AND THE UNITED STATES, 1795-1805. UK USA-45 ATTIT ...HIST/WRIT BIBLIOG 18/19 MADISON/J WAR/1812. PAGE 115 A2357
DIPLOM COLONIAL WAR

B55
SVARLIEN O.,AN INTRODUCTION TO THE LAW OF NATIONS. SEA AIR INT/ORG NAT/G CHIEF ADMIN AGREE WAR PRIVIL ORD/FREE SOVEREIGN...BIBLIOG 16/20. PAGE 140 A2868
INT/LAW DIPLOM

B55
TROTIER A.H.,DOCTORAL DISSERTATIONS ACCEPTED BY AMERICAN UNIVERSITIES 1954-55. SECT DIPLOM HEALTH ...ART/METH GEOG INT/LAW SOC LING CHARTS 20. PAGE 145 A2968
BIBLIOG ACADEM USA+45 WRITING

B55
UNESCO,BIBLIOGRAPHIC SERVICES THROUGHOUT THE WORLD (VOLS. I AND II). WOR+45 DIPLOM CONTROL 20 UNESCO. PAGE 148 A3018
BIBLIOG INT/ORG COM/IND

B55
VINSON J.C.,THE PARCHMENT PEACE: THE UNITED STATES SENATE AND THE WASHINGTON CONFERENCE, 1921-1922. USA-45 INT/ORG DELIB/GP PLAN ARMS/CONT GOV/REL ISOLAT PEACE ATTIT SOVEREIGN...INT/LAW BIBLIOG 20 SENATE PRESIDENT CONGRESS LEAGUE/NAT CHINJAP. PAGE 159 A3242
POLICY DIPLOM NAT/G LEGIS

B55
WOODWARD E.L.,DOCUMENTS ON BRITISH FOREIGN POLICY 1919-39 (9 VOLS.). EUR+WWI UK WOR-45 INT/ORG WAR 20. PAGE 167 A3392
BIBLIOG DIPLOM

C55
APTER D.E.,"THE GOLD COAST IN TRANSITION." AFR CONSTN LOC/G LEGIS DIPLOM COLONIAL CONTROL GOV/REL ...CHARTS BIBLIOG 20 CMN/WLTH. PAGE 8 A0170
ORD/FREE REPRESENT PARL/PROC NAT/G

B56
BEALE H.K.,THEODORE ROOSEVELT AND THE RISE OF AMERICA TO WORLD POWER. USA-45 BAL/PWR COLONIAL DRIVE PERSON PWR...POLICY BIBLIOG 20 ROOSEVLT/T PRESIDENT. PAGE 12 A0238
DIPLOM CHIEF BIOG

B56
CHANG C.J.,THE MINORITY GROUPS OF YUNN AN AND CHINESE POLITICAL EXPANSION INTO SOUTHEAST ASIA (DOCTORAL THESIS). ASIA CHINA/COM S/ASIA FORCES TEC/DEV DIPLOM EDU/PROP...GEOG BIBLIOG 20. PAGE 26 A0520
GP/REL REGION DOMIN MARXISM

B56
DEGRAS J.,THE COMMUNIST INTERNATIONAL, 1919-1943: DOCUMENTS (3 VOLS.). EX/STRUC...ANTHOL BIBLIOG 20. PAGE 36 A0723
COM DIPLOM POLICY POL/PAR

B56
GUNTHER F.,BUCHERKUNDE ZUR WELTGESCHICHTE VON UNTERGANG DES ROMISCHEN WELTREICHES BIS ZUR GEGENWART. WOR+45 WOR-45 LEAD PERSON. PAGE 58 A1193
BIBLIOG DIPLOM NAT/G TREND

B56
JUAN T.L.,ECONOMIC AND SOCIAL DEVELOPMENT OF MODERN CHINA: A BIBLIOGRAPHICAL GUIDE. ASIA AGRI COM/IND DIST/IND FINAN INDUS DIPLOM...STAT 20. PAGE 75 A1541
BIBLIOG SOC

B56
SIPKOV I.,LEGAL SOURCES AND BIBLIOGRAPHY OF BULGARIA. BULGARIA COM LEGIS WRITING ADJUD CT/SYS ...INT/LAW TREATY 20. PAGE 134 A2736
BIBLIOG LAW TOTALISM MARXISM

B56
SNELL J.L.,THE MEANING OF YALTA: BIG THREE DIPLOMACY AND THE NEW BALANCE OF POWER. EUR+WWI GERMANY USA-45 USSR FORCES PLAN BAL/PWR DIPLOM WAR CHOOSE PEACE...CHARTS BIBLIOG 20 UN CHINJAP ROOSEVLT/F. PAGE 134 A2749
CONFER CHIEF POLICY PROB/SOLV

B56
SPEECKAERT G.P.,INTERNATIONAL INSTITUTIONS AND INTERNATIONAL ORGANIZATIONS. PROF/ORG DELIB/GP KNOWL 19/20. PAGE 136 A2776
BIBLIOG INT/ORG DIPLOM VOL/ASSN

B56
UN HEADQUARTERS LIBRARY,BIBLIOGRAPHY OF INDUSTRIALIZATION IN UNDERDEVELOPED COUNTRIES (BIBLIOGRAPHICAL SERIES NO. 6). WOR+45 R+D ACADEM INT/ORG NAT/G. PAGE 147 A3002
BIBLIOG ECO/UNDEV TEC/DEV

B56
UNITED NATIONS,BIBLIOGRAPHY ON INDUSTRIALIZATION IN UNDER-DEVELOPED COUNTRIES. WOR+45 R+D INT/ORG NAT/G FOR/AID ADMIN LEAD 20 UN. PAGE 149 A3036
BIBLIOG ECO/UNDEV INDUS TEC/DEV

B56
US DEPARTMENT OF STATE,ECONOMIC PROBLEMS OF UNDERDEVELOPED AREAS (PAMPHLET). AFR ASIA ISLAM
BIBLIOG ECO/UNDEV

L/A+17C AGRI FINAN INDUS INT/ORG LABOR INT/TRADE ...PSY SOC 20. PAGE 151 A3090 TEC/DEV R+D

B56
VON BECKERATH E.,HANDWORTERBUCH DER SOCIALWISSENSCHAFTEN (II VOLS.). EUR+WWI GERMANY POL/PAR WORKER DIPLOM LEAD CHOOSE SUFF WEALTH...SOC 20. PAGE 159 A3249 BIBLIOG INT/TRADE NAT/G ECO/DEV

B56
VON HARPE W.,DIE SOWJETUNION FINNLAND UND SKANDANAVIEN, 1945-1955. EUR+WWI FINLAND GERMANY USSR WAR INGP/REL ORD/FREE SOVEREIGN MARXISM ...POLICY GOV/COMP BIBLIOG 20 STALIN/J. PAGE 160 A3252 DIPLOM COM NEUTRAL BAL/PWR

B56
WATKINS J.T.,GENERAL INTERNATIONAL ORGANIZATION: A SOURCE BOOK. 19/20 LEAGUE/NAT UN. PAGE 162 A3292 BIBLIOG DIPLOM INT/ORG WRITING

B56
WILSON P.,GOVERNMENT AND POLITICS OF INDIA AND PAKISTAN: 1885-1955; A BIBLIOGRAPHY OF WORKS IN WESTERN LANGUAGES. INDIA PAKISTAN CONSTN LOC/G POL/PAR FORCES DIPLOM ADMIN WAR CHOOSE...BIOG CON/ANAL 19/20. PAGE 165 A3361 BIBLIOG COLONIAL NAT/G S/ASIA

C56
DUPUY R.E.,"MILITARY HERITAGE OF AMERICA." USA+45 USA-45 TEC/DEV DIPLOM ROUTINE...POLICY TREND CHARTS IDEA/COMP BIBLIOG COLD/WAR. PAGE 39 A0804 FORCES WAR CONCPT

C56
VAGTS A.,"DEFENSE AND DIPLOMACY: THE SOLDIER AND THE CONDUCT OF FOREIGN RELATIONS." OP/RES CONFER DETER WAR PEACE RESPECT...POLICY DECISION CONCPT BIBLIOG 17/20. PAGE 158 A3209 DIPLOM FORCES HIST/WRIT

B57
BEERS H.P.,THE FRENCH IN NORTH AMERICA. FRANCE USA-45...TIME/SEQ BIBLIOG. PAGE 12 A0247 HIST/WRIT DIPLOM BIOG WRITING

B57
BISHOP O.B.,PUBLICATIONS OF THE GOVERNMENTS OF NOVA SCOTIA, PRINCE EDWARD ISLAND, NEW BRUNSWICK 1758-1952. CANADA UK ADMIN COLONIAL LEAD...POLICY 18/20. PAGE 14 A0293 BIBLIOG NAT/G DIPLOM

B57
CARIBBEAN COMMISSION,A CATALOGUE OF CARIBBEAN COMMISSION PUBLICATIONS (PAMPHLET). WEST/IND CULTURE ECO/UNDEV LOC/G DIPLOM SOC. PAGE 24 A0483 BIBLIOG L/A+17C INT/ORG NAT/G

B57
HALD M.,A SELECTED BIBLIOGRAPHY ON ECONOMIC DEVELOPMENT AND FOREIGN AID. INT/ORG PROB/SOLV ...SOC 20. PAGE 59 A1222 BIBLIOG ECO/UNDEV TEC/DEV FOR/AID

B57
HODGKIN T.,NATIONALISM IN COLONIAL AFRICA. STRATA STRUCT MUNIC NAT/G POL/PAR LEGIS ATTIT SOVEREIGN ...POLICY TREND BIBLIOG 20. PAGE 66 A1351 AFR COLONIAL NAT/LISM DIPLOM

B57
NEUMANN F.,THE DEMOCRATIC AND THE AUTHORITARIAN STATE: ESSAYS IN POLITICAL AND LEGAL THEORY. USA+45 USA-45 CONTROL REV GOV/REL PEACE ALL/IDEOS ...INT/LAW CONCPT GEN/LAWS BIBLIOG 20. PAGE 108 A2221 DOMIN NAT/G ORD/FREE POLICY

B57
UNESCO,A REGISTER OF LEGAL DOCUMENTATION IN THE WORLD (2ND ED.). CT/SYS...JURID IDEA/COMP METH/COMP NAT/COMP 20. PAGE 148 A3019 BIBLIOG LAW INT/LAW CONSTN

B57
UNESCO,WORLD LIST OF SOCIAL SCIENCE PERIODICALS (2ND ED.). WOR+45 20 UN. PAGE 148 A3020 BIBLIOG SOC INT/ORG

B57
WILSON P.,SOUTH ASIA; A SELECTED BIBLIOGRAPHY ON INDIA, PAKISTAN, CEYLON (PAMPHLET). CEYLON INDIA PAKISTAN LAW ECO/UNDEV PLAN DIPLOM 20. PAGE 165 A3362 BIBLIOG S/ASIA CULTURE NAT/G

C57
BEERS H.P.,"THE FRENCH IN NORTH AFRICA: A BIBLIOGRAPHICAL GUIDE TO FRENCH ARCHIVES, REPRODUCTIONS, AND RESEARCH MISSIONS." AFR CANADA FRANCE USA-45 NAT/LISM ATTIT 20. PAGE 12 A0248 BIBLIOG DIPLOM COLONIAL

C57
TANG P.S.H.,"COMMUNIST CHINA TODAY: DOMESTIC AND FOREIGN POLICIES." CHINA/COM COM S/ASIA USSR STRATA FORCES DIPLOM EDU/PROP COERCE GOV/REL...POLICY MAJORIT BIBLIOG 20. PAGE 141 A2886 POL/PAR LEAD ADMIN CONSTN

B58
ALEXANDROWICZ,A BIBLIOGRAPHY OF INDIAN LAW. INDIA S/ASIA CONSTN CT/SYS...INT/LAW 19/20. PAGE 6 A0113 BIBLIOG LAW ADJUD JURID

B58
DEUTSCHE GESCHAFT VOLKERRECHT,DIE VOLKERRECHTLICHEN DISSERTATIONEN AN DEN WESTDEUTSCHEN UNIVERSITATEN, 1945-1957. GERMANY/W NAT/G DIPLOM ADJUD CT/SYS ...POLICY 20. PAGE 37 A0748 BIBLIOG INT/LAW ACADEM JURID

B58
HUNT B.I.,BIPARTISANSHIP: A CASE STUDY OF THE FOREIGN ASSISTANCE PROGRAM, 1947-56 (DOCTORAL THESIS). USA+45 INT/ORG CONSULT LEGIS TEC/DEV ...BIBLIOG PRESIDENT TREATY NATO TRUMAN/HS EISNHWR/DD CONGRESS. PAGE 69 A1418 FOR/AID POL/PAR GP/REL DIPLOM

B58
KENNAN G.F.,THE DECISION TO INTERVENE: SOVIET-AMERICAN RELATIONS, 1917-1920 (VOL. II). CZECHOSLVK EUR+WWI USA-45 USSR ELITES NAT/G FORCES PROB/SOLV REV WAR TOTALISM PWR...CHARTS BIBLIOG 20 TREATY PRESIDENT CHINJAP. PAGE 78 A1588 DIPLOM POLICY ATTIT

B58
MASON H.L.,TOYNBEE'S APPROACH TO WORLD POLITICS. AFR USA+45 USSR LAW WAR NAT/LISM ALL/IDEOS...HUM BIBLIOG. PAGE 95 A1957 DIPLOM CONCPT PHIL/SCI SECT

B58
MEYRIAT J.,ETUDES DES BIBLIOGRAPHIES COURANTES DES PUBLICATIONS OFFICIELLES NATIONALES. WOR+45 DIPLOM CONTROL 20 UNESCO. PAGE 100 A2056 BIBLIOG COM/IND NAT/G

B58
NEAL F.W.,TITOISM IN ACTION. COM YUGOSLAVIA AGRI LOC/G DIPLOM TOTALISM...BIBLIOG 20 TITO/MARSH. PAGE 107 A2206 MARXISM POL/PAR CHIEF ADMIN

B58
PALYI M.,MANAGED MONEY AT THE CROSSROADS: THE EUROPEAN EXPERIENCE. WOR+45 WOR-45 TEC/DEV DIPLOM INT/TRADE DEMAND WEALTH...CHARTS BIBLIOG 19/20 EUROPE GOLD/STAND SILVER. PAGE 113 A2324 FINAN ECO/TAC ECO/DEV PRODUC

B58
PAN AMERICAN UNION,REPERTORIO DE PUBLICACIONES PERIODICAS ACTUALES LATINO-AMERICANAS. CULTURE ECO/UNDEV ADMIN LEAD GOV/REL 20 OAS. PAGE 113 A2326 BIBLIOG L/A+17C NAT/G DIPLOM

B58
SCHOEDER P.W.,THE AXIS ALLIANCE AND JAPANESE-AMERICAN RELATIONS 1941. ASIA GERMANY UK USA-45 PEACE ATTIT...POLICY BIBLIOG 20 CHINJAP TREATY. PAGE 129 A2641 AGREE DIPLOM WAR

B58
SEYID MUHAMMAD V.A.,THE LEGAL FRAMEWORK OF WORLD TRADE. WOR+45 INT/ORG DIPLOM CONTROL...BIBLIOG 20 TREATY UN IMF GATT. PAGE 131 A2689 INT/LAW VOL/ASSN INT/TRADE TARIFFS

B58
UNIV KARACHI INST PUB BUS ADM,PUBLICATIONS OF THE GOVERNMENT OF PAKISTAN 1947-1957. PAKISTAN S/ASIA DIPLOM COLONIAL ATTIT 20. PAGE 149 A3040 BIBLIOG NAT/G POLICY

B58
US DEPARTMENT OF STATE,PUBLICATIONS OF THE DEPARTMENT OF STATE, JANUARY 1,1953 TO DECEMBER 31, 1957. AGRI INT/ORG FORCES FOR/AID EDU/PROP ARMS/CONT NUC/PWR ATTIT 20 DEPT/STATE OAS UN NATO. PAGE 151 A3092 BIBLIOG DIPLOM

B58
YUAN TUNG-LI,CHINA IN WESTERN LITERATURE. SECT DIPLOM...ART/METH GEOG JURID SOC BIOG CON/ANAL. PAGE 169 A3440 BIBLIOG ASIA CULTURE HUM

L58
HYVARINEN R.,"MONISTIC AND PLURALISTIC INTERPRETATIONS IN THE STUDY OF INTERNATIONAL POLITICS." COLONIAL REGION RACE/REL DISCRIM TOTALISM SOVEREIGN...INT/LAW PHIL/SCI CONCPT BIBLIOG 20. PAGE 70 A1429 DIPLOM PLURISM INT/ORG METH

C58
BLANCHARD W.,"THAILAND." THAILAND CULTURE AGRI FINAN INDUS FAM LABOR INT/TRADE ATTIT...GEOG HEAL SOC BIBLIOG 20. PAGE 15 A0307 NAT/G DIPLOM ECO/UNDEV S/ASIA

C58
CARTER G.M.,"THE POLITICS OF INEQUALITY: SOUTH AFRICA SINCE 1948." SOUTH/AFR CONSTN DIPLOM EDU/PROP REPRESENT DISCRIM ATTIT...POLICY PREDICT CHARTS BIBLIOG 20. PAGE 25 A0504 RACE/REL POL/PAR CHOOSE DOMIN

C58
FIFIELD R.H.,"THE DIPLOMACY OF SOUTHEAST ASIA: 1945-1958." INT/ORG NAT/G COLONIAL REGION...CHARTS BIBLIOG 20 UN. PAGE 45 A0927 S/ASIA DIPLOM NAT/LISM

C58
GOLAY J.F.,"THE FOUNDING OF THE FEDERAL REPUBLIC OF GERMANY." GERMANY/W CONSTN EX/STRUC DIPLOM ADMIN CHOOSE...DECISION BIBLIOG 20. PAGE 53 A1088 FEDERAL NAT/G PARL/PROC POL/PAR

C58
RAJAN M.S.,"UNITED NATIONS AND DOMESTIC JURISDICTION." WOR+45 WOR-45 PARL/PROC...IDEA/COMP BIBLIOG 20 UN. PAGE 119 A2434 INT/LAW DIPLOM CONSTN INT/ORG

C58
WILDING N.,"AN ENCYCLOPEDIA OF PARLIAMENT." UK LAW CONSTN CHIEF PROB/SOLV DIPLOM DEBATE WAR INGP/REL PARL/PROC POL/PAR

PRIVIL...BIBLIOG DICTIONARY 13/20 CMN/WLTH PARLIAMENT. PAGE 164 A3349
NAT/G ADMIN

B59
BUNDESMIN FUR VERTRIEBENE,ZEITTAFEL DER VORGESCHICHTE UND DES ABLAUFS DER VERTREIBUNG SOWIE DER UNTERBRINGUNG UND EINGLIEDERUNG DER (2 VOLS.). GERMANY/E GERMANY/W NAT/G PROVS PROB/SOLV DIPLOM PARL/PROC ATTIT...BIBLIOG SOC/INTEG 20 MIGRATION PARLIAMENT. PAGE 21 A0431
JURID GP/REL INT/LAW

B59
KARUNAKARAN K.P.,INDIA IN WORLD AFFAIRS, 1952-1958 (VOL. II). INDIA ECO/UNDEV SECT FOR/AID INT/TRADE ADJUD NEUTRAL REV WAR DISCRIM ORD/FREE MARXISM ...BIBLIOG 20. PAGE 77 A1569
DIPLOM INT/ORG S/ASIA COLONIAL

B59
LINK R.G.,ENGLISH THEORIES OF ECONOMIC FLUCTUATIONS: 1815-1848. FRANCE UK AGRI WORKER DIPLOM PRICE TASK WAR DEMAND PRODUC...POLICY BIBLIOG 18 MALTHUS MILL/JS WILSON/J. PAGE 89 A1826
IDEA/COMP ECO/DEV WEALTH EQUILIB

B59
LOPEZ M.M.,CATALOGOS DE PUBLICACIONES PERIODICAS MEXICANAS. L/A+17C CULTURE NAT/G DIPLOM 20 MEXIC/AMER. PAGE 91 A1861
BIBLIOG PRESS CON/ANAL

B59
MAYER A.J.,POLITICAL ORIGINS OF THE NEW DIPLOMACY, 1917-1918. EUR+WWI MOD/EUR USA-45 WAR PWR...POLICY INT/LAW BIBLIOG. PAGE 97 A1983
TREND DIPLOM

B59
OKINSHEVICH L.A.,LATIN AMERICA IN SOVIET WRITINGS, 1945-1958: A BIBLIOGRAPHY. USSR LAW ECO/UNDEV LABOR DIPLOM EDU/PROP REV...GEOG SOC 20. PAGE 111 A2287
BIBLIOG WRITING COM L/A+17C

B59
PANAMERICAN UNION,PUBLICATIONS: PAU AND OFFICIAL RECORDS OF THE OAS, IN ENGLISH, SPANISH, PORTUGUESE, AND FRENCH, 1958-59. NAT/G ATTIT...SOC 20 OAS. PAGE 113 A2328
BIBLIOG L/A+17C INT/LAW DIPLOM

B59
PHADINIS U.,DOCUMENTS ON ASIAN AFFAIRS: A SELECT BIBLIOGRAPHY. ASIA...SOC 20. PAGE 116 A2372
BIBLIOG NAT/G DIPLOM

B59
SHANNON D.A.,THE DECLINE OF AMERICAN COMMUNISM; A HISTORY OF THE COMMUNIST PARTY OF THE UNITED STATES SINCE 1945. USA+45 LAW SOCIETY LABOR NAT/G WORKER DIPLOM EDU/PROP LEAD...POLICY BIBLIOG 20 KHRUSH/N NEGRO AFL/CIO COLD/WAR COM/PARTY. PAGE 131 A2692
MARXISM POL/PAR ATTIT POPULISM

B59
STOVEL J.A.,CANADA IN THE WORLD ECONOMY. CANADA PRICE DEMAND...STAT CHARTS BIBLIOG 20 VINER/J. PAGE 139 A2838
INT/TRADE BAL/PAY FINAN ECO/TAC

B59
THOMAS D.H.,GUIDE TO THE DIPLOMATIC ARCHIVES OF WESTERN EUROPE. EUR+WWI ELITES INT/ORG NAT/G BAL/PWR INT/TRADE PEACE. PAGE 143 A2921
BIBLIOG DIPLOM CONFER

B59
UNION OF INTERNATIONAL ASSNS,DIRECTORY OF PERIODICALS PUBLISHED BY INTERNATIONAL ORGANIZATIONS (2ND ED.)....INDEX 20. PAGE 148 A3027
BIBLIOG INT/ORG DIPLOM VOL/ASSN

B59
YOUNG J.,CHECKLIST OF MICROFILM REPRODUCTIONS OF SELECTED ARCHIVES OF THE JAPANESE ARMY, NAVY, AND OTHER GOVT AGENCIES, 1868-1945. DELIB/GP LEGIS DIPLOM EDU/PROP CIVMIL/REL 19/20 CHINJAP. PAGE 169 A3436
BIBLIOG ASIA FORCES WAR

C59
KULSKI W.W.,"PEACEFUL COEXISTENCE." USSR ECO/UNDEV INT/ORG POL/PAR EDU/PROP COLONIAL CONTROL REV NAT/LISM PEACE PWR MARXISM...BIBLIOG 20. PAGE 83 A1692
COM DIPLOM DOMIN

B60
BYRD E.M. JR.,TREATIES AND EXECUTIVE AGREEMENTS IN THE UNITED STATES: THEIR SEPARATE ROLES AND LIMITATIONS. USA+45 USA-45 EX/STRUC TARIFFS CT/SYS GOV/REL FEDERAL...IDEA/COMP BIBLIOG SUPREME/CT SENATE CONGRESS. PAGE 23 A0461
CHIEF INT/LAW DIPLOM

B60
CENTRAL ASIAN RESEARCH CENTRE,RUSSIA LOOKS AT AFRICA (PAMPHLET). AFR USSR COLONIAL RACE/REL...HUM 19/20 STALIN/J. PAGE 25 A0511
BIBLIOG MARXISM TREND DIPLOM

B60
DE HERRERA C.D.,LISTA BIBLIOGRAFICA DE LOS TRABAJOS DE GRADUACION Y TESIS PRESENTADOS EN LA UNIVERSIDAD, 1939-1960. PANAMA DIPLOM LEAD...SOC 20. PAGE 35 A0703
BIBLIOG L/A+17C NAT/G ACADEM

B60
EMERSON R.,FROM EMPIRE TO NATION: THE RISE TO SELF-ASSERTION OF ASIAN AND AFRICAN PEOPLES. S/ASIA CULTURE NAT/G SECT DIPLOM ATTIT SOVEREIGN MARXISM ...POLICY BIBLIOG 19/20. PAGE 41 A0847
NAT/LISM COLONIAL AFR ASIA

B60
ENGELMAN F.L.,THE PEACE OF CHRISTMAS EVE. UK USA-45 NAT/G FORCES CONFER PERS/REL...AUD/VIS BIBLIOG 19 TREATY. PAGE 42 A0853
WAR PEACE DIPLOM PERSON

B60
FEIS H.,BETWEEN WAR AND PEACE: THE POTSDAM CONFERENCE. EUR+WWI NAT/G DELIB/GP PROB/SOLV REPAR WAR CIVMIL/REL...BIBLIOG 20. PAGE 45 A0911
DIPLOM CONFER BAL/PWR

B60
FLORES R.H.,CATALOGO DE TESIS DOCTORALES DE LAS FACULTADES DE LA UNIVERSIDAD DE EL SALVADOR. EL/SALVADR LAW DIPLOM ADMIN LEAD GOV/REL...SOC 19/20. PAGE 47 A0954
BIBLIOG ACADEM L/A+17C NAT/G

B60
HARVARD LAW SCHOOL LIBRARY,CURRENT LEGAL BIBLIOGRAPHY. USA+45 CONSTN LEGIS ADJUD CT/SYS POLICY. PAGE 62 A1279
BIBLIOG JURID LAW INT/LAW

B60
HEYSE T.,PROBLEMS FONCIERS ET REGIME DES TERRES (ASPECTS ECONOMIQUES, JURIDIQUES ET SOCIAUX). AFR CONGO/BRAZ INT/ORG DIPLOM SOVEREIGN...GEOG TREATY 20. PAGE 64 A1325
BIBLIOG AGRI ECO/UNDEV LEGIS

B60
MC CLELLAN G.S.,INDIA. CHINA/COM INDIA CONSTN ELITES STRATA AGRI POL/PAR FOR/AID ARMS/CONT REV MARXISM...CENSUS BIBLIOG 20 COLD/WAR GANDHI/M NEHRU/J. PAGE 97 A1990
DIPLOM NAT/G SOCIETY ECO/UNDEV

B60
PHILLIPS J.F.V.,KWAME NKRUMAH AND THE FUTURE OF AFRICA. FUT GHANA ISLAM ECO/UNDEV CHIEF DIPLOM COLONIAL RACE/REL NAT/LISM...TREND IDEA/COMP BIBLIOG 20 NKRUMAH/K. PAGE 116 A2376
BIOG LEAD SOVEREIGN AFR

B60
SOBEL R.,THE ORIGINS OF INTERVENTIONISM: THE UNITED STATES AND THE RUSSO-FINNISH WAR. FINLAND USA-45 USSR LEGIS ATTIT RIGID/FLEX...BIBLIOG 20 INTERVENT. PAGE 135 A2755
DIPLOM WAR PROB/SOLV NEUTRAL

B60
SZTARAY Z.,BIBLIOGRAPHY ON HUNGARY. HUNGARY MOD/EUR CULTURE INDUS SECT DIPLOM REV...ART/METH SOC LING 18/20. PAGE 141 A2879
BIBLIOG NAT/G COM MARXISM

B60
THEOBOLD R.,THE NEW NATIONS OF WEST AFRICA. GHANA NIGERIA CULTURE INT/ORG ECO/TAC FOR/AID COLONIAL RACE/REL POPULISM...ANTHOL BIBLIOG 20 UN. PAGE 143 A2916
AFR SOVEREIGN ECO/UNDEV DIPLOM

B60
TURNER G.B.,NATIONAL SECURITY IN THE NUCLEAR AGE. KOREA USA+45 PLAN DIPLOM ARMS/CONT DETER WAR WEAPON ...BIBLIOG 20 COLD/WAR NATO. PAGE 146 A2982
NAT/G POLICY FORCES NUC/PWR

B60
VAN HOOGSTRATE D.J.,AMERICAN FOREIGN POLICY: REALISTS AND IDEALISTS: A CATHOLIC INTERPRETATION. BAL/PWR FOR/AID ARMS/CONT GOV/REL PEACE LOVE MORAL SOVEREIGN CATHISM...BIBLIOG 20. PAGE 158 A3213
CATH DIPLOM POLICY IDEA/COMP

C60
COX R.H.,"LOCKE ON WAR AND PEACE." UK DIPLOM DOMIN PWR...BIOG IDEA/COMP BIBLIOG 18. PAGE 32 A0646
CONCPT NAT/G PEACE WAR

C60
FITZSIMMONS T.,"USSR: ITS PEOPLE, ITS SOCIETY, ITS CULTURE." USSR FAM SECT DIPLOM EDU/PROP ADMIN RACE/REL ATTIT...POLICY CHARTS BIBLIOG 20. PAGE 46 A0944
CULTURE STRUCT SOCIETY COM

C60
WRIGGINS W.H.,"CEYLON: DILEMMAS OF A NEW NATION." ASIA CEYLON CONSTN STRUCT POL/PAR SECT FORCES DIPLOM GOV/REL NAT/LISM...CHARTS BIBLIOG 20. PAGE 167 A3399
PROB/SOLV NAT/G ECO/UNDEV

N60
ERDMAN P.E.,COMMON MARKETS AND FREE TRADE AREAS (PAMPHLET). USA+45 MARKET INT/ORG TEC/DEV DIPLOM UTIL...CON/ANAL CHARTS BIBLIOG 20 EEC OEEC. PAGE 42 A0859
TREND PROB/SOLV INT/TRADE ECO/DEV

B61
ANSPRENGER F.,POLITIK IM SCHWARZEN AFRIKA. FRANCE NAT/G DIPLOM REGION REV NAT/LISM...CHARTS BIBLIOG 19/20. PAGE 8 A0164
AFR COLONIAL SOVEREIGN

B61
BRENNAN D.G.,ARMS CONTROL, DISARMAMENT, AND NATIONAL SECURITY. WOR+45 NAT/G FORCES CREATE PROB/SOLV PARTIC WAR PEACE...DECISION INT/LAW ANTHOL BIBLIOG 20. PAGE 18 A0372
ARMS/CONT ORD/FREE DIPLOM POLICY

B61
COLLISON R.L.,BIBLIOGRAPHICAL SERVICES THROUGHOUT THE WORLD: 1950-59 (VOL. 9). WOR+45 INT/ORG EDU/PROP PRESS WRITING ADMIN CENTRAL 20 UNESCO. PAGE 28 A0568
BIBLIOG COM/IND DIPLOM

B61
CONOVER H.F.,SERIALS FOR AFRICAN STUDIES. ECO/UNDEV DIPLOM LEAD NAT/LISM ATTIT...SOC 20. PAGE 30 A0604
BIBLIOG AFR NAT/G

B61
DEAN V.M.,BUILDERS OF EMERGING NATIONS. WOR+45
NAT/G

ECO/UNDEV ECO/TAC NEUTRAL TOTALISM ORD/FREE PWR ...BIOG AUD/VIS IDEA/COMP BIBLIOG 20 COLD/WAR. PAGE 35 A0719 — CHIEF POLICY DIPLOM

B61
DIMOCK M.E.,BUSINESS AND GOVERNMENT (4TH ED.). AGRI FINAN OP/RES PLAN BUDGET DIPLOM LOBBY NUC/PWR NEW/LIB SOCISM...POLICY BIBLIOG 20. PAGE 37 A0765 — NAT/G INDUS LABOR ECO/TAC

B61
GRASES P.,ESTUDIOS BIBLIOGRAFICOS. VENEZUELA...SOC 20. PAGE 55 A1130 — BIBLIOG NAT/G DIPLOM L/A+17C

B61
GURTOO D.H.N.,INDIA'S BALANCE OF PAYMENTS (1920-1960). INDIA FINAN DIPLOM FOR/AID INT/TRADE PRICE COLONIAL...CHARTS BIBLIOG 20. PAGE 58 A1197 — BAL/PAY STAT ECO/TAC ECO/UNDEV

B61
HARRISON J.P.,GUIDE TO MATERIALS ON LATIN AMERICA IN THE NATIONAL ARCHIVES (2 VOLS.). USA+45 ECO/UNDEV FINAN LOC/G FORCES 20. PAGE 62 A1271 — BIBLIOG L/A+17C NAT/G DIPLOM

B61
HISTORICAL RESEARCH INSTITUTE,A SHORT BIBLIOGRAPHY OF INDO-MUSLIM HISTORY. INDIA S/ASIA DIPLOM EDU/PROP COLONIAL LEAD NAT/LISM ATTIT...BIOG 19/20. PAGE 65 A1343 — BIBLIOG NAT/G SECT POL/PAR

B61
LANDSKROY W.A.,OFFICIAL SERIAL PUBLICATIONS RELATING TO ECONOMIC DEVELOPMENT IN AFRICA SOUTH OF THE SAHARA (PAMPHLET). AFR UK R+D ACT/RES 20 UN. PAGE 84 A1720 — BIBLIOG ECO/UNDEV COLONIAL INT/ORG

B61
LEGISLATIVE REFERENCE SERVICE,WORLD COMMUNIST MOVEMENT: SELECTIVE CHRONOLOGY, 1818-1957 (4 VOLS.). COM WOR+45 WOR-45 POL/PAR LEAD 19/20. PAGE 86 A1766 — BIBLIOG DIPLOM TIME/SEQ MARXISM

B61
LERCHE C.O. JR.,FOREIGN POLICY OF THE AMERICAN PEOPLE (REV. ED.). USA+45 USSR FORCES TEC/DEV EDU/PROP WAR PRODUC ORD/FREE MARXISM...POLICY TREND BIBLIOG 20 COLD/WAR. PAGE 87 A1781 — DECISION PLAN PEACE DIPLOM

B61
NEWMAN R.P.,RECOGNITION OF COMMUNIST CHINA? A STUDY IN ARGUMENT. CHINA/COM NAT/G PROB/SOLV RATIONAL ...INT/LAW LOG IDEA/COMP BIBLIOG 20. PAGE 108 A2226 — MARXISM ATTIT DIPLOM POLICY

B61
NOLLAU G.,INTERNATIONAL COMMUNISM AND WORLD REVOLUTION; HISTORY AND METHODS (TRANS. BY VICTOR ANDERSEN). COM WORKER DIPLOM CONFER INGP/REL ...CONCPT BIBLIOG 20 STALIN/J LENIN/VI COMINTERN COMINFORM WORLD/CONG. PAGE 110 A2249 — MARXISM POL/PAR INT/ORG REV

B61
PEASLEE A.J.,INTERNATIONAL GOVERNMENTAL ORGANIZATIONS (2 VOLS.). CONSTN VOL/ASSN DIPLOM ...GP/COMP 20 UN OAS EEC EFTA ECSC. PAGE 114 A2345 — BIBLIOG INT/ORG INDEX LAW

B61
SOCIAL SCIENCE SERIALS IN SPECIAL LIBRARIES IN THE NEW YORK AREA; A SELECTED LIST. R+D ACADEM EDU/PROP WRITING...PSY 20. PAGE 119 A2448 — BIBLIOG DIPLOM SOC

B61
ROBINS D.B.,EVOLVING UNITED STATES POLICIES TOWARD THE EMERGING NATIONS OF ASIA AND AFRICA (PAMPHLET). ISLAM ECO/UNDEV INT/ORG CONSULT CREATE PLAN TEC/DEV FOR/AID CONFER ALL/VALS 20 KENNEDY/JF EISNHWR/DD UN AID. PAGE 122 A2501 — AFR S/ASIA DIPLOM BIBLIOG

B61
ROBINSON M.E.,EDUCATION FOR SOCIAL CHANGE: ESTABLISHING INSTITUTES OF PUBLIC AND BUSINESS ADMINISTRATION ABROAD (PAMPHLET). WOR+45 SOCIETY ACADEM CONFER INGP/REL ROLE...SOC CHARTS BIBLIOG 20 ICA. PAGE 122 A2506 — FOR/AID EDU/PROP MGT ADJUST

B61
ROSENAU J.N.,INTERNATIONAL POLITICS AND FOREIGN POLICY: A READER IN RESEARCH AND THEORY. ELITES ATTIT SOVEREIGN...DECISION CHARTS HYPO/EXP GAME SIMUL ANTHOL BIBLIOG METH 20. PAGE 124 A2531 — ACT/RES DIPLOM CONCPT POLICY

B61
ROSENAU J.N.,PUBLIC OPINION AND FOREIGN POLICY; AN OPERATIONAL FORMULA. USA+45 COM/IND OP/RES EDU/PROP LOBBY CROWD...CON/ANAL BIBLIOG 20. PAGE 124 A2532 — ATTIT PRESS DIPLOM

B61
SCHMIDT H.,VERTEIDIGUNG ODER VERGELTUNG. COM CUBA GERMANY/W USSR FORCES DIPLOM ARMS/CONT DETER NUC/PWR...POLICY CHARTS HYPO/EXP SIMUL BIBLIOG 20 NATO COLD/WAR. PAGE 128 A2630 — PLAN WAR BAL/PWR ORD/FREE

B61
SCHNAPPER B.,LA POLITIQUE ET LE COMMERCE FRANCAIS DANS LE GOLFE DE GUINEE DE 1838 A 1871. FRANCE GUINEA UK SEA EXTR/IND NAT/G DELIB/GP LEGIS ADMIN ORD/FREE...POLICY GEOG CENSUS CHARTS BIBLIOG 19. PAGE 129 A2636 — COLONIAL INT/TRADE DOMIN AFR

B61
SOKOL A.E.,SEAPOWER IN THE NUCLEAR AGE. USA+45 USSR DIST/IND FORCES INT/TRADE DETER WAR...POLICY NAT/COMP BIBLIOG COLD/WAR. PAGE 135 A2763 — SEA PWR WEAPON NUC/PWR

B61
SSU-YU T.,JAPANESE STUDIES ON JAPAN AND THE FAR EAST: A SHORT BIOGRAPHICAL AND BIBLIOGRAPHICAL INTRODUCTION. ASIA CULTURE ECO/UNDEV NAT/G DIPLOM 20 CHINJAP. PAGE 136 A2795 — BIBLIOG SOC

B61
STARK H.,SOCIAL AND ECONOMIC FRONTIERS IN LATIN AMERICA (2ND ED.). CUBA FUT CULTURE AGRI INDUS ECO/TAC PRODUC ATTIT MARXISM...NAT/COMP BIBLIOG T 20. PAGE 137 A2807 — L/A+17C SOCIETY DIPLOM ECO/UNDEV

B61
UAR MINISTRY OF CULTURE,A BIBLIOGRAPHICAL LIST OF AL MAGHRIB. ALGERIA ISLAM MOROCCO UAR SECT INT/TRADE COLONIAL 19/20 TUNIS. PAGE 146 A2987 — BIBLIOG DIPLOM GEOG

B61
UAR MINISTRY OF CULTURE,A BIBLIOGRAPHICAL LIST OF LIBYA. ISLAM LIBYA DIPLOM COLONIAL REV WAR 19/20. PAGE 146 A2988 — BIBLIOG GEOG SECT NAT/LISM

B61
UAR MINISTRY OF CULTURE,A BIBLIOGRAPHICAL LIST OF TUNISIA. ISLAM CULTURE NAT/G EDU/PROP COLONIAL ...GEOG 19/20 TUNIS. PAGE 146 A2989 — BIBLIOG DIPLOM SECT

B61
US SENATE COMM GOVT OPERATIONS,ORGANIZING FOR NATIONAL SECURITY. COM USA+45 BUDGET DIPLOM DETER NUC/PWR WAR WEAPON ORD/FREE...BIBLIOG 20 COLD/WAR. PAGE 156 A3172 — POLICY PLAN FORCES COERCE

B61
WINTER R.C.,BLUEPRINTS FOR INDEPENDENCE. WOR+45 INT/ORG DIPLOM COLONIAL CONTROL REV WAR PWR ...BIBLIOG 20 UN. PAGE 165 A3367 — NAT/G ECO/UNDEV SOVEREIGN CONSTN

B61
YUAN TUNG-LI,A GUIDE TO DOCTORAL DISSERTATIONS BY CHINESE STUDENTS IN AMERICA, 1905-1960. ASIA CULTURE SOCIETY ECO/UNDEV NAT/G PROB/SOLV DIPLOM LEAD ATTIT...HUM SOC STAT 20. PAGE 169 A3441 — BIBLIOG ACADEM ACT/RES OP/RES

B62
AIR FORCE ACADEMY LIBRARY,INTERNATIONAL ORGANIZATIONS AND MILITARY SECURITY SYSTEMS (PAMPHLET) (SPECIAL BIBLIOGRAPHY SERIES, NUMBER 25). DIPLOM FOR/AID INT/TRADE NUC/PWR PEACE 20 UN NATO OAS SEATO LEAGUE/NAT. PAGE 5 A0104 — BIBLIOG INT/ORG FORCES DETER

B62
BIBLIOTHEQUE PALAIS DE LA PAIX,CATALOGUE OF THE PEACE PALACE LIBRARY, SUPPLEMENT 1937-1952 (7 VOLS.). WOR+45 WOR-45 INT/ORG NAT/G ADJUD WAR PEACE ...JURID 20. PAGE 14 A0285 — BIBLIOG INT/LAW DIPLOM

B62
BLAUSTEIN A.P.,MANUAL ON FOREIGN LEGAL PERIODICALS AND THEIR INDEX. WOR+45 DIPLOM 20. PAGE 15 A0310 — BIBLIOG INDEX LAW JURID

B62
BROWN L.C.,LATIN AMERICA, A BIBLIOGRAPHY. EX/STRUC ADMIN LEAD ATTIT...POLICY 20. PAGE 20 A0405 — BIBLIOG L/A+17C DIPLOM NAT/G

B62
COLLISON R.L.,BIBLIOGRAPHIES, SUBJECT AND NATIONAL: A GUIDE TO THEIR CONTENTS, ARRANGEMENT, AND USE (2ND REV. ED.). SECT DIPLOM...ART/METH GEOG HUM PHIL/SCI SOC MATH BIOG 20. PAGE 28 A0569 — BIBLIOG/A CON/ANAL BIBLIOG

B62
DAVAR F.C.,IRAN AND INDIA THROUGH THE AGES. INDIA IRAN ELITES SECT CREATE ORD/FREE...LING BIBLIOG. PAGE 34 A0683 — NAT/COMP DIPLOM CULTURE

B62
DIAZ J.S.,MANUAL DE BIBLIOGRAFIA DE LA LITERATURA ESPANOLA. PRE/AMER SPAIN ECO/UNDEV DIPLOM LEAD ATTIT...SOC 15/20. PAGE 37 A0755 — BIBLIOG L/A+17C NAT/G COLONIAL

B62
FATOUROS A.A.,GOVERNMENT GUARANTEES TO FOREIGN INVESTORS. WOR+45 ECO/UNDEV INDUS WORKER ADJUD ...NAT/COMP BIBLIOG TREATY. PAGE 44 A0903 — NAT/G FINAN INT/TRADE ECO/DEV

B62
GUTTMAN A.,THE WOUND IN THE HEART: AMERICA AND THE SPANISH CIVIL WAR. SPAIN USA-45 POL/PAR LEGIS ECO/TAC CHOOSE ANOMIE ATTIT MARXISM...POLICY ANARCH BIBLIOG 20 ROOSEVLT/F. PAGE 58 A1198 — ALL/IDEOS WAR DIPLOM CATHISM

B62
HUTTENBACK R.A.,BRITISH RELATIONS WITH THE SIND, 1799-1843. FRANCE INDIA UK FORCES...POLICY CHARTS BIBLIOG 18/19 SIND. PAGE 69 A1425 — COLONIAL DIPLOM DOMIN S/ASIA

B62
INGHAM K.,A HISTORY OF EAST AFRICA. NAT/G DIPLOM ADMIN WAR NAT/LISM...SOC BIOG BIBLIOG. PAGE 70 — AFR CONSTN

A1439 COLONIAL

B62
JORDAN A.A. JR.,FOREIGN AID AND THE DEFENSE OF SOUTHEAST ASIA. PAKISTAN VIETNAM/S FINAN PLAN BUDGET ECO/TAC DETER WAR ORD/FREE...POLICY DECISION CENSUS CHARTS BIBLIOG 20. PAGE 75 A1535
FOR/AID S/ASIA FORCES ECO/UNDEV

B62
KENT G.O.,A CATALOG OF FILES AND MICROFILMS OF THE GERMAN FOREIGN MINISTRY ARCHIVES, 1920-1945 (3 VOLS.). GERMANY WOR-45 WRITING WAR 20. PAGE 78 A1595
BIBLIOG NAT/G DIPLOM FASCISM

B62
KIDDER F.E.,THESES ON PAN AMERICAN TOPICS. LAW CULTURE NAT/G SECT DIPLOM HEALTH...ART/METH GEOG SOC 13/20. PAGE 79 A1615
BIBLIOG CHRIST-17C L/A+17C SOCIETY

B62
LAUERHAUSS L.,COMMUNISM IN LATIN AMERICA: THE POST-WAR YEARS (1945 -1960) (PAPER). INTELL STRATA ECO/UNDEV AGRI WORKER FOR/AID INT/TRADE COLONIAL GUERRILLA 20. PAGE 85 A1745
BIBLIOG L/A+17C MARXISM REV

B62
PERRE J.,LES MUTATIONS DE LA GUERRE MODERNE: DE LA REVOLUTION FRANCAISE A LA REVOLUTION NUCLEAIRE. DIPLOM ARMS/CONT DEATH REV WEAPON GP/REL PEACE ATTIT...STAT PREDICT BIBLIOG 18/20 WWI. PAGE 115 A2365
WAR FORCES NUC/PWR

B62
SCHUMAN F.L.,THE COLD WAR: RETROSPECT AND PROSPECT. FUT USA+45 USSR WOR+45 BAL/PWR EDU/PROP ARMS/CONT ATTIT...MAJORIT IDEA/COMP ANTHOL BIBLIOG 20 COLD/WAR. PAGE 129 A2651
MARXISM TEC/DEV DIPLOM NUC/PWR

B62
SCOTT W.E.,ALLIANCE AGAINST HITLER. EUR+WWI FRANCE GERMANY USSR BAL/PWR LEAD TOTALISM PWR FASCISM MARXISM...POLICY BIBLIOG 20 HITLER/A. PAGE 131 A2675
WAR DIPLOM FORCES

B62
SHAPIRO D.,A SELECT BIBLIOGRAPHY OF WORKS IN ENGLISH ON RUSSIAN HISTORY, 1801-1917. COM USSR STRATA FORCES EDU/PROP ADMIN REV RACE/REL ATTIT 19/20. PAGE 131 A2693
BIBLIOG DIPLOM COLONIAL

B62
SHAW C.,LEGAL PROBLEMS IN INTERNATIONAL TRADE AND INVESTMENT. WOR+45 ECO/DEV ECO/UNDEV MARKET DIPLOM TAX INCOME ROLE...ANTHOL BIBLIOG 20 TREATY UN IMF GATT. PAGE 132 A2698
INT/LAW INT/TRADE FINAN ECO/TAC

B62
SPIRO H.J.,POLITICS IN AFRICA: PROSPECTS SOUTH OF THE SAHARA. INT/ORG KIN FORCES LEGIS PROB/SOLV COERCE RACE/REL FEDERAL...TREND CHARTS BIBLIOG 20. PAGE 136 A2790
AFR NAT/LISM DIPLOM

B62
STARR R.E.,POLAND 1944-1962: THE SOVIETIZATION OF A CAPTIVE PEOPLE. COM POLAND USSR POL/PAR SECT LEGIS DIPLOM DOMIN EDU/PROP CHOOSE ORD/FREE...POLICY CHARTS BIBLIOG 20. PAGE 137 A2808
MARXISM NAT/G TOTALISM NAT/COMP

B62
TAYLOR D.,THE BRITISH IN AFRICA. UK CULTURE ECO/UNDEV INDUS DIPLOM INT/TRADE ADMIN WAR RACE/REL ORD/FREE SOVEREIGN...POLICY BIBLIOG 15/20 CMN/WLTH. PAGE 142 A2898
AFR COLONIAL DOMIN

B62
UNECA LIBRARY,BOOKS ON AFRICA IN THE UNECA LIBRARY. WOR+45 AGRI INT/ORG NAT/G PLAN WRITING REGION...SOC STAT UN. PAGE 147 A3008
BIBLIOG AFR ECO/UNDEV TEC/DEV

B62
UNECA LIBRARY,NEW ACQUISITIONS IN THE UNECA LIBRARY. LAW NAT/G PLAN PROB/SOLV TEC/DEV ADMIN REGION...GEOG SOC 20 UN. PAGE 147 A3009
BIBLIOG AFR ECO/UNDEV INT/ORG

B62
UNESCO,GENERAL CATALOGUE OF UNESCO PUBLICATIONS AND UNESCO SPONSORED PUBLICATIONS, 1946-1959. WOR+45 ...POLICY ART/METH HUM PHIL/SCI UN. PAGE 148 A3022
BIBLIOG INT/ORG ECO/UNDEV SOC

B62
US LIBRARY OF CONGRESS,A LIST OF AMERICAN DOCTORAL DISSERTATIONS ON AFRICA. SOCIETY SECT DIPLOM EDU/PROP ADMIN...GEOG 19/20. PAGE 155 A3157
BIBLIOG AFR ACADEM CULTURE

B62
WEIDNER E.W.,THE WORLD ROLE OF UNIVERSITIES. USA+45 WOR+45 SECT ACT/RES PROB/SOLV GIVE EFFICIENCY KNOWL ...LING CHARTS BIBLIOG 20. PAGE 162 A3297
ACADEM EDU/PROP DIPLOM POLICY

B62
WELLEQUET J.,LE CONGO BELGE ET LA WELTPOLITIK (1894-1914. GERMANY DOMIN EDU/PROP WAR ATTIT ...BIBLIOG T CONGO/LEOP. PAGE 163 A3314
ADMIN DIPLOM GP/REL COLONIAL

L62
SCHWERIN K.,"LAW LIBRARIES AND FOREIGN LAW COLLECTION IN THE USA." USA+45 USA-45...INT/LAW STAT 20. PAGE 130 A2667
BIBLIOG LAW ACADEM

ADMIN

C62
DUFFY J.,"PORTUGAL IN AFRICA." PORTUGAL SIER/LEONE INDUS WORKER INT/TRADE WAR CONSERVE...CATH GEOG TREND 16/20. PAGE 39 A0795
BIBLIOG RACE/REL ECO/UNDEV COLONIAL

C62
LILLICH R.B.,"INTERNATIONAL CLAIMS: THEIR ADJUDICATION BY NATIONAL COMMISSIONS." WOR+45 WOR-45 NAT/G ADJUD...JURID BIBLIOG 18/20. PAGE 89 A1817
INT/LAW DIPLOM PROB/SOLV

C62
ROBINSON J.A.,"CONGRESS AND FOREIGN POLICY-MAKING: A STUDY IN LEGISLATIVE INFLUENCE AND INITIATIVE." USA+45 CHIEF DELIB/GP CREATE CONTROL EXEC GOV/REL PERCEPT...TREND BIBLIOG 20 CONGRESS. PAGE 122 A2505
LEGIS DIPLOM POLICY DECISION

B63
ADLER G.J.,BRITISH INDIA'S NORTHERN FRONTIER: 1865-95. AFGHANISTN RUSSIA UK PROVS COLONIAL COERCE PEACE...GEOG CHARTS BIBLIOG 19 TREATY. PAGE 4 A0091
S/ASIA FORCES DIPLOM POLICY

B63
AFRICAN BIBLIOGRAPHIC CENTER,THE SCENE IS GUINEA AND THE PERSONAGE IS SEKOU TOURE: A SELECTED CURRENT READING LIST, 1959-1962 (PAMPHLET). GUINEA ECO/UNDEV CHIEF FOR/AID COLONIAL...BIOG 20. PAGE 5 A0095
BIBLIOG AFR POL/PAR COM

B63
AFRICAN BIBLIOGRAPHIC CENTER,THE SCENE IS KENYA AND THE PERSONAGE IS TOM MBOYA: A SELECTED CURRENT READING LIST FROM 1956-1962 (PAMPHLET). ECO/UNDEV LABOR POL/PAR CHIEF COLONIAL CHOOSE NAT/LISM ORD/FREE 20. PAGE 5 A0096
BIBLIOG DIPLOM AFR NAT/G

B63
BISHOP O.B.,PUBLICATIONS OF THE GOVERNMENT OF THE PROVINCE OF CANADA 1841-1867. CANADA DIPLOM COLONIAL LEAD...POLICY 18. PAGE 14 A0294
BIBLIOG NAT/G ATTIT

B63
BUTTS R.F.,AMERICAN EDUCATION IN INTERNATIONAL DEVELOPMENT. USA+45 WOR+45 INTELL SCHOOL DIPLOM EDU/PROP...BIBLIOG 20. PAGE 23 A0457
ACADEM FOR/AID CONSULT ECO/UNDEV

B63
COMISION DE HISTORIO,GUIA DE LOS DOCUMENTOS MICROFOTOGRAFIADOS POR LA UNIDAD MOVIL DE LA UNESCO. SOCIETY ECO/UNDEV INT/ORG ADMIN...SOC 20 UNESCO. PAGE 28 A0573
BIBLIOG NAT/G L/A+17C DIPLOM

B63
ELIAS T.O.,GOVERNMENT AND POLITICS IN AFRICA. CONSTN CULTURE SOCIETY NAT/G POL/PAR DIPLOM REPRESENT PERSON...SOC TREND BIBLIOG 4/20. PAGE 41 A0837
AFR NAT/LISM COLONIAL LAW

B63
HALASZ DE BEKY I.L.,A BIBLIOGRAPHY OF THE HUNGARIAN REVOLUTION 1956. COM HUNGARY USSR DIPLOM COERCE MARXISM...POLICY AUD/VIS 20 UN COLD/WAR. PAGE 59 A1221
BIBLIOG REV FORCES ATTIT

B63
HONORD S.,PUBLIC RELATIONS IN ADMINISTRATION. WOR+45 NAT/G...SOC/WK BIBLIOG 20. PAGE 67 A1379
PRESS DIPLOM MGT METH/COMP

B63
JUDD P.,AFRICAN INDEPENDENCE: THE EXPLODING EMERGENCE OF THE NEW AFRICAN NATIONS. AFR UK LAW CONSTN CULTURE KIN DIPLOM ATTIT...CHARTS BIBLIOG 20 UN DEGAULLE/C NEGRO THIRD/WRLD. PAGE 75 A1542
ORD/FREE POLICY DOMIN LOC/G

B63
KORBEL J.,POLAND BETWEEN EAST AND WEST: SOVIET AND GERMAN DIPLOMACY TOWARD POLAND 1919-1933. EUR+WWI GERMANY POLAND USSR FORCES AGREE WAR SOVEREIGN ...BIBLIOG 20 TREATY. PAGE 81 A1670
BAL/PWR DIPLOM DOMIN NAT/LISM

B63
LAFEBER W.,THE NEW EMPIRE: AN INTERPRETATION OF AMERICAN EXPANSION, 1860-1898. USA-45 CONSTN NAT/LISM SOVEREIGN...TREND BIBLIOG 19/20. PAGE 84 A1711
INDUS NAT/G DIPLOM CAP/ISM

B63
LANOUE G.R.,A BIBLIOGRAPHY OF DOCTORAL DISSERTATIONS ON POLITICS AND RELIGION. USA+45 USA-45 CONSTN PROVS DIPLOM CT/SYS MORAL...POLICY JURID CONCPT 20. PAGE 84 A1728
BIBLIOG NAT/G LOC/G SECT

B63
LERCHE C.O. JR.,AMERICA IN WORLD AFFAIRS. COM UK USA+45 INT/ORG FORCES ECO/TAC INT/TRADE EDU/PROP WAR NAT/LISM PEACE...BIBLIOG 18/20 UN CONGRESS PRESIDENT COLD/WAR. PAGE 87 A1783
NAT/G DIPLOM PLAN

B63
LIVNEH E.,ISRAEL LEGAL BIBLIOGRAPHY IN EUROPEAN LANGUAGES. ISRAEL LOC/G JUDGE TAX...INT/LAW 20. PAGE 90 A1846
BIBLIOG LAW NAT/G CONSTN

B63
LYONS F.S.L.,INTERNATIONALISM IN EUROPE 1815-1914. LAW AGRI COM/IND DIST/IND LABOR SECT INT/TRADE TARIFFS...BIBLIOG 19/20. PAGE 92 A1880
DIPLOM MOD/EUR INT/ORG

B63
MILLER W.J.,THE MEANING OF COMMUNISM. USSR SOCIETY ECO/DEV EX/STRUC WORKER TEC/DEV ADMIN TOTALISM ...POLICY CONCPT CHARTS BIBLIOG T 20 COLD/WAR LENIN/VI STALIN/J. PAGE 101 A2080
MARXISM TRADIT DIPLOM NAT/G

B63
PADELFORD N.J.,AFRICA AND WORLD ORDER. AFR COLONIAL SOVEREIGN...ANTHOL BIBLIOG 20 UN UNIFICA COMMONWLTH. PAGE 113 A2312
DIPLOM NAT/G ORD/FREE

B63
PANAMERICAN UNION,DOCUMENTOS OFICIALES DE LA ORGANIZACION DE LOS ESTADOS AMERICANOS, INDICE Y LISTA (VOL. III, 1962). L/A+17C DELIB/GP INT/TRADE EDU/PROP REGION NUC/PWR...HEAL INT/LAW SOC/WK 20 OAS. PAGE 113 A2329
BIBLIOG INT/ORG DIPLOM

B63
PEREZ ORTIZ R.,ANUARIO BIBLIOGRAFICO COLOMBIANO, 1961. AGRI...INT/LAW JURID SOC LING 20 COLOMB. PAGE 115 A2354
BIBLIOG L/A+17C NAT/G

B63
SCHRADER R.,SCIENCE AND POLICY. WOR+45 ECO/DEV ECO/UNDEV R+D FORCES PLAN DIPLOM GOV/REL TECHRACY BIBLIOG. PAGE 129 A2644
TEC/DEV NAT/G POLICY ADMIN

B63
THIEN T.T.,INDIA AND SOUTHEAST ASIA 1947-1960. COM INDIA S/ASIA SECT DELIB/GP FOR/AID RACE/REL NAT/LISM SOCISM...CHARTS BIBLIOG 20 UN NEHRU/J TREATY. PAGE 143 A2917
DRIVE DIPLOM POLICY

B63
UAR MINISTRY OF CULTURE,A BIBLIOGRAPHICAL LIST OF ARABIAN PENINSULA. ISLAM SAUDI/ARAB YEMEN FINAN NAT/G DIPLOM 19/20. PAGE 146 A2990
BIBLIOG GEOG INDUS SECT

B63
US DEPARTMENT OF STATE,POLITICAL BEHAVIOR--A LIST OF CURRENT STUDIES. USA+45 COM/IND DIPLOM LEAD PERS/REL DRIVE PERCEPT KNOWL...DECISION SIMUL METH. PAGE 151 A3093
BIBLIOG METH/COMP GP/REL ATTIT

B63
WALKER A.A.,OFFICIAL PUBLICATIONS OF SIERRA LEONE AND GAMBIA. GAMBIA SIER/LEONE UK LAW CONSTN LEGIS PLAN BUDGET DIPLOM...SOC SAMP CON/ANAL 20. PAGE 160 A3262
BIBLIOG NAT/G COLONIAL ADMIN

C63
ATTIA G.E.O.,"LES FORCES ARMEES DES NATIONS UNIES EN COREE ET AU MOYENORIENT." KOREA CONSTN DELIB/GP LEGIS PWR...IDEA/COMP NAT/COMP BIBLIOG UN SUEZ. PAGE 10 A0194
FORCES NAT/G INT/LAW

C63
CHARLETON W.G.,"THE REVOLUTION IN AMERICAN FOREIGN POLICY." COM PROB/SOLV FOR/AID DOMIN COLONIAL NEUTRAL DETER WAR ISOLAT NAT/LISM...BIBLIOG 19/20 UN COLD/WAR NATO. PAGE 26 A0523
DIPLOM INT/ORG BAL/PWR

C63
SCHMITT K.M.,"EVOLUTION OR CHAOS: DYNAMICS OF LATIN AMERICAN GOVERNMENT AND POLITICS." L/A+17C AGRI FINAN CAP/ISM EXEC LEAD BAL/PAY TOTALISM ATTIT ...TREND BIBLIOG 20. PAGE 129 A2635
DIPLOM POLICY POL/PAR LOBBY

N63
LIBRARY HUNGARIAN ACADEMY SCI,HUNGARIAN PUBLICATIONS ON ASIA AND AFRICA, 1950-1962: A SELECTED BIBLIOGRAPHY (PAMPHLET). AFR ASIA HUNGARY S/ASIA ECO/UNDEV NAT/G EDU/PROP ATTIT 20 UNESCO. PAGE 88 A1807
BIBLIOG REGION DIPLOM WRITING

B64
ANDREWS D.H.,LATIN AMERICA: A BIBLIOGRAPHY OF PAPERBACK BOOKS. SECT INT/TRADE EDU/PROP WAR GOV/REL ADJUST NAT/LISM ATTIT...ART/METH LING BIOG 20. PAGE 8 A0160
BIBLIOG L/A+17C CULTURE NAT/G

B64
CHENG C.,ECONOMIC RELATIONS BETWEEN PEKING AND MOSCOW: 1949-63. ASIA CHINA/COM COM USSR FINAN INDUS CONSULT TEC/DEV INT/TRADE...PREDICT CHARTS BIBLIOG 20. PAGE 26 A0527
DIPLOM FOR/AID MARXISM

B64
CORFO,CHILE, A SELECTED BIBLIOGRAPHY IN ENGLISH (PAMPHLET). CHILE DIPLOM...SOC 20. PAGE 31 A0623
BIBLIOG NAT/G POLICY L/A+17C

B64
FREUD A.,OF HUMAN SOVEREIGNTY. WOR+45 INDUS SECT ECO/TAC CRIME CHOOSE ATTIT MORAL MARXISM...POLICY BIBLIOG 20. PAGE 49 A0998
NAT/LISM DIPLOM WAR PEACE

B64
FREYMOND J.,WESTERN EUROPE SINCE THE WAR. COM EUR+WWI USA+45 DIPLOM...BIBLIOG 20 NATO UN EEC. PAGE 49 A1001
INT/ORG POLICY ECO/DEV ECO/TAC

B64
GRZYBOWSKI K.,THE SOCIALIST COMMONWEALTH OF NATIONS: ORGANIZATIONS AND INSTITUTIONS. FORCES DIPLOM INT/TRADE ADJUD ADMIN LEAD WAR MARXISM SOCISM...BIBLIOG 20 COMECON WARSAW/P. PAGE 58 A1185
INT/LAW COM REGION INT/ORG

B64
HAMBRIDGE G.,DYNAMICS OF DEVELOPMENT. AGRI FINAN INDUS LABOR INT/TRADE EDU/PROP ADMIN LEAD OWN HEALTH...ANTHOL BIBLIOG 20. PAGE 61 A1245
ECO/UNDEV ECO/TAC OP/RES ACT/RES

B64
HARMON R.B.,BIBLIOGRAPHY OF BIBLIOGRAPHIES IN POLITICAL SCIENCE (MIMEOGRAPHED PAPER: LIMITED EDITION). WOR+45 WOR-45 INT/ORG POL/PAR GOV/REL ALL/IDEOS...INT/LAW JURID MGT 19/20. PAGE 61 A1260
BIBLIOG NAT/G DIPLOM LOC/G

B64
IBERO-AMERICAN INSTITUTES,IBEROAMERICANA. STRUCT ADMIN SOC. PAGE 70 A1430
BIBLIOG L/A+17C NAT/G DIPLOM

B64
JACKSON W.V.,LIBRARY GUIDE FOR BRAZILIAN STUDIES. BRAZIL USA+45 STRUCT DIPLOM ADMIN...SOC 20. PAGE 72 A1481
BIBLIOG L/A+17C NAT/G LOC/G

B64
KIS T.I.,LES PAYS DE L'EUROPE DE L'EST: LEURS RAPPORTS MUTUELS ET LE PROBLEME DE LEUR INTEGRATION DANS L'ORBITE DE L'USSR. EUR+WWI RUSSIA USSR INT/ORG NAT/G REV ATTIT...JURID SOC BIBLIOG WARSAW/P COMECON EUROPE/E. PAGE 80 A1638
DIPLOM COM MARXISM REGION

B64
LEGGE J.D.,INDONESIA. INDONESIA ELITES ECO/UNDEV POL/PAR CHIEF FORCES INT/TRADE COERCE CHOOSE ORD/FREE...SOC CHARTS BIBLIOG 16/20 CHINJAP. PAGE 86 A1765
S/ASIA DOMIN NAT/LISM POLICY

B64
MUSSO AMBROSI L.A.,BIBLIOGRAFIA DE BIBLIOGRAFIAS URUGUAYAS. URUGUAY DIPLOM ADMIN ATTIT...SOC 20. PAGE 106 A2185
BIBLIOG NAT/G L/A+17C PRESS

B64
NEWCOMER H.A.,INTERNATIONAL AIDS TO OVERSEAS INVESTMENTS AND TRADE. ECO/UNDEV TARIFFS PROFIT ...BIBLIOG 20 GATT UN. PAGE 108 A2225
INT/TRADE FINAN DIPLOM FOR/AID

B64
NICOL D.,AFRICA - A SUBJECTIVE VIEW. AFR INT/ORG PLAN ADMIN COLONIAL PARL/PROC PARTIC REGION GOV/REL LITERACY ATTIT...BIBLIOG 20 CIVIL/SERV. PAGE 109 A2230
NAT/G LEAD CULTURE ACADEM

B64
PERKINS D.,THE AMERICAN DEMOCRACY: ITS RISE TO POWER. ASIA USSR LAW CULTURE FINAN EDU/PROP COLONIAL CHOOSE...POLICY CHARTS BIBLIOG WORSHIP PRESIDENT 15/20 NEGRO. PAGE 115 A2362
LOC/G ECO/TAC WAR DIPLOM

B64
RICHARDSON I.L.,BIBLIOGRAFIA BRASILEIRA DE ADMINISTRACAO PUBLICA E ASSUNTOS CORRELATOS. BRAZIL CONSTN FINAN LOC/G NAT/G POL/PAR PLAN DIPLOM RECEIVE ATTIT...METH 20. PAGE 121 A2474
BIBLIOG MGT ADMIN LAW

B64
RUSSELL R.B.,UNITED NATIONS EXPERIENCE WITH MILITARY FORCES: POLITICAL AND LEGAL ASPECTS. AFR KOREA WOR+45 LEGIS PROB/SOLV ADMIN CONTROL EFFICIENCY PEACE...POLICY INT/LAW BIBLIOG UN. PAGE 126 A2576
FORCES DIPLOM SANCTION ORD/FREE

B64
SEGUNDO-SANCHEZ M.,OBRAS (2 VOLS.). VENEZUELA EX/STRUC DIPLOM ADMIN 19/20. PAGE 131 A2682
BIBLIOG LEAD NAT/G L/A+17C

B64
SPECTOR S.D.,A CHECKLIST OF PAPERBOUND BOOKS ON RUSSIA. USSR SECT DIPLOM EDU/PROP HEALTH...PHIL/SCI PSY SOC SOC/WK WORSHIP 20. PAGE 135 A2775
BIBLIOG COM PERF/ART

B64
STEWART C.F.,A BIBLIOGRAPHY OF INTERNATIONAL BUSINESS. WOR+45 FINAN LG/CO NAT/G PLAN ECO/TAC TARIFFS...DECISION MGT GP/COMP NAT/COMP 20 EEC. PAGE 138 A2824
BIBLIOG INT/ORG OP/RES INT/TRADE

B64
STILLMAN E.O.,THE POLITICS OF HYSTERIA: THE SOURCES OF TWENTIETH-CENTURY CONFLICT. WOR+45 WOR-45 CULTURE ECO/UNDEV PLAN CAP/ISM WAR MARXISM ...PREDICT BIBLIOG 20 COLD/WAR. PAGE 138 A2828
DIPLOM IDEA/COMP COLONIAL CONTROL

B64
TREADGOLD D.W.,THE DEVELOPMENT OF THE USSR. COM USSR ECO/DEV CREATE BAL/PWR DEBATE COLONIAL TOTALISM...HUM ANTHOL BIBLIOG 19/20. PAGE 145 A2960
MARXISM CONSERVE DIPLOM DOMIN

B64
TURNER M.C.,LIBROS EN VENTA EN HISPANOAMERICA Y ESPANA. SPAIN LAW CONSTN CULTURE ADMIN LEAD...HUM SOC 20. PAGE 146 A2983
BIBLIOG L/A+17C NAT/G DIPLOM

B64
UAR NATIONAL LIBRARY,A BIBLIOGRAPHICAL LIST OF WORKS ABOUT PALESTINE AND JORDAN (2ND ED.). ISRAEL JORDAN SECT DIPLOM...SOC 20 JEWS. PAGE 146 A2991
BIBLIOG ISLAM

B64
WALLBANK T.W.,DOCUMENTS ON MODERN AFRICA. NAT/G COLONIAL GP/REL ATTIT PWR...BIBLIOG 19/20. PAGE 160 A3267
AFR NAT/LISM ECO/UNDEV DIPLOM

B64
WRIGHT T.P. JR.,AMERICAN SUPPORT OF FREE ELECTIONS ABROAD. USA+45 USA-45 DOMIN LEAD NEUTRAL MARXISM ...POLICY TIME/SEQ BIBLIOG 19/20 COLD/WAR INTERVENT. PAGE 168 A3420
DIPLOM CHOOSE L/A+17C POPULISM

S64
"FURTHER READING." INDIA PAKISTAN SECT WAR PEACE ATTIT...POLICY 20. PAGE 3 A0067
BIBLIOG GP/REL DIPLOM NAT/G

S64
PRASAD B.,"SURVEY OF RECENT RESEARCH: STUDIES ON INDIA'S FOREIGN POLIC AND RELATIONS." ASIA INDIA PAKISTAN USA+45 NAT/G INT/TRADE GOV/REL 20 UN CMN/WLTH. PAGE 117 A2406
BIBLIOG DIPLOM ROLE POLICY

C64
EASTON S.C.,"THE RISE AND FALL OF WESTERN COLONIALISM." AFR ISLAM L/A+17C ECO/UNDEV REV NAT/LISM...CHARTS BIBLIOG 15/20. PAGE 40 A0817
COLONIAL DIPLOM ORD/FREE WAR

C64
SCHRAMM W.,"MASS MEDIA AND NATIONAL DEVELOPMENT: THE ROLE OF INFORMATION IN DEVELOPING COUNTRIES." FINAN R+D ACT/RES PLAN TEC/DEV DIPLOM CHOOSE SUPEGO ORD/FREE...BIBLIOG 20. PAGE 129 A2645
ECO/UNDEV COM/IND EDU/PROP MAJORIT

B65
AIR UNIVERSITY LIBRARY,LATIN AMERICA, SELECTED REFERENCES. ECO/UNDEV FORCES EDU/PROP MARXISM 20 OAS. PAGE 5 A0106
BIBLIOG L/A+17C NAT/G DIPLOM

B65
ALBRECHT-CARRIE R.,THE MEANING OF THE FIRST WORLD WAR. MOD/EUR USA-45 INT/ORG BAL/PWR PEACE ATTIT LAISSEZ MARXISM...CONCPT BIBLIOG 19/20 LEAGUE/NAT WWI. PAGE 5 A0110
DIPLOM WAR

B65
AMERICAN ECONOMIC ASSOCIATION,INDEX OF ECONOMIC JOURNALS 1886-1965 (7 VOLS.). UK USA+45 USA-45 AGRI FINAN PLAN ECO/TAC INT/TRADE ADMIN...STAT CENSUS 19/20. PAGE 7 A0145
BIBLIOG WRITING INDUS

B65
CALLEO D.P.,EUROPE'S FUTURE: THE GRAND ALTERNATIVES. UK INT/ORG DIPLOM PWR SOVEREIGN ...CONCPT IDEA/COMP NAT/COMP BIBLIOG 20 EEC EUROPE DEGAULLE/C NATO. PAGE 23 A0468
FUT EUR+WWI FEDERAL NAT/LISM

B65
COLLINS H.,KARL MARX AND THE BRITISH LABOUR MOVEMENT; YEARS OF THE FIRST INTERNATIONAL. FRANCE SWITZERLND UK CAP/ISM WAR...MARXIST IDEA/COMP BIBLIOG 19. PAGE 28 A0567
MARXISM LABOR INT/ORG REV

B65
FALK R.A.,THE AFTERMATH OF SABBATINO: BACKGROUND PAPERS AND PROCEEDINGS OF SEVENTH HAMMARSKJOLD FORUM. USA+45 LAW ACT/RES ADJUD ROLE...BIBLIOG 20 EXPROPRIAT SABBATINO HARLAN/JM. PAGE 44 A0891
SOVEREIGN CT/SYS INT/LAW OWN

B65
FRIEDMANN W.,AN INTRODUCTION TO WORLD POLITICS (5TH ED.). WOR+45 ECO/UNDEV BAL/PWR FOR/AID INT/TRADE PEACE...STAT CENSUS CHARTS BIBLIOG T 20 COLD/WAR UN THIRD/WRLD. PAGE 49 A1003
DIPLOM INT/ORG PROB/SOLV

B65
GILBERT M.,THE EUROPEAN POWERS 1900-45. EUR+WWI ITALY MOD/EUR USSR REV WAR PWR ALL/IDEOS FASCISM ...AUD/VIS CHARTS BIBLIOG 20. PAGE 52 A1069
DIPLOM NAT/G POLICY BAL/PWR

B65
HAGRAS K.M.,UNITED NATIONS CONFERENCE ON TRADE AND DEVELOPMENT: A CASE STUDY OF UN DIPLOMACY. CONSULT ACT/RES TEC/DEV FOR/AID INT/TRADE...BIBLIOG 20 UN LEAGUE/NAT UNCTAD. PAGE 59 A1213
INT/ORG ADMIN DELIB/GP DIPLOM

B65
HALPERIN E.,NATIONALISM AND COMMUNISM. CHILE L/A+17C CAP/ISM EDU/PROP CHOOSE DISCRIM SOCISM ...BIBLIOG 20 COM/PARTY. PAGE 60 A1236
NAT/LISM MARXISM POL/PAR REV

B65
HARMON R.B.,POLITICAL SCIENCE: A BIBLIOGRAPHICAL GUIDE TO THE LITERATURE. WOR+45 WOR-45 R+D INT/ORG LOC/G NAT/G DIPLOM ADMIN...CONCPT METH. PAGE 61 A1261
BIBLIOG POL/PAR LAW GOV/COMP

B65
HISPANIC SOCIETY OF AMERICA,CATALOGUE (10 VOLS.). PORTUGAL PRE/AMER SPAIN NAT/G ADMIN...POLICY SOC 15/20. PAGE 65 A1341
BIBLIOG L/A+17C COLONIAL DIPLOM

B65
IRIYE A.,AFTER IMPERIALISM; THE SEARCH FOR A NEW ORDER IN THE FAR EAST 1921-1931. USA-45 USSR DOMIN AGREE COLONIAL REV PWR...BIBLIOG DICTIONARY 20 CHINJAP. PAGE 72 A1468
DIPLOM ASIA SOVEREIGN

B65
JADOS S.S.,DOCUMENTS ON RUSSIAN-AMERICAN RELATIONS: WASHINGTON TO EISENHOWER. USA+45 USA-45 USSR INT/ORG LEGIS INT/TRADE WAR PEACE...ANTHOL BIBLIOG 18/20 PRESIDENT. PAGE 73 A1488
DIPLOM CHIEF CONTROL

B65
JOHNSTONE A.,UNITED STATES DIRECT INVESTMENT IN FRANCE: AN INVESTIGATION OF THE FRENCH CHARGES. FRANCE USA+45 ECO/DEV INDUS LG/CO NAT/G ECO/TAC CONTROL WEALTH...BIBLIOG 20 INTERVENT. PAGE 75 A1529
FINAN DIPLOM POLICY SOVEREIGN

B65
LERCHE C.O.,THE COLD WAR AND AFTER. AFR COM S/ASIA USA+45 USSR NUC/PWR SOVEREIGN MARXISM...TIME/SEQ TREND BIBLIOG 20 COLD/WAR. PAGE 87 A1784
DIPLOM BAL/PWR IDEA/COMP

B65
LINDBLOM C.E.,THE INTELLIGENCE OF DEMOCRACY; DECISION MAKING THROUGH MUTUAL ADJUSTMENT. WOR+45 SOCIETY NAT/G PROB/SOLV DOMIN PARTIC GP/REL ORD/FREE...POLICY IDEA/COMP BIBLIOG 20. PAGE 89 A1821
PLURISM DECISION ADJUST DIPLOM

B65
LOEWENHEIM F.L.,PEACE OR APPEASEMENT? HITLER, CHAMBERLAIN AND THE MUNICH CRISIS. MUNIC DELIB/GP WAR TOTALISM ATTIT SOVEREIGN...TIME/SEQ ANTHOL BIBLIOG 20 HITLER/A CHAMBRLN/N. PAGE 90 A1851
DIPLOM LEAD PEACE

B65
MACDONALD R.W.,THE LEAGUE OF ARAB STATES: A STUDY IN THE DYNAMICS OF REGIONAL ORGANIZATION. ISRAEL UAR USSR FINAN INT/ORG DELIB/GP ECO/TAC AGREE NEUTRAL ORD/FREE PWR...DECISION BIBLIOG 20 TREATY UN. PAGE 92 A1888
ISLAM REGION DIPLOM ADMIN

B65
MEDIVA J.T.,LA IMPRENTA EN MEXICO, 1539-1821 (8 VOLS.). SOCIETY ECO/UNDEV DIPLOM COLONIAL GP/REL 16/19 MEXIC/AMER. PAGE 99 A2031
BIBLIOG WRITING NAT/G L/A+17C

B65
MEHROTRA S.R.,INDIA AND THE COMMONWEALTH 1885-1929. INDIA UK INT/ORG VOL/ASSN GP/REL ATTIT...POLICY BIBLIOG 19/20 CMN/WLTH. PAGE 99 A2034
DIPLOM NAT/G POL/PAR NAT/LISM

B65
MEYERHOFF A.E.,THE STRATEGY OF PERSUASION: THE USE OF ADVERTISING SKILLS IN FIGHTING THE COLD WAR. USA+45 USSR PLAN ATTIT DRIVE...BIBLIOG 20 COLD/WAR. PAGE 100 A2054
EDU/PROP SERV/IND METH/COMP DIPLOM

B65
MONCONDUIT F.,LA COMMISSION EUROPEENNE DES DROITS DE L'HOMME. DIPLOM AGREE GP/REL ORD/FREE PWR ...BIBLIOG 20 TREATY. PAGE 102 A2103
INT/LAW INT/ORG ADJUD JURID

B65
MOODY M.,CATALOG OF INTERNATIONAL LAW AND RELATIONS (20 VOLS.). WOR+45 INT/ORG NAT/G ADJUD ADMIN CT/SYS POLICY. PAGE 103 A2117
BIBLIOG INT/LAW DIPLOM

B65
NATIONAL BOOK CENTRE PAKISTAN,BOOKS ON PAKISTAN: A BIBLIOGRAPHY. PAKISTAN CULTURE DIPLOM ADMIN ATTIT ...MAJORIT SOC CONCPT 20. PAGE 107 A2201
BIBLIOG CONSTN S/ASIA NAT/G

B65
NATIONAL CENTRAL LIBRARY,LATIN AMERICAN ECONOMIC AND SOCIAL SERIALS. UK SOCIETY NAT/G PLAN PROB/SOLV ...SOC 20. PAGE 107 A2202
BIBLIOG INT/TRADE ECO/UNDEV L/A+17C

B65
O'CONNELL M.R.,IRISH POLITICS AND SOCIAL CONFLICT IN THE AGE OF THE AMERICAN REVOLUTION. FRANCE IRELAND MOD/EUR STRATA SECT LEGIS DIPLOM INT/TRADE DOMIN REV WAR...BIBLIOG 18 PARLIAMENT. PAGE 111 A2268
CATHISM ATTIT NAT/G DELIB/GP

B65
PANJAB U EXTENSION LIBRARY,INDIAN NEWS INDEX. INDIA ECO/UNDEV INDUS INT/ORG SCHOOL FORCES ADJUD WAR ATTIT WEALTH 20. PAGE 114 A2333
BIBLIOG PRESS WRITING DIPLOM

B65
ROTBERG R.I.,A POLITICAL HISTORY OF TROPICAL AFRICA. EX/STRUC DIPLOM INT/TRADE DOMIN ADMIN RACE/REL NAT/LISM PWR SOVEREIGN...GEOG TIME/SEQ BIBLIOG 1/20. PAGE 124 A2545
AFR CULTURE COLONIAL

B65
SCOTT A.M.,THE REVOLUTION IN STATECRAFT: INFORMAL PENETRATION. WOR+45 WOR-45 CULTURE INT/ORG FORCES ECO/TAC ROUTINE...BIBLIOG 20. PAGE 130 A2670
DIPLOM EDU/PROP FOR/AID

B65
SHUKRI A.,THE CONCEPT OF SELF-DETERMINATION IN THE UNITED NATIONS. WOR+45 DIPLOM INT/TRADE SANCTION NAT/LISM...BIBLIOG 20 UN. PAGE 132 A2709
COLONIAL INT/ORG INT/LAW SOVEREIGN

B65
SMITH A.L. JR.,THE DEUTSCHTUM OF NAZI GERMANY AND THE UNITED STATES. GERMANY USA-45 DIPLOM ATTIT FASCISM...BIBLIOG 20 MIGRATION NAZI. PAGE 134 A2744
INGP/REL NAT/LISM STRANGE DELIB/GP

B65
SPEECKAERT G.P.,SELECT BIBLIOGRAPHY ON INTERNATIONAL ORGANIZATION, 1885-1964. WOR+45 WOR-45 EX/STRUC DIPLOM ADMIN REGION 19/20 UN. PAGE 136 A2777
BIBLIOG INT/ORG GEN/LAWS STRATA

B65
THAYER F.C. JR.,AIR TRANSPORT POLICY AND NATIONAL SECURITY: A POLITICAL, ECONOMIC, AND MILITARY ANALYSIS. DIST/IND OP/RES PLAN TEC/DEV DIPLOM DETER WAR COST EFFICIENCY...POLICY BIBLIOG 20 DEPT/DEFEN FAA CAB. PAGE 142 A2908
AIR FORCES CIVMIL/REL ORD/FREE

B65
US LIBRARY OF CONGRESS,A DIRECTORY OF INFORMATION RESOURCES IN THE UNITED STATES: SOCIAL SCIENCES. USA+45 ACADEM INT/ORG LABOR PROF/ORG PUB/INST SCHOOL SECT 20. PAGE 155 A3159
BIBLIOG R+D COMPUT/IR

B65
VAN DEN BERGHE P.L.,AFRICA: SOCIAL PROBLEMS OF CHANGE AND CONFLICT. ELITES STRATA ECO/UNDEV KIN MUNIC DIPLOM GP/REL RACE/REL NAT/LISM...ANTHOL BIBLIOG 20. PAGE 158 A3210
SOC CULTURE AFR STRUCT

B65
VON GLAHN G.,LAW AMONG NATIONS: AN INTRODUCTION TO PUBLIC INTERNATIONAL LAW. WOR+45 WOR-45 INT/ORG NAT/G CREATE ADJUD WAR...GEOG CLASSIF TREND BIBLIOG. PAGE 160 A3250
ACADEM INT/LAW GEN/LAWS LAW

B65
WALKER A.A.,THE RHODESIAS AND NYASALAND: A GUIDE TO OFFICIAL PUBLICATIONS. RHODESIA UK OP/RES PLAN PROB/SOLV DIPLOM...POLICY SOC CON/ANAL 19/20 NYASALAND. PAGE 160 A3263
BIBLIOG NAT/G COLONIAL AFR

B65
WEAVER J.N.,THE INTERNATIONAL DEVELOPMENT ASSOCIATION: A NEW APPROACH TO FOREIGN AID. USA+45 NAT/G OP/RES PLAN PROB/SOLV WEALTH...CHARTS BIBLIOG 20 UN. PAGE 162 A3295
FOR/AID INT/ORG ECO/UNDEV FINAN

B65
WHITE G.M.,THE USE OF EXPERTS BY INTERNATIONAL TRIBUNALS. WOR+45 WOR-45 INT/ORG NAT/G PAY ADJUD COST...OBS BIBLIOG 20. PAGE 164 A3334
INT/LAW ROUTINE CONSULT CT/SYS

B65
WINT G.,COMMUNIST CHINA'S CRUSADE: MAO'S ROAD TO POWER AND THE NEW CAMPAIGN FOR WORLD REVOLUTION. ASIA CHINA/COM USA+45 USSR NAT/G POL/PAR DOMIN COERCE WAR PWR...POLICY CHARTS IDEA/COMP BIBLIOG 20 MAO. PAGE 165 A3364
DIPLOM MARXISM REV COLONIAL

B65
WITHERELL J.W.,MADAGASCAR AND ADJACENT ISLANDS; A GUIDE TO OFFICIAL PUBLICATIONS (PAMPHLET). FRANCE MADAGASCAR S/ASIA UK LAW OP/RES PLAN DIPLOM ...POLICY CON/ANAL 19/20. PAGE 165 A3371
BIBLIOG COLONIAL LOC/G ADMIN

L65
LOFTUS M.L.,"INTERNATIONAL MONETARY FUND, 1962-1965: A SELECTED BIBLIOGRAPHY." WOR+45 PLAN BUDGET INCOME PROFIT WEALTH. PAGE 90 A1852
BIBLIOG FINAN INT/TRADE INT/ORG

L65
MATTHEWS D.G.,"A CURRENT BIBLIOGRAPHY ON SUDANESE AFFAIRS; A SELECT BIBLIOGRAPHY FROM 1960-1964." SUDAN LAW CULTURE AGRI FINAN INDUS LABOR POL/PAR TEC/DEV FOR/AID RACE/REL LITERACY...LING 20. PAGE 96 A1970
BIBLIOG ECO/UNDEV NAT/G DIPLOM

S65
"FURTHER READING." INDIA USSR FORCES ATTIT SOCISM 20. PAGE 3 A0068
BIBLIOG DIPLOM MARXISM

S65
"FURTHER READING." INDIA ADMIN COLONIAL WAR GOV/REL ATTIT 20. PAGE 3 A0069
BIBLIOG DIPLOM NAT/G POLICY

S65
AFRICAN BIBLIOGRAPHIC CENTER,"US TREATIES AND AGREEMENTS WITH COUNTRIES IN AFRICA, 1957 TO MID-1963." AFR USA+45 AGRI FINAN FORCES TEC/DEV CAP/ISM FOR/AID 20. PAGE 5 A0097
BIBLIOG DIPLOM INT/ORG INT/TRADE

S65
DOSSICK J.J.,"DOCTORAL DISSERTATIONS ON RUSSIA, THE SOVIET UNION, AND EASTERN EUROPE." USSR ACADEM DIPLOM EDU/PROP MARXISM 19/20 COLD/WAR. PAGE 38 A0775
BIBLIOG HUM SOC

S65
GANGAL S.C.,"SURVEY OF RECENT RESEARCH: INDIA AND THE COMMONWEALTH" INDIA UK NAT/G INT/TRADE PARTIC GOV/REL ROLE 20 CMN/WLTH. PAGE 51 A1039
BIBLIOG POLICY REGION DIPLOM

S65
MERRITT R.L.,"SELECTED ARTICLES AND DOCUMENTS ON INTERNATIONAL LAW AND RELATIONS." WOR+45 INT/ORG FORCES INT/TRADE. PAGE 100 A2045
BIBLIOG DIPLOM INT/LAW GOV/REL

S65
PRABHAKAR P.,"SURVEY OF RESEARCH AND SOURCE MATERIALS; THE SINO-INDIAN BORDER DISPUTE." CHINA/COM INDIA LAW NAT/G PLAN BAL/PWR WAR...POLICY 20 COLD/WAR. PAGE 117 A2404
BIBLIOG ASIA S/ASIA DIPLOM

C65
BURTON J.W.,"INTERNATIONAL RELATIONS: A GENERAL THEORY." WOR+45 NAT/G CREATE BAL/PWR NEUTRAL COERCE DETER ADJUST...TREND IDEA/COMP GEN/METH BIBLIOG. PAGE 22 A0447
DIPLOM GEN/LAWS ACT/RES ORD/FREE

C65
MARK M.,"BEYOND SOVEREIGNTY." WOR+45 WOR-45 ECO/UNDEV BAL/PWR INT/TRADE NUC/PWR REV WAR MARXISM NEW/LIB BIBLIOG. PAGE 95 A1942
NAT/LISM NAT/G DIPLOM INTELL

C65
SCHEINGOLD S.A.,"THE RULE OF LAW IN EUROPEAN INTEGRATION: THE PATH OF THE SCHUMAN PLAN." EUR+WWI JUDGE ADJUD FEDERAL ATTIT PWR...RECORD INT BIBLIOG EEC ECSC. PAGE 128 A2621
INT/LAW CT/SYS REGION CENTRAL

C65
SEARA M.V.,"COSMIC INTERNATIONAL LAW." LAW ACADEM ACT/RES DIPLOM COLONIAL CONTROL NUC/PWR SOVEREIGN ...GEN/LAWS BIBLIOG UN. PAGE 131 A2678
SPACE INT/LAW IDEA/COMP INT/ORG

C65
WUORINEN J.H.,"SCANDINAVIA." DENMARK FINLAND ICELAND NORWAY SWEDEN SOCIETY AGRI POL/PAR DELIB/GP DIPLOM INT/TRADE NEUTRAL WAR...CHARTS TREATY 20. PAGE 168 A3423
BIBLIOG NAT/G POLICY

B66
ASAMOAH O.Y.,THE LEGAL SIGNIFICANCE OF THE DECLARATIONS OF THE GENERAL ASSEMBLY OF THE UNITED NATIONS. WOR+45 CREATE CONTROL...BIBLIOG 20 UN. PAGE 9 A0184
INT/LAW INT/ORG DIPLOM

B66
BROWN J.F.,THE NEW EASTERN EUROPE. ALBANIA BULGARIA HUNGARY POLAND ROMANIA CULTURE AGRI POL/PAR WAR NAT/LISM MARXISM...CHARTS BIBLIOG 20. PAGE 20 A0404
DIPLOM COM NAT/G ECO/UNDEV

B66
BROWN L.C.,STATE AND SOCIETY IN INDEPENDENT NORTH AFRICA. ALGERIA LIBYA MOROCCO AGRI INDUS INT/ORG POL/PAR SECT PLAN DIPLOM COLONIAL...LING NAT/COMP ANTHOL BIBLIOG 20 TUNIS MUSLIM. PAGE 20 A0406
NAT/G SOCIETY CULTURE ECO/UNDEV

B66
CANNING HOUSE LIBRARY,AUTHOR AND SUBJECT CATALOGUES OF THE CANNING HOUSE LIBRARY (5 VOLS.). UK CULTURE LEAD...SOC 19/20. PAGE 24 A0478
BIBLIOG L/A+17C NAT/G DIPLOM

B66
CLENDENON C.,AMERICANS IN AFRICA 1865-1900. AFR USA-45 ECO/UNDEV SECT REV RACE/REL CONSERVE ...TRADIT GEOG BIBLIOG 16/18. PAGE 27 A0549
DIPLOM COLONIAL INT/TRADE

B66
CONNEL-SMITH G.,THE INTERAMERICAN SYSTEM. CUBA L/A+17C DELIB/GP FOR/AID COLONIAL PEACE PWR MARXISM ...BIBLIOG 19/20 OAS. PAGE 29 A0586
DIPLOM INT/TRADE REGION INT/ORG

B66
EKIRCH A.A. JR.,IDEAS, IDEALS, AND AMERICAN DIPLOMACY. USA+45 USA-45 INT/ORG DOMIN COLONIAL ARMS/CONT DETER ISOLAT NAT/LISM...MAJORIT BIBLIOG 19/20 COLD/WAR. PAGE 41 A0834
DIPLOM LEAD PEACE

B66
EPSTEIN F.T.,THE AMERICAN BIBLIOGRAPHY OF RUSSIAN AND EAST EUROPEAN STUDIES FOR 1964. USSR LOC/G NAT/G POL/PAR FORCES ADMIN ARMS/CONT...JURID CONCPT 20 UN. PAGE 42 A0855
BIBLIOG COM MARXISM DIPLOM

B66
ESTHUS R.A.,THEODORE ROOSEVELT AND JAPAN. ASIA USA-45 FORCES CONFER WAR SOVEREIGN...BIBLIOG 20 CHINJAP. PAGE 42 A0864
DIPLOM DELIB/GP

B66
FALL B.B.,VIET-NAM WITNESS, 1953-66. S/ASIA VIETNAM SECT PROB/SOLV COLONIAL GUERRILLA...CHARTS BIBLIOG 20. PAGE 44 A0895
MARXIST WAR DIPLOM

B66
FARWELL G.,MASK OF ASIA: THE PHILIPPINES. PHILIPPINE SECT DIPLOM ATTIT...SOC RECORD PREDICT BIBLIOG 20. PAGE 44 A0901
S/ASIA CULTURE

B66
GRAHAM I.C.C.,PUBLICATIONS OF THE SOCIAL SCIENCE DEPARTMENT, THE RAND CORPORATION, 1948-1966. USSR WOR+45 NAT/G ARMS/CONT DETER WAR NAT/LISM...SOC GOV/COMP. PAGE 55 A1127
BIBLIOG DIPLOM NUC/PWR FORCES

B66
HARMON R.B.,SOURCES AND PROBLEMS OF BIBLIOGRAPHY IN POLITICAL SCIENCE (PAMPHLET). INT/ORG LOC/G MUNIC POL/PAR ADMIN GOV/REL ALL/IDEOS...JURID MGT CONCPT 19/20. PAGE 61 A1262
BIBLIOG DIPLOM INT/LAW NAT/G

B66
HOFMANN L.,UNITED STATES AND CANADIAN PUBLICATIONS ON AFRICA IN 1964. LAW AGRI INDUS SCHOOL...HUM SOC 20. PAGE 66 A1360
BIBLIOG AFR DIPLOM

B66
HOLT R.T.,THE POLITICAL BASIS OF ECONOMIC DEVELOPMENT. STRATA STRUCT NAT/G DIPLOM ADMIN...SOC NAT/COMP BIBLIOG 20. PAGE 67 A1376
ECO/TAC GOV/COMP CONSTN EX/STRUC

B66
KANET R.E.,THE SOVIET UNION AND SUB-SAHARAN AFRICA: COMMUNIST POLICY TOWARD AFRICA, 1917-1965. AFR USSR ECO/UNDEV TEC/DEV EDU/PROP TASK DISCRIM PEACE WEALTH ALL/IDEOS...CHARTS BIBLIOG SOC/INTEG 19/20 NEGRO UN INTERVENT. PAGE 76 A1555
DIPLOM ECO/TAC MARXISM

B66
KIM Y.K.,PATTERNS OF COMPETITIVE COEXISTENCE: USA VS. USSR. USA+45 USSR ECO/DEV ECO/UNDEV INT/ORG FOR/AID INT/TRADE ARMS/CONT...BIBLIOG 20 COLD/WAR. PAGE 79 A1618
DIPLOM PEACE BAL/PWR DETER

B66
LEIGH M.B.,CHECK LIST OF HOLDINGS ON BORNEO IN THE CORNELL UNIVERSITY LIBRARIES (PAMPHLET). BORNEO MALAYSIA LAW CONSTN GP/REL SOC. PAGE 86 A1769
BIBLIOG S/ASIA DIPLOM NAT/G

B66
MCINTYRE W.D.,COLONIES INTO COMMONWEALTH. UK CONSTN VOL/ASSN DOMIN CONTROL...BIBLIOG 18/20 CMN/WLTH. PAGE 98 A2012
DIPLOM INT/ORG COLONIAL SOVEREIGN

B66
MIKESELL R.F.,PUBLIC INTERNATIONAL LENDING FOR DEVELOPMENT. WOR+45 WOR-45 DELIB/GP...TIME/SEQ CHARTS BIBLIOG 20. PAGE 101 A2070
INT/ORG FOR/AID ECO/UNDEV FINAN

B66
MULLER C.F.J.,A SELECT BIBLIOGRAPHY OF SOUTH AFRICAN HISTORY; A GUIDE FOR HISTORICAL RESEARCH. SOUTH/AFR UK LAW CONSTN SOCIETY STRUCT AGRI SECT DIPLOM COLONIAL LEAD RACE/REL...POLICY 17/20 NEGRO. PAGE 106 A2167
BIBLIOG AFR NAT/G

B66
NEUMANN R.G.,THE GOVERNMENT OF THE GERMAN FEDERAL REPUBLIC. EUR+WWI GERMANY/W LOC/G EX/STRUC LEGIS CT/SYS INGP/REL PWR...BIBLIOG 20 ADENAUER/K. PAGE 108 A2222
NAT/G POL/PAR DIPLOM CONSTN

B66
NIJHOFF M.,ANNUAIRE EUROPEEN (VOL. XII). INT/TRADE REGION PEACE 20 EFTA EEC ECSC EURATOM. PAGE 109 A2241
BIBLIOG INT/ORG EUR+WWI DIPLOM

B66
OHLIN G.,FOREIGN AID POLICIES RECONSIDERED. ECO/DEV ECO/UNDEV VOL/ASSN CONSULT PLAN CONTROL ATTIT ...CONCPT CHARTS BIBLIOG 20. PAGE 111 A2286
FOR/AID DIPLOM GIVE

B66
RIESELBACH L.N.,THE ROOTS OF ISOLATIONISM* CONGRESSIONAL VOTING AND PRESIDENTIAL LEADERSHIP IN FOREIGN POLICY. POL/PAR LEGIS DIPLOM EDU/PROP LEAD REGION REPRESENT...SOC STAT IDEA/COMP HYPO/EXP BIBLIOG 19/20 CONGRESS. PAGE 121 A2477
ISOLAT CHOOSE CHIEF POLICY

B66
RISTIC D.N.,YUGOSLAVIA'S REVOLUTION OF 1941. EUR+WWI YUGOSLAVIA NAT/G WAR ORD/FREE...RECORD BIBLIOG 20 HITLER/A TREATY. PAGE 121 A2484
REV ATTIT FASCISM DIPLOM

B66
SINGH L.P.,THE POLITICS OF ECONOMIC COOPERATION IN ASIA; A STUDY OF ASIAN INTERNATIONAL ORGANIZATIONS. ASIA INT/ORG ACT/RES PLAN GP/REL...POLICY GP/COMP BIBLIOG 20 UN SEATO. PAGE 133 A2733
ECO/UNDEV ECO/TAC REGION DIPLOM

B66
SKILLING H.G.,THE GOVERNMENTS OF COMMUNIST EAST EUROPE. COM EUR+WWI ELITES FORCES DIPLOM ECO/TAC CONTROL HABITAT SOCISM...DECISION BIBLIOG 20 EUROPE/E COM/PARTY. PAGE 134 A2738
MARXISM NAT/COMP GP/COMP DOMIN

B66
SOCIAL SCIENCE RESEARCH COUN,BIBLIOGRAPHY OF RESEARCH IN THE SOCIAL SCIENCES IN AUSTRALIA 1957-1960. LAW R+D DIPLOM 20 AUSTRAL. PAGE 135 A2758
BIBLIOG SOC PSY

B66
TINKER H.,SOUTH ASIA. UK LAW ECO/UNDEV AGRI ACADEM SECT DIPLOM EDU/PROP REV WEALTH ALL/IDEOS...CHARTS BIBLIOG GANDHI/M NEHRU/J. PAGE 144 A2945
S/ASIA COLONIAL TREND

B66
TYSON G.,NEHRU: THE YEARS OF POWER. INDIA UK STRATA ECO/UNDEV FINAN SECT TASK WAR ORD/FREE MARXISM ...POLICY BIBLIOG 20 NEHRU/J. PAGE 146 A2985
CHIEF PWR DIPLOM NAT/G

B66
UNITED NATIONS,INTERNATIONAL SPACE BIBLIOGRAPHY. FUT INT/ORG TEC/DEV DIPLOM ARMS/CONT NUC/PWR ...JURID SOC UN. PAGE 149 A3037
BIBLIOG SPACE PEACE R+D

B66
US LIBRARY OF CONGRESS,NIGERIA: A GUIDE TO OFFICIAL PUBLICATIONS. CAMEROON NIGERIA UK DIPLOM...POLICY 19/20 UN LEAGUE/NAT. PAGE 155 A3160
BIBLIOG ADMIN NAT/G COLONIAL

B66
VYAS R.,DAWNING ON THE CAPITOL: US CONGRESS AND INDIA. INDIA S/ASIA USA+45 ELITES ECO/DEV ECO/UNDEV PLAN FOR/AID...BIBLIOG 20 CONGRESS. PAGE 160 A3256
POLICY LEGIS NAT/G DIPLOM

B66
ZEINE Z.N.,THE EMERGENCE OF ARAB NATIONALISM (REV. ED.). TURKEY UK NAT/G SECT TEC/DEV LEAD REV WAR AGE/Y ROLE ORD/FREE...TRADIT CHARTS BIBLIOG 20 ARABS OTTOMAN. PAGE 170 A3451
ISLAM NAT/LISM DIPLOM

L66
BARMAN R.K.,"INDO-PAKISTANI RELATIONS 1947-1965: A SELECTED BIBLIOGRAPHY." INDIA PAKISTAN NAT/G 20. PAGE 11 A0223
BIBLIOG DIPLOM S/ASIA

L66
SEYLER W.C.,"DOCTORAL DISSERTATIONS IN POLITICAL SCIENCE IN UNIVERSITIES OF THE UNITED STATES AND CANADA." INT/ORG LOC/G ADMIN...INT/LAW MGT GOV/COMP. PAGE 131 A2690
BIBLIOG LAW NAT/G

S66
"RESEARCH WORK 1965-1966." NEW/ZEALND ELITES ACADEM LOC/G MUNIC POL/PAR PROVS DIPLOM COLONIAL...SOC 20 AUSTRAL. PAGE 4 A0073
BIBLIOG NAT/G CULTURE S/ASIA

S66
"WORLD BANK CONVENTION ON INVESTMENT DISPUTES; A BIBLIOGRAPH ICAL NOTE." VOL/ASSN CONSULT CAP/ISM DIPLOM INT/TRADE 20 SENATE PRESIDENT. PAGE 4 A0074
BIBLIOG ADJUD FINAN INT/ORG

S66
"FURTHER READING." INDIA LEAD ATTIT...CONCPT 20. PAGE 4 A0075
BIBLIOG NAT/G DIPLOM POLICY

S66
AFRICAN BIBLIOGRAPHIC CENTER,"A DESCRIPTIVE STUDY OF CURRENT AFRICAN FOREIGN RELATIONS." COM CULTURE INT/ORG SECT RACE/REL DISCRIM ATTIT 20. PAGE 5 A0099
BIBLIOG DIPLOM AFR

S66
AFRICAN BIBLIOGRAPHIC CENTER,"THE NEW AFRO-ASIAN STATES IN PERSPECTIVE, 1960-1963: A SELECT BIBLIOGRAPHY." AFR ASIA CULTURE SOCIETY INT/ORG LABOR TEC/DEV LITERACY 20 UN. PAGE 5 A0100
BIBLIOG DIPLOM FOR/AID INT/TRADE

S66
MATTHEWS D.G.,"ETHIOPIAN OUTLINE: A BIBLIOGRAPHIC RESEARCH GUIDE." ETHIOPIA LAW STRUCT ECO/UNDEV AGRI LABOR SECT CHIEF DELIB/GP EX/STRUC ADMIN...LING ORG/CHARTS 20. PAGE 96 A1972
BIBLIOG NAT/G DIPLOM POL/PAR

S66
MERRITT R.L.,"SELECTED ARTICLES AND DOCUMENTS ON COMPARATIVE GOVERNMENT AND CROSS-NATIONAL RESEARCH." AFR ASIA EUR+WWI L/A+17C MOD/EUR ELITES R+D ACT/RES DIPLOM PWR...SOC CONCPT 18/20. PAGE 100 A2046
BIBLIOG GOV/COMP NAT/G GOV/REL

C66
BLAISDELL D.C.,"INTERNATIONAL ORGANIZATION." FUT WOR+45 ECO/DEV DELIB/GP FORCES EFFICIENCY PEACE ORD/FREE...INT/LAW 20 UN LEAGUE/NAT NATO. PAGE 15 A0304
BIBLIOG INT/ORG DIPLOM ARMS/CONT

C66
DUROSELLE J.B.,"LE CONFLIT DE TRIESTE 1943-1954: ETUDES DE CAS DE CONFLITS INTERNATIONAUX III." ITALY USA+45 YUGOSLAVIA ELITES DELIB/GP PLAN ADJUST ...POLICY GEOG CHARTS IDEA/COMP TIME 20 TREATY UN COLD/WAR. PAGE 40 A0810
BIBLIOG WAR DIPLOM GEN/LAWS

C66
KULSKI W.W.,"DEGAULLE AND THE WORLD: THE FOREIGN POLICY OF THE FIFTH FRENCH REPUBLIC." FRANCE ECO/UNDEV POL/PAR BAL/PWR DETER NUC/PWR ATTIT PWR ...RECORD BIBLIOG DEGAULLE NATO EEC. PAGE 83 A1694
POLICY SOVEREIGN PERSON DIPLOM

C66
WINT G.,"ASIA: A HANDBOOK." ASIA S/ASIA INDUS LABOR SECT PRESS RACE/REL MARXISM...STAT CHARTS BIBLIOG 20. PAGE 165 A3366
ECO/UNDEV DIPLOM NAT/G SOCIETY

B67
AMERICAN BIBLIOGRAPHICAL CTR,LIST OF PERIODICALS: AMERICA:HISTORY AND LIFE AND HISTORICAL ABSTRACTS (BIBLIOGRAPHY AND REFERENCE SERIES NO. 3). USA+45 CULTURE DIPLOM 18/20. PAGE 7 A0142
BIBLIOG USA-45

B67
ANDREATTA L.,VIETNAM, A CHECKLIST. S/ASIA VIETNAM PRESS PEACE ATTIT...POLICY 20. PAGE 8 A0159
BIBLIOG DIPLOM WAR

B67
BLOM-COOPER L.,THE LITERATURE OF THE LAW AND THE LANGUAGE OF THE LAW (2 VOLS.). CANADA ISRAEL UK WOR+45 WOR-45 JUDGE CT/SYS ATTIT...CRIMLGY JURID ANTHOL CMN/WLTH. PAGE 15 A0312
BIBLIOG LAW INT/LAW ADJUD

B67
CECIL L.,ALBERT BALLIN; BUSINESS AND POLITICS IN IMPERIAL GERMANY 1888-1918. GERMANY UK INT/TRADE LEAD WAR PERS/REL ADJUST PWR WEALTH...MGT BIBLIOG 19/20. PAGE 25 A0510
DIPLOM CONSTN ECO/DEV TOP/EX

B67
CHO S.S.,KOREA IN WORLD POLITICS 1940-1950; AN EVALUATION OF AMERICAN RESPONSIBILITY. KOREA USA+45 USSR CONSTN INT/ORG NAT/G FORCES FOR/AID ANOMIE SUPEGO MARXISM...DECISION BIBLIOG 20. PAGE 26 A0533
POLICY DIPLOM PROB/SOLV WAR

B67
DOSSICK J.J.,DOCTORAL RESEARCH ON PUERTO RICO AND PUERTO RICANS. PUERT/RICO USA+45 USA-45 ADMIN 20. PAGE 38 A0776 — BIBLIOG CONSTN POL/PAR DIPLOM

B67
EUROPA-ARCHIV,DEUTSCHES AND AUSLANDISCHES SCHRIFTTUM ZU DEN REGIONALEN SICHERHEITSVEREINBARUNGEN 1945-1956. WOR+45 FORCES BAL/PWR REGION. PAGE 43 A0875 — BIBLIOG INT/ORG PEACE DETER

B67
FRASER-TYTLER W.K.,AFGHANISTAN: A STUDY OF POLITICAL DEVELOPMENTS IN CENTRAL AND SOUTHERN ASIA (3RD ED.). AFGHANISTN INDIA KIN FOR/AID PWR ...BIBLIOG. PAGE 48 A0990 — DIPLOM NAT/G CONSTN GEOG

B67
GRIFFITH SB I.I.,THE CHINESE PEOPLE'S LIBERATION ARMY. CHINA/COM DIPLOM DOMIN GUERRILLA NUC/PWR REV ...CHARTS BIBLIOG 20. PAGE 57 A1163 — FORCES CIVMIL/REL NAT/LISM PWR

B67
HALPERIN M.H.,CONTEMPORARY MILITARY STRATEGY. ASIA CHINA/COM USA+45 USSR INT/ORG FORCES ACT/RES PLAN TEC/DEV BAL/PWR COERCE WAR...METH/COMP BIBLIOG 20 NATO. PAGE 60 A1240 — DIPLOM NUC/PWR DETER ARMS/CONT

B67
HOLSTI K.J.,INTERNATIONAL POLITICS* A FRAMEWORK FOR ANALYSIS. WOR+45 WOR-45 NAT/G EDU/PROP DETER WAR WEAPON PWR BIBLIOG. PAGE 67 A1372 — DIPLOM BARGAIN POLICY INT/LAW

B67
INTERNATIONAL LABOUR OFFICE,SUBJECT GUIDE TO PUBLICATIONS OF THE INTERNATIONAL LABOUR OFFICE, 1919-1964. DIPLOM 20. PAGE 71 A1457 — BIBLIOG LABOR INT/ORG WORKER

B67
ISENBERG I.,FRANCE UNDER DE GAULLE (THE REFERENCE SHELF VOL. 39 NO. 1). EUR+WWI FRANCE ECO/DEV ...BIBLIOG 20 DEGAULLE/C NATO EEC. PAGE 72 A1469 — ATTIT DIPLOM POLICY CHIEF

B67
LANDEN R.G.,OMAN SINCE 1856: DISRUPTIVE MODERNIZATION IN A TRADITIONAL ARAB SOCIETY. UK DIST/IND EXTR/IND SECT DIPLOM INT/TRADE...SOC LING CHARTS BIBLIOG 19/20. PAGE 84 A1714 — ISLAM CULTURE ECO/UNDEV NAT/G

B67
PIKE F.B.,FREEDOM AND REFORM IN LATIN AMERICA. BRAZIL URUGUAY CONSTN CULTURE SECT DIPLOM EDU/PROP PARTIC DRIVE ALL/VALS CATHISM...GEOG ANTHOL BIBLIOG REFORMERS BOLIV. PAGE 116 A2379 — L/A+17C ORD/FREE ECO/UNDEV REV

B67
POGANY A.H.,POLITICAL SCIENCE AND INTERNATIONAL RELATIONS, BOOKS RECOMMENDED FOR AMERICAN CATHOLIC COLLEGE LIBRARIES. INT/ORG LOC/G NAT/G FORCES BAL/PWR ECO/TAC NUC/PWR...CATH INT/LAW TREATY 20. PAGE 117 A2393 — BIBLIOG DIPLOM

B67
RALSTON D.B.,THE ARMY OF THE REPUBLIC; THE PLACE OF THE MILITARY IN THE POLITICAL EVOLUTION OF FRANCE 1871-1914. FRANCE MOD/EUR EX/STRUC LEGIS TOP/EX DIPLOM ADMIN WAR GP/REL ROLE...BIBLIOG 19/20. PAGE 119 A2436 — FORCES NAT/G CIVMIL/REL POLICY

B67
SAYEED K.B.,THE POLITICAL SYSTEM OF PAKISTAN. PAKISTAN DIPLOM REGION CHOOSE ORD/FREE...BIBLIOG 20. PAGE 127 A2609 — NAT/G POL/PAR CONSTN SECT

B67
SCOTT A.M.,THE FUNCTIONING OF THE INTERNATIONAL POLITICAL SYSTEM. INT/ORG OP/RES PROB/SOLV COERCE WAR EQUILIB...METH/CNCPT BIBLIOG. PAGE 130 A2671 — DIPLOM DECISION BAL/PWR

B67
SINGER D.,QUANTITATIVE INTERNATIONAL POLITICS* INSIGHTS AND EVIDENCE. WOR+45 WOR-45 PARTIC WAR INGP/REL ATTIT PERSON ROLE...PREDICT BIBLIOG 19/20 UN SENATE. PAGE 133 A2722 — DIPLOM NAT/G INT/ORG DECISION

B67
US DEPARTMENT OF STATE,FOREIGN AFFAIRS RESEARCH (PAMPHLET). USA+45 WOR+45 ACADEM NAT/G...PSY SOC CHARTS 20. PAGE 152 A3100 — BIBLIOG INDEX R+D DIPLOM

B67
US DEPARTMENT OF STATE,TREATIES IN FORCE. USA+45 WOR+45 AGREE WAR PEACE 20 TREATY. PAGE 152 A3101 — BIBLIOG DIPLOM INT/ORG DETER

C67
GEHLEN M.P.,"THE POLITICS OF COEXISTENCE: SOVIET METHODS AND MOTIVES." COM USSR NAT/G INT/TRADE EDU/PROP ARMS/CONT DETER KNOWL...CHARTS IDEA/COMP 20 COLD/WAR. PAGE 52 A1056 — BIBLIOG PEACE DIPLOM MARXISM

C67
LING D.L.,"TUNISIA: FROM PROTECTORATE TO REPUBLIC." CULTURE NAT/G POL/PAR CHIEF DIPLOM COERCE WAR PWR ...BIBLIOG 19/20 TUNIS. PAGE 89 A1825 — AFR NAT/LISM COLONIAL PROB/SOLV

C67
SPANIER J.W.,"WORLD POLITICS IN AN AGE OF REVOLUTION." COM WOR+45 FORCES COERCE WAR NAT/LISM SOVEREIGN...POLICY BIBLIOG 20. PAGE 135 A2772 — DIPLOM TEC/DEV REV ECO/UNDEV

B68
ANTWERP-INST UNIVERSITAIRE,BIBLIOGRAPHIC COMPENDIUM: DEVELOPING COUNTRIES (ANTWERP-INST UNIVERSITAIRE DES TERRITOIRES D'OUTRE-MER). AFR EUR+WWI SOCIETY AGRI FINAN NEIGH VOL/ASSN PROB/SOLV TEC/DEV FOR/AID INT/TRADE 20. PAGE 8 A0166 — BIBLIOG ECO/UNDEV DIPLOM PLAN

B82
POOLE W.F.,INDEX TO PERIODICAL LITERATURE. LOC/G NAT/G DIPLOM ADMIN...HUM PHIL/SCI SOC 19. PAGE 117 A2396 — BIBLIOG USA-45 ALL/VALS SOCIETY

B93
ROYAL GEOGRAPHIC SOCIETY,BIBLIOGRAPHY OF BARBARY STATES (4 SUPPLEMENTARY PAPERS). ALGERIA LIBYA MOROCCO SOCIETY STRUCT DIPLOM LEAD 14/19 TUNIS. PAGE 125 A2555 — BIBLIOG ISLAM NAT/G COLONIAL

C93
PLAYFAIR R.L.,"A BIBLIOGRAPHY OF MOROCCO." MOROCCO CULTURE AGRI FORCES DIPLOM WAR HEALTH...GEOG JURID SOC CHARTS. PAGE 116 A2387 — BIBLIOG ISLAM MEDIT-7

BIBLIOG/A....BIBLIOGRAPHY OVER 50 ITEMS ANNOTATED

N
AMERICAN DOCUMENTATION INST,DOCUMENTATION ABSTRACTS. WOR+45 NAT/G COMPUTER CREATE TEC/DEV DIPLOM EDU/PROP REGION KNOWL...PHIL/SCI CLASSIF LING. PAGE 7 A0143 — BIBLIOG/A AUTOMAT COMPUT/IR R+D

N
CONOVER H.F.,WORLD GOVERNMENT: A LIST OF SELECTED REFERENCES (PAMPHLET). WOR+45 PROB/SOLV ARMS/CONT WAR PEACE 20 UN. PAGE 29 A0589 — BIBLIOG/A NUC/PWR INT/ORG DIPLOM

N
LIBRARY INTERNATIONAL REL,INTERNATIONAL INFORMATION SERVICE. WOR+45 CULTURE INT/ORG FORCES...GEOG HUM SOC. PAGE 88 A1808 — BIBLIOG/A DIPLOM INT/TRADE INT/LAW

N
MONPIED E.,BIBLIOGRAPHIE FEDERALISTE: ARTICLES ET DOCUMENTS PUBLIES DANS LES PERIODIQUES PARUS EN FRANCE NOV. 1945-OCT. 1950. EUR+WWI WOR+45 ADMIN REGION ATTIT MARXISM PACIFISM 20 EEC. PAGE 103 A2108 — BIBLIOG/A FEDERAL CENTRAL INT/ORG

N
UNIVERSITY OF FLORIDA LIBRARY,DOORS TO LATIN AMERICA; RECENT BOOKS AND PAMPHLETS. CONSTN CULTURE SOCIETY ECO/UNDEV COLONIAL LEAD GOV/REL NAT/LISM ATTIT...HUM SOC 20. PAGE 149 A3047 — BIBLIOG/A L/A+17C DIPLOM NAT/G

B
CURRENT THOUGHT ON PEACE AND WAR. WOR+45 INT/ORG FORCES PROB/SOLV DIPLOM NUC/PWR PERCEPT...POLICY SOC 20 UN NATO. PAGE 1 A0008 — BIBLIOG/A PEACE ATTIT WAR

B
UN DEPARTMENT SOCIAL AFFAIRS,SOCIAL WELFARE INFORMATION SERIES: CURRENT LITERATURE AND NATIONAL CONFERENCES. WOR+45 INDUS SERV/IND INT/ORG CONSULT ACT/RES WEALTH...HEAL UN. PAGE 147 A2997 — BIBLIOG/A SOC/WK DIPLOM ADMIN

N
AFRICANA NEWSLETTER. ECO/UNDEV ACADEM SECT DIPLOM PRESS COLONIAL NAT/LISM 20. PAGE 1 A0001 — BIBLIOG/A AFR NAT/G

N
AMERICAN JOURNAL OF INTERNATIONAL LAW. WOR+45 WOR-45 CONSTN INT/ORG NAT/G CT/SYS ARMS/CONT WAR ...DECISION JURID NAT/COMP 20. PAGE 1 A0002 — BIBLIOG/A INT/LAW DIPLOM ADJUD

N
AMERICAN POLITICAL SCIENCE REVIEW. USA+45 USA-45 WOR+45 WOR-45 INT/ORG ADMIN...INT/LAW PHIL/SCI CONCPT METH 20 UN. PAGE 1 A0003 — BIBLIOG/A DIPLOM NAT/G GOV/COMP

N
ANNALS OF THE AMERICAN ACADEMY OF POLITICAL AND SOCIAL SCIENCE. AFR ASIA S/ASIA WOR+45 POL/PAR DIPLOM CRIME REV...SOC BIOG 20. PAGE 1 A0004 — BIBLIOG/A NAT/G CULTURE ATTIT

N
BULLETIN ANALYTIQUE DE DOCUMENTATION POLITIQUE, ECONOMIQUE, ET SOCIAL CONTEMPORAIRE. FRANCE WOR+45 SOCIETY ECO/DEV ECO/UNDEV INT/ORG LOC/G PROB/SOLV FOR/AID LEAD REGION SOC. PAGE 1 A0006 — BIBLIOG/A DIPLOM NAT/COMP NAT/G

N
CANADIAN GOVERNMENT PUBLICATIONS (1955-). CANADA AGRI FINAN LABOR FORCES INT/TRADE HEALTH...JURID 20 PARLIAMENT. PAGE 1 A0007 — BIBLIOG/A NAT/G DIPLOM INT/ORG

N
INTERNATIONAL AFFAIRS. WOR+45 WOR-45 ECO/UNDEV INT/ORG NAT/G PROB/SOLV FOR/AID WAR...POLICY 20. — BIBLIOG/A DIPLOM

PAGE 1 A0009 INT/LAW INT/TRADE N

INTERNATIONAL BOOK NEWS, 1928-1934. ECO/UNDEV FINAN INDUS LABOR INT/TRADE CONFER ADJUD COLONIAL...HEAL SOC/WK CHARTS 20 LEAGUE/NAT. PAGE 1 A0010 BIBLIOG/A DIPLOM INT/LAW INT/ORG N

INTERNATIONAL REVIEW OF ADMINISTRATIVE SCIENCES. WOR+45 WOR-45 STRATA ECO/DEV ECO/UNDEV CREATE PLAN PROB/SOLV DIPLOM CONTROL REPRESENT...MGT 20. PAGE 1 A0011 BIBLIOG/A ADMIN INT/ORG NAT/G N

INTERNATIONAL STUDIES. ASIA S/ASIA WOR+45 ECO/UNDEV INT/ORG NAT/G LEAD ATTIT WEALTH...SOC 20. PAGE 1 A0012 BIBLIOG/A DIPLOM INT/LAW INT/TRADE N

JOURNAL OF CONFLICT RESOLUTION. FUT WOR+45 INT/ORG NAT/G FORCES CREATE PROB/SOLV ARMS/CONT NUC/PWR WEAPON SOC. PAGE 1 A0014 BIBLIOG/A DIPLOM WAR N

JOURNAL OF MODERN HISTORY. WOR+45 WOR-45 LEAD WAR ...TIME/SEQ TREND NAT/COMP 20. PAGE 1 A0016 BIBLIOG/A DIPLOM NAT/G N

JOURNAL OF POLITICS. USA+45 USA-45 CONSTN POL/PAR EX/STRUC LEGIS PROB/SOLV DIPLOM CT/SYS CHOOSE RACE/REL 20. PAGE 1 A0017 BIBLIOG/A NAT/G LAW LOC/G N

MIDWEST JOURNAL OF POLITICAL SCIENCE. USA+45 CONSTN ECO/DEV LEGIS PROB/SOLV CT/SYS LEAD GOV/REL ATTIT POLICY. PAGE 1 A0020 BIBLIOG/A NAT/G DIPLOM POL/PAR N

POLITICAL SCIENCE QUARTERLY. USA+45 USA-45 LAW CONSTN ECO/DEV INT/ORG LOC/G POL/PAR LEGIS LEAD NUC/PWR...CONCPT 20. PAGE 1 A0023 BIBLIOG/A NAT/G DIPLOM POLICY N

REVIEW OF POLITICS. WOR+45 WOR-45 CONSTN LEGIS PROB/SOLV ADMIN LEAD ALL/IDEOS...PHIL/SCI 20. PAGE 2 A0024 BIBLIOG/A DIPLOM INT/ORG NAT/G N

SOCIAL RESEARCH. WOR+45 WOR-45 R+D LEAD GP/REL ATTIT...SOC TREND 20. PAGE 2 A0025 BIBLIOG/A DIPLOM NAT/G SOCIETY N

AFRICAN RESEARCH BULLETIN. AFR CULTURE NAT/G COLONIAL...SOC 20. PAGE 2 A0026 BIBLIOG/A DIPLOM PRESS N

CHINA QUARTERLY. COM AGRI INDUS ACADEM POL/PAR INT/TRADE CONFER GOV/REL...TIME/SEQ CON/ANAL INDEX 20. PAGE 2 A0032 BIBLIOG/A ASIA DIPLOM POLICY N

DOCUMENTATION ECONOMIQUE: REVUE BIBLIOGRAPHIQUE DE SYNTHESE. WOR+45 COM/IND FINAN BUDGET DIPLOM...GEOG 20. PAGE 2 A0033 BIBLIOG/A SOC N

HANDBOOK OF LATIN AMERICAN STUDIES. LAW CULTURE ECO/UNDEV POL/PAR ADMIN LEAD...SOC 20. PAGE 2 A0035 BIBLIOG/A L/A+17C NAT/G DIPLOM N

LATIN AMERICA IN PERIODICAL LITERATURE. LAW TEC/DEV DIPLOM RECEIVE EDU/PROP...GEOG HUM MGT 20. PAGE 2 A0037 BIBLIOG/A L/A+17C SOCIETY ECO/UNDEV N

REVUE FRANCAISE DE SCIENCE POLITIQUE. FRANCE UK ...BIBLIOG/A 20. PAGE 2 A0040 NAT/G DIPLOM CONCPT ROUTINE N

THE WORLD OF LEARNING. INTELL ACT/RES EDU/PROP 20 UNESCO. PAGE 2 A0045 BIBLIOG/A ACADEM R+D INT/ORG N

SCHOLARLY BOOKS IN AMERICA; A QUARTERLY BIBLIOGRAPHY OF UNIVERSITY PRESS PUBLICATIONS. WOR+45 AGRI COM/IND NAT/G HEALTH...GEOG PHIL/SCI PSY SOC LING 20. PAGE 3 A0046 BIBLIOG/A LAW MUNIC DIPLOM N

JAHRBUCH DER DISSERTATIONEN. GERMANY/W WOR+45 ...TREND 20. PAGE 3 A0048 BIBLIOG/A NAT/G ACADEM DIPLOM N

"PROLOG",DIGEST OF THE SOVIET UKRANIAN PRESS. USSR LAW AGRI INDUS PROVS SCHOOL DIPLOM GOV/REL ATTIT ...HUM LING 20. PAGE 4 A0081 BIBLIOG/A NAT/G PRESS COM N

AFRICAN BIBLIOGRAPHIC CENTER,A CURRENT BIBLIOGRAPHY ON AFRICAN AFFAIRS. LAW CULTURE ECO/UNDEV LABOR SECT DIPLOM FOR/AID COLONIAL NAT/LISM...LING 20. PAGE 5 A0094 BIBLIOG/A AFR NAT/G REGION N

AIR UNIVERSITY LIBRARY,INDEX TO MILITARY PERIODICALS. FUT SPACE WOR+45 REGION ARMS/CONT NUC/PWR WAR PEACE INT/LAW. PAGE 5 A0105 BIBLIOG/A FORCES NAT/G DIPLOM N

AMER COUNCIL OF LEARNED SOCIET,THE ACLS CONSTITUENT SOCIETY JOURNAL PROJECT. FUT USA+45 LAW NAT/G PLAN DIPLOM PHIL/SCI. PAGE 7 A0134 BIBLIOG/A HUM COMPUT/IR COMPUTER N

AMERICAN ECONOMIC ASSOCIATION,THE JOURNAL OF ECONOMIC ABSTRACTS. ECO/UNDEV MARKET LABOR DIPLOM ...MGT CONCPT METH 20. PAGE 7 A0144 BIBLIOG/A R+D FINAN N

ASIA FOUNDATION,LIBRARY NOTES. LAW CONSTN CULTURE SOCIETY ECO/UNDEV INT/ORG NAT/G COLONIAL LEAD REGION NAT/LISM ATTIT 20 UN. PAGE 9 A0189 BIBLIOG/A ASIA S/ASIA DIPLOM N

ATLANTIC INSTITUTE,ATLANTIC STUDIES. COM EUR+WWI USA+45 CULTURE STRUCT ECO/DEV FORCES LEAD ARMS/CONT ...INT/LAW JURID SOC. PAGE 10 A0193 BIBLIOG/A DIPLOM POLICY GOV/REL N

CARNEGIE ENDOWMENT,CURRENT RESEARCH IN INTERNATIONAL AFFAIRS: SELECTED BIBLIOGRAPHY OF WORK IN PROGRESS BY PRIVATE RESEARCH AGENCIES. WOR+45 NAT/G ACT/RES GOV/COMP. PAGE 24 A0488 BIBLIOG/A DIPLOM R+D N

CORDIER H.,BIBLIOTECA SINICA. SOCIETY STRUCT SECT DIPLOM COLONIAL...GEOG SOC CON/ANAL. PAGE 30 A0618 BIBLIOG/A NAT/G CULTURE ASIA N

FOREIGN TRADE LIBRARY,NEW TITLES RECEIVED IN THE LIBRARY. WOR+45 ECO/UNDEV FINAN NAT/G PLAN TEC/DEV BUDGET ECO/TAC TARIFFS GOV/REL STAT. PAGE 47 A0964 BIBLIOG/A INT/TRADE INDUS ECO/DEV N

INSTITUTE OF HISPANIC STUDIES,HISPANIC AMERICAN REPORT. EUR+WWI SPAIN LAW CONSTN ECO/UNDEV POL/PAR EX/STRUC LEGIS LEAD...HUM SOC 20. PAGE 70 A1445 BIBLIOG/A L/A+17C NAT/G DIPLOM N

KYRIAK T.E.,ASIAN DEVELOPMENTS: A BIBLIOGRAPHY. INDONESIA KOREA/N VIETNAM/N CULTURE SOCIETY ECO/UNDEV NAT/G DIPLOM...SOC TREND 20 MONGOLIA. PAGE 83 A1699 BIBLIOG/A ALL/IDEOS S/ASIA ASIA N

KYRIAK T.E.,CHINA: A BIBLIOGRAPHY. ASIA CHINA/COM AGRI FINAN INDUS NAT/G INT/TRADE PRESS...SOC 20. PAGE 83 A1700 BIBLIOG/A MARXISM TOP/EX POL/PAR N

KYRIAK T.E.,EAST EUROPE: BIBLIOGRAPHY--INDEX TO US JPRS RESEARCH TRANSLATIONS. ALBANIA BULGARIA COM CZECHOSLVK HUNGARY POLAND ROMANIA AGRI EXTR/IND FINAN SERV/IND INT/TRADE WEAPON...GEOG MGT SOC 20. PAGE 83 A1701 BIBLIOG/A PRESS MARXISM INDUS N

KYRIAK T.E.,SOVIET UNION: BIBLIOGRAPHY INDEX TO US JPRS RESEARCH TRANSLATIONS. USSR ECO/DEV AGRI COM/IND CONSTRUC DIST/IND EXTR/IND PROC/MFG R+D INT/TRADE...SOC 20. PAGE 83 A1703 BIBLIOG/A INDUS MARXISM PRESS N

LA DOCUMENTATION FRANCAISE,CHRONOLOGIE INTERNATIONAL. FRANCE WOR+45 CHIEF PROB/SOLV BAL/PWR CONFER LEAD...POLICY CON/ANAL 20. PAGE 83 A1705 BIBLIOG/A DIPLOM TIME/SEQ N

MCSPADDEN J.W.,THE AMERICAN STATESMAN'S YEARBOOK. WOR-45 LAW CONSTN AGRI FINAN DEBATE ADMIN PARL/PROC ...CHARTS BIBLIOG/A 20. PAGE 99 A2025 DIPLOM NAT/G PROVS LEGIS N

MURRA R.O.,POST-WAR PROBLEMS: A CURRENT LIST OF UNITED STATES GOVERNMENT PUBLICATIONS (PAMPHLET). WOR+45 SOCIETY FINAN INT/ORG SCHOOL WORKER TEC/DEV ECO/TAC...SOC 20. PAGE 106 A2180 BIBLIOG/A ADJUST AGRI INDUS N

TURNER R.K.,BIBLIOGRAPHY ON WORLD ORGANIZATION. INT/TRADE CT/SYS ARMS/CONT WEALTH...INT/LAW 20. PAGE 146 A2984 BIBLIOG/A INT/ORG PEACE WAR N

UNIVERSITY MICROFILMS INC,DISSERTATION ABSTRACTS: ABSTRACTS OF DISSERTATIONS AND MONOGRAPHS IN MICROFILM. CANADA DIPLOM ADMIN...INDEX 20. PAGE 149 BIBLIOG/A ACADEM PRESS

A3045 WRITING N

US BUREAU OF THE CENSUS,BIBLIOGRAPHY OF SOCIAL SCIENCE PERIODICALS AND MONOGRAPH SERIES. WOR+45 LAW DIPLOM EDU/PROP HEALTH...PSY SOC LING STAT. PAGE 150 A3058 BIBLIOG/A CULTURE NAT/G SOCIETY N

US CONSULATE GENERAL HONG KONG,REVIEW OF THE HONG KONG CHINESE PRESS. ECO/UNDEV LOC/G NAT/G PLAN DIPLOM EDU/PROP LEAD GP/REL MARXISM...POLICY INDEX 20. PAGE 150 A3073 BIBLIOG/A ASIA PRESS ATTIT N

US CONSULATE GENERAL HONG KONG,CURRENT BACKGROUND. CHINA/COM ECO/UNDEV LOC/G NAT/G PLAN DIPLOM EDU/PROP LEAD REV ATTIT...POLICY INDEX 20. PAGE 151 A3074 BIBLIOG/A MARXIST ASIA PRESS N

US CONSULATE GENERAL HONG KONG,SURVEY OF CHINA MAINLAND PRESS. CHINA/COM ECO/UNDEV LOC/G NAT/G PLAN DIPLOM EDU/PROP LEAD REV ATTIT...POLICY INDEX 20. PAGE 151 A3075 BIBLIOG/A MARXIST ASIA PRESS N

US CONSULATE GENERAL HONG KONG,US CONSULATE GENERAL, HONG KONG, PRESS SUMMARIES. CHINA/COM ECO/UNDEV LOC/G NAT/G PLAN DIPLOM EDU/PROP LEAD REV ATTIT...POLICY INDEX 20. PAGE 151 A3076 BIBLIOG/A MARXIST ASIA PRESS N

US DEPARTMENT OF STATE,ABSTRACTS OF COMPLETED DOCTORAL DISSERTATIONS FOR THE ACADEMIC YEAR 1950-1951. WOR+45 WOR-45 ACADEM POL/PAR ECO/TAC ...POLICY SOC 19/20. PAGE 151 A3078 BIBLIOG/A DIPLOM INT/ORG NAT/G N

US SUPERINTENDENT OF DOCUMENTS,FOREIGN RELATIONS OF THE UNITED STATES; PUBLICATIONS RELATING TO FOREIGN COUNTRIES (PRICE LIST 65). UAR USA+45 VIETNAM ECO/UNDEV VOL/ASSN FOR/AID EDU/PROP ARMS/CONT HEALTH MARXISM...POLICY INT/LAW UN NATO. PAGE 157 A3201 BIBLIOG/A DIPLOM INT/ORG NAT/G N

US SUPERINTENDENT OF DOCUMENTS,GOVERNMENT PERIODICALS AND SUBSCRIPTION SERVICES (PRICE LIST 36). LAW WORKER CT/SYS HEALTH. PAGE 157 A3202 BIBLIOG/A USA+45 NAT/G DIPLOM N

US SUPERINTENDENT OF DOCUMENTS,TARIFF AND TAXATION (PRICE LIST 37). USA+45 LAW INT/TRADE ADJUD ADMIN CT/SYS INCOME OWN...DECISION GATT. PAGE 157 A3204 BIBLIOG/A TAX TARIFFS NAT/G B00

GRIFFIN A.P.C.,LIST OF BOOKS RELATING TO THE THEORY OF COLONIZATION, GOVERNMENT OF DEPENDENCIES, PROTECTORATES, AND RELATED TOPICS. FRANCE GERMANY ITALY SPAIN UK USA-45 WOR-45 ECO/TAC ADMIN CONTROL REGION NAT/LISM ALL/VALS PWR...INT/LAW SOC 16/19. PAGE 56 A1149 BIBLIOG/A COLONIAL GOV/REL DOMIN B01

GRIFFIN A.P.C.,LIST OF BOOKS ON SAMOA (PAMPHLET). GERMANY S/ASIA UK USA-45 WOR-45 ECO/UNDEV REGION ALL/VALS ORD/FREE ALL/IDEOS...GEOG INT/LAW 19 SAMOA GUAM. PAGE 56 A1150 BIBLIOG/A COLONIAL DIPLOM B05

AMES J.G.,COMPREHENSIVE INDEX TO THE PUBLICATIONS OF THE UNITED STATES GOVERNMENT , 1881-1893. USA-45 CONSTN POL/PAR DELIB/GP TOP/EX DIPLOM PARL/PROC INGP/REL...INDEX 19 CONGRESS. PAGE 8 A0153 BIBLIOG/A LEGIS NAT/G GOV/REL B05

GRIFFIN A.P.C.,LIST OF REFERENCES ON THE US CONSULAR SERVICE (PAMPHLET). FRANCE GERMANY SPAIN UK USA-45 WOR-45 OP/RES DOMIN ADMIN FEEDBACK ROUTINE GOV/REL...DECISION 19. PAGE 56 A1153 BIBLIOG/A NAT/G DIPLOM CONSULT B06

GRIFFIN A.P.C.,SELECT LIST OF REFERENCES ON THE BRITISH TARIFF MOVEMENT. MOD/EUR UK BAL/PWR BARGAIN ECO/TAC LAISSEZ 20. PAGE 56 A1154 BIBLIOG/A INT/TRADE TARIFFS COLONIAL B07

GRIFFIN A.P.C.,LIST OF WORKS RELATING TO THE FRENCH ALLIANCE IN THE AMERICAN REVOLUTION. FRANCE FORCES DIPLOM 18 PRE/US/AM. PAGE 56 A1155 BIBLIOG/A REV WAR B08

GRIFFIN A.P.C.,LIST OF REFERENCES ON INTERNATIONAL ARBITRATION. FRANCE L/A+17C USA-45 WOR-45 DIPLOM CONFER COLONIAL ARMS/CONT BAL/PAY EQUILIB SOVEREIGN ...DECISION 19/20 MEXIC/AMER. PAGE 56 A1156 BIBLIOG/A INT/ORG INT/LAW DELIB/GP B10

GRIFFIN A.P.C.,LIST OF REFERENCES ON RECIPROCITY (2ND REV. ED.). CANADA CUBA UK USA-45 WOR-45 NAT/G TARIFFS CONFER COLONIAL CONTROL SANCTION CONSEN ALL/VALS...DECISION 19/20. PAGE 56 A1157 BIBLIOG/A VOL/ASSN DIPLOM REPAR B10

MENDELSSOHN S.,SOUTH AFRICAN BIBLIOGRAPHY (2 VOLS.). SOUTH/AFR EXTR/IND LABOR SECT DIPLOM INT/TRADE COLONIAL RACE/REL DISCRIM...GEOG 20. PAGE 99 A2038 BIBLIOG/A AFR NAT/G NAT/LISM B17

DOS SANTOS M.,BIBLIOGRAPHIA GERAL, A DESCRIPCAO BIBLIOGRAFICA DE LIVROS TANTO DE AUTORES PORTUGUEZES COMO BRASILEIROS... BRAZIL PORTUGAL NAT/G LEAD GP/REL 15/20. PAGE 38 A0774 BIBLIOG/A L/A+17C DIPLOM COLONIAL B17

MEYER H.H.B.,THE UNITED STATES AT WAR, ORGANIZATIONS AND LITERATURE. USA-45 AGRI FINAN INDUS CHIEF FORCES DIPLOM FOR/AID INT/TRADE...SOC 20 PRESIDENT. PAGE 100 A2050 BIBLIOG/A WAR NAT/G VOL/ASSN B19

LONDON SCHOOL ECONOMICS-POL,ANNUAL DIGEST OF PUBLIC INTERNATIONAL LAW CASES. INT/ORG MUNIC NAT/G PROVS ADMIN NEUTRAL WAR GOV/REL PRIVIL 20. PAGE 91 A1858 BIBLIOG/A INT/LAW ADJUD DIPLOM B19

MEYER H.H.B.,SELECT LIST OF REFERENCES ON ECONOMIC RECONSTRUCTION: INCLUDING REPORTS OF THE BRITISH MINISTRY OF RECONSTRUCTION. UK LABOR PLAN PROB/SOLV ECO/TAC INT/TRADE WAR DEMAND PRODUC 20. PAGE 100 A2051 BIBLIOG/A EUR+WWI ECO/DEV WORKER B22

MYERS D.P.,MANUAL OF COLLECTIONS OF TREATIES AND OF COLLECTIONS RELATING TO TREATIES. MOD/EUR INT/ORG LEGIS WRITING ADMIN SOVEREIGN...INT/LAW 19/20. PAGE 106 A2186 BIBLIOG/A DIPLOM CONFER B25

GODET M.,INDEX BIBLIOGRAPHICUS: INTERNATIONAL CATALOGUE OF SOURCES OF CURRENT BIBLIOGRAPHIC INFORMATION. EUR+WWI MOD/EUR SOCIETY SECT TAX ...JURID PHIL/SCI SOC MATH. PAGE 53 A1085 BIBLIOG/A DIPLOM EDU/PROP LAW B30

SCHNEIDER G.,HANDBUCH DER BIBLIOGRAPHIE. GERMANY WOR-45 CULTURE SOCIETY LEAD. PAGE 129 A2637 BIBLIOG/A NAT/G DIPLOM B31

BORCHARD E.H.,GUIDE TO THE LAW AND LEGAL LITERATURE OF FRANCE. FRANCE FINAN INDUS LABOR SECT LEGIS ADMIN COLONIAL CRIME OWN...INT/LAW 20. PAGE 17 A0337 BIBLIOG/A LAW CONSTN METH C32

MARRARO H.R.,"AMERICAN OPINION ON THE UNIFICATION OF ITALY." ITALY MOD/EUR USA-45 FORCES DIPLOM PRESS REV CATHISM...BIOG 19 PRESIDENT. PAGE 95 A1944 BIBLIOG/A NAT/LISM ATTIT ORD/FREE B33

AMERICAN FOREIGN LAW ASSN,BIOGRAPHICAL NOTES ON THE LAWS AND LEGAL LITERATURE OF URUGUAY AND CURACAO. URUGUAY CONSTN FINAN SECT FORCES JUDGE DIPLOM INT/TRADE ADJUD CT/SYS CRIME 20. PAGE 7 A0147 BIBLIOG/A LAW JURID ADMIN B33

MATTHEWS M.A.,THE AMERICAN INSTITUTE OF INTERNATIONAL LAW AND THE CODIFICATION OF INTERNATIONAL LAW (PAMPHLET). USA-45 CONSTN ADJUD CT/SYS...JURID 20. PAGE 96 A1973 BIBLIOG/A INT/LAW L/A+17C DIPLOM B34

US TARIFF COMMISSION,THE TARIFF; A BIBLIOGRAPHY: A SELECT LIST OF REFERENCES. USA-45 LAW DIPLOM TAX ADMIN...POLICY TREATY 20. PAGE 157 A3208 BIBLIOG/A TARIFFS ECO/TAC B35

FOREIGN AFFAIRS BIBLIOGRAPHY: A SELECTED AND ANNOTATED LIST OF BOOKS ON INTERNATIONAL RELATIONS 1919-1962 (4 VOLS.). CONSTN FORCES COLONIAL ARMS/CONT WAR NAT/LISM PEACE ATTIT DRIVE...POLICY INT/LAW 20. PAGE 3 A0050 BIBLIOG/A DIPLOM INT/ORG B35

BEMIS S.F.,GUIDE TO THE DIPLOMATIC HISTORY OF THE UNITED STATES, 17751921. NAT/G LEGIS TOP/EX PROB/SOLV CAP/ISM INT/TRADE TARIFFS ADJUD ...CON/ANAL 18/20. PAGE 13 A0264 BIBLIOG/A DIPLOM USA-45 B35

LANGER W.L.,THE DIPLOMACY OF IMPERIALISM 1890-1902. FRANCE GERMANY ITALY UK WOR-45 BAL/PWR INT/TRADE LEGIT ADJUD CONTROL WAR PWR SOVEREIGN...CHARTS BIBLIOG/A 19/20. PAGE 84 A1726 DIPLOM COLONIAL DOMIN B36

MATTHEWS M.A.,DIPLOMACY: SELECT LIST ON DIPLOMACY, DIPLOMATIC AND CONSULAR PRACTICE, AND FOREIGN OFFICE ORGANIZATION (PAMPHLET). EUR+WWI MOD/EUR USA-45 WOR-45...INT/LAW 20. PAGE 96 A1974 BIBLIOG/A DIPLOM NAT/G B36

MATTHEWS M.A.,INTERNATIONAL LAW: SELECT LIST OF WORKS IN ENGLISH ON PUBLIC INTERNATIONAL LAW: WITH COLLECTIONS OF CASES AND OPINIONS. CHRIST-17C EUR+WWI MOD/EUR WOR-45 CONSTN ADJUD JURID. PAGE 96 A1975 BIBLIOG/A INT/LAW ATTIT DIPLOM B37

BOURNE H.E.,THE WORLD WAR: A LIST OF THE MORE IMPORTANT BOOKS PUBLISHED BEFORE 1937 (PAMPHLET). EUR+WWI NAT/G DIPLOM ATTIT SOC. PAGE 17 A0351 BIBLIOG/A WAR FORCES PLAN B37

GALLOWAY G.B.,AMERICAN PAMPHLET LITERATURE OF PUBLIC AFFAIRS (PAMPHLET). USA-45 ECO/DEV LABOR ADMIN...MGT 20. PAGE 51 A1034 BIBLIOG/A PLAN DIPLOM NAT/G B37

SCHUSTER E.,GUIDE TO LAW AND LEGAL LITERATURE OF BIBLIOG/A

CENTRAL AMERICAN REPUBLICS. L/A+17C INT/ORG ADJUD SANCTION CRIME...JURID 19/20. PAGE 129 A2654 — REGION CT/SYS LAW

B38
MATTHEWS M.A.,FEDERALISM: SELECT LIST OF REFERENCES ON FEDERAL GOVERNMENT REGIONALISM...EXAMPLES OF FEDERATIONS (PAMPHLET). WOR-45 CONSTN INT/ORG NAT/G 19/20 OAS LEAGUE/NAT. PAGE 96 A1976 — BIBLIOG/A FEDERAL REGION DIPLOM

B40
THE GUIDE TO CATHOLIC LITERATURE, 1888-1940. ALL/VALS...POLICY MYSTIC HUM PHIL/SCI 19/20. PAGE 3 A0051 — BIBLIOG/A CATHISM DIPLOM CULTURE

B40
BROWN A.D.,PANAMA CANAL AND PANAMA CANAL ZONE: A SELECTED LIST OF REFERENCES. PANAMA NAT/G SCHOOL DIPLOM HEALTH...GEOG SOC 20 CANAL/ZONE. PAGE 19 A0397 — BIBLIOG/A ECO/UNDEV

B40
CONOVER H.F.,FOREIGN RELATIONS OF THE UNITED STATES: A LIST OF RECENT BOOKS (PAMPHLET). ASIA CANADA L/A+17C UK INT/ORG INT/TRADE TARIFFS NEUTRAL WAR PEACE...INT/LAW CON/ANAL 20 CHINJAP. PAGE 29 A0592 — BIBLIOG/A USA-45 DIPLOM

B40
FULLER G.H.,A LIST OF BIBLIOGRAPHIES ON PROPAGANDA (PAMPHLET). MOD/EUR USA-45 CONSULT ACT/RES PRESS FEEDBACK TASK WAR ATTIT PWR...CON/ANAL METH/COMP 20. PAGE 50 A1020 — BIBLIOG/A EDU/PROP DOMIN DIPLOM

B40
NAFZIGER R.O.,INTERNATIONAL NEWS AND THE PRESS: COMMUNICATIONS, ORGANIZATION OF NEWS-GATHERING INTERNATIONAL AFFAIRS AND FOREIGN... COM/IND FORCES WAR ATTIT...POLICY 20. PAGE 107 A2191 — BIBLIOG/A PRESS DIPLOM EDU/PROP

C40
FAHS C.B.,"GOVERNMENT IN JAPAN." FINAN FORCES LEGIS TOP/EX BUDGET INT/TRADE EDU/PROP SOVEREIGN ...CON/ANAL BIBLIOG/A 20 CHINJAP. PAGE 43 A0884 — ASIA DIPLOM NAT/G ADMIN

B41
WHITAKER A.P.,THE UNITED STATES AND THE INDEPENDENCE OF LATIN AMERICA, 1800-1830. PORTUGAL SPAIN USA-45 COLONIAL REGION SOVEREIGN...POLICY TIME/SEQ BIBLIOG/A 18/20. PAGE 163 A3329 — DIPLOM L/A+17C CONCPT ORD/FREE

B42
CONOVER H.F.,NEW ZEALAND: A SELECTED LIST OF REFERENCES (PAMPHLET). NEW/ZEALND ECO/UNDEV AGRI INDUS LABOR NAT/G SCHOOL FORCES DIPLOM COLONIAL WAR ...HUM 20. PAGE 29 A0595 — BIBLIOG/A S/ASIA CULTURE

B42
FULLER G.H.,DEFENSE FINANCING: A SUPPLEMENTARY LIST OF REFERENCES (PAMPHLET). CANADA UK USA-45 ECO/DEV NAT/G DELIB/GP BUDGET ADJUD ARMS/CONT WEAPON COST PEACE PWR 20 AUSTRAL CHINJAP CONGRESS. PAGE 50 A1021 — BIBLIOG/A FINAN FORCES DIPLOM

B42
PAGINSKY P.,GERMAN WORKS RELATING TO AMERICA, 1493-1800; A LIST COMPILED FROM THE COLLECTIONS OF THE NEW YORK PUBLIC LIBRARY. GERMANY PRE/AMER CULTURE COLONIAL ATTIT...POLICY SOC 15/19. PAGE 113 A2317 — BIBLIOG/A NAT/G L/A+17C DIPLOM

B42
US LIBRARY OF CONGRESS,ECONOMICS OF WAR (APRIL 1941-MARCH 1942). WOR-45 FINAN INDUS LOC/G NAT/G PLAN BUDGET RATION COST DEMAND...POLICY 20. PAGE 154 A3146 — BIBLIOG/A INT/TRADE ECO/TAC WAR

B42
US LIBRARY OF CONGRESS,POSTWAR PLANNING AND RECONSTRUCTION: APRIL-DECEMBER 1942 (SUPPLEMENT 1). WOR+45 SOCIETY INT/ORG DIPLOM...SOC PREDICT 20 UN. PAGE 154 A3147 — BIBLIOG/A WAR PEACE PLAN

B43
BROWN A.D.,GREECE: SELECTED LIST OF REFERENCES. GREECE ECO/UNDEV AGRI FINAN INDUS LABOR SECT TEC/DEV INT/TRADE LEAD...SOC 20. PAGE 20 A0399 — BIBLIOG/A WAR DIPLOM NAT/G

B43
FULLER G.F.,FOREIGN RELIEF AND REHABILITATION (PAMPHLET). FUT GERMANY UK USA-45 INT/ORG PROB/SOLV DIPLOM FOR/AID ADMIN ADJUST PEACE ALL/VALS...SOC/WK 20 UN JEWS. PAGE 50 A1018 — BIBLIOG/A PLAN GIVE WAR

B43
GRIERSON P.,BOOKS ON SOVIET RUSSIA 1917-42: A BIBLIOGRAPHY AND A GUIDE TO READING. USSR CULTURE ELITES NAT/G PLAN DIPLOM REV...GEOG 20. PAGE 56 A1148 — BIBLIOG/A COM MARXISM LEAD

B43
ST LEGER A.,SELECTION OF WORKS FOR AN UNDERSTANDING OF WORLD AFFAIRS SINCE 1914. WOR-45 INT/ORG CREATE BAL/PWR REV ADJUST 20. PAGE 137 A2796 — BIBLIOG/A WAR SOCIETY DIPLOM

B43
US LIBRARY OF CONGRESS,POLITICAL DEVELOPMENTS AND THE WAR: APRIL-DECEMBER 1942 (SUPPLEMENT 1). WOR-45 CONSTN NAT/G POL/PAR CREATE RECEIVE EDU/PROP ATTIT 20. PAGE 154 A3148 — BIBLIOG/A WAR DIPLOM

B44
FULLER G.H.,TURKEY: A SELECTED LIST OF REFERENCES. ISLAM TURKEY CULTURE ECO/UNDEV AGRI DIPLOM NAT/LISM CONSERVE...GEOG HUM INT/LAW SOC 7/20 MAPS. PAGE 50 A1024 — BIBLIOG/A ALL/VALS

N45
INDIA QUARTERLY, A JOURNAL OF INTERNATIONAL AFFAIRS. INDIA LAW CONSTN ECO/UNDEV INT/ORG POL/PAR COLONIAL LEAD PARL/PROC WAR ATTIT...SOC 20 CMN/WLTH. PAGE 3 A0053 — BIBLIOG/A S/ASIA DIPLOM NAT/G

B45
CLAGETT H.L.,COMMUNIST CHINA: RUTHLESS ENEMY OR PAPER TIGER (PAMPHLET). CHINA/COM ECO/UNDEV AGRI INDUS NAT/G POL/PAR ECO/TAC INT/TRADE GUERRILLA ATTIT...CHARTS NAT/COMP ORG/CHARTS 20. PAGE 26 A0540 — BIBLIOG/A MARXISM DIPLOM COERCE

B45
GALLOWAY E.,ABSTRACTS OF POSTWAR LITERATURE (VOL. IV) JAN.-JULY, 1945 NOS. 901-1074. POLAND USA+45 USSR WOR+45 INDUS LABOR PLAN ECO/TAC INT/TRADE TAX EDU/PROP ADMIN COLONIAL INT/LAW. PAGE 51 A1033 — BIBLIOG/A NUC/PWR NAT/G DIPLOM

B45
HARVARD WIDENER LIBRARY,INDOCHINA: A SELECTED LIST OF REFERENCES. CAMBODIA FRANCE S/ASIA VIETNAM COLONIAL...POLICY 19/20. PAGE 62 A1282 — BIBLIOG/A ACADEM DIPLOM NAT/G

B45
MACMINN N.,BIBLIOGRAPHY OF THE PUBLISHED WRITINGS OF JOHN STUART MILL. MOD/EUR UK CAP/ISM DIPLOM KNOWL...EPIST CONCPT 19 MILL/JS. PAGE 93 A1901 — BIBLIOG/A SOCIETY INGP/REL LAISSEZ

B45
PERAZA SARAUSA F.,BIBLIOGRAFIAS CUBANAS. CUBA CULTURE ECO/UNDEV AGRI EDU/PROP PRESS CIVMIL/REL ...POLICY GEOG PHIL/SCI BIOG 19/20. PAGE 115 A2353 — BIBLIOG/A L/A+17C NAT/G DIPLOM

B45
ROGERS W.C.,INTERNATIONAL ADMINISTRATION: A BIBLIOGRAPHY (PUBLICATION NO 92; A PAMPHLET). WOR-45 INT/ORG LOC/G NAT/G CENTRAL 20. PAGE 123 A2514 — BIBLIOG/A ADMIN MGT DIPLOM

B45
VANCE H.L.,GUIDE TO THE LAW AND LEGAL LITERATURE OF MEXICO. LAW CONSTN FINAN LABOR FORCES ADJUD ADMIN ...CRIMLGY PHIL/SCI CON/ANAL 20 MEXIC/AMER. PAGE 158 A3217 — BIBLIOG/A INT/LAW JURID CT/SYS

B45
WOOLBERT R.G.,FOREIGN AFFAIRS BIBLIOGRAPHY, 1932-1942. INT/ORG SECT INT/TRADE COLONIAL RACE/REL NAT/LISM...GEOG INT/LAW GOV/COMP IDEA/COMP 20. PAGE 167 A3393 — BIBLIOG/A DIPLOM WAR

B46
GRIFFIN G.G.,A GUIDE TO MANUSCRIPTS RELATING TO AMERICAN HISTORY IN BRITISH DEPOSITORIES. CANADA IRELAND MOD/EUR UK USA-45 LAW DIPLOM ADMIN COLONIAL WAR NAT/LISM SOVEREIGN...GEOG INT/LAW 15/19 CMN/WLTH. PAGE 56 A1159 — BIBLIOG/A ALL/VALS NAT/G

B46
SCANLON H.L.,INTERNATIONAL LAW: A SELECTIVE LIST OF WORKS IN ENGLISH ON PUBLIC INTERNATIONAL LAW (A PAMPHLET). CHRIST-17C EUR+WWI MOD/EUR WOR-45 CT/SYS ...JURID 20. PAGE 127 A2613 — BIBLIOG/A INT/LAW ADJUD DIPLOM

N46
HOBBS C.C.,SOUTHEAST ASIA, 1935-45: A SELECTED LIST OF REFERENCE BOOKS (PAMPHLET). S/ASIA AGRI INDUS NAT/G SECT DIPLOM WAR...ART/METH GEOG SOC LING 20. PAGE 65 A1346 — BIBLIOG/A CULTURE HABITAT

B47
CONOVER H.F.,NON-SELF-GOVERNING AREAS. BELGIUM FRANCE ITALY UK WOR+45 CULTURE ECO/UNDEV INT/ORG LOC/G NAT/G ECO/TAC INT/TRADE ADMIN HEALTH...SOC UN. PAGE 30 A0601 — BIBLIOG/A COLONIAL DIPLOM

B47
US LIBRARY OF CONGRESS,POSTWAR PLANNING AND RECONSTRUCTION: JANUARY-MARCH 1943. WOR+45 SOCIETY INT/ORG DIPLOM...SOC PREDICT 20. PAGE 154 A3149 — BIBLIOG/A WAR PEACE PLAN

B48
FLOREN LOZANO L.,BIBLIOGRAFIA DE LA BIBLIOGRAFIA DOMINICANA. DOMIN/REP NAT/G DIPLOM EDU/PROP CIVMIL/REL...POLICY ART/METH GEOG PHIL/SCI HIST/WRIT 20. PAGE 47 A0952 — BIBLIOG/A BIOG L/A+17C CULTURE

B48
HOWARD J.E.,PARLIAMENT AND FOREIGN POLICY IN FRANCE. FRANCE CONSTN DELIB/GP BUDGET ADMIN PARL/PROC CHOOSE...BIBLIOG/A 20 PARLIAMENT. PAGE 68 A1399 — LEGIS CONTROL DIPLOM ATTIT

B48
JONES H.D.,UNESCO: A SELECTED LIST OF REFERENCES. CULTURE CREATE PEACE ATTIT DRIVE 20 UNESCO UN. PAGE 75 A1531 — BIBLIOG/A INT/ORG DIPLOM EDU/PROP

B48
MINISTERE FINANCES ET ECO,BULLETIN BIBLIOGRAPHIQUE. AFR EUR+WWI FRANCE CULTURE STRUCT FINAN NAT/G ACT/RES INT/TRADE ADMIN REGION PRODUC STAT. — BIBLIOG/A ECO/UNDEV TEC/DEV

PAGE 102 A2088 COLONIAL

B48
NEUBURGER O.,GUIDE TO OFFICIAL PUBLICATIONS OF THE OTHER AMERICAN REPUBLICS: VENEZUELA (VOL. XIX). VENEZUELA FINAN LEGIS PLAN BUDGET DIPLOM CT/SYS PARL/PROC 19/20. PAGE 108 A2219
BIBLIOG/A NAT/G CONSTN LAW

B49
THE CURRENT DIGEST OF THE SOVIET PRESS. USSR WOR+45 LOC/G NAT/G DIPLOM EDU/PROP...MARXIST 20. PAGE 3 A0056
BIBLIOG/A COM ATTIT PRESS

B49
BEHRENDT R.F.,MODERN LATIN AMERICA IN SOCIAL SCIENCE LITERATURE. STRUCT ECO/UNDEV SCHOOL DIPLOM INT/TRADE EDU/PROP...GEOG 20. PAGE 12 A0250
BIBLIOG/A SOC L/A+17C

B49
BOZZA T.,SCRITTORI POLITICI ITALIANI DAL 1550 AL 1650. CHRIST-17C ITALY DIPLOM DOMIN 16/17. PAGE 18 A0365
BIBLIOG/A NAT/G CONCPT WRITING

B49
US DEPARTMENT OF STATE,SOVIET BIBLIOGRAPHY (PAMPHLET). CHINA/COM COM USSR LAW AGRI INT/ORG ECO/TAC EDU/PROP...POLICY GEOG 20. PAGE 151 A3084
BIBLIOG/A MARXISM CULTURE DIPLOM

B50
BEHRENDT R.F.,MODERN LATIN AMERICA IN SOCIAL SCIENCE LITERATURE (SUPPLEMENTS I AND II). STRUCT ECO/UNDEV SCHOOL DIPLOM INT/TRADE...GEOG 20. PAGE 12 A0251
BIBLIOG/A SOC L/A+17C

B50
BROWN E.S.,MANUAL OF GOVERNMENT PUBLICATIONS. WOR+45 WOR-45 CONSTN INT/ORG MUNIC PROVS DIPLOM ADMIN 20. PAGE 20 A0401
BIBLIOG/A NAT/G LAW

B50
CORNELL U DEPT ASIAN STUDIES,SOUTHEAST ASIA PROGRAM DATA PAPER. BURMA CAMBODIA INDONESIA MALAYSIA VIETNAM SOCIETY STRUCT NAT/G SECT DIPLOM FOR/AID PWR WEALTH...SOC 20. PAGE 31 A0625
BIBLIOG/A CULTURE S/ASIA ECO/UNDEV

B50
COUNCIL BRITISH NATIONAL BIB,BRITISH NATIONAL BIBLIOGRAPHY. UK AGRI CONSTRUC PERF/ART POL/PAR SECT CREATE INT/TRADE LEAD...HUM JURID PHIL/SCI 20. PAGE 31 A0637
BIBLIOG/A NAT/G TEC/DEV DIPLOM

B50
DAVIS E.P.,PERIODICALS OF INTERNATIONAL ORGANIZATIONS; PART I, THE UN AND SPECIALIZED AGENCIES; PART II, INTER-AMERICAN ORGS. CULTURE AGRI FINAN INDUS LABOR INT/TRADE...GEOG HEAL STAT 20 UN OAS UNESCO. PAGE 34 A0689
BIBLIOG/A INT/ORG DIPLOM L/A+17C

B50
MONPIED E.,BIBLIOGRAPHIE FEDERALISTE: OUVRAGES CHOISIS (VOL. I, MIMEOGRAPHED PAPER). EUR+WWI DIPLOM ADMIN REGION ATTIT PACIFISM SOCISM...INT/LAW 19/20. PAGE 103 A2109
BIBLIOG/A FEDERAL CENTRAL INT/ORG

B50
MUGRIDGE D.H.,AMERICAN HISTORY AND CIVILIZATION: LIST OF GUIDES AND ANNOTATED OR SELECTIVE BIBLIOGRAPHIES. NAT/G SECT DIPLOM RACE/REL DISCRIM ATTIT...ART/METH SOC 18/20. PAGE 105 A2164
BIBLIOG/A USA-45 SOCIETY

B50
PERHAM M.,COLONIAL GOVERNMENT: ANNOTATED READING LIST ON BRITISH COLONIAL GOVERNMENT. UK WOR+45 WOR-45 ECO/UNDEV INT/ORG LEGIS FOR/AID INT/TRADE DOMIN ADMIN REV 20. PAGE 115 A2356
BIBLIOG/A COLONIAL GOV/REL NAT/G

B50
US LIBRARY OF CONGRESS,THE UNITED STATES AND EUROPE: BIBLIOGRAPHY OF THOUGHT EXPRESSED IN AMERICAN PUBLICATIONS DURING 1950. EUR+WWI GERMANY USA+45 USSR INT/ORG DIPLOM COLONIAL SOVEREIGN ...POLICY 20 COLD/WAR UN BERLIN/BLO. PAGE 154 A3150
BIBLIOG/A SOC ATTIT

N51
MONPIED E.,FEDERALIST BIBLIOGRAPHY: ARTICLES AND DOCUMENTS PUBLISHED IN BRITISH PERIODICALS 1945-1951 (MIMEOGRAPHED). EUR+WWI UK WOR+45 DIPLOM REGION ATTIT SOCISM...INT/LAW 20. PAGE 103 A2110
BIBLIOG/A INT/ORG FEDERAL CENTRAL

B51
CORMACK M.,SELECTED PAMPHLETS ON THE UNITED NATIONS AND INTERNATIONAL RELATIONS (PAMPHLET). USA+45 R+D EX/STRUC PROB/SOLV ROUTINE...POLICY CON/ANAL 20 UN NATO. PAGE 31 A0624
BIBLIOG/A NAT/G INT/ORG DIPLOM

B51
US DEPARTMENT OF STATE,LIVRES AMERICAINS TRADUITS EN FRANCAIS ET LIVRES FRANCAIS SUR LES ETATS-UNIS D'AMERIQUE (2ND ED.). FRANCE USA+45 SECT DIPLOM EDU/PROP LEISURE...ART/METH GEOG HUM 20. PAGE 151 A3086
BIBLIOG/A SOC

B51
US DEPARTMENT OF STATE,POINT FOUR, NEAR EAST AND AFRICA, A SELECTED BIBLIOGRAPHY OF STUDIES ON ECONOMICALLY UNDERDEVELOPED COUNTRIES. AGRI COM/IND FINAN INDUS PLAN INT/TRADE...SOC TREND 20. PAGE 151 A3087
BIBLIOG/A AFR S/ASIA ISLAM

B51
US LIBRARY OF CONGRESS,PUBLIC AFFAIRS ABSTRACTS. USA+45 INT/ORG INT/TRADE ARMS/CONT...NAT/COMP 20 CONGRESS. PAGE 155 A3151
BIBLIOG/A DIPLOM POLICY

B51
US LIBRARY OF CONGRESS,EAST EUROPEAN ACCESSIONS LIST (VOL. I). POL/PAR DIPLOM ADMIN LEAD 20. PAGE 155 A3152
BIBLIOG/A COM SOCIETY NAT/G

B51
WABEKE B.H.,A GUIDE TO DUTCH BIBLIOGRAPHIES. BELGIUM INDONESIA NETHERLAND DIPLOM INT/TRADE WAR NAT/LISM KNOWL...ART/METH HUM JURID CON/ANAL 14/20. PAGE 160 A3257
BIBLIOG/A NAT/G CULTURE COLONIAL

B52
DUNN F.S.,CURRENT RESEARCH IN INTERNATIONAL AFFAIRS. UK USA+45...POLICY TREATY. PAGE 39 A0801
BIBLIOG/A DIPLOM INT/LAW

B52
GURLAND A.R.L.,POLITICAL SCIENCE IN WESTERN GERMANY: THOUGHTS AND WRITINGS, 1950-1952 (PAMPHLET). EUR+WWI GERMANY/W ELITES SOCIETY NAT/G NAT/LISM TOTALISM 20. PAGE 58 A1196
BIBLIOG/A DIPLOM CIVMIL/REL FASCISM

B52
SMITH C.M.,INTERNATIONAL COMMUNICATION AND POLITICAL WARFARE: AN ANNOTATED BIBLIOGRAPHY (A PAPER). WOR+45 INTELL R+D NAT/G FORCES ACT/RES DIPLOM COERCE ALL/IDEOS. PAGE 134 A2745
BIBLIOG/A EDU/PROP WAR COM/IND

B52
SPENCER F.A.,WAR AND POSTWAR GREECE: AN ANALYSIS BASED ON GREEK WRITINGS. GREECE SOCIETY NAT/G POL/PAR FORCES CREATE DIPLOM LEAD MARXISM...SOC 20. PAGE 136 A2784
BIBLIOG/A WAR REV

B52
THOM J.M.,GUIDE TO RESEARCH MATERIAL IN POLITICAL SCIENCE (PAMPHLET). ELITES LOC/G MUNIC NAT/G LEGIS DIPLOM ADJUD CIVMIL/REL GOV/REL PWR MGT. PAGE 143 A2919
BIBLIOG/A KNOWL

B52
US LIBRARY OF CONGRESS,EGYPT AND THE ANGLO-EGYPTIAN SUDAN: A SELECTIVE GUIDE TO BACKGROUND READING (PAMPHLET). SUDAN UAR UK DIPLOM...POLICY 20. PAGE 155 A3153
BIBLIOG/A COLONIAL ISLAM NAT/G

N52
COORDINATING COMM DOC SOC SCI,INTERNATIONAL REPERTORY OF SOCIAL SCIENCE DOCUMENTATION CENTERS (PAMPHLET). ACT/RES OP/RES WRITING KNOWL...CON/ANAL METH. PAGE 30 A0610
BIBLIOG/A R+D NAT/G INT/ORG

B53
LANDHEER B.,FUNDAMENTALS OF PUBLIC INTERNATIONAL LAW (SELECTIVE BIBLIOGRAPHIES OF THE LIBRARY OF THE PEACE PALACE, VOL. I; PAMPH). INT/ORG OP/RES PEACE ...IDEA/COMP 20. PAGE 84 A1715
BIBLIOG/A INT/LAW DIPLOM PHIL/SCI

B53
LARSEN K.,NATIONAL BIBLIOGRAPHIC SERVICES: THEIR CREATION AND OPERATION. WOR+45 COM/IND CREATE PLAN DIPLOM PRESS ADMIN ROUTINE...MGT UNESCO. PAGE 85 A1733
BIBLIOG/A INT/ORG WRITING

B53
MANSERGH N.,DOCUMENTS AND SPEECHES ON BRITISH COMMONWEALTH AFFAIRS 1931-1952. INDIA IRELAND PAKISTAN UK CONSTN POL/PAR CHIEF FORCES COLONIAL ORD/FREE SOVEREIGN...JURID 20 COMMONWLTH. PAGE 94 A1929
BIBLIOG/A DIPLOM ECO/TAC

B53
SCHAAF R.W.,DOCUMENTS OF INTERNATIONAL MEETINGS. AGRI INDUS ACADEM DIPLOM NUC/PWR RACE/REL AGE/Y HEALTH...SOC 20. PAGE 127 A2614
BIBLIOG/A DELIB/GP INT/ORG POLICY

B53
SHIRATO I.,JAPANESE SOURCES ON THE HISTORY OF THE CHINESE COMMUNIST MOVEMENT (PAMPHLET). CHINA/COM USSR CONSTRUC NAT/G POL/PAR FORCES DIPLOM DOMIN EDU/PROP CONTROL WAR TOTALISM SOCISM 20. PAGE 132 A2702
BIBLIOG/A MARXISM ECO/UNDEV

B53
UNESCO,GUIDE DES CENTRES NATIONAUX D'INFORMATION BIBLIOGRAPHIQUE (VOL. III). WOR+45 INT/ORG NAT/G 20 UNESCO. PAGE 148 A3017
BIBLIOG/A COM/IND DIPLOM

B54
KENWORTHY L.S.,FREE AND INEXPENSIVE MATERIALS ON WORLD AFFAIRS (PAMPHLET). WOR+45 CULTURE ECO/UNDEV INT/TRADE ARMS/CONT NUC/PWR UN. PAGE 78 A1597
BIBLIOG/A NAT/G INT/ORG DIPLOM

B54
LANDHEER B.,RECOGNITION IN INTERNATIONAL LAW (SELECTIVE BIBLIOGRAPHIES OF THE LIBRARY OF THE PEACE PALACE, VOL. II; PAMPHLET). NAT/G LEGIT SANCTION 20. PAGE 84 A1716
BIBLIOG/A INT/LAW INT/ORG DIPLOM

B54
SHARMA J.S.,MAHATMA GANDHI: A DESCRIPTIVE BIBLIOGRAPHY. INDIA S/ASIA PROB/SOLV DIPLOM COLONIAL WAR NAT/LISM PEACE ATTIT PERSON SOVEREIGN ...CONCPT 20 GANDHI/M. PAGE 132 A2695
BIBLIOG/A BIOG CHIEF LEAD

B54
TOTOK W.,HANDBUCH DER BIBLIOGRAPHISCHEN NACHSCHLAGEWERKE. GERMANY LAW CULTURE ADMIN...SOC 20. PAGE 144 A2952
BIBLIOG/A NAT/G DIPLOM POLICY

BERLE A.A. JR.,"THE 20TH CENTURY CAPITALIST REVOLUTION." ECO/DEV NAT/G DIPLOM PRICE CONTROL ATTIT...BIBLIOG/A 20. PAGE 14 A0275 — C54 LG/CO CAP/ISM MGT PWR

JAPANESE STUDIES OF MODERN CHINA. ASIA DIPLOM LEAD REV MARXISM 19/20 CHINJAP. PAGE 43 A0885 — B55 BIBLIOG/A SOC

INSTITUTE POLITISCHE WISSEN,POLITISCHE LITERATUR (3 VOLS.). INT/ORG LEAD WAR PEACE...CONCPT TREND NAT/COMP 20. PAGE 70 A1446 — B55 BIBLIOG/A NAT/G DIPLOM POLICY

PLISCHKE E.,AMERICAN FOREIGN RELATIONS: A BIBLIOGRAPHY OF OFFICIAL SOURCES. USA+45 USA-45 INT/ORG FORCES PRESS WRITING DEBATE EXEC...POLICY INT/LAW 18/20 CONGRESS. PAGE 116 A2390 — B55 BIBLIOG/A DIPLOM NAT/G

PYRAH G.B.,IMPERIAL POLICY AND SOUTH AFRICA 1902-1910. SOUTH/AFR UK NAT/G WAR DISCRIM...CONCPT CHARTS BIBLIOG/A 19/20 CMN/WLTH. PAGE 118 A2421 — B55 DIPLOM COLONIAL POLICY RACE/REL

QUAN K.L.,INTRODUCTION TO ASIA: A SELECTIVE GUIDE TO BACKGROUND READING. ECO/UNDEV NAT/G PROB/SOLV DIPLOM ATTIT 20. PAGE 118 A2424 — B55 BIBLIOG/A S/ASIA CULTURE ASIA

UN ECONOMIC AND SOCIAL COUNCIL,BIBLIOGRAPHY OF PUBLICATIONS OF THE UN AND SPECIALIZED AGENCIES IN THE SOCIAL WELFARE FIELD, 1946-1952. WOR+45 FAM INT/ORG MUNIC ACT/RES PLAN PROB/SOLV EDU/PROP AGE/C AGE/Y HABITAT...HEAL UN. PAGE 147 A3000 — B55 BIBLIOG/A SOC/WK ADMIN WEALTH

UN HEADQUARTERS LIBRARY,BIBLIOQRAPHIE DE LA CHARTE DES NATIONS UNIES. CHINA/COM KOREA WOR+45 VOL/ASSN CONFER ADMIN COERCE PEACE ATTIT ORD/FREE SOVEREIGN ...INT/LAW 20 UNESCO UN. PAGE 147 A3001 — B55 BIBLIOG/A INT/ORG DIPLOM

BEARDSLEY S.W.,HUMAN RELATIONS IN INTERNATIONAL AFFAIRS: A GUIDE TO SIGNIFICANT INTERPRETATION AND RESEARCH. UNIV PERS/REL NAT/LISM DRIVE PERSON ...POLICY PSY SOC CON/ANAL IDEA/COMP 20. PAGE 12 A0241 — B56 BIBLIOG/A ATTIT CULTURE DIPLOM

BUREAU OF PUBLIC AFFAIRS,AMERICAN FOREIGN POLICY: CURRENT DOCUMENTS. COM USA+45 USSR WOR+45 DELIB/GP FOR/AID INT/TRADE ARMS/CONT NUC/PWR ALL/VALS ALL/IDEOS...DECISION 20 NATO. PAGE 21 A0434 — B56 BIBLIOG/A DIPLOM POLICY

CONOVER H.F.,A GUIDE TO BIBLIOGRAPHIC TOOLS FOR RESEARCH IN FOREIGN AFFAIRS. AFR ASIA COM EUR+WWI WOR+45 BAL/PWR CON/ANAL. PAGE 30 A0602 — B56 BIBLIOG/A R+D DIPLOM INT/ORG

ESTEP R.,AN AIR POWER BIBLIOGRAPHY. USA+45 TEC/DEV BUDGET DIPLOM EDU/PROP DETER CIVMIL/REL...DECISION INT/LAW 20. PAGE 42 A0862 — B56 BIBLIOG/A FORCES WEAPON PLAN

IRIKURA J.K.,SOUTHEAST ASIA: SELECTED ANNOTATED BIBLIOGRAPHY OF JAPANESE PUBLICATIONS. CULTURE ADMIN RACE/REL 20 CHINJAP. PAGE 71 A1466 — B56 BIBLIOG/A S/ASIA DIPLOM

PHILIPPINE STUDIES PROGRAM,SELECTED BIBLIOGRAPHY ON THE PHILIPPINES, TOPICALLY ARRANGED AND ANNOTATED. PHILIPPINE SECT DIPLOM COLONIAL LEAD...SOC 18/20. PAGE 116 A2375 — B56 BIBLIOG/A S/ASIA NAT/G ECO/UNDEV

UNDERHILL F.H.,THE BRITISH COMMONWEALTH: AN EXPERIMENT IN CO-OPERATION AMONG NATIONS. CANADA UK WOR+45 WOR-45 INT/ORG COLONIAL UTIL SOVEREIGN CONSERVE...OLD/LIB SOC/EXP BIBLIOG/A 19/20 CMN/WLTH. PAGE 147 A3007 — B56 VOL/ASSN NAT/LISM DIPLOM

US LIBRARY OF CONGRESS,UNITED STATES DIRECT ECONOMIC AID TO FOREIGN COUNTRIES: A COLLECTION OF EXCERPTS AND A BIBLIOGRAPHY (PAMPHLET). USA+45 PRESS DEBATE...ANTHOL BIBLIOG/A CONGRESS. PAGE 155 A3154 — B56 FOR/AID POLICY DIPLOM ECO/UNDEV

WILBUR C.M.,DOCUMENTS ON COMMUNISM, NATIONALISM, AND SOVIET ADVISERS IN CHINA, 1918-1927. CHINA/COM USSR STRUCT DIPLOM LEAD NAT/LISM...BIBLIOG/A 20. PAGE 164 A3343 — B56 REV POL/PAR MARXISM COM

WU E.,LEADERS OF TWENTIETH-CENTURY CHINA; AN ANNOTATED BIBLIOGRAPHY OF SELECTED CHINESE BIOGRAPHICAL WORKS IN HOOVER LIBRARY. ASIA INDUS POL/PAR DIPLOM ADMIN REV WAR...HUM MGT 20. PAGE 168 A3422 — B56 BIBLIOG/A BIOG INTELL CHIEF

BYRNES R.F.,BIBLIOGRAPHY OF AMERICAN PUBLICATIONS ON EAST CENTRAL EUROPE, 1945-1957 (VOL. XXII). SECT DIPLOM EDU/PROP RACE/REL...ART/METH GEOG JURID SOC LING 20 JEWS. PAGE 23 A0462 — B57 BIBLIOG/A COM MARXISM NAT/G

CONOVER H.F.,NORTH AND NORTHEAST AFRICA; A SELECTED ANNOTATED LIST OF WRITINGS. ALGERIA MOROCCO SUDAN UAR CULTURE INT/ORG PROB/SOLV ADJUD NAT/LISM PWR WEALTH...SOC 20 UN. PAGE 30 A0603 — B57 BIBLIOG/A DIPLOM AFR ECO/UNDEV

MOYER K.E.,FROM IRAN TO MORROCCO; FROM TURKEY TO THE SUDAN: A SELECTED AND ANNOTATED BIBLIOGRAPHY OF NORTH AFRICA AND NEAR EAST... ISLAM DIPLOM EDU/PROP 20. PAGE 105 A2162 — B57 BIBLIOG/A ECO/UNDEV SECT NAT/G

YAMADA H.,ANNALS OF THE SOCIAL SCIENCES. WOR+45 WOR-45 LAW CULTURE SOCIETY STRUCT DIPLOM...EPIST PSY CONCPT 15/20. PAGE 168 A3428 — B57 BIBLIOG/A TREND IDEA/COMP SOC

BIBLIOGRAPHY OF NEW GUIDES AND AIDS TO PUBLIC DOCUMENTS USE, 1953-1956 (PAMPHLET). WOR+45 MUNIC DIPLOM...CON/ANAL CHARTS METH. PAGE 164 A3347 — N57 BIBLIOG/A NAT/G LOC/G INT/ORG

HUMPHREYS R.A.,LATIN AMERICAN HISTORY: A GUIDE TO THE LITERATURE IN ENGLISH. CULTURE NAT/G DIPLOM BIOG. PAGE 69 A1417 — B58 BIBLIOG/A L/A+17C

MACLES L.M.,LES SOURCES DU TRAVAIL BIBLIOGRAPHIQUE (3 VOLS.). FRANCE WOR+45 DIPLOM...GEOG PHIL/SCI SOC 20. PAGE 93 A1897 — B58 BIBLIOG/A NAT/G HUM

MASON J.B.,THAILAND BIBLIOGRAPHY. S/ASIA THAILAND CULTURE EDU/PROP ADMIN...GEOG SOC LING 20. PAGE 95 A1958 — B58 BIBLIOG/A ECO/UNDEV DIPLOM NAT/G

UNESCO,REPERTORIO DE PUBLICACIONES PERIODICAS ACTUALES LATINO AMERICANAS (VOL. VIII). LAW DIPLOM GP/REL...PHIL/SCI SOC 20 UNESCO. PAGE 148 A3021 — B58 BIBLIOG/A COM/IND L/A+17C

TRAGER F.N.,"A SELECTED AND ANNOTATED BIBLIOGRAPHY ON ECONOMIC DEVELOPMENT, 1953-1957." WOR+45 AGRI FINAN INDUS MARKET LABOR MUNIC WORKER PLAN INT/TRADE PRODUC CENSUS. PAGE 145 A2958 — L58 BIBLIOG/A ECO/UNDEV ECO/DEV

BUTTINGER J.,"THE SMALLER DRAGON; A POLITICAL HISTORY OF VIETNAM." VIETNAM SECT DIPLOM CIVMIL/REL ISOLAT NAT/LISM...BIBLIOG/A 3/20. PAGE 22 A0455 — C58 COLONIAL DOMIN SOVEREIGN REV

CAREW-HUNT R.C.,BOOKS ON COMMUNISM. NAT/G POL/PAR DIPLOM REV...BIOG 19/20. PAGE 24 A0481 — B59 BIBLIOG/A MARXISM COM ASIA

HAZLEWOOD A.,THE ECONOMICS OF "UNDER-DEVELOPED" AREAS. WOR+45 DIST/IND EXTR/IND FINAN INDUS MARKET PLAN FOR/AID...GEOG 20. PAGE 63 A1302 — B59 BIBLIOG/A ECO/UNDEV AGRI INT/TRADE

INTERAMERICAN CULTURAL COUN,LISTA DE LIBROS REPRESENTAVOS DE AMERICA. CULTURE DIPLOM ADMIN 20. PAGE 71 A1448 — B59 BIBLIOG/A NAT/G L/A+17C SOC

NAHM A.C.,JAPANESE PENETRATION OF KOREA, 1894-1910. ASIA KOREA NAT/G...POLICY 20 CHINJAP. PAGE 107 A2192 — B59 BIBLIOG/A DIPLOM WAR COLONIAL

LEWIS P.R.,LITERATURE OF THE SOCIAL SCIENCES: AN INTRODUCTORY SURVEY AND GUIDE. UK LAW INDUS DIPLOM INT/TRADE ADMIN...MGT 19/20. PAGE 88 A1802 — B60 BIBLIOG/A SOC

MEYRIAT J.,LA SCIENCE POLITIQUE EN FRANCE, 1945-1958; BIBLIOGRAPHIES FRANCAISES DE SCIENCES SOCIALES (VOL. I). EUR+WWI FRANCE POL/PAR DIPLOM ADMIN CHOOSE ATTIT...IDEA/COMP METH/COMP NAT/COMP 20. PAGE 100 A2057 — B60 BIBLIOG/A NAT/G CONCPT PHIL/SCI

MOUSKHELY M.,L'URSS ET LES PAYS DE L'EST. ASIA COM S/ASIA USSR PRESS...SOC 20. PAGE 105 A2156 — B60 BIBLIOG/A DIPLOM ATTIT

MUGRIDGE D.H.,A GUIDE TO THE STUDY OF THE UNITED STATES OF AMERICA: REPRESENTATIVE BOOKS REFLECTING THE DEVELOPMENT OF AMERICAN LIFE. USA+45 USA-45 CONSTN POL/PAR FORCES DIPLOM PRESS CHOOSE...SOC 17/20. PAGE 105 A2165 — B60 BIBLIOG/A CULTURE NAT/G POLICY

PRITTIE T.,GERMANY DIVIDED: THE LEGACY OF THE NAZI ERA. EUR+WWI GERMANY RACE/REL SUPEGO...PSY AUD/VIS BIBLIOG/A 20 NAZI. PAGE 118 A2414 — B60 STERTYP PERSON ATTIT DIPLOM

QUBAIN F.I.,INSIDE THE ARAB MIND: A BIBLIOGRAPHIC SURVEY OF LITERATURE IN ARABIC ON ARAB NATIONALISM — B60 BIBLIOG/A FEDERAL

AND UNITY. ISLAM POL/PAR SECT LEAD SOVEREIGN MARXISM SOCISM. PAGE 118 A2425 DIPLOM NAT/LISM

B60
TABORN P.,RECORDS OF THE HEADQUARTERS, UNITED NATIONS COMMAND (PRELIMINARY INVENTORIES; PAPER). WOR+45 DIPLOM CONFER PEACE ATTIT...POLICY UN. PAGE 141 A2881 BIBLIOG/A WAR ARMS/CONT INT/ORG

B60
UNITED WORLD FEDERALISTS,UNITED WORLD FEDERALISTS; PANORAMA OF RECENT BOOKS, FILMS, AND JOURNALS ON WORLD FEDERATION, THE UN, AND WORLD PEACE. CULTURE ECO/UNDEV PROB/SOLV FOR/AID ARMS/CONT NUC/PWR ...INT/LAW PHIL/SCI 20 UN. PAGE 149 A3039 BIBLIOG/A DIPLOM INT/ORG PEACE

B60
US DEPARTMENT OF THE ARMY,DISARMAMENT: A BIBLIOGRAPHIC RECORD: 1916-1960. DETER WAR WEAPON PEACE 20 UN LEAGUE/NAT COLD/WAR NATO. PAGE 152 A3103 BIBLIOG/A ARMS/CONT NUC/PWR DIPLOM

S60
BRODY R.A.,"DETERRENCE STRATEGIES: AN ANNOTATED BIBLIOGRAPHY." WOR+45 PLAN ARMS/CONT NUC/PWR WAR WEAPON DECISION. PAGE 19 A0383 BIBLIOG/A FORCES DETER DIPLOM

C60
HAZARD J.N.,"THE SOVIET SYSTEM OF GOVERNMENT." USSR SOCIETY INDUS NAT/G POL/PAR DIPLOM CT/SYS...JURID CHARTS BIBLIOG/A 20. PAGE 63 A1298 COM NAT/COMP STRUCT ADMIN

N60
INTERNATIONAL FEDN DOCUMENTTN,BIBLIOGRAPHY OF DIRECTORIES OF SOURCES OF INFORMATION (PAMPHLET). WOR+45 R+D INT/ORG NAT/G TEC/DEV DIPLOM. PAGE 71 A1456 BIBLIOG/A ECO/DEV ECO/UNDEV

B61
BURDETTE F.L.,POLITICAL SCIENCE: A SELECTED BIBLIOGRAPHY OF BOOKS IN PRINT, WITH ANNOTATIONS (PAMPHLET). LAW LOC/G NAT/G POL/PAR PROVS DIPLOM EDU/PROP ADMIN CHOOSE ATTIT 20. PAGE 21 A0432 BIBLIOG/A GOV/COMP CONCPT ROUTINE

B61
CARNELL F.,THE POLITICS OF THE NEW STATES: A SELECT ANNOTATED BIBLIOGRAPHY WITH SPECIAL REFERENCE TO THE COMMONWEALTH. CONSTN ELITES LABOR NAT/G POL/PAR EX/STRUC DIPLOM ADJUD ADMIN...GOV/COMP 20 COMMONWLTH. PAGE 24 A0496 BIBLIOG/A AFR ASIA COLONIAL

B61
CONFERENCE ATLANTIC COMMUNITY,AN INTRODUCTORY BIBLIOGRAPHY. COM WOR+45 FORCES DIPLOM ECO/TAC WAR ...INT/LAW HIST/WRIT COLD/WAR NATO. PAGE 29 A0584 BIBLIOG/A CON/ANAL INT/ORG

B61
DETHINE P.,BIBLIOGRAPHIE DES ASPECTS ECONOMIQUES ET SOCIAUX DE L'INDUSTRIALISATION EN AFRIQUE. AFR FINAN LABOR FOR/AID...SOC 20. PAGE 36 A0734 BIBLIOG/A ECO/UNDEV INDUS TEC/DEV

B61
HOLDSWORTH M.,SOVIET AFRICAN STUDIES 1918-1959. USSR ACADEM NAT/G DIPLOM REGION KNOWL 20. PAGE 66 A1366 BIBLIOG/A AFR HABITAT NAT/COMP

B61
LEHMAN R.L.,AFRICA SOUTH OF THE SAHARA (PAMPHLET). DIPLOM COLONIAL NAT/LISM. PAGE 86 A1768 BIBLIOG/A AFR CULTURE NAT/G

B61
PALMER N.D.,THE INDIAN POLITICAL SYSTEM. INDIA ECO/UNDEV SECT CHIEF COLONIAL CHOOSE ALL/IDEOS SOCISM...CHARTS BIBLIOG/A 20. PAGE 113 A2322 NAT/LISM POL/PAR NAT/G DIPLOM

B61
THEOBALD R.,THE CHALLENGE OF ABUNDANCE. USA+45 WOR+45 MARKET DIPLOM FOR/AID REV PRODUC UTOPIA SUPEGO...POLICY TREND BIBLIOG/A 20. PAGE 142 A2913 WELF/ST ECO/UNDEV PROB/SOLV ECO/TAC

B61
US LIBRARY OF CONGRESS,WORLD COMMUNIST MOVEMENT. USA+45 USSR WOR+45 INT/ORG DIPLOM REV ATTIT 19/20. PAGE 155 A3155 BIBLIOG/A EDU/PROP MARXISM POL/PAR

B61
WARD R.E.,JAPANESE POLITICAL SCIENCE: A GUIDE TO JAPANESE REFERENCE AND RESEARCH MATERIALS (2ND ED.). LAW CONSTN STRATA NAT/G POL/PAR DELIB/GP LEGIS ADMIN CHOOSE GP/REL...INT/LAW 19/20 CHINJAP. PAGE 161 A3282 BIBLIOG/A PHIL/SCI

B61
ZIMMERMAN I.,A GUIDE TO CURRENT LATIN AMERICAN PERIODICALS: HUMANITIES AND SOCIAL SCIENCES. LABOR SECT EDU/PROP...GEOG HUM SOC LING STAT NAT/COMP 20. PAGE 170 A3452 BIBLIOG/A DIPLOM L/A+17C PHIL/SCI

S61
"CRITERIA FOR ALLOCATING INVESTMENT RESOURCES AMONG VARIOUS FIELDS OF DEVELOPMENT IN UNDERDEVELOPED ECONOMIES." ASIA AGRI INT/ORG CAP/ISM BAL/PAY EFFICIENCY PROFIT WEALTH...STAT 20 UN. PAGE 3 A0061 BIBLIOG/A ECO/UNDEV PLAN TEC/DEV

B62
BRIMMER B.,A GUIDE TO THE USE OF UNITED NATIONS DOCUMENTS. WOR+45 ECO/UNDEV AGRI EX/STRUC FORCES PROB/SOLV ADMIN WAR PEACE WEALTH...POLICY UN. PAGE 19 A0378 BIBLIOG/A INT/ORG DIPLOM

B62
COLLISON R.L.,BIBLIOGRAPHIES, SUBJECT AND NATIONAL: A GUIDE TO THEIR CONTENTS, ARRANGEMENT, AND USE (2ND REV. ED.). SECT DIPLOM...ART/METH GEOG HUM PHIL/SCI SOC MATH BIOG 20. PAGE 28 A0569 BIBLIOG/A CON/ANAL BIBLIOG

B62
COSTA RICA UNIVERSIDAD BIBL,LISTA DE TESIS DE GRADO DE LA UNIVERSIDAD DE COSTA RICA. COSTA/RICA LAW LOC/G ADMIN LEAD...SOC 20. PAGE 31 A0631 BIBLIOG/A NAT/G DIPLOM ECO/UNDEV

B62
DELANEY R.F.,THE LITERATURE OF COMMUNISM IN AMERICA. COM USA+45 USA-45 INT/ORG LABOR NAT/G POL/PAR INGP/REL...MAJORIT 20. PAGE 36 A0727 BIBLIOG/A MARXISM EDU/PROP IDEA/COMP

B62
HENDRICKS D.,PAMPHLETS ON THE FIRST WORLD WAR: AN ANNOTATED BIBLIOGRAPHY (OCCASIONAL PAPER NO. 79). GERMANY WOR-45 EDU/PROP NAT/LISM ATTIT PWR ALL/IDEOS 20. PAGE 64 A1314 BIBLIOG/A WAR DIPLOM NAT/G

B62
KIRPICEVA I.K.,HANDBUCH DER RUSSISCHEN UND SOWJETISCHEN BIBLIOGRAPHIEN (5 VOLS.). USSR STRUCT ECO/DEV DIPLOM LEAD ATTIT 18/20. PAGE 80 A1637 BIBLIOG/A NAT/G MARXISM COM

B62
KYRIAK T.E.,INTERNATIONAL COMMUNIST DEVELOPMENTS 1957-1961: INDEX TO TRANSLATIONS FROM AFRICA, ASIA, LATIN AMERICA, WEST EUROPE. COM WOR+45 NAT/G WORKER DIPLOM NAT/LISM. PAGE 83 A1704 BIBLIOG/A MARXISM LABOR POL/PAR

B62
LEOPOLD R.W.,THE GROWTH OF AMERICAN FOREIGN POLICY: A HISTORY. USA+45 USA-45 EX/STRUC LEGIS INT/TRADE WAR...CHARTS BIBLIOG/A T 18/20. PAGE 87 A1780 NAT/G DIPLOM POLICY

B62
LERNER M.,THE AGE OF OVERKILL: A PREFACE TO WORLD POLITICS. USA+45 USSR WOR+45 SOCIETY ECO/UNDEV BAL/PWR NEUTRAL PARTIC REV ALL/IDEOS MARXISM ...BIBLIOG/A 20. PAGE 87 A1787 DIPLOM NUC/PWR PWR DEATH

B62
US DEPARTMENT OF THE ARMY,AFRICA: ITS PROBLEMS AND PROSPECTS. CHINA/COM USSR INT/ORG FOR/AID COLONIAL LEAD FEDERAL DRIVE SOVEREIGN MARXISM...GEOG 20 COLD/WAR. PAGE 152 A3104 BIBLIOG/A AFR NAT/LISM DIPLOM

B62
US DEPARTMENT OF THE ARMY,GUIDE TO JAPANESE MONOGRAPHS AND JAPANESE STUDIES ON MANCHURIA: 1945-1960. CHINA/COM NAT/G DIPLOM LEAD COERCE WAR ...CHARTS 19/20 CHINJAP. PAGE 152 A3105 BIBLIOG/A FORCES ASIA S/ASIA

B62
US LIBRARY OF CONGRESS,UNITED STATES AND CANADIAN PUBLICATIONS ON AFRICA IN 1960. CANADA USA+45 CULTURE TEC/DEV DIPLOM FOR/AID RACE/REL...GEOG HUM SOC SOC/WK LING 20. PAGE 155 A3156 BIBLIOG/A AFR

B62
VIET J.,INTERNATIONAL COOPERATION AND PROGRAMMES OF ECONOMIC AND SOCIAL DEVELOPMENT. TEC/DEV FOR/AID DOMIN COLONIAL PEACE WEALTH 20 UNESCO. PAGE 159 A3232 BIBLIOG/A INT/ORG DIPLOM ECO/UNDEV

L62
"HIGHER EDUCATION AND ECONOMIC AND SOCIAL DEVELOPMENT IN LATIN AMERICA: A BIBLIOGRAPHY." L/A+17C SOCIETY ECO/UNDEV PROF/ORG DIPLOM CONFER ...SOC 20. PAGE 3 A0062 BIBLIOG/A ACADEM INTELL EDU/PROP

B63
FABER K.,DIE NATIONALISTISCHE PUBLIZISTIK DEUTSCHLANDS VON 1866 BIS 1871 (2 VOLS.). EUR+WWI GERMANY DIPLOM EDU/PROP 19. PAGE 43 A0881 BIBLIOG/A NAT/G NAT/LISM POL/PAR

B63
GRAEBNER N.A.,THE COLD WAR: IDEOLOGICAL CONFLICT OR POWER STRUGGLE? USSR WOR+45 WOR-45 PROB/SOLV EDU/PROP ARMS/CONT REV NAT/LISM PEACE ORD/FREE ...IDEA/COMP ANTHOL BIBLIOG/A 20 COLD/WAR. PAGE 55 A1123 DIPLOM BAL/PWR MARXISM

B63
HALPERIN M.H.,LIMITED WAR IN A NUCLEAR AGE. CUBA KOREA USA+45 USSR INT/ORG FORCES PLAN DIPLOM DETER PWR...BIBLIOG/A 20. PAGE 60 A1238 WAR NUC/PWR CONTROL WEAPON

B63
KATZ S.M.,A SELECTED LIST OF US READINGS ON DEVELOPMENT. AGRI COM/IND DIST/IND INDUS LABOR PLAN FOR/AID EDU/PROP HEALTH...POLICY SOC/WK 20. PAGE 77 A1571 BIBLIOG/A ECO/UNDEV TEC/DEV ACT/RES

B63
LIU K.C.,AMERICANS AND CHINESE: A HISTORICAL ESSAY AND BIBLIOGRAPHY. ASIA USA+45 USA-45 SOCIETY SECT 18/20. PAGE 90 A1845 BIBLIOG/A GP/REL DIPLOM ATTIT

B63
MANSERGH N.,DOCUMENTS AND SPEECHES ON COMMONWEALTH AFFAIRS 1952-1962. CANADA INDIA PAKISTAN UK CONSTN BIBLIOG/A FEDERAL

FORCES ECO/TAC EDU/PROP COLONIAL DETER WAR ORD/FREE SOVEREIGN...POLICY 20 AUSTRAL. PAGE 94 A1932
INT/TRADE DIPLOM

B63
PRESTON W. JR.,ALIENS AND DISSENTERS: FEDERAL SUPPRESSION OF RADICALS 1903-1933. USA-45 DIPLOM ADJUD REPRESENT RACE/REL MAJORITY...BIBLIOG/A 19/20. PAGE 117 A2409
DISCRIM GP/REL INGP/REL ATTIT

B63
US DEPARTMENT OF THE ARMY,SOVIET RUSSIA: STRATEGIC SURVEY (PAMPHLET). USSR POL/PAR PLAN DOMIN EDU/PROP ARMS/CONT GUERRILLA WAR WEAPON...TREND CHARTS ORG/CHARTS 20. PAGE 152 A3106
BIBLIOG/A MARXISM DIPLOM COERCE

B63
US DEPARTMENT OF THE ARMY,US OVERSEAS BASES: PRESENT STATUS AND FUTURE PROSPECTS (PAMPHLET). USA+45 DIPLOM NUC/PWR ATTIT ORD/FREE...POLICY CHARTS 20. PAGE 152 A3107
BIBLIOG/A WAR BAL/PWR DETER

B64
BAILEY T.A.,A DIPLOMATIC HISTORY OF THE AMERICAN PEOPLE (7TH ED.). USA+45 USA-45 FOR/AID COLONIAL PARL/PROC WAR...CHARTS BIBLIOG/A T 18/20. PAGE 10 A0208
DIPLOM NAT/G

B64
BLANCHARD C.H.,KOREAN WAR BIBLIOGRAPHY. KOREA FAM BAL/PWR RATION MURDER WEAPON MARXISM...CHARTS 20. PAGE 15 A0306
BIBLIOG/A WAR DIPLOM FORCES

B64
COHEN M.L.,SELECTED BIBLIOGRAPHY OF FOREIGN AND INTERNATIONAL LAW....IDEA/COMP METH/COMP 20. PAGE 28 A0562
BIBLIOG/A JURID LAW INT/LAW

B64
DIAS R.W.M.,A BIBLIOGRAPHY OF JURISPRUDENCE (2ND ED.). VOL/ASSN LEGIS ADJUD CT/SYS OWN...INT/LAW 18/20. PAGE 37 A0754
BIBLIOG/A JURID LAW CONCPT

B64
EMBREE A.T.,A GUIDE TO PAPERBACKS ON ASIA; SELECTED AND ANNOTATED (PAMPHLET). CULTURE SOCIETY ECO/UNDEV SECT DIPLOM COLONIAL MARXISM...SOC 20. PAGE 41 A0845
BIBLIOG/A ASIA S/ASIA NAT/G

B64
GESELLSCHAFT RECHTSVERGLEICH,BIBLIOGRAPHIE DES DEUTSCHEN RECHTS (BIBLIOGRAPHY OF GERMAN LAW, TRANS. BY COURTLAND PETERSON). GERMANY FINAN INDUS LABOR SECT FORCES CT/SYS PARL/PROC CRIME...INT/LAW SOC NAT/COMP 20. PAGE 52 A1066
BIBLIOG/A JURID CONSTN ADMIN

B64
GJUPANOVIC H.,LEGAL SOURCES AND BIBLIOGRAPHY OF YUGOSLAVIA. COM YUGOSLAVIA LAW LEGIS DIPLOM ADMIN PARL/PROC REGION CRIME CENTRAL 20. PAGE 53 A1078
BIBLIOG/A JURID CONSTN ADJUD

B64
HAZLEWOOD A.,THE ECONOMICS OF DEVELOPMENT: AN ANNOTATED LIST OF BOOKS AND ARTICLES PUBLISHED 1958-1962. AGRI FINAN INDUS LABOR NAT/G DIPLOM INT/TRADE INCOME...MGT 20. PAGE 63 A1303
BIBLIOG/A ECO/UNDEV TEC/DEV

B64
KNIGHT R.,BIBLIOGRAPHY ON INCOME AND WEALTH, 1957-1960 (VOL VIII). WOR+45 ECO/DEV FINAN INT/TRADE...GOV/COMP METH/COMP. PAGE 80 A1652
BIBLIOG/A ECO/UNDEV WEALTH INCOME

B64
KNOX V.H.,PUBLIC FINANCE: INFORMATION SOURCES. USA+45 DIPLOM ADMIN GOV/REL COST...POLICY 20. PAGE 81 A1657
BIBLIOG/A FINAN TAX BUDGET

B64
KOLARZ W.,BOOKS ON COMMUNISM. USSR WOR+45 CULTURE NAT/G POL/PAR DIPLOM LEAD...CONCPT GOV/COMP IDEA/COMP. PAGE 81 A1667
BIBLIOG/A SOCIETY COM MARXISM

B64
MAHAR J.M.,INDIA: A CRITICAL BIBLIOGRAPHY. INDIA PAKISTAN CULTURE ECO/UNDEV LOC/G POL/PAR SECT PROB/SOLV DIPLOM ADMIN COLONIAL PARL/PROC ATTIT 20. PAGE 93 A1906
BIBLIOG/A S/ASIA NAT/G LEAD

B64
MATTHEWS D.G.,A CURRENT VIEW OF AFRICANA (PAMPHLET). CULTURE ECO/UNDEV DIPLOM RACE/REL ATTIT 20. PAGE 96 A1968
BIBLIOG/A AFR NAT/G NAT/LISM

B64
ROBERTS HL,FOREIGN AFFAIRS BIBLIOGRAPHY, 1952-1962. ECO/DEV SECT PLAN FOR/AID INT/TRADE ARMS/CONT NAT/LISM ATTIT...INT/LAW GOV/COMP IDEA/COMP 20. PAGE 122 A2495
BIBLIOG/A DIPLOM INT/ORG WAR

B64
SZLADITS C.,BIBLIOGRAPHY ON FOREIGN AND COMPARATIVE LAW: BOOKS AND ARTICLES IN ENGLISH (SUPPLEMENT 1962). FINAN INDUS JUDGE LICENSE ADMIN CT/SYS PARL/PROC OWN...INT/LAW CLASSIF METH/COMP NAT/COMP 20. PAGE 141 A2877
BIBLIOG/A JURID ADJUD LAW

B64
WILLIAMS S.P.,TOWARD A GENUINE WORLD SECURITY SYSTEM (PAMPHLET). WOR+45 INT/ORG FORCES PLAN NUC/PWR ORD/FREE...INT/LAW CONCPT UN PRESIDENT. PAGE 165 A3353
BIBLIOG/A ARMS/CONT DIPLOM PEACE

B64
WITHERELL J.W.,OFFICIAL PUBLICATIONS OF FRENCH EQUATORIAL AFRICA, FRENCH CAMEROONS, AND TOGO, 1946-1958 (PAMPHLET). CAMEROON CHAD FRANCE GABON TOGO LAW ECO/UNDEV EXTR/IND INT/TRADE...GEOG HEAL 20. PAGE 165 A3370
BIBLIOG/A AFR NAT/G ADMIN

S64
HORECKY P.L.,"LIBRARY OF CONGRESS PUBLICATIONS IN AID OF USSR AND EAST EUROPEAN RESEARCH." BULGARIA CZECHOSLVK POLAND USSR YUGOSLAVIA NAT/G POL/PAR DIPLOM ADMIN GOV/REL...CLASSIF 20. PAGE 67 A1382
BIBLIOG/A COM MARXISM

B65
PEACE RESEARCH ABSTRACTS. FUT WOR+45 R+D INT/ORG NAT/G PLAN TEC/DEV BAL/PWR DIPLOM FOR/AID NUC/PWR HEALTH. PAGE 4 A0072
BIBLIOG/A PEACE ARMS/CONT WAR

B65
AUVADE R.,BIBLIOGRAPHIE CRITIQUE DES OEUVRES PARUES SUR L'INDOCHINE FRANCAISE: UN SIECLE D'HISTOIRE ET D'ENSEIGNEMENT. VIETNAM DIPLOM...SOC 20. PAGE 10 A0198
BIBLIOG/A R+D ACADEM COLONIAL

B65
BRIDGMAN J.,GERMAN AFRICA: A SELECT ANNOTATED BIBLIOGRAPHY. AFR AGRI DIPLOM REPAR WAR FASCISM 20. PAGE 18 A0374
BIBLIOG/A COLONIAL NAT/G EDU/PROP

B65
CHUNG Y.S.,KOREA: A SELECTED BIBLIOGRAPHY 1959-1963. ASIA KOREA NAT/G DIPLOM 20. PAGE 26 A0537
BIBLIOG/A SOC

B65
FLYNN A.H.,WORLD UNDERSTANDING: A SELECTED BIBLIOGRAPHY. WOR+45 PROB/SOLV BAL/PWR DIPLOM EFFICIENCY PEACE UN. PAGE 47 A0956
BIBLIOG/A INT/ORG EDU/PROP ROUTINE

B65
FORM W.H.,INDUSTRIAL RELATIONS AND SOCIAL CHANGE IN LATIN AMERICA. L/A+17C AGRI LABOR NAT/G PLAN PROB/SOLV DIPLOM...MGT SOC ANTHOL BIBLIOG/A METH 20. PAGE 47 A0966
INDUS GP/REL NAT/COMP ECO/UNDEV

B65
FRASER S.,GOVERNMENTAL POLICY AND INTERNATIONAL EDUCATION. CHINA/COM COM USA+45 WOR+45 CONTROL MARXISM...ANTHOL BIBLIOG/A 20 UN. PAGE 48 A0989
EDU/PROP DIPLOM POLICY NAT/G

B65
INTERNATIONAL SOCIAL SCI COUN,SOCIAL SCIENCES IN THE USSR. USSR ECO/DEV AGRI FINAN INDUS PLAN CAP/ISM...INT/LAW PHIL/SCI PSY SOC 20. PAGE 71 A1460
BIBLIOG/A ACT/RES MARXISM JURID

B65
MCCOLL G.D.,THE AUSTRALIAN BALANCE OF PAYMENTS. UK USA+45 AGRI WORKER DIPLOM EQUILIB PRODUC...STAT TREND CHARTS BIBLIOG/A 20 AUSTRAL. PAGE 97 A2001
ECO/DEV BAL/PAY INT/TRADE COST

B65
MOSKOWITZ H.,US SECURITY, ARMS CONTROL, AND DISARMAMENT 1961-1965. FORCES DIPLOM DETER WAR WEAPON...CHARTS 20 UN COLD/WAR NATO. PAGE 105 A2154
BIBLIOG/A ARMS/CONT NUC/PWR PEACE

B65
MOSTECKY V.,SOVIET LEGAL BIBLIOGRAPHY. USSR LEGIS PRESS WRITING CONFER ADJUD CT/SYS REV MARXISM ...INT/LAW JURID DICTIONARY 20. PAGE 105 A2155
BIBLIOG/A LAW COM CONSTN

B65
MOWRY G.E.,THE URBAN NATION 1920-1960. USA+45 USA-45 SOCIETY ECO/DEV MUNIC FOR/AID INT/TRADE AUTOMAT...BIBLIOG/A 20. PAGE 105 A2161
TEC/DEV NAT/G TOTALISM DIPLOM

B65
NEWBURY C.W.,BRITISH POLICY TOWARDS WEST AFRICA: SELECT DOCUMENTS 1786-1874. AFR UK INT/TRADE DOMIN ADMIN COLONIAL CT/SYS COERCE ORD/FREE...BIBLIOG/A 18/19. PAGE 108 A2224
DIPLOM POLICY NAT/G WRITING

B65
REQUA E.G.,THE DEVELOPING NATIONS: A GUIDE TO INFORMATION SOURCES CONCERNING THEIR ECON, POLIT, TECHNICAL, AND SOCIAL PROBLEMS. AFR ASIA ISLAM L/A+17C INDUS INT/ORG CONSULT PLAN PROB/SOLV...SOC 20 UN. PAGE 120 A2466
BIBLIOG/A ECO/UNDEV FOR/AID TEC/DEV

B65
SABLE M.H.,PERIODICALS FOR LATIN AMERICAN ECONOMIC DEVELOPMENT, TRADE, AND FINANCE: AN ANNOTATED BIBLIOGRAPHY (A PAMPHLET). ECO/TAC PRODUC PROFIT ...STAT NAT/COMP 20 OAS. PAGE 126 A2583
BIBLIOG/A L/A+17C ECO/UNDEV INT/TRADE

B65
SANDERSON G.N.,ENGLAND, EUROPE, AND THE UPPER NILE 1882-1899. ISLAM MOD/EUR UAR UK CHIEF...POLICY CHARTS BIBLIOG/A 19 ARABS NEGRO. PAGE 127 A2600
AFR DIPLOM COLONIAL

B65
UNIVERSAL REFERENCE SYSTEM,INTERNATIONAL AFFAIRS: VOLUME I IN THE POLITICAL SCIENCE, GOVERNMENT, AND
BIBLIOG/A GEN/METH

PUBLIC POLICY SERIES....DECISION ECOMETRIC GEOG INT/LAW JURID MGT PHIL/SCI PSY SOC. PAGE 149 A3041
COMPUT/IR DIPLOM

B65
US DEPARTMENT OF DEFENSE,US SECURITY ARMS CONTROL, AND DISARMAMENT 1961-1965 (PAMPHLET). CHINA/COM COM GERMANY/W ISRAEL SPACE USA+45 USSR WOR+45 FORCES EDU/PROP DETER EQUILIB PEACE ALL/VALS...GOV/COMP 20 NATO. PAGE 151 A3077
BIBLIOG/A ARMS/CONT NUC/PWR DIPLOM

B65
US DEPARTMENT OF THE ARMY,NUCLEAR WEAPONS AND THE ATLANTIC ALLIANCE: A BIBLIOGRAPHIC SURVEY. ASIA COM EUR+WWI USA+45 FORCES DIPLOM WEAPON...STAT 20 NATO. PAGE 152 A3108
BIBLIOG/A ARMS/CONT NUC/PWR BAL/PWR

B65
US LIBRARY OF CONGRESS,RARE BOOKS DIVISION: GUIDE TO ITS COLLECTION AND SERVICES. LOC/G SECT WAR. PAGE 155 A3158
BIBLIOG/A NAT/G DIPLOM

B65
WILGUS A.C.,HISTORIES AND HISTORIANS OF HISPANIC AMERICA (REPRINT ED.). CHRIST-17C SECT DIPLOM REV 16/20. PAGE 164 A3350
BIBLIOG/A L/A+17C REGION COLONIAL

L65
MATTHEWS D.G.,"A CURRENT BIBLIOGRAPHY ON ETHIOPIAN AFFAIRS: A SELECT BIBLIOGRAPHY FROM 1950-1964." ETHIOPIA LAW CULTURE ECO/UNDEV INDUS LABOR SECT FORCES DIPLOM CIVMIL/REL RACE/REL...LING STAT 20. PAGE 96 A1969
BIBLIOG/A ADMIN POL/PAR NAT/G

L65
MATTHEWS D.G.,"LE TIERS MONDE: A SELECT AND PRELIMINARY BIBLIOGRAPHIC SURVEY OF MANPOWER IN DEVELOPING COUNTRIES, 1960-1964." AFR ISLAM L/A+17C INDUS PLAN PROB/SOLV TEC/DEV INT/TRADE EFFICIENCY WEALTH...STAT 20. PAGE 96 A1971
BIBLIOG/A ECO/UNDEV LABOR WORKER

C65
SCHWEBEL M.,"BEHAVIORAL SCIENCE AND HUMAN SURVIVAL." FORCES ARMS/CONT COERCE NUC/PWR WAR GP/REL NAT/LISM PERCEPT...POLICY PSY ANTHOL BIBLIOG/A 20 COLD/WAR. PAGE 130 A2662
PEACE ACT/RES DIPLOM HEAL

C65
US AIR FORCE ACADEMY,"AMERICAN DEFENSE POLICY." COM INT/ORG TEC/DEV FOR/AID ARMS/CONT DETER NUC/PWR ...POLICY DECISION CONCPT ANTHOL BIBLIOG/A 20 COLD/WAR NATO. PAGE 149 A3054
PLAN FORCES WAR COERCE

B66
BESTERMAN T.,A WORLD BIBLIOGRAPHY OF BIBLIOGRAPHIES (4TH ED.). WOR+45 WOR-45 LAW INT/ORG ADMIN CON/ANAL. PAGE 14 A0282
BIBLIOG/A DIPLOM

B66
DAVIDSON A.B.,RUSSIA AND AFRICA. USSR AGRI INT/TRADE...GEOG BIBLIOG/A 18/20. PAGE 34 A0687
MARXISM COLONIAL RACE/REL DIPLOM

B66
DOUMA J.,BIBLIOGRAPHY ON THE INTERNATIONAL COURT INCLUDING THE PERMANENT COURT, 1918-1964. WOR+45 WOR-45 DELIB/GP WAR PRIVIL...JURID NAT/COMP 20 UN LEAGUE/NAT. PAGE 38 A0780
BIBLIOG/A INT/ORG CT/SYS DIPLOM

B66
EMBREE A.T.,ASIA: A GUIDE TO BASIC BOOKS (PAMPHLET). ECO/UNDEV SECT FORCES DIPLOM ALL/IDEOS ...SOC 20. PAGE 41 A0846
BIBLIOG/A ASIA S/ASIA NAT/G

B66
GLAZER M.,THE FEDERAL GOVERNMENT AND THE UNIVERSITY. CHILE PROB/SOLV DIPLOM GIVE ADMIN WAR ...POLICY SOC 20. PAGE 53 A1079
BIBLIOG/A NAT/G PLAN ACADEM

B66
HALLET R.,PEOPLE AND PROGRESS IN WEST AFRICA: AN INTRODUCTION TO THE PROBLEMS OF DEVELOPMENT. COM/IND INDUS KIN DIPLOM FOR/AID INT/TRADE HEALTH ...GEOG TREND CHARTS BIBLIOG/A 20 AFRICA/W. PAGE 60 A1233
AFR SOCIETY ECO/UNDEV ECO/TAC

B66
KEYES J.G.,A BIBLIOGRAPHY OF WESTERN LANGUAGE PUBLICATIONS CONCERNING NORTH VIETNAM IN THE CORNELL LIBRARY. VIETNAM/N NAT/G FORCES TEC/DEV DIPLOM LEAD RACE/REL...GEOG SOC 20. PAGE 78 A1603
BIBLIOG/A CULTURE ECO/UNDEV S/ASIA

B66
MEERHAEGHE M.,INTERNATIONAL ECONOMIC INSTITUTIONS. EUR+WWI FINAN INDUS MARKET PLAN TARIFFS BAL/PAY EQUILIB...POLICY BIBLIOG/A 20 GATT OEEC EEC IBRD EURCOALSTL. PAGE 99 A2032
ECO/TAC ECO/DEV INT/TRADE INT/ORG

B66
SPULBER N.,THE STATE AND ECONOMIC DEVELOPMENT IN EASTERN EUROPE. BULGARIA COM CZECHOSLVK HUNGARY POLAND YUGOSLAVIA CULTURE PLAN CAP/ISM INT/TRADE CONTROL...POLICY CHARTS METH/COMP BIBLIOG/A 19/20. PAGE 136 A2793
ECO/DEV ECO/UNDEV NAT/G TOTALISM

B66
SZLADITS C.,A BIBLIOGRAPHY ON FOREIGN AND COMPARATIVE LAW (SUPPLEMENT 1964). FINAN FAM LABOR LG/CO LEGIS JUDGE ADMIN CRIME...CRIMLGY 20. PAGE 141 A2878
BIBLIOG/A CT/SYS INT/LAW

B66
US DEPARTMENT OF STATE,RESEARCH ON AFRICA (EXTERNAL RESEARCH LIST NO 5-25). LAW CULTURE ECO/UNDEV POL/PAR DIPLOM EDU/PROP LEAD REGION MARXISM...GEOG LING WORSHIP 20. PAGE 152 A3094
BIBLIOG/A ASIA S/ASIA NAT/G

B66
US DEPARTMENT OF STATE,RESEARCH ON THE AMERICAN REPUBLICS (EXTERNAL RESEARCH LIST NO 6-25). CULTURE SOCIETY POL/PAR DIPLOM EDU/PROP MARXISM WORSHIP 20 OAS. PAGE 152 A3095
BIBLIOG/A L/A+17C REGION NAT/G

B66
US DEPARTMENT OF STATE,RESEARCH ON THE MIDDLE EAST (EXTERNAL RESEARCH LIST NO 4-25). GREECE ISRAEL SYRIA UAR YEMEN CULTURE SOCIETY POL/PAR SECT DIPLOM EDU/PROP WAR NAT/LISM...GEOG GOV/COMP 20. PAGE 152 A3096
BIBLIOG/A ISLAM NAT/G REGION

B66
US DEPARTMENT OF STATE,RESEARCH ON THE USSR AND EASTERN EUROPE (EXTERNAL RESEARCH LIST NO 1-25). USSR LAW CULTURE SOCIETY NAT/G TEC/DEV DIPLOM EDU/PROP REGION...GEOG LING. PAGE 152 A3097
BIBLIOG/A EUR+WWI COM MARXISM

B66
US DEPARTMENT OF STATE,RESEARCH ON WESTERN EUROPE, GREAT BRITAIN, AND CANADA (EXTERNAL RESEARCH LIST NO 3-25). CANADA GERMANY/W UK LAW CULTURE NAT/G POL/PAR FORCES EDU/PROP REGION MARXISM...GEOG SOC WORSHIP 20 CMN/WLTH. PAGE 152 A3098
BIBLIOG/A EUR+WWI DIPLOM

B66
US DEPARTMENT OF THE ARMY,COMMUNIST CHINA: A STRATEGIC SURVEY: A BIBLIOGRAPHY (PAMPHLET NO. 20-67). CHINA/COM COM INDIA USSR NAT/G POL/PAR EX/STRUC FORCES NUC/PWR REV ATTIT...POLICY GEOG CHARTS. PAGE 152 A3109
BIBLIOG/A MARXISM S/ASIA DIPLOM

B66
US DEPARTMENT OF THE ARMY,SOUTH ASIA: A STRATEGIC SURVEY (PAMPHLET NO. 550-3). AFGHANISTN INDIA NEPAL PAKISTAN ECO/UNDEV INT/ORG POL/PAR FORCES FOR/AID INT/TRADE LEAD WAR...POLICY SOC TREND 20. PAGE 152 A3110
BIBLIOG/A S/ASIA DIPLOM NAT/G

L66
AMERICAN ECONOMIC REVIEW,"SIXTY-THIRD LIST OF DOCTORAL DISSERTATIONS IN POLITICAL ECONOMY IN AMERICAN UNIVERSITIES AND COLLEGES." ECO/DEV AGRI FINAN LABOR WORKER PLAN BUDGET INT/TRADE ADMIN DEMAND...MGT STAT 20. PAGE 7 A0146
BIBLIOG/A CONCPT ACADEM

S66
AFRICAN BIBLIOGRAPHIC CENTER,"A CURRENT VIEW OF AFRICANA: A SELECT AND ANNOTATED BIBLIOGRAPHICAL PUBLISHING GUIDE, 1965-1966." AFR CULTURE INDUS LABOR SECT FOR/AID ADMIN COLONIAL REV RACE/REL SOCISM...LING 20. PAGE 5 A0098
BIBLIOG/A NAT/G TEC/DEV POL/PAR

S66
ERB GF,"THE UNITED NATIONS CONFERENCE ON TRADE AND DEVELOPMENT (UNCTAD): A SELECTED CURRENT READING LIST." FINAN FOR/AID CONFER 20 UN. PAGE 42 A0858
BIBLIOG/A INT/TRADE ECO/UNDEV INT/ORG

S66
GRUNDY K.W.,"RECENT CONTRIBUTIONS TO THE STUDY OF AFRICAN POLITICAL THOUGHT." DIPLOM NAT/LISM ALL/IDEOS...NEW/IDEA GOV/COMP 20. PAGE 58 A1182
BIBLIOG/A AFR ATTIT IDEA/COMP

S66
O'BRIEN W.V.,"EVENTS AND TRENDS: PATTERNS OF AFRICAN INTERNATIONAL POLITICAL BEHAVIOR." CULTURE SOCIETY NAT/G NAT/LISM SOCISM. PAGE 111 A2267
BIBLIOG/A AFR TREND DIPLOM

C66
ZAWODNY J.K.,"GUIDE TO THE STUDY OF INTERNATIONAL RELATIONS." OP/RES PRESS...STAT INT 20. PAGE 169 A3449
BIBLIOG/A DIPLOM INT/LAW INT/ORG

B67
BARANSON J.,TECHNOLOGY FOR UNDERDEVELOPED AREAS: AN ANNOTATED BIBLIOGRAPHY. FUT WOR+45 CULTURE INDUS INT/ORG CREATE PROB/SOLV INT/TRADE EDU/PROP AUTOMAT ...CONCPT METH. PAGE 11 A0218
BIBLIOG/A ECO/UNDEV TEC/DEV R+D

B67
CRABBS R.F.,UNITED STATES HIGHER EDUCATION AND WORLD AFFAIRS. WOR+45 R+D ACADEM...POLICY 20. PAGE 32 A0650
BIBLIOG/A NAT/G EDU/PROP DIPLOM

B67
SABLE M.H.,A GUIDE TO LATIN AMERICAN STUDIES (2 VOLS). CONSTN FINAN INT/ORG LABOR MUNIC POL/PAR FORCES CAP/ISM FOR/AID ADMIN MARXISM SOCISM OAS. PAGE 126 A2584
BIBLIOG/A L/A+17C DIPLOM NAT/LISM

B67
SHAFFER H.G.,THE COMMUNIST WORLD: MARXIST AND NON-MARXIST VIEWS. WOR+45 SOCIETY DIPLOM ECO/TAC CONTROL SOCISM...MARXIST ANTHOL BIBLIOG/A 20. PAGE 131 A2691
MARXISM NAT/COMP IDEA/COMP COM

B67
THORNE C.,THE APPROACH OF WAR, 1938-1939. EUR+WWI POL/PAR CHIEF FORCES LEAD DRIVE PWR FASCISM ...BIBLIOG/A 20 HITLER/A. PAGE 144 A2936
DIPLOM WAR ELITES

B67
UNIVERSAL REFERENCE SYSTEM,BIBLIOGRAPHY OF BIBLIOGRAPHIES IN POLITICAL SCIENCE, GOVERNMENT, AND PUBLIC POLICY (VOLUME III). WOR+45 WOR-45 LAW ADMIN...SOC CON/ANAL COMPUT/IR GEN/METH. PAGE 149 A3042
BIBLIOG/A NAT/G DIPLOM POLICY

B67
UNIVERSAL REFERENCE SYSTEM,ECONOMIC REGULATION, BUSINESS, AND GOVERNMENT (VOLUME VIII). WOR+45 WOR-45 ECO/DEV ECO/UNDEV FINAN LABOR TEC/DEV ECO/TAC INT/TRADE GOV/REL...POLICY COMPUT/IR. PAGE 149 A3043
BIBLIOG/A CONTROL NAT/G

B67
UNIVERSAL REFERENCE SYSTEM,LAW, JURISPRUDENCE, AND JUDICIAL PROCESS (VOLUME VII). WOR+45 WOR-45 CONSTN NAT/G LEGIS JUDGE CT/SYS...INT/LAW COMPUT/IR GEN/METH METH. PAGE 149 A3044
BIBLIOG/A LAW JURID ADJUD

B67
US DEPARTMENT OF THE ARMY,CIVILIAN IN PEACE, SOLDIER IN WAR: A BIBLIOGRAPHIC SURVEY OF THE ARMY AND AIR NATIONAL GUARD (PAMPHLET, NOS. 130-2). USA+45 USA-45 LOC/G NAT/G PROVS LEGIS PLAN ADMIN ATTIT ORD/FREE...POLICY 19/20. PAGE 152 A3111
BIBLIOG/A FORCES ROLE DIPLOM

B67
US SUPERINTENDENT OF DOCUMENTS,LIBRARY OF CONGRESS (PRICE LIST 83). AFR ASIA EUR+WWI USA-45 USSR NAT/G DIPLOM CONFER CT/SYS WAR...DECISION PHIL/SCI CLASSIF 19/20 CONGRESS PRESIDENT. PAGE 157 A3205
BIBLIOG/A USA+45 AUTOMAT LAW

S67
AFRICAN BIBLIOGRAPHIC CENTER,"THE SWORD AND GOVERNMENT: A PRELIMINARY AND SELECTED BIBLIOGRAPHICAL GUIDE TO AFRICAN MILITARY AFFAIRS; PART I." AFR USA+45 USSR INT/ORG POL/PAR FOR/AID COLONIAL ARMS/CONT PWR 20 UN. PAGE 5 A0101
BIBLIOG/A FORCES CIVMIL/REL DIPLOM

S67
ROTBERG R.I.,"COLONIALISM AND AFTER: THE POLITICAL LITERATURE OF CENTRAL AFRICA - A BIBLIOGRAPHIC ESSAY." AFR CHIEF EX/STRUC REV INGP/REL RACE/REL SOVEREIGN 20. PAGE 124 A2546
BIBLIOG/A COLONIAL DIPLOM NAT/G

C67
HUDSON G.F.,"THE HARD AND BITTER PEACE; WORLD POLITICS SINCE 1945." ASIA COM S/ASIA USSR WOR+45 COLONIAL WAR...TREND BIBLIOG/A 20 COLD/WAR UN. PAGE 68 A1405
DIPLOM INT/ORG ARMS/CONT BAL/PWR

N67
US SUPERINTENDENT OF DOCUMENTS,SPACE: MISSILES, THE MOON, NASA, AND SATELLITES (PRICE LIST 79A). USA+45 COM/IND R+D NAT/G DIPLOM EDU/PROP ADMIN CONTROL HEALTH...POLICY SIMUL NASA CONGRESS. PAGE 157 A3206
BIBLIOG/A SPACE TEC/DEV PEACE

B97
US DEPARTMENT OF STATE,CATALOGUE OF WORKS RELATING TO THE LAW OF NATIONS AND DIPLOMACY IN THE LIBRARY OF THE DEPARTMENT OF STATE (PAMPHLET). WOR-45 NAT/G ADJUD CT/SYS...INT/LAW JURID 19. PAGE 152 A3102
BIBLIOG/A DIPLOM LAW

B98
GRIFFIN A.P.C.,LIST OF BOOKS RELATING TO CUBA (PAMPHLET). CUBA L/A+17C USA-45 INT/TRADE DOMIN WAR GP/REL ALL/VALS...GEOG SOC CHARTS 19/20. PAGE 56 A1158
BIBLIOG/A NAT/G COLONIAL

BIBLIOTHEQUE PALAIS DE LA PAIX A0285

BICAMERALISM....SEE LEGIS, CONGRESS, HOUSE/REP, SENATE

BIERZANECK R. A0286

BIEVILLE MARC D.E. A0721

BIGELOW K.W. A0608

BIGLER/W....WILLIAM BIGLER

BILL/RIGHT....BILL OF RIGHTS

BILLERBECK K. A0287

BINANI G.D. A0288

BINDER L. A0289

BINNS/JJ....JOSEPH J. BINNS

BIO/SOC....BIO-SOCIAL PROCESSES, DRUGS, SEXUALITY

B42
TOLMAN E.C.,DRIVES TOWARD WAR. UNIV PLAN DIPLOM ECO/TAC COERCE PERS/REL ADJUST HAPPINESS BIO/SOC HEREDITY HEALTH KNOWL. PAGE 144 A2947
PSY WAR UTOPIA DRIVE

C51
LEONARD L.L.,"INTERNATIONAL ORGANIZATION (1ST ED.)" WOR+45 FINAN DELIB/GP ECO/TAC GIVE DOMIN SANCTION PEACE BIO/SOC ORD/FREE...INT/LAW 20 UN LEAGUE/NAT. PAGE 87 A1779
BIBLIOG POLICY DIPLOM INT/ORG

B55
KROPOTKIN P.,MUTUAL AID, A FACTOR OF EVOLUTION (1902). UNIV ADJUST ATTIT HEREDITY PERSON LOVE DARWIN/C. PAGE 82 A1687
INGP/REL SOCIETY GEN/LAWS BIO/SOC

B56
SPROUT H.,MAN-MILIEU RELATIONSHIP HYPOTHESES IN THE CONTEXT OF INTERNATIONAL POLITICS. UNIV PROB/SOLV BIO/SOC PERSON...DECISION GEOG SOC METH/CNCPT PREDICT 20. PAGE 136 A2792
HABITAT DIPLOM CONCPT DRIVE

S59
PUGWASH CONFERENCE,"ON BIOLOGICAL AND CHEMICAL WARFARE." WOR+45 SOCIETY PROC/MFG INT/ORG FORCES EDU/PROP ADJUD RIGID/FLEX ORD/FREE PWR...DECISION PSY NEW/IDEA MATH VAL/FREE 20. PAGE 118 A2417
ACT/RES BIO/SOC WAR WEAPON

B60
US HOUSE COMM. SCI. ASTRONAUT.,OCEAN SCIENCES AND NATIONAL SECURITY. FUT SEA ECO/DEV EXTR/IND INT/ORG NAT/G FORCES ACT/RES TEC/DEV ECO/TAC COERCE WAR BIO/SOC KNOWL PWR...CONCPT RECORD LAB/EXP 20. PAGE 154 A3141
R+D ORD/FREE

B62
CALDER R.,COMMON SENSE ABOUT A STARVING WORLD. WOR+45 STRATA ECO/DEV PLAN GP/REL BIO/SOC HABITAT ...POLICY GEOG STAT RECORD 20 UN BIRTH/CON. PAGE 23 A0466
FOR/AID CENSUS ECO/UNDEV AGRI

B64
COHEN M.,LAW AND POLITICS IN SPACE: SPECIFIC AND URGENT PROBLEMS IN THE LAW OF OUTER SPACE. CHINA/COM COM USA+45 USSR WOR+45 COM/IND INT/ORG NAT/G LEGIT NUC/PWR ATTIT BIO/SOC...JURID CONCPT CONGRESS 20 STALIN/J. PAGE 28 A0561
DELIB/GP LAW INT/LAW SPACE

B66
HOEVELER H.J.,INTERNATIONALE BEKAMPFUNG DES VERBRECHENS. AUSTRIA SWITZERLND WOR+45 INT/ORG CONTROL BIO/SOC...METH/COMP NAT/COMP 20 MAFIA SCOT/YARD FBI. PAGE 66 A1352
CRIMLGY CRIME DIPLOM INT/LAW

B67
RUSSELL B.,WAR CRIMES IN VIETNAM. USA+45 VIETNAM FORCES DIPLOM WEAPON RACE/REL DISCRIM ISOLAT BIO/SOC 20 COLD/WAR RUSSELL/B. PAGE 126 A2574
WAR CRIME ATTIT POLICY

BIOG....BIOGRAPHY (INCLUDES PSYCHOANALYSIS)

N
TOSCANO M.,THE HISTORY OF TREATIES AND INTERNATIONAL POLITICS (REV. ED.). WOR-45 AGREE WAR ...BIOG 19/20 TREATY WWI. PAGE 144 A2951
DIPLOM INT/ORG

N
ANNALS OF THE AMERICAN ACADEMY OF POLITICAL AND SOCIAL SCIENCE. AFR ASIA S/ASIA WOR+45 POL/PAR DIPLOM CRIME REV...SOC BIOG 20. PAGE 1 A0004
BIBLIOG/A NAT/G CULTURE ATTIT

N
MIDDLE EAST JOURNAL. CULTURE SECT DIPLOM LEAD GOV/REL ATTIT...POLICY PHIL/SCI SOC LING BIOG 20. PAGE 1 A0019
BIBLIOG ISLAM NAT/G ECO/UNDEV

N
AMERICAN BIBLIOGRAPHIC SERVICE,INTERNATIONAL GUIDE TO INDIC STUDIES - A QUARTERLY INDEX TO PERIODICAL LITERATURE. INDIA CULTURE NAT/G DIPLOM...EPIST SOC BIOG 20. PAGE 7 A0140
BIBLIOG S/ASIA CON/ANAL

N
EUROPA PUBLICATIONS LIMITED,THE EUROPA YEAR BOOK. CONSTN FINAN INDUS POL/PAR DIPLOM TV CT/SYS...STAT BIOG CHARTS WORSHIP 20. PAGE 43 A0874
BIBLIOG NAT/G PRESS INT/ORG

B08
ARON R.,WAR AND INDUSTRIAL SOCIETY. EUR+WWI MOD/EUR WOR+45 WOR-45 CONSTN SOCIETY INT/ORG POL/PAR VOL/ASSN DIPLOM INT/TRADE PEACE ATTIT...BIOG GEN/LAWS 19/20. PAGE 9 A0178
ECO/DEV WAR

B19
VANDERPOL A.,LA DOCTRINE SCOLASTIQUE DU DROIT DE GUERRE. CHRIST-17C FORCES DIPLOM LEGIT SUPEGO MORAL ...BIOG AQUINAS/T SUAREZ/F CHRISTIAN. PAGE 158 A3220
WAR SECT INT/LAW

B20
HALDANE R.B.,BEFORE THE WAR. MOD/EUR SOCIETY INT/ORG NAT/G DELIB/GP PLAN DOMIN EDU/PROP LEGIT ADMIN COERCE ATTIT DRIVE MORAL ORD/FREE PWR...SOC CONCPT SELF/OBS RECORD BIOG TIME/SEQ. PAGE 60 A1223
POLICY DIPLOM UK

B21
STUART G.H.,FRENCH FOREIGN POLICY. CONSTN INT/ORG NAT/G POL/PAR EX/STRUC FORCES PLAN ECO/TAC DOMIN EDU/PROP ADJUD COERCE ATTIT DRIVE RIGID/FLEX ALL/VALS...POLICY OBS RECORD BIOG TIME/SEQ TREND. PAGE 139 A2852
MOD/EUR DIPLOM FRANCE

C32
MARRARO H.R.,"AMERICAN OPINION ON THE UNIFICATION OF ITALY." ITALY MOD/EUR USA-45 FORCES DIPLOM PRESS REV CATHISM...BIOG 19 PRESIDENT. PAGE 95 A1944
BIBLIOG/A NAT/LISM ATTIT ORD/FREE

C37
ROWAN R.W.,"THE STORY OF THE SECRET SERVICE." WOR-45 REV...BIOG BIBLIOG. PAGE 124 A2552
WAR COERCE

DIPLOM

B39
NICOLSON H.,CURZON: THE LAST PHASE, 1919-1925. UK NAT/G DELIB/GP TOP/EX ROUTINE WAR RIGID/FLEX ...METH/CNCPT 20 CURZON/GN. PAGE 109 A2231
POLICY DIPLOM BIOG

B45
CONOVER H.F.,THE NAZI STATE: WAR CRIMES AND WAR CRIMINALS. GERMANY CULTURE NAT/G SECT FORCES DIPLOM INT/TRADE EDU/PROP...INT/LAW BIOG HIST/WRIT TIME/SEQ 20. PAGE 30 A0600
BIBLIOG WAR CRIME

B45
PERAZA SARAUSA F.,BIBLIOGRAFIAS CUBANAS. CUBA CULTURE ECO/UNDEV AGRI EDU/PROP PRESS CIVMIL/REL ...POLICY GEOG PHIL/SCI BIOG 19/20. PAGE 115 A2353
BIBLIOG/A L/A+17C NAT/G DIPLOM

B48
BELOFF M.,THOMAS JEFFERSON AND AMERICAN DEMOCRACY. USA-45 NAT/G DIPLOM GOV/REL PEACE 18/19 JEFFERSN/T PRESIDENT VIRGINIA. PAGE 13 A0258
BIOG CHIEF REV

B48
CHURCHILL W.,THE GATHERING STORM. UK WOR-45 INT/ORG NAT/G FORCES TOP/EX DIPLOM ECO/TAC COERCE ATTIT ORD/FREE PWR WEALTH...POLICY SELF/OBS RECORD NAZI PARLIAMENT 20. PAGE 26 A0538
BIOG

B48
FLOREN LOZANO L.,BIBLIOGRAFIA DE LA BIBLIOGRAFIA DOMINICANA. DOMIN/REP NAT/G DIPLOM EDU/PROP CIVMIL/REL...POLICY ART/METH GEOG PHIL/SCI HIST/WRIT 20. PAGE 47 A0952
BIBLIOG/A BIOG L/A+17C CULTURE

B49
STETTINIUS E.R.,ROOSEVELT AND THE RUSSIANS: THE YALTA CONFERENCE. UK USSR WOR+45 WOR-45 INT/ORG VOL/ASSN TOP/EX ACT/RES EDU/PROP PEACE ATTIT DRIVE PERSON SUPEGO PWR...POLICY CONCPT MYTH OBS TIME/SEQ AUD/VIS COLD/WAR 20 CHURCHLL/W YALTA ROOSEVLT/F. PAGE 138 A2819
DIPLOM DELIB/GP BIOG

B50
CHURCHILL W.,TRIUMPH AND TRAGEDY. UK WOR-45 INT/ORG NAT/G DELIB/GP FORCES TOP/EX DIPLOM COERCE CHOOSE ATTIT ORD/FREE PWR WEALTH...SELF/OBS CHARTS NAZI 20. PAGE 26 A0539
BIOG PEACE WAR

B53
BRETTON H.L.,STRESEMANN AND THE REVISION OF VERSAILLES: A FIGHT FOR REASON. EUR+WWI GERMANY FORCES BUDGET ARMS/CONT WAR SUPEGO...BIBLIOG 20 TREATY VERSAILLES STRESEMN/G. PAGE 18 A0373
POLICY DIPLOM BIOG

B53
COUSINS N.,WHO SPEAKS FOR MAN. GERMANY KOREA WOR+45 SOCIETY INT/ORG NAT/G CREATE EDU/PROP HEALTH KNOWL LOVE MORAL...OBS SELF/OBS BIOG HYPO/EXP TOT/POP 20 CHINJAP. PAGE 32 A0642
ATTIT WAR PEACE

B53
CRAIG G.A.,THE DIPLOMATS 1919-1939. WAR PEACE ATTIT ...POLICY BIOG 20. PAGE 32 A0651
DIPLOM ELITES FASCISM

B54
COUDENHOVE-KALERGI,AN IDEA CONQUERS THE WORLD. EUR+WWI MOD/EUR USA-45 CONSTN FAM CREATE EDU/PROP ATTIT PERSON KNOWL...CONCPT SELF/OBS TIME/SEQ. PAGE 31 A0635
INT/ORG BIOG DIPLOM

B54
MITCHELL P.,AFRICAN AFTERTHOUGHTS. UGANDA CONSTN NAT/G ADJUD COERCE WAR 20 WWI MAU/MAU. PAGE 102 A2090
BIOG CHIEF COLONIAL DOMIN

B54
SHARMA J.S.,MAHATMA GANDHI: A DESCRIPTIVE BIBLIOGRAPHY. INDIA S/ASIA PROB/SOLV DIPLOM COLONIAL WAR NAT/LISM PEACE ATTIT PERSON SOVEREIGN ...CONCPT 20 GANDHI/M. PAGE 132 A2695
BIBLIOG/A BIOG CHIEF LEAD

B56
BEALE H.K.,THEODORE ROOSEVELT AND THE RISE OF AMERICA TO WORLD POWER. USA-45 BAL/PWR COLONIAL DRIVE PERSON PWR...POLICY BIBLIOG 20 ROOSEVLT/T PRESIDENT. PAGE 12 A0238
DIPLOM CHIEF BIOG

B56
GEORGE A.L.,WOODROW WILSON AND COLONEL HOUSE. WOR-45 CONSTN FACE/GP INT/ORG NAT/G POL/PAR CONSULT LEGIT EXEC COERCE CHOOSE ATTIT DRIVE PERSON MORAL ORD/FREE PWR RESPECT...POLICY MGT PSY OBS RECORD INT LEAGUE/NAT. PAGE 52 A1060
USA-45 BIOG DIPLOM

B56
WILSON P.,GOVERNMENT AND POLITICS OF INDIA AND PAKISTAN: 1885-1955; A BIBLIOGRAPHY OF WORKS IN WESTERN LANGUAGES. INDIA PAKISTAN CONSTN LOC/G POL/PAR FORCES DIPLOM ADMIN WAR CHOOSE...BIOG CON/ANAL 19/20. PAGE 165 A3361
BIBLIOG COLONIAL NAT/G S/ASIA

B56
WU E.,LEADERS OF TWENTIETH-CENTURY CHINA; AN ANNOTATED BIBLIOGRAPHY OF SELECTED CHINESE BIOGRAPHICAL WORKS IN HOOVER LIBRARY. ASIA INDUS POL/PAR DIPLOM ADMIN REV WAR...HUM MGT 20. PAGE 168 A3422
BIBLIOG/A BIOG INTELL CHIEF

B57
BEAL J.R.,JOHN FOSTER DULLES, A BIOGRAPHY. USA+45 USSR WOR+45 CONSTN INT/ORG NAT/G EX/STRUC LEGIT ADMIN NUC/PWR DISPL PERSON ORD/FREE PWR SKILL ...POLICY PSY OBS RECORD COLD/WAR UN 20 DULLES/JF. PAGE 12 A0237
BIOG DIPLOM

B57
BEERS H.P.,THE FRENCH IN NORTH AMERICA. FRANCE USA-45...TIME/SEQ BIBLIOG. PAGE 12 A0247
HIST/WRIT DIPLOM BIOG WRITING

B57
TOMASIC D.A.,NATIONAL COMMUNISM AND SOVIET STRATEGY. UK USSR YUGOSLAVIA NAT/G POL/PAR CHIEF CREATE DOMIN REV WAR PWR...BIOG TREND 20 TITO/MARSH STALIN/J. PAGE 144 A2948
COM NAT/LISM MARXISM DIPLOM

B58
HUMPHREYS R.A.,LATIN AMERICAN HISTORY: A GUIDE TO THE LITERATURE IN ENGLISH. CULTURE NAT/G DIPLOM BIOG. PAGE 69 A1417
BIBLIOG/A L/A+17C

B58
YUAN TUNG-LI,CHINA IN WESTERN LITERATURE. SECT DIPLOM...ART/METH GEOG JURID SOC BIOG CON/ANAL. PAGE 169 A3440
BIBLIOG ASIA CULTURE HUM

B59
CAREW-HUNT R.C.,BOOKS ON COMMUNISM. NAT/G POL/PAR DIPLOM REV...BIOG 19/20. PAGE 24 A0481
BIBLIOG/A MARXISM COM ASIA

B60
EINSTEIN A.,EINSTEIN ON PEACE. FUT WOR+45 WOR-45 SOCIETY NAT/G PLAN BAL/PWR CAP/ISM DIPLOM ARMS/CONT DETER NAT/LISM...POLICY RELATIV HUM PHIL/SCI CONCPT BIOG COLD/WAR LEAGUE/NAT NAZI. PAGE 41 A0829
INT/ORG ATTIT NUC/PWR PEACE

B60
JAECKH A.,WELTSAAT; ERLEBTES UND ERSTREBTES. GERMANY WOR+45 WOR-45 PLAN WAR...POLICY OBS/ENVIR NAT/COMP PERS/COMP 20. PAGE 73 A1489
BIOG NAT/G SELF/OBS DIPLOM

B60
MORISON E.E.,TURMOIL AND TRADITION: A STUDY OF THE LIFE AND TIMES OF HENRY L. STIMSON. USA+45 USA-45 POL/PAR CHIEF DELIB/GP FORCES BAL/PWR DIPLOM ARMS/CONT WAR PEACE 19/20 STIMSON/HL ROOSEVLT/F TAFT/WH HOOVER/H REPUBLICAN. PAGE 104 A2142
BIOG NAT/G EX/STRUC

B60
PHILLIPS J.F.V.,KWAME NKRUMAH AND THE FUTURE OF AFRICA. FUT GHANA ISLAM ECO/UNDEV CHIEF DIPLOM COLONIAL RACE/REL NAT/LISM...TREND IDEA/COMP BIBLIOG 20 NKRUMAH/K. PAGE 116 A2376
BIOG LEAD SOVEREIGN AFR

B60
SCANLON D.G.,INTERNATIONAL EDUCATION: A DOCUMENTARY HISTORY. ADMIN CONTROL ATTIT PERCEPT...BIOG ANTHOL METH 20. PAGE 127 A2612
EDU/PROP INT/ORG NAT/COMP DIPLOM

C60
COX R.H.,"LOCKE ON WAR AND PEACE." UK DIPLOM DOMIN PWR...BIOG IDEA/COMP BIBLIOG 18. PAGE 32 A0646
CONCPT NAT/G PEACE WAR

B61
ACHESON D.,SKETCHES FROM LIFE. WOR+45 20 CHURCHLL/W EDEN/A ADENAUER/K SALAZAR/A. PAGE 4 A0085
BIOG LEAD CHIEF DIPLOM

B61
BARNES W.,THE FOREIGN SERVICE OF THE UNITED STATES. USA+45 USA-45 CONSTN INT/ORG POL/PAR CONSULT DELIB/GP LEGIS DOMIN EDU/PROP EXEC ATTIT RIGID/FLEX ORD/FREE PWR...POLICY CONCPT STAT OBS RECORD BIOG TIME/SEQ TREND. PAGE 11 A0224
NAT/G MGT DIPLOM

B61
DEAN V.M.,BUILDERS OF EMERGING NATIONS. WOR+45 ECO/UNDEV ECO/TAC NEUTRAL TOTALISM ORD/FREE PWR ...BIOG AUD/VIS IDEA/COMP BIBLIOG 20 COLD/WAR. PAGE 35 A0719
NAT/G CHIEF POLICY DIPLOM

B61
GRAEBNER N.,AN UNCERTAIN TRADITION: AMERICAN SECRETARIES OF STATE IN THE 20TH CENTURY. USA+45 CONSTN INT/ORG NAT/G DELIB/GP TOP/EX BAL/PWR DOMIN LEGIT ADMIN ARMS/CONT ATTIT DRIVE PERSON SUPEGO ORD/FREE PWR...GEN/LAWS VAL/FREE CONGRESS. PAGE 55 A1121
USA-45 BIOG DIPLOM

B61
HISTORICAL RESEARCH INSTITUTE,A SHORT BIBLIOGRAPHY OF INDO-MUSLIM HISTORY. INDIA S/ASIA DIPLOM EDU/PROP COLONIAL LEAD NAT/LISM ATTIT...BIOG 19/20. PAGE 65 A1343
BIBLIOG NAT/G SECT POL/PAR

B61
MILLER R.I.,DAG HAMMARSKJOLD AND CRISES DIPLOMACY. WOR+45 NAT/G PROB/SOLV LEAD ROLE...DECISION BIOG UN HAMMARSK/D. PAGE 101 A2079
DIPLOM INT/ORG CHIEF

S61
VIRALLY M.,"VERS UNE REFORME DU SECRETARIAT DES NATIONS UNIES." FUT WOR+45 CONSTN ECO/DEV TOP/EX BAL/PWR ADMIN ALL/VALS...CONCPT BIOG UN VAL/FREE 20. PAGE 159 A3243
INT/ORG INTELL DIPLOM

B62
COLLISON R.L.,BIBLIOGRAPHIES, SUBJECT AND NATIONAL: A GUIDE TO THEIR CONTENTS, ARRANGEMENT, AND USE (2ND REV. ED.). SECT DIPLOM...ART/METH GEOG HUM PHIL/SCI SOC MATH BIOG 20. PAGE 28 A0569
BIBLIOG/A CON/ANAL BIBLIOG

B62
INGHAM K.,A HISTORY OF EAST AFRICA. NAT/G DIPLOM ADMIN WAR NAT/LISM...SOC BIOG BIBLIOG. PAGE 70 A1439
AFR CONSTN COLONIAL

B62
SCHRODER P.M.,METTERNICH'S DIPLOMACY AT ITS ZENITH, 1820-1823. MOD/EUR ELITES INT/ORG VOL/ASSN DELIB/GP ECO/TAC EDU/PROP DISPL PWR SOVEREIGN...POLICY CONCPT GEN/LAWS 19 METTRNCH/K. PAGE 129 A2647
ORD/FREE BIOG BAL/PWR DIPLOM

L62
STEIN E.,"MR HAMMARSKJOLD, THE CHARTER LAW AND THE FUTURE ROLE OF THE UNITED NATIONS SECRETARY-GENERAL." WOR+45 CONSTN INT/ORG DELIB/GP FORCES TOP/EX BAL/PWR LEGIT ROUTINE RIGID/FLEX PWR ...POLICY JURID OBS STERTYP UN COLD/WAR 20 HAMMARSK/D. PAGE 137 A2815
CONCPT BIOG

B63
AFRICAN BIBLIOGRAPHIC CENTER,THE SCENE IS GUINEA AND THE PERSONAGE IS SEKOU TOURE: A SELECTED CURRENT READING LIST, 1959-1962 (PAMPHLET). GUINEA ECO/UNDEV CHIEF FOR/AID COLONIAL...BIOG 20. PAGE 5 A0095
BIBLIOG AFR POL/PAR COM

B63
LOOMIE A.J.,THE SPANISH ELIZABETHANS: THE ENGLISH EXILES AT THE COURT OF PHILIP II. SPAIN UK WAR INGP/REL DRIVE HABITAT CATHISM...BIOG 16/17 MIGRATION. PAGE 91 A1860
NAT/G STRANGE POLICY DIPLOM

B63
QUAISON-SACKEY A.,AFRICA UNBOUND: REFLECTIONS OF AN AFRICAN STATESMAN. ISLAM CULTURE INTELL INT/ORG POL/PAR TOP/EX DOMIN EDU/PROP LEGIT ATTIT PERSON ...CONCPT OBS TIME/SEQ CHARTS STERTYP 20 UN. PAGE 118 A2423
AFR BIOG

B63
TUCKER R.C.,THE SOVIET POLITICAL MIND. WOR+45 ELITES INT/ORG NAT/G POL/PAR PLAN DIPLOM ECO/TAC DOMIN ADMIN NUC/PWR REV DRIVE PERSON SUPEGO PWR WEALTH...POLICY MGT PSY CONCPT OBS BIOG TREND COLD/WAR MARX/KARL 20. PAGE 145 A2972
COM TOP/EX USSR

B63
WHITNEY T.P.,KHRUSHCHEV SPEAKS. USSR AGRI LEAD ...BIOG ANTHOL 20 KHRUSH/N STALIN/J ESPIONAGE. PAGE 164 A3339
DIPLOM MARXISM CHIEF

S63
MATHUR P.N.,"GAINS IN ECONOMIC GROWTH FROM INTERNATIONAL TRADE." USA-45 ECO/DEV FINAN INDUS ATTIT WEALTH...MATH QUANT STAT BIOG TREND GEN/LAWS WORK 20. PAGE 96 A1966
MARKET ECO/TAC CAP/ISM INT/TRADE

B64
ANDREWS D.H.,LATIN AMERICA: A BIBLIOGRAPHY OF PAPERBACK BOOKS. SECT INT/TRADE EDU/PROP WAR GOV/REL ADJUST NAT/LISM ATTIT...ART/METH LING BIOG 20. PAGE 8 A0160
BIBLIOG L/A+17C CULTURE NAT/G

B64
EHRENBURG I.,THE WAR: 1941-1945 (VOL. V OF "MEN, YEARS - LIFE," TRANS. BY TATIANA SHEBUNINA). GERMANY USSR PRESS WRITING PERS/REL PEACE ANOMIE ATTIT PERSON...CONCPT RECORD BIOG 20 STALIN/J HITLER/A. PAGE 40 A0827
WAR DIPLOM COM MARXIST

B64
HARPER F.,OUT OF CHINA. CHINA/COM ELITES STRATA ATTIT PERSON...BIOG 20 MAO HONG/KONG MIGRATION. PAGE 62 A1264
HABITAT DEEP/INT DIPLOM MARXISM

B64
JENSEN D.L.,DIPLOMACY AND DOGMATISM. FRANCE SPAIN REV WAR PERSON CATHISM...POLICY BIOG 16. PAGE 74 A1513
DIPLOM ATTIT SECT

B64
REMAK J.,THE GENTLE CRITIC: THEODOR FONTANE AND GERMAN POLITICS, 1848-1898. GERMANY PRUSSIA CULTURE ELITES BAL/PWR DIPLOM WRITING GOV/REL...HUM BIOG 19 BISMARCK/O JUNKER FONTANE/T. PAGE 120 A2465
PERSON SOCIETY WORKER CHIEF

B64
SULLIVAN G.,THE STORY OF THE PEACE CORPS. USA+45 WOR+45 INTELL FACE/GP NAT/G SCHOOL VOL/ASSN CONSULT EX/STRUC PLAN EDU/PROP ADMIN ATTIT DRIVE ALL/VALS ...POLICY HEAL SOC CONCPT INT QU BIOG TREND SOC/EXP WORK. PAGE 140 A2861
INT/ORG ECO/UNDEV FOR/AID PEACE

B64
THANT U.,TOWARD WORLD PEACE. DELIB/GP TEC/DEV EDU/PROP WAR SOVEREIGN...INT/LAW 20 UN MID/EAST. PAGE 142 A2907
DIPLOM BIOG PEACE COERCE

S64
KHAN M.Z.,"THE PRESIDENT OF THE GENERAL ASSEMBLY." WOR+45 CONSTN DELIB/GP EDU/PROP LEGIT ROUTINE PWR RESPECT SKILL...DECISION SOC BIOG TREND UN 20. PAGE 78 A1609
INT/ORG TOP/EX

B65
ADENAUER K.,MEMOIRS 1945-53. EUR+WWI GERMANY/W ECO/DEV CHIEF FORCES ECO/TAC WAR GOV/REL PWR SOVEREIGN 20 NATO ADENAUER/K. PAGE 4 A0088
BIOG DIPLOM NAT/G PERS/REL

B65
ADENAUER K.,MEINE ERINNERUNGEN, 1945-53 (VOL. I), 1953-55 (VOL. II). EUR+WWI GERMANY CHIEF FORCES PROB/SOLV DIPLOM ARMS/CONT INGP/REL PEACE SOVEREIGN ...OBS/ENVIR RECORD 20. PAGE 4 A0089
NAT/G BIOG SELF/OBS

B65
EISENHOWER D.D.,WAGING PEACE 1956-61: THE WHITE HOUSE YEARS. USA+45 DIPLOM LEAD INGP/REL RACE/REL PEACE ATTIT...TRADIT TIME/SEQ 20 EISNHWR/DD PRESIDENT COLD/WAR CIV/RIGHTS BERLIN. PAGE 41 A0833
TOP/EX BIOG ORD/FREE POLICY

B65
HART B.H.L.,THE MEMOIRS OF CAPTAIN LIDDELL HART (VOL. I). UK NAT/G PLAN TEC/DEV DIPLOM ADMIN WEAPON GOV/REL PERS/REL ATTIT PWR FASCISM...POLICY 20. PAGE 62 A1274
FORCES BIOG LEAD WAR

B65
MENON K.P.S.,MANY WORLDS. INDIA BAL/PWR CAP/ISM COLONIAL REV ORD/FREE PWR MARXISM...POLICY 20 COLD/WAR. PAGE 100 A2042
BIOG DIPLOM NAT/G

B66
DONALD A.D.,JOHN F. KENNEDY AND THE NEW FRONTIER. LEGIS DIPLOM DISCRIM PEACE PWR 20. PAGE 38 A0771
LEAD CHIEF BIOG EFFICIENCY

B66
LENT H.B.,THE PEACE CORPS: AMBASSADORS OF GOOD WILL. USA+45 ECO/UNDEV...INT TESTS BIOG AUD/VIS SOC/INTEG 20 PEACE/CORP. PAGE 87 A1776
VOL/ASSN FOR/AID DIPLOM CONSULT

B66
SPEARS E.L.,TWO MEN WHO SAVED FRANCE: PETAIN AND DE GAULLE. FRANCE CONSTN FORCES DIPLOM WAR PERSON 20 WWI PETAIN/HP DEGAULLE/C. PAGE 135 A2773
BIOG LEAD CHIEF NAT/G

B66
VIEN N.C.,SEEKING THE TRUTH. FRANCE VIETNAM AGRI ADMIN WAR...BIOG 20 BAO/DAI INTERVENT. PAGE 159 A3231
NAT/G CONSULT CONSTN

B67
ATTWOOD W.,THE REDS AND THE BLACKS. AFR POL/PAR CHOOSE GOV/REL RACE/REL NAT/LISM...BIOG 20. PAGE 10 A0195
DIPLOM PWR MARXISM

B67
JAGAN C.,THE WEST ON TRIAL. GUYANA CONSTN ECO/UNDEV DIPLOM COERCE PWR SOVEREIGN...BIOG 20. PAGE 73 A1490
SOCISM CREATE PLAN COLONIAL

B67
MAW B.,BREAKTHROUGH IN BURMA: MEMOIRS OF A REVOLUTION, 1939-1946. BURMA UK FORCES PROB/SOLV DIPLOM FOR/AID DOMIN LEAD...BIOG 20. PAGE 97 A1980
REV ORD/FREE NAT/LISM COLONIAL

B67
WILLIS F.R.,DE GAULLE: ANACHRONISM, REALIST, OR PROPHET? FRANCE POL/PAR FORCES DIPLOM WAR PEACE ROLE ORD/FREE...POLICY IDEA/COMP ANTHOL 20 DEGAULLE/C. PAGE 165 A3356
BIOG PERSON CHIEF LEAD

BIRCH/SOC....JOHN BIRCH SOCIETY

B66
WELCH R.H.W.,THE NEW AMERICANISM, AND OTHER SPEECHES AND ESSAYS. USA+45 ACADEM POL/PAR SCHOOL VOL/ASSN FORCES CAP/ISM TAX REV DISCRIM 20 CIV/RIGHTS COLD/WAR BIRCH/SOC. PAGE 163 A3313
DIPLOM FASCISM MARXISM RACE/REL

BIRDSALL P. A0290

BIRMINGHAM D. A0291

BIRTH/CON....BIRTH CONTROL POLICIES AND TECHNIQUES

N19
HAUSER P.M.,WORLD POPULATION PROBLEMS (PAMPHLET). USA+45 WOR+45 ECO/DEV ECO/UNDEV FAM ACT/RES PLAN PROB/SOLV FOR/AID GIVE EATING...CHARTS 20 BIRTH/CON RESOURCE/N. PAGE 63 A1289
CONTROL CENSUS ATTIT PREDICT

N19
NATIONAL ACADEMY OF SCIENCES,THE GROWTH OF WORLD POPULATION: ANALYSIS OF THE PROBLEMS AND RECOMMENDATIONS FOR RESEARCH AND TRAINING (PAMPHLET). WOR+45 CULTURE ECO/UNDEV EDU/PROP MARRIAGE AGE HEALTH...ANTHOL 20 BIRTH/CON. PAGE 107 A2199
CENSUS PLAN FAM INT/ORG

B60
VOGT W.,PEOPLE: CHALLENGE TO SURVIVAL. WOR+45 ECO/DEV ECO/UNDEV FAM INT/ORG NAT/G PLAN PROB/SOLV FOR/AID GIVE EATING 20 BIRTH/CON. PAGE 159 A3247
CENSUS CONTROL ATTIT TEC/DEV

B62
CALDER R.,COMMON SENSE ABOUT A STARVING WORLD. WOR+45 STRATA ECO/DEV PLAN GP/REL BIO/SOC HABITAT ...POLICY GEOG STAT RECORD 20 UN BIRTH/CON. PAGE 23
FOR/AID CENSUS ECO/UNDEV

A0466 AGRI

B66
UN ECAFE,ADMINISTRATIVE ASPECTS OF FAMILY PLANNING PROGRAMMES (PAMPHLET). ASIA THAILAND WOR+45 VOL/ASSN PROB/SOLV BUDGET FOR/AID EDU/PROP CONFER CONTROL GOV/REL TIME 20 UN BIRTH/CON. PAGE 147 A2999 PLAN CENSUS FAM ADMIN

B66
US SENATE COMM GOVT OPERATIONS,POPULATION CRISIS. USA+45 ECO/DEV ECO/UNDEV AGRI SECT DELIB/GP PROB/SOLV FOR/AID REPRESENT ATTIT...GEOG CHARTS 20 CONGRESS DEPT/STATE DEPT/HEW BIRTH/CON. PAGE 156 A3178 CENSUS CONTROL LEGIS CONSULT

BISHOP D.G. A0292

BISHOP O.B. A0293,A0294

BISMARCK/O....OTTO VON BISMARCK

B27
BRANDENBURG E.,FROM BISMARCK TO THE WORLD WAR; A HISTORY OF GERMAN FOREIGN POLICY, 1870-1914 (TRANS. BY ANNIE ELIZABETH ADAMS). GERMANY MOD/EUR FORCES AGREE PWR 19/20 TREATY CHAMBRLN/J WWI BISMARCK/O. PAGE 18 A0368 DIPLOM POLICY WAR

B29
LANGER W.L.,THE FRANCO-RUSSIAN ALLIANCE: 1890-1894. FRANCE MOD/EUR UK USSR NAT/G CHIEF FORCES BAL/PWR AGREE WAR PEACE PWR...TIME/SEQ TREATY 19 BISMARCK/O. PAGE 84 A1724 DIPLOM

B58
CRAIG G.A.,FROM BISMARCK TO ADENAUER: ASPECTS OF GERMAN STATECRAFT. GERMANY INTELL FORCES ECO/TAC CONFER COERCE WAR GP/REL ORD/FREE PWR CONSERVE 19/20 BISMARCK/O ADENAUER/K. PAGE 32 A0653 DIPLOM LEAD NAT/G

B62
SCHMIDT-VOLKMAR E.,DER KULTURKAMPF IN DEUTSCHLAND 1871-1890. GERMANY PRUSSIA SOCIETY STRUCT SECT DIPLOM GP/REL NAT/LISM 19 CHURCH/STA BISMARCK/O. PAGE 128 A2632 POL/PAR CATHISM ATTIT NAT/G

B64
REMAK J.,THE GENTLE CRITIC: THEODOR FONTANE AND GERMAN POLITICS, 1848-1898. GERMANY PRUSSIA CULTURE ELITES BAL/PWR DIPLOM WRITING GOV/REL...HUM BIOG 19 BISMARCK/O JUNKER FONTANE/T. PAGE 120 A2465 PERSON SOCIETY WORKER CHIEF

B66
CRAIG G.A.,WAR, POLITICS, AND DIPLOMACY. PRUSSIA CONSTN FORCES CIVMIL/REL TOTALISM PWR 19/20 BISMARCK/O DULLES/JF NAPOLEON/B. PAGE 32 A0654 WAR DIPLOM BAL/PWR

BISSAINTHE M. A0295

BLACK C.E. A0296

BLACK E.R. A0297

BLACK J.E. A0298

BLACK/EUG....EUGENE BLACK

B66
US SENATE COMM ON FOREIGN REL,ASIAN DEVELOPMENT BANK ACT. USA+45 LAW DIPLOM...CHARTS 20 BLACK/EUG S/EASTASIA. PAGE 156 A3186 FOR/AID FINAN ECO/UNDEV S/ASIA

BLACK/HL....HUGO L. BLACK

BLACK/MUS....BLACK MUSLIMS

BLACK/PWR....BLACK POWER; SEE ALSO NEGRO

BLACK/ZION....BLACK ZIONISM

BLACKETT P.M.S. A0299,A0300

BLACKMER D.L.M. A2082

BLACKSTN/W....SIR WILLIAM BLACKSTONE

BLACKSTOCK P.W. A0301,A0302

BLACKSTONE, SIR WILLIAM....SEE BLACKSTN/W

BLAISDELL D.C. A0303,A0304

BLAKE J.W. A0305

BLANCHARD C.H. A0306

BLANCHARD W. A0307

BLANSHARD P. A0308,A0309

BLAUSTEIN A.P. A0310

BLOCH/E....ERNEST BLOCH

BLOCH-MORHANGE J. A0311

BLOM-COOPER L. A0312

BLOOMFIELD L.M. A0314

BLOOMFIELD L.P. A0313,A0316,A0317,A0318,A0319,A0320,A0321

BLUM A.A. A0966

BLUM L. A0322,A0323

BLUM Y.Z. A0324

BMA....BRITISH MEDICAL ASSOCIATION

BOARD....SEE DELIB/GP

BOARD/MDCN....BOARD ON MEDICINE

BOAS/FRANZ....FRANZ BOAS

BODENHEIMER E. A0325

BODENHEIMER S.J. A0326

BODIN/JEAN....JEAN BODIN

BOER/WAR....BOER WAR

B99
BROOKS S.,BRITAIN AND THE BOERS. AFR SOUTH/AFR UK CULTURE INSPECT LEGIT...INT/LAW 19/20 BOER/WAR. PAGE 19 A0396 WAR DIPLOM NAT/G

BOESCH E.E. A0283

BOGARDUS E.S. A0327

BOGARDUS....BOGARDUS SCALE

BOGART L. A0328

BOGGS S.W. A0329

BOHATTA H. A0330

BOHME/H....HELMUT BOHME

BOHN L. A0331

BOISSIER P. A0332

BOKOR-SZEGO H. A0333

BOLIVIA....SEE ALSO L/A+17C

B66
GARNER W.R.,THE CHACO DISPUTE; A STUDY OF PRESTIGE DIPLOMACY. L/A+17C PARAGUAY USA-45 INT/ORG AGREE PEACE...TIME/SEQ 20 BOLIV LEAGUE/NAT ARGEN CHACO/WAR. PAGE 51 A1050 WAR DIPLOM CONCPT PWR

B67
PIKE F.B.,FREEDOM AND REFORM IN LATIN AMERICA. BRAZIL URUGUAY CONSTN CULTURE SECT DIPLOM EDU/PROP PARTIC DRIVE ALL/VALS CATHISM...GEOG ANTHOL BIBLIOG REFORMERS BOLIV. PAGE 116 A2379 L/A+17C ORD/FREE ECO/UNDEV REV

S67
HEATH D.B.,"BOLIVIA UNDER BARRIENTOS." L/A+17C NAT/G CHIEF DIPLOM ECO/TAC...POLICY 20 BOLIV. PAGE 64 A1306 ECO/UNDEV POL/PAR REV CONSTN

BOLIVAR/S ....SIMON BOLIVAR

N19
LANGE O.R.,"DISARMAMENT ECONOMIC GROWTH AND INTERNATIONAL CO-OPERATION" (PAMPHLET). WOR+45 DIST/IND PLAN INT/TRADE GIVE TASK DETER WEALTH SOCISM 18/19 BOLIVAR/S. PAGE 84 A1723 ARMS/CONT DIPLOM ECO/DEV ECO/UNDEV

BOLIVIA....BOLIVIA; SEE ALSO L/A+17C

BOLSHEVISM....BOLSHEVISM AND BOLSHEVISTS

B59
GOLDWIN R.A.,READINGS IN RUSSIAN FOREIGN POLICY. HUNGARY USSR YUGOSLAVIA ELITES INT/ORG NAT/G REV WAR NAT/LISM PERSON SOCISM...CHARTS 20 MAPS BOLSHEVISM. PAGE 53 A1095 COM MARXISM DIPLOM POLICY

S61
TUCKER R.C.,"TOWARDS A COMPARATIVE POLITICS OF MOVEMENT-REGIMES" (BMR)" USSR CONSTN NAT/G CREATE PROB/SOLV DIPLOM DOMIN REV...GP/COMP IDEA/COMP METH 20 STALIN/J BOLSHEVISM. PAGE 145 A2971
MARXISM POLICY GEN/LAWS PWR

B64
LENSEN G.A.,REVELATIONS OF A RUSSIAN DIPLOMAT: THE MEMOIRS OF DMITRII I. ABRIKOSSOV. ASIA MOD/EUR RUSSIA USA-45 ELITES ACADEM CHIEF FORCES REV WAR PWR CONSERVE MARXISM 19/20 ABRIKSSV/D CHINJAP BOLSHEVISM. PAGE 87 A1775
DIPLOM POLICY OBS

BONAPART/L....LOUIS BONAPARTE (KING OF HOLLAND)

BONNEFOUS M. A0334

BONNET H. A0335

BONTOC....BONTOC, A MOUNTAIN TRIBE OF LUZON, PHILIPPINES

BOONE/DANL....DANIEL BOONE

BORBA DE MORAES R. A0336

BORCHARD E.M. A0337,A0338

BORDEN/R....SIR ROBERT BORDEN

B66
WILSON H.A.,THE IMPERIAL POLICY OF SIR ROBERT BORDEN. CANADA UK ELITES INT/ORG VOL/ASSN CONTROL LEAD WAR ROLE 20 CMN/WLTH BORDEN/R. PAGE 165 A3360
INGP/REL COLONIAL CONSTN CHIEF

BORGESE G. A0339,A0340

BORGESE G.A. A0339, A0340, A0341

BORKENAU F. A0342

BORNEO....SEE ALSO S/ASIA

B66
LEIGH M.B.,CHECK LIST OF HOLDINGS ON BORNEO IN THE CORNELL UNIVERSITY LIBRARIES (PAMPHLET). BORNEO MALAYSIA LAW CONSTN GP/REL SOC. PAGE 86 A1769
BIBLIOG S/ASIA DIPLOM NAT/G

BORNSTEIN J. A0343

BOSCH/JUAN....JUAN BOSCH

BOSSISM....BOSSISM; MONOPOLY OF POLITICAL POWER (U.S.)

BOSTON....BOSTON, MASSACHUSETTS

B67
JOHNSON A.M.,BOSTON CAPITALISTS AND WESTERN RAILROADS: A STUDY IN THE NINETEENTH CENTURY RAILROAD INVESTMENT PROCESS. CREATE BARGAIN INT/TRADE GAMBLE KNOWL 19 BOSTON. PAGE 74 A1519
FINAN DIST/IND CAP/ISM ECO/UNDEV

BOTSWANA....BOTSWANA

BOUDET P. A0344

BOULDER....BOULDER, COLORADO

BOULDING K.E. A0345,A0346,A0347,A0348,A0349

BOUQUET A.C. A2262

BOURASSA/H....HENRI BOURASSA

BOURBON-BUSSET J. A0350

BOURGEOIS R. A0344

BOURGUIBA

B62
BAULIN J.,THE ARAB ROLE IN AFRICA. AFR ALGERIA FUT ISLAM MOROCCO UAR COLONIAL NEUTRAL REV...SOC 20 TUNIS BOURGUIBA. PAGE 12 A0235
NAT/LISM DIPLOM NAT/G SECT

BOURNE H.E. A0351

BOUSCAREN A.T. A0352

BOWETT D.W. A0353,A0354

BOWIE R. A0355,A0356

BOWIE R.R. A0357

BOWKER R.R. A1806

BOWLES C. A0358,A0359,A0360,A0361

BOXER/REBL....BOXER REBELLION

B55
TAN C.C.,THE BOXER CATASTROPHE. ASIA UK USSR ELITES POL/PAR VOL/ASSN FORCES PROB/SOLV DIPLOM ADMIN COLONIAL NAT/LISM PEACE TREATY 19/20 BOXER/REBL. PAGE 141 A2885
REV NAT/G WAR

BOYCE A.N. A0362

BOYD A. A0363

BOYD F. A0363

BOYD J.P. A0364

BOZZA T. A0365

BRACKETT R.D. A0366

BRACKMAN A.C. A0367

BRADLEY/FH....FRANCIS HERBERT BRADLEY

BRAHMIN....BRAHMIN CASTE

BRAINWASHING....SEE EDU/PROP

BRANDEIS/L....LOUIS BRANDEIS

BRANDENBURG E. A0368

BRANNAN/C....CHARLES BRANNAN (SECRETARY OF AGRICULTURE)

BRAZIL....SEE ALSO L/A+17C

B17
DOS SANTOS M.,BIBLIOGRAPHIA GERAL, A DESCRIPCAO BIBLIOGRAFICA DE LIVROS TANTO DE AUTORES PORTUGUEZES COMO BRASILEIROS... BRAZIL PORTUGAL NAT/G LEAD GP/REL 15/20. PAGE 38 A0774
BIBLIOG/A L/A+17C DIPLOM COLONIAL

N19
BARROS J.F.P.,THE INTERNATIONAL POLICE: THE USE OF FORCE IN THE STRUCTURE OF PEACE (PAMPHLET). BRAZIL WOR+45 WOR-45 FORCES DISCRIM NAT/LISM ORD/FREE SOVEREIGN...POLICY NEW/IDEA WORSHIP 20. PAGE 11 A0229
PEACE INT/ORG COERCE BAL/PWR

B32
EAGLETON C.,INTERNATIONAL GOVERNMENT. BRAZIL FRANCE GERMANY ITALY UK USSR WOR-45 DELIB/GP TOP/EX PLAN ECO/TAC EDU/PROP LEGIT ADJUD REGION ARMS/CONT COERCE ATTIT PWR...GEOG MGT VAL/FREE LEAGUE/NAT 20. PAGE 40 A0816
INT/ORG JURID DIPLOM INT/LAW

B42
SIMOES DOS REIS A.,BIBLIOGRAFIA DAS BIBLIOGRAFIAS BRASILEIRAS. BRAZIL ADMIN COLONIAL 20. PAGE 133 A2717
BIBLIOG NAT/G DIPLOM L/A+17C

B49
BORBA DE MORAES R.,MANUAL BIBLIOGRAFICO DE ESTUDOS BRASILEIROS. BRAZIL DIPLOM ADMIN LEAD...SOC 20. PAGE 17 A0336
BIBLIOG L/A+17C NAT/G ECO/UNDEV

B50
FIGANIERE J.C.,BIBLIOTHECA HISTORICA PORTUGUEZA. BRAZIL PORTUGAL SECT ADMIN. PAGE 45 A0929
BIBLIOG NAT/G DIPLOM COLONIAL

B60
MENEZES A.J.,O BRASIL E O MUNDO ASIO-AFRICANO (REV. ED.). AFR ASIA BRAZIL WOR+45 INT/TRADE ORD/FREE PWR SOVEREIGN...POLICY 20. PAGE 99 A2040
DIPLOM BAL/PWR LEAD ECO/UNDEV

B61
HADDAD J.A.,REVOLUCAO CUBANA E REVOLUCAO BRASILEIRA. BRAZIL CUBA L/A+17C STRATA AGRI WORKER EDU/PROP REGION...POLICY NAT/COMP 20. PAGE 59 A1210
REV ORD/FREE DIPLOM ECO/UNDEV

B62
LEVY H.V.,LIBERDADE E JUSTICA SOCIAL (2ND ED.). BRAZIL COM L/A+17C USSR INT/ORG PARTIC GP/REL WEALTH 20 UN COM/PARTY. PAGE 88 A1798
ORD/FREE MARXISM CAP/ISM LAW

B63
GUIMARAES A.P.,INFLACAO E MONOPOLIO NO BRASIL. BRAZIL FINAN NAT/G PLAN PAY...METH/COMP 20. PAGE 58 A1189
ECO/UNDEV PRICE INT/TRADE BAL/PAY

B63
MENEZES A.J.,SUBDESENVOLVIMENTO E POLITICA INTERNACIONAL. BRAZIL WOR+45 PLAN CONTROL LEAD NAT/LISM ORD/FREE 20 THIRD/WRLD. PAGE 99 A2041 ECO/UNDEV DIPLOM POLICY BAL/PWR

B63
ROBOCK S.H.,OVERVIEW OF TOTAL BRAZILIAN SETTING, NEWER REGIONAL PATTERNS NING AND FOREIGN AID. BRAZIL ECO/UNDEV AGRI FINAN INDUS INT/ORG INCOME UTIL...CHARTS 20. PAGE 122 A2507 ECO/TAC REGION PLAN FOR/AID

B63
THORELLI H.B.,INTOP: INTERNATIONAL OPERATIONS SIMULATION: PLAYER'S MANUAL. BRAZIL FINAN OP/RES ADMIN GP/REL INGP/REL PRODUC PERCEPT...DECISION MGT EEC. PAGE 144 A2935 GAME INT/TRADE EDU/PROP LG/CO

B64
ALVIM J.C.,A REVOLUCAO SEM RUMO. BRAZIL NAT/G BAL/PWR DIPLOM INT/TRADE PARTIC WEALTH...POLICY SOC SOC/INTEG 20. PAGE 6 A0132 REV CIVMIL/REL ECO/UNDEV ORD/FREE

B64
HOROWITZ I.L.,REVOLUTION IN BRAZIL. BRAZIL L/A+17C ELITES STRATA NAT/G BAL/PWR PARTIC ATTIT 20. PAGE 68 A1388 ECO/UNDEV DIPLOM POLICY ORD/FREE

B64
JACKSON W.V.,LIBRARY GUIDE FOR BRAZILIAN STUDIES. BRAZIL USA+45 STRUCT DIPLOM ADMIN...SOC 20. PAGE 72 A1481 BIBLIOG L/A+17C NAT/G LOC/G

B64
MAIER J.,POLITICS OF CHANGE IN LATIN AMERICA. BRAZIL L/A+17C STRATA INT/ORG NAT/G POL/PAR FOR/AID REV 20. PAGE 93 A1907 SOCIETY NAT/LISM DIPLOM REGION

B64
RICHARDSON I.L.,BIBLIOGRAFIA BRASILEIRA DE ADMINISTRACAO PUBLICA E ASSUNTOS CORRELATOS. BRAZIL CONSTN FINAN LOC/G NAT/G POL/PAR PLAN DIPLOM RECEIVE ATTIT...METH 20. PAGE 121 A2474 BIBLIOG MGT ADMIN LAW

B64
SINGER H.W.,INTERNATIONAL DEVELOPMENT: GROWTH AND CHANGE. AFR BRAZIL L/A+17C WOR+45 CULTURE AGRI INDUS NAT/G ACT/RES ECO/TAC EDU/PROP WEALTH...GEOG CONCPT METH/CNCPT STAT HYPO/EXP WORK TOT/POP 20. PAGE 133 A2723 FINAN ECO/UNDEV FOR/AID INT/TRADE

B64
WITHERS W.,THE ECONOMIC CRISIS IN LATIN AMERICA. BRAZIL CHILE STRATA AGRI DIPLOM FOR/AID PWR SOCISM ...POLICY 20 MEXIC/AMER ARGEN. PAGE 166 A3372 L/A+17C ECO/UNDEV CAP/ISM ALL/IDEOS

B65
RODRIGUES J.H.,BRAZIL AND AFRICA. AFR BRAZIL PORTUGAL UK USA+45 USA-45 CULTURE ECO/UNDEV INT/ORG INT/TRADE RACE/REL ORD/FREE 15/20 UN MISCEGEN. PAGE 123 A2513 DIPLOM COLONIAL POLICY ATTIT

B67
PIKE F.B.,FREEDOM AND REFORM IN LATIN AMERICA. BRAZIL URUGUAY CONSTN CULTURE SECT DIPLOM EDU/PROP PARTIC DRIVE ALL/VALS CATHISM...GEOG ANTHOL BIBLIOG REFORMERS BOLIV. PAGE 116 A2379 L/A+17C ORD/FREE ECO/UNDEV REV

S67
BURNS E.B.,"TRADITIONS AND VARIATIONS IN BRAZILIAN FOREIGN POLICY." BRAZIL L/A+17C POL/PAR INT/TRADE COLONIAL INGP/REL ATTIT ORD/FREE PWR 20. PAGE 22 A0443 DIPLOM NAT/LISM CREATE

S67
LEFF N.H.,"EXPORT STAGNATION AND AUTARKIC DEVELOPMENT IN BRAZIL, 19471962." BRAZIL ECO/TAC TARIFFS 20. PAGE 86 A1764 BAL/PAY INT/TRADE WEALTH DIPLOM

BRECHER M. A0369

BREGMAN A. A0370

BREHON....BREHON LAW (ANCIENT CELTIC)

BREMBECK C.S. A1256

BRENNAN D.G. A0371,A0372

BRETTON H.L. A0373

BRIAND/A....ARISTIDE BRIAND

B52
FERRELL R.H.,PEACE IN THEIR TIME. FRANCE UK USA-45 INT/ORG NAT/G FORCES CREATE AGREE ARMS/CONT COERCE WAR TREATY 20 WILSON/W LEAGUE/NAT BRIAND/A. PAGE 45 A0920 PEACE DIPLOM

BRIDGEPORT....BRIDGEPORT, CONNECTICUT

BRIDGMAN J. A0374

BRIERLY J.L. A0375,A0376,A0377

BRIMMER B. A0378

BRINKMANN C. A3249

BRISBY L. A1576

BRIT/COLUM....BRITISH COLUMBIA, CANADA

BRITISH COMMONWEALTH OF NATIONS....SEE COMMONWLTH

BRITISH MEDICAL ASSOCIATION....SEE BMA

BRITISH COMMONWEALTH REL CONF A0379

BRITTEN M. A2976

BRODIE B. A0380,A0381

BRODY H. A0382

BRODY R.A. A0383,A3228

BROEKMEIJER M.W.J. A0384, A0385

BROGAN D.W. A0386

BROMBERGER M. A0387

BROMBERGER S. A0387

BROMKE A. A0388,A0389

BROOK D. A0390

BROOK/EDGR....EDGAR H. BROOKES

BROOKES E.H. A0391

BROOKINGS INSTITUTION A0392,A0393,A0394,A0395

BROOKINGS....BROOKINGS INSTITUTION, THE

BROOKS S. A0396

BROWN A.D. A0397,A0398,A0399

BROWN B.E. A0400

BROWN E.S. A0401

BROWN H. A0402

BROWN J.F. A0403,A0404

BROWN L.C. A0405,A0406

BROWN S. A0407

BROWN W.A. A0186

BROWN W.N. A0408

BROWN/JOHN....JOHN BROWN

BROWNELL/H....HERBERT BROWNELL

BROWNLIE I. A0409

BRUNER J.S. A0410

BRYAN/WJ....WILLIAM JENNINGS BRYAN

BRYANT A. A0411

BRYCE J. A0412,A0413

BRYCE/J....JAMES BRYCE

BRYNES A. A0414

BRZEZINSKI Z.K. A0415,A0416,A0417,A0418,A0419,A0420

BRZEZNSK/Z....ZBIGNIEW K. BRZEZINSKI

BUCHAN A. A0421,A0422,A0423

BUCHANAN W. A0424,A0425

BUCHANAN/J....PRESIDENT JAMES BUCHANAN

BUCHMANN J. A0426

BUCK P.W. A0427

BUCKLEY/WF....WILLIAM F. BUCKLEY

BUDDHISM....BUDDHISM

B55
THOMPSON V.,MINORITY PROBLEMS IN SOUTHEAST ASIA. CAMBODIA CHINA/COM LAOS S/ASIA KIN NAT/G SECT PROB/SOLV EDU/PROP REGION GP/REL RACE/REL MARXISM ...SOC 20 BUDDHISM UN. PAGE 143 A2933
INGP/REL GEOG DIPLOM STRUCT

S66
DINH TRANS V.A.N.,"VIETNAM: A THIRD WAY" S/ASIA USA+45 USSR VIETNAM VIETNAM/S NAT/G SECT FORCES CAP/ISM DIPLOM COLONIAL NEUTRAL MARXISM SOCISM 20 BUDDHISM UNIFICA. PAGE 38 A0766
WAR PLAN ORD/FREE SOCIALIST

BUDGET....BUDGETING, BUDGETS, FISCAL PLANNING

N
DOCUMENTATION ECONOMIQUE: REVUE BIBLIOGRAPHIQUE DE SYNTHESE. WOR+45 COM/IND FINAN BUDGET DIPLOM...GEOG 20. PAGE 2 A0033
BIBLIOG/A SOC

N
FOREIGN TRADE LIBRARY,NEW TITLES RECEIVED IN THE LIBRARY. WOR+45 ECO/UNDEV FINAN NAT/G PLAN TEC/DEV BUDGET ECO/TAC TARIFFS GOV/REL STAT. PAGE 47 A0964
BIBLIOG/A INT/TRADE INDUS ECO/DEV

N
IMF AND IBRD, JOINT LIBRARY,LIST OF RECENT ADDITIONS. WOR+45 ECO/DEV ECO/UNDEV BUDGET FOR/AID RATION...CONCPT IDEA/COMP. PAGE 70 A1434
BIBLIOG INT/ORG INT/TRADE FINAN

N
IMF AND IBRD, JOINT LIBRARY,LIST OF RECENT PERIODICAL ARTICLES. WOR+45 ECO/DEV ECO/UNDEV BUDGET FOR/AID RATION...CONCPT IDEA/COMP. PAGE 70 A1435
BIBLIOG INT/ORG INT/TRADE FINAN

N
UNITED NATIONS,OFFICIAL RECORDS OF THE UNITED NATIONS' GENERAL ASSEMBLY. WOR+45 BUDGET DIPLOM ADMIN 20 UN. PAGE 148 A3033
INT/ORG DELIB/GP INT/LAW WRITING

B14
DE BLOCH J.,THE FUTURE OF WAR IN ITS TECHNICAL, ECONOMIC, AND POLITICAL RELATIONS (1899). MOD/EUR TEC/DEV BUDGET INT/TRADE DETER GUERRILLA WEAPON COST PEACE 20. PAGE 34 A0698
WAR BAL/PWR PREDICT FORCES

N19
MASON E.S.,THE DIPLOMACY OF ECONOMIC ASSISTANCE (PAMPHLET). INDIA PAKISTAN USA+45 ECO/UNDEV NAT/G BUDGET ATTIT...POLICY 20. PAGE 95 A1955
FOR/AID DIPLOM FINAN

B37
UNION OF SOUTH AFRICA,REPORT CONCERNING ADMINISTRATION OF SOUTH WEST AFRICA (6 VOLS.). SOUTH/AFR INDUS PUB/INST FORCES LEGIS BUDGET DIPLOM EDU/PROP ADJUD CT/SYS...GEOG CHARTS 20 AFRICA/SW LEAGUE/NAT. PAGE 148 A3028
NAT/G ADMIN COLONIAL CONSTN

C40
FAHS C.B.,"GOVERNMENT IN JAPAN." FINAN FORCES LEGIS TOP/EX BUDGET INT/TRADE EDU/PROP SOVEREIGN ...CON/ANAL BIBLIOG/A 20 CHINJAP. PAGE 43 A0884
ASIA DIPLOM NAT/G ADMIN

B42
FULLER G.H.,DEFENSE FINANCING: A SUPPLEMENTARY LIST OF REFERENCES (PAMPHLET). CANADA UK USA-45 ECO/DEV NAT/G DELIB/GP BUDGET ADJUD ARMS/CONT WEAPON COST PEACE PWR 20 AUSTRAL CHINJAP CONGRESS. PAGE 50 A1021
BIBLIOG/A FINAN FORCES DIPLOM

B42
US LIBRARY OF CONGRESS,ECONOMICS OF WAR (APRIL 1941-MARCH 1942). WOR-45 FINAN INDUS LOC/G NAT/G PLAN BUDGET RATION COST DEMAND...POLICY 20. PAGE 154 A3146
BIBLIOG/A INT/TRADE ECO/TAC WAR

B43
CONOVER H.F.,SOVIET RUSSIA: SELECTED LIST OF REFERENCES. USSR CULTURE INDUS NAT/G TOP/EX TEC/DEV BUDGET WAR CIVMIL/REL EFFICIENCY MARXISM 20. PAGE 29 A0597
BIBLIOG ECO/DEV COM DIPLOM

B48
HOWARD J.E.,PARLIAMENT AND FOREIGN POLICY IN FRANCE. FRANCE CONSTN DELIB/GP BUDGET ADMIN PARL/PROC CHOOSE...BIBLIOG/A 20 PARLIAMENT. PAGE 68 A1399
LEGIS CONTROL DIPLOM ATTIT

B48
NEUBURGER O.,GUIDE TO OFFICIAL PUBLICATIONS OF THE OTHER AMERICAN REPUBLICS: VENEZUELA (VOL. XIX). VENEZUELA FINAN LEGIS PLAN BUDGET DIPLOM CT/SYS PARL/PROC 19/20. PAGE 108 A2219
BIBLIOG/A NAT/G CONSTN LAW

B51
US HOUSE COMM APPROPRIATIONS,MUTUAL SECURITY PROGRAM APPROPRIATIONS FOR 1952: HEARINGS BEFORE A SUBCOMMITTEE OF THE COMMITTEE ON APPROPRIATIONS. KOREA L/A+17C ECO/DEV ECO/UNDEV INT/ORG INSPECT BAL/PWR DIPLOM DEBATE WAR...POLICY STAT ASIA/S 20 CONGRESS NATO COLD/WAR MID/EAST. PAGE 153 A3118
LEGIS FORCES BUDGET FOR/AID

B52
US MUTUAL SECURITY AGENCY,U. S. TECHNICAL AND ECONOMIC ASSISTANCE IN THE FAR EAST (PAMPHLET). ASIA BURMA INDONESIA PHILIPPINE TAIWAN THAILAND USA+45 AGRI INDUS PLAN EDU/PROP ADMIN HEALTH. PAGE 155 A3161
FOR/AID TEC/DEV ECO/UNDEV BUDGET

B53
BRETTON H.L.,STRESEMANN AND THE REVISION OF VERSAILLES: A FIGHT FOR REASON. EUR+WWI GERMANY FORCES BUDGET ARMS/CONT WAR SUPEGO...BIBLIOG 20 TREATY VERSAILLES STRESEMN/G. PAGE 18 A0373
POLICY DIPLOM BIOG

B54
BECKEL G.,WORKSHOPS FOR THE WORLD; THE SPECIALIZED AGENCIES OF THE UN. WOR+45 AGRI DIST/IND CREATE TEC/DEV BUDGET CONTROL TASK WEALTH...CHARTS ORG/CHARTS 20 UN CASEBOOK. PAGE 12 A0246
INT/ORG DIPLOM PEACE CON/ANAL

B55
OECD,MARSHALL PLAN IN TURKEY. TURKEY USA+45 COM/IND CONSTRUC SERV/IND FORCES BUDGET...STAT 20 MARSHL/PLN. PAGE 111 A2277
FOR/AID ECO/UNDEV AGRI INDUS

B56
ESTEP R.,AN AIR POWER BIBLIOGRAPHY. USA+45 TEC/DEV BUDGET DIPLOM EDU/PROP DETER CIVMIL/REL...DECISION INT/LAW 20. PAGE 42 A0862
BIBLIOG/A FORCES WEAPON PLAN

B57
US PRES CITIZEN ADVISERS,REPORT TO THE PRESIDENT ON THE MUTUAL SECURITY PROGRAM. COM USA+45 WOR+45 FINAN INDUS PLAN BUDGET CAP/ISM DIPLOM FOR/AID INT/TRADE REGION 20 SECUR/PROG. PAGE 155 A3163
BAL/PWR FORCES INT/ORG ECO/TAC

B58
ROCKEFELLER BROTH FUND INC,INTERNATIONAL SECURITY - THE MILITARY ASPECT. USA+45 INT/ORG NAT/G BUDGET ARMS/CONT WAR WEAPON PEACE ORD/FREE 20 NATO. PAGE 123 A2511
NUC/PWR DETER FORCES DIPLOM

B58
US OPERATIONS MISSION TO VIET,BUILDING ECONOMIC STRENGTH (PAMPHLET). USA+45 VIETNAM/S INDUS TEC/DEV BUDGET ADMIN EATING HEALTH...STAT 20. PAGE 155 A3162
FOR/AID ECO/UNDEV AGRI EDU/PROP

N58
US HOUSE COMM FOREIGN AFFAIRS,HEARINGS ON DRAFT LEGISLATION TO AMEND FURTHER THE MUTUAL SECURITY ACT OF 1954 (PAMPHLET). USA+45 CONSULT FORCES BUDGET DIPLOM DETER COST ORD/FREE...JURID 20 DEPT/DEFEN UN DEPT/STATE. PAGE 153 A3123
LEGIS DELIB/GP CONFER WEAPON

N58
US HOUSE COMM FOREIGN AFFAIRS,HEARINGS ON REVIEW OF THE MUTUAL SECURITY PROGRAMS; EXAMINATION OF SELECTED PROJECTS IN FORMOSA AND PAKISTAN (PAMPHLET). ASIA PAKISTAN TAIWAN INDUS CONSULT DELIB/GP LEGIS BUDGET CONFER DEBATE 20. PAGE 153 A3125
FOR/AID ECO/UNDEV DIPLOM ECO/TAC

B59
AIR FORCE ACADEMY ASSEMBLY '59,INTERNATIONAL STABILITY AND PROGRESS (PAMPHLET). USA+45 USSR ECO/UNDEV PROB/SOLV BUDGET DIPLOM ADMIN DETER COST ATTIT...TREND 20. PAGE 5 A0103
FOR/AID FORCES WAR PLAN

B59
US PRES COMM STUDY MIL ASSIST,COMPOSITE REPORT. USA+45 ECO/UNDEV PLAN BUDGET DIPLOM EFFICIENCY ...POLICY MGT 20. PAGE 155 A3164
FOR/AID FORCES WEAPON ORD/FREE

B59
WENTHOLT W.,SOME COMMENTS ON THE LIQUIDATION OF THE EUROPEAN PAYMENT UNION AND RELATED PROBLEMS (PAMPHLET). WOR+45 PLAN BUDGET PRICE CONTROL 20 EEC GOLD/STAND. PAGE 163 A3319
FINAN ECO/DEV INT/ORG ECO/TAC

B60
KENEN P.B.,BRITISH MONETARY POLICY AND THE BALANCE OF PAYMENTS 1951-57. UK PLAN BUDGET ECO/TAC INT/TRADE PAY PRICE COST ATTIT 20. PAGE 77 A1585
BAL/PAY PROB/SOLV FINAN NAT/G

B60
STOLPER W.F.,GERMANY BETWEEN EAST AND WEST: THE ECONOMICS OF COMPETITIVE COEXISTENCE. FUT GERMANY/E GERMANY/W WOR+45 FINAN POL/PAR BUDGET ECO/TAC FOR/AID INT/TRADE...STAT CHARTS METH/COMP 20 COLD/WAR. PAGE 138 A2832
ECO/DEV DIPLOM GOV/COMP BAL/PWR

B60
US HOUSE COMM FOREIGN AFFAIRS,HEARINGS ON A BILL TO AMEND FURTHER THE MUTUAL SECURITY ACT OF 1954. USA+45 CONSULT FORCES BUDGET FOR/AID CONFER DETER ...CHARTS 20 DEPT/DEFEN DEPT/STATE UNEF. PAGE 153 A3127
DIPLOM ORD/FREE DELIB/GP LEGIS

B60
US HOUSE COMM GOVT OPERATIONS,OPERATIONS OF THE
FINAN

DEVELOPMENT LOAN FUND: HEARINGS (COMMITTEE ON GOVERNMENT OPERATIONS). USA+45 PLAN BUDGET DIPLOM GOV/REL COST...CHARTS 20 CONGRESS DEPT/STATE AID. PAGE 154 A3137
FOR/AID ECO/TAC EFFICIENCY

B61
DIMOCK M.E.,BUSINESS AND GOVERNMENT (4TH ED.). AGRI FINAN OP/RES PLAN BUDGET DIPLOM LOBBY NUC/PWR NEW/LIB SOCISM...POLICY BIBLIOG 20. PAGE 37 A0765
NAT/G INDUS LABOR ECO/TAC

B61
NATIONAL BANK OF LIBYA,INFLATION IN LIBYA (PAMPHLET). LIBYA SOCIETY NAT/G PLAN INT/TRADE ...STAT CHARTS 20 GOLD/STAND. PAGE 107 A2200
ECO/TAC ECO/UNDEV FINAN BUDGET

B61
OEEC,LIBERALISATION OF CURRENT INVISIBLES AND CAPITAL MOVEMENTS BY THE OEEC (PAMPHLET). WOR+45 ECO/DEV BUDGET ECO/TAC ORD/FREE 20. PAGE 111 A2282
FINAN INT/ORG INT/TRADE BAL/PAY

B61
SINGER J.D.,FINANCING INTERNATIONAL ORGANIZATION: THE UNITED NATIONS BUDGET PROCESS. WOR+45 FINAN ACT/RES CREATE PLAN BUDGET ECO/TAC ADMIN ROUTINE ATTIT KNOWL...DECISION METH/CNCPT TIME/SEQ UN 20. PAGE 133 A2726
INT/ORG MGT

B61
TRIFFIN R.,GOLD AND THE DOLLAR CRISIS: THE FUTURE OF CONVERTIBILITY. USA+45 USA-45 INT/ORG PROB/SOLV BUDGET INT/TRADE PRICE...STAT CHARTS 19/20 GOLD/STAND. PAGE 145 A2963
FINAN ECO/DEV ECO/TAC BAL/PAY

B61
US HOUSE COMM APPROPRIATIONS,INTER-AMERICAN PROGRAMS FOR 1961: DENIAL OF 1962 BUDGET INFORMATION. CHILE L/A+17C USA+45 FINAN CONSULT BUDGET ADJUD COST EFFICIENCY WEALTH...POLICY CHARTS 20 CONGRESS. PAGE 153 A3119
LEGIS FOR/AID DELIB/GP ECO/UNDEV

B61
US SENATE COMM GOVT OPERATIONS,ORGANIZING FOR NATIONAL SECURITY. COM USA+45 BUDGET DIPLOM DETER NUC/PWR WAR WEAPON ORD/FREE...BIBLIOG 20 COLD/WAR. PAGE 156 A3172
POLICY PLAN FORCES COERCE

B62
FORD A.G.,THE GOLD STANDARD 1880-1914: BRITAIN AND ARGENTINA. UK ECO/UNDEV INT/TRADE ADMIN GOV/REL DEMAND EFFICIENCY...STAT CHARTS 19/20 ARGEN GOLD/STAND. PAGE 47 A0960
FINAN ECO/TAC BUDGET BAL/PAY

B62
JORDAN A.A. JR.,FOREIGN AID AND THE DEFENSE OF SOUTHEAST ASIA. PAKISTAN VIETNAM/S FINAN PLAN BUDGET ECO/TAC DETER WAR ORD/FREE...POLICY DECISION CENSUS CHARTS BIBLIOG 20. PAGE 75 A1535
FOR/AID S/ASIA FORCES ECO/UNDEV

B62
LUTZ F.A.,GELD UND WAHRUNG. MARKET LABOR BUDGET 20 GOLD/STAND EUROPE. PAGE 92 A1875
ECO/TAC FINAN DIPLOM POLICY

B62
THEOBALD R.,NATIONAL DEVELOPMENT EFFORTS (PAMPHLET). WOR+45 AGRI BUDGET FOR/AID INT/TRADE TAX 20. PAGE 142 A2914
ECO/UNDEV PLAN BAL/PAY WEALTH

B63
FATEMI N.S.,THE DOLLAR CRISIS. USA+45 INDUS NAT/G LEGIS BUDGET TAX COST...CHARTS METH/COMP 20 EEC. PAGE 44 A0902
PROB/SOLV BAL/PAY FOR/AID PLAN

B63
INTERNATIONAL MONETARY FUND,COMPENSATORY FINANCING OF EXPORT FLUCTUATIONS (PAMPHLET). WOR+45 ECO/DEV ECO/UNDEV INT/ORG WEALTH...TREND 20 IMF MONEY. PAGE 71 A1459
BAL/PAY FINAN BUDGET INT/TRADE

B63
UN SECRETARY GENERAL,PLANNING FOR ECONOMIC DEVELOPMENT. ECO/UNDEV FINAN BUDGET INT/TRADE TARIFFS TAX ADMIN 20 UN. PAGE 147 A3005
PLAN ECO/TAC MGT NAT/COMP

B63
US AGENCY INTERNATIONAL DEV,US FOREIGN ASSISTANCE AND ASSISTANCE FROM INTERNATIONAL ORGANIZATIONS. USA+45 WOR+45 ECO/UNDEV AGRI NAT/G TEC/DEV BUDGET. PAGE 149 A3050
FOR/AID INT/ORG CHARTS STAT

B63
US CONGRESS JOINT ECO COMM,THE UNITED STATES BALANCE OF PAYMENTS. USA+45 DELIB/GP BUDGET PRICE PRODUC 20 CONGRESS GOLD/STAND MONEY. PAGE 150 A3067
BAL/PAY INT/TRADE FINAN ECO/TAC

B63
US SENATE COMM GOVT OPERATIONS,REPORT OF A STUDY OF US FOREIGN AID IN TEN MIDDLE EASTERN AND AFRICAN COUNTRIES. AFR ISLAM USA+45 FORCES PLAN BUDGET DIPLOM TAX DETER WEALTH...STAT CHARTS 20 CONGRESS AID MID/EAST. PAGE 156 A3174
FOR/AID EFFICIENCY ECO/TAC FINAN

B63
WALKER A.A.,OFFICIAL PUBLICATIONS OF SIERRA LEONE AND GAMBIA. GAMBIA SIER/LEONE UK LAW CONSTN LEGIS PLAN BUDGET DIPLOM...SOC SAMP CON/ANAL 20. PAGE 160 A3262
BIBLIOG NAT/G COLONIAL ADMIN

L63
PADELFORD N.J.,"FINANCIAL CRISIS AND THE UNITED NATIONS." FUT USSR WOR+45 LAW CONSTN FINAN INT/ORG DELIB/GP FORCES PLAN BUDGET DIPLOM COST WEALTH ...STAT CHARTS UN CONGO 20. PAGE 113 A2311
CREATE ECO/TAC

N63
US COMM STRENG SEC FREE WORLD,THE SCOPE AND DISTRIBUTION OF UNITED STATES MILITARY AND ECONOMIC ASSISTANCE PROGRAMS (PAMPHLET). USA+45 PLAN BAL/PWR BUDGET DIPLOM CONTROL CIVMIL/REL ATTIT. PAGE 150 A3059
DELIB/GP POLICY FOR/AID ORD/FREE

B64
FATOUROS A.A.,CANADA'S OVERSEAS AID. CANADA WOR+45 ECO/DEV FINAN NAT/G BUDGET ECO/TAC CONFER ADMIN 20. PAGE 44 A0904
FOR/AID DIPLOM ECO/UNDEV POLICY

B64
KNOX V.H.,PUBLIC FINANCE: INFORMATION SOURCES. USA+45 DIPLOM ADMIN GOV/REL COST...POLICY 20. PAGE 81 A1657
BIBLIOG/A FINAN TAX BUDGET

B64
OECD,DEVELOPMENT ASSISTANCE EFFORTS - POLICIES OF THE MEMBERS. AGRI INDUS BUDGET...GEOG NAT/COMP 20 OECD. PAGE 111 A2280
INT/ORG FOR/AID ECO/UNDEV TEC/DEV

B64
OECD,THE FLOW OF FINANCIAL RESOURCES TO LESS DEVELOPED COUNTRIES 1956-1963. WOR+45 FINAN CAP/ISM ...POLICY STAT 20. PAGE 111 A2281
FOR/AID BUDGET INT/ORG ECO/UNDEV

B64
SCHWARTZ M.D.,CONFERENCE ON SPACE SCIENCE AND SPACE LAW. FUT COM/IND NAT/G FORCES ACT/RES PLAN BUDGET DIPLOM NUC/PWR WEAPON...POLICY ANTHOL 20. PAGE 130 A2658
SPACE LAW PEACE TEC/DEV

B64
US AGENCY INTERNATIONAL DEV,REPORT TO CONGRESS ON THE FOREIGN ASSISTANCE PROGRAM. AFR ASIA L/A+17C USA+45 INT/ORG VOL/ASSN FORCES CAP/ISM ADMIN WEAPON. PAGE 149 A3052
FOR/AID ECO/UNDEV TEC/DEV BUDGET

B64
US HOUSE COMM GOVT OPERATIONS,US OWNED FOREIGN CURRENCIES: HEARINGS (COMMITTEE ON GOVERNMENT OPERATIONS). INDIA ECO/DEV PLAN BUDGET TAX DEMAND EFFICIENCY 20 AID CONGRESS. PAGE 154 A3138
FINAN ECO/TAC FOR/AID OWN

S64
CARNEGIE ENDOWMENT INT. PEACE,"ADMINISTRATION AND BUDGET (ISSUES BEFORE THE NINETEENTH GENERAL ASSEMBLY)." WOR+45 FINAN BUDGET ECO/TAC ROUTINE COST...STAT RECORD UN. PAGE 24 A0495
INT/ORG ADMIN

B65
ANALYSIS AND ASSESSMENT OF THE ECONOMIC EFFECTS: PUBLIC LAW 480 TITLE I PROGRAM TURKEY. INDIA TURKEY USA+45 AGRI NAT/G PLAN BUDGET DIPLOM COST EFFICIENCY...CHARTS 20. PAGE 3 A0070
ECO/TAC FOR/AID FINAN ECO/UNDEV

B65
FRUTKIN A.W.,SPACE AND THE INTERNATIONAL COOPERATION YEAR: A NATIONAL CHALLENGE (PAMPHLET). EUR+WWI USA+45 FINAN TEC/DEV BUDGET...MGT 20 NASA. PAGE 49 A1011
SPACE INDUS NAT/G DIPLOM

B65
OGILVY-WEBB M.,THE GOVERNMENT EXPLAINS: A STUDY OF THE INFORMATION SERVICES. UK DELIB/GP LEGIS WORKER BUDGET DIPLOM 20. PAGE 111 A2284
EDU/PROP ATTIT NAT/G ADMIN

B65
US BUREAU OF THE BUDGET,THE BALANCE OF PAYMENTS STATISTICS OF THE UNITED STATES: A REVIEW AND APPRAISAL. USA+45 FINAN NAT/G PROB/SOLV DIPLOM. PAGE 150 A3057
BAL/PAY STAT METH/COMP BUDGET

B65
US CONGRESS JT ATOM ENRGY COMM,ATOMIC ENERGY LEGISLATION THROUGH 89TH CONGRESS, 1ST SESSION. USA+45 LAW INT/ORG DELIB/GP BUDGET DIPLOM 20 AEC CONGRESS CASEBOOK EURATOM IAEA. PAGE 150 A3071
NUC/PWR FORCES PEACE LEGIS

B65
US SENATE COMM ON FOREIGN REL,HEARINGS ON THE FOREIGN ASSISTANCE PROGRAM. AFR ASIA L/A+17C USA+45 WOR+45 FORCES TEC/DEV BUDGET CONTROL WEAPON ORD/FREE 20 UN CONGRESS SEC/STATE. PAGE 156 A3183
FOR/AID DIPLOM INT/ORG ECO/UNDEV

L65
LOFTUS M.L.,"INTERNATIONAL MONETARY FUND, 1962-1965: A SELECTED BIBLIOGRAPHY." WOR+45 PLAN BUDGET INCOME PROFIT WEALTH. PAGE 90 A1852
BIBLIOG FINAN INT/TRADE INT/ORG

B66
HAYER T.,FRENCH AID. AFR FRANCE AGRI FINAN BUDGET ADMIN WAR PRODUC...CHARTS 18/20 THIRD/WRLD OVRSEA/DEV. PAGE 63 A1295
TEC/DEV COLONIAL FOR/AID ECO/UNDEV

B66
INTERNATIONAL ECO POLICY ASSN,THE UNITED STATES BALANCE OF PAYMENTS. INT/ORG NAT/G PROB/SOLV BUDGET DIPLOM INT/TRADE WEALTH 20. PAGE 71 A1454
BAL/PAY ECO/TAC POLICY

FINAN

B66
KINDLEBERGER C.P.,EUROPE AND THE DOLLAR. EUR+WWI FRANCE GERMANY/W USA+45 CONSTN INT/ORG DIPLOM INT/TRADE...ANTHOL 20 GOLD/STAND. PAGE 79 A1623 BAL/PAY BUDGET FINAN ECO/DEV

B66
LUARD E.,THE EVOLUTION OF INTERNATIONAL ORGANIZATIONS. UK WOR+45 BUDGET INT/TRADE WAR BAL/PAY PEACE ORD/FREE...POLICY 19/20 EEC ILO LEAGUE/NAT UN. PAGE 91 A1871 INT/ORG EFFICIENCY CREATE TREND

B66
ROBERTSON D.J.,THE BRITISH BALANCE OF PAYMENTS. UK WOR+45 INDUS BUDGET TAX ADJUST...CHARTS ANTHOL 20. PAGE 122 A2500 FINAN BAL/PAY ECO/DEV INT/TRADE

B66
UN ECAFE,ADMINISTRATIVE ASPECTS OF FAMILY PLANNING PROGRAMMES (PAMPHLET). ASIA THAILAND WOR+45 VOL/ASSN PROB/SOLV BUDGET FOR/AID EDU/PROP CONFER CONTROL GOV/REL TIME 20 UN BIRTH/CON. PAGE 147 A2999 PLAN CENSUS FAM ADMIN

B66
US HOUSE COMM APPROPRIATIONS,HEARINGS ON FOREIGN OPERATIONS AND RELATED AGENCIES APPROPRIATIONS. CUBA USA+45 VOL/ASSN DELIB/GP DIPLOM CONFER ORD/FREE 20 CONGRESS MIGRATION INT/AM/DEV PEACE/CORP. PAGE 153 A3120 FOR/AID BUDGET ECO/UNDEV FORCES

B66
US HOUSE COMM GOVT OPERATIONS,AN INVESTIGATION OF THE US ECONOMIC AND MILITARY ASSISTANCE PROGRAMS IN VIETNAM. USA+45 VIETNAM/S SOCIETY CONSTRUC FINAN FORCES BUDGET INT/TRADE PEACE HEALTH...MGT HOUSE/REP AID. PAGE 154 A3139 FOR/AID ECO/UNDEV WAR INSPECT

B66
US SENATE COMM ON FOREIGN REL,HEARINGS ON S 2859 AND S 2861. USA+45 WOR+45 FORCES BUDGET CAP/ISM ADMIN DETER WEAPON TOTALISM...NAT/COMP 20 UN CONGRESS. PAGE 156 A3185 FOR/AID DIPLOM ORD/FREE ECO/UNDEV

L66
AMERICAN ECONOMIC REVIEW,"SIXTY-THIRD LIST OF DOCTORAL DISSERTATIONS IN POLITICAL ECONOMY IN AMERICAN UNIVERSITIES AND COLLEGES." ECO/DEV AGRI FINAN LABOR WORKER PLAN BUDGET INT/TRADE ADMIN DEMAND...MGT STAT 20. PAGE 7 A0146 BIBLIOG/A CONCPT ACADEM

N66
EOMMITTEE ECONOMIC DEVELOPMENT,THE DOLLAR AND THE WORLD MONETARY SYSTEM: A STATEMENT ON NATIONAL POLICY (PAMPHLET). USA+45 NAT/G PLAN PROB/SOLV BUDGET ECO/TAC FOR/AID INCOME...POLICY 20 GOLD/STAND EUROPE. PAGE 42 A0854 FINAN BAL/PAY DIPLOM ECO/DEV

B67
O'LEARY M.K.,THE POLITICS OF AMERICAN FOREIGN AID. USA+45 POL/PAR CHIEF BUDGET EDU/PROP LOBBY CONGRESS. PAGE 111 A2270 FOR/AID DIPLOM PARL/PROC ATTIT

B67
US AGENCY INTERNATIONAL DEV,PROPOSED FOREIGN AID PROGRAM FOR 1968: SUMMARY PRESENTATION TO THE CONGRESS. AFR S/ASIA USA+45 AGRI TEC/DEV DIPLOM ECO/TAC BAL/PAY COST HEALTH KNOWL SKILL 20 AID CONGRESS. PAGE 149 A3053 ECO/UNDEV BUDGET FOR/AID STAT

L67
DEVADHAR Y.C.,"THE ROLE OF FOREIGN PRIVATE CAPITAL IN INDIA'S ECONOMIC DEVELOPMENT* ASSESSMENT OF POLICY AND PERFORMANCE." INDIA INDUS PLAN TEC/DEV BUDGET DIPLOM ECO/TAC BAL/PAY PRODUC WEALTH ...CHARTS 20. PAGE 37 A0750 CAP/ISM FOR/AID POLICY ACT/RES

S67
ANTHEM T.,"CYPRUS* WHAT NOW?" CYPRUS GREECE TURKEY NAT/G BUDGET MAJORITY 20 NATO. PAGE 8 A0165 DIPLOM COERCE INT/TRADE ADJUD

S67
MOBERG E.,"THE EFFECT OF SECURITY POLICY MEASURES: DISCUSSION RELATED TO SWEDEN'S SECURITY POLICY." SWEDEN PLAN PROB/SOLV DIPLOM GOV/REL MORAL...CHARTS 20. PAGE 102 A2092 POLICY ORD/FREE BUDGET FINAN

BUELL R. A0428

BUENOS/AIR....BUENOS AIRES, ARGENTINA

BUGANDA....BUGANDA, UGANDA

BUKHARIN/N....NIKOLAI BUKHARIN

BULGARIA....BULGARIA; SEE ALSO COM

N
KYRIAK T.E.,EAST EUROPE: BIBLIOGRAPHY--INDEX TO US JPRS RESEARCH TRANSLATIONS. ALBANIA BULGARIA COM CZECHOSLVK HUNGARY POLAND ROMANIA AGRI EXTR/IND FINAN SERV/IND INT/TRADE WEAPON...GEOG MGT SOC 20. PAGE 83 A1701 BIBLIOG/A PRESS MARXISM INDUS

B18
KERNER R.J.,SLAVIC EUROPE: A SELECTED BIBLIOGRAPHY IN THE WESTERN EUROPEAN LANGUAGES. BULGARIA CZECHOSLVK GERMANY/E POLAND RUSSIA YUGOSLAVIA NAT/G DIPLOM MARXISM...LING 19/20. PAGE 78 A1598 BIBLIOG SOCIETY CULTURE COM

B43
CONOVER H.F.,THE BALKANS: A SELECTED LIST OF REFERENCES. ALBANIA BULGARIA ROMANIA YUGOSLAVIA INT/ORG PROB/SOLV DIPLOM LEGIT CONFER ADJUD WAR NAT/LISM PEACE PWR 20 LEAGUE/NAT. PAGE 29 A0596 BIBLIOG EUR+WWI

B56
SIPKOV I.,LEGAL SOURCES AND BIBLIOGRAPHY OF BULGARIA. BULGARIA COM LEGIS WRITING ADJUD CT/SYS ...INT/LAW TREATY 20. PAGE 134 A2736 BIBLIOG LAW TOTALISM MARXISM

B59
ETSCHMANN R.,DIE WAHRUNGS- UND DEVISENPOLITIK DES OSTBLOCKS UND IHRE AUSWIRKUNGEN AUF DIE WIRTSCHAFTSBEZIEHUNGEN ZWISCHEN OST U WEST. BULGARIA CZECHOSLVK HUNGARY POLAND USSR MARKET NAT/G PLAN DIPLOM...NAT/COMP 20. PAGE 42 A0867 ECO/TAC FINAN POLICY INT/TRADE

B62
JELAVICH C.,TSARIST RUSSIA AND BALKAN NATIONALISM. BULGARIA MOD/EUR RUSSIA DOMIN GOV/REL...GEOG 19 SERBIA. PAGE 73 A1503 NAT/LISM DIPLOM WAR

L64
BARROS J.,"THE GREEK-BULGARIAN INCIDENT OF 1925: THE LEAGUE OF NATIONS AND THE GREAT POWERS." BULGARIA EUR+WWI NAT/G FORCES ECO/TAC EDU/PROP LEGIT ROUTINE COERCE WAR PEACE DRIVE PWR...JURID CONCPT METH/CNCPT GEN/LAWS GEN/METH LEAGUE/NAT TOT/POP 20. PAGE 11 A0228 INT/ORG ORD/FREE DIPLOM

S64
HORECKY P.L.,"LIBRARY OF CONGRESS PUBLICATIONS IN AID OF USSR AND EAST EUROPEAN RESEARCH." BULGARIA CZECHOSLVK POLAND USSR YUGOSLAVIA NAT/G POL/PAR DIPLOM ADMIN GOV/REL...CLASSIF 20. PAGE 67 A1382 BIBLIOG/A COM MARXISM

B66
BROWN J.F.,THE NEW EASTERN EUROPE. ALBANIA BULGARIA HUNGARY POLAND ROMANIA CULTURE AGRI POL/PAR WAR NAT/LISM MARXISM...CHARTS BIBLIOG 20. PAGE 20 A0404 DIPLOM COM NAT/G ECO/UNDEV

B66
SPULBER N.,THE STATE AND ECONOMIC DEVELOPMENT IN EASTERN EUROPE. BULGARIA COM CZECHOSLVK HUNGARY POLAND YUGOSLAVIA CULTURE PLAN CAP/ISM INT/TRADE CONTROL...POLICY CHARTS METH/COMP BIBLIOG/A 19/20. PAGE 136 A2793 ECO/DEV ECO/UNDEV NAT/G TOTALISM

S67
EGBERT D.D.,"POLITICS AND ART IN COMMUNIST BULGARIA" BULGARIA COM USSR CULTURE DIPLOM INGP/REL TOTALISM...TREND 20. PAGE 40 A0825 CREATE ART/METH CONTROL MARXISM

BULL H. A0429

BULLITT/WC....WILLIAM C. BULLITT

BULLOUGH V.L. A0430

BUNCHE/R....RALPH BUNCHE

BUNDESMIN FUR VERTRIEBENE A0431

BUNDY/M....MCGEORGE BUNDY

B62
US SENATE COMM GOVT OPERATIONS,ADMINISTRATION OF NATIONAL SECURITY. USA+45 CHIEF PLAN PROB/SOLV TEC/DEV DIPLOM ATTIT...POLICY DECISION 20 KENNEDY/JF RUSK/D MCNAMARA/R BUNDY/M HERTER/C. PAGE 156 A3173 ORD/FREE ADMIN NAT/G CONTROL

BUR/BUDGET....BUREAU OF THE BUDGET

BUR/STNDRD....BUREAU OF STANDARDS

BURAGR/ECO....BUREAU OF AGRICULTURAL ECONOMICS

BURDETTE F.L. A0432

BUREAU OF AGRICULTURAL ECONOMICS....SEE BURAGR/ECO

BUREAU ECONOMIC RES LAT AM A0433

BUREAU OF PUBLIC AFFAIRS A0434

BUREAUCRCY....BUREAUCRACY; SEE ALSO ADMIN

S26
COHEN P.A.,"WANG T'AO AND INCIPIENT CHINESE NAT/LISM

NATIONALISM." ASIA ADMIN ATTIT 19/20 BUREAUCRCY. PAGE 28 A0563 — ISOLAT CONSERVE DIPLOM

BURGANDA....SEE ALSO AFR

S55

DE SMITH S.A.,"CONSTITUTIONAL MONARCHY IN BURGANDA." AFR UGANDA UK STRUCT CHIEF REGION INGP/REL ADJUST NAT/LISM SOVEREIGN CONSERVE ...POLICY 19/20 BURGANDA. PAGE 35 A0712 — NAT/G DIPLOM CONSTN COLONIAL

BURKE E. A0435,A0436

BURKE F.G. A0437

BURKE W.T. A2007

BURKE/EDM....EDMUND BURKE

BURKS D.D. A2635

BURMA....BURMA

B48

PELCOVITS N.A.,OLD CHINA HANDS AND THE FOREIGN OFFICE. ASIA BURMA UK ECO/UNDEV NAT/G ECO/TAC FOR/AID TARIFFS DOMIN COLONIAL GOV/REL SOVEREIGN 19 HONG/KONG TREATY. PAGE 114 A2348 — INT/TRADE ATTIT DIPLOM

B50

CORNELL U DEPT ASIAN STUDIES,SOUTHEAST ASIA PROGRAM DATA PAPER. BURMA CAMBODIA INDONESIA MALAYSIA VIETNAM SOCIETY STRUCT NAT/G SECT DIPLOM FOR/AID PWR WEALTH...SOC 20. PAGE 31 A0625 — BIBLIOG/A CULTURE S/ASIA ECO/UNDEV

B52

US MUTUAL SECURITY AGENCY,U. S. TECHNICAL AND ECONOMIC ASSISTANCE IN THE FAR EAST (PAMPHLET). ASIA BURMA INDONESIA PHILIPPINE TAIWAN THAILAND USA+45 AGRI INDUS PLAN EDU/PROP ADMIN HEALTH. PAGE 155 A3161 — FOR/AID TEC/DEV ECO/UNDEV BUDGET

B56

BALL W.M.,NATIONALISM AND COMMUNISM IN EAST ASIA. ASIA BURMA EUR+WWI KOREA USA+45 ECO/UNDEV NAT/G POL/PAR DIPLOM ECO/TAC FOR/AID EDU/PROP COERCE RACE/REL NAT/LISM DRIVE SOVEREIGN...TREND 20 CHINJAP. PAGE 11 A0214 — S/ASIA ATTIT

B60

LEVIN J.V.,THE EXPORT ECONOMIES: THEIR PATTERN OF DEVELOPMENT IN HISTORICAL PERSPECTIVE. BURMA PERU AGRI WORKER COLONIAL COST DEMAND INCOME 20. PAGE 88 A1795 — INT/TRADE ECO/UNDEV BAL/PAY EXTR/IND

B61

SYATAUW J.J.G.,SOME NEWLY ESTABLISHED ASIAN STATES AND THE DEVELOPMENT OF INTERNATIONAL LAW. BURMA CEYLON INDIA INDONESIA ECO/UNDEV COLONIAL NEUTRAL WAR PEACE SOVEREIGN...CHARTS 19/20. PAGE 140 A2873 — INT/LAW ADJUST SOCIETY S/ASIA

S63

GORDON B.,"ECONOMIC IMPEDIMENTS TO REGIONALISM IN SOUTH EAST ASIA." BURMA FUT S/ASIA THAILAND USA+45 AGRI INDUS R+D NAT/G PLAN ECO/TAC WEALTH...STAT CONT/OBS 20. PAGE 54 A1110 — VOL/ASSN ECO/UNDEV INT/TRADE REGION

C66

TARLING N.,"A CONCISE HISTORY OF SOUTHEAST ASIA." BURMA CAMBODIA LAOS S/ASIA THAILAND VIETNAM ECO/UNDEV POL/PAR FORCES ADMIN REV WAR CIVMIL/REL ORD/FREE MARXISM SOCISM 13/20. PAGE 141 A2890 — COLONIAL DOMIN INT/TRADE NAT/LISM

B67

MAW B.,BREAKTHROUGH IN BURMA: MEMOIRS OF A REVOLUTION, 1939-1946. BURMA UK FORCES PROB/SOLV DIPLOM FOR/AID DOMIN LEAD...BIOG 20. PAGE 97 A1980 — REV ORD/FREE NAT/LISM COLONIAL

BURNET A. A0438

BURNS A. A0439

BURNS A.L. A0440,A0441,A1310,A1562

BURNS C.D. A0442

BURNS E.B. A0443

BURNS E.L.M. A0444

BURR R.N. A0445

BURR/AARON....AARON BURR

BURTON J.W. A0446,A0447

BURTON M.E. A0448

BURUNDI....SEE ALSO AFR

BUSHONG A.D. A1615

BUSINESS CYCLE....SEE ECO, FINAN

BUSINESS MANAGEMENT....SEE MGT

BUSS C. A0449

BUSSCHAU W.J. A0450

BUTLER G. A0451

BUTLER N.M. A0452

BUTLER R. A3392

BUTLER W.E. A2155

BUTOW R.J.C. A0453

BUTT R. A0454

BUTTINGER J. A0455,A0456

BUTTS R.F. A0457

BUTWELL R. A0458

BUTZ O. A0459

BYNKERSHOEK C. A0460

BYRD E.M. A0461

BYRNES R.F. A0462

BYZANTINE....BYZANTINE EMPIRE

CAB....CIVIL AERONAUTICS BOARD

C

B65

THAYER F.C. JR.,AIR TRANSPORT POLICY AND NATIONAL SECURITY: A POLITICAL, ECONOMIC, AND MILITARY ANALYSIS. DIST/IND OP/RES PLAN TEC/DEV DIPLOM DETER WAR COST EFFICIENCY...POLICY BIBLIOG 20 DEPT/DEFEN FAA CAB. PAGE 142 A2908 — AIR FORCES CIVMIL/REL ORD/FREE

CABINET....SEE ALSO EX/STRUC, DELIB/GP, CONSULT

CADWELL R. A0463

CAESAR/JUL....JULIUS CAESAR

CAHIER P. A0464,A0465

CAIRO....CAIRO, EGYPT

CALCUTTA....CALCUTTA, INDIA

CALDER R. A0466,A0467

CALHOUN/JC....JOHN C. CALHOUN

CALIFORNIA....CALIFORNIA

CALLEO D.P. A0468

CALVIN/J....JOHN CALVIN

B63

MONTER W.,THE GOVERNMENT OF GENEVA, 1536-1605 (DOCTORAL THESIS). SWITZERLND DIPLOM LEAD ORD/FREE SOVEREIGN 16/17 CALVIN/J ROME. PAGE 103 A2112 — SECT FINAN LOC/G ADMIN

CALVO SERER R. A0469

CALVOCORESSI P. A0470,A0471

CAMB/SOMER....CAMBRIDGE-SOMERVILLE YOUTH STUDY

CAMBODIA....SEE ALSO S/ASIA

B45

HARVARD WIDENER LIBRARY,INDOCHINA: A SELECTED LIST OF REFERENCES. CAMBODIA FRANCE S/ASIA VIETNAM COLONIAL...POLICY 19/20. PAGE 62 A1282 — BIBLIOG/A ACADEM DIPLOM NAT/G

B50

CORNELL U DEPT ASIAN STUDIES,SOUTHEAST ASIA PROGRAM DATA PAPER. BURMA CAMBODIA INDONESIA MALAYSIA VIETNAM SOCIETY STRUCT NAT/G SECT DIPLOM FOR/AID PWR WEALTH...SOC 20. PAGE 31 A0625 — BIBLIOG/A CULTURE S/ASIA ECO/UNDEV

B55

THOMPSON V.,MINORITY PROBLEMS IN SOUTHEAST ASIA. CAMBODIA CHINA/COM LAOS S/ASIA KIN NAT/G SECT — INGP/REL GEOG

PROB/SOLV EDU/PROP REGION GP/REL RACE/REL MARXISM ...SOC 20 BUDDHISM UN. PAGE 143 A2933 — DIPLOM STRUCT

B58
US HOUSE COMM GOVT OPERATIONS,HEARINGS BEFORE A SUBCOMMITTEE OF THE COMMITTEE ON GOVERNMENT OPERATIONS. CAMBODIA PHILIPPINE USA+45 CONSTRUC TEC/DEV ADMIN CONTROL WEAPON EFFICIENCY HOUSE/REP. PAGE 154 A3135 — FOR/AID DIPLOM ORD/FREE ECO/UNDEV

S62
DIHN N.Q.,"L'INTERNATIONALISATION DU MEKONG." CAMBODIA LAOS VIETNAM WOR+45 INT/ORG NAT/G VOL/ASSN PEACE HEALTH...CONCPT TIME/SEQ CHARTS METH VAL/FREE 20. PAGE 37 A0761 — S/ASIA DELIB/GP

C66
TARLING N.,"A CONCISE HISTORY OF SOUTHEAST ASIA." BURMA CAMBODIA LAOS S/ASIA THAILAND VIETNAM ECO/UNDEV POL/PAR FORCES ADMIN REV WAR CIVMIL/REL ORD/FREE MARXISM SOCISM 13/20. PAGE 141 A2890 — COLONIAL DOMIN INT/TRADE NAT/LISM

CAMBRAY P.G. A2114

CAMELOT....PROJECT CAMELOT (CHILE)

CAMERON J. A0472

CAMEROON....SEE ALSO AFR

B63
GARDINIER D.E.,CAMEROON: UNITED NATIONS CHALLENGE TO FRENCH POLICY. AFR CAMEROON FRANCE NAT/G LEGIS CONTROL SOVEREIGN 20 UN. PAGE 51 A1042 — DIPLOM POLICY INT/ORG COLONIAL

B64
WITHERELL J.W.,OFFICIAL PUBLICATIONS OF FRENCH EQUATORIAL AFRICA, FRENCH CAMEROONS, AND TOGO, 1946-1958 (PAMPHLET). CAMEROON CHAD FRANCE GABON TOGO LAW ECO/UNDEV EXTR/IND INT/TRADE...GEOG HEAL 20. PAGE 165 A3370 — BIBLIOG/A AFR NAT/G ADMIN

B66
US LIBRARY OF CONGRESS,NIGERIA: A GUIDE TO OFFICIAL PUBLICATIONS. CAMEROON NIGERIA UK DIPLOM...POLICY 19/20 UN LEAGUE/NAT. PAGE 155 A3160 — BIBLIOG ADMIN NAT/G COLONIAL

CAMPAIGNE J.G. A0473

CAMPBELL A. A0254

CAMPBELL J.C. A0474,A0475

CANAD/CRWN....CANADIAN CROWN CORPORATIONS

CANADA....SEE ALSO COMMONWLTH

N
CANADIAN GOVERNMENT PUBLICATIONS (1955-). CANADA AGRI FINAN LABOR FORCES INT/TRADE HEALTH...JURID 20 PARLIAMENT. PAGE 1 A0007 — BIBLIOG/A NAT/G DIPLOM INT/ORG

N
UNIVERSITY MICROFILMS INC,DISSERTATION ABSTRACTS: ABSTRACTS OF DISSERTATIONS AND MONOGRAPHS IN MICROFILM. CANADA DIPLOM ADMIN...INDEX 20. PAGE 149 A3045 — BIBLIOG/A ACADEM PRESS WRITING

B10
GRIFFIN A.P.C.,LIST OF REFERENCES ON RECIPROCITY (2ND REV. ED.). CANADA CUBA UK USA-45 WOR-45 NAT/G TARIFFS CONFER COLONIAL CONTROL SANCTION CONSEN ALL/VALS...DECISION 19/20. PAGE 56 A1157 — BIBLIOG/A VOL/ASSN DIPLOM REPAR

N19
MASSEY V.,CANADIANS AND THEIR COMMONWEALTH: THE ROMANES LECTURE DELIVERED IN THE SHELDONIAN THEATRE JUNE 1, 1961 (PAMPHLET). CANADA UK CULTURE ECO/DEV REPRESENT NAT/LISM PEACE PWR CONSERVE 20 CMN/WLTH. PAGE 96 A1959 — ATTIT DIPLOM NAT/G SOVEREIGN

N19
TAYLOR T.G.,CANADA'S ROLE IN GEOPOLITICS (PAMPHLET). CANADA FUT USSR COLONIAL REGION WEALTH ...CHARTS 20. PAGE 142 A2901 — GEOG DIPLOM SOCIETY ECO/DEV

B26
LEWIN E.,RECENT PUBLICATIONS IN THE LIBRARY OF THE ROYAL COLONIAL INSTITUTE (PAMPHLET). CANADA UK EX/STRUC PARL/PROC NAT/LISM SOVEREIGN 20 CMN/WLTH PARLIAMENT. PAGE 88 A1799 — BIBLIOG COLONIAL CONSTN DIPLOM

B28
CORBETT P.E.,CANADA AND WORLD POLITICS. LAW CULTURE SOCIETY STRUCT MARKET INT/ORG FORCES ACT/RES PLAN ECO/TAC LEGIT ORD/FREE PWR RESPECT...SOC CONCPT TIME/SEQ TREND CMN/WLTH 20 LEAGUE/NAT. PAGE 30 A0612 — NAT/G CANADA

B40
CONOVER H.F.,FOREIGN RELATIONS OF THE UNITED STATES: A LIST OF RECENT BOOKS (PAMPHLET). ASIA CANADA L/A+17C UK INT/ORG INT/TRADE TARIFFS NEUTRAL WAR PEACE...INT/LAW CON/ANAL 20 CHINJAP. PAGE 29 A0592 — BIBLIOG/A USA-45 DIPLOM

B42
FULLER G.H.,DEFENSE FINANCING: A SUPPLEMENTARY LIST OF REFERENCES (PAMPHLET). CANADA UK USA-45 ECO/DEV NAT/G DELIB/GP BUDGET ADJUD ARMS/CONT WEAPON COST PEACE PWR 20 AUSTRAL CHINJAP CONGRESS. PAGE 50 A1021 — BIBLIOG/A FINAN FORCES DIPLOM

B46
GRIFFIN G.G.,A GUIDE TO MANUSCRIPTS RELATING TO AMERICAN HISTORY IN BRITISH DEPOSITORIES. CANADA IRELAND MOD/EUR UK USA-45 LAW DIPLOM ADMIN COLONIAL WAR NAT/LISM SOVEREIGN...GEOG INT/LAW 15/19 CMN/WLTH. PAGE 56 A1159 — BIBLIOG/A ALL/VALS NAT/G

B47
HILL M.,IMMUNITIES AND PRIVILEGES OF INTERNATIONAL OFFICIALS. CANADA EUR+WWI NETHERLAND SWITZERLND LAW LEGIS DIPLOM LEGIT RESPECT...TIME/SEQ LEAGUE/NAT UN VAL/FREE 20. PAGE 65 A1330 — INT/ORG ADMIN

B56
UNDERHILL F.H.,THE BRITISH COMMONWEALTH: AN EXPERIMENT IN CO-OPERATION AMONG NATIONS. CANADA UK WOR+45 WOR-45 INT/ORG COLONIAL UTIL SOVEREIGN CONSERVE...OLD/LIB SOC/EXP BIBLIOG/A 19/20 CMN/WLTH. PAGE 147 A3007 — VOL/ASSN NAT/LISM DIPLOM

B57
BISHOP O.B.,PUBLICATIONS OF THE GOVERNMENTS OF NOVA SCOTIA, PRINCE EDWARD ISLAND, NEW BRUNSWICK 1758-1952. CANADA UK ADMIN COLONIAL LEAD...POLICY 18/20. PAGE 14 A0293 — BIBLIOG NAT/G DIPLOM

C57
BEERS H.P.,"THE FRENCH IN NORTH AFRICA: A BIBLIOGRAPHICAL GUIDE TO FRENCH ARCHIVES, REPRODUCTIONS, AND RESEARCH MISSIONS." AFR CANADA FRANCE USA-45 NAT/LISM ATTIT 20. PAGE 12 A0248 — BIBLIOG DIPLOM COLONIAL

B59
STOVEL J.A.,CANADA IN THE WORLD ECONOMY. CANADA PRICE DEMAND...STAT CHARTS BIBLIOG 20 VINER/J. PAGE 139 A2838 — INT/TRADE BAL/PAY FINAN ECO/TAC

B60
CONN S.,THE FRAMEWORK OF HEMISPHERE DEFENSE. CANADA L/A+17C USA-45 NAT/G FORCES BAL/PWR DOMIN WAR PEACE DISPL PWR RESPECT...PLURIST CONCPT HIST/WRIT HYPO/EXP MEXIC/AMER 20 ROOSEVLT/F. PAGE 29 A0585 — USA+45 INT/ORG DIPLOM

B60
MINIFIE J.M.,PEACEMAKER OR POWDER-MONKEY. CANADA INT/ORG NAT/G FORCES LEAD WAR...PREDICT 20. PAGE 102 A2086 — DIPLOM POLICY NEUTRAL PEACE

B61
WILLOUGHBY W.R.,THE ST LAWRENCE WATERWAY: A STUDY IN POLITICS AND DIPLOMACY. USA+45 ECO/DEV COM/IND INT/ORG CONSULT DELIB/GP ACT/RES TEC/DEV DIPLOM ECO/TAC ROUTINE...TIME/SEQ 20. PAGE 165 A3357 — LEGIS INT/TRADE CANADA DIST/IND

S61
ANGLIN D.,"UNITED STATES OPPOSITION TO CANADIAN MEMBERSHIP IN THE PAN AMERICAN UNION: A CANADIAN VIEW." L/A+17C UK USA+45 VOL/ASSN DELIB/GP EX/STRUC PLAN DIPLOM DOMIN REGION ATTIT RIGID/FLEX PWR ...RELATIV CONCPT STERTYP CMN/WLTH OAS 20. PAGE 8 A0162 — INT/ORG CANADA

B62
US LIBRARY OF CONGRESS,UNITED STATES AND CANADIAN PUBLICATIONS ON AFRICA IN 1960. CANADA USA+45 CULTURE TEC/DEV DIPLOM FOR/AID RACE/REL...GEOG HUM SOC SOC/WK LING 20. PAGE 155 A3156 — BIBLIOG/A AFR

B63
BISHOP O.B.,PUBLICATIONS OF THE GOVERNMENT OF THE PROVINCE OF CANADA 1841-1867. CANADA DIPLOM COLONIAL LEAD...POLICY 18. PAGE 14 A0294 — BIBLIOG NAT/G ATTIT

B63
DEENER D.R.,CANADA - UNITED STATES TREATY RELATIONS. CANADA USA+45 USA-45 NAT/G FORCES PLAN PROB/SOLV AGREE NUC/PWR...TREND 18/20 TREATY. PAGE 35 A0722 — DIPLOM INT/LAW POLICY

B63
MANSERGH N.,DOCUMENTS AND SPEECHES ON COMMONWEALTH AFFAIRS 1952-1962. CANADA INDIA PAKISTAN UK CONSTN FORCES ECO/TAC EDU/PROP COLONIAL DETER WAR ORD/FREE SOVEREIGN...POLICY 20 AUSTRAL. PAGE 94 A1932 — BIBLIOG/A FEDERAL INT/TRADE DIPLOM

S63
HARNETTY P.,"CANADA, SOUTH AFRICA AND THE COMMONWEALTH." CANADA SOUTH/AFR LAW INT/ORG VOL/ASSN DELIB/GP LEGIS TOP/EX ECO/TAC LEGIT DRIVE MORAL...CONCPT CMN/WLTH 20. PAGE 62 A1263 — AFR ATTIT

B64
THE SPECIAL COMMONWEALTH AFRICAN ASSISTANCE PLAN. AFR CANADA INDIA NIGERIA UK FINAN SCHOOL...CHARTS 20 COMMONWLTH. PAGE 3 A0065 — ECO/UNDEV TREND FOR/AID ADMIN

B64
CURRIE D.P.,FEDERALISM AND THE NEW NATIONS OF AFRICA. CANADA USA+45 INT/TRADE TAX GP/REL ...NAT/COMP SOC/INTEG 20. PAGE 33 A0667 — FEDERAL AFR ECO/UNDEV

INT/LAW

B64
DICKEY J.S.,THE UNITED STATES AND CANADA. CANADA USA+45...SOC 20. PAGE 37 A0756
DIPLOM TREND GOV/COMP PROB/SOLV

B64
FATOUROS A.A.,CANADA'S OVERSEAS AID. CANADA WOR+45 ECO/DEV FINAN NAT/G BUDGET ECO/TAC CONFER ADMIN 20. PAGE 44 A0904
FOR/AID DIPLOM ECO/UNDEV POLICY

B65
SOPER T.,EVOLVING COMMONWEALTH. AFR CANADA INDIA IRELAND UK LAW CONSTN POL/PAR DOMIN CONTROL WAR PWR ...AUD/VIS 18/20 COMMONWLTH OEEC. PAGE 135 A2769
INT/ORG COLONIAL VOL/ASSN

B66
SPICER K.,A SAMARITAN STATE? AFR CANADA INDIA PAKISTAN UK USA+45 FINAN INDUS PRODUC...CHARTS 20 NATO. PAGE 136 A2787
DIPLOM FOR/AID ECO/DEV ADMIN

B66
US DEPARTMENT OF STATE,RESEARCH ON WESTERN EUROPE, GREAT BRITAIN, AND CANADA (EXTERNAL RESEARCH LIST NO 3-25). CANADA GERMANY/W UK LAW CULTURE NAT/G POL/PAR FORCES EDU/PROP REGION MARXISM...GEOG SOC WORSHIP 20 CMN/WLTH. PAGE 152 A3098
BIBLIOG/A EUR+WWI DIPLOM

B66
WILSON H.A.,THE IMPERIAL POLICY OF SIR ROBERT BORDEN. CANADA UK ELITES INT/ORG VOL/ASSN CONTROL LEAD WAR ROLE 20 CMN/WLTH BORDEN/R. PAGE 165 A3360
INGP/REL COLONIAL CONSTN CHIEF

B67
BLOM-COOPER L.,THE LITERATURE OF THE LAW AND THE LANGUAGE OF THE LAW (2 VOLS.). CANADA ISRAEL UK WOR+45 WOR-45 JUDGE CT/SYS ATTIT...CRIMLGY JURID ANTHOL CMN/WLTH. PAGE 15 A0312
BIBLIOG LAW INT/LAW ADJUD

B67
PIPER D.C.,THE INTERNATIONAL LAW OF THE GREAT LAKES. CANADA EXTR/IND MUNIC LICENSE ARMS/CONT CRIME...GEOG 19/20. PAGE 116 A2381
CONCPT DIPLOM INT/LAW

B67
SCHWARTZ M.A.,PUBLIC OPINION AND CANADIAN IDENTITY. CANADA SOCIETY LOC/G DIPLOM ADMIN LEAD REGION GP/REL SAMP. PAGE 130 A2657
ATTIT NAT/G NAT/LISM POL/PAR

S67
TACKABERRY R.B.,"ORGANIZING AND TRAINING PEACE-KEEPING FORCES* THE CANADIAN VIEW." CANADA PLAN DIPLOM CONFER ADJUD ADMIN CIVMIL/REL 20 UN. PAGE 141 A2882
PEACE FORCES INT/ORG CONSULT

CANAL/ZONE....PANAMA CANAL ZONE

B40
BROWN A.D.,PANAMA CANAL AND PANAMA CANAL ZONE: A SELECTED LIST OF REFERENCES. PANAMA NAT/G SCHOOL DIPLOM HEALTH...GEOG SOC 20 CANAL/ZONE. PAGE 19 A0397
BIBLIOG/A ECO/UNDEV

B64
DUBOIS J.,DANGER OVER PANAMA. FUT PANAMA SCHOOL PROB/SOLV EDU/PROP MARXISM...POLICY 19/20 TREATY INTERVENT CANAL/ZONE. PAGE 39 A0790
DIPLOM COERCE

CANELAS O.A. A0476

CANFIELD L.H. A0477

CANNING HOUSE LIBRARY A0478

CANNON/JG....JOSEPH G. CANNON

CANON/LAW....CANON LAW

CANTRIL/H....HADLEY CANTRIL

CAP/ISM....CAPITALISM

B00
MOCKLER-FERRYMAN A.,BRITISH WEST AFRICA. FRANCE GERMANY NIGER SIER/LEONE UK CULTURE DIPLOM WAR RACE/REL PRODUC PROFIT WEALTH...POLICY PREDICT 19. PAGE 102 A2095
AFR COLONIAL INT/TRADE CAP/ISM

B02
SEELEY J.R.,THE EXPANSION OF ENGLAND. MOD/EUR S/ASIA UK CULTURE NAT/G FORCES PLAN DOMIN EDU/PROP COLONIAL ROUTINE ATTIT ALL/VALS SOVEREIGN...CONCPT HIST/WRIT PARLIAMENT 18 CMN/WLTH. PAGE 131 A2679
INT/ORG ACT/RES CAP/ISM INDIA

B08
LABRIOLA A.,ESSAYS ON THE MATERIALISTIC CONCEPTION OF HISTORY. STRATA POL/PAR CAP/ISM DIPLOM INT/TRADE WAR 20. PAGE 83 A1706
MARXIST WORKER REV COLONIAL

B19
SUMNER W.G.,WAR AND OTHER ESSAYS. USA-45 DELIB/GP DIPLOM TARIFFS COLONIAL PEACE SOVEREIGN 20. PAGE 140 A2864
INT/TRADE ORD/FREE CAP/ISM ECO/TAC

N19
DEANE H.,THE WAR IN VIETNAM (PAMPHLET). CHINA/COM VIETNAM BAL/PWR DIPLOM ECO/TAC SOCISM INTERVENT COLD/WAR INTERVENT COLD/WAR. PAGE 35 A0720
WAR SOCIALIST MORAL CAP/ISM

N19
MARCUS W.,US PRIVATE INVESTMENT AND ECONOMIC AID IN UNDERDEVELOPED COUNTRIES (PAMPHLET). USA+45 LG/CO NAT/G CAP/ISM EDU/PROP 20. PAGE 94 A1937
FOR/AID ECO/UNDEV FINAN PLAN

B32
HANSEN A.H.,ECONOMIC STABILIZATION IN AN UNBALANCED WORLD. COM EUR+WWI USA-45 WOR-45 AGRI FINAN INDUS MARKET INT/ORG LABOR VOL/ASSN EDU/PROP ATTIT HEALTH KNOWL WEALTH...HIST/WRIT TREND VAL/FREE 20. PAGE 61 A1253
NAT/G ECO/DEV CAP/ISM SOCISM

B32
LENIN V.I.,THE WAR AND THE SECOND INTERNATIONAL. COM MOD/EUR USSR CAP/ISM DIPLOM NAT/LISM ATTIT MARXISM...CONCPT 20. PAGE 87 A1772
POL/PAR WAR SOCISM INT/ORG

B34
GRAHAM F.D.,PROTECTIVE TARIFFS. FUT USA+45 WOR-45 INDUS MARKET VOL/ASSN PLAN CAP/ISM ECO/TAC PEACE ATTIT DRIVE HEALTH ORD/FREE...OBS TREND GEN/LAWS 20. PAGE 55 A1124
INT/ORG TARIFFS

B35
BEMIS S.F.,GUIDE TO THE DIPLOMATIC HISTORY OF THE UNITED STATES, 17751921. NAT/G LEGIS TOP/EX PROB/SOLV CAP/ISM INT/TRADE TARIFFS ADJUD ...CON/ANAL 18/20. PAGE 13 A0264
BIBLIOG/A DIPLOM USA-45

B35
STALEY E.,WAR AND THE PRIVATE INVESTOR. UNIV WOR-45 INTELL SOCIETY INT/ORG NAT/G TOP/EX CAP/ISM ECO/TAC WAR ATTIT ALL/VALS...INT TIME/SEQ TREND CON/ANAL WORK TOT/POP 20. PAGE 137 A2799
FINAN INT/TRADE DIPLOM

B37
VINER J.,STUDIES IN THE THEORY OF INTERNATIONAL TRADE. WOR-45 CONSTN ECO/DEV AGRI INDUS MARKET INT/ORG LABOR NAT/G ECO/TAC TARIFFS COLONIAL ATTIT WEALTH...POLICY CONCPT MATH STAT OBS SAMP TREND GEN/LAWS MARX/KARL 20. PAGE 159 A3236
CAP/ISM INT/TRADE

B39
LENIN V.I.,IMPERIALISM: THE HIGHEST STAGE OF CAPITALISM. USSR WOR-45 DIST/IND INT/TRADE ATTIT MARXISM SOCISM...CHARTS 20. PAGE 87 A1773
MARXIST CAP/ISM COLONIAL DOMIN

C40
NORMAN E.H.,"JAPAN'S EMERGENCE AS A MODERN STATE: POLITICAL AND ECONOMIC PROBLEMS OF THE MEIJI PERIOD." CONSTN STRATA AGRI INDUS POL/PAR TEC/DEV CAP/ISM CIVMIL/REL...BIBLIOG 19/20 CHINJAP. PAGE 110 A2250
CENTRAL DIPLOM POLICY NAT/LISM

B42
CROWE S.E.,THE BERLIN WEST AFRICA CONFERENCE, 1884-85. GERMANY ELITES MARKET INT/ORG DELIB/GP FORCES PROB/SOLV BAL/PWR CAP/ISM DOMIN COLONIAL ...INT/LAW 19. PAGE 33 A0664
AFR CONFER INT/TRADE DIPLOM

L42
SHOTWELL J.,"LESSON OF THE LAST WORLD WAR." EUR+WWI MOD/EUR USA-45 SOCIETY ECO/UNDEV INDUS VOL/ASSN CONSULT ACT/RES CREATE CAP/ISM INT/TRADE DRIVE ALL/VALS...CONCPT NEW/IDEA SELF/OBS GEN/LAWS LEAGUE/NAT NAZI 20. PAGE 132 A2708
INT/ORG ORD/FREE

B44
WEIGERT H.W.,COMPASS OF THE WORLD, A SYMPOSIUM ON POLITICAL GEOGRAPHY. EUR+WWI FUT MOD/EUR S/ASIA USA-45 WOR-45 SOCIETY AGRI INDUS MARKET ECO/TAC INT/TRADE PERSON 20. PAGE 162 A3298
TEC/DEV CAP/ISM RUSSIA GEOG

B45
MACMINN N.,BIBLIOGRAPHY OF THE PUBLISHED WRITINGS OF JOHN STUART MILL. MOD/EUR UK CAP/ISM DIPLOM KNOWL...EPIST CONCPT 19 MILL/JS. PAGE 93 A1901
BIBLIOG/A SOCIETY INGP/REL LAISSEZ

B47
BORGESE G.,COMMON CAUSE. LAW CONSTN SOCIETY STRATA ECO/DEV INT/ORG POL/PAR FORCES LEGIS TOP/EX CAP/ISM DIPLOM ADMIN EXEC ATTIT PWR 20. PAGE 17 A0339
WOR+45 NAT/G SOVEREIGN REGION

B48
GRAHAM F.D.,THE THEORY OF INTERNATIONAL VALUES. FUT WOR+45 WOR-45 ECO/DEV FINAN INT/ORG PLAN TEC/DEV CAP/ISM DIPLOM ECO/TAC TARIFFS ROUTINE BAL/PAY DRIVE PWR WEALTH SOCISM...POLICY STAT HYPO/EXP GEN/LAWS 20. PAGE 55 A1125
NEW/IDEA INT/TRADE

B49
FORD FOUNDATION,REPORT OF THE STUDY FOR THE FORD FOUNDATION ON POLICY AND PROGRAM. SOCIETY R+D ACT/RES CAP/ISM FOR/AID EDU/PROP ADMIN KNOWL ...POLICY PSY SOC 20. PAGE 47 A0961
WEALTH GEN/LAWS

N50
SCHAPIRO J.S.,THE WORLD IN CRISES: POLITICAL AND SOCIAL MOVEMENTS IN THE TWENTIETH CENTURY. USA+45 INT/ORG LABOR PLAN CAP/ISM DIPLOM COLONIAL PEACE TOTALISM ATTIT LAISSEZ...BIBLIOG 20 COLD/WAR. PAGE 128 A2618
NAT/LISM TEC/DEV REV WAR

B54
STALEY E.,THE FUTURE OF UNDERDEVELOPED COUNTRIES: POLITICAL IMPLICATIONS OF ECONOMIC DEVELOPMENT. COM FUT USA+45 SOCIETY ECO/UNDEV CREATE PLAN CAP/ISM ATTIT DRIVE MARXISM SOCISM...POLICY CONCPT CHARTS COLD/WAR 20. PAGE 137 A2801
EDU/PROP ECO/TAC FOR/AID

C54
BERLE A.A. JR.,"THE 20TH CENTURY CAPITALIST REVOLUTION." ECO/DEV NAT/G DIPLOM PRICE CONTROL ATTIT...BIBLIOG/A 20. PAGE 14 A0275
LG/CO CAP/ISM MGT PWR

B55
O3HEVSS E.,WIRTSCHAFTSSYSTEME UND INTERNATIONALER HANDEL. ECO/DEV FINAN MARKET DIPLOM ECO/TAC COST ...METH/COMP NAT/COMP 20. PAGE 112 A2306
CAP/ISM SOCISM INT/TRADE IDEA/COMP

B55
SEMJONOW J.M.,DIE FASCHISTISCHE GEOPOLITIK IM DIENSTE DES AMERIKANISCHEN IMPERIALISMUS. USA+45 USA-45 CAP/ISM PEACE ORD/FREE MARXISM SOCISM ...POLICY GEOG 20. PAGE 131 A2684
DIPLOM COERCE FASCISM WAR

B56
KNORR K.E.,RUBLE DIPLOMACY: CHALLENGE TO AMERICAN FOREIGN AID(PAMPHLET). CHINA/COM USA+45 USSR PLAN TEC/DEV CAP/ISM INT/TRADE DOMIN EDU/PROP CONTROL LEAD 20 COLD/WAR. PAGE 81 A1654
ECO/UNDEV COM DIPLOM FOR/AID

B57
ALEXANDER L.M.,WORLD POLITICAL PATTERNS. NAT/G PROVS CAP/ISM DIPLOM COLONIAL NAT/LISM...POLICY GEOG CHARTS METH/COMP NAT/COMP 20. PAGE 5 A0111
CONTROL METH GOV/COMP

B57
MCNEILL W.H.,GREECE: AMERICAN AID IN ACTION. GREECE UK USA+45 FINAN CAP/ISM INT/TRADE BAL/PAY PRODUC WEALTH...POLICY METH/COMP 20. PAGE 99 A2022
FOR/AID DIPLOM ECO/UNDEV

B57
US PRES CITIZEN ADVISERS,REPORT TO THE PRESIDENT ON THE MUTUAL SECURITY PROGRAM. COM USA+45 WOR+45 FINAN INDUS PLAN BUDGET CAP/ISM DIPLOM FOR/AID INT/TRADE REGION 20 SECUR/PROG. PAGE 155 A3163
BAL/PWR FORCES INT/ORG ECO/TAC

B58
APPADORAI A.,THE USE OF FORCE IN INTERNATIONAL RELATIONS. WOR+45 CULTURE ECO/UNDEV CAP/ISM ARMS/CONT REV WAR ATTIT PERSON SOVEREIGN MARXISM ...INT/LAW PACIFIST 20 UN INTERVENT THIRD/WRLD COLD/WAR. PAGE 8 A0169
PEACE FEDERAL INT/ORG

B58
AVRAMOVIC D.,POSTWAR GROWTH IN INTERNATIONAL INDEBTEDNESS. WOR+45 AGRI INDUS CAP/ISM PRICE INCOME...NAT/COMP 20 GOLD/STAND SILVER. PAGE 10 A0199
INT/TRADE FINAN COST BAL/PAY

B58
VARG P.A.,MISSIONARIES, CHINESE, AND DIPLOMATS: THE AMERICAN PROTESTANT MISSIONARY MOVEMENT IN CHINA, 1890-1952. ASIA ECO/UNDEV NAT/G PROB/SOLV CAP/ISM EDU/PROP COLONIAL NAT/LISM ATTIT MARXISM...NAT/COMP STERTYP 20 CHINJAP PROTESTANT MISSION. PAGE 158 A3221
CULTURE DIPLOM SECT

B59
NOVE A.,COMMUNIST ECONOMIC STRATEGY: SOVIET GROWTH AND CAPABILITIES. USSR AGRI LABOR PLAN TEC/DEV CAP/ISM INT/TRADE EFFICIENCY MARXISM 20 THIRD/WRLD. PAGE 110 A2257
FOR/AID ECO/TAC DIPLOM INDUS

S59
SOLDATI A.,"EOCNOMIC DISINTEGRATION IN EUROPE." EUR+WWI FUT WOR+45 INDUS INT/ORG NAT/G CAP/ISM WEALTH...NEW/IDEA OBS TREND CHARTS EEC 20. PAGE 135 A2764
FINAN ECO/TAC

B60
APTHEKER H.,DISARMAMENT AND THE AMERICAN ECONOMY: A SYMPOSIUM. FUT USA+45 ECO/DEV DIST/IND FINAN INDUS PROC/MFG LABOR NAT/G POL/PAR CONSULT PLAN CAP/ISM INT/TRADE PEACE ATTIT MORAL WEALTH...TREND GEN/LAWS TOT/POP 20. PAGE 9 A0172
MARXIST ARMS/CONT

B60
CAMPAIGNE J.G.,AMERICAN MIGHT AND SOVIET MYTH. COM EUR+WWI ECO/DEV ECO/UNDEV INT/ORG NAT/G CAP/ISM ECO/TAC FOR/AID EDU/PROP ATTIT PWR WEALTH...POLICY CONCPT MYTH TREND STERTYP GEN/LAWS COLD/WAR. PAGE 23 A0473
USA+45 DOMIN DIPLOM USSR

B60
EINSTEIN A.,EINSTEIN ON PEACE. FUT WOR+45 WOR-45 SOCIETY NAT/G PLAN BAL/PWR CAP/ISM DIPLOM ARMS/CONT DETER NAT/LISM...POLICY RELATIV HUM PHIL/SCI CONCPT BIOG COLD/WAR LEAGUE/NAT NAZI. PAGE 41 A0829
INT/ORG ATTIT NUC/PWR PEACE

B60
HOFFMANN P.G.,ONE HUNDRED COUNTRIES, ONE AND ONE QUARTER BILLION PEOPLE. MARKET INT/ORG TEC/DEV CAP/ISM...GEOG CHARTS METH/COMP 20 UN. PAGE 66 A1354
FOR/AID ECO/TAC ECO/UNDEV INT/TRADE

B60
KHRUSHCHEV N.,FOR VICTORY IN PEACEFUL COMPETITION WITH CAPITALISM. COM FUT USSR WOR+45 CONSTN SOCIETY INDUS INT/ORG DELIB/GP PLAN BAL/PWR DIPLOM PERSON MARXISM...MARXIST WORK 20 COLD/WAR. PAGE 79 A1611
TOP/EX PWR CAP/ISM SOCISM

B60
LERNER A.P.,THE ECONOMICS OF CONTROL. USA+45 ECO/UNDEV INT/ORG ACT/RES PLAN CAP/ISM INT/TRADE ATTIT WEALTH...SOC MATH STAT GEN/LAWS INDEX 20. PAGE 87 A1785
ECO/DEV ROUTINE ECO/TAC SOCISM

S60
FRANKEL S.H.,"ECONOMIC ASPECTS OF POLITICAL INDEPENDENCE IN AFRICA." AFR FUT SOCIETY ECO/UNDEV COM/IND FINAN LEGIS PLAN TEC/DEV CAP/ISM ECO/TAC INT/TRADE ADMIN ATTIT DRIVE RIGID/FLEX PWR WEALTH ...MGT NEW/IDEA MATH TIME/SEQ VAL/FREE 20. PAGE 48 A0984
NAT/G FOR/AID

S60
MIKESELL R.F.,"AMERICA'S ECONOMIC RESPONSIBILITY AS A GREAT POWER." COM FUT USA+45 USSR WOR+45 INT/ORG PLAN ECO/TAC FOR/AID EDU/PROP CHOOSE WEALTH ...POLICY 20. PAGE 101 A2069
ECO/UNDEV BAL/PWR CAP/ISM

B61
AUBREY H.G.,COEXISTENCE: ECONOMIC CHALLENGE AND RESPONSE. USSR WOR+45 ACT/RES BAL/PWR CAP/ISM DIPLOM ECO/TAC FOR/AID INT/TRADE PEACE SOCISM ...METH/COMP NAT/COMP COLD/WAR. PAGE 10 A0196
POLICY ECO/UNDEV PLAN COM

B61
BONNEFOUS M.,EUROPE ET TIERS MONDE. EUR+WWI SOCIETY INT/ORG NAT/G VOL/ASSN ACT/RES TEC/DEV CAP/ISM ECO/TAC ATTIT ORD/FREE SOVEREIGN...POLICY CONCPT TREND 20. PAGE 16 A0334
AFR ECO/UNDEV FOR/AID INT/TRADE

B61
GANGULI B.N.,ECONOMIC INTEGRATION. FINAN LABOR CAP/ISM DIPLOM WEALTH...NAT/COMP 20. PAGE 51 A1041
ECO/TAC METH/CNCPT EQUILIB ECO/UNDEV

B61
MORRAY J.P.,FROM YALTA TO DISARMAMENT: COLD WAR DEBATE. USA+45 CAP/ISM FOR/AID CONTROL NUC/PWR 20 UN COLD/WAR CHURCHLL/W. PAGE 104 A2145
MARXIST ARMS/CONT DIPLOM BAL/PWR

B61
PERLO V.,EL IMPERIALISMO NORTHEAMERICANO. USA+45 USA-45 FINAN CAP/ISM DIPLOM DOMIN CONTROL DISCRIM 19/20. PAGE 115 A2363
SOCIALIST ECO/DEV INT/TRADE ECO/TAC

S61
"CRITERIA FOR ALLOCATING INVESTMENT RESOURCES AMONG VARIOUS FIELDS OF DEVELOPMENT IN UNDERDEVELOPED ECONOMIES." ASIA AGRI INT/ORG CAP/ISM BAL/PAY EFFICIENCY PROFIT WEALTH...STAT 20 UN. PAGE 3 A0061
BIBLIOG/A ECO/UNDEV PLAN TEC/DEV

S61
WHELAN J.G.,"KHRUSHCHEV AND THE BALANCE OF WORLD POWER." FUT WOR+45 INT/ORG VOL/ASSN CAP/ISM DIPLOM SKILL...POLICY COLD/WAR 20 KHRUSH/N. PAGE 163 A3328
COM PWR BAL/PWR USSR

B62
FRIEDMANN W.,METHODS AND POLICIES OF PRINCIPAL DONOR COUNTRIES IN PUBLIC INTERNATIONAL DEVELOPMENT FINANCING: PRELIMINARY APPRAISAL. FRANCE GERMANY/W UK USA+45 USSR WOR+45 FINAN TEC/DEV CAP/ISM DIPLOM ECO/TAC ATTIT 20 EEC. PAGE 49 A1002
INT/ORG FOR/AID NAT/COMP ADMIN

B62
LEVY H.V.,LIBERDADE E JUSTICA SOCIAL (2ND ED.). BRAZIL COM L/A+17C USSR INT/ORG PARTIC GP/REL WEALTH 20 UN COM/PARTY. PAGE 88 A1798
ORD/FREE MARXISM CAP/ISM LAW

B62
MOUSSA P.,THE UNDERPRIVILEGED NATIONS. FINAN INT/ORG PLAN PROB/SOLV CAP/ISM GIVE TASK WEALTH ...POLICY SOC 20. PAGE 105 A2159
ECO/UNDEV NAT/G DIPLOM FOR/AID

B62
POSTON R.W.,DEMOCRACY SPEAKS MANY TONGUES. L/A+17C USA+45 ECO/UNDEV ACT/RES ECO/TAC ADMIN ORD/FREE ...METH/COMP 20. PAGE 117 A2397
FOR/AID DIPLOM CAP/ISM MARXISM

B62
ROY P.A.,SOUTH WIND RED. L/A+17C USA+45 ECO/UNDEV NAT/G CAP/ISM MARXISM SOCISM...OLD/LIB GEOG RECORD INT CENSUS 20 COLD/WAR. PAGE 125 A2554
DIPLOM INDUS POLICY ECO/TAC

B63
HYDE D.,THE PEACEFUL ASSAULT. COM UAR USSR ECO/DEV ECO/UNDEV NAT/G POL/PAR CAP/ISM PWR 20. PAGE 69 A1427
MARXISM CONTROL ECO/TAC DIPLOM

B63
LAFEBER W.,THE NEW EMPIRE: AN INTERPRETATION OF AMERICAN EXPANSION, 1860-1898. USA-45 CONSTN NAT/LISM SOVEREIGN...TREND BIBLIOG 19/20. PAGE 84 A1711
INDUS NAT/G DIPLOM CAP/ISM

B63
LANGE O.,ECONOMIC DEVELOPMENT, PLANNING, AND INTERNATIONAL COOPERATION. UAR WOR+45 FINAN CAP/ISM
ECO/UNDEV DIPLOM

PERS/REL 20. PAGE 84 A1722 INT/TRADE PLAN

B63
PATRA A.C.,THE ADMINISTRATION OF JUSTICE UNDER THE EAST INDIA COMPANY IN BENGAL, BIHAR AND ORISSA. INDIA UK LG/CO CAP/ISM INT/TRADE ADJUD COLONIAL CONTROL CT/SYS...POLICY 20. PAGE 114 A2341 ADMIN JURID CONCPT

B63
ROSSI M.,THE THIRD WORLD. FUT WOR+45 INT/ORG NAT/G CAP/ISM COLONIAL PEACE PWR MARXISM 20 UN THIRD/WRLD. PAGE 124 A2542 ECO/UNDEV DIPLOM BAL/PWR NEUTRAL

B63
THEOBALD R.,FREE MEN AND FREE MARKETS. USA+45 USA-45 ECO/DEV NAT/G TEC/DEV DIPLOM INT/TRADE INCOME ORD/FREE WEALTH...TREND 19/20 KEYNES/JM. PAGE 143 A2915 CONCPT ECO/TAC CAP/ISM MARKET

B63
VON HALLER A.,DIE LETZTEN WOLLEN DIE ERSTEN SEIN. AFR S/ASIA INT/TRADE REV ORD/FREE SOVEREIGN 20. PAGE 160 A3251 FOR/AID ECO/UNDEV MARXISM CAP/ISM

S63
MATHUR P.N.,"GAINS IN ECONOMIC GROWTH FROM INTERNATIONAL TRADE." USA-45 ECO/DEV FINAN INDUS ATTIT WEALTH...MATH QUANT STAT BIOG TREND GEN/LAWS WORK 20. PAGE 96 A1966 MARKET ECO/TAC CAP/ISM INT/TRADE

C63
SCHMITT K.M.,"EVOLUTION OR CHAOS: DYNAMICS OF LATIN AMERICAN GOVERNMENT AND POLITICS." L/A+17C AGRI FINAN CAP/ISM EXEC LEAD BAL/PAY TOTALISM ATTIT ...TREND BIBLIOG 20. PAGE 129 A2635 DIPLOM POLICY POL/PAR LOBBY

B64
DUTT R.P.,THE INTERNATIONALE. COM WOR+45 WOR-45 WORKER CAP/ISM WAR ATTIT...TREND GEN/LAWS 18/20 COM/PARTY. PAGE 40 A0813 ALL/IDEOS INT/ORG MARXIST ORD/FREE

B64
GIBSON J.S.,IDEOLOGY AND WORLD AFFAIRS. FUT WOR+45 ECO/UNDEV NAT/G CAP/ISM TOTALISM ORD/FREE FASCISM MARXISM 20. PAGE 52 A1067 ALL/IDEOS DIPLOM POLICY IDEA/COMP

B64
MEYER F.S.,WHAT IS CONSERVATISM? USA+45 NAT/G FORCES DIPLOM ORD/FREE IDEA/COMP. PAGE 100 A2048 CONSERVE CONCPT EDU/PROP CAP/ISM

B64
NEHEMKIS P.,LATIN AMERICA: MYTH AND REALITY. INDUS INT/ORG MUNIC PROB/SOLV CAP/ISM DIPLOM REV...SOC 20. PAGE 108 A2211 REGION MYTH L/A+17C ECO/UNDEV

B64
OECD,THE FLOW OF FINANCIAL RESOURCES TO LESS DEVELOPED COUNTRIES 1956-1963. WOR+45 FINAN CAP/ISM ...POLICY STAT 20. PAGE 111 A2281 FOR/AID BUDGET INT/ORG ECO/UNDEV

B64
RANIS G.,THE UNITED STATES AND THE DEVELOPING ECONOMIES. COM USA+45 AGRI FINAN TEC/DEV CAP/ISM ECO/TAC INT/TRADE...POLICY METH/COMP ANTHOL 20 AID. PAGE 119 A2441 ECO/UNDEV DIPLOM FOR/AID

B64
STANKIEWICZ W.J.,POLITICAL THOUGHT SINCE WORLD WAR II. WOR+45 CAP/ISM DIPLOM COLONIAL COERCE REV REPRESENT ADJUST ANOMIE ALL/IDEOS 20. PAGE 137 A2804 IDEA/COMP DOMIN ORD/FREE AUTHORIT

B64
STILLMAN E.O.,THE POLITICS OF HYSTERIA: THE SOURCES OF TWENTIETH-CENTURY CONFLICT. WOR+45 WOR-45 CULTURE ECO/UNDEV PLAN CAP/ISM WAR MARXISM ...PREDICT BIBLIOG 20 COLD/WAR. PAGE 138 A2828 DIPLOM IDEA/COMP COLONIAL CONTROL

B64
US AGENCY INTERNATIONAL DEV,REPORT TO CONGRESS ON THE FOREIGN ASSISTANCE PROGRAM. AFR ASIA L/A+17C USA+45 INT/ORG VOL/ASSN FORCES CAP/ISM ADMIN WEAPON. PAGE 149 A3052 FOR/AID ECO/UNDEV TEC/DEV BUDGET

B64
WITHERS W.,THE ECONOMIC CRISIS IN LATIN AMERICA. BRAZIL CHILE STRATA AGRI DIPLOM FOR/AID PWR SOCISM ...POLICY 20 MEXIC/AMER ARGEN. PAGE 166 A3372 L/A+17C ECO/UNDEV CAP/ISM ALL/IDEOS

L64
ARMENGALD A.,"ECONOMIE ET COEXISTENCE." COM EUR+WWI FUT USA+45 WOR+45 ECO/DEV ECO/UNDEV FINAN INT/ORG NAT/G EXEC CHOOSE ATTIT ALL/VALS...POLICY RELATIV DECISION TREND SOC/EXP COLD/WAR WORK 20. PAGE 9 A0173 MARKET ECO/TAC CAP/ISM

S64
KARPOV P.V.,"PEACEFUL COEXISTENCE AND INTERNATIONAL LAW." WOR+45 LAW SOCIETY INT/ORG VOL/ASSN FORCES CREATE CAP/ISM DIPLOM ADJUD NUC/PWR PEACE MORAL ORD/FREE PWR MARXISM...MARXIST JURID CONCPT OBS TREND COLD/WAR MARX/KARL 20. PAGE 77 A1568 COM ATTIT INT/LAW USSR

S64
MCCREARY E.A.,"THOSE AMERICAN MANAGERS DON'T IMPRESS EUROPE." EUR+WWI USA+45 CULTURE STRATA ECO/DEV TOP/EX INT/TRADE ATTIT DRIVE PERSON RIGID/FLEX...CONCPT 20. PAGE 98 A2003 MARKET ACT/RES BAL/PAY CAP/ISM

S64
SALVADORI M.,"EL CAPITALISMO EN LA EUROPA DE LA POSGUERRA." INT/ORG NAT/G POL/PAR PLAN ECO/TAC ATTIT ORD/FREE WEALTH...HIST/WRIT COLD/WAR EEC 20. PAGE 127 A2596 EUR+WWI ECO/DEV CAP/ISM

B65
BROOKINGS INSTITUTION,BROOKINGS PAPERS ON PUBLIC POLICY. USA+45 ECO/UNDEV LEGIS CAP/ISM ECO/TAC TAX EDU/PROP CONTROL APPORT 20. PAGE 19 A0395 DIPLOM FOR/AID POLICY FINAN

B65
COLLINS H.,KARL MARX AND THE BRITISH LABOUR MOVEMENT; YEARS OF THE FIRST INTERNATIONAL. FRANCE SWITZERLND UK CAP/ISM WAR...MARXIST IDEA/COMP BIBLIOG 19. PAGE 28 A0567 MARXISM LABOR INT/ORG REV

B65
DU BOIS W.E.B.,THE WORLD AND AFRICA. USA+45 CAP/ISM DISCRIM STRANGE SOCISM...TIME/SEQ TREND IDEA/COMP 19/20 NEGRO. PAGE 39 A0789 AFR DIPLOM COLONIAL CULTURE

B65
HALPERIN E.,NATIONALISM AND COMMUNISM. CHILE L/A+17C CAP/ISM EDU/PROP CHOOSE DISCRIM SOCISM ...BIBLIOG 20 COM/PARTY. PAGE 60 A1236 NAT/LISM MARXISM POL/PAR REV

B65
INTERNATIONAL SOCIAL SCI COUN,SOCIAL SCIENCES IN THE USSR. USSR ECO/DEV AGRI FINAN INDUS PLAN CAP/ISM...INT/LAW PHIL/SCI PSY SOC 20. PAGE 71 A1460 BIBLIOG/A ACT/RES MARXISM JURID

B65
MENON K.P.S.,MANY WORLDS. INDIA BAL/PWR CAP/ISM COLONIAL REV ORD/FREE PWR MARXISM...POLICY 20 COLD/WAR. PAGE 100 A2042 BIOG DIPLOM NAT/G

S65
AFRICAN BIBLIOGRAPHIC CENTER,"US TREATIES AND AGREEMENTS WITH COUNTRIES IN AFRICA, 1957 TO MID-1963." AFR USA+45 AGRI FINAN FORCES TEC/DEV CAP/ISM FOR/AID 20. PAGE 5 A0097 BIBLIOG DIPLOM INT/ORG INT/TRADE

B66
EDWARDS C.D.,TRADE REGULATIONS OVERSEAS. IRELAND NEW/ZEALND SOUTH/AFR NAT/G CAP/ISM TARIFFS CONTROL ...POLICY JURID 20 EEC CHINJAP. PAGE 40 A0823 INT/TRADE DIPLOM INT/LAW ECO/TAC

B66
PASSIN H.,THE UNITED STATES AND JAPAN. USA+45 INDUS CAP/ISM...TREND 20 CHINJAP TREATY. PAGE 114 A2337 DIPLOM INT/TRADE ECO/DEV ECO/TAC

B66
SPULBER N.,THE STATE AND ECONOMIC DEVELOPMENT IN EASTERN EUROPE. BULGARIA COM CZECHOSLVK HUNGARY POLAND YUGOSLAVIA CULTURE PLAN CAP/ISM INT/TRADE CONTROL...POLICY CHARTS METH/COMP BIBLIOG/A 19/20. PAGE 136 A2793 ECO/DEV ECO/UNDEV NAT/G TOTALISM

B66
US SENATE COMM ON FOREIGN REL,HEARINGS ON S 2859 AND S 2861. USA+45 WOR+45 FORCES BUDGET CAP/ISM ADMIN DETER WEAPON TOTALISM...NAT/COMP 20 UN CONGRESS. PAGE 156 A3185 FOR/AID DIPLOM ORD/FREE ECO/UNDEV

B66
WELCH R.H.W.,THE NEW AMERICANISM, AND OTHER SPEECHES AND ESSAYS. USA+45 ACADEM POL/PAR SCHOOL VOL/ASSN FORCES CAP/ISM TAX REV DISCRIM 20 CIV/RIGHTS COLD/WAR BIRCH/SOC. PAGE 163 A3313 DIPLOM FASCISM MARXISM RACE/REL

B66
ZISCHKA A.,WAR ES EIN WUNDER? GERMANY/W ECO/DEV FINAN LG/CO BARGAIN CAP/ISM FOR/AID RATION 20 MARSHL/PLN. PAGE 170 A3456 ECO/TAC INT/TRADE INDUS WAR

S66
"WORLD BANK CONVENTION ON INVESTMENT DISPUTES; A BIBLIOGRAPH ICAL NOTE." VOL/ASSN CONSULT CAP/ISM DIPLOM INT/TRADE 20 SENATE PRESIDENT. PAGE 4 A0074 BIBLIOG ADJUD FINAN INT/ORG

S66
DINH TRANS V.A.N.,"VIETNAM: A THIRD WAY" S/ASIA USA+45 USSR VIETNAM VIETNAM/S NAT/G SECT FORCES CAP/ISM DIPLOM COLONIAL NEUTRAL MARXISM SOCISM 20 BUDDHISM UNIFICA. PAGE 38 A0766 WAR PLAN ORD/FREE SOCIALIST

S66
DUROSELLE J.B.,"THE FUTURE OF THE ATLANTIC COMMUNITY." EUR+WWI USA+45 USSR NAT/G CAP/ISM REGION DETER NUC/PWR ATTIT MARXISM...INT/LAW 20 NATO. PAGE 40 A0811 FUT DIPLOM MYTH POLICY

B67
AUBREY H.G.,ATLANTIC ECONOMIC COOPERATION. ECO/DEV INDUS VOL/ASSN PROB/SOLV DIPLOM INT/TRADE TARIFFS CONFER 20. PAGE 10 A0197 INT/ORG ECO/TAC TEC/DEV CAP/ISM

B67
DILLARD D.,ECONOMIC DEVELOPMENT OF THE NORTH ATLANTIC COMMUNITY. EUR+WWI MOD/EUR USA+45 USA-45 ECO/DEV INT/TRADE

ECO/UNDEV LABOR CAP/ISM WAR BAL/PAY...NAT/COMP 15/20. PAGE 37 A0763 — INDUS DIPLOM

B67
FILENE P.G.,AMERICANS AND THE SOVIET EXPERIMENT, 1917-1933. USA-45 USSR INTELL NAT/G CAP/ISM DIPLOM EDU/PROP PRESS REV SOCISM...PSY 20. PAGE 45 A0930 — ATTIT RIGID/FLEX MARXISM SOCIETY

B67
JOHNSON A.M.,BOSTON CAPITALISTS AND WESTERN RAILROADS: A STUDY IN THE NINETEENTH CENTURY RAILROAD INVESTMENT PROCESS. CREATE BARGAIN INT/TRADE GAMBLE KNOWL 19 BOSTON. PAGE 74 A1519 — FINAN DIST/IND CAP/ISM ECO/UNDEV

B67
SABLE M.H.,A GUIDE TO LATIN AMERICAN STUDIES (2 VOLS). CONSTN FINAN INT/ORG LABOR MUNIC POL/PAR FORCES CAP/ISM FOR/AID ADMIN MARXISM SOCISM OAS. PAGE 126 A2584 — BIBLIOG/A L/A+17C DIPLOM NAT/LISM

L67
DEVADHAR Y.C.,"THE ROLE OF FOREIGN PRIVATE CAPITAL IN INDIA'S ECONOMIC DEVELOPMENT* ASSESSMENT OF POLICY AND PERFORMANCE." INDIA INDUS PLAN TEC/DEV BUDGET DIPLOM ECO/TAC BAL/PAY PRODUC WEALTH ...CHARTS 20. PAGE 37 A0750 — CAP/ISM FOR/AID POLICY ACT/RES

S67
FELDMAN H.,"AID AS IMPERIALISM?" INDIA PAKISTAN UK USA+45 BAL/PWR CAP/ISM DIPLOM ECO/TAC DOMIN BAL/PAY WEALTH...POLICY 20. PAGE 45 A0914 — COLONIAL FOR/AID S/ASIA ECO/UNDEV

S67
FRENCH D.S.,"DOES THE U.S. EXPLOIT THE DEVELOPING NATIONS?" INT/ORG NAT/G CAP/ISM BAL/PAY WEALTH POLICY. PAGE 49 A0997 — ECO/UNDEV INT/TRADE ECO/TAC COLONIAL

S67
KIERNAN V.G.,"INDIA AND THE LABOUR PARTY." INDIA UK CAP/ISM GP/REL EFFICIENCY NAT/LISM PWR SOCISM ...SOCIALIST TIME/SEQ 20. PAGE 79 A1616 — COLONIAL DIPLOM POL/PAR ECO/UNDEV

S67
KINGSLEY R.E.,"THE US BUSINESS IMAGE IN LATIN AMERICA." L/A+17C USA+45 NAT/G TEC/DEV CAP/ISM FOR/AID DOMIN EDU/PROP...CONCPT LING IDEA/COMP 20. PAGE 79 A1626 — ATTIT LOVE DIPLOM ECO/UNDEV

S67
PERLO V.,"NEW DIMENSIONS IN EAST-WEST TRADE." UK USA+45 USSR WOR+45 ECO/DEV NAT/G CAP/ISM PEACE WEALTH LAISSEZ...SOCIALIST MGT 20. PAGE 115 A2364 — BAL/PWR ECO/TAC INT/TRADE

S67
PEUKERT W.,"WEST GERMANY'S 'RED TRADE'." COM GERMANY INDUS CAP/ISM DOMIN SANCTION DEMAND PEACE UTIL...MARXIST 20 COLD/WAR. PAGE 115 A2371 — DIPLOM ECO/TAC INT/TRADE

S67
ROMANOVSKY S.,"MISUSE OF CULTURAL COOPERATION." USA+45 INTELL DIPLOM DOMIN ATTIT COLD/WAR. PAGE 123 A2518 — EDU/PROP POLICY MARXISM CAP/ISM

S67
SCHUMANN H.,"IMPERIALISMUS-KRITIK UND KOLONIALISMUS-FORSCHUNG." GERMANY/E DIPLOM SOVEREIGN...SOC HIST/WRIT 20. PAGE 129 A2652 — COLONIAL ATTIT DOMIN CAP/ISM

CAPE/HOPE....CAPE OF GOOD HOPE

CAPITAL....SEE FINAN,

CAPITALISM....SEE CAP/ISM

CAPODIST/J....JOHN CAPODISTRIAS

CAPONE/AL....AL CAPONE

CARDINALL A.W. A0479

CARDOZA M.H. A0480

CARDOZA/JN....JACOB N. CARDOZA

CAREW-HUNT R.C. A0481

CARIBBEAN COMMISSION A0482,A0483

CARIBBEAN....CARIBBEAN

B43
BROWN A.D.,BRITISH POSSESSIONS IN THE CARIBBEAN AREA: A SELECTED LIST OF REFERENCES. UK NAT/G DIPLOM...GEOG 20 CARIBBEAN. PAGE 20 A0398 — BIBLIOG COLONIAL ECO/UNDEV L/A+17C

S62
SPRINGER H.W.,"FEDERATION IN THE CARIBBEAN: AN ATTEMPT THAT FAILED." L/A+17C ECO/UNDEV INT/ORG POL/PAR PROVS LEGIS CREATE PLAN LEGIT ADMIN FEDERAL ATTIT DRIVE PERSON ORD/FREE PWR...POLICY GEOG PSY CONCPT OBS CARIBBEAN CMN/WLTH 20. PAGE 136 A2791 — VOL/ASSN NAT/G REGION

B65
DEMAS W.G.,THE ECONOMICS OF DEVELOPMENT IN SMALL COUNTRIES WITH SPECIAL REFERENCE TO THE CARIBBEAN. WOR+45 BAL/PAY DEMAND EFFICIENCY PRODUC...GEOG CARIBBEAN. PAGE 36 A0731 — ECO/UNDEV PLAN WEALTH INT/TRADE

CARLETON W.G. A0484

CARLO A.M. A0485

CARLSTON K.S. A0486,A0487

CARMICHAEL J. A2875

CARNEG/COM....CARNEGIE COMMISSION

CARNEGIE ENDOWMENT INT. PEACE A0488,A0489,A0490,A0491,A0492,, A0493,A0494,A0495

CARNELL F. A0496

CARPOZI G.J. A1421

CARR E.H. A0497,A0498,A0499

CARRANZA/V....VENUSTIANZO CARRANZA

B67
TEITELBAUM L.M.,WOODROW WILSON AND THE MEXICAN REVOLUTION 1913-1916: A HISTORY OF UNITED STATES-MEXICAN RELATIONS. USA-45 CHIEF TOP/EX WAR 20 MEXIC/AMER WILSON/W VILLA/P CARRANZA/V. PAGE 142 A2902 — REV DIPLOM

CARRINGTON C.E. A0500,A0501

CARROLL H.N. A0502

CARROLL K.J. A0503

CARTER G.M. A0504

CASADIO F.A. A2102

CASE STUDIES....CARRIED UNDER THE SPECIAL TECHNIQUES USED, OR TOPICS COVERED

CASEBOOK....CASEBOOK, SUCH AS LEGAL OR SOCIOLOGICAL CASEBOOK

B38
HAGUE PERMANENT CT INTL JUSTIC,WORLD COURT REPORTS: COLLECTION OF THE JUDGEMENTS ORDERS AND OPINIONS VOLUME 3 1932-35. WOR-45 LAW DELIB/GP CONFER WAR PEACE ATTIT...DECISION ANTHOL 20 WORLD/CT CASEBOOK. PAGE 59 A1214 — INT/ORG CT/SYS DIPLOM ADJUD

B43
HAGUE PERMANENT CT INTL JUSTIC,WORLD COURT REPORTS: COLLECTION OF THE JUDGEMENTS ORDERS AND OPINIONS VOLUME 4 1936-42. WOR-45 CONFER PEACE ATTIT ...DECISION JURID ANTHOL 20 WORLD/CT CASEBOOK. PAGE 59 A1215 — INT/ORG CT/SYS DIPLOM ADJUD

B54
BECKEL G.,WORKSHOPS FOR THE WORLD; THE SPECIALIZED AGENCIES OF THE UN. WOR+45 AGRI DIST/IND CREATE TEC/DEV BUDGET CONTROL TASK WEALTH...CHARTS ORG/CHARTS 20 UN CASEBOOK. PAGE 12 A0246 — INT/ORG DIPLOM PEACE CON/ANAL

B65
US CONGRESS JT ATOM ENRGY COMM,ATOMIC ENERGY LEGISLATION THROUGH 89TH CONGRESS, 1ST SESSION. USA+45 LAW INT/ORG DELIB/GP BUDGET DIPLOM 20 AEC CONGRESS CASEBOOK EURATOM IAEA. PAGE 150 A3071 — NUC/PWR FORCES PEACE LEGIS

B66
GROSS F.,WORLD POLITICS AND TENSION AREAS. CHINA/COM SOMALIA VENEZUELA COERCE GP/REL RACE/REL ATTIT HABITAT 19/20 CASEBOOK NEWYORK/C. PAGE 57 A1173 — DIPLOM WAR PROB/SOLV

B66
NANTWI E.K.,THE ENFORCEMENT OF INTERNATIONAL JUDICIAL DECISIONS AND ARBITAL AWARDS IN PUBLIC INTERNATIONAL LAW. WOR+45 WOR-45 JUDGE PROB/SOLV DIPLOM CT/SYS SUPEGO MORAL PWR RESPECT...METH/CNCPT 18/20 CASEBOOK. PAGE 107 A2196 — INT/LAW ADJUD SOVEREIGN INT/ORG

CASEY R.G. A0505

CASSELL F. A0506

CASTANEDA J. A0507

CASTE....SEE INDIA + STRATA, HINDU

CASTLE E.W. A0508

CASTRO/F....FIDEL CASTRO

B59
NUNEZ JIMENEZ A.,LA LIBERACION DE LAS ISLAS. CUBA L/A+17C USA+45 LAW CHIEF PLAN DIPLOM FOR/AID OWN WEALTH 20 CASTRO/F. PAGE 110 A2261
AGRI REV ECO/UNDEV NAT/G

B62
WILLIAMS W.A.,THE UNITED STATES, CUBA, AND CASTRO: AN ESSAY ON THE DYNAMICS OF REVOLUTION AND THE DISSOLUTION OF EMPIRE. CUBA USA+45 AGRI VOL/ASSN DIPLOM ECO/TAC DOMIN COERCE...POLICY 20 EISNHWR/DD CIA KENNEDY/JF CASTRO/F. PAGE 165 A3354
REV CONSTN COM LEAD

B63
PACHTER H.M.,COLLISION COURSE; THE CUBAN MISSILE CRISIS AND COEXISTENCE. CUBA USA+45 DIPLOM ARMS/CONT PEACE MARXISM...DECISION INT/LAW 20 COLD/WAR KHRUSH/N KENNEDY/JF CASTRO/F. PAGE 112 A2307
WAR BAL/PWR NUC/PWR DETER

B65
MALLIN J.,FORTRESS CUBA; RUSSIA'S AMERICAN BASE. COM CUBA L/A+17C FORCES PLAN DIPLOM LEAD REV WAR ...POLICY 20 CASTRO/F GUEVARA/C INTERVENT. PAGE 93 A1914
MARXISM CHIEF GUERRILLA DOMIN

CATEGORY (AS CONCEPT)....SEE METH/CNCPT

CATH....ROMAN CATHOLIC

B24
GENTILI A.,DE LEGATIONIBUS. CHRIST-17C NAT/G SECT CONSULT LEGIT...POLICY CATH JURID CONCPT MYTH. PAGE 52 A1058
DIPLOM INT/LAW INT/ORG LAW

C44
SUAREZ F.,"ON WAR" (1621) IN SELECTIONS FROM THREE WORKS, VOL. I." NAT/G SECT CHIEF DIPLOM LEGIT MORAL PWR...POLICY INT/LAW 17. PAGE 140 A2859
WAR REV ORD/FREE CATH

B60
VAN HOOGSTRATE D.J.,AMERICAN FOREIGN POLICY: REALISTS AND IDEALISTS: A CATHOLIC INTERPRETATION. BAL/PWR FOR/AID ARMS/CONT GOV/REL PEACE LOVE MORAL SOVEREIGN CATHISM...BIBLIOG 20. PAGE 158 A3213
CATH DIPLOM POLICY IDEA/COMP

S60
O'BRIEN W.,"THE ROLE OF FORCE IN THE INTERNATIONAL JURIDICAL ORDER." WOR+45 NAT/G FORCES DOMIN ADJUD ARMS/CONT DETER NUC/PWR WAR ATTIT PWR...CATH INT/LAW JURID CONCPT TREND STERTYP GEN/LAWS 20. PAGE 110 A2266
INT/ORG COERCE

B62
ALIX C.,LE SAINT-SIEGE ET LES NATIONALISMES EN EUROPE 1870-1960. COM GERMANY IRELAND ITALY SOCIETY SECT TOTALISM RIGID/FLEX MORAL 19/20. PAGE 6 A0122
CATH NAT/LISM ATTIT DIPLOM

C62
DUFFY J.,"PORTUGAL IN AFRICA." PORTUGAL SIER/LEONE INDUS WORKER INT/TRADE WAR CONSERVE...CATH GEOG TREND 16/20. PAGE 39 A0795
BIBLIOG RACE/REL ECO/UNDEV COLONIAL

B64
CEPEDE M.,POPULATION AND FOOD. USA+45 STRUCT ECO/UNDEV FAM PLAN TEC/DEV FOR/AID CONTROL...CATH SOC TREND 19/20. PAGE 25 A0513
FUT GEOG AGRI CENSUS

B66
HORMANN K.,PEACE AND MODERN WAR IN THE JUDGEMENT OF THE CHURCH. INT/ORG FORCES EDU/PROP ATTIT 20. PAGE 67 A1384
PEACE WAR CATH MORAL

B67
POGANY A.H.,POLITICAL SCIENCE AND INTERNATIONAL RELATIONS, BOOKS RECOMMENDED FOR AMERICAN CATHOLIC COLLEGE LIBRARIES. INT/ORG LOC/G NAT/G FORCES BAL/PWR ECO/TAC NUC/PWR...CATH INT/LAW TREATY 20. PAGE 117 A2393
BIBLIOG DIPLOM

CATHISM....ROMAN CATHOLICISM

C32
MARRARO H.R.,"AMERICAN OPINION ON THE UNIFICATION OF ITALY." ITALY MOD/EUR USA-45 FORCES DIPLOM PRESS REV CATHISM...BIOG 19 PRESIDENT. PAGE 95 A1944
BIBLIOG/A NAT/LISM ATTIT ORD/FREE

B40
THE GUIDE TO CATHOLIC LITERATURE, 1888-1940. ALL/VALS...POLICY MYSTIC HUM PHIL/SCI 19/20. PAGE 3 A0051
BIBLIOG/A CATHISM DIPLOM CULTURE

B43
MC DOWELL R.B.,IRISH PUBLIC OPINION, 1750-1800. IRELAND CONSTN VOL/ASSN WORKER ORD/FREE CATHISM CONSERVE...POLICY IDEA/COMP BIBLIOG 18/ PARLIAMENT. PAGE 97 A1992
ATTIT NAT/G DIPLOM REV

B51
BISSAINTHE M.,DICTIONNAIRE DE BIBLIOGRAPHIE HAITIENNE. HAITI ELITES AGRI LEGIS DIPLOM INT/TRADE WRITING ORD/FREE CATHISM...ART/METH GEOG 19/20 NEGRO TREATY. PAGE 15 A0295
BIBLIOG L/A+17C SOCIETY NAT/G

B59
RICE E.A.,THE DIPLOMATIC RELATIONS BETWEEN THE UNITED STATES AND MEXICO 1925-1929. USA-45 NAT/G DOMIN PEACE ORD/FREE CATHISM 20 MEXIC/AMER. PAGE 121 A2472
DIPLOM SECT POLICY

B59
TARDIFF G.,LA LIBERTAD; LA LIBERTAD DE EXPRESION, IDEALES Y REALIDADES AMERICANAS. ISLAM INT/ORG PROB/SOLV PRESS CONFER PARTIC CATHISM...INT/LAW SOC/INTEG UN MID/EAST. PAGE 141 A2889
ORD/FREE ATTIT DIPLOM CONCPT

B60
ENGEL-JANOSI F.,OSTERREICH UND DER VATIKAN (2 VOLS). AUSTRIA VATICAN NAT/LISM PEACE PERSON CATHISM 20. PAGE 42 A0852
DIPLOM ATTIT WAR

B60
VAN HOOGSTRATE D.J.,AMERICAN FOREIGN POLICY: REALISTS AND IDEALISTS: A CATHOLIC INTERPRETATION. BAL/PWR FOR/AID ARMS/CONT GOV/REL PEACE LOVE MORAL SOVEREIGN CATHISM...BIBLIOG 20. PAGE 158 A3213
CATH DIPLOM POLICY IDEA/COMP

B62
BLANSHARD P.,FREEDOM AND CATHOLIC POWER IN SPAIN AND PORTUGAL: AN AMERICAN INTERPRETATION. AFR PORTUGAL SPAIN USA+45 LAW LABOR DIPLOM EDU/PROP DISCRIM ISOLAT TOTALISM 20 CHURCH/STA. PAGE 15 A0309
GP/REL FASCISM CATHISM PWR

B62
GUTTMAN A.,THE WOUND IN THE HEART: AMERICA AND THE SPANISH CIVIL WAR. SPAIN USA-45 POL/PAR LEGIS ECO/TAC CHOOSE ANOMIE ATTIT MARXISM...POLICY ANARCH BIBLIOG 20 ROOSEVLT/F. PAGE 58 A1198
ALL/IDEOS WAR DIPLOM CATHISM

B62
SCHMIDT-VOLKMAR E.,DER KULTURKAMPF IN DEUTSCHLAND 1871-1890. GERMANY PRUSSIA SOCIETY STRUCT SECT DIPLOM GP/REL NAT/LISM 19 CHURCH/STA BISMARCK/O. PAGE 128 A2632
POL/PAR CATHISM ATTIT NAT/G

B63
LOOMIE A.J.,THE SPANISH ELIZABETHANS: THE ENGLISH EXILES AT THE COURT OF PHILIP II. SPAIN UK WAR INGP/REL DRIVE HABITAT CATHISM...BIOG 16/17 MIGRATION. PAGE 91 A1860
NAT/G STRANGE POLICY DIPLOM

B63
RAVENS J.P.,STAAT UND KATHOLISCHE KIRCHE IN PREUSSENS POLNISCHEN TEILUNGSGEBIETEN. GERMANY POLAND PRUSSIA PROVS DIPLOM EDU/PROP DEBATE NAT/LISM...JURID 18 CHURCH/STA. PAGE 119 A2451
GP/REL CATHISM SECT NAT/G

B64
JENSEN D.L.,DIPLOMACY AND DOGMATISM. FRANCE SPAIN REV WAR PERSON CATHISM...POLICY BIOG 16. PAGE 74 A1513
DIPLOM ATTIT SECT

B65
O'CONNELL M.R.,IRISH POLITICS AND SOCIAL CONFLICT IN THE AGE OF THE AMERICAN REVOLUTION. FRANCE IRELAND MOD/EUR STRATA SECT LEGIS DIPLOM INT/TRADE DOMIN REV WAR...BIBLIOG 18 PARLIAMENT. PAGE 111 A2268
CATHISM ATTIT NAT/G DELIB/GP

B66
ENTWICKLUNGSPOLITIK - HANDBUCH UND LEXIKON. MARKET SECT DIPLOM INT/TRADE EDU/PROP CATHISM 20. PAGE 14 A0283
ECO/UNDEV FOR/AID ECO/TAC PLAN

B67
KATZ R.,DEATH IN ROME. EUR+WWI ITALY POL/PAR DIPLOM LEAD ATTIT PERSON ROLE CATHISM. PAGE 77 A1570
WAR MURDER FORCES DEATH

B67
PIKE F.B.,FREEDOM AND REFORM IN LATIN AMERICA. BRAZIL URUGUAY CONSTN CULTURE SECT DIPLOM EDU/PROP PARTIC DRIVE ALL/VALS CATHISM...GEOG ANTHOL BIBLIOG REFORMERS BOLIV. PAGE 116 A2379
L/A+17C ORD/FREE ECO/UNDEV REV

CATHOLICISM....SEE CATH, CATHISM

CAUCUS....SEE PARL/PROC

CBS A0509

CECIL L. A0510

CED....COMMITTEE FOR ECONOMIC DEVELOPMENT

CENSORSHIP....SEE EDU/PROP

CENSUS....POPULATION ENUMERATION

N19
HAUSER P.M.,WORLD POPULATION PROBLEMS (PAMPHLET). USA+45 WOR+45 ECO/DEV ECO/UNDEV FAM ACT/RES PLAN PROB/SOLV FOR/AID GIVE EATING...CHARTS 20 BIRTH/CON RESOURCE/N. PAGE 63 A1289
CONTROL CENSUS ATTIT PREDICT

N19
NATIONAL ACADEMY OF SCIENCES,THE GROWTH OF WORLD POPULATION: ANALYSIS OF THE PROBLEMS AND
CENSUS PLAN

RECOMMENDATIONS FOR RESEARCH AND TRAINING (PAMPHLET). WOR+45 CULTURE ECO/UNDEV EDU/PROP MARRIAGE AGE HEALTH...ANTHOL 20 BIRTH/CON. PAGE 107 A2199 — FAM INT/ORG

B44
DAVIS H.E.,PIONEERS IN WORLD ORDER. WOR-45 CONSTN ECO/TAC DOMIN EDU/PROP LEGIT ADJUD ADMIN ARMS/CONT CHOOSE KNOWL ORD/FREE...POLICY JURID SOC STAT OBS CENSUS TIME/SEQ ANTHOL LEAGUE/NAT 20. PAGE 34 A0691 — INT/ORG ROUTINE

B46
GAULD W.A.,MAN, NATURE, AND TIME, AN INTRODUCTION TO WORLD STUDY. WOR-45 CULTURE CREATE DIPLOM GP/REL DRIVE...SOC LING CENSUS CHARTS TIME 18/20. PAGE 52 A1054 — HABITAT PERSON

B48
KULISCHER E.M.,EUROPE ON THE MOVE: WAR AND POPULATION CHANGES, 1917-1947. COM EUR+WWI FUT GERMANY USSR DIST/IND PLAN INT/TRADE CONTROL WAR DRIVE...CENSUS TREND COLD/WAR 20. PAGE 82 A1690 — ECO/TAC GEOG

B57
DRUCKER P.F.,AMERICA'S NEXT TWENTY YEARS. USA+45 DIST/IND ACADEM MUNIC SCHOOL DIPLOM ECO/TAC AUTOMAT HABITAT HEALTH...SOC/WK TREND 20 URBAN/RNWL PUB/TRANS. PAGE 39 A0788 — WORKER FOR/AID CENSUS GEOG

B58
WIGGINS J.W.,FOREIGN AID REEXAMINED: A CRITICAL APPRAISAL. CHINA/COM INDONESIA USA+45 FINAN INT/TRADE REGION NAT/LISM ATTIT...CENSUS 20. PAGE 164 A3342 — FOR/AID DIPLOM ECO/UNDEV SOVEREIGN

L58
TRAGER F.N.,"A SELECTED AND ANNOTATED BIBLIOGRAPHY ON ECONOMIC DEVELOPMENT, 1953-1957." WOR+45 AGRI FINAN INDUS MARKET LABOR MUNIC WORKER PLAN INT/TRADE PRODUC CENSUS. PAGE 145 A2958 — BIBLIOG/A ECO/UNDEV ECO/DEV

B60
ASPREMONT-LYNDEN H.,RAPPORT SUR L'ADMINISTRATION BELGE DU RUANDA-URUNDI PENDANT L'ANNEE 1959. BELGIUM RWANDA AGRI INDUS DIPLOM ECO/TAC INT/TRADE DOMIN ADMIN RACE/REL...GEOG CENSUS 20 UN. PAGE 9 A0192 — AFR COLONIAL ECO/UNDEV INT/ORG

B60
LE GHAIT E.,NO CARTE BLANCHE TO CAPRICORN; THE FOLLY OF NUCLEAR WAR. WOR+45 INT/ORG BAL/PWR DIPLOM RISK COERCE...CENSUS 20 NATO. PAGE 86 A1754 — DETER NUC/PWR PLAN DECISION

B60
MC CLELLAN G.S.,INDIA. CHINA/COM INDIA CONSTN ELITES STRATA AGRI POL/PAR FOR/AID ARMS/CONT REV MARXISM...CENSUS BIBLIOG 20 COLD/WAR GANDHI/M NEHRU/J. PAGE 97 A1990 — DIPLOM NAT/G SOCIETY ECO/UNDEV

B60
THE ECONOMIST (LONDON),THE COMMONWEALTH AND EUROPE. EUR+WWI WOR+45 AGRI FINAN INCOME...STAT CENSUS CHARTS CMN/WLTH EEC. PAGE 142 A2911 — INT/TRADE INDUS INT/ORG NAT/COMP

B60
VOGT W.,PEOPLE: CHALLENGE TO SURVIVAL. WOR+45 ECO/DEV ECO/UNDEV FAM INT/ORG NAT/G PLAN PROB/SOLV FOR/AID GIVE EATING 20 BIRTH/CON. PAGE 159 A3247 — CENSUS CONTROL ATTIT TEC/DEV

B61
SCHNAPPER B.,LA POLITIQUE ET LE COMMERCE FRANCAIS DANS LE GOLFE DE GUINEE DE 1838 A 1871. FRANCE GUINEA UK SEA EXTR/IND NAT/G DELIB/GP LEGIS ADMIN ORD/FREE...POLICY GEOG CENSUS CHARTS BIBLIOG 19. PAGE 129 A2636 — COLONIAL INT/TRADE DOMIN AFR

B62
CALDER R.,COMMON SENSE ABOUT A STARVING WORLD. WOR+45 STRATA ECO/DEV PLAN GP/REL BIO/SOC HABITAT ...POLICY GEOG STAT RECORD 20 UN BIRTH/CON. PAGE 23 A0466 — FOR/AID CENSUS ECO/UNDEV AGRI

B62
JORDAN A.A. JR.,FOREIGN AID AND THE DEFENSE OF SOUTHEAST ASIA. PAKISTAN VIETNAM/S FINAN PLAN BUDGET ECO/TAC DETER WAR ORD/FREE...POLICY DECISION CENSUS CHARTS BIBLIOG 20. PAGE 75 A1535 — FOR/AID S/ASIA FORCES ECO/UNDEV

B62
ROY P.A.,SOUTH WIND RED. L/A+17C USA+45 ECO/UNDEV NAT/G CAP/ISM MARXISM SOCISM...OLD/LIB GEOG RECORD INT CENSUS 20 COLD/WAR. PAGE 125 A2554 — DIPLOM INDUS POLICY ECO/TAC

B63
GREAT BRITAIN CENTRAL OFF INF,CONSULTATION AND CO-OPERATION IN THE COMMONWEALTH. LAW R+D FORCES PLAN EDU/PROP CONFER INGP/REL...GEOG CENSUS 19/20 CMN/WLTH. PAGE 55 A1133 — DIPLOM DELIB/GP VOL/ASSN REGION

B64
CEPEDE M.,POPULATION AND FOOD. USA+45 STRUCT ECO/UNDEV FAM PLAN TEC/DEV FOR/AID CONTROL...CATH SOC TREND 19/20. PAGE 25 A0513 — FUT GEOG AGRI CENSUS

B64
JANOWITZ M.,THE MILITARY IN THE POLITICAL DEVELOPMENT OF NEW NATIONS: AN ESSAY IN COMPARATIVE ANALYSIS. AFR ASIA ISLAM L/A+17C S/ASIA USA+45 ECO/UNDEV INT/ORG NAT/G POL/PAR DELIB/GP PLAN ECO/TAC DOMIN LEGIT COERCE ATTIT DRIVE RESPECT ...SOC CONCPT CENSUS VAL/FREE. PAGE 73 A1495 — FORCES PWR

B64
WRIGHT Q.,A STUDY OF WAR. LAW NAT/G PROB/SOLV BAL/PWR NAT/LISM PEACE ATTIT SOVEREIGN...CENSUS SOC/INTEG. PAGE 168 A3419 — WAR CONCPT DIPLOM CONTROL

B65
WHITE HOUSE CONFERENCE ON INTERNATIONAL COOPERATION(VOL.II). SPACE WOR+45 EXTR/IND INT/ORG LABOR WORKER NUC/PWR PEACE AGE/Y...CENSUS ANTHOL 20 RESOURCE/N URBAN/RNWL PUB/TRANS. PAGE 3 A0071 — R+D CONFER TEC/DEV DIPLOM

B65
AMERICAN ECONOMIC ASSOCIATION,INDEX OF ECONOMIC JOURNALS 1886-1965 (7 VOLS.). UK USA+45 USA-45 AGRI FINAN PLAN ECO/TAC INT/TRADE ADMIN...STAT CENSUS 19/20. PAGE 7 A0145 — BIBLIOG WRITING INDUS

B65
FRIEDMANN W.,AN INTRODUCTION TO WORLD POLITICS (5TH ED.). WOR+45 ECO/UNDEV BAL/PWR FOR/AID INT/TRADE PEACE...STAT CENSUS CHARTS BIBLIOG T 20 COLD/WAR UN THIRD/WRLD. PAGE 49 A1003 — DIPLOM INT/ORG PROB/SOLV

B65
WINT G.,ASIA: A HANDBOOK. ASIA COM INDIA USSR CULTURE INTELL NAT/G...GEOG STAT CENSUS NAT/COMP WORSHIP 20 TREATY CHINJAP. PAGE 165 A3365 — DIPLOM SOC

B66
THOMPSON J.H.,MODERNIZATION OF THE ARAB WORLD. FUT ISRAEL STRUCT ECO/UNDEV DIPLOM INGP/REL ATTIT ...CENSUS ANTHOL 20 ARABS. PAGE 143 A2926 — ADJUST ISLAM PROB/SOLV NAT/COMP

B66
UN ECAFE,ADMINISTRATIVE ASPECTS OF FAMILY PLANNING PROGRAMMES (PAMPHLET). ASIA THAILAND WOR+45 VOL/ASSN PROB/SOLV BUDGET FOR/AID EDU/PROP CONFER CONTROL GOV/REL TIME 20 UN BIRTH/CON. PAGE 147 A2999 — PLAN CENSUS FAM ADMIN

B66
US SENATE COMM GOVT OPERATIONS,POPULATION CRISIS. USA+45 ECO/DEV ECO/UNDEV AGRI SECT DELIB/GP PROB/SOLV FOR/AID REPRESENT ATTIT...GEOG CHARTS 20 CONGRESS DEPT/STATE DEPT/HEW BIRTH/CON. PAGE 156 A3178 — CENSUS CONTROL LEGIS CONSULT

S67
KRISTENSEN T.,"THE SOUTH AS AN INDUSTRIAL POWER." FUT WOR+45 ECO/DEV AGRI INDUS TEC/DEV...CENSUS TREND CHARTS 20. PAGE 82 A1686 — DIPLOM ECO/UNDEV PREDICT PRODUC

B86
MAS LATRIE L.,RELATIONS ET COMMERCE DE L'AFRIQUE SEPTENTRIONALE OU MAGREB AVEC LES NATIONS CHRETIENNES AU MOYEN AGE. CULTURE CHIEF FORCES WAR ...SOC CENSUS TREATY 10/16. PAGE 95 A1954 — ISLAM SECT DIPLOM INT/TRADE

CENTER/PAR....CENTER PARTY (ALL NATIONS)

CENTO....CENTRAL TREATY ORGANIZATION

S61
BURNET A.,"TOO MANY ALLIES." COM EUR+WWI UK WOR+45 WOR-45 ACT/RES PLAN DISPL PWR SKILL...TIME/SEQ 20 CMN/WLTH SEATO NATO CENTO. PAGE 22 A0438 — VOL/ASSN INT/ORG DIPLOM

CENTRAL AFRICAN REPUBLIC....SEE CENTRL/AFR

CENTRAL INTELLIGENCE AGENCY....SEE CIA

CENTRAL TREATY ORGANIZATION....SEE CENTO

CENTRAL....CENTRALIZATION

N
MONPIED E.,BIBLIOGRAPHIE FEDERALISTE: ARTICLES ET DOCUMENTS PUBLIES DANS LES PERIODIQUES PARUS EN FRANCE NOV. 1945-OCT. 1950. EUR+WWI WOR+45 ADMIN REGION ATTIT MARXISM PACIFISM 20 EEC. PAGE 103 A2108 — BIBLIOG/A FEDERAL CENTRAL INT/ORG

B15
HOBSON J.A.,TOWARDS INTERNATIONAL GOVERNMENT. MOD/EUR STRUCT ECO/TAC EDU/PROP ADJUD ALL/VALS ...SOCIALIST CONCPT GEN/LAWS TOT/POP 20. PAGE 65 A1347 — FUT INT/ORG CENTRAL

N19
FANI-KAYODE R.,BLACKISM (PAMPHLET). AFR WOR+45 INT/ORG BAL/PWR CONTROL CENTRAL...DECISION 20 UN. PAGE 44 A0896 — RACE/REL ECO/UNDEV REGION DIPLOM

B36
HARVARD BUREAU ECO RES LAT AM,THE ECONOMIC LITERATURE OF LATIN AMERICA: A TENTATIVE BIBLIOGRAPHY. NAT/G TARIFFS CENTRAL COST DEMAND 20. PAGE 62 A1277 — BIBLIOG ECO/UNDEV L/A+17C INT/TRADE

C39
REISCHAUER R.,"JAPAN'S GOVERNMENT--POLITICS." — NAT/G

CONSTN STRATA POL/PAR FORCES LEGIS DIPLOM ADMIN EXEC CENTRAL...POLICY BIBLIOG 20 CHINJAP. PAGE 120 A2462
S/ASIA CONCPT ROUTINE

C40
NORMAN E.H.,"JAPAN'S EMERGENCE AS A MODERN STATE: POLITICAL AND ECONOMIC PROBLEMS OF THE MEIJI PERIOD." CONSTN STRATA AGRI INDUS POL/PAR TEC/DEV CAP/ISM CIVMIL/REL...BIBLIOG 19/20 CHINJAP. PAGE 110 A2250
CENTRAL DIPLOM POLICY NAT/LISM

B45
ROGERS W.C.,INTERNATIONAL ADMINISTRATION: A BIBLIOGRAPHY (PUBLICATION NO 92; A PAMPHLET). WOR-45 INT/ORG LOC/G NAT/G CENTRAL 20. PAGE 123 A2514
BIBLIOG/A ADMIN MGT DIPLOM

B50
DULLES J.F.,WAR OR PEACE. CHINA/COM USA+45 USSR INT/ORG SECT FORCES PLAN NUC/PWR WAR CENTRAL MARXISM...POLICY 20 UN ROOSEVLT/F STALIN/J. PAGE 39 A0797
PEACE DIPLOM TREND ORD/FREE

B50
MONPIED E.,BIBLIOGRAPHIE FEDERALISTE: OUVRAGES CHOISIS (VOL. I, MIMEOGRAPHED PAPER). EUR+WWI DIPLOM ADMIN REGION ATTIT PACIFISM SOCISM...INT/LAW 19/20. PAGE 103 A2109
BIBLIOG/A FEDERAL CENTRAL INT/ORG

N51
MONPIED E.,FEDERALIST BIBLIOGRAPHY: ARTICLES AND DOCUMENTS PUBLISHED IN BRITISH PERIODICALS 1945-1951 (MIMEOGRAPHED). EUR+WWI UK WOR+45 DIPLOM REGION ATTIT SOCISM...INT/LAW 20. PAGE 103 A2110
BIBLIOG/A INT/ORG FEDERAL CENTRAL

B55
HOGAN W.N.,INTERNATIONAL CONFLICT AND COLLECTIVE SECURITY: THE PRINCIPLE OF CONCERN IN INTERNATIONAL ORGANIZATION. CONSTN EX/STRUC BAL/PWR DIPLOM ADJUD CONTROL CENTRAL CONSEN PEACE...INT/LAW CONCPT METH/COMP 20 UN LEAGUE/NAT. PAGE 66 A1361
INT/ORG WAR ORD/FREE FORCES

B60
AMERICAN ASSEMBLY COLUMBIA U,THE SECRETARY OF STATE. USA+45 ELITES NAT/G PLAN ADMIN GOV/REL CENTRAL ATTIT...POLICY MGT 20 SEC/STATE CONGRESS PRESIDENT. PAGE 7 A0136
DELIB/GP EX/STRUC GP/REL DIPLOM

B60
ROPKE W.,A HUMANE ECONOMY. CULTURE ECO/DEV FINAN INDUS GP/REL CENTRAL WEALTH...GEOG SOC IDEA/COMP 20 EEC. PAGE 123 A2525
ECO/TAC INT/ORG DIPLOM ORD/FREE

B61
COLLISON R.L.,BIBLIOGRAPHICAL SERVICES THROUGHOUT THE WORLD: 1950-59 (VOL. 9). WOR+45 INT/ORG EDU/PROP PRESS WRITING ADMIN CENTRAL 20 UNESCO. PAGE 28 A0568
BIBLIOG COM/IND DIPLOM

B62
EVANS M.S.,THE FRINGE ON TOP. USSR EX/STRUC FORCES DIPLOM ECO/TAC PEACE CONSERVE SOCISM...TREND 20 KENNEDY/JF. PAGE 43 A0877
NAT/G PWR CENTRAL POLICY

B64
GJUPANOVIC H.,LEGAL SOURCES AND BIBLIOGRAPHY OF YUGOSLAVIA. COM YUGOSLAVIA LAW LEGIS DIPLOM ADMIN PARL/PROC REGION CRIME CENTRAL 20. PAGE 53 A1078
BIBLIOG/A JURID CONSTN ADJUD

B64
LISKA G.,EUROPE ASCENDANT. EUR+WWI ECO/DEV FORCES INT/TRADE MARXISM 20 EEC. PAGE 90 A1838
DIPLOM BAL/PWR TARIFFS CENTRAL

S64
BARKUN M.,"CONFLICT RESOLUTION THROUGH IMPLICIT MEDIATION." UNIV BARGAIN CONSEN FEDERAL JURID. PAGE 11 A0222
CONSULT CENTRAL INT/LAW IDEA/COMP

C65
SCHEINGOLD S.A.,"THE RULE OF LAW IN EUROPEAN INTEGRATION: THE PATH OF THE SCHUMAN PLAN." EUR+WWI JUDGE ADJUD FEDERAL ATTIT PWR...RECORD INT BIBLIOG EEC ECSC. PAGE 128 A2621
INT/LAW CT/SYS REGION CENTRAL

B66
LONDON K.,EASTERN EUROPE IN TRANSITION. CHINA/COM USSR DOMIN COLONIAL CENTRAL RIGID/FLEX PWR...SOC ANTHOL 20. PAGE 91 A1855
SOVEREIGN COM NAT/LISM DIPLOM

B67
ZUCKERMAN S.,SCIENTISTS AND WAR. ELITES INDUS DIPLOM CENTRAL EFFICIENCY KNOWL 20. PAGE 170 A3459
R+D CONSULT ACT/RES GP/REL

S67
DAVIS H.B.,"LENIN AND NATIONALISM: THE REDIRECTION OF THE MARXIST THEORY OF NATIONALISM." COM MOD/EUR USSR STRATA INT/ORG PLAN DOMIN COLONIAL FEDERAL ...TREND 20. PAGE 34 A0690
NAT/LISM MARXISM ATTIT CENTRAL

S67
NEUCHTERLEIN D.E.,"THAILAND* ANOTHER VIETNAM?" THAILAND ECO/UNDEV DIPLOM ADMIN REGION CENTRAL NAT/LISM...POLICY 20. PAGE 108 A2220
WAR GUERRILLA S/ASIA NAT/G

S67
SAPP B.B.,"TRIBAL CULTURES AND COMMUNISM." AFR USA+45 STRATA DIPLOM FOR/AID REGION CENTRAL ATTIT AUTHORIT RIGID/FLEX KNOWL. PAGE 127 A2604
KIN MARXISM ECO/UNDEV STRUCT

S67
WEIL G.L.,"THE MERGER OF THE INSTITUTIONS OF THE EUROPEAN COMMUNITIES" EUR+WWI ECO/DEV INT/TRADE CONSEN PLURISM...DECISION MGT 20 EEC EURATOM ECSC TREATY. PAGE 162 A3300
ECO/TAC INT/ORG CENTRAL INT/LAW

S67
WEIL G.L.,"THE EUROPEAN COMMUNITY* WHAT LIES BEYOND THE POINT OF NO RETURN?" VOL/ASSN PROB/SOLV DIPLOM REGION INGP/REL CENTRAL PWR 20 EEC. PAGE 162 A3301
INT/ORG ECO/DEV INT/TRADE PREDICT

S67
ZARTMAN I.W.,"AFRICA AS A SUBORDINATE STATE SYSTEM IN INTERNATIONAL RELATIONS." LAW BAL/PWR REGION CENTRAL...GEOG 20. PAGE 169 A3447
DIPLOM INT/ORG CONSTN AFR

CENTRAL ASIAN RESEARCH CENTRE A0511

CENTRAL/AM....CENTRAL AMERICA

CENTRL/AFR....CENTRAL AFRICAN REPUBLIC

B54
COOKSON J.,BEFORE THE AFRICAN STORM. BELGIUM CENTRL/AFR FRANCE UK ECO/UNDEV POL/PAR CREATE BAL/PWR RACE/REL NAT/LISM ORD/FREE CONSERVE MARXISM SOC/INTEG 20 CONGO/LEOP. PAGE 30 A0607
COLONIAL REV DISCRIM DIPLOM

CENTRO PARA EL DESARROLLO A0512

CEPEDE M. A0513

CERAMI C.A. A0514

CERMAK/AJ....ANTON J. CERMAK

CEWA....CEWA (AFRICAN TRIBE)

CEYLON....CEYLON

B51
JENNINGS I.,THE COMMONWEALTH IN ASIA. CEYLON INDIA PAKISTAN CULTURE STRATA NAT/G LEGIS DIPLOM COLONIAL ATTIT...DECISION 20 CMN/WLTH. PAGE 74 A1507
CONSTN INT/ORG POLICY PLAN

B51
JENNINGS S.I.,THE COMMONWEALTH IN ASIA. CEYLON INDIA PAKISTAN S/ASIA UK CONSTN CULTURE SOCIETY STRATA STRUCT NAT/G POL/PAR EDU/PROP LEAD WAR 20 CMN/WLTH. PAGE 74 A1510
NAT/LISM REGION COLONIAL DIPLOM

B57
WILSON P.,SOUTH ASIA; A SELECTED BIBLIOGRAPHY ON INDIA, PAKISTAN, CEYLON (PAMPHLET). CEYLON INDIA PAKISTAN LAW ECO/UNDEV PLAN DIPLOM 20. PAGE 165 A3362
BIBLIOG S/ASIA CULTURE NAT/G

B58
JENNINGS I.,PROBLEMS OF THE NEW COMMONWEALTH. CEYLON INDIA PAKISTAN S/ASIA ECO/UNDEV INT/ORG LOC/G DIPLOM ECO/TAC INT/TRADE COLONIAL RACE/REL DISCRIM 20 COMMONWLTH PARLIAMENT. PAGE 74 A1508
NAT/LISM NEUTRAL FOR/AID POL/PAR

B58
JENNINGS W.I.,PROBLEMS OF THE NEW COMMONWEALTH. CEYLON INDIA MALAYSIA PAKISTAN ECO/UNDEV VOL/ASSN RACE/REL NAT/LISM ROLE 20 CMN/WLTH. PAGE 74 A1511
GP/REL INGP/REL COLONIAL INT/ORG

B60
JEFFRIES C.,TRANSFER OF POWER: PROBLEMS OF THE PASSAGE TO SELFGOVERNMENT. CEYLON GHANA MALAYSIA NIGERIA UK INT/ORG CONSULT DELIB/GP LEGIS DIPLOM CONFER PARL/PROC 20. PAGE 73 A1502
SOVEREIGN COLONIAL ORD/FREE NAT/G

B60
SALETORE B.A.,INDIA'S DIPLOMATIC RELATIONS WITH THE EAST. ASIA CEYLON INDIA NEPAL S/ASIA CULTURE 7/14 PERSIA. PAGE 126 A2591
DIPLOM NAT/COMP ETIQUET

B60
WOLF C.,FOREIGN AID: THEORY AND PRACTICE IN SOUTHERN ASIA. CEYLON INDONESIA PHILIPPINE S/ASIA CULTURE STRATA ECO/UNDEV PLAN EDU/PROP ATTIT ...METH/CNCPT MATH QUANT STAT CONT/OBS TIME/SEQ SIMUL TOT/POP 20. PAGE 166 A3378
ACT/RES ECO/TAC FOR/AID

C60
WRIGGINS W.H.,"CEYLON: DILEMMAS OF A NEW NATION." ASIA CEYLON CONSTN STRUCT POL/PAR SECT FORCES DIPLOM GOV/REL NAT/LISM...CHARTS BIBLIOG 20. PAGE 167 A3399
PROB/SOLV NAT/G ECO/UNDEV

B61
SYATAUW J.J.G.,SOME NEWLY ESTABLISHED ASIAN STATES AND THE DEVELOPMENT OF INTERNATIONAL LAW. BURMA CEYLON INDIA INDONESIA ECO/UNDEV COLONIAL NEUTRAL WAR PEACE SOVEREIGN...CHARTS 19/20. PAGE 140 A2873
INT/LAW ADJUST SOCIETY S/ASIA

B64
RAGHAVAN M.D.,INDIA IN CEYLONESE HISTORY, SOCIETY AND CULTURE. CEYLON INDIA S/ASIA LAW SOCIETY INT/TRADE ATTIT...ART/METH JURID SOC LING 20. PAGE 119 A2433
DIPLOM CULTURE SECT STRUCT

CHACO/WAR....CHACO WAR

B66
GARNER W.R.,THE CHACO DISPUTE; A STUDY OF PRESTIGE DIPLOMACY. L/A+17C PARAGUAY USA-45 INT/ORG AGREE PEACE...TIME/SEQ 20 BOLIV LEAGUE/NAT ARGEN CHACO/WAR. PAGE 51 A1050
WAR DIPLOM CONCPT PWR

CHAD....SEE ALSO AFR

B64
WITHERELL J.W.,OFFICIAL PUBLICATIONS OF FRENCH EQUATORIAL AFRICA, FRENCH CAMEROONS, AND TOGO, 1946-1958 (PAMPHLET). CAMEROON CHAD FRANCE GABON TOGO LAW ECO/UNDEV EXTR/IND INT/TRADE...GEOG HEAL 20. PAGE 165 A3370
BIBLIOG/A AFR NAT/G ADMIN

CHAKRAVARTI P.C. A0515

CHALLENER R.D. A2982

CHALUPA V. A0516

CHAMBERLAIN L.H. A0517

CHAMBERS/J....JORDAN CHAMBERS

CHAMBR/DEP....CHAMBER OF DEPUTIES (FRANCE)

CHAMBRLN/J....JOSEPH CHAMBERLAIN

B27
BRANDENBURG E.,FROM BISMARCK TO THE WORLD WAR; A HISTORY OF GERMAN FOREIGN POLICY, 1870-1914 (TRANS. BY ANNIE ELIZABETH ADAMS). GERMANY MOD/EUR FORCES AGREE PWR 19/20 TREATY CHAMBRLN/J WWI BISMARCK/O. PAGE 18 A0368
DIPLOM POLICY WAR

CHAMBRLN/N....NEVILLE CHAMBERLAIN

B65
LOEWENHEIM F.L.,PEACE OR APPEASEMENT? HITLER, CHAMBERLAIN AND THE MUNICH CRISIS. MUNIC DELIB/GP WAR TOTALISM ATTIT SOVEREIGN...TIME/SEQ ANTHOL BIBLIOG 20 HITLER/A CHAMBRLN/N. PAGE 90 A1851
DIPLOM LEAD PEACE

CHAND A. A0518

CHANDLER E.H.S. A0519

CHANG C.J. A0520

CHANG H. A0521

CHANGE (AS GOAL)....SEE ORD/FREE

CHANGE (AS INNOVATION)....SEE CREATE

CHANGE (SOCIAL MOBILITY)....SEE GEOG, STRATA

CHARACTER....SEE PERSON

CHARISMA....CHARISMA

CHARLES/I....CHARLES I OF ENGLAND

CHARLESWORTH J.C. A0522

CHARLETON W.G. A0523

CHARTISM....CHARTISM

CHARTS....GRAPHS, CHARTS, DIAGRAMS, MAPS

CHASE E.P. A0524

CHASE/S....STUART CHASE

CHATEAUB/F....VICOMTE FRANCOIS RENE DE CHATEAUBRIAND

CHATTANOOG....CHATTANOOGA, TENNESSEE

CHECKS AND BALANCES SYSTEM....SEE BAL/PWR

CHEEVER D.S. A0525

CHEN/YUN....CH'EN YUN

CHENERY H.B. A0526

CHENG C. A0527

CHIANG....CHIANG KAI-SHEK

CHICAGO....CHICAGO, ILLINOIS

CHIDZERO B.T.G. A0528

CHIEF....PRESIDENT, MONARCH, PRESIDENCY, PREMIER, CHIEF OFFICER OF ANY GOVERNMENT

N
LA DOCUMENTATION FRANCAISE,CHRONOLOGIE INTERNATIONAL. FRANCE WOR+45 CHIEF PROB/SOLV BAL/PWR CONFER LEAD...POLICY CON/ANAL 20. PAGE 83 A1705
BIBLIOG/A DIPLOM TIME/SEQ

B02
MOREL E.D.,AFFAIRS OF WEST AFRICA. UK FINAN INDUS FAM KIN SECT CHIEF WORKER DIPLOM RACE/REL LITERACY HEALTH...CHARTS 18/20 AFRICA/W NEGRO. PAGE 104 A2129
COLONIAL ADMIN AFR

B14
HASSE A.R.,INDEX TO UNITED STATES DOCUMENTS RELATING TO FOREIGN AFFAIRS, 1828-1861 (3 VOLS.). USA-45 CHIEF 19 CONGRESS. PAGE 63 A1285
INDEX DIPLOM LEGIS

B17
DE VICTORIA F.,DE INDIS ET DE JURE BELLI (1557) IN F. DE VICTORIA, DE INDIS ET DE JURE BELLI REFLECTIONES. UNIV NAT/G SECT CHIEF PARTIC COERCE PEACE MORAL...POLICY 16 INDIAN/AM CHRISTIAN CONSCN/OBJ. PAGE 35 A0715
WAR INT/LAW OWN

B17
MEYER H.H.B.,THE UNITED STATES AT WAR, ORGANIZATIONS AND LITERATURE. USA-45 AGRI FINAN INDUS CHIEF FORCES DIPLOM FOR/AID INT/TRADE...SOC 20 PRESIDENT. PAGE 100 A2050
BIBLIOG/A WAR NAT/G VOL/ASSN

N17
BURKE E.,THOUGHTS ON THE PROSPECT OF A REGICIDE PEACE (PAMPHLET). FRANCE UK SECT DOMIN MURDER PEACE ORD/FREE SOVEREIGN POPULISM...POLICY GOV/COMP IDEA/COMP 18 JACOBINISM COEXIST. PAGE 21 A0435
REV CHIEF NAT/G DIPLOM

B19
ROUSSEAU J.J.,A LASTING PEACE. INT/ORG NAT/G CHIEF DIPLOM DETER WAR POLICY. PAGE 124 A2550
PLAN PEACE UTIL

B19
SUTHERLAND G.,CONSTITUTIONAL POWER AND WORLD AFFAIRS. CONSTN STRUCT INT/ORG NAT/G CHIEF LEGIS ACT/RES PLAN GOV/REL ALL/VALS...OBS TIME/SEQ CONGRESS VAL/FREE 20 PRESIDENT. PAGE 140 A2866
USA-45 EXEC DIPLOM

N19
GRANT N.,COMMUNIST PSYCHOLOGICAL OFFENSIVE: DISTORTION IN THE TRANSLATION OF OFFICIAL DOCUMENTS (PAMPHLET). USSR POL/PAR CHIEF FOR/AID PRESS WRITING COLONIAL LEAD WAR PEACE 20 KHRUSH/N. PAGE 55 A1129
MARXISM DIPLOM EDU/PROP

N19
MEZERIK A.G.,U-2 AND OPEN SKIES (PAMPHLET). USA+45 USSR INT/ORG CHIEF FORCES PLAN EDU/PROP CONTROL SANCTION ARMS/CONT 20 UN EISNHWR/DD. PAGE 100 A2060
DIPLOM RISK DEBATE

B29
LANGER W.L.,THE FRANCO-RUSSIAN ALLIANCE: 1890-1894. FRANCE MOD/EUR UK USSR NAT/G CHIEF FORCES BAL/PWR AGREE WAR PEACE PWR...TIME/SEQ TREATY 19 BISMARCK/O. PAGE 84 A1724
DIPLOM

B35
MARRIOTT J.A.,DICTATORSHIP AND DEMOCRACY. GERMANY GREECE UK CHIEF DIPLOM DOMIN LEGIT PEACE ORD/FREE CONSERVE...TREND ROME HITLER/A. PAGE 95 A1946
TOTALISM POPULISM PLURIST NAT/G

B38
GRISWOLD A.W.,THE FAR EASTERN POLICY OF THE UNITED STATES. ASIA S/ASIA USA-45 INT/ORG INT/TRADE WAR NAT/LISM...BIBLIOG 19/20 LEAGUE/NAT ROOSEVLT/T ROOSEVLT/F WILSON/W TREATY. PAGE 57 A1166
DIPLOM POLICY CHIEF

B38
SAINT-PIERRE C.I.,SCHEME FOR LASTING PEACE (TRANS. BY H. BELLOT). INDUS NAT/G CHIEF FORCES INT/TRADE CT/SYS WAR PWR SOVEREIGN WEALTH...POLICY 18. PAGE 126 A2587
INT/ORG PEACE AGREE INT/LAW

B39
KOHN H.,REVOLUTIONS AND DICTATORSHIPS. COM EUR+WWI ISLAM MOD/EUR NAT/G CHIEF FORCES WAR CIVMIL/REL PWR MARXISM 18/20. PAGE 81 A1661
NAT/LISM TOTALISM REV FASCISM

B41
BIRDSALL P.,VERSAILLES TWENTY YEARS AFTER. MOD/EUR POL/PAR CHIEF CONSULT FORCES LEGIS REPAR PEACE ORD/FREE...BIBLIOG 20 PRESIDENT TREATY. PAGE 14 A0290
DIPLOM NAT/LISM WAR

B44
RUDIN H.R.,ARMISTICE 1918. FRANCE GERMANY MOD/EUR UK USA-45 NAT/G CHIEF DELIB/GP FORCES BAL/PWR REPAR ARMS/CONT 20 WILSON/W TREATY. PAGE 125 A2566
AGREE WAR PEACE DIPLOM

L44
WRIGHT Q.,"THE US AND INTERNATIONAL AGREEMENTS." FUT USA-45 CONSTN INTELL INT/ORG LOC/G NAT/G CHIEF CONSULT EX/STRUC DIPLOM LEGIT DRIVE PERCEPT PWR ...CONCPT CONGRESS 20. PAGE 167 A3407
DELIB/GP TOP/EX PEACE

C44
SUAREZ F.,"ON WAR" (1621) IN SELECTIONS FROM THREE WORKS, VOL. I." NAT/G SECT CHIEF DIPLOM LEGIT MORAL PWR...POLICY INT/LAW 17. PAGE 140 A2859
WAR REV ORD/FREE CATH

B48
BELOFF M.,THOMAS JEFFERSON AND AMERICAN DEMOCRACY. USA-45 NAT/G DIPLOM GOV/REL PEACE 18/19 JEFFERSN/T PRESIDENT VIRGINIA. PAGE 13 A0258
BIOG CHIEF REV

L49
HEINDEL R.H.,"THE NORTH ATLANTIC TREATY IN THE UNITED STATES SENATE." CONSTN POL/PAR CHIEF DEBATE LEAD ROUTINE WAR PEACE...CHARTS UN SENATE NATO. PAGE 64 A1309
DECISION PARL/PROC LEGIS INT/ORG

B50
GUERRANT E.O.,ROOSEVELT'S GOOD NEIGHBOR POLICY. L/A+17C USA+45 USA-45 FOR/AID...IDEA/COMP 20 ROOSEVLT/F TRUMAN/HS. PAGE 58 A1187
DIPLOM NAT/G CHIEF POLICY

B52
FIFIELD R.H.,WOODROW WILSON AND THE FAR EAST. ASIA CHIEF BAL/PWR CONFER COLONIAL ARMS/CONT WAR ...TIME/SEQ NAT/COMP BIBLIOG 19/20 WILSON/W LEAGUE/NAT PRESIDENT. PAGE 45 A0926
DIPLOM DELIB/GP INT/ORG

L52
WRIGHT Q.,"CONGRESS AND THE TREATY-MAKING POWER." USA+45 WOR+45 CONSTN INTELL NAT/G CHIEF CONSULT EX/STRUC LEGIS TOP/EX CREATE GOV/REL DISPL DRIVE RIGID/FLEX...TREND TOT/POP CONGRESS CONGRESS 20 TREATY. PAGE 167 A3408
ROUTINE DIPLOM INT/LAW DELIB/GP

C52
FIFIELD R.H.,"WOODROW WILSON AND THE FAR EAST." ASIA CHIEF DELIB/GP BAL/PWR CONFER COLONIAL ARMS/CONT WAR...TIME/SEQ NAT/COMP 19/20 WILSON/W LEAGUE/NAT. PAGE 45 A0925
BIBLIOG DIPLOM INT/ORG

B53
MANSERGH N.,DOCUMENTS AND SPEECHES ON BRITISH COMMONWEALTH AFFAIRS 1931-1952. INDIA IRELAND PAKISTAN UK CONSTN POL/PAR CHIEF FORCES COLONIAL ORD/FREE SOVEREIGN...JURID 20 COMMONWLTH. PAGE 94 A1929
BIBLIOG/A DIPLOM ECO/TAC

B53
MATLOFF M.,STRATEGIC PLANNING FOR COALITION WARFARE. UK USA-45 CHIEF DIPLOM EXEC GOV/REL ...METH/COMP 20. PAGE 96 A1967
WAR PLAN DECISION FORCES

B54
BUTOW R.J.C.,JAPAN'S DECISION TO SURRENDER. USA-45 USSR CHIEF FORCES DOMIN NUC/PWR...BIBLIOG 20 TREATY CHINJAP. PAGE 22 A0453
ELITES DIPLOM WAR PEACE

B54
MITCHELL P.,AFRICAN AFTERTHOUGHTS. UGANDA CONSTN NAT/G ADJUD COERCE WAR 20 WWI MAU/MAU. PAGE 102 A2090
BIOG CHIEF COLONIAL DOMIN

B54
SHARMA J.S.,MAHATMA GANDHI: A DESCRIPTIVE BIBLIOGRAPHY. INDIA S/ASIA PROB/SOLV DIPLOM COLONIAL WAR NAT/LISM PEACE ATTIT PERSON SOVEREIGN ...CONCPT 20 GANDHI/M. PAGE 132 A2695
BIBLIOG/A BIOG CHIEF LEAD

B55
ALFIERI D.,DICTATORS FACE TO FACE. NAT/G TOP/EX DIPLOM EXEC COERCE ORD/FREE FASCISM...POLICY OBS 20 HITLER/A MUSSOLIN/B. PAGE 6 A0116
WAR CHIEF TOTALISM PERS/REL

B55
CRAIG G.A.,THE POLITICS OF THE PRUSSIAN ARMY 1640-1945. CHRIST-17C EUR+WWI MOD/EUR PRUSSIA STRUCT DIPLOM ADMIN REV WAR...SOC BIBLIOG 17/20. PAGE 32 A0652
FORCES NAT/G ROLE CHIEF

B55
SVARLIEN O.,AN INTRODUCTION TO THE LAW OF NATIONS. SEA AIR INT/ORG NAT/G CHIEF ADMIN AGREE WAR PRIVIL ORD/FREE SOVEREIGN...BIBLIOG 16/20. PAGE 140 A2868
INT/LAW DIPLOM

S55
DE SMITH S.A.,"CONSTITUTIONAL MONARCHY IN BURGANDA." AFR UGANDA UK STRUCT CHIEF REGION INGP/REL ADJUST NAT/LISM SOVEREIGN CONSERVE ...POLICY 19/20 BURGANDA. PAGE 35 A0712
NAT/G DIPLOM CONSTN COLONIAL

B56
BEALE H.K.,THEODORE ROOSEVELT AND THE RISE OF AMERICA TO WORLD POWER. USA-45 BAL/PWR COLONIAL DRIVE PERSON PWR...POLICY BIBLIOG 20 ROOSEVLT/T PRESIDENT. PAGE 12 A0238
DIPLOM CHIEF BIOG

B56
KOENIG L.W.,THE TRUMAN ADMINISTRATION: ITS PRINCIPLES AND PRACTICE. USA+45 POL/PAR CHIEF LEGIS DIPLOM DEATH NUC/PWR WAR CIVMIL/REL PEACE ...DECISION 20 TRUMAN/HS PRESIDENT TREATY. PAGE 81 A1658
ADMIN POLICY EX/STRUC GOV/REL

B56
SNELL J.L.,THE MEANING OF YALTA: BIG THREE DIPLOMACY AND THE NEW BALANCE OF POWER. EUR+WWI GERMANY USA-45 USSR FORCES PLAN BAL/PWR DIPLOM WAR CHOOSE PEACE...CHARTS BIBLIOG 20 UN CHINJAP ROOSEVLT/F. PAGE 134 A2749
CONFER CHIEF POLICY PROB/SOLV

B56
WU E.,LEADERS OF TWENTIETH-CENTURY CHINA; AN ANNOTATED BIBLIOGRAPHY OF SELECTED CHINESE BIOGRAPHICAL WORKS IN HOOVER LIBRARY. ASIA INDUS POL/PAR DIPLOM ADMIN REV WAR...HUM MGT 20. PAGE 168 A3422
BIBLIOG/A BIOG INTELL CHIEF

B57
DUDDEN A.P.,WOODROW WILSON AND THE WORLD OF TODAY. USA-45 NAT/G PROVS CONTROL PARTIC WAR ISOLAT PWR SKILL...PERS/COMP ANTHOL 19/20 WILSON/W UN LEAGUE/NAT WWI. PAGE 39 A0794
CHIEF DIPLOM POL/PAR LEAD

B57
JASZI O.,AGAINST THE TYRANT. WOR+45 WOR-45 CONSTN DIPLOM CONTROL PARTIC REV WAR...CONCPT. PAGE 73 A1498
TOTALISM ORD/FREE CHIEF MURDER

B57
RUMEU DE ARMAS A.,ESPANA EEN EL AFRICA ATLANTICA. AFR CHRIST-17C PORTUGAL SPAIN DIPLOM ECO/TAC CONTROL 14/16 AFRICA/W. PAGE 125 A2568
NAT/G COLONIAL CHIEF PWR

B57
TOMASIC D.A.,NATIONAL COMMUNISM AND SOVIET STRATEGY. UK USSR YUGOSLAVIA NAT/G POL/PAR CHIEF CREATE DOMIN REV WAR PWR...BIOG TREND 20 TITO/MARSH STALIN/J. PAGE 144 A2948
COM NAT/LISM MARXISM DIPLOM

B58
NEAL F.W.,TITOISM IN ACTION. COM YUGOSLAVIA AGRI LOC/G DIPLOM TOTALISM...BIBLIOG 20 TITO/MARSH. PAGE 107 A2206
MARXISM POL/PAR CHIEF ADMIN

B58
NEHRU J.,SPEECHES. INDIA ECO/UNDEV AGRI INDUS INT/ORG POL/PAR DIPLOM FOR/AID NAT/LISM...ANTHOL 20. PAGE 108 A2213
PLAN CHIEF COLONIAL NEUTRAL

L58
HAVILAND H.F.,"FOREIGN AID AND THE POLICY PROCESS: 1957." USA+45 FACE/GP POL/PAR VOL/ASSN CHIEF DELIB/GP ACT/RES LEGIT EXEC GOV/REL ATTIT DRIVE PWR ...POLICY TESTS CONGRESS 20. PAGE 63 A1291
LEGIS PLAN FOR/AID

S58
ROTHFELS H.,"THE GERMAN RESISTANCE IN ITS INTERNATIONAL ASPECTS" (BMR)" EUR+WWI GERMANY UNIV CHIEF DIPLOM WAR NAT/LISM ATTIT...POLICY 20 HITLER/A NAZI. PAGE 124 A2548
VOL/ASSN MORAL FASCISM CIVMIL/REL

C58
WILDING N.,"AN ENCYCLOPEDIA OF PARLIAMENT." UK LAW CONSTN CHIEF PROB/SOLV DIPLOM DEBATE WAR INGP/REL PRIVIL...BIBLIOG DICTIONARY 13/20 CMN/WLTH PARLIAMENT. PAGE 164 A3349
PARL/PROC POL/PAR NAT/G ADMIN

B59
DAWSON R.H.,THE DECISION TO AID RUSSIA* FOREIGN POLICY AND DOMESTIC POLITICS. GERMANY USSR CHIEF EX/STRUC LEGIS TOP/EX PROB/SOLV WAR ATTIT...POLICY CONGRESS. PAGE 34 A0695
DECISION DELIB/GP DIPLOM FOR/AID

B59
DEHIO L.,GERMANY AND WORLD POLITICS IN THE TWENTIETH CENTURY. EUR+WWI FRANCE GERMANY MOD/EUR UK USSR NAT/G CHIEF BAL/PWR DOMIN COLONIAL CONTROL LEAD...IDEA/COMP 20 VERSAILLES. PAGE 36 A0724
DIPLOM WAR NAT/LISM SOVEREIGN

B59
GILBERT R.,GENOCIDE IN TIBET. ASIA SECT CHIEF DIPLOM 20. PAGE 52 A1072
MARXISM MURDER WAR GP/REL

B59
NUNEZ JIMENEZ A.,LA LIBERACION DE LAS ISLAS. CUBA L/A+17C USA+45 LAW CHIEF PLAN DIPLOM FOR/AID OWN WEALTH 20 CASTRO/F. PAGE 110 A2261
AGRI REV ECO/UNDEV NAT/G

B59
ROBINSON J.A.,THE MONRONEY RESOULUTION: CONGRESSIONAL INITIATIVE IN FOREIGN POLICY MAKING. USA+45 POL/PAR TOP/EX DIPLOM INT/TRADE 20 CONGRESS WORLD/BANK INTL/DEV. PAGE 122 A2504
LEGIS FINAN ECO/UNDEV CHIEF

B59
VINACKE H.M.,A HISTORY OF THE FAR EAST IN MODERN TIMES (6TH ED.). KOREA S/ASIA USSR CONSTN CULTURE STRATA ECO/UNDEV NAT/G CHIEF FOR/AID INT/TRADE GP/REL...SOC NAT/COMP 19/20 CHINJAP. PAGE 159 A3235
STRUCT ASIA

B60
BYRD E.M. JR.,TREATIES AND EXECUTIVE AGREEMENTS IN THE UNITED STATES: THEIR SEPARATE ROLES AND LIMITATIONS. USA+45 USA-45 EX/STRUC TARIFFS CT/SYS GOV/REL FEDERAL...IDEA/COMP BIBLIOG SUPREME/CT SENATE CONGRESS. PAGE 23 A0461
CHIEF INT/LAW DIPLOM

B60
DE GAULLE C.,THE EDGE OF THE SWORD. EUR+WWI FRANCE ELITES CHIEF DIPLOM ROLE...REALPOL TRADIT. PAGE 34
FORCES SUPEGO

A0701 LEAD WAR

B60
KHRUSHCHEV N.S.,KHRUSHCHEV IN AMERICA. USA+45 USSR INT/TRADE EDU/PROP PRESS PEACE...MARXIST RECORD INT 20 COLD/WAR KHRUSH/N. PAGE 79 A1613
MARXISM CHIEF DIPLOM

B60
MORISON E.E.,TURMOIL AND TRADITION: A STUDY OF THE LIFE AND TIMES OF HENRY L. STIMSON. USA+45 USA-45 POL/PAR CHIEF DELIB/GP FORCES BAL/PWR DIPLOM ARMS/CONT WAR PEACE 19/20 STIMSON/HL ROOSEVLT/F TAFT/WH HOOVER/H REPUBLICAN. PAGE 104 A2142
BIOG NAT/G EX/STRUC

B60
MOSELY P.E.,THE KREMLIN AND WORLD POLITICS. EUR+WWI GERMANY USA+45 USSR CHIEF TOP/EX BAL/PWR DOMIN PEACE PWR...METH 20 COLD/WAR STALIN/J EUROPE/E. PAGE 105 A2151
COM DIPLOM POLICY WAR

B60
PHILLIPS J.F.V.,KWAME NKRUMAH AND THE FUTURE OF AFRICA. FUT GHANA ISLAM ECO/UNDEV CHIEF DIPLOM COLONIAL RACE/REL NAT/LISM...TREND IDEA/COMP BIBLIOG 20 NKRUMAH/K. PAGE 116 A2376
BIOG LEAD SOVEREIGN AFR

B60
PRICE D.,THE SECRETARY OF STATE. USA+45 CONSTN ELITES INTELL CHIEF EX/STRUC TOP/EX LEGIT ATTIT PWR SKILL...DECISION 20 CONGRESS. PAGE 117 A2410
CONSULT DIPLOM INT/LAW

B61
ACHESON D.,SKETCHES FROM LIFE. WOR+45 20 CHURCHLL/W EDEN/A ADENAUER/K SALAZAR/A. PAGE 4 A0085
BIOG LEAD CHIEF DIPLOM

B61
DEAN V.M.,BUILDERS OF EMERGING NATIONS. WOR+45 ECO/UNDEV ECO/TAC NEUTRAL TOTALISM ORD/FREE PWR ...BIOG AUD/VIS IDEA/COMP BIBLIOG 20 COLD/WAR. PAGE 35 A0719
NAT/G CHIEF POLICY DIPLOM

B61
MILLER R.I.,DAG HAMMARSKJOLD AND CRISES DIPLOMACY. WOR+45 NAT/G PROB/SOLV LEAD ROLE...DECISION BIOG UN HAMMARSK/D. PAGE 101 A2079
DIPLOM INT/ORG CHIEF

B61
PALMER N.D.,THE INDIAN POLITICAL SYSTEM. INDIA ECO/UNDEV SECT CHIEF COLONIAL CHOOSE ALL/IDEOS SOCISM...CHARTS BIBLIOG/A 20. PAGE 113 A2322
NAT/LISM POL/PAR NAT/G DIPLOM

B61
PANIKKAR K.M.,THE VOICE OF FREEDOM: SELECTED SPEECHES OF PANDIT MOTILAL NEHRU. INDIA UK CONSTN FINAN FORCES LEGIS DIPLOM TAX COLONIAL...POLICY MAJORIT ANTHOL 20 NEHRU/PM. PAGE 114 A2331
NAT/LISM ORD/FREE CHIEF NAT/G

B61
PANIKKAR K.M.,REVOLUTION IN AFRICA. AFR GUINEA ECO/UNDEV POL/PAR DIPLOM COLONIAL EXEC LEAD SOVEREIGN...CHARTS 20. PAGE 114 A2332
NAT/LISM NAT/G CHIEF

B61
SCOTT A.M.,POLITICS, USA; CASES ON THE AMERICAN DEMOCRATIC PROCESS. USA+45 CHIEF FORCES DIPLOM LOBBY CHOOSE RACE/REL FEDERAL ATTIT...JURID ANTHOL T 20 PRESIDENT CONGRESS CIVIL/LIB. PAGE 130 A2669
CT/SYS CONSTN NAT/G PLAN

B62
DUROSELLE J.B.,HISTOIRE DIPLOMATIQUE DE 1919 A NOS JOURS (3RD ED.). FRANCE INT/ORG CHIEF FORCES CONFER ARMS/CONT WAR PEACE ORD/FREE...T TREATY 20 COLD/WAR. PAGE 39 A0807
DIPLOM WOR+45 WOR-45

B62
HARARI M.,GOVERNMENT AND POLITICS OF THE MIDDLE EAST. ISLAM USA+45 NAT/G SECT CHIEF ADMIN ORD/FREE 20. PAGE 61 A1257
DIPLOM ECO/UNDEV TEC/DEV POLICY

B62
JEWELL M.E.,SENATORIAL POLITICS AND FOREIGN POLICY. NAT/G POL/PAR CHIEF DELIB/GP TOP/EX FOR/AID EDU/PROP ROUTINE ATTIT PWR SKILL...MAJORIT METH/CNCPT TIME/SEQ CONGRESS 20 PRESIDENT. PAGE 74 A1516
USA+45 LEGIS DIPLOM

B62
KENNEDY J.F.,TO TURN THE TIDE. SPACE AGRI INT/ORG FORCES TEC/DEV ADMIN NUC/PWR PEACE WEALTH...ANTHOL 20 KENNEDY/JF CIV/RIGHTS. PAGE 78 A1592
DIPLOM CHIEF POLICY NAT/G

B62
TOURE S.,THE INTERNATIONAL POLICY OF THE DEMOCRATIC PARTY OF GUINEA (VOL. VII). AFR ALGERIA GHANA GUINEA MALI CONSTN VOL/ASSN CHIEF WAR PEACE ATTIT ...WELF/ST 20 DEMOCRAT. PAGE 144 A2953
DIPLOM POLICY POL/PAR NEW/LIB

B62
US SENATE COMM GOVT OPERATIONS,ADMINISTRATION OF NATIONAL SECURITY. USA+45 CHIEF PLAN PROB/SOLV TEC/DEV DIPLOM ATTIT...POLICY DECISION 20 KENNEDY/JF RUSK/D MCNAMARA/R BUNDY/M HERTER/C. PAGE 156 A3173
ORD/FREE ADMIN NAT/G CONTROL

C62
BACON F.,"OF EMPIRE" (1612) IN F. BACON, ESSAYS." ELITES NAT/G PROB/SOLV DIPLOM ADMIN CONTROL WEALTH 16/17 KING. PAGE 10 A0201
PWR CHIEF DOMIN GEN/LAWS

C62
ROBINSON J.A.,"CONGRESS AND FOREIGN POLICY-MAKING: A STUDY IN LEGISLATIVE INFLUENCE AND INITIATIVE." USA+45 CHIEF DELIB/GP CREATE CONTROL EXEC GOV/REL PERCEPT...TREND BIBLIOG 20 CONGRESS. PAGE 122 A2505
LEGIS DIPLOM POLICY DECISION

B63
AFRICAN BIBLIOGRAPHIC CENTER,THE SCENE IS GUINEA AND THE PERSONAGE IS SEKOU TOURE: A SELECTED CURRENT READING LIST, 1959-1962 (PAMPHLET). GUINEA ECO/UNDEV CHIEF FOR/AID COLONIAL...BIOG 20. PAGE 5 A0095
BIBLIOG AFR POL/PAR COM

B63
AFRICAN BIBLIOGRAPHIC CENTER,THE SCENE IS KENYA AND THE PERSONAGE IS TOM MBOYA: A SELECTED CURRENT READING LIST FROM 1956-1962 (PAMPHLET). ECO/UNDEV LABOR POL/PAR CHIEF COLONIAL CHOOSE NAT/LISM ORD/FREE 20. PAGE 5 A0096
BIBLIOG DIPLOM AFR NAT/G

B63
BLOCH-MORHANGE J.,VINGT ANNEES D'HISTOIRE CONTEMPORAINE. FORCES FOR/AID CONFER LEAD 20 COLD/WAR. PAGE 15 A0311
WAR DIPLOM INT/ORG CHIEF

B63
DALLIN A.,DIVERSITY IN INTERNATIONAL COMMUNISM: A DOCUMENTARY RECORD, 1961-1963. CHINA/COM CHIEF PRESS WRITING DEBATE LEAD...POLICY ANTHOL 20. PAGE 33 A0677
COM DIPLOM POL/PAR CONFER

B63
ERHARD L.,THE ECONOMICS OF SUCCESS. GERMANY/W WOR+45 LABOR CHIEF TAX REGION COST DEMAND ANTHOL. PAGE 42 A0860
ECO/DEV INT/TRADE PLAN DIPLOM

B63
GRIFFITH W.E.,ALBANIA AND THE SINO-SOVIET RIFT. ALBANIA CHINA/COM USSR POL/PAR CHIEF LEGIS DIPLOM DOMIN ATTIT PWR...POLICY 20 KHRUSH/N MAO. PAGE 57 A1161
EDU/PROP MARXISM NAT/LISM GOV/REL

B63
HONEY P.J.,COMMUNISM IN NORTH VIETNAM: ITS ROLE IN THE SINO-SOVIET DISPUTE. CHINA/COM INDIA USSR VIETNAM/N AGRI POL/PAR LEGIS ECO/TAC WAR PEACE ATTIT...GEOG IDEA/COMP 20. PAGE 67 A1378
POLICY MARXISM CHIEF DIPLOM

B63
KLEIMAN R.,ATLANTIC CRISIS; AMERICAN DIPLOMACY CONFRONTS A RESURGENT EUROPE. EUR+WWI USA+45 ECO/DEV AGRI NAT/G CHIEF FORCES PLAN LEAD ATTIT ...CONCPT 20 NATO KENNEDY/JF DEGAULLE/C EEC JOHNSON/LB. PAGE 80 A1648
DIPLOM REGION POLICY

B63
MALIK C.,MAN IN THE STRUGGLE FOR PEACE. USSR WOR+45 CHIEF PLAN PROB/SOLV PARTIC NUC/PWR REV ORD/FREE ...IDEA/COMP METH/COMP 20 UN COLD/WAR. PAGE 93 A1912
PEACE MARXISM DIPLOM EDU/PROP

B63
WHITNEY T.P.,KHRUSHCHEV SPEAKS. USSR AGRI LEAD ...BIOG ANTHOL 20 KHRUSH/N STALIN/J ESPIONAGE. PAGE 164 A3339
DIPLOM MARXISM CHIEF

B64
AFRO ASIAN SOLIDARITY AGAINST IMPERIALISM. AFR ISLAM S/ASIA ECO/UNDEV NAT/G POL/PAR TOP/EX PRESS ...INT ANTHOL 20 CHOU/ENLAI. PAGE 3 A0066
MARXISM DIPLOM EDU/PROP CHIEF

B64
DAVIES U.P. JR.,FOREIGN AND OTHER AFFAIRS. EUR+WWI L/A+17C S/ASIA USA+45 ECO/UNDEV CHIEF PLAN ECO/TAC PWR MARXISM 20 KENNEDY/JF UN. PAGE 34 A0688
DIPLOM NAT/G POLICY FOR/AID

B64
HALPERIN S.W.,MUSSOLINI AND ITALIAN FASCISM. ITALY NAT/G POL/PAR SECT ECO/TAC LEAD PWR SOCISM...POLICY 20 MUSSOLIN/B. PAGE 60 A1241
FASCISM NAT/LISM EDU/PROP CHIEF

B64
LEGGE J.D.,INDONESIA. INDONESIA ELITES ECO/UNDEV POL/PAR CHIEF FORCES INT/TRADE COERCE CHOOSE ORD/FREE...SOC CHARTS BIBLIOG 16/20 CHINJAP. PAGE 86 A1765
S/ASIA DOMIN NAT/LISM POLICY

B64
LENSEN G.A.,REVELATIONS OF A RUSSIAN DIPLOMAT: THE MEMOIRS OF DMITRII I. ABRIKOSSOV. ASIA MOD/EUR RUSSIA USA-45 ELITES ACADEM CHIEF FORCES REV WAR PWR CONSERVE MARXISM 19/20 ABRIKSSV/D CHINJAP BOLSHEVISM. PAGE 87 A1775
DIPLOM POLICY OBS

B64
NEWBURY C.W.,THE WEST AFRICAN COMMONWEALTH. CONSTN INTELL ECO/UNDEV VOL/ASSN CHIEF DELIB/GP LEGIS INT/TRADE COLONIAL FEDERAL ATTIT 20 COMMONWLTH AFRICA/W. PAGE 108 A2223
INT/ORG SOVEREIGN GOV/REL AFR

B64
REMAK J.,THE GENTLE CRITIC: THEODOR FONTANE AND GERMAN POLITICS, 1848-1898. GERMANY PRUSSIA CULTURE ELITES BAL/PWR DIPLOM WRITING GOV/REL...HUM BIOG 19 BISMARCK/O JUNKER FONTANE/T. PAGE 120 A2465
PERSON SOCIETY WORKER CHIEF

B64
SARROS P.P.,CONGRESS AND THE NEW DIPLOMACY: THE FORMULATION OF MUTUAL SECURITY POLICY: 1953-60
DIPLOM POL/PAR

(THESIS). USA+45 CHIEF EX/STRUC REGION ROUTINE CHOOSE GOV/REL PEACE ROLE...POLICY 20 PRESIDENT CONGRESS. PAGE 127 A2606
NAT/G

B64
UNITED ARAB REPUBLIC,TOWARDS THE SECOND AFRICAN SUMMIT ASSEMBLY. AFR UAR CONSTN VOL/ASSN CHIEF PLAN DIPLOM AGREE 20 NASSER/G AFR/STATES. PAGE 148 A3030
CONFER DELIB/GP INT/ORG POLICY

B64
US SENATE COMM GOVT OPERATIONS,THE SECRETARY OF STATE AND THE AMBASSADOR. USA+45 CHIEF CONSULT EX/STRUC FORCES PLAN ADMIN EXEC INGP/REL ROLE ...ANTHOL 20 PRESIDENT DEPT/STATE. PAGE 156 A3175
DIPLOM DELIB/GP NAT/G

B64
US SENATE COMM GOVT OPERATIONS,ADMINISTRATION OF NATIONAL SECURITY. USA+45 CHIEF TOP/EX PLAN DIPLOM CONTROL PEACE...POLICY DECISION 20 PRESIDENT CONGRESS. PAGE 156 A3176
ADMIN FORCES ORD/FREE NAT/G

B64
WARREN S.,THE PRESIDENT AS WORLD LEADER. USA+45 WOR+45 ELITES COM/IND INT/ORG NAT/G VOL/ASSN CHIEF EX/STRUC LEGIT COERCE ATTIT PERSON RIGID/FLEX...INT TIME/SEQ COLD/WAR 20 ROOSEVLT/F TRUMAN/HS EISNHWR/DD KENNEDY/JF. PAGE 161 A3286
TOP/EX PWR DIPLOM

S64
RUSK D.,"THE MAKING OF FOREIGN POLICY" USA+45 CHIEF DELIB/GP WORKER PROB/SOLV ADMIN ATTIT PWR ...DECISION 20 DEPT/STATE RUSK/D GOLDMAN/E. PAGE 125 A2570
DIPLOM INT POLICY

B65
ADENAUER K.,MEMOIRS 1945-53. EUR+WWI GERMANY/W ECO/DEV CHIEF FORCES ECO/TAC WAR GOV/REL PWR SOVEREIGN 20 NATO ADENAUER/K. PAGE 4 A0088
BIOG DIPLOM NAT/G PERS/REL

B65
ADENAUER K.,MEINE ERINNERUNGEN, 1945-53 (VOL. I), 1953-55 (VOL. II). EUR+WWI GERMANY CHIEF FORCES PROB/SOLV DIPLOM ARMS/CONT INGP/REL PEACE SOVEREIGN ...OBS/ENVIR RECORD 20. PAGE 4 A0089
NAT/G BIOG SELF/OBS

B65
HAIGHT D.E.,THE PRESIDENT; ROLES AND POWERS. USA+45 USA-45 POL/PAR PLAN DIPLOM CHOOSE PERS/REL PWR 18/20 PRESIDENT CONGRESS. PAGE 59 A1217
CHIEF LEGIS TOP/EX EX/STRUC

B65
JADOS S.S.,DOCUMENTS ON RUSSIAN-AMERICAN RELATIONS: WASHINGTON TO EISENHOWER. USA+45 USA-45 USSR INT/ORG LEGIS INT/TRADE WAR PEACE...ANTHOL BIBLIOG 18/20 PRESIDENT. PAGE 73 A1488
DIPLOM CHIEF CONTROL

B65
MALLIN J.,FORTRESS CUBA; RUSSIA'S AMERICAN BASE. COM CUBA L/A+17C FORCES PLAN DIPLOM LEAD REV WAR ...POLICY 20 CASTRO/F GUEVARA/C INTERVENT. PAGE 93 A1914
MARXISM CHIEF GUERRILLA DOMIN

B65
MANSFIELD P.,NASSER'S EGYPT. AFR ISLAM UAR ECO/UNDEV AGRI COLONIAL SOVEREIGN...CHARTS 20 NASSER/G MID/EAST. PAGE 94 A1934
CHIEF ECO/TAC DIPLOM POLICY

B65
MCSHERRY J.E.,RUSSIA AND THE UNITED STATES UNDER EISENHOWER, KHRUSHCHEV, AND KENNEDY. USSR EX/STRUC TOP/EX PRESS WAR...POLICY TREND 20. PAGE 99 A2024
DIPLOM CHIEF NAT/G PEACE

B65
MIDDLETON D.,CRISIS IN THE WEST. EUR+WWI FUT WOR+45 CHIEF PLAN ECO/TAC LEAD REGION NUC/PWR NAT/LISM MARXISM 20 COLD/WAR NATO EEC. PAGE 101 A2068
INT/ORG DIPLOM NAT/G POLICY

B65
MUNGER E.S.,NOTES ON THE FORMATION OF SOUTH AFRICAN FOREIGN POLICY. ACADEM POL/PAR SECT CHIEF DELIB/GP FORCES LEGIS PRESS ATTIT...TREND 20 NEGRO. PAGE 106 A2170
AFR DOMIN POLICY DIPLOM

B65
SANDERSON G.N.,ENGLAND, EUROPE, AND THE UPPER NILE 1882-1899. ISLAM MOD/EUR UAR UK CHIEF...POLICY CHARTS BIBLIOG/A 19 ARABS NEGRO. PAGE 127 A2600
AFR DIPLOM COLONIAL

B65
WEISNER J.B.,WHERE SCIENCE AND POLITICS MEET. USA+45 ECO/DEV R+D FORCES PROB/SOLV DIPLOM FOR/AID CONTROL...PHIL/SCI PRESIDENT KENNEDY/JF JOHNSON/LB. PAGE 163 A3310
CHIEF NAT/G POLICY TEC/DEV

B66
DONALD A.D.,JOHN F. KENNEDY AND THE NEW FRONTIER. LEGIS DIPLOM DISCRIM PEACE PWR 20. PAGE 38 A0771
LEAD CHIEF BIOG EFFICIENCY

B66
EUBANK K.,THE SUMMIT CONFERENCES. EUR+WWI USA+45 USA-45 MUNIC BAL/PWR WAR PEACE PWR...POLICY AUD/VIS 20 GENEVA/CON TEHERAN YALTA POTSDAM. PAGE 43 A0872
CONFER NAT/G CHIEF DIPLOM

B66
HERZ M.F.,BEGINNINGS OF THE COLD WAR. COM POLAND USA+45 USSR INT/ORG NAT/G CHIEF FOR/AID DOMIN CONFER AGREE WAR PEACE 20 STALIN/J COLD/WAR UN. PAGE 64 A1321
DIPLOM

B66
MOORE R.J.,SIR CHARLES WOOD'S INDIAN POLICY: 1853-66. INDIA POL/PAR CHIEF DELIB/GP DIPLOM CONTROL LEAD WOOD/CHAS. PAGE 103 A2124
COLONIAL ADMIN CONSULT DECISION

B66
RIESELBACH L.N.,THE ROOTS OF ISOLATIONISM* CONGRESSIONAL VOTING AND PRESIDENTIAL LEADERSHIP IN FOREIGN POLICY. POL/PAR LEGIS DIPLOM EDU/PROP LEAD REGION REPRESENT...SOC STAT IDEA/COMP HYPO/EXP BIBLIOG 19/20 CONGRESS. PAGE 121 A2477
ISOLAT CHOOSE CHIEF POLICY

B66
SANDERS R.E.,SPAIN AND THE UNITED NATIONS 1945-1950. SPAIN CHIEF DIPLOM CONFER SANCTION ATTIT ...POLICY 20 UN COLD/WAR. PAGE 127 A2599
INT/ORG FASCISM GP/REL STRANGE

B66
SINGER L.,ALLE LITTEN AN GROSSENWAHN: VON WOODROW WILSON BIS MAO TSE-TUNG. ASIA UK USSR INT/ORG DELIB/GP BAL/PWR DOMIN ATTIT PERSON 20 WILSON/W ROOSEVLT/F. PAGE 133 A2731
DIPLOM TOTALISM WAR CHIEF

B66
SPEARS E.L.,TWO MEN WHO SAVED FRANCE: PETAIN AND DE GAULLE. FRANCE CONSTN FORCES DIPLOM WAR PERSON 20 WWI PETAIN/HP DEGAULLE/C. PAGE 135 A2773
BIOG LEAD CHIEF NAT/G

B66
TYSON G.,NEHRU: THE YEARS OF POWER. INDIA UK STRATA ECO/UNDEV FINAN SECT TASK WAR ORD/FREE MARXISM ...POLICY BIBLIOG 20 NEHRU/J. PAGE 146 A2985
CHIEF PWR DIPLOM NAT/G

B66
US CONGRESS JOINT ECO COMM,NEW APPROACH TO UNITED STATES INTERNATIONAL ECONOMIC POLICY. USA+45 WOR+45 CHIEF DELIB/GP CONFER...CHARTS 20 CONGRESS MONEY. PAGE 150 A3070
DIPLOM ECO/TAC BAL/PAY FINAN

B66
WILSON H.A.,THE IMPERIAL POLICY OF SIR ROBERT BORDEN. CANADA UK ELITES INT/ORG VOL/ASSN CONTROL LEAD WAR ROLE 20 CMN/WLTH BORDEN/R. PAGE 165 A3360
INGP/REL COLONIAL CONSTN CHIEF

S66
GAMER R.E.,"URGENT SINGAPORE, PATIENT MALAYSIA." MALAYSIA S/ASIA ECO/UNDEV POL/PAR CHIEF TARIFFS TAX CONTROL LEAD REGION PWR 20 SINGAPORE. PAGE 51 A1036
DIPLOM NAT/G POLICY ECO/TAC

S66
MATTHEWS D.G.,"ETHIOPIAN OUTLINE: A BIBLIOGRAPHIC RESEARCH GUIDE." ETHIOPIA LAW STRUCT ECO/UNDEV AGRI LABOR SECT CHIEF DELIB/GP EX/STRUC ADMIN...LING ORG/CHARTS 20. PAGE 96 A1972
BIBLIOG NAT/G DIPLOM POL/PAR

B67
BRZEZINSKI Z.K.,THE SOVIET BLOC: UNITY AND CONFLICT (2ND ED., REV., ENLARGED). COM POLAND USSR INTELL CHIEF EX/STRUC CONTROL EXEC GOV/REL PWR MARXISM ...TREND IDEA/COMP 20 LENIN/VI MARX/KARL STALIN/J. PAGE 21 A0420
NAT/G DIPLOM

B67
ISENBERG I.,FRANCE UNDER DE GAULLE (THE REFERENCE SHELF VOL. 39 NO. 1). EUR+WWI FRANCE ECO/DEV ...BIBLIOG 20 DEGAULLE/C NATO EEC. PAGE 72 A1469
ATTIT DIPLOM POLICY CHIEF

B67
O'LEARY M.K.,THE POLITICS OF AMERICAN FOREIGN AID. USA+45 POL/PAR CHIEF BUDGET EDU/PROP LOBBY CONGRESS. PAGE 111 A2270
FOR/AID DIPLOM PARL/PROC ATTIT

B67
TEITELBAUM L.M.,WOODROW WILSON AND THE MEXICAN REVOLUTION 1913-1916: A HISTORY OF UNITED STATES-MEXICAN RELATIONS. USA-45 CHIEF TOP/EX WAR 20 MEXIC/AMER WILSON/W VILLA/P CARRANZA/V. PAGE 142 A2902
REV DIPLOM

B67
THORNE C.,THE APPROACH OF WAR, 1938-1939. EUR+WWI POL/PAR CHIEF FORCES LEAD DRIVE PWR FASCISM ...BIBLIOG/A 20 HITLER/A. PAGE 144 A2936
DIPLOM WAR ELITES

B67
WILLIS F.R.,DE GAULLE: ANACHRONISM, REALIST, OR PROPHET? FRANCE POL/PAR FORCES DIPLOM WAR PEACE ROLE ORD/FREE...POLICY IDEA/COMP ANTHOL 20 DEGAULLE/C. PAGE 165 A3356
BIOG PERSON CHIEF LEAD

L67
KOMESAR N.K.,"PRESIDENTIAL AMENDMENT & TERMINATION OF TREATIES* THE CASE OF THE WARSAW CONVENTION." POLAND USA+45 NAT/G CHIEF PROB/SOLV DIPLOM PWR 20 CONGRESS. PAGE 81 A1669
TOP/EX LEGIS CONSTN LICENSE

S67
BUTT R.,"THE COMMON MARKET AND CONSERVATIVE POLITICS, 1961-2." UK CHIEF DIPLOM ECO/TAC INT/TRADE CONFER DEBATE REGION ATTIT...POLICY 20 EEC. PAGE 22 A0454
EUR+WWI INT/ORG POL/PAR

S67
HALL M.,"GERMANY, EAST AND WEST* DANGER AT THE
NAT/LISM

CROSSROADS." GERMANY ELITES CHIEF FORCES DIPLOM ECO/TAC REPAR ARMS/CONT...SOCIALIST 20. PAGE 60 A1227 — ATTIT FASCISM WEAPON

S67
HEATH D.B.,"BOLIVIA UNDER BARRIENTOS." L/A+17C NAT/G CHIEF DIPLOM ECO/TAC...POLICY 20 BOLIV. PAGE 64 A1306 — ECO/UNDEV POL/PAR REV CONSTN

S67
KRAUS J.,"A MARXIST IN GHANA." GHANA ELITES CHIEF PROB/SOLV TEC/DEV DIPLOM ECO/TAC COLONIAL PARTIC PWR 20 NKRUMAH/K. PAGE 82 A1676 — MARXISM PLAN ATTIT CREATE

S67
LACOUTRE J.,"HO CHI MINH." CHINA/COM USSR VIETNAM/N NAT/G CHIEF TOP/EX LEAD NEUTRAL...REALPOL PREDICT 20. PAGE 83 A1708 — NAT/LISM MARXISM REV DIPLOM

S67
MEYER J.,"CUBA S'ENFERME DANS SA REVOLUTION." CHINA/COM CUBA USSR NAT/G TOP/EX DIPLOM LEAD ATTIT ...PREDICT 20. PAGE 100 A2053 — MARXISM REV CHIEF NAT/LISM

S67
ROTBERG R.I.,"COLONIALISM AND AFTER: THE POLITICAL LITERATURE OF CENTRAL AFRICA - A BIBLIOGRAPHIC ESSAY." AFR CHIEF EX/STRUC REV INGP/REL RACE/REL SOVEREIGN 20. PAGE 124 A2546 — BIBLIOG/A COLONIAL DIPLOM NAT/G

C67
LING D.L.,"TUNISIA: FROM PROTECTORATE TO REPUBLIC." CULTURE NAT/G POL/PAR CHIEF DIPLOM COERCE WAR PWR ...BIBLIOG 19/20 TUNIS. PAGE 89 A1825 — AFR NAT/LISM COLONIAL PROB/SOLV

B86
MAS LATRIE L.,RELATIONS ET COMMERCE DE L'AFRIQUE SEPTENTRIONALE OU MAGREB AVEC LES NATIONS CHRETIENNES AU MOYEN AGE. CULTURE CHIEF FORCES WAR ...SOC CENSUS TREATY 10/16. PAGE 95 A1954 — ISLAM SECT DIPLOM INT/TRADE

B96
DE VATTEL E.,THE LAW OF NATIONS. AGRI FINAN CHIEF DIPLOM INT/TRADE AGREE OWN ALL/VALS MORAL ORD/FREE SOVEREIGN...GEN/LAWS 18 NATURL/LAW WOLFF/C. PAGE 35 A0714 — LAW CONCPT NAT/G INT/LAW

CHILDREN....SEE AGE/C

CHILDS J.B. A0529

CHILDS J.R. A0530

CHILDS/RS....RICHARD SPENCER CHILDS

CHILE....SEE ALSO L/A+17C

B29
DE REPARAZ G.,GEOGRAFIA Y POLITICA. CHILE SPAIN USSR NAT/G DIPLOM REV MARXISM...POLICY 19/20. PAGE 35 A0709 — GEOG MOD/EUR

B58
ALMEYDA M.C.,REFLEXIONES POLITICAS. CHILE L/A+17C USA+45 INT/ORG POL/PAR ECO/TAC PARTIC ATTIT 20. PAGE 6 A0128 — ECO/UNDEV REGION DIPLOM INT/TRADE

B61
US HOUSE COMM APPROPRIATIONS,INTER-AMERICAN PROGRAMS FOR 1961: DENIAL OF 1962 BUDGET INFORMATION. CHILE L/A+17C USA+45 FINAN CONSULT BUDGET ADJUD COST EFFICIENCY WEALTH...POLICY CHARTS 20 CONGRESS. PAGE 153 A3119 — LEGIS FOR/AID DELIB/GP ECO/UNDEV

B63
PIKE F.B.,CHILE AND THE UNITED STATES 1880-1962: THE EMERGENCE OF CHILE'S CRISIS AND THE CHALLENGE TO US DIPLOMACY. CHILE COM USA+45 USA-45 SOCIETY STRATA ECO/UNDEV...MYTH 19/20. PAGE 116 A2378 — FOR/AID DIPLOM ATTIT STRUCT

B64
CORFO,CHILE, A SELECTED BIBLIOGRAPHY IN ENGLISH (PAMPHLET). CHILE DIPLOM...SOC 20. PAGE 31 A0623 — BIBLIOG NAT/G POLICY L/A+17C

B64
KALDOR N.,ESSAYS ON ECONOMIC POLICY (VOL. II). CHILE GERMANY INDIA FINAN...GOV/COMP METH/COMP 20 KEYNES/JM. PAGE 76 A1551 — BAL/PAY INT/TRADE METH/CNCPT ECO/UNDEV

B64
WITHERS W.,THE ECONOMIC CRISIS IN LATIN AMERICA. BRAZIL CHILE STRATA AGRI DIPLOM FOR/AID PWR SOCISM ...POLICY 20 MEXIC/AMER ARGEN. PAGE 166 A3372 — L/A+17C ECO/UNDEV CAP/ISM ALL/IDEOS

B65
HALPERIN E.,NATIONALISM AND COMMUNISM. CHILE L/A+17C CAP/ISM EDU/PROP CHOOSE DISCRIM SOCISM ...BIBLIOG 20 COM/PARTY. PAGE 60 A1236 — NAT/LISM MARXISM POL/PAR REV

B66
GLAZER M.,THE FEDERAL GOVERNMENT AND THE UNIVERSITY. CHILE PROB/SOLV DIPLOM GIVE ADMIN WAR ...POLICY SOC 20. PAGE 53 A1079 — BIBLIOG/A NAT/G PLAN ACADEM

CHINA....CHINA IN GENERAL; SEE ALSO ASIA ,CHINA/COM, TAIWAN

S64
LEVI W.,"CHINA AND THE UNITED NATIONS." ASIA CHINA CHINA/COM WOR+45 WOR-45 CONSTN NAT/G DELIB/GP EX/STRUC FORCES ACT/RES EDU/PROP PWR...POLICY RECORD TIME/SEQ GEN/LAWS UN COLD/WAR 20. PAGE 88 A1794 — INT/ORG ATTIT NAT/LISM

CHINA INSTITUTE OF AMERICA. A0531

CHINA/COM....COMMUNIST CHINA

N
PEKING REVIEW. CHINA/COM CULTURE AGRI INDUS DIPLOM EDU/PROP GUERRILLA ATTIT MARXISM...BIBLIOG 20. PAGE 1 A0022 — MARXIST NAT/G POL/PAR PRESS

N
KYRIAK T.E.,CHINA: A BIBLIOGRAPHY. ASIA CHINA/COM AGRI FINAN INDUS NAT/G INT/TRADE PRESS...SOC 20. PAGE 83 A1700 — BIBLIOG/A MARXISM TOP/EX POL/PAR

N
US CONSULATE GENERAL HONG KONG,CURRENT BACKGROUND. CHINA/COM ECO/UNDEV LOC/G NAT/G PLAN DIPLOM EDU/PROP LEAD REV ATTIT...POLICY INDEX 20. PAGE 151 A3074 — BIBLIOG/A MARXIST ASIA PRESS

N
US CONSULATE GENERAL HONG KONG,SURVEY OF CHINA MAINLAND PRESS. CHINA/COM ECO/UNDEV LOC/G NAT/G PLAN DIPLOM EDU/PROP LEAD REV ATTIT...POLICY INDEX 20. PAGE 151 A3075 — BIBLIOG/A MARXIST ASIA PRESS

N
US CONSULATE GENERAL HONG KONG,US CONSULATE GENERAL, HONG KONG, PRESS SUMMARIES. CHINA/COM ECO/UNDEV LOC/G NAT/G PLAN DIPLOM EDU/PROP LEAD REV ATTIT...POLICY INDEX 20. PAGE 151 A3076 — BIBLIOG/A MARXIST ASIA PRESS

N19
DEANE H.,THE WAR IN VIETNAM (PAMPHLET). CHINA/COM VIETNAM BAL/PWR DIPLOM ECO/TAC SOCISM INTERVENT COLD/WAR INTERVENT COLD/WAR. PAGE 35 A0720 — WAR SOCIALIST MORAL CAP/ISM

B45
CLAGETT H.L.,COMMUNIST CHINA: RUTHLESS ENEMY OR PAPER TIGER (PAMPHLET). CHINA/COM ECO/UNDEV AGRI INDUS NAT/G POL/PAR ECO/TAC INT/TRADE GUERRILLA ATTIT...CHARTS NAT/COMP ORG/CHARTS 20. PAGE 26 A0540 — BIBLIOG/A MARXISM DIPLOM COERCE

B48
CLYDE P.H.,THE FAR EAST: A HISTORY OF THE IMPACT OF THE WEST ON EASTERN ASIA. CHINA/COM CULTURE INT/TRADE DOMIN COLONIAL WAR PWR...CHARTS BIBLIOG 19/20 CHINJAP. PAGE 27 A0554 — DIPLOM ASIA

B49
US DEPARTMENT OF STATE,SOVIET BIBLIOGRAPHY (PAMPHLET). CHINA/COM COM USSR LAW AGRI INT/ORG ECO/TAC EDU/PROP...POLICY GEOG 20. PAGE 151 A3084 — BIBLIOG/A MARXISM CULTURE DIPLOM

B50
DULLES J.F.,WAR OR PEACE. CHINA/COM USA+45 USSR INT/ORG SECT FORCES PLAN NUC/PWR WAR CENTRAL MARXISM...POLICY 20 UN ROOSEVLT/F STALIN/J. PAGE 39 A0797 — PEACE DIPLOM TREND ORD/FREE

B52
RIGGS F.W.,FORMOSA UNDER CHINESE NATIONALIST RULE. CHINA/COM USA+45 CONSTN AGRI FINAN LABOR LOC/G NAT/G POL/PAR FORCES HEALTH KNOWL...STAT WORK VAL/FREE 20. PAGE 121 A2479 — ASIA FOR/AID DIPLOM

B53
SHIRATO I.,JAPANESE SOURCES ON THE HISTORY OF THE CHINESE COMMUNIST MOVEMENT (PAMPHLET). CHINA/COM USSR CONSTRUC NAT/G POL/PAR FORCES DIPLOM DOMIN EDU/PROP CONTROL WAR TOTALISM SOCISM 20. PAGE 132 A2702 — BIBLIOG/A MARXISM ECO/UNDEV

B55
THOMPSON V.,MINORITY PROBLEMS IN SOUTHEAST ASIA. CAMBODIA CHINA/COM LAOS S/ASIA KIN NAT/G SECT PROB/SOLV EDU/PROP REGION GP/REL RACE/REL MARXISM ...SOC 20 BUDDHISM UN. PAGE 143 A2933 — INGP/REL GEOG DIPLOM STRUCT

B55
UN HEADQUARTERS LIBRARY,BIBLIOQRAPHIE DE LA CHARTE DES NATIONS UNIES. CHINA/COM KOREA WOR+45 VOL/ASSN CONFER ADMIN COERCE PEACE ATTIT ORD/FREE SOVEREIGN ...INT/LAW 20 UNESCO UN. PAGE 147 A3001 — BIBLIOG/A INT/ORG DIPLOM

L55
ROSTOW W.W.,"RUSSIA AND CHINA UNDER COMMUNISM." CHINA/COM USSR INTELL STRUCT INT/ORG NAT/G POL/PAR TOP/EX ACT/RES PLAN ADMIN ATTIT ALL/VALS MARXISM ...CONCPT OBS TIME/SEQ TREND GOV/COMP VAL/FREE 20. PAGE 124 A2543 — COM ASIA

B56
BROOK D.,THE UNITED NATIONS AND CHINA DILEMMA. CHINA/COM FUT WOR+45 ECO/UNDEV NAT/G DELIB/GP ACT/RES DIPLOM ROUTINE NAT/LISM TOTALISM ATTIT DRIVE...CONCPT OBS TIME/SEQ UN TOT/POP TIME UN 20. PAGE 19 A0390
ASIA INT/ORG BAL/PWR

B56
CHANG C.J.,THE MINORITY GROUPS OF YUNN AN AND CHINESE POLITICAL EXPANSION INTO SOUTHEAST ASIA (DOCTORAL THESIS). ASIA CHINA/COM S/ASIA FORCES TEC/DEV DIPLOM EDU/PROP...GEOG BIBLIOG 20. PAGE 26 A0520
GP/REL REGION DOMIN MARXISM

B56
KNORR K.E.,RUBLE DIPLOMACY: CHALLENGE TO AMERICAN FOREIGN AID(PAMPHLET). CHINA/COM USA+45 USSR PLAN TEC/DEV CAP/ISM INT/TRADE DOMIN EDU/PROP CONTROL LEAD 20 COLD/WAR. PAGE 81 A1654
ECO/UNDEV COM DIPLOM FOR/AID

B56
ROBERTS H.L.,RUSSIA AND AMERICA. CHINA/COM S/ASIA USSR FORCES TEC/DEV FOR/AID NUC/PWR ALL/IDEOS ...MAJORIT TREND NAT/COMP 20 COLD/WAR UN NATO. PAGE 122 A2494
DIPLOM INT/ORG BAL/PWR TOTALISM

B56
WILBUR C.M.,DOCUMENTS ON COMMUNISM, NATIONALISM, AND SOVIET ADVISERS IN CHINA, 1918-1927. CHINA/COM USSR STRUCT DIPLOM LEAD NAT/LISM...BIBLIOG/A 20. PAGE 164 A3343
REV POL/PAR MARXISM COM

C57
TANG P.S.H.,"COMMUNIST CHINA TODAY: DOMESTIC AND FOREIGN POLICIES." CHINA/COM COM S/ASIA USSR STRATA FORCES DIPLOM EDU/PROP COERCE GOV/REL...POLICY MAJORIT BIBLIOG 20. PAGE 141 A2886
POL/PAR LEAD ADMIN CONSTN

B58
ANGELL N.,DEFENCE AND THE ENGLISH-SPEAKING ROLE. CHINA/COM UK USSR INT/ORG FORCES EDU/PROP NEUTRAL NUC/PWR NAT/LISM PEACE TOTALISM 20 COLD/WAR COEXIST. PAGE 8 A0161
DIPLOM WAR MARXISM ORD/FREE

B58
BOWLES C.,IDEAS, PEOPLE AND PEACE. ASIA CHINA/COM FUT INDIA USA+45 USSR ECO/UNDEV INT/ORG LEAD TASK MARXISM 20 NATO UN COLD/WAR. PAGE 18 A0359
PEACE POLICY NAT/G DIPLOM

B58
WIGGINS J.W.,FOREIGN AID REEXAMINED: A CRITICAL APPRAISAL. CHINA/COM INDONESIA USA+45 FINAN INT/TRADE REGION NAT/LISM ATTIT...CENSUS 20. PAGE 164 A3342
FOR/AID DIPLOM ECO/UNDEV SOVEREIGN

B59
CHINA INSTITUTE OF AMERICA.,CHINA AND THE UNITED NATIONS. CHINA/COM FUT STRUCT EDU/PROP LEGIT ADMIN ATTIT KNOWL ORD/FREE PWR...OBS RECORD STAND/INT TIME/SEQ UN LEAGUE/NAT UNESCO 20. PAGE 26 A0531
ASIA INT/ORG

B59
STRAUSZ-HUPE R.,PROTRACTED CONFLICT. CHINA/COM KOREA WOR+45 INT/ORG FORCES ACT/RES ECO/TAC LEGIT COERCE DRIVE PERCEPT KNOWL PWR...PSY CONCPT RECORD GEN/METH COLD/WAR VAL/FREE 20. PAGE 139 A2847
COM PLAN USSR

S59
KRIPALANI A.J.B.,"FOR PRINCIPLED NEUTRALITY." CHINA/COM INDIA S/ASIA PLAN ECO/TAC RIGID/FLEX MORAL PWR...MYSTIC SOC RECORD 20 GANDHI/M. PAGE 82 A1684
ATTIT FOR/AID DIPLOM

S59
QUIGLEY H.S.,"TOWARD REAPPRAISAL OF OUR CHINA POLICY." CHINA/COM USA+45 INT/ORG PLAN ECO/TAC PERCEPT ORD/FREE...DECISION PSY CON/ANAL GEN/METH VAL/FREE 20. PAGE 118 A2427
ASIA KNOWL DIPLOM

B60
FISCHER L.,THE SOVIETS IN WORLD AFFAIRS. CHINA/COM COM EUR+WWI USSR INT/ORG CONFER LEAD ARMS/CONT REV PWR...CHARTS 20 TREATY VERSAILLES. PAGE 46 A0938
DIPLOM NAT/G POLICY MARXISM

B60
KARDELJE,SOCIALISM AND WAR. CHINA/COM WOR+45 YUGOSLAVIA DIPLOM EDU/PROP ATTIT...POLICY CONCPT IDEA/COMP COLD/WAR. PAGE 76 A1565
MARXIST WAR MARXISM BAL/PWR

B60
MC CLELLAN G.S.,INDIA. CHINA/COM INDIA CONSTN ELITES STRATA AGRI POL/PAR FOR/AID ARMS/CONT REV MARXISM...CENSUS BIBLIOG 20 COLD/WAR GANDHI/M NEHRU/J. PAGE 97 A1990
DIPLOM NAT/G SOCIETY ECO/UNDEV

B60
MORAES F.,THE REVOLT IN TIBET. ASIA CHINA/COM INDIA CULTURE CONTROL COERCE WAR TOTALISM...POLICY SOC WORSHIP 20 TIBET INTERVENT. PAGE 104 A2127
COLONIAL FORCES DIPLOM ORD/FREE

B60
SPEER J.P.,FOR WHAT PURPOSE? CHINA/COM USSR CONSTN PROB/SOLV DIPLOM CONTROL TASK WAR NAT/LISM WORSHIP 20 UN. PAGE 136 A2778
PEACE SECT SUPEGO ALL/IDEOS

B60
WHITING A.S.,CHINA CROSSES THE YALU: THE DECISION TO ENTER THE KOREAN WAR. ASIA CHINA/COM KOREA ECO/UNDEV R+D INT/ORG TOP/EX ACT/RES BAL/PWR ATTIT PWR...GEN/METH 20. PAGE 164 A3338
PLAN COERCE WAR

S60
GINSBURGS G.,"PEKING-LHASA-NEW DELHI." CHINA/COM FUT INDIA S/ASIA KIN NAT/G PROVS SECT FORCES BAL/PWR ECO/TAC DOMIN EDU/PROP LEGIT ADMIN REGION GUERRILLA PWR...TREND TIBET 20. PAGE 52 A1074
ASIA COERCE DIPLOM

B61
DALLIN D.J.,SOVIET FOREIGN POLICY AFTER STALIN. ASIA CHINA/COM EUR+WWI GERMANY IRAN UK YUGOSLAVIA INT/ORG NAT/G VOL/ASSN FORCES TOP/EX BAL/PWR DOMIN EDU/PROP COERCE ATTIT PWR 20. PAGE 33 A0679
COM DIPLOM USSR

B61
HUDSON G.F.,THE SINO-SOVIET DISPUTE. CHINA/COM USSR INTELL INT/TRADE DEBATE REV...IDEA/COMP 20. PAGE 68 A1404
DIPLOM MARXISM PRESS ATTIT

B61
LETHBRIDGE H.J.,CHINA'S URBAN COMMUNES. CHINA/COM FUT ECO/UNDEV DIPLOM EDU/PROP DEMAND INCOME MARXISM ...POLICY 20. PAGE 87 A1790
MUNIC CONTROL ECO/TAC NAT/G

B61
MENDEL D.H. JR.,THE JAPANESE PEOPLE AND FOREIGN POLICY. CHINA/COM KOREA USA+45 USSR SOCIETY FORCES CHOOSE 20 CHINJAP. PAGE 99 A2037
NAT/G DIPLOM POLICY ATTIT

B61
NEWMAN R.P.,RECOGNITION OF COMMUNIST CHINA? A STUDY IN ARGUMENT. CHINA/COM NAT/G PROB/SOLV RATIONAL ...INT/LAW LOG IDEA/COMP BIBLIOG 20. PAGE 108 A2226
MARXISM ATTIT DIPLOM POLICY

B61
WARNER D.,HURRICANE FROM CHINA. ASIA CHINA/COM FUT L/A+17C USA+45 CULTURE NAT/G FORCES TOP/EX FOR/AID DRIVE PWR...CONCPT TIME/SEQ SEATO WORK 20. PAGE 161 A3284
ATTIT TREND REV

S61
BARNET R.,"RUSSIA, CHINA, AND THE WORLD: THE SOVIET ATTITUDE ON DISARMAMENT (PART 3)." ASIA CHINA/COM FUT INT/ORG NAT/G POL/PAR VOL/ASSN ARMS/CONT ATTIT ...POLICY CONCPT TIME/SEQ TREND TOT/POP VAL/FREE 20. PAGE 11 A0226
COM PLAN TOTALISM USSR

S61
DANIELS R.V.,"THE CHINESE REVOLUTION IN RUSSIAN PERSPECTIVE." ASIA CHINA/COM COM USSR INTELL INT/ORG TOP/EX REV TOTALISM PWR...POLICY WORK VAL/FREE 20. PAGE 33 A0680
POL/PAR PLAN

S61
ZAGORIA D.S.,"SINO-SOVIET FRICTION IN UNDERDEVELOPED AREAS." ASIA CHINA/COM COM ACT/RES PLAN ATTIT ORD/FREE PWR COLD/WAR 20. PAGE 169 A3443
ECO/UNDEV ECO/TAC INT/TRADE USSR

S61
ZAGORIA D.S.,"THE FUTURE OF SINO-SOVIET RELATIONS." CHINA/COM INT/ORG NAT/G POL/PAR VOL/ASSN ACT/RES PLAN PERSON...METH/CNCPT TIME/SEQ TOT/POP VAL/FREE 20 MAO KHRUSH/N. PAGE 169 A3444
ASIA COM TOTALISM USSR

B62
CLUBB O.E. JR.,THE UNITED STATES AND THE SINO-SOVIET BLOC IN SOUTHEAST ASIA. ASIA CHINA/COM COM USA+45 USSR ECO/UNDEV INT/ORG NAT/G FORCES TOP/EX PLAN ECO/TAC DOMIN COERCE GUERRILLA ATTIT RIGID/FLEX...POLICY OBS TREND 20. PAGE 27 A0553
S/ASIA PWR BAL/PWR DIPLOM

B62
DUROSELLE J.B.,LES NOUVEAUX ETATS DANS LES RELATIONS INTERNATIONALES. AFR CHINA/COM FRANCE MOROCCO S/ASIA USSR ECO/UNDEV INT/ORG PLAN ECO/TAC EDU/PROP ATTIT DRIVE...TREND TOT/POP TUNIS 20. PAGE 39 A0806
NAT/G CONSTN DIPLOM

B62
FRIEDRICH-EBERT-STIFTUNG,THE SOVIET BLOC AND DEVELOPING COUNTRIES. CHINA/COM COM GERMANY/E USSR WOR+45 ECO/UNDEV INT/ORG NAT/G TEC/DEV NEUTRAL PWR ...POLICY 20. PAGE 49 A1008
MARXISM DIPLOM ECO/TAC FOR/AID

B62
HOOK S.,WORLD COMMUNISM: KEY DOCUMENTARY MATERIAL. CHINA/COM L/A+17C USA+45 USSR POL/PAR DIPLOM COLONIAL REV WAR...ANTHOL 20 MARX/KARL LENIN/VI COM/PARTY. PAGE 67 A1380
MARXISM COM GEN/LAWS NAT/G

B62
KLUCKHOHN F.L.,THE NAKED RISE OF COMMUNISM. CHINA/COM COM USSR WOR+45 CONSTN POL/PAR PLAN CONTROL LEAD NEUTRAL CONSERVE 20 STALIN/J EUROPE/E COM/PARTY. PAGE 80 A1650
MARXISM IDEA/COMP DIPLOM DOMIN

B62
LAQUEUR W.,THE FUTURE OF COMMUNIST SOCIETY. CHINA/COM USSR LAW ECO/DEV NAT/G POL/PAR PLAN PROB/SOLV DIPLOM LEAD...POLICY CONCPT IDEA/COMP ANTHOL 20. PAGE 85 A1731
MARXISM COM FUT SOCIETY

B62
LAQUEUR W.,POLYCENTRISM. CHINA/COM COM USSR WOR+45 INT/ORG NAT/G ECO/TAC DOMIN LEAD ATTIT PWR SOVEREIGN...ANTHOL 20. PAGE 85 A1732
MARXISM DIPLOM BAL/PWR POLICY

B62
LESSING P.,AFRICA'S RED HARVEST. AFR CHINA/COM COM
NAT/LISM

USSR ECO/UNDEV BAL/PWR DIPLOM CONTROL PWR 20 COLD/WAR INTERVENT. PAGE 87 A1789
MARXISM FOR/AID EDU/PROP

B62
MACKENTOSH J.M.,STRATEGY AND TACTICS OF SOVIET FOREIGN POLICY. CHINA/COM FUT USA+45 WOR+45 INT/ORG PLAN DOMIN LEGIT ROUTINE COERCE NUC/PWR WAR ATTIT DRIVE ORD/FREE PWR...CONCPT OBS TIME/SEQ TREND GEN/METH COLD/WAR 20. PAGE 92 A1894
COM POLICY DIPLOM USSR

B62
MODELSKI G.,SEATO-SIX STUDIES. ASIA CHINA/COM INDIA S/ASIA INT/ORG NAT/G ECO/TAC DETER ATTIT ORD/FREE PWR...TIME/SEQ COLD/WAR TOT/POP 20 SEATO. PAGE 102 A2098
MARKET ECO/UNDEV INT/TRADE

B62
SNYDER L.L.D.,THE IMPERIALISM READER. AFR ASIA CHINA/COM COM EUR+WWI FUT MOD/EUR USA+45 WOR+45 WOR-45 INT/ORG COLONIAL SOVEREIGN CMN/WLTH OAS 20. PAGE 134 A2751
DOMIN PWR DIPLOM

B62
US DEPARTMENT OF THE ARMY,AFRICA: ITS PROBLEMS AND PROSPECTS. CHINA/COM USSR INT/ORG FOR/AID COLONIAL LEAD FEDERAL DRIVE SOVEREIGN MARXISM...GEOG 20 COLD/WAR. PAGE 152 A3104
BIBLIOG/A AFR NAT/LISM DIPLOM

B62
US DEPARTMENT OF THE ARMY,GUIDE TO JAPANESE MONOGRAPHS AND JAPANESE STUDIES ON MANCHURIA: 1945-1960. CHINA/COM NAT/G DIPLOM LEAD COERCE WAR ...CHARTS 19/20 CHINJAP. PAGE 152 A3105
BIBLIOG/A FORCES ASIA S/ASIA

S62
BRZEZINSKI Z.K.,"PEACEFUL ENGAGEMENT IN COMMUNIST DISUNITY." ASIA CHINA/COM USA+45 USSR NAT/G TOP/EX CREATE ECO/TAC FOR/AID DOMIN ATTIT PERCEPT RIGID/FLEX PWR...PSY 20. PAGE 20 A0417
COM DIPLOM TOTALISM

S62
FOCSANEANU L.,"LES GRANDS TRAITES DE LA REPUBLIQUE POPULAIRE DE CHINE." ASIA CHINA/COM COM USSR WOR+45 INT/ORG NAT/G POL/PAR ACT/RES PLAN DIPLOM EDU/PROP ...CONCPT TIME/SEQ 20 TREATY. PAGE 47 A0957
VOL/ASSN TOTALISM

S62
LONDON K.,"SINO-SOVIET RELATIONS IN THE CONTEXT OF THE 'WORLD SOCIALIST SYSTEM'." ASIA CHINA/COM COM USSR INT/ORG NAT/G TOP/EX BAL/PWR DIPLOM DOMIN ATTIT PERCEPT RIGID/FLEX PWR MARXISM...METH/CNCPT TREND 20. PAGE 91 A1854
DELIB/GP CONCPT SOCISM

S62
SPECTOR I.,"SOVIET POLICY IN ASIA: A REAPPRAISAL." ASIA CHINA/COM COM INDIA INDONESIA ECO/UNDEV INT/ORG DOMIN EDU/PROP REGION RESPECT...CONCPT TREND TOT/POP COLD/WAR 20 CHINJAP. PAGE 135 A2774
S/ASIA PWR FOR/AID USSR

S62
THOMAS J.R.T.,"SOVIET BEHAVIOR IN THE QUEMOY CRISES OF 1958." CHINA/COM FUT USSR WOR+45 INT/ORG VOL/ASSN FORCES PLAN BAL/PWR DOMIN COERCE NUC/PWR REV WAR ATTIT DRIVE ORD/FREE...POLICY OBS RECORD COLD/WAR FOR/POL 20. PAGE 143 A2923
COM PWR

B63
DALLIN A.,DIVERSITY IN INTERNATIONAL COMMUNISM: A DOCUMENTARY RECORD, 1961-1963. CHINA/COM CHIEF PRESS WRITING DEBATE LEAD...POLICY ANTHOL 20. PAGE 33 A0677
COM DIPLOM POL/PAR CONFER

B63
FRANKEL J.,THE MAKING OF FOREIGN POLICY: AN ANALYSIS OF DECISION-MAKING. CHINA/COM EUR+WWI USA+45 ELITES INTELL FORCES LEGIS PLAN ATTIT ALL/VALS MORAL CONSERVE...GOV/COMP 20 PRESIDENT UN TREATY. PAGE 48 A0981
POLICY DECISION PROB/SOLV DIPLOM

B63
GRIFFITH W.E.,ALBANIA AND THE SINO-SOVIET RIFT. ALBANIA CHINA/COM USSR POL/PAR CHIEF LEGIS DIPLOM DOMIN ATTIT PWR...POLICY 20 KHRUSH/N MAO. PAGE 57 A1161
EDU/PROP MARXISM NAT/LISM GOV/REL

B63
HAMM H.,ALBANIA - CHINA'S BEACHHEAD IN EUROPE. ALBANIA CHINA/COM USSR YUGOSLAVIA ELITES SOCIETY POL/PAR DELIB/GP FORCES ECO/TAC COERCE ISOLAT PEACE MARXISM...IDEA/COMP 20 MAO. PAGE 61 A1248
DIPLOM REV NAT/G POLICY

B63
HONEY P.J.,COMMUNISM IN NORTH VIETNAM: ITS ROLE IN THE SINO-SOVIET DISPUTE. CHINA/COM INDIA USSR VIETNAM/N AGRI POL/PAR LEGIS ECO/TAC WAR PEACE ATTIT...GEOG IDEA/COMP 20. PAGE 67 A1378
POLICY MARXISM CHIEF DIPLOM

B63
RUSSELL B.,UNARMED VICTORY. CHINA/COM CUBA INDIA USA+45 WAR MARXISM...POLICY IDEA/COMP 20 KHRUSH/N COLD/WAR. PAGE 125 A2573
DIPLOM ATTIT SOCISM ORD/FREE

S63
ETIENNE G.,"'LOIS OBJECTIVES' ET PROBLEMES DE DEVELOPPEMENT DANS LE CONTEXTE CHINE-URSS." ASIA CHINA/COM COM FUT STRUCT INT/ORG VOL/ASSN TOP/EX TEC/DEV ECO/TAC ATTIT RIGID/FLEX...GEOG MGT TIME/SEQ TOT/POP 20. PAGE 42 A0866
TOTALISM USSR

S63
GUPTA S.C.,"INDIA AND THE SOVIET UNION." CHINA/COM COM INDIA S/ASIA VOL/ASSN TOP/EX FOR/AID EDU/PROP PEACE PWR...RECORD COLD/WAR 20. PAGE 58 A1195
DISPL MYTH USSR

S63
SPINELLI A.,"IL TRATTATO DI MOSCA E I PROBLEMI DELLA COESISTENZA PACIFICA." CHINA/COM COM FRANCE FUT WOR+45 INT/ORG VOL/ASSN PEACE...POLICY MYTH 20. PAGE 136 A2788
ATTIT ARMS/CONT TOTALISM

S63
WEISSBERG G.,"MAPS AS EVIDENCE IN INTERNATIONAL BOUNDARY DISPUTES: A REAPPRAISAL." CHINA/COM EUR+WWI INDIA MOD/EUR S/ASIA INT/ORG NAT/G LEGIT PERCEPT...JURID CHARTS 20. PAGE 163 A3311
LAW GEOG SOVEREIGN

S63
WOLF C.,"SOME ASPECTS OF THE 'VALUE' OF LESS-DEVELOPED COUNTRIES TO THE UNITED STATES." ASIA CHINA/COM COM USA+45 USSR ECO/UNDEV BAL/PWR ECO/TAC FOR/AID DOMIN EDU/PROP ATTIT PWR...POLICY METH/CNCPT CONT/OBS TREND CHARTS 20. PAGE 166 A3379
CONCPT GEN/LAWS DIPLOM

N63
PATEL H.M.,THE DEFENCE OF INDIA (PAMPHLET). CHINA/COM INDIA PAKISTAN WOR+45 TEC/DEV BAL/PWR DIPLOM CONTROL WAR. PAGE 114 A2340
FORCES POLICY SOVEREIGN DETER

B64
CHENG C.,ECONOMIC RELATIONS BETWEEN PEKING AND MOSCOW: 1949-63. ASIA CHINA/COM COM USSR FINAN INDUS CONSULT TEC/DEV INT/TRADE...PREDICT CHARTS BIBLIOG 20. PAGE 26 A0527
DIPLOM FOR/AID MARXISM

B64
COHEN M.,LAW AND POLITICS IN SPACE: SPECIFIC AND URGENT PROBLEMS IN THE LAW OF OUTER SPACE. CHINA/COM COM USA+45 USSR WOR+45 COM/IND INT/ORG NAT/G LEGIT NUC/PWR ATTIT BIO/SOC...JURID CONCPT CONGRESS 20 STALIN/J. PAGE 28 A0561
DELIB/GP LAW INT/LAW SPACE

B64
DUROSELLE J.B.,LA COMMUNAUTE INTERNATIONALE FACE AUX JEUNES ETATS. CHINA/COM COM S/ASIA USSR INT/ORG ROLE...ANTHOL 20 UN SEATO THIRD/WRLD. PAGE 40 A0808
DIPLOM COLONIAL ECO/UNDEV SOVEREIGN

B64
HAMRELL S.,THE SOVIET BLOC, CHINA, AND AFRICA. AFR CHINA/COM COM USSR ECO/UNDEV EDU/PROP 20. PAGE 61 A1249
MARXISM DIPLOM CONTROL FOR/AID

B64
HARPER F.,OUT OF CHINA. CHINA/COM ELITES STRATA ATTIT PERSON...BIOG 20 MAO HONG/KONG MIGRATION. PAGE 62 A1264
HABITAT DEEP/INT DIPLOM MARXISM

B64
LATOURETTE K.S.,CHINA. ASIA CHINA/COM FUT USSR ECO/UNDEV ECO/TAC WAR 19/20. PAGE 85 A1744
MARXISM NAT/G POLICY DIPLOM

B64
LENS S.,THE FUTILE CRUSADE. ASIA CHINA/COM L/A+17C USA+45 USSR WOR+45 ECO/DEV BAL/PWR DIPLOM NUC/PWR WAR NAT/LISM PEACE 20 COLD/WAR PRESIDENT CIA. PAGE 87 A1774
ORD/FREE ANOMIE COM MARXISM

B64
ROSENAU J.N.,INTERNATIONAL ASPECTS OF CIVIL STRIFE. CHINA/COM CUBA EUR+WWI USA+45 USSR BAL/PWR EDU/PROP NEUTRAL COERCE MORAL...NAT/COMP 20 COLD/WAR UN. PAGE 124 A2533
POLICY DIPLOM REV WAR

B64
SAKAI R.K.,STUDIES ON ASIA, 1964. ASIA CHINA/COM ISRAEL MALAYSIA S/ASIA USA+45 USSR ECO/UNDEV FAM POL/PAR SECT CONSULT NAT/LISM...POLICY SOC 20 CHINJAP. PAGE 126 A2588
PWR DIPLOM

B64
ZEBOT C.A.,THE ECONOMICS OF COMPETITIVE COEXISTENCE. CHINA/COM USSR WOR+45 FINAN MARKET FOR/AID PRICE DEMAND EQUILIB WEALTH ALL/IDEOS 20. PAGE 169 A3450
TEC/DEV DIPLOM METH/COMP

S64
DE GAULLE C.,"FRENCH WORLD VIEW." AFR ASIA CHINA/COM EUR+WWI ISLAM ECO/UNDEV INT/ORG NAT/G VOL/ASSN ACT/RES DIPLOM ECO/TAC EDU/PROP ATTIT DRIVE WEALTH 20. PAGE 35 A0702
TOP/EX PWR FOR/AID FRANCE

S64
DELGADO J.,"EL MOMENTO POLITICO HISPANOAMERICA." CHINA/COM FUT PANAMA USA+45 USSR INT/ORG NAT/G POL/PAR FORCES DOMIN REGION COERCE ATTIT ALL/VALS ...TRADIT CONCPT COLD/WAR 20. PAGE 36 A0728
L/A+17C EDU/PROP NAT/LISM

S64
DEVILLERS P.H.,"L'URSS, LA CHINE ET LES ORIGINES DE LA GUERRE DE COREE." ASIA CHINA/COM COM USSR INT/ORG ECO/TAC EDU/PROP ATTIT RIGID/FLEX PWR...STAND/INT HIST/WRIT COLD/WAR 20. PAGE 37 A0751
WOR+45 KOREA

S64
LEVI W.,"CHINA AND THE UNITED NATIONS." ASIA CHINA CHINA/COM WOR+45 WOR-45 CONSTN NAT/G DELIB/GP EX/STRUC FORCES ACT/RES EDU/PROP PWR...POLICY RECORD TIME/SEQ GEN/LAWS UN COLD/WAR 20. PAGE 88 A1794
INT/ORG ATTIT NAT/LISM

B65
BROMKE A.,THE COMMUNIST STATES AT THE CROSSROADS
COM

BETWEEN MOSCOW AND PEKING. CHINA/COM USSR INGP/REL NAT/LISM TOTALISM 20. PAGE 19 A0389
DIPLOM MARXISM REGION

B65
FRASER S.,GOVERNMENTAL POLICY AND INTERNATIONAL EDUCATION. CHINA/COM COM USA+45 WOR+45 CONTROL MARXISM...ANTHOL BIBLIOG/A 20 UN. PAGE 48 A0989
EDU/PROP DIPLOM POLICY NAT/G

B65
RAPPAPORT A.,ISSUES IN AMERICAN DIPLOMACY: WORLD POWER AND LEADERSHIP SINCE 1895 (VOL. II). CHINA/COM EUR+WWI L/A+17C USA+45 USA-45 NAT/G ECO/TAC DOMIN CONFER LEAD NUC/PWR WEAPON...DECISION 19/20 WILSON/W ROOSEVLT/F CHINJAP. PAGE 119 A2447
WAR POLICY DIPLOM

B65
US DEPARTMENT OF DEFENSE,US SECURITY ARMS CONTROL, AND DISARMAMENT 1961-1965 (PAMPHLET). CHINA/COM COM GERMANY/W ISRAEL SPACE USA+45 USSR WOR+45 FORCES EDU/PROP DETER EQUILIB PEACE ALL/VALS...GOV/COMP 20 NATO. PAGE 151 A3077
BIBLIOG/A ARMS/CONT NUC/PWR DIPLOM

B65
US SENATE COMM ON JUDICIARY,REFUGEE PROBLEMS IN SOUTH VIETNAM AND LAOS: HEARINGS BEFORE SUBCOMMITTEE TO INVESTIGATE PROBLEMS OF REFUGEES, ESCAPEES. CHINA/COM LAOS USA+45 VIETNAM/S PROB/SOLV DIPLOM GOV/REL GP/REL EFFICIENCY ORD/FREE...POLICY GEOG 20 CONGRESS MIGRATION. PAGE 157 A3194
STRANGE HABITAT FOR/AID CIVMIL/REL

B65
WINT G.,COMMUNIST CHINA'S CRUSADE: MAO'S ROAD TO POWER AND THE NEW CAMPAIGN FOR WORLD REVOLUTION. ASIA CHINA/COM USA+45 USSR NAT/G POL/PAR DOMIN COERCE WAR PWR...POLICY CHARTS IDEA/COMP BIBLIOG 20 MAO. PAGE 165 A3364
DIPLOM MARXISM REV COLONIAL

S65
FLEMING D.F.,"CAN PAX AMERICANA SUCCEED?" ASIA CHINA/COM EUR+WWI USSR VIETNAM BAL/PWR DIPLOM DOMIN COERCE GOV/REL 20. PAGE 46 A0948
DECISION ATTIT ECO/TAC

S65
HOLSTI O.R.,"EAST-WEST CONFLICT AND SINO-SOVIET RELATIONS" CHINA/COM USSR COMPUTER REGION DECISION. PAGE 67 A1373
VOL/ASSN DIPLOM CON/ANAL COM

S65
PRABHAKAR P.,"SURVEY OF RESEARCH AND SOURCE MATERIALS; THE SINO-INDIAN BORDER DISPUTE." CHINA/COM INDIA LAW NAT/G PLAN BAL/PWR WAR...POLICY 20 COLD/WAR. PAGE 117 A2404
BIBLIOG ASIA S/ASIA DIPLOM

S65
RAY H.,"THE POLICY OF RUSSIA TOWARDS SINO-INDIAN CONFLICT." ASIA CHINA/COM COM INDIA USSR NAT/G TOP/EX FOR/AID EDU/PROP NEUTRAL COERCE PEACE RIGID/FLEX PWR...METH/CNCPT TIME/SEQ VAL/FREE 20. PAGE 120 A2452
S/ASIA ATTIT DIPLOM WAR

B66
SUPPLEMENTAL FOREIGN ASSISTANCE FISCAL YEAR 1966: VIETNAM. CHINA/COM COM S/ASIA USA+45 VIETNAM EXTR/IND FINAN DIPLOM TAX GUERRILLA HABITAT ORD/FREE...STAT CHARTS 20 SENATE PRESIDENT. PAGE 4 A0077
CONFER LEGIS WAR FOR/AID

B66
BRACKMAN A.C.,SOUTHEAST ASIA'S SECOND FRONT: THE POWER STRUGGLE IN THE MALAY ARCHIPELAGO. CHINA/COM INDONESIA MALAYSIA ECO/UNDEV INT/ORG NAT/G FORCES DIPLOM EDU/PROP REGION COERCE GUERRILLA AUTHORIT POPULISM...MAJORIT 20 KENNEDY/JF SEATO. PAGE 18 A0367
S/ASIA MARXISM REV

B66
FITZGERALD C.P.,THE BIRTH OF COMMUNIST CHINA (2ND ED.). ASIA CHINA/COM STRUCT BAL/PWR DIPLOM ECO/TAC INT/TRADE WEALTH 20. PAGE 46 A0942
REV MARXISM ECO/UNDEV

B66
GROSS F.,WORLD POLITICS AND TENSION AREAS. CHINA/COM SOMALIA VENEZUELA COERCE GP/REL RACE/REL ATTIT HABITAT 19/20 CASEBOOK NEWYORK/C. PAGE 57 A1173
DIPLOM WAR PROB/SOLV

B66
HALPERIN M.H.,CHINA AND NUCLEAR PROLIFERATION (PAMPHLET). CHINA/COM FUT INDIA USA+45 USSR ARMS/CONT WAR 20 CHINJAP. PAGE 60 A1239
NUC/PWR FORCES POLICY DIPLOM

B66
JACK H.A.,RELIGION AND PEACE: PAPERS FROM THE NATIONAL INTER-RELIGIOUS CONFERENCE ON PEACE, WASHINGTON, 1966. CHINA/COM USA+45 VIETNAM WOR+45 FORCES FOR/AID LEAD PERS/REL. PAGE 72 A1472
PEACE SECT SUPEGO DIPLOM

B66
LONDON K.,EASTERN EUROPE IN TRANSITION. CHINA/COM USSR DOMIN COLONIAL CENTRAL RIGID/FLEX PWR...SOC ANTHOL 20. PAGE 91 A1855
SOVEREIGN COM NAT/LISM DIPLOM

B66
MORRIS B.S.,INTERNATIONAL COMMUNISM AND AMERICAN POLICY. CHINA/COM USA+45 USSR INT/ORG POL/PAR GP/REL NAT/LISM ATTIT PERCEPT 20. PAGE 105 A2147
DIPLOM POLICY MARXISM

B66
US DEPARTMENT OF THE ARMY,COMMUNIST CHINA: A STRATEGIC SURVEY: A BIBLIOGRAPHY (PAMPHLET NO. 20-67). CHINA/COM COM INDIA USSR NAT/G POL/PAR EX/STRUC FORCES NUC/PWR REV ATTIT...POLICY GEOG CHARTS. PAGE 152 A3109
BIBLIOG/A MARXISM S/ASIA DIPLOM

B66
ZABLOCKI C.J.,SINO-SOVIET RIVALRY. AFR ASIA CHINA/COM CUBA EUR+WWI L/A+17C USA+45 USSR WOR+45 POL/PAR FORCES COERCE NUC/PWR...GOV/COMP IDEA/COMP 20 MAO KHRUSH/N. PAGE 169 A3442
DIPLOM MARXISM COM

L66
MCDOUGAL M.S.,"CHINESE PARTICIPATION IN THE UNITED NATIONS: THE LEGAL IMPERATIVES OF A NEGOTIATED SOLUTION" CHINA/COM WOR+45 VOL/ASSN DIPLOM PARTIC ...DECISION IDEA/COMP 20 UN. PAGE 98 A2010
INT/ORG REPRESENT POLICY PROB/SOLV

S66
CHIU H.,"COMMUNIST CHINA'S ATTITUDE TOWARD INTERNATIONAL LAW" CHINA/COM USSR LAW CONSTN DIPLOM GP/REL 20 LENIN/VI. PAGE 26 A0532
INT/LAW MARXISM CONCPT IDEA/COMP

S66
CRANMER-BYNG J.L.,"THE CHINESE ATTITUDE TOWARDS EXTERNAL RELATIONS." ASIA CHINA/COM EXEC NAT/LISM MARXISM...POLICY 20. PAGE 32 A0660
ATTIT DIPLOM NAT/G

N66
US HOUSE COMM FOREIGN AFFAIRS,UNITED STATES POLICY TOWARD ASIA (PAMPHLET). CHINA/COM USA+45 USSR VIETNAM INT/ORG NAT/G PWR MARXISM 20 UN. PAGE 154 A3133
POLICY ASIA DIPLOM PLAN

B67
GRIFFITH SB I.I.,THE CHINESE PEOPLE'S LIBERATION ARMY. CHINA/COM DIPLOM DOMIN GUERRILLA NUC/PWR REV ...CHARTS BIBLIOG 20. PAGE 57 A1163
FORCES CIVMIL/REL NAT/LISM PWR

B67
HALPERIN M.H.,CONTEMPORARY MILITARY STRATEGY. ASIA CHINA/COM USA+45 USSR INT/ORG FORCES ACT/RES PLAN TEC/DEV BAL/PWR COERCE WAR...METH/COMP BIBLIOG 20 NATO. PAGE 60 A1240
DIPLOM NUC/PWR DETER ARMS/CONT

B67
KAROL K.S.,CHINA, THE OTHER COMMUNISM (TRANS. BY TOM BAISTOW). CHINA/COM CULTURE INDUS FORCES DIPLOM EDU/PROP CONTROL EXEC NUC/PWR ATTIT...SOC CHARTS 20. PAGE 77 A1567
NAT/G POL/PAR MARXISM INGP/REL

B67
SALISBURY H.E.,ORBIT OF CHINA. ASIA CHINA/COM DIPLOM PEACE PWR 20. PAGE 126 A2593
EDU/PROP OBS INT ARMS/CONT

S67
"CHINESE STATEMENT ON NUCLEAR PROLIFERATION." CHINA/COM USA+45 USSR DOMIN COLONIAL PWR. PAGE 4 A0078
NUC/PWR BAL/PWR ARMS/CONT DIPLOM

S67
ADIE W.A.C.,"CHINA'S 'SECOND LIBERATION'." CHINA/COM SOCIETY WORKER DIPLOM TASK 20 MAO. PAGE 4 A0090
MARXISM REV INGP/REL ANOMIE

S67
EISENDRATH C.,"THE OUTER SPACE TREATY." CHINA/COM COM USA+45 DIPLOM CONTROL NUC/PWR...INT/LAW 20 UN COLD/WAR TREATY. PAGE 41 A0831
SPACE INT/ORG PEACE ARMS/CONT

S67
FARQUHAR D.M.,"CHINESE COMMUNIST ASSESSMENTS OF A FOREIGN CONQUEST DYNASTY." CHINA/COM DIPLOM CONTROL ...METH 20. PAGE 44 A0900
MARXISM HIST/WRIT POLICY COLONIAL

S67
LACOUTRE J.,"HO CHI MINH." CHINA/COM USSR VIETNAM/N NAT/G CHIEF TOP/EX LEAD NEUTRAL...REALPOL PREDICT 20. PAGE 83 A1708
NAT/LISM MARXISM REV DIPLOM

S67
MEYER J.,"CUBA S'ENFERME DANS SA REVOLUTION." CHINA/COM CUBA USSR NAT/G TOP/EX DIPLOM LEAD ATTIT ...PREDICT 20. PAGE 100 A2053
MARXISM REV CHIEF NAT/LISM

S67
TERRILL R.,"THE SIEGE MENTALITY." CHINA/COM NAT/G FORCES DIPLOM REV EFFICIENCY NAT/LISM MARXISM ...TREND 20. PAGE 142 A2904
EDU/PROP WAR DOMIN

S67
WALKER R.L.,"THE WEST AND THE 'NEW ASIA'." CHINA/COM ECO/UNDEV DIPLOM...PREDICT 20. PAGE 160 A3266
ASIA INT/TRADE COLONIAL REGION

CHINESE/AM....CHINESE IMMIGRANTS TO US AND THEIR DESCENDANTS

CHITTAGONG....CHITTAGONG HILL TRIBES

CHIU H. A0532

CHO S.S. A0533

CHOICE (IN DECISION-MAKING)....SEE PROB/SOLV

CHONCHOL J. A2716

CHOOSE....CHOICE, ELECTION

N
JOURNAL OF POLITICS. USA+45 USA-45 CONSTN POL/PAR EX/STRUC LEGIS PROB/SOLV DIPLOM CT/SYS CHOOSE RACE/REL 20. PAGE 1 A0017 — BIBLIOG/A NAT/G LAW LOC/G

C06
MONTGOMERY H.,"A DICTIONARY OF POLITICAL PHRASES AND ILLUSIONS WITH A SHORT BIBLIOGRAPHY." EUR+WWI MOD/EUR UK AGRI LABOR LOC/G NAT/G COLONIAL CHOOSE RACE/REL. PAGE 103 A2114 — BIBLIOG DICTIONARY POLICY DIPLOM

N19
MEZERIK A.G.,COLONIALISM AND THE UNITED NATIONS (PAMPHLET). WOR+45 NAT/G ADMIN LEAD WAR CHOOSE EFFICIENCY PEACE ATTIT ORD/FREE...POLICY CHARTS UN COLD/WAR. PAGE 100 A2061 — COLONIAL DIPLOM BAL/PWR INT/ORG

B26
INTERNATIONAL BIBLIOGRAPHY OF POLITICAL SCIENCE. WOR+45 NAT/G POL/PAR EX/STRUC LEGIS CT/SYS LEAD CHOOSE GOV/REL ATTIT...PHIL/SCI 20. PAGE 3 A0049 — BIBLIOG DIPLOM CONCPT ADMIN

B32
FLEMMING D.,THE UNITED STATES AND THE LEAGUE OF NATIONS, 1918-1920. FUT USA-45 NAT/G LEGIS TOP/EX DEBATE CHOOSE PEACE ATTIT SOVEREIGN...TIME/SEQ CON/ANAL CONGRESS LEAGUE/NAT 20 TREATY. PAGE 46 A0950 — INT/ORG EDU/PROP

B33
REID H.D.,RECUEIL DES COURS; TOME 45: LES SERVITUDES INTERNATIONALES III. FRANCE CONSTN DELIB/GP PRESS CONTROL REV WAR CHOOSE PEACE MORAL MARITIME TREATY. PAGE 120 A2457 — ORD/FREE DIPLOM LAW

B33
WAMBAUCH S.,PLEBISCITES SINCE THE WORLD WAR: WITH A COLLECTION OF OFFICIAL DOCUMENTS. WOR-45 COLONIAL SANCTION...MAJORIT DECISION CHARTS BIBLIOG 19/20 WWI. PAGE 161 A3272 — DIPLOM CONSTN NAT/G CHOOSE

B38
RAPPARD W.E.,THE CRISIS OF DEMOCRACY. EUR+WWI UNIV WOR-45 CULTURE SOCIETY ECO/DEV INT/ORG POL/PAR ACT/RES EDU/PROP EXEC CHOOSE ATTIT ALL/VALS...SOC OBS HIST/WRIT TIME/SEQ LEAGUE/NAT NAZI TOT/POP 20. PAGE 119 A2449 — NAT/G CONCPT

B44
DAVIS H.E.,PIONEERS IN WORLD ORDER. WOR-45 CONSTN ECO/TAC DOMIN EDU/PROP LEGIT ADJUD ADMIN ARMS/CONT CHOOSE KNOWL ORD/FREE...POLICY JURID SOC STAT OBS CENSUS TIME/SEQ ANTHOL LEAGUE/NAT 20. PAGE 34 A0691 — INT/ORG ROUTINE

B46
BLUM L.,FOR ALL MANKIND (TRANS. BY W. PICKLES). FRANCE GERMANY USSR LAW SOCIETY STRUCT POL/PAR WORKER DIPLOM DOMIN CHOOSE ORD/FREE FASCISM 20. PAGE 16 A0323 — POPULISM SOCIALIST NAT/G WAR

B47
HEIMANN E.,FREEDOM AND ORDER: LESSONS FROM THE WAR. WOR-45 CONSTN FORCES CHOOSE CIVMIL/REL PERSON ALL/IDEOS SOCISM...SOC IDEA/COMP WORSHIP 20. PAGE 64 A1308 — NAT/G SOCIETY ORD/FREE DIPLOM

L47
HISS D.,"UNITED STATES PARTICIPATION IN THE UNITED NATIONS." USA+45 EX/STRUC PLAN DIPLOM ROUTINE CHOOSE...PLURIST UN 20. PAGE 65 A1342 — INT/ORG PWR

B48
HOWARD J.E.,PARLIAMENT AND FOREIGN POLICY IN FRANCE. FRANCE CONSTN DELIB/GP BUDGET ADMIN PARL/PROC CHOOSE...BIBLIOG/A 20 PARLIAMENT. PAGE 68 A1399 — LEGIS CONTROL DIPLOM ATTIT

B50
CHURCHILL W.,TRIUMPH AND TRAGEDY. UK WOR-45 INT/ORG NAT/G DELIB/GP FORCES TOP/EX DIPLOM COERCE CHOOSE ATTIT ORD/FREE PWR WEALTH...SELF/OBS CHARTS NAZI 20. PAGE 26 A0539 — BIOG PEACE WAR

B50
JIMENEZ E.,VOTING AND HANDLING OF DISPUTES IN THE SECURITY COUNCIL. WOR+45 CONSTN INT/ORG DIPLOM LEGIT DETER CHOOSE MORAL ORD/FREE PWR...JURID TIME/SEQ COLD/WAR UN 20. PAGE 74 A1517 — DELIB/GP ROUTINE

L50
US SENATE COMM. GOVT. OPER.,"REVISION OF THE UN CHARTER." FUT USA+45 WOR+45 CONSTN ECO/DEV ECO/UNDEV NAT/G DELIB/GP ACT/RES CREATE PLAN EXEC ROUTINE CHOOSE ALL/VALS...POLICY CONCPT CONGRESS UN TOT/POP 20 COLD/WAR. PAGE 157 A3196 — INT/ORG LEGIS PEACE

B51
RAPPAPORT A.,THE BRITISH PRESS AND WILSONIAN NEUTRALITY. UK WOR-45 SEA POL/PAR WAR CHOOSE PEACE ATTIT PERCEPT...GEOG 20 WILSON/W. PAGE 119 A2446 — PRESS DIPLOM NEUTRAL POLICY

S51
BELKNAP G.,"POLITICAL PARTY IDENTIFICATION AND ATTITUDES TOWARD FOREIGN POLICY" (BMR)" USA+45 — POL/PAR ATTIT

VOL/ASSN CONTROL CHOOSE...STAT INT CHARTS 20. PAGE 12 A0254 — POLICY DIPLOM

B53
STOUT H.M.,BRITISH GOVERNMENT. UK FINAN LOC/G POL/PAR DELIB/GP DIPLOM ADMIN COLONIAL CHOOSE ORD/FREE...JURID BIBLIOG 20 COMMONWLTH. PAGE 139 A2837 — NAT/G PARL/PROC CONSTN NEW/LIB

B55
JOY C.T.,HOW COMMUNISTS NEGOTIATE. COM USA+45 CONSTN CULTURE ECO/UNDEV NAT/G CONSULT DELIB/GP FORCES PLAN ECO/TAC DOMIN EDU/PROP LEGIT EXEC ROUTINE COERCE WAR CHOOSE PEACE ATTIT RIGID/FLEX ORD/FREE PWR...POLICY 20. PAGE 75 A1539 — ASIA INT/ORG DIPLOM

B56
GEORGE A.L.,WOODROW WILSON AND COLONEL HOUSE. WOR-45 CONSTN FACE/GP INT/ORG NAT/G POL/PAR CONSULT LEGIT EXEC COERCE CHOOSE ATTIT DRIVE PERSON MORAL ORD/FREE PWR RESPECT...POLICY MGT PSY OBS RECORD INT LEAGUE/NAT. PAGE 52 A1060 — USA-45 BIOG DIPLOM

B56
SNELL J.L.,THE MEANING OF YALTA: BIG THREE DIPLOMACY AND THE NEW BALANCE OF POWER. EUR+WWI GERMANY USA-45 USSR FORCES PLAN BAL/PWR DIPLOM WAR CHOOSE PEACE...CHARTS BIBLIOG 20 UN CHINJAP ROOSEVLT/F. PAGE 134 A2749 — CONFER CHIEF POLICY PROB/SOLV

B56
SOHN L.B.,BASIC DOCUMENTS OF THE UNITED NATIONS. WOR+45 LAW INT/ORG LEGIT EXEC ROUTINE CHOOSE PWR ...JURID CONCPT GEN/LAWS ANTHOL UN TOT/POP OAS FAO ILO 20. PAGE 135 A2761 — DELIB/GP CONSTN

B56
VON BECKERATH E.,HANDWORTERBUCH DER SOCIALWISSENSCHAFTEN (II VOLS.). EUR+WWI GERMANY POL/PAR WORKER DIPLOM LEAD CHOOSE SUFF WEALTH...SOC 20. PAGE 159 A3249 — BIBLIOG INT/TRADE NAT/G ECO/DEV

B56
WILSON P.,GOVERNMENT AND POLITICS OF INDIA AND PAKISTAN: 1885-1955; A BIBLIOGRAPHY OF WORKS IN WESTERN LANGUAGES. INDIA PAKISTAN CONSTN LOC/G POL/PAR FORCES DIPLOM ADMIN WAR CHOOSE...BIOG CON/ANAL 19/20. PAGE 165 A3361 — BIBLIOG COLONIAL NAT/G S/ASIA

B58
HOLT R.T.,RADIO FREE EUROPE. FUT USA+45 CULTURE ECO/DEV INT/ORG KIN POL/PAR SECT FORCES ACT/RES DIPLOM COERCE REV CHOOSE PEACE ATTIT PWR...MAJORIT CONCPT COLD/WAR WORK 20 RFE. PAGE 67 A1374 — COM EDU/PROP COM/IND

L58
INT. SOC. SCI. BULL.,"TECHNIQUES OF MEDIATION AND CONCILIATION." EUR+WWI USA+45 SOCIETY INDUS INT/ORG LABOR NAT/G LEGIS DIPLOM EDU/PROP CHOOSE ATTIT RIGID/FLEX...JURID CONCPT GEN/LAWS 20. PAGE 70 A1447 — VOL/ASSN DELIB/GP INT/LAW

S58
BLAISDELL D.C.,"PRESSURE GROUPS, FOREIGN POLICIES, AND INTERNATIONAL POLITICS." USA+45 WOR+45 INT/ORG PLAN DOMIN EDU/PROP LEGIT ADMIN ROUTINE CHOOSE ...DECISION MGT METH/CNCPT CON/ANAL 20. PAGE 15 A0303 — PROF/ORG PWR

S58
BURNS A.L.,"THE INTERNATIONAL CONSEQUENCES OF EXPECTING SURPRISE." WOR+45 INT/ORG NAT/G FORCES DIPLOM COERCE NUC/PWR WAR CHOOSE ORD/FREE ...METH/CNCPT STYLE OBS STERTYP TOT/POP VAL/FREE. PAGE 22 A0440 — PLAN PWR DETER

S58
STAAR R.F.,"ELECTIONS IN COMMUNIST POLAND." EUR+WWI SOCIETY INT/ORG NAT/G POL/PAR LEGIS ACT/RES ECO/TAC EDU/PROP ADJUD ADMIN ROUTINE COERCE TOTALISM ATTIT ORD/FREE PWR 20. PAGE 137 A2797 — COM CHOOSE POLAND

C58
CARTER G.M.,"THE POLITICS OF INEQUALITY: SOUTH AFRICA SINCE 1948." SOUTH/AFR CONSTN DIPLOM EDU/PROP REPRESENT DISCRIM ATTIT...POLICY PREDICT CHARTS BIBLIOG 20. PAGE 25 A0504 — RACE/REL POL/PAR CHOOSE DOMIN

C58
GOLAY J.F.,"THE FOUNDING OF THE FEDERAL REPUBLIC OF GERMANY." GERMANY/W CONSTN EX/STRUC DIPLOM ADMIN CHOOSE...DECISION BIBLIOG 20. PAGE 53 A1088 — FEDERAL NAT/G PARL/PROC POL/PAR

B59
BOWLES C.,THE COMING POLITICAL BREAKTHROUGH. USA+45 ECO/DEV EX/STRUC ATTIT...CONCPT OBS 20. PAGE 18 A0360 — DIPLOM CHOOSE PREDICT POL/PAR

B59
PAGAN B.,HISTORIA DE LOS PARTIDOS POLITICOS PUERTORRIQUENOS 1898-1956. PUERT/RICO PROVS DIPLOM DOMIN EDU/PROP PARTIC 20. PAGE 113 A2316 — POL/PAR CHOOSE COLONIAL PWR

S59
ZAUBERMAN A.,"SOVIET BLOC ECONOMIC INTEGRATION." COM CULTURE INTELL ECO/DEV INDUS TOP/EX ACT/RES PLAN ECO/TAC INT/TRADE ROUTINE CHOOSE ATTIT ...TIME/SEQ 20. PAGE 169 A3448 — MARKET INT/ORG USSR TOTALISM

B60
DAVIDS J.,AMERICA AND THE WORLD OF OUR TIME: UNITED — USA+45

STATES DIPLOMACY IN THE TWENTIETH CENTURY. USA-45 SOCIETY ECO/DEV INT/ORG NAT/G POL/PAR FORCES ECO/TAC DOMIN EDU/PROP EXEC COERCE WAR CHOOSE ATTIT PERSON ORD/FREE...CONCPT TIME/SEQ TOT/POP 20. PAGE 34 A0686 PWR DIPLOM

B60
HOLT R.T.,STRATEGIC PSYCHOLOGICAL OPERATIONS AND AMERICAN FOREIGN POLICY. ITALY USA+45 FOR/AID DOMIN RUMOR ADMIN TASK WAR CHOOSE ATTIT ALL/IDEOS...PSY COLD/WAR. PAGE 67 A1375 EDU/PROP ACT/RES DIPLOM POLICY

B60
HOVET T. JR.,BLOC POLITICS IN THE UNITED NATIONS. WOR+45...POLICY STAT CHARTS METH UN. PAGE 68 A1396 LOBBY INT/ORG DIPLOM CHOOSE

B60
JACOBSON H.K.,AMERICAN FOREIGN POLICY. COM EUR+WWI USA+45 USA-45 ECO/DEV ECO/UNDEV INT/ORG NAT/G INT/TRADE EDU/PROP COLONIAL CHOOSE MARXISM 20 NATO. PAGE 72 A1485 POL/PAR PWR DIPLOM

B60
MEYRIAT J.,LA SCIENCE POLITIQUE EN FRANCE, 1945-1958; BIBLIOGRAPHIES FRANCAISES DE SCIENCES SOCIALES (VOL. I). EUR+WWI FRANCE POL/PAR DIPLOM ADMIN CHOOSE ATTIT...IDEA/COMP METH/COMP NAT/COMP 20. PAGE 100 A2057 BIBLIOG/A NAT/G CONCPT PHIL/SCI

B60
MUGRIDGE D.H.,A GUIDE TO THE STUDY OF THE UNITED STATES OF AMERICA: REPRESENTATIVE BOOKS REFLECTING THE DEVELOPMENT OF AMERICAN LIFE. USA+45 USA-45 CONSTN POL/PAR FORCES DIPLOM PRESS CHOOSE...SOC 17/20. PAGE 105 A2165 BIBLIOG/A CULTURE NAT/G POLICY

B60
THE AFRICA 1960 COMMITTEE,MANDATE IN TRUST; THE PROBLEM OF SOUTH WEST AFRICA. GERMANY STRUCT REGION SANCTION CHOOSE DISCRIM...INT/LAW 20 AFRICA/SW UN LEAGUE/NAT TRUST/TERR. PAGE 142 A2910 NAT/G DIPLOM COLONIAL RACE/REL

L60
HAAS E.B.,"CONSENSUS FORMATION IN THE COUNCIL OF EUROPE." EUR+WWI NAT/G DELIB/GP DIPLOM REGION CHOOSE PWR SOVEREIGN...RELATIV NEW/IDEA QUANT CHARTS INDEX TOT/POP OEEC 20 COUNCL/EUR. PAGE 59 A1206 POL/PAR INT/ORG STAT

S60
COHEN A.,"THE NEW AFRICA AND THE UN." FUT ECO/UNDEV NAT/G ECO/TAC INT/TRADE CHOOSE ATTIT ORD/FREE PWR ...POLICY METH/CNCPT OBS TREND CON/ANAL GEN/LAWS TOT/POP VAL/FREE UN 20. PAGE 27 A0558 AFR INT/ORG BAL/PWR FOR/AID

S60
FITZGIBBON R.H.,"DICTATORSHIP AND DEMOCRACY IN LATIN AMERICA." FUT ECO/DEV ECO/UNDEV INT/ORG LOC/G NAT/G TOP/EX PLAN TEC/DEV ECO/TAC CHOOSE ATTIT DRIVE PERSON ALL/VALS OAS TOT/POP 20. PAGE 46 A0943 L/A+17C ACT/RES INT/TRADE

S60
MIKESELL R.F.,"AMERICA'S ECONOMIC RESPONSIBILITY AS A GREAT POWER." COM FUT USA+45 USSR WOR+45 INT/ORG PLAN ECO/TAC FOR/AID EDU/PROP CHOOSE WEALTH ...POLICY 20. PAGE 101 A2069 ECO/UNDEV BAL/PWR CAP/ISM

S60
RIESELBACH Z.N.,"QUANTITATIVE TECHNIQUES FOR STUDYING VOTING BEHAVIOR IN THE UNITED NATIONS GENERAL ASSEMBLY." FUT S/ASIA USA+45 INT/ORG BAL/PWR DIPLOM ECO/TAC FOR/AID ADMIN PWR...POLICY METH/CNCPT METH UN 20. PAGE 121 A2478 QUANT CHOOSE

B61
BURDETTE F.L.,POLITICAL SCIENCE: A SELECTED BIBLIOGRAPHY OF BOOKS IN PRINT, WITH ANNOTATIONS (PAMPHLET). LAW LOC/G NAT/G POL/PAR PROVS DIPLOM EDU/PROP ADMIN CHOOSE ATTIT 20. PAGE 21 A0432 BIBLIOG/A GOV/COMP CONCPT ROUTINE

B61
FUCHS G.,GEGEN HITLER UND HENLEIN. CZECHOSLVK GERMANY DIPLOM CHOOSE GP/REL TOTALISM SOVEREIGN 20 HITLER/A. PAGE 50 A1013 FASCISM WORKER POL/PAR NAT/LISM

B61
GRAEBNER N.,THE NEW ISOLATIONISM: A STUDY IN POLITICS AND FOREIGN POLICY SINCE 1960. USA+45 INT/ORG LOC/G NAT/G POL/PAR LEGIS BAL/PWR EDU/PROP CHOOSE ATTIT PERSON ORD/FREE 20 TRUMAN/HS EISNHWR/DD. PAGE 55 A1120 EXEC PWR DIPLOM

B61
MENDEL D.H. JR.,THE JAPANESE PEOPLE AND FOREIGN POLICY. CHINA/COM KOREA USA+45 USSR SOCIETY FORCES CHOOSE 20 CHINJAP. PAGE 99 A2037 NAT/G DIPLOM POLICY ATTIT

B61
PALMER N.D.,THE INDIAN POLITICAL SYSTEM. INDIA ECO/UNDEV SECT CHIEF COLONIAL CHOOSE ALL/IDEOS SOCISM...CHARTS BIBLIOG/A 20. PAGE 113 A2322 NAT/LISM POL/PAR NAT/G DIPLOM

B61
SCOTT A.M.,POLITICS, USA; CASES ON THE AMERICAN DEMOCRATIC PROCESS. USA+45 CHIEF FORCES DIPLOM LOBBY CHOOSE RACE/REL FEDERAL ATTIT...JURID ANTHOL T 20 PRESIDENT CONGRESS CIVIL/LIB. PAGE 130 A2669 CT/SYS CONSTN NAT/G PLAN

B61
TETENS T.H.,THE NEW GERMANY AND THE OLD NAZIS. EUR+WWI GERMANY/W USA+45 NAT/G CRIME CHOOSE RACE/REL TOTALISM AGE/Y ATTIT 20 JEWS NAZI ADENAUER/K. PAGE 142 A2905 FASCISM DIPLOM FOR/AID POL/PAR

B61
WARD R.E.,JAPANESE POLITICAL SCIENCE: A GUIDE TO JAPANESE REFERENCE AND RESEARCH MATERIALS (2ND ED.). LAW CONSTN STRATA NAT/G POL/PAR DELIB/GP LEGIS ADMIN CHOOSE GP/REL...INT/LAW 19/20 CHINJAP. PAGE 161 A3282 BIBLIOG/A PHIL/SCI

S61
ROSTOW W.W.,"THE FUTURE OF FOREIGN AID." COM FUT WOR+45 ECO/DEV INDUS INT/ORG NAT/G CONSULT ACT/RES PLAN DOMIN LEGIT CHOOSE RIGID/FLEX ALL/VALS ...MAJORIT CONCPT TREND TOT/POP 20. PAGE 124 A2544 ECO/UNDEV ECO/TAC FOR/AID

S61
TANNENBAUM F.,"THE UNITED STATES AND LATIN AMERICA." FUT USA+45 NAT/G FOR/AID CHOOSE ATTIT ALL/VALS VAL/FREE 20. PAGE 141 A2888 L/A+17C ECO/DEV DIPLOM

B62
ABOSCH H.,THE MENACE OF THE MIRACLE: GERMANY FROM HITLER TO ADENAUER. EUR+WWI GERMANY/W CULTURE FORCES PRESS NUC/PWR WAR CHOOSE 20 HITLER/A ADENAUER/K. PAGE 4 A0082 DIPLOM PEACE POLICY

B62
BRYANT A.,A CHOICE FOR DESTINY: COMMONWEALTH AND THE COMMON MARKET. EUR+WWI FUT UK INT/TRADE COLONIAL ATTIT SOVEREIGN 20 CMN/WLTH EEC. PAGE 20 A0411 INT/ORG VOL/ASSN DIPLOM CHOOSE

B62
BUCHMANN J.,L'AFRIQUE NOIRE INDEPENDANTE. POL/PAR DIPLOM COLONIAL PARTIC CHOOSE GP/REL ATTIT ORD/FREE WEALTH NEGRO. PAGE 21 A0426 AFR NAT/LISM DECISION

B62
GUTTMAN A.,THE WOUND IN THE HEART: AMERICA AND THE SPANISH CIVIL WAR. SPAIN USA-45 POL/PAR LEGIS ECO/TAC CHOOSE ANOMIE ATTIT MARXISM...POLICY ANARCH BIBLIOG 20 ROOSEVLT/F. PAGE 58 A1198 ALL/IDEOS WAR DIPLOM CATHISM

B62
HATCH J.,AFRICA TODAY-AND TOMORROW: AN OUTLINE OF BASIC FACTS AND MAJOR PROBLEMS. AFR FUT ISLAM STRATA ECO/UNDEV INT/ORG NAT/G POL/PAR DELIB/GP TOP/EX EDU/PROP LEGIT CHOOSE ATTIT...TIME/SEQ TOT/POP COLD/WAR 20. PAGE 63 A1287 PLAN CONSTN NAT/LISM

B62
OSGOOD C.E.,AN ALTERNATIVE TO WAR OR SURRENDER. FUT UNIV CULTURE INTELL SOCIETY R+D INT/ORG CONSULT DELIB/GP ACT/RES PLAN CHOOSE ATTIT PERCEPT KNOWL ...PHIL/SCI PSY SOC TREND GEN/LAWS 20. PAGE 112 A2300 ORD/FREE EDU/PROP PEACE WAR

B62
ROSENNE S.,THE WORLD COURT: WHAT IT IS AND HOW IT WORKS. WOR+45 WOR-45 LAW CONSTN JUDGE EDU/PROP LEGIT ROUTINE CHOOSE PEACE ORD/FREE...JURID OBS TIME/SEQ CHARTS UN TOT/POP VAL/FREE 20. PAGE 124 A2538 INT/ORG ADJUD INT/LAW

B62
STARR R.E.,POLAND 1944-1962: THE SOVIETIZATION OF A CAPTIVE PEOPLE. COM POLAND USSR POL/PAR SECT LEGIS DIPLOM DOMIN EDU/PROP CHOOSE ORD/FREE...POLICY CHARTS BIBLIOG 20. PAGE 137 A2808 MARXISM NAT/G TOTALISM NAT/COMP

L62
BAILEY S.D.,"THE TROIKA AND THE FUTURE OF THE UN." CONSTN CREATE LEGIT EXEC CHOOSE ORD/FREE PWR ...CONCPT NEW/IDEA UN COLD/WAR 20. PAGE 10 A0206 FUT INT/ORG USSR

S62
GAREAU F.H.,"BLOC POLITICS IN WEST AFRICA." AFR CONGO/BRAZ GHANA GUINEA MALI WOR+45 STRUCT ECO/UNDEV INT/ORG VOL/ASSN CHOOSE ORD/FREE PWR UN 20. PAGE 51 A1048 NAT/G NAT/LISM

S62
GUETZKOW H.,"THE POTENTIAL OF CASE STUDY IN ANALYZING INTERNATIONAL CONFLICT." EUR+WWI FUT GERMANY INTELL SOCIETY STRUCT INT/ORG LOC/G NAT/G CONSULT CREATE PLAN CHOOSE ATTIT RIGID/FLEX ...POLICY SAAR 20. PAGE 58 A1188 EDU/PROP METH/CNCPT COERCE FRANCE

S62
TRUMAN D.,"THE DOMESTIC POLITICS OF FOREIGN AID." USA+45 WOR+45 NAT/G POL/PAR LEGIS DIPLOM ECO/TAC EDU/PROP ADMIN CHOOSE ATTIT PWR CONGRESS 20 CONGRESS. PAGE 145 A2970 ROUTINE FOR/AID

B63
AFRICAN BIBLIOGRAPHIC CENTER,THE SCENE IS KENYA AND THE PERSONAGE IS TOM MBOYA: A SELECTED CURRENT READING LIST FROM 1956-1962 (PAMPHLET). ECO/UNDEV LABOR POL/PAR CHIEF COLONIAL CHOOSE NAT/LISM ORD/FREE 20. PAGE 5 A0096 BIBLIOG DIPLOM AFR NAT/G

B63
FRANZ G.,TEILUNG UND WIEDERVEREINIGUNG. GERMANY IRELAND ITALY NETHERLAND POLAND CULTURE BAL/PWR CHOOSE NAT/LISM ORD/FREE SOVEREIGN 19/20. PAGE 48 A0987 DIPLOM WAR NAT/COMP ATTIT

B63
HOVET T. JR.,AFRICA IN THE UNITED NATIONS. AFR DELIB/GP EDU/PROP LOBBY CHOOSE ORD/FREE PWR RESPECT INT/ORG USSR

SKILL...STAT TIME/SEQ CON/ANAL CHARTS STERTYP VAL/FREE 20 UN. PAGE 68 A1397

S63
LIPSHART A.,"THE ANALYSIS OF BLOC VOTING IN THE GENERAL ASSEMBLY." L/A+17C WOR+45 ACT/RES INGP/REL ...POLICY DECISION NEW/IDEA STAT IDEA/COMP UN. PAGE 90 A1832
CHOOSE INT/ORG DELIB/GP

S63
MODELSKI G.,"STUDY OF ALLIANCES." WOR+45 WOR-45 INT/ORG NAT/G FORCES LEGIT ADMIN CHOOSE ALL/VALS PWR SKILL...INT/LAW CONCPT GEN/LAWS 20 TREATY. PAGE 102 A2099
VOL/ASSN CON/ANAL DIPLOM

S63
SINGER M.R.,"ELECTIONS WITHIN THE UNITED NATIONS: AN EXPERIMENTAL STUDY UTILIZING STATISTICAL ANALYSIS." USA+45 WOR+45 DIPLOM ECO/TAC COERCE PWR WEALTH...STAT CHARTS SIMUL GEN/LAWS COLD/WAR VAL/FREE UN 20. PAGE 133 A2732
INT/ORG CHOOSE

S63
WELLS H.,"THE OAS AND THE DOMINICAN ELECTIONS." L/A+17C INT/ORG NAT/G POL/PAR TEC/DEV ECO/TAC EDU/PROP PERCEPT...TIME/SEQ OAS TOT/POP 20. PAGE 163 A3317
CONSULT CHOOSE DOMIN/REP

B64
BUTWELL R.,SOUTHEAST ASIA TODAY - AND TOMORROW. NAT/G COLONIAL LEAD REGION WAR CHOOSE WEALTH MARXISM 20. PAGE 23 A0458
S/ASIA DIPLOM ECO/UNDEV NAT/LISM

B64
ETZIONI A.,WINNING WITHOUT WAR. FUT MOD/EUR USA+45 WOR+45 ECO/DEV ECO/UNDEV INT/ORG NAT/G FORCES TOP/EX PLAN TEC/DEV ECO/TAC DOMIN EDU/PROP LEGIT COERCE CHOOSE ATTIT MORAL ORD/FREE RESPECT WEALTH MAJORIT. PAGE 43 A0871
PWR TREND DIPLOM USSR

B64
FREUD A.,OF HUMAN SOVEREIGNTY. WOR+45 INDUS SECT ECO/TAC CRIME CHOOSE ATTIT MORAL MARXISM...POLICY BIBLIOG 20. PAGE 49 A0998
NAT/LISM DIPLOM WAR PEACE

B64
LEGGE J.D.,INDONESIA. INDONESIA ELITES ECO/UNDEV POL/PAR CHIEF FORCES INT/TRADE COERCE CHOOSE ORD/FREE...SOC CHARTS BIBLIOG 16/20 CHINJAP. PAGE 86 A1765
S/ASIA DOMIN NAT/LISM POLICY

B64
MORGAN T.,GOLDWATER EITHER/OR; A SELF-PORTRAIT BASED UPON HIS OWN WORDS. USA+45 CONSTN AGRI LABOR DIPLOM RACE/REL WEALTH POPULISM...POLICY MAJORIT 20 GOLDWATR/B REPUBLICAN. PAGE 104 A2131
LEAD POL/PAR CHOOSE ATTIT

B64
PERKINS D.,THE AMERICAN DEMOCRACY: ITS RISE TO POWER. ASIA USSR LAW CULTURE FINAN EDU/PROP COLONIAL CHOOSE...POLICY CHARTS BIBLIOG WORSHIP PRESIDENT 15/20 NEGRO. PAGE 115 A2362
LOC/G ECO/TAC WAR DIPLOM

B64
SARROS P.P.,CONGRESS AND THE NEW DIPLOMACY: THE FORMULATION OF MUTUAL SECURITY POLICY: 1953-60 (THESIS). USA+45 CHIEF EX/STRUC REGION ROUTINE CHOOSE GOV/REL PEACE ROLE...POLICY 20 PRESIDENT CONGRESS. PAGE 127 A2606
DIPLOM POL/PAR NAT/G

B64
WRIGHT T.P. JR.,AMERICAN SUPPORT OF FREE ELECTIONS ABROAD. USA+45 USA-45 DOMIN LEAD NEUTRAL MARXISM ...POLICY TIME/SEQ BIBLIOG 19/20 COLD/WAR INTERVENT. PAGE 168 A3420
DIPLOM CHOOSE L/A+17C POPULISM

L64
ARMENGALD A.,"ECONOMIE ET COEXISTENCE." COM EUR+WWI FUT USA+45 WOR+45 ECO/DEV ECO/UNDEV FINAN INT/ORG NAT/G EXEC CHOOSE ATTIT ALL/VALS...POLICY RELATIV DECISION TREND SOC/EXP COLD/WAR WORK 20. PAGE 9 A0173
MARKET ECO/TAC CAP/ISM

S64
JACK H.,"NONALIGNMENT AND A TEST BAN AGREEMENT: THE ROLE OF THE NON-ALIGNED STATES." WOR+45 INT/ORG CONSULT DOMIN EDU/PROP LEGIT CHOOSE PEACE ATTIT DRIVE KNOWL ORD/FREE...TREND CHARTS GEN/LAWS UN VAL/FREE 20. PAGE 72 A1471
PWR CONCPT NUC/PWR

S64
MAZRUI A.A.,"THE UNITED NATIONS AND SOME AFRICAN POLITICAL ATTITUDES." ECO/TAC FOR/AID DOMIN ROUTINE CHOOSE ATTIT DRIVE MORAL PWR RESPECT WEALTH...PSY CONCPT OBS TREND UN VAL/FREE 20. PAGE 97 A1987
AFR INT/ORG SOVEREIGN

C64
SCHRAMM W.,"MASS MEDIA AND NATIONAL DEVELOPMENT: THE ROLE OF INFORMATION IN DEVELOPING COUNTRIES." FINAN R+D ACT/RES PLAN TEC/DEV DIPLOM CHOOSE SUPEGO ORD/FREE...BIBLIOG 20. PAGE 129 A2645
ECO/UNDEV COM/IND EDU/PROP MAJORIT

B65
FAGG J.E.,CUBA, HAITI, AND THE DOMINICAN REPUBLIC. CUBA DOMIN/REP HAITI L/A+17C NAT/G DIPLOM ECO/TAC DOMIN CHOOSE AUTHORIT ROLE SOVEREIGN POPULISM 17/20. PAGE 43 A0883
COLONIAL ECO/UNDEV REV GOV/COMP

B65
HAIGHT D.E.,THE PRESIDENT; ROLES AND POWERS. USA+45 USA-45 POL/PAR PLAN DIPLOM CHOOSE PERS/REL PWR 18/20 PRESIDENT CONGRESS. PAGE 59 A1217
CHIEF LEGIS TOP/EX EX/STRUC

B65
HALPERIN E.,NATIONALISM AND COMMUNISM. CHILE L/A+17C CAP/ISM EDU/PROP CHOOSE DISCRIM SOCISM ...BIBLIOG 20 COM/PARTY. PAGE 60 A1236
NAT/LISM MARXISM POL/PAR REV

B66
CANFIELD L.H.,THE PRESIDENCY OF WOODROW WILSON: PRELUDE TO A WORLD IN CRISIS. USA-45 ADJUD NEUTRAL WAR CHOOSE INGP/REL PEACE ORD/FREE 20 WILSON/W PRESIDENT TREATY LEAGUE/NAT. PAGE 24 A0477
PERSON POLICY DIPLOM GOV/REL

B66
CLARK G.,WORLD PEACE THROUGH WORLD LAW; TWO ALTERNATIVE PLANS. WOR+45 DELIB/GP FORCES TAX CONFER ADJUD SANCTION ARMS/CONT WAR CHOOSE PRIVIL 20 UN COLD/WAR. PAGE 27 A0541
INT/LAW PEACE PLAN INT/ORG

B66
COLE A.B.,SOCIALIST PARTIES IN POSTWAR JAPAN. STRATA AGRI LABOR PLAN DIPLOM ECO/TAC AGREE LEAD CHOOSE ATTIT...CHARTS 20 CHINJAP SOC/DEMPAR. PAGE 28 A0566
POL/PAR POLICY SOCISM NAT/G

B66
GERARD-LIBOIS J.,KATANGA SECESSION. INT/ORG FORCES DIPLOM ADMIN CONTROL WAR CHOOSE PWR...CHARTS 20 KATANGA TSHOMBE/M UN. PAGE 52 A1062
NAT/G REGION ORD/FREE REV

B66
LONG B.,THE WAR DIARY OF BRECKINRIDGE LONG: SELECTIONS FROM THE YEARS 1939-1944. USA-45 INT/ORG FORCES FOR/AID CHOOSE 20. PAGE 91 A1859
DIPLOM WAR DELIB/GP

B66
RIESELBACH L.N.,THE ROOTS OF ISOLATIONISM* CONGRESSIONAL VOTING AND PRESIDENTIAL LEADERSHIP IN FOREIGN POLICY. POL/PAR LEGIS DIPLOM EDU/PROP LEAD REGION REPRESENT...SOC STAT IDEA/COMP HYPO/EXP BIBLIOG 19/20 CONGRESS. PAGE 121 A2477
ISOLAT CHOOSE CHIEF POLICY

B66
WEINSTEIN F.B.,VIETNAM'S UNHELD ELECTIONS: THE FAILURE TO CARRY OUT THE 1956 REUNIFICATION ELECTIONS... (MONOGRAPH). VIETNAM/S VIETNAM/N LEGIT CONFER ADJUD WAR PEACE 20 TREATY GENEVA/CON UNIFICA. PAGE 162 A3306
AGREE NAT/G CHOOSE DIPLOM

B67
ATTWOOD W.,THE REDS AND THE BLACKS. AFR POL/PAR CHOOSE GOV/REL RACE/REL NAT/LISM...BIOG 20. PAGE 10 A0195
DIPLOM PWR MARXISM

B67
ROSENAU J.N.,DOMESTIC SOURCES OF FOREIGN POLICY. WOR+45 STRATA COM/IND MUNIC POL/PAR LOBBY PARTIC REGION ATTIT...PSY SOC COLD/WAR. PAGE 124 A2534
DIPLOM POLICY NAT/G CHOOSE

B67
SAYEED K.B.,THE POLITICAL SYSTEM OF PAKISTAN. PAKISTAN DIPLOM REGION CHOOSE ORD/FREE...BIBLIOG 20. PAGE 127 A2609
NAT/G POL/PAR CONSTN SECT

S67
MUDGE G.A.,"DOMESTIC POLICIES AND UN ACTIVITIES* THE CASE OF RHODESIA AND THE REPUBLIC OF SOUTH AFRICA." RHODESIA SOUTH/AFR POL/PAR LEAD SANCTION CHOOSE RACE/REL CONSEN DISCRIM ATTIT...INT/LAW UN PARLIAMENT 20. PAGE 105 A2163
AFR NAT/G POLICY

S67
SENCOURT R.,"FOREIGN POLICY* AN HISTORIC RECTIFICATION." EUR+WWI UK DIPLOM EDU/PROP LEAD WAR CHOOSE PERS/REL...METH/COMP PARLIAMENT. PAGE 131 A2685
POLICY POL/PAR NAT/G

S67
SPENCER R.,"GERMANY AFTER THE AUTUMN CRISIS." GERMANY CHOOSE GP/REL PERS/REL. PAGE 136 A2785
DIPLOM POL/PAR PROB/SOLV

CHOPER J.H. A1849

CHOU/ENLAI....CHOU EN-LAI

B64
AFRO ASIAN SOLIDARITY AGAINST IMPERIALISM. AFR ISLAM S/ASIA ECO/UNDEV NAT/G POL/PAR TOP/EX PRESS ...INT ANTHOL 20 CHOU/ENLAI. PAGE 3 A0066
MARXISM DIPLOM EDU/PROP CHIEF

CHOWDHURI R.N. A0534

CHRIS/DEM....CHRISTIAN DEMOCRATIC PARTY (ALL NATIONS)

CHRISTENSEN A.N. A0535

CHRISTIAN....CHRISTIAN BELIEFS OR CHURCHES

B17
DE VICTORIA F.,DE INDIS ET DE JURE BELLI (1557) IN F. DE VICTORIA, DE INDIS ET DE JURE BELLI REFLECTIONES. UNIV NAT/G SECT CHIEF PARTIC COERCE
WAR INT/LAW OWN

PEACE MORAL...POLICY 16 INDIAN/AM CHRISTIAN CONSCN/OBJ. PAGE 35 A0715

B19
VANDERPOL A.,LA DOCTRINE SCOLASTIQUE DU DROIT DE GUERRE. CHRIST-17C FORCES DIPLOM LEGIT SUPEGO MORAL ...BIOG AQUINAS/T SUAREZ/F CHRISTIAN. PAGE 158 A3220
WAR SECT INT/LAW

N19
HALPERN M.,THE MORALITY AND POLITICS OF INTERVENTION (PAMPHLET). USA+45 INT/ORG FORCES ECO/TAC MORAL ORD/FREE 20 INTERVENT CHRISTIAN. PAGE 61 A1243
POLICY DIPLOM SOVEREIGN DOMIN

B40
NIEBUHR R.,CHRISTIANITY AND POWER POLITICS. WOR-45 SECT DIPLOM GP/REL SUPEGO ALL/IDEOS WORSHIP 20 CHRISTIAN. PAGE 109 A2234
PARTIC PEACE MORAL

B47
NIEBUHR R.,THE CHILDREN OF LIGHT AND THE CHILDREN OF DARKNESS: A VINDICATION OF DEMOCRACY AND CRITIQUE OF TRADITIONAL DEFENSE. UNIV STRUCT NAT/G SECT INGP/REL OWN PEACE ORD/FREE MARXISM ...IDEA/COMP GEN/LAWS 20 CHRISTIAN. PAGE 109 A2235
POPULISM DIPLOM NEIGH GP/REL

B59
NIEBUHR R.,NATIONS AND EMPIRES. WOR+45 INT/ORG COLONIAL NUC/PWR TOTALISM UTOPIA ORD/FREE MARXISM WORSHIP 20 COLD/WAR PROTESTANT CHRISTIAN. PAGE 109 A2237
DIPLOM NAT/G POLICY PWR

CHRIST-17C.... CHRISTENDOM TO 1700

B00
GROTIUS H.,DE JURE BELLI AC PACIS. CHRIST-17C UNIV LAW SOCIETY PROVS LEGIT PEACE PERCEPT MORAL PWR ...CONCPT CON/ANAL GEN/LAWS. PAGE 57 A1180
JURID INT/LAW WAR

B00
OMAN C.,A HISTORY OF THE ART OF WAR: THE MIDDLE AGES FROM THE FOURTH TO THE FOURTEENTH CENTURY. CHRIST-17C MEDIT-7 CULTURE SOCIETY INT/ORG ROUTINE PERSON...CONT/OBS HIST/WRIT CHARTS VAL/FREE. PAGE 112 A2291
FORCES SKILL WAR

B19
VANDERPOL A.,LA DOCTRINE SCOLASTIQUE DU DROIT DE GUERRE. CHRIST-17C FORCES DIPLOM LEGIT SUPEGO MORAL ...BIOG AQUINAS/T SUAREZ/F CHRISTIAN. PAGE 158 A3220
WAR SECT INT/LAW

B22
BRYCE J.,INTERNATIONAL RELATIONS. CHRIST-17C EUR+WWI MOD/EUR CULTURE INTELL NAT/G DELIB/GP CREATE BAL/PWR DIPLOM ATTIT DRIVE RIGID/FLEX ALL/VALS...PLURIST JURID CONCPT TIME/SEQ GEN/LAWS TOT/POP. PAGE 20 A0412
INT/ORG POLICY

B24
GENTILI A.,DE LEGATIONIBUS. CHRIST-17C NAT/G SECT CONSULT LEGIT...POLICY CATH JURID CONCPT MYTH. PAGE 52 A1058
DIPLOM INT/LAW INT/ORG LAW

B30
BYNKERSHOEK C.,QUAESTIONUM JURIS PUBLICI LIBRI DUO. CHRIST-17C MOD/EUR CONSTN ELITES SOCIETY NAT/G PROVS EX/STRUC FORCES TOP/EX BAL/PWR DIPLOM ATTIT MORAL...TRADIT CONCPT. PAGE 23 A0460
INT/ORG LAW NAT/LISM INT/LAW

B32
BRYCE J.,THE HOLY ROMAN EMPIRE. GERMANY ITALY MOD/EUR CULTURE SOCIETY STRUCT INT/ORG NAT/G SECT DIPLOM DOMIN WAR SUPEGO ALL/VALS SOVEREIGN...GEOG SOC TIME/SEQ CHARTS STERTYP. PAGE 20 A0413
CHRIST-17C NAT/LISM

B35
BUREAU ECONOMIC RES LAT AM,THE ECONOMIC LITERATURE OF LATIN AMERICA (2 VOLS.). CHRIST-17C AGRI DIST/IND EXTR/IND INDUS WORKER INT/TRADE...GEOG 16/20. PAGE 21 A0433
BIBLIOG L/A+17C ECO/UNDEV FINAN

B36
MATTHEWS M.A.,INTERNATIONAL LAW: SELECT LIST OF WORKS IN ENGLISH ON PUBLIC INTERNATIONAL LAW: WITH COLLECTIONS OF CASES AND OPINIONS. CHRIST-17C EUR+WWI MOD/EUR WOR-45 CONSTN ADJUD JURID. PAGE 96 A1975
BIBLIOG/A INT/LAW ATTIT DIPLOM

B37
THOMPSON J.W.,SECRET DIPLOMACY: A RECORD OF ESPIONAGE AND DOUBLE-DEALING: 1500-1815. CHRIST-17C MOD/EUR NAT/G WRITING RISK MORAL...ANTHOL BIBLIOG 16/19 ESPIONAGE. PAGE 143 A2927
DIPLOM CRIME

B41
GRISMER R.,A NEW BIBLIOGRAPHY OF THE LITERATURES OF SPAIN AND SPANISH AMERICA. CHRIST-17C MOD/EUR PRE/AMER SPAIN CULTURE DIPLOM EDU/PROP...ART/METH GEOG HUM PHIL/SCI 20. PAGE 57 A1165
BIBLIOG LAW NAT/G ECO/UNDEV

B46
SCANLON H.L.,INTERNATIONAL LAW: A SELECTIVE LIST OF WORKS IN ENGLISH ON PUBLIC INTERNATIONAL LAW (A PAMPHLET). CHRIST-17C EUR+WWI MOD/EUR WOR-45 CT/SYS ...JURID 20. PAGE 127 A2613
BIBLIOG/A INT/LAW ADJUD DIPLOM

B49
BOZZA T.,SCRITTORI POLITICI ITALIANI DAL 1550 AL 1650. CHRIST-17C ITALY DIPLOM DOMIN 16/17. PAGE 18 A0365
BIBLIOG/A NAT/G CONCPT

WRITING

B54
NUSSBAUM D.,A CONCISE HISTORY OF THE LAW OF NATIONS. ASIA CHRIST-17C EUR+WWI ISLAM MEDIT-7 MOD/EUR S/ASIA UNIV WOR+45 WOR-45 SOCIETY STRUCT EXEC ATTIT ALL/VALS...CONCPT HIST/WRIT TIME/SEQ. PAGE 110 A2263
INT/ORG LAW PEACE INT/LAW

B55
CRAIG G.A.,THE POLITICS OF THE PRUSSIAN ARMY 1640-1945. CHRIST-17C EUR+WWI MOD/EUR PRUSSIA STRUCT DIPLOM ADMIN REV WAR...SOC BIBLIOG 17/20. PAGE 32 A0652
FORCES NAT/G ROLE CHIEF

B57
RUMEU DE ARMAS A.,ESPANA EEN EL AFRICA ATLANTICA. AFR CHRIST-17C PORTUGAL SPAIN DIPLOM ECO/TAC CONTROL 14/16 AFRICA/W. PAGE 125 A2568
NAT/G COLONIAL CHIEF PWR

B60
NURTY K.S.,STUDIES IN PROBLEMS OF PEACE. CHRIST-17C MOD/EUR S/ASIA WOR+45 WOR-45 INT/ORG NAT/G SECT COERCE REV NAT/LISM ALL/VALS...CONCPT MYTH TIME/SEQ. PAGE 110 A2262
POLICY PEACE PACIFISM ORD/FREE

B62
KIDDER F.E.,THESES ON PAN AMERICAN TOPICS. LAW CULTURE NAT/G SECT DIPLOM HEALTH...ART/METH GEOG SOC 13/20. PAGE 79 A1615
BIBLIOG CHRIST-17C L/A+17C SOCIETY

B62
WOETZEL R.K.,THE NURENBERG TRIALS IN INTERNATIONAL LAW. CHRIST-17C MOD/EUR WOR+45 SOCIETY NAT/G DELIB/GP DOMIN LEGIT ROUTINE ATTIT DRIVE PERSON SUPEGO MORAL ORD/FREE...POLICY MAJORIT JURID PSY SOC SELF/OBS RECORD NAZI TOT/POP. PAGE 166 A3376
INT/ORG ADJUD WAR

S62
JOHNSON O.H.,"THE ENGLISH TRADITION IN INTERNATIONAL LAW." CHRIST-17C MOD/EUR EDU/PROP LEGIT CT/SYS ORD/FREE...JURID CONCPT TIME/SEQ. PAGE 75 A1526
LAW INT/LAW UK

S63
LOPEZIBOR J.,"L'EUROPE, FORME DE VIE." CHRIST-17C EUR+WWI FUT MOD/EUR SOCIETY INT/ORG SECT EDU/PROP ATTIT RIGID/FLEX ALL/VALS...POLICY HUM SOC TIME/SEQ TREND GEN/LAWS. PAGE 91 A1862
NAT/G CULTURE

S63
WRIGHT Q.,"DECLINE OF CLASSIC DIPLOMACY." CHRIST-17C EUR+WWI MOD/EUR WOR+45 WOR-45 INT/ORG NAT/G DELIB/GP BAL/PWR ATTIT PWR...HIST/WRIT LEAGUE/NAT. PAGE 168 A3418
TEC/DEV CONCPT DIPLOM

B65
WILGUS A.C.,HISTORIES AND HISTORIANS OF HISPANIC AMERICA (REPRINT ED.). CHRIST-17C SECT DIPLOM REV 16/20. PAGE 164 A3350
BIBLIOG/A L/A+17C REGION COLONIAL

B67
ADAMS A.E.,AN ATLAS OF RUSSIAN AND EAST EUROPEAN HISTORY. CHRIST-17C COM MOD/EUR INDUS SECT FORCES DIPLOM COLONIAL REV WAR 4/20. PAGE 4 A0086
CHARTS REGION TREND

CHRONOLOGY....SEE TIME/SEQ

CHUKWUEMEKA N. A0536

CHUNG Y.S. A0537

CHURCH....SEE SECT

CHURCH/STA....CHURCH-STATE RELATIONS (ALL NATIONS)

B53
MARITAIN J.,L'HOMME ET L'ETAT. SECT DIPLOM GP/REL PEACE ORD/FREE...IDEA/COMP 17/20 CHURCH/STA NATURL/LAW. PAGE 95 A1940
CONCPT NAT/G SOVEREIGN COERCE

B56
JAMESON J.F.,THE AMERICAN REVOLUTION CONSIDERED AS A SOCIAL MOVEMENT. USA-45 AGRI FINAN SECT INT/TRADE REPRESENT SUFF INGP/REL RACE/REL DISCRIM...MAJORIT 18/19 CHURCH/STA. PAGE 73 A1494
ORD/FREE REV FEDERAL CONSTN

B62
BLANSHARD P.,FREEDOM AND CATHOLIC POWER IN SPAIN AND PORTUGAL: AN AMERICAN INTERPRETATION. AFR PORTUGAL SPAIN USA+45 LAW LABOR DIPLOM EDU/PROP DISCRIM ISOLAT TOTALISM 20 CHURCH/STA. PAGE 15 A0309
GP/REL FASCISM CATHISM PWR

B62
SCHMIDT-VOLKMAR E.,DER KULTURKAMPF IN DEUTSCHLAND 1871-1890. GERMANY PRUSSIA SOCIETY STRUCT SECT DIPLOM GP/REL NAT/LISM 19 CHURCH/STA BISMARCK/O. PAGE 128 A2632
POL/PAR CATHISM ATTIT NAT/G

B63
RAVENS J.P.,STAAT UND KATHOLISCHE KIRCHE IN PREUSSENS POLNISCHEN TEILUNGSGEBIETEN. GERMANY POLAND PRUSSIA PROVS DIPLOM EDU/PROP DEBATE NAT/LISM...JURID 18 CHURCH/STA. PAGE 119 A2451
GP/REL CATHISM SECT NAT/G

CHURCHILL W. A0538,A0539

CHURCHLL/W....SIR WINSTON CHURCHILL

B49
STETTINIUS E.R.,ROOSEVELT AND THE RUSSIANS: THE YALTA CONFERENCE. UK USSR WOR+45 WOR-45 INT/ORG VOL/ASSN TOP/EX ACT/RES EDU/PROP PEACE ATTIT DRIVE PERSON SUPEGO PWR...POLICY CONCPT MYTH OBS TIME/SEQ AUD/VIS COLD/WAR 20 CHURCHLL/W YALTA ROOSEVLT/F. PAGE 138 A2819
DIPLOM DELIB/GP BIOG

B61
ACHESON D.,SKETCHES FROM LIFE. WOR+45 20 CHURCHLL/W EDEN/A ADENAUER/K SALAZAR/A. PAGE 4 A0085
BIOG LEAD CHIEF DIPLOM

B61
MORRAY J.P.,FROM YALTA TO DISARMAMENT: COLD WAR DEBATE. USA+45 CAP/ISM FOR/AID CONTROL NUC/PWR 20 UN COLD/WAR CHURCHLL/W. PAGE 104 A2145
MARXIST ARMS/CONT DIPLOM BAL/PWR

B61
WRINCH P.,THE MILITARY STRATEGY OF WINSTON CHURCHILL. UK WOR-45 SEA VOL/ASSN TEC/DEV BAL/PWR LEAD WAR PEACE ATTIT...POLICY 20 CHURCHLL/W. PAGE 168 A3421
CIVMIL/REL FORCES PLAN DIPLOM

CIA....CENTRAL INTELLIGENCE AGENCY

L52
HILSMAN R. JR.,"INTELLIGENCE AND POLICY MAKING IN FOREIGN AFFAIRS." USA+45 CONSULT ACT/RES DIPLOM EDU/PROP ROUTINE PEACE PERCEPT PWR SKILL...POLICY MGT HYPO/EXP CONGRESS 20 CIA. PAGE 65 A1333
PROF/ORG SIMUL WAR

B62
WILLIAMS W.A.,THE UNITED STATES, CUBA, AND CASTRO: AN ESSAY ON THE DYNAMICS OF REVOLUTION AND THE DISSOLUTION OF EMPIRE. CUBA USA+45 AGRI VOL/ASSN DIPLOM ECO/TAC DOMIN COERCE...POLICY 20 EISNHWR/DD CIA KENNEDY/JF CASTRO/F. PAGE 165 A3354
REV CONSTN COM LEAD

B64
BLACKSTOCK P.W.,THE STRATEGY OF SUBVERSION. USA+45 FORCES EDU/PROP ADMIN COERCE GOV/REL...DECISION MGT 20 DEPT/DEFEN CIA DEPT/STATE. PAGE 15 A0301
ORD/FREE DIPLOM CONTROL

B64
LENS S.,THE FUTILE CRUSADE. ASIA CHINA/COM L/A+17C USA+45 USSR WOR+45 ECO/DEV BAL/PWR DIPLOM NUC/PWR WAR NAT/LISM PEACE 20 COLD/WAR PRESIDENT CIA. PAGE 87 A1774
ORD/FREE ANOMIE COM MARXISM

CICERO....CICERO

CINCINNATI....CINCINNATI, OHIO

CINEMA....SEE FILM

CITIES....SEE MUNIC

CITIZENSHP....CITIZENSHIP

CITY/MGT....CITY MANAGEMENT, CITY MANAGERS; SEE ALSO MUNIC, ADMIN, MGT, LOC/G

CIV/DEFENS....CIVIL DEFENSE (SYSTEMS, PLANNING, AND

CIV/DISOBD....CIVIL DISOBEDIENCE

CIV/RIGHTS....CIVIL RIGHTS: CONTEMPORARY CIVIL RIGHTS MOVEMENTS; SEE ALSO RACE/REL, CONSTN + LAW

B62
BOWLES C.,THE CONSCIENCE OF A LIBERAL. COM USA+45 WOR+45 STRUCT LOC/G NAT/G FORCES LEGIS GOV/REL DISCRIM 20 UN CIV/RIGHTS. PAGE 18 A0361
DIPLOM POLICY

B62
KENNEDY J.F.,TO TURN THE TIDE. SPACE AGRI INT/ORG FORCES TEC/DEV ADMIN NUC/PWR PEACE WEALTH...ANTHOL 20 KENNEDY/JF CIV/RIGHTS. PAGE 78 A1592
DIPLOM CHIEF POLICY NAT/G

B65
EISENHOWER D.D.,WAGING PEACE 1956-61: THE WHITE HOUSE YEARS. USA+45 DIPLOM LEAD INGP/REL RACE/REL PEACE ATTIT...TRADIT TIME/SEQ 20 EISNHWR/DD PRESIDENT COLD/WAR CIV/RIGHTS BERLIN. PAGE 41 A0833
TOP/EX BIOG ORD/FREE POLICY

B65
LYONS G.M.,AMERICA: PURPOSE AND POWER. UK USA+45 FINAN INDUS MARKET WORKER TEC/DEV DIPLOM AUTOMAT NUC/PWR WAR RACE/REL ORD/FREE 20 EEC CONGRESS SUPREME/CT CIV/RIGHTS. PAGE 92 A1881
PWR PROB/SOLV ECO/DEV TASK

B66
WELCH R.H.W.,THE NEW AMERICANISM, AND OTHER SPEECHES AND ESSAYS. USA+45 ACADEM POL/PAR SCHOOL VOL/ASSN FORCES CAP/ISM TAX REV DISCRIM 20 CIV/RIGHTS COLD/WAR BIRCH/SOC. PAGE 163 A3313
DIPLOM FASCISM MARXISM RACE/REL

CIVIL AERONAUTICS BOARD....SEE CAB

CIVIL DISOBEDIENCE....SEE CIV/DISOBD

CIVIL RIGHTS....SEE CIV/RIGHTS

CIVIL SERVICE....SEE ADMIN

CIVIL/CODE....CIVIL CODE (FRANCE)

CIVIL/LAW....CIVIL LAW

CIVIL/LIB....CIVIL LIBERTIES; SEE ALSO CONSTN + LAW

B61
SCOTT A.M.,POLITICS, USA; CASES ON THE AMERICAN DEMOCRATIC PROCESS. USA+45 CHIEF FORCES DIPLOM LOBBY CHOOSE RACE/REL FEDERAL ATTIT...JURID ANTHOL T 20 PRESIDENT CONGRESS CIVIL/LIB. PAGE 130 A2669
CT/SYS CONSTN NAT/G PLAN

CIVIL/SERV....CIVIL SERVICE; SEE ALSO ADMIN

B48
CHILDS J.R.,AMERICAN FOREIGN SERVICE. USA+45 SOCIETY NAT/G ROUTINE GOV/REL 20 DEPT/STATE CIVIL/SERV. PAGE 26 A0530
DIPLOM ADMIN GP/REL

B63
US SENATE COMM APPROPRIATIONS,PERSONNEL ADMINISTRATION AND OPERATIONS OF AGENCY FOR INTERNATIONAL DEVELOPMENT: SPECIAL HEARING. FINAN LEAD COST UTIL SKILL...CHARTS 20 CONGRESS AID CIVIL/SERV. PAGE 155 A3170
ADMIN FOR/AID EFFICIENCY DIPLOM

B64
NICOL D.,AFRICA - A SUBJECTIVE VIEW. AFR INT/ORG PLAN ADMIN COLONIAL PARL/PROC PARTIC REGION GOV/REL LITERACY ATTIT...BIBLIOG 20 CIVIL/SERV. PAGE 109 A2230
NAT/G LEAD CULTURE ACADEM

CIVIL/WAR....CIVIL WAR

L00
HISTORICUS,"LETTERS AND SOME QUESTIONS OF INTERNATIONAL LAW." FRANCE NETHERLAND UK USA-45 WOR-45 LAW NAT/G COERCE...SOC CONCPT GEN/LAWS TOT/POP 19 CIVIL/WAR. PAGE 65 A1344
WEALTH JURID WAR INT/LAW

B63
PECQUET P.,THE DIPLOMACY OF THE CONFEDERATE CABINET OF RICHMOND AND ITS AGENTS ABROAD (LIMITED ED.). MOD/EUR USA-45 LEAD...OBS 19 CIVIL/WAR SOUTH/US. PAGE 114 A2347
DIPLOM WAR ORD/FREE

CIVIL-MILITARY RELATIONS....SEE CIVMIL/REL

CIVMIL/REL....CIVIL-MILITARY RELATIONS

N19
ZLOTNICK M.,WEAPONS IN SPACE (PAMPHLET). FUT WOR+45 TEC/DEV DIPLOM ARMS/CONT CIVMIL/REL PEACE HABITAT ...CONCPT NEW/IDEA CHARTS. PAGE 170 A3457
SPACE WEAPON NUC/PWR WAR

B39
KOHN H.,REVOLUTIONS AND DICTATORSHIPS. COM EUR+WWI ISLAM MOD/EUR NAT/G CHIEF FORCES WAR CIVMIL/REL PWR MARXISM 18/20. PAGE 81 A1661
NAT/LISM TOTALISM REV FASCISM

C40
NORMAN E.H.,"JAPAN'S EMERGENCE AS A MODERN STATE: POLITICAL AND ECONOMIC PROBLEMS OF THE MEIJI PERIOD." CONSTN STRATA AGRI INDUS POL/PAR TEC/DEV CAP/ISM CIVMIL/REL...BIBLIOG 19/20 CHINJAP. PAGE 110 A2250
CENTRAL DIPLOM POLICY NAT/LISM

S41
LASSWELL H.D.,"THE GARRISON STATE" (BMR)" FUT WOR+45 ELITES INTELL FORCES ECO/TAC DOMIN EDU/PROP COERCE INGP/REL 20. PAGE 85 A1739
NAT/G DIPLOM PWR CIVMIL/REL

B43
CONOVER H.F.,SOVIET RUSSIA: SELECTED LIST OF REFERENCES. USSR CULTURE INDUS NAT/G TOP/EX TEC/DEV BUDGET WAR CIVMIL/REL EFFICIENCY MARXISM 20. PAGE 29 A0597
BIBLIOG ECO/DEV COM DIPLOM

B44
FULLER G.H.,MILITARY GOVERNMENT: A LIST OF REFERENCES (A PAMPHLET). ITALY UK USA-45 WOR-45 LAW FORCES DOMIN ADMIN ARMS/CONT ORD/FREE PWR ...DECISION 20 CHINJAP. PAGE 50 A1023
BIBLIOG DIPLOM CIVMIL/REL SOVEREIGN

B45
CONOVER H.F.,THE GOVERNMENTS OF THE MAJOR FOREIGN POWERS: A BIBLIOGRAPHY. FRANCE GERMANY ITALY UK USSR CONSTN LOC/G POL/PAR EX/STRUC FORCES ADMIN CT/SYS CIVMIL/REL TOTALISM...POLICY 19/20. PAGE 29 A0598
BIBLIOG NAT/G DIPLOM

B45
CONOVER H.F.,ITALY: ECONOMICS, POLITICS AND MILITARY AFFAIRS, 1940-1945. ITALY ELITES NAT/G POL/PAR EX/STRUC TOP/EX DIPLOM DOMIN CONTROL COERCE
BIBLIOG TOTALISM FORCES

WAR CIVMIL/REL EFFICIENCY 20. PAGE 29 A0599
B45

PERAZA SARAUSA F.,BIBLIOGRAFIAS CUBANAS. CUBA CULTURE ECO/UNDEV AGRI EDU/PROP PRESS CIVMIL/REL ...POLICY GEOG PHIL/SCI BIOG 19/20. PAGE 115 A2353
BIBLIOG/A L/A+17C NAT/G DIPLOM
B47

HEIMANN E.,FREEDOM AND ORDER: LESSONS FROM THE WAR. WOR-45 CONSTN FORCES CHOOSE CIVMIL/REL PERSON ALL/IDEOS SOCISM...SOC IDEA/COMP WORSHIP 20. PAGE 64 A1308
NAT/G SOCIETY ORD/FREE DIPLOM
B48

FLOREN LOZANO L.,BIBLIOGRAFIA DE LA BIBLIOGRAFIA DOMINICANA. DOMIN/REP NAT/G DIPLOM EDU/PROP CIVMIL/REL...POLICY ART/METH GEOG PHIL/SCI HIST/WRIT 20. PAGE 47 A0952
BIBLIOG/A BIOG L/A+17C CULTURE
B49

JACKSON R.H.,INTERNATIONAL CONFERENCE ON MILITARY TRIALS. FRANCE GERMANY UK USA+45 USSR VOL/ASSN DELIB/GP REPAR ADJUD CT/SYS CRIME WAR 20 WAR/TRIAL. PAGE 72 A1479
DIPLOM INT/ORG INT/LAW CIVMIL/REL
C49

YANAGA C.,"JAPAN SINCE PERRY." S/ASIA CULTURE ECO/DEV FORCES WAR 19/20 CHINJAP. PAGE 168 A3430
DIPLOM POL/PAR CIVMIL/REL NAT/LISM
B52

GURLAND A.R.L.,POLITICAL SCIENCE IN WESTERN GERMANY: THOUGHTS AND WRITINGS, 1950-1952 (PAMPHLET). EUR+WWI GERMANY/W ELITES SOCIETY NAT/G NAT/LISM TOTALISM 20. PAGE 58 A1196
BIBLIOG/A DIPLOM CIVMIL/REL FASCISM
B52

THOM J.M.,GUIDE TO RESEARCH MATERIAL IN POLITICAL SCIENCE (PAMPHLET). ELITES LOC/G MUNIC NAT/G LEGIS DIPLOM ADJUD CIVMIL/REL GOV/REL PWR MGT. PAGE 143 A2919
BIBLIOG/A KNOWL
B54

SAPIN B.M.,THE ROLE OF THE MILITARY IN AMERICAN FOREIGN POLICY. USA+45 INT/ORG PROB/SOLV DETER NUC/PWR ATTIT PWR...BIBLIOG 20 NATO. PAGE 127 A2602
DIPLOM POLICY CIVMIL/REL NAT/G
B55

VIGON J.,TEORIA DEL MILITARISMO. NAT/G DIPLOM COLONIAL COERCE GUERRILLA CIVMIL/REL NAT/LISM MORAL ALL/IDEOS PACIFISM 18/20. PAGE 159 A3234
FORCES PHIL/SCI WAR POLICY
B56

ESTEP R.,AN AIR POWER BIBLIOGRAPHY. USA+45 TEC/DEV BUDGET DIPLOM EDU/PROP DETER CIVMIL/REL...DECISION INT/LAW 20. PAGE 42 A0862
BIBLIOG/A FORCES WEAPON PLAN
B56

KOENIG L.W.,THE TRUMAN ADMINISTRATION: ITS PRINCIPLES AND PRACTICE. USA+45 POL/PAR CHIEF LEGIS DIPLOM DEATH NUC/PWR WAR CIVMIL/REL PEACE ...DECISION 20 TRUMAN/HS PRESIDENT TREATY. PAGE 81 A1658
ADMIN POLICY EX/STRUC GOV/REL
B58

GAVIN J.M.,WAR AND PEACE IN THE SPACE AGE. SPACE USA+45 USSR FORCES PLAN TEC/DEV BAL/PWR DIPLOM ARMS/CONT WEAPON CIVMIL/REL...CHARTS GP/COMP 20 NATO COLD/WAR. PAGE 52 A1055
WAR DETER NUC/PWR PEACE
S58

ROTHFELS H.,"THE GERMAN RESISTANCE IN ITS INTERNATIONAL ASPECTS" (BMR)" EUR+WWI GERMANY UNIV CHIEF DIPLOM WAR NAT/LISM ATTIT...POLICY 20 HITLER/A NAZI. PAGE 124 A2548
VOL/ASSN MORAL FASCISM CIVMIL/REL
C58

BUTTINGER J.,"THE SMALLER DRAGON; A POLITICAL HISTORY OF VIETNAM." VIETNAM SECT DIPLOM CIVMIL/REL ISOLAT NAT/LISM...BIBLIOG/A 3/20. PAGE 22 A0455
COLONIAL DOMIN SOVEREIGN REV
B59

AMERICAN FRIENDS OF VIETNAM,AID TO VIETNAM: AN AMERICAN SUCCESS STORY (PAMPHLET). ASIA FUT USA+45 VIETNAM ECO/UNDEV WAR CIVMIL/REL GOV/REL...ANTHOL 20. PAGE 7 A0148
DIPLOM NAT/G FOR/AID FORCES
B59

STERNBERG F.,THE MILITARY AND INDUSTRIAL REVOLUTION OF OUR TIME. USA+45 USSR WOR+45 WORKER COMPUTER PLAN TEC/DEV NUC/PWR GP/REL...POLICY NAT/COMP 20. PAGE 138 A2818
DIPLOM FORCES INDUS CIVMIL/REL
B59

YOUNG J.,CHECKLIST OF MICROFILM REPRODUCTIONS OF SELECTED ARCHIVES OF THE JAPANESE ARMY, NAVY, AND OTHER GOVT AGENCIES, 1868-1945. DELIB/GP LEGIS DIPLOM EDU/PROP CIVMIL/REL 19/20 CHINJAP. PAGE 169 A3436
BIBLIOG ASIA FORCES WAR
B60

BROOKINGS INSTITUTION,UNITED STATES FOREIGN POLICY: STUDY NO 9: THE FORMULATION AND ADMINISTRATION OF UNITED STATES FOREIGN POLICY. USA+45 WOR+45 EX/STRUC LEGIS BAL/PWR FOR/AID EDU/PROP CIVMIL/REL GOV/REL...INT COLD/WAR. PAGE 19 A0394
DIPLOM INT/ORG CREATE
B60

FEIS H.,BETWEEN WAR AND PEACE: THE POTSDAM CONFERENCE. EUR+WWI NAT/G DELIB/GP PROB/SOLV REPAR WAR CIVMIL/REL...BIBLIOG 20. PAGE 45 A0911
DIPLOM CONFER BAL/PWR
B61

US SENATE COMM ON FOREIGN RELS,INTERNATIONAL DEVELOPMENT AND SECURITY: HEARINGS ON BILL (2 VOLS.). ECO/UNDEV FINAN FORCES REV COST WEALTH ...CHARTS 20 AID PRESIDENT. PAGE 157 A3191
FOR/AID CIVMIL/REL ORD/FREE ECO/TAC
B61

WOOD B.,THE MAKING OF THE GOOD NEIGHBOR POLICY. L/A+17C USA-45 COERCE CIVMIL/REL DISCRIM. PAGE 166 A3389
DIPLOM DELIB/GP POLICY
B61

WRINCH P.,THE MILITARY STRATEGY OF WINSTON CHURCHILL. UK WOR-45 SEA VOL/ASSN TEC/DEV B/L/PWR LEAD WAR PEACE ATTIT...POLICY 20 CHURCHLL/W. PAGE 168 A3421
CIVMIL/REL FORCES PLAN DIPLOM
B62

MORTON L.,STRATEGY AND COMMAND: THE FIRST TWO YEARS. USA-45 NAT/G CONTROL EXEC LEAD WEAPON CIVMIL/REL PWR...POLICY AUD/VIS CHARTS 20 CHINJAP. PAGE 105 A2150
WAR FORCES PLAN DIPLOM
B62

THOMSON G.P.,NUCLEAR ENERGY IN BRITAIN DURING THE LAST WAR: THE CHERWELL SIMON LECTURE (MONOGRAPH). UK R+D CONSULT FORCES PLAN DIPLOM TASK CIVMIL/REL ROLE...PHIL/SCI NEW/IDEA LAB/EXP 20 MAUD. PAGE 143 A2934
CREATE TEC/DEV WAR NUC/PWR
B63

ELLERT R.B.,NATO 'FAIR TRIAL' SAFEGUARDS: PRECURSOR TO AN INTERNATIONAL BILL OF PROCEDURAL RIGHTS. WOR+45 FORCES CRIME CIVMIL/REL ATTIT ORD/FREE 20 NATO. PAGE 41 A0841
JURID INT/LAW INT/ORG CT/SYS
B63

GALLAGHER M.P.,THE SOVIET HISTORY OF WORLD WAR II. EUR+WWI USSR DIPLOM DOMIN WRITING CONTROL WAR MARXISM...PSY TIME/SEQ 20 STALIN/J. PAGE 50 A1031
CIVMIL/REL EDU/PROP HIST/WRIT PRESS
B63

JOYCE W.,THE PROPAGANDA GAP. USA+45 COM/IND ACADEM DOMIN FEEDBACK REV CIVMIL/REL...REALPOL COLD/WAR. PAGE 75 A1540
EDU/PROP PERCEPT BAL/PWR DIPLOM
B63

US SENATE,DOCUMENTS ON INTERNATIONAL AS"ECTS OF EXPLORATION AND USE OF OUTER SPACE, 1954-62: STAFF REPORT FOR COMM AERON SPACE SCI. USA+45 USSR LEGIS LEAD CIVMIL/REL PEACE...POLICY INT/LAW ANTHOL 20 CONGRESS NASA KHRUSH/N. PAGE 155 A3165
SPACE UTIL GOV/REL DIPLOM
N63

US COMM STRENG SEC FREE WORLD,THE SCOPE AND DISTRIBUTION OF UNITED STATES MILITARY AND ECONOMIC ASSISTANCE PROGRAMS (PAMPHLET). USA+45 PLAN BAL/PWR BUDGET DIPLOM CONTROL CIVMIL/REL ATTIT. PAGE 150 A3059
DELIB/GP POLICY FOR/AID ORD/FREE
B64

ALVIM J.C.,A REVOLUCAO SEM RUMO. BRAZIL NAT/G BAL/PWR DIPLOM INT/TRADE PARTIC WEALTH...POLICY SOC SOC/INTEG 20. PAGE 6 A0132
REV CIVMIL/REL ECO/UNDEV ORD/FREE
B64

EPSTEIN H.M.,REVOLT IN THE CONGO. AFR CONGO/BRAZ WOR+45 NAT/G FORCES DOMIN WAR CIVMIL/REL INGP/REL MARXISM...RECORD GP/COMP 20 CONGO/LEOP UN. PAGE 42 A0856
REV COLONIAL NAT/LISM DIPLOM
B64

LIEVWEN E.,GENERALS VS PRESIDENTS: WEOMILITARISM IN LATIN AMERICA. L/A+17C FORCES DIPLOM FOR/AID LEAD ...NAT/COMP 20 PRESIDENT. PAGE 89 A1813
CIVMIL/REL REV CONSERVE ORD/FREE
B64

REES D.,KOREA: THE LIMITED WAR. ASIA KOREA WOR+45 NAT/G CIVMIL/REL PERS/REL PERSON...POLICY CHARTS 20 UN TRUMAN/HS MACARTHR/D. PAGE 120 A2455
DIPLOM WAR INT/ORG FORCES
B64

SINGH N.,THE DEFENCE MECHANISM OF THE MODERN STATE. COM UK USA+45 CONSTN INT/ORG NUC/PWR WAR INGP/REL ROLE 20 DEPT/DEFEN COMMONWLTH. PAGE 134 A2735
FORCES TOP/EX NAT/G CIVMIL/REL
B64

US AIR FORCE ACADEMY ASSEMBLY,OUTER SPACE: FINAL REPORT APRIL 1-4, 1964. FUT USA+45 WOR+45 LAW DELIB/GP CONFER ARMS/CONT WAR PEACE ATTIT MORAL ...ANTHOL 20 NASA. PAGE 150 A3055
SPACE CIVMIL/REL NUC/PWR DIPLOM
B65

KAHN H.,ON ESCALATION; METAPHORS AND SCENARIOS. FORCES DIPLOM ARMS/CONT WAR CIVMIL/REL...INT/LAW 20. PAGE 76 A1548
NUC/PWR ACT/RES INT/ORG ORD/FREE
B65

THAYER F.C. JR.,AIR TRANSPORT POLICY AND NATIONAL SECURITY: A POLITICAL, ECONOMIC, AND MILITARY ANALYSIS. DIST/IND OP/RES PLAN TEC/DEV DIPLOM DETER WAR COST EFFICIENCY...POLICY BIBLIOG 20 DEPT/DEFEN FAA CAB. PAGE 142 A2908
AIR FORCES CIVMIL/REL ORD/FREE

B65
US SENATE,US INTERNATIONAL SPACE PROGRAMS, 1959-65: STAFF REPORT FOR COMM ON AERONAUTICAL AND SPACE SCIENCES. WOR+45 VOL/ASSN CIVMIL/REL 20 CONGRESS NASA TREATY. PAGE 155 A3166
SPACE DIPLOM PLAN GOV/REL

B65
US SENATE COMM ON JUDICIARY,REFUGEE PROBLEMS IN SOUTH VIETNAM AND LAOS: HEARINGS BEFORE SUBCOMMITTEE TO INVESTIGATE PROBLEMS OF REFUGEES, ESCAPEES. CHINA/COM LAOS USA+45 VIETNAM/S PROB/SOLV DIPLOM GOV/REL GP/REL EFFICIENCY ORD/FREE...POLICY GEOG 20 CONGRESS MIGRATION. PAGE 157 A3194
STRANGE HABITAT FOR/AID CIVMIL/REL

L65
MATTHEWS D.G.,"A CURRENT BIBLIOGRAPHY ON ETHIOPIAN AFFAIRS: A SELECT BIBLIOGRAPHY FROM 1950-1964." ETHIOPIA LAW CULTURE ECO/UNDEV INDUS LABOR SECT FORCES DIPLOM CIVMIL/REL RACE/REL...LING STAT 20. PAGE 96 A1969
BIBLIOG/A ADMIN POL/PAR NAT/G

B66
CLAUSEWITZ C.V.,ON WAR (VOL. III). UNIV EDU/PROP ...POLICY DECISION METH 18/20. PAGE 27 A0548
WAR FORCES PLAN CIVMIL/REL

B66
CRAIG G.A.,WAR, POLITICS, AND DIPLOMACY. PRUSSIA CONSTN FORCES CIVMIL/REL TOTALISM PWR 19/20 BISMARCK/O DULLES/JF NAPOLEON/B. PAGE 32 A0654
WAR DIPLOM BAL/PWR

B66
DAVIS V.,POSTWAR DEFENSE POLICY AND THE US NAVY, 1943-1946. USA+45 DIPLOM CONFER LEAD ATTIT...POLICY IDEA/COMP 20 NAVY. PAGE 34 A0692
FORCES PLAN PROB/SOLV CIVMIL/REL

B66
HORELICK A.L.,STRATEGIC POWER AND SOVIET FOREIGN POLICY. CUBA USSR FORCES PLAN CIVMIL/REL...POLICY DECISION 20 COLD/WAR. PAGE 67 A1383
DIPLOM BAL/PWR DETER NUC/PWR

B66
MCKAY V.,AFRICAN DIPLOMACY STUDIES IN THE DETERMINANTS OF FOREIGN POLICY. AFR SOUTH/AFR CULTURE NEUTRAL REGION SOVEREIGN...INT/LAW GOV/COMP ANTHOL 20. PAGE 98 A2013
ECO/UNDEV RACE/REL CIVMIL/REL DIPLOM

B66
SAPIN B.M.,THE MAKING OF UNITED STATES FOREIGN POLICY. USA+45 INT/ORG DELIB/GP FORCES PLAN ECO/TAC CIVMIL/REL PRESIDENT. PAGE 127 A2603
DIPLOM EX/STRUC DECISION NAT/G

C66
TARLING N.,"A CONCISE HISTORY OF SOUTHEAST ASIA." BURMA CAMBODIA LAOS S/ASIA THAILAND VIETNAM ECO/UNDEV POL/PAR FORCES ADMIN REV WAR CIVMIL/REL ORD/FREE MARXISM SOCISM 13/20. PAGE 141 A2890
COLONIAL DOMIN INT/TRADE NAT/LISM

B67
BURNS E.L.M.,MEGAMURDER. WOR+45 LAW INT/ORG NAT/G BAL/PWR DIPLOM DETER MURDER WEAPON CIVMIL/REL PEACE ...INT/LAW TREND 20. PAGE 22 A0444
FORCES PLAN WAR NUC/PWR

B67
GRIFFITH SB I.I.,THE CHINESE PEOPLE'S LIBERATION ARMY. CHINA/COM DIPLOM DOMIN GUERRILLA NUC/PWR REV ...CHARTS BIBLIOG 20. PAGE 57 A1163
FORCES CIVMIL/REL NAT/LISM PWR

B67
RALSTON D.B.,THE ARMY OF THE REPUBLIC; THE PLACE OF THE MILITARY IN THE POLITICAL EVOLUTION OF FRANCE 1871-1914. FRANCE MOD/EUR EX/STRUC LEGIS TOP/EX DIPLOM ADMIN WAR GP/REL ROLE...BIBLIOG 19/20. PAGE 119 A2436
FORCES NAT/G CIVMIL/REL POLICY

B67
SALISBURY H.E.,BEHIND THE LINES - HANOI. VIETNAM/N NAT/G GUERRILLA CIVMIL/REL NAT/LISM KNOWL 20. PAGE 126 A2592
WAR PROB/SOLV DIPLOM OBS

S67
AFRICAN BIBLIOGRAPHIC CENTER,"THE SWORD AND GOVERNMENT: A PRELIMINARY AND SELECTED BIBLIOGRAPHICAL GUIDE TO AFRICAN MILITARY AFFAIRS; PART I." AFR USA+45 USSR INT/ORG POL/PAR FOR/AID COLONIAL ARMS/CONT PWR 20 UN. PAGE 5 A0101
BIBLIOG/A FORCES CIVMIL/REL DIPLOM

S67
GODUNSKY Y.,"'APOSTLES OF PEACE' IN LATIN AMERICA." L/A+17C USA+45 BAL/PWR DIPLOM FOR/AID DOMIN COLONIAL CIVMIL/REL MARXIST. PAGE 53 A1086
ECO/UNDEV REV VOL/ASSN EDU/PROP

S67
PAUKER G.J.,"TOWARD A NEW ORDER IN INDONESIA." COM INDONESIA S/ASIA ECO/UNDEV POL/PAR EX/STRUC TOP/EX BAL/PWR ECO/TAC FOR/AID DOMIN NAT/LISM AUTHORIT ORD/FREE PWR 20. PAGE 114 A2342
REV NAT/G DIPLOM CIVMIL/REL

S67
TACKABERRY R.B.,"ORGANIZING AND TRAINING PEACE-KEEPING FORCES* THE CANADIAN VIEW." CANADA PLAN DIPLOM CONFER ADJUD ADMIN CIVMIL/REL 20 UN. PAGE 141 A2882
PEACE FORCES INT/ORG CONSULT

CLAGETT H.L. A0540,A3217

CLAN....SEE KIN

CLARK G. A0541

CLARK S.V.O. A0542

CLARK W. A0543

CLARK/JB....JOHN BATES CLARK

CLARKE D.E. A0374

CLASS DIVISION....SEE STRATA

CLASS, SOCIAL....SEE STRATA

CLASSIF....CLASSIFICATION, TYPOLOGY, SET THEORY

N
AMERICAN DOCUMENTATION INST,DOCUMENTATION ABSTRACTS. WOR+45 NAT/G COMPUTER CREATE TEC/DEV DIPLOM EDU/PROP REGION KNOWL...PHIL/SCI CLASSIF LING. PAGE 7 A0143
BIBLIOG/A AUTOMAT COMPUT/IR R+D

S55
WRIGHT Q.,"THE PEACEFUL ADJUSTMENT OF INTERNATIONAL RELATIONS: PROBLEMS AND RESEARCH APPROACHES." UNIV INTELL EDU/PROP ADJUD ROUTINE KNOWL SKILL...INT/LAW JURID PHIL/SCI CLASSIF 20. PAGE 167 A3411
R+D METH/CNCPT PEACE

B64
SZLADITS C.,BIBLIOGRAPHY ON FOREIGN AND COMPARATIVE LAW: BOOKS AND ARTICLES IN ENGLISH (SUPPLEMENT 1962). FINAN INDUS JUDGE LICENSE ADMIN CT/SYS PARL/PROC OWN...INT/LAW CLASSIF METH/COMP NAT/COMP 20. PAGE 141 A2877
BIBLIOG/A JURID ADJUD LAW

S64
HORECKY P.L.,"LIBRARY OF CONGRESS PUBLICATIONS IN AID OF USSR AND EAST EUROPEAN RESEARCH." BULGARIA CZECHOSLVK POLAND USSR YUGOSLAVIA NAT/G POL/PAR DIPLOM ADMIN GOV/REL...CLASSIF 20. PAGE 67 A1382
BIBLIOG/A COM MARXISM

B65
VON GLAHN G.,LAW AMONG NATIONS: AN INTRODUCTION TO PUBLIC INTERNATIONAL LAW. WOR+45 WOR-45 INT/ORG NAT/G CREATE ADJUD WAR...GEOG CLASSIF TREND BIBLIOG. PAGE 160 A3250
ACADEM INT/LAW GEN/LAWS LAW

B67
US SUPERINTENDENT OF DOCUMENTS,LIBRARY OF CONGRESS (PRICE LIST 83). AFR ASIA EUR+WWI USA-45 USSR NAT/G DIPLOM CONFER CT/SYS WAR...DECISION PHIL/SCI CLASSIF 19/20 CONGRESS PRESIDENT. PAGE 157 A3205
BIBLIOG/A USA+45 AUTOMAT LAW

CLAUDE I. A0544,A0545,A0546,A0547

CLAUSEWITZ C.V. A0548

CLAUSWTZ/K....KARL VON CLAUSEWITZ

CLEMENCE/G....GEORGES CLEMENCEAU

CLEMENS W.C. A0321

CLEMSON....CLEMSON UNIVERSITY

CLENDENON C. A0549

CLEVELAND H. A0550,A0551

CLEVELAND....CLEVELAND, OHIO

CLEVELND/G....PRESIDENT GROVER CLEVELAND

CLIENT....CLIENTS, CLIENTELE (BUT NOT CUSTOMERS)

CLIFFORD/C....CLARK CLIFFORD

CLINGHAM T.A. A0552

CLIQUES....SEE FACE/GP

CLUBB O.E. A0553

CLUBS....SEE VOL/ASSN, FACE/GP

CLYDE P.H. A0554

CMA....CANADIAN MEDICAL ASSOCIATION

CMN/WLTH....BRITISH COMMONWEALTH OF NATIONS; SEE ALSO VOL/ASSN, APPROPRIATE NATIONS, COMMONWLTH

N
PUBLISHERS' CIRCULAR, THE OFFICIAL ORGAN OF THE PUBLISHERS' ASSOCIATION OF GREAT BRITAIN AND IRELAND. EUR+WWI MOD/EUR UK LAW PROB/SOLV DIPLOM COLONIAL ATTIT...HUM 19/20 CMN/WLTH. PAGE 2 A0039
BIBLIOG NAT/G WRITING LEAD

N
MINISTRY OF OVERSEAS DEVELOPME,TECHNICAL CO-OPERATION -- A BIBLIOGRAPHY. UK LAW SOCIETY DIPLOM ECO/TAC FOR/AID...STAT 20 CMN/WLTH. PAGE 102 A2089
BIBLIOG TEC/DEV ECO/DEV NAT/G

B02
SEELEY J.R.,THE EXPANSION OF ENGLAND. MOD/EUR S/ASIA UK CULTURE NAT/G FORCES PLAN DOMIN EDU/PROP COLONIAL ROUTINE ATTIT ALL/VALS SOVEREIGN...CONCPT HIST/WRIT PARLIAMENT 18 CMN/WLTH. PAGE 131 A2679
INT/ORG ACT/RES CAP/ISM INDIA

N19
MASSEY V.,CANADIANS AND THEIR COMMONWEALTH: THE ROMANES LECTURE DELIVERED IN THE SHELDONIAN THEATRE JUNE 1, 1961 (PAMPHLET). CANADA UK CULTURE ECO/DEV REPRESENT NAT/LISM PEACE PWR CONSERVE 20 CMN/WLTH. PAGE 96 A1959
ATTIT DIPLOM NAT/G SOVEREIGN

B26
LEWIN E.,RECENT PUBLICATIONS IN THE LIBRARY OF THE ROYAL COLONIAL INSTITUTE (PAMPHLET). CANADA UK EX/STRUC PARL/PROC NAT/LISM SOVEREIGN 20 CMN/WLTH PARLIAMENT. PAGE 88 A1799
BIBLIOG COLONIAL CONSTN DIPLOM

B27
GOOCH G.P.,ENGLISH DEMOCRATIC IDEAS IN THE SEVENTEENTH CENTURY (2ND ED.). UK LAW SECT FORCES DIPLOM LEAD PARL/PROC REV ATTIT AUTHORIT...ANARCH CONCPT 17 PARLIAMENT CMN/WLTH REFORMERS. PAGE 54 A1100
IDEA/COMP MAJORIT EX/STRUC CONSERVE

B28
CORBETT P.E.,CANADA AND WORLD POLITICS. LAW CULTURE SOCIETY STRUCT MARKET INT/ORG FORCES ACT/RES PLAN ECO/TAC LEGIT ORD/FREE PWR RESPECT...SOC CONCPT TIME/SEQ TREND CMN/WLTH 20 LEAGUE/NAT. PAGE 30 A0612
NAT/G CANADA

B28
HALL W.P.,EMPIRE TO COMMONWEALTH. FUT WOR-45 CONSTN ECO/DEV ECO/UNDEV INT/ORG PROVS PLAN DIPLOM EDU/PROP ADMIN COLONIAL PEACE PERSON ALL/VALS ...POLICY GEOG SOC OBS RECORD TREND CMN/WLTH PARLIAMENT 19/20. PAGE 60 A1229
VOL/ASSN NAT/G UK

B28
HURST C.,GREAT BRITAIN AND THE DOMINIONS. EUR+WWI CULTURE ECO/DEV INT/ORG NAT/G DIPLOM ECO/TAC COLONIAL ATTIT PWR SOVEREIGN...TIME/SEQ GEN/LAWS TOT/POP VAL/FREE 20 CMN/WLTH. PAGE 69 A1420
VOL/ASSN DOMIN UK

B36
ROBINSON H.,DEVELOPMENT OF THE BRITISH EMPIRE. WOR-45 CULTURE SOCIETY STRUCT ECO/DEV ECO/UNDEV INT/ORG VOL/ASSN FORCES CREATE PLAN DOMIN EDU/PROP ADMIN COLONIAL PWR WEALTH...POLICY GEOG CHARTS CMN/WLTH 16/20. PAGE 122 A2503
NAT/G HIST/WRIT UK

B39
MARRIOTT J.,COMMONWEALTH OR ANARCHY: A SURVEY OF PROJECTS OF PEACE. WOR-45 STRATA DOMIN ATTIT ORD/FREE PWR...TRADIT TIME/SEQ GEN/METH 16/20 CMN/WLTH. PAGE 95 A1945
FUT INT/ORG PEACE

L44
HAILEY,"THE FUTURE OF COLONIAL PEOPLES." WOR-45 CONSTN CULTURE ECO/UNDEV AGRI MARKET INT/ORG NAT/G SECT CONSULT ECO/TAC LEGIT ADMIN NAT/LISM ALL/VALS ...SOC OBS TREND STERTYP CMN/WLTH LEAGUE/NAT PARLIAMENT 20. PAGE 59 A1218
PLAN CONCPT DIPLOM UK

N45
INDIA QUARTERLY, A JOURNAL OF INTERNATIONAL AFFAIRS. INDIA LAW CONSTN ECO/UNDEV INT/ORG POL/PAR COLONIAL LEAD PARL/PROC WAR ATTIT...SOC 20 CMN/WLTH. PAGE 3 A0053
BIBLIOG/A S/ASIA DIPLOM NAT/G

B45
ELTON G.E.,IMPERIAL COMMONWEALTH. INDIA UK DIPLOM DOMIN WAR NAT/LISM SOVEREIGN...TRADIT CHARTS T 15/20 CMN/WLTH AUSTRAL PRE/US/AM. PAGE 41 A0844
REGION CONCPT COLONIAL

B46
GRIFFIN G.G.,A GUIDE TO MANUSCRIPTS RELATING TO AMERICAN HISTORY IN BRITISH DEPOSITORIES. CANADA IRELAND MOD/EUR UK USA-45 LAW DIPLOM ADMIN COLONIAL WAR NAT/LISM SOVEREIGN...GEOG INT/LAW 15/19 CMN/WLTH. PAGE 56 A1159
BIBLIOG/A ALL/VALS NAT/G

B51
CARRINGTON C.E.,THE LIQUIDATION OF THE BRITISH EMPIRE. AFR NAT/G INT/TRADE COLONIAL RACE/REL ATTIT ORD/FREE...POLICY NAT/COMP 20 CMN/WLTH. PAGE 25 A0501
SOVEREIGN NAT/LISM DIPLOM GP/REL

B51
JENNINGS I.,THE COMMONWEALTH IN ASIA. CEYLON INDIA PAKISTAN CULTURE STRATA NAT/G LEGIS DIPLOM COLONIAL ATTIT...DECISION 20 CMN/WLTH. PAGE 74 A1507
CONSTN INT/ORG POLICY PLAN

B51
JENNINGS S.I.,THE COMMONWEALTH IN ASIA. CEYLON INDIA PAKISTAN S/ASIA UK CONSTN CULTURE SOCIETY STRATA STRUCT NAT/G POL/PAR EDU/PROP LEAD WAR 20 CMN/WLTH. PAGE 74 A1510
NAT/LISM REGION COLONIAL DIPLOM

B55
PYRAH G.B.,IMPERIAL POLICY AND SOUTH AFRICA 1902-1910. SOUTH/AFR UK NAT/G WAR DISCRIM...CONCPT CHARTS BIBLIOG/A 19/20 CMN/WLTH. PAGE 118 A2421
DIPLOM COLONIAL POLICY RACE/REL

S55
HALLETT D.,"THE HISTORY AND STRUCTURE OF OEEC." EUR+WWI USA+45 CONSTN INDUS INT/ORG NAT/G DELIB/GP ACT/RES PLAN ORD/FREE WEALTH...CONCPT OEEC 20 CMN/WLTH. PAGE 60 A1234
VOL/ASSN ECO/DEV

C55
APTER D.E.,"THE GOLD COAST IN TRANSITION." AFR CONSTN LOC/G LEGIS DIPLOM COLONIAL CONTROL GOV/REL ...CHARTS BIBLIOG 20 CMN/WLTH. PAGE 8 A0170
ORD/FREE REPRESENT PARL/PROC NAT/G

B56
UNDERHILL F.H.,THE BRITISH COMMONWEALTH: AN EXPERIMENT IN CO-OPERATION AMONG NATIONS. CANADA UK WOR+45 WOR-45 INT/ORG COLONIAL UTIL SOVEREIGN CONSERVE...OLD/LIB SOC/EXP BIBLIOG/A 19/20 CMN/WLTH. PAGE 147 A3007
VOL/ASSN NAT/LISM DIPLOM

B56
WEIS P.,NATIONALITY AND STATELESSNESS IN INTERNATIONAL LAW. UK WOR+45 WOR-45 LAW CONSTN NAT/G DIPLOM EDU/PROP LEGIT ROUTINE RIGID/FLEX ...JURID RECORD CMN/WLTH 20. PAGE 162 A3309
INT/ORG SOVEREIGN INT/LAW

B57
BUCK P.W.,CONTOL OF FOREIGN RELATIONS IN MODERN NATIONS. FRANCE L/A+17C NETHERLAND USSR WOR+45 INT/ORG TOP/EX BAL/PWR DOMIN EDU/PROP COERCE PEACE ATTIT...CONCPT TREND 20 CMN/WLTH. PAGE 21 A0427
NAT/G PWR DIPLOM

B57
BURNS A.,IN DEFENCE OF COLONIES; BRITISH COLONIAL TERRITORIES IN INTERNATIONAL AFFAIRS. UK ECO/UNDEV PLAN DOMIN SOVEREIGN...MAJORIT 18/20 CMN/WLTH INTERVENT. PAGE 22 A0439
COLONIAL POLICY ATTIT DIPLOM

B58
INDIAN COUNCIL WORLD AFFAIRS,DEFENCE AND SECURITY IN THE INDIAN OCEAN AREA. INDIA S/ASIA CULTURE CONSULT DELIB/GP FORCES PROB/SOLV DIPLOM INT/TRADE 20 CMN/WLTH. PAGE 70 A1438
GEOG HABITAT ECO/UNDEV ORD/FREE

B58
JENNINGS W.I.,PROBLEMS OF THE NEW COMMONWEALTH. CEYLON INDIA MALAYSIA PAKISTAN ECO/UNDEV VOL/ASSN RACE/REL NAT/LISM ROLE 20 CMN/WLTH. PAGE 74 A1511
GP/REL INGP/REL COLONIAL INT/ORG

B58
MANSERGH N.,COMMONWEALTH PERSPECTIVES. GHANA UK LAW VOL/ASSN CONFER HEALTH SOVEREIGN...GEOG CHARTS ANTHOL 20 CMN/WLTH AUSTRAL. PAGE 94 A1930
DIPLOM COLONIAL INT/ORG INGP/REL

B58
MANSERGH N.,SURVEY OF BRITISH COMMONWEALTH AFFAIRS: PROBLEMS OF WARTIME CO-OPERATION AND POST-WAR CHANGE 1939-1952. INDIA IRELAND S/ASIA CONSTN INT/ORG BAL/PWR COLONIAL NEUTRAL WAR ADJUST PEACE ROLE ORD/FREE...CHARTS 20 CMN/WLTH NATO UN. PAGE 94 A1931
VOL/ASSN CONSEN PROB/SOLV INGP/REL

B58
MOORE B.T.,NATO AND THE FUTURE OF EUROPE. EUR+WWI FUT USA+45 ECO/DEV INDUS MARKET NAT/G VOL/ASSN FORCES DIPLOM NUC/PWR ORD/FREE...CONCPT CHARTS ORG/CHARTS CMN/WLTH 20 NATO. PAGE 103 A2122
INT/ORG REGION

C58
WILDING N.,"AN ENCYCLOPEDIA OF PARLIAMENT." UK LAW CONSTN CHIEF PROB/SOLV DIPLOM DEBATE WAR INGP/REL PRIVIL...BIBLIOG DICTIONARY 13/20 CMN/WLTH PARLIAMENT. PAGE 164 A3349
PARL/PROC POL/PAR NAT/G ADMIN

B59
JONES A.C.,NEW FABIAN COLONIAL ESSAYS. UK SOCIETY POL/PAR EDU/PROP ADMIN ORD/FREE SOVEREIGN SOCISM ...ANTHOL 20 CMN/WLTH LABOR/PAR. PAGE 75 A1530
COLONIAL INT/ORG INGP/REL DOMIN

B59
TUNSTALL W.C.B.,THE COMMONWEALTH AND REGIONAL DEFENCE (PAMPHLET). UK LAW VOL/ASSN PLAN AGREE REGION WAR ORD/FREE 20 CMN/WLTH NATO SEATO TREATY. PAGE 146 A2977
INT/ORG FORCES DIPLOM

B60
ALLEN H.C.,THE ANGLO-AMERICAN PREDICAMENT: THE BRITISH COMMONWEALTH, THE UNITED STATES AND EUROPEAN UNITY. EUR+WWI FUT UK USA+45 WOR+45 ECO/DEV NAT/G PLAN DETER...CONCPT OBS TIME/SEQ TREND COLD/WAR VAL/FREE CMN/WLTH 20. PAGE 6 A0123
INT/ORG PWR BAL/PWR

B60
THE ECONOMIST (LONDON),THE COMMONWEALTH AND EUROPE. EUR+WWI WOR+45 AGRI FINAN INCOME...STAT CENSUS CHARTS CMN/WLTH EEC. PAGE 142 A2911
INT/TRADE INDUS INT/ORG NAT/COMP

B60
WHEARE K.C.,THE CONSTITUTIONAL STRUCTURE OF THE COMMONWEALTH. UK EX/STRUC DIPLOM DOMIN ADMIN COLONIAL CONTROL LEAD INGP/REL SUPEGO 20 CMN/WLTH. PAGE 163 A3325
CONSTN INT/ORG VOL/ASSN SOVEREIGN

B61
BELOFF M.,NEW DIMENSIONS IN FOREIGN POLICY: A STUDY IN BRITISH ADMINISTRATION. UK NAT/G ATTIT RIGID/FLEX ORD/FREE...GEN/LAWS EUR+WWI CMN/WLTH EEC 20. PAGE 13 A0260
INT/ORG DIPLOM

B61
CHIDZERO B.T.G.,TANGANYIKA AND INTERNATIONAL
ECO/UNDEV

TRUSTEESHIP. AFR WOR+45 WOR-45 ECO/DEV INT/ORG ECO/TAC DOMIN COLONIAL...RECORD CHARTS 20 TANGANYIKA CMN/WLTH. PAGE 26 A0528 CONSTN

S61
ANGLIN D.,"UNITED STATES OPPOSITION TO CANADIAN MEMBERSHIP IN THE PAN AMERICAN UNION: A CANADIAN VIEW." L/A+17C UK USA+45 VOL/ASSN DELIB/GP EX/STRUC PLAN DIPLOM DOMIN REGION ATTIT RIGID/FLEX PWR ...RELATIV CONCPT STERTYP CMN/WLTH OAS 20. PAGE 8 A0162 INT/ORG CANADA

S61
BURNET A.,"TOO MANY ALLIES." COM EUR+WWI UK WOR+45 WOR-45 ACT/RES PLAN DISPL PWR SKILL...TIME/SEQ 20 CMN/WLTH SEATO NATO CENTO. PAGE 22 A0438 VOL/ASSN INT/ORG DIPLOM

S61
RAY J.,"THE EUROPEAN FREE-TRADE ASSOCIATION AND ITS IMPACT ON INDIA'S TRADE." EUR+WWI FRANCE GERMANY INDIA S/ASIA UK NAT/G VOL/ASSN PLAN INT/TRADE ROUTINE WEALTH...STAT CHARTS CMN/WLTH EEC OEEC 20 EFTA. PAGE 120 A2453 ECO/DEV ECO/TAC

S61
WEST F.J.,"THE NEW GUINEA QUESTION: AN AUSTRALIAN VIEW." WOR+45 INT/ORG VOL/ASSN LEGIT PERCEPT ...POLICY TIME/SEQ AUSTRAL VAL/FREE 20 CMN/WLTH. PAGE 163 A3320 S/ASIA ECO/UNDEV

B62
BRYANT A.,A CHOICE FOR DESTINY: COMMONWEALTH AND THE COMMON MARKET. EUR+WWI FUT UK INT/TRADE COLONIAL ATTIT SOVEREIGN 20 CMN/WLTH EEC. PAGE 20 A0411 INT/ORG VOL/ASSN DIPLOM CHOOSE

B62
HETHERINGTON H.,SOME ASPECTS OF THE BRITISH EXPERIMENT IN DEMOCRACY. UK DIPLOM COLONIAL ...CONCPT 20 CMN/WLTH. PAGE 64 A1322 EDU/PROP AFR POPULISM SOC/EXP

B62
PAKISTAN MINISTRY OF FINANCE,FOREIGN ECONOMIC AID: A REVIEW OF FOREIGN ECONOMIC AID TO PAKISTAN. EUR+WWI PAKISTAN UK USA+45 USSR ECO/UNDEV INT/ORG DELIB/GP DIPLOM ECO/TAC...CHARTS CMN/WLTH CHINJAP. PAGE 113 A2318 FOR/AID RECEIVE WEALTH FINAN

B62
SNYDER L.L.D.,THE IMPERIALISM READER. AFR ASIA CHINA/COM COM EUR+WWI FUT MOD/EUR USA+45 WOR+45 WOR-45 INT/ORG COLONIAL SOVEREIGN CMN/WLTH OAS 20. PAGE 134 A2751 DOMIN PWR DIPLOM

B62
TAYLOR D.,THE BRITISH IN AFRICA. UK CULTURE ECO/UNDEV INDUS DIPLOM INT/TRADE ADMIN WAR RACE/REL ORD/FREE SOVEREIGN...POLICY BIBLIOG 15/20 CMN/WLTH. PAGE 142 A2898 AFR COLONIAL DOMIN

S62
MILLAR T.B.,"THE COMMONWEALTH AND THE UNITED NATIONS." FUT WOR+45 STRUCT NAT/G VOL/ASSN CONSULT DELIB/GP EDU/PROP LEGIT ATTIT...POLICY CONCPT TREND CMN/WLTH UN 20. PAGE 101 A2072 INT/ORG

S62
SCOTT J.B.,"ANGLO-SOVIET TRADE AND ITS EFFECTS ON THE COMMONWEALTH." COM FUT UK USSR WOR+45 ECO/DEV MARKET INT/ORG CONSULT WEALTH...POLICY TREND CMN/WLTH 20. PAGE 130 A2673 NAT/G ECO/TAC

S62
SPRINGER H.W.,"FEDERATION IN THE CARIBBEAN: AN ATTEMPT THAT FAILED." L/A+17C ECO/UNDEV INT/ORG POL/PAR PROVS LEGIS CREATE PLAN LEGIT ADMIN FEDERAL ATTIT DRIVE PERSON ORD/FREE PWR...POLICY GEOG PSY CONCPT OBS CARIBBEAN CMN/WLTH 20. PAGE 136 A2791 VOL/ASSN NAT/G REGION

S62
THOMPSON D.,"THE UNITED KINGDOM AND THE TREATY OF ROME." EUR+WWI INT/ORG NAT/G DELIB/GP LEGIS INT/TRADE RIGID/FLEX...CONCPT EEC PARLIAMENT CMN/WLTH 20. PAGE 143 A2925 ADJUD JURID

B63
GREAT BRITAIN CENTRAL OFF INF,CONSULTATION AND CO-OPERATION IN THE COMMONWEALTH. LAW R+D FORCES PLAN EDU/PROP CONFER INGP/REL...GEOG CENSUS 19/20 CMN/WLTH. PAGE 55 A1133 DIPLOM DELIB/GP VOL/ASSN REGION

S63
BELOFF M.,"BRITAIN, EUROPE AND THE ATLANTIC COMMUNITY." EUR+WWI ELITES NAT/G VOL/ASSN TOP/EX ATTIT ORD/FREE PWR SOVEREIGN WEALTH EEC TOT/POP VAL/FREE CMN/WLTH 20. PAGE 13 A0262 INT/ORG ECO/DEV UK

S63
HARNETTY P.,"CANADA, SOUTH AFRICA AND THE COMMONWEALTH." CANADA SOUTH/AFR LAW INT/ORG VOL/ASSN DELIB/GP LEGIS TOP/EX ECO/TAC LEGIT DRIVE MORAL...CONCPT CMN/WLTH 20. PAGE 62 A1263 AFR ATTIT

S63
SHONFIELD A.,"AFTER BRUSSELS." EUR+WWI FRANCE GERMANY UK ECO/DEV DIST/IND MARKET VOL/ASSN DELIB/GP CREATE INT/TRADE ATTIT RIGID/FLEX...RECORD TREND GEN/LAWS EEC CMN/WLTH 20. PAGE 132 A2705 PLAN ECO/TAC

B64
ARNOLD G.,TOWARDS PEACE AND A MULTIRACIAL COMMONWEALTH. UK TEC/DEV BAL/PWR COLONIAL GP/REL NAT/LISM PEACE SOVEREIGN...POLICY SOC/INTEG 20 CMN/WLTH. PAGE 9 A0175 DIPLOM INT/TRADE FOR/AID ORD/FREE

B64
DE SMITH S.A.,THE NEW COMMONWEALTH AND ITS CONSTITUTIONS. AFR CYPRUS PAKISTAN S/ASIA INT/ORG NAT/G LEGIS LEGIT RIGID/FLEX PWR...CONCPT TIME/SEQ CMN/WLTH 20. PAGE 35 A0713 EX/STRUC CONSTN SOVEREIGN

B64
EAYRS J.,THE COMMONWEALTH AND SUEZ: A DOCUMENTARY SURVEY. FRANCE ISLAM VOL/ASSN FORCES CONFER COLONIAL WAR INGP/REL 20 CMN/WLTH SUEZ UN. PAGE 40 A0818 DIPLOM NAT/LISM DIST/IND SOVEREIGN

B64
ESTHUS R.A.,FROM ENMITY TO ALLIANCE: US AUSTRALIAN RELATIONS. S/ASIA DIST/IND VOL/ASSN FORCES ATTIT 20 AUSTRAL TREATY CMN/WLTH. PAGE 42 A0863 DIPLOM WAR INT/TRADE FOR/AID

B64
GREAT BRITAIN CENTRAL OFF INF,CONSTITUTIONAL DEVELOPMENT IN THE COMMONWEALTH. VOL/ASSN PLAN DIPLOM COLONIAL INGP/REL NAT/LISM ORD/FREE PWR 17/20 CMN/WLTH. PAGE 55 A1135 REGION CONSTN NAT/G SOVEREIGN

B64
WAINHOUSE D.W.,REMNANTS OF EMPIRE: THE UNITED NATIONS AND THE END OF COLONIALISM. FUT PORTUGAL WOR+45 NAT/G CONSULT DOMIN LEGIT ADMIN ROUTINE ATTIT ORD/FREE...POLICY JURID RECORD INT TIME/SEQ UN CMN/WLTH 20. PAGE 160 A3260 INT/ORG TREND COLONIAL

L64
SYMONDS R.,"REFLECTIONS IN LOCALISATION." AFR S/ASIA UK STRATA INT/ORG NAT/G SCHOOL EDU/PROP LEGIT KNOWL ORD/FREE PWR RESPECT CMN/WLTH 20. PAGE 140 A2874 ADMIN MGT COLONIAL

S64
CARNEGIE ENDOWMENT INT. PEACE,"COLONIAL COUNTRIES AND PEOPLES (ISSUES BEFORE THE NINETEENTH GENERAL ASSEMBLY)." AFR ISLAM L/A+17C WOR+45 DELIB/GP LEGIS ECO/TAC EDU/PROP NAT/LISM PEACE ALL/VALS...RECORD UN CMN/WLTH 20. PAGE 24 A0491 INT/ORG ECO/UNDEV COLONIAL

S64
GROSS J.A.,"WHITEHALL AND THE COMMONWEALTH." EUR+WWI MOD/EUR INT/ORG NAT/G CONSULT DELIB/GP LEGIS DOMIN ADMIN COLONIAL ROUTINE PWR CMN/WLTH 19/20. PAGE 57 A1174 EX/STRUC ATTIT TREND

S64
PRASAD B.,"SURVEY OF RECENT RESEARCH: STUDIES ON INDIA'S FOREIGN POLIC AND RELATIONS." ASIA INDIA PAKISTAN USA+45 NAT/G INT/TRADE GOV/REL 20 UN CMN/WLTH. PAGE 117 A2406 BIBLIOG DIPLOM ROLE POLICY

B65
MEHROTRA S.R.,INDIA AND THE COMMONWEALTH 1885-1929. INDIA UK INT/ORG VOL/ASSN GP/REL ATTIT...POLICY BIBLIOG 19/20 CMN/WLTH. PAGE 99 A2034 DIPLOM NAT/G POL/PAR NAT/LISM

B65
MILLER J.D.B.,THE COMMONWEALTH IN THE WORLD (3RD ED.). CONSTN COLONIAL PWR SOVEREIGN 20 CMN/WLTH. PAGE 101 A2077 VOL/ASSN INT/ORG INGP/REL DIPLOM

B65
WILLIAMSON J.A.,GREAT BRITAIN AND THE COMMONWEALTH. UK DOMIN COLONIAL INGP/REL...POLICY 18/20 CMN/WLTH. PAGE 165 A3355 NAT/G DIPLOM INT/ORG SOVEREIGN

S65
GANGAL S.C.,"SURVEY OF RECENT RESEARCH: INDIA AND THE COMMONWEALTH" INDIA UK NAT/G INT/TRADE PARTIC GOV/REL ROLE 20 CMN/WLTH. PAGE 51 A1039 BIBLIOG POLICY REGION DIPLOM

B66
HAMILTON W.B.,A DECADE OF THE COMMONWEALTH, 1955-1964. UK LAW ELITES FINAN FOR/AID CONFER COLONIAL PWR...GEOG CHARTS ANTHOL 20 CMN/WLTH UN. PAGE 61 A1247 INT/ORG INGP/REL DIPLOM NAT/G

B66
INTERNATIONAL ECONOMIC ASSN,STABILITY AND PROGRESS IN THE WORLD ECONOMY: THE FIRST CONGRESS OF THE INTERNATIONAL ECONOMIC ASSOCIATION. WOR+45 ECO/DEV ECO/UNDEV DELIB/GP FOR/AID BAL/PAY...TREND CMN/WLTH 20. PAGE 71 A1455 INT/TRADE

B66
MCINTYRE W.D.,COLONIES INTO COMMONWEALTH. UK CONSTN VOL/ASSN DOMIN CONTROL...BIBLIOG 18/20 CMN/WLTH. PAGE 98 A2012 DIPLOM INT/ORG COLONIAL SOVEREIGN

B66
THORNTON A.P.,THE IMPERIAL IDEA AND ITS ENEMIES. UK WOR+45 WOR-45 NAT/G PLAN DOMIN CONTROL WAR ATTIT PWR...TREND CHARTS 19/20 CMN/WLTH. PAGE 144 A2937 COLONIAL DIPLOM

B66
US DEPARTMENT OF STATE,RESEARCH ON WESTERN EUROPE, GREAT BRITAIN, AND CANADA (EXTERNAL RESEARCH LIST NO 3-25). CANADA GERMANY/W UK LAW CULTURE NAT/G POL/PAR FORCES EDU/PROP REGION MARXISM...GEOG SOC WORSHIP 20 CMN/WLTH. PAGE 152 A3098 BIBLIOG/A EUR+WWI DIPLOM

B66
WILSON H.A.,THE IMPERIAL POLICY OF SIR ROBERT INGP/REL

BORDEN. CANADA UK ELITES INT/ORG VOL/ASSN CONTROL LEAD WAR ROLE 20 CMN/WLTH BORDEN/R. PAGE 165 A3360 COLONIAL CONSTN CHIEF

B67
BLOM-COOPER L.,THE LITERATURE OF THE LAW AND THE LANGUAGE OF THE LAW (2 VOLS.). CANADA ISRAEL UK WOR+45 WOR-45 JUDGE CT/SYS ATTIT...CRIMLGY JURID ANTHOL CMN/WLTH. PAGE 15 A0312 BIBLIOG LAW INT/LAW ADJUD

S67
ROCKE J.R.M.,"THE BRITISH EXPORT BATTLE FOR THE CARIBBEAN" GP/REL...POLICY 20 CMN/WLTH. PAGE 122 A2510 INT/TRADE DIPLOM MARKET ECO/TAC

COALITIONS....SEE VOL/ASSN+POL

COASTGUARD....COAST GUARD

COBB/HOWLL....HOWELL COBB

COBLENZ C. A2464

COCHRANE J.D. A0555

COERCE....COERCION, VIOLENCE; SEE ALSO FORCES, PROCESSES AND PRACTICES INDEX, PART G, P. XIII

N
BACKGROUND; JOURNAL OF INTERNATIONAL STUDIES ASSOCIATION. INT/ORG FORCES ACT/RES EDU/PROP COERCE NAT/LISM PEACE ATTIT...INT/LAW CONCPT 20. PAGE 1 A0005 BIBLIOG DIPLOM POLICY

B00
DARBY W.E.,INTERNATIONAL TRIBUNALS. WOR-45 NAT/G ECO/TAC DOMIN LEGIT CT/SYS COERCE ORD/FREE PWR SOVEREIGN JURID. PAGE 33 A0681 INT/ORG ADJUD PEACE INT/LAW

B00
HOLLAND T.E.,STUDIES IN INTERNATIONAL LAW. TURKEY USSR WOR-45 CONSTN NAT/G DIPLOM DOMIN LEGIT COERCE WAR PEACE ORD/FREE PWR SOVEREIGN...JURID CHARTS 20 PARLIAMENT SUEZ TREATY. PAGE 66 A1367 INT/ORG LAW INT/LAW

B00
MORRIS H.C.,THE HISTORY OF COLONIZATION. WOR+45 WOR-45 ECO/DEV ECO/UNDEV INT/ORG ACT/RES PLAN ECO/TAC LEGIT ROUTINE COERCE ATTIT DRIVE ALL/VALS ...GEOG TREND 19. PAGE 105 A2148 DOMIN SOVEREIGN COLONIAL

L00
HISTORICUS,"LETTERS AND SOME QUESTIONS OF INTERNATIONAL LAW." FRANCE NETHERLAND UK USA-45 WOR-45 LAW NAT/G COERCE...SOC CONCPT GEN/LAWS TOT/POP 19 CIVIL/WAR. PAGE 65 A1344 WEALTH JURID WAR INT/LAW

B03
MOREL E.D.,THE BRITISH CASE IN FRENCH CONGO. CONGO/BRAZ FRANCE UK COERCE MORAL WEALTH...POLICY INT/LAW 20 CONGO/LEOP. PAGE 104 A2130 DIPLOM INT/TRADE COLONIAL AFR

B09
HOLLAND T.E.,LETTERS UPON WAR AND NEUTRALITY. WOR-45 NAT/G FORCES JUDGE ECO/TAC LEGIT CT/SYS NEUTRAL ROUTINE COERCE...JURID TIME/SEQ 20. PAGE 67 A1368 LAW INT/LAW INT/ORG WAR

B17
DE VICTORIA F.,DE INDIS ET DE JURE BELLI (1557) IN F. DE VICTORIA, DE INDIS ET DE JURE BELLI REFLECTIONES. UNIV NAT/G SECT CHIEF PARTIC COERCE PEACE MORAL...POLICY 16 INDIAN/AM CHRISTIAN CONSCN/OBJ. PAGE 35 A0715 WAR INT/LAW OWN

N19
BARROS J.F.P.,THE INTERNATIONAL POLICE: THE USE OF FORCE IN THE STRUCTURE OF PEACE (PAMPHLET). BRAZIL WOR+45 WOR-45 FORCES DISCRIM NAT/LISM ORD/FREE SOVEREIGN...POLICY NEW/IDEA WORSHIP 20. PAGE 11 A0229 PEACE INT/ORG COERCE BAL/PWR

N19
FREEMAN H.A.,COERCION OF STATES IN FEDERAL UNIONS (PAMPHLET). WOR-45 DIPLOM CONTROL COERCE PEACE ORD/FREE...GOV/COMP METH/COMP NAT/COMP PACIFIST 20. PAGE 49 A0994 FEDERAL WAR INT/ORG PACIFISM

B20
HALDANE R.B.,BEFORE THE WAR. MOD/EUR SOCIETY INT/ORG NAT/G DELIB/GP PLAN DOMIN EDU/PROP LEGIT ADMIN COERCE ATTIT DRIVE MORAL ORD/FREE PWR...SOC CONCPT SELF/OBS RECORD BIOG TIME/SEQ. PAGE 60 A1223 POLICY DIPLOM UK

B20
WOOLF L.,EMPIRE AND COMMERCE IN AFRICA. EUR+WWI MOD/EUR FINAN INDUS MARKET INT/ORG PLAN COERCE ATTIT DRIVE PWR WEALTH...CONCPT TIME/SEQ TREND CHARTS 20. PAGE 167 A3394 AFR DOMIN COLONIAL SOVEREIGN

B21
STUART G.H.,FRENCH FOREIGN POLICY. CONSTN INT/ORG NAT/G POL/PAR EX/STRUC FORCES PLAN ECO/TAC DOMIN EDU/PROP ADJUD COERCE ATTIT DRIVE RIGID/FLEX ALL/VALS...POLICY OBS RECORD BIOG TIME/SEQ TREND. PAGE 139 A2852 MOD/EUR DIPLOM FRANCE

B27
LAUTERPACHT H.,PRIVATE LAW SOURCES AND ANALOGIES OF INTERNATIONAL LAW. WOR-45 NAT/G DELIB/GP LEGIT COERCE ATTIT ORD/FREE PWR SOVEREIGN...JURID CONCPT HIST/WRIT TIME/SEQ GEN/METH LEAGUE/NAT 20. PAGE 85 A1748 INT/ORG ADJUD PEACE INT/LAW

B28
HOWARD-ELLIS C.,THE ORIGIN, STRUCTURE AND WORKING OF THE LEAGUE OF NATIONS. EUR+WWI MOD/EUR USA-45 CONSTN FORCES LEGIS ECO/TAC LEGIT COERCE ORD/FREE ...JURID SOC CONCPT LEAGUE/NAT 20 ILO ICJ. PAGE 68 A1401 INT/ORG ADJUD

B28
STUART G.H.,LATIN AMERICA AND THE UNITED STATES. USA-45 ECO/UNDEV INT/ORG NAT/G POL/PAR PLAN DOMIN EDU/PROP COLONIAL REGION COERCE ATTIT ALL/VALS ...POLICY GEOG TREND 19/20. PAGE 139 A2853 L/A+17C DIPLOM

B29
CONWELL-EVANS T.P.,THE LEAGUE COUNCIL IN ACTION. EUR+WWI TURKEY UK USSR WOR-45 INT/ORG FORCES JUDGE ECO/TAC EDU/PROP LEGIT ROUTINE ARMS/CONT COERCE ATTIT PWR...MAJORIT GEOG JURID CONCPT LEAGUE/NAT TOT/POP VAL/FREE TUNIS 20. PAGE 30 A0605 DELIB/GP INT/LAW

B32
EAGLETON C.,INTERNATIONAL GOVERNMENT. BRAZIL FRANCE GERMANY ITALY UK USSR WOR-45 DELIB/GP TOP/EX PLAN ECO/TAC EDU/PROP LEGIT ADJUD REGION ARMS/CONT COERCE ATTIT PWR...GEOG MGT VAL/FREE LEAGUE/NAT 20. PAGE 40 A0816 INT/ORG JURID DIPLOM INT/LAW

B33
DAHLIN E.,FRENCH AND GERMAN PUBLIC OPINION ON DECLARED WAR AIMS 1914-1918. BELGIUM FRANCE GERMANY NAT/G POL/PAR DIPLOM COERCE REV WAR PEACE 20 WWI WILSON/W. PAGE 33 A0674 ATTIT EDU/PROP DOMIN NAT/COMP

B33
LAUTERPACHT H.,THE FUNCTION OF LAW IN THE INTERNATIONAL COMMUNITY. WOR-45 NAT/G FORCES CREATE DOMIN LEGIT COERCE WAR PEACE ATTIT ORD/FREE PWR SOVEREIGN...JURID CONCPT METH/CNCPT TIME/SEQ GEN/LAWS GEN/METH LEAGUE/NAT TOT/POP VAL/FREE 20. PAGE 85 A1749 INT/ORG LAW INT/LAW

B35
WEINBERG A.K.,MANIFEST DESTINY: A STUDY OF NATIONALIST EXPANSIONISM IN AMERICAN HISTORY. USA+45 USA-45 FORCES DIPLOM COLONIAL WAR ATTIT 18/20 INTERVENT. PAGE 162 A3305 NAT/LISM GEOG COERCE NAT/G

B36
BRIERLY J.L.,THE LAW OF NATIONS (2ND ED.). WOR+45 WOR-45 INT/ORG AGREE CONTROL COERCE WAR NAT/LISM PEACE PWR 16/20 TREATY LEAGUE/NAT. PAGE 18 A0375 DIPLOM INT/LAW NAT/G

B36
THWAITE D.,THE SEETHING AFRICAN POT: A STUDY OF BLACK NATIONALISM 1882-1935. ETHIOPIA SECT VOL/ASSN COERCE GUERRILLA MURDER DISCRIM MARXISM...PSY TIME/SEQ 18/20 NEGRO. PAGE 144 A2939 NAT/LISM AFR RACE/REL DIPLOM

B37
KOHN H.,FORCE OR REASON; ISSUES OF THE TWENTIETH CENTURY. WOR+45 NAT/G DIPLOM WAR DRIVE ORD/FREE ALL/IDEOS FASCISM PLURISM...POLICY IDEA/COMP 20. PAGE 81 A1660 COERCE DOMIN RATIONAL COLONIAL

C37
ROWAN R.W.,"THE STORY OF THE SECRET SERVICE." WOR-45 REV...BIOG BIBLIOG. PAGE 124 A2552 WAR COERCE DIPLOM

B38
FLEMMING D.,THE UNITED STATES AND WORLD ORGANIZATION, 1920-1933. ASIA FUT WOR-45 NAT/G TOP/EX DIPLOM ECO/TAC EDU/PROP LEGIT COERCE WAR ...TIME/SEQ LEAGUE/NAT 20 CHINJAP. PAGE 47 A0951 USA-45 INT/ORG PEACE

B38
HOBSON J.A.,IMPERIALISM. MOD/EUR UK WOR-45 CULTURE ECO/UNDEV NAT/G VOL/ASSN PLAN EDU/PROP LEGIT REGION COERCE ATTIT PWR...POLICY PLURIST TIME/SEQ GEN/LAWS 19/20. PAGE 66 A1348 DOMIN ECO/TAC BAL/PWR COLONIAL

B38
PETTEE G.S.,THE PROCESS OF REVOLUTION. COM FRANCE ITALY MOD/EUR RUSSIA SPAIN WOR-45 ELITES INTELL SOCIETY STRATA STRUCT INT/ORG NAT/G POL/PAR ACT/RES PLAN EDU/PROP LEGIT EXEC...SOC MYTH TIME/SEQ TOT/POP 18/20. PAGE 115 A2370 COERCE CONCPT REV

B39
DULLES J.,WAR, PEACE AND CHANGE. FRANCE ITALY UK USA-45 WOR-45 LAW INT/ORG NAT/G SECT VOL/ASSN FORCES TOP/EX DOMIN ARMS/CONT COERCE ATTIT PERSON RIGID/FLEX MORAL PWR...JURID STERTYP TOT/POP LEAGUE/NAT 20. PAGE 39 A0796 EDU/PROP TOTALISM WAR

B39
ROBBINS L.,ECONOMIC CAUSES OF WAR. WOR-45 ECO/DEV ECO/UNDEV INT/ORG NAT/G TEC/DEV DIPLOM DOMIN COLONIAL ATTIT DRIVE PWR WEALTH...POLICY CONCPT OBS SAMP TREND CON/ANAL GEN/LAWS MARX/KARL 20. PAGE 122 A2493 COERCE ECO/TAC WAR

B39
ZIMMERN A.,THE LEAGUE OF NATIONS AND THE RULE OF LAW. WOR-45 STRUCT NAT/G DELIB/GP EX/STRUC BAL/PWR INT/ORG LAW

DOMIN LEGIT COERCE ORD/FREE PWR...POLICY RECORD LEAGUE/NAT TOT/POP VAL/FREE 20 LEAGUE/NAT. PAGE 170 A3453 — DIPLOM

B39
ZIMMERN A.,MODERN POLITICAL DOCTRINE. WOR-45 CULTURE SOCIETY ECO/UNDEV DELIB/GP EX/STRUC CREATE DOMIN COERCE NAT/LISM ATTIT RIGID/FLEX ORD/FREE PWR WEALTH...POLICY CONCPT OBS TIME/SEQ TREND TOT/POP LEAGUE/NAT 20. PAGE 170 A3454 — NAT/G ECO/TAC BAL/PWR INT/TRADE

L39
NEARING S.,"A WARLESS WORLD." FUT WOR-45 SOCIETY INT/ORG NAT/G EX/STRUC PLAN DOMIN WAR ATTIT DRIVE PWR...POLICY PSY CONCPT OBS TREND HYPO/EXP MARX/KARL 20 MARX/KARL LENIN/VI. PAGE 108 A2210 — COERCE PEACE

B41
NIEMEYER G.,LAW WITHOUT FORCE: THE FUNCTION OF POLITICS IN INTERNATIONAL LAW. PLAN INSPECT DIPLOM REPAR LEGIT ADJUD WAR ORD/FREE...IDEA/COMP METH/COMP GEN/LAWS 20. PAGE 109 A2240 — COERCE LAW PWR INT/LAW

B41
SCHWARZENBERGER G.,POWER POLITICS: AN INTRODUCTION TO THE STUDY OF INTERNATIONAL RELATIONS AND POST-WAR PLANNING. INT/ORG FORCES COERCE WAR FEDERAL PEACE MORAL...POLICY CONCPT CON/ANAL BIBLIOG 20. PAGE 130 A2660 — DIPLOM UTOPIA PWR

S41
LASSWELL H.D.,"THE GARRISON STATE" (BMR)" FUT WOR+45 ELITES INTELL FORCES ECO/TAC DOMIN EDU/PROP COERCE INGP/REL 20. PAGE 85 A1739 — NAT/G DIPLOM PWR CIVMIL/REL

B42
TOLMAN E.C.,DRIVES TOWARD WAR. UNIV PLAN DIPLOM ECO/TAC COERCE PERS/REL ADJUST HAPPINESS BIO/SOC HEREDITY HEALTH KNOWL. PAGE 144 A2947 — PSY WAR UTOPIA DRIVE

B43
MICAUD C.A.,THE FRENCH RIGHT AND NAZI GERMANY 1933-1939: A STUDY OF PUBLIC OPINION. GERMANY UK USSR POL/PAR ARMS/CONT COERCE DETER PEACE RIGID/FLEX PWR MARXISM...FASCIST TREND 20 LEAGUE/NAT TREATY. PAGE 101 A2065 — DIPLOM AGREE

B43
SERENI A.P.,THE ITALIAN CONCEPTION OF INTERNATIONAL LAW. EUR+WWI MOD/EUR INT/ORG NAT/G DOMIN COERCE ORD/FREE FASCISM...OBS/ENVIR TREND 20. PAGE 131 A2686 — LAW TIME/SEQ INT/LAW ITALY

B43
US DEPARTMENT OF STATE,NATIONAL SOCIALISM; BASIC PRINCIPLES, THEIR APPLICATION BY THE NAZI PARTY'S FOREIGN ORGANIZATION... GERMANY WOR-45 ECO/DEV LOC/G POL/PAR FORCES DIPLOM DOMIN COLONIAL ARMS/CONT COERCE NAT/LISM PWR 20 NAZI. PAGE 151 A3081 — FASCISM SOCISM NAT/G TOTALISM

B45
CLAGETT H.L.,COMMUNIST CHINA: RUTHLESS ENEMY OR PAPER TIGER (PAMPHLET). CHINA/COM ECO/UNDEV AGRI INDUS NAT/G POL/PAR ECO/TAC INT/TRADE GUERRILLA ATTIT...CHARTS NAT/COMP ORG/CHARTS 20. PAGE 26 A0540 — BIBLIOG/A MARXISM DIPLOM COERCE

B45
CONOVER H.F.,ITALY: ECONOMICS, POLITICS AND MILITARY AFFAIRS, 1940-1945. ITALY ELITES NAT/G POL/PAR EX/STRUC TOP/EX DIPLOM DOMIN CONTROL COERCE WAR CIVMIL/REL EFFICIENCY 20. PAGE 29 A0599 — BIBLIOG TOTALISM FORCES

B45
TINGSTERN H.,PEACE AND SECURITY AFTER WW II. WOR-45 DELIB/GP TOP/EX LEGIT CT/SYS COERCE PEACE ATTIT PERCEPT...CONCPT LEAGUE/NAT 20. PAGE 144 A2943 — INT/ORG ORD/FREE WAR INT/LAW

B45
WEST R.,CONSCIENCE AND SOCIETY: A STUDY OF THE PSYCHOLOGICAL PREREQUISITES OF LAW AND ORDER. FUT UNIV LAW SOCIETY STRUCT DIPLOM WAR PERS/REL SUPEGO ...SOC 20. PAGE 163 A3321 — COERCE INT/LAW ORD/FREE PERSON

B46
KEETON G.W.,MAKING INTERNATIONAL LAW WORK. FUT WOR-45 NAT/G DELIB/GP FORCES LEGIT COERCE PEACE ATTIT RIGID/FLEX ORD/FREE PWR...JURID CONCPT HIST/WRIT GEN/METH LEAGUE/NAT 20. PAGE 77 A1578 — INT/ORG ADJUD INT/LAW

B47
BROOKINGS INST.,MAJOR PROBLEMS OF UNITED STATES FOREIGN POLICY. USA+45 WOR+45 STRUCT ECO/DEV ECO/UNDEV INT/ORG NAT/G POL/PAR VOL/ASSN DELIB/GP FORCES ECO/TAC LEGIT COERCE ORD/FREE PWR WEALTH ...POLICY STAT TREND CHARTS TOT/POP. PAGE 19 A0392 — ACT/RES DIPLOM

B47
PERKINS D.,THE UNITED STATES AND THE CARIBBEAN. CUBA DOMIN/REP GUATEMALA HAITI PANAMA CULTURE ECO/UNDEV FOR/AID ADMIN COERCE HABITAT...POLICY 19/20. PAGE 115 A2359 — DIPLOM L/A+17C USA-45

B48
CHURCHILL W.,THE GATHERING STORM. UK WOR-45 INT/ORG NAT/G FORCES TOP/EX DIPLOM ECO/TAC COERCE ATTIT ORD/FREE PWR WEALTH...POLICY SELF/OBS RECORD NAZI PARLIAMENT 20. PAGE 26 A0538 — BIOG

B48
DURBIN E.F.M.,THE POLITICS OF DEMOCRATIC SOCIALISM; AN ESSAY ON SOCIAL POLICY. STRATA POL/PAR PLAN COERCE DRIVE PERSON PWR MARXISM...CHARTS METH/COMP. PAGE 39 A0805 — SOCIALIST POPULISM POLICY SOCIETY

B49
KAFKA G.,FREIHEIT UND ANARCHIE. SECT COERCE DETER WAR ATTIT...IDEA/COMP 20 NATO. PAGE 75 A1545 — CONCPT ORD/FREE JURID INT/ORG

B49
OGBURN W.,TECHNOLOGY AND INTERNATIONAL RELATIONS. WOR+45 WOR-45 ECO/DEV CREATE PLAN ECO/TAC EDU/PROP COERCE PWR SKILL WEALTH...TECHNIC PSY SOC NEW/IDEA CHARTS TOT/POP 20. PAGE 111 A2283 — TEC/DEV DIPLOM INT/ORG

B50
BERLE A.A.,NATURAL SELECTION OF POLITICAL FORCES. FUT WOR+45 WOR-45 CULTURE SOCIETY INT/ORG NAT/G FORCES EDU/PROP LEGIT COERCE...CONCPT HIST/WRIT TREND 20. PAGE 13 A0274 — POL/PAR BAL/PWR DIPLOM

B50
CHASE E.P.,THE UNITED NATIONS IN ACTION. WOR+45 CONSTN DELIB/GP LEGIT ROUTINE COERCE PEACE ORD/FREE PWR...CON/ANAL GEN/LAWS UN 20. PAGE 26 A0524 — INT/ORG STRUCT ARMS/CONT

B50
CHURCHILL W.,TRIUMPH AND TRAGEDY. UK WOR-45 INT/ORG NAT/G DELIB/GP FORCES TOP/EX DIPLOM COERCE CHOOSE ATTIT ORD/FREE PWR WEALTH...SELF/OBS CHARTS NAZI 20. PAGE 26 A0539 — BIOG PEACE WAR

B50
DE ARECHAGA E.J.,VOTING AND THE HANDLING OF DISPUTES IN THE SECURITY COUNCIL. WOR+45 CONSTN DIPLOM COERCE ORD/FREE...RECORD CON/ANAL GEN/METH COLD/WAR UN 20. PAGE 34 A0696 — INT/ORG PWR

B50
GATZKE H.W.,GERMANY'S DRIVE TO THE WEST. BELGIUM GERMANY MOD/EUR AGRI INDUS POL/PAR FORCES DOMIN AGREE CONTROL REGION COERCE 20 TREATY WWI. PAGE 51 A1053 — WAR POLICY NAT/G DIPLOM

B50
LINCOLN G.,ECONOMICS OF NATIONAL SECURITY. USA+45 ELITES COM/IND DIST/IND INDUS NAT/G VOL/ASSN DELIB/GP EX/STRUC FOR/AID EDU/PROP COERCE NUC/PWR WAR ATTIT KNOWL ORD/FREE PWR COLD/WAR TOT/POP VAL/FREE 20. PAGE 89 A1818 — FORCES ECO/TAC

B51
BLANSHARD P.,COMMUNISM, DEMOCRACY AND CATHOLIC POWER. USSR VATICAN WOR+45 WOR-45 CULTURE ELITES INTELL SOCIETY STRUCT INT/ORG POL/PAR EDU/PROP COERCE ATTIT KNOWL PWR MARXISM...CONCPT COLD/WAR 20. PAGE 15 A0308 — COM SECT TOTALISM

B52
FERRELL R.H.,PEACE IN THEIR TIME. FRANCE UK USA-45 INT/ORG NAT/G FORCES CREATE AGREE ARMS/CONT COERCE WAR TREATY 20 WILSON/W LEAGUE/NAT BRIAND/A. PAGE 45 A0920 — PEACE DIPLOM

B52
LIPPMANN W.,ISOLATION AND ALLIANCES: AN AMERICAN SPEAKS TO THE BRITISH. USA+45 USA-45 INT/ORG AGREE COERCE DETER WAR PEACE MORAL 20 TREATY INTERVENT. PAGE 89 A1829 — DIPLOM SOVEREIGN COLONIAL ATTIT

B52
SMITH C.M.,INTERNATIONAL COMMUNICATION AND POLITICAL WARFARE: AN ANNOTATED BIBLIOGRAPHY (A PAPER). WOR+45 INTELL R+D NAT/G FORCES ACT/RES DIPLOM COERCE ALL/IDEOS. PAGE 134 A2745 — BIBLIOG/A EDU/PROP WAR COM/IND

B53
BARBER H.W.,FOREIGN POLICIES OF THE UNITED STATES. USA+45 USA-45 WOR+45 INT/ORG NAT/G EX/STRUC ECO/TAC DOMIN EDU/PROP LEGIT COERCE KNOWL PWR COLD/WAR COLD/WAR 20. PAGE 11 A0219 — CONCPT DIPLOM

B53
LANGER W.L.,THE UNDECLARED WAR, 1940-1941. EUR+WWI GERMANY USA-45 USSR AIR FORCES TEC/DEV CONFER CONTROL COERCE PERCEPT ORD/FREE PWR 20 CHINJAP EUROPE. PAGE 84 A1727 — WAR POLICY DIPLOM

B53
MARITAIN J.,L'HOMME ET L'ETAT. SECT DIPLOM GP/REL PEACE ORD/FREE...IDEA/COMP 17/20 CHURCH/STA NATURL/LAW. PAGE 95 A1940 — CONCPT NAT/G SOVEREIGN COERCE

B53
THAYER P.W.,SOUTHEAST ASIA IN THE COMING WORLD. ASIA S/ASIA USA+45 USA-45 SOCIETY INT/ORG ACT/RES ECO/TAC EDU/PROP COERCE TOTALISM ALL/VALS...JURID 20. PAGE 142 A2909 — ECO/UNDEV ATTIT FOR/AID DIPLOM

B53
ZIMMERN A.,THE AMERICAN ROAD TO PEACE. USA+45 LAW INT/ORG NAT/G EX/STRUC TOP/EX EDU/PROP LEGIT COERCE PEACE ATTIT ORD/FREE PWR...CONCPT TIME/SEQ LEAGUE/NAT TOT/POP VAL/FREE 20 UN. PAGE 170 A3455 — USA-45 DIPLOM

B54
ARON R.,CENTURY OF TOTAL WAR. FUT WOR+45 WOR-45 SOCIETY INT/ORG NAT/G FORCES TOP/EX CREATE BAL/PWR DOMIN EDU/PROP COERCE DETER PEACE TOTALISM PWR ...TIME/SEQ TREND COLD/WAR TOT/POP VAL/FREE — ATTIT WAR

LEAGUE/NAT 20. PAGE 9 A0179

B54
CHEEVER D.S.,ORGANIZING FOR PEACE. FUT WOR+45 WOR-45 STRATA STRUCT NAT/G CREATE DIPLOM LEGIT REGION COERCE DETER PEACE ATTIT DRIVE ALL/VALS ...TIME/SEQ TREND UN LEAGUE/NAT. PAGE 26 A0525 — INT/ORG

B54
MITCHELL P.,AFRICAN AFTERTHOUGHTS. UGANDA CONSTN NAT/G ADJUD COERCE WAR 20 WWI MAU/MAU. PAGE 102 A2090 — BIOG CHIEF COLONIAL DOMIN

L54
CHARLESWORTH J.C.,"AMERICA AND A NEW ASIA." ASIA INDIA ISLAM S/ASIA USA+45 USA-45 ECO/UNDEV NAT/G POL/PAR FORCES FOR/AID DOMIN EDU/PROP COERCE DRIVE ALL/VALS MARXISM SOCISM TOT/POP 20. PAGE 26 A0522 — ECO/TAC DIPLOM NAT/LISM

B55
ALFIERI D.,DICTATORS FACE TO FACE. NAT/G TOP/EX DIPLOM EXEC COERCE ORD/FREE FASCISM...POLICY OBS 20 HITLER/A MUSSOLIN/B. PAGE 6 A0116 — WAR CHIEF TOTALISM PERS/REL

B55
JOY C.T.,HOW COMMUNISTS NEGOTIATE. COM USA+45 CONSTN CULTURE ECO/UNDEV NAT/G CONSULT DELIB/GP FORCES PLAN ECO/TAC DOMIN EDU/PROP LEGIT EXEC ROUTINE COERCE WAR CHOOSE PEACE ATTIT RIGID/FLEX ORD/FREE PWR...POLICY 20. PAGE 75 A1539 — ASIA INT/ORG DIPLOM

B55
SEMJONOW J.M.,DIE FASCHISTISCHE GEOPOLITIK IM DIENSTE DES AMERIKANISCHEN IMPERIALISMUS. USA+45 USA-45 CAP/ISM PEACE ORD/FREE MARXISM SOCISM ...POLICY GEOG 20. PAGE 131 A2684 — DIPLOM COERCE FASCISM WAR

B55
SNYDER R.C.,AMERICAN FOREIGN POLICY. USA+45 USA-45 WOR+45 WOR-45 CONSTN INT/ORG POL/PAR VOL/ASSN DELIB/GP LEGIS CREATE DOMIN EDU/PROP EXEC COERCE ATTIT DRIVE ORD/FREE PWR...MGT OBS RECORD TIME/SEQ TREND. PAGE 134 A2752 — NAT/G DIPLOM

B55
UN HEADQUARTERS LIBRARY,BIBLIOQRAPHIE DE LA CHARTE DES NATIONS UNIES. CHINA/COM KOREA WOR+45 VOL/ASSN CONFER ADMIN COERCE PEACE ATTIT ORD/FREE SOVEREIGN ...INT/LAW 20 UNESCO UN. PAGE 147 A3001 — BIBLIOG/A INT/ORG DIPLOM

B55
VIGON J.,TEORIA DEL MILITARISMO. NAT/G DIPLOM COLONIAL COERCE GUERRILLA CIVMIL/REL NAT/LISM MORAL ALL/IDEOS PACIFISM 18/20. PAGE 159 A3234 — FORCES PHIL/SCI WAR POLICY

B56
BALL W.M.,NATIONALISM AND COMMUNISM IN EAST ASIA. ASIA BURMA EUR+WWI KOREA USA+45 ECO/UNDEV NAT/G POL/PAR DIPLOM ECO/TAC FOR/AID EDU/PROP COERCE RACE/REL NAT/LISM DRIVE SOVEREIGN...TREND 20 CHINJAP. PAGE 11 A0214 — S/ASIA ATTIT

B56
BLACKETT P.M.S.,ATOMIC WEAPONS AND EAST-WEST RELATIONS. FUT WOR+45 INT/ORG DELIB/GP COERCE ATTIT RIGID/FLEX KNOWL...RELATIV HIST/WRIT TREND GEN/METH COLD/WAR 20. PAGE 15 A0299 — FORCES PWR ARMS/CONT NUC/PWR

B56
GEORGE A.L.,WOODROW WILSON AND COLONEL HOUSE. WOR-45 CONSTN FACE/GP INT/ORG NAT/G POL/PAR CONSULT LEGIT EXEC COERCE CHOOSE ATTIT DRIVE PERSON MORAL ORD/FREE PWR RESPECT...POLICY MGT PSY OBS RECORD INT LEAGUE/NAT. PAGE 52 A1060 — USA-45 BIOG DIPLOM

B56
HAAS E.B.,DYNAMICS OF INTERNATIONAL RELATIONS. WOR-45 ELITES INT/ORG VOL/ASSN EX/STRUC FORCES ECO/TAC DOMIN LEGIT COERCE ATTIT PERSON PWR ...CONCPT TIME/SEQ CHARTS COLD/WAR 20. PAGE 58 A1202 — WOR+45 NAT/G DIPLOM

B56
REITZEL W.,UNITED STATES FOREIGN POLICY, 1945-1955. USA+45 WOR+45 CONSTN INT/ORG EDU/PROP LEGIT EXEC COERCE NUC/PWR PEACE ATTIT ORD/FREE PWR...DECISION CONCPT OBS RECORD TIME/SEQ TREND COLD/WAR UN CONGRESS. PAGE 120 A2464 — NAT/G POLICY DIPLOM

B56
US DEPARTMENT OF STATE,THE SUEZ CANAL PROBLEM; JULY 26-SEPTEMBER 22, 1956. UAR WOR+45 BAL/PWR COERCE NAT/LISM ATTIT ORD/FREE SOVEREIGN 20 SUEZ. PAGE 151 A3091 — DIPLOM CONFER INT/TRADE

B56
WHITAKER A.P.,ARGENTINE UPHEAVAL. STRUCT FORCES DIPLOM COERCE PWR 20 ARGEN. PAGE 164 A3332 — REV POL/PAR STRATA NAT/G

B56
WOLFF R.L.,THE BALKANS IN OUR TIME. ALBANIA FUT MOD/EUR USSR YUGOSLAVIA CULTURE INT/ORG SECT DIPLOM EDU/PROP COERCE WAR ORD/FREE...CHARTS 4/20 BALKANS COMINFORM. PAGE 166 A3388 — GEOG COM

B57
BLOOMFIELD L.M.,EGYPT, ISRAEL AND THE GULF OF AQABA: IN INTERNATIONAL LAW. LAW NAT/G CONSULT FORCES PLAN ECO/TAC ROUTINE COERCE ATTIT DRIVE PERCEPT PERSON RIGID/FLEX LOVE PWR WEALTH...GEOG CONCPT MYTH TREND. PAGE 15 A0314 — ISLAM INT/LAW UAR

B57
BROMBERGER M.,LES SECRETS DE L'EXPEDITION D'EGYPTE. FRANCE ISLAM UAR UK USA+45 USSR WOR+45 INT/ORG NAT/G FORCES BAL/PWR ECO/TAC DOMIN WAR NAT/LISM ATTIT PWR SOVEREIGN...MAJORIT TIME/SEQ CHARTS SUEZ COLD/WAR 20. PAGE 19 A0387 — COERCE DIPLOM

B57
BUCK P.W.,CONTOL OF FOREIGN RELATIONS IN MODERN NATIONS. FRANCE L/A+17C NETHERLAND USSR WOR+45 INT/ORG TOP/EX BAL/PWR DOMIN EDU/PROP COERCE PEACE ATTIT...CONCPT TREND 20 CMN/WLTH. PAGE 21 A0427 — NAT/G PWR DIPLOM

B57
COMM. STUDY ORGAN. PEACE,STRENGTHENING THE UNITED NATIONS. FUT USA+45 WOR+45 CONSTN NAT/G DELIB/GP FORCES LEGIS ECO/TAC LEGIT COERCE PEACE...JURID CONCPT UN COLD/WAR 20. PAGE 28 A0580 — INT/ORG ORD/FREE

B57
FURNISS E.S.,AMERICAN MILITARY POLICY: STRATEGIC ASPECTS OF WORLD POLITICAL GEOGRAPHY. COM EUR+WWI ISLAM L/A+17C USA+45 WOR+45 INT/ORG ACT/RES ARMS/CONT COERCE NUC/PWR ATTIT PWR...GEOG NEW/IDEA VAL/FREE COLD/WAR 20. PAGE 50 A1027 — FORCES DIPLOM

B57
KENNAN G.F.,RUSSIA, THE ATOM AND THE WEST. COM EUR+WWI FUT WOR+45 SOCIETY ECO/DEV FORCES DIPLOM ECO/TAC DOMIN EDU/PROP COERCE NUC/PWR ATTIT DRIVE ORD/FREE PWR...POLICY OBS TIME/SEQ TREND COLD/WAR NATO 20. PAGE 77 A1574 — NAT/G INT/ORG USSR

B57
KISSINGER H.A.,NUCLEAR WEAPONS AND FOREIGN POLICY. FUT USA+45 WOR+45 INT/ORG FORCES ACT/RES TEC/DEV DIPLOM ARMS/CONT COERCE ATTIT KNOWL PWR...DECISION GEOG CHARTS 20. PAGE 80 A1640 — PLAN DETER NUC/PWR

B57
LEFEVER E.W.,ETHICS AND UNITED STATUS FOREIGN POLICY. SOCIETY INT/ORG NAT/G ACT/RES DIPLOM EDU/PROP COERCE ATTIT MORAL...TREND GEN/LAWS COLD/WAR 20. PAGE 86 A1762 — USA+45 CULTURE CONCPT POLICY

L57
HAAS E.B.,"REGIONAL INTEGRATION AND NATIONAL POLICY." WOR+45 VOL/ASSN DELIB/GP EX/STRUC ECO/TAC DOMIN EDU/PROP LEGIT COERCE ATTIT PERCEPT KNOWL ...TIME/SEQ COLD/WAR 20 UN. PAGE 59 A1203 — INT/ORG ORD/FREE REGION

S57
DEUTSCH K.W.,"MASS COMMUNICATIONS AND THE LOSS OF FREEDOM IN NATIONAL DECISION MAKING." FUT WOR+45 SOCIETY COM/IND INT/ORG NAT/G ACT/RES CREATE TEC/DEV EDU/PROP MAJORITY PERCEPT...METH/CNCPT 20. PAGE 36 A0737 — COERCE DECISION WAR

S57
HOAG M.W.,"ECONOMIC PROBLEMS OF ALLIANCE." COM EUR+WWI WOR+45 ECO/DEV ECO/UNDEV NAT/G VOL/ASSN FORCES PLAN TEC/DEV DIPLOM COERCE ORD/FREE PWR WEALTH...DECISION GEN/LAWS NATO COLD/WAR. PAGE 65 A1345 — INT/ORG ECO/TAC

S57
SPEIER H.,"SOVIET ATOMIC BLACKMAIL AND THE NORTH ATLANTIC ALLIANCE." EUR+WWI USA+45 USSR INT/ORG NAT/G FORCES DIPLOM DRIVE ORD/FREE PWR NATO VAL/FREE COLD/WAR 20. PAGE 136 A2781 — COM COERCE NUC/PWR

S57
WRIGHT Q.,"THE VALUE OF CONFLICT RESOLUTION OF A GENERAL DISCIPLINE OF INTERNATIONAL RELATIONS." WOR+45 SOCIETY INT/ORG NAT/G FORCES TOP/EX PLAN TEC/DEV ECO/TAC DOMIN LEGIT COERCE ATTIT PWR ...GEN/METH COLD/WAR VAL/FREE. PAGE 168 A3412 — ORD/FREE SOC DIPLOM

C57
TANG P.S.H.,"COMMUNIST CHINA TODAY: DOMESTIC AND FOREIGN POLICIES." CHINA/COM COM S/ASIA USSR STRATA FORCES DIPLOM EDU/PROP COERCE GOV/REL...POLICY MAJORIT BIBLIOG 20. PAGE 141 A2886 — POL/PAR LEAD ADMIN CONSTN

B58
ARON R.,ON WAR: ATOMIC WEAPONS AND GLOBAL DIPLOMACY (TRANS. BY TERENCE KILMARTIN). WOR+45 SOCIETY FORCES BAL/PWR WAR WEAPON PERSON...SOC 20. PAGE 9 A0182 — ARMS/CONT NUC/PWR COERCE DIPLOM

B58
BOWETT D.W.,SELF-DEFENSE IN INTERNATIONAL LAW. EUR+WWI MOD/EUR WOR+45 WOR-45 SOCIETY INT/ORG CONSULT DIPLOM LEGIT COERCE ATTIT ORD/FREE...JURID 20 UN. PAGE 17 A0353 — ADJUD CONCPT WAR INT/LAW

B58
CAMPBELL J.C.,DEFENSE OF THE MIDDLE EAST: PROBLEMS OF AMERICAN POLICY. ISLAM USA+45 INT/ORG NAT/G EX/STRUC FORCES ECO/TAC DOMIN EDU/PROP LEGIT REGION COERCE...METH/CNCPT COLD/WAR TOT/POP 20. PAGE 23 A0474 — TOP/EX ORD/FREE DIPLOM

B58
CRAIG G.A.,FROM BISMARCK TO ADENAUER: ASPECTS OF GERMAN STATECRAFT. GERMANY INTELL FORCES ECO/TAC CONFER COERCE WAR GP/REL ORD/FREE PWR CONSERVE 19/20 BISMARCK/O ADENAUER/K. PAGE 32 A0653 — DIPLOM LEAD NAT/G

B58
DUCLOUX L.,FROM BLACKMAIL TO TREASON. FRANCE PLAN — COERCE

DIPLOM EDU/PROP PRESS RUMOR NAT/LISM...CRIMLGY 20. PAGE 39 A0793 — CRIME NAT/G PWR

B58
HOLT R.T.,RADIO FREE EUROPE. FUT USA+45 CULTURE ECO/DEV INT/ORG KIN POL/PAR SECT FORCES ACT/RES DIPLOM COERCE REV CHOOSE PEACE ATTIT PWR...MAJORIT CONCPT COLD/WAR WORK 20 RFE. PAGE 67 A1374 — COM EDU/PROP COM/IND

B58
JENKS C.W.,THE COMMON LAW OF MANKIND. EUR+WWI MOD/EUR SPACE WOR+45 INT/ORG BAL/PWR ARMS/CONT COERCE SUPEGO MORAL...TREND 20. PAGE 73 A1505 — JURID SOVEREIGN

B58
SCHUMAN F.,INTERNATIONAL POLITICS. WOR+45 WOR-45 INTELL NAT/G FORCES DOMIN LEGIT COERCE NUC/PWR ATTIT DISPL ORD/FREE PWR SOVEREIGN...POLICY CONCPT GEN/LAWS SUEZ 20. PAGE 129 A2650 — FUT INT/ORG NAT/LISM DIPLOM

B58
SLICK T.,PERMANENT PEACE: A CHECK AND BALANCE PLAN. FUT WOR+45 NAT/G FORCES CREATE PLAN EDU/PROP LEGIT ADJUD COERCE NAT/LISM RIGID/FLEX MORAL...HUM CONCPT METH/CNCPT NEW/IDEA TREND CHARTS TOT/POP 20. PAGE 134 A2742 — INT/ORG ORD/FREE PEACE ARMS/CONT

L58
SNYDER R.N.,"THE UNITED STATES DECISION TO RESIST AGGRESSION IN KOREA." ASIA KOREA S/ASIA USA+45 USA-45 WOR+45 INT/ORG DELIB/GP BAL/PWR COERCE PWR ...CONCPT REC/INT RESIST/INT COLD/WAR 20. PAGE 134 A2753 — QUANT METH/CNCPT DIPLOM

S58
BURNS A.L.,"THE INTERNATIONAL CONSEQUENCES OF EXPECTING SURPRISE." WOR+45 INT/ORG NAT/G FORCES DIPLOM COERCE NUC/PWR WAR CHOOSE ORD/FREE ...METH/CNCPT STYLE OBS STERTYP TOT/POP VAL/FREE. PAGE 22 A0440 — PLAN PWR DETER

S58
SINGER J.D.,"THREAT PERCEPTION AND THE ARMAMENT TENSION DILEMMA." WOR+45 WOR-45 ELITES INT/ORG NAT/G DELIB/GP PLAN LEGIT COERCE DETER ATTIT RIGID/FLEX PWR...DECISION PSY 20. PAGE 133 A2724 — PERCEPT ARMS/CONT BAL/PWR

S58
STAAR R.F.,"ELECTIONS IN COMMUNIST POLAND." EUR+WWI SOCIETY INT/ORG NAT/G POL/PAR LEGIS ACT/RES ECO/TAC EDU/PROP ADJUD ADMIN ROUTINE COERCE TOTALISM ATTIT ORD/FREE PWR 20. PAGE 137 A2797 — COM CHOOSE POLAND

S58
THOMPSON K.W.,"NATIONAL SECURITY IN A NUCLEAR AGE." USA+45 WOR+45 SOCIETY INT/ORG NAT/G TOP/EX DIPLOM DOMIN EDU/PROP LEGIT ARMS/CONT COERCE ORD/FREE ...TREND STERTYP TOT/POP VAL/FREE COLD/WAR 20. PAGE 143 A2929 — FORCES PWR BAL/PWR

B59
BRODIE B.,STRATEGY IN THE MISSILE AGE. FUT WOR+45 CONSULT PLAN COERCE DETER RIGID/FLEX PWR...CONCPT TIME/SEQ TREND 20. PAGE 19 A0381 — ACT/RES FORCES ARMS/CONT NUC/PWR

B59
CHALUPA V.,RISE AND DEVELOPMENT OF A TOTALITARIAN STATE. CZECHOSLVK USSR STRUCT INT/ORG WORKER DIPLOM ECO/TAC COERCE NAT/LISM ATTIT...POLICY 20 COM/PARTY. PAGE 25 A0516 — TOTALISM MARXISM REV POL/PAR

B59
COMM. STUDY ORGAN. PEACE,ORGANIZING PEACE IN THE NUCLEAR AGE. FUT CONSULT DELIB/GP DOMIN ADJUD ROUTINE COERCE ORD/FREE...TECHNIC INT/LAW JURID NEW/IDEA UN COLD/WAR 20. PAGE 29 A0581 — INT/ORG ACT/RES NUC/PWR

B59
COUDENHOVE-KALERGI,FROM WAR TO PEACE. USA+45 USSR WOR+45 WOR-45 LAW INT/ORG NAT/G LEGIT COERCE LOVE ...POLICY PLURIST METH/CNCPT STERTYP TOT/POP UN 20 NATO. PAGE 31 A0636 — FUT ORD/FREE

B59
FOX W.T.R.,THEORETICAL ASPECTS OF INTERNATIONAL RELATIONS. WOR+45 INT/ORG NAT/G POL/PAR CONSULT PLAN ECO/TAC DOMIN EDU/PROP LEGIT EXEC COERCE PWR WEALTH...RELATIV CONCPT 20. PAGE 48 A0975 — DELIB/GP ANTHOL

B59
GOODRICH L.,THE UNITED NATIONS. WOR+45 CONSTN STRUCT ACT/RES LEGIT COERCE KNOWL ORD/FREE PWR ...GEN/LAWS UN 20. PAGE 54 A1104 — INT/ORG ROUTINE

B59
HERZ J.H.,INTERNATIONAL POLITICS IN THE ATOMIC AGE. FUT USA+45 WOR+45 WOR-45 SOCIETY NAT/G FORCES PLAN COERCE DETER ATTIT DRIVE ORD/FREE PWR...TREND COLD/WAR 20. PAGE 64 A1319 — INT/ORG ARMS/CONT NUC/PWR

B59
KNIERIEM A.,THE NUREMBERG TRIALS. EUR+WWI GERMANY VOL/ASSN LEAD COERCE WAR INGP/REL TOTALISM SUPEGO ORD/FREE...CONCPT METH/COMP. PAGE 80 A1651 — INT/LAW CRIME PARTIC JURID

B59
KULSKI W.W.,PEACEFUL CO-EXISTENCE: AN ANALYSIS OF SOVIET FOREIGN POLICY. WOR+45 INTELL SOCIETY ECO/UNDEV POL/PAR EDU/PROP COERCE DRIVE RIGID/FLEX PWR SKILL...PSY CONCPT HIST/WRIT CON/ANAL GEN/METH WORK VAL/FREE 20. PAGE 83 A1691 — PLAN DIPLOM USSR

B59
STRAUSZ-HUPE R.,PROTRACTED CONFLICT. CHINA/COM KOREA WOR+45 INT/ORG FORCES ACT/RES ECO/TAC LEGIT COERCE DRIVE PERCEPT KNOWL PWR...PSY CONCPT RECORD GEN/METH COLD/WAR VAL/FREE 20. PAGE 139 A2847 — COM PLAN USSR

L59
KAPLAN M.A.,"SOME PROBLEMS IN THE STRATEGIC ANALYSIS OF INTERNATIONAL POLITICS." UNIV R+D INT/ORG CREATE PLAN DIPLOM EDU/PROP COERCE DISPL PWR...METH/CNCPT NEW/IDEA HYPO/EXP TOT/POP 20. PAGE 76 A1561 — DECISION BAL/PWR

S59
CARLSTON K.S.,"NATIONALIZATION: AN ANALYTIC APPROACH." WOR+45 INT/ORG ECO/TAC DOMIN LEGIT ADJUD COERCE ORD/FREE PWR WEALTH SOCISM...JURID CONCPT TREND STERTYP TOT/POP VAL/FREE 20. PAGE 24 A0486 — INDUS NAT/G NAT/LISM SOVEREIGN

S59
LASSWELL H.D.,"UNIVERSALITY IN PERSPECTIVE." FUT UNIV SOCIETY CONSULT TOP/EX PLAN EDU/PROP ADJUD ROUTINE ARMS/CONT COERCE PEACE ATTIT PERSON ALL/VALS. PAGE 85 A1741 — INT/ORG JURID TOTALISM

S59
SOHN L.B.,"THE DEFINITION OF AGGRESSION." FUT LAW FORCES LEGIT ADJUD ROUTINE COERCE ORD/FREE PWR ...MAJORIT JURID QUANT COLD/WAR 20. PAGE 135 A2762 — INT/ORG CT/SYS DETER SOVEREIGN

B60
BARNET R.,WHO WANTS DISARMAMENT. COM EUR+WWI USA+45 USSR INT/ORG NAT/G BAL/PWR DIPLOM EDU/PROP COERCE DETER NUC/PWR WAR WEAPON ATTIT PWR...TIME/SEQ COLD/WAR CONGRESS 20. PAGE 11 A0225 — PLAN FORCES ARMS/CONT

B60
BROWN H.,COMMUNITY OF FEAR. FORCES TEC/DEV ARMS/CONT COERCE PEACE 20. PAGE 20 A0402 — NUC/PWR WAR DIPLOM DETER

B60
BUCHAN A.,NATO IN THE 1960'S. EUR+WWI USA+45 WOR+45 INT/ORG ACT/RES PLAN LEGIT COERCE DETER ATTIT DRIVE RIGID/FLEX ORD/FREE...METH/CNCPT TIME/SEQ TREND GEN/LAWS COLD/WAR 20 NATO. PAGE 21 A0421 — VOL/ASSN FORCES ARMS/CONT SOVEREIGN

B60
DAVIDS J.,AMERICA AND THE WORLD OF OUR TIME: UNITED STATES DIPLOMACY IN THE TWENTIETH CENTURY. USA-45 SOCIETY ECO/DEV INT/ORG NAT/G POL/PAR FORCES ECO/TAC DOMIN EDU/PROP EXEC COERCE WAR CHOOSE ATTIT PERSON ORD/FREE...CONCPT TIME/SEQ TOT/POP 20. PAGE 34 A0686 — USA+45 PWR DIPLOM

B60
ENGEL J.,THE SECURITY OF THE FREE WORLD. USSR WOR+45 STRATA STRUCT ECO/DEV ECO/UNDEV INT/ORG DELIB/GP FORCES DOMIN LEGIT ADJUD EXEC ARMS/CONT COERCE...POLICY CONCPT NEW/IDEA TIME/SEQ GEN/LAWS COLD/WAR WORK UN 20 NATO. PAGE 42 A0851 — COM TREND DIPLOM

B60
FURNIA A.H.,THE DIPLOMACY OF APPEASEMENT: ANGLO-FRENCH RELATIONS AND THE PRELUDE TO WORLD WAR II 1931-1938. FRANCE GERMANY UK ELITES NAT/G DELIB/GP FORCES WAR PEACE RIGID/FLEX 20. PAGE 50 A1026 — DIPLOM BAL/PWR COERCE

B60
JENNINGS R.,PROGRESS OF INTERNATIONAL LAW. FUT WOR+45 WOR-45 SOCIETY NAT/G VOL/ASSN DELIB/GP DIPLOM EDU/PROP LEGIT COERCE ATTIT DRIVE MORAL ORD/FREE...JURID CONCPT OBS TIME/SEQ TREND GEN/LAWS. PAGE 74 A1509 — INT/ORG LAW INT/LAW

B60
LE GHAIT E.,NO CARTE BLANCHE TO CAPRICORN; THE FOLLY OF NUCLEAR WAR. WOR+45 INT/ORG BAL/PWR DIPLOM RISK COERCE...CENSUS 20 NATO. PAGE 86 A1754 — DETER NUC/PWR PLAN DECISION

B60
LIEUWEN E.,ARMS AND POLITICS IN LATIN AMERICA. FUT USA+45 USA-45 ECO/UNDEV INT/ORG NAT/G FORCES DIPLOM COERCE ATTIT ALL/VALS VAL/FREE OAS 20. PAGE 88 A1811 — L/A+17C FOR/AID

B60
MORAES F.,THE REVOLT IN TIBET. ASIA CHINA/COM INDIA CULTURE CONTROL COERCE WAR TOTALISM...POLICY SOC WORSHIP 20 TIBET INTERVENT. PAGE 104 A2127 — COLONIAL FORCES DIPLOM ORD/FREE

B60
NURTY K.S.,STUDIES IN PROBLEMS OF PEACE. CHRIST-17C MOD/EUR S/ASIA WOR+45 WOR-45 INT/ORG NAT/G SECT COERCE REV NAT/LISM ALL/VALS...CONCPT MYTH TIME/SEQ. PAGE 110 A2262 — POLICY PEACE PACIFISM ORD/FREE

B60
SETON-WATSON H.,NEITHER WAR NOR PEACE. ASIA USSR WOR+45 ELITES INT/ORG NAT/G EX/STRUC FORCES BAL/PWR ECO/TAC EDU/PROP COERCE NAT/LISM ORD/FREE WEALTH TOT/POP 20. PAGE 131 A2688 — ATTIT PWR DIPLOM TOTALISM

B60
TAYLOR M.D.,THE UNCERTAIN TRUMPET. USA+45 USSR WOR+45 INT/ORG NAT/G CONSULT DOMIN COERCE NUC/PWR WAR ATTIT ORD/FREE PWR...POLICY CONCPT TREND GEN/METH COLD/WAR UN NATO 20. PAGE 142 A2900 — PLAN FORCES DIPLOM

B60
US HOUSE COMM. SCI. ASTRONAUT.,OCEAN SCIENCES AND NATIONAL SECURITY. FUT SEA ECO/DEV EXTR/IND INT/ORG NAT/G FORCES ACT/RES TEC/DEV ECO/TAC COERCE WAR BIO/SOC KNOWL PWR...CONCPT RECORD LAB/EXP 20. PAGE 154 A3141 R+D ORD/FREE

B60
WHITING A.S.,CHINA CROSSES THE YALU: THE DECISION TO ENTER THE KOREAN WAR. ASIA CHINA/COM KOREA ECO/UNDEV R+D INT/ORG TOP/EX ACT/RES BAL/PWR ATTIT PWR...GEN/METH 20. PAGE 164 A3338 PLAN COERCE WAR

L60
BRENNAN D.G.,"SETTING AND GOALS OF ARMS CONTROL." FUT USA+45 USSR WOR+45 INTELL INT/ORG NAT/G VOL/ASSN CONSULT PLAN DIPLOM ECO/TAC ADMIN KNOWL PWR...POLICY CONCPT TREND COLD/WAR 20. PAGE 18 A0371 FORCES COERCE ARMS/CONT DETER

L60
HOLTON G.,"ARMS CONTROL." FUT WOR+45 CULTURE INT/ORG NAT/G FORCES TOP/EX PLAN EDU/PROP COERCE ATTIT RIGID/FLEX ORD/FREE...POLICY PHIL/SCI SOC TREND COLD/WAR. PAGE 67 A1377 ACT/RES CONSULT ARMS/CONT NUC/PWR

L60
JACOB P.E.,"THE DISARMAMENT CONSENSUS." USA+45 USSR WOR+45 INT/ORG NAT/G ACT/RES TEC/DEV BAL/PWR EDU/PROP ADMIN COERCE DETER NUC/PWR CONSEN RIGID/FLEX PWR...CONCPT RECORD CHARTS COLD/WAR 20. PAGE 72 A1482 DELIB/GP ATTIT ARMS/CONT

L60
KUNZ J.,"SANCTIONS IN INTERNATIONAL LAW." WOR+45 WOR-45 LEGIT ARMS/CONT COERCE PEACE ATTIT ...METH/CNCPT TIME/SEQ TREND 20. PAGE 83 A1695 INT/ORG ADJUD INT/LAW

L60
LAUTERPACHT E.,"THE UNITED NATIONS EMERGENCY FORCE." R+D LEGIT ROUTINE COERCE KNOWL ORD/FREE SKILL...JURID UN 20. PAGE 85 A1746 INT/ORG FORCES

L60
NOGEE J.L.,"THE DIPLOMACY OF DISARMAMENT." WOR+45 INT/ORG NAT/G CONSULT DELIB/GP TOP/EX BAL/PWR DIPLOM EDU/PROP COERCE DETER WEAPON PEACE ATTIT ...RECORD TIME/SEQ TOT/POP VAL/FREE COLD/WAR 20. PAGE 109 A2246 PWR ORD/FREE ARMS/CONT NUC/PWR

S60
DOUGHERTY J.E.,"KEY TO SECURITY: DISARMAMENT OR ARMS STABILITY." COM USA+45 USSR INT/ORG NAT/G CREATE EDU/PROP COERCE DETER ATTIT PWR...DECISION CONCPT MYTH NEW/IDEA TREND 20 COLD/WAR. PAGE 38 A0777 FORCES ORD/FREE ARMS/CONT NUC/PWR

S60
GINSBURGS G.,"PEKING-LHASA-NEW DELHI." CHINA/COM FUT INDIA S/ASIA KIN NAT/G PROVS SECT FORCES BAL/PWR ECO/TAC DOMIN EDU/PROP LEGIT ADMIN REGION GUERRILLA PWR...TREND TIBET 20. PAGE 52 A1074 ASIA COERCE DIPLOM

S60
HAVILAND H.F.,"PROBLEMS OF AMERICAN FOREIGN POLICY." ASIA COM USA+45 WOR+45 INT/ORG NAT/G CONSULT ECO/TAC FOR/AID DOMIN COERCE NUC/PWR ATTIT DRIVE ORD/FREE PWR RESPECT SKILL...POLICY GEOG OBS SAMP TREND GEN/METH METH COLD/WAR UN 20. PAGE 63 A1292 ECO/UNDEV FORCES DIPLOM

S60
IKLE F.C.,"NTH COUNTRIES AND DISARMAMENT." WOR+45 DELIB/GP ECO/TAC DOMIN EDU/PROP LEGIT ROUTINE COERCE RIGID/FLEX ORD/FREE...MARXIST TREND 20. PAGE 70 A1432 FUT INT/ORG ARMS/CONT NUC/PWR

S60
KALUODA J.,"COMMUNIST STRATEGY IN LATIN AMERICA." L/A+17C USA+45 INT/ORG NAT/G POL/PAR DIPLOM ECO/TAC EDU/PROP COERCE WEALTH...CONCPT OAS COLD/WAR 20. PAGE 76 A1553 COM PWR CUBA

S60
KENNAN G.F.,"PEACEFUL CO-EXISTENCE: A WESTERN VIEW." COM EUR+WWI USA+45 USSR WOR+45 PLAN BAL/PWR DIPLOM INT/TRADE PWR...POLICY CONCPT OBS HIST/WRIT TREND GEN/LAWS COLD/WAR 20 KHRUSH/N. PAGE 78 A1589 ATTIT COERCE

S60
MORGENSTERN O.,"GOAL: AN ARMED, INSPECTED, OPEN WORLD." COM EUR+WWI USA+45 R+D INT/ORG NAT/G TEC/DEV BAL/PWR COERCE NUC/PWR ORD/FREE PWR...TREND 20. PAGE 104 A2133 FORCES CONCPT ARMS/CONT DETER

S60
MUNRO L.,"CAN THE UNITED NATIONS ENFORCE PEACE." WOR+45 LAW INT/ORG VOL/ASSN BAL/PWR LEGIT ARMS/CONT COERCE DETER PEACE PWR...CONCPT REC/INT TREND UN 20 HAMMARSK/D. PAGE 106 A2173 FORCES ORD/FREE

S60
O'BRIEN W.,"THE ROLE OF FORCE IN THE INTERNATIONAL JURIDICAL ORDER." WOR+45 NAT/G FORCES DOMIN ADJUD ARMS/CONT DETER NUC/PWR WAR ATTIT PWR...CATH INT/LAW JURID CONCPT TREND STERTYP GEN/LAWS 20. PAGE 110 A2266 INT/ORG COERCE

S60
SCHACHTER O.,"THE ENFORCEMENT OF INTERNATIONAL JUDICIAL AND ARBITRAL DECISIONS." WOR+45 NAT/G ECO/TAC DOMIN LEGIT ROUTINE COERCE ATTIT DRIVE ALL/VALS PWR...METH/CNCPT TREND TOT/POP 20 UN. PAGE 128 A2615 INT/ORG ADJUD INT/LAW

S60
THOMPSON K.W.,"MORAL PURPOSE IN FOREIGN POLICY: REALITIES AND ILLUSIONS." WOR+45 WOR-45 LAW CULTURE SOCIETY INT/ORG PLAN ADJUD ADMIN COERCE RIGID/FLEX SUPEGO KNOWL ORD/FREE PWR...SOC TREND SOC/EXP TOT/POP 20. PAGE 143 A2930 MORAL JURID DIPLOM

B61
ANAND R.P.,COMPULSORY JURISDICTION OF INTERNATIONAL COURT OF JUSTICE. FUT WOR+45 SOCIETY PLAN LEGIT ADJUD ATTIT DRIVE PERSON ORD/FREE...JURID CONCPT TREND 20 ICJ. PAGE 8 A0156 INT/ORG COERCE INT/LAW

B61
BISHOP D.G.,THE ADMINISTRATION OF BRITISH FOREIGN RELATIONS. EUR+WWI MOD/EUR INT/ORG NAT/G POL/PAR DELIB/GP LEGIS TOP/EX ECO/TAC DOMIN EDU/PROP ADMIN COERCE 20. PAGE 14 A0292 ROUTINE PWR DIPLOM UK

B61
DALLIN D.J.,SOVIET FOREIGN POLICY AFTER STALIN. ASIA CHINA/COM EUR+WWI GERMANY IRAN UK YUGOSLAVIA INT/ORG NAT/G VOL/ASSN FORCES TOP/EX BAL/PWR DOMIN EDU/PROP COERCE ATTIT PWR 20. PAGE 33 A0679 COM DIPLOM USSR

B61
LARSON A.,WHEN NATIONS DISAGREE. USA+45 WOR+45 INT/ORG ADJUD COERCE CRIME OWN SOVEREIGN...POLICY JURID 20. PAGE 85 A1734 INT/LAW DIPLOM WAR

B61
LIPPMANN W.,THE COMING TESTS WITH RUSSIA. COM CUBA GERMANY USSR FORCES CONTROL NEUTRAL COERCE NUC/PWR REV WAR PWR...INT 20 KHRUSH/N BERLIN. PAGE 89 A1830 BAL/PWR DIPLOM MARXISM ARMS/CONT

B61
MCDOUGAL M.S.,LAW AND MINIMUM WORLD PUBLIC ORDER. WOR+45 SOCIETY NAT/G DELIB/GP EDU/PROP LEGIT ADJUD COERCE ATTIT PERSON...JURID CONCPT RECORD TREND TOT/POP 20. PAGE 98 A2006 INT/ORG ORD/FREE INT/LAW

B61
STONE J.,QUEST FOR SURVIVAL. WOR+45 NAT/G VOL/ASSN LEGIT ADMIN ARMS/CONT COERCE DISPL ORD/FREE PWR ...POLICY INT/LAW JURID COLD/WAR 20. PAGE 139 A2836 INT/ORG ADJUD SOVEREIGN

B61
US SENATE COMM GOVT OPERATIONS,ORGANIZING FOR NATIONAL SECURITY. COM USA+45 BUDGET DIPLOM DETER NUC/PWR WAR WEAPON ORD/FREE...BIBLIOG 20 COLD/WAR. PAGE 156 A3172 POLICY PLAN FORCES COERCE

B61
WOOD B.,THE MAKING OF THE GOOD NEIGHBOR POLICY. L/A+17C USA-45 COERCE CIVMIL/REL DISCRIM. PAGE 166 A3389 DIPLOM DELIB/GP POLICY

L61
CLAUDE I.,"THE UNITED NATIONS AND THE USE OF FORCE." FUT WOR+45 SOCIETY DIPLOM EDU/PROP LEGIT ADMIN ROUTINE COERCE WAR PEACE ORD/FREE...CONCPT TREND UN 20. PAGE 27 A0545 INT/ORG FORCES

L61
HALPERIN M.H.,"NUCLEAR WEAPONS AND LIMITED WARS." FUT UNIV WOR+45 INTELL SOCIETY ECO/DEV ACT/RES DRIVE PERCEPT RIGID/FLEX...CONCPT TIME/SEQ TREND TOT/POP 20. PAGE 60 A1237 PLAN COERCE NUC/PWR WAR

L61
HILSMAN R. JR.,"THE NEW COMMUNIST TACTIC: PRECIS-INTERNAL WAR." COM FUT USA+45 ECO/UNDEV POL/PAR FOR/AID RIGID/FLEX ALL/VALS...TREND COLD/WAR 20. PAGE 65 A1334 FORCES COERCE USSR GUERRILLA

L61
HOYT E.C.,"UNITED STATES REACTION TO THE KOREAN ATTACK." COM KOREA USA+45 CONSTN DELIB/GP FORCES PLAN ECO/TAC DOMIN EDU/PROP LEGIT ROUTINE COERCE WAR ATTIT DISPL RIGID/FLEX ORD/FREE PWR...POLICY INT/LAW TREND UN 20. PAGE 68 A1402 ASIA INT/ORG BAL/PWR DIPLOM

S61
BRZEZINSKI Z.K.,"THE ORGANIZATION OF THE COMMUNIST CAMP." COM CZECHOSLVK COM/IND NAT/G DELIB/GP INT/TRADE DOMIN EDU/PROP EXEC ROUTINE COERCE ATTIT PWR...MGT CONCPT TIME/SEQ CHARTS VAL/FREE 20 TREATY. PAGE 20 A0416 VOL/ASSN DIPLOM USSR

S61
MIKSCHE F.O.,"DEFENSE ORGANIZATION FOR WESTERN EUROPE." USA+45 INT/ORG NAT/G VOL/ASSN ACT/RES DOMIN LEGIT COERCE ORD/FREE PWR...RELATIV TREND 20 NATO. PAGE 101 A2071 EUR+WWI FORCES WEAPON NUC/PWR

S61
TRAMPE G.,"DIE FORM DER DIPLOMATIC ALS POLITSCHE WAFFE." WOR+45 WOR-45 SOCIETY STRATA INT/ORG NAT/G ACT/RES PLAN ECO/TAC EDU/PROP COERCE WAR ATTIT RIGID/FLEX...DECISION CONCPT TREND. PAGE 145 A2959 CONSULT PWR DIPLOM

B62
BELL C.,NEGOTIATION FROM STRENGTH. WOR+45 FACE/GP INT/ORG DELIB/GP FORCES PLAN DOMIN COERCE NUC/PWR PEACE DRIVE PWR...POLICY LOG OBS RECORD INT SAMP TREND COLD/WAR 20. PAGE 13 A0255 NAT/G CONCPT DIPLOM

B62
BLACKETT P.M.S.,STUDIES OF WAR: NUCLEAR AND CONVENTIONAL. EUR+WWI USA+45 DELIB/GP ACT/RES CREATE PLAN TEC/DEV LEGIT COERCE WAR ORD/FREE PWR ...POLICY TECHNIC TIME/SEQ 20. PAGE 15 A0300 INT/ORG FORCES ARMS/CONT NUC/PWR

B62
BOULDING K.E.,CONFLICT AND DEFENSE: A GENERAL THEORY. FUT SOCIETY INT/ORG NAT/G CREATE BAL/PWR COERCE NAT/LISM DRIVE ALL/VALS...PLURIST DECISION CONCPT METH/CNCPT TREND HYPO/EXP TOT/POP 20. PAGE 17 A0347
MATH SIMUL PEACE WAR

B62
BURTON J.W.,PEACE THEORY: PRECONDITIONS OF DISARMAMENT. COM EUR+WWI USA+45 NAT/G FORCES BAL/PWR DIPLOM ECO/TAC EDU/PROP REGION COERCE DETER PEACE ATTIT PWR TOT/POP COLD/WAR 20. PAGE 22 A0446
INT/ORG PLAN ARMS/CONT

B62
CALVOCORESSI P.,WORLD ORDER AND NEW STATES: PROBLEMS OF KEEPING THE PEACE. AFR EUR+WWI S/ASIA ELITES NAT/G ECO/TAC FOR/AID EDU/PROP COERCE ATTIT DRIVE ALL/VALS...GEN/LAWS COLD/WAR 20 UN. PAGE 23 A0471
INT/ORG PEACE

B62
CARLSTON K.S.,LAW AND ORGANIZATION IN WORLD SOCIETY. WOR+45 FINAN ECO/TAC DOMIN LEGIT CT/SYS ROUTINE COERCE ORD/FREE PWR WEALTH...PLURIST DECISION JURID MGT METH/CNCPT GEN/LAWS 20. PAGE 24 A0487
INT/ORG LAW

B62
CLUBB O.E. JR.,THE UNITED STATES AND THE SINO-SOVIET BLOC IN SOUTHEAST ASIA. ASIA CHINA/COM COM USA+45 USSR ECO/UNDEV INT/ORG NAT/G FORCES TOP/EX PLAN ECO/TAC DOMIN COERCE GUERRILLA ATTIT RIGID/FLEX...POLICY OBS TREND 20. PAGE 27 A0553
S/ASIA PWR BAL/PWR DIPLOM

B62
DEHIO L.,THE PRECARIOUS BALANCE: FOUR CENTURIES OF THE EUROPEAN POWER STRUGGLE. FRANCE GERMANY SPAIN NAT/G DOMIN PWR...GOV/COMP 8/20. PAGE 36 A0725
BAL/PWR WAR DIPLOM COERCE

B62
FORBES H.W.,THE STRATEGY OF DISARMAMENT. FUT WOR+45 INT/ORG VOL/ASSN CONSULT ARMS/CONT COERCE NUC/PWR WAR DRIVE RIGID/FLEX ORD/FREE PWR...POLICY CONCPT OBS TREND STERTYP 20. PAGE 47 A0959
PLAN FORCES DIPLOM

B62
GRAEBNER N.,COLD WAR DIPLOMACY 1945-1960. WOR+45 INT/ORG ECO/TAC EDU/PROP COERCE ORD/FREE PWR WEALTH ...HIST/WRIT TOT/POP VAL/FREE COLD/WAR 20. PAGE 55 A1122
USA+45 DIPLOM

B62
KING G.,THE UNITED NATIONS IN THE CONGO: A QUEST FOR PEACE. WOR+45 NAT/G CONSULT FORCES LEGIT COERCE WAR ORD/FREE...JURID METH/CNCPT OBS INT HIST/WRIT TIME/SEQ CONGO UN 20 COLD/WAR. PAGE 79 A1624
AFR INT/ORG

B62
MACKENTOSH J.M.,STRATEGY AND TACTICS OF SOVIET FOREIGN POLICY. CHINA/COM FUT USA+45 WOR+45 INT/ORG PLAN DOMIN LEGIT ROUTINE COERCE NUC/PWR WAR ATTIT DRIVE ORD/FREE PWR...CONCPT OBS TIME/SEQ TREND GEN/METH COLD/WAR 20. PAGE 92 A1894
COM POLICY DIPLOM USSR

B62
MORGENTHAU H.J.,POLITICS IN THE TWENTIETH CENTURY: IMPASSE OF AMERICAN FOREIGN POLICY. FUT GERMANY USA+45 USSR WOR+45 INT/ORG NAT/G ACT/RES PLAN FOR/AID EDU/PROP LEGIT COERCE WAR PWR...TIME/SEQ TREND COLD/WAR 20. PAGE 104 A2138
SKILL DIPLOM

B62
MULLEY F.W.,THE POLITICS OF WESTERN DEFENSE. EUR+WWI USA-45 WOR+45 VOL/ASSN EX/STRUC FORCES COERCE DETER PEACE ATTIT ORD/FREE PWR...RECORD TIME/SEQ CHARTS COLD/WAR 20 NATO. PAGE 106 A2168
INT/ORG DELIB/GP NUC/PWR

B62
NEAL F.W.,WAR AND PEACE AND GERMANY. EUR+WWI USSR STRUCT INT/ORG NAT/G FORCES DOMIN EDU/PROP LEGIT EXEC COERCE ORD/FREE...HUM SOC NEW/IDEA OBS TIME/SEQ TOT/POP COLD/WAR 20 BERLIN. PAGE 108 A2208
USA+45 POLICY DIPLOM GERMANY

B62
QUIRK R.E.,AN AFFAIR OF HONOR: WOODROW WILSON AND THE OCCUPATION OF VERACRUZ. L/A+17C USA-45 COLONIAL SUPEGO PWR 20 WILSON/W MEXIC/AMER. PAGE 118 A2428
DOMIN DIPLOM COERCE PROB/SOLV

B62
SOMMER T.,DEUTSCHLAND UND JAPAN ZWISCHEN DEN MACHTEN. GERMANY DELIB/GP BAL/PWR AGREE COERCE TOTALISM PWR 20 CHINJAP TREATY. PAGE 135 A2765
DIPLOM WAR ATTIT

B62
SPIRO H.J.,POLITICS IN AFRICA: PROSPECTS SOUTH OF THE SAHARA. INT/ORG KIN FORCES LEGIS PROB/SOLV COERCE RACE/REL FEDERAL...TREND CHARTS BIBLIOG 20. PAGE 136 A2790
AFR NAT/LISM DIPLOM

B62
TRISKA J.F.,THE THEORY, LAW, AND POLICY OF SOVIET TREATIES. WOR+45 WOR-45 CONSTN INT/ORG NAT/G VOL/ASSN DOMIN LEGIT COERCE ATTIT PWR RESPECT ...POLICY JURID CONCPT OBS SAMP TIME/SEQ TREND GEN/LAWS 20. PAGE 145 A2966
COM LAW INT/LAW USSR

B62
US DEPARTMENT OF THE ARMY,GUIDE TO JAPANESE MONOGRAPHS AND JAPANESE STUDIES ON MANCHURIA: 1945-1960. CHINA/COM NAT/G DIPLOM LEAD COERCE WAR ...CHARTS 19/20 CHINJAP. PAGE 152 A3105
BIBLIOG/A FORCES ASIA S/ASIA

B62
WILLIAMS W.A.,THE UNITED STATES, CUBA, AND CASTRO: AN ESSAY ON THE DYNAMICS OF REVOLUTION AND THE DISSOLUTION OF EMPIRE. CUBA USA+45 AGRI VOL/ASSN DIPLOM ECO/TAC DOMIN COERCE...POLICY 20 EISNHWR/DD CIA KENNEDY/JF CASTRO/F. PAGE 165 A3354
REV CONSTN COM LEAD

L62
PETKOFF D.K.,"RECOGNITION AND NON-RECOGNITION OF STATES AND GOVERNMENTS IN INTERNATIONAL LAW." ASIA COM USA+45 WOR+45 NAT/G ACT/RES DIPLOM DOMIN LEGIT COERCE ORD/FREE PWR...CONCPT GEN/LAWS 20. PAGE 115 A2369
INT/ORG LAW INT/LAW

L62
ULYSSES,"THE INTERNATIONAL AIMS AND POLICIES OF THE SOVIET UNION: THE NEW CONCEPTS AND STRATEGY OF KHRUSHCHEV." FUT USSR WOR+45 SOCIETY INT/ORG NAT/G POL/PAR FORCES TOP/EX PLAN DOMIN EDU/PROP COERCE ATTIT PERSON PWR...TREND COLD/WAR 20 KHRUSH/N. PAGE 146 A2994
COM POLICY BAL/PWR DIPLOM

S62
CRANE R.D.,"LAW AND STRATEGY IN SPACE." FUT USA+45 WOR+45 AIR LAW INT/ORG NAT/G FORCES ACT/RES PLAN BAL/PWR LEGIT ARMS/CONT COERCE ORD/FREE...POLICY INT/LAW JURID SOC/EXP 20 TREATY. PAGE 32 A0656
CONCPT SPACE

S62
CROAN M.,"POLYCENTRISM: COMMUNIST INTERNATIONAL RELATIONS." ASIA STRUCT INT/ORG NAT/G POL/PAR CONSULT PLAN DOMIN EDU/PROP COERCE ATTIT RIGID/FLEX SOCISM...POLICY CONCPT TREND CON/ANAL GEN/LAWS MARX/KARL. PAGE 33 A0663
COM CREATE DIPLOM NAT/LISM

S62
DRACHKOVITCH M.M.,"THE EMERGING PATTERN OF YUGOSLAV-SOVIET RELATIONS." COM FUT USSR WOR+45 INT/ORG ECO/TAC FOR/AID DOMIN COERCE ATTIT PERSON ORD/FREE PWR...TIME/SEQ 20 TITO/MARSH KHRUSH/N STALIN/J. PAGE 38 A0783
TOP/EX DIPLOM YUGOSLAVIA

S62
FALK R.A.,"THE REALITY OF INTERNATIONAL LAW." WOR+45 NAT/G LEGIT COERCE DETER WAR MORAL ORD/FREE PWR SOVEREIGN...JURID CONCPT VAL/FREE COLD/WAR 20. PAGE 43 A0887
INT/ORG ADJUD NUC/PWR INT/LAW

S62
GREENSPAN M.,"INTERNATIONAL LAW AND ITS PROTECTION FOR PARTICIPANTS IN UNCONVENTIONAL WARFARE." WOR+45 LAW INT/ORG NAT/G POL/PAR COERCE REV ORD/FREE ...INT/LAW TOT/POP 20. PAGE 56 A1143
FORCES JURID GUERRILLA WAR

S62
GUETZKOW H.,"THE POTENTIAL OF CASE STUDY IN ANALYZING INTERNATIONAL CONFLICT." EUR+WWI FUT GERMANY INTELL SOCIETY STRUCT INT/ORG LOC/G NAT/G CONSULT CREATE PLAN CHOOSE ATTIT RIGID/FLEX ...POLICY SAAR 20. PAGE 58 A1188
EDU/PROP METH/CNCPT COERCE FRANCE

S62
JACOBSON H.K.,"THE UNITED NATIONS AND COLONIALISM: A TENTATIVE APPRAISAL." AFR FUT S/ASIA USA+45 USSR WOR+45 NAT/G DELIB/GP PLAN DIPLOM ECO/TAC DOMIN ADMIN ROUTINE COERCE ATTIT RIGID/FLEX ORD/FREE PWR ...OBS STERTYP UN 20. PAGE 73 A1486
INT/ORG CONCPT COLONIAL

S62
KOLARZ W.,"THE IMPACT OF COMMUNISM ON WEST AFRICA." AFR FUT SOCIETY INT/ORG NAT/G CREATE PLAN DOMIN EDU/PROP COERCE NAT/LISM ATTIT RIGID/FLEX SOCISM ...POLICY CONCPT TREND MARX/KARL 20. PAGE 81 A1666
COM POL/PAR COLONIAL

S62
RUSSETT B.M.,"CAUSE, SURPRISE, AND NO ESCAPE." FUT WOR-45 CULTURE SOCIETY INT/ORG FORCES TEC/DEV BAL/PWR EDU/PROP ARMS/CONT NUC/PWR WAR WEAPON PEACE KNOWL ORD/FREE PWR...POLICY CONCPT RECORD TIME/SEQ TREND GEN/LAWS 20 WWI. PAGE 126 A2578
COERCE DIPLOM

S62
SINGER J.D.,"STABLE DETERRENCE AND ITS LIMITS." FUT WOR+45 R+D INT/ORG CONSULT ACT/RES TEC/DEV ARMS/CONT COERCE DRIVE PERCEPT RIGID/FLEX ORD/FREE PWR...MYTH SIMUL TOT/POP 20. PAGE 133 A2728
NAT/G FORCES DETER NUC/PWR

S62
STRACHEY J.,"COMMUNIST INTENTIONS." ASIA USSR YUGOSLAVIA INT/ORG NAT/G FORCES DOMIN EDU/PROP COERCE NUC/PWR NAT/LISM PEACE RIGID/FLEX PWR MARXISM...CONCPT MYTH OBS TIME/SEQ TREND COLD/WAR TOT/POP 20. PAGE 139 A2843
COM ATTIT WAR

S62
THOMAS J.R.T.,"SOVIET BEHAVIOR IN THE QUEMOY CRISES OF 1958." CHINA/COM FUT USSR WOR+45 INT/ORG VOL/ASSN FORCES PLAN BAL/PWR DOMIN COERCE NUC/PWR REV WAR ATTIT DRIVE ORD/FREE...POLICY OBS RECORD COLD/WAR FOR/POL 20. PAGE 143 A2923
COM PWR

S62
TOWSTER J.,"THE USSR AND THE USA: CHALLENGE AND RESPONSE." COM GERMANY USA+45 USSR WOR+45 ECO/UNDEV INT/ORG VOL/ASSN EX/STRUC FORCES TOP/EX CREATE PLAN TEC/DEV DIPLOM ECO/TAC EDU/PROP COLONIAL COERCE PWR ...GEN/METH COLD/WAR 20 KENNEDY/JF. PAGE 145 A2956
ACT/RES GEN/LAWS

B63
ABSHIRE D.M.,NATIONAL SECURITY: POLITICAL, MILITARY, AND ECONOMIC STRATEGIES IN THE DECADE AHEAD. ASIA COM USA+45 WOR+45 ECO/DEV ECO/UNDEV
FUT ACT/RES BAL/PWR

INT/ORG DELIB/GP FORCES ECO/TAC COERCE ATTIT RIGID/FLEX HEALTH ORD/FREE PWR WEALTH...POLICY STAT CHARTS ANTHOL COLD/WAR VAL/FREE. PAGE 4 A0083

B63
ADLER G.J.,BRITISH INDIA'S NORTHERN FRONTIER: 1865-95. AFGHANISTN RUSSIA UK PROVS COLONIAL COERCE PEACE...GEOG CHARTS BIBLIOG 19 TREATY. PAGE 4 A0091
S/ASIA FORCES DIPLOM POLICY

B63
BROWN W.N.,THE UNITED STATES AND INDIA AND PAKISTAN (REV. ED.). INDIA PAKISTAN S/ASIA WOR+45 POL/PAR SECT INT/TRADE COLONIAL COERCE DISCRIM. PAGE 20 A0408
DIPLOM ECO/UNDEV SOVEREIGN STRUCT

B63
BRZEZINSKI Z.K.,AFRICA AND THE COMMUNIST WORLD. AFR ASIA COM CULTURE SOCIETY INT/ORG DELIB/GP ACT/RES ECO/TAC COERCE ORD/FREE PWR WEALTH...STAT TOT/POP VAL/FREE 20. PAGE 21 A0418
ATTIT EDU/PROP DIPLOM USSR

B63
BURNS A.L.,PEACE-KEEPING BY U.N.FORCES - FROM SUEZ TO THE CONGO. AFR FUT ISLAM ISRAEL USSR WOR+45 NAT/G DELIB/GP BAL/PWR DOMIN LEGIT EXEC COERCE PEACE ATTIT PWR RESPECT SOVEREIGN...CONCPT UN 20. PAGE 22 A0441
INT/ORG FORCES ORD/FREE

B63
FIFIELD R.H.,SOUTHEAST ASIA IN UNITED STATES POLICY. S/ASIA USA+45 ECO/UNDEV NAT/G DIPLOM ECO/TAC ADMIN COERCE ORD/FREE...POLICY MAJORIT 20. PAGE 45 A0928
INT/ORG PWR

B63
FLORES E.,LAND REFORM AND THE ALLIANCE FOR PROGRESS (PAMPHLET). L/A+17C USA+45 STRUCT ECO/UNDEV NAT/G WORKER CREATE PLAN ECO/TAC COERCE REV 20. PAGE 47 A0953
AGRI INT/ORG DIPLOM POLICY

B63
HALASZ DE BEKY I.L.,A BIBLIOGRAPHY OF THE HUNGARIAN REVOLUTION 1956. COM HUNGARY USSR DIPLOM COERCE MARXISM...POLICY AUD/VIS 20 UN COLD/WAR. PAGE 59 A1221
BIBLIOG REV FORCES ATTIT

B63
HAMM H.,ALBANIA - CHINA'S BEACHHEAD IN EUROPE. ALBANIA CHINA/COM USSR YUGOSLAVIA ELITES SOCIETY POL/PAR DELIB/GP FORCES ECO/TAC COERCE ISOLAT PEACE MARXISM...IDEA/COMP 20 MAO. PAGE 61 A1248
DIPLOM REV NAT/G POLICY

B63
HENDERSON W.,SOUTHEAST ASIA: PROBLEMS OF UNITED STATES POLICY. COM S/ASIA CULTURE STRATA ECO/UNDEV INT/ORG DELIB/GP ACT/RES ECO/TAC DOMIN EDU/PROP LEGIT COERCE ATTIT ALL/VALS...STAT TIME/SEQ ANTHOL VAL/FREE 20. PAGE 64 A1313
ASIA USA+45 DIPLOM

B63
HINSLEY F.H.,POWER AND THE PURSUIT OF PEACE. WOR+45 WOR-45 PLAN RIGID/FLEX ALL/VALS ALL/IDEOS...POLICY DECISION INT/LAW 12/20 ROUSSEAU/J KANT/I BENTHAM/J LEAGUE/NAT. PAGE 65 A1338
DIPLOM CONSTN PEACE COERCE

B63
JAIRAZBHOY R.A.,FOREIGN INFLUENCE IN ANCIENT INDIA. INDIA ELITES SECT DIPLOM EDU/PROP COLONIAL REGION GP/REL...ART/METH LING WORSHIP +/14 GRECO/ROMN MESOPOTAM PERSIA PARTH/SASS. PAGE 73 A1491
CULTURE SOCIETY COERCE DOMIN

B63
LERCHE C.O. JR.,CONCEPTS OF INTERNATIONAL POLITICS. WOR+45 WOR-45 LAW DELIB/GP EX/STRUC TEC/DEV ECO/TAC INT/TRADE LEGIT ROUTINE COERCE ATTIT ORD/FREE PWR RESPECT...STERTYP GEN/LAWS VAL/FREE. PAGE 87 A1782
INT/ORG WAR

B63
MBOYA T.,FREEDOM AND AFTER. AFR LABOR POL/PAR DIPLOM EDU/PROP COERCE SOCISM 20. PAGE 97 A1989
COLONIAL ECO/UNDEV NAT/LISM INT/ORG

B63
NORTH R.C.,CONTENT ANALYSIS: A HANDBOOK WITH APPLICATIONS FOR THE STUDY OF INTERNATIONAL CRISIS. ASIA COM EUR+WWI MOD/EUR INT/ORG TEC/DEV DOMIN EDU/PROP ROUTINE COERCE PERCEPT RIGID/FLEX ALL/VALS ...QUANT TESTS CON/ANAL SIMUL GEN/LAWS VAL/FREE. PAGE 110 A2252
METH/CNCPT COMPUT/IR USSR

B63
ROSECRANCE R.N.,ACTION AND REACTION IN WORLD POLITICS. FUT WOR-45 SOCIETY DELIB/GP ACT/RES CREATE DIPLOM ECO/TAC DOMIN EDU/PROP COERCE ATTIT PERSON SUPEGO ORD/FREE PWR...CHARTS SIMUL LEAGUE/NAT VAL/FREE UN 19/20. PAGE 123 A2529
WOR+45 INT/ORG BAL/PWR

B63
SCHMELTZ G.W.,LA POLITIQUE MONDIALE CONTEMPORAINE. SOCIETY ECO/UNDEV INDUS INT/ORG NAT/G POL/PAR CONSULT DELIB/GP PLAN TEC/DEV ECO/TAC DOMIN EDU/PROP ROUTINE COERCE PERCEPT PERSON LOVE SKILL ...SOC RECORD TOT/POP. PAGE 128 A2629
WOR+45 COLONIAL

B63
THUCYDIDES,THE PELOPONESIAN WARS. MEDIT-7 CULTURE INT/ORG NAT/G FORCES TOP/EX PLAN ROUTINE PWR ...CONCPT. PAGE 144 A2938
ATTIT COERCE WAR

B63
US DEPARTMENT OF THE ARMY,SOVIET RUSSIA: STRATEGIC SURVEY (PAMPHLET). USSR POL/PAR PLAN DOMIN EDU/PROP ARMS/CONT GUERRILLA WAR WEAPON...TREND CHARTS ORG/CHARTS 20. PAGE 152 A3106
BIBLIOG/A MARXISM DIPLOM COERCE

B63
VOSS E.H.,NUCLEAR AMBUSH: THE TEST-BAN TRAP. WOR+45 COM/IND INT/ORG NAT/G DELIB/GP FORCES LEGIS TOP/EX ACT/RES DOMIN EDU/PROP LEGIT ROUTINE COERCE ATTIT PERCEPT RIGID/FLEX HEALTH MORAL ORD/FREE PWR. PAGE 160 A3255
TEC/DEV HIST/WRIT ARMS/CONT NUC/PWR

L63
LISSITZYN O.J.,"INTERNATIONAL LAW IN A DIVIDED WORLD." FUT WOR+45 CONSTN CULTURE ECO/DEV ECO/UNDEV DIST/IND NAT/G FORCES ECO/TAC LEGIT ADJUD ADMIN COERCE ATTIT HEALTH MORAL ORD/FREE PWR RESPECT WEALTH VAL/FREE. PAGE 90 A1841
INT/ORG LAW

L63
PHELPS J.,"STUDIES IN DETERRENCE VIII: MILITARY STABILITARY AND ARMS CONTROL: A CRITICAL SURVEY." FUT WOR+45 INT/ORG ACT/RES EDU/PROP COERCE NUC/PWR WAR HEALTH PWR...POLICY TECHNIC TREND SIMUL TOT/POP 20. PAGE 116 A2373
FORCES ORD/FREE ARMS/CONT DETER

L63
SCHELLING T.C.,"STRATEGIC PROBLEMS OF AN INTERNATIONAL ARMED FORCE." WOR+45 ECO/DEV INT/ORG NAT/G PLAN BAL/PWR LEGIT ARMS/CONT COERCE DETER ORD/FREE PWR...POLICY CONCPT COLD/WAR 20. PAGE 128 A2624
CREATE FORCES

S63
BLOOMFIELD L.P.,"INTERNATIONAL FORCE IN A DISARMING BUT REVOLUTIONARY WORLD." INT/ORG COERCE REV DRIVE PWR...CONCPT STERTYP GEN/LAWS 20. PAGE 16 A0318
FORCES ORD/FREE ARMS/CONT GUERRILLA

S63
BLOOMFIELD L.P.,"HEADQUARTERS-FIELD RELATIONS: SOME NOTES ON THE BEGINNING AND END OF ONUC." AFR INT/ORG ROUTINE COERCE WAR WEAPON UN CONGO 20. PAGE 16 A0319
FORCES ORD/FREE

S63
BRZEZINSKI Z.,"SOVIET QUIESCENCE." EUR+WWI USA+45 USSR FORCES CREATE PLAN COERCE DETER WAR ATTIT 20 TREATY EUROPE. PAGE 20 A0415
DIPLOM ARMS/CONT NUC/PWR AGREE

S63
BULLOUGH V.L.,"THE ROMAN EMPIRE VS PERSIA, 363-502: A STUDY OF SUCCESSFUL DETERRENCE." NAT/G PLAN DIPLOM ORD/FREE PWR...TIME/SEQ COLD/WAR VAL/FREE 4/6 PERSIA ROM/EMP. PAGE 21 A0430
MEDIT-7 COERCE DETER

S63
DICKS H.V.,"NATIONAL LOYALTY, IDENTITY, AND THE INTERNATIONAL SOLDIER." FUT NAT/G COERCE ATTIT DRIVE PERCEPT PERSON RIGID/FLEX SUPEGO ALL/VALS ...PSY VAL/FREE. PAGE 37 A0758
INT/ORG FORCES

S63
HUMPHREY H.H.,"REGIONAL ARMS CONTROL AGREEMENTS." WOR+45 FORCES PLAN LEGIT COERCE ATTIT HEALTH ORD/FREE...HUM METH/CNCPT MYTH OBS INT TREND TOT/POP 20. PAGE 69 A1416
L/A+17C INT/ORG ARMS/CONT REGION

S63
NICHOLAS H.G.,"UN PEACE FORCES AND THE CHANGING GLOBE: THE LESSONS OF SUEZ AND CONGO." FUT WOR+45 CONSTN INT/ORG CONSULT DELIB/GP TOP/EX CREATE DIPLOM DOMIN LEGIT COERCE WAR PERSON RIGID/FLEX PWR UN SUEZ CONGO UNEF 20. PAGE 109 A2229
ACT/RES FORCES

S63
SINGER M.R.,"ELECTIONS WITHIN THE UNITED NATIONS: AN EXPERIMENTAL STUDY UTILIZING STATISTICAL ANALYSIS." USA+45 WOR+45 DIPLOM ECO/TAC COERCE PWR WEALTH...STAT CHARTS SIMUL GEN/LAWS COLD/WAR VAL/FREE UN 20. PAGE 133 A2732
INT/ORG CHOOSE

S63
SONNENFELDT H.,"FOREIGN POLICY FROM MALENKOV TO KHRUSHCHEV." WOR+45 NAT/G FORCES BAL/PWR DIPLOM ECO/TAC COERCE ATTIT PWR...CONCPT HIST/WRIT COLD/WAR 20. PAGE 135 A2768
COM DOMIN FOR/AID USSR

B64
BARKER A.J.,SUEZ: THE SEVEN DAY WAR. EUR+WWI ISLAM UAR INT/ORG NAT/G PLAN DIPLOM ECO/TAC DOMIN NAT/LISM DRIVE RIGID/FLEX PWR SOVEREIGN...POLICY JURID TREND CHARTS SUEZ UN 20. PAGE 11 A0221
FORCES COERCE UK

B64
BLACKSTOCK P.W.,THE STRATEGY OF SUBVERSION. USA+45 FORCES EDU/PROP ADMIN COERCE GOV/REL...DECISION MGT 20 DEPT/DEFEN CIA DEPT/STATE. PAGE 15 A0301
ORD/FREE DIPLOM CONTROL

B64
DEITCHMAN S.J.,LIMITED WAR AND AMERICAN DEFENSE POLICY. USA+45 WOR+45 INT/ORG NAT/G PLAN TEC/DEV COERCE NUC/PWR RIGID/FLEX PWR SKILL...DECISION METH/CNCPT TIME/SEQ TOT/POP COLD/WAR 20. PAGE 36 A0726
FORCES WAR WEAPON

B64
DEUTSCHE GES AUSWARTIGE POL,STRATEGIE UND ABRUSTUNGSPOLITIK DER SOWJETUNION. USSR TEC/DEV DIPLOM COERCE DETER WEAPON...POLICY PSY 20 ABM/DEFSYS. PAGE 37 A0747
NUC/PWR WAR FORCES ARMS/CONT

B64
DUBOIS J.,DANGER OVER PANAMA. FUT PANAMA SCHOOL PROB/SOLV EDU/PROP MARXISM...POLICY 19/20 TREATY
DIPLOM COERCE

INTERVENT CANAL/ZONE. PAGE 39 A0790

B64
ETZIONI A.,WINNING WITHOUT WAR. FUT MOD/EUR USA+45 WOR+45 ECO/DEV ECO/UNDEV INT/ORG NAT/G FORCES TOP/EX PLAN TEC/DEV ECO/TAC DOMIN EDU/PROP LEGIT COERCE CHOOSE ATTIT MORAL ORD/FREE RESPECT WEALTH MAJORIT. PAGE 43 A0871
PWR TREND DIPLOM USSR

B64
FALL B.,STREET WITHOUT JOY. FRANCE USA+45 DIPLOM ECO/TAC FOR/AID GUERRILLA REV WEAPON...TREND 20. PAGE 44 A0894
WAR S/ASIA FORCES COERCE

B64
FISHER R.,INTERNATIONAL CONFLICT AND BEHAVIORAL SCIENCE: THE CRAIGVILLE PAPERS. COM FUT USA+45 WOR+45 NAT/G DELIB/GP EX/STRUC FORCES ECO/TAC DOMIN EDU/PROP LEGIT COERCE ATTIT PERCEPT ORD/FREE PWR RESPECT...PSY SOC VAL/FREE. PAGE 46 A0940
INT/ORG PLAN DIPLOM

B64
FRYDENSBERG P.,PEACE-KEEPING: EXPERIENCE AND EVALUATION: THE OSLO PAPERS. NORWAY FORCES PLAN CONTROL...INT/LAW 20 UN. PAGE 49 A1012
INT/ORG DIPLOM PEACE COERCE

B64
IRISH M.D.,WORLD PRESSURES ON AMERICAN FOREIGN POLICY. ASIA COM L/A+17C SOUTH/AFR UK WOR+45 ECO/DEV ECO/UNDEV COLONIAL SANCTION COERCE REV TOTALISM...ANTHOL 20 COLD/WAR EUROPE/W INTERVENT. PAGE 72 A1467
DIPLOM POLICY

B64
JACOB P.E.,THE INTEGRATION OF POLITICAL COMMUNITIES. USA+45 WOR+45 CULTURE LOC/G MUNIC NAT/G CREATE PLAN LEGIT REGION COERCE ALL/VALS ...POLICY GEOG PSY SOC TREND HYPO/EXP GEN/LAWS VAL/FREE 20. PAGE 72 A1483
INT/ORG METH/CNCPT SIMUL STAT

B64
JANOWITZ M.,THE MILITARY IN THE POLITICAL DEVELOPMENT OF NEW NATIONS: AN ESSAY IN COMPARATIVE ANALYSIS. AFR ASIA ISLAM L/A+17C S/ASIA USA+45 ECO/UNDEV INT/ORG NAT/G POL/PAR DELIB/GP PLAN ECO/TAC DOMIN LEGIT COERCE ATTIT DRIVE RESPECT ...SOC CONCPT CENSUS VAL/FREE. PAGE 73 A1495
FORCES PWR

B64
KIMMINICH O.,RUSTUNG UND POLITISCHE SPANNUNG. INDUS ARMS/CONT COERCE NAT/LISM PEACE PERSON ORD/FREE ...POLICY GEOG 20. PAGE 79 A1619
DIPLOM FORCES WEAPON WAR

B64
LEGGE J.D.,INDONESIA. INDONESIA ELITES ECO/UNDEV POL/PAR CHIEF FORCES INT/TRADE COERCE CHOOSE ORD/FREE...SOC CHARTS BIBLIOG 16/20 CHINJAP. PAGE 86 A1765
S/ASIA DOMIN NAT/LISM POLICY

B64
LEGUM C.,SOUTH AFRICA: CRISIS FOR THE WEST. SOUTH/AFR COERCE DISCRIM ATTIT...TREND 20 INTERVENT. PAGE 86 A1767
RACE/REL STRATA DIPLOM PROB/SOLV

B64
ROSECRANCE R.N.,THE DISPERSION OF NUCLEAR WEAPONS: STRATEGY AND POLITICS. ASIA COM FUT S/ASIA USA+45 INT/ORG NAT/G DELIB/GP FORCES ACT/RES TEC/DEV BAL/PWR COERCE DETER ATTIT RIGID/FLEX ORD/FREE ...POLICY CHARTS VAL/FREE. PAGE 123 A2530
EUR+WWI PWR PEACE

B64
ROSENAU J.N.,INTERNATIONAL ASPECTS OF CIVIL STRIFE. CHINA/COM CUBA EUR+WWI USA+45 USSR BAL/PWR EDU/PROP NEUTRAL COERCE MORAL...NAT/COMP 20 COLD/WAR UN. PAGE 124 A2533
POLICY DIPLOM REV WAR

B64
STANGER R.J.,ESSAYS ON INTERVENTION. PLAN PROB/SOLV BAL/PWR ADJUD COERCE WAR ROLE PWR...INT/LAW CONCPT 20 UN INTERVENT. PAGE 137 A2803
SOVEREIGN DIPLOM POLICY LEGIT

B64
STANKIEWICZ W.J.,POLITICAL THOUGHT SINCE WORLD WAR II. WOR+45 CAP/ISM DIPLOM COLONIAL COERCE REV REPRESENT ADJUST ANOMIE ALL/IDEOS 20. PAGE 137 A2804
IDEA/COMP DOMIN ORD/FREE AUTHORIT

B64
THANT U.,TOWARD WORLD PEACE. DELIB/GP TEC/DEV EDU/PROP WAR SOVEREIGN...INT/LAW 20 UN MID/EAST. PAGE 142 A2907
DIPLOM BIOG PEACE COERCE

B64
TONG T.,UNITED STATES DIPLOMACY IN CHINA, 1844-1860. ASIA USA-45 ECO/UNDEV ECO/TAC COERCE GP/REL...INT/LAW 19 TREATY. PAGE 144 A2949
DIPLOM INT/TRADE COLONIAL

B64
WARREN S.,THE PRESIDENT AS WORLD LEADER. USA+45 WOR+45 ELITES COM/IND INT/ORG NAT/G VOL/ASSN CHIEF EX/STRUC LEGIT COERCE ATTIT PERSON RIGID/FLEX...INT TIME/SEQ COLD/WAR 20 ROOSEVLT/F TRUMAN/HS EISNHWR/DD KENNEDY/JF. PAGE 161 A3286
TOP/EX PWR DIPLOM

B64
WEINTRAUB S.,THE WAR IN THE WARDS. KOREA/N WOR+45 DIPLOM COERCE ORD/FREE SKILL 20 TREATY. PAGE 162 A3308
EDU/PROP PEACE CROWD PUB/INST

L64
BARROS J.,"THE GREEK-BULGARIAN INCIDENT OF 1925: THE LEAGUE OF NATIONS AND THE GREAT POWERS." BULGARIA EUR+WWI NAT/G FORCES ECO/TAC EDU/PROP LEGIT ROUTINE COERCE WAR PEACE DRIVE PWR...JURID CONCPT METH/CNCPT GEN/LAWS GEN/METH LEAGUE/NAT TOT/POP 20. PAGE 11 A0228
INT/ORG ORD/FREE DIPLOM

L64
BERKS R.N.,"THE US AND WEAPONS CONTROL." WOR+45 LAW INT/ORG NAT/G LEGIS EXEC COERCE PEACE ATTIT RIGID/FLEX ALL/VALS PWR...POLICY TOT/POP 20. PAGE 13 A0273
USA+45 PLAN ARMS/CONT

L64
CARNEGIE ENDOWMENT INT. PEACE,"POLITICAL QUESTIONS (ISSUES BEFORE THE NINETEENTH GENERAL ASSEMBLY)." SPACE WOR+45 CONSTN FINAN NAT/G CONSULT DELIB/GP FORCES LEGIS TEC/DEV EDU/PROP LEGIT ARMS/CONT COERCE NUC/PWR ATTIT ALL/VALS...CONCPT OBS UN COLD/WAR 20. PAGE 24 A0490
INT/ORG PEACE

L64
CLAUDE I.,"THE OAS, THE UN, AND THE UNITED STATES." L/A+17C USA+45 CONSTN NAT/G DELIB/GP DOMIN EDU/PROP LEGIT REGION COERCE ORD/FREF PWR...TIME/SEQ TREND STERTYP OAS UN 20. PAGE 27 A0546
INT/ORG POLICY

L64
HOFFMANN S.,"EUROPE'S IDENTITY CRISIS: BETWEEN THE PAST AND AMERICA." EUR+WWI FUT USA+45 INT/ORG NAT/G LEGIT RIGID/FLEX ALL/VALS...RELATIV TOT/POP 20. PAGE 66 A1358
COERCE POLICY

L64
WARD C.,"THE 'NEW MYTHS' AND 'OLD REALITIES' OF NUCLEAR WAR." COM FUT USA+45 USSR WOR+45 INT/ORG NAT/G DOMIN LEGIT EXEC ATTIT PERCEPT ALL/VALS ...POLICY RELATIV PSY MYTH TREND 20. PAGE 161 A3280
FORCES COERCE ARMS/CONT NUC/PWR

S64
ASHRAF S.,"INDIA AND WORLD AFFAIRS: AN ANNUAL BIBLIOGRAPHY, 1962." WOR+45 LAW ECO/UNDEV INT/ORG FORCES PLAN ECO/TAC COERCE ORD/FREE PWR WEALTH ...HIST/WRIT VAL/FREE. PAGE 9 A0188
S/ASIA NAT/G

S64
COFFEY J.,"THE SOVIET VIEW OF A DISARMED WORLD." COM USA+45 INT/ORG NAT/G EX/STRUC EDU/PROP COERCE PERCEPT ORD/FREE PWR...TREND STERTYP VAL/FREE 20 UN. PAGE 27 A0556
FORCES ATTIT ARMS/CONT USSR

S64
CRANE R.D.,"BASIC PRINCIPLES IN SOVIET SPACE LAW." FUT WOR+45 AIR INT/ORG DIPLOM DOMIN ARMS/CONT COERCE NUC/PWR PEACE ATTIT DRIVE PWR...INT/LAW METH/CNCPT NEW/IDEA OBS TREND GEN/LAWS VAL/FREE MARX/KARL 20. PAGE 32 A0659
COM LAW USSR SPACE

S64
DELGADO J.,"EL MOMENTO POLITICO HISPANOAMERICA." CHINA/COM FUT PANAMA USA+45 USSR INT/ORG NAT/G POL/PAR FORCES DOMIN REGION COERCE ATTIT ALL/VALS ...TRADIT CONCPT COLD/WAR 20. PAGE 36 A0728
L/A+17C EDU/PROP NAT/LISM

S64
FALK S.L.,"DISARMAMENT IN HISTORICAL PERSPECTIVE." WOR-45 NAT/G PLAN NUC/PWR PEACE ORD/FREE PWR ...TIME/SEQ AUD/VIS VAL/FREE LEAGUE/NAT 20. PAGE 44 A0892
INT/ORG COERCE ARMS/CONT

S64
GARDNER R.N.,"THE SOVIET UNION AND THE UNITED NATIONS." WOR+45 FINAN POL/PAR VOL/ASSN FORCES ECO/TAC DOMIN EDU/PROP LEGIT ADJUD ADMIN ARMS/CONT COERCE ATTIT ALL/VALS...POLICY MAJORIT CONCPT OBS TIME/SEQ TREND STERTYP UN. PAGE 51 A1046
COM INT/ORG USSR

S64
GINSBURGS G.,"WARS OF NATIONAL LIBERATION - THE SOVIET THESIS." COM USSR WOR+45 WOR-45 LAW CULTURE INT/ORG DIPLOM LEGIT COLONIAL GUERRILLA WAR NAT/LISM ATTIT PERSON MORAL PWR...JURID OBS TREND MARX/KARL 20. PAGE 53 A1075
COERCE CONCPT INT/LAW REV

S64
HOWARD M.,"MILITARY POWER AND INTERNATIONAL ORDER." WOR+45 SOCIETY INT/ORG NAT/G BAL/PWR DOMIN COERCE NUC/PWR WEAPON PWR...NEW/IDEA 20. PAGE 68 A1400
FORCES ATTIT WAR

S64
KISSINGER H.A.,"COALITION DIPLOMACY IN A NUCLEAR AGE." COM EUR+WWI USA+45 WOR+45 INT/ORG NAT/G FORCES ACT/RES DOMIN LEGIT COERCE PERCEPT ALL/VALS ...POLICY TOT/POP 20. PAGE 80 A1644
CONSULT ATTIT DIPLOM NUC/PWR

S64
KOTANI H.,"PEACE-KEEPING: PROBLEMS FOR SMALLER COUNTRIES." FUT WOR+45 NAT/G ACT/RES PLAN DOMIN EDU/PROP COERCE ALL/VALS...POLICY UN TOT/POP 20. PAGE 82 A1673
INT/ORG FORCES

S64
MOORE W.E.,"PREDICTING DISCONTINUITIES IN SOCIAL CHANGE." UNIV WOR+45 ECO/DEV ECO/UNDEV INT/ORG NAT/G COERCE ALL/VALS...METH/CNCPT TIME/SEQ TREND TOT/POP VAL/FREE 20. PAGE 103 A2125
SOCIETY GEN/LAWS REV

S64
REIDY J.W.,"LATIN AMERICA AND THE ATLANTIC TRIANGLE." EUR+WWI FUT USA+45 INT/ORG NAT/G REGION
L/A+17C WEALTH

COERCE ORD/FREE PWR...TIME/SEQ VAL/FREE 20. PAGE 120 A2458 — POLICY

S64
VANDENBOSCH A.,"THE SMALL STATES IN INTERNATIONAL POLITICS AND ORGANIZATION." EUR+WWI MOD/EUR WOR+45 WOR-45 CONSTN DELIB/GP COERCE ORD/FREE PWR ...TIME/SEQ GEN/LAWS VAL/FREE LEAGUE/NAT UN 19/20. PAGE 158 A3219 — NAT/G INT/ORG DIPLOM

S64
WASKOW A.I.,"NEW ROADS TO A WORLD WITHOUT WAR." FUT WOR+45 CULTURE INTELL SOCIETY NAT/G DOMIN LEGIT EXEC COERCE PEACE ATTIT DISPL PERCEPT RIGID/FLEX ALL/VALS...POLICY RELATIV SOC NEW/IDEA 20. PAGE 161 A3288 — INT/ORG FORCES

B65
COOPER S.,BEHIND THE GOLDEN CURTAIN: A VIEW OF THE USA. UK USA+45 SECT EDU/PROP COERCE LEISURE ORD/FREE WEALTH 20. PAGE 30 A0609 — SOCIETY DIPLOM ATTIT ACT/RES

B65
GEORGE M.,THE WARPED VISION. EUR+WWI UK NAT/G POL/PAR LEGIS PARL/PROC SANCTION COERCE WAR GOV/REL PEACE RESPECT 20 CONSRV/PAR. PAGE 52 A1061 — LEAD ATTIT DIPLOM POLICY

B65
GRETTON P.,MARITIME STRATEGY - A STUDY OF DEFENSE PROBLEMS. ASIA UK USSR DIPLOM COERCE DETER NUC/PWR WEAPON...CONCPT NAT/COMP 20. PAGE 56 A1147 — FORCES PLAN WAR SEA

B65
LARUS J.,FROM COLLECTIVE SECURITY TO PREVENTIVE DIPLOMACY. FUT FORCES PROB/SOLV DEBATE AGREE COERCE WAR PWR...ANTHOL 20 LEAGUE/NAT UN. PAGE 85 A1736 — INT/ORG PEACE DIPLOM ORD/FREE

B65
NEWBURY C.W.,BRITISH POLICY TOWARDS WEST AFRICA: SELECT DOCUMENTS 1786-1874. AFR UK INT/TRADE DOMIN ADMIN COLONIAL CT/SYS COERCE ORD/FREE...BIBLIOG/A 18/19. PAGE 108 A2224 — DIPLOM POLICY NAT/G WRITING

B65
RANSOM H.H.,AN AMERICAN FOREIGN POLICY READER. USA+45 FORCES EDU/PROP COERCE NUC/PWR WAR PEACE ...DECISION 20. PAGE 119 A2443 — NAT/G DIPLOM POLICY

B65
ROSENBERG A.,DEMOCRACY AND SOCIALISM. COM EUR+WWI FRANCE MOD/EUR STRUCT INT/ORG NAT/G POL/PAR TOP/EX EDU/PROP COERCE PERSON PWR FASCISM MARXISM...CONCPT TIME/SEQ MARX/KARL 19/20. PAGE 124 A2535 — ATTIT

B65
THOMAS A.V.,NONINTERVENTION: THE LAW AND ITS IMPORT IN THE AMERICAS. L/A+17C USA+45 USA-45 WOR+45 DIPLOM ADJUD...JURID IDEA/COMP 20 UN INTERVENT. PAGE 143 A2920 — INT/LAW PWR COERCE

B65
WINT G.,COMMUNIST CHINA'S CRUSADE: MAO'S ROAD TO POWER AND THE NEW CAMPAIGN FOR WORLD REVOLUTION. ASIA CHINA/COM USA+45 USSR NAT/G POL/PAR DOMIN COERCE WAR PWR...POLICY CHARTS IDEA/COMP BIBLIOG 20 MAO. PAGE 165 A3364 — DIPLOM MARXISM REV COLONIAL

L65
TUCKER R.W.,"PEACE AND WAR." UNIV CULTURE SOCIETY INT/ORG NAT/G ACT/RES DOMIN DETER WAR ATTIT DISPL ...POLICY CONCPT MYTH GEN/LAWS 20. PAGE 145 A2975 — PWR COERCE ARMS/CONT PEACE

S65
FLEMING D.F.,"CAN PAX AMERICANA SUCCEED?" ASIA CHINA/COM EUR+WWI USSR VIETNAM BAL/PWR DIPLOM DOMIN COERCE GOV/REL 20. PAGE 46 A0948 — DECISION ATTIT ECO/TAC

S65
KHOURI F.J.,"THE JORDON RIVER CONTROVERSY." LAW SOCIETY ECO/UNDEV AGRI FINAN INDUS SECT FORCES ACT/RES PLAN TEC/DEV ECO/TAC EDU/PROP COERCE ATTIT DRIVE PERCEPT RIGID/FLEX ALL/VALS...GEOG SOC MYTH WORK. PAGE 78 A1610 — ISLAM INT/ORG ISRAEL JORDAN

S65
RAY H.,"THE POLICY OF RUSSIA TOWARDS SINO-INDIAN CONFLICT." ASIA CHINA/COM COM INDIA USSR NAT/G TOP/EX FOR/AID EDU/PROP NEUTRAL COERCE PEACE RIGID/FLEX PWR...METH/CNCPT TIME/SEQ VAL/FREE 20. PAGE 120 A2452 — S/ASIA ATTIT DIPLOM WAR

S65
ROGGER H.,"EAST GERMANY: STABLE OR IMMOBILE." COM EUR+WWI GERMANY/E NAT/G INT/TRADE DOMIN EDU/PROP COERCE TOTALISM COLD/WAR 20. PAGE 123 A2516 — TOP/EX RIGID/FLEX GERMANY

C65
BURTON J.W.,"INTERNATIONAL RELATIONS: A GENERAL THEORY." WOR+45 NAT/G CREATE BAL/PWR NEUTRAL COERCE DETER ADJUST...TREND IDEA/COMP GEN/METH BIBLIOG. PAGE 22 A0447 — DIPLOM GEN/LAWS ACT/RES ORD/FREE

C65
SCHWEBEL M.,"BEHAVIORAL SCIENCE AND HUMAN SURVIVAL." FORCES ARMS/CONT COERCE NUC/PWR WAR GP/REL NAT/LISM PERCEPT...POLICY PSY ANTHOL BIBLIOG/A 20 COLD/WAR. PAGE 130 A2662 — PEACE ACT/RES DIPLOM HEAL

C65
US AIR FORCE ACADEMY,"AMERICAN DEFENSE POLICY." COM INT/ORG TEC/DEV FOR/AID ARMS/CONT DETER NUC/PWR ...POLICY DECISION CONCPT ANTHOL BIBLIOG/A 20 COLD/WAR NATO. PAGE 149 A3054 — PLAN FORCES WAR COERCE

B66
BRACKMAN A.C.,SOUTHEAST ASIA'S SECOND FRONT: THE POWER STRUGGLE IN THE MALAY ARCHIPELAGO. CHINA/COM INDONESIA MALAYSIA ECO/UNDEV INT/ORG NAT/G FORCES DIPLOM EDU/PROP REGION COERCE GUERRILLA AUTHORIT POPULISM...MAJORIT 20 KENNEDY/JF SEATO. PAGE 18 A0367 — S/ASIA MARXISM REV

B66
EWING L.L.,THE REFERENCE HANDBOOK OF THE ARMED FORCES OF THE WORLD. WOR+45 ECO/TAC FOR/AID COERCE WAR PWR 20. PAGE 43 A0879 — FORCES STAT DIPLOM PLAN

B66
GROSS F.,WORLD POLITICS AND TENSION AREAS. CHINA/COM SOMALIA VENEZUELA COERCE GP/REL RACE/REL ATTIT HABITAT 19/20 CASEBOOK NEWYORK/C. PAGE 57 A1173 — DIPLOM WAR PROB/SOLV

B66
OBERMANN E.,VERTEIDIGUNG PER FREIHEIT. GERMANY/W WOR+45 INT/ORG COERCE NUC/PWR WEAPON MARXISM 20 UN NATO WARSAW/P TREATY. PAGE 111 A2273 — FORCES ORD/FREE WAR PEACE

B66
VON BORCH H.,FRIEDE TROTZ KRIEG. GERMANY USSR WOR+45 PEACE ANOMIE ATTIT 20. PAGE 112 A2305 — DIPLOM NUC/PWR WAR COERCE

B66
SMITH D.M.,AMERICAN INTERVENTION, 1917. GERMANY UK USA-45 SEA FORCES DIPLOM INT/TRADE EDU/PROP COERCE WEAPON PEACE 20 WILSON/W WWI. PAGE 134 A2746 — WAR ATTIT POLICY NEUTRAL

B66
WAINHOUSE D.W.,INTERNATIONAL PEACE OBSERVATION: A HISTORY AND FORECAST. INT/ORG PROB/SOLV BAL/PWR AGREE ARMS/CONT COERCE NUC/PWR...PREDICT METH/COMP 20 UN LEAGUE/NAT OAS TREATY. PAGE 160 A3261 — PEACE DIPLOM

B66
ZABLOCKI C.J.,SINO-SOVIET RIVALRY. AFR ASIA CHINA/COM CUBA EUR+WWI L/A+17C USA+45 USSR WOR+45 POL/PAR FORCES COERCE NUC/PWR...GOV/COMP IDEA/COMP 20 MAO KHRUSH/N. PAGE 169 A3442 — DIPLOM MARXISM COM

B67
HALPERIN M.H.,CONTEMPORARY MILITARY STRATEGY. ASIA CHINA/COM USA+45 USSR INT/ORG FORCES ACT/RES PLAN TEC/DEV BAL/PWR COERCE WAR...METH/COMP BIBLIOG 20 NATO. PAGE 60 A1240 — DIPLOM NUC/PWR DETER ARMS/CONT

B67
JAGAN C.,THE WEST ON TRIAL. GUYANA CONSTN ECO/UNDEV DIPLOM COERCE PWR SOVEREIGN...BIOG 20. PAGE 73 A1490 — SOCISM CREATE PLAN COLONIAL

B67
LAWYERS COMM AMER POLICY VIET,VIETNAM AND INTERNATIONAL LAW: AN ANALYSIS OF THE LEGALITY OF THE US MILITARY INVOLVEMENT. VIETNAM LAW INT/ORG COERCE WEAPON PEACE ORD/FREE 20 UN SEATO TREATY. PAGE 86 A1753 — INT/LAW DIPLOM ADJUD WAR

B67
MEHDI M.T.,PEACE IN THE MIDDLE EAST. ISRAEL SOCIETY NAT/G PLAN EDU/PROP NAT/LISM DRIVE...IDEA/COMP 20 JEWS. PAGE 99 A2033 — ISLAM DIPLOM GP/REL COERCE

B67
SCOTT A.M.,THE FUNCTIONING OF THE INTERNATIONAL POLITICAL SYSTEM. INT/ORG OP/RES PROB/SOLV COERCE WAR EQUILIB...METH/CNCPT BIBLIOG. PAGE 130 A2671 — DIPLOM DECISION BAL/PWR

B67
WAELDER R.,PROGRESS AND REVOLUTION* A STUDY OF THE ISSUES OF OUR AGE. WOR+45 WOR-45 BAL/PWR DIPLOM COERCE ROLE MORAL ALL/IDEOS...IDEA/COMP NAT/COMP 19/20. PAGE 160 A3259 — PWR NAT/G REV TEC/DEV

L67
MACDONALD R.S.J.,"THE RESORT TO ECONOMIC COERCION BY INTERNATIONAL POLITICAL ORGANIZATIONS." CUBA ETHIOPIA RHODESIA SOUTH/AFR NAT/G FOR/AID INT/TRADE DOMIN CONTROL SANCTION...DECISION LEAGUE/NAT UN OAS 20. PAGE 92 A1887 — INT/ORG COERCE ECO/TAC DIPLOM

S67
ABT J.J.,"WORLD OF SENATOR FULBRIGHT." VIETNAM WOR+45 COERCE DETER REV ORD/FREE MARXISM...MARXIST 20. PAGE 4 A0084 — DIPLOM PLAN PWR

S67
ANTHEM T.,"CYPRUS* WHAT NOW?" CYPRUS GREECE TURKEY NAT/G BUDGET MAJORITY 20 NATO. PAGE 8 A0165 — DIPLOM COERCE INT/TRADE ADJUD

S67
FRANKEL M.,"THE WAR IN VIETNAM." VIETNAM ECO/UNDEV DIPLOM CONFER INGP/REL PEACE PWR...POLICY PREDICT 20. PAGE 48 A0982 — WAR COERCE PLAN GUERRILLA

S67
FRANKLIN W.O.,"CLAUSEWITZ ON LIMITED WAR." VIETNAM WOR+45 WOR-45 PROB/SOLV DIPLOM ECO/TAC DOMIN COLONIAL...METH/COMP 19/20. PAGE 48 A0986
COERCE WAR PLAN GUERRILLA

S67
KIPP K.,"DIE POLITISCHE BEDEUTUNG DER 'GEGENKUSTE' DARGESTELLT AM BEISPIEL DER USA IM 20. JAHRHUNDERT" USA+45 USA-45 SEA NAT/G CONTROL COERCE WAR...POLICY GEOG 20. PAGE 79 A1629
FORCES ORD/FREE DIPLOM DETER

S67
KYLE K.,"BACKGROUND TO THE CRISIS" ISLAM ISRAEL UAR UK USSR NAT/G PROB/SOLV LEGIT CONTROL REGION STRANGE MORAL 20 JEWS. PAGE 83 A1698
DIPLOM POLICY SOVEREIGN COERCE

S67
SHOEMAKER R.L.,"JAPANESE ARMY AND THE WEST." ASIA ELITES EX/STRUC DIPLOM DOMIN EDU/PROP COERCE ATTIT AUTHORIT PWR 1/20 CHINJAP. PAGE 132 A2703
FORCES TEC/DEV WAR TOTALISM

C67
LING D.L.,"TUNISIA: FROM PROTECTORATE TO REPUBLIC." CULTURE NAT/G POL/PAR CHIEF DIPLOM COERCE WAR PWR ...BIBLIOG 19/20 TUNIS. PAGE 89 A1825
AFR NAT/LISM COLONIAL PROB/SOLV

C67
SPANIER J.W.,"WORLD POLITICS IN AN AGE OF REVOLUTION." COM WOR+45 FORCES COERCE WAR NAT/LISM SOVEREIGN...POLICY BIBLIOG 20. PAGE 135 A2772
DIPLOM TEC/DEV REV ECO/UNDEV

B96
SMITH A.,LECTURES ON JUSTICE, POLICE, REVENUE AND ARMS (1763). UK LAW FAM FORCES TARIFFS AGREE COERCE INCOME OWN WEALTH LAISSEZ...GEN/LAWS 17/18. PAGE 134 A2743
DIPLOM JURID OLD/LIB TAX

COERCION....SEE COERCE

COEXIST....COEXISTENCE; SEE ALSO COLD/WAR, PEACE

N17
BURKE E.,THOUGHTS ON THE PROSPECT OF A REGICIDE PEACE (PAMPHLET). FRANCE UK SECT DOMIN MURDER PEACE ORD/FREE SOVEREIGN POPULISM...POLICY GOV/COMP IDEA/COMP 18 JACOBINISM COEXIST. PAGE 21 A0435
REV CHIEF NAT/G DIPLOM

B58
ANGELL N.,DEFENCE AND THE ENGLISH-SPEAKING ROLE. CHINA/COM UK USSR INT/ORG FORCES EDU/PROP NEUTRAL NUC/PWR NAT/LISM PEACE TOTALISM 20 COLD/WAR COEXIST. PAGE 8 A0161
DIPLOM WAR MARXISM ORD/FREE

COEXISTENCE....SEE COLD/WAR, COEXIST

COFFEY J. A0556

COFFIN F.M. A0557

COFFIN/WS....WILLIAM SLOANE COFFIN, JR.

COGNITION....SEE PERCEPT

COGNITIVE DISSONANCE....SEE PERCEPT, ROLE

COHEN A. A0558

COHEN B.C. A0559

COHEN M. A0560,A0561

COHEN M.L. A0562

COHEN P.A. A0563

COHESION....SEE CONSEN

COHN K. A0564

COLBY C.C. A0565

COLD/WAR....COLD WAR

N
WEINTAL E.,FACING THE BRINK* AN INTIMATE STUDY OF CRISIS DIPLOMACY. CYPRUS FRANCE USA+45 USSR VIETNAM YEMEN INT/ORG NAT/G...POLICY DECISION PREDICT COLD/WAR PRESIDENT NATO 20. PAGE 162 A3307
DIPLOM

N/R
FULBRIGHT J.W.,THE ARROGANCE OF POWER. USA+45 WOR+45 ECO/UNDEV ACADEM LEGIS ECO/TAC FOR/AID PEACE ROLE ORD/FREE PWR 20 COLD/WAR CONGRESS. PAGE 50 A1014
DIPLOM POLICY REV

NCO
CARRINGTON C.E.,THE COMMONWEALTH IN AFRICA (PAMPHLET). UK STRUCT NAT/G COLONIAL REPRESENT GOV/REL RACE/REL NAT/LISM...MAJORIT 20 EEC NEGRO COLD/WAR. PAGE 25 A0500
ECO/UNDEV AFR DIPLOM PLAN

N19
DEANE H.,THE WAR IN VIETNAM (PAMPHLET). CHINA/COM VIETNAM BAL/PWR DIPLOM ECO/TAC SOCISM INTERVENT COLD/WAR INTERVENT COLD/WAR. PAGE 35 A0720
WAR SOCIALIST MORAL CAP/ISM

N19
DEANE H.,THE WAR IN VIETNAM (PAMPHLET). CHINA/COM VIETNAM BAL/PWR DIPLOM ECO/TAC SOCISM INTERVENT COLD/WAR INTERVENT COLD/WAR. PAGE 35 A0720
WAR SOCIALIST MORAL CAP/ISM

N19
HAJDA J.,THE COLD WAR VIEWED AS A SOCIOLOGICAL PROBLEM (PAMPHLET). COM CZECHOSLVK EUR+WWI SOCIETY PLAN EDU/PROP CONTROL TASK ATTIT MARXISM...POLICY 20 COLD/WAR MIGRATION. PAGE 59 A1220
DIPLOM LEAD PWR NAT/G

N19
MEZERIK A.G.,COLONIALISM AND THE UNITED NATIONS (PAMPHLET). WOR+45 NAT/G ADMIN LEAD WAR CHOOSE EFFICIENCY PEACE ATTIT ORD/FREE...POLICY CHARTS UN COLD/WAR. PAGE 100 A2061
COLONIAL DIPLOM BAL/PWR INT/ORG

B45
STRAUSZ-HUPE R.,THE BALANCE OF TOMORROW: POWER AND FOREIGN POLICY IN THE UNITED STATES. FUT USA+45 ECO/DEV EXTR/IND INT/ORG FORCES BAL/PWR REGION NUC/PWR...GEOG CHARTS 20 COLD/WAR EUROPE/W. PAGE 139 A2845
DIPLOM PWR POLICY WAR

L47
COMM. STUDY ORGAN. PEACE,"SECURITY THROUGH THE UNITED NATIONS." COM FUT WOR+45 TOP/EX ACT/RES BAL/PWR ARMS/CONT NUC/PWR...CONCPT GEN/LAWS UN TOT/POP COLD/WAR 20. PAGE 28 A0577
INT/ORG ORD/FREE PEACE

N47
FOX W.T.R.,UNITED STATES POLICY IN A TWO POWER WORLD. COM USA+45 USSR FORCES DOMIN AGREE NEUTRAL NUC/PWR ORD/FREE SOVEREIGN 20 COLD/WAR TREATY EUROPE/W INTERVENT. PAGE 48 A0972
DIPLOM FOR/AID POLICY

B48
KULISCHER E.M.,EUROPE ON THE MOVE: WAR AND POPULATION CHANGES, 1917-1947. COM EUR+WWI FUT GERMANY USSR DIST/IND PLAN INT/TRADE CONTROL WAR DRIVE...CENSUS TREND COLD/WAR 20. PAGE 82 A1690
ECO/TAC GEOG

B48
MORGENTHAL H.J.,POLITICS AMONG NATIONS: THE STRUGGLE FOR POWER AND PEACE. FUT WOR+45 INT/ORG OP/RES PROB/SOLV BAL/PWR CONTROL ATTIT MORAL ...INT/LAW BIBLIOG 20 COLD/WAR. PAGE 104 A2135
DIPLOM PEACE PWR POLICY

B48
US DEPARTMENT OF STATE,FOREIGN AFFAIRS HIGHLIGHTS (NEWSLETTER). COM USA+45 INT/ORG PLAN BAL/PWR WAR PWR...BIBLIOG 20 COLD/WAR NATO UN DEPT/STATE. PAGE 151 A3083
DIPLOM NAT/G POLICY

B49
ROSENHAUPT H.W.,HOW TO WAGE PEACE. USA+45 SOCIETY STRATA STRUCT R+D INT/ORG POL/PAR LEGIS ACT/RES CREATE PLAN EDU/PROP ADMIN EXEC ATTIT ALL/VALS ...TIME/SEQ TREND COLD/WAR 20. PAGE 124 A2536
INTELL CONCPT DIPLOM

B49
STETTINIUS E.R.,ROOSEVELT AND THE RUSSIANS: THE YALTA CONFERENCE. UK USSR WOR+45 WOR-45 INT/ORG VOL/ASSN TOP/EX ACT/RES EDU/PROP PEACE ATTIT DRIVE PERSON SUPEGO PWR...POLICY CONCPT MYTH OBS TIME/SEQ AUD/VIS COLD/WAR 20 CHURCHLL/W YALTA ROOSEVLT/F. PAGE 138 A2819
DIPLOM DELIB/GP BIOG

B50
ALMOND G.A.,THE AMERICAN PEOPLE AND FOREIGN POLICY. USA+45 USA-45 CULTURE SOCIETY STRUCT CONSEN PERSON PWR POPULISM...TIME/SEQ TREND 20 COLD/WAR. PAGE 6 A0129
ATTIT DIPLOM DECISION ELITES

B50
BROOKINGS INSTITUTION,MAJOR PROBLEMS OF UNITED STATES FOREIGN POLICY. AFR ASIA INDIA UK USA+45 USSR BAL/PWR FOR/AID WAR PEACE TOTALISM MARXISM SOCISM 20 CHINJAP COLD/WAR. PAGE 19 A0393
DIPLOM POLICY ORD/FREE

B50
DE ARECHAGA E.J.,VOTING AND THE HANDLING OF DISPUTES IN THE SECURITY COUNCIL. WOR+45 CONSTN DIPLOM COERCE ORD/FREE...RECORD CON/ANAL GEN/METH COLD/WAR UN 20. PAGE 34 A0696
INT/ORG PWR

B50
JIMENEZ E.,VOTING AND HANDLING OF DISPUTES IN THE SECURITY COUNCIL. WOR+45 CONSTN INT/ORG DIPLOM LEGIT DETER CHOOSE MORAL ORD/FREE PWR...JURID TIME/SEQ COLD/WAR UN 20. PAGE 74 A1517
DELIB/GP ROUTINE

B50
LINCOLN G.,ECONOMICS OF NATIONAL SECURITY. USA+45 ELITES COM/IND DIST/IND INDUS NAT/G VOL/ASSN DELIB/GP EX/STRUC FOR/AID EDU/PROP COERCE NUC/PWR WAR ATTIT KNOWL ORD/FREE PWR COLD/WAR TOT/POP VAL/FREE 20. PAGE 89 A1818
FORCES ECO/TAC

B50
US LIBRARY OF CONGRESS,THE UNITED STATES AND EUROPE: BIBLIOGRAPHY OF THOUGHT EXPRESSED IN AMERICAN PUBLICATIONS DURING 1950. EUR+WWI GERMANY USA+45 USSR INT/ORG DIPLOM COLONIAL SOVEREIGN ...POLICY 20 COLD/WAR UN BERLIN/BLO. PAGE 154 A3150
BIBLIOG/A SOC ATTIT

L50
US SENATE COMM. GOVT. OPER.,"REVISION OF THE UN CHARTER." FUT USA+45 WOR+45 CONSTN ECO/DEV ECO/UNDEV NAT/G DELIB/GP ACT/RES CREATE PLAN EXEC ROUTINE CHOOSE ALL/VALS...POLICY CONCPT CONGRESS UN TOT/POP 20 COLD/WAR. PAGE 157 A3196
INT/ORG LEGIS PEACE

N50
SCHAPIRO J.S.,THE WORLD IN CRISES: POLITICAL AND SOCIAL MOVEMENTS IN THE TWENTIETH CENTURY. USA+45 INT/ORG LABOR PLAN CAP/ISM DIPLOM COLONIAL PEACE TOTALISM ATTIT LAISSEZ...BIBLIOG 20 COLD/WAR. PAGE 128 A2618
NAT/LISM TEC/DEV REV WAR

B51
BLANSHARD P.,COMMUNISM, DEMOCRACY AND CATHOLIC POWER. USSR VATICAN WOR+45 WOR-45 CULTURE ELITES INTELL SOCIETY STRUCT INT/ORG POL/PAR EDU/PROP COERCE ATTIT KNOWL PWR MARXISM...CONCPT COLD/WAR 20. PAGE 15 A0308
COM SECT TOTALISM

B51
MACLAURIN J.,THE UNITED NATIONS AND POWER POLITICS. WOR+45 CONSULT EDU/PROP LEGIT ADJUD EXEC MORAL ORD/FREE...HUM JURID CONCPT RECORD TIME/SEQ UN COLD/WAR 20. PAGE 93 A1896
INT/ORG ROUTINE

B51
US HOUSE COMM APPROPRIATIONS,MUTUAL SECURITY PROGRAM APPROPRIATIONS FOR 1952: HEARINGS BEFORE A SUBCOMMITTEE OF THE COMMITTEE ON APPROPRIATIONS. KOREA L/A+17C ECO/DEV ECO/UNDEV INT/ORG INSPECT BAL/PWR DIPLOM DEBATE WAR...POLICY STAT ASIA/S 20 CONGRESS NATO COLD/WAR MID/EAST. PAGE 153 A3118
LEGIS FORCES BUDGET FOR/AID

B52
BARR S.,CITIZENS OF THE WORLD. USA+45 WOR+45 CULTURE FORCES LEGIS ACT/RES BAL/PWR LEGIT PEACE ATTIT ORD/FREE PWR...PLURIST CONCPT OBS TIME/SEQ COLD/WAR 20. PAGE 11 A0227
NAT/G INT/ORG DIPLOM

B52
HOSELITZ B.F.,THE PROGRESS OF UNDERDEVELOPED AREAS. FUT WOR+45 WOR-45 ECO/DEV ECO/TAC INT/TRADE WEALTH ...SOC TREND GEN/LAWS TOT/POP VAL/FREE COLD/WAR 20. PAGE 68 A1391
ECO/UNDEV PLAN FOR/AID

L52
NIEBUHR R.,"THE MORAL IMPLICATIONS OF LOYALTY TO THE UNITED NATIONS." WOR+45 WOR-45 SOCIETY ECO/DEV INT/ORG VOL/ASSN PEACE ATTIT PERSON LOVE ORD/FREE PWR RESPECT...CONCPT UN TOT/POP COLD/WAR UNESCO 20. PAGE 109 A2236
SUPEGO GEN/LAWS

B53
BARBER H.W.,FOREIGN POLICIES OF THE UNITED STATES. USA+45 USA-45 WOR+45 INT/ORG NAT/G EX/STRUC ECO/TAC DOMIN EDU/PROP LEGIT COERCE KNOWL PWR COLD/WAR COLD/WAR 20. PAGE 11 A0219
CONCPT DIPLOM

B53
BARBER H.W.,FOREIGN POLICIES OF THE UNITED STATES. USA+45 USA-45 WOR+45 INT/ORG NAT/G EX/STRUC ECO/TAC DOMIN EDU/PROP LEGIT COERCE KNOWL PWR COLD/WAR COLD/WAR 20. PAGE 11 A0219
CONCPT DIPLOM

B53
MENDE T.,WORLD POWER IN THE BALANCE. FUT USA+45 USSR WOR-45 ECO/DEV ECO/TAC INT/TRADE EDU/PROP UTOPIA ATTIT...HUM CONCPT TREND COLD/WAR TOT/POP 20. PAGE 99 A2036
WOR+45 PWR BAL/PWR

S53
BOULDING K.E.,"ECONOMIC ISSUES IN INTERNATIONAL CONFLICT." WOR+45 ECO/DEV NAT/G TOP/EX DIPLOM ECO/TAC DOMIN ATTIT WEALTH...MAJORIT OBS/ENVIR TREND GEN/LAWS COLD/WAR TOT/POP 20. PAGE 17 A0345
PWR FOR/AID

B54
ARON R.,CENTURY OF TOTAL WAR. FUT WOR+45 WOR-45 SOCIETY INT/ORG NAT/G FORCES TOP/EX CREATE BAL/PWR DOMIN EDU/PROP COERCE DETER PEACE TOTALISM PWR ...TIME/SEQ TREND COLD/WAR TOT/POP VAL/FREE LEAGUE/NAT 20. PAGE 9 A0179
ATTIT WAR

B54
BUTZ O.,GERMANY: DILEMMA FOR AMERICAN POLICY. GERMANY USA+45 USA-45 USSR WOR+45 INT/ORG FORCES NUC/PWR EFFICIENCY PEACE PWR...GOV/COMP 20 COLD/WAR. PAGE 23 A0459
DIPLOM NAT/G WAR POLICY

B54
KENNAN G.F.,REALITIES OF AMERICAN FOREIGN POLICY. USA+45 INT/ORG NUC/PWR TOTALISM 20 COLD/WAR. PAGE 77 A1586
DIPLOM BAL/PWR DECISION DETER

B54
MILLARD E.L.,FREEDOM IN A FEDERAL WORLD. FUT WOR+45 VOL/ASSN TOP/EX LEGIT ROUTINE FEDERAL PEACE ATTIT DISPL ORD/FREE PWR...MAJORIT INT/LAW JURID TREND COLD/WAR 20. PAGE 101 A2073
INT/ORG CREATE ADJUD BAL/PWR

B54
STALEY E.,THE FUTURE OF UNDERDEVELOPED COUNTRIES: POLITICAL IMPLICATIONS OF ECONOMIC DEVELOPMENT. COM FUT USA+45 SOCIETY ECO/UNDEV CREATE PLAN CAP/ISM ATTIT DRIVE MARXISM SOCISM...POLICY CONCPT CHARTS COLD/WAR 20. PAGE 137 A2801
EDU/PROP ECO/TAC FOR/AID

B54
STONE J.,LEGAL CONTROLS OF INTERNATIONAL CONFLICT: A TREATISE ON THE DYNAMICS OF DISPUTES AND WAR LAW. WOR+45 WOR-45 NAT/G DIPLOM CT/SYS SOVEREIGN...JURID CONCPT METH/CNCPT GEN/LAWS TOT/POP VAL/FREE COLD/WAR LEAGUE/NAT 20. PAGE 138 A2834
INT/ORG LAW WAR INT/LAW

B54
STRAUSZ-HUPE R.,INTERNATIONAL RELATIONS IN THE AGE OF THE CONFLICT BETWEEN DEMOCRACY AND DICTATORSHIP (2ND ED.). INT/ORG BAL/PWR EDU/PROP ADMIN WAR PEACE PWR...CONCPT CHARTS BIBLIOG 20 COLD/WAR UN LEAGUE/NAT. PAGE 139 A2846
DIPLOM POPULISM MARXISM

S54
FOX W.T.R.,"CIVIL-MILITARY RELATIONS." USA+45 USA-45 R+D ACT/RES DIPLOM INT/TRADE EDU/PROP DETER DISPL DRIVE ORD/FREE...METH/CNCPT TREND COLD/WAR 20. PAGE 48 A0974
POLICY FORCES PLAN SOCIETY

S54
WOLFERS A.,"COLLECTIVE SECURITY AND THE WAR IN KOREA." ASIA KOREA USA+45 INT/ORG DIPLOM ROUTINE ...GEN/LAWS UN COLD/WAR 20. PAGE 166 A3381
ACT/RES LEGIT

B55
JONES J.M.,THE FIFTEEN WEEKS (FEBRUARY 21-JUNE 5, 1947). EUR+WWI USA+45 PROB/SOLV BAL/PWR...POLICY TIME/SEQ 20 COLD/WAR MARSHL/PLN TRUMAN/HS WASHING/DC. PAGE 75 A1532
DIPLOM ECO/TAC FOR/AID

B55
MOCH J.,HUMAN FOLLY: DISARM OR PERISH. USA+45 WOR+45 SOCIETY INT/ORG NAT/G ACT/RES EDU/PROP ATTIT PERSON KNOWL ORD/FREE PWR...MAJORIT TOT/POP COLD/WAR 20. PAGE 102 A2093
FUT DELIB/GP ARMS/CONT NUC/PWR

B55
TANNENBAUM F.,THE AMERICAN TRADITION IN FOREIGN POLICY. USA+45 USA-45 CONSTN INT/ORG NAT/G POL/PAR VOL/ASSN TOP/EX LEGIT DRIVE ORD/FREE PWR...CONCPT GEN/LAWS CONGRESS LEAGUE/NAT COLD/WAR OAS 18/20. PAGE 141 A2887
TIME/SEQ

B56
BLACKETT P.M.S.,ATOMIC WEAPONS AND EAST-WEST RELATIONS. FUT WOR+45 INT/ORG DELIB/GP COERCE ATTIT RIGID/FLEX KNOWL...RELATIV HIST/WRIT TREND GEN/METH COLD/WAR 20. PAGE 15 A0299
FORCES PWR ARMS/CONT NUC/PWR

B56
BOWLES C.,AFRICA'S CHALLENGE TO AMERICA. USA+45 ECO/UNDEV NAT/G LEGIS COLONIAL CONTROL REV ORD/FREE SOVEREIGN 20 COLD/WAR. PAGE 18 A0358
AFR DIPLOM POLICY FOR/AID

B56
GILBERT R.,COMPETITIVE COEXISTENCE: THE NEW SOVIET CHALLENGE. WORKER DIPLOM WAR ORD/FREE 20 COLD/WAR. PAGE 52 A1071
NUC/PWR DOMIN MARXISM PEACE

B56
GOODRICH L.,KOREA: A STUDY OF US POLICY IN THE UNITED NATIONS. ASIA USA+45 STRUCT CONSULT DELIB/GP ATTIT DRIVE PWR...JURID GEN/LAWS COLD/WAR 20 UN. PAGE 54 A1103
INT/ORG DIPLOM KOREA

B56
HAAS E.B.,DYNAMICS OF INTERNATIONAL RELATIONS. WOR-45 ELITES INT/ORG VOL/ASSN EX/STRUC FORCES ECO/TAC DOMIN LEGIT COERCE ATTIT PERSON PWR ...CONCPT TIME/SEQ CHARTS COLD/WAR 20. PAGE 58 A1202
WOR+45 NAT/G DIPLOM

B56
KIRK G.,THE CHANGING ENVIRONMENT OF INTERNATIONAL RELATIONS. ASIA S/ASIA USA+45 WOR+45 ECO/UNDEV INT/ORG NAT/G FOR/AID EDU/PROP PEACE KNOWL ...PLURIST COLD/WAR TOT/POP 20. PAGE 80 A1634
FUT EXEC DIPLOM

B56
KNORR K.E.,RUBLE DIPLOMACY: CHALLENGE TO AMERICAN FOREIGN AID(PAMPHLET). CHINA/COM USA+45 USSR PLAN TEC/DEV CAP/ISM INT/TRADE DOMIN EDU/PROP CONTROL LEAD 20 COLD/WAR. PAGE 81 A1654
ECO/UNDEV COM DIPLOM FOR/AID

B56
REITZEL W.,UNITED STATES FOREIGN POLICY, 1945-1955. USA+45 WOR+45 CONSTN INT/ORG EDU/PROP LEGIT EXEC COERCE NUC/PWR PEACE ATTIT ORD/FREE PWR...DECISION CONCPT OBS RECORD TIME/SEQ TREND COLD/WAR UN CONGRESS. PAGE 120 A2464
NAT/G POLICY DIPLOM

B56
ROBERTS H.L.,RUSSIA AND AMERICA. CHINA/COM S/ASIA USSR FORCES TEC/DEV FOR/AID NUC/PWR ALL/IDEOS ...MAJORIT TREND NAT/COMP 20 COLD/WAR UN NATO. PAGE 122 A2494
DIPLOM INT/ORG BAL/PWR TOTALISM

S56
POTTER P.B.,"NEUTRALITY, 1955." WOR+45 WOR-45 INT/ORG NAT/G WAR ATTIT...POLICY IDEA/COMP 17/20 LEAGUE/NAT UN COLD/WAR. PAGE 117 A2399
NEUTRAL INT/LAW DIPLOM CONCPT

C56
DUPUY R.E.,"MILITARY HERITAGE OF AMERICA." USA+45 USA-45 TEC/DEV DIPLOM ROUTINE...POLICY TREND CHARTS IDEA/COMP BIBLIOG COLD/WAR. PAGE 39 A0804
FORCES WAR CONCPT

B57
BEAL J.R.,JOHN FOSTER DULLES, A BIOGRAPHY. USA+45 USSR WOR+45 CONSTN INT/ORG NAT/G EX/STRUC LEGIT ADMIN NUC/PWR DISPL PERSON ORD/FREE PWR SKILL ...POLICY PSY OBS RECORD COLD/WAR UN 20 DULLES/JF. PAGE 12 A0237
BIOG DIPLOM

B57
BROMBERGER M.,LES SECRETS DE L'EXPEDITION D'EGYPTE. FRANCE ISLAM UAR UK USA+45 USSR WOR+45 INT/ORG NAT/G FORCES BAL/PWR ECO/TAC DOMIN WAR NAT/LISM ATTIT PWR SOVEREIGN...MAJORIT TIME/SEQ CHARTS SUEZ COLD/WAR 20. PAGE 19 A0387
COERCE DIPLOM

B57
COMM. STUDY ORGAN. PEACE,STRENGTHENING THE UNITED NATIONS. FUT USA+45 WOR+45 CONSTN NAT/G DELIB/GP FORCES LEGIS ECO/TAC LEGIT COERCE PEACE...JURID CONCPT UN COLD/WAR 20. PAGE 28 A0580
INT/ORG ORD/FREE

B57
DE VISSCHER C.,THEORY AND REALITY IN PUBLIC INTERNATIONAL LAW. WOR+45 WOR-45 SOCIETY NAT/G CT/SYS ATTIT MORAL ORD/FREE PWR...JURID CONCPT METH/CNCPT TIME/SEQ GEN/LAWS LEAGUE/NAT TOT/POP VAL/FREE COLD/WAR. PAGE 35 A0716
INT/ORG LAW INT/LAW

B57
FURNISS E.S.,AMERICAN MILITARY POLICY: STRATEGIC ASPECTS OF WORLD POLITICAL GEOGRAPHY. COM EUR+WWI ISLAM L/A+17C USA+45 WOR+45 INT/ORG ACT/RES ARMS/CONT COERCE NUC/PWR ATTIT PWR...GEOG NEW/IDEA VAL/FREE COLD/WAR 20. PAGE 50 A1027
FORCES DIPLOM

B57
HOLCOMBE A.N.,STRENGTHENING THE UNITED NATIONS. USA+45 ACT/RES CREATE PLAN EDU/PROP ATTIT PERCEPT PWR...METH/CNCPT CONT/OBS RECORD UN COLD/WAR 20. PAGE 66 A1365
INT/ORG ROUTINE

B57
KENNAN G.F.,RUSSIA, THE ATOM AND THE WEST. COM EUR+WWI FUT WOR+45 SOCIETY ECO/DEV FORCES DIPLOM ECO/TAC DOMIN EDU/PROP COERCE NUC/PWR ATTIT DRIVE ORD/FREE PWR...POLICY OBS TIME/SEQ TREND COLD/WAR NATO 20. PAGE 77 A1574
NAT/G INT/ORG USSR

B57
LEFEVER E.W.,ETHICS AND UNITED STATUS FOREIGN POLICY. SOCIETY INT/ORG NAT/G ACT/RES DIPLOM EDU/PROP COERCE ATTIT MORAL...TREND GEN/LAWS COLD/WAR 20. PAGE 86 A1762
USA+45 CULTURE CONCPT POLICY

B57
SPEIER H.,GERMAN REARMAMENT AND ATOMIC WAR: THE VIEWS OF GERMAN MILITARY AND POLITICAL LEADERS. FUT WOR+45 INT/ORG NAT/G WEAPON ATTIT PWR...INT QU TOT/POP VAL/FREE COLD/WAR 20. PAGE 136 A2780
TOP/EX FORCES NUC/PWR GERMANY

L57
FURNISS E.S.,"SOME PERSPECTIVES ON AMERICAN MILITARY ASSISTANCE." USA+45 WOR+45 ECO/UNDEV INT/ORG ECO/TAC ORD/FREE...GEOG TIME/SEQ TREND COLD/WAR 20. PAGE 50 A1028
FORCES FOR/AID WEAPON

L57
HAAS E.B.,"REGIONAL INTEGRATION AND NATIONAL POLICY." WOR+45 VOL/ASSN DELIB/GP EX/STRUC ECO/TAC DOMIN EDU/PROP LEGIT COERCE ATTIT PERCEPT KNOWL ...TIME/SEQ COLD/WAR 20 UN. PAGE 59 A1203
INT/ORG ORD/FREE REGION

S57
HOAG M.W.,"ECONOMIC PROBLEMS OF ALLIANCE." COM EUR+WWI WOR+45 ECO/DEV ECO/UNDEV NAT/G VOL/ASSN FORCES PLAN TEC/DEV DIPLOM COERCE ORD/FREE PWR WEALTH...DECISION GEN/LAWS NATO COLD/WAR. PAGE 65 A1345
INT/ORG ECO/TAC

S57
SPEIER H.,"SOVIET ATOMIC BLACKMAIL AND THE NORTH ATLANTIC ALLIANCE." EUR+WWI USA+45 USSR INT/ORG NAT/G FORCES DIPLOM DRIVE ORD/FREE PWR NATO VAL/FREE COLD/WAR 20. PAGE 136 A2781
COM COERCE NUC/PWR

S57
WRIGHT Q.,"THE VALUE OF CONFLICT RESOLUTION OF A GENERAL DISCIPLINE OF INTERNATIONAL RELATIONS." WOR+45 SOCIETY INT/ORG NAT/G FORCES TOP/EX PLAN TEC/DEV ECO/TAC DOMIN LEGIT COERCE ATTIT PWR ...GEN/METH COLD/WAR VAL/FREE. PAGE 168 A3412
ORD/FREE SOC DIPLOM

B58
ANGELL N.,DEFENCE AND THE ENGLISH-SPEAKING ROLE. CHINA/COM UK USSR INT/ORG FORCES EDU/PROP NEUTRAL NUC/PWR NAT/LISM PEACE TOTALISM 20 COLD/WAR COEXIST. PAGE 8 A0161
DIPLOM WAR MARXISM ORD/FREE

B58
APPADORAI A.,THE USE OF FORCE IN INTERNATIONAL RELATIONS. WOR+45 CULTURE ECO/UNDEV CAP/ISM ARMS/CONT REV WAR ATTIT PERSON SOVEREIGN MARXISM ...INT/LAW PACIFIST 20 UN INTERVENT THIRD/WRLD COLD/WAR. PAGE 8 A0169
PEACE FEDERAL INT/ORG

B58
BOWLES C.,IDEAS, PEOPLE AND PEACE. ASIA CHINA/COM FUT INDIA USA+45 USSR ECO/UNDEV INT/ORG LEAD TASK MARXISM 20 NATO UN COLD/WAR. PAGE 18 A0359
PEACE POLICY NAT/G DIPLOM

B58
CAMPBELL J.C.,DEFENSE OF THE MIDDLE EAST: PROBLEMS OF AMERICAN POLICY. ISLAM USA+45 INT/ORG NAT/G EX/STRUC FORCES ECO/TAC DOMIN EDU/PROP LEGIT REGION COERCE...METH/CNCPT COLD/WAR TOT/POP 20. PAGE 23 A0474
TOP/EX ORD/FREE DIPLOM

B58
GAVIN J.M.,WAR AND PEACE IN THE SPACE AGE. SPACE USA+45 USSR FORCES PLAN TEC/DEV BAL/PWR DIPLOM ARMS/CONT WEAPON CIVMIL/REL...CHARTS GP/COMP 20 NATO COLD/WAR. PAGE 52 A1055
WAR DETER NUC/PWR PEACE

B58
HAUSER P.H.,POPULATION AND WORLD POLITICS. FUT WOR+45 WOR-45 AGRI DIST/IND INDUS INT/ORG PLAN ECO/TAC DISPL HEALTH COLD/WAR 20. PAGE 63 A1288
NAT/G ECO/UNDEV FOR/AID

B58
HOLT R.T.,RADIO FREE EUROPE. FUT USA+45 CULTURE ECO/DEV INT/ORG KIN POL/PAR SECT FORCES ACT/RES DIPLOM COERCE REV CHOOSE PEACE ATTIT PWR...MAJORIT CONCPT COLD/WAR WORK 20 RFE. PAGE 67 A1374
COM EDU/PROP COM/IND

B58
MILLIS W.,FOREIGN POLICY AND THE FREE SOCIETY. USA+45 WOR+45 SOCIETY NAT/G FORCES BAL/PWR FOR/AID EDU/PROP DETER ATTIT PWR 20 COLD/WAR. PAGE 102 A2084
DIPLOM POLICY ORD/FREE CONSULT

B58
NATIONAL PLANNING ASSOCIATION,1970 WITHOUT ARMS CONTROL (PAMPHLET). WOR+45 PROB/SOLV TEC/DEV DIPLOM CONFER DETER NUC/PWR WAR...CHARTS 20 COLD/WAR. PAGE 107 A2204
ARMS/CONT ORD/FREE WEAPON PREDICT

B58
NOEL-BAKER D.,THE ARMS RACE. WOR+45 NAT/G DELIB/GP ACT/RES TEC/DEV EDU/PROP NUC/PWR ATTIT KNOWL PWR ...CONCPT OBS LEAGUE/NAT 20 COLD/WAR. PAGE 109 A2245
FUT INT/ORG ARMS/CONT PEACE

B58
RIGGS R.,POLITICS IN THE UNITED NATIONS: A STUDY OF UNITED STATES INFLUENCE IN THE GENERAL ASSEMBLY. USA+45 WOR+45 LEGIS TOP/EX CREATE BAL/PWR DIPLOM DOMIN EDU/PROP COLONIAL ROUTINE ATTIT RIGID/FLEX PWR...CONCPT OBS HIST/WRIT CHARTS STERTYP GEN/LAWS UN COLD/WAR 20. PAGE 121 A2480
INT/ORG

L58
SNYDER R.N.,"THE UNITED STATES DECISION TO RESIST AGGRESSION IN KOREA." ASIA KOREA S/ASIA USA+45 USA-45 WOR+45 INT/ORG DELIB/GP BAL/PWR COERCE PWR ...CONCPT REC/INT RESIST/INT COLD/WAR 20. PAGE 134 A2753
QUANT METH/CNCPT DIPLOM

S58
BOGART L.,"MEASURING THE EFFECTIVENESS OF AN OVERSEAS INFORMATION CAMPAIGN." EUR+WWI GREECE USA+45 INT/ORG MUNIC PLAN DIPLOM PEACE PERCEPT RIGID/FLEX KNOWL...TECHNIC PSY SOC NEW/IDEA CONT/OBS REC/INT STAND/INT SAMP/SIZ COLD/WAR 20. PAGE 16 A0328
ATTIT EDU/PROP

S58
BOURBON-BUSSET J.,"HOW DECISIONS ARE MADE IN FOREIGN POLITICS: PSYCHOLOGY IN INTERNATIONAL POLITICS." WOR+45 NAT/G SECT REGION WAR MORAL ...CONCPT OBS STERTYP GEN/LAWS TOT/POP COLD/WAR 20. PAGE 17 A0350
INT/ORG DELIB/GP DIPLOM

S58
DAVENPORT J.,"ARMS AND THE WELFARE STATE." INTELL STRUCT FORCES CREATE ECO/TAC FOR/AID DOMIN LEGIT ADMIN WAR ORD/FREE PWR...POLICY SOC CONCPT MYTH OBS TREND COLD/WAR TOT/POP 20. PAGE 34 A0685
USA+45 NAT/G USSR

S58
THOMPSON K.W.,"NATIONAL SECURITY IN A NUCLEAR AGE." USA+45 WOR+45 SOCIETY INT/ORG NAT/G TOP/EX DIPLOM DOMIN EDU/PROP LEGIT ARMS/CONT COERCE ORD/FREE ...TREND STERTYP TOT/POP VAL/FREE COLD/WAR 20. PAGE 143 A2929
FORCES PWR BAL/PWR

B59
BALL M.M.,NATO AND THE EUROPEAN MOVEMENT. EUR+WWI USA+45 INT/ORG FORCES BAL/PWR EDU/PROP LEGIT REGION ATTIT ORD/FREE PWR...STAT OBS TIME/SEQ TREND CHARTS ORG/CHARTS STERTYP COLD/WAR EEC OEEC 20 NATO. PAGE 10 A0212
DELIB/GP STRUCT

B59
COMM. STUDY ORGAN. PEACE,ORGANIZING PEACE IN THE NUCLEAR AGE. FUT CONSULT DELIB/GP DOMIN ADJUD ROUTINE COERCE ORD/FREE...TECHNIC INT/LAW JURID NEW/IDEA UN COLD/WAR 20. PAGE 29 A0581
INT/ORG ACT/RES NUC/PWR

B59
FREE L.A.,SIX ALLIES AND A NEUTRAL. ASIA COM EUR+WWI FRANCE GERMANY/W INDIA S/ASIA UK USA+45 INT/ORG NAT/G NUC/PWR PEACE ATTIT PERCEPT RIGID/FLEX ALL/VALS...STAT REC/INT COLD/WAR 20 CHINJAP. PAGE 48 A0992
PSY DIPLOM

B59
GORDENKER L.,THE UNITED NATIONS AND THE PEACEFUL UNIFICATION OF KOREA. ASIA LAW LOC/G CONSULT ACT/RES DIPLOM DOMIN LEGIT ADJUD ADMIN ORD/FREE SOVEREIGN...INT GEN/METH UN COLD/WAR 20. PAGE 54 A1109
DELIB/GP KOREA INT/ORG

B59
GOULD L.P.,THE PRICE OF SURVIVAL. EUR+WWI SPACE USA+45 FORCES ECO/TAC NUC/PWR WAR ORD/FREE MARXISM ...IDEA/COMP 20 COLD/WAR NATO. PAGE 54 A1117
POLICY PROB/SOLV DIPLOM PEACE

B59
HERZ J.H.,INTERNATIONAL POLITICS IN THE ATOMIC AGE. FUT USA+45 WOR+45 WOR-45 SOCIETY NAT/G FORCES PLAN COERCE DETER ATTIT DRIVE ORD/FREE PWR...TREND COLD/WAR 20. PAGE 64 A1319
INT/ORG ARMS/CONT NUC/PWR

B59
HUGHES E.M.,AMERICA THE VINCIBLE. USA+45 FOR/AID ARMS/CONT NUC/PWR PERS/REL RATIONAL ATTIT ALL/VALS 20 COLD/WAR. PAGE 69 A1413
ORD/FREE DIPLOM WAR

B59
LAQUER W.Z.,THE SOVIET UNION AND THE MIDDLE EAST. COM UAR USSR ECO/UNDEV NAT/G VOL/ASSN ECO/TAC EDU/PROP COLONIAL EXEC PWR...TIME/SEQ TREND COLD/WAR 20. PAGE 85 A1730
ISLAM DRIVE FOR/AID NAT/LISM

B59
NIEBUHR R.,NATIONS AND EMPIRES. WOR+45 INT/ORG COLONIAL NUC/PWR TOTALISM UTOPIA ORD/FREE MARXISM WORSHIP 20 COLD/WAR PROTESTANT CHRISTIAN. PAGE 109 A2237
DIPLOM NAT/G POLICY PWR

B59
SHANNON D.A.,THE DECLINE OF AMERICAN COMMUNISM; A HISTORY OF THE COMMUNIST PARTY OF THE UNITED STATES SINCE 1945. USA+45 LAW SOCIETY LABOR NAT/G WORKER DIPLOM EDU/PROP LEAD...POLICY BIBLIOG 20 KHRUSH/N NEGRO AFL/CIO COLD/WAR COM/PARTY. PAGE 131 A2692
MARXISM POL/PAR ATTIT POPULISM

B59
STRAUSZ-HUPE R.,PROTRACTED CONFLICT. CHINA/COM KOREA WOR+45 INT/ORG FORCES ACT/RES ECO/TAC LEGIT COERCE DRIVE PERCEPT KNOWL PWR...PSY CONCPT RECORD GEN/METH COLD/WAR VAL/FREE 20. PAGE 139 A2847
COM PLAN USSR

B59
THOMAS N.,THE PREREQUISITES FOR PEACE. ASIA EUR+WWI FUT ISLAM S/ASIA WOR+45 FORCES PLAN BAL/PWR EDU/PROP LEGIT ATTIT PWR...SOCIALIST CONCPT COLD/WAR 20 UN. PAGE 143 A2924
INT/ORG ORD/FREE ARMS/CONT PEACE

B59
WOLFERS A.,ALLIANCE POLICY IN THE COLD WAR. COM INT/ORG FORCES COLONIAL CONTROL NUC/PWR 20 NATO UN COLD/WAR. PAGE 166 A3384
DIPLOM DETER BAL/PWR

B59
YRARRAZAVAL E.,AMERICA LATINE EN LA GUERRA FRIA. EUR+WWI L/A+17C USA+45 USSR WOR+45 INDUS INT/ORG NAT/LISM...POLICY COLD/WAR. PAGE 169 A3439
REGION DIPLOM ECO/UNDEV INT/TRADE

L59
GARDNER R.N.,"NEW DIRECTIONS IN UNITED STATES FOREIGN ECONOMIC POLICY." USA+45 CONSULT...GEN/LAWS GEN/METH COLD/WAR 20. PAGE 51 A1044
ECO/UNDEV ECO/TAC FOR/AID DIPLOM

S59
FISCHER L.,"THE SOVIET-AMERICAN ANTAGONISM: HOW WILL IT END." CONSTN CULTURE PLAN TEC/DEV RIGID/FLEX SUPEGO ORD/FREE...MARXIST DECISION PSY CONCPT CON/ANAL GEN/LAWS VAL/FREE 20 COLD/WAR. PAGE 46 A0936
USA+45 PWR DIPLOM USSR

S59
HOFFMANN S.,"IMPLEMENTATION OF INTERNATIONAL INSTRUMENTS ON HUMAN RIGHTS." WOR+45 VOL/ASSN DELIB/GP JUDGE EDU/PROP LEGIT ROUTINE PEACE COLD/WAR 20. PAGE 66 A1355
INT/ORG MORAL

S59
KISSINGER H.A.,"THE SEARCH FOR STABILITY." COM GERMANY MOD/EUR USA+45 USA-45 USSR INT/ORG ARMS/CONT NUC/PWR ORD/FREE PWR COLD/WAR 20 NATO. PAGE 80 A1641
FUT ATTIT BAL/PWR

S59
SAYEGH F.,"ARAB NATIONALISM AND SOVIET-AMERICAN RELATIONS." ISLAM USA+45 ECO/UNDEV PLAN ECO/TAC LEGIT NAT/LISM DRIVE PERCEPT KNOWL PWR...DECISION CONCPT STAT RECORD TREND CON/ANAL VAL/FREE 20 COLD/WAR. PAGE 127 A2610
DIPLOM USSR

S59
SOHN L.B.,"THE DEFINITION OF AGGRESSION." FUT LAW FORCES LEGIT ADJUD ROUTINE COERCE ORD/FREE PWR ...MAJORIT JURID QUANT COLD/WAR 20. PAGE 135 A2762
INT/ORG CT/SYS DETER SOVEREIGN

B60
ALLEN H.C.,THE ANGLO-AMERICAN PREDICAMENT: THE BRITISH COMMONWEALTH, THE UNITED STATES AND EUROPEAN UNITY. EUR+WWI FUT UK USA+45 WOR+45 ECO/DEV NAT/G PLAN DETER...CONCPT OBS TIME/SEQ TREND COLD/WAR VAL/FREE CMN/WLTH 20. PAGE 6 A0123
INT/ORG PWR BAL/PWR

B60
BAILEY S.D.,THE GENERAL ASSEMBLY OF THE UNITED NATIONS. FUT WOR+45 STRUCT LEGIS ACT/RES PLAN EDU/PROP LEGIT ADMIN EXEC PEACE ATTIT HEALTH PWR ...CONCPT TREND CHARTS GEN/LAWS UN TOT/POP VAL/FREE COLD/WAR 20. PAGE 10 A0204
INT/ORG DELIB/GP DIPLOM

B60
BARNET R.,WHO WANTS DISARMAMENT. COM EUR+WWI USA+45 USSR INT/ORG NAT/G BAL/PWR DIPLOM EDU/PROP COERCE DETER NUC/PWR WAR WEAPON ATTIT PWR...TIME/SEQ COLD/WAR CONGRESS 20. PAGE 11 A0225
PLAN FORCES ARMS/CONT

B60
BROOKINGS INSTITUTION,UNITED STATES FOREIGN POLICY: STUDY NO 9: THE FORMULATION AND ADMINISTRATION OF UNITED STATES FOREIGN POLICY. USA+45 WOR+45 EX/STRUC LEGIS BAL/PWR FOR/AID EDU/PROP CIVMIL/REL GOV/REL...INT COLD/WAR. PAGE 19 A0394
DIPLOM INT/ORG CREATE

B60
BUCHAN A.,NATO IN THE 1960'S. EUR+WWI USA+45 WOR+45 INT/ORG ACT/RES PLAN LEGIT COERCE DETER ATTIT DRIVE RIGID/FLEX ORD/FREE...METH/CNCPT TIME/SEQ TREND GEN/LAWS COLD/WAR 20 NATO. PAGE 21 A0421
VOL/ASSN FORCES ARMS/CONT SOVEREIGN

B60
CAMPAIGNE J.G.,AMERICAN MIGHT AND SOVIET MYTH. COM EUR+WWI ECO/DEV ECO/UNDEV INT/ORG NAT/G CAP/ISM ECO/TAC FOR/AID EDU/PROP ATTIT PWR WEALTH...POLICY CONCPT MYTH TREND STERTYP GEN/LAWS COLD/WAR. PAGE 23 A0473
USA+45 DOMIN DIPLOM USSR

B60
DEUTSCHER I.,THE GREAT CONTEST: RUSSIA AND THE WEST. USA+45 USSR SOCIETY INDUS ARMS/CONT ATTIT ...CONCPT IDEA/COMP 20 COLD/WAR. PAGE 37 A0749
PEACE DIPLOM PWR

B60
DUCHACEK I.D.,CONFLICT AND COOPERATION AMONG NATIONS. WOR+45 WOR-45 SOCIETY NAT/G DOMIN DETER PWR SKILL COLD/WAR 20. PAGE 39 A0791
INT/ORG BAL/PWR DIPLOM

B60
EINSTEIN A.,EINSTEIN ON PEACE. FUT WOR+45 WOR-45 SOCIETY NAT/G PLAN BAL/PWR CAP/ISM DIPLOM ARMS/CONT DETER NAT/LISM...POLICY RELATIV HUM PHIL/SCI CONCPT BIOG COLD/WAR LEAGUE/NAT NAZI. PAGE 41 A0829
INT/ORG ATTIT NUC/PWR PEACE

B60
ENGEL J.,THE SECURITY OF THE FREE WORLD. USSR WOR+45 STRATA STRUCT ECO/DEV ECO/UNDEV INT/ORG DELIB/GP FORCES DOMIN LEGIT ADJUD EXEC ARMS/CONT COERCE...POLICY CONCPT NEW/IDEA TIME/SEQ GEN/LAWS COLD/WAR WORK UN 20 NATO. PAGE 42 A0851
COM TREND DIPLOM

B60
FISCHER L.,RUSSIA, AMERICA, AND THE WORLD. FUT USA+45 USSR WOR+45 FORCES PLAN BAL/PWR ECO/TAC FOR/AID NEUTRAL TASK NUC/PWR PWR 20 COLD/WAR. PAGE 46 A0937
DIPLOM POLICY MARXISM ECO/UNDEV

B60
FRANCK P.G.,AFGHANISTAN: BETWEEN EAST AND WEST. AFGHANISTN USA+45 USSR ECO/UNDEV PLAN ADMIN ROUTINE ATTIT PWR...STAT OBS CHARTS TOT/POP COLD/WAR 20. PAGE 48 A0978
ECO/TAC TREND FOR/AID

B60
HOLT R.T.,STRATEGIC PSYCHOLOGICAL OPERATIONS AND AMERICAN FOREIGN POLICY. ITALY USA+45 FOR/AID DOMIN RUMOR ADMIN TASK WAR CHOOSE ATTIT ALL/IDEOS...PSY COLD/WAR. PAGE 67 A1375
EDU/PROP ACT/RES DIPLOM POLICY

B60
KARDELJE,SOCIALISM AND WAR. CHINA/COM WOR+45 YUGOSLAVIA DIPLOM EDU/PROP ATTIT...POLICY CONCPT IDEA/COMP COLD/WAR. PAGE 76 A1565
MARXIST WAR MARXISM BAL/PWR

B60
KENEN P.B.,GIANT AMONG NATIONS: PROBLEMS IN UNITED STATES FOREIGN ECONOMIC POLICY. USA+45 FINAN DIPLOM TARIFFS BAL/PAY WEALTH 20 COLD/WAR. PAGE 77 A1584
FOR/AID ECO/UNDEV INT/TRADE PLAN

B60
KHRUSHCHEV N.,FOR VICTORY IN PEACEFUL COMPETITION WITH CAPITALISM. COM FUT USSR WOR+45 CONSTN SOCIETY INDUS INT/ORG DELIB/GP PLAN BAL/PWR DIPLOM PERSON MARXISM...MARXIST WORK 20 COLD/WAR. PAGE 79 A1611
TOP/EX PWR CAP/ISM SOCISM

B60
KHRUSHCHEV N.S.,KHRUSHCHEV IN AMERICA. USA+45 USSR INT/TRADE EDU/PROP PRESS PEACE...MARXIST RECORD INT 20 COLD/WAR KHRUSH/N. PAGE 79 A1613
MARXISM CHIEF DIPLOM

B60
LISKA G.,THE NEW STATECRAFT. WOR+45 WOR-45 LEGIS DIPLOM ADMIN ATTIT PWR WEALTH...HIST/WRIT TREND COLD/WAR 20. PAGE 90 A1837
ECO/TAC CONCPT FOR/AID

B60
MC CLELLAN G.S.,INDIA. CHINA/COM INDIA CONSTN ELITES STRATA AGRI POL/PAR FOR/AID ARMS/CONT REV MARXISM...CENSUS BIBLIOG 20 COLD/WAR GANDHI/M NEHRU/J. PAGE 97 A1990
DIPLOM NAT/G SOCIETY ECO/UNDEV

B60
MCCLELLAND C.A.,NUCLEAR WEAPONS, MISSILES, AND FUTURE WAR: PROBLEM FOR THE SIXTIES. WOR+45 FORCES ARMS/CONT DETER MARXISM...POLICY ANTHOL COLD/WAR. PAGE 97 A1998
DIPLOM NUC/PWR WAR WEAPON

B60
MONTGOMERY B.L.,AN APPROACH TO SANITY; A STUDY OF EAST-WEST RELATIONS. CONFER WAR EFFICIENCY ATTIT ...POLICY 20 NATO COLD/WAR KHRUSH/N. PAGE 103 A2113
DIPLOM INT/ORG BAL/PWR DETER

B60
MOSELY P.E.,THE KREMLIN AND WORLD POLITICS. EUR+WWI GERMANY USA+45 USSR CHIEF TOP/EX BAL/PWR DOMIN PEACE PWR...METH 20 COLD/WAR STALIN/J EUROPE/E. PAGE 105 A2151
COM DIPLOM POLICY WAR

B60
SPEIER H.,DIVIDED BERLIN: THE ANATOMY OF SOVIET POLITICAL BLACKMAIL. COM GERMANY USA+45 USSR WOR+45 NAT/G TOP/EX DOMIN EDU/PROP ALL/VALS...POLICY CONCPT COLD/WAR 20 U-2. PAGE 136 A2782
INT/ORG ACT/RES DIPLOM

B60
STOLPER W.F.,GERMANY BETWEEN EAST AND WEST: THE ECONOMICS OF COMPETITIVE COEXISTENCE. FUT GERMANY/E GERMANY/W WOR+45 FINAN POL/PAR BUDGET ECO/TAC FOR/AID INT/TRADE...STAT CHARTS METH/COMP 20
ECO/DEV DIPLOM GOV/COMP BAL/PWR

COLD/WAR. PAGE 138 A2832

B60
TAYLOR M.D.,THE UNCERTAIN TRUMPET. USA+45 USSR WOR+45 INT/ORG NAT/G CONSULT DOMIN COERCE NUC/PWR WAR ATTIT ORD/FREE PWR...POLICY CONCPT TREND GEN/METH COLD/WAR UN NATO 20. PAGE 142 A2900
PLAN FORCES DIPLOM

B60
TURNER G.B.,NATIONAL SECURITY IN THE NUCLEAR AGE. KOREA USA+45 PLAN DIPLOM ARMS/CONT DETER WAR WEAPON ...BIBLIOG 20 COLD/WAR NATO. PAGE 146 A2982
NAT/G POLICY FORCES NUC/PWR

B60
US DEPARTMENT OF THE ARMY,DISARMAMENT: A BIBLIOGRAPHIC RECORD: 1916-1960. DETER WAR WEAPON PEACE 20 UN LEAGUE/NAT COLD/WAR NATO. PAGE 152 A3103
BIBLIOG/A ARMS/CONT NUC/PWR DIPLOM

L60
BRENNAN D.G.,"SETTING AND GOALS OF ARMS CONTROL." FUT USA+45 USSR WOR+45 INTELL INT/ORG NAT/G VOL/ASSN CONSULT PLAN DIPLOM ECO/TAC ADMIN KNOWL PWR...POLICY CONCPT TREND COLD/WAR 20. PAGE 18 A0371
FORCES COERCE ARMS/CONT DETER

L60
FERNBACH A.P.,"SOVIET COEXISTENCE STRATEGY." WOR+45 PROF/ORG VOL/ASSN DIPLOM DOMIN EDU/PROP ATTIT DRIVE PERSON PWR SKILL WEALTH...POLICY OBS SAMP TREND STERTYP ILO WORK COLD/WAR 420. PAGE 45 A0919
LABOR INT/ORG USSR

L60
HOLTON G.,"ARMS CONTROL." FUT WOR+45 CULTURE INT/ORG NAT/G FORCES TOP/EX PLAN EDU/PROP COERCE ATTIT RIGID/FLEX ORD/FREE...POLICY PHIL/SCI SOC TREND COLD/WAR. PAGE 67 A1377
ACT/RES CONSULT ARMS/CONT NUC/PWR

L60
JACOB P.E.,"THE DISARMAMENT CONSENSUS." USA+45 USSR WOR+45 INT/ORG NAT/G ACT/RES TEC/DEV BAL/PWR EDU/PROP ADMIN COERCE DETER NUC/PWR CONSEN RIGID/FLEX PWR...CONCPT RECORD CHARTS COLD/WAR 20. PAGE 72 A1482
DELIB/GP ATTIT ARMS/CONT

L60
NOGEE J.L.,"THE DIPLOMACY OF DISARMAMENT." WOR+45 INT/ORG NAT/G CONSULT DELIB/GP TOP/EX BAL/PWR DIPLOM EDU/PROP COERCE DETER WEAPON PEACE ATTIT ...RECORD TIME/SEQ TOT/POP VAL/FREE COLD/WAR 20. PAGE 109 A2246
PWR ORD/FREE ARMS/CONT NUC/PWR

S60
DOUGHERTY J.E.,"KEY TO SECURITY: DISARMAMENT OR ARMS STABILITY." COM USA+45 USSR INT/ORG NAT/G CREATE EDU/PROP COERCE DETER ATTIT PWR...DECISION CONCPT MYTH NEW/IDEA TREND 20 COLD/WAR. PAGE 38 A0777
FORCES ORD/FREE ARMS/CONT NUC/PWR

S60
HAVILAND H.F.,"PROBLEMS OF AMERICAN FOREIGN POLICY." ASIA COM USA+45 WOR+45 INT/ORG NAT/G CONSULT ECO/TAC FOR/AID DOMIN COERCE NUC/PWR ATTIT DRIVE ORD/FREE PWR RESPECT SKILL...POLICY GEOG OBS SAMP TREND GEN/METH METH COLD/WAR UN 20. PAGE 63 A1292
ECO/UNDEV FORCES DIPLOM

S60
JACOBSON H.K.,"THE USSR AND ILO." COM STRUCT ECO/DEV ECO/UNDEV CONSULT DELIB/GP ECO/TAC ILO WORK COLD/WAR 20. PAGE 72 A1484
INT/ORG LABOR USSR

S60
KALUODA J.,"COMMUNIST STRATEGY IN LATIN AMERICA." L/A+17C USA+45 INT/ORG NAT/G POL/PAR DIPLOM ECO/TAC EDU/PROP COERCE WEALTH...CONCPT OAS COLD/WAR 20. PAGE 76 A1553
COM PWR CUBA

S60
KENNAN G.F.,"PEACEFUL CO-EXISTENCE: A WESTERN VIEW." COM EUR+WWI USA+45 USSR WOR+45 PLAN BAL/PWR DIPLOM INT/TRADE PWR...POLICY CONCPT OBS HIST/WRIT TREND GEN/LAWS COLD/WAR 20 KHRUSH/N. PAGE 78 A1589
ATTIT COERCE

S60
KISTIAKOWSKY G.B.,"SCIENCE AND FOREIGN AFFAIRS." FUT WOR+45 NAT/G PROF/ORG PLAN ECO/TAC EDU/PROP NUC/PWR...TREND COLD/WAR 20. PAGE 80 A1645
CONSULT TEC/DEV FOR/AID DIPLOM

S60
LYON P.,"NEUTRALITY AND THE EMERGENCE OF THE CONCEPT OF NEUTRALISM." WOR+45 WOR-45 INT/ORG NAT/G BAL/PWR NEUTRAL ATTIT PWR...POLICY TIME/SEQ TREND COLD/WAR TOT/POP VAL/FREE 20 UN. PAGE 92 A1878
CONCPT

S60
MURPHY J.C.,"INTERNATIONAL INVESTMENT AND THE NATIONAL INTEREST." WOR+45 WOR-45 ECO/DEV ECO/UNDEV NAT/G ACT/RES...CHARTS TOT/POP COLD/WAR 20. PAGE 106 A2179
FINAN WEALTH FOR/AID

S60
PETERSON E.N.,"HISTORICAL SCHOLARSHIP AND WORLD UNITY." FUT UNIV WOR-45 CULTURE INTELL INT/ORG NAT/G ACT/RES EDU/PROP ATTIT PERCEPT RIGID/FLEX ...NEW/IDEA OBS HIST/WRIT TREND COLD/WAR TOT/POP 20. PAGE 115 A2367
PLAN KNOWL NAT/LISM

S60
POTTER P.B.,"RELATIVE VALUES OF INTERNATIONAL RELATIONS, LAW, AND ORGANIZATIONS." WOR+45 NAT/G LEGIT ADJUD ORD/FREE...CONCPT TOT/POP COLD/WAR 20. PAGE 117 A2401
INT/ORG LEGIS DIPLOM INT/LAW

S60
RHYNE C.S.,"LAW AS AN INSTRUMENT FOR PEACE." FUT WOR+45 PLAN LEGIT ROUTINE ARMS/CONT NUC/PWR ATTIT ORD/FREE...JURID METH/CNCPT TREND CON/ANAL HYPO/EXP COLD/WAR 20. PAGE 120 A2471
ADJUD EDU/PROP INT/LAW PEACE

S60
RUSSEL R.W.,"ROLES FOR PSYCHOLOGISTS IN THE MAINTENANCE OF PEACE." FUT USA+45 CULTURE INT/ORG DIPLOM FOR/AID EDU/PROP ATTIT KNOWL MORAL PWR ...POLICY SOC COLD/WAR 20. PAGE 125 A2572
PSY GEN/METH

S60
WRIGHT Q.,"LEGAL ASPECTS OF THE U-2 INCIDENT." COM USA+45 USSR STRUCT NAT/G FORCES PLAN TEC/DEV ADJUD RIGID/FLEX MORAL ORD/FREE...DECISION INT/LAW JURID PSY TREND GEN/LAWS COLD/WAR VAL/FREE 20 U-2. PAGE 168 A3413
PWR POLICY SPACE

B61
AUBREY H.G.,COEXISTENCE: ECONOMIC CHALLENGE AND RESPONSE. USSR WOR+45 ACT/RES BAL/PWR CAP/ISM DIPLOM ECO/TAC FOR/AID INT/TRADE PEACE SOCISM ...METH/COMP NAT/COMP COLD/WAR. PAGE 10 A0196
POLICY ECO/UNDEV PLAN COM

B61
BECHHOEFER B.G.,POSTWAR NEGOTIATIONS FOR ARMS CONTROL. COM EUR+WWI USSR INT/ORG NAT/G ACT/RES BAL/PWR DIPLOM ECO/TAC EDU/PROP ADMIN REGION DETER NUC/PWR WAR WEAPON PEACE ATTIT PWR...POLICY TIME/SEQ COLD/WAR CONGRESS 20. PAGE 12 A0244
USA+45 ARMS/CONT

B61
BULL H.,THE CONTROL OF THE ARMS RACE. COM USA+45 INT/ORG NAT/G PLAN TEC/DEV DIPLOM ATTIT...RELATIV DECISION CONCPT SELF/OBS TREND CON/ANAL GEN/METH 20 COLD/WAR. PAGE 21 A0429
FORCES PWR ARMS/CONT NUC/PWR

B61
CONFERENCE ATLANTIC COMMUNITY,AN INTRODUCTORY BIBLIOGRAPHY. COM WOR+45 FORCES DIPLOM ECO/TAC WAR ...INT/LAW HIST/WRIT COLD/WAR NATO. PAGE 29 A0584
BIBLIOG/A CON/ANAL INT/ORG

B61
DEAN V.M.,BUILDERS OF EMERGING NATIONS. WOR+45 ECO/UNDEV ECO/TAC NEUTRAL TOTALISM ORD/FREE PWR ...BIOG AUD/VIS IDEA/COMP BIBLIOG 20 COLD/WAR. PAGE 35 A0719
NAT/G CHIEF POLICY DIPLOM

B61
EISENHOWER D.D.,PEACE WITH JUSTICE: SELECTED ADDRESSES. USSR PARTIC ARMS/CONT MORAL...TRADIT CONCPT GEN/LAWS ANTHOL 20 PRESIDENT COLD/WAR. PAGE 41 A0832
PEACE DIPLOM EDU/PROP POLICY

B61
FLEMING D.F.,THE COLD WAR AND ITS ORIGINS: 1950-1960 (VOL. II). ASIA FUT HUNGARY POLAND WOR+45 TEC/DEV DOMIN NUC/PWR REV PEACE...T 20 COLD/WAR EISNHWR/DD SUEZ. PAGE 46 A0946
MARXISM DIPLOM BAL/PWR

B61
FLEMING D.F.,THE COLD WAR AND ITS ORIGINS: 1917-1950 (VOL. I). ASIA USSR WOR+45 WOR-45 TEC/DEV FOR/AID NUC/PWR REV WAR PEACE FASCISM...T 20 COLD/WAR NATO BERLIN/BLO. PAGE 46 A0947
DIPLOM MARXISM BAL/PWR

B61
FULLER J.F.C.,THE CONDUCT OF WAR, 1789-1961. FRANCE RUSSIA SOCIETY NAT/G FORCES PROB/SOLV AGREE NUC/PWR WEAPON PEACE...SOC 18/20 TREATY COLD/WAR. PAGE 50 A1025
WAR POLICY REV ROLE

B61
HARDT J.P.,THE COLD WAR ECONOMIC GAP. USA+45 USSR ECO/DEV FORCES INT/TRADE NUC/PWR PWR 20 COLD/WAR. PAGE 61 A1258
DIPLOM ECO/TAC NAT/COMP POLICY

B61
HENKIN L.,ARMS CONTROL: ISSUES FOR THE PUBLIC. EUR+WWI FUT USA+45 USSR INT/ORG NAT/G DIPLOM EDU/PROP DETER NUC/PWR ATTIT PWR...CONCPT RECORD HIST/WRIT TIME/SEQ TOT/POP COLD/WAR 20. PAGE 64 A1316
WOR+45 DELIB/GP ARMS/CONT

B61
KERTESZ S.D.,AMERICAN DIPLOMACY IN A NEW ERA. COM S/ASIA UK USA+45 FORCES PROB/SOLV BAL/PWR ECO/TAC ADMIN COLONIAL WAR PEACE ORD/FREE 20 NATO CONGRESS UN COLD/WAR. PAGE 78 A1601
ANTHOL DIPLOM TREND

B61
KISSINGER H.A.,THE NECESSITY FOR CHOICE. FUT USA+45 ECO/UNDEV NAT/G PLAN BAL/PWR ECO/TAC ARMS/CONT DETER NUC/PWR ATTIT...POLICY CONCPT RECORD GEN/LAWS COLD/WAR 20. PAGE 80 A1642
TOP/EX TREND DIPLOM

B61
LERCHE C.O. JR.,FOREIGN POLICY OF THE AMERICAN PEOPLE (REV. ED.). USA+45 USSR FORCES TEC/DEV EDU/PROP WAR PRODUC ORD/FREE MARXISM...POLICY TREND BIBLIOG 20 COLD/WAR. PAGE 87 A1781
DECISION PLAN PEACE DIPLOM

B61
LUKACS J.,A HISTORY OF THE COLD WAR. ASIA COM EUR+WWI USA+45 USA-45 INT/ORG NAT/G DELIB/GP ACT/RES BAL/PWR DIPLOM DOMIN EDU/PROP LEGIT DRIVE ORD/FREE...TREND COLD/WAR 20. PAGE 91 A1872
PWR TIME/SEQ USSR

B61
NOLLAU G.,INTERNATIONAL COMMUNISM AND WORLD REVOLUTION: HISTORY AND METHODS. RUSSIA USSR
COM REV

INT/ORG NAT/G POL/PAR VOL/ASSN FORCES BAL/PWR DIPLOM EXEC REGION WAR ATTIT PWR MARXISM...CONCPT TIME/SEQ COLD/WAR 19/20. PAGE 102 A2100

B61
MORLEY L.,THE PATCHWORK HISTORY OF FOREIGN AID. KOREA/S USA+45 USSR LAW FINAN INT/ORG TEC/DEV BAL/PWR GIVE 20 COLD/WAR NATO. PAGE 104 A2144 FOR/AID ECO/UNDEV FORCES DIPLOM

B61
MORRAY J.P.,FROM YALTA TO DISARMAMENT: COLD WAR DEBATE. USA+45 CAP/ISM FOR/AID CONTROL NUC/PWR 20 UN COLD/WAR CHURCHLL/W. PAGE 104 A2145 MARXIST ARMS/CONT DIPLOM BAL/PWR

B61
NOGEE J.L.,SOVIET POLICY TOWARD INTERNATIONAL CONTROL OF ATOMIC ENERGY. COM USA+45 WOR+45 INTELL NAT/G ACT/RES DIPLOM EDU/PROP NUC/PWR TOTALISM PERCEPT KNOWL PWR...TIME/SEQ COLD/WAR 20. PAGE 109 A2247 INT/ORG ATTIT ARMS/CONT USSR

B61
OAKES J.B.,THE EDGE OF FREEDOM. EUR+WWI USA+45 USSR ECO/UNDEV BAL/PWR DIPLOM DOMIN COLONIAL PWR MARXISM POPULISM...IDEA/COMP 20 COLD/WAR. PAGE 111 A2271 AFR ORD/FREE SOVEREIGN NEUTRAL

B61
PECKERT J.,DIE GROSSEN UND DIE KLEINEN MAECHTE. COM GERMANY/W ECO/DEV ECO/UNDEV NAT/G WAR RACE/REL PEACE...POLICY GP/COMP GOV/COMP 20 COLD/WAR. PAGE 114 A2346 DIPLOM ECO/TAC BAL/PWR

B61
RIENOW R.,CONTEMPORARY INTERNATIONAL POLITICS. WOR+45 INT/ORG BAL/PWR EDU/PROP COLONIAL NEUTRAL REGION WAR PEACE...INT/LAW 20 COLD/WAR UN. PAGE 121 A2476 DIPLOM PWR POLICY NAT/G

B61
SCHMIDT H.,VERTEIDIGUNG ODER VERGELTUNG. COM CUBA GERMANY/W USSR FORCES DIPLOM ARMS/CONT DETER NUC/PWR...POLICY CHARTS HYPO/EXP SIMUL BIBLIOG 20 NATO COLD/WAR. PAGE 128 A2630 PLAN WAR BAL/PWR ORD/FREE

B61
SLESSOR J.,WHAT PRICE COEXISTENCE? COM INT/ORG NAT/G FORCES COLONIAL ARMS/CONT WAR...POLICY TREND 20 NATO COLD/WAR. PAGE 134 A2741 DIPLOM PEACE WOR+45 NUC/PWR

B61
SOKOL A.E.,SEAPOWER IN THE NUCLEAR AGE. USA+45 USSR DIST/IND FORCES INT/TRADE DETER WAR...POLICY NAT/COMP BIBLIOG COLD/WAR. PAGE 135 A2763 SEA PWR WEAPON NUC/PWR

B61
STILLMAN E.,THE NEW POLITICS: AMERICA AND THE END OF THE POSTWAR WORLD. FUT WOR+45 CULTURE SOCIETY ECO/UNDEV INT/ORG NAT/G FORCES TOP/EX ACT/RES DIPLOM EDU/PROP LEGIT ROUTINE DETER ATTIT ORD/FREE PWR...OBS STERTYP COLD/WAR TOT/POP VAL/FREE. PAGE 138 A2827 USA+45 PLAN

B61
STONE J.,QUEST FOR SURVIVAL. WOR+45 NAT/G VOL/ASSN LEGIT ADMIN ARMS/CONT COERCE DISPL ORD/FREE PWR ...POLICY INT/LAW JURID COLD/WAR 20. PAGE 139 A2836 INT/ORG ADJUD SOVEREIGN

B61
STRAUSZ-HUPE R.,A FORWARD STRATEGY FOR AMERICA. FUT WOR+45 ECO/DEV INT/ORG NAT/G POL/PAR DELIB/GP FORCES ACT/RES CREATE ECO/TAC DOMIN EDU/PROP ATTIT DRIVE PWR...MAJORIT CONCPT STAT OBS TIME/SEQ TREND COLD/WAR TOT/POP. PAGE 139 A2848 USA+45 PLAN DIPLOM

B61
US SENATE COMM GOVT OPERATIONS,ORGANIZING FOR NATIONAL SECURITY. COM USA+45 BUDGET DIPLOM DETER NUC/PWR WAR WEAPON ORD/FREE...BIBLIOG 20 COLD/WAR. PAGE 156 A3172 POLICY PLAN FORCES COERCE

B61
WRIGHT Q.,THE ROLE OF INTERNATIONAL LAW IN THE ELIMINATION OF WAR. FUT WOR+45 WOR-45 NAT/G BAL/PWR DIPLOM DOMIN LEGIT PWR...POLICY INT/LAW JURID CONCPT TIME/SEQ TREND GEN/LAWS COLD/WAR 20. PAGE 168 A3414 INT/ORG ADJUD ARMS/CONT

L61
HILSMAN R. JR.,"THE NEW COMMUNIST TACTIC: PRECIS-INTERNAL WAR." COM FUT USA+45 ECO/UNDEV POL/PAR FOR/AID RIGID/FLEX ALL/VALS...TREND COLD/WAR 20. PAGE 65 A1334 FORCES COERCE USSR GUERRILLA

L61
TAUBENFELD H.J.,"A REGIME FOR OUTER SPACE." FUT UNIV R+D ACT/RES PLAN BAL/PWR LEGIT ARMS/CONT ORD/FREE...POLICY JURID TREND UN TOT/POP 20 COLD/WAR. PAGE 142 A2894 INT/ORG ADJUD SPACE

S61
CARLETON W.G.,"AMERICAN FOREIGN POLICY: MYTHS AND REALITIES." FUT USA+45 WOR+45 ECO/UNDEV INT/ORG EX/STRUC ARMS/CONT NUC/PWR WAR ATTIT...POLICY CONCPT CONT/OBS GEN/METH COLD/WAR TOT/POP 20. PAGE 24 A0484 PLAN MYTH DIPLOM

S61
DELLA PORT G.,"PROBLEMI E PROSPETTIVE DI COESISTENZA FRA ORIENTE ED OCCIDENTE, (PART 3)." COM FUT WOR+45 NAT/G BAL/PWR FOR/AID BAL/PAY PWR WEALTH...SOC CONCPT GEN/LAWS COLD/WAR 20. PAGE 36 A0729 INT/TRADE

S61
GOODWIN G.L.,"THE EXPANDING UNITED NATIONS: 2-DIPLOMATIC PRESSURES AND TECHNIQUES." COM ECO/UNDEV TOP/EX BAL/PWR DIPLOM DOMIN...POLICY CONCPT UN COLD/WAR 20. PAGE 54 A1108 INT/ORG PWR

S61
JACKSON E.,"CONSTITUTIONAL DEVELOPMENTS OF THE UNITED NATIONS: THE GROWTH OF ITS EXECUTIVE CAPACITY." FUT WOR+45 CONSTN STRUCT ACT/RES PLAN ALL/VALS...NEW/IDEA OBS COLD/WAR UN 20. PAGE 72 A1475 INT/ORG EXEC

S61
KRANNHALS H.V.,"COMMAND INTEGRATION WITHIN THE WARSAW PACT." COM USSR WOR+45 DELIB/GP EDU/PROP ...CONCPT AUD/VIS CHARTS COLD/WAR TOT/POP VAL/FREE 20 TREATY WARSAW/P. PAGE 82 A1675 INT/ORG FORCES TOTALISM

S61
LIPSON L.,"AN ARGUMENT ON THE LEGALITY OF RECONNAISSANCE STATELLITES." COM USA+45 USSR WOR+45 AIR INTELL NAT/G CONSULT PLAN DIPLOM LEGIT ROUTINE ATTIT...INT/LAW JURID CONCPT METH/CNCPT TREND COLD/WAR 20. PAGE 90 A1833 INT/ORG LAW SPACE

S61
WHELAN J.G.,"KHRUSHCHEV AND THE BALANCE OF WORLD POWER." FUT WOR+45 INT/ORG VOL/ASSN CAP/ISM DIPLOM SKILL...POLICY COLD/WAR 20 KHRUSH/N. PAGE 163 A3328 COM PWR BAL/PWR USSR

S61
ZAGORIA D.S.,"SINO-SOVIET FRICTION IN UNDERDEVELOPED AREAS." ASIA CHINA/COM COM ACT/RES PLAN ATTIT ORD/FREE PWR COLD/WAR 20. PAGE 169 A3443 ECO/UNDEV ECO/TAC INT/TRADE USSR

B62
APATHEKER H.,AMERICAN FOREIGN POLICY AND THE COLD WAR. USA+45 NAT/G POL/PAR COLONIAL NAT/LISM SOVEREIGN MARXISM SOCISM 20 COLD/WAR MARX/KARL LENIN/VI INTERVENT. PAGE 8 A0167 DIPLOM WAR PEACE

B62
BAILEY S.D.,THE SECRETARIAT OF THE UNITED NATIONS. FUT WOR+45 DELIB/GP PLAN BAL/PWR DOMIN EDU/PROP ADMIN PEACE ATTIT PWR...DECISION CONCPT TREND CON/ANAL CHARTS UN VAL/FREE COLD/WAR 20. PAGE 10 A0205 INT/ORG EXEC DIPLOM

B62
BEATON L.,THE SPREAD OF NUCLEAR WEAPONS. WOR+45 NAT/G PLAN PROB/SOLV DIPLOM ECO/TAC DETER...POLICY 20 COLD/WAR. PAGE 12 A0242 ARMS/CONT NUC/PWR TEC/DEV FUT

B62
BELL C.,NEGOTIATION FROM STRENGTH. WOR+45 FACE/GP INT/ORG DELIB/GP FORCES PLAN DOMIN COERCE NUC/PWR PEACE DRIVE PWR...POLICY LOG OBS RECORD INT SAMP TREND COLD/WAR 20. PAGE 13 A0255 NAT/G CONCPT DIPLOM

B62
BURTON J.W.,PEACE THEORY: PRECONDITIONS OF DISARMAMENT. COM EUR+WWI USA+45 NAT/G FORCES BAL/PWR DIPLOM ECO/TAC EDU/PROP REGION COERCE DETER PEACE ATTIT PWR TOT/POP COLD/WAR 20. PAGE 22 A0446 INT/ORG PLAN ARMS/CONT

B62
CALVOCORESSI P.,WORLD ORDER AND NEW STATES: PROBLEMS OF KEEPING THE PEACE. AFR EUR+WWI S/ASIA ELITES NAT/G ECO/TAC FOR/AID EDU/PROP COERCE ATTIT DRIVE ALL/VALS...GEN/LAWS COLD/WAR 20 UN. PAGE 23 A0471 INT/ORG PEACE

B62
COUNCIL ON WORLD TENSIONS,A STUDY OF WORLD TENSIONS AND DEVELOPMENT. WOR+45 ECO/DEV ECO/UNDEV INT/ORG PLAN DIPLOM ECO/TAC EDU/PROP ATTIT KNOWL ORD/FREE PWR WEALTH...CONCPT TREND CHARTS STERTYP COLD/WAR TOT/POP 20. PAGE 31 A0640 TEC/DEV SOC

B62
DALLIN A.,THE SOVIET UNION AT THE UNITED NATIONS: AN INQUIRY INTO SOVIET MOTIVES AND OBJECTIVES. ACT/RES EDU/PROP LEGIT ATTIT KNOWL PWR...POLICY RECORD HIST/WRIT TIME/SEQ TREND ORG/CHARTS GEN/METH COLD/WAR FAO 20 UN. PAGE 33 A0675 COM INT/ORG USSR

B62
DUROSELLE J.B.,HISTOIRE DIPLOMATIQUE DE 1919 A NOS JOURS (3RD ED.). FRANCE INT/ORG CHIEF FORCES CONFER ARMS/CONT WAR PEACE ORD/FREE...T TREATY 20 COLD/WAR. PAGE 39 A0807 DIPLOM WOR+45 WOR-45

B62
ELLIOTT J.R.,THE APPEAL OF COMMUNISM IN THE UNDERDEVELOPED NATIONS. USSR WOR+45 INT/ORG NAT/G DIPLOM DOMIN EDU/PROP ROUTINE ATTIT RIGID/FLEX ORD/FREE PWR WEALTH MARXISM...POLICY SOC METH/CNCPT MYTH TOT/POP COLD/WAR 20. PAGE 41 A0842 COM ECO/UNDEV

B62
GRAEBNER N.,COLD WAR DIPLOMACY 1945-1960. WOR+45 INT/ORG ECO/TAC EDU/PROP COERCE ORD/FREE PWR WEALTH ...HIST/WRIT TOT/POP VAL/FREE COLD/WAR 20. PAGE 55 A1122 USA+45 DIPLOM

B62
HATCH J.,AFRICA TODAY-AND TOMORROW: AN OUTLINE OF BASIC FACTS AND MAJOR PROBLEMS. AFR FUT ISLAM STRATA ECO/UNDEV INT/ORG NAT/G POL/PAR DELIB/GP TOP/EX EDU/PROP LEGIT CHOOSE ATTIT...TIME/SEQ TOT/POP COLD/WAR 20. PAGE 63 A1287
PLAN CONSTN NAT/LISM

B62
HUNTINGTON S.P.,CHANGING PATTERNS OF MILITARY POLITICS. EUR+WWI L/A+17C S/ASIA USA+45 WOR+45 CULTURE INT/ORG NAT/G CONSULT PLAN DOMIN EDU/PROP LEGIT DETER WAR ATTIT PERSON PWR...DECISION CONCPT SIMUL GEN/LAWS ANTHOL COLD/WAR 20. PAGE 69 A1419
FORCES RIGID/FLEX

B62
KAHN H.,THINKING ABOUT THE UNTHINKABLE. FUT USA+45 LAW NAT/G CONSULT FORCES ACT/RES CREATE PLAN TEC/DEV BAL/PWR DIPLOM EDU/PROP ARMS/CONT DETER ATTIT...CONCPT OBS TREND COLD/WAR 20. PAGE 76 A1547
INT/ORG ORD/FREE NUC/PWR PEACE

B62
KING G.,THE UNITED NATIONS IN THE CONGO: A QUEST FOR PEACE. WOR+45 NAT/G CONSULT FORCES LEGIT COERCE WAR ORD/FREE...JURID METH/CNCPT OBS INT HIST/WRIT TIME/SEQ CONGO UN 20 COLD/WAR. PAGE 79 A1624
AFR INT/ORG

B62
LAWSON R.,INTERNATIONAL REGIONAL ORGANIZATIONS. WOR+45 NAT/G VOL/ASSN CONSULT LEGIS EDU/PROP LEGIT ADMIN EXEC ROUTINE HEALTH PWR WEALTH...JURID EEC COLD/WAR 20 UN. PAGE 86 A1752
INT/ORG DELIB/GP REGION

B62
LESSING P.,AFRICA'S RED HARVEST. AFR CHINA/COM COM USSR ECO/UNDEV BAL/PWR DIPLOM CONTROL PWR 20 COLD/WAR INTERVENT. PAGE 87 A1789
NAT/LISM MARXISM FOR/AID EDU/PROP

B62
MACKENTOSH J.M.,STRATEGY AND TACTICS OF SOVIET FOREIGN POLICY. CHINA/COM FUT USA+45 WOR+45 INT/ORG PLAN DOMIN LEGIT ROUTINE COERCE NUC/PWR WAR ATTIT DRIVE ORD/FREE PWR...CONCPT OBS TIME/SEQ TREND GEN/METH COLD/WAR 20. PAGE 92 A1894
COM POLICY DIPLOM USSR

B62
MANDER J.,BERLIN: HOSTAGE FOR THE WEST. FUT GERMANY WOR+45 FOR/AID RISK ATTIT ORD/FREE 20 BERLIN COLD/WAR. PAGE 93 A1916
DIPLOM BAL/PWR DOMIN DETER

B62
MODELSKI G.,SEATO-SIX STUDIES. ASIA CHINA/COM INDIA S/ASIA INT/ORG NAT/G ECO/TAC DETER ATTIT ORD/FREE PWR...TIME/SEQ COLD/WAR TOT/POP 20 SEATO. PAGE 102 A2098
MARKET ECO/UNDEV INT/TRADE

B62
MONCRIEFF A.,THE STRATEGY OF SURVIVAL. UK FORCES BAL/PWR CONFER DETER WAR...ANTHOL 20 COLD/WAR. PAGE 102 A2104
PLAN DECISION DIPLOM ARMS/CONT

B62
MORGENSTERN O.,STRATEGIE - HEUTE (2ND ED.). USA+45 USSR ECO/DEV DELIB/GP WAR PEACE ORD/FREE...GOV/COMP NAT/COMP 20 COLD/WAR NATO. PAGE 104 A2134
NUC/PWR DIPLOM FORCES TEC/DEV

B62
MORGENTHAU H.J.,POLITICS IN THE TWENTIETH CENTURY: IMPASSE OF AMERICAN FOREIGN POLICY. FUT GERMANY USA+45 USSR WOR+45 INT/ORG NAT/G ACT/RES PLAN FOR/AID EDU/PROP LEGIT COERCE WAR PWR...TIME/SEQ TREND COLD/WAR 20. PAGE 104 A2138
SKILL DIPLOM

B62
MORGENTHAU H.J.,POLITICS IN THE 20TH CENTURY: RESTORATION OF AMERICAN POLITICS. ASIA GERMANY USA+45 USSR WOR+45 NAT/G PLAN EDU/PROP LEGIT NUC/PWR ATTIT PWR SKILL...CONCPT TREND COLD/WAR 20. PAGE 104 A2139
INT/ORG DIPLOM

B62
MULLEY F.W.,THE POLITICS OF WESTERN DEFENSE. EUR+WWI USA-45 WOR+45 VOL/ASSN EX/STRUC FORCES COERCE DETER PEACE ATTIT ORD/FREE PWR...RECORD TIME/SEQ CHARTS COLD/WAR 20 NATO. PAGE 106 A2168
INT/ORG DELIB/GP NUC/PWR

B62
NEAL F.W.,WAR AND PEACE AND GERMANY. EUR+WWI USSR STRUCT INT/ORG NAT/G FORCES DOMIN EDU/PROP LEGIT EXEC COERCE ORD/FREE...HUM SOC NEW/IDEA OBS TIME/SEQ TOT/POP COLD/WAR 20 BERLIN. PAGE 108 A2208
USA+45 POLICY DIPLOM GERMANY

B62
ROY P.A.,SOUTH WIND RED. L/A+17C USA+45 ECO/UNDEV NAT/G CAP/ISM MARXISM SOCISM...OLD/LIB GEOG RECORD INT CENSUS 20 COLD/WAR. PAGE 125 A2554
DIPLOM INDUS POLICY ECO/TAC

B62
SCHUMAN F.L.,THE COLD WAR: RETROSPECT AND PROSPECT. FUT USA+45 USSR WOR+45 BAL/PWR EDU/PROP ARMS/CONT ATTIT...MAJORIT IDEA/COMP ANTHOL BIBLIOG 20 COLD/WAR. PAGE 129 A2651
MARXISM TEC/DEV DIPLOM NUC/PWR

B62
SCHWARZENBERGER G.,THE FRONTIERS OF INTERNATIONAL LAW. WOR+45 WOR-45 NAT/G LEGIT CT/SYS ROUTINE MORAL ORD/FREE PWR...JURID SOC GEN/METH 20 COLD/WAR. PAGE 130 A2661
INT/ORG LAW INT/LAW

B62
SINGER J.D.,DETERRENCE, ARMS CONTROL AND DISARMAMENT: TOWARD A SYNTHESIS IN NATIONAL SECURITY POLICY. COM USA+45 INT/ORG BAL/PWR DETER ORD/FREE...POLICY COLD/WAR 20. PAGE 133 A2727
FUT ACT/RES ARMS/CONT

B62
SNOW J.H.,GOVERNMENT BY TREASON. USA+45 USA-45 LEGIS DIPLOM FOR/AID GIVE CONTROL WEALTH MARXISM ...MAJORIT 20 CONGRESS COLD/WAR. PAGE 134 A2750
FINAN TAX PWR POLICY

B62
SPANIER J.W.,THE POLITICS OF DISARMAMENT. COM USA+45 USSR EDU/PROP ATTIT ORD/FREE PWR RESPECT ...MYTH RECORD 20 COLD/WAR. PAGE 135 A2771
INT/ORG DELIB/GP ARMS/CONT

B62
STRACHEY J.,ON THE PREVENTION OF WAR. FUT WOR+45 INT/ORG NAT/G ACT/RES PLAN BAL/PWR DOMIN EDU/PROP PEACE ATTIT...POLICY TREND TOT/POP COLD/WAR 20 UN. PAGE 139 A2842
FORCES ORD/FREE ARMS/CONT NUC/PWR

B62
US DEPARTMENT OF THE ARMY,AFRICA: ITS PROBLEMS AND PROSPECTS. CHINA/COM USSR INT/ORG FOR/AID COLONIAL LEAD FEDERAL DRIVE SOVEREIGN MARXISM...GEOG 20 COLD/WAR. PAGE 152 A3104
BIBLIOG/A AFR NAT/LISM DIPLOM

B62
WRIGHT Q.,PREVENTING WORLD WAR THREE. FUT WOR+45 CULTURE INT/ORG NAT/G CONSULT FORCES ADMIN ARMS/CONT DRIVE RIGID/FLEX ORD/FREE SOVEREIGN ...POLICY CONCPT TREND STERTYP COLD/WAR 20. PAGE 168 A3416
CREATE ATTIT

B62
YALEN R.,REGIONALISM AND WORLD ORDER. EUR+WWI WOR+45 WOR-45 INT/ORG VOL/ASSN DELIB/GP FORCES TOP/EX BAL/PWR DIPLOM DOMIN REGION ARMS/CONT PWR ...JURID HYPO/EXP COLD/WAR 20. PAGE 168 A3427
ORD/FREE POLICY

L62
BAILEY S.D.,"THE TROIKA AND THE FUTURE OF THE UN." CONSTN CREATE LEGIT EXEC CHOOSE ORD/FREE PWR ...CONCPT NEW/IDEA UN COLD/WAR 20. PAGE 10 A0206
FUT INT/ORG USSR

L62
STEIN E.,"MR HAMMARSKJOLD, THE CHARTER LAW AND THE FUTURE ROLE OF THE UNITED NATIONS SECRETARY-GENERAL." WOR+45 CONSTN INT/ORG DELIB/GP FORCES TOP/EX BAL/PWR LEGIT ROUTINE RIGID/FLEX PWR ...POLICY JURID OBS STERTYP UN COLD/WAR 20 HAMMARSK/D. PAGE 137 A2815
CONCPT BIOG

L62
ULYSSES,"THE INTERNATIONAL AIMS AND POLICIES OF THE SOVIET UNION: THE NEW CONCEPTS AND STRATEGY OF KHRUSHCHEV." FUT USSR WOR+45 SOCIETY INT/ORG NAT/G POL/PAR FORCES TOP/EX PLAN DOMIN EDU/PROP COERCE ATTIT PERSON PWR...TREND COLD/WAR 20 KHRUSH/N. PAGE 146 A2994
COM POLICY BAL/PWR DIPLOM

S62
BOULDING K.E.,"THE PREVENTION OF WORLD WAR THREE." FUT WOR+45 INT/ORG PLAN BAL/PWR PEACE ORD/FREE PWR ...NEW/IDEA TREND TOT/POP COLD/WAR 20. PAGE 17 A0348
VOL/ASSN NAT/G ARMS/CONT DIPLOM

S62
DALLIN A.,"THE SOVIET VIEW OF THE UNITED NATIONS." WOR+45 VOL/ASSN TOP/EX DIPLOM DOMIN EDU/PROP LEGIT ATTIT RIGID/FLEX PWR...CONCPT OBS HIST/WRIT TIME/SEQ STERTYP GEN/LAWS COLD/WAR UN 20. PAGE 33 A0676
COM INT/ORG USSR

S62
FALK R.A.,"THE REALITY OF INTERNATIONAL LAW." WOR+45 NAT/G LEGIT COERCE DETER WAR MORAL ORD/FREE PWR SOVEREIGN...JURID CONCPT VAL/FREE COLD/WAR 20. PAGE 43 A0887
INT/ORG ADJUD NUC/PWR INT/LAW

S62
FENWICK C.G.,"ISSUES AT PUNTA DEL ESTE: NON-INTERVENTION VS COLLECTIVE SECURITY." L/A+17C USA+45 VOL/ASSN DELIB/GP ECO/TAC LEGIT ADJUD REGION ORD/FREE OAS COLD/WAR 20. PAGE 45 A0917
INT/ORG CUBA

S62
FINKELSTEIN L.S.,"THE UNITED NATIONS AND ORGANIZATIONS FOR CONTROL OF ARMAMENT." FUT WOR+45 VOL/ASSN DELIB/GP TOP/EX CREATE EDU/PROP LEGIT ADJUD NUC/PWR ATTIT RIGID/FLEX ORD/FREE...POLICY DECISION CONCPT OBS TREND GEN/LAWS TOT/POP COLD/WAR. PAGE 46 A0933
INT/ORG PWR ARMS/CONT

S62
HOFFMANN S.,"RESTRAINTS AND CHOICES IN AMERICAN FOREIGN POLICY." USA-45 INT/ORG NAT/G PLAN ARMS/CONT ATTIT...POLICY CONCPT OBS TREND GEN/METH COLD/WAR 20. PAGE 66 A1356
USA+45 ORD/FREE DIPLOM

S62
LISSITZYN O.J.,"SOME LEGAL IMPLICATIONS OF THE U-2 AND RB-47 INCIDENTS." FUT USA+45 USSR WOR+45 AIR NAT/G DIPLOM LEGIT MORAL ORD/FREE SOVEREIGN...JURID GEN/LAWS GEN/METH COLD/WAR 20 U-2. PAGE 90 A1840
LAW CONCPT SPACE INT/LAW

S62
MCWHINNEY E.,"CO-EXISTENCE, THE CUBA CRISIS, AND COLD WAR-INTERNATIONAL WAR." CUBA USA+45 USSR WOR+45 NAT/G TOP/EX BAL/PWR DIPLOM DOMIN LEGIT PEACE RIGID/FLEX ORD/FREE...STERTYP COLD/WAR 20.
CONCPT INT/LAW

PAGE 99 A2026

S62

SPECTOR I.,"SOVIET POLICY IN ASIA: A REAPPRAISAL." ASIA CHINA/COM COM INDIA INDONESIA ECO/UNDEV INT/ORG DOMIN EDU/PROP REGION RESPECT...CONCPT TREND TOT/POP COLD/WAR 20 CHINJAP. PAGE 135 A2774 S/ASIA PWR FOR/AID USSR

S62

STRACHEY J.,"COMMUNIST INTENTIONS." ASIA USSR YUGOSLAVIA INT/ORG NAT/G FORCES DOMIN EDU/PROP COERCE NUC/PWR NAT/LISM PEACE RIGID/FLEX PWR MARXISM...CONCPT MYTH OBS TIME/SEQ TREND COLD/WAR TOT/POP 20. PAGE 139 A2843 COM ATTIT WAR

S62

THOMAS J.R.T.,"SOVIET BEHAVIOR IN THE QUEMOY CRISES OF 1958." CHINA/COM FUT USSR WOR+45 INT/ORG VOL/ASSN FORCES PLAN BAL/PWR DOMIN COERCE NUC/PWR REV WAR ATTIT DRIVE ORD/FREE...POLICY OBS RECORD COLD/WAR FOR/POL 20. PAGE 143 A2923 COM PWR

S62

TOWSTER J.,"THE USSR AND THE USA: CHALLENGE AND RESPONSE." COM GERMANY USA+45 USSR WOR+45 ECO/UNDEV INT/ORG VOL/ASSN EX/STRUC FORCES TOP/EX CREATE PLAN TEC/DEV DIPLOM ECO/TAC EDU/PROP COLONIAL COERCE PWR ...GEN/METH COLD/WAR 20 KENNEDY/JF. PAGE 145 A2956 ACT/RES GEN/LAWS

B63

ABSHIRE D.M.,NATIONAL SECURITY: POLITICAL, MILITARY, AND ECONOMIC STRATEGIES IN THE DECADE AHEAD. ASIA COM USA+45 WOR+45 ECO/DEV ECO/UNDEV INT/ORG DELIB/GP FORCES ECO/TAC COERCE ATTIT RIGID/FLEX HEALTH ORD/FREE PWR WEALTH...POLICY STAT CHARTS ANTHOL COLD/WAR VAL/FREE. PAGE 4 A0083 FUT ACT/RES BAL/PWR

B63

BLOCH-MORHANGE J.,VINGT ANNEES D'HISTOIRE CONTEMPORAINE. FORCES FOR/AID CONFER LEAD 20 COLD/WAR. PAGE 15 A0311 WAR DIPLOM INT/ORG CHIEF

B63

CROZIER B.,THE MORNING AFTER; A STUDY OF INDEPENDENCE. WOR+45 EX/STRUC PLAN BAL/PWR COLONIAL GP/REL 20 COLD/WAR. PAGE 33 A0666 SOVEREIGN NAT/LISM NAT/G DIPLOM

B63

DUNN F.S.,PEACE-MAKING AND THE SETTLEMENT WITH JAPAN. ASIA USA+45 USA-45 FORCES BAL/PWR ECO/TAC CONFER WAR PWR SOVEREIGN 20 CHINJAP COLD/WAR TREATY. PAGE 39 A0802 POLICY PEACE PLAN DIPLOM

B63

GONZALEZ PEDRERO E.,ANATOMIA DE UN CONFLICTO. WOR+45 ECO/DEV ECO/UNDEV ECO/TAC FOR/AID CONTROL ARMS/CONT GOV/REL...NAT/COMP 20 COLD/WAR. PAGE 54 A1099 DIPLOM DETER BAL/PWR

B63

GRAEBNER N.A.,THE COLD WAR: IDEOLOGICAL CONFLICT OR POWER STRUGGLE? USSR WOR+45 WOR-45 PROB/SOLV EDU/PROP ARMS/CONT REV NAT/LISM PEACE ORD/FREE ...IDEA/COMP ANTHOL BIBLIOG/A 20 COLD/WAR. PAGE 55 A1123 DIPLOM BAL/PWR MARXISM

B63

HALASZ DE BEKY I.L.,A BIBLIOGRAPHY OF THE HUNGARIAN REVOLUTION 1956. COM HUNGARY USSR DIPLOM COERCE MARXISM...POLICY AUD/VIS 20 UN COLD/WAR. PAGE 59 A1221 BIBLIOG REV FORCES ATTIT

B63

JOYCE W.,THE PROPAGANDA GAP. USA+45 COM/IND ACADEM DOMIN FEEDBACK REV CIVMIL/REL...REALPOL COLD/WAR. PAGE 75 A1540 EDU/PROP PERCEPT BAL/PWR DIPLOM

B63

KHRUSHCHEV N.S.,THE NEW CONTENT OF PEACEFUL COEXISTENCE IN THE NUCLEAR AGE. GERMANY/E WORKER NUC/PWR REV SOCISM 20 COLD/WAR. PAGE 79 A1614 MARXISM POL/PAR PEACE DIPLOM

B63

LERCHE C.O. JR.,AMERICA IN WORLD AFFAIRS. COM UK USA+45 INT/ORG FORCES ECO/TAC INT/TRADE EDU/PROP WAR NAT/LISM PEACE...BIBLIOG 18/20 UN CONGRESS PRESIDENT COLD/WAR. PAGE 87 A1783 NAT/G DIPLOM PLAN

B63

LYON P.,NEUTRALISM. ECO/UNDEV EDU/PROP COLONIAL ALL/IDEOS...IDEA/COMP 20 COLD/WAR UN. PAGE 92 A1879 NAT/COMP NAT/LISM DIPLOM NEUTRAL

B63

MALIK C.,MAN IN THE STRUGGLE FOR PEACE. USSR WOR+45 CHIEF PLAN PROB/SOLV PARTIC NUC/PWR REV ORD/FREE ...IDEA/COMP METH/COMP 20 UN COLD/WAR. PAGE 93 A1912 PEACE MARXISM DIPLOM EDU/PROP

B63

MILLER W.J.,THE MEANING OF COMMUNISM. USSR SOCIETY ECO/DEV EX/STRUC WORKER TEC/DEV ADMIN TOTALISM ...POLICY CONCPT CHARTS BIBLIOG T 20 COLD/WAR LENIN/VI STALIN/J. PAGE 101 A2080 MARXISM TRADIT DIPLOM NAT/G

B63

MULLENBACH P.,CIVILIAN NUCLEAR POWER: ECONOMIC ISSUES AND POLICY FORMATION. FINAN INT/ORG DELIB/GP ACT/RES ECO/TAC ATTIT SUPEGO HEALTH ORD/FREE PWR ...POLICY CONCPT MATH STAT CHARTS VAL/FREE 20 COLD/WAR. PAGE 105 A2166 USA+45 ECO/DEV NUC/PWR

B63

PACHTER H.M.,COLLISION COURSE; THE CUBAN MISSILE CRISIS AND COEXISTENCE. CUBA USA+45 DIPLOM ARMS/CONT PEACE MARXISM...DECISION INT/LAW 20 COLD/WAR KHRUSH/N KENNEDY/JF CASTRO/F. PAGE 112 A2307 WAR BAL/PWR NUC/PWR DETER

B63

ROSS H.,THE COLD WAR: CONTAINMENT AND ITS CRITICSS. WOR+45 POL/PAR BAL/PWR ECO/TAC PEACE ORD/FREE ...POLICY IDEA/COMP ANTHOL T 20 COLD/WAR DULLES/JF TRUMAN/HS EISNHWR/DD. PAGE 124 A2541 MARXISM ARMS/CONT DIPLOM

B63

RUSK D.,THE WINDS OF FREEDOM. S/ASIA SOUTH/AFR INT/ORG FORCES NUC/PWR PEACE ORD/FREE 20 UN COLD/WAR. PAGE 125 A2569 DIPLOM FOR/AID INT/TRADE

B63

RUSSELL B.,UNARMED VICTORY. CHINA/COM CUBA INDIA USA+45 WAR MARXISM...POLICY IDEA/COMP 20 KHRUSH/N COLD/WAR. PAGE 125 A2573 DIPLOM ATTIT SOCISM ORD/FREE

B63

STEVENSON A.E.,LOOKING OUTWARD: YEARS OF CRISIS AT THE UNITED NATIONS. COM CUBA USA+45 WOR+45 SOCIETY NAT/G EX/STRUC ACT/RES LEGIT COLONIAL ATTIT PERSON SUPEGO ALL/VALS...POLICY HUM UN COLD/WAR CONGO 20. PAGE 138 A2823 INT/ORG CONCPT ARMS/CONT

B63

TUCKER R.C.,THE SOVIET POLITICAL MIND. WOR+45 ELITES INT/ORG NAT/G POL/PAR PLAN DIPLOM ECO/TAC DOMIN ADMIN NUC/PWR REV DRIVE PERSON SUPEGO PWR WEALTH...POLICY MGT PSY CONCPT OBS BIOG TREND COLD/WAR MARX/KARL 20. PAGE 145 A2972 COM TOP/EX USSR

B63

VAN SLYCK P.,PEACE: THE CONTROL OF NATIONAL POWER. CUBA WOR+45 FINAN NAT/G FORCES PROB/SOLV TEC/DEV BAL/PWR ADMIN CONTROL ORD/FREE...POLICY INT/LAW UN COLD/WAR TREATY. PAGE 158 A3214 ARMS/CONT PEACE INT/ORG DIPLOM

B63

WESTERFIELD H.,THE INSTRUMENTS OF AMERICA'S FOREIGN POLICY. WOR+45 ECO/DEV NAT/G CONSULT EX/STRUC LEGIS BAL/PWR FOR/AID INT/TRADE DOMIN EDU/PROP LEGIT ATTIT KNOWL ORD/FREE PWR WEALTH...OBS COLD/WAR TOT/POP VAL/FREE. PAGE 163 A3322 USA+45 INT/ORG DIPLOM

B63

WHITTON J.B.,PROPAGANDA AND THE COLD WAR. USA+45 USSR INDUS NAT/G PLAN WRITING EFFICIENCY...POLICY 20 COLD/WAR. PAGE 164 A3341 ATTIT EDU/PROP COM/IND DIPLOM

L63

RUSSETT B.M.,"TOWARD A MODEL OF COMPETITIVE INTERNATIONAL POLITICS." USA+45 WOR+45 INT/ORG NAT/G POL/PAR VOL/ASSN LEGIS BAL/PWR DIPLOM LEGIT PWR...CONCPT CONT/OBS STERTYP GEN/LAWS TOT/POP COLD/WAR 20 UN. PAGE 126 A2579 ATTIT EDU/PROP

L63

SCHELLING T.C.,"STRATEGIC PROBLEMS OF AN INTERNATIONAL ARMED FORCE." WOR+45 ECO/DEV INT/ORG NAT/G PLAN BAL/PWR LEGIT ARMS/CONT COERCE DETER ORD/FREE PWR...POLICY CONCPT COLD/WAR 20. PAGE 128 A2624 CREATE FORCES

S63

ALEXANDER R.,"LATIN AMERICA AND THE COMMUNIST BLOC." ASIA COM CUBA L/A+17C USA+45 USSR NAT/G VOL/ASSN TEC/DEV FOR/AID LEGIT PWR WEALTH COLD/WAR 20. PAGE 6 A0112 ECO/UNDEV RECORD

S63

BOHN L.,"WHOSE NUCLEAR TEST: NON-PHYSICAL INSPECTION AND TEST BAN." WOR+45 R+D INT/ORG VOL/ASSN ORD/FREE...GEN/LAWS GEN/METH COLD/WAR 20. PAGE 16 A0331 ADJUD ARMS/CONT TEC/DEV NUC/PWR

S63

BULLOUGH V.L.,"THE ROMAN EMPIRE VS PERSIA, 363-502: A STUDY OF SUCCESSFUL DETERRENCE." NAT/G PLAN DIPLOM ORD/FREE PWR...TIME/SEQ COLD/WAR VAL/FREE 4/6 PERSIA ROM/EMP. PAGE 21 A0430 MEDIT-7 COERCE DETER

S63

COSER L.,"AMERICA AND THE WORLD REVOLUTION." COM FUT USA+45 WOR+45 INTELL SOCIETY NAT/G ECO/TAC EDU/PROP ALL/VALS SOCISM...PSY GEN/LAWS TOT/POP 20 COLD/WAR. PAGE 31 A0629 ECO/UNDEV PLAN FOR/AID DIPLOM

S63

GROSSER A.,"FRANCE AND GERMANY IN THE ATLANTIC COMMUNITY." INT/ORG NAT/G TOP/EX DIPLOM REGION PEACE ATTIT ORD/FREE PWR...CONCPT RECORD TIME/SEQ GEN/LAWS VAL/FREE COLD/WAR 20. PAGE 57 A1178 EUR+WWI VOL/ASSN FRANCE GERMANY

S63

GUPTA S.C.,"INDIA AND THE SOVIET UNION." CHINA/COM COM INDIA S/ASIA VOL/ASSN TOP/EX FOR/AID EDU/PROP PEACE PWR...RECORD COLD/WAR 20. PAGE 58 A1195 DISPL MYTH USSR

S63

HAVILAND H.F.,"BUILDING A POLITICAL COMMUNITY." EUR+WWI FUT UK USA+45 ECO/DEV ECO/UNDEV INT/ORG NAT/G DELIB/GP BAL/PWR ECO/TAC NEUTRAL ROUTINE ATTIT PWR WEALTH...CONCPT COLD/WAR TOT/POP 20. VOL/ASSN DIPLOM

PAGE 63 A1293

S63
HOLBO P.S.,"COLD WAR DRIFT IN LATIN AMERICA." CUBA L/A+17C USA+45 USA-45 INT/ORG NAT/G NEIGH VOL/ASSN ACT/RES PLAN ECO/TAC ATTIT RIGID/FLEX ALL/VALS ...RECORD TIME/SEQ OAS LAFTA 20 COLD/WAR. PAGE 66 A1363
DELIB/GP CREATE FOR/AID

S63
MANGONE G.,"THE UNITED NATIONS AND UNITED STATES FOREIGN POLICY." USA+45 WOR+45 ECO/UNDEV NAT/G DIPLOM LEGIT ROUTINE ATTIT DRIVE...TIME/SEQ UN COLD/WAR 20. PAGE 94 A1922
INT/ORG ECO/TAC FOR/AID

S63
NADLER E.B.,"SOME ECONOMIC DISADVANTAGES OF THE ARMS RACE." USA+45 INDUS R+D FORCES PLAN TEC/DEV ECO/TAC FOR/AID EDU/PROP PWR WEALTH...TREND COLD/WAR 20. PAGE 107 A2190
ECO/DEV MGT BAL/PAY

S63
NOGEE J.L.,"PROPOGANDA AND NEGOTIATION: THE CASE OF THE TEN NATION DISARMAMENT COMMITTEE." COM EUR+WWI USA+45 VOL/ASSN DELIB/GP FORCES DIPLOM DOMIN LEGIT PWR...METH/CNCPT STERTYP COLD/WAR VAL/FREE 20. PAGE 110 A2248
INT/ORG EDU/PROP ARMS/CONT

S63
SINGER M.R.,"ELECTIONS WITHIN THE UNITED NATIONS: AN EXPERIMENTAL STUDY UTILIZING STATISTICAL ANALYSIS." USA+45 WOR+45 DIPLOM ECO/TAC COERCE PWR WEALTH...STAT CHARTS SIMUL GEN/LAWS COLD/WAR VAL/FREE UN 20. PAGE 133 A2732
INT/ORG CHOOSE

S63
SONNENFELDT H.,"FOREIGN POLICY FROM MALENKOV TO KHRUSHCHEV." WOR+45 NAT/G FORCES BAL/PWR DIPLOM ECO/TAC COERCE ATTIT PWR...CONCPT HIST/WRIT COLD/WAR 20. PAGE 135 A2768
COM DOMIN FOR/AID USSR

S63
WOLFERS A.,"INTEGRATION IN THE WEST: THE CONFLICT OF PERSPECTIVES." EUR+WWI USA+45 ECO/DEV INT/ORG DELIB/GP CREATE TEC/DEV DIPLOM ATTIT PWR...CONCPT HIST/WRIT TREND GEN/LAWS COLD/WAR EEC 20. PAGE 166 A3386
RIGID/FLEX ECO/TAC

C63
CHARLETON W.G.,"THE REVOLUTION IN AMERICAN FOREIGN POLICY." COM PROB/SOLV FOR/AID DOMIN COLONIAL NEUTRAL DETER WAR ISOLAT NAT/LISM...BIBLIOG 19/20 UN COLD/WAR NATO. PAGE 26 A0523
DIPLOM INT/ORG BAL/PWR

B64
DALLIN A.,THE SOVIET UNION, ARMS CONTROL AND DISARMAMENT. COM INT/ORG VOL/ASSN EX/STRUC DIPLOM NUC/PWR ATTIT PWR TOT/POP COLD/WAR 20. PAGE 33 A0678
ORD/FREE ARMS/CONT USSR

B64
DEITCHMAN S.J.,LIMITED WAR AND AMERICAN DEFENSE POLICY. USA+45 WOR+45 INT/ORG NAT/G PLAN TEC/DEV COERCE NUC/PWR RIGID/FLEX PWR SKILL...DECISION METH/CNCPT TIME/SEQ TOT/POP COLD/WAR 20. PAGE 36 A0726
FORCES WAR WEAPON

B64
FULBRIGHT J.W.,OLD MYTHS AND NEW REALITIES. USA+45 USSR LEGIS INT/TRADE DETER ATTIT...POLICY 20 COLD/WAR TREATY. PAGE 50 A1016
DIPLOM INT/ORG ORD/FREE

B64
IRISH M.D.,WORLD PRESSURES ON AMERICAN FOREIGN POLICY. ASIA COM L/A+17C SOUTH/AFR UK WOR+45 ECO/DEV ECO/UNDEV COLONIAL SANCTION COERCE REV TOTALISM...ANTHOL 20 COLD/WAR EUROPE/W INTERVENT. PAGE 72 A1467
DIPLOM POLICY

B64
KEEP J.,CONTEMPORARY HISTORY IN THE SOVIET MIRROR. COM USSR POL/PAR CREATE DIPLOM AGREE WAR ATTIT ...MYTH TREND ANTHOL 20 COLD/WAR STALIN/J MARX/KARL LENIN/VI. PAGE 77 A1576
HIST/WRIT METH MARXISM IDEA/COMP

B64
KENNEDY J.F.,THE BURDEN AND THE GLORY. FUT USA+45 TEC/DEV ECO/TAC EDU/PROP ARMS/CONT MURDER RACE/REL PEACE...ANTHOL 20 KENNEDY/JF COLD/WAR NATO PRESIDENT. PAGE 78 A1593
ADMIN POLICY GOV/REL DIPLOM

B64
LENS S.,THE FUTILE CRUSADE. ASIA CHINA/COM L/A+17C USA+45 USSR WOR+45 ECO/DEV BAL/PWR DIPLOM NUC/PWR WAR NAT/LISM PEACE 20 COLD/WAR PRESIDENT CIA. PAGE 87 A1774
ORD/FREE ANOMIE COM MARXISM

B64
LUARD E.,THE COLD WAR: A RE-APPRAISAL. FUT USSR WOR+45 FORCES NUC/PWR NAT/LISM ORD/FREE SOVEREIGN ...INT 20 COLD/WAR STALIN/J TREATY UN. PAGE 91 A1870
DIPLOM WAR PEACE TOTALISM

B64
MCWHINNEY E.,"PEACEFUL COEXISTENCE" AND SOVIET-WESTERN INTERNATIONAL LAW. USSR DIPLOM LEAD...JURID 20 COLD/WAR. PAGE 99 A2027
PEACE IDEA/COMP INT/LAW ATTIT

B64
ROSENAU J.N.,INTERNATIONAL ASPECTS OF CIVIL STRIFE. CHINA/COM CUBA EUR+WWI USA+45 USSR BAL/PWR EDU/PROP NEUTRAL COERCE MORAL...NAT/COMP 20 COLD/WAR UN. PAGE 124 A2533
POLICY DIPLOM REV WAR

B64
STILLMAN E.O.,THE POLITICS OF HYSTERIA: THE SOURCES OF TWENTIETH-CENTURY CONFLICT. WOR+45 WOR-45 CULTURE ECO/UNDEV PLAN CAP/ISM WAR MARXISM ...PREDICT BIBLIOG 20 COLD/WAR. PAGE 138 A2828
DIPLOM IDEA/COMP COLONIAL CONTROL

B64
VOELKMANN K.,HERRSCHER VON MORGEN? BAL/PWR COLONIAL NEUTRAL REGION RACE/REL ALL/VALS SOVEREIGN...RECORD 20 COLD/WAR THIRD/WRLD. PAGE 159 A3246
DIPLOM ECO/UNDEV CONTROL NAT/COMP

B64
WARREN S.,THE PRESIDENT AS WORLD LEADER. USA+45 WOR+45 ELITES COM/IND INT/ORG NAT/G VOL/ASSN CHIEF EX/STRUC LEGIT COERCE ATTIT PERSON RIGID/FLEX...INT TIME/SEQ COLD/WAR 20 ROOSEVLT/F TRUMAN/HS EISNHWR/DD KENNEDY/JF. PAGE 161 A3286
TOP/EX PWR DIPLOM

B64
WOODHOUSE C.M.,THE NEW CONCERT OF NATIONS. WOR+45 ECO/DEV ECO/UNDEV NAT/G BAL/PWR ECO/TAC NAT/LISM PWR SOVEREIGN ALL/IDEOS 20 UN COLD/WAR. PAGE 166 A3391
DIPLOM MORAL FOR/AID COLONIAL

B64
WRIGHT T.P. JR.,AMERICAN SUPPORT OF FREE ELECTIONS ABROAD. USA+45 USA-45 DOMIN LEAD NEUTRAL MARXISM ...POLICY TIME/SEQ BIBLIOG 19/20 COLD/WAR INTERVENT. PAGE 168 A3420
DIPLOM CHOOSE L/A+17C POPULISM

L64
ARMENGALD A.,"ECONOMIE ET COEXISTENCE." COM EUR+WWI FUT USA+45 WOR+45 ECO/DEV ECO/UNDEV FINAN INT/ORG NAT/G EXEC CHOOSE ATTIT ALL/VALS...POLICY RELATIV DECISION TREND SOC/EXP COLD/WAR WORK 20. PAGE 9 A0173
MARKET ECO/TAC CAP/ISM

L64
CAMPBELL J.C.,"THE MIDDLE EAST IN THE MUTED COLD WAR." COM EUR+WWI UAR USA+45 USSR STRUCT ECO/UNDEV NAT/G VOL/ASSN EX/STRUC TOP/EX DIPLOM ECO/TAC EDU/PROP...TIME/SEQ COLD/WAR 20. PAGE 23 A0475
ISLAM FOR/AID NAT/LISM

L64
CARNEGIE ENDOWMENT INT. PEACE,"POLITICAL QUESTIONS (ISSUES BEFORE THE NINETEENTH GENERAL ASSEMBLY)." SPACE WOR+45 CONSTN FINAN NAT/G CONSULT DELIB/GP FORCES LEGIS TEC/DEV EDU/PROP LEGIT ARMS/CONT COERCE NUC/PWR ATTIT ALL/VALS...CONCPT OBS UN COLD/WAR 20. PAGE 24 A0490
INT/ORG PEACE

L64
MILLIS W.,"THE DEMILITARIZED WORLD." COM USA+45 USSR WOR+45 CONSTN NAT/G EX/STRUC PLAN LEGIT ATTIT DRIVE...CONCPT TIME/SEQ STERTYP TOT/POP COLD/WAR 20. PAGE 102 A2085
FUT INT/ORG BAL/PWR PEACE

S64
ARMSTRONG J.A.,"THE SOVIET-AMERICAN CONFRONTATION: A NEW STAGE?" CUBA USA+45 USSR PLAN PROB/SOLV INT/TRADE CONTROL ARMS/CONT NUC/PWR MARXISM 20 COLD/WAR INTERVENT. PAGE 9 A0174
DIPLOM POLICY INSPECT

S64
BEIM D.,"THE COMMUNIST BLOC AND THE FOREIGN-AID GAME." WOR+45 NAT/G PLAN ROUTINE ATTIT KNOWL ORD/FREE...DECISION QUANT CONT/OBS TIME/SEQ CHARTS GAME SIMUL COLD/WAR 20. PAGE 12 A0252
COM ECO/UNDEV ECO/TAC FOR/AID

S64
DELGADO J.,"EL MOMENTO POLITICO HISPANOAMERICA." CHINA/COM FUT PANAMA USA+45 USSR INT/ORG NAT/G POL/PAR FORCES DOMIN REGION COERCE ATTIT ALL/VALS ...TRADIT CONCPT COLD/WAR 20. PAGE 36 A0728
L/A+17C EDU/PROP NAT/LISM

S64
DEVILLERS P.H.,"L'URSS, LA CHINE ET LES ORIGINES DE LA GUERRE DE COREE." ASIA CHINA/COM USSR INT/ORG ECO/TAC EDU/PROP ATTIT RIGID/FLEX PWR...STAND/INT HIST/WRIT COLD/WAR 20. PAGE 37 A0751
WOR+45 KOREA

S64
GARMARNIKOW M.,"INFLUENCE-BUYING IN WEST AFRICA." COM FUT USSR INTELL NAT/G PLAN TEC/DEV ECO/TAC DOMIN EDU/PROP REGION NAT/LISM ATTIT DRIVE ALL/VALS SOVEREIGN...POLICY PSY SOC CONCPT TREND STERTYP WORK COLD/WAR 20. PAGE 51 A1049
AFR ECO/UNDEV FOR/AID SOCISM

S64
GROSSER A.,"Y A-T-IL UN CONFLIT FRANCO-AMERICAIN." EUR+WWI USA+45 INT/ORG NAT/G PLAN BAL/PWR DIPLOM EDU/PROP NUC/PWR ATTIT DRIVE ORD/FREE PWR...CONCPT OBS TIME/SEQ TREND STERTYP VAL/FREE COLD/WAR. PAGE 57 A1179
VOL/ASSN NAT/LISM FRANCE

S64
HOFFMANN S.,"CE QU'EN PENSENT LES AMERICAINS." EUR+WWI INT/ORG VOL/ASSN PLAN BAL/PWR DIPLOM DOMIN EDU/PROP REGION ARMS/CONT DRIVE ORD/FREE PWR ...POLICY CONCPT OBS TREND STERTYP COLD/WAR VAL/FREE 20. PAGE 66 A1357
USA+45 ATTIT FRANCE

S64
KARPOV P.V.,"PEACEFUL COEXISTENCE AND INTERNATIONAL LAW." WOR+45 LAW SOCIETY INT/ORG VOL/ASSN FORCES CREATE CAP/ISM DIPLOM ADJUD NUC/PWR PEACE MORAL ORD/FREE PWR MARXISM...MARXIST JURID CONCPT OBS TREND COLD/WAR MARX/KARL 20. PAGE 77 A1568
COM ATTIT INT/LAW USSR

S64
LERNER W.,"THE HISTORICAL ORIGINS OF THE SOVIET DOCTRINE OF PEACEFUL COEXISTENCE." COM USSR INT/ORG
EDU/PROP DIPLOM

NAT/G VOL/ASSN PLAN PEACE ATTIT RIGID/FLEX PWR MARXISM...TIME/SEQ COLD/WAR 20. PAGE 87 A1788

S64
LEVI W.,"CHINA AND THE UNITED NATIONS." ASIA CHINA CHINA/COM WOR+45 WOR-45 CONSTN NAT/G DELIB/GP EX/STRUC FORCES ACT/RES EDU/PROP PWR...POLICY RECORD TIME/SEQ GEN/LAWS UN COLD/WAR 20. PAGE 88 A1794 — INT/ORG ATTIT NAT/LISM

S64
LIPSON L.,"PEACEFUL COEXISTENCE." COM USSR WOR+45 LAW INT/ORG DIPLOM LEGIT ADJUD ORD/FREE...CONCPT OBS TREND GEN/LAWS VAL/FREE COLD/WAR 20. PAGE 90 A1834 — ATTIT JURID INT/LAW PEACE

S64
MCGHEE G.C.,"EAST-WEST RELATIONS TODAY." WOR+45 PROB/SOLV BAL/PWR PEACE 20 COLD/WAR. PAGE 98 A2011 — IDEA/COMP DIPLOM ADJUD

S64
PADELFORD N.J.,"THE ORGANIZATION OF AFRICAN UNITY." ECO/UNDEV INT/ORG PLAN BAL/PWR DIPLOM ECO/TAC NAT/LISM ORD/FREE PWR WEALTH...CONCPT TREND STERTYP VAL/FREE COLD/WAR 20. PAGE 113 A2313 — AFR VOL/ASSN REGION

S64
SALVADORI M.,"EL CAPITALISMO EN LA EUROPA DE LA POSGUERRA." INT/ORG NAT/G POL/PAR PLAN ECO/TAC ATTIT ORD/FREE WEALTH...HIST/WRIT COLD/WAR EEC 20. PAGE 127 A2596 — EUR+WWI ECO/DEV CAP/ISM

S64
TINKER H.,"POLITICS IN SOUTHEAST ASIA." INT/ORG NAT/G CREATE PLAN TEC/DEV GUERRILLA KNOWL ORD/FREE COLD/WAR. PAGE 144 A2944 — S/ASIA ACT/RES REGION

B65
CORDIER A.W.,THE QUEST FOR PEACE. WOR+45 NAT/G PLAN BAL/PWR ECO/TAC ARMS/CONT NUC/PWR PWR...ANTHOL UN COLD/WAR. PAGE 30 A0617 — PEACE DIPLOM POLICY INT/ORG

B65
EISENHOWER D.D.,WAGING PEACE 1956-61: THE WHITE HOUSE YEARS. USA+45 DIPLOM LEAD INGP/REL RACE/REL PEACE ATTIT...TRADIT TIME/SEQ 20 EISNHWR/DD PRESIDENT COLD/WAR CIV/RIGHTS BERLIN. PAGE 41 A0833 — TOP/EX BIOG ORD/FREE POLICY

B65
FRIEDMANN W.,AN INTRODUCTION TO WORLD POLITICS (5TH ED.). WOR+45 ECO/UNDEV BAL/PWR FOR/AID INT/TRADE PEACE...STAT CENSUS CHARTS BIBLIOG T 20 COLD/WAR UN THIRD/WRLD. PAGE 49 A1003 — DIPLOM INT/ORG PROB/SOLV

B65
HUSS P.J.,RED SPIES IN THE UN. CZECHOSLVK USA+45 USSR COM/IND FORCES EDU/PROP NUC/PWR MARXISM 20 UN COLD/WAR. PAGE 69 A1421 — PEACE INT/ORG BAL/PWR DIPLOM

B65
LERCHE C.O.,THE COLD WAR AND AFTER. AFR COM S/ASIA USA+45 USSR NUC/PWR SOVEREIGN MARXISM...TIME/SEQ TREND BIBLIOG 20 COLD/WAR. PAGE 87 A1784 — DIPLOM BAL/PWR IDEA/COMP

B65
LIEUWEN E.,U.S. POLICY IN LATIN AMERICA: A SHORT HISTORY. L/A+17C USA+45 USA-45 DELIB/GP ECO/TAC 19/20 COLD/WAR MONROE/DOC. PAGE 89 A1812 — DIPLOM COLONIAL NAT/G FOR/AID

B65
MENON K.P.S.,MANY WORLDS. INDIA BAL/PWR CAP/ISM COLONIAL REV ORD/FREE PWR MARXISM...POLICY 20 COLD/WAR. PAGE 100 A2042 — BIOG DIPLOM NAT/G

B65
MEYERHOFF A.E.,THE STRATEGY OF PERSUASION: THE USE OF ADVERTISING SKILLS IN FIGHTING THE COLD WAR. USA+45 USSR PLAN ATTIT DRIVE...BIBLIOG 20 COLD/WAR. PAGE 100 A2054 — EDU/PROP SERV/IND METH/COMP DIPLOM

B65
MIDDLETON D.,CRISIS IN THE WEST. EUR+WWI FUT WOR+45 CHIEF PLAN ECO/TAC LEAD REGION NUC/PWR NAT/LISM MARXISM 20 COLD/WAR NATO EEC. PAGE 101 A2068 — INT/ORG DIPLOM NAT/G POLICY

B65
MOSKOWITZ H.,US SECURITY, ARMS CONTROL, AND DISARMAMENT 1961-1965. FORCES DIPLOM DETER WAR WEAPON...CHARTS 20 UN COLD/WAR NATO. PAGE 105 A2154 — BIBLIOG/A ARMS/CONT NUC/PWR PEACE

B65
PENNICK JL J.R.,THE POLITICS OF AMERICAN SCIENCE, 1939 TO THE PRESENT. USA+45 USA-45 INTELL TEC/DEV DIPLOM NEW/LIB...ANTHOL 20 COLD/WAR. PAGE 114 A2349 — POLICY ADMIN PHIL/SCI NAT/G

B65
TREFOUSSE H.L.,THE COLD WAR: A BOOK OF DOCUMENTS. ASIA L/A+17C USSR WOR+45 WOR-45 ECO/TAC FOR/AID ARMS/CONT NUC/PWR PEACE ORD/FREE...ANTHOL 20 COLD/WAR KENNEDY/JF EISNHWR/DD. PAGE 145 A2961 — BAL/PWR DIPLOM MARXISM

L65
KAPLAN M.A.,"OLD REALITIES AND NEW MYTHS." USA+45 WOR+45 INT/ORG NAT/G TOP/EX ACT/RES BAL/PWR ECO/TAC EDU/PROP LEGIT RIGID/FLEX ALL/VALS...RECORD COLD/WAR 20. PAGE 76 A1564 — ATTIT MYTH DIPLOM

L65
RUBIN A.P.,"UNITED STATES CONTEMPORARY PRACTICE RELATING TO INTERNATIONAL LAW." USA+45 WOR+45 CONSTN INT/ORG NAT/G DELIB/GP EX/STRUC DIPLOM DOMIN CT/SYS ROUTINE ORD/FREE...CONCPT COLD/WAR 20. PAGE 125 A2558 — LAW LEGIT INT/LAW

S65
DOSSICK J.J.,"DOCTORAL DISSERTATIONS ON RUSSIA, THE SOVIET UNION, AND EASTERN EUROPE." USSR ACADEM DIPLOM EDU/PROP MARXISM 19/20 COLD/WAR. PAGE 38 A0775 — BIBLIOG HUM SOC

S65
GROSS L.,"PROBLEMS OF INTERNATIONAL ADJUDICATION AND COMPLIANCE WITH INTERNATIONAL LAW: SOME SIMPLE SOLUTIONS." WOR+45 SOCIETY NAT/G DOMIN LEGIT ADJUD CT/SYS RIGID/FLEX HEALTH PWR...JURID NEW/IDEA COLD/WAR 20. PAGE 57 A1177 — LAW METH/CNCPT INT/LAW

S65
HAZARD J.N.,"CO-EXISTENCE LAW BOWS OUT." WOR+45 R+D INT/ORG VOL/ASSN CONSULT DELIB/GP ACT/RES CREATE PEACE KNOWL...JURID CONCPT COLD/WAR VAL/FREE 20. PAGE 63 A1300 — PROF/ORG ADJUD

S65
HELMREICH E.C.,"KADAR'S HUNGARY." COM EUR+WWI HUNGARY USSR INTELL ECO/DEV AGRI INT/ORG TOP/EX DOMIN ALL/VALS WORK COLD/WAR 20. PAGE 64 A1311 — NAT/G RIGID/FLEX TOTALISM

S65
PRABHAKAR P.,"SURVEY OF RESEARCH AND SOURCE MATERIALS; THE SINO-INDIAN BORDER DISPUTE." CHINA/COM INDIA LAW NAT/G PLAN BAL/PWR WAR...POLICY 20 COLD/WAR. PAGE 117 A2404 — BIBLIOG ASIA S/ASIA DIPLOM

S65
ROGGER H.,"EAST GERMANY: STABLE OR IMMOBILE." COM EUR+WWI GERMANY/E NAT/G INT/TRADE DOMIN EDU/PROP COERCE TOTALISM COLD/WAR 20. PAGE 123 A2516 — TOP/EX RIGID/FLEX GERMANY

C65
SCHWEBEL M.,"BEHAVIORAL SCIENCE AND HUMAN SURVIVAL." FORCES ARMS/CONT COERCE NUC/PWR WAR GP/REL NAT/LISM PERCEPT...POLICY PSY ANTHOL BIBLIOG/A 20 COLD/WAR. PAGE 130 A2662 — PEACE ACT/RES DIPLOM HEAL

C65
US AIR FORCE ACADEMY,"AMERICAN DEFENSE POLICY." COM INT/ORG TEC/DEV FOR/AID ARMS/CONT DETER NUC/PWR ...POLICY DECISION CONCPT ANTHOL BIBLIOG/A 20 COLD/WAR NATO. PAGE 149 A3054 — PLAN FORCES WAR COERCE

B66
BLACKSTOCK P.W.,AGENTS OF DECEIT: FRAUDS, FORGERIES AND POLITICAL INTRIGUES AMONG NATIONS. USSR EDU/PROP WRITING KNOWL 18/20 COLD/WAR KENNAN/G. PAGE 15 A0302 — CON/ANAL DIPLOM HIST/WRIT

B66
CLARK G.,WORLD PEACE THROUGH WORLD LAW; TWO ALTERNATIVE PLANS. WOR+45 DELIB/GP FORCES TAX CONFER ADJUD SANCTION ARMS/CONT WAR CHOOSE PRIVIL 20 UN COLD/WAR. PAGE 27 A0541 — INT/LAW PEACE PLAN INT/ORG

B66
CROWLEY D.W.,THE BACKGROUND TO CURRENT AFFAIRS. UK WOR+45 INT/ORG BAL/PWR NUC/PWR ATTIT ROLE 20 COLD/WAR. PAGE 33 A0665 — DIPLOM PWR POLICY

B66
DAENIKER G.,STRATEGIE DES KLEIN STAATS. SWITZERLND ACT/RES CREATE DIPLOM NEUTRAL DETER WAR WEAPON PWR SOVEREIGN...IDEA/COMP 20 COLD/WAR. PAGE 33 A0673 — NUC/PWR PLAN FORCES NAT/G

B66
EKIRCH A.A. JR.,IDEAS, IDEALS, AND AMERICAN DIPLOMACY. USA+45 USA-45 INT/ORG DOMIN COLONIAL ARMS/CONT DETER ISOLAT NAT/LISM...MAJORIT BIBLIOG 19/20 COLD/WAR. PAGE 41 A0834 — DIPLOM LEAD PEACE

B66
FRANK E.,LAWMAKERS IN A CHANGING WORLD. FRANCE UK USSR WOR+45 PARTIC EFFICIENCY ROLE ALL/IDEOS ...CHARTS ANTHOL PARLIAMENT 20 UN COLD/WAR. PAGE 48 A0979 — GOV/COMP LEGIS NAT/G DIPLOM

B66
HERZ M.F.,BEGINNINGS OF THE COLD WAR. COM POLAND USA+45 USSR INT/ORG NAT/G CHIEF FOR/AID DOMIN CONFER AGREE WAR PEACE 20 STALIN/J COLD/WAR UN. PAGE 64 A1321 — DIPLOM

B66
HORELICK A.L.,STRATEGIC POWER AND SOVIET FOREIGN POLICY. CUBA USSR FORCES PLAN CIVMIL/REL...POLICY DECISION 20 COLD/WAR. PAGE 67 A1383 — DIPLOM BAL/PWR DETER NUC/PWR

B66
KIM Y.K.,PATTERNS OF COMPETITIVE COEXISTENCE: USA VS. USSR. USA+45 USSR ECO/DEV ECO/UNDEV INT/ORG FOR/AID INT/TRADE ARMS/CONT...BIBLIOG 20 COLD/WAR. PAGE 79 A1618 — DIPLOM PEACE BAL/PWR DETER

B66
MARTIN L.W.,DIPLOMACY IN MODERN EUROPEAN HISTORY. EUR+WWI MOD/EUR INT/ORG NAT/G EX/STRUC ROUTINE WAR PEACE TOTALISM PWR 15/20 COLD/WAR EUROPE/W. PAGE 95 A1953 — DIPLOM POLICY

B66
MAY E.R.,ANXIETY AND AFFLUENCE: 1945-1965. USA+45 DIPLOM FOR/AID ARMS/CONT RACE/REL CONSEN...ANTHOL 20 COLD/WAR KENNEDY/JF EISNHWR/DD TRUMAN/HS — ANOMIE ECO/DEV NUC/PWR

BERLIN/BLO. PAGE 97 A1982 — WEALTH

B66
MC LELLAN D.S.,THE COLD WAR IN TRANSITION. USSR WOR+45 CONTROL LEAD NUC/PWR NAT/LISM SOVEREIGN 20 COLD/WAR THIRD/WRLD. PAGE 97 A1994
BAL/PWR DETER DIPLOM POLICY

B66
SANDERS R.E.,SPAIN AND THE UNITED NATIONS 1945-1950. SPAIN CHIEF DIPLOM CONFER SANCTION ATTIT ...POLICY 20 UN COLD/WAR. PAGE 127 A2599
INT/ORG FASCISM GP/REL STRANGE

B66
SOBEL L.A.,SOUTH VIETNAM: US-COMMUNIST CONFRONTATION IN SOUTHEAST ASIA 1961-65. VIETNAM FOR/AID CROWD DETER REV PEACE...GEOG 20 INTERVENT DIEM COLD/WAR. PAGE 134 A2754
WAR TIME/SEQ FORCES NAT/G

B66
WARBURG J.P.,THE UNITED STATES IN THE POSTWAR WORLD. USA+45 ECO/TAC...POLICY 20 COLD/WAR. PAGE 161 A3277
FOR/AID DIPLOM PLAN ADMIN

B66
WELCH R.H.W.,THE NEW AMERICANISM, AND OTHER SPEECHES AND ESSAYS. USA+45 ACADEM POL/PAR SCHOOL VOL/ASSN FORCES CAP/ISM TAX REV DISCRIM 20 CIV/RIGHTS COLD/WAR BIRCH/SOC. PAGE 163 A3313
DIPLOM FASCISM MARXISM RACE/REL

B66
WESTWOOD A.F.,FOREIGN AID IN A FOREIGN POLICY FRAMEWORK. AFR ASIA INDIA IRAN L/A+17C USA+45 USSR ECO/UNDEV AGRI FORCES LEGIS PLAN PROB/SOLV ...DECISION 20 COLD/WAR. PAGE 163 A3324
FOR/AID DIPLOM POLICY ECO/TAC

C66
DUROSELLE J.B.,"LE CONFLIT DE TRIESTE 1943-1954: ETUDES DE CAS DE CONFLITS INTERNATIONAUX III." ITALY USA+45 YUGOSLAVIA ELITES DELIB/GP PLAN ADJUST ...POLICY GEOG CHARTS IDEA/COMP TIME 20 TREATY UN COLD/WAR. PAGE 40 A0810
BIBLIOG WAR DIPLOM GEN/LAWS

B67
MACRIDIS R.C.,FOREIGN POLICY IN WORLD POLITICS (3RD ED.). EX/STRUC BAL/PWR COLONIAL NAT/LISM SKILL SOVEREIGN WEALTH...CONCPT TIME/SEQ ANTHOL 20 COLD/WAR. PAGE 93 A1902
DIPLOM POLICY NAT/G IDEA/COMP

B67
MCCLINTOCK R.,THE MEANING OF LIMITED WAR. FUT WOR+45 NAT/G FORCES GUERRILLA REV...POLICY SAMP/SIZ TREND NAT/COMP 45 COLD/WAR. PAGE 97 A1999
WAR NUC/PWR BAL/PWR DIPLOM

B67
PADELFORD N.J.,THE DYNAMICS OF INTERNATIONAL POLITICS (2ND ED.). WOR+45 LAW INT/ORG FORCES TEC/DEV REGION NAT/LISM PEACE ATTIT PWR ALL/IDEOS UN COLD/WAR NATO TREATY. PAGE 113 A2314
DIPLOM NAT/G POLICY DECISION

B67
ROACH J.R.,THE UNITED STATES AND THE ATLANTIC COMMUNITY; ISSUES AND PROSPECTS. WOR+45 TEC/DEV ECO/TAC COLONIAL REGION PEACE ROLE...ANTHOL NATO COLD/WAR EEC. PAGE 121 A2491
INT/ORG POLICY ADJUST DIPLOM

B67
ROSENAU J.N.,DOMESTIC SOURCES OF FOREIGN POLICY. WOR+45 STRATA COM/IND MUNIC POL/PAR LOBBY PARTIC REGION ATTIT...PSY SOC COLD/WAR. PAGE 124 A2534
DIPLOM POLICY NAT/G CHOOSE

B67
RUSSELL B.,WAR CRIMES IN VIETNAM. USA+45 VIETNAM FORCES DIPLOM WEAPON RACE/REL DISCRIM ISOLAT BIO/SOC 20 COLD/WAR RUSSELL/B. PAGE 126 A2574
WAR CRIME ATTIT POLICY

S67
APEL H.,"LES NOUVEAUX ASPECTS DE LA POLITIQUE ETRANGERE ALLEMANDE." EUR+WWI GERMANY POL/PAR BAL/PWR ECO/TAC INT/TRADE NUC/PWR NAT/LISM PEACE ...POLICY 20 EEC COLD/WAR. PAGE 8 A0168
DIPLOM INT/ORG FEDERAL

S67
CARROLL K.J.,"SECOND STEP TOWARD ARMS CONTROL." WOR+45 INT/ORG VOL/ASSN FORCES PROB/SOLV RISK WEAPON 20 COLD/WAR. PAGE 25 A0503
ARMS/CONT DIPLOM PLAN NUC/PWR

S67
EISENDRATH C.,"THE OUTER SPACE TREATY." CHINA/COM COM USA+45 DIPLOM CONTROL NUC/PWR...INT/LAW 20 UN COLD/WAR TREATY. PAGE 41 A0831
SPACE INT/ORG PEACE ARMS/CONT

S67
KRUSCHE H.,"THE STRIVING OF THE KIESINGER-STRAUS GOVERNMENT FOR NUCLEAR WEAPONS IS A THREAT TO EUROPEAN SECURITY." EUR+WWI GERMANY BAL/PWR SANCTION WEAPON PEACE ORD/FREE...MARXIST 20 NATO COLD/WAR. PAGE 82 A1688
ARMS/CONT INT/ORG NUC/PWR DIPLOM

S67
PEUKERT W.,"WEST GERMANY'S 'RED TRADE'." COM GERMANY INDUS CAP/ISM DOMIN SANCTION DEMAND PEACE UTIL...MARXIST 20 COLD/WAR. PAGE 115 A2371
DIPLOM ECO/TAC INT/TRADE

S67
REINTANZ G.,"THE SPACE TREATY." WOR+45 DIPLOM CONTROL ARMS/CONT NUC/PWR WAR...MARXIST 20 COLD/WAR UN TREATY. PAGE 120 A2461
SPACE INT/LAW INT/ORG

PEACE

S67
ROMANOVSKY S.,"MISUSE OF CULTURAL COOPERATION." USA+45 INTELL DIPLOM DOMIN ATTIT COLD/WAR. PAGE 123 A2518
EDU/PROP POLICY MARXISM CAP/ISM

S67
STEEL R.,"BEYOND THE POWER BLOCS." USA+45 USSR ECO/UNDEV NEUTRAL NUC/PWR NAT/LISM ATTIT...GEOG NATO WARSAW/P COLD/WAR. PAGE 137 A2811
DIPLOM TREND BAL/PWR PLAN

S67
STEELE R.,"A TASTE FOR INTERVENTION." USA+45 FOR/AID INT/TRADE EDU/PROP COLONIAL WAR PWR...TREND 20 COLD/WAR. PAGE 137 A2812
POLICY DIPLOM DOMIN ATTIT

S67
WILPERT C.,"A LOOK IN THE MIRROR AND OVER THE WALL." GERMANY POL/PAR...KNO/TEST COLD/WAR. PAGE 165 A3358
NAT/G PLAN DIPLOM ATTIT

C67
GEHLEN M.P.,"THE POLITICS OF COEXISTENCE: SOVIET METHODS AND MOTIVES." COM USSR NAT/G INT/TRADE EDU/PROP ARMS/CONT DETER KNOWL...CHARTS IDEA/COMP 20 COLD/WAR. PAGE 52 A1056
BIBLIOG PEACE DIPLOM MARXISM

C67
HUDSON G.F.,"THE HARD AND BITTER PEACE; WORLD POLITICS SINCE 1945." ASIA COM S/ASIA USSR WOR+45 COLONIAL WAR...TREND BIBLIOG/A 20 COLD/WAR UN. PAGE 68 A1405
DIPLOM INT/ORG ARMS/CONT BAL/PWR

COLE A.B. A0566

COLE/GEO....GEORGE COLE

COLLECTIVE BARGAINING....SEE BARGAIN+LABOR+GP/REL

COLLECTIVE SECURITY....SEE FORCES

COLLINS H. A0567

COLLINS R. A0549

COLLISON R.L. A0568,A0569

COLOMBIA....SEE ALSO L/A+17C

B63
PEREZ ORTIZ R.,ANUARIO BIBLIOGRAFICO COLOMBIANO, 1961. AGRI...INT/LAW JURID SOC LING 20 COLOMB. PAGE 115 A2354
BIBLIOG L/A+17C NAT/G

B66
CURRIE L.,ACCELERATING DEVELOPMENT: THE NECESSITY AND MEANS. COLOMBIA USA+45 INDUS DIPLOM EFFICIENCY WEALTH...METH/CNCPT NEW/IDEA 20. PAGE 33 A0668
PLAN ECO/UNDEV FOR/AID TEC/DEV

S67
FABREGA J.,"ANTECEDENTES EXTRANJEROS EN LA CONSTITUCION PANAMENA." CUBA L/A+17C PANAMA URUGUAY EX/STRUC LEGIS DIPLOM ORD/FREE 19/20 COLOMB MEXIC/AMER. PAGE 43 A0882
CONSTN JURID NAT/G PARL/PROC

COLOMBOS C.J. A0570

COLONIAL AMERICA....SEE PRE/US/AM, PRE/AMER

COLONIAL....COLONIALISM; SEE ALSO DOMIN

N
INDIAN COUNCIL WORLD AFFAIRS,SELECT ARTICLES ON CURRENT AFFAIRS (BIBLIOGRAPHICAL SERIES: 7). AFR ASIA COM EUR+WWI S/ASIA UK COLONIAL NUC/PWR PEACE ATTIT...INT/LAW SOC 20. PAGE 70 A1437
BIBLIOG DIPLOM INT/ORG ECO/UNDEV

N
INTERNATIONAL COMN JURISTS,AFRICAN CONFERENCE ON THE RULE OF LAW. AFR INT/ORG LEGIS DIPLOM CONFER COLONIAL ORD/FREE...CONCPT METH/COMP 20. PAGE 71 A1452
CT/SYS JURID DELIB/GP

N
UNIVERSITY OF FLORIDA LIBRARY,DOORS TO LATIN AMERICA; RECENT BOOKS AND PAMPHLETS. CONSTN CULTURE SOCIETY ECO/UNDEV COLONIAL LEAD GOV/REL NAT/LISM ATTIT...HUM SOC 20. PAGE 149 A3047
BIBLIOG/A L/A+17C DIPLOM NAT/G

N
AFRICANA NEWSLETTER. ECO/UNDEV ACADEM SECT DIPLOM PRESS COLONIAL NAT/LISM 20. PAGE 1 A0001
BIBLIOG/A AFR NAT/G

N
INTERNATIONAL BOOK NEWS, 1928-1934. ECO/UNDEV FINAN INDUS LABOR INT/TRADE CONFER ADJUD COLONIAL...HEAL
BIBLIOG/A DIPLOM

SOC/WK CHARTS 20 LEAGUE/NAT. PAGE 1 A0010
INT/LAW INT/ORG

N
AFRICAN RESEARCH BULLETIN. AFR CULTURE NAT/G COLONIAL...SOC 20. PAGE 2 A0026
BIBLIOG/A DIPLOM PRESS

N
PUBLISHERS' CIRCULAR, THE OFFICIAL ORGAN OF THE PUBLISHERS' ASSOCIATION OF GREAT BRITAIN AND IRELAND. EUR+WWI MOD/EUR UK LAW PROB/SOLV DIPLOM COLONIAL ATTIT...HUM 19/20 CMN/WLTH. PAGE 2 A0039
BIBLIOG NAT/G WRITING LEAD

N
AFRICAN BIBLIOGRAPHIC CENTER,A CURRENT BIBLIOGRAPHY ON AFRICAN AFFAIRS. LAW CULTURE ECO/UNDEV LABOR SECT DIPLOM FOR/AID COLONIAL NAT/LISM...LING 20. PAGE 5 A0094
BIBLIOG/A AFR NAT/G REGION

N
ASIA FOUNDATION,LIBRARY NOTES. LAW CONSTN CULTURE SOCIETY ECO/UNDEV INT/ORG NAT/G COLONIAL LEAD REGION NAT/LISM ATTIT 20 UN. PAGE 9 A0189
BIBLIOG/A ASIA S/ASIA DIPLOM

N
CORDIER H.,BIBLIOTECA SINICA. SOCIETY STRUCT SECT DIPLOM COLONIAL...GEOG SOC CON/ANAL. PAGE 30 A0618
BIBLIOG/A NAT/G CULTURE ASIA

N
DOHERTY D.K.,PRELIMINARY BIBLIOGRAPHY OF COLONIZATION AND SETTLEMENT IN LATIN AMERICA AND ANGLO-AMERICA. L/A+17C PRE/AMER USA-45 ECO/UNDEV NAT/G 15/20. PAGE 38 A0768
BIBLIOG COLONIAL ADMIN DIPLOM

N
HOOVER INSTITUTION,UNITED STATES AND CANADIAN PUBLICATIONS ON AFRICA. CULTURE ECO/UNDEV AGRI TEC/DEV EDU/PROP COLONIAL RACE/REL NAT/LISM ATTIT HEALTH...SOC SOC/WK 20. PAGE 67 A1381
BIBLIOG DIPLOM NAT/G AFR

NCO
CARRINGTON C.E.,THE COMMONWEALTH IN AFRICA (PAMPHLET). UK STRUCT NAT/G COLONIAL REPRESENT GOV/REL RACE/REL NAT/LISM...MAJORIT 20 EEC NEGRO COLD/WAR. PAGE 25 A0500
ECO/UNDEV AFR DIPLOM PLAN

B00
GRIFFIN A.P.C.,LIST OF BOOKS RELATING TO THE THEORY OF COLONIZATION, GOVERNMENT OF DEPENDENCIES, PROTECTORATES, AND RELATED TOPICS. FRANCE GERMANY ITALY SPAIN UK USA-45 WOR-45 ECO/TAC ADMIN CONTROL REGION NAT/LISM ALL/VALS PWR...INT/LAW SOC 16/19. PAGE 56 A1149
BIBLIOG/A COLONIAL GOV/REL DOMIN

B00
MOCKLER-FERRYMAN A.,BRITISH WEST AFRICA. FRANCE GERMANY NIGER SIER/LEONE UK CULTURE DIPLOM WAR RACE/REL PRODUC PROFIT WEALTH...POLICY PREDICT 19. PAGE 102 A2095
AFR COLONIAL INT/TRADE CAP/ISM

B00
MORRIS H.C.,THE HISTORY OF COLONIZATION. WOR+45 WOR-45 ECO/DEV ECO/UNDEV INT/ORG ACT/RES PLAN ECO/TAC LEGIT ROUTINE COERCE ATTIT DRIVE ALL/VALS ...GEOG TREND 19. PAGE 105 A2148
DOMIN SOVEREIGN COLONIAL

B00
VOLPICELLI Z.,RUSSIA ON THE PACIFIC AND THE SIBERIAN RAILWAY. MOD/EUR ECO/UNDEV INT/ORG FORCES PLAN DOMIN COLONIAL ROUTINE ATTIT ALL/VALS...OBS HIST/WRIT TIME/SEQ TREND CON/ANAL AUD/VIS CHARTS 18/19. PAGE 159 A3248
NAT/G ACT/RES RUSSIA

B01
GRIFFIN A.P.C.,LIST OF BOOKS ON SAMOA (PAMPHLET). GERMANY S/ASIA UK USA-45 WOR-45 ECO/UNDEV REGION ALL/VALS ORD/FREE ALL/IDEOS...GEOG INT/LAW 19 SAMOA GUAM. PAGE 56 A1150
BIBLIOG/A COLONIAL DIPLOM

B01
HART A.B.,AMERICAN HISTORY TOLD BY CONTEMPORARIES. UK CULTURE FINAN SECT FORCES DIPLOM TAX RUMOR CT/SYS REV GOV/REL GP/REL...ANTHOL 17/18 PRE/US/AM FEDERALIST. PAGE 62 A1273
USA-45 COLONIAL SOVEREIGN

B02
MOREL E.D.,AFFAIRS OF WEST AFRICA. UK FINAN INDUS FAM KIN SECT CHIEF WORKER DIPLOM RACE/REL LITERACY HEALTH...CHARTS 18/20 AFRICA/W NEGRO. PAGE 104 A2129
COLONIAL ADMIN AFR

B02
SEELEY J.R.,THE EXPANSION OF ENGLAND. MOD/EUR S/ASIA UK CULTURE NAT/G FORCES PLAN DOMIN EDU/PROP COLONIAL ROUTINE ATTIT ALL/VALS SOVEREIGN...CONCPT HIST/WRIT PARLIAMENT 18 CMN/WLTH. PAGE 131 A2679
INT/ORG ACT/RES CAP/ISM INDIA

B03
FORTESCUE G.K.,SUBJECT INDEX OF THE MODERN WORKS ADDED TO THE LIBRARY OF THE BRITISH MUSEUM IN THE YEARS 1881-1900 (3 VOLS.). UK LAW CONSTN FINAN NAT/G FORCES INT/TRADE COLONIAL 19. PAGE 47 A0968
BIBLIOG INDEX WRITING

B03
GRIFFIN A.P.C.,SELECT LIST OF REFERENCES ON THE MONROE DOCTRINE (PAMPHLET). L/A+17C NAT/G TOP/EX 19/20. PAGE 56 A1151
BIBLIOG DIPLOM COLONIAL

B03
GRIFFIN A.P.C.,LISTS PUBLISHED 1902-03: ANGLO-SAXON INTERESTS (PAMPHLET). UK USA-45 ELITES SOCIETY DIPLOM ISOLAT 19/20. PAGE 56 A1152
BIBLIOG COLONIAL RACE/REL DOMIN

B03
MOREL E.D.,THE BRITISH CASE IN FRENCH CONGO. CONGO/BRAZ FRANCE UK COERCE MORAL WEALTH...POLICY INT/LAW 20 CONGO/LEOP. PAGE 104 A2130
DIPLOM INT/TRADE COLONIAL AFR

B06
GRIFFIN A.P.C.,SELECT LIST OF REFERENCES ON THE BRITISH TARIFF MOVEMENT. MOD/EUR UK BAL/PWR BARGAIN ECO/TAC LAISSEZ 20. PAGE 56 A1154
BIBLIOG/A INT/TRADE TARIFFS COLONIAL

C06
MONTGOMERY H.,"A DICTIONARY OF POLITICAL PHRASES AND ILLUSIONS WITH A SHORT BIBLIOGRAPHY." EUR+WWI MOD/EUR UK AGRI LABOR LOC/G NAT/G COLONIAL CHOOSE RACE/REL. PAGE 103 A2114
BIBLIOG DICTIONARY POLICY DIPLOM

B08
GRIFFIN A.P.C.,LIST OF REFERENCES ON INTERNATIONAL ARBITRATION. FRANCE L/A+17C USA-45 WOR-45 DIPLOM CONFER COLONIAL ARMS/CONT BAL/PAY EQUILIB SOVEREIGN ...DECISION 19/20 MEXIC/AMER. PAGE 56 A1156
BIBLIOG/A INT/ORG INT/LAW DELIB/GP

B08
LABRIOLA A.,ESSAYS ON THE MATERIALISTIC CONCEPTION OF HISTORY. STRATA POL/PAR CAP/ISM DIPLOM INT/TRADE WAR 20. PAGE 83 A1706
MARXIST WORKER REV COLONIAL

B09
FREMANTLE H.E.S.,THE NEW NATION, A SURVEY OF THE CONDITION AND PROSPECTS OF SOUTH AFRICA. SOUTH/AFR CONSTN POL/PAR DIPLOM DOMIN COLONIAL WEALTH...SOC TREND 19. PAGE 49 A0996
NAT/LISM SOVEREIGN RACE/REL REGION

B10
GRIFFIN A.P.C.,LIST OF REFERENCES ON RECIPROCITY (2ND REV. ED.). CANADA CUBA UK USA-45 WOR-45 NAT/G TARIFFS CONFER COLONIAL CONTROL SANCTION CONSEN ALL/VALS...DECISION 19/20. PAGE 56 A1157
BIBLIOG/A VOL/ASSN DIPLOM REPAR

B10
MENDELSSOHN S.,SOUTH AFRICAN BIBLIOGRAPHY (2 VOLS.). SOUTH/AFR EXTR/IND LABOR SECT DIPLOM INT/TRADE COLONIAL RACE/REL DISCRIM...GEOG 20. PAGE 99 A2038
BIBLIOG/A AFR NAT/G NAT/LISM

B14
HARRIS N.D.,INTERVENTION AND COLONIZATION IN AFRICA. BELGIUM FRANCE GERMANY MOD/EUR PORTUGAL UK ECO/UNDEV BAL/PWR DOMIN CONTROL PWR...GEOG 19/20. PAGE 62 A1267
AFR COLONIAL DIPLOM

B17
DOS SANTOS M.,BIBLIOGRAPHIA GERAL, A DESCRIPCAO BIBLIOGRAFICA DE LIVROS TANTO DE AUTORES PORTUGUEZES COMO BRASILEIROS... BRAZIL PORTUGAL NAT/G LEAD GP/REL 15/20. PAGE 38 A0774
BIBLIOG/A L/A+17C DIPLOM COLONIAL

B19
SUMNER W.G.,WAR AND OTHER ESSAYS. USA-45 DELIB/GP DIPLOM TARIFFS COLONIAL PEACE SOVEREIGN 20. PAGE 140 A2864
INT/TRADE ORD/FREE CAP/ISM ECO/TAC

N19
ASIAN-AFRICAN CONFERENCE,SELECTED DOCUMENTS OF THE BANDUNG CONFERENCE (PAMPHLET). S/ASIA PLAN ECO/TAC CONFER REGION REV NAT/LISM 20. PAGE 9 A0191
NEUTRAL ECO/UNDEV COLONIAL DIPLOM

N19
BENTHAM J.,A PLAN FOR AN UNIVERSAL AND PERPETUAL PEACE (1838) (PAMPHLET). NAT/G FORCES BAL/PWR INT/TRADE ADMIN AGREE CT/SYS ARMS/CONT SOVEREIGN WEALTH GEN/LAWS. PAGE 13 A0269
INT/ORG INT/LAW PEACE COLONIAL

N19
GRANT N.,COMMUNIST PSYCHOLOGICAL OFFENSIVE: DISTORTION IN THE TRANSLATION OF OFFICIAL DOCUMENTS (PAMPHLET). USSR POL/PAR CHIEF FOR/AID PRESS WRITING COLONIAL LEAD WAR PEACE 20 KHRUSH/N. PAGE 55 A1129
MARXISM DIPLOM EDU/PROP

N19
HANNA A.J.,EUROPEAN RULE IN AFRICA (PAMPHLET). BELGIUM FRANCE MOD/EUR UK WOR+45 WOR-45 ECO/UNDEV NAT/G PARTIC SOVEREIGN...NAT/COMP 19/20. PAGE 61 A1252
DIPLOM COLONIAL AFR NAT/LISM

N19
LISKA G.,THE GREATER MAGHREB: FROM INDEPENDENCE TO UNITY? (PAMPHLET). ALGERIA ISLAM MOROCCO PROB/SOLV BAL/PWR CONFER COLONIAL REPRESENT NAT/LISM 20 TUNIS. PAGE 90 A1835
ECO/UNDEV REGION DIPLOM DOMIN

N19
MEZERIK A.G.,COLONIALISM AND THE UNITED NATIONS (PAMPHLET). WOR+45 NAT/G ADMIN LEAD WAR CHOOSE EFFICIENCY PEACE ATTIT ORD/FREE...POLICY CHARTS UN COLD/WAR. PAGE 100 A2061
COLONIAL DIPLOM BAL/PWR INT/ORG

N19
PROVISIONS SECTION OAU,ORGANIZATION OF AFRICAN UNITY: BASIC DOCUMENTS AND RESOLUTIONS (PAMPHLET). AFR CULTURE ECO/UNDEV DIPLOM ECO/TAC EDU/PROP COLONIAL ARMS/CONT NUC/PWR RACE/REL DISCRIM NAT/LISM 20 UN OAU. PAGE 118 A2415
CONSTN EX/STRUC SOVEREIGN INT/ORG

N19
SALKEVER L.R.,SUB-SAHARA AFRICA (PAMPHLET). AFR
ECO/UNDEV

USSR EXTR/IND NAT/G SCHOOL DIPLOM COLONIAL WEALTH ...GEOG CHARTS 16/20. PAGE 127 A2594
TEC/DEV TASK INT/TRADE

N19
TAYLOR T.G.,CANADA'S ROLE IN GEOPOLITICS (PAMPHLET). CANADA FUT USSR COLONIAL REGION WEALTH ...CHARTS 20. PAGE 142 A2901
GEOG DIPLOM SOCIETY ECO/DEV

N19
VELYAMINOV G.,AFRICA AND THE COMMON MARKET (PAMPHLET). AFR MARKET VOL/ASSN ECO/TAC COLONIAL ORD/FREE...SOCIALIST 20 THIRD/WRLD. PAGE 158 A3227
INT/ORG INT/TRADE SOVEREIGN ECO/UNDEV

B20
WOOLF L.,EMPIRE AND COMMERCE IN AFRICA. EUR+WWI MOD/EUR FINAN INDUS MARKET INT/ORG PLAN COERCE ATTIT DRIVE PWR WEALTH...CONCPT TIME/SEQ TREND CHARTS 20. PAGE 167 A3394
AFR DOMIN COLONIAL SOVEREIGN

C25
MOON P.T.,"SYLLABUS ON INTERNATIONAL RELATIONS." EUR+WWI MOD/EUR USA-45 FORCES COLONIAL WAR WEAPON NAT/LISM...POLICY BIBLIOG T 19/20. PAGE 103 A2120
INT/ORG DIPLOM NAT/G

B26
LEWIN E.,RECENT PUBLICATIONS IN THE LIBRARY OF THE ROYAL COLONIAL INSTITUTE (PAMPHLET). CANADA UK EX/STRUC PARL/PROC NAT/LISM SOVEREIGN 20 CMN/WLTH PARLIAMENT. PAGE 88 A1799
BIBLIOG COLONIAL CONSTN DIPLOM

B27
HARRIS N.D.,EUROPE AND AFRICA. BELGIUM FRANCE GERMANY MOD/EUR PORTUGAL UK ECO/UNDEV BAL/PWR PWR ...GEOG 19/20. PAGE 62 A1268
AFR COLONIAL DIPLOM

B27
PARRINGTON V.L.,MAIN CURRENTS IN AMERICAN THOUGHT (VOL.I). USA-45 AGRI POL/PAR DIPLOM TAX REGION REV 17/18 FRANKLIN/B JEFFERSN/T. PAGE 114 A2336
COLONIAL SECT FEEDBACK ALL/IDEOS

B28
HALL W.P.,EMPIRE TO COMMONWEALTH. FUT WOR-45 CONSTN ECO/DEV ECO/UNDEV INT/ORG PROVS PLAN DIPLOM EDU/PROP ADMIN COLONIAL PEACE PERSON ALL/VALS ...POLICY GEOG SOC OBS RECORD TREND CMN/WLTH PARLIAMENT 19/20. PAGE 60 A1229
VOL/ASSN NAT/G UK

B28
HURST C.,GREAT BRITAIN AND THE DOMINIONS. EUR+WWI CULTURE ECO/DEV INT/ORG NAT/G DIPLOM ECO/TAC COLONIAL ATTIT PWR SOVEREIGN...TIME/SEQ GEN/LAWS TOT/POP VAL/FREE 20 CMN/WLTH. PAGE 69 A1420
VOL/ASSN DOMIN UK

B28
STUART G.H.,LATIN AMERICA AND THE UNITED STATES. USA-45 ECO/UNDEV INT/ORG NAT/G POL/PAR PLAN DOMIN EDU/PROP COLONIAL REGION COERCE ATTIT ALL/VALS ...POLICY GEOG TREND 19/20. PAGE 139 A2853
L/A+17C DIPLOM

B29
BOUDET P.,BIBLIOGRAPHIE DE L'INDOCHINE FRANCAISE. S/ASIA VIETNAM SECT...GEOG LING 20. PAGE 17 A0344
BIBLIOG ADMIN COLONIAL DIPLOM

B30
SMUTS J.C.,AFRICA AND SOME WORLD PROBLEMS. RHODESIA SOUTH/AFR CULTURE ECO/UNDEV INDUS INT/ORG SECT PROB/SOLV REGION GOV/REL DISCRIM ATTIT 19/20 LEAGUE/NAT LIVNGSTN/D NEGRO. PAGE 134 A2748
LEGIS AFR COLONIAL RACE/REL

B31
BORCHARD E.H.,GUIDE TO THE LAW AND LEGAL LITERATURE OF FRANCE. FRANCE FINAN INDUS LABOR SECT LEGIS ADMIN COLONIAL CRIME OWN...INT/LAW 20. PAGE 17 A0337
BIBLIOG/A LAW CONSTN METH

B32
CARDINALL AW,A BIBLIOGRAPHY OF THE GOLD COAST. AFR UK NAT/G EX/STRUC ATTIT...POLICY 19/20. PAGE 24 A0479
BIBLIOG ADMIN COLONIAL DIPLOM

B33
WAMBAUCH S.,PLEBISCITES SINCE THE WORLD WAR: WITH A COLLECTION OF OFFICIAL DOCUMENTS. WOR-45 COLONIAL SANCTION...MAJORIT DECISION CHARTS BIBLIOG 19/20 WWI. PAGE 161 A3272
DIPLOM CONSTN NAT/G CHOOSE

B34
LOVELL R.I.,THE STRUGGLE FOR SOUTH AFRICA, 1875-1899. GERMANY RHODESIA SOUTH/AFR UK NAT/G ECO/TAC HABITAT WEALTH...POLICY 19. PAGE 91 A1866
COLONIAL DIPLOM WAR GP/REL

B35
FOREIGN AFFAIRS BIBLIOGRAPHY: A SELECTED AND ANNOTATED LIST OF BOOKS ON INTERNATIONAL RELATIONS 1919-1962 (4 VOLS.). CONSTN FORCES COLONIAL ARMS/CONT WAR NAT/LISM PEACE ATTIT DRIVE...POLICY INT/LAW 20. PAGE 3 A0050
BIBLIOG/A DIPLOM INT/ORG

B35
LANGER W.L.,THE DIPLOMACY OF IMPERIALISM 1890-1902. FRANCE GERMANY ITALY UK WOR-45 BAL/PWR INT/TRADE LEGIT ADJUD CONTROL WAR PWR SOVEREIGN...CHARTS BIBLIOG/A 19/20. PAGE 84 A1726
DIPLOM COLONIAL DOMIN

B35
WEINBERG A.K.,MANIFEST DESTINY: A STUDY OF NATIONALIST EXPANSIONISM IN AMERICAN HISTORY.
NAT/LISM GEOG

USA+45 USA-45 FORCES DIPLOM COLONIAL WAR ATTIT 18/20 INTERVENT. PAGE 162 A3305
COERCE NAT/G

B36
BOYCE A.N.,EUROPE AND SOUTH AFRICA. FRANCE GERMANY ITALY SOUTH/AFR UK INDUS NAT/G CONTROL REV WAR NAT/LISM...CONCPT HIST/WRIT 20. PAGE 18 A0362
COLONIAL GOV/COMP NAT/COMP DIPLOM

B36
ROBINSON H.,DEVELOPMENT OF THE BRITISH EMPIRE. WOR-45 CULTURE SOCIETY STRUCT ECO/DEV ECO/UNDEV INT/ORG VOL/ASSN FORCES CREATE PLAN DOMIN EDU/PROP ADMIN COLONIAL PWR WEALTH...POLICY GEOG CHARTS CMN/WLTH 16/20. PAGE 122 A2503
NAT/G HIST/WRIT UK

B36
VARLEY D.H.,A BIBLIOGRAPHY OF ITALIAN COLONISATION IN AFRICA WITH A SECTION ON ABYSSINIA. AFR ETHIOPIA ITALY LIBYA SOMALIA AGRI FINAN LABOR TEC/DEV DIPLOM INT/TRADE RACE/REL DISCRIM 19/20. PAGE 158 A3222
BIBLIOG COLONIAL ADMIN LAW

B37
BLAKE J.W.,EUROPEAN BEGINNINGS IN WEST AFRICA 1454-1578. FRANCE GUINEA PORTUGAL UK PWR WEALTH 16/16 AFRICA/W. PAGE 15 A0305
DIPLOM COLONIAL INT/TRADE DOMIN

B37
DE KIEWIET C.W.,THE IMPERIAL FACTOR IN SOUTH AFRICA. AFR SOUTH/AFR UK WAR...POLICY SOC 19. PAGE 35 A0705
DIPLOM COLONIAL CULTURE

B37
KOHN H.,FORCE OR REASON; ISSUES OF THE TWENTIETH CENTURY. WOR+45 NAT/G DIPLOM WAR DRIVE ORD/FREE ALL/IDEOS FASCISM PLURISM...POLICY IDEA/COMP 20. PAGE 81 A1660
COERCE DOMIN RATIONAL COLONIAL

B37
ROYAL INST. INT. AFF.,THE COLONIAL PROBLEM. WOR-45 LAW ECO/DEV ECO/UNDEV NAT/G PLAN ECO/TAC EDU/PROP ADMIN ATTIT ALL/VALS...CONCPT 20. PAGE 125 A2556
INT/ORG ACT/RES SOVEREIGN COLONIAL

B37
UNION OF SOUTH AFRICA,REPORT CONCERNING ADMINISTRATION OF SOUTH WEST AFRICA (6 VOLS.). SOUTH/AFR INDUS PUB/INST FORCES LEGIS BUDGET DIPLOM EDU/PROP ADJUD CT/SYS...GEOG CHARTS 20 AFRICA/SW LEAGUE/NAT. PAGE 148 A3028
NAT/G ADMIN COLONIAL CONSTN

B37
VINER J.,STUDIES IN THE THEORY OF INTERNATIONAL TRADE. WOR-45 CONSTN ECO/DEV AGRI INDUS MARKET INT/ORG LABOR NAT/G ECO/TAC TARIFFS COLONIAL ATTIT WEALTH...POLICY CONCPT MATH STAT OBS SAMP TREND GEN/LAWS MARX/KARL 20. PAGE 159 A3236
CAP/ISM INT/TRADE

B38
FRANKEL S.H.,CAPITAL INVESTMENT IN AFRICA. AFR EUR+WWI RHODESIA SOUTH/AFR UK FINAN FOR/AID COLONIAL DEMAND UTIL WEALTH...METH/CNCPT CHARTS 20 CONGO/LEOP. PAGE 48 A0983
ECO/UNDEV EXTR/IND DIPLOM PRODUC

B38
HOBSON J.A.,IMPERIALISM. MOD/EUR UK WOR-45 CULTURE ECO/UNDEV NAT/G VOL/ASSN PLAN EDU/PROP LEGIT REGION COERCE ATTIT PWR...POLICY PLURIST TIME/SEQ GEN/LAWS 19/20. PAGE 66 A1348
DOMIN ECO/TAC BAL/PWR COLONIAL

B39
FURNIVALL J.S.,NETHERLANDS INDIA. INDIA NETHERLAND CULTURE INDUS NAT/G DIPLOM ADMIN WEALTH...POLICY CHARTS 17/20. PAGE 50 A1029
COLONIAL ECO/UNDEV SOVEREIGN PLURISM

B39
LENIN V.I.,IMPERIALISM: THE HIGHEST STAGE OF CAPITALISM. USSR WOR-45 DIST/IND INT/TRADE ATTIT MARXISM SOCISM...CHARTS 20. PAGE 87 A1773
MARXIST CAP/ISM COLONIAL DOMIN

B39
ROBBINS L.,ECONOMIC CAUSES OF WAR. WOR-45 ECO/DEV ECO/UNDEV INT/ORG NAT/G TEC/DEV DIPLOM DOMIN COLONIAL ATTIT DRIVE PWR WEALTH...POLICY CONCPT OBS SAMP TREND CON/ANAL GEN/LAWS MARX/KARL 20. PAGE 122 A2493
COERCE ECO/TAC WAR

B40
ITALIAN LIBRARY OF INFORMATION: OUTLINE STUDIES (VOL. V). ITALY LIBYA CONTROL...FASCIST 20. PAGE 3 A0052
COLONIAL DIPLOM ECO/TAC POLICY

B41
PERHAM M.,AFRICANS AND BRITISH RULE. AFR UK ECO/TAC CONTROL GP/REL ATTIT 20. PAGE 115 A2355
DIPLOM COLONIAL ADMIN ECO/UNDEV

B41
WHITAKER A.P.,THE UNITED STATES AND THE INDEPENDENCE OF LATIN AMERICA, 1800-1830. PORTUGAL SPAIN USA-45 COLONIAL REGION SOVEREIGN...POLICY TIME/SEQ BIBLIOG/A 18/20. PAGE 163 A3329
DIPLOM L/A+17C CONCPT ORD/FREE

B42
CONOVER H.F.,FRENCH COLONIES IN AFRICA: A LIST OF REFERENCES. ALGERIA FRANCE MOROCCO SOMALIA SUDAN CULTURE AGRI LOC/G SECT FORCES DIPLOM INT/TRADE NAT/LISM HEALTH...CON/ANAL 20. PAGE 29 A0594
BIBLIOG AFR ECO/UNDEV COLONIAL

B42
CONOVER H.F.,NEW ZEALAND: A SELECTED LIST OF REFERENCES (PAMPHLET). NEW/ZEALND ECO/UNDEV AGRI INDUS LABOR NAT/G SCHOOL FORCES DIPLOM COLONIAL WAR ...HUM 20. PAGE 29 A0595
BIBLIOG/A S/ASIA CULTURE

B42
CROWE S.E.,THE BERLIN WEST AFRICA CONFERENCE, 1884-85. GERMANY ELITES MARKET INT/ORG DELIB/GP FORCES PROB/SOLV BAL/PWR CAP/ISM DOMIN COLONIAL ...INT/LAW 19. PAGE 33 A0664
AFR CONFER INT/TRADE DIPLOM

B42
JOSHI P.S.,THE TYRANNY OF COLOUR. INDIA SOUTH/AFR UK ECO/UNDEV NAT/G POL/PAR DIPLOM ECO/TAC WAR ...POLICY 19/20. PAGE 75 A1538
COLONIAL DISCRIM RACE/REL

B42
PAGINSKY P.,GERMAN WORKS RELATING TO AMERICA, 1493-1800; A LIST COMPILED FROM THE COLLECTIONS OF THE NEW YORK PUBLIC LIBRARY. GERMANY PRE/AMER CULTURE COLONIAL ATTIT...POLICY SOC 15/19. PAGE 113 A2317
BIBLIOG/A NAT/G L/A+17C DIPLOM

B42
SIMOES DOS REIS A.,BIBLIOGRAFIA DAS BIBLIOGRAFIAS BRASILEIRAS. BRAZIL ADMIN COLONIAL 20. PAGE 133 A2717
BIBLIOG NAT/G DIPLOM L/A+17C

B43
BEMIS S.F.,THE LATIN AMERICAN POLICY OF THE UNITED STATES: AN HISTORICAL INTERPRETATION. INT/ORG AGREE COLONIAL WAR PEACE ATTIT ORD/FREE...POLICY INT/LAW CHARTS 18/20 MEXIC/AMER WILSON/W MONROE/DOC. PAGE 13 A0265
DIPLOM SOVEREIGN USA-45 L/A+17C

B43
BROWN A.D.,BRITISH POSSESSIONS IN THE CARIBBEAN AREA: A SELECTED LIST OF REFERENCES. UK NAT/G DIPLOM...GEOG 20 CARIBBEAN. PAGE 20 A0398
BIBLIOG COLONIAL ECO/UNDEV L/A+17C

B43
LEWIN E.,ROYAL EMPIRE SOCIETY BIBLIOGRAPHIES NO. 9: SUB-SAHARA AFRICA. ECO/UNDEV TEC/DEV DIPLOM ADMIN COLONIAL LEAD 20. PAGE 88 A1800
BIBLIOG AFR NAT/G SOCIETY

B43
MAISEL A.Q.,AFRICA: FACTS AND FORECASTS. WOR+45 INT/ORG CONTROL RACE/REL SOVEREIGN...PREDICT CHARTS 20. PAGE 93 A1910
AFR WAR DIPLOM COLONIAL

B43
US DEPARTMENT OF STATE,NATIONAL SOCIALISM; BASIC PRINCIPLES, THEIR APPLICATION BY THE NAZI PARTY'S FOREIGN ORGANIZATION... GERMANY WOR-45 ECO/DEV LOC/G POL/PAR FORCES DIPLOM DOMIN COLONIAL ARMS/CONT COERCE NAT/LISM PWR 20 NAZI. PAGE 151 A3081
FASCISM SOCISM NAT/G TOTALISM

B43
WALKER E.A.,BRITAIN AND SOUTH AFRICA. SOUTH/AFR POL/PAR GP/REL RACE/REL ATTIT ORD/FREE 17/20. PAGE 160 A3264
COLONIAL WAR DIPLOM SOVEREIGN

B44
RAGATZ L.J.,LITERATURE OF EUROPEAN IMPERIALISM. ECO/TAC INT/TRADE DOMIN GOV/REL DEMAND NAT/LISM PWR WEALTH 19/20. PAGE 119 A2432
BIBLIOG COLONIAL INT/ORG ECO/UNDEV

C44
VAN VALKENBURG S.,"ELEMENTS OF POLITICAL GEOGRAPHY." FRANCE COM/IND INDUS NAT/G SECT RACE/REL...LING TREND GEN/LAWS BIBLIOG 20. PAGE 158 A3215
GEOG DIPLOM COLONIAL

N45
INDIA QUARTERLY, A JOURNAL OF INTERNATIONAL AFFAIRS. INDIA LAW CONSTN ECO/UNDEV INT/ORG POL/PAR COLONIAL LEAD PARL/PROC WAR ATTIT...SOC 20 CMN/WLTH. PAGE 3 A0053
BIBLIOG/A S/ASIA DIPLOM NAT/G

B45
ELTON G.E.,IMPERIAL COMMONWEALTH. INDIA UK DIPLOM DOMIN WAR NAT/LISM SOVEREIGN...TRADIT CHARTS T 15/20 CMN/WLTH AUSTRAL PRE/US/AM. PAGE 41 A0844
REGION CONCPT COLONIAL

B45
GALLOWAY E.,ABSTRACTS OF POSTWAR LITERATURE (VOL. IV) JAN.-JULY, 1945 NOS. 901-1074. POLAND USA+45 USSR WOR+45 INDUS LABOR PLAN ECO/TAC INT/TRADE TAX EDU/PROP ADMIN COLONIAL INT/LAW. PAGE 51 A1033
BIBLIOG/A NUC/PWR NAT/G DIPLOM

B45
HARVARD WIDENER LIBRARY,INDOCHINA: A SELECTED LIST OF REFERENCES. CAMBODIA FRANCE S/ASIA VIETNAM COLONIAL...POLICY 19/20. PAGE 62 A1282
BIBLIOG/A ACADEM DIPLOM NAT/G

B45
UNCIO CONFERENCE LIBRARY,SHORT TITLE CLASSIFIED CATALOG. WOR-45 DOMIN COLONIAL WAR...SOC/WK 20 LEAGUE/NAT UN. PAGE 147 A3006
BIBLIOG DIPLOM INT/ORG INT/LAW

B45
WING D.,SHORT-TITLE CATALOGUE OF BOOKS PRINTED IN THE BRITISH ISLES, AND OF ENGLISH BOOKS PRINTED OVERSEAS; 1641-1700 (3 VOLS.). UK USA-45 LAW DIPLOM ADMIN COLONIAL LEAD ATTIT 17. PAGE 165 A3363
BIBLIOG MOD/EUR NAT/G

B45
WOOLBERT R.G.,FOREIGN AFFAIRS BIBLIOGRAPHY, 1932-1942. INT/ORG SECT INT/TRADE COLONIAL RACE/REL NAT/LISM...GEOG INT/LAW GOV/COMP IDEA/COMP 20. PAGE 167 A3393
BIBLIOG/A DIPLOM WAR

B46
GRIFFIN G.G.,A GUIDE TO MANUSCRIPTS RELATING TO AMERICAN HISTORY IN BRITISH DEPOSITORIES. CANADA IRELAND MOD/EUR UK USA-45 LAW DIPLOM ADMIN COLONIAL WAR NAT/LISM SOVEREIGN...GEOG INT/LAW 15/19 CMN/WLTH. PAGE 56 A1159
BIBLIOG/A ALL/VALS NAT/G

B47
CONOVER H.F.,NON-SELF-GOVERNING AREAS. BELGIUM FRANCE ITALY UK WOR+45 CULTURE ECO/UNDEV INT/ORG LOC/G NAT/G ECO/TAC INT/TRADE ADMIN HEALTH...SOC UN. PAGE 30 A0601
BIBLIOG/A COLONIAL DIPLOM

B48
GUIDE TO THE RECORDS IN THE NATIONAL ARCHIVES. ECO/UNDEV ADMIN COLONIAL 16/20. PAGE 3 A0055
BIBLIOG NAT/G L/A+17C DIPLOM

B48
CLYDE P.H.,THE FAR EAST: A HISTORY OF THE IMPACT OF THE WEST ON EASTERN ASIA. CHINA/COM CULTURE INT/TRADE DOMIN COLONIAL WAR PWR...CHARTS BIBLIOG 19/20 CHINJAP. PAGE 27 A0554
DIPLOM ASIA

B48
LOGAN R.W.,THE AFRICAN MANDATES IN WORLD POLITICS. EUR+WWI GERMANY ISLAM INT/ORG BARGAIN...POLICY INT/LAW 20. PAGE 90 A1853
WAR COLONIAL AFR DIPLOM

B48
MINISTERE FINANCES ET ECO,BULLETIN BIBLIOGRAPHIQUE. AFR EUR+WWI FRANCE CULTURE STRUCT FINAN NAT/G ACT/RES INT/TRADE ADMIN REGION PRODUC STAT. PAGE 102 A2088
BIBLIOG/A ECO/UNDEV TEC/DEV COLONIAL

B48
PELCOVITS N.A.,OLD CHINA HANDS AND THE FOREIGN OFFICE. ASIA BURMA UK ECO/UNDEV NAT/G ECO/TAC FOR/AID TARIFFS DOMIN COLONIAL GOV/REL SOVEREIGN 19 HONG/KONG TREATY. PAGE 114 A2348
INT/TRADE ATTIT DIPLOM

B49
HINDEN R.,EMPIRE AND AFTER. UK POL/PAR BAL/PWR DIPLOM INT/TRADE WAR NAT/LISM PWR 17/20. PAGE 65 A1335
NAT/G COLONIAL ATTIT POLICY

B49
MANSERGH N.,THE COMING OF THE FIRST WORLD WAR: A STUDY IN EUROPEAN BALANCE, 1878-1914. GERMANY MOD/EUR VOL/ASSN COLONIAL CONTROL PWR 19/20 TREATY. PAGE 94 A1928
DIPLOM WAR BAL/PWR

B50
CHUKWUEMEKA N.,AFRICAN DEPENDENCIES: A CHALLENGE TO WESTERN DEMOCRACY. NIGERIA ECO/DEV INDUS FOR/AID INT/TRADE DOMIN 20. PAGE 26 A0536
DIPLOM ECO/UNDEV COLONIAL AFR

B50
FIGANIERE J.C.,BIBLIOTHECA HISTORICA PORTUGUEZA. BRAZIL PORTUGAL SECT ADMIN. PAGE 45 A0929
BIBLIOG NAT/G DIPLOM COLONIAL

B50
GLEASON J.H.,THE GENESIS OF RUSSOPHOBIA IN GREAT BRITAIN: A STUDY OF THE INTERACTION OF POLICY AND OPINION. ASIA RUSSIA UK NAT/G AGREE CONTROL REV WAR LOVE PWR TREATY 19. PAGE 53 A1080
DIPLOM POLICY DOMIN COLONIAL

B50
MOCKFORD J.,SOUTH-WEST AFRICA AND THE INTERNATIONAL COURT (PAMPHLET). AFR GERMANY SOUTH/AFR UK ECO/UNDEV DIPLOM CONTROL DISCRIM...DECISION JURID 20 AFRICA/SW. PAGE 102 A2094
COLONIAL SOVEREIGN INT/LAW DOMIN

B50
PERHAM M.,COLONIAL GOVERNMENT: ANNOTATED READING LIST ON BRITISH COLONIAL GOVERNMENT. UK WOR+45 WOR-45 ECO/UNDEV INT/ORG LEGIS FOR/AID INT/TRADE DOMIN ADMIN REV 20. PAGE 115 A2356
BIBLIOG/A COLONIAL GOV/REL NAT/G

B50
US LIBRARY OF CONGRESS,THE UNITED STATES AND EUROPE: BIBLIOGRAPHY OF THOUGHT EXPRESSED IN AMERICAN PUBLICATIONS DURING 1950. EUR+WWI GERMANY USA+45 USSR INT/ORG DIPLOM COLONIAL SOVEREIGN ...POLICY 20 COLD/WAR UN BERLIN/BLO. PAGE 154 A3150
BIBLIOG/A SOC ATTIT

N50
SCHAPIRO J.S.,THE WORLD IN CRISES: POLITICAL AND SOCIAL MOVEMENTS IN THE TWENTIETH CENTURY. USA+45 INT/ORG LABOR PLAN CAP/ISM DIPLOM COLONIAL PEACE TOTALISM ATTIT LAISSEZ...BIBLIOG 20 COLD/WAR. PAGE 128 A2618
NAT/LISM TEC/DEV REV WAR

B51
CATALOGO GENERAL DE LA LIBRERIA ESPANOLA E HISPANOAMERICANA 1901-1930; AUTORES (5 VOLS., 1932-1951). SPAIN COLONIAL GOV/REL...SOC 20. PAGE 3 A0058
BIBLIOG L/A+17C DIPLOM NAT/G

B51
BROGAN D.W.,THE PRICE OF REVOLUTION. FRANCE USA+45
REV

USA-45 USSR CONSTN NAT/G DIPLOM COLONIAL NAT/LISM ORD/FREE POPULISM...CONCPT 18/20 PRE/US/AM. PAGE 19 A0386 — METH/COMP COST MARXISM

B51
CARRINGTON C.E.,THE LIQUIDATION OF THE BRITISH EMPIRE. AFR NAT/G INT/TRADE COLONIAL RACE/REL ATTIT ORD/FREE...POLICY NAT/COMP 20 CMN/WLTH. PAGE 25 A0501 — SOVEREIGN NAT/LISM DIPLOM GP/REL

B51
JENNINGS I.,THE COMMONWEALTH IN ASIA. CEYLON INDIA PAKISTAN CULTURE STRATA NAT/G LEGIS DIPLOM COLONIAL ATTIT...DECISION 20 CMN/WLTH. PAGE 74 A1507 — CONSTN INT/ORG POLICY PLAN

B51
JENNINGS S.I.,THE COMMONWEALTH IN ASIA. CEYLON INDIA PAKISTAN S/ASIA UK CONSTN CULTURE SOCIETY STRATA STRUCT NAT/G POL/PAR EDU/PROP LEAD WAR 20 CMN/WLTH. PAGE 74 A1510 — NAT/LISM REGION COLONIAL DIPLOM

B51
LEONARD L.L.,INTERNATIONAL ORGANIZATION. WOR+45 WOR-45 EX/STRUC FORCES LEGIS ECO/TAC INT/TRADE COLONIAL ARMS/CONT...SOC/WK GOV/COMP BIBLIOG. PAGE 87 A1778 — NAT/G DIPLOM INT/ORG DELIB/GP

B51
WABEKE B.H.,A GUIDE TO DUTCH BIBLIOGRAPHIES. BELGIUM INDONESIA NETHERLAND DIPLOM INT/TRADE WAR NAT/LISM KNOWL...ART/METH HUM JURID CON/ANAL 14/20. PAGE 160 A3257 — BIBLIOG/A NAT/G CULTURE COLONIAL

C51
GRUNDER G.A.,"THE PHILIPPINES AND THE UNITED STATES." PHILIPPINE S/ASIA USA-45 NAT/G POL/PAR ADMIN SOVEREIGN...TIME/SEQ BIBLIOG 20. PAGE 57 A1181 — COLONIAL POLICY DIPLOM ECO/TAC

B52
FIFIELD R.H.,WOODROW WILSON AND THE FAR EAST. ASIA CHIEF BAL/PWR CONFER COLONIAL ARMS/CONT WAR ...TIME/SEQ NAT/COMP BIBLIOG 19/20 WILSON/W LEAGUE/NAT PRESIDENT. PAGE 45 A0926 — DIPLOM DELIB/GP INT/ORG

B52
LIPPMANN W.,ISOLATION AND ALLIANCES: AN AMERICAN SPEAKS TO THE BRITISH. USA+45 USA-45 INT/ORG AGREE COERCE DETER WAR PEACE MORAL 20 TREATY INTERVENT. PAGE 89 A1829 — DIPLOM SOVEREIGN COLONIAL ATTIT

B52
US LIBRARY OF CONGRESS,EGYPT AND THE ANGLO-EGYPTIAN SUDAN: A SELECTIVE GUIDE TO BACKGROUND READING (PAMPHLET). SUDAN UAR UK DIPLOM...POLICY 20. PAGE 155 A3153 — BIBLIOG/A COLONIAL ISLAM NAT/G

S52
HAAS E.B.,"THE RECONCILIATION OF CONFLICT, COLONIAL POLICY AIMS: ACCEPTANCE OF THE LEAGUE OF NATIONS MANDATE SYSTEM." FRANCE GERMANY UK WOR+45 WOR-45 LEGIT ATTIT DRIVE ORD/FREE...OLD/LIB INT SYS/QU TIME/SEQ TREND LEAGUE/NAT 20. PAGE 58 A1201 — INT/ORG COLONIAL

C52
FIFIELD R.H.,"WOODROW WILSON AND THE FAR EAST." ASIA CHIEF DELIB/GP BAL/PWR CONFER COLONIAL ARMS/CONT WAR...TIME/SEQ NAT/COMP 19/20 WILSON/W LEAGUE/NAT. PAGE 45 A0925 — BIBLIOG DIPLOM INT/ORG

B53
ELAHI K.N.,A GUIDE TO WORKS OF REFERENCE PUBLISHED IN PAKISTAN (PAMPHLET). PAKISTAN DIPLOM COLONIAL LEAD. PAGE 41 A0835 — BIBLIOG S/ASIA NAT/G

B53
MANSERGH N.,DOCUMENTS AND SPEECHES ON BRITISH COMMONWEALTH AFFAIRS 1931-1952. INDIA IRELAND PAKISTAN UK CONSTN POL/PAR CHIEF FORCES COLONIAL ORD/FREE SOVEREIGN...JURID 20 COMMONWLTH. PAGE 94 A1929 — BIBLIOG/A DIPLOM ECO/TAC

B53
ROSCIO J.G.,OBRAS. L/A+17C SPAIN DIPLOM REV WAR NAT/LISM TOTALISM PWR SOVEREIGN 19. PAGE 123 A2527 — ORD/FREE COLONIAL NAT/G PHIL/SCI

B53
STOUT H.M.,BRITISH GOVERNMENT. UK FINAN LOC/G POL/PAR DELIB/GP DIPLOM ADMIN COLONIAL CHOOSE ORD/FREE...JURID BIBLIOG 20 COMMONWLTH. PAGE 139 A2837 — NAT/G PARL/PROC CONSTN NEW/LIB

B54
COOKSON J.,BEFORE THE AFRICAN STORM. BELGIUM CENTRL/AFR FRANCE UK ECO/UNDEV POL/PAR CREATE BAL/PWR RACE/REL NAT/LISM ORD/FREE CONSERVE MARXISM SOC/INTEG 20 CONGO/LEOP. PAGE 30 A0607 — COLONIAL REV DISCRIM DIPLOM

B54
MITCHELL P.,AFRICAN AFTERTHOUGHTS. UGANDA CONSTN NAT/G ADJUD COERCE WAR 20 WWI MAU/MAU. PAGE 102 A2090 — BIOG CHIEF COLONIAL DOMIN

B54
SHARMA J.S.,MAHATMA GANDHI: A DESCRIPTIVE BIBLIOGRAPHY. INDIA S/ASIA PROB/SOLV DIPLOM COLONIAL WAR NAT/LISM PEACE ATTIT PERSON SOVEREIGN ...CONCPT 20 GANDHI/M. PAGE 132 A2695 — BIBLIOG/A BIOG CHIEF LEAD

B55
PANT Y.P.,PLANNING IN UNDERDEVELOPED ECONOMIES. INDIA NEPAL INT/TRADE COLONIAL SOVEREIGN ALL/IDEOS ...TIME/SEQ METH/COMP 20. PAGE 114 A2334 — ECO/UNDEV PLAN ECO/TAC DIPLOM

B55
PERKINS B.,THE FIRST RAPPROCHEMENTS: ENGLAND AND THE UNITED STATES, 1795-1805. UK USA-45 ATTIT ...HIST/WRIT BIBLIOG 18/19 MADISON/J WAR/1812. PAGE 115 A2357 — DIPLOM COLONIAL WAR

B55
PYRAH G.B.,IMPERIAL POLICY AND SOUTH AFRICA 1902-1910. SOUTH/AFR UK NAT/G WAR DISCRIM...CONCPT CHARTS BIBLIOG/A 19/20 CMN/WLTH. PAGE 118 A2421 — DIPLOM COLONIAL POLICY RACE/REL

B55
STILLMAN C.W.,AFRICA IN THE MODERN WORLD. AFR USA+45 WOR+45 INT/TRADE COLONIAL PARTIC REGION GOV/REL RACE/REL 20. PAGE 138 A2826 — ECO/UNDEV DIPLOM POLICY STRUCT

B55
STUART G.H.,LATIN AMERICA AND THE UNITED STATES (5TH ED.). L/A+17C USA+45 USA-45 INT/TRADE COLONIAL ...POLICY CHARTS T 19/20. PAGE 140 A2856 — NAT/G DIPLOM

B55
TAN C.C.,THE BOXER CATASTROPHE. ASIA UK USSR ELITES POL/PAR VOL/ASSN FORCES PROB/SOLV DIPLOM ADMIN COLONIAL NAT/LISM PEACE TREATY 19/20 BOXER/REBL. PAGE 141 A2885 — REV NAT/G WAR

B55
VIGON J.,TEORIA DEL MILITARISMO. NAT/G DIPLOM COLONIAL COERCE GUERRILLA CIVMIL/REL NAT/LISM MORAL ALL/IDEOS PACIFISM 18/20. PAGE 159 A3234 — FORCES PHIL/SCI WAR POLICY

S55
DE SMITH S.A.,"CONSTITUTIONAL MONARCHY IN BURGANDA." AFR UGANDA UK STRUCT CHIEF REGION INGP/REL ADJUST NAT/LISM SOVEREIGN CONSERVE ...POLICY 19/20 BURGANDA. PAGE 35 A0712 — NAT/G DIPLOM CONSTN COLONIAL

C55
APTER D.E.,"THE GOLD COAST IN TRANSITION." AFR CONSTN LOC/G LEGIS DIPLOM COLONIAL CONTROL GOV/REL ...CHARTS BIBLIOG 20 CMN/WLTH. PAGE 8 A0170 — ORD/FREE REPRESENT PARL/PROC NAT/G

B56
BEALE H.K.,THEODORE ROOSEVELT AND THE RISE OF AMERICA TO WORLD POWER. USA-45 BAL/PWR COLONIAL DRIVE PERSON PWR...POLICY BIBLIOG 20 ROOSEVLT/T PRESIDENT. PAGE 12 A0238 — DIPLOM CHIEF BIOG

B56
BOWLES C.,AFRICA'S CHALLENGE TO AMERICA. USA+45 ECO/UNDEV NAT/G LEGIS COLONIAL CONTROL REV ORD/FREE SOVEREIGN 20 COLD/WAR. PAGE 18 A0358 — AFR DIPLOM POLICY FOR/AID

B56
GREECE PRESBEIA U.S.,BRITISH OPINION ON CYPRUS. CYPRUS UK FORCES DIPLOM INT/TRADE DOMIN GOV/REL ORD/FREE SOVEREIGN...POLICY 20. PAGE 55 A1137 — ATTIT COLONIAL LEGIS PRESS

B56
PHILIPPINE STUDIES PROGRAM,SELECTED BIBLIOGRAPHY ON THE PHILIPPINES, TOPICALLY ARRANGED AND ANNOTATED. PHILIPPINE SECT DIPLOM COLONIAL LEAD...SOC 18/20. PAGE 116 A2375 — BIBLIOG/A S/ASIA NAT/G ECO/UNDEV

B56
UNDERHILL F.H.,THE BRITISH COMMONWEALTH: AN EXPERIMENT IN CO-OPERATION AMONG NATIONS. CANADA UK WOR+45 WOR-45 INT/ORG COLONIAL UTIL SOVEREIGN CONSERVE...OLD/LIB SOC/EXP BIBLIOG/A 19/20 CMN/WLTH. PAGE 147 A3007 — VOL/ASSN NAT/LISM DIPLOM

B56
WILSON P.,GOVERNMENT AND POLITICS OF INDIA AND PAKISTAN: 1885-1955; A BIBLIOGRAPHY OF WORKS IN WESTERN LANGUAGES. INDIA PAKISTAN CONSTN LOC/G POL/PAR FORCES DIPLOM ADMIN WAR CHOOSE...BIOG CON/ANAL 19/20. PAGE 165 A3361 — BIBLIOG COLONIAL NAT/G S/ASIA

B57
ALEXANDER L.M.,WORLD POLITICAL PATTERNS. NAT/G PROVS CAP/ISM DIPLOM COLONIAL NAT/LISM...POLICY GEOG CHARTS METH/COMP NAT/COMP 20. PAGE 5 A0111 — CONTROL METH GOV/COMP

B57
BISHOP O.B.,PUBLICATIONS OF THE GOVERNMENTS OF NOVA SCOTIA, PRINCE EDWARD ISLAND, NEW BRUNSWICK 1758-1952. CANADA UK ADMIN COLONIAL LEAD...POLICY 18/20. PAGE 14 A0293 — BIBLIOG NAT/G DIPLOM

B57
BURNS A.,IN DEFENCE OF COLONIES; BRITISH COLONIAL TERRITORIES IN INTERNATIONAL AFFAIRS. UK ECO/UNDEV PLAN DOMIN SOVEREIGN...MAJORIT 18/20 CMN/WLTH INTERVENT. PAGE 22 A0439 — COLONIAL POLICY ATTIT DIPLOM

B57
HODGKIN T.,NATIONALISM IN COLONIAL AFRICA. STRATA STRUCT MUNIC NAT/G POL/PAR LEGIS ATTIT SOVEREIGN ...POLICY TREND BIBLIOG 20. PAGE 66 A1351 — AFR COLONIAL NAT/LISM DIPLOM

B57
PALMER N.D.,INTERNATIONAL RELATIONS. WOR+45 INT/ORG NAT/G ECO/TAC EDU/PROP COLONIAL WAR PWR SOVEREIGN — DIPLOM BAL/PWR

...POLICY T 20 TREATY. PAGE 113 A2321 NAT/COMP

B57
RUMEU DE ARMAS A.,ESPANA EEN EL AFRICA ATLANTICA. AFR CHRIST-17C PORTUGAL SPAIN DIPLOM ECO/TAC CONTROL 14/16 AFRICA/W. PAGE 125 A2568 NAT/G COLONIAL CHIEF PWR

C57
BEERS H.P.,"THE FRENCH IN NORTH AFRICA: A BIBLIOGRAPHICAL GUIDE TO FRENCH ARCHIVES, REPRODUCTIONS, AND RESEARCH MISSIONS." AFR CANADA FRANCE USA-45 NAT/LISM ATTIT 20. PAGE 12 A0248 BIBLIOG DIPLOM COLONIAL

B58
GROBLER J.H.,AFRICA'S DESTINY. AFR EUR+WWI SOUTH/AFR UK USA+45 ELITES KIN LOC/G DIPLOM DISCRIM ATTIT CONSERVE MARXISM 20 ROOSEVLT/T NEGRO. PAGE 57 A1168 POLICY ORD/FREE COLONIAL CONSTN

B58
JENNINGS I.,PROBLEMS OF THE NEW COMMONWEALTH. CEYLON INDIA PAKISTAN S/ASIA ECO/UNDEV INT/ORG LOC/G DIPLOM ECO/TAC INT/TRADE COLONIAL RACE/REL DISCRIM 20 COMMONWLTH PARLIAMENT. PAGE 74 A1508 NAT/LISM NEUTRAL FOR/AID POL/PAR

B58
JENNINGS W.I.,PROBLEMS OF THE NEW COMMONWEALTH. CEYLON INDIA MALAYSIA PAKISTAN ECO/UNDEV VOL/ASSN RACE/REL NAT/LISM ROLE 20 CMN/WLTH. PAGE 74 A1511 GP/REL INGP/REL COLONIAL INT/ORG

B58
MANSERGH N.,COMMONWEALTH PERSPECTIVES. GHANA UK LAW VOL/ASSN CONFER HEALTH SOVEREIGN...GEOG CHARTS ANTHOL 20 CMN/WLTH AUSTRAL. PAGE 94 A1930 DIPLOM COLONIAL INT/ORG INGP/REL

B58
MANSERGH N.,SURVEY OF BRITISH COMMONWEALTH AFFAIRS: PROBLEMS OF WARTIME CO-OPERATION AND POST-WAR CHANGE 1939-1952. INDIA IRELAND S/ASIA CONSTN INT/ORG BAL/PWR COLONIAL NEUTRAL WAR ADJUST PEACE ROLE ORD/FREE...CHARTS 20 CMN/WLTH NATO UN. PAGE 94 A1931 VOL/ASSN CONSEN PROB/SOLV INGP/REL

B58
NEHRU J.,SPEECHES. INDIA ECO/UNDEV AGRI INDUS INT/ORG POL/PAR DIPLOM FOR/AID NAT/LISM...ANTHOL 20. PAGE 108 A2213 PLAN CHIEF COLONIAL NEUTRAL

B58
RIGGS R.,POLITICS IN THE UNITED NATIONS: A STUDY OF UNITED STATES INFLUENCE IN THE GENERAL ASSEMBLY. USA+45 WOR+45 LEGIS TOP/EX CREATE BAL/PWR DIPLOM DOMIN EDU/PROP COLONIAL ROUTINE ATTIT RIGID/FLEX PWR...CONCPT OBS HIST/WRIT CHARTS STERTYP GEN/LAWS UN COLD/WAR 20. PAGE 121 A2480 INT/ORG

B58
TILLION G.,ALGERIA: THE REALITIES. ALGERIA FRANCE ISLAM CULTURE STRATA PROB/SOLV DOMIN REV NAT/LISM WEALTH MARXISM...GEOG 20. PAGE 144 A2940 ECO/UNDEV SOC COLONIAL DIPLOM

B58
UNIV KARACHI INST PUB BUS ADM,PUBLICATIONS OF THE GOVERNMENT OF PAKISTAN 1947-1957. PAKISTAN S/ASIA DIPLOM COLONIAL ATTIT 20. PAGE 149 A3040 BIBLIOG NAT/G POLICY

B58
VARG P.A.,MISSIONARIES, CHINESE, AND DIPLOMATS: THE AMERICAN PROTESTANT MISSIONARY MOVEMENT IN CHINA, 1890-1952. ASIA ECO/UNDEV NAT/G PROB/SOLV CAP/ISM EDU/PROP COLONIAL NAT/LISM ATTIT MARXISM...NAT/COMP STERTYP 20 CHINJAP PROTESTANT MISSION. PAGE 158 A3221 CULTURE DIPLOM SECT

L58
HYVARINEN R.,"MONISTIC AND PLURALISTIC INTERPRETATIONS IN THE STUDY OF INTERNATIONAL POLITICS." COLONIAL REGION RACE/REL DISCRIM TOTALISM SOVEREIGN...INT/LAW PHIL/SCI CONCPT BIBLIOG 20. PAGE 70 A1429 DIPLOM PLURISM INT/ORG METH

C58
BUTTINGER J.,"THE SMALLER DRAGON; A POLITICAL HISTORY OF VIETNAM." VIETNAM SECT DIPLOM CIVMIL/REL ISOLAT NAT/LISM...BIBLIOG/A 3/20. PAGE 22 A0455 COLONIAL DOMIN SOVEREIGN REV

C58
FIFIELD R.H.,"THE DIPLOMACY OF SOUTHEAST ASIA: 1945-1958." INT/ORG NAT/G COLONIAL REGION...CHARTS BIBLIOG 20 UN. PAGE 45 A0927 S/ASIA DIPLOM NAT/LISM

B59
ALWAN M.,ALGERIA BEFORE THE UNITED NATIONS. AFR ASIA FRANCE ISLAM S/ASIA CONSTN SOCIETY STRUCT INT/ORG NAT/G ECO/TAC ADMIN COLONIAL NAT/LISM ATTIT PWR...DECISION TREND 420 UN. PAGE 7 A0133 PLAN RIGID/FLEX DIPLOM ALGERIA

B59
ARON R.,IMPERIALISM AND COLONIALISM (PAMPHLET). WOR+45 WOR-45 ECO/TAC CONTROL REV ORD/FREE 19/20. PAGE 9 A0183 COLONIAL DOMIN ECO/UNDEV DIPLOM

B59
BLOOMFIELD L.P.,WESTERN EUROPE AND THE UN - TRENDS AND PROSPECTS. EUR+WWI BAL/PWR DIPLOM ECO/TAC COLONIAL ATTIT PWR...POLICY 20 UN EUROPE/W. PAGE 16 A0316 INT/ORG TREND FUT NAT/G

B59
DEHIO L.,GERMANY AND WORLD POLITICS IN THE TWENTIETH CENTURY. EUR+WWI FRANCE GERMANY MOD/EUR UK USSR NAT/G CHIEF BAL/PWR DOMIN COLONIAL CONTROL LEAD...IDEA/COMP 20 VERSAILLES. PAGE 36 A0724 DIPLOM WAR NAT/LISM SOVEREIGN

B59
EGYPTIAN SOCIETY OF INT LAW,THE MONROVIA CONFERENCE (PAMPHLET). AFR ALGERIA FRANCE UAR CONFER REGION NUC/PWR WAR DISCRIM 20 SAHARA AFR/STATES. PAGE 40 A0826 COLONIAL SOVEREIGN RACE/REL DIPLOM

B59
JACKSON B.W.,FIVE IDEAS THAT CHANGE THE WORLD. FUT WOR+45 WOR-45 ECO/UNDEV INDUS DIPLOM DOMIN CONTROL ...IDEA/COMP 20. PAGE 72 A1473 MARXISM NAT/LISM COLONIAL ECO/TAC

B59
JONES A.C.,NEW FABIAN COLONIAL ESSAYS. UK SOCIETY POL/PAR EDU/PROP ADMIN ORD/FREE SOVEREIGN SOCISM ...ANTHOL 20 CMN/WLTH LABOR/PAR. PAGE 75 A1530 COLONIAL INT/ORG INGP/REL DOMIN

B59
KARUNAKARAN K.P.,INDIA IN WORLD AFFAIRS, 1952-1958 (VOL. II). INDIA ECO/UNDEV SECT FOR/AID INT/TRADE ADJUD NEUTRAL REV WAR DISCRIM ORD/FREE MARXISM ...BIBLIOG 20. PAGE 77 A1569 DIPLOM INT/ORG S/ASIA COLONIAL

B59
LAQUER W.Z.,THE SOVIET UNION AND THE MIDDLE EAST. COM UAR USSR ECO/UNDEV NAT/G VOL/ASSN ECO/TAC EDU/PROP COLONIAL EXEC PWR...TIME/SEQ TREND COLD/WAR 20. PAGE 85 A1730 ISLAM DRIVE FOR/AID NAT/LISM

B59
MAC MILLAN W.M.,THE ROAD TO SELF-RULE. SOUTH/AFR UK CULTURE SOCIETY AGRI LABOR NAT/G INT/TRADE CONTROL GP/REL...SOC 19/20. PAGE 92 A1884 AFR COLONIAL SOVEREIGN POLICY

B59
NAHM A.C.,JAPANESE PENETRATION OF KOREA, 1894-1910. ASIA KOREA NAT/G...POLICY 20 CHINJAP. PAGE 107 A2192 BIBLIOG/A DIPLOM WAR COLONIAL

B59
NIEBUHR R.,NATIONS AND EMPIRES. WOR+45 INT/ORG COLONIAL NUC/PWR TOTALISM UTOPIA ORD/FREE MARXISM WORSHIP 20 COLD/WAR PROTESTANT CHRISTIAN. PAGE 109 A2237 DIPLOM NAT/G POLICY PWR

B59
PAGAN B.,HISTORIA DE LOS PARTIDOS POLITICOS PUERTORRIQUENOS 1898-1956. PUERT/RICO PROVS DIPLOM DOMIN EDU/PROP PARTIC 20. PAGE 113 A2316 POL/PAR CHOOSE COLONIAL PWR

B59
WARD B.,5 IDEAS THAT CHANGE THE WORLD. WOR+45 WOR-45 SOCIETY STRUCT AGRI INDUS INT/ORG NAT/G FORCES ACT/RES ARMS/CONT TOTALISM ATTIT DRIVE GEN/LAWS. PAGE 161 A3278 ECO/UNDEV ALL/VALS NAT/LISM COLONIAL

B59
WOLFERS A.,ALLIANCE POLICY IN THE COLD WAR. COM INT/ORG FORCES COLONIAL CONTROL NUC/PWR 20 NATO UN COLD/WAR. PAGE 166 A3384 DIPLOM DETER BAL/PWR

C59
KULSKI W.W.,"PEACEFUL COEXISTENCE." USSR ECO/UNDEV INT/ORG POL/PAR EDU/PROP COLONIAL CONTROL REV NAT/LISM PEACE PWR MARXISM...BIBLIOG 20. PAGE 83 A1692 COM DIPLOM DOMIN

B60
ASPREMONT-LYNDEN H.,RAPPORT SUR L'ADMINISTRATION BELGE DU RUANDA-URUNDI PENDANT L'ANNEE 1959. BELGIUM RWANDA AGRI INDUS DIPLOM ECO/TAC INT/TRADE DOMIN ADMIN RACE/REL...GEOG CENSUS 20 UN. PAGE 9 A0192 AFR COLONIAL ECO/UNDEV INT/ORG

B60
CENTRAL ASIAN RESEARCH CENTRE,RUSSIA LOOKS AT AFRICA (PAMPHLET). AFR USSR COLONIAL RACE/REL...HUM 19/20 STALIN/J. PAGE 25 A0511 BIBLIOG MARXISM TREND DIPLOM

B60
EMERSON R.,FROM EMPIRE TO NATION: THE RISE TO SELF-ASSERTION OF ASIAN AND AFRICAN PEOPLES. S/ASIA CULTURE NAT/G SECT DIPLOM ATTIT SOVEREIGN MARXISM ...POLICY BIBLIOG 19/20. PAGE 41 A0847 NAT/LISM COLONIAL AFR ASIA

B60
GLUBB J.B.,WAR IN THE DESERT: AN R.A.F. FRONTIER CAMPAIGN. SAUDI/ARAB UK KIN SECT LEAD...GEOG 20 RAF. PAGE 53 A1083 COLONIAL WAR FORCES DIPLOM

B60
JACOBSON H.K.,AMERICAN FOREIGN POLICY. COM EUR+WWI USA+45 USA-45 ECO/DEV ECO/UNDEV INT/ORG NAT/G INT/TRADE EDU/PROP COLONIAL CHOOSE MARXISM 20 NATO. PAGE 72 A1485 POL/PAR PWR DIPLOM

B60
JEFFRIES C.,TRANSFER OF POWER: PROBLEMS OF THE PASSAGE TO SELFGOVERNMENT. CEYLON GHANA MALAYSIA NIGERIA UK INT/ORG CONSULT DELIB/GP LEGIS DIPLOM CONFER PARL/PROC 20. PAGE 73 A1502 SOVEREIGN COLONIAL ORD/FREE NAT/G

B60
LATIFI D.,INDIA AND UNITED STATES AID. ASIA INDIA UK USA+45 AGRI FINAN INDUS COLONIAL ORD/FREE SOVEREIGN WEALTH...METH/COMP 20. PAGE 85 A1743
FOR/AID DIPLOM ECO/UNDEV

B60
LEVIN J.V.,THE EXPORT ECONOMIES: THEIR PATTERN OF DEVELOPMENT IN HISTORICAL PERSPECTIVE. BURMA PERU AGRI WORKER COLONIAL COST DEMAND INCOME 20. PAGE 88 A1795
INT/TRADE ECO/UNDEV BAL/PAY EXTR/IND

B60
MORAES F.,THE REVOLT IN TIBET. ASIA CHINA/COM INDIA CULTURE CONTROL COERCE WAR TOTALISM...POLICY SOC WORSHIP 20 TIBET INTERVENT. PAGE 104 A2127
COLONIAL FORCES DIPLOM ORD/FREE

B60
PENTONY D.E.,THE UNDERDEVELOPED LANDS. FUT WOR+45 CULTURE AGRI FINAN INDUS MARKET INT/ORG LABOR NAT/G VOL/ASSN CONSULT TEC/DEV ECO/TAC EDU/PROP COLONIAL ATTIT WEALTH...OBS RECORD SAMP TREND GEN/METH WORK UN 20. PAGE 115 A2351
ECO/UNDEV POLICY FOR/AID INT/TRADE

B60
PHILLIPS J.F.V.,KWAME NKRUMAH AND THE FUTURE OF AFRICA. FUT GHANA ISLAM ECO/UNDEV CHIEF DIPLOM COLONIAL RACE/REL NAT/LISM...TREND IDEA/COMP BIBLIOG 20 NKRUMAH/K. PAGE 116 A2376
BIOG LEAD SOVEREIGN AFR

B60
STRACHEY J.,THE END OF EMPIRE. UK WOR+45 WOR-45 DIPLOM INT/TRADE DOMIN ADJUST ORD/FREE WEALTH ...SOCIALIST GOV/COMP TIME COMMONWLTH. PAGE 139 A2841
COLONIAL ECO/DEV BAL/PWR LAISSEZ

B60
THE AFRICA 1960 COMMITTEE,MANDATE IN TRUST; THE PROBLEM OF SOUTH WEST AFRICA. GERMANY STRUCT REGION SANCTION CHOOSE DISCRIM...INT/LAW 20 AFRICA/SW UN LEAGUE/NAT TRUST/TERR. PAGE 142 A2910
NAT/G DIPLOM COLONIAL RACE/REL

B60
THEOBOLD R.,THE NEW NATIONS OF WEST AFRICA. GHANA NIGERIA CULTURE INT/ORG ECO/TAC FOR/AID COLONIAL RACE/REL POPULISM...ANTHOL BIBLIOG 20 UN. PAGE 143 A2916
AFR SOVEREIGN ECO/UNDEV DIPLOM

B60
WHEARE K.C.,THE CONSTITUTIONAL STRUCTURE OF THE COMMONWEALTH. UK EX/STRUC DIPLOM DOMIN ADMIN COLONIAL CONTROL LEAD INGP/REL SUPEGO 20 CMN/WLTH. PAGE 163 A3325
CONSTN INT/ORG VOL/ASSN SOVEREIGN

B60
WODDIS J.,AFRICA: THE ROOTS OF REVOLT. SOUTH/AFR WORKER INT/TRADE RACE/REL DISCRIM ORD/FREE 20. PAGE 166 A3374
COLONIAL SOVEREIGN WAR ECO/UNDEV

B61
ANSPRENGER F.,POLITIK IM SCHWARZEN AFRIKA. FRANCE NAT/G DIPLOM REGION REV NAT/LISM...CHARTS BIBLIOG 19/20. PAGE 8 A0164
AFR COLONIAL SOVEREIGN

B61
CAMERON J.,THE AFRICAN REVOLUTION. AFR UK ECO/UNDEV POL/PAR REGION RACE/REL DISCRIM PWR CONSERVE ...CONCPT SOC/INTEG 20 NEGRO. PAGE 23 A0472
REV COLONIAL ORD/FREE DIPLOM

B61
CARNELL F.,THE POLITICS OF THE NEW STATES: A SELECT ANNOTATED BIBLIOGRAPHY WITH SPECIAL REFERENCE TO THE COMMONWEALTH. CONSTN ELITES LABOR NAT/G POL/PAR EX/STRUC DIPLOM ADJUD ADMIN...GOV/COMP 20 COMMONWLTH. PAGE 24 A0496
BIBLIOG/A AFR ASIA COLONIAL

B61
CHIDZERO B.T.G.,TANGANYIKA AND INTERNATIONAL TRUSTEESHIP. AFR WOR+45 WOR-45 ECO/DEV INT/ORG ECO/TAC DOMIN COLONIAL...RECORD CHARTS 20 TANGANYIKA CMN/WLTH. PAGE 26 A0528
ECO/UNDEV CONSTN

B61
GURTOO D.H.N.,INDIA'S BALANCE OF PAYMENTS (1920-1960). INDIA FINAN DIPLOM FOR/AID INT/TRADE PRICE COLONIAL...CHARTS BIBLIOG 20. PAGE 58 A1197
BAL/PAY STAT ECO/TAC ECO/UNDEV

B61
HISTORICAL RESEARCH INSTITUTE,A SHORT BIBLIOGRAPHY OF INDO-MUSLIM HISTORY. INDIA S/ASIA DIPLOM EDU/PROP COLONIAL LEAD NAT/LISM ATTIT...BIOG 19/20. PAGE 65 A1343
BIBLIOG NAT/G SECT POL/PAR

B61
KERTESZ S.D.,AMERICAN DIPLOMACY IN A NEW ERA. COM S/ASIA UK USA+45 FORCES PROB/SOLV BAL/PWR ECO/TAC ADMIN COLONIAL WAR PEACE ORD/FREE 20 NATO CONGRESS UN COLD/WAR. PAGE 78 A1601
ANTHOL DIPLOM TREND

B61
LANDSKROY W.A.,OFFICIAL SERIAL PUBLICATIONS RELATING TO ECONOMIC DEVELOPMENT IN AFRICA SOUTH OF THE SAHARA (PAMPHLET). AFR UK R+D ACT/RES 20 UN. PAGE 84 A1720
BIBLIOG ECO/UNDEV COLONIAL INT/ORG

B61
LEHMAN R.L.,AFRICA SOUTH OF THE SAHARA (PAMPHLET). DIPLOM COLONIAL NAT/LISM. PAGE 86 A1768
BIBLIOG/A AFR CULTURE NAT/G

B61
MACLURE M.,AFRICA: THE POLITICAL PATTERN. SOUTH/AFR CULTURE LEGIS DIPLOM COLONIAL RACE/REL 20. PAGE 93 A1898
AFR POLICY NAT/G

B61
MATTHEWS T.,WAR IN ALGERIA. ALGERIA FRANCE CONTROL ATTIT SOVEREIGN 20. PAGE 96 A1978
REV COLONIAL DIPLOM WAR

B61
OAKES J.B.,THE EDGE OF FREEDOM. EUR+WWI USA+45 USSR ECO/UNDEV BAL/PWR DIPLOM DOMIN COLONIAL PWR MARXISM POPULISM...IDEA/COMP 20 COLD/WAR. PAGE 111 A2271
AFR ORD/FREE SOVEREIGN NEUTRAL

B61
PALMER N.D.,THE INDIAN POLITICAL SYSTEM. INDIA ECO/UNDEV SECT CHIEF COLONIAL CHOOSE ALL/IDEOS SOCISM...CHARTS BIBLIOG/A 20. PAGE 113 A2322
NAT/LISM POL/PAR NAT/G DIPLOM

B61
PANIKKAR K.M.,THE VOICE OF FREEDOM: SELECTED SPEECHES OF PANDIT MOTILAL NEHRU. INDIA UK CONSTN FINAN FORCES LEGIS DIPLOM TAX COLONIAL...POLICY MAJORIT ANTHOL 20 NEHRU/PM. PAGE 114 A2331
NAT/LISM ORD/FREE CHIEF NAT/G

B61
PANIKKAR K.M.,REVOLUTION IN AFRICA. AFR GUINEA ECO/UNDEV POL/PAR DIPLOM COLONIAL EXEC LEAD SOVEREIGN...CHARTS 20. PAGE 114 A2332
NAT/LISM NAT/G CHIEF

B61
PERKINS D.,THE UNITED STATES AND LATIN AMERICAN. L/A+17C USA+45 USA-45 STRUCT COLONIAL REV ORD/FREE 19/20. PAGE 115 A2360
DIPLOM INT/TRADE NAT/G

B61
RICE G.W.,THE SOVIET POSITION ON DEPENDENT TERRITORIES IN THE UNITED NATIONS (THESIS, OHIO STATE UNIVERSITY). USSR PLAN SOVEREIGN...POLICY 20 UN. PAGE 121 A2473
INT/ORG COM DIPLOM COLONIAL

B61
RIENOW R.,CONTEMPORARY INTERNATIONAL POLITICS. WOR+45 INT/ORG BAL/PWR EDU/PROP COLONIAL NEUTRAL REGION WAR PEACE...INT/LAW 20 COLD/WAR UN. PAGE 121 A2476
DIPLOM PWR POLICY NAT/G

B61
SCHNAPPER B.,LA POLITIQUE ET LE COMMERCE FRANCAIS DANS LE GOLFE DE GUINEE DE 1838 A 1871. FRANCE GUINEA UK SEA EXTR/IND NAT/G DELIB/GP LEGIS ADMIN ORD/FREE...POLICY GEOG CENSUS CHARTS BIBLIOG 19. PAGE 129 A2636
COLONIAL INT/TRADE DOMIN AFR

B61
SLESSOR J.,WHAT PRICE COEXISTENCE? COM INT/ORG NAT/G FORCES COLONIAL ARMS/CONT WAR...POLICY TREND 20 NATO COLD/WAR. PAGE 134 A2741
DIPLOM PEACE WOR+45 NUC/PWR

B61
SYATAUW J.J.G.,SOME NEWLY ESTABLISHED ASIAN STATES AND THE DEVELOPMENT OF INTERNATIONAL LAW. BURMA CEYLON INDIA INDONESIA ECO/UNDEV COLONIAL NEUTRAL WAR PEACE SOVEREIGN...CHARTS 19/20. PAGE 140 A2873
INT/LAW ADJUST SOCIETY S/ASIA

B61
UAR MINISTRY OF CULTURE,A BIBLIOGRAPHICAL LIST OF AL MAGHRIB. ALGERIA ISLAM MOROCCO UAR SECT INT/TRADE COLONIAL 19/20 TUNIS. PAGE 146 A2987
BIBLIOG DIPLOM GEOG

B61
UAR MINISTRY OF CULTURE,A BIBLIOGRAPHICAL LIST OF LIBYA. ISLAM LIBYA DIPLOM COLONIAL REV WAR 19/20. PAGE 146 A2988
BIBLIOG GEOG SECT NAT/LISM

B61
UAR MINISTRY OF CULTURE,A BIBLIOGRAPHICAL LIST OF TUNISIA. ISLAM CULTURE NAT/G EDU/PROP COLONIAL ...GEOG 19/20 TUNIS. PAGE 146 A2989
BIBLIOG DIPLOM SECT

B61
WALLERSTEIN I.M.,AFRICA; THE POLITICS OF INDEPENDENCE. AFR SOCIETY STRUCT LEAD PARL/PROC PARTIC GP/REL...POLICY 20. PAGE 160 A3269
ECO/UNDEV DIPLOM COLONIAL ORD/FREE

B61
WARD B.J.,INDIA AND THE WEST. INDIA UK USA+45 INT/TRADE GIVE COLONIAL ATTIT MARXISM 19/20. PAGE 161 A3279
PLAN ECO/UNDEV ECO/TAC FOR/AID

B61
WINTER R.C.,BLUEPRINTS FOR INDEPENDENCE. WOR+45 INT/ORG DIPLOM COLONIAL CONTROL REV WAR PWR ...BIBLIOG 20 UN. PAGE 165 A3367
NAT/G ECO/UNDEV SOVEREIGN CONSTN

B62
APATHEKER H.,AMERICAN FOREIGN POLICY AND THE COLD WAR. USA+45 NAT/G POL/PAR COLONIAL NAT/LISM SOVEREIGN MARXISM SOCISM 20 COLD/WAR MARX/KARL LENIN/VI INTERVENT. PAGE 8 A0167
DIPLOM WAR PEACE

B62
BAULIN J.,THE ARAB ROLE IN AFRICA. AFR ALGERIA FUT ISLAM MOROCCO UAR COLONIAL NEUTRAL REV...SOC 20 TUNIS BOURGUIBA. PAGE 12 A0235
NAT/LISM DIPLOM NAT/G SECT

B62
BRYANT A.,A CHOICE FOR DESTINY: COMMONWEALTH AND THE COMMON MARKET. EUR+WWI FUT UK INT/TRADE COLONIAL ATTIT SOVEREIGN 20 CMN/WLTH EEC. PAGE 20 A0411
INT/ORG VOL/ASSN DIPLOM CHOOSE

B62
BUCHMANN J.,L'AFRIQUE NOIRE INDEPENDANTE. POL/PAR DIPLOM COLONIAL PARTIC CHOOSE GP/REL ATTIT ORD/FREE WEALTH NEGRO. PAGE 21 A0426
AFR NAT/LISM DECISION

B62
CADWELL R.,COMMUNISM IN THE MODERN WORLD. USSR WOR+45 SOCIETY AGRI INDUS INT/ORG SECT EDU/PROP COLONIAL PEACE...SOC 20. PAGE 23 A0463
COM DIPLOM POLICY CONCPT

B62
DIAZ J.S.,MANUAL DE BIBLIOGRAFIA DE LA LITERATURA ESPANOLA. PRE/AMER SPAIN ECO/UNDEV DIPLOM LEAD ATTIT...SOC 15/20. PAGE 37 A0755
BIBLIOG L/A+17C NAT/G COLONIAL

B62
GUENA Y.,HISTORIQUE DE LA COMMUNAUTE. FUT ECO/UNDEV NAT/G PLAN EDU/PROP COLONIAL REGION NAT/LISM ALL/VALS SOVEREIGN...CONCPT OBS CHARTS 20. PAGE 58 A1186
AFR VOL/ASSN FOR/AID FRANCE

B62
HETHERINGTON H.,SOME ASPECTS OF THE BRITISH EXPERIMENT IN DEMOCRACY. UK DIPLOM COLONIAL ...CONCPT 20 CMN/WLTH. PAGE 64 A1322
EDU/PROP AFR POPULISM SOC/EXP

B62
HOOK S.,WORLD COMMUNISM: KEY DOCUMENTARY MATERIAL. CHINA/COM L/A+17C USA+45 USSR POL/PAR DIPLOM COLONIAL REV WAR...ANTHOL 20 MARX/KARL LENIN/VI COM/PARTY. PAGE 67 A1380
MARXISM COM GEN/LAWS NAT/G

B62
HUTTENBACK R.A.,BRITISH RELATIONS WITH THE SIND, 1799-1843. FRANCE INDIA UK FORCES...POLICY CHARTS BIBLIOG 18/19 SIND. PAGE 69 A1425
COLONIAL DIPLOM DOMIN S/ASIA

B62
INGHAM K.,A HISTORY OF EAST AFRICA. NAT/G DIPLOM ADMIN WAR NAT/LISM...SOC BIOG BIBLIOG. PAGE 70 A1439
AFR CONSTN COLONIAL

B62
KENT R.K.,FROM MADAGASCAR TO THE MALAGASY REPUBLIC. FRANCE MADAGASCAR DIPLOM NAT/LISM ORD/FREE...MGT 18/20. PAGE 78 A1596
COLONIAL SOVEREIGN REV POL/PAR

B62
LAUERHAUSS L.,COMMUNISM IN LATIN AMERICA: THE POST-WAR YEARS (1945 -1960) (PAPER). INTELL STRATA ECO/UNDEV AGRI WORKER FOR/AID INT/TRADE COLONIAL GUERRILLA 20. PAGE 85 A1745
BIBLIOG L/A+17C MARXISM REV

B62
MONTGOMERY J.D.,THE POLITICS OF FOREIGN AID: AMERICAN EXPERIENCE IN SOUTHEAST ASIA. S/ASIA USA+45 NAT/G PROB/SOLV COLONIAL 20. PAGE 103 A2115
FOR/AID DIPLOM GOV/REL GIVE

B62
QUIRK R.E.,AN AFFAIR OF HONOR: WOODROW WILSON AND THE OCCUPATION OF VERACRUZ. L/A+17C USA-45 COLONIAL SUPEGO PWR 20 WILSON/W MEXIC/AMER. PAGE 118 A2428
DOMIN DIPLOM COERCE PROB/SOLV

B62
RIMALOV V.V.,ECONOMIC COOPERATION BETWEEN USSR AND UNDERDEVELOPED COUNTRIES. USSR FINAN TEC/DEV INT/TRADE DOMIN EDU/PROP COLONIAL NAT/LISM DRIVE SOVEREIGN...AUD/VIS 20. PAGE 121 A2482
FOR/AID PLAN ECO/UNDEV DIPLOM

B62
SELOSOEMARDJAN O.,SOCIAL CHANGES IN JOGJAKARTA. INDONESIA NETHERLAND ELITES STRATA STRUCT FAM POL/PAR CREATE DIPLOM INT/TRADE EDU/PROP ADMIN GOV/REL...SOC 20 JAVA CHINJAP. PAGE 131 A2683
ECO/UNDEV CULTURE REV COLONIAL

B62
SHAPIRO D.,A SELECT BIBLIOGRAPHY OF WORKS IN ENGLISH ON RUSSIAN HISTORY, 1801-1917. COM USSR STRATA FORCES EDU/PROP ADMIN REV RACE/REL ATTIT 19/20. PAGE 131 A2693
BIBLIOG DIPLOM COLONIAL

B62
SNYDER L.L.D.,THE IMPERIALISM READER. AFR ASIA CHINA/COM COM EUR+WWI FUT MOD/EUR USA+45 WOR+45 WOR-45 INT/ORG COLONIAL SOVEREIGN CMN/WLTH OAS 20. PAGE 134 A2751
DOMIN PWR DIPLOM

B62
TAYLOR D.,THE BRITISH IN AFRICA. UK CULTURE ECO/UNDEV INDUS DIPLOM INT/TRADE ADMIN WAR RACE/REL ORD/FREE SOVEREIGN...POLICY BIBLIOG 15/20 CMN/WLTH. PAGE 142 A2898
AFR COLONIAL DOMIN

B62
US DEPARTMENT OF THE ARMY,AFRICA: ITS PROBLEMS AND PROSPECTS. CHINA/COM USSR INT/ORG FOR/AID COLONIAL LEAD FEDERAL DRIVE SOVEREIGN MARXISM...GEOG 20 COLD/WAR. PAGE 152 A3104
BIBLIOG/A AFR NAT/LISM DIPLOM

B62
VIET J.,INTERNATIONAL COOPERATION AND PROGRAMMES OF ECONOMIC AND SOCIAL DEVELOPMENT. TEC/DEV FOR/AID DOMIN COLONIAL PEACE WEALTH 20 UNESCO. PAGE 159 A3232
BIBLIOG/A INT/ORG DIPLOM ECO/UNDEV

B62
WELLEQUET J.,LE CONGO BELGE ET LA WELTPOLITIK (1894-1914. GERMANY DOMIN EDU/PROP WAR ATTIT ...BIBLIOG T CONGO/LEOP. PAGE 163 A3314
ADMIN DIPLOM GP/REL COLONIAL

L62
CORET A.,"LES PROVINCES PORTUGALLES D'OUTREMER ET L'ONU." AFR PORTUGAL S/ASIA WOR+45 LOC/G NAT/G DOMIN...CONCPT TIME/SEQ UN 20 GOA. PAGE 31 A0620
INT/ORG SOVEREIGN COLONIAL

L62
MURACCIOLE L.,"LA LOI FONDAMENTALE DE LA REPUBLIQUE DU CONGO." WOR+45 SOCIETY ECO/UNDEV INT/ORG NAT/G LEGIS PLAN LEGIT ADJUD COLONIAL ROUTINE ATTIT SOVEREIGN 20 CONGO. PAGE 106 A2174
AFR CONSTN

S62
CORET A.,"LA DECLARATION DE L'ASSEMBLEE GENERAL DE L'ONU SUR L'OCTROI DE L'INDEPENDENCE AUX PAYS ET AUX PEUPLES." AFR ASIA ISLAM NIGERIA S/ASIA USSR WOR+45 ECO/UNDEV NAT/G DELIB/GP COLONIAL ALL/VALS ...CONCPT TIME/SEQ TREND UN TOT/POP 20 MEXIC/AMER. PAGE 31 A0621
INT/ORG STRUCT SOVEREIGN

S62
JACOBSON H.K.,"THE UNITED NATIONS AND COLONIALISM: A TENTATIVE APPRAISAL." AFR FUT S/ASIA USA+45 USSR WOR+45 NAT/G DELIB/GP PLAN DIPLOM ECO/TAC DOMIN ADMIN ROUTINE COERCE ATTIT RIGID/FLEX ORD/FREE PWR ...OBS STERTYP UN 20. PAGE 73 A1486
INT/ORG CONCPT COLONIAL

S62
KOLARZ W.,"THE IMPACT OF COMMUNISM ON WEST AFRICA." AFR FUT SOCIETY INT/ORG NAT/G CREATE PLAN DOMIN EDU/PROP COERCE NAT/LISM ATTIT RIGID/FLEX SOCISM ...POLICY CONCPT TREND MARX/KARL 20. PAGE 81 A1666
COM POL/PAR COLONIAL

S62
PIQUEMAL M.,"LES PROBLEMES DES UNIONS D'ETATS EN AFRIQUE NOIRE." FRANCE SOCIETY INT/ORG NAT/G DELIB/GP PLAN LEGIT ADMIN COLONIAL ROUTINE ATTIT ORD/FREE PWR...GEOG METH/CNCPT 20. PAGE 116 A2382
AFR ECO/UNDEV REGION

S62
RUBINSTEIN A.Z.,"RUSSIA AND THE UNCOMMITTED NATIONS." AFR INDIA ISLAM L/A+17C LAOS S/ASIA ELITES ECO/UNDEV INT/ORG KIN CREATE PLAN TEC/DEV NAT/LISM RIGID/FLEX PWR WEALTH...METH/CNCPT TIME/SEQ GEN/LAWS WORK. PAGE 125 A2562
ECO/TAC TREND COLONIAL USSR

S62
TOWSTER J.,"THE USSR AND THE USA: CHALLENGE AND RESPONSE." COM GERMANY USA+45 USSR WOR+45 ECO/UNDEV INT/ORG VOL/ASSN EX/STRUC FORCES TOP/EX CREATE PLAN TEC/DEV DIPLOM ECO/TAC EDU/PROP COLONIAL COERCE PWR ...GEN/METH COLD/WAR 20 KENNEDY/JF. PAGE 145 A2956
ACT/RES GEN/LAWS

S62
VASAK K.,"DE LA CONVENTION EUROPEENNE A LA CONVENTION AFRICAINE DES DROITS DE L'HOMME." AFR ISLAM WOR+45 LAW CONSTN ECO/UNDEV INT/ORG PERCEPT ALL/VALS 20. PAGE 158 A3223
DELIB/GP CONCPT COLONIAL

C62
DUFFY J.,"PORTUGAL IN AFRICA." PORTUGAL SIER/LEONE INDUS WORKER INT/TRADE WAR CONSERVE...CATH GEOG TREND 16/20. PAGE 39 A0795
BIBLIOG RACE/REL ECO/UNDEV COLONIAL

B63
BRITISH AID. UK AGRI DIST/IND INDUS SCHOOL TEC/DEV INT/TRADE COLONIAL DEMAND...TREND CHARTS 20. PAGE 3 A0064
FOR/AID ECO/UNDEV NAT/G FINAN

B63
ADLER G.J.,BRITISH INDIA'S NORTHERN FRONTIER: 1865-95. AFGHANISTN RUSSIA UK PROVS COLONIAL COERCE PEACE...GEOG CHARTS BIBLIOG 19 TREATY. PAGE 4 A0091
S/ASIA FORCES DIPLOM POLICY

B63
AFRICAN BIBLIOGRAPHIC CENTER,THE SCENE IS GUINEA AND THE PERSONAGE IS SEKOU TOURE: A SELECTED CURRENT READING LIST, 1959-1962 (PAMPHLET). GUINEA ECO/UNDEV CHIEF FOR/AID COLONIAL...BIOG 20. PAGE 5 A0095
BIBLIOG AFR POL/PAR COM

B63
AFRICAN BIBLIOGRAPHIC CENTER,THE SCENE IS KENYA AND THE PERSONAGE IS TOM MBOYA: A SELECTED CURRENT READING LIST FROM 1956-1962 (PAMPHLET). ECO/UNDEV LABOR POL/PAR CHIEF COLONIAL CHOOSE NAT/LISM ORD/FREE 20. PAGE 5 A0096
BIBLIOG DIPLOM AFR NAT/G

B63
BISHOP O.B.,PUBLICATIONS OF THE GOVERNMENT OF THE PROVINCE OF CANADA 1841-1867. CANADA DIPLOM COLONIAL LEAD...POLICY 18. PAGE 14 A0294
BIBLIOG NAT/G ATTIT

B63
BRECHER M.,THE NEW STATES OF ASIA. ASIA S/ASIA INT/ORG BAL/PWR COLONIAL NEUTRAL ORD/FREE PWR 20 UN. PAGE 18 A0369
NAT/G ECO/UNDEV DIPLOM POLICY

B63
BROWN W.N.,THE UNITED STATES AND INDIA AND PAKISTAN (REV. ED.). INDIA PAKISTAN S/ASIA WOR+45 POL/PAR SECT INT/TRADE COLONIAL COERCE DISCRIM. PAGE 20
DIPLOM ECO/UNDEV SOVEREIGN

A0408 STRUCT

B63
CANELAS O.A.,RADIOGRAFIA DE LA ALIANZA PARA EL ATRASO. L/A+17C USA+45 ECO/TAC DOMIN COLONIAL NAT/LISM...SOCIALIST NAT/COMP 20. PAGE 23 A0476 REV DIPLOM ECO/UNDEV REGION

B63
CROZIER B.,THE MORNING AFTER; A STUDY OF INDEPENDENCE. WOR+45 EX/STRUC PLAN BAL/PWR COLONIAL GP/REL 20 COLD/WAR. PAGE 33 A0666 SOVEREIGN NAT/LISM NAT/G DIPLOM

B63
DECOTTIGNIES R.,LES NATIONALITES AFRICAINES. AFR NAT/G PROB/SOLV DIPLOM COLONIAL ORD/FREE...CHARTS GOV/COMP 20. PAGE 35 A0721 NAT/LISM JURID LEGIS LAW

B63
ELIAS T.O.,GOVERNMENT AND POLITICS IN AFRICA. CONSTN CULTURE SOCIETY NAT/G POL/PAR DIPLOM REPRESENT PERSON...SOC TREND BIBLIOG 4/20. PAGE 41 A0837 AFR NAT/LISM COLONIAL LAW

B63
ETHIOPIAN MINISTRY INFORMATION,AFRICAN SUMMIT CONFERENCE ADDIS ABABA, ETHIOPIA, 1963. ETHIOPIA DELIB/GP COLONIAL NAT/LISM...POLICY DECISION 20. PAGE 42 A0865 AFR CONFER REGION DIPLOM

B63
GARDINIER D.E.,CAMEROON: UNITED NATIONS CHALLENGE TO FRENCH POLICY. AFR CAMEROON FRANCE NAT/G LEGIS CONTROL SOVEREIGN 20 UN. PAGE 51 A1042 DIPLOM POLICY INT/ORG COLONIAL

B63
GILBERT M.,THE APPEASERS. COM GERMANY UK PLAN ECO/TAC COLONIAL CONTROL EXEC ORD/FREE PWR FASCISM 20 PARLIAMENT. PAGE 52 A1068 DIPLOM WAR POLICY DECISION

B63
HAILEY L.,THE REPUBLIC OF SOUTH AFRICA AND THE HIGH COMMISSION TERRITORIES. AFR SOUTH/AFR UK INT/ORG NAT/G PROVS RACE/REL SOVEREIGN...CHARTS 19/20 COMMONWLTH. PAGE 59 A1219 COLONIAL DIPLOM ATTIT

B63
HARGREAVES J.D.,PRELUDE TO THE PARTITION OF WEST AFRICA. AFR. PAGE 61 A1259 COLONIAL DIPLOM POLICY

B63
HUSSEY W.D.,THE BRITISH EMPIRE AND COMMONWEALTH 1500 TO 1961. UK USA-45 SOCIETY ECO/UNDEV NAT/G VOL/ASSN INT/TRADE DOMIN CONTROL WAR PWR ...DICTIONARY 16/20 COMMONWLTH TRUST/TERR. PAGE 69 A1422 COLONIAL SOVEREIGN INT/ORG

B63
JAIRAZBHOY R.A.,FOREIGN INFLUENCE IN ANCIENT INDIA. INDIA ELITES SECT DIPLOM EDU/PROP COLONIAL REGION GP/REL...ART/METH LING WORSHIP +/14 GRECO/ROMN MESOPOTAM PERSIA PARTH/SASS. PAGE 73 A1491 CULTURE SOCIETY COERCE DOMIN

B63
JENNINGS W.I.,DEMOCRACY IN AFRICA. UK CULTURE STRUCT ECO/UNDEV DIPLOM COLONIAL GP/REL ADJUST NAT/LISM ORD/FREE...GOV/COMP 20 THIRD/WRLD. PAGE 74 A1512 PROB/SOLV AFR CONSTN POPULISM

B63
LEE C.,THE POLITICS OF KOREAN NATIONALISM. KOREA S/ASIA DIPLOM REV WAR 14/20 CHINJAP. PAGE 86 A1759 NAT/LISM SOVEREIGN COLONIAL

B63
LYON P.,NEUTRALISM. ECO/UNDEV EDU/PROP COLONIAL ALL/IDEOS...IDEA/COMP 20 COLD/WAR UN. PAGE 92 A1879 NAT/COMP NAT/LISM DIPLOM NEUTRAL

B63
MANSERGH N.,DOCUMENTS AND SPEECHES ON COMMONWEALTH AFFAIRS 1952-1962. CANADA INDIA PAKISTAN UK CONSTN FORCES ECO/TAC EDU/PROP COLONIAL DETER WAR ORD/FREE SOVEREIGN...POLICY 20 AUSTRAL. PAGE 94 A1932 BIBLIOG/A FEDERAL INT/TRADE DIPLOM

B63
MBOYA T.,FREEDOM AND AFTER. AFR LABOR POL/PAR DIPLOM EDU/PROP COERCE SOCISM 20. PAGE 97 A1989 COLONIAL ECO/UNDEV NAT/LISM INT/ORG

B63
MENDES C.,NACIONALISMO E DESENVOLVIMENTO. AFR ASIA L/A+17C STRATA INT/TRADE COLONIAL. PAGE 99 A2039 NAT/LISM ECO/UNDEV DIPLOM REV

B63
PADELFORD N.J.,AFRICA AND WORLD ORDER. AFR COLONIAL SOVEREIGN...ANTHOL BIBLIOG 20 UN UNIFICA COMMONWLTH. PAGE 113 A2312 DIPLOM NAT/G ORD/FREE

B63
PATRA A.C.,THE ADMINISTRATION OF JUSTICE UNDER THE EAST INDIA COMPANY IN BENGAL, BIHAR AND ORISSA. INDIA UK LG/CO CAP/ISM INT/TRADE ADJUD COLONIAL CONTROL CT/SYS...POLICY 20. PAGE 114 A2341 ADMIN JURID CONCPT

B63
RIUKIN A.,THE AFRICAN PRESENCE IN WORLD AFFAIRS. AFR WOR+45 ECO/UNDEV AGRI INT/ORG BAL/PWR ECO/TAC COLONIAL NEUTRAL NAT/LISM PEACE SOVEREIGN 20 UN. PAGE 121 A2486 DIPLOM NAT/G POLICY PWR

B63
ROSSI M.,THE THIRD WORLD. FUT WOR+45 INT/ORG NAT/G CAP/ISM COLONIAL PEACE PWR MARXISM 20 UN THIRD/WRLD. PAGE 124 A2542 ECO/UNDEV DIPLOM BAL/PWR NEUTRAL

B63
SCHMELTZ G.W.,LA POLITIQUE MONDIALE CONTEMPORAINE. SOCIETY ECO/UNDEV INDUS INT/ORG NAT/G POL/PAR CONSULT DELIB/GP PLAN TEC/DEV ECO/TAC DOMIN EDU/PROP ROUTINE COERCE PERCEPT PERSON LOVE SKILL ...SOC RECORD TOT/POP. PAGE 128 A2629 WOR+45 COLONIAL

B63
STEVENSON A.E.,LOOKING OUTWARD: YEARS OF CRISIS AT THE UNITED NATIONS. COM CUBA USA+45 WOR+45 SOCIETY NAT/G EX/STRUC ACT/RES LEGIT COLONIAL ATTIT PERSON SUPEGO ALL/VALS...POLICY HUM UN COLD/WAR CONGO 20. PAGE 138 A2823 INT/ORG CONCPT ARMS/CONT

B63
WALKER A.A.,OFFICIAL PUBLICATIONS OF SIERRA LEONE AND GAMBIA. GAMBIA SIER/LEONE UK LAW CONSTN LEGIS PLAN BUDGET DIPLOM...SOC SAMP CON/ANAL 20. PAGE 160 A3262 BIBLIOG NAT/G COLONIAL ADMIN

B63
WILCOX W.A.,PAKISTAN; THE CONSOLIDATION OF A NATION. INDIA PAKISTAN CONSTN SECT PROB/SOLV COLONIAL PARTIC GP/REL FEDERAL...POLICY 19/20. PAGE 164 A3348 NAT/LISM ECO/UNDEV DIPLOM STRUCT

S63
CHAKRAVARTI P.C.,"INDIAN NON-ALIGNMENT AND UNITED STATES POLICY." ASIA INDIA S/ASIA USA+45 CULTURE ECO/UNDEV NAT/G VOL/ASSN DELIB/GP TOP/EX FOR/AID NEUTRAL...POLICY HUM CONCPT RECORD GEN/LAWS 20. PAGE 25 A0515 ATTIT ALL/VALS COLONIAL DIPLOM

S63
ROUGEMONT D.,"LES NOUVELLES CHANCES DE L'EUROPE." EUR+WWI FUT ECO/DEV INT/ORG NAT/G ACT/RES PLAN TEC/DEV EDU/PROP ADMIN COLONIAL FEDERAL ATTIT PWR SKILL...TREND 20. PAGE 124 A2549 ECO/UNDEV PERCEPT

C63
CHARLETON W.G.,"THE REVOLUTION IN AMERICAN FOREIGN POLICY." COM PROB/SOLV FOR/AID DOMIN COLONIAL NEUTRAL DETER WAR ISOLAT NAT/LISM...BIBLIOG 19/20 UN COLD/WAR NATO. PAGE 26 A0523 DIPLOM INT/ORG BAL/PWR

B64
ARNOLD G.,TOWARDS PEACE AND A MULTIRACIAL COMMONWEALTH. UK TEC/DEV BAL/PWR COLONIAL GP/REL NAT/LISM PEACE SOVEREIGN...POLICY SOC/INTEG 20 CMN/WLTH. PAGE 9 A0175 DIPLOM INT/TRADE FOR/AID ORD/FREE

B64
BAILEY T.A.,A DIPLOMATIC HISTORY OF THE AMERICAN PEOPLE (7TH ED.). USA+45 USA-45 FOR/AID COLONIAL PARL/PROC WAR...CHARTS BIBLIOG/A T 18/20. PAGE 10 A0208 DIPLOM NAT/G

B64
BURKE F.G.,AFRICA'S QUEST FOR ORDER. AFR CULTURE KIN MUNIC NAT/G DIPLOM COLONIAL REV DISCRIM NAT/LISM AGE/Y 20. PAGE 21 A0437 ORD/FREE CONSEN RACE/REL LEAD

B64
BUTWELL R.,SOUTHEAST ASIA TODAY - AND TOMORROW. NAT/G COLONIAL LEAD REGION WAR CHOOSE WEALTH MARXISM 20. PAGE 23 A0458 S/ASIA DIPLOM ECO/UNDEV NAT/LISM

B64
CASEY R.G.,THE FUTURE OF THE COMMONWEALTH. INDIA PAKISTAN UK ECO/UNDEV INT/ORG TEC/DEV COLONIAL SUPEGO 20 EEC AUSTRAL. PAGE 25 A0505 DIPLOM SOVEREIGN NAT/LISM FOR/AID

B64
COX R.,PAN-AFRICANISM IN PRACTICE. AFR DIPLOM CONFER RACE/REL ROLE SOVEREIGN...POLICY 20 PANAF/FREE. PAGE 32 A0645 ORD/FREE COLONIAL REGION NAT/LISM

B64
DESHMUKH C.D.,THE COMMONWEALTH AS INDIA SEES IT. INDIA UK ECO/UNDEV TEC/DEV INT/TRADE GP/REL RACE/REL SOVEREIGN SOC/INTEG 19/20 COMMONWLTH. PAGE 36 A0733 DIPLOM COLONIAL NAT/LISM ATTIT

B64
DONOUGHUE B.,BRITISH POLITICS AND THE AMERICAN REVOLUTION: THE PATH TO WAR 1773-75. UK USA-45 NAT/G LEGIS WAR 18 PRE/US/AM. PAGE 38 A0772 DIPLOM POLICY COLONIAL REV

B64
DUROSELLE J.B.,LA COMMUNAUTE INTERNATIONALE FACE AUX JEUNES ETATS. CHINA/COM COM S/ASIA USSR INT/ORG ROLE...ANTHOL 20 UN SEATO THIRD/WRLD. PAGE 40 A0808 DIPLOM COLONIAL ECO/UNDEV SOVEREIGN

B64
DUROSELLE J.B.,POLITIQUES NATIONALES ENVERS LES JEUNES ETATS. FRANCE ISRAEL ITALY UK USA+45 USSR YUGOSLAVIA ECO/DEV FINAN ECO/TAC INT/TRADE ADMIN PWR 20. PAGE 40 A0809 DIPLOM ECO/UNDEV COLONIAL DOMIN

B64
EAYRS J.,THE COMMONWEALTH AND SUEZ: A DOCUMENTARY SURVEY. FRANCE ISLAM VOL/ASSN FORCES CONFER COLONIAL WAR INGP/REL 20 CMN/WLTH SUEZ UN. PAGE 40 A0818
DIPLOM NAT/LISM DIST/IND SOVEREIGN

B64
EMBREE A.T.,A GUIDE TO PAPERBACKS ON ASIA; SELECTED AND ANNOTATED (PAMPHLET). CULTURE SOCIETY ECO/UNDEV SECT DIPLOM COLONIAL MARXISM...SOC 20. PAGE 41 A0845
BIBLIOG/A ASIA S/ASIA NAT/G

B64
EPSTEIN H.M.,REVOLT IN THE CONGO. AFR CONGO/BRAZ WOR+45 NAT/G FORCES DOMIN WAR CIVMIL/REL INGP/REL MARXISM...RECORD GP/COMP 20 CONGO/LEOP UN. PAGE 42 A0856
REV COLONIAL NAT/LISM DIPLOM

B64
GREAT BRITAIN CENTRAL OFF INF,CONSTITUTIONAL DEVELOPMENT IN THE COMMONWEALTH. VOL/ASSN PLAN DIPLOM COLONIAL INGP/REL NAT/LISM ORD/FREE PWR 17/20 CMN/WLTH. PAGE 55 A1135
REGION CONSTN NAT/G SOVEREIGN

B64
IRISH M.D.,WORLD PRESSURES ON AMERICAN FOREIGN POLICY. ASIA COM L/A+17C SOUTH/AFR UK WOR+45 ECO/DEV ECO/UNDEV COLONIAL SANCTION COERCE REV TOTALISM...ANTHOL 20 COLD/WAR EUROPE/W INTERVENT. PAGE 72 A1467
DIPLOM POLICY

B64
KITCHEN H.,A HANDBOOK OF AFRICAN AFFAIRS. ECO/UNDEV CREATE DIPLOM COLONIAL RACE/REL...ART/METH GEOG CHARTS 20. PAGE 80 A1646
AFR NAT/G INT/ORG FORCES

B64
KOLARZ W.,COMMUNISM AND COLONIALISM. AFR ASIA USSR DISCRIM ATTIT ORD/FREE SOVEREIGN SOC/INTEG 20. PAGE 81 A1668
EDU/PROP DIPLOM TOTALISM COLONIAL

B64
LUTHULI A.,AFRICA'S FREEDOM. KIN LABOR POL/PAR SCHOOL DIPLOM NEUTRAL REGION REV NAT/LISM PWR WEALTH SOCISM SOC/INTEG 20. PAGE 92 A1874
AFR ECO/UNDEV COLONIAL

B64
MACKESY P.,THE WAR FOR AMERICA, 1775-1783. UK FORCES DIPLOM...POLICY 18. PAGE 93 A1895
WAR COLONIAL LEAD REV

B64
MAHAR J.M.,INDIA: A CRITICAL BIBLIOGRAPHY. INDIA PAKISTAN CULTURE ECO/UNDEV LOC/G POL/PAR SECT PROB/SOLV DIPLOM ADMIN COLONIAL PARL/PROC ATTIT 20. PAGE 93 A1906
BIBLIOG/A S/ASIA NAT/G LEAD

B64
NEWBURY C.W.,THE WEST AFRICAN COMMONWEALTH. CONSTN INTELL ECO/UNDEV VOL/ASSN CHIEF DELIB/GP LEGIS INT/TRADE COLONIAL FEDERAL ATTIT 20 COMMONWLTH AFRICA/W. PAGE 108 A2223
INT/ORG SOVEREIGN GOV/REL AFR

B64
NICOL D.,AFRICA - A SUBJECTIVE VIEW. AFR INT/ORG PLAN ADMIN COLONIAL PARL/PROC PARTIC REGION GOV/REL LITERACY ATTIT...BIBLIOG 20 CIVIL/SERV. PAGE 109 A2230
NAT/G LEAD CULTURE ACADEM

B64
PENNOCK J.R.,SELF-GOVERNMENT IN MODERNIZING NATIONS. AFR COM USA+45 ECO/DEV POL/PAR PROB/SOLV DIPLOM ECO/TAC COLONIAL REV POPULISM SOCISM 20. PAGE 114 A2350
ECO/UNDEV POLICY SOVEREIGN NAT/G

B64
PERKINS D.,THE AMERICAN DEMOCRACY: ITS RISE TO POWER. ASIA USSR LAW CULTURE FINAN EDU/PROP COLONIAL CHOOSE...POLICY CHARTS BIBLIOG WORSHIP PRESIDENT 15/20 NEGRO. PAGE 115 A2362
LOC/G ECO/TAC WAR DIPLOM

B64
QUIGG P.W.,AFRICA: A FOREIGN AFFAIRS READER. AFR FRANCE PORTUGAL UK DIPLOM LEAD PARL/PROC MARXISM ...MAJORIT METH/CNCPT GOV/COMP IDEA/COMP ANTHOL 19/20. PAGE 118 A2426
COLONIAL SOVEREIGN NAT/LISM RACE/REL

B64
STANKIEWICZ W.J.,POLITICAL THOUGHT SINCE WORLD WAR II. WOR+45 CAP/ISM DIPLOM COLONIAL COERCE REV REPRESENT ADJUST ANOMIE ALL/IDEOS 20. PAGE 137 A2804
IDEA/COMP DOMIN ORD/FREE AUTHORIT

B64
STILLMAN E.O.,THE POLITICS OF HYSTERIA: THE SOURCES OF TWENTIETH-CENTURY CONFLICT. WOR+45 WOR-45 CULTURE ECO/UNDEV PLAN CAP/ISM WAR MARXISM ...PREDICT BIBLIOG 20 COLD/WAR. PAGE 138 A2828
DIPLOM IDEA/COMP COLONIAL CONTROL

B64
TONG T.,UNITED STATES DIPLOMACY IN CHINA, 1844-1860. ASIA USA-45 ECO/UNDEV ECO/TAC COERCE GP/REL...INT/LAW 19 TREATY. PAGE 144 A2949
DIPLOM INT/TRADE COLONIAL

B64
TREADGOLD D.W.,THE DEVELOPMENT OF THE USSR. COM USSR ECO/DEV CREATE BAL/PWR DEBATE COLONIAL TOTALISM...HUM ANTHOL BIBLIOG 19/20. PAGE 145 A2960
MARXISM CONSERVE DIPLOM DOMIN

B64
VOELKMANN K.,HERRSCHER VON MORGEN? BAL/PWR COLONIAL NEUTRAL REGION RACE/REL ALL/VALS SOVEREIGN...RECORD 20 COLD/WAR THIRD/WRLD. PAGE 159 A3246
DIPLOM ECO/UNDEV CONTROL NAT/COMP

B64
WAINHOUSE D.W.,REMNANTS OF EMPIRE: THE UNITED NATIONS AND THE END OF COLONIALISM. FUT PORTUGAL WOR+45 NAT/G CONSULT DOMIN LEGIT ADMIN ROUTINE ATTIT ORD/FREE...POLICY JURID RECORD INT TIME/SEQ UN CMN/WLTH 20. PAGE 160 A3260
INT/ORG TREND COLONIAL

B64
WALLBANK T.W.,DOCUMENTS ON MODERN AFRICA. NAT/G COLONIAL GP/REL ATTIT PWR...BIBLIOG 19/20. PAGE 160 A3267
AFR NAT/LISM ECO/UNDEV DIPLOM

B64
WOODHOUSE C.M.,THE NEW CONCERT OF NATIONS. WOR+45 ECO/DEV ECO/UNDEV NAT/G BAL/PWR ECO/TAC NAT/LISM PWR SOVEREIGN ALL/IDEOS 20 UN COLD/WAR. PAGE 166 A3391
DIPLOM MORAL FOR/AID COLONIAL

L64
SYMONDS R.,"REFLECTIONS IN LOCALISATION." AFR S/ASIA UK STRATA INT/ORG NAT/G SCHOOL EDU/PROP LEGIT KNOWL ORD/FREE PWR RESPECT CMN/WLTH 20. PAGE 140 A2874
ADMIN MGT COLONIAL

S64
CARNEGIE ENDOWMENT INT. PEACE,"COLONIAL COUNTRIES AND PEOPLES (ISSUES BEFORE THE NINETEENTH GENERAL ASSEMBLY)." AFR ISLAM L/A+17C WOR+45 DELIB/GP LEGIS ECO/TAC EDU/PROP NAT/LISM PEACE ALL/VALS...RECORD UN CMN/WLTH 20. PAGE 24 A0491
INT/ORG ECO/UNDEV COLONIAL

S64
GINSBURGS G.,"WARS OF NATIONAL LIBERATION - THE SOVIET THESIS." COM USSR WOR+45 WOR-45 LAW CULTURE INT/ORG DIPLOM LEGIT COLONIAL GUERRILLA WAR NAT/LISM ATTIT PERSON MORAL PWR...JURID OBS TREND MARX/KARL 20. PAGE 53 A1075
COERCE CONCPT INT/LAW REV

S64
GROSS J.A.,"WHITEHALL AND THE COMMONWEALTH." EUR+WWI MOD/EUR INT/ORG NAT/G CONSULT DELIB/GP LEGIS DOMIN ADMIN COLONIAL ROUTINE PWR CMN/WLTH 19/20. PAGE 57 A1174
EX/STRUC ATTIT TREND

S64
MARTELLI G.,"PORTUGAL AND THE UNITED NATIONS." AFR EUR+WWI ELITES INT/ORG NAT/G PROVS PLAN DIPLOM ECO/TAC DOMIN COLONIAL RIGID/FLEX MORAL ORD/FREE PWR WEALTH...MYTH UN 20. PAGE 95 A1947
ATTIT PORTUGAL

C64
EASTON S.C.,"THE RISE AND FALL OF WESTERN COLONIALISM." AFR ISLAM L/A+17C ECO/UNDEV REV NAT/LISM...CHARTS BIBLIOG 15/20. PAGE 40 A0817
COLONIAL DIPLOM ORD/FREE WAR

B65
AUVADE R.,BIBLIOGRAPHIE CRITIQUE DES OEUVRES PARUES SUR L'INDOCHINE FRANCAISE: UN SIECLE D'HISTOIRE ET D'ENSEIGNEMENT. VIETNAM DIPLOM...SOC 20. PAGE 10 A0198
BIBLIOG/A R+D ACADEM COLONIAL

B65
BRIDGMAN J.,GERMAN AFRICA: A SELECT ANNOTATED BIBLIOGRAPHY. AFR AGRI DIPLOM REPAR WAR FASCISM 20. PAGE 18 A0374
BIBLIOG/A COLONIAL NAT/G EDU/PROP

B65
COWEN Z.,THE BRITISH COMMONWEALTH OF NATIONS IN A CHANGING WORLD. UK ECO/UNDEV INT/ORG ECO/TAC INT/TRADE COLONIAL WAR GP/REL RACE/REL SOVEREIGN SOC/INTEG 20 TREATY EEC COMMONWLTH. PAGE 32 A0644
JURID DIPLOM PARL/PROC NAT/LISM

B65
DU BOIS W.E.B.,THE WORLD AND AFRICA. USA+45 CAP/ISM DISCRIM STRANGE SOCISM...TIME/SEQ TREND IDEA/COMP 19/20 NEGRO. PAGE 39 A0789
AFR DIPLOM COLONIAL CULTURE

B65
EMERSON R.,THE POLITICAL AWAKENING OF AFRICA. ECO/UNDEV INT/ORG COLONIAL RACE/REL ORD/FREE MARXISM...TREND ANTHOL 20. PAGE 42 A0849
AFR NAT/LISM DIPLOM POL/PAR

B65
FAGG J.E.,CUBA, HAITI, AND THE DOMINICAN REPUBLIC. CUBA DOMIN/REP HAITI L/A+17C NAT/G DIPLOM ECO/TAC DOMIN CHOOSE AUTHORIT ROLE SOVEREIGN POPULISM 17/20. PAGE 43 A0883
COLONIAL ECO/UNDEV REV GOV/COMP

B65
FANON F.,STUDIES IN A DYING COLONIALISM. ALGERIA FRANCE STRATA FAM DIPLOM DOMIN WAR RACE/REL DISCRIM HEALTH 20. PAGE 44 A0897
NAT/LISM COLONIAL REV SOVEREIGN

B65
GRAHAM G.S.,THE POLITICS OF NAVAL SUPREMACY; STUDIES IN BRITISH MARITIME ASCENDANCY. UK SEA NAT/G BAL/PWR LEAD WAR WEAPON PEACE...POLICY 18/19 COMMONWLTH. PAGE 55 A1126
FORCES PWR COLONIAL DIPLOM

B65
HISPANIC SOCIETY OF AMERICA,CATALOGUE (10 VOLS.). PORTUGAL PRE/AMER SPAIN NAT/G ADMIN...POLICY SOC 15/20. PAGE 65 A1341
BIBLIOG L/A+17C COLONIAL DIPLOM

B65
INGRAM D.,COMMONWEALTH FOR A COLOUR-BLIND WORLD. AFR INDIA UK STRATA ECO/UNDEV VOL/ASSN CREATE PLAN CONFER COLONIAL ORD/FREE SOC/INTEG 20 COMMONWLTH. PAGE 70 A1441
RACE/REL INT/ORG INGP/REL PROB/SOLV

B65
IRIYE A.,AFTER IMPERIALISM; THE SEARCH FOR A NEW ORDER IN THE FAR EAST 1921-1931. USA-45 USSR DOMIN AGREE COLONIAL REV PWR...BIBLIOG DICTIONARY 20 CHINJAP. PAGE 72 A1468
DIPLOM ASIA SOVEREIGN

B65
JALEE P.,THE PILLAGE OF THE THIRD WORLD (TRANS. BY MARY KLOPPER). WOR+45 AGRI INDUS ECO/TAC FOR/AID COLONIAL CONTROL PRODUC PWR WEALTH...STAT CHARTS 20 RESOURCE/N. PAGE 73 A1493
ECO/UNDEV DOMIN INT/TRADE DIPLOM

B65
KIRKWOOD K.,BRITAIN AND AFRICA. AFR UK ECO/UNDEV ECO/TAC WAR NAT/LISM SOVEREIGN 19/20. PAGE 80 A1636
NAT/G DIPLOM POLICY COLONIAL

B65
LEE M.,THE UNITED NATIONS AND WORLD REALITIES. ECO/UNDEV FORCES WAR PEACE ATTIT ROLE WEALTH 20 UN. PAGE 86 A1761
INT/ORG COLONIAL ARMS/CONT DIPLOM

B65
LIEUWEN E.,U.S. POLICY IN LATIN AMERICA: A SHORT HISTORY. L/A+17C USA+45 USA-45 DELIB/GP ECO/TAC 19/20 COLD/WAR MONROE/DOC. PAGE 89 A1812
DIPLOM COLONIAL NAT/G FOR/AID

B65
MANSFIELD P.,NASSER'S EGYPT. AFR ISLAM UAR ECO/UNDEV AGRI COLONIAL SOVEREIGN...CHARTS 20 NASSER/G MID/EAST. PAGE 94 A1934
CHIEF ECO/TAC DIPLOM POLICY

B65
MEDIVA J.T.,LA IMPRENTA EN MEXICO, 1539-1821 (8 VOLS.). SOCIETY ECO/UNDEV DIPLOM COLONIAL GP/REL 16/19 MEXIC/AMER. PAGE 99 A2031
BIBLIOG WRITING NAT/G L/A+17C

B65
MENON K.P.S.,MANY WORLDS. INDIA BAL/PWR CAP/ISM COLONIAL REV ORD/FREE PWR MARXISM...POLICY 20 COLD/WAR. PAGE 100 A2042
BIOG DIPLOM NAT/G

B65
MILLER J.D.B.,THE COMMONWEALTH IN THE WORLD (3RD ED.). CONSTN COLONIAL PWR SOVEREIGN 20 CMN/WLTH. PAGE 101 A2077
VOL/ASSN INT/ORG INGP/REL DIPLOM

B65
MOLNAR T.,AFRICA: A POLITICAL TRAVELOGUE. STRUCT ECO/UNDEV DIPLOM EDU/PROP LEAD RACE/REL MARXISM 20 INTERVENT EUROPE. PAGE 102 A2101
COLONIAL AFR ORD/FREE

B65
MORRIS R.B.,THE PEACEMAKERS; THE GREAT POWERS AND AMERICAN INDEPENDENCE. BAL/PWR CONFER COLONIAL NEUTRAL PEACE ORD/FREE TREATY 18 PRE/US/AM. PAGE 105 A2149
SOVEREIGN REV DIPLOM

B65
NEWBURY C.W.,BRITISH POLICY TOWARDS WEST AFRICA: SELECT DOCUMENTS 1786-1874. AFR UK INT/TRADE DOMIN ADMIN COLONIAL CT/SYS COERCE ORD/FREE...BIBLIOG/A 18/19. PAGE 108 A2224
DIPLOM POLICY NAT/G WRITING

B65
NKRUMAH K.,NEO-COLONIALISM: THE LAST STAGE OF IMPERIALISM. AFR INT/ORG WORKER FOR/AID INT/TRADE EDU/PROP GOV/REL NAT/LISM SOVEREIGN POPULISM SOCISM ...SOCIALIST 20 THIRD/WRLD INTRVN/ECO. PAGE 109 A2243
COLONIAL DIPLOM ECO/UNDEV ECO/TAC

B65
QURESHI I.H.,THE STRUGGLE FOR PAKISTAN. INDIA PAKISTAN UK CULTURE LEGIS DIPLOM EDU/PROP COLONIAL ATTIT SOVEREIGN 19/20 MUSLIM. PAGE 118 A2429
GP/REL RACE/REL WAR SECT

B65
RODRIGUES J.H.,BRAZIL AND AFRICA. AFR BRAZIL PORTUGAL UK USA+45 USA-45 CULTURE ECO/UNDEV INT/ORG INT/TRADE RACE/REL ORD/FREE 15/20 UN MISCEGEN. PAGE 123 A2513
DIPLOM COLONIAL POLICY ATTIT

B65
ROMEIN J.,THE ASIAN CENTURY. ASIA COM S/ASIA DIPLOM COLONIAL TIME 20. PAGE 123 A2519
REV NAT/LISM CULTURE MARXISM

B65
ROTBERG R.I.,A POLITICAL HISTORY OF TROPICAL AFRICA. EX/STRUC DIPLOM INT/TRADE DOMIN ADMIN RACE/REL NAT/LISM PWR SOVEREIGN...GEOG TIME/SEQ BIBLIOG 1/20. PAGE 124 A2545
AFR CULTURE COLONIAL

B65
RUBINSTEIN A.,THE CHALLENGE OF POLITICS: IDEAS AND ISSUES. BAL/PWR COLONIAL WAR TOTALISM ORD/FREE PWR MARXISM SOCISM...INT/LAW 20. PAGE 125 A2561
NAT/G SOVEREIGN DIPLOM NAT/LISM

B65
SANDERSON G.N.,ENGLAND, EUROPE, AND THE UPPER NILE 1882-1899. ISLAM MOD/EUR UAR UK CHIEF...POLICY CHARTS BIBLIOG/A 19 ARABS NEGRO. PAGE 127 A2600
AFR DIPLOM COLONIAL

B65
SHUKRI A.,THE CONCEPT OF SELF-DETERMINATION IN THE UNITED NATIONS. WOR+45 DIPLOM INT/TRADE SANCTION NAT/LISM...BIBLIOG 20 UN. PAGE 132 A2709
COLONIAL INT/ORG INT/LAW SOVEREIGN

B65
SOPER T.,EVOLVING COMMONWEALTH. AFR CANADA INDIA IRELAND UK LAW CONSTN POL/PAR DOMIN CONTROL WAR PWR ...AUD/VIS 18/20 COMMONWLTH OEEC. PAGE 135 A2769
INT/ORG COLONIAL VOL/ASSN

B65
SPENCE J.E.,REPUBLIC UNDER PRESSURE: A STUDY OF SOUTH AFRICAN FOREIGN POLICY. SOUTH/AFR ADMIN COLONIAL GOV/REL RACE/REL DISCRIM NAT/LISM ATTIT ROLE...TREND 20 NEGRO. PAGE 136 A2783
DIPLOM POLICY AFR

B65
SULZBERGER C.L.,UNFINISHED REVOLUTION. USA+45 WOR+45 INT/ORG TEC/DEV BAL/PWR FOR/AID COLONIAL NEUTRAL PWR SOVEREIGN MARXISM 20. PAGE 140 A2863
DIPLOM ECO/UNDEV POLICY NAT/G

B65
WALKER A.A.,THE RHODESIAS AND NYASALAND: A GUIDE TO OFFICIAL PUBLICATIONS. RHODESIA UK OP/RES PLAN PROB/SOLV DIPLOM...POLICY SOC CON/ANAL 19/20 NYASALAND. PAGE 160 A3263
BIBLIOG NAT/G COLONIAL AFR

B65
WILGUS A.C.,HISTORIES AND HISTORIANS OF HISPANIC AMERICA (REPRINT ED.). CHRIST-17C SECT DIPLOM REV 16/20. PAGE 164 A3350
BIBLIOG/A L/A+17C REGION COLONIAL

B65
WILLIAMSON J.A.,GREAT BRITAIN AND THE COMMONWEALTH. UK DOMIN COLONIAL INGP/REL...POLICY 18/20 CMN/WLTH. PAGE 165 A3355
NAT/G DIPLOM INT/ORG SOVEREIGN

B65
WINT G.,COMMUNIST CHINA'S CRUSADE: MAO'S ROAD TO POWER AND THE NEW CAMPAIGN FOR WORLD REVOLUTION. ASIA CHINA/COM USA+45 USSR NAT/G POL/PAR DOMIN COERCE WAR PWR...POLICY CHARTS IDEA/COMP BIBLIOG 20 MAO. PAGE 165 A3364
DIPLOM MARXISM REV COLONIAL

B65
WITHERELL J.W.,MADAGASCAR AND ADJACENT ISLANDS; A GUIDE TO OFFICIAL PUBLICATIONS (PAMPHLET). FRANCE MADAGASCAR S/ASIA UK LAW OP/RES PLAN DIPLOM ...POLICY CON/ANAL 19/20. PAGE 165 A3371
BIBLIOG COLONIAL LOC/G ADMIN

S65
"FURTHER READING." INDIA ADMIN COLONIAL WAR GOV/REL ATTIT 20. PAGE 3 A0069
BIBLIOG DIPLOM NAT/G POLICY

S65
RODNEY W.,"THE ENTENTE STATES OF WEST AFRICA." AFR FRANCE USA+45 POL/PAR SCHOOL FORCES ECO/TAC COLONIAL PWR 20 AFRICA/W. PAGE 123 A2512
DIPLOM POLICY NAT/G ECO/UNDEV

C65
SEARA M.V.,"COSMIC INTERNATIONAL LAW." LAW ACADEM ACT/RES DIPLOM COLONIAL CONTROL NUC/PWR SOVEREIGN ...GEN/LAWS BIBLIOG UN. PAGE 131 A2678
SPACE INT/LAW IDEA/COMP INT/ORG

B66
AMERICAN ASSEMBLY COLUMBIA U,THE UNITED STATES AND THE PHILIPPINES. PHILIPPINE S/ASIA USA+45 USA-45 SOCIETY FORCES INT/TRADE...POLICY 20. PAGE 7 A0138
COLONIAL DIPLOM NAT/LISM

B66
BIRMINGHAM D.,TRADE AND CONFLICT IN ANGOLA. PORTUGAL CULTURE FORCES DIPLOM GP/REL PROFIT HABITAT NAT/COMP. PAGE 14 A0291
WAR INT/TRADE ECO/UNDEV COLONIAL

B66
BROWN L.C.,STATE AND SOCIETY IN INDEPENDENT NORTH AFRICA. ALGERIA LIBYA MOROCCO AGRI INDUS INT/ORG POL/PAR SECT PLAN DIPLOM COLONIAL...LING NAT/COMP ANTHOL BIBLIOG 20 TUNIS MUSLIM. PAGE 20 A0406
NAT/G SOCIETY CULTURE ECO/UNDEV

B66
CLENDENON C.,AMERICANS IN AFRICA 1865-1900. AFR USA-45 ECO/UNDEV SECT REV RACE/REL CONSERVE ...TRADIT GEOG BIBLIOG 16/18. PAGE 27 A0549
DIPLOM COLONIAL INT/TRADE

B66
CONNEL-SMITH G.,THE INTERAMERICAN SYSTEM. CUBA L/A+17C DELIB/GP FOR/AID COLONIAL PEACE PWR MARXISM ...BIBLIOG 19/20 OAS. PAGE 29 A0586
DIPLOM INT/TRADE REGION INT/ORG

B66
COPLIN W.D.,THE FUNCTIONS OF INTERNATIONAL LAW. WOR+45 ECO/DEV ECO/UNDEV ADJUD COLONIAL WAR OWN SOVEREIGN...POLICY GEN/LAWS 20. PAGE 30 A0611
INT/LAW DIPLOM INT/ORG

B66
DAVIDSON A.B.,RUSSIA AND AFRICA. USSR AGRI INT/TRADE...GEOG BIBLIOG/A 18/20. PAGE 34 A0687
MARXISM COLONIAL RACE/REL DIPLOM

B66
EKIRCH A.A. JR.,IDEAS, IDEALS, AND AMERICAN
DIPLOM

DIPLOMACY. USA+45 USA-45 INT/ORG DOMIN COLONIAL ARMS/CONT DETER ISOLAT NAT/LISM...MAJORIT BIBLIOG 19/20 COLD/WAR. PAGE 41 A0834
LEAD
PEACE

B66
FABAR R.,THE VISION AND THE NEED: LATE VICTORIAN IMPERIALIST AIMS. MOD/EUR UK WOR-45 CULTURE NAT/G DIPLOM...TIME/SEQ METH/COMP 19 KIPLING/R COMMONWLTH. PAGE 43 A0880
COLONIAL
CONCPT
ADMIN
ATTIT

B66
FALL B.B.,VIET-NAM WITNESS, 1953-66. S/ASIA VIETNAM SECT PROB/SOLV COLONIAL GUERRILLA...CHARTS BIBLIOG 20. PAGE 44 A0895
MARXIST
WAR
DIPLOM

B66
FERKISS V.C.,AFRICA'S SEARCH FOR IDENTITY. AFR USA+45 CULTURE ECO/UNDEV INT/ORG NAT/G COLONIAL MARXISM 20. PAGE 45 A0918
NAT/LISM
SOVEREIGN
DIPLOM
ROLE

B66
GRENVILLE J.A.S.,POLITICS, STRATEGY, AND AMERICAN DEMOCRACY: STUDIES IN FOREIGN POLICY, 1873-1917. CUBA PHILIPPINE SPAIN USA-45 VENEZUELA ELITES NAT/G CREATE PARTIC WAR RIGID/FLEX ORD/FREE...DECISION TREND 19/20 HAWAII. PAGE 56 A1146
DIPLOM
COLONIAL
POLICY

B66
HAMILTON W.B.,A DECADE OF THE COMMONWEALTH, 1955-1964. UK LAW ELITES FINAN FOR/AID CONFER COLONIAL PWR...GEOG CHARTS ANTHOL 20 CMN/WLTH UN. PAGE 61 A1247
INT/ORG
INGP/REL
DIPLOM
NAT/G

B66
HAYER T.,FRENCH AID. AFR FRANCE AGRI FINAN BUDGET ADMIN WAR PRODUC...CHARTS 18/20 THIRD/WRLD OVRSEA/DEV. PAGE 63 A1295
TEC/DEV
COLONIAL
FOR/AID
ECO/UNDEV

B66
HUTTENBACK R.A.,BRITISH IMPERIAL EXPERIENCE. S/ASIA UK WOR-45 INT/ORG TEC/DEV...CHARTS 16/20 COMMONWLTH MERCANTLST. PAGE 69 A1424
COLONIAL
TIME/SEQ
INT/TRADE

B66
LENGYEL E.,AFRICA: PAST, PRESENT, AND FUTURE. FUT SOUTH/AFR COLONIAL RACE/REL SOVEREIGN...GEOG AUD/VIS CHARTS T 20 CONGO/LEOP NEGRO. PAGE 87 A1771
AFR
CONSTN
ECO/UNDEV

B66
LONDON K.,EASTERN EUROPE IN TRANSITION. CHINA/COM USSR DOMIN COLONIAL CENTRAL RIGID/FLEX PWR...SOC ANTHOL 20. PAGE 91 A1855
SOVEREIGN
COM
NAT/LISM
DIPLOM

B66
MCINTYRE W.D.,COLONIES INTO COMMONWEALTH. UK CONSTN VOL/ASSN DOMIN CONTROL...BIBLIOG 18/20 CMN/WLTH. PAGE 98 A2012
DIPLOM
INT/ORG
COLONIAL
SOVEREIGN

B66
MOORE R.J.,SIR CHARLES WOOD'S INDIAN POLICY: 1853-66. INDIA POL/PAR CHIEF DELIB/GP DIPLOM CONTROL LEAD WOOD/CHAS. PAGE 103 A2124
COLONIAL
ADMIN
CONSULT
DECISION

B66
MULLER C.F.J.,A SELECT BIBLIOGRAPHY OF SOUTH AFRICAN HISTORY; A GUIDE FOR HISTORICAL RESEARCH. SOUTH/AFR UK LAW CONSTN SOCIETY STRUCT AGRI SECT DIPLOM COLONIAL LEAD RACE/REL...POLICY 17/20 NEGRO. PAGE 106 A2167
BIBLIOG
AFR
NAT/G

B66
O'CONNER A.M.,AN ECONOMIC GEOGRAPHY OF EAST AFRICA. AFR TANZANIA UGANDA AGRI WORKER INT/TRADE COLONIAL GOV/REL...CHARTS METH/COMP 20 AFRICA/E. PAGE 111 A2269
ECO/UNDEV
EXTR/IND
GEOG
HABITAT

B66
SCHATTEN F.,COMMUNISM IN AFRICA. AFR GHANA GUINEA MALI CULTURE ECO/UNDEV LABOR SECT ECO/TAC EDU/PROP REV 20. PAGE 128 A2619
COLONIAL
NAT/LISM
MARXISM
DIPLOM

B66
THORNTON A.P.,THE IMPERIAL IDEA AND ITS ENEMIES. UK WOR+45 WOR-45 NAT/G PLAN DOMIN CONTROL WAR ATTIT PWR...TREND CHARTS 19/20 CMN/WLTH. PAGE 144 A2937
COLONIAL
DIPLOM

B66
TINKER H.,SOUTH ASIA. UK LAW ECO/UNDEV AGRI ACADEM SECT DIPLOM EDU/PROP REV WEALTH ALL/IDEOS...CHARTS BIBLIOG GANDHI/M NEHRU/J. PAGE 144 A2945
S/ASIA
COLONIAL
TREND

B66
US LIBRARY OF CONGRESS,NIGERIA: A GUIDE TO OFFICIAL PUBLICATIONS. CAMEROON NIGERIA UK DIPLOM...POLICY 19/20 UN LEAGUE/NAT. PAGE 155 A3160
BIBLIOG
ADMIN
NAT/G
COLONIAL

B66
WELCH C.E.,DREAM OF UNITY; PAN-AFRICANISM AND POLITICAL UNIFICATION IN WEST AFRICA. AFR ECO/UNDEV CONFER COLONIAL LEAD...INT/LAW 20. PAGE 163 A3312
INT/ORG
REGION
NAT/LISM
DIPLOM

B66
WILSON H.A.,THE IMPERIAL POLICY OF SIR ROBERT BORDEN. CANADA UK ELITES INT/ORG VOL/ASSN CONTROL LEAD WAR ROLE 20 CMN/WLTH BORDEN/R. PAGE 165 A3360
INGP/REL
COLONIAL
CONSTN
CHIEF

S66
"RESEARCH WORK 1965-1966." NEW/ZEALND ELITES ACADEM LOC/G MUNIC POL/PAR PROVS DIPLOM COLONIAL...SOC 20 AUSTRAL. PAGE 4 A0073
BIBLIOG
NAT/G
CULTURE
S/ASIA

S66
AFRICAN BIBLIOGRAPHIC CENTER,"A CURRENT VIEW OF AFRICANA: A SELECT AND ANNOTATED BIBLIOGRAPHICAL PUBLISHING GUIDE, 1965-1966." AFR CULTURE INDUS LABOR SECT FOR/AID ADMIN COLONIAL REV RACE/REL SOCISM...LING 20. PAGE 5 A0098
BIBLIOG/A
NAT/G
TEC/DEV
POL/PAR

S66
DINH TRANS V.A.N.,"VIETNAM: A THIRD WAY" S/ASIA USA+45 USSR VIETNAM VIETNAM/S NAT/G SECT FORCES CAP/ISM DIPLOM COLONIAL NEUTRAL MARXISM SOCISM 20 BUDDHISM UNIFICA. PAGE 38 A0766
WAR
PLAN
ORD/FREE
SOCIALIST

S66
GREEN L.C.,"RHODESIAN OIL: BOOTLEGGERS OR PIRATES?" AFR RHODESIA UK WOR+45 INT/ORG NAT/G DIPLOM LEGIT COLONIAL SOVEREIGN 20 UN OAU. PAGE 55 A1139
INT/TRADE
SANCTION
INT/LAW
POLICY

S66
MANSERGH N.,"THE PARTITION OF INDIA IN RETROSPECT." INDIA PAKISTAN S/ASIA UK DIPLOM COLONIAL GP/REL PWR 20. PAGE 94 A1933
NAT/G
PARL/PROC
POLICY
POL/PAR

S66
PRATT R.C.,"AFRICAN REACTIONS TO THE RHODESIAN CRISIS." RHODESIA UK LAW DIPLOM...POLICY 20. PAGE 117 A2408
ATTIT
AFR
COLONIAL
RACE/REL

C66
TARLING N.,"A CONCISE HISTORY OF SOUTHEAST ASIA." BURMA CAMBODIA LAOS S/ASIA THAILAND VIETNAM ECO/UNDEV POL/PAR FORCES ADMIN REV WAR CIVMIL/REL ORD/FREE MARXISM SOCISM 13/20. PAGE 141 A2890
COLONIAL
DOMIN
INT/TRADE
NAT/LISM

B67
ADAMS A.E.,AN ATLAS OF RUSSIAN AND EAST EUROPEAN HISTORY. CHRIST-17C COM MOD/EUR INDUS SECT FORCES DIPLOM COLONIAL REV WAR 4/20. PAGE 4 A0086
CHARTS
REGION
TREND

B67
DE BLIJ H.J.,SYSTEMATIC POLITICAL GEOGRAPHY. WOR+45 STRUCT INT/ORG NAT/G EDU/PROP ADMIN COLONIAL ROUTINE ORD/FREE PWR...IDEA/COMP T 20. PAGE 34 A0697
GEOG
CONCPT
METH

B67
JAGAN C.,THE WEST ON TRIAL. GUYANA CONSTN ECO/UNDEV DIPLOM COERCE PWR SOVEREIGN...BIOG 20. PAGE 73 A1490
SOCISM
CREATE
PLAN
COLONIAL

B67
KNOLES G.H.,THE RESPONSIBILITIES OF POWER, 1900-1929. USA-45 SOCIETY SECT JUDGE COLONIAL REPRESENT WEALTH POPULISM...IDEA/COMP ANTHOL PRESIDENT 20 LEAGUE/NAT. PAGE 81 A1653
PWR
DIPLOM
NAT/LISM
WAR

B67
MACRIDIS R.C.,FOREIGN POLICY IN WORLD POLITICS (3RD ED.). EX/STRUC BAL/PWR COLONIAL NAT/LISM SKILL SOVEREIGN WEALTH...CONCPT TIME/SEQ ANTHOL 20 COLD/WAR. PAGE 93 A1902
DIPLOM
POLICY
NAT/G
IDEA/COMP

B67
MAW B.,BREAKTHROUGH IN BURMA: MEMOIRS OF A REVOLUTION, 1939-1946. BURMA UK FORCES PROB/SOLV DIPLOM FOR/AID DOMIN LEAD...BIOG 20. PAGE 97 A1980
REV
ORD/FREE
NAT/LISM
COLONIAL

B67
MAZRUI A.A.,TOWARDS A PAX AFRICANA. AFR STRUCT ECO/UNDEV NAT/G DIPLOM COLONIAL REGION WAR ATTIT 20. PAGE 97 A1988
PEACE
FORCES
PROB/SOLV
SOVEREIGN

B67
MCNELLY T.,SOURCES IN MODERN EAST ASIAN HISTORY AND POLITICS. KOREA VIETNAM CULTURE DIPLOM COLONIAL REV WAR PWR ALL/IDEOS MARXISM...ANTHOL 20 CHINJAP. PAGE 99 A2023
NAT/COMP
ASIA
S/ASIA
SOCIETY

B67
MEYNAUD J.,TRADE UNIONISM IN AFRICA; A STUDY OF ITS GROWTH AND ORIENTATION (TRANS. BY ANGELA BRENCH). INT/ORG PROB/SOLV COLONIAL PWR...TIME/SEQ TREND ILO. PAGE 100 A2055
LABOR
AFR
NAT/LISM
ORD/FREE

B67
MILLER J.D.B.,THE POLITICS OF THE THIRD WORLD. AFR S/ASIA 20 UN. PAGE 101 A2078
INT/ORG
DIPLOM
COLONIAL
SOVEREIGN

B67
NYERERE J.K.,FREEDOM AND UNITY/UHURU NA UMOJA: A SELECTION FROM WRITINGS AND SPEECHES, 1952-65. TANZANIA ELITES ECO/UNDEV INT/ORG NAT/G CREATE DIPLOM COLONIAL REGION RACE/REL...ANTHOL 20. PAGE 110 A2265
SOVEREIGN
AFR
TREND
ORD/FREE

B67
ROACH J.R.,THE UNITED STATES AND THE ATLANTIC COMMUNITY; ISSUES AND PROSPECTS. WOR+45 TEC/DEV ECO/TAC COLONIAL REGION PEACE ROLE...ANTHOL NATO COLD/WAR EEC. PAGE 121 A2491
INT/ORG
POLICY
ADJUST
DIPLOM

B67
STEVENS R.P.,LESOTHO, BATSWANA, AND SWAZILAND* THE FORMER HIGH COMMISSION TERRITORIES IN SOUTHERN AFRICA. ECO/DEV KIN POL/PAR HIST/WRIT. PAGE 138 A2821
COLONIAL DIPLOM ORD/FREE

S67
"CHINESE STATEMENT ON NUCLEAR PROLIFERATION." CHINA/COM USA+45 USSR DOMIN COLONIAL PWR. PAGE 4 A0078
NUC/PWR BAL/PWR ARMS/CONT DIPLOM

S67
AFRICAN BIBLIOGRAPHIC CENTER,"THE SWORD AND GOVERNMENT: A PRELIMINARY AND SELECTED BIBLIOGRAPHICAL GUIDE TO AFRICAN MILITARY AFFAIRS; PART I." AFR USA+45 USSR INT/ORG POL/PAR FOR/AID COLONIAL ARMS/CONT PWR 20 UN. PAGE 5 A0101
BIBLIOG/A FORCES CIVMIL/REL DIPLOM

S67
BURNS E.B.,"TRADITIONS AND VARIATIONS IN BRAZILIAN FOREIGN POLICY." BRAZIL L/A+17C POL/PAR INT/TRADE COLONIAL INGP/REL ATTIT ORD/FREE PWR 20. PAGE 22 A0443
DIPLOM NAT/LISM CREATE

S67
CHAND A.,"INDIA AND TANZANIA." INDIA TANZANIA TEC/DEV ECO/TAC FOR/AID COLONIAL PEACE UTIL WEALTH ...GOV/COMP 20. PAGE 25 A0518
ECO/UNDEV NEUTRAL DIPLOM PLAN

S67
CONNOR W.,"SELF-DETERMINATION: THE NEW PHASE." WOR+45 WOR-45 CULTURE INT/ORG COLONIAL 19/20. PAGE 29 A0588
NAT/LISM SOVEREIGN INGP/REL GP/REL

S67
D'AMATO D.,"LEGAL ASPECTS OF THE FRENCH NUCLEAR TESTS." FRANCE WOR+45 ACT/RES COLONIAL RISK GOV/REL EQUILIB ORD/FREE PWR DECISION. PAGE 33 A0672
INT/LAW DIPLOM NUC/PWR ADJUD

S67
DAVIS H.B.,"LENIN AND NATIONALISM: THE REDIRECTION OF THE MARXIST THEORY OF NATIONALISM." COM MOD/EUR USSR STRATA INT/ORG PLAN DOMIN COLONIAL FEDERAL ...TREND 20. PAGE 34 A0690
NAT/LISM MARXISM ATTIT CENTRAL

S67
FARQUHAR D.M.,"CHINESE COMMUNIST ASSESSMENTS OF A FOREIGN CONQUEST DYNASTY." CHINA/COM DIPLOM CONTROL ...METH 20. PAGE 44 A0900
MARXISM HIST/WRIT POLICY COLONIAL

S67
FAWCETT J.E.S.,"GIBRALTAR* THE LEGAL ISSUES." SPAIN UK INT/ORG BAL/PWR LICENSE CONFER SANCTION PRIVIL ...JURID CHARTS 20. PAGE 44 A0905
INT/LAW DIPLOM COLONIAL ADJUD

S67
FELDMAN H.,"AID AS IMPERIALISM?" INDIA PAKISTAN UK USA+45 BAL/PWR CAP/ISM DIPLOM ECO/TAC DOMIN BAL/PAY WEALTH...POLICY 20. PAGE 45 A0914
COLONIAL FOR/AID S/ASIA ECO/UNDEV

S67
FRANKLIN W.O.,"CLAUSEWITZ ON LIMITED WAR." VIETNAM WOR+45 WOR-45 PROB/SOLV DIPLOM ECO/TAC DOMIN COLONIAL...METH/COMP 19/20. PAGE 48 A0986
COERCE WAR PLAN GUERRILLA

S67
FRENCH D.S.,"DOES THE U.S. EXPLOIT THE DEVELOPING NATIONS?" INT/ORG NAT/G CAP/ISM BAL/PAY WEALTH POLICY. PAGE 49 A0997
ECO/UNDEV INT/TRADE ECO/TAC COLONIAL

S67
GODUNSKY Y.,"'APOSTLES OF PEACE' IN LATIN AMERICA." L/A+17C USA+45 BAL/PWR DIPLOM FOR/AID DOMIN COLONIAL CIVMIL/REL MARXIST. PAGE 53 A1086
ECO/UNDEV REV VOL/ASSN EDU/PROP

S67
GRUNDY K.W.,"AFRICA IN THE WORLD ARENA." ECO/UNDEV BAL/PWR FOR/AID NEUTRAL REV NAT/LISM GOV/COMP. PAGE 58 A1183
AFR DIPLOM INT/ORG COLONIAL

S67
KIERNAN V.G.,"INDIA AND THE LABOUR PARTY." INDIA UK CAP/ISM GP/REL EFFICIENCY NAT/LISM PWR SOCISM ...SOCIALIST TIME/SEQ 20. PAGE 79 A1616
COLONIAL DIPLOM POL/PAR ECO/UNDEV

S67
KRAUS J.,"A MARXIST IN GHANA." GHANA ELITES CHIEF PROB/SOLV TEC/DEV DIPLOM ECO/TAC COLONIAL PARTIC PWR 20 NKRUMAH/K. PAGE 82 A1676
MARXISM PLAN ATTIT CREATE

S67
ROSE S.,"ASIAN NATIONALISM* THE SECOND STAGE." ASIA COM ECO/UNDEV NAT/G PROB/SOLV DIPLOM FOR/AID DOMIN NEUTRAL REGION TASK...METH/COMP 20. PAGE 123 A2528
NAT/LISM S/ASIA BAL/PWR COLONIAL

S67
ROTBERG R.I.,"COLONIALISM AND AFTER: THE POLITICAL LITERATURE OF CENTRAL AFRICA - A BIBLIOGRAPHIC ESSAY." AFR CHIEF EX/STRUC REV INGP/REL RACE/REL SOVEREIGN 20. PAGE 124 A2546
BIBLIOG/A COLONIAL DIPLOM NAT/G

S67
SCHUMANN H.,"IMPERIALISMUS-KRITIK UND KOLONIALISMUS-FORSCHUNG." GERMANY/E DIPLOM SOVEREIGN...SOC HIST/WRIT 20. PAGE 129 A2652
COLONIAL ATTIT DOMIN CAP/ISM

S67
STEELE R.,"A TASTE FOR INTERVENTION." USA+45 FOR/AID INT/TRADE EDU/PROP COLONIAL WAR PWR...TREND 20 COLD/WAR. PAGE 137 A2812
POLICY DIPLOM DOMIN ATTIT

S67
WALKER R.L.,"THE WEST AND THE 'NEW ASIA'." CHINA/COM ECO/UNDEV DIPLOM...PREDICT 20. PAGE 160 A3266
ASIA INT/TRADE COLONIAL REGION

S67
WILLIAMS B.H.,"FREEDOM AS A SLOGAN IN INTERNATIONAL CONFLICT." VIETNAM DIPLOM COLONIAL. PAGE 164 A3351
EDU/PROP ORD/FREE WAR PWR

C67
HUDSON G.F.,"THE HARD AND BITTER PEACE; WORLD POLITICS SINCE 1945." ASIA COM S/ASIA USSR WOR+45 COLONIAL WAR...TREND BIBLIOG/A 20 COLD/WAR UN. PAGE 68 A1405
DIPLOM INT/ORG ARMS/CONT BAL/PWR

C67
LING D.L.,"TUNISIA: FROM PROTECTORATE TO REPUBLIC." CULTURE NAT/G POL/PAR CHIEF DIPLOM COERCE WAR PWR ...BIBLIOG 19/20 TUNIS. PAGE 89 A1825
AFR NAT/LISM COLONIAL PROB/SOLV

C83
BURKE E.,"RESOLUTIONS FOR CONCILIATION WITH AMERICA" (1775), IN E. BURKE, COLLECTED WORKS, VOL. 2." UK USA-45 FORCES INT/TRADE TARIFFS TAX SANCTION PEACE...POLICY 18 PRE/US/AM. PAGE 21 A0436
COLONIAL WAR SOVEREIGN ECO/TAC

B90
HOSMAR J.K.,A SHORT HISTORY OF ANGLO-SAXON FREEDOM. UK USA-45 ROMAN/EMP NAT/G EX/STRUC LEGIS COLONIAL REV NAT/LISM POPULISM PARLIAMENT ANGLO/SAX MAGNA/CART. PAGE 68 A1394
CONSTN ORD/FREE DIPLOM PARL/PROC

B93
ROYAL GEOGRAPHIC SOCIETY,BIBLIOGRAPHY OF BARBARY STATES (4 SUPPLEMENTARY PAPERS). ALGERIA LIBYA MOROCCO SOCIETY STRUCT DIPLOM LEAD 14/19 TUNIS. PAGE 125 A2555
BIBLIOG ISLAM NAT/G COLONIAL

B98
GRIFFIN A.P.C.,LIST OF BOOKS RELATING TO CUBA (PAMPHLET). CUBA L/A+17C USA-45 INT/TRADE DOMIN WAR GP/REL ALL/VALS...GEOG SOC CHARTS 19/20. PAGE 56 A1158
BIBLIOG/A NAT/G COLONIAL

COLORADO....COLORADO

COLUMBIA U SCHOOL OF LAW A0571,A0572
COLUMBIA U BUR APPL SOC RES A2403
COLUMBIA/U....COLUMBIA UNIVERSITY

COM....COMMUNIST COUNTRIES, EXCEPT CHINA; SEE ALSO APPROPRIATE NATIONS, MARXISM

N
INDIAN COUNCIL WORLD AFFAIRS,SELECT ARTICLES ON CURRENT AFFAIRS (BIBLIOGRAPHICAL SERIES: 7). AFR ASIA COM EUR+WWI S/ASIA UK COLONIAL NUC/PWR PEACE ATTIT...INT/LAW SOC 20. PAGE 70 A1437
BIBLIOG DIPLOM INT/ORG ECO/UNDEV

N
NEUE POLITISCHE LITERATUR. AFR ASIA EUR+WWI GERMANY RUSSIA SOCIETY ECO/DEV ECO/UNDEV PLAN PROB/SOLV LEAD MARXISM...PHIL/SCI CONCPT 20. PAGE 1 A0021
BIBLIOG DIPLOM COM NAT/G

N
CHINA QUARTERLY. COM AGRI INDUS ACADEM POL/PAR INT/TRADE CONFER GOV/REL...TIME/SEQ CON/ANAL INDEX 20. PAGE 2 A0032
BIBLIOG/A ASIA DIPLOM POLICY

N
AVTOREFERATY DISSERTATSII. USSR INTELL ACADEM NAT/G DIPLOM GOV/REL KNOWL CONCPT. PAGE 3 A0047
BIBLIOG MARXISM MARXIST COM

N
"PROLOG",DIGEST OF THE SOVIET UKRANIAN PRESS. USSR LAW AGRI INDUS PROVS SCHOOL DIPLOM GOV/REL ATTIT ...HUM LING 20. PAGE 4 A0081
BIBLIOG/A NAT/G PRESS COM

N
ATLANTIC INSTITUTE,ATLANTIC STUDIES. COM EUR+WWI USA+45 CULTURE STRUCT ECO/DEV FORCES LEAD ARMS/CONT ...INT/LAW JURID SOC. PAGE 10 A0193
BIBLIOG/A DIPLOM POLICY GOV/REL

N
KYRIAK T.E.,EAST EUROPE: BIBLIOGRAPHY--INDEX TO US JPRS RESEARCH TRANSLATIONS. ALBANIA BULGARIA COM CZECHOSLVK HUNGARY POLAND ROMANIA AGRI EXTR/IND FINAN SERV/IND INT/TRADE WEAPON...GEOG MGT SOC 20. PAGE 83 A1701
BIBLIOG/A PRESS MARXISM INDUS

N
US LIBRARY OF CONGRESS,EAST EUROPEAN ACCESSIONS INDEX. NAT/G ISOLAT ATTIT KNOWL...POLICY 20. PAGE 154 A3144
BIBLIOG COM MARXIST DIPLOM

B18
KERNER R.J.,SLAVIC EUROPE: A SELECTED BIBLIOGRAPHY IN THE WESTERN EUROPEAN LANGUAGES. BULGARIA CZECHOSLVK GERMANY/E POLAND RUSSIA YUGOSLAVIA NAT/G DIPLOM MARXISM...LING 19/20. PAGE 78 A1598
BIBLIOG SOCIETY CULTURE COM

N19
HAJDA J.,THE COLD WAR VIEWED AS A SOCIOLOGICAL PROBLEM (PAMPHLET). COM CZECHOSLVK EUR+WWI SOCIETY PLAN EDU/PROP CONTROL TASK ATTIT MARXISM...POLICY 20 COLD/WAR MIGRATION. PAGE 59 A1220
DIPLOM LEAD PWR NAT/G

B32
HANSEN A.H.,ECONOMIC STABILIZATION IN AN UNBALANCED WORLD. COM EUR+WWI USA-45 WOR-45 AGRI FINAN INDUS MARKET INT/ORG LABOR VOL/ASSN EDU/PROP ATTIT HEALTH KNOWL WEALTH...HIST/WRIT TREND VAL/FREE 20. PAGE 61 A1253
NAT/G ECO/DEV CAP/ISM SOCISM

B32
LENIN V.I.,THE WAR AND THE SECOND INTERNATIONAL. COM MOD/EUR USSR CAP/ISM DIPLOM NAT/LISM ATTIT MARXISM...CONCPT 20. PAGE 87 A1772
POL/PAR WAR SOCISM INT/ORG

B38
HARPER S.N.,THE GOVERNMENT OF THE SOVIET UNION. COM USSR LAW CONSTN ECO/DEV PLAN TEC/DEV DIPLOM INT/TRADE ADMIN REV NAT/LISM...POLICY 20. PAGE 62 A1265
MARXISM NAT/G LEAD POL/PAR

B38
PETTEE G.S.,THE PROCESS OF REVOLUTION. COM FRANCE ITALY MOD/EUR RUSSIA SPAIN WOR-45 ELITES INTELL SOCIETY STRATA STRUCT INT/ORG NAT/G POL/PAR ACT/RES PLAN EDU/PROP LEGIT EXEC...SOC MYTH TIME/SEQ TOT/POP 18/20. PAGE 115 A2370
COERCE CONCPT REV

B39
KOHN H.,REVOLUTIONS AND DICTATORSHIPS. COM EUR+WWI ISLAM MOD/EUR NAT/G CHIEF FORCES WAR CIVMIL/REL PWR MARXISM 18/20. PAGE 81 A1661
NAT/LISM TOTALISM REV FASCISM

B39
WHEELER-BENNET J.W.,THE FORGOTTEN PEACE: BREST-LITOVSK. COM GERMANY USSR TOP/EX AGREE WAR PWR ...BIBLIOG 20 TREATY LENIN/VI UKRAINE. PAGE 163 A3326
PEACE DIPLOM CONFER

S42
SHOTWELL J.,"AFTER THE WAR." COM EUR+WWI USA+45 USA-45 NAT/G DIPLOM INT/TRADE ARMS/CONT SOVEREIGN ...CONCPT LEAGUE/NAT TOT/POP FAO 20. PAGE 132 A2707
FUT INT/ORG PEACE

B43
CONOVER H.F.,SOVIET RUSSIA: SELECTED LIST OF REFERENCES. USSR CULTURE INDUS NAT/G TOP/EX TEC/DEV BUDGET WAR CIVMIL/REL EFFICIENCY MARXISM 20. PAGE 29 A0597
BIBLIOG ECO/DEV COM DIPLOM

B43
GRIERSON P.,BOOKS ON SOVIET RUSSIA 1917-42: A BIBLIOGRAPHY AND A GUIDE TO READING. USSR CULTURE ELITES NAT/G PLAN DIPLOM REV...GEOG 20. PAGE 56 A1148
BIBLIOG/A COM MARXISM LEAD

B46
BIBLIOGRAFIIA DISSERTATSII: DOKTORSKIE DISSERTATSII ZA 19411944 (2 VOLS.). COM USSR LAW POL/PAR DIPLOM ADMIN LEAD...PHIL/SCI SOC 20. PAGE 3 A0054
BIBLIOG ACADEM KNOWL MARXIST

B46
BRODIE B.,THE OBSOLETE WEAPON: ATOMIC POWER AND WORLD ORDER. COM USA+45 USSR WOR+45 DELIB/GP PLAN ORD/FREE PWR...CONCPT TIME/SEQ TREND UN 20. PAGE 19 A0380
INT/ORG TEC/DEV ARMS/CONT NUC/PWR

L47
COMM. STUDY ORGAN. PEACE,"SECURITY THROUGH THE UNITED NATIONS." COM FUT WOR+45 TOP/EX ACT/RES BAL/PWR ARMS/CONT NUC/PWR...CONCPT GEN/LAWS UN TOT/POP COLD/WAR 20. PAGE 28 A0577
INT/ORG ORD/FREE PEACE

N47
FOX W.T.R.,UNITED STATES POLICY IN A TWO POWER WORLD. COM USA+45 USSR FORCES DOMIN AGREE NEUTRAL NUC/PWR ORD/FREE SOVEREIGN 20 COLD/WAR TREATY EUROPE/W INTERVENT. PAGE 48 A0972
DIPLOM FOR/AID POLICY

B48
KULISCHER E.M.,EUROPE ON THE MOVE: WAR AND POPULATION CHANGES, 1917-1947. COM EUR+WWI FUT GERMANY USSR DIST/IND PLAN INT/TRADE CONTROL WAR DRIVE...CENSUS TREND COLD/WAR 20. PAGE 82 A1690
ECO/TAC GEOG

B48
US DEPARTMENT OF STATE,FOREIGN AFFAIRS HIGHLIGHTS (NEWSLETTER). COM USA+45 INT/ORG PLAN BAL/PWR WAR PWR...BIBLIOG 20 COLD/WAR NATO UN DEPT/STATE. PAGE 151 A3083
DIPLOM NAT/G POLICY

B49
THE CURRENT DIGEST OF THE SOVIET PRESS. USSR WOR+45 LOC/G NAT/G DIPLOM EDU/PROP...MARXIST 20. PAGE 3 A0056
BIBLIOG/A COM ATTIT PRESS

B49
MARITAIN J.,HUMAN RIGHTS: COMMENTS AND INTERPRETATIONS. COM UNIV WOR+45 LAW CONSTN CULTURE SOCIETY ECO/DEV ECO/UNDEV SCHOOL DELIB/GP EDU/PROP ATTIT PERCEPT ALL/VALS...HUM SOC TREND UNESCO 20. PAGE 95 A1939
INT/ORG CONCPT

B49
US DEPARTMENT OF STATE,SOVIET BIBLIOGRAPHY (PAMPHLET). CHINA/COM COM USSR LAW AGRI INT/ORG ECO/TAC EDU/PROP...POLICY GEOG 20. PAGE 151 A3084
BIBLIOG/A MARXISM CULTURE DIPLOM

B50
BARGHOORN F.C.,THE SOVIET IMAGE OF THE UNITED STATES: A STUDY IN DISTORTION. COM USSR DOMIN WAR NAT/LISM TOTALISM SOCISM...PSY 20. PAGE 11 A0220
PROB/SOLV EDU/PROP DIPLOM ATTIT

S50
WITTFOGEL K.A.,"RUSSIA AND ASIA: PROBLEMS OF CONTEMPORARY AREA STUDIES AND INTERNATIONAL RELATIONS." ASIA COM USA+45 SOCIETY NAT/G DIPLOM ECO/TAC FOR/AID EDU/PROP KNOWL...HIST/WRIT TOT/POP 20. PAGE 166 A3373
ECO/DEV ADMIN RUSSIA USSR

B51
BLANSHARD P.,COMMUNISM, DEMOCRACY AND CATHOLIC POWER. USSR VATICAN WOR+45 WOR-45 CULTURE ELITES INTELL SOCIETY STRUCT INT/ORG POL/PAR EDU/PROP COERCE ATTIT KNOWL PWR MARXISM...CONCPT COLD/WAR 20. PAGE 15 A0308
COM SECT TOTALISM

B51
BORKENAU F.,EUROPEAN COMMUNISM. COM EUR+WWI GERMANY SPAIN USSR INT/ORG PLAN REV WAR ATTIT 20 STALIN/J HITLER/A. PAGE 17 A0342
MARXISM POLICY DIPLOM NAT/G

B51
US LIBRARY OF CONGRESS,EAST EUROPEAN ACCESSIONS LIST (VOL. I). POL/PAR DIPLOM ADMIN LEAD 20. PAGE 155 A3152
BIBLIOG/A COM SOCIETY NAT/G

B51
WHITE L.C.,INTERNATIONAL NON-GOVERNMENTAL ORGANIZATIONS. AFR ASIA COM EUR+WWI USA+45 WOR+45 INT/ORG DIPLOM INT/TRADE ALL/VALS...HUM FAO ILO EEC 20. PAGE 164 A3337
VOL/ASSN CONSULT

L51
ULAM A.B.,"THE COMIMFORM AND THE PEOPLE'S DEMOCRACIES." EUR+WWI WOR+45 STRUCT NAT/G POL/PAR TOP/EX ACT/RES PLAN ECO/TAC DOMIN ATTIT ALL/VALS ...HIST/WRIT TIME/SEQ 20 COMINFORM. PAGE 146 A2992
COM INT/ORG USSR TOTALISM

S51
CONNERY R.H.,"THE MUTUAL DEFENSE ASSISTANCE PROGRAM." COM EUR+WWI KOREA USA+45 NAT/G VOL/ASSN CREATE PLAN BAL/PWR EDU/PROP PERCEPT...POLICY DECISION CONCPT NATO 20. PAGE 29 A0587
INT/ORG FORCES FOR/AID

C51
BEST H.,"THE SOVIET STATE AND ITS INCEPTION." USSR CULTURE INDUS DIPLOM WEALTH...GEOG SOC BIBLIOG 20. PAGE 14 A0281
COM GEN/METH REV MARXISM

B52
MACARTHUR D.,REVITALIZING A NATION. ASIA COM FUT KOREA WOR+45 NAT/G FOR/AID TAX GIVE WAR ATTIT SOCISM 20 CHINJAP EUROPE. PAGE 92 A1885
LEAD FORCES TOP/EX POLICY

B52
U OF MICH SURVEY RESEARCH CTR,AMERICA'S ROLE IN WORLD AFFAIRS. ASIA COM EUR+WWI USA+45 USSR FOR/AID WAR AUTHORIT ORD/FREE...DEEP/QU 20. PAGE 146 A2986
DIPLOM NAT/G ROLE POLICY

B52
ULAM A.B.,TITOISM AND THE COMINFORM. USSR WOR+45 STRUCT INT/ORG NAT/G ACT/RES PLAN EXEC ATTIT DRIVE ALL/VALS...CONCPT OBS VAL/FREE 20 COMINTERN TITO/MARSH. PAGE 146 A2993
COM POL/PAR TOTALISM YUGOSLAVIA

B52
US DEPARTMENT OF STATE,RESEARCH ON EASTERN EUROPE (EXCLUDING USSR). EUR+WWI LAW ECO/DEV NAT/G PROB/SOLV DIPLOM ADMIN LEAD MARXISM...TREND 19/20. PAGE 151 A3088
BIBLIOG R+D ACT/RES COM

B53
FEIS H.,THE CHINA TANGLE. ASIA COM USA+45 USA-45 FORCES ECO/TAC REV ATTIT 20 INTERVENT. PAGE 45 A0910
POLICY DIPLOM WAR FOR/AID

S53
LINCOLN G.,"FACTORS DETERMINING ARMS AID." COM FUT USA+45 USSR WOR+45 ECO/DEV NAT/G CONSULT PLAN TEC/DEV DIPLOM DOMIN EDU/PROP PERCEPT PWR ...DECISION CONCPT TREND MARX/KARL 20. PAGE 89 A1819
FORCES POLICY BAL/PWR FOR/AID

B54
STALEY E.,THE FUTURE OF UNDERDEVELOPED COUNTRIES: POLITICAL IMPLICATIONS OF ECONOMIC DEVELOPMENT. COM FUT USA+45 SOCIETY ECO/UNDEV CREATE PLAN CAP/ISM ATTIT DRIVE MARXISM SOCISM...POLICY CONCPT CHARTS COLD/WAR 20. PAGE 137 A2801
EDU/PROP ECO/TAC FOR/AID

B55
JOY C.T.,HOW COMMUNISTS NEGOTIATE. COM USA+45 CONSTN CULTURE ECO/UNDEV NAT/G CONSULT DELIB/GP FORCES PLAN ECO/TAC DOMIN EDU/PROP LEGIT EXEC ROUTINE COERCE WAR CHOOSE PEACE ATTIT RIGID/FLEX ORD/FREE PWR...POLICY 20. PAGE 75 A1539
ASIA INT/ORG DIPLOM

L55
ROSTOW W.W.,"RUSSIA AND CHINA UNDER COMMUNISM." CHINA/COM USSR INTELL STRUCT INT/ORG NAT/G POL/PAR TOP/EX ACT/RES PLAN ADMIN ATTIT ALL/VALS MARXISM ...CONCPT OBS TIME/SEQ TREND GOV/COMP VAL/FREE 20. PAGE 124 A2543
COM ASIA

B56
BUREAU OF PUBLIC AFFAIRS,AMERICAN FOREIGN POLICY: CURRENT DOCUMENTS. COM USA+45 USSR WOR+45 DELIB/GP FOR/AID INT/TRADE ARMS/CONT NUC/PWR ALL/VALS ALL/IDEOS...DECISION 20 NATO. PAGE 21 A0434
BIBLIOG/A DIPLOM POLICY

B56
CONOVER H.F.,A GUIDE TO BIBLIOGRAPHIC TOOLS FOR RESEARCH IN FOREIGN AFFAIRS. AFR ASIA COM EUR+WWI WOR+45 BAL/PWR CON/ANAL. PAGE 30 A0602
BIBLIOG/A R+D DIPLOM INT/ORG

B56
DEGRAS J.,THE COMMUNIST INTERNATIONAL, 1919-1943: DOCUMENTS (3 VOLS.). EX/STRUC...ANTHOL BIBLIOG 20. PAGE 36 A0723
COM DIPLOM POLICY POL/PAR

B56
KNORR K.E.,RUBLE DIPLOMACY: CHALLENGE TO AMERICAN FOREIGN AID(PAMPHLET). CHINA/COM USA+45 USSR PLAN TEC/DEV CAP/ISM INT/TRADE DOMIN EDU/PROP CONTROL LEAD 20 COLD/WAR. PAGE 81 A1654
ECO/UNDEV COM DIPLOM FOR/AID

B56
SIPKOV I.,LEGAL SOURCES AND BIBLIOGRAPHY OF BULGARIA. BULGARIA COM LEGIS WRITING ADJUD CT/SYS ...INT/LAW TREATY 20. PAGE 134 A2736
BIBLIOG LAW TOTALISM MARXISM

B56
VON HARPE W.,DIE SOWJETUNION FINNLAND UND SKANDANAVIEN, 1945-1955. EUR+WWI FINLAND GERMANY USSR WAR INGP/REL ORD/FREE SOVEREIGN MARXISM ...POLICY GOV/COMP BIBLIOG 20 STALIN/J. PAGE 160 A3252
DIPLOM COM NEUTRAL BAL/PWR

B56
WATT D.C.,BRITAIN AND THE SUEZ CANAL. COM UAR UK ...INT/LAW 20 SUEZ TREATY. PAGE 162 A3294
DIPLOM INT/TRADE DIST/IND NAT/G

B56
WILBUR C.M.,DOCUMENTS ON COMMUNISM, NATIONALISM, AND SOVIET ADVISERS IN CHINA, 1918-1927. CHINA/COM USSR STRUCT DIPLOM LEAD NAT/LISM...BIBLIOG/A 20. PAGE 164 A3343
REV POL/PAR MARXISM COM

B56
WOLFF R.L.,THE BALKANS IN OUR TIME. ALBANIA FUT MOD/EUR USSR YUGOSLAVIA CULTURE INT/ORG SECT DIPLOM EDU/PROP COERCE WAR ORD/FREE...CHARTS 4/20 BALKANS COMINFORM. PAGE 166 A3388
GEOG COM

B57
BYRNES R.F.,BIBLIOGRAPHY OF AMERICAN PUBLICATIONS ON EAST CENTRAL EUROPE, 1945-1957 (VOL. XXII). SECT DIPLOM EDU/PROP RACE/REL...ART/METH GEOG JURID SOC LING 20 JEWS. PAGE 23 A0462
BIBLIOG/A COM MARXISM NAT/G

B57
CRABB C.,BIPARTISAN FOREIGN POLICY: MYTH OR REALITY. ASIA COM EUR+WWI ISLAM USA+45 USA-45 INT/ORG NAT/G LEGIS TOP/EX PWR CONGRESS 20. PAGE 32 A0649
POL/PAR ATTIT DIPLOM

B57
FURNISS E.S.,AMERICAN MILITARY POLICY: STRATEGIC ASPECTS OF WORLD POLITICAL GEOGRAPHY. COM EUR+WWI ISLAM L/A+17C USA+45 WOR+45 INT/ORG ACT/RES ARMS/CONT COERCE NUC/PWR ATTIT PWR...GEOG NEW/IDEA VAL/FREE COLD/WAR 20. PAGE 50 A1027
FORCES DIPLOM

B57
KENNAN G.F.,RUSSIA, THE ATOM AND THE WEST. COM EUR+WWI FUT WOR+45 SOCIETY ECO/DEV FORCES DIPLOM ECO/TAC DOMIN EDU/PROP COERCE NUC/PWR ATTIT DRIVE ORD/FREE PWR...POLICY OBS TIME/SEQ TREND COLD/WAR NATO 20. PAGE 77 A1574
NAT/G INT/ORG USSR

B57
TOMASIC D.A.,NATIONAL COMMUNISM AND SOVIET STRATEGY. UK USSR YUGOSLAVIA NAT/G POL/PAR CHIEF CREATE DOMIN REV WAR PWR...BIOG TREND 20 TITO/MARSH STALIN/J. PAGE 144 A2948
COM NAT/LISM MARXISM DIPLOM

B57
US PRES CITIZEN ADVISERS,REPORT TO THE PRESIDENT ON THE MUTUAL SECURITY PROGRAM. COM USA+45 WOR+45 FINAN INDUS PLAN BUDGET CAP/ISM DIPLOM FOR/AID INT/TRADE REGION 20 SECUR/PROG. PAGE 155 A3163
BAL/PWR FORCES INT/ORG ECO/TAC

S57
ALLEN R.L.,"UNITED NATIONS TECHNICAL ASSISTANCE: SOVIET AND EAST-EUROPEAN PARTICIPATION." COM WOR+45 AGRI INDUS INT/ORG NAT/G FOR/AID SKILL UN 20. PAGE 6 A0124
ECO/UNDEV TEC/DEV USSR

S57
HOAG M.W.,"ECONOMIC PROBLEMS OF ALLIANCE." COM EUR+WWI WOR+45 ECO/DEV ECO/UNDEV NAT/G VOL/ASSN FORCES PLAN TEC/DEV DIPLOM COERCE ORD/FREE PWR WEALTH...DECISION GEN/LAWS NATO COLD/WAR. PAGE 65 A1345
INT/ORG ECO/TAC

S57
SPEIER H.,"SOVIET ATOMIC BLACKMAIL AND THE NORTH ATLANTIC ALLIANCE." EUR+WWI USA+45 USSR INT/ORG NAT/G FORCES DIPLOM DRIVE ORD/FREE PWR NATO VAL/FREE COLD/WAR 20. PAGE 136 A2781
COM COERCE NUC/PWR

C57
TANG P.S.H.,"COMMUNIST CHINA TODAY: DOMESTIC AND FOREIGN POLICIES." CHINA/COM COM S/ASIA USSR STRATA FORCES DIPLOM EDU/PROP COERCE GOV/REL...POLICY MAJORIT BIBLIOG 20. PAGE 141 A2886
POL/PAR LEAD ADMIN CONSTN

B58
BERLINER J.S.,SOVIET ECONOMIC AID: THE AID AND TRADE POLICY IN UNDERDEVELOPED COUNTRIES. AFR COM ISLAM L/A+17C S/ASIA USSR ECO/DEV DIST/IND FINAN MARKET INT/ORG ACT/RES PLAN BAL/PWR WEAPON PWR WEALTH...CHARTS 20. PAGE 14 A0277
ECO/UNDEV ECO/TAC FOR/AID

B58
GARTHOFF R.L.,SOVIET STRATEGY IN THE NUCLEAR AGE. FUT USSR R+D INT/ORG NAT/G ACT/RES TEC/DEV DOMIN DETER WAR ATTIT PWR...RELATIV METH/CNCPT SELF/OBS TREND CON/ANAL STERTYP GEN/LAWS 20. PAGE 51 A1052
COM FORCES BAL/PWR NUC/PWR

B58
HOLT R.T.,RADIO FREE EUROPE. FUT USA+45 CULTURE ECO/DEV INT/ORG KIN POL/PAR SECT FORCES ACT/RES DIPLOM COERCE REV CHOOSE PEACE ATTIT PWR...MAJORIT CONCPT COLD/WAR WORK 20 RFE. PAGE 67 A1374
COM EDU/PROP COM/IND

B58
NEAL F.W.,TITOISM IN ACTION. COM YUGOSLAVIA AGRI LOC/G DIPLOM TOTALISM...BIBLIOG 20 TITO/MARSH. PAGE 107 A2206
MARXISM POL/PAR CHIEF ADMIN

B58
PALMER E.E.,THE COMMUNIST CHALLENGE. COM USA+45 USA-45 ECO/DEV ECO/UNDEV NEUTRAL ORD/FREE POPULISM ...CONCPT NAT/COMP ANTHOL 19/20 LENIN/VI STALIN/J MAO MARX/KARL COM/PARTY. PAGE 113 A2320
MARXISM DIPLOM IDEA/COMP POLICY

S58
STAAR R.F.,"ELECTIONS IN COMMUNIST POLAND." EUR+WWI SOCIETY INT/ORG NAT/G POL/PAR LEGIS ACT/RES ECO/TAC EDU/PROP ADJUD ADMIN ROUTINE COERCE TOTALISM ATTIT ORD/FREE PWR 20. PAGE 137 A2797
COM CHOOSE POLAND

B59
CAREW-HUNT R.C.,BOOKS ON COMMUNISM. NAT/G POL/PAR DIPLOM REV...BIOG 19/20. PAGE 24 A0481
BIBLIOG/A MARXISM COM ASIA

B59
FREE L.A.,SIX ALLIES AND A NEUTRAL. ASIA COM EUR+WWI FRANCE GERMANY/W INDIA S/ASIA UK USA+45 INT/ORG NAT/G NUC/PWR PEACE ATTIT PERCEPT RIGID/FLEX ALL/VALS...STAT REC/INT COLD/WAR 20 CHINJAP. PAGE 48 A0992
PSY DIPLOM

B59
GOLDWIN R.A.,READINGS IN RUSSIAN FOREIGN POLICY. HUNGARY USSR YUGOSLAVIA ELITES INT/ORG NAT/G REV WAR NAT/LISM PERSON SOCISM...CHARTS 20 MAPS BOLSHEVISM. PAGE 53 A1095
COM MARXISM DIPLOM POLICY

B59
LAQUER W.Z.,THE SOVIET UNION AND THE MIDDLE EAST. COM UAR USSR ECO/UNDEV NAT/G VOL/ASSN ECO/TAC EDU/PROP COLONIAL EXEC PWR...TIME/SEQ TREND COLD/WAR 20. PAGE 85 A1730
ISLAM DRIVE FOR/AID NAT/LISM

B59
MODELSKI G.,ATOMIC ENERGY IN THE COMMUNIST BLOC. FUT INT/ORG CONSULT FORCES ACT/RES PLAN KNOWL SKILL ...PHIL/SCI STAT CHARTS 20. PAGE 102 A2096
TEC/DEV NUC/PWR USSR COM

B59
OKINSHEVICH L.A.,LATIN AMERICA IN SOVIET WRITINGS, 1945-1958: A BIBLIOGRAPHY. USSR LAW ECO/UNDEV LABOR DIPLOM EDU/PROP REV...GEOG SOC 20. PAGE 111 A2287
BIBLIOG WRITING COM L/A+17C

B59
STRAUSZ-HUPE R.,PROTRACTED CONFLICT. CHINA/COM KOREA WOR+45 INT/ORG FORCES ACT/RES ECO/TAC LEGIT COERCE DRIVE PERCEPT KNOWL PWR...PSY CONCPT RECORD GEN/METH COLD/WAR VAL/FREE 20. PAGE 139 A2847
COM PLAN USSR

B59
WOLFERS A.,ALLIANCE POLICY IN THE COLD WAR. COM INT/ORG FORCES COLONIAL CONTROL NUC/PWR 20 NATO UN COLD/WAR. PAGE 166 A3384
DIPLOM DETER BAL/PWR

S59
BROMKE A.,"DISENGAGEMENT IN EAST EUROPE." COM USSR INT/ORG DIPLOM EDU/PROP NEUTRAL NUC/PWR DRIVE RIGID/FLEX PWR...PSY CONCPT CON/ANAL GEN/METH VAL/FREE 20. PAGE 19 A0388
BAL/PWR

S59
KISSINGER H.A.,"THE SEARCH FOR STABILITY." COM GERMANY MOD/EUR USA+45 USA-45 USSR INT/ORG ARMS/CONT NUC/PWR ORD/FREE PWR COLD/WAR 20 NATO.
FUT ATTIT BAL/PWR

PAGE 80 A1641

S59

ZAUBERMAN A.,"SOVIET BLOC ECONOMIC INTEGRATION." COM CULTURE INTELL ECO/DEV INDUS TOP/EX ACT/RES PLAN ECO/TAC INT/TRADE ROUTINE CHOOSE ATTIT ...TIME/SEQ 20. PAGE 169 A3448 — MARKET INT/ORG USSR TOTALISM

C59

KULSKI W.W.,"PEACEFUL COEXISTENCE." USSR ECO/UNDEV INT/ORG POL/PAR EDU/PROP COLONIAL CONTROL REV NAT/LISM PEACE PWR MARXISM...BIBLIOG 20. PAGE 83 A1692 — COM DIPLOM DOMIN

B60

ALLEN R.L.,SOVIET ECONOMIC WARFARE. USSR FINAN INDUS NAT/G PLAN TEC/DEV FOR/AID DETER WEALTH ...TREND GEN/LAWS 20. PAGE 6 A0126 — COM ECO/TAC

B60

BARNET R.,WHO WANTS DISARMAMENT. COM EUR+WWI USA+45 USSR INT/ORG NAT/G BAL/PWR DIPLOM EDU/PROP COERCE DETER NUC/PWR WAR WEAPON ATTIT PWR...TIME/SEQ COLD/WAR CONGRESS 20. PAGE 11 A0225 — PLAN FORCES ARMS/CONT

B60

BILLERBECK K.,SOVIET BLOC FOREIGN AID TO UNDERDEVELOPED COUNTRIES. COM FUT USSR FINAN FORCES TEC/DEV DIPLOM INT/TRADE EDU/PROP NUC/PWR...TREND 20. PAGE 14 A0287 — FOR/AID ECO/UNDEV ECO/TAC MARXISM

B60

CAMPAIGNE J.G.,AMERICAN MIGHT AND SOVIET MYTH. COM EUR+WWI ECO/DEV ECO/UNDEV INT/ORG NAT/G CAP/ISM ECO/TAC FOR/AID EDU/PROP ATTIT PWR WEALTH...POLICY CONCPT MYTH TREND STERTYP GEN/LAWS COLD/WAR. PAGE 23 A0473 — USA+45 DOMIN DIPLOM USSR

B60

ENGEL J.,THE SECURITY OF THE FREE WORLD. USSR WOR+45 STRATA STRUCT ECO/DEV ECO/UNDEV INT/ORG DELIB/GP FORCES DOMIN LEGIT ADJUD EXEC ARMS/CONT COERCE...POLICY CONCPT NEW/IDEA TIME/SEQ GEN/LAWS COLD/WAR WORK UN 20 NATO. PAGE 42 A0851 — COM TREND DIPLOM

B60

FISCHER L.,THE SOVIETS IN WORLD AFFAIRS. CHINA/COM COM EUR+WWI USSR INT/ORG CONFER LEAD ARMS/CONT REV PWR...CHARTS 20 TREATY VERSAILLES. PAGE 46 A0938 — DIPLOM NAT/G POLICY MARXISM

B60

FOOTMAN D.,INTERNATIONAL COMMUNISM. ASIA EUR+WWI FRANCE FUT GERMANY MOD/EUR S/ASIA USA-45 WOR+45 WOR-45 INTELL LABOR TOTALISM MARXISM WORK 20. PAGE 47 A0958 — COM INT/ORG STRUCT REV

B60

JACOBSON H.K.,AMERICAN FOREIGN POLICY. COM EUR+WWI USA+45 USA-45 ECO/DEV ECO/UNDEV INT/ORG NAT/G INT/TRADE EDU/PROP COLONIAL CHOOSE MARXISM 20 NATO. PAGE 72 A1485 — POL/PAR PWR DIPLOM

B60

KENNAN G.F.,RUSSIA AND THE WEST. ASIA COM EUR+WWI GERMANY UK USA+45 USA-45 USSR INT/ORG NAT/G VOL/ASSN DOMIN REV WAR PWR...TIME/SEQ 20. PAGE 78 A1590 — EXEC DIPLOM

B60

KHRUSHCHEV N.,FOR VICTORY IN PEACEFUL COMPETITION WITH CAPITALISM. COM FUT USSR WOR+45 CONSTN SOCIETY INDUS INT/ORG DELIB/GP PLAN BAL/PWR DIPLOM PERSON MARXISM...MARXIST WORK 20 COLD/WAR. PAGE 79 A1611 — TOP/EX PWR CAP/ISM SOCISM

B60

MCKINNEY R.,REVIEW OF THE INTERNATIONAL ATOMIC POLICIES AND PROGRAMS OF THE UNITED STATES (5 VOLS.). COM FUT USA+45 ECO/DEV ECO/UNDEV INT/ORG DELIB/GP PLAN ADMIN 20 THIRD/WRLD. PAGE 98 A2016 — NUC/PWR PEACE DIPLOM POLICY

B60

MOSELY P.E.,THE KREMLIN AND WORLD POLITICS. EUR+WWI GERMANY USA+45 USSR CHIEF TOP/EX BAL/PWR DOMIN PEACE PWR...METH 20 COLD/WAR STALIN/J EUROPE/E. PAGE 105 A2151 — COM DIPLOM POLICY WAR

B60

MOUSKHELY M.,L'URSS ET LES PAYS DE L'EST. ASIA COM S/ASIA USSR PRESS...SOC 20. PAGE 105 A2156 — BIBLIOG/A DIPLOM ATTIT

B60

SPEIER H.,DIVIDED BERLIN: THE ANATOMY OF SOVIET POLITICAL BLACKMAIL. COM GERMANY USA+45 USSR WOR+45 NAT/G TOP/EX DOMIN EDU/PROP ALL/VALS...POLICY CONCPT COLD/WAR 20 U-2. PAGE 136 A2782 — INT/ORG ACT/RES DIPLOM

B60

SZTARAY Z.,BIBLIOGRAPHY ON HUNGARY. HUNGARY MOD/EUR CULTURE INDUS SECT DIPLOM REV...ART/METH SOC LING 18/20. PAGE 141 A2879 — BIBLIOG NAT/G COM MARXISM

S60

DOUGHERTY J.E.,"KEY TO SECURITY: DISARMAMENT OR ARMS STABILITY." COM USA+45 USSR INT/ORG NAT/G CREATE EDU/PROP COERCE DETER ATTIT PWR...DECISION CONCPT MYTH NEW/IDEA TREND 20 COLD/WAR. PAGE 38 A0777 — FORCES ORD/FREE ARMS/CONT NUC/PWR

S60

GOODMAN E.,"THE CRY OF NATIONAL LIBERATION: RECENT SOVIET ATTITUDES TOWARDS NATIONAL SELF-DETERMINATION." COM INT/ORG LEGIS ROUTINE PWR ...TIME/SEQ CON/ANAL STERTYP GEN/LAWS 20 UN. PAGE 54 A1101 — ATTIT EDU/PROP SOVEREIGN USSR

S60

GRACIA-MORA M.R.,"INTERNATIONAL RESPONSIBILITY FOR SUBVERSIVE ACTIVITIES AND HOSTILE PROPAGANDA BY PRIVATE PERSONS AGAINST." COM EUR+WWI L/A+17C UK USA+45 USSR WOR-45 CONSTN NAT/G LEGIT ADJUD REV PEACE TOTALISM ORD/FREE...INT/LAW 20. PAGE 55 A1119 — INT/ORG JURID SOVEREIGN

S60

HAVILAND H.F.,"PROBLEMS OF AMERICAN FOREIGN POLICY." ASIA COM USA+45 WOR+45 INT/ORG NAT/G CONSULT ECO/TAC FOR/AID DOMIN COERCE NUC/PWR ATTIT DRIVE ORD/FREE PWR RESPECT SKILL...POLICY GEOG OBS SAMP TREND GEN/METH METH COLD/WAR UN 20. PAGE 63 A1292 — ECO/UNDEV FORCES DIPLOM

S60

JACOBSON H.K.,"THE USSR AND ILO." COM STRUCT ECO/DEV ECO/UNDEV CONSULT DELIB/GP ECO/TAC ILO WORK COLD/WAR 20. PAGE 72 A1484 — INT/ORG LABOR USSR

S60

KALUODA J.,"COMMUNIST STRATEGY IN LATIN AMERICA." L/A+17C USA+45 INT/ORG NAT/G POL/PAR DIPLOM ECO/TAC EDU/PROP COERCE WEALTH...CONCPT OAS COLD/WAR 20. PAGE 76 A1553 — COM PWR CUBA

S60

KENNAN G.F.,"PEACEFUL CO-EXISTENCE: A WESTERN VIEW." COM EUR+WWI USA+45 USSR WOR+45 PLAN BAL/PWR DIPLOM INT/TRADE PWR...POLICY CONCPT OBS HIST/WRIT TREND GEN/LAWS COLD/WAR 20 KHRUSH/N. PAGE 78 A1589 — ATTIT COERCE

S60

MIKESELL R.F.,"AMERICA'S ECONOMIC RESPONSIBILITY AS A GREAT POWER." COM FUT USA+45 USSR WOR+45 INT/ORG PLAN ECO/TAC FOR/AID EDU/PROP CHOOSE WEALTH ...POLICY 20. PAGE 101 A2069 — ECO/UNDEV BAL/PWR CAP/ISM

S60

MORGENSTERN O.,"GOAL: AN ARMED, INSPECTED, OPEN WORLD." COM EUR+WWI USA+45 R+D INT/ORG NAT/G TEC/DEV BAL/PWR COERCE NUC/PWR ORD/FREE PWR...TREND 20. PAGE 104 A2133 — FORCES CONCPT ARMS/CONT DETER

S60

OWEN C.F.,"US AND SOVIET RELATIONS WITH UNDERDEVELOPED COUNTRIES: LATIN AMERICA-A CASE STUDY." AFR COM L/A+17C USA+45 USSR EXTR/IND MARKET TEC/DEV DIPLOM ECO/TAC NAT/LISM ORD/FREE PWR ...TREND WORK 20. PAGE 112 A2303 — ECO/UNDEV DRIVE INT/TRADE

S60

PYE L.W.,"SOVIET AND AMERICAN STYLES IN FOREIGN AID." COM USA+45 USSR WOR+45 NAT/G PLAN ECO/TAC ROUTINE RIGID/FLEX...POLICY CONCPT TREND GEN/LAWS TOT/POP 20. PAGE 118 A2419 — ECO/UNDEV ATTIT FOR/AID

S60

WRIGHT Q.,"LEGAL ASPECTS OF THE U-2 INCIDENT." COM USA+45 USSR STRUCT NAT/G FORCES PLAN TEC/DEV ADJUD RIGID/FLEX MORAL ORD/FREE...DECISION INT/LAW JURID PSY TREND GEN/LAWS COLD/WAR VAL/FREE 20 U-2. PAGE 168 A3413 — PWR POLICY SPACE

C60

FITZSIMMONS T.,"USSR: ITS PEOPLE, ITS SOCIETY, ITS CULTURE." USSR FAM SECT DIPLOM EDU/PROP ADMIN RACE/REL ATTIT...POLICY CHARTS BIBLIOG 20. PAGE 46 A0944 — CULTURE STRUCT SOCIETY COM

C60

HAZARD J.N.,"THE SOVIET SYSTEM OF GOVERNMENT." USSR SOCIETY INDUS NAT/G POL/PAR DIPLOM CT/SYS...JURID CHARTS BIBLIOG/A 20. PAGE 63 A1298 — COM NAT/COMP STRUCT ADMIN

B61

AMORY J.F.,AROUND THE EDGE OF WAR: A NEW APPROACH TO THE PROBLEMS OF AMERICAN FOREIGN POLICY. COM L/A+17C USA+45 USSR FOR/AID EDU/PROP AGREE CONTROL ARMS/CONT NUC/PWR WAR PWR...IDEA/COMP 20 TREATY ESPIONAGE. PAGE 8 A0154 — NAT/G DIPLOM POLICY

B61

AUBREY H.G.,COEXISTENCE: ECONOMIC CHALLENGE AND RESPONSE. USSR WOR+45 ACT/RES BAL/PWR CAP/ISM DIPLOM ECO/TAC FOR/AID INT/TRADE PEACE SOCISM ...METH/COMP NAT/COMP COLD/WAR. PAGE 10 A0196 — POLICY ECO/UNDEV PLAN COM

B61

BECHHOEFER B.G.,POSTWAR NEGOTIATIONS FOR ARMS CONTROL. COM EUR+WWI USSR INT/ORG NAT/G ACT/RES BAL/PWR DIPLOM ECO/TAC EDU/PROP ADMIN REGION DETER NUC/PWR WAR WEAPON PEACE ATTIT PWR...POLICY TIME/SEQ COLD/WAR CONGRESS 20. PAGE 12 A0244 — USA+45 ARMS/CONT

B61

BULL H.,THE CONTROL OF THE ARMS RACE. COM USA+45 INT/ORG NAT/G PLAN TEC/DEV DIPLOM ATTIT...RELATIV DECISION CONCPT SELF/OBS TREND CON/ANAL GEN/METH 20 COLD/WAR. PAGE 21 A0429 — FORCES PWR ARMS/CONT NUC/PWR

B61

CONFERENCE ATLANTIC COMMUNITY,AN INTRODUCTORY BIBLIOGRAPHY. COM WOR+45 FORCES DIPLOM ECO/TAC WAR ...INT/LAW HIST/WRIT COLD/WAR NATO. PAGE 29 A0584 — BIBLIOG/A CON/ANAL INT/ORG

B61

DALLIN D.J.,SOVIET FOREIGN POLICY AFTER STALIN. ASIA CHINA/COM EUR+WWI GERMANY IRAN UK YUGOSLAVIA INT/ORG NAT/G VOL/ASSN FORCES TOP/EX BAL/PWR DOMIN — COM DIPLOM USSR

EDU/PROP COERCE ATTIT PWR 20. PAGE 33 A0679

B61
KERTESZ S.D.,AMERICAN DIPLOMACY IN A NEW ERA. COM S/ASIA UK USA+45 FORCES PROB/SOLV BAL/PWR ECO/TAC ADMIN COLONIAL WAR PEACE ORD/FREE 20 NATO CONGRESS UN COLD/WAR. PAGE 78 A1601 — ANTHOL DIPLOM TREND

B61
LEGISLATIVE REFERENCE SERVICE,WORLD COMMUNIST MOVEMENT: SELECTIVE CHRONOLOGY, 1818-1957 (4 VOLS.). COM WOR+45 WOR-45 POL/PAR LEAD 19/20. PAGE 86 A1766 — BIBLIOG DIPLOM TIME/SEQ MARXISM

B61
LIPPMANN W.,THE COMING TESTS WITH RUSSIA. COM CUBA GERMANY USSR FORCES CONTROL NEUTRAL COERCE NUC/PWR REV WAR PWR...INT 20 KHRUSH/N BERLIN. PAGE 89 A1830 — BAL/PWR DIPLOM MARXISM ARMS/CONT

B61
LUKACS J.,A HISTORY OF THE COLD WAR. ASIA COM EUR+WWI USA+45 USA-45 INT/ORG NAT/G DELIB/GP ACT/RES BAL/PWR DIPLOM DOMIN EDU/PROP LEGIT DRIVE ORD/FREE...TREND COLD/WAR 20. PAGE 91 A1872 — PWR TIME/SEQ USSR

B61
NOLLAU G.,INTERNATIONAL COMMUNISM AND WORLD REVOLUTION: HISTORY AND METHODS. RUSSIA USSR INT/ORG NAT/G POL/PAR VOL/ASSN FORCES BAL/PWR DIPLOM EXEC REGION WAR ATTIT PWR MARXISM...CONCPT TIME/SEQ COLD/WAR 19/20. PAGE 102 A2100 — COM REV

B61
NOGEE J.L.,SOVIET POLICY TOWARD INTERNATIONAL CONTROL OF ATOMIC ENERGY. COM USA+45 WOR+45 INTELL NAT/G ACT/RES DIPLOM EDU/PROP NUC/PWR TOTALISM PERCEPT KNOWL PWR...TIME/SEQ COLD/WAR 20. PAGE 109 A2247 — INT/ORG ATTIT ARMS/CONT USSR

B61
NOLLAU G.,INTERNATIONAL COMMUNISM AND WORLD REVOLUTION; HISTORY AND METHODS (TRANS. BY VICTOR ANDERSEN). COM WORKER DIPLOM CONFER INGP/REL ...CONCPT BIBLIOG 20 STALIN/J LENIN/VI COMINTERN COMINFORM WORLD/CONG. PAGE 110 A2249 — MARXISM POL/PAR INT/ORG REV

B61
OVERSTREET H.,THE WAR CALLED PEACE. USSR WOR+45 COM/IND INT/ORG POL/PAR BAL/PWR EDU/PROP PEACE ATTIT...CONCPT 20 KHRUSH/N. PAGE 112 A2302 — DIPLOM COM POLICY LEAD

B61
PECKERT J.,DIE GROSSEN UND DIE KLEINEN MAECHTE. COM GERMANY/W ECO/DEV ECO/UNDEV NAT/G WAR RACE/REL PEACE...POLICY GP/COMP GOV/COMP 20 COLD/WAR. PAGE 114 A2346 — DIPLOM ECO/TAC BAL/PWR

B61
RICE G.W.,THE SOVIET POSITION ON DEPENDENT TERRITORIES IN THE UNITED NATIONS (THESIS, OHIO STATE UNIVERSITY). USSR PLAN SOVEREIGN...POLICY 20 UN. PAGE 121 A2473 — INT/ORG COM DIPLOM COLONIAL

B61
SCHIEDER T.,DOCUMENTS ON THE EXPULSION OF THE GERMANS FROM EASTERN-CENTRAL-EUROPE (VOL. II/III). COM EUR+WWI GERMANY HUNGARY ROMANIA USSR DIPLOM RACE/REL 20 MIGRATION. PAGE 128 A2625 — GEOG CULTURE

B61
SCHMIDT H.,VERTEIDIGUNG ODER VERGELTUNG. COM CUBA GERMANY/W USSR FORCES DIPLOM ARMS/CONT DETER NUC/PWR...POLICY CHARTS HYPO/EXP SIMUL BIBLIOG 20 NATO COLD/WAR. PAGE 128 A2630 — PLAN WAR BAL/PWR ORD/FREE

B61
SLESSOR J.,WHAT PRICE COEXISTENCE? COM INT/ORG NAT/G FORCES COLONIAL ARMS/CONT WAR...POLICY TREND 20 NATO COLD/WAR. PAGE 134 A2741 — DIPLOM PEACE WOR+45 NUC/PWR

B61
US SENATE COMM GOVT OPERATIONS,ORGANIZING FOR NATIONAL SECURITY. COM USA+45 BUDGET DIPLOM DETER NUC/PWR WAR WEAPON ORD/FREE...BIBLIOG 20 COLD/WAR. PAGE 156 A3172 — POLICY PLAN FORCES COERCE

L61
HILSMAN R. JR.,"THE NEW COMMUNIST TACTIC: PRECIS-INTERNAL WAR." COM FUT USA+45 ECO/UNDEV POL/PAR FOR/AID RIGID/FLEX ALL/VALS...TREND COLD/WAR 20. PAGE 65 A1334 — FORCES COERCE USSR GUERRILLA

L61
HOYT E.C.,"UNITED STATES REACTION TO THE KOREAN ATTACK." COM KOREA USA+45 CONSTN DELIB/GP FORCES PLAN ECO/TAC DOMIN EDU/PROP LEGIT ROUTINE COERCE WAR ATTIT DISPL RIGID/FLEX ORD/FREE PWR...POLICY INT/LAW TREND UN 20. PAGE 68 A1402 — ASIA INT/ORG BAL/PWR DIPLOM

S61
BARNET R.,"RUSSIA, CHINA, AND THE WORLD: THE SOVIET ATTITUDE ON DISARMAMENT (PART 3)." ASIA CHINA/COM FUT INT/ORG NAT/G POL/PAR VOL/ASSN ARMS/CONT ATTIT ...POLICY CONCPT TIME/SEQ TREND TOT/POP VAL/FREE 20. PAGE 11 A0226 — COM PLAN TOTALISM USSR

S61
BRZEZINSKI Z.K.,"THE ORGANIZATION OF THE COMMUNIST CAMP." COM CZECHOSLVK COM/IND NAT/G DELIB/GP INT/TRADE DOMIN EDU/PROP EXEC ROUTINE COERCE ATTIT PWR...MGT CONCPT TIME/SEQ CHARTS VAL/FREE 20 TREATY. PAGE 20 A0416 — VOL/ASSN DIPLOM USSR

S61
BURNET A.,"TOO MANY ALLIES." COM EUR+WWI UK WOR+45 WOR-45 ACT/RES PLAN DISPL PWR SKILL...TIME/SEQ 20 CMN/WLTH SEATO NATO CENTO. PAGE 22 A0438 — VOL/ASSN INT/ORG DIPLOM

S61
DANIELS R.V.,"THE CHINESE REVOLUTION IN RUSSIAN PERSPECTIVE." ASIA CHINA/COM COM USSR INTELL INT/ORG TOP/EX REV TOTALISM PWR...POLICY WORK VAL/FREE 20. PAGE 33 A0680 — POL/PAR PLAN

S61
DELLA PORT G.,"PROBLEMI E PROSPETTIVE DI COESISTENZA FRA ORIENTE ED OCCIDENTE, (PART 3)." COM FUT WOR+45 NAT/G BAL/PWR FOR/AID BAL/PAY PWR WEALTH...SOC CONCPT GEN/LAWS COLD/WAR 20. PAGE 36 A0729 — INT/TRADE

S61
GOODWIN G.L.,"THE EXPANDING UNITED NATIONS: 2-DIPLOMATIC PRESSURES AND TECHNIQUES." COM ECO/UNDEV TOP/EX BAL/PWR DIPLOM DOMIN...POLICY CONCPT UN COLD/WAR 20. PAGE 54 A1108 — INT/ORG PWR

S61
JUVILER P.H.,"INTERPARLIAMENTARY CONTACTS IN SOVIET FOREIGN POLICY." COM FUT WOR+45 WOR-45 SOCIETY CONSULT ACT/RES DIPLOM ADMIN PEACE ATTIT RIGID/FLEX WEALTH...WELF/ST SOC TOT/POP CONGRESS 19/20. PAGE 75 A1543 — INT/ORG DELIB/GP USSR

S61
KRANNHALS H.V.,"COMMAND INTEGRATION WITHIN THE WARSAW PACT." COM USSR WOR+45 DELIB/GP EDU/PROP ...CONCPT AUD/VIS CHARTS COLD/WAR TOT/POP VAL/FREE 20 TREATY WARSAW/P. PAGE 82 A1675 — INT/ORG FORCES TOTALISM

S61
LIPSON L.,"AN ARGUMENT ON THE LEGALITY OF RECONNAISSANCE STATELLITES." COM USA+45 USSR WOR+45 AIR INTELL NAT/G CONSULT PLAN DIPLOM LEGIT ROUTINE ATTIT...INT/LAW JURID CONCPT METH/CNCPT TREND COLD/WAR 20. PAGE 90 A1833 — INT/ORG LAW SPACE

S61
NOVE A.,"THE SOVIET MODEL AND UNDERDEVELOPED COUNTRIES." COM FUT USSR WOR+45 CULTURE ECO/DEV POL/PAR FOR/AID EDU/PROP ADMIN MORAL WEALTH ...POLICY RECORD HIST/WRIT 20. PAGE 110 A2258 — ECO/UNDEV PLAN

S61
ROSTOW W.W.,"THE FUTURE OF FOREIGN AID." COM FUT WOR+45 ECO/DEV INDUS INT/ORG NAT/G CONSULT ACT/RES PLAN DOMIN LEGIT CHOOSE RIGID/FLEX ALL/VALS ...MAJORIT CONCPT TREND TOT/POP 20. PAGE 124 A2544 — ECO/UNDEV ECO/TAC FOR/AID

S61
VERNON R.,"A TRADE POLICY FOR THE 1960'S." COM FUT USA+45 WOR+45 ECO/DEV ECO/UNDEV FINAN TOP/EX ACT/RES...WELF/ST METH/CNCPT CONT/OBS TOT/POP 20. PAGE 159 A3229 — PLAN INT/TRADE

S61
WHELAN J.G.,"KHRUSHCHEV AND THE BALANCE OF WORLD POWER." FUT WOR+45 INT/ORG VOL/ASSN CAP/ISM DIPLOM SKILL...POLICY COLD/WAR 20 KHRUSH/N. PAGE 163 A3328 — COM PWR BAL/PWR USSR

S61
ZAGORIA D.S.,"SINO-SOVIET FRICTION IN UNDERDEVELOPED AREAS." ASIA CHINA/COM COM ACT/RES PLAN ATTIT ORD/FREE PWR COLD/WAR 20. PAGE 169 A3443 — ECO/UNDEV ECO/TAC INT/TRADE USSR

S61
ZAGORIA D.S.,"THE FUTURE OF SINO-SOVIET RELATIONS." CHINA/COM COM INT/ORG NAT/G POL/PAR VOL/ASSN ACT/RES PLAN PERSON...METH/CNCPT TIME/SEQ TOT/POP VAL/FREE 20 MAO KHRUSH/N. PAGE 169 A3444 — ASIA COM TOTALISM USSR

B62
ALIX C.,LE SAINT-SIEGE ET LES NATIONALISMES EN EUROPE 1870-1960. COM GERMANY IRELAND ITALY SOCIETY SECT TOTALISM RIGID/FLEX MORAL 19/20. PAGE 6 A0122 — CATH NAT/LISM ATTIT DIPLOM

B62
ARNOLD H.J.P.,AID FOR DEVELOPING COUNTRIES. COM EUR+WWI USA+45 USSR WOR+45 EDU/PROP ATTIT DRIVE PWR WEALTH...TREND CHARTS STERTYP NAT/ 20. PAGE 9 A0177 — ECO/UNDEV ECO/TAC FOR/AID

B62
BOUSCAREN A.T.,SOVIET FOREIGN POLICY: A PATTERN OF PERSISTANCE. WOR+45 WOR-45 SOCIETY STRUCT INT/ORG POL/PAR CREATE PLAN EDU/PROP ROUTINE ATTIT RIGID/FLEX...POLICY CONCPT RECORD HIST/WRIT TIME/SEQ MARX/KARL 20. PAGE 17 A0352 — COM NAT/G DIPLOM USSR

B62
BOWLES C.,THE CONSCIENCE OF A LIBERAL. COM USA+45 WOR+45 STRUCT LOC/G NAT/G FORCES LEGIS GOV/REL DISCRIM 20 UN CIV/RIGHTS. PAGE 18 A0361 — DIPLOM POLICY

B62
BURTON J.W.,PEACE THEORY: PRECONDITIONS OF DISARMAMENT. COM EUR+WWI USA+45 NAT/G FORCES BAL/PWR DIPLOM ECO/TAC EDU/PROP REGION COERCE DETER PEACE ATTIT PWR TOT/POP COLD/WAR 20. PAGE 22 A0446 — INT/ORG PLAN ARMS/CONT

B62
CADWELL R.,COMMUNISM IN THE MODERN WORLD. USSR WOR+45 SOCIETY AGRI INDUS INT/ORG SECT EDU/PROP COLONIAL PEACE...SOC 20. PAGE 23 A0463 — COM DIPLOM POLICY

CONCPT

B62
CLUBB O.E. JR.,THE UNITED STATES AND THE SINO-SOVIET BLOC IN SOUTHEAST ASIA. ASIA CHINA/COM COM USA+45 USSR ECO/UNDEV INT/ORG NAT/G FORCES TOP/EX PLAN ECO/TAC DOMIN COERCE GUERRILLA ATTIT RIGID/FLEX...POLICY OBS TREND 20. PAGE 27 A0553
S/ASIA PWR BAL/PWR DIPLOM

B62
DALLIN A.,THE SOVIET UNION AT THE UNITED NATIONS: AN INQUIRY INTO SOVIET MOTIVES AND OBJECTIVES. ACT/RES EDU/PROP LEGIT ATTIT KNOWL PWR...POLICY RECORD HIST/WRIT TIME/SEQ TREND ORG/CHARTS GEN/METH COLD/WAR FAO 20 UN. PAGE 33 A0675
COM INT/ORG USSR

B62
DELANEY R.F.,THE LITERATURE OF COMMUNISM IN AMERICA. COM USA+45 USA-45 INT/ORG LABOR NAT/G POL/PAR INGP/REL...MAJORIT 20. PAGE 36 A0727
BIBLIOG/A MARXISM EDU/PROP IDEA/COMP

B62
DOUGLAS W.O.,DEMOCRACY'S MANIFESTO. COM USA+45 ECO/UNDEV INT/ORG FORCES PLAN NEUTRAL TASK MARXISM ...JURID 20 NATO SEATO. PAGE 38 A0779
DIPLOM POLICY NAT/G ORD/FREE

B62
ELLIOTT J.R.,THE APPEAL OF COMMUNISM IN THE UNDERDEVELOPED NATIONS. USSR WOR+45 INT/ORG NAT/G DIPLOM DOMIN EDU/PROP ROUTINE ATTIT RIGID/FLEX ORD/FREE PWR WEALTH MARXISM...POLICY SOC METH/CNCPT MYTH TOT/POP COLD/WAR 20. PAGE 41 A0842
COM ECO/UNDEV

B62
FRIEDRICH-EBERT-STIFTUNG,THE SOVIET BLOC AND DEVELOPING COUNTRIES. CHINA/COM COM GERMANY/E USSR WOR+45 ECO/UNDEV INT/ORG NAT/G TEC/DEV NEUTRAL PWR ...POLICY 20. PAGE 49 A1008
MARXISM DIPLOM ECO/TAC FOR/AID

B62
GILPIN R.,AMERICAN SCIENTISTS AND NUCLEAR WEAPONS POLICY. COM FUT USA+45 WOR+45 INT/ORG NAT/G PROF/ORG CONSULT FORCES CREATE TEC/DEV BAL/PWR EDU/PROP ARMS/CONT WAR PERCEPT KNOWL MORAL PWR ...PHIL/SCI SOC CONCPT GEN/LAWS 20. PAGE 52 A1073
INTELL ATTIT DETER NUC/PWR

B62
GYORGY A.,PROBLEMS IN INTERNATIONAL RELATIONS. COM CT/SYS NUC/PWR ALL/IDEOS 20 UN EEC ECSC. PAGE 58 A1199
DIPLOM NEUTRAL BAL/PWR REV

B62
HOOK S.,WORLD COMMUNISM: KEY DOCUMENTARY MATERIAL. CHINA/COM L/A+17C USA+45 USSR POL/PAR DIPLOM COLONIAL REV WAR...ANTHOL 20 MARX/KARL LENIN/VI COM/PARTY. PAGE 67 A1380
MARXISM COM GEN/LAWS NAT/G

B62
KIRPICEVA I.K.,HANDBUCH DER RUSSISCHEN UND SOWJETISCHEN BIBLIOGRAPHIEN (5 VOLS.). USSR STRUCT ECO/DEV DIPLOM LEAD ATTIT 18/20. PAGE 80 A1637
BIBLIOG/A NAT/G MARXISM COM

B62
KLUCKHOHN F.L.,THE NAKED RISE OF COMMUNISM. CHINA/COM COM USSR WOR+45 CONSTN POL/PAR PLAN CONTROL LEAD NEUTRAL CONSERVE 20 STALIN/J EUROPE/E COM/PARTY. PAGE 80 A1650
MARXISM IDEA/COMP DIPLOM DOMIN

B62
KYRIAK T.E.,INTERNATIONAL COMMUNIST DEVELOPMENTS 1957-1961: INDEX TO TRANSLATIONS FROM AFRICA, ASIA, LATIN AMERICA, WEST EUROPE. COM WOR+45 NAT/G WORKER DIPLOM NAT/LISM. PAGE 83 A1704
BIBLIOG/A MARXISM LABOR POL/PAR

B62
LAQUEUR W.,THE FUTURE OF COMMUNIST SOCIETY. CHINA/COM USSR LAW ECO/DEV NAT/G POL/PAR PLAN PROB/SOLV DIPLOM LEAD...POLICY CONCPT IDEA/COMP ANTHOL 20. PAGE 85 A1731
MARXISM COM FUT SOCIETY

B62
LAQUEUR W.,POLYCENTRISM. CHINA/COM COM USSR WOR+45 INT/ORG NAT/G ECO/TAC DOMIN LEAD ATTIT PWR SOVEREIGN...ANTHOL 20. PAGE 85 A1732
MARXISM DIPLOM BAL/PWR POLICY

B62
LEFEVER E.W.,ARMS AND ARMS CONTROL. COM USA+45 INT/ORG TEC/DEV DIPLOM ORD/FREE 20. PAGE 86 A1763
ATTIT PWR ARMS/CONT BAL/PWR

B62
LESSING P.,AFRICA'S RED HARVEST. AFR CHINA/COM COM USSR ECO/UNDEV BAL/PWR DIPLOM CONTROL PWR 20 COLD/WAR INTERVENT. PAGE 87 A1789
NAT/LISM MARXISM FOR/AID EDU/PROP

B62
LEVY H.V.,LIBERDADE E JUSTICA SOCIAL (2ND ED.). BRAZIL COM L/A+17C USSR INT/ORG PARTIC GP/REL WEALTH 20 UN COM/PARTY. PAGE 88 A1798
ORD/FREE MARXISM CAP/ISM LAW

B62
MACKENTOSH J.M.,STRATEGY AND TACTICS OF SOVIET FOREIGN POLICY. CHINA/COM FUT USA+45 WOR+45 INT/ORG PLAN DOMIN LEGIT ROUTINE COERCE NUC/PWR WAR ATTIT DRIVE ORD/FREE PWR...CONCPT OBS TIME/SEQ TREND GEN/METH COLD/WAR 20. PAGE 92 A1894
COM POLICY DIPLOM USSR

B62
MCKENNA J.,DIPLOMATIC PROTEST IN FOREIGN POLICY: ANALYSIS AND CASE STUDIES. COM USA+45 WOR+45 INT/ORG PUB/INST DELIB/GP TOP/EX ACT/RES PLAN LEGIT ATTIT 20. PAGE 98 A2014
NAT/G POLICY DIPLOM

B62
SHAPIRO D.,A SELECT BIBLIOGRAPHY OF WORKS IN ENGLISH ON RUSSIAN HISTORY, 1801-1917. COM USSR STRATA FORCES EDU/PROP ADMIN REV RACE/REL ATTIT 19/20. PAGE 131 A2693
BIBLIOG DIPLOM COLONIAL

B62
SINGER J.D.,DETERRENCE, ARMS CONTROL AND DISARMAMENT: TOWARD A SYNTHESIS IN NATIONAL SECURITY POLICY. COM USA+45 INT/ORG BAL/PWR DETER ORD/FREE...POLICY COLD/WAR 20. PAGE 133 A2727
FUT ACT/RES ARMS/CONT

B62
SNYDER L.L.D.,THE IMPERIALISM READER. AFR ASIA CHINA/COM COM EUR+WWI FUT MOD/EUR USA+45 WOR+45 WOR-45 INT/ORG COLONIAL SOVEREIGN CMN/WLTH OAS 20. PAGE 134 A2751
DOMIN PWR DIPLOM

B62
SPANIER J.W.,THE POLITICS OF DISARMAMENT. COM USA+45 USSR EDU/PROP ATTIT ORD/FREE PWR RESPECT ...MYTH RECORD 20 COLD/WAR. PAGE 135 A2771
INT/ORG DELIB/GP ARMS/CONT

B62
STARR R.E.,POLAND 1944-1962: THE SOVIETIZATION OF A CAPTIVE PEOPLE. COM POLAND USSR POL/PAR SECT LEGIS DIPLOM DOMIN EDU/PROP CHOOSE ORD/FREE...POLICY CHARTS BIBLIOG 20. PAGE 137 A2808
MARXISM NAT/G TOTALISM NAT/COMP

B62
TRISKA J.F.,THE THEORY, LAW, AND POLICY OF SOVIET TREATIES. WOR+45 WOR-45 CONSTN INT/ORG NAT/G VOL/ASSN DOMIN LEGIT COERCE ATTIT PWR RESPECT ...POLICY JURID CONCPT OBS SAMP TIME/SEQ TREND GEN/LAWS 20. PAGE 145 A2966
COM LAW INT/LAW USSR

B62
WILLIAMS W.A.,THE UNITED STATES, CUBA, AND CASTRO: AN ESSAY ON THE DYNAMICS OF REVOLUTION AND THE DISSOLUTION OF EMPIRE. CUBA USA+45 AGRI VOL/ASSN DIPLOM ECO/TAC DOMIN COERCE...POLICY 20 EISNHWR/DD CIA KENNEDY/JF CASTRO/F. PAGE 165 A3354
REV CONSTN COM LEAD

L62
PETKOFF D.K.,"RECOGNITION AND NON-RECOGNITION OF STATES AND GOVERNMENTS IN INTERNATIONAL LAW." ASIA COM USA+45 WOR+45 NAT/G ACT/RES DIPLOM DOMIN LEGIT COERCE ORD/FREE PWR...CONCPT GEN/LAWS 20. PAGE 115 A2369
INT/ORG LAW INT/LAW

L62
ULYSSES,"THE INTERNATIONAL AIMS AND POLICIES OF THE SOVIET UNION: THE NEW CONCEPTS AND STRATEGY OF KHRUSHCHEV." FUT USSR WOR+45 SOCIETY INT/ORG NAT/G POL/PAR FORCES TOP/EX PLAN DOMIN EDU/PROP COERCE ATTIT PERSON PWR...TREND COLD/WAR 20 KHRUSH/N. PAGE 146 A2994
COM POLICY BAL/PWR DIPLOM

S62
BOKOR-SZEGO H.,"LA CONVENTION DE BELGRADE ET LE REGIME DU DANUBE." COM EUR+WWI WOR+45 STRUCT POL/PAR VOL/ASSN PLAN EDU/PROP WEALTH...TIME/SEQ 20. PAGE 16 A0333
INT/ORG TOTALISM YUGOSLAVIA

S62
BROWN B.E.,"L'ONU ABANDONNE LA HONGRIE." COM USSR WOR+45 CONSTN NAT/G POL/PAR DELIB/GP ACT/RES TEC/DEV PWR...TIME/SEQ 20 UN. PAGE 20 A0400
INT/ORG TOTALISM HUNGARY POLICY

S62
BRZEZINSKI Z.K.,"PEACEFUL ENGAGEMENT IN COMMUNIST DISUNITY." ASIA CHINA/COM USA+45 USSR NAT/G TOP/EX CREATE ECO/TAC FOR/AID DOMIN ATTIT PERCEPT RIGID/FLEX PWR...PSY 20. PAGE 20 A0417
COM DIPLOM TOTALISM

S62
CRANE R.D.,"SOVIET ATTITUDE TOWARD INTERNATIONAL SPACE LAW." COM FUT USA+45 USSR AIR CONSTN DELIB/GP DOMIN PWR...JURID TREND TOT/POP 20. PAGE 32 A0657
LAW ATTIT INT/LAW SPACE

S62
CROAN M.,"POLYCENTRISM: COMMUNIST INTERNATIONAL RELATIONS." ASIA STRUCT INT/ORG NAT/G POL/PAR CONSULT PLAN DOMIN EDU/PROP COERCE ATTIT RIGID/FLEX SOCISM...POLICY CONCPT TREND CON/ANAL GEN/LAWS MARX/KARL. PAGE 33 A0663
COM CREATE DIPLOM NAT/LISM

S62
DALLIN A.,"THE SOVIET VIEW OF THE UNITED NATIONS." WOR+45 VOL/ASSN TOP/EX DIPLOM DOMIN EDU/PROP LEGIT ATTIT RIGID/FLEX PWR...CONCPT OBS HIST/WRIT TIME/SEQ STERTYP GEN/LAWS COLD/WAR UN 20. PAGE 33 A0676
COM INT/ORG USSR

S62
DRACHKOVITCH M.M.,"THE EMERGING PATTERN OF YUGOSLAV-SOVIET RELATIONS." COM FUT USSR WOR+45 INT/ORG ECO/TAC FOR/AID DOMIN COERCE ATTIT PERSON ORD/FREE PWR...TIME/SEQ 20 TITO/MARSH KHRUSH/N STALIN/J. PAGE 38 A0783
TOP/EX DIPLOM YUGOSLAVIA

S62
FOCSANEANU L.,"LES GRANDS TRAITES DE LA REPUBLIQUE POPULAIRE DE CHINE." ASIA CHINA/COM COM USSR WOR+45 INT/ORG NAT/G POL/PAR ACT/RES PLAN DIPLOM EDU/PROP
VOL/ASSN TOTALISM

...CONCPT TIME/SEQ 20 TREATY. PAGE 47 A0957

S62
FOSTER W.C.,"ARMS CONTROL AND DISARMAMENT IN A DIVIDED WORLD." COM FUT USA+45 USSR WOR+45 INTELL INT/ORG NAT/G VOL/ASSN CONSULT CREATE PLAN TEC/DEV EDU/PROP LEGIT NUC/PWR ATTIT RIGID/FLEX...CONCPT TREND TOT/POP 20 UN. PAGE 47 A0971
DELIB/GP POLICY ARMS/CONT DIPLOM

S62
KOLARZ W.,"THE IMPACT OF COMMUNISM ON WEST AFRICA." AFR FUT SOCIETY INT/ORG NAT/G CREATE PLAN DOMIN EDU/PROP COERCE NAT/LISM ATTIT RIGID/FLEX SOCISM ...POLICY CONCPT TREND MARX/KARL 20. PAGE 81 A1666
COM POL/PAR COLONIAL

S62
LONDON K.,"SINO-SOVIET RELATIONS IN THE CONTEXT OF THE 'WORLD SOCIALIST SYSTEM'." ASIA CHINA/COM COM USSR INT/ORG NAT/G TOP/EX BAL/PWR DIPLOM DOMIN ATTIT PERCEPT RIGID/FLEX PWR MARXISM...METH/CNCPT TREND 20. PAGE 91 A1854
DELIB/GP CONCPT SOCISM

S62
NANES A.,"DISARMAMENT: THE LAST SEVEN YEARS." COM EUR+WWI USA+45 USSR INT/ORG FORCES TOP/EX CREATE LEGIT NUC/PWR DISPL ORD/FREE...CONCPT TIME/SEQ CON/ANAL 20. PAGE 107 A2195
DELIB/GP RIGID/FLEX ARMS/CONT

S62
SCOTT J.B.,"ANGLO-SOVIET TRADE AND ITS EFFECTS ON THE COMMONWEALTH." COM FUT UK USSR WOR+45 ECO/DEV MARKET INT/ORG CONSULT WEALTH...POLICY TREND CMN/WLTH 20. PAGE 130 A2673
NAT/G ECO/TAC

S62
SPECTOR I.,"SOVIET POLICY IN ASIA: A REAPPRAISAL." ASIA CHINA/COM COM INDIA INDONESIA ECO/UNDEV INT/ORG DOMIN EDU/PROP REGION RESPECT...CONCPT TREND TOT/POP COLD/WAR 20 CHINJAP. PAGE 135 A2774
S/ASIA PWR FOR/AID USSR

S62
STRACHEY J.,"COMMUNIST INTENTIONS." ASIA USSR YUGOSLAVIA INT/ORG NAT/G FORCES DOMIN EDU/PROP COERCE NUC/PWR NAT/LISM PEACE RIGID/FLEX PWR MARXISM...CONCPT MYTH OBS TIME/SEQ TREND COLD/WAR TOT/POP 20. PAGE 139 A2843
COM ATTIT WAR

S62
THOMAS J.R.T.,"SOVIET BEHAVIOR IN THE QUEMOY CRISES OF 1958." CHINA/COM FUT USSR WOR+45 INT/ORG VOL/ASSN FORCES PLAN BAL/PWR DOMIN COERCE NUC/PWR REV WAR ATTIT DRIVE ORD/FREE...POLICY OBS RECORD COLD/WAR FOR/POL 20. PAGE 143 A2923
COM PWR

S62
TOWSTER J.,"THE USSR AND THE USA: CHALLENGE AND RESPONSE." COM GERMANY USA+45 USSR WOR+45 ECO/UNDEV INT/ORG VOL/ASSN EX/STRUC FORCES TOP/EX CREATE PLAN TEC/DEV DIPLOM ECO/TAC EDU/PROP COLONIAL COERCE PWR ...GEN/METH COLD/WAR 20 KENNEDY/JF. PAGE 145 A2956
ACT/RES GEN/LAWS

B63
ABSHIRE D.M.,NATIONAL SECURITY: POLITICAL, MILITARY, AND ECONOMIC STRATEGIES IN THE DECADE AHEAD. ASIA COM USA+45 WOR+45 ECO/DEV ECO/UNDEV INT/ORG DELIB/GP FORCES ECO/TAC COERCE ATTIT RIGID/FLEX HEALTH ORD/FREE PWR WEALTH...POLICY STAT CHARTS ANTHOL COLD/WAR VAL/FREE. PAGE 4 A0083
FUT ACT/RES BAL/PWR

B63
AFRICAN BIBLIOGRAPHIC CENTER,THE SCENE IS GUINEA AND THE PERSONAGE IS SEKOU TOURE: A SELECTED CURRENT READING LIST, 1959-1962 (PAMPHLET). GUINEA ECO/UNDEV CHIEF FOR/AID COLONIAL...BIOG 20. PAGE 5 A0095
BIBLIOG AFR POL/PAR COM

B63
BRZEZINSKI Z.K.,AFRICA AND THE COMMUNIST WORLD. AFR ASIA COM CULTURE SOCIETY INT/ORG DELIB/GP ACT/RES ECO/TAC COERCE ORD/FREE PWR WEALTH...STAT TOT/POP VAL/FREE 20. PAGE 21 A0418
ATTIT EDU/PROP DIPLOM USSR

B63
DALLIN A.,DIVERSITY IN INTERNATIONAL COMMUNISM: A DOCUMENTARY RECORD, 1961-1963. CHINA/COM CHIEF PRESS WRITING DEBATE LEAD...POLICY ANTHOL 20. PAGE 33 A0677
COM DIPLOM POL/PAR CONFER

B63
FULBRIGHT J.W.,PROSPECTS FOR THE WEST. COM USA+45 USSR INT/ORG NAT/G SCHOOL PROB/SOLV NUC/PWR WAR PEACE ORD/FREE...PREDICT METH/COMP 20 DEGAULLE/C. PAGE 50 A1015
DIPLOM BAL/PWR CONCPT POLICY

B63
GILBERT M.,THE APPEASERS. COM GERMANY UK PLAN ECO/TAC COLONIAL CONTROL EXEC ORD/FREE PWR FASCISM 20 PARLIAMENT. PAGE 52 A1068
DIPLOM WAR POLICY DECISION

B63
GOLDWIN R.A.,FOREIGN AND MILITARY POLICY. COM USSR WOR+45 ECO/DEV INT/ORG FORCES PLAN ECO/TAC REGION ARMS/CONT MARXISM 20 UN. PAGE 54 A1097
DIPLOM POLICY PWR NAT/G

B63
HALASZ DE BEKY I.L.,A BIBLIOGRAPHY OF THE HUNGARIAN REVOLUTION 1956. COM HUNGARY USSR DIPLOM COERCE MARXISM...POLICY AUD/VIS 20 UN COLD/WAR. PAGE 59 A1221
BIBLIOG REV FORCES ATTIT

B63
HENDERSON W.,SOUTHEAST ASIA: PROBLEMS OF UNITED STATES POLICY. COM S/ASIA CULTURE STRATA ECO/UNDEV INT/ORG DELIB/GP ACT/RES ECO/TAC DOMIN EDU/PROP LEGIT COERCE ATTIT ALL/VALS...STAT`TIME/SEQ ANTHOL VAL/FREE 20. PAGE 64 A1313
ASIA USA+45 DIPLOM

B63
HYDE D.,THE PEACEFUL ASSAULT. COM UAR USSR ECO/DEV ECO/UNDEV NAT/G POL/PAR CAP/ISM PWR 20. PAGE 69 A1427
MARXISM CONTROL ECO/TAC DIPLOM

B63
JACOBSON H.K.,THE USSR AND THE UN'S ECONOMIC AND SOCIAL ACTIVITIES. COM WOR+45 DELIB/GP ACT/RES ECO/TAC EDU/PROP RIGID/FLEX SUPEGO HEALTH PWR SKILL ...POLICY CHARTS GEN/METH VAL/FREE UNESCO 20 UN. PAGE 73 A1487
INT/ORG ATTIT USSR

B63
LERCHE C.O. JR.,AMERICA IN WORLD AFFAIRS. COM UK USA+45 INT/ORG FORCES ECO/TAC INT/TRADE EDU/PROP WAR NAT/LISM PEACE...BIBLIOG 18/20 UN CONGRESS PRESIDENT COLD/WAR. PAGE 87 A1783
NAT/G DIPLOM PLAN

B63
NORTH R.C.,CONTENT ANALYSIS: A HANDBOOK WITH APPLICATIONS FOR THE STUDY OF INTERNATIONAL CRISIS. ASIA COM EUR+WWI MOD/EUR INT/ORG TEC/DEV DOMIN EDU/PROP ROUTINE COERCE PERCEPT RIGID/FLEX ALL/VALS ...QUANT TESTS CON/ANAL SIMUL GEN/LAWS VAL/FREE. PAGE 110 A2252
METH/CNCPT COMPUT/IR USSR

B63
PIKE F.B.,CHILE AND THE UNITED STATES 1880-1962: THE EMERGENCE OF CHILE'S CRISIS AND THE CHALLENGE TO US DIPLOMACY. CHILE COM USA+45 USA-45 SOCIETY STRATA ECO/UNDEV...MYTH 19/20. PAGE 116 A2378
FOR/AID DIPLOM ATTIT STRUCT

B63
SMITH J.E.,THE DEFENSE OF BERLIN. COM GUATEMALA WOR+45 ECO/TAC ADMIN NEUTRAL ATTIT ORD/FREE SOVEREIGN...DECISION 20 DEPT/STATE. PAGE 134 A2747
DIPLOM FORCES BAL/PWR PLAN

B63
STEVENSON A.E.,LOOKING OUTWARD: YEARS OF CRISIS AT THE UNITED NATIONS. COM CUBA USA+45 WOR+45 SOCIETY NAT/G EX/STRUC ACT/RES LEGIT COLONIAL ATTIT PERSON SUPEGO ALL/VALS...POLICY HUM UN COLD/WAR CONGO 20. PAGE 138 A2823
INT/ORG CONCPT ARMS/CONT

B63
SWEARER H.R.,CONTEMPORARY COMMUNISM: THEORY AND PRACTICE. COM USSR SOCIETY ECO/DEV POL/PAR FORCES PLAN ADMIN LEAD NAT/LISM...POLICY ANTHOL 20 LENIN/VI COM/PARTY. PAGE 140 A2869
MARXISM CONCPT DIPLOM NAT/G

B63
THIEN T.T.,INDIA AND SOUTHEAST ASIA 1947-1960. COM INDIA S/ASIA SECT DELIB/GP FOR/AID RACE/REL NAT/LISM SOCISM...CHARTS BIBLIOG 20 UN NEHRU/J TREATY. PAGE 143 A2917
DRIVE DIPLOM POLICY

B63
TUCKER R.C.,THE SOVIET POLITICAL MIND. WOR+45 ELITES INT/ORG NAT/G POL/PAR PLAN DIPLOM ECO/TAC DOMIN ADMIN NUC/PWR REV DRIVE PERSON SUPEGO PWR WEALTH...POLICY MGT PSY CONCPT OBS BIOG TREND COLD/WAR MARX/KARL 20. PAGE 145 A2972
COM TOP/EX USSR

L63
MOUSKHELY M.,"LE BLOC COMMUNISTE ET LA COMMUNAUTE ECONOMIQUE EUROPEENNE." AFR COM EUR+WWI FUT USSR WOR+45 INTELL ECO/UNDEV LABOR POL/PAR NUC/PWR RIGID/FLEX...TIME/SEQ ORG/CHARTS EEC TOT/POP 20. PAGE 105 A2158
INT/ORG ECO/DEV

L63
SZASZY E.,"L'EVOLUTION DES PRINCIPES GENERAUX DU DROIT INTERNATIONAL PRIVE DANS LES PAYS DE DEMOCRATIE POPULAIRE." COM FUT WOR+45 LAW ECO/DEV PERF/ART POL/PAR PROF/ORG ECO/TAC INT/TRADE EDU/PROP ATTIT RIGID/FLEX ALL/VALS SOCISM...JURID TREND GEN/LAWS WORK 20. PAGE 141 A2876
DIPLOM TOTALISM INT/LAW INT/ORG

S63
ALEXANDER R.,"LATIN AMERICA AND THE COMMUNIST BLOC." ASIA COM CUBA L/A+17C USA+45 USSR NAT/G VOL/ASSN TEC/DEV FOR/AID LEGIT PWR WEALTH COLD/WAR 20. PAGE 6 A0112
ECO/UNDEV RECORD

S63
BECHHOEFER B.G.,"UNITED NATIONS PROCEDURES IN CASE OF VIOLATIONS OF DISARMAMENT AGREEMENTS." COM USA+45 USSR LAW CONSTN NAT/G EX/STRUC FORCES LEGIS BAL/PWR EDU/PROP CT/SYS ARMS/CONT ORD/FREE PWR ...POLICY STERTYP UN VAL/FREE 20. PAGE 12 A0245
INT/ORG DELIB/GP

S63
COSER L.,"AMERICA AND THE WORLD REVOLUTION." COM FUT USA+45 WOR+45 INTELL SOCIETY NAT/G ECO/TAC EDU/PROP ALL/VALS SOCISM...PSY GEN/LAWS TOT/POP 20 COLD/WAR. PAGE 31 A0629
ECO/UNDEV PLAN FOR/AID DIPLOM

S63
DARLING F.C.,"THE GEOPOLITICS OF AMERICAN FOREIGN POLITICS IN ASIA." COM S/ASIA USA+45 USSR ECO/UNDEV NAT/G VOL/ASSN CONSULT PLAN GUERRILLA...STAT TOT/POP 20. PAGE 34 A0682
FORCES ECO/TAC FOR/AID DIPLOM

S63
ETIENNE G.,"'LOIS OBJECTIVES' ET PROBLEMES DE DEVELOPPEMENT DANS LE CONTEXTE CHINE-URSS." ASIA
TOTALISM USSR

CHINA/COM COM FUT STRUCT INT/ORG VOL/ASSN TOP/EX TEC/DEV ECO/TAC ATTIT RIGID/FLEX...GEOG MGT TIME/SEQ TOT/POP 20. PAGE 42 A0866

S63
GIRAUD E.,"L'INTERDICTION DU RECOURS A LA FORCE, LA THEORIE ET LA PRATIQUE DES NATIONS UNIES." ALGERIA COM CUBA HUNGARY WOR+45 ADJUD TOTALISM ATTIT RIGID/FLEX PWR...POLICY JURID CONCPT UN 20 CONGO. PAGE 53 A1077
INT/ORG FORCES DIPLOM

S63
GUPTA S.C.,"INDIA AND THE SOVIET UNION." CHINA/COM COM INDIA S/ASIA VOL/ASSN TOP/EX FOR/AID EDU/PROP PEACE PWR...RECORD COLD/WAR 20. PAGE 58 A1195
DISPL MYTH USSR

S63
HORVATH J.,"MOSCOW'S AID PROGRAM: THE PERFORMANCE SO FAR." COM FUT USSR WOR+45 ECO/DEV FINAN PLAN TEC/DEV FOR/AID EDU/PROP ATTIT ORD/FREE PWR WEALTH ...POLICY STAT CHARTS VAL/FREE 20. PAGE 68 A1389
ECO/UNDEV ECO/TAC

S63
MACWHINNEY E.,"LES CONCEPT SOVIETIQUE DE 'COEXISTENCE PACIFIQUE' ET LES RAPPORTS JURIDIQUES ENTRE L'URSS ET LES ETATS OCIDENTAUX." COM FUT WOR+45 LAW CULTURE INTELL POL/PAR ACT/RES BAL/PWR ...INT/LAW 20. PAGE 93 A1903
NAT/G CONCPT DIPLOM USSR

S63
NEIDLE A.F.,"PEACE KEEPING AND DISARMAMENT." COM USA+45 USSR WOR+45 INT/ORG NAT/G BAL/PWR EDU/PROP LEGIT ATTIT PWR 20. PAGE 108 A2214
DELIB/GP ACT/RES ARMS/CONT PEACE

S63
NOGEE J.L.,"PROPOGANDA AND NEGOTIATION: THE CASE OF THE TEN NATION DISARMAMENT COMMITTEE." COM EUR+WWI USA+45 VOL/ASSN DELIB/GP FORCES DIPLOM DOMIN LEGIT PWR...METH/CNCPT STERTYP COLD/WAR VAL/FREE 20. PAGE 110 A2248
INT/ORG EDU/PROP ARMS/CONT

S63
PHELPS J.,"INFORMATION AND ARMS CONTROL." COM SPACE USA+45 USSR WOR+45 R+D INT/ORG NAT/G DELIB/GP DIPLOM ORD/FREE...CONCPT 20. PAGE 116 A2374
KNOWL ARMS/CONT NUC/PWR

S63
RAMERIE L.,"TENSION AU SEIN DU COMECON: LE CAS ROUMAIN." COM EUR+WWI USSR WOR+45 ECO/DEV DIST/IND NAT/G POL/PAR VOL/ASSN EDU/PROP TOTALISM ATTIT WEALTH...TIME/SEQ 20 COMECON. PAGE 119 A2438
INT/ORG ECO/TAC INT/TRADE ROMANIA

S63
SONNENFELDT H.,"FOREIGN POLICY FROM MALENKOV TO KHRUSHCHEV." WOR+45 NAT/G FORCES BAL/PWR DIPLOM ECO/TAC COERCE ATTIT PWR...CONCPT HIST/WRIT COLD/WAR 20. PAGE 135 A2768
COM DOMIN FOR/AID USSR

S63
SPINELLI A.,"IL TRATTATO DI MOSCA E I PROBLEMI DELLA COESISTENZA PACIFICA." CHINA/COM COM FRANCE FUT WOR+45 INT/ORG VOL/ASSN PEACE...POLICY MYTH 20. PAGE 136 A2788
ATTIT ARMS/CONT TOTALISM

S63
WOLF C.,"SOME ASPECTS OF THE 'VALUE' OF LESS-DEVELOPED COUNTRIES TO THE UNITED STATES." ASIA CHINA/COM COM USA+45 USSR ECO/UNDEV BAL/PWR ECO/TAC FOR/AID DOMIN EDU/PROP ATTIT PWR...POLICY METH/CNCPT CONT/OBS TREND CHARTS 20. PAGE 166 A3379
CONCPT GEN/LAWS DIPLOM

C63
CHARLETON W.G.,"THE REVOLUTION IN AMERICAN FOREIGN POLICY." COM PROB/SOLV FOR/AID DOMIN COLONIAL NEUTRAL DETER WAR ISOLAT NAT/LISM...BIBLIOG 19/20 UN COLD/WAR NATO. PAGE 26 A0523
DIPLOM INT/ORG BAL/PWR

B64
BELL C.,THE DEBATABLE ALLIANCE. COM UK USA+45 NAT/G FORCES PLAN BAL/PWR NUC/PWR WAR ATTIT...GOV/COMP 20. PAGE 13 A0256
DIPLOM PWR PEACE POLICY

B64
CHENG C.,ECONOMIC RELATIONS BETWEEN PEKING AND MOSCOW: 1949-63. ASIA CHINA/COM COM USSR FINAN INDUS CONSULT TEC/DEV INT/TRADE...PREDICT CHARTS BIBLIOG 20. PAGE 26 A0527
DIPLOM FOR/AID MARXISM

B64
COFFIN F.M.,WITNESS FOR AID. COM EUR+WWI USA+45 DIPLOM GP/REL CONSEN ORD/FREE MARXISM...NEW/IDEA 20 CONGRESS AID. PAGE 27 A0557
FOR/AID ECO/UNDEV DELIB/GP PLAN

B64
COHEN M.,LAW AND POLITICS IN SPACE: SPECIFIC AND URGENT PROBLEMS IN THE LAW OF OUTER SPACE. CHINA/COM COM USA+45 USSR WOR+45 COM/IND INT/ORG NAT/G LEGIT NUC/PWR ATTIT BIO/SOC...JURID CONCPT CONGRESS 20 STALIN/J. PAGE 28 A0561
DELIB/GP LAW INT/LAW SPACE

B64
DALLIN A.,THE SOVIET UNION, ARMS CONTROL AND DISARMAMENT. COM INT/ORG VOL/ASSN EX/STRUC DIPLOM NUC/PWR ATTIT PWR TOT/POP COLD/WAR 20. PAGE 33 A0678
ORD/FREE ARMS/CONT USSR

B64
DUROSELLE J.B.,LA COMMUNAUTE INTERNATIONALE FACE AUX JEUNES ETATS. CHINA/COM COM S/ASIA USSR INT/ORG ROLE...ANTHOL 20 UN SEATO THIRD/WRLD. PAGE 40 A0808
DIPLOM COLONIAL ECO/UNDEV SOVEREIGN

B64
DUTT R.P.,THE INTERNATIONALE. COM WOR+45 WOR-45 WORKER CAP/ISM WAR ATTIT...TREND GEN/LAWS 18/20 COM/PARTY. PAGE 40 A0813
ALL/IDEOS INT/ORG MARXIST ORD/FREE

B64
EHRENBURG I.,THE WAR: 1941-1945 (VOL. V OF "MEN, YEARS - LIFE," TRANS. BY TATIANA SHEBUNINA). GERMANY USSR PRESS WRITING PERS/REL PEACE ANOMIE ATTIT PERSON...CONCPT RECORD BIOG 20 STALIN/J HITLER/A. PAGE 40 A0827
WAR DIPLOM COM MARXIST

B64
FISHER R.,INTERNATIONAL CONFLICT AND BEHAVIORAL SCIENCE: THE CRAIGVILLE PAPERS. COM FUT USA+45 WOR+45 NAT/G DELIB/GP EX/STRUC FORCES ECO/TAC DOMIN EDU/PROP LEGIT COERCE ATTIT PERCEPT ORD/FREE PWR RESPECT...PSY SOC VAL/FREE. PAGE 46 A0940
INT/ORG PLAN DIPLOM

B64
FREYMOND J.,WESTERN EUROPE SINCE THE WAR. COM EUR+WWI USA+45 DIPLOM...BIBLIOG 20 NATO UN EEC. PAGE 49 A1001
INT/ORG POLICY ECO/DEV ECO/TAC

B64
GJUPANOVIC H.,LEGAL SOURCES AND BIBLIOGRAPHY OF YUGOSLAVIA. COM YUGOSLAVIA LAW LEGIS DIPLOM ADMIN PARL/PROC REGION CRIME CENTRAL 20. PAGE 53 A1078
BIBLIOG/A JURID CONSTN ADJUD

B64
GRIFFITH W.E.,COMMUNISM IN EUROPE (2 VOLS.). CZECHOSLVK USSR WOR+45 WOR-45 YUGOSLAVIA INGP/REL MARXISM SOCISM...ANTHOL 20 EUROPE/E. PAGE 57 A1162
COM POL/PAR DIPLOM GOV/COMP

B64
GRZYBOWSKI K.,THE SOCIALIST COMMONWEALTH OF NATIONS: ORGANIZATIONS AND INSTITUTIONS. FORCES DIPLOM INT/TRADE ADJUD ADMIN LEAD WAR MARXISM SOCISM...BIBLIOG 20 COMECON WARSAW/P. PAGE 58 A1185
INT/LAW COM REGION INT/ORG

B64
HAMRELL S.,THE SOVIET BLOC, CHINA, AND AFRICA. AFR CHINA/COM COM USSR ECO/UNDEV EDU/PROP 20. PAGE 61 A1249
MARXISM DIPLOM CONTROL FOR/AID

B64
IKLE F.C.,HOW NATIONS NEGOTIATE. COM EUR+WWI USA+45 INTELL INT/ORG VOL/ASSN DELIB/GP ACT/RES CREATE DOMIN EDU/PROP ADJUD ROUTINE ATTIT PERSON ORD/FREE RESPECT SKILL...PSY SOC OBS VAL/FREE. PAGE 70 A1433
NAT/G PWR POLICY

B64
IRISH M.D.,WORLD PRESSURES ON AMERICAN FOREIGN POLICY. ASIA COM L/A+17C SOUTH/AFR UK WOR+45 ECO/DEV ECO/UNDEV COLONIAL SANCTION COERCE REV TOTALISM...ANTHOL 20 COLD/WAR EUROPE/W INTERVENT. PAGE 72 A1467
DIPLOM POLICY

B64
KEEP J.,CONTEMPORARY HISTORY IN THE SOVIET MIRROR. COM USSR POL/PAR CREATE DIPLOM AGREE WAR ATTIT ...MYTH TREND ANTHOL 20 COLD/WAR STALIN/J MARX/KARL LENIN/VI. PAGE 77 A1576
HIST/WRIT METH MARXISM IDEA/COMP

B64
KIS T.I.,LES PAYS DE L'EUROPE DE L'EST: LEURS RAPPORTS MUTUELS ET LE PROBLEME DE LEUR INTEGRATION DANS L'ORBITE DE L'USSR. EUR+WWI RUSSIA USSR INT/ORG NAT/G REV ATTIT...JURID SOC BIBLIOG WARSAW/P COMECON EUROPE/E. PAGE 80 A1638
DIPLOM COM MARXISM REGION

B64
KOLARZ W.,BOOKS ON COMMUNISM. USSR WOR+45 CULTURE NAT/G POL/PAR DIPLOM LEAD...CONCPT GOV/COMP IDEA/COMP. PAGE 81 A1667
BIBLIOG/A SOCIETY COM MARXISM

B64
LENS S.,THE FUTILE CRUSADE. ASIA CHINA/COM L/A+17C USA+45 USSR WOR+45 ECO/DEV BAL/PWR DIPLOM NUC/PWR WAR NAT/LISM PEACE 20 COLD/WAR PRESIDENT CIA. PAGE 87 A1774
ORD/FREE ANOMIE COM MARXISM

B64
MAUD J.,AID FOR DEVELOPING COUNTRIES. COM EUR+WWI UK INT/TRADE ORD/FREE...GOV/COMP 20. PAGE 96 A1979
FOR/AID DIPLOM ECO/TAC ECO/UNDEV

B64
PENNOCK J.R.,SELF-GOVERNMENT IN MODERNIZING NATIONS. AFR COM USA+45 ECO/DEV POL/PAR PROB/SOLV DIPLOM ECO/TAC COLONIAL REV POPULISM SOCISM 20. PAGE 114 A2350
ECO/UNDEV POLICY SOVEREIGN NAT/G

B64
RANIS G.,THE UNITED STATES AND THE DEVELOPING ECONOMIES. COM USA+45 AGRI FINAN TEC/DEV CAP/ISM ECO/TAC INT/TRADE...POLICY METH/COMP ANTHOL 20 AID. PAGE 119 A2441
ECO/UNDEV DIPLOM FOR/AID

B64
ROCK V.P.,A STRATEGY OF INTERDEPENDENCE. COM USSR WOR+45 NAT/G FORCES PROB/SOLV TEC/DEV DETER WAR ORD/FREE...CONCPT NEW/IDEA METH/COMP 20. PAGE 122 A2509
DIPLOM NUC/PWR PEACE POLICY

B64
ROSECRANCE R.N.,THE DISPERSION OF NUCLEAR WEAPONS:
EUR+WWI

STRATEGY AND POLITICS. ASIA COM FUT S/ASIA USA+45 INT/ORG NAT/G DELIB/GP FORCES ACT/RES TEC/DEV BAL/PWR COERCE DETER ATTIT RIGID/FLEX ORD/FREE ...POLICY CHARTS VAL/FREE. PAGE 123 A2530
PWR PEACE

B64
RUBINSTEIN A.Z.,THE SOVIETS IN INTERNATIONAL ORGANIZATIONS: CHANGING POLICY TOWARD DEVELOPING COUNTRIES, 1953-1963. COM DELIB/GP ACT/RES ECO/TAC EDU/PROP ADMIN ATTIT ORD/FREE PWR...INT VAL/FREE UN 20. PAGE 125 A2563
ECO/UNDEV INT/ORG USSR

B64
SINGH N.,THE DEFENCE MECHANISM OF THE MODERN STATE. COM UK USA+45 CONSTN INT/ORG NUC/PWR WAR INGP/REL ROLE 20 DEPT/DEFEN COMMONWLTH. PAGE 134 A2735
FORCES TOP/EX NAT/G CIVMIL/REL

B64
SPECTOR S.D.,A CHECKLIST OF PAPERBOUND BOOKS ON RUSSIA. USSR SECT DIPLOM EDU/PROP HEALTH...PHIL/SCI PSY SOC SOC/WK WORSHIP 20. PAGE 135 A2775
BIBLIOG COM PERF/ART

B64
TREADGOLD D.W.,THE DEVELOPMENT OF THE USSR. COM USSR ECO/DEV CREATE BAL/PWR DEBATE COLONIAL TOTALISM...HUM ANTHOL BIBLIOG 19/20. PAGE 145 A2960
MARXISM CONSERVE DIPLOM DOMIN

L64
ARMENGALD A.,"ECONOMIE ET COEXISTENCE." COM EUR+WWI FUT USA+45 WOR+45 ECO/DEV ECO/UNDEV FINAN INT/ORG NAT/G EXEC CHOOSE ATTIT ALL/VALS...POLICY RELATIV DECISION TREND SOC/EXP COLD/WAR WORK 20. PAGE 9 A0173
MARKET ECO/TAC CAP/ISM

L64
CAMPBELL J.C.,"THE MIDDLE EAST IN THE MUTED COLD WAR." COM EUR+WWI UAR USA+45 USSR STRUCT ECO/UNDEV NAT/G VOL/ASSN EX/STRUC TOP/EX DIPLOM ECO/TAC EDU/PROP...TIME/SEQ COLD/WAR 20. PAGE 23 A0475
ISLAM FOR/AID NAT/LISM

L64
KORBONSKI A.,"COMECON." ASIA ECO/DEV ECO/UNDEV ECO/TAC BAL/PAY NAT/LISM 20 COMECON. PAGE 81 A1671
COM INT/ORG INT/TRADE

L64
MILLIS W.,"THE DEMILITARIZED WORLD." COM USA+45 USSR WOR+45 CONSTN NAT/G EX/STRUC PLAN LEGIT ATTIT DRIVE...CONCPT TIME/SEQ STERTYP TOT/POP COLD/WAR 20. PAGE 102 A2085
FUT INT/ORG BAL/PWR PEACE

L64
POUNDS N.J.G.,"THE POLITICS OF PARTITION." AFR ASIA COM EUR+WWI FUT ISLAM S/ASIA USA-45 LAW ECO/DEV ECO/UNDEV AGRI INDUS INT/ORG POL/PAR PROVS SECT FORCES TOP/EX EDU/PROP LEGIT ATTIT MORAL ORD/FREE PWR RESPECT WEALTH. PAGE 117 A2402
NAT/G NAT/LISM

L64
WARD C.,"THE 'NEW MYTHS' AND 'OLD REALITIES' OF NUCLEAR WAR." COM FUT USA+45 USSR WOR+45 INT/ORG NAT/G DOMIN LEGIT EXEC ATTIT PERCEPT ALL/VALS ...POLICY RELATIV PSY MYTH TREND 20. PAGE 161 A3280
FORCES COERCE ARMS/CONT NUC/PWR

S64
BEIM D.,"THE COMMUNIST BLOC AND THE FOREIGN-AID GAME." WOR+45 NAT/G PLAN ROUTINE ATTIT KNOWL ORD/FREE...DECISION QUANT CONT/OBS TIME/SEQ CHARTS GAME SIMUL COLD/WAR 20. PAGE 12 A0252
COM ECO/UNDEV ECO/TAC FOR/AID

S64
COFFEY J.,"THE SOVIET VIEW OF A DISARMED WORLD." COM USA+45 INT/ORG NAT/G EX/STRUC EDU/PROP COERCE PERCEPT ORD/FREE PWR...TREND STERTYP VAL/FREE 20 UN. PAGE 27 A0556
FORCES ATTIT ARMS/CONT USSR

S64
CRANE R.D.,"BASIC PRINCIPLES IN SOVIET SPACE LAW." FUT WOR+45 AIR INT/ORG DIPLOM DOMIN ARMS/CONT COERCE NUC/PWR PEACE ATTIT DRIVE PWR...INT/LAW METH/CNCPT NEW/IDEA OBS TREND GEN/LAWS VAL/FREE MARX/KARL 20. PAGE 32 A0659
COM LAW USSR SPACE

S64
GARDNER R.N.,"THE SOVIET UNION AND THE UNITED NATIONS." WOR+45 FINAN POL/PAR VOL/ASSN FORCES ECO/TAC DOMIN EDU/PROP LEGIT ADJUD ADMIN ARMS/CONT COERCE ATTIT ALL/VALS...POLICY MAJORIT CONCPT OBS TIME/SEQ TREND STERTYP UN. PAGE 51 A1046
COM INT/ORG USSR

S64
GARMARNIKOW M.,"INFLUENCE-BUYING IN WEST AFRICA." COM FUT USSR INTELL NAT/G PLAN TEC/DEV ECO/TAC DOMIN EDU/PROP REGION NAT/LISM ATTIT DRIVE ALL/VALS SOVEREIGN...POLICY PSY SOC CONCPT TREND STERTYP WORK COLD/WAR 20. PAGE 51 A1049
AFR ECO/UNDEV FOR/AID SOCISM

S64
GINSBURGS G.,"WARS OF NATIONAL LIBERATION - THE SOVIET THESIS." COM USSR WOR+45 WOR-45 LAW CULTURE INT/ORG DIPLOM LEGIT COLONIAL GUERRILLA WAR NAT/LISM ATTIT PERSON MORAL PWR...JURID OBS TREND MARX/KARL 20. PAGE 53 A1075
COERCE CONCPT INT/LAW REV

S64
GRZYBOWSKI K.,"INTERNATIONAL ORGANIZATIONS FROM THE SOVIET POINT OF VIEW." WOR+45 WOR-45 CULTURE ECO/DEV VOL/ASSN EDU/PROP ATTIT RIGID/FLEX KNOWL ...SOC OBS TIME/SEQ TREND GEN/LAWS VAL/FREE ILO UN 20. PAGE 58 A1184
COM INT/ORG DIPLOM USSR

S64
HORECKY P.L.,"LIBRARY OF CONGRESS PUBLICATIONS IN AID OF USSR AND EAST EUROPEAN RESEARCH." BULGARIA CZECHOSLVK POLAND USSR YUGOSLAVIA NAT/G POL/PAR DIPLOM ADMIN GOV/REL...CLASSIF 20. PAGE 67 A1382
BIBLIOG/A COM MARXISM

S64
KARPOV P.V.,"PEACEFUL COEXISTENCE AND INTERNATIONAL LAW." WOR+45 LAW SOCIETY INT/ORG VOL/ASSN FORCES CREATE CAP/ISM DIPLOM ADJUD NUC/PWR PEACE MORAL ORD/FREE PWR MARXISM...MARXIST JURID CONCPT OBS TREND COLD/WAR MARX/KARL 20. PAGE 77 A1568
COM ATTIT INT/LAW USSR

S64
KISSINGER H.A.,"COALITION DIPLOMACY IN A NUCLEAR AGE." COM EUR+WWI USA+45 WOR+45 INT/ORG NAT/G FORCES ACT/RES DOMIN LEGIT COERCE PERCEPT ALL/VALS ...POLICY TOT/POP 20. PAGE 80 A1644
CONSULT ATTIT DIPLOM NUC/PWR

S64
LERNER W.,"THE HISTORICAL ORIGINS OF THE SOVIET DOCTRINE OF PEACEFUL COEXISTENCE." COM USSR INT/ORG NAT/G VOL/ASSN PLAN PEACE ATTIT RIGID/FLEX PWR MARXISM...TIME/SEQ COLD/WAR 20. PAGE 87 A1788
EDU/PROP DIPLOM

S64
LIPSON L.,"PEACEFUL COEXISTENCE." COM USSR WOR+45 LAW INT/ORG DIPLOM LEGIT ADJUD ORD/FREE...CONCPT OBS TREND GEN/LAWS VAL/FREE COLD/WAR 20. PAGE 90 A1834
ATTIT JURID INT/LAW PEACE

S64
MAGGS P.B.,"SOVIET VIEWPOINT ON NUCLEAR WEAPONS IN INTERNATIONAL LAW." USSR WOR+45 INT/ORG FORCES DIPLOM ARMS/CONT ATTIT ORD/FREE PWR...POLICY JURID CONCPT OBS TREND CON/ANAL GEN/LAWS VAL/FREE 20. PAGE 93 A1905
COM LAW INT/LAW NUC/PWR

S64
PESELT B.M.,"COMMUNIST ECONOMIC OFFENSIVE." WOR+45 SOCIETY INT/ORG PLAN ECO/TAC DOMIN EDU/PROP ATTIT PERSON PWR WEALTH...TREND CHARTS 20. PAGE 115 A2366
COM ECO/UNDEV FOR/AID USSR

S64
RUBINSTEIN A.Z.,"THE SOVIET IMAGE OF WESTERN EUROPE." COM EUR+WWI FRANCE GERMANY GERMANY/W USA+45 USSR INT/ORG NAT/G VOL/ASSN FORCES TOP/EX BAL/PWR EDU/PROP ORD/FREE PWR...MYTH RECORD NATO EEC 20. PAGE 125 A2564
RIGID/FLEX ATTIT

S64
TRISKA J.F.,"SOVIET TREATY LAW: A QUANTITATIVE ANALYSIS." WOR+45 LAW ECO/UNDEV AGRI COM/IND INDUS CREATE TEC/DEV DIPLOM ATTIT PWR WEALTH...JURID SAMP TIME/SEQ TREND CHARTS VAL/FREE 20 TREATY. PAGE 145 A2967
COM ECO/TAC INT/LAW USSR

B65
BROMKE A.,THE COMMUNIST STATES AT THE CROSSROADS BETWEEN MOSCOW AND PEKING. CHINA/COM USSR INGP/REL NAT/LISM TOTALISM 20. PAGE 19 A0389
COM DIPLOM MARXISM REGION

B65
DAVISON W.P.,INTERNATIONAL POLITICAL COMMUNICATION. COM USA+45 WOR+45 CULTURE ECO/UNDEV NAT/G PROB/SOLV PRESS TV ADMIN 20 FILM. PAGE 34 A0693
EDU/PROP DIPLOM PERS/REL COM/IND

B65
FRASER S.,GOVERNMENTAL POLICY AND INTERNATIONAL EDUCATION. CHINA/COM COM USA+45 WOR+45 CONTROL MARXISM...ANTHOL BIBLIOG/A 20 UN. PAGE 48 A0989
EDU/PROP DIPLOM POLICY NAT/G

B65
JOHNSON H.G.,THE WORLD ECONOMY AT THE CROSSROADS. COM WOR-45 ECO/DEV AGRI INDUS INT/TRADE REGION NAT/LISM 20. PAGE 74 A1523
FINAN DIPLOM INT/ORG ECO/UNDEV

B65
LERCHE C.O.,THE COLD WAR AND AFTER. AFR COM S/ASIA USA+45 USSR NUC/PWR SOVEREIGN MARXISM...TIME/SEQ TREND BIBLIOG 20 COLD/WAR. PAGE 87 A1784
DIPLOM BAL/PWR IDEA/COMP

B65
MALLIN J.,FORTRESS CUBA; RUSSIA'S AMERICAN BASE. COM CUBA L/A+17C FORCES PLAN DIPLOM LEAD REV WAR ...POLICY 20 CASTRO/F GUEVARA/C INTERVENT. PAGE 93 A1914
MARXISM CHIEF GUERRILLA DOMIN

B65
MOSTECKY V.,SOVIET LEGAL BIBLIOGRAPHY. USSR LEGIS PRESS WRITING CONFER ADJUD CT/SYS REV MARXISM ...INT/LAW JURID DICTIONARY 20. PAGE 105 A2155
BIBLIOG/A LAW COM CONSTN

B65
ROMEIN J.,THE ASIAN CENTURY. ASIA COM S/ASIA DIPLOM COLONIAL TIME 20. PAGE 123 A2519
REV NAT/LISM CULTURE MARXISM

B65
ROSENBERG A.,DEMOCRACY AND SOCIALISM. COM EUR+WWI FRANCE MOD/EUR STRUCT INT/ORG NAT/G POL/PAR TOP/EX EDU/PROP COERCE PERSON PWR FASCISM MARXISM...CONCPT TIME/SEQ MARX/KARL 19/20. PAGE 124 A2535
ATTIT

B65
US DEPARTMENT OF DEFENSE,US SECURITY ARMS CONTROL, AND DISARMAMENT 1961-1965 (PAMPHLET). CHINA/COM COM
BIBLIOG/A ARMS/CONT

GERMANY/W ISRAEL SPACE USA+45 USSR WOR+45 FORCES EDU/PROP DETER EQUILIB PEACE ALL/VALS...GOV/COMP 20 NATO. PAGE 151 A3077
NUC/PWR DIPLOM

B65
US DEPARTMENT OF THE ARMY,NUCLEAR WEAPONS AND THE ATLANTIC ALLIANCE: A BIBLIOGRAPHIC SURVEY. ASIA COM EUR+WWI USA+45 FORCES DIPLOM WEAPON...STAT 20 NATO. PAGE 152 A3108
BIBLIOG/A ARMS/CONT NUC/PWR BAL/PWR

B65
WINT G.,ASIA: A HANDBOOK. ASIA COM INDIA USSR CULTURE INTELL NAT/G...GEOG STAT CENSUS NAT/COMP WORSHIP 20 TREATY CHINJAP. PAGE 165 A3365
DIPLOM SOC

S65
HELMREICH E.C.,"KADAR'S HUNGARY." COM EUR+WWI HUNGARY USSR INTELL ECO/DEV AGRI INT/ORG TOP/EX DOMIN ALL/VALS WORK COLD/WAR 20. PAGE 64 A1311
NAT/G RIGID/FLEX TOTALISM

S65
HOLSTI O.R.,"EAST-WEST CONFLICT AND SINO-SOVIET RELATIONS" CHINA/COM USSR COMPUTER REGION DECISION. PAGE 67 A1373
VOL/ASSN DIPLOM CON/ANAL COM

S65
KORBONSKI A.,"USA POLICY IN EAST EUROPE." COM EUR+WWI GERMANY USA+45 CULTURE ECO/UNDEV EDU/PROP RIGID/FLEX WEALTH 20. PAGE 82 A1672
ACT/RES ECO/TAC FOR/AID

S65
RAY H.,"THE POLICY OF RUSSIA TOWARDS SINO-INDIAN CONFLICT." ASIA CHINA/COM COM INDIA USSR NAT/G TOP/EX FOR/AID EDU/PROP NEUTRAL COERCE PEACE RIGID/FLEX PWR...METH/CNCPT TIME/SEQ VAL/FREE 20. PAGE 120 A2452
S/ASIA ATTIT DIPLOM WAR

S65
ROGGER H.,"EAST GERMANY: STABLE OR IMMOBILE." COM EUR+WWI GERMANY/E NAT/G INT/TRADE DOMIN EDU/PROP COERCE TOTALISM COLD/WAR 20. PAGE 123 A2516
TOP/EX RIGID/FLEX GERMANY

C65
US AIR FORCE ACADEMY,"AMERICAN DEFENSE POLICY." COM INT/ORG TEC/DEV FOR/AID ARMS/CONT DETER NUC/PWR ...POLICY DECISION CONCPT ANTHOL BIBLIOG/A 20 COLD/WAR NATO. PAGE 149 A3054
PLAN FORCES WAR COERCE

B66
SUPPLEMENTAL FOREIGN ASSISTANCE FISCAL YEAR 1966: VIETNAM. CHINA/COM COM S/ASIA USA+45 VIETNAM EXTR/IND FINAN DIPLOM TAX GUERRILLA HABITAT ORD/FREE...STAT CHARTS 20 SENATE PRESIDENT. PAGE 4 A0077
CONFER LEGIS WAR FOR/AID

B66
BLOOMFIELD L.P.,KHRUSHCHEV AND THE ARMS RACE. USA+45 USSR ECO/DEV BAL/PWR EDU/PROP CONFER NUC/PWR ATTIT...CHARTS 20 KHRUSH/N. PAGE 16 A0321
ARMS/CONT COM POLICY DIPLOM

B66
BROWN J.F.,THE NEW EASTERN EUROPE. ALBANIA BULGARIA HUNGARY POLAND ROMANIA CULTURE AGRI POL/PAR WAR NAT/LISM MARXISM...CHARTS BIBLIOG 20. PAGE 20 A0404
DIPLOM COM NAT/G ECO/UNDEV

B66
EPSTEIN F.T.,THE AMERICAN BIBLIOGRAPHY OF RUSSIAN AND EAST EUROPEAN STUDIES FOR 1964. USSR LOC/G NAT/G POL/PAR FORCES ADMIN ARMS/CONT...JURID CONCPT 20 UN. PAGE 42 A0855
BIBLIOG COM MARXISM DIPLOM

B66
HERZ M.F.,BEGINNINGS OF THE COLD WAR. COM POLAND USA+45 USSR INT/ORG NAT/G CHIEF FOR/AID DOMIN CONFER AGREE WAR PEACE 20 STALIN/J COLD/WAR UN. PAGE 64 A1321
DIPLOM

B66
INTL CONF ON WORLD POLITICS-5,EASTERN EUROPE IN TRANSITION. EUR+WWI USSR ECO/TAC NAT/LISM ATTIT SOVEREIGN...CHARTS ANTHOL 20 TREATY WARSAW/P. PAGE 71 A1463
COM NAT/COMP MARXISM DIPLOM

B66
LONDON K.,EASTERN EUROPE IN TRANSITION. CHINA/COM USSR DOMIN COLONIAL CENTRAL RIGID/FLEX PWR...SOC ANTHOL 20. PAGE 91 A1855
SOVEREIGN COM NAT/LISM DIPLOM

B66
SKILLING H.G.,THE GOVERNMENTS OF COMMUNIST EAST EUROPE. COM EUR+WWI ELITES FORCES DIPLOM ECO/TAC CONTROL HABITAT SOCISM...DECISION BIBLIOG 20 EUROPE/E COM/PARTY. PAGE 134 A2738
MARXISM NAT/COMP GP/COMP DOMIN

B66
SPULBER N.,THE STATE AND ECONOMIC DEVELOPMENT IN EASTERN EUROPE. BULGARIA COM CZECHOSLVK HUNGARY POLAND YUGOSLAVIA CULTURE PLAN CAP/ISM INT/TRADE CONTROL...POLICY CHARTS METH/COMP BIBLIOG/A 19/20. PAGE 136 A2793
ECO/DEV ECO/UNDEV NAT/G TOTALISM

B66
US DEPARTMENT OF STATE,RESEARCH ON THE USSR AND EASTERN EUROPE (EXTERNAL RESEARCH LIST NO 1-25). USSR LAW CULTURE SOCIETY NAT/G TEC/DEV DIPLOM EDU/PROP REGION...GEOG LING. PAGE 152 A3097
BIBLIOG/A EUR+WWI COM MARXISM

B66
US DEPARTMENT OF THE ARMY,COMMUNIST CHINA: A STRATEGIC SURVEY: A BIBLIOGRAPHY (PAMPHLET NO. 20-67). CHINA/COM COM INDIA USSR NAT/G POL/PAR EX/STRUC FORCES NUC/PWR REV ATTIT...POLICY GEOG CHARTS. PAGE 152 A3109
BIBLIOG/A MARXISM S/ASIA DIPLOM

B66
US SENATE COMM ON FOREIGN REL,UNITED STATES POLICY TOWARD EUROPE (AND RELATED MATTERS). COM EUR+WWI GERMANY PROB/SOLV REGION NUC/PWR WAR NAT/LISM PEACE PWR...NAT/COMP 20 NATO CONGRESS DEGAULLE/C. PAGE 156 A3184
DIPLOM INT/ORG POLICY WOR+45

B66
WESTIN A.F.,VIEWS OF AMERICA. COM USA+45 USSR SOCIETY ECO/UNDEV POL/PAR ECO/TAC GP/REL STRANGE MARXISM...MARXIST 20. PAGE 163 A3323
CONCPT ATTIT DIPLOM IDEA/COMP

B66
ZABLOCKI C.J.,SINO-SOVIET RIVALRY. AFR ASIA CHINA/COM CUBA EUR+WWI L/A+17C USA+45 USSR WOR+45 POL/PAR FORCES COERCE NUC/PWR...GOV/COMP IDEA/COMP 20 MAO KHRUSH/N. PAGE 169 A3442
DIPLOM MARXISM COM

S66
AFRICAN BIBLIOGRAPHIC CENTER,"A DESCRIPTIVE STUDY OF CURRENT AFRICAN FOREIGN RELATIONS." COM CULTURE INT/ORG SECT RACE/REL DISCRIM ATTIT 20. PAGE 5 A0099
BIBLIOG DIPLOM AFR

S66
FRIEND A.,"THE MIDDLE EAST CRISIS" COM ISLAM ISRAEL SYRIA UAR USA+45 USSR FORCES PLAN FOR/AID CONTROL ORD/FREE PWR...SOCIALIST TIME/SEQ 20 NASSER/G. PAGE 49 A1009
WAR INT/ORG DIPLOM PEACE

S66
SKILLING H.G.,"THE RUMANIAN NATIONAL COURSE." COM EUR+WWI ROMANIA NAT/G ECO/TAC PWR 20. PAGE 134 A2739
NAT/LISM POLICY DIPLOM MARXISM

B67
ADAMS A.E.,AN ATLAS OF RUSSIAN AND EAST EUROPEAN HISTORY. CHRIST-17C COM MOD/EUR INDUS SECT FORCES DIPLOM COLONIAL REV WAR 4/20. PAGE 4 A0086
CHARTS REGION TREND

B67
BRZEZINSKI Z.K.,THE SOVIET BLOC: UNITY AND CONFLICT (2ND ED., REV., ENLARGED). COM POLAND USSR INTELL CHIEF EX/STRUC CONTROL EXEC GOV/REL PWR MARXISM ...TREND IDEA/COMP 20 LENIN/VI MARX/KARL STALIN/J. PAGE 21 A0420
NAT/G DIPLOM

B67
SHAFFER H.G.,THE COMMUNIST WORLD: MARXIST AND NON-MARXIST VIEWS. WOR+45 SOCIETY DIPLOM ECO/TAC CONTROL SOCISM...MARXIST ANTHOL BIBLIOG/A 20. PAGE 131 A2691
MARXISM NAT/COMP IDEA/COMP COM

L67
"POLITICAL PARTIES ON FOREIGN POLICY IN THE INTER-ELECTION YEARS 1962-66." ASIA COM INDIA USA+45 PLAN ATTIT...DECISION 20. PAGE 4 A0079
POL/PAR DIPLOM POLICY

S67
BREGMAN A.,"WHITHER RUSSIA?" COM RUSSIA INTELL POL/PAR DIPLOM PARTIC NAT/LISM TOTALISM ATTIT ORD/FREE 20. PAGE 18 A0370
MARXISM ELITES ADMIN CREATE

S67
DAVIS H.B.,"LENIN AND NATIONALISM: THE REDIRECTION OF THE MARXIST THEORY OF NATIONALISM." COM MOD/EUR USSR STRATA INT/ORG PLAN DOMIN COLONIAL FEDERAL ...TREND 20. PAGE 34 A0690
NAT/LISM MARXISM ATTIT CENTRAL

S67
EGBERT D.D.,"POLITICS AND ART IN COMMUNIST BULGARIA" BULGARIA COM USSR CULTURE DIPLOM INGP/REL TOTALISM...TREND 20. PAGE 40 A0825
CREATE ART/METH CONTROL MARXISM

S67
EISENDRATH C.,"THE OUTER SPACE TREATY." CHINA/COM COM USA+45 DIPLOM CONTROL NUC/PWR...INT/LAW 20 UN COLD/WAR TREATY. PAGE 41 A0831
SPACE INT/ORG PEACE ARMS/CONT

S67
FALKOWSKI M.,"SOCIALIST ECONOMISTS AND THE DEVELOPING COUNTRIES." COM PLAN TEC/DEV ROUTINE DEMAND EFFICIENCY PRODUC WEALTH...MARXIST TREND GEN/METH. PAGE 44 A0893
DIPLOM SOCISM ECO/UNDEV INDUS

S67
KAISER R.G.,"THE TRUMAN DOCTRINE* HOW IT ALL BEGAN." COM EUR+WWI USA+45 R+D INT/ORG BAL/PWR ECO/TAC PEACE TRUMAN/DOC. PAGE 76 A1550
DIPLOM ECO/UNDEV FOR/AID

S67
MOSELY P.E.,"EASTERN EUROPE IN WORLD POWER POLITICS: WHERE DE-STALINIZATION HAS LED." ECO/UNDEV NAT/LISM 20. PAGE 105 A2153
COM NAT/G DIPLOM MARXISM

S67
PAUKER G.J.,"TOWARD A NEW ORDER IN INDONESIA." COM INDONESIA S/ASIA ECO/UNDEV POL/PAR EX/STRUC TOP/EX BAL/PWR ECO/TAC FOR/AID DOMIN NAT/LISM AUTHORIT ORD/FREE PWR 20. PAGE 114 A2342
REV NAT/G DIPLOM CIVMIL/REL

S67
PEUKERT W.,"WEST GERMANY'S 'RED TRADE'." COM GERMANY INDUS CAP/ISM DOMIN SANCTION DEMAND PEACE UTIL...MARXIST 20 COLD/WAR. PAGE 115 A2371
DIPLOM ECO/TAC INT/TRADE

S67
ROSE S.,"ASIAN NATIONALISM* THE SECOND STAGE." ASIA COM ECO/UNDEV NAT/G PROB/SOLV DIPLOM FOR/AID DOMIN NEUTRAL REGION TASK...METH/COMP 20. PAGE 123 A2528
NAT/LISM S/ASIA BAL/PWR COLONIAL

C67
GEHLEN M.P.,"THE POLITICS OF COEXISTENCE: SOVIET METHODS AND MOTIVES." COM USSR NAT/G INT/TRADE EDU/PROP ARMS/CONT DETER KNOWL...CHARTS IDEA/COMP 20 COLD/WAR. PAGE 52 A1056
BIBLIOG PEACE DIPLOM MARXISM

C67
HUDSON G.F.,"THE HARD AND BITTER PEACE; WORLD POLITICS SINCE 1945." ASIA COM S/ASIA USSR WOR+45 COLONIAL WAR...TREND BIBLIOG/A 20 COLD/WAR UN. PAGE 68 A1405
DIPLOM INT/ORG ARMS/CONT BAL/PWR

C67
SPANIER J.W.,"WORLD POLITICS IN AN AGE OF REVOLUTION." COM WOR+45 FORCES COERCE WAR NAT/LISM SOVEREIGN...POLICY BIBLIOG 20. PAGE 135 A2772
DIPLOM TEC/DEV REV ECO/UNDEV

COM/IND....COMMUNICATIONS INDUSTRY

N
DOCUMENTATION ECONOMIQUE: REVUE BIBLIOGRAPHIQUE DE SYNTHESE. WOR+45 COM/IND FINAN BUDGET DIPLOM...GEOG 20. PAGE 2 A0033
BIBLIOG/A SOC

N
INDIA: A REFERENCE ANNUAL. INDIA CULTURE COM/IND R+D FORCES PLAN RECEIVE EDU/PROP HEALTH...STAT CHARTS BIBLIOG 20. PAGE 2 A0036
CONSTN LABOR INT/ORG

N
SCHOLARLY BOOKS IN AMERICA; A QUARTERLY BIBLIOGRAPHY OF UNIVERSITY PRESS PUBLICATIONS. WOR+45 AGRI COM/IND NAT/G HEALTH...GEOG PHIL/SCI PSY SOC LING 20. PAGE 3 A0046
BIBLIOG/A LAW MUNIC DIPLOM

N
KYRIAK T.E.,SOVIET UNION: BIBLIOGRAPHY INDEX TO US JPRS RESEARCH TRANSLATIONS. USSR ECO/DEV AGRI COM/IND CONSTRUC DIST/IND EXTR/IND PROC/MFG R+D INT/TRADE...SOC 20. PAGE 83 A1703
BIBLIOG/A INDUS MARXISM PRESS

N19
MORGENSTERN O.,THE COMMAND AND CONTROL STRUCTURE (PAMPHLET). USSR COM/IND INT/ORG WEAPON PEACE UTIL ...TREND 20 NATO. PAGE 104 A2132
CONTROL FORCES EFFICIENCY PLAN

B36
HUGENDUBEL P.,DIE KRIEGSMACHE DER FRANZOSISCHEN PRESSE. FRANCE GERMANY MOD/EUR COM/IND NAT/G DIPLOM DOMIN PWR 20. PAGE 69 A1412
PRESS EDU/PROP WAR ATTIT

B40
NAFZIGER R.O.,INTERNATIONAL NEWS AND THE PRESS: COMMUNICATIONS, ORGANIZATION OF NEWS-GATHERING INTERNATIONAL AFFAIRS AND FOREIGN... COM/IND FORCES WAR ATTIT...POLICY 20. PAGE 107 A2191
BIBLIOG/A PRESS DIPLOM EDU/PROP

B41
BAUMANN G.,GRUNDLAGEN UND PRAXIS DER INTERNATIONALEN PROPAGANDA. FRANCE GERMANY UK CULTURE COM/IND PRESS PWR...PSY METH/COMP 20. PAGE 12 A0236
EDU/PROP DOMIN ATTIT DIPLOM

C44
VAN VALKENBURG S.,"ELEMENTS OF POLITICAL GEOGRAPHY." FRANCE COM/IND INDUS NAT/G SECT RACE/REL...LING TREND GEN/LAWS BIBLIOG 20. PAGE 158 A3215
GEOG DIPLOM COLONIAL

B48
GRIFFITH E.S.,RESEARCH IN POLITICAL SCIENCE: THE WORK OF PANELS OF RESEARCH COMMITTEE, APSA. WOR+45 WOR-45 COM/IND R+D FORCES ACT/RES WAR...GOV/COMP ANTHOL 20. PAGE 56 A1160
BIBLIOG PHIL/SCI DIPLOM JURID

B48
LINEBARGER P.,PSYCHOLOGICAL WARFARE. NAT/G PLAN DIPLOM DOMIN ATTIT...POLICY CONCPT EXHIBIT 20 WWI. PAGE 89 A1824
EDU/PROP PSY WAR COM/IND

B50
LINCOLN G.,ECONOMICS OF NATIONAL SECURITY. USA+45 ELITES COM/IND DIST/IND INDUS NAT/G VOL/ASSN DELIB/GP EX/STRUC FOR/AID EDU/PROP COERCE NUC/PWR WAR ATTIT KNOWL ORD/FREE PWR COLD/WAR TOT/POP VAL/FREE 20. PAGE 89 A1818
FORCES ECO/TAC

B51
US DEPARTMENT OF STATE,POINT FOUR, NEAR EAST AND AFRICA, A SELECTED BIBLIOGRAPHY OF STUDIES ON ECONOMICALLY UNDERDEVELOPED COUNTRIES. AGRI COM/IND FINAN INDUS PLAN INT/TRADE...SOC TREND 20. PAGE 151 A3087
BIBLIOG/A AFR S/ASIA ISLAM

B52
SMITH C.M.,INTERNATIONAL COMMUNICATION AND POLITICAL WARFARE: AN ANNOTATED BIBLIOGRAPHY (A PAPER). WOR+45 INTELL R+D NAT/G FORCES ACT/RES DIPLOM COERCE ALL/IDEOS. PAGE 134 A2745
BIBLIOG/A EDU/PROP WAR COM/IND

B53
LARSEN K.,NATIONAL BIBLIOGRAPHIC SERVICES: THEIR CREATION AND OPERATION. WOR+45 COM/IND CREATE PLAN DIPLOM PRESS ADMIN ROUTINE...MGT UNESCO. PAGE 85 A1733
BIBLIOG/A INT/ORG WRITING

B53
UNESCO,GUIDE DES CENTRES NATIONAUX D'INFORMATION BIBLIOGRAPHIQUE (VOL. III). WOR+45 INT/ORG NAT/G 20 UNESCO. PAGE 148 A3017
BIBLIOG/A COM/IND DIPLOM

B54
BINANI G.D.,INDIA AT A GLANCE (REV. ED.). INDIA COM/IND FINAN INDUS LABOR PROVS SCHOOL PLAN DIPLOM INT/TRADE ADMIN...JURID 20. PAGE 14 A0288
INDEX CON/ANAL NAT/G ECO/UNDEV

B55
MALCLES L.N.,BIBLIOGRAPHICAL SERVICES THROUGHOUT THE WORLD (VOL. 4). WOR+45 INT/ORG VOL/ASSN DIPLOM PRESS WRITING 20 UNESCO. PAGE 93 A1911
BIBLIOG ROUTINE COM/IND

B55
OECD,MARSHALL PLAN IN TURKEY. TURKEY USA+45 COM/IND CONSTRUC SERV/IND FORCES BUDGET...STAT 20 MARSHL/PLN. PAGE 111 A2277
FOR/AID ECO/UNDEV AGRI INDUS

B55
STEPHENS O.,FACTS TO A CANDID WORLD. USA+45 WOR+45 COM/IND EX/STRUC PRESS ROUTINE EFFICIENCY ATTIT ...PSY 20. PAGE 138 A2817
EDU/PROP PHIL/SCI NAT/G DIPLOM

B55
UNESCO,BIBLIOGRAPHIC SERVICES THROUGHOUT THE WORLD (VOLS. I AND II). WOR+45 DIPLOM CONTROL 20 UNESCO. PAGE 148 A3018
BIBLIOG INT/ORG COM/IND

B56
JUAN T.L.,ECONOMIC AND SOCIAL DEVELOPMENT OF MODERN CHINA: A BIBLIOGRAPHICAL GUIDE. ASIA AGRI COM/IND DIST/IND FINAN INDUS DIPLOM...STAT 20. PAGE 75 A1541
BIBLIOG SOC

B57
ASHER R.E.,THE UNITED NATIONS AND ECONOMIC AND SOCIAL COOPERATION. ECO/UNDEV COM/IND DIST/IND FINAN PLAN PROB/SOLV INT/TRADE TASK WEALTH...SOC 20 UN. PAGE 9 A0186
INT/ORG DIPLOM FOR/AID

B57
WASSENBERGH H.A.,POST-WAR INTERNATIONAL CIVIL AVIATION POLICY AND THE LAW OF THE AIR. WOR+45 AIR INT/ORG DOMIN LEGIT PEACE ORD/FREE...POLICY JURID NEW/IDEA OBS TIME/SEQ TREND CHARTS 20 TREATY. PAGE 162 A3290
COM/IND NAT/G INT/LAW

S57
DEUTSCH K.W.,"MASS COMMUNICATIONS AND THE LOSS OF FREEDOM IN NATIONAL DECISION MAKING." FUT WOR+45 SOCIETY COM/IND INT/ORG NAT/G ACT/RES CREATE TEC/DEV EDU/PROP MAJORITY PERCEPT...METH/CNCPT 20. PAGE 36 A0737
COERCE DECISION WAR

B58
HOLT R.T.,RADIO FREE EUROPE. FUT USA+45 CULTURE ECO/DEV INT/ORG KIN POL/PAR SECT FORCES ACT/RES DIPLOM COERCE REV CHOOSE PEACE ATTIT PWR...MAJORIT CONCPT COLD/WAR WORK 20 RFE. PAGE 67 A1374
COM EDU/PROP COM/IND

B58
MEYRIAT J.,ETUDES DES BIBLIOGRAPHIES COURANTES DES PUBLICATIONS OFFICIELLES NATIONALES. WOR+45 DIPLOM CONTROL 20 UNESCO. PAGE 100 A2056
BIBLIOG COM/IND NAT/G

B58
UNESCO,REPERTORIO DE PUBLICACIONES PERIODICAS ACTUALES LATINO AMERICANAS (VOL. VIII). LAW DIPLOM GP/REL...PHIL/SCI SOC 20 UNESCO. PAGE 148 A3021
BIBLIOG/A COM/IND L/A+17C

L59
GRANDIN T.,"THE POLITICAL USE OF THE RADIO." EUR+WWI SOCIETY INT/ORG DIPLOM CONTROL ATTIT ORD/FREE...CONCPT STAT RECORD SAMP GEN/LAWS TOT/POP 20. PAGE 55 A1128
COM/IND EDU/PROP NAT/LISM

S60
FRANKEL S.H.,"ECONOMIC ASPECTS OF POLITICAL INDEPENDENCE IN AFRICA." AFR FUT SOCIETY ECO/UNDEV COM/IND FINAN LEGIS PLAN TEC/DEV CAP/ISM ECO/TAC INT/TRADE ADMIN ATTIT DRIVE RIGID/FLEX PWR WEALTH ...MGT NEW/IDEA MATH TIME/SEQ VAL/FREE 20. PAGE 48 A0984
NAT/G FOR/AID

S60
RIVKIN A.,"AFRICAN ECONOMIC DEVELOPMENT: ADVANCED TECHNOLOGY AND THE STAGES OF GROWTH." CULTURE ECO/UNDEV AGRI COM/IND EXTR/IND PLAN ECO/TAC ATTIT DRIVE RIGID/FLEX SKILL WEALTH...MGT SOC GEN/LAWS WORK TOT/POP 20. PAGE 121 A2487
AFR TEC/DEV FOR/AID

B61
CALVOCORESSI P.,SOUTH AFRICA AND WORLD OPINION. SOUTH/AFR WOR+45 COM/IND INT/ORG 20. PAGE 23 A0470
ATTIT DISCRIM RACE/REL DIPLOM

B61
COLLISON R.L.,BIBLIOGRAPHICAL SERVICES THROUGHOUT THE WORLD: 1950-59 (VOL. 9). WOR+45 INT/ORG EDU/PROP PRESS WRITING ADMIN CENTRAL 20 UNESCO. PAGE 28 A0568
BIBLIOG COM/IND DIPLOM

B61
INTERNATIONAL BANK RECONST DEV,THE WORLD BANK IN AFRICA: SUMMARY OF ACTIVITIES. AGRI COM/IND DIST/IND EXTR/IND INDUS TAX COST...CHARTS 20.
FINAN ECO/UNDEV INT/ORG

PAGE 71 A1450 AFR

B61
MICHAEL D.N.,PROPOSED STUDIES ON THE IMPLICATIONS OF PEACEFUL SPACE ACTIVITIES FOR HUMAN AFFAIRS. COM/IND INDUS FORCES DIPLOM PEACE PERSON...PSY SOC 20. PAGE 101 A2066 FUT SPACE ACT/RES PROB/SOLV

B61
OVERSTREET H.,THE WAR CALLED PEACE. USSR WOR+45 COM/IND INT/ORG POL/PAR BAL/PWR EDU/PROP PEACE ATTIT...CONCPT 20 KHRUSH/N. PAGE 112 A2302 DIPLOM COM POLICY LEAD

B61
ROSENAU J.N.,PUBLIC OPINION AND FOREIGN POLICY; AN OPERATIONAL FORMULA. USA+45 COM/IND OP/RES EDU/PROP LOBBY CROWD...CON/ANAL BIBLIOG 20. PAGE 124 A2532 ATTIT PRESS DIPLOM

B61
WILLOUGHBY W.R.,THE ST LAWRENCE WATERWAY: A STUDY IN POLITICS AND DIPLOMACY. USA+45 ECO/DEV COM/IND INT/ORG CONSULT DELIB/GP ACT/RES TEC/DEV DIPLOM ECO/TAC ROUTINE...TIME/SEQ 20. PAGE 165 A3357 LEGIS INT/TRADE CANADA DIST/IND

S61
BRZEZINSKI Z.K.,"THE ORGANIZATION OF THE COMMUNIST CAMP." COM CZECHOSLVK COM/IND NAT/G DELIB/GP INT/TRADE DOMIN EDU/PROP EXEC ROUTINE COERCE ATTIT PWR...MGT CONCPT TIME/SEQ CHARTS VAL/FREE 20 TREATY. PAGE 20 A0416 VOL/ASSN DIPLOM USSR

B62
THANT U.,THE UNITED NATIONS' DEVELOPMENT DECADE: PROPOSALS FOR ACTION. WOR+45 SOCIETY ECO/UNDEV AGRI COM/IND FINAN R+D MUNIC SCHOOL VOL/ASSN CONSULT PLAN TEC/DEV ECO/TAC EDU/PROP ADMIN ROUTINE RIGID/FLEX...MGT SOC CONCPT UNESCO UN TOT/POP VAL/FREE. PAGE 142 A2906 INT/ORG ALL/VALS

B62
US CONGRESS,COMMUNICATIONS SATELLITE LEGISLATION: HEARINGS BEFORE COMM ON AERON AND SPACE SCIENCES ON BILLS S2550 AND 2814. WOR+45 LAW VOL/ASSN PLAN DIPLOM CONTROL OWN PEACE...NEW/IDEA CONGRESS NASA. PAGE 150 A3062 SPACE COM/IND ADJUD GOV/REL

S62
ALGER C.F.,"THE EXTERNAL BUREAUCRACY IN UNITED STATES FOREIGN AFFAIRS." USA+45 WOR+45 SOCIETY COM/IND INT/ORG NAT/G CONSULT EX/STRUC ACT/RES ...MGT SOC CONCPT TREND 20. PAGE 6 A0118 ADMIN ATTIT DIPLOM

B63
GORDON G.N.,THE IDEA INVADERS. USA+45 USSR CULTURE COM/IND DIPLOM PRESS TV TOTALISM MARXISM 20. PAGE 54 A1113 EDU/PROP ATTIT ORD/FREE CONTROL

B63
JOYCE W.,THE PROPAGANDA GAP. USA+45 COM/IND ACADEM DOMIN FEEDBACK REV CIVMIL/REL...REALPOL COLD/WAR. PAGE 75 A1540 EDU/PROP PERCEPT BAL/PWR DIPLOM

B63
KATZ S.M.,A SELECTED LIST OF US READINGS ON DEVELOPMENT. AGRI COM/IND DIST/IND INDUS LABOR PLAN FOR/AID EDU/PROP HEALTH...POLICY SOC/WK 20. PAGE 77 A1571 BIBLIOG/A ECO/UNDEV TEC/DEV ACT/RES

B63
LYONS F.S.L.,INTERNATIONALISM IN EUROPE 1815-1914. LAW AGRI COM/IND DIST/IND LABOR SECT INT/TRADE TARIFFS...BIBLIOG 19/20. PAGE 92 A1880 DIPLOM MOD/EUR INT/ORG

B63
US DEPARTMENT OF STATE,POLITICAL BEHAVIOR--A LIST OF CURRENT STUDIES. USA+45 COM/IND DIPLOM LEAD PERS/REL DRIVE PERCEPT KNOWL...DECISION SIMUL METH. PAGE 151 A3093 BIBLIOG METH/COMP GP/REL ATTIT

B63
VOSS E.H.,NUCLEAR AMBUSH: THE TEST-BAN TRAP. WOR+45 COM/IND INT/ORG NAT/G DELIB/GP FORCES LEGIS TOP/EX ACT/RES DOMIN EDU/PROP LEGIT ROUTINE COERCE ATTIT PERCEPT RIGID/FLEX HEALTH MORAL ORD/FREE PWR. PAGE 160 A3255 TEC/DEV HIST/WRIT ARMS/CONT NUC/PWR

B63
WHITTON J.B.,PROPAGANDA AND THE COLD WAR. USA+45 USSR INDUS NAT/G PLAN WRITING EFFICIENCY...POLICY 20 COLD/WAR. PAGE 164 A3341 ATTIT EDU/PROP COM/IND DIPLOM

S63
COUTY P.,"L'ASSISTANCE POUR LE DEVELOPPEMENT: POINT DE VUE SCANDINAVES." EUR+WWI FINLAND FUT SWEDEN WOR+45 ECO/DEV ECO/UNDEV COM/IND LABOR NAT/G PROF/ORG ACT/RES SKILL WEALTH TOT/POP 20. PAGE 32 A0643 FINAN ROUTINE FOR/AID

S63
GARDNER R.N.,"COOPERATION IN OUTER SPACE." FUT USSR WOR+45 AIR LAW COM/IND CONSULT DELIB/GP CREATE KNOWL 20 TREATY. PAGE 51 A1045 INT/ORG ACT/RES PEACE SPACE

B64
COHEN M.,LAW AND POLITICS IN SPACE: SPECIFIC AND URGENT PROBLEMS IN THE LAW OF OUTER SPACE. CHINA/COM COM USA+45 USSR WOR+45 COM/IND INT/ORG NAT/G LEGIT NUC/PWR ATTIT BIO/SOC...JURID CONCPT CONGRESS 20 STALIN/J. PAGE 28 A0561 DELIB/GP LAW INT/LAW SPACE

B64
NASA,PROCEEDINGS OF CONFERENCE ON THE LAW OF SPACE AND OF SATELLITE COMMUNICATIONS: CHICAGO 1963. FUT WOR+45 DELIB/GP PROB/SOLV TEC/DEV CONFER ADJUD NUC/PWR...POLICY IDEA/COMP 20 NASA. PAGE 107 A2197 SPACE COM/IND LAW DIPLOM

B64
OWEN W.,STRATEGY FOR MOBILITY. FUT WOR+45 WOR-45 DIST/IND INT/ORG NAT/G DELIB/GP PLAN TEC/DEV ECO/TAC ORD/FREE PWR WEALTH...STAT TIME/SEQ VAL/FREE 20. PAGE 112 A2304 COM/IND ECO/UNDEV

B64
RUSSET B.M.,WORLD HANDBOOK OF POLITICAL AND SOCIAL INDICATORS. WOR+45 COM/IND ADMIN WEALTH...GEOG 20. PAGE 126 A2577 DIPLOM STAT NAT/G NAT/COMP

B64
SCHWARTZ M.D.,CONFERENCE ON SPACE SCIENCE AND SPACE LAW. FUT COM/IND NAT/G FORCES ACT/RES PLAN BUDGET DIPLOM NUC/PWR WEAPON...POLICY ANTHOL 20. PAGE 130 A2658 SPACE LAW PEACE TEC/DEV

B64
UNESCO,WORLD COMMUNICATIONS: PRESS, RADIO, TELEVISION, FILM (4TH ED.). WOR+45 DIPLOM TV PEACE ...NAT/COMP SOC/INTEG 20 FILM. PAGE 148 A3023 COM/IND EDU/PROP PRESS TEC/DEV

B64
WARREN S.,THE PRESIDENT AS WORLD LEADER. USA+45 WOR+45 ELITES COM/IND INT/ORG NAT/G VOL/ASSN CHIEF EX/STRUC LEGIT COERCE ATTIT PERSON RIGID/FLEX...INT TIME/SEQ COLD/WAR 20 ROOSEVLT/F TRUMAN/HS EISNHWR/DD KENNEDY/JF. PAGE 161 A3286 TOP/EX PWR DIPLOM

S64
TRISKA J.F.,"SOVIET TREATY LAW: A QUANTITATIVE ANALYSIS." WOR+45 LAW ECO/UNDEV AGRI COM/IND INDUS CREATE TEC/DEV DIPLOM ATTIT PWR WEALTH...JURID SAMP TIME/SEQ TREND CHARTS VAL/FREE 20 TREATY. PAGE 145 A2967 COM ECO/TAC INT/LAW USSR

C64
SCHRAMM W.,"MASS MEDIA AND NATIONAL DEVELOPMENT: THE ROLE OF INFORMATION IN DEVELOPING COUNTRIES." FINAN R+D ACT/RES PLAN TEC/DEV DIPLOM CHOOSE SUPEGO ORD/FREE...BIBLIOG 20. PAGE 129 A2645 ECO/UNDEV COM/IND EDU/PROP MAJORIT

B65
DAVISON W.P.,INTERNATIONAL POLITICAL COMMUNICATION. COM USA+45 WOR+45 CULTURE ECO/UNDEV NAT/G PROB/SOLV PRESS TV ADMIN 20 FILM. PAGE 34 A0693 EDU/PROP DIPLOM PERS/REL COM/IND

B65
DOMENACH J.M.,LA PROPAGANDE POLITIQUE. COM/IND INT/ORG POL/PAR DOMIN RIGID/FLEX FASCISM MARXISM ...PSY 20. PAGE 38 A0770 ATTIT EDU/PROP TEC/DEV MYTH

B65
HUSS P.J.,RED SPIES IN THE UN. CZECHOSLVK USA+45 USSR COM/IND FORCES EDU/PROP NUC/PWR MARXISM 20 UN COLD/WAR. PAGE 69 A1421 PEACE INT/ORG BAL/PWR DIPLOM

B65
SABLE M.H.,MASTER DIRECTORY FOR LATIN AMERICA. AGRI COM/IND FINAN R+D ACADEM LABOR NAT/G POL/PAR VOL/ASSN INT/TRADE EDU/PROP 20. PAGE 126 A2582 INDEX L/A+17C INT/ORG DIPLOM

B65
UNESCO,HANDBOOK OF INTERNATIONAL EXCHANGES. COM/IND R+D ACADEM PROF/ORG VOL/ASSN CREATE TEC/DEV EDU/PROP AGREE 20 TREATY. PAGE 148 A3025 INDEX INT/ORG DIPLOM PRESS

B66
HALLET R.,PEOPLE AND PROGRESS IN WEST AFRICA: AN INTRODUCTION TO THE PROBLEMS OF DEVELOPMENT. COM/IND INDUS KIN DIPLOM FOR/AID INT/TRADE HEALTH ...GEOG TREND CHARTS BIBLIOG/A 20 AFRICA/W. PAGE 60 A1233 AFR SOCIETY ECO/UNDEV ECO/TAC

B67
HOHENBERG J.,BETWEEN TWO WORLDS. ASIA S/ASIA USA+45 PRESS TV PERS/REL ISOLAT...INT CHARTS METH/COMP 20. PAGE 66 A1362 COM/IND DIPLOM EFFICIENCY KNOWL

B67
MURTY B.S.,PROPAGANDA AND WORLD PUBLIC ORDER. FUT WOR+45 COM/IND INT/ORG PROB/SOLV ATTIT KNOWL ORD/FREE...POLICY UN. PAGE 106 A2183 EDU/PROP DIPLOM CONTROL JURID

B67
ROSENAU J.N.,DOMESTIC SOURCES OF FOREIGN POLICY. WOR+45 STRATA COM/IND MUNIC POL/PAR LOBBY PARTIC REGION ATTIT...PSY SOC COLD/WAR. PAGE 124 A2534 DIPLOM POLICY NAT/G CHOOSE

S67
DOYLE S.E.,"COMMUNICATION SATELLITES* INTERNAL ORGANIZATION FOR DEVELOPMENT AND CONTROL." USA+45 R+D ACT/RES DIPLOM NAT/LISM...POLICY INT/LAW PREDICT UN. PAGE 38 A0781 TEC/DEV SPACE COM/IND INT/ORG

S67
KELLY F.K.,"A PROPOSAL FOR AN ANNUAL REPORT ON THE STATE OF MANKIND." FUT INTELL COM/IND INT/ORG SOCIETY UNIV

CREATE PROB/SOLV PERS/REL...CONCPT 20 UN. PAGE 77 A1579 ATTIT NEW/IDEA

S67
RAMSEY J.A.,"THE STATUS OF INTERNATIONAL COPYRIGHTS." WOR+45 CREATE TEC/DEV DIPLOM CONFER CONTROL SANCTION OWN...POLICY JURID. PAGE 119 A2439 INT/LAW INT/ORG COM/IND PRESS

N67
US SUPERINTENDENT OF DOCUMENTS,SPACE: MISSILES, THE MOON, NASA, AND SATELLITES (PRICE LIST 79A). USA+45 COM/IND R+D NAT/G DIPLOM EDU/PROP ADMIN CONTROL HEALTH...POLICY SIMUL NASA CONGRESS. PAGE 157 A3206 BIBLIOG/A SPACE TEC/DEV PEACE

COM/PARTY....COMMUNIST PARTY (ALL NATIONS)

B58
PALMER E.E.,THE COMMUNIST CHALLENGE. COM USA+45 USA-45 ECO/DEV ECO/UNDEV NEUTRAL ORD/FREE POPULISM ...CONCPT NAT/COMP ANTHOL 19/20 LENIN/VI STALIN/J MAO MARX/KARL COM/PARTY. PAGE 113 A2320 MARXISM DIPLOM IDEA/COMP POLICY

B59
CHALUPA V.,RISE AND DEVELOPMENT OF A TOTALITARIAN STATE. CZECHOSLVK USSR STRUCT INT/ORG WORKER DIPLOM ECO/TAC COERCE NAT/LISM ATTIT...POLICY 20 COM/PARTY. PAGE 25 A0516 TOTALISM MARXISM REV POL/PAR

B59
SHANNON D.A.,THE DECLINE OF AMERICAN COMMUNISM; A HISTORY OF THE COMMUNIST PARTY OF THE UNITED STATES SINCE 1945. USA+45 LAW SOCIETY LABOR NAT/G WORKER DIPLOM EDU/PROP LEAD...POLICY BIBLIOG 20 KHRUSH/N NEGRO AFL/CIO COLD/WAR COM/PARTY. PAGE 131 A2692 MARXISM POL/PAR ATTIT POPULISM

B62
HOOK S.,WORLD COMMUNISM: KEY DOCUMENTARY MATERIAL. CHINA/COM L/A+17C USA+45 USSR POL/PAR DIPLOM COLONIAL REV WAR...ANTHOL 20 MARX/KARL LENIN/VI COM/PARTY. PAGE 67 A1380 MARXISM COM GEN/LAWS NAT/G

B62
KLUCKHOHN F.L.,THE NAKED RISE OF COMMUNISM. CHINA/COM COM USSR WOR+45 CONSTN POL/PAR PLAN CONTROL LEAD NEUTRAL CONSERVE 20 STALIN/J EUROPE/E COM/PARTY. PAGE 80 A1650 MARXISM IDEA/COMP DIPLOM DOMIN

B62
LEVY H.V.,LIBERDADE E JUSTICA SOCIAL (2ND ED.). BRAZIL COM L/A+17C USSR INT/ORG PARTIC GP/REL WEALTH 20 UN COM/PARTY. PAGE 88 A1798 ORD/FREE MARXISM CAP/ISM LAW

B63
NORTH R.C.,M. N. ROY'S MISSION TO CHINA: THE COMMUNIST-KUOMINTANG SPLIT OF 1927. ASIA USSR STRATA LEGIS WORKER LEAD REV ATTIT ROLE SOCISM 20 ROY/MN COM/PARTY. PAGE 110 A2253 POL/PAR MARXISM DIPLOM

B63
SWEARER H.R.,CONTEMPORARY COMMUNISM: THEORY AND PRACTICE. COM USSR SOCIETY ECO/DEV POL/PAR FORCES PLAN ADMIN LEAD NAT/LISM...POLICY ANTHOL 20 LENIN/VI COM/PARTY. PAGE 140 A2869 MARXISM CONCPT DIPLOM NAT/G

B64
CALVO SERER R.,LAS NUEVAS DEMOCRACIAS. AFR ASIA ISLAM USA+45 WOR+45 BAL/PWR DOMIN PARTIC INGP/REL AUTHORIT POPULISM...CONCPT 20 COM/PARTY. PAGE 23 A0469 ORD/FREE MARXISM DIPLOM POLICY

B64
DUTT R.P.,THE INTERNATIONALE. COM WOR+45 WOR-45 WORKER CAP/ISM WAR ATTIT...TREND GEN/LAWS 18/20 COM/PARTY. PAGE 40 A0813 ALL/IDEOS INT/ORG MARXIST ORD/FREE

B65
HALPERIN E.,NATIONALISM AND COMMUNISM. CHILE L/A+17C CAP/ISM EDU/PROP CHOOSE DISCRIM SOCISM ...BIBLIOG 20 COM/PARTY. PAGE 60 A1236 NAT/LISM MARXISM POL/PAR REV

B66
SAGER P.,MOSKAUS HAND IN INDIEN. INDIA USSR DIPLOM DOMIN...PSY CONCPT 20 COM/PARTY. PAGE 126 A2586 PRESS EDU/PROP METH POL/PAR

B66
SKILLING H.G.,THE GOVERNMENTS OF COMMUNIST EAST EUROPE. COM EUR+WWI ELITES FORCES DIPLOM ECO/TAC CONTROL HABITAT SOCISM...DECISION BIBLIOG 20 EUROPE/E COM/PARTY. PAGE 134 A2738 MARXISM NAT/COMP GP/COMP DOMIN

B66
WOHL R.,FRENCH COMMUNISM IN THE MAKING 1914-1924. FRANCE USSR LEAD REV...IDEA/COMP 20 COM/PARTY. PAGE 166 A3377 MARXISM WORKER DIPLOM

COM/SCITEC....COMMITTEE ON SCIENCE AND TECHNOLOGY (OF

COMECON....COMMUNIST ECONOMIC ORGANIZATION EAST EUROPE

S63
RAMERIE L.,"TENSION AU SEIN DU COMECON: LE CAS ROUMAIN." COM EUR+WWI USSR WOR+45 ECO/DEV DIST/IND NAT/G POL/PAR VOL/ASSN EDU/PROP TOTALISM ATTIT WEALTH...TIME/SEQ 20 COMECON. PAGE 119 A2438 INT/ORG ECO/TAC INT/TRADE ROMANIA

B64
GRZYBOWSKI K.,THE SOCIALIST COMMONWEALTH OF NATIONS: ORGANIZATIONS AND INSTITUTIONS. FORCES DIPLOM INT/TRADE ADJUD ADMIN LEAD WAR MARXISM SOCISM...BIBLIOG 20 COMECON WARSAW/P. PAGE 58 A1185 INT/LAW COM REGION INT/ORG

B64
KIS T.I.,LES PAYS DE L'EUROPE DE L'EST: LEURS RAPPORTS MUTUELS ET LE PROBLEME DE LEUR INTEGRATION DANS L'ORBITE DE L'USSR. EUR+WWI RUSSIA USSR INT/ORG NAT/G REV ATTIT...JURID SOC BIBLIOG WARSAW/P COMECON EUROPE/E. PAGE 80 A1638 DIPLOM COM MARXISM REGION

L64
KORBONSKI A.,"COMECON." ASIA ECO/DEV ECO/UNDEV ECO/TAC BAL/PAY NAT/LISM 20 COMECON. PAGE 81 A1671 COM INT/ORG INT/TRADE

COMINFORM....COMMUNIST INFORMATION BUREAU

L51
ULAM A.B.,"THE COMIMFORM AND THE PEOPLE'S DEMOCRACIES." EUR+WWI WOR+45 STRUCT NAT/G POL/PAR TOP/EX ACT/RES PLAN ECO/TAC DOMIN ATTIT ALL/VALS ...HIST/WRIT TIME/SEQ 20 COMINFORM. PAGE 146 A2992 COM INT/ORG USSR TOTALISM

B56
WOLFF R.L.,THE BALKANS IN OUR TIME. ALBANIA FUT MOD/EUR USSR YUGOSLAVIA CULTURE INT/ORG SECT DIPLOM EDU/PROP COERCE WAR ORD/FREE...CHARTS 4/20 BALKANS COMINFORM. PAGE 166 A3388 GEOG COM

B61
NOLLAU G.,INTERNATIONAL COMMUNISM AND WORLD REVOLUTION; HISTORY AND METHODS (TRANS. BY VICTOR ANDERSEN). COM WORKER DIPLOM CONFER INGP/REL ...CONCPT BIBLIOG 20 STALIN/J LENIN/VI COMINTERN COMINFORM WORLD/CONG. PAGE 110 A2249 MARXISM POL/PAR INT/ORG REV

COMINTERN....COMMUNIST THIRD INTERNATIONAL

B52
ULAM A.B.,TITOISM AND THE COMINFORM. USSR WOR+45 STRUCT INT/ORG NAT/G ACT/RES PLAN EXEC ATTIT DRIVE ALL/VALS...CONCPT OBS VAL/FREE 20 COMINTERN TITO/MARSH. PAGE 146 A2993 COM POL/PAR TOTALISM YUGOSLAVIA

B61
NOLLAU G.,INTERNATIONAL COMMUNISM AND WORLD REVOLUTION; HISTORY AND METHODS (TRANS. BY VICTOR ANDERSEN). COM WORKER DIPLOM CONFER INGP/REL ...CONCPT BIBLIOG 20 STALIN/J LENIN/VI COMINTERN COMINFORM WORLD/CONG. PAGE 110 A2249 MARXISM POL/PAR INT/ORG REV

B66
DRACHOVITCH M.M.,THE COMINTERN HISTORICAL HIGHLIGHTS. USSR INT/ORG EX/STRUC LEGIT LEAD GUERRILLA...ANTHOL 20 COMINTERN LENIN/VI. PAGE 38 A0784 DIPLOM REV MARXISM PERSON

S66
MCNEAL R.H.,"THE LEGACY OF THE COMINTERN." USSR WOR+45 WOR-45 PROB/SOLV DIPLOM CONFER CONTROL LEAD WAR 20 STALIN/J COMINTERN. PAGE 98 A2020 MARXISM INT/ORG POL/PAR PWR

COMISION DE HISTORIO A0573

COMM. STUDY ORGAN. PEACE A0574,A0575,A0576,A0577,A0578,A0579, A0580,A0581

COMM/SPACE....COMMITTEE ON SPACE RESEARCH

COMMANDS....SEE LEAD, DOMIN

COMMISSIONS....SEE CONFER, DELIB/GP

COMMITTEE FOR ECONOMIC DEVELOPMENT....SEE CED

COMMITTEES....SEE CONFER, DELIB/GP

COMMON/LAW....COMMON LAW

COMMONWEALTH OF WORLD CITIZENS A0582

COMMONWEALTH....SEE COMMONWLTH

COMMONWLTH....BRITISH COMMONWEALTH OF NATIONS; SEE ALSO VOL/ASSN, APPROPRIATE NATIONS, CMN/WLTH

B53
MANSERGH N.,DOCUMENTS AND SPEECHES ON BRITISH COMMONWEALTH AFFAIRS 1931-1952. INDIA IRELAND PAKISTAN UK CONSTN POL/PAR CHIEF FORCES COLONIAL ORD/FREE SOVEREIGN...JURID 20 COMMONWLTH. PAGE 94 A1929 BIBLIOG/A DIPLOM ECO/TAC

B53
STOUT H.M.,BRITISH GOVERNMENT. UK FINAN LOC/G POL/PAR DELIB/GP DIPLOM ADMIN COLONIAL CHOOSE ORD/FREE...JURID BIBLIOG 20 COMMONWLTH. PAGE 139 NAT/G PARL/PROC CONSTN

A2837 — NEW/LIB

B58
JENNINGS I.,PROBLEMS OF THE NEW COMMONWEALTH. CEYLON INDIA PAKISTAN S/ASIA ECO/UNDEV INT/ORG LOC/G DIPLOM ECO/TAC INT/TRADE COLONIAL RACE/REL DISCRIM 20 COMMONWLTH PARLIAMENT. PAGE 74 A1508
NAT/LISM NEUTRAL FOR/AID POL/PAR

B60
STRACHEY J.,THE END OF EMPIRE. UK WOR+45 WOR-45 DIPLOM INT/TRADE DOMIN ADJUST ORD/FREE WEALTH ...SOCIALIST GOV/COMP TIME COMMONWLTH. PAGE 139 A2841
COLONIAL ECO/DEV BAL/PWR LAISSEZ

B61
CARNELL F.,THE POLITICS OF THE NEW STATES: A SELECT ANNOTATED BIBLIOGRAPHY WITH SPECIAL REFERENCE TO THE COMMONWEALTH. CONSTN ELITES LABOR NAT/G POL/PAR EX/STRUC DIPLOM ADJUD ADMIN...GOV/COMP 20 COMMONWLTH. PAGE 24 A0496
BIBLIOG/A AFR ASIA COLONIAL

B63
CONF ON FUTURE OF COMMONWEALTH,THE FUTURE OF THE COMMONWEALTH. UK ECO/UNDEV AGRI EDU/PROP ADMIN SOC/INTEG 20 COMMONWLTH. PAGE 29 A0583
DIPLOM RACE/REL ORD/FREE TEC/DEV

B63
HAILEY L.,THE REPUBLIC OF SOUTH AFRICA AND THE HIGH COMMISSION TERRITORIES. AFR SOUTH/AFR UK INT/ORG NAT/G PROVS RACE/REL SOVEREIGN...CHARTS 19/20 COMMONWLTH. PAGE 59 A1219
COLONIAL DIPLOM ATTIT

B63
HUSSEY W.D.,THE BRITISH EMPIRE AND COMMONWEALTH 1500 TO 1961. UK USA-45 SOCIETY ECO/UNDEV NAT/G VOL/ASSN INT/TRADE DOMIN CONTROL WAR PWR ...DICTIONARY 16/20 COMMONWLTH TRUST/TERR. PAGE 69 A1422
COLONIAL SOVEREIGN INT/ORG

B63
PADELFORD N.J.,AFRICA AND WORLD ORDER. AFR COLONIAL SOVEREIGN...ANTHOL BIBLIOG 20 UN UNIFICA COMMONWLTH. PAGE 113 A2312
DIPLOM NAT/G ORD/FREE

B64
THE SPECIAL COMMONWEALTH AFRICAN ASSISTANCE PLAN. AFR CANADA INDIA NIGERIA UK FINAN SCHOOL...CHARTS 20 COMMONWLTH. PAGE 3 A0065
ECO/UNDEV TREND FOR/AID ADMIN

B64
DESHMUKH C.D.,THE COMMONWEALTH AS INDIA SEES IT. INDIA UK ECO/UNDEV TEC/DEV INT/TRADE GP/REL RACE/REL SOVEREIGN SOC/INTEG 19/20 COMMONWLTH. PAGE 36 A0733
DIPLOM COLONIAL NAT/LISM ATTIT

B64
NEWBURY C.W.,THE WEST AFRICAN COMMONWEALTH. CONSTN INTELL ECO/UNDEV VOL/ASSN CHIEF DELIB/GP LEGIS INT/TRADE COLONIAL FEDERAL ATTIT 20 COMMONWLTH AFRICA/W. PAGE 108 A2223
INT/ORG SOVEREIGN GOV/REL AFR

B64
SINGH N.,THE DEFENCE MECHANISM OF THE MODERN STATE. COM UK USA+45 CONSTN INT/ORG NUC/PWR WAR INGP/REL ROLE 20 DEPT/DEFEN COMMONWLTH. PAGE 134 A2735
FORCES TOP/EX NAT/G CIVMIL/REL

N64
GREAT BRITAIN CENTRAL OFF INF,THE COLOMBO PLAN (PAMPHLET). ASIA S/ASIA USA+45 VOL/ASSN...CHARTS 20 COMMONWLTH RESOURCE/N. PAGE 55 A1134
FOR/AID PLAN INT/ORG ECO/UNDEV

B65
COWEN Z.,THE BRITISH COMMONWEALTH OF NATIONS IN A CHANGING WORLD. UK ECO/UNDEV INT/ORG ECO/TAC INT/TRADE COLONIAL WAR GP/REL RACE/REL SOVEREIGN SOC/INTEG 20 TREATY EEC COMMONWLTH. PAGE 32 A0644
JURID DIPLOM PARL/PROC NAT/LISM

B65
GRAHAM G.S.,THE POLITICS OF NAVAL SUPREMACY; STUDIES IN BRITISH MARITIME ASCENDANCY. UK SEA NAT/G BAL/PWR LEAD WAR WEAPON PEACE...POLICY 18/19 COMMONWLTH. PAGE 55 A1126
FORCES PWR COLONIAL DIPLOM

B65
INGRAM D.,COMMONWEALTH FOR A COLOUR-BLIND WORLD. AFR INDIA UK STRATA ECO/UNDEV VOL/ASSN CREATE PLAN CONFER COLONIAL ORD/FREE SOC/INTEG 20 COMMONWLTH. PAGE 70 A1441
RACE/REL INT/ORG INGP/REL PROB/SOLV

B65
SOPER T.,EVOLVING COMMONWEALTH. AFR CANADA INDIA IRELAND UK LAW CONSTN POL/PAR DOMIN CONTROL WAR PWR ...AUD/VIS 18/20 COMMONWLTH OEEC. PAGE 135 A2769
INT/ORG COLONIAL VOL/ASSN

B66
FABAR R.,THE VISION AND THE NEED: LATE VICTORIAN IMPERIALIST AIMS. MOD/EUR UK WOR-45 CULTURE NAT/G DIPLOM...TIME/SEQ METH/COMP 19 KIPLING/R COMMONWLTH. PAGE 43 A0880
COLONIAL CONCPT ADMIN ATTIT

B66
HUTTENBACK R.A.,BRITISH IMPERIAL EXPERIENCE. S/ASIA UK WOR-45 INT/ORG TEC/DEV...CHARTS 16/20 COMMONWLTH MERCANTLST. PAGE 69 A1424
COLONIAL TIME/SEQ INT/TRADE

COMMUN/DEV....COMMUNITY DEVELOPMENT MOVEMENT IN INDIA

COMMUNES....COMMUNES

COMMUNICATION, MASS....SEE EDU/PROP

COMMUNICATION, PERSONAL....SEE PERS/REL

COMMUNICATION, POLITICAL....SEE EDU/PROP

COMMUNICATIONS INDUSTRY....SEE COM/IND

COMMUNISM....SEE MARXISM

COMMUNIST CHINA....SEE CHINA/COM

COMMUNIST COUNTRIES (EXCEPT CHINA)....SEE COM

COMMUNIST ECONOMIC ORGANIZATION....SEE COMECON

COMMUNIST INFORMATION BUREAU....SEE COMINFORM

COMMUNIST THIRD INTERNATIONAL....SEE COMINTERN

COMMUNITY....SEE NEIGH

COMPANY, LARGE....SEE LG/CO

COMPANY, SMALL....SEE SML/CO

COMPARATIVE....SEE APPROPRIATE COMPARATIVE ANALYSIS INDEX

COMPETITION....SEE APPROPRIATE RELATIONS AND VALUES INDEXES

COMPNY/ACT....COMPANIES ACT (U.K., 1882)

COMPUT/IR....INFORMATION RETRIEVAL

N
AMERICAN DOCUMENTATION INST,DOCUMENTATION ABSTRACTS. WOR+45 NAT/G COMPUTER CREATE TEC/DEV DIPLOM EDU/PROP REGION KNOWL...PHIL/SCI CLASSIF LING. PAGE 7 A0143
BIBLIOG/A AUTOMAT COMPUT/IR R+D

N
AMER COUNCIL OF LEARNED SOCIET,THE ACLS CONSTITUENT SOCIETY JOURNAL PROJECT. FUT USA+45 LAW NAT/G PLAN DIPLOM PHIL/SCI. PAGE 7 A0134
BIBLIOG/A HUM COMPUT/IR COMPUTER

N
KYRIAK T.E.,INTERNATIONAL DEVELOPMENTS: A BIBLIOGRAPHY (SERIAL). WOR+45...COMPUT/IR AUD/VIS CHARTS. PAGE 83 A1702
BIBLIOG NAT/G DIPLOM

B60
STEIN E.,AMERICAN ENTERPRISE IN THE EUROPEAN COMMON MARKET: A LEGAL PROFILE. EUR+WWI FUT USA+45 SOCIETY STRUCT ECO/DEV NAT/G VOL/ASSN CONSULT PLAN TEC/DEV ECO/TAC INT/TRADE ADMIN ATTIT RIGID/FLEX PWR...MGT NEW/IDEA STAT TREND COMPUT/IR SIMUL EEC 20. PAGE 137 A2814
MARKET ADJUD INT/LAW

B60
WOETZEL R.K.,THE INTERNATIONAL CONTROL OF AIRSPACE AND OUTERSPACE. FUT WOR+45 AIR CONSTN STRUCT CONSULT PLAN TEC/DEV ADJUD RIGID/FLEX KNOWL ORD/FREE PWR...TECHNIC GEOG MGT NEW/IDEA TREND COMPUT/IR VAL/FREE 20 TREATY. PAGE 166 A3375
INT/ORG JURID SPACE INT/LAW

B63
NORTH R.C.,CONTENT ANALYSIS: A HANDBOOK WITH APPLICATIONS FOR THE STUDY OF INTERNATIONAL CRISIS. ASIA COM EUR+WWI MOD/EUR INT/ORG TEC/DEV DOMIN EDU/PROP ROUTINE COERCE PERCEPT RIGID/FLEX ALL/VALS ...QUANT TESTS CON/ANAL SIMUL GEN/LAWS VAL/FREE. PAGE 110 A2252
METH/CNCPT COMPUT/IR USSR

B65
UNIVERSAL REFERENCE SYSTEM,INTERNATIONAL AFFAIRS: VOLUME I IN THE POLITICAL SCIENCE, GOVERNMENT, AND PUBLIC POLICY SERIES....DECISION ECOMETRIC GEOG INT/LAW JURID MGT PHIL/SCI PSY SOC. PAGE 149 A3041
BIBLIOG/A GEN/METH COMPUT/IR DIPLOM

B65
US LIBRARY OF CONGRESS,A DIRECTORY OF INFORMATION RESOURCES IN THE UNITED STATES: SOCIAL SCIENCES. USA+45 ACADEM INT/ORG LABOR PROF/ORG PUB/INST SCHOOL SECT 20. PAGE 155 A3159
BIBLIOG R+D COMPUT/IR

B66
KUENNE R.E.,THE POLARIS MISSILE STRIKE* A GENERAL ECONOMIC SYSTEMS ANALYSIS. USA+45 USSR NAT/G BAL/PWR ARMS/CONT WAR...MATH PROBABIL COMPUT/IR CHARTS HYPO/EXP SIMUL. PAGE 82 A1689
NUC/PWR FORCES DETER DIPLOM

B67
UNIVERSAL REFERENCE SYSTEM,BIBLIOGRAPHY OF BIBLIOGRAPHIES IN POLITICAL SCIENCE, GOVERNMENT, AND PUBLIC POLICY (VOLUME III). WOR+45 WOR-45 LAW ADMIN...SOC CON/ANAL COMPUT/IR GEN/METH. PAGE 149 A3042
BIBLIOG/A NAT/G DIPLOM POLICY

B67
UNIVERSAL REFERENCE SYSTEM,ECONOMIC REGULATION, BUSINESS, AND GOVERNMENT (VOLUME VIII). WOR+45 WOR-45 ECO/DEV ECO/UNDEV FINAN LABOR TEC/DEV ECO/TAC INT/TRADE GOV/REL...POLICY COMPUT/IR. PAGE 149 A3043
BIBLIOG/A CONTROL NAT/G

B67
UNIVERSAL REFERENCE SYSTEM,LAW, JURISPRUDENCE, AND JUDICIAL PROCESS (VOLUME VII). WOR+45 WOR-45 CONSTN NAT/G LEGIS JUDGE CT/SYS...INT/LAW COMPUT/IR GEN/METH METH. PAGE 149 A3044
BIBLIOG/A LAW JURID ADJUD

COMPUTER....COMPUTER TECHNIQUES AND TECHNOLOGY

N
AMERICAN DOCUMENTATION INST,DOCUMENTATION ABSTRACTS. WOR+45 NAT/G COMPUTER CREATE TEC/DEV DIPLOM EDU/PROP REGION KNOWL...PHIL/SCI CLASSIF LING. PAGE 7 A0143
BIBLIOG/A AUTOMAT COMPUT/IR R+D

N
AMER COUNCIL OF LEARNED SOCIET,THE ACLS CONSTITUENT SOCIETY JOURNAL PROJECT. FUT USA+45 LAW NAT/G PLAN DIPLOM PHIL/SCI. PAGE 7 A0134
BIBLIOG/A HUM COMPUT/IR COMPUTER

B59
STERNBERG F.,THE MILITARY AND INDUSTRIAL REVOLUTION OF OUR TIME. USA+45 USSR WOR+45 WORKER COMPUTER PLAN TEC/DEV NUC/PWR GP/REL...POLICY NAT/COMP 20. PAGE 138 A2818
DIPLOM FORCES INDUS CIVMIL/REL

S65
HOLSTI O.R.,"EAST-WEST CONFLICT AND SINO-SOVIET RELATIONS" CHINA/COM USSR COMPUTER REGION DECISION. PAGE 67 A1373
VOL/ASSN DIPLOM CON/ANAL COM

COMTE/A....AUGUST COMTE

CON/ANAL....QUANTITATIVE CONTENT ANALYSIS

N
AUSTRALIAN PUBLIC AFFAIRS INFORMATION SERVICE. LAW ...HEAL HUM MGT SOC CON/ANAL 20 AUSTRAL. PAGE 2 A0028
BIBLIOG NAT/G CULTURE DIPLOM

N
CHINA QUARTERLY. COM AGRI INDUS ACADEM POL/PAR INT/TRADE CONFER GOV/REL...TIME/SEQ CON/ANAL INDEX 20. PAGE 2 A0032
BIBLIOG/A ASIA DIPLOM POLICY

N
AMERICAN BIBLIOGRAPHIC SERVICE,INTERNATIONAL GUIDE TO INDIC STUDIES - A QUARTERLY INDEX TO PERIODICAL LITERATURE. INDIA CULTURE NAT/G DIPLOM...EPIST SOC BIOG 20. PAGE 7 A0140
BIBLIOG S/ASIA CON/ANAL

N
AMERICAN BIBLIOGRAPHIC SERVICE,QUARTERLY CHECKLIST OF ORIENTAL STUDIES. CULTURE LOC/G NAT/G DIPLOM ...HIST/WRIT CON/ANAL 20. PAGE 7 A0141
BIBLIOG S/ASIA ASIA

N
CORDIER H.,BIBLIOTECA SINICA. SOCIETY STRUCT SECT DIPLOM COLONIAL...GEOG SOC CON/ANAL. PAGE 30 A0618
BIBLIOG/A NAT/G CULTURE ASIA

N
COUNCIL ON FOREIGN RELATIONS,DOCUMENTS ON AMERICAN FOREIGN RELATIONS. INT/ORG ECO/TAC NUC/PWR WAR WEAPON...POLICY CON/ANAL CHARTS 20 OAS UN. PAGE 31 A0639
BIBLIOG USA+45 USA-45 DIPLOM

N
LA DOCUMENTATION FRANCAISE,CHRONOLOGIE INTERNATIONAL. FRANCE WOR+45 CHIEF PROB/SOLV BAL/PWR CONFER LEAD...POLICY CON/ANAL 20. PAGE 83 A1705
BIBLIOG/A DIPLOM TIME/SEQ

N
LEYPOLOT F.,AMERICAN CATALOGUE OF BOOKS, 1876-1910 (19 VOLS.). NAT/G DIPLOM...CON/ANAL 19/20. PAGE 88 A1806
BIBLIOG USA-45 PROF/ORG PROC/MFG

N
LONDON LIBRARY ASSOCIATION,ATHENAEUM SUBJECT INDEX. 1915-1918. NAT/G DIPLOM NAT/LISM 20. PAGE 91 A1857
BIBLIOG CON/ANAL SOC

N
UNITED NATIONS,YEARBOOK OF THE INTERNATIONAL LAW COMMISSION....CON/ANAL 20 UN. PAGE 149 A3035
BIBLIOG INT/ORG INT/LAW DELIB/GP

N
WORLD PEACE FOUNDATION,DOCUMENTS OF INTERNATIONAL ORGANIZATIONS: A SELECTED BIBLIOGRAPHY. WOR+45 WOR-45 AGRI FINAN ACT/RES OP/RES INT/TRADE ADMIN ...CON/ANAL 20 UN UNESCO LEAGUE/NAT. PAGE 167 A3396
BIBLIOG DIPLOM INT/ORG REGION

B00
GROTIUS H.,DE JURE BELLI AC PACIS. CHRIST-17C UNIV LAW SOCIETY PROVS LEGIT PEACE PERCEPT MORAL PWR ...CONCPT CON/ANAL GEN/LAWS. PAGE 57 A1180
JURID INT/LAW WAR

B00
VOLPICELLI Z.,RUSSIA ON THE PACIFIC AND THE SIBERIAN RAILWAY. MOD/EUR ECO/UNDEV INT/ORG FORCES PLAN DOMIN COLONIAL ROUTINE ATTIT ALL/VALS...OBS HIST/WRIT TIME/SEQ TREND CON/ANAL AUD/VIS CHARTS 18/19. PAGE 159 A3248
NAT/G ACT/RES RUSSIA

B11
PHILLIPSON C.,THE INTERNATIONAL LAW AND CUSTOM OF ANCIENT GREECE AND ROME. MEDIT-7 UNIV INTELL SOCIETY STRUCT NAT/G LEGIS EXEC PERSON...CONCPT OBS CON/ANAL ROM/EMP. PAGE 116 A2377
INT/ORG LAW INT/LAW

B22
REINSCH P.,SECRET DIPLOMACY: HOW FAR CAN IT BE ELIMINATED. FUT WOR-45 CULTURE INT/ORG NAT/G EDU/PROP WAR...MYTH HIST/WRIT CON/ANAL 20. PAGE 120 A2460
RIGID/FLEX PWR DIPLOM

B31
STUART G.H.,THE INTERNATIONAL CITY OF TANGIER. AFR EUR+WWI MOD/EUR MOROCCO CONSTN PROVS CREATE PLAN LEGIT PEACE ORD/FREE PWR...INT/LAW OBS TIME/SEQ CON/ANAL 20 TANGIER. PAGE 139 A2854
LOC/G INT/ORG DIPLOM SOVEREIGN

B32
FLEMMING D.,THE UNITED STATES AND THE LEAGUE OF NATIONS, 1918-1920. FUT USA-45 NAT/G LEGIS TOP/EX DEBATE CHOOSE PEACE ATTIT SOVEREIGN...TIME/SEQ CON/ANAL CONGRESS LEAGUE/NAT 20 TREATY. PAGE 46 A0950
INT/ORG EDU/PROP

B35
BEMIS S.F.,GUIDE TO THE DIPLOMATIC HISTORY OF THE UNITED STATES, 17751921. NAT/G LEGIS TOP/EX PROB/SOLV CAP/ISM INT/TRADE TARIFFS ADJUD ...CON/ANAL 18/20. PAGE 13 A0264
BIBLIOG/A DIPLOM USA-45

B35
STALEY E.,WAR AND THE PRIVATE INVESTOR. UNIV WOR-45 INTELL SOCIETY INT/ORG NAT/G TOP/EX CAP/ISM ECO/TAC WAR ATTIT ALL/VALS...INT TIME/SEQ TREND CON/ANAL WORK TOT/POP 20. PAGE 137 A2799
FINAN INT/TRADE DIPLOM

B39
ROBBINS L.,ECONOMIC CAUSES OF WAR. WOR-45 ECO/DEV ECO/UNDEV INT/ORG NAT/G TEC/DEV DIPLOM DOMIN COLONIAL ATTIT DRIVE PWR WEALTH...POLICY CONCPT OBS SAMP TREND CON/ANAL GEN/LAWS MARX/KARL 20. PAGE 122 A2493
COERCE ECO/TAC WAR

C39
HADDOW A.,"POLITICAL SCIENCE IN AMERICAN COLLEGES AND UNIVERSITIES 1636-1900." CONSTN MORAL...POLICY INT/LAW CON/ANAL BIBLIOG T 17/20. PAGE 59 A1211
USA-45 LAW ACADEM KNOWL

B40
CONOVER H.F.,A BRIEF LIST OF REFERENCES ON WESTERN HEMISPHERE DEFENSE (PAMPHLET). USA-45 NAT/G CONSULT DELIB/GP FORCES BAL/PWR CONFER DETER...PREDICT CON/ANAL 20. PAGE 29 A0591
BIBLIOG DIPLOM PLAN INT/ORG

B40
CONOVER H.F.,FOREIGN RELATIONS OF THE UNITED STATES: A LIST OF RECENT BOOKS (PAMPHLET). ASIA CANADA L/A+17C UK INT/ORG INT/TRADE TARIFFS NEUTRAL WAR PEACE...INT/LAW CON/ANAL 20 CHINJAP. PAGE 29 A0592
BIBLIOG/A USA-45 DIPLOM

B40
FULLER G.H.,A LIST OF BIBLIOGRAPHIES ON PROPAGANDA (PAMPHLET). MOD/EUR USA-45 CONSULT ACT/RES PRESS FEEDBACK TASK WAR ATTIT PWR...CON/ANAL METH/COMP 20. PAGE 50 A1020
BIBLIOG/A EDU/PROP DOMIN DIPLOM

C40
FAHS C.B.,"GOVERNMENT IN JAPAN." FINAN FORCES LEGIS TOP/EX BUDGET INT/TRADE EDU/PROP SOVEREIGN ...CON/ANAL BIBLIOG/A 20 CHINJAP. PAGE 43 A0884
ASIA DIPLOM NAT/G ADMIN

B41
MCCLURE W.,INTERNATIONAL EXECUTIVE AGREEMENTS. USA-45 WOR-45 INT/ORG NAT/G DELIB/GP ADJUD ROUTINE ORD/FREE PWR...TIME/SEQ TREND CON/ANAL. PAGE 97 A2000
TOP/EX DIPLOM

B41
SCHWARZENBERGER G.,POWER POLITICS: AN INTRODUCTION TO THE STUDY OF INTERNATIONAL RELATIONS AND POST-WAR PLANNING. INT/ORG FORCES COERCE WAR FEDERAL PEACE MORAL...POLICY CONCPT CON/ANAL BIBLIOG 20. PAGE 130 A2660
DIPLOM UTOPIA PWR

B42
CONOVER H.F.,FRENCH COLONIES IN AFRICA: A LIST OF REFERENCES. ALGERIA FRANCE MOROCCO SOMALIA SUDAN CULTURE AGRI LOC/G SECT FORCES DIPLOM INT/TRADE NAT/LISM HEALTH...CON/ANAL 20. PAGE 29 A0594
BIBLIOG AFR ECO/UNDEV COLONIAL

B43
LIPPMANN W.,US FOREIGN POLICY: SHIELD OF THE REPUBLIC. USA-45 WOR-45 CULTURE INT/ORG POL/PAR CREATE BAL/PWR DOMIN EDU/PROP WAR ORD/FREE PWR ...PLURIST CONCPT TREND CON/ANAL 20. PAGE 89 A1827
NAT/G DIPLOM PEACE

L44
CORWIN E.S.,"THE CONSTITUTION AND WORLD ORGANIZATION." FUT USA+45 USA-45 NAT/G EX/STRUC LEGIS PEACE KNOWL...CON/ANAL UN 20. PAGE 31 A0627
INT/ORG CONSTN SOVEREIGN

B45
VANCE H.L.,GUIDE TO THE LAW AND LEGAL LITERATURE OF MEXICO. LAW CONSTN FINAN LABOR FORCES ADJUD ADMIN ...CRIMLGY PHIL/SCI CON/ANAL 20 MEXIC/AMER. PAGE 158 A3217
BIBLIOG/A INT/LAW JURID CT/SYS

C46
GOODRICH L.M.,"CHARTER OF THE UNITED NATIONS: COMMENTARY AND DOCUMENTS." EX/STRUC ADMIN...INT/LAW
CONSTN INT/ORG

CON/ANAL BIBLIOG 20 UN. PAGE 54 A1106 DIPLOM

B47
DE HUSZAR G.B.,PERSISTENT INTERNATIONAL ISSUES. WOR+45 WOR-45 AGRI INDUS INT/ORG PROB/SOLV EFFICIENCY WEALTH...CON/ANAL ANTHOL UN. PAGE 35 A0704 DIPLOM PEACE ECO/TAC FOR/AID

S49
FOX W.T.R.,"INTERWAR INTERNATIONAL RELATIONS RESEARCH: THE AMERICAN EXPERIENCE." USA+45 USA-45 INTELL INT/ORG VOL/ASSN OP/RES ATTIT SKILL ...TIME/SEQ LEAGUE/NAT 20. PAGE 48 A0973 ACT/RES CON/ANAL

B50
CHASE E.P.,THE UNITED NATIONS IN ACTION. WOR+45 CONSTN DELIB/GP LEGIT ROUTINE COERCE PEACE ORD/FREE PWR...CON/ANAL GEN/LAWS UN 20. PAGE 26 A0524 INT/ORG STRUCT ARMS/CONT

B50
DE ARECHAGA E.J.,VOTING AND THE HANDLING OF DISPUTES IN THE SECURITY COUNCIL. WOR+45 CONSTN DIPLOM COERCE ORD/FREE...RECORD CON/ANAL GEN/METH COLD/WAR UN 20. PAGE 34 A0696 INT/ORG PWR

B50
LAUTERPACHT H.,INTERNATIONAL LAW AND HUMAN RIGHTS. USA+45 CONSTN STRUCT INT/ORG ACT/RES EDU/PROP PEACE PERSON ALL/VALS...CONCPT CON/ANAL GEN/LAWS UN 20. PAGE 86 A1750 DELIB/GP LAW INT/LAW

B51
CORMACK M.,SELECTED PAMPHLETS ON THE UNITED NATIONS AND INTERNATIONAL RELATIONS (PAMPHLET). USA+45 R+D EX/STRUC PROB/SOLV ROUTINE...POLICY CON/ANAL 20 UN NATO. PAGE 31 A0624 BIBLIOG/A NAT/G INT/ORG DIPLOM

B51
KELSEN H.,THE LAW OF THE UNITED NATIONS. WOR+45 STRUCT RIGID/FLEX ORD/FREE...INT/LAW JURID CONCPT CON/ANAL GEN/METH UN TOT/POP VAL/FREE 20. PAGE 77 A1581 INT/ORG ADJUD

B51
WABEKE B.H.,A GUIDE TO DUTCH BIBLIOGRAPHIES. BELGIUM INDONESIA NETHERLAND DIPLOM INT/TRADE WAR NAT/LISM KNOWL...ART/METH HUM JURID CON/ANAL 14/20. PAGE 160 A3257 BIBLIOG/A NAT/G CULTURE COLONIAL

L51
KELSEN H.,"RECENT TRENDS IN THE LAW OF THE UNITED NATIONS." KOREA WOR+45 CONSTN LEGIS DIPLOM LEGIT DETER WAR RIGID/FLEX HEALTH ORD/FREE RESPECT ...JURID CON/ANAL UN VAL/FREE 20 NATO. PAGE 77 A1582 INT/ORG LAW INT/LAW

N52
COORDINATING COMM DOC SOC SCI,INTERNATIONAL REPERTORY OF SOCIAL SCIENCE DOCUMENTATION CENTERS (PAMPHLET). ACT/RES OP/RES WRITING KNOWL...CON/ANAL METH. PAGE 30 A0610 BIBLIOG/A R+D NAT/G INT/ORG

B53
BORGESE G.,FOUNDATIONS OF THE WORLD REPUBLIC. FUT SOCIETY NAT/G CREATE LEGIT PERSON MORAL...MAJORIT CON/ANAL LEAGUE/NAT TOT/POP 20. PAGE 17 A0340 INT/ORG CONSTN PEACE

B53
NEISSER H.,NATIONAL INCOMES AND INTERNATIONAL TRADE. FRANCE GERMANY SWEDEN UK USA-45 EXTR/IND FINAN INDUS TEC/DEV PRICE BAL/PAY EQUILIB INCOME WEALTH...CHARTS METH 19 CHINJAP. PAGE 108 A2215 INT/TRADE PRODUC MARKET CON/ANAL

B54
BECKEL G.,WORKSHOPS FOR THE WORLD; THE SPECIALIZED AGENCIES OF THE UN. WOR+45 AGRI DIST/IND CREATE TEC/DEV BUDGET CONTROL TASK WEALTH...CHARTS ORG/CHARTS 20 UN CASEBOOK. PAGE 12 A0246 INT/ORG DIPLOM PEACE CON/ANAL

B54
BINANI G.D.,INDIA AT A GLANCE (REV. ED.). INDIA COM/IND FINAN INDUS LABOR PROVS SCHOOL PLAN DIPLOM INT/TRADE ADMIN...JURID 20. PAGE 14 A0288 INDEX CON/ANAL NAT/G ECO/UNDEV

S54
DODD S.C.,"THE SCIENTIFIC MEASUREMENT OF FITNESS FOR SELF-GOVERNMENT." FUT CONSTN ECO/UNDEV INT/ORG PLAN PWR...CONCPT QUANT CON/ANAL SOC/EXP UN LEAGUE/NAT 20. PAGE 38 A0767 NAT/G STAT SOVEREIGN

B56
BEARDSLEY S.W.,HUMAN RELATIONS IN INTERNATIONAL AFFAIRS: A GUIDE TO SIGNIFICANT INTERPRETATION AND RESEARCH. UNIV PERS/REL NAT/LISM DRIVE PERSON ...POLICY PSY SOC CON/ANAL IDEA/COMP 20. PAGE 12 A0241 BIBLIOG/A ATTIT CULTURE DIPLOM

B56
CONOVER H.F.,A GUIDE TO BIBLIOGRAPHIC TOOLS FOR RESEARCH IN FOREIGN AFFAIRS. AFR ASIA COM EUR+WWI WOR+45 BAL/PWR CON/ANAL. PAGE 30 A0602 BIBLIOG/A R+D DIPLOM INT/ORG

B56
LOVEDAY A.,REFLECTIONS ON INTERNATIONAL ADMINISTRATION. WOR+45 WOR-45 DELIB/GP ACT/RES ADMIN EXEC ROUTINE DRIVE...METH/CNCPT TIME/SEQ CON/ANAL SIMUL TOT/POP 20. PAGE 91 A1865 INT/ORG MGT

B56
WILSON P.,GOVERNMENT AND POLITICS OF INDIA AND PAKISTAN: 1885-1955; A BIBLIOGRAPHY OF WORKS IN WESTERN LANGUAGES. INDIA PAKISTAN CONSTN LOC/G POL/PAR FORCES DIPLOM ADMIN WAR CHOOSE...BIOG CON/ANAL 19/20. PAGE 165 A3361 BIBLIOG COLONIAL NAT/G S/ASIA

B57
ROSENNE S.,THE INTERNATIONAL COURT OF JUSTICE. WOR+45 LAW DOMIN LEGIT PEACE PWR SOVEREIGN...JURID CONCPT RECORD TIME/SEQ CON/ANAL CHARTS UN TOT/POP VAL/FREE LEAGUE/NAT 20 ICJ. PAGE 124 A2537 INT/ORG CT/SYS INT/LAW

N57
BIBLIOGRAPHY OF NEW GUIDES AND AIDS TO PUBLIC DOCUMENTS USE, 1953-1956 (PAMPHLET). WOR+45 MUNIC DIPLOM...CON/ANAL CHARTS METH. PAGE 164 A3347 BIBLIOG/A NAT/G LOC/G INT/ORG

B58
GARTHOFF R.L.,SOVIET STRATEGY IN THE NUCLEAR AGE. FUT USSR R+D INT/ORG NAT/G ACT/RES TEC/DEV DOMIN DETER WAR ATTIT PWR...RELATIV METH/CNCPT SELF/OBS TREND CON/ANAL STERTYP GEN/LAWS 20. PAGE 51 A1052 COM FORCES BAL/PWR NUC/PWR

B58
JAPANESE ASSOCIATION INT. LAW,JAPAN AND THE UNITED NATIONS. SOCIETY ROUTINE ATTIT DRIVE PERCEPT RIGID/FLEX ORD/FREE...METH/CNCPT CON/ANAL CHINJAP UN. PAGE 73 A1497 ASIA INT/ORG

B58
YUAN TUNG-LI,CHINA IN WESTERN LITERATURE. SECT DIPLOM...ART/METH GEOG JURID SOC BIOG CON/ANAL. PAGE 169 A3440 BIBLIOG ASIA CULTURE HUM

S58
BLAISDELL D.C.,"PRESSURE GROUPS, FOREIGN POLICIES, AND INTERNATIONAL POLITICS." USA+45 WOR+45 INT/ORG PLAN DOMIN EDU/PROP LEGIT ADMIN ROUTINE CHOOSE ...DECISION MGT METH/CNCPT CON/ANAL 20. PAGE 15 A0303 PROF/ORG PWR

S58
LASSWELL H.D.,"THE SCIENTIFIC STUDY OF INTERNATIONAL RELATIONS." USA+45 INT/ORG CREATE EDU/PROP DETER ATTIT PERCEPT PWR...DECISION CONCPT METH/CNCPT STYLE CON/ANAL 20. PAGE 85 A1740 PHIL/SCI GEN/METH DIPLOM

B59
KULSKI W.W.,PEACEFUL CO-EXISTENCE: AN ANALYSIS OF SOVIET FOREIGN POLICY. WOR+45 INTELL SOCIETY ECO/UNDEV POL/PAR EDU/PROP COERCE DRIVE RIGID/FLEX PWR SKILL...PSY CONCPT HIST/WRIT CON/ANAL GEN/METH WORK VAL/FREE 20. PAGE 83 A1691 PLAN DIPLOM USSR

B59
LOPEZ M.M.,CATALOGOS DE PUBLICACIONES PERIODICAS MEXICANAS. L/A+17C CULTURE NAT/G DIPLOM 20 MEXIC/AMER. PAGE 91 A1861 BIBLIOG PRESS CON/ANAL

B59
MATHISEN T.,METHODOLOGY IN THE STUDY OF INTERNATIONAL RELATIONS. FUT WOR+45 SOCIETY INT/ORG NAT/G POL/PAR WAR PEACE KNOWL PWR...RELATIV CONCPT METH/CNCPT TREND HYPO/EXP METH TOT/POP 20. PAGE 96 A1965 GEN/METH CON/ANAL DIPLOM CREATE

S59
BAILEY S.D.,"THE FUTURE COMPOSITION OF THE TRUSTEESHIP COUNCIL." FUT WOR+45 CONSTN VOL/ASSN ADMIN ATTIT PWR...OBS TREND CON/ANAL VAL/FREE UN 20. PAGE 10 A0203 INT/ORG NAT/LISM SOVEREIGN

S59
BROMKE A.,"DISENGAGEMENT IN EAST EUROPE." COM USSR INT/ORG DIPLOM EDU/PROP NEUTRAL NUC/PWR DRIVE RIGID/FLEX PWR...PSY CONCPT CON/ANAL GEN/METH VAL/FREE 20. PAGE 19 A0388 BAL/PWR

S59
FISCHER L.,"THE SOVIET-AMERICAN ANTAGONISM: HOW WILL IT END." CONSTN CULTURE PLAN TEC/DEV RIGID/FLEX SUPEGO ORD/FREE...MARXIST DECISION PSY CONCPT CON/ANAL GEN/LAWS VAL/FREE 20 COLD/WAR. PAGE 46 A0936 USA+45 PWR DIPLOM USSR

S59
KINDLEBERGER C.P.,"UNITED STATES ECONOMIC FOREIGN POLICY: RESEARCH REQUIREMENTS FOR 1965." FUT USA+45 WOR+45 DIST/IND MARKET INT/ORG ECO/TAC INT/TRADE WEALTH...OBS TREND CON/ANAL GEN/LAWS VAL/FREE 20. PAGE 79 A1621 FINAN ECO/DEV FOR/AID

S59
KOHN L.Y.,"ISRAEL AND NEW NATION STATES OF ASIA AND AFRICA." AFR ASIA FUT S/ASIA VOL/ASSN TEC/DEV NAT/LISM RIGID/FLEX SKILL WEALTH...RELATIV OBS TREND CON/ANAL 20. PAGE 81 A1663 ECO/UNDEV ECO/TAC FOR/AID ISRAEL

S59
PADELFORD N.J.,"REGIONAL COOPERATION IN THE SOUTH PACIFIC: THE SOUTH PACIFIC COMMISSION." FUT NEW/ZEALND UK WOR+45 CULTURE ECO/UNDEV LOC/G VOL/ASSN...OBS CON/ANAL UNESCO VAL/FREE AUSTRAL 20. PAGE 112 A2308 INT/ORG ADMIN

S59
QUIGLEY H.S.,"TOWARD REAPPRAISAL OF OUR CHINA POLICY." CHINA/COM USA+45 INT/ORG PLAN ECO/TAC PERCEPT ORD/FREE...DECISION PSY CON/ANAL GEN/METH VAL/FREE 20. PAGE 118 A2427 ASIA KNOWL DIPLOM

S59
SAYEGH F.,"ARAB NATIONALISM AND SOVIET-AMERICAN RELATIONS." ISLAM USA+45 ECO/UNDEV PLAN ECO/TAC LEGIT NAT/LISM DRIVE PERCEPT KNOWL PWR...DECISION CONCPT STAT RECORD TREND CON/ANAL VAL/FREE 20 DIPLOM USSR

COLD/WAR. PAGE 127 A2610

S59
STOESSINGER J.G.,"THE INTERNATIONAL ATOMIC ENERGY AGENCY: THE FIRST PHASE." FUT WOR+45 NAT/G VOL/ASSN DELIB/GP BAL/PWR LEGIT ADMIN ROUTINE PWR...OBS CON/ANAL GEN/LAWS VAL/FREE 20 IAEA. PAGE 138 A2829 INT/ORG ECO/DEV FOR/AID NUC/PWR

B60
PLAMENATZ J.,ON ALIEN RULE AND SELF-GOVERNMENT. AFR FUT S/ASIA WOR+45 CULTURE SOCIETY ECO/UNDEV INT/ORG DOMIN EDU/PROP ATTIT RIGID/FLEX ALL/VALS...POLICY CONCPT OBS TREND CON/ANAL GEN/LAWS TOT/POP VAL/FREE. PAGE 116 A2386 NAT/G CONSTN NAT/LISM SOVEREIGN

L60
DEUTSCH K.W.,"TOWARD AN INVENTORY OF BASIC TRENDS AND PATTERNS IN COMPARATIVE AND INTERNATIONAL POLITICS." UNIV WOR+45 SOCIETY STRUCT INT/ORG NAT/G CREATE PLAN EDU/PROP KNOWL...PHIL/SCI METH/CNCPT STAT SELF/OBS OBS/ENVIR SAMP TREND CON/ANAL CHARTS SOC/EXP GEN/METH 20. PAGE 36 A0739 R+D PERCEPT

S60
COHEN A.,"THE NEW AFRICA AND THE UN." FUT ECO/UNDEV NAT/G ECO/TAC INT/TRADE CHOOSE ATTIT ORD/FREE PWR ...POLICY METH/CNCPT OBS TREND CON/ANAL GEN/LAWS TOT/POP VAL/FREE UN 20. PAGE 27 A0558 AFR INT/ORG BAL/PWR FOR/AID

S60
GOODMAN E.,"THE CRY OF NATIONAL LIBERATION: RECENT SOVIET ATTITUDES TOWARDS NATIONAL SELF-DETERMINATION." COM INT/ORG LEGIS ROUTINE PWR ...TIME/SEQ CON/ANAL STERTYP GEN/LAWS 20 UN. PAGE 54 A1101 ATTIT EDU/PROP SOVEREIGN USSR

S60
NANES A.,"THE EUROPEAN COMMUNITY AND THE UNITED STATES: EVOLVING RELATIONS." EUR+WWI USA+45 WOR+45 ECO/UNDEV MARKET NAT/G DELIB/GP PLAN LEGIT ATTIT PWR WEALTH...CONCPT STAT TIME/SEQ CON/ANAL EEC OEEC 20 EURATOM. PAGE 107 A2194 INT/ORG REGION

S60
RHYNE C.S.,"LAW AS AN INSTRUMENT FOR PEACE." FUT WOR+45 PLAN LEGIT ROUTINE ARMS/CONT NUC/PWR ATTIT ORD/FREE...JURID METH/CNCPT TREND CON/ANAL HYPO/EXP COLD/WAR 20. PAGE 120 A2471 ADJUD EDU/PROP INT/LAW PEACE

N60
ERDMAN P.E.,COMMON MARKETS AND FREE TRADE AREAS (PAMPHLET). USA+45 MARKET INT/ORG TEC/DEV DIPLOM UTIL...CON/ANAL CHARTS BIBLIOG 20 EEC OEEC. PAGE 42 A0859 TREND PROB/SOLV INT/TRADE ECO/DEV

B61
BULL H.,THE CONTROL OF THE ARMS RACE. COM USA+45 INT/ORG NAT/G PLAN TEC/DEV DIPLOM ATTIT...RELATIV DECISION CONCPT SELF/OBS TREND CON/ANAL GEN/METH 20 COLD/WAR. PAGE 21 A0429 FORCES PWR ARMS/CONT NUC/PWR

B61
CONFERENCE ATLANTIC COMMUNITY,AN INTRODUCTORY BIBLIOGRAPHY. COM WOR+45 FORCES DIPLOM ECO/TAC WAR ...INT/LAW HIST/WRIT COLD/WAR NATO. PAGE 29 A0584 BIBLIOG/A CON/ANAL INT/ORG

B61
DIA M.,THE AFRICAN NATIONS AND WORLD SOLIDARITY. ISLAM CULTURE ELITES ECO/DEV ECO/UNDEV INT/ORG NAT/G PLAN ECO/TAC INT/TRADE EDU/PROP NAT/LISM ATTIT DRIVE ORD/FREE WEALTH...SOCIALIST CONCPT CON/ANAL GEN/LAWS TOT/POP 20. PAGE 37 A0753 AFR REGION SOCISM

B61
ROSENAU J.N.,PUBLIC OPINION AND FOREIGN POLICY; AN OPERATIONAL FORMULA. USA+45 COM/IND OP/RES EDU/PROP LOBBY CROWD...CON/ANAL BIBLIOG 20. PAGE 124 A2532 ATTIT PRESS DIPLOM

B62
BAILEY S.D.,THE SECRETARIAT OF THE UNITED NATIONS. FUT WOR+45 DELIB/GP PLAN BAL/PWR DOMIN EDU/PROP ADMIN PEACE ATTIT PWR...DECISION CONCPT TREND CON/ANAL CHARTS UN VAL/FREE COLD/WAR 20. PAGE 10 A0205 INT/ORG EXEC DIPLOM

B62
COLLISON R.L.,BIBLIOGRAPHIES, SUBJECT AND NATIONAL: A GUIDE TO THEIR CONTENTS, ARRANGEMENT, AND USE (2ND REV. ED.). SECT DIPLOM...ART/METH GEOG HUM PHIL/SCI SOC MATH BIOG 20. PAGE 28 A0569 BIBLIOG/A CON/ANAL BIBLIOG

B62
NICHOLAS H.G.,THE UNITED NATIONS AS A POLITICAL INSTITUTION. WOR+45 CONSTN EX/STRUC ACT/RES LEGIT PERCEPT KNOWL PWR...CONCPT TIME/SEQ CON/ANAL ORG/CHARTS UN 20. PAGE 109 A2228 INT/ORG ROUTINE

S62
CROAN M.,"POLYCENTRISM: COMMUNIST INTERNATIONAL RELATIONS." ASIA STRUCT INT/ORG NAT/G POL/PAR CONSULT PLAN DOMIN EDU/PROP COERCE ATTIT RIGID/FLEX SOCISM...POLICY CONCPT TREND CON/ANAL GEN/LAWS MARX/KARL. PAGE 33 A0663 COM CREATE DIPLOM NAT/LISM

S62
MILLIKEN M.,"NEW AND OLD CRITERIA FOR AID." WOR+45 ECO/DEV ECO/UNDEV ACT/RES PLAN ATTIT KNOWL...TREND CON/ANAL SIMUL GEN/METH 20. PAGE 102 A2083 USA+45 ECO/TAC FOR/AID

S62
NANES A.,"DISARMAMENT: THE LAST SEVEN YEARS." COM EUR+WWI USA+45 USSR INT/ORG FORCES TOP/EX CREATE LEGIT NUC/PWR DISPL ORD/FREE...CONCPT TIME/SEQ CON/ANAL 20. PAGE 107 A2195 DELIB/GP RIGID/FLEX ARMS/CONT

B63
HOVET T. JR.,AFRICA IN THE UNITED NATIONS. AFR DELIB/GP EDU/PROP LOBBY CHOOSE ORD/FREE PWR RESPECT SKILL...STAT TIME/SEQ CON/ANAL CHARTS STERTYP VAL/FREE 20 UN. PAGE 68 A1397 INT/ORG USSR

B63
NORTH R.C.,CONTENT ANALYSIS: A HANDBOOK WITH APPLICATIONS FOR THE STUDY OF INTERNATIONAL CRISIS. ASIA COM EUR+WWI MOD/EUR INT/ORG TEC/DEV DOMIN EDU/PROP ROUTINE COERCE PERCEPT RIGID/FLEX ALL/VALS ...QUANT TESTS CON/ANAL SIMUL GEN/LAWS VAL/FREE. PAGE 110 A2252 METH/CNCPT COMPUT/IR USSR

B63
WALKER A.A.,OFFICIAL PUBLICATIONS OF SIERRA LEONE AND GAMBIA. GAMBIA SIER/LEONE UK LAW CONSTN LEGIS PLAN BUDGET DIPLOM...SOC SAMP CON/ANAL 20. PAGE 160 A3262 BIBLIOG NAT/G COLONIAL ADMIN

S63
GANDOLFI A.,"LES ACCORDS DE COOPERATION EN MATIERE DE POLITIQUE ETRANGERE ENTRE LA FRANCE ET LES NOUVEAUX ETATS AFRICAINS ET." AFR ISLAM MADAGASCAR WOR+45 ECO/DEV INT/ORG NAT/G DELIB/GP ECO/TAC ALL/VALS...CON/ANAL 20. PAGE 51 A1038 VOL/ASSN ECO/UNDEV DIPLOM FRANCE

S63
MODELSKI G.,"STUDY OF ALLIANCES." WOR+45 WOR-45 INT/ORG NAT/G FORCES LEGIT ADMIN CHOOSE ALL/VALS PWR SKILL...INT/LAW CONCPT GEN/LAWS 20 TREATY. PAGE 102 A2099 VOL/ASSN CON/ANAL DIPLOM

B64
CZERNIN F.,VERSAILLES - 1919. EUR+WWI USA-45 FACE/GP POL/PAR VOL/ASSN DELIB/GP TOP/EX CREATE BAL/PWR DIPLOM LEGIT NAT/LISM PEACE ATTIT RIGID/FLEX ORD/FREE PWR...CON/ANAL LEAGUE/NAT 20 VERSAILLES. PAGE 33 A0671 INT/ORG STRUCT

B64
GRODZINS M.,THE ATOMIC AGE: FORTY-FIVE SCIENTISTS AND SCHOLARS SPEAK ON NATIONAL AND WORLD AFFAIRS. FUT USA+45 WOR+45 R+D INT/ORG NAT/G CONSULT TEC/DEV EDU/PROP ATTIT PERSON ORD/FREE...HUM CONCPT TIME/SEQ CON/ANAL. PAGE 57 A1169 INTELL ARMS/CONT NUC/PWR

L64
RIPLEY R.B.,"INTERAGENCY COMMITTEES AND INCREMENTALISM: THE CASE OF AID TO INDIA." INDIA USA+45 INTELL NAT/G DELIB/GP ACT/RES DIPLOM ROUTINE NAT/LISM ATTIT PWR...SOC CONCPT NEW/IDEA TIME/SEQ CON/ANAL VAL/FREE 20. PAGE 121 A2483 EXEC MGT FOR/AID

S64
HICKEY D.,"THE PHILOSOPHICAL ARGUMENT FOR WORLD GOVERNMENT." WOR+45 SOCIETY ACT/RES PLAN LEGIT ADJUD PEACE PERCEPT PERSON ORD/FREE...HUM JURID PHIL/SCI METH/CNCPT CON/ANAL STERTYP GEN/LAWS TOT/POP 20. PAGE 65 A1327 FUT INT/ORG

S64
KOJIMA K.,"THE PATTERN OF INTERNATIONAL TRADE AMONG ADVANCED COUNTRIES." EUR+WWI UK USA+45 WOR+45 MARKET NAT/G ECO/TAC WEALTH...MATH STAT CON/ANAL CHARTS EEC CHINJAP 20 CHINJAP. PAGE 81 A1665 ECO/DEV TREND INT/TRADE

S64
MAGGS P.B.,"SOVIET VIEWPOINT ON NUCLEAR WEAPONS IN INTERNATIONAL LAW." USSR WOR+45 INT/ORG FORCES DIPLOM ARMS/CONT ATTIT ORD/FREE PWR...POLICY JURID CONCPT OBS TREND CON/ANAL GEN/LAWS VAL/FREE 20. PAGE 93 A1905 COM LAW INT/LAW NUC/PWR

S64
TAUBENFELD R.K.,"INDEPENDENT REVENUE FOR THE UNITED NATIONS." WOR+45 SOCIETY STRUCT INDUS NAT/G CONSULT ACT/RES PLAN ECO/TAC LEGIT WEALTH...DECISION CON/ANAL GEN/METH UN 20. PAGE 142 A2896 INT/ORG FINAN

B65
WALKER A.A.,THE RHODESIAS AND NYASALAND: A GUIDE TO OFFICIAL PUBLICATIONS. RHODESIA UK OP/RES PLAN PROB/SOLV DIPLOM...POLICY SOC CON/ANAL 19/20 NYASALAND. PAGE 160 A3263 BIBLIOG NAT/G COLONIAL AFR

B65
WITHERELL J.W.,MADAGASCAR AND ADJACENT ISLANDS; A GUIDE TO OFFICIAL PUBLICATIONS (PAMPHLET). FRANCE MADAGASCAR S/ASIA UK LAW OP/RES PLAN DIPLOM ...POLICY CON/ANAL 19/20. PAGE 165 A3371 BIBLIOG COLONIAL LOC/G ADMIN

S65
HOLSTI O.R.,"EAST-WEST CONFLICT AND SINO-SOVIET RELATIONS" CHINA/COM USSR COMPUTER REGION DECISION. PAGE 67 A1373 VOL/ASSN DIPLOM CON/ANAL COM

B66
BESTERMAN T.,A WORLD BIBLIOGRAPHY OF BIBLIOGRAPHIES (4TH ED.). WOR+45 WOR-45 LAW INT/ORG ADMIN CON/ANAL. PAGE 14 A0282 BIBLIOG/A DIPLOM

B66
BLACKSTOCK P.W.,AGENTS OF DECEIT: FRAUDS, FORGERIES AND POLITICAL INTRIGUES AMONG NATIONS. USSR EDU/PROP WRITING KNOWL 18/20 COLD/WAR KENNAN/G. PAGE 15 A0302 CON/ANAL DIPLOM HIST/WRIT

B67
UNIVERSAL REFERENCE SYSTEM,BIBLIOGRAPHY OF BIBLIOGRAPHIES IN POLITICAL SCIENCE, GOVERNMENT, AND PUBLIC POLICY (VOLUME III). WOR+45 WOR-45 LAW BIBLIOG/A NAT/G DIPLOM

ADMIN...SOC CON/ANAL COMPUT/IR GEN/METH. PAGE 149 A3042 POLICY

S67
MANN F.A.,"THE BRETTON WOODS AGREEMENT IN THE ENGLISH COURTS." UK JUDGE ADJUD CT/SYS...JURID PREDICT CON/ANAL 20. PAGE 94 A1923 LAW INT/LAW CONSTN

S67
OLIVIER G.,"ASPECTS JURIDIQUES DE L'ADOPTION DU TRAITE CECA A LA CRISE CHARBONNIERE (SUITE ET FIN)" LAW DIST/IND PLAN DIPLOM RATION PRICE ADMIN COST DEMAND...POLICY CON/ANAL ECSC TREATY. PAGE 112 A2288 INT/TRADE INT/ORG EXTR/IND CONSTN

CON/INTERP....CONSTITUTIONAL INTERPRETATION

CONCEN/CMP....CONCENTRATION CAMPS

CONCPT....SUBJECT-MATTER CONCEPTS

CONDEMNATN....CONDEMNATION OF LAND OR PROPERTY

CONDOTTIER....CONDOTTIERI - HIRED MILITIA

CONF ON FUTURE OF COMMONWEALTH A0583

CONFER....CONFERENCES; SEE ALSO DELIB/GP

N
INTERNATIONAL COMN JURISTS,AFRICAN CONFERENCE ON THE RULE OF LAW. AFR INT/ORG LEGIS DIPLOM CONFER COLONIAL ORD/FREE...CONCPT METH/COMP 20. PAGE 71 A1452 CT/SYS JURID DELIB/GP

N
INTERNATIONAL BOOK NEWS, 1928-1934. ECO/UNDEV FINAN INDUS LABOR INT/TRADE CONFER ADJUD COLONIAL...HEAL SOC/WK CHARTS 20 LEAGUE/NAT. PAGE 1 A0010 BIBLIOG/A DIPLOM INT/LAW INT/ORG

N
CHINA QUARTERLY. COM AGRI INDUS ACADEM POL/PAR INT/TRADE CONFER GOV/REL...TIME/SEQ CON/ANAL INDEX 20. PAGE 2 A0032 BIBLIOG/A ASIA DIPLOM POLICY

N
LA DOCUMENTATION FRANCAISE,CHRONOLOGIE INTERNATIONAL. FRANCE WOR+45 CHIEF PROB/SOLV BAL/PWR CONFER LEAD...POLICY CON/ANAL 20. PAGE 83 A1705 BIBLIOG/A DIPLOM TIME/SEQ

N
UNITED NATIONS,OFFICIAL RECORDS OF THE ECONOMIC AND SOCIAL COUNCIL OF THE UNITED NATIONS. WOR+45 DIPLOM INT/TRADE CONFER...SOC SOC/WK 20 UN UNESCO. PAGE 148 A3031 INT/ORG DELIB/GP WRITING

N
UNITED NATIONS,OFFICIAL RECORDS OF THE UNITED NATIONS' ATOMIC ENERGY COMMISSION - DISARMAMENT COMMISSION. WOR+45 TEC/DEV DIPLOM WRITING NUC/PWR 20 UN. PAGE 148 A3032 ARMS/CONT INT/ORG DELIB/GP CONFER

NLO
WHITE J.A.,THE DIPLOMACY OF THE RUSSO-JAPANESE WAR. ASIA KOREA RUSSIA FORCES CONFER CONTROL PEACE ...BIBLIOG 19 CHINJAP. PAGE 164 A3336 DIPLOM WAR BAL/PWR

B08
GRIFFIN A.P.C.,LIST OF REFERENCES ON INTERNATIONAL ARBITRATION. FRANCE L/A+17C USA-45 WOR-45 DIPLOM CONFER COLONIAL ARMS/CONT BAL/PAY EQUILIB SOVEREIGN ...DECISION 19/20 MEXIC/AMER. PAGE 56 A1156 BIBLIOG/A INT/ORG INT/LAW DELIB/GP

B10
GRIFFIN A.P.C.,LIST OF REFERENCES ON RECIPROCITY (2ND REV. ED.). CANADA CUBA UK USA-45 WOR-45 NAT/G TARIFFS CONFER COLONIAL CONTROL SANCTION CONSEN ALL/VALS...DECISION 19/20. PAGE 56 A1157 BIBLIOG/A VOL/ASSN DIPLOM REPAR

N19
ASIAN-AFRICAN CONFERENCE,SELECTED DOCUMENTS OF THE BANDUNG CONFERENCE (PAMPHLET). S/ASIA PLAN ECO/TAC CONFER REGION REV NAT/LISM 20. PAGE 9 A0191 NEUTRAL ECO/UNDEV COLONIAL DIPLOM

N19
LISKA G.,THE GREATER MAGHREB: FROM INDEPENDENCE TO UNITY? (PAMPHLET). ALGERIA ISLAM MOROCCO PROB/SOLV BAL/PWR CONFER COLONIAL REPRESENT NAT/LISM 20 TUNIS. PAGE 90 A1835 ECO/UNDEV REGION DIPLOM DOMIN

N19
MEZERIK A.G.,ATOM TESTS AND RADIATION HAZARDS (PAMPHLET). WOR+45 INT/ORG DIPLOM DETER 20 UN TREATY. PAGE 100 A2059 NUC/PWR ARMS/CONT CONFER HEALTH

N19
UNITED ARAB REPUBLIC,THE PROBLEM OF THE PALESTINIAN REFUGEES (PAMPHLET). ISRAEL UAR LAW PROB/SOLV EDU/PROP CONFER ADJUD CONTROL NAT/LISM HEALTH 20 JEWS UN MIGRATION. PAGE 148 A3029 STRANGE GP/REL INGP/REL DIPLOM

B22
MYERS D.P.,MANUAL OF COLLECTIONS OF TREATIES AND OF COLLECTIONS RELATING TO TREATIES. MOD/EUR INT/ORG LEGIS WRITING ADMIN SOVEREIGN...INT/LAW 19/20. PAGE 106 A2186 BIBLIOG/A DIPLOM CONFER

L22
DORE R.,"BIBLIOGRAPHIE DES 'LIVRES JAUNES' A LA DATE DU 1ER JANVIER 1922." FRANCE CONFER 19/20. PAGE 38 A0773 BIBLIOG DIPLOM INT/ORG

B28
LAPRADELLE,ANNUAIRE DE LA VIE INTERNATIONALE: POLITIQUE, ECONOMIQUE, JURIDIQUE. INT/ORG CONFER ARMS/CONT 20. PAGE 85 A1729 BIBLIOG DIPLOM INT/LAW

B38
GREGORY W.,INTERNATIONAL CONGRESSES AND CONFERENCES 1840-1937: A UNION LIST OF THEIR PUBLICATIONS AVAILABLE IN US AND CANADA. WOR-45 LEGIS ATTIT ...POLICY 19/20. PAGE 56 A1145 BIBLIOG INT/ORG CONFER

B38
HAGUE PERMANENT CT INTL JUSTIC,WORLD COURT REPORTS: COLLECTION OF THE JUDGEMENTS ORDERS AND OPINIONS VOLUME 3 1932-35. WOR-45 LAW DELIB/GP CONFER WAR PEACE ATTIT...DECISION ANTHOL 20 WORLD/CT CASEBOOK. PAGE 59 A1214 INT/ORG CT/SYS DIPLOM ADJUD

B39
WHEELER-BENNET J.W.,THE FORGOTTEN PEACE: BREST-LITOVSK. COM GERMANY USSR TOP/EX AGREE WAR PWR ...BIBLIOG 20 TREATY LENIN/VI UKRAINE. PAGE 163 A3326 PEACE DIPLOM CONFER

B40
CONOVER H.F.,A BRIEF LIST OF REFERENCES ON WESTERN HEMISPHERE DEFENSE (PAMPHLET). USA-45 NAT/G CONSULT DELIB/GP FORCES BAL/PWR CONFER DETER...PREDICT CON/ANAL 20. PAGE 29 A0591 BIBLIOG DIPLOM PLAN INT/ORG

B42
CROWE S.E.,THE BERLIN WEST AFRICA CONFERENCE, 1884-85. GERMANY ELITES MARKET INT/ORG DELIB/GP FORCES PROB/SOLV BAL/PWR CAP/ISM DOMIN COLONIAL ...INT/LAW 19. PAGE 33 A0664 AFR CONFER INT/TRADE DIPLOM

B43
CONOVER H.F.,THE BALKANS: A SELECTED LIST OF REFERENCES. ALBANIA BULGARIA ROMANIA YUGOSLAVIA INT/ORG PROB/SOLV DIPLOM LEGIT CONFER ADJUD WAR NAT/LISM PEACE PWR 20 LEAGUE/NAT. PAGE 29 A0596 BIBLIOG EUR+WWI

B43
HAGUE PERMANENT CT INTL JUSTIC,WORLD COURT REPORTS: COLLECTION OF THE JUDGEMENTS ORDERS AND OPINIONS VOLUME 4 1936-42. WOR-45 CONFER PEACE ATTIT ...DECISION JURID ANTHOL 20 WORLD/CT CASEBOOK. PAGE 59 A1215 INT/ORG CT/SYS DIPLOM ADJUD

B47
SOCIAL SCIENCE RESEARCH COUN,PUBLIC REACTION TO THE ATOMIC BOMB AND WORLD AFFAIRS. SOCIETY CONFER ARMS/CONT...STAT QU SAMP CHARTS 20. PAGE 135 A2757 ATTIT NUC/PWR DIPLOM WAR

B52
FIFIELD R.H.,WOODROW WILSON AND THE FAR EAST. ASIA CHIEF BAL/PWR CONFER COLONIAL ARMS/CONT WAR ...TIME/SEQ NAT/COMP BIBLIOG 19/20 WILSON/W LEAGUE/NAT PRESIDENT. PAGE 45 A0926 DIPLOM DELIB/GP INT/ORG

C52
FIFIELD R.H.,"WOODROW WILSON AND THE FAR EAST." ASIA CHIEF DELIB/GP BAL/PWR CONFER COLONIAL ARMS/CONT WAR...TIME/SEQ NAT/COMP 19/20 WILSON/W LEAGUE/NAT. PAGE 45 A0925 BIBLIOG DIPLOM INT/ORG

B53
KANTOR H.,A BIBLIOGRAPHY OF UNPUBLISHED DOCTORAL DISSERTATIONS AND MASTERS' THESES DEALING WITH GOVTS, POL, INT REL OF LAT AM. L/A+17C INT/ORG POL/PAR ACT/RES OP/RES CONFER ATTIT...INT/LAW PHIL/SCI 20. PAGE 76 A1556 BIBLIOG ACADEM DIPLOM NAT/G

B53
LANGER W.L.,THE UNDECLARED WAR, 1940-1941. EUR+WWI GERMANY USA-45 USSR AIR FORCES TEC/DEV CONFER CONTROL COERCE PERCEPT ORD/FREE PWR 20 CHINJAP EUROPE. PAGE 84 A1727 WAR POLICY DIPLOM

B55
UN HEADQUARTERS LIBRARY,BIBLIOGRAPHIE DE LA CHARTE DES NATIONS UNIES. CHINA/COM KOREA WOR+45 VOL/ASSN CONFER ADMIN COERCE PEACE ATTIT ORD/FREE SOVEREIGN ...INT/LAW 20 UNESCO UN. PAGE 147 A3001 BIBLIOG/A INT/ORG DIPLOM

B56
SNELL J.L.,THE MEANING OF YALTA: BIG THREE DIPLOMACY AND THE NEW BALANCE OF POWER. EUR+WWI GERMANY USA-45 USSR FORCES PLAN BAL/PWR DIPLOM WAR CHOOSE PEACE...CHARTS BIBLIOG 20 UN CHINJAP ROOSEVLT/F. PAGE 134 A2749 CONFER CHIEF POLICY PROB/SOLV

B56
TOYNBEE A.,THE WAR AND THE NEUTRALS. L/A+17C PORTUGAL SPAIN SWEDEN SWITZERLND TURKEY WOR+45 WOR-45 ECO/TAC CONFER CONTROL REGION 20. PAGE 145 A2957 NEUTRAL WAR INT/TRADE DIPLOM

B56
US DEPARTMENT OF STATE,THE SUEZ CANAL PROBLEM; JULY 26-SEPTEMBER 22, 1956. UAR WOR+45 BAL/PWR COERCE NAT/LISM ATTIT ORD/FREE SOVEREIGN 20 SUEZ. PAGE 151 DIPLOM CONFER INT/TRADE

A3091

C56
VAGTS A.,"DEFENSE AND DIPLOMACY: THE SOLDIER AND THE CONDUCT OF FOREIGN RELATIONS." OP/RES CONFER DETER WAR PEACE RESPECT...POLICY DECISION CONCPT BIBLIOG 17/20. PAGE 158 A3209 — DIPLOM FORCES HIST/WRIT

B57
US SENATE COMM ON JUDICIARY,HEARING BEFORE SUBCOMMITTEE ON COMMITTEE OF JUDICIARY, UNITED STATES SENATE: S. J. RES. 3. USA+45 NAT/G CONSULT DELIB/GP DIPLOM ADJUD LOBBY REPRESENT 20 CONGRESS TREATY. PAGE 157 A3192 — LEGIS CONSTN CONFER AGREE

B57
US SENATE SPEC COMM FOR AID,COMPILATION OF STUDIES AND SURVEYS. AFR ASIA L/A+17C USA+45 ECO/UNDEV AGRI INT/ORG CONSULT TEC/DEV CONFER TOTALISM...NAT/COMP 20 CONGRESS. PAGE 157 A3197 — FOR/AID DIPLOM ORD/FREE DELIB/GP

N57
US SENATE SPECIAL COMM FOR AFF,REPORT OF THE SPECIAL COMMITTEE TO STUDY THE FOREIGN AID PROGRAM (PAMPHLET). USA+45 CONSULT DELIB/GP LEGIS PLAN TEC/DEV CONFER SUPEGO CONGRESS. PAGE 157 A3199 — FOR/AID ORD/FREE ECO/UNDEV DIPLOM

B58
CRAIG G.A.,FROM BISMARCK TO ADENAUER: ASPECTS OF GERMAN STATECRAFT. GERMANY INTELL FORCES ECO/TAC CONFER COERCE WAR GP/REL ORD/FREE PWR CONSERVE 19/20 BISMARCK/O ADENAUER/K. PAGE 32 A0653 — DIPLOM LEAD NAT/G

B58
MANSERGH N.,COMMONWEALTH PERSPECTIVES. GHANA UK LAW VOL/ASSN CONFER HEALTH SOVEREIGN...GEOG CHARTS ANTHOL 20 CMN/WLTH AUSTRAL. PAGE 94 A1930 — DIPLOM COLONIAL INT/ORG INGP/REL

B58
NATIONAL PLANNING ASSOCIATION,1970 WITHOUT ARMS CONTROL (PAMPHLET). WOR+45 PROB/SOLV TEC/DEV DIPLOM CONFER DETER NUC/PWR WAR...CHARTS 20 COLD/WAR. PAGE 107 A2204 — ARMS/CONT ORD/FREE WEAPON PREDICT

B58
UN INTL CONF ON PEACEFUL USE,PROGRESS IN ATOMIC ENERGY (VOL. I). WOR+45 R+D PLAN TEC/DEV CONFER CONTROL PEACE SKILL...CHARTS ANTHOL 20 UN BAGHDAD. PAGE 147 A3003 — NUC/PWR DIPLOM WORKER EDU/PROP

N58
US HOUSE COMM FOREIGN AFFAIRS,HEARINGS ON DRAFT LEGISLATION TO AMEND FURTHER THE MUTUAL SECURITY ACT OF 1954 (PAMPHLET). USA+45 CONSULT FORCES BUDGET DIPLOM DETER COST ORD/FREE...JURID 20 DEPT/DEFEN UN DEPT/STATE. PAGE 153 A3123 — LEGIS DELIB/GP CONFER WEAPON

N58
US HOUSE COMM FOREIGN AFFAIRS,HEARINGS ON THE FAR EAST AND THE PACIFIC (PAMPHLET). LAOS USA+45 NAT/G CONSULT FORCES CONFER DEBATE ORD/FREE 20. PAGE 153 A3124 — FOR/AID DIPLOM DELIB/GP LEGIS

N58
US HOUSE COMM FOREIGN AFFAIRS,HEARINGS ON REVIEW OF THE MUTUAL SECURITY PROGRAMS; EXAMINATION OF SELECTED PROJECTS IN FORMOSA AND PAKISTAN (PAMPHLET). ASIA PAKISTAN TAIWAN INDUS CONSULT DELIB/GP LEGIS BUDGET CONFER DEBATE 20. PAGE 153 A3125 — FOR/AID ECO/UNDEV DIPLOM ECO/TAC

B59
EGYPTIAN SOCIETY OF INT LAW,THE MONROVIA CONFERENCE (PAMPHLET). AFR ALGERIA FRANCE UAR CONFER REGION NUC/PWR WAR DISCRIM 20 SAHARA AFR/STATES. PAGE 40 A0826 — COLONIAL SOVEREIGN RACE/REL DIPLOM

B59
HALEY A.G.,FIRST COLLOQUIUM ON THE LAW OF OUTER SPACE. WOR+45 INT/ORG ACT/RES PLAN BAL/PWR CONFER ATTIT PWR...POLICY JURID CHARTS ANTHOL 20. PAGE 60 A1225 — SPACE LAW SOVEREIGN CONTROL

B59
TARDIFF G.,LA LIBERTAD; LA LIBERTAD DE EXPRESION, IDEALES Y REALIDADES AMERICANAS. ISLAM INT/ORG PROB/SOLV PRESS CONFER PARTIC CATHISM...INT/LAW SOC/INTEG UN MID/EAST. PAGE 141 A2889 — ORD/FREE ATTIT DIPLOM CONCPT

B59
THOMAS D.H.,GUIDE TO THE DIPLOMATIC ARCHIVES OF WESTERN EUROPE. EUR+WWI ELITES INT/ORG NAT/G BAL/PWR INT/TRADE PEACE. PAGE 143 A2921 — BIBLIOG DIPLOM CONFER

N59
US HOUSE COMM FOREIGN AFFAIRS,HEARINGS ON DRAFT LEGISLATION TO AMEND FURTHER THE MUTUAL SECURITY ACT OF 1954 (PAMPHLET). USA+45 USSR CONSULT DELIB/GP FORCES ECO/TAC CONFER...POLICY 20 CONGRESS. PAGE 153 A3126 — DIPLOM FOR/AID ORD/FREE LEGIS

B60
ENGELMAN F.L.,THE PEACE OF CHRISTMAS EVE. UK USA-45 NAT/G FORCES CONFER PERS/REL...AUD/VIS BIBLIOG 19 TREATY. PAGE 42 A0853 — WAR PEACE DIPLOM PERSON

B60
FEIS H.,BETWEEN WAR AND PEACE: THE POTSDAM CONFERENCE. EUR+WWI NAT/G DELIB/GP PROB/SOLV REPAR WAR CIVMIL/REL...BIBLIOG 20. PAGE 45 A0911 — DIPLOM CONFER BAL/PWR

B60
FISCHER L.,THE SOVIETS IN WORLD AFFAIRS. CHINA/COM COM EUR+WWI USSR INT/ORG CONFER LEAD ARMS/CONT REV PWR...CHARTS 20 TREATY VERSAILLES. PAGE 46 A0938 — DIPLOM NAT/G POLICY MARXISM

B60
JEFFRIES C.,TRANSFER OF POWER: PROBLEMS OF THE PASSAGE TO SELFGOVERNMENT. CEYLON GHANA MALAYSIA NIGERIA UK INT/ORG CONSULT DELIB/GP LEGIS DIPLOM CONFER PARL/PROC 20. PAGE 73 A1502 — SOVEREIGN COLONIAL ORD/FREE NAT/G

B60
MONTGOMERY B.L.,AN APPROACH TO SANITY; A STUDY OF EAST-WEST RELATIONS. CONFER WAR EFFICIENCY ATTIT ...POLICY 20 NATO COLD/WAR KHRUSH/N. PAGE 103 A2113 — DIPLOM INT/ORG BAL/PWR DETER

B60
TABORN P.,RECORDS OF THE HEADQUARTERS, UNITED NATIONS COMMAND (PRELIMINARY INVENTORIES; PAPER). WOR+45 DIPLOM CONFER PEACE ATTIT...POLICY UN. PAGE 141 A2881 — BIBLIOG/A WAR ARMS/CONT INT/ORG

B60
US HOUSE COMM FOREIGN AFFAIRS,HEARINGS ON A BILL TO AMEND FURTHER THE MUTUAL SECURITY ACT OF 1954. USA+45 CONSULT FORCES BUDGET FOR/AID CONFER DETER ...CHARTS 20 DEPT/DEFEN DEPT/STATE UNEF. PAGE 153 A3127 — DIPLOM ORD/FREE DELIB/GP LEGIS

B61
NOLLAU G.,INTERNATIONAL COMMUNISM AND WORLD REVOLUTION; HISTORY AND METHODS (TRANS. BY VICTOR ANDERSEN). COM WORKER DIPLOM CONFER INGP/REL ...CONCPT BIBLIOG 20 STALIN/J LENIN/VI COMINTERN COMINFORM WORLD/CONG. PAGE 110 A2249 — MARXISM POL/PAR INT/ORG REV

B61
ROBINS D.B.,EVOLVING UNITED STATES POLICIES TOWARD THE EMERGING NATIONS OF ASIA AND AFRICA (PAMPHLET). ISLAM ECO/UNDEV INT/ORG CONSULT CREATE PLAN TEC/DEV FOR/AID CONFER ALL/VALS 20 KENNEDY/JF EISNHWR/DD UN AID. PAGE 122 A2501 — AFR S/ASIA DIPLOM BIBLIOG

B61
ROBINSON M.E.,EDUCATION FOR SOCIAL CHANGE: ESTABLISHING INSTITUTES OF PUBLIC AND BUSINESS ADMINISTRATION ABROAD (PAMPHLET). WOR+45 SOCIETY ACADEM CONFER INGP/REL ROLE...SOC CHARTS BIBLIOG 20 ICA. PAGE 122 A2506 — FOR/AID EDU/PROP MGT ADJUST

B61
US HOUSE COMM FOREIGN AFFAIRS,THE INTERNATIONAL DEVELOPMENT AND SECURITY ACT: HEARINGS BEFORE COMMITTEE ON FOREIGN AFFAIRS, HOUSE OF REP: HR7372. USA+45 AGRI INT/ORG NAT/G CONSULT DELIB/GP DIPLOM ECO/TAC INT/TRADE LOBBY REPRESENT 20 MCNAMARA/R DILLON/D RUSK/D CONGRESS. PAGE 153 A3128 — FOR/AID CONFER LEGIS ECO/UNDEV

B62
DUROSELLE J.B.,HISTOIRE DIPLOMATIQUE DE 1919 A NOS JOURS (3RD ED.). FRANCE INT/ORG CHIEF FORCES CONFER ARMS/CONT WAR PEACE ORD/FREE...T TREATY 20 COLD/WAR. PAGE 39 A0807 — DIPLOM WOR+45 WOR-45

B62
MONCRIEFF A.,THE STRATEGY OF SURVIVAL. UK FORCES BAL/PWR CONFER DETER WAR...ANTHOL 20 COLD/WAR. PAGE 102 A2104 — PLAN DECISION DIPLOM ARMS/CONT

B62
PERKINS D.,AMERICA'S QUEST FOR PEACE. USA+45 WOR+45 DIPLOM CONFER NAT/LISM ATTIT 20 UN TREATY. PAGE 115 A2361 — INT/LAW INT/ORG ARMS/CONT PEACE

B62
SCHMITT H.A.,THE PATH TO EUROPEAN UNITY. EUR+WWI USA+45 PLAN TEC/DEV DIPLOM FOR/AID CONFER...INT/LAW 20 EEC EURCOALSTL MARSHL/PLN UNIFICA. PAGE 128 A2634 — INT/ORG INT/TRADE REGION ECO/DEV

L62
"HIGHER EDUCATION AND ECONOMIC AND SOCIAL DEVELOPMENT IN LATIN AMERICA: A BIBLIOGRAPHY." L/A+17C SOCIETY ECO/UNDEV PROF/ORG DIPLOM CONFER ...SOC 20. PAGE 3 A0062 — BIBLIOG/A ACADEM INTELL EDU/PROP

B63
BLOCH-MORHANGE J.,VINGT ANNEES D'HISTOIRE CONTEMPORAINE. FORCES FOR/AID CONFER LEAD 20 COLD/WAR. PAGE 15 A0311 — WAR DIPLOM INT/ORG CHIEF

B63
DALLIN A.,DIVERSITY IN INTERNATIONAL COMMUNISM: A DOCUMENTARY RECORD, 1961-1963. CHINA/COM CHIEF PRESS WRITING DEBATE LEAD...POLICY ANTHOL 20. PAGE 33 A0677 — COM DIPLOM POL/PAR CONFER

B63
DUNN F.S.,PEACE-MAKING AND THE SETTLEMENT WITH JAPAN. ASIA USA+45 USA-45 FORCES BAL/PWR ECO/TAC CONFER WAR PWR SOVEREIGN 20 CHINJAP COLD/WAR TREATY. PAGE 39 A0802 — POLICY PEACE PLAN DIPLOM

B63
ETHIOPIAN MINISTRY INFORMATION,AFRICAN SUMMIT CONFERENCE ADDIS ABABA, ETHIOPIA, 1963. ETHIOPIA DELIB/GP COLONIAL NAT/LISM...POLICY DECISION 20. PAGE 42 A0865 — AFR CONFER REGION DIPLOM

B63
GREAT BRITAIN CENTRAL OFF INF,CONSULTATION AND CO- — DIPLOM

OPERATION IN THE COMMONWEALTH. LAW R+D FORCES PLAN EDU/PROP CONFER INGP/REL...GEOG CENSUS 19/20 CMN/WLTH. PAGE 55 A1133
DELIB/GP VOL/ASSN REGION

B63
NICOLSON H.,DIPLOMACY (3RD ED.). INT/ORG NAT/G CONSULT DELIB/GP CONFER 19/20 LEAGUE/NAT UN. PAGE 109 A2232
DIPLOM CONCPT NAT/COMP

B63
UNITED STATES GOVERNMENT,REPORT TO THE INTER-AMERICAN ECONOMIC AND SOCIAL COUNCIL. L/A+17C INDUS PLAN INT/TRADE TARIFFS CONFER...CHARTS 20 LAFTA. PAGE 149 A3038
FOR/AID ECO/TAC ECO/UNDEV DIPLOM

B63
US CONGRESS JOINT ECO COMM,THE UNITED STATES BALANCE OF PAYMENTS. USA+45 DELIB/GP CONFER...MATH PREDICT CHARTS 20 CONGRESS. PAGE 150 A3068
BAL/PAY ECO/TAC INT/TRADE CONSULT

B63
US HOUSE COMM FOREIGN AFFAIRS,HEARINGS ON H.R. 5490 TO AMEND FURTHER THE FOREIGN ASSISTANCE ACT OF 1961. CUBA EUR+WWI INDIA INT/ORG DELIB/GP LEGIS DIPLOM CONFER ORD/FREE 20 DEPT/STATE DEPT/DEFEN UN. PAGE 153 A3129
FOR/AID INT/TRADE FORCES WEAPON

B64
COX R.,PAN-AFRICANISM IN PRACTICE. AFR DIPLOM CONFER RACE/REL ROLE SOVEREIGN...POLICY 20 PANAF/FREE. PAGE 32 A0645
ORD/FREE COLONIAL REGION NAT/LISM

B64
EAYRS J.,THE COMMONWEALTH AND SUEZ: A DOCUMENTARY SURVEY. FRANCE ISLAM VOL/ASSN FORCES CONFER COLONIAL WAR INGP/REL 20 CMN/WLTH SUEZ UN. PAGE 40 A0818
DIPLOM NAT/LISM DIST/IND SOVEREIGN

B64
FATOUROS A.A.,CANADA'S OVERSEAS AID. CANADA WOR+45 ECO/DEV FINAN NAT/G BUDGET ECO/TAC CONFER ADMIN 20. PAGE 44 A0904
FOR/AID DIPLOM ECO/UNDEV POLICY

B64
NASA,PROCEEDINGS OF CONFERENCE ON THE LAW OF SPACE AND OF SATELLITE COMMUNICATIONS: CHICAGO 1963. FUT WOR+45 DELIB/GP PROB/SOLV TEC/DEV CONFER ADJUD NUC/PWR...POLICY IDEA/COMP 20 NASA. PAGE 107 A2197
SPACE COM/IND LAW DIPLOM

B64
UNITED ARAB REPUBLIC,TOWARDS THE SECOND AFRICAN SUMMIT ASSEMBLY. AFR UAR CONSTN VOL/ASSN CHIEF PLAN DIPLOM AGREE 20 NASSER/G AFR/STATES. PAGE 148 A3030
CONFER DELIB/GP INT/ORG POLICY

B64
US AIR FORCE ACADEMY ASSEMBLY,OUTER SPACE: FINAL REPORT APRIL 1-4, 1964. FUT USA+45 WOR+45 LAW DELIB/GP CONFER ARMS/CONT WAR PEACE ATTIT MORAL ...ANTHOL 20 NASA. PAGE 150 A3055
SPACE CIVMIL/REL NUC/PWR DIPLOM

B64
US HOUSE COMM FOREIGN AFFAIRS,HEARINGS ON H.R. 10502 TO AMEND FURTHER THE FOREIGN ASSISTANCE ACT OF 1961. AFR ASIA L/A+17C INT/ORG CONSULT DELIB/GP TEC/DEV ECO/TAC EDU/PROP CONFER 20 UN NATO CONGRESS AID. PAGE 153 A3130
FOR/AID DIPLOM ORD/FREE ECO/UNDEV

B65
WHITE HOUSE CONFERENCE ON INTERNATIONAL COOPERATION(VOL.II). SPACE WOR+45 EXTR/IND INT/ORG LABOR WORKER NUC/PWR PEACE AGE/Y...CENSUS ANTHOL 20 RESOURCE/N URBAN/RNWL PUB/TRANS. PAGE 3 A0071
R+D CONFER TEC/DEV DIPLOM

B65
EDUCATION AND WORLD AFFAIRS,THE UNIVERSITY LOOKS ABROAD: APPROACHES TO WORLD AFFAIRS AT SIX AMERICAN UNIVERSITIES. USA+45 CREATE EDU/PROP CONFER LEAD KNOWL 20 CORNELL/U MICH/STA/U STANFORD/U TULANE/U WISCONSN/U. PAGE 40 A0822
ACADEM DIPLOM ATTIT GP/COMP

B65
INGRAM D.,COMMONWEALTH FOR A COLOUR-BLIND WORLD. AFR INDIA UK STRATA ECO/UNDEV VOL/ASSN CREATE PLAN CONFER COLONIAL ORD/FREE SOC/INTEG 20 COMMONWLTH. PAGE 70 A1441
RACE/REL INT/ORG INGP/REL PROB/SOLV

B65
MORGENTHAU H.,MORGENTHAU DIARY (CHINA) (2 VOLS.). ASIA USA+45 USA-45 LAW DELIB/GP EX/STRUC PLAN FOR/AID INT/TRADE CONFER WAR MARXISM 20 CHINJAP. PAGE 104 A2136
DIPLOM ADMIN

B65
MORRIS R.B.,THE PEACEMAKERS; THE GREAT POWERS AND AMERICAN INDEPENDENCE. BAL/PWR CONFER COLONIAL NEUTRAL PEACE ORD/FREE TREATY 18 PRE/US/AM. PAGE 105 A2149
SOVEREIGN REV DIPLOM

B65
MOSTECKY V.,SOVIET LEGAL BIBLIOGRAPHY. USSR LEGIS PRESS WRITING CONFER ADJUD CT/SYS REV MARXISM ...INT/LAW JURID DICTIONARY 20. PAGE 105 A2155
BIBLIOG/A LAW COM CONSTN

B65
RAPPAPORT A.,ISSUES IN AMERICAN DIPLOMACY: WORLD POWER AND LEADERSHIP SINCE 1895 (VOL. II). CHINA/COM EUR+WWI L/A+17C USA+45 USA-45 NAT/G ECO/TAC DOMIN CONFER LEAD NUC/PWR WEAPON...DECISION 19/20 WILSON/W ROOSEVLT/F CHINJAP. PAGE 119 A2447
WAR POLICY DIPLOM

B65
STOETZER O.C.,THE ORGANIZATION OF AMERICAN STATES. L/A+17C EX/STRUC FOR/AID CONFER PARL/PROC ORD/FREE SOVEREIGN...POLICY INT/LAW 20 OAS. PAGE 138 A2831
INT/ORG REGION DIPLOM BAL/PWR

B65
US HOUSE COMM FOREIGN AFFAIRS,HEARINGS ON DRAFT BILL TO AMEND FURTHER THE FOREIGN ASSISTANCE ACT OF 1961. AFR ASIA L/A+17C USA+45 INT/ORG DELIB/GP TEC/DEV ECO/TAC CONFER TOTALISM 20 CONGRESS AID. PAGE 153 A3131
FOR/AID ECO/UNDEV DIPLOM ORD/FREE

B65
WEILER J.,L'ECONOMIE INTERNATIONALE DEPUIS 1950. WOR+45 DIPLOM TARIFFS CONFER...POLICY TREATY. PAGE 162 A3302
FINAN INT/TRADE REGION FOR/AID

B66
SUPPLEMENTAL FOREIGN ASSISTANCE FISCAL YEAR 1966: VIETNAM. CHINA/COM COM S/ASIA USA+45 VIETNAM EXTR/IND FINAN DIPLOM TAX GUERRILLA HABITAT ORD/FREE...STAT CHARTS 20 SENATE PRESIDENT. PAGE 4 A0077
CONFER LEGIS WAR FOR/AID

B66
BEAUFRE A.,NATO AND EUROPE. WOR+45 PLAN CONFER EXEC NUC/PWR ATTIT...POLICY 20 NATO EUROPE. PAGE 12 A0243
INT/ORG DETER DIPLOM ADMIN

B66
BLOOMFIELD L.P.,KHRUSHCHEV AND THE ARMS RACE. USA+45 USSR ECO/DEV BAL/PWR EDU/PROP CONFER NUC/PWR ATTIT...CHARTS 20 KHRUSH/N. PAGE 16 A0321
ARMS/CONT COM POLICY DIPLOM

B66
CLARK G.,WORLD PEACE THROUGH WORLD LAW; TWO ALTERNATIVE PLANS. WOR+45 DELIB/GP FORCES TAX CONFER ADJUD SANCTION ARMS/CONT WAR CHOOSE PRIVIL 20 UN COLD/WAR. PAGE 27 A0541
INT/LAW PEACE PLAN INT/ORG

B66
DAVIS V.,POSTWAR DEFENSE POLICY AND THE US NAVY, 1943-1946. USA+45 DIPLOM CONFER LEAD ATTIT...POLICY IDEA/COMP 20 NAVY. PAGE 34 A0692
FORCES PLAN PROB/SOLV CIVMIL/REL

B66
ESTHUS R.A.,THEODORE ROOSEVELT AND JAPAN. ASIA USA-45 FORCES CONFER WAR SOVEREIGN...BIBLIOG 20 CHINJAP. PAGE 42 A0864
DIPLOM DELIB/GP

B66
EUBANK K.,THE SUMMIT CONFERENCES. EUR+WWI USA+45 USA-45 MUNIC BAL/PWR WAR PEACE PWR...POLICY AUD/VIS 20 GENEVA/CON TEHERAN YALTA POTSDAM. PAGE 43 A0872
CONFER NAT/G CHIEF DIPLOM

B66
EWING B.G.,PEACE THROUGH NEGOTIATION: THE AUSTRIAN EXPERIENCE. AUSTRIA USSR VIETNAM CONFER CONTROL DETER WAR ATTIT HEALTH PWR...POLICY 20. PAGE 43 A0878
PEACE DIPLOM MARXISM

B66
FREUND L.,POLITISCHE WAFFEN. EUR+WWI GERMANY CONSULT FORCES CONFER NUC/PWR 20. PAGE 49 A1000
EDU/PROP DIPLOM ATTIT

B66
HAMILTON W.B.,A DECADE OF THE COMMONWEALTH, 1955-1964. UK LAW ELITES FINAN FOR/AID CONFER COLONIAL PWR...GEOG CHARTS ANTHOL 20 CMN/WLTH UN. PAGE 61 A1247
INT/ORG INGP/REL DIPLOM NAT/G

B66
HANSEN G.H.,AFRO-ASIA AND NON-ALIGNMENT. AFR ASIA S/ASIA NEUTRAL MORAL 20. PAGE 61 A1255
DIPLOM CONFER POLICY NAT/LISM

B66
HERZ M.F.,BEGINNINGS OF THE COLD WAR. COM POLAND USA+45 USSR INT/ORG NAT/G CHIEF FOR/AID DOMIN CONFER AGREE WAR PEACE 20 STALIN/J COLD/WAR UN. PAGE 64 A1321
DIPLOM

B66
KAREFA-SMART J.,AFRICA: PROGRESS THROUGH COOPERATION. AFR FINAN TEC/DEV DIPLOM FOR/AID EDU/PROP CONFER REGION GP/REL WEALTH...HEAL SOC/INTEG 20. PAGE 76 A1566
ORD/FREE ECO/UNDEV VOL/ASSN PLAN

B66
LEE L.T.,VIENNA CONVENTION ON CONSULAR RELATIONS. WOR+45 LAW INT/ORG CONFER GP/REL PRIVIL...INT/LAW 20 TREATY VIENNA/CNV. PAGE 86 A1760
AGREE DIPLOM ADMIN

B66
SANDERS R.E.,SPAIN AND THE UNITED NATIONS 1945-1950. SPAIN CHIEF DIPLOM CONFER SANCTION ATTIT ...POLICY 20 UN COLD/WAR. PAGE 127 A2599
INT/ORG FASCISM GP/REL STRANGE

B66
UN ECAFE,ADMINISTRATIVE ASPECTS OF FAMILY PLANNING PROGRAMMES (PAMPHLET). ASIA THAILAND WOR+45 VOL/ASSN PROB/SOLV BUDGET FOR/AID EDU/PROP CONFER CONTROL GOV/REL TIME 20 UN BIRTH/CON. PAGE 147 A2999
PLAN CENSUS FAM ADMIN

B66
US CONGRESS JOINT ECO COMM,NEW APPROACH TO UNITED STATES INTERNATIONAL ECONOMIC POLICY. USA+45 WOR+45 CHIEF DELIB/GP CONFER...CHARTS 20 CONGRESS MONEY. PAGE 150 A3070 DIPLOM ECO/TAC BAL/PAY FINAN

B66
US HOUSE COMM APPROPRIATIONS,HEARINGS ON FOREIGN OPERATIONS AND RELATED AGENCIES APPROPRIATIONS. CUBA USA+45 VOL/ASSN DELIB/GP DIPLOM CONFER ORD/FREE 20 CONGRESS MIGRATION INT/AM/DEV PEACE/CORP. PAGE 153 A3120 FOR/AID BUDGET ECO/UNDEV FORCES

B66
US HOUSE COMM FOREIGN AFFAIRS,UNITED STATES - SOUTH AFRICAN RELATIONS. SOUTH/AFR USA+45 NAT/G CONSULT DELIB/GP LEGIS CONFER SANCTION RACE/REL ATTIT 20 CONGRESS. PAGE 154 A3134 DISCRIM DIPLOM POLICY PARL/PROC

B66
WEINSTEIN F.B.,VIETNAM'S UNHELD ELECTIONS: THE FAILURE TO CARRY OUT THE 1956 REUNIFICATION ELECTIONS... (MONOGRAPH). VIETNAM/S VIETNAM/N LEGIT CONFER ADJUD WAR PEACE 20 TREATY GENEVA/CON UNIFICA. PAGE 162 A3306 AGREE NAT/G CHOOSE DIPLOM

B66
WELCH C.E.,DREAM OF UNITY; PAN-AFRICANISM AND POLITICAL UNIFICATION IN WEST AFRICA. AFR ECO/UNDEV CONFER COLONIAL LEAD...INT/LAW 20. PAGE 163 A3312 INT/ORG REGION NAT/LISM DIPLOM

S66
ERB GF,"THE UNITED NATIONS CONFERENCE ON TRADE AND DEVELOPMENT (UNCTAD): A SELECTED CURRENT READING LIST." FINAN FOR/AID CONFER 20 UN. PAGE 42 A0858 BIBLIOG/A INT/TRADE ECO/UNDEV INT/ORG

S66
MCNEAL R.H.,"THE LEGACY OF THE COMINTERN." USSR WOR+45 WOR-45 PROB/SOLV DIPLOM CONFER CONTROL LEAD WAR 20 STALIN/J COMINTERN. PAGE 98 A2020 MARXISM INT/ORG POL/PAR PWR

B67
AUBREY H.G.,ATLANTIC ECONOMIC COOPERATION. ECO/DEV INDUS VOL/ASSN PROB/SOLV DIPLOM INT/TRADE TARIFFS CONFER 20. PAGE 10 A0197 INT/ORG ECO/TAC TEC/DEV CAP/ISM

B67
BLOOMFIELD L.,THE UNITED NATIONS AND US FOREIGN POLICY. USA+45 DIPLOM LEAD ARMS/CONT DETER PWR 20 UN. PAGE 15 A0313 INT/ORG PLAN CONFER IDEA/COMP

B67
FINE S.,RECENT AMERICA* CONFLICTING INTERPRETATIONS OF THE GREAT ISSUES (2ND ED.). USA+45 USA-45 POL/PAR SECT CONFER NUC/PWR WAR ATTIT...POLICY TREND ANTHOL PRESIDENT 20. PAGE 46 A0931 IDEA/COMP DIPLOM NAT/G

B67
UNESCO,PRINCIPLES AND PROBLEMS OF NATIONAL SCIENCE POLICIES. WOR+45 ECO/DEV ECO/UNDEV R+D INT/ORG PROB/SOLV CONFER...PHIL/SCI CHARTS 20 UNESCO UN. PAGE 148 A3026 NAT/COMP POLICY TEC/DEV CREATE

B67
US SUPERINTENDENT OF DOCUMENTS,LIBRARY OF CONGRESS (PRICE LIST 83). AFR ASIA EUR+WWI USA-45 USSR NAT/G DIPLOM CONFER CT/SYS WAR...DECISION PHIL/SCI CLASSIF 19/20 CONGRESS PRESIDENT. PAGE 157 A3205 BIBLIOG/A USA+45 AUTOMAT LAW

L67
ANAND R.P.,"SOVEREIGN EQUALITY OF STATES IN INTERNATIONAL LAW." UNIV DIPLOM DOMIN CONFER DEBATE SANCTION ATTIT UN. PAGE 8 A0157 INT/LAW INT/ORG CONCPT POLICY

L67
GENEVEY P.,"LE DESARMEMENT APRES LE TRAITE DE VERSAILLES." EUR+WWI GERMANY INT/ORG PROB/SOLV CONFER WAR...POLICY PREDICT 20. PAGE 52 A1057 ARMS/CONT PEACE DIPLOM FORCES

S67
BUTT R.,"THE COMMON MARKET AND CONSERVATIVE POLITICS, 1961-2." UK CHIEF DIPLOM ECO/TAC INT/TRADE CONFER DEBATE REGION ATTIT...POLICY 20 EEC. PAGE 22 A0454 EUR+WWI INT/ORG POL/PAR

S67
CLINGHAM T.A. JR.,"LEGISLATIVE FLOTSAM AND INTERNATIONAL ACTION IN THE 'YARMOUTH CASTLE'S' WAKE." WOR+45 PROB/SOLV CONFER COST HEALTH...POLICY INT/LAW CONGRESS. PAGE 27 A0552 DIPLOM DIST/IND INT/ORG LAW

S67
COSGROVE C.A.,"AGRICULTURE, FINANCE AND POLITICS IN THE EUROPEAN COMMUNITY." EUR+WWI DIST/IND MARKET INT/ORG VOL/ASSN DELIB/GP TEC/DEV BAL/PWR BARGAIN ECO/TAC RATION CONFER 20 EEC. PAGE 31 A0630 ECO/DEV DIPLOM AGRI INT/TRADE

S67
DE ROUGEMENT D.,"THE CAMPAIGN OF THE EUROPEAN CONGRESSES." ELITES INTELL DIPLOM ECO/TAC CONFER PEACE...POLICY PREDICT. PAGE 35 A0710 EUR+WWI REGION FEDERAL INT/ORG

S67
FAWCETT J.E.S.,"GIBRALTAR* THE LEGAL ISSUES." SPAIN UK INT/ORG BAL/PWR LICENSE CONFER SANCTION PRIVIL ...JURID CHARTS 20. PAGE 44 A0905 INT/LAW DIPLOM COLONIAL ADJUD

S67
FOREIGN POLICY ASSOCIATION,"US CONCERN FOR WORLD LAW." USA+45 WOR+45 DELIB/GP JUDGE BAL/PWR CONFER PEACE ORD/FREE 20 UN. PAGE 47 A0962 INT/LAW INT/ORG DIPLOM ARMS/CONT

S67
FRANK I.,"NEW PERSPECTIVES ON TRADE AND DEVELOPMENT." PROB/SOLV BARGAIN DIPLOM FOR/AID CONFER GP/REL WEALTH 20 UN GATT. PAGE 48 A0980 ECO/UNDEV INT/ORG INT/TRADE ECO/TAC

S67
FRANKEL M.,"THE WAR IN VIETNAM." VIETNAM ECO/UNDEV DIPLOM CONFER INGP/REL PEACE PWR...POLICY PREDICT 20. PAGE 48 A0982 WAR COERCE PLAN GUERRILLA

S67
JOHNSTON D.M.,"LAW, TECHNOLOGY AND THE SEA." WOR+45 PLAN PROB/SOLV TEC/DEV CONFER ADJUD ORD/FREE ...POLICY JURID. PAGE 75 A1528 INT/LAW INT/ORG DIPLOM NEUTRAL

S67
RAMSEY J.A.,"THE STATUS OF INTERNATIONAL COPYRIGHTS." WOR+45 CREATE TEC/DEV DIPLOM CONFER CONTROL SANCTION OWN...POLICY JURID. PAGE 119 A2439 INT/LAW INT/ORG COM/IND PRESS

S67
SCHACTER O.,"SCIENTIFIC ADVANCES AND INTERNATIONAL LAWMAKING." FUT R+D PLAN PROB/SOLV CONFER CONTROL ...POLICY PREDICT 20 UN. PAGE 128 A2617 TEC/DEV INT/LAW INT/ORG ACT/RES

S67
SHARP G.,"THE NEED OF A FUNCTIONAL SUBSTITUTE FOR WAR." FUT UNIV WOR+45 CULTURE SOCIETY INT/ORG CONSULT DELIB/GP ACT/RES CREATE BAL/PWR CONFER ARMS/CONT NUC/PWR 20. PAGE 132 A2696 PEACE WAR DIPLOM PROB/SOLV

S67
SHERSHNEV Y.,"THE KENNEDY ROUND* PLANS AND REALITY." EUR+WWI USA+45 INT/ORG DIPLOM TARIFFS DOMIN CONFER PWR...MARXIST PREDICT. PAGE 132 A2701 ECO/TAC ECO/DEV INT/TRADE BAL/PWR

S67
TACKABERRY R.B.,"ORGANIZING AND TRAINING PEACE-KEEPING FORCES* THE CANADIAN VIEW." CANADA PLAN DIPLOM CONFER ADJUD ADMIN CIVMIL/REL 20 UN. PAGE 141 A2882 PEACE FORCES INT/ORG CONSULT

S67
VAN DUSEN H.P.,"HAMMARSKOLD IN THE WORLD'S SERVICE." DIPLOM CONFER LEAD PEACE STRANGE UTOPIA MORAL SKILL OBJECTIVE...INT/LAW SELF/OBS 20. PAGE 158 A3211 INT/ORG CONSULT TOP/EX NEUTRAL

S67
VLASCIC I.A.,"THE SPACE TREATY* A PRELIMINARY EVALUATION." FUT USSR WOR+45 R+D ACT/RES TEC/DEV DIPLOM CONFER ARMS/CONT PEACE...PREDICT UN TREATY. PAGE 159 A3245 SPACE INT/LAW INT/ORG NEUTRAL

S67
WASHBURN A.M.,"NUCLEAR PROLIFERATION IN A REVOLUTIONARY INTERNATIONAL SYSTEM." WOR+45 NAT/G DELIB/GP PLAN TEC/DEV...POLICY 20. PAGE 161 A3287 ARMS/CONT NUC/PWR DIPLOM CONFER

CONFERENCE ATLANTIC COMMUNITY A0584

CONFERENCES....SEE CONFER, DELIB/GP

CONFIDENCE, PERSONAL....SEE SUPEGO

CONFLICT, MILITARY....SEE WAR, FORCES+COERCE

CONFLICT, PERSONAL....SEE PERS/REL, ROLE

CONFLICT....CONFLICT THEORY

CONFORMITY....SEE CONSEN, DOMIN

CONFRONTATION....SEE CONFRONTN

CONFRONTN....CONFRONTATION

CONFUCIUS....CONFUCIUS

B58
CHANG H.,WITHIN THE FOUR SEAS. ASIA WAR MORAL MARXISM...IDEA/COMP NAT/COMP 20 CONFUCIUS. PAGE 26 A0521 PEACE DIPLOM KNOWL CULTURE

CONGO....CONGO, PRE-INDEPENDENCE OR GENERAL

S61
MILLER E.,"LEGAL ASPECTS OF UN ACTION IN THE CONGO." AFR CULTURE ADMIN PEACE DRIVE RIGID/FLEX ORD/FREE...WELF/ST JURID OBS UN CONGO 20. PAGE 101 A2076 INT/ORG LEGIT

B62
KING G.,THE UNITED NATIONS IN THE CONGO: A QUEST FOR PEACE. WOR+45 NAT/G CONSULT FORCES LEGIT COERCE WAR ORD/FREE...JURID METH/CNCPT OBS INT HIST/WRIT TIME/SEQ CONGO UN 20 COLD/WAR. PAGE 79 A1624 AFR INT/ORG

L62
MURACCIOLE L.,"LA LOI FONDAMENTALE DE LA REPUBLIQUE DU CONGO." WOR+45 SOCIETY ECO/UNDEV INT/ORG NAT/G LEGIS PLAN LEGIT ADJUD COLONIAL ROUTINE ATTIT SOVEREIGN 20 CONGO. PAGE 106 A2174 AFR CONSTN

B63
STEVENSON A.E.,LOOKING OUTWARD: YEARS OF CRISIS AT THE UNITED NATIONS. COM CUBA USA+45 WOR+45 SOCIETY NAT/G EX/STRUC ACT/RES LEGIT COLONIAL ATTIT PERSON SUPEGO ALL/VALS...POLICY HUM UN COLD/WAR CONGO 20. PAGE 138 A2823 INT/ORG CONCPT ARMS/CONT

L63
PADELFORD N.J.,"FINANCIAL CRISIS AND THE UNITED NATIONS." FUT USSR WOR+45 LAW CONSTN FINAN INT/ORG DELIB/GP FORCES PLAN BUDGET DIPLOM COST WEALTH ...STAT CHARTS UN CONGO 20. PAGE 113 A2311 CREATE ECO/TAC

S63
BLOOMFIELD L.P.,"HEADQUARTERS-FIELD RELATIONS: SOME NOTES ON THE BEGINNING AND END OF ONUC." AFR INT/ORG ROUTINE COERCE WAR WEAPON UN CONGO 20. PAGE 16 A0319 FORCES ORD/FREE

S63
GIRAUD E.,"L'INTERDICTION DU RECOURS A LA FORCE, LA THEORIE ET LA PRATIQUE DES NATIONS UNIES." ALGERIA COM CUBA HUNGARY WOR+45 ADJUD TOTALISM ATTIT RIGID/FLEX PWR...POLICY JURID CONCPT UN 20 CONGO. PAGE 53 A1077 INT/ORG FORCES DIPLOM

S63
MURRAY J.N.,"UNITED NATIONS PEACE-KEEPING AND PROBLEMS OF POLITICAL CONTROL." FUT WOR+45 CONSTN DELIB/GP FORCES TOP/EX ACT/RES CREATE LEGIT PEACE PWR...METH/CNCPT CONGO UN 20. PAGE 106 A2182 INT/ORG ORD/FREE

S63
NICHOLAS H.G.,"UN PEACE FORCES AND THE CHANGING GLOBE: THE LESSONS OF SUEZ AND CONGO." FUT WOR+45 CONSTN INT/ORG CONSULT DELIB/GP TOP/EX CREATE DIPLOM DOMIN LEGIT COERCE WAR PERSON RIGID/FLEX PWR UN SUEZ CONGO UNEF 20. PAGE 109 A2229 ACT/RES FORCES

CONGO/BRAZ....CONGO, BRAZZAVILLE; SEE ALSO AFR

B03
MOREL E.D.,THE BRITISH CASE IN FRENCH CONGO. CONGO/BRAZ FRANCE UK COERCE MORAL WEALTH...POLICY INT/LAW 20 CONGO/LEOP. PAGE 104 A2130 DIPLOM INT/TRADE COLONIAL AFR

B60
HEYSE T.,PROBLEMS FONCIERS ET REGIME DES TERRES (ASPECTS ECONOMIQUES, JURIDIQUES ET SOCIAUX). AFR CONGO/BRAZ INT/ORG DIPLOM SOVEREIGN...GEOG TREATY 20. PAGE 64 A1325 BIBLIOG AGRI ECO/UNDEV LEGIS

B62
FAO,FOOD AND AGRICULTURE ORGANIZATION AFRICAN SURVEY. AFR CONGO/BRAZ GHANA STRATA AGRI INT/ORG TEC/DEV FOR/AID INT/TRADE RACE/REL DEMAND EFFICIENCY PRODUC...GEOG 20 UN CONGO/LEOP. PAGE 44 A0898 ECO/TAC WEALTH EXTR/IND ECO/UNDEV

S62
GAREAU F.H.,"BLOC POLITICS IN WEST AFRICA." AFR CONGO/BRAZ GHANA GUINEA MALI WOR+45 STRUCT ECO/UNDEV INT/ORG VOL/ASSN CHOOSE ORD/FREE PWR UN 20. PAGE 51 A1048 NAT/G NAT/LISM

B64
EPSTEIN H.M.,REVOLT IN THE CONGO. AFR CONGO/BRAZ WOR+45 NAT/G FORCES DOMIN WAR CIVMIL/REL INGP/REL MARXISM...RECORD GP/COMP 20 CONGO/LEOP UN. PAGE 42 A0856 REV COLONIAL NAT/LISM DIPLOM

CONGO/KINS....CONGO, KINSHASA; SEE ALSO AFR

B03
MOREL E.D.,THE BRITISH CASE IN FRENCH CONGO. CONGO/BRAZ FRANCE UK COERCE MORAL WEALTH...POLICY INT/LAW 20 CONGO/LEOP. PAGE 104 A2130 DIPLOM INT/TRADE COLONIAL AFR

B38
FRANKEL S.H.,CAPITAL INVESTMENT IN AFRICA. AFR EUR+WWI RHODESIA SOUTH/AFR UK FINAN FOR/AID COLONIAL DEMAND UTIL WEALTH...METH/CNCPT CHARTS 20 CONGO/LEOP. PAGE 48 A0983 ECO/UNDEV EXTR/IND DIPLOM PRODUC

B54
COOKSON J.,BEFORE THE AFRICAN STORM. BELGIUM CENTRL/AFR FRANCE UK ECO/UNDEV POL/PAR CREATE BAL/PWR RACE/REL NAT/LISM ORD/FREE CONSERVE MARXISM SOC/INTEG 20 CONGO/LEOP. PAGE 30 A0607 COLONIAL REV DISCRIM DIPLOM

B62
FAO,FOOD AND AGRICULTURE ORGANIZATION AFRICAN SURVEY. AFR CONGO/BRAZ GHANA STRATA AGRI INT/ORG TEC/DEV FOR/AID INT/TRADE RACE/REL DEMAND EFFICIENCY PRODUC...GEOG 20 UN CONGO/LEOP. PAGE 44 A0898 ECO/TAC WEALTH EXTR/IND ECO/UNDEV

B62
WELLEQUET J.,LE CONGO BELGE ET LA WELTPOLITIK (1894-1914. GERMANY DOMIN EDU/PROP WAR ATTIT ...BIBLIOG T CONGO/LEOP. PAGE 163 A3314 ADMIN DIPLOM GP/REL COLONIAL

B64
EPSTEIN H.M.,REVOLT IN THE CONGO. AFR CONGO/BRAZ WOR+45 NAT/G FORCES DOMIN WAR CIVMIL/REL INGP/REL MARXISM...RECORD GP/COMP 20 CONGO/LEOP UN. PAGE 42 A0856 REV COLONIAL NAT/LISM DIPLOM

B66
LENGYEL E.,AFRICA: PAST, PRESENT, AND FUTURE. FUT SOUTH/AFR COLONIAL RACE/REL SOVEREIGN...GEOG AUD/VIS CHARTS T 20 CONGO/LEOP NEGRO. PAGE 87 A1771 AFR CONSTN ECO/UNDEV

CONGRESS....CONGRESS (ALL NATIONS); SEE ALSO LEGIS, HOUSE/REP, SENATE, DELIB/GP

N
US SUPERINTENDENT OF DOCUMENTS,CATALOGUE OF PUBLIC DOCUMENTS OF CONGRESS AND OF ALL DEPARTMENTS OF THE GOVERNMENT OF THE UNITED STATES. DIPLOM ATTIT ...POLICY DICTIONARY 20 CONGRESS. PAGE 157 A3200 BIBLIOG NAT/G WRITING USA-45

N
US SUPERINTENDENT OF DOCUMENTS,MONTHLY CATALOG OF UNITED STATES GOVERNMENT PUBLICATIONS. USA+45 USA-45 AGRI LABOR FORCES INT/TRADE TARIFFS TAX EDU/PROP CT/SYS ARMS/CONT RACE/REL 19/20 CONGRESS PRESIDENT. PAGE 157 A3203 BIBLIOG NAT/G VOL/ASSN POLICY

N/R
FULBRIGHT J.W.,THE ARROGANCE OF POWER. USA+45 WOR+45 ECO/UNDEV ACADEM LEGIS ECO/TAC FOR/AID PEACE ROLE ORD/FREE PWR 20 COLD/WAR CONGRESS. PAGE 50 A1014 DIPLOM POLICY REV

B04
CRANDALL S.B.,TREATIES: THEIR MAKING AND ENFORCEMENT. MOD/EUR USA-45 CONSTN INT/ORG NAT/G LEGIS EDU/PROP LEGIT EXEC PEACE KNOWL MORAL...JURID CONGRESS 19/20 TREATY. PAGE 32 A0655 LAW

B05
AMES J.G.,COMPREHENSIVE INDEX TO THE PUBLICATIONS OF THE UNITED STATES GOVERNMENT , 1881-1893. USA-45 CONSTN POL/PAR DELIB/GP TOP/EX DIPLOM PARL/PROC INGP/REL...INDEX 19 CONGRESS. PAGE 8 A0153 BIBLIOG/A LEGIS NAT/G GOV/REL

B14
HASSE A.R.,INDEX TO UNITED STATES DOCUMENTS RELATING TO FOREIGN AFFAIRS, 1828-1861 (3 VOLS.). USA-45 CHIEF 19 CONGRESS. PAGE 63 A1285 INDEX DIPLOM LEGIS

B17
MEYER H.H.B.,LIST OF REFERENCES ON EMBARGOES (PAMPHLET). USA-45 AGRI DIPLOM WRITING DEBATE WEAPON...INT/LAW 18/20 CONGRESS. PAGE 100 A2049 BIBLIOG DIST/IND ECO/TAC INT/TRADE

B17
UPTON E.,THE MILITARY POLICY OF THE US. USA-45 STRUCT INT/ORG EXEC ATTIT PERCEPT...MGT CONCPT OBS HIST/WRIT CHARTS CONGRESS 18/20. PAGE 149 A3049 FORCES SKILL WAR

B19
SUTHERLAND G.,CONSTITUTIONAL POWER AND WORLD AFFAIRS. CONSTN STRUCT INT/ORG NAT/G CHIEF LEGIS ACT/RES PLAN GOV/REL ALL/VALS...OBS TIME/SEQ CONGRESS VAL/FREE 20 PRESIDENT. PAGE 140 A2866 USA-45 EXEC DIPLOM

B30
FLEMMING D.,THE TREATY VETO OF THE AMERICAN SENATE. FUT USA+45 USA-45 CONSTN INT/ORG NAT/G TOP/EX LEGIT GOV/REL PWR...POLICY MAJORIT CONCPT OBS TIME/SEQ CONGRESS 20. PAGE 46 A0949 LEGIS RIGID/FLEX

B32
FLEMMING D.,THE UNITED STATES AND THE LEAGUE OF NATIONS, 1918-1920. FUT USA-45 NAT/G LEGIS TOP/EX DEBATE CHOOSE PEACE ATTIT SOVEREIGN...TIME/SEQ CON/ANAL CONGRESS LEAGUE/NAT 20 TREATY. PAGE 46 A0950 INT/ORG EDU/PROP

B42
FULLER G.H.,DEFENSE FINANCING: A SUPPLEMENTARY LIST OF REFERENCES (PAMPHLET). CANADA UK USA-45 ECO/DEV NAT/G DELIB/GP BUDGET ADJUD ARMS/CONT WEAPON COST PEACE PWR 20 AUSTRAL CHINJAP CONGRESS. PAGE 50 A1021 BIBLIOG/A FINAN FORCES DIPLOM

B44
WHITTON J.B.,THE SECOND CHANCE: AMERICA AND THE PEACE. EUR+WWI USA-45 SOCIETY STRUCT INT/ORG NAT/G LEGIT EXEC WAR ALL/VALS...SOC CONCPT TIME/SEQ TREND CONGRESS 20. PAGE 164 A3340 LEGIS PEACE

L44
WRIGHT Q.,"THE US AND INTERNATIONAL AGREEMENTS." FUT USA-45 CONSTN INTELL INT/ORG LOC/G NAT/G CHIEF CONSULT EX/STRUC DIPLOM LEGIT DRIVE PERCEPT PWR ...CONCPT CONGRESS 20. PAGE 167 A3407 DELIB/GP TOP/EX PEACE

B49
US SENATE COMM ON FOREIGN REL,A DECADE OF AMERICAN FOREIGN POLICY; BASIC DOCUMENTS, 1941-49. USA+45 BIBLIOG DIPLOM

USA-45 NAT/G 20 CONGRESS. PAGE 156 A3179 POLICY
B50

MCCAMY J.,THE ADMINISTRATION OF AMERICAN FOREIGN AFFAIRS. USA+45 SOCIETY INT/ORG NAT/G ACT/RES PLAN INT/TRADE EDU/PROP ADJUD ALL/VALS...METH/CNCPT TIME/SEQ CONGRESS 20. PAGE 97 A1996 EXEC STRUCT DIPLOM
B50

US DEPARTMENT OF STATE,POINT FOUR: COOPERATIVE PROGRAM FOR AID IN THE DEVELOPMENT OF ECONOMICALLY UNDERDEVELOPED AREAS. WOR+45 AGRI INDUS INT/ORG PLAN TEC/DEV DIPLOM EDU/PROP ADMIN PEACE PRODUC WEALTH 20 CONGRESS UN. PAGE 151 A3085 ECO/UNDEV FOR/AID FINAN INT/TRADE
L50

US SENATE COMM. GOVT. OPER.,"REVISION OF THE UN CHARTER." FUT USA+45 WOR+45 CONSTN ECO/DEV ECO/UNDEV NAT/G DELIB/GP ACT/RES CREATE PLAN EXEC ROUTINE CHOOSE ALL/VALS...POLICY CONCPT CONGRESS UN TOT/POP 20 COLD/WAR. PAGE 157 A3196 INT/ORG LEGIS PEACE
B51

US HOUSE COMM APPROPRIATIONS,MUTUAL SECURITY PROGRAM APPROPRIATIONS FOR 1952: HEARINGS BEFORE A SUBCOMMITTEE OF THE COMMITTEE ON APPROPRIATIONS. KOREA L/A+17C ECO/DEV ECO/UNDEV INT/ORG INSPECT BAL/PWR DIPLOM DEBATE WAR...POLICY STAT ASIA/S 20 CONGRESS NATO COLD/WAR MID/EAST. PAGE 153 A3118 LEGIS FORCES BUDGET FOR/AID
B51

US LIBRARY OF CONGRESS,PUBLIC AFFAIRS ABSTRACTS. USA+45 INT/ORG INT/TRADE ARMS/CONT...NAT/COMP 20 CONGRESS. PAGE 155 A3151 BIBLIOG/A DIPLOM POLICY
L52

HILSMAN R. JR.,"INTELLIGENCE AND POLICY MAKING IN FOREIGN AFFAIRS." USA+45 CONSULT ACT/RES DIPLOM EDU/PROP ROUTINE PEACE PERCEPT PWR SKILL...POLICY MGT HYPO/EXP CONGRESS 20 CIA. PAGE 65 A1333 PROF/ORG SIMUL WAR
L52

WRIGHT Q.,"CONGRESS AND THE TREATY-MAKING POWER." USA+45 WOR+45 CONSTN INTELL NAT/G CHIEF CONSULT EX/STRUC LEGIS TOP/EX CREATE GOV/REL DISPL DRIVE RIGID/FLEX...TREND TOT/POP CONGRESS CONGRESS 20 TREATY. PAGE 167 A3408 ROUTINE DIPLOM INT/LAW DELIB/GP
L52

WRIGHT Q.,"CONGRESS AND THE TREATY-MAKING POWER." USA+45 WOR+45 CONSTN INTELL NAT/G CHIEF CONSULT EX/STRUC LEGIS TOP/EX CREATE GOV/REL DISPL DRIVE RIGID/FLEX...TREND TOT/POP CONGRESS CONGRESS 20 TREATY. PAGE 167 A3408 ROUTINE DIPLOM INT/LAW DELIB/GP
S52

SCHWEBEL S.M.,"THE SECRETARY-GENERAL OF THE UN." FUT INTELL CONSULT DELIB/GP ADMIN PEACE ATTIT ...JURID MGT CONCPT TREND UN CONGRESS 20. PAGE 130 A2663 INT/ORG TOP/EX
B55

PLISCHKE E.,AMERICAN FOREIGN RELATIONS: A BIBLIOGRAPHY OF OFFICIAL SOURCES. USA+45 USA-45 INT/ORG FORCES PRESS WRITING DEBATE EXEC...POLICY INT/LAW 18/20 CONGRESS. PAGE 116 A2390 BIBLIOG/A DIPLOM NAT/G
B55

TANNENBAUM F.,THE AMERICAN TRADITION IN FOREIGN POLICY. USA+45 USA-45 CONSTN INT/ORG NAT/G POL/PAR VOL/ASSN TOP/EX LEGIT DRIVE ORD/FREE PWR...CONCPT GEN/LAWS CONGRESS LEAGUE/NAT COLD/WAR OAS 18/20. PAGE 141 A2887 TIME/SEQ
B55

VINSON J.C.,THE PARCHMENT PEACE: THE UNITED STATES SENATE AND THE WASHINGTON CONFERENCE, 1921-1922. USA-45 INT/ORG DELIB/GP PLAN ARMS/CONT GOV/REL ISOLAT PEACE ATTIT SOVEREIGN...INT/LAW BIBLIOG 20 SENATE PRESIDENT CONGRESS LEAGUE/NAT CHINJAP. PAGE 159 A3242 POLICY DIPLOM NAT/G LEGIS
B56

REITZEL W.,UNITED STATES FOREIGN POLICY, 1945-1955. USA+45 WOR+45 CONSTN INT/ORG EDU/PROP LEGIT EXEC COERCE NUC/PWR PEACE ATTIT ORD/FREE PWR...DECISION CONCPT OBS RECORD TIME/SEQ TREND COLD/WAR UN CONGRESS. PAGE 120 A2464 NAT/G POLICY DIPLOM
B56

US HOUSE COMM FOREIGN AFFAIRS,SURVEY OF ACTIVITIES OF THE COMMITTEE ON FOREIGN AFFAIRS HOUSE OF REPRESENTATIVES: 84TH THROUGH 86TH CONGRESS. USA+45 LAW ADJUD...POLICY STAT CHARTS 20 CONGRESS HOUSE/REP. PAGE 153 A3122 LEGIS DELIB/GP NAT/G DIPLOM
B56

US LIBRARY OF CONGRESS,UNITED STATES DIRECT ECONOMIC AID TO FOREIGN COUNTRIES: A COLLECTION OF EXCERPTS AND A BIBLIOGRAPHY (PAMPHLET). USA+45 PRESS DEBATE...ANTHOL BIBLIOG/A CONGRESS. PAGE 155 A3154 FOR/AID POLICY DIPLOM ECO/UNDEV
B57

CRABB C.,BIPARTISAN FOREIGN POLICY: MYTH OR REALITY. ASIA COM EUR+WWI ISLAM USA+45 USA-45 INT/ORG NAT/G LEGIS TOP/EX PWR CONGRESS 20. PAGE 32 A0649 POL/PAR ATTIT DIPLOM
B57

US SENATE COMM ON JUDICIARY,HEARING BEFORE SUBCOMMITTEE ON COMMITTEE OF JUDICIARY, UNITED STATES SENATE: S. J. RES. 3. USA+45 NAT/G CONSULT DELIB/GP DIPLOM ADJUD LOBBY REPRESENT 20 CONGRESS TREATY. PAGE 157 A3192 LEGIS CONSTN CONFER AGREE
B57

US SENATE SPEC COMM FOR AID,COMPILATION OF STUDIES AND SURVEYS. AFR ASIA L/A+17C USA+45 ECO/UNDEV AGRI INT/ORG CONSULT TEC/DEV CONFER TOTALISM...NAT/COMP 20 CONGRESS. PAGE 157 A3197 FOR/AID DIPLOM ORD/FREE DELIB/GP
B57

US SENATE SPEC COMM FOR AID,HEARINGS BEFORE THE SPECIAL COMMITTEE TO STUDY THE FOREIGN AID PROGRAM. USA+45 USSR ECO/UNDEV INT/ORG FORCES WEAPON TOTALISM ATTIT SUPEGO...NAT/COMP CONGRESS. PAGE 157 A3198 FOR/AID DIPLOM ORD/FREE TEC/DEV
N57

US SENATE SPECIAL COMM FOR AFF,REPORT OF THE SPECIAL COMMITTEE TO STUDY THE FOREIGN AID PROGRAM (PAMPHLET). USA+45 CONSULT DELIB/GP LEGIS PLAN TEC/DEV CONFER SUPEGO CONGRESS. PAGE 157 A3199 FOR/AID ORD/FREE ECO/UNDEV DIPLOM
B58

CARROLL H.N.,THE HOUSE OF REPRESENTATIVES AND FOREIGN AFFAIRS. USA+45 USA-45 NAT/G POL/PAR DIPLOM FOR/AID LEGIT ROUTINE PWR...TIME/SEQ CONGRESS. PAGE 25 A0502 DELIB/GP LEGIS
B58

HENKIN L.,ARMS CONTROL AND INSPECTION IN AMERICAN LAW. LAW CONSTN INT/ORG LOC/G MUNIC NAT/G PROVS EDU/PROP LEGIT EXEC NUC/PWR KNOWL ORD/FREE...OBS TOT/POP CONGRESS 20. PAGE 64 A1315 USA+45 JURID ARMS/CONT
B58

HUNT B.I.,BIPARTISANSHIP: A CASE STUDY OF THE FOREIGN ASSISTANCE PROGRAM, 1947-56 (DOCTORAL THESIS). USA+45 INT/ORG CONSULT LEGIS TEC/DEV ...BIBLIOG PRESIDENT TREATY NATO TRUMAN/HS EISNHWR/DD CONGRESS. PAGE 69 A1418 FOR/AID POL/PAR GP/REL DIPLOM
L58

HAVILAND H.F.,"FOREIGN AID AND THE POLICY PROCESS: 1957." USA+45 FACE/GP POL/PAR VOL/ASSN CHIEF DELIB/GP ACT/RES LEGIT EXEC GOV/REL ATTIT DRIVE PWR ...POLICY TESTS CONGRESS 20. PAGE 63 A1291 LEGIS PLAN FOR/AID
B59

DAWSON R.H.,THE DECISION TO AID RUSSIA* FOREIGN POLICY AND DOMESTIC POLITICS. GERMANY USSR CHIEF EX/STRUC LEGIS TOP/EX PROB/SOLV WAR ATTIT...POLICY CONGRESS. PAGE 34 A0695 DECISION DELIB/GP DIPLOM FOR/AID
B59

ROBINSON J.A.,THE MONRONEY RESOULUTION: CONGRESSIONAL INITIATIVE IN FOREIGN POLICY MAKING. USA+45 POL/PAR TOP/EX DIPLOM INT/TRADE 20 CONGRESS WORLD/BANK INTL/DEV. PAGE 122 A2504 LEGIS FINAN ECO/UNDEV CHIEF
B59

US GENERAL ACCOUNTING OFFICE,EXAM OF ECONOMIC AND TECHNICAL ASSISTANCE PROGRAM FOR INDIA INT'NAT'L COOP ADMIN REPORT TO CONGRESS 1955-1958. INDIA USA+45 ECO/UNDEV FINAN PLAN DIPLOM COST UTIL WEALTH ...CHARTS 20 CONGRESS AID. PAGE 153 A3114 FOR/AID EFFICIENCY ECO/TAC TEC/DEV
N59

US HOUSE COMM FOREIGN AFFAIRS,HEARINGS ON DRAFT LEGISLATION TO AMEND FURTHER THE MUTUAL SECURITY ACT OF 1954 (PAMPHLET). USA+45 USSR CONSULT DELIB/GP FORCES ECO/TAC CONFER...POLICY 20 CONGRESS. PAGE 153 A3126 DIPLOM FOR/AID ORD/FREE LEGIS
B60

AMERICAN ASSEMBLY COLUMBIA U,THE SECRETARY OF STATE. USA+45 ELITES NAT/G PLAN ADMIN GOV/REL CENTRAL ATTIT...POLICY MGT 20 SEC/STATE CONGRESS PRESIDENT. PAGE 7 A0136 DELIB/GP EX/STRUC GP/REL DIPLOM
B60

BARNET R.,WHO WANTS DISARMAMENT. COM EUR+WWI USA+45 USSR INT/ORG NAT/G BAL/PWR DIPLOM EDU/PROP COERCE DETER NUC/PWR WAR WEAPON ATTIT PWR...TIME/SEQ COLD/WAR CONGRESS 20. PAGE 11 A0225 PLAN FORCES ARMS/CONT
B60

BYRD E.M. JR.,TREATIES AND EXECUTIVE AGREEMENTS IN THE UNITED STATES: THEIR SEPARATE ROLES AND LIMITATIONS. USA+45 USA-45 EX/STRUC TARIFFS CT/SYS GOV/REL FEDERAL...IDEA/COMP BIBLIOG SUPREME/CT SENATE CONGRESS. PAGE 23 A0461 CHIEF INT/LAW DIPLOM
B60

PRICE D.,THE SECRETARY OF STATE. USA+45 CONSTN ELITES INTELL CHIEF EX/STRUC TOP/EX LEGIT ATTIT PWR SKILL...DECISION 20 CONGRESS. PAGE 117 A2410 CONSULT DIPLOM INT/LAW
B60

US HOUSE COMM GOVT OPERATIONS,OPERATIONS OF THE DEVELOPMENT LOAN FUND: HEARINGS (COMMITTEE ON GOVERNMENT OPERATIONS). USA+45 PLAN BUDGET DIPLOM GOV/REL COST...CHARTS 20 CONGRESS DEPT/STATE AID. PAGE 154 A3137 FINAN FOR/AID ECO/TAC EFFICIENCY
B61

BECHHOEFER B.G.,POSTWAR NEGOTIATIONS FOR ARMS CONTROL. COM EUR+WWI USSR INT/ORG NAT/G ACT/RES BAL/PWR DIPLOM ECO/TAC EDU/PROP ADMIN REGION DETER NUC/PWR WAR WEAPON PEACE ATTIT PWR...POLICY TIME/SEQ COLD/WAR CONGRESS 20. PAGE 12 A0244 USA+45 ARMS/CONT
B61

GRAEBNER N.,AN UNCERTAIN TRADITION: AMERICAN SECRETARIES OF STATE IN THE 20TH CENTURY. USA+45 USA-45 BIOG

CONSTN INT/ORG NAT/G DELIB/GP TOP/EX BAL/PWR DOMIN LEGIT ADMIN ARMS/CONT ATTIT DRIVE PERSON SUPEGO ORD/FREE PWR...GEN/LAWS VAL/FREE CONGRESS. PAGE 55 A1121 DIPLOM

B61
KERTESZ S.D.,AMERICAN DIPLOMACY IN A NEW ERA. COM S/ASIA UK USA+45 FORCES PROB/SOLV BAL/PWR ECO/TAC ADMIN COLONIAL WAR PEACE ORD/FREE 20 NATO CONGRESS UN COLD/WAR. PAGE 78 A1601 ANTHOL DIPLOM TREND

B61
SCOTT A.M.,POLITICS, USA; CASES ON THE AMERICAN DEMOCRATIC PROCESS. USA+45 CHIEF FORCES DIPLOM LOBBY CHOOSE RACE/REL FEDERAL ATTIT...JURID ANTHOL T 20 PRESIDENT CONGRESS CIVIL/LIB. PAGE 130 A2669 CT/SYS CONSTN NAT/G PLAN

B61
US CONGRESS JOINT ECO COMM,INTERNATIONAL PAYMENTS IMBALANCES AND NEED FOR STRENGTHENING INTERNATIONAL FINANCIAL ARRANGEMENTS. USA+45 WOR+45 DELIB/GP DIPLOM INT/TRADE...CHARTS 20 CONGRESS OEEC. PAGE 150 A3063 BAL/PAY INT/ORG FINAN PROB/SOLV

B61
US HOUSE COMM APPROPRIATIONS,INTER-AMERICAN PROGRAMS FOR 1961: DENIAL OF 1962 BUDGET INFORMATION. CHILE L/A+17C USA+45 FINAN CONSULT BUDGET ADJUD COST EFFICIENCY WEALTH...POLICY CHARTS 20 CONGRESS. PAGE 153 A3119 LEGIS FOR/AID DELIB/GP ECO/UNDEV

B61
US HOUSE COMM FOREIGN AFFAIRS,THE INTERNATIONAL DEVELOPMENT AND SECURITY ACT: HEARINGS BEFORE COMMITTEE ON FOREIGN AFFAIRS, HOUSE OF REP: HR7372. USA+45 AGRI INT/ORG NAT/G CONSULT DELIB/GP DIPLOM ECO/TAC INT/TRADE LOBBY REPRESENT 20 MCNAMARA/R DILLON/D RUSK/D CONGRESS. PAGE 153 A3128 FOR/AID CONFER LEGIS ECO/UNDEV

S61
JUVILER P.H.,"INTERPARLIAMENTARY CONTACTS IN SOVIET FOREIGN POLICY." COM FUT WOR+45 WOR-45 SOCIETY CONSULT ACT/RES DIPLOM ADMIN PEACE ATTIT RIGID/FLEX WEALTH...WELF/ST SOC TOT/POP CONGRESS 19/20. PAGE 75 A1543 INT/ORG DELIB/GP USSR

B62
JEWELL M.E.,SENATORIAL POLITICS AND FOREIGN POLICY. NAT/G POL/PAR CHIEF DELIB/GP TOP/EX FOR/AID EDU/PROP ROUTINE ATTIT PWR SKILL...MAJORIT METH/CNCPT TIME/SEQ CONGRESS 20 PRESIDENT. PAGE 74 A1516 USA+45 LEGIS DIPLOM

B62
RIVKIN A.,AFRICA AND THE WEST. AFR EUR+WWI FUT ISLAM ISRAEL USA+45 SOCIETY INT/ORG FORCES CREATE PLAN FOR/AID EDU/PROP ATTIT...CONCPT TREND EEC 20 CONGRESS UN. PAGE 121 A2488 ECO/UNDEV ECO/TAC

B62
SNOW J.H.,GOVERNMENT BY TREASON. USA+45 USA-45 LEGIS DIPLOM FOR/AID GIVE CONTROL WEALTH MARXISM ...MAJORIT 20 CONGRESS COLD/WAR. PAGE 134 A2750 FINAN TAX PWR POLICY

B62
US CONGRESS,LEGISLATIVE HISTORY OF UNITED STATES TAX CONVENTIONS(VOL. 1). USA+45 USA-45 DELIB/GP WEALTH...CHARTS 20 CONGRESS. PAGE 150 A3061 TAX LEGIS LAW DIPLOM

B62
US CONGRESS,COMMUNICATIONS SATELLITE LEGISLATION: HEARINGS BEFORE COMM ON AERON AND SPACE SCIENCES ON BILLS S2550 AND 2814. WOR+45 LAW VOL/ASSN PLAN DIPLOM CONTROL OWN PEACE...NEW/IDEA CONGRESS NASA. PAGE 150 A3062 SPACE COM/IND ADJUD GOV/REL

B62
US CONGRESS JOINT ECO COMM,FACTORS AFFECTING THE UNITED STATES BALANCE OF PAYMENTS. USA+45 DELIB/GP PLAN DIPLOM FOR/AID PRODUC WEALTH...CHARTS 20 CONGRESS OEEC. PAGE 150 A3064 BAL/PAY INT/TRADE ECO/TAC FINAN

B62
US CONGRESS JOINT ECO COMM,ECONOMIC DEVELOPMENTS IN SOUTH AMERICA. USA+45 SOCIETY FINAN NAT/G PROB/SOLV TEC/DEV INT/TRADE TAX EFFICIENCY PRODUC ATTIT ...POLICY 20 CONGRESS SOUTH/AMER. PAGE 150 A3065 L/A+17C ECO/UNDEV FOR/AID DIPLOM

B62
US SENATE COMM ON JUDICIARY,CONSTITUTIONAL RIGHTS OF MILITARY PERSONNEL. USA+45 USA-45 FORCES DIPLOM WAR CONGRESS. PAGE 157 A3193 CONSTN ORD/FREE JURID CT/SYS

S62
TRUMAN D.,"THE DOMESTIC POLITICS OF FOREIGN AID." USA+45 WOR+45 NAT/G POL/PAR LEGIS DIPLOM ECO/TAC EDU/PROP ADMIN CHOOSE ATTIT PWR CONGRESS 20 CONGRESS. PAGE 145 A2970 ROUTINE FOR/AID

S62
TRUMAN D.,"THE DOMESTIC POLITICS OF FOREIGN AID." USA+45 WOR+45 NAT/G POL/PAR LEGIS DIPLOM ECO/TAC EDU/PROP ADMIN CHOOSE ATTIT PWR CONGRESS 20 CONGRESS. PAGE 145 A2970 ROUTINE FOR/AID

C62
ROBINSON J.A.,"CONGRESS AND FOREIGN POLICY-MAKING: A STUDY IN LEGISLATIVE INFLUENCE AND INITIATIVE." USA+45 CHIEF DELIB/GP CREATE CONTROL EXEC GOV/REL PERCEPT...TREND BIBLIOG 20 CONGRESS. PAGE 122 A2505 LEGIS DIPLOM POLICY DECISION

B63
DRACHKOVITCH,UNITED STATES AID TO YUGOSLAVIA AND POLAND. POLAND USA+45 YUGOSLAVIA LEGIS EXEC TOTALISM MARXISM 20 CONGRESS. PAGE 38 A0782 FOR/AID POLICY DIPLOM ATTIT

B63
LERCHE C.O. JR.,AMERICA IN WORLD AFFAIRS. COM UK USA+45 INT/ORG FORCES ECO/TAC INT/TRADE EDU/PROP WAR NAT/LISM PEACE...BIBLIOG 18/20 UN CONGRESS PRESIDENT COLD/WAR. PAGE 87 A1783 NAT/G DIPLOM PLAN

B63
US CONGRESS JOINT ECO COMM,DISCRIMINATORY OCEAN FREIGHT RATES AND BALANCE OF PAYMENTS. USA+45 SEA DELIB/GP DISCRIM...CHARTS 20 CONGRESS. PAGE 150 A3066 BAL/PAY DIST/IND PRICE INT/TRADE

B63
US CONGRESS JOINT ECO COMM,THE UNITED STATES BALANCE OF PAYMENTS. USA+45 DELIB/GP BUDGET PRICE PRODUC 20 CONGRESS GOLD/STAND MONEY. PAGE 150 A3067 BAL/PAY INT/TRADE FINAN ECO/TAC

B63
US CONGRESS JOINT ECO COMM,THE UNITED STATES BALANCE OF PAYMENTS. USA+45 DELIB/GP CONFER...MATH PREDICT CHARTS 20 CONGRESS. PAGE 150 A3068 BAL/PAY ECO/TAC INT/TRADE CONSULT

B63
US HOUSE COMM BANKING-CURR,RECENT CHANGES IN MONETARY POLICY AND BALANCE OF PAYMENTS PROBLEMS. USA+45 DELIB/GP PLAN DIPLOM...CHARTS 20 CONGRESS. PAGE 153 A3121 BAL/PAY FINAN ECO/TAC POLICY

B63
US SENATE,DOCUMENTS ON INTERNATIONAL AS"ECTS OF EXPLORATION AND USE OF OUTER SPACE, 1954-62: STAFF REPORT FOR COMM AERON SPACE SCI. USA+45 USSR LEGIS LEAD CIVMIL/REL PEACE...POLICY INT/LAW ANTHOL 20 CONGRESS NASA KHRUSH/N. PAGE 155 A3165 SPACE UTIL GOV/REL DIPLOM

B63
US SENATE COMM APPROPRIATIONS,PERSONNEL ADMINISTRATION AND OPERATIONS OF AGENCY FOR INTERNATIONAL DEVELOPMENT: SPECIAL HEARING. FINAN LEAD COST UTIL SKILL...CHARTS 20 CONGRESS AID CIVIL/SERV. PAGE 155 A3170 ADMIN FOR/AID EFFICIENCY DIPLOM

B63
US SENATE COMM GOVT OPERATIONS,REPORT OF A STUDY OF US FOREIGN AID IN TEN MIDDLE EASTERN AND AFRICAN COUNTRIES. AFR ISLAM USA+45 FORCES PLAN BUDGET DIPLOM TAX DETER WEALTH...STAT CHARTS 20 CONGRESS AID MID/EAST. PAGE 156 A3174 FOR/AID EFFICIENCY ECO/TAC FINAN

B63
US SENATE COMM ON FOREIGN REL,HEARINGS ON S 1276 A BILL TO AMEND FURTHER THE FOREIGN ASSISTANCE ACT OF 1961. USA+45 WOR+45 INDUS INT/ORG FORCES TAX WEAPON SUPEGO...NAT/COMP 20 UN CONGRESS PRESIDENT. PAGE 156 A3182 FOR/AID DIPLOM ECO/UNDEV ORD/FREE

S63
WYZNER E.,"NIEKTORE ASPEKTY PRAWNE FINANSOWANIA OPERACJI ONZ W KONGO I NA BEIZKIM WSCHODZIE." S/ASIA CONSTN FINAN INT/ORG TOP/EX...TIME/SEQ UN 20 CONGRESS. PAGE 168 A3426 FORCES JURID DIPLOM

B64
COFFIN F.M.,WITNESS FOR AID. COM EUR+WWI USA+45 DIPLOM GP/REL CONSEN ORD/FREE MARXISM...NEW/IDEA 20 CONGRESS AID. PAGE 27 A0557 FOR/AID ECO/UNDEV DELIB/GP PLAN

B64
COHEN M.,LAW AND POLITICS IN SPACE: SPECIFIC AND URGENT PROBLEMS IN THE LAW OF OUTER SPACE. CHINA/COM COM USA+45 USSR WOR+45 COM/IND INT/ORG NAT/G LEGIT NUC/PWR ATTIT BIO/SOC...JURID CONCPT CONGRESS 20 STALIN/J. PAGE 28 A0561 DELIB/GP LAW INT/LAW SPACE

B64
MASON E.S.,FOREIGN AID AND FOREIGN POLICY. USA+45 AGRI INDUS NAT/G EX/STRUC ACT/RES RIGID/FLEX ALL/VALS...POLICY GEN/LAWS MARSHL/PLN CONGRESS 20. PAGE 95 A1956 ECO/UNDEV ECO/TAC FOR/AID DIPLOM

B64
REUSS H.S.,THE CRITICAL DECADE - AN ECONOMIC POLICY FOR AMERICA AND THE FREE WORLD. USA+45 FINAN POL/PAR WORKER PLAN DIPLOM ECO/TAC TARIFFS BAL/PAY ...POLICY 20 CONGRESS GOLD/STAND. PAGE 120 A2468 FOR/AID INT/TRADE LABOR LEGIS

B64
SARROS P.P.,CONGRESS AND THE NEW DIPLOMACY: THE FORMULATION OF MUTUAL SECURITY POLICY: 1953-60 (THESIS). USA+45 CHIEF EX/STRUC REGION ROUTINE CHOOSE GOV/REL PEACE ROLE...POLICY 20 PRESIDENT CONGRESS. PAGE 127 A2606 DIPLOM POL/PAR NAT/G

B64
US HOUSE COMM FOREIGN AFFAIRS,HEARINGS ON H.R. 10502 TO AMEND FURTHER THE FOREIGN ASSISTANCE ACT OF 1961. AFR ASIA L/A+17C INT/ORG CONSULT DELIB/GP TEC/DEV ECO/TAC EDU/PROP CONFER 20 UN NATO CONGRESS AID. PAGE 153 A3130 FOR/AID DIPLOM ORD/FREE ECO/UNDEV

B64
US HOUSE COMM GOVT OPERATIONS,US OWNED FOREIGN CURRENCIES: HEARINGS (COMMITTEE ON GOVERNMENT OPERATIONS). INDIA ECO/DEV PLAN BUDGET TAX DEMAND FINAN ECO/TAC FOR/AID

EFFICIENCY 20 AID CONGRESS. PAGE 154 A3138 — OWN

B64
US HOUSE COMM ON JUDICIARY,IMMIGRATION HEARINGS. DELIB/GP STRANGE HABITAT...GEOG JURID 20 CONGRESS MIGRATION. PAGE 154 A3140 — NAT/G POLICY DIPLOM NAT/LISM

B64
US SENATE COMM GOVT OPERATIONS,ADMINISTRATION OF NATIONAL SECURITY. USA+45 CHIEF TOP/EX PLAN DIPLOM CONTROL PEACE...POLICY DECISION 20 PRESIDENT CONGRESS. PAGE 156 A3176 — ADMIN FORCES ORD/FREE NAT/G

S64
DERWINSKI E.J.,"THE COST OF THE INTERNATIONAL COFFEE AGREEMENT." L/A+17C USA+45 WOR+45 ECO/UNDEV NAT/G VOL/ASSN LEGIS DIPLOM ECO/TAC FOR/AID LEGIT ATTIT...TIME/SEQ CONGRESS 20 TREATY. PAGE 36 A0732 — MARKET DELIB/GP INT/TRADE

S64
WOOD H.B.,"STRETCHING YOUR FOREIGN-AID DOLLAR." USA+45 WOR+45 CONSULT EDU/PROP ATTIT WEALTH...OBS TOT/POP CONGRESS 20. PAGE 166 A3390 — ECO/UNDEV MGT FOR/AID

B65
HAIGHT D.E.,THE PRESIDENT; ROLES AND POWERS. USA+45 USA-45 POL/PAR PLAN DIPLOM CHOOSE PERS/REL PWR 18/20 PRESIDENT CONGRESS. PAGE 59 A1217 — CHIEF LEGIS TOP/EX EX/STRUC

B65
LYONS G.M.,AMERICA: PURPOSE AND POWER. UK USA+45 FINAN INDUS MARKET WORKER TEC/DEV DIPLOM AUTOMAT NUC/PWR WAR RACE/REL ORD/FREE 20 EEC CONGRESS SUPREME/CT CIV/RIGHTS. PAGE 92 A1881 — PWR PROB/SOLV ECO/DEV TASK

B65
US CONGRESS JOINT ECO COMM,GUIDELINES FOR INTERNATIONAL MONETARY REFORM. USA+45 WOR+45 DELIB/GP BAL/PAY 20 CONGRESS IMF MONEY. PAGE 150 A3069 — DIPLOM FINAN PLAN INT/ORG

B65
US CONGRESS JT ATOM ENRGY COMM,ATOMIC ENERGY LEGISLATION THROUGH 89TH CONGRESS, 1ST SESSION. USA+45 LAW INT/ORG DELIB/GP BUDGET DIPLOM 20 AEC CONGRESS CASEBOOK EURATOM IAEA. PAGE 150 A3071 — NUC/PWR FORCES PEACE LEGIS

B65
US HOUSE COMM FOREIGN AFFAIRS,HEARINGS ON DRAFT BILL TO AMEND FURTHER THE FOREIGN ASSISTANCE ACT OF 1961. AFR ASIA L/A+17C USA+45 INT/ORG DELIB/GP TEC/DEV ECO/TAC CONFER TOTALISM 20 CONGRESS AID. PAGE 153 A3131 — FOR/AID ECO/UNDEV DIPLOM ORD/FREE

B65
US SENATE,US INTERNATIONAL SPACE PROGRAMS, 1959-65: STAFF REPORT FOR COMM ON AERONAUTICAL AND SPACE SCIENCES. WOR+45 VOL/ASSN CIVMIL/REL 20 CONGRESS NASA TREATY. PAGE 155 A3166 — SPACE DIPLOM PLAN GOV/REL

B65
US SENATE COMM BANKING CURR,BALANCE OF PAYMENTS - 1965. USA+45 ECO/TAC PRICE WEALTH...CHARTS 20 CONGRESS GOLD/STAND. PAGE 156 A3171 — BAL/PAY FINAN DIPLOM INT/TRADE

B65
US SENATE COMM ON FOREIGN REL,HEARINGS ON THE FOREIGN ASSISTANCE PROGRAM. AFR ASIA L/A+17C USA+45 WOR+45 FORCES TEC/DEV BUDGET CONTROL WEAPON ORD/FREE 20 UN CONGRESS SEC/STATE. PAGE 156 A3183 — FOR/AID DIPLOM INT/ORG ECO/UNDEV

B65
US SENATE COMM ON JUDICIARY,REFUGEE PROBLEMS IN SOUTH VIETNAM AND LAOS: HEARINGS BEFORE SUBCOMMITTEE TO INVESTIGATE PROBLEMS OF REFUGEES, ESCAPEES. CHINA/COM LAOS USA+45 VIETNAM/S PROB/SOLV DIPLOM GOV/REL GP/REL EFFICIENCY ORD/FREE...POLICY GEOG 20 CONGRESS MIGRATION. PAGE 157 A3194 — STRANGE HABITAT FOR/AID CIVMIL/REL

B65
US SENATE COMM ON JUDICIARY,ANTITRUST EXEMPTIONS FOR AGREEMENTS RELATING TO BALANCE OF PAYMENTS. FINAN ECO/TAC CONTROL WEALTH...POLICY 20 CONGRESS. PAGE 157 A3195 — BAL/PAY ADJUD MARKET INT/TRADE

B66
RIESELBACH L.N.,THE ROOTS OF ISOLATIONISM* CONGRESSIONAL VOTING AND PRESIDENTIAL LEADERSHIP IN FOREIGN POLICY. POL/PAR LEGIS DIPLOM EDU/PROP LEAD REGION REPRESENT...SOC STAT IDEA/COMP HYPO/EXP BIBLIOG 19/20 CONGRESS. PAGE 121 A2477 — ISOLAT CHOOSE CHIEF POLICY

B66
US CONGRESS JOINT ECO COMM,NEW APPROACH TO UNITED STATES INTERNATIONAL ECONOMIC POLICY. USA+45 WOR+45 CHIEF DELIB/GP CONFER...CHARTS 20 CONGRESS MONEY. PAGE 150 A3070 — DIPLOM ECO/TAC BAL/PAY FINAN

B66
US HOUSE COMM APPROPRIATIONS,HEARINGS ON FOREIGN OPERATIONS AND RELATED AGENCIES APPROPRIATIONS. CUBA USA+45 VOL/ASSN DELIB/GP DIPLOM CONFER ORD/FREE 20 CONGRESS MIGRATION INT/AM/DEV PEACE/CORP. PAGE 153 A3120 — FOR/AID BUDGET ECO/UNDEV FORCES

B66
US HOUSE COMM FOREIGN AFFAIRS,HEARINGS ON HR 12449 A BILL TO AMEND FURTHER THE FOREIGN ASSISTANCE ACT OF 1961. AFR ASIA L/A+17C USA+45 VIETNAM INT/ORG TEC/DEV INT/TRADE ATTIT ORD/FREE 20 UN NATO CONGRESS AID. PAGE 154 A3132 — FOR/AID ECO/TAC ECO/UNDEV DIPLOM

B66
US HOUSE COMM FOREIGN AFFAIRS,UNITED STATES - SOUTH AFRICAN RELATIONS. SOUTH/AFR USA+45 NAT/G CONSULT DELIB/GP LEGIS CONFER SANCTION RACE/REL ATTIT 20 CONGRESS. PAGE 154 A3134 — DISCRIM DIPLOM POLICY PARL/PROC

B66
US SENATE COMM GOVT OPERATIONS,POPULATION CRISIS. USA+45 ECO/DEV ECO/UNDEV AGRI SECT DELIB/GP PROB/SOLV FOR/AID REPRESENT ATTIT...GEOG CHARTS 20 CONGRESS DEPT/STATE DEPT/HEW BIRTH/CON. PAGE 156 A3178 — CENSUS CONTROL LEGIS CONSULT

B66
US SENATE COMM ON FOREIGN REL,UNITED STATES POLICY TOWARD EUROPE (AND RELATED MATTERS). COM EUR+WWI GERMANY PROB/SOLV REGION NUC/PWR WAR NAT/LISM PEACE PWR...NAT/COMP 20 NATO CONGRESS DEGAULLE/C. PAGE 156 A3184 — DIPLOM INT/ORG POLICY WOR+45

B66
US SENATE COMM ON FOREIGN REL,HEARINGS ON S 2859 AND S 2861. USA+45 WOR+45 FORCES BUDGET CAP/ISM ADMIN DETER WEAPON TOTALISM...NAT/COMP 20 UN CONGRESS. PAGE 156 A3185 — FOR/AID DIPLOM ORD/FREE ECO/UNDEV

B66
VYAS R.,DAWNING ON THE CAPITOL: US CONGRESS AND INDIA. INDIA S/ASIA USA+45 ELITES ECO/DEV ECO/UNDEV PLAN FOR/AID...BIBLIOG 20 CONGRESS. PAGE 160 A3256 — POLICY LEGIS NAT/G DIPLOM

B67
O'LEARY M.K.,THE POLITICS OF AMERICAN FOREIGN AID. USA+45 POL/PAR CHIEF BUDGET EDU/PROP LOBBY CONGRESS. PAGE 111 A2270 — FOR/AID DIPLOM PARL/PROC ATTIT

B67
US AGENCY INTERNATIONAL DEV,PROPOSED FOREIGN AID PROGRAM FOR 1968: SUMMARY PRESENTATION TO THE CONGRESS. AFR S/ASIA USA+45 AGRI TEC/DEV DIPLOM ECO/TAC BAL/PAY COST HEALTH KNOWL SKILL 20 AID CONGRESS. PAGE 149 A3053 — ECO/UNDEV BUDGET FOR/AID STAT

B67
US SENATE COMM ON FOREIGN REL,HUMAN RIGHTS CONVENTIONS. USA+45 LABOR VOL/ASSN DELIB/GP DOMIN ADJUD REPRESENT...INT/LAW MGT CONGRESS. PAGE 156 A3189 — LEGIS ORD/FREE WORKER LOBBY

B67
US SUPERINTENDENT OF DOCUMENTS,LIBRARY OF CONGRESS (PRICE LIST 83). AFR ASIA EUR+WWI USA-45 USSR NAT/G DIPLOM CONFER CT/SYS WAR...DECISION PHIL/SCI CLASSIF 19/20 CONGRESS PRESIDENT. PAGE 157 A3205 — BIBLIOG/A USA+45 AUTOMAT LAW

L67
KOMESAR N.K.,"PRESIDENTIAL AMENDMENT & TERMINATION OF TREATIES* THE CASE OF THE WARSAW CONVENTION." POLAND USA+45 NAT/G CHIEF PROB/SOLV DIPLOM PWR 20 CONGRESS. PAGE 81 A1669 — TOP/EX LEGIS CONSTN LICENSE

S67
CLINGHAM T.A. JR.,"LEGISLATIVE FLOTSAM AND INTERNATIONAL ACTION IN THE 'YARMOUTH CASTLE'S' WAKE." WOR+45 PROB/SOLV CONFER COST HEALTH...POLICY INT/LAW CONGRESS. PAGE 27 A0552 — DIPLOM DIST/IND INT/ORG LAW

N67
US SUPERINTENDENT OF DOCUMENTS,SPACE: MISSILES, THE MOON, NASA, AND SATELLITES (PRICE LIST 79A). USA+45 COM/IND R+D NAT/G DIPLOM EDU/PROP ADMIN CONTROL HEALTH...POLICY SIMUL NASA CONGRESS. PAGE 157 A3206 — BIBLIOG/A SPACE TEC/DEV PEACE

CONGRESS/P....CONGRESS PARTY (ALL NATIONS)

CONN S. A0585

CONNECTICT....CONNECTICUT

CONNEL-SMITH G. A0586

CONNERY R.H. A0587

CONNOR W. A0588

CONOVER H.F. A0589,A0590,A0591,A0592,A0593,A0594,A0595,A0596 , A0597,A0598,A0599,A0600,A0601,A0602,A0603,A0604

CONRAD/JOS....JOSEPH CONRAD

CONSCIENCE....SEE SUPEGO

CONSCN/OBJ....CONSCIENTIOUS OBJECTION TO WAR AND KILLING

B17
DE VICTORIA F.,DE INDIS ET DE JURE BELLI (1557) IN F. DE VICTORIA, DE INDIS ET DE JURE BELLI REFLECTIONES. UNIV NAT/G SECT CHIEF PARTIC COERCE PEACE MORAL...POLICY 16 INDIAN/AM CHRISTIAN CONSCN/OBJ. PAGE 35 A0715 — WAR INT/LAW OWN

B57
PETERSON H.C.,OPPONENTS OF WAR 1917-1918. USA-45 POL/PAR DOMIN ORD/FREE PWR PACIFISM SOCISM 20 IWW CONSCN/OBJ. PAGE 115 A2368 — WAR PEACE ATTIT EDU/PROP

B66
MAYER P.,THE PACIFIST CONSCIENCE. SECT CREATE ARMS/CONT WAR RACE/REL ATTIT LOVE...ANTHOL PACIFIST WORSHIP FREUD/S GANDHI/M LAO/TZU KING/MAR/L CONSCN/OBJ. PAGE 97 A1984 — DIPLOM PACIFISM SUPEGO

CONSCRIPTN....CONSCRIPTION

CONSEN....CONSENSUS

B10
GRIFFIN A.P.C.,LIST OF REFERENCES ON RECIPROCITY (2ND REV. ED.). CANADA CUBA UK USA-45 WOR-45 NAT/G TARIFFS CONFER COLONIAL CONTROL SANCTION CONSEN ALL/VALS...DECISION 19/20. PAGE 56 A1157 — BIBLIOG/A VOL/ASSN DIPLOM REPAR

B50
ALMOND G.A.,THE AMERICAN PEOPLE AND FOREIGN POLICY. USA+45 USA-45 CULTURE SOCIETY STRUCT CONSEN PERSON PWR POPULISM...TIME/SEQ TREND 20 COLD/WAR. PAGE 6 A0129 — ATTIT DIPLOM DECISION ELITES

B55
HOGAN W.N.,INTERNATIONAL CONFLICT AND COLLECTIVE SECURITY: THE PRINCIPLE OF CONCERN IN INTERNATIONAL ORGANIZATION. CONSTN EX/STRUC BAL/PWR DIPLOM ADJUD CONTROL CENTRAL CONSEN PEACE...INT/LAW CONCPT METH/COMP 20 UN LEAGUE/NAT. PAGE 66 A1361 — INT/ORG WAR ORD/FREE FORCES

B57
FRASER L.,PROPAGANDA. GERMANY USSR WOR+45 WOR-45 NAT/G POL/PAR CONTROL FEEDBACK LOBBY CROWD WAR CONSEN NAT/LISM 20. PAGE 48 A0988 — EDU/PROP FASCISM MARXISM DIPLOM

B58
MANSERGH N.,SURVEY OF BRITISH COMMONWEALTH AFFAIRS: PROBLEMS OF WARTIME CO-OPERATION AND POST-WAR CHANGE 1939-1952. INDIA IRELAND S/ASIA CONSTN INT/ORG BAL/PWR COLONIAL NEUTRAL WAR ADJUST PEACE ROLE ORD/FREE...CHARTS 20 CMN/WLTH NATO UN. PAGE 94 A1931 — VOL/ASSN CONSEN PROB/SOLV INGP/REL

L60
JACOB P.E.,"THE DISARMAMENT CONSENSUS." USA+45 USSR WOR+45 INT/ORG NAT/G ACT/RES TEC/DEV BAL/PWR EDU/PROP ADMIN COERCE DETER NUC/PWR CONSEN RIGID/FLEX PWR...CONCPT RECORD CHARTS COLD/WAR 20. PAGE 72 A1482 — DELIB/GP ATTIT ARMS/CONT

B62
MOON P.,DIVIDE AND QUIT. INDIA PAKISTAN STRATA DELIB/GP PLAN DIPLOM REPRESENT GP/REL INGP/REL CONSEN DISCRIM...OBS 20. PAGE 103 A2119 — WAR REGION ISOLAT SECT

B63
HARTLEY A.,A STATE OF ENGLAND. UK ELITES SOCIETY ACADEM NAT/G SCHOOL INGP/REL CONSEN ORD/FREE NEW/LIB...POLICY 20. PAGE 62 A1275 — DIPLOM ATTIT INTELL ECO/DEV

B64
BURKE F.G.,AFRICA'S QUEST FOR ORDER. AFR CULTURE KIN MUNIC NAT/G DIPLOM COLONIAL REV DISCRIM NAT/LISM AGE/Y 20. PAGE 21 A0437 — ORD/FREE CONSEN RACE/REL LEAD

B64
COFFIN F.M.,WITNESS FOR AID. COM EUR+WWI USA+45 DIPLOM GP/REL CONSEN ORD/FREE MARXISM...NEW/IDEA 20 CONGRESS AID. PAGE 27 A0557 — FOR/AID ECO/UNDEV DELIB/GP PLAN

S64
BARKUN M.,"CONFLICT RESOLUTION THROUGH IMPLICIT MEDIATION." UNIV BARGAIN CONSEN FEDERAL JURID. PAGE 11 A0222 — CONSULT CENTRAL INT/LAW IDEA/COMP

S65
SPAAK P.H.,"THE SEARCH FOR CONSENSUS: A NEW EFFORT TO BUILD EUROPE." FRANCE GERMANY ECO/DEV NAT/G CONSULT FORCES PLAN EDU/PROP REGION CONSEN ATTIT ...SOC METH/CNCPT OBS TREND EEC NATO WORK 20. PAGE 135 A2770 — EUR+WWI INT/ORG

B66
MAY E.R.,ANXIETY AND AFFLUENCE: 1945-1965. USA+45 DIPLOM FOR/AID ARMS/CONT RACE/REL CONSEN...ANTHOL 20 COLD/WAR KENNEDY/JF EISNHWR/DD TRUMAN/HS BERLIN/BLO. PAGE 97 A1982 — ANOMIE ECO/DEV NUC/PWR WEALTH

L67
LISSITZYN O.J.,"TREATIES AND CHANGED CIRCUMSTANCES (REBUS SIC STANTIBUS)" WOR+45 CONSEN...JURID 20. PAGE 90 A1842 — AGREE DIPLOM INT/LAW

S67
HODGE G.,"THE RISE AND DEMISE OF THE UN TECHNICAL ASSISTANCE ADMINISTRATION." RISK TASK INGP/REL CONSEN EFFICIENCY 20 UN. PAGE 66 A1349 — ADMIN TEC/DEV EX/STRUC INT/ORG

S67
MUDGE G.A.,"DOMESTIC POLICIES AND UN ACTIVITIES* THE CASE OF RHODESIA AND THE REPUBLIC OF SOUTH AFRICA." RHODESIA SOUTH/AFR POL/PAR LEAD SANCTION CHOOSE RACE/REL CONSEN DISCRIM ATTIT...INT/LAW UN PARLIAMENT 20. PAGE 105 A2163 — AFR NAT/G POLICY

S67
RABIER J.-R.,"THE EUROPEAN IDEA AND NATIONAL PUBLIC OPINIONS." ACT/RES PLAN DIPLOM PARTIC CONSEN ATTIT PERCEPT...DECISION CHARTS. PAGE 118 A2430 — POLICY FEDERAL EUR+WWI PROB/SOLV

S67
WEIL G.L.,"THE MERGER OF THE INSTITUTIONS OF THE EUROPEAN COMMUNITIES" EUR+WWI ECO/DEV INT/TRADE CONSEN PLURISM...DECISION MGT 20 EEC EURATOM ECSC TREATY. PAGE 162 A3300 — ECO/TAC INT/ORG CENTRAL INT/LAW

CONSENSUS....SEE CONSEN

CONSERVATISM....SEE CONSERVE

CONSERVE....TRADITIONALISM

C05
DUNNING W.A.,"HISTORY OF POLITICAL THEORIES FROM LUTHER TO MONTESQUIEU." LAW NAT/G SECT DIPLOM REV WAR ORD/FREE SOVEREIGN CONSERVE...TRADIT BIBLIOG 16/18. PAGE 39 A0803 — PHIL/SCI CONCPT GEN/LAWS

N19
MASSEY V.,CANADIANS AND THEIR COMMONWEALTH: THE ROMANES LECTURE DELIVERED IN THE SHELDONIAN THEATRE JUNE 1, 1961 (PAMPHLET). CANADA UK CULTURE ECO/DEV REPRESENT NAT/LISM PEACE PWR CONSERVE 20 CMN/WLTH. PAGE 96 A1959 — ATTIT DIPLOM NAT/G SOVEREIGN

S26
COHEN P.A.,"WANG T'AO AND INCIPIENT CHINESE NATIONALISM." ASIA ADMIN ATTIT 19/20 BUREAUCRCY. PAGE 28 A0563 — NAT/LISM ISOLAT CONSERVE DIPLOM

B27
GOOCH G.P.,ENGLISH DEMOCRATIC IDEAS IN THE SEVENTEENTH CENTURY (2ND ED.). UK LAW SECT FORCES DIPLOM LEAD PARL/PROC REV ATTIT AUTHORIT...ANARCH CONCPT 17 PARLIAMENT CMN/WLTH REFORMERS. PAGE 54 A1100 — IDEA/COMP MAJORIT EX/STRUC CONSERVE

B33
FERRERO G.,PEACE AND WAR (TRANS. BY BERTHA PRITCHARD). CULTURE FINAN SECT ATTIT SUPEGO MORAL ORD/FREE CONSERVE POPULISM SOCISM POLICY. PAGE 45 A0922 — WAR PEACE DIPLOM PROB/SOLV

B35
MARRIOTT J.A.,DICTATORSHIP AND DEMOCRACY. GERMANY GREECE UK CHIEF DIPLOM DOMIN LEGIT PEACE ORD/FREE CONSERVE...TREND ROME HITLER/A. PAGE 95 A1946 — TOTALISM POPULISM PLURIST NAT/G

B43
MC DOWELL R.B.,IRISH PUBLIC OPINION, 1750-1800. IRELAND CONSTN VOL/ASSN WORKER ORD/FREE CATHISM CONSERVE...POLICY IDEA/COMP BIBLIOG 18/ PARLIAMENT. PAGE 97 A1992 — ATTIT NAT/G DIPLOM REV

B44
FULLER G.H.,TURKEY: A SELECTED LIST OF REFERENCES. ISLAM TURKEY CULTURE ECO/UNDEV AGRI DIPLOM NAT/LISM CONSERVE...GEOG HUM INT/LAW SOC 7/20 MAPS. PAGE 50 A1024 — BIBLIOG/A ALL/VALS

B45
NELSON M.F.,KOREA AND THE OLD ORDERS IN EASTERN ASIA. ASIA FRANCE KOREA RUSSIA DELIB/GP INT/TRADE DOMIN CONTROL WAR ORD/FREE...POLICY BIBLIOG. PAGE 108 A2218 — DIPLOM BAL/PWR ATTIT CONSERVE

C45
NELSON M.F.,"KOREA AND THE OLD ORDERS IN EASTERN ASIA." KOREA WOR-45 DELIB/GP INT/TRADE DOMIN CONTROL WAR ATTIT ORD/FREE CONSERVE...POLICY TREATY. PAGE 108 A2217 — BIBLIOG DIPLOM BAL/PWR ASIA

B54
COOKSON J.,BEFORE THE AFRICAN STORM. BELGIUM CENTRL/AFR FRANCE UK ECO/UNDEV POL/PAR CREATE BAL/PWR RACE/REL NAT/LISM ORD/FREE CONSERVE MARXISM SOC/INTEG 20 CONGO/LEOP. PAGE 30 A0607 — COLONIAL REV DISCRIM DIPLOM

S55
DE SMITH S.A.,"CONSTITUTIONAL MONARCHY IN BURGANDA." AFR UGANDA UK STRUCT CHIEF REGION INGP/REL ADJUST NAT/LISM SOVEREIGN CONSERVE ...POLICY 19/20 BURGANDA. PAGE 35 A0712 — NAT/G DIPLOM CONSTN COLONIAL

B56
UNDERHILL F.H.,THE BRITISH COMMONWEALTH: AN EXPERIMENT IN CO-OPERATION AMONG NATIONS. CANADA UK WOR+45 WOR-45 INT/ORG COLONIAL UTIL SOVEREIGN CONSERVE...OLD/LIB SOC/EXP BIBLIOG/A 19/20 CMN/WLTH. PAGE 147 A3007 — VOL/ASSN NAT/LISM DIPLOM

B58
CRAIG G.A.,FROM BISMARCK TO ADENAUER: ASPECTS OF GERMAN STATECRAFT. GERMANY INTELL FORCES ECO/TAC CONFER COERCE WAR GP/REL ORD/FREE PWR CONSERVE 19/20 BISMARCK/O ADENAUER/K. PAGE 32 A0653 — DIPLOM LEAD NAT/G

B58
GROBLER J.H.,AFRICA'S DESTINY. AFR EUR+WWI SOUTH/AFR UK USA+45 ELITES KIN LOC/G DIPLOM DISCRIM ATTIT CONSERVE MARXISM 20 ROOSEVLT/T NEGRO. PAGE 57 A1168 — POLICY ORD/FREE COLONIAL CONSTN

B61
CAMERON J.,THE AFRICAN REVOLUTION. AFR UK ECO/UNDEV POL/PAR REGION RACE/REL DISCRIM PWR CONSERVE ...CONCPT SOC/INTEG 20 NEGRO. PAGE 23 A0472
REV COLONIAL ORD/FREE DIPLOM

B62
EVANS M.S.,THE FRINGE ON TOP. USSR EX/STRUC FORCES DIPLOM ECO/TAC PEACE CONSERVE SOCISM...TREND 20 KENNEDY/JF. PAGE 43 A0877
NAT/G PWR CENTRAL POLICY

B62
GOLDWATER B.M.,WHY NOT VICTORY? A FRESH LOOK AT AMERICAN FOREIGN POLICY. USA+45 WOR+45 FOR/AID LEAD ARMS/CONT WAR PEACE ATTIT ORD/FREE PWR MARXISM ...INT/LAW 20 TREATY ECHR COUNCL/EUR. PAGE 53 A1092
DIPLOM POLICY CONSERVE NAT/LISM

B62
KLUCKHOHN F.L.,THE NAKED RISE OF COMMUNISM. CHINA/COM COM USSR WOR+45 CONSTN POL/PAR PLAN CONTROL LEAD NEUTRAL CONSERVE 20 STALIN/J EUROPE/E COM/PARTY. PAGE 80 A1650
MARXISM IDEA/COMP DIPLOM DOMIN

C62
DUFFY J.,"PORTUGAL IN AFRICA." PORTUGAL SIER/LEONE INDUS WORKER INT/TRADE WAR CONSERVE...CATH GEOG TREND 16/20. PAGE 39 A0795
BIBLIOG RACE/REL ECO/UNDEV COLONIAL

B63
FRANKEL J.,THE MAKING OF FOREIGN POLICY: AN ANALYSIS OF DECISION-MAKING. CHINA/COM EUR+WWI USA+45 ELITES INTELL FORCES LEGIS PLAN ATTIT ALL/VALS MORAL CONSERVE...GOV/COMP 20 PRESIDENT UN TREATY. PAGE 48 A0981
POLICY DECISION PROB/SOLV DIPLOM

B64
LENSEN G.A.,REVELATIONS OF A RUSSIAN DIPLOMAT: THE MEMOIRS OF DMITRII I. ABRIKOSSOV. ASIA MOD/EUR RUSSIA USA-45 ELITES ACADEM CHIEF FORCES REV WAR PWR CONSERVE MARXISM 19/20 ABRIKSSV/D CHINJAP BOLSHEVISM. PAGE 87 A1775
DIPLOM POLICY OBS

B64
LIEVWEN E.,GENERALS VS PRESIDENTS: WEOMILITARISM IN LATIN AMERICA. L/A+17C FORCES DIPLOM FOR/AID LEAD ...NAT/COMP 20 PRESIDENT. PAGE 89 A1813
CIVMIL/REL REV CONSERVE ORD/FREE

B64
MEYER F.S.,WHAT IS CONSERVATISM? USA+45 NAT/G FORCES DIPLOM ORD/FREE IDEA/COMP. PAGE 100 A2048
CONSERVE CONCPT EDU/PROP CAP/ISM

B64
TREADGOLD D.W.,THE DEVELOPMENT OF THE USSR. COM USSR ECO/DEV CREATE BAL/PWR DEBATE COLONIAL TOTALISM...HUM ANTHOL BIBLIOG 19/20. PAGE 145 A2960
MARXISM CONSERVE DIPLOM DOMIN

B66
CLENDENON C.,AMERICANS IN AFRICA 1865-1900. AFR USA-45 ECO/UNDEV SECT REV RACE/REL CONSERVE ...TRADIT GEOG BIBLIOG 16/18. PAGE 27 A0549
DIPLOM COLONIAL INT/TRADE

CONSRV/PAR....CONSERVATIVE PARTY (ALL NATIONS)

B54
EPSTEIN L.D.,BRITAIN - UNEASY ALLY. KOREA UK USA+45 NAT/G POL/PAR ECO/TAC FOR/AID INT/TRADE WAR LABOR/PAR CONSRV/PAR. PAGE 42 A0857
DIPLOM ATTIT POLICY NAT/COMP

B65
GEORGE M.,THE WARPED VISION. EUR+WWI UK NAT/G POL/PAR LEGIS PARL/PROC SANCTION COERCE WAR GOV/REL PEACE RESPECT 20 CONSRV/PAR. PAGE 52 A1061
LEAD ATTIT DIPLOM POLICY

CONSTITUTION....SEE CONSTN

CONSTN....CONSTITUTIONS

N
SABIN J.,BIBLIOTHECA AMERICANA: A DICTIONARY OF BOOKS RELATING TO AMERICA, FROM ITS DISCOVERY TO THE PRESENT TIME(29 VOLS.). CONSTN CULTURE SOCIETY ECO/DEV LOC/G EDU/PROP NAT/LISM...POLICY GEOG SOC 19. PAGE 126 A2581
BIBLIOG L/A+17C DIPLOM NAT/G

N
UNIVERSITY OF FLORIDA LIBRARY,DOORS TO LATIN AMERICA; RECENT BOOKS AND PAMPHLETS. CONSTN CULTURE SOCIETY ECO/UNDEV COLONIAL LEAD GOV/REL NAT/LISM ATTIT...HUM SOC 20. PAGE 149 A3047
BIBLIOG/A L/A+17C DIPLOM NAT/G

N
AMERICAN JOURNAL OF INTERNATIONAL LAW. WOR+45 WOR-45 CONSTN INT/ORG NAT/G CT/SYS ARMS/CONT WAR ...DECISION JURID NAT/COMP 20. PAGE 1 A0002
BIBLIOG/A INT/LAW DIPLOM ADJUD

N
JOURNAL OF POLITICS. USA+45 USA-45 CONSTN POL/PAR EX/STRUC LEGIS PROB/SOLV DIPLOM CT/SYS CHOOSE RACE/REL 20. PAGE 1 A0017
BIBLIOG/A NAT/G LAW LOC/G

N
LITERATUR-VERZEICHNIS DER POLITISCHEN WISSENSCHAFTEN. GERMANY/W WOR+45 CONSTN SOCIETY ECO/DEV INT/ORG POL/PAR LEAD REPRESENT GOV/REL GP/REL...POLICY PHIL/SCI. PAGE 1 A0018
BIBLIOG EUR+WWI DIPLOM NAT/G

N
MIDWEST JOURNAL OF POLITICAL SCIENCE. USA+45 CONSTN ECO/DEV LEGIS PROB/SOLV CT/SYS LEAD GOV/REL ATTIT POLICY. PAGE 1 A0020
BIBLIOG/A NAT/G DIPLOM POL/PAR

N
POLITICAL SCIENCE QUARTERLY. USA+45 USA-45 LAW CONSTN ECO/DEV INT/ORG LOC/G POL/PAR LEGIS LEAD NUC/PWR...CONCPT 20. PAGE 1 A0023
BIBLIOG/A NAT/G DIPLOM POLICY

N
REVIEW OF POLITICS. WOR+45 WOR-45 CONSTN LEGIS PROB/SOLV ADMIN LEAD ALL/IDEOS...PHIL/SCI 20. PAGE 2 A0024
BIBLIOG/A DIPLOM INT/ORG NAT/G

N
BIBLIOGRAPHIE DER SOZIALWISSENSCHAFTEN. WOR-45 CONSTN SOCIETY ECO/DEV ECO/UNDEV DIPLOM LEAD WAR PEACE...PHIL/SCI SOC 19/20. PAGE 2 A0030
BIBLIOG LAW CONCPT NAT/G

N
INDIA: A REFERENCE ANNUAL. INDIA CULTURE COM/IND R+D FORCES PLAN RECEIVE EDU/PROP HEALTH...STAT CHARTS BIBLIOG 20. PAGE 2 A0036
CONSTN LABOR INT/ORG

N
THE JAPAN SCIENCE REVIEW: LAW AND POLITICS: LIST OF BOOKS AND ARTICLES ON LAW AND POLITICS. CONSTN AGRI INDUS LABOR DIPLOM TAX ADMIN CRIME...INT/LAW SOC 20 CHINJAP. PAGE 2 A0042
BIBLIOG LAW S/ASIA PHIL/SCI

N
ASIA FOUNDATION,LIBRARY NOTES. LAW CONSTN CULTURE SOCIETY ECO/UNDEV INT/ORG NAT/G COLONIAL LEAD REGION NAT/LISM ATTIT 20 UN. PAGE 9 A0189
BIBLIOG/A ASIA S/ASIA DIPLOM

N
EUROPA PUBLICATIONS LIMITED,THE EUROPA YEAR BOOK. CONSTN FINAN INDUS POL/PAR DIPLOM TV CT/SYS...STAT BIOG CHARTS WORSHIP 20. PAGE 43 A0874
BIBLIOG NAT/G PRESS INT/ORG

N
HARVARD LAW SCHOOL LIBRARY,ANNUAL LEGAL BIBLIOGRAPHY. USA+45 CONSTN LEGIS ADJUD CT/SYS ...POLICY 20. PAGE 62 A1278
BIBLIOG JURID LAW INT/LAW

N
INSTITUTE OF HISPANIC STUDIES,HISPANIC AMERICAN REPORT. EUR+WWI SPAIN LAW CONSTN ECO/UNDEV POL/PAR EX/STRUC LEGIS LEAD...HUM SOC 20. PAGE 70 A1445
BIBLIOG/A L/A+17C NAT/G DIPLOM

N
MCSPADDEN J.W.,THE AMERICAN STATESMAN'S YEARBOOK. WOR-45 LAW CONSTN AGRI FINAN DEBATE ADMIN PARL/PROC ...CHARTS BIBLIOG/A 20. PAGE 99 A2025
DIPLOM NAT/G PROVS LEGIS

B00
HOLLAND T.E.,STUDIES IN INTERNATIONAL LAW. TURKEY USSR WOR-45 CONSTN NAT/G DIPLOM DOMIN LEGIT COERCE WAR PEACE ORD/FREE PWR SOVEREIGN...JURID CHARTS 20 PARLIAMENT SUEZ TREATY. PAGE 66 A1367
INT/ORG LAW INT/LAW

B03
FORTESCUE G.K.,SUBJECT INDEX OF THE MODERN WORKS ADDED TO THE LIBRARY OF THE BRITISH MUSEUM IN THE YEARS 1881-1900 (3 VOLS.). UK LAW CONSTN FINAN NAT/G FORCES INT/TRADE COLONIAL 19. PAGE 47 A0968
BIBLIOG INDEX WRITING

B04
CRANDALL S.B.,TREATIES: THEIR MAKING AND ENFORCEMENT. MOD/EUR USA-45 CONSTN INT/ORG NAT/G LEGIS EDU/PROP LEGIT EXEC PEACE KNOWL MORAL...JURID CONGRESS 19/20 TREATY. PAGE 32 A0655
LAW

B05
AMES J.G.,COMPREHENSIVE INDEX TO THE PUBLICATIONS OF THE UNITED STATES GOVERNMENT , 1881-1893. USA-45 CONSTN POL/PAR DELIB/GP TOP/EX DIPLOM PARL/PROC INGP/REL...INDEX 19 CONGRESS. PAGE 8 A0153
BIBLIOG/A LEGIS NAT/G GOV/REL

B08
ARON R.,WAR AND INDUSTRIAL SOCIETY. EUR+WWI MOD/EUR WOR+45 WOR-45 CONSTN SOCIETY INT/ORG POL/PAR VOL/ASSN DIPLOM INT/TRADE PEACE ATTIT...BIOG GEN/LAWS 19/20. PAGE 9 A0178
ECO/DEV WAR

B09
FREMANTLE H.E.S.,THE NEW NATION, A SURVEY OF THE CONDITION AND PROSPECTS OF SOUTH AFRICA. SOUTH/AFR CONSTN POL/PAR DIPLOM DOMIN COLONIAL WEALTH...SOC TREND 19. PAGE 49 A0996
NAT/LISM SOVEREIGN RACE/REL REGION

B19
SUTHERLAND G.,CONSTITUTIONAL POWER AND WORLD AFFAIRS. CONSTN STRUCT INT/ORG NAT/G CHIEF LEGIS ACT/RES PLAN GOV/REL ALL/VALS...OBS TIME/SEQ CONGRESS VAL/FREE 20 PRESIDENT. PAGE 140 A2866
USA-45 EXEC DIPLOM

N19
PROVISIONS SECTION OAU,ORGANIZATION OF AFRICAN
CONSTN

UNITY: BASIC DOCUMENTS AND RESOLUTIONS (PAMPHLET). EX/STRUC
AFR CULTURE ECO/UNDEV DIPLOM ECO/TAC EDU/PROP SOVEREIGN
COLONIAL ARMS/CONT NUC/PWR RACE/REL DISCRIM INT/ORG
NAT/LISM 20 UN OAU. PAGE 118 A2415

B20
MEYER H.H.B.,LIST OF REFERENCES ON THE TREATY- BIBLIOG
MAKING POWER. USA-45 CONTROL PWR...INT/LAW TIME/SEQ DIPLOM
18/20 TREATY. PAGE 100 A2052 CONSTN

B20
VINOGRADOFF P.,OUTLINES OF HISTORICAL JURISPRUDENCE JURID
(2 VOLS.). GREECE MEDIT-7 LAW CONSTN FACE/GP FAM METH
KIN MUNIC CRIME OWN...INT/LAW IDEA/COMP BIBLIOG.
PAGE 159 A3241

B21
STUART G.H.,FRENCH FOREIGN POLICY. CONSTN INT/ORG MOD/EUR
NAT/G POL/PAR EX/STRUC FORCES PLAN ECO/TAC DOMIN DIPLOM
EDU/PROP ADJUD COERCE ATTIT DRIVE RIGID/FLEX FRANCE
ALL/VALS...POLICY OBS RECORD BIOG TIME/SEQ TREND.
PAGE 139 A2852

B22
WRIGHT Q.,THE CONTROL OF AMERICAN FOREIGN NAT/G
RELATIONS. USA-45 WOR-45 CONSTN INT/ORG CONSULT EXEC
LEGIS LEGIT ROUTINE ORD/FREE PWR...POLICY JURID DIPLOM
CONCPT METH/CNCPT RECORD LEAGUE/NAT 20. PAGE 167
A3402

B24
HALL W.E.,A TREATISE ON INTERNATIONAL LAW. WOR-45 PWR
CONSTN INT/ORG NAT/G DIPLOM ORD/FREE LEAGUE/NAT 20 JURID
TREATY. PAGE 60 A1228 WAR
INT/LAW

B26
LEWIN E.,RECENT PUBLICATIONS IN THE LIBRARY OF THE BIBLIOG
ROYAL COLONIAL INSTITUTE (PAMPHLET). CANADA UK COLONIAL
EX/STRUC PARL/PROC NAT/LISM SOVEREIGN 20 CMN/WLTH CONSTN
PARLIAMENT. PAGE 88 A1799 DIPLOM

B28
HALL W.P.,EMPIRE TO COMMONWEALTH. FUT WOR-45 CONSTN VOL/ASSN
ECO/DEV ECO/UNDEV INT/ORG PROVS PLAN DIPLOM NAT/G
EDU/PROP ADMIN COLONIAL PEACE PERSON ALL/VALS UK
...POLICY GEOG SOC OBS RECORD TREND CMN/WLTH
PARLIAMENT 19/20. PAGE 60 A1229

B28
HOWARD-ELLIS C.,THE ORIGIN, STRUCTURE AND WORKING INT/ORG
OF THE LEAGUE OF NATIONS. EUR+WWI MOD/EUR USA-45 ADJUD
CONSTN FORCES LEGIS ECO/TAC LEGIT COERCE ORD/FREE
...JURID SOC CONCPT LEAGUE/NAT 20 ILO ICJ. PAGE 68
A1401

B28
MAIR L.P.,THE PROTECTION OF MINORITIES. EUR+WWI LAW
WOR-45 CONSTN INT/ORG NAT/G LEGIT CT/SYS GP/REL SOVEREIGN
RACE/REL DISCRIM ORD/FREE RESPECT...JURID CONCPT
TIME/SEQ 20. PAGE 93 A1909

C28
WARD P.W.,"SOVEREIGNTY: A STUDY OF A CONTEMPORARY SOVEREIGN
POLITICAL NOTION." CONSTN NAT/G DIPLOM REPRESENT CONCPT
PLURISM...IDEA/COMP BIBLIOG. PAGE 161 A3281 NAT/LISM

B29
BUELL R.,INTERNATIONAL RELATIONS. WOR+45 WOR-45 INT/ORG
CONSTN STRATA FORCES TOP/EX ADMIN ATTIT DRIVE BAL/PWR
SUPEGO MORAL ORD/FREE PWR SOVEREIGN...JURID SOC DIPLOM
CONCPT 20. PAGE 21 A0428

B30
BYNKERSHOEK C.,QUAESTIONUM JURIS PUBLICI LIBRI DUO. INT/ORG
CHRIST-17C MOD/EUR CONSTN ELITES SOCIETY NAT/G LAW
PROVS EX/STRUC FORCES TOP/EX BAL/PWR DIPLOM ATTIT NAT/LISM
MORAL...TRADIT CONCPT. PAGE 23 A0460 INT/LAW

B30
FLEMMING D.,THE TREATY VETO OF THE AMERICAN SENATE. LEGIS
FUT USA+45 USA-45 CONSTN INT/ORG NAT/G TOP/EX LEGIT RIGID/FLEX
GOV/REL PWR...POLICY MAJORIT CONCPT OBS TIME/SEQ
CONGRESS 20. PAGE 46 A0949

B30
WRIGHT Q.,MANDATES UNDER THE LEAGUE OF NATIONS. INT/ORG
WOR-45 CONSTN ECO/DEV ECO/UNDEV NAT/G DELIB/GP LAW
TOP/EX LEGIT ALL/VALS...JURID CONCPT LEAGUE/NAT 20. INT/LAW
PAGE 167 A3403

B31
BORCHARD E.H.,GUIDE TO THE LAW AND LEGAL LITERATURE BIBLIOG/A
OF FRANCE. FRANCE FINAN INDUS LABOR SECT LEGIS LAW
ADMIN COLONIAL CRIME OWN...INT/LAW 20. PAGE 17 CONSTN
A0337 METH

B31
STUART G.H.,THE INTERNATIONAL CITY OF TANGIER. AFR LOC/G
EUR+WWI MOD/EUR MOROCCO CONSTN PROVS CREATE PLAN INT/ORG
LEGIT PEACE ORD/FREE PWR...INT/LAW OBS TIME/SEQ DIPLOM
CON/ANAL 20 TANGIER. PAGE 139 A2854 SOVEREIGN

B32
MORLEY F.,THE SOCIETY OF NATIONS. EUR+WWI UNIV INT/ORG
WOR-45 LAW CONSTN ACT/RES PLAN EDU/PROP LEGIT CONCPT
ROUTINE...POLICY TIME/SEQ LEAGUE/NAT TOT/POP 20.
PAGE 104 A2143

B33
AMERICAN FOREIGN LAW ASSN,BIOGRAPHICAL NOTES ON THE BIBLIOG/A
LAWS AND LEGAL LITERATURE OF URUGUAY AND CURACAO. LAW
URUGUAY CONSTN FINAN SECT FORCES JUDGE DIPLOM JURID
INT/TRADE ADJUD CT/SYS CRIME 20. PAGE 7 A0147 ADMIN

B33
MATTHEWS M.A.,THE AMERICAN INSTITUTE OF BIBLIOG/A
INTERNATIONAL LAW AND THE CODIFICATION OF INT/LAW
INTERNATIONAL LAW (PAMPHLET). USA-45 CONSTN ADJUD L/A+17C
CT/SYS...JURID 20. PAGE 96 A1973 DIPLOM

B33
REID H.D.,RECUEIL DES COURS; TOME 45: LES ORD/FREE
SERVITUDES INTERNATIONALES III. FRANCE CONSTN DIPLOM
DELIB/GP PRESS CONTROL REV WAR CHOOSE PEACE MORAL LAW
MARITIME TREATY. PAGE 120 A2457

B33
WAMBAUCH S.,PLEBISCITES SINCE THE WORLD WAR: WITH A DIPLOM
COLLECTION OF OFFICIAL DOCUMENTS. WOR-45 COLONIAL CONSTN
SANCTION...MAJORIT DECISION CHARTS BIBLIOG 19/20 NAT/G
WWI. PAGE 161 A3272 CHOOSE

B35
FOREIGN AFFAIRS BIBLIOGRAPHY: A SELECTED AND BIBLIOG/A
ANNOTATED LIST OF BOOKS ON INTERNATIONAL RELATIONS DIPLOM
1919-1962 (4 VOLS.). CONSTN FORCES COLONIAL INT/ORG
ARMS/CONT WAR NAT/LISM PEACE ATTIT DRIVE...POLICY
INT/LAW 20. PAGE 3 A0050

B35
KENNEDY W.P.,THE LAW AND CUSTOM OF THE SOUTH CT/SYS
AFRICAN CONSTITUTION. AFR SOUTH/AFR KIN LOC/G PROVS CONSTN
DIPLOM ADJUD ADMIN EXEC 20. PAGE 78 A1594 JURID
PARL/PROC

B36
MATTHEWS M.A.,INTERNATIONAL LAW: SELECT LIST OF BIBLIOG/A
WORKS IN ENGLISH ON PUBLIC INTERNATIONAL LAW: WITH INT/LAW
COLLECTIONS OF CASES AND OPINIONS. CHRIST-17C ATTIT
EUR+WWI MOD/EUR WOR-45 CONSTN ADJUD JURID. PAGE 96 DIPLOM
A1975

B37
UNION OF SOUTH AFRICA,REPORT CONCERNING NAT/G
ADMINISTRATION OF SOUTH WEST AFRICA (6 VOLS.). ADMIN
SOUTH/AFR INDUS PUB/INST FORCES LEGIS BUDGET DIPLOM COLONIAL
EDU/PROP ADJUD CT/SYS...GEOG CHARTS 20 AFRICA/SW CONSTN
LEAGUE/NAT. PAGE 148 A3028

B37
VINER J.,STUDIES IN THE THEORY OF INTERNATIONAL CAP/ISM
TRADE. WOR-45 CONSTN ECO/DEV AGRI INDUS MARKET INT/TRADE
INT/ORG LABOR NAT/G ECO/TAC TARIFFS COLONIAL ATTIT
WEALTH...POLICY CONCPT MATH STAT OBS SAMP TREND
GEN/LAWS MARX/KARL 20. PAGE 159 A3236

B38
HARPER S.N.,THE GOVERNMENT OF THE SOVIET UNION. COM MARXISM
USSR LAW CONSTN ECO/DEV PLAN TEC/DEV DIPLOM NAT/G
INT/TRADE ADMIN REV NAT/LISM...POLICY 20. PAGE 62 LEAD
A1265 POL/PAR

B38
MATTHEWS M.A.,FEDERALISM: SELECT LIST OF REFERENCES BIBLIOG/A
ON FEDERAL GOVERNMENT REGIONALISM...EXAMPLES OF FEDERAL
FEDERATIONS (PAMPHLET). WOR-45 CONSTN INT/ORG NAT/G REGION
19/20 OAS LEAGUE/NAT. PAGE 96 A1976 DIPLOM

C39
HADDOW A.,"POLITICAL SCIENCE IN AMERICAN COLLEGES USA-45
AND UNIVERSITIES 1636-1900." CONSTN MORAL...POLICY LAW
INT/LAW CON/ANAL BIBLIOG T 17/20. PAGE 59 A1211 ACADEM
KNOWL

C39
REISCHAUER R.,"JAPAN'S GOVERNMENT--POLITICS." NAT/G
CONSTN STRATA POL/PAR FORCES LEGIS DIPLOM ADMIN S/ASIA
EXEC CENTRAL...POLICY BIBLIOG 20 CHINJAP. PAGE 120 CONCPT
A2462 ROUTINE

C40
NORMAN E.H.,"JAPAN'S EMERGENCE AS A MODERN STATE: CENTRAL
POLITICAL AND ECONOMIC PROBLEMS OF THE MEIJI DIPLOM
PERIOD." CONSTN STRATA AGRI INDUS POL/PAR TEC/DEV POLICY
CAP/ISM CIVMIL/REL...BIBLIOG 19/20 CHINJAP. NAT/LISM
PAGE 110 A2250

B41
BURTON M.E.,THE ASSEMBLY OF THE LEAGUE OF NATIONS. DELIB/GP
WOR-45 CONSTN SOCIETY STRUCT INT/ORG NAT/G CREATE EX/STRUC
ATTIT RIGID/FLEX PWR...POLICY TIME/SEQ LEAGUE/NAT DIPLOM
20. PAGE 22 A0448

B43
MC DOWELL R.B.,IRISH PUBLIC OPINION, 1750-1800. ATTIT
IRELAND CONSTN VOL/ASSN WORKER ORD/FREE CATHISM NAT/G
CONSERVE...POLICY IDEA/COMP BIBLIOG 18/ PARLIAMENT. DIPLOM
PAGE 97 A1992 REV

B43
US LIBRARY OF CONGRESS,POLITICAL DEVELOPMENTS AND BIBLIOG/A
THE WAR: APRIL-DECEMBER 1942 (SUPPLEMENT 1). WOR-45 WAR
CONSTN NAT/G POL/PAR CREATE RECEIVE EDU/PROP ATTIT DIPLOM
20. PAGE 154 A3148

B44
BRIERLY J.L.,THE OUTLOOK FOR INTERNATIONAL LAW. FUT INT/ORG
WOR-45 CONSTN NAT/G VOL/ASSN FORCES ECO/TAC DOMIN LAW
LEGIT ADJUD ROUTINE PEACE ORD/FREE...INT/LAW JURID
METH LEAGUE/NAT 20. PAGE 18 A0376

B44
DAVIS H.E.,PIONEERS IN WORLD ORDER. WOR-45 CONSTN INT/ORG
ECO/TAC DOMIN EDU/PROP LEGIT ADJUD ADMIN ARMS/CONT ROUTINE
CHOOSE KNOWL ORD/FREE...POLICY JURID SOC STAT OBS
CENSUS TIME/SEQ ANTHOL LEAGUE/NAT 20. PAGE 34 A0691

B44
PUTTKAMMER E.W.,WAR AND THE LAW. UNIV USA-45 CONSTN CULTURE SOCIETY NAT/G POL/PAR ROUTINE ALL/VALS ...JURID CONCPT OBS WORK VAL/FREE 20. PAGE 118 A2418
INT/ORG LAW WAR INT/LAW

L44
CORWIN E.S.,"THE CONSTITUTION AND WORLD ORGANIZATION." FUT USA+45 USA-45 NAT/G EX/STRUC LEGIS PEACE KNOWL...CON/ANAL UN 20. PAGE 31 A0627
INT/ORG CONSTN SOVEREIGN

L44
HAILEY,"THE FUTURE OF COLONIAL PEOPLES." WOR-45 CONSTN CULTURE ECO/UNDEV AGRI MARKET INT/ORG NAT/G SECT CONSULT ECO/TAC LEGIT ADMIN NAT/LISM ALL/VALS ...SOC OBS TREND STERTYP CMN/WLTH LEAGUE/NAT PARLIAMENT 20. PAGE 59 A1218
PLAN CONCPT DIPLOM UK

L44
WRIGHT Q.,"THE US AND INTERNATIONAL AGREEMENTS." FUT USA-45 CONSTN INTELL INT/ORG LOC/G NAT/G CHIEF CONSULT EX/STRUC DIPLOM LEGIT DRIVE PERCEPT PWR ...CONCPT CONGRESS 20. PAGE 167 A3407
DELIB/GP TOP/EX PEACE

S44
WRIGHT Q.,"CONSTITUTIONAL PROCEDURES OF THE US FOR CARRYING OUT OBLIGATIONS FOR MILITARY SANCTIONS." EUR+WWI FUT USA-45 WOR-45 CONSTN INTELL NAT/G CONSULT EX/STRUC LEGIS ROUTINE DRIVE...POLICY JURID CONCPT OBS TREND TOT/POP 20. PAGE 167 A3406
TOP/EX FORCES INT/LAW WAR

N45
INDIA QUARTERLY, A JOURNAL OF INTERNATIONAL AFFAIRS. INDIA LAW CONSTN ECO/UNDEV INT/ORG POL/PAR COLONIAL LEAD PARL/PROC WAR ATTIT...SOC 20 CMN/WLTH. PAGE 3 A0053
BIBLIOG/A S/ASIA DIPLOM NAT/G

B45
CONOVER H.F.,THE GOVERNMENTS OF THE MAJOR FOREIGN POWERS: A BIBLIOGRAPHY. FRANCE GERMANY ITALY UK USSR CONSTN LOC/G POL/PAR EX/STRUC FORCES ADMIN CT/SYS CIVMIL/REL TOTALISM...POLICY 19/20. PAGE 29 A0598
BIBLIOG NAT/G DIPLOM

B45
RANSHOFFEN-WERTHEIMER EF,THE INTERNATIONAL SECRETARIAT: A GREAT EXPERIMENT IN INTERNATIONAL ADMINISTRATION. EUR+WWI FUT CONSTN FACE/GP CONSULT DELIB/GP ACT/RES ADMIN ROUTINE PEACE ORD/FREE...MGT RECORD ORG/CHARTS LEAGUE/NAT WORK 20. PAGE 119 A2442
INT/ORG EXEC

B45
VANCE H.L.,GUIDE TO THE LAW AND LEGAL LITERATURE OF MEXICO. LAW CONSTN FINAN LABOR FORCES ADJUD ADMIN ...CRIMLGY PHIL/SCI CON/ANAL 20 MEXIC/AMER. PAGE 158 A3217
BIBLIOG/A INT/LAW JURID CT/SYS

S46
DOUGLAS W.O.,"SYMPOSIUM ON WORLD ORGANIZATION." FUT USA+45 WOR+45 CONSTN SOCIETY NAT/G PLAN EDU/PROP LEGIT RIGID/FLEX KNOWL...INT/LAW JURID STERTYP TOT/POP 20. PAGE 38 A0778
INT/ORG LAW

C46
GOODRICH L.M.,"CHARTER OF THE UNITED NATIONS: COMMENTARY AND DOCUMENTS." EX/STRUC ADMIN...INT/LAW CON/ANAL BIBLIOG 20 UN. PAGE 54 A1106
CONSTN INT/ORG DIPLOM

B47
BORGESE G.,COMMON CAUSE. LAW CONSTN SOCIETY STRATA ECO/DEV INT/ORG POL/PAR FORCES LEGIS TOP/EX CAP/ISM DIPLOM ADMIN EXEC ATTIT PWR 20. PAGE 17 A0339
WOR+45 NAT/G SOVEREIGN REGION

B47
HEIMANN E.,FREEDOM AND ORDER: LESSONS FROM THE WAR. WOR-45 CONSTN FORCES CHOOSE CIVMIL/REL PERSON ALL/IDEOS SOCISM...SOC IDEA/COMP WORSHIP 20. PAGE 64 A1308
NAT/G SOCIETY ORD/FREE DIPLOM

B48
CHAMBERLAIN L.H.,AMERICAN FOREIGN POLICY. FUT USA+45 USA-45 WOR+45 WOR-45 NAT/G LEGIS TOP/EX ECO/TAC FOR/AID EDU/PROP EXEC ATTIT ORD/FREE ...JURID TREND TOT/POP 20. PAGE 25 A0517
CONSTN DIPLOM

B48
FENWICK C.G.,INTERNATIONAL LAW. WOR+45 WOR-45 CONSTN NAT/G LEGIT CT/SYS REGION...CONCPT LEAGUE/NAT UN 20. PAGE 45 A0916
INT/ORG JURID INT/LAW

B48
HOWARD J.E.,PARLIAMENT AND FOREIGN POLICY IN FRANCE. FRANCE CONSTN DELIB/GP BUDGET ADMIN PARL/PROC CHOOSE...BIBLIOG/A 20 PARLIAMENT. PAGE 68 A1399
LEGIS CONTROL DIPLOM ATTIT

B48
NEUBURGER O.,GUIDE TO OFFICIAL PUBLICATIONS OF THE OTHER AMERICAN REPUBLICS: VENEZUELA (VOL. XIX). VENEZUELA FINAN LEGIS PLAN BUDGET DIPLOM CT/SYS PARL/PROC 19/20. PAGE 108 A2219
BIBLIOG/A NAT/G CONSTN LAW

S48
GROSS L.,"THE PEACE OF WESTPHALIA, 1648-1948." WOR+45 WOR-45 CONSTN BAL/PWR FEDERAL 17/20 TREATY WESTPHALIA. PAGE 57 A1175
INT/LAW AGREE CONCPT DIPLOM

B49
HEADLAM-MORLEY,BIBLIOGRAPHY IN POLITICS FOR THE HONOUR SCHOOL OF PHILOSOPHY, POLITICS AND ECONOMICS (PAMPHLET). UK CONSTN LABOR MUNIC DIPLOM ADMIN 19/20. PAGE 64 A1305
BIBLIOG NAT/G PHIL/SCI GOV/REL

B49
MARITAIN J.,HUMAN RIGHTS: COMMENTS AND INTERPRETATIONS. COM UNIV WOR+45 LAW CONSTN CULTURE SOCIETY ECO/DEV ECO/UNDEV SCHOOL DELIB/GP EDU/PROP ATTIT PERCEPT ALL/VALS...HUM SOC TREND UNESCO 20. PAGE 95 A1939
INT/ORG CONCPT

L49
COMM. STUDY ORGAN. PEACE,"A TEN YEAR RECORD, 1939-1949." FUT WOR+45 LAW R+D CONSULT DELIB/GP CREATE LEGIT ROUTINE ORD/FREE...TIME/SEQ UN 20. PAGE 28 A0578
INT/ORG CONSTN PEACE

L49
HEINDEL R.H.,"THE NORTH ATLANTIC TREATY IN THE UNITED STATES SENATE." CONSTN POL/PAR CHIEF DEBATE LEAD ROUTINE WAR PEACE...CHARTS UN SENATE NATO. PAGE 64 A1309
DECISION PARL/PROC LEGIS INT/ORG

B50
BROWN E.S.,MANUAL OF GOVERNMENT PUBLICATIONS. WOR+45 WOR-45 CONSTN INT/ORG MUNIC PROVS DIPLOM ADMIN 20. PAGE 20 A0401
BIBLIOG/A NAT/G LAW

B50
CHASE E.P.,THE UNITED NATIONS IN ACTION. WOR+45 CONSTN DELIB/GP LEGIT ROUTINE COERCE PEACE ORD/FREE PWR...CON/ANAL GEN/LAWS UN 20. PAGE 26 A0524
INT/ORG STRUCT ARMS/CONT

B50
DE ARECHAGA E.J.,VOTING AND THE HANDLING OF DISPUTES IN THE SECURITY COUNCIL. WOR+45 CONSTN DIPLOM COERCE ORD/FREE...RECORD CON/ANAL GEN/METH COLD/WAR UN 20. PAGE 34 A0696
INT/ORG PWR

B50
JIMENEZ E.,VOTING AND HANDLING OF DISPUTES IN THE SECURITY COUNCIL. WOR+45 CONSTN INT/ORG DIPLOM LEGIT DETER CHOOSE MORAL ORD/FREE PWR...JURID TIME/SEQ COLD/WAR UN 20. PAGE 74 A1517
DELIB/GP ROUTINE

B50
LAUTERPACHT H.,INTERNATIONAL LAW AND HUMAN RIGHTS. USA+45 CONSTN STRUCT INT/ORG ACT/RES EDU/PROP PEACE PERSON ALL/VALS...CONCPT CON/ANAL GEN/LAWS UN 20. PAGE 86 A1750
DELIB/GP LAW INT/LAW

B50
MACIVER R.M.,GREAT EXPRESSIONS OF HUMAN RIGHTS. LAW CONSTN CULTURE INTELL SOCIETY R+D INT/ORG ATTIT DRIVE...JURID OBS HIST/WRIT GEN/LAWS. PAGE 92 A1891
UNIV CONCPT

B50
ROSS A.,CONSTITUTION OF THE UNITED NATIONS. CONSTN CONSULT DELIB/GP ECO/TAC...INT/LAW JURID 20 UN LEAGUE/NAT. PAGE 124 A2540
PEACE DIPLOM ORD/FREE INT/ORG

B50
SOHN L.B.,CASES AND OTHER MATERIALS ON WORLD LAW. FUT WOR+45 LAW INT/ORG...INT/LAW JURID METH/CNCPT 20 UN. PAGE 135 A2760
CT/SYS CONSTN

L50
US SENATE COMM. GOVT. OPER.,"REVISION OF THE UN CHARTER." FUT USA+45 WOR+45 CONSTN ECO/DEV ECO/UNDEV NAT/G DELIB/GP ACT/RES CREATE PLAN EXEC ROUTINE CHOOSE ALL/VALS...POLICY CONCPT CONGRESS UN TOT/POP 20 COLD/WAR. PAGE 157 A3196
INT/ORG LEGIS PEACE

B51
BROGAN D.W.,THE PRICE OF REVOLUTION. FRANCE USA+45 USA-45 USSR CONSTN NAT/G DIPLOM COLONIAL NAT/LISM ORD/FREE POPULISM...CONCPT 18/20 PRE/US/AM. PAGE 19 A0386
REV METH/COMP COST MARXISM

B51
CHRISTENSEN A.N.,THE EVOLUTION OF LATIN AMERICAN GOVERNMENT: A BOOK OF READINGS. ECO/UNDEV INDUS LOC/G POL/PAR EX/STRUC LEGIS FOR/AID CT/SYS ...SOC/WK 20 SOUTH/AMER. PAGE 26 A0535
NAT/G CONSTN DIPLOM L/A+17C

B51
JENNINGS I.,THE COMMONWEALTH IN ASIA. CEYLON INDIA PAKISTAN CULTURE STRATA NAT/G LEGIS DIPLOM COLONIAL ATTIT...DECISION 20 CMN/WLTH. PAGE 74 A1507
CONSTN INT/ORG POLICY PLAN

B51
JENNINGS S.I.,THE COMMONWEALTH IN ASIA. CEYLON INDIA PAKISTAN S/ASIA UK CONSTN CULTURE SOCIETY STRATA STRUCT NAT/G POL/PAR EDU/PROP LEAD WAR 20 CMN/WLTH. PAGE 74 A1510
NAT/LISM REGION COLONIAL DIPLOM

B51
SWISHER C.B.,THE THEORY AND PRACTICE OF AMERICAN NATIONAL GOVERNMENT. CULTURE LEGIS DIPLOM ADJUD ADMIN WAR PEACE ORD/FREE...MAJORIT 17/20. PAGE 140 A2872
CONSTN NAT/G GOV/REL GEN/LAWS

B51
UNESCO,FREEDOM AND CULTURE. FUT WOR+45 CONSTN CULTURE PERF/ART VOL/ASSN EDU/PROP PEACE ATTIT ALL/VALS SOVEREIGN...POLICY MAJORIT CONCPT TREND STERTYP GEN/LAWS UN TOT/POP 20. PAGE 147 A3013
INT/ORG SOCIETY

B51
WELLES S.,SEVEN DECISIONS THAT SHAPED HISTORY. ASIA FRANCE FUT USA+45 WOR+45 WOR-45 CONSTN STRUCT INT/ORG NAT/G ACT/RES EDU/PROP DRIVE...POLICY CONCPT TIME/SEQ TREND TOT/POP UN 20 CHINJAP. PAGE 163 A3315
USA-45 DIPLOM WAR

L51
KELSEN H.,"RECENT TRENDS IN THE LAW OF THE UNITED NATIONS." KOREA WOR+45 CONSTN LEGIS DIPLOM LEGIT DETER WAR RIGID/FLEX HEALTH ORD/FREE RESPECT ...JURID CON/ANAL UN VAL/FREE 20 NATO. PAGE 77 A1582
INT/ORG LAW INT/LAW

B52
FLECHTHEIM O.K.,FUNDAMENTALS OF POLITICAL SCIENCE. WOR+45 WOR-45 LAW POL/PAR EX/STRUC LEGIS ADJUD ATTIT PWR...INT/LAW. PAGE 46 A0945
NAT/G DIPLOM IDEA/COMP CONSTN

B52
KELSEN H.,PRINCIPLES OF INTERNATIONAL LAW. WOR+45 WOR-45 INT/ORG ORD/FREE...JURID GEN/LAWS TOT/POP 20. PAGE 77 A1583
ADJUD CONSTN INT/LAW

B52
RIGGS F.W.,FORMOSA UNDER CHINESE NATIONALIST RULE. CHINA/COM USA+45 CONSTN AGRI FINAN LABOR LOC/G NAT/G POL/PAR FORCES HEALTH KNOWL...STAT WORK VAL/FREE 20. PAGE 121 A2479
ASIA FOR/AID DIPLOM

B52
VANDENBOSCH A.,THE UN: BACKGROUND, ORGANIZATION, FUNCTIONS, ACTIVITIES. WOR+45 LAW CONSTN STRUCT INT/ORG CONSULT BAL/PWR EDU/PROP EXEC ALL/VALS ...POLICY CONCPT UN 20. PAGE 158 A3218
DELIB/GP TIME/SEQ PEACE

B52
WALTERS F.P.,A HISTORY OF THE LEAGUE OF NATIONS. EUR+WWI CONSTN NAT/G LEGIS TOP/EX ACT/RES PLAN EDU/PROP LEGIT ROUTINE ATTIT...TREND LEAGUE/NAT 20 CHINJAP. PAGE 161 A3271
INT/ORG TIME/SEQ NAT/LISM

L52
WRIGHT Q.,"CONGRESS AND THE TREATY-MAKING POWER." USA+45 WOR+45 CONSTN INTELL NAT/G CHIEF CONSULT EX/STRUC LEGIS TOP/EX CREATE GOV/REL DISPL DRIVE RIGID/FLEX...TREND TOT/POP CONGRESS CONGRESS 20 TREATY. PAGE 167 A3408
ROUTINE DIPLOM INT/LAW DELIB/GP

S52
MASTERS R.D.,"RUSSIA AND THE UNITED NATIONS." FUT USA+45 USSR WOR+45 CONSTN VOL/ASSN DELIB/GP TOP/EX CREATE DIPLOM ADMIN...TREND STERTYP UN 20. PAGE 96 A1962
INT/ORG PWR

B53
BORGESE G.,FOUNDATIONS OF THE WORLD REPUBLIC. FUT SOCIETY NAT/G CREATE LEGIT PERSON MORAL...MAJORIT CON/ANAL LEAGUE/NAT TOT/POP 20. PAGE 17 A0340
INT/ORG CONSTN PEACE

B53
MANSERGH N.,DOCUMENTS AND SPEECHES ON BRITISH COMMONWEALTH AFFAIRS 1931-1952. INDIA IRELAND PAKISTAN UK CONSTN POL/PAR CHIEF FORCES COLONIAL ORD/FREE SOVEREIGN...JURID 20 COMMONWLTH. PAGE 94 A1929
BIBLIOG/A DIPLOM ECO/TAC

B53
OPPENHEIM L.,INTERNATIONAL LAW: A TREATISE (7TH ED., 2 VOLS.). LAW CONSTN PROB/SOLV INT/TRADE ADJUD AGREE NEUTRAL WAR ORD/FREE SOVEREIGN...BIBLIOG 20 LEAGUE/NAT UN ILO. PAGE 112 A2294
INT/LAW INT/ORG DIPLOM

B53
STOUT H.M.,BRITISH GOVERNMENT. UK FINAN LOC/G POL/PAR DELIB/GP DIPLOM ADMIN COLONIAL CHOOSE ORD/FREE...JURID BIBLIOG 20 COMMONWLTH. PAGE 139 A2837
NAT/G PARL/PROC CONSTN NEW/LIB

B54
COUDENHOVE-KALERGI,AN IDEA CONQUERS THE WORLD. EUR+WWI MOD/EUR USA-45 CONSTN FAM CREATE EDU/PROP ATTIT PERSON KNOWL...CONCPT SELF/OBS TIME/SEQ. PAGE 31 A0635
INT/ORG BIOG DIPLOM

B54
MITCHELL P.,AFRICAN AFTERTHOUGHTS. UGANDA CONSTN NAT/G ADJUD COERCE WAR 20 WWI MAU/MAU. PAGE 102 A2090
BIOG CHIEF COLONIAL DOMIN

B54
US SENATE COMM ON FOREIGN REL,REVIEW OF THE UNITED NATIONS CHARTER: A COLLECTION OF DOCUMENTS. LEGIS DIPLOM ADMIN ARMS/CONT WAR REPRESENT SOVEREIGN ...INT/LAW 20 UN. PAGE 156 A3180
BIBLIOG CONSTN INT/ORG DEBATE

B54
WHITAKER A.P.,THE WESTERN HEMISPHERE IDEA. USA+45 USA-45 CONSTN INT/ORG NAT/G DIPLOM SOVEREIGN...GEOG TIME/SEQ OAS 19/20 MONROE/DOC. PAGE 164 A3331
L/A+17C CONCPT REGION

S54
DODD S.C.,"THE SCIENTIFIC MEASUREMENT OF FITNESS FOR SELF-GOVERNMENT." FUT CONSTN ECO/UNDEV INT/ORG PLAN PWR...CONCPT QUANT CON/ANAL SOC/EXP UN LEAGUE/NAT 20. PAGE 38 A0767
NAT/G STAT SOVEREIGN

C54
BOWIE R.R.,"STUDIES IN FEDERALISM." AGRI FINAN LABOR EX/STRUC FORCES LEGIS DIPLOM INT/TRADE ADJUD ...BIBLIOG 20 EEC. PAGE 17 A0357
FEDERAL EUR+WWI INT/ORG CONSTN

B55
BUSS C.,THE FAR EAST: A HISTORY OF RECENT AND CONTEMPORARY INTERNATIONAL RELATIONS IN EAST ASIA. WOR+45 WOR-45 CONSTN INT/ORG NAT/G BAL/PWR ATTIT PWR SOVEREIGN...GEOG JURID SOC CONCPT METH/CNCPT 19/20. PAGE 22 A0449
ASIA DIPLOM

B55
GOODRICH L.,THE UNITED NATIONS AND THE MAINTENANCE OF INTERNATIONAL PEACE AND SECURITY. WOR+45 CONSTN ACT/RES CREATE PLAN PERCEPT PWR...ORG/CHARTS GEN/LAWS UN 20. PAGE 54 A1102
INT/ORG ORD/FREE ARMS/CONT PEACE

B55
HOGAN W.N.,INTERNATIONAL CONFLICT AND COLLECTIVE SECURITY: THE PRINCIPLE OF CONCERN IN INTERNATIONAL ORGANIZATION. CONSTN EX/STRUC BAL/PWR DIPLOM ADJUD CONTROL CENTRAL CONSEN PEACE...INT/LAW CONCPT METH/COMP 20 UN LEAGUE/NAT. PAGE 66 A1361
INT/ORG WAR ORD/FREE FORCES

B55
JAPAN MOMBUSHO DAIGAKU GAKIYUT,BIBLIOGRAPHY OF THE STUDIES ON LAW AND POLITICS (PAMPHLET). CONSTN INDUS LABOR DIPLOM TAX ADMIN...CRIMLGY INT/LAW 20 CHINJAP. PAGE 73 A1496
BIBLIOG LAW PHIL/SCI

B55
JOY C.T.,HOW COMMUNISTS NEGOTIATE. COM USA+45 CONSTN CULTURE ECO/UNDEV NAT/G CONSULT DELIB/GP FORCES PLAN ECO/TAC DOMIN EDU/PROP LEGIT EXEC ROUTINE COERCE WAR CHOOSE PEACE ATTIT RIGID/FLEX ORD/FREE PWR...POLICY 20. PAGE 75 A1539
ASIA INT/ORG DIPLOM

B55
LANDHEER B.,EUROPEAN YEARBOOK, 1955. CONSTN ECO/DEV DIST/IND FINAN DELIB/GP ECO/TAC DETER NUC/PWR ...BIBLIOG 20 EEC. PAGE 84 A1717
EUR+WWI INT/ORG GOV/REL INT/TRADE

B55
SNYDER R.C.,AMERICAN FOREIGN POLICY. USA+45 USA-45 WOR+45 WOR-45 CONSTN INT/ORG POL/PAR VOL/ASSN DELIB/GP LEGIS CREATE DOMIN EDU/PROP EXEC COERCE ATTIT DRIVE ORD/FREE PWR...MGT OBS RECORD TIME/SEQ TREND. PAGE 134 A2752
NAT/G DIPLOM

B55
TANNENBAUM F.,THE AMERICAN TRADITION IN FOREIGN POLICY. USA+45 USA-45 CONSTN INT/ORG NAT/G POL/PAR VOL/ASSN TOP/EX LEGIT DRIVE ORD/FREE PWR...CONCPT GEN/LAWS CONGRESS LEAGUE/NAT COLD/WAR OAS 18/20. PAGE 141 A2887
TIME/SEQ

B55
WILCOX F.O.,PROPOSALS FOR CHANGES IN THE UNITED NATIONS. WOR+45 CONSTN ACT/RES CREATE LEGIT ATTIT ORD/FREE...CONCPT ORG/CHARTS UN TOT/POP 20. PAGE 164 A3344
INT/ORG STRUCT

S55
DE SMITH S.A.,"CONSTITUTIONAL MONARCHY IN BURGANDA." AFR UGANDA UK STRUCT CHIEF REGION INGP/REL ADJUST NAT/LISM SOVEREIGN CONSERVE ...POLICY 19/20 BURGANDA. PAGE 35 A0712
NAT/G DIPLOM CONSTN COLONIAL

S55
HALLETT D.,"THE HISTORY AND STRUCTURE OF OEEC." EUR+WWI USA+45 CONSTN INDUS INT/ORG NAT/G DELIB/GP ACT/RES PLAN ORD/FREE WEALTH...CONCPT OEEC 20 CMN/WLTH. PAGE 60 A1234
VOL/ASSN ECO/DEV

C55
APTER D.E.,"THE GOLD COAST IN TRANSITION." AFR CONSTN LOC/G LEGIS DIPLOM COLONIAL CONTROL GOV/REL ...CHARTS BIBLIOG 20 CMN/WLTH. PAGE 8 A0170
ORD/FREE REPRESENT PARL/PROC NAT/G

B56
COMMONWEALTH OF WORLD CITIZENS,THE BIRTH OF A WORLD PEOPLE. WOR+45 CONSTN PROB/SOLV CONTROL TASK WAR GP/REL UTOPIA PWR...POLICY NEW/IDEA 20. PAGE 29 A0582
DIPLOM VOL/ASSN PEACE INT/ORG

B56
GEORGE A.L.,WOODROW WILSON AND COLONEL HOUSE. WOR-45 CONSTN FACE/GP INT/ORG NAT/G POL/PAR CONSULT LEGIT EXEC COERCE CHOOSE ATTIT DRIVE PERSON MORAL ORD/FREE PWR RESPECT...POLICY MGT PSY OBS RECORD INT LEAGUE/NAT. PAGE 52 A1060
USA-45 BIOG DIPLOM

B56
JAMESON J.F.,THE AMERICAN REVOLUTION CONSIDERED AS A SOCIAL MOVEMENT. USA-45 AGRI FINAN SECT INT/TRADE REPRESENT SUFF INGP/REL RACE/REL DISCRIM...MAJORIT 18/19 CHURCH/STA. PAGE 73 A1494
ORD/FREE REV FEDERAL CONSTN

B56
REITZEL W.,UNITED STATES FOREIGN POLICY, 1945-1955. USA+45 WOR+45 CONSTN INT/ORG EDU/PROP LEGIT EXEC COERCE NUC/PWR PEACE ATTIT ORD/FREE PWR...DECISION CONCPT OBS RECORD TIME/SEQ TREND COLD/WAR UN CONGRESS. PAGE 120 A2464
NAT/G POLICY DIPLOM

B56
SOHN L.B.,BASIC DOCUMENTS OF THE UNITED NATIONS. WOR+45 LAW INT/ORG LEGIT EXEC ROUTINE CHOOSE PWR ...JURID CONCPT GEN/LAWS ANTHOL UN TOT/POP OAS FAO ILO 20. PAGE 135 A2761
DELIB/GP CONSTN

B56
WEIS P.,NATIONALITY AND STATELESSNESS IN INTERNATIONAL LAW. UK WOR+45 WOR-45 LAW CONSTN NAT/G DIPLOM EDU/PROP LEGIT ROUTINE RIGID/FLEX ...JURID RECORD CMN/WLTH 20. PAGE 162 A3309
INT/ORG SOVEREIGN INT/LAW

B56
WILSON P.,GOVERNMENT AND POLITICS OF INDIA AND PAKISTAN: 1885-1955; A BIBLIOGRAPHY OF WORKS IN WESTERN LANGUAGES. INDIA PAKISTAN CONSTN LOC/G POL/PAR FORCES DIPLOM ADMIN WAR CHOOSE...BIOG
BIBLIOG COLONIAL NAT/G S/ASIA

CON/ANAL 19/20. PAGE 165 A3361

B57
BEAL J.R.,JOHN FOSTER DULLES, A BIOGRAPHY. USA+45 USSR WOR+45 CONSTN INT/ORG NAT/G EX/STRUC LEGIT ADMIN NUC/PWR DISPL PERSON ORD/FREE PWR SKILL ...POLICY PSY OBS RECORD COLD/WAR UN 20 DULLES/JF. PAGE 12 A0237 — BIOG DIPLOM

B57
COMM. STUDY ORGAN. PEACE,STRENGTHENING THE UNITED NATIONS. FUT USA+45 WOR+45 CONSTN NAT/G DELIB/GP FORCES LEGIS ECO/TAC LEGIT COERCE PEACE...JURID CONCPT UN COLD/WAR 20. PAGE 28 A0580 — INT/ORG ORD/FREE

B57
JASZI O.,AGAINST THE TYRANT. WOR+45 WOR-45 CONSTN DIPLOM CONTROL PARTIC REV WAR...CONCPT. PAGE 73 A1498 — TOTALISM ORD/FREE CHIEF MURDER

B57
MATECKI B.,ESTABLISHMENT OF THE INTERNATIONAL FINANCE CORPORATION AND UNITED STATES POLICY. USA+45 WOR+45 CONSTN NAT/G CREATE RIGID/FLEX KNOWL ...METH/CNCPT TIME/SEQ SIMUL TOT/POP 20 INTL/FINAN. PAGE 96 A1964 — FINAN INT/ORG DIPLOM

B57
MURRAY J.N.,THE UNITED NATIONS TRUSTEESHIP SYSTEM. AFR WOR+45 CONSTN CONSULT LEGIS EDU/PROP LEGIT EXEC ROUTINE...INT TIME/SEQ SOMALI UN 20. PAGE 106 A2181 — INT/ORG DELIB/GP

B57
UNESCO,A REGISTER OF LEGAL DOCUMENTATION IN THE WORLD (2ND ED.). CT/SYS...JURID IDEA/COMP METH/COMP NAT/COMP 20. PAGE 148 A3019 — BIBLIOG LAW INT/LAW CONSTN

B57
US SENATE COMM ON JUDICIARY,HEARING BEFORE SUBCOMMITTEE ON COMMITTEE OF JUDICIARY, UNITED STATES SENATE: S. J. RES. 3. USA+45 NAT/G CONSULT DELIB/GP DIPLOM ADJUD LOBBY REPRESENT 20 CONGRESS TREATY. PAGE 157 A3192 — LEGIS CONSTN CONFER AGREE

C57
TANG P.S.H.,"COMMUNIST CHINA TODAY: DOMESTIC AND FOREIGN POLICIES." CHINA/COM COM S/ASIA USSR STRATA FORCES DIPLOM EDU/PROP COERCE GOV/REL...POLICY MAJORIT BIBLIOG 20. PAGE 141 A2886 — POL/PAR LEAD ADMIN CONSTN

B58
ALEXANDROWICZ,A BIBLIOGRAPHY OF INDIAN LAW. INDIA S/ASIA CONSTN CT/SYS...INT/LAW 19/20. PAGE 6 A0113 — BIBLIOG LAW ADJUD JURID

B58
GROBLER J.H.,AFRICA'S DESTINY. AFR EUR+WWI SOUTH/AFR UK USA+45 ELITES KIN LOC/G DIPLOM DISCRIM ATTIT CONSERVE MARXISM 20 ROOSEVLT/T NEGRO. PAGE 57 A1168 — POLICY ORD/FREE COLONIAL CONSTN

B58
HENKIN L.,ARMS CONTROL AND INSPECTION IN AMERICAN LAW. LAW CONSTN INT/ORG LOC/G MUNIC NAT/G PROVS EDU/PROP LEGIT EXEC NUC/PWR KNOWL ORD/FREE...OBS TOT/POP CONGRESS 20. PAGE 64 A1315 — USA+45 JURID ARMS/CONT

B58
MANSERGH N.,SURVEY OF BRITISH COMMONWEALTH AFFAIRS: PROBLEMS OF WARTIME CO-OPERATION AND POST-WAR CHANGE 1939-1952. INDIA IRELAND S/ASIA CONSTN INT/ORG BAL/PWR COLONIAL NEUTRAL WAR ADJUST PEACE ROLE ORD/FREE...CHARTS 20 CMN/WLTH NATO UN. PAGE 94 A1931 — VOL/ASSN CONSEN PROB/SOLV INGP/REL

B58
RUSSELL R.B.,A HISTORY OF THE UNITED NATIONS CHARTER: THE ROLE OF THE UNITED STATES. SOCIETY NAT/G CONSULT DOMIN LEGIT ATTIT ORD/FREE PWR ...POLICY JURID CONCPT UN LEAGUE/NAT. PAGE 126 A2575 — USA-45 INT/ORG CONSTN

B58
STONE J.,AGGRESSION AND WORLD ORDER: A CRITIQUE OF UNITED NATIONS THEORIES OF AGGRESSION. LAW CONSTN DELIB/GP PROB/SOLV BAL/PWR DIPLOM DEBATE ADJUD CRIME PWR...POLICY IDEA/COMP 20 UN SUEZ LEAGUE/NAT. PAGE 138 A2835 — ORD/FREE INT/ORG WAR CONCPT

S58
ELKIN A.B.,"OEEC-ITS STRUCTURE AND POWERS." EUR+WWI CONSTN INDUS INT/ORG NAT/G VOL/ASSN DELIB/GP ACT/RES PLAN ORD/FREE WEALTH...CHARTS ORG/CHARTS OEEC 20. PAGE 41 A0839 — ECO/DEV EX/STRUC

C58
CARTER G.M.,"THE POLITICS OF INEQUALITY: SOUTH AFRICA SINCE 1948." SOUTH/AFR CONSTN DIPLOM EDU/PROP REPRESENT DISCRIM ATTIT...POLICY PREDICT CHARTS BIBLIOG 20. PAGE 25 A0504 — RACE/REL POL/PAR CHOOSE DOMIN

C58
GOLAY J.F.,"THE FOUNDING OF THE FEDERAL REPUBLIC OF GERMANY." GERMANY/W CONSTN EX/STRUC DIPLOM ADMIN CHOOSE...DECISION BIBLIOG 20. PAGE 53 A1088 — FEDERAL NAT/G PARL/PROC POL/PAR

C58
RAJAN M.S.,"UNITED NATIONS AND DOMESTIC JURISDICTION." WOR+45 WOR-45 PARL/PROC...IDEA/COMP BIBLIOG 20 UN. PAGE 119 A2434 — INT/LAW DIPLOM CONSTN

INT/ORG

C58
WILDING N.,"AN ENCYCLOPEDIA OF PARLIAMENT." UK LAW CONSTN CHIEF PROB/SOLV DIPLOM DEBATE WAR INGP/REL PRIVIL...BIBLIOG DICTIONARY 13/20 CMN/WLTH PARLIAMENT. PAGE 164 A3349 — PARL/PROC POL/PAR NAT/G ADMIN

B59
ALWAN M.,ALGERIA BEFORE THE UNITED NATIONS. AFR ASIA FRANCE ISLAM S/ASIA CONSTN SOCIETY STRUCT INT/ORG NAT/G ECO/TAC ADMIN COLONIAL NAT/LISM ATTIT PWR...DECISION TREND 420 UN. PAGE 7 A0133 — PLAN RIGID/FLEX DIPLOM ALGERIA

B59
CORBETT P.E.,LAW IN DIPLOMACY. UK USA+45 USSR CONSTN SOCIETY INT/ORG JUDGE LEGIT ATTIT ORD/FREE TOT/POP LEAGUE/NAT 20. PAGE 30 A0616 — NAT/G ADJUD JURID DIPLOM

B59
GOODRICH L.,THE UNITED NATIONS. WOR+45 CONSTN STRUCT ACT/RES LEGIT COERCE KNOWL ORD/FREE PWR ...GEN/LAWS UN 20. PAGE 54 A1104 — INT/ORG ROUTINE

B59
HALLE L.J.,DREAM AND REALITY: ASPECTS OF AMERICAN FOREIGN POLICY. USA+45 CONSTN CONSULT PROB/SOLV NAT/LISM PERSON. PAGE 60 A1230 — POLICY MYTH DIPLOM NAT/G

B59
VINACKE H.M.,A HISTORY OF THE FAR EAST IN MODERN TIMES (6TH ED.). KOREA S/ASIA USSR CONSTN CULTURE STRATA ECO/UNDEV NAT/G CHIEF FOR/AID INT/TRADE GP/REL...SOC NAT/COMP 19/20 CHINJAP. PAGE 159 A3235 — STRUCT ASIA

L59
BEGUIN B.,"ILO AND THE TRIPARTITE SYSTEM." EUR+WWI WOR+45 WOR-45 CONSTN ECO/DEV ECO/UNDEV INDUS INT/ORG NAT/G VOL/ASSN DELIB/GP PLAN TEC/DEV LEGIT ORD/FREE WEALTH...CONCPT TIME/SEQ WORK ILO 20. PAGE 12 A0249 — LABOR

L59
WOLFERS A.,"ACTORS IN INTERNATIONAL POLITICS. IN (FOX,WTR. THEORETICAL ASPECTS OF INTERNATIONAL." FUT WOR+45 CONSTN INT/ORG NAT/G CREATE...CONCPT 20. PAGE 166 A3383 — PERSON PWR DIPLOM

S59
BAILEY S.D.,"THE FUTURE COMPOSITION OF THE TRUSTEESHIP COUNCIL." FUT WOR+45 CONSTN VOL/ASSN ADMIN ATTIT PWR...OBS TREND CON/ANAL VAL/FREE UN 20. PAGE 10 A0203 — INT/ORG NAT/LISM SOVEREIGN

S59
FISCHER L.,"THE SOVIET-AMERICAN ANTAGONISM: HOW WILL IT END." CONSTN CULTURE PLAN TEC/DEV RIGID/FLEX SUPEGO ORD/FREE...MARXIST DECISION PSY CONCPT CON/ANAL GEN/LAWS VAL/FREE 20 COLD/WAR. PAGE 46 A0936 — USA+45 PWR DIPLOM USSR

B60
DUMON F.,LA COMMUNAUTE FRANCO-AFRO-MALGACHE: SES ORIGINES, SES INSTITUTIONS, SON EVOLUTION. FRANCE MADAGASCAR POL/PAR DIPLOM ADMIN ATTIT...TREND T 20. PAGE 39 A0798 — JURID INT/ORG AFR CONSTN

B60
HARVARD LAW SCHOOL LIBRARY,CURRENT LEGAL BIBLIOGRAPHY. USA+45 CONSTN LEGIS ADJUD CT/SYS POLICY. PAGE 62 A1279 — BIBLIOG JURID LAW INT/LAW

B60
KHRUSHCHEV N.,FOR VICTORY IN PEACEFUL COMPETITION WITH CAPITALISM. COM FUT USSR WOR+45 CONSTN SOCIETY INDUS INT/ORG DELIB/GP PLAN BAL/PWR DIPLOM PERSON MARXISM...MARXIST WORK 20 COLD/WAR. PAGE 79 A1611 — TOP/EX PWR CAP/ISM SOCISM

B60
MC CLELLAN G.S.,INDIA. CHINA/COM INDIA CONSTN ELITES STRATA AGRI POL/PAR FOR/AID ARMS/CONT REV MARXISM...CENSUS BIBLIOG 20 COLD/WAR GANDHI/M NEHRU/J. PAGE 97 A1990 — DIPLOM NAT/G SOCIETY ECO/UNDEV

B60
MUGRIDGE D.H.,A GUIDE TO THE STUDY OF THE UNITED STATES OF AMERICA: REPRESENTATIVE BOOKS REFLECTING THE DEVELOPMENT OF AMERICAN LIFE. USA+45 USA-45 CONSTN POL/PAR FORCES DIPLOM PRESS CHOOSE...SOC 17/20. PAGE 105 A2165 — BIBLIOG/A CULTURE NAT/G POLICY

B60
MUNRO L.,UNITED NATIONS, HOPE FOR A DIVIDED WORLD. FUT WOR+45 CONSTN DELIB/GP CREATE TEC/DEV DIPLOM EDU/PROP LEGIT PEACE ATTIT HEALTH ORD/FREE PWR ...CONCPT TREND UN VAL/FREE 20. PAGE 106 A2172 — INT/ORG ROUTINE

B60
PLAMENATZ J.,ON ALIEN RULE AND SELF-GOVERNMENT. AFR FUT S/ASIA WOR+45 CULTURE SOCIETY ECO/UNDEV INT/ORG DOMIN EDU/PROP ATTIT RIGID/FLEX ALL/VALS...POLICY CONCPT OBS TREND CON/ANAL GEN/LAWS TOT/POP VAL/FREE. PAGE 116 A2386 — NAT/G CONSTN NAT/LISM SOVEREIGN

B60
PRICE D.,THE SECRETARY OF STATE. USA+45 CONSTN ELITES INTELL CHIEF EX/STRUC TOP/EX LEGIT ATTIT PWR SKILL...DECISION 20 CONGRESS. PAGE 117 A2410 — CONSULT DIPLOM INT/LAW

B60
SPEER J.P.,FOR WHAT PURPOSE? CHINA/COM USSR CONSTN PROB/SOLV DIPLOM CONTROL TASK WAR NAT/LISM WORSHIP — PEACE SECT

20 UN. PAGE 136 A2778 SUPEGO ALL/IDEOS

B60
THEOBALD R.,THE RICH AND THE POOR: A STUDY OF THE ECONOMICS OF RISING EXPECTATIONS. WOR+45 CONSTN ECO/DEV ECO/UNDEV INT/ORG NAT/G PLAN FOR/AID ROUTINE BAL/PAY ORD/FREE PWR WEALTH...GEOG TREND WORK 20. PAGE 142 A2912 ECO/TAC INT/TRADE

B60
WHEARE K.C.,THE CONSTITUTIONAL STRUCTURE OF THE COMMONWEALTH. UK EX/STRUC DIPLOM DOMIN ADMIN COLONIAL CONTROL LEAD INGP/REL SUPEGO 20 CMN/WLTH. PAGE 163 A3325 CONSTN INT/ORG VOL/ASSN SOVEREIGN

B60
WOETZEL R.K.,THE INTERNATIONAL CONTROL OF AIRSPACE AND OUTERSPACE. FUT WOR+45 AIR CONSTN STRUCT CONSULT PLAN TEC/DEV ADJUD RIGID/FLEX KNOWL ORD/FREE PWR...TECHNIC GEOG MGT NEW/IDEA TREND COMPUT/IR VAL/FREE 20 TREATY. PAGE 166 A3375 INT/ORG JURID SPACE INT/LAW

L60
DEAN A.W.,"SECOND GENEVA CONFERENCE OF THE LAW OF THE SEA: THE FIGHT FOR FREEDOM OF THE SEAS." FUT USA+45 USSR WOR+45 WOR-45 SEA CONSTN STRUCT PLAN INT/TRADE ADJUD ADMIN ORD/FREE...DECISION RECORD TREND GEN/LAWS 20 TREATY. PAGE 35 A0717 INT/ORG JURID INT/LAW

S60
CLARK W.,"NEW FORCES IN THE UN." FUT UK WOR+45 CONSTN BAL/PWR DIPLOM DRIVE PWR SKILL...CONCPT TREND UN TOT/POP 20. PAGE 27 A0543 INT/ORG ECO/UNDEV SOVEREIGN

S60
GOODRICH L.,"GEOGRAPHICAL DISTRIBUTION OF THE STAFF OF THE UN SECRETARIAT." FUT WOR+45 CONSTN BAL/PWR DIPLOM EDU/PROP LEGIT ROUTINE RIGID/FLEX...CHARTS UN 20. PAGE 54 A1105 INT/ORG EX/STRUC

S60
GRACIA-MORA M.R.,"INTERNATIONAL RESPONSIBILITY FOR SUBVERSIVE ACTIVITIES AND HOSTILE PROPAGANDA BY PRIVATE PERSONS AGAINST." COM EUR+WWI L/A+17C UK USA+45 USSR WOR-45 CONSTN NAT/G LEGIT ADJUD REV PEACE TOTALISM ORD/FREE...INT/LAW 20. PAGE 55 A1119 INT/ORG JURID SOVEREIGN

S60
PADELFORD N.J.,"POLITICS AND CHANGE IN THE SECURITY COUNCIL." FUT WOR+45 CONSTN NAT/G EX/STRUC LEGIS ORD/FREE...CONCPT CHARTS UN 20. PAGE 113 A2309 INT/ORG DELIB/GP

S60
SCHWELB E.,"INTERNATIONAL CONVENTIONS ON HUMAN RIGHTS." FUT WOR+45 LAW CONSTN CULTURE SOCIETY STRUCT VOL/ASSN DELIB/GP PLAN ADJUD SUPEGO LOVE MORAL...SOC CONCPT STAT RECORD HIST/WRIT TREND 20 UN. PAGE 130 A2664 INT/ORG HUM

S60
SWIFT R.,"THE UNITED NATIONS AND ITS PUBLIC." WOR+45 CONSTN FINAN CONSULT DELIB/GP ACT/RES ADMIN ROUTINE RIGID/FLEX SKILL UN 20. PAGE 140 A2870 INT/ORG EDU/PROP

C60
WRIGGINS W.H.,"CEYLON: DILEMMAS OF A NEW NATION." ASIA CEYLON CONSTN STRUCT POL/PAR SECT FORCES DIPLOM GOV/REL NAT/LISM...CHARTS BIBLIOG 20. PAGE 167 A3399 PROB/SOLV NAT/G ECO/UNDEV

B61
BAINS J.S.,STUDIES IN POLITICAL SCIENCE. INDIA WOR+45 WOR-45 CONSTN BAL/PWR ADJUD ADMIN PARL/PROC SOVEREIGN...SOC METH/COMP ANTHOL 17/20 UN. PAGE 10 A0209 DIPLOM INT/LAW NAT/G

B61
BARNES W.,THE FOREIGN SERVICE OF THE UNITED STATES. USA+45 USA-45 CONSTN INT/ORG POL/PAR CONSULT DELIB/GP LEGIS DOMIN EDU/PROP EXEC ATTIT RIGID/FLEX ORD/FREE PWR...POLICY CONCPT STAT OBS RECORD BIOG TIME/SEQ TREND. PAGE 11 A0224 NAT/G MGT DIPLOM

B61
CARNELL F.,THE POLITICS OF THE NEW STATES: A SELECT ANNOTATED BIBLIOGRAPHY WITH SPECIAL REFERENCE TO THE COMMONWEALTH. CONSTN ELITES LABOR NAT/G POL/PAR EX/STRUC DIPLOM ADJUD ADMIN...GOV/COMP 20 COMMONWLTH. PAGE 24 A0496 BIBLIOG/A AFR ASIA COLONIAL

B61
CHIDZERO B.T.G.,TANGANYIKA AND INTERNATIONAL TRUSTEESHIP. AFR WOR+45 WOR-45 ECO/DEV INT/ORG ECO/TAC DOMIN COLONIAL...RECORD CHARTS 20 TANGANYIKA CMN/WLTH. PAGE 26 A0528 ECO/UNDEV CONSTN

B61
GRAEBNER N.,AN UNCERTAIN TRADITION: AMERICAN SECRETARIES OF STATE IN THE 20TH CENTURY. USA+45 CONSTN INT/ORG NAT/G DELIB/GP TOP/EX BAL/PWR DOMIN LEGIT ADMIN ARMS/CONT ATTIT DRIVE PERSON SUPEGO ORD/FREE PWR...GEN/LAWS VAL/FREE CONGRESS. PAGE 55 A1121 USA-45 BIOG DIPLOM

B61
MECHAM J.L.,THE UNITED STATES AND INTER-AMERICAN SECURITY, 1889-1960. L/A+17C USA+45 USA-45 CONSTN FORCES INT/TRADE PEACE TOTALISM ATTIT...JURID 19/20 UN OAS. PAGE 99 A2030 DIPLOM WAR ORD/FREE INT/ORG

B61
PANIKKAR K.M.,THE VOICE OF FREEDOM: SELECTED SPEECHES OF PANDIT MOTILAL NEHRU. INDIA UK CONSTN FINAN FORCES LEGIS DIPLOM TAX COLONIAL...POLICY MAJORIT ANTHOL 20 NEHRU/PM. PAGE 114 A2331 NAT/LISM ORD/FREE CHIEF NAT/G

B61
PEASLEE A.J.,INTERNATIONAL GOVERNMENT ORGANIZATIONS, CONSTITUTIONAL DOCUMENTS. WOR+45 WOR-45 CONSTN VOL/ASSN DELIB/GP EX/STRUC ROUTINE KNOWL TOT/POP 20. PAGE 114 A2344 INT/ORG STRUCT

B61
PEASLEE A.J.,INTERNATIONAL GOVERNMENTAL ORGANIZATIONS (2 VOLS.). CONSTN VOL/ASSN DIPLOM ...GP/COMP 20 UN OAS EEC EFTA ECSC. PAGE 114 A2345 BIBLIOG INT/ORG INDEX LAW

B61
SCOTT A.M.,POLITICS, USA; CASES ON THE AMERICAN DEMOCRATIC PROCESS. USA+45 CHIEF FORCES DIPLOM LOBBY CHOOSE RACE/REL FEDERAL ATTIT...JURID ANTHOL T 20 PRESIDENT CONGRESS CIVIL/LIB. PAGE 130 A2669 CT/SYS CONSTN NAT/G PLAN

B61
SHARP W.R.,FIELD ADMINISTRATION IN THE UNITED NATION SYSTEM: THE CONDUCT OF INTERNATIONAL ECONOMIC AND SOCIAL PROGRAMS. FUT WOR+45 CONSTN SOCIETY ECO/UNDEV R+D DELIB/GP ACT/RES PLAN TEC/DEV EDU/PROP EXEC ROUTINE HEALTH WEALTH...HUM CONCPT CHARTS METH ILO UNESCO VAL/FREE UN 20. PAGE 132 A2697 INT/ORG CONSULT

B61
WARD R.E.,JAPANESE POLITICAL SCIENCE: A GUIDE TO JAPANESE REFERENCE AND RESEARCH MATERIALS (2ND ED.). LAW CONSTN STRATA NAT/G POL/PAR DELIB/GP LEGIS ADMIN CHOOSE GP/REL...INT/LAW 19/20 CHINJAP. PAGE 161 A3282 BIBLIOG/A PHIL/SCI

B61
WECHSLER H.,PRINCIPLES, POLITICS AND FUNDAMENTAL LAW: SELECTED ESSAYS. USA+45 USA-45 LAW SOCIETY NAT/G PROVS DELIB/GP EX/STRUC ACT/RES LEGIT PERSON KNOWL PWR...JURID 20 NUREMBERG. PAGE 162 A3296 CT/SYS CONSTN INT/LAW

B61
WINTER R.C.,BLUEPRINTS FOR INDEPENDENCE. WOR+45 INT/ORG DIPLOM COLONIAL CONTROL REV WAR PWR ...BIBLIOG 20 UN. PAGE 165 A3367 NAT/G ECO/UNDEV SOVEREIGN CONSTN

B61
YDIT M.,INTERNATIONALISED TERRITORIES. FUT WOR+45 WOR-45 CONSTN VOL/ASSN CREATE PLAN LEGIT PEACE ORD/FREE...GEOG INT/LAW JURID SOC NEW/IDEA OBS RECORD SAMP TIME/SEQ TREND 19/20 BERLIN. PAGE 169 A3431 LOC/G INT/ORG DIPLOM SOVEREIGN

L61
HOYT E.C.,"UNITED STATES REACTION TO THE KOREAN ATTACK." COM KOREA USA+45 CONSTN DELIB/GP FORCES PLAN ECO/TAC DOMIN EDU/PROP LEGIT ROUTINE COERCE WAR ATTIT DISPL RIGID/FLEX ORD/FREE PWR...POLICY INT/LAW TREND UN 20. PAGE 68 A1402 ASIA INT/ORG BAL/PWR DIPLOM

S61
ALGER C.F.,"NON-RESOLUTION CONSEQUENCES OF THE UNITED NATIONS AND THEIR EFFECT ON INTERNATIONAL CONFLICT." WOR+45 CONSTN ECO/DEV NAT/G CONSULT DELIB/GP TOP/EX ACT/RES PLAN DIPLOM EDU/PROP ROUTINE ATTIT ALL/VALS...INT/LAW TOT/POP UN 20. PAGE 6 A0117 INT/ORG DRIVE BAL/PWR

S61
JACKSON E.,"CONSTITUTIONAL DEVELOPMENTS OF THE UNITED NATIONS: THE GROWTH OF ITS EXECUTIVE CAPACITY." FUT WOR+45 CONSTN STRUCT ACT/RES PLAN ALL/VALS...NEW/IDEA OBS COLD/WAR UN 20. PAGE 72 A1475 INT/ORG EXEC

S61
JACKSON E.,"THE FUTURE DEVELOPMENT OF THE UNITED NATIONS: SOME SUGGESTIONS FOR RESEARCH." FUT LAW CONSTN ECO/DEV FINAN PEACE WEALTH...WELF/ST CONCPT UN 20. PAGE 72 A1476 INT/ORG PWR

S61
TUCKER R.C.,"TOWARDS A COMPARATIVE POLITICS OF MOVEMENT-REGIMES" (BMR)" USSR CONSTN NAT/G CREATE PROB/SOLV DIPLOM DOMIN REV...GP/COMP IDEA/COMP METH 20 STALIN/J BOLSHEVISM. PAGE 145 A2971 MARXISM POLICY GEN/LAWS PWR

S61
VIRALLY M.,"VERS UNE REFORME DU SECRETARIAT DES NATIONS UNIES." FUT WOR+45 CONSTN ECO/DEV TOP/EX BAL/PWR ADMIN ALL/VALS...CONCPT BIOG UN VAL/FREE 20. PAGE 159 A3243 INT/ORG INTELL DIPLOM

B62
ALTHING F.A.M.,EUROPEAN ORGANIZATIONS AND FOREIGN RELATIONS OF STATES: A COMPARATIVE ANALYSIS OF DECISION-MAKING. EUR+WWI CONSTN ELITES BAL/PWR INT/TRADE SOVEREIGN TREATY. PAGE 6 A0131 DELIB/GP INT/ORG DECISION DIPLOM

B62
DUROSELLE J.B.,LES NOUVEAUX ETATS DANS LES RELATIONS INTERNATIONALES. AFR CHINA/COM FRANCE MOROCCO S/ASIA USSR ECO/UNDEV INT/ORG PLAN ECO/TAC EDU/PROP ATTIT DRIVE...TREND TOT/POP TUNIS 20. PAGE 39 A0806 NAT/G CONSTN DIPLOM

B62
HATCH J.,AFRICA TODAY-AND TOMORROW: AN OUTLINE OF BASIC FACTS AND MAJOR PROBLEMS. AFR FUT ISLAM STRATA ECO/UNDEV INT/ORG NAT/G POL/PAR DELIB/GP PLAN CONSTN NAT/LISM

TOP/EX EDU/PROP LEGIT CHOOSE ATTIT...TIME/SEQ TOT/POP COLD/WAR 20. PAGE 63 A1287

B62

INGHAM K.,A HISTORY OF EAST AFRICA. NAT/G DIPLOM ADMIN WAR NAT/LISM...SOC BIOG BIBLIOG. PAGE 70 A1439 — AFR CONSTN COLONIAL

B62

KLUCKHOHN F.L.,THE NAKED RISE OF COMMUNISM. CHINA/COM COM USSR WOR+45 CONSTN POL/PAR PLAN CONTROL LEAD NEUTRAL CONSERVE 20 STALIN/J EUROPE/E COM/PARTY. PAGE 80 A1650 — MARXISM IDEA/COMP DIPLOM DOMIN

B62

NICHOLAS H.G.,THE UNITED NATIONS AS A POLITICAL INSTITUTION. WOR+45 CONSTN EX/STRUC ACT/RES LEGIT PERCEPT KNOWL PWR...CONCPT TIME/SEQ CON/ANAL ORG/CHARTS UN 20. PAGE 109 A2228 — INT/ORG ROUTINE

B62

ROSENNE S.,THE WORLD COURT: WHAT IT IS AND HOW IT WORKS. WOR+45 WOR-45 LAW CONSTN JUDGE EDU/PROP LEGIT ROUTINE CHOOSE PEACE ORD/FREE...JURID OBS TIME/SEQ CHARTS UN TOT/POP VAL/FREE 20. PAGE 124 A2538 — INT/ORG ADJUD INT/LAW

B62

TOURE S.,THE INTERNATIONAL POLICY OF THE DEMOCRATIC PARTY OF GUINEA (VOL. VII). AFR ALGERIA GHANA GUINEA MALI CONSTN VOL/ASSN CHIEF WAR PEACE ATTIT ...WELF/ST 20 DEMOCRAT. PAGE 144 A2953 — DIPLOM POLICY POL/PAR NEW/LIB

B62

TRISKA J.F.,THE THEORY, LAW, AND POLICY OF SOVIET TREATIES. WOR+45 WOR-45 CONSTN INT/ORG NAT/G VOL/ASSN DOMIN LEGIT COERCE ATTIT PWR RESPECT ...POLICY JURID CONCPT OBS SAMP TIME/SEQ TREND GEN/LAWS 20. PAGE 145 A2966 — COM LAW INT/LAW USSR

B62

US SENATE COMM ON JUDICIARY,CONSTITUTIONAL RIGHTS OF MILITARY PERSONNEL. USA+45 USA-45 FORCES DIPLOM WAR CONGRESS. PAGE 157 A3193 — CONSTN ORD/FREE JURID CT/SYS

B62

WILLIAMS W.A.,THE UNITED STATES, CUBA, AND CASTRO: AN ESSAY ON THE DYNAMICS OF REVOLUTION AND THE DISSOLUTION OF EMPIRE. CUBA USA+45 AGRI VOL/ASSN DIPLOM ECO/TAC DOMIN COERCE...POLICY 20 EISNHWR/DD CIA KENNEDY/JF CASTRO/F. PAGE 165 A3354 — REV CONSTN COM LEAD

L62

BAILEY S.D.,"THE TROIKA AND THE FUTURE OF THE UN." CONSTN CREATE LEGIT EXEC CHOOSE ORD/FREE PWR ...CONCPT NEW/IDEA UN COLD/WAR 20. PAGE 10 A0206 — FUT INT/ORG USSR

L62

MALINOWSKI W.R.,"CENTRALIZATION AND DE-CENTRALIZATION IN THE UNITED NATIONS' ECONOMIC AND SOCIAL ACTIVITIES." WOR+45 CONSTN ECO/UNDEV INT/ORG VOL/ASSN DELIB/GP ECO/TAC EDU/PROP ADMIN RIGID/FLEX ...OBS CHARTS UNESCO UN EEC OAS OEEC 20. PAGE 93 A1913 — CREATE GEN/LAWS

L62

MURACCIOLE L.,"LA LOI FONDAMENTALE DE LA REPUBLIQUE DU CONGO." WOR+45 SOCIETY ECO/UNDEV INT/ORG NAT/G LEGIS PLAN LEGIT ADJUD COLONIAL ROUTINE ATTIT SOVEREIGN 20 CONGO. PAGE 106 A2174 — AFR CONSTN

L62

STEIN E.,"MR HAMMARSKJOLD, THE CHARTER LAW AND THE FUTURE ROLE OF THE UNITED NATIONS SECRETARY-GENERAL." WOR+45 CONSTN INT/ORG DELIB/GP FORCES TOP/EX BAL/PWR LEGIT ROUTINE RIGID/FLEX PWR ...POLICY JURID OBS STERTYP UN COLD/WAR 20 HAMMARSK/D. PAGE 137 A2815 — CONCPT BIOG

S62

BROWN B.E.,"L'ONU ABANDONNE LA HONGRIE." COM USSR WOR+45 CONSTN NAT/G POL/PAR DELIB/GP ACT/RES TEC/DEV PWR...TIME/SEQ 20 UN. PAGE 20 A0400 — INT/ORG TOTALISM HUNGARY POLICY

S62

CRANE R.D.,"SOVIET ATTITUDE TOWARD INTERNATIONAL SPACE LAW." COM FUT USA+45 USSR AIR CONSTN DELIB/GP DOMIN PWR...JURID TREND TOT/POP 20. PAGE 32 A0657 — LAW ATTIT INT/LAW SPACE

S62

MONNIER J.P.,"LA SUCCESSION D'ETATS EN MATIERE DE RESPONSABILITE INTERNATIONALE." UNIV CONSTN INTELL SOCIETY ADJUD ROUTINE PERCEPT SUPEGO...GEN/LAWS TOT/POP 20. PAGE 103 A2107 — NAT/G JURID INT/LAW

S62

VASAK K.,"DE LA CONVENTION EUROPEENNE A LA CONVENTION AFRICAINE DES DROITS DE L'HOMME." AFR ISLAM WOR+45 LAW CONSTN ECO/UNDEV INT/ORG PERCEPT ALL/VALS 20. PAGE 158 A3223 — DELIB/GP CONCPT COLONIAL

S62

VIGNES D.,"L'AUTORITE DES TRAITES INTERNATIONAUX EN DROIT INTERNE." EUR+WWI UNIV LAW CONSTN INTELL NAT/G POL/PAR DIPLOM ATTIT PERCEPT ALL/VALS ...POLICY INT/LAW JURID CONCPT TIME/SEQ 20 TREATY. PAGE 159 A3233 — STRUCT LEGIT FRANCE

C62

BACON F.,"OF THE TRUE GREATNESS OF KINGDOMS AND ESTATES" (1612) IN F. BACON, ESSAYS." ELITES FORCES DOMIN EDU/PROP LEGIT...POLICY GEN/LAWS 16/17 TREATY. PAGE 10 A0200 — WAR PWR DIPLOM CONSTN

B63

BOWETT D.W.,THE LAW OF INTERNATIONAL INSTITUTIONS. WOR+45 WOR-45 CONSTN DELIB/GP EX/STRUC JUDGE EDU/PROP LEGIT CT/SYS EXEC ROUTINE RIGID/FLEX ORD/FREE PWR...JURID CONCPT ORG/CHARTS GEN/METH LEAGUE/NAT OAS OEEC 20 UN. PAGE 17 A0354 — INT/ORG ADJUD DIPLOM

B63

ELIAS T.O.,GOVERNMENT AND POLITICS IN AFRICA. CONSTN CULTURE SOCIETY NAT/G POL/PAR DIPLOM REPRESENT PERSON...SOC TREND BIBLIOG 4/20. PAGE 41 A0837 — AFR NAT/LISM COLONIAL LAW

B63

HINSLEY F.H.,POWER AND THE PURSUIT OF PEACE. WOR+45 WOR-45 PLAN RIGID/FLEX ALL/VALS ALL/IDEOS...POLICY DECISION INT/LAW 12/20 ROUSSEAU/J KANT/I BENTHAM/J LEAGUE/NAT. PAGE 65 A1338 — DIPLOM CONSTN PEACE COERCE

B63

JENNINGS W.I.,DEMOCRACY IN AFRICA. UK CULTURE STRUCT ECO/UNDEV DIPLOM COLONIAL GP/REL ADJUST NAT/LISM ORD/FREE...GOV/COMP 20 THIRD/WRLD. PAGE 74 A1512 — PROB/SOLV AFR CONSTN POPULISM

B63

JUDD P.,AFRICAN INDEPENDENCE: THE EXPLODING EMERGENCE OF THE NEW AFRICAN NATIONS. AFR UK LAW CONSTN CULTURE KIN DIPLOM ATTIT...CHARTS BIBLIOG 20 UN DEGAULLE/C NEGRO THIRD/WRLD. PAGE 75 A1542 — ORD/FREE POLICY DOMIN LOC/G

B63

LAFEBER W.,THE NEW EMPIRE: AN INTERPRETATION OF AMERICAN EXPANSION, 1860-1898. USA-45 CONSTN NAT/LISM SOVEREIGN...TREND BIBLIOG 19/20. PAGE 84 A1711 — INDUS NAT/G DIPLOM CAP/ISM

B63

LANOUE G.R.,A BIBLIOGRAPHY OF DOCTORAL DISSERTATIONS ON POLITICS AND RELIGION. USA+45 USA-45 CONSTN PROVS DIPLOM CT/SYS MORAL...POLICY JURID CONCPT 20. PAGE 84 A1728 — BIBLIOG NAT/G LOC/G SECT

B63

LIVNEH E.,ISRAEL LEGAL BIBLIOGRAPHY IN EUROPEAN LANGUAGES. ISRAEL LOC/G JUDGE TAX...INT/LAW 20. PAGE 90 A1846 — BIBLIOG LAW NAT/G CONSTN

B63

MANSERGH N.,DOCUMENTS AND SPEECHES ON COMMONWEALTH AFFAIRS 1952-1962. CANADA INDIA PAKISTAN UK CONSTN FORCES ECO/TAC EDU/PROP COLONIAL DETER WAR ORD/FREE SOVEREIGN...POLICY 20 AUSTRAL. PAGE 94 A1932 — BIBLIOG/A FEDERAL INT/TRADE DIPLOM

B63

MAYNE R.,THE COMMUNITY OF EUROPE. UK CONSTN NAT/G CONSULT DELIB/GP CREATE PLAN ECO/TAC LEGIT ADMIN ROUTINE ORD/FREE PWR WEALTH...CONCPT TIME/SEQ EEC EURATOM 20. PAGE 97 A1985 — EUR+WWI INT/ORG REGION

B63

ROBERTSON A.H.,HUMAN RIGHTS IN EUROPE. CONSTN SOCIETY INT/ORG NAT/G VOL/ASSN DELIB/GP ACT/RES PLAN ADJUD REGION ROUTINE ATTIT LOVE ORD/FREE RESPECT...JURID SOC CONCPT SOC/EXP UN 20. PAGE 122 A2498 — EUR+WWI PERSON

B63

WALKER A.A.,OFFICIAL PUBLICATIONS OF SIERRA LEONE AND GAMBIA. GAMBIA SIER/LEONE UK LAW CONSTN LEGIS PLAN BUDGET DIPLOM...SOC SAMP CON/ANAL 20. PAGE 160 A3262 — BIBLIOG NAT/G COLONIAL ADMIN

B63

WILCOX W.A.,PAKISTAN; THE CONSOLIDATION OF A NATION. INDIA PAKISTAN CONSTN SECT PROB/SOLV COLONIAL PARTIC GP/REL FEDERAL...POLICY 19/20. PAGE 164 A3348 — NAT/LISM ECO/UNDEV DIPLOM STRUCT

L63

LISSITZYN O.J.,"INTERNATIONAL LAW IN A DIVIDED WORLD." FUT WOR+45 CONSTN CULTURE ECO/DEV ECO/UNDEV DIST/IND NAT/G FORCES ECO/TAC LEGIT ADJUD ADMIN COERCE ATTIT HEALTH MORAL ORD/FREE PWR RESPECT WEALTH VAL/FREE. PAGE 90 A1841 — INT/ORG LAW

L63

PADELFORD N.J.,"FINANCIAL CRISIS AND THE UNITED NATIONS." FUT USSR WOR+45 LAW CONSTN FINAN INT/ORG DELIB/GP FORCES PLAN BUDGET DIPLOM COST WEALTH ...STAT CHARTS UN CONGO 20. PAGE 113 A2311 — CREATE ECO/TAC

S63

BECHHOEFER B.G.,"UNITED NATIONS PROCEDURES IN CASE OF VIOLATIONS OF DISARMAMENT AGREEMENTS." COM USA+45 USSR LAW CONSTN NAT/G EX/STRUC FORCES LEGIS BAL/PWR EDU/PROP CT/SYS ARMS/CONT ORD/FREE PWR ...POLICY STERTYP UN VAL/FREE 20. PAGE 12 A0245 — INT/ORG DELIB/GP

S63

CAHIER P.,"LE DROIT INTERNE DES ORGANISATIONS INTERNATIONALES." UNIV CONSTN SOCIETY ECO/DEV R+D NAT/G TOP/EX LEGIT ATTIT PERCEPT...TIME/SEQ 19/20. PAGE 23 A0464 — INT/ORG JURID DIPLOM INT/LAW

S63

GROSS F.,"THE US NATIONAL INTEREST AND THE UN." FUT CONSTN NAT/G DELIB/GP CREATE DIPLOM RIGID/FLEX ORD/FREE...CONCPT GEN/LAWS 20 UN. PAGE 57 A1172 — USA+45 INT/ORG PEACE

S63
MURRAY J.N.,"UNITED NATIONS PEACE-KEEPING AND PROBLEMS OF POLITICAL CONTROL." FUT WOR+45 CONSTN DELIB/GP FORCES TOP/EX ACT/RES CREATE LEGIT PEACE PWR...METH/CNCPT CONGO UN 20. PAGE 106 A2182 INT/ORG ORD/FREE

S63
NICHOLAS H.G.,"UN PEACE FORCES AND THE CHANGING GLOBE: THE LESSONS OF SUEZ AND CONGO." FUT WOR+45 CONSTN INT/ORG CONSULT DELIB/GP TOP/EX CREATE DIPLOM DOMIN LEGIT COERCE WAR PERSON RIGID/FLEX PWR UN SUEZ CONGO UNEF 20. PAGE 109 A2229 ACT/RES FORCES

S63
WYZNER E.,"NIEKTORE ASPEKTY PRAWNE FINANSOWANIA OPERACJI ONZ W KONGO I NA BEIZKIM WSCHODZIE." S/ASIA CONSTN FINAN INT/ORG TOP/EX...TIME/SEQ UN 20 CONGRESS. PAGE 168 A3426 FORCES JURID DIPLOM

C63
ATTIA G.E.O.,"LES FORCES ARMEES DES NATIONS UNIES EN COREE ET AU MOYENORIENT." KOREA CONSTN DELIB/GP LEGIS PWR...IDEA/COMP NAT/COMP BIBLIOG UN SUEZ. PAGE 10 A0194 FORCES NAT/G INT/LAW

B64
APTER D.E.,IDEOLOGY AND DISCONTENT. FUT WOR+45 CONSTN CULTURE INTELL SOCIETY STRUCT INT/ORG NAT/G DELIB/GP LEGIS CREATE PLAN TEC/DEV EDU/PROP EXEC PERCEPT PERSON RIGID/FLEX ALL/VALS...POLICY TOT/POP. PAGE 8 A0171 ACT/RES ATTIT

B64
DE SMITH S.A.,THE NEW COMMONWEALTH AND ITS CONSTITUTIONS. AFR CYPRUS PAKISTAN S/ASIA INT/ORG NAT/G LEGIS LEGIT RIGID/FLEX PWR...CONCPT TIME/SEQ CMN/WLTH 20. PAGE 35 A0713 EX/STRUC CONSTN SOVEREIGN

B64
GESELLSCHAFT RECHTSVERGLEICH,BIBLIOGRAPHIE DES DEUTSCHEN RECHTS (BIBLIOGRAPHY OF GERMAN LAW, TRANS. BY COURTLAND PETERSON). GERMANY FINAN INDUS LABOR SECT FORCES CT/SYS PARL/PROC CRIME...INT/LAW SOC NAT/COMP 20. PAGE 52 A1066 BIBLIOG/A JURID CONSTN ADMIN

B64
GJUPANOVIC H.,LEGAL SOURCES AND BIBLIOGRAPHY OF YUGOSLAVIA. COM YUGOSLAVIA LAW LEGIS DIPLOM ADMIN PARL/PROC REGION CRIME CENTRAL 20. PAGE 53 A1078 BIBLIOG/A JURID CONSTN ADJUD

B64
GREAT BRITAIN CENTRAL OFF INF,CONSTITUTIONAL DEVELOPMENT IN THE COMMONWEALTH. VOL/ASSN PLAN DIPLOM COLONIAL INGP/REL NAT/LISM ORD/FREE PWR 17/20 CMN/WLTH. PAGE 55 A1135 REGION CONSTN NAT/G SOVEREIGN

B64
LOCKHART W.B.,CASES AND MATERIALS ON CONSTITUTIONAL RIGHTS AND LIBERTIES. USA+45 FORCES LEGIS DIPLOM PRESS CONTROL CRIME WAR PWR...AUD/VIS T WORSHIP 20 NEGRO. PAGE 90 A1849 ORD/FREE CONSTN NAT/G

B64
MORGAN T.,GOLDWATER EITHER/OR; A SELF-PORTRAIT BASED UPON HIS OWN WORDS. USA+45 CONSTN AGRI LABOR DIPLOM RACE/REL WEALTH POPULISM...POLICY MAJORIT 20 GOLDWATR/B REPUBLICAN. PAGE 104 A2131 LEAD POL/PAR CHOOSE ATTIT

B64
NEWBURY C.W.,THE WEST AFRICAN COMMONWEALTH. CONSTN INTELL ECO/UNDEV VOL/ASSN CHIEF DELIB/GP LEGIS INT/TRADE COLONIAL FEDERAL ATTIT 20 COMMONWLTH AFRICA/W. PAGE 108 A2223 INT/ORG SOVEREIGN GOV/REL AFR

B64
RICHARDSON I.L.,BIBLIOGRAFIA BRASILEIRA DE ADMINISTRACAO PUBLICA E ASSUNTOS CORRELATOS. BRAZIL CONSTN FINAN LOC/G NAT/G POL/PAR PLAN DIPLOM RECEIVE ATTIT...METH 20. PAGE 121 A2474 BIBLIOG MGT ADMIN LAW

B64
SINGH N.,THE DEFENCE MECHANISM OF THE MODERN STATE. COM UK USA+45 CONSTN INT/ORG NUC/PWR WAR INGP/REL ROLE 20 DEPT/DEFEN COMMONWLTH. PAGE 134 A2735 FORCES TOP/EX NAT/G CIVMIL/REL

B64
STOESSINGER J.G.,FINANCING THE UNITED NATIONS SYSTEM. FUT WOR+45 CONSTN NAT/G VOL/ASSN DELIB/GP EX/STRUC ECO/TAC LEGIT CT/SYS PWR WEALTH...STAT TIME/SEQ TREND CHARTS VAL/FREE. PAGE 138 A2830 FINAN INT/ORG

B64
TURNER M.C.,LIBROS EN VENTA EN HISPANOAMERICA Y ESPANA. SPAIN LAW CONSTN CULTURE ADMIN LEAD...HUM SOC 20. PAGE 146 A2983 BIBLIOG L/A+17C NAT/G DIPLOM

B64
UN PUB. INFORM. ORGAN.,EVERY MAN'S UNITED NATIONS. UNIV WOR+45 CONSTN CULTURE SOCIETY ECO/DEV ECO/UNDEV NAT/G ACT/RES PLAN ECO/TAC INT/TRADE EDU/PROP LEGIT PEACE ATTIT ALL/VALS...POLICY HUM INT/LAW CONCPT CHARTS UN TOT/POP 20. PAGE 147 A3004 INT/ORG ROUTINE

B64
UNITED ARAB REPUBLIC,TOWARDS THE SECOND AFRICAN SUMMIT ASSEMBLY. AFR UAR CONSTN VOL/ASSN CHIEF PLAN DIPLOM AGREE 20 NASSER/G AFR/STATES. PAGE 148 A3030 CONFER DELIB/GP INT/ORG POLICY

B64
VECCHIO G.D.,L'ETAT ET LE DROIT. ITALY CONSTN EX/STRUC LEGIS DIPLOM CT/SYS...JURID 20 UN. PAGE 158 A3225 NAT/G SOVEREIGN CONCPT INT/LAW

L64
CARNEGIE ENDOWMENT INT. PEACE,"POLITICAL QUESTIONS (ISSUES BEFORE THE NINETEENTH GENERAL ASSEMBLY)." SPACE WOR+45 CONSTN FINAN NAT/G CONSULT DELIB/GP FORCES LEGIS TEC/DEV EDU/PROP LEGIT ARMS/CONT COERCE NUC/PWR ATTIT ALL/VALS...CONCPT OBS UN COLD/WAR 20. PAGE 24 A0490 INT/ORG PEACE

L64
CLAUDE I.,"THE OAS, THE UN, AND THE UNITED STATES." L/A+17C USA+45 CONSTN NAT/G DELIB/GP DOMIN EDU/PROP LEGIT REGION COERCE ORD/FREE PWR...TIME/SEQ TREND STERTYP OAS UN 20. PAGE 27 A0546 INT/ORG POLICY

L64
MANZER R.A.,"THE UNITED NATIONS SPECIAL FUND." WOR+45 CONSTN ECO/UNDEV NAT/G TOP/EX LEGIT WEALTH ...CHARTS UN 20. PAGE 94 A1936 FINAN INT/ORG

L64
MILLIS W.,"THE DEMILITARIZED WORLD." COM USA+45 USSR WOR+45 CONSTN NAT/G EX/STRUC PLAN LEGIT ATTIT DRIVE...CONCPT TIME/SEQ STERTYP TOT/POP COLD/WAR 20. PAGE 102 A2085 FUT INT/ORG BAL/PWR PEACE

L64
WORLD PEACE FOUNDATION,"INTERNATIONAL ORGANIZATIONS: SUMMARY OF ACTIVITIES." INDIA PAKISTAN TURKEY WOR+45 CONSTN CONSULT EX/STRUC ECO/TAC EDU/PROP LEGIT ORD/FREE...JURID SOC UN 20 CYPRESS. PAGE 167 A3397 INT/ORG ROUTINE

S64
CARNEGIE ENDOWMENT INT. PEACE,"HUMAN RIGHTS (ISSUES BEFORE THE NINETEENTH GENERAL ASSEMBLY)." AFR WOR+45 LAW CONSTN NAT/G EDU/PROP GP/REL DISCRIM PEACE ATTIT MORAL ORD/FREE...INT/LAW PSY CONCPT RECORD UN 20. PAGE 24 A0492 INT/ORG PERSON RACE/REL

S64
CARNEGIE ENDOWMENT INT. PEACE,"LEGAL QUESTIONS (ISSUES BEFORE THE NINETEENTH GENERAL ASSEMBLY)." WOR+45 CONSTN NAT/G DELIB/GP ADJUD PEACE MORAL ORD/FREE...RECORD UN 20 TREATY. PAGE 24 A0494 INT/ORG LAW INT/LAW

S64
KHAN M.Z.,"THE PRESIDENT OF THE GENERAL ASSEMBLY." WOR+45 CONSTN DELIB/GP EDU/PROP LEGIT ROUTINE PWR RESPECT SKILL...DECISION SOC BIOG TREND UN 20. PAGE 78 A1609 INT/ORG TOP/EX

S64
LEVI W.,"CHINA AND THE UNITED NATIONS." ASIA CHINA CHINA/COM WOR+45 WOR-45 CONSTN NAT/G DELIB/GP EX/STRUC FORCES ACT/RES EDU/PROP PWR...POLICY RECORD TIME/SEQ GEN/LAWS UN COLD/WAR 20. PAGE 88 A1794 INT/ORG ATTIT NAT/LISM

S64
VANDENBOSCH A.,"THE SMALL STATES IN INTERNATIONAL POLITICS AND ORGANIZATION." EUR+WWI MOD/EUR WOR+45 WOR-45 CONSTN DELIB/GP COERCE ORD/FREE PWR ...TIME/SEQ GEN/LAWS VAL/FREE LEAGUE/NAT UN 19/20. PAGE 158 A3219 NAT/G INT/ORG DIPLOM

B65
MILLER J.D.B.,THE COMMONWEALTH IN THE WORLD (3RD ED.). CONSTN COLONIAL PWR SOVEREIGN 20 CMN/WLTH. PAGE 101 A2077 VOL/ASSN INT/ORG INGP/REL DIPLOM

B65
MOSTECKY V.,SOVIET LEGAL BIBLIOGRAPHY. USSR LEGIS PRESS WRITING CONFER ADJUD CT/SYS REV MARXISM ...INT/LAW JURID DICTIONARY 20. PAGE 105 A2155 BIBLIOG/A LAW COM CONSTN

B65
NATIONAL BOOK CENTRE PAKISTAN,BOOKS ON PAKISTAN: A BIBLIOGRAPHY. PAKISTAN CULTURE DIPLOM ADMIN ATTIT ...MAJORIT SOC CONCPT 20. PAGE 107 A2201 BIBLIOG CONSTN S/ASIA NAT/G

B65
SOPER T.,EVOLVING COMMONWEALTH. AFR CANADA INDIA IRELAND UK LAW CONSTN POL/PAR DOMIN CONTROL WAR PWR ...AUD/VIS 18/20 COMMONWLTH OEEC. PAGE 135 A2769 INT/ORG COLONIAL VOL/ASSN

B65
VONGLAHN G.,LAW AMONG NATIONS: AN INTRODUCTION TO PUBLIC INTERNATIONAL LAW. UNIV WOR+45 LAW INT/ORG NAT/G LEGIT EXEC RIGID/FLEX...CONCPT TIME/SEQ GEN/LAWS UN TOT/POP 20. PAGE 160 A3253 CONSTN JURID INT/LAW

B65
WEIL G.L.,A HANDBOOK ON THE EUROPEAN ECONOMIC COMMUNITY. BELGIUM EUR+WWI FRANCE GERMANY/W ITALY CONSTN ECO/DEV CREATE PARTIC GP/REL...DECISION MGT CHARTS 20 EEC. PAGE 162 A3299 INT/TRADE INT/ORG TEC/DEV INT/LAW

L65
RUBIN A.P.,"UNITED STATES CONTEMPORARY PRACTICE RELATING TO INTERNATIONAL LAW." USA+45 WOR+45 CONSTN INT/ORG NAT/G DELIB/GP EX/STRUC DIPLOM DOMIN CT/SYS ROUTINE ORD/FREE...CONCPT COLD/WAR 20. PAGE 125 A2558 LAW LEGIT INT/LAW

S65
STEIN E.,"TOWARD SUPREMACY OF TREATY-CONSTITUTION BY JUDICIAL FIAT: ON THE MARGIN OF THE COSTA CASE." ADJUD CONSTN

EUR+WWI ITALY WOR+45 INT/ORG NAT/G LEGIT REGION NAT/LISM PWR...JURID CONCPT TREND TOT/POP VAL/FREE 20. PAGE 138 A2816 [SOVEREIGN INT/LAW]

B66 AMERICAN JOURNAL COMP LAW,THE AMERICAN JOURNAL OF COMPARATIVE LAW READER. EUR+WWI USA+45 USA-45 LAW CONSTN LOC/G MUNIC NAT/G DIPLOM...ANTHOL 20 SUPREME/CT EURCT/JUST. PAGE 7 A0151 [IDEA/COMP JURID INT/LAW CT/SYS]

B66 CRAIG G.A.,WAR, POLITICS, AND DIPLOMACY. PRUSSIA CONSTN FORCES CIVMIL/REL TOTALISM PWR 19/20 BISMARCK/O DULLES/JF NAPOLEON/B. PAGE 32 A0654 [WAR DIPLOM BAL/PWR]

B66 GUPTA S.,KASHMIR - A STUDY IN INDIA-PAKISTAN RELATIONS. INDIA KASHMIR PAKISTAN CONSTN INT/ORG REV RACE/REL NAT/LISM 20 UN MUSLIM/LG. PAGE 58 A1194 [DIPLOM GP/REL SOVEREIGN WAR]

B66 HOLT R.T.,THE POLITICAL BASIS OF ECONOMIC DEVELOPMENT. STRATA STRUCT NAT/G DIPLOM ADMIN...SOC NAT/COMP BIBLIOG 20. PAGE 67 A1376 [ECO/TAC GOV/COMP CONSTN EX/STRUC]

B66 KINDLEBERGER C.P.,EUROPE AND THE DOLLAR. EUR+WWI FRANCE GERMANY/W USA+45 CONSTN INT/ORG DIPLOM INT/TRADE...ANTHOL 20 GOLD/STAND. PAGE 79 A1623 [BAL/PAY BUDGET FINAN ECO/DEV]

B66 LEIGH M.B.,CHECK LIST OF HOLDINGS ON BORNEO IN THE CORNELL UNIVERSITY LIBRARIES (PAMPHLET). BORNEO MALAYSIA LAW CONSTN GP/REL SOC. PAGE 86 A1769 [BIBLIOG S/ASIA DIPLOM NAT/G]

B66 LENGYEL E.,AFRICA: PAST, PRESENT, AND FUTURE. FUT SOUTH/AFR COLONIAL RACE/REL SOVEREIGN...GEOG AUD/VIS CHARTS T 20 CONGO/LEOP NEGRO. PAGE 87 A1771 [AFR CONSTN ECO/UNDEV]

B66 MCINTYRE W.D.,COLONIES INTO COMMONWEALTH. UK CONSTN VOL/ASSN DOMIN CONTROL...BIBLIOG 18/20 CMN/WLTH. PAGE 98 A2012 [DIPLOM INT/ORG COLONIAL SOVEREIGN]

B66 MULLER C.F.J.,A SELECT BIBLIOGRAPHY OF SOUTH AFRICAN HISTORY; A GUIDE FOR HISTORICAL RESEARCH. SOUTH/AFR UK LAW CONSTN SOCIETY STRUCT AGRI SECT DIPLOM COLONIAL LEAD RACE/REL...POLICY 17/20 NEGRO. PAGE 106 A2167 [BIBLIOG AFR NAT/G]

B66 NEUMANN R.G.,THE GOVERNMENT OF THE GERMAN FEDERAL REPUBLIC. EUR+WWI GERMANY/W LOC/G EX/STRUC LEGIS CT/SYS INGP/REL PWR...BIBLIOG 20 ADENAUER/K. PAGE 108 A2222 [NAT/G POL/PAR DIPLOM CONSTN]

B66 SPEARS E.L.,TWO MEN WHO SAVED FRANCE: PETAIN AND DE GAULLE. FRANCE CONSTN FORCES DIPLOM WAR PERSON 20 WWI PETAIN/HP DEGAULLE/C. PAGE 135 A2773 [BIOG LEAD CHIEF NAT/G]

B66 SPINELLI A.,THE EUROCRATS; CONFLICT AND CRISIS IN THE EUROPEAN COMMUNITY (TRANS. BY C. GROVE HAINES). EUR+WWI MARKET POL/PAR ECO/TAC PARL/PROC EEC OEEC ECSC EURATOM. PAGE 136 A2789 [INT/ORG INGP/REL CONSTN ADMIN]

B66 VIEN N.C.,SEEKING THE TRUTH. FRANCE VIETNAM AGRI ADMIN WAR...BIOG 20 BAO/DAI INTERVENT. PAGE 159 A3231 [NAT/G CONSULT CONSTN]

B66 WILSON H.A.,THE IMPERIAL POLICY OF SIR ROBERT BORDEN. CANADA UK ELITES INT/ORG VOL/ASSN CONTROL LEAD WAR ROLE 20 CMN/WLTH BORDEN/R. PAGE 165 A3360 [INGP/REL COLONIAL CONSTN CHIEF]

S66 CHIU H.,"COMMUNIST CHINA'S ATTITUDE TOWARD INTERNATIONAL LAW" CHINA/COM USSR LAW CONSTN DIPLOM GP/REL 20 LENIN/VI. PAGE 26 A0532 [INT/LAW MARXISM CONCPT IDEA/COMP]

B67 CECIL L.,ALBERT BALLIN; BUSINESS AND POLITICS IN IMPERIAL GERMANY 1888-1918. GERMANY UK INT/TRADE LEAD WAR PERS/REL ADJUST PWR WEALTH...MGT BIBLIOG 19/20. PAGE 25 A0510 [DIPLOM CONSTN ECO/DEV TOP/EX]

B67 CHO S.S.,KOREA IN WORLD POLITICS 1940-1950; AN EVALUATION OF AMERICAN RESPONSIBILITY. KOREA USA+45 USSR CONSTN INT/ORG NAT/G FORCES FOR/AID ANOMIE SUPEGO MARXISM...DECISION BIBLIOG 20. PAGE 26 A0533 [POLICY DIPLOM PROB/SOLV WAR]

B67 DOSSICK J.J.,DOCTORAL RESEARCH ON PUERTO RICO AND PUERTO RICANS. PUERT/RICO USA+45 USA-45 ADMIN 20. PAGE 38 A0776 [BIBLIOG CONSTN POL/PAR DIPLOM]

B67 FRASER-TYTLER W.K.,AFGHANISTAN: A STUDY OF POLITICAL DEVELOPMENTS IN CENTRAL AND SOUTHERN ASIA (3RD ED.). AFGHANISTN INDIA KIN FOR/AID PWR ...BIBLIOG. PAGE 48 A0990 [DIPLOM NAT/G CONSTN GEOG]

B67 JAGAN C.,THE WEST ON TRIAL. GUYANA CONSTN ECO/UNDEV DIPLOM COERCE PWR SOVEREIGN...BIOG 20. PAGE 73 A1490 [SOCISM CREATE PLAN COLONIAL]

B67 PIKE F.B.,FREEDOM AND REFORM IN LATIN AMERICA. BRAZIL URUGUAY CONSTN CULTURE SECT DIPLOM EDU/PROP PARTIC DRIVE ALL/VALS CATHISM...GEOG ANTHOL BIBLIOG REFORMERS BOLIV. PAGE 116 A2379 [L/A+17C ORD/FREE ECO/UNDEV REV]

B67 SABLE M.H.,A GUIDE TO LATIN AMERICAN STUDIES (2 VOLS). CONSTN FINAN INT/ORG LABOR MUNIC POL/PAR FORCES CAP/ISM FOR/AID ADMIN MARXISM SOCISM OAS. PAGE 126 A2584 [BIBLIOG/A L/A+17C DIPLOM NAT/LISM]

B67 SAYEED K.B.,THE POLITICAL SYSTEM OF PAKISTAN. PAKISTAN DIPLOM REGION CHOOSE ORD/FREE...BIBLIOG 20. PAGE 127 A2609 [NAT/G POL/PAR CONSTN SECT]

B67 UNIVERSAL REFERENCE SYSTEM,LAW, JURISPRUDENCE, AND JUDICIAL PROCESS (VOLUME VII). WOR+45 WOR-45 CONSTN NAT/G LEGIS JUDGE CT/SYS...INT/LAW COMPUT/IR GEN/METH METH. PAGE 149 A3044 [BIBLIOG/A LAW JURID ADJUD]

B67 WATERS M.,THE UNITED NATIONS* INTERNATIONAL ORGANIZATION AND ADMINISTRATION. WOR+45 EX/STRUC FORCES DIPLOM LEAD REGION ARMS/CONT REPRESENT INGP/REL ROLE...METH/COMP ANTHOL 20 UN LEAGUE/NAT. PAGE 162 A3291 [CONSTN INT/ORG ADMIN ADJUD]

L67 CAHIERS P.,"LE RECOURS EN CONSTATATION DE MANQUEMENTS DES ETATS MEMBRES DEVANT LA COUR DES COMMUNAUTES EUROPEENNES." LAW PROB/SOLV DIPLOM ADMIN CT/SYS SANCTION ATTIT...POLICY DECISION JURID ECSC EEC. PAGE 23 A0465 [INT/ORG CONSTN ROUTINE ADJUD]

L67 GOLD J.,"INTERPRETATION BY THE INTERNATIONAL MONETARY FUND OF ITS ARTICLES OF AGREEMENT." INT/TRADE ADJUD ATTIT...POLICY JURID. PAGE 53 A1089 [CONSTN INT/ORG LAW DIPLOM]

L67 KOMESAR N.K.,"PRESIDENTIAL AMENDMENT & TERMINATION OF TREATIES* THE CASE OF THE WARSAW CONVENTION." POLAND USA+45 NAT/G CHIEF PROB/SOLV DIPLOM PWR 20 CONGRESS. PAGE 81 A1669 [TOP/EX LEGIS CONSTN LICENSE]

S67 BLUM Y.Z.,"INDONESIA'S RETURN TO THE UNITED NATIONS." INDONESIA ADJUD SANCTION REPRESENT ...JURID 20 UN. PAGE 16 A0324 [CONSTN LAW DIPLOM INT/ORG]

S67 ECKHARDT A.R.,"SILENCE IN THE CHURCHES." ISRAEL WOR+45 CONSTN GP/REL DISCRIM DRIVE JEWS. PAGE 40 A0820 [SECT ATTIT DIPLOM ISLAM]

S67 FABREGA J.,"ANTECEDENTES EXTRANJEROS EN LA CONSTITUCION PANAMENA." CUBA L/A+17C PANAMA URUGUAY EX/STRUC LEGIS DIPLOM ORD/FREE 19/20 COLOMB MEXIC/AMER. PAGE 43 A0882 [CONSTN JURID NAT/G PARL/PROC]

S67 HEATH D.B.,"BOLIVIA UNDER BARRIENTOS." L/A+17C NAT/G CHIEF DIPLOM ECO/TAC...POLICY 20 BOLIV. PAGE 64 A1306 [ECO/UNDEV POL/PAR REV CONSTN]

S67 MANN F.A.,"THE BRETTON WOODS AGREEMENT IN THE ENGLISH COURTS." UK JUDGE ADJUD CT/SYS...JURID PREDICT CON/ANAL 20. PAGE 94 A1923 [LAW INT/LAW CONSTN]

S67 OLIVIER G.,"ASPECTS JURIDIQUES DE L'ADOPTION DU TRAITE CECA A LA CRISE CHARBONNIERE (SUITE ET FIN)" LAW DIST/IND PLAN DIPLOM RATION PRICE ADMIN COST DEMAND...POLICY CON/ANAL ECSC TREATY. PAGE 112 A2288 [INT/TRADE INT/ORG EXTR/IND CONSTN]

S67 ZARTMAN I.W.,"AFRICA AS A SUBORDINATE STATE SYSTEM IN INTERNATIONAL RELATIONS." LAW BAL/PWR REGION CENTRAL...GEOG 20. PAGE 169 A3447 [DIPLOM INT/ORG CONSTN AFR]

B90 HOSMAR J.K.,A SHORT HISTORY OF ANGLO-SAXON FREEDOM. UK USA-45 ROMAN/EMP NAT/G EX/STRUC LEGIS COLONIAL REV NAT/LISM POPULISM PARLIAMENT ANGLO/SAX MAGNA/CART. PAGE 68 A1394 [CONSTN ORD/FREE DIPLOM PARL/PROC]

CONSTN/CNV....CONSTITUTIONAL CONVENTION

CONSTRUC....CONSTRUCTION INDUSTRY

N KYRIAK T.E.,SOVIET UNION: BIBLIOGRAPHY INDEX TO US JPRS RESEARCH TRANSLATIONS. USSR ECO/DEV AGRI COM/IND CONSTRUC DIST/IND EXTR/IND PROC/MFG R+D [BIBLIOG/A INDUS MARXISM]

INT/TRADE...SOC 20. PAGE 83 A1703
PRESS

B50
COUNCIL BRITISH NATIONAL BIB,BRITISH NATIONAL BIBLIOGRAPHY. UK AGRI CONSTRUC PERF/ART POL/PAR SECT CREATE INT/TRADE LEAD...HUM JURID PHIL/SCI 20. PAGE 31 A0637
BIBLIOG/A NAT/G TEC/DEV DIPLOM

B53
SHIRATO I.,JAPANESE SOURCES ON THE HISTORY OF THE CHINESE COMMUNIST MOVEMENT (PAMPHLET). CHINA/COM USSR CONSTRUC NAT/G POL/PAR FORCES DIPLOM DOMIN EDU/PROP CONTROL WAR TOTALISM SOCISM 20. PAGE 132 A2702
BIBLIOG/A MARXISM ECO/UNDEV

B55
OECD,MARSHALL PLAN IN TURKEY. TURKEY USA+45 COM/IND CONSTRUC SERV/IND FORCES BUDGET...STAT 20 MARSHL/PLN. PAGE 111 A2277
FOR/AID ECO/UNDEV AGRI INDUS

B58
US HOUSE COMM GOVT OPERATIONS,HEARINGS BEFORE A SUBCOMMITTEE OF THE COMMITTEE ON GOVERNMENT OPERATIONS. CAMBODIA PHILIPPINE USA+45 CONSTRUC TEC/DEV ADMIN CONTROL WEAPON EFFICIENCY HOUSE/REP. PAGE 154 A3135
FOR/AID DIPLOM ORD/FREE ECO/UNDEV

B66
US HOUSE COMM GOVT OPERATIONS,AN INVESTIGATION OF THE US ECONOMIC AND MILITARY ASSISTANCE PROGRAMS IN VIETNAM. USA+45 VIETNAM/S SOCIETY CONSTRUC FINAN FORCES BUDGET INT/TRADE PEACE HEALTH...MGT HOUSE/REP AID. PAGE 154 A3139
FOR/AID ECO/UNDEV WAR INSPECT

CONSTRUCTION INDUSTRY....SEE CONSTRUC

CONSULT....CONSULTANTS

B
UN DEPARTMENT SOCIAL AFFAIRS,SOCIAL WELFARE INFORMATION SERIES: CURRENT LITERATURE AND NATIONAL CONFERENCES. WOR+45 INDUS SERV/IND INT/ORG CONSULT ACT/RES WEALTH...HEAL UN. PAGE 147 A2997
BIBLIOG/A SOC/WK DIPLOM ADMIN

B05
GRIFFIN A.P.C.,LIST OF REFERENCES ON THE US CONSULAR SERVICE (PAMPHLET). FRANCE GERMANY SPAIN UK USA-45 WOR-45 OP/RES DOMIN ADMIN FEEDBACK ROUTINE GOV/REL...DECISION 19. PAGE 56 A1153
BIBLIOG/A NAT/G DIPLOM CONSULT

S17
ROOT E.,"THE EFFECT OF DEMOCRACY ON INTERNATIONAL LAW." USA-45 WOR-45 INTELL SOCIETY INT/ORG NAT/G CONSULT ACT/RES CREATE PLAN EDU/PROP PEACE SKILL ...CONCPT METH/CNCPT OBS 20. PAGE 123 A2523
LEGIS JURID INT/LAW

B19
DE CALLIERES F.,THE PRACTICE OF DIPLOMACY. MOD/EUR INT/ORG NAT/G DELIB/GP LEGIS TOP/EX DOMIN ATTIT KNOWL LEAGUE/NAT 20. PAGE 34 A0699
CONSULT ACT/RES DIPLOM INT/LAW

B22
WRIGHT Q.,THE CONTROL OF AMERICAN FOREIGN RELATIONS. USA-45 WOR-45 CONSTN INT/ORG CONSULT LEGIS LEGIT ROUTINE ORD/FREE PWR...POLICY JURID CONCPT METH/CNCPT RECORD LEAGUE/NAT 20. PAGE 167 A3402
NAT/G EXEC DIPLOM

B24
GENTILI A.,DE LEGATIONIBUS. CHRIST-17C NAT/G SECT CONSULT LEGIT...POLICY CATH JURID CONCPT MYTH. PAGE 52 A1058
DIPLOM INT/LAW INT/ORG LAW

B31
STOWELL E.C.,INTERNATIONAL LAW. FUT UNIV WOR-45 SOCIETY CONSULT EX/STRUC FORCES ACT/RES PLAN DIPLOM EDU/PROP LEGIT DISPL PWR SKILL...POLICY CONCPT OBS TREND TOT/POP 20. PAGE 139 A2839
INT/ORG ROUTINE INT/LAW

B32
WRIGHT Q.,GOLD AND MONETARY STABILIZATION. FUT USA-45 WOR-45 INTELL ECO/DEV INT/ORG NAT/G CONSULT PLAN ECO/TAC ADMIN ATTIT WEALTH...CONCPT TREND 20. PAGE 167 A3404
FINAN POLICY

B33
LANGER W.L.,FOREIGN AFFAIRS BIBLIOGRAPHY. WOR-45 INT/ORG CONSULT EDU/PROP ROUTINE NAT/LISM ATTIT SOVEREIGN...STAT RECORD GEN/METH LEAGUE/NAT TOT/POP. PAGE 84 A1725
KNOWL

B33
OHLIN B.,INTERREGIONAL AND INTERNATIONAL TRADE. USA-45 WOR-45 CULTURE FINAN MARKET CONSULT PLAN ECO/TAC ATTIT WEALTH...CONCPT MATH TOT/POP 20. PAGE 111 A2285
INT/ORG ECO/DEV INT/TRADE REGION

B38
WARE E.E.,THE STUDY OF INTERNATIONAL RELATIONS IN THE UNITED STATES. USA+45 USA-45 WOR-45 INTELL SERV/IND INT/ORG NAT/G PROF/ORG SECT CONSULT INT/TRADE EDU/PROP ARMS/CONT...CONCPT 20. PAGE 161 A3283
KNOWL DIPLOM

B39
MAXWELL B.W.,INTERNATIONAL RELATIONS. EUR+WWI WOR-45 NAT/G CONSULT DIPLOM LEGIT ADJUD NAT/LISM ATTIT ORD/FREE SOVEREIGN...JURID LEAGUE/NAT TOT/POP VAL/FREE 20. PAGE 97 A1981
INT/ORG

B40
CONOVER H.F.,A BRIEF LIST OF REFERENCES ON WESTERN HEMISPHERE DEFENSE (PAMPHLET). USA-45 NAT/G CONSULT DELIB/GP FORCES BAL/PWR CONFER DETER...PREDICT CON/ANAL 20. PAGE 29 A0591
BIBLIOG DIPLOM PLAN INT/ORG

B40
FULLER G.H.,A LIST OF BIBLIOGRAPHIES ON PROPAGANDA (PAMPHLET). MOD/EUR USA-45 CONSULT ACT/RES PRESS FEEDBACK TASK WAR ATTIT PWR...CON/ANAL METH/COMP 20. PAGE 50 A1020
BIBLIOG/A EDU/PROP DOMIN DIPLOM

B40
MIDDLEBUSH F.,ELEMENTS OF INTERNATIONAL RELATIONS. WOR-45 PROVS CONSULT EDU/PROP LEGIT WAR NAT/LISM ATTIT KNOWL MORAL ORD/FREE PWR...JURID LEAGUE/NAT TOT/POP VAL/FREE. PAGE 101 A2067
NAT/G INT/ORG PEACE DIPLOM

B41
BIRDSALL P.,VERSAILLES TWENTY YEARS AFTER. MOD/EUR POL/PAR CHIEF CONSULT FORCES LEGIS REPAR PEACE ORD/FREE...BIBLIOG 20 PRESIDENT TREATY. PAGE 14 A0290
DIPLOM NAT/LISM WAR

L42
SHOTWELL J.,"LESSON OF THE LAST WORLD WAR." EUR+WWI MOD/EUR USA-45 SOCIETY ECO/UNDEV INDUS VOL/ASSN CONSULT EX/STRUC CREATE CAP/ISM INT/TRADE DRIVE ALL/VALS...CONCPT NEW/IDEA SELF/OBS GEN/LAWS LEAGUE/NAT NAZI 20. PAGE 132 A2708
INT/ORG ORD/FREE

L44
HAILEY,"THE FUTURE OF COLONIAL PEOPLES." WOR-45 CONSTN CULTURE ECO/UNDEV AGRI MARKET INT/ORG NAT/G SECT CONSULT ECO/TAC LEGIT ADMIN NAT/LISM ALL/VALS ...SOC OBS TREND STERTYP CMN/WLTH LEAGUE/NAT PARLIAMENT 20. PAGE 59 A1218
PLAN CONCPT DIPLOM UK

L44
WRIGHT Q.,"THE US AND INTERNATIONAL AGREEMENTS." FUT USA-45 CONSTN INTELL INT/ORG LOC/G NAT/G CHIEF CONSULT EX/STRUC DIPLOM LEGIT DRIVE PERCEPT PWR ...CONCPT CONGRESS 20. PAGE 167 A3407
DELIB/GP TOP/EX PEACE

S44
WRIGHT Q.,"CONSTITUTIONAL PROCEDURES OF THE US FOR CARRYING OUT OBLIGATIONS FOR MILITARY SANCTIONS." EUR+WWI FUT USA-45 WOR-45 CONSTN INTELL NAT/G CONSULT EX/STRUC LEGIS ROUTINE DRIVE...POLICY JURID CONCPT OBS TREND TOT/POP 20. PAGE 167 A3406
TOP/EX FORCES INT/LAW WAR

B45
RANSHOFFEN-WERTHEIMER EF,THE INTERNATIONAL SECRETARIAT: A GREAT EXPERIMENT IN INTERNATIONAL ADMINISTRATION. EUR+WWI FUT CONSTN FACE/GP CONSULT DELIB/GP ACT/RES ADMIN ROUTINE PEACE ORD/FREE...MGT RECORD ORG/CHARTS LEAGUE/NAT WORK 20. PAGE 119 A2442
INT/ORG EXEC

S46
SILBERNER E.,"THE PROBLEM OF WAR IN NINETEENTH CENTURY ECONOMIC THOUGHT." EUR+WWI MOD/EUR UNIV LAW ECO/DEV ECO/UNDEV FINAN INDUS MARKET INT/ORG NAT/G CONSULT FORCES...CONCPT GEN/LAWS GEN/METH 19. PAGE 133 A2715
ATTIT ECO/TAC WAR

B47
GORDON D.L.,THE HIDDEN WEAPON: THE STORY OF ECONOMIC WARFARE. EUR+WWI USA-45 LAW FINAN INDUS NAT/G CONSULT FORCES PLAN DOMIN PWR WEALTH ...INT/LAW CONCPT OBS TOT/POP NAZI 20. PAGE 54 A1112
INT/ORG ECO/TAC INT/TRADE WAR

B47
KIRK G.,THE STUDY OF INTERNATIONAL RELATIONS. FUT USA-45 R+D ACADEM INT/ORG CONSULT DELIB/GP INT/TRADE EDU/PROP PEACE RIGID/FLEX KNOWL VAL/FREE 20. PAGE 80 A1632
USA+45 DIPLOM

L47
BRUNER J.S.,"TOWARD A COMMON GROUND-INTERNATIONAL SOCIAL SCIENCE." FUT WOR+45 INTELL R+D NAT/G VOL/ASSN CONSULT DELIB/GP ACT/RES CREATE PLAN TEC/DEV ATTIT ORD/FREE...PSY SOC CONCPT ANTHOL UNESCO 20. PAGE 20 A0410
INT/ORG KNOWL

L49
COMM. STUDY ORGAN. PEACE,"A TEN YEAR RECORD, 1939-1949." FUT WOR+45 LAW R+D CONSULT DELIB/GP CREATE LEGIT ROUTINE ORD/FREE...TIME/SEQ UN 20. PAGE 28 A0578
INT/ORG CONSTN PEACE

B50
ROSS A.,CONSTITUTION OF THE UNITED NATIONS. CONSTN CONSULT DELIB/GP ECO/TAC...INT/LAW JURID 20 UN LEAGUE/NAT. PAGE 124 A2540
PEACE DIPLOM ORD/FREE INT/ORG

S50
UNESCO,"MEETING ON UNIVERSITY TEACHING OF INTERNATIONAL RELATIONS." FUT WOR+45 R+D VOL/ASSN CONSULT PLAN EDU/PROP ATTIT...CONCPT TREND 20. PAGE 147 A3012
INT/ORG KNOWL DIPLOM

B51
MACLAURIN J.,THE UNITED NATIONS AND POWER POLITICS. WOR+45 CONSULT EDU/PROP LEGIT ADJUD EXEC MORAL ORD/FREE...HUM JURID CONCPT RECORD TIME/SEQ UN COLD/WAR 20. PAGE 93 A1896
INT/ORG ROUTINE

B51
PRICE D.K.,THE NEW DIMENSIONS OF DIPLOMACY: THE ORGANIZATION OF THE US GOVERNMENT FOR ITS NEW ROLE
DIPLOM GP/REL

IN WORLD AFFAIRS (PAMPHLET). USA+45 WOR+45 INT/ORG VOL/ASSN CONSULT DELIB/GP PLAN PROB/SOLV 20 PRESIDENT. PAGE 117 A2411
NAT/G

B51
WHITE L.C.,INTERNATIONAL NON-GOVERNMENTAL ORGANIZATIONS. AFR ASIA COM EUR+WWI USA+45 WOR+45 INT/ORG DIPLOM INT/TRADE ALL/VALS...HUM FAO ILO EEC 20. PAGE 164 A3337
VOL/ASSN CONSULT

B52
VANDENBOSCH A.,THE UN: BACKGROUND, ORGANIZATION, FUNCTIONS, ACTIVITIES. WOR+45 LAW CONSTN STRUCT INT/ORG CONSULT BAL/PWR EDU/PROP EXEC ALL/VALS ...POLICY CONCPT UN 20. PAGE 158 A3218
DELIB/GP TIME/SEQ PEACE

L52
HILSMAN R. JR.,"INTELLIGENCE AND POLICY MAKING IN FOREIGN AFFAIRS." USA+45 CONSULT ACT/RES DIPLOM EDU/PROP ROUTINE PEACE PERCEPT PWR SKILL...POLICY MGT HYPO/EXP CONGRESS 20 CIA. PAGE 65 A1333
PROF/ORG SIMUL WAR

L52
WRIGHT Q.,"CONGRESS AND THE TREATY-MAKING POWER." USA+45 WOR+45 CONSTN INTELL NAT/G CHIEF CONSULT EX/STRUC LEGIS TOP/EX CREATE GOV/REL DISPL DRIVE RIGID/FLEX...TREND TOT/POP CONGRESS CONGRESS 20 TREATY. PAGE 167 A3408
ROUTINE DIPLOM INT/LAW DELIB/GP

S52
SCHWEBEL S.M.,"THE SECRETARY-GENERAL OF THE UN." FUT INTELL CONSULT DELIB/GP ADMIN PEACE ATTIT ...JURID MGT CONCPT TREND UN CONGRESS 20. PAGE 130 A2663
INT/ORG TOP/EX

B53
COHEN B.C.,CITIZEN EDUCATION IN WORLD AFFAIRS. USA+45 INT/ORG VOL/ASSN CONSULT ATTIT PWR...INT TIME/SEQ 20. PAGE 27 A0559
KNOWL EDU/PROP DIPLOM

B53
MACMAHON A.W.,ADMINISTRATION IN FOREIGN AFFAIRS. NAT/G CONSULT DELIB/GP LEGIS ACT/RES CREATE ADMIN EXEC RIGID/FLEX PWR...METH/CNCPT TIME/SEQ TOT/POP VAL/FREE 20. PAGE 93 A1899
USA+45 ROUTINE FOR/AID DIPLOM

S53
LINCOLN G.,"FACTORS DETERMINING ARMS AID." COM FUT USA+45 USSR WOR+45 ECO/DEV NAT/G CONSULT PLAN TEC/DEV DIPLOM DOMIN EDU/PROP PERCEPT PWR ...DECISION CONCPT TREND MARX/KARL 20. PAGE 89 A1819
FORCES POLICY BAL/PWR FOR/AID

B54
MANNING C.A.W.,THE UNIVERSITY TEACHING OF SOCIAL SCIENCES: INTERNATIONAL RELATIONS. WOR+45 INTELL STRATA R+D ACADEM INT/ORG NAT/G CONSULT DELIB/GP ACT/RES EDU/PROP NAT/LISM ATTIT...POLICY CONT/OBS HYPO/EXP VAL/FREE LEAGUE/NAT UNESCO 20. PAGE 94 A1925
KNOWL PHIL/SCI DIPLOM

L54
OPLER M.E.,"SOCIAL ASPECTS OF TECHNICAL ASSISTANCE IN OPERATION." WOR+45 VOL/ASSN CREATE PLAN TEC/DEV EDU/PROP ALL/VALS...METH/CNCPT OBS RECORD TREND UN 20. PAGE 112 A2292
INT/ORG CONSULT FOR/AID

B55
COMM. STUDY ORGAN. PEACE,REPORTS. WOR-45 ECO/DEV ECO/UNDEV VOL/ASSN CONSULT FORCES PLAN TEC/DEV DOMIN EDU/PROP NUC/PWR ATTIT PWR WEALTH...JURID STERTYP FAO ILO 20 UN. PAGE 28 A0579
WOR+45 INT/ORG ARMS/CONT

B55
JOY C.T.,HOW COMMUNISTS NEGOTIATE. COM USA+45 CONSTN CULTURE ECO/UNDEV NAT/G CONSULT DELIB/GP FORCES PLAN ECO/TAC DOMIN EDU/PROP LEGIT EXEC ROUTINE COERCE WAR CHOOSE PEACE ATTIT RIGID/FLEX ORD/FREE PWR...POLICY 20. PAGE 75 A1539
ASIA INT/ORG DIPLOM

S55
TORRE M.,"PSYCHIATRIC OBSERVATIONS OF INTERNATIONAL CONFERENCES." WOR+45 INT/ORG PROF/ORG VOL/ASSN CONSULT EDU/PROP ROUTINE ATTIT DRIVE KNOWL...PSY METH/CNCPT OBS/ENVIR STERTYP 20. PAGE 144 A2950
DELIB/GP OBS DIPLOM

B56
GEORGE A.L.,WOODROW WILSON AND COLONEL HOUSE. WOR-45 CONSTN FACE/GP INT/ORG NAT/G POL/PAR CONSULT LEGIT EXEC COERCE CHOOSE ATTIT DRIVE PERSON MORAL ORD/FREE PWR RESPECT...POLICY MGT PSY OBS RECORD INT LEAGUE/NAT. PAGE 52 A1060
USA-45 BIOG DIPLOM

B56
GOODRICH L.,KOREA: A STUDY OF US POLICY IN THE UNITED NATIONS. ASIA USA+45 STRUCT CONSULT DELIB/GP ATTIT DRIVE PWR...JURID GEN/LAWS COLD/WAR 20 UN. PAGE 54 A1103
INT/ORG DIPLOM KOREA

B56
HOUSTON J.A.,LATIN AMERICA IN THE UNITED NATIONS. CONSULT DIPLOM LEGIT ROUTINE ATTIT ORD/FREE PWR ...JURID OBS RECORD TIME/SEQ CHARTS 20 UN. PAGE 68 A1395
L/A+17C INT/ORG INT/LAW REGION

S56
CUTLER R.,"THE DEVELOPMENT OF THE NATIONAL SECURITY COUNCIL." USA+45 INTELL CONSULT EX/STRUC DIPLOM LEAD 20 TRUMAN/HS EISNHWR/DD NSC. PAGE 33 A0670
ORD/FREE DELIB/GP PROB/SOLV NAT/G

S56
GORDON L.,"THE ORGANIZATION FOR EUROPEAN ECONOMIC COOPERATION." EUR+WWI INDUS INT/ORG NAT/G CONSULT DELIB/GP ACT/RES CREATE PLAN TEC/DEV EDU/PROP LEGIT WEALTH OEEC 20. PAGE 54 A1114
VOL/ASSN ECO/DEV

B57
ASHER R.E.,THE UNITED NATIONS AND THE PROMOTION OF THE GENERAL WELFARE. WOR+45 WOR-45 ECO/UNDEV EX/STRUC ACT/RES PLAN EDU/PROP ROUTINE HEALTH...HUM CONCPT CHARTS UNESCO UN ILO 20. PAGE 9 A0185
INT/ORG CONSULT

B57
BLOOMFIELD L.M.,EGYPT, ISRAEL AND THE GULF OF AQABA: IN INTERNATIONAL LAW. LAW NAT/G CONSULT FORCES PLAN ECO/TAC ROUTINE COERCE ATTIT DRIVE PERCEPT PERSON RIGID/FLEX LOVE PWR WEALTH...GEOG CONCPT MYTH TREND. PAGE 15 A0314
ISLAM INT/LAW UAR

B57
LAVES W.H.C.,UNESCO. FUT WOR+45 NAT/G CONSULT DELIB/GP TEC/DEV ECO/TAC EDU/PROP PEACE ORD/FREE ...CONCPT TIME/SEQ TREND UNESCO VAL/FREE 20. PAGE 86 A1751
INT/ORG KNOWL

B57
MURRAY J.N.,THE UNITED NATIONS TRUSTEESHIP SYSTEM. AFR WOR+45 CONSTN CONSULT LEGIS EDU/PROP LEGIT EXEC ROUTINE...INT TIME/SEQ SOMALI UN 20. PAGE 106 A2181
INT/ORG DELIB/GP

B57
TRIFFIN R.,EUROPE AND THE MONEY MUDDLE. USA+45 INT/ORG NAT/G CONSULT PLAN ECO/TAC EXEC ROUTINE BAL/PAY WEALTH...METH/CNCPT OBS TREND CHARTS STERTYP GEN/METH EEC VAL/FREE ECSC. PAGE 145 A2962
EUR+WWI ECO/DEV REGION

B57
US SENATE COMM ON JUDICIARY,HEARING BEFORE SUBCOMMITTEE ON COMMITTEE OF JUDICIARY, UNITED STATES SENATE: S. J. RES. 3. USA+45 NAT/G CONSULT DELIB/GP DIPLOM ADJUD LOBBY REPRESENT 20 CONGRESS TREATY. PAGE 157 A3192
LEGIS CONSTN CONFER AGREE

B57
US SENATE SPEC COMM FOR AID,COMPILATION OF STUDIES AND SURVEYS. AFR ASIA L/A+17C USA+45 ECO/UNDEV AGRI INT/ORG CONSULT TEC/DEV CONFER TOTALISM...NAT/COMP 20 CONGRESS. PAGE 157 A3197
FOR/AID DIPLOM ORD/FREE DELIB/GP

L57
WARREN S.,"FOREIGN AID AND FOREIGN POLICY." USA+45 WOR+45 WOR-45 DIST/IND INDUS MARKET CONSULT CREATE DIPLOM EDU/PROP LEGIT ATTIT RIGID/FLEX...TIME/SEQ GEN/LAWS WORK 20. PAGE 161 A3285
ECO/UNDEV ALL/VALS ECO/TAC FOR/AID

S57
ELDER R.E.,"THE PUBLIC STUDIES DIVISION OF THE DEPARTMENT OF STATE: PUBLIC OPINION ANALYSTS IN THE FORMULATION AND CONDUCT OF." INT/ORG CONSULT DOMIN EDU/PROP ADMIN ATTIT PWR...CONCPT OBS TIME/SEQ VAL/FREE 20. PAGE 41 A0836
USA+45 NAT/G DIPLOM

N57
US SENATE SPECIAL COMM FOR AFF,REPORT OF THE SPECIAL COMMITTEE TO STUDY THE FOREIGN AID PROGRAM (PAMPHLET). USA+45 CONSULT DELIB/GP LEGIS PLAN TEC/DEV CONFER SUPEGO CONGRESS. PAGE 157 A3199
FOR/AID ORD/FREE ECO/UNDEV DIPLOM

B58
BOWETT D.W.,SELF-DEFENSE IN INTERNATIONAL LAW. EUR+WWI MOD/EUR WOR+45 WOR-45 SOCIETY INT/ORG CONSULT DIPLOM LEGIT COERCE ATTIT ORD/FREE...JURID 20 UN. PAGE 17 A0353
ADJUD CONCPT WAR INT/LAW

B58
GANGE J.,UNIVERSITY RESEARCH ON INTERNATIONAL AFFAIRS. USA+45 ACADEM INT/ORG CONSULT CREATE EXEC ROUTINE...QUANT STAT INT STERTYP GEN/METH TOT/POP VAL/FREE 20. PAGE 51 A1040
R+D MGT DIPLOM

B58
HUNT B.I.,BIPARTISANSHIP: A CASE STUDY OF THE FOREIGN ASSISTANCE PROGRAM, 1947-56 (DOCTORAL THESIS). USA+45 INT/ORG CONSULT LEGIS TEC/DEV ...BIBLIOG PRESIDENT TREATY NATO TRUMAN/HS EISNHWR/DD CONGRESS. PAGE 69 A1418
FOR/AID POL/PAR GP/REL DIPLOM

B58
INDIAN COUNCIL WORLD AFFAIRS,DEFENCE AND SECURITY IN THE INDIAN OCEAN AREA. INDIA S/ASIA CULTURE CONSULT DELIB/GP FORCES PROB/SOLV DIPLOM INT/TRADE 20 CMN/WLTH. PAGE 70 A1438
GEOG HABITAT ECO/UNDEV ORD/FREE

B58
MARTIN L.J.,INTERNATIONAL PROPAGANDA: ITS LEGAL AND DIPLOMATIC CONTROL. UK USA+45 USSR CONSULT DELIB/GP DOMIN CONTROL 20. PAGE 95 A1951
EDU/PROP DIPLOM INT/LAW ATTIT

B58
MELMAN S.,INSPECTION FOR DISARMAMENT. USA+45 WOR+45 SOCIETY INT/ORG NAT/G CONSULT ACT/RES PLAN EDU/PROP CONTROL DETER PEACE ATTIT PERSON KNOWL...PSY STAT OBS CHARTS TOT/POP VAL/FREE 20. PAGE 99 A2035
FUT ORD/FREE ARMS/CONT NUC/PWR

B58
MILLIS W.,FOREIGN POLICY AND THE FREE SOCIETY. USA+45 WOR+45 SOCIETY NAT/G FORCES BAL/PWR FOR/AID EDU/PROP DETER ATTIT PWR 20 COLD/WAR. PAGE 102 A2084
DIPLOM POLICY ORD/FREE CONSULT

B58
RUSSELL R.B.,A HISTORY OF THE UNITED NATIONS CHARTER: THE ROLE OF THE UNITED STATES. SOCIETY NAT/G CONSULT DOMIN LEGIT ATTIT ORD/FREE PWR ...POLICY JURID CONCPT UN LEAGUE/NAT. PAGE 126 A2575
USA-45 INT/ORG CONSTN

S58
MCDOUGAL M.S.,"PERSPECTIVES FOR A LAW OF OUTER SPACE." FUT WOR+45 AIR CONSULT DELIB/GP TEC/DEV CT/SYS ORD/FREE...POLICY JURID 20 UN. PAGE 98 A2004 INT/ORG SPACE INT/LAW

N58
US HOUSE COMM FOREIGN AFFAIRS,HEARINGS ON DRAFT LEGISLATION TO AMEND FURTHER THE MUTUAL SECURITY ACT OF 1954 (PAMPHLET). USA+45 CONSULT FORCES BUDGET DIPLOM DETER COST ORD/FREE...JURID 20 DEPT/DEFEN UN DEPT/STATE. PAGE 153 A3123 LEGIS DELIB/GP CONFER WEAPON

N58
US HOUSE COMM FOREIGN AFFAIRS,HEARINGS ON THE FAR EAST AND THE PACIFIC (PAMPHLET). LAOS USA+45 NAT/G CONSULT FORCES CONFER DEBATE ORD/FREE 20. PAGE 153 A3124 FOR/AID DIPLOM DELIB/GP LEGIS

N58
US HOUSE COMM FOREIGN AFFAIRS,HEARINGS ON REVIEW OF THE MUTUAL SECURITY PROGRAMS; EXAMINATION OF SELECTED PROJECTS IN FORMOSA AND PAKISTAN (PAMPHLET). ASIA PAKISTAN TAIWAN INDUS CONSULT DELIB/GP LEGIS BUDGET CONFER DEBATE 20. PAGE 153 A3125 FOR/AID ECO/UNDEV DIPLOM ECO/TAC

B59
BRODIE B.,STRATEGY IN THE MISSILE AGE. FUT WOR+45 CONSULT PLAN COERCE DETER RIGID/FLEX PWR...CONCPT TIME/SEQ TREND 20. PAGE 19 A0381 ACT/RES FORCES ARMS/CONT NUC/PWR

B59
COMM. STUDY ORGAN. PEACE,ORGANIZING PEACE IN THE NUCLEAR AGE. FUT CONSULT DELIB/GP DOMIN ADJUD ROUTINE COERCE ORD/FREE...TECHNIC INT/LAW JURID NEW/IDEA UN COLD/WAR 20. PAGE 29 A0581 INT/ORG ACT/RES NUC/PWR

B59
DIEBOLD W. JR.,THE SCHUMAN PLAN: A STUDY IN ECONOMIC COOPERATION, 1950-1959. EUR+WWI FRANCE GERMANY USA+45 EXTR/IND CONSULT DELIB/GP PLAN DIPLOM ECO/TAC INT/TRADE ROUTINE ORD/FREE WEALTH ...METH/CNCPT STAT CONT/OBS INT TIME/SEQ ECSC 20. PAGE 37 A0759 INT/ORG REGION

B59
FOX W.T.R.,THEORETICAL ASPECTS OF INTERNATIONAL RELATIONS. WOR+45 INT/ORG NAT/G POL/PAR CONSULT PLAN ECO/TAC DOMIN EDU/PROP LEGIT EXEC COERCE PWR WEALTH...RELATIV CONCPT 20. PAGE 48 A0975 DELIB/GP ANTHOL

B59
GORDENKER L.,THE UNITED NATIONS AND THE PEACEFUL UNIFICATION OF KOREA. ASIA LAW LOC/G CONSULT ACT/RES DIPLOM DOMIN LEGIT ADJUD ADMIN ORD/FREE SOVEREIGN...INT GEN/METH UN COLD/WAR 20. PAGE 54 A1109 DELIB/GP KOREA INT/ORG

B59
HALLE L.J.,DREAM AND REALITY: ASPECTS OF AMERICAN FOREIGN POLICY. USA+45 CONSTN CONSULT PROB/SOLV NAT/LISM PERSON. PAGE 60 A1230 POLICY MYTH DIPLOM NAT/G

B59
MACIVER R.M.,THE NATIONS AND THE UN. WOR+45 NAT/G CONSULT ADJUD ADMIN ALL/VALS...CONCPT DEEP/QU UN TOT/POP UNESCO 20. PAGE 92 A1892 INT/ORG ATTIT DIPLOM

B59
MODELSKI G.,ATOMIC ENERGY IN THE COMMUNIST BLOC. FUT INT/ORG CONSULT FORCES ACT/RES PLAN KNOWL SKILL ...PHIL/SCI STAT CHARTS 20. PAGE 102 A2096 TEC/DEV NUC/PWR USSR COM

B59
REIFF H.,THE UNITED STATES AND THE TREATY LAW OF THE SEA. USA+45 USA-45 SEA SOCIETY INT/ORG CONSULT DELIB/GP LEGIS DIPLOM LEGIT ATTIT ORD/FREE PWR WEALTH...GEOG JURID TOT/POP 20 TREATY. PAGE 120 A2459 ADJUD INT/LAW

B59
SIMPSON J.L.,INTERNATIONAL ARBITRATION: LAW AND PRACTICE. WOR+45 WOR-45 INT/ORG DELIB/GP ADJUD PEACE MORAL ORD/FREE...METH 18/20. PAGE 133 A2720 INT/LAW DIPLOM CT/SYS CONSULT

B59
STANFORD RESEARCH INSTITUTE,POSSIBLE NONMILITARY SCIENTIFIC DEVELOPMENTS AND THEIR POTENTIAL IMPACT ON FOREIGN POLICY PROBLEMS OF THE UNITED. FUT USA+45 INT/ORG PROF/ORG CONSULT ACT/RES CREATE PLAN PEACE KNOWL SKILL...TECHNIC PHIL/SCI NEW/IDEA UNESCO 20. PAGE 137 A2802 R+D TEC/DEV

L59
GARDNER R.N.,"NEW DIRECTIONS IN UNITED STATES FOREIGN ECONOMIC POLICY." USA+45 CONSULT...GEN/LAWS GEN/METH COLD/WAR 20. PAGE 51 A1044 ECO/UNDEV ECO/TAC FOR/AID DIPLOM

L59
MCDOUGAL M.S.,"THE IDENTIFICATION AND APPRAISAL OF DIVERSE SYSTEMS OF PUBLIC ORDER (BMR)" WOR+45 NAT/G CONSULT EDU/PROP POLICY. PAGE 98 A2005 INT/LAW DIPLOM ALL/IDEOS

S59
FOX W.T.R.,"THE USES OF INTERNATIONAL RELATIONS THEORY. IN (FOX, THE THEORETICAL ASPECTS OF INTERNATIONAL RELATIONS,. WOR+45 INTELL SOCIETY STRATA INT/ORG CONSULT ACT/RES PWR...POLICY 20. PAGE 48 A0976 PLAN DIPLOM METH/CNCPT

S59
LASSWELL H.D.,"UNIVERSALITY IN PERSPECTIVE." FUT UNIV SOCIETY CONSULT TOP/EX PLAN EDU/PROP ADJUD ROUTINE ARMS/CONT COERCE PEACE ATTIT PERSON ALL/VALS. PAGE 85 A1741 INT/ORG JURID TOTALISM

S59
REUBENS E.D.,"THE BASIS FOR REORIENATION OF AMERICAN FOREIGN AID POLICY." USA+45 USSR STRUCT INT/ORG CONSULT ECO/TAC ADMIN DRIVE MORAL ORD/FREE PWR WEALTH...RELATIV MATH STAT TREND GEN/LAWS VAL/FREE 20. PAGE 120 A2467 ECO/UNDEV PLAN FOR/AID DIPLOM

N59
US HOUSE COMM FOREIGN AFFAIRS,HEARINGS ON DRAFT LEGISLATION TO AMEND FURTHER THE MUTUAL SECURITY ACT OF 1954 (PAMPHLET). USA+45 USSR CONSULT DELIB/GP FORCES ECO/TAC CONFER...POLICY 20 CONGRESS. PAGE 153 A3126 DIPLOM FOR/AID ORD/FREE LEGIS

B60
ARMS CONTROL. FUT UNIV WOR+45 INTELL R+D INT/ORG NAT/G VOL/ASSN CONSULT CREATE EDU/PROP PEACE...HUM GEN/LAWS TOT/POP 20. PAGE 3 A0060 DELIB/GP ORD/FREE ARMS/CONT NUC/PWR

B60
APTHEKER H.,DISARMAMENT AND THE AMERICAN ECONOMY: A SYMPOSIUM. FUT USA+45 ECO/DEV DIST/IND FINAN INDUS PROC/MFG LABOR NAT/G POL/PAR CONSULT PLAN CAP/ISM INT/TRADE PEACE ATTIT MORAL WEALTH...TREND GEN/LAWS TOT/POP 20. PAGE 9 A0172 MARXIST ARMS/CONT

B60
BLACK E.R.,THE DIPLOMACY OF ECONOMIC DEVELOPMENT. WOR+45 CONSULT PLAN TEC/DEV DIPLOM ECO/TAC FOR/AID ...CONCPT TREND 20. PAGE 15 A0297 ECO/UNDEV ACT/RES

B60
CARNEGIE ENDOWMENT INT. PEACE,PERSPECTIVES ON PEACE - 1910-1960. WOR+45 WOR-45 INTELL INT/ORG CONSULT ACT/RES EDU/PROP ATTIT KNOWL ORD/FREE...TIME/SEQ TREND EEC OAS UNESCO NAZI 20. PAGE 24 A0489 FUT CONCPT ARMS/CONT PEACE

B60
JEFFRIES C.,TRANSFER OF POWER: PROBLEMS OF THE PASSAGE TO SELFGOVERNMENT. CEYLON GHANA MALAYSIA NIGERIA UK INT/ORG CONSULT DELIB/GP LEGIS DIPLOM CONFER PARL/PROC 20. PAGE 73 A1502 SOVEREIGN COLONIAL ORD/FREE NAT/G

B60
PENTONY D.E.,THE UNDERDEVELOPED LANDS. FUT WOR+45 CULTURE AGRI FINAN INDUS MARKET INT/ORG LABOR NAT/G VOL/ASSN CONSULT TEC/DEV ECO/TAC EDU/PROP COLONIAL ATTIT WEALTH...OBS RECORD SAMP TREND GEN/METH WORK UN 20. PAGE 115 A2351 ECO/UNDEV POLICY FOR/AID INT/TRADE

B60
PRICE D.,THE SECRETARY OF STATE. USA+45 CONSTN ELITES INTELL CHIEF EX/STRUC TOP/EX LEGIT ATTIT PWR SKILL...DECISION 20 CONGRESS. PAGE 117 A2410 CONSULT DIPLOM INT/LAW

B60
STEIN E.,AMERICAN ENTERPRISE IN THE EUROPEAN COMMON MARKET: A LEGAL PROFILE. EUR+WWI FUT USA+45 SOCIETY STRUCT ECO/DEV NAT/G VOL/ASSN CONSULT PLAN TEC/DEV ECO/TAC INT/TRADE ADMIN ATTIT RIGID/FLEX PWR...MGT NEW/IDEA STAT TREND COMPUT/IR SIMUL EEC 20. PAGE 137 A2814 MARKET ADJUD INT/LAW

B60
TAYLOR M.D.,THE UNCERTAIN TRUMPET. USA+45 USSR WOR+45 INT/ORG NAT/G CONSULT DOMIN COERCE NUC/PWR WAR ATTIT ORD/FREE PWR...POLICY CONCPT TREND GEN/METH COLD/WAR UN NATO 20. PAGE 142 A2900 PLAN FORCES DIPLOM

B60
US HOUSE COMM FOREIGN AFFAIRS,HEARINGS ON A BILL TO AMEND FURTHER THE MUTUAL SECURITY ACT OF 1954. USA+45 CONSULT FORCES BUDGET FOR/AID CONFER DETER ...CHARTS 20 DEPT/DEFEN DEPT/STATE UNEF. PAGE 153 A3127 DIPLOM ORD/FREE DELIB/GP LEGIS

B60
WOETZEL R.K.,THE INTERNATIONAL CONTROL OF AIRSPACE AND OUTERSPACE. FUT WOR+45 AIR CONSTN STRUCT CONSULT PLAN TEC/DEV ADJUD RIGID/FLEX KNOWL ORD/FREE PWR...TECHNIC GEOG MGT NEW/IDEA TREND COMPUT/IR VAL/FREE 20 TREATY. PAGE 166 A3375 INT/ORG JURID SPACE INT/LAW

L60
BRENNAN D.G.,"SETTING AND GOALS OF ARMS CONTROL." FUT USA+45 USSR WOR+45 INTELL INT/ORG NAT/G VOL/ASSN CONSULT PLAN DIPLOM ECO/TAC ADMIN KNOWL PWR...POLICY CONCPT TREND COLD/WAR 20. PAGE 18 A0371 FORCES COERCE ARMS/CONT DETER

L60
HOLTON G.,"ARMS CONTROL." FUT WOR+45 CULTURE INT/ORG NAT/G FORCES TOP/EX PLAN EDU/PROP COERCE ATTIT RIGID/FLEX ORD/FREE...POLICY PHIL/SCI SOC TREND COLD/WAR. PAGE 67 A1377 ACT/RES CONSULT ARMS/CONT NUC/PWR

L60
NOGEE J.L.,"THE DIPLOMACY OF DISARMAMENT." WOR+45 INT/ORG NAT/G CONSULT DELIB/GP TOP/EX BAL/PWR DIPLOM EDU/PROP COERCE DETER WEAPON PEACE ATTIT ...RECORD TIME/SEQ TOT/POP VAL/FREE COLD/WAR 20. PAGE 109 A2246 PWR ORD/FREE ARMS/CONT NUC/PWR

S60
HAVILAND H.F.,"PROBLEMS OF AMERICAN FOREIGN ECO/UNDEV

POLICY." ASIA COM USA+45 WOR+45 INT/ORG NAT/G CONSULT ECO/TAC FOR/AID DOMIN COERCE NUC/PWR ATTIT DRIVE ORD/FREE PWR RESPECT SKILL...POLICY GEOG OBS SAMP TREND GEN/METH METH COLD/WAR UN 20. PAGE 63 A1292 FORCES DIPLOM

S60
JACOBSON H.K.,"THE USSR AND ILO." COM STRUCT ECO/DEV ECO/UNDEV CONSULT DELIB/GP ECO/TAC ILO WORK COLD/WAR 20. PAGE 72 A1484 INT/ORG LABOR USSR

S60
KAPLAN M.A.,"THEORETICAL ANALYSIS OF THE BALANCE OF POWER." FUT USA+45 WOR+45 INTELL ECO/DEV INT/ORG NAT/G CONSULT TOP/EX ACT/RES PLAN TEC/DEV ATTIT ALL/VALS...METH/CNCPT TOT/POP 20. PAGE 76 A1562 CREATE NEW/IDEA DIPLOM NUC/PWR

S60
KISTIAKOWSKY G.B.,"SCIENCE AND FOREIGN AFFAIRS." FUT WOR+45 NAT/G PROF/ORG PLAN ECO/TAC EDU/PROP NUC/PWR...TREND COLD/WAR 20. PAGE 80 A1645 CONSULT TEC/DEV FOR/AID DIPLOM

S60
OSGOOD C.E.,"COGNITIVE DYNAMICS IN THE CONDUCT OF HUMAN AFFAIRS." USA+45 INTELL INT/ORG CONSULT PLAN ATTIT PERSON...PSY CHARTS HYPO/EXP 20. PAGE 112 A2299 R+D SOCIETY

S60
SWIFT R.,"THE UNITED NATIONS AND ITS PUBLIC." WOR+45 CONSTN FINAN CONSULT DELIB/GP ACT/RES ADMIN ROUTINE RIGID/FLEX SKILL UN 20. PAGE 140 A2870 INT/ORG EDU/PROP

B61
BARNES W.,THE FOREIGN SERVICE OF THE UNITED STATES. USA+45 USA-45 CONSTN INT/ORG POL/PAR CONSULT DELIB/GP LEGIS DOMIN EDU/PROP EXEC ATTIT RIGID/FLEX ORD/FREE PWR...POLICY CONCPT STAT OBS RECORD BIOG TIME/SEQ TREND. PAGE 11 A0224 NAT/G MGT DIPLOM

B61
FRIEDMANN W.G.,JOINT INTERNATIONAL BUSINESS VENTURES. ASIA ISLAM L/A+17C ECO/DEV DIST/IND FINAN PROC/MFG FACE/GP LG/CO NAT/G VOL/ASSN CONSULT EX/STRUC PLAN ADMIN ROUTINE WEALTH...OLD/LIB WORK 20. PAGE 49 A1004 ECO/UNDEV INT/TRADE

B61
HARRISON S.,INDIA AND THE UNITED STATES. FUT S/ASIA USA+45 WOR+45 INTELL ECO/DEV ECO/UNDEV AGRI INDUS INT/ORG NAT/G CONSULT EX/STRUC TOP/EX PLAN ECO/TAC NEUTRAL ALL/VALS...MGT TOT/POP 20. PAGE 62 A1272 DELIB/GP ACT/RES FOR/AID INDIA

B61
ROBINS D.B.,EVOLVING UNITED STATES POLICIES TOWARD THE EMERGING NATIONS OF ASIA AND AFRICA (PAMPHLET). ISLAM ECO/UNDEV INT/ORG CONSULT CREATE PLAN TEC/DEV FOR/AID CONFER ALL/VALS 20 KENNEDY/JF EISNHWR/DD UN AID. PAGE 122 A2501 AFR S/ASIA DIPLOM BIBLIOG

B61
SHARP W.R.,FIELD ADMINISTRATION IN THE UNITED NATION SYSTEM: THE CONDUCT OF INTERNATIONAL ECONOMIC AND SOCIAL PROGRAMS. FUT WOR+45 CONSTN SOCIETY ECO/UNDEV R+D DELIB/GP ACT/RES PLAN TEC/DEV EDU/PROP EXEC ROUTINE HEALTH WEALTH...HUM CONCPT CHARTS METH ILO UNESCO VAL/FREE UN 20. PAGE 132 A2697 INT/ORG CONSULT

B61
US HOUSE COMM APPROPRIATIONS,INTER-AMERICAN PROGRAMS FOR 1961: DENIAL OF 1962 BUDGET INFORMATION. CHILE L/A+17C USA+45 FINAN CONSULT BUDGET ADJUD COST EFFICIENCY WEALTH...POLICY CHARTS 20 CONGRESS. PAGE 153 A3119 LEGIS FOR/AID DELIB/GP ECO/UNDEV

B61
US HOUSE COMM FOREIGN AFFAIRS,THE INTERNATIONAL DEVELOPMENT AND SECURITY ACT: HEARINGS BEFORE COMMITTEE ON FOREIGN AFFAIRS, HOUSE OF REP: HR7372. USA+45 AGRI INT/ORG NAT/G CONSULT DELIB/GP DIPLOM ECO/TAC INT/TRADE LOBBY REPRESENT 20 MCNAMARA/R DILLON/D RUSK/D CONGRESS. PAGE 153 A3128 FOR/AID CONFER LEGIS ECO/UNDEV

B61
WILLOUGHBY W.R.,THE ST LAWRENCE WATERWAY: A STUDY IN POLITICS AND DIPLOMACY. USA+45 ECO/DEV COM/IND INT/ORG CONSULT DELIB/GP ACT/RES TEC/DEV DIPLOM ECO/TAC ROUTINE...TIME/SEQ 20. PAGE 165 A3357 LEGIS INT/TRADE CANADA DIST/IND

L61
SAND P.T.,"AN HISTORICAL SURVEY OF INTERNATIONAL AIR LAW SINCE 1944." USA+45 USA-45 WOR+45 WOR-45 SOCIETY ECO/DEV NAT/G CONSULT EX/STRUC ACT/RES PLAN LEGIT ROUTINE...JURID CONCPT METH/CNCPT TREND 20. PAGE 127 A2598 INT/ORG LAW INT/LAW SPACE

S61
ALGER C.F.,"NON-RESOLUTION CONSEQUENCES OF THE UNITED NATIONS AND THEIR EFFECT ON INTERNATIONAL CONFLICT." WOR+45 CONSTN ECO/DEV NAT/G CONSULT DELIB/GP TOP/EX ACT/RES PLAN DIPLOM EDU/PROP ROUTINE ATTIT ALL/VALS...INT/LAW TOT/POP UN 20. PAGE 6 A0117 INT/ORG DRIVE BAL/PWR

S61
GALBRAITH J.K.,"A POSITIVE APPROACH TO ECONOMIC AID." FUT USA+45 INTELL NAT/G CONSULT ACT/RES DIPLOM ECO/TAC EDU/PROP ATTIT KNOWL PWR WEALTH ...SOC STERTYP 20. PAGE 50 A1030 ECO/UNDEV ROUTINE FOR/AID

S61
JUVILER P.H.,"INTERPARLIAMENTARY CONTACTS IN SOVIET FOREIGN POLICY." COM FUT WOR+45 WOR-45 SOCIETY CONSULT ACT/RES DIPLOM ADMIN PEACE ATTIT RIGID/FLEX WEALTH...WELF/ST SOC TOT/POP CONGRESS 19/20. PAGE 75 A1543 INT/ORG DELIB/GP USSR

S61
LIPSON L.,"AN ARGUMENT ON THE LEGALITY OF RECONNAISSANCE STATELLITES." COM USA+45 USSR WOR+45 AIR INTELL NAT/G CONSULT PLAN DIPLOM LEGIT ROUTINE ATTIT...INT/LAW JURID CONCPT METH/CNCPT TREND COLD/WAR 20. PAGE 90 A1833 INT/ORG LAW SPACE

S61
ROSTOW W.W.,"THE FUTURE OF FOREIGN AID." COM FUT WOR+45 ECO/DEV INDUS INT/ORG NAT/G CONSULT ACT/RES PLAN DOMIN LEGIT CHOOSE RIGID/FLEX ALL/VALS ...MAJORIT CONCPT TREND TOT/POP 20. PAGE 124 A2544 ECO/UNDEV ECO/TAC FOR/AID

S61
TRAMPE G.,"DIE FORM DER DIPLOMATIC ALS POLITSCHE WAFFE." WOR+45 WOR-45 SOCIETY STRATA INT/ORG NAT/G ACT/RES PLAN ECO/TAC EDU/PROP COERCE WAR ATTIT RIGID/FLEX...DECISION CONCPT TREND. PAGE 145 A2959 CONSULT PWR DIPLOM

B62
ALEXANDROWICZ C.H.,WORLD ECONOMIC AGENCIES: LAW AND PRACTICE. WOR+45 DIST/IND FINAN LABOR CONSULT INT/TRADE TARIFFS REPRESENT HEALTH...JURID 20 UN GATT EEC OAS ECSC. PAGE 6 A0115 INT/LAW INT/ORG DIPLOM ADJUD

B62
CARDOZA M.H.,DIPLOMATS IN INTERNATIONAL COOPERATION: STEPCHILDREN OF THE FOREIGN SERVICE. EUR+WWI USA+45 NAT/G CONSULT ACT/RES EDU/PROP ROUTINE RIGID/FLEX KNOWL SKILL...SOC OBS TIME/SEQ EEC OEEC NATO 20. PAGE 24 A0480 INT/ORG METH/CNCPT DIPLOM

B62
DREIER J.C.,THE ORGANIZATION OF AMERICAN STATES AND THE HEMISPHERE CRISIS. CUBA USA+45 CULTURE STRATA NAT/G VOL/ASSN CONSULT FORCES ACT/RES CREATE DIPLOM ECO/TAC FOR/AID ALL/VALS...POLICY OBS OAS 20. PAGE 38 A0786 L/A+17C CONCPT

B62
FORBES H.W.,THE STRATEGY OF DISARMAMENT. FUT WOR+45 INT/ORG VOL/ASSN CONSULT ARMS/CONT COERCE NUC/PWR WAR DRIVE RIGID/FLEX ORD/FREE PWR...POLICY CONCPT OBS TREND STERTYP 20. PAGE 47 A0959 PLAN FORCES DIPLOM

B62
GILPIN R.,AMERICAN SCIENTISTS AND NUCLEAR WEAPONS POLICY. COM FUT USA+45 WOR+45 INT/ORG NAT/G PROF/ORG CONSULT FORCES CREATE TEC/DEV BAL/PWR EDU/PROP ARMS/CONT WAR PERCEPT KNOWL MORAL PWR ...PHIL/SCI SOC CONCPT GEN/LAWS 20. PAGE 52 A1073 INTELL ATTIT DETER NUC/PWR

B62
HUNTINGTON S.P.,CHANGING PATTERNS OF MILITARY POLITICS. EUR+WWI L/A+17C S/ASIA USA+45 WOR+45 CULTURE INT/ORG NAT/G CONSULT PLAN DOMIN EDU/PROP LEGIT DETER WAR ATTIT PERSON PWR...DECISION CONCPT SIMUL GEN/LAWS ANTHOL COLD/WAR 20. PAGE 69 A1419 FORCES RIGID/FLEX

B62
KAHN H.,THINKING ABOUT THE UNTHINKABLE. FUT USA+45 LAW NAT/G CONSULT FORCES ACT/RES CREATE PLAN TEC/DEV BAL/PWR DIPLOM EDU/PROP ARMS/CONT DETER ATTIT...CONCPT OBS TREND COLD/WAR 20. PAGE 76 A1547 INT/ORG ORD/FREE NUC/PWR PEACE

B62
KING G.,THE UNITED NATIONS IN THE CONGO: A QUEST FOR PEACE. WOR+45 NAT/G CONSULT FORCES LEGIT COERCE WAR ORD/FREE...JURID METH/CNCPT OBS INT HIST/WRIT TIME/SEQ CONGO UN 20 COLD/WAR. PAGE 79 A1624 AFR INT/ORG

B62
LAWSON R.,INTERNATIONAL REGIONAL ORGANIZATIONS. WOR+45 NAT/G VOL/ASSN CONSULT LEGIS EDU/PROP LEGIT ADMIN EXEC ROUTINE HEALTH PWR WEALTH...JURID EEC COLD/WAR 20 UN. PAGE 86 A1752 INT/ORG DELIB/GP REGION

B62
MCDOUGAL M.S.,THE PUBLIC ORDER OF THE OCEANS. WOR+45 WOR-45 SEA INT/ORG NAT/G CONSULT DELIB/GP DIPLOM LEGIT PEACE RIGID/FLEX...GEOG INT/LAW JURID RECORD TOT/POP 20 TREATY. PAGE 98 A2007 ADJUD ORD/FREE

B62
OSGOOD C.E.,AN ALTERNATIVE TO WAR OR SURRENDER. FUT UNIV CULTURE INTELL SOCIETY R+D INT/ORG CONSULT DELIB/GP ACT/RES PLAN CHOOSE ATTIT PERCEPT KNOWL ...PHIL/SCI PSY SOC TREND GEN/LAWS 20. PAGE 112 A2300 ORD/FREE EDU/PROP PEACE WAR

B62
ROBINSON A.D.,DUTCH ORGANIZED AGRICULTURE IN INTERNATIONAL POLITICS, 1945-1960. EUR+WWI NETHERLAND STRUCT ECO/DEV NAT/G VOL/ASSN CONSULT DELIB/GP PLAN TEC/DEV INT/TRADE EDU/PROP ATTIT RIGID/FLEX ALL/VALS...NEW/IDEA TREND EEC 20. PAGE 122 A2502 AGRI INT/ORG

B62
SAVORD R.,AMERICAN AGENCIES INTERESTED IN INTERNATIONAL AFFAIRS. USA-45 R+D NAT/G VOL/ASSN ACT/RES EDU/PROP KNOWL...CONCPT 20. PAGE 127 A2608 INT/ORG CONSULT DIPLOM

B62
SCHWARTZ L.E.,INTERNATIONAL ORGANIZATIONS AND SPACE COOPERATION. VOL/ASSN CONSULT CREATE TEC/DEV INT/ORG DIPLOM

SANCTION...POLICY INT/LAW PHIL/SCI 20 UN. PAGE 130 A2656 R+D SPACE

B62
STRAUSS L.L.,MEN AND DECISIONS. USA+45 USA-45 USSR CONSULT FORCES TOP/EX WAR PEACE 20. PAGE 139 A2844 DECISION PWR NUC/PWR DIPLOM

B62
THANT U.,THE UNITED NATIONS' DEVELOPMENT DECADE: PROPOSALS FOR ACTION. WOR+45 SOCIETY ECO/UNDEV AGRI COM/IND FINAN R+D MUNIC SCHOOL VOL/ASSN CONSULT PLAN TEC/DEV ECO/TAC EDU/PROP ADMIN ROUTINE RIGID/FLEX...MGT SOC CONCPT UNESCO UN TOT/POP VAL/FREE. PAGE 142 A2906 INT/ORG ALL/VALS

B62
THOMSON G.P.,NUCLEAR ENERGY IN BRITAIN DURING THE LAST WAR: THE CHERWELL SIMON LECTURE (MONOGRAPH). UK R+D CONSULT FORCES PLAN DIPLOM TASK CIVMIL/REL ROLE...PHIL/SCI NEW/IDEA LAB/EXP 20 MAUD. PAGE 143 A2934 CREATE TEC/DEV WAR NUC/PWR

B62
WRIGHT Q.,PREVENTING WORLD WAR THREE. FUT WOR+45 CULTURE INT/ORG NAT/G CONSULT FORCES ADMIN ARMS/CONT DRIVE RIGID/FLEX ORD/FREE SOVEREIGN ...POLICY CONCPT TREND STERTYP COLD/WAR 20. PAGE 168 A3416 CREATE ATTIT

L62
GROSS L.,"IMMUNITIES AND PRIVILEGES OF DELIGATIONS TO THE UNITED NATIONS." USA+45 WOR+45 STRATA NAT/G VOL/ASSN CONSULT DIPLOM EDU/PROP ROUTINE RESPECT ...POLICY INT/LAW CONCPT UN 20. PAGE 57 A1176 INT/ORG LAW ELITES

L62
MURACCIOLE L.,"LA BANQUE CENTRALE DES ETATS DE L'AFRIQUE DE L'OUEST." AFR LAW ECO/UNDEV INT/ORG NAT/G CONSULT ECO/TAC ROUTINE...CHARTS 20. PAGE 106 A2175 ISLAM FINAN INT/TRADE

S62
ALGER C.F.,"THE EXTERNAL BUREAUCRACY IN UNITED STATES FOREIGN AFFAIRS." USA+45 WOR+45 SOCIETY COM/IND INT/ORG NAT/G CONSULT EX/STRUC ACT/RES ...MGT SOC CONCPT TREND 20. PAGE 6 A0118 ADMIN ATTIT DIPLOM

S62
CROAN M.,"POLYCENTRISM: COMMUNIST INTERNATIONAL RELATIONS." ASIA STRUCT INT/ORG NAT/G POL/PAR CONSULT PLAN DOMIN EDU/PROP COERCE ATTIT RIGID/FLEX SOCISM...POLICY CONCPT TREND CON/ANAL GEN/LAWS MARX/KARL. PAGE 33 A0663 COM CREATE DIPLOM NAT/LISM

S62
FOSTER W.C.,"ARMS CONTROL AND DISARMAMENT IN A DIVIDED WORLD." COM FUT USA+45 USSR WOR+45 INTELL INT/ORG NAT/G VOL/ASSN CONSULT CREATE PLAN TEC/DEV EDU/PROP LEGIT NUC/PWR ATTIT RIGID/FLEX...CONCPT TREND TOT/POP 20 UN. PAGE 47 A0971 DELIB/GP POLICY ARMS/CONT DIPLOM

S62
GUETZKOW H.,"THE POTENTIAL OF CASE STUDY IN ANALYZING INTERNATIONAL CONFLICT." EUR+WWI FUT GERMANY INTELL SOCIETY STRUCT INT/ORG LOC/G NAT/G CONSULT CREATE PLAN CHOOSE ATTIT RIGID/FLEX ...POLICY SAAR 20. PAGE 58 A1188 EDU/PROP METH/CNCPT COERCE FRANCE

S62
MILLAR T.B.,"THE COMMONWEALTH AND THE UNITED NATIONS." FUT WOR+45 STRUCT NAT/G VOL/ASSN CONSULT DELIB/GP EDU/PROP LEGIT ATTIT...POLICY CONCPT TREND CMN/WLTH UN 20. PAGE 101 A2072 INT/ORG

S62
NORTH R.C.,"DECISION MAKING IN CRISIS: AN INTRODUCTION." WOR+45 WOR-45 NAT/G CONSULT DELIB/GP TEC/DEV PERCEPT KNOWL...POLICY DECISION PSY METH/CNCPT CONT/OBS TREND VAL/FREE 20. PAGE 110 A2251 INT/ORG ROUTINE DIPLOM

S62
SCHACHTER O.,"DAG HAMMARSKJOLD AND THE RELATION OF LAW TO POLITICS." FUT WOR+45 INT/ORG CONSULT PLAN TEC/DEV BAL/PWR DIPLOM LEGIT ATTIT PERCEPT ORD/FREE ...POLICY JURID CONCPT OBS TESTS STERTYP GEN/LAWS 20 HAMMARSK/D. PAGE 128 A2616 ACT/RES ADJUD

S62
SCHILLING W.R.,"SCIENTISTS, FOREIGN POLICY AND POLITICS." WOR+45 WOR-45 INTELL INT/ORG CONSULT TOP/EX ACT/RES PLAN ADMIN KNOWL...CONCPT OBS TREND LEAGUE/NAT 20. PAGE 128 A2627 NAT/G TEC/DEV DIPLOM NUC/PWR

S62
SCOTT J.B.,"ANGLO-SOVIET TRADE AND ITS EFFECTS ON THE COMMONWEALTH." COM FUT UK USSR WOR+45 ECO/DEV MARKET INT/ORG CONSULT WEALTH...POLICY TREND CMN/WLTH 20. PAGE 130 A2673 NAT/G ECO/TAC

S62
SINGER J.D.,"STABLE DETERRENCE AND ITS LIMITS." FUT WOR+45 R+D INT/ORG CONSULT ACT/RES TEC/DEV ARMS/CONT COERCE DRIVE PERCEPT RIGID/FLEX ORD/FREE PWR...MYTH SIMUL TOT/POP 20. PAGE 133 A2728 NAT/G FORCES DETER NUC/PWR

S62
SPENSER J.H.,"AFRICA AT THE UNITED NATIONS: SOME OBSERVATIONS." FUT ECO/UNDEV NAT/G CONSULT DELIB/GP PLAN BAL/PWR ECO/TAC EDU/PROP ATTIT RIGID/FLEX HEALTH ORD/FREE PWR WEALTH...POLICY CONCPT OBS TREND STERTYP GEN/METH UN VAL/FREE. PAGE 136 A2786 AFR INT/ORG REGION

B63
BOISSIER P.,HISTORIE DU COMITE INTERNATIONAL DE LA CROIX ROUGE. MOD/EUR WOR-45 CONSULT FORCES PLAN DIPLOM EDU/PROP ADMIN MORAL ORD/FREE...SOC CONCPT RECORD TIME/SEQ GEN/LAWS TOT/POP VAL/FREE 19/20. PAGE 16 A0332 INT/ORG HEALTH ARMS/CONT WAR

B63
BUTTS R.F.,AMERICAN EDUCATION IN INTERNATIONAL DEVELOPMENT. USA+45 WOR+45 INTELL SCHOOL DIPLOM EDU/PROP...BIBLIOG 20. PAGE 23 A0457 ACADEM FOR/AID CONSULT ECO/UNDEV

B63
MAYNE R.,THE COMMUNITY OF EUROPE. UK CONSTN NAT/G CONSULT DELIB/GP CREATE PLAN ECO/TAC LEGIT ADMIN ROUTINE ORD/FREE PWR WEALTH...CONCPT TIME/SEQ EEC EURATOM 20. PAGE 97 A1985 EUR+WWI INT/ORG REGION

B63
NICOLSON H.,DIPLOMACY (3RD ED.). INT/ORG NAT/G CONSULT DELIB/GP CONFER 19/20 LEAGUE/NAT UN. PAGE 109 A2232 DIPLOM CONCPT NAT/COMP

B63
SCHMELTZ G.W.,LA POLITIQUE MONDIALE CONTEMPORAINE. SOCIETY ECO/UNDEV INDUS INT/ORG NAT/G POL/PAR CONSULT DELIB/GP PLAN TEC/DEV ECO/TAC DOMIN EDU/PROP ROUTINE COERCE PERCEPT PERSON LOVE SKILL ...SOC RECORD TOT/POP. PAGE 128 A2629 WOR+45 COLONIAL

B63
US CONGRESS JOINT ECO COMM,THE UNITED STATES BALANCE OF PAYMENTS. USA+45 DELIB/GP CONFER...MATH PREDICT CHARTS 20 CONGRESS. PAGE 150 A3068 BAL/PAY ECO/TAC INT/TRADE CONSULT

B63
WESTERFIELD H.,THE INSTRUMENTS OF AMERICA'S FOREIGN POLICY. WOR+45 ECO/DEV NAT/G CONSULT EX/STRUC LEGIS BAL/PWR FOR/AID INT/TRADE DOMIN EDU/PROP LEGIT ATTIT KNOWL ORD/FREE PWR WEALTH...OBS COLD/WAR TOT/POP VAL/FREE. PAGE 163 A3322 USA+45 INT/ORG DIPLOM

L63
SINGER J.D.,"WEAPONS MANAGEMENT IN WORLD POLITICS: PROCEEDINGS OF THE INTERNATIONAL ARMS CONTROL SYMPOSIUM, DECEMBER, 1962." FUT WOR+45 SOCIETY ECO/DEV INDUS INT/ORG DELIB/GP FORCES ACT/RES ECO/TAC EDU/PROP ARMS/CONT SUPEGO HEALTH ORD/FREE PWR SKILL...POLICY CHARTS SIMUL ANTHOL VAL/FREE 20. PAGE 133 A2729 CONSULT ATTIT DIPLOM NUC/PWR

S63
DARLING F.C.,"THE GEOPOLITICS OF AMERICAN FOREIGN POLITICS IN ASIA." COM S/ASIA USA+45 USSR ECO/UNDEV NAT/G VOL/ASSN CONSULT PLAN GUERRILLA...STAT TOT/POP 20. PAGE 34 A0682 FORCES ECO/TAC FOR/AID DIPLOM

S63
GARDNER R.N.,"COOPERATION IN OUTER SPACE." FUT USSR WOR+45 AIR LAW COM/IND CONSULT DELIB/GP CREATE KNOWL 20 TREATY. PAGE 51 A1045 INT/ORG ACT/RES PEACE SPACE

S63
NICHOLAS H.G.,"UN PEACE FORCES AND THE CHANGING GLOBE: THE LESSONS OF SUEZ AND CONGO." FUT WOR+45 CONSTN INT/ORG CONSULT DELIB/GP TOP/EX CREATE DIPLOM DOMIN LEGIT COERCE WAR PERSON RIGID/FLEX PWR UN SUEZ CONGO UNEF 20. PAGE 109 A2229 ACT/RES FORCES

S63
SCHMIDT W.E.,"THE CASE AGAINST COMMODITY AGREEMENTS." FUT L/A+17C STRATA CONSULT PLAN ECO/TAC EDU/PROP ATTIT DRIVE RIGID/FLEX WEALTH ...MYTH 20. PAGE 128 A2631 ECO/UNDEV ACT/RES INT/TRADE

S63
SCHOFLING J.A.,"EFTA: THE OTHER EUROPE." ECO/DEV MARKET CONSULT ECO/TAC WEALTH...TIME/SEQ EEC OEEC 20 EFTA. PAGE 129 A2642 EUR+WWI INT/ORG REGION

S63
TALLON D.,"L'ETUDE DU DROIT COMPARE COMME MOYEN DE RECHERCHER LES MATIERES SUSCEPTIBLES D'UNIFICATION INTERNATIONALE." WOR+45 LAW SOCIETY VOL/ASSN CONSULT LEGIT CT/SYS RIGID/FLEX KNOWL 20. PAGE 141 A2884 INT/ORG JURID INT/LAW

S63
VINER J.,"REPORT OF THE CLAY COMMITTEE ON FOREIGN AID: A SYMPOSIUM." USA+45 WOR+45 NAT/G CONSULT PLAN BAL/PWR ATTIT WEALTH...MGT CONCPT TOT/POP 20. PAGE 159 A3240 ACT/RES ECO/TAC FOR/AID

S63
WALKER H.,"THE INTERNATIONAL LAW OF COMMODITY AGREEMENTS." FUT WOR+45 ECO/DEV ECO/UNDEV FINAN INT/ORG NAT/G CONSULT CREATE PLAN ECO/TAC ATTIT PERCEPT...CONCPT GEN/LAWS TOT/POP GATT 20. PAGE 160 A3265 MARKET VOL/ASSN INT/LAW INT/TRADE

S63
WELLS H.,"THE OAS AND THE DOMINICAN ELECTIONS." L/A+17C INT/ORG NAT/G POL/PAR TEC/DEV ECO/TAC EDU/PROP PERCEPT...TIME/SEQ OAS TOT/POP 20. PAGE 163 A3317 CONSULT CHOOSE DOMIN/REP

B64
AHLUWALIA K.,THE LEGAL STATUS, PRIVILEGES AND IMMUNITIES OF SPECIALIZED AGENCIES OF UN AND PRIVIL DIPLOM

CERTAIN OTHER INTERNATIONAL ORGANIZATIONS. WOR+45 LAW CONSULT DELIB/GP FORCES. PAGE 5 A0102
INT/ORG INT/LAW

B64
CHENG C.,ECONOMIC RELATIONS BETWEEN PEKING AND MOSCOW: 1949-63. ASIA CHINA/COM COM USSR FINAN INDUS CONSULT TEC/DEV INT/TRADE...PREDICT CHARTS BIBLIOG 20. PAGE 26 A0527
DIPLOM FOR/AID MARXISM

B64
GRODZINS M.,THE ATOMIC AGE: FORTY-FIVE SCIENTISTS AND SCHOLARS SPEAK ON NATIONAL AND WORLD AFFAIRS. FUT USA+45 WOR+45 R+D INT/ORG NAT/G CONSULT TEC/DEV EDU/PROP ATTIT PERSON ORD/FREE...HUM CONCPT TIME/SEQ CON/ANAL. PAGE 57 A1169
INTELL ARMS/CONT NUC/PWR

B64
SAKAI R.K.,STUDIES ON ASIA, 1964. ASIA CHINA/COM ISRAEL MALAYSIA S/ASIA USA+45 USSR ECO/UNDEV FAM POL/PAR SECT CONSULT NAT/LISM...POLICY SOC 20 CHINJAP. PAGE 126 A2588
PWR DIPLOM

B64
SULLIVAN G.,THE STORY OF THE PEACE CORPS. USA+45 WOR+45 INTELL FACE/GP NAT/G SCHOOL VOL/ASSN CONSULT EX/STRUC PLAN EDU/PROP ADMIN ATTIT DRIVE ALL/VALS ...POLICY HEAL SOC CONCPT INT QU BIOG TREND SOC/EXP WORK. PAGE 140 A2861
INT/ORG ECO/UNDEV FOR/AID PEACE

B64
US HOUSE COMM FOREIGN AFFAIRS,HEARINGS ON H.R. 10502 TO AMEND FURTHER THE FOREIGN ASSISTANCE ACT OF 1961. AFR ASIA L/A+17C INT/ORG CONSULT DELIB/GP TEC/DEV ECO/TAC EDU/PROP CONFER 20 UN NATO CONGRESS AID. PAGE 153 A3130
FOR/AID DIPLOM ORD/FREE ECO/UNDEV

B64
US SENATE COMM GOVT OPERATIONS,THE SECRETARY OF STATE AND THE AMBASSADOR. USA+45 CHIEF CONSULT EX/STRUC FORCES PLAN ADMIN EXEC INGP/REL ROLE ...ANTHOL 20 PRESIDENT DEPT/STATE. PAGE 156 A3175
DIPLOM DELIB/GP NAT/G

B64
WAINHOUSE D.W.,REMNANTS OF EMPIRE: THE UNITED NATIONS AND THE END OF COLONIALISM. FUT PORTUGAL WOR+45 NAT/G CONSULT DOMIN LEGIT ADMIN ROUTINE ATTIT ORD/FREE...POLICY JURID RECORD INT TIME/SEQ UN CMN/WLTH 20. PAGE 160 A3260
INT/ORG TREND COLONIAL

L64
CARNEGIE ENDOWMENT INT. PEACE,"POLITICAL QUESTIONS (ISSUES BEFORE THE NINETEENTH GENERAL ASSEMBLY)." SPACE WOR+45 CONSTN FINAN NAT/G CONSULT DELIB/GP FORCES LEGIS TEC/DEV EDU/PROP LEGIT ARMS/CONT COERCE NUC/PWR ATTIT ALL/VALS...CONCPT OBS UN COLD/WAR 20. PAGE 24 A0490
INT/ORG PEACE

L64
CURTIS G.L.,"THE UNITED NATIONS OBSERVER GROUP IN LEBANON." ISLAM USA+45 NAT/G CONSULT ACT/RES PLAN BAL/PWR LEGIT ATTIT KNOWL...HIST/WRIT UN 20 UN. PAGE 33 A0669
INT/ORG FORCES DIPLOM LEBANON

L64
HERZ J.H.,"THE RELEVANCY AND IRRELEVANCY OF APPEASEMENT." WOR+45 INT/ORG CONSULT TOP/EX LEGIT ATTIT SUPEGO ORD/FREE...POLICY SOC GEN/LAWS 20. PAGE 64 A1320
ACT/RES RIGID/FLEX

L64
LLOYD W.B.,"PEACE REQUIRES PEACEMAKERS." AFR INDIA S/ASIA SWITZERLND WOR+45 INT/ORG VOL/ASSN PLAN PERSON PWR 20. PAGE 90 A1848
CONSULT PEACE

L64
WORLD PEACE FOUNDATION,"INTERNATIONAL ORGANIZATIONS: SUMMARY OF ACTIVITIES." INDIA PAKISTAN TURKEY WOR+45 CONSTN CONSULT EX/STRUC ECO/TAC EDU/PROP LEGIT ORD/FREE...JURID SOC UN 20 CYPRESS. PAGE 167 A3397
INT/ORG ROUTINE

S64
BARKUN M.,"CONFLICT RESOLUTION THROUGH IMPLICIT MEDIATION." UNIV BARGAIN CONSEN FEDERAL JURID. PAGE 11 A0222
CONSULT CENTRAL INT/LAW IDEA/COMP

S64
GROSS J.A.,"WHITEHALL AND THE COMMONWEALTH." EUR+WWI MOD/EUR INT/ORG NAT/G CONSULT DELIB/GP LEGIS DOMIN ADMIN COLONIAL ROUTINE PWR CMN/WLTH 19/20. PAGE 57 A1174
EX/STRUC ATTIT TREND

S64
HOSKYNS C.,"THE AFRICAN STATES AND THE UNITED NATIONS: 1958-1964." SOUTH/AFR NAT/G VOL/ASSN CONSULT BAL/PWR EDU/PROP MORAL ORD/FREE PWR ...CONCPT TREND UN 20. PAGE 68 A1393
AFR INT/ORG DIPLOM

S64
HUELIN D.,"ECONOMIC INTEGRATION IN LATIN AMERICAN: PROGRESS AND PROBLEMS." L/A+17C ECO/DEV AGRI DIST/IND FINAN INDUS NAT/G VOL/ASSN CONSULT DELIB/GP EX/STRUC ACT/RES PLAN TEC/DEV ECO/TAC ROUTINE BAL/PAY WEALTH WORK 20. PAGE 69 A1411
MARKET ECO/UNDEV INT/TRADE

S64
JACK H.,"NONALIGNMENT AND A TEST BAN AGREEMENT: THE ROLE OF THE NON-ALIGNED STATES." WOR+45 INT/ORG CONSULT DOMIN EDU/PROP LEGIT CHOOSE PEACE ATTIT DRIVE KNOWL ORD/FREE...TREND CHARTS GEN/LAWS UN VAL/FREE 20. PAGE 72 A1471
PWR CONCPT NUC/PWR

S64
JORDAN A.,"POLITICAL COMMUNICATION: THE THIRD DIMENSION OF STRATEGY." USA+45 WOR+45 INT/ORG NAT/G CONSULT FORCES PLAN LEGIT EXEC PERCEPT ALL/VALS ...POLICY RELATIV PSY NEW/IDEA AUD/VIS EXHIBIT TOT/POP 20. PAGE 75 A1534
EDU/PROP RIGID/FLEX ATTIT

S64
KISSINGER H.A.,"COALITION DIPLOMACY IN A NUCLEAR AGE." COM EUR+WWI USA+45 WOR+45 INT/ORG NAT/G FORCES ACT/RES DOMIN LEGIT COERCE PERCEPT ALL/VALS ...POLICY TOT/POP 20. PAGE 80 A1644
CONSULT ATTIT DIPLOM NUC/PWR

S64
MOWER A.G.,"THE OFFICIAL PRESSURE GROUP OF THE COUNCIL OF EUROPE'S CONSULATIVE ASSEMBLY." EUR+WWI SOCIETY STRUCT FINAN CONSULT ECO/TAC ADMIN ROUTINE ATTIT PWR WEALTH...STAT CHARTS 20 COUNCL/EUR. PAGE 105 A2160
INT/ORG EDU/PROP

S64
TAUBENFELD R.K.,"INDEPENDENT REVENUE FOR THE UNITED NATIONS." WOR+45 SOCIETY STRUCT INDUS NAT/G CONSULT ACT/RES PLAN ECO/TAC LEGIT WEALTH...DECISION CON/ANAL GEN/METH UN 20. PAGE 142 A2896
INT/ORG FINAN

S64
WOOD H.B.,"STRETCHING YOUR FOREIGN-AID DOLLAR." USA+45 WOR+45 CONSULT EDU/PROP ATTIT WEALTH...OBS TOT/POP CONGRESS 20. PAGE 166 A3390
ECO/UNDEV MGT FOR/AID

B65
HAGRAS K.M.,UNITED NATIONS CONFERENCE ON TRADE AND DEVELOPMENT: A CASE STUDY OF UN DIPLOMACY. CONSULT ACT/RES TEC/DEV FOR/AID INT/TRADE...BIBLIOG 20 UN LEAGUE/NAT UNCTAD. PAGE 59 A1213
INT/ORG ADMIN DELIB/GP DIPLOM

B65
REQUA E.G.,THE DEVELOPING NATIONS: A GUIDE TO INFORMATION SOURCES CONCERNING THEIR ECON, POLIT, TECHNICAL, AND SOCIAL PROBLEMS. AFR ASIA ISLAM L/A+17C INDUS INT/ORG CONSULT PLAN PROB/SOLV...SOC 20 UN. PAGE 120 A2466
BIBLIOG/A ECO/UNDEV FOR/AID TEC/DEV

B65
US SENATE COMM AERO SPACE SCI,INTERNATIONAL COOPERATION AND ORGANIZATION FOR OUTER SPACE. FUT USA+45 WOR+45 PROF/ORG VOL/ASSN CONSULT DELIB/GP PLAN TEC/DEV ARMS/CONT GP/REL PEACE 20 UN NASA. PAGE 155 A3167
DIPLOM SPACE R+D NAT/G

B65
WHITE G.M.,THE USE OF EXPERTS BY INTERNATIONAL TRIBUNALS. WOR+45 WOR-45 INT/ORG NAT/G PAY ADJUD COST...OBS BIBLIOG 20. PAGE 164 A3334
INT/LAW ROUTINE CONSULT CT/SYS

S65
HAZARD J.N.,"CO-EXISTENCE LAW BOWS OUT." WOR+45 R+D INT/ORG VOL/ASSN CONSULT DELIB/GP ACT/RES CREATE PEACE KNOWL...JURID CONCPT COLD/WAR VAL/FREE 20. PAGE 63 A1300
PROF/ORG ADJUD

S65
MERRITT R.L.,"WOODROW WILSON AND THE 'GREAT AND SOLEMN REFERENDUM,' 1920." USA-45 SOCIETY NAT/G CONSULT LEGIS ACT/RES PLAN DOMIN EDU/PROP ROUTINE ATTIT DISPL DRIVE PERSON RIGID/FLEX MORAL ORD/FREE ...PSY SOC CONCPT MYTH LEAGUE/NAT. PAGE 100 A2044
INT/ORG TOP/EX DIPLOM

S65
QUADE Q.L.,"THE TRUMAN ADMINISTRATION AND THE SEPARATION OF POWERS: THE CASE OF THE MARSHALL PLAN." SOCIETY INT/ORG NAT/G CONSULT DELIB/GP LEGIS PLAN ECO/TAC ROUTINE DRIVE PERCEPT RIGID/FLEX ORD/FREE PWR WEALTH...DECISION GEOG NEW/IDEA TREND 20 TRUMAN/HS. PAGE 118 A2422
USA+45 ECO/UNDEV DIPLOM

S65
SPAAK P.H.,"THE SEARCH FOR CONSENSUS: A NEW EFFORT TO BUILD EUROPE." FRANCE GERMANY ECO/DEV NAT/G CONSULT FORCES PLAN EDU/PROP REGION CONSEN ATTIT ...SOC METH/CNCPT OBS TREND EEC NATO WORK 20. PAGE 135 A2770
EUR+WWI INT/ORG

B66
FREUND L.,POLITISCHE WAFFEN. EUR+WWI GERMANY CONSULT FORCES CONFER NUC/PWR 20. PAGE 49 A1000
EDU/PROP DIPLOM ATTIT

B66
LENT H.B.,THE PEACE CORPS: AMBASSADORS OF GOOD WILL. USA+45 ECO/UNDEV...INT TESTS BIOG AUD/VIS SOC/INTEG 20 PEACE/CORP. PAGE 87 A1776
VOL/ASSN FOR/AID DIPLOM CONSULT

B66
MOORE R.J.,SIR CHARLES WOOD'S INDIAN POLICY: 1853-66. INDIA POL/PAR CHIEF DELIB/GP DIPLOM CONTROL LEAD WOOD/CHAS. PAGE 103 A2124
COLONIAL ADMIN CONSULT DECISION

B66
OHLIN G.,FOREIGN AID POLICIES RECONSIDERED. ECO/DEV ECO/UNDEV VOL/ASSN CONSULT PLAN CONTROL ATTIT ...CONCPT CHARTS BIBLIOG 20. PAGE 111 A2286
FOR/AID DIPLOM GIVE

B66
US HOUSE COMM FOREIGN AFFAIRS,UNITED STATES - SOUTH AFRICAN RELATIONS. SOUTH/AFR USA+45 NAT/G CONSULT DELIB/GP LEGIS CONFER SANCTION RACE/REL ATTIT 20 CONGRESS. PAGE 154 A3134
DISCRIM DIPLOM POLICY PARL/PROC

B66
US SENATE COMM AERO SPACE SCI,SOVIET SPACE PROGRAMS, 1962-65; GOALS AND PURPOSES, ACHIEVEMENTS, PLANS, AND INTERNATIONAL IMPLICATIONS. USA+45 USSR R+D FORCES PLAN EDU/PROP PRESS ADJUD ARMS/CONT ATTIT MARXISM. PAGE 155 A3168
CONSULT SPACE FUT DIPLOM

B66
US SENATE COMM GOVT OPERATIONS,POPULATION CRISIS. USA+45 ECO/DEV ECO/UNDEV AGRI SECT DELIB/GP PROB/SOLV FOR/AID REPRESENT ATTIT...GEOG CHARTS 20 CONGRESS DEPT/STATE DEPT/HEW BIRTH/CON. PAGE 156 A3178
CENSUS CONTROL LEGIS CONSULT

B66
VIEN N.C.,SEEKING THE TRUTH. FRANCE VIETNAM AGRI ADMIN WAR...BIOG 20 BAO/DAI INTERVENT. PAGE 159 A3231
NAT/G CONSULT CONSTN

S66
"WORLD BANK CONVENTION ON INVESTMENT DISPUTES; A BIBLIOGRAPH ICAL NOTE." VOL/ASSN CONSULT CAP/ISM DIPLOM INT/TRADE 20 SENATE PRESIDENT. PAGE 4 A0074
BIBLIOG ADJUD FINAN INT/ORG

S66
ORVIK N.,"NATO: THE ROLE OF THE SMALL MEMBERS." EUR+WWI FUT USA+45 CONSULT FORCES PROB/SOLV ARMS/CONT DETER NUC/PWR PWR 20 NATO. PAGE 112 A2298
NAT/G DIPLOM INT/ORG POLICY

B67
HIRSCHMAN A.O.,DEVELOPMENT PROJECTS OBSERVED. INDUS INT/ORG CONSULT EX/STRUC CREATE OP/RES ECO/TAC DEMAND...POLICY MGT METH/COMP 20 WORLD/BANK. PAGE 65 A1339
ECO/UNDEV R+D FINAN PLAN

B67
ZUCKERMAN S.,SCIENTISTS AND WAR. ELITES INDUS DIPLOM CENTRAL EFFICIENCY KNOWL 20. PAGE 170 A3459
R+D CONSULT ACT/RES GP/REL

S67
CRAWFORD E.T.,"FOREIGN AREA RESEARCH: A BACKGROUND STATEMENT." USA+45 CONSULT DELIB/GP DIPLOM. PAGE 32 A0661
INTELL NAT/G POLICY ACT/RES

S67
GLOBERSON A.,"SOCIAL GROWTH IN THE DEVELOPING COUNTRIES." CULTURE SOCIETY CONSULT PROB/SOLV SOC. PAGE 53 A1082
ECO/UNDEV FOR/AID EDU/PROP PLAN

S67
JOHNSON D.H.N.,"THE SOUTH-WEST AFRICA CASES." AFR ETHIOPIA LIBERIA SOUTH/AFR CONSULT JUDGE BAL/PWR 20. PAGE 74 A1521
INT/LAW DIPLOM INT/ORG ADJUD

S67
SHARP G.,"THE NEED OF A FUNCTIONAL SUBSTITUTE FOR WAR." FUT UNIV WOR+45 CULTURE SOCIETY INT/ORG CONSULT DELIB/GP ACT/RES CREATE BAL/PWR CONFER ARMS/CONT NUC/PWR 20. PAGE 132 A2696
PEACE WAR DIPLOM PROB/SOLV

S67
TACKABERRY R.B.,"ORGANIZING AND TRAINING PEACE-KEEPING FORCES* THE CANADIAN VIEW." CANADA PLAN DIPLOM CONFER ADJUD ADMIN CIVMIL/REL 20 UN. PAGE 141 A2882
PEACE FORCES INT/ORG CONSULT

S67
VAN DUSEN H.P.,"HAMMARSKOLD IN THE WORLD'S SERVICE." DIPLOM CONFER LEAD PEACE STRANGE UTOPIA MORAL SKILL OBJECTIVE...INT/LAW SELF/OBS 20. PAGE 158 A3211
INT/ORG CONSULT TOP/EX NEUTRAL

CONSULTANTS....SEE CONSULT

CONSUMER....SEE MARKET, ECO

CONT/OBS....CONTROLLED DIRECT OBSERVATION

B00
OMAN C.,A HISTORY OF THE ART OF WAR: THE MIDDLE AGES FROM THE FOURTH TO THE FOURTEENTH CENTURY. CHRIST-17C MEDIT-7 CULTURE SOCIETY INT/ORG ROUTINE PERSON...CONT/OBS HIST/WRIT CHARTS VAL/FREE. PAGE 112 A2291
FORCES SKILL WAR

B22
POTTER P.B.,AN INTRODUCTION TO THE STUDY OF INTERNATIONAL ORGANIZATION. WOR-45 ACT/RES CREATE EDU/PROP ROUTINE PERCEPT KNOWL...CONT/OBS RECORD GEN/LAWS TOT/POP VAL/FREE 20. PAGE 117 A2398
INT/ORG CONCPT

B53
MACK R.T.,RAISING THE WORLDS STANDARD OF LIVING. IRAN INT/ORG VOL/ASSN EX/STRUC ECO/TAC WEALTH...MGT METH/CNCPT STAT CONT/OBS INT TOT/POP VAL/FREE 20 UN. PAGE 92 A1893
WOR+45 FOR/AID INT/TRADE

B54
MANNING C.A.W.,THE UNIVERSITY TEACHING OF SOCIAL SCIENCES: INTERNATIONAL RELATIONS. WOR+45 INTELL STRATA R+D ACADEM INT/ORG NAT/G CONSULT DELIB/GP ACT/RES EDU/PROP NAT/LISM ATTIT...POLICY CONT/OBS HYPO/EXP VAL/FREE LEAGUE/NAT UNESCO 20. PAGE 94 A1925
KNOWL PHIL/SCI DIPLOM

B57
HOLCOMBE A.N.,STRENGTHENING THE UNITED NATIONS. USA+45 ACT/RES CREATE PLAN EDU/PROP ATTIT PERCEPT PWR...METH/CNCPT CONT/OBS RECORD UN COLD/WAR 20. PAGE 66 A1365
INT/ORG ROUTINE

S58
BOGART L.,"MEASURING THE EFFECTIVENESS OF AN OVERSEAS INFORMATION CAMPAIGN." EUR+WWI GREECE USA+45 INT/ORG MUNIC PLAN DIPLOM PEACE PERCEPT RIGID/FLEX KNOWL...TECHNIC PSY SOC NEW/IDEA CONT/OBS REC/INT STAND/INT SAMP/SIZ COLD/WAR 20. PAGE 16 A0328
ATTIT EDU/PROP

B59
DIEBOLD W. JR.,THE SCHUMAN PLAN: A STUDY IN ECONOMIC COOPERATION, 1950-1959. EUR+WWI FRANCE GERMANY USA+45 EXTR/IND CONSULT DELIB/GP PLAN DIPLOM ECO/TAC INT/TRADE ROUTINE ORD/FREE WEALTH ...METH/CNCPT STAT CONT/OBS INT TIME/SEQ ECSC 20. PAGE 37 A0759
INT/ORG REGION

S59
BOULDING K.E.,"NATIONAL IMAGES AND INTERNATIONAL SYSTEMS." FUT WOR+45 CULTURE INT/ORG TOP/EX ROUTINE ...METH/CNCPT MYTH CONT/OBS TREND HYPO/EXP GEN/METH TOT/POP 20. PAGE 17 A0346
NAT/G DIPLOM

B60
SHONFIELD A.,THE ATTACK ON WORLD POVERTY. WOR+45 ECO/DEV ECO/UNDEV FINAN VOL/ASSN PLAN EDU/PROP DRIVE KNOWL WEALTH...CONT/OBS STAND/INT ORG/CHARTS TOT/POP UNESCO 20. PAGE 132 A2704
INT/ORG ECO/TAC FOR/AID INT/TRADE

B60
WOLF C.,FOREIGN AID: THEORY AND PRACTICE IN SOUTHERN ASIA. CEYLON INDONESIA PHILIPPINE S/ASIA CULTURE STRATA ECO/UNDEV PLAN EDU/PROP ATTIT ...METH/CNCPT MATH QUANT STAT CONT/OBS TIME/SEQ SIMUL TOT/POP 20. PAGE 166 A3378
ACT/RES ECO/TAC FOR/AID

S60
MORALES C.J.,"TRADE AND ECONOMIC INTEGRATION IN LATIN AMERICA." FUT L/A+17C LAW STRATA ECO/UNDEV DIST/IND INDUS LABOR NAT/G LEGIS ECO/TAC ADMIN RIGID/FLEX WEALTH...CONCPT NEW/IDEA CONT/OBS TIME/SEQ WORK 20. PAGE 104 A2128
FINAN INT/TRADE REGION

B61
KNORR K.E.,THE INTERNATIONAL SYSTEM. FUT SOCIETY INT/ORG NAT/G PLAN BAL/PWR DIPLOM WAR PWR ...DECISION METH/CNCPT CONT/OBS GAME METH UN 20. PAGE 81 A1655
ACT/RES SIMUL ECO/UNDEV

S61
CARLETON W.G.,"AMERICAN FOREIGN POLICY: MYTHS AND REALITIES." FUT USA+45 WOR+45 ECO/UNDEV INT/ORG EX/STRUC ARMS/CONT NUC/PWR WAR ATTIT...POLICY CONCPT CONT/OBS GEN/METH COLD/WAR TOT/POP 20. PAGE 24 A0484
PLAN MYTH DIPLOM

S61
HAZARD J.N.,"CODIFYING PEACEFUL COEXISTANCE." FUT INTELL INT/ORG TEC/DEV PEACE HEALTH...INT/LAW CONT/OBS 20. PAGE 63 A1299
VOL/ASSN JURID

S61
VERNON R.,"A TRADE POLICY FOR THE 1960'S." COM FUT USA+45 WOR+45 ECO/DEV ECO/UNDEV FINAN TOP/EX ACT/RES...WELF/ST METH/CNCPT CONT/OBS TOT/POP 20. PAGE 159 A3229
PLAN INT/TRADE

S62
NORTH R.C.,"DECISION MAKING IN CRISIS: AN INTRODUCTION." WOR+45 WOR-45 NAT/G CONSULT DELIB/GP TEC/DEV PERCEPT KNOWL...POLICY DECISION PSY METH/CNCPT CONT/OBS TREND VAL/FREE 20. PAGE 110 A2251
INT/ORG ROUTINE DIPLOM

L63
RUSSETT B.M.,"TOWARD A MODEL OF COMPETITIVE INTERNATIONAL POLITICS." USA+45 WOR+45 INT/ORG NAT/G POL/PAR VOL/ASSN LEGIS BAL/PWR DIPLOM LEGIT PWR...CONCPT CONT/OBS STERTYP GEN/LAWS TOT/POP COLD/WAR 20 UN. PAGE 126 A2579
ATTIT EDU/PROP

S63
GORDON B.,"ECONOMIC IMPEDIMENTS TO REGIONALISM IN SOUTH EAST ASIA." BURMA FUT S/ASIA THAILAND USA+45 AGRI INDUS R+D NAT/G PLAN ECO/TAC WEALTH...STAT CONT/OBS 20. PAGE 54 A1110
VOL/ASSN ECO/UNDEV INT/TRADE REGION

S63
WOLF C.,"SOME ASPECTS OF THE 'VALUE' OF LESS-DEVELOPED COUNTRIES TO THE UNITED STATES." ASIA CHINA/COM COM USA+45 USSR ECO/UNDEV BAL/PWR ECO/TAC FOR/AID DOMIN EDU/PROP ATTIT PWR...POLICY METH/CNCPT CONT/OBS TREND CHARTS 20. PAGE 166 A3379
CONCPT GEN/LAWS DIPLOM

S64
BEIM D.,"THE COMMUNIST BLOC AND THE FOREIGN-AID GAME." WOR+45 NAT/G PLAN ROUTINE ATTIT KNOWL ORD/FREE...DECISION QUANT CONT/OBS TIME/SEQ CHARTS GAME SIMUL COLD/WAR 20. PAGE 12 A0252
COM ECO/UNDEV ECO/TAC FOR/AID

CONTEMPT....SEE RESPECT

CONTENT ANALYSIS....SEE CON/ANAL

CONTROL....CONTROL OF HUMAN GROUP OPERATIONS

N
INTERNATIONAL REVIEW OF ADMINISTRATIVE SCIENCES. WOR+45 WOR-45 STRATA ECO/DEV ECO/UNDEV CREATE PLAN PROB/SOLV DIPLOM CONTROL REPRESENT...MGT 20. PAGE 1 A0011
BIBLIOG/A ADMIN INT/ORG NAT/G

BLI
MOOR C.C.,HOW TO USE UNITED NATIONS DOCUMENTS (PAPER). WOR+45 ACADEM CONTROL 20 UN. PAGE 103 A2121
BIBLIOG METH INT/ORG

NLO
WHITE J.A.,THE DIPLOMACY OF THE RUSSO-JAPANESE WAR. ASIA KOREA RUSSIA FORCES CONFER CONTROL PEACE ...BIBLIOG 19 CHINJAP. PAGE 164 A3336
DIPLOM WAR BAL/PWR

B00
GRIFFIN A.P.C.,LIST OF BOOKS RELATING TO THE THEORY OF COLONIZATION, GOVERNMENT OF DEPENDENCIES, PROTECTORATES, AND RELATED TOPICS. FRANCE GERMANY ITALY SPAIN UK USA-45 WOR-45 ECO/TAC ADMIN CONTROL REGION NAT/LISM ALL/VALS PWR...INT/LAW SOC 16/19. PAGE 56 A1149
BIBLIOG/A COLONIAL GOV/REL DOMIN

B10
GRIFFIN A.P.C.,LIST OF REFERENCES ON RECIPROCITY (2ND REV. ED.). CANADA CUBA UK USA-45 WOR-45 NAT/G TARIFFS CONFER COLONIAL CONTROL SANCTION CONSEN ALL/VALS...DECISION 19/20. PAGE 56 A1157
BIBLIOG/A VOL/ASSN DIPLOM REPAR

B14
HARRIS N.D.,INTERVENTION AND COLONIZATION IN AFRICA. BELGIUM FRANCE GERMANY MOD/EUR PORTUGAL UK ECO/UNDEV BAL/PWR DOMIN CONTROL PWR...GEOG 19/20. PAGE 62 A1267
AFR COLONIAL DIPLOM

N19
FANI-KAYODE R.,BLACKISM (PAMPHLET). AFR WOR+45 INT/ORG BAL/PWR CONTROL CENTRAL...DECISION 20 UN. PAGE 44 A0896
RACE/REL ECO/UNDEV REGION DIPLOM

N19
FRANCK P.G.,AFGHANISTAN BETWEEN EAST AND WEST: THE ECONOMICS OF COMPETITIVE COEXISTENCE (PAMPHLET). AFGHANISTN USA+45 USA-45 USSR INDUS ECO/TAC INT/TRADE CONTROL NEUTRAL ORD/FREE MARXISM...GEOG 20 UN. PAGE 48 A0977
FOR/AID PLAN DIPLOM ECO/UNDEV

N19
FREEMAN H.A.,COERCION OF STATES IN FEDERAL UNIONS (PAMPHLET). WOR-45 DIPLOM CONTROL COERCE PEACE ORD/FREE...GOV/COMP METH/COMP NAT/COMP PACIFIST 20. PAGE 49 A0994
FEDERAL WAR INT/ORG PACIFISM

N19
HAJDA J.,THE COLD WAR VIEWED AS A SOCIOLOGICAL PROBLEM (PAMPHLET). COM CZECHOSLVK EUR+WWI SOCIETY PLAN EDU/PROP CONTROL TASK ATTIT MARXISM...POLICY 20 COLD/WAR MIGRATION. PAGE 59 A1220
DIPLOM LEAD PWR NAT/G

N19
HAUSER P.M.,WORLD POPULATION PROBLEMS (PAMPHLET). USA+45 WOR+45 ECO/DEV ECO/UNDEV FAM ACT/RES PLAN PROB/SOLV FOR/AID GIVE EATING...CHARTS 20 BIRTH/CON RESOURCE/N. PAGE 63 A1289
CONTROL CENSUS ATTIT PREDICT

N19
JACKSON R.G.A.,THE CASE FOR AN INTERNATIONAL DEVELOPMENT AUTHORITY (PAMPHLET). WOR+45 ECO/DEV DIPLOM GIVE CONTROL GP/REL EFFICIENCY NAT/LISM SOVEREIGN 20. PAGE 72 A1478
FOR/AID INT/ORG ECO/UNDEV ADMIN

N19
MEZERIK A.G.,U-2 AND OPEN SKIES (PAMPHLET). USA+45 USSR INT/ORG CHIEF FORCES PLAN EDU/PROP CONTROL SANCTION ARMS/CONT 20 UN EISNHWR/DD. PAGE 100 A2060
DIPLOM RISK DEBATE

N19
MEZERIK AG,OUTER SPACE: UN, US, USSR (PAMPHLET). USSR DELIB/GP FORCES DETER NUC/PWR SOVEREIGN ...POLICY 20 UN TREATY. PAGE 101 A2063
SPACE CONTROL DIPLOM INT/ORG

N19
MORGENSTERN O.,THE COMMAND AND CONTROL STRUCTURE (PAMPHLET). USSR COM/IND INT/ORG WEAPON PEACE UTIL ...TREND 20 NATO. PAGE 104 A2132
CONTROL FORCES EFFICIENCY PLAN

N19
UNITED ARAB REPUBLIC,THE PROBLEM OF THE PALESTINIAN REFUGEES (PAMPHLET). ISRAEL UAR LAW PROB/SOLV EDU/PROP CONFER ADJUD CONTROL NAT/LISM HEALTH 20 JEWS UN MIGRATION. PAGE 148 A3029
STRANGE GP/REL INGP/REL DIPLOM

B20
MEYER H.H.B.,LIST OF REFERENCES ON THE TREATY-MAKING POWER. USA-45 CONTROL PWR...INT/LAW TIME/SEQ 18/20 TREATY. PAGE 100 A2052
BIBLIOG DIPLOM CONSTN

B29
STURZO L.,THE INTERNATIONAL COMMUNITY AND THE RIGHT OF WAR (TRANS. BY BARBARA BARCLAY CARTER). CULTURE CREATE PROB/SOLV DIPLOM ADJUD CONTROL PEACE PERSON ORD/FREE...INT/LAW IDEA/COMP PACIFIST 20 LEAGUE/NAT. PAGE 140 A2858
INT/ORG PLAN WAR CONCPT

B33
REID H.D.,RECUEIL DES COURS; TOME 45: LES SERVITUDES INTERNATIONALES III. FRANCE CONSTN DELIB/GP PRESS CONTROL REV WAR CHOOSE PEACE MORAL MARITIME TREATY. PAGE 120 A2457
ORD/FREE DIPLOM LAW

B35
LANGER W.L.,THE DIPLOMACY OF IMPERIALISM 1890-1902. FRANCE GERMANY ITALY UK WOR-45 BAL/PWR INT/TRADE LEGIT ADJUD CONTROL WAR PWR SOVEREIGN...CHARTS BIBLIOG/A 19/20. PAGE 84 A1726
DIPLOM COLONIAL DOMIN

B36
BOYCE A.N.,EUROPE AND SOUTH AFRICA. FRANCE GERMANY ITALY SOUTH/AFR UK INDUS NAT/G CONTROL REV WAR NAT/LISM...CONCPT HIST/WRIT 20. PAGE 18 A0362
COLONIAL GOV/COMP NAT/COMP DIPLOM

B36
BRIERLY J.L.,THE LAW OF NATIONS (2ND ED.). WOR+45 WOR-45 INT/ORG AGREE CONTROL COERCE WAR NAT/LISM PEACE PWR 16/20 TREATY LEAGUE/NAT. PAGE 18 A0375
DIPLOM INT/LAW NAT/G

B39
CARR E.H.,PROPAGANDA IN INTERNATIONAL POLITICS (PAMPHLET). EUR+WWI GERMANY MOD/EUR NAT/G AGREE WAR MORAL...POLICY 20 TREATY. PAGE 24 A0497
DIPLOM EDU/PROP CONTROL ATTIT

B39
THOMAS J.A.,THE HOUSE OF COMMONS, 1832-1901; A STUDY OF ITS ECONOMIC AND FUNCTIONAL CHARACTER. UK LAW STRATA FINAN DIPLOM CONTROL LEAD LOBBY REPRESENT WEALTH...POLICY STAT BIBLIOG 19/20 PARLIAMENT. PAGE 143 A2922
PARL/PROC LEGIS POL/PAR ECO/DEV

B40
ITALIAN LIBRARY OF INFORMATION: OUTLINE STUDIES (VOL. V). ITALY LIBYA CONTROL...FASCIST 20. PAGE 3 A0052
COLONIAL DIPLOM ECO/TAC POLICY

B41
PERHAM M.,AFRICANS AND BRITISH RULE. AFR UK ECO/TAC CONTROL GP/REL ATTIT 20. PAGE 115 A2355
DIPLOM COLONIAL ADMIN ECO/UNDEV

B42
BORNSTEIN J.,ACTION AGAINST THE ENEMY'S MIND. EUR+WWI GERMANY USA-45 DIPLOM DOMIN PRESS LEAD GP/REL DISCRIM PERCEPT FASCISM MARXISM 20 JEWS NAZI ANTI/SEMIT. PAGE 17 A0343
EDU/PROP PSY WAR CONTROL

B43
MAISEL A.Q.,AFRICA: FACTS AND FORECASTS. WOR+45 INT/ORG CONTROL RACE/REL SOVEREIGN...PREDICT CHARTS 20. PAGE 93 A1910
AFR WAR DIPLOM COLONIAL

B43
VINER J.,TRADE RELATIONS BETWEEN FREE-MARKET AND CONTROLLED ECONOMIES. WOR-45 MARKET PLAN TARIFFS DEMAND...POLICY STAT 20. PAGE 159 A3237
INT/TRADE DIPLOM CONTROL NAT/G

C43
BENTHAM J.,"PRINCIPLES OF INTERNATIONAL LAW" IN J. BOWRING, ED., THE WORKS OF JEREMY BENTHAM." UNIV NAT/G PLAN PROB/SOLV DIPLOM CONTROL SANCTION MORAL ORD/FREE PWR SOVEREIGN 19. PAGE 13 A0270
INT/LAW JURID WAR PEACE

B45
CONOVER H.F.,ITALY: ECONOMICS, POLITICS AND MILITARY AFFAIRS, 1940-1945. ITALY ELITES NAT/G POL/PAR EX/STRUC TOP/EX DIPLOM DOMIN CONTROL COERCE WAR CIVMIL/REL EFFICIENCY 20. PAGE 29 A0599
BIBLIOG TOTALISM FORCES

B45
HORN O.B.,BRITISH PUBLIC OPINION AND THE FIRST PARTITION OF POLAND. POLAND UK LEGIS PRESS RUMOR CONTROL PARTIC NAT/LISM SOVEREIGN 18/19. PAGE 67 A1385
DIPLOM POLICY ATTIT NAT/G

B45
NELSON M.F.,KOREA AND THE OLD ORDERS IN EASTERN ASIA. ASIA FRANCE KOREA RUSSIA DELIB/GP INT/TRADE DOMIN CONTROL WAR ORD/FREE...POLICY BIBLIOG. PAGE 108 A2218
DIPLOM BAL/PWR ATTIT CONSERVE

C45
NELSON M.F.,"KOREA AND THE OLD ORDERS IN EASTERN ASIA." KOREA WOR-45 DELIB/GP INT/TRADE DOMIN CONTROL WAR ATTIT ORD/FREE CONSERVE...POLICY TREATY. PAGE 108 A2217
BIBLIOG DIPLOM BAL/PWR ASIA

B48
HOWARD J.E.,PARLIAMENT AND FOREIGN POLICY IN FRANCE. FRANCE CONSTN DELIB/GP BUDGET ADMIN PARL/PROC CHOOSE...BIBLIOG/A 20 PARLIAMENT. PAGE 68 A1399
LEGIS CONTROL DIPLOM ATTIT

B48
KULISCHER E.M.,EUROPE ON THE MOVE: WAR AND POPULATION CHANGES, 1917-1947. COM EUR+WWI FUT GERMANY USSR DIST/IND PLAN INT/TRADE CONTROL WAR DRIVE...CENSUS TREND COLD/WAR 20. PAGE 82 A1690
ECO/TAC GEOG

B48
MORGENTHAL H.J.,POLITICS AMONG NATIONS: THE STRUGGLE FOR POWER AND PEACE. FUT WOR+45 INT/ORG OP/RES PROB/SOLV BAL/PWR CONTROL ATTIT MORAL ...INT/LAW BIBLIOG 20 COLD/WAR. PAGE 104 A2135
DIPLOM PEACE PWR POLICY

B49
MANSERGH N.,THE COMING OF THE FIRST WORLD WAR: A STUDY IN EUROPEAN BALANCE, 1878-1914. GERMANY MOD/EUR VOL/ASSN COLONIAL CONTROL PWR 19/20 TREATY. PAGE 94 A1928
DIPLOM WAR BAL/PWR

B50
DE RUSETT A.,STRENGTHENING THE FRAMEWORK OF PEACE. WOR+45 VOL/ASSN FORCES CREATE INSPECT ADJUD CONTROL WAR EQUILIB FEDERAL ORD/FREE 20 UN EUROPE. PAGE 35 A0711
INT/ORG DIPLOM PEACE METH/COMP

B50
GATZKE H.W.,GERMANY'S DRIVE TO THE WEST. BELGIUM GERMANY MOD/EUR AGRI INDUS POL/PAR FORCES DOMIN AGREE CONTROL REGION COERCE 20 TREATY WWI. PAGE 51 A1053
WAR POLICY NAT/G DIPLOM

B50
GLEASON J.H.,THE GENESIS OF RUSSOPHOBIA IN GREAT BRITAIN: A STUDY OF THE INTERACTION OF POLICY AND OPINION. ASIA RUSSIA UK NAT/G AGREE CONTROL REV WAR LOVE PWR TREATY 19. PAGE 53 A1080
DIPLOM POLICY DOMIN COLONIAL

B50
MOCKFORD J.,SOUTH-WEST AFRICA AND THE INTERNATIONAL COURT (PAMPHLET). AFR GERMANY SOUTH/AFR UK ECO/UNDEV DIPLOM CONTROL DISCRIM...DECISION JURID 20 AFRICA/SW. PAGE 102 A2094
COLONIAL SOVEREIGN INT/LAW DOMIN

B51
CORBETT P.E.,LAW AND SOCIETY IN THE RELATIONS OF STATES. FUT WOR+45 WOR-45 CONTROL WAR PEACE PWR ...POLICY JURID 16/20 TREATY. PAGE 30 A0615
INT/LAW DIPLOM INT/ORG

S51
BELKNAP G.,"POLITICAL PARTY IDENTIFICATION AND ATTITUDES TOWARD FOREIGN POLICY" (BMR)" USA+45 VOL/ASSN CONTROL CHOOSE...STAT INT CHARTS 20. PAGE 12 A0254
POL/PAR ATTIT POLICY DIPLOM

B53
LANGER W.L.,THE UNDECLARED WAR, 1940-1941. EUR+WWI GERMANY USA-45 USSR AIR FORCES TEC/DEV CONFER CONTROL COERCE PERCEPT ORD/FREE PWR 20 CHINJAP EUROPE. PAGE 84 A1727
WAR POLICY DIPLOM

B53
SHIRATO I.,JAPANESE SOURCES ON THE HISTORY OF THE CHINESE COMMUNIST MOVEMENT (PAMPHLET). CHINA/COM USSR CONSTRUC NAT/G POL/PAR FORCES DIPLOM DOMIN EDU/PROP CONTROL WAR TOTALISM SOCISM 20. PAGE 132 A2702
BIBLIOG/A MARXISM ECO/UNDEV

B53
SQUIRES J.D.,BRITISH PROPAGANDA AT HOME AND IN THE UNITED STATES FROM 1914 TO 1917. UK NAT/G PROB/SOLV DOMIN PRESS EFFICIENCY...PSY PREDICT 20 WWI INTERVENT PSY/WAR. PAGE 136 A2794
EDU/PROP CONTROL WAR DIPLOM

B54
BECKEL G.,WORKSHOPS FOR THE WORLD; THE SPECIALIZED AGENCIES OF THE UN. WOR+45 AGRI DIST/IND CREATE TEC/DEV BUDGET CONTROL TASK WEALTH...CHARTS ORG/CHARTS 20 UN CASEBOOK. PAGE 12 A0246
INT/ORG DIPLOM PEACE CON/ANAL

B54
BUCHANAN W.,AN INTERNATIONAL POLICE FORCE AND PUBLIC OPINION IN THE UNITED STATES, 1939-1953. USA+45 PROB/SOLV CONTROL ATTIT ORD/FREE...STAT TREND 20. PAGE 21 A0425
IDEA/COMP FORCES DIPLOM PLAN

B54
SALVEMINI G.,PRELUDE TO WORLD WAR II. ITALY MOD/EUR INT/ORG BAL/PWR EDU/PROP CONTROL TOTALISM...TREND NAT/COMP BIBLIOG 19 HITLER/A LEAGUE/NAT MUSSOLIN/B. PAGE 127 A2597
WAR FASCISM LEAD PWR

B54
TAYLOR A.J.P.,THE STRUGGLE FOR MASTERY IN EUROPE 1848-1918. MOD/EUR VOL/ASSN FORCES BAL/PWR DOMIN CONTROL PEACE MORAL 19/20 TREATY EUROPE WWI. PAGE 142 A2897
DIPLOM WAR PWR

C54
BERLE A.A. JR.,"THE 20TH CENTURY CAPITALIST REVOLUTION." ECO/DEV NAT/G DIPLOM PRICE CONTROL ATTIT...BIBLIOG/A 20. PAGE 14 A0275
LG/CO CAP/ISM MGT PWR

B55
HOGAN W.N.,INTERNATIONAL CONFLICT AND COLLECTIVE SECURITY: THE PRINCIPLE OF CONCERN IN INTERNATIONAL ORGANIZATION. CONSTN EX/STRUC BAL/PWR DIPLOM ADJUD CONTROL CENTRAL CONSEN PEACE...INT/LAW CONCPT METH/COMP 20 UN LEAGUE/NAT. PAGE 66 A1361
INT/ORG WAR ORD/FREE FORCES

B55
ROWE C.,VOLTAIRE AND THE STATE. FRANCE MOD/EUR BAL/PWR CONTROL TASK SUPEGO ORD/FREE PWR...CONCPT 18 VOLTAIRE. PAGE 125 A2553
NAT/G DIPLOM NAT/LISM ATTIT

B55
UNESCO,BIBLIOGRAPHIC SERVICES THROUGHOUT THE WORLD (VOLS. I AND II). WOR+45 DIPLOM CONTROL 20 UNESCO. PAGE 148 A3018
BIBLIOG INT/ORG COM/IND

C55
APTER D.E.,"THE GOLD COAST IN TRANSITION." AFR CONSTN LOC/G LEGIS DIPLOM COLONIAL CONTROL GOV/REL ...CHARTS BIBLIOG 20 CMN/WLTH. PAGE 8 A0170
ORD/FREE REPRESENT PARL/PROC NAT/G

B56
BOWLES C.,AFRICA'S CHALLENGE TO AMERICA. USA+45 ECO/UNDEV NAT/G LEGIS COLONIAL CONTROL REV ORD/FREE SOVEREIGN 20 COLD/WAR. PAGE 18 A0358
AFR DIPLOM POLICY FOR/AID

B56
COMMONWEALTH OF WORLD CITIZENS,THE BIRTH OF A WORLD PEOPLE. WOR+45 CONSTN PROB/SOLV CONTROL TASK WAR GP/REL UTOPIA PWR...POLICY NEW/IDEA 20. PAGE 29 A0582
DIPLOM VOL/ASSN PEACE INT/ORG

B56
KNORR K.E.,RUBLE DIPLOMACY: CHALLENGE TO AMERICAN FOREIGN AID(PAMPHLET). CHINA/COM USA+45 USSR PLAN TEC/DEV CAP/ISM INT/TRADE DOMIN EDU/PROP CONTROL LEAD 20 COLD/WAR. PAGE 81 A1654
ECO/UNDEV COM DIPLOM FOR/AID

B56
TOYNBEE A.,THE WAR AND THE NEUTRALS. L/A+17C PORTUGAL SPAIN SWEDEN SWITZERLND TURKEY WOR+45 WOR-45 ECO/TAC CONFER CONTROL REGION 20. PAGE 145 A2957
NEUTRAL WAR INT/TRADE DIPLOM

B57
ALEXANDER L.M.,WORLD POLITICAL PATTERNS. NAT/G PROVS CAP/ISM DIPLOM COLONIAL NAT/LISM...POLICY GEOG CHARTS METH/COMP NAT/COMP 20. PAGE 5 A0111
CONTROL METH GOV/COMP

B57
DUDDEN A.P.,WOODROW WILSON AND THE WORLD OF TODAY. USA-45 NAT/G PROVS CONTROL PARTIC WAR ISOLAT PWR SKILL...PERS/COMP ANTHOL 19/20 WILSON/W UN LEAGUE/NAT WWI. PAGE 39 A0794
CHIEF DIPLOM POL/PAR LEAD

B57
FRASER L.,PROPAGANDA. GERMANY USSR WOR+45 WOR-45 NAT/G POL/PAR CONTROL FEEDBACK LOBBY CROWD WAR CONSEN NAT/LISM 20. PAGE 48 A0988
EDU/PROP FASCISM MARXISM DIPLOM

B57
FREUND G.,UNHOLY ALLIANCE. EUR+WWI GERMANY USSR FORCES ECO/TAC CONTROL WAR PWR...TREND TREATY. PAGE 49 A0999
DIPLOM PLAN POLICY

B57
JASZI O.,AGAINST THE TYRANT. WOR+45 WOR-45 CONSTN DIPLOM CONTROL PARTIC REV WAR...CONCPT. PAGE 73 A1498
TOTALISM ORD/FREE CHIEF MURDER

B57
NEUMANN F.,THE DEMOCRATIC AND THE AUTHORITARIAN STATE: ESSAYS IN POLITICAL AND LEGAL THEORY. USA+45 USA-45 CONTROL REV GOV/REL PEACE ALL/IDEOS ...INT/LAW CONCPT GEN/LAWS BIBLIOG 20. PAGE 108 A2221
DOMIN NAT/G ORD/FREE POLICY

B57
RUMEU DE ARMAS A.,ESPANA EEN EL AFRICA ATLANTICA. AFR CHRIST-17C PORTUGAL SPAIN DIPLOM ECO/TAC CONTROL 14/16 AFRICA/W. PAGE 125 A2568
NAT/G COLONIAL CHIEF PWR

B57
SINEY M.C.,THE ALLIED BLOCKADE OF GERMANY: 1914-1916. EUR+WWI GERMANY MOD/EUR USA-45 DIPLOM CONTROL NEUTRAL PWR 20. PAGE 133 A2721
DETER INT/TRADE INT/LAW WAR

B57
US COMMISSION GOVT SECURITY,RECOMMENDATIONS; AREA: IMMIGRANT PROGRAM. USA+45 LAW WORKER DIPLOM EDU/PROP WRITING ADMIN PEACE ATTIT...CONCPT ANTHOL 20 MIGRATION SUBVERT. PAGE 150 A3060
POLICY CONTROL PLAN NAT/G

B58
KENNAN G.F.,RUSSIA, THE ATOM AND THE WEST. USA+45 USSR INT/ORG ARMS/CONT MARXISM 20 NATO. PAGE 77 A1587
BAL/PWR NUC/PWR CONTROL DIPLOM

B58
MARTIN L.J.,INTERNATIONAL PROPAGANDA: ITS LEGAL AND DIPLOMATIC CONTROL. UK USA+45 USSR CONSULT DELIB/GP DOMIN CONTROL 20. PAGE 95 A1951
EDU/PROP DIPLOM INT/LAW ATTIT

B58
MELMAN S.,INSPECTION FOR DISARMAMENT. USA+45 WOR+45 SOCIETY INT/ORG NAT/G CONSULT ACT/RES PLAN EDU/PROP CONTROL DETER PEACE ATTIT PERSON KNOWL...PSY STAT OBS CHARTS TOT/POP VAL/FREE 20. PAGE 99 A2035
FUT ORD/FREE ARMS/CONT NUC/PWR

B58
MEYRIAT J.,ETUDES DES BIBLIOGRAPHIES COURANTES DES PUBLICATIONS OFFICIELLES NATIONALES. WOR+45 DIPLOM CONTROL 20 UNESCO. PAGE 100 A2056
BIBLIOG COM/IND NAT/G

B58
SEYID MUHAMMAD V.A.,THE LEGAL FRAMEWORK OF WORLD TRADE. WOR+45 INT/ORG DIPLOM CONTROL...BIBLIOG 20 TREATY UN IMF GATT. PAGE 131 A2689
INT/LAW VOL/ASSN INT/TRADE TARIFFS

B58
SOC OF COMP LEGIS AND INT LAW,THE LAW OF THE SEA... (PAMPHLET). WOR+45 NAT/G INT/TRADE ADJUD CONTROL NUC/PWR WAR PEACE ATTIT ORD/FREE...JURID CHARTS 20 UN TREATY RESOURCE/N. PAGE 135 A2756
INT/LAW INT/ORG DIPLOM SEA

B58
UN INTL CONF ON PEACEFUL USE,PROGRESS IN ATOMIC ENERGY (VOL. I). WOR+45 R+D PLAN TEC/DEV CONFER CONTROL PEACE SKILL...CHARTS ANTHOL 20 UN BAGHDAD. PAGE 147 A3003
NUC/PWR DIPLOM WORKER EDU/PROP

B58
US HOUSE COMM GOVT OPERATIONS,HEARINGS BEFORE A SUBCOMMITTEE OF THE COMMITTEE ON GOVERNMENT
FOR/AID DIPLOM

OPERATIONS. CAMBODIA PHILIPPINE USA+45 CONSTRUC TEC/DEV ADMIN CONTROL WEAPON EFFICIENCY HOUSE/REP. PAGE 154 A3135 — ORD/FREE ECO/UNDEV

B59
ARON R.,IMPERIALISM AND COLONIALISM (PAMPHLET). WOR+45 WOR-45 ECO/TAC CONTROL REV ORD/FREE 19/20. PAGE 9 A0183 — COLONIAL DOMIN ECO/UNDEV DIPLOM

B59
DEHIO L.,GERMANY AND WORLD POLITICS IN THE TWENTIETH CENTURY. EUR+WWI FRANCE GERMANY MOD/EUR UK USSR NAT/G CHIEF BAL/PWR DOMIN COLONIAL CONTROL LEAD...IDEA/COMP 20 VERSAILLES. PAGE 36 A0724 — DIPLOM WAR NAT/LISM SOVEREIGN

B59
HALEY A.G.,FIRST COLLOQUIUM ON THE LAW OF OUTER SPACE. WOR+45 INT/ORG ACT/RES PLAN BAL/PWR CONFER ATTIT PWR...POLICY JURID CHARTS ANTHOL 20. PAGE 60 A1225 — SPACE LAW SOVEREIGN CONTROL

B59
HARRIMAN A.,PEACE WITH RUSSIA? USA+45 USSR SOCIETY ECO/TAC CONTROL TOTALISM ATTIT MARXISM...POLICY 20 STALIN/J KHRUSH/N. PAGE 62 A1266 — DIPLOM PEACE NAT/G TASK

B59
HARVARD UNIVERSITY LAW SCHOOL,INTERNATIONAL PROBLEMS OF FINANCIAL PROTECTION AGAINST NUCLEAR RISK. WOR+45 NAT/G DELIB/GP PROB/SOLV DIPLOM CONTROL ATTIT...POLICY INT/LAW MATH 20. PAGE 62 A1281 — NUC/PWR ADJUD INDUS FINAN

B59
JACKSON B.W.,FIVE IDEAS THAT CHANGE THE WORLD. FUT WOR+45 WOR-45 ECO/UNDEV INDUS DIPLOM DOMIN CONTROL ...IDEA/COMP 20. PAGE 72 A1473 — MARXISM NAT/LISM COLONIAL ECO/TAC

B59
MAC MILLAN W.M.,THE ROAD TO SELF-RULE. SOUTH/AFR UK CULTURE SOCIETY AGRI LABOR NAT/G INT/TRADE CONTROL GP/REL...SOC 19/20. PAGE 92 A1884 — AFR COLONIAL SOVEREIGN POLICY

B59
COLUMBIA U BUR APPL SOC RES,ATTITUDES OF PROMINENT AMERICANS TOWARD "WORLD PEACE THROUGH WORLD LAW" (SUPRA-NATL ORGANIZATION FOR WAR PREVENTION). USA+45 USSR ELITES FORCES PLAN PROB/SOLV CONTROL WAR PWR...POLICY SOC QU IDEA/COMP 20 UN. PAGE 117 A2403 — ATTIT ACT/RES INT/LAW STAT

B59
WENTHOLT W.,SOME COMMENTS ON THE LIQUIDATION OF THE EUROPEAN PAYMENT UNION AND RELATED PROBLEMS (PAMPHLET). WOR+45 PLAN BUDGET PRICE CONTROL 20 EEC GOLD/STAND. PAGE 163 A3319 — FINAN ECO/DEV INT/ORG ECO/TAC

B59
WOLFERS A.,ALLIANCE POLICY IN THE COLD WAR. COM INT/ORG FORCES COLONIAL CONTROL NUC/PWR 20 NATO UN COLD/WAR. PAGE 166 A3384 — DIPLOM DETER BAL/PWR

L59
GRANDIN T.,"THE POLITICAL USE OF THE RADIO." EUR+WWI SOCIETY INT/ORG DIPLOM CONTROL ATTIT ORD/FREE...CONCPT STAT RECORD SAMP GEN/LAWS TOT/POP 20. PAGE 55 A1128 — COM/IND EDU/PROP NAT/LISM

C59
KULSKI W.W.,"PEACEFUL COEXISTENCE." USSR ECO/UNDEV INT/ORG POL/PAR EDU/PROP COLONIAL CONTROL REV NAT/LISM PEACE PWR MARXISM...BIBLIOG 20. PAGE 83 A1692 — COM DIPLOM DOMIN

B60
MORAES F.,THE REVOLT IN TIBET. ASIA CHINA/COM INDIA CULTURE CONTROL COERCE WAR TOTALISM...POLICY SOC WORSHIP 20 TIBET INTERVENT. PAGE 104 A2127 — COLONIAL FORCES DIPLOM ORD/FREE

B60
SCANLON D.G.,INTERNATIONAL EDUCATION: A DOCUMENTARY HISTORY. ADMIN CONTROL ATTIT PERCEPT...BIOG ANTHOL METH 20. PAGE 127 A2612 — EDU/PROP INT/ORG NAT/COMP DIPLOM

B60
SPEER J.P.,FOR WHAT PURPOSE? CHINA/COM USSR CONSTN PROB/SOLV DIPLOM CONTROL TASK WAR NAT/LISM WORSHIP 20 UN. PAGE 136 A2778 — PEACE SECT SUPEGO ALL/IDEOS

B60
VOGT W.,PEOPLE: CHALLENGE TO SURVIVAL. WOR+45 ECO/DEV ECO/UNDEV FAM INT/ORG NAT/G PLAN PROB/SOLV FOR/AID GIVE EATING 20 BIRTH/CON. PAGE 159 A3247 — CENSUS CONTROL ATTIT TEC/DEV

B60
WHEARE K.C.,THE CONSTITUTIONAL STRUCTURE OF THE COMMONWEALTH. UK EX/STRUC DIPLOM DOMIN ADMIN COLONIAL CONTROL LEAD INGP/REL SUPEGO 20 CMN/WLTH. PAGE 163 A3325 — CONSTN INT/ORG VOL/ASSN SOVEREIGN

B61
AMORY J.F.,AROUND THE EDGE OF WAR: A NEW APPROACH TO THE PROBLEMS OF AMERICAN FOREIGN POLICY. COM L/A+17C USA+45 USSR FOR/AID EDU/PROP AGREE CONTROL ARMS/CONT NUC/PWR WAR PWR...IDEA/COMP 20 TREATY ESPIONAGE. PAGE 8 A0154 — NAT/G DIPLOM POLICY

B61
GOLDWERT M.,CONSTABULARY IN THE DOMINICAN REPUBLIC AND NICARAGUA. DOMIN/REP L/A+17C NICARAGUA USA-45 NAT/G PLAN CONTROL TASK REV...POLICY 20 INTERVENT. PAGE 53 A1093 — DIPLOM PEACE FORCES

B61
HARRIS S.E.,THE DOLLAR IN CRISIS. USA+45 MARKET INT/ORG ECO/TAC PRICE CONTROL WEALTH...METH/COMP ANTHOL 20 GOLD/STAND. PAGE 62 A1269 — BAL/PAY DIPLOM FINAN INT/TRADE

B61
LETHBRIDGE H.J.,CHINA'S URBAN COMMUNES. CHINA/COM FUT ECO/UNDEV DIPLOM EDU/PROP DEMAND INCOME MARXISM ...POLICY 20. PAGE 87 A1790 — MUNIC CONTROL ECO/TAC NAT/G

B61
LIPPMANN W.,THE COMING TESTS WITH RUSSIA. COM CUBA GERMANY USSR FORCES CONTROL NEUTRAL COERCE NUC/PWR REV WAR PWR...INT 20 KHRUSH/N BERLIN. PAGE 89 A1830 — BAL/PWR DIPLOM MARXISM ARMS/CONT

B61
MATTHEWS T.,WAR IN ALGERIA. ALGERIA FRANCE CONTROL ATTIT SOVEREIGN 20. PAGE 96 A1978 — REV COLONIAL DIPLOM WAR

B61
MORRAY J.P.,FROM YALTA TO DISARMAMENT: COLD WAR DEBATE. USA+45 CAP/ISM FOR/AID CONTROL NUC/PWR 20 UN COLD/WAR CHURCHLL/W. PAGE 104 A2145 — MARXIST ARMS/CONT DIPLOM BAL/PWR

B61
PERLO V.,EL IMPERIALISMO NORTHEAMERICANO. USA+45 USA-45 FINAN CAP/ISM DIPLOM DOMIN CONTROL DISCRIM 19/20. PAGE 115 A2363 — SOCIALIST ECO/DEV INT/TRADE ECO/TAC

B61
US GENERAL ACCOUNTING OFFICE,EXAMINATION OF ECONOMIC AND TECHNICAL ASSISTANCE PROGRAM FOR IRAN. IRAN USA+45 AGRI INDUS DIPLOM CONTROL COST 20. PAGE 153 A3115 — FOR/AID ADMIN TEC/DEV ECO/UNDEV

B61
WINTER R.C.,BLUEPRINTS FOR INDEPENDENCE. WOR+45 INT/ORG DIPLOM COLONIAL CONTROL REV WAR PWR ...BIBLIOG 20 UN. PAGE 165 A3367 — NAT/G ECO/UNDEV SOVEREIGN CONSTN

B62
EBENSTEIN W.,TWO WAYS OF LIFE. USA+45 CULTURE ECO/DEV PLAN EDU/PROP CONTROL ORD/FREE...GOV/COMP IDEA/COMP T 20 MARX/KARL ENGELS/F LENIN/VI LOCKE/JOHN MILL/JS. PAGE 40 A0819 — MARXISM POPULISM ECO/TAC DIPLOM

B62
KING-HALL S.,POWER POLITICS IN THE NUCLEAR AGE: A POLICY FOR BRITAIN. UK WOR+45 PLAN ECO/TAC CONTROL RISK ARMS/CONT MORAL PWR RESPECT...OLD/LIB 20. PAGE 79 A1625 — BAL/PWR NUC/PWR POLICY DIPLOM

B62
KLUCKHOHN F.L.,THE NAKED RISE OF COMMUNISM. CHINA/COM COM USSR WOR+45 CONSTN POL/PAR PLAN CONTROL LEAD NEUTRAL CONSERVE 20 STALIN/J EUROPE/E COM/PARTY. PAGE 80 A1650 — MARXISM IDEA/COMP DIPLOM DOMIN

B62
LESSING P.,AFRICA'S RED HARVEST. AFR CHINA/COM COM USSR ECO/UNDEV BAL/PWR DIPLOM CONTROL PWR 20 COLD/WAR INTERVENT. PAGE 87 A1789 — NAT/LISM MARXISM FOR/AID EDU/PROP

B62
MORTON L.,STRATEGY AND COMMAND: THE FIRST TWO YEARS. USA-45 NAT/G CONTROL EXEC LEAD WEAPON CIVMIL/REL PWR...POLICY AUD/VIS CHARTS 20 CHINJAP. PAGE 105 A2150 — WAR FORCES PLAN DIPLOM

B62
NOBECOURT R.G.,LES SECRETS DE LA PROPAGANDE EN FRANCE OCCUPEE. FRANCE ELITES NAT/G DIPLOM GP/REL NAT/LISM TOTALISM ORD/FREE 20 VICHY VICHY. PAGE 109 A2244 — METH/COMP EDU/PROP WAR CONTROL

B62
SNOW J.H.,GOVERNMENT BY TREASON. USA+45 USA-45 LEGIS DIPLOM FOR/AID GIVE CONTROL WEALTH MARXISM ...MAJORIT 20 CONGRESS COLD/WAR. PAGE 134 A2750 — FINAN TAX PWR POLICY

B62
US CONGRESS,COMMUNICATIONS SATELLITE LEGISLATION: HEARINGS BEFORE COMM ON AERON AND SPACE SCIENCES ON BILLS S2550 AND 2814. WOR+45 LAW VOL/ASSN PLAN DIPLOM CONTROL OWN PEACE...NEW/IDEA CONGRESS NASA. PAGE 150 A3062 — SPACE COM/IND ADJUD GOV/REL

B62
US SENATE COMM GOVT OPERATIONS,ADMINISTRATION OF NATIONAL SECURITY. USA+45 CHIEF PLAN PROB/SOLV TEC/DEV DIPLOM ATTIT...POLICY DECISION 20 KENNEDY/JF RUSK/D MCNAMARA/R BUNDY/M HERTER/C. PAGE 156 A3173 — ORD/FREE ADMIN NAT/G CONTROL

B62
WADSWORTH J.J.,THE PRICE OF PEACE. WOR+45 TEC/DEV CONTROL NUC/PWR PEACE ATTIT TREATY 20. PAGE 160 A3258 — DIPLOM INT/ORG ARMS/CONT

POLICY

C62

BACON F.,"OF EMPIRE" (1612) IN F. BACON, ESSAYS." ELITES NAT/G PROB/SOLV DIPLOM ADMIN CONTROL WEALTH 16/17 KING. PAGE 10 A0201 — PWR CHIEF DOMIN GEN/LAWS

C62

ROBINSON J.A.,"CONGRESS AND FOREIGN POLICY-MAKING: A STUDY IN LEGISLATIVE INFLUENCE AND INITIATIVE." USA+45 CHIEF DELIB/GP CREATE CONTROL EXEC GOV/REL PERCEPT...TREND BIBLIOG 20 CONGRESS. PAGE 122 A2505 — LEGIS DIPLOM POLICY DECISION

B63

GALLAGHER M.P.,THE SOVIET HISTORY OF WORLD WAR II. EUR+WWI USSR DIPLOM DOMIN WRITING CONTROL WAR MARXISM...PSY TIME/SEQ 20 STALIN/J. PAGE 50 A1031 — CIVMIL/REL EDU/PROP HIST/WRIT PRESS

B63

GARDINIER D.E.,CAMEROON: UNITED NATIONS CHALLENGE TO FRENCH POLICY. AFR CAMEROON FRANCE NAT/G LEGIS CONTROL SOVEREIGN 20 UN. PAGE 51 A1042 — DIPLOM POLICY INT/ORG COLONIAL

B63

GILBERT M.,THE APPEASERS. COM GERMANY UK PLAN ECO/TAC COLONIAL CONTROL EXEC ORD/FREE PWR FASCISM 20 PARLIAMENT. PAGE 52 A1068 — DIPLOM WAR POLICY DECISION

B63

GONZALEZ PEDRERO E.,ANATOMIA DE UN CONFLICTO. WOR+45 ECO/DEV ECO/UNDEV ECO/TAC FOR/AID CONTROL ARMS/CONT GOV/REL...NAT/COMP 20 COLD/WAR. PAGE 54 A1099 — DIPLOM DETER BAL/PWR

B63

GORDON G.N.,THE IDEA INVADERS. USA+45 USSR CULTURE COM/IND DIPLOM PRESS TV TOTALISM MARXISM 20. PAGE 54 A1113 — EDU/PROP ATTIT ORD/FREE CONTROL

B63

HALPERIN M.H.,LIMITED WAR IN A NUCLEAR AGE. CUBA KOREA USA+45 USSR INT/ORG FORCES PLAN DIPLOM DETER PWR...BIBLIOG/A 20. PAGE 60 A1238 — WAR NUC/PWR CONTROL WEAPON

B63

HUSSEY W.D.,THE BRITISH EMPIRE AND COMMONWEALTH 1500 TO 1961. UK USA-45 SOCIETY ECO/UNDEV NAT/G VOL/ASSN INT/TRADE DOMIN CONTROL WAR PWR ...DICTIONARY 16/20 COMMONWLTH TRUST/TERR. PAGE 69 A1422 — COLONIAL SOVEREIGN INT/ORG

B63

HYDE D.,THE PEACEFUL ASSAULT. COM UAR USSR ECO/DEV ECO/UNDEV NAT/G POL/PAR CAP/ISM PWR 20. PAGE 69 A1427 — MARXISM CONTROL ECO/TAC DIPLOM

B63

MARITANO N.,AN ALLIANCE FOR PROGRESS. FUT L/A+17C USA+45 CULTURE ECO/UNDEV NAT/G PLAN CONTROL POLICY. PAGE 95 A1941 — DIPLOM INT/ORG ECO/TAC FOR/AID

B63

MENEZES A.J.,SUBDESENVOLVIMENTO E POLITICA INTERNACIONAL. BRAZIL WOR+45 PLAN CONTROL LEAD NAT/LISM ORD/FREE 20 THIRD/WRLD. PAGE 99 A2041 — ECO/UNDEV DIPLOM POLICY BAL/PWR

B63

PATRA A.C.,THE ADMINISTRATION OF JUSTICE UNDER THE EAST INDIA COMPANY IN BENGAL, BIHAR AND ORISSA. INDIA UK LG/CO CAP/ISM INT/TRADE ADJUD COLONIAL CONTROL CT/SYS...POLICY 20. PAGE 114 A2341 — ADMIN JURID CONCPT

B63

RAO V.K.R.,FOREIGN AID AND INDIA'S ECONOMIC DEVELOPMENT. INDIA INT/ORG PROB/SOLV TEC/DEV ECO/TAC CONTROL WEALTH...TREND 20. PAGE 119 A2445 — FOR/AID ECO/UNDEV RECEIVE DIPLOM

B63

VAN SLYCK P.,PEACE: THE CONTROL OF NATIONAL POWER. CUBA WOR+45 FINAN NAT/G FORCES PROB/SOLV TEC/DEV BAL/PWR ADMIN CONTROL ORD/FREE...POLICY INT/LAW UN COLD/WAR TREATY. PAGE 158 A3214 — ARMS/CONT PEACE INT/ORG DIPLOM

N63

PATEL H.M.,THE DEFENCE OF INDIA (PAMPHLET). CHINA/COM INDIA PAKISTAN WOR+45 TEC/DEV BAL/PWR DIPLOM CONTROL WAR. PAGE 114 A2340 — FORCES POLICY SOVEREIGN DETER

N63

US COMM STRENG SEC FREE WORLD,THE SCOPE AND DISTRIBUTION OF UNITED STATES MILITARY AND ECONOMIC ASSISTANCE PROGRAMS (PAMPHLET). USA+45 PLAN BAL/PWR BUDGET DIPLOM CONTROL CIVMIL/REL ATTIT. PAGE 150 A3059 — DELIB/GP POLICY FOR/AID ORD/FREE

B64

BLACKSTOCK P.W.,THE STRATEGY OF SUBVERSION. USA+45 FORCES EDU/PROP ADMIN COERCE GOV/REL...DECISION MGT 20 DEPT/DEFEN CIA DEPT/STATE. PAGE 15 A0301 — ORD/FREE DIPLOM CONTROL

B64

CEPEDE M.,POPULATION AND FOOD. USA+45 STRUCT ECO/UNDEV FAM PLAN TEC/DEV FOR/AID CONTROL...CATH SOC TREND 19/20. PAGE 25 A0513 — FUT GEOG AGRI

CENSUS

B64

FINER H.,DULLES OVER SUEZ. FRANCE FUT UAR UK WOR+45 NAT/G PROB/SOLV CONTROL NUC/PWR WAR 20 DULLES/JF SUEZ. PAGE 46 A0932 — DIPLOM POLICY REC/INT

B64

FRYDENSBERG P.,PEACE-KEEPING: EXPERIENCE AND EVALUATION: THE OSLO PAPERS. NORWAY FORCES PLAN CONTROL...INT/LAW 20 UN. PAGE 49 A1012 — INT/ORG DIPLOM PEACE COERCE

B64

HAMRELL S.,THE SOVIET BLOC, CHINA, AND AFRICA. AFR CHINA/COM COM USSR ECO/UNDEV EDU/PROP 20. PAGE 61 A1249 — MARXISM DIPLOM CONTROL FOR/AID

B64

HANSEN B.,INTERNATIONAL LIQUIDITY. USA+45 INT/ORG ECO/TAC PRICE CONTROL WEALTH...POLICY 20. PAGE 61 A1254 — BAL/PAY INT/TRADE DIPLOM FINAN

B64

KAUFMANN W.W.,THE MC NAMARA STRATEGY. TOP/EX INSPECT BAL/PWR DIPLOM CONTROL DETER GUERRILLA NUC/PWR WEAPON COST PWR...METH/COMP 20 MCNAMARA/R KENNEDY/JF JOHNSON/LB NATO DEPT/DEFEN. PAGE 77 A1572 — FORCES WAR PLAN PROB/SOLV

B64

LOCKHART W.B.,CASES AND MATERIALS ON CONSTITUTIONAL RIGHTS AND LIBERTIES. USA+45 FORCES LEGIS DIPLOM PRESS CONTROL CRIME WAR PWR...AUD/VIS T WORSHIP 20 NEGRO. PAGE 90 A1849 — ORD/FREE CONSTN NAT/G

B64

RUSSELL R.B.,UNITED NATIONS EXPERIENCE WITH MILITARY FORCES: POLITICAL AND LEGAL ASPECTS. AFR KOREA WOR+45 LEGIS PROB/SOLV ADMIN CONTROL EFFICIENCY PEACE...POLICY INT/LAW BIBLIOG UN. PAGE 126 A2576 — FORCES DIPLOM SANCTION ORD/FREE

B64

STILLMAN E.O.,THE POLITICS OF HYSTERIA: THE SOURCES OF TWENTIETH-CENTURY CONFLICT. WOR+45 WOR-45 CULTURE ECO/UNDEV PLAN CAP/ISM WAR MARXISM ...PREDICT BIBLIOG 20 COLD/WAR. PAGE 138 A2828 — DIPLOM IDEA/COMP COLONIAL CONTROL

B64

TAUBENFELD H.J.,SPACE AND SOCIETY. USA+45 LAW FORCES CREATE TEC/DEV ADJUD CONTROL COST PEACE ...PREDICT ANTHOL 20. PAGE 142 A2895 — SPACE SOCIETY ADJUST DIPLOM

B64

TULLY A.,WHERE DID YOUR MONEY GO. USA+45 USSR ECO/UNDEV ADMIN EFFICIENCY WEALTH...METH/COMP 20. PAGE 146 A2976 — FOR/AID DIPLOM CONTROL

B64

US SENATE COMM GOVT OPERATIONS,ADMINISTRATION OF NATIONAL SECURITY. USA+45 CHIEF TOP/EX PLAN DIPLOM CONTROL PEACE...POLICY DECISION 20 PRESIDENT CONGRESS. PAGE 156 A3176 — ADMIN FORCES ORD/FREE NAT/G

B64

VOELKMANN K.,HERRSCHER VON MORGEN? BAL/PWR COLONIAL NEUTRAL REGION RACE/REL ALL/VALS SOVEREIGN...RECORD 20 COLD/WAR THIRD/WRLD. PAGE 159 A3246 — DIPLOM ECO/UNDEV CONTROL NAT/COMP

B64

WRIGHT Q.,A STUDY OF WAR. LAW NAT/G PROB/SOLV BAL/PWR NAT/LISM PEACE ATTIT SOVEREIGN...CENSUS SOC/INTEG. PAGE 168 A3419 — WAR CONCPT DIPLOM CONTROL

S64

ARMSTRONG J.A.,"THE SOVIET-AMERICAN CONFRONTATION: A NEW STAGE?" CUBA USA+45 USSR PLAN PROB/SOLV INT/TRADE CONTROL ARMS/CONT NUC/PWR MARXISM 20 COLD/WAR INTERVENT. PAGE 9 A0174 — DIPLOM POLICY INSPECT

B65

BROOKINGS INSTITUTION,BROOKINGS PAPERS ON PUBLIC POLICY. USA+45 ECO/UNDEV LEGIS CAP/ISM ECO/TAC TAX EDU/PROP CONTROL APPORT 20. PAGE 19 A0395 — DIPLOM FOR/AID POLICY FINAN

B65

FRASER S.,GOVERNMENTAL POLICY AND INTERNATIONAL EDUCATION. CHINA/COM COM USA+45 WOR+45 CONTROL MARXISM...ANTHOL BIBLIOG/A 20 UN. PAGE 48 A0989 — EDU/PROP DIPLOM POLICY NAT/G

B65

JADOS S.S.,DOCUMENTS ON RUSSIAN-AMERICAN RELATIONS: WASHINGTON TO EISENHOWER. USA+45 USA-45 USSR INT/ORG LEGIS INT/TRADE WAR PEACE...ANTHOL BIBLIOG 18/20 PRESIDENT. PAGE 73 A1488 — DIPLOM CHIEF CONTROL

B65

JALEE P.,THE PILLAGE OF THE THIRD WORLD (TRANS. BY MARY KLOPPER). WOR+45 AGRI INDUS ECO/TAC FOR/AID COLONIAL CONTROL PRODUC PWR WEALTH...STAT CHARTS 20 RESOURCE/N. PAGE 73 A1493 — ECO/UNDEV DOMIN INT/TRADE DIPLOM

B65

JOHNSTON D.M.,THE INTERNATIONAL LAW OF FISHERIES: A FRAMEWORK FOR POLICYORIENTED INQUIRIES. WOR+45 ACT/RES PLAN PROB/SOLV CONTROL SOVEREIGN. PAGE 75 A1527 — CONCPT EXTR/IND JURID DIPLOM

B65
JOHNSTONE A.,UNITED STATES DIRECT INVESTMENT IN FRANCE: AN INVESTIGATION OF THE FRENCH CHARGES. FRANCE USA+45 ECO/DEV INDUS LG/CO NAT/G ECO/TAC CONTROL WEALTH...BIBLIOG 20 INTERVENT. PAGE 75 A1529
FINAN DIPLOM POLICY SOVEREIGN

B65
SILVA SOLAR J.,EL DESARROLLO DE LA NUEVA SOCIEDAD EN AMERICA. L/A+17C SOCIETY AGRI PROB/SOLV DIPLOM PARTIC GP/REL OWN...POLICY SOC 20 REFORMERS. PAGE 133 A2716
STRUCT ECO/UNDEV REGION CONTROL

B65
SOPER T.,EVOLVING COMMONWEALTH. AFR CANADA INDIA IRELAND UK LAW CONSTN POL/PAR DOMIN CONTROL WAR PWR ...AUD/VIS 18/20 COMMONWLTH OEEC. PAGE 135 A2769
INT/ORG COLONIAL VOL/ASSN

B65
STEWART I.G.,AFRICAN PRIMARY PRODUCTS AND INTERNATIONAL TRADE. ECO/UNDEV AGRI FINAN DIPLOM CONTROL 20. PAGE 138 A2825
AFR INT/TRADE INT/ORG

B65
US SENATE COMM ON FOREIGN REL,HEARINGS ON THE FOREIGN ASSISTANCE PROGRAM. AFR ASIA L/A+17C USA+45 WOR+45 FORCES TEC/DEV BUDGET CONTROL WEAPON ORD/FREE 20 UN CONGRESS SEC/STATE. PAGE 156 A3183
FOR/AID DIPLOM INT/ORG ECO/UNDEV

B65
US SENATE COMM ON JUDICIARY,ANTITRUST EXEMPTIONS FOR AGREEMENTS RELATING TO BALANCE OF PAYMENTS. FINAN ECO/TAC CONTROL WEALTH...POLICY 20 CONGRESS. PAGE 157 A3195
BAL/PAY ADJUD MARKET INT/TRADE

B65
WASKOW A.I.,KEEPING THE WORLD DISARMED. AFR GERMANY/E DIPLOM CONTROL WAR 20 UN. PAGE 161 A3289
ARMS/CONT PEACE FORCES PROB/SOLV

B65
WEISNER J.B.,WHERE SCIENCE AND POLITICS MEET. USA+45 ECO/DEV R+D FORCES PROB/SOLV DIPLOM FOR/AID CONTROL...PHIL/SCI PRESIDENT KENNEDY/JF JOHNSON/LB. PAGE 163 A3310
CHIEF NAT/G POLICY TEC/DEV

C65
SEARA M.V.,"COSMIC INTERNATIONAL LAW." LAW ACADEM ACT/RES DIPLOM COLONIAL CONTROL NUC/PWR SOVEREIGN ...GEN/LAWS BIBLIOG UN. PAGE 131 A2678
SPACE INT/LAW IDEA/COMP INT/ORG

B66
AMERICAN ASSEMBLY COLUMBIA U,A WORLD OF NUCLEAR POWERS? FUT WOR+45 ECO/DEV BAL/PWR ECO/TAC CONTROL RISK EFFICIENCY ATTIT PWR...METH/COMP ANTHOL 20. PAGE 7 A0137
NUC/PWR DIPLOM TEC/DEV ARMS/CONT

B66
ASAMOAH O.Y.,THE LEGAL SIGNIFICANCE OF THE DECLARATIONS OF THE GENERAL ASSEMBLY OF THE UNITED NATIONS. WOR+45 CREATE CONTROL...BIBLIOG 20 UN. PAGE 9 A0184
INT/LAW INT/ORG DIPLOM

B66
BRYNES A.,WE GIVE TO CONQUER. USA+45 USSR STRATA ECO/UNDEV INT/ORG NAT/G DIPLOM DRIVE...TREND IDEA/COMP 20. PAGE 20 A0414
FOR/AID CONTROL GIVE WAR

B66
EDWARDS C.D.,TRADE REGULATIONS OVERSEAS. IRELAND NEW/ZEALND SOUTH/AFR NAT/G CAP/ISM TARIFFS CONTROL ...POLICY JURID 20 EEC CHINJAP. PAGE 40 A0823
INT/TRADE DIPLOM INT/LAW ECO/TAC

B66
EWING B.G.,PEACE THROUGH NEGOTIATION: THE AUSTRIAN EXPERIENCE. AUSTRIA USSR VIETNAM CONFER CONTROL DETER WAR ATTIT HEALTH PWR...POLICY 20. PAGE 43 A0878
PEACE DIPLOM MARXISM

B66
FREIDEL F.,AMERICAN ISSUES IN THE TWENTIETH CENTURY. SOCIETY FINAN ECO/TAC FOR/AID CONTROL NUC/PWR WAR RACE/REL PEACE ATTIT...ANTHOL T 20 WILSON/W ROOSEVLT/F KENNEDY/JF TRUMAN/HS. PAGE 49 A0995
DIPLOM POLICY NAT/G ORD/FREE

B66
GERARD-LIBOIS J.,KATANGA SECESSION. INT/ORG FORCES DIPLOM ADMIN CONTROL WAR CHOOSE PWR...CHARTS 20 KATANGA TSHOMBE/M UN. PAGE 52 A1062
NAT/G REGION ORD/FREE REV

B66
HOEVELER H.J.,INTERNATIONALE BEKAMPFUNG DES VERBRECHENS. AUSTRIA SWITZERLND WOR+45 INT/ORG CONTROL BIO/SOC...METH/COMP NAT/COMP 20 MAFIA SCOT/YARD FBI. PAGE 66 A1352
CRIMLGY CRIME DIPLOM INT/LAW

B66
KNORR K.E.,ON THE USES OF MILITARY POWER IN THE NUCLEAR AGE. WOR+45 INT/ORG TEC/DEV ADMIN CONTROL WAR COST 20. PAGE 81 A1656
FORCES DIPLOM DETER NUC/PWR

B66
MC LELLAN D.S.,THE COLD WAR IN TRANSITION. USSR WOR+45 CONTROL LEAD NUC/PWR NAT/LISM SOVEREIGN 20 COLD/WAR THIRD/WRLD. PAGE 97 A1994
BAL/PWR DETER DIPLOM POLICY

B66
MCINTYRE W.D.,COLONIES INTO COMMONWEALTH. UK CONSTN VOL/ASSN DOMIN CONTROL...BIBLIOG 18/20 CMN/WLTH. PAGE 98 A2012
DIPLOM INT/ORG COLONIAL SOVEREIGN

B66
MOORE R.J.,SIR CHARLES WOOD'S INDIAN POLICY: 1853-66. INDIA POL/PAR CHIEF DELIB/GP DIPLOM CONTROL LEAD WOOD/CHAS. PAGE 103 A2124
COLONIAL ADMIN CONSULT DECISION

B66
NIEDERGANG M.,LA REVOLUTION DE SAINT-DOMINGUE. DOMIN/REP INT/ORG NAT/G CONTROL LEAD GP/REL ORD/FREE MARXISM 20. PAGE 109 A2239
REV FORCES DIPLOM

B66
OHLIN G.,FOREIGN AID POLICIES RECONSIDERED. ECO/DEV ECO/UNDEV VOL/ASSN CONSULT PLAN CONTROL ATTIT ...CONCPT CHARTS BIBLIOG 20. PAGE 111 A2286
FOR/AID DIPLOM GIVE

B66
PAN S.,VIETNAM CRISIS. ASIA FRANCE USA+45 USA-45 VIETNAM CULTURE SOCIETY INT/ORG ECO/TAC AGREE CONTROL WAR MARXISM 20. PAGE 113 A2325
ECO/UNDEV POLICY DIPLOM NAT/COMP

B66
SKILLING H.G.,THE GOVERNMENTS OF COMMUNIST EAST EUROPE. COM EUR+WWI ELITES FORCES DIPLOM ECO/TAC CONTROL HABITAT SOCISM...DECISION BIBLIOG 20 EUROPE/E COM/PARTY. PAGE 134 A2738
MARXISM NAT/COMP GP/COMP DOMIN

B66
SPULBER N.,THE STATE AND ECONOMIC DEVELOPMENT IN EASTERN EUROPE. BULGARIA COM CZECHOSLVK HUNGARY POLAND YUGOSLAVIA CULTURE PLAN CAP/ISM INT/TRADE CONTROL...POLICY CHARTS METH/COMP BIBLIOG/A 19/20. PAGE 136 A2793
ECO/DEV ECO/UNDEV NAT/G TOTALISM

B66
THORNTON A.P.,THE IMPERIAL IDEA AND ITS ENEMIES. UK WOR+45 WOR-45 NAT/G PLAN DOMIN CONTROL WAR ATTIT PWR...TREND CHARTS 19/20 CMN/WLTH. PAGE 144 A2937
COLONIAL DIPLOM

B66
TRIFFIN R.,THE BALANCE OF PAYMENTS AND THE FOREIGN INVESTMENT POSITION OF THE UNITED STATES. USA+45 INT/ORG INT/TRADE PRICE CONTROL...POLICY 20 GOLD/STAND. PAGE 145 A2965
BAL/PAY DIPLOM FINAN ECO/TAC

B66
UN ECAFE,ADMINISTRATIVE ASPECTS OF FAMILY PLANNING PROGRAMMES (PAMPHLET). ASIA THAILAND WOR+45 VOL/ASSN PROB/SOLV BUDGET FOR/AID EDU/PROP CONFER CONTROL GOV/REL TIME 20 UN BIRTH/CON. PAGE 147 A2999
PLAN CENSUS FAM ADMIN

B66
US SENATE COMM GOVT OPERATIONS,POPULATION CRISIS. USA+45 ECO/DEV ECO/UNDEV AGRI SECT DELIB/GP PROB/SOLV FOR/AID REPRESENT ATTIT...GEOG CHARTS 20 CONGRESS DEPT/STATE DEPT/HEW BIRTH/CON. PAGE 156 A3178
CENSUS CONTROL LEGIS CONSULT

B66
WILSON H.A.,THE IMPERIAL POLICY OF SIR ROBERT BORDEN. CANADA UK ELITES INT/ORG VOL/ASSN CONTROL LEAD WAR ROLE 20 CMN/WLTH BORDEN/R. PAGE 165 A3360
INGP/REL COLONIAL CONSTN CHIEF

S66
FRIEND A.,"THE MIDDLE EAST CRISIS" COM ISLAM ISRAEL SYRIA UAR USA+45 USSR FORCES PLAN FOR/AID CONTROL ORD/FREE PWR...SOCIALIST TIME/SEQ 20 NASSER/G. PAGE 49 A1009
WAR INT/ORG DIPLOM PEACE

S66
GAMER R.E.,"URGENT SINGAPORE, PATIENT MALAYSIA." MALAYSIA S/ASIA ECO/UNDEV POL/PAR CHIEF TARIFFS TAX CONTROL LEAD REGION PWR 20 SINGAPORE. PAGE 51 A1036
DIPLOM NAT/G POLICY ECO/TAC

S66
MCNEAL R.H.,"THE LEGACY OF THE COMINTERN." USSR WOR+45 WOR-45 PROB/SOLV DIPLOM CONFER CONTROL LEAD WAR 20 STALIN/J COMINTERN. PAGE 98 A2020
MARXISM INT/ORG POL/PAR PWR

B67
BRZEZINSKI Z.K.,THE SOVIET BLOC: UNITY AND CONFLICT (2ND ED., REV., ENLARGED). COM POLAND USSR INTELL CHIEF EX/STRUC CONTROL EXEC GOV/REL PWR MARXISM ...TREND IDEA/COMP 20 LENIN/VI MARX/KARL STALIN/J. PAGE 21 A0420
NAT/G DIPLOM

B67
KAROL K.S.,CHINA, THE OTHER COMMUNISM (TRANS. BY TOM BAISTOW). CHINA/COM CULTURE INDUS FORCES DIPLOM EDU/PROP CONTROL EXEC NUC/PWR ATTIT...SOC CHARTS 20. PAGE 77 A1567
NAT/G POL/PAR MARXISM INGP/REL

B67
MURTY B.S.,PROPAGANDA AND WORLD PUBLIC ORDER. FUT WOR+45 COM/IND INT/ORG PROB/SOLV ATTIT KNOWL ORD/FREE...POLICY UN. PAGE 106 A2183
EDU/PROP DIPLOM CONTROL JURID

B67
RUEFF J.,BALANCE OF PAYMENTS. WOR+45 FINAN TEC/DEV DIPLOM TARIFFS PRICE CONTROL...POLICY CONCPT IDEA/COMP. PAGE 125 A2567
INT/TRADE BAL/PAY ECO/TAC NAT/COMP

B67
SHAFFER H.G.,THE COMMUNIST WORLD: MARXIST AND NON-MARXIST VIEWS. WOR+45 SOCIETY DIPLOM ECO/TAC CONTROL SOCISM...MARXIST ANTHOL BIBLIOG/A 20. PAGE 131 A2691 MARXISM NAT/COMP IDEA/COMP COM

B67
UNIVERSAL REFERENCE SYSTEM,ECONOMIC REGULATION, BUSINESS, AND GOVERNMENT (VOLUME VIII). WOR+45 WOR-45 ECO/DEV ECO/UNDEV FINAN LABOR TEC/DEV ECO/TAC INT/TRADE GOV/REL...POLICY COMPUT/IR. PAGE 149 A3043 BIBLIOG/A CONTROL NAT/G

L67
"RESTRICTIVE SOVEREIGN IMMUNITY, THE STATE DEPARTMENT, AND THE COURTS." USA+45 USA-45 EX/STRUC DIPLOM ADJUD CONTROL GOV/REL 19/20 DEPT/STATE SUPREME/CT. PAGE 4 A0080 SOVEREIGN ORD/FREE PRIVIL CT/SYS

L67
MACDONALD R.S.J.,"THE RESORT TO ECONOMIC COERCION BY INTERNATIONAL POLITICAL ORGANIZATIONS." CUBA ETHIOPIA RHODESIA SOUTH/AFR NAT/G FOR/AID INT/TRADE DOMIN CONTROL SANCTION...DECISION LEAGUE/NAT UN OAS 20. PAGE 92 A1887 INT/ORG COERCE ECO/TAC DIPLOM

S67
EGBERT D.D.,"POLITICS AND ART IN COMMUNIST BULGARIA" BULGARIA COM USSR CULTURE DIPLOM INGP/REL TOTALISM...TREND 20. PAGE 40 A0825 CREATE ART/METH CONTROL MARXISM

S67
EISENDRATH C.,"THE OUTER SPACE TREATY." CHINA/COM COM USA+45 DIPLOM CONTROL NUC/PWR...INT/LAW 20 UN COLD/WAR TREATY. PAGE 41 A0831 SPACE INT/ORG PEACE ARMS/CONT

S67
FARQUHAR D.M.,"CHINESE COMMUNIST ASSESSMENTS OF A FOREIGN CONQUEST DYNASTY." CHINA/COM DIPLOM CONTROL ...METH 20. PAGE 44 A0900 MARXISM HIST/WRIT POLICY COLONIAL

S67
HUDSON R.,"WAS THIS WAR NECESSARY? THE UN AND THE MIDDLE EAST" WOR+45 STRUCT DIPLOM DOMIN CONTROL REPRESENT PWR...NEW/IDEA 20 UN MID/EAST. PAGE 69 A1410 DELIB/GP INT/ORG PROB/SOLV PEACE

S67
KIPP K.,"DIE POLITISCHE BEDEUTUNG DER 'GEGENKUSTE' DARGESTELLT AM BEISPIEL DER USA IM 20. JAHRHUNDERT" USA+45 USA-45 SEA NAT/G CONTROL COERCE WAR...POLICY GEOG 20. PAGE 79 A1629 FORCES ORD/FREE DIPLOM DETER

S67
KYLE K.,"BACKGROUND TO THE CRISIS" ISLAM ISRAEL UAR UK USSR NAT/G PROB/SOLV LEGIT CONTROL REGION STRANGE MORAL 20 JEWS. PAGE 83 A1698 DIPLOM POLICY SOVEREIGN COERCE

S67
LOSMAN D.L.,"FOREIGN AID, SOCIALISM AND THE EMERGING COUNTRIES" WOR+45 ADMIN CONTROL PWR 20. PAGE 91 A1864 ECO/UNDEV FOR/AID SOC

S67
RAMSEY J.A.,"THE STATUS OF INTERNATIONAL COPYRIGHTS." WOR+45 CREATE TEC/DEV DIPLOM CONFER CONTROL SANCTION OWN...POLICY JURID. PAGE 119 A2439 INT/LAW INT/ORG COM/IND PRESS

S67
REINTANZ G.,"THE SPACE TREATY." WOR+45 DIPLOM CONTROL ARMS/CONT NUC/PWR WAR...MARXIST 20 COLD/WAR UN TREATY. PAGE 120 A2461 SPACE INT/LAW INT/ORG PEACE

S67
SCHACTER O.,"SCIENTIFIC ADVANCES AND INTERNATIONAL LAWMAKING." FUT R+D PLAN PROB/SOLV CONFER CONTROL ...POLICY PREDICT 20 UN. PAGE 128 A2617 TEC/DEV INT/LAW INT/ORG ACT/RES

S67
SHULMAN M.D.,"'EUROPE' VERSUS 'DETENTE'." USA+45 USSR INT/ORG CONTROL ARMS/CONT DETER 20. PAGE 132 A2711 DIPLOM BAL/PWR NUC/PWR

N67
US SUPERINTENDENT OF DOCUMENTS,SPACE: MISSILES, THE MOON, NASA, AND SATELLITES (PRICE LIST 79A). USA+45 COM/IND R+D NAT/G DIPLOM EDU/PROP ADMIN CONTROL HEALTH...POLICY SIMUL NASA CONGRESS. PAGE 157 A3206 BIBLIOG/A SPACE TEC/DEV PEACE

N67
US SENATE COMM ON FOREIGN REL,ARMS SALES AND FOREIGN POLICY (PAMPHLET). FINAN FOR/AID CONTROL 20. PAGE 156 A3187 ARMS/CONT ADMIN OP/RES DIPLOM

B91
SIDGWICK H.,THE ELEMENTS OF POLITICS. LOC/G NAT/G LEGIS DIPLOM ADJUD CONTROL EXEC PARL/PROC REPRESENT GOV/REL SOVEREIGN ALL/IDEOS 19 MILL/JS BENTHAM/J. PAGE 132 A2713 POLICY LAW CONCPT

CONTROLLED DIRECT OBSERVATION....SEE CONT/OBS

CONV/LEASE....CONVICT LEASE SYSTEM IN SOUTH

CONVENTIONAL....SEE CONVNTL

CONVNTL....CONVENTIONAL

CONWELL-EVANS T.P. A0605

COOK T. A0606

COOKSON J. A0607

COOLIDGE/C....CALVIN COOLIDGE

COOMBS P.H. A0608

COOPER S. A0609

COOPERATION....SEE AGREE

COOPERATIVE....SEE VOL/ASSN

COORDINATING COMM DOC SOC SCI A0610

COORDINATION....SEE CENTRAL

COPLIN W.D. A0611

COPYRIGHT....COPYRIGHT

CORBETT P.E. A0612,A0613,A0614,A0615,A0616

CORDIER A.W. A0617

CORDIER H. A0618

CORE....CONGRESS OF RACIAL EQUALITY

CORET A. A0619,A0620,A0621,A0622

CORFO A0623

CORMACK M. A0624

CORN/LAWS....CORN LAWS (U.K.)

CORNELL U DEPT ASIAN STUDIES A0625

CORNELL UNIVERSITY LIBRARY A0626

CORNELL/U....CORNELL UNIVERSITY

B65
EDUCATION AND WORLD AFFAIRS,THE UNIVERSITY LOOKS ABROAD: APPROACHES TO WORLD AFFAIRS AT SIX AMERICAN UNIVERSITIES. USA+45 CREATE EDU/PROP CONFER LEAD KNOWL 20 CORNELL/U MICH/STA/U STANFORD/U TULANE/U WISCONSN/U. PAGE 40 A0822 ACADEM DIPLOM ATTIT GP/COMP

CORONATIONS....SEE INAUGURATE

CORPORATN....CORPORATION

CORRECTIONAL INSTITUTION....SEE PUB/INST

CORREL....STATISTICAL CORRELATIONS

S67
VERBA S.,"PUBLIC OPINION AND THE WAR IN VIETNAM." USA+45 VIETNAM DIPLOM WAR...CORREL STAT QU CHARTS 20. PAGE 158 A3228 ATTIT KNO/TEST NAT/G PLAN

CORWIN E.S. A0627

CORY R.H. A0628

COSER L. A0629

COSGROVE C.A. A0630

COST....ECONOMIC VALUE; SEE ALSO PROFIT,

B14
DE BLOCH J.,THE FUTURE OF WAR IN ITS TECHNICAL, ECONOMIC, AND POLITICAL RELATIONS (1899). MOD/EUR TEC/DEV BUDGET INT/TRADE DETER GUERRILLA WEAPON COST PEACE 20. PAGE 34 A0698 WAR BAL/PWR PREDICT FORCES

B17
VEBLEN T.B.,AN INQUIRY INTO THE NATURE OF PEACE AND THE TERMS OF ITS PERPETUATION. UNIV STRATA FINAN EDU/PROP PRICE COST DISCRIM NAT/LISM MORAL ORD/FREE PACIFIST 20 WORLDUNITY. PAGE 158 A3224 PEACE DIPLOM WAR NAT/G

B36
HARVARD BUREAU ECO RES LAT AM,THE ECONOMIC LITERATURE OF LATIN AMERICA: A TENTATIVE BIBLIOGRAPHY. NAT/G TARIFFS CENTRAL COST DEMAND 20. PAGE 62 A1277 BIBLIOG ECO/UNDEV L/A+17C INT/TRADE

B42
FULLER G.H.,DEFENSE FINANCING: A SUPPLEMENTARY LIST OF REFERENCES (PAMPHLET). CANADA UK USA-45 ECO/DEV NAT/G DELIB/GP BUDGET ADJUD ARMS/CONT WEAPON COST PEACE PWR 20 AUSTRAL CHINJAP CONGRESS. PAGE 50 A1021
BIBLIOG/A FINAN FORCES DIPLOM

B42
US LIBRARY OF CONGRESS,ECONOMICS OF WAR (APRIL 1941-MARCH 1942). WOR-45 FINAN INDUS LOC/G NAT/G PLAN BUDGET RATION COST DEMAND...POLICY 20. PAGE 154 A3146
BIBLIOG/A INT/TRADE ECO/TAC WAR

B51
BROGAN D.W.,THE PRICE OF REVOLUTION. FRANCE USA+45 USA-45 USSR CONSTN NAT/G DIPLOM COLONIAL NAT/LISM ORD/FREE POPULISM...CONCPT 18/20 PRE/US/AM. PAGE 19 A0386
REV METH/COMP COST MARXISM

B55
O3HEVSS E.,WIRTSCHAFTSSYSTEME UND INTERNATIONALER HANDEL. ECO/DEV FINAN MARKET DIPLOM ECO/TAC COST ...METH/COMP NAT/COMP 20. PAGE 112 A2306
CAP/ISM SOCISM INT/TRADE IDEA/COMP

B56
KRAUS O.,THEORIE DER ZWISCHENSTAATLICHEN WIRTSCHAFTSBEZIEHUNGEN. TARIFFS WAR COST 20. PAGE 82 A1677
INT/TRADE DIPLOM BAL/PAY ECO/TAC

B58
AVRAMOVIC D.,POSTWAR GROWTH IN INTERNATIONAL INDEBTEDNESS. WOR+45 AGRI INDUS CAP/ISM PRICE INCOME...NAT/COMP 20 GOLD/STAND SILVER. PAGE 10 A0199
INT/TRADE FINAN COST BAL/PAY

N58
US HOUSE COMM FOREIGN AFFAIRS,HEARINGS ON DRAFT LEGISLATION TO AMEND FURTHER THE MUTUAL SECURITY ACT OF 1954 (PAMPHLET). USA+45 CONSULT FORCES BUDGET DIPLOM DETER COST ORD/FREE...JURID 20 DEPT/DEFEN UN DEPT/STATE. PAGE 153 A3123
LEGIS DELIB/GP CONFER WEAPON

B59
AIR FORCE ACADEMY ASSEMBLY '59,INTERNATIONAL STABILITY AND PROGRESS (PAMPHLET). USA+45 USSR ECO/UNDEV PROB/SOLV BUDGET DIPLOM ADMIN DETER COST ATTIT...TREND 20. PAGE 5 A0103
FOR/AID FORCES WAR PLAN

B59
CHANDLER E.H.S.,THE HIGH TOWER OF REFUGE: THE INSPIRING STORY OF REFUGEE RELIEF THROUGHOUT THE WORLD. WOR+45 NEIGH SECT WORKER PROB/SOLV DIPLOM ECO/TAC EDU/PROP COST HABITAT. PAGE 25 A0519
GIVE WEALTH STRANGE INT/ORG

B59
US GENERAL ACCOUNTING OFFICE,EXAM OF ECONOMIC AND TECHNICAL ASSISTANCE PROGRAM FOR INDIA INT'NAT'L COOP ADMIN REPORT TO CONGRESS 1955-1958. INDIA USA+45 ECO/UNDEV FINAN PLAN DIPLOM COST UTIL WEALTH ...CHARTS 20 CONGRESS AID. PAGE 153 A3114
FOR/AID EFFICIENCY ECO/TAC TEC/DEV

B60
KENEN P.B.,BRITISH MONETARY POLICY AND THE BALANCE OF PAYMENTS 1951-57. UK PLAN BUDGET ECO/TAC INT/TRADE PAY PRICE COST ATTIT 20. PAGE 77 A1585
BAL/PAY PROB/SOLV FINAN NAT/G

B60
LEVIN J.V.,THE EXPORT ECONOMIES: THEIR PATTERN OF DEVELOPMENT IN HISTORICAL PERSPECTIVE. BURMA PERU AGRI WORKER COLONIAL COST DEMAND INCOME 20. PAGE 88 A1795
INT/TRADE ECO/UNDEV BAL/PAY EXTR/IND

B60
US HOUSE COMM GOVT OPERATIONS,OPERATIONS OF THE DEVELOPMENT LOAN FUND: HEARINGS (COMMITTEE ON GOVERNMENT OPERATIONS). USA+45 PLAN BUDGET DIPLOM GOV/REL COST...CHARTS 20 CONGRESS DEPT/STATE AID. PAGE 154 A3137
FINAN FOR/AID ECO/TAC EFFICIENCY

B60
US SENATE COMM ON FOREIGN REL,SITUATION IN VIETNAM (2 VOLS.). USA+45 VIETNAM ECO/TAC COST SENATE DEPT/STATE. PAGE 156 A3181
FOR/AID PLAN EFFICIENCY INSPECT

B61
INTERNATIONAL BANK RECONST DEV,THE WORLD BANK IN AFRICA: SUMMARY OF ACTIVITIES. AGRI COM/IND DIST/IND EXTR/IND INDUS TAX COST...CHARTS 20. PAGE 71 A1450
FINAN ECO/UNDEV INT/ORG AFR

B61
LIEFMANN-KEIL E.,OKONOMISCHE THEORIE DER SOZIALPOLITIK. INT/ORG LABOR WORKER COST INCOME NEW/LIB...CONCPT SOC/INTEG 20. PAGE 88 A1810
ECO/DEV INDUS NAT/G SOC/WK

B61
US GENERAL ACCOUNTING OFFICE,EXAMINATION OF ECONOMIC AND TECHNICAL ASSISTANCE PROGRAM FOR IRAN. IRAN USA+45 AGRI INDUS DIPLOM CONTROL COST 20. PAGE 153 A3115
FOR/AID ADMIN TEC/DEV ECO/UNDEV

B61
US HOUSE COMM APPROPRIATIONS,INTER-AMERICAN PROGRAMS FOR 1961: DENIAL OF 1962 BUDGET INFORMATION. CHILE L/A+17C USA+45 FINAN CONSULT BUDGET ADJUD COST EFFICIENCY WEALTH...POLICY CHARTS 20 CONGRESS. PAGE 153 A3119
LEGIS FOR/AID DELIB/GP ECO/UNDEV

B61
US SENATE COMM ON FOREIGN RELS,INTERNATIONAL DEVELOPMENT AND SECURITY: HEARINGS ON BILL (2 VOLS.). ECO/UNDEV FINAN FORCES REV COST WEALTH ...CHARTS 20 AID PRESIDENT. PAGE 157 A3191
FOR/AID CIVMIL/REL ORD/FREE ECO/TAC

B62
HOLMAN A.G.,SOME MEASURES AND INTERPRETATIONS OF EFFECTS OF US FOREIGN ENTERPRISES ON US BALANCE OF PAYMENTS. USA+45 COST INCOME WEALTH...MATH CHARTS 20. PAGE 67 A1371
BAL/PAY INT/TRADE FINAN ECO/TAC

B62
KINDLEBERGER C.P.,FOREIGN TRADE AND THE NATIONAL ECONOMY. WOR+45 ECO/DEV ECO/UNDEV ECO/TAC COST DEMAND 20. PAGE 79 A1622
INT/TRADE GOV/COMP BAL/PAY POLICY

B63
ERHARD L.,THE ECONOMICS OF SUCCESS. GERMANY/W WOR+45 LABOR CHIEF TAX REGION COST DEMAND ANTHOL. PAGE 42 A0860
ECO/DEV INT/TRADE PLAN DIPLOM

B63
FATEMI N.S.,THE DOLLAR CRISIS. USA+45 INDUS NAT/G LEGIS BUDGET TAX COST...CHARTS METH/COMP 20 EEC. PAGE 44 A0902
PROB/SOLV BAL/PAY FOR/AID PLAN

B63
US SENATE COMM APPROPRIATIONS,PERSONNEL ADMINISTRATION AND OPERATIONS OF AGENCY FOR INTERNATIONAL DEVELOPMENT: SPECIAL HEARING. FINAN LEAD COST UTIL SKILL...CHARTS 20 CONGRESS AID CIVIL/SERV. PAGE 155 A3170
ADMIN FOR/AID EFFICIENCY DIPLOM

L63
PADELFORD N.J.,"FINANCIAL CRISIS AND THE UNITED NATIONS." FUT USSR WOR+45 LAW CONSTN FINAN INT/ORG DELIB/GP FORCES PLAN BUDGET DIPLOM COST WEALTH ...STAT CHARTS UN CONGO 20. PAGE 113 A2311
CREATE ECO/TAC

B64
KAUFMANN W.W.,THE MC NAMARA STRATEGY. TOP/EX INSPECT BAL/PWR DIPLOM CONTROL DETER GUERRILLA NUC/PWR WEAPON COST PWR...METH/COMP 20 MCNAMARA/R KENNEDY/JF JOHNSON/LB NATO DEPT/DEFEN. PAGE 77 A1572
FORCES WAR PLAN PROB/SOLV

B64
KNOX V.H.,PUBLIC FINANCE: INFORMATION SOURCES. USA+45 DIPLOM ADMIN GOV/REL COST...POLICY 20. PAGE 81 A1657
BIBLIOG/A FINAN TAX BUDGET

B64
MYINT H.,THE ECONOMICS OF THE DEVELOPING COUNTRIES. WOR+45 AGRI PLAN COST...POLICY GEOG 20 MONEY. PAGE 107 A2187
ECO/UNDEV INT/TRADE EXTR/IND FINAN

B64
TAUBENFELD H.J.,SPACE AND SOCIETY. USA+45 LAW FORCES CREATE TEC/DEV ADJUD CONTROL COST PEACE ...PREDICT ANTHOL 20. PAGE 142 A2895
SPACE SOCIETY ADJUST DIPLOM

S64
CARNEGIE ENDOWMENT INT. PEACE,"ADMINISTRATION AND BUDGET (ISSUES BEFORE THE NINETEENTH GENERAL ASSEMBLY)." WOR+45 FINAN BUDGET ECO/TAC ROUTINE COST...STAT RECORD UN. PAGE 24 A0495
INT/ORG ADMIN

B65
ANALYSIS AND ASSESSMENT OF THE ECONOMIC EFFECTS: PUBLIC LAW 480 TITLE I PROGRAM TURKEY. INDIA TURKEY USA+45 AGRI NAT/G PLAN BUDGET DIPLOM COST EFFICIENCY...CHARTS 20. PAGE 3 A0070
ECO/TAC FOR/AID FINAN ECO/UNDEV

B65
HASSON J.A.,THE ECONOMICS OF NUCLEAR POWER. INDIA UK USA+45 WOR+45 INT/ORG TEC/DEV COST...SOC STAT CHARTS 20 EURATOM. PAGE 63 A1286
NUC/PWR INDUS ECO/DEV METH

B65
MCCOLL G.D.,THE AUSTRALIAN BALANCE OF PAYMENTS. UK USA+45 AGRI WORKER DIPLOM EQUILIB PRODUC...STAT TREND CHARTS BIBLIOG/A 20 AUSTRAL. PAGE 97 A2001
ECO/DEV BAL/PAY INT/TRADE COST

B65
THAYER F.C. JR.,AIR TRANSPORT POLICY AND NATIONAL SECURITY: A POLITICAL, ECONOMIC, AND MILITARY ANALYSIS. DIST/IND OP/RES PLAN TEC/DEV DIPLOM DETER WAR COST EFFICIENCY...POLICY BIBLIOG 20 DEPT/DEFEN FAA CAB. PAGE 142 A2908
AIR FORCES CIVMIL/REL ORD/FREE

B65
WHITE G.M.,THE USE OF EXPERTS BY INTERNATIONAL TRIBUNALS. WOR+45 WOR-45 INT/ORG NAT/G PAY ADJUD COST...OBS BIBLIOG 20. PAGE 164 A3334
INT/LAW ROUTINE CONSULT CT/SYS

B66
INTL ATOMIC ENERGY AGENCY,INTERNATIONAL CONVENTIONS ON CIVIL LIABILITY FOR NUCLEAR DAMAGE. FUT WOR+45 ADJUD WAR COST PEACE SOVEREIGN...JURID 20. PAGE 71 A1462
DIPLOM INT/ORG DELIB/GP NUC/PWR

B66
KNORR K.E.,ON THE USES OF MILITARY POWER IN THE NUCLEAR AGE. WOR+45 INT/ORG TEC/DEV ADMIN CONTROL
FORCES DIPLOM

WAR COST 20. PAGE 81 A1656 DETER NUC/PWR

B66
MURPHY G.G.,SOVIET MONGOLIA: A STUDY OF THE OLDEST POLITICAL SATELLITE. USSR STRATA STRUCT COST INCOME ATTIT SOCISM 20. PAGE 106 A2177 DIPLOM ECO/TAC PLAN DOMIN

B67
US AGENCY INTERNATIONAL DEV,PROPOSED FOREIGN AID PROGRAM FOR 1968: SUMMARY PRESENTATION TO THE CONGRESS. AFR S/ASIA USA+45 AGRI TEC/DEV DIPLOM ECO/TAC BAL/PAY COST HEALTH KNOWL SKILL 20 AID CONGRESS. PAGE 149 A3053 ECO/UNDEV BUDGET FOR/AID STAT

S67
CLINGHAM T.A. JR.,"LEGISLATIVE FLOTSAM AND INTERNATIONAL ACTION IN THE 'YARMOUTH CASTLE'S' WAKE." WOR+45 PROB/SOLV CONFER COST HEALTH...POLICY INT/LAW CONGRESS. PAGE 27 A0552 DIPLOM DIST/IND INT/ORG LAW

S67
OLIVIER G.,"ASPECTS JURIDIQUES DE L'ADOPTION DU TRAITE CECA A LA CRISE CHARBONNIERE (SUITE ET FIN)" LAW DIST/IND PLAN DIPLOM RATION PRICE ADMIN COST DEMAND...POLICY CON/ANAL ECSC TREATY. PAGE 112 A2288 INT/TRADE INT/ORG EXTR/IND CONSTN

COSTA RICA UNIVERSIDAD BIBL A0631

COSTA/RICA....SEE ALSO L/A+17C

B62
COSTA RICA UNIVERSIDAD BIBL,LISTA DE TESIS DE GRADO DE LA UNIVERSIDAD DE COSTA RICA. COSTA/RICA LAW LOC/G ADMIN LEAD...SOC 20. PAGE 31 A0631 BIBLIOG/A NAT/G DIPLOM ECO/UNDEV

COTTRELL A.J. A0632

COTTRELL L.S. A0633

COTTRELL W.F. A0634

COUDENHOVE-KALERGI A0635,A0636

COUGHLIN/C....CHARLES EDWARD COUGHLIN

COUNCIL BRITISH NATIONAL BIB A0637

COUNCIL OF EUROPE A0638

COUNCIL ON FOREIGN RELATIONS A0639

COUNCIL ON WORLD TENSIONS A0640,A0641

COUNCL/EUR....COUNCIL OF EUROPE

B49
BOYD A.,WESTERN UNION: A STUDY OF THE TREND TOWARD EUROPEAN UNITY. FUT REGION NAT/LISM...POLICY IDEA/COMP BIBLIOG 14/20 OEEC ERASMUS/D COUNCL/EUR FULBRGHT/J NATO. PAGE 18 A0363 DIPLOM AGREE TREND INT/ORG

L60
HAAS E.B.,"CONSENSUS FORMATION IN THE COUNCIL OF EUROPE." EUR+WWI NAT/G DELIB/GP DIPLOM REGION CHOOSE PWR SOVEREIGN...RELATIV NEW/IDEA QUANT CHARTS INDEX TOT/POP OEEC 20 COUNCL/EUR. PAGE 59 A1206 POL/PAR INT/ORG STAT

S61
HAAS E.B.,"INTERNATIONAL INTEGRATION: THE EUROPEAN AND THE UNIVERSAL PROCESS." EUR+WWI FUT WOR+45 NAT/G EX/STRUC ATTIT DRIVE ORD/FREE PWR...CONCPT GEN/LAWS OEEC 20 NATO COUNCL/EUR. PAGE 59 A1207 INT/ORG TREND REGION

B62
GOLDWATER B.M.,WHY NOT VICTORY? A FRESH LOOK AT AMERICAN FOREIGN POLICY. USA+45 WOR+45 FOR/AID LEAD ARMS/CONT WAR PEACE ATTIT ORD/FREE PWR MARXISM ...INT/LAW 20 TREATY ECHR COUNCL/EUR. PAGE 53 A1092 DIPLOM POLICY CONSERVE NAT/LISM

B64
ECONOMIDES C.P.,LE POUVOIR DE DECISION DES ORGANISATIONS INTERNATIONALES EUROPEENNES. DIPLOM DOMIN INGP/REL EFFICIENCY...INT/LAW JURID 20 NATO OEEC EEC COUNCL/EUR EURATOM. PAGE 40 A0821 INT/ORG PWR DECISION GP/COMP

S64
MOWER A.G.,"THE OFFICIAL PRESSURE GROUP OF THE COUNCIL OF EUROPE'S CONSULATIVE ASSEMBLY." EUR+WWI SOCIETY STRUCT FINAN CONSULT ECO/TAC ADMIN ROUTINE ATTIT PWR WEALTH...STAT CHARTS 20 COUNCL/EUR. PAGE 105 A2160 INT/ORG EDU/PROP

COUNCL/MGR....COUNCIL-MANAGER SYSTEM OF LOCAL GOVERNMENT

COUNTIES....SEE LOC/G

COUNTY AGRICULTURAL AGENT....SEE COUNTY/AGT

COUNTY/AGT....COUNTY AGRICULTURAL AGENT

COURAGE....SEE DRIVE

COURT SYSTEMS....SEE CT/SYS

COURT/DIST....DISTRICT COURTS

COUSINS N. A0642

COUTY P. A0643

COWEN Z. A0644

COWPER/W....WILLIAM COWPER

COX R. A0645

COX R.H. A0646,A0647

COYLE D.C. A0648

CRABB C. A0649

CRABBS R.F. A0650

CRAIG G.A. A0651,A0652,A0653,A0654

CRANDALL S.B. A0655

CRANE R.D. A0656,A0657,A0658,A0659

CRANMER-BYNG J.L. A0660

CRAWFORD E.T. A0661

CREATE....CREATIVE PROCESSES

N
AMERICAN DOCUMENTATION INST,DOCUMENTATION ABSTRACTS. WOR+45 NAT/G COMPUTER CREATE TEC/DEV DIPLOM EDU/PROP REGION KNOWL...PHIL/SCI CLASSIF LING. PAGE 7 A0143 BIBLIOG/A AUTOMAT COMPUT/IR R+D

N
INTERNATIONAL REVIEW OF ADMINISTRATIVE SCIENCES. WOR+45 WOR-45 STRATA ECO/DEV ECO/UNDEV CREATE PLAN PROB/SOLV DIPLOM CONTROL REPRESENT...MGT 20. PAGE 1 A0011 BIBLIOG/A ADMIN INT/ORG NAT/G

N
JOURNAL OF CONFLICT RESOLUTION. FUT WOR+45 INT/ORG NAT/G FORCES CREATE PROB/SOLV ARMS/CONT NUC/PWR WEAPON SOC. PAGE 1 A0014 BIBLIOG/A DIPLOM WAR

S17
ROOT E.,"THE EFFECT OF DEMOCRACY ON INTERNATIONAL LAW." USA-45 WOR-45 INTELL SOCIETY INT/ORG NAT/G CONSULT ACT/RES CREATE PLAN EDU/PROP PEACE SKILL ...CONCPT METH/CNCPT OBS 20. PAGE 123 A2523 LEGIS JURID INT/LAW

B20
BURNS C.D.,INTERNATIONAL POLITICS. WOR-45 CULTURE SOCIETY ECO/UNDEV NAT/G VOL/ASSN DELIB/GP ACT/RES CREATE DOMIN EDU/PROP LEGIT ATTIT DRIVE RIGID/FLEX ALL/VALS...PLURIST PSY CONCPT TREND. PAGE 22 A0442 INT/ORG PEACE SOVEREIGN

B21
BALFOUR A.J.,ESSAYS SPECULATIVE AND POLITICAL. SEA CULTURE CREATE WAR NAT/LISM PEACE LOVE...ART/METH INT/LAW CONCPT ANTHOL 20 JEWS. PAGE 10 A0211 PHIL/SCI SOCIETY DIPLOM

B22
BRYCE J.,INTERNATIONAL RELATIONS. CHRIST-17C EUR+WWI MOD/EUR CULTURE INTELL NAT/G DELIB/GP CREATE BAL/PWR DIPLOM ATTIT DRIVE RIGID/FLEX ALL/VALS...PLURIST JURID CONCPT TIME/SEQ GEN/LAWS TOT/POP. PAGE 20 A0412 INT/ORG POLICY

B22
FICHTE J.G.,ADDRESSES TO THE GERMAN NATION. GERMANY PRUSSIA ELITES NAT/G SECT CREATE INT/TRADE HEREDITY ...ART/METH LING 19 FRANK/PARL. PAGE 45 A0923 NAT/LISM CULTURE EDU/PROP REGION

B22
POTTER P.B.,AN INTRODUCTION TO THE STUDY OF INTERNATIONAL ORGANIZATION. WOR-45 ACT/RES CREATE EDU/PROP ROUTINE PERCEPT KNOWL...CONT/OBS RECORD GEN/LAWS TOT/POP VAL/FREE 20. PAGE 117 A2398 INT/ORG CONCPT

B29
STURZO L.,THE INTERNATIONAL COMMUNITY AND THE RIGHT OF WAR (TRANS. BY BARBARA BARCLAY CARTER). CULTURE CREATE PROB/SOLV DIPLOM ADJUD CONTROL PEACE PERSON ORD/FREE...INT/LAW IDEA/COMP PACIFIST 20 LEAGUE/NAT. PAGE 140 A2858 INT/ORG PLAN WAR CONCPT

B31
BEALES A.C.,THE HISTORY OF PEACE. WOR-45 VOL/ASSN DELIB/GP CREATE PLAN EDU/PROP ATTIT MORAL ...TIME/SEQ VAL/FREE 19/20. PAGE 12 A0239 INT/ORG ARMS/CONT PEACE

B31
STUART G.H.,THE INTERNATIONAL CITY OF TANGIER. AFR EUR+WWI MOD/EUR MOROCCO CONSTN PROVS CREATE PLAN LEGIT PEACE ORD/FREE PWR...INT/LAW OBS TIME/SEQ CON/ANAL 20 TANGIER. PAGE 139 A2854
LOC/G INT/ORG DIPLOM SOVEREIGN

B33
LAUTERPACHT H.,THE FUNCTION OF LAW IN THE INTERNATIONAL COMMUNITY. WOR-45 NAT/G FORCES CREATE DOMIN LEGIT COERCE WAR PEACE ATTIT ORD/FREE PWR SOVEREIGN...JURID CONCPT METH/CNCPT TIME/SEQ GEN/LAWS GEN/METH LEAGUE/NAT TOT/POP VAL/FREE 20. PAGE 85 A1749
INT/ORG LAW INT/LAW

B34
EINSTEIN A.,THE WORLD AS I SEE IT. WOR-45 INTELL R+D INT/ORG NAT/G SECT VOL/ASSN FORCES CREATE EDU/PROP LEGIT ARMS/CONT WAR WEAPON NAT/LISM ALL/VALS...POLICY CONCPT 20. PAGE 41 A0828
SOCIETY PHIL/SCI DIPLOM PACIFISM

B36
ROBINSON H.,DEVELOPMENT OF THE BRITISH EMPIRE. WOR-45 CULTURE SOCIETY STRUCT ECO/DEV ECO/UNDEV INT/ORG VOL/ASSN FORCES CREATE PLAN DOMIN EDU/PROP ADMIN COLONIAL PWR WEALTH...POLICY GEOG CHARTS CMN/WLTH 16/20. PAGE 122 A2503
NAT/G HIST/WRIT UK

B38
MCNAIR A.D.,THE LAW OF TREATIES: BRITISH PRACTICE AND OPINIONS. UK CREATE DIPLOM LEGIT WRITING ADJUD WAR...INT/LAW JURID TREATY. PAGE 98 A2018
AGREE LAW CT/SYS NAT/G

B39
ZIMMERN A.,MODERN POLITICAL DOCTRINE. WOR-45 CULTURE SOCIETY ECO/UNDEV DELIB/GP EX/STRUC CREATE DOMIN COERCE NAT/LISM ATTIT RIGID/FLEX ORD/FREE PWR WEALTH...POLICY CONCPT OBS TIME/SEQ TREND TOT/POP LEAGUE/NAT 20. PAGE 170 A3454
NAT/G ECO/TAC BAL/PWR INT/TRADE

B41
BURTON M.E.,THE ASSEMBLY OF THE LEAGUE OF NATIONS. WOR-45 CONSTN SOCIETY STRUCT INT/ORG NAT/G CREATE ATTIT RIGID/FLEX PWR...POLICY TIME/SEQ LEAGUE/NAT 20. PAGE 22 A0448
DELIB/GP EX/STRUC DIPLOM

S41
WRIGHT Q.,"FUNDAMENTAL PROBLEMS OF INTERNATIONAL ORGANIZATION." UNIV WOR-45 STRUCT FORCES ACT/RES CREATE DOMIN EDU/PROP LEGIT REGION NAT/LISM ORD/FREE PWR RESPECT SOVEREIGN...JURID SOC CONCPT METH/CNCPT TIME/SEQ 20. PAGE 167 A3405
INT/ORG ATTIT PEACE

B42
BONNET H.,THE UNITED NATIONS, WHAT THEY ARE, WHAT THEY MAY BECOME. FUT WOR-45 CREATE BAL/PWR ECO/TAC PWR...TREND GEN/LAWS 20. PAGE 16 A0335
INT/ORG ORD/FREE

L42
SHOTWELL J.,"LESSON OF THE LAST WORLD WAR." EUR+WWI MOD/EUR USA-45 SOCIETY ECO/UNDEV INDUS VOL/ASSN CONSULT ACT/RES CREATE CAP/ISM INT/TRADE DRIVE ALL/VALS...CONCPT NEW/IDEA SELF/OBS GEN/LAWS LEAGUE/NAT NAZI 20. PAGE 132 A2708
INT/ORG ORD/FREE

B43
LIPPMANN W.,US FOREIGN POLICY: SHIELD OF THE REPUBLIC. USA-45 WOR-45 CULTURE INT/ORG POL/PAR CREATE BAL/PWR DOMIN EDU/PROP WAR ORD/FREE PWR ...PLURIST CONCPT TREND CON/ANAL 20. PAGE 89 A1827
NAT/G DIPLOM PEACE

B43
ST LEGER A.,SELECTION OF WORKS FOR AN UNDERSTANDING OF WORLD AFFAIRS SINCE 1914. WOR-45 INT/ORG CREATE BAL/PWR REV ADJUST 20. PAGE 137 A2796
BIBLIOG/A WAR SOCIETY DIPLOM

B43
US LIBRARY OF CONGRESS,POLITICAL DEVELOPMENTS AND THE WAR: APRIL-DECEMBER 1942 (SUPPLEMENT 1). WOR-45 CONSTN NAT/G POL/PAR CREATE RECEIVE EDU/PROP ATTIT 20. PAGE 154 A3148
BIBLIOG/A WAR DIPLOM

B44
ADLER M.J.,HOW TO THINK ABOUT WAR AND PEACE. WOR-45 LAW SOCIETY EX/STRUC DIPLOM KNOWL ORD/FREE...POLICY TREND GEN/LAWS 20. PAGE 4 A0092
INT/ORG CREATE ARMS/CONT PEACE

B44
BARTLETT R.J.,THE LEAGUE TO ENFORCE PEACE. FUT USA-45 NAT/G POL/PAR CREATE EDU/PROP ADMIN RIGID/FLEX PWR...CONCPT TREND GEN/METH LEAGUE/NAT 20. PAGE 11 A0231
INT/ORG ORD/FREE DIPLOM

B45
BEVERIDGE W.,THE PRICE OF PEACE. GERMANY UK WOR+45 WOR-45 NAT/G FORCES CREATE LEGIT REGION WAR ATTIT KNOWL ORD/FREE PWR...POLICY NEW/IDEA GEN/LAWS LEAGUE/NAT 20 TREATY. PAGE 14 A0284
INT/ORG TREND PEACE

B45
KANDELL I.L.,UNITED STATES ACTIVITIES IN INTERNATIONAL CULTURAL RELATIONS. INT/ORG NAT/G VOL/ASSN CREATE DIPLOM EDU/PROP ATTIT RIGID/FLEX KNOWL...PLURIST CONCPT OBS TREND GEN/LAWS TOT/POP UNESCO 20. PAGE 76 A1554
USA-45 CULTURE

B46
GAULD W.A.,MAN, NATURE, AND TIME, AN INTRODUCTION TO WORLD STUDY. WOR-45 CULTURE CREATE DIPLOM GP/REL DRIVE...SOC LING CENSUS CHARTS TIME 18/20. PAGE 52 A1054
HABITAT PERSON

L47
BRUNER J.S.,"TOWARD A COMMON GROUND-INTERNATIONAL SOCIAL SCIENCE." FUT WOR+45 INTELL R+D NAT/G VOL/ASSN CONSULT DELIB/GP ACT/RES CREATE PLAN TEC/DEV ATTIT ORD/FREE...PSY SOC CONCPT ANTHOL UNESCO 20. PAGE 20 A0410
INT/ORG KNOWL

S47
RADVANYI L.,"PROBLEMS OF INTERNATIONAL OPINION SURVEYS." WOR+45 INT/ORG NAT/G CREATE ATTIT...PSY SOC METH/CNCPT REC/INT KNO/TEST SAMP/SIZ METH VAL/FREE 20. PAGE 118 A2431
QU/SEMANT SAMP DIPLOM

B48
JONES H.D.,UNESCO: A SELECTED LIST OF REFERENCES. CULTURE CREATE PEACE ATTIT DRIVE 20 UNESCO UN. PAGE 75 A1531
BIBLIOG/A INT/ORG DIPLOM EDU/PROP

B49
OGBURN W.,TECHNOLOGY AND INTERNATIONAL RELATIONS. WOR+45 WOR-45 ECO/DEV CREATE PLAN ECO/TAC EDU/PROP COERCE PWR SKILL WEALTH...TECHNIC PSY SOC NEW/IDEA CHARTS TOT/POP 20. PAGE 111 A2283
TEC/DEV DIPLOM INT/ORG

B49
ROSENHAUPT H.W.,HOW TO WAGE PEACE. USA+45 SOCIETY STRATA STRUCT R+D INT/ORG POL/PAR LEGIS ACT/RES CREATE PLAN EDU/PROP ADMIN EXEC ATTIT ALL/VALS ...TIME/SEQ TREND COLD/WAR 20. PAGE 124 A2536
INTELL CONCPT DIPLOM

L49
COMM. STUDY ORGAN. PEACE,"A TEN YEAR RECORD, 1939-1949." FUT WOR+45 LAW R+D CONSULT DELIB/GP CREATE LEGIT ROUTINE ORD/FREE...TIME/SEQ UN 20. PAGE 28 A0578
INT/ORG CONSTN PEACE

B50
COUNCIL BRITISH NATIONAL BIB,BRITISH NATIONAL BIBLIOGRAPHY. UK AGRI CONSTRUC PERF/ART POL/PAR SECT CREATE INT/TRADE LEAD...HUM JURID PHIL/SCI 20. PAGE 31 A0637
BIBLIOG/A NAT/G TEC/DEV DIPLOM

B50
DE RUSETT A.,STRENGTHENING THE FRAMEWORK OF PEACE. WOR+45 VOL/ASSN FORCES CREATE INSPECT ADJUD CONTROL WAR EQUILIB FEDERAL ORD/FREE 20 UN EUROPE. PAGE 35 A0711
INT/ORG DIPLOM PEACE METH/COMP

L50
US SENATE COMM. GOVT. OPER.,"REVISION OF THE UN CHARTER." FUT USA+45 WOR+45 CONSTN ECO/DEV ECO/UNDEV NAT/G DELIB/GP ACT/RES CREATE PLAN EXEC ROUTINE CHOOSE ALL/VALS...POLICY CONCPT CONGRESS UN TOT/POP 20 COLD/WAR. PAGE 157 A3196
INT/ORG LEGIS PEACE

L51
MANGONE G.,"THE IDEA AND PRACTICE OF WORLD GOVERNMENT." FUT WOR+45 WOR-45 ECO/DEV LEGIS CREATE LEGIT ROUTINE ATTIT MORAL PWR WEALTH...CONCPT GEN/LAWS 20. PAGE 94 A1920
INT/ORG SOCIETY INT/LAW

S51
CONNERY R.H.,"THE MUTUAL DEFENSE ASSISTANCE PROGRAM." COM EUR+WWI KOREA USA+45 NAT/G VOL/ASSN CREATE PLAN BAL/PWR EDU/PROP PERCEPT...POLICY DECISION CONCPT NATO 20. PAGE 29 A0587
INT/ORG FORCES FOR/AID

B52
FERRELL R.H.,PEACE IN THEIR TIME. FRANCE UK USA-45 INT/ORG NAT/G FORCES CREATE AGREE ARMS/CONT COERCE WAR TREATY 20 WILSON/W LEAGUE/NAT BRIAND/A. PAGE 45 A0920
PEACE DIPLOM

B52
SPENCER F.A.,WAR AND POSTWAR GREECE: AN ANALYSIS BASED ON GREEK WRITINGS. GREECE SOCIETY NAT/G POL/PAR FORCES CREATE DIPLOM LEAD MARXISM...SOC 20. PAGE 136 A2784
BIBLIOG/A WAR REV

L52
WRIGHT Q.,"CONGRESS AND THE TREATY-MAKING POWER." USA+45 WOR+45 CONSTN INTELL NAT/G CHIEF CONSULT EX/STRUC LEGIS TOP/EX CREATE GOV/REL DISPL DRIVE RIGID/FLEX...TREND TOT/POP CONGRESS CONGRESS 20 TREATY. PAGE 167 A3408
ROUTINE DIPLOM INT/LAW DELIB/GP

S52
MASTERS R.D.,"RUSSIA AND THE UNITED NATIONS." FUT USA+45 USSR WOR+45 CONSTN VOL/ASSN DELIB/GP TOP/EX CREATE DIPLOM ADMIN...TREND STERTYP UN 20. PAGE 96 A1962
INT/ORG PWR

S52
SCHUMAN F.,"INTERNATIONAL IDEALS AND THE NATIONAL INTEREST." WOR+45 WOR-45 INT/ORG VOL/ASSN DELIB/GP CREATE BAL/PWR DOMIN PEACE PERSON MORAL PWR SOVEREIGN...POLICY GEN/LAWS TOT/POP LEAGUE/NAT 20. PAGE 129 A2648
ATTIT CONCPT

B53
BORGESE G.,FOUNDATIONS OF THE WORLD REPUBLIC. FUT SOCIETY NAT/G CREATE LEGIT PERSON MORAL...MAJORIT CON/ANAL LEAGUE/NAT TOT/POP 20. PAGE 17 A0340
INT/ORG CONSTN PEACE

B53
COUSINS N.,WHO SPEAKS FOR MAN. GERMANY KOREA WOR+45 SOCIETY INT/ORG NAT/G CREATE EDU/PROP HEALTH KNOWL LOVE MORAL...OBS SELF/OBS BIOG HYPO/EXP TOT/POP 20 CHINJAP. PAGE 32 A0642
ATTIT WAR PEACE

B53
LARSEN K.,NATIONAL BIBLIOGRAPHIC SERVICES: THEIR CREATION AND OPERATION. WOR+45 COM/IND CREATE PLAN
BIBLIOG/A INT/ORG

DIPLOM PRESS ADMIN ROUTINE...MGT UNESCO. PAGE 85 A1733 WRITING

B53
MACMAHON A.W.,ADMINISTRATION IN FOREIGN AFFAIRS. NAT/G CONSULT DELIB/GP LEGIS ACT/RES CREATE ADMIN EXEC RIGID/FLEX PWR...METH/CNCPT TIME/SEQ TOT/POP VAL/FREE 20. PAGE 93 A1899 USA+45 ROUTINE FOR/AID DIPLOM

S53
MANNING C.A.W.,"THE PRETENTIONS OF INTERNATIONAL RELATIONS." WOR+45 SOCIETY CREATE EDU/PROP ATTIT PERSON KNOWL...GEN/LAWS TOT/POP VAL/FREE 20. PAGE 94 A1924 INT/ORG DIPLOM UK

B54
ARON R.,CENTURY OF TOTAL WAR. FUT WOR+45 WOR-45 SOCIETY INT/ORG NAT/G FORCES TOP/EX CREATE BAL/PWR DOMIN EDU/PROP COERCE DETER PEACE TOTALISM PWR ...TIME/SEQ TREND COLD/WAR TOT/POP VAL/FREE LEAGUE/NAT 20. PAGE 9 A0179 ATTIT WAR

B54
BECKEL G.,WORKSHOPS FOR THE WORLD; THE SPECIALIZED AGENCIES OF THE UN. WOR+45 AGRI DIST/IND CREATE TEC/DEV BUDGET CONTROL TASK WEALTH...CHARTS ORG/CHARTS 20 UN CASEBOOK. PAGE 12 A0246 INT/ORG DIPLOM PEACE CON/ANAL

B54
CHEEVER D.S.,ORGANIZING FOR PEACE. FUT WOR+45 WOR-45 STRATA STRUCT NAT/G CREATE DIPLOM LEGIT REGION COERCE DETER PEACE ATTIT DRIVE ALL/VALS ...TIME/SEQ TREND UN LEAGUE/NAT. PAGE 26 A0525 INT/ORG

B54
COOKSON J.,BEFORE THE AFRICAN STORM. BELGIUM CENTRL/AFR FRANCE UK ECO/UNDEV POL/PAR CREATE BAL/PWR RACE/REL NAT/LISM ORD/FREE CONSERVE MARXISM SOC/INTEG 20 CONGO/LEOP. PAGE 30 A0607 COLONIAL REV DISCRIM DIPLOM

B54
COUDENHOVE-KALERGI,AN IDEA CONQUERS THE WORLD. EUR+WWI MOD/EUR USA-45 CONSTN FAM CREATE EDU/PROP ATTIT PERSON KNOWL...CONCPT SELF/OBS TIME/SEQ. PAGE 31 A0635 INT/ORG BIOG DIPLOM

B54
MANGONE G.,A SHORT HISTORY OF INTERNATIONAL ORGANIZATION. MOD/EUR USA+45 USA-45 WOR+45 WOR-45 LAW LEGIS CREATE LEGIT ROUTINE RIGID/FLEX PWR ...JURID CONCPT OBS TIME/SEQ STERTYP GEN/LAWS UN TOT/POP VAL/FREE 18/20. PAGE 94 A1921 INT/ORG INT/LAW

B54
MILLARD E.L.,FREEDOM IN A FEDERAL WORLD. FUT WOR+45 VOL/ASSN TOP/EX LEGIT ROUTINE FEDERAL PEACE ATTIT DISPL ORD/FREE PWR...MAJORIT INT/LAW JURID TREND COLD/WAR 20. PAGE 101 A2073 INT/ORG CREATE ADJUD BAL/PWR

B54
NORTHROP F.S.C.,EUROPEAN UNION AND UNITED STATES FOREIGN POLICY: A STUDY IN SOCIOLOGICAL JURISPRUDENCE. EUR+WWI MOD/EUR USA+45 SOCIETY STRUCT NAT/G CREATE ECO/TAC DOMIN EDU/PROP REGION ATTIT RIGID/FLEX HEALTH ORD/FREE WEALTH ...METH/CNCPT TIME/SEQ TREND. PAGE 110 A2256 INT/ORG SOC DIPLOM

B54
STALEY E.,THE FUTURE OF UNDERDEVELOPED COUNTRIES: POLITICAL IMPLICATIONS OF ECONOMIC DEVELOPMENT. COM FUT USA+45 SOCIETY ECO/UNDEV CREATE PLAN CAP/ISM ATTIT DRIVE MARXISM SOCISM...POLICY CONCPT CHARTS COLD/WAR 20. PAGE 137 A2801 EDU/PROP ECO/TAC FOR/AID

B54
STREIT C.K.,FREEDOM AGAINST ITSELF. LAW SOCIETY DIPLOM UTOPIA PWR SOVEREIGN ALL/IDEOS 17/20 NATO UN. PAGE 139 A2850 ORD/FREE CREATE INT/ORG CONCPT

B54
WRIGHT Q.,PROBLEMS OF STABILITY AND PROGRESS IN INTERNATIONAL RELATIONSHIPS. FUT WOR+45 WOR-45 SOCIETY LEGIS CREATE TEC/DEV ECO/TAC EDU/PROP ADJUD WAR PEACE ORD/FREE PWR...KNO/TEST TREND GEN/LAWS 20. PAGE 167 A3409 INT/ORG CONCPT DIPLOM

L54
OPLER M.E.,"SOCIAL ASPECTS OF TECHNICAL ASSISTANCE IN OPERATION." WOR+45 VOL/ASSN CREATE PLAN TEC/DEV EDU/PROP ALL/VALS...METH/CNCPT OBS RECORD TREND UN 20. PAGE 112 A2292 INT/ORG CONSULT FOR/AID

B55
GOODRICH L.,THE UNITED NATIONS AND THE MAINTENANCE OF INTERNATIONAL PEACE AND SECURITY. WOR+45 CONSTN ACT/RES CREATE PLAN PERCEPT PWR...ORG/CHARTS GEN/LAWS UN 20. PAGE 54 A1102 INT/ORG ORD/FREE ARMS/CONT PEACE

B55
SNYDER R.C.,AMERICAN FOREIGN POLICY. USA+45 USA-45 WOR+45 WOR-45 CONSTN INT/ORG POL/PAR VOL/ASSN DELIB/GP LEGIS CREATE DOMIN EDU/PROP EXEC COERCE ATTIT DRIVE ORD/FREE PWR...MGT OBS RECORD TIME/SEQ TREND. PAGE 134 A2752 NAT/G DIPLOM

B55
WILCOX F.O.,PROPOSALS FOR CHANGES IN THE UNITED NATIONS. WOR+45 CONSTN ACT/RES CREATE LEGIT ATTIT ORD/FREE...CONCPT ORG/CHARTS UN TOT/POP 20. PAGE 164 A3344 INT/ORG STRUCT

B56
JESSUP P.C.,TRANSNATIONAL LAW. FUT WOR+45 JUDGE CREATE ADJUD ORD/FREE...CONCPT VAL/FREE 20. PAGE 74 A1515 LAW JURID INT/LAW

B56
WOLFERS A.,THE ANGLO-AMERICAN TRADITION IN FOREIGN AFFAIRS. UK USA+45 WOR-45 CULTURE SOCIETY ECO/DEV INT/ORG NAT/G CREATE PLAN BAL/PWR ECO/TAC EDU/PROP PEACE DISPL DRIVE...TREND GEN/LAWS 20. PAGE 166 A3382 ATTIT CONCPT DIPLOM

S56
GORDON L.,"THE ORGANIZATION FOR EUROPEAN ECONOMIC COOPERATION." EUR+WWI INDUS INT/ORG NAT/G CONSULT DELIB/GP ACT/RES CREATE PLAN TEC/DEV EDU/PROP LEGIT WEALTH OEEC 20. PAGE 54 A1114 VOL/ASSN ECO/DEV

B57
DEUTSCH K.W.,POLITICAL COMMUNITY AND THE NORTH ATLANTIC AREA: INTERNATIONAL ORGANIZATION IN THE LIGHT OF HISTORICAL EXPERIENCE. MOD/EUR USA+45 USA-45 SOCIETY FORCES TOP/EX CREATE PLAN DIPLOM DOMIN EDU/PROP LEGIT ATTIT ORD/FREE PWR...SAMP/SIZ TIME/SEQ CHARTS TOT/POP. PAGE 36 A0736 EUR+WWI INT/ORG PEACE REGION

B57
HOLCOMBE A.N.,STRENGTHENING THE UNITED NATIONS. USA+45 ACT/RES CREATE PLAN EDU/PROP ATTIT PERCEPT PWR...METH/CNCPT CONT/OBS RECORD UN COLD/WAR 20. PAGE 66 A1365 INT/ORG ROUTINE

B57
MATECKI B.,ESTABLISHMENT OF THE INTERNATIONAL FINANCE CORPORATION AND UNITED STATES POLICY. USA+45 WOR+45 CONSTN NAT/G CREATE RIGID/FLEX KNOWL ...METH/CNCPT TIME/SEQ SIMUL TOT/POP 20 INTL/FINAN. PAGE 96 A1964 FINAN INT/ORG DIPLOM

B57
TOMASIC D.A.,NATIONAL COMMUNISM AND SOVIET STRATEGY. UK USSR YUGOSLAVIA NAT/G POL/PAR CHIEF CREATE DOMIN REV WAR PWR...BIOG TREND 20 TITO/MARSH STALIN/J. PAGE 144 A2948 COM NAT/LISM MARXISM DIPLOM

L57
WARREN S.,"FOREIGN AID AND FOREIGN POLICY." USA+45 WOR+45 WOR-45 DIST/IND INDUS MARKET CONSULT CREATE DIPLOM EDU/PROP LEGIT ATTIT RIGID/FLEX...TIME/SEQ GEN/LAWS WORK 20. PAGE 161 A3285 ECO/UNDEV ALL/VALS ECO/TAC FOR/AID

S57
DEUTSCH K.W.,"MASS COMMUNICATIONS AND THE LOSS OF FREEDOM IN NATIONAL DECISION MAKING." FUT WOR+45 SOCIETY COM/IND INT/ORG NAT/G ACT/RES CREATE TEC/DEV EDU/PROP MAJORITY PERCEPT...METH/CNCPT 20. PAGE 36 A0737 COERCE DECISION WAR

B58
GANGE J.,UNIVERSITY RESEARCH ON INTERNATIONAL AFFAIRS. USA+45 ACADEM INT/ORG CONSULT CREATE EXEC ROUTINE...QUANT STAT INT STERTYP GEN/METH TOT/POP VAL/FREE 20. PAGE 51 A1040 R+D MGT DIPLOM

B58
RIGGS R.,POLITICS IN THE UNITED NATIONS: A STUDY OF UNITED STATES INFLUENCE IN THE GENERAL ASSEMBLY. USA+45 WOR+45 LEGIS TOP/EX CREATE BAL/PWR DIPLOM DOMIN EDU/PROP COLONIAL ROUTINE ATTIT RIGID/FLEX PWR...CONCPT OBS HIST/WRIT CHARTS STERTYP GEN/LAWS UN COLD/WAR 20. PAGE 121 A2480 INT/ORG

B58
SLICK T.,PERMANENT PEACE: A CHECK AND BALANCE PLAN. FUT WOR+45 NAT/G FORCES CREATE PLAN EDU/PROP LEGIT ADJUD COERCE NAT/LISM RIGID/FLEX MORAL...HUM CONCPT METH/CNCPT NEW/IDEA TREND CHARTS TOT/POP 20. PAGE 134 A2742 INT/ORG ORD/FREE PEACE ARMS/CONT

S58
ANDERSON N.,"INTERNATIONAL SEMINARS: AN ANALYSIS AND AN EVALUATION." WOR+45 R+D ACT/RES CREATE PLAN REGION ATTIT KNOWL SKILL...SOC REC/INT PERS/TEST CHARTS 20. PAGE 8 A0158 INT/ORG DELIB/GP

S58
DAVENPORT J.,"ARMS AND THE WELFARE STATE." INTELL STRUCT FORCES CREATE ECO/TAC FOR/AID DOMIN LEGIT ADMIN WAR ORD/FREE PWR...POLICY SOC CONCPT MYTH OBS TREND COLD/WAR TOT/POP 20. PAGE 34 A0685 USA+45 NAT/G USSR

S58
LASSWELL H.D.,"THE SCIENTIFIC STUDY OF INTERNATIONAL RELATIONS." USA+45 INT/ORG CREATE EDU/PROP DETER ATTIT PERCEPT PWR...DECISION CONCPT METH/CNCPT STYLE CON/ANAL 20. PAGE 85 A1740 PHIL/SCI GEN/METH DIPLOM

S58
SONDERMANN F.A.,"SOCIOLOGY AND INTERNATIONAL RELATIONS." WOR+45 CULTURE SOCIETY INT/ORG NAT/G CREATE ATTIT DRIVE PERSON RIGID/FLEX...PSY SOC 20. PAGE 135 A2767 PLAN NEW/IDEA PEACE

B59
MATHISEN T.,METHODOLOGY IN THE STUDY OF INTERNATIONAL RELATIONS. FUT WOR+45 SOCIETY INT/ORG NAT/G POL/PAR WAR PEACE KNOWL PWR...RELATIV CONCPT METH/CNCPT TREND HYPO/EXP METH TOT/POP 20. PAGE 96 A1965 GEN/METH CON/ANAL DIPLOM CREATE

B59
STANFORD RESEARCH INSTITUTE,POSSIBLE NONMILITARY SCIENTIFIC DEVELOPMENTS AND THEIR POTENTIAL IMPACT ON FOREIGN POLICY PROBLEMS OF THE UNITED. FUT USA+45 INT/ORG PROF/ORG CONSULT ACT/RES CREATE PLAN R+D TEC/DEV

PEACE KNOWL SKILL...TECHNIC PHIL/SCI NEW/IDEA UNESCO 20. PAGE 137 A2802

KAPLAN M.A.,"SOME PROBLEMS IN THE STRATEGIC ANALYSIS OF INTERNATIONAL POLITICS." UNIV R+D INT/ORG CREATE PLAN DIPLOM EDU/PROP COERCE DISPL PWR...METH/CNCPT NEW/IDEA HYPO/EXP TOT/POP 20. PAGE 76 A1561 — L59 — DECISION BAL/PWR

WOLFERS A.,"ACTORS IN INTERNATIONAL POLITICS. IN (FOX,WTR. THEORETICAL ASPECTS OF INTERNATIONAL." FUT WOR+45 CONSTN INT/ORG NAT/G CREATE...CONCPT 20. PAGE 166 A3383 — L59 — PERSON PWR DIPLOM

HARTT J.,"ANTARCTICA: ITS IMMEDIATE PRACTICALITIES." FUT USA+45 USSR WOR+45 INT/ORG NAT/G CREATE TEC/DEV REGION KNOWL WEALTH...GEOG 20 ANTARTICA. PAGE 62 A1276 — S59 — VOL/ASSN ORD/FREE DIPLOM

ARMS CONTROL. FUT UNIV WOR+45 INTELL R+D INT/ORG NAT/G VOL/ASSN CONSULT CREATE EDU/PROP PEACE...HUM GEN/LAWS TOT/POP 20. PAGE 3 A0060 — B60 — DELIB/GP ORD/FREE ARMS/CONT NUC/PWR

BROOKINGS INSTITUTION,UNITED STATES FOREIGN POLICY: STUDY NO 9: THE FORMULATION AND ADMINISTRATION OF UNITED STATES FOREIGN POLICY. USA+45 WOR+45 EX/STRUC LEGIS BAL/PWR FOR/AID EDU/PROP CIVMIL/REL GOV/REL...INT COLD/WAR. PAGE 19 A0394 — B60 — DIPLOM INT/ORG CREATE

LANDHEER B.,ETHICAL VALUES IN INTERNATIONAL DECISION-MAKING. FUT LAW SOCIETY INT/ORG NAT/G DELIB/GP CREATE NAT/LISM ATTIT PERSON...DECISION CONCPT LEAGUE/NAT TOT/POP 20. PAGE 84 A1718 — B60 — HYPO/EXP POLICY PEACE

MUNRO L.,UNITED NATIONS, HOPE FOR A DIVIDED WORLD. FUT WOR+45 CONSTN DELIB/GP CREATE TEC/DEV DIPLOM EDU/PROP LEGIT PEACE ATTIT HEALTH ORD/FREE PWR ...CONCPT TREND UN VAL/FREE 20. PAGE 106 A2172 — B60 — INT/ORG ROUTINE

DEUTSCH K.W.,"TOWARD AN INVENTORY OF BASIC TRENDS AND PATTERNS IN COMPARATIVE AND INTERNATIONAL POLITICS." UNIV WOR+45 SOCIETY STRUCT INT/ORG NAT/G CREATE PLAN EDU/PROP KNOWL...PHIL/SCI METH/CNCPT STAT SELF/OBS OBS/ENVIR SAMP TREND CON/ANAL CHARTS SOC/EXP GEN/METH 20. PAGE 36 A0739 — L60 — R+D PERCEPT

BOGARDUS E.S.,"THE SOCIOLOGY OF A STRUCTURED PEACE." FUT SOCIETY CREATE DIPLOM EDU/PROP ADJUD ROUTINE ATTIT RIGID/FLEX KNOWL ORD/FREE RESPECT ...POLICY INT/LAW JURID NEW/IDEA SELF/OBS TOT/POP 20 UN. PAGE 16 A0327 — S60 — INT/ORG SOC NAT/LISM PEACE

DOUGHERTY J.E.,"KEY TO SECURITY: DISARMAMENT OR ARMS STABILITY." COM USA+45 USSR INT/ORG NAT/G CREATE EDU/PROP COERCE DETER ATTIT PWR...DECISION CONCPT MYTH NEW/IDEA TREND 20 COLD/WAR. PAGE 38 A0777 — S60 — FORCES ORD/FREE ARMS/CONT NUC/PWR

EFIMENCO N.M.,"CATEGORIES OF INTERNATIONAL INTEGRATION." UNIV WOR+45 INT/ORG NAT/G ACT/RES CREATE PEACE...CONCPT TREND 20. PAGE 40 A0824 — S60 — PLAN BAL/PWR SOVEREIGN

HAYTON R.D.,"THE ANTARCTIC SETTLEMENT OF 1959." FUT USA+45 WOR+45 WOR-45 STRUCT R+D INT/ORG EX/STRUC CREATE TEC/DEV LEGIT PEACE ATTIT SOVEREIGN ...TIME/SEQ 20 TREATY IGY. PAGE 63 A1297 — S60 — DELIB/GP JURID DIPLOM REGION

KAPLAN M.A.,"THEORETICAL ANALYSIS OF THE BALANCE OF POWER." FUT USA+45 WOR+45 INTELL ECO/DEV INT/ORG NAT/G CONSULT TOP/EX ACT/RES PLAN TEC/DEV ATTIT ALL/VALS...METH/CNCPT TOT/POP 20. PAGE 76 A1562 — S60 — CREATE NEW/IDEA DIPLOM NUC/PWR

BRENNAN D.G.,ARMS CONTROL, DISARMAMENT, AND NATIONAL SECURITY. WOR+45 NAT/G FORCES CREATE PROB/SOLV PARTIC WAR PEACE...DECISION INT/LAW ANTHOL BIBLIOG 20. PAGE 18 A0372 — B61 — ARMS/CONT ORD/FREE DIPLOM POLICY

ROBINS D.B.,EVOLVING UNITED STATES POLICIES TOWARD THE EMERGING NATIONS OF ASIA AND AFRICA (PAMPHLET). ISLAM ECO/UNDEV INT/ORG CONSULT CREATE PLAN TEC/DEV FOR/AID CONFER ALL/VALS 20 KENNEDY/JF EISNHWR/DD UN AID. PAGE 122 A2501 — B61 — AFR S/ASIA DIPLOM BIBLIOG

SINGER J.D.,FINANCING INTERNATIONAL ORGANIZATION: THE UNITED NATIONS BUDGET PROCESS. WOR+45 FINAN ACT/RES CREATE PLAN BUDGET ECO/TAC ADMIN ROUTINE ATTIT KNOWL...DECISION METH/CNCPT TIME/SEQ UN 20. PAGE 133 A2726 — B61 — INT/ORG MGT

STRAUSZ-HUPE R.,A FORWARD STRATEGY FOR AMERICA. FUT WOR+45 ECO/DEV INT/ORG NAT/G POL/PAR DELIB/GP FORCES ACT/RES CREATE ECO/TAC DOMIN EDU/PROP ATTIT DRIVE PWR...MAJORIT CONCPT STAT OBS TIME/SEQ TREND COLD/WAR TOT/POP. PAGE 139 A2848 — B61 — USA+45 PLAN DIPLOM

YDIT M.,INTERNATIONALISED TERRITORIES. FUT WOR+45 WOR-45 CONSTN VOL/ASSN CREATE PLAN LEGIT PEACE ORD/FREE...GEOG INT/LAW JURID SOC NEW/IDEA OBS RECORD SAMP TIME/SEQ TREND 19/20 BERLIN. PAGE 169 A3431 — B61 — LOC/G INT/ORG DIPLOM SOVEREIGN

BARALL M.,"THE UNITED STATES GOVERNMENT RESPONDS." L/A+17C USA+45 SOCIETY NAT/G CREATE PLAN DIPLOM ECO/TAC ATTIT DRIVE RIGID/FLEX KNOWL SKILL WEALTH ...METH/CNCPT TIME/SEQ GEN/METH 20. PAGE 11 A0217 — S61 — ECO/UNDEV ACT/RES FOR/AID

SINGER J.D.,"THE LEVEL OF ANALYSIS: PROBLEMS IN INTERNATIONAL RELATIONS." FUT INTELL R+D INT/ORG CREATE EDU/PROP...METH/CNCPT HYPO/EXP GEN/METH METH VAL/FREE. PAGE 133 A2725 — S61 — SOCIETY SOC DIPLOM

TUCKER R.C.,"TOWARDS A COMPARATIVE POLITICS OF MOVEMENT-REGIMES" (BMR)" USSR CONSTN NAT/G CREATE PROB/SOLV DIPLOM DOMIN REV...GP/COMP IDEA/COMP METH 20 STALIN/J BOLSHEVISM. PAGE 145 A2971 — S61 — MARXISM POLICY GEN/LAWS PWR

BLACKETT P.M.S.,STUDIES OF WAR: NUCLEAR AND CONVENTIONAL. EUR+WWI USA+45 DELIB/GP ACT/RES CREATE PLAN TEC/DEV LEGIT COERCE WAR ORD/FREE PWR ...POLICY TECHNIC TIME/SEQ 20. PAGE 15 A0300 — B62 — INT/ORG FORCES ARMS/CONT NUC/PWR

BOULDING K.E.,CONFLICT AND DEFENSE: A GENERAL THEORY. FUT SOCIETY INT/ORG NAT/G CREATE BAL/PWR COERCE NAT/LISM DRIVE ALL/VALS...PLURIST DECISION CONCPT METH/CNCPT TREND HYPO/EXP TOT/POP 20. PAGE 17 A0347 — B62 — MATH SIMUL PEACE WAR

BOUSCAREN A.T.,SOVIET FOREIGN POLICY: A PATTERN OF PERSISTANCE. WOR+45 WOR-45 SOCIETY STRUCT INT/ORG POL/PAR CREATE PLAN EDU/PROP ROUTINE ATTIT RIGID/FLEX...POLICY CONCPT RECORD HIST/WRIT TIME/SEQ MARX/KARL 20. PAGE 17 A0352 — B62 — COM NAT/G DIPLOM USSR

DAVAR F.C.,IRAN AND INDIA THROUGH THE AGES. INDIA IRAN ELITES SECT CREATE ORD/FREE...LING BIBLIOG. PAGE 34 A0683 — B62 — NAT/COMP DIPLOM CULTURE

DREIER J.C.,THE ORGANIZATION OF AMERICAN STATES AND THE HEMISPHERE CRISIS. CUBA USA+45 CULTURE STRATA NAT/G VOL/ASSN CONSULT FORCES ACT/RES CREATE DIPLOM ECO/TAC FOR/AID ALL/VALS...POLICY OBS OAS 20. PAGE 38 A0786 — B62 — L/A+17C CONCPT

GILPIN R.,AMERICAN SCIENTISTS AND NUCLEAR WEAPONS POLICY. COM FUT USA+45 WOR+45 INT/ORG NAT/G PROF/ORG CONSULT FORCES CREATE TEC/DEV BAL/PWR EDU/PROP ARMS/CONT WAR PERCEPT KNOWL MORAL PWR ...PHIL/SCI SOC CONCPT GEN/LAWS 20. PAGE 52 A1073 — B62 — INTELL ATTIT DETER NUC/PWR

KAHN H.,THINKING ABOUT THE UNTHINKABLE. FUT USA+45 LAW NAT/G CONSULT FORCES ACT/RES CREATE PLAN TEC/DEV BAL/PWR DIPLOM EDU/PROP ARMS/CONT DETER ATTIT...CONCPT OBS TREND COLD/WAR 20. PAGE 76 A1547 — B62 — INT/ORG ORD/FREE NUC/PWR PEACE

RIVKIN A.,AFRICA AND THE WEST. AFR EUR+WWI FUT ISLAM ISRAEL USA+45 SOCIETY INT/ORG FORCES CREATE PLAN FOR/AID EDU/PROP ATTIT...CONCPT TREND EEC 20 CONGRESS UN. PAGE 121 A2488 — B62 — ECO/UNDEV ECO/TAC

SCHWARTZ L.E.,INTERNATIONAL ORGANIZATIONS AND SPACE COOPERATION. VOL/ASSN CONSULT CREATE TEC/DEV SANCTION...POLICY INT/LAW PHIL/SCI 20 UN. PAGE 130 A2656 — B62 — INT/ORG DIPLOM R+D SPACE

SELOSOEMARDJAN O.,SOCIAL CHANGES IN JOGJAKARTA. INDONESIA NETHERLAND ELITES STRATA STRUCT FAM POL/PAR CREATE DIPLOM INT/TRADE EDU/PROP ADMIN GOV/REL...SOC 20 JAVA CHINJAP. PAGE 131 A2683 — B62 — ECO/UNDEV CULTURE REV COLONIAL

THOMSON G.P.,NUCLEAR ENERGY IN BRITAIN DURING THE LAST WAR: THE CHERWELL SIMON LECTURE (MONOGRAPH). UK R+D CONSULT FORCES PLAN DIPLOM TASK CIVMIL/REL ROLE...PHIL/SCI NEW/IDEA LAB/EXP 20 MAUD. PAGE 143 A2934 — B62 — CREATE TEC/DEV WAR NUC/PWR

WRIGHT Q.,PREVENTING WORLD WAR THREE. FUT WOR+45 CULTURE INT/ORG NAT/G CONSULT FORCES ADMIN ARMS/CONT DRIVE RIGID/FLEX ORD/FREE SOVEREIGN ...POLICY CONCPT TREND STERTYP COLD/WAR 20. PAGE 168 A3416 — B62 — CREATE ATTIT

BAILEY S.D.,"THE TROIKA AND THE FUTURE OF THE UN." CONSTN CREATE LEGIT EXEC CHOOSE ORD/FREE PWR ...CONCPT NEW/IDEA UN COLD/WAR 20. PAGE 10 A0206 — L62 — FUT INT/ORG USSR

MALINOWSKI W.R.,"CENTRALIZATION AND DE-CENTRALIZATION IN THE UNITED NATIONS' ECONOMIC AND SOCIAL ACTIVITIES." WOR+45 CONSTN ECO/UNDEV INT/ORG VOL/ASSN DELIB/GP ECO/TAC EDU/PROP ADMIN RIGID/FLEX ...OBS CHARTS UNESCO UN EEC OAS OEEC 20. PAGE 93 — L62 — CREATE GEN/LAWS

A1913

S62

BELSHAW C.,"TRAINING AND RECRUITMENT: SOME PRINCIPLES OF INTERNATIONAL AID." FUT WOR+45 SOCIETY INT/ORG NAT/G CREATE PLAN TEC/DEV ECO/TAC FOR/AID EDU/PROP ATTIT PERCEPT...HUM UN FAO ILO UNESCO 20. PAGE 13 A0263 — VOL/ASSN ECO/UNDEV

S62

BRZEZINSKI Z.K.,"PEACEFUL ENGAGEMENT IN COMMUNIST DISUNITY." ASIA CHINA/COM USA+45 USSR NAT/G TOP/EX CREATE ECO/TAC FOR/AID DOMIN ATTIT PERCEPT RIGID/FLEX PWR...PSY 20. PAGE 20 A0417 — COM DIPLOM TOTALISM

S62

CROAN M.,"POLYCENTRISM: COMMUNIST INTERNATIONAL RELATIONS." ASIA STRUCT INT/ORG NAT/G POL/PAR CONSULT PLAN DOMIN EDU/PROP COERCE ATTIT RIGID/FLEX SOCISM...POLICY CONCPT TREND CON/ANAL GEN/LAWS MARX/KARL. PAGE 33 A0663 — COM CREATE DIPLOM NAT/LISM

S62

FINKELSTEIN L.S.,"THE UNITED NATIONS AND ORGANIZATIONS FOR CONTROL OF ARMAMENT." FUT WOR+45 VOL/ASSN DELIB/GP TOP/EX CREATE EDU/PROP LEGIT ADJUD NUC/PWR ATTIT RIGID/FLEX ORD/FREE...POLICY DECISION CONCPT OBS TREND GEN/LAWS TOT/POP COLD/WAR. PAGE 46 A0933 — INT/ORG PWR ARMS/CONT

S62

FOSTER W.C.,"ARMS CONTROL AND DISARMAMENT IN A DIVIDED WORLD." COM FUT USA+45 USSR WOR+45 INTELL INT/ORG NAT/G VOL/ASSN CONSULT CREATE PLAN TEC/DEV EDU/PROP LEGIT NUC/PWR ATTIT RIGID/FLEX...CONCPT TREND TOT/POP 20 UN. PAGE 47 A0971 — DELIB/GP POLICY ARMS/CONT DIPLOM

S62

GUETZKOW H.,"THE POTENTIAL OF CASE STUDY IN ANALYZING INTERNATIONAL CONFLICT." EUR+WWI FUT GERMANY INTELL SOCIETY STRUCT INT/ORG LOC/G NAT/G CONSULT CREATE PLAN CHOOSE ATTIT RIGID/FLEX ...POLICY SAAR 20. PAGE 58 A1188 — EDU/PROP METH/CNCPT COERCE FRANCE

S62

KOLARZ W.,"THE IMPACT OF COMMUNISM ON WEST AFRICA." AFR FUT SOCIETY INT/ORG NAT/G CREATE PLAN DOMIN EDU/PROP COERCE NAT/LISM ATTIT RIGID/FLEX SOCISM ...POLICY CONCPT TREND MARX/KARL 20. PAGE 81 A1666 — COM POL/PAR COLONIAL

S62

MARIAS J.,"A PROGRAM FOR EUROPE." EUR+WWI INT/ORG NAT/G PLAN DIPLOM DOMIN PWR...STERTYP TOT/POP 20. PAGE 95 A1938 — VOL/ASSN CREATE REGION

S62

NANES A.,"DISARMAMENT: THE LAST SEVEN YEARS." COM EUR+WWI USA+45 USSR INT/ORG FORCES TOP/EX CREATE LEGIT NUC/PWR DISPL ORD/FREE...CONCPT TIME/SEQ CON/ANAL 20. PAGE 107 A2195 — DELIB/GP RIGID/FLEX ARMS/CONT

S62

RUBINSTEIN A.Z.,"RUSSIA AND THE UNCOMMITTED NATIONS." AFR INDIA ISLAM L/A+17C LAOS S/ASIA ELITES ECO/UNDEV INT/ORG KIN CREATE PLAN TEC/DEV NAT/LISM RIGID/FLEX PWR WEALTH...METH/CNCPT TIME/SEQ GEN/LAWS WORK. PAGE 125 A2562 — ECO/TAC TREND COLONIAL USSR

S62

SPRINGER H.W.,"FEDERATION IN THE CARIBBEAN: AN ATTEMPT THAT FAILED." L/A+17C ECO/UNDEV INT/ORG POL/PAR PROVS LEGIS CREATE PLAN LEGIT ADMIN FEDERAL ATTIT DRIVE PERSON ORD/FREE PWR...POLICY GEOG PSY CONCPT OBS CARIBBEAN CMN/WLTH 20. PAGE 136 A2791 — VOL/ASSN NAT/G REGION

S62

TOWSTER J.,"THE USSR AND THE USA: CHALLENGE AND RESPONSE." COM GERMANY USA+45 USSR WOR+45 ECO/UNDEV INT/ORG VOL/ASSN EX/STRUC FORCES TOP/EX CREATE PLAN TEC/DEV DIPLOM ECO/TAC EDU/PROP COLONIAL COERCE PWR ...GEN/METH COLD/WAR 20 KENNEDY/JF. PAGE 145 A2956 — ACT/RES GEN/LAWS

C62

ROBINSON J.A.,"CONGRESS AND FOREIGN POLICY-MAKING: A STUDY IN LEGISLATIVE INFLUENCE AND INITIATIVE." USA+45 CHIEF DELIB/GP CREATE CONTROL EXEC GOV/REL PERCEPT...TREND BIBLIOG 20 CONGRESS. PAGE 122 A2505 — LEGIS DIPLOM POLICY DECISION

B63

FLORES E.,LAND REFORM AND THE ALLIANCE FOR PROGRESS (PAMPHLET). L/A+17C USA+45 STRUCT ECO/UNDEV NAT/G WORKER CREATE PLAN ECO/TAC COERCE REV 20. PAGE 47 A0953 — AGRI INT/ORG DIPLOM POLICY

B63

HALEY A.G.,SPACE LAW AND GOVERNMENT. FUT USA+45 WOR+45 LEGIS ACT/RES CREATE ATTIT RIGID/FLEX ORD/FREE PWR SOVEREIGN...POLICY JURID CONCPT CHARTS VAL/FREE 20. PAGE 60 A1226 — INT/ORG LAW SPACE

B63

MAYNE R.,THE COMMUNITY OF EUROPE. UK CONSTN NAT/G CONSULT DELIB/GP CREATE PLAN ECO/TAC LEGIT ADMIN ROUTINE ORD/FREE PWR WEALTH...CONCPT TIME/SEQ EEC EURATOM 20. PAGE 97 A1985 — EUR+WWI INT/ORG REGION

B63

OECD,SCIENCE AND THE POLICIES OF GOVERNMENTS: THE IMPLICATIONS OF SCIENCE AND TECHNOLOGY FOR NATL AND INTL AFFAIRS. WOR+45 INT/ORG EDU/PROP AUTOMAT ...POLICY PHIL/SCI 20. PAGE 111 A2279 — CREATE TEC/DEV DIPLOM NAT/G

B63

ROSECRANCE R.N.,ACTION AND REACTION IN WORLD POLITICS. FUT WOR-45 SOCIETY DELIB/GP ACT/RES CREATE DIPLOM ECO/TAC DOMIN EDU/PROP COERCE ATTIT PERSON SUPEGO ORD/FREE PWR...CHARTS SIMUL LEAGUE/NAT VAL/FREE UN 19/20. PAGE 123 A2529 — WOR+45 INT/ORG BAL/PWR

B63

ROSNER G.,THE UNITED NATIONS EMERGENCY FORCE. FRANCE ISRAEL UAR UK WOR+45 CREATE WAR PEACE ORD/FREE PWR...INT/LAW JURID HIST/WRIT TIME/SEQ UN. PAGE 124 A2539 — INT/ORG FORCES

L63

PADELFORD N.J.,"FINANCIAL CRISIS AND THE UNITED NATIONS." FUT USSR WOR+45 LAW CONSTN FINAN INT/ORG DELIB/GP FORCES PLAN BUDGET DIPLOM COST WEALTH ...STAT CHARTS UN CONGO 20. PAGE 113 A2311 — CREATE ECO/TAC

L63

SCHELLING T.C.,"STRATEGIC PROBLEMS OF AN INTERNATIONAL ARMED FORCE." WOR+45 ECO/DEV INT/ORG NAT/G PLAN BAL/PWR LEGIT ARMS/CONT COERCE DETER ORD/FREE PWR...POLICY CONCPT COLD/WAR 20. PAGE 128 A2624 — CREATE FORCES

L63

WILCOX F.O.,"THE ATLANTIC COMMUNITY: PROGRESS AND PROSPECTS." EUR+WWI FUT USA+45 WOR+45 SOCIETY CREATE ECO/TAC EDU/PROP LEGIT REGION ATTIT ALL/VALS ...POLICY ANTHOL VAL/FREE 20. PAGE 164 A3346 — INT/ORG ACT/RES

S63

BRZEZINSKI Z.,"SOVIET QUIESCENCE." EUR+WWI USA+45 USSR FORCES CREATE PLAN COERCE DETER WAR ATTIT 20 TREATY EUROPE. PAGE 20 A0415 — DIPLOM ARMS/CONT NUC/PWR AGREE

S63

GARDNER R.N.,"COOPERATION IN OUTER SPACE." FUT USSR WOR+45 AIR LAW COM/IND CONSULT DELIB/GP CREATE KNOWL 20 TREATY. PAGE 51 A1045 — INT/ORG ACT/RES PEACE SPACE

S63

GROSS F.,"THE US NATIONAL INTEREST AND THE UN." FUT CONSTN NAT/G DELIB/GP CREATE DIPLOM RIGID/FLEX ORD/FREE...CONCPT GEN/LAWS 20 UN. PAGE 57 A1172 — USA+45 INT/ORG PEACE

S63

HOLBO P.S.,"COLD WAR DRIFT IN LATIN AMERICA." CUBA L/A+17C USA+45 USA-45 INT/ORG NAT/G NEIGH VOL/ASSN ACT/RES PLAN ECO/TAC ATTIT RIGID/FLEX ALL/VALS ...RECORD TIME/SEQ OAS LAFTA 20 COLD/WAR. PAGE 66 A1363 — DELIB/GP CREATE FOR/AID

S63

KRAVIS I.B.,"THE POLITICAL ARITHMETIC OF INTERNATIONAL BURDENSHARING." FUT USA+45 WOR+45 FINAN DELIB/GP ACT/RES CREATE TEC/DEV ATTIT PWR WEALTH...POLICY MATH STAT VAL/FREE 20. PAGE 82 A1681 — INT/ORG ECO/TAC

S63

MORGENTHAU H.J.,"THE POLITICAL CONDITIONS FOR AN INTERNATIONAL POLICE FORCE." FUT WOR+45 CREATE LEGIT ADMIN PEACE ORD/FREE 20. PAGE 104 A2141 — INT/ORG FORCES ARMS/CONT DETER

S63

MURRAY J.N.,"UNITED NATIONS PEACE-KEEPING AND PROBLEMS OF POLITICAL CONTROL." FUT WOR+45 CONSTN DELIB/GP FORCES TOP/EX ACT/RES CREATE LEGIT PEACE PWR...METH/CNCPT CONGO UN 20. PAGE 106 A2182 — INT/ORG ORD/FREE

S63

NICHOLAS H.G.,"UN PEACE FORCES AND THE CHANGING GLOBE: THE LESSONS OF SUEZ AND CONGO." FUT WOR+45 CONSTN INT/ORG CONSULT DELIB/GP TOP/EX CREATE DIPLOM DOMIN LEGIT COERCE WAR PERSON RIGID/FLEX PWR UN SUEZ CONGO UNEF 20. PAGE 109 A2229 — ACT/RES FORCES

S63

PINCUS J.,"THE COST OF FOREIGN AID." WOR+45 ECO/DEV FINAN NAT/G VOL/ASSN CREATE ECO/TAC EDU/PROP WEALTH ...METH/CNCPT STAT CHARTS HYPO/EXP TOT/POP VAL/FREE 20. PAGE 116 A2380 — USA+45 ECO/UNDEV FOR/AID

S63

SHONFIELD A.,"AFTER BRUSSELS." EUR+WWI FRANCE GERMANY UK ECO/DEV DIST/IND MARKET VOL/ASSN DELIB/GP CREATE INT/TRADE ATTIT RIGID/FLEX...RECORD TREND GEN/LAWS EEC CMN/WLTH 20. PAGE 132 A2705 — PLAN ECO/TAC

S63

WALKER H.,"THE INTERNATIONAL LAW OF COMMODITY AGREEMENTS." FUT WOR+45 ECO/DEV ECO/UNDEV FINAN INT/ORG NAT/G CONSULT CREATE PLAN ECO/TAC ATTIT PERCEPT...CONCPT GEN/LAWS TOT/POP GATT 20. PAGE 160 A3265 — MARKET VOL/ASSN INT/LAW INT/TRADE

S63

WOLFERS A.,"INTEGRATION IN THE WEST: THE CONFLICT OF PERSPECTIVES." EUR+WWI USA+45 ECO/DEV INT/ORG DELIB/GP CREATE TEC/DEV DIPLOM ATTIT PWR...CONCPT HIST/WRIT TREND GEN/LAWS COLD/WAR EEC 20. PAGE 166 A3386 — RIGID/FLEX ECO/TAC

B64

APTER D.E.,IDEOLOGY AND DISCONTENT. FUT WOR+45 CONSTN CULTURE INTELL SOCIETY STRUCT INT/ORG NAT/G DELIB/GP LEGIS CREATE PLAN TEC/DEV EDU/PROP EXEC PERCEPT PERSON RIGID/FLEX ALL/VALS...POLICY TOT/POP. PAGE 8 A0171 — ACT/RES ATTIT

B64
CZERNIN F.,VERSAILLES - 1919. EUR+WWI USA-45 FACE/GP POL/PAR VOL/ASSN DELIB/GP TOP/EX CREATE BAL/PWR DIPLOM LEGIT NAT/LISM PEACE ATTIT RIGID/FLEX ORD/FREE PWR...CON/ANAL LEAGUE/NAT 20 VERSAILLES. PAGE 33 A0671
INT/ORG STRUCT

B64
GOWING M.,BRITAIN AND ATOMIC ENERGY 1939-1945. FRANCE UK USA+45 USA-45 NAT/G CREATE...PHIL/SCI 20 AEA. PAGE 54 A1118
NUC/PWR DIPLOM TEC/DEV

B64
IKLE F.C.,HOW NATIONS NEGOTIATE. COM EUR+WWI USA+45 INTELL INT/ORG VOL/ASSN DELIB/GP ACT/RES CREATE DOMIN EDU/PROP ADJUD ROUTINE ATTIT PERSON ORD/FREE RESPECT SKILL...PSY SOC OBS VAL/FREE. PAGE 70 A1433
NAT/G PWR POLICY

B64
JACOB P.E.,THE INTEGRATION OF POLITICAL COMMUNITIES. USA+45 WOR+45 CULTURE LOC/G MUNIC NAT/G CREATE PLAN LEGIT REGION COERCE ALL/VALS ...POLICY GEOG PSY SOC TREND HYPO/EXP GEN/LAWS VAL/FREE 20. PAGE 72 A1483
INT/ORG METH/CNCPT SIMUL STAT

B64
KEEP J.,CONTEMPORARY HISTORY IN THE SOVIET MIRROR. COM USSR POL/PAR CREATE DIPLOM AGREE WAR ATTIT ...MYTH TREND ANTHOL 20 COLD/WAR STALIN/J MARX/KARL LENIN/VI. PAGE 77 A1576
HIST/WRIT METH MARXISM IDEA/COMP

B64
KITCHEN H.,A HANDBOOK OF AFRICAN AFFAIRS. ECO/UNDEV CREATE DIPLOM COLONIAL RACE/REL...ART/METH GEOG CHARTS 20. PAGE 80 A1646
AFR NAT/G INT/ORG FORCES

B64
PRAKASH B.,INDIA AND THE WORLD. INDIA INT/ORG CREATE ORD/FREE...POLICY TREND 20. PAGE 117 A2405
DIPLOM PEACE ATTIT

B64
TAUBENFELD H.J.,SPACE AND SOCIETY. USA+45 LAW FORCES CREATE TEC/DEV ADJUD CONTROL COST PEACE ...PREDICT ANTHOL 20. PAGE 142 A2895
SPACE SOCIETY ADJUST DIPLOM

B64
TREADGOLD D.W.,THE DEVELOPMENT OF THE USSR. COM USSR ECO/DEV CREATE BAL/PWR DEBATE COLONIAL TOTALISM...HUM ANTHOL BIBLIOG 19/20. PAGE 145 A2960
MARXISM CONSERVE DIPLOM DOMIN

L64
CARNEGIE ENDOWMENT INT. PEACE,"ECONOMIC AND SOCIAL QUESTION (ISSUES BEFORE THE NINETEENTH GENERAL ASSEMBLY)." WOR+45 ECO/DEV ECO/UNDEV INDUS R+D DELIB/GP CREATE PLAN TEC/DEV ECO/TAC FOR/AID BAL/PAY...RECORD UN 20. PAGE 24 A0493
INT/ORG INT/TRADE

L64
HAAS E.B.,"ECONOMICS AND DIFFERENTIAL PATTERNS OF POLITICAL INTEGRATION: PROJECTIONS ABOUT UNITY IN LATIN AMERICA." SOCIETY NAT/G DELIB/GP ACT/RES CREATE PLAN ECO/TAC REGION ROUTINE ATTIT DRIVE PWR WEALTH...CONCPT TREND CHARTS LAFTA 20. PAGE 59 A1208
L/A+17C INT/ORG MARKET

S64
KARPOV P.V.,"PEACEFUL COEXISTENCE AND INTERNATIONAL LAW." WOR+45 LAW SOCIETY INT/ORG VOL/ASSN FORCES CREATE CAP/ISM DIPLOM ADJUD NUC/PWR PEACE MORAL ORD/FREE PWR MARXISM...MARXIST JURID CONCPT OBS TREND COLD/WAR MARX/KARL 20. PAGE 77 A1568
COM ATTIT INT/LAW USSR

S64
SCHWELB E.,"OPERATION OF THE EUROPEAN CONVENTION ON HUMAN RIGHTS." EUR+WWI LAW SOCIETY CREATE EDU/PROP ADJUD ADMIN PEACE ATTIT ORD/FREE PWR...POLICY INT/LAW CONCPT OBS GEN/LAWS UN VAL/FREE ILO 20 ECHR. PAGE 130 A2665
INT/ORG MORAL

S64
TINKER H.,"POLITICS IN SOUTHEAST ASIA." INT/ORG NAT/G CREATE PLAN TEC/DEV GUERRILLA KNOWL ORD/FREE COLD/WAR. PAGE 144 A2944
S/ASIA ACT/RES REGION

S64
TOUVAL S.,"THE SOMALI REPUBLIC." AFR ISLAM SOMALIA FAM KIN NAT/G CREATE FOR/AID LEGIT ATTIT ALL/VALS ...RECORD TREND 20. PAGE 144 A2954
ECO/UNDEV RIGID/FLEX

S64
TRISKA J.F.,"SOVIET TREATY LAW: A QUANTITATIVE ANALYSIS." WOR+45 LAW ECO/UNDEV AGRI COM/IND INDUS CREATE TEC/DEV DIPLOM ATTIT PWR WEALTH...JURID SAMP TIME/SEQ TREND CHARTS VAL/FREE 20 TREATY. PAGE 145 A2967
COM ECO/TAC INT/LAW USSR

B65
EDUCATION AND WORLD AFFAIRS,THE UNIVERSITY LOOKS ABROAD: APPROACHES TO WORLD AFFAIRS AT SIX AMERICAN UNIVERSITIES. USA+45 CREATE EDU/PROP CONFER LEAD KNOWL 20 CORNELL/U MICH/STA/U STANFORD/U TULANE/U WISCONSN/U. PAGE 40 A0822
ACADEM DIPLOM ATTIT GP/COMP

B65
HALLE L.J.,THE SOCIETY OF MAN. WOR+45 WOR-45 EDU/PROP NAT/LISM MARXISM CONCPT. PAGE 60 A1231
DIPLOM PHIL/SCI CREATE SOCIETY

B65
HOSELITZ B.F.,ECONOMICS AND THE IDEA OF MANKIND. UNIV ECO/DEV ECO/UNDEV DIST/IND INDUS INT/ORG NAT/G ACT/RES ECO/TAC WEALTH...CONCPT STAT. PAGE 68 A1392
CREATE INT/TRADE

B65
INGRAM D.,COMMONWEALTH FOR A COLOUR-BLIND WORLD. AFR INDIA UK STRATA ECO/UNDEV VOL/ASSN CREATE PLAN CONFER COLONIAL ORD/FREE SOC/INTEG 20 COMMONWLTH. PAGE 70 A1441
RACE/REL INT/ORG INGP/REL PROB/SOLV

B65
UNESCO,HANDBOOK OF INTERNATIONAL EXCHANGES. COM/IND R+D ACADEM PROF/ORG VOL/ASSN CREATE TEC/DEV EDU/PROP AGREE 20 TREATY. PAGE 148 A3025
INDEX INT/ORG DIPLOM PRESS

B65
VON GLAHN G.,LAW AMONG NATIONS: AN INTRODUCTION TO PUBLIC INTERNATIONAL LAW. WOR+45 WOR-45 INT/ORG NAT/G CREATE ADJUD WAR...GEOG CLASSIF TREND BIBLIOG. PAGE 160 A3250
ACADEM INT/LAW GEN/LAWS LAW

B65
WEIL G.L.,A HANDBOOK ON THE EUROPEAN ECONOMIC COMMUNITY. BELGIUM EUR+WWI FRANCE GERMANY/W ITALY CONSTN ECO/DEV CREATE PARTIC GP/REL...DECISION MGT CHARTS 20 EEC. PAGE 162 A3299
INT/TRADE INT/ORG TEC/DEV INT/LAW

S65
AMRAM P.W.,"REPORT ON THE TENTH SESSION OF THE HAGUE CONFERENCE ON PRIVATE INTERNATIONAL LAW." USA+45 WOR+45 INT/ORG CREATE LEGIT ADJUD ALL/VALS ...JURID CONCPT METH/CNCPT OBS GEN/METH 20. PAGE 8 A0155
VOL/ASSN DELIB/GP INT/LAW

S65
BROWN S.,"AN ALTERNATIVE TO THE GRAND DESIGN." EUR+WWI FUT USA+45 INT/ORG NAT/G EX/STRUC FORCES CREATE BAL/PWR DOMIN RIGID/FLEX ORD/FREE PWR ...NEW/IDEA RECORD EEC NATO 20. PAGE 20 A0407
VOL/ASSN CONCPT DIPLOM

S65
HAZARD J.N.,"CO-EXISTENCE LAW BOWS OUT." WOR+45 R+D INT/ORG VOL/ASSN CONSULT DELIB/GP ACT/RES CREATE PEACE KNOWL...JURID CONCPT COLD/WAR VAL/FREE 20. PAGE 63 A1300
PROF/ORG ADJUD

C65
BURTON J.W.,"INTERNATIONAL RELATIONS: A GENERAL THEORY." WOR+45 NAT/G CREATE BAL/PWR NEUTRAL COERCE DETER ADJUST...TREND IDEA/COMP GEN/METH BIBLIOG. PAGE 22 A0447
DIPLOM GEN/LAWS ACT/RES ORD/FREE

B66
ASAMOAH O.Y.,THE LEGAL SIGNIFICANCE OF THE DECLARATIONS OF THE GENERAL ASSEMBLY OF THE UNITED NATIONS. WOR+45 CREATE CONTROL...BIBLIOG 20 UN. PAGE 9 A0184
INT/LAW INT/ORG DIPLOM

B66
BOULDING K.E.,THE IMPACT OF THE SOCIAL SCIENCES. UNIV LAW SOCIETY CREATE PROB/SOLV...TREND WORSHIP. PAGE 17 A0349
SOC DIPLOM

B66
DAENIKER G.,STRATEGIE DES KLEIN STAATS. SWITZERLND ACT/RES CREATE DIPLOM NEUTRAL DETER WAR WEAPON PWR SOVEREIGN...IDEA/COMP 20 COLD/WAR. PAGE 33 A0673
NUC/PWR PLAN FORCES NAT/G

B66
FINKLE J.L.,POLITICAL DEVELOPMENT AND SOCIAL CHANGE. WOR+45 CULTURE NAT/G OP/RES PROB/SOLV DIPLOM ECO/TAC INGP/REL...METH/COMP ANTHOL 20. PAGE 46 A0934
ECO/UNDEV SOCIETY CREATE

B66
GRENVILLE J.A.S.,POLITICS, STRATEGY, AND AMERICAN DEMOCRACY: STUDIES IN FOREIGN POLICY, 1873-1917. CUBA PHILIPPINE SPAIN USA-45 VENEZUELA ELITES NAT/G CREATE PARTIC WAR RIGID/FLEX ORD/FREE...DECISION TREND 19/20 HAWAII. PAGE 56 A1146
DIPLOM COLONIAL POLICY

B66
LUARD E.,THE EVOLUTION OF INTERNATIONAL ORGANIZATIONS. UK WOR+45 BUDGET INT/TRADE WAR BAL/PAY PEACE ORD/FREE...POLICY 19/20 EEC ILO LEAGUE/NAT UN. PAGE 91 A1871
INT/ORG EFFICIENCY CREATE TREND

B66
MAYER P.,THE PACIFIST CONSCIENCE. SECT CREATE ARMS/CONT WAR RACE/REL ATTIT LOVE...ANTHOL PACIFIST WORSHIP FREUD/S GANDHI/M LAO/TZU KING/MAR/L CONSCN/OBJ. PAGE 97 A1984
DIPLOM PACIFISM SUPEGO

B67
BARANSON J.,TECHNOLOGY FOR UNDERDEVELOPED AREAS: AN ANNOTATED BIBLIOGRAPHY. FUT WOR+45 CULTURE INDUS INT/ORG CREATE PROB/SOLV INT/TRADE EDU/PROP AUTOMAT ...CONCPT METH. PAGE 11 A0218
BIBLIOG/A ECO/UNDEV TEC/DEV R+D

B67
HIRSCHMAN A.O.,DEVELOPMENT PROJECTS OBSERVED. INDUS INT/ORG CONSULT EX/STRUC CREATE OP/RES ECO/TAC DEMAND...POLICY MGT METH/COMP 20 WORLD/BANK. PAGE 65 A1339
ECO/UNDEV R+D FINAN PLAN

B67
JAGAN C.,THE WEST ON TRIAL. GUYANA CONSTN ECO/UNDEV DIPLOM COERCE PWR SOVEREIGN...BIOG 20. PAGE 73 A1490
SOCISM CREATE PLAN COLONIAL

B67
JOHNSON A.M.,BOSTON CAPITALISTS AND WESTERN RAILROADS: A STUDY IN THE NINETEENTH CENTURY RAILROAD INVESTMENT PROCESS. CREATE BARGAIN INT/TRADE GAMBLE KNOWL 19 BOSTON. PAGE 74 A1519
FINAN DIST/IND CAP/ISM ECO/UNDEV

B67
NYERERE J.K.,FREEDOM AND UNITY/UHURU NA UMOJA: A SELECTION FROM WRITINGS AND SPEECHES, 1952-65. TANZANIA ELITES ECO/UNDEV INT/ORG NAT/G CREATE DIPLOM COLONIAL REGION RACE/REL...ANTHOL 20. PAGE 110 A2265
SOVEREIGN AFR TREND ORD/FREE

B67
UNESCO,PRINCIPLES AND PROBLEMS OF NATIONAL SCIENCE POLICIES. WOR+45 ECO/DEV ECO/UNDEV R+D INT/ORG PROB/SOLV CONFER...PHIL/SCI CHARTS 20 UNESCO UN. PAGE 148 A3026
NAT/COMP POLICY TEC/DEV CREATE

S67
BREGMAN A.,"WHITHER RUSSIA?" COM RUSSIA INTELL POL/PAR DIPLOM PARTIC NAT/LISM TOTALISM ATTIT ORD/FREE 20. PAGE 18 A0370
MARXISM ELITES ADMIN CREATE

S67
BURNS E.B.,"TRADITIONS AND VARIATIONS IN BRAZILIAN FOREIGN POLICY." BRAZIL L/A+17C POL/PAR INT/TRADE COLONIAL INGP/REL ATTIT ORD/FREE PWR 20. PAGE 22 A0443
DIPLOM NAT/LISM CREATE

S67
EGBERT D.D.,"POLITICS AND ART IN COMMUNIST BULGARIA" BULGARIA COM USSR CULTURE DIPLOM INGP/REL TOTALISM...TREND 20. PAGE 40 A0825
CREATE ART/METH CONTROL MARXISM

S67
KELLY F.K.,"A PROPOSAL FOR AN ANNUAL REPORT ON THE STATE OF MANKIND." FUT INTELL COM/IND INT/ORG CREATE PROB/SOLV PERS/REL...CONCPT 20 UN. PAGE 77 A1579
SOCIETY UNIV ATTIT NEW/IDEA

S67
KRAUS J.,"A MARXIST IN GHANA." GHANA ELITES CHIEF PROB/SOLV TEC/DEV DIPLOM ECO/TAC COLONIAL PARTIC PWR 20 NKRUMAH/K. PAGE 82 A1676
MARXISM PLAN ATTIT CREATE

S67
RAMSEY J.A.,"THE STATUS OF INTERNATIONAL COPYRIGHTS." WOR+45 CREATE TEC/DEV DIPLOM CONFER CONTROL SANCTION OWN...POLICY JURID. PAGE 119 A2439
INT/LAW INT/ORG COM/IND PRESS

S67
SHARP G.,"THE NEED OF A FUNCTIONAL SUBSTITUTE FOR WAR." FUT UNIV WOR+45 CULTURE SOCIETY INT/ORG CONSULT DELIB/GP ACT/RES CREATE BAL/PWR CONFER ARMS/CONT NUC/PWR 20. PAGE 132 A2696
PEACE WAR DIPLOM PROB/SOLV

CREDIT....CREDIT

CREMEANS C. A0662

CRIME....SEE ALSO ANOMIE

N
ANNALS OF THE AMERICAN ACADEMY OF POLITICAL AND SOCIAL SCIENCE. AFR ASIA S/ASIA WOR+45 POL/PAR DIPLOM CRIME REV...SOC BIOG 20. PAGE 1 A0004
BIBLIOG/A NAT/G CULTURE ATTIT

N
THE JAPAN SCIENCE REVIEW: LAW AND POLITICS: LIST OF BOOKS AND ARTICLES ON LAW AND POLITICS. CONSTN AGRI INDUS LABOR DIPLOM TAX ADMIN CRIME...INT/LAW SOC 20 CHINJAP. PAGE 2 A0042
BIBLIOG LAW S/ASIA PHIL/SCI

B20
VINOGRADOFF P.,OUTLINES OF HISTORICAL JURISPRUDENCE (2 VOLS.). GREECE MEDIT-7 LAW CONSTN FACE/GP FAM KIN MUNIC CRIME OWN...INT/LAW IDEA/COMP BIBLIOG. PAGE 159 A3241
JURID METH

B31
BORCHARD E.H.,GUIDE TO THE LAW AND LEGAL LITERATURE OF FRANCE. FRANCE FINAN INDUS LABOR SECT LEGIS ADMIN COLONIAL CRIME OWN...INT/LAW 20. PAGE 17 A0337
BIBLIOG/A LAW CONSTN METH

B33
AMERICAN FOREIGN LAW ASSN,BIOGRAPHICAL NOTES ON THE LAWS AND LEGAL LITERATURE OF URUGUAY AND CURACAO. URUGUAY CONSTN FINAN SECT FORCES JUDGE DIPLOM INT/TRADE ADJUD CT/SYS CRIME 20. PAGE 7 A0147
BIBLIOG/A LAW JURID ADMIN

B37
SCHUSTER E.,GUIDE TO LAW AND LEGAL LITERATURE OF CENTRAL AMERICAN REPUBLICS. L/A+17C INT/ORG ADJUD SANCTION CRIME...JURID 19/20. PAGE 129 A2654
BIBLIOG/A REGION CT/SYS LAW

B37
THOMPSON J.W.,SECRET DIPLOMACY: A RECORD OF ESPIONAGE AND DOUBLE-DEALING: 1500-1815. CHRIST-17C MOD/EUR NAT/G WRITING RISK MORAL...ANTHOL BIBLIOG 16/19 ESPIONAGE. PAGE 143 A2927
DIPLOM CRIME

B45
CONOVER H.F.,THE NAZI STATE: WAR CRIMES AND WAR CRIMINALS. GERMANY CULTURE NAT/G SECT FORCES DIPLOM INT/TRADE EDU/PROP...INT/LAW BIOG HIST/WRIT TIME/SEQ 20. PAGE 30 A0600
BIBLIOG WAR CRIME

B49
JACKSON R.H.,INTERNATIONAL CONFERENCE ON MILITARY TRIALS. FRANCE GERMANY UK USA+45 USSR VOL/ASSN DELIB/GP REPAR ADJUD CT/SYS CRIME WAR 20 WAR/TRIAL. PAGE 72 A1479
DIPLOM INT/ORG INT/LAW CIVMIL/REL

B57
INSTITUT DE DROIT INTL,TABLEAU GENERAL DES RESOLUTIONS (1873-1956). LAW NEUTRAL CRIME WAR MARRIAGE PEACE...JURID 19/20. PAGE 70 A1442
INT/LAW DIPLOM ORD/FREE ADJUD

B58
DUCLOUX L.,FROM BLACKMAIL TO TREASON. FRANCE PLAN DIPLOM EDU/PROP PRESS RUMOR NAT/LISM...CRIMLGY 20. PAGE 39 A0793
COERCE CRIME NAT/G PWR

B58
STONE J.,AGGRESSION AND WORLD ORDER: A CRITIQUE OF UNITED NATIONS THEORIES OF AGGRESSION. LAW CONSTN DELIB/GP PROB/SOLV BAL/PWR DIPLOM DEBATE ADJUD CRIME PWR...POLICY IDEA/COMP 20 UN SUEZ LEAGUE/NAT. PAGE 138 A2835
ORD/FREE INT/ORG WAR CONCPT

B59
KNIERIEM A.,THE NUREMBERG TRIALS. EUR+WWI GERMANY VOL/ASSN LEAD COERCE WAR INGP/REL TOTALISM SUPEGO ORD/FREE...CONCPT METH/COMP. PAGE 80 A1651
INT/LAW CRIME PARTIC JURID

B59
PANHUYS H.F.,THE ROLE OF NATIONALITY IN INTERNATIONAL LAW. ADJUD CRIME WAR STRANGE...JURID TREND. PAGE 114 A2330
INT/LAW NAT/LISM INGP/REL

B59
VORSPAN A.,JUSTICE AND JUDAISM. FAM DIPLOM ECO/TAC EDU/PROP CRIME RACE/REL MARRIAGE ANOMIE ATTIT ORD/FREE...POLICY 20 UN. PAGE 160 A3254
SECT CULTURE ACT/RES GP/REL

B61
LARSON A.,WHEN NATIONS DISAGREE. USA+45 WOR+45 INT/ORG ADJUD COERCE CRIME OWN SOVEREIGN...POLICY JURID 20. PAGE 85 A1734
INT/LAW DIPLOM WAR

B61
TETENS T.H.,THE NEW GERMANY AND THE OLD NAZIS. EUR+WWI GERMANY/W USA+45 NAT/G CRIME CHOOSE RACE/REL TOTALISM AGE/Y ATTIT 20 JEWS NAZI ADENAUER/K. PAGE 142 A2905
FASCISM DIPLOM FOR/AID POL/PAR

S62
GRAVEN J.,"LE MOUVEAU DROIT PENAL INTERNATIONAL." UNIV STRUCT LEGIS ACT/RES CRIME ATTIT PERCEPT PERSON...JURID CONCPT 20. PAGE 55 A1132
CT/SYS PUB/INST INT/ORG INT/LAW

B63
ELLERT R.B.,NATO 'FAIR TRIAL' SAFEGUARDS: PRECURSOR TO AN INTERNATIONAL BILL OF PROCEDURAL RIGHTS. WOR+45 FORCES CRIME CIVMIL/REL ATTIT ORD/FREE 20 NATO. PAGE 41 A0841
JURID INT/LAW INT/ORG CT/SYS

B64
FREUD A.,OF HUMAN SOVEREIGNTY. WOR+45 INDUS SECT ECO/TAC CRIME CHOOSE ATTIT MORAL MARXISM...POLICY BIBLIOG 20. PAGE 49 A0998
NAT/LISM DIPLOM WAR PEACE

B64
GESELLSCHAFT RECHTSVERGLEICH,BIBLIOGRAPHIE DES DEUTSCHEN RECHTS (BIBLIOGRAPHY OF GERMAN LAW, TRANS. BY COURTLAND PETERSON). GERMANY FINAN INDUS LABOR SECT FORCES CT/SYS PARL/PROC CRIME...INT/LAW SOC NAT/COMP 20. PAGE 52 A1066
BIBLIOG/A JURID CONSTN ADMIN

B64
GJUPANOVIC H.,LEGAL SOURCES AND BIBLIOGRAPHY OF YUGOSLAVIA. COM YUGOSLAVIA LAW LEGIS DIPLOM ADMIN PARL/PROC REGION CRIME CENTRAL 20. PAGE 53 A1078
BIBLIOG/A JURID CONSTN ADJUD

B64
LOCKHART W.B.,CASES AND MATERIALS ON CONSTITUTIONAL RIGHTS AND LIBERTIES. USA+45 FORCES LEGIS DIPLOM PRESS CONTROL CRIME WAR PWR...AUD/VIS T WORSHIP 20 NEGRO. PAGE 90 A1849
ORD/FREE CONSTN NAT/G

B65
LAFAVE W.R.,LAW AND SOVIET SOCIETY. EX/STRUC DIPLOM DOMIN EDU/PROP PRESS ADMIN CRIME OWN MARXISM 20 KHRUSH/N. PAGE 84 A1710
JURID CT/SYS ADJUD GOV/REL

B66
HOEVELER H.J.,INTERNATIONALE BEKAMPFUNG DES VERBRECHENS. AUSTRIA SWITZERLND WOR+45 INT/ORG CONTROL BIO/SOC...METH/COMP NAT/COMP 20 MAFIA SCOT/YARD FBI. PAGE 66 A1352
CRIMLGY CRIME DIPLOM INT/LAW

B66
SZLADITS C.,A BIBLIOGRAPHY ON FOREIGN AND COMPARATIVE LAW (SUPPLEMENT 1964). FINAN FAM LABOR LG/CO LEGIS JUDGE ADMIN CRIME...CRIMLGY 20. PAGE 141 A2878
BIBLIOG/A CT/SYS INT/LAW

B67
BODENHEIMER E.,TREATISE ON JUSTICE. INT/ORG NAT/G PUB/INST ACT/RES RISK CRIME INGP/REL DISCRIM DRIVE LAISSEZ 20. PAGE 16 A0325
ALL/VALS STRUCT JURID

CONCPT

B67
PIPER D.C.,THE INTERNATIONAL LAW OF THE GREAT LAKES. CANADA EXTR/IND MUNIC LICENSE ARMS/CONT CRIME...GEOG 19/20. PAGE 116 A2381 — CONCPT DIPLOM INT/LAW

B67
RUSSELL B.,WAR CRIMES IN VIETNAM. USA+45 VIETNAM FORCES DIPLOM WEAPON RACE/REL DISCRIM ISOLAT BIO/SOC 20 COLD/WAR RUSSELL/B. PAGE 126 A2574 — WAR CRIME ATTIT POLICY

S67
COHN K.,"CRIMES AGAINST HUMANITY." GERMANY INT/ORG SANCTION ATTIT ORD/FREE...MARXIST CRIMLGY 20 UN. PAGE 28 A0564 — WAR INT/LAW CRIME ADJUD

CRIMINOLOGY....SEE CRIMLGY

CRIMLGY....CRIMINOLOGY

B45
VANCE H.L.,GUIDE TO THE LAW AND LEGAL LITERATURE OF MEXICO. LAW CONSTN FINAN LABOR FORCES ADJUD ADMIN ...CRIMLGY PHIL/SCI CON/ANAL 20 MEXIC/AMER. PAGE 158 A3217 — BIBLIOG/A INT/LAW JURID CT/SYS

B55
JAPAN MOMBUSHO DAIGAKU GAKIYUT,BIBLIOGRAPHY OF THE STUDIES ON LAW AND POLITICS (PAMPHLET). CONSTN INDUS LABOR DIPLOM TAX ADMIN...CRIMLGY INT/LAW 20 CHINJAP. PAGE 73 A1496 — BIBLIOG LAW PHIL/SCI

B58
DUCLOUX L.,FROM BLACKMAIL TO TREASON. FRANCE PLAN DIPLOM EDU/PROP PRESS RUMOR NAT/LISM...CRIMLGY 20. PAGE 39 A0793 — COERCE CRIME NAT/G PWR

B65
UNESCO,INTERNATIONAL ORGANIZATIONS IN THE SOCIAL SCIENCES(REV. ED.). LAW ADMIN ATTIT...CRIMLGY GEOG INT/LAW PSY SOC STAT 20 UNESCO. PAGE 148 A3024 — INT/ORG R+D PROF/ORG ACT/RES

B66
HOEVELER H.J.,INTERNATIONALE BEKAMPFUNG DES VERBRECHENS. AUSTRIA SWITZERLND WOR+45 INT/ORG CONTROL BIO/SOC...METH/COMP NAT/COMP 20 MAFIA SCOT/YARD FBI. PAGE 66 A1352 — CRIMLGY CRIME DIPLOM INT/LAW

B66
SZLADITS C.,A BIBLIOGRAPHY ON FOREIGN AND COMPARATIVE LAW (SUPPLEMENT 1964). FINAN FAM LABOR LG/CO LEGIS JUDGE ADMIN CRIME...CRIMLGY 20. PAGE 141 A2878 — BIBLIOG/A CT/SYS INT/LAW

B67
BLOM-COOPER L.,THE LITERATURE OF THE LAW AND THE LANGUAGE OF THE LAW (2 VOLS.). CANADA ISRAEL UK WOR+45 WOR-45 JUDGE CT/SYS ATTIT...CRIMLGY JURID ANTHOL CMN/WLTH. PAGE 15 A0312 — BIBLIOG LAW INT/LAW ADJUD

S67
COHN K.,"CRIMES AGAINST HUMANITY." GERMANY INT/ORG SANCTION ATTIT ORD/FREE...MARXIST CRIMLGY 20 UN. PAGE 28 A0564 — WAR INT/LAW CRIME ADJUD

CRIMNL/LAW....CRIMINAL LAW

CROAN M. A0663

CROMWELL/O....OLIVER CROMWELL

CROSS-PRESSURES .... SEE ROLE

CROWD....MOB BEHAVIOR, MASS BEHAVIOR

B28
PLAYNE C.E.,THE PRE-WAR MIND IN BRITAIN. GERMANY MOD/EUR UK STRATA SECT DIPLOM EDU/PROP CROWD SUFF ...POLICY ANARCH PSY SOC IDEA/COMP 20 WWI. PAGE 116 A2388 — PRESS WAR DOMIN ATTIT

B57
FRASER L.,PROPAGANDA. GERMANY USSR WOR+45 WOR-45 NAT/G POL/PAR CONTROL FEEDBACK LOBBY CROWD WAR CONSEN NAT/LISM 20. PAGE 48 A0988 — EDU/PROP FASCISM MARXISM DIPLOM

B61
ROSENAU J.N.,PUBLIC OPINION AND FOREIGN POLICY; AN OPERATIONAL FORMULA. USA+45 COM/IND OP/RES EDU/PROP LOBBY CROWD...CON/ANAL BIBLIOG 20. PAGE 124 A2532 — ATTIT PRESS DIPLOM

B64
WEINTRAUB S.,THE WAR IN THE WARDS. KOREA/N WOR+45 DIPLOM COERCE ORD/FREE SKILL 20 TREATY. PAGE 162 A3308 — EDU/PROP PEACE CROWD PUB/INST

B66
SOBEL L.A.,SOUTH VIETNAM: US-COMMUNIST CONFRONTATION IN SOUTHEAST ASIA 1961-65. VIETNAM FOR/AID CROWD DETER REV PEACE...GEOG 20 INTERVENT DIEM COLD/WAR. PAGE 134 A2754 — WAR TIME/SEQ FORCES NAT/G

CROWE S.E. A0664

CROWLEY D.W. A0665

CROZIER B. A0666

CRUMP/ED....EDWARD H. CRUMP

CRUSADES....CRUSADES, CRUSADERS OF HOLY WARS; ALSO KNIGHTS

CT/APPEALS....COURT OF APPEALS AND APPELLATE COURT SYSTEM

CT/SYS....COURT SYSTEMS

N
INTERNATIONAL COMN JURISTS,AFRICAN CONFERENCE ON THE RULE OF LAW. AFR INT/ORG LEGIS DIPLOM CONFER COLONIAL ORD/FREE...CONCPT METH/COMP 20. PAGE 71 A1452 — CT/SYS JURID DELIB/GP

N
AMERICAN JOURNAL OF INTERNATIONAL LAW. WOR+45 WOR-45 CONSTN INT/ORG NAT/G CT/SYS ARMS/CONT WAR ...DECISION JURID NAT/COMP 20. PAGE 1 A0002 — BIBLIOG/A INT/LAW DIPLOM ADJUD

N
JOURNAL OF POLITICS. USA+45 USA-45 CONSTN POL/PAR EX/STRUC LEGIS PROB/SOLV DIPLOM CT/SYS CHOOSE RACE/REL 20. PAGE 1 A0017 — BIBLIOG/A NAT/G LAW LOC/G

N
MIDWEST JOURNAL OF POLITICAL SCIENCE. USA+45 CONSTN ECO/DEV LEGIS PROB/SOLV CT/SYS LEAD GOV/REL ATTIT POLICY. PAGE 1 A0020 — BIBLIOG/A NAT/G DIPLOM POL/PAR

N
ARBITRATION JOURNAL. WOR+45 LAW INDUS JUDGE DIPLOM CT/SYS INGP/REL 20. PAGE 2 A0027 — BIBLIOG MGT LABOR ADJUD

N
EUROPA PUBLICATIONS LIMITED,THE EUROPA YEAR BOOK. CONSTN FINAN INDUS POL/PAR DIPLOM TV CT/SYS...STAT BIOG CHARTS WORSHIP 20. PAGE 43 A0874 — BIBLIOG NAT/G PRESS INT/ORG

N
HARVARD LAW SCHOOL LIBRARY,ANNUAL LEGAL BIBLIOGRAPHY. USA+45 CONSTN LEGIS ADJUD CT/SYS ...POLICY 20. PAGE 62 A1278 — BIBLIOG JURID LAW INT/LAW

N
HARVARD UNIVERSITY LAW LIBRARY,CATALOG OF INTERNATIONAL LAW AND RELATIONS. WOR+45 WOR-45 INT/ORG NAT/G JUDGE DIPLOM INT/TRADE ADJUD CT/SYS 19/20. PAGE 62 A1280 — BIBLIOG INT/LAW JURID

N
TURNER R.K.,BIBLIOGRAPHY ON WORLD ORGANIZATION. INT/TRADE CT/SYS ARMS/CONT WEALTH...INT/LAW 20. PAGE 146 A2984 — BIBLIOG/A INT/ORG PEACE WAR

N
US SUPERINTENDENT OF DOCUMENTS,GOVERNMENT PERIODICALS AND SUBSCRIPTION SERVICES (PRICE LIST 36). LAW WORKER CT/SYS HEALTH. PAGE 157 A3202 — BIBLIOG/A USA+45 NAT/G DIPLOM

N
US SUPERINTENDENT OF DOCUMENTS,MONTHLY CATALOG OF UNITED STATES GOVERNMENT PUBLICATIONS. USA+45 USA-45 AGRI LABOR FORCES INT/TRADE TARIFFS TAX EDU/PROP CT/SYS ARMS/CONT RACE/REL 19/20 CONGRESS PRESIDENT. PAGE 157 A3203 — BIBLIOG NAT/G VOL/ASSN POLICY

N
US SUPERINTENDENT OF DOCUMENTS,TARIFF AND TAXATION (PRICE LIST 37). USA+45 LAW INT/TRADE ADJUD ADMIN CT/SYS INCOME OWN...DECISION GATT. PAGE 157 A3204 — BIBLIOG/A TAX TARIFFS NAT/G

B00
DARBY W.E.,INTERNATIONAL TRIBUNALS. WOR-45 NAT/G ECO/TAC DOMIN LEGIT CT/SYS COERCE ORD/FREE PWR SOVEREIGN JURID. PAGE 33 A0681 — INT/ORG ADJUD PEACE INT/LAW

B01
HART A.B.,AMERICAN HISTORY TOLD BY CONTEMPORARIES. UK CULTURE FINAN SECT FORCES DIPLOM TAX RUMOR CT/SYS REV GOV/REL GP/REL...ANTHOL 17/18 PRE/US/AM FEDERALIST. PAGE 62 A1273 — USA-45 COLONIAL SOVEREIGN

B09
HOLLAND T.E.,LETTERS UPON WAR AND NEUTRALITY. WOR-45 NAT/G FORCES JUDGE ECO/TAC LEGIT CT/SYS NEUTRAL ROUTINE COERCE...JURID TIME/SEQ 20. PAGE 67 A1368 — LAW INT/LAW INT/ORG WAR

L16
WRIGHT Q.,"THE ENFORCEMENT OF INTERNATIONAL LAW THROUGH MUNICIPAL LAW IN THE US." USA-45 LOC/G NAT/G PUB/INST FORCES LEGIT CT/SYS PERCEPT ALL/VALS ...JURID 20. PAGE 167 A3401 — INT/ORG LAW INT/LAW WAR

N19
BENTHAM J.,A PLAN FOR AN UNIVERSAL AND PERPETUAL PEACE (1838) (PAMPHLET). NAT/G FORCES BAL/PWR INT/TRADE ADMIN AGREE CT/SYS ARMS/CONT SOVEREIGN WEALTH GEN/LAWS. PAGE 13 A0269
INT/ORG INT/LAW PEACE COLONIAL

B21
OPPENHEIM L.,THE FUTURE OF INTERNATIONAL LAW. EUR+WWI MOD/EUR LAW LEGIS JUDGE LEGIT ORD/FREE ...JURID TIME/SEQ GEN/LAWS 20. PAGE 112 A2293
INT/ORG CT/SYS INT/LAW

L25
HUDSON M.,"THE PERMANENT COURT OF INTERNATIONAL JUSTICE AND THE QUESTION OF AMERICAN PARTICIPATION." WOR-45 LEGIT CT/SYS ORD/FREE ...JURID CONCPT TIME/SEQ GEN/LAWS VAL/FREE 20 ICJ. PAGE 68 A1406
INT/ORG ADJUD DIPLOM INT/LAW

B26
INTERNATIONAL BIBLIOGRAPHY OF POLITICAL SCIENCE. WOR+45 NAT/G POL/PAR EX/STRUC LEGIS CT/SYS LEAD CHOOSE GOV/REL ATTIT...PHIL/SCI 20. PAGE 3 A0049
BIBLIOG DIPLOM CONCPT ADMIN

B28
MAIR L.P.,THE PROTECTION OF MINORITIES. EUR+WWI WOR-45 CONSTN INT/ORG NAT/G LEGIT CT/SYS GP/REL RACE/REL DISCRIM ORD/FREE RESPECT...JURID CONCPT TIME/SEQ 20. PAGE 93 A1909
LAW SOVEREIGN

B33
AMERICAN FOREIGN LAW ASSN,BIOGRAPHICAL NOTES ON THE LAWS AND LEGAL LITERATURE OF URUGUAY AND CURACAO. URUGUAY CONSTN FINAN SECT FORCES JUDGE DIPLOM INT/TRADE ADJUD CT/SYS CRIME 20. PAGE 7 A0147
BIBLIOG/A LAW JURID ADMIN

B33
MATTHEWS M.A.,THE AMERICAN INSTITUTE OF INTERNATIONAL LAW AND THE CODIFICATION OF INTERNATIONAL LAW (PAMPHLET). USA-45 CONSTN ADJUD CT/SYS...JURID 20. PAGE 96 A1973
BIBLIOG/A INT/LAW L/A+17C DIPLOM

B35
HUDSON M.,BY PACIFIC MEANS. WOR-45 EDU/PROP ORD/FREE...CONCPT TIME/SEQ GEN/LAWS LEAGUE/NAT TOT/POP 20 TREATY. PAGE 68 A1407
INT/ORG CT/SYS PEACE

B35
KENNEDY W.P.,THE LAW AND CUSTOM OF THE SOUTH AFRICAN CONSTITUTION. AFR SOUTH/AFR KIN LOC/G PROVS DIPLOM ADJUD ADMIN EXEC 20. PAGE 78 A1594
CT/SYS CONSTN JURID PARL/PROC

B36
HUDSON M.O.,INTERNATIONAL LEGISLATION: 1929-1931. WOR-45 SEA AIR AGRI FINAN LABOR DIPLOM ECO/TAC REPAR CT/SYS ARMS/CONT WAR WEAPON...JURID 20 TREATY LEAGUE/NAT. PAGE 69 A1409
INT/LAW PARL/PROC ADJUD LAW

B37
KETCHAM E.H.,PRELIMINARY SELECT BIBLIOGRAPHY OF INTERNATIONAL LAW (PAMPHLET). WOR-45 LAW INT/ORG NAT/G PROB/SOLV CT/SYS NEUTRAL WAR 19/20. PAGE 78 A1602
BIBLIOG DIPLOM ADJUD INT/LAW

B37
SCHUSTER E.,GUIDE TO LAW AND LEGAL LITERATURE OF CENTRAL AMERICAN REPUBLICS. L/A+17C INT/ORG ADJUD SANCTION CRIME...JURID 19/20. PAGE 129 A2654
BIBLIOG/A REGION CT/SYS LAW

B37
UNION OF SOUTH AFRICA,REPORT CONCERNING ADMINISTRATION OF SOUTH WEST AFRICA (6 VOLS.). SOUTH/AFR INDUS PUB/INST FORCES LEGIS BUDGET DIPLOM EDU/PROP ADJUD CT/SYS...GEOG CHARTS 20 AFRICA/SW LEAGUE/NAT. PAGE 148 A3028
NAT/G ADMIN COLONIAL CONSTN

B38
HAGUE PERMANENT CT INTL JUSTIC,WORLD COURT REPORTS: COLLECTION OF THE JUDGEMENTS ORDERS AND OPINIONS VOLUME 3 1932-35. WOR-45 LAW DELIB/GP CONFER WAR PEACE ATTIT...DECISION ANTHOL 20 WORLD/CT CASEBOOK. PAGE 59 A1214
INT/ORG CT/SYS DIPLOM ADJUD

B38
MCNAIR A.D.,THE LAW OF TREATIES: BRITISH PRACTICE AND OPINIONS. UK CREATE DIPLOM LEGIT WRITING ADJUD WAR...INT/LAW JURID TREATY. PAGE 98 A2018
AGREE LAW CT/SYS NAT/G

B38
SAINT-PIERRE C.I.,SCHEME FOR LASTING PEACE (TRANS. BY H. BELLOT). INDUS NAT/G CHIEF FORCES INT/TRADE CT/SYS WAR PWR SOVEREIGN WEALTH...POLICY 18. PAGE 126 A2587
INT/ORG PEACE AGREE INT/LAW

B43
HAGUE PERMANENT CT INTL JUSTIC,WORLD COURT REPORTS: COLLECTION OF THE JUDGEMENTS ORDERS AND OPINIONS VOLUME 4 1936-42. WOR-45 CONFER PEACE ATTIT ...DECISION JURID ANTHOL 20 WORLD/CT CASEBOOK. PAGE 59 A1215
INT/ORG CT/SYS DIPLOM ADJUD

B45
CONOVER H.F.,THE GOVERNMENTS OF THE MAJOR FOREIGN POWERS: A BIBLIOGRAPHY. FRANCE GERMANY ITALY UK USSR CONSTN LOC/G POL/PAR EX/STRUC FORCES ADMIN CT/SYS CIVMIL/REL TOTALISM...POLICY 19/20. PAGE 29 A0598
BIBLIOG NAT/G DIPLOM

B45
TINGSTERN H.,PEACE AND SECURITY AFTER WW II. WOR-45 DELIB/GP TOP/EX LEGIT CT/SYS COERCE PEACE ATTIT PERCEPT...CONCPT LEAGUE/NAT 20. PAGE 144 A2943
INT/ORG ORD/FREE WAR INT/LAW

B45
VANCE H.L.,GUIDE TO THE LAW AND LEGAL LITERATURE OF MEXICO. LAW CONSTN FINAN LABOR FORCES ADJUD ADMIN ...CRIMLGY PHIL/SCI CON/ANAL 20 MEXIC/AMER. PAGE 158 A3217
BIBLIOG/A INT/LAW JURID CT/SYS

B46
SCANLON H.L.,INTERNATIONAL LAW: A SELECTIVE LIST OF WORKS IN ENGLISH ON PUBLIC INTERNATIONAL LAW (A PAMPHLET). CHRIST-17C EUR+WWI MOD/EUR WOR-45 CT/SYS ...JURID 20. PAGE 127 A2613
BIBLIOG/A INT/LAW ADJUD DIPLOM

B47
HYDE C.C.,INTERNATIONAL LAW, CHIEFLY AS INTERPRETED AND APPLIED BY THE UNITED STATES (3 VOLS., 2ND REV. ED.). USA-45 WOR+45 WOR-45 INT/ORG CT/SYS WAR NAT/LISM PEACE ORD/FREE...JURID 19/20 TREATY. PAGE 69 A1426
INT/LAW DIPLOM NAT/G POLICY

B47
INTERNATIONAL COURT OF JUSTICE,CHARTER OF THE UNITED NATIONS, STATUTE AND RULES OF COURT AND OTHER CONSTITUTIONAL DOCUMENTS. SWITZERLND LAW ADJUD INGP/REL...JURID 20 ICJ UN. PAGE 71 A1453
INT/LAW INT/ORG CT/SYS DIPLOM

B48
FENWICK C.G.,INTERNATIONAL LAW. WOR+45 WOR-45 CONSTN NAT/G LEGIT CT/SYS REGION...CONCPT LEAGUE/NAT UN 20. PAGE 45 A0916
INT/ORG JURID INT/LAW

B48
NEUBURGER O.,GUIDE TO OFFICIAL PUBLICATIONS OF THE OTHER AMERICAN REPUBLICS: VENEZUELA (VOL. XIX). VENEZUELA FINAN LEGIS PLAN BUDGET DIPLOM CT/SYS PARL/PROC 19/20. PAGE 108 A2219
BIBLIOG/A NAT/G CONSTN LAW

B49
JACKSON R.H.,INTERNATIONAL CONFERENCE ON MILITARY TRIALS. FRANCE GERMANY UK USA+45 USSR VOL/ASSN DELIB/GP REPAR ADJUD CT/SYS CRIME WAR 20 WAR/TRIAL. PAGE 72 A1479
DIPLOM INT/ORG INT/LAW CIVMIL/REL

B50
SOHN L.B.,CASES AND OTHER MATERIALS ON WORLD LAW. FUT WOR+45 LAW INT/ORG...INT/LAW JURID METH/CNCPT 20 UN. PAGE 135 A2760
CT/SYS CONSTN

B51
CHRISTENSEN A.N.,THE EVOLUTION OF LATIN AMERICAN GOVERNMENT: A BOOK OF READINGS. ECO/UNDEV INDUS LOC/G POL/PAR EX/STRUC LEGIS FOR/AID CT/SYS ...SOC/WK 20 SOUTH/AMER. PAGE 26 A0535
NAT/G CONSTN DIPLOM L/A+17C

L51
WHITAKER A.P.,"DEVELOPMENT OF AMERICAN REGIONALISM: THE ORGANIZATION OF AMERICAN STATES." L/A+17C USA+45 VOL/ASSN DELIB/GP FORCES TOP/EX ACT/RES ECO/TAC CT/SYS REGION PEACE ALL/VALS OAS 20. PAGE 163 A3330
INT/ORG TIME/SEQ DETER

B53
ORFIELD L.B.,THE GROWTH OF SCANDINAVIAN LAW. DENMARK ICELAND NORWAY SWEDEN LAW DIPLOM...BIBLIOG 9/20. PAGE 112 A2296
JURID CT/SYS NAT/G

B54
STONE J.,LEGAL CONTROLS OF INTERNATIONAL CONFLICT: A TREATISE ON THE DYNAMICS OF DISPUTES AND WAR LAW. WOR+45 WOR-45 NAT/G DIPLOM CT/SYS SOVEREIGN...JURID CONCPT METH/CNCPT GEN/LAWS TOT/POP VAL/FREE COLD/WAR LEAGUE/NAT 20. PAGE 138 A2834
INT/ORG LAW WAR INT/LAW

B56
SIPKOV I.,LEGAL SOURCES AND BIBLIOGRAPHY OF BULGARIA. BULGARIA COM LEGIS WRITING ADJUD CT/SYS ...INT/LAW TREATY 20. PAGE 134 A2736
BIBLIOG LAW TOTALISM MARXISM

B57
DE VISSCHER C.,THEORY AND REALITY IN PUBLIC INTERNATIONAL LAW. WOR+45 WOR-45 SOCIETY NAT/G CT/SYS ATTIT MORAL ORD/FREE PWR...JURID CONCPT METH/CNCPT TIME/SEQ GEN/LAWS LEAGUE/NAT TOT/POP VAL/FREE COLD/WAR. PAGE 35 A0716
INT/ORG LAW INT/LAW

B57
JENKS C.W.,THE INTERNATIONAL PROTECTION OF TRADE UNION FREEDOM. FUT WOR+45 WOR-45 VOL/ASSN DELIB/GP CT/SYS REGION ROUTINE...JURID METH/CNCPT RECORD TIME/SEQ CHARTS ILO WORK OAS 20. PAGE 73 A1504
LABOR INT/ORG

B57
ROSENNE S.,THE INTERNATIONAL COURT OF JUSTICE. WOR+45 LAW DOMIN LEGIT PEACE PWR SOVEREIGN...JURID CONCPT RECORD TIME/SEQ CON/ANAL CHARTS UN TOT/POP VAL/FREE LEAGUE/NAT 20 ICJ. PAGE 124 A2537
INT/ORG CT/SYS INT/LAW

B57
UNESCO,A REGISTER OF LEGAL DOCUMENTATION IN THE WORLD (2ND ED.). CT/SYS...JURID IDEA/COMP METH/COMP NAT/COMP 20. PAGE 148 A3019
BIBLIOG LAW INT/LAW CONSTN

B58
ALEXANDROWICZ,A BIBLIOGRAPHY OF INDIAN LAW. INDIA S/ASIA CONSTN CT/SYS...INT/LAW 19/20. PAGE 6 A0113
BIBLIOG LAW ADJUD JURID

B58
DEUTSCHE GESCHAFT VOLKERRECHT,DIE VOLKERRECHTLICHEN DISSERTATIONEN AN DEN WESTDEUTSCHEN UNIVERSITATEN,
BIBLIOG INT/LAW

1945-1957. GERMANY/W NAT/G DIPLOM ADJUD CT/SYS ...POLICY 20. PAGE 37 A0748 — ACADEM JURID

S58
MCDOUGAL M.S.,"PERSPECTIVES FOR A LAW OF OUTER SPACE." FUT WOR+45 AIR CONSULT DELIB/GP TEC/DEV CT/SYS ORD/FREE...POLICY JURID 20 UN. PAGE 98 A2004 — INT/ORG SPACE INT/LAW

B59
SCHNEIDER J.,TREATY-MAKING POWER OF INTERNATIONAL ORGANIZATIONS. FUT WOR+45 WOR-45 LAW NAT/G JUDGE DIPLOM LEGIT CT/SYS ORD/FREE PWR...INT/LAW JURID GEN/LAWS TOT/POP UNESCO 20 TREATY. PAGE 129 A2639 — INT/ORG ROUTINE

B59
SIMPSON J.L.,INTERNATIONAL ARBITRATION: LAW AND PRACTICE. WOR+45 WOR-45 INT/ORG DELIB/GP ADJUD PEACE MORAL ORD/FREE...METH 18/20. PAGE 133 A2720 — INT/LAW DIPLOM CT/SYS CONSULT

S59
SOHN L.B.,"THE DEFINITION OF AGGRESSION." FUT LAW FORCES LEGIT ADJUD ROUTINE COERCE ORD/FREE PWR ...MAJORIT JURID QUANT COLD/WAR 20. PAGE 135 A2762 — INT/ORG CT/SYS DETER SOVEREIGN

B60
BYRD E.M. JR.,TREATIES AND EXECUTIVE AGREEMENTS IN THE UNITED STATES: THEIR SEPARATE ROLES AND LIMITATIONS. USA+45 USA-45 EX/STRUC TARIFFS CT/SYS GOV/REL FEDERAL...IDEA/COMP BIBLIOG SUPREME/CT SENATE CONGRESS. PAGE 23 A0461 — CHIEF INT/LAW DIPLOM

B60
HARVARD LAW SCHOOL LIBRARY,CURRENT LEGAL BIBLIOGRAPHY. USA+45 CONSTN LEGIS ADJUD CT/SYS POLICY. PAGE 62 A1279 — BIBLIOG JURID LAW INT/LAW

C60
HAZARD J.N.,"THE SOVIET SYSTEM OF GOVERNMENT." USSR SOCIETY INDUS NAT/G POL/PAR DIPLOM CT/SYS...JURID CHARTS BIBLIOG/A 20. PAGE 63 A1298 — COM NAT/COMP STRUCT ADMIN

B61
SCOTT A.M.,POLITICS, USA; CASES ON THE AMERICAN DEMOCRATIC PROCESS. USA+45 CHIEF FORCES DIPLOM LOBBY CHOOSE RACE/REL FEDERAL ATTIT...JURID ANTHOL T 20 PRESIDENT CONGRESS CIVIL/LIB. PAGE 130 A2669 — CT/SYS CONSTN NAT/G PLAN

B61
WECHSLER H.,PRINCIPLES, POLITICS AND FUNDAMENTAL LAW: SELECTED ESSAYS. USA+45 USA-45 LAW SOCIETY NAT/G PROVS DELIB/GP EX/STRUC ACT/RES LEGIT PERSON KNOWL PWR...JURID 20 NUREMBERG. PAGE 162 A3296 — CT/SYS CONSTN INT/LAW

B62
CARLSTON K.S.,LAW AND ORGANIZATION IN WORLD SOCIETY. WOR+45 FINAN ECO/TAC DOMIN LEGIT CT/SYS ROUTINE COERCE ORD/FREE PWR WEALTH...PLURIST DECISION JURID MGT METH/CNCPT GEN/LAWS 20. PAGE 24 A0487 — INT/ORG LAW

B62
GYORGY A.,PROBLEMS IN INTERNATIONAL RELATIONS. COM CT/SYS NUC/PWR ALL/IDEOS 20 UN EEC ECSC. PAGE 58 A1199 — DIPLOM NEUTRAL BAL/PWR REV

B62
LILLICH R.B.,INTERNATIONAL CLAIMS: THEIR ADJUDICATION BY NATIONAL COMMISSIONS. WOR+45 WOR-45 INT/ORG LEGIT CT/SYS TOT/POP 20. PAGE 89 A1816 — ADJUD JURID INT/LAW

B62
SCHWARZENBERGER G.,THE FRONTIERS OF INTERNATIONAL LAW. WOR+45 WOR-45 NAT/G LEGIT CT/SYS ROUTINE MORAL ORD/FREE PWR...JURID SOC GEN/METH 20 COLD/WAR. PAGE 130 A2661 — INT/ORG LAW INT/LAW

B62
US SENATE COMM ON JUDICIARY,CONSTITUTIONAL RIGHTS OF MILITARY PERSONNEL. USA+45 USA-45 FORCES DIPLOM WAR CONGRESS. PAGE 157 A3193 — CONSTN ORD/FREE JURID CT/SYS

S62
GRAVEN J.,"LE MOUVEAU DROIT PENAL INTERNATIONAL." UNIV STRUCT LEGIS ACT/RES CRIME ATTIT PERCEPT PERSON...JURID CONCPT 20. PAGE 55 A1132 — CT/SYS PUB/INST INT/ORG INT/LAW

S62
JOHNSON O.H.,"THE ENGLISH TRADITION IN INTERNATIONAL LAW." CHRIST-17C MOD/EUR EDU/PROP LEGIT CT/SYS ORD/FREE...JURID CONCPT TIME/SEQ. PAGE 75 A1526 — LAW INT/LAW UK

B63
BOWETT D.W.,THE LAW OF INTERNATIONAL INSTITUTIONS. WOR+45 WOR-45 CONSTN DELIB/GP EX/STRUC JUDGE EDU/PROP LEGIT CT/SYS EXEC ROUTINE RIGID/FLEX ORD/FREE PWR...JURID CONCPT ORG/CHARTS GEN/METH LEAGUE/NAT OAS OEEC 20 UN. PAGE 17 A0354 — INT/ORG ADJUD DIPLOM

B63
ELLERT R.B.,NATO 'FAIR TRIAL' SAFEGUARDS: PRECURSOR TO AN INTERNATIONAL BILL OF PROCEDURAL RIGHTS. WOR+45 FORCES CRIME CIVMIL/REL ATTIT ORD/FREE 20 NATO. PAGE 41 A0841 — JURID INT/LAW INT/ORG CT/SYS

B63
LANOUE G.R.,A BIBLIOGRAPHY OF DOCTORAL DISSERTATIONS ON POLITICS AND RELIGION. USA+45 CONSTN PROVS DIPLOM CT/SYS MORAL...POLICY JURID CONCPT 20. PAGE 84 A1728 — BIBLIOG NAT/G LOC/G SECT

B63
PATRA A.C.,THE ADMINISTRATION OF JUSTICE UNDER THE EAST INDIA COMPANY IN BENGAL, BIHAR AND ORISSA. INDIA UK LG/CO CAP/ISM INT/TRADE ADJUD COLONIAL CONTROL CT/SYS...POLICY 20. PAGE 114 A2341 — ADMIN JURID CONCPT

S63
BECHHOEFER B.G.,"UNITED NATIONS PROCEDURES IN CASE OF VIOLATIONS OF DISARMAMENT AGREEMENTS." COM USA+45 USSR LAW CONSTN NAT/G EX/STRUC FORCES LEGIS BAL/PWR EDU/PROP CT/SYS ARMS/CONT ORD/FREE PWR ...POLICY STERTYP UN VAL/FREE 20. PAGE 12 A0245 — INT/ORG DELIB/GP

S63
TALLON D.,"L'ETUDE DU DROIT COMPARE COMME MOYEN DE RECHERCHER LES MATIERES SUSCEPTIBLES D'UNIFICATION INTERNATIONALE." WOR+45 LAW SOCIETY VOL/ASSN CONSULT LEGIT CT/SYS RIGID/FLEX KNOWL 20. PAGE 141 A2884 — INT/ORG JURID INT/LAW

B64
DIAS R.W.M.,A BIBLIOGRAPHY OF JURISPRUDENCE (2ND ED.). VOL/ASSN LEGIS ADJUD CT/SYS OWN...INT/LAW 18/20. PAGE 37 A0754 — BIBLIOG/A JURID LAW CONCPT

B64
FALK R.A.,THE ROLE OF DOMESTIC COURTS IN THE INTERNATIONAL LEGAL ORDER. FUT WOR+45 INT/ORG NAT/G JUDGE EDU/PROP LEGIT CT/SYS...POLICY RELATIV JURID CONCPT GEN/LAWS 20. PAGE 43 A0889 — LAW INT/LAW

B64
GESELLSCHAFT RECHTSVERGLEICH,BIBLIOGRAPHIE DES DEUTSCHEN RECHTS (BIBLIOGRAPHY OF GERMAN LAW, TRANS. BY COURTLAND PETERSON). GERMANY FINAN INDUS LABOR SECT FORCES CT/SYS PARL/PROC CRIME...INT/LAW SOC NAT/COMP 20. PAGE 52 A1066 — BIBLIOG/A JURID CONSTN ADMIN

B64
SCHECHTER A.H.,INTERPRETATION OF AMBIGUOUS DOCUMENTS BY INTERNATIONAL ADMINISTRATIVE TRIBUNALS. WOR+45 EX/STRUC INT/TRADE CT/SYS SOVEREIGN 20 UN ILO EURCT/JUST. PAGE 128 A2620 — INT/LAW DIPLOM INT/ORG ADJUD

B64
STOESSINGER J.G.,FINANCING THE UNITED NATIONS SYSTEM. FUT WOR+45 CONSTN NAT/G VOL/ASSN DELIB/GP EX/STRUC ECO/TAC LEGIT CT/SYS PWR WEALTH...STAT TIME/SEQ TREND CHARTS VAL/FREE. PAGE 138 A2830 — FINAN INT/ORG

B64
SZLADITS C.,BIBLIOGRAPHY ON FOREIGN AND COMPARATIVE LAW: BOOKS AND ARTICLES IN ENGLISH (SUPPLEMENT 1962). FINAN INDUS JUDGE LICENSE ADMIN CT/SYS PARL/PROC OWN...INT/LAW CLASSIF METH/COMP NAT/COMP 20. PAGE 141 A2877 — BIBLIOG/A JURID ADJUD LAW

B64
VECCHIO G.D.,L'ETAT ET LE DROIT. ITALY CONSTN EX/STRUC LEGIS DIPLOM CT/SYS...JURID 20 UN. PAGE 158 A3225 — NAT/G SOVEREIGN CONCPT INT/LAW

B65
FALK R.A.,THE AFTERMATH OF SABBATINO: BACKGROUND PAPERS AND PROCEEDINGS OF SEVENTH HAMMARSKJOLD FORUM. USA+45 LAW ACT/RES ADJUD ROLE...BIBLIOG 20 EXPROPRIAT SABBATINO HARLAN/JM. PAGE 44 A0891 — SOVEREIGN CT/SYS INT/LAW OWN

B65
LAFAVE W.R.,LAW AND SOVIET SOCIETY. EX/STRUC DIPLOM DOMIN EDU/PROP PRESS ADMIN CRIME OWN MARXISM 20 KHRUSH/N. PAGE 84 A1710 — JURID CT/SYS ADJUD GOV/REL

B65
MOODY M.,CATALOG OF INTERNATIONAL LAW AND RELATIONS (20 VOLS.). WOR+45 INT/ORG NAT/G ADJUD ADMIN CT/SYS POLICY. PAGE 103 A2117 — BIBLIOG INT/LAW DIPLOM

B65
MOSTECKY V.,SOVIET LEGAL BIBLIOGRAPHY. USSR LEGIS PRESS WRITING CONFER ADJUD CT/SYS REV MARXISM ...INT/LAW JURID DICTIONARY 20. PAGE 105 A2155 — BIBLIOG/A LAW COM CONSTN

B65
NEWBURY C.W.,BRITISH POLICY TOWARDS WEST AFRICA: SELECT DOCUMENTS 1786-1874. AFR UK INT/TRADE DOMIN ADMIN COLONIAL CT/SYS COERCE ORD/FREE...BIBLIOG/A 18/19. PAGE 108 A2224 — DIPLOM POLICY NAT/G WRITING

B65
WHITE G.M.,THE USE OF EXPERTS BY INTERNATIONAL TRIBUNALS. WOR+45 WOR-45 INT/ORG NAT/G PAY ADJUD COST...OBS BIBLIOG 20. PAGE 164 A3334 — INT/LAW ROUTINE CONSULT CT/SYS

L65
RUBIN A.P.,"UNITED STATES CONTEMPORARY PRACTICE RELATING TO INTERNATIONAL LAW." USA+45 WOR+45 CONSTN INT/ORG NAT/G DELIB/GP EX/STRUC DIPLOM DOMIN CT/SYS ROUTINE ORD/FREE...CONCPT COLD/WAR 20. PAGE 125 A2558 — LAW LEGIT INT/LAW

S65
GROSS L.,"PROBLEMS OF INTERNATIONAL ADJUDICATION AND COMPLIANCE WITH INTERNATIONAL LAW: SOME SIMPLE SOLUTIONS." WOR+45 SOCIETY NAT/G DOMIN LEGIT ADJUD CT/SYS RIGID/FLEX HEALTH PWR...JURID NEW/IDEA — LAW METH/CNCPT INT/LAW

COLD/WAR 20. PAGE 57 A1177

C65
SCHEINGOLD S.A.,"THE RULE OF LAW IN EUROPEAN INTEGRATION: THE PATH OF THE SCHUMAN PLAN." EUR+WWI JUDGE ADJUD FEDERAL ATTIT PWR...RECORD INT BIBLIOG EEC ECSC. PAGE 128 A2621
INT/LAW CT/SYS REGION CENTRAL

B66
AMERICAN JOURNAL COMP LAW,THE AMERICAN JOURNAL OF COMPARATIVE LAW READER. EUR+WWI USA+45 USA-45 LAW CONSTN LOC/G MUNIC NAT/G DIPLOM...ANTHOL 20 SUPREME/CT EURCT/JUST. PAGE 7 A0151
IDEA/COMP JURID INT/LAW CT/SYS

B66
COUNCIL OF EUROPE,EUROPEAN CONVENTION ON HUMAN RIGHTS - COLLECTED TEXTS (5TH ED.). EUR+WWI DIPLOM ADJUD CT/SYS...INT/LAW 20 ECHR. PAGE 31 A0638
ORD/FREE DELIB/GP INT/ORG JURID

B66
DOUMA J.,BIBLIOGRAPHY ON THE INTERNATIONAL COURT INCLUDING THE PERMANENT COURT, 1918-1964. WOR+45 WOR-45 DELIB/GP WAR PRIVIL...JURID NAT/COMP 20 UN LEAGUE/NAT. PAGE 38 A0780
BIBLIOG/A INT/ORG CT/SYS DIPLOM

B66
NANTWI E.K.,THE ENFORCEMENT OF INTERNATIONAL JUDICIAL DECISIONS AND ARBITAL AWARDS IN PUBLIC INTERNATIONAL LAW. WOR+45 WOR-45 JUDGE PROB/SOLV DIPLOM CT/SYS SUPEGO MORAL PWR RESPECT...METH/CNCPT 18/20 CASEBOOK. PAGE 107 A2196
INT/LAW ADJUD SOVEREIGN INT/ORG

B66
NEUMANN R.G.,THE GOVERNMENT OF THE GERMAN FEDERAL REPUBLIC. EUR+WWI GERMANY/W LOC/G EX/STRUC LEGIS CT/SYS INGP/REL PWR...BIBLIOG 20 ADENAUER/K. PAGE 108 A2222
NAT/G POL/PAR DIPLOM CONSTN

B66
SZLADITS C.,A BIBLIOGRAPHY ON FOREIGN AND COMPARATIVE LAW (SUPPLEMENT 1964). FINAN FAM LABOR LG/CO LEGIS JUDGE ADMIN CRIME...CRIMLGY 20. PAGE 141 A2878
BIBLIOG/A CT/SYS INT/LAW

B67
BLOM-COOPER L.,THE LITERATURE OF THE LAW AND THE LANGUAGE OF THE LAW (2 VOLS.). CANADA ISRAEL UK WOR+45 WOR-45 JUDGE CT/SYS ATTIT...CRIMLGY JURID ANTHOL CMN/WLTH. PAGE 15 A0312
BIBLIOG LAW INT/LAW ADJUD

B67
UNIVERSAL REFERENCE SYSTEM,LAW, JURISPRUDENCE, AND JUDICIAL PROCESS (VOLUME VII). WOR+45 WOR-45 CONSTN NAT/G LEGIS JUDGE CT/SYS...INT/LAW COMPUT/IR GEN/METH METH. PAGE 149 A3044
BIBLIOG/A LAW JURID ADJUD

B67
US SUPERINTENDENT OF DOCUMENTS,LIBRARY OF CONGRESS (PRICE LIST 83). AFR ASIA EUR+WWI USA-45 USSR NAT/G DIPLOM CONFER CT/SYS WAR...DECISION PHIL/SCI CLASSIF 19/20 CONGRESS PRESIDENT. PAGE 157 A3205
BIBLIOG/A USA+45 AUTOMAT LAW

L67
"RESTRICTIVE SOVEREIGN IMMUNITY, THE STATE DEPARTMENT, AND THE COURTS." USA+45 USA-45 EX/STRUC DIPLOM ADJUD CONTROL GOV/REL 19/20 DEPT/STATE SUPREME/CT. PAGE 4 A0080
SOVEREIGN ORD/FREE PRIVIL CT/SYS

L67
CAHIERS P.,"LE RECOURS EN CONSTATATION DE MANQUEMENTS DES ETATS MEMBRES DEVANT LA COUR DES COMMUNAUTES EUROPEENNES." LAW PROB/SOLV DIPLOM ADMIN CT/SYS SANCTION ATTIT...POLICY DECISION JURID ECSC EEC. PAGE 23 A0465
INT/ORG CONSTN ROUTINE ADJUD

S67
MANN F.A.,"THE BRETTON WOODS AGREEMENT IN THE ENGLISH COURTS." UK JUDGE ADJUD CT/SYS...JURID PREDICT CON/ANAL 20. PAGE 94 A1923
LAW INT/LAW CONSTN

B97
US DEPARTMENT OF STATE,CATALOGUE OF WORKS RELATING TO THE LAW OF NATIONS AND DIPLOMACY IN THE LIBRARY OF THE DEPARTMENT OF STATE (PAMPHLET). WOR-45 NAT/G ADJUD CT/SYS...INT/LAW JURID 19. PAGE 152 A3102
BIBLIOG/A DIPLOM LAW

CTS/WESTM....COURTS OF WESTMINSTER HALL

CUBA....SEE ALSO L/A+17C

B10
GRIFFIN A.P.C.,LIST OF REFERENCES ON RECIPROCITY (2ND REV. ED.). CANADA CUBA UK USA-45 WOR-45 NAT/G TARIFFS CONFER COLONIAL CONTROL SANCTION CONSEN ALL/VALS...DECISION 19/20. PAGE 56 A1157
BIBLIOG/A VOL/ASSN DIPLOM REPAR

B45
PERAZA SARAUSA F.,BIBLIOGRAFIAS CUBANAS. CUBA CULTURE ECO/UNDEV AGRI EDU/PROP PRESS CIVMIL/REL ...POLICY GEOG PHIL/SCI BIOG 19/20. PAGE 115 A2353
BIBLIOG/A L/A+17C NAT/G DIPLOM

B47
PERKINS D.,THE UNITED STATES AND THE CARIBBEAN. CUBA DOMIN/REP GUATEMALA HAITI PANAMA CULTURE ECO/UNDEV FOR/AID ADMIN COERCE HABITAT...POLICY 19/20. PAGE 115 A2359
DIPLOM L/A+17C USA-45

B59
NUNEZ JIMENEZ A.,LA LIBERACION DE LAS ISLAS. CUBA L/A+17C USA+45 LAW CHIEF PLAN DIPLOM FOR/AID OWN WEALTH 20 CASTRO/F. PAGE 110 A2261
AGRI REV ECO/UNDEV NAT/G

S60
KALUODA J.,"COMMUNIST STRATEGY IN LATIN AMERICA." L/A+17C USA+45 INT/ORG NAT/G POL/PAR DIPLOM ECO/TAC EDU/PROP COERCE WEALTH...CONCPT OAS COLD/WAR 20. PAGE 76 A1553
COM PWR CUBA

B61
HADDAD J.A.,REVOLUCAO CUBANA E REVOLUCAO BRASILEIRA. BRAZIL CUBA L/A+17C STRATA AGRI WORKER EDU/PROP REGION...POLICY NAT/COMP 20. PAGE 59 A1210
REV ORD/FREE DIPLOM ECO/UNDEV

B61
LIPPMANN W.,THE COMING TESTS WITH RUSSIA. COM CUBA GERMANY USSR FORCES CONTROL NEUTRAL COERCE NUC/PWR REV WAR PWR...INT 20 KHRUSH/N BERLIN. PAGE 89 A1830
BAL/PWR DIPLOM MARXISM ARMS/CONT

B61
SCHMIDT H.,VERTEIDIGUNG ODER VERGELTUNG. COM CUBA GERMANY/W USSR FORCES DIPLOM ARMS/CONT DETER NUC/PWR...POLICY CHARTS HYPO/EXP SIMUL BIBLIOG 20 NATO COLD/WAR. PAGE 128 A2630
PLAN WAR BAL/PWR ORD/FREE

B61
STARK H.,SOCIAL AND ECONOMIC FRONTIERS IN LATIN AMERICA (2ND ED.). CUBA FUT CULTURE AGRI INDUS ECO/TAC PRODUC ATTIT MARXISM...NAT/COMP BIBLIOG T 20. PAGE 137 A2807
L/A+17C SOCIETY DIPLOM ECO/UNDEV

B62
DREIER J.C.,THE ORGANIZATION OF AMERICAN STATES AND THE HEMISPHERE CRISIS. CUBA USA+45 CULTURE STRATA NAT/G VOL/ASSN CONSULT FORCES ACT/RES CREATE DIPLOM ECO/TAC FOR/AID ALL/VALS...POLICY OBS OAS 20. PAGE 38 A0786
L/A+17C CONCPT

B62
MORRAY J.P.,THE SECOND REVOLUTION IN CUBA. CUBA AGRI LABOR POL/PAR DIPLOM FOR/AID GUERRILLA TOTALISM MARXISM 20. PAGE 104 A2146
REV MARXIST ECO/TAC NAT/LISM

B62
WILLIAMS W.A.,THE UNITED STATES, CUBA, AND CASTRO: AN ESSAY ON THE DYNAMICS OF REVOLUTION AND THE DISSOLUTION OF EMPIRE. CUBA USA+45 AGRI VOL/ASSN DIPLOM ECO/TAC DOMIN COERCE...POLICY 20 EISNHWR/DD CIA KENNEDY/JF CASTRO/F. PAGE 165 A3354
REV CONSTN COM LEAD

L62
NIZARD L.,"CUBAN QUESTION AND SECURITY COUNCIL." L/A+17C USA+45 ECO/UNDEV NAT/G POL/PAR DELIB/GP ECO/TAC PWR...RELATIV OBS TIME/SEQ TREND GEN/LAWS UN 20 UN. PAGE 109 A2242
INT/ORG JURID DIPLOM CUBA

S62
FENWICK C.G.,"ISSUES AT PUNTA DEL ESTE: NON-INTERVENTION VS COLLECTIVE SECURITY." L/A+17C USA+45 VOL/ASSN DELIB/GP ECO/TAC LEGIT ADJUD REGION ORD/FREE OAS COLD/WAR 20. PAGE 45 A0917
INT/ORG CUBA

S62
MCWHINNEY E.,"CO-EXISTENCE, THE CUBA CRISIS, AND COLD WAR-INTERNATIONAL WAR." CUBA USA+45 USSR WOR+45 NAT/G TOP/EX BAL/PWR DIPLOM DOMIN LEGIT PEACE RIGID/FLEX ORD/FREE...STERTYP COLD/WAR 20. PAGE 99 A2026
CONCPT INT/LAW

B63
HALPERIN M.H.,LIMITED WAR IN A NUCLEAR AGE. CUBA KOREA USA+45 USSR INT/ORG FORCES PLAN DIPLOM DETER PWR...BIBLIOG/A 20. PAGE 60 A1238
WAR NUC/PWR CONTROL WEAPON

B63
PACHTER H.M.,COLLISION COURSE; THE CUBAN MISSILE CRISIS AND COEXISTENCE. CUBA USA+45 DIPLOM ARMS/CONT PEACE MARXISM...DECISION INT/LAW 20 COLD/WAR KHRUSH/N KENNEDY/JF CASTRO/F. PAGE 112 A2307
WAR BAL/PWR NUC/PWR DETER

B63
RUSSELL B.,UNARMED VICTORY. CHINA/COM CUBA INDIA USA+45 WAR MARXISM...POLICY IDEA/COMP 20 KHRUSH/N COLD/WAR. PAGE 125 A2573
DIPLOM ATTIT SOCISM ORD/FREE

B63
STEVENSON A.E.,LOOKING OUTWARD: YEARS OF CRISIS AT THE UNITED NATIONS. COM CUBA USA+45 WOR+45 SOCIETY NAT/G EX/STRUC ACT/RES LEGIT COLONIAL ATTIT PERSON SUPEGO ALL/VALS...POLICY HUM UN COLD/WAR CONGO 20. PAGE 138 A2823
INT/ORG CONCPT ARMS/CONT

B63
US HOUSE COMM FOREIGN AFFAIRS,HEARINGS ON H.R. 5490 TO AMEND FURTHER THE FOREIGN ASSISTANCE ACT OF 1961. CUBA EUR+WWI INDIA INT/ORG DELIB/GP LEGIS DIPLOM CONFER ORD/FREE 20 DEPT/STATE DEPT/DEFEN UN. PAGE 153 A3129
FOR/AID INT/TRADE FORCES WEAPON

B63
VAN SLYCK P.,PEACE: THE CONTROL OF NATIONAL POWER. CUBA WOR+45 FINAN NAT/G FORCES PROB/SOLV TEC/DEV BAL/PWR ADMIN CONTROL ORD/FREE...POLICY INT/LAW UN COLD/WAR TREATY. PAGE 158 A3214
ARMS/CONT PEACE INT/ORG DIPLOM

L63
CRANE R.D.,"THE CUBAN CRISIS: A STRATEGIC ANALYSIS OF AMERICAN AND SOVIET POLICY." CUBA USA+45 USSR BAL/PWR RISK DETER NUC/PWR PERCEPT ORD/FREE 20.
DIPLOM POLICY FORCES

PAGE 32 A0658

S63
ALEXANDER R.,"LATIN AMERICA AND THE COMMUNIST BLOC." ASIA COM CUBA L/A+17C USA+45 USSR NAT/G VOL/ASSN TEC/DEV FOR/AID LEGIT PWR WEALTH COLD/WAR 20. PAGE 6 A0112
ECO/UNDEV RECORD

S63
GIRAUD E.,"L'INTERDICTION DU RECOURS A LA FORCE, LA THEORIE ET LA PRATIQUE DES NATIONS UNIES." ALGERIA COM CUBA HUNGARY WOR+45 ADJUD TOTALISM ATTIT RIGID/FLEX PWR...POLICY JURID CONCPT UN 20 CONGO. PAGE 53 A1077
INT/ORG FORCES DIPLOM

S63
HOLBO P.S.,"COLD WAR DRIFT IN LATIN AMERICA." CUBA L/A+17C USA+45 USA-45 INT/ORG NAT/G NEIGH VOL/ASSN ACT/RES PLAN ECO/TAC ATTIT RIGID/FLEX ALL/VALS ...RECORD TIME/SEQ OAS LAFTA 20 COLD/WAR. PAGE 66 A1363
DELIB/GP CREATE FOR/AID

S63
MCDOUGAL M.S.,"THE SOVIET-CUBAN QUARANTINE AND SELF-DEFENSE." CUBA USA+45 USSR WOR+45 INT/ORG NAT/G BAL/PWR NUC/PWR ATTIT...JURID CONCPT. PAGE 98 A2008
ORD/FREE LEGIT SOVEREIGN

B64
ROSENAU J.N.,INTERNATIONAL ASPECTS OF CIVIL STRIFE. CHINA/COM CUBA EUR+WWI USA+45 USSR BAL/PWR EDU/PROP NEUTRAL COERCE MORAL...NAT/COMP 20 COLD/WAR UN. PAGE 124 A2533
POLICY DIPLOM REV WAR

S64
ARMSTRONG J.A.,"THE SOVIET-AMERICAN CONFRONTATION: A NEW STAGE?" CUBA USA+45 USSR PLAN PROB/SOLV INT/TRADE CONTROL ARMS/CONT NUC/PWR MARXISM 20 COLD/WAR INTERVENT. PAGE 9 A0174
DIPLOM POLICY INSPECT

B65
FAGG J.E.,CUBA, HAITI, AND THE DOMINICAN REPUBLIC. CUBA DOMIN/REP HAITI L/A+17C NAT/G DIPLOM ECO/TAC DOMIN CHOOSE AUTHORIT ROLE SOVEREIGN POPULISM 17/20. PAGE 43 A0883
COLONIAL ECO/UNDEV REV GOV/COMP

B65
MALLIN J.,FORTRESS CUBA; RUSSIA'S AMERICAN BASE. COM CUBA L/A+17C FORCES PLAN DIPLOM LEAD REV WAR ...POLICY 20 CASTRO/F GUEVARA/C INTERVENT. PAGE 93 A1914
MARXISM CHIEF GUERRILLA DOMIN

S65
MAC CHESNEY B.,"SOME COMMENTS ON THE 'QUARANTINE' OF CUBA." USA+45 WOR+45 NAT/G BAL/PWR DIPLOM LEGIT ROUTINE ATTIT ORD/FREE...JURID METH/CNCPT 20. PAGE 92 A1883
INT/ORG LAW CUBA USSR

B66
CONNEL-SMITH G.,THE INTERAMERICAN SYSTEM. CUBA L/A+17C DELIB/GP FOR/AID COLONIAL PEACE PWR MARXISM ...BIBLIOG 19/20 OAS. PAGE 29 A0586
DIPLOM INT/TRADE REGION INT/ORG

B66
GRENVILLE J.A.S.,POLITICS, STRATEGY, AND AMERICAN DEMOCRACY: STUDIES IN FOREIGN POLICY, 1873-1917. CUBA PHILIPPINE SPAIN USA-45 VENEZUELA ELITES NAT/G CREATE PARTIC WAR RIGID/FLEX ORD/FREE...DECISION TREND 19/20 HAWAII. PAGE 56 A1146
DIPLOM COLONIAL POLICY

B66
HORELICK A.L.,STRATEGIC POWER AND SOVIET FOREIGN POLICY. CUBA USSR FORCES PLAN CIVMIL/REL...POLICY DECISION 20 COLD/WAR. PAGE 67 A1383
DIPLOM BAL/PWR DETER NUC/PWR

B66
US HOUSE COMM APPROPRIATIONS,HEARINGS ON FOREIGN OPERATIONS AND RELATED AGENCIES APPROPRIATIONS. CUBA USA+45 VOL/ASSN DELIB/GP DIPLOM CONFER ORD/FREE 20 CONGRESS MIGRATION INT/AM/DEV PEACE/CORP. PAGE 153 A3120
FOR/AID BUDGET ECO/UNDEV FORCES

B66
ZABLOCKI C.J.,SINO-SOVIET RIVALRY. AFR ASIA CHINA/COM COM CUBA EUR+WWI L/A+17C USA+45 USSR WOR+45 POL/PAR FORCES COERCE NUC/PWR...GOV/COMP IDEA/COMP 20 MAO KHRUSH/N. PAGE 169 A3442
DIPLOM MARXISM COM

L67
MACDONALD R.S.J.,"THE RESORT TO ECONOMIC COERCION BY INTERNATIONAL POLITICAL ORGANIZATIONS." CUBA ETHIOPIA RHODESIA SOUTH/AFR NAT/G FOR/AID INT/TRADE DOMIN CONTROL SANCTION...DECISION LEAGUE/NAT UN OAS 20. PAGE 92 A1887
INT/ORG COERCE ECO/TAC DIPLOM

S67
FABREGA J.,"ANTECEDENTES EXTRANJEROS EN LA CONSTITUCION PANAMENA." CUBA L/A+17C PANAMA URUGUAY EX/STRUC LEGIS DIPLOM ORD/FREE 19/20 COLOMB MEXIC/AMER. PAGE 43 A0882
CONSTN JURID NAT/G PARL/PROC

S67
MEYER J.,"CUBA S'ENFERME DANS SA REVOLUTION." CHINA/COM CUBA USSR NAT/G TOP/EX DIPLOM LEAD ATTIT ...PREDICT 20. PAGE 100 A2053
MARXISM REV CHIEF NAT/LISM

B98
GRIFFIN A.P.C.,LIST OF BOOKS RELATING TO CUBA (PAMPHLET). CUBA L/A+17C USA-45 INT/TRADE DOMIN WAR GP/REL ALL/VALS...GEOG SOC CHARTS 19/20. PAGE 56 A1158
BIBLIOG/A NAT/G COLONIAL

CUBAN CRISIS....SEE INT/REL+APPROPRIATE NATIONS+COLD WAR

CULTS....SEE SECT

CULTUR/REV....CULTURAL REVOLUTION IN CHINA

CULTURAL REVOLUTION IN CHINA....SEE CULTUR/REV

CULTURE....CULTURAL PATTERNS

CURLEY/JM....JAMES M. CURLEY

CURRIE D.P. A0667

CURRIE L. A0668

CURTIS G.L. A0669

CURZON/GN....GEORGE NATHANIEL CURZON

B39
NICOLSON H.,CURZON: THE LAST PHASE, 1919-1925. UK NAT/G DELIB/GP TOP/EX ROUTINE WAR RIGID/FLEX ...METH/CNCPT 20 CURZON/GN. PAGE 109 A2231
POLICY DIPLOM BIOG

CUTLER R. A0670

CYBERNETICS....SEE FEEDBACK, SIMUL, CONTROL

CYCLES....SEE TIME/SEQ

CYPRUS....SEE ALSO APPROPRIATE TIME/SPACE/CULTURE INDEX

N
WEINTAL E.,FACING THE BRINK* AN INTIMATE STUDY OF CRISIS DIPLOMACY. CYPRUS FRANCE USA+45 USSR VIETNAM YEMEN INT/ORG NAT/G...POLICY DECISION PREDICT COLD/WAR PRESIDENT NATO 20. PAGE 162 A3307
DIPLOM

B56
GREECE PRESBEIA U.S.,BRITISH OPINION ON CYPRUS. CYPRUS UK FORCES DIPLOM INT/TRADE DOMIN GOV/REL ORD/FREE SOVEREIGN...POLICY 20. PAGE 55 A1137
ATTIT COLONIAL LEGIS PRESS

B64
DE SMITH S.A.,THE NEW COMMONWEALTH AND ITS CONSTITUTIONS. AFR CYPRUS PAKISTAN S/ASIA INT/ORG NAT/G LEGIS LEGIT RIGID/FLEX PWR...CONCPT TIME/SEQ CMN/WLTH 20. PAGE 35 A0713
EX/STRUC CONSTN SOVEREIGN

L64
WORLD PEACE FOUNDATION,"INTERNATIONAL ORGANIZATIONS: SUMMARY OF ACTIVITIES." INDIA PAKISTAN TURKEY WOR+45 CONSTN CONSULT EX/STRUC ECO/TAC EDU/PROP LEGIT ORD/FREE...JURID SOC UN 20 CYPRESS. PAGE 167 A3397
INT/ORG ROUTINE

S67
ANTHEM T.,"CYPRUS* WHAT NOW?" CYPRUS GREECE TURKEY NAT/G BUDGET MAJORITY 20 NATO. PAGE 8 A0165
DIPLOM COERCE INT/TRADE ADJUD

CZECHOSLVK....CZECHOSLOVAKIA; SEE ALSO COM

N
KYRIAK T.E.,EAST EUROPE: BIBLIOGRAPHY--INDEX TO US JPRS RESEARCH TRANSLATIONS. ALBANIA BULGARIA COM CZECHOSLVK HUNGARY POLAND ROMANIA AGRI EXTR/IND FINAN SERV/IND INT/TRADE WEAPON...GEOG MGT SOC 20. PAGE 83 A1701
BIBLIOG/A PRESS MARXISM INDUS

B18
KERNER R.J.,SLAVIC EUROPE: A SELECTED BIBLIOGRAPHY IN THE WESTERN EUROPEAN LANGUAGES. BULGARIA CZECHOSLVK GERMANY/E POLAND RUSSIA YUGOSLAVIA NAT/G DIPLOM MARXISM...LING 19/20. PAGE 78 A1598
BIBLIOG SOCIETY CULTURE COM

N19
HAJDA J.,THE COLD WAR VIEWED AS A SOCIOLOGICAL PROBLEM (PAMPHLET). COM CZECHOSLVK EUR+WWI SOCIETY PLAN EDU/PROP CONTROL TASK ATTIT MARXISM...POLICY 20 COLD/WAR MIGRATION. PAGE 59 A1220
DIPLOM LEAD PWR NAT/G

B48
NAMIER L.B.,DIPLOMATIC PRELUDE 1938-1939. CZECHOSLVK EUR+WWI GERMANY POLAND UK FORCES DOMIN PWR 20 HITLER/A. PAGE 107 A2193
WAR TOTALISM DIPLOM

B54
REYNOLDS P.A.,BRITISH FOREIGN POLICY IN THE INTER-WAR YEARS. CZECHOSLVK GERMANY POLAND UK USA-45 POL/PAR FORCES ECO/TAC ARMS/CONT WAR ATTIT 20. PAGE 120 A2470
DIPLOM POLICY NAT/G

B58
KENNAN G.F.,THE DECISION TO INTERVENE: SOVIET-AMERICAN RELATIONS, 1917-1920 (VOL. II). CZECHOSLVK EUR+WWI USA-45 USSR ELITES NAT/G FORCES PROB/SOLV
DIPLOM POLICY ATTIT

REV WAR TOTALISM PWR...CHARTS BIBLIOG 20 TREATY PRESIDENT CHINJAP. PAGE 78 A1588

B59
CHALUPA V.,RISE AND DEVELOPMENT OF A TOTALITARIAN STATE. CZECHOSLVK USSR STRUCT INT/ORG WORKER DIPLOM ECO/TAC COERCE NAT/LISM ATTIT...POLICY 20 COM/PARTY. PAGE 25 A0516
TOTALISM MARXISM REV POL/PAR

B59
ETSCHMANN R.,DIE WAHRUNGS- UND DEVISENPOLITIK DES OSTBLOCKS UND IHRE AUSWIRKUNGEN AUF DIE WIRTSCHAFTSBEZIEHUNGEN ZWISCHEN OST U WEST. BULGARIA CZECHOSLVK HUNGARY POLAND USSR MARKET NAT/G PLAN DIPLOM...NAT/COMP 20. PAGE 42 A0867
ECO/TAC FINAN POLICY INT/TRADE

B61
FUCHS G.,GEGEN HITLER UND HENLEIN. CZECHOSLVK GERMANY DIPLOM CHOOSE GP/REL TOTALISM SOVEREIGN 20 HITLER/A. PAGE 50 A1013
FASCISM WORKER POL/PAR NAT/LISM

S61
BRZEZINSKI Z.K.,"THE ORGANIZATION OF THE COMMUNIST CAMP." COM CZECHOSLVK COM/IND NAT/G DELIB/GP INT/TRADE DOMIN EDU/PROP EXEC ROUTINE COERCE ATTIT PWR...MGT CONCPT TIME/SEQ CHARTS VAL/FREE 20 TREATY. PAGE 20 A0416
VOL/ASSN DIPLOM USSR

B64
GRIFFITH W.E.,COMMUNISM IN EUROPE (2 VOLS.). CZECHOSLVK USSR WOR+45 WOR-45 YUGOSLAVIA INGP/REL MARXISM SOCISM...ANTHOL 20 EUROPE/E. PAGE 57 A1162
COM POL/PAR DIPLOM GOV/COMP

S64
HORECKY P.L.,"LIBRARY OF CONGRESS PUBLICATIONS IN AID OF USSR AND EAST EUROPEAN RESEARCH." BULGARIA CZECHOSLVK POLAND USSR YUGOSLAVIA NAT/G POL/PAR DIPLOM ADMIN GOV/REL...CLASSIF 20. PAGE 67 A1382
BIBLIOG/A COM MARXISM

B65
HUSS P.J.,RED SPIES IN THE UN. CZECHOSLVK USA+45 USSR COM/IND FORCES EDU/PROP NUC/PWR MARXISM 20 UN COLD/WAR. PAGE 69 A1421
PEACE INT/ORG BAL/PWR DIPLOM

B66
LAMBERG R.F.,PRAG UND DIE DRITTE WELT. AFR ASIA CZECHOSLVK L/A+17C MARKET TEC/DEV ECO/TAC REV ATTIT 20 TREATY. PAGE 84 A1713
DIPLOM ECO/UNDEV INT/TRADE FOR/AID

B66
SPULBER N.,THE STATE AND ECONOMIC DEVELOPMENT IN EASTERN EUROPE. BULGARIA COM CZECHOSLVK HUNGARY POLAND YUGOSLAVIA CULTURE PLAN CAP/ISM INT/TRADE CONTROL...POLICY CHARTS METH/COMP BIBLIOG/A 19/20. PAGE 136 A2793
ECO/DEV ECO/UNDEV NAT/G TOTALISM

CZERNIN F. A0671

D

D'AMATO D. A0672

DAC....DEVELOPMENT ASSISTANCE COMMITTEE (PART OF OECD)

DAENIKER G. A0673

DAHLIN E. A0674

DAHOMEY....SEE ALSO AFR

DAKAR....DAKAR, SENEGAL

DALLIN A. A0675,A0676,A0677,A0678

DALLIN D.J. A0679

DANGERFIELD R. A1112

DANIEL/Y....YULI DANIEL

DANIELS R.V. A0680

DANTE....DANTE ALIGHIERI

B37
BORGESE G.A.,GOLIATH: THE MARCH OF FASCISM. GERMANY ITALY LAW POL/PAR SECT DIPLOM SOCISM...JURID MYTH 20 DANTE MACHIAVELL MUSSOLIN/B. PAGE 17 A0341
POLICY NAT/LISM FASCISM NAT/G

B57
ALIGHIERI D.,ON WORLD GOVERNMENT. ROMAN/EMP LAW SOCIETY INT/ORG NAT/G POL/PAR ADJUD WAR GP/REL PEACE WORSHIP 15 WORLDUNITY DANTE. PAGE 6 A0121
POLICY CONCPT DIPLOM SECT

DARBY W.E. A0681

DARLING F.C. A0682

DARWIN/C....CHARLES DARWIN

B55
KROPOTKIN P.,MUTUAL AID, A FACTOR OF EVOLUTION (1902). UNIV ADJUST ATTIT HEREDITY PERSON LOVE DARWIN/C. PAGE 82 A1687
INGP/REL SOCIETY GEN/LAWS BIO/SOC

DATA ANALYSIS....SEE CON/ANAL, STAT, MATH, COMPUTER

DAVAR F.C. A0683

DAVEE R. A0684

DAVENPORT J. A0685

DAVENPORT M.W.S. A1681

DAVID P.T. A0587

DAVIDS J. A0686

DAVIDSON A.B. A0687

DAVIES U.P. A0688

DAVIS E.P. A0689

DAVIS H.B. A0690

DAVIS H.E. A0691

DAVIS V. A0692

DAVIS/JEFF....JEFFERSON DAVIS

DAVIS/W....WARREN DAVIS

DAVISON W.P. A0693

DAWSON K.H. A0694

DAWSON R.H. A0695

DE ARECHAGA E.J. A0696

DE BLIJ H.J. A0697

DE BLOCH J. A0698

DE CALLIERES F. A0699

DE CONDE A. A0700

DE GAULLE C. A0701,A0702

DE HERRERA C.D. A0703

DE HUSZAR G.B. A0704

DE KIEWIET C.W. A0705

DE MADARIAGA S. A0706,A0707

DE MARTENS G.F. A0708

DE REPARAZ G. A0709

DE ROUGEMENT D. A0710

DE RUSETT A. A0711

DE SMITH S.A. A0712,A0713

DE VATTEL E. A0714

DE VICTORIA F. A0715

DE VISSCHER C. A0716

DEAN A.W. A0717

DEAN V.M. A0718,A0719

DEANE H. A0720

DEATH....DEATH

B56
KOENIG L.W.,THE TRUMAN ADMINISTRATION: ITS PRINCIPLES AND PRACTICE. USA+45 POL/PAR CHIEF LEGIS DIPLOM DEATH NUC/PWR WAR CIVMIL/REL PEACE ...DECISION 20 TRUMAN/HS PRESIDENT TREATY. PAGE 81 A1658
ADMIN POLICY EX/STRUC GOV/REL

B62
LERNER M.,THE AGE OF OVERKILL: A PREFACE TO WORLD POLITICS. USA+45 USSR WOR+45 SOCIETY ECO/UNDEV BAL/PWR NEUTRAL PARTIC REV ALL/IDEOS MARXISM ...BIBLIOG/A 20. PAGE 87 A1787
DIPLOM NUC/PWR PWR DEATH

B62
PERRE J.,LES MUTATIONS DE LA GUERRE MODERNE: DE LA REVOLUTION FRANCAISE A LA REVOLUTION NUCLEAIRE. DIPLOM ARMS/CONT DEATH REV WEAPON GP/REL PEACE ATTIT...STAT PREDICT BIBLIOG 18/20 WWI. PAGE 115 A2365
WAR FORCES NUC/PWR

B67
KATZ R.,DEATH IN ROME. EUR+WWI ITALY POL/PAR DIPLOM LEAD ATTIT PERSON ROLE CATHISM. PAGE 77 A1570
WAR MURDER FORCES DEATH

DEBATE....ORGANIZED COLLECTIVE ARGUMENT

N
MCSPADDEN J.W.,THE AMERICAN STATESMAN'S YEARBOOK. WOR-45 LAW CONSTN AGRI FINAN DEBATE ADMIN PARL/PROC ...CHARTS BIBLIOG/A 20. PAGE 99 A2025
DIPLOM NAT/G PROVS LEGIS

B17
MEYER H.H.B.,LIST OF REFERENCES ON EMBARGOES (PAMPHLET). USA-45 AGRI DIPLOM WRITING DEBATE WEAPON...INT/LAW 18/20 CONGRESS. PAGE 100 A2049
BIBLIOG DIST/IND ECO/TAC INT/TRADE

N19
MEZERIK A.G.,U-2 AND OPEN SKIES (PAMPHLET). USA+45 USSR INT/ORG CHIEF FORCES PLAN EDU/PROP CONTROL SANCTION ARMS/CONT 20 UN EISNHWR/DD. PAGE 100 A2060
DIPLOM RISK DEBATE

B32
FLEMMING D.,THE UNITED STATES AND THE LEAGUE OF NATIONS, 1918-1920. FUT USA-45 NAT/G LEGIS TOP/EX DEBATE CHOOSE PEACE ATTIT SOVEREIGN...TIME/SEQ CON/ANAL CONGRESS LEAGUE/NAT 20 TREATY. PAGE 46 A0950
INT/ORG EDU/PROP

B49
GROB F.,THE RELATIVITY OF WAR AND PEACE: A STUDY IN LAW, HISTORY, AND POLLTICS. WOR+45 WOR-45 LAW DIPLOM DEBATE...CONCPT LING IDEA/COMP BIBLIOG 18/20. PAGE 57 A1167
WAR PEACE INT/LAW STYLE

L49
HEINDEL R.H.,"THE NORTH ATLANTIC TREATY IN THE UNITED STATES SENATE." CONSTN POL/PAR CHIEF DEBATE LEAD ROUTINE WAR PEACE...CHARTS UN SENATE NATO. PAGE 64 A1309
DECISION PARL/PROC LEGIS INT/ORG

B51
US HOUSE COMM APPROPRIATIONS,MUTUAL SECURITY PROGRAM APPROPRIATIONS FOR 1952: HEARINGS BEFORE A SUBCOMMITTEE OF THE COMMITTEE ON APPROPRIATIONS. KOREA L/A+17C ECO/DEV ECO/UNDEV INT/ORG INSPECT BAL/PWR DIPLOM DEBATE WAR...POLICY STAT ASIA/S 20 CONGRESS NATO COLD/WAR MID/EAST. PAGE 153 A3118
LEGIS FORCES BUDGET FOR/AID

B54
US SENATE COMM ON FOREIGN REL,REVIEW OF THE UNITED NATIONS CHARTER: A COLLECTION OF DOCUMENTS. LEGIS DIPLOM ADMIN ARMS/CONT WAR REPRESENT SOVEREIGN ...INT/LAW 20 UN. PAGE 156 A3180
BIBLIOG CONSTN INT/ORG DEBATE

B55
PLISCHKE E.,AMERICAN FOREIGN RELATIONS: A BIBLIOGRAPHY OF OFFICIAL SOURCES. USA+45 USA-45 INT/ORG FORCES PRESS WRITING DEBATE EXEC...POLICY INT/LAW 18/20 CONGRESS. PAGE 116 A2390
BIBLIOG/A DIPLOM NAT/G

B56
US LIBRARY OF CONGRESS,UNITED STATES DIRECT ECONOMIC AID TO FOREIGN COUNTRIES: A COLLECTION OF EXCERPTS AND A BIBLIOGRAPHY (PAMPHLET). USA+45 PRESS DEBATE...ANTHOL BIBLIOG/A CONGRESS. PAGE 155 A3154
FOR/AID POLICY DIPLOM ECO/UNDEV

B58
STONE J.,AGGRESSION AND WORLD ORDER: A CRITIQUE OF UNITED NATIONS THEORIES OF AGGRESSION. LAW CONSTN DELIB/GP PROB/SOLV BAL/PWR DIPLOM DEBATE ADJUD CRIME PWR...POLICY IDEA/COMP 20 UN SUEZ LEAGUE/NAT. PAGE 138 A2835
ORD/FREE INT/ORG WAR CONCPT

C58
WILDING N.,"AN ENCYCLOPEDIA OF PARLIAMENT." UK LAW CONSTN CHIEF PROB/SOLV DIPLOM DEBATE WAR INGP/REL PRIVIL...BIBLIOG DICTIONARY 13/20 CMN/WLTH PARLIAMENT. PAGE 164 A3349
PARL/PROC POL/PAR NAT/G ADMIN

N58
US HOUSE COMM FOREIGN AFFAIRS,HEARINGS ON THE FAR EAST AND THE PACIFIC (PAMPHLET). LAOS USA+45 NAT/G CONSULT FORCES CONFER DEBATE ORD/FREE 20. PAGE 153 A3124
FOR/AID DIPLOM DELIB/GP LEGIS

N58
US HOUSE COMM FOREIGN AFFAIRS,HEARINGS ON REVIEW OF THE MUTUAL SECURITY PROGRAMS; EXAMINATION OF SELECTED PROJECTS IN FORMOSA AND PAKISTAN (PAMPHLET). ASIA PAKISTAN TAIWAN INDUS CONSULT DELIB/GP LEGIS BUDGET CONFER DEBATE 20. PAGE 153 A3125
FOR/AID ECO/UNDEV DIPLOM ECO/TAC

B61
HUDSON G.F.,THE SINO-SOVIET DISPUTE. CHINA/COM USSR INTELL INT/TRADE DEBATE REV...IDEA/COMP 20. PAGE 68 A1404
DIPLOM MARXISM PRESS ATTIT

B63
DALLIN A.,DIVERSITY IN INTERNATIONAL COMMUNISM: A DOCUMENTARY RECORD, 1961-1963. CHINA/COM CHIEF PRESS WRITING DEBATE LEAD...POLICY ANTHOL 20. PAGE 33 A0677
COM DIPLOM POL/PAR CONFER

B63
RAVENS J.P.,STAAT UND KATHOLISCHE KIRCHE IN PREUSSENS POLNISCHEN TEILUNGSGEBIETEN. GERMANY POLAND PRUSSIA PROVS DIPLOM EDU/PROP DEBATE NAT/LISM...JURID 18 CHURCH/STA. PAGE 119 A2451
GP/REL CATHISM SECT NAT/G

B64
TREADGOLD D.W.,THE DEVELOPMENT OF THE USSR. COM USSR ECO/DEV CREATE BAL/PWR DEBATE COLONIAL TOTALISM...HUM ANTHOL BIBLIOG 19/20. PAGE 145 A2960
MARXISM CONSERVE DIPLOM DOMIN

B65
LARUS J.,FROM COLLECTIVE SECURITY TO PREVENTIVE DIPLOMACY. FUT FORCES PROB/SOLV DEBATE AGREE COERCE WAR PWR...ANTHOL 20 LEAGUE/NAT UN. PAGE 85 A1736
INT/ORG PEACE DIPLOM ORD/FREE

L67
ANAND R.P.,"SOVEREIGN EQUALITY OF STATES IN INTERNATIONAL LAW." UNIV DIPLOM DOMIN CONFER DEBATE SANCTION ATTIT UN. PAGE 8 A0157
INT/LAW INT/ORG CONCPT POLICY

L67
BODENHEIMER S.J.,"THE 'POLITICAL UNION' DEBATE IN EUROPE* A CASE STUDY IN INTERGOVERNMENTAL DIPLOMACY." EUR+WWI FUT NAT/G FORCES PLAN DEBATE SOVEREIGN...CONCPT PREDICT EEC NATO. PAGE 16 A0326
DIPLOM REGION INT/ORG

S67
BUTT R.,"THE COMMON MARKET AND CONSERVATIVE POLITICS, 1961-2." UK CHIEF DIPLOM ECO/TAC INT/TRADE CONFER DEBATE REGION ATTIT...POLICY 20 EEC. PAGE 22 A0454
EUR+WWI INT/ORG POL/PAR

DEBS/E....EUGENE DEBS

DEBT....PUBLIC DEBT, INCLUDING NATIONAL DEBT;

DECISION....DECISION-MAKING AND GAME THEORY; SEE ALSO GAME

N
WEINTAL E.,FACING THE BRINK* AN INTIMATE STUDY OF CRISIS DIPLOMACY. CYPRUS FRANCE USA+45 USSR VIETNAM YEMEN INT/ORG NAT/G...POLICY DECISION PREDICT COLD/WAR PRESIDENT NATO 20. PAGE 162 A3307
DIPLOM

N
AMERICAN JOURNAL OF INTERNATIONAL LAW. WOR+45 WOR-45 CONSTN INT/ORG NAT/G CT/SYS ARMS/CONT WAR ...DECISION JURID NAT/COMP 20. PAGE 1 A0002
BIBLIOG/A INT/LAW DIPLOM ADJUD

N
US SUPERINTENDENT OF DOCUMENTS,TARIFF AND TAXATION (PRICE LIST 37). USA+45 LAW INT/TRADE ADJUD ADMIN CT/SYS INCOME OWN...DECISION GATT. PAGE 157 A3204
BIBLIOG/A TAX TARIFFS NAT/G

B05
GRIFFIN A.P.C.,LIST OF REFERENCES ON THE US CONSULAR SERVICE (PAMPHLET). FRANCE GERMANY SPAIN UK USA-45 WOR-45 OP/RES DOMIN ADMIN FEEDBACK ROUTINE GOV/REL...DECISION 19. PAGE 56 A1153
BIBLIOG/A NAT/G DIPLOM CONSULT

B08
GRIFFIN A.P.C.,LIST OF REFERENCES ON INTERNATIONAL ARBITRATION. FRANCE L/A+17C USA-45 WOR-45 DIPLOM CONFER COLONIAL ARMS/CONT BAL/PAY EQUILIB SOVEREIGN ...DECISION 19/20 MEXIC/AMER. PAGE 56 A1156
BIBLIOG/A INT/ORG INT/LAW DELIB/GP

B10
GRIFFIN A.P.C.,LIST OF REFERENCES ON RECIPROCITY (2ND REV. ED.). CANADA CUBA UK USA-45 WOR-45 NAT/G TARIFFS CONFER COLONIAL CONTROL SANCTION CONSEN ALL/VALS...DECISION 19/20. PAGE 56 A1157
BIBLIOG/A VOL/ASSN DIPLOM REPAR

N19
FANI-KAYODE R.,BLACKISM (PAMPHLET). AFR WOR+45 INT/ORG BAL/PWR CONTROL CENTRAL...DECISION 20 UN. PAGE 44 A0896
RACE/REL ECO/UNDEV REGION DIPLOM

B33
WAMBAUCH S.,PLEBISCITES SINCE THE WORLD WAR: WITH A COLLECTION OF OFFICIAL DOCUMENTS. WOR-45 COLONIAL SANCTION...MAJORIT DECISION CHARTS BIBLIOG 19/20 WWI. PAGE 161 A3272
DIPLOM CONSTN NAT/G CHOOSE

B38
HAGUE PERMANENT CT INTL JUSTIC,WORLD COURT REPORTS: COLLECTION OF THE JUDGEMENTS ORDERS AND OPINIONS VOLUME 3 1932-35. WOR-45 LAW DELIB/GP CONFER WAR PEACE ATTIT...DECISION ANTHOL 20 WORLD/CT CASEBOOK. PAGE 59 A1214
INT/ORG CT/SYS DIPLOM ADJUD

B40
WOLFERS A.,BRITAIN AND FRANCE BETWEEN TWO WORLD WARS. FRANCE UK INT/ORG NAT/G PLAN BARGAIN ECO/TAC AGREE ISOLAT ALL/IDEOS...DECISION GEOG 20 TREATY VERSAILLES INTERVENT. PAGE 166 A3380
DIPLOM WAR POLICY

B43
HAGUE PERMANENT CT INTL JUSTIC,WORLD COURT REPORTS:
INT/ORG

COLLECTION OF THE JUDGEMENTS ORDERS AND OPINIONS VOLUME 4 1936-42. WOR-45 CONFER PEACE ATTIT ...DECISION JURID ANTHOL 20 WORLD/CT CASEBOOK. PAGE 59 A1215 CT/SYS DIPLOM ADJUD

B44
FULLER G.H.,MILITARY GOVERNMENT: A LIST OF REFERENCES (A PAMPHLET). ITALY UK USA-45 WOR-45 LAW FORCES DOMIN ADMIN ARMS/CONT ORD/FREE PWR ...DECISION 20 CHINJAP. PAGE 50 A1023 BIBLIOG DIPLOM CIVMIL/REL SOVEREIGN

B48
WHEELER-BENNETT J.W.,MUNICH: PROLOGUE TO TRAGEDY. EUR+WWI FRANCE GERMANY UK PLAN PROB/SOLV SOVEREIGN ...POLICY DECISION 20 HITLER/A. PAGE 163 A3327 DIPLOM WAR PEACE

L49
HEINDEL R.H.,"THE NORTH ATLANTIC TREATY IN THE UNITED STATES SENATE." CONSTN POL/PAR CHIEF DEBATE LEAD ROUTINE WAR PEACE...CHARTS UN SENATE NATO. PAGE 64 A1309 DECISION PARL/PROC LEGIS INT/ORG

B50
ALMOND G.A.,THE AMERICAN PEOPLE AND FOREIGN POLICY. USA+45 USA-45 CULTURE SOCIETY STRUCT CONSEN PERSON PWR POPULISM...TIME/SEQ TREND 20 COLD/WAR. PAGE 6 A0129 ATTIT DIPLOM DECISION ELITES

B50
MOCKFORD J.,SOUTH-WEST AFRICA AND THE INTERNATIONAL COURT (PAMPHLET). AFR GERMANY SOUTH/AFR UK ECO/UNDEV DIPLOM CONTROL DISCRIM...DECISION JURID 20 AFRICA/SW. PAGE 102 A2094 COLONIAL SOVEREIGN INT/LAW DOMIN

B51
JENNINGS I.,THE COMMONWEALTH IN ASIA. CEYLON INDIA PAKISTAN CULTURE STRATA NAT/G LEGIS DIPLOM COLONIAL ATTIT...DECISION 20 CMN/WLTH. PAGE 74 A1507 CONSTN INT/ORG POLICY PLAN

S51
CONNERY R.H.,"THE MUTUAL DEFENSE ASSISTANCE PROGRAM." COM EUR+WWI KOREA USA+45 NAT/G VOL/ASSN CREATE PLAN BAL/PWR EDU/PROP PERCEPT...POLICY DECISION CONCPT NATO 20. PAGE 29 A0587 INT/ORG FORCES FOR/AID

B53
MATLOFF M.,STRATEGIC PLANNING FOR COALITION WARFARE. UK USA-45 CHIEF DIPLOM EXEC GOV/REL ...METH/COMP 20. PAGE 96 A1967 WAR PLAN DECISION FORCES

B53
MCNEILL W.H.,AMERICA, BRITAIN, AND RUSSIA; THEIR COOPERATION AND CONFLICT. UK USA-45 USSR ECO/DEV ECO/UNDEV FORCES PLAN ADMIN AGREE PERS/REL ...DECISION 20 TREATY. PAGE 98 A2021 WAR DIPLOM DOMIN

S53
LINCOLN G.,"FACTORS DETERMINING ARMS AID." COM FUT USA+45 USSR WOR+45 ECO/DEV NAT/G CONSULT PLAN TEC/DEV DIPLOM DOMIN EDU/PROP PERCEPT PWR ...DECISION CONCPT TREND MARX/KARL 20. PAGE 89 A1819 FORCES POLICY BAL/PWR FOR/AID

B54
GROSS F.,FOREIGN POLICY ANALYSIS. USA+45 TOP/EX PLAN INGP/REL ATTIT TECHRACY...CONCPT 20. PAGE 57 A1171 POLICY DIPLOM DECISION EDU/PROP

B54
KENNAN G.F.,REALITIES OF AMERICAN FOREIGN POLICY. USA+45 INT/ORG NUC/PWR TOTALISM 20 COLD/WAR. PAGE 77 A1586 DIPLOM BAL/PWR DECISION DETER

B56
BUREAU OF PUBLIC AFFAIRS,AMERICAN FOREIGN POLICY: CURRENT DOCUMENTS. COM USA+45 USSR WOR+45 DELIB/GP FOR/AID INT/TRADE ARMS/CONT NUC/PWR ALL/VALS ALL/IDEOS...DECISION 20 NATO. PAGE 21 A0434 BIBLIOG/A DIPLOM POLICY

B56
ESTEP R.,AN AIR POWER BIBLIOGRAPHY. USA+45 TEC/DEV BUDGET DIPLOM EDU/PROP DETER CIVMIL/REL...DECISION INT/LAW 20. PAGE 42 A0862 BIBLIOG/A FORCES WEAPON PLAN

B56
KOENIG L.W.,THE TRUMAN ADMINISTRATION: ITS PRINCIPLES AND PRACTICE. USA+45 POL/PAR CHIEF LEGIS DIPLOM DEATH NUC/PWR WAR CIVMIL/REL PEACE ...DECISION 20 TRUMAN/HS PRESIDENT TREATY. PAGE 81 A1658 ADMIN POLICY EX/STRUC GOV/REL

B56
REITZEL W.,UNITED STATES FOREIGN POLICY, 1945-1955. USA+45 WOR+45 CONSTN INT/ORG EDU/PROP LEGIT EXEC COERCE NUC/PWR PEACE ATTIT ORD/FREE PWR...DECISION CONCPT OBS RECORD TIME/SEQ TREND COLD/WAR UN CONGRESS. PAGE 120 A2464 NAT/G POLICY DIPLOM

B56
SPROUT H.,MAN-MILIEU RELATIONSHIP HYPOTHESES IN THE CONTEXT OF INTERNATIONAL POLITICS. UNIV PROB/SOLV BIO/SOC PERSON...DECISION GEOG SOC METH/CNCPT PREDICT 20. PAGE 136 A2792 HABITAT DIPLOM CONCPT DRIVE

C56
VAGTS A.,"DEFENSE AND DIPLOMACY: THE SOLDIER AND THE CONDUCT OF FOREIGN RELATIONS." OP/RES CONFER DETER WAR PEACE RESPECT...POLICY DECISION CONCPT BIBLIOG 17/20. PAGE 158 A3209 DIPLOM FORCES HIST/WRIT

B57
CASTLE E.W.,THE GREAT GIVEAWAY: THE REALITIES OF FOREIGN AID. USA+45 DIPLOM EDU/PROP NEUTRAL ...DECISION 20. PAGE 25 A0508 FOR/AID GIVE ECO/UNDEV PROB/SOLV

B57
KAPLAN M.A.,SYSTEM AND PROCESS OF INTERNATIONAL POLITICS. FUT WOR+45 WOR-45 SOCIETY PLAN BAL/PWR ADMIN ATTIT PERSON RIGID/FLEX PWR SOVEREIGN ...DECISION TREND VAL/FREE. PAGE 76 A1560 INT/ORG DIPLOM

B57
KISSINGER H.A.,NUCLEAR WEAPONS AND FOREIGN POLICY. FUT USA+45 WOR+45 INT/ORG FORCES ACT/RES TEC/DEV DIPLOM ARMS/CONT COERCE ATTIT KNOWL PWR...DECISION GEOG CHARTS 20. PAGE 80 A1640 PLAN DETER NUC/PWR

S57
DEUTSCH K.W.,"MASS COMMUNICATIONS AND THE LOSS OF FREEDOM IN NATIONAL DECISION MAKING." FUT WOR+45 SOCIETY COM/IND INT/ORG NAT/G ACT/RES CREATE TEC/DEV EDU/PROP MAJORITY PERCEPT...METH/CNCPT 20. PAGE 36 A0737 COERCE DECISION WAR

S57
HOAG M.W.,"ECONOMIC PROBLEMS OF ALLIANCE." COM EUR+WWI WOR+45 ECO/DEV ECO/UNDEV NAT/G VOL/ASSN FORCES PLAN TEC/DEV DIPLOM COERCE ORD/FREE PWR WEALTH...DECISION GEN/LAWS NATO COLD/WAR. PAGE 65 A1345 INT/ORG ECO/TAC

S57
SCHELLING T.C.,"BARGAINING COMMUNICATION, AND LIMITED WAR." UNIV WOR+45 FACE/GP INT/ORG NAT/G FORCES ACT/RES WAR PERCEPT ALL/VALS...PSY OBS PROJ/TEST CHARTS HYPO/EXP GEN/LAWS TOT/POP 20. PAGE 128 A2622 ROUTINE DECISION

B58
PALMER E.E.,AMERICAN FOREIGN POLICY. USA+45 CULTURE ECO/UNDEV NAT/G PLAN GIVE BAL/PAY ORD/FREE WEALTH POPULISM...DECISION ANTHOL 20. PAGE 113 A2319 DIPLOM ECO/TAC POLICY

S58
BLAISDELL D.C.,"PRESSURE GROUPS, FOREIGN POLICIES, AND INTERNATIONAL POLITICS." USA+45 WOR+45 INT/ORG PLAN DOMIN EDU/PROP LEGIT ADMIN ROUTINE CHOOSE ...DECISION MGT METH/CNCPT CON/ANAL 20. PAGE 15 A0303 PROF/ORG PWR

S58
LASSWELL H.D.,"THE SCIENTIFIC STUDY OF INTERNATIONAL RELATIONS." USA+45 INT/ORG CREATE EDU/PROP DETER ATTIT PERCEPT PWR...DECISION CONCPT METH/CNCPT STYLE CON/ANAL 20. PAGE 85 A1740 PHIL/SCI GEN/METH DIPLOM

S58
SINGER J.D.,"THREAT PERCEPTION AND THE ARMAMENT TENSION DILEMMA." WOR+45 WOR-45 ELITES INT/ORG NAT/G DELIB/GP PLAN LEGIT COERCE DETER ATTIT RIGID/FLEX PWR...DECISION PSY 20. PAGE 133 A2724 PERCEPT ARMS/CONT BAL/PWR

C58
GOLAY J.F.,"THE FOUNDING OF THE FEDERAL REPUBLIC OF GERMANY." GERMANY/W CONSTN EX/STRUC DIPLOM ADMIN CHOOSE...DECISION BIBLIOG 20. PAGE 53 A1088 FEDERAL NAT/G PARL/PROC POL/PAR

B59
ALWAN M.,ALGERIA BEFORE THE UNITED NATIONS. AFR ASIA FRANCE ISLAM S/ASIA CONSTN SOCIETY STRUCT INT/ORG NAT/G ECO/TAC ADMIN COLONIAL NAT/LISM ATTIT PWR...DECISION TREND 420 UN. PAGE 7 A0133 PLAN RIGID/FLEX DIPLOM ALGERIA

B59
DAWSON R.H.,THE DECISION TO AID RUSSIA* FOREIGN POLICY AND DOMESTIC POLITICS. GERMANY USSR CHIEF EX/STRUC LEGIS TOP/EX PROB/SOLV WAR ATTIT...POLICY CONGRESS. PAGE 34 A0695 DECISION DELIB/GP DIPLOM FOR/AID

L59
KAPLAN M.A.,"SOME PROBLEMS IN THE STRATEGIC ANALYSIS OF INTERNATIONAL POLITICS." UNIV R+D INT/ORG CREATE PLAN DIPLOM EDU/PROP COERCE DISPL PWR...METH/CNCPT NEW/IDEA HYPO/EXP TOT/POP 20. PAGE 76 A1561 DECISION BAL/PWR

S59
FISCHER L.,"THE SOVIET-AMERICAN ANTAGONISM: HOW WILL IT END." CONSTN CULTURE PLAN TEC/DEV RIGID/FLEX SUPEGO ORD/FREE...MARXIST DECISION PSY CONCPT CON/ANAL GEN/LAWS VAL/FREE 20 COLD/WAR. PAGE 46 A0936 USA+45 PWR DIPLOM USSR

S59
PUGWASH CONFERENCE,"ON BIOLOGICAL AND CHEMICAL WARFARE." WOR+45 SOCIETY PROC/MFG INT/ORG FORCES EDU/PROP ADJUD RIGID/FLEX ORD/FREE PWR...DECISION PSY NEW/IDEA MATH VAL/FREE 20. PAGE 118 A2417 ACT/RES BIO/SOC WAR WEAPON

S59
QUIGLEY H.S.,"TOWARD REAPPRAISAL OF OUR CHINA POLICY." CHINA/COM USA+45 INT/ORG PLAN ECO/TAC PERCEPT ORD/FREE...DECISION PSY CON/ANAL GEN/METH VAL/FREE 20. PAGE 118 A2427 ASIA KNOWL DIPLOM

S59
SAYEGH F.,"ARAB NATIONALISM AND SOVIET-AMERICAN RELATIONS." ISLAM USA+45 ECO/UNDEV PLAN ECO/TAC LEGIT NAT/LISM DRIVE PERCEPT KNOWL PWR...DECISION CONCPT STAT RECORD TREND CON/ANAL VAL/FREE 20 COLD/WAR. PAGE 127 A2610 DIPLOM USSR

B60
HOFFMANN S.H.,CONTEMPORARY THEORY IN INTERNATIONAL DIPLOM
RELATIONS. RATIONAL...SOC METH/CNCPT METH/COMP METH
SIMUL ANTHOL 20. PAGE 66 A1359 PHIL/SCI
DECISION

B60
KINGSTON-MCCLOUG E.,DEFENSE; POLICY AND STRATEGY. FORCES
UK SEA AIR TEC/DEV DIPLOM ADMIN LEAD WAR ORD/FREE PLAN
...CHARTS 20. PAGE 79 A1627 POLICY
DECISION

B60
LANDHEER B.,ETHICAL VALUES IN INTERNATIONAL HYPO/EXP
DECISION-MAKING. FUT LAW SOCIETY INT/ORG NAT/G POLICY
DELIB/GP CREATE NAT/LISM ATTIT PERSON...DECISION PEACE
CONCPT LEAGUE/NAT TOT/POP 20. PAGE 84 A1718

B60
LE GHAIT E.,NO CARTE BLANCHE TO CAPRICORN; THE DETER
FOLLY OF NUCLEAR WAR. WOR+45 INT/ORG BAL/PWR DIPLOM NUC/PWR
RISK COERCE...CENSUS 20 NATO. PAGE 86 A1754 PLAN
DECISION

B60
PRICE D.,THE SECRETARY OF STATE. USA+45 CONSTN CONSULT
ELITES INTELL CHIEF EX/STRUC TOP/EX LEGIT ATTIT PWR DIPLOM
SKILL...DECISION 20 CONGRESS. PAGE 117 A2410 INT/LAW

L60
DEAN A.W.,"SECOND GENEVA CONFERENCE OF THE LAW OF INT/ORG
THE SEA: THE FIGHT FOR FREEDOM OF THE SEAS." FUT JURID
USA+45 USSR WOR+45 WOR-45 SEA CONSTN STRUCT PLAN INT/LAW
INT/TRADE ADJUD ADMIN ORD/FREE...DECISION RECORD
TREND GEN/LAWS 20 TREATY. PAGE 35 A0717

S60
BRODY R.A.,"DETERRENCE STRATEGIES: AN ANNOTATED BIBLIOG/A
BIBLIOGRAPHY." WOR+45 PLAN ARMS/CONT NUC/PWR WAR FORCES
WEAPON DECISION. PAGE 19 A0383 DETER
DIPLOM

S60
DOUGHERTY J.E.,"KEY TO SECURITY: DISARMAMENT OR FORCES
ARMS STABILITY." COM USA+45 USSR INT/ORG NAT/G ORD/FREE
CREATE EDU/PROP COERCE DETER ATTIT PWR...DECISION ARMS/CONT
CONCPT MYTH NEW/IDEA TREND 20 COLD/WAR. PAGE 38 NUC/PWR
A0777

S60
WRIGHT Q.,"LEGAL ASPECTS OF THE U-2 INCIDENT." COM PWR
USA+45 USSR STRUCT NAT/G FORCES PLAN TEC/DEV ADJUD POLICY
RIGID/FLEX MORAL ORD/FREE...DECISION INT/LAW JURID SPACE
PSY TREND GEN/LAWS COLD/WAR VAL/FREE 20 U-2.
PAGE 168 A3413

B61
BRENNAN D.G.,ARMS CONTROL, DISARMAMENT, AND ARMS/CONT
NATIONAL SECURITY. WOR+45 NAT/G FORCES CREATE ORD/FREE
PROB/SOLV PARTIC WAR PEACE...DECISION INT/LAW DIPLOM
ANTHOL BIBLIOG 20. PAGE 18 A0372 POLICY

B61
BULL H.,THE CONTROL OF THE ARMS RACE. COM USA+45 FORCES
INT/ORG NAT/G PLAN TEC/DEV DIPLOM ATTIT...RELATIV PWR
DECISION CONCPT SELF/OBS TREND CON/ANAL GEN/METH 20 ARMS/CONT
COLD/WAR. PAGE 21 A0429 NUC/PWR

B61
GALLOIS P.,THE BALANCE OF TERROR: STRATEGY FOR THE PLAN
NUCLEAR AGE. FUT WOR+45 INT/ORG FORCES TOP/EX DETER DECISION
WAR ATTIT RIGID/FLEX ORD/FREE PWR...HYPO/EXP 20. DIPLOM
PAGE 50 A1032 NUC/PWR

B61
KNORR K.E.,THE INTERNATIONAL SYSTEM. FUT SOCIETY ACT/RES
INT/ORG NAT/G PLAN BAL/PWR DIPLOM WAR PWR SIMUL
...DECISION METH/CNCPT CONT/OBS GAME METH UN 20. ECO/UNDEV
PAGE 81 A1655

B61
LERCHE C.O. JR.,FOREIGN POLICY OF THE AMERICAN DECISION
PEOPLE (REV. ED.). USA+45 USSR FORCES TEC/DEV PLAN
EDU/PROP WAR PRODUC ORD/FREE MARXISM...POLICY TREND PEACE
BIBLIOG 20 COLD/WAR. PAGE 87 A1781 DIPLOM

B61
MILLER R.I.,DAG HAMMARSKJOLD AND CRISES DIPLOMACY. DIPLOM
WOR+45 NAT/G PROB/SOLV LEAD ROLE...DECISION BIOG UN INT/ORG
HAMMARSK/D. PAGE 101 A2079 CHIEF

B61
ROSENAU J.N.,INTERNATIONAL POLITICS AND FOREIGN ACT/RES
POLICY: A READER IN RESEARCH AND THEORY. ELITES DIPLOM
ATTIT SOVEREIGN...DECISION CHARTS HYPO/EXP GAME CONCPT
SIMUL ANTHOL BIBLIOG METH 20. PAGE 124 A2531 POLICY

B61
SINGER J.D.,FINANCING INTERNATIONAL ORGANIZATION: INT/ORG
THE UNITED NATIONS BUDGET PROCESS. WOR+45 FINAN MGT
ACT/RES CREATE PLAN BUDGET ECO/TAC ADMIN ROUTINE
ATTIT KNOWL...DECISION METH/CNCPT TIME/SEQ UN 20.
PAGE 133 A2726

S61
TRAMPE G.,"DIE FORM DER DIPLOMATIC ALS POLITSCHE CONSULT
WAFFE." WOR+45 WOR-45 SOCIETY STRATA INT/ORG NAT/G PWR
ACT/RES PLAN ECO/TAC EDU/PROP COERCE WAR ATTIT DIPLOM
RIGID/FLEX...DECISION CONCPT TREND. PAGE 145 A2959

B62
ALTHING F.A.M.,EUROPEAN ORGANIZATIONS AND FOREIGN DELIB/GP
RELATIONS OF STATES: A COMPARATIVE ANALYSIS OF INT/ORG
DECISION-MAKING. EUR+WWI CONSTN ELITES BAL/PWR DECISION
INT/TRADE SOVEREIGN TREATY. PAGE 6 A0131 DIPLOM

B62
BAILEY S.D.,THE SECRETARIAT OF THE UNITED NATIONS. INT/ORG
FUT WOR+45 DELIB/GP PLAN BAL/PWR DOMIN EDU/PROP EXEC
ADMIN PEACE ATTIT PWR...DECISION CONCPT TREND DIPLOM
CON/ANAL CHARTS UN VAL/FREE COLD/WAR 20. PAGE 10
A0205

B62
BOULDING K.E.,CONFLICT AND DEFENSE: A GENERAL MATH
THEORY. FUT SOCIETY INT/ORG NAT/G CREATE BAL/PWR SIMUL
COERCE NAT/LISM DRIVE ALL/VALS...PLURIST DECISION PEACE
CONCPT METH/CNCPT TREND HYPO/EXP TOT/POP 20. WAR
PAGE 17 A0347

B62
BUCHMANN J.,L'AFRIQUE NOIRE INDEPENDANTE. POL/PAR AFR
DIPLOM COLONIAL PARTIC CHOOSE GP/REL ATTIT ORD/FREE NAT/LISM
WEALTH NEGRO. PAGE 21 A0426 DECISION

B62
CARLSTON K.S.,LAW AND ORGANIZATION IN WORLD INT/ORG
SOCIETY. WOR+45 FINAN ECO/TAC DOMIN LEGIT CT/SYS LAW
ROUTINE COERCE ORD/FREE PWR WEALTH...PLURIST
DECISION JURID MGT METH/CNCPT GEN/LAWS 20. PAGE 24
A0487

B62
HADWEN J.G.,HOW UNITED NATIONS DECISIONS ARE MADE. INT/ORG
WOR+45 LAW EDU/PROP LEGIT ADMIN PWR...DECISION ROUTINE
SELF/OBS GEN/LAWS UN 20. PAGE 59 A1212

B62
HUNTINGTON S.P.,CHANGING PATTERNS OF MILITARY FORCES
POLITICS. EUR+WWI L/A+17C S/ASIA USA+45 WOR+45 RIGID/FLEX
CULTURE INT/ORG NAT/G CONSULT PLAN DOMIN EDU/PROP
LEGIT DETER WAR ATTIT PERSON PWR...DECISION CONCPT
SIMUL GEN/LAWS ANTHOL COLD/WAR 20. PAGE 69 A1419

B62
JORDAN A.A. JR.,FOREIGN AID AND THE DEFENSE OF FOR/AID
SOUTHEAST ASIA. PAKISTAN VIETNAM/S FINAN PLAN S/ASIA
BUDGET ECO/TAC DETER WAR ORD/FREE...POLICY DECISION FORCES
CENSUS CHARTS BIBLIOG 20. PAGE 75 A1535 ECO/UNDEV

B62
MONCRIEFF A.,THE STRATEGY OF SURVIVAL. UK FORCES PLAN
BAL/PWR CONFER DETER WAR...ANTHOL 20 COLD/WAR. DECISION
PAGE 102 A2104 DIPLOM
ARMS/CONT

B62
STRAUSS L.L.,MEN AND DECISIONS. USA+45 USA-45 USSR DECISION
CONSULT FORCES TOP/EX WAR PEACE 20. PAGE 139 A2844 PWR
NUC/PWR
DIPLOM

B62
US SENATE COMM GOVT OPERATIONS,ADMINISTRATION OF ORD/FREE
NATIONAL SECURITY. USA+45 CHIEF PLAN PROB/SOLV ADMIN
TEC/DEV DIPLOM ATTIT...POLICY DECISION 20 NAT/G
KENNEDY/JF RUSK/D MCNAMARA/R BUNDY/M HERTER/C. CONTROL
PAGE 156 A3173

S62
FINKELSTEIN L.S.,"THE UNITED NATIONS AND INT/ORG
ORGANIZATIONS FOR CONTROL OF ARMAMENT." FUT WOR+45 PWR
VOL/ASSN DELIB/GP TOP/EX CREATE EDU/PROP LEGIT ARMS/CONT
ADJUD NUC/PWR ATTIT RIGID/FLEX ORD/FREE...POLICY
DECISION CONCPT OBS TREND GEN/LAWS TOT/POP
COLD/WAR. PAGE 46 A0933

S62
NORTH R.C.,"DECISION MAKING IN CRISIS: AN INT/ORG
INTRODUCTION." WOR+45 WOR-45 NAT/G CONSULT DELIB/GP ROUTINE
TEC/DEV PERCEPT KNOWL...POLICY DECISION PSY DIPLOM
METH/CNCPT CONT/OBS TREND VAL/FREE 20. PAGE 110
A2251

C62
ROBINSON J.A.,"CONGRESS AND FOREIGN POLICY-MAKING: LEGIS
A STUDY IN LEGISLATIVE INFLUENCE AND INITIATIVE." DIPLOM
USA+45 CHIEF DELIB/GP CREATE CONTROL EXEC GOV/REL POLICY
PERCEPT...TREND BIBLIOG 20 CONGRESS. PAGE 122 A2505 DECISION

B63
ETHIOPIAN MINISTRY INFORMATION,AFRICAN SUMMIT AFR
CONFERENCE ADDIS ABABA, ETHIOPIA, 1963. ETHIOPIA CONFER
DELIB/GP COLONIAL NAT/LISM...POLICY DECISION 20. REGION
PAGE 42 A0865 DIPLOM

B63
FRANKEL J.,THE MAKING OF FOREIGN POLICY: AN POLICY
ANALYSIS OF DECISION-MAKING. CHINA/COM EUR+WWI DECISION
USA+45 ELITES INTELL FORCES LEGIS PLAN ATTIT PROB/SOLV
ALL/VALS MORAL CONSERVE...GOV/COMP 20 PRESIDENT UN DIPLOM
TREATY. PAGE 48 A0981

B63
GILBERT M.,THE APPEASERS. COM GERMANY UK PLAN DIPLOM
ECO/TAC COLONIAL CONTROL EXEC ORD/FREE PWR FASCISM WAR
20 PARLIAMENT. PAGE 52 A1068 POLICY
DECISION

B63
HINSLEY F.H.,POWER AND THE PURSUIT OF PEACE. WOR+45 DIPLOM
WOR-45 PLAN RIGID/FLEX ALL/VALS ALL/IDEOS...POLICY CONSTN
DECISION INT/LAW 12/20 ROUSSEAU/J KANT/I BENTHAM/J PEACE
LEAGUE/NAT. PAGE 65 A1338 COERCE

B63
LINDBERG L.,POLITICAL DYNAMICS OF EUROPEAN ECONOMIC MARKET
INTEGRATION. EUR+WWI ECO/DEV INT/ORG VOL/ASSN ECO/TAC

DELIB/GP ADMIN WEALTH...DECISION EEC 20. PAGE 89 A1820

B63
MCDOUGAL M.S.,LAW AND PUBLIC ORDER IN SPACE. FUT USA+45 ACT/RES TEC/DEV ADJUD...POLICY INT/LAW JURID 20. PAGE 98 A2009 SPACE ORD/FREE DIPLOM DECISION

B63
PACHTER H.M.,COLLISION COURSE; THE CUBAN MISSILE CRISIS AND COEXISTENCE. CUBA USA+45 DIPLOM ARMS/CONT PEACE MARXISM...DECISION INT/LAW 20 COLD/WAR KHRUSH/N KENNEDY/JF CASTRO/F. PAGE 112 A2307 WAR BAL/PWR NUC/PWR DETER

B63
SMITH J.E.,THE DEFENSE OF BERLIN. COM GUATEMALA WOR+45 ECO/TAC ADMIN NEUTRAL ATTIT ORD/FREE SOVEREIGN...DECISION 20 DEPT/STATE. PAGE 134 A2747 DIPLOM FORCES BAL/PWR PLAN

B63
THORELLI H.B.,INTOP: INTERNATIONAL OPERATIONS SIMULATION: PLAYER'S MANUAL. BRAZIL FINAN OP/RES ADMIN GP/REL INGP/REL PRODUC PERCEPT...DECISION MGT EEC. PAGE 144 A2935 GAME INT/TRADE EDU/PROP LG/CO

B63
US DEPARTMENT OF STATE,POLITICAL BEHAVIOR--A LIST OF CURRENT STUDIES. USA+45 COM/IND DIPLOM LEAD PERS/REL DRIVE PERCEPT KNOWL...DECISION SIMUL METH. PAGE 151 A3093 BIBLIOG METH/COMP GP/REL ATTIT

S63
CLEVELAND H.,"CRISIS DIPLOMACY." USA+45 WOR+45 LAW FORCES TASK NUC/PWR PWR 20. PAGE 27 A0551 DECISION DIPLOM PROB/SOLV POLICY

S63
LIPSHART A.,"THE ANALYSIS OF BLOC VOTING IN THE GENERAL ASSEMBLY." L/A+17C WOR+45 ACT/RES INGP/REL ...POLICY DECISION NEW/IDEA STAT IDEA/COMP UN. PAGE 90 A1832 CHOOSE INT/ORG DELIB/GP

B64
BLACKSTOCK P.W.,THE STRATEGY OF SUBVERSION. USA+45 FORCES EDU/PROP ADMIN COERCE GOV/REL...DECISION MGT 20 DEPT/DEFEN CIA DEPT/STATE. PAGE 15 A0301 ORD/FREE DIPLOM CONTROL

B64
DEITCHMAN S.J.,LIMITED WAR AND AMERICAN DEFENSE POLICY. USA+45 WOR+45 INT/ORG NAT/G PLAN TEC/DEV COERCE NUC/PWR RIGID/FLEX PWR SKILL...DECISION METH/CNCPT TIME/SEQ TOT/POP COLD/WAR 20. PAGE 36 A0726 FORCES WAR WEAPON

B64
ECONOMIDES C.P.,LE POUVOIR DE DECISION DES ORGANISATIONS INTERNATIONALES EUROPEENNES. DIPLOM DOMIN INGP/REL EFFICIENCY...INT/LAW JURID 20 NATO OEEC EEC COUNCL/EUR EURATOM. PAGE 40 A0821 INT/ORG PWR DECISION GP/COMP

B64
HARRISON H.V.,THE ROLE OF THEORY IN INTERNATIONAL RELATIONS. UNIV WOR+45 R+D INT/ORG NAT/G PERCEPT KNOWL...DECISION CONCPT GEN/METH METH 20. PAGE 62 A1270 METH/CNCPT HYPO/EXP DIPLOM

B64
KULSKI W.W.,INTERNATIONAL POLITICS IN A REVOLUTIONARY AGE. NEUTRAL NAT/LISM...POLICY DECISION INT/LAW CONCPT 20 UN. PAGE 83 A1693 DIPLOM WAR NUC/PWR INT/ORG

B64
STEWART C.F.,A BIBLIOGRAPHY OF INTERNATIONAL BUSINESS. WOR+45 FINAN LG/CO NAT/G PLAN ECO/TAC TARIFFS...DECISION MGT GP/COMP NAT/COMP 20 EEC. PAGE 138 A2824 BIBLIOG INT/ORG OP/RES INT/TRADE

B64
US SENATE COMM GOVT OPERATIONS,ADMINISTRATION OF NATIONAL SECURITY. USA+45 CHIEF TOP/EX PLAN DIPLOM CONTROL PEACE...POLICY DECISION 20 PRESIDENT CONGRESS. PAGE 156 A3176 ADMIN FORCES ORD/FREE NAT/G

L64
ARMENGALD A.,"ECONOMIE ET COEXISTENCE." COM EUR+WWI FUT USA+45 WOR+45 ECO/DEV ECO/UNDEV FINAN INT/ORG NAT/G EXEC CHOOSE ATTIT ALL/VALS...POLICY RELATIV DECISION TREND SOC/EXP COLD/WAR WORK 20. PAGE 9 A0173 MARKET ECO/TAC CAP/ISM

S64
BEIM D.,"THE COMMUNIST BLOC AND THE FOREIGN-AID GAME." WOR+45 NAT/G PLAN ROUTINE ATTIT KNOWL ORD/FREE...DECISION QUANT CONT/OBS TIME/SEQ CHARTS GAME SIMUL COLD/WAR 20. PAGE 12 A0252 COM ECO/UNDEV ECO/TAC FOR/AID

S64
GARDNER R.N.,"GATT AND THE UNITED NATIONS CONFERENCE ON TRADE AND DEVELOPMENT." USA+45 WOR+45 SOCIETY ECO/UNDEV MARKET NAT/G DELIB/GP ACT/RES PLAN ECO/TAC TARIFFS EDU/PROP ROUTINE DRIVE RIGID/FLEX WEALTH...DECISION MGT TREND UN TOT/POP 20 GATT. PAGE 51 A1047 INT/ORG INT/TRADE

S64
KHAN M.Z.,"THE PRESIDENT OF THE GENERAL ASSEMBLY." WOR+45 CONSTN DELIB/GP EDU/PROP LEGIT ROUTINE PWR RESPECT SKILL...DECISION SOC BIOG TREND UN 20. PAGE 78 A1609 INT/ORG TOP/EX

S64
RUSK D.,"THE MAKING OF FOREIGN POLICY" USA+45 CHIEF DELIB/GP WORKER PROB/SOLV ADMIN ATTIT PWR ...DECISION 20 DEPT/STATE RUSK/D GOLDMAN/E. PAGE 125 A2570 DIPLOM INT POLICY

S64
TAUBENFELD R.K.,"INDEPENDENT REVENUE FOR THE UNITED NATIONS." WOR+45 SOCIETY STRUCT INDUS NAT/G CONSULT ACT/RES PLAN ECO/TAC LEGIT WEALTH...DECISION CON/ANAL GEN/METH UN 20. PAGE 142 A2896 INT/ORG FINAN

B65
FRANKLAND N.,THE BOMBING OFFENSIVE AGAINST GERMANY. GERMANY UK TEC/DEV DIPLOM WAR...METH/COMP 20. PAGE 48 A0985 WEAPON PLAN DECISION FORCES

B65
LINDBLOM C.E.,THE INTELLIGENCE OF DEMOCRACY; DECISION MAKING THROUGH MUTUAL ADJUSTMENT. WOR+45 SOCIETY NAT/G PROB/SOLV DOMIN PARTIC GP/REL ORD/FREE...POLICY IDEA/COMP BIBLIOG 20. PAGE 89 A1821 PLURISM DECISION ADJUST DIPLOM

B65
MACDONALD R.W.,THE LEAGUE OF ARAB STATES: A STUDY IN THE DYNAMICS OF REGIONAL ORGANIZATION. ISRAEL UAR USSR FINAN INT/ORG DELIB/GP ECO/TAC AGREE NEUTRAL ORD/FREE PWR...DECISION BIBLIOG 20 TREATY UN. PAGE 92 A1888 ISLAM REGION DIPLOM ADMIN

B65
RANSOM H.H.,AN AMERICAN FOREIGN POLICY READER. USA+45 FORCES EDU/PROP COERCE NUC/PWR WAR PEACE ...DECISION 20. PAGE 119 A2443 NAT/G DIPLOM POLICY

B65
RAPPAPORT A.,ISSUES IN AMERICAN DIPLOMACY: WORLD POWER AND LEADERSHIP SINCE 1895 (VOL. II). CHINA/COM EUR+WWI L/A+17C USA+45 USA-45 NAT/G ECO/TAC DOMIN CONFER LEAD NUC/PWR WEAPON...DECISION 19/20 WILSON/W ROOSEVLT/F CHINJAP. PAGE 119 A2447 WAR POLICY DIPLOM

B65
RUBINSTEIN A.Z.,THE CHALLENGE OF POLITICS: IDEAS AND ISSUES (2ND ED.). UNIV ELITES SOCIETY EX/STRUC BAL/PWR PARL/PROC AUTHORIT...DECISION ANTHOL 20. PAGE 125 A2565 NAT/G DIPLOM GP/REL ORD/FREE

B65
UNIVERSAL REFERENCE SYSTEM,INTERNATIONAL AFFAIRS: VOLUME I IN THE POLITICAL SCIENCE, GOVERNMENT, AND PUBLIC POLICY SERIES....DECISION ECOMETRIC GEOG INT/LAW JURID MGT PHIL/SCI PSY SOC. PAGE 149 A3041 BIBLIOG/A GEN/METH COMPUT/IR DIPLOM

B65
WEIL G.L.,A HANDBOOK ON THE EUROPEAN ECONOMIC COMMUNITY. BELGIUM EUR+WWI FRANCE GERMANY/W ITALY CONSTN ECO/DEV CREATE PARTIC GP/REL...DECISION MGT CHARTS 20 EEC. PAGE 162 A3299 INT/TRADE INT/ORG TEC/DEV INT/LAW

S65
FLEMING D.F.,"CAN PAX AMERICANA SUCCEED?" ASIA CHINA/COM EUR+WWI USSR VIETNAM BAL/PWR DIPLOM DOMIN COERCE GOV/REL 20. PAGE 46 A0948 DECISION ATTIT ECO/TAC

S65
HOLSTI O.R.,"EAST-WEST CONFLICT AND SINO-SOVIET RELATIONS" CHINA/COM USSR COMPUTER REGION DECISION. PAGE 67 A1373 VOL/ASSN DIPLOM CON/ANAL COM

S65
QUADE Q.L.,"THE TRUMAN ADMINISTRATION AND THE SEPARATION OF POWERS: THE CASE OF THE MARSHALL PLAN." SOCIETY INT/ORG NAT/G CONSULT DELIB/GP LEGIS PLAN ECO/TAC ROUTINE DRIVE PERCEPT RIGID/FLEX ORD/FREE PWR WEALTH...DECISION GEOG NEW/IDEA TREND 20 TRUMAN/HS. PAGE 118 A2422 USA+45 ECO/UNDEV DIPLOM

C65
US AIR FORCE ACADEMY,"AMERICAN DEFENSE POLICY." COM INT/ORG TEC/DEV FOR/AID ARMS/CONT DETER NUC/PWR ...POLICY DECISION CONCPT ANTHOL BIBLIOG/A 20 COLD/WAR NATO. PAGE 149 A3054 PLAN FORCES WAR COERCE

B66
CLAUSEWITZ C.V.,ON WAR (VOL. III). UNIV EDU/PROP ...POLICY DECISION METH 18/20. PAGE 27 A0548 WAR FORCES PLAN CIVMIL/REL

B66
ERICKSON J.,THE MILITARY-TECHNICAL REVOLUTION. USA+45 WOR+45 INT/ORG PLAN ATTIT...DECISION ANTHOL 20. PAGE 42 A0861 DIPLOM DETER POLICY NUC/PWR

B66
GRENVILLE J.A.S.,POLITICS, STRATEGY, AND AMERICAN DEMOCRACY: STUDIES IN FOREIGN POLICY, 1873-1917. CUBA PHILIPPINE SPAIN USA-45 VENEZUELA ELITES NAT/G CREATE PARTIC WAR RIGID/FLEX ORD/FREE...DECISION TREND 19/20 HAWAII. PAGE 56 A1146 DIPLOM COLONIAL POLICY

B66
HORELICK A.L.,STRATEGIC POWER AND SOVIET FOREIGN POLICY. CUBA USSR FORCES PLAN CIVMIL/REL...POLICY DECISION 20 COLD/WAR. PAGE 67 A1383 DIPLOM BAL/PWR DETER NUC/PWR

B66
MC CLELLAND C.A.,THEORY AND THE INTERNATIONAL DIPLOM

SYSTEM. EDU/PROP PWR...DECISION SOC METH. PAGE 97 A1991 METH/CNCPT ACT/RES R+D

B66
MOORE R.J.,SIR CHARLES WOOD'S INDIAN POLICY: 1853-66. INDIA POL/PAR CHIEF DELIB/GP DIPLOM CONTROL LEAD WOOD/CHAS. PAGE 103 A2124 COLONIAL ADMIN CONSULT DECISION

B66
SAPIN B.M.,THE MAKING OF UNITED STATES FOREIGN POLICY. USA+45 INT/ORG DELIB/GP FORCES PLAN ECO/TAC CIVMIL/REL PRESIDENT. PAGE 127 A2603 DIPLOM EX/STRUC DECISION NAT/G

B66
SKILLING H.G.,THE GOVERNMENTS OF COMMUNIST EAST EUROPE. COM EUR+WWI ELITES FORCES DIPLOM ECO/TAC CONTROL HABITAT SOCISM...DECISION BIBLIOG 20 EUROPE/E COM/PARTY. PAGE 134 A2738 MARXISM NAT/COMP GP/COMP DOMIN

B66
STADLER K.R.,THE BIRTH OF THE AUSTRIAN REPUBLIC, 1918-1921. AUSTRIA PLAN TASK PEACE...POLICY DECISION 20. PAGE 137 A2798 NAT/G DIPLOM WAR DELIB/GP

B66
WESTWOOD A.F.,FOREIGN AID IN A FOREIGN POLICY FRAMEWORK. AFR ASIA INDIA IRAN L/A+17C USA+45 USSR ECO/UNDEV AGRI FORCES LEGIS PLAN PROB/SOLV ...DECISION 20 COLD/WAR. PAGE 163 A3324 FOR/AID DIPLOM POLICY ECO/TAC

L66
MCDOUGAL M.S.,"CHINESE PARTICIPATION IN THE UNITED NATIONS: THE LEGAL IMPERATIVES OF A NEGOTIATED SOLUTION" CHINA/COM WOR+45 VOL/ASSN DIPLOM PARTIC ...DECISION IDEA/COMP 20 UN. PAGE 98 A2010 INT/ORG REPRESENT POLICY PROB/SOLV

B67
CHO S.S.,KOREA IN WORLD POLITICS 1940-1950; AN EVALUATION OF AMERICAN RESPONSIBILITY. KOREA USA+45 USSR CONSTN INT/ORG NAT/G FORCES FOR/AID ANOMIE SUPEGO MARXISM...DECISION BIBLIOG 20. PAGE 26 A0533 POLICY DIPLOM PROB/SOLV WAR

B67
ROBINSON R.D.,INTERNATIONAL MANAGEMENT. USA+45 FINAN R+D PLAN PRODUC...DECISION T. PAGE 92 A1882 INT/TRADE MGT INT/LAW MARKET

B67
PADELFORD N.J.,THE DYNAMICS OF INTERNATIONAL POLITICS (2ND ED.). WOR+45 LAW INT/ORG FORCES TEC/DEV REGION NAT/LISM PEACE ATTIT PWR ALL/IDEOS UN COLD/WAR NATO TREATY. PAGE 113 A2314 DIPLOM NAT/G POLICY DECISION

B67
SCOTT A.M.,THE FUNCTIONING OF THE INTERNATIONAL POLITICAL SYSTEM. INT/ORG OP/RES PROB/SOLV COERCE WAR EQUILIB...METH/CNCPT BIBLIOG. PAGE 130 A2671 DIPLOM DECISION BAL/PWR

B67
SINGER D.,QUANTITATIVE INTERNATIONAL POLITICS* INSIGHTS AND EVIDENCE. WOR+45 WOR-45 PARTIC WAR INGP/REL ATTIT PERSON ROLE...PREDICT BIBLIOG 19/20 UN SENATE. PAGE 133 A2722 DIPLOM NAT/G INT/ORG DECISION

B67
US SUPERINTENDENT OF DOCUMENTS,LIBRARY OF CONGRESS (PRICE LIST 83). AFR ASIA EUR+WWI USA-45 USSR NAT/G DIPLOM CONFER CT/SYS WAR...DECISION PHIL/SCI CLASSIF 19/20 CONGRESS PRESIDENT. PAGE 157 A3205 BIBLIOG/A USA+45 AUTOMAT LAW

L67
"POLITICAL PARTIES ON FOREIGN POLICY IN THE INTER-ELECTION YEARS 1962-66." ASIA COM INDIA USA+45 PLAN ATTIT...DECISION 20. PAGE 4 A0079 POL/PAR DIPLOM POLICY

L67
CAHIERS P.,"LE RECOURS EN CONSTATATION DE MANQUEMENTS DES ETATS MEMBRES DEVANT LA COUR DES COMMUNAUTES EUROPEENNES." LAW PROB/SOLV DIPLOM ADMIN CT/SYS SANCTION ATTIT...POLICY DECISION JURID ECSC EEC. PAGE 23 A0465 INT/ORG CONSTN ROUTINE ADJUD

L67
MACDONALD R.S.J.,"THE RESORT TO ECONOMIC COERCION BY INTERNATIONAL POLITICAL ORGANIZATIONS." CUBA ETHIOPIA RHODESIA SOUTH/AFR NAT/G FOR/AID INT/TRADE DOMIN CONTROL SANCTION...DECISION LEAGUE/NAT UN OAS 20. PAGE 92 A1887 INT/ORG COERCE ECO/TAC DIPLOM

L67
MOORE N.,"THE LAWFULNESS OF MILITARY ASSISTANCE TO THE REPUBLIC OF VIET NAM." USA+45 VIETNAM WOR+45 FOR/AID DOMIN DETER WAR WEAPON...DECISION INT/LAW 20 UN. PAGE 103 A2123 PWR DIPLOM FORCES GOV/REL

S67
D'AMATO D.,"LEGAL ASPECTS OF THE FRENCH NUCLEAR TESTS." FRANCE WOR+45 ACT/RES COLONIAL RISK GOV/REL EQUILIB ORD/FREE PWR DECISION. PAGE 33 A0672 INT/LAW DIPLOM NUC/PWR ADJUD

S67
ODA S.,"THE NORMALIZATION OF RELATIONS BETWEEN JAPAN AND THE REPUBLIC OF KOREA." NAT/G BAL/PWR REPAR INT/LAW. PAGE 111 A2276 DIPLOM LEGIS DECISION

S67
RABIER J.-R.,"THE EUROPEAN IDEA AND NATIONAL PUBLIC OPINIONS." ACT/RES PLAN DIPLOM PARTIC CONSEN ATTIT PERCEPT...DECISION CHARTS. PAGE 118 A2430 POLICY FEDERAL EUR+WWI PROB/SOLV

S67
SUINN R.M.,"THE DISARMAMENT FANTASY* PSYCHOLOGICAL FACTORS THAT MAY PRODUCE WARFARE." DIPLOM RISK ARMS/CONT DETER ANOMIE PERSON GAME. PAGE 140 A2860 DECISION NUC/PWR WAR PSY

S67
WEIL G.L.,"THE MERGER OF THE INSTITUTIONS OF THE EUROPEAN COMMUNITIES" EUR+WWI ECO/DEV INT/TRADE CONSEN PLURISM...DECISION MGT 20 EEC EURATOM ECSC TREATY. PAGE 162 A3300 ECO/TAC INT/ORG CENTRAL INT/LAW

DECISION-MAKING, DISIPLINE....SEE DECISION

DECISION-MAKING, INDIVIDUAL....SEE PROB/SOLV,

DECISION-MAKING, PROCEDURAL....SEE PROB/SOLV

DECISION-MAKING, THEORY....SEE GAME

DECLAR/IND....DECLARATION OF INDEPENDENCE (U.S.)

DECOTTIGNIES R. A0721

DEENER D.R. A0722

DEEP/INT....DEPTH INTERVIEWS

B64
HARPER F.,OUT OF CHINA. CHINA/COM ELITES STRATA ATTIT PERSON...BIOG 20 MAO HONG/KONG MIGRATION. PAGE 62 A1264 HABITAT DEEP/INT DIPLOM MARXISM

DEEP/QU....DEPTH QUESTIONNAIRES

S51
GYR J.,"ANALYSIS OF COMMITTEE MEMBER BEHAVIOUR IN FOUR CULTURES." ASIA ISLAM L/A+17C USA+45 INT/ORG VOL/ASSN LEGIT ATTIT...INT DEEP/QU SAMP CHARTS 20. PAGE 58 A1200 DELIB/GP CULTURE

B52
U OF MICH SURVEY RESEARCH CTR,AMERICA'S ROLE IN WORLD AFFAIRS. ASIA COM EUR+WWI USA+45 USSR FOR/AID WAR AUTHORIT ORD/FREE...DEEP/QU 20. PAGE 146 A2986 DIPLOM NAT/G ROLE POLICY

B59
MACIVER R.M.,THE NATIONS AND THE UN. WOR+45 NAT/G CONSULT ADJUD ADMIN ALL/VALS...CONCPT DEEP/QU UN TOT/POP UNESCO 20. PAGE 92 A1892 INT/ORG ATTIT DIPLOM

S63
VEROFF J.,"AFRICAN STUDENTS IN THE UNITED STATES." AFR USA+45 CULTURE ACT/RES FOR/AID PEACE ATTIT KNOWL...SOC RECORD DEEP/QU SYS/QU CHARTS STERTYP TOT/POP 20. PAGE 159 A3230 PERCEPT RIGID/FLEX RACE/REL

DEFENSE....SEE DETER, PLAN, FORCES, WAR, COERCE

DEFENSE DEPARTMENT....SEE DEPT/DEFEN

DEFINETT/B....BRUNO DEFINETTI

DEFLATION....DEFLATION

DEGAULLE/C....CHARLES DE GAULLE

B63
FULBRIGHT J.W.,PROSPECTS FOR THE WEST. COM USA+45 USSR INT/ORG NAT/G SCHOOL PROB/SOLV NUC/PWR WAR PEACE ORD/FREE...PREDICT METH/COMP 20 DEGAULLE/C. PAGE 50 A1015 DIPLOM BAL/PWR CONCPT POLICY

B63
JUDD P.,AFRICAN INDEPENDENCE: THE EXPLODING EMERGENCE OF THE NEW AFRICAN NATIONS. AFR UK LAW CONSTN CULTURE KIN DIPLOM ATTIT...CHARTS BIBLIOG 20 UN DEGAULLE/C NEGRO THIRD/WRLD. PAGE 75 A1542 ORD/FREE POLICY DOMIN LOC/G

B63
KLEIMAN R.,ATLANTIC CRISIS; AMERICAN DIPLOMACY CONFRONTS A RESURGENT EUROPE. EUR+WWI USA+45 ECO/DEV AGRI NAT/G CHIEF FORCES PLAN LEAD ATTIT ...CONCPT 20 NATO KENNEDY/JF DEGAULLE/C EEC JOHNSON/LB. PAGE 80 A1648 DIPLOM REGION POLICY

S63
KAWALKOWSKI A.,"POUR UNE EUROPE INDEPENDENTE ET REUNIFIEE." EUR+WWI FUT USA+45 USSR WOR+45 ECO/DEV PROC/MFG INT/ORG NAT/G ACT/RES TEC/DEV FEDERAL RIGID/FLEX...CONCPT METH/CNCPT OEEC TOT/POP 20 DEGAULLE/C. PAGE 77 A1573 R+D PLAN NUC/PWR

S63
MULLEY F.W.,"NUCLEAR WEAPONS: CHALLENGE TO NATIONAL SOVEREIGNTY." EUR+WWI FRANCE UK USA+45 VOL/ASSN EX/STRUC FORCES TOP/EX ACT/RES REGION DRIVE PWR 20 NATO DEGAULLE/C. PAGE 106 A2169 INT/ORG ATTIT DIPLOM NUC/PWR

B65
CALLEO D.P.,EUROPE'S FUTURE: THE GRAND ALTERNATIVES. UK INT/ORG DIPLOM PWR SOVEREIGN ...CONCPT IDEA/COMP NAT/COMP BIBLIOG 20 EEC EUROPE DEGAULLE/C NATO. PAGE 23 A0468 — FUT EUR+WWI FEDERAL NAT/LISM

B66
SPEARS E.L.,TWO MEN WHO SAVED FRANCE: PETAIN AND DE GAULLE. FRANCE CONSTN FORCES DIPLOM WAR PERSON 20 WWI PETAIN/HP DEGAULLE/C. PAGE 135 A2773 — BIOG LEAD CHIEF NAT/G

B66
US SENATE COMM ON FOREIGN REL,UNITED STATES POLICY TOWARD EUROPE (AND RELATED MATTERS). COM EUR+WWI GERMANY PROB/SOLV REGION NUC/PWR WAR NAT/LISM PEACE PWR...NAT/COMP 20 NATO CONGRESS DEGAULLE/C. PAGE 156 A3184 — DIPLOM INT/ORG POLICY WOR+45

C66
KULSKI W.W.,"DEGAULLE AND THE WORLD: THE FOREIGN POLICY OF THE FIFTH FRENCH REPUBLIC." FRANCE ECO/UNDEV POL/PAR BAL/PWR DETER NUC/PWR ATTIT PWR ...RECORD BIBLIOG DEGAULLE NATO EEC. PAGE 83 A1694 — POLICY SOVEREIGN PERSON DIPLOM

B67
ISENBERG I.,FRANCE UNDER DE GAULLE (THE REFERENCE SHELF VOL. 39 NO. 1). EUR+WWI FRANCE ECO/DEV ...BIBLIOG 20 DEGAULLE/C NATO EEC. PAGE 72 A1469 — ATTIT DIPLOM POLICY CHIEF

B67
WILLIS F.R.,DE GAULLE: ANACHRONISM, REALIST, OR PROPHET? FRANCE POL/PAR FORCES DIPLOM WAR PEACE ROLE ORD/FREE...POLICY IDEA/COMP ANTHOL 20 DEGAULLE/C. PAGE 165 A3356 — BIOG PERSON CHIEF LEAD

DEGRAS J. A0723

DEHIO L. A0724,A0725

DEITCHMAN S.J. A0726

DEITY....DEITY: GOD AND GODS

B16
PUFENDORF S.,LAW OF NATURE AND OF NATIONS (ABRIDGED). UNIV LAW NAT/G DIPLOM AGREE WAR PERSON ALL/VALS PWR...POLICY 18 DEITY NATURL/LAW. PAGE 118 A2416 — CONCPT INT/LAW SECT MORAL

DELANEY R.F. A0727

DELAWARE....DELAWARE

DELEGATION OF POWER....SEE EX/STRUC

DELGADO J. A0728

DELIB/GP....CONFERENCES, COMMITTEES, BOARDS, CABINETS

N
INTERNATIONAL COMN JURISTS,AFRICAN CONFERENCE ON THE RULE OF LAW. AFR INT/ORG LEGIS DIPLOM CONFER COLONIAL ORD/FREE...CONCPT METH/COMP 20. PAGE 71 A1452 — CT/SYS JURID DELIB/GP

N
UNITED NATIONS,OFFICIAL RECORDS OF THE ECONOMIC AND SOCIAL COUNCIL OF THE UNITED NATIONS. WOR+45 DIPLOM INT/TRADE CONFER...SOC SOC/WK 20 UN UNESCO. PAGE 148 A3031 — INT/ORG DELIB/GP WRITING

N
UNITED NATIONS,OFFICIAL RECORDS OF THE UNITED NATIONS' ATOMIC ENERGY COMMISSION - DISARMAMENT COMMISSION. WOR+45 TEC/DEV DIPLOM WRITING NUC/PWR 20 UN. PAGE 148 A3032 — ARMS/CONT INT/ORG DELIB/GP CONFER

N
UNITED NATIONS,OFFICIAL RECORDS OF THE UNITED NATIONS' GENERAL ASSEMBLY. WOR+45 BUDGET DIPLOM ADMIN 20 UN. PAGE 148 A3033 — INT/ORG DELIB/GP INT/LAW WRITING

N
UNITED NATIONS,YEARBOOK OF THE INTERNATIONAL LAW COMMISSION....CON/ANAL 20 UN. PAGE 149 A3035 — BIBLIOG INT/ORG INT/LAW DELIB/GP

B05
AMES J.G.,COMPREHENSIVE INDEX TO THE PUBLICATIONS OF THE UNITED STATES GOVERNMENT , 1881-1893. USA-45 CONSTN POL/PAR DELIB/GP TOP/EX DIPLOM PARL/PROC INGP/REL...INDEX 19 CONGRESS. PAGE 8 A0153 — BIBLIOG/A LEGIS NAT/G GOV/REL

B08
GRIFFIN A.P.C.,LIST OF REFERENCES ON INTERNATIONAL ARBITRATION. FRANCE L/A+17C USA-45 WOR-45 DIPLOM CONFER COLONIAL ARMS/CONT BAL/PAY EQUILIB SOVEREIGN ...DECISION 19/20 MEXIC/AMER. PAGE 56 A1156 — BIBLIOG/A INT/ORG INT/LAW DELIB/GP

B15
FARIES J.C.,THE RISE OF INTERNATIONALISM. ASIA MOD/EUR NAT/G VOL/ASSN DELIB/GP BAL/PWR EDU/PROP ARMS/CONT RIGID/FLEX TREND. PAGE 44 A0899 — INT/ORG DIPLOM PEACE

B19
DE CALLIERES F.,THE PRACTICE OF DIPLOMACY. MOD/EUR INT/ORG NAT/G DELIB/GP LEGIS TOP/EX DOMIN ATTIT KNOWL LEAGUE/NAT 20. PAGE 34 A0699 — CONSULT ACT/RES DIPLOM INT/LAW

B19
SUMNER W.G.,WAR AND OTHER ESSAYS. USA-45 DELIB/GP DIPLOM TARIFFS COLONIAL PEACE SOVEREIGN 20. PAGE 140 A2864 — INT/TRADE ORD/FREE CAP/ISM ECO/TAC

B19
US DEPARTMENT OF STATE,A TENTATIVE LIST OF TREATY COLLECTIONS. WOR-45 BAL/PWR INT/TRADE TARIFFS WAR PEACE ORD/FREE 20. PAGE 151 A3080 — ANTHOL DIPLOM DELIB/GP

N19
MEZERIK AG,OUTER SPACE: UN, US, USSR (PAMPHLET). USSR DELIB/GP FORCES DETER NUC/PWR SOVEREIGN ...POLICY 20 UN TREATY. PAGE 101 A2063 — SPACE CONTROL DIPLOM INT/ORG

B20
BURNS C.D.,INTERNATIONAL POLITICS. WOR-45 CULTURE SOCIETY ECO/UNDEV NAT/G VOL/ASSN DELIB/GP ACT/RES CREATE DOMIN EDU/PROP LEGIT ATTIT DRIVE RIGID/FLEX ALL/VALS...PLURIST PSY CONCPT TREND. PAGE 22 A0442 — INT/ORG PEACE SOVEREIGN

B20
HALDANE R.B.,BEFORE THE WAR. MOD/EUR SOCIETY INT/ORG NAT/G DELIB/GP PLAN DOMIN EDU/PROP LEGIT ADMIN COERCE ATTIT DRIVE MORAL ORD/FREE PWR...SOC CONCPT SELF/OBS RECORD BIOG TIME/SEQ. PAGE 60 A1223 — POLICY DIPLOM UK

B22
BRYCE J.,INTERNATIONAL RELATIONS. CHRIST-17C EUR+WWI MOD/EUR CULTURE INTELL NAT/G DELIB/GP CREATE BAL/PWR DIPLOM ATTIT DRIVE RIGID/FLEX ALL/VALS...PLURIST JURID CONCPT TIME/SEQ GEN/LAWS TOT/POP. PAGE 20 A0412 — INT/ORG POLICY

B26
INSTITUT INTERMEDIAIRE INTL,REPERTOIRE GENERAL DES TRAITES ET AUTRES ACTES DIPLOMATIQUES CONCLUS DEPUIS 1895 JUSQU'EN 1920. MOD/EUR WOR-45 INT/ORG VOL/ASSN DELIB/GP INT/TRADE WAR TREATY 19/20. PAGE 70 A1443 — BIBLIOG DIPLOM

B27
LAUTERPACHT H.,PRIVATE LAW SOURCES AND ANALOGIES OF INTERNATIONAL LAW. WOR-45 NAT/G DELIB/GP LEGIT COERCE ATTIT ORD/FREE PWR SOVEREIGN...JURID CONCPT HIST/WRIT TIME/SEQ GEN/METH LEAGUE/NAT 20. PAGE 85 A1748 — INT/ORG ADJUD PEACE INT/LAW

B28
MILLER D.H.,THE DRAFTING OF THE COVENANT. UNIV WOR-45 INTELL NAT/G DELIB/GP PLAN ECO/TAC LEGIT WAR ATTIT PERCEPT...CONCPT TIME/SEQ LEAGUE/NAT TOT/POP 20. PAGE 101 A2074 — INT/ORG STRUCT PEACE

B29
CONWELL-EVANS T.P.,THE LEAGUE COUNCIL IN ACTION. EUR+WWI TURKEY UK USSR WOR-45 INT/ORG FORCES JUDGE ECO/TAC EDU/PROP LEGIT ROUTINE ARMS/CONT COERCE ATTIT PWR...MAJORIT GEOG JURID CONCPT LEAGUE/NAT TOT/POP VAL/FREE TUNIS 20. PAGE 30 A0605 — DELIB/GP INT/LAW

B29
DUNN F.,THE PRACTICE AND PROCEDURE OF INTERNATIONAL CONFERENCES. WOR-45 NAT/G DELIB/GP BAL/PWR LEGIT EXEC ROUTINE PEACE ORD/FREE RESPECT...JURID CONCPT METH/CNCPT OBS RECORD TIME/SEQ 20. PAGE 39 A0799 — INT/ORG DIPLOM

B30
WRIGHT Q.,MANDATES UNDER THE LEAGUE OF NATIONS. WOR-45 CONSTN ECO/DEV ECO/UNDEV NAT/G DELIB/GP TOP/EX LEGIT ALL/VALS...JURID CONCPT LEAGUE/NAT 20. PAGE 167 A3403 — INT/ORG LAW INT/LAW

B31
BEALES A.C.,THE HISTORY OF PEACE. WOR-45 VOL/ASSN DELIB/GP CREATE PLAN EDU/PROP ATTIT MORAL ...TIME/SEQ VAL/FREE 19/20. PAGE 12 A0239 — INT/ORG ARMS/CONT PEACE

B31
GREAVES H.R.G.,THE LEAGUE COMMITTEES AND WORLD ORDER. WOR-45 DELIB/GP EX/STRUC EDU/PROP ALL/VALS LEAGUE/NAT VAL/FREE 20. PAGE 55 A1136 — INT/ORG DIPLOM ROUTINE

B31
HILL N.,INTERNATIONAL ADMINISTRATION. WOR-45 DELIB/GP DIPLOM EDU/PROP ALL/VALS...MGT TIME/SEQ LEAGUE/NAT TOT/POP VAL/FREE 20. PAGE 65 A1331 — INT/ORG ADMIN

B32
EAGLETON C.,INTERNATIONAL GOVERNMENT. BRAZIL FRANCE GERMANY ITALY UK USSR WOR-45 DELIB/GP TOP/EX PLAN ECO/TAC EDU/PROP LEGIT ADJUD REGION ARMS/CONT COERCE ATTIT PWR...GEOG MGT VAL/FREE LEAGUE/NAT 20. PAGE 40 A0816 — INT/ORG JURID DIPLOM INT/LAW

B33
REID H.D.,RECUEIL DES COURS; TOME 45: LES SERVITUDES INTERNATIONALES III. FRANCE CONSTN DELIB/GP PRESS CONTROL REV WAR CHOOSE PEACE MORAL MARITIME TREATY. PAGE 120 A2457 — ORD/FREE DIPLOM LAW

B35
CONOVER H.F.,A SELECTED LIST OF REFERENCES ON THE DIPLOMATIC & TRADE RELATIONS OF THE US WITH THE USSR, 1919-1935 (PAMPHLET). USA-45 USSR DELIB/GP — BIBLIOG DIPLOM INT/TRADE

LEGIS OP/RES PROB/SOLV BAL/PWR BARGAIN 20. PAGE 29 A0590

B38
HAGUE PERMANENT CT INTL JUSTIC,WORLD COURT REPORTS: COLLECTION OF THE JUDGEMENTS ORDERS AND OPINIONS VOLUME 3 1932-35. WOR-45 LAW DELIB/GP CONFER WAR PEACE ATTIT...DECISION ANTHOL 20 WORLD/CT CASEBOOK. PAGE 59 A1214 INT/ORG CT/SYS DIPLOM ADJUD

B39
BENES E.,INTERNATIONAL SECURITY. GERMANY UK NAT/G DELIB/GP PLAN BAL/PWR ATTIT ORD/FREE PWR LEAGUE/NAT 20 TREATY. PAGE 13 A0267 EUR+WWI INT/ORG WAR

B39
NICOLSON H.,CURZON: THE LAST PHASE, 1919-1925. UK NAT/G DELIB/GP TOP/EX ROUTINE WAR RIGID/FLEX ...METH/CNCPT 20 CURZON/GN. PAGE 109 A2231 POLICY DIPLOM BIOG

B39
ZIMMERN A.,THE LEAGUE OF NATIONS AND THE RULE OF LAW. WOR-45 STRUCT NAT/G DELIB/GP EX/STRUC BAL/PWR DOMIN LEGIT COERCE ORD/FREE PWR...POLICY RECORD LEAGUE/NAT TOT/POP VAL/FREE 20 LEAGUE/NAT. PAGE 170 A3453 INT/ORG LAW DIPLOM

B39
ZIMMERN A.,MODERN POLITICAL DOCTRINE. WOR-45 CULTURE SOCIETY ECO/UNDEV DELIB/GP EX/STRUC CREATE DOMIN COERCE NAT/LISM ATTIT RIGID/FLEX ORD/FREE PWR WEALTH...POLICY CONCPT OBS TIME/SEQ TREND TOT/POP LEAGUE/NAT 20. PAGE 170 A3454 NAT/G ECO/TAC BAL/PWR INT/TRADE

B40
CONOVER H.F.,A BRIEF LIST OF REFERENCES ON WESTERN HEMISPHERE DEFENSE (PAMPHLET). USA-45 NAT/G CONSULT DELIB/GP FORCES BAL/PWR CONFER DETER...PREDICT CON/ANAL 20. PAGE 29 A0591 BIBLIOG DIPLOM PLAN INT/ORG

B41
BURTON M.E.,THE ASSEMBLY OF THE LEAGUE OF NATIONS. WOR-45 CONSTN SOCIETY STRUCT INT/ORG NAT/G CREATE ATTIT RIGID/FLEX PWR...POLICY TIME/SEQ LEAGUE/NAT 20. PAGE 22 A0448 DELIB/GP EX/STRUC DIPLOM

B41
MCCLURE W.,INTERNATIONAL EXECUTIVE AGREEMENTS. USA-45 WOR-45 INT/ORG NAT/G DELIB/GP ADJUD ROUTINE ORD/FREE PWR...TIME/SEQ TREND CON/ANAL. PAGE 97 A2000 TOP/EX DIPLOM

L41
COMM. STUDY ORGAN. PEACE,"PRELIMINARY REPORT." WOR-45 SOCIETY DELIB/GP PLAN LEGIT WAR ORD/FREE ...CONCPT TOT/POP 20. PAGE 28 A0574 INT/ORG ACT/RES PEACE

B42
CORBETT P.E.,POST WAR WORLDS. ASIA EUR+WWI FUT S/ASIA USA-45 ECO/DEV ECO/UNDEV NAT/G DELIB/GP FORCES PLAN ROUTINE ATTIT PWR 20. PAGE 30 A0613 WOR-45 INT/ORG

B42
CROWE S.E.,THE BERLIN WEST AFRICA CONFERENCE, 1884-85. GERMANY ELITES MARKET INT/ORG DELIB/GP FORCES PROB/SOLV BAL/PWR CAP/ISM DOMIN COLONIAL ...INT/LAW 19. PAGE 33 A0664 AFR CONFER INT/TRADE DIPLOM

B42
FULLER G.H.,DEFENSE FINANCING: A SUPPLEMENTARY LIST OF REFERENCES (PAMPHLET). CANADA UK USA-45 ECO/DEV NAT/G DELIB/GP BUDGET ADJUD ARMS/CONT WEAPON COST PEACE PWR 20 AUSTRAL CHINJAP CONGRESS. PAGE 50 A1021 BIBLIOG/A FINAN FORCES DIPLOM

B42
KELSEN H.,LAW AND PEACE IN INTERNATIONAL RELATIONS. FUT WOR-45 NAT/G DELIB/GP DIPLOM LEGIT RIGID/FLEX ORD/FREE SOVEREIGN...JURID CONCPT TREND STERTYP GEN/LAWS LEAGUE/NAT 20. PAGE 77 A1580 INT/ORG ADJUD PEACE INT/LAW

B44
COMM. STUDY ORGAN. PEACE,UNITED NATIONS GUARDS AND TECHNICAL FIELD SERVICES. WOR+45 DELIB/GP EDU/PROP DRIVE PWR SKILL...CONCPT GEN/LAWS UN TOT/POP 20. PAGE 28 A0576 INT/ORG FORCES PEACE

B44
RUDIN H.R.,ARMISTICE 1918. FRANCE GERMANY MOD/EUR UK USA-45 NAT/G CHIEF DELIB/GP FORCES BAL/PWR REPAR ARMS/CONT 20 WILSON/W TREATY. PAGE 125 A2566 AGREE WAR PEACE DIPLOM

L44
WRIGHT Q.,"THE US AND INTERNATIONAL AGREEMENTS." FUT USA-45 CONSTN INTELL INT/ORG LOC/G NAT/G CHIEF CONSULT EX/STRUC DIPLOM LEGIT DRIVE PERCEPT PWR ...CONCPT CONGRESS 20. PAGE 167 A3407 DELIB/GP TOP/EX PEACE

B45
NELSON M.F.,KOREA AND THE OLD ORDERS IN EASTERN ASIA. ASIA FRANCE KOREA RUSSIA DELIB/GP INT/TRADE DOMIN CONTROL WAR ORD/FREE...POLICY BIBLIOG. PAGE 108 A2218 DIPLOM BAL/PWR ATTIT CONSERVE

B45
PASTUHOV V.D.,A GUIDE TO THE PRACTICE OF INTERNATIONAL CONFERENCES. WOR+45 PLAN LEGIT ORD/FREE...MGT OBS RECORD VAL/FREE ILO LEAGUE/NAT 20. PAGE 114 A2338 INT/ORG DELIB/GP

B45
RANSHOFFEN-WERTHEIMER EF,THE INTERNATIONAL SECRETARIAT: A GREAT EXPERIMENT IN INTERNATIONAL ADMINISTRATION. EUR+WWI FUT CONSTN FACE/GP CONSULT DELIB/GP ACT/RES ADMIN ROUTINE PEACE ORD/FREE...MGT RECORD ORG/CHARTS LEAGUE/NAT WORK 20. PAGE 119 A2442 INT/ORG EXEC

B45
TINGSTERN H.,PEACE AND SECURITY AFTER WW II. WOR-45 DELIB/GP TOP/EX LEGIT CT/SYS COERCE PEACE ATTIT PERCEPT...CONCPT LEAGUE/NAT 20. PAGE 144 A2943 INT/ORG ORD/FREE WAR INT/LAW

C45
NELSON M.F.,"KOREA AND THE OLD ORDERS IN EASTERN ASIA." KOREA WOR-45 DELIB/GP INT/TRADE DOMIN CONTROL WAR ATTIT ORD/FREE CONSERVE...POLICY TREATY. PAGE 108 A2217 BIBLIOG DIPLOM BAL/PWR ASIA

B46
BRODIE B.,THE OBSOLETE WEAPON: ATOMIC POWER AND WORLD ORDER. COM USA+45 USSR WOR+45 DELIB/GP PLAN ORD/FREE PWR...CONCPT TIME/SEQ TREND UN 20. PAGE 19 A0380 INT/ORG TEC/DEV ARMS/CONT NUC/PWR

B46
KEETON G.W.,MAKING INTERNATIONAL LAW WORK. FUT WOR-45 NAT/G DELIB/GP FORCES LEGIT COERCE PEACE ATTIT RIGID/FLEX ORD/FREE PWR...JURID CONCPT HIST/WRIT GEN/METH LEAGUE/NAT 20. PAGE 77 A1578 INT/ORG ADJUD INT/LAW

B46
MITRANY D.,A WORKING PEACE SYSTEM. WOR+45 WOR-45 ECO/DEV INT/ORG NAT/G DELIB/GP ECO/TAC REGION ATTIT RIGID/FLEX...TREND GEN/LAWS LEAGUE/NAT 20. PAGE 102 A2091 VOL/ASSN PLAN PEACE SOVEREIGN

B47
BROOKINGS INST.,MAJOR PROBLEMS OF UNITED STATES FOREIGN POLICY. USA+45 WOR+45 STRUCT ECO/DEV ECO/UNDEV INT/ORG NAT/G POL/PAR VOL/ASSN DELIB/GP FORCES ECO/TAC LEGIT COERCE ORD/FREE PWR WEALTH ...POLICY STAT TREND CHARTS TOT/POP. PAGE 19 A0392 ACT/RES DIPLOM

B47
KIRK G.,THE STUDY OF INTERNATIONAL RELATIONS. FUT USA-45 R+D ACADEM INT/ORG CONSULT DELIB/GP INT/TRADE EDU/PROP PEACE RIGID/FLEX KNOWL VAL/FREE 20. PAGE 80 A1632 USA+45 DIPLOM

B47
MANDER L.,FOUNDATIONS OF MODERN WORLD SOCIETY. WOR+45 DELIB/GP ECO/TAC INT/TRADE EDU/PROP ALL/VALS ...TIME/SEQ GEN/LAWS TOT/POP VAL/FREE ILO 20. PAGE 94 A1917 INT/ORG EX/STRUC DIPLOM

L47
BRUNER J.S.,"TOWARD A COMMON GROUND-INTERNATIONAL SOCIAL SCIENCE." FUT WOR+45 INTELL R+D NAT/G VOL/ASSN CONSULT DELIB/GP ACT/RES CREATE PLAN TEC/DEV ATTIT ORD/FREE...PSY SOC CONCPT ANTHOL UNESCO 20. PAGE 20 A0410 INT/ORG KNOWL

B48
HOWARD J.E.,PARLIAMENT AND FOREIGN POLICY IN FRANCE. FRANCE CONSTN DELIB/GP BUDGET ADMIN PARL/PROC CHOOSE...BIBLIOG/A 20 PARLIAMENT. PAGE 68 A1399 LEGIS CONTROL DIPLOM ATTIT

B48
JESSUP P.C.,A MODERN LAW OF NATIONS. FUT WOR+45 WOR-45 SOCIETY NAT/G DELIB/GP LEGIS BAL/PWR EDU/PROP LEGIT PWR...INT/LAW JURID TIME/SEQ LEAGUE/NAT 20. PAGE 74 A1514 INT/ORG ADJUD

B49
JACKSON R.H.,INTERNATIONAL CONFERENCE ON MILITARY TRIALS. FRANCE GERMANY UK USA+45 USSR VOL/ASSN DELIB/GP REPAR ADJUD CT/SYS CRIME WAR 20 WAR/TRIAL. PAGE 72 A1479 DIPLOM INT/ORG INT/LAW CIVMIL/REL

B49
MARITAIN J.,HUMAN RIGHTS: COMMENTS AND INTERPRETATIONS. COM UNIV WOR+45 LAW CONSTN CULTURE SOCIETY ECO/DEV ECO/UNDEV SCHOOL DELIB/GP EDU/PROP ATTIT PERCEPT ALL/VALS...HUM SOC TREND UNESCO 20. PAGE 95 A1939 INT/ORG CONCPT

B49
STETTINIUS E.R.,ROOSEVELT AND THE RUSSIANS: THE YALTA CONFERENCE. UK USSR WOR+45 WOR-45 INT/ORG VOL/ASSN TOP/EX ACT/RES EDU/PROP PEACE ATTIT DRIVE PERSON SUPEGO PWR...POLICY CONCPT MYTH OBS TIME/SEQ AUD/VIS COLD/WAR 20 CHURCHLL/W YALTA ROOSEVLT/F. PAGE 138 A2819 DIPLOM DELIB/GP BIOG

L49
COMM. STUDY ORGAN. PEACE,"A TEN YEAR RECORD, 1939-1949." FUT WOR+45 LAW R+D CONSULT DELIB/GP CREATE LEGIT ROUTINE ORD/FREE...TIME/SEQ UN 20. PAGE 28 A0578 INT/ORG CONSTN PEACE

B50
CHASE E.P.,THE UNITED NATIONS IN ACTION. WOR+45 CONSTN DELIB/GP LEGIT ROUTINE COERCE PEACE ORD/FREE PWR...CON/ANAL GEN/LAWS UN 20. PAGE 26 A0524 INT/ORG STRUCT ARMS/CONT

B50
CHURCHILL W.,TRIUMPH AND TRAGEDY. UK WOR-45 INT/ORG NAT/G DELIB/GP FORCES TOP/EX DIPLOM COERCE CHOOSE ATTIT ORD/FREE PWR WEALTH...SELF/OBS CHARTS NAZI 20. PAGE 26 A0539 BIOG PEACE WAR

B50
JIMENEZ E.,VOTING AND HANDLING OF DISPUTES IN THE SECURITY COUNCIL. WOR+45 CONSTN INT/ORG DIPLOM LEGIT DETER CHOOSE MORAL ORD/FREE PWR...JURID DELIB/GP ROUTINE

TIME/SEQ COLD/WAR UN 20. PAGE 74 A1517

B50
LAUTERPACHT H.,INTERNATIONAL LAW AND HUMAN RIGHTS. USA+45 CONSTN STRUCT INT/ORG ACT/RES EDU/PROP PEACE PERSON ALL/VALS...CONCPT CON/ANAL GEN/LAWS UN 20. PAGE 86 A1750
DELIB/GP LAW INT/LAW

B50
LINCOLN G.,ECONOMICS OF NATIONAL SECURITY. USA+45 ELITES COM/IND DIST/IND INDUS NAT/G VOL/ASSN DELIB/GP EX/STRUC FOR/AID EDU/PROP COERCE NUC/PWR WAR ATTIT KNOWL ORD/FREE PWR COLD/WAR TOT/POP VAL/FREE 20. PAGE 89 A1818
FORCES ECO/TAC

B50
ROSS A.,CONSTITUTION OF THE UNITED NATIONS. CONSTN CONSULT DELIB/GP ECO/TAC...INT/LAW JURID 20 UN LEAGUE/NAT. PAGE 124 A2540
PEACE DIPLOM ORD/FREE INT/ORG

L50
US SENATE COMM. GOVT. OPER.,"REVISION OF THE UN CHARTER." FUT USA+45 WOR+45 CONSTN ECO/DEV ECO/UNDEV NAT/G DELIB/GP ACT/RES CREATE PLAN EXEC ROUTINE CHOOSE ALL/VALS...POLICY CONCPT CONGRESS UN TOT/POP 20 COLD/WAR. PAGE 157 A3196
INT/ORG LEGIS PEACE

B51
HAVILAND H.F.,THE POLITICAL ROLE OF THE GENERAL ASSEMBLY. WOR+45 DELIB/GP EDU/PROP PEACE RIGID/FLEX PWR...CONCPT TIME/SEQ GEN/LAWS UN VAL/FREE 20. PAGE 63 A1290
INT/ORG ORD/FREE DIPLOM

B51
LEONARD L.L.,INTERNATIONAL ORGANIZATION. WOR+45 WOR-45 EX/STRUC FORCES LEGIS ECO/TAC INT/TRADE COLONIAL ARMS/CONT...SOC/WK GOV/COMP BIBLIOG. PAGE 87 A1778
NAT/G DIPLOM INT/ORG DELIB/GP

B51
PRICE D.K.,THE NEW DIMENSIONS OF DIPLOMACY: THE ORGANIZATION OF THE US GOVERNMENT FOR ITS NEW ROLE IN WORLD AFFAIRS (PAMPHLET). USA+45 WOR+45 INT/ORG VOL/ASSN CONSULT DELIB/GP PLAN PROB/SOLV 20 PRESIDENT. PAGE 117 A2411
DIPLOM GP/REL NAT/G

L51
WHITAKER A.P.,"DEVELOPMENT OF AMERICAN REGIONALISM: THE ORGANIZATION OF AMERICAN STATES." L/A+17C USA+45 VOL/ASSN DELIB/GP FORCES TOP/EX ACT/RES ECO/TAC CT/SYS REGION PEACE ALL/VALS OAS 20. PAGE 163 A3330
INT/ORG TIME/SEQ DETER

S51
GYR J.,"ANALYSIS OF COMMITTEE MEMBER BEHAVIOUR IN FOUR CULTURES." ASIA ISLAM L/A+17C USA+45 INT/ORG VOL/ASSN LEGIT ATTIT...INT DEEP/QU SAMP CHARTS 20. PAGE 58 A1200
DELIB/GP CULTURE

C51
LEONARD L.L.,"INTERNATIONAL ORGANIZATION (1ST ED.)" WOR+45 FINAN DELIB/GP ECO/TAC GIVE DOMIN SANCTION PEACE BIO/SOC ORD/FREE...INT/LAW 20 UN LEAGUE/NAT. PAGE 87 A1779
BIBLIOG POLICY DIPLOM INT/ORG

B52
FIFIELD R.H.,WOODROW WILSON AND THE FAR EAST. ASIA CHIEF BAL/PWR CONFER COLONIAL ARMS/CONT WAR ...TIME/SEQ NAT/COMP BIBLIOG 19/20 WILSON/W LEAGUE/NAT PRESIDENT. PAGE 45 A0926
DIPLOM DELIB/GP INT/ORG

B52
JACKSON E.,MEETING OF THE MINDS: A WAY TO PEACE THROUGH MEDIATION. WOR+45 INDUS INT/ORG NAT/G DELIB/GP DIPLOM EDU/PROP LEGIT ORD/FREE...NEW/IDEA SELF/OBS TIME/SEQ CHARTS GEN/LAWS TOT/POP 20 UN TREATY. PAGE 72 A1474
LABOR JUDGE

B52
MANTOUX E.,THE CARTHAGINIAN PEACE. GERMANY WOR-45 SOCIETY FINAN INT/ORG DELIB/GP FORCES PLAN LEGIT ...CONCPT TIME/SEQ 20 KEYNES/JM HITLER/A. PAGE 94 A1935
ECO/DEV INT/TRADE WAR

B52
VANDENBOSCH A.,THE UN: BACKGROUND, ORGANIZATION, FUNCTIONS, ACTIVITIES. WOR+45 LAW CONSTN STRUCT INT/ORG CONSULT BAL/PWR EDU/PROP EXEC ALL/VALS ...POLICY CONCPT UN 20. PAGE 158 A3218
DELIB/GP TIME/SEQ PEACE

L52
WRIGHT Q.,"CONGRESS AND THE TREATY-MAKING POWER." USA+45 WOR+45 CONSTN INTELL NAT/G CHIEF CONSULT EX/STRUC LEGIS TOP/EX CREATE GOV/REL DISPL DRIVE RIGID/FLEX...TREND TOT/POP CONGRESS CONGRESS 20 TREATY. PAGE 167 A3408
ROUTINE DIPLOM INT/LAW DELIB/GP

S52
MASTERS R.D.,"RUSSIA AND THE UNITED NATIONS." FUT USA+45 USSR WOR+45 CONSTN VOL/ASSN DELIB/GP TOP/EX CREATE DIPLOM ADMIN...TREND STERTYP UN 20. PAGE 96 A1962
INT/ORG PWR

S52
SCHUMAN F.,"INTERNATIONAL IDEALS AND THE NATIONAL INTEREST." WOR+45 WOR-45 INT/ORG VOL/ASSN DELIB/GP CREATE BAL/PWR DOMIN PEACE PERSON MORAL PWR SOVEREIGN...POLICY GEN/LAWS TOT/POP LEAGUE/NAT 20. PAGE 129 A2648
ATTIT CONCPT

S52
SCHWEBEL S.M.,"THE SECRETARY-GENERAL OF THE UN." FUT INTELL CONSULT DELIB/GP ADMIN PEACE ATTIT ...JURID MGT CONCPT TREND UN CONGRESS 20. PAGE 130 A2663
INT/ORG TOP/EX

C52
FIFIELD R.H.,"WOODROW WILSON AND THE FAR EAST." ASIA CHIEF DELIB/GP BAL/PWR CONFER COLONIAL ARMS/CONT WAR...TIME/SEQ NAT/COMP 19/20 WILSON/W LEAGUE/NAT. PAGE 45 A0925
BIBLIOG DIPLOM INT/ORG

C52
STUART G.H.,"AMERICAN DIPLOMATIC AND CONSULAR PRACTICE (2ND ED.)" EUR+WWI MOD/EUR USA-45 DELIB/GP INT/TRADE ADJUD...BIBLIOG 20. PAGE 140 A2855
DIPLOM ADMIN INT/ORG

B53
MACMAHON A.W.,ADMINISTRATION IN FOREIGN AFFAIRS. NAT/G CONSULT DELIB/GP LEGIS ACT/RES CREATE ADMIN EXEC RIGID/FLEX PWR...METH/CNCPT TIME/SEQ TOT/POP VAL/FREE 20. PAGE 93 A1899
USA+45 ROUTINE FOR/AID DIPLOM

B53
SCHAAF R.W.,DOCUMENTS OF INTERNATIONAL MEETINGS. AGRI INDUS ACADEM DIPLOM NUC/PWR RACE/REL AGE/Y HEALTH...SOC 20. PAGE 127 A2614
BIBLIOG/A DELIB/GP INT/ORG POLICY

B53
STOUT H.M.,BRITISH GOVERNMENT. UK FINAN LOC/G POL/PAR DELIB/GP DIPLOM ADMIN COLONIAL CHOOSE ORD/FREE...JURID BIBLIOG 20 COMMONWLTH. PAGE 139 A2837
NAT/G PARL/PROC CONSTN NEW/LIB

L53
UNESCO,"THE TECHNIQUE OF INTERNATIONAL CONFERENCES." WOR+45 INT/ORG VOL/ASSN EDU/PROP ROUTINE ATTIT DRIVE KNOWL ORD/FREE...SOC UNESCO 20. PAGE 148 A3016
DELIB/GP ACT/RES

B54
MANNING C.A.W.,THE UNIVERSITY TEACHING OF SOCIAL SCIENCES: INTERNATIONAL RELATIONS. WOR+45 INTELL STRATA R+D ACADEM INT/ORG NAT/G CONSULT DELIB/GP ACT/RES EDU/PROP NAT/LISM ATTIT...POLICY CONT/OBS HYPO/EXP VAL/FREE LEAGUE/NAT UNESCO 20. PAGE 94 A1925
KNOWL PHIL/SCI DIPLOM

B55
BURR R.N.,DOCUMENTS ON INTER-AMERICAN COOPERATION: VOL. I, 1810-1881; VOL. II, 1881-1948. DELIB/GP BAL/PWR INT/TRADE REPRESENT NAT/LISM PEACE HABITAT ORD/FREE PWR SOVEREIGN...INT/LAW 20 OAS. PAGE 22 A0445
BIBLIOG DIPLOM INT/ORG L/A+17C

B55
CHOWDHURI R.N.,INTERNATIONAL MANDATES AND TRUSTEESHIP SYSTEMS. WOR+45 STRUCT ECO/UNDEV INT/ORG LEGIS DOMIN EDU/PROP LEGIT ADJUD EXEC PWR ...CONCPT TIME/SEQ UN 20. PAGE 26 A0534
DELIB/GP PLAN SOVEREIGN

B55
JOY C.T.,HOW COMMUNISTS NEGOTIATE. COM USA+45 CONSTN CULTURE ECO/UNDEV NAT/G CONSULT DELIB/GP FORCES PLAN ECO/TAC DOMIN EDU/PROP LEGIT EXEC ROUTINE COERCE WAR CHOOSE PEACE ATTIT RIGID/FLEX ORD/FREE PWR...POLICY 20. PAGE 75 A1539
ASIA INT/ORG DIPLOM

B55
LANDHEER B.,EUROPEAN YEARBOOK, 1955. CONSTN ECO/DEV DIST/IND FINAN DELIB/GP ECO/TAC DETER NUC/PWR ...BIBLIOG 20 EEC. PAGE 84 A1717
EUR+WWI INT/ORG GOV/REL INT/TRADE

B55
MOCH J.,HUMAN FOLLY: DISARM OR PERISH. USA+45 WOR+45 SOCIETY INT/ORG NAT/G ACT/RES EDU/PROP ATTIT PERSON KNOWL ORD/FREE PWR...MAJORIT TOT/POP COLD/WAR 20. PAGE 102 A2093
FUT DELIB/GP ARMS/CONT NUC/PWR

B55
SNYDER R.C.,AMERICAN FOREIGN POLICY. USA+45 USA-45 WOR+45 WOR-45 CONSTN INT/ORG POL/PAR VOL/ASSN DELIB/GP LEGIS CREATE DOMIN EDU/PROP EXEC COERCE ATTIT DRIVE ORD/FREE PWR...MGT OBS RECORD TIME/SEQ TREND. PAGE 134 A2752
NAT/G DIPLOM

B55
VINSON J.C.,THE PARCHMENT PEACE: THE UNITED STATES SENATE AND THE WASHINGTON CONFERENCE, 1921-1922. USA-45 INT/ORG DELIB/GP PLAN ARMS/CONT GOV/REL ISOLAT PEACE ATTIT SOVEREIGN...INT/LAW BIBLIOG 20 SENATE PRESIDENT CONGRESS LEAGUE/NAT CHINJAP. PAGE 159 A3242
POLICY DIPLOM NAT/G LEGIS

S55
HALLETT D.,"THE HISTORY AND STRUCTURE OF OEEC." EUR+WWI USA+45 CONSTN INDUS INT/ORG NAT/G DELIB/GP ACT/RES PLAN ORD/FREE WEALTH...CONCPT OEEC 20 CMN/WLTH. PAGE 60 A1234
VOL/ASSN ECO/DEV

S55
TORRE M.,"PSYCHIATRIC OBSERVATIONS OF INTERNATIONAL CONFERENCES." WOR+45 INT/ORG PROF/ORG VOL/ASSN CONSULT EDU/PROP ROUTINE ATTIT DRIVE KNOWL...PSY METH/CNCPT OBS/ENVIR STERTYP 20. PAGE 144 A2950
DELIB/GP OBS DIPLOM

B56
BLACKETT P.M.S.,ATOMIC WEAPONS AND EAST-WEST RELATIONS. FUT WOR+45 INT/ORG DELIB/GP COERCE ATTIT RIGID/FLEX KNOWL...RELATIV HIST/WRIT TREND GEN/METH COLD/WAR 20. PAGE 15 A0299
FORCES PWR ARMS/CONT NUC/PWR

B56
BROOK D.,THE UNITED NATIONS AND CHINA DILEMMA. CHINA/COM FUT WOR+45 ECO/UNDEV NAT/G DELIB/GP
ASIA INT/ORG

ACT/RES DIPLOM ROUTINE NAT/LISM TOTALISM ATTIT DRIVE...CONCPT OBS TIME/SEQ UN TOT/POP TIME UN 20. PAGE 19 A0390 — BAL/PWR

B56
BUREAU OF PUBLIC AFFAIRS,AMERICAN FOREIGN POLICY: CURRENT DOCUMENTS. COM USA+45 USSR WOR+45 DELIB/GP FOR/AID INT/TRADE ARMS/CONT NUC/PWR ALL/VALS ALL/IDEOS...DECISION 20 NATO. PAGE 21 A0434 — BIBLIOG/A DIPLOM POLICY

B56
FOSTER J.G.,BRITAIN IN WESTERN EUROPE: WEU AND THE ATLANTIC ALLIANCE. EUR+WWI FRANCE GERMANY GERMANY/W ITALY UK STRATA NAT/G DELIB/GP ECO/TAC ORD/FREE PWR ...TRADIT TIME/SEQ TREND OEEC PARLIAMENT 20 EUROPE/W. PAGE 47 A0969 — INT/ORG FORCES WEAPON

B56
GOODRICH L.,KOREA: A STUDY OF US POLICY IN THE UNITED NATIONS. ASIA USA+45 STRUCT CONSULT DELIB/GP ATTIT DRIVE PWR...JURID GEN/LAWS COLD/WAR 20 UN. PAGE 54 A1103 — INT/ORG DIPLOM KOREA

B56
LOVEDAY A.,REFLECTIONS ON INTERNATIONAL ADMINISTRATION. WOR+45 WOR-45 DELIB/GP ACT/RES ADMIN EXEC ROUTINE DRIVE...METH/CNCPT TIME/SEQ CON/ANAL SIMUL TOT/POP 20. PAGE 91 A1865 — INT/ORG MGT

B56
SOHN L.B.,BASIC DOCUMENTS OF THE UNITED NATIONS. WOR+45 LAW INT/ORG LEGIT EXEC ROUTINE CHOOSE PWR ...JURID CONCPT GEN/LAWS ANTHOL UN TOT/POP OAS FAO ILO 20. PAGE 135 A2761 — DELIB/GP CONSTN

B56
SPEECKAERT G.P.,INTERNATIONAL INSTITUTIONS AND INTERNATIONAL ORGANIZATIONS. PROF/ORG DELIB/GP KNOWL 19/20. PAGE 136 A2776 — BIBLIOG INT/ORG DIPLOM VOL/ASSN

B56
US HOUSE COMM FOREIGN AFFAIRS,SURVEY OF ACTIVITIES OF THE COMMITTEE ON FOREIGN AFFAIRS HOUSE OF REPRESENTATIVES: 84TH THROUGH 86TH CONGRESS. USA+45 LAW ADJUD...POLICY STAT CHARTS 20 CONGRESS HOUSE/REP. PAGE 153 A3122 — LEGIS DELIB/GP NAT/G DIPLOM

S56
CUTLER R.,"THE DEVELOPMENT OF THE NATIONAL SECURITY COUNCIL." USA+45 INTELL CONSULT EX/STRUC DIPLOM LEAD 20 TRUMAN/HS EISNHWR/DD NSC. PAGE 33 A0670 — ORD/FREE DELIB/GP PROB/SOLV NAT/G

S56
GORDON L.,"THE ORGANIZATION FOR EUROPEAN ECONOMIC COOPERATION." EUR+WWI INDUS INT/ORG NAT/G CONSULT DELIB/GP ACT/RES CREATE PLAN TEC/DEV EDU/PROP LEGIT WEALTH OEEC 20. PAGE 54 A1114 — VOL/ASSN ECO/DEV

B57
BRODY H.,UN DIARY: THE SEARCH FOR PEACE. HUNGARY WOR+45 DELIB/GP ROUTINE REV WAR ORD/FREE...AUD/VIS 20 UN SUEZ. PAGE 19 A0382 — INT/ORG PEACE DIPLOM POLICY

B57
COMM. STUDY ORGAN. PEACE,STRENGTHENING THE UNITED NATIONS. FUT USA+45 WOR+45 CONSTN NAT/G DELIB/GP FORCES LEGIS ECO/TAC LEGIT COERCE PEACE...JURID CONCPT UN COLD/WAR 20. PAGE 28 A0580 — INT/ORG ORD/FREE

B57
JENKS C.W.,THE INTERNATIONAL PROTECTION OF TRADE UNION FREEDOM. FUT WOR+45 WOR-45 VOL/ASSN DELIB/GP CT/SYS REGION ROUTINE...JURID METH/CNCPT RECORD TIME/SEQ CHARTS ILO WORK OAS 20. PAGE 73 A1504 — LABOR INT/ORG

B57
LAVES W.H.C.,UNESCO. FUT WOR+45 NAT/G CONSULT DELIB/GP TEC/DEV ECO/TAC EDU/PROP PEACE ORD/FREE ...CONCPT TIME/SEQ TREND UNESCO VAL/FREE 20. PAGE 86 A1751 — INT/ORG KNOWL

B57
MILLIKAN M.F.,A PROPOSAL: KEY TO AN EFFECTIVE FOREIGN POLICY. USA+45 AGRI FINAN DELIB/GP DIPLOM REPRESENT MAJORITY...NEW/IDEA CHARTS. PAGE 101 A2081 — FOR/AID GIVE ECO/UNDEV PLAN

B57
MURRAY J.N.,THE UNITED NATIONS TRUSTEESHIP SYSTEM. AFR WOR+45 CONSTN CONSULT LEGIS EDU/PROP LEGIT EXEC ROUTINE...INT TIME/SEQ SOMALI UN 20. PAGE 106 A2181 — INT/ORG DELIB/GP

B57
US SENATE COMM ON JUDICIARY,HEARING BEFORE SUBCOMMITTEE ON COMMITTEE OF JUDICIARY, UNITED STATES SENATE: S. J. RES. 3. USA+45 NAT/G CONSULT DELIB/GP DIPLOM ADJUD LOBBY REPRESENT 20 CONGRESS TREATY. PAGE 157 A3192 — LEGIS CONSTN CONFER AGREE

B57
US SENATE SPEC COMM FOR AID,COMPILATION OF STUDIES AND SURVEYS. AFR ASIA L/A+17C USA+45 ECO/UNDEV AGRI INT/ORG CONSULT TEC/DEV CONFER TOTALISM...NAT/COMP 20 CONGRESS. PAGE 157 A3197 — FOR/AID DIPLOM ORD/FREE DELIB/GP

L57
HAAS E.B.,"REGIONAL INTEGRATION AND NATIONAL POLICY." WOR+45 VOL/ASSN DELIB/GP EX/STRUC ECO/TAC DOMIN EDU/PROP LEGIT COERCE ATTIT PERCEPT KNOWL ...TIME/SEQ COLD/WAR 20 UN. PAGE 59 A1203 — INT/ORG ORD/FREE REGION

N57
US SENATE SPECIAL COMM FOR AFF.REPORT OF THE SPECIAL COMMITTEE TO STUDY THE FOREIGN AID PROGRAM (PAMPHLET). USA+45 CONSULT DELIB/GP LEGIS PLAN TEC/DEV CONFER SUPEGO CONGRESS. PAGE 157 A3199 — FOR/AID ORD/FREE ECO/UNDEV DIPLOM

B58
CARROLL H.N.,THE HOUSE OF REPRESENTATIVES AND FOREIGN AFFAIRS. USA+45 USA-45 NAT/G POL/PAR DIPLOM FOR/AID LEGIT ROUTINE PWR...TIME/SEQ CONGRESS. PAGE 25 A0502 — DELIB/GP LEGIS

B58
INDIAN COUNCIL WORLD AFFAIRS,DEFENCE AND SECURITY IN THE INDIAN OCEAN AREA. INDIA S/ASIA CULTURE CONSULT DELIB/GP FORCES PROB/SOLV DIPLOM INT/TRADE 20 CMN/WLTH. PAGE 70 A1438 — GEOG HABITAT ECO/UNDEV ORD/FREE

B58
MARTIN L.J.,INTERNATIONAL PROPAGANDA: ITS LEGAL AND DIPLOMATIC CONTROL. UK USA+45 USSR CONSULT DELIB/GP DOMIN CONTROL 20. PAGE 95 A1951 — EDU/PROP DIPLOM INT/LAW ATTIT

B58
NOEL-BAKER D.,THE ARMS RACE. WOR+45 NAT/G DELIB/GP ACT/RES TEC/DEV EDU/PROP NUC/PWR ATTIT KNOWL PWR ...CONCPT OBS LEAGUE/NAT 20 COLD/WAR. PAGE 109 A2245 — FUT INT/ORG ARMS/CONT PEACE

B58
STONE J.,AGGRESSION AND WORLD ORDER: A CRITIQUE OF UNITED NATIONS THEORIES OF AGGRESSION. LAW CONSTN DELIB/GP PROB/SOLV BAL/PWR DIPLOM DEBATE ADJUD CRIME PWR...POLICY IDEA/COMP 20 UN SUEZ LEAGUE/NAT. PAGE 138 A2835 — ORD/FREE INT/ORG WAR CONCPT

L58
HAVILAND H.F.,"FOREIGN AID AND THE POLICY PROCESS: 1957." USA+45 FACE/GP POL/PAR VOL/ASSN CHIEF DELIB/GP ACT/RES LEGIT EXEC GOV/REL ATTIT DRIVE PWR ...POLICY TESTS CONGRESS 20. PAGE 63 A1291 — LEGIS PLAN FOR/AID

L58
INT. SOC. SCI. BULL.,"TECHNIQUES OF MEDIATION AND CONCILIATION." EUR+WWI USA+45 SOCIETY INDUS INT/ORG LABOR NAT/G LEGIS DIPLOM EDU/PROP CHOOSE ATTIT RIGID/FLEX...JURID CONCPT GEN/LAWS 20. PAGE 70 A1447 — VOL/ASSN DELIB/GP INT/LAW

L58
SNYDER R.N.,"THE UNITED STATES DECISION TO RESIST AGGRESSION IN KOREA." ASIA KOREA S/ASIA USA+45 USA-45 WOR+45 INT/ORG DELIB/GP BAL/PWR COERCE PWR ...CONCPT REC/INT RESIST/INT COLD/WAR 20. PAGE 134 A2753 — QUANT METH/CNCPT DIPLOM

S58
ANDERSON N.,"INTERNATIONAL SEMINARS: AN ANALYSIS AND AN EVALUATION." WOR+45 R+D ACT/RES CREATE PLAN REGION ATTIT KNOWL SKILL...SOC REC/INT PERS/TEST CHARTS 20. PAGE 8 A0158 — INT/ORG DELIB/GP

S58
BOURBON-BUSSET J.,"HOW DECISIONS ARE MADE IN FOREIGN POLITICS: PSYCHOLOGY IN INTERNATIONAL POLITICS." WOR+45 NAT/G SECT REGION WAR MORAL ...CONCPT OBS STERTYP GEN/LAWS TOT/POP COLD/WAR 20. PAGE 17 A0350 — INT/ORG DELIB/GP DIPLOM

S58
ELKIN A.B.,"OEEC-ITS STRUCTURE AND POWERS." EUR+WWI CONSTN INDUS INT/ORG NAT/G VOL/ASSN DELIB/GP ACT/RES PLAN ORD/FREE WEALTH...CHARTS ORG/CHARTS OEEC 20. PAGE 41 A0839 — ECO/DEV EX/STRUC

S58
MCDOUGAL M.S.,"PERSPECTIVES FOR A LAW OF OUTER SPACE." FUT WOR+45 AIR CONSULT DELIB/GP TEC/DEV CT/SYS ORD/FREE...POLICY JURID 20 UN. PAGE 98 A2004 — INT/ORG SPACE INT/LAW

S58
SINGER J.D.,"THREAT PERCEPTION AND THE ARMAMENT TENSION DILEMMA." WOR+45 WOR-45 ELITES INT/ORG NAT/G DELIB/GP PLAN LEGIT COERCE DETER ATTIT RIGID/FLEX PWR...DECISION PSY 20. PAGE 133 A2724 — PERCEPT ARMS/CONT BAL/PWR

N58
US HOUSE COMM FOREIGN AFFAIRS,HEARINGS ON DRAFT LEGISLATION TO AMEND FURTHER THE MUTUAL SECURITY ACT OF 1954 (PAMPHLET). USA+45 CONSULT FORCES BUDGET DIPLOM DETER COST ORD/FREE...JURID 20 DEPT/DEFEN UN DEPT/STATE. PAGE 153 A3123 — LEGIS DELIB/GP CONFER WEAPON

N58
US HOUSE COMM FOREIGN AFFAIRS,HEARINGS ON THE FAR EAST AND THE PACIFIC (PAMPHLET). LAOS USA+45 NAT/G CONSULT FORCES CONFER DEBATE ORD/FREE 20. PAGE 153 A3124 — FOR/AID DIPLOM DELIB/GP LEGIS

N58
US HOUSE COMM FOREIGN AFFAIRS,HEARINGS ON REVIEW OF THE MUTUAL SECURITY PROGRAMS; EXAMINATION OF SELECTED PROJECTS IN FORMOSA AND PAKISTAN (PAMPHLET). ASIA PAKISTAN TAIWAN INDUS CONSULT DELIB/GP LEGIS BUDGET CONFER DEBATE 20. PAGE 153 A3125 — FOR/AID ECO/UNDEV DIPLOM ECO/TAC

B59
BALL M.M.,NATO AND THE EUROPEAN MOVEMENT. EUR+WWI USA+45 INT/ORG FORCES BAL/PWR EDU/PROP LEGIT REGION ATTIT ORD/FREE PWR...STAT OBS TIME/SEQ TREND CHARTS ORG/CHARTS STERTYP COLD/WAR EEC OEEC 20 NATO. — DELIB/GP STRUCT

PAGE 10 A0212
NUC/PWR

B59
COMM. STUDY ORGAN. PEACE,ORGANIZING PEACE IN THE NUCLEAR AGE. FUT CONSULT DELIB/GP DOMIN ADJUD ROUTINE COERCE ORD/FREE...TECHNIC INT/LAW JURID NEW/IDEA UN COLD/WAR 20. PAGE 29 A0581
INT/ORG ACT/RES NUC/PWR

B59
DAWSON R.H.,THE DECISION TO AID RUSSIA* FOREIGN POLICY AND DOMESTIC POLITICS. GERMANY USSR CHIEF EX/STRUC LEGIS TOP/EX PROB/SOLV WAR ATTIT...POLICY CONGRESS. PAGE 34 A0695
DECISION DELIB/GP DIPLOM FOR/AID

B59
DIEBOLD W. JR.,THE SCHUMAN PLAN: A STUDY IN ECONOMIC COOPERATION, 1950-1959. EUR+WWI FRANCE GERMANY USA+45 EXTR/IND CONSULT DELIB/GP PLAN DIPLOM ECO/TAC INT/TRADE ROUTINE ORD/FREE WEALTH ...METH/CNCPT STAT CONT/OBS INT TIME/SEQ ECSC 20. PAGE 37 A0759
INT/ORG REGION

B59
FOX W.T.R.,THEORETICAL ASPECTS OF INTERNATIONAL RELATIONS. WOR+45 INT/ORG NAT/G POL/PAR CONSULT PLAN ECO/TAC DOMIN EDU/PROP LEGIT EXEC COERCE PWR WEALTH...RELATIV CONCPT 20. PAGE 48 A0975
DELIB/GP ANTHOL

B59
GORDENKER L.,THE UNITED NATIONS AND THE PEACEFUL UNIFICATION OF KOREA. ASIA LAW LOC/G CONSULT ACT/RES DIPLOM DOMIN LEGIT ADJUD ADMIN ORD/FREE SOVEREIGN...INT GEN/METH UN COLD/WAR 20. PAGE 54 A1109
DELIB/GP KOREA INT/ORG

B59
GREENSPAN M.,THE MODERN LAW OF LAND WARFARE. WOR+45 INT/ORG NAT/G DELIB/GP FORCES ATTIT...POLICY HYPO/EXP STERTYP 20. PAGE 56 A1142
ADJUD PWR WAR

B59
HARVARD UNIVERSITY LAW SCHOOL,INTERNATIONAL PROBLEMS OF FINANCIAL PROTECTION AGAINST NUCLEAR RISK. WOR+45 NAT/G DELIB/GP PROB/SOLV DIPLOM CONTROL ATTIT...POLICY INT/LAW MATH 20. PAGE 62 A1281
NUC/PWR ADJUD INDUS FINAN

B59
REIFF H.,THE UNITED STATES AND THE TREATY LAW OF THE SEA. USA+45 USA-45 SEA SOCIETY INT/ORG CONSULT DELIB/GP LEGIS DIPLOM LEGIT ATTIT ORD/FREE PWR WEALTH...GEOG JURID TOT/POP 20 TREATY. PAGE 120 A2459
ADJUD INT/LAW

B59
SIMPSON J.L.,INTERNATIONAL ARBITRATION: LAW AND PRACTICE. WOR+45 WOR-45 INT/ORG DELIB/GP ADJUD PEACE MORAL ORD/FREE...METH 18/20. PAGE 133 A2720
INT/LAW DIPLOM CT/SYS CONSULT

B59
YOUNG J.,CHECKLIST OF MICROFILM REPRODUCTIONS OF SELECTED ARCHIVES OF THE JAPANESE ARMY, NAVY, AND OTHER GOVT AGENCIES, 1868-1945. DELIB/GP LEGIS DIPLOM EDU/PROP CIVMIL/REL 19/20 CHINJAP. PAGE 169 A3436
BIBLIOG ASIA FORCES WAR

L59
BEGUIN B.,"ILO AND THE TRIPARTITE SYSTEM." EUR+WWI WOR+45 WOR-45 CONSTN ECO/DEV ECO/UNDEV INDUS INT/ORG NAT/G VOL/ASSN DELIB/GP PLAN TEC/DEV LEGIT ORD/FREE WEALTH...CONCPT TIME/SEQ WORK ILO 20. PAGE 12 A0249
LABOR

S59
BELOFF M.,"NATIONAL GOVERNMENT AND INTERNATIONAL GOVERNMENT." WOR+45 R+D DELIB/GP ACT/RES PLAN PWR ...GEN/METH VAL/FREE EEC OEEC 20. PAGE 13 A0259
NAT/G INT/ORG DIPLOM

S59
HARVEY M.F.,"THE PALESTINE REFUGEE PROBLEM: ELEMENTS OF A SOLUTION." ISLAM LAW INT/ORG DELIB/GP TOP/EX ECO/TAC ROUTINE DRIVE HEALTH LOVE ORD/FREE PWR WEALTH...MAJORIT FAO 20. PAGE 62 A1283
ACT/RES LEGIT PEACE ISRAEL

S59
HOFFMANN S.,"IMPLEMENTATION OF INTERNATIONAL INSTRUMENTS ON HUMAN RIGHTS." WOR+45 VOL/ASSN DELIB/GP JUDGE EDU/PROP LEGIT ROUTINE PEACE COLD/WAR 20. PAGE 66 A1355
INT/ORG MORAL

S59
POTTER P.B.,"OBSTACLES AND ALTERNATIVES TO INTERNATIONAL LAW." WOR+45 NAT/G VOL/ASSN DELIB/GP BAL/PWR DOMIN ROUTINE...JURID VAL/FREE 20. PAGE 117 A2400
INT/ORG LAW DIPLOM INT/LAW

S59
STOESSINGER J.G.,"THE INTERNATIONAL ATOMIC ENERGY AGENCY: THE FIRST PHASE." FUT WOR+45 NAT/G VOL/ASSN DELIB/GP BAL/PWR LEGIT ADMIN ROUTINE PWR...OBS CON/ANAL GEN/LAWS VAL/FREE 20 IAEA. PAGE 138 A2829
INT/ORG ECO/DEV FOR/AID NUC/PWR

N59
US HOUSE COMM FOREIGN AFFAIRS,HEARINGS ON DRAFT LEGISLATION TO AMEND FURTHER THE MUTUAL SECURITY ACT OF 1954 (PAMPHLET). USA+45 USSR CONSULT DELIB/GP FORCES ECO/TAC CONFER...POLICY 20 CONGRESS. PAGE 153 A3126
DIPLOM FOR/AID ORD/FREE LEGIS

B60
ARMS CONTROL. FUT UNIV WOR+45 INTELL R+D INT/ORG NAT/G VOL/ASSN CONSULT CREATE EDU/PROP PEACE...HUM GEN/LAWS TOT/POP 20. PAGE 3 A0060
DELIB/GP ORD/FREE ARMS/CONT

B60
AMERICAN ASSEMBLY COLUMBIA U,THE SECRETARY OF STATE. USA+45 ELITES NAT/G PLAN ADMIN GOV/REL CENTRAL ATTIT...POLICY MGT 20 SEC/STATE CONGRESS PRESIDENT. PAGE 7 A0136
DELIB/GP EX/STRUC GP/REL DIPLOM

B60
BAILEY S.D.,THE GENERAL ASSEMBLY OF THE UNITED NATIONS. FUT WOR+45 STRUCT LEGIS ACT/RES PLAN EDU/PROP LEGIT ADMIN EXEC PEACE ATTIT HEALTH PWR ...CONCPT TREND CHARTS GEN/LAWS UN TOT/POP VAL/FREE COLD/WAR 20. PAGE 10 A0204
INT/ORG DELIB/GP DIPLOM

B60
ENGEL J.,THE SECURITY OF THE FREE WORLD. USSR WOR+45 STRATA STRUCT ECO/DEV ECO/UNDEV INT/ORG DELIB/GP FORCES DOMIN LEGIT ADJUD EXEC ARMS/CONT COERCE...POLICY CONCPT NEW/IDEA TIME/SEQ GEN/LAWS COLD/WAR WORK UN 20 NATO. PAGE 42 A0851
COM TREND DIPLOM

B60
FEIS H.,BETWEEN WAR AND PEACE: THE POTSDAM CONFERENCE. EUR+WWI NAT/G DELIB/GP PROB/SOLV REPAR WAR CIVMIL/REL...BIBLIOG 20. PAGE 45 A0911
DIPLOM CONFER BAL/PWR

B60
FURNIA A.H.,THE DIPLOMACY OF APPEASEMENT: ANGLO-FRENCH RELATIONS AND THE PRELUDE TO WORLD WAR II 1931-1938. FRANCE GERMANY UK ELITES NAT/G DELIB/GP FORCES WAR PEACE RIGID/FLEX 20. PAGE 50 A1026
DIPLOM BAL/PWR COERCE

B60
JEFFRIES C.,TRANSFER OF POWER: PROBLEMS OF THE PASSAGE TO SELFGOVERNMENT. CEYLON GHANA MALAYSIA NIGERIA UK INT/ORG CONSULT DELIB/GP LEGIS DIPLOM CONFER PARL/PROC 20. PAGE 73 A1502
SOVEREIGN COLONIAL ORD/FREE NAT/G

B60
JENNINGS R.,PROGRESS OF INTERNATIONAL LAW. FUT WOR+45 WOR-45 SOCIETY NAT/G VOL/ASSN DELIB/GP DIPLOM EDU/PROP LEGIT COERCE ATTIT DRIVE MORAL ORD/FREE...JURID CONCPT OBS TIME/SEQ TREND GEN/LAWS. PAGE 74 A1509
INT/ORG LAW INT/LAW

B60
KHRUSHCHEV N.,FOR VICTORY IN PEACEFUL COMPETITION WITH CAPITALISM. COM FUT USSR WOR+45 CONSTN SOCIETY INDUS INT/ORG DELIB/GP PLAN BAL/PWR DIPLOM PERSON MARXISM...MARXIST WORK 20 COLD/WAR. PAGE 79 A1611
TOP/EX PWR CAP/ISM SOCISM

B60
LANDHEER B.,ETHICAL VALUES IN INTERNATIONAL DECISION-MAKING. FUT LAW SOCIETY INT/ORG NAT/G DELIB/GP CREATE NAT/LISM ATTIT PERSON...DECISION CONCPT LEAGUE/NAT TOT/POP 20. PAGE 84 A1718
HYPO/EXP POLICY PEACE

B60
LISTER L.,EUROPE'S COAL AND STEEL COMMUNITY. FRANCE GERMANY STRUCT ECO/DEV EXTR/IND INDUS MARKET NAT/G DELIB/GP ECO/TAC INT/TRADE EDU/PROP ATTIT RIGID/FLEX ORD/FREE PWR WEALTH...CONCPT STAT TIME/SEQ CHARTS ECSC 20. PAGE 90 A1843
EUR+WWI INT/ORG REGION

B60
MCKINNEY R.,REVIEW OF THE INTERNATIONAL ATOMIC POLICIES AND PROGRAMS OF THE UNITED STATES (5 VOLS.). COM FUT USA+45 ECO/DEV ECO/UNDEV INT/ORG DELIB/GP PLAN ADMIN 20 THIRD/WRLD. PAGE 98 A2016
NUC/PWR PEACE DIPLOM POLICY

B60
MORISON E.E.,TURMOIL AND TRADITION: A STUDY OF THE LIFE AND TIMES OF HENRY L. STIMSON. USA+45 USA-45 POL/PAR CHIEF DELIB/GP FORCES BAL/PWR DIPLOM ARMS/CONT WAR PEACE 19/20 STIMSON/HL ROOSEVLT/F TAFT/WH HOOVER/H REPUBLICAN. PAGE 104 A2142
BIOG NAT/G EX/STRUC

B60
MUNRO L.,UNITED NATIONS, HOPE FOR A DIVIDED WORLD. FUT WOR+45 CONSTN DELIB/GP CREATE TEC/DEV DIPLOM EDU/PROP LEGIT PEACE ATTIT HEALTH ORD/FREE PWR ...CONCPT TREND UN VAL/FREE 20. PAGE 106 A2172
INT/ORG ROUTINE

B60
PAN AMERICAN UNION,FIFTH MEETING OF CONSULTATION OF MINISTERS OF FOREIGN AFFAIRS OF AMERICAN STATES. L/A+17C FORCES PLAN PROB/SOLV ADJUD PEACE...POLICY INT/LAW 20 OAS. PAGE 113 A2327
INT/ORG DIPLOM DELIB/GP ECO/UNDEV

B60
SCHLESINGER J.R.,THE POLITICAL ECONOMY OF NATIONAL SECURITY. USA+45 USSR WOR+45 ECO/DEV ECO/UNDEV NAT/G DELIB/GP TOP/EX BAL/PWR DIPLOM INT/TRADE ATTIT PWR...STERTYP TOT/POP 20. PAGE 128 A2628
PLAN ECO/TAC

B60
US HOUSE COMM FOREIGN AFFAIRS,HEARINGS ON A BILL TO AMEND FURTHER THE MUTUAL SECURITY ACT OF 1954. USA+45 CONSULT FORCES BUDGET FOR/AID CONFER DETER ...CHARTS 20 DEPT/DEFEN DEPT/STATE UNEF. PAGE 153 A3127
DIPLOM ORD/FREE DELIB/GP LEGIS

L60
HAAS E.B.,"CONSENSUS FORMATION IN THE COUNCIL OF EUROPE." EUR+WWI NAT/G DELIB/GP DIPLOM REGION CHOOSE PWR SOVEREIGN...RELATIV NEW/IDEA QUANT CHARTS INDEX TOT/POP OEEC 20 COUNCL/EUR. PAGE 59 A1206
POL/PAR INT/ORG STAT

L60
JACOB P.E.,"THE DISARMAMENT CONSENSUS." USA+45 USSR WOR+45 INT/ORG NAT/G ACT/RES TEC/DEV BAL/PWR EDU/PROP ADMIN COERCE DETER NUC/PWR CONSEN
DELIB/GP ATTIT ARMS/CONT

RIGID/FLEX PWR...CONCPT RECORD CHARTS COLD/WAR 20. PAGE 72 A1482

L60
NOGEE J.L.,"THE DIPLOMACY OF DISARMAMENT." WOR+45 INT/ORG NAT/G CONSULT DELIB/GP TOP/EX BAL/PWR DIPLOM EDU/PROP COERCE DETER WEAPON PEACE ATTIT ...RECORD TIME/SEQ TOT/POP VAL/FREE COLD/WAR 20. PAGE 109 A2246 — PWR ORD/FREE ARMS/CONT NUC/PWR

S60
DYSON F.J.,"THE FUTURE DEVELOPMENT OF NUCLEAR WEAPONS." FUT WOR+45 DELIB/GP ACT/RES PLAN DETER WEAPON ATTIT PWR...POLICY 20. PAGE 40 A0815 — INT/ORG ARMS/CONT NUC/PWR

S60
HAYTON R.D.,"THE ANTARCTIC SETTLEMENT OF 1959." FUT USA+45 WOR+45 WOR-45 STRUCT R+D INT/ORG EX/STRUC CREATE TEC/DEV LEGIT PEACE ATTIT SOVEREIGN ...TIME/SEQ 20 TREATY IGY. PAGE 63 A1297 — DELIB/GP JURID DIPLOM REGION

S60
IKLE F.C.,"NTH COUNTRIES AND DISARMAMENT." WOR+45 DELIB/GP ECO/TAC DOMIN EDU/PROP LEGIT ROUTINE COERCE RIGID/FLEX ORD/FREE...MARXIST TREND 20. PAGE 70 A1432 — FUT INT/ORG ARMS/CONT NUC/PWR

S60
JACOBSON H.K.,"THE USSR AND ILO." COM STRUCT ECO/DEV ECO/UNDEV CONSULT DELIB/GP ECO/TAC ILO WORK COLD/WAR 20. PAGE 72 A1484 — INT/ORG LABOR USSR

S60
MARTIN E.M.,"NEW TRENDS IN UNITED STATES ECONOMIC FOREIGN POLICY." USA+45 INTELL DELIB/GP FOR/AID INT/TRADE ROUTINE BAL/PAY...RELATIV 20. PAGE 95 A1949 — NAT/G PLAN DIPLOM

S60
MORA J.A.,"THE ORGANIZATION OF AMERICAN STATES." USA+45 LAW ECO/UNDEV VOL/ASSN DELIB/GP PLAN BAL/PWR EDU/PROP ADMIN DRIVE RIGID/FLEX ORD/FREE WEALTH ...TIME/SEQ GEN/LAWS OAS 20. PAGE 103 A2126 — L/A+17C INT/ORG REGION

S60
NANES A.,"THE EUROPEAN COMMUNITY AND THE UNITED STATES: EVOLVING RELATIONS." EUR+WWI USA+45 WOR+45 ECO/UNDEV MARKET NAT/G DELIB/GP PLAN LEGIT ATTIT PWR WEALTH...CONCPT STAT TIME/SEQ CON/ANAL EEC OEEC 20 EURATOM. PAGE 107 A2194 — INT/ORG REGION

S60
PADELFORD N.J.,"POLITICS AND CHANGE IN THE SECURITY COUNCIL." FUT WOR+45 CONSTN NAT/G EX/STRUC LEGIS ORD/FREE...CONCPT CHARTS UN 20. PAGE 113 A2309 — INT/ORG DELIB/GP

S60
SCHWELB E.,"INTERNATIONAL CONVENTIONS ON HUMAN RIGHTS." FUT WOR+45 LAW CONSTN CULTURE SOCIETY STRUCT VOL/ASSN DELIB/GP PLAN ADJUD SUPEGO LOVE MORAL...SOC CONCPT STAT RECORD HIST/WRIT TREND 20 UN. PAGE 130 A2664 — INT/ORG HUM

S60
SWIFT R.,"THE UNITED NATIONS AND ITS PUBLIC." WOR+45 CONSTN FINAN CONSULT DELIB/GP ACT/RES ADMIN ROUTINE RIGID/FLEX SKILL UN 20. PAGE 140 A2870 — INT/ORG EDU/PROP

B61
BARNES W.,THE FOREIGN SERVICE OF THE UNITED STATES. USA+45 USA-45 CONSTN INT/ORG POL/PAR CONSULT DELIB/GP LEGIS DOMIN EDU/PROP EXEC ATTIT RIGID/FLEX ORD/FREE PWR...POLICY CONCPT STAT OBS RECORD BIOG TIME/SEQ TREND. PAGE 11 A0224 — NAT/G MGT DIPLOM

B61
BISHOP D.G.,THE ADMINISTRATION OF BRITISH FOREIGN RELATIONS. EUR+WWI MOD/EUR INT/ORG NAT/G POL/PAR DELIB/GP LEGIS TOP/EX ECO/TAC DOMIN EDU/PROP ADMIN COERCE 20. PAGE 14 A0292 — ROUTINE PWR DIPLOM UK

B61
GRAEBNER N.,AN UNCERTAIN TRADITION: AMERICAN SECRETARIES OF STATE IN THE 20TH CENTURY. USA+45 CONSTN INT/ORG NAT/G DELIB/GP TOP/EX BAL/PWR DOMIN LEGIT ADMIN ARMS/CONT ATTIT DRIVE PERSON SUPEGO ORD/FREE PWR...GEN/LAWS VAL/FREE CONGRESS. PAGE 55 A1121 — USA-45 BIOG DIPLOM

B61
HARRISON S.,INDIA AND THE UNITED STATES. FUT S/ASIA USA+45 WOR+45 INTELL ECO/DEV ECO/UNDEV AGRI INDUS INT/ORG NAT/G CONSULT EX/STRUC TOP/EX PLAN ECO/TAC NEUTRAL ALL/VALS...MGT TOT/POP 20. PAGE 62 A1272 — DELIB/GP ACT/RES FOR/AID INDIA

B61
HENKIN L.,ARMS CONTROL: ISSUES FOR THE PUBLIC. EUR+WWI FUT USA+45 USSR INT/ORG NAT/G DIPLOM EDU/PROP DETER NUC/PWR ATTIT PWR...CONCPT RECORD HIST/WRIT TIME/SEQ TOT/POP COLD/WAR 20. PAGE 64 A1316 — WOR+45 DELIB/GP ARMS/CONT

B61
LUKACS J.,A HISTORY OF THE COLD WAR. ASIA COM EUR+WWI USA+45 USA-45 INT/ORG NAT/G DELIB/GP ACT/RES BAL/PWR DIPLOM DOMIN EDU/PROP LEGIT DRIVE ORD/FREE...TREND COLD/WAR 20. PAGE 91 A1872 — PWR TIME/SEQ USSR

B61
MCDOUGAL M.S.,LAW AND MINIMUM WORLD PUBLIC ORDER. WOR+45 SOCIETY NAT/G DELIB/GP EDU/PROP LEGIT ADJUD COERCE ATTIT PERSON...JURID CONCPT RECORD TREND TOT/POP 20. PAGE 98 A2006 — INT/ORG ORD/FREE INT/LAW

B61
PEASLEE A.J.,INTERNATIONAL GOVERNMENT ORGANIZATIONS, CONSTITUTIONAL DOCUMENTS. WOR+45 WOR-45 CONSTN VOL/ASSN DELIB/GP EX/STRUC ROUTINE KNOWL TOT/POP 20. PAGE 114 A2344 — INT/ORG STRUCT

B61
ROBERTSON A.H.,THE LAW OF INTERNATIONAL INSTITUTIONS IN EUROPE. EUR+WWI MOD/EUR INT/ORG NAT/G VOL/ASSN DELIB/GP...JURID TIME/SEQ TOT/POP 20 TREATY. PAGE 122 A2497 — RIGID/FLEX ORD/FREE

B61
SCHNAPPER B.,LA POLITIQUE ET LE COMMERCE FRANCAIS DANS LE GOLFE DE GUINEE DE 1838 A 1871. FRANCE GUINEA UK SEA EXTR/IND NAT/G DELIB/GP LEGIS ADMIN ORD/FREE...POLICY GEOG CENSUS CHARTS BIBLIOG 19. PAGE 129 A2636 — COLONIAL INT/TRADE DOMIN AFR

B61
SHARP W.R.,FIELD ADMINISTRATION IN THE UNITED NATION SYSTEM: THE CONDUCT OF INTERNATIONAL ECONOMIC AND SOCIAL PROGRAMS. FUT WOR+45 CONSTN SOCIETY ECO/UNDEV R+D DELIB/GP ACT/RES PLAN TEC/DEV EDU/PROP EXEC ROUTINE HEALTH WEALTH...HUM CONCPT CHARTS METH ILO UNESCO VAL/FREE UN 20. PAGE 132 A2697 — INT/ORG CONSULT

B61
STRAUSZ-HUPE R.,A FORWARD STRATEGY FOR AMERICA. FUT WOR+45 ECO/DEV INT/ORG NAT/G POL/PAR DELIB/GP FORCES ACT/RES CREATE ECO/TAC DOMIN EDU/PROP ATTIT DRIVE PWR...MAJORIT CONCPT STAT OBS TIME/SEQ TREND COLD/WAR TOT/POP. PAGE 139 A2848 — USA+45 PLAN DIPLOM

B61
US CONGRESS JOINT ECO COMM,INTERNATIONAL PAYMENTS IMBALANCES AND NEED FOR STRENGTHENING INTERNATIONAL FINANCIAL ARRANGEMENTS. USA+45 WOR+45 DELIB/GP DIPLOM INT/TRADE...CHARTS 20 CONGRESS OEEC. PAGE 150 A3063 — BAL/PAY INT/ORG FINAN PROB/SOLV

B61
US HOUSE COMM APPROPRIATIONS,INTER-AMERICAN PROGRAMS FOR 1961: DENIAL OF 1962 BUDGET INFORMATION. CHILE L/A+17C USA+45 FINAN CONSULT BUDGET ADJUD COST EFFICIENCY WEALTH...POLICY CHARTS 20 CONGRESS. PAGE 153 A3119 — LEGIS FOR/AID DELIB/GP ECO/UNDEV

B61
US HOUSE COMM FOREIGN AFFAIRS,THE INTERNATIONAL DEVELOPMENT AND SECURITY ACT: HEARINGS BEFORE COMMITTEE ON FOREIGN AFFAIRS, HOUSE OF REP: HR7372. USA+45 AGRI INT/ORG NAT/G CONSULT DELIB/GP DIPLOM ECO/TAC INT/TRADE LOBBY REPRESENT 20 MCNAMARA/R DILLON/D RUSK/D CONGRESS. PAGE 153 A3128 — FOR/AID CONFER LEGIS ECO/UNDEV

B61
WARD R.E.,JAPANESE POLITICAL SCIENCE: A GUIDE TO JAPANESE REFERENCE AND RESEARCH MATERIALS (2ND ED.). LAW CONSTN STRATA NAT/G POL/PAR DELIB/GP LEGIS ADMIN CHOOSE GP/REL...INT/LAW 19/20 CHINJAP. PAGE 161 A3282 — BIBLIOG/A PHIL/SCI

B61
WECHSLER H.,PRINCIPLES, POLITICS AND FUNDAMENTAL LAW: SELECTED ESSAYS. USA+45 USA-45 LAW SOCIETY NAT/G PROVS DELIB/GP EX/STRUC ACT/RES LEGIT PERSON KNOWL PWR...JURID 20 NUREMBERG. PAGE 162 A3296 — CT/SYS CONSTN INT/LAW

B61
WILLOUGHBY W.R.,THE ST LAWRENCE WATERWAY: A STUDY IN POLITICS AND DIPLOMACY. USA+45 ECO/DEV COM/IND INT/ORG CONSULT DELIB/GP ACT/RES TEC/DEV DIPLOM ECO/TAC ROUTINE...TIME/SEQ 20. PAGE 165 A3357 — LEGIS INT/TRADE CANADA DIST/IND

B61
WOOD B.,THE MAKING OF THE GOOD NEIGHBOR POLICY. L/A+17C USA-45 COERCE CIVMIL/REL DISCRIM. PAGE 166 A3389 — DIPLOM DELIB/GP POLICY

L61
HOYT E.C.,"UNITED STATES REACTION TO THE KOREAN ATTACK." COM KOREA USA+45 CONSTN DELIB/GP FORCES PLAN ECO/TAC DOMIN EDU/PROP LEGIT ROUTINE COERCE WAR ATTIT DISPL RIGID/FLEX ORD/FREE PWR...POLICY INT/LAW TREND UN 20. PAGE 68 A1402 — ASIA INT/ORG BAL/PWR DIPLOM

S61
ALGER C.F.,"NON-RESOLUTION CONSEQUENCES OF THE UNITED NATIONS AND THEIR EFFECT ON INTERNATIONAL CONFLICT." WOR+45 CONSTN ECO/DEV NAT/G CONSULT DELIB/GP TOP/EX ACT/RES PLAN DIPLOM EDU/PROP ROUTINE ATTIT ALL/VALS...INT/LAW TOT/POP UN 20. PAGE 6 A0117 — INT/ORG DRIVE BAL/PWR

S61
ANGLIN D.,"UNITED STATES OPPOSITION TO CANADIAN MEMBERSHIP IN THE PAN AMERICAN UNION: A CANADIAN VIEW." L/A+17C UK USA+45 VOL/ASSN DELIB/GP EX/STRUC PLAN DIPLOM DOMIN REGION ATTIT RIGID/FLEX PWR ...RELATIV CONCPT STERTYP CMN/WLTH OAS 20. PAGE 8 A0162 — INT/ORG CANADA

S61
BRZEZINSKI Z.K.,"THE ORGANIZATION OF THE COMMUNIST CAMP." COM CZECHOSLVK COM/IND NAT/G DELIB/GP INT/TRADE DOMIN EDU/PROP EXEC ROUTINE COERCE ATTIT PWR...MGT CONCPT TIME/SEQ CHARTS VAL/FREE 20 TREATY. PAGE 20 A0416 — VOL/ASSN DIPLOM USSR

S61
CLAUDE I.,"THE MANAGEMENT OF POWER IN THE CHANGING UNITED NATIONS." WOR+45 PERCEPT UN TOT/POP VAL/FREE 20. PAGE 27 A0544
INT/ORG DELIB/GP BAL/PWR

S61
JUVILER P.H.,"INTERPARLIAMENTARY CONTACTS IN SOVIET FOREIGN POLICY." COM FUT WOR+45 WOR-45 SOCIETY CONSULT ACT/RES DIPLOM ADMIN PEACE ATTIT RIGID/FLEX WEALTH...WELF/ST SOC TOT/POP CONGRESS 19/20. PAGE 75 A1543
INT/ORG DELIB/GP USSR

S61
KRANNHALS H.V.,"COMMAND INTEGRATION WITHIN THE WARSAW PACT." COM USSR WOR+45 DELIB/GP EDU/PROP ...CONCPT AUD/VIS CHARTS COLD/WAR TOT/POP VAL/FREE 20 TREATY WARSAW/P. PAGE 82 A1675
INT/ORG FORCES TOTALISM

S61
LANFALUSSY A.,"EUROPE'S PROGRESS: DUE TO COMMON MARKET." EUR+WWI ECO/DEV DELIB/GP PLAN ECO/TAC ROUTINE WEALTH...GEOG TREND EEC 20. PAGE 84 A1721
INT/ORG MARKET

S61
PADELFORD N.J.,"POLITICS AND THE FUTURE OF ECOSOC." AFR S/ASIA ECO/UNDEV INDUS NAT/G DELIB/GP ACT/RES ORD/FREE WEALTH...CONCPT CHARTS UN 20 ECOSOC. PAGE 113 A2310
INT/ORG TEC/DEV

B62
ALTHING F.A.M.,EUROPEAN ORGANIZATIONS AND FOREIGN RELATIONS OF STATES: A COMPARATIVE ANALYSIS OF DECISION-MAKING. EUR+WWI CONSTN ELITES BAL/PWR INT/TRADE SOVEREIGN TREATY. PAGE 6 A0131
DELIB/GP INT/ORG DECISION DIPLOM

B62
BAILEY S.D.,THE SECRETARIAT OF THE UNITED NATIONS. FUT WOR+45 DELIB/GP PLAN BAL/PWR DOMIN EDU/PROP ADMIN PEACE ATTIT PWR...DECISION CONCPT TREND CON/ANAL CHARTS UN VAL/FREE COLD/WAR 20. PAGE 10 A0205
INT/ORG EXEC DIPLOM

B62
BELL C.,NEGOTIATION FROM STRENGTH. WOR+45 FACE/GP INT/ORG DELIB/GP FORCES PLAN DOMIN COERCE NUC/PWR PEACE DRIVE PWR...POLICY LOG OBS RECORD INT SAMP TREND COLD/WAR 20. PAGE 13 A0255
NAT/G CONCPT DIPLOM

B62
BLACKETT P.M.S.,STUDIES OF WAR: NUCLEAR AND CONVENTIONAL. EUR+WWI USA+45 DELIB/GP ACT/RES CREATE PLAN TEC/DEV LEGIT COERCE WAR ORD/FREE PWR ...POLICY TECHNIC TIME/SEQ 20. PAGE 15 A0300
INT/ORG FORCES ARMS/CONT NUC/PWR

B62
HATCH J.,AFRICA TODAY-AND TOMORROW: AN OUTLINE OF BASIC FACTS AND MAJOR PROBLEMS. AFR FUT ISLAM STRATA ECO/UNDEV INT/ORG NAT/G POL/PAR DELIB/GP TOP/EX EDU/PROP LEGIT CHOOSE ATTIT...TIME/SEQ TOT/POP COLD/WAR 20. PAGE 63 A1287
PLAN CONSTN NAT/LISM

B62
JEWELL M.E.,SENATORIAL POLITICS AND FOREIGN POLICY. NAT/G POL/PAR CHIEF DELIB/GP TOP/EX FOR/AID EDU/PROP ROUTINE ATTIT PWR SKILL...MAJORIT METH/CNCPT TIME/SEQ CONGRESS 20 PRESIDENT. PAGE 74 A1516
USA+45 LEGIS DIPLOM

B62
LAWSON R.,INTERNATIONAL REGIONAL ORGANIZATIONS. WOR+45 NAT/G VOL/ASSN CONSULT LEGIS EDU/PROP LEGIT ADMIN EXEC ROUTINE HEALTH PWR WEALTH...JURID EEC COLD/WAR 20 UN. PAGE 86 A1752
INT/ORG DELIB/GP REGION

B62
MCDOUGAL M.S.,THE PUBLIC ORDER OF THE OCEANS. WOR+45 WOR-45 SEA INT/ORG NAT/G CONSULT DELIB/GP DIPLOM LEGIT PEACE RIGID/FLEX...GEOG INT/LAW JURID RECORD TOT/POP 20 TREATY. PAGE 98 A2007
ADJUD ORD/FREE

B62
MCKENNA J.,DIPLOMATIC PROTEST IN FOREIGN POLICY: ANALYSIS AND CASE STUDIES. COM USA+45 WOR+45 INT/ORG PUB/INST DELIB/GP TOP/EX ACT/RES PLAN LEGIT ATTIT 20. PAGE 98 A2014
NAT/G POLICY DIPLOM

B62
MOON P.,DIVIDE AND QUIT. INDIA PAKISTAN STRATA DELIB/GP PLAN DIPLOM REPRESENT GP/REL INGP/REL CONSEN DISCRIM...OBS 20. PAGE 103 A2119
WAR REGION ISOLAT SECT

B62
MORGENSTERN O.,STRATEGIE - HEUTE (2ND ED.). USA+45 USSR ECO/DEV DELIB/GP WAR PEACE ORD/FREE...GOV/COMP NAT/COMP 20 COLD/WAR NATO. PAGE 104 A2134
NUC/PWR DIPLOM FORCES TEC/DEV

B62
MULLEY F.W.,THE POLITICS OF WESTERN DEFENSE. EUR+WWI USA-45 WOR+45 VOL/ASSN EX/STRUC FORCES COERCE DETER PEACE ATTIT ORD/FREE PWR...RECORD TIME/SEQ CHARTS COLD/WAR 20 NATO. PAGE 106 A2168
INT/ORG DELIB/GP NUC/PWR

B62
OSGOOD C.E.,AN ALTERNATIVE TO WAR OR SURRENDER. FUT UNIV CULTURE INTELL SOCIETY R+D INT/ORG CONSULT DELIB/GP ACT/RES PLAN CHOOSE ATTIT PERCEPT KNOWL ...PHIL/SCI PSY SOC TREND GEN/LAWS 20. PAGE 112 A2300
ORD/FREE EDU/PROP PEACE WAR

B62
PAKISTAN MINISTRY OF FINANCE,FOREIGN ECONOMIC AID: A REVIEW OF FOREIGN ECONOMIC AID TO PAKISTAN. EUR+WWI PAKISTAN UK USA+45 USSR ECO/UNDEV INT/ORG DELIB/GP DIPLOM ECO/TAC...CHARTS CMN/WLTH CHINJAP. PAGE 113 A2318
FOR/AID RECEIVE WEALTH FINAN

B62
ROBINSON A.D.,DUTCH ORGANIZED AGRICULTURE IN INTERNATIONAL POLITICS, 1945-1960. EUR+WWI NETHERLAND STRUCT ECO/DEV NAT/G VOL/ASSN CONSULT DELIB/GP PLAN TEC/DEV INT/TRADE EDU/PROP ATTIT RIGID/FLEX ALL/VALS...NEW/IDEA TREND EEC 20. PAGE 122 A2502
AGRI INT/ORG

B62
ROOSEVELT J.,THE LIBERAL PAPERS. USA+45 WOR+45 ECO/DEV INT/ORG DELIB/GP ACT/RES PROB/SOLV DETER ATTIT...TREND IDEA/COMP ANTHOL. PAGE 123 A2520
DIPLOM NEW/LIB POLICY FORCES

B62
SCHRODER P.M.,METTERNICH'S DIPLOMACY AT ITS ZENITH, 1820-1823. MOD/EUR ELITES INT/ORG VOL/ASSN DELIB/GP ECO/TAC EDU/PROP DISPL PWR SOVEREIGN...POLICY CONCPT GEN/LAWS 19 METTRNCH/K. PAGE 129 A2647
ORD/FREE BIOG BAL/PWR DIPLOM

B62
SOMMER T.,DEUTSCHLAND UND JAPAN ZWISCHEN DEN MACHTEN. GERMANY DELIB/GP BAL/PWR AGREE COERCE TOTALISM PWR 20 CHINJAP TREATY. PAGE 135 A2765
DIPLOM WAR ATTIT

B62
SPANIER J.W.,THE POLITICS OF DISARMAMENT. COM USA+45 USSR EDU/PROP ATTIT ORD/FREE PWR RESPECT ...MYTH RECORD 20 COLD/WAR. PAGE 135 A2771
INT/ORG DELIB/GP ARMS/CONT

B62
US CONGRESS,LEGISLATIVE HISTORY OF UNITED STATES TAX CONVENTIONS(VOL. 1). USA+45 USA-45 DELIB/GP WEALTH...CHARTS 20 CONGRESS. PAGE 150 A3061
TAX LEGIS LAW DIPLOM

B62
US CONGRESS JOINT ECO COMM,FACTORS AFFECTING THE UNITED STATES BALANCE OF PAYMENTS. USA+45 DELIB/GP PLAN DIPLOM FOR/AID PRODUC WEALTH...CHARTS 20 CONGRESS OEEC. PAGE 150 A3064
BAL/PAY INT/TRADE ECO/TAC FINAN

B62
WOETZEL R.K.,THE NURENBERG TRIALS IN INTERNATIONAL LAW. CHRIST-17C MOD/EUR WOR+45 SOCIETY NAT/G DELIB/GP DOMIN LEGIT ROUTINE ATTIT DRIVE PERSON SUPEGO MORAL ORD/FREE...POLICY MAJORIT JURID PSY SOC SELF/OBS RECORD NAZI TOT/POP. PAGE 166 A3376
INT/ORG ADJUD WAR

B62
YALEN R.,REGIONALISM AND WORLD ORDER. EUR+WWI WOR+45 WOR-45 INT/ORG VOL/ASSN DELIB/GP FORCES TOP/EX BAL/PWR DIPLOM DOMIN REGION ARMS/CONT PWR ...JURID HYPO/EXP COLD/WAR 20. PAGE 168 A3427
ORD/FREE POLICY

L62
MALINOWSKI W.R.,"CENTRALIZATION AND DE-CENTRALIZATION IN THE UNITED NATIONS' ECONOMIC AND SOCIAL ACTIVITIES." WOR+45 CONSTN ECO/UNDEV INT/ORG VOL/ASSN DELIB/GP ECO/TAC EDU/PROP ADMIN RIGID/FLEX ...OBS CHARTS UNESCO UN EEC OAS OEEC 20. PAGE 93 A1913
CREATE GEN/LAWS

L62
NIZARD L.,"CUBAN QUESTION AND SECURITY COUNCIL." L/A+17C USA+45 ECO/UNDEV NAT/G POL/PAR DELIB/GP ECO/TAC PWR...RELATIV OBS TIME/SEQ TREND GEN/LAWS UN 20 UN. PAGE 109 A2242
INT/ORG JURID DIPLOM CUBA

L62
STEIN E.,"MR HAMMARSKJOLD, THE CHARTER LAW AND THE FUTURE ROLE OF THE UNITED NATIONS SECRETARY-GENERAL." WOR+45 CONSTN INT/ORG DELIB/GP FORCES TOP/EX BAL/PWR LEGIT ROUTINE RIGID/FLEX PWR ...POLICY JURID OBS STERTYP UN COLD/WAR 20 HAMMARSK/D. PAGE 137 A2815
CONCPT BIOG

S62
BERKES R.N.B.,"THE NEW FRONTIER IN THE UN." FUT USA+45 WOR+45 INT/ORG DELIB/GP NAT/LISM PERCEPT RESPECT UN OAS 20. PAGE 13 A0272
GEN/LAWS DIPLOM

S62
BROWN B.E.,"L'ONU ABANDONNE LA HONGRIE." COM USSR WOR+45 CONSTN NAT/G POL/PAR DELIB/GP ACT/RES TEC/DEV PWR...TIME/SEQ 20 UN. PAGE 20 A0400
INT/ORG TOTALISM HUNGARY POLICY

S62
CORET A.,"LE STATUT DE L'ILE CHRISTMAS DE L'OCEAN INDIEN." FUT S/ASIA ECO/DEV ECO/UNDEV VOL/ASSN DELIB/GP PLAN...RELATIV OBS TIME/SEQ TREND AUSTRAL 20. PAGE 30 A0619
NAT/G INT/ORG NEW/ZEALND

S62
CORET A.,"LA DECLARATION DE L'ASSEMBLEE GENERAL DE L'ONU SUR L'OCTROI DE L'INDEPENDENCE AUX PAYS ET AUX PEUPLES." AFR ASIA ISLAM NIGERIA S/ASIA USSR WOR+45 ECO/UNDEV NAT/G DELIB/GP COLONIAL ALL/VALS ...CONCPT TIME/SEQ TREND UN TOT/POP 20 MEXIC/AMER. PAGE 31 A0621
INT/ORG STRUCT SOVEREIGN

S62
CRANE R.D.,"SOVIET ATTITUDE TOWARD INTERNATIONAL SPACE LAW." COM FUT USA+45 USSR AIR CONSTN DELIB/GP DOMIN PWR...JURID TREND TOT/POP 20. PAGE 32 A0657
LAW ATTIT INT/LAW SPACE

S62
DIHN N.Q.,"L'INTERNATIONALISATION DU MEKONG."
S/ASIA

CAMBODIA LAOS VIETNAM WOR+45 INT/ORG NAT/G VOL/ASSN DELIB/GP PEACE HEALTH...CONCPT TIME/SEQ CHARTS METH VAL/FREE 20. PAGE 37 A0761

S62
FENWICK C.G.,"ISSUES AT PUNTA DEL ESTE: NON-INTERVENTION VS COLLECTIVE SECURITY." L/A+17C USA+45 VOL/ASSN DELIB/GP ECO/TAC LEGIT ADJUD REGION ORD/FREE OAS COLD/WAR 20. PAGE 45 A0917 INT/ORG CUBA

S62
FINKELSTEIN L.S.,"THE UNITED NATIONS AND ORGANIZATIONS FOR CONTROL OF ARMAMENT." FUT WOR+45 VOL/ASSN DELIB/GP TOP/EX CREATE EDU/PROP LEGIT ADJUD NUC/PWR ATTIT RIGID/FLEX ORD/FREE...POLICY DECISION CONCPT OBS TREND GEN/LAWS TOT/POP COLD/WAR. PAGE 46 A0933 INT/ORG PWR ARMS/CONT

S62
FOSTER W.C.,"ARMS CONTROL AND DISARMAMENT IN A DIVIDED WORLD." COM FUT USA+45 USSR WOR+45 INTELL INT/ORG NAT/G VOL/ASSN CONSULT CREATE PLAN TEC/DEV EDU/PROP LEGIT NUC/PWR ATTIT RIGID/FLEX...CONCPT TREND TOT/POP 20 UN. PAGE 47 A0971 DELIB/GP POLICY ARMS/CONT DIPLOM

S62
JACOBSON H.K.,"THE UNITED NATIONS AND COLONIALISM: A TENTATIVE APPRAISAL." AFR FUT S/ASIA USA+45 USSR WOR+45 NAT/G DELIB/GP PLAN DIPLOM ECO/TAC DOMIN ADMIN ROUTINE COERCE ATTIT RIGID/FLEX ORD/FREE PWR ...OBS STERTYP UN 20. PAGE 73 A1486 INT/ORG CONCPT COLONIAL

S62
LONDON K.,"SINO-SOVIET RELATIONS IN THE CONTEXT OF THE 'WORLD SOCIALIST SYSTEM'." ASIA CHINA/COM COM USSR INT/ORG NAT/G TOP/EX BAL/PWR DIPLOM DOMIN ATTIT PERCEPT RIGID/FLEX PWR MARXISM...METH/CNCPT TREND 20. PAGE 91 A1854 DELIB/GP CONCPT SOCISM

S62
MANGIN G.,"LES ACCORDS DE COOPERATION EN MATIERE DE JUSTICE ENTRE LA FRANCE ET LES ETATS AFRICAINS ET MALGACHE." AFR ISLAM WOR+45 STRUCT ECO/UNDEV NAT/G DELIB/GP PERCEPT ALL/VALS...JURID MGT TIME/SEQ 20. PAGE 94 A1919 INT/ORG LAW FRANCE

S62
MILLAR T.B.,"THE COMMONWEALTH AND THE UNITED NATIONS." FUT WOR+45 STRUCT NAT/G VOL/ASSN CONSULT DELIB/GP EDU/PROP LEGIT ATTIT...POLICY CONCPT TREND CMN/WLTH UN 20. PAGE 101 A2072 INT/ORG

S62
MORGENTHAU H.J.,"A POLITICAL THEORY OF FOREIGN AID." ECO/UNDEV NAT/G DELIB/GP PLAN ECO/TAC EDU/PROP EXEC ORD/FREE RESPECT WEALTH...METH/CNCPT TREND 20. PAGE 104 A2140 USA+45 PHIL/SCI FOR/AID

S62
NANES A.,"DISARMAMENT: THE LAST SEVEN YEARS." COM EUR+WWI USA+45 USSR INT/ORG FORCES TOP/EX CREATE LEGIT NUC/PWR DISPL ORD/FREE...CONCPT TIME/SEQ CON/ANAL 20. PAGE 107 A2195 DELIB/GP RIGID/FLEX ARMS/CONT

S62
NORTH R.C.,"DECISION MAKING IN CRISIS: AN INTRODUCTION." WOR+45 WOR-45 NAT/G CONSULT DELIB/GP TEC/DEV PERCEPT KNOWL...POLICY DECISION PSY METH/CNCPT CONT/OBS TREND VAL/FREE 20. PAGE 110 A2251 INT/ORG ROUTINE DIPLOM

S62
ORBAN M.,"L'EUROPE EN FORMATION ET SES PROBLEMES." EUR+WWI FUT WOR+45 WOR-45 INTELL STRUCT DELIB/GP ACT/RES FEDERAL RIGID/FLEX WEALTH...CONCPT TIME/SEQ OEEC 20. PAGE 112 A2295 INT/ORG PLAN REGION

S62
PIQUEMAL M.,"LES PROBLEMES DES UNIONS D'ETATS EN AFRIQUE NOIRE." FRANCE SOCIETY INT/ORG NAT/G DELIB/GP PLAN LEGIT ADMIN COLONIAL ROUTINE ATTIT ORD/FREE PWR...GEOG METH/CNCPT 20. PAGE 116 A2382 AFR ECO/UNDEV REGION

S62
SPENSER J.H.,"AFRICA AT THE UNITED NATIONS: SOME OBSERVATIONS." FUT ECO/UNDEV NAT/G CONSULT DELIB/GP PLAN BAL/PWR ECO/TAC EDU/PROP ATTIT RIGID/FLEX HEALTH ORD/FREE PWR WEALTH...POLICY CONCPT OBS TREND STERTYP GEN/METH UN VAL/FREE. PAGE 136 A2786 AFR INT/ORG REGION

S62
THOMPSON D.,"THE UNITED KINGDOM AND THE TREATY OF ROME." EUR+WWI INT/ORG NAT/G DELIB/GP LEGIS INT/TRADE RIGID/FLEX...CONCPT EEC PARLIAMENT CMN/WLTH 20. PAGE 143 A2925 ADJUD JURID

S62
VASAK K.,"DE LA CONVENTION EUROPEENNE A LA CONVENTION AFRICAINE DES DROITS DE L'HOMME." AFR ISLAM WOR+45 LAW CONSTN ECO/UNDEV INT/ORG PERCEPT ALL/VALS 20. PAGE 158 A3223 DELIB/GP CONCPT COLONIAL

C62
ROBINSON J.A.,"CONGRESS AND FOREIGN POLICY-MAKING: A STUDY IN LEGISLATIVE INFLUENCE AND INITIATIVE." USA+45 CHIEF DELIB/GP CREATE CONTROL EXEC GOV/REL PERCEPT...TREND BIBLIOG 20 CONGRESS. PAGE 122 A2505 LEGIS DIPLOM POLICY DECISION

B63
ABSHIRE D.M.,NATIONAL SECURITY: POLITICAL, MILITARY, AND ECONOMIC STRATEGIES IN THE DECADE AHEAD. ASIA COM USA+45 WOR+45 ECO/DEV ECO/UNDEV INT/ORG DELIB/GP FORCES ECO/TAC COERCE ATTIT RIGID/FLEX HEALTH ORD/FREE PWR WEALTH...POLICY STAT CHARTS ANTHOL COLD/WAR VAL/FREE. PAGE 4 A0083 FUT ACT/RES BAL/PWR

B63
BOWETT D.W.,THE LAW OF INTERNATIONAL INSTITUTIONS. WOR+45 WOR-45 CONSTN DELIB/GP EX/STRUC JUDGE EDU/PROP LEGIT CT/SYS EXEC ROUTINE RIGID/FLEX ORD/FREE PWR...JURID CONCPT ORG/CHARTS GEN/METH LEAGUE/NAT OAS OEEC 20 UN. PAGE 17 A0354 INT/ORG ADJUD DIPLOM

B63
BRZEZINSKI Z.K.,AFRICA AND THE COMMUNIST WORLD. AFR ASIA COM CULTURE SOCIETY INT/ORG DELIB/GP ACT/RES ECO/TAC COERCE ORD/FREE PWR WEALTH...STAT TOT/POP VAL/FREE 20. PAGE 21 A0418 ATTIT EDU/PROP DIPLOM USSR

B63
BURNS A.L.,PEACE-KEEPING BY U.N.FORCES - FROM SUEZ TO THE CONGO. AFR FUT ISLAM ISRAEL USSR WOR+45 NAT/G DELIB/GP BAL/PWR DOMIN LEGIT EXEC COERCE PEACE ATTIT PWR RESPECT SOVEREIGN...CONCPT UN 20. PAGE 22 A0441 INT/ORG FORCES ORD/FREE

B63
COLUMBIA U SCHOOL OF LAW,PUBLIC INTERNATIONAL DEVELOPMENT FINANCING IN SENEGAL. SENEGAL FINAN DELIB/GP GIVE EFFICIENCY...CHARTS GOV/COMP ANTHOL 20. PAGE 28 A0571 FOR/AID PLAN RECEIVE ECO/UNDEV

B63
ETHIOPIAN MINISTRY INFORMATION,AFRICAN SUMMIT CONFERENCE ADDIS ABABA, ETHIOPIA, 1963. ETHIOPIA DELIB/GP COLONIAL NAT/LISM...POLICY DECISION 20. PAGE 42 A0865 AFR CONFER REGION DIPLOM

B63
GREAT BRITAIN CENTRAL OFF INF,CONSULTATION AND CO-OPERATION IN THE COMMONWEALTH. LAW R+D FORCES PLAN EDU/PROP CONFER INGP/REL...GEOG CENSUS 19/20 CMN/WLTH. PAGE 55 A1133 DIPLOM DELIB/GP VOL/ASSN REGION

B63
HAMM H.,ALBANIA - CHINA'S BEACHHEAD IN EUROPE. ALBANIA CHINA/COM USSR YUGOSLAVIA ELITES SOCIETY POL/PAR DELIB/GP FORCES ECO/TAC COERCE ISOLAT PEACE MARXISM...IDEA/COMP 20 MAO. PAGE 61 A1248 DIPLOM REV NAT/G POLICY

B63
HENDERSON W.,SOUTHEAST ASIA: PROBLEMS OF UNITED STATES POLICY. COM S/ASIA CULTURE STRATA ECO/UNDEV INT/ORG DELIB/GP ACT/RES ECO/TAC DOMIN EDU/PROP LEGIT COERCE ATTIT ALL/VALS...STAT TIME/SEQ ANTHOL VAL/FREE 20. PAGE 64 A1313 ASIA USA+45 DIPLOM

B63
HOVET T. JR.,AFRICA IN THE UNITED NATIONS. AFR DELIB/GP EDU/PROP LOBBY CHOOSE ORD/FREE PWR RESPECT SKILL...STAT TIME/SEQ CON/ANAL CHARTS STERTYP VAL/FREE 20 UN. PAGE 68 A1397 INT/ORG USSR

B63
JACOBSON H.K.,THE USSR AND THE UN'S ECONOMIC AND SOCIAL ACTIVITIES. COM WOR+45 DELIB/GP ACT/RES ECO/TAC EDU/PROP RIGID/FLEX SUPEGO HEALTH PWR SKILL ...POLICY CHARTS GEN/METH VAL/FREE UNESCO 20 UN. PAGE 73 A1487 INT/ORG ATTIT USSR

B63
KRAVIS I.B.,DOMESTIC INTERESTS AND INTERNATIONAL OBLIGATIONS: SAFEGUARDS IN INTERNATIONAL TRADE ORGANIZATIONS. EUR+WWI USA+45 WOR+45 FINAN DELIB/GP ATTIT RIGID/FLEX HEALTH...STAT EEC VAL/FREE OEEC ECSC 20. PAGE 82 A1680 INT/ORG ECO/TAC INT/TRADE

B63
LADOR-LEDERER J.J.,INTERNATIONAL NON-GOVERNMENTAL ORGANIZATIONS: A STUDY IN AUTONOMOUS ORGANIZATION AND IUS GENTIUM. LAW DELIB/GP LEGIS DIPLOM 20. PAGE 83 A1709 INT/ORG INT/LAW INGP/REL VOL/ASSN

B63
LERCHE C.O. JR.,CONCEPTS OF INTERNATIONAL POLITICS. WOR+45 WOR-45 LAW DELIB/GP EX/STRUC TEC/DEV ECO/TAC INT/TRADE LEGIT ROUTINE COERCE ATTIT ORD/FREE PWR RESPECT...STERTYP GEN/LAWS VAL/FREE. PAGE 87 A1782 INT/ORG WAR

B63
LILIENTHAL D.E.,CHANGE, HOPE, AND THE BOMB. USA+45 WOR+45 R+D INT/ORG NAT/G DELIB/GP FORCES ACT/RES DETER RIGID/FLEX ORD/FREE...POLICY CONCPT OBS AEC 20. PAGE 89 A1815 ATTIT MYTH ARMS/CONT NUC/PWR

B63
LINDBERG L.,POLITICAL DYNAMICS OF EUROPEAN ECONOMIC INTEGRATION. EUR+WWI ECO/DEV INT/ORG VOL/ASSN DELIB/GP ADMIN WEALTH...DECISION EEC 20. PAGE 89 A1820 MARKET ECO/TAC

B63
MAYNE R.,THE COMMUNITY OF EUROPE. UK CONSTN NAT/G CONSULT DELIB/GP CREATE PLAN ECO/TAC LEGIT ADMIN ROUTINE ORD/FREE PWR WEALTH...CONCPT TIME/SEQ EEC EURATOM 20. PAGE 97 A1985 EUR+WWI INT/ORG REGION

B63
MULLENBACH P.,CIVILIAN NUCLEAR POWER: ECONOMIC ISSUES AND POLICY FORMATION. FINAN INT/ORG DELIB/GP ACT/RES ECO/TAC ATTIT SUPEGO HEALTH ORD/FREE PWR ...POLICY CONCPT MATH STAT CHARTS VAL/FREE 20 COLD/WAR. PAGE 105 A2166 USA+45 ECO/DEV NUC/PWR

B63
NICOLSON H.,DIPLOMACY (3RD ED.). INT/ORG NAT/G CONSULT DELIB/GP CONFER 19/20 LEAGUE/NAT UN. DIPLOM CONCPT

PAGE 109 A2232 NAT/COMP

B63
PANAMERICAN UNION,DOCUMENTOS OFICIALES DE LA ORGANIZACION DE LOS ESTADOS AMERICANOS, INDICE Y LISTA (VOL. III, 1962). L/A+17C DELIB/GP INT/TRADE EDU/PROP REGION NUC/PWR...HEAL INT/LAW SOC/WK 20 OAS. PAGE 113 A2329 BIBLIOG INT/ORG DIPLOM

B63
ROBERTSON A.H.,HUMAN RIGHTS IN EUROPE. CONSTN SOCIETY INT/ORG NAT/G VOL/ASSN DELIB/GP ACT/RES PLAN ADJUD REGION ROUTINE ATTIT LOVE ORD/FREE RESPECT...JURID SOC CONCPT SOC/EXP UN 20. PAGE 122 A2498 EUR+WWI PERSON

B63
ROSECRANCE R.N.,ACTION AND REACTION IN WORLD POLITICS. FUT WOR-45 SOCIETY DELIB/GP ACT/RES CREATE DIPLOM ECO/TAC DOMIN EDU/PROP COERCE ATTIT PERSON SUPEGO ORD/FREE PWR...CHARTS SIMUL LEAGUE/NAT VAL/FREE UN 19/20. PAGE 123 A2529 WOR+45 INT/ORG BAL/PWR

B63
SCHMELTZ G.W.,LA POLITIQUE MONDIALE CONTEMPORAINE. SOCIETY ECO/UNDEV INDUS INT/ORG NAT/G POL/PAR CONSULT DELIB/GP PLAN TEC/DEV ECO/TAC DOMIN EDU/PROP ROUTINE COERCE PERCEPT PERSON LOVE SKILL ...SOC RECORD TOT/POP. PAGE 128 A2629 WOR+45 COLONIAL

B63
THIEN T.T.,INDIA AND SOUTHEAST ASIA 1947-1960. COM INDIA S/ASIA SECT DELIB/GP FOR/AID RACE/REL NAT/LISM SOCISM...CHARTS BIBLIOG 20 UN NEHRU/J TREATY. PAGE 143 A2917 DRIVE DIPLOM POLICY

B63
US CONGRESS JOINT ECO COMM,DISCRIMINATORY OCEAN FREIGHT RATES AND BALANCE OF PAYMENTS. USA+45 SEA DELIB/GP DISCRIM...CHARTS 20 CONGRESS. PAGE 150 A3066 BAL/PAY DIST/IND PRICE INT/TRADE

B63
US CONGRESS JOINT ECO COMM,THE UNITED STATES BALANCE OF PAYMENTS. USA+45 DELIB/GP BUDGET PRICE PRODUC 20 CONGRESS GOLD/STAND MONEY. PAGE 150 A3067 BAL/PAY INT/TRADE FINAN ECO/TAC

B63
US CONGRESS JOINT ECO COMM,THE UNITED STATES BALANCE OF PAYMENTS. USA+45 DELIB/GP CONFER...MATH PREDICT CHARTS 20 CONGRESS. PAGE 150 A3068 BAL/PAY ECO/TAC INT/TRADE CONSULT

B63
US HOUSE COMM BANKING-CURR,RECENT CHANGES IN MONETARY POLICY AND BALANCE OF PAYMENTS PROBLEMS. USA+45 DELIB/GP PLAN DIPLOM...CHARTS 20 CONGRESS. PAGE 153 A3121 BAL/PAY FINAN ECO/TAC POLICY

B63
US HOUSE COMM FOREIGN AFFAIRS,HEARINGS ON H.R. 5490 TO AMEND FURTHER THE FOREIGN ASSISTANCE ACT OF 1961. CUBA EUR+WWI INDIA INT/ORG DELIB/GP LEGIS DIPLOM CONFER ORD/FREE 20 DEPT/STATE DEPT/DEFEN UN. PAGE 153 A3129 FOR/AID INT/TRADE FORCES WEAPON

B63
VOSS E.H.,NUCLEAR AMBUSH: THE TEST-BAN TRAP. WOR+45 COM/IND INT/ORG NAT/G DELIB/GP FORCES LEGIS TOP/EX ACT/RES DOMIN EDU/PROP LEGIT ROUTINE COERCE ATTIT PERCEPT RIGID/FLEX HEALTH MORAL ORD/FREE PWR. PAGE 160 A3255 TEC/DEV HIST/WRIT ARMS/CONT NUC/PWR

L63
PADELFORD N.J.,"FINANCIAL CRISIS AND THE UNITED NATIONS." FUT USSR WOR+45 LAW CONSTN FINAN INT/ORG DELIB/GP FORCES PLAN BUDGET DIPLOM COST WEALTH ...STAT CHARTS UN CONGO 20. PAGE 113 A2311 CREATE ECO/TAC

L63
PRINCETON UNIV. CONFERENCE,"ARAB DEVELOPMENT IN THE EMERGING INTERNATIONAL ECONOMY." FUT USA+45 DIST/IND FINAN DELIB/GP PLAN ECO/TAC WEALTH VAL/FREE 20. PAGE 118 A2413 ISLAM ECO/UNDEV FOR/AID INT/TRADE

L63
SINGER J.D.,"WEAPONS MANAGEMENT IN WORLD POLITICS: PROCEEDINGS OF THE INTERNATIONAL ARMS CONTROL SYMPOSIUM, DECEMBER, 1962." FUT WOR+45 SOCIETY ECO/DEV INDUS INT/ORG DELIB/GP FORCES ACT/RES ECO/TAC EDU/PROP ARMS/CONT SUPEGO HEALTH ORD/FREE PWR SKILL...POLICY CHARTS SIMUL ANTHOL VAL/FREE 20. PAGE 133 A2729 CONSULT ATTIT DIPLOM NUC/PWR

L63
ZARTMAN I.W.,"THE SAHARA--BRIDGE OR BARRIER." ISLAM CULTURE SOCIETY NAT/G DELIB/GP DOMIN EDU/PROP LEGIT ATTIT...HIST/WRIT TIME/SEQ CHARTS TOT/POP VAL/FREE 20. PAGE 169 A3445 INT/ORG PWR NAT/LISM

S63
ANGUILE G.,"CIVILISATION DU PLAN DANS L'EUROPE ET L'AFRIQUE DE DEMAIN." AFR EUR+WWI GABON ECO/DEV FINAN MARKET DELIB/GP ECO/TAC WEALTH...TREND 20. PAGE 8 A0163 ECO/UNDEV PLAN INT/TRADE

S63
BECHHOEFER B.G.,"UNITED NATIONS PROCEDURES IN CASE OF VIOLATIONS OF DISARMAMENT AGREEMENTS." COM USA+45 USSR LAW CONSTN NAT/G EX/STRUC FORCES LEGIS BAL/PWR EDU/PROP CT/SYS ARMS/CONT ORD/FREE PWR ...POLICY STERTYP UN VAL/FREE 20. PAGE 12 A0245 INT/ORG DELIB/GP

S63
CHAKRAVARTI P.C.,"INDIAN NON-ALIGNMENT AND UNITED STATES POLICY." ASIA INDIA S/ASIA USA+45 CULTURE ECO/UNDEV NAT/G VOL/ASSN DELIB/GP TOP/EX FOR/AID NEUTRAL...POLICY HUM CONCPT RECORD GEN/LAWS 20. PAGE 25 A0515 ATTIT ALL/VALS COLONIAL DIPLOM

S63
EMERSON R.,"THE ATLANTIC COMMUNITY AND THE EMERGING COUNTRIES." FUT WOR+45 ECO/DEV ECO/UNDEV R+D NAT/G DELIB/GP BAL/PWR ECO/TAC EDU/PROP ROUTINE ORD/FREE PWR WEALTH...POLICY CONCPT TREND GEN/METH EEC 20 NATO. PAGE 42 A0848 ATTIT INT/TRADE

S63
ETZIONI A.,"EUROPEAN UNIFICATION: A STRATEGY OF CHANGE." EUR+WWI CULTURE ECO/DEV DELIB/GP ACT/RES ECO/TAC EDU/PROP ATTIT ORD/FREE PWR SKILL WEALTH ...STAT TIME/SEQ EEC TOT/POP VAL/FREE 20. PAGE 42 A0869 INT/ORG RIGID/FLEX

S63
ETZIONI A.,"EUROPEAN UNIFICATION AND PERSPECTIVES ON SOVEREIGNTY." EUR+WWI FUT DELIB/GP TEC/DEV ECO/TAC EDU/PROP DETER NUC/PWR ATTIT DRIVE ORD/FREE PWR WEALTH...CONCPT RECORD TIME/SEQ EEC VAL/FREE 20. PAGE 43 A0870 INT/ORG ECO/DEV SOVEREIGN

S63
GANDOLFI A.,"LES ACCORDS DE COOPERATION EN MATIERE DE POLITIQUE ETRANGERE ENTRE LA FRANCE ET LES NOUVEAUX ETATS AFRICAINS ET." AFR ISLAM MADAGASCAR WOR+45 ECO/DEV INT/ORG NAT/G DELIB/GP ECO/TAC ALL/VALS...CON/ANAL 20. PAGE 51 A1038 VOL/ASSN ECO/UNDEV DIPLOM FRANCE

S63
GARDNER R.N.,"COOPERATION IN OUTER SPACE." FUT USSR WOR+45 AIR LAW COM/IND CONSULT DELIB/GP CREATE KNOWL 20 TREATY. PAGE 51 A1045 INT/ORG ACT/RES PEACE SPACE

S63
GROSS F.,"THE US NATIONAL INTEREST AND THE UN." FUT CONSTN NAT/G DELIB/GP CREATE DIPLOM RIGID/FLEX ORD/FREE...CONCPT GEN/LAWS 20 UN. PAGE 57 A1172 USA+45 INT/ORG PEACE

S63
HALLSTEIN W.,"THE EUROPEAN COMMUNITY AND ATLANTIC PARTNERSHIP." EUR+WWI USA+45 MARKET NAT/G VOL/ASSN DELIB/GP ARMS/CONT NUC/PWR ATTIT PWR...CONCPT STAT TIME/SEQ TREND OEEC 20 EEC. PAGE 60 A1235 INT/ORG ECO/TAC UK

S63
HARNETTY P.,"CANADA, SOUTH AFRICA AND THE COMMONWEALTH." CANADA SOUTH/AFR LAW INT/ORG VOL/ASSN DELIB/GP LEGIS TOP/EX ECO/TAC LEGIT DRIVE MORAL...CONCPT CMN/WLTH 20. PAGE 62 A1263 AFR ATTIT

S63
HAVILAND H.F.,"BUILDING A POLITICAL COMMUNITY." EUR+WWI FUT UK USA+45 ECO/DEV ECO/UNDEV INT/ORG NAT/G DELIB/GP BAL/PWR ECO/TAC NEUTRAL ROUTINE ATTIT PWR WEALTH...CONCPT COLD/WAR TOT/POP 20. PAGE 63 A1293 VOL/ASSN DIPLOM

S63
HOLBO P.S.,"COLD WAR DRIFT IN LATIN AMERICA." CUBA L/A+17C USA+45 USA-45 INT/ORG NAT/G NEIGH VOL/ASSN ACT/RES PLAN ECO/TAC ATTIT RIGID/FLEX ALL/VALS ...RECORD TIME/SEQ OAS LAFTA 20 COLD/WAR. PAGE 66 A1363 DELIB/GP CREATE FOR/AID

S63
KRAVIS I.B.,"THE POLITICAL ARITHMETIC OF INTERNATIONAL BURDENSHARING." FUT USA+45 WOR+45 FINAN DELIB/GP ACT/RES CREATE TEC/DEV ATTIT PWR WEALTH...POLICY MATH STAT VAL/FREE 20. PAGE 82 A1681 INT/ORG ECO/TAC

S63
LIPSHART A.,"THE ANALYSIS OF BLOC VOTING IN THE GENERAL ASSEMBLY." L/A+17C WOR+45 ACT/RES INGP/REL ...POLICY DECISION NEW/IDEA STAT IDEA/COMP UN. PAGE 90 A1832 CHOOSE INT/ORG DELIB/GP

S63
MURRAY J.N.,"UNITED NATIONS PEACE-KEEPING AND PROBLEMS OF POLITICAL CONTROL." FUT WOR+45 CONSTN DELIB/GP FORCES TOP/EX ACT/RES CREATE LEGIT PEACE PWR...METH/CNCPT CONGO UN 20. PAGE 106 A2182 INT/ORG ORD/FREE

S63
NEIDLE A.F.,"PEACE KEEPING AND DISARMAMENT." COM USA+45 USSR WOR+45 INT/ORG NAT/G BAL/PWR EDU/PROP LEGIT ATTIT PWR 20. PAGE 108 A2214 DELIB/GP ACT/RES ARMS/CONT PEACE

S63
NICHOLAS H.G.,"UN PEACE FORCES AND THE CHANGING GLOBE: THE LESSONS OF SUEZ AND CONGO." FUT WOR+45 CONSTN INT/ORG CONSULT DELIB/GP TOP/EX CREATE DIPLOM DOMIN LEGIT COERCE WAR PERSON RIGID/FLEX PWR UN SUEZ CONGO UNEF 20. PAGE 109 A2229 ACT/RES FORCES

S63
NOGEE J.L.,"PROPOGANDA AND NEGOTIATION: THE CASE OF THE TEN NATION DISARMAMENT COMMITTEE." COM EUR+WWI USA+45 VOL/ASSN DELIB/GP FORCES DIPLOM DOMIN LEGIT PWR...METH/CNCPT STERTYP COLD/WAR VAL/FREE 20. PAGE 110 A2248 INT/ORG EDU/PROP ARMS/CONT

S63
NYE J.S. JR.,"EAST AFRICAN ECONOMIC INTEGRATION." ECO/UNDEV

AFR UGANDA PROVS DELIB/GP PLAN ECO/TAC INT/TRADE ADMIN ROUTINE ORD/FREE PWR WEALTH...OBS TIME/SEQ VAL/FREE 20. PAGE 110 A2264 INT/ORG

S63

PHELPS J.,"INFORMATION AND ARMS CONTROL." COM SPACE USA+45 USSR WOR+45 R+D INT/ORG NAT/G DELIB/GP DIPLOM ORD/FREE...CONCPT 20. PAGE 116 A2374 KNOWL ARMS/CONT NUC/PWR

S63

SHONFIELD A.,"AFTER BRUSSELS." EUR+WWI FRANCE GERMANY UK ECO/DEV DIST/IND MARKET VOL/ASSN DELIB/GP CREATE INT/TRADE ATTIT RIGID/FLEX...RECORD TREND GEN/LAWS EEC CMN/WLTH 20. PAGE 132 A2705 PLAN ECO/TAC

S63

WOLFERS A.,"INTEGRATION IN THE WEST: THE CONFLICT OF PERSPECTIVES." EUR+WWI USA+45 ECO/DEV INT/ORG DELIB/GP CREATE TEC/DEV DIPLOM ATTIT PWR...CONCPT HIST/WRIT TREND GEN/LAWS COLD/WAR EEC 20. PAGE 166 A3386 RIGID/FLEX ECO/TAC

S63

WRIGHT Q.,"DECLINE OF CLASSIC DIPLOMACY." CHRIST-17C EUR+WWI MOD/EUR WOR+45 WOR-45 INT/ORG NAT/G DELIB/GP BAL/PWR ATTIT PWR...HIST/WRIT LEAGUE/NAT. PAGE 168 A3418 TEC/DEV CONCPT DIPLOM

C63

ATTIA G.E.O.,"LES FORCES ARMEES DES NATIONS UNIES EN COREE ET AU MOYENORIENT." KOREA CONSTN DELIB/GP LEGIS PWR...IDEA/COMP NAT/COMP BIBLIOG UN SUEZ. PAGE 10 A0194 FORCES NAT/G INT/LAW

N63

US COMM STRENG SEC FREE WORLD,THE SCOPE AND DISTRIBUTION OF UNITED STATES MILITARY AND ECONOMIC ASSISTANCE PROGRAMS (PAMPHLET). USA+45 PLAN BAL/PWR BUDGET DIPLOM CONTROL CIVMIL/REL ATTIT. PAGE 150 A3059 DELIB/GP POLICY FOR/AID ORD/FREE

B64

AHLUWALIA K.,THE LEGAL STATUS, PRIVILEGES AND IMMUNITIES OF SPECIALIZED AGENCIES OF UN AND CERTAIN OTHER INTERNATIONAL ORGANIZATIONS. WOR+45 LAW CONSULT DELIB/GP FORCES. PAGE 5 A0102 PRIVIL DIPLOM INT/ORG INT/LAW

B64

APTER D.E.,IDEOLOGY AND DISCONTENT. FUT WOR+45 CONSTN CULTURE INTELL SOCIETY STRUCT INT/ORG NAT/G DELIB/GP LEGIS CREATE PLAN TEC/DEV EDU/PROP EXEC PERCEPT PERSON RIGID/FLEX ALL/VALS...POLICY TOT/POP. PAGE 8 A0171 ACT/RES ATTIT

B64

CLAUDE I.,SWORDS INTO PLOWSHARES. FUT WOR+45 WOR-45 DELIB/GP EX/STRUC LEGIT ATTIT ORD/FREE...CONCPT TIME/SEQ TREND UN TOT/POP 20. PAGE 27 A0547 INT/ORG STRUCT

B64

COFFIN F.M.,WITNESS FOR AID. COM EUR+WWI USA+45 DIPLOM GP/REL CONSEN ORD/FREE MARXISM...NEW/IDEA 20 CONGRESS AID. PAGE 27 A0557 FOR/AID ECO/UNDEV DELIB/GP PLAN

B64

COHEN M.,LAW AND POLITICS IN SPACE: SPECIFIC AND URGENT PROBLEMS IN THE LAW OF OUTER SPACE. CHINA/COM COM USA+45 USSR WOR+45 COM/IND INT/ORG NAT/G LEGIT NUC/PWR ATTIT BIO/SOC...JURID CONCPT CONGRESS 20 STALIN/J. PAGE 28 A0561 DELIB/GP LAW INT/LAW SPACE

B64

COTTRELL A.J.,THE POLITICS OF THE ATLANTIC ALLIANCE. EUR+WWI USA+45 INT/ORG NAT/G DELIB/GP EX/STRUC BAL/PWR DIPLOM REGION DETER ATTIT ORD/FREE ...CONCPT RECORD GEN/LAWS GEN/METH NATO 20. PAGE 31 A0632 VOL/ASSN FORCES

B64

CZERNIN F.,VERSAILLES - 1919. EUR+WWI USA-45 FACE/GP POL/PAR VOL/ASSN DELIB/GP TOP/EX CREATE BAL/PWR DIPLOM LEGIT NAT/LISM PEACE ATTIT RIGID/FLEX ORD/FREE PWR...CON/ANAL LEAGUE/NAT 20 VERSAILLES. PAGE 33 A0671 INT/ORG STRUCT

B64

FISHER R.,INTERNATIONAL CONFLICT AND BEHAVIORAL SCIENCE: THE CRAIGVILLE PAPERS. COM FUT USA+45 WOR+45 NAT/G DELIB/GP EX/STRUC FORCES ECO/TAC DOMIN EDU/PROP LEGIT COERCE ATTIT PERCEPT ORD/FREE PWR RESPECT...PSY SOC VAL/FREE. PAGE 46 A0940 INT/ORG PLAN DIPLOM

B64

IKLE F.C.,HOW NATIONS NEGOTIATE. COM EUR+WWI USA+45 INTELL INT/ORG VOL/ASSN DELIB/GP ACT/RES CREATE DOMIN EDU/PROP ADJUD ROUTINE ATTIT PERSON ORD/FREE RESPECT SKILL...PSY SOC OBS VAL/FREE. PAGE 70 A1433 NAT/G PWR POLICY

B64

JANOWITZ M.,THE MILITARY IN THE POLITICAL DEVELOPMENT OF NEW NATIONS: AN ESSAY IN COMPARATIVE ANALYSIS. AFR ASIA ISLAM L/A+17C S/ASIA USA+45 ECO/UNDEV INT/ORG NAT/G POL/PAR DELIB/GP PLAN ECO/TAC DOMIN LEGIT COERCE ATTIT DRIVE RESPECT ...SOC CONCPT CENSUS VAL/FREE. PAGE 73 A1495 FORCES PWR

B64

MARKHAM J.W.,THE COMMON MARKET: FRIEND OR COMPETITOR. EUR+WWI FUT USA+45 INT/ORG LG/CO NAT/G VOL/ASSN DELIB/GP EX/STRUC PLAN TARIFFS ORD/FREE PWR WEALTH...POLICY STAT TREND EEC VAL/FREE 20. PAGE 95 A1943 ECO/DEV ECO/TAC

B64

NASA,PROCEEDINGS OF CONFERENCE ON THE LAW OF SPACE AND OF SATELLITE COMMUNICATIONS: CHICAGO 1963. FUT WOR+45 DELIB/GP PROB/SOLV TEC/DEV CONFER ADJUD NUC/PWR...POLICY IDEA/COMP 20 NASA. PAGE 107 A2197 SPACE COM/IND LAW DIPLOM

B64

NEWBURY C.W.,THE WEST AFRICAN COMMONWEALTH. CONSTN INTELL ECO/UNDEV VOL/ASSN CHIEF DELIB/GP LEGIS INT/TRADE COLONIAL FEDERAL ATTIT 20 COMMONWLTH AFRICA/W. PAGE 108 A2223 INT/ORG SOVEREIGN GOV/REL AFR

B64

OWEN W.,STRATEGY FOR MOBILITY. FUT WOR+45 WOR-45 DIST/IND INT/ORG NAT/G DELIB/GP PLAN TEC/DEV ECO/TAC ORD/FREE PWR WEALTH...STAT TIME/SEQ VAL/FREE 20. PAGE 112 A2304 COM/IND ECO/UNDEV

B64

ROSECRANCE R.N.,THE DISPERSION OF NUCLEAR WEAPONS: STRATEGY AND POLITICS. ASIA COM FUT S/ASIA USA+45 INT/ORG NAT/G DELIB/GP FORCES ACT/RES TEC/DEV BAL/PWR COERCE DETER ATTIT RIGID/FLEX ORD/FREE ...POLICY CHARTS VAL/FREE. PAGE 123 A2530 EUR+WWI PWR PEACE

B64

RUBINSTEIN A.Z.,THE SOVIETS IN INTERNATIONAL ORGANIZATIONS: CHANGING POLICY TOWARD DEVELOPING COUNTRIES, 1953-1963. COM DELIB/GP ACT/RES ECO/TAC EDU/PROP ADMIN ATTIT ORD/FREE PWR...INT VAL/FREE UN 20. PAGE 125 A2563 ECO/UNDEV INT/ORG USSR

B64

SCHWELB E.,HUMAN RIGHTS AND THE INTERNATIONAL COMMUNITY. WOR+45 WOR-45 NAT/G SECT DELIB/GP DIPLOM PEACE RESPECT TREATY 20 UN. PAGE 130 A2666 INT/ORG ORD/FREE INT/LAW

B64

STOESSINGER J.G.,FINANCING THE UNITED NATIONS SYSTEM. FUT WOR+45 CONSTN NAT/G VOL/ASSN DELIB/GP EX/STRUC ECO/TAC LEGIT CT/SYS PWR WEALTH...STAT TIME/SEQ TREND CHARTS VAL/FREE. PAGE 138 A2830 FINAN INT/ORG

B64

THANT U.,TOWARD WORLD PEACE. DELIB/GP TEC/DEV EDU/PROP WAR SOVEREIGN...INT/LAW 20 UN MID/EAST. PAGE 142 A2907 DIPLOM BIOG PEACE COERCE

B64

UNITED ARAB REPUBLIC,TOWARDS THE SECOND AFRICAN SUMMIT ASSEMBLY. AFR UAR CONSTN VOL/ASSN CHIEF PLAN DIPLOM AGREE 20 NASSER/G AFR/STATES. PAGE 148 A3030 CONFER DELIB/GP INT/ORG POLICY

B64

US AIR FORCE ACADEMY ASSEMBLY,OUTER SPACE: FINAL REPORT APRIL 1-4, 1964. FUT USA+45 WOR+45 LAW DELIB/GP CONFER ARMS/CONT WAR PEACE ATTIT MORAL ...ANTHOL 20 NASA. PAGE 150 A3055 SPACE CIVMIL/REL NUC/PWR DIPLOM

B64

US HOUSE COMM FOREIGN AFFAIRS,HEARINGS ON H.R. 10502 TO AMEND FURTHER THE FOREIGN ASSISTANCE ACT OF 1961. AFR ASIA L/A+17C INT/ORG CONSULT DELIB/GP TEC/DEV ECO/TAC EDU/PROP CONFER 20 UN NATO CONGRESS AID. PAGE 153 A3130 FOR/AID DIPLOM ORD/FREE ECO/UNDEV

B64

US HOUSE COMM ON JUDICIARY,IMMIGRATION HEARINGS. DELIB/GP STRANGE HABITAT...GEOG JURID 20 CONGRESS MIGRATION. PAGE 154 A3140 NAT/G POLICY DIPLOM NAT/LISM

B64

US SENATE COMM GOVT OPERATIONS,THE SECRETARY OF STATE AND THE AMBASSADOR. USA+45 CHIEF CONSULT EX/STRUC FORCES PLAN ADMIN EXEC INGP/REL ROLE ...ANTHOL 20 PRESIDENT DEPT/STATE. PAGE 156 A3175 DIPLOM DELIB/GP NAT/G

L64

CARNEGIE ENDOWMENT INT. PEACE,"POLITICAL QUESTIONS (ISSUES BEFORE THE NINETEENTH GENERAL ASSEMBLY)." SPACE WOR+45 CONSTN FINAN NAT/G CONSULT DELIB/GP FORCES LEGIS TEC/DEV EDU/PROP LEGIT ARMS/CONT COERCE NUC/PWR ATTIT ALL/VALS...CONCPT OBS UN COLD/WAR 20. PAGE 24 A0490 INT/ORG PEACE

L64

CARNEGIE ENDOWMENT INT. PEACE,"ECONOMIC AND SOCIAL QUESTION (ISSUES BEFORE THE NINETEENTH GENERAL ASSEMBLY)." WOR+45 ECO/DEV ECO/UNDEV INDUS R+D DELIB/GP CREATE PLAN TEC/DEV ECO/TAC FOR/AID BAL/PAY...RECORD UN 20. PAGE 24 A0493 INT/ORG INT/TRADE

L64

CLAUDE I.,"THE OAS, THE UN, AND THE UNITED STATES." L/A+17C USA+45 CONSTN NAT/G DELIB/GP DOMIN EDU/PROP LEGIT REGION COERCE ORD/FREE PWR...TIME/SEQ TREND STERTYP OAS UN 20. PAGE 27 A0546 INT/ORG POLICY

L64

HAAS E.B.,"ECONOMICS AND DIFFERENTIAL PATTERNS OF POLITICAL INTEGRATION: PROJECTIONS ABOUT UNITY IN LATIN AMERICA." SOCIETY NAT/G DELIB/GP ACT/RES CREATE PLAN ECO/TAC REGION ROUTINE ATTIT DRIVE PWR WEALTH...CONCPT TREND CHARTS LAFTA 20. PAGE 59 A1208 L/A+17C INT/ORG MARKET

L64

RIPLEY R.B.,"INTERAGENCY COMMITTEES AND INCREMENTALISM: THE CASE OF AID TO INDIA." INDIA USA+45 INTELL NAT/G DELIB/GP ACT/RES DIPLOM ROUTINE EXEC MGT FOR/AID

NAT/LISM ATTIT PWR...SOC CONCPT NEW/IDEA TIME/SEQ CON/ANAL VAL/FREE 20. PAGE 121 A2483

S64
CARNEGIE ENDOWMENT INT. PEACE,"COLONIAL COUNTRIES AND PEOPLES (ISSUES BEFORE THE NINETEENTH GENERAL ASSEMBLY)." AFR ISLAM L/A+17C WOR+45 DELIB/GP LEGIS ECO/TAC EDU/PROP NAT/LISM PEACE ALL/VALS...RECORD UN CMN/WLTH 20. PAGE 24 A0491
INT/ORG ECO/UNDEV COLONIAL

S64
CARNEGIE ENDOWMENT INT. PEACE,"LEGAL QUESTIONS (ISSUES BEFORE THE NINETEENTH GENERAL ASSEMBLY)." WOR+45 CONSTN NAT/G DELIB/GP ADJUD PEACE MORAL ORD/FREE...RECORD UN 20 TREATY. PAGE 24 A0494
INT/ORG LAW INT/LAW

S64
COCHRANE J.D.,"US ATTITUDES TOWARD CENTRAL-AMERICAN INTEGRATION." L/A+17C USA+45 ECO/UNDEV FACE/GP VOL/ASSN DELIB/GP ECO/TAC INT/TRADE EDU/PROP RIGID/FLEX ORD/FREE WEALTH...TIME/SEQ TOT/POP 20. PAGE 27 A0555
NAT/G ATTIT REGION

S64
DERWINSKI E.J.,"THE COST OF THE INTERNATIONAL COFFEE AGREEMENT." L/A+17C USA+45 WOR+45 ECO/UNDEV NAT/G VOL/ASSN LEGIS DIPLOM ECO/TAC FOR/AID LEGIT ATTIT...TIME/SEQ CONGRESS 20 TREATY. PAGE 36 A0732
MARKET DELIB/GP INT/TRADE

S64
GARDNER R.N.,"GATT AND THE UNITED NATIONS CONFERENCE ON TRADE AND DEVELOPMENT." USA+45 WOR+45 SOCIETY ECO/UNDEV MARKET NAT/G DELIB/GP ACT/RES PLAN ECO/TAC TARIFFS EDU/PROP ROUTINE DRIVE RIGID/FLEX WEALTH...DECISION MGT TREND UN TOT/POP 20 GATT. PAGE 51 A1047
INT/ORG INT/TRADE

S64
GROSS J.A.,"WHITEHALL AND THE COMMONWEALTH." EUR+WWI MOD/EUR INT/ORG NAT/G CONSULT DELIB/GP LEGIS DOMIN ADMIN COLONIAL ROUTINE PWR CMN/WLTH 19/20. PAGE 57 A1174
EX/STRUC ATTIT TREND

S64
HOVET T. JR.,"THE ROLE OF AFRICA IN THE UNITED NATIONS." FUT WOR+45 NAT/G DELIB/GP DOMIN EDU/PROP LEGIT ORD/FREE PWR RESPECT SKILL...OBS TIME/SEQ TREND VAL/FREE UN 20. PAGE 68 A1398
AFR INT/ORG DIPLOM

S64
HUELIN D.,"ECONOMIC INTEGRATION IN LATIN AMERICAN: PROGRESS AND PROBLEMS." L/A+17C ECO/DEV AGRI DIST/IND FINAN INDUS NAT/G VOL/ASSN CONSULT DELIB/GP EX/STRUC ACT/RES PLAN TEC/DEV ECO/TAC ROUTINE BAL/PAY WEALTH WORK 20. PAGE 69 A1411
MARKET ECO/UNDEV INT/TRADE

S64
KHAN M.Z.,"ISLAM AND INTERNATIONAL RELATIONS." FUT WOR+45 LAW CULTURE SOCIETY NAT/G SECT DELIB/GP FORCES EDU/PROP ATTIT PERSON SUPEGO ALL/VALS ...POLICY PSY CONCPT MYTH HIST/WRIT GEN/LAWS. PAGE 78 A1608
ISLAM INT/ORG DIPLOM

S64
KHAN M.Z.,"THE PRESIDENT OF THE GENERAL ASSEMBLY." WOR+45 CONSTN DELIB/GP EDU/PROP LEGIT ROUTINE PWR RESPECT SKILL...DECISION SOC BIOG TREND UN 20. PAGE 78 A1609
INT/ORG TOP/EX

S64
LEVI W.,"CHINA AND THE UNITED NATIONS." ASIA CHINA CHINA/COM WOR+45 WOR-45 CONSTN NAT/G DELIB/GP EX/STRUC FORCES ACT/RES EDU/PROP PWR...POLICY RECORD TIME/SEQ GEN/LAWS UN COLD/WAR 20. PAGE 88 A1794
INT/ORG ATTIT NAT/LISM

S64
RUSK D.,"THE MAKING OF FOREIGN POLICY" USA+45 CHIEF DELIB/GP WORKER PROB/SOLV ADMIN ATTIT PWR ...DECISION 20 DEPT/STATE RUSK/D GOLDMAN/E. PAGE 125 A2570
DIPLOM INT POLICY

S64
SAAB H.,"THE ARAB SEARCH FOR A FEDERAL UNION." SOCIETY INT/ORG NAT/G DELIB/GP FORCES ACT/RES TEC/DEV ECO/TAC DOMIN LEGIT REGION ROUTINE ATTIT DRIVE RIGID/FLEX ALL/VALS...SOC CONCPT NEW/IDEA TIME/SEQ TREND. PAGE 126 A2580
ISLAM PLAN

S64
SKUBISZEWSKI K.,"FORMS OF PARTICIPATION OF INTERNATIONAL ORGANIZATION IN THE LAW MAKING PROCESS." FUT WOR+45 NAT/G DELIB/GP DOMIN LEGIT KNOWL PWR...JURID TREND 20. PAGE 134 A2740
INT/ORG LAW INT/LAW

S64
VANDENBOSCH A.,"THE SMALL STATES IN INTERNATIONAL POLITICS AND ORGANIZATION." EUR+WWI MOD/EUR WOR+45 WOR-45 CONSTN DELIB/GP COERCE ORD/FREE PWR ...TIME/SEQ GEN/LAWS VAL/FREE LEAGUE/NAT UN 19/20. PAGE 158 A3219
NAT/G INT/ORG DIPLOM

B65
FORGAC A.A.,NEW DIPLOMACY AND THE UNITED NATIONS. FRANCE GERMANY UK USSR INT/ORG DELIB/GP EX/STRUC PEACE...INT/LAW CONCPT UN. PAGE 47 A0965
DIPLOM ETIQUET NAT/G

B65
HAGRAS K.M.,UNITED NATIONS CONFERENCE ON TRADE AND DEVELOPMENT: A CASE STUDY OF UN DIPLOMACY. CONSULT ACT/RES TEC/DEV FOR/AID INT/TRADE...BIBLIOG 20 UN LEAGUE/NAT UNCTAD. PAGE 59 A1213
INT/ORG ADMIN DELIB/GP DIPLOM

B65
LIEUWEN E.,U.S. POLICY IN LATIN AMERICA: A SHORT HISTORY. L/A+17C USA+45 USA-45 DELIB/GP ECO/TAC 19/20 COLD/WAR MONROE/DOC. PAGE 89 A1812
DIPLOM COLONIAL NAT/G FOR/AID

B65
LOEWENHEIM F.L.,PEACE OR APPEASEMENT? HITLER, CHAMBERLAIN AND THE MUNICH CRISIS. MUNIC DELIB/GP WAR TOTALISM ATTIT SOVEREIGN...TIME/SEQ ANTHOL BIBLIOG 20 HITLER/A CHAMBRLN/N. PAGE 90 A1851
DIPLOM LEAD PEACE

B65
MACDONALD R.W.,THE LEAGUE OF ARAB STATES: A STUDY IN THE DYNAMICS OF REGIONAL ORGANIZATION. ISRAEL UAR USSR FINAN INT/ORG DELIB/GP ECO/TAC AGREE NEUTRAL ORD/FREE PWR...DECISION BIBLIOG 20 TREATY UN. PAGE 92 A1888
ISLAM REGION DIPLOM ADMIN

B65
MEAGHER R.F.,PUBLIC INTERNATIONAL DEVELOPMENT FINANCING IN SUDAN. SUDAN FINAN DELIB/GP GIVE ...CHARTS GOV/COMP 20. PAGE 99 A2029
FOR/AID PLAN RECEIVE ECO/UNDEV

B65
MORGENTHAU H.,MORGENTHAU DIARY (CHINA) (2 VOLS.). ASIA USA+45 USA-45 LAW DELIB/GP EX/STRUC PLAN FOR/AID INT/TRADE CONFER WAR MARXISM 20 CHINJAP. PAGE 104 A2136
DIPLOM ADMIN

B65
MUNGER E.S.,NOTES ON THE FORMATION OF SOUTH AFRICAN FOREIGN POLICY. ACADEM POL/PAR SECT CHIEF DELIB/GP FORCES LEGIS PRESS ATTIT...TREND 20 NEGRO. PAGE 106 A2170
AFR DOMIN POLICY DIPLOM

B65
O'CONNELL M.R.,IRISH POLITICS AND SOCIAL CONFLICT IN THE AGE OF THE AMERICAN REVOLUTION. FRANCE IRELAND MOD/EUR STRATA SECT LEGIS DIPLOM INT/TRADE DOMIN REV WAR...BIBLIOG 18 PARLIAMENT. PAGE 111 A2268
CATHISM ATTIT NAT/G DELIB/GP

B65
OGILVY-WEBB M.,THE GOVERNMENT EXPLAINS: A STUDY OF THE INFORMATION SERVICES. UK DELIB/GP LEGIS WORKER BUDGET DIPLOM 20. PAGE 111 A2284
EDU/PROP ATTIT NAT/G ADMIN

B65
SMITH A.L. JR.,THE DEUTSCHTUM OF NAZI GERMANY AND THE UNITED STATES. GERMANY USA-45 DIPLOM ATTIT FASCISM...BIBLIOG 20 MIGRATION NAZI. PAGE 134 A2744
INGP/REL NAT/LISM STRANGE DELIB/GP

B65
US CONGRESS JOINT ECO COMM,GUIDELINES FOR INTERNATIONAL MONETARY REFORM. USA+45 WOR+45 DELIB/GP BAL/PAY 20 CONGRESS IMF MONEY. PAGE 150 A3069
DIPLOM FINAN PLAN INT/ORG

B65
US CONGRESS JT ATOM ENRGY COMM,ATOMIC ENERGY LEGISLATION THROUGH 89TH CONGRESS, 1ST SESSION. USA+45 LAW INT/ORG DELIB/GP BUDGET DIPLOM 20 AEC CONGRESS CASEBOOK EURATOM IAEA. PAGE 150 A3071
NUC/PWR FORCES PEACE LEGIS

B65
US HOUSE COMM FOREIGN AFFAIRS,HEARINGS ON DRAFT BILL TO AMEND FURTHER THE FOREIGN ASSISTANCE ACT OF 1961. AFR ASIA L/A+17C USA+45 INT/ORG DELIB/GP TEC/DEV ECO/TAC CONFER TOTALISM 20 CONGRESS AID. PAGE 153 A3131
FOR/AID ECO/UNDEV DIPLOM ORD/FREE

B65
US SENATE COMM AERO SPACE SCI,INTERNATIONAL COOPERATION AND ORGANIZATION FOR OUTER SPACE. FUT USA+45 WOR+45 PROF/ORG VOL/ASSN CONSULT DELIB/GP PLAN TEC/DEV ARMS/CONT GP/REL PEACE 20 UN NASA. PAGE 155 A3167
DIPLOM SPACE R+D NAT/G

B65
US SENATE COMM GOVT OPERATIONS,ADMINISTRATION OF NATIONAL SECURITY. USA+45 DELIB/GP ADMIN ROLE ...POLICY CHARTS SENATE. PAGE 156 A3177
NAT/G ORD/FREE DIPLOM PROB/SOLV

L65
RUBIN A.P.,"UNITED STATES CONTEMPORARY PRACTICE RELATING TO INTERNATIONAL LAW." USA+45 WOR+45 CONSTN INT/ORG NAT/G DELIB/GP EX/STRUC DIPLOM DOMIN CT/SYS ROUTINE ORD/FREE...CONCPT COLD/WAR 20. PAGE 125 A2558
LAW LEGIT INT/LAW

S65
AMRAM P.W.,"REPORT ON THE TENTH SESSION OF THE HAGUE CONFERENCE ON PRIVATE INTERNATIONAL LAW." USA+45 WOR+45 INT/ORG CREATE LEGIT ADJUD ALL/VALS ...JURID CONCPT METH/CNCPT OBS GEN/METH 20. PAGE 8 A0155
VOL/ASSN DELIB/GP INT/LAW

S65
HAZARD J.N.,"CO-EXISTENCE LAW BOWS OUT." WOR+45 R+D INT/ORG VOL/ASSN CONSULT DELIB/GP ACT/RES CREATE PEACE KNOWL...JURID CONCPT COLD/WAR VAL/FREE 20. PAGE 63 A1300
PROF/ORG ADJUD

S65
QUADE Q.L.,"THE TRUMAN ADMINISTRATION AND THE SEPARATION OF POWERS: THE CASE OF THE MARSHALL PLAN." SOCIETY INT/ORG NAT/G CONSULT DELIB/GP LEGIS PLAN ECO/TAC ROUTINE DRIVE PERCEPT RIGID/FLEX
USA+45 ECO/UNDEV DIPLOM

ORD/FREE PWR WEALTH...DECISION GEOG NEW/IDEA TREND 20 TRUMAN/HS. PAGE 118 A2422

C65
WUORINEN J.H.,"SCANDINAVIA." DENMARK FINLAND ICELAND NORWAY SWEDEN SOCIETY AGRI POL/PAR DELIB/GP DIPLOM INT/TRADE NEUTRAL WAR...CHARTS TREATY 20. PAGE 168 A3423 — BIBLIOG NAT/G POLICY

B66
CLARK G.,WORLD PEACE THROUGH WORLD LAW; TWO ALTERNATIVE PLANS. WOR+45 DELIB/GP FORCES TAX CONFER ADJUD SANCTION ARMS/CONT WAR CHOOSE PRIVIL 20 UN COLD/WAR. PAGE 27 A0541 — INT/LAW PEACE PLAN INT/ORG

B66
CONNEL-SMITH G.,THE INTERAMERICAN SYSTEM. CUBA L/A+17C DELIB/GP FOR/AID COLONIAL PEACE PWR MARXISM ...BIBLIOG 19/20 OAS. PAGE 29 A0586 — DIPLOM INT/TRADE REGION INT/ORG

B66
COUNCIL OF EUROPE,EUROPEAN CONVENTION ON HUMAN RIGHTS - COLLECTED TEXTS (5TH ED.). EUR+WWI DIPLOM ADJUD CT/SYS...INT/LAW 20 ECHR. PAGE 31 A0638 — ORD/FREE DELIB/GP INT/ORG JURID

B66
COYLE D.C.,THE UNITED NATIONS AND HOW IT WORKS. ECO/UNDEV DELIB/GP BAL/PWR EDU/PROP ARMS/CONT NUC/PWR WAR 20 UN. PAGE 32 A0648 — INT/ORG PEACE DIPLOM INT/TRADE

B66
DOUMA J.,BIBLIOGRAPHY ON THE INTERNATIONAL COURT INCLUDING THE PERMANENT COURT, 1918-1964. WOR+45 WOR-45 DELIB/GP WAR PRIVIL...JURID NAT/COMP 20 UN LEAGUE/NAT. PAGE 38 A0780 — BIBLIOG/A INT/ORG CT/SYS DIPLOM

B66
ESTHUS R.A.,THEODORE ROOSEVELT AND JAPAN. ASIA USA-45 FORCES CONFER WAR SOVEREIGN...BIBLIOG 20 CHINJAP. PAGE 42 A0864 — DIPLOM DELIB/GP

B66
INTERNATIONAL ECONOMIC ASSN,STABILITY AND PROGRESS IN THE WORLD ECONOMY: THE FIRST CONGRESS OF THE INTERNATIONAL ECONOMIC ASSOCIATION. WOR+45 ECO/DEV ECO/UNDEV DELIB/GP FOR/AID BAL/PAY...TREND CMN/WLTH 20. PAGE 71 A1455 — INT/TRADE

B66
INTL ATOMIC ENERGY AGENCY,INTERNATIONAL CONVENTIONS ON CIVIL LIABILITY FOR NUCLEAR DAMAGE. FUT WOR+45 ADJUD WAR COST PEACE SOVEREIGN...JURID 20. PAGE 71 A1462 — DIPLOM INT/ORG DELIB/GP NUC/PWR

B66
LALL A.,MODERN INTERNATIONAL NEGOTIATION: PRINCIPLES AND PRACTICE. WOR+45 INT/ORG DELIB/GP PROB/SOLV DETER...INT/LAW TREATY. PAGE 84 A1712 — DIPLOM ECO/TAC ATTIT

B66
LATHAM E.,THE COMMUNIST CONTROVERSY IN WASHINGTON. USA+45 USA-45 DELIB/GP EX/STRUC LEGIS DIPLOM NAT/LISM MARXISM 20. PAGE 85 A1742 — POL/PAR TOTALISM ORD/FREE NAT/G

B66
LEAGUE OF WOMEN VOTERS OF US,FOREIGN AID AT THE CROSSROADS. USA+45 WOR+45 DELIB/GP PROB/SOLV DIPLOM INT/TRADE RECEIVE BAL/PAY...CHARTS 20 UN. PAGE 86 A1756 — FOR/AID GIVE ECO/UNDEV PLAN

B66
LONG B.,THE WAR DIARY OF BRECKINRIDGE LONG: SELECTIONS FROM THE YEARS 1939-1944. USA-45 INT/ORG FORCES FOR/AID CHOOSE 20. PAGE 91 A1859 — DIPLOM WAR DELIB/GP

B66
MIKESELL R.F.,PUBLIC INTERNATIONAL LENDING FOR DEVELOPMENT. WOR+45 WOR-45 DELIB/GP...TIME/SEQ CHARTS BIBLIOG 20. PAGE 101 A2070 — INT/ORG FOR/AID ECO/UNDEV FINAN

B66
MOORE R.J.,SIR CHARLES WOOD'S INDIAN POLICY: 1853-66. INDIA POL/PAR CHIEF DELIB/GP DIPLOM CONTROL LEAD WOOD/CHAS. PAGE 103 A2124 — COLONIAL ADMIN CONSULT DECISION

B66
POLLACK R.S.,THE INDIVIDUAL'S RIGHTS AND INTERNATIONAL ORGANIZATION. LAW INT/ORG DELIB/GP SUPEGO...JURID SOC/INTEG 20 TREATY UN. PAGE 117 A2394 — INT/LAW ORD/FREE DIPLOM PERSON

B66
SAPIN B.M.,THE MAKING OF UNITED STATES FOREIGN POLICY. USA+45 INT/ORG DELIB/GP FORCES PLAN ECO/TAC CIVMIL/REL PRESIDENT. PAGE 127 A2603 — DIPLOM EX/STRUC DECISION NAT/G

B66
SINGER L.,ALLE LITTEN AN GROSSENWAHN: VON WOODROW WILSON BIS MAO TSE-TUNG. ASIA UK USSR INT/ORG DELIB/GP BAL/PWR DOMIN ATTIT PERSON 20 WILSON/W ROOSEVLT/F. PAGE 133 A2731 — DIPLOM TOTALISM WAR CHIEF

B66
STADLER K.R.,THE BIRTH OF THE AUSTRIAN REPUBLIC, 1918-1921. AUSTRIA PLAN TASK PEACE...POLICY DECISION 20. PAGE 137 A2798 — NAT/G DIPLOM WAR DELIB/GP

B66
US CONGRESS JOINT ECO COMM,NEW APPROACH TO UNITED STATES INTERNATIONAL ECONOMIC POLICY. USA+45 WOR+45 CHIEF DELIB/GP CONFER...CHARTS 20 CONGRESS MONEY. PAGE 150 A3070 — DIPLOM ECO/TAC BAL/PAY FINAN

B66
US HOUSE COMM APPROPRIATIONS,HEARINGS ON FOREIGN OPERATIONS AND RELATED AGENCIES APPROPRIATIONS. CUBA USA+45 VOL/ASSN DELIB/GP DIPLOM CONFER ORD/FREE 20 CONGRESS MIGRATION INT/AM/DEV PEACE/CORP. PAGE 153 A3120 — FOR/AID BUDGET ECO/UNDEV FORCES

B66
US HOUSE COMM FOREIGN AFFAIRS,UNITED STATES - SOUTH AFRICAN RELATIONS. SOUTH/AFR USA+45 NAT/G CONSULT DELIB/GP LEGIS CONFER SANCTION RACE/REL ATTIT 20 CONGRESS. PAGE 154 A3134 — DISCRIM DIPLOM POLICY PARL/PROC

B66
US SENATE COMM GOVT OPERATIONS,POPULATION CRISIS. USA+45 ECO/DEV ECO/UNDEV AGRI SECT DELIB/GP PROB/SOLV FOR/AID REPRESENT ATTIT...GEOG CHARTS 20 CONGRESS DEPT/STATE DEPT/HEW BIRTH/CON. PAGE 156 A3178 — CENSUS CONTROL LEGIS CONSULT

S66
MATTHEWS D.G.,"ETHIOPIAN OUTLINE: A BIBLIOGRAPHIC RESEARCH GUIDE." ETHIOPIA LAW STRUCT ECO/UNDEV AGRI LABOR SECT CHIEF DELIB/GP EX/STRUC ADMIN...LING ORG/CHARTS 20. PAGE 96 A1972 — BIBLIOG NAT/G DIPLOM POL/PAR

C66
BLAISDELL D.C.,"INTERNATIONAL ORGANIZATION." FUT WOR+45 ECO/DEV DELIB/GP FORCES EFFICIENCY PEACE ORD/FREE...INT/LAW 20 UN LEAGUE/NAT NATO. PAGE 15 A0304 — BIBLIOG INT/ORG DIPLOM ARMS/CONT

C66
DUROSELLE J.B.,"LE CONFLIT DE TRIESTE 1943-1954: ETUDES DE CAS DE CONFLITS INTERNATIONAUX III." ITALY USA+45 YUGOSLAVIA ELITES DELIB/GP PLAN ADJUST ...POLICY GEOG CHARTS IDEA/COMP TIME 20 TREATY UN COLD/WAR. PAGE 40 A0810 — BIBLIOG WAR DIPLOM GEN/LAWS

B67
MCBRIDE J.H.,THE TEST BAN TREATY: MILITARY, TECHNOLOGICAL, AND POLITICAL IMPLICATIONS. USA+45 USSR DELIB/GP FORCES LEGIS TEC/DEV BAL/PWR TREATY. PAGE 97 A1995 — ARMS/CONT DIPLOM NUC/PWR

B67
US SENATE COMM AERO SPACE SCI,TREATY ON PRINCIPLES GOVERNING ACTIVITIES OF STATES IN EXPLORATION AND USE OF OUTER SPACE, INCLUDING...BODIES. DELIB/GP FORCES LEGIS DIPLOM...JURID 20 DEPT/STATE NASA DEPT/DEFEN UN. PAGE 155 A3169 — SPACE INT/LAW ORD/FREE PEACE

B67
US SENATE COMM ON FOREIGN REL,HUMAN RIGHTS CONVENTIONS. USA+45 LABOR VOL/ASSN DELIB/GP DOMIN ADJUD REPRESENT...INT/LAW MGT CONGRESS. PAGE 156 A3189 — LEGIS ORD/FREE WORKER LOBBY

L67
GRAUBARD S.R.,"TOWARD THE YEAR 2000: WORK IN PROGRESS." FUT ACADEM SECT DELIB/GP DIPLOM EDU/PROP AGE/Y PERSON ROLE...PSY ANTHOL. PAGE 55 A1131 — PREDICT PROB/SOLV SOCIETY CULTURE

S67
COSGROVE C.A.,"AGRICULTURE, FINANCE AND POLITICS IN THE EUROPEAN COMMUNITY." EUR+WWI DIST/IND MARKET INT/ORG VOL/ASSN DELIB/GP TEC/DEV BAL/PWR BARGAIN ECO/TAC RATION CONFER 20 EEC. PAGE 31 A0630 — ECO/DEV DIPLOM AGRI INT/TRADE

S67
CRAWFORD E.T.,"FOREIGN AREA RESEARCH: A BACKGROUND STATEMENT." USA+45 CONSULT DELIB/GP DIPLOM. PAGE 32 A0661 — INTELL NAT/G POLICY ACT/RES

S67
FELD B.T.,"A PLEDGE* NO FIRST USE." DELIB/GP BAL/PWR DOMIN DETER. PAGE 45 A0913 — ARMS/CONT NUC/PWR DIPLOM PEACE

S67
FOREIGN POLICY ASSOCIATION,"US CONCERN FOR WORLD LAW." USA+45 WOR+45 DELIB/GP JUDGE BAL/PWR CONFER PEACE ORD/FREE 20 UN. PAGE 47 A0962 — INT/LAW INT/ORG DIPLOM ARMS/CONT

S67
HAZARD J.N.,"POST-DISARMAMENT INTERNATIONAL LAW." FUT USSR WOR+45 INT/ORG DELIB/GP FORCES DETER EQUILIB SOVEREIGN MARXISM 20 UN. PAGE 63 A1301 — INT/LAW ARMS/CONT PWR PLAN

S67
HUDSON R.,"WAS THIS WAR NECESSARY? THE UN AND THE MIDDLE EAST" WOR+45 STRUCT DIPLOM DOMIN CONTROL REPRESENT PWR...NEW/IDEA 20 UN MID/EAST. PAGE 69 A1410 — DELIB/GP INT/ORG PROB/SOLV PEACE

S67
SHARP G.,"THE NEED OF A FUNCTIONAL SUBSTITUTE FOR WAR." FUT UNIV WOR+45 CULTURE SOCIETY INT/ORG CONSULT DELIB/GP ACT/RES CREATE BAL/PWR CONFER ARMS/CONT NUC/PWR 20. PAGE 132 A2696 — PEACE WAR DIPLOM PROB/SOLV

S67
WASHBURN A.M.,"NUCLEAR PROLIFERATION IN A — ARMS/CONT

REVOLUTIONARY INTERNATIONAL SYSTEM." WOR+45 NAT/G DELIB/GP PLAN TEC/DEV...POLICY 20. PAGE 161 A3287
NUC/PWR DIPLOM CONFER

DELLA PORT G. A0729

DELZELL C.F. A0730

DEMAND....ECONOMIC DEMAND

B19
MEYER H.H.B.,SELECT LIST OF REFERENCES ON ECONOMIC RECONSTRUCTION: INCLUDING REPORTS OF THE BRITISH MINISTRY OF RECONSTRUCTION. UK LABOR PLAN PROB/SOLV ECO/TAC INT/TRADE WAR DEMAND PRODUC 20. PAGE 100 A2051
BIBLIOG/A EUR+WWI ECO/DEV WORKER

B36
HARVARD BUREAU ECO RES LAT AM,THE ECONOMIC LITERATURE OF LATIN AMERICA: A TENTATIVE BIBLIOGRAPHY. NAT/G TARIFFS CENTRAL COST DEMAND 20. PAGE 62 A1277
BIBLIOG ECO/UNDEV L/A+17C INT/TRADE

B38
FRANKEL S.H.,CAPITAL INVESTMENT IN AFRICA. AFR EUR+WWI RHODESIA SOUTH/AFR UK FINAN FOR/AID COLONIAL DEMAND UTIL WEALTH...METH/CNCPT CHARTS 20 CONGO/LEOP. PAGE 48 A0983
ECO/UNDEV EXTR/IND DIPLOM PRODUC

B42
US LIBRARY OF CONGRESS,ECONOMICS OF WAR (APRIL 1941-MARCH 1942). WOR-45 FINAN INDUS LOC/G NAT/G PLAN BUDGET RATION COST DEMAND...POLICY 20. PAGE 154 A3146
BIBLIOG/A INT/TRADE ECO/TAC WAR

B43
VINER J.,TRADE RELATIONS BETWEEN FREE-MARKET AND CONTROLLED ECONOMIES. WOR-45 MARKET PLAN TARIFFS DEMAND...POLICY STAT 20. PAGE 159 A3237
INT/TRADE DIPLOM CONTROL NAT/G

B44
RAGATZ L.J.,LITERATURE OF EUROPEAN IMPERIALISM. ECO/TAC INT/TRADE DOMIN GOV/REL DEMAND NAT/LISM PWR WEALTH 19/20. PAGE 119 A2432
BIBLIOG COLONIAL INT/ORG ECO/UNDEV

B58
PALYI M.,MANAGED MONEY AT THE CROSSROADS: THE EUROPEAN EXPERIENCE. WOR+45 WOR-45 TEC/DEV DIPLOM INT/TRADE DEMAND WEALTH...CHARTS BIBLIOG 19/20 EUROPE GOLD/STAND SILVER. PAGE 113 A2324
FINAN ECO/TAC ECO/DEV PRODUC

B59
LINK R.G.,ENGLISH THEORIES OF ECONOMIC FLUCTUATIONS: 1815-1848. FRANCE UK AGRI WORKER DIPLOM PRICE TASK WAR DEMAND PRODUC...POLICY BIBLIOG 18 MALTHUS MILL/JS WILSON/J. PAGE 89 A1826
IDEA/COMP ECO/DEV WEALTH EQUILIB

B59
STOVEL J.A.,CANADA IN THE WORLD ECONOMY. CANADA PRICE DEMAND...STAT CHARTS BIBLIOG 20 VINER/J. PAGE 139 A2838
INT/TRADE BAL/PAY FINAN ECO/TAC

B60
LEVIN J.V.,THE EXPORT ECONOMIES: THEIR PATTERN OF DEVELOPMENT IN HISTORICAL PERSPECTIVE. BURMA PERU AGRI WORKER COLONIAL COST DEMAND INCOME 20. PAGE 88 A1795
INT/TRADE ECO/UNDEV BAL/PAY EXTR/IND

B61
LETHBRIDGE H.J.,CHINA'S URBAN COMMUNES. CHINA/COM FUT ECO/UNDEV DIPLOM EDU/PROP DEMAND INCOME MARXISM ...POLICY 20. PAGE 87 A1790
MUNIC CONTROL ECO/TAC NAT/G

B61
OECD,STATISTICS OF BALANCE OF PAYMENTS 1950-61. WOR+45 FINAN ECO/TAC INT/TRADE DEMAND WEALTH...STAT NAT/COMP 20 OEEC OECD. PAGE 111 A2278
BAL/PAY ECO/DEV INT/ORG CHARTS

B62
FAO,FOOD AND AGRICULTURE ORGANIZATION AFRICAN SURVEY. AFR CONGO/BRAZ GHANA STRATA AGRI INT/ORG TEC/DEV FOR/AID INT/TRADE RACE/REL DEMAND EFFICIENCY PRODUC...GEOG 20 UN CONGO/LEOP. PAGE 44 A0898
ECO/TAC WEALTH EXTR/IND ECO/UNDEV

B62
FORD A.G.,THE GOLD STANDARD 1880-1914: BRITAIN AND ARGENTINA. UK ECO/UNDEV INT/TRADE ADMIN GOV/REL DEMAND EFFICIENCY...STAT CHARTS 19/20 ARGEN GOLD/STAND. PAGE 47 A0960
FINAN ECO/TAC BUDGET BAL/PAY

B62
KINDLEBERGER C.P.,FOREIGN TRADE AND THE NATIONAL ECONOMY. WOR+45 ECO/DEV ECO/UNDEV ECO/TAC COST DEMAND 20. PAGE 79 A1622
INT/TRADE GOV/COMP BAL/PAY POLICY

B63
BRITISH AID. UK AGRI DIST/IND INDUS SCHOOL TEC/DEV INT/TRADE COLONIAL DEMAND...TREND CHARTS 20. PAGE 3 A0064
FOR/AID ECO/UNDEV NAT/G FINAN

B63
EL-NAGGAR S.,FOREIGN AID TO UNITED ARAB REPUBLIC. UAR USA+45 USSR AGRI FINAN INDUS FORCES EATING DEMAND...CHARTS METH/COMP 20 RESOURCE/N AID. PAGE 41 A0838
FOR/AID ECO/UNDEV RECEIVE PLAN

B63
ERHARD L.,THE ECONOMICS OF SUCCESS. GERMANY/W WOR+45 LABOR CHIEF TAX REGION COST DEMAND ANTHOL. PAGE 42 A0860
ECO/DEV INT/TRADE PLAN DIPLOM

B63
PAENSON I.,SYSTEMATIC GLOSSARY ENGLISH, FRENCH, SPANISH, RUSSIAN OF SELECTED ECONOMIC AND SOCIAL TERMS. WOR+45 FINAN LABOR INT/TRADE DEMAND PRODUC 20. PAGE 113 A2315
DICTIONARY SOC LING

B63
SALENT W.S.,THE UNITED STATES BALANCE OF PAYMENTS IN 1968. EUR+WWI UK USA+45 AGRI R+D LABOR FORCES PRODUC...GEOG CONCPT CHARTS 20 CHINJAP EEC. PAGE 126 A2589
BAL/PAY DEMAND FINAN INT/TRADE

B64
MC GOVERN G.S.,WAR AGAINST WANT. USA+45 AGRI DIPLOM INT/TRADE GIVE RECEIVE DEMAND HEALTH 20 KENNEDY/JF FOOD/PEACE. PAGE 97 A1993
FOR/AID ECO/DEV POLICY EATING

B64
US HOUSE COMM GOVT OPERATIONS,US OWNED FOREIGN CURRENCIES: HEARINGS (COMMITTEE ON GOVERNMENT OPERATIONS). INDIA ECO/DEV PLAN BUDGET TAX DEMAND EFFICIENCY 20 AID CONGRESS. PAGE 154 A3138
FINAN ECO/TAC FOR/AID OWN

B64
ZEBOT C.A.,THE ECONOMICS OF COMPETITIVE COEXISTENCE. CHINA/COM USSR WOR+45 FINAN MARKET FOR/AID PRICE DEMAND EQUILIB WEALTH ALL/IDEOS 20. PAGE 169 A3450
TEC/DEV DIPLOM METH/COMP

B65
DEMAS W.G.,THE ECONOMICS OF DEVELOPMENT IN SMALL COUNTRIES WITH SPECIAL REFERENCE TO THE CARIBBEAN. WOR+45 BAL/PAY DEMAND EFFICIENCY PRODUC...GEOG CARIBBEAN. PAGE 36 A0731
ECO/UNDEV PLAN WEALTH INT/TRADE

B65
MURUMBI J.,PROBLEMS OF ECONOMIC DEVELOPMENT IN EAST AFRICA. FINAN INDUS WORKER TEC/DEV INT/TRADE TAX DEMAND EFFICIENCY PRODUC SOCISM...TREND CHARTS 20 AFRICA/E. PAGE 106 A2184
AGRI ECO/TAC ECO/UNDEV PROC/MFG

B65
ROLFE S.E.,GOLD AND WORLD POWER. UK USA+45 WOR-45 INDUS WORKER INT/TRADE DEMAND...MGT CHARTS 20 GOLD/STAND. PAGE 123 A2517
BAL/PAY EQUILIB ECO/TAC DIPLOM

B66
KEENLEYSIDE H.L.,INTERNATIONAL AID: A SUMMARY. AFR INDIA S/ASIA UK STRATA EXTR/IND TEC/DEV ADMIN RACE/REL DEMAND NAT/LISM WEALTH...TREND CHINJAP. PAGE 77 A1575
ECO/UNDEV FOR/AID DIPLOM TASK

L66
AMERICAN ECONOMIC REVIEW,"SIXTY-THIRD LIST OF DOCTORAL DISSERTATIONS IN POLITICAL ECONOMY IN AMERICAN UNIVERSITIES AND COLLEGES." ECO/DEV AGRI FINAN LABOR WORKER PLAN BUDGET INT/TRADE ADMIN DEMAND...MGT STAT 20. PAGE 7 A0146
BIBLIOG/A CONCPT ACADEM

B67
HIRSCHMAN A.O.,DEVELOPMENT PROJECTS OBSERVED. INDUS INT/ORG CONSULT EX/STRUC CREATE OP/RES ECO/TAC DEMAND...POLICY MGT METH/COMP 20 WORLD/BANK. PAGE 65 A1339
ECO/UNDEV R+D FINAN PLAN

S67
FALKOWSKI M.,"SOCIALIST ECONOMISTS AND THE DEVELOPING COUNTRIES." COM PLAN TEC/DEV ROUTINE DEMAND EFFICIENCY PRODUC WEALTH...MARXIST TREND GEN/METH. PAGE 44 A0893
DIPLOM SOCISM ECO/UNDEV INDUS

S67
LEVI M.,"LES DIFFICULTES ECONOMIQUES DE LA GRANDE-BRETAGNE." UK INT/ORG TEC/DEV BARGAIN DIPLOM DOMIN REPRESENT DEMAND WEALTH...POLICY 20 EEC. PAGE 88 A1792
BAL/PAY INT/TRADE PRODUC

S67
OLIVIER G.,"ASPECTS JURIDIQUES DE L'ADOPTION DU TRAITE CECA A LA CRISE CHARBONNIERE (SUITE ET FIN)" LAW DIST/IND PLAN DIPLOM RATION PRICE ADMIN COST DEMAND...POLICY CON/ANAL ECSC TREATY. PAGE 112 A2288
INT/TRADE INT/ORG EXTR/IND CONSTN

S67
PEUKERT W.,"WEST GERMANY'S 'RED TRADE'." COM GERMANY INDUS CAP/ISM DOMIN SANCTION DEMAND PEACE UTIL...MARXIST 20 COLD/WAR. PAGE 115 A2371
DIPLOM ECO/TAC INT/TRADE

S67
WINTHROP H.,"CONTEMPORARY ECONOMIC DEHUMANIZATION* SOME DIFFICULTIES SURROUNDING ITS REDUCTION." USA+45 WOR+45 ACT/RES PROB/SOLV DIPLOM ROUTINE DEMAND UTIL. PAGE 165 A3368
TEC/DEV SOCIETY WEALTH

DEMAS W.G. A0731

DEMOCRACY....SEE MAJORIT, **POPULISM, NEW/LIB**

DEMOCRAT....DEMOCRATIC PARTY (ALL NATIONS)

B27
SIEGFRIED A.,AMERICA COMES OF AGE: A FRENCH ANALYSIS (TRANS. BY H.H. HEMMING AND DORIS HEMMING). FRANCE UK POL/PAR WORKER TEC/DEV DIPLOM REGION RACE/REL ADJUST PRODUC HEREDITY...TIME/SEQ GP/COMP SOC/INTEG 20 DEMOCRAT REPUBLICAN KKK. PAGE 132 A2714 — USA-45 CULTURE ECO/DEV SOC

B62
TOURE S.,THE INTERNATIONAL POLICY OF THE DEMOCRATIC PARTY OF GUINEA (VOL. VII). AFR ALGERIA GHANA GUINEA MALI CONSTN VOL/ASSN CHIEF WAR PEACE ATTIT ...WELF/ST 20 DEMOCRAT. PAGE 144 A2953 — DIPLOM POLICY POL/PAR NEW/LIB

B64
JOHNSON L.B.,MY HOPE FOR AMERICA. FUT USA+45 USSR LAW PLAN DIPLOM GIVE INCOME PEACE ATTIT ORD/FREE WEALTH 20 JOHNSON/LB PRESIDENT DEMOCRAT. PAGE 74 A1525 — POLICY POL/PAR NAT/G GOV/REL

DEMOGRAPHY....SEE GEOG

DENMARK....SEE ALSO APPROPRIATE TIME/SPACE/CULTURE INDEX

B53
ORFIELD L.B.,THE GROWTH OF SCANDINAVIAN LAW. DENMARK ICELAND NORWAY SWEDEN LAW DIPLOM...BIBLIOG 9/20. PAGE 112 A2296 — JURID CT/SYS NAT/G

C65
WUORINEN J.H.,"SCANDINAVIA." DENMARK FINLAND ICELAND NORWAY SWEDEN SOCIETY AGRI POL/PAR DELIB/GP DIPLOM INT/TRADE NEUTRAL WAR...CHARTS TREATY 20. PAGE 168 A3423 — BIBLIOG NAT/G POLICY

DENVER....DENVER, COLORADO

DEPARTMENT HEADS...SEE EX/STRUC, TOP/EX

DEPORT....DEPORTATION

DEPRESSION....ECONOMIC DEPRESSION

B35
SIMONDS F.H.,THE GREAT POWERS IN WORLD POLITICS. FRANCE GERMANY UK WOR-45 INT/ORG NAT/G ARMS/CONT PEACE FASCISM...POLICY GEOG 20 DEPRESSION NAZI. PAGE 133 A2718 — DIPLOM WEALTH WAR

DEPT/AGRI....U.S. DEPARTMENT OF AGRICULTURE

DEPT/COM....U.S. DEPARTMENT OF COMMERCE

DEPT/DEFEN....U.S. DEPARTMENT OF DEFENSE

N58
US HOUSE COMM FOREIGN AFFAIRS,HEARINGS ON DRAFT LEGISLATION TO AMEND FURTHER THE MUTUAL SECURITY ACT OF 1954 (PAMPHLET). USA+45 CONSULT FORCES BUDGET DIPLOM DETER COST ORD/FREE...JURID 20 DEPT/DEFEN UN DEPT/STATE. PAGE 153 A3123 — LEGIS DELIB/GP CONFER WEAPON

B59
VAN WAGENEN R.W.,SOME VIEWS OF AMERICAN DEFENSE OFFICIALS ABOUT THE UNITED NATIONS (PAPER). FUT USA+45 NAT/G DIPLOM WAR EFFICIENCY PEACE...POLICY INT 20 UN DEPT/DEFEN. PAGE 158 A3216 — INT/ORG LEAD ATTIT FORCES

B60
US HOUSE COMM FOREIGN AFFAIRS,HEARINGS ON A BILL TO AMEND FURTHER THE MUTUAL SECURITY ACT OF 1954. USA+45 CONSULT FORCES BUDGET FOR/AID CONFER DETER ...CHARTS 20 DEPT/DEFEN DEPT/STATE UNEF. PAGE 153 A3127 — DIPLOM ORD/FREE DELIB/GP LEGIS

B63
US HOUSE COMM FOREIGN AFFAIRS,HEARINGS ON H.R. 5490 TO AMEND FURTHER THE FOREIGN ASSISTANCE ACT OF 1961. CUBA EUR+WWI INDIA INT/ORG DELIB/GP LEGIS DIPLOM CONFER ORD/FREE 20 DEPT/STATE DEPT/DEFEN UN. PAGE 153 A3129 — FOR/AID INT/TRADE FORCES WEAPON

B64
BLACKSTOCK P.W.,THE STRATEGY OF SUBVERSION. USA+45 FORCES EDU/PROP ADMIN COERCE GOV/REL...DECISION MGT 20 DEPT/DEFEN CIA DEPT/STATE. PAGE 15 A0301 — ORD/FREE DIPLOM CONTROL

B64
KAUFMANN W.W.,THE MC NAMARA STRATEGY. TOP/EX INSPECT BAL/PWR DIPLOM CONTROL DETER GUERRILLA NUC/PWR WEAPON COST PWR...METH/COMP 20 MCNAMARA/R KENNEDY/JF JOHNSON/LB NATO DEPT/DEFEN. PAGE 77 A1572 — FORCES WAR PLAN PROB/SOLV

B64
SINGH N.,THE DEFENCE MECHANISM OF THE MODERN STATE. COM UK USA+45 CONSTN INT/ORG NUC/PWR WAR INGP/REL ROLE 20 DEPT/DEFEN COMMONWLTH. PAGE 134 A2735 — FORCES TOP/EX NAT/G CIVMIL/REL

B65
THAYER F.C., JR.,AIR TRANSPORT POLICY AND NATIONAL SECURITY: A POLITICAL, ECONOMIC, AND MILITARY ANALYSIS. DIST/IND OP/RES PLAN TEC/DEV DIPLOM DETER WAR COST EFFICIENCY...POLICY BIBLIOG 20 DEPT/DEFEN FAA CAB. PAGE 142 A2908 — AIR FORCES CIVMIL/REL ORD/FREE

B67
US SENATE COMM AERO SPACE SCI,TREATY ON PRINCIPLES GOVERNING ACTIVITIES OF STATES IN EXPLORATION AND USE OF OUTER SPACE, INCLUDING...BODIES. DELIB/GP FORCES LEGIS DIPLOM...JURID 20 DEPT/STATE NASA DEPT/DEFEN UN. PAGE 155 A3169 — SPACE INT/LAW ORD/FREE PEACE

DEPT/HEW....U.S. DEPARTMENT OF HEALTH, EDUCATION, AND WELFARE

B66
US SENATE COMM GOVT OPERATIONS,POPULATION CRISIS. USA+45 ECO/DEV ECO/UNDEV AGRI SECT DELIB/GP PROB/SOLV FOR/AID REPRESENT ATTIT...GEOG CHARTS 20 CONGRESS DEPT/STATE DEPT/HEW BIRTH/CON. PAGE 156 A3178 — CENSUS CONTROL LEGIS CONSULT

DEPT/HUD....U.S. DEPARTMENT OF HOUSING AND URBAN DEVELOPMENT

DEPT/INTER....U.S. DEPARTMENT OF THE INTERIOR

DEPT/JUST....U.S. DEPARTMENT OF JUSTICE

DEPT/LABOR....U.S. DEPARTMENT OF LABOR AND INDUSTRY

DEPT/STATE....U.S. DEPARTMENT OF STATE

B48
CHILDS J.R.,AMERICAN FOREIGN SERVICE. USA+45 SOCIETY NAT/G ROUTINE GOV/REL 20 DEPT/STATE CIVIL/SERV. PAGE 26 A0530 — DIPLOM ADMIN GP/REL

B48
US DEPARTMENT OF STATE,FOREIGN AFFAIRS HIGHLIGHTS (NEWSLETTER). COM USA+45 INT/ORG PLAN BAL/PWR WAR PWR...BIBLIOG 20 COLD/WAR NATO UN DEPT/STATE. PAGE 151 A3083 — DIPLOM NAT/G POLICY

B54
US DEPARTMENT OF STATE,PUBLICATIONS OF THE DEPARTMENT OF STATE, OCTOBER 1,1929 TO JANUARY 1, 1953. AGRI INT/ORG FORCES FOR/AID EDU/PROP ARMS/CONT NUC/PWR ATTIT 20 DEPT/STATE OAS UN NATO. PAGE 151 A3089 — BIBLIOG DIPLOM

B58
US DEPARTMENT OF STATE,PUBLICATIONS OF THE DEPARTMENT OF STATE, JANUARY 1,1953 TO DECEMBER 31, 1957. AGRI INT/ORG FORCES FOR/AID EDU/PROP ARMS/CONT NUC/PWR ATTIT 20 DEPT/STATE OAS UN NATO. PAGE 151 A3092 — BIBLIOG DIPLOM

N58
US HOUSE COMM FOREIGN AFFAIRS,HEARINGS ON DRAFT LEGISLATION TO AMEND FURTHER THE MUTUAL SECURITY ACT OF 1954 (PAMPHLET). USA+45 CONSULT FORCES BUDGET DIPLOM DETER COST ORD/FREE...JURID 20 DEPT/DEFEN UN DEPT/STATE. PAGE 153 A3123 — LEGIS DELIB/GP CONFER WEAPON

B60
US HOUSE COMM FOREIGN AFFAIRS,HEARINGS ON A BILL TO AMEND FURTHER THE MUTUAL SECURITY ACT OF 1954. USA+45 CONSULT FORCES BUDGET FOR/AID CONFER DETER ...CHARTS 20 DEPT/DEFEN DEPT/STATE UNEF. PAGE 153 A3127 — DIPLOM ORD/FREE DELIB/GP LEGIS

B60
US HOUSE COMM GOVT OPERATIONS,OPERATIONS OF THE DEVELOPMENT LOAN FUND: HEARINGS (COMMITTEE ON GOVERNMENT OPERATIONS). USA+45 PLAN BUDGET DIPLOM GOV/REL COST...CHARTS 20 CONGRESS DEPT/STATE AID. PAGE 154 A3137 — FINAN FOR/AID ECO/TAC EFFICIENCY

B60
US SENATE COMM ON FOREIGN REL,SITUATION IN VIETNAM (2 VOLS.). USA+45 VIETNAM ECO/TAC COST SENATE DEPT/STATE. PAGE 156 A3181 — FOR/AID PLAN EFFICIENCY INSPECT

B63
GORDON L.,A NEW DEAL FOR LATIN AMERICA. L/A+17C USA+45 CULTURE NAT/G TEC/DEV DIPLOM FOR/AID REGION TASK...POLICY 20 DEPT/STATE. PAGE 54 A1115 — ECO/UNDEV ECO/TAC INT/ORG PLAN

B63
SMITH J.E.,THE DEFENSE OF BERLIN. COM GUATEMALA WOR+45 ECO/TAC ADMIN NEUTRAL ATTIT ORD/FREE SOVEREIGN...DECISION 20 DEPT/STATE. PAGE 134 A2747 — DIPLOM FORCES BAL/PWR PLAN

B63
US HOUSE COMM FOREIGN AFFAIRS,HEARINGS ON H.R. 5490 TO AMEND FURTHER THE FOREIGN ASSISTANCE ACT OF 1961. CUBA EUR+WWI INDIA INT/ORG DELIB/GP LEGIS DIPLOM CONFER ORD/FREE 20 DEPT/STATE DEPT/DEFEN UN. PAGE 153 A3129 — FOR/AID INT/TRADE FORCES WEAPON

B64
BLACKSTOCK P.W.,THE STRATEGY OF SUBVERSION. USA+45 FORCES EDU/PROP ADMIN COERCE GOV/REL...DECISION MGT 20 DEPT/DEFEN CIA DEPT/STATE. PAGE 15 A0301 — ORD/FREE DIPLOM CONTROL

B64
US SENATE COMM GOVT OPERATIONS,THE SECRETARY OF STATE AND THE AMBASSADOR. USA+45 CHIEF CONSULT EX/STRUC FORCES PLAN ADMIN EXEC INGP/REL ROLE ...ANTHOL 20 PRESIDENT DEPT/STATE. PAGE 156 A3175 — DIPLOM DELIB/GP NAT/G

S64
RUSK D.,"THE MAKING OF FOREIGN POLICY" USA+45 CHIEF DELIB/GP WORKER PROB/SOLV ADMIN ATTIT PWR ...DECISION 20 DEPT/STATE RUSK/D GOLDMAN/E. PAGE 125 A2570
DIPLOM INT POLICY

B66
US SENATE COMM GOVT OPERATIONS,POPULATION CRISIS. USA+45 ECO/DEV ECO/UNDEV AGRI SECT DELIB/GP PROB/SOLV FOR/AID REPRESENT ATTIT...GEOG CHARTS 20 CONGRESS DEPT/STATE DEPT/HEW BIRTH/CON. PAGE 156 A3178
CENSUS CONTROL LEGIS CONSULT

B67
US SENATE COMM AERO SPACE SCI,TREATY ON PRINCIPLES GOVERNING ACTIVITIES OF STATES IN EXPLORATION AND USE OF OUTER SPACE, INCLUDING...BODIES. DELIB/GP FORCES LEGIS DIPLOM...JURID 20 DEPT/STATE NASA DEPT/DEFEN UN. PAGE 155 A3169
SPACE INT/LAW ORD/FREE PEACE

L67
"RESTRICTIVE SOVEREIGN IMMUNITY, THE STATE DEPARTMENT, AND THE COURTS." USA+45 USA-45 EX/STRUC DIPLOM ADJUD CONTROL GOV/REL 19/20 DEPT/STATE SUPREME/CT. PAGE 4 A0080
SOVEREIGN ORD/FREE PRIVIL CT/SYS

DEPT/TREAS....U.S. DEPARTMENT OF THE TREASURY

DERWINSKI E.J. A0732

DESCARTE/R....RENE DESCARTES

DESEGREGATION....SEE NEGRO, SOUTH/US, RACE/REL, SOC/INTEG, CIV/RIGHTS, DISCRIM, MISCEGEN, ISOLAT, SCHOOL, STRANGE

DESHMUKH C.D. A0733

DESSALIN/J....JEAN-JACQUES DESSALINES

DESTALIN....DE-STALINIZATION

DETER....DETERRENCE; SEE ALSO PWR, PLAN

B14
DE BLOCH J.,THE FUTURE OF WAR IN ITS TECHNICAL, ECONOMIC, AND POLITICAL RELATIONS (1899). MOD/EUR TEC/DEV BUDGET INT/TRADE DETER GUERRILLA WEAPON COST PEACE 20. PAGE 34 A0698
WAR BAL/PWR PREDICT FORCES

B19
ROUSSEAU J.J.,A LASTING PEACE. INT/ORG NAT/G CHIEF DIPLOM DETER WAR POLICY. PAGE 124 A2550
PLAN PEACE UTIL

N19
LANGE O.R.,"DISARMAMENT ECONOMIC GROWTH AND INTERNATIONAL CO-OPERATION" (PAMPHLET). WOR+45 DIST/IND PLAN INT/TRADE GIVE TASK DETER WEALTH SOCISM 18/19 BOLIVAR/S. PAGE 84 A1723
ARMS/CONT DIPLOM ECO/DEV ECO/UNDEV

N19
MEZERIK A.G.,ATOM TESTS AND RADIATION HAZARDS (PAMPHLET). WOR+45 INT/ORG DIPLOM DETER 20 UN TREATY. PAGE 100 A2059
NUC/PWR ARMS/CONT CONFER HEALTH

N19
MEZERIK AG,OUTER SPACE: UN, US, USSR (PAMPHLET). USSR DELIB/GP FORCES DETER NUC/PWR SOVEREIGN ...POLICY 20 UN TREATY. PAGE 101 A2063
SPACE CONTROL DIPLOM INT/ORG

B40
CONOVER H.F.,A BRIEF LIST OF REFERENCES ON WESTERN HEMISPHERE DEFENSE (PAMPHLET). USA-45 NAT/G CONSULT DELIB/GP FORCES BAL/PWR CONFER DETER...PREDICT CON/ANAL 20. PAGE 29 A0591
BIBLIOG DIPLOM PLAN INT/ORG

B43
MICAUD C.A.,THE FRENCH RIGHT AND NAZI GERMANY 1933-1939: A STUDY OF PUBLIC OPINION. GERMANY UK USSR POL/PAR ARMS/CONT COERCE DETER PEACE RIGID/FLEX PWR MARXISM...FASCIST TREND 20 LEAGUE/NAT TREATY. PAGE 101 A2065
DIPLOM AGREE

L46
MASTERS D.,"ONE WORLD OR NONE." FUT WOR+45 INTELL INT/ORG ACT/RES EDU/PROP DETER ATTIT RIGID/FLEX SUPEGO KNOWL...STAT TREND ORG/CHARTS 20. PAGE 96 A1960
POLICY PHIL/SCI ARMS/CONT NUC/PWR

B49
KAFKA G.,FREIHEIT UND ANARCHIE. SECT COERCE DETER WAR ATTIT...IDEA/COMP 20 NATO. PAGE 75 A1545
CONCPT ORD/FREE JURID INT/ORG

B50
JIMENEZ E.,VOTING AND HANDLING OF DISPUTES IN THE SECURITY COUNCIL. WOR+45 CONSTN INT/ORG DIPLOM LEGIT DETER CHOOSE MORAL ORD/FREE PWR...JURID TIME/SEQ COLD/WAR UN 20. PAGE 74 A1517
DELIB/GP ROUTINE

L51
KELSEN H.,"RECENT TRENDS IN THE LAW OF THE UNITED NATIONS." KOREA WOR+45 CONSTN LEGIS DIPLOM LEGIT DETER WAR RIGID/FLEX HEALTH ORD/FREE RESPECT ...JURID CON/ANAL UN VAL/FREE 20 NATO. PAGE 77 A1582
INT/ORG LAW INT/LAW

L51
WHITAKER A.P.,"DEVELOPMENT OF AMERICAN REGIONALISM: THE ORGANIZATION OF AMERICAN STATES." L/A+17C USA+45 VOL/ASSN DELIB/GP FORCES TOP/EX ACT/RES ECO/TAC CT/SYS REGION PEACE ALL/VALS OAS 20. PAGE 163 A3330
INT/ORG TIME/SEQ DETER

B52
LIPPMANN W.,ISOLATION AND ALLIANCES: AN AMERICAN SPEAKS TO THE BRITISH. USA+45 USA-45 INT/ORG AGREE COERCE DETER WAR PEACE MORAL 20 TREATY INTERVENT. PAGE 89 A1829
DIPLOM SOVEREIGN COLONIAL ATTIT

B54
ARON R.,CENTURY OF TOTAL WAR. FUT WOR+45 WOR-45 SOCIETY INT/ORG NAT/G FORCES TOP/EX CREATE BAL/PWR DOMIN EDU/PROP COERCE DETER PEACE TOTALISM PWR ...TIME/SEQ TREND COLD/WAR TOT/POP VAL/FREE LEAGUE/NAT 20. PAGE 9 A0179
ATTIT WAR

B54
CHEEVER D.S.,ORGANIZING FOR PEACE. FUT WOR+45 WOR-45 STRATA STRUCT NAT/G CREATE DIPLOM LEGIT REGION COERCE DETER PEACE ATTIT DRIVE ALL/VALS ...TIME/SEQ TREND UN LEAGUE/NAT. PAGE 26 A0525
INT/ORG

B54
KENNAN G.F.,REALITIES OF AMERICAN FOREIGN POLICY. USA+45 INT/ORG NUC/PWR TOTALISM 20 COLD/WAR. PAGE 77 A1586
DIPLOM BAL/PWR DECISION DETER

B54
SAPIN B.M.,THE ROLE OF THE MILITARY IN AMERICAN FOREIGN POLICY. USA+45 INT/ORG PROB/SOLV DETER NUC/PWR ATTIT PWR...BIBLIOG 20 NATO. PAGE 127 A2602
DIPLOM POLICY CIVMIL/REL NAT/G

S54
FOX W.T.R.,"CIVIL-MILITARY RELATIONS." USA+45 USA-45 R+D ACT/RES DIPLOM INT/TRADE EDU/PROP DETER DISPL DRIVE ORD/FREE...METH/CNCPT TREND COLD/WAR 20. PAGE 48 A0974
POLICY FORCES PLAN SOCIETY

B55
COTTRELL W.F.,ENERGY AND SOCIETY. FUT WOR+45 WOR-45 ECO/DEV ECO/UNDEV INT/ORG NAT/G DETER ORD/FREE PWR SKILL WEALTH...SOC TIME/SEQ TOT/POP VAL/FREE 20. PAGE 31 A0634
TEC/DEV BAL/PWR PEACE

B55
LANDHEER B.,EUROPEAN YEARBOOK, 1955. CONSTN ECO/DEV DIST/IND FINAN DELIB/GP ECO/TAC DETER NUC/PWR ...BIBLIOG 20 EEC. PAGE 84 A1717
EUR+WWI INT/ORG GOV/REL INT/TRADE

B56
ESTEP R.,AN AIR POWER BIBLIOGRAPHY. USA+45 TEC/DEV BUDGET DIPLOM EDU/PROP DETER CIVMIL/REL...DECISION INT/LAW 20. PAGE 42 A0862
BIBLIOG/A FORCES WEAPON PLAN

C56
VAGTS A.,"DEFENSE AND DIPLOMACY: THE SOLDIER AND THE CONDUCT OF FOREIGN RELATIONS." OP/RES CONFER DETER WAR PEACE RESPECT...POLICY DECISION CONCPT BIBLIOG 17/20. PAGE 158 A3209
DIPLOM FORCES HIST/WRIT

B57
ARON R.,FRANCE DEFEATS EDC. EUR+WWI GERMANY LEGIS DIPLOM DOMIN EDU/PROP ADMIN...HIST/WRIT 20. PAGE 9 A0180
INT/ORG FORCES DETER FRANCE

B57
KISSINGER H.A.,NUCLEAR WEAPONS AND FOREIGN POLICY. FUT USA+45 WOR+45 INT/ORG FORCES ACT/RES TEC/DEV DIPLOM ARMS/CONT COERCE ATTIT KNOWL PWR...DECISION GEOG CHARTS 20. PAGE 80 A1640
PLAN DETER NUC/PWR

B57
LISKA G.,INTERNATIONAL EQUILIBRIUM. WOR+45 WOR-45 SOCIETY INT/ORG FORCES DETER ATTIT ORD/FREE PWR ...GEN/LAWS 19/20. PAGE 90 A1836
NAT/G BAL/PWR REGION DIPLOM

B57
NEHRU J.,MILITARY ALLIANCE (PAMPHLET). INDIA WOR+45 NAT/G PLAN DETER NUC/PWR WAR...POLICY ANTHOL NEHRU/J SEATO UN. PAGE 108 A2212
INT/ORG DIPLOM FORCES PEACE

B57
REISS J.,GEORGE KENNANS POLITIK DER EINDAMMUNG. USSR NAT/G FORCES TOTALISM ATTIT ORD/FREE...POLICY 20 NATO TRUMAN/HS MARSHL/PLN KENNAN/G. PAGE 120 A2463
DIPLOM DETER PEACE

B57
SINEY M.C.,THE ALLIED BLOCKADE OF GERMANY: 1914-1916. EUR+WWI GERMANY MOD/EUR USA-45 DIPLOM CONTROL NEUTRAL PWR 20. PAGE 133 A2721
DETER INT/TRADE INT/LAW WAR

B58
GARTHOFF R.L.,SOVIET STRATEGY IN THE NUCLEAR AGE. FUT USSR R+D INT/ORG NAT/G ACT/RES TEC/DEV DOMIN DETER WAR ATTIT PWR...RELATIV METH/CNCPT SELF/OBS TREND CON/ANAL STERTYP GEN/LAWS 20. PAGE 51 A1052
COM FORCES BAL/PWR NUC/PWR

B58
GAVIN J.M.,WAR AND PEACE IN THE SPACE AGE. SPACE USA+45 USSR FORCES PLAN TEC/DEV BAL/PWR DIPLOM ARMS/CONT WEAPON CIVMIL/REL...CHARTS GP/COMP 20
WAR DETER NUC/PWR

NATO COLD/WAR. PAGE 52 A1055 PEACE

B58
MELMAN S.,INSPECTION FOR DISARMAMENT. USA+45 WOR+45 FUT
SOCIETY INT/ORG NAT/G CONSULT ACT/RES PLAN EDU/PROP ORD/FREE
CONTROL DETER PEACE ATTIT PERSON KNOWL...PSY STAT ARMS/CONT
OBS CHARTS TOT/POP VAL/FREE 20. PAGE 99 A2035 NUC/PWR

B58
MILLIS W.,FOREIGN POLICY AND THE FREE SOCIETY. DIPLOM
USA+45 WOR+45 SOCIETY NAT/G FORCES BAL/PWR FOR/AID POLICY
EDU/PROP DETER ATTIT PWR 20 COLD/WAR. PAGE 102 ORD/FREE
A2084 CONSULT

B58
NATIONAL PLANNING ASSOCIATION,1970 WITHOUT ARMS ARMS/CONT
CONTROL (PAMPHLET). WOR+45 PROB/SOLV TEC/DEV DIPLOM ORD/FREE
CONFER DETER NUC/PWR WAR...CHARTS 20 COLD/WAR. WEAPON
PAGE 107 A2204 PREDICT

B58
ROCKEFELLER BROTH FUND INC,INTERNATIONAL SECURITY - NUC/PWR
THE MILITARY ASPECT. USA+45 INT/ORG NAT/G BUDGET DETER
ARMS/CONT WAR WEAPON PEACE ORD/FREE 20 NATO. FORCES
PAGE 123 A2511 DIPLOM

S58
BURNS A.L.,"THE INTERNATIONAL CONSEQUENCES OF PLAN
EXPECTING SURPRISE." WOR+45 INT/ORG NAT/G FORCES PWR
DIPLOM COERCE NUC/PWR WAR CHOOSE ORD/FREE DETER
...METH/CNCPT STYLE OBS STERTYP TOT/POP VAL/FREE.
PAGE 22 A0440

S58
LASSWELL H.D.,"THE SCIENTIFIC STUDY OF PHIL/SCI
INTERNATIONAL RELATIONS." USA+45 INT/ORG CREATE GEN/METH
EDU/PROP DETER ATTIT PERCEPT PWR...DECISION CONCPT DIPLOM
METH/CNCPT STYLE CON/ANAL 20. PAGE 85 A1740

S58
SINGER J.D.,"THREAT PERCEPTION AND THE ARMAMENT PERCEPT
TENSION DILEMMA." WOR+45 WOR-45 ELITES INT/ORG ARMS/CONT
NAT/G DELIB/GP PLAN LEGIT COERCE DETER ATTIT BAL/PWR
RIGID/FLEX PWR...DECISION PSY 20. PAGE 133 A2724

N58
US HOUSE COMM FOREIGN AFFAIRS,HEARINGS ON DRAFT LEGIS
LEGISLATION TO AMEND FURTHER THE MUTUAL SECURITY DELIB/GP
ACT OF 1954 (PAMPHLET). USA+45 CONSULT FORCES CONFER
BUDGET DIPLOM DETER COST ORD/FREE...JURID 20 WEAPON
DEPT/DEFEN UN DEPT/STATE. PAGE 153 A3123

B59
AIR FORCE ACADEMY ASSEMBLY '59,INTERNATIONAL FOR/AID
STABILITY AND PROGRESS (PAMPHLET). USA+45 USSR FORCES
ECO/UNDEV PROB/SOLV BUDGET DIPLOM ADMIN DETER COST WAR
ATTIT...TREND 20. PAGE 5 A0103 PLAN

B59
BRODIE B.,STRATEGY IN THE MISSILE AGE. FUT WOR+45 ACT/RES
CONSULT PLAN COERCE DETER RIGID/FLEX PWR...CONCPT FORCES
TIME/SEQ TREND 20. PAGE 19 A0381 ARMS/CONT
NUC/PWR

B59
EMME E.M.,THE IMPACT OF AIR POWER - NATIONAL DETER
SECURITY AND WORLD POLITICS. USA+45 USSR FORCES AIR
DIPLOM WEAPON PEACE TOTALISM...POLICY NAT/COMP 20 WAR
EUROPE. PAGE 42 A0850 ORD/FREE

B59
HERZ J.H.,INTERNATIONAL POLITICS IN THE ATOMIC AGE. INT/ORG
FUT USA+45 WOR+45 WOR-45 SOCIETY NAT/G FORCES PLAN ARMS/CONT
COERCE DETER ATTIT DRIVE ORD/FREE PWR...TREND NUC/PWR
COLD/WAR 20. PAGE 64 A1319

B59
WOLFERS A.,ALLIANCE POLICY IN THE COLD WAR. COM DIPLOM
INT/ORG FORCES COLONIAL CONTROL NUC/PWR 20 NATO UN DETER
COLD/WAR. PAGE 166 A3384 BAL/PWR

S59
SOHN L.B.,"THE DEFINITION OF AGGRESSION." FUT LAW INT/ORG
FORCES LEGIT ADJUD ROUTINE COERCE ORD/FREE PWR CT/SYS
...MAJORIT JURID QUANT COLD/WAR 20. PAGE 135 A2762 DETER
SOVEREIGN

S59
WARBURG J.P.,"THE CENTRAL EUROPEAN CRISIS: A PLAN
PROPOSAL FOR WESTERN INITIATIVE." EUR+WWI INT/ORG GERMANY
NAT/G LEGIT DETER WAR...CONCPT BER/BLOC UN 20.
PAGE 161 A3276

N59
BRITISH COMMONWEALTH REL CONF,EXTRACTS FROM THE DIPLOM
PROCEEDINGS OF THE SIXTH UNOFFICIAL CONFERENCE PARL/PROC
(PAMPHLET). GHANA INDIA RHODESIA UK FINAN FORCES INT/TRADE
DETER FEDERAL...LING 20 PARLIAMENT. PAGE 19 A0379 ORD/FREE

B60
ALLEN H.C.,THE ANGLO-AMERICAN PREDICAMENT: THE INT/ORG
BRITISH COMMONWEALTH, THE UNITED STATES AND PWR
EUROPEAN UNITY. EUR+WWI FUT UK USA+45 WOR+45 BAL/PWR
ECO/DEV NAT/G PLAN DETER...CONCPT OBS TIME/SEQ
TREND COLD/WAR VAL/FREE CMN/WLTH 20. PAGE 6 A0123

B60
ALLEN R.L.,SOVIET ECONOMIC WARFARE. USSR FINAN COM
INDUS NAT/G PLAN TEC/DEV FOR/AID DETER WEALTH ECO/TAC
...TREND GEN/LAWS 20. PAGE 6 A0126

B60
BARNET R.,WHO WANTS DISARMAMENT. COM EUR+WWI USA+45 PLAN
USSR INT/ORG NAT/G BAL/PWR DIPLOM EDU/PROP COERCE FORCES
DETER NUC/PWR WAR WEAPON ATTIT PWR...TIME/SEQ ARMS/CONT
COLD/WAR CONGRESS 20. PAGE 11 A0225

B60
BROWN H.,COMMUNITY OF FEAR. FORCES TEC/DEV NUC/PWR
ARMS/CONT COERCE PEACE 20. PAGE 20 A0402 WAR
DIPLOM
DETER

B60
BUCHAN A.,NATO IN THE 1960'S. EUR+WWI USA+45 WOR+45 VOL/ASSN
INT/ORG ACT/RES PLAN LEGIT COERCE DETER ATTIT DRIVE FORCES
RIGID/FLEX ORD/FREE...METH/CNCPT TIME/SEQ TREND ARMS/CONT
GEN/LAWS COLD/WAR 20 NATO. PAGE 21 A0421 SOVEREIGN

B60
DUCHACEK I.D.,CONFLICT AND COOPERATION AMONG INT/ORG
NATIONS. WOR+45 WOR-45 SOCIETY NAT/G DOMIN DETER BAL/PWR
PWR SKILL COLD/WAR 20. PAGE 39 A0791 DIPLOM

B60
EINSTEIN A.,EINSTEIN ON PEACE. FUT WOR+45 WOR-45 INT/ORG
SOCIETY NAT/G PLAN BAL/PWR CAP/ISM DIPLOM ARMS/CONT ATTIT
DETER NAT/LISM...POLICY RELATIV HUM PHIL/SCI CONCPT NUC/PWR
BIOG COLD/WAR LEAGUE/NAT NAZI. PAGE 41 A0829 PEACE

B60
FOREIGN POLICY CLEARING HOUSE,STRATEGY FOR THE DIPLOM
60'S. FUT USA+45 WOR+45 ECO/UNDEV FORCES BAL/PWR NAT/G
TASK ARMS/CONT DETER PWR MARXISM 20 SENATE. PAGE 47 POLICY
A0963 ACT/RES

B60
LE GHAIT E.,NO CARTE BLANCHE TO CAPRICORN; THE DETER
FOLLY OF NUCLEAR WAR. WOR+45 INT/ORG BAL/PWR DIPLOM NUC/PWR
RISK COERCE...CENSUS 20 NATO. PAGE 86 A1754 PLAN
DECISION

B60
MCCLELLAND C.A.,NUCLEAR WEAPONS, MISSILES, AND DIPLOM
FUTURE WAR: PROBLEM FOR THE SIXTIES. WOR+45 FORCES NUC/PWR
ARMS/CONT DETER MARXISM...POLICY ANTHOL COLD/WAR. WAR
PAGE 97 A1998 WEAPON

B60
MONTGOMERY B.L.,AN APPROACH TO SANITY; A STUDY OF DIPLOM
EAST-WEST RELATIONS. CONFER WAR EFFICIENCY ATTIT INT/ORG
...POLICY 20 NATO COLD/WAR KHRUSH/N. PAGE 103 A2113 BAL/PWR
DETER

B60
THOMPSON K.W.,POLITICAL REALISM AND THE CRISIS IN PLAN
WORLD POLITICS. USA+45 USA-45 SOCIETY INT/ORG NAT/G HUM
LEGIS TOP/EX LEGIT DETER ATTIT ORD/FREE PWR BAL/PWR
...GEN/LAWS TOT/POP 20. PAGE 143 A2931 DIPLOM

B60
TURNER G.B.,NATIONAL SECURITY IN THE NUCLEAR AGE. NAT/G
KOREA USA+45 PLAN DIPLOM ARMS/CONT DETER WAR WEAPON POLICY
...BIBLIOG 20 COLD/WAR NATO. PAGE 146 A2982 FORCES
NUC/PWR

B60
US DEPARTMENT OF THE ARMY,DISARMAMENT: A BIBLIOG/A
BIBLIOGRAPHIC RECORD: 1916-1960. DETER WAR WEAPON ARMS/CONT
PEACE 20 UN LEAGUE/NAT COLD/WAR NATO. PAGE 152 NUC/PWR
A3103 DIPLOM

B60
US HOUSE COMM FOREIGN AFFAIRS,HEARINGS ON A BILL TO DIPLOM
AMEND FURTHER THE MUTUAL SECURITY ACT OF 1954. ORD/FREE
USA+45 CONSULT FORCES BUDGET FOR/AID CONFER DETER DELIB/GP
...CHARTS 20 DEPT/DEFEN DEPT/STATE UNEF. PAGE 153 LEGIS
A3127

L60
BRENNAN D.G.,"SETTING AND GOALS OF ARMS CONTROL." FORCES
FUT USA+45 USSR WOR+45 INTELL INT/ORG NAT/G COERCE
VOL/ASSN CONSULT PLAN DIPLOM ECO/TAC ADMIN KNOWL ARMS/CONT
PWR...POLICY CONCPT TREND COLD/WAR 20. PAGE 18 DETER
A0371

L60
JACOB P.E.,"THE DISARMAMENT CONSENSUS." USA+45 USSR DELIB/GP
WOR+45 INT/ORG NAT/G ACT/RES TEC/DEV BAL/PWR ATTIT
EDU/PROP ADMIN COERCE DETER NUC/PWR CONSEN ARMS/CONT
RIGID/FLEX PWR...CONCPT RECORD CHARTS COLD/WAR 20.
PAGE 72 A1482

L60
NOGEE J.L.,"THE DIPLOMACY OF DISARMAMENT." WOR+45 PWR
INT/ORG NAT/G CONSULT DELIB/GP TOP/EX BAL/PWR ORD/FREE
DIPLOM EDU/PROP COERCE DETER WEAPON PEACE ATTIT ARMS/CONT
...RECORD TIME/SEQ TOT/POP VAL/FREE COLD/WAR 20. NUC/PWR
PAGE 109 A2246

S60
BRODY R.A.,"DETERRENCE STRATEGIES: AN ANNOTATED BIBLIOG/A
BIBLIOGRAPHY." WOR+45 PLAN ARMS/CONT NUC/PWR WAR FORCES
WEAPON DECISION. PAGE 19 A0383 DETER
DIPLOM

S60
DOUGHERTY J.E.,"KEY TO SECURITY: DISARMAMENT OR FORCES
ARMS STABILITY." COM USA+45 USSR INT/ORG NAT/G ORD/FREE
CREATE EDU/PROP COERCE DETER ATTIT PWR...DECISION ARMS/CONT
CONCPT MYTH NEW/IDEA TREND 20 COLD/WAR. PAGE 38 NUC/PWR
A0777

S60
DYSON F.J.,"THE FUTURE DEVELOPMENT OF NUCLEAR INT/ORG
WEAPONS." FUT WOR+45 DELIB/GP ACT/RES PLAN DETER ARMS/CONT
WEAPON ATTIT PWR...POLICY 20. PAGE 40 A0815 NUC/PWR

S60
MORGENSTERN O.,"GOAL: AN ARMED, INSPECTED, OPEN FORCES

WORLD." COM EUR+WWI USA+45 R+D INT/ORG NAT/G TEC/DEV BAL/PWR COERCE NUC/PWR ORD/FREE PWR...TREND 20. PAGE 104 A2133 CONCPT ARMS/CONT DETER

S60
MUNRO L.,"CAN THE UNITED NATIONS ENFORCE PEACE." WOR+45 LAW INT/ORG VOL/ASSN BAL/PWR LEGIT ARMS/CONT COERCE DETER PEACE PWR...CONCPT REC/INT TREND UN 20 HAMMARSK/D. PAGE 106 A2173 FORCES ORD/FREE

S60
O'BRIEN W.,"THE ROLE OF FORCE IN THE INTERNATIONAL JURIDICAL ORDER." WOR+45 NAT/G FORCES DOMIN ADJUD ARMS/CONT DETER NUC/PWR WAR ATTIT PWR...CATH INT/LAW JURID CONCPT TREND STERTYP GEN/LAWS 20. PAGE 110 A2266 INT/ORG COERCE

B61
BECHHOEFER B.G.,POSTWAR NEGOTIATIONS FOR ARMS CONTROL. COM EUR+WWI USSR INT/ORG NAT/G ACT/RES BAL/PWR DIPLOM ECO/TAC EDU/PROP ADMIN REGION DETER NUC/PWR WAR WEAPON PEACE ATTIT PWR...POLICY TIME/SEQ COLD/WAR CONGRESS 20. PAGE 12 A0244 USA+45 ARMS/CONT

B61
DELZELL C.F.,MUSSOLINI'S ENEMIES - THE ITALIAN ANTI-FASCIST RESISTANCE. ITALY DIPLOM PRESS DETER WAR TOTALISM ORD/FREE MARXISM 20. PAGE 36 A0730 FASCISM GP/REL POL/PAR REV

B61
GALLOIS P.,THE BALANCE OF TERROR: STRATEGY FOR THE NUCLEAR AGE. FUT WOR+45 INT/ORG FORCES TOP/EX DETER WAR ATTIT RIGID/FLEX ORD/FREE PWR...HYPO/EXP 20. PAGE 50 A1032 PLAN DECISION DIPLOM NUC/PWR

B61
HANCOCK W.K.,FOUR STUDIES OF WAR AND PEACE IN THIS CENTURY. FUT WOR+45 WOR-45 ACT/RES LEGIT DETER HEALTH...TREND ANTHOL TOT/POP VAL/FREE UN 20. PAGE 61 A1250 INT/ORG POLICY ARMS/CONT

B61
HENKIN L.,ARMS CONTROL: ISSUES FOR THE PUBLIC. EUR+WWI FUT USA+45 USSR INT/ORG NAT/G DIPLOM EDU/PROP DETER NUC/PWR ATTIT PWR...CONCPT RECORD HIST/WRIT TIME/SEQ TOT/POP COLD/WAR 20. PAGE 64 A1316 WOR+45 DELIB/GP ARMS/CONT

B61
KISSINGER H.A.,THE NECESSITY FOR CHOICE. FUT USA+45 ECO/UNDEV NAT/G PLAN BAL/PWR ECO/TAC ARMS/CONT DETER NUC/PWR ATTIT...POLICY CONCPT RECORD GEN/LAWS COLD/WAR 20. PAGE 80 A1642 TOP/EX TREND DIPLOM

B61
SCHMIDT H.,VERTEIDIGUNG ODER VERGELTUNG. COM CUBA GERMANY/W USSR FORCES DIPLOM ARMS/CONT DETER NUC/PWR...POLICY CHARTS HYPO/EXP SIMUL BIBLIOG 20 NATO COLD/WAR. PAGE 128 A2630 PLAN WAR BAL/PWR ORD/FREE

B61
SOKOL A.E.,SEAPOWER IN THE NUCLEAR AGE. USA+45 USSR DIST/IND FORCES INT/TRADE DETER WAR...POLICY NAT/COMP BIBLIOG COLD/WAR. PAGE 135 A2763 SEA PWR WEAPON NUC/PWR

B61
STILLMAN E.,THE NEW POLITICS: AMERICA AND THE END OF THE POSTWAR WORLD. FUT WOR+45 CULTURE SOCIETY ECO/UNDEV INT/ORG NAT/G FORCES TOP/EX ACT/RES DIPLOM EDU/PROP LEGIT ROUTINE DETER ATTIT ORD/FREE PWR...OBS STERTYP COLD/WAR TOT/POP VAL/FREE. PAGE 138 A2827 USA+45 PLAN

B61
US SENATE COMM GOVT OPERATIONS,ORGANIZING FOR NATIONAL SECURITY. COM USA+45 BUDGET DIPLOM DETER NUC/PWR WAR WEAPON ORD/FREE...BIBLIOG 20 COLD/WAR. PAGE 156 A3172 POLICY PLAN FORCES COERCE

L61
WRIGHT Q.,"STUDIES IN DETERRENCE: LIMITED WARS AND THE ROLE OF SEABORNE WEAPONS SYSTEMS." FUT USA+45 WOR+45 SEA INT/ORG NAT/G FORCES ACT/RES WAR WEAPON ORD/FREE TOT/POP 20. PAGE 168 A3415 TEC/DEV SKILL BAL/PWR DETER

S61
LEWY G.,"SUPERIOR ORDERS, NUCLEAR WARFARE AND THE DICTATES OF CONSCIENCE: THE DILEMMA OF MILITARY OBEDIENCE IN THE ATOMIC." FUT UNIV WOR+45 INTELL SOCIETY FORCES TOP/EX ACT/RES ADMIN ROUTINE NUC/PWR PERCEPT RIGID/FLEX ALL/VALS...POLICY CONCPT 20. PAGE 88 A1805 DETER INT/ORG LAW INT/LAW

S61
MACHOWSKI K.,"SELECTED PROBLEMS OF NATIONAL SOVEREIGNTY WITH REFERENCE TO THE LAW OF OUTER SPACE." FUT WOR+45 AIR LAW INTELL SOCIETY ECO/DEV PLAN EDU/PROP DETER DRIVE PERCEPT SOVEREIGN ...POLICY INT/LAW OBS TREND TOT/POP 20. PAGE 92 A1889 UNIV ACT/RES NUC/PWR SPACE

B62
AIR FORCE ACADEMY LIBRARY,INTERNATIONAL ORGANIZATIONS AND MILITARY SECURITY SYSTEMS (PAMPHLET) (SPECIAL BIBLIOGRAPHY SERIES, NUMBER 25). DIPLOM FOR/AID INT/TRADE NUC/PWR PEACE 20 UN NATO OAS SEATO LEAGUE/NAT. PAGE 5 A0104 BIBLIOG INT/ORG FORCES DETER

B62
BEATON L.,THE SPREAD OF NUCLEAR WEAPONS. WOR+45 NAT/G PLAN PROB/SOLV DIPLOM ECO/TAC DETER...POLICY 20 COLD/WAR. PAGE 12 A0242 ARMS/CONT NUC/PWR TEC/DEV FUT

B62
BURTON J.W.,PEACE THEORY: PRECONDITIONS OF DISARMAMENT. COM EUR+WWI USA+45 NAT/G FORCES BAL/PWR DIPLOM ECO/TAC EDU/PROP REGION COERCE DETER PEACE ATTIT PWR TOT/POP COLD/WAR 20. PAGE 22 A0446 INT/ORG PLAN ARMS/CONT

B62
GILPIN R.,AMERICAN SCIENTISTS AND NUCLEAR WEAPONS POLICY. COM FUT USA+45 WOR+45 INT/ORG NAT/G PROF/ORG CONSULT FORCES CREATE TEC/DEV BAL/PWR EDU/PROP ARMS/CONT WAR PERCEPT KNOWL MORAL PWR ...PHIL/SCI SOC CONCPT GEN/LAWS 20. PAGE 52 A1073 INTELL ATTIT DETER NUC/PWR

B62
HUNTINGTON S.P.,CHANGING PATTERNS OF MILITARY POLITICS. EUR+WWI L/A+17C S/ASIA USA+45 WOR+45 CULTURE INT/ORG NAT/G CONSULT PLAN DOMIN EDU/PROP LEGIT DETER WAR ATTIT PERSON PWR...DECISION CONCPT SIMUL GEN/LAWS ANTHOL COLD/WAR 20. PAGE 69 A1419 FORCES RIGID/FLEX

B62
JORDAN A.A. JR.,FOREIGN AID AND THE DEFENSE OF SOUTHEAST ASIA. PAKISTAN VIETNAM/S FINAN PLAN BUDGET ECO/TAC DETER WAR ORD/FREE...POLICY DECISION CENSUS CHARTS BIBLIOG 20. PAGE 75 A1535 FOR/AID S/ASIA FORCES ECO/UNDEV

B62
KAHN H.,THINKING ABOUT THE UNTHINKABLE. FUT USA+45 LAW NAT/G CONSULT FORCES ACT/RES CREATE PLAN TEC/DEV BAL/PWR DIPLOM EDU/PROP ARMS/CONT DETER ATTIT...CONCPT OBS TREND COLD/WAR 20. PAGE 76 A1547 INT/ORG ORD/FREE NUC/PWR PEACE

B62
MANDER J.,BERLIN: HOSTAGE FOR THE WEST. FUT GERMANY WOR+45 FOR/AID RISK ATTIT ORD/FREE 20 BERLIN COLD/WAR. PAGE 93 A1916 DIPLOM BAL/PWR DOMIN DETER

B62
MODELSKI G.,SEATO-SIX STUDIES. ASIA CHINA/COM INDIA S/ASIA INT/ORG NAT/G ECO/TAC DETER ATTIT ORD/FREE PWR...TIME/SEQ COLD/WAR TOT/POP 20 SEATO. PAGE 102 A2098 MARKET ECO/UNDEV INT/TRADE

B62
MONCRIEFF A.,THE STRATEGY OF SURVIVAL. UK FORCES BAL/PWR CONFER DETER WAR...ANTHOL 20 COLD/WAR. PAGE 102 A2104 PLAN DECISION DIPLOM ARMS/CONT

B62
MULLEY F.W.,THE POLITICS OF WESTERN DEFENSE. EUR+WWI USA-45 WOR+45 VOL/ASSN EX/STRUC FORCES COERCE DETER PEACE ATTIT ORD/FREE PWR...RECORD TIME/SEQ CHARTS COLD/WAR 20 NATO. PAGE 106 A2168 INT/ORG DELIB/GP NUC/PWR

B62
OSGOOD R.E.,NATO: THE ENTANGLING ALLIANCE. USA+45 WOR+45 VOL/ASSN FORCES TOP/EX PLAN DETER WEAPON DRIVE RIGID/FLEX ORD/FREE PWR...TREND 20 NATO. PAGE 112 A2301 INT/ORG ARMS/CONT PEACE

B62
ROOSEVELT J.,THE LIBERAL PAPERS. USA+45 WOR+45 ECO/DEV INT/ORG DELIB/GP ACT/RES PROB/SOLV DETER ATTIT...TREND IDEA/COMP ANTHOL. PAGE 123 A2520 DIPLOM NEW/LIB POLICY FORCES

B62
SINGER J.D.,DETERRENCE, ARMS CONTROL AND DISARMAMENT: TOWARD A SYNTHESIS IN NATIONAL SECURITY POLICY. COM USA+45 INT/ORG BAL/PWR DETER ORD/FREE...POLICY COLD/WAR 20. PAGE 133 A2727 FUT ACT/RES ARMS/CONT

S62
FALK R.A.,"THE REALITY OF INTERNATIONAL LAW." WOR+45 NAT/G LEGIT COERCE DETER WAR MORAL ORD/FREE PWR SOVEREIGN...JURID CONCPT VAL/FREE COLD/WAR 20. PAGE 43 A0887 INT/ORG ADJUD NUC/PWR INT/LAW

S62
SINGER J.D.,"STABLE DETERRENCE AND ITS LIMITS." FUT WOR+45 R+D INT/ORG CONSULT ACT/RES TEC/DEV ARMS/CONT COERCE DRIVE PERCEPT RIGID/FLEX ORD/FREE PWR...MYTH SIMUL TOT/POP 20. PAGE 133 A2728 NAT/G FORCES DETER NUC/PWR

B63
BAILEY S.D.,THE UNITED NATIONS: A SHORT POLITICAL GUIDE. FUT PROB/SOLV LEAD...INT/LAW 20 UN. PAGE 10 A0207 INT/ORG PEACE DETER DIPLOM

B63
FALK R.A.,LAW, MORALITY, AND WAR IN THE CONTEMPORARY WORLD. WOR+45 LAW INT/ORG EX/STRUC FORCES EDU/PROP LEGIT DETER NUC/PWR MORAL ORD/FREE ...JURID TOT/POP 20. PAGE 43 A0888 ADJUD ARMS/CONT PEACE INT/LAW

B63
GONZALEZ PEDRERO E.,ANATOMIA DE UN CONFLICTO. WOR+45 ECO/DEV ECO/UNDEV ECO/TAC FOR/AID CONTROL ARMS/CONT GOV/REL...NAT/COMP 20 COLD/WAR. PAGE 54 A1099 DIPLOM DETER BAL/PWR

B63
HALPERIN M.H.,LIMITED WAR IN A NUCLEAR AGE. CUBA KOREA USA+45 USSR INT/ORG FORCES PLAN DIPLOM DETER PWR...BIBLIOG/A 20. PAGE 60 A1238 WAR NUC/PWR CONTROL WEAPON

B63
LILIENTHAL D.E.,CHANGE, HOPE, AND THE BOMB. USA+45 ATTIT

WOR+45 R+D INT/ORG NAT/G DELIB/GP FORCES ACT/RES DETER RIGID/FLEX ORD/FREE...POLICY CONCPT OBS AEC 20. PAGE 89 A1815 MYTH ARMS/CONT NUC/PWR

B63
MANSERGH N.,DOCUMENTS AND SPEECHES ON COMMONWEALTH AFFAIRS 1952-1962. CANADA INDIA PAKISTAN UK CONSTN FORCES ECO/TAC EDU/PROP COLONIAL DETER WAR ORD/FREE SOVEREIGN...POLICY 20 AUSTRAL. PAGE 94 A1932 BIBLIOG/A FEDERAL INT/TRADE DIPLOM

B63
PACHTER H.M.,COLLISION COURSE; THE CUBAN MISSILE CRISIS AND COEXISTENCE. CUBA USA+45 DIPLOM ARMS/CONT PEACE MARXISM...DECISION INT/LAW 20 COLD/WAR KHRUSH/N KENNEDY/JF CASTRO/F. PAGE 112 A2307 WAR BAL/PWR NUC/PWR DETER

B63
US DEPARTMENT OF THE ARMY,US OVERSEAS BASES: PRESENT STATUS AND FUTURE PROSPECTS (PAMPHLET). USA+45 DIPLOM NUC/PWR ATTIT ORD/FREE...POLICY CHARTS 20. PAGE 152 A3107 BIBLIOG/A WAR BAL/PWR DETER

B63
US SENATE COMM GOVT OPERATIONS,REPORT OF A STUDY OF US FOREIGN AID IN TEN MIDDLE EASTERN AND AFRICAN COUNTRIES. AFR ISLAM USA+45 FORCES PLAN BUDGET DIPLOM TAX DETER WEALTH...STAT CHARTS 20 CONGRESS AID MID/EAST. PAGE 156 A3174 FOR/AID EFFICIENCY ECO/TAC FINAN

L63
CRANE R.D.,"THE CUBAN CRISIS: A STRATEGIC ANALYSIS OF AMERICAN AND SOVIET POLICY." CUBA USA+45 USSR BAL/PWR RISK DETER NUC/PWR PERCEPT ORD/FREE 20. PAGE 32 A0658 DIPLOM POLICY FORCES

L63
PHELPS J.,"STUDIES IN DETERRENCE VIII: MILITARY STABILITARY AND ARMS CONTROL: A CRITICAL SURVEY." FUT WOR+45 INT/ORG ACT/RES EDU/PROP COERCE NUC/PWR WAR HEALTH PWR...POLICY TECHNIC TREND SIMUL TOT/POP 20. PAGE 116 A2373 FORCES ORD/FREE ARMS/CONT DETER

L63
SCHELLING T.C.,"STRATEGIC PROBLEMS OF AN INTERNATIONAL ARMED FORCE." WOR+45 ECO/DEV INT/ORG NAT/G PLAN BAL/PWR LEGIT ARMS/CONT COERCE DETER ORD/FREE PWR...POLICY CONCPT COLD/WAR 20. PAGE 128 A2624 CREATE FORCES

S63
BRZEZINSKI Z.,"SOVIET QUIESCENCE." EUR+WWI USA+45 USSR FORCES CREATE PLAN COERCE DETER WAR ATTIT 20 TREATY EUROPE. PAGE 20 A0415 DIPLOM ARMS/CONT NUC/PWR AGREE

S63
BULLOUGH V.L.,"THE ROMAN EMPIRE VS PERSIA, 363-502: A STUDY OF SUCCESSFUL DETERRENCE." NAT/G PLAN DIPLOM ORD/FREE PWR...TIME/SEQ COLD/WAR VAL/FREE 4/6 PERSIA ROM/EMP. PAGE 21 A0430 MEDIT-7 COERCE DETER

S63
ETZIONI A.,"EUROPEAN UNIFICATION AND PERSPECTIVES ON SOVEREIGNTY." EUR+WWI FUT DELIB/GP TEC/DEV ECO/TAC EDU/PROP DETER NUC/PWR ATTIT DRIVE ORD/FREE PWR WEALTH...CONCPT RECORD TIME/SEQ EEC VAL/FREE 20. PAGE 43 A0870 INT/ORG ECO/DEV SOVEREIGN

S63
KINTNER W.R.,"THE PROJECTED EUROPEAN UNION AND AMERICAN RESPONSIBILITIES." EUR+WWI USA+45 STRATA INT/ORG NAT/G DOMIN DETER NUC/PWR ATTIT ORD/FREE PWR 20 NATO. PAGE 79 A1628 FUT FORCES DIPLOM REGION

S63
MEYROWITZ H.,"LES JURISTES DEVANT L'ARME NUCLAIRE." FUT WOR+45 INTELL SOCIETY BAL/PWR DETER WAR...JURID CONCPT 20. PAGE 100 A2058 ACT/RES ADJUD INT/LAW NUC/PWR

S63
MORGENTHAU H.J.,"THE POLITICAL CONDITIONS FOR AN INTERNATIONAL POLICE FORCE." FUT WOR+45 CREATE LEGIT ADMIN PEACE ORD/FREE 20. PAGE 104 A2141 INT/ORG FORCES ARMS/CONT DETER

C63
CHARLETON W.G.,"THE REVOLUTION IN AMERICAN FOREIGN POLICY." COM PROB/SOLV FOR/AID DOMIN COLONIAL NEUTRAL DETER WAR ISOLAT NAT/LISM...BIBLIOG 19/20 UN COLD/WAR NATO. PAGE 26 A0523 DIPLOM INT/ORG BAL/PWR

N63
PATEL H.M.,THE DEFENCE OF INDIA (PAMPHLET). CHINA/COM INDIA PAKISTAN WOR+45 TEC/DEV BAL/PWR DIPLOM CONTROL WAR. PAGE 114 A2340 FORCES POLICY SOVEREIGN DETER

B64
COTTRELL A.J.,THE POLITICS OF THE ATLANTIC ALLIANCE. EUR+WWI USA+45 INT/ORG NAT/G DELIB/GP EX/STRUC BAL/PWR DIPLOM REGION DETER ATTIT ORD/FREE ...CONCPT RECORD GEN/LAWS GEN/METH NATO 20. PAGE 31 A0632 VOL/ASSN FORCES

B64
DEUTSCHE GES AUSWARTIGE POL,STRATEGIE UND ABRUSTUNGSPOLITIK DER SOWJETUNION. USSR TEC/DEV DIPLOM COERCE DETER WEAPON...POLICY PSY 20 ABM/DEFSYS. PAGE 37 A0747 NUC/PWR WAR FORCES ARMS/CONT

B64
FULBRIGHT J.W.,OLD MYTHS AND NEW REALITIES. USA+45 DIPLOM

USSR LEGIS INT/TRADE DETER ATTIT...POLICY 20 COLD/WAR TREATY. PAGE 50 A1016 INT/ORG ORD/FREE

B64
HEKHUIS D.J.,INTERNATIONAL STABILITY: MILITARY, ECONOMIC AND POLITICAL DIMENSIONS. FUT WOR+45 LAW ECO/UNDEV INT/ORG NAT/G VOL/ASSN FORCES ACT/RES BAL/PWR PWR WEALTH...STAT UN 20. PAGE 64 A1310 TEC/DEV DETER REGION

B64
KAUFMANN W.W.,THE MC NAMARA STRATEGY. TOP/EX INSPECT BAL/PWR DIPLOM CONTROL DETER GUERRILLA NUC/PWR WEAPON COST PWR...METH/COMP 20 MCNAMARA/R KENNEDY/JF JOHNSON/LB NATO DEPT/DEFEN. PAGE 77 A1572 FORCES WAR PLAN PROB/SOLV

B64
ROCK V.P.,A STRATEGY OF INTERDEPENDENCE. COM USSR WOR+45 NAT/G FORCES PROB/SOLV TEC/DEV DETER WAR ORD/FREE...CONCPT NEW/IDEA METH/COMP 20. PAGE 122 A2509 DIPLOM NUC/PWR PEACE POLICY

B64
ROSECRANCE R.N.,THE DISPERSION OF NUCLEAR WEAPONS: STRATEGY AND POLITICS. ASIA COM FUT S/ASIA USA+45 INT/ORG NAT/G DELIB/GP FORCES ACT/RES TEC/DEV BAL/PWR COERCE DETER ATTIT RIGID/FLEX ORD/FREE ...POLICY CHARTS VAL/FREE. PAGE 123 A2530 EUR+WWI PWR PEACE

B65
GRETTON P.,MARITIME STRATEGY - A STUDY OF DEFENSE PROBLEMS. ASIA UK USSR DIPLOM COERCE DETER NUC/PWR WEAPON...CONCPT NAT/COMP 20. PAGE 56 A1147 FORCES PLAN WAR SEA

B65
MOSKOWITZ H.,US SECURITY, ARMS CONTROL, AND DISARMAMENT 1961-1965. FORCES DIPLOM DETER WAR WEAPON...CHARTS 20 UN COLD/WAR NATO. PAGE 105 A2154 BIBLIOG/A ARMS/CONT NUC/PWR PEACE

B65
SEABURY P.,BALANCE OF POWER. INT/ORG DETER PEACE ATTIT...INT/LAW. PAGE 131 A2677 BAL/PWR DIPLOM WAR

B65
THAYER F.C. JR.,AIR TRANSPORT POLICY AND NATIONAL SECURITY: A POLITICAL, ECONOMIC, AND MILITARY ANALYSIS. DIST/IND OP/RES PLAN TEC/DEV DIPLOM DETER WAR COST EFFICIENCY...POLICY BIBLIOG 20 DEPT/DEFEN FAA CAB. PAGE 142 A2908 AIR FORCES CIVMIL/REL ORD/FREE

B65
US DEPARTMENT OF DEFENSE,US SECURITY ARMS CONTROL, AND DISARMAMENT 1961-1965 (PAMPHLET). CHINA/COM COM GERMANY/W ISRAEL SPACE USA+45 USSR WOR+45 FORCES EDU/PROP DETER EQUILIB PEACE ALL/VALS...GOV/COMP 20 NATO. PAGE 151 A3077 BIBLIOG/A ARMS/CONT NUC/PWR DIPLOM

L65
TUCKER R.W.,"PEACE AND WAR." UNIV CULTURE SOCIETY INT/ORG NAT/G ACT/RES DOMIN DETER WAR ATTIT DISPL ...POLICY CONCPT MYTH GEN/LAWS 20. PAGE 145 A2975 PWR COERCE ARMS/CONT PEACE

C65
BURTON J.W.,"INTERNATIONAL RELATIONS: A GENERAL THEORY." WOR+45 NAT/G CREATE BAL/PWR NEUTRAL COERCE DETER ADJUST...TREND IDEA/COMP GEN/METH BIBLIOG. PAGE 22 A0447 DIPLOM GEN/LAWS ACT/RES ORD/FREE

C65
US AIR FORCE ACADEMY,"AMERICAN DEFENSE POLICY." COM INT/ORG TEC/DEV FOR/AID ARMS/CONT DETER NUC/PWR ...POLICY DECISION CONCPT ANTHOL BIBLIOG/A 20 COLD/WAR NATO. PAGE 149 A3054 PLAN FORCES WAR COERCE

B66
BEAUFRE A.,NATO AND EUROPE. WOR+45 PLAN CONFER EXEC NUC/PWR ATTIT...POLICY 20 NATO EUROPE. PAGE 12 A0243 INT/ORG DETER DIPLOM ADMIN

B66
DAENIKER G.,STRATEGIE DES KLEIN STAATS. SWITZERLND ACT/RES CREATE DIPLOM NEUTRAL DETER WAR WEAPON PWR SOVEREIGN...IDEA/COMP 20 COLD/WAR. PAGE 33 A0673 NUC/PWR PLAN FORCES NAT/G

B66
EKIRCH A.A. JR.,IDEAS, IDEALS, AND AMERICAN DIPLOMACY. USA+45 USA-45 INT/ORG DOMIN COLONIAL ARMS/CONT DETER ISOLAT NAT/LISM...MAJORIT BIBLIOG 19/20 COLD/WAR. PAGE 41 A0834 DIPLOM LEAD PEACE

B66
ERICKSON J.,THE MILITARY-TECHNICAL REVOLUTION. USA+45 WOR+45 INT/ORG PLAN ATTIT...DECISION ANTHOL 20. PAGE 42 A0861 DIPLOM DETER POLICY NUC/PWR

B66
EWING B.G.,PEACE THROUGH NEGOTIATION: THE AUSTRIAN EXPERIENCE. AUSTRIA USSR VIETNAM CONFER CONTROL DETER WAR ATTIT HEALTH PWR...POLICY 20. PAGE 43 A0878 PEACE DIPLOM MARXISM

B66
GRAHAM I.C.C.,PUBLICATIONS OF THE SOCIAL SCIENCE DEPARTMENT, THE RAND CORPORATION, 1948-1966. USSR WOR+45 NAT/G ARMS/CONT DETER WAR NAT/LISM...SOC GOV/COMP. PAGE 55 A1127 BIBLIOG DIPLOM NUC/PWR FORCES

B66
HORELICK A.L.,STRATEGIC POWER AND SOVIET FOREIGN POLICY. CUBA USSR FORCES PLAN CIVMIL/REL...POLICY DECISION 20 COLD/WAR. PAGE 67 A1383
DIPLOM BAL/PWR DETER NUC/PWR

B66
KIM Y.K.,PATTERNS OF COMPETITIVE COEXISTENCE: USA VS. USSR. USA+45 USSR ECO/DEV ECO/UNDEV INT/ORG FOR/AID INT/TRADE ARMS/CONT...BIBLIOG 20 COLD/WAR. PAGE 79 A1618
DIPLOM PEACE BAL/PWR DETER

B66
KNORR K.E.,ON THE USES OF MILITARY POWER IN THE NUCLEAR AGE. WOR+45 INT/ORG TEC/DEV ADMIN CONTROL WAR COST 20. PAGE 81 A1656
FORCES DIPLOM DETER NUC/PWR

B66
KUENNE R.E.,THE POLARIS MISSILE STRIKE* A GENERAL ECONOMIC SYSTEMS ANALYSIS. USA+45 USSR NAT/G BAL/PWR ARMS/CONT WAR...MATH PROBABIL COMPUT/IR CHARTS HYPO/EXP SIMUL. PAGE 82 A1689
NUC/PWR FORCES DETER DIPLOM

B66
LALL A.,MODERN INTERNATIONAL NEGOTIATION: PRINCIPLES AND PRACTICE. WOR+45 INT/ORG DELIB/GP PROB/SOLV DETER...INT/LAW TREATY. PAGE 84 A1712
DIPLOM ECO/TAC ATTIT

B66
MC LELLAN D.S.,THE COLD WAR IN TRANSITION. USSR WOR+45 CONTROL LEAD NUC/PWR NAT/LISM SOVEREIGN 20 COLD/WAR THIRD/WRLD. PAGE 97 A1994
BAL/PWR DETER DIPLOM POLICY

B66
SALTER L.M.,RESOLUTION OF INTERNATIONAL CONFLICT. USA+45 INT/ORG SECT DIPLOM ECO/TAC FOR/AID DETER NUC/PWR WAR 20. PAGE 127 A2595
PROB/SOLV PEACE INT/LAW POLICY

B66
SCHWARZ U.,AMERICAN STRATEGY: A NEW PERSPECTIVE. USA+45 USA-45 INT/ORG TEC/DEV BAL/PWR DIPLOM LEAD ARMS/CONT DETER NUC/PWR WAR 20 NATO. PAGE 130 A2659
NAT/G POLICY FORCES PWR

B66
SOBEL L.A.,SOUTH VIETNAM: US-COMMUNIST CONFRONTATION IN SOUTHEAST ASIA 1961-65. VIETNAM FOR/AID CROWD DETER REV PEACE...GEOG 20 INTERVENT DIEM COLD/WAR. PAGE 134 A2754
WAR TIME/SEQ FORCES NAT/G

B66
US SENATE COMM ON FOREIGN REL,HEARINGS ON S 2859 AND S 2861. USA+45 WOR+45 FORCES BUDGET CAP/ISM ADMIN DETER WEAPON TOTALISM...NAT/COMP 20 UN CONGRESS. PAGE 156 A3185
FOR/AID DIPLOM ORD/FREE ECO/UNDEV

S66
DUROSELLE J.B.,"THE FUTURE OF THE ATLANTIC COMMUNITY." EUR+WWI USA+45 USSR NAT/G CAP/ISM REGION DETER NUC/PWR ATTIT MARXISM...INT/LAW 20 NATO. PAGE 40 A0811
FUT DIPLOM MYTH POLICY

S66
ORVIK N.,"NATO: THE ROLE OF THE SMALL MEMBERS." EUR+WWI FUT USA+45 CONSULT FORCES PROB/SOLV ARMS/CONT DETER NUC/PWR PWR 20 NATO. PAGE 112 A2298
NAT/G DIPLOM INT/ORG POLICY

S66
SHERMAN M.,"GUARANTEES AND NUCLEAR SPREAD." USA+45 WOR+45 INT/ORG PLAN DETER WAR ORD/FREE 20 NATO. PAGE 132 A2700
DIPLOM POLICY NAT/G NUC/PWR

C66
KULSKI W.W.,"DEGAULLE AND THE WORLD: THE FOREIGN POLICY OF THE FIFTH FRENCH REPUBLIC." FRANCE ECO/UNDEV POL/PAR BAL/PWR DETER NUC/PWR ATTIT PWR ...RECORD BIBLIOG DEGAULLE NATO EEC. PAGE 83 A1694
POLICY SOVEREIGN PERSON DIPLOM

B67
BLOOMFIELD L.,THE UNITED NATIONS AND US FOREIGN POLICY. USA+45 DIPLOM LEAD ARMS/CONT DETER PWR 20 UN. PAGE 15 A0313
INT/ORG PLAN CONFER IDEA/COMP

B67
BURNS E.L.M.,MEGAMURDER. WOR+45 LAW INT/ORG NAT/G BAL/PWR DIPLOM DETER MURDER WEAPON CIVMIL/REL PEACE ...INT/LAW TREND 20. PAGE 22 A0444
FORCES PLAN WAR NUC/PWR

B67
EUROPA-ARCHIV,DEUTSCHES AND AUSLANDISCHES SCHRIFTTUM ZU DEN REGIONALEN SICHERHEITSVEREINBARUNGEN 1945-1956. WOR+45 FORCES BAL/PWR REGION. PAGE 43 A0875
BIBLIOG INT/ORG PEACE DETER

B67
HALPERIN M.H.,CONTEMPORARY MILITARY STRATEGY. ASIA CHINA/COM USA+45 USSR INT/ORG FORCES ACT/RES PLAN TEC/DEV BAL/PWR COERCE WAR...METH/COMP BIBLIOG 20 NATO. PAGE 60 A1240
DIPLOM NUC/PWR DETER ARMS/CONT

B67
HOLSTI K.J.,INTERNATIONAL POLITICS* A FRAMEWORK FOR ANALYSIS. WOR+45 WOR-45 NAT/G EDU/PROP DETER WAR WEAPON PWR BIBLIOG. PAGE 67 A1372
DIPLOM BARGAIN POLICY INT/LAW

B67
US DEPARTMENT OF STATE,TREATIES IN FORCE. USA+45 WOR+45 AGREE WAR PEACE 20 TREATY. PAGE 152 A3101
BIBLIOG DIPLOM INT/ORG DETER

L67
MOORE N.,"THE LAWFULNESS OF MILITARY ASSISTANCE TO THE REPUBLIC OF VIET NAM." USA+45 VIETNAM WOR+45 FOR/AID DOMIN DETER WAR WEAPON...DECISION INT/LAW 20 UN. PAGE 103 A2123
PWR DIPLOM FORCES GOV/REL

S67
ABT J.J.,"WORLD OF SENATOR FULBRIGHT." VIETNAM WOR+45 COERCE DETER REV ORD/FREE MARXISM...MARXIST 20. PAGE 4 A0084
DIPLOM PLAN PWR

S67
FELD B.T.,"A PLEDGE* NO FIRST USE." DELIB/GP BAL/PWR DOMIN DETER. PAGE 45 A0913
ARMS/CONT NUC/PWR DIPLOM PEACE

S67
HAZARD J.N.,"POST-DISARMAMENT INTERNATIONAL LAW." FUT USSR WOR+45 INT/ORG DELIB/GP FORCES DETER EQUILIB SOVEREIGN MARXISM 20 UN. PAGE 63 A1301
INT/LAW ARMS/CONT PWR PLAN

S67
JACKSON W.G.F.,"NUCLEAR PROLIFERATION AND THE GREAT POWERS." FUT UK WOR+45 INT/ORG DOMIN ARMS/CONT DETER ORD/FREE PACIFIST. PAGE 72 A1480
NUC/PWR ATTIT BAL/PWR NAT/LISM

S67
KAHN H.,"CRITERIA FOR LONG-RANGE NUCLEAR CONTROL POLICIES." WOR+45 INT/ORG TEC/DEV DOMIN DETER WAR WEAPON ISOLAT ORD/FREE POLICY. PAGE 76 A1549
NUC/PWR ARMS/CONT BAL/PWR DIPLOM

S67
KIPP K.,"DIE POLITISCHE BEDEUTUNG DER 'GEGENKUSTE' DARGESTELLT AM BEISPIEL DER USA IM 20. JAHRHUNDERT" USA+45 USA-45 SEA NAT/G CONTROL COERCE WAR...POLICY GEOG 20. PAGE 79 A1629
FORCES ORD/FREE DIPLOM DETER

S67
SHULMAN M.D.,"'EUROPE' VERSUS 'DETENTE'." USA+45 USSR INT/ORG CONTROL ARMS/CONT DETER 20. PAGE 132 A2711
DIPLOM BAL/PWR NUC/PWR

S67
SUINN R.M.,"THE DISARMAMENT FANTASY* PSYCHOLOGICAL FACTORS THAT MAY PRODUCE WARFARE." DIPLOM RISK ARMS/CONT DETER ANOMIE PERSON GAME. PAGE 140 A2860
DECISION NUC/PWR WAR PSY

C67
GEHLEN M.P.,"THE POLITICS OF COEXISTENCE: SOVIET METHODS AND MOTIVES." COM USSR NAT/G INT/TRADE EDU/PROP ARMS/CONT DETER KNOWL...CHARTS IDEA/COMP 20 COLD/WAR. PAGE 52 A1056
BIBLIOG PEACE DIPLOM MARXISM

DETERRENCE....SEE DETER

DETHINE P. A0734

DETROIT....DETROIT, MICHIGAN

DEUTSCH K.W. A0735,A0736,A0737,A0738,A0739,A0740,A0741,A0742

DEUTSCHE BIBLIOTH FRANKF A M A0743

DEUTSCHE BUCHEREI A0744,A0745,A0746

DEUTSCHE GES AUSWARTIGE POL A0747

DEUTSCHE GESCHAFT VOLKERRECHT A0748

DEUTSCHER I. A0749

DEV/ASSIST....DEVELOPMENT AND ASSISTANCE COMMITTEE

DEVADHAR Y.C. A0750

DEVELOPMENT....SEE CREATE+ECO/UNDEV

DEVELOPMENT AND ASSISTANCE COMMITTEE....SEE DEV/ASSIST

DEVELOPMNT....HUMAN DEVELOPMENTAL CHANGE, PSYCHOLOGICAL AND PHYSIOLOGICAL

DEVIANT BEHAVIOR....SEE ANOMIE, CRIME

DEVILLERS P.H. A0751

DEWEY J. A0752

DEWEY/JOHN....JOHN DEWEY

DEWEY/THOM....THOMAS DEWEY

DIA M. A0753

DIAS R.W.M. A0754

DIAZ J.S. A0755

DIAZ/P....PORFIRIO DIAZ

DIBBLE C. A1549

DICKEY J.S. A0756

DICKINSON E. A0757

DICKS H.V. A0758

DICTIONARY....DICTIONARY

N
US SUPERINTENDENT OF DOCUMENTS,CATALOGUE OF PUBLIC DOCUMENTS OF CONGRESS AND OF ALL DEPARTMENTS OF THE GOVERNMENT OF THE UNITED STATES. DIPLOM ATTIT ...POLICY DICTIONARY 20 CONGRESS. PAGE 157 A3200
BIBLIOG NAT/G WRITING USA-45

C06
MONTGOMERY H.,"A DICTIONARY OF POLITICAL PHRASES AND ILLUSIONS WITH A SHORT BIBLIOGRAPHY." EUR+WWI MOD/EUR UK AGRI LABOR LOC/G NAT/G COLONIAL CHOOSE RACE/REL. PAGE 103 A2114
BIBLIOG DICTIONARY POLICY DIPLOM

C58
WILDING N.,"AN ENCYCLOPEDIA OF PARLIAMENT." UK LAW CONSTN CHIEF PROB/SOLV DIPLOM DEBATE WAR INGP/REL PRIVIL...BIBLIOG DICTIONARY 13/20 CMN/WLTH PARLIAMENT. PAGE 164 A3349
PARL/PROC POL/PAR NAT/G ADMIN

B63
HUSSEY W.D.,THE BRITISH EMPIRE AND COMMONWEALTH 1500 TO 1961. UK USA-45 SOCIETY ECO/UNDEV NAT/G VOL/ASSN INT/TRADE DOMIN CONTROL WAR PWR ...DICTIONARY 16/20 COMMONWLTH TRUST/TERR. PAGE 69 A1422
COLONIAL SOVEREIGN INT/ORG

B63
PAENSON I.,SYSTEMATIC GLOSSARY ENGLISH, FRENCH, SPANISH, RUSSIAN OF SELECTED ECONOMIC AND SOCIAL TERMS. WOR+45 FINAN LABOR INT/TRADE DEMAND PRODUC 20. PAGE 113 A2315
DICTIONARY SOC LING

B65
IRIYE A.,AFTER IMPERIALISM; THE SEARCH FOR A NEW ORDER IN THE FAR EAST 1921-1931. USA-45 USSR DOMIN AGREE COLONIAL REV PWR...BIBLIOG DICTIONARY 20 CHINJAP. PAGE 72 A1468
DIPLOM ASIA SOVEREIGN

B65
MOSTECKY V.,SOVIET LEGAL BIBLIOGRAPHY. USSR LEGIS PRESS WRITING CONFER ADJUD CT/SYS REV MARXISM ...INT/LAW JURID DICTIONARY 20. PAGE 105 A2155
BIBLIOG/A LAW COM CONSTN

B66
WOOLLEY H.B.,MEASURING TRANSACTIONS BETWEEN WORLD AREAS. WOR+45 FINAN...STAT NET/THEORY CHARTS DICTIONARY 20 GOLD/STAND. PAGE 167 A3395
INT/TRADE BAL/PAY DIPLOM ECOMETRIC

B67
TROTSKY L.,PROBLEMS OF THE CHINESE REVOLUTION (3RD ED. TRANS. BY MAX SCHACTMAN). ASIA USSR DIPLOM MARXISM SOCISM...IDEA/COMP ANTHOL DICTIONARY 20 STALIN/J. PAGE 145 A2969
MARXIST REV

DIDEROT/D....DENIS DIDEROT

DIEBOLD W. A0759,A0760

DIEM....NGO DINH DIEM

B66
SOBEL L.A.,SOUTH VIETNAM: US-COMMUNIST CONFRONTATION IN SOUTHEAST ASIA 1961-65. VIETNAM FOR/AID CROWD DETER REV PEACE...GEOG 20 INTERVENT DIEM COLD/WAR. PAGE 134 A2754
WAR TIME/SEQ FORCES NAT/G

DIHN N.Q. A0761

DILLA H.M. A0762

DILLARD D. A0763

DILLON D.R. A0764

DILLON/D ....DOUGLAS DILLON

B61
US HOUSE COMM FOREIGN AFFAIRS,THE INTERNATIONAL DEVELOPMENT AND SECURITY ACT: HEARINGS BEFORE COMMITTEE ON FOREIGN AFFAIRS, HOUSE OF REP: HR7372. USA+45 AGRI INT/ORG NAT/G CONSULT DELIB/GP DIPLOM ECO/TAC INT/TRADE LOBBY REPRESENT 20 MCNAMARA/R DILLON/D RUSK/D CONGRESS. PAGE 153 A3128
FOR/AID CONFER LEGIS ECO/UNDEV

DIMOCK M.E. A0765

DINH TRAN VAN A0766

DIPLOM....DIPLOMACY

DIPLOMACY....SEE DIPLOM

DIRECT/NAT....DIRECTORY NATIONAL (IRELAND)

DIRECTORY NATIONAL (IRELAND)....SEE DIRECT/NAT

DIRKSEN/E....EVERETT DIRKSEN

DISARMAMENT....SEE ARMS/CONT

DISCIPLINE....SEE EDU/PROP, CONTROL

DISCRIM....DISCRIMINATION; SEE ALSO GP/REL, RACE/REL, ISOLAT

B10
MENDELSSOHN S.,SOUTH AFRICAN BIBLIOGRAPHY (2 VOLS.). SOUTH/AFR EXTR/IND LABOR SECT DIPLOM INT/TRADE COLONIAL RACE/REL DISCRIM...GEOG 20. PAGE 99 A2038
BIBLIOG/A AFR NAT/G NAT/LISM

B17
VEBLEN T.B.,AN INQUIRY INTO THE NATURE OF PEACE AND THE TERMS OF ITS PERPETUATION. UNIV STRATA FINAN EDU/PROP PRICE COST DISCRIM NAT/LISM MORAL ORD/FREE PACIFIST 20 WORLDUNITY. PAGE 158 A3224
PEACE DIPLOM WAR NAT/G

N19
BARROS J.F.P.,THE INTERNATIONAL POLICE: THE USE OF FORCE IN THE STRUCTURE OF PEACE (PAMPHLET). BRAZIL WOR+45 WOR-45 FORCES DISCRIM NAT/LISM ORD/FREE SOVEREIGN...POLICY NEW/IDEA WORSHIP 20. PAGE 11 A0229
PEACE INT/ORG COERCE BAL/PWR

N19
PROVISIONS SECTION OAU,ORGANIZATION OF AFRICAN UNITY: BASIC DOCUMENTS AND RESOLUTIONS (PAMPHLET). AFR CULTURE ECO/UNDEV DIPLOM ECO/TAC EDU/PROP COLONIAL ARMS/CONT NUC/PWR RACE/REL DISCRIM NAT/LISM 20 UN OAU. PAGE 118 A2415
CONSTN EX/STRUC SOVEREIGN INT/ORG

B28
MAIR L.P.,THE PROTECTION OF MINORITIES. EUR+WWI WOR-45 CONSTN INT/ORG NAT/G LEGIT CT/SYS GP/REL RACE/REL DISCRIM ORD/FREE RESPECT...JURID CONCPT TIME/SEQ 20. PAGE 93 A1909
LAW SOVEREIGN

B30
SMUTS J.C.,AFRICA AND SOME WORLD PROBLEMS. RHODESIA SOUTH/AFR CULTURE ECO/UNDEV INDUS INT/ORG SECT PROB/SOLV REGION GOV/REL DISCRIM ATTIT 19/20 LEAGUE/NAT LIVNGSTN/D NEGRO. PAGE 134 A2748
LEGIS AFR COLONIAL RACE/REL

B36
THWAITE D.,THE SEETHING AFRICAN POT: A STUDY OF BLACK NATIONALISM 1882-1935. ETHIOPIA SECT VOL/ASSN COERCE GUERRILLA MURDER DISCRIM MARXISM...PSY TIME/SEQ 18/20 NEGRO. PAGE 144 A2939
NAT/LISM AFR RACE/REL DIPLOM

B36
VARLEY D.H.,A BIBLIOGRAPHY OF ITALIAN COLONISATION IN AFRICA WITH A SECTION ON ABYSSINIA. AFR ETHIOPIA ITALY LIBYA SOMALIA AGRI FINAN LABOR TEC/DEV DIPLOM INT/TRADE RACE/REL DISCRIM 19/20. PAGE 158 A3222
BIBLIOG COLONIAL ADMIN LAW

B37
TUPPER E.,JAPAN IN AMERICAN PUBLIC OPINION. USA-45 POL/PAR VOL/ASSN INT/TRADE DISCRIM...BIBLIOG 20 CHINJAP TREATY. PAGE 146 A2979
ATTIT IDEA/COMP DIPLOM PRESS

C37
TUPPER E.,"JAPAN IN AMERICAN PUBLIC OPINION." USA+45 POL/PAR VOL/ASSN INT/TRADE DISCRIM ...IDEA/COMP 20 CHINJAP. PAGE 146 A2978
BIBLIOG ATTIT DIPLOM PRESS

B42
BORNSTEIN J.,ACTION AGAINST THE ENEMY'S MIND. EUR+WWI GERMANY USA-45 DIPLOM DOMIN PRESS LEAD GP/REL DISCRIM PERCEPT FASCISM MARXISM 20 JEWS NAZI ANTI/SEMIT. PAGE 17 A0343
EDU/PROP PSY WAR CONTROL

B42
JOSHI P.S.,THE TYRANNY OF COLOUR. INDIA SOUTH/AFR UK ECO/UNDEV NAT/G POL/PAR DIPLOM ECO/TAC WAR ...POLICY 19/20. PAGE 75 A1538
COLONIAL DISCRIM RACE/REL

B50
MOCKFORD J.,SOUTH-WEST AFRICA AND THE INTERNATIONAL COURT (PAMPHLET). AFR GERMANY SOUTH/AFR UK ECO/UNDEV DIPLOM CONTROL DISCRIM...DECISION JURID 20 AFRICA/SW. PAGE 102 A2094
COLONIAL SOVEREIGN INT/LAW DOMIN

B50
MUGRIDGE D.H.,AMERICAN HISTORY AND CIVILIZATION: LIST OF GUIDES AND ANNOTATED OR SELECTIVE BIBLIOGRAPHIES. NAT/G SECT DIPLOM RACE/REL DISCRIM ATTIT...ART/METH SOC 18/20. PAGE 105 A2164
BIBLIOG/A USA-45 SOCIETY

B54
COOKSON J.,BEFORE THE AFRICAN STORM. BELGIUM CENTRL/AFR FRANCE UK ECO/UNDEV POL/PAR CREATE BAL/PWR RACE/REL NAT/LISM ORD/FREE CONSERVE MARXISM SOC/INTEG 20 CONGO/LEOP. PAGE 30 A0607
COLONIAL REV DISCRIM DIPLOM

B55
PYRAH G.B.,IMPERIAL POLICY AND SOUTH AFRICA 1902-1910. SOUTH/AFR UK NAT/G WAR DISCRIM...CONCPT CHARTS BIBLIOG/A 19/20 CMN/WLTH. PAGE 118 A2421
DIPLOM COLONIAL POLICY RACE/REL

B56
JAMESON J.F.,THE AMERICAN REVOLUTION CONSIDERED AS A SOCIAL MOVEMENT. USA-45 AGRI FINAN SECT INT/TRADE REPRESENT SUFF INGP/REL RACE/REL DISCRIM...MAJORIT 18/19 CHURCH/STA. PAGE 73 A1494
ORD/FREE REV FEDERAL CONSTN

B58
GROBLER J.H.,AFRICA'S DESTINY. AFR EUR+WWI SOUTH/AFR UK USA+45 ELITES KIN LOC/G DIPLOM DISCRIM ATTIT CONSERVE MARXISM 20 ROOSEVLT/T NEGRO. PAGE 57 A1168
POLICY ORD/FREE COLONIAL CONSTN

B58
JENNINGS I.,PROBLEMS OF THE NEW COMMONWEALTH. CEYLON INDIA PAKISTAN S/ASIA ECO/UNDEV INT/ORG LOC/G DIPLOM ECO/TAC INT/TRADE COLONIAL RACE/REL DISCRIM 20 COMMONWLTH PARLIAMENT. PAGE 74 A1508
NAT/LISM NEUTRAL FOR/AID POL/PAR

L58
HYVARINEN R.,"MONISTIC AND PLURALISTIC INTERPRETATIONS IN THE STUDY OF INTERNATIONAL POLITICS." COLONIAL REGION RACE/REL DISCRIM TOTALISM SOVEREIGN...INT/LAW PHIL/SCI CONCPT BIBLIOG 20. PAGE 70 A1429
DIPLOM PLURISM INT/ORG METH

C58
CARTER G.M.,"THE POLITICS OF INEQUALITY: SOUTH AFRICA SINCE 1948." SOUTH/AFR CONSTN DIPLOM EDU/PROP REPRESENT DISCRIM ATTIT...POLICY PREDICT CHARTS BIBLIOG 20. PAGE 25 A0504
RACE/REL POL/PAR CHOOSE DOMIN

B59
EGYPTIAN SOCIETY OF INT LAW,THE MONROVIA CONFERENCE (PAMPHLET). AFR ALGERIA FRANCE UAR CONFER REGION NUC/PWR WAR DISCRIM 20 SAHARA AFR/STATES. PAGE 40 A0826
COLONIAL SOVEREIGN RACE/REL DIPLOM

B59
KARUNAKARAN K.P.,INDIA IN WORLD AFFAIRS, 1952-1958 (VOL. II). INDIA ECO/UNDEV SECT FOR/AID INT/TRADE ADJUD NEUTRAL REV WAR DISCRIM ORD/FREE MARXISM ...BIBLIOG 20. PAGE 77 A1569
DIPLOM INT/ORG S/ASIA COLONIAL

B60
STEVENSON A.E.,PUTTING FIRST THINGS FIRST. USA+45 INT/ORG NEIGH FOR/AID DISCRIM...ANTHOL 20. PAGE 138 A2822
DIPLOM ECO/UNDEV ORD/FREE EDU/PROP

B60
THE AFRICA 1960 COMMITTEE,MANDATE IN TRUST; THE PROBLEM OF SOUTH WEST AFRICA. GERMANY STRUCT REGION SANCTION CHOOSE DISCRIM...INT/LAW 20 AFRICA/SW UN LEAGUE/NAT TRUST/TERR. PAGE 142 A2910
NAT/G DIPLOM COLONIAL RACE/REL

B60
WODDIS J.,AFRICA: THE ROOTS OF REVOLT. SOUTH/AFR WORKER INT/TRADE RACE/REL DISCRIM ORD/FREE 20. PAGE 166 A3374
COLONIAL SOVEREIGN WAR ECO/UNDEV

B61
CALVOCORESSI P.,SOUTH AFRICA AND WORLD OPINION. SOUTH/AFR WOR+45 COM/IND INT/ORG 20. PAGE 23 A0470
ATTIT DISCRIM RACE/REL DIPLOM

B61
CAMERON J.,THE AFRICAN REVOLUTION. AFR UK ECO/UNDEV POL/PAR REGION RACE/REL DISCRIM PWR CONSERVE ...CONCPT SOC/INTEG 20 NEGRO. PAGE 23 A0472
REV COLONIAL ORD/FREE DIPLOM

B61
PERLO V.,EL IMPERIALISMO NORTHEAMERICANO. USA+45 USA-45 FINAN CAP/ISM DIPLOM DOMIN CONTROL DISCRIM 19/20. PAGE 115 A2363
SOCIALIST ECO/DEV INT/TRADE ECO/TAC

B61
WOOD B.,THE MAKING OF THE GOOD NEIGHBOR POLICY. L/A+17C USA-45 COERCE CIVMIL/REL DISCRIM. PAGE 166 A3389
DIPLOM DELIB/GP POLICY

B62
BLANSHARD P.,FREEDOM AND CATHOLIC POWER IN SPAIN AND PORTUGAL: AN AMERICAN INTERPRETATION. AFR PORTUGAL SPAIN USA+45 LAW LABOR DIPLOM EDU/PROP DISCRIM ISOLAT TOTALISM 20 CHURCH/STA. PAGE 15 A0309
GP/REL FASCISM CATHISM PWR

B62
BOWLES C.,THE CONSCIENCE OF A LIBERAL. COM USA+45 WOR+45 STRUCT LOC/G NAT/G FORCES LEGIS GOV/REL DISCRIM 20 UN CIV/RIGHTS. PAGE 18 A0361
DIPLOM POLICY

B62
MOON P.,DIVIDE AND QUIT. INDIA PAKISTAN STRATA DELIB/GP PLAN DIPLOM REPRESENT GP/REL INGP/REL CONSEN DISCRIM...OBS 20. PAGE 103 A2119
WAR REGION ISOLAT SECT

B63
BROWN W.N.,THE UNITED STATES AND INDIA AND PAKISTAN (REV. ED.). INDIA PAKISTAN S/ASIA WOR+45 POL/PAR SECT INT/TRADE COLONIAL COERCE DISCRIM. PAGE 20 A0408
DIPLOM ECO/UNDEV SOVEREIGN STRUCT

B63
PRESTON W. JR.,ALIENS AND DISSENTERS: FEDERAL SUPPRESSION OF RADICALS 1903-1933. USA-45 DIPLOM ADJUD REPRESENT RACE/REL MAJORITY...BIBLIOG/A 19/20. PAGE 117 A2409
DISCRIM GP/REL INGP/REL ATTIT

B63
US CONGRESS JOINT ECO COMM,DISCRIMINATORY OCEAN FREIGHT RATES AND BALANCE OF PAYMENTS. USA+45 SEA DELIB/GP DISCRIM...CHARTS 20 CONGRESS. PAGE 150 A3066
BAL/PAY DIST/IND PRICE INT/TRADE

B64
BURKE F.G.,AFRICA'S QUEST FOR ORDER. AFR CULTURE KIN MUNIC NAT/G DIPLOM COLONIAL REV DISCRIM NAT/LISM AGE/Y 20. PAGE 21 A0437
ORD/FREE CONSEN RACE/REL LEAD

B64
KOLARZ W.,COMMUNISM AND COLONIALISM. AFR ASIA USSR DISCRIM ATTIT ORD/FREE SOVEREIGN SOC/INTEG 20. PAGE 81 A1668
EDU/PROP DIPLOM TOTALISM COLONIAL

B64
LEGUM C.,SOUTH AFRICA: CRISIS FOR THE WEST. SOUTH/AFR COERCE DISCRIM ATTIT...TREND 20 INTERVENT. PAGE 86 A1767
RACE/REL STRATA DIPLOM PROB/SOLV

B64
MARTIN J.J.,AMERICAN LIBERALISM AND WORLD POLITICS, 1931-41 (2 VOLS.). GERMANY USA-45 POL/PAR DISCRIM NAT/LISM PEACE RATIONAL ATTIT RIGID/FLEX MARXISM PACIFISM 20. PAGE 95 A1950
NEW/LIB DIPLOM NAT/G POLICY

B64
SEGAL R.,SANCTIONS AGAINST SOUTH AFRICA. AFR SOUTH/AFR NAT/G INT/TRADE RACE/REL PEACE PWR ...INT/LAW ANTHOL 20 UN. PAGE 131 A2681
SANCTION DISCRIM ECO/TAC POLICY

S64
CARNEGIE ENDOWMENT INT. PEACE,"HUMAN RIGHTS (ISSUES BEFORE THE NINETEENTH GENERAL ASSEMBLY)." AFR WOR+45 LAW CONSTN NAT/G EDU/PROP GP/REL DISCRIM PEACE ATTIT MORAL ORD/FREE...INT/LAW PSY CONCPT RECORD UN 20. PAGE 24 A0492
INT/ORG PERSON RACE/REL

B65
BRACKETT R.D.,PATHWAYS TO PEACE. SECT VOL/ASSN GP/REL PERS/REL DISCRIM...LING 20 UN PEACE/CORP. PAGE 18 A0366
PEACE INT/ORG EDU/PROP PARTIC

B65
DU BOIS W.E.B.,THE WORLD AND AFRICA. USA+45 CAP/ISM DISCRIM STRANGE SOCISM...TIME/SEQ TREND IDEA/COMP 19/20 NEGRO. PAGE 39 A0789
AFR DIPLOM COLONIAL CULTURE

B65
FANON F.,STUDIES IN A DYING COLONIALISM. ALGERIA FRANCE STRATA FAM DIPLOM DOMIN WAR RACE/REL DISCRIM HEALTH 20. PAGE 44 A0897
NAT/LISM COLONIAL REV SOVEREIGN

B65
HALPERIN E.,NATIONALISM AND COMMUNISM. CHILE L/A+17C CAP/ISM EDU/PROP CHOOSE DISCRIM SOCISM ...BIBLIOG 20 COM/PARTY. PAGE 60 A1236
NAT/LISM MARXISM POL/PAR REV

B65
LEISS A.C.,APARTHEID AND UNITED NATIONS COLLECTIVE MEASURES. SOUTH/AFR ECO/UNDEV EXTR/IND FORCES WORKER ECO/TAC FOR/AID INT/TRADE WEALTH...TREND CHARTS 20 UN NEGRO. PAGE 86 A1770
DISCRIM RACE/REL STRATA DIPLOM

B65
SPENCE J.E.,REPUBLIC UNDER PRESSURE: A STUDY OF SOUTH AFRICAN FOREIGN POLICY. SOUTH/AFR ADMIN COLONIAL GOV/REL RACE/REL DISCRIM NAT/LISM ATTIT ROLE...TREND 20 NEGRO. PAGE 136 A2783
DIPLOM POLICY AFR

B66
DONALD A.D.,JOHN F. KENNEDY AND THE NEW FRONTIER. LEGIS DIPLOM DISCRIM PEACE PWR 20. PAGE 38 A0771
LEAD CHIEF BIOG EFFICIENCY

B66
KANET R.E.,THE SOVIET UNION AND SUB-SAHARAN AFRICA: COMMUNIST POLICY TOWARD AFRICA, 1917-1965. AFR USSR ECO/UNDEV TEC/DEV EDU/PROP TASK DISCRIM PEACE WEALTH ALL/IDEOS...CHARTS BIBLIOG SOC/INTEG 19/20 NEGRO UN INTERVENT. PAGE 76 A1555
DIPLOM ECO/TAC MARXISM

B66
US HOUSE COMM FOREIGN AFFAIRS,UNITED STATES - SOUTH AFRICAN RELATIONS. SOUTH/AFR USA+45 NAT/G CONSULT DELIB/GP LEGIS CONFER SANCTION RACE/REL ATTIT 20 CONGRESS. PAGE 154 A3134
DISCRIM DIPLOM POLICY PARL/PROC

B66
WELCH R.H.W.,THE NEW AMERICANISM, AND OTHER SPEECHES AND ESSAYS. USA+45 ACADEM POL/PAR SCHOOL VOL/ASSN FORCES CAP/ISM TAX REV DISCRIM 20 CIV/RIGHTS COLD/WAR BIRCH/SOC. PAGE 163 A3313
DIPLOM FASCISM MARXISM RACE/REL

S66
AFRICAN BIBLIOGRAPHIC CENTER,"A DESCRIPTIVE STUDY OF CURRENT AFRICAN FOREIGN RELATIONS." COM CULTURE INT/ORG SECT RACE/REL DISCRIM ATTIT 20. PAGE 5 A0099
BIBLIOG DIPLOM AFR

B67
BODENHEIMER E.,TREATISE ON JUSTICE. INT/ORG NAT/G PUB/INST ACT/RES RISK CRIME INGP/REL DISCRIM DRIVE LAISSEZ 20. PAGE 16 A0325
ALL/VALS STRUCT JURID

CONCPT

B67
RUSSELL B.,WAR CRIMES IN VIETNAM. USA+45 VIETNAM FORCES DIPLOM WEAPON RACE/REL DISCRIM ISOLAT BIO/SOC 20 COLD/WAR RUSSELL/B. PAGE 126 A2574
WAR CRIME ATTIT POLICY

S67
ECKHARDT A.R.,"SILENCE IN THE CHURCHES." ISRAEL WOR+45 CONSTN GP/REL DISCRIM DRIVE JEWS. PAGE 40 A0820
SECT ATTIT DIPLOM ISLAM

S67
MUDGE G.A.,"DOMESTIC POLICIES AND UN ACTIVITIES* THE CASE OF RHODESIA AND THE REPUBLIC OF SOUTH AFRICA." RHODESIA SOUTH/AFR POL/PAR LEAD SANCTION CHOOSE RACE/REL CONSEN DISCRIM ATTIT...INT/LAW UN PARLIAMENT 20. PAGE 105 A2163
AFR NAT/G POLICY

S67
ROWAN C.T.,"NEW FRONTIERS IN RACE RELATIONS." USA+45 NAT/G DIPLOM 20. PAGE 124 A2551
RACE/REL DISCRIM POLICY PROB/SOLV

DISCRIMINATION....SEE DISCRIM

DISEASE....SEE HEALTH

DISPL....DISPLACEMENT AND PROJECTION

B31
STOWELL E.C.,INTERNATIONAL LAW. FUT UNIV WOR-45 SOCIETY CONSULT EX/STRUC FORCES ACT/RES PLAN DIPLOM EDU/PROP LEGIT DISPL PWR SKILL...POLICY CONCPT OBS TREND TOT/POP 20. PAGE 139 A2839
INT/ORG ROUTINE INT/LAW

B39
WILSON G.G.,HANDBOOK OF INTERNATIONAL LAW. FUT UNIV USA-45 WOR-45 SOCIETY LEGIT ATTIT DISPL DRIVE ALL/VALS...INT/LAW TIME/SEQ TREND. PAGE 165 A3359
INT/ORG LAW CONCPT WAR

B40
MILLER E.,THE NEUROSES OF WAR. UNIV INTELL SOCIETY INT/ORG NAT/G EDU/PROP DISPL DRIVE PERCEPT PERSON RIGID/FLEX...SOC TIME/SEQ 20. PAGE 101 A2075
HEALTH PSY WAR

S51
BUCHANAN W.,"STEREOTYPES AND TENSIONS AS REVEALED BY THE UNESCO INTERNATIONAL POLL." WOR+45 INT/ORG ATTIT DISPL PERCEPT RIGID/FLEX...INT TESTS SAMP 20. PAGE 21 A0424
R+D STERTYP

B52
SCHUMAN F.,THE COMMONWEALTH OF MAN. WOR+45 WOR-45 LAW CULTURE ELITES SOCIETY FAM INT/ORG NAT/G VOL/ASSN TOP/EX PLAN BAL/PWR LEGIT ATTIT DISPL DRIVE...POLICY MYTH TREND TOT/POP ILO OEEC 20. PAGE 129 A2649
CONCPT GEN/LAWS

L52
WRIGHT Q.,"CONGRESS AND THE TREATY-MAKING POWER." USA+45 WOR+45 CONSTN INTELL NAT/G CHIEF CONSULT EX/STRUC LEGIS TOP/EX CREATE GOV/REL DISPL DRIVE RIGID/FLEX...TREND TOT/POP CONGRESS CONGRESS 20 TREATY. PAGE 167 A3408
ROUTINE DIPLOM INT/LAW DELIB/GP

B54
MILLARD E.L.,FREEDOM IN A FEDERAL WORLD. FUT WOR+45 VOL/ASSN TOP/EX LEGIT ROUTINE FEDERAL PEACE ATTIT DISPL ORD/FREE PWR...MAJORIT INT/LAW JURID TREND COLD/WAR 20. PAGE 101 A2073
INT/ORG CREATE ADJUD BAL/PWR

S54
FOX W.T.R.,"CIVIL-MILITARY RELATIONS." USA+45 USA-45 R+D ACT/RES DIPLOM INT/TRADE EDU/PROP DETER DISPL DRIVE ORD/FREE...METH/CNCPT TREND COLD/WAR 20. PAGE 48 A0974
POLICY FORCES PLAN SOCIETY

B56
WOLFERS A.,THE ANGLO-AMERICAN TRADITION IN FOREIGN AFFAIRS. UK USA+45 WOR-45 CULTURE SOCIETY ECO/DEV INT/ORG NAT/G CREATE PLAN BAL/PWR ECO/TAC EDU/PROP PEACE DISPL DRIVE...TREND GEN/LAWS 20. PAGE 166 A3382
ATTIT CONCPT DIPLOM

B57
BEAL J.R.,JOHN FOSTER DULLES, A BIOGRAPHY. USA+45 USSR WOR+45 CONSTN INT/ORG NAT/G EX/STRUC LEGIT ADMIN NUC/PWR DISPL PERSON ORD/FREE PWR SKILL ...POLICY PSY OBS RECORD COLD/WAR UN 20 DULLES/JF. PAGE 12 A0237
BIOG DIPLOM

B57
STRACHEY A.,THE UNCONSCIOUS MOTIVES OF WAR; A PSYCHO-ANALYTICAL CONTRIBUTION. UNIV SOCIETY DIPLOM DREAM GP/REL ADJUST ATTIT DISPL PERCEPT PERSON KNOWL MORAL. PAGE 139 A2840
WAR DRIVE LOVE PSY

B58
HAUSER P.H.,POPULATION AND WORLD POLITICS. FUT WOR+45 WOR-45 AGRI DIST/IND INDUS INT/ORG PLAN ECO/TAC DISPL HEALTH COLD/WAR 20. PAGE 63 A1288
NAT/G ECO/UNDEV FOR/AID

B58
SCHUMAN F.,INTERNATIONAL POLITICS. WOR+45 WOR-45 INTELL NAT/G FORCES DOMIN LEGIT COERCE NUC/PWR ATTIT DISPL ORD/FREE PWR SOVEREIGN...POLICY CONCPT GEN/LAWS SUEZ 20. PAGE 129 A2650
FUT INT/ORG NAT/LISM DIPLOM

L59
KAPLAN M.A.,"SOME PROBLEMS IN THE STRATEGIC ANALYSIS OF INTERNATIONAL POLITICS." UNIV R+D INT/ORG CREATE PLAN DIPLOM EDU/PROP COERCE DISPL PWR...METH/CNCPT NEW/IDEA HYPO/EXP TOT/POP 20. PAGE 76 A1561
DECISION BAL/PWR

B60
CONN S.,THE FRAMEWORK OF HEMISPHERE DEFENSE. CANADA L/A+17C USA-45 NAT/G FORCES BAL/PWR DOMIN WAR PEACE DISPL PWR RESPECT...PLURIST CONCPT HIST/WRIT HYPO/EXP MEXIC/AMER 20 ROOSEVLT/F. PAGE 29 A0585
USA+45 INT/ORG DIPLOM

B61
STONE J.,QUEST FOR SURVIVAL. WOR+45 NAT/G VOL/ASSN LEGIT ADMIN ARMS/CONT COERCE DISPL ORD/FREE PWR ...POLICY INT/LAW JURID COLD/WAR 20. PAGE 139 A2836
INT/ORG ADJUD SOVEREIGN

L61
HOYT E.C.,"UNITED STATES REACTION TO THE KOREAN ATTACK." COM KOREA USA+45 CONSTN DELIB/GP FORCES PLAN ECO/TAC DOMIN EDU/PROP LEGIT ROUTINE COERCE WAR ATTIT DISPL RIGID/FLEX ORD/FREE PWR...POLICY INT/LAW TREND UN 20. PAGE 68 A1402
ASIA INT/ORG BAL/PWR DIPLOM

S61
BURNET A.,"TOO MANY ALLIES." COM EUR+WWI UK WOR+45 WOR-45 ACT/RES PLAN DISPL PWR SKILL...TIME/SEQ 20 CMN/WLTH SEATO NATO CENTO. PAGE 22 A0438
VOL/ASSN INT/ORG DIPLOM

B62
SCHRODER P.M.,METTERNICH'S DIPLOMACY AT ITS ZENITH, 1820-1823. MOD/EUR ELITES INT/ORG VOL/ASSN DELIB/GP ECO/TAC EDU/PROP DISPL PWR SOVEREIGN...POLICY CONCPT GEN/LAWS 19 METTRNCH/K. PAGE 129 A2647
ORD/FREE BIOG BAL/PWR DIPLOM

S62
NANES A.,"DISARMAMENT: THE LAST SEVEN YEARS." COM EUR+WWI USA+45 USSR INT/ORG FORCES TOP/EX CREATE LEGIT NUC/PWR DISPL ORD/FREE...CONCPT TIME/SEQ CON/ANAL 20. PAGE 107 A2195
DELIB/GP RIGID/FLEX ARMS/CONT

S63
GUPTA S.C.,"INDIA AND THE SOVIET UNION." CHINA/COM COM INDIA S/ASIA VOL/ASSN TOP/EX FOR/AID EDU/PROP PEACE PWR...RECORD COLD/WAR 20. PAGE 58 A1195
DISPL MYTH USSR

S63
SHWADRAN B.,"MIDDLE EAST OIL, 1962." ISLAM USSR ECO/DEV DIST/IND INDUS PLAN BAL/PWR DISPL DRIVE ...POLICY STAT TREND GEN/LAWS EEC OEEC 20 OIL. PAGE 132 A2712
MARKET ECO/TAC INT/TRADE

B64
TAYLOR E.,RICHER BY ASIA. S/ASIA CULTURE VOL/ASSN ACT/RES ATTIT DISPL PERSON ALL/VALS...INT/LAW MYTH SELF/OBS 20. PAGE 142 A2899
SOCIETY RIGID/FLEX INDIA

S64
WASKOW A.I.,"NEW ROADS TO A WORLD WITHOUT WAR." FUT WOR+45 CULTURE INTELL SOCIETY NAT/G DOMIN LEGIT EXEC COERCE PEACE ATTIT DISPL PERCEPT RIGID/FLEX ALL/VALS...POLICY RELATIV SOC NEW/IDEA 20. PAGE 161 A3288
INT/ORG FORCES

L65
TUCKER R.W.,"PEACE AND WAR." UNIV CULTURE SOCIETY INT/ORG NAT/G ACT/RES DOMIN DETER WAR ATTIT DISPL ...POLICY CONCPT MYTH GEN/LAWS 20. PAGE 145 A2975
PWR COERCE ARMS/CONT PEACE

S65
MERRITT R.L.,"WOODROW WILSON AND THE 'GREAT AND SOLEMN REFERENDUM,' 1920." USA-45 SOCIETY NAT/G CONSULT LEGIS ACT/RES PLAN DOMIN EDU/PROP ROUTINE ATTIT DISPL DRIVE PERSON RIGID/FLEX MORAL ORD/FREE ...PSY SOC CONCPT MYTH LEAGUE/NAT. PAGE 100 A2044
INT/ORG TOP/EX DIPLOM

DISPLACEMENT....SEE DISPL

DISPUTE, RESOLUTION OF....SEE ADJUD

DISRAELI/B....BENJAMIN DISRAELI

DIST/IND....DISTRIBUTIVE SYSTEM

N
KYRIAK T.E.,SOVIET UNION: BIBLIOGRAPHY INDEX TO US JPRS RESEARCH TRANSLATIONS. USSR ECO/DEV AGRI COM/IND CONSTRUC DIST/IND EXTR/IND PROC/MFG R+D INT/TRADE...SOC 20. PAGE 83 A1703
BIBLIOG/A INDUS MARXISM PRESS

B17
MEYER H.H.B.,LIST OF REFERENCES ON EMBARGOES (PAMPHLET). USA-45 AGRI DIPLOM WRITING DEBATE WEAPON...INT/LAW 18/20 CONGRESS. PAGE 100 A2049
BIBLIOG DIST/IND ECO/TAC INT/TRADE

N19
LANGE O.R.,"DISARMAMENT ECONOMIC GROWTH AND INTERNATIONAL CO-OPERATION" (PAMPHLET). WOR+45 DIST/IND PLAN INT/TRADE GIVE TASK DETER WEALTH SOCISM 18/19 BOLIVAR/S. PAGE 84 A1723
ARMS/CONT DIPLOM ECO/DEV ECO/UNDEV

B35
BUREAU ECONOMIC RES LAT AM,THE ECONOMIC LITERATURE OF LATIN AMERICA (2 VOLS.). CHRIST-17C AGRI DIST/IND EXTR/IND INDUS WORKER INT/TRADE...GEOG 16/20. PAGE 21 A0433
BIBLIOG L/A+17C ECO/UNDEV FINAN

B39
LENIN V.I.,IMPERIALISM: THE HIGHEST STAGE OF
MARXIST

CAPITALISM. USSR WOR-45 DIST/IND INT/TRADE ATTIT MARXISM SOCISM...CHARTS 20. PAGE 87 A1773
CAP/ISM COLONIAL DOMIN

B48
KULISCHER E.M.,EUROPE ON THE MOVE: WAR AND POPULATION CHANGES, 1917-1947. COM EUR+WWI FUT GERMANY USSR DIST/IND PLAN INT/TRADE CONTROL WAR DRIVE...CENSUS TREND COLD/WAR 20. PAGE 82 A1690
ECO/TAC GEOG

B50
LINCOLN G.,ECONOMICS OF NATIONAL SECURITY. USA+45 ELITES COM/IND DIST/IND INDUS NAT/G VOL/ASSN DELIB/GP EX/STRUC FOR/AID EDU/PROP COERCE NUC/PWR WAR ATTIT KNOWL ORD/FREE PWR COLD/WAR TOT/POP VAL/FREE 20. PAGE 89 A1818
FORCES ECO/TAC

B52
ALEXANDROWICZ C.H.,INTERNATIONAL ECONOMIC ORGANIZATION. WOR+45 ECO/DEV ECO/UNDEV DIST/IND FINAN MARKET PLAN ECO/TAC LEGIT DRIVE WEALTH ...POLICY CONCPT QUANT OBS TIME/SEQ GEN/LAWS WORK EEC ILO OEEC UNESCO 20. PAGE 6 A0114
INT/ORG INT/TRADE

B54
BECKEL G.,WORKSHOPS FOR THE WORLD; THE SPECIALIZED AGENCIES OF THE UN. WOR+45 AGRI DIST/IND CREATE TEC/DEV BUDGET CONTROL TASK WEALTH...CHARTS ORG/CHARTS 20 UN CASEBOOK. PAGE 12 A0246
INT/ORG DIPLOM PEACE CON/ANAL

B55
LANDHEER B.,EUROPEAN YEARBOOK, 1955. CONSTN ECO/DEV DIST/IND FINAN DELIB/GP ECO/TAC DETER NUC/PWR ...BIBLIOG 20 EEC. PAGE 84 A1717
EUR+WWI INT/ORG GOV/REL INT/TRADE

B56
JUAN T.L.,ECONOMIC AND SOCIAL DEVELOPMENT OF MODERN CHINA: A BIBLIOGRAPHICAL GUIDE. ASIA AGRI COM/IND DIST/IND FINAN INDUS DIPLOM...STAT 20. PAGE 75 A1541
BIBLIOG SOC

B56
WATT D.C.,BRITAIN AND THE SUEZ CANAL. COM UAR UK ...INT/LAW 20 SUEZ TREATY. PAGE 162 A3294
DIPLOM INT/TRADE DIST/IND NAT/G

B57
ASHER R.E.,THE UNITED NATIONS AND ECONOMIC AND SOCIAL COOPERATION. ECO/UNDEV COM/IND DIST/IND FINAN PLAN PROB/SOLV INT/TRADE TASK WEALTH...SOC 20 UN. PAGE 9 A0186
INT/ORG DIPLOM FOR/AID

B57
DRUCKER P.F.,AMERICA'S NEXT TWENTY YEARS. USA+45 DIST/IND ACADEM MUNIC SCHOOL DIPLOM ECO/TAC AUTOMAT HABITAT HEALTH...SOC/WK TREND 20 URBAN/RNWL PUB/TRANS. PAGE 39 A0788
WORKER FOR/AID CENSUS GEOG

L57
WARREN S.,"FOREIGN AID AND FOREIGN POLICY." USA+45 WOR+45 WOR-45 DIST/IND INDUS MARKET CONSULT CREATE DIPLOM EDU/PROP LEGIT ATTIT RIGID/FLEX...TIME/SEQ GEN/LAWS WORK 20. PAGE 161 A3285
ECO/UNDEV ALL/VALS ECO/TAC FOR/AID

B58
BERLINER J.S.,SOVIET ECONOMIC AID: THE AID AND TRADE POLICY IN UNDERDEVELOPED COUNTRIES. AFR COM ISLAM L/A+17C S/ASIA USSR ECO/DEV DIST/IND FINAN MARKET INT/ORG ACT/RES PLAN BAL/PWR WEAPON PWR WEALTH...CHARTS 20. PAGE 14 A0277
ECO/UNDEV ECO/TAC FOR/AID

B58
HAUSER P.H.,POPULATION AND WORLD POLITICS. FUT WOR+45 AGRI DIST/IND INDUS INT/ORG PLAN ECO/TAC DISPL HEALTH COLD/WAR 20. PAGE 63 A1288
NAT/G ECO/UNDEV FOR/AID

B59
HAZLEWOOD A.,THE ECONOMICS OF "UNDER-DEVELOPED" AREAS. WOR+45 DIST/IND EXTR/IND FINAN INDUS MARKET PLAN FOR/AID...GEOG 20. PAGE 63 A1302
BIBLIOG/A ECO/UNDEV AGRI INT/TRADE

L59
MURPHY J.C.,"SOME IMPLICATIONS OF EUROPE'S COMMON MARKET. IN (COOK P, ECONOMIC DEVELOPMENT AND INTERNATIONAL TRADE.." EUR+WWI ECO/DEV DIST/IND INDUS NAT/G PLAN ECO/TAC INT/TRADE WEALTH...STAT TREND OEEC TOT/POP 20 EEC. PAGE 106 A2178
MARKET INT/ORG REGION

S59
KINDLEBERGER C.P.,"UNITED STATES ECONOMIC FOREIGN POLICY: RESEARCH REQUIREMENTS FOR 1965." FUT USA+45 WOR+45 DIST/IND MARKET INT/ORG ECO/TAC INT/TRADE WEALTH...OBS TREND CON/ANAL GEN/LAWS VAL/FREE 20. PAGE 79 A1621
FINAN ECO/DEV FOR/AID

B60
APTHEKER H.,DISARMAMENT AND THE AMERICAN ECONOMY: A SYMPOSIUM. FUT USA+45 ECO/DEV DIST/IND FINAN INDUS PROC/MFG LABOR NAT/G POL/PAR CONSULT PLAN CAP/ISM INT/TRADE PEACE ATTIT MORAL WEALTH...TREND GEN/LAWS TOT/POP 20. PAGE 9 A0172
MARXIST ARMS/CONT

S60
"THE EMERGING COMMON MARKETS IN LATIN AMERICA." FUT L/A+17C STRATA DIST/IND INDUS LABOR NAT/G LEGIS ECO/TAC ADMIN RIGID/FLEX HEALTH...NEW/IDEA TIME/SEQ OAS 20. PAGE 3 A0059
FINAN ECO/UNDEV INT/TRADE

S60
KREININ M.E.,"THE 'OUTER-SEVEN' AND EUROPEAN INTEGRATION." EUR+WWI FRANCE GERMANY ITALY UK ECO/DEV DIST/IND INT/TRADE DRIVE WEALTH...MYTH CHARTS EEC OEEC 20. PAGE 82 A1682
ECO/TAC GEN/LAWS

S60
MORALES C.J.,"TRADE AND ECONOMIC INTEGRATION IN LATIN AMERICA." FUT L/A+17C LAW STRATA ECO/UNDEV DIST/IND INDUS LABOR NAT/G LEGIS ECO/TAC ADMIN RIGID/FLEX WEALTH...CONCPT NEW/IDEA CONT/OBS TIME/SEQ WORK 20. PAGE 104 A2128
FINAN INT/TRADE REGION

B61
FRIEDMANN W.G.,JOINT INTERNATIONAL BUSINESS VENTURES. ASIA ISLAM L/A+17C ECO/DEV DIST/IND FINAN PROC/MFG FACE/GP LG/CO NAT/G VOL/ASSN CONSULT EX/STRUC PLAN ADMIN ROUTINE WEALTH...OLD/LIB WORK 20. PAGE 49 A1004
ECO/UNDEV INT/TRADE

B61
INTERNATIONAL BANK RECONST DEV,THE WORLD BANK IN AFRICA: SUMMARY OF ACTIVITIES. AGRI COM/IND DIST/IND EXTR/IND INDUS TAX COST...CHARTS 20. PAGE 71 A1450
FINAN ECO/UNDEV INT/ORG AFR

B61
KITZINGER V.W.,THE CHALLENGE OF THE COMMON MARKET. EUR+WWI ECO/DEV DIST/IND PLAN ECO/TAC INT/TRADE LEGIT ATTIT PWR WEALTH...TIME/SEQ TREND CHARTS EEC 20. PAGE 80 A1647
MARKET INT/ORG UK

B61
SOKOL A.E.,SEAPOWER IN THE NUCLEAR AGE. USA+45 USSR DIST/IND FORCES INT/TRADE DETER WAR...POLICY NAT/COMP BIBLIOG COLD/WAR. PAGE 135 A2763
SEA PWR WEAPON NUC/PWR

B61
WILLOUGHBY W.R.,THE ST LAWRENCE WATERWAY: A STUDY IN POLITICS AND DIPLOMACY. USA+45 ECO/DEV COM/IND INT/ORG CONSULT DELIB/GP ACT/RES TEC/DEV DIPLOM ECO/TAC ROUTINE...TIME/SEQ 20. PAGE 165 A3357
LEGIS INT/TRADE CANADA DIST/IND

S61
DEUTSCH K.W.,"NATIONAL INDUSTRIALIZATION AND THE DECLINING SHARE OF THE INTERNATIONAL ECONOMIC SECTOR." EUR+WWI FUT WOR+45 WOR-45 MARKET PLAN EDU/PROP WEALTH...WELF/ST OBS TESTS 20. PAGE 36 A0740
DIST/IND ECO/DEV INT/TRADE

B62
ALEXANDROWICZ C.H.,WORLD ECONOMIC AGENCIES: LAW AND PRACTICE. WOR+45 DIST/IND FINAN LABOR CONSULT INT/TRADE TARIFFS REPRESENT HEALTH...JURID 20 UN GATT EEC OAS ECSC. PAGE 6 A0115
INT/LAW INT/ORG DIPLOM ADJUD

B63
BRITISH AID. UK AGRI DIST/IND INDUS SCHOOL TEC/DEV INT/TRADE COLONIAL DEMAND...TREND CHARTS 20. PAGE 3 A0064
FOR/AID ECO/UNDEV NAT/G FINAN

B63
KATZ S.M.,A SELECTED LIST OF US READINGS ON DEVELOPMENT. AGRI COM/IND DIST/IND INDUS LABOR PLAN FOR/AID EDU/PROP HEALTH...POLICY SOC/WK 20. PAGE 77 A1571
BIBLIOG/A ECO/UNDEV TEC/DEV ACT/RES

B63
LYONS F.S.L.,INTERNATIONALISM IN EUROPE 1815-1914. LAW AGRI COM/IND DIST/IND LABOR SECT INT/TRADE TARIFFS...BIBLIOG 19/20. PAGE 92 A1880
DIPLOM MOD/EUR INT/ORG

B63
US CONGRESS JOINT ECO COMM,DISCRIMINATORY OCEAN FREIGHT RATES AND BALANCE OF PAYMENTS. USA+45 SEA DELIB/GP DISCRIM...CHARTS 20 CONGRESS. PAGE 150 A3066
BAL/PAY DIST/IND PRICE INT/TRADE

L63
LISSITZYN O.J.,"INTERNATIONAL LAW IN A DIVIDED WORLD." FUT WOR+45 CONSTN CULTURE ECO/DEV ECO/UNDEV DIST/IND NAT/G FORCES ECO/TAC LEGIT ADJUD ADMIN COERCE ATTIT HEALTH MORAL ORD/FREE PWR RESPECT WEALTH VAL/FREE. PAGE 90 A1841
INT/ORG LAW

L63
PRINCETON UNIV. CONFERENCE,"ARAB DEVELOPMENT IN THE EMERGING INTERNATIONAL ECONOMY." FUT USA+45 DIST/IND FINAN DELIB/GP PLAN ECO/TAC WEALTH VAL/FREE 20. PAGE 118 A2413
ISLAM ECO/UNDEV FOR/AID INT/TRADE

S63
DIEBOLD W. JR.,"THE NEW SITUATION OF INTERNATIONAL TRADE POLICY." EUR+WWI FRANCE FUT UK USA+45 WOR+45 DIST/IND PLAN INT/TRADE EDU/PROP PWR WEALTH ...RECORD TREND GEN/LAWS EEC VAL/FREE 20. PAGE 37 A0760
MARKET ECO/TAC

S63
RAMERIE L.,"TENSION AU SEIN DU COMECON: LE CAS ROUMAIN." COM EUR+WWI USSR WOR+45 ECO/DEV DIST/IND NAT/G POL/PAR VOL/ASSN EDU/PROP TOTALISM ATTIT WEALTH...TIME/SEQ 20 COMECON. PAGE 119 A2438
INT/ORG ECO/TAC INT/TRADE ROMANIA

S63
SHONFIELD A.,"AFTER BRUSSELS." EUR+WWI FRANCE GERMANY UK ECO/DEV DIST/IND MARKET VOL/ASSN DELIB/GP CREATE INT/TRADE ATTIT RIGID/FLEX...RECORD TREND GEN/LAWS EEC CMN/WLTH 20. PAGE 132 A2705
PLAN ECO/TAC

S63
SHWADRAN B.,"MIDDLE EAST OIL, 1962." ISLAM USSR ECO/DEV DIST/IND INDUS PLAN BAL/PWR DISPL DRIVE ...POLICY STAT TREND GEN/LAWS EEC OEEC 20 OIL. PAGE 132 A2712
MARKET ECO/TAC INT/TRADE

B64
EAYRS J.,THE COMMONWEALTH AND SUEZ: A DOCUMENTARY SURVEY. FRANCE ISLAM VOL/ASSN FORCES CONFER COLONIAL WAR INGP/REL 20 CMN/WLTH SUEZ UN. PAGE 40 A0818 — DIPLOM NAT/LISM DIST/IND SOVEREIGN

B64
ESTHUS R.A.,FROM ENMITY TO ALLIANCE: US AUSTRALIAN RELATIONS. S/ASIA DIST/IND VOL/ASSN FORCES ATTIT 20 AUSTRAL TREATY CMN/WLTH. PAGE 42 A0863 — DIPLOM WAR INT/TRADE FOR/AID

B64
KRETZSCHMAR W.W.,AUSLANDSHILFE ALS MITTEL DER AUSSENWIRTSCHAFTS- UND AUSSENPOLITIK. ASIA GERMANY/W UK USA+45 SOCIETY STRUCT ECO/UNDEV LOBBY EFFICIENCY 20. PAGE 82 A1683 — FOR/AID DIPLOM AGRI DIST/IND

B64
OWEN W.,STRATEGY FOR MOBILITY. FUT WOR+45 WOR-45 DIST/IND INT/ORG NAT/G DELIB/GP PLAN TEC/DEV ECO/TAC ORD/FREE PWR WEALTH...STAT TIME/SEQ VAL/FREE 20. PAGE 112 A2304 — COM/IND ECO/UNDEV

S64
HUELIN D.,"ECONOMIC INTEGRATION IN LATIN AMERICAN: PROGRESS AND PROBLEMS." L/A+17C ECO/DEV AGRI DIST/IND FINAN INDUS NAT/G VOL/ASSN CONSULT DELIB/GP EX/STRUC ACT/RES PLAN TEC/DEV ECO/TAC ROUTINE BAL/PAY WEALTH WORK 20. PAGE 69 A1411 — MARKET ECO/UNDEV INT/TRADE

B65
HOSELITZ B.F.,ECONOMICS AND THE IDEA OF MANKIND. UNIV ECO/DEV ECO/UNDEV DIST/IND INDUS INT/ORG NAT/G ACT/RES ECO/TAC WEALTH...CONCPT STAT. PAGE 68 A1392 — CREATE INT/TRADE

B65
THAYER F.C. JR.,AIR TRANSPORT POLICY AND NATIONAL SECURITY: A POLITICAL, ECONOMIC, AND MILITARY ANALYSIS. DIST/IND OP/RES PLAN TEC/DEV DIPLOM DETER WAR COST EFFICIENCY...POLICY BIBLIOG 20 DEPT/DEFEN FAA CAB. PAGE 142 A2908 — AIR FORCES CIVMIL/REL ORD/FREE

L65
WIONCZEK M.,"LATIN AMERICA FREE TRADE ASSOCIATION." AGRI DIST/IND FINAN INDUS INT/ORG LABOR NAT/G TEC/DEV ECO/TAC HEALTH SKILL WEALTH...POLICY RELATIV MGT LAFTA 20. PAGE 165 A3369 — L/A+17C MARKET REGION

B67
JOHNSON A.M.,BOSTON CAPITALISTS AND WESTERN RAILROADS: A STUDY IN THE NINETEENTH CENTURY RAILROAD INVESTMENT PROCESS. CREATE BARGAIN INT/TRADE GAMBLE KNOWL 19 BOSTON. PAGE 74 A1519 — FINAN DIST/IND CAP/ISM ECO/UNDEV

B67
LANDEN R.G.,OMAN SINCE 1856: DISRUPTIVE MODERNIZATION IN A TRADITIONAL ARAB SOCIETY. UK DIST/IND EXTR/IND SECT DIPLOM INT/TRADE...SOC LING CHARTS BIBLIOG 19/20. PAGE 84 A1714 — ISLAM CULTURE ECO/UNDEV NAT/G

S67
CLINGHAM T.A. JR.,"LEGISLATIVE FLOTSAM AND INTERNATIONAL ACTION IN THE 'YARMOUTH CASTLE'S' WAKE." WOR+45 PROB/SOLV CONFER COST HEALTH...POLICY INT/LAW CONGRESS. PAGE 27 A0552 — DIPLOM DIST/IND INT/ORG LAW

S67
COSGROVE C.A.,"AGRICULTURE, FINANCE AND POLITICS IN THE EUROPEAN COMMUNITY." EUR+WWI DIST/IND MARKET INT/ORG VOL/ASSN DELIB/GP TEC/DEV BAL/PWR BARGAIN ECO/TAC RATION CONFER 20 EEC. PAGE 31 A0630 — ECO/DEV DIPLOM AGRI INT/TRADE

S67
OLIVIER G.,"ASPECTS JURIDIQUES DE L'ADOPTION DU TRAITE CECA A LA CRISE CHARBONNIERE (SUITE ET FIN)" LAW DIST/IND PLAN DIPLOM RATION PRICE ADMIN COST DEMAND...POLICY CON/ANAL ECSC TREATY. PAGE 112 A2288 — INT/TRADE INT/ORG EXTR/IND CONSTN

DISTRIBUTIVE SYSTEM....SEE DIST/IND

DISTRICT OF COLUMBIA....SEE WASHING/DC

DISTRICTING...SEE APPORT

DIVORCE....DIVORCE

DIXON/YATE....DIXON-YATES BILL

DOC/ANAL....CONVENTIONAL CONTENT ANALYSIS

DODD S.C. A0767

DODD/TJ....SENATOR THOMAS J. DODD

DOHERTY D.K. A0768

DOLE C.F. A0769

DOMENACH J.M. A0770

DOMIN....DOMINATION THROUGH USE OF ESTABLISHED POWER

B00
DARBY W.E.,INTERNATIONAL TRIBUNALS. WOR-45 NAT/G ECO/TAC DOMIN LEGIT CT/SYS COERCE ORD/FREE PWR SOVEREIGN JURID. PAGE 33 A0681 — INT/ORG ADJUD PEACE INT/LAW

B00
GRIFFIN A.P.C.,LIST OF BOOKS RELATING TO THE THEORY OF COLONIZATION, GOVERNMENT OF DEPENDENCIES, PROTECTORATES, AND RELATED TOPICS. FRANCE GERMANY ITALY SPAIN UK USA-45 WOR-45 ECO/TAC ADMIN CONTROL REGION NAT/LISM ALL/VALS PWR...INT/LAW SOC 16/19. PAGE 56 A1149 — BIBLIOG/A COLONIAL GOV/REL DOMIN

B00
HOLLAND T.E.,STUDIES IN INTERNATIONAL LAW. TURKEY USSR WOR-45 CONSTN NAT/G DIPLOM DOMIN LEGIT COERCE WAR PEACE ORD/FREE PWR SOVEREIGN...JURID CHARTS 20 PARLIAMENT SUEZ TREATY. PAGE 66 A1367 — INT/ORG LAW INT/LAW

B00
MORRIS H.C.,THE HISTORY OF COLONIZATION. WOR+45 WOR-45 ECO/DEV ECO/UNDEV INT/ORG ACT/RES PLAN ECO/TAC LEGIT ROUTINE COERCE ATTIT DRIVE ALL/VALS ...GEOG TREND 19. PAGE 105 A2148 — DOMIN SOVEREIGN COLONIAL

B00
VOLPICELLI Z.,RUSSIA ON THE PACIFIC AND THE SIBERIAN RAILWAY. MOD/EUR ECO/UNDEV INT/ORG FORCES PLAN DOMIN COLONIAL ROUTINE ATTIT ALL/VALS...OBS HIST/WRIT TIME/SEQ TREND CON/ANAL AUD/VIS CHARTS 18/19. PAGE 159 A3248 — NAT/G ACT/RES RUSSIA

B02
SEELEY J.R.,THE EXPANSION OF ENGLAND. MOD/EUR S/ASIA UK CULTURE NAT/G FORCES PLAN DOMIN EDU/PROP COLONIAL ROUTINE ATTIT ALL/VALS SOVEREIGN...CONCPT HIST/WRIT PARLIAMENT 18 CMN/WLTH. PAGE 131 A2679 — INT/ORG ACT/RES CAP/ISM INDIA

B03
GRIFFIN A.P.C.,LISTS PUBLISHED 1902-03: ANGLO-SAXON INTERESTS (PAMPHLET). UK USA-45 ELITES SOCIETY DIPLOM ISOLAT 19/20. PAGE 56 A1152 — BIBLIOG COLONIAL RACE/REL DOMIN

B05
GRIFFIN A.P.C.,LIST OF REFERENCES ON THE US CONSULAR SERVICE (PAMPHLET). FRANCE GERMANY SPAIN UK USA-45 WOR-45 OP/RES DOMIN ADMIN FEEDBACK ROUTINE GOV/REL...DECISION 19. PAGE 56 A1153 — BIBLIOG/A NAT/G DIPLOM CONSULT

B09
FREMANTLE H.E.S.,THE NEW NATION, A SURVEY OF THE CONDITION AND PROSPECTS OF SOUTH AFRICA. SOUTH/AFR CONSTN POL/PAR DIPLOM DOMIN COLONIAL WEALTH...SOC TREND 19. PAGE 49 A0996 — NAT/LISM SOVEREIGN RACE/REL REGION

B14
HARRIS N.D.,INTERVENTION AND COLONIZATION IN AFRICA. BELGIUM FRANCE GERMANY MOD/EUR PORTUGAL UK ECO/UNDEV BAL/PWR DOMIN CONTROL PWR...GEOG 19/20. PAGE 62 A1267 — AFR COLONIAL DIPLOM

N17
BURKE E.,THOUGHTS ON THE PROSPECT OF A REGICIDE PEACE (PAMPHLET). FRANCE UK SECT DOMIN MURDER PEACE ORD/FREE SOVEREIGN POPULISM...POLICY GOV/COMP IDEA/COMP 18 JACOBINISM COEXIST. PAGE 21 A0435 — REV CHIEF NAT/G DIPLOM

B19
DE CALLIERES F.,THE PRACTICE OF DIPLOMACY. MOD/EUR INT/ORG NAT/G DELIB/GP LEGIS TOP/EX DOMIN ATTIT KNOWL LEAGUE/NAT 20. PAGE 34 A0699 — CONSULT ACT/RES DIPLOM INT/LAW

N19
HALPERN M.,THE MORALITY AND POLITICS OF INTERVENTION (PAMPHLET). USA+45 INT/ORG FORCES ECO/TAC MORAL ORD/FREE 20 INTERVENT CHRISTIAN. PAGE 61 A1243 — POLICY DIPLOM SOVEREIGN DOMIN

N19
LISKA G.,THE GREATER MAGHREB: FROM INDEPENDENCE TO UNITY? (PAMPHLET). ALGERIA ISLAM MOROCCO PROB/SOLV BAL/PWR CONFER COLONIAL REPRESENT NAT/LISM 20 TUNIS. PAGE 90 A1835 — ECO/UNDEV REGION DIPLOM DOMIN

B20
BURNS C.D.,INTERNATIONAL POLITICS. WOR-45 CULTURE SOCIETY ECO/UNDEV NAT/G VOL/ASSN DELIB/GP ACT/RES CREATE DOMIN EDU/PROP LEGIT ATTIT DRIVE RIGID/FLEX ALL/VALS...PLURIST PSY CONCPT TREND. PAGE 22 A0442 — INT/ORG PEACE SOVEREIGN

B20
HALDANE R.B.,BEFORE THE WAR. MOD/EUR SOCIETY INT/ORG NAT/G DELIB/GP PLAN DOMIN EDU/PROP LEGIT ADMIN COERCE ATTIT DRIVE MORAL ORD/FREE PWR...SOC CONCPT SELF/OBS RECORD BIOG TIME/SEQ. PAGE 60 A1223 — POLICY DIPLOM UK

B20
WOOLF L.,EMPIRE AND COMMERCE IN AFRICA. EUR+WWI MOD/EUR FINAN INDUS MARKET INT/ORG PLAN COERCE ATTIT DRIVE PWR WEALTH...CONCPT TIME/SEQ TREND CHARTS 20. PAGE 167 A3394 — AFR DOMIN COLONIAL SOVEREIGN

B21
STUART G.H.,FRENCH FOREIGN POLICY. CONSTN INT/ORG NAT/G POL/PAR EX/STRUC FORCES PLAN ECO/TAC DOMIN EDU/PROP ADJUD COERCE ATTIT DRIVE RIGID/FLEX ALL/VALS...POLICY OBS RECORD BIOG TIME/SEQ TREND. PAGE 139 A2852 — MOD/EUR DIPLOM FRANCE

B23
KADEN E.H.,DER POLITISCHE CHARAKTER DER FRANZOSISCHEN KULTURPROPAGANDA AM RHEIN. FRANCE MOD/EUR DOMIN PRESS...GEOG METH/COMP 20. PAGE 75 — EDU/PROP ATTIT DIPLOM

A1544 NAT/G

B28
HUBER G.,DIE FRANZOSISCHE PROPAGANDA IM WELTKRIEG GEGEN DEUTSCHLAND 1914 BIS 1918. FRANCE GERMANY MOD/EUR DIPLOM WAR...EXHIBIT 20 WWI. PAGE 68 A1403 EDU/PROP ATTIT DOMIN PRESS

B28
HURST C.,GREAT BRITAIN AND THE DOMINIONS. EUR+WWI CULTURE ECO/DEV INT/ORG NAT/G DIPLOM ECO/TAC COLONIAL ATTIT PWR SOVEREIGN...TIME/SEQ GEN/LAWS TOT/POP VAL/FREE 20 CMN/WLTH. PAGE 69 A1420 VOL/ASSN DOMIN UK

B28
PLAYNE C.E.,THE PRE-WAR MIND IN BRITAIN. GERMANY MOD/EUR UK STRATA SECT DIPLOM EDU/PROP CROWD SUFF ...POLICY ANARCH PSY SOC IDEA/COMP 20 WWI. PAGE 116 A2388 PRESS WAR DOMIN ATTIT

B28
STUART G.H.,LATIN AMERICA AND THE UNITED STATES. USA-45 ECO/UNDEV INT/ORG NAT/G POL/PAR PLAN DOMIN EDU/PROP COLONIAL REGION COERCE ATTIT ALL/VALS ...POLICY GEOG TREND 19/20. PAGE 139 A2853 L/A+17C DIPLOM

B31
HODGES C.,THE BACKGROUND OF INTERNATIONAL RELATIONS. WOR-45 SOCIETY ECO/DEV ECO/UNDEV INT/ORG DIPLOM DOMIN EDU/PROP LEGIT WAR ATTIT DRIVE PERSON ALL/VALS...CONCPT METH/CNCPT TIME/SEQ CHARTS WORK LEAGUE/NAT 19/20. PAGE 66 A1350 NAT/G BAL/PWR

B32
BRYCE J.,THE HOLY ROMAN EMPIRE. GERMANY ITALY MOD/EUR CULTURE SOCIETY STRUCT INT/ORG NAT/G SECT DIPLOM DOMIN WAR SUPEGO ALL/VALS SOVEREIGN...GEOG SOC TIME/SEQ CHARTS STERTYP. PAGE 20 A0413 CHRIST-17C NAT/LISM

B33
DAHLIN E.,FRENCH AND GERMAN PUBLIC OPINION ON DECLARED WAR AIMS 1914-1918. BELGIUM FRANCE GERMANY NAT/G POL/PAR DIPLOM COERCE REV WAR PEACE 20 WWI WILSON/W. PAGE 33 A0674 ATTIT EDU/PROP DOMIN NAT/COMP

B33
LAUTERPACHT H.,THE FUNCTION OF LAW IN THE INTERNATIONAL COMMUNITY. WOR-45 NAT/G FORCES CREATE DOMIN LEGIT COERCE WAR PEACE ATTIT ORD/FREE PWR SOVEREIGN...JURID CONCPT METH/CNCPT TIME/SEQ GEN/LAWS GEN/METH LEAGUE/NAT TOT/POP VAL/FREE 20. PAGE 85 A1749 INT/ORG LAW INT/LAW

B35
LANGER W.L.,THE DIPLOMACY OF IMPERIALISM 1890-1902. FRANCE GERMANY ITALY UK WOR-45 BAL/PWR INT/TRADE LEGIT ADJUD CONTROL WAR PWR SOVEREIGN...CHARTS BIBLIOG/A 19/20. PAGE 84 A1726 DIPLOM COLONIAL DOMIN

B35
MARRIOTT J.A.,DICTATORSHIP AND DEMOCRACY. GERMANY GREECE UK CHIEF DIPLOM DOMIN LEGIT PEACE ORD/FREE CONSERVE...TREND ROME HITLER/A. PAGE 95 A1946 TOTALISM POPULISM PLURIST NAT/G

B36
HUGENDUBEL P.,DIE KRIEGSMACHE DER FRANZOSISCHEN PRESSE. FRANCE GERMANY MOD/EUR COM/IND NAT/G DIPLOM DOMIN PWR 20. PAGE 69 A1412 PRESS EDU/PROP WAR ATTIT

B36
METZ I.,DIE DEUTSCHE FLOTTE IN DER ENGLISCHEN PRESSE, DER NAVY SCARE VOM WINTER 1904/05. GERMANY UK FORCES DIPLOM WAR 20 NAVY. PAGE 100 A2047 EDU/PROP ATTIT DOMIN PRESS

B36
ROBINSON H.,DEVELOPMENT OF THE BRITISH EMPIRE. WOR-45 CULTURE SOCIETY STRUCT ECO/DEV ECO/UNDEV INT/ORG VOL/ASSN FORCES CREATE PLAN DOMIN EDU/PROP ADMIN COLONIAL PWR WEALTH...POLICY GEOG CHARTS CMN/WLTH 16/20. PAGE 122 A2503 NAT/G HIST/WRIT UK

B37
BLAKE J.W.,EUROPEAN BEGINNINGS IN WEST AFRICA 1454-1578. FRANCE GUINEA PORTUGAL UK PWR WEALTH 16/16 AFRICA/W. PAGE 15 A0305 DIPLOM COLONIAL INT/TRADE DOMIN

B37
KOHN H.,FORCE OR REASON; ISSUES OF THE TWENTIETH CENTURY. WOR+45 NAT/G DIPLOM WAR DRIVE ORD/FREE ALL/IDEOS FASCISM PLURISM...POLICY IDEA/COMP 20. PAGE 81 A1660 COERCE DOMIN RATIONAL COLONIAL

B38
HOBSON J.A.,IMPERIALISM. MOD/EUR UK WOR-45 CULTURE ECO/UNDEV NAT/G VOL/ASSN PLAN EDU/PROP LEGIT REGION COERCE ATTIT PWR...POLICY PLURIST TIME/SEQ GEN/LAWS 19/20. PAGE 66 A1348 DOMIN ECO/TAC BAL/PWR COLONIAL

B39
DULLES J.,WAR, PEACE AND CHANGE. FRANCE ITALY UK USA-45 WOR-45 LAW INT/ORG NAT/G SECT VOL/ASSN FORCES TOP/EX DOMIN ARMS/CONT COERCE ATTIT PERSON RIGID/FLEX MORAL PWR...JURID STERTYP TOT/POP LEAGUE/NAT 20. PAGE 39 A0796 EDU/PROP TOTALISM WAR

B39
FULLER G.H.,A SELECTED LIST OF REFERENCES ON THE EXPANSION OF THE US NAVY, 1933-1939 (PAMPHLET). MOD/EUR USA-45 NAT/G PLAN DIPLOM DOMIN RISK ARMS/CONT EQUILIB PWR 20 NAVY. PAGE 50 A1019 BIBLIOG FORCES WEAPON WAR

B39
LENIN V.I.,IMPERIALISM: THE HIGHEST STAGE OF CAPITALISM. USSR WOR-45 DIST/IND INT/TRADE ATTIT MARXISM SOCISM...CHARTS 20. PAGE 87 A1773 MARXIST CAP/ISM COLONIAL DOMIN

B39
MARRIOTT J.,COMMONWEALTH OR ANARCHY: A SURVEY OF PROJECTS OF PEACE. WOR-45 STRATA DOMIN ATTIT ORD/FREE PWR...TRADIT TIME/SEQ GEN/METH 16/20 CMN/WLTH. PAGE 95 A1945 FUT INT/ORG PEACE

B39
ROBBINS L.,ECONOMIC CAUSES OF WAR. WOR-45 ECO/DEV ECO/UNDEV INT/ORG NAT/G TEC/DEV DIPLOM DOMIN COLONIAL ATTIT DRIVE PWR WEALTH...POLICY CONCPT OBS SAMP TREND CON/ANAL GEN/LAWS MARX/KARL 20. PAGE 122 A2493 COERCE ECO/TAC WAR

B39
ZIMMERN A.,THE LEAGUE OF NATIONS AND THE RULE OF LAW. WOR-45 STRUCT NAT/G DELIB/GP EX/STRUC BAL/PWR DOMIN LEGIT COERCE ORD/FREE PWR...POLICY RECORD LEAGUE/NAT TOT/POP VAL/FREE 20 LEAGUE/NAT. PAGE 170 A3453 INT/ORG LAW DIPLOM

B39
ZIMMERN A.,MODERN POLITICAL DOCTRINE. WOR-45 CULTURE SOCIETY ECO/UNDEV DELIB/GP EX/STRUC CREATE DOMIN COERCE NAT/LISM ATTIT RIGID/FLEX ORD/FREE PWR WEALTH...POLICY CONCPT OBS TIME/SEQ TREND TOT/POP LEAGUE/NAT 20. PAGE 170 A3454 NAT/G ECO/TAC BAL/PWR INT/TRADE

L39
NEARING S.,"A WARLESS WORLD." FUT WOR-45 SOCIETY INT/ORG NAT/G EX/STRUC PLAN DOMIN WAR ATTIT DRIVE PWR...POLICY PSY CONCPT OBS TREND HYPO/EXP MARX/KARL 20 MARX/KARL LENIN/VI. PAGE 108 A2210 COERCE PEACE

B40
FULLER G.H.,A LIST OF BIBLIOGRAPHIES ON PROPAGANDA (PAMPHLET). MOD/EUR USA-45 CONSULT ACT/RES PRESS FEEDBACK TASK WAR ATTIT PWR...CON/ANAL METH/COMP 20. PAGE 50 A1020 BIBLIOG/A EDU/PROP DOMIN DIPLOM

B40
WANDERSCHECK H.,FRANKREICHS PROPAGANDA GEGEN DEUTSCHLAND. FRANCE GERMANY MOD/EUR UK NAT/G DIPLOM WAR 20 JEWS. PAGE 161 A3273 EDU/PROP ATTIT DOMIN PRESS

S40
FLORIN J.,"BOLSHEVIST AND NATIONAL SOCIALIST DOCTRINES OF INTERNATIONAL LAW." EUR+WWI GERMANY USSR R+D INT/ORG NAT/G DIPLOM DOMIN EDU/PROP SOCISM ...CONCPT TIME/SEQ 20. PAGE 47 A0955 LAW ATTIT TOTALISM INT/LAW

B41
BAUMANN G.,GRUNDLAGEN UND PRAXIS DER INTERNATIONALEN PROPAGANDA. FRANCE GERMANY UK CULTURE COM/IND PRESS PWR...PSY METH/COMP 20. PAGE 12 A0236 EDU/PROP DOMIN ATTIT DIPLOM

S41
LASSWELL H.D.,"THE GARRISON STATE" (BMR)" FUT WOR+45 ELITES INTELL FORCES ECO/TAC DOMIN EDU/PROP COERCE INGP/REL 20. PAGE 85 A1739 NAT/G DIPLOM PWR CIVMIL/REL

S41
WRIGHT Q.,"FUNDAMENTAL PROBLEMS OF INTERNATIONAL ORGANIZATION." UNIV WOR-45 STRUCT FORCES ACT/RES CREATE DOMIN EDU/PROP LEGIT REGION NAT/LISM ORD/FREE PWR RESPECT SOVEREIGN...JURID SOC CONCPT METH/CNCPT TIME/SEQ 20. PAGE 167 A3405 INT/ORG ATTIT PEACE

B42
BORNSTEIN J.,ACTION AGAINST THE ENEMY'S MIND. EUR+WWI GERMANY USA-45 DIPLOM DOMIN PRESS LEAD GP/REL DISCRIM PERCEPT FASCISM MARXISM 20 JEWS NAZI ANTI/SEMIT. PAGE 17 A0343 EDU/PROP PSY WAR CONTROL

B42
CROWE S.E.,THE BERLIN WEST AFRICA CONFERENCE, 1884-85. GERMANY ELITES MARKET INT/ORG DELIB/GP FORCES PROB/SOLV BAL/PWR CAP/ISM DOMIN COLONIAL ...INT/LAW 19. PAGE 33 A0664 AFR CONFER INT/TRADE DIPLOM

B42
JACKSON M.V.,EUROPEAN POWERS AND SOUTH-EAST AFRICA: A STUDY OF INTERNATIONAL RELATIONS ON SOUTH-EAST COAST OF AFRICA, 1796-1856. AFR FRANCE PORTUGAL SOUTH/AFR UK USA-45 FORCES INT/TRADE PWR...CHARTS BIBLIOG 18/19 TREATY. PAGE 72 A1477 DOMIN POLICY ORD/FREE DIPLOM

B43
LIPPMANN W.,US FOREIGN POLICY: SHIELD OF THE REPUBLIC. USA-45 WOR-45 CULTURE INT/ORG POL/PAR CREATE BAL/PWR DOMIN EDU/PROP WAR ORD/FREE PWR ...PLURIST CONCPT TREND CON/ANAL 20. PAGE 89 A1827 NAT/G DIPLOM PEACE

B43
SERENI A.P.,THE ITALIAN CONCEPTION OF INTERNATIONAL LAW. EUR+WWI MOD/EUR INT/ORG NAT/G DOMIN COERCE ORD/FREE FASCISM...OBS/ENVIR TREND 20. PAGE 131 A2686 LAW TIME/SEQ INT/LAW ITALY

B43
US DEPARTMENT OF STATE,NATIONAL SOCIALISM; BASIC PRINCIPLES, THEIR APPLICATION BY THE NAZI PARTY'S FOREIGN ORGANIZATION... GERMANY WOR-45 ECO/DEV LOC/G POL/PAR FORCES DIPLOM DOMIN COLONIAL ARMS/CONT COERCE NAT/LISM PWR 20 NAZI. PAGE 151 FASCISM SOCISM NAT/G TOTALISM

B44
BRIERLY J.L.,THE OUTLOOK FOR INTERNATIONAL LAW. FUT WOR-45 CONSTN NAT/G VOL/ASSN FORCES ECO/TAC DOMIN LEGIT ADJUD ROUTINE PEACE ORD/FREE...INT/LAW JURID METH LEAGUE/NAT 20. PAGE 18 A0376
INT/ORG
LAW

B44
DAVIS H.E.,PIONEERS IN WORLD ORDER. WOR-45 CONSTN ECO/TAC DOMIN EDU/PROP LEGIT ADJUD ADMIN ARMS/CONT CHOOSE KNOWL ORD/FREE...POLICY JURID SOC STAT OBS CENSUS TIME/SEQ ANTHOL LEAGUE/NAT 20. PAGE 34 A0691
INT/ORG
ROUTINE

B44
FULLER G.H.,MILITARY GOVERNMENT: A LIST OF REFERENCES (A PAMPHLET). ITALY UK USA-45 WOR-45 LAW FORCES DOMIN ADMIN ARMS/CONT ORD/FREE PWR ...DECISION 20 CHINJAP. PAGE 50 A1023
BIBLIOG
DIPLOM
CIVMIL/REL
SOVEREIGN

B44
RAGATZ L.J.,LITERATURE OF EUROPEAN IMPERIALISM. ECO/TAC INT/TRADE DOMIN GOV/REL DEMAND NAT/LISM PWR WEALTH 19/20. PAGE 119 A2432
BIBLIOG
COLONIAL
INT/ORG
ECO/UNDEV

B45
CONOVER H.F.,ITALY: ECONOMICS, POLITICS AND MILITARY AFFAIRS, 1940-1945. ITALY ELITES NAT/G POL/PAR EX/STRUC TOP/EX DIPLOM DOMIN CONTROL COERCE WAR CIVMIL/REL EFFICIENCY 20. PAGE 29 A0599
BIBLIOG
TOTALISM
FORCES

B45
ELTON G.E.,IMPERIAL COMMONWEALTH. INDIA UK DIPLOM DOMIN WAR NAT/LISM SOVEREIGN...TRADIT CHARTS T 15/20 CMN/WLTH AUSTRAL PRE/US/AM. PAGE 41 A0844
REGION
CONCPT
COLONIAL

B45
HILL N.,CLAIMS TO TERRITORY IN INTERNATIONAL LAW AND RELATIONS. WOR-45 NAT/G DOMIN EDU/PROP LEGIT REGION ROUTINE ORD/FREE PWR WEALTH...GEOG INT/LAW JURID 20. PAGE 65 A1332
INT/ORG
ADJUD
SOVEREIGN

B45
NELSON M.F.,KOREA AND THE OLD ORDERS IN EASTERN ASIA. ASIA FRANCE KOREA RUSSIA DELIB/GP INT/TRADE DOMIN CONTROL WAR ORD/FREE...POLICY BIBLIOG. PAGE 108 A2218
DIPLOM
BAL/PWR
ATTIT
CONSERVE

B45
UNCIO CONFERENCE LIBRARY,SHORT TITLE CLASSIFIED CATALOG. WOR-45 DOMIN COLONIAL WAR...SOC/WK 20 LEAGUE/NAT UN. PAGE 147 A3006
BIBLIOG
DIPLOM
INT/ORG
INT/LAW

C45
NELSON M.F.,"KOREA AND THE OLD ORDERS IN EASTERN ASIA." KOREA WOR-45 DELIB/GP INT/TRADE DOMIN CONTROL WAR ATTIT ORD/FREE CONSERVE...POLICY TREATY. PAGE 108 A2217
BIBLIOG
DIPLOM
BAL/PWR
ASIA

B46
BLUM L.,FOR ALL MANKIND (TRANS. BY W. PICKLES). FRANCE GERMANY USSR LAW SOCIETY STRUCT POL/PAR WORKER DIPLOM DOMIN CHOOSE ORD/FREE FASCISM 20. PAGE 16 A0323
POPULISM
SOCIALIST
NAT/G
WAR

B47
GORDON D.L.,THE HIDDEN WEAPON: THE STORY OF ECONOMIC WARFARE. EUR+WWI USA-45 LAW FINAN INDUS NAT/G CONSULT FORCES PLAN DOMIN PWR WEALTH ...INT/LAW CONCPT OBS TOT/POP NAZI 20. PAGE 54 A1112
INT/ORG
ECO/TAC
INT/TRADE
WAR

N47
FOX W.T.R.,UNITED STATES POLICY IN A TWO POWER WORLD. COM USA+45 USSR FORCES DOMIN AGREE NEUTRAL NUC/PWR ORD/FREE SOVEREIGN 20 COLD/WAR TREATY EUROPE/W INTERVENT. PAGE 48 A0972
DIPLOM
FOR/AID
POLICY

B48
CLYDE P.H.,THE FAR EAST: A HISTORY OF THE IMPACT OF THE WEST ON EASTERN ASIA. CHINA/COM CULTURE INT/TRADE DOMIN COLONIAL WAR PWR...CHARTS BIBLIOG 19/20 CHINJAP. PAGE 27 A0554
DIPLOM
ASIA

B48
LINEBARGER P.,PSYCHOLOGICAL WARFARE. NAT/G PLAN DIPLOM DOMIN ATTIT...POLICY CONCPT EXHIBIT 20 WWI. PAGE 89 A1824
EDU/PROP
PSY
WAR
COM/IND

B48
NAMIER L.B.,DIPLOMATIC PRELUDE 1938-1939. CZECHOSLVK EUR+WWI GERMANY POLAND UK FORCES DOMIN PWR 20 HITLER/A. PAGE 107 A2193
WAR
TOTALISM
DIPLOM

B48
PELCOVITS N.A.,OLD CHINA HANDS AND THE FOREIGN OFFICE. ASIA BURMA UK ECO/UNDEV NAT/G ECO/TAC FOR/AID TARIFFS DOMIN COLONIAL GOV/REL SOVEREIGN 19 HONG/KONG TREATY. PAGE 114 A2348
INT/TRADE
ATTIT
DIPLOM

B49
BOZZA T.,SCRITTORI POLITICI ITALIANI DAL 1550 AL 1650. CHRIST-17C ITALY DIPLOM DOMIN 16/17. PAGE 18 A0365
BIBLIOG/A
NAT/G
CONCPT
WRITING

B50
BARGHOORN F.C.,THE SOVIET IMAGE OF THE UNITED STATES: A STUDY IN DISTORTION. COM USSR DOMIN WAR NAT/LISM TOTALISM SOCISM...PSY 20. PAGE 11 A0220
PROB/SOLV
EDU/PROP
DIPLOM
ATTIT

B50
CHUKWUEMEKA N.,AFRICAN DEPENDENCIES: A CHALLENGE TO WESTERN DEMOCRACY. NIGERIA ECO/DEV INDUS FOR/AID INT/TRADE DOMIN 20. PAGE 26 A0536
DIPLOM
ECO/UNDEV
COLONIAL
AFR

B50
GATZKE H.W.,GERMANY'S DRIVE TO THE WEST. BELGIUM GERMANY MOD/EUR AGRI INDUS POL/PAR FORCES DOMIN AGREE CONTROL REGION COERCE 20 TREATY WWI. PAGE 51 A1053
WAR
POLICY
NAT/G
DIPLOM

B50
GLEASON J.H.,THE GENESIS OF RUSSOPHOBIA IN GREAT BRITAIN: A STUDY OF THE INTERACTION OF POLICY AND OPINION. ASIA RUSSIA UK NAT/G AGREE CONTROL REV WAR LOVE PWR TREATY 19. PAGE 53 A1080
DIPLOM
POLICY
DOMIN
COLONIAL

B50
MOCKFORD J.,SOUTH-WEST AFRICA AND THE INTERNATIONAL COURT (PAMPHLET). AFR GERMANY SOUTH/AFR UK ECO/UNDEV DIPLOM CONTROL DISCRIM...DECISION JURID 20 AFRICA/SW. PAGE 102 A2094
COLONIAL
SOVEREIGN
INT/LAW
DOMIN

B50
PERHAM M.,COLONIAL GOVERNMENT: ANNOTATED READING LIST ON BRITISH COLONIAL GOVERNMENT. UK WOR+45 WOR-45 ECO/UNDEV INT/ORG LEGIS FOR/AID INT/TRADE DOMIN ADMIN REV 20. PAGE 115 A2356
BIBLIOG/A
COLONIAL
GOV/REL
NAT/G

L51
ULAM A.B.,"THE COMIMFORM AND THE PEOPLE'S DEMOCRACIES." EUR+WWI WOR+45 STRUCT NAT/G POL/PAR TOP/EX ACT/RES PLAN ECO/TAC DOMIN ATTIT ALL/VALS ...HIST/WRIT TIME/SEQ 20 COMINFORM. PAGE 146 A2992
COM
INT/ORG
USSR
TOTALISM

C51
LEONARD L.L.,"INTERNATIONAL ORGANIZATION (1ST ED.)" WOR+45 FINAN DELIB/GP ECO/TAC GIVE DOMIN SANCTION PEACE BIO/SOC ORD/FREE...INT/LAW 20 UN LEAGUE/NAT. PAGE 87 A1779
BIBLIOG
POLICY
DIPLOM
INT/ORG

B52
SHULIM J.I.,THE OLD DOMINION AND NAPOLEON BONAPARTE. POL/PAR DOMIN PRESS REV WAR 18/19 VIRGINIA. PAGE 132 A2710
ATTIT
PROVS
EDU/PROP
DIPLOM

B52
SKALWEIT S.,FRANKREICH UND FRIEDRICH DER GROSSE. FRANCE GERMANY PRUSSIA NAT/G DOMIN WAR 18 FREDERICK. PAGE 134 A2737
ATTIT
EDU/PROP
DIPLOM
SOC

S52
SCHUMAN F.,"INTERNATIONAL IDEALS AND THE NATIONAL INTEREST." WOR+45 WOR-45 INT/ORG VOL/ASSN DELIB/GP CREATE BAL/PWR DOMIN PEACE PERSON MORAL PWR SOVEREIGN...POLICY GEN/LAWS TOT/POP LEAGUE/NAT 20. PAGE 129 A2648
ATTIT
CONCPT

B53
BARBER H.W.,FOREIGN POLICIES OF THE UNITED STATES. USA+45 USA-45 WOR+45 INT/ORG NAT/G EX/STRUC ECO/TAC DOMIN EDU/PROP LEGIT COERCE KNOWL PWR COLD/WAR COLD/WAR 20. PAGE 11 A0219
CONCPT
DIPLOM

B53
MCNEILL W.H.,AMERICA, BRITAIN, AND RUSSIA; THEIR COOPERATION AND CONFLICT. UK USA-45 USSR ECO/DEV ECO/UNDEV FORCES PLAN ADMIN AGREE PERS/REL ...DECISION 20 TREATY. PAGE 98 A2021
WAR
DIPLOM
DOMIN

B53
SHIRATO I.,JAPANESE SOURCES ON THE HISTORY OF THE CHINESE COMMUNIST MOVEMENT (PAMPHLET). CHINA/COM USSR CONSTRUC NAT/G POL/PAR FORCES DIPLOM DOMIN EDU/PROP CONTROL WAR TOTALISM SOCISM 20. PAGE 132 A2702
BIBLIOG/A
MARXISM
ECO/UNDEV

B53
SQUIRES J.D.,BRITISH PROPAGANDA AT HOME AND IN THE UNITED STATES FROM 1914 TO 1917. UK NAT/G PROB/SOLV DOMIN PRESS EFFICIENCY...PSY PREDICT 20 WWI INTERVENT PSY/WAR. PAGE 136 A2794
EDU/PROP
CONTROL
WAR
DIPLOM

S53
BOULDING K.E.,"ECONOMIC ISSUES IN INTERNATIONAL CONFLICT." WOR+45 ECO/DEV NAT/G TOP/EX DIPLOM ECO/TAC DOMIN ATTIT WEALTH...MAJORIT OBS/ENVIR TREND GEN/LAWS COLD/WAR TOT/POP 20. PAGE 17 A0345
PWR
FOR/AID

S53
LINCOLN G.,"FACTORS DETERMINING ARMS AID." COM FUT USA+45 USSR WOR+45 ECO/DEV NAT/G CONSULT PLAN TEC/DEV DIPLOM DOMIN EDU/PROP PERCEPT PWR ...DECISION CONCPT TREND MARX/KARL 20. PAGE 89 A1819
FORCES
POLICY
BAL/PWR
FOR/AID

C53
DEUTSCH K.W.,"NATIONALISM AND SOCIAL COMMUNICATION: AN INQUIRY INTO THE FOUNDATIONS OF NATIONALITY." CULTURE STRUCT DIPLOM DOMIN ATTIT ORD/FREE SOVEREIGN...SOC STAT CHARTS IDEA/COMP BIBLIOG. PAGE 36 A0735
NAT/LISM
CONCPT
PERCEPT
STRATA

B54
ARON R.,CENTURY OF TOTAL WAR. FUT WOR+45 WOR-45 SOCIETY INT/ORG NAT/G FORCES TOP/EX CREATE BAL/PWR DOMIN EDU/PROP COERCE DETER PEACE TOTALISM PWR ...TIME/SEQ TREND COLD/WAR TOT/POP VAL/FREE LEAGUE/NAT 20. PAGE 9 A0179
ATTIT
WAR

B54
BUTOW R.J.C.,JAPAN'S DECISION TO SURRENDER. USA-45 USSR CHIEF FORCES DOMIN NUC/PWR...BIBLIOG 20 TREATY CHINJAP. PAGE 22 A0453
ELITES DIPLOM WAR PEACE

B54
MITCHELL P.,AFRICAN AFTERTHOUGHTS. UGANDA CONSTN NAT/G ADJUD COERCE WAR 20 WWI MAU/MAU. PAGE 102 A2090
BIOG CHIEF COLONIAL DOMIN

B54
NORTHROP F.S.C.,EUROPEAN UNION AND UNITED STATES FOREIGN POLICY: A STUDY IN SOCIOLOGICAL JURISPRUDENCE. EUR+WWI MOD/EUR USA+45 SOCIETY STRUCT NAT/G CREATE ECO/TAC DOMIN EDU/PROP REGION ATTIT RIGID/FLEX HEALTH ORD/FREE WEALTH ...METH/CNCPT TIME/SEQ TREND. PAGE 110 A2256
INT/ORG SOC DIPLOM

B54
TAYLOR A.J.P.,THE STRUGGLE FOR MASTERY IN EUROPE 1848-1918. MOD/EUR VOL/ASSN FORCES BAL/PWR DOMIN CONTROL PEACE MORAL 19/20 TREATY EUROPE WWI. PAGE 142 A2897
DIPLOM WAR PWR

L54
CHARLESWORTH J.C.,"AMERICA AND A NEW ASIA." ASIA INDIA ISLAM S/ASIA USA+45 USA-45 ECO/UNDEV NAT/G POL/PAR FORCES FOR/AID DOMIN EDU/PROP COERCE DRIVE ALL/VALS MARXISM SOCISM TOT/POP 20. PAGE 26 A0522
ECO/TAC DIPLOM NAT/LISM

B55
CHOWDHURI R.N.,INTERNATIONAL MANDATES AND TRUSTEESHIP SYSTEMS. WOR+45 STRUCT ECO/UNDEV INT/ORG LEGIS DOMIN EDU/PROP LEGIT ADJUD EXEC PWR ...CONCPT TIME/SEQ UN 20. PAGE 26 A0534
DELIB/GP PLAN SOVEREIGN

B55
COMM. STUDY ORGAN. PEACE,REPORTS. WOR-45 ECO/DEV ECO/UNDEV VOL/ASSN CONSULT FORCES PLAN TEC/DEV DOMIN EDU/PROP NUC/PWR ATTIT PWR WEALTH...JURID STERTYP FAO ILO 20 UN. PAGE 28 A0579
WOR+45 INT/ORG ARMS/CONT

B55
JOY C.T.,HOW COMMUNISTS NEGOTIATE. COM USA+45 CONSTN CULTURE ECO/UNDEV NAT/G CONSULT DELIB/GP FORCES PLAN ECO/TAC DOMIN EDU/PROP LEGIT EXEC ROUTINE COERCE WAR CHOOSE PEACE ATTIT RIGID/FLEX ORD/FREE PWR...POLICY 20. PAGE 75 A1539
ASIA INT/ORG DIPLOM

B55
SNYDER R.C.,AMERICAN FOREIGN POLICY. USA+45 USA-45 WOR+45 WOR-45 CONSTN INT/ORG POL/PAR VOL/ASSN DELIB/GP LEGIS CREATE DOMIN EDU/PROP EXEC COERCE ATTIT DRIVE ORD/FREE PWR...MGT OBS RECORD TIME/SEQ TREND. PAGE 134 A2752
NAT/G DIPLOM

B56
CHANG C.J.,THE MINORITY GROUPS OF YUNN AN AND CHINESE POLITICAL EXPANSION INTO SOUTHEAST ASIA (DOCTORAL THESIS). ASIA CHINA/COM S/ASIA FORCES TEC/DEV DIPLOM EDU/PROP...GEOG BIBLIOG 20. PAGE 26 A0520
GP/REL REGION DOMIN MARXISM

B56
GILBERT R.,COMPETITIVE COEXISTENCE: THE NEW SOVIET CHALLENGE. WORKER DIPLOM WAR ORD/FREE 20 COLD/WAR. PAGE 52 A1071
NUC/PWR DOMIN MARXISM PEACE

B56
GREECE PRESBEIA U.S.,BRITISH OPINION ON CYPRUS. CYPRUS UK FORCES DIPLOM INT/TRADE DOMIN GOV/REL ORD/FREE SOVEREIGN...POLICY 20. PAGE 55 A1137
ATTIT COLONIAL LEGIS PRESS

B56
HAAS E.B.,DYNAMICS OF INTERNATIONAL RELATIONS. WOR-45 ELITES INT/ORG VOL/ASSN EX/STRUC FORCES ECO/TAC DOMIN LEGIT COERCE ATTIT PERSON PWR ...CONCPT TIME/SEQ CHARTS COLD/WAR 20. PAGE 58 A1202
WOR+45 NAT/G DIPLOM

B56
KNORR K.E.,RUBLE DIPLOMACY: CHALLENGE TO AMERICAN FOREIGN AID(PAMPHLET). CHINA/COM USA+45 USSR PLAN TEC/DEV CAP/ISM INT/TRADE DOMIN EDU/PROP CONTROL LEAD 20 COLD/WAR. PAGE 81 A1654
ECO/UNDEV COM DIPLOM FOR/AID

B57
ARON R.,FRANCE DEFEATS EDC. EUR+WWI GERMANY LEGIS DIPLOM DOMIN EDU/PROP ADMIN...HIST/WRIT 20. PAGE 9 A0180
INT/ORG FORCES DETER FRANCE

B57
BERLE A.A.,TIDES OF CRISIS: A PRIMER OF FOREIGN RELATIONS. USA+45 WOR+45 DOMIN NUC/PWR NAT/LISM PWR ...CONCPT STERTYP GEN/LAWS 20 UN. PAGE 14 A0276
INT/ORG TREND PEACE

B57
BROMBERGER M.,LES SECRETS DE L'EXPEDITION D'EGYPTE. FRANCE ISLAM UAR UK USA+45 USSR WOR+45 INT/ORG NAT/G FORCES BAL/PWR ECO/TAC DOMIN WAR NAT/LISM ATTIT PWR SOVEREIGN...MAJORIT TIME/SEQ CHARTS SUEZ COLD/WAR 20. PAGE 19 A0387
COERCE DIPLOM

B57
BUCK P.W.,CONTOL OF FOREIGN RELATIONS IN MODERN NATIONS. FRANCE L/A+17C NETHERLAND USSR WOR+45 INT/ORG TOP/EX BAL/PWR DOMIN EDU/PROP COERCE PEACE ATTIT...CONCPT TREND 20 CMN/WLTH. PAGE 21 A0427
NAT/G PWR DIPLOM

B57
BURNS A.,IN DEFENCE OF COLONIES; BRITISH COLONIAL TERRITORIES IN INTERNATIONAL AFFAIRS. UK ECO/UNDEV PLAN DOMIN SOVEREIGN...MAJORIT 18/20 CMN/WLTH INTERVENT. PAGE 22 A0439
COLONIAL POLICY ATTIT DIPLOM

B57
DEUTSCH K.W.,POLITICAL COMMUNITY AND THE NORTH ATLANTIC AREA: INTERNATIONAL ORGANIZATION IN THE LIGHT OF HISTORICAL EXPERIENCE. MOD/EUR USA+45 USA-45 SOCIETY FORCES TOP/EX CREATE PLAN DIPLOM DOMIN EDU/PROP LEGIT ATTIT ORD/FREE PWR...SAMP/SIZ TIME/SEQ CHARTS TOT/POP. PAGE 36 A0736
EUR+WWI INT/ORG PEACE REGION

B57
KENNAN G.F.,RUSSIA, THE ATOM AND THE WEST. COM EUR+WWI FUT WOR+45 SOCIETY ECO/DEV FORCES DIPLOM ECO/TAC DOMIN EDU/PROP COERCE NUC/PWR ATTIT DRIVE ORD/FREE PWR...POLICY OBS TIME/SEQ TREND COLD/WAR NATO 20. PAGE 77 A1574
NAT/G INT/ORG USSR

B57
NEUMANN F.,THE DEMOCRATIC AND THE AUTHORITARIAN STATE: ESSAYS IN POLITICAL AND LEGAL THEORY. USA+45 USA-45 CONTROL REV GOV/REL PEACE ALL/IDEOS ...INT/LAW CONCPT GEN/LAWS BIBLIOG 20. PAGE 108 A2221
DOMIN NAT/G ORD/FREE POLICY

B57
PETERSON H.C.,OPPONENTS OF WAR 1917-1918. USA-45 POL/PAR DOMIN ORD/FREE PWR PACIFISM SOCISM 20 IWW CONSCN/OBJ. PAGE 115 A2368
WAR PEACE ATTIT EDU/PROP

B57
ROSENNE S.,THE INTERNATIONAL COURT OF JUSTICE. WOR+45 LAW DOMIN LEGIT PEACE PWR SOVEREIGN...JURID CONCPT RECORD TIME/SEQ CON/ANAL CHARTS UN TOT/POP VAL/FREE LEAGUE/NAT 20 ICJ. PAGE 124 A2537
INT/ORG CT/SYS INT/LAW

B57
TOMASIC D.A.,NATIONAL COMMUNISM AND SOVIET STRATEGY. UK USSR YUGOSLAVIA NAT/G POL/PAR CHIEF CREATE DOMIN REV WAR PWR...BIOG TREND 20 TITO/MARSH STALIN/J. PAGE 144 A2948
COM NAT/LISM MARXISM DIPLOM

B57
WASSENBERGH H.A.,POST-WAR INTERNATIONAL CIVIL AVIATION POLICY AND THE LAW OF THE AIR. WOR+45 AIR INT/ORG DOMIN LEGIT PEACE ORD/FREE...POLICY JURID NEW/IDEA OBS TIME/SEQ TREND CHARTS 20 TREATY. PAGE 162 A3290
COM/IND NAT/G INT/LAW

L57
HAAS E.B.,"REGIONAL INTEGRATION AND NATIONAL POLICY." WOR+45 VOL/ASSN DELIB/GP EX/STRUC ECO/TAC DOMIN EDU/PROP LEGIT COERCE ATTIT PERCEPT KNOWL ...TIME/SEQ COLD/WAR 20 UN. PAGE 59 A1203
INT/ORG ORD/FREE REGION

S57
ELDER R.E.,"THE PUBLIC STUDIES DIVISION OF THE DEPARTMENT OF STATE: PUBLIC OPINION ANALYSTS IN THE FORMULATION AND CONDUCT OF." INT/ORG CONSULT DOMIN EDU/PROP ADMIN ATTIT PWR...CONCPT OBS TIME/SEQ VAL/FREE 20. PAGE 41 A0836
USA+45 NAT/G DIPLOM

S57
WRIGHT Q.,"THE VALUE OF CONFLICT RESOLUTION OF A GENERAL DISCIPLINE OF INTERNATIONAL RELATIONS." WOR+45 SOCIETY INT/ORG NAT/G FORCES TOP/EX PLAN TEC/DEV ECO/TAC DOMIN LEGIT COERCE ATTIT PWR ...GEN/METH COLD/WAR VAL/FREE. PAGE 168 A3412
ORD/FREE SOC DIPLOM

B58
CAMPBELL J.C.,DEFENSE OF THE MIDDLE EAST: PROBLEMS OF AMERICAN POLICY. ISLAM USA+45 INT/ORG NAT/G EX/STRUC FORCES ECO/TAC DOMIN EDU/PROP LEGIT REGION COERCE...METH/CNCPT COLD/WAR TOT/POP 20. PAGE 23 A0474
TOP/EX ORD/FREE DIPLOM

B58
GARTHOFF R.L.,SOVIET STRATEGY IN THE NUCLEAR AGE. FUT USSR R+D INT/ORG NAT/G ACT/RES TEC/DEV DOMIN DETER WAR ATTIT PWR...RELATIV METH/CNCPT SELF/OBS TREND CON/ANAL STERTYP GEN/LAWS 20. PAGE 51 A1052
COM FORCES BAL/PWR NUC/PWR

B58
MARTIN L.J.,INTERNATIONAL PROPAGANDA: ITS LEGAL AND DIPLOMATIC CONTROL. UK USA+45 USSR CONSULT DELIB/GP DOMIN CONTROL 20. PAGE 95 A1951
EDU/PROP DIPLOM INT/LAW ATTIT

B58
ORGANSKI A.F.K.,WORLD POLITICS. FUT WOR+45 SOCIETY STRUCT NAT/G BAL/PWR ECO/TAC DOMIN NAT/LISM ATTIT KNOWL ORD/FREE PWR...CONCPT METH/CNCPT TREND STERTYP GEN/LAWS TOT/POP 20. PAGE 112 A2297
INT/ORG DIPLOM

B58
RIGGS R.,POLITICS IN THE UNITED NATIONS: A STUDY OF UNITED STATES INFLUENCE IN THE GENERAL ASSEMBLY. USA+45 WOR+45 LEGIS TOP/EX CREATE BAL/PWR DIPLOM DOMIN EDU/PROP COLONIAL ROUTINE ATTIT RIGID/FLEX PWR...CONCPT OBS HIST/WRIT CHARTS STERTYP GEN/LAWS UN COLD/WAR 20. PAGE 121 A2480
INT/ORG

B58
RUSSELL R.B.,A HISTORY OF THE UNITED NATIONS CHARTER: THE ROLE OF THE UNITED STATES. SOCIETY NAT/G CONSULT DOMIN LEGIT ATTIT ORD/FREE PWR ...POLICY JURID CONCPT UN LEAGUE/NAT. PAGE 126 A2575
USA-45 INT/ORG CONSTN

B58
SCHUMAN F.,INTERNATIONAL POLITICS. WOR+45 WOR-45 INTELL NAT/G FORCES DOMIN LEGIT COERCE NUC/PWR ATTIT DISPL ORD/FREE PWR SOVEREIGN...POLICY CONCPT GEN/LAWS SUEZ 20. PAGE 129 A2650
FUT INT/ORG NAT/LISM DIPLOM

B58
TILLION G.,ALGERIA: THE REALITIES. ALGERIA FRANCE ISLAM CULTURE STRATA PROB/SOLV DOMIN REV NAT/LISM WEALTH MARXISM...GEOG 20. PAGE 144 A2940
ECO/UNDEV SOC COLONIAL DIPLOM

S58
BLAISDELL D.C.,"PRESSURE GROUPS, FOREIGN POLICIES, AND INTERNATIONAL POLITICS." USA+45 WOR+45 INT/ORG PLAN DOMIN EDU/PROP LEGIT ADMIN ROUTINE CHOOSE ...DECISION MGT METH/CNCPT CON/ANAL 20. PAGE 15 A0303
PROF/ORG PWR

S58
DAVENPORT J.,"ARMS AND THE WELFARE STATE." INTELL STRUCT FORCES CREATE ECO/TAC FOR/AID DOMIN LEGIT ADMIN WAR ORD/FREE PWR...POLICY SOC CONCPT MYTH OBS TREND COLD/WAR TOT/POP 20. PAGE 34 A0685
USA+45 NAT/G USSR

S58
THOMPSON K.W.,"NATIONAL SECURITY IN A NUCLEAR AGE." USA+45 WOR+45 SOCIETY INT/ORG NAT/G TOP/EX DIPLOM DOMIN EDU/PROP LEGIT ARMS/CONT COERCE ORD/FREE ...TREND STERTYP TOT/POP VAL/FREE COLD/WAR 20. PAGE 143 A2929
FORCES PWR BAL/PWR

C58
BUTTINGER J.,"THE SMALLER DRAGON; A POLITICAL HISTORY OF VIETNAM." VIETNAM SECT DIPLOM CIVMIL/REL ISOLAT NAT/LISM...BIBLIOG/A 3/20. PAGE 22 A0455
COLONIAL DOMIN SOVEREIGN REV

C58
CARTER G.M.,"THE POLITICS OF INEQUALITY: SOUTH AFRICA SINCE 1948." SOUTH/AFR CONSTN DIPLOM EDU/PROP REPRESENT DISCRIM ATTIT...POLICY PREDICT CHARTS BIBLIOG 20. PAGE 25 A0504
RACE/REL POL/PAR CHOOSE DOMIN

B59
ARON R.,IMPERIALISM AND COLONIALISM (PAMPHLET). WOR+45 WOR-45 ECO/TAC CONTROL REV ORD/FREE 19/20. PAGE 9 A0183
COLONIAL DOMIN ECO/UNDEV DIPLOM

B59
COMM. STUDY ORGAN. PEACE,ORGANIZING PEACE IN THE NUCLEAR AGE. FUT CONSULT DELIB/GP DOMIN ADJUD ROUTINE COERCE ORD/FREE...TECHNIC INT/LAW JURID NEW/IDEA UN COLD/WAR 20. PAGE 29 A0581
INT/ORG ACT/RES NUC/PWR

B59
DEHIO L.,GERMANY AND WORLD POLITICS IN THE TWENTIETH CENTURY. EUR+WWI FRANCE GERMANY MOD/EUR UK USSR NAT/G CHIEF BAL/PWR DOMIN COLONIAL CONTROL LEAD...IDEA/COMP 20 VERSAILLES. PAGE 36 A0724
DIPLOM WAR NAT/LISM SOVEREIGN

B59
FOX W.T.R.,THEORETICAL ASPECTS OF INTERNATIONAL RELATIONS. WOR+45 INT/ORG NAT/G POL/PAR CONSULT PLAN ECO/TAC DOMIN EDU/PROP LEGIT EXEC COERCE PWR WEALTH...RELATIV CONCPT 20. PAGE 48 A0975
DELIB/GP ANTHOL

B59
GORDENKER L.,THE UNITED NATIONS AND THE PEACEFUL UNIFICATION OF KOREA. ASIA LAW LOC/G CONSULT ACT/RES DIPLOM DOMIN LEGIT ADJUD ADMIN ORD/FREE SOVEREIGN...INT GEN/METH UN COLD/WAR 20. PAGE 54 A1109
DELIB/GP KOREA INT/ORG

B59
JACKSON B.W.,FIVE IDEAS THAT CHANGE THE WORLD. FUT WOR+45 WOR-45 ECO/UNDEV INDUS DIPLOM DOMIN CONTROL ...IDEA/COMP 20. PAGE 72 A1473
MARXISM NAT/LISM COLONIAL ECO/TAC

B59
JONES A.C.,NEW FABIAN COLONIAL ESSAYS. UK SOCIETY POL/PAR EDU/PROP ADMIN ORD/FREE SOVEREIGN SOCISM ...ANTHOL 20 CMN/WLTH LABOR/PAR. PAGE 75 A1530
COLONIAL INT/ORG INGP/REL DOMIN

B59
JOSEPH F.M.,AS OTHERS SEE US: THE UNITED STATES THROUGH FOREIGN EYES. AFR EUR+WWI ISLAM L/A+17C S/ASIA USA+45 CULTURE SOCIETY ECO/DEV ECO/UNDEV INT/ORG NAT/G DIPLOM ECO/TAC REV ATTIT RIGID/FLEX HEALTH ORD/FREE WEALTH 20. PAGE 75 A1537
RESPECT DOMIN NAT/LISM SOVEREIGN

B59
KIRCHHEIMER O.,GEGENWARTSPROBLEME DER ASYLGEWAHRUNG. DOMIN GP/REL ATTIT...NAT/COMP 20. PAGE 79 A1630
DIPLOM INT/LAW JURID ORD/FREE

B59
PAGAN B.,HISTORIA DE LOS PARTIDOS POLITICOS PUERTORRIQUENOS 1898-1956. PUERT/RICO PROVS DIPLOM DOMIN EDU/PROP PARTIC 20. PAGE 113 A2316
POL/PAR CHOOSE COLONIAL PWR

B59
RICE E.A.,THE DIPLOMATIC RELATIONS BETWEEN THE UNITED STATES AND MEXICO 1925-1929. USA-45 NAT/G DOMIN PEACE ORD/FREE CATHISM 20 MEXIC/AMER. PAGE 121 A2472
DIPLOM SECT POLICY

S59
CARLSTON K.S.,"NATIONALIZATION: AN ANALYTIC APPROACH." WOR+45 INT/ORG ECO/TAC DOMIN LEGIT ADJUD COERCE ORD/FREE PWR WEALTH SOCISM...JURID CONCPT TREND STERTYP TOT/POP VAL/FREE 20. PAGE 24 A0486
INDUS NAT/G NAT/LISM SOVEREIGN

S59
POTTER P.B.,"OBSTACLES AND ALTERNATIVES TO INTERNATIONAL LAW." WOR+45 NAT/G VOL/ASSN DELIB/GP BAL/PWR DOMIN ROUTINE...JURID VAL/FREE 20. PAGE 117 A2400
INT/ORG LAW DIPLOM INT/LAW

S59
SUTTON F.X.,"REPRESENTATION AND THE NATURE OF POLITICAL SYSTEMS." UNIV WOR-45 CULTURE SOCIETY STRATA INT/ORG FORCES JUDGE DOMIN LEGIT EXEC REGION REPRESENT ATTIT ORD/FREE RESPECT...SOC HIST/WRIT TIME/SEQ. PAGE 140 A2867
NAT/G CONCPT

C59
KULSKI W.W.,"PEACEFUL COEXISTENCE." USSR ECO/UNDEV INT/ORG POL/PAR EDU/PROP COLONIAL CONTROL REV NAT/LISM PEACE PWR MARXISM...BIBLIOG 20. PAGE 83 A1692
COM DIPLOM DOMIN

B60
ALBRECHT-CARRIE R.,FRANCE, EUROPE AND THE TWO WORLD WARS. EUR+WWI FRANCE GERMANY MOD/EUR UK ECO/DEV NAT/G FORCES BAL/PWR DOMIN ARMS/CONT PEACE PWR 20 TREATY EUROPE. PAGE 5 A0109
DIPLOM WAR

B60
ASPREMONT-LYNDEN H.,RAPPORT SUR L'ADMINISTRATION BELGE DU RUANDA-URUNDI PENDANT L'ANNEE 1959. BELGIUM RWANDA AGRI INDUS DIPLOM ECO/TAC INT/TRADE DOMIN ADMIN RACE/REL...GEOG CENSUS 20 UN. PAGE 9 A0192
AFR COLONIAL ECO/UNDEV INT/ORG

B60
CAMPAIGNE J.G.,AMERICAN MIGHT AND SOVIET MYTH. COM EUR+WWI ECO/DEV ECO/UNDEV INT/ORG NAT/G CAP/ISM ECO/TAC FOR/AID EDU/PROP ATTIT PWR WEALTH...POLICY CONCPT MYTH TREND STERTYP GEN/LAWS COLD/WAR. PAGE 23 A0473
USA+45 DOMIN DIPLOM USSR

B60
CONN S.,THE FRAMEWORK OF HEMISPHERE DEFENSE. CANADA L/A+17C USA-45 NAT/G FORCES BAL/PWR DOMIN WAR PEACE DISPL PWR RESPECT...PLURIST CONCPT HIST/WRIT HYPO/EXP MEXIC/AMER 20 ROOSEVLT/F. PAGE 29 A0585
USA+45 INT/ORG DIPLOM

B60
DAVIDS J.,AMERICA AND THE WORLD OF OUR TIME: UNITED STATES DIPLOMACY IN THE TWENTIETH CENTURY. USA-45 SOCIETY ECO/DEV INT/ORG NAT/G POL/PAR FORCES ECO/TAC DOMIN EDU/PROP EXEC COERCE WAR CHOOSE ATTIT PERSON ORD/FREE...CONCPT TIME/SEQ TOT/POP 20. PAGE 34 A0686
USA+45 PWR DIPLOM

B60
DUCHACEK I.D.,CONFLICT AND COOPERATION AMONG NATIONS. WOR+45 WOR-45 SOCIETY NAT/G DOMIN DETER PWR SKILL COLD/WAR 20. PAGE 39 A0791
INT/ORG BAL/PWR DIPLOM

B60
ENGEL J.,THE SECURITY OF THE FREE WORLD. USSR WOR+45 STRATA STRUCT ECO/DEV ECO/UNDEV INT/ORG DELIB/GP FORCES DOMIN LEGIT ADJUD EXEC ARMS/CONT COERCE...POLICY CONCPT NEW/IDEA TIME/SEQ GEN/LAWS COLD/WAR WORK UN 20 NATO. PAGE 42 A0851
COM TREND DIPLOM

B60
HAAS E.B.,THE COMPARATIVE STUDY OF THE UNITED NATIONS. WOR+45 NAT/G DOMIN LEGIT ROUTINE PEACE ORD/FREE PWR UN VAL/FREE 20. PAGE 59 A1205
INT/ORG DIPLOM

B60
HOLT R.T.,STRATEGIC PSYCHOLOGICAL OPERATIONS AND AMERICAN FOREIGN POLICY. ITALY USA+45 FOR/AID DOMIN RUMOR ADMIN TASK WAR CHOOSE ATTIT ALL/IDEOS...PSY COLD/WAR. PAGE 67 A1375
EDU/PROP ACT/RES DIPLOM POLICY

B60
KENNAN G.F.,RUSSIA AND THE WEST. ASIA COM EUR+WWI GERMANY UK USA+45 USA-45 USSR INT/ORG NAT/G VOL/ASSN DOMIN REV WAR PWR...TIME/SEQ 20. PAGE 78 A1590
EXEC DIPLOM

B60
LINDSAY K.,EUROPEAN ASSEMBLIES: THE EXPERIMENTAL PERIOD 1949-1959. EUR+WWI ECO/DEV NAT/G POL/PAR LEGIS TOP/EX ACT/RES PLAN ECO/TAC DOMIN LEGIT ROUTINE ATTIT DRIVE ORD/FREE PWR SKILL...SOC CONCPT TREND CHARTS GEN/LAWS VAL/FREE. PAGE 89 A1823
VOL/ASSN INT/ORG REGION

B60
MOSELY P.E.,THE KREMLIN AND WORLD POLITICS. EUR+WWI GERMANY USA+45 USSR CHIEF TOP/EX BAL/PWR DOMIN PEACE PWR...METH 20 COLD/WAR STALIN/J EUROPE/E. PAGE 105 A2151
COM DIPLOM POLICY WAR

B60
PLAMENATZ J.,ON ALIEN RULE AND SELF-GOVERNMENT. AFR FUT S/ASIA WOR+45 CULTURE SOCIETY ECO/UNDEV INT/ORG DOMIN EDU/PROP ATTIT RIGID/FLEX ALL/VALS...POLICY CONCPT OBS TREND CON/ANAL GEN/LAWS TOT/POP VAL/FREE. PAGE 116 A2386
NAT/G CONSTN NAT/LISM SOVEREIGN

B60
SETHE P.,SCHICKSALSSTUNDEN DER WELTGESCHICHTE (6TH ED.). NAT/G BAL/PWR DOMIN REV PWR...NAT/COMP 16/20. PAGE 131 A2687
DIPLOM WAR PEACE

B60
SPEIER H.,DIVIDED BERLIN: THE ANATOMY OF SOVIET POLITICAL BLACKMAIL. COM GERMANY USA+45 USSR WOR+45
INT/ORG ACT/RES

NAT/G TOP/EX DOMIN EDU/PROP ALL/VALS...POLICY CONCPT COLD/WAR 20 U-2. PAGE 136 A2782 — DIPLOM

B60
STRACHEY J.,THE END OF EMPIRE. UK WOR+45 WOR-45 DIPLOM INT/TRADE DOMIN ADJUST ORD/FREE WEALTH ...SOCIALIST GOV/COMP TIME COMMONWLTH. PAGE 139 A2841 — COLONIAL ECO/DEV BAL/PWR LAISSEZ

B60
TAYLOR M.D.,THE UNCERTAIN TRUMPET. USA+45 USSR WOR+45 INT/ORG NAT/G CONSULT DOMIN COERCE NUC/PWR WAR ATTIT ORD/FREE PWR...POLICY CONCPT TREND GEN/METH COLD/WAR UN NATO 20. PAGE 142 A2900 — PLAN FORCES DIPLOM

B60
WHEARE K.C.,THE CONSTITUTIONAL STRUCTURE OF THE COMMONWEALTH. UK EX/STRUC DIPLOM DOMIN ADMIN COLONIAL CONTROL LEAD INGP/REL SUPEGO 20 CMN/WLTH. PAGE 163 A3325 — CONSTN INT/ORG VOL/ASSN SOVEREIGN

L60
FERNBACH A.P.,"SOVIET COEXISTENCE STRATEGY." WOR+45 PROF/ORG VOL/ASSN DIPLOM DOMIN EDU/PROP ATTIT DRIVE PERSON PWR SKILL WEALTH...POLICY OBS SAMP TREND STERTYP ILO WORK COLD/WAR 420. PAGE 45 A0919 — LABOR INT/ORG USSR

S60
GINSBURGS G.,"PEKING-LHASA-NEW DELHI." CHINA/COM FUT INDIA S/ASIA KIN NAT/G PROVS SECT FORCES BAL/PWR ECO/TAC DOMIN EDU/PROP LEGIT ADMIN REGION GUERRILLA PWR...TREND TIBET 20. PAGE 52 A1074 — ASIA COERCE DIPLOM

S60
GULICK E.U.,"OUR BALANCE OF POWER SYSTEM IN PERSPECTIVE." FUT WOR+45 WOR-45 ECO/DEV DOMIN ROUTINE NUC/PWR PEACE PWR WEALTH...PLURIST CONCPT HIST/WRIT GEN/METH TOT/POP 20. PAGE 58 A1191 — INT/ORG TREND ARMS/CONT BAL/PWR

S60
HAVILAND H.F.,"PROBLEMS OF AMERICAN FOREIGN POLICY." ASIA COM USA+45 WOR+45 INT/ORG NAT/G CONSULT ECO/TAC FOR/AID DOMIN COERCE NUC/PWR ATTIT DRIVE ORD/FREE PWR RESPECT SKILL...POLICY GEOG OBS SAMP TREND GEN/METH METH COLD/WAR UN 20. PAGE 63 A1292 — ECO/UNDEV FORCES DIPLOM

S60
IKLE F.C.,"NTH COUNTRIES AND DISARMAMENT." WOR+45 DELIB/GP ECO/TAC DOMIN EDU/PROP LEGIT ROUTINE COERCE RIGID/FLEX ORD/FREE...MARXIST TREND 20. PAGE 70 A1432 — FUT INT/ORG ARMS/CONT NUC/PWR

S60
MAGATHAN W.,"SOME BASES OF WEST GERMAN MILITARY POLICY." EUR+WWI FUT INT/ORG TOP/EX ECO/TAC DOMIN DRIVE ORD/FREE PWR...TRADIT GEOG OBS TREND. PAGE 93 A1904 — NAT/G FORCES GERMANY

S60
O'BRIEN W.,"THE ROLE OF FORCE IN THE INTERNATIONAL JURIDICAL ORDER." WOR+45 NAT/G FORCES DOMIN ADJUD ARMS/CONT DETER NUC/PWR WAR ATTIT PWR...CATH INT/LAW JURID CONCPT TREND STERTYP GEN/LAWS 20. PAGE 110 A2266 — INT/ORG COERCE

S60
SCHACHTER O.,"THE ENFORCEMENT OF INTERNATIONAL JUDICIAL AND ARBITRAL DECISIONS." WOR+45 NAT/G ECO/TAC DOMIN LEGIT ROUTINE COERCE ATTIT DRIVE ALL/VALS PWR...METH/CNCPT TREND TOT/POP 20 UN. PAGE 128 A2615 — INT/ORG ADJUD INT/LAW

C60
COX R.H.,"LOCKE ON WAR AND PEACE." UK DIPLOM DOMIN PWR...BIOG IDEA/COMP BIBLIOG 18. PAGE 32 A0646 — CONCPT NAT/G PEACE WAR

B61
BARNES W.,THE FOREIGN SERVICE OF THE UNITED STATES. USA+45 USA-45 CONSTN INT/ORG POL/PAR CONSULT DELIB/GP LEGIS DOMIN EDU/PROP EXEC ATTIT RIGID/FLEX ORD/FREE PWR...POLICY CONCPT STAT OBS RECORD BIOG TIME/SEQ TREND. PAGE 11 A0224 — NAT/G MGT DIPLOM

B61
BISHOP D.G.,THE ADMINISTRATION OF BRITISH FOREIGN RELATIONS. EUR+WWI MOD/EUR INT/ORG NAT/G POL/PAR DELIB/GP LEGIS TOP/EX ECO/TAC DOMIN EDU/PROP ADMIN COERCE 20. PAGE 14 A0292 — ROUTINE PWR DIPLOM UK

B61
CHIDZERO B.T.G.,TANGANYIKA AND INTERNATIONAL TRUSTEESHIP. AFR WOR+45 WOR-45 ECO/DEV INT/ORG ECO/TAC DOMIN COLONIAL...RECORD CHARTS 20 TANGANYIKA CMN/WLTH. PAGE 26 A0528 — ECO/UNDEV CONSTN

B61
DALLIN D.J.,SOVIET FOREIGN POLICY AFTER STALIN. ASIA CHINA/COM EUR+WWI GERMANY IRAN UK YUGOSLAVIA INT/ORG NAT/G VOL/ASSN FORCES TOP/EX BAL/PWR DOMIN EDU/PROP COERCE ATTIT PWR 20. PAGE 33 A0679 — COM DIPLOM USSR

B61
FLEMING D.F.,THE COLD WAR AND ITS ORIGINS: 1950-1960 (VOL. II). ASIA FUT HUNGARY POLAND WOR+45 TEC/DEV DOMIN NUC/PWR REV PEACE...T 20 COLD/WAR EISNHWR/DD SUEZ. PAGE 46 A0946 — MARXISM DIPLOM BAL/PWR

B61
GRAEBNER N.,AN UNCERTAIN TRADITION: AMERICAN SECRETARIES OF STATE IN THE 20TH CENTURY. USA+45 CONSTN INT/ORG NAT/G DELIB/GP TOP/EX BAL/PWR DOMIN LEGIT ADMIN ARMS/CONT ATTIT DRIVE PERSON SUPEGO ORD/FREE PWR...GEN/LAWS VAL/FREE CONGRESS. PAGE 55 A1121 — USA-45 BIOG DIPLOM

B61
LUKACS J.,A HISTORY OF THE COLD WAR. ASIA COM EUR+WWI USA+45 USA-45 INT/ORG NAT/G DELIB/GP ACT/RES BAL/PWR DIPLOM DOMIN EDU/PROP LEGIT DRIVE ORD/FREE...TREND COLD/WAR 20. PAGE 91 A1872 — PWR TIME/SEQ USSR

B61
OAKES J.B.,THE EDGE OF FREEDOM. EUR+WWI USA+45 USSR ECO/UNDEV BAL/PWR DIPLOM DOMIN COLONIAL PWR MARXISM POPULISM...IDEA/COMP 20 COLD/WAR. PAGE 111 A2271 — AFR ORD/FREE SOVEREIGN NEUTRAL

B61
PERLO V.,EL IMPERIALISMO NORTHEAMERICANO. USA+45 USA-45 FINAN CAP/ISM DIPLOM DOMIN CONTROL DISCRIM 19/20. PAGE 115 A2363 — SOCIALIST ECO/DEV INT/TRADE ECO/TAC

B61
SCHNAPPER B.,LA POLITIQUE ET LE COMMERCE FRANCAIS DANS LE GOLFE DE GUINEE DE 1838 A 1871. FRANCE GUINEA UK SEA EXTR/IND NAT/G DELIB/GP LEGIS ADMIN ORD/FREE...POLICY GEOG CENSUS CHARTS BIBLIOG 19. PAGE 129 A2636 — COLONIAL INT/TRADE DOMIN AFR

B61
STRAUSZ-HUPE R.,A FORWARD STRATEGY FOR AMERICA. FUT WOR+45 ECO/DEV INT/ORG NAT/G POL/PAR DELIB/GP FORCES ACT/RES CREATE ECO/TAC DOMIN EDU/PROP ATTIT DRIVE PWR...MAJORIT CONCPT STAT OBS TIME/SEQ TREND COLD/WAR TOT/POP. PAGE 139 A2848 — USA+45 PLAN DIPLOM

B61
WRIGHT Q.,THE ROLE OF INTERNATIONAL LAW IN THE ELIMINATION OF WAR. FUT WOR+45 WOR-45 NAT/G BAL/PWR DIPLOM DOMIN LEGIT PWR...POLICY INT/LAW JURID CONCPT TIME/SEQ TREND GEN/LAWS COLD/WAR 20. PAGE 168 A3414 — INT/ORG ADJUD ARMS/CONT

L61
HOYT E.C.,"UNITED STATES REACTION TO THE KOREAN ATTACK." COM KOREA USA+45 CONSTN DELIB/GP FORCES PLAN ECO/TAC DOMIN EDU/PROP LEGIT ROUTINE COERCE WAR ATTIT DISPL RIGID/FLEX ORD/FREE PWR...POLICY INT/LAW TREND UN 20. PAGE 68 A1402 — ASIA INT/ORG BAL/PWR DIPLOM

S61
ANGLIN D.,"UNITED STATES OPPOSITION TO CANADIAN MEMBERSHIP IN THE PAN AMERICAN UNION: A CANADIAN VIEW." L/A+17C UK USA+45 VOL/ASSN DELIB/GP EX/STRUC PLAN DIPLOM DOMIN REGION ATTIT RIGID/FLEX PWR ...RELATIV CONCPT STERTYP CMN/WLTH OAS 20. PAGE 8 A0162 — INT/ORG CANADA

S61
BRZEZINSKI Z.K.,"THE ORGANIZATION OF THE COMMUNIST CAMP." COM CZECHOSLVK COM/IND NAT/G DELIB/GP INT/TRADE DOMIN EDU/PROP EXEC ROUTINE COERCE ATTIT PWR...MGT CONCPT TIME/SEQ CHARTS VAL/FREE 20 TREATY. PAGE 20 A0416 — VOL/ASSN DIPLOM USSR

S61
GOODWIN G.L.,"THE EXPANDING UNITED NATIONS: 2-DIPLOMATIC PRESSURES AND TECHNIQUES." COM ECO/UNDEV TOP/EX BAL/PWR DIPLOM DOMIN...POLICY CONCPT UN COLD/WAR 20. PAGE 54 A1108 — INT/ORG PWR

S61
MIKSCHE F.O.,"DEFENSE ORGANIZATION FOR WESTERN EUROPE." USA+45 INT/ORG NAT/G VOL/ASSN ACT/RES DOMIN LEGIT COERCE ORD/FREE PWR...RELATIV TREND 20 NATO. PAGE 101 A2071 — EUR+WWI FORCES WEAPON NUC/PWR

S61
ROSTOW W.W.,"THE FUTURE OF FOREIGN AID." COM FUT WOR+45 ECO/DEV INDUS INT/ORG NAT/G CONSULT ACT/RES PLAN DOMIN LEGIT CHOOSE RIGID/FLEX ALL/VALS ...MAJORIT CONCPT TREND TOT/POP 20. PAGE 124 A2544 — ECO/UNDEV ECO/TAC FOR/AID

S61
TUCKER R.C.,"TOWARDS A COMPARATIVE POLITICS OF MOVEMENT-REGIMES" (BMR)" USSR CONSTN NAT/G CREATE PROB/SOLV DIPLOM DOMIN REV...GP/COMP IDEA/COMP METH 20 STALIN/J BOLSHEVISM. PAGE 145 A2971 — MARXISM POLICY GEN/LAWS PWR

B62
BAILEY S.D.,THE SECRETARIAT OF THE UNITED NATIONS. FUT WOR+45 DELIB/GP PLAN BAL/PWR DOMIN EDU/PROP ADMIN PEACE ATTIT PWR...DECISION CONCPT TREND CON/ANAL CHARTS UN VAL/FREE COLD/WAR 20. PAGE 10 A0205 — INT/ORG EXEC DIPLOM

B62
BELL C.,NEGOTIATION FROM STRENGTH. WOR+45 FACE/GP INT/ORG DELIB/GP FORCES PLAN DOMIN COERCE NUC/PWR PEACE DRIVE PWR...POLICY LOG OBS RECORD INT SAMP TREND COLD/WAR 20. PAGE 13 A0255 — NAT/G CONCPT DIPLOM

B62
CARLSTON K.S.,LAW AND ORGANIZATION IN WORLD SOCIETY. WOR+45 FINAN ECO/TAC DOMIN LEGIT CT/SYS ROUTINE COERCE ORD/FREE PWR WEALTH...PLURIST DECISION JURID MGT METH/CNCPT GEN/LAWS 20. PAGE 24 A0487 — INT/ORG LAW

B62
CLUBB O.E. JR.,THE UNITED STATES AND THE SINO-SOVIET BLOC IN SOUTHEAST ASIA. ASIA CHINA/COM COM USA+45 USSR ECO/UNDEV INT/ORG NAT/G FORCES TOP/EX — S/ASIA PWR BAL/PWR

PLAN ECO/TAC DOMIN COERCE GUERRILLA ATTIT RIGID/FLEX...POLICY OBS TREND 20. PAGE 27 A0553 — DIPLOM

B62
DEHIO L.,THE PRECARIOUS BALANCE: FOUR CENTURIES OF THE EUROPEAN POWER STRUGGLE. FRANCE GERMANY SPAIN NAT/G DOMIN PWR...GOV/COMP 8/20. PAGE 36 A0725 — BAL/PWR WAR DIPLOM COERCE

B62
ELLIOTT J.R.,THE APPEAL OF COMMUNISM IN THE UNDERDEVELOPED NATIONS. USSR WOR+45 INT/ORG NAT/G DIPLOM DOMIN EDU/PROP ROUTINE ATTIT RIGID/FLEX ORD/FREE PWR WEALTH MARXISM...POLICY SOC METH/CNCPT MYTH TOT/POP COLD/WAR 20. PAGE 41 A0842 — COM ECO/UNDEV

B62
HUNTINGTON S.P.,CHANGING PATTERNS OF MILITARY POLITICS. EUR+WWI L/A+17C S/ASIA USA+45 WOR+45 CULTURE INT/ORG NAT/G CONSULT PLAN DOMIN EDU/PROP LEGIT DETER WAR ATTIT PERSON PWR...DECISION CONCPT SIMUL GEN/LAWS ANTHOL COLD/WAR 20. PAGE 69 A1419 — FORCES RIGID/FLEX

B62
HUTTENBACK R.A.,BRITISH RELATIONS WITH THE SIND, 1799-1843. FRANCE INDIA UK FORCES...POLICY CHARTS BIBLIOG 18/19 SIND. PAGE 69 A1425 — COLONIAL DIPLOM DOMIN S/ASIA

B62
JELAVICH C.,TSARIST RUSSIA AND BALKAN NATIONALISM. BULGARIA MOD/EUR RUSSIA DOMIN GOV/REL...GEOG 19 SERBIA. PAGE 73 A1503 — NAT/LISM DIPLOM WAR

B62
KLUCKHOHN F.L.,THE NAKED RISE OF COMMUNISM. CHINA/COM COM USSR WOR+45 CONSTN POL/PAR PLAN CONTROL LEAD NEUTRAL CONSERVE 20 STALIN/J EUROPE/E COM/PARTY. PAGE 80 A1650 — MARXISM IDEA/COMP DIPLOM DOMIN

B62
LAQUEUR W.,POLYCENTRISM. CHINA/COM COM USSR WOR+45 INT/ORG NAT/G ECO/TAC DOMIN LEAD ATTIT PWR SOVEREIGN...ANTHOL 20. PAGE 85 A1732 — MARXISM DIPLOM BAL/PWR POLICY

B62
MACKENTOSH J.M.,STRATEGY AND TACTICS OF SOVIET FOREIGN POLICY. CHINA/COM FUT USA+45 WOR+45 INT/ORG PLAN DOMIN LEGIT ROUTINE COERCE NUC/PWR WAR ATTIT DRIVE ORD/FREE PWR...CONCPT OBS TIME/SEQ TREND GEN/METH COLD/WAR 20. PAGE 92 A1894 — COM POLICY DIPLOM USSR

B62
MANDER J.,BERLIN: HOSTAGE FOR THE WEST. FUT GERMANY WOR+45 FOR/AID RISK ATTIT ORD/FREE 20 BERLIN COLD/WAR. PAGE 93 A1916 — DIPLOM BAL/PWR DOMIN DETER

B62
NEAL F.W.,WAR AND PEACE AND GERMANY. EUR+WWI USSR STRUCT INT/ORG NAT/G FORCES DOMIN EDU/PROP LEGIT EXEC COERCE ORD/FREE...HUM SOC NEW/IDEA OBS TIME/SEQ TOT/POP COLD/WAR 20 BERLIN. PAGE 108 A2208 — USA+45 POLICY DIPLOM GERMANY

B62
QUIRK R.E.,AN AFFAIR OF HONOR: WOODROW WILSON AND THE OCCUPATION OF VERACRUZ. L/A+17C USA-45 COLONIAL SUPEGO PWR 20 WILSON/W MEXIC/AMER. PAGE 118 A2428 — DOMIN DIPLOM COERCE PROB/SOLV

B62
RIMALOV V.V.,ECONOMIC COOPERATION BETWEEN USSR AND UNDERDEVELOPED COUNTRIES. USSR FINAN TEC/DEV INT/TRADE DOMIN EDU/PROP COLONIAL NAT/LISM DRIVE SOVEREIGN...AUD/VIS 20. PAGE 121 A2482 — FOR/AID PLAN ECO/UNDEV DIPLOM

B62
SNYDER L.L.D.,THE IMPERIALISM READER. AFR ASIA CHINA/COM COM EUR+WWI FUT MOD/EUR USA+45 WOR+45 WOR-45 INT/ORG COLONIAL SOVEREIGN CMN/WLTH OAS 20. PAGE 134 A2751 — DOMIN PWR DIPLOM

B62
STARR R.E.,POLAND 1944-1962: THE SOVIETIZATION OF A CAPTIVE PEOPLE. COM POLAND USSR POL/PAR SECT LEGIS DIPLOM DOMIN EDU/PROP CHOOSE ORD/FREE...POLICY CHARTS BIBLIOG 20. PAGE 137 A2808 — MARXISM NAT/G TOTALISM NAT/COMP

B62
STRACHEY J.,ON THE PREVENTION OF WAR. FUT WOR+45 INT/ORG NAT/G ACT/RES PLAN BAL/PWR DOMIN EDU/PROP PEACE ATTIT...POLICY TREND TOT/POP COLD/WAR 20 UN. PAGE 139 A2842 — FORCES ORD/FREE ARMS/CONT NUC/PWR

B62
TAYLOR D.,THE BRITISH IN AFRICA. UK CULTURE ECO/UNDEV INDUS DIPLOM INT/TRADE ADMIN WAR RACE/REL ORD/FREE SOVEREIGN...POLICY BIBLIOG 15/20 CMN/WLTH. PAGE 142 A2898 — AFR COLONIAL DOMIN

B62
TRISKA J.F.,THE THEORY, LAW, AND POLICY OF SOVIET TREATIES. WOR+45 WOR-45 CONSTN INT/ORG NAT/G VOL/ASSN DOMIN LEGIT COERCE ATTIT PWR RESPECT ...POLICY JURID CONCPT OBS SAMP TIME/SEQ TREND GEN/LAWS 20. PAGE 145 A2966 — COM LAW INT/LAW USSR

B62
VIET J.,INTERNATIONAL COOPERATION AND PROGRAMMES OF ECONOMIC AND SOCIAL DEVELOPMENT. TEC/DEV FOR/AID DOMIN COLONIAL PEACE WEALTH 20 UNESCO. PAGE 159 A3232 — BIBLIOG/A INT/ORG DIPLOM ECO/UNDEV

B62
WELLEQUET J.,LE CONGO BELGE ET LA WELTPOLITIK (1894-1914. GERMANY DOMIN EDU/PROP WAR ATTIT ...BIBLIOG T CONGO/LEOP. PAGE 163 A3314 — ADMIN DIPLOM GP/REL COLONIAL

B62
WILLIAMS W.A.,THE UNITED STATES, CUBA, AND CASTRO: AN ESSAY ON THE DYNAMICS OF REVOLUTION AND THE DISSOLUTION OF EMPIRE. CUBA USA+45 AGRI VOL/ASSN DIPLOM ECO/TAC DOMIN COERCE...POLICY 20 EISNHWR/DD CIA KENNEDY/JF CASTRO/F. PAGE 165 A3354 — REV CONSTN COM LEAD

B62
WOETZEL R.K.,THE NURENBERG TRIALS IN INTERNATIONAL LAW. CHRIST-17C MOD/EUR WOR+45 SOCIETY NAT/G DELIB/GP DOMIN LEGIT ROUTINE ATTIT DRIVE PERSON SUPEGO MORAL ORD/FREE...POLICY MAJORIT JURID PSY SOC SELF/OBS RECORD NAZI TOT/POP. PAGE 166 A3376 — INT/ORG ADJUD WAR

B62
WOLFERS A.,DISCORD AND COLLABORATION: ESSAYS ON INTERNATIONAL POLITICS. WOR+45 CULTURE SOCIETY INT/ORG NAT/G BAL/PWR DIPLOM DOMIN NAT/LISM PEACE PWR...POLICY CONCPT STYLE RECORD TREND GEN/LAWS 20. PAGE 166 A3385 — ATTIT ORD/FREE

B62
YALEN R.,REGIONALISM AND WORLD ORDER. EUR+WWI WOR+45 WOR-45 INT/ORG VOL/ASSN DELIB/GP FORCES TOP/EX BAL/PWR DIPLOM DOMIN REGION ARMS/CONT PWR ...JURID HYPO/EXP COLD/WAR 20. PAGE 168 A3427 — ORD/FREE POLICY

L62
CORET A.,"LES PROVINCES PORTUGALLES D'OUTREMER ET L'ONU." AFR PORTUGAL S/ASIA WOR+45 LOC/G NAT/G DOMIN...CONCPT TIME/SEQ UN 20 GOA. PAGE 31 A0620 — INT/ORG SOVEREIGN COLONIAL

L62
PETKOFF D.K.,"RECOGNITION AND NON-RECOGNITION OF STATES AND GOVERNMENTS IN INTERNATIONAL LAW." ASIA COM USA+45 WOR+45 NAT/G ACT/RES DIPLOM DOMIN LEGIT COERCE ORD/FREE PWR...CONCPT GEN/LAWS 20. PAGE 115 A2369 — INT/ORG LAW INT/LAW

L62
ULYSSES,"THE INTERNATIONAL AIMS AND POLICIES OF THE SOVIET UNION: THE NEW CONCEPTS AND STRATEGY OF KHRUSHCHEV." FUT USSR WOR+45 SOCIETY INT/ORG NAT/G POL/PAR FORCES TOP/EX PLAN DOMIN EDU/PROP COERCE ATTIT PERSON PWR...TREND COLD/WAR 20 KHRUSH/N. PAGE 146 A2994 — COM POLICY BAL/PWR DIPLOM

S62
BRZEZINSKI Z.K.,"PEACEFUL ENGAGEMENT IN COMMUNIST DISUNITY." ASIA CHINA/COM COM USA+45 USSR NAT/G TOP/EX CREATE ECO/TAC FOR/AID DOMIN ATTIT PERCEPT RIGID/FLEX PWR...PSY 20. PAGE 20 A0417 — COM DIPLOM TOTALISM

S62
CRANE R.D.,"SOVIET ATTITUDE TOWARD INTERNATIONAL SPACE LAW." COM FUT USA+45 USSR AIR CONSTN DELIB/GP DOMIN PWR...JURID TREND TOT/POP 20. PAGE 32 A0657 — LAW ATTIT INT/LAW SPACE

S62
CROAN M.,"POLYCENTRISM: COMMUNIST INTERNATIONAL RELATIONS." ASIA STRUCT INT/ORG NAT/G POL/PAR CONSULT PLAN DOMIN EDU/PROP COERCE ATTIT RIGID/FLEX SOCISM...POLICY CONCPT TREND CON/ANAL GEN/LAWS MARX/KARL. PAGE 33 A0663 — COM CREATE DIPLOM NAT/LISM

S62
DALLIN A.,"THE SOVIET VIEW OF THE UNITED NATIONS." WOR+45 VOL/ASSN TOP/EX DIPLOM DOMIN EDU/PROP LEGIT ATTIT RIGID/FLEX PWR...CONCPT OBS HIST/WRIT TIME/SEQ STERTYP GEN/LAWS COLD/WAR UN 20. PAGE 33 A0676 — COM INT/ORG USSR

S62
DE MADARIAGA S.,"TOWARD THE UNITED STATES OF EUROPE." EUR+WWI PLAN DOMIN FEDERAL ATTIT PWR SOVEREIGN...GEOG TOT/POP 20. PAGE 35 A0707 — FUT INT/ORG

S62
DRACHKOVITCH M.M.,"THE EMERGING PATTERN OF YUGOSLAV-SOVIET RELATIONS." COM FUT USSR WOR+45 INT/ORG ECO/TAC FOR/AID DOMIN COERCE ATTIT PERSON ORD/FREE PWR...TIME/SEQ 20 TITO/MARSH KHRUSH/N STALIN/J. PAGE 38 A0783 — TOP/EX DIPLOM YUGOSLAVIA

S62
JACOBSON H.K.,"THE UNITED NATIONS AND COLONIALISM: A TENTATIVE APPRAISAL." AFR FUT S/ASIA USA+45 USSR WOR+45 NAT/G DELIB/GP PLAN DIPLOM ECO/TAC DOMIN ADMIN ROUTINE COERCE ATTIT RIGID/FLEX ORD/FREE PWR ...OBS STERTYP UN 20. PAGE 73 A1486 — INT/ORG CONCPT COLONIAL

S62
KOLARZ W.,"THE IMPACT OF COMMUNISM ON WEST AFRICA." AFR FUT SOCIETY INT/ORG NAT/G CREATE PLAN DOMIN EDU/PROP COERCE NAT/LISM ATTIT RIGID/FLEX SOCISM ...POLICY CONCPT TREND MARX/KARL 20. PAGE 81 A1666 — COM POL/PAR COLONIAL

S62
LONDON K.,"SINO-SOVIET RELATIONS IN THE CONTEXT OF THE 'WORLD SOCIALIST SYSTEM'." ASIA CHINA/COM COM USSR INT/ORG NAT/G TOP/EX BAL/PWR DIPLOM DOMIN ATTIT PERCEPT RIGID/FLEX PWR MARXISM...METH/CNCPT TREND 20. PAGE 91 A1854 — DELIB/GP CONCPT SOCISM

S62
MARIAS J.,"A PROGRAM FOR EUROPE." EUR+WWI INT/ORG — VOL/ASSN

NAT/G PLAN DIPLOM DOMIN PWR...STERTYP TOT/POP 20. PAGE 95 A1938 CREATE REGION

S62
MCWHINNEY E.,"CO-EXISTENCE, THE CUBA CRISIS, AND COLD WAR-INTERNATIONAL WAR." CUBA USA+45 USSR WOR+45 NAT/G TOP/EX BAL/PWR DIPLOM DOMIN LEGIT PEACE RIGID/FLEX ORD/FREE...STERTYP COLD/WAR 20. PAGE 99 A2026 CONCPT INT/LAW

S62
SPECTOR I.,"SOVIET POLICY IN ASIA: A REAPPRAISAL." ASIA CHINA/COM COM INDIA INDONESIA ECO/UNDEV INT/ORG DOMIN EDU/PROP REGION RESPECT...CONCPT TREND TOT/POP COLD/WAR 20 CHINJAP. PAGE 135 A2774 S/ASIA PWR FOR/AID USSR

S62
STRACHEY J.,"COMMUNIST INTENTIONS." ASIA USSR YUGOSLAVIA INT/ORG NAT/G FORCES DOMIN EDU/PROP COERCE NUC/PWR NAT/LISM PEACE RIGID/FLEX PWR MARXISM...CONCPT MYTH OBS TIME/SEQ TREND COLD/WAR TOT/POP 20. PAGE 139 A2843 COM ATTIT WAR

S62
THOMAS J.R.T.,"SOVIET BEHAVIOR IN THE QUEMOY CRISES OF 1958." CHINA/COM FUT USSR WOR+45 INT/ORG VOL/ASSN FORCES PLAN BAL/PWR DOMIN COERCE NUC/PWR REV WAR ATTIT DRIVE ORD/FREE...POLICY OBS RECORD COLD/WAR FOR/POL 20. PAGE 143 A2923 COM PWR

C62
BACON F.,"OF THE TRUE GREATNESS OF KINGDOMS AND ESTATES" (1612) IN F. BACON, ESSAYS." ELITES FORCES DOMIN EDU/PROP LEGIT...POLICY GEN/LAWS 16/17 TREATY. PAGE 10 A0200 WAR PWR DIPLOM CONSTN

C62
BACON F.,"OF EMPIRE" (1612) IN F. BACON, ESSAYS." ELITES NAT/G PROB/SOLV DIPLOM ADMIN CONTROL WEALTH 16/17 KING. PAGE 10 A0201 PWR CHIEF DOMIN GEN/LAWS

B63
BURNS A.L.,PEACE-KEEPING BY U.N.FORCES - FROM SUEZ TO THE CONGO. AFR FUT ISLAM ISRAEL USSR WOR+45 NAT/G DELIB/GP BAL/PWR DOMIN LEGIT EXEC COERCE PEACE ATTIT PWR RESPECT SOVEREIGN...CONCPT UN 20. PAGE 22 A0441 INT/ORG FORCES ORD/FREE

B63
CANELAS O.A.,RADIOGRAFIA DE LA ALIANZA PARA EL ATRASO. L/A+17C USA+45 ECO/TAC DOMIN COLONIAL NAT/LISM...SOCIALIST NAT/COMP 20. PAGE 23 A0476 REV DIPLOM ECO/UNDEV REGION

B63
GALLAGHER M.P.,THE SOVIET HISTORY OF WORLD WAR II. EUR+WWI USSR DIPLOM DOMIN WRITING CONTROL WAR MARXISM...PSY TIME/SEQ 20 STALIN/J. PAGE 50 A1031 CIVMIL/REL EDU/PROP HIST/WRIT PRESS

B63
GRIFFITH W.E.,ALBANIA AND THE SINO-SOVIET RIFT. ALBANIA CHINA/COM USSR POL/PAR CHIEF LEGIS DIPLOM DOMIN ATTIT PWR...POLICY 20 KHRUSH/N MAO. PAGE 57 A1161 EDU/PROP MARXISM NAT/LISM GOV/REL

B63
HENDERSON W.,SOUTHEAST ASIA: PROBLEMS OF UNITED STATES POLICY. COM S/ASIA CULTURE STRATA ECO/UNDEV INT/ORG DELIB/GP ACT/RES ECO/TAC DOMIN EDU/PROP LEGIT COERCE ATTIT ALL/VALS...STAT TIME/SEQ ANTHOL VAL/FREE 20. PAGE 64 A1313 ASIA USA+45 DIPLOM

B63
HUSSEY W.D.,THE BRITISH EMPIRE AND COMMONWEALTH 1500 TO 1961. UK USA-45 SOCIETY ECO/UNDEV NAT/G VOL/ASSN INT/TRADE DOMIN CONTROL WAR PWR ...DICTIONARY 16/20 COMMONWLTH TRUST/TERR. PAGE 69 A1422 COLONIAL SOVEREIGN INT/ORG

B63
JAIRAZBHOY R.A.,FOREIGN INFLUENCE IN ANCIENT INDIA. INDIA ELITES SECT DIPLOM EDU/PROP COLONIAL REGION GP/REL...ART/METH LING WORSHIP +/14 GRECO/ROMN MESOPOTAM PERSIA PARTH/SASS. PAGE 73 A1491 CULTURE SOCIETY COERCE DOMIN

B63
JOYCE W.,THE PROPAGANDA GAP. USA+45 COM/IND ACADEM DOMIN FEEDBACK REV CIVMIL/REL...REALPOL COLD/WAR. PAGE 75 A1540 EDU/PROP PERCEPT BAL/PWR DIPLOM

B63
JUDD P.,AFRICAN INDEPENDENCE: THE EXPLODING EMERGENCE OF THE NEW AFRICAN NATIONS. AFR UK LAW CONSTN CULTURE KIN DIPLOM ATTIT...CHARTS BIBLIOG 20 UN DEGAULLE/C NEGRO THIRD/WRLD. PAGE 75 A1542 ORD/FREE POLICY DOMIN LOC/G

B63
KHADDURI M.,MODERN LIBYA: A STUDY IN POLITICAL DEVELOPMENT. EUR+WWI ISLAM LIBYA ELITES INT/ORG POL/PAR FORCES DIPLOM FOR/AID DOMIN EDU/PROP LEGIT NAT/LISM DRIVE RIGID/FLEX SKILL...CONCPT TIME/SEQ TREND 20. PAGE 78 A1606 NAT/G STRUCT

B63
KORBEL J.,POLAND BETWEEN EAST AND WEST: SOVIET AND GERMAN DIPLOMACY TOWARD POLAND 1919-1933. EUR+WWI GERMANY POLAND USSR FORCES AGREE WAR SOVEREIGN ...BIBLIOG 20 TREATY. PAGE 81 A1670 BAL/PWR DIPLOM DOMIN NAT/LISM

B63
MOSELY P.E.,THE SOVIET UNION, 1922-1962: A FOREIGN AFFAIRS READER. ASIA POLAND USSR CULTURE INTELL AGRI POL/PAR WORKER INT/TRADE DOMIN WAR NAT/LISM MARXISM SOCISM 20 KHRUSH/N. PAGE 105 A2152 PWR POLICY DIPLOM

B63
NORTH R.C.,CONTENT ANALYSIS: A HANDBOOK WITH APPLICATIONS FOR THE STUDY OF INTERNATIONAL CRISIS. ASIA COM EUR+WWI MOD/EUR INT/ORG TEC/DEV DOMIN EDU/PROP ROUTINE COERCE PERCEPT RIGID/FLEX ALL/VALS ...QUANT TESTS CON/ANAL SIMUL GEN/LAWS VAL/FREE. PAGE 110 A2252 METH/CNCPT COMPUT/IR USSR

B63
QUAISON-SACKEY A.,AFRICA UNBOUND: REFLECTIONS OF AN AFRICAN STATESMAN. ISLAM CULTURE INTELL INT/ORG POL/PAR TOP/EX DOMIN EDU/PROP LEGIT ATTIT PERSON ...CONCPT OBS TIME/SEQ CHARTS STERTYP 20 UN. PAGE 118 A2423 AFR BIOG

B63
ROSECRANCE R.N.,ACTION AND REACTION IN WORLD POLITICS. FUT WOR-45 SOCIETY DELIB/GP ACT/RES CREATE DIPLOM ECO/TAC DOMIN EDU/PROP COERCE ATTIT PERSON SUPEGO ORD/FREE PWR...CHARTS SIMUL LEAGUE/NAT VAL/FREE UN 19/20. PAGE 123 A2529 WOR+45 INT/ORG BAL/PWR

B63
SCHMELTZ G.W.,LA POLITIQUE MONDIALE CONTEMPORAINE. SOCIETY ECO/UNDEV INDUS INT/ORG NAT/G POL/PAR CONSULT DELIB/GP PLAN TEC/DEV ECO/TAC DOMIN EDU/PROP ROUTINE COERCE PERCEPT PERSON LOVE SKILL ...SOC RECORD TOT/POP. PAGE 128 A2629 WOR+45 COLONIAL

B63
TUCKER R.C.,THE SOVIET POLITICAL MIND. WOR+45 ELITES INT/ORG NAT/G POL/PAR PLAN DIPLOM ECO/TAC DOMIN ADMIN NUC/PWR REV DRIVE PERSON SUPEGO PWR WEALTH...POLICY MGT PSY CONCPT OBS BIOG TREND COLD/WAR MARX/KARL 20. PAGE 145 A2972 COM TOP/EX USSR

B63
US DEPARTMENT OF THE ARMY,SOVIET RUSSIA: STRATEGIC SURVEY (PAMPHLET). USSR POL/PAR PLAN DOMIN EDU/PROP ARMS/CONT GUERRILLA WAR WEAPON...TREND CHARTS ORG/CHARTS 20. PAGE 152 A3106 BIBLIOG/A MARXISM DIPLOM COERCE

B63
VOSS E.H.,NUCLEAR AMBUSH: THE TEST-BAN TRAP. WOR+45 COM/IND INT/ORG NAT/G DELIB/GP FORCES LEGIS TOP/EX ACT/RES DOMIN EDU/PROP LEGIT ROUTINE COERCE ATTIT PERCEPT RIGID/FLEX HEALTH MORAL ORD/FREE PWR. PAGE 160 A3255 TEC/DEV HIST/WRIT ARMS/CONT NUC/PWR

B63
WESTERFIELD H.,THE INSTRUMENTS OF AMERICA'S FOREIGN POLICY. WOR+45 ECO/DEV NAT/G CONSULT EX/STRUC LEGIS BAL/PWR FOR/AID INT/TRADE DOMIN EDU/PROP LEGIT ATTIT KNOWL ORD/FREE PWR WEALTH...OBS COLD/WAR TOT/POP VAL/FREE. PAGE 163 A3322 USA+45 INT/ORG DIPLOM

L63
ZARTMAN I.W.,"THE SAHARA--BRIDGE OR BARRIER." ISLAM CULTURE SOCIETY NAT/G DELIB/GP DOMIN EDU/PROP LEGIT ATTIT...HIST/WRIT TIME/SEQ CHARTS TOT/POP VAL/FREE 20. PAGE 169 A3445 INT/ORG PWR NAT/LISM

S63
KINTNER W.R.,"THE PROJECTED EUROPEAN UNION AND AMERICAN RESPONSIBILITIES." EUR+WWI USA+45 STRATA INT/ORG NAT/G DOMIN DETER NUC/PWR ATTIT ORD/FREE PWR 20 NATO. PAGE 79 A1628 FUT FORCES DIPLOM REGION

S63
MAZRUI A.A.,"ON THE CONCEPT 'WE ARE ALL AFRICANS'." AFR CULTURE KIN LOC/G NAT/G DOMIN EDU/PROP LEGIT ATTIT PERCEPT PERSON KNOWL ORD/FREE...TIME/SEQ TOT/POP 20. PAGE 97 A1986 PROVS INT/ORG NAT/LISM

S63
NICHOLAS H.G.,"UN PEACE FORCES AND THE CHANGING GLOBE: THE LESSONS OF SUEZ AND CONGO." FUT WOR+45 CONSTN INT/ORG CONSULT DELIB/GP TOP/EX CREATE DIPLOM DOMIN LEGIT COERCE WAR PERSON RIGID/FLEX PWR UN SUEZ CONGO UNEF 20. PAGE 109 A2229 ACT/RES FORCES

S63
NOGEE J.L.,"PROPOGANDA AND NEGOTIATION: THE CASE OF THE TEN NATION DISARMAMENT COMMITTEE." COM EUR+WWI USA+45 VOL/ASSN DELIB/GP FORCES DIPLOM DOMIN LEGIT PWR...METH/CNCPT STERTYP COLD/WAR VAL/FREE 20. PAGE 110 A2248 INT/ORG EDU/PROP ARMS/CONT

S63
SONNENFELDT H.,"FOREIGN POLICY FROM MALENKOV TO KHRUSHCHEV." WOR+45 NAT/G FORCES BAL/PWR DIPLOM ECO/TAC COERCE ATTIT PWR...CONCPT HIST/WRIT COLD/WAR 20. PAGE 135 A2768 COM DOMIN FOR/AID USSR

S63
WOLF C.,"SOME ASPECTS OF THE 'VALUE' OF LESS-DEVELOPED COUNTRIES TO THE UNITED STATES." ASIA CHINA/COM COM USA+45 USSR ECO/UNDEV BAL/PWR ECO/TAC FOR/AID DOMIN EDU/PROP ATTIT PWR...POLICY METH/CNCPT CONT/OBS TREND CHARTS 20. PAGE 166 A3379 CONCPT GEN/LAWS DIPLOM

C63
CHARLETON W.G.,"THE REVOLUTION IN AMERICAN FOREIGN POLICY." COM PROB/SOLV FOR/AID DOMIN COLONIAL NEUTRAL DETER WAR ISOLAT NAT/LISM...BIBLIOG 19/20 UN COLD/WAR NATO. PAGE 26 A0523 DIPLOM INT/ORG BAL/PWR

B64
BARKER A.J.,SUEZ: THE SEVEN DAY WAR. EUR+WWI ISLAM FORCES

UAR INT/ORG NAT/G PLAN DIPLOM ECO/TAC DOMIN NAT/LISM DRIVE RIGID/FLEX PWR SOVEREIGN...POLICY JURID TREND CHARTS SUEZ UN 20. PAGE 11 A0221
COERCE UK

B64

CALVO SERER R.,LAS NUEVAS DEMOCRACIAS. AFR ASIA ISLAM USA+45 WOR+45 BAL/PWR DOMIN PARTIC INGP/REL AUTHORIT POPULISM...CONCPT 20 COM/PARTY. PAGE 23 A0469
ORD/FREE MARXISM DIPLOM POLICY

B64

DUROSELLE J.B.,POLITIQUES NATIONALES ENVERS LES JEUNES ETATS. FRANCE ISRAEL ITALY UK USA+45 USSR YUGOSLAVIA ECO/DEV FINAN ECO/TAC INT/TRADE ADMIN PWR 20. PAGE 40 A0809
DIPLOM ECO/UNDEV COLONIAL DOMIN

B64

ECONOMIDES C.P.,LE POUVOIR DE DECISION DES ORGANISATIONS INTERNATIONALES EUROPEENNES. DIPLOM DOMIN INGP/REL EFFICIENCY...INT/LAW JURID 20 NATO OEEC EEC COUNCL/EUR EURATOM. PAGE 40 A0821
INT/ORG PWR DECISION GP/COMP

B64

EPSTEIN H.M.,REVOLT IN THE CONGO. AFR CONGO/BRAZ WOR+45 NAT/G FORCES DOMIN WAR CIVMIL/REL INGP/REL MARXISM...RECORD GP/COMP 20 CONGO/LEOP UN. PAGE 42 A0856
REV COLONIAL NAT/LISM DIPLOM

B64

ETZIONI A.,WINNING WITHOUT WAR. FUT MOD/EUR USA+45 WOR+45 ECO/DEV ECO/UNDEV INT/ORG NAT/G FORCES TOP/EX PLAN TEC/DEV ECO/TAC DOMIN EDU/PROP LEGIT COERCE CHOOSE ATTIT MORAL ORD/FREE RESPECT WEALTH MAJORIT. PAGE 43 A0871
PWR TREND DIPLOM USSR

B64

FISHER R.,INTERNATIONAL CONFLICT AND BEHAVIORAL SCIENCE: THE CRAIGVILLE PAPERS. COM FUT USA+45 WOR+45 NAT/G DELIB/GP EX/STRUC FORCES ECO/TAC DOMIN EDU/PROP LEGIT COERCE ATTIT PERCEPT ORD/FREE PWR RESPECT...PSY SOC VAL/FREE. PAGE 46 A0940
INT/ORG PLAN DIPLOM

B64

HALPERN J.M.,GOVERNMENT, POLITICS, AND SOCIAL STRUCTURE IN LAOS. LAOS CULTURE SOCIETY STRATA STRUCT FAM DIPLOM DOMIN MARXISM...INT GOV/COMP WORSHIP SOC/INTEG 20. PAGE 60 A1242
NAT/G SOC LOC/G

B64

IKLE F.C.,HOW NATIONS NEGOTIATE. COM EUR+WWI USA+45 INTELL INT/ORG VOL/ASSN DELIB/GP ACT/RES CREATE DOMIN EDU/PROP ADJUD ROUTINE ATTIT PERSON ORD/FREE RESPECT SKILL...PSY SOC OBS VAL/FREE. PAGE 70 A1433
NAT/G PWR POLICY

B64

JANOWITZ M.,THE MILITARY IN THE POLITICAL DEVELOPMENT OF NEW NATIONS: AN ESSAY IN COMPARATIVE ANALYSIS. AFR ASIA ISLAM L/A+17C S/ASIA USA+45 ECO/UNDEV INT/ORG NAT/G POL/PAR DELIB/GP PLAN ECO/TAC DOMIN LEGIT COERCE ATTIT DRIVE RESPECT ...SOC CONCPT CENSUS VAL/FREE. PAGE 73 A1495
FORCES PWR

B64

LEGGE J.D.,INDONESIA. INDONESIA ELITES ECO/UNDEV POL/PAR CHIEF FORCES INT/TRADE COERCE CHOOSE ORD/FREE...SOC CHARTS BIBLIOG 16/20 CHINJAP. PAGE 86 A1765
S/ASIA DOMIN NAT/LISM POLICY

B64

STANKIEWICZ W.J.,POLITICAL THOUGHT SINCE WORLD WAR II. WOR+45 CAP/ISM DIPLOM COLONIAL COERCE REV REPRESENT ADJUST ANOMIE ALL/IDEOS 20. PAGE 137 A2804
IDEA/COMP DOMIN ORD/FREE AUTHORIT

B64

TREADGOLD D.W.,THE DEVELOPMENT OF THE USSR. COM USSR ECO/DEV CREATE BAL/PWR DEBATE COLONIAL TOTALISM...HUM ANTHOL BIBLIOG 19/20. PAGE 145 A2960
MARXISM CONSERVE DIPLOM DOMIN

B64

WAINHOUSE D.W.,REMNANTS OF EMPIRE: THE UNITED NATIONS AND THE END OF COLONIALISM. FUT PORTUGAL WOR+45 NAT/G CONSULT DOMIN LEGIT ADMIN ROUTINE ATTIT ORD/FREE...POLICY JURID RECORD INT TIME/SEQ UN CMN/WLTH 20. PAGE 160 A3260
INT/ORG TREND COLONIAL

B64

WRIGHT T.P. JR.,AMERICAN SUPPORT OF FREE ELECTIONS ABROAD. USA+45 USA-45 DOMIN LEAD NEUTRAL MARXISM ...POLICY TIME/SEQ BIBLIOG 19/20 COLD/WAR INTERVENT. PAGE 168 A3420
DIPLOM CHOOSE L/A+17C POPULISM

L64

CLAUDE I.,"THE OAS, THE UN, AND THE UNITED STATES." L/A+17C USA+45 CONSTN NAT/G DELIB/GP DOMIN EDU/PROP LEGIT REGION COERCE ORD/FREE PWR...TIME/SEQ TREND STERTYP OAS UN 20. PAGE 27 A0546
INT/ORG POLICY

L64

WARD C.,"THE 'NEW MYTHS' AND 'OLD REALITIES' OF NUCLEAR WAR." COM FUT USA+45 USSR WOR+45 INT/ORG NAT/G DOMIN LEGIT EXEC ATTIT PERCEPT ALL/VALS ...POLICY RELATIV PSY MYTH TREND 20. PAGE 161 A3280
FORCES COERCE ARMS/CONT NUC/PWR

S64

CRANE R.D.,"BASIC PRINCIPLES IN SOVIET SPACE LAW." FUT WOR+45 AIR INT/ORG DIPLOM DOMIN ARMS/CONT COERCE NUC/PWR PEACE ATTIT DRIVE PWR...INT/LAW METH/CNCPT NEW/IDEA OBS TREND GEN/LAWS VAL/FREE MARX/KARL 20. PAGE 32 A0659
COM LAW USSR SPACE

S64

DELGADO J.,"EL MOMENTO POLITICO HISPANOAMERICA."
L/A+17C

CHINA/COM FUT PANAMA USA+45 USSR INT/ORG NAT/G POL/PAR FORCES DOMIN REGION COERCE ATTIT ALL/VALS ...TRADIT CONCPT COLD/WAR 20. PAGE 36 A0728
EDU/PROP NAT/LISM

S64

GARDNER R.N.,"THE SOVIET UNION AND THE UNITED NATIONS." WOR+45 FINAN POL/PAR VOL/ASSN FORCES ECO/TAC DOMIN EDU/PROP LEGIT ADJUD ADMIN ARMS/CONT COERCE ATTIT ALL/VALS...POLICY MAJORIT CONCPT OBS TIME/SEQ TREND STERTYP UN. PAGE 51 A1046
COM INT/ORG USSR

S64

GARMARNIKOW M.,"INFLUENCE-BUYING IN WEST AFRICA." COM FUT USSR INTELL NAT/G PLAN TEC/DEV ECO/TAC DOMIN EDU/PROP REGION NAT/LISM ATTIT DRIVE ALL/VALS SOVEREIGN...POLICY PSY SOC CONCPT TREND STERTYP WORK COLD/WAR 20. PAGE 51 A1049
AFR ECO/UNDEV FOR/AID SOCISM

S64

GROSS J.A.,"WHITEHALL AND THE COMMONWEALTH." EUR+WWI MOD/EUR INT/ORG NAT/G CONSULT DELIB/GP LEGIS DOMIN ADMIN COLONIAL ROUTINE PWR CMN/WLTH 19/20. PAGE 57 A1174
EX/STRUC ATTIT TREND

S64

HOFFMANN S.,"CE QU'EN PENSENT LES AMERICAINS." EUR+WWI INT/ORG VOL/ASSN PLAN BAL/PWR DIPLOM DOMIN EDU/PROP REGION ARMS/CONT DRIVE ORD/FREE PWR ...POLICY CONCPT OBS TREND STERTYP COLD/WAR VAL/FREE 20. PAGE 66 A1357
USA+45 ATTIT FRANCE

S64

HOVET T. JR.,"THE ROLE OF AFRICA IN THE UNITED NATIONS." FUT WOR+45 NAT/G DELIB/GP DOMIN EDU/PROP LEGIT ORD/FREE PWR RESPECT SKILL...OBS TIME/SEQ TREND VAL/FREE UN 20. PAGE 68 A1398
AFR INT/ORG DIPLOM

S64

HOWARD M.,"MILITARY POWER AND INTERNATIONAL ORDER." WOR+45 SOCIETY INT/ORG NAT/G BAL/PWR DOMIN COERCE NUC/PWR WEAPON PWR...NEW/IDEA 20. PAGE 68 A1400
FORCES ATTIT WAR

S64

JACK H.,"NONALIGNMENT AND A TEST BAN AGREEMENT: THE ROLE OF THE NON-ALIGNED STATES." WOR+45 INT/ORG CONSULT DOMIN EDU/PROP LEGIT CHOOSE PEACE ATTIT DRIVE KNOWL ORD/FREE...TREND CHARTS GEN/LAWS UN VAL/FREE 20. PAGE 72 A1471
PWR CONCPT NUC/PWR

S64

KISSINGER H.A.,"COALITION DIPLOMACY IN A NUCLEAR AGE." COM EUR+WWI USA+45 WOR+45 INT/ORG NAT/G FORCES ACT/RES DOMIN LEGIT COERCE PERCEPT ALL/VALS ...POLICY TOT/POP 20. PAGE 80 A1644
CONSULT ATTIT DIPLOM NUC/PWR

S64

KOTANI H.,"PEACE-KEEPING: PROBLEMS FOR SMALLER COUNTRIES." FUT WOR+45 NAT/G ACT/RES PLAN DOMIN EDU/PROP COERCE ALL/VALS...POLICY UN TOT/POP 20. PAGE 82 A1673
INT/ORG FORCES

S64

MARTELLI G.,"PORTUGAL AND THE UNITED NATIONS." AFR EUR+WWI ELITES INT/ORG NAT/G PROVS PLAN DIPLOM ECO/TAC DOMIN COLONIAL RIGID/FLEX MORAL ORD/FREE PWR WEALTH...MYTH UN 20. PAGE 95 A1947
ATTIT PORTUGAL

S64

MAZRUI A.A.,"THE UNITED NATIONS AND SOME AFRICAN POLITICAL ATTITUDES." ECO/TAC FOR/AID DOMIN ROUTINE CHOOSE ATTIT DRIVE MORAL PWR RESPECT WEALTH...PSY CONCPT OBS TREND UN VAL/FREE 20. PAGE 97 A1987
AFR INT/ORG SOVEREIGN

S64

PESELT B.M.,"COMMUNIST ECONOMIC OFFENSIVE." WOR+45 SOCIETY INT/ORG PLAN ECO/TAC DOMIN EDU/PROP ATTIT PERSON PWR WEALTH...TREND CHARTS 20. PAGE 115 A2366
COM ECO/UNDEV FOR/AID USSR

S64

SAAB H.,"THE ARAB SEARCH FOR A FEDERAL UNION." SOCIETY INT/ORG NAT/G DELIB/GP FORCES ACT/RES TEC/DEV ECO/TAC DOMIN LEGIT REGION ROUTINE ATTIT DRIVE RIGID/FLEX ALL/VALS...SOC CONCPT NEW/IDEA TIME/SEQ TREND. PAGE 126 A2580
ISLAM PLAN

S64

SINGH N.,"THE CONTEMPORARY PRACTICE OF INDIA IN THE FIELD OF INTERNATIONAL LAW." INDIA S/ASIA INT/ORG NAT/G DOMIN EDU/PROP LEGIT KNOWL...CONCPT TOT/POP 20. PAGE 133 A2734
LAW ATTIT DIPLOM INT/LAW

S64

SKUBISZEWSKI K.,"FORMS OF PARTICIPATION OF INTERNATIONAL ORGANIZATION IN THE LAW MAKING PROCESS." FUT WOR+45 NAT/G DELIB/GP DOMIN LEGIT KNOWL PWR...JURID TREND 20. PAGE 134 A2740
INT/ORG LAW INT/LAW

S64

WASKOW A.I.,"NEW ROADS TO A WORLD WITHOUT WAR." FUT WOR+45 CULTURE INTELL SOCIETY NAT/G DOMIN LEGIT EXEC COERCE PEACE ATTIT DISPL PERCEPT RIGID/FLEX ALL/VALS...POLICY RELATIV SOC NEW/IDEA 20. PAGE 161 A3288
INT/ORG FORCES

B65

DOMENACH J.M.,LA PROPAGANDE POLITIQUE. COM/IND INT/ORG POL/PAR DOMIN RIGID/FLEX FASCISM MARXISM ...PSY 20. PAGE 38 A0770
ATTIT EDU/PROP TEC/DEV MYTH

B65

FAGG J.E.,CUBA, HAITI, AND THE DOMINICAN REPUBLIC. CUBA DOMIN/REP HAITI L/A+17C NAT/G DIPLOM ECO/TAC
COLONIAL ECO/UNDEV

DOMIN CHOOSE AUTHORIT ROLE SOVEREIGN POPULISM 17/20. PAGE 43 A0883 REV GOV/COMP

B65
FANON F.,STUDIES IN A DYING COLONIALISM. ALGERIA FRANCE STRATA FAM DIPLOM DOMIN WAR RACE/REL DISCRIM HEALTH 20. PAGE 44 A0897 NAT/LISM COLONIAL REV SOVEREIGN

B65
IRIYE A.,AFTER IMPERIALISM; THE SEARCH FOR A NEW ORDER IN THE FAR EAST 1921-1931. USA-45 USSR DOMIN AGREE COLONIAL REV PWR...BIBLIOG DICTIONARY 20 CHINJAP. PAGE 72 A1468 DIPLOM ASIA SOVEREIGN

B65
JALEE P.,THE PILLAGE OF THE THIRD WORLD (TRANS. BY MARY KLOPPER). WOR+45 AGRI INDUS ECO/TAC FOR/AID COLONIAL CONTROL PRODUC PWR WEALTH...STAT CHARTS 20 RESOURCE/N. PAGE 73 A1493 ECO/UNDEV DOMIN INT/TRADE DIPLOM

B65
LAFAVE W.R.,LAW AND SOVIET SOCIETY. EX/STRUC DIPLOM DOMIN EDU/PROP PRESS ADMIN CRIME OWN MARXISM 20 KHRUSH/N. PAGE 84 A1710 JURID CT/SYS ADJUD GOV/REL

B65
LINDBLOM C.E.,THE INTELLIGENCE OF DEMOCRACY; DECISION MAKING THROUGH MUTUAL ADJUSTMENT. WOR+45 SOCIETY NAT/G PROB/SOLV DOMIN PARTIC GP/REL ORD/FREE...POLICY IDEA/COMP BIBLIOG 20. PAGE 89 A1821 PLURISM DECISION ADJUST DIPLOM

B65
MALLIN J.,FORTRESS CUBA; RUSSIA'S AMERICAN BASE. COM CUBA L/A+17C FORCES PLAN DIPLOM LEAD REV WAR ...POLICY 20 CASTRO/F GUEVARA/C INTERVENT. PAGE 93 A1914 MARXISM CHIEF GUERRILLA DOMIN

B65
MUNGER E.S.,NOTES ON THE FORMATION OF SOUTH AFRICAN FOREIGN POLICY. ACADEM POL/PAR SECT CHIEF DELIB/GP FORCES LEGIS PRESS ATTIT...TREND 20 NEGRO. PAGE 106 A2170 AFR DOMIN POLICY DIPLOM

B65
NEWBURY C.W.,BRITISH POLICY TOWARDS WEST AFRICA: SELECT DOCUMENTS 1786-1874. AFR UK INT/TRADE DOMIN ADMIN COLONIAL CT/SYS COERCE ORD/FREE...BIBLIOG/A 18/19. PAGE 108 A2224 DIPLOM POLICY NAT/G WRITING

B65
O'CONNELL M.R.,IRISH POLITICS AND SOCIAL CONFLICT IN THE AGE OF THE AMERICAN REVOLUTION. FRANCE IRELAND MOD/EUR STRATA SECT LEGIS DIPLOM INT/TRADE DOMIN REV WAR...BIBLIOG 18 PARLIAMENT. PAGE 111 A2268 CATHISM ATTIT NAT/G DELIB/GP

B65
RAPPAPORT A.,ISSUES IN AMERICAN DIPLOMACY: WORLD POWER AND LEADERSHIP SINCE 1895 (VOL. II). CHINA/COM EUR+WWI L/A+17C USA+45 USA-45 NAT/G ECO/TAC DOMIN CONFER LEAD NUC/PWR WEAPON...DECISION 19/20 WILSON/W ROOSEVLT/F CHINJAP. PAGE 119 A2447 WAR POLICY DIPLOM

B65
ROTBERG R.I.,A POLITICAL HISTORY OF TROPICAL AFRICA. EX/STRUC DIPLOM INT/TRADE DOMIN ADMIN RACE/REL NAT/LISM PWR SOVEREIGN...GEOG TIME/SEQ BIBLIOG 1/20. PAGE 124 A2545 AFR CULTURE COLONIAL

B65
SOPER T.,EVOLVING COMMONWEALTH. AFR CANADA INDIA IRELAND UK LAW CONSTN POL/PAR DOMIN CONTROL WAR PWR ...AUD/VIS 18/20 COMMONWLTH OEEC. PAGE 135 A2769 INT/ORG COLONIAL VOL/ASSN

B65
WILLIAMSON J.A.,GREAT BRITAIN AND THE COMMONWEALTH. UK DOMIN COLONIAL INGP/REL...POLICY 18/20 CMN/WLTH. PAGE 165 A3355 NAT/G DIPLOM INT/ORG SOVEREIGN

B65
WINT G.,COMMUNIST CHINA'S CRUSADE: MAO'S ROAD TO POWER AND THE NEW CAMPAIGN FOR WORLD REVOLUTION. ASIA CHINA/COM USA+45 USSR NAT/G POL/PAR DOMIN COERCE WAR PWR...POLICY CHARTS IDEA/COMP BIBLIOG 20 MAO. PAGE 165 A3364 DIPLOM MARXISM REV COLONIAL

L65
RUBIN A.P.,"UNITED STATES CONTEMPORARY PRACTICE RELATING TO INTERNATIONAL LAW." USA+45 WOR+45 CONSTN INT/ORG NAT/G DELIB/GP EX/STRUC DIPLOM DOMIN CT/SYS ROUTINE ORD/FREE...CONCPT COLD/WAR 20. PAGE 125 A2558 LAW LEGIT INT/LAW

L65
TUCKER R.W.,"PEACE AND WAR." UNIV CULTURE SOCIETY INT/ORG NAT/G ACT/RES DOMIN DETER WAR ATTIT DISPL ...POLICY CONCPT MYTH GEN/LAWS 20. PAGE 145 A2975 PWR COERCE ARMS/CONT PEACE

S65
BROWN S.,"AN ALTERNATIVE TO THE GRAND DESIGN." EUR+WWI FUT USA+45 INT/ORG NAT/G EX/STRUC FORCES CREATE BAL/PWR DOMIN RIGID/FLEX ORD/FREE PWR ...NEW/IDEA RECORD EEC NATO 20. PAGE 20 A0407 VOL/ASSN CONCPT DIPLOM

S65
FLEMING D.F.,"CAN PAX AMERICANA SUCCEED?" ASIA CHINA/COM EUR+WWI USSR VIETNAM BAL/PWR DIPLOM DOMIN COERCE GOV/REL 20. PAGE 46 A0948 DECISION ATTIT ECO/TAC

S65
GROSS L.,"PROBLEMS OF INTERNATIONAL ADJUDICATION AND COMPLIANCE WITH INTERNATIONAL LAW: SOME SIMPLE SOLUTIONS." WOR+45 SOCIETY NAT/G DOMIN LEGIT ADJUD CT/SYS RIGID/FLEX HEALTH PWR...JURID NEW/IDEA COLD/WAR 20. PAGE 57 A1177 LAW METH/CNCPT INT/LAW

S65
HELMREICH E.C.,"KADAR'S HUNGARY." COM EUR+WWI HUNGARY USSR INTELL ECO/DEV AGRI INT/ORG TOP/EX DOMIN ALL/VALS WORK COLD/WAR 20. PAGE 64 A1311 NAT/G RIGID/FLEX TOTALISM

S65
MERRITT R.L.,"WOODROW WILSON AND THE 'GREAT AND SOLEMN REFERENDUM,' 1920." USA-45 SOCIETY NAT/G CONSULT LEGIS ACT/RES PLAN DOMIN EDU/PROP ROUTINE ATTIT DISPL DRIVE PERSON RIGID/FLEX MORAL ORD/FREE ...PSY SOC CONCPT MYTH LEAGUE/NAT. PAGE 100 A2044 INT/ORG TOP/EX DIPLOM

S65
PLISCHKE E.,"INTEGRATING BERLIN AND THE FEDERAL REPUBLIC OF GERMANY." EUR+WWI GERMANY/W LEGIS TEC/DEV DOMIN ORD/FREE PWR...JURID 20 BERLIN. PAGE 117 A2392 DIPLOM NAT/G MUNIC

S65
ROGGER H.,"EAST GERMANY: STABLE OR IMMOBILE." COM EUR+WWI GERMANY/E NAT/G INT/TRADE DOMIN EDU/PROP COERCE TOTALISM COLD/WAR 20. PAGE 123 A2516 TOP/EX RIGID/FLEX GERMANY

B66
EKIRCH A.A. JR.,IDEAS, IDEALS, AND AMERICAN DIPLOMACY. USA+45 USA-45 INT/ORG DOMIN COLONIAL ARMS/CONT DETER ISOLAT NAT/LISM...MAJORIT BIBLIOG 19/20 COLD/WAR. PAGE 41 A0834 DIPLOM LEAD PEACE

B66
HERZ M.F.,BEGINNINGS OF THE COLD WAR. COM POLAND USA+45 USSR INT/ORG NAT/G CHIEF FOR/AID DOMIN CONFER AGREE WAR PEACE 20 STALIN/J COLD/WAR UN. PAGE 64 A1321 DIPLOM

B66
LONDON K.,EASTERN EUROPE IN TRANSITION. CHINA/COM USSR DOMIN COLONIAL CENTRAL RIGID/FLEX PWR...SOC ANTHOL 20. PAGE 91 A1855 SOVEREIGN COM NAT/LISM DIPLOM

B66
MCINTYRE W.D.,COLONIES INTO COMMONWEALTH. UK CONSTN VOL/ASSN DOMIN CONTROL...BIBLIOG 18/20 CMN/WLTH. PAGE 98 A2012 DIPLOM INT/ORG COLONIAL SOVEREIGN

B66
MURPHY G.G.,SOVIET MONGOLIA: A STUDY OF THE OLDEST POLITICAL SATELLITE. USSR STRATA STRUCT COST INCOME ATTIT SOCISM 20. PAGE 106 A2177 DIPLOM ECO/TAC PLAN DOMIN

B66
SAGER P.,MOSKAUS HAND IN INDIEN. INDIA USSR DIPLOM DOMIN...PSY CONCPT 20 COM/PARTY. PAGE 126 A2586 PRESS EDU/PROP METH POL/PAR

B66
SINGER L.,ALLE LITTEN AN GROSSENWAHN: VON WOODROW WILSON BIS MAO TSE-TUNG. ASIA UK USSR INT/ORG DELIB/GP BAL/PWR DOMIN ATTIT PERSON 20 WILSON/W ROOSEVLT/F. PAGE 133 A2731 DIPLOM TOTALISM WAR CHIEF

B66
SKILLING H.G.,THE GOVERNMENTS OF COMMUNIST EAST EUROPE. COM EUR+WWI ELITES FORCES DIPLOM ECO/TAC CONTROL HABITAT SOCISM...DECISION BIBLIOG 20 EUROPE/E COM/PARTY. PAGE 134 A2738 MARXISM NAT/COMP GP/COMP DOMIN

B66
THORNTON A.P.,THE IMPERIAL IDEA AND ITS ENEMIES. UK WOR+45 WOR-45 NAT/G PLAN DOMIN CONTROL WAR ATTIT PWR...TREND CHARTS 19/20 CMN/WLTH. PAGE 144 A2937 COLONIAL DIPLOM

C66
TARLING N.,"A CONCISE HISTORY OF SOUTHEAST ASIA." BURMA CAMBODIA LAOS S/ASIA THAILAND VIETNAM ECO/UNDEV POL/PAR FORCES ADMIN REV WAR CIVMIL/REL ORD/FREE MARXISM SOCISM 13/20. PAGE 141 A2890 COLONIAL DOMIN INT/TRADE NAT/LISM

B67
GRIFFITH SB I.I.,THE CHINESE PEOPLE'S LIBERATION ARMY. CHINA/COM DIPLOM DOMIN GUERRILLA NUC/PWR REV ...CHARTS BIBLIOG 20. PAGE 57 A1163 FORCES CIVMIL/REL NAT/LISM PWR

B67
MAW B.,BREAKTHROUGH IN BURMA: MEMOIRS OF A REVOLUTION, 1939-1946. BURMA UK FORCES PROB/SOLV DIPLOM FOR/AID DOMIN LEAD...BIOG 20. PAGE 97 A1980 REV ORD/FREE NAT/LISM COLONIAL

B67
US SENATE COMM ON FOREIGN REL,HUMAN RIGHTS CONVENTIONS. USA+45 LABOR VOL/ASSN DELIB/GP DOMIN ADJUD REPRESENT...INT/LAW MGT CONGRESS. PAGE 156 A3189 LEGIS ORD/FREE WORKER LOBBY

L67
ANAND R.P.,"SOVEREIGN EQUALITY OF STATES IN INTERNATIONAL LAW." UNIV DIPLOM DOMIN CONFER DEBATE SANCTION ATTIT UN. PAGE 8 A0157 INT/LAW INT/ORG CONCPT POLICY

L67
MACDONALD R.S.J.,"THE RESORT TO ECONOMIC COERCION INT/ORG

BY INTERNATIONAL POLITICAL ORGANIZATIONS." CUBA ETHIOPIA RHODESIA SOUTH/AFR NAT/G FOR/AID INT/TRADE DOMIN CONTROL SANCTION...DECISION LEAGUE/NAT UN OAS 20. PAGE 92 A1887
COERCE ECO/TAC DIPLOM

L67
MOORE N.,"THE LAWFULNESS OF MILITARY ASSISTANCE TO THE REPUBLIC OF VIET NAM." USA+45 VIETNAM WOR+45 FOR/AID DOMIN DETER WAR WEAPON...DECISION INT/LAW 20 UN. PAGE 103 A2123
PWR DIPLOM FORCES GOV/REL

S67
"CHINESE STATEMENT ON NUCLEAR PROLIFERATION." CHINA/COM USA+45 USSR DOMIN COLONIAL PWR. PAGE 4 A0078
NUC/PWR BAL/PWR ARMS/CONT DIPLOM

S67
DAVIS H.B.,"LENIN AND NATIONALISM: THE REDIRECTION OF THE MARXIST THEORY OF NATIONALISM." COM MOD/EUR USSR STRATA INT/ORG PLAN DOMIN COLONIAL FEDERAL ...TREND 20. PAGE 34 A0690
NAT/LISM MARXISM ATTIT CENTRAL

S67
FELD B.T.,"A PLEDGE* NO FIRST USE." DELIB/GP BAL/PWR DOMIN DETER. PAGE 45 A0913
ARMS/CONT NUC/PWR DIPLOM PEACE

S67
FELDMAN H.,"AID AS IMPERIALISM?" INDIA PAKISTAN UK USA+45 BAL/PWR CAP/ISM DIPLOM ECO/TAC DOMIN BAL/PAY WEALTH...POLICY 20. PAGE 45 A0914
COLONIAL FOR/AID S/ASIA ECO/UNDEV

S67
FRANKLIN W.O.,"CLAUSEWITZ ON LIMITED WAR." VIETNAM WOR+45 WOR-45 PROB/SOLV DIPLOM ECO/TAC DOMIN COLONIAL...METH/COMP 19/20. PAGE 48 A0986
COERCE WAR PLAN GUERRILLA

S67
GODUNSKY Y.,"'APOSTLES OF PEACE' IN LATIN AMERICA." L/A+17C USA+45 BAL/PWR DIPLOM FOR/AID DOMIN COLONIAL CIVMIL/REL MARXIST. PAGE 53 A1086
ECO/UNDEV REV VOL/ASSN EDU/PROP

S67
HUDSON R.,"WAS THIS WAR NECESSARY? THE UN AND THE MIDDLE EAST" WOR+45 STRUCT DIPLOM DOMIN CONTROL REPRESENT PWR...NEW/IDEA 20 UN MID/EAST. PAGE 69 A1410
DELIB/GP INT/ORG PROB/SOLV PEACE

S67
JACKSON W.G.F.,"NUCLEAR PROLIFERATION AND THE GREAT POWERS." FUT UK WOR+45 INT/ORG DOMIN ARMS/CONT DETER ORD/FREE PACIFIST. PAGE 72 A1480
NUC/PWR ATTIT BAL/PWR NAT/LISM

S67
KAHN H.,"CRITERIA FOR LONG-RANGE NUCLEAR CONTROL POLICIES." WOR+45 INT/ORG TEC/DEV DOMIN DETER WAR WEAPON ISOLAT ORD/FREE POLICY. PAGE 76 A1549
NUC/PWR ARMS/CONT BAL/PWR DIPLOM

S67
KINGSLEY R.E.,"THE US BUSINESS IMAGE IN LATIN AMERICA." L/A+17C USA+45 NAT/G TEC/DEV CAP/ISM FOR/AID DOMIN EDU/PROP...CONCPT LING IDEA/COMP 20. PAGE 79 A1626
ATTIT LOVE DIPLOM ECO/UNDEV

S67
LEVI M.,"LES DIFFICULTES ECONOMIQUES DE LA GRANDE-BRETAGNE." UK INT/ORG TEC/DEV BARGAIN DIPLOM DOMIN REPRESENT DEMAND WEALTH...POLICY 20 EEC. PAGE 88 A1792
BAL/PAY INT/TRADE PRODUC

S67
PAUKER G.J.,"TOWARD A NEW ORDER IN INDONESIA." COM INDONESIA S/ASIA ECO/UNDEV POL/PAR EX/STRUC TOP/EX BAL/PWR ECO/TAC FOR/AID DOMIN NAT/LISM AUTHORIT ORD/FREE PWR 20. PAGE 114 A2342
REV NAT/G DIPLOM CIVMIL/REL

S67
PEUKERT W.,"WEST GERMANY'S 'RED TRADE'." COM GERMANY INDUS CAP/ISM DOMIN SANCTION DEMAND PEACE UTIL...MARXIST 20 COLD/WAR. PAGE 115 A2371
DIPLOM ECO/TAC INT/TRADE

S67
ROMANOVSKY S.,"MISUSE OF CULTURAL COOPERATION." USA+45 INTELL DIPLOM DOMIN ATTIT COLD/WAR. PAGE 123 A2518
EDU/PROP POLICY MARXISM CAP/ISM

S67
ROSE S.,"ASIAN NATIONALISM* THE SECOND STAGE." ASIA COM ECO/UNDEV NAT/G PROB/SOLV DIPLOM FOR/AID DOMIN NEUTRAL REGION TASK...METH/COMP 20. PAGE 123 A2528
NAT/LISM S/ASIA BAL/PWR COLONIAL

S67
SARBADHIKARI P.,"A NOTE ON THE DOMESTIC CRISIS OF NON-ALIGNMENT." ELITES INTELL ECO/UNDEV FOR/AID DOMIN. PAGE 127 A2605
NEUTRAL WEALTH TOTALISM BAL/PWR

S67
SCHUMANN H.,"IMPERIALISMUS-KRITIK UND KOLONIALISMUS-FORSCHUNG." GERMANY/E DIPLOM SOVEREIGN...SOC HIST/WRIT 20. PAGE 129 A2652
COLONIAL ATTIT DOMIN CAP/ISM

S67
SHERSHNEV Y.,"THE KENNEDY ROUND* PLANS AND REALITY." EUR+WWI USA+45 INT/ORG DIPLOM TARIFFS DOMIN CONFER PWR...MARXIST PREDICT. PAGE 132 A2701
ECO/TAC ECO/DEV INT/TRADE BAL/PWR

S67
SHOEMAKER R.L.,"JAPANESE ARMY AND THE WEST." ASIA ELITES EX/STRUC DIPLOM DOMIN EDU/PROP COERCE ATTIT AUTHORIT PWR 1/20 CHINJAP. PAGE 132 A2703
FORCES TEC/DEV WAR TOTALISM

S67
STEELE R.,"A TASTE FOR INTERVENTION." USA+45 FOR/AID INT/TRADE EDU/PROP COLONIAL WAR PWR...TREND 20 COLD/WAR. PAGE 137 A2812
POLICY DIPLOM DOMIN ATTIT

S67
TERRILL R.,"THE SIEGE MENTALITY." CHINA/COM NAT/G FORCES DIPLOM REV EFFICIENCY NAT/LISM MARXISM ...TREND 20. PAGE 142 A2904
EDU/PROP WAR DOMIN

S67
YEFROMEV A.,"THE TRUE FACE OF THE WEST GERMAN NATIONAL-DEMOCRATS." GERMANY/W NAT/G DOMIN LEAD SANCTION WAR ATTIT PERSON...MARXIST 20. PAGE 169 A3433
POL/PAR TOTALISM PARL/PROC DIPLOM

B98
GRIFFIN A.P.C.,LIST OF BOOKS RELATING TO CUBA (PAMPHLET). CUBA L/A+17C USA-45 INT/TRADE DOMIN WAR GP/REL ALL/VALS...GEOG SOC CHARTS 19/20. PAGE 56 A1158
BIBLIOG/A NAT/G COLONIAL

DOMIN/REP....DOMINICAN REPUBLIC; SEE ALSO L/A + 17C

B47
PERKINS D.,THE UNITED STATES AND THE CARIBBEAN. CUBA DOMIN/REP GUATEMALA HAITI PANAMA CULTURE ECO/UNDEV FOR/AID ADMIN COERCE HABITAT...POLICY 19/20. PAGE 115 A2359
DIPLOM L/A+17C USA-45

B48
FLOREN LOZANO L.,BIBLIOGRAFIA DE LA BIBLIOGRAFIA DOMINICANA. DOMIN/REP NAT/G DIPLOM EDU/PROP CIVMIL/REL...POLICY ART/METH GEOG PHIL/SCI HIST/WRIT 20. PAGE 47 A0952
BIBLIOG/A BIOG L/A+17C CULTURE

B61
GOLDWERT M.,CONSTABULARY IN THE DOMINICAN REPUBLIC AND NICARAGUA. DOMIN/REP L/A+17C NICARAGUA USA-45 NAT/G PLAN CONTROL TASK REV...POLICY 20 INTERVENT. PAGE 53 A1093
DIPLOM PEACE FORCES

S63
WELLS H.,"THE OAS AND THE DOMINICAN ELECTIONS." L/A+17C INT/ORG NAT/G POL/PAR TEC/DEV ECO/TAC EDU/PROP PERCEPT...TIME/SEQ OAS TOT/POP 20. PAGE 163 A3317
CONSULT CHOOSE DOMIN/REP

B65
FAGG J.E.,CUBA, HAITI, AND THE DOMINICAN REPUBLIC. CUBA DOMIN/REP HAITI L/A+17C NAT/G DIPLOM ECO/TAC DOMIN CHOOSE AUTHORIT ROLE SOVEREIGN POPULISM 17/20. PAGE 43 A0883
COLONIAL ECO/UNDEV REV GOV/COMP

B66
NIEDERGANG M.,LA REVOLUTION DE SAINT-DOMINGUE. DOMIN/REP INT/ORG NAT/G CONTROL LEAD GP/REL ORD/FREE MARXISM 20. PAGE 109 A2239
REV FORCES DIPLOM

DOMINATION....SEE DOMIN

DOMINICAN REPUBLIC....SEE DOMIN/REP

DOMINO....THE DOMINO THEORY

DONALD A.D. A0771

DONNELLY/I....IGNATIUS DONNELLY

DONOUGHUE B. A0772

DORE R. A0773

DOS SANTOS M. A0774

DOSSICK J.J. A0775,A0776

DOSTOYEV/F....FYODOR DOSTOYEVSKY

DOUGHERTY J.E. A0632,A0777

DOUGLAS W.O. A0778,A0779

DOUGLAS/P....PAUL DOUGLAS

DOUGLAS/WO....WILLIAM O. DOUGLAS

DOUMA J. A0780

DOYLE S.E. A0781

DRACHKOVITCH A0782 ,A0783,A0784

DRAKE S.T.C. A0785

DRAPER/HAL....HAL DRAPER

DREAM....DREAMING

B57
STRACHEY A.,THE UNCONSCIOUS MOTIVES OF WAR; A PSYCHO-ANALYTICAL CONTRIBUTION. UNIV SOCIETY DIPLOM DREAM GP/REL ADJUST ATTIT DISPL PERCEPT PERSON KNOWL MORAL. PAGE 139 A2840 — WAR DRIVE LOVE PSY

DREIER J.C. A0786,A0787

DREYFUS/A....ALFRED DREYFUS OR DREYFUS AFFAIR

DRIVE....DRIVE AND MORALE

B00
LORIMER J.,THE INSTITUTES OF THE LAW OF NATIONS. WOR-45 CULTURE SOCIETY NAT/G VOL/ASSN DIPLOM LEGIT WAR PEACE DRIVE ORD/FREE SOVEREIGN...CONCPT RECORD INT TREND HYPO/EXP GEN/METH TOT/POP VAL/FREE 20. PAGE 91 A1863 — INT/ORG LAW INT/LAW

B00
MORRIS H.C.,THE HISTORY OF COLONIZATION. WOR+45 WOR-45 ECO/DEV ECO/UNDEV INT/ORG ACT/RES PLAN ECO/TAC LEGIT ROUTINE COERCE ATTIT DRIVE ALL/VALS ...GEOG TREND 19. PAGE 105 A2148 — DOMIN SOVEREIGN COLONIAL

N19
STEUBER F.A.,THE CONTRIBUTION OF SWITZERLAND TO THE ECONOMIC AND SOCIAL DEVELOPMENT OF LOW-INCOME COUNTRIES (PAMPHLET). SWITZERLND FINAN NAT/G VOL/ASSN INT/TRADE DRIVE...CHARTS 20. PAGE 138 A2820 — FOR/AID ECO/UNDEV PLAN DIPLOM

B20
BURNS C.D.,INTERNATIONAL POLITICS. WOR-45 CULTURE SOCIETY ECO/UNDEV NAT/G VOL/ASSN DELIB/GP ACT/RES CREATE DOMIN EDU/PROP LEGIT ATTIT DRIVE RIGID/FLEX ALL/VALS...PLURIST PSY CONCPT TREND. PAGE 22 A0442 — INT/ORG PEACE SOVEREIGN

B20
HALDANE R.B.,BEFORE THE WAR. MOD/EUR SOCIETY INT/ORG NAT/G DELIB/GP PLAN DOMIN EDU/PROP LEGIT ADMIN COERCE ATTIT DRIVE MORAL ORD/FREE PWR...SOC CONCPT SELF/OBS RECORD BIOG TIME/SEQ. PAGE 60 A1223 — POLICY DIPLOM UK

B20
WOOLF L.,EMPIRE AND COMMERCE IN AFRICA. EUR+WWI MOD/EUR FINAN INDUS MARKET INT/ORG PLAN COERCE ATTIT DRIVE PWR WEALTH...CONCPT TIME/SEQ TREND CHARTS 20. PAGE 167 A3394 — AFR DOMIN COLONIAL SOVEREIGN

B21
STUART G.H.,FRENCH FOREIGN POLICY. CONSTN INT/ORG NAT/G POL/PAR EX/STRUC FORCES PLAN ECO/TAC DOMIN EDU/PROP ADJUD COERCE ATTIT DRIVE RIGID/FLEX ALL/VALS...POLICY OBS RECORD BIOG TIME/SEQ TREND. PAGE 139 A2852 — MOD/EUR DIPLOM FRANCE

B22
BRYCE J.,INTERNATIONAL RELATIONS. CHRIST-17C EUR+WWI MOD/EUR CULTURE INTELL NAT/G DELIB/GP CREATE BAL/PWR DIPLOM ATTIT DRIVE RIGID/FLEX ALL/VALS...PLURIST JURID CONCPT TIME/SEQ GEN/LAWS TOT/POP. PAGE 20 A0412 — INT/ORG POLICY

C28
SCHNEIDER H.W.,"MAKING THE FASCIST STATE." ITALY CULTURE LABOR DIPLOM REV WAR NAT/LISM TOTALISM ATTIT DRIVE SOCISM...BIBLIOG PARLIAMENT 20. PAGE 129 A2638 — FASCISM POLICY POL/PAR

B29
BUELL R.,INTERNATIONAL RELATIONS. WOR+45 WOR-45 CONSTN STRATA FORCES TOP/EX ADMIN ATTIT DRIVE SUPEGO MORAL ORD/FREE PWR SOVEREIGN...JURID SOC CONCPT 20. PAGE 21 A0428 — INT/ORG BAL/PWR DIPLOM

B31
HODGES C.,THE BACKGROUND OF INTERNATIONAL RELATIONS. WOR-45 SOCIETY ECO/DEV ECO/UNDEV INT/ORG DIPLOM DOMIN EDU/PROP LEGIT WAR ATTIT DRIVE PERSON ALL/VALS...CONCPT METH/CNCPT TIME/SEQ CHARTS WORK LEAGUE/NAT 19/20. PAGE 66 A1350 — NAT/G BAL/PWR

B34
GRAHAM F.D.,PROTECTIVE TARIFFS. FUT USA+45 WOR-45 INDUS MARKET VOL/ASSN PLAN CAP/ISM ECO/TAC PEACE ATTIT DRIVE HEALTH ORD/FREE...OBS TREND GEN/LAWS 20. PAGE 55 A1124 — INT/ORG TARIFFS

B35
FOREIGN AFFAIRS BIBLIOGRAPHY: A SELECTED AND ANNOTATED LIST OF BOOKS ON INTERNATIONAL RELATIONS 1919-1962 (4 VOLS.). CONSTN FORCES COLONIAL ARMS/CONT WAR NAT/LISM PEACE ATTIT DRIVE...POLICY INT/LAW 20. PAGE 3 A0050 — BIBLIOG/A DIPLOM INT/ORG

B37
KOHN H.,FORCE OR REASON; ISSUES OF THE TWENTIETH CENTURY. WOR+45 NAT/G DIPLOM WAR DRIVE ORD/FREE ALL/IDEOS FASCISM PLURISM...POLICY IDEA/COMP 20. PAGE 81 A1660 — COERCE DOMIN RATIONAL COLONIAL

B39
ROBBINS L.,ECONOMIC CAUSES OF WAR. WOR-45 ECO/DEV ECO/UNDEV INT/ORG NAT/G TEC/DEV DIPLOM DOMIN COLONIAL ATTIT DRIVE PWR WEALTH...POLICY CONCPT OBS SAMP TREND CON/ANAL GEN/LAWS MARX/KARL 20. PAGE 122 A2493 — COERCE ECO/TAC WAR

B39
WILSON G.G.,HANDBOOK OF INTERNATIONAL LAW. FUT UNIV USA-45 WOR-45 SOCIETY LEGIT ATTIT DISPL DRIVE ALL/VALS...INT/LAW TIME/SEQ TREND. PAGE 165 A3359 — INT/ORG LAW CONCPT WAR

L39
NEARING S.,"A WARLESS WORLD." FUT WOR-45 SOCIETY INT/ORG NAT/G EX/STRUC PLAN DOMIN WAR ATTIT DRIVE PWR...POLICY PSY CONCPT OBS TREND HYPO/EXP MARX/KARL 20 MARX/KARL LENIN/VI. PAGE 108 A2210 — COERCE PEACE

B40
MILLER E.,THE NEUROSES OF WAR. UNIV INTELL SOCIETY INT/ORG NAT/G EDU/PROP DISPL DRIVE PERCEPT PERSON RIGID/FLEX...SOC TIME/SEQ 20. PAGE 101 A2075 — HEALTH PSY WAR

B40
RAPPARD W.E.,THE QUEST FOR PEACE. UNIV USA-45 WOR-45 SOCIETY INT/ORG NAT/G PLAN EXEC ROUTINE WAR ATTIT DRIVE ALL/VALS...POLICY CONCPT OBS TIME/SEQ LEAGUE/NAT TOT/POP 20. PAGE 119 A2450 — EUR+WWI ACT/RES PEACE

B42
TOLMAN E.C.,DRIVES TOWARD WAR. UNIV PLAN DIPLOM ECO/TAC COERCE PERS/REL ADJUST HAPPINESS BIO/SOC HEREDITY HEALTH KNOWL. PAGE 144 A2947 — PSY WAR UTOPIA DRIVE

L42
SHOTWELL J.,"LESSON OF THE LAST WORLD WAR." EUR+WWI MOD/EUR USA-45 SOCIETY ECO/UNDEV INDUS VOL/ASSN CONSULT ACT/RES CREATE CAP/ISM INT/TRADE DRIVE ALL/VALS...CONCPT NEW/IDEA SELF/OBS GEN/LAWS LEAGUE/NAT NAZI 20. PAGE 132 A2708 — INT/ORG ORD/FREE

S42
TURNER F.J.,"AMERICAN SECTIONALISM AND WORLD ORGANIZATION." EUR+WWI UNIV USA-45 WOR-45 INTELL ECO/DEV TOP/EX ACT/RES PLAN EDU/PROP LEGIT ALL/VALS ...CONCPT NEW/IDEA OBS TREND LEAGUE/NAT TOT/POP 20. PAGE 146 A2981 — INT/ORG DRIVE BAL/PWR

B43
HEMLEBEN S.J.,PLANS FOR WORLD PEACE THROUGH SIX CENTURIES. WOR-45 EDU/PROP DRIVE PWR...CONCPT TIME/SEQ GEN/LAWS TOT/POP LEAGUE/NAT 14/20. PAGE 64 A1312 — INT/ORG PEACE

B44
COMM. STUDY ORGAN. PEACE,UNITED NATIONS GUARDS AND TECHNICAL FIELD SERVICES. WOR+45 DELIB/GP EDU/PROP DRIVE PWR SKILL...CONCPT GEN/LAWS UN TOT/POP 20. PAGE 28 A0576 — INT/ORG FORCES PEACE

B44
MACIVER R.M.,TOWARDS AN ABIDING PEACE. USA-45 ECO/TAC EDU/PROP DRIVE ORD/FREE PWR WEALTH...CONCPT TIME/SEQ GEN/METH TOT/POP 20. PAGE 92 A1890 — INT/ORG PEACE INT/LAW

L44
WRIGHT Q.,"THE US AND INTERNATIONAL AGREEMENTS." FUT USA-45 CONSTN INTELL INT/ORG LOC/G NAT/G CHIEF CONSULT EX/STRUC DIPLOM LEGIT DRIVE PERCEPT PWR ...CONCPT CONGRESS 20. PAGE 167 A3407 — DELIB/GP TOP/EX PEACE

S44
WRIGHT Q.,"CONSTITUTIONAL PROCEDURES OF THE US FOR CARRYING OUT OBLIGATIONS FOR MILITARY SANCTIONS." EUR+WWI FUT USA-45 WOR-45 CONSTN INTELL NAT/G CONSULT EX/STRUC LEGIS ROUTINE DRIVE...POLICY JURID CONCPT OBS TREND TOT/POP 20. PAGE 167 A3406 — TOP/EX FORCES INT/LAW WAR

B46
GAULD W.A.,MAN, NATURE, AND TIME, AN INTRODUCTION TO WORLD STUDY. WOR-45 CULTURE CREATE DIPLOM GP/REL DRIVE...SOC LING CENSUS CHARTS TIME 18/20. PAGE 52 A1054 — HABITAT PERSON

B48
DURBIN E.F.M.,THE POLITICS OF DEMOCRATIC SOCIALISM; AN ESSAY ON SOCIAL POLICY. STRATA POL/PAR PLAN COERCE DRIVE PERSON PWR MARXISM...CHARTS METH/COMP. PAGE 39 A0805 — SOCIALIST POPULISM POLICY SOCIETY

B48
GRAHAM F.D.,THE THEORY OF INTERNATIONAL VALUES. FUT WOR+45 WOR-45 ECO/DEV FINAN INT/ORG PLAN TEC/DEV CAP/ISM DIPLOM ECO/TAC TARIFFS ROUTINE BAL/PAY DRIVE PWR WEALTH SOCISM...POLICY STAT HYPO/EXP GEN/LAWS 20. PAGE 55 A1125 — NEW/IDEA INT/TRADE

B48
JONES H.D.,UNESCO: A SELECTED LIST OF REFERENCES. CULTURE CREATE PEACE ATTIT DRIVE 20 UNESCO UN. PAGE 75 A1531 — BIBLIOG/A INT/ORG DIPLOM EDU/PROP

B48
KULISCHER E.M.,EUROPE ON THE MOVE: WAR AND POPULATION CHANGES, 1917-1947. COM EUR+WWI FUT GERMANY USSR DIST/IND PLAN INT/TRADE CONTROL WAR DRIVE...CENSUS TREND COLD/WAR 20. PAGE 82 A1690 — ECO/TAC GEOG

B48
VISSON A.,AS OTHERS SEE US. EUR+WWI FRANCE UK USA+45 CULTURE INTELL SOCIETY STRATA NAT/G POL/PAR FOR/AID ATTIT DRIVE LOVE ORD/FREE RESPECT WEALTH ...PLURIST SOC OBS TOT/POP 20. PAGE 159 A3244 — USA-45 PERCEPT

B49
GORER G.,THE PEOPLE OF GREAT RUSSIA: A PSYCHOLOGICAL STUDY. RUSSIA USSR NAT/G DIPLOM LEAD AGE/C ANOMIE ATTIT DRIVE...POLICY 20. PAGE 54 A1116 — ISOLAT PERSON PSY SOCIETY

B49
SINGER K.,THE IDEA OF CONFLICT. UNIV INTELL INT/ORG NAT/G PLAN ROUTINE ATTIT DRIVE ALL/VALS...POLICY CONCPT TIME/SEQ. PAGE 133 A2730 — ACT/RES SOC

B49
STETTINIUS E.R.,ROOSEVELT AND THE RUSSIANS: THE YALTA CONFERENCE. UK USSR WOR+45 WOR-45 INT/ORG VOL/ASSN TOP/EX ACT/RES EDU/PROP PEACE ATTIT DRIVE PERSON SUPEGO PWR...POLICY CONCPT MYTH OBS TIME/SEQ AUD/VIS COLD/WAR 20 CHURCHLL/W YALTA ROOSEVLT/F. PAGE 138 A2819 — DIPLOM DELIB/GP BIOG

B50
MACIVER R.M.,GREAT EXPRESSIONS OF HUMAN RIGHTS. LAW CONSTN CULTURE INTELL SOCIETY R+D INT/ORG ATTIT DRIVE...JURID OBS HIST/WRIT GEN/LAWS. PAGE 92 A1891 — UNIV CONCPT

B51
MCKEON R.,DEMOCRACY IN A WORLD OF TENSION. UNIV LAW INTELL STRUCT R+D INT/ORG SCHOOL EDU/PROP LEGIT ATTIT DRIVE PERCEPT PERSON...POLICY JURID PSY SOC CONCPT METH/CNCPT OBS UNESCO TOT/POP VAL/FREE. PAGE 98 A2015 — SOCIETY ALL/VALS ORD/FREE

B51
WELLES S.,SEVEN DECISIONS THAT SHAPED HISTORY. ASIA FRANCE FUT USA+45 WOR+45 WOR-45 CONSTN STRUCT INT/ORG NAT/G ACT/RES EDU/PROP DRIVE...POLICY CONCPT TIME/SEQ TREND TOT/POP UN 20 CHINJAP. PAGE 163 A3315 — USA-45 DIPLOM WAR

B52
ALEXANDROWICZ C.H.,INTERNATIONAL ECONOMIC ORGANIZATION. WOR+45 ECO/DEV ECO/UNDEV DIST/IND FINAN MARKET PLAN ECO/TAC LEGIT DRIVE WEALTH ...POLICY CONCPT QUANT OBS TIME/SEQ GEN/LAWS WORK EEC ILO OEEC UNESCO 20. PAGE 6 A0114 — INT/ORG INT/TRADE

B52
SCHUMAN F.,THE COMMONWEALTH OF MAN. WOR+45 WOR-45 LAW CULTURE ELITES SOCIETY FAM INT/ORG NAT/G VOL/ASSN TOP/EX PLAN BAL/PWR LEGIT ATTIT DISPL DRIVE...POLICY MYTH TREND TOT/POP ILO OEEC 20. PAGE 129 A2649 — CONCPT GEN/LAWS

B52
ULAM A.B.,TITOISM AND THE COMINFORM. USSR WOR+45 STRUCT INT/ORG NAT/G ACT/RES PLAN EXEC ATTIT DRIVE ALL/VALS...CONCPT OBS VAL/FREE 20 COMINTERN TITO/MARSH. PAGE 146 A2993 — COM POL/PAR TOTALISM YUGOSLAVIA

L52
THOMPSON K.W.,"THE STUDY OF INTERNATIONAL POLITICS: A SURVEY OF TRENDS AND DEVELOPMENTS." UNIV USA+45 WOR+45 WOR-45 SOCIETY ECO/DEV R+D ACT/RES PLAN ROUTINE ATTIT DRIVE PERCEPT PERSON...CONCPT OBS TREND GEN/LAWS TOT/POP. PAGE 143 A2928 — INT/ORG BAL/PWR DIPLOM

L52
WRIGHT Q.,"CONGRESS AND THE TREATY-MAKING POWER." USA+45 WOR+45 CONSTN INTELL NAT/G CHIEF CONSULT EX/STRUC LEGIS TOP/EX CREATE GOV/REL DISPL DRIVE RIGID/FLEX...TREND TOT/POP CONGRESS CONGRESS 20 TREATY. PAGE 167 A3408 — ROUTINE DIPLOM INT/LAW DELIB/GP

S52
HAAS E.B.,"THE RECONCILIATION OF CONFLICT, COLONIAL POLICY AIMS: ACCEPTANCE OF THE LEAGUE OF NATIONS MANDATE SYSTEM." FRANCE GERMANY UK WOR+45 WOR-45 LEGIT ATTIT DRIVE ORD/FREE...OLD/LIB INT SYS/QU TIME/SEQ TREND LEAGUE/NAT 20. PAGE 58 A1201 — INT/ORG COLONIAL

L53
UNESCO,"THE TECHNIQUE OF INTERNATIONAL CONFERENCES." WOR+45 INT/ORG VOL/ASSN EDU/PROP ROUTINE ATTIT DRIVE KNOWL ORD/FREE...SOC UNESCO 20. PAGE 148 A3016 — DELIB/GP ACT/RES

B54
CHEEVER D.S.,ORGANIZING FOR PEACE. FUT WOR+45 WOR-45 STRATA STRUCT NAT/G CREATE DIPLOM LEGIT REGION COERCE DETER PEACE ATTIT DRIVE ALL/VALS ...TIME/SEQ TREND UN LEAGUE/NAT. PAGE 26 A0525 — INT/ORG

B54
STALEY E.,THE FUTURE OF UNDERDEVELOPED COUNTRIES: POLITICAL IMPLICATIONS OF ECONOMIC DEVELOPMENT. COM FUT USA+45 SOCIETY ECO/UNDEV CREATE PLAN CAP/ISM ATTIT DRIVE MARXISM SOCISM...POLICY CONCPT CHARTS COLD/WAR 20. PAGE 137 A2801 — EDU/PROP ECO/TAC FOR/AID

L54
CHARLESWORTH J.C.,"AMERICA AND A NEW ASIA." ASIA INDIA ISLAM S/ASIA USA+45 USA-45 ECO/UNDEV NAT/G POL/PAR FORCES FOR/AID DOMIN EDU/PROP COERCE DRIVE ALL/VALS MARXISM SOCISM TOT/POP 20. PAGE 26 A0522 — ECO/TAC DIPLOM NAT/LISM

S54
FOX W.T.R.,"CIVIL-MILITARY RELATIONS." USA+45 USA-45 R+D ACT/RES DIPLOM INT/TRADE EDU/PROP DETER DISPL DRIVE ORD/FREE...METH/CNCPT TREND COLD/WAR 20. PAGE 48 A0974 — POLICY FORCES PLAN SOCIETY

B55
SNYDER R.C.,AMERICAN FOREIGN POLICY. USA+45 USA-45 WOR+45 WOR-45 CONSTN INT/ORG POL/PAR VOL/ASSN DELIB/GP LEGIS CREATE DOMIN EDU/PROP EXEC COERCE ATTIT DRIVE ORD/FREE PWR...MGT OBS RECORD TIME/SEQ TREND. PAGE 134 A2752 — NAT/G DIPLOM

B55
TANNENBAUM F.,THE AMERICAN TRADITION IN FOREIGN POLICY. USA+45 USA-45 CONSTN INT/ORG NAT/G POL/PAR VOL/ASSN TOP/EX LEGIT DRIVE ORD/FREE PWR...CONCPT GEN/LAWS CONGRESS LEAGUE/NAT COLD/WAR OAS 18/20. PAGE 141 A2887 — TIME/SEQ

S55
TORRE M.,"PSYCHIATRIC OBSERVATIONS OF INTERNATIONAL CONFERENCES." WOR+45 INT/ORG PROF/ORG VOL/ASSN CONSULT EDU/PROP ROUTINE ATTIT DRIVE KNOWL...PSY METH/CNCPT OBS/ENVIR STERTYP 20. PAGE 144 A2950 — DELIB/GP OBS DIPLOM

B56
BALL W.M.,NATIONALISM AND COMMUNISM IN EAST ASIA. ASIA BURMA EUR+WWI KOREA USA+45 ECO/UNDEV NAT/G POL/PAR DIPLOM ECO/TAC FOR/AID EDU/PROP COERCE RACE/REL NAT/LISM DRIVE SOVEREIGN...TREND 20 CHINJAP. PAGE 11 A0214 — S/ASIA ATTIT

B56
BEALE H.K.,THEODORE ROOSEVELT AND THE RISE OF AMERICA TO WORLD POWER. USA-45 BAL/PWR COLONIAL DRIVE PERSON PWR...POLICY BIBLIOG 20 ROOSEVLT/T PRESIDENT. PAGE 12 A0238 — DIPLOM CHIEF BIOG

B56
BEARDSLEY S.W.,HUMAN RELATIONS IN INTERNATIONAL AFFAIRS: A GUIDE TO SIGNIFICANT INTERPRETATION AND RESEARCH. UNIV PERS/REL NAT/LISM DRIVE PERSON ...POLICY PSY SOC CON/ANAL IDEA/COMP 20. PAGE 12 A0241 — BIBLIOG/A ATTIT CULTURE DIPLOM

B56
BROOK D.,THE UNITED NATIONS AND CHINA DILEMMA. CHINA/COM FUT WOR+45 ECO/UNDEV NAT/G DELIB/GP ACT/RES DIPLOM ROUTINE NAT/LISM TOTALISM ATTIT DRIVE...CONCPT OBS TIME/SEQ UN TOT/POP TIME UN 20. PAGE 19 A0390 — ASIA INT/ORG BAL/PWR

B56
GEORGE A.L.,WOODROW WILSON AND COLONEL HOUSE. WOR-45 CONSTN FACE/GP INT/ORG NAT/G POL/PAR CONSULT LEGIT EXEC COERCE CHOOSE ATTIT DRIVE PERSON MORAL ORD/FREE PWR RESPECT...POLICY MGT PSY OBS RECORD INT LEAGUE/NAT. PAGE 52 A1060 — USA-45 BIOG DIPLOM

B56
GOODRICH L.,KOREA: A STUDY OF US POLICY IN THE UNITED NATIONS. ASIA USA+45 STRUCT CONSULT DELIB/GP ATTIT DRIVE PWR...JURID GEN/LAWS COLD/WAR 20 UN. PAGE 54 A1103 — INT/ORG DIPLOM KOREA

B56
LOVEDAY A.,REFLECTIONS ON INTERNATIONAL ADMINISTRATION. WOR+45 WOR-45 DELIB/GP ACT/RES ADMIN EXEC ROUTINE DRIVE...METH/CNCPT TIME/SEQ CON/ANAL SIMUL TOT/POP 20. PAGE 91 A1865 — INT/ORG MGT

B56
SPROUT H.,MAN-MILIEU RELATIONSHIP HYPOTHESES IN THE CONTEXT OF INTERNATIONAL POLITICS. UNIV PROB/SOLV BIO/SOC PERSON...DECISION GEOG SOC METH/CNCPT PREDICT 20. PAGE 136 A2792 — HABITAT DIPLOM CONCPT DRIVE

B56
WOLFERS A.,THE ANGLO-AMERICAN TRADITION IN FOREIGN AFFAIRS. UK USA+45 WOR-45 CULTURE SOCIETY ECO/DEV INT/ORG NAT/G CREATE PLAN BAL/PWR ECO/TAC EDU/PROP PEACE DISPL DRIVE...TREND GEN/LAWS 20. PAGE 166 A3382 — ATTIT CONCPT DIPLOM

B57
BLOOMFIELD L.M.,EGYPT, ISRAEL AND THE GULF OF AQABA: IN INTERNATIONAL LAW. LAW NAT/G CONSULT FORCES PLAN ECO/TAC ROUTINE COERCE ATTIT DRIVE PERCEPT PERSON RIGID/FLEX LOVE PWR WEALTH...GEOG CONCPT MYTH TREND. PAGE 15 A0314 — ISLAM INT/LAW UAR

B57
DEAN V.M.,THE NATURE OF THE NON-WESTERN WORLD. AFR ASIA L/A+17C S/ASIA CULTURE SOCIETY STRATA ECO/DEV DIPLOM ECO/TAC FOR/AID ATTIT DRIVE ALL/VALS ...RELATIV SOC CONCPT TIME/SEQ TREND TOT/POP 20. PAGE 35 A0718 — ECO/UNDEV STERTYP NAT/LISM

B57
KENNAN G.F.,RUSSIA, THE ATOM AND THE WEST. COM EUR+WWI FUT WOR+45 SOCIETY ECO/DEV FORCES DIPLOM ECO/TAC DOMIN EDU/PROP COERCE NUC/PWR ATTIT DRIVE ORD/FREE PWR...POLICY OBS TIME/SEQ TREND COLD/WAR NATO 20. PAGE 77 A1574 — NAT/G INT/ORG USSR

B57
STRACHEY A.,THE UNCONSCIOUS MOTIVES OF WAR; A PSYCHO-ANALYTICAL CONTRIBUTION. UNIV SOCIETY DIPLOM DREAM GP/REL ADJUST ATTIT DISPL PERCEPT PERSON KNOWL MORAL. PAGE 139 A2840 — WAR DRIVE LOVE PSY

S57
SPEIER H.,"SOVIET ATOMIC BLACKMAIL AND THE NORTH ATLANTIC ALLIANCE." EUR+WWI USA+45 USSR INT/ORG NAT/G FORCES DIPLOM DRIVE ORD/FREE PWR NATO VAL/FREE COLD/WAR 20. PAGE 136 A2781 — COM COERCE NUC/PWR

B58
HAAS E.B.,THE UNITING OF EUROPE. EUR+WWI INT/ORG NAT/G POL/PAR TOP/EX ECO/TAC EDU/PROP LEGIT FEDERAL NAT/LISM DRIVE RIGID/FLEX ORD/FREE PWR PLURISM — VOL/ASSN ECO/DEV

...POLICY CONCPT INT GEN/LAWS ECSC EEC 20. PAGE 59 A1204

B58
JAPANESE ASSOCIATION INT. LAW,JAPAN AND THE UNITED NATIONS. SOCIETY ROUTINE ATTIT DRIVE PERCEPT RIGID/FLEX ORD/FREE...METH/CNCPT CON/ANAL CHINJAP UN. PAGE 73 A1497 ASIA INT/ORG

B58
KINDLEBERGER C.P.,INTERNATIONAL ECONOMICS. WOR+45 WOR-45 ECO/DEV ECO/UNDEV FINAN VOL/ASSN ACT/RES DIPLOM ECO/TAC LEGIT REGION ATTIT DRIVE ORD/FREE WEALTH...POLICY STAT TREND GEN/LAWS EEC ECSC OEEC 20. PAGE 79 A1620 INT/ORG BAL/PWR TARIFFS

L58
HAVILAND H.F.,"FOREIGN AID AND THE POLICY PROCESS: 1957." USA+45 FACE/GP POL/PAR VOL/ASSN CHIEF DELIB/GP ACT/RES LEGIT EXEC GOV/REL ATTIT DRIVE PWR ...POLICY TESTS CONGRESS 20. PAGE 63 A1291 LEGIS PLAN FOR/AID

S58
SONDERMANN F.A.,"SOCIOLOGY AND INTERNATIONAL RELATIONS." WOR+45 CULTURE SOCIETY INT/ORG NAT/G CREATE ATTIT DRIVE PERSON RIGID/FLEX...PSY SOC 20. PAGE 135 A2767 PLAN NEW/IDEA PEACE

B59
ALLEN R.L.,SOVIET INFLUENCE IN LATIN AMERICA. ECO/UNDEV FINAN PROC/MFG NAT/G TEC/DEV EDU/PROP EXEC ROUTINE ATTIT DRIVE PERSON ALL/VALS PWR...STAT CHARTS WORK 20. PAGE 6 A0125 L/A+17C ECO/TAC INT/TRADE USSR

B59
HERZ J.H.,INTERNATIONAL POLITICS IN THE ATOMIC AGE. FUT USA+45 WOR+45 WOR-45 SOCIETY NAT/G FORCES PLAN COERCE DETER ATTIT DRIVE ORD/FREE PWR...TREND COLD/WAR 20. PAGE 64 A1319 INT/ORG ARMS/CONT NUC/PWR

B59
KULSKI W.W.,PEACEFUL CO-EXISTENCE: AN ANALYSIS OF SOVIET FOREIGN POLICY. WOR+45 INTELL SOCIETY ECO/UNDEV POL/PAR EDU/PROP COERCE DRIVE RIGID/FLEX PWR SKILL...PSY CONCPT HIST/WRIT CON/ANAL GEN/METH WORK VAL/FREE 20. PAGE 83 A1691 PLAN DIPLOM USSR

B59
LAQUER W.Z.,THE SOVIET UNION AND THE MIDDLE EAST. COM UAR USSR ECO/UNDEV NAT/G VOL/ASSN ECO/TAC EDU/PROP COLONIAL EXEC PWR...TIME/SEQ TREND COLD/WAR 20. PAGE 85 A1730 ISLAM DRIVE FOR/AID NAT/LISM

B59
STRAUSZ-HUPE R.,PROTRACTED CONFLICT. CHINA/COM KOREA WOR+45 INT/ORG FORCES ACT/RES ECO/TAC LEGIT COERCE DRIVE PERCEPT KNOWL PWR...PSY CONCPT RECORD GEN/METH COLD/WAR VAL/FREE 20. PAGE 139 A2847 COM PLAN USSR

B59
WARD B.,5 IDEAS THAT CHANGE THE WORLD. WOR+45 WOR-45 SOCIETY STRUCT AGRI INDUS INT/ORG NAT/G FORCES ACT/RES ARMS/CONT TOTALISM ATTIT DRIVE GEN/LAWS. PAGE 161 A3278 ECO/UNDEV ALL/VALS NAT/LISM COLONIAL

S59
BROMKE A.,"DISENGAGEMENT IN EAST EUROPE." COM USSR INT/ORG DIPLOM EDU/PROP NEUTRAL NUC/PWR DRIVE RIGID/FLEX PWR...PSY CONCPT CON/ANAL GEN/METH VAL/FREE 20. PAGE 19 A0388 BAL/PWR

S59
HARVEY M.F.,"THE PALESTINE REFUGEE PROBLEM: ELEMENTS OF A SOLUTION." ISLAM LAW INT/ORG DELIB/GP TOP/EX ECO/TAC ROUTINE DRIVE HEALTH LOVE ORD/FREE PWR WEALTH...MAJORIT FAO 20. PAGE 62 A1283 ACT/RES LEGIT PEACE ISRAEL

S59
REUBENS E.D.,"THE BASIS FOR REORIENATION OF AMERICAN FOREIGN AID POLICY." USA+45 USSR STRUCT INT/ORG CONSULT ECO/TAC ADMIN DRIVE MORAL ORD/FREE PWR WEALTH...RELATIV MATH STAT TREND GEN/LAWS VAL/FREE 20. PAGE 120 A2467 ECO/UNDEV PLAN FOR/AID DIPLOM

S59
SAYEGH F.,"ARAB NATIONALISM AND SOVIET-AMERICAN RELATIONS." ISLAM USA+45 ECO/UNDEV PLAN ECO/TAC LEGIT NAT/LISM DRIVE PERCEPT KNOWL PWR...DECISION CONCPT STAT RECORD TREND CON/ANAL VAL/FREE 20 COLD/WAR. PAGE 127 A2610 DIPLOM USSR

B60
BUCHAN A.,NATO IN THE 1960'S. EUR+WWI USA+45 WOR+45 INT/ORG ACT/RES PLAN LEGIT COERCE DETER ATTIT DRIVE RIGID/FLEX ORD/FREE...METH/CNCPT TIME/SEQ TREND GEN/LAWS COLD/WAR 20 NATO. PAGE 21 A0421 VOL/ASSN FORCES ARMS/CONT SOVEREIGN

B60
JENNINGS R.,PROGRESS OF INTERNATIONAL LAW. FUT WOR+45 WOR-45 SOCIETY NAT/G VOL/ASSN DELIB/GP DIPLOM EDU/PROP LEGIT COERCE ATTIT DRIVE MORAL ORD/FREE...JURID CONCPT OBS TIME/SEQ TREND GEN/LAWS. PAGE 74 A1509 INT/ORG LAW INT/LAW

B60
LINDSAY K.,EUROPEAN ASSEMBLIES: THE EXPERIMENTAL PERIOD 1949-1959. EUR+WWI ECO/DEV NAT/G POL/PAR LEGIS TOP/EX ACT/RES PLAN ECO/TAC DOMIN LEGIT ROUTINE ATTIT DRIVE ORD/FREE PWR SKILL...SOC CONCPT TREND CHARTS GEN/LAWS VAL/FREE. PAGE 89 A1823 VOL/ASSN INT/ORG REGION

B60
SHONFIELD A.,THE ATTACK ON WORLD POVERTY. WOR+45 ECO/DEV ECO/UNDEV FINAN VOL/ASSN PLAN EDU/PROP INT/ORG ECO/TAC

DRIVE KNOWL WEALTH...CONT/OBS STAND/INT ORG/CHARTS TOT/POP UNESCO 20. PAGE 132 A2704 FOR/AID INT/TRADE

L60
FERNBACH A.P.,"SOVIET COEXISTENCE STRATEGY." WOR+45 PROF/ORG VOL/ASSN DIPLOM DOMIN EDU/PROP ATTIT DRIVE PERSON PWR SKILL WEALTH...POLICY OBS SAMP TREND STERTYP ILO WORK COLD/WAR 420. PAGE 45 A0919 LABOR INT/ORG USSR

S60
BOWIE R.,"POLICY FORMATION IN AMERICAN FOREIGN POLICY." FUT USA+45 WOR+45 STRUCT ECO/DEV INT/ORG POL/PAR LEGIS ACT/RES EXEC ALL/VALS...POLICY OBS VAL/FREE 20. PAGE 17 A0355 PLAN DRIVE DIPLOM

S60
CLARK W.,"NEW FORCES IN THE UN." FUT UK WOR+45 CONSTN BAL/PWR DIPLOM DRIVE PWR SKILL...CONCPT TREND UN TOT/POP 20. PAGE 27 A0543 INT/ORG ECO/UNDEV SOVEREIGN

S60
FITZGIBBON R.H.,"DICTATORSHIP AND DEMOCRACY IN LATIN AMERICA." FUT ECO/DEV ECO/UNDEV INT/ORG LOC/G NAT/G TOP/EX PLAN TEC/DEV ECO/TAC CHOOSE ATTIT DRIVE PERSON ALL/VALS OAS TOT/POP 20. PAGE 46 A0943 L/A+17C ACT/RES INT/TRADE

S60
FRANKEL S.H.,"ECONOMIC ASPECTS OF POLITICAL INDEPENDENCE IN AFRICA." AFR FUT SOCIETY ECO/UNDEV COM/IND FINAN LEGIS PLAN TEC/DEV CAP/ISM ECO/TAC INT/TRADE ADMIN ATTIT DRIVE RIGID/FLEX PWR WEALTH ...MGT NEW/IDEA MATH TIME/SEQ VAL/FREE 20. PAGE 48 A0984 NAT/G FOR/AID

S60
GARNICK D.H.,"ON THE ECONOMIC FEASIBILITY OF A MIDDLE EASTERN COMMON MARKET." AFR ISLAM CULTURE INDUS NAT/G PLAN TEC/DEV ECO/TAC ADMIN ATTIT DRIVE RIGID/FLEX...PLURIST STAT TREND GEN/LAWS 20. PAGE 51 A1051 MARKET INT/TRADE

S60
HAVILAND H.F.,"PROBLEMS OF AMERICAN FOREIGN POLICY." ASIA COM USA+45 WOR+45 INT/ORG NAT/G CONSULT ECO/TAC FOR/AID DOMIN COERCE NUC/PWR ATTIT DRIVE ORD/FREE PWR RESPECT SKILL...POLICY GEOG OBS SAMP TREND GEN/METH METH COLD/WAR UN 20. PAGE 63 A1292 ECO/UNDEV FORCES DIPLOM

S60
KREININ M.E.,"THE 'OUTER-SEVEN' AND EUROPEAN INTEGRATION." EUR+WWI FRANCE GERMANY ITALY UK ECO/DEV DIST/IND INT/TRADE DRIVE WEALTH...MYTH CHARTS EEC OEEC 20. PAGE 82 A1682 ECO/TAC GEN/LAWS

S60
MAGATHAN W.,"SOME BASES OF WEST GERMAN MILITARY POLICY." EUR+WWI FUT INT/ORG TOP/EX ECO/TAC DOMIN DRIVE ORD/FREE PWR...TRADIT GEOG OBS TREND. PAGE 93 A1904 NAT/G FORCES GERMANY

S60
MORA J.A.,"THE ORGANIZATION OF AMERICAN STATES." USA+45 LAW ECO/UNDEV VOL/ASSN DELIB/GP PLAN BAL/PWR EDU/PROP ADMIN DRIVE RIGID/FLEX ORD/FREE WEALTH ...TIME/SEQ GEN/LAWS OAS 20. PAGE 103 A2126 L/A+17C INT/ORG REGION

S60
OWEN C.F.,"US AND SOVIET RELATIONS WITH UNDERDEVELOPED COUNTRIES: LATIN AMERICA-A CASE STUDY." AFR COM L/A+17C USA+45 USSR EXTR/IND MARKET TEC/DEV DIPLOM ECO/TAC NAT/LISM ORD/FREE PWR ...TREND WORK 20. PAGE 112 A2303 ECO/UNDEV DRIVE INT/TRADE

S60
RIVKIN A.,"AFRICAN ECONOMIC DEVELOPMENT: ADVANCED TECHNOLOGY AND THE STAGES OF GROWTH." CULTURE ECO/UNDEV AGRI COM/IND EXTR/IND PLAN ECO/TAC ATTIT DRIVE RIGID/FLEX SKILL WEALTH...MGT SOC GEN/LAWS WORK TOT/POP 20. PAGE 121 A2487 AFR TEC/DEV FOR/AID

S60
SCHACHTER O.,"THE ENFORCEMENT OF INTERNATIONAL JUDICIAL AND ARBITRAL DECISIONS." WOR+45 NAT/G ECO/TAC DOMIN LEGIT ROUTINE COERCE ATTIT DRIVE ALL/VALS PWR...METH/CNCPT TREND TOT/POP 20 UN. PAGE 128 A2615 INT/ORG ADJUD INT/LAW

B61
ANAND R.P.,COMPULSORY JURISDICTION OF INTERNATIONAL COURT OF JUSTICE. FUT WOR+45 SOCIETY PLAN LEGIT ADJUD ATTIT DRIVE PERSON ORD/FREE...JURID CONCPT TREND 20 ICJ. PAGE 8 A0156 INT/ORG COERCE INT/LAW

B61
DIA M.,THE AFRICAN NATIONS AND WORLD SOLIDARITY. ISLAM CULTURE ELITES ECO/DEV ECO/UNDEV INT/ORG NAT/G PLAN ECO/TAC INT/TRADE EDU/PROP NAT/LISM ATTIT DRIVE ORD/FREE WEALTH...SOCIALIST CONCPT CON/ANAL GEN/LAWS TOT/POP 20. PAGE 37 A0753 AFR REGION SOCISM

B61
GRAEBNER N.,AN UNCERTAIN TRADITION: AMERICAN SECRETARIES OF STATE IN THE 20TH CENTURY. USA+45 CONSTN INT/ORG NAT/G DELIB/GP TOP/EX BAL/PWR DOMIN LEGIT ADMIN ARMS/CONT ATTIT DRIVE PERSON SUPEGO ORD/FREE PWR...GEN/LAWS VAL/FREE CONGRESS. PAGE 55 A1121 USA-45 BIOG DIPLOM

B61
HASAN H.S.,PAKISTAN AND THE UN. ISLAM WOR+45 ECO/DEV ECO/UNDEV NAT/G TOP/EX ECO/TAC FOR/AID EDU/PROP ADMIN DRIVE PERCEPT...OBS TIME/SEQ UN 20. INT/ORG ATTIT PAKISTAN

PAGE 62 A1284

B61
LUKACS J.,A HISTORY OF THE COLD WAR. ASIA COM EUR+WWI USA+45 USA-45 INT/ORG NAT/G DELIB/GP ACT/RES BAL/PWR DIPLOM DOMIN EDU/PROP LEGIT DRIVE ORD/FREE...TREND COLD/WAR 20. PAGE 91 A1872
PWR TIME/SEQ USSR

B61
STRAUSZ-HUPE R.,A FORWARD STRATEGY FOR AMERICA. FUT WOR+45 ECO/DEV INT/ORG NAT/G POL/PAR DELIB/GP FORCES ACT/RES CREATE ECO/TAC DOMIN EDU/PROP ATTIT DRIVE PWR...MAJORIT CONCPT STAT OBS TIME/SEQ TREND COLD/WAR TOT/POP. PAGE 139 A2848
USA+45 PLAN DIPLOM

B61
WARNER D.,HURRICANE FROM CHINA. ASIA CHINA/COM FUT L/A+17C USA+45 CULTURE NAT/G FORCES TOP/EX FOR/AID DRIVE PWR...CONCPT TIME/SEQ SEATO WORK 20. PAGE 161 A3284
ATTIT TREND REV

L61
HALPERIN M.H.,"NUCLEAR WEAPONS AND LIMITED WARS." FUT UNIV WOR+45 INTELL SOCIETY ECO/DEV ACT/RES DRIVE PERCEPT RIGID/FLEX...CONCPT TIME/SEQ TREND TOT/POP 20. PAGE 60 A1237
PLAN COERCE NUC/PWR WAR

S61
ALGER C.F.,"NON-RESOLUTION CONSEQUENCES OF THE UNITED NATIONS AND THEIR EFFECT ON INTERNATIONAL CONFLICT." WOR+45 CONSTN ECO/DEV NAT/G CONSULT DELIB/GP TOP/EX ACT/RES PLAN DIPLOM EDU/PROP ROUTINE ATTIT ALL/VALS...INT/LAW TOT/POP UN 20. PAGE 6 A0117
INT/ORG DRIVE BAL/PWR

S61
BARALL M.,"THE UNITED STATES GOVERNMENT RESPONDS." L/A+17C USA+45 SOCIETY NAT/G CREATE PLAN DIPLOM ECO/TAC ATTIT DRIVE RIGID/FLEX KNOWL SKILL WEALTH ...METH/CNCPT TIME/SEQ GEN/METH 20. PAGE 11 A0217
ECO/UNDEV ACT/RES FOR/AID

S61
HAAS E.B.,"INTERNATIONAL INTEGRATION: THE EUROPEAN AND THE UNIVERSAL PROCESS." EUR+WWI FUT WOR+45 NAT/G EX/STRUC ATTIT DRIVE ORD/FREE PWR...CONCPT GEN/LAWS OEEC 20 NATO COUNCL/EUR. PAGE 59 A1207
INT/ORG TREND REGION

S61
HEILBRONER R.L.,"DYNAMICS OF FOREIGN AID: PROBLEMS OF UNDERDEVELOPED NATIONS PLAGUE ASSISTANCE PROGRAM." FUT USA+45 WOR+45 STRATA NAT/G PLAN TEC/DEV ATTIT DRIVE WEALTH WORK 20. PAGE 64 A1307
ECO/UNDEV ECO/TAC FOR/AID

S61
MACHOWSKI K.,"SELECTED PROBLEMS OF NATIONAL SOVEREIGNTY WITH REFERENCE TO THE LAW OF OUTER SPACE." FUT WOR+45 AIR LAW INTELL SOCIETY ECO/DEV PLAN EDU/PROP DETER DRIVE PERCEPT SOVEREIGN ...POLICY INT/LAW OBS TREND TOT/POP 20. PAGE 92 A1889
UNIV ACT/RES NUC/PWR SPACE

S61
MILLER E.,"LEGAL ASPECTS OF UN ACTION IN THE CONGO." AFR CULTURE ADMIN PEACE DRIVE RIGID/FLEX ORD/FREE...WELF/ST JURID OBS UN CONGO 20. PAGE 101 A2076
INT/ORG LEGIT

S61
TAUBENFELD H.J.,"OUTER SPACE--PAST POLITICS AND FUTURE POLICY." FUT USA+45 USA-45 WOR+45 AIR INTELL STRUCT ECO/DEV NAT/G TOP/EX ACT/RES ADMIN ROUTINE NUC/PWR ATTIT DRIVE...CONCPT TIME/SEQ TREND TOT/POP 20. PAGE 141 A2892
PLAN SPACE INT/ORG

B62
ARNOLD H.J.P.,AID FOR DEVELOPING COUNTRIES. COM EUR+WWI USA+45 USSR WOR+45 EDU/PROP ATTIT DRIVE PWR WEALTH...TREND CHARTS STERTYP NAT/ 20. PAGE 9 A0177
ECO/UNDEV ECO/TAC FOR/AID

B62
BELL C.,NEGOTIATION FROM STRENGTH. WOR+45 FACE/GP INT/ORG DELIB/GP FORCES PLAN DOMIN COERCE NUC/PWR PEACE DRIVE PWR...POLICY LOG OBS RECORD INT SAMP TREND COLD/WAR 20. PAGE 13 A0255
NAT/G CONCPT DIPLOM

B62
BOULDING K.E.,CONFLICT AND DEFENSE: A GENERAL THEORY. FUT SOCIETY INT/ORG NAT/G CREATE BAL/PWR COERCE NAT/LISM DRIVE ALL/VALS...PLURIST DECISION CONCPT METH/CNCPT TREND HYPO/EXP TOT/POP 20. PAGE 17 A0347
MATH SIMUL PEACE WAR

B62
CALVOCORESSI P.,WORLD ORDER AND NEW STATES: PROBLEMS OF KEEPING THE PEACE. AFR EUR+WWI S/ASIA ELITES NAT/G ECO/TAC FOR/AID EDU/PROP COERCE ATTIT DRIVE ALL/VALS...GEN/LAWS COLD/WAR 20 UN. PAGE 23 A0471
INT/ORG PEACE

B62
DUROSELLE J.B.,LES NOUVEAUX ETATS DANS LES RELATIONS INTERNATIONALES. AFR CHINA/COM FRANCE MOROCCO S/ASIA USSR ECO/UNDEV INT/ORG PLAN ECO/TAC EDU/PROP ATTIT DRIVE...TREND TOT/POP TUNIS 20. PAGE 39 A0806
NAT/G CONSTN DIPLOM

B62
FORBES H.W.,THE STRATEGY OF DISARMAMENT. FUT WOR+45 INT/ORG VOL/ASSN CONSULT ARMS/CONT COERCE NUC/PWR WAR DRIVE RIGID/FLEX ORD/FREE PWR...POLICY CONCPT OBS TREND STERTYP 20. PAGE 47 A0959
PLAN FORCES DIPLOM

B62
HUMPHREY D.D.,THE UNITED STATES AND THE COMMON MARKET. USA+45 INDUS MARKET INT/ORG PLAN EDU/PROP BAL/PAY DRIVE PWR WEALTH...TREND STERTYP EEC 20. PAGE 69 A1415
ATTIT ECO/TAC

B62
KRAFT J.,THE GRAND DESIGN. EUR+WWI USA+45 AGRI FINAN INDUS MARKET INT/ORG NAT/G PLAN ECO/TAC TARIFFS REGION DRIVE ORD/FREE WEALTH...POLICY OBS TREND EEC 20. PAGE 82 A1674
VOL/ASSN ECO/DEV INT/TRADE

B62
LEWIS J.P.,QUIET CRISIS IN INDIA. INDIA USA+45 CULTURE ECO/UNDEV AGRI INDUS PROC/MFG NAT/G PLAN TEC/DEV DRIVE PWR SKILL WEALTH...MYTH 20. PAGE 88 A1801
S/ASIA ECO/TAC FOR/AID

B62
MACKENTOSH J.M.,STRATEGY AND TACTICS OF SOVIET FOREIGN POLICY. CHINA/COM FUT USA+45 WOR+45 INT/ORG PLAN DOMIN LEGIT ROUTINE COERCE NUC/PWR WAR ATTIT DRIVE ORD/FREE PWR...CONCPT OBS TIME/SEQ TREND GEN/METH COLD/WAR 20. PAGE 92 A1894
COM POLICY DIPLOM USSR

B62
OSGOOD R.E.,NATO: THE ENTANGLING ALLIANCE. USA+45 WOR+45 VOL/ASSN FORCES TOP/EX PLAN DETER WEAPON DRIVE RIGID/FLEX ORD/FREE PWR...TREND 20 NATO. PAGE 112 A2301
INT/ORG ARMS/CONT PEACE

B62
RIMALOV V.V.,ECONOMIC COOPERATION BETWEEN USSR AND UNDERDEVELOPED COUNTRIES. USSR FINAN TEC/DEV INT/TRADE DOMIN EDU/PROP COLONIAL NAT/LISM DRIVE SOVEREIGN...AUD/VIS 20. PAGE 121 A2482
FOR/AID PLAN ECO/UNDEV DIPLOM

B62
US DEPARTMENT OF THE ARMY,AFRICA: ITS PROBLEMS AND PROSPECTS. CHINA/COM USSR INT/ORG FOR/AID COLONIAL LEAD FEDERAL DRIVE SOVEREIGN MARXISM...GEOG 20 COLD/WAR. PAGE 152 A3104
BIBLIOG/A AFR NAT/LISM DIPLOM

B62
WOETZEL R.K.,THE NURENBERG TRIALS IN INTERNATIONAL LAW. CHRIST-17C MOD/EUR WOR+45 SOCIETY NAT/G DELIB/GP DOMIN LEGIT ROUTINE ATTIT DRIVE PERSON SUPEGO MORAL ORD/FREE...POLICY MAJORIT JURID PSY SOC SELF/OBS RECORD NAZI TOT/POP. PAGE 166 A3376
INT/ORG ADJUD WAR

B62
WRIGHT Q.,PREVENTING WORLD WAR THREE. FUT WOR+45 CULTURE INT/ORG NAT/G CONSULT FORCES ADMIN ARMS/CONT DRIVE RIGID/FLEX ORD/FREE SOVEREIGN ...POLICY CONCPT TREND STERTYP COLD/WAR 20. PAGE 168 A3416
CREATE ATTIT

S62
DEUTSCH K.W.,"TOWARDS WESTERN EUROPEAN INTEGRATION: AN INTERIM ASSESSMENT." EUR+WWI STRUCT ECO/DEV INT/ORG ECO/TAC INT/TRADE EDU/PROP PEACE ATTIT DRIVE PWR SOVEREIGN...PSY SOC TIME/SEQ CHARTS STERTYP 20. PAGE 36 A0741
VOL/ASSN RIGID/FLEX REGION

S62
FISCHER G.,"UNE NOUVELLE ORGANIZATION REGIONALE: L'ASA." S/ASIA WOR+45 ECO/UNDEV VOL/ASSN PERCEPT RIGID/FLEX...TIME/SEQ 20 ASA. PAGE 46 A0935
INT/ORG DRIVE REGION

S62
PYE L.W.,"THE POLITICAL IMPULSES AND FANTASIES BEHIND FOREIGN AID." FUT USA+45 ECO/UNDEV DIPLOM ECO/TAC ROUTINE DRIVE KNOWL...SOC METH/CNCPT NEW/IDEA TREND HYPO/EXP STERTYP GEN/METH 20. PAGE 118 A2420
ACT/RES ATTIT FOR/AID

S62
SINGER J.D.,"STABLE DETERRENCE AND ITS LIMITS." FUT WOR+45 R+D INT/ORG CONSULT ACT/RES TEC/DEV ARMS/CONT COERCE DRIVE PERCEPT RIGID/FLEX ORD/FREE PWR...MYTH SIMUL TOT/POP 20. PAGE 133 A2728
NAT/G FORCES DETER NUC/PWR

S62
SPRINGER H.W.,"FEDERATION IN THE CARIBBEAN: AN ATTEMPT THAT FAILED." L/A+17C ECO/UNDEV INT/ORG POL/PAR PROVS LEGIS CREATE PLAN LEGIT ADMIN FEDERAL ATTIT DRIVE PERSON ORD/FREE PWR...POLICY GEOG PSY CONCPT OBS CARIBBEAN CMN/WLTH 20. PAGE 136 A2791
VOL/ASSN NAT/G REGION

S62
THOMAS J.R.T.,"SOVIET BEHAVIOR IN THE QUEMOY CRISES OF 1958." CHINA/COM FUT USSR WOR+45 INT/ORG VOL/ASSN FORCES PLAN BAL/PWR DOMIN COERCE NUC/PWR REV WAR ATTIT DRIVE ORD/FREE...POLICY OBS RECORD COLD/WAR FOR/POL 20. PAGE 143 A2923
COM PWR

B63
CREMEANS C.,THE ARABS AND THE WORLD: NASSER'S ARAB NATIONALIST POLICY. FUT ISLAM UAR USA+45 SOCIETY STRATA NAT/G POL/PAR PLAN DIPLOM EDU/PROP LEGIT DRIVE ALL/VALS...INT TIME/SEQ CHARTS 20 NASSER/G. PAGE 33 A0662
TOP/EX ATTIT REGION NAT/LISM

B63
KHADDURI M.,MODERN LIBYA: A STUDY IN POLITICAL DEVELOPMENT. EUR+WWI ISLAM LIBYA ELITES INT/ORG POL/PAR FORCES DIPLOM FOR/AID DOMIN EDU/PROP LEGIT NAT/LISM DRIVE RIGID/FLEX SKILL...CONCPT TIME/SEQ TREND 20. PAGE 78 A1606
NAT/G STRUCT

B63
LOOMIE A.J.,THE SPANISH ELIZABETHANS: THE ENGLISH EXILES AT THE COURT OF PHILIP II. SPAIN UK WAR INGP/REL DRIVE HABITAT CATHISM...BIOG 16/17 MIGRATION. PAGE 91 A1860
NAT/G STRANGE POLICY DIPLOM

B63
STROMBERG R.N.,COLLECTIVE SECURITY AND AMERICAN FOREIGN POLICY FROM THE LEAGUE OF NATIONS TO NATO. USA+45 USA-45 WOR-45 INT/ORG VOL/ASSN EX/STRUC FORCES LEGIT ROUTINE DRIVE...CONCPT TREND UN LEAGUE/NAT 20 NATO. PAGE 139 A2851
ORD/FREE TIME/SEQ DIPLOM

B63
THIEN T.T.,INDIA AND SOUTHEAST ASIA 1947-1960. COM INDIA S/ASIA SECT DELIB/GP FOR/AID RACE/REL NAT/LISM SOCISM...CHARTS BIBLIOG 20 UN NEHRU/J TREATY. PAGE 143 A2917
DRIVE DIPLOM POLICY

B63
TUCKER R.C.,THE SOVIET POLITICAL MIND. WOR+45 ELITES INT/ORG NAT/G POL/PAR PLAN DIPLOM ECO/TAC DOMIN ADMIN NUC/PWR REV DRIVE PERSON SUPEGO PWR WEALTH...POLICY MGT PSY CONCPT OBS BIOG TREND COLD/WAR MARX/KARL 20. PAGE 145 A2972
COM TOP/EX USSR

B63
US DEPARTMENT OF STATE,POLITICAL BEHAVIOR--A LIST OF CURRENT STUDIES. USA+45 COM/IND DIPLOM LEAD PERS/REL DRIVE PERCEPT KNOWL...DECISION SIMUL METH. PAGE 151 A3093
BIBLIOG METH/COMP GP/REL ATTIT

S63
ALPHAND H.,"FRANCE AND HER ALLIES." EUR+WWI UK USA+45 ECO/DEV INT/ORG NAT/G VOL/ASSN FORCES TOP/EX DIPLOM ECO/TAC LEGIT ATTIT DRIVE ORD/FREE PWR WEALTH...STAT EEC TOT/POP 20. PAGE 6 A0130
ACT/RES FRANCE

S63
BLOOMFIELD L.P.,"INTERNATIONAL FORCE IN A DISARMING BUT REVOLUTIONARY WORLD." INT/ORG COERCE REV DRIVE PWR...CONCPT STERTYP GEN/LAWS 20. PAGE 16 A0318
FORCES ORD/FREE ARMS/CONT GUERRILLA

S63
DICKS H.V.,"NATIONAL LOYALTY, IDENTITY, AND THE INTERNATIONAL SOLDIER." FUT NAT/G COERCE ATTIT DRIVE PERCEPT PERSON RIGID/FLEX SUPEGO ALL/VALS ...PSY VAL/FREE. PAGE 37 A0758
INT/ORG FORCES

S63
ETZIONI A.,"EUROPEAN UNIFICATION AND PERSPECTIVES ON SOVEREIGNTY." EUR+WWI FUT DELIB/GP TEC/DEV ECO/TAC EDU/PROP DETER NUC/PWR ATTIT DRIVE ORD/FREE PWR WEALTH...CONCPT RECORD TIME/SEQ EEC VAL/FREE 20. PAGE 43 A0870
INT/ORG ECO/DEV SOVEREIGN

S63
HARNETTY P.,"CANADA, SOUTH AFRICA AND THE COMMONWEALTH." CANADA SOUTH/AFR LAW INT/ORG VOL/ASSN DELIB/GP LEGIS TOP/EX ECO/TAC LEGIT DRIVE MORAL...CONCPT CMN/WLTH 20. PAGE 62 A1263
AFR ATTIT

S63
KISSINGER H.A.,"STRAINS ON THE ALLIANCE." EUR+WWI FRANCE GERMANY GERMANY/W USA+45 ECO/DEV INT/ORG NAT/G TOP/EX EDU/PROP NUC/PWR ATTIT PWR...PSY TREND 20. PAGE 80 A1643
VOL/ASSN DRIVE DIPLOM

S63
MANGONE G.,"THE UNITED NATIONS AND UNITED STATES FOREIGN POLICY." USA+45 WOR+45 ECO/UNDEV NAT/G DIPLOM LEGIT ROUTINE ATTIT DRIVE...TIME/SEQ UN COLD/WAR 20. PAGE 94 A1922
INT/ORG ECO/TAC FOR/AID

S63
MULLEY F.W.,"NUCLEAR WEAPONS: CHALLENGE TO NATIONAL SOVEREIGNTY." EUR+WWI FRANCE UK USA+45 VOL/ASSN EX/STRUC FORCES TOP/EX ACT/RES REGION DRIVE PWR 20 NATO DEGAULLE/C. PAGE 106 A2169
INT/ORG ATTIT DIPLOM NUC/PWR

S63
SCHMIDT W.E.,"THE CASE AGAINST COMMODITY AGREEMENTS." FUT L/A+17C STRATA CONSULT PLAN ECO/TAC EDU/PROP ATTIT DRIVE RIGID/FLEX WEALTH ...MYTH 20. PAGE 128 A2631
ECO/UNDEV ACT/RES INT/TRADE

S63
SHWADRAN B.,"MIDDLE EAST OIL, 1962." ISLAM USSR ECO/DEV DIST/IND INDUS PLAN BAL/PWR DISPL DRIVE ...POLICY STAT TREND GEN/LAWS EEC OEEC 20 OIL. PAGE 132 A2712
MARKET ECO/TAC INT/TRADE

B64
ADAMS V.,THE PEACE CORPS IN ACTION. USA+45 VOL/ASSN EX/STRUC GOV/REL PERCEPT ORD/FREE...OBS 20 KENNEDY/JF PEACE/CORP. PAGE 4 A0087
DIPLOM FOR/AID PERSON DRIVE

B64
AMERICAN ASSEMBLY,THE UNITED STATES AND THE MIDDLE EAST. ISRAEL USA+45 STRUCT ECO/DEV ECO/UNDEV INT/ORG NAT/G SCHOOL SECT VOL/ASSN EX/STRUC TEC/DEV NAT/LISM...SOC 20. PAGE 7 A0135
ISLAM DRIVE REGION

B64
BARKER A.J.,SUEZ: THE SEVEN DAY WAR. EUR+WWI ISLAM UAR INT/ORG NAT/G PLAN DIPLOM ECO/TAC DOMIN NAT/LISM DRIVE RIGID/FLEX PWR SOVEREIGN...POLICY JURID TREND CHARTS SUEZ UN 20. PAGE 11 A0221
FORCES COERCE UK

B64
BINDER L.,THE IDEOLOGICAL REVOLUTION IN THE MIDDLE EAST. ISLAM STRUCT INT/ORG KIN SECT EX/STRUC TOP/EX PLAN ATTIT DRIVE RIGID/FLEX PWR...MYTH TOT/POP 20. PAGE 14 A0289
POL/PAR NAT/G NAT/LISM

B64
JANOWITZ M.,THE MILITARY IN THE POLITICAL DEVELOPMENT OF NEW NATIONS: AN ESSAY IN COMPARATIVE ANALYSIS. AFR ASIA ISLAM L/A+17C S/ASIA USA+45 ECO/UNDEV INT/ORG NAT/G POL/PAR DELIB/GP PLAN ECO/TAC DOMIN LEGIT COERCE ATTIT DRIVE RESPECT ...SOC CONCPT CENSUS VAL/FREE. PAGE 73 A1495
FORCES PWR

B64
RAMAZANI R.K.,THE MIDDLE EAST AND THE EUROPEAN COMMON MARKET. EUR+WWI ISLAM ECO/DEV EXTR/IND MARKET PROC/MFG INT/ORG NAT/G TEC/DEV ECO/TAC REGION DRIVE WEALTH...STAT CHARTS EEC TOT/POP 20. PAGE 119 A2437
ECO/UNDEV ATTIT INT/TRADE

B64
SULLIVAN G.,THE STORY OF THE PEACE CORPS. USA+45 WOR+45 INTELL FACE/GP NAT/G SCHOOL VOL/ASSN CONSULT EX/STRUC PLAN EDU/PROP ADMIN ATTIT DRIVE ALL/VALS ...POLICY HEAL SOC CONCPT INT QU BIOG TREND SOC/EXP WORK. PAGE 140 A2861
INT/ORG ECO/UNDEV FOR/AID PEACE

B64
WYTHE G.,THE UNITED STATES AND INTER-AMERICAN RELATIONS: A CONTEMPORARY APPRAISAL. L/A+17C USA+45 ECO/UNDEV INT/ORG NAT/G VOL/ASSN INT/TRADE EDU/PROP DRIVE...SOC TREND OAS UN 20. PAGE 168 A3425
ATTIT ECO/TAC FOR/AID

L64
BARROS J.,"THE GREEK-BULGARIAN INCIDENT OF 1925: THE LEAGUE OF NATIONS AND THE GREAT POWERS." BULGARIA EUR+WWI NAT/G FORCES ECO/TAC EDU/PROP LEGIT ROUTINE COERCE WAR PEACE DRIVE PWR...JURID CONCPT METH/CNCPT GEN/LAWS GEN/METH LEAGUE/NAT TOT/POP 20. PAGE 11 A0228
INT/ORG ORD/FREE DIPLOM

L64
HAAS E.B.,"ECONOMICS AND DIFFERENTIAL PATTERNS OF POLITICAL INTEGRATION: PROJECTIONS ABOUT UNITY IN LATIN AMERICA." SOCIETY NAT/G DELIB/GP ACT/RES CREATE PLAN ECO/TAC REGION ROUTINE ATTIT DRIVE PWR WEALTH...CONCPT TREND CHARTS LAFTA 20. PAGE 59 A1208
L/A+17C INT/ORG MARKET

L64
MILLIS W.,"THE DEMILITARIZED WORLD." COM USA+45 USSR WOR+45 CONSTN NAT/G EX/STRUC PLAN LEGIT ATTIT DRIVE...CONCPT TIME/SEQ STERTYP TOT/POP COLD/WAR 20. PAGE 102 A2085
FUT INT/ORG BAL/PWR PEACE

S64
CRANE R.D.,"BASIC PRINCIPLES IN SOVIET SPACE LAW." FUT WOR+45 AIR INT/ORG DIPLOM DOMIN ARMS/CONT COERCE NUC/PWR PEACE ATTIT DRIVE PWR...INT/LAW METH/CNCPT NEW/IDEA OBS TREND GEN/LAWS VAL/FREE MARX/KARL 20. PAGE 32 A0659
COM LAW USSR SPACE

S64
DE GAULLE C.,"FRENCH WORLD VIEW." AFR ASIA CHINA/COM EUR+WWI ISLAM ECO/UNDEV INT/ORG NAT/G VOL/ASSN ACT/RES DIPLOM ECO/TAC EDU/PROP ATTIT DRIVE WEALTH 20. PAGE 35 A0702
TOP/EX PWR FOR/AID FRANCE

S64
GARDNER R.N.,"GATT AND THE UNITED NATIONS CONFERENCE ON TRADE AND DEVELOPMENT." USA+45 WOR+45 SOCIETY ECO/UNDEV MARKET NAT/G DELIB/GP ACT/RES PLAN ECO/TAC TARIFFS EDU/PROP ROUTINE DRIVE RIGID/FLEX WEALTH...DECISION MGT TREND UN TOT/POP 20 GATT. PAGE 51 A1047
INT/ORG INT/TRADE

S64
GARMARNIKOW M.,"INFLUENCE-BUYING IN WEST AFRICA." COM FUT USSR INTELL NAT/G PLAN TEC/DEV ECO/TAC DOMIN EDU/PROP REGION NAT/LISM ATTIT DRIVE ALL/VALS SOVEREIGN...POLICY PSY SOC CONCPT TREND STERTYP WORK COLD/WAR 20. PAGE 51 A1049
AFR ECO/UNDEV FOR/AID SOCISM

S64
GREENBERG S.,"JUDAISM AND WORLD JUSTICE." MEDIT-7 WOR+45 LAW CULTURE SOCIETY INT/ORG NAT/G FORCES EDU/PROP ATTIT DRIVE PERSON SUPEGO ALL/VALS ...POLICY PSY CONCPT GEN/LAWS JEWS. PAGE 55 A1140
SECT JURID PEACE

S64
GROSSER A.,"Y A-T-IL UN CONFLIT FRANCO-AMERICAIN." EUR+WWI USA+45 INT/ORG NAT/G PLAN BAL/PWR DIPLOM EDU/PROP NUC/PWR ATTIT DRIVE ORD/FREE PWR...CONCPT OBS TIME/SEQ TREND STERTYP VAL/FREE COLD/WAR. PAGE 57 A1179
VOL/ASSN NAT/LISM FRANCE

S64
HOFFMANN S.,"CE QU'EN PENSENT LES AMERICAINS." EUR+WWI INT/ORG VOL/ASSN PLAN BAL/PWR DIPLOM DOMIN EDU/PROP REGION ARMS/CONT DRIVE ORD/FREE PWR ...POLICY CONCPT OBS TREND STERTYP COLD/WAR VAL/FREE 20. PAGE 66 A1357
USA+45 ATTIT FRANCE

S64
JACK H.,"NONALIGNMENT AND A TEST BAN AGREEMENT: THE ROLE OF THE NON-ALIGNED STATES." WOR+45 INT/ORG CONSULT DOMIN EDU/PROP LEGIT CHOOSE PEACE ATTIT DRIVE KNOWL ORD/FREE...TREND CHARTS GEN/LAWS UN VAL/FREE 20. PAGE 72 A1471
PWR CONCPT NUC/PWR

S64
MAZRUI A.A.,"THE UNITED NATIONS AND SOME AFRICAN POLITICAL ATTITUDES." ECO/TAC FOR/AID DOMIN ROUTINE CHOOSE ATTIT DRIVE MORAL PWR RESPECT WEALTH...PSY CONCPT OBS TREND UN VAL/FREE 20. PAGE 97 A1987
AFR INT/ORG SOVEREIGN

S64
MCCREARY E.A.,"THOSE AMERICAN MANAGERS DON'T IMPRESS EUROPE." EUR+WWI USA+45 CULTURE STRATA ECO/DEV TOP/EX INT/TRADE ATTIT DRIVE PERSON
MARKET ACT/RES BAL/PAY

RIGID/FLEX...CONCPT 20. PAGE 98 A2003 CAP/ISM

S64
SAAB H.,"THE ARAB SEARCH FOR A FEDERAL UNION." SOCIETY INT/ORG NAT/G DELIB/GP FORCES ACT/RES TEC/DEV ECO/TAC DOMIN LEGIT REGION ROUTINE ATTIT DRIVE RIGID/FLEX ALL/VALS...SOC CONCPT NEW/IDEA TIME/SEQ TREND. PAGE 126 A2580 ISLAM PLAN

S64
ZARTMAN I.W.,"LES RELATIONS ENTRE LA FRANCE ET L'ALGERIA DEPUIS LES ACCORDS D'EVIAN." EUR+WWI FUT ISLAM CULTURE AGRI EXTR/IND FINAN INDUS POL/PAR DIPLOM ECO/TAC FOR/AID PEACE ATTIT DRIVE ALL/VALS ...TIME/SEQ VAL/FREE 20. PAGE 169 A3446 ECO/UNDEV ALGERIA FRANCE

B65
LEVENSTEIN A.,FREEDOM'S ADVOCATE - A TWENTY-FIVE YEAR CHRONICLE. USA+45 POL/PAR LEGIS DIPLOM WAR PEACE TOTALISM DRIVE MARXISM 20 FREEDOM/HS. PAGE 87 A1791 ORD/FREE VOL/ASSN POLICY ATTIT

B65
MEYERHOFF A.E.,THE STRATEGY OF PERSUASION: THE USE OF ADVERTISING SKILLS IN FIGHTING THE COLD WAR. USA+45 USSR PLAN ATTIT DRIVE...BIBLIOG 20 COLD/WAR. PAGE 100 A2054 EDU/PROP SERV/IND METH/COMP DIPLOM

S65
KHOURI F.J.,"THE JORDON RIVER CONTROVERSY." LAW SOCIETY ECO/UNDEV AGRI FINAN INDUS SECT FORCES ACT/RES PLAN TEC/DEV ECO/TAC EDU/PROP COERCE ATTIT DRIVE PERCEPT RIGID/FLEX ALL/VALS...GEOG SOC MYTH WORK. PAGE 78 A1610 ISLAM INT/ORG ISRAEL JORDAN

S65
MERRITT R.L.,"WOODROW WILSON AND THE 'GREAT AND SOLEMN REFERENDUM,' 1920." USA-45 SOCIETY NAT/G CONSULT LEGIS ACT/RES PLAN DOMIN EDU/PROP ROUTINE ATTIT DISPL DRIVE PERSON RIGID/FLEX MORAL ORD/FREE ...PSY SOC CONCPT MYTH LEAGUE/NAT. PAGE 100 A2044 INT/ORG TOP/EX DIPLOM

S65
QUADE Q.L.,"THE TRUMAN ADMINISTRATION AND THE SEPARATION OF POWERS: THE CASE OF THE MARSHALL PLAN." SOCIETY INT/ORG NAT/G CONSULT DELIB/GP LEGIS PLAN ECO/TAC ROUTINE DRIVE PERCEPT RIGID/FLEX ORD/FREE PWR WEALTH...DECISION GEOG NEW/IDEA TREND 20 TRUMAN/HS. PAGE 118 A2422 USA+45 ECO/UNDEV DIPLOM

B66
BRYNES A.,WE GIVE TO CONQUER. USA+45 USSR STRATA ECO/UNDEV INT/ORG NAT/G DIPLOM DRIVE...TREND IDEA/COMP 20. PAGE 20 A0414 FOR/AID CONTROL GIVE WAR

B67
BODENHEIMER E.,TREATISE ON JUSTICE. INT/ORG NAT/G PUB/INST ACT/RES RISK CRIME INGP/REL DISCRIM DRIVE LAISSEZ 20. PAGE 16 A0325 ALL/VALS STRUCT JURID CONCPT

B67
MEHDI M.T.,PEACE IN THE MIDDLE EAST. ISRAEL SOCIETY NAT/G PLAN EDU/PROP NAT/LISM DRIVE...IDEA/COMP 20 JEWS. PAGE 99 A2033 ISLAM DIPLOM GP/REL COERCE

B67
PIKE F.B.,FREEDOM AND REFORM IN LATIN AMERICA. BRAZIL URUGUAY CONSTN CULTURE SECT DIPLOM EDU/PROP PARTIC DRIVE ALL/VALS CATHISM...GEOG ANTHOL BIBLIOG REFORMERS BOLIV. PAGE 116 A2379 L/A+17C ORD/FREE ECO/UNDEV REV

B67
THORNE C.,THE APPROACH OF WAR, 1938-1939. EUR+WWI POL/PAR CHIEF FORCES LEAD DRIVE PWR FASCISM ...BIBLIOG/A 20 HITLER/A. PAGE 144 A2936 DIPLOM WAR ELITES

S67
ECKHARDT A.R.,"SILENCE IN THE CHURCHES." ISRAEL WOR+45 CONSTN GP/REL DISCRIM DRIVE JEWS. PAGE 40 A0820 SECT ATTIT DIPLOM ISLAM

DRUCKER P.F. A0788

DRUG ADDICTION....SEE BIO/SOC, ANOMIE, CRIME

DU BOIS W.E.B. A0789

DUBCEK/A....ALEXANDER DUBCEK

DUBOIS J. A0790

DUBOIS/J....JULES DUBOIS

DUBOIS/WEB....W.E.B. DUBOIS

DUCHACEK I.D. A0791

DUCLOS P. A0792

DUCLOUX L. A0793

DUDDEN A.P. A0794

DUFFY J. A0795

DUGUIT/L....LEON DUGUIT

DUHRING/E....EUGEN DUHRING

DUIGNAN P. A0549

DULLES J.F. A0796, A0797

DULLES/JF....JOHN FOSTER DULLES

B57
BEAL J.R.,JOHN FOSTER DULLES, A BIOGRAPHY. USA+45 USSR WOR+45 CONSTN INT/ORG NAT/G EX/STRUC LEGIT ADMIN NUC/PWR DISPL PERSON ORD/FREE PWR SKILL ...POLICY PSY OBS RECORD COLD/WAR UN 20 DULLES/JF. PAGE 12 A0237 BIOG DIPLOM

B63
ROSS H.,THE COLD WAR: CONTAINMENT AND ITS CRITICSS. WOR+45 POL/PAR BAL/PWR ECO/TAC PEACE ORD/FREE ...POLICY IDEA/COMP ANTHOL T 20 COLD/WAR DULLES/JF TRUMAN/HS EISNHWR/DD. PAGE 124 A2541 MARXISM ARMS/CONT DIPLOM

B64
FINER H.,DULLES OVER SUEZ. FRANCE FUT UAR UK WOR+45 NAT/G PROB/SOLV CONTROL NUC/PWR WAR 20 DULLES/JF SUEZ. PAGE 46 A0932 DIPLOM POLICY REC/INT

B66
CRAIG G.A.,WAR, POLITICS, AND DIPLOMACY. PRUSSIA CONSTN FORCES CIVMIL/REL TOTALISM PWR 19/20 BISMARCK/O DULLES/JF NAPOLEON/B. PAGE 32 A0654 WAR DIPLOM BAL/PWR

DUMON F. A0798

DUNN F.S. A0799, A0800, A0801, A0802

DUNNING W.A. A0803

DUPONT....DUPONT CORPORATION (E.I. DUPONT DE NEMOURS)

DUPUY R.E. A0804

DUPUY T.N. A0804

DURBIN E.F.M. A0805

DURKHEIM/E....EMIL DURKHEIM

DUROSELLE J.B. A0806,A0807,A0808,A0809,A0810,A0811

DUTOIT B. A0812

DUTT R.P. A0813

DUTY....SEE SUPEGO

DUVERGER/M....MAURICE DUVERGER

DYCK H.V. A0814

DYSON F.J. A0815

E

EACM....EAST AFRICAN COMMON MARKET

S61
OCHENG D.,"ECONOMIC FORCES AND UGANDA'S FOREIGN POLICY." AFR UGANDA INT/TRADE TARIFFS INCOME SOVEREIGN WEALTH 20 EACM EEC TANGANYIKA. PAGE 111 A2274 ECO/TAC DIPLOM ECO/UNDEV INT/ORG

EAGLETON C. A0816

EAST AFRICA....SEE AFRICA/E

EAST GERMANY....SEE GERMANY/E

EASTERN EUROPE....SEE EUROPE/E

EASTON S.C. A0817

EATING....EATING, CUISINE

N19
HAUSER P.M.,WORLD POPULATION PROBLEMS (PAMPHLET). USA+45 WOR+45 ECO/DEV ECO/UNDEV FAM ACT/RES PLAN PROB/SOLV FOR/AID GIVE EATING...CHARTS 20 BIRTH/CON RESOURCE/N. PAGE 63 A1289 CONTROL CENSUS ATTIT PREDICT

B58
US OPERATIONS MISSION TO VIET,BUILDING ECONOMIC STRENGTH (PAMPHLET). USA+45 VIETNAM/S INDUS TEC/DEV BUDGET ADMIN EATING HEALTH...STAT 20. PAGE 155 A3162 FOR/AID ECO/UNDEV AGRI EDU/PROP

B60
VOGT W.,PEOPLE: CHALLENGE TO SURVIVAL. WOR+45 ECO/DEV ECO/UNDEV FAM INT/ORG NAT/G PLAN PROB/SOLV FOR/AID GIVE EATING 20 BIRTH/CON. PAGE 159 A3247
CENSUS CONTROL ATTIT TEC/DEV

B63
EL-NAGGAR S.,FOREIGN AID TO UNITED ARAB REPUBLIC. UAR USA+45 USSR AGRI FINAN INDUS FORCES EATING DEMAND...CHARTS METH/COMP 20 RESOURCE/N AID. PAGE 41 A0838
FOR/AID ECO/UNDEV RECEIVE PLAN

B63
US GOVERNMENT,REPORT TO INTER-AMERICAN ECONOMIC AND SOCIAL COUNCIL AT SECOND ANNUAL MEETING. L/A+17C USA+45 VOL/ASSN TEC/DEV DIPLOM TAX EATING EFFICIENCY HEALTH...STAT CHARTS 20 AID. PAGE 153 A3116
ECO/TAC FOR/AID FINAN PLAN

B64
MC GOVERN G.S.,WAR AGAINST WANT. USA+45 AGRI DIPLOM INT/TRADE GIVE RECEIVE DEMAND HEALTH 20 KENNEDY/JF FOOD/PEACE. PAGE 97 A1993
FOR/AID ECO/DEV POLICY EATING

B66
MOOMAW I.W.,THE CHALLENGE OF HUNGER. USA+45 PLAN ADMIN EATING 20. PAGE 103 A2118
FOR/AID DIPLOM ECO/UNDEV ECO/TAC

EAYRS J. A0818

EBENSTEIN W. A0819

EBERHART S. A0633

ECHR....EUROPEAN CONVENTION ON HUMAN RIGHTS

B62
GOLDWATER B.M.,WHY NOT VICTORY? A FRESH LOOK AT AMERICAN FOREIGN POLICY. USA+45 WOR+45 FOR/AID LEAD ARMS/CONT WAR PEACE ATTIT ORD/FREE PWR MARXISM ...INT/LAW 20 TREATY ECHR COUNCL/EUR. PAGE 53 A1092
DIPLOM POLICY CONSERVE NAT/LISM

S64
SCHWELB E.,"OPERATION OF THE EUROPEAN CONVENTION ON HUMAN RIGHTS." EUR+WWI LAW SOCIETY CREATE EDU/PROP ADJUD ADMIN PEACE ATTIT ORD/FREE PWR...POLICY INT/LAW CONCPT OBS GEN/LAWS UN VAL/FREE ILO 20 ECHR. PAGE 130 A2665
INT/ORG MORAL

B66
COUNCIL OF EUROPE,EUROPEAN CONVENTION ON HUMAN RIGHTS - COLLECTED TEXTS (5TH ED.). EUR+WWI DIPLOM ADJUD CT/SYS...INT/LAW 20 ECHR. PAGE 31 A0638
ORD/FREE DELIB/GP INT/ORG JURID

ECKARDT A.L. A0820

ECKHARDT A.R. A0820

ECKSTEIN A. A0740

ECO....ECONOMICS

ECO/DEV....ECONOMIC SYSTEM IN DEVELOPED COUNTRIES

ECO/TAC....ECONOMIC MEASURES

N
JOURNAL OF INTERNATIONAL AFFAIRS. WOR+45 ECO/UNDEV POL/PAR ECO/TAC WAR PEACE PERSON ALL/IDEOS ...INT/LAW TREND. PAGE 1 A0015
BIBLIOG DIPLOM INT/ORG NAT/G

N
COUNCIL ON FOREIGN RELATIONS,DOCUMENTS ON AMERICAN FOREIGN RELATIONS. INT/ORG ECO/TAC NUC/PWR WAR WEAPON...POLICY CON/ANAL CHARTS 20 OAS UN. PAGE 31 A0639
BIBLIOG USA+45 USA-45 DIPLOM

N
FOREIGN TRADE LIBRARY,NEW TITLES RECEIVED IN THE LIBRARY. WOR+45 ECO/UNDEV FINAN NAT/G PLAN TEC/DEV BUDGET ECO/TAC TARIFFS GOV/REL STAT. PAGE 47 A0964
BIBLIOG/A INT/TRADE INDUS ECO/DEV

N
MINISTRY OF OVERSEAS DEVELOPME,TECHNICAL CO-OPERATION -- A BIBLIOGRAPHY. UK LAW SOCIETY DIPLOM ECO/TAC FOR/AID...STAT 20 CMN/WLTH. PAGE 102 A2089
BIBLIOG TEC/DEV ECO/DEV NAT/G

N
MURRA R.O.,POST-WAR PROBLEMS: A CURRENT LIST OF UNITED STATES GOVERNMENT PUBLICATIONS (PAMPHLET). WOR+45 SOCIETY FINAN INT/ORG SCHOOL WORKER TEC/DEV ECO/TAC...SOC 20. PAGE 106 A2180
BIBLIOG/A ADJUST AGRI INDUS

N
US DEPARTMENT OF STATE,ABSTRACTS OF COMPLETED DOCTORAL DISSERTATIONS FOR THE ACADEMIC YEAR 1950-1951. WOR+45 WOR-45 ACADEM POL/PAR ECO/TAC ...POLICY SOC 19/20. PAGE 151 A3078
BIBLIOG/A DIPLOM INT/ORG NAT/G

N/R
FULBRIGHT J.W.,THE ARROGANCE OF POWER. USA+45 WOR+45 ECO/UNDEV ACADEM LEGIS ECO/TAC FOR/AID PEACE ROLE ORD/FREE PWR 20 COLD/WAR CONGRESS. PAGE 50 A1014
DIPLOM POLICY REV

B00
DARBY W.E.,INTERNATIONAL TRIBUNALS. WOR-45 NAT/G ECO/TAC DOMIN LEGIT CT/SYS COERCE ORD/FREE PWR SOVEREIGN JURID. PAGE 33 A0681
INT/ORG ADJUD PEACE INT/LAW

B00
GRIFFIN A.P.C.,LIST OF BOOKS RELATING TO THE THEORY OF COLONIZATION, GOVERNMENT OF DEPENDENCIES, PROTECTORATES, AND RELATED TOPICS. FRANCE GERMANY ITALY SPAIN UK USA-45 WOR-45 ECO/TAC ADMIN CONTROL REGION NAT/LISM ALL/VALS PWR...INT/LAW SOC 16/19. PAGE 56 A1149
BIBLIOG/A COLONIAL GOV/REL DOMIN

B00
MORRIS H.C.,THE HISTORY OF COLONIZATION. WOR+45 WOR-45 ECO/DEV ECO/UNDEV INT/ORG ACT/RES PLAN ECO/TAC LEGIT ROUTINE COERCE ATTIT DRIVE ALL/VALS ...GEOG TREND 19. PAGE 105 A2148
DOMIN SOVEREIGN COLONIAL

B06
GRIFFIN A.P.C.,SELECT LIST OF REFERENCES ON THE BRITISH TARIFF MOVEMENT. MOD/EUR UK BAL/PWR BARGAIN ECO/TAC LAISSEZ 20. PAGE 56 A1154
BIBLIOG/A INT/TRADE TARIFFS COLONIAL

B09
HOLLAND T.E.,LETTERS UPON WAR AND NEUTRALITY. WOR-45 NAT/G FORCES JUDGE ECO/TAC LEGIT CT/SYS NEUTRAL ROUTINE COERCE...JURID TIME/SEQ 20. PAGE 67 A1368
LAW INT/LAW INT/ORG WAR

B15
HOBSON J.A.,TOWARDS INTERNATIONAL GOVERNMENT. MOD/EUR STRUCT ECO/TAC EDU/PROP ADJUD ALL/VALS ...SOCIALIST CONCPT GEN/LAWS TOT/POP 20. PAGE 65 A1347
FUT INT/ORG CENTRAL

B17
MEYER H.H.B.,LIST OF REFERENCES ON EMBARGOES (PAMPHLET). USA-45 AGRI DIPLOM WRITING DEBATE WEAPON...INT/LAW 18/20 CONGRESS. PAGE 100 A2049
BIBLIOG DIST/IND ECO/TAC INT/TRADE

B19
KEYNES J.M.,THE ECONOMIC CONSEQUENCES OF THE PEACE. FUT GERMANY MOD/EUR RUSSIA UK USA-45 CULTURE ECO/DEV FINAN INDUS INT/ORG TOP/EX ECO/TAC ROUTINE WAR ATTIT PERCEPT ALL/VALS...OLD/LIB MYTH OBS TIME/SEQ TREND 20 TREATY. PAGE 78 A1605
EUR+WWI SOCIETY PEACE

B19
MEYER H.H.B.,SELECT LIST OF REFERENCES ON ECONOMIC RECONSTRUCTION: INCLUDING REPORTS OF THE BRITISH MINISTRY OF RECONSTRUCTION. UK LABOR PLAN PROB/SOLV ECO/TAC INT/TRADE WAR DEMAND PRODUC 20. PAGE 100 A2051
BIBLIOG/A EUR+WWI ECO/DEV WORKER

B19
SUMNER W.G.,WAR AND OTHER ESSAYS. USA-45 DELIB/GP DIPLOM TARIFFS COLONIAL PEACE SOVEREIGN 20. PAGE 140 A2864
INT/TRADE ORD/FREE CAP/ISM ECO/TAC

N19
ASIAN-AFRICAN CONFERENCE,SELECTED DOCUMENTS OF THE BANDUNG CONFERENCE (PAMPHLET). S/ASIA PLAN ECO/TAC CONFER REGION REV NAT/LISM 20. PAGE 9 A0191
NEUTRAL ECO/UNDEV COLONIAL DIPLOM

N19
BASCH A.,THE FUTURE OF FOREIGN LENDING FOR DEVELOPMENT (PAMPHLET). WOR+45 ECO/UNDEV FINAN INT/ORG ECO/TAC ATTIT...PREDICT 20. PAGE 11 A0232
FOR/AID ECO/DEV DIPLOM GIVE

N19
DEANE H.,THE WAR IN VIETNAM (PAMPHLET). CHINA/COM VIETNAM BAL/PWR DIPLOM ECO/TAC SOCISM INTERVENT COLD/WAR INTERVENT COLD/WAR. PAGE 35 A0720
WAR SOCIALIST MORAL CAP/ISM

N19
FRANCK P.G.,AFGHANISTAN BETWEEN EAST AND WEST: THE ECONOMICS OF COMPETITIVE COEXISTENCE (PAMPHLET). AFGHANISTN USA+45 USA-45 USSR INDUS ECO/TAC INT/TRADE CONTROL NEUTRAL ORD/FREE MARXISM...GEOG 20 UN. PAGE 48 A0977
FOR/AID PLAN DIPLOM ECO/UNDEV

N19
HALPERN M.,THE MORALITY AND POLITICS OF INTERVENTION (PAMPHLET). USA+45 INT/ORG FORCES ECO/TAC MORAL ORD/FREE 20 INTERVENT CHRISTIAN. PAGE 61 A1243
POLICY DIPLOM SOVEREIGN DOMIN

N19
KUWAIT ARABIA,KUWAIT FUND FOR ARAB ECONOMIC DEVELOPMENT (PAMPHLET). ISLAM KUWAIT UAR ECO/UNDEV LEGIS ECO/TAC WEALTH 20. PAGE 83 A1697
FOR/AID DIPLOM FINAN ADMIN

N19
PROVISIONS SECTION OAU,ORGANIZATION OF AFRICAN UNITY: BASIC DOCUMENTS AND RESOLUTIONS (PAMPHLET). AFR CULTURE ECO/UNDEV DIPLOM ECO/TAC EDU/PROP COLONIAL ARMS/CONT NUC/PWR RACE/REL DISCRIM NAT/LISM 20 UN OAU. PAGE 118 A2415
CONSTN EX/STRUC SOVEREIGN INT/ORG

N19
VELYAMINOV G.,AFRICA AND THE COMMON MARKET
INT/ORG

(PAMPHLET). AFR MARKET VOL/ASSN ECO/TAC COLONIAL ORD/FREE...SOCIALIST 20 THIRD/WRLD. PAGE 158 A3227
INT/TRADE
SOVEREIGN
ECO/UNDEV

B21

STUART G.H.,FRENCH FOREIGN POLICY. CONSTN INT/ORG NAT/G POL/PAR EX/STRUC FORCES PLAN ECO/TAC DOMIN EDU/PROP ADJUD COERCE ATTIT DRIVE RIGID/FLEX ALL/VALS...POLICY OBS RECORD BIOG TIME/SEQ TREND. PAGE 139 A2852
MOD/EUR
DIPLOM
FRANCE

B28

CORBETT P.E.,CANADA AND WORLD POLITICS. LAW CULTURE SOCIETY STRUCT MARKET INT/ORG FORCES ACT/RES PLAN ECO/TAC LEGIT ORD/FREE PWR RESPECT...SOC CONCPT TIME/SEQ TREND CMN/WLTH 20 LEAGUE/NAT. PAGE 30 A0612
NAT/G
CANADA

B28

HOWARD-ELLIS C.,THE ORIGIN, STRUCTURE AND WORKING OF THE LEAGUE OF NATIONS. EUR+WWI MOD/EUR USA-45 CONSTN FORCES LEGIS ECO/TAC LEGIT COERCE ORD/FREE ...JURID SOC CONCPT LEAGUE/NAT 20 ILO ICJ. PAGE 68 A1401
INT/ORG
ADJUD

B28

HURST C.,GREAT BRITAIN AND THE DOMINIONS. EUR+WWI CULTURE ECO/DEV INT/ORG NAT/G DIPLOM ECO/TAC COLONIAL ATTIT PWR SOVEREIGN...TIME/SEQ GEN/LAWS TOT/POP VAL/FREE 20 CMN/WLTH. PAGE 69 A1420
VOL/ASSN
DOMIN
UK

B28

MILLER D.H.,THE DRAFTING OF THE COVENANT. UNIV WOR-45 INTELL NAT/G DELIB/GP PLAN ECO/TAC LEGIT WAR ATTIT PERCEPT...CONCPT TIME/SEQ LEAGUE/NAT TOT/POP 20. PAGE 101 A2074
INT/ORG
STRUCT
PEACE

B29

CONWELL-EVANS T.P.,THE LEAGUE COUNCIL IN ACTION. EUR+WWI TURKEY UK USSR WOR-45 INT/ORG FORCES JUDGE ECO/TAC EDU/PROP LEGIT ROUTINE ARMS/CONT COERCE ATTIT PWR...MAJORIT GEOG JURID CONCPT LEAGUE/NAT TOT/POP VAL/FREE TUNIS 20. PAGE 30 A0605
DELIB/GP
INT/LAW

B32

EAGLETON C.,INTERNATIONAL GOVERNMENT. BRAZIL FRANCE GERMANY ITALY UK USSR WOR-45 DELIB/GP TOP/EX PLAN ECO/TAC EDU/PROP LEGIT ADJUD REGION ARMS/CONT COERCE ATTIT PWR...GEOG MGT VAL/FREE LEAGUE/NAT 20. PAGE 40 A0816
INT/ORG
JURID
DIPLOM
INT/LAW

B32

WRIGHT Q.,GOLD AND MONETARY STABILIZATION. FUT USA-45 WOR-45 INTELL ECO/DEV INT/ORG NAT/G CONSULT PLAN ECO/TAC ADMIN ATTIT WEALTH...CONCPT TREND 20. PAGE 167 A3404
FINAN
POLICY

B33

OHLIN B.,INTERREGIONAL AND INTERNATIONAL TRADE. USA-45 WOR-45 CULTURE FINAN MARKET CONSULT PLAN ECO/TAC ATTIT WEALTH...CONCPT MATH TOT/POP 20. PAGE 111 A2285
INT/ORG
ECO/DEV
INT/TRADE
REGION

B34

GRAHAM F.D.,PROTECTIVE TARIFFS. FUT USA+45 WOR-45 INDUS MARKET VOL/ASSN PLAN CAP/ISM ECO/TAC PEACE ATTIT DRIVE HEALTH ORD/FREE...OBS TREND GEN/LAWS 20. PAGE 55 A1124
INT/ORG
TARIFFS

B34

LOVELL R.I.,THE STRUGGLE FOR SOUTH AFRICA, 1875-1899. GERMANY RHODESIA SOUTH/AFR UK NAT/G ECO/TAC HABITAT WEALTH...POLICY 19. PAGE 91 A1866
COLONIAL
DIPLOM
WAR
GP/REL

B34

US TARIFF COMMISSION,THE TARIFF; A BIBLIOGRAPHY: A SELECT LIST OF REFERENCES. USA-45 LAW DIPLOM TAX ADMIN...POLICY TREATY 20. PAGE 157 A3208
BIBLIOG/A
TARIFFS
ECO/TAC

B35

STALEY E.,WAR AND THE PRIVATE INVESTOR. UNIV WOR-45 INTELL SOCIETY INT/ORG NAT/G TOP/EX CAP/ISM ECO/TAC WAR ATTIT ALL/VALS...INT TIME/SEQ TREND CON/ANAL WORK TOT/POP 20. PAGE 137 A2799
FINAN
INT/TRADE
DIPLOM

B36

HUDSON M.O.,INTERNATIONAL LEGISLATION: 1929-1931. WOR-45 SEA AIR AGRI FINAN LABOR DIPLOM ECO/TAC REPAR CT/SYS ARMS/CONT WAR WEAPON...JURID 20 TREATY LEAGUE/NAT. PAGE 69 A1409
INT/LAW
PARL/PROC
ADJUD
LAW

B37

ROBBINS L.,ECONOMIC PLANNING AND INTERNATIONAL ORDER. WOR-45 SOCIETY FINAN INDUS NAT/G ECO/TAC ROUTINE WEALTH...SOC TIME/SEQ GEN/METH WORK 20 KEYNES/JM. PAGE 122 A2492
INT/ORG
PLAN
INT/TRADE

B37

ROYAL INST. INT. AFF.,THE COLONIAL PROBLEM. WOR-45 LAW ECO/DEV ECO/UNDEV NAT/G PLAN ECO/TAC EDU/PROP ADMIN ATTIT ALL/VALS...CONCPT 20. PAGE 125 A2556
INT/ORG
ACT/RES
SOVEREIGN
COLONIAL

B37

VINER J.,STUDIES IN THE THEORY OF INTERNATIONAL TRADE. WOR-45 CONSTN ECO/DEV AGRI INDUS MARKET INT/ORG LABOR NAT/G ECO/TAC TARIFFS COLONIAL ATTIT WEALTH...POLICY CONCPT MATH STAT OBS SAMP TREND GEN/LAWS MARX/KARL 20. PAGE 159 A3236
CAP/ISM
INT/TRADE

B38

COLBY C.C.,GEOGRAPHICAL ASPECTS OF INTERNATIONAL RELATIONS. WOR-45 ECO/DEV ECO/UNDEV AGRI EXTR/IND INDUS MARKET R+D INT/ORG NAT/G TEC/DEV ECO/TAC INT/TRADE NAT/LISM WEALTH...METH/CNCPT CHARTS GEN/LAWS 20. PAGE 28 A0565
PLAN
GEOG
DIPLOM

B38

FLEMMING D.,THE UNITED STATES AND WORLD ORGANIZATION, 1920-1933. ASIA FUT WOR-45 NAT/G TOP/EX DIPLOM ECO/TAC EDU/PROP LEGIT COERCE WAR ...TIME/SEQ LEAGUE/NAT 20 CHINJAP. PAGE 47 A0951
USA-45
INT/ORG
PEACE

B38

HOBSON J.A.,IMPERIALISM. MOD/EUR UK WOR-45 CULTURE ECO/UNDEV NAT/G VOL/ASSN PLAN EDU/PROP LEGIT REGION COERCE ATTIT PWR...POLICY PLURIST TIME/SEQ GEN/LAWS 19/20. PAGE 66 A1348
DOMIN
ECO/TAC
BAL/PWR
COLONIAL

B39

ROBBINS L.,ECONOMIC CAUSES OF WAR. WOR-45 ECO/DEV ECO/UNDEV INT/ORG NAT/G TEC/DEV DIPLOM DOMIN COLONIAL ATTIT DRIVE PWR WEALTH...POLICY CONCPT OBS SAMP TREND CON/ANAL GEN/LAWS MARX/KARL 20. PAGE 122 A2493
COERCE
ECO/TAC
WAR

B39

STALEY E.,WORLD ECONOMY IN TRANSITION. WOR-45 SOCIETY INT/ORG PROF/ORG ECO/TAC ATTIT WEALTH ...METH/CNCPT TREND GEN/LAWS 20. PAGE 137 A2800
TEC/DEV
INT/TRADE

B39

ZIMMERN A.,MODERN POLITICAL DOCTRINE. WOR-45 CULTURE SOCIETY ECO/UNDEV DELIB/GP EX/STRUC CREATE DOMIN COERCE NAT/LISM ATTIT RIGID/FLEX ORD/FREE PWR WEALTH...POLICY CONCPT OBS TIME/SEQ TREND TOT/POP LEAGUE/NAT 20. PAGE 170 A3454
NAT/G
ECO/TAC
BAL/PWR
INT/TRADE

B40

ITALIAN LIBRARY OF INFORMATION: OUTLINE STUDIES (VOL. V). ITALY LIBYA CONTROL...FASCIST 20. PAGE 3 A0052
COLONIAL
DIPLOM
ECO/TAC
POLICY

B40

CARR E.H.,THE TWENTY YEARS' CRISIS 1919-1939. FUT WOR-45 BAL/PWR ECO/TAC LEGIT TOTALISM ATTIT ALL/VALS...POLICY JURID CONCPT TIME/SEQ TREND GEN/LAWS TOT/POP 20. PAGE 24 A0498
INT/ORG
DIPLOM
PEACE

B40

WOLFERS A.,BRITAIN AND FRANCE BETWEEN TWO WORLD WARS. FRANCE UK INT/ORG NAT/G PLAN BARGAIN ECO/TAC AGREE ISOLAT ALL/IDEOS...DECISION GEOG 20 TREATY VERSAILLES INTERVENT. PAGE 166 A3380
DIPLOM
WAR
POLICY

B41

PERHAM M.,AFRICANS AND BRITISH RULE. AFR UK ECO/TAC CONTROL GP/REL ATTIT 20. PAGE 115 A2355
DIPLOM
COLONIAL
ADMIN
ECO/UNDEV

L41

COMM. STUDY ORGAN. PEACE,"ORGANIZATION OF PEACE." USA-45 WOR-45 STRATA NAT/G ACT/RES DIPLOM ECO/TAC EDU/PROP ADJUD ATTIT ORD/FREE PWR...SOC CONCPT ANTHOL LEAGUE/NAT 20. PAGE 28 A0575
INT/ORG
PLAN
PEACE

S41

LASSWELL H.D.,"THE GARRISON STATE" (BMR)" FUT WOR+45 ELITES INTELL FORCES ECO/TAC DOMIN EDU/PROP COERCE INGP/REL 20. PAGE 85 A1739
NAT/G
DIPLOM
PWR
CIVMIL/REL

B42

BONNET H.,THE UNITED NATIONS, WHAT THEY ARE, WHAT THEY MAY BECOME. FUT WOR-45 CREATE BAL/PWR ECO/TAC PWR...TREND GEN/LAWS 20. PAGE 16 A0335
INT/ORG
ORD/FREE

B42

FEILCHENFELD E.H.,THE INTERNATIONAL ECONOMIC LAW OF BELLIGERENT OCCUPATION. EUR+WWI MOD/EUR USA-45 INT/ORG DIPLOM ADJUD ARMS/CONT LEAGUE/NAT 20. PAGE 44 A0907
ECO/TAC
INT/LAW
WAR

B42

HAMBRO C.J.,HOW TO WIN THE PEACE. ECO/TAC EDU/PROP ADJUD PERSON ALL/VALS...SOCIALIST TREND GEN/LAWS 20. PAGE 61 A1246
FUT
INT/ORG
PEACE

B42

JOSHI P.S.,THE TYRANNY OF COLOUR. INDIA SOUTH/AFR UK ECO/UNDEV NAT/G POL/PAR DIPLOM ECO/TAC WAR ...POLICY 19/20. PAGE 75 A1538
COLONIAL
DISCRIM
RACE/REL

B42

TOLMAN E.C.,DRIVES TOWARD WAR. UNIV PLAN DIPLOM ECO/TAC COERCE PERS/REL ADJUST HAPPINESS BIO/SOC HEREDITY HEALTH KNOWL. PAGE 144 A2947
PSY
WAR
UTOPIA
DRIVE

B42

US LIBRARY OF CONGRESS,ECONOMICS OF WAR (APRIL 1941-MARCH 1942). WOR-45 FINAN INDUS LOC/G NAT/G PLAN BUDGET RATION COST DEMAND...POLICY 20. PAGE 154 A3146
BIBLIOG/A
INT/TRADE
ECO/TAC
WAR

B44

BRIERLY J.L.,THE OUTLOOK FOR INTERNATIONAL LAW. FUT WOR-45 CONSTN NAT/G VOL/ASSN FORCES ECO/TAC DOMIN LEGIT ADJUD ROUTINE PEACE ORD/FREE...INT/LAW JURID METH LEAGUE/NAT 20. PAGE 18 A0376
INT/ORG
LAW

B44

DAVIS H.E.,PIONEERS IN WORLD ORDER. WOR-45 CONSTN ECO/TAC DOMIN EDU/PROP LEGIT ADJUD ADMIN ARMS/CONT CHOOSE KNOWL ORD/FREE...POLICY JURID SOC STAT OBS CENSUS TIME/SEQ ANTHOL LEAGUE/NAT 20. PAGE 34 A0691
INT/ORG
ROUTINE

B44
MACIVER R.M.,TOWARDS AN ABIDING PEACE. USA-45 ECO/TAC EDU/PROP DRIVE ORD/FREE PWR WEALTH...CONCPT TIME/SEQ GEN/METH TOT/POP 20. PAGE 92 A1890 — INT/ORG PEACE INT/LAW

B44
RAGATZ L.J.,LITERATURE OF EUROPEAN IMPERIALISM. ECO/TAC INT/TRADE DOMIN GOV/REL DEMAND NAT/LISM PWR WEALTH 19/20. PAGE 119 A2432 — BIBLIOG COLONIAL INT/ORG ECO/UNDEV

B44
WEIGERT H.W.,COMPASS OF THE WORLD, A SYMPOSIUM ON POLITICAL GEOGRAPHY. EUR+WWI FUT MOD/EUR S/ASIA USA-45 WOR-45 SOCIETY AGRI INDUS MARKET ECO/TAC INT/TRADE PERSON 20. PAGE 162 A3298 — TEC/DEV CAP/ISM RUSSIA GEOG

L44
HAILEY,"THE FUTURE OF COLONIAL PEOPLES." WOR-45 CONSTN CULTURE ECO/UNDEV AGRI MARKET INT/ORG NAT/G SECT CONSULT ECO/TAC LEGIT ADMIN NAT/LISM ALL/VALS ...SOC OBS TREND STERTYP CMN/WLTH LEAGUE/NAT PARLIAMENT 20. PAGE 59 A1218 — PLAN CONCPT DIPLOM UK

B45
CLAGETT H.L.,COMMUNIST CHINA: RUTHLESS ENEMY OR PAPER TIGER (PAMPHLET). CHINA/COM ECO/UNDEV AGRI INDUS NAT/G POL/PAR ECO/TAC INT/TRADE GUERRILLA ATTIT...CHARTS NAT/COMP ORG/CHARTS 20. PAGE 26 A0540 — BIBLIOG/A MARXISM DIPLOM COERCE

B45
GALLOWAY E.,ABSTRACTS OF POSTWAR LITERATURE (VOL. IV) JAN.-JULY, 1945 NOS. 901-1074. POLAND USA+45 USSR WOR+45 INDUS LABOR PLAN ECO/TAC INT/TRADE TAX EDU/PROP ADMIN COLONIAL INT/LAW. PAGE 51 A1033 — BIBLIOG/A NUC/PWR NAT/G DIPLOM

B46
MITRANY D.,A WORKING PEACE SYSTEM. WOR+45 WOR-45 ECO/DEV INT/ORG NAT/G DELIB/GP ECO/TAC REGION ATTIT RIGID/FLEX...TREND GEN/LAWS LEAGUE/NAT 20. PAGE 102 A2091 — VOL/ASSN PLAN PEACE SOVEREIGN

S46
SILBERNER E.,"THE PROBLEM OF WAR IN NINETEENTH CENTURY ECONOMIC THOUGHT." EUR+WWI MOD/EUR UNIV LAW ECO/DEV ECO/UNDEV FINAN INDUS MARKET INT/ORG NAT/G CONSULT FORCES...CONCPT GEN/LAWS GEN/METH 19. PAGE 133 A2715 — ATTIT ECO/TAC WAR

B47
BROOKINGS INST.,MAJOR PROBLEMS OF UNITED STATES FOREIGN POLICY. USA+45 WOR+45 STRUCT ECO/DEV ECO/UNDEV INT/ORG NAT/G POL/PAR VOL/ASSN DELIB/GP FORCES ECO/TAC LEGIT COERCE ORD/FREE PWR WEALTH ...POLICY STAT TREND CHARTS TOT/POP. PAGE 19 A0392 — ACT/RES DIPLOM

B47
CONOVER H.F.,NON-SELF-GOVERNING AREAS. BELGIUM FRANCE ITALY UK WOR+45 CULTURE ECO/UNDEV INT/ORG LOC/G NAT/G ECO/TAC INT/TRADE ADMIN HEALTH...SOC UN. PAGE 30 A0601 — BIBLIOG/A COLONIAL DIPLOM

B47
DE HUSZAR G.B.,PERSISTENT INTERNATIONAL ISSUES. WOR+45 WOR-45 AGRI INDUS INT/ORG PROB/SOLV EFFICIENCY WEALTH...CON/ANAL ANTHOL UN. PAGE 35 A0704 — DIPLOM PEACE ECO/TAC FOR/AID

B47
FEIS H.,SEEN FROM E A, THREE INTERNATIONAL EPISODES. EUR+WWI ITALY USA-45 WOR-45 AGRI INT/ORG NAT/G INT/TRADE LEGIT EXEC ATTIT ORD/FREE...POLICY LEAGUE/NAT TOT/POP 20 OIL. PAGE 44 A0908 — EXTR/IND ECO/TAC DIPLOM

B47
GORDON D.L.,THE HIDDEN WEAPON: THE STORY OF ECONOMIC WARFARE. EUR+WWI USA-45 LAW FINAN INDUS NAT/G CONSULT FORCES PLAN DOMIN PWR WEALTH ...INT/LAW CONCPT OBS TOT/POP NAZI 20. PAGE 54 A1112 — INT/ORG ECO/TAC INT/TRADE WAR

B47
MANDER L.,FOUNDATIONS OF MODERN WORLD SOCIETY. WOR+45 DELIB/GP ECO/TAC INT/TRADE EDU/PROP ALL/VALS ...TIME/SEQ GEN/LAWS TOT/POP VAL/FREE ILO 20. PAGE 94 A1917 — INT/ORG EX/STRUC DIPLOM

B47
TOWLE L.W.,INTERNATIONAL TRADE AND COMMERCIAL POLICY. WOR+45 LAW ECO/DEV FINAN INDUS NAT/G ECO/TAC WEALTH...TIME/SEQ ILO 20. PAGE 144 A2955 — MARKET INT/ORG INT/TRADE

B48
CHAMBERLAIN L.H.,AMERICAN FOREIGN POLICY. FUT USA+45 USA-45 WOR+45 WOR-45 NAT/G LEGIS TOP/EX ECO/TAC FOR/AID EDU/PROP EXEC ATTIT ORD/FREE ...JURID TREND TOT/POP 20. PAGE 25 A0517 — CONSTN DIPLOM

B48
CHURCHILL W.,THE GATHERING STORM. UK WOR-45 INT/ORG NAT/G FORCES TOP/EX DIPLOM ECO/TAC COERCE ATTIT ORD/FREE PWR WEALTH...POLICY SELF/OBS RECORD NAZI PARLIAMENT 20. PAGE 26 A0538 — BIOG

B48
GRAHAM F.D.,THE THEORY OF INTERNATIONAL VALUES. FUT WOR+45 WOR-45 ECO/DEV FINAN INT/ORG PLAN TEC/DEV CAP/ISM DIPLOM ECO/TAC TARIFFS ROUTINE BAL/PAY DRIVE PWR WEALTH SOCISM...POLICY STAT HYPO/EXP GEN/LAWS 20. PAGE 55 A1125 — NEW/IDEA INT/TRADE

B48
KULISCHER E.M.,EUROPE ON THE MOVE: WAR AND POPULATION CHANGES, 1917-1947. COM EUR+WWI FUT GERMANY USSR DIST/IND PLAN INT/TRADE CONTROL WAR DRIVE...CENSUS TREND COLD/WAR 20. PAGE 82 A1690 — ECO/TAC GEOG

B48
PELCOVITS N.A.,OLD CHINA HANDS AND THE FOREIGN OFFICE. ASIA BURMA UK ECO/UNDEV NAT/G ECO/TAC FOR/AID TARIFFS DOMIN COLONIAL GOV/REL SOVEREIGN 19 HONG/KONG TREATY. PAGE 114 A2348 — INT/TRADE ATTIT DIPLOM

B49
OGBURN W.,TECHNOLOGY AND INTERNATIONAL RELATIONS. WOR+45 WOR-45 ECO/DEV CREATE PLAN ECO/TAC EDU/PROP COERCE PWR SKILL WEALTH...TECHNIC PSY SOC NEW/IDEA CHARTS TOT/POP 20. PAGE 111 A2283 — TEC/DEV DIPLOM INT/ORG

B49
US DEPARTMENT OF STATE,SOVIET BIBLIOGRAPHY (PAMPHLET). CHINA/COM COM USSR LAW AGRI INT/ORG ECO/TAC EDU/PROP...POLICY GEOG 20. PAGE 151 A3084 — BIBLIOG/A MARXISM CULTURE DIPLOM

B50
LEVI W.,FUNDAMENTALS OF WORLD ORGANIZATION. WOR+45 WOR-45 CULTURE ECO/TAC GIVE RECEIVE PERSON WEALTH ...METH/COMP 19/20 UN LEAGUE/NAT. PAGE 88 A1793 — INT/ORG PEACE ORD/FREE DIPLOM

B50
LINCOLN G.,ECONOMICS OF NATIONAL SECURITY. USA+45 ELITES COM/IND DIST/IND INDUS NAT/G VOL/ASSN DELIB/GP EX/STRUC FOR/AID EDU/PROP COERCE NUC/PWR WAR ATTIT KNOWL ORD/FREE PWR COLD/WAR TOT/POP VAL/FREE 20. PAGE 89 A1818 — FORCES ECO/TAC

B50
ROSS A.,CONSTITUTION OF THE UNITED NATIONS. CONSTN CONSULT DELIB/GP ECO/TAC...INT/LAW JURID 20 UN LEAGUE/NAT. PAGE 124 A2540 — PEACE DIPLOM ORD/FREE INT/ORG

S50
WITTFOGEL K.A.,"RUSSIA AND ASIA: PROBLEMS OF CONTEMPORARY AREA STUDIES AND INTERNATIONAL RELATIONS." ASIA COM USA+45 SOCIETY NAT/G DIPLOM ECO/TAC FOR/AID EDU/PROP KNOWL...HIST/WRIT TOT/POP 20. PAGE 166 A3373 — ECO/DEV ADMIN RUSSIA USSR

C50
ELLSWORTH P.T.,"INTERNATIONAL ECONOMY." ECO/DEV ECO/UNDEV FINAN LABOR DIPLOM FOR/AID TARIFFS BAL/PAY EQUILIB NAT/LISM OPTIMAL...INT/LAW 20 ILO GATT. PAGE 41 A0843 — BIBLIOG INT/TRADE ECO/TAC INT/ORG

B51
LEONARD L.L.,INTERNATIONAL ORGANIZATION. WOR+45 WOR-45 EX/STRUC FORCES LEGIS ECO/TAC INT/TRADE COLONIAL ARMS/CONT...SOC/WK GOV/COMP BIBLIOG. PAGE 87 A1778 — NAT/G DIPLOM INT/ORG DELIB/GP

B51
VINER J.,INTERNATIONAL ECONOMICS. USA-45 WOR-45 ECO/DEV INDUS NAT/G ECO/TAC ALL/VALS...TIME/SEQ 20. PAGE 159 A3238 — FINAN INT/ORG WAR INT/TRADE

L51
ULAM A.B.,"THE COMIMFORM AND THE PEOPLE'S DEMOCRACIES." EUR+WWI WOR+45 STRUCT NAT/G POL/PAR TOP/EX ACT/RES PLAN ECO/TAC DOMIN ATTIT ALL/VALS ...HIST/WRIT TIME/SEQ 20 COMINFORM. PAGE 146 A2992 — COM INT/ORG USSR TOTALISM

L51
WHITAKER A.P.,"DEVELOPMENT OF AMERICAN REGIONALISM: THE ORGANIZATION OF AMERICAN STATES." L/A+17C USA+45 VOL/ASSN DELIB/GP FORCES TOP/EX ACT/RES ECO/TAC CT/SYS REGION PEACE ALL/VALS OAS 20. PAGE 163 A3330 — INT/ORG TIME/SEQ DETER

C51
GRUNDER G.A.,"THE PHILIPPINES AND THE UNITED STATES." PHILIPPINE S/ASIA USA-45 NAT/G POL/PAR ADMIN SOVEREIGN...TIME/SEQ BIBLIOG 20. PAGE 57 A1181 — COLONIAL POLICY DIPLOM ECO/TAC

C51
LEONARD L.L.,"INTERNATIONAL ORGANIZATION (1ST ED.)" WOR+45 FINAN DELIB/GP ECO/TAC GIVE DOMIN SANCTION PEACE BIO/SOC ORD/FREE...INT/LAW 20 UN LEAGUE/NAT. PAGE 87 A1779 — BIBLIOG POLICY DIPLOM INT/ORG

B52
ALEXANDROWICZ C.H.,INTERNATIONAL ECONOMIC ORGANIZATION. WOR+45 ECO/DEV ECO/UNDEV DIST/IND FINAN MARKET PLAN ECO/TAC LEGIT DRIVE WEALTH ...POLICY CONCPT QUANT OBS TIME/SEQ GEN/LAWS WORK EEC ILO OEEC UNESCO 20. PAGE 6 A0114 — INT/ORG INT/TRADE

B52
HOSELITZ B.F.,THE PROGRESS OF UNDERDEVELOPED AREAS. FUT WOR+45 ECO/DEV ECO/TAC INT/TRADE WEALTH ...SOC TREND GEN/LAWS TOT/POP VAL/FREE COLD/WAR 20. PAGE 68 A1391 — ECO/UNDEV PLAN FOR/AID

B53
BARBER H.W.,FOREIGN POLICIES OF THE UNITED STATES. USA+45 USA-45 WOR+45 INT/ORG NAT/G EX/STRUC ECO/TAC DOMIN EDU/PROP LEGIT COERCE KNOWL PWR COLD/WAR COLD/WAR 20. PAGE 11 A0219 — CONCPT DIPLOM

B53
FEIS H.,THE CHINA TANGLE. ASIA COM USA+45 USA-45 FORCES ECO/TAC REV ATTIT 20 INTERVENT. PAGE 45 A0910 — POLICY DIPLOM WAR

FOR/AID

B53
MACK R.T.,RAISING THE WORLDS STANDARD OF LIVING. IRAN INT/ORG VOL/ASSN EX/STRUC ECO/TAC WEALTH...MGT METH/CNCPT STAT CONT/OBS INT TOT/POP VAL/FREE 20 UN. PAGE 92 A1893
WOR+45 FOR/AID INT/TRADE

B53
MANSERGH N.,DOCUMENTS AND SPEECHES ON BRITISH COMMONWEALTH AFFAIRS 1931-1952. INDIA IRELAND PAKISTAN UK CONSTN POL/PAR CHIEF FORCES COLONIAL ORD/FREE SOVEREIGN...JURID 20 COMMONWLTH. PAGE 94 A1929
BIBLIOG/A DIPLOM ECO/TAC

B53
MENDE T.,WORLD POWER IN THE BALANCE. FUT USA+45 USSR WOR-45 ECO/DEV ECO/TAC INT/TRADE EDU/PROP UTOPIA ATTIT...HUM CONCPT TREND COLD/WAR TOT/POP 20. PAGE 99 A2036
WOR+45 PWR BAL/PWR

B53
THAYER P.W.,SOUTHEAST ASIA IN THE COMING WORLD. ASIA S/ASIA USA+45 USA-45 SOCIETY INT/ORG ACT/RES ECO/TAC EDU/PROP COERCE TOTALISM ALL/VALS...JURID 20. PAGE 142 A2909
ECO/UNDEV ATTIT FOR/AID DIPLOM

S53
BOULDING K.E.,"ECONOMIC ISSUES IN INTERNATIONAL CONFLICT." WOR+45 ECO/DEV NAT/G TOP/EX DIPLOM ECO/TAC DOMIN ATTIT WEALTH...MAJORIT OBS/ENVIR TREND GEN/LAWS COLD/WAR TOT/POP 20. PAGE 17 A0345
PWR FOR/AID

B54
EPSTEIN L.D.,BRITAIN - UNEASY ALLY. KOREA UK USA+45 NAT/G POL/PAR ECO/TAC FOR/AID INT/TRADE WAR LABOR/PAR CONSRV/PAR. PAGE 42 A0857
DIPLOM ATTIT POLICY NAT/COMP

B54
GERMANY FOREIGN MINISTRY,DOCUMENTS ON GERMAN FOREIGN POLICY 1918-1945, SERIES C (1933-1937) VOLS. I-V. GERMANY MOD/EUR FORCES PLAN ECO/TAC ...FASCIST CHARTS ANTHOL 20. PAGE 52 A1065
NAT/G DIPLOM POLICY

B54
NORTHROP F.S.C.,EUROPEAN UNION AND UNITED STATES FOREIGN POLICY: A STUDY IN SOCIOLOGICAL JURISPRUDENCE. EUR+WWI MOD/EUR USA+45 SOCIETY STRUCT NAT/G CREATE ECO/TAC DOMIN EDU/PROP REGION ATTIT RIGID/FLEX HEALTH ORD/FREE WEALTH ...METH/CNCPT TIME/SEQ TREND. PAGE 110 A2256
INT/ORG SOC DIPLOM

B54
REYNOLDS P.A.,BRITISH FOREIGN POLICY IN THE INTER-WAR YEARS. CZECHOSLVK GERMANY POLAND UK USA-45 POL/PAR FORCES ECO/TAC ARMS/CONT WAR ATTIT 20. PAGE 120 A2470
DIPLOM POLICY NAT/G

B54
STALEY E.,THE FUTURE OF UNDERDEVELOPED COUNTRIES: POLITICAL IMPLICATIONS OF ECONOMIC DEVELOPMENT. COM FUT USA+45 SOCIETY ECO/UNDEV CREATE PLAN CAP/ISM ATTIT DRIVE MARXISM SOCISM...POLICY CONCPT CHARTS COLD/WAR 20. PAGE 137 A2801
EDU/PROP ECO/TAC FOR/AID

B54
TINBERGEN J.,INTERNATIONAL ECONOMIC INTEGRATION. WOR+45 WOR-45 ECO/UNDEV NAT/G ECO/TAC BAL/PAY ...METH/CNCPT STAT TIME/SEQ GEN/METH OEEC 20. PAGE 144 A2941
INT/ORG ECO/DEV INT/TRADE

B54
WRIGHT Q.,PROBLEMS OF STABILITY AND PROGRESS IN INTERNATIONAL RELATIONSHIPS. FUT WOR+45 WOR-45 SOCIETY LEGIS CREATE TEC/DEV ECO/TAC EDU/PROP ADJUD WAR PEACE ORD/FREE PWR...KNO/TEST TREND GEN/LAWS 20. PAGE 167 A3409
INT/ORG CONCPT DIPLOM

L54
CHARLESWORTH J.C.,"AMERICA AND A NEW ASIA." ASIA INDIA ISLAM S/ASIA USA+45 USA-45 ECO/UNDEV NAT/G POL/PAR FORCES FOR/AID DOMIN EDU/PROP COERCE DRIVE ALL/VALS MARXISM SOCISM TOT/POP 20. PAGE 26 A0522
ECO/TAC DIPLOM NAT/LISM

B55
ARNOLD G.L.,THE PATTERN OF WORLD CONFLICT. USA+45 INT/ORG ECO/TAC INT/TRADE PEACE 20 EUROPE. PAGE 9 A0176
DIPLOM BAL/PWR NAT/LISM PLAN

B55
JONES J.M.,THE FIFTEEN WEEKS (FEBRUARY 21-JUNE 5, 1947). EUR+WWI USA+45 PROB/SOLV BAL/PWR...POLICY TIME/SEQ 20 COLD/WAR MARSHL/PLN TRUMAN/HS WASHING/DC. PAGE 75 A1532
DIPLOM ECO/TAC FOR/AID

B55
JOY C.T.,HOW COMMUNISTS NEGOTIATE. COM USA+45 CONSTN CULTURE ECO/UNDEV NAT/G CONSULT DELIB/GP FORCES PLAN ECO/TAC DOMIN EDU/PROP LEGIT EXEC ROUTINE COERCE WAR CHOOSE PEACE ATTIT RIGID/FLEX ORD/FREE PWR...POLICY 20. PAGE 75 A1539
ASIA INT/ORG DIPLOM

B55
LANDHEER B.,EUROPEAN YEARBOOK, 1955. CONSTN ECO/DEV DIST/IND FINAN DELIB/GP ECO/TAC DETER NUC/PWR ...BIBLIOG 20 EEC. PAGE 84 A1717
EUR+WWI INT/ORG GOV/REL INT/TRADE

B55
MYRDAL A.R.,AMERICA'S ROLE IN INTERNATIONAL SOCIAL WELFARE. FUT WOR+45 SOCIETY R+D VOL/ASSN ECO/TAC EDU/PROP HEALTH KNOWL WEALTH...SOC CHARTS ORG/CHARTS TOT/POP 20. PAGE 107 A2188
PLAN SKILL FOR/AID

B55
O3HEVSS E.,WIRTSCHAFTSSYSTEME UND INTERNATIONALER HANDEL. ECO/DEV FINAN MARKET DIPLOM ECO/TAC COST ...METH/COMP NAT/COMP 20. PAGE 112 A2306
CAP/ISM SOCISM INT/TRADE IDEA/COMP

B55
PANT Y.P.,PLANNING IN UNDERDEVELOPED ECONOMIES. INDIA NEPAL INT/TRADE COLONIAL SOVEREIGN ALL/IDEOS ...TIME/SEQ METH/COMP 20. PAGE 114 A2334
ECO/UNDEV PLAN ECO/TAC DIPLOM

B55
WRIGHT Q.,THE STUDY OF INTERNATIONAL RELATIONS. WOR+45 WOR-45 SOCIETY ECO/TAC INT/TRADE EDU/PROP ALL/VALS...CONCPT GEN/METH 20. PAGE 167 A3410
INT/ORG DIPLOM

L55
KISER M.,"ORGANIZATION OF AMERICAN STATES." L/A+17C USA+45 ECO/UNDEV INT/ORG NAT/G PLAN TEC/DEV DIPLOM ECO/TAC INT/TRADE EDU/PROP ADMIN ALL/VALS...POLICY MGT RECORD ORG/CHARTS OAS 20. PAGE 80 A1639
VOL/ASSN ECO/DEV REGION

B56
BALL W.M.,NATIONALISM AND COMMUNISM IN EAST ASIA. ASIA BURMA EUR+WWI KOREA USA+45 ECO/UNDEV NAT/G POL/PAR DIPLOM ECO/TAC FOR/AID EDU/PROP COERCE RACE/REL NAT/LISM DRIVE SOVEREIGN...TREND 20 CHINJAP. PAGE 11 A0214
S/ASIA ATTIT

B56
FORSTMANN A.,DIE GRUNDLAGEN DER AUSSENWIRTSCHAFTSTHEORIE. ECO/TAC TARIFFS PRICE WAR ...NAT/COMP 20. PAGE 47 A0967
INT/TRADE CONCPT DIPLOM ECO/DEV

B56
FOSTER J.G.,BRITAIN IN WESTERN EUROPE: WEU AND THE ATLANTIC ALLIANCE. EUR+WWI FRANCE GERMANY GERMANY/W ITALY UK STRATA NAT/G DELIB/GP ECO/TAC ORD/FREE PWR ...TRADIT TIME/SEQ TREND OEEC PARLIAMENT 20 EUROPE/W. PAGE 47 A0969
INT/ORG FORCES WEAPON

B56
HAAS E.B.,DYNAMICS OF INTERNATIONAL RELATIONS. WOR-45 ELITES INT/ORG VOL/ASSN EX/STRUC FORCES ECO/TAC DOMIN LEGIT COERCE ATTIT PERSON PWR ...CONCPT TIME/SEQ CHARTS COLD/WAR 20. PAGE 58 A1202
WOR+45 NAT/G DIPLOM

B56
KRAUS O.,THEORIE DER ZWISCHENSTAATLICHEN WIRTSCHAFTSBEZIEHUNGEN. TARIFFS WAR COST 20. PAGE 82 A1677
INT/TRADE DIPLOM BAL/PAY ECO/TAC

B56
TOYNBEE A.,THE WAR AND THE NEUTRALS. L/A+17C PORTUGAL SPAIN SWEDEN SWITZERLND TURKEY WOR+45 WOR-45 ECO/TAC CONFER CONTROL REGION 20. PAGE 145 A2957
NEUTRAL WAR INT/TRADE DIPLOM

B56
WOLFERS A.,THE ANGLO-AMERICAN TRADITION IN FOREIGN AFFAIRS. UK USA+45 WOR-45 CULTURE SOCIETY ECO/DEV INT/ORG NAT/G CREATE PLAN BAL/PWR ECO/TAC EDU/PROP PEACE DISPL DRIVE...TREND GEN/LAWS 20. PAGE 166 A3382
ATTIT CONCPT DIPLOM

B57
ARON R.,L'UNIFICATION ECONOMIQUE DE L'EUROPE. EUR+WWI SWITZERLND UK INT/ORG NAT/G REGION NAT/LISM ORD/FREE PWR...CONCPT METH/CNCPT OBS TREND STERTYP GEN/LAWS EEC 20. PAGE 9 A0181
VOL/ASSN ECO/TAC

B57
BLOOMFIELD L.M.,EGYPT, ISRAEL AND THE GULF OF AQABA: IN INTERNATIONAL LAW. LAW NAT/G CONSULT FORCES PLAN ECO/TAC ROUTINE COERCE ATTIT DRIVE PERCEPT PERSON RIGID/FLEX LOVE PWR WEALTH...GEOG CONCPT MYTH TREND. PAGE 15 A0314
ISLAM INT/LAW UAR

B57
BROMBERGER M.,LES SECRETS DE L'EXPEDITION D'EGYPTE. FRANCE ISLAM UAR UK USA+45 USSR WOR+45 INT/ORG NAT/G FORCES BAL/PWR ECO/TAC DOMIN WAR NAT/LISM ATTIT PWR SOVEREIGN...MAJORIT TIME/SEQ CHARTS SUEZ COLD/WAR 20. PAGE 19 A0387
COERCE DIPLOM

B57
COMM. STUDY ORGAN. PEACE,STRENGTHENING THE UNITED NATIONS. FUT USA+45 WOR+45 CONSTN NAT/G DELIB/GP FORCES LEGIS ECO/TAC LEGIT COERCE PEACE...JURID CONCPT UN COLD/WAR 20. PAGE 28 A0580
INT/ORG ORD/FREE

B57
DEAN V.M.,THE NATURE OF THE NON-WESTERN WORLD. AFR ASIA L/A+17C S/ASIA CULTURE SOCIETY STRATA ECO/DEV DIPLOM ECO/TAC FOR/AID ATTIT DRIVE ALL/VALS ...RELATIV SOC CONCPT TIME/SEQ TREND TOT/POP 20. PAGE 35 A0718
ECO/UNDEV STERTYP NAT/LISM

B57
DRUCKER P.F.,AMERICA'S NEXT TWENTY YEARS. USA+45 DIST/IND ACADEM MUNIC SCHOOL DIPLOM ECO/TAC AUTOMAT HABITAT HEALTH...SOC/WK TREND 20 URBAN/RNWL PUB/TRANS. PAGE 39 A0788
WORKER FOR/AID CENSUS GEOG

B57
FREUND G.,UNHOLY ALLIANCE. EUR+WWI GERMANY USSR FORCES ECO/TAC CONTROL WAR PWR...TREND TREATY. PAGE 49 A0999
DIPLOM PLAN POLICY

B57

KENNAN G.F.,RUSSIA, THE ATOM AND THE WEST. COM EUR+WWI FUT WOR+45 SOCIETY ECO/DEV FORCES DIPLOM ECO/TAC DOMIN EDU/PROP COERCE NUC/PWR ATTIT DRIVE ORD/FREE PWR...POLICY OBS TIME/SEQ TREND COLD/WAR NATO 20. PAGE 77 A1574

NAT/G INT/ORG USSR

B57

LAVES W.H.C.,UNESCO. FUT WOR+45 NAT/G CONSULT DELIB/GP TEC/DEV ECO/TAC EDU/PROP PEACE ORD/FREE ...CONCPT TIME/SEQ TREND UNESCO VAL/FREE 20. PAGE 86 A1751

INT/ORG KNOWL

B57

PALMER N.D.,INTERNATIONAL RELATIONS. WOR+45 INT/ORG NAT/G ECO/TAC EDU/PROP COLONIAL WAR PWR SOVEREIGN ...POLICY T 20 TREATY. PAGE 113 A2321

DIPLOM BAL/PWR NAT/COMP

B57

RUMEU DE ARMAS A.,ESPANA EEN EL AFRICA ATLANTICA. AFR CHRIST-17C PORTUGAL SPAIN DIPLOM ECO/TAC CONTROL 14/16 AFRICA/W. PAGE 125 A2568

NAT/G COLONIAL CHIEF PWR

B57

TRIFFIN R.,EUROPE AND THE MONEY MUDDLE. USA+45 INT/ORG NAT/G CONSULT PLAN ECO/TAC EXEC ROUTINE BAL/PAY WEALTH...METH/CNCPT OBS TREND CHARTS STERTYP GEN/METH EEC VAL/FREE ECSC. PAGE 145 A2962

EUR+WWI ECO/DEV REGION

B57

US PRES CITIZEN ADVISERS,REPORT TO THE PRESIDENT ON THE MUTUAL SECURITY PROGRAM. COM USA+45 WOR+45 FINAN INDUS PLAN BUDGET CAP/ISM DIPLOM FOR/AID INT/TRADE REGION 20 SECUR/PROG. PAGE 155 A3163

BAL/PWR FORCES INT/ORG ECO/TAC

L57

FURNISS E.S.,"SOME PERSPECTIVES ON AMERICAN MILITARY ASSISTANCE." USA+45 WOR+45 ECO/UNDEV INT/ORG ECO/TAC ORD/FREE...GEOG TIME/SEQ TREND COLD/WAR 20. PAGE 50 A1028

FORCES FOR/AID WEAPON

L57

HAAS E.B.,"REGIONAL INTEGRATION AND NATIONAL POLICY." WOR+45 VOL/ASSN DELIB/GP EX/STRUC ECO/TAC DOMIN EDU/PROP LEGIT COERCE ATTIT PERCEPT KNOWL ...TIME/SEQ COLD/WAR 20 UN. PAGE 59 A1203

INT/ORG ORD/FREE REGION

L57

WARREN S.,"FOREIGN AID AND FOREIGN POLICY." USA+45 WOR+45 WOR-45 DIST/IND INDUS MARKET CONSULT CREATE DIPLOM EDU/PROP LEGIT ATTIT RIGID/FLEX...TIME/SEQ GEN/LAWS WORK 20. PAGE 161 A3285

ECO/UNDEV ALL/VALS ECO/TAC FOR/AID

S57

HOAG M.W.,"ECONOMIC PROBLEMS OF ALLIANCE." COM EUR+WWI WOR+45 ECO/DEV ECO/UNDEV NAT/G VOL/ASSN FORCES PLAN TEC/DEV DIPLOM COERCE ORD/FREE PWR WEALTH...DECISION GEN/LAWS NATO COLD/WAR. PAGE 65 A1345

INT/ORG ECO/TAC

S57

WRIGHT Q.,"THE VALUE OF CONFLICT RESOLUTION OF A GENERAL DISCIPLINE OF INTERNATIONAL RELATIONS." WOR+45 SOCIETY INT/ORG NAT/G FORCES TOP/EX PLAN TEC/DEV ECO/TAC DOMIN LEGIT COERCE ATTIT PWR ...GEN/METH COLD/WAR VAL/FREE. PAGE 168 A3412

ORD/FREE SOC DIPLOM

B58

ALMEYDA M.C.,REFLEXIONES POLITICAS. CHILE L/A+17C USA+45 INT/ORG POL/PAR ECO/TAC PARTIC ATTIT 20. PAGE 6 A0128

ECO/UNDEV REGION DIPLOM INT/TRADE

B58

BERLINER J.S.,SOVIET ECONOMIC AID: THE AID AND TRADE POLICY IN UNDERDEVELOPED COUNTRIES. AFR COM ISLAM L/A+17C S/ASIA USSR ECO/DEV DIST/IND FINAN MARKET INT/ORG ACT/RES PLAN BAL/PWR WEAPON PWR WEALTH...CHARTS 20. PAGE 14 A0277

ECO/UNDEV ECO/TAC FOR/AID

B58

CAMPBELL J.C.,DEFENSE OF THE MIDDLE EAST: PROBLEMS OF AMERICAN POLICY. ISLAM USA+45 INT/ORG NAT/G EX/STRUC FORCES ECO/TAC DOMIN EDU/PROP LEGIT REGION COERCE...METH/CNCPT COLD/WAR TOT/POP 20. PAGE 23 A0474

TOP/EX ORD/FREE DIPLOM

B58

CRAIG G.A.,FROM BISMARCK TO ADENAUER: ASPECTS OF GERMAN STATECRAFT. GERMANY INTELL FORCES ECO/TAC CONFER COERCE WAR GP/REL ORD/FREE PWR CONSERVE 19/20 BISMARCK/O ADENAUER/K. PAGE 32 A0653

DIPLOM LEAD NAT/G

B58

HAAS E.B.,THE UNITING OF EUROPE. EUR+WWI INT/ORG NAT/G POL/PAR TOP/EX ECO/TAC EDU/PROP LEGIT FEDERAL NAT/LISM DRIVE RIGID/FLEX ORD/FREE PWR PLURISM ...POLICY CONCPT INT GEN/LAWS ECSC EEC 20. PAGE 59 A1204

VOL/ASSN ECO/DEV

B58

HAUSER P.H.,POPULATION AND WORLD POLITICS. FUT WOR+45 WOR-45 AGRI DIST/IND INDUS INT/ORG PLAN ECO/TAC DISPL HEALTH COLD/WAR 20. PAGE 63 A1288

NAT/G ECO/UNDEV FOR/AID

B58

IMLAH A.H.,ECONOMIC ELEMENTS IN THE PAX BRITANNICA. MOD/EUR USA+45 USA-45 ECO/DEV INT/ORG NAT/G BAL/PWR ECO/TAC PEACE ATTIT PWR WEALTH...STAT CHARTS VAL/FREE 19. PAGE 70 A1436

MARKET UK

B58

JENNINGS I.,PROBLEMS OF THE NEW COMMONWEALTH. CEYLON INDIA PAKISTAN S/ASIA ECO/UNDEV INT/ORG LOC/G DIPLOM ECO/TAC INT/TRADE COLONIAL RACE/REL DISCRIM 20 COMMONWLTH PARLIAMENT. PAGE 74 A1508

NAT/LISM NEUTRAL FOR/AID POL/PAR

B58

KINDLEBERGER C.P.,INTERNATIONAL ECONOMICS. WOR+45 WOR-45 ECO/DEV ECO/UNDEV FINAN VOL/ASSN ACT/RES DIPLOM ECO/TAC LEGIT REGION ATTIT DRIVE ORD/FREE WEALTH...POLICY STAT TREND GEN/LAWS EEC ECSC OEEC 20. PAGE 79 A1620

INT/ORG BAL/PWR TARIFFS

B58

ORGANSKI A.F.K.,WORLD POLITICS. FUT WOR+45 SOCIETY STRUCT NAT/G BAL/PWR ECO/TAC DOMIN NAT/LISM ATTIT KNOWL ORD/FREE PWR...CONCPT METH/CNCPT TREND STERTYP GEN/LAWS TOT/POP 20. PAGE 112 A2297

INT/ORG DIPLOM

B58

PALMER E.E.,AMERICAN FOREIGN POLICY. USA+45 CULTURE ECO/UNDEV NAT/G PLAN GIVE BAL/PAY ORD/FREE WEALTH POPULISM...DECISION ANTHOL 20. PAGE 113 A2319

DIPLOM ECO/TAC POLICY

B58

PALYI M.,MANAGED MONEY AT THE CROSSROADS: THE EUROPEAN EXPERIENCE. WOR+45 WOR-45 TEC/DEV DIPLOM INT/TRADE DEMAND WEALTH...CHARTS BIBLIOG 19/20 EUROPE GOLD/STAND SILVER. PAGE 113 A2324

FINAN ECO/TAC ECO/DEV PRODUC

B58

SCITOUSKY T.,ECONOMIC THEORY AND WESTERN EUROPEAN INTEGRATION. EUR+WWI INT/ORG ACT/RES INT/TRADE REGION BAL/PAY WEALTH...METH/CNCPT STAT CHARTS GEN/METH ECSC TOT/POP EEC OEEC 20. PAGE 130 A2668

ECO/TAC

S58

DAVENPORT J.,"ARMS AND THE WELFARE STATE." INTELL STRUCT FORCES CREATE ECO/TAC FOR/AID DOMIN LEGIT ADMIN WAR ORD/FREE PWR...POLICY SOC CONCPT MYTH OBS TREND COLD/WAR TOT/POP 20. PAGE 34 A0685

USA+45 NAT/G USSR

S58

JORDAN A.,"MILITARY ASSISTANCE AND NATIONAL POLICY." ASIA FUT USA+45 WOR+45 ECO/DEV ECO/UNDEV INT/ORG NAT/G PLAN ECO/TAC ROUTINE WEAPON ATTIT RIGID/FLEX PWR...CONCPT TREND 20. PAGE 75 A1533

FORCES POLICY FOR/AID DIPLOM

S58

STAAR R.F.,"ELECTIONS IN COMMUNIST POLAND." EUR+WWI SOCIETY INT/ORG NAT/G POL/PAR LEGIS ACT/RES ECO/TAC EDU/PROP ADJUD ADMIN ROUTINE COERCE TOTALISM ATTIT ORD/FREE PWR 20. PAGE 137 A2797

COM CHOOSE POLAND

N58

US HOUSE COMM FOREIGN AFFAIRS,HEARINGS ON REVIEW OF THE MUTUAL SECURITY PROGRAMS; EXAMINATION OF SELECTED PROJECTS IN FORMOSA AND PAKISTAN (PAMPHLET). ASIA PAKISTAN TAIWAN INDUS CONSULT DELIB/GP LEGIS BUDGET CONFER DEBATE 20. PAGE 153 A3125

FOR/AID ECO/UNDEV DIPLOM ECO/TAC

B59

ALLEN R.L.,SOVIET INFLUENCE IN LATIN AMERICA. ECO/UNDEV FINAN PROC/MFG NAT/G TEC/DEV EDU/PROP EXEC ROUTINE ATTIT DRIVE PERSON ALL/VALS PWR...STAT CHARTS WORK 20. PAGE 6 A0125

L/A+17C ECO/TAC INT/TRADE USSR

B59

ALWAN M.,ALGERIA BEFORE THE UNITED NATIONS. AFR ASIA FRANCE ISLAM S/ASIA CONSTN SOCIETY STRUCT INT/ORG NAT/G ECO/TAC ADMIN COLONIAL NAT/LISM ATTIT PWR...DECISION TREND 420 UN. PAGE 7 A0133

PLAN RIGID/FLEX DIPLOM ALGERIA

B59

ARON R.,IMPERIALISM AND COLONIALISM (PAMPHLET). WOR+45 WOR-45 ECO/TAC CONTROL REV ORD/FREE 19/20. PAGE 9 A0183

COLONIAL DOMIN ECO/UNDEV DIPLOM

B59

BLOOMFIELD L.P.,WESTERN EUROPE AND THE UN - TRENDS AND PROSPECTS. EUR+WWI BAL/PWR DIPLOM ECO/TAC COLONIAL ATTIT PWR...POLICY 20 UN EUROPE/W. PAGE 16 A0316

INT/ORG TREND FUT NAT/G

B59

CHALUPA V.,RISE AND DEVELOPMENT OF A TOTALITARIAN STATE. CZECHOSLVK USSR STRUCT INT/ORG WORKER DIPLOM ECO/TAC COERCE NAT/LISM ATTIT...POLICY 20 COM/PARTY. PAGE 25 A0516

TOTALISM MARXISM REV POL/PAR

B59

CHANDLER E.H.S.,THE HIGH TOWER OF REFUGE: THE INSPIRING STORY OF REFUGEE RELIEF THROUGHOUT THE WORLD. WOR+45 NEIGH SECT WORKER PROB/SOLV DIPLOM ECO/TAC EDU/PROP COST HABITAT. PAGE 25 A0519

GIVE WEALTH STRANGE INT/ORG

B59

DIEBOLD W. JR.,THE SCHUMAN PLAN: A STUDY IN ECONOMIC COOPERATION, 1950-1959. EUR+WWI FRANCE GERMANY USA+45 EXTR/IND CONSULT DELIB/GP PLAN DIPLOM ECO/TAC INT/TRADE ROUTINE ORD/FREE WEALTH ...METH/CNCPT STAT CONT/OBS INT TIME/SEQ ECSC 20. PAGE 37 A0759

INT/ORG REGION

B59

ETSCHMANN R.,DIE WAHRUNGS- UND DEVISENPOLITIK DES OSTBLOCKS UND IHRE AUSWIRKUNGEN AUF DIE WIRTSCHAFTSBEZIEHUNGEN ZWISCHEN OST U WEST. BULGARIA CZECHOSLVK HUNGARY POLAND USSR MARKET NAT/G PLAN DIPLOM...NAT/COMP 20. PAGE 42 A0867

ECO/TAC FINAN POLICY INT/TRADE

B59

FOX W.T.R.,THEORETICAL ASPECTS OF INTERNATIONAL RELATIONS. WOR+45 INT/ORG NAT/G POL/PAR CONSULT

DELIB/GP ANTHOL

PLAN ECO/TAC DOMIN EDU/PROP LEGIT EXEC COERCE PWR WEALTH...RELATIV CONCPT 20. PAGE 48 A0975

B59
GOULD L.P.,THE PRICE OF SURVIVAL. EUR+WWI SPACE USA+45 FORCES ECO/TAC NUC/PWR WAR ORD/FREE MARXISM ...IDEA/COMP 20 COLD/WAR NATO. PAGE 54 A1117
POLICY PROB/SOLV DIPLOM PEACE

B59
HARRIMAN A.,PEACE WITH RUSSIA? USA+45 USSR SOCIETY ECO/TAC CONTROL TOTALISM ATTIT MARXISM...POLICY 20 STALIN/J KHRUSH/N. PAGE 62 A1266
DIPLOM PEACE NAT/G TASK

B59
HEWES T.,EQUALITY OF OPPORTUNITY - THE AMERICAN IDEAL AND KEY TO WORLD PEACE. USA+45 NAT/G OWN WEALTH ALL/IDEOS SOCISM...CONCPT 20. PAGE 64 A1323
POLICY PEACE ECO/TAC DIPLOM

B59
JACKSON B.W.,FIVE IDEAS THAT CHANGE THE WORLD. FUT WOR+45 WOR-45 ECO/UNDEV INDUS DIPLOM DOMIN CONTROL ...IDEA/COMP 20. PAGE 72 A1473
MARXISM NAT/LISM COLONIAL ECO/TAC

B59
JOSEPH F.M.,AS OTHERS SEE US: THE UNITED STATES THROUGH FOREIGN EYES. AFR EUR+WWI ISLAM L/A+17C S/ASIA USA+45 CULTURE SOCIETY ECO/DEV ECO/UNDEV INT/ORG NAT/G DIPLOM ECO/TAC REV ATTIT RIGID/FLEX HEALTH ORD/FREE WEALTH 20. PAGE 75 A1537
RESPECT DOMIN NAT/LISM SOVEREIGN

B59
LAQUER W.Z.,THE SOVIET UNION AND THE MIDDLE EAST. COM UAR USSR ECO/UNDEV NAT/G VOL/ASSN ECO/TAC EDU/PROP COLONIAL EXEC PWR...TIME/SEQ TREND COLD/WAR 20. PAGE 85 A1730
ISLAM DRIVE FOR/AID NAT/LISM

B59
MEZERK A.G.,FINANCIAL ASSISTANCE FOR ECONOMIC DEVELOPMENT. WOR+45 INDUS DIPLOM INT/TRADE...CHARTS GOV/COMP UN. PAGE 101 A2064
FOR/AID FINAN ECO/TAC ECO/UNDEV

B59
NOVE A.,COMMUNIST ECONOMIC STRATEGY: SOVIET GROWTH AND CAPABILITIES. USSR AGRI LABOR PLAN TEC/DEV CAP/ISM INT/TRADE EFFICIENCY MARXISM 20 THIRD/WRLD. PAGE 110 A2257
FOR/AID ECO/TAC DIPLOM INDUS

B59
ROBERTSON A.H.,EUROPEAN INSTITUTIONS: COOPERATION, INTEGRATION, UNIFICATION. EUR+WWI FINAN INT/ORG FORCES INT/TRADE TARIFFS 20 EEC EURATOM ECSC NATO TREATY. PAGE 122 A2496
ECO/DEV DIPLOM INDUS ECO/TAC

B59
SANNWALD R.E.,ECONOMIC INTEGRATION: THEORETICAL ASSUMPTIONS AND CONSEQUENCES OF EUROPEAN UNIFICATION. EUR+WWI FUT FINAN INDUS VOL/ASSN ACT/RES ECO/TAC...PLURIST EEC OEEC 20. PAGE 127 A2601
INT/ORG ECO/DEV INT/TRADE

B59
STOVEL J.A.,CANADA IN THE WORLD ECONOMY. CANADA PRICE DEMAND...STAT CHARTS BIBLIOG 20 VINER/J. PAGE 139 A2838
INT/TRADE BAL/PAY FINAN ECO/TAC

B59
STRAUSZ-HUPE R.,PROTRACTED CONFLICT. CHINA/COM KOREA WOR+45 INT/ORG FORCES ACT/RES ECO/TAC LEGIT COERCE DRIVE PERCEPT KNOWL PWR...PSY CONCPT RECORD GEN/METH COLD/WAR VAL/FREE 20. PAGE 139 A2847
COM PLAN USSR

B59
US GENERAL ACCOUNTING OFFICE,EXAM OF ECONOMIC AND TECHNICAL ASSISTANCE PROGRAM FOR INDIA INT'NAT'L COOP ADMIN REPORT TO CONGRESS 1955-1958. INDIA USA+45 ECO/UNDEV FINAN PLAN DIPLOM COST UTIL WEALTH ...CHARTS 20 CONGRESS AID. PAGE 153 A3114
FOR/AID EFFICIENCY ECO/TAC TEC/DEV

B59
VORSPAN A.,JUSTICE AND JUDAISM. FAM DIPLOM ECO/TAC EDU/PROP CRIME RACE/REL MARRIAGE ANOMIE ATTIT ORD/FREE...POLICY 20 UN. PAGE 160 A3254
SECT CULTURE ACT/RES GP/REL

B59
WENTHOLT W.,SOME COMMENTS ON THE LIQUIDATION OF THE EUROPEAN PAYMENT UNION AND RELATED PROBLEMS (PAMPHLET). WOR+45 PLAN BUDGET PRICE CONTROL 20 EEC GOLD/STAND. PAGE 163 A3319
FINAN ECO/DEV INT/ORG ECO/TAC

L59
GARDNER R.N.,"NEW DIRECTIONS IN UNITED STATES FOREIGN ECONOMIC POLICY." USA+45 CONSULT...GEN/LAWS GEN/METH COLD/WAR 20. PAGE 51 A1044
ECO/UNDEV ECO/TAC FOR/AID DIPLOM

L59
MURPHY J.C.,"SOME IMPLICATIONS OF EUROPE'S COMMON MARKET. IN (COOK P, ECONOMIC DEVELOPMENT AND INTERNATIONAL TRADE,." EUR+WWI ECO/DEV DIST/IND INDUS NAT/G PLAN ECO/TAC INT/TRADE WEALTH...STAT TREND OEEC TOT/POP 20 EEC. PAGE 106 A2178
MARKET INT/ORG REGION

L59
WURFEL D.,"FOREIGN AID AND SOCIAL REFORM IN POLITICAL DEVELOPMENT" (BMR)" PHILIPPINE USA+45 WOR+45 SOCIETY POL/PAR ACT/RES TEC/DEV DIPLOM 20. PAGE 168 A3424
FOR/AID PROB/SOLV ECO/TAC ECO/UNDEV

S59
CARLSTON K.S.,"NATIONALIZATION: AN ANALYTIC APPROACH." WOR+45 INT/ORG ECO/TAC DOMIN LEGIT ADJUD COERCE ORD/FREE PWR WEALTH SOCISM...JURID CONCPT TREND STERTYP TOT/POP VAL/FREE 20. PAGE 24 A0486
INDUS NAT/G NAT/LISM SOVEREIGN

S59
HARVEY M.F.,"THE PALESTINE REFUGEE PROBLEM: ELEMENTS OF A SOLUTION." ISLAM LAW INT/ORG DELIB/GP TOP/EX ECO/TAC ROUTINE DRIVE HEALTH LOVE ORD/FREE PWR WEALTH...MAJORIT FAO 20. PAGE 62 A1283
ACT/RES LEGIT PEACE ISRAEL

S59
KINDLEBERGER C.P.,"UNITED STATES ECONOMIC FOREIGN POLICY: RESEARCH REQUIREMENTS FOR 1965." FUT USA+45 WOR+45 DIST/IND MARKET INT/ORG ECO/TAC INT/TRADE WEALTH...OBS TREND CON/ANAL GEN/LAWS VAL/FREE 20. PAGE 79 A1621
FINAN ECO/DEV FOR/AID

S59
KOHN L.Y.,"ISRAEL AND NEW NATION STATES OF ASIA AND AFRICA." AFR ASIA FUT S/ASIA VOL/ASSN TEC/DEV NAT/LISM RIGID/FLEX SKILL WEALTH...RELATIV OBS TREND CON/ANAL 20. PAGE 81 A1663
ECO/UNDEV ECO/TAC FOR/AID ISRAEL

S59
KRIPALANI A.J.B.,"FOR PRINCIPLED NEUTRALITY." CHINA/COM INDIA S/ASIA PLAN ECO/TAC RIGID/FLEX MORAL PWR...MYSTIC SOC RECORD 20 GANDHI/M. PAGE 82 A1684
ATTIT FOR/AID DIPLOM

S59
PLAZA G.,"FOR A REGIONAL MARKET IN LATIN AMERICA." FUT L/A+17C CULTURE INDUS NAT/G ECO/TAC INT/TRADE ATTIT WEALTH...NEW/IDEA TREND OAS 20. PAGE 116 A2389
MARKET INT/ORG REGION

S59
QUIGLEY H.S.,"TOWARD REAPPRAISAL OF OUR CHINA POLICY." CHINA/COM USA+45 INT/ORG PLAN ECO/TAC PERCEPT ORD/FREE...DECISION PSY CON/ANAL GEN/METH VAL/FREE 20. PAGE 118 A2427
ASIA KNOWL DIPLOM

S59
REUBENS E.D.,"THE BASIS FOR REORIENATION OF AMERICAN FOREIGN AID POLICY." USA+45 USSR STRUCT INT/ORG CONSULT ECO/TAC ADMIN DRIVE MORAL ORD/FREE PWR WEALTH...RELATIV MATH STAT TREND GEN/LAWS VAL/FREE 20. PAGE 120 A2467
ECO/UNDEV PLAN FOR/AID DIPLOM

S59
SAYEGH F.,"ARAB NATIONALISM AND SOVIET-AMERICAN RELATIONS." ISLAM USA+45 ECO/UNDEV PLAN ECO/TAC LEGIT NAT/LISM DRIVE PERCEPT KNOWL PWR...DECISION CONCPT STAT RECORD TREND CON/ANAL VAL/FREE 20 COLD/WAR. PAGE 127 A2610
DIPLOM USSR

S59
SIMONS H.,"WORLD-WIDE CAPABILITIES FOR PRODUCTION AND CONTROL OF NUCLEAR WEAPONS." FUT WOR+45 INDUS INT/ORG NAT/G ECO/TAC ATTIT PWR SKILL...TREND CHARTS VAL/FREE 20. PAGE 133 A2719
TEC/DEV ARMS/CONT NUC/PWR

S59
SOLDATI A.,"EOCNOMIC DISINTEGRATION IN EUROPE." EUR+WWI FUT WOR+45 INDUS INT/ORG NAT/G CAP/ISM WEALTH...NEW/IDEA OBS TREND CHARTS EEC 20. PAGE 135 A2764
FINAN ECO/TAC

S59
TIPTON J.B.,"PARTICIPATION OF THE UNITED STATES IN THE INTERNATIONAL LABOR ORGANIZATION." USA+45 LAW STRUCT ECO/DEV ECO/UNDEV INDUS TEC/DEV ECO/TAC ADMIN PERCEPT ORD/FREE SKILL...STAT HIST/WRIT GEN/METH ILO WORK 20. PAGE 144 A2946
LABOR INT/ORG

S59
ZAUBERMAN A.,"SOVIET BLOC ECONOMIC INTEGRATION." COM CULTURE INTELL ECO/DEV INDUS TOP/EX ACT/RES PLAN ECO/TAC INT/TRADE ROUTINE CHOOSE ATTIT ...TIME/SEQ 20. PAGE 169 A3448
MARKET INT/ORG USSR TOTALISM

N59
US HOUSE COMM FOREIGN AFFAIRS,HEARINGS ON DRAFT LEGISLATION TO AMEND FURTHER THE MUTUAL SECURITY ACT OF 1954 (PAMPHLET). USA+45 USSR CONSULT DELIB/GP FORCES ECO/TAC CONFER...POLICY 20 CONGRESS. PAGE 153 A3126
DIPLOM FOR/AID ORD/FREE LEGIS

B60
ALLEN R.L.,SOVIET ECONOMIC WARFARE. USSR FINAN INDUS NAT/G PLAN TEC/DEV FOR/AID DETER WEALTH ...TREND GEN/LAWS 20. PAGE 6 A0126
COM ECO/TAC

B60
ASPREMONT-LYNDEN H.,RAPPORT SUR L'ADMINISTRATION BELGE DU RUANDA-URUNDI PENDANT L'ANNEE 1959. BELGIUM RWANDA AGRI INDUS DIPLOM ECO/TAC INT/TRADE DOMIN ADMIN RACE/REL...GEOG CENSUS 20 UN. PAGE 9 A0192
AFR COLONIAL ECO/UNDEV INT/ORG

B60
BILLERBECK K.,SOVIET BLOC FOREIGN AID TO UNDERDEVELOPED COUNTRIES. COM FUT USSR FINAN FORCES TEC/DEV DIPLOM INT/TRADE EDU/PROP NUC/PWR...TREND 20. PAGE 14 A0287
FOR/AID ECO/UNDEV ECO/TAC MARXISM

B60
BLACK E.R.,THE DIPLOMACY OF ECONOMIC DEVELOPMENT. WOR+45 CONSULT PLAN TEC/DEV DIPLOM ECO/TAC FOR/AID ...CONCPT TREND 20. PAGE 15 A0297
ECO/UNDEV ACT/RES

B60
CAMPAIGNE J.G.,AMERICAN MIGHT AND SOVIET MYTH. COM
USA+45

EUR+WWI ECO/DEV ECO/UNDEV INT/ORG NAT/G CAP/ISM ECO/TAC FOR/AID EDU/PROP ATTIT PWR WEALTH...POLICY CONCPT MYTH TREND STERTYP GEN/LAWS COLD/WAR. PAGE 23 A0473 — DOMIN DIPLOM USSR

B60
DAVIDS J.,AMERICA AND THE WORLD OF OUR TIME: UNITED STATES DIPLOMACY IN THE TWENTIETH CENTURY. USA-45 SOCIETY ECO/DEV INT/ORG NAT/G POL/PAR FORCES ECO/TAC DOMIN EDU/PROP EXEC COERCE WAR CHOOSE ATTIT PERSON ORD/FREE...CONCPT TIME/SEQ TOT/POP 20. PAGE 34 A0686 — USA+45 PWR DIPLOM

B60
FISCHER L.,RUSSIA, AMERICA, AND THE WORLD. FUT USA+45 USSR WOR+45 FORCES PLAN BAL/PWR ECO/TAC FOR/AID NEUTRAL TASK NUC/PWR PWR 20 COLD/WAR. PAGE 46 A0937 — DIPLOM POLICY MARXISM ECO/UNDEV

B60
FRANCK P.G.,AFGHANISTAN: BETWEEN EAST AND WEST. AFGHANISTN USA+45 USSR ECO/UNDEV PLAN ADMIN ROUTINE ATTIT PWR...STAT OBS CHARTS TOT/POP COLD/WAR 20. PAGE 48 A0978 — ECO/TAC TREND FOR/AID

B60
HAHN W.F.,AMERICAN STRATEGY FOR THE NUCLEAR AGE. USA+45 NAT/G TEC/DEV ECO/TAC FOR/AID ARMS/CONT NUC/PWR ORD/FREE MARXISM...ANTHOL 20. PAGE 59 A1216 — DIPLOM PLAN PEACE

B60
HOFFMANN P.G.,ONE HUNDRED COUNTRIES, ONE AND ONE QUARTER BILLION PEOPLE. MARKET INT/ORG TEC/DEV CAP/ISM...GEOG CHARTS METH/COMP 20 UN. PAGE 66 A1354 — FOR/AID ECO/TAC ECO/UNDEV INT/TRADE

B60
KENEN P.B.,BRITISH MONETARY POLICY AND THE BALANCE OF PAYMENTS 1951-57. UK PLAN BUDGET ECO/TAC INT/TRADE PAY PRICE COST ATTIT 20. PAGE 77 A1585 — BAL/PAY PROB/SOLV FINAN NAT/G

B60
KRISTENSEN T.,THE ECONOMIC WORLD BALANCE. FUT WOR+45 CULTURE ECO/DEV BAL/PWR INT/TRADE REGION PWR WEALTH...STAT TREND CHARTS 20. PAGE 82 A1685 — ECO/UNDEV ECO/TAC FOR/AID

B60
LERNER A.P.,THE ECONOMICS OF CONTROL. USA+45 ECO/UNDEV INT/ORG ACT/RES PLAN CAP/ISM INT/TRADE ATTIT WEALTH...SOC MATH STAT GEN/LAWS INDEX 20. PAGE 87 A1785 — ECO/DEV ROUTINE ECO/TAC SOCISM

B60
LINDSAY K.,EUROPEAN ASSEMBLIES: THE EXPERIMENTAL PERIOD 1949-1959. EUR+WWI ECO/DEV NAT/G POL/PAR LEGIS TOP/EX ACT/RES PLAN ECO/TAC DOMIN LEGIT ROUTINE ATTIT DRIVE ORD/FREE PWR SKILL...SOC CONCPT TREND CHARTS GEN/LAWS VAL/FREE. PAGE 89 A1823 — VOL/ASSN INT/ORG REGION

B60
LISKA G.,THE NEW STATECRAFT. WOR+45 WOR-45 LEGIS DIPLOM ADMIN ATTIT PWR WEALTH...HIST/WRIT TREND COLD/WAR 20. PAGE 90 A1837 — ECO/TAC CONCPT FOR/AID

B60
LISTER L.,EUROPE'S COAL AND STEEL COMMUNITY. FRANCE GERMANY STRUCT ECO/DEV EXTR/IND INDUS MARKET NAT/G DELIB/GP ECO/TAC INT/TRADE EDU/PROP ATTIT RIGID/FLEX ORD/FREE PWR WEALTH...CONCPT STAT TIME/SEQ CHARTS ECSC 20. PAGE 90 A1843 — EUR+WWI INT/ORG REGION

B60
PENTONY D.E.,THE UNDERDEVELOPED LANDS. FUT WOR+45 CULTURE AGRI FINAN INDUS MARKET INT/ORG LABOR NAT/G VOL/ASSN CONSULT TEC/DEV ECO/TAC EDU/PROP COLONIAL ATTIT WEALTH...OBS RECORD SAMP TREND GEN/METH WORK UN 20. PAGE 115 A2351 — ECO/UNDEV POLICY FOR/AID INT/TRADE

B60
PENTONY D.E.,UNITED STATES FOREIGN AID. INDIA LAOS USA+45 ECO/UNDEV INT/TRADE ADMIN PEACE ATTIT ...POLICY METH/COMP ANTHOL 20. PAGE 115 A2352 — FOR/AID DIPLOM ECO/TAC

B60
PRINCETON U CONFERENCE,CURRENT PROBLEMS IN NORTH AFRICA. ALGERIA LIBYA MOROCCO USA+45 EXTR/IND POL/PAR PROB/SOLV DIPLOM ECO/TAC WAR...ANTHOL 20 TUNIS. PAGE 118 A2412 — POLICY ECO/UNDEV NAT/G

B60
RITNER P.,THE DEATH OF AFRICA. USA+45 ECO/UNDEV DIPLOM ECO/TAC REGION RACE/REL NAT/LISM ORD/FREE ...POLICY 20 NEGRO. PAGE 121 A2485 — AFR SOCIETY FUT TASK

B60
ROPKE W.,A HUMANE ECONOMY. CULTURE ECO/DEV FINAN INDUS GP/REL CENTRAL WEALTH...GEOG SOC IDEA/COMP 20 EEC. PAGE 123 A2525 — ECO/TAC INT/ORG DIPLOM ORD/FREE

B60
SCHLESINGER J.R.,THE POLITICAL ECONOMY OF NATIONAL SECURITY. USA+45 USSR WOR+45 ECO/DEV ECO/UNDEV NAT/G DELIB/GP TOP/EX BAL/PWR DIPLOM INT/TRADE ATTIT PWR...STERTYP TOT/POP 20. PAGE 128 A2628 — PLAN ECO/TAC

B60
SETON-WATSON H.,NEITHER WAR NOR PEACE. ASIA USSR WOR+45 ELITES INT/ORG NAT/G EX/STRUC FORCES BAL/PWR ECO/TAC EDU/PROP COERCE NAT/LISM ORD/FREE WEALTH TOT/POP 20. PAGE 131 A2688 — ATTIT PWR DIPLOM TOTALISM

B60
SHONFIELD A.,THE ATTACK ON WORLD POVERTY. WOR+45 ECO/DEV ECO/UNDEV FINAN VOL/ASSN PLAN EDU/PROP DRIVE KNOWL WEALTH...CONT/OBS STAND/INT ORG/CHARTS TOT/POP UNESCO 20. PAGE 132 A2704 — INT/ORG ECO/TAC FOR/AID INT/TRADE

B60
STEIN E.,AMERICAN ENTERPRISE IN THE EUROPEAN COMMON MARKET: A LEGAL PROFILE. EUR+WWI FUT USA+45 SOCIETY STRUCT ECO/DEV NAT/G VOL/ASSN CONSULT PLAN TEC/DEV ECO/TAC INT/TRADE ADMIN ATTIT RIGID/FLEX PWR...MGT NEW/IDEA STAT TREND COMPUT/IR SIMUL EEC 20. PAGE 137 A2814 — MARKET ADJUD INT/LAW

B60
STOLPER W.F.,GERMANY BETWEEN EAST AND WEST: THE ECONOMICS OF COMPETITIVE COEXISTENCE. FUT GERMANY/E GERMANY/W WOR+45 FINAN POL/PAR BUDGET ECO/TAC FOR/AID INT/TRADE...STAT CHARTS METH/COMP 20 COLD/WAR. PAGE 138 A2832 — ECO/DEV DIPLOM GOV/COMP BAL/PWR

B60
THEOBALD R.,THE RICH AND THE POOR: A STUDY OF THE ECONOMICS OF RISING EXPECTATIONS. WOR+45 CONSTN ECO/DEV ECO/UNDEV INT/ORG NAT/G PLAN FOR/AID ROUTINE BAL/PAY ORD/FREE PWR WEALTH...GEOG TREND WORK 20. PAGE 142 A2912 — ECO/TAC INT/TRADE

B60
THEOBOLD R.,THE NEW NATIONS OF WEST AFRICA. GHANA NIGERIA CULTURE INT/ORG ECO/TAC FOR/AID COLONIAL RACE/REL POPULISM...ANTHOL BIBLIOG 20 UN. PAGE 143 A2916 — AFR SOVEREIGN ECO/UNDEV DIPLOM

B60
US HOUSE COMM GOVT OPERATIONS,OPERATIONS OF THE DEVELOPMENT LOAN FUND: HEARINGS (COMMITTEE ON GOVERNMENT OPERATIONS). USA+45 PLAN BUDGET DIPLOM GOV/REL COST...CHARTS 20 CONGRESS DEPT/STATE AID. PAGE 154 A3137 — FINAN FOR/AID ECO/TAC EFFICIENCY

B60
US HOUSE COMM. SCI. ASTRONAUT.,OCEAN SCIENCES AND NATIONAL SECURITY. FUT SEA ECO/DEV EXTR/IND INT/ORG NAT/G FORCES ACT/RES TEC/DEV ECO/TAC COERCE WAR BIO/SOC KNOWL PWR...CONCPT RECORD LAB/EXP 20. PAGE 154 A3141 — R+D ORD/FREE

B60
US SENATE COMM ON FOREIGN REL,SITUATION IN VIETNAM (2 VOLS.). USA+45 VIETNAM ECO/TAC COST SENATE DEPT/STATE. PAGE 156 A3181 — FOR/AID PLAN EFFICIENCY INSPECT

B60
WOLF C.,FOREIGN AID: THEORY AND PRACTICE IN SOUTHERN ASIA. CEYLON INDONESIA PHILIPPINE S/ASIA CULTURE STRATA ECO/UNDEV PLAN EDU/PROP ATTIT ...METH/CNCPT MATH QUANT STAT CONT/OBS TIME/SEQ SIMUL TOT/POP 20. PAGE 166 A3378 — ACT/RES ECO/TAC FOR/AID

L60
BRENNAN D.G.,"SETTING AND GOALS OF ARMS CONTROL." FUT USA+45 USSR WOR+45 INTELL INT/ORG NAT/G VOL/ASSN CONSULT PLAN DIPLOM ECO/TAC ADMIN KNOWL PWR...POLICY CONCPT TREND COLD/WAR 20. PAGE 18 A0371 — FORCES COERCE ARMS/CONT DETER

S60
"THE EMERGING COMMON MARKETS IN LATIN AMERICA." FUT L/A+17C STRATA DIST/IND INDUS LABOR NAT/G LEGIS ECO/TAC ADMIN RIGID/FLEX HEALTH...NEW/IDEA TIME/SEQ OAS 20. PAGE 3 A0059 — FINAN ECO/UNDEV INT/TRADE

S60
COHEN A.,"THE NEW AFRICA AND THE UN." FUT ECO/UNDEV NAT/G ECO/TAC INT/TRADE CHOOSE ATTIT ORD/FREE PWR ...POLICY METH/CNCPT OBS TREND CON/ANAL GEN/LAWS TOT/POP VAL/FREE UN 20. PAGE 27 A0558 — AFR INT/ORG BAL/PWR FOR/AID

S60
FITZGIBBON R.H.,"DICTATORSHIP AND DEMOCRACY IN LATIN AMERICA." FUT ECO/DEV ECO/UNDEV INT/ORG LOC/G NAT/G TOP/EX PLAN TEC/DEV ECO/TAC CHOOSE ATTIT DRIVE PERSON ALL/VALS OAS TOT/POP 20. PAGE 46 A0943 — L/A+17C ACT/RES INT/TRADE

S60
FRANKEL S.H.,"ECONOMIC ASPECTS OF POLITICAL INDEPENDENCE IN AFRICA." AFR FUT SOCIETY ECO/UNDEV COM/IND FINAN LEGIS PLAN TEC/DEV CAP/ISM ECO/TAC INT/TRADE ADMIN ATTIT DRIVE RIGID/FLEX PWR WEALTH ...MGT NEW/IDEA MATH TIME/SEQ VAL/FREE 20. PAGE 48 A0984 — NAT/G FOR/AID

S60
GARNICK D.H.,"ON THE ECONOMIC FEASIBILITY OF A MIDDLE EASTERN COMMON MARKET." AFR ISLAM CULTURE INDUS NAT/G PLAN TEC/DEV ECO/TAC ADMIN ATTIT DRIVE RIGID/FLEX...PLURIST STAT TREND GEN/LAWS 20. PAGE 51 A1051 — MARKET INT/TRADE

S60
GINSBURGS G.,"PEKING-LHASA-NEW DELHI." CHINA/COM FUT INDIA S/ASIA KIN NAT/G PROVS SECT FORCES BAL/PWR ECO/TAC DOMIN EDU/PROP LEGIT ADMIN REGION GUERRILLA PWR...TREND TIBET 20. PAGE 52 A1074 — ASIA COERCE DIPLOM

S60
HAVILAND H.F.,"PROBLEMS OF AMERICAN FOREIGN POLICY." ASIA COM USA+45 WOR+45 INT/ORG NAT/G CONSULT ECO/TAC FOR/AID DOMIN COERCE NUC/PWR ATTIT DRIVE ORD/FREE PWR RESPECT SKILL...POLICY GEOG OBS — ECO/UNDEV FORCES DIPLOM

SAMP TREND GEN/METH METH COLD/WAR UN 20. PAGE 63 A1292

S60
IKLE F.C.,"NTH COUNTRIES AND DISARMAMENT." WOR+45 DELIB/GP ECO/TAC DOMIN EDU/PROP LEGIT ROUTINE COERCE RIGID/FLEX ORD/FREE...MARXIST TREND 20. PAGE 70 A1432 — FUT INT/ORG ARMS/CONT NUC/PWR

S60
JACOBSON H.K.,"THE USSR AND ILO." COM STRUCT ECO/DEV ECO/UNDEV CONSULT DELIB/GP ECO/TAC ILO WORK COLD/WAR 20. PAGE 72 A1484 — INT/ORG LABOR USSR

S60
KALUODA J.,"COMMUNIST STRATEGY IN LATIN AMERICA." L/A+17C USA+45 INT/ORG NAT/G POL/PAR DIPLOM ECO/TAC EDU/PROP COERCE WEALTH...CONCPT OAS COLD/WAR 20. PAGE 76 A1553 — COM PWR CUBA

S60
KISTIAKOWSKY G.B.,"SCIENCE AND FOREIGN AFFAIRS." FUT WOR+45 NAT/G PROF/ORG PLAN ECO/TAC EDU/PROP NUC/PWR...TREND COLD/WAR 20. PAGE 80 A1645 — CONSULT TEC/DEV FOR/AID DIPLOM

S60
KREININ M.E.,"THE 'OUTER-SEVEN' AND EUROPEAN INTEGRATION." EUR+WWI FRANCE GERMANY ITALY UK ECO/DEV DIST/IND INT/TRADE DRIVE WEALTH...MYTH CHARTS EEC OEEC 20. PAGE 82 A1682 — ECO/TAC GEN/LAWS

S60
LINDHOLM R.W.,"ACCELERATED DEVELOPMENT WITH A MINIMUM OF FOREIGN AID AND ECONOMIC CONTROLS." SOCIETY INDUS ECO/TAC WEALTH...CONCPT 20. PAGE 89 A1822 — ECO/DEV FINAN FOR/AID

S60
MAGATHAN W.,"SOME BASES OF WEST GERMAN MILITARY POLICY." EUR+WWI FUT INT/ORG TOP/EX ECO/TAC DOMIN DRIVE ORD/FREE PWR...TRADIT GEOG OBS TREND. PAGE 93 A1904 — NAT/G FORCES GERMANY

S60
MIKESELL R.F.,"AMERICA'S ECONOMIC RESPONSIBILITY AS A GREAT POWER." COM FUT USA+45 USSR WOR+45 INT/ORG PLAN ECO/TAC FOR/AID EDU/PROP CHOOSE WEALTH ...POLICY 20. PAGE 101 A2069 — ECO/UNDEV BAL/PWR CAP/ISM

S60
MORALES C.J.,"TRADE AND ECONOMIC INTEGRATION IN LATIN AMERICA." FUT L/A+17C LAW STRATA ECO/UNDEV DIST/IND INDUS LABOR NAT/G LEGIS ECO/TAC ADMIN RIGID/FLEX WEALTH...CONCPT NEW/IDEA CONT/OBS TIME/SEQ WORK 20. PAGE 104 A2128 — FINAN INT/TRADE REGION

S60
OWEN C.F.,"US AND SOVIET RELATIONS WITH UNDERDEVELOPED COUNTRIES: LATIN AMERICA-A CASE STUDY." AFR COM L/A+17C USA+45 USSR EXTR/IND MARKET TEC/DEV DIPLOM ECO/TAC NAT/LISM ORD/FREE PWR ...TREND WORK 20. PAGE 112 A2303 — ECO/UNDEV DRIVE INT/TRADE

S60
PYE L.W.,"SOVIET AND AMERICAN STYLES IN FOREIGN AID." COM USA+45 USSR WOR+45 NAT/G PLAN ECO/TAC ROUTINE RIGID/FLEX...POLICY CONCPT TREND GEN/LAWS TOT/POP 20. PAGE 118 A2419 — ECO/UNDEV ATTIT FOR/AID

S60
RICHTER J.H.,"TOWARDS AN INTERNATIONAL POLICY ON AGRICULTURAL TRADE." EUR+WWI USA+45 ECO/DEV NAT/G PLAN ECO/TAC ATTIT PWR WEALTH...CONCPT GEN/LAWS 20. PAGE 121 A2475 — AGRI INT/ORG

S60
RIESELBACH Z.N.,"QUANTITATIVE TECHNIQUES FOR STUDYING VOTING BEHAVIOR IN THE UNITED NATIONS GENERAL ASSEMBLY." FUT S/ASIA USA+45 INT/ORG BAL/PWR DIPLOM ECO/TAC FOR/AID ADMIN PWR...POLICY METH/CNCPT METH UN 20. PAGE 121 A2478 — QUANT CHOOSE

S60
RIVKIN A.,"AFRICAN ECONOMIC DEVELOPMENT: ADVANCED TECHNOLOGY AND THE STAGES OF GROWTH." CULTURE ECO/UNDEV AGRI COM/IND EXTR/IND PLAN ECO/TAC ATTIT DRIVE RIGID/FLEX SKILL WEALTH...MGT SOC GEN/LAWS WORK TOT/POP 20. PAGE 121 A2487 — AFR TEC/DEV FOR/AID

S60
SCHACHTER O.,"THE ENFORCEMENT OF INTERNATIONAL JUDICIAL AND ARBITRAL DECISIONS." WOR+45 NAT/G ECO/TAC DOMIN LEGIT ROUTINE COERCE ATTIT DRIVE ALL/VALS PWR...METH/CNCPT TREND TOT/POP 20 UN. PAGE 128 A2615 — INT/ORG ADJUD INT/LAW

B61
AUBREY H.G.,COEXISTENCE: ECONOMIC CHALLENGE AND RESPONSE. USSR WOR+45 ACT/RES BAL/PWR CAP/ISM DIPLOM ECO/TAC FOR/AID INT/TRADE PEACE SOCISM ...METH/COMP NAT/COMP COLD/WAR. PAGE 10 A0196 — POLICY ECO/UNDEV PLAN COM

B61
BECHHOEFER B.G.,POSTWAR NEGOTIATIONS FOR ARMS CONTROL. COM EUR+WWI USSR INT/ORG NAT/G ACT/RES BAL/PWR DIPLOM ECO/TAC EDU/PROP ADMIN REGION DETER NUC/PWR WAR WEAPON PEACE ATTIT PWR...POLICY TIME/SEQ COLD/WAR CONGRESS 20. PAGE 12 A0244 — USA+45 ARMS/CONT

B61
BISHOP D.G.,THE ADMINISTRATION OF BRITISH FOREIGN RELATIONS. EUR+WWI MOD/EUR INT/ORG NAT/G POL/PAR DELIB/GP LEGIS TOP/EX ECO/TAC DOMIN EDU/PROP ADMIN COERCE 20. PAGE 14 A0292 — ROUTINE PWR DIPLOM UK

B61
BONNEFOUS M.,EUROPE ET TIERS MONDE. EUR+WWI SOCIETY INT/ORG NAT/G VOL/ASSN ACT/RES TEC/DEV CAP/ISM ECO/TAC ATTIT ORD/FREE SOVEREIGN...POLICY CONCPT TREND 20. PAGE 16 A0334 — AFR ECO/UNDEV FOR/AID INT/TRADE

B61
CHIDZERO B.T.G.,TANGANYIKA AND INTERNATIONAL TRUSTEESHIP. AFR WOR+45 WOR-45 ECO/DEV INT/ORG ECO/TAC DOMIN COLONIAL...RECORD CHARTS 20 TANGANYIKA CMN/WLTH. PAGE 26 A0528 — ECO/UNDEV CONSTN

B61
CONFERENCE ATLANTIC COMMUNITY,AN INTRODUCTORY BIBLIOGRAPHY. COM WOR+45 FORCES DIPLOM ECO/TAC WAR ...INT/LAW HIST/WRIT COLD/WAR NATO. PAGE 29 A0584 — BIBLIOG/A CON/ANAL INT/ORG

B61
DEAN V.M.,BUILDERS OF EMERGING NATIONS. WOR+45 ECO/UNDEV ECO/TAC NEUTRAL TOTALISM ORD/FREE PWR ...BIOG AUD/VIS IDEA/COMP BIBLIOG 20 COLD/WAR. PAGE 35 A0719 — NAT/G CHIEF POLICY DIPLOM

B61
DIA M.,THE AFRICAN NATIONS AND WORLD SOLIDARITY. ISLAM CULTURE ELITES ECO/DEV ECO/UNDEV INT/ORG NAT/G PLAN ECO/TAC INT/TRADE EDU/PROP NAT/LISM ATTIT DRIVE ORD/FREE WEALTH...SOCIALIST CONCPT CON/ANAL GEN/LAWS TOT/POP 20. PAGE 37 A0753 — AFR REGION SOCISM

B61
DIMOCK M.E.,BUSINESS AND GOVERNMENT (4TH ED.). AGRI FINAN OP/RES PLAN BUDGET DIPLOM LOBBY NUC/PWR NEW/LIB SOCISM...POLICY BIBLIOG 20. PAGE 37 A0765 — NAT/G INDUS LABOR ECO/TAC

B61
EINZIG P.,A DYNAMIC THEORY OF FORWARD EXCHANGE. FUT WOR+45 WOR-45 INT/TRADE BAL/PAY WEALTH...OLD/LIB NEW/IDEA OBS TREND 20. PAGE 41 A0830 — FINAN ECO/TAC

B61
GANGULI B.N.,ECONOMIC INTEGRATION. FINAN LABOR CAP/ISM DIPLOM WEALTH...NAT/COMP 20. PAGE 51 A1041 — ECO/TAC METH/CNCPT EQUILIB ECO/UNDEV

B61
GURTOO D.H.N.,INDIA'S BALANCE OF PAYMENTS (1920-1960). INDIA FINAN DIPLOM FOR/AID INT/TRADE PRICE COLONIAL...CHARTS BIBLIOG 20. PAGE 58 A1197 — BAL/PAY STAT ECO/TAC ECO/UNDEV

B61
HARDT J.P.,THE COLD WAR ECONOMIC GAP. USA+45 USSR ECO/DEV FORCES INT/TRADE NUC/PWR PWR 20 COLD/WAR. PAGE 61 A1258 — DIPLOM ECO/TAC NAT/COMP POLICY

B61
HARRIS S.E.,THE DOLLAR IN CRISIS. USA+45 MARKET INT/ORG ECO/TAC PRICE CONTROL WEALTH...METH/COMP ANTHOL 20 GOLD/STAND. PAGE 62 A1269 — BAL/PAY DIPLOM FINAN INT/TRADE

B61
HARRISON S.,INDIA AND THE UNITED STATES. FUT S/ASIA USA+45 WOR+45 INTELL ECO/DEV ECO/UNDEV AGRI INDUS INT/ORG NAT/G CONSULT EX/STRUC TOP/EX PLAN ECO/TAC NEUTRAL ALL/VALS...MGT TOT/POP 20. PAGE 62 A1272 — DELIB/GP ACT/RES FOR/AID INDIA

B61
HASAN H.S.,PAKISTAN AND THE UN. ISLAM WOR+45 ECO/DEV ECO/UNDEV NAT/G TOP/EX ECO/TAC FOR/AID EDU/PROP ADMIN DRIVE PERCEPT...OBS TIME/SEQ UN 20. PAGE 62 A1284 — INT/ORG ATTIT PAKISTAN

B61
KERTESZ S.D.,AMERICAN DIPLOMACY IN A NEW ERA. COM S/ASIA UK USA+45 FORCES PROB/SOLV BAL/PWR ECO/TAC ADMIN COLONIAL WAR PEACE ORD/FREE 20 NATO CONGRESS UN COLD/WAR. PAGE 78 A1601 — ANTHOL DIPLOM TREND

B61
KISSINGER H.A.,THE NECESSITY FOR CHOICE. FUT USA+45 ECO/UNDEV NAT/G PLAN BAL/PWR ECO/TAC ARMS/CONT DETER NUC/PWR ATTIT...POLICY CONCPT RECORD GEN/LAWS COLD/WAR 20. PAGE 80 A1642 — TOP/EX TREND DIPLOM

B61
KITZINGER V.W.,THE CHALLENGE OF THE COMMON MARKET. EUR+WWI ECO/DEV DIST/IND PLAN ECO/TAC INT/TRADE LEGIT ATTIT PWR WEALTH...TIME/SEQ TREND CHARTS EEC 20. PAGE 80 A1647 — MARKET INT/ORG UK

B61
LETHBRIDGE H.J.,CHINA'S URBAN COMMUNES. CHINA/COM FUT ECO/UNDEV DIPLOM EDU/PROP DEMAND INCOME MARXISM ...POLICY 20. PAGE 87 A1790 — MUNIC CONTROL ECO/TAC NAT/G

B61
NATIONAL BANK OF LIBYA,INFLATION IN LIBYA (PAMPHLET). LIBYA SOCIETY NAT/G PLAN INT/TRADE ...STAT CHARTS 20 GOLD/STAND. PAGE 107 A2200 — ECO/TAC ECO/UNDEV FINAN BUDGET

B61
NEAL F.W.,US FOREIGN POLICY AND THE SOVIET UNION. USA+45 USSR INT/ORG ECO/TAC ARMS/CONT MAJORITY NAT/LISM ATTIT RESPECT MARXISM 20. PAGE 108 A2207 — DIPLOM POLICY PEACE

B61
OECD,STATISTICS OF BALANCE OF PAYMENTS 1950-61. — BAL/PAY

WOR+45 FINAN ECO/TAC INT/TRADE DEMAND WEALTH...STAT NAT/COMP 20 OEEC OECD. PAGE 111 A2278 — ECO/DEV INT/ORG CHARTS

B61
OEEC,LIBERALISATION OF CURRENT INVISIBLES AND CAPITAL MOVEMENTS BY THE OEEC (PAMPHLET). WOR+45 ECO/DEV BUDGET ECO/TAC ORD/FREE 20. PAGE 111 A2282 — FINAN INT/ORG INT/TRADE BAL/PAY

B61
PECKERT J.,DIE GROSSEN UND DIE KLEINEN MAECHTE. COM GERMANY/W ECO/DEV ECO/UNDEV NAT/G WAR RACE/REL PEACE...POLICY GP/COMP GOV/COMP 20 COLD/WAR. PAGE 114 A2346 — DIPLOM ECO/TAC BAL/PWR

B61
PERLO V.,EL IMPERIALISMO NORTHEAMERICANO. USA+45 USA-45 FINAN CAP/ISM DIPLOM DOMIN CONTROL DISCRIM 19/20. PAGE 115 A2363 — SOCIALIST ECO/DEV INT/TRADE ECO/TAC

B61
SCAMMEL W.M.,INTERNATIONAL MONETARY POLICY. WOR+45 WOR-45 ACT/RES ECO/TAC LEGIT WEALTH...GEN/METH UN 20. PAGE 127 A2611 — INT/ORG FINAN BAL/PAY

B61
SCHWARTZ H.,THE RED PHOENIX: RUSSIA SINCE WORLD WAR II. USA+45 WOR+45 ELITES POL/PAR TEC/DEV ECO/TAC MARXISM. PAGE 130 A2655 — DIPLOM NAT/G ECO/DEV

B61
SINGER J.D.,FINANCING INTERNATIONAL ORGANIZATION: THE UNITED NATIONS BUDGET PROCESS. WOR+45 FINAN ACT/RES CREATE PLAN BUDGET ECO/TAC ADMIN ROUTINE ATTIT KNOWL...DECISION METH/CNCPT TIME/SEQ UN 20. PAGE 133 A2726 — INT/ORG MGT

B61
STARK H.,SOCIAL AND ECONOMIC FRONTIERS IN LATIN AMERICA (2ND ED.). CUBA FUT CULTURE AGRI INDUS ECO/TAC PRODUC ATTIT MARXISM...NAT/COMP BIBLIOG T 20. PAGE 137 A2807 — L/A+17C SOCIETY DIPLOM ECO/UNDEV

B61
STRAUSZ-HUPE R.,A FORWARD STRATEGY FOR AMERICA. FUT WOR+45 ECO/DEV INT/ORG NAT/G POL/PAR DELIB/GP FORCES ACT/RES CREATE ECO/TAC DOMIN EDU/PROP ATTIT DRIVE PWR...MAJORIT CONCPT STAT OBS TIME/SEQ TREND COLD/WAR TOT/POP. PAGE 139 A2848 — USA+45 PLAN DIPLOM

B61
THEOBALD R.,THE CHALLENGE OF ABUNDANCE. USA+45 WOR+45 MARKET DIPLOM FOR/AID REV PRODUC UTOPIA SUPEGO...POLICY TREND BIBLIOG/A 20. PAGE 142 A2913 — WELF/ST ECO/UNDEV PROB/SOLV ECO/TAC

B61
TRIFFIN R.,GOLD AND THE DOLLAR CRISIS: THE FUTURE OF CONVERTIBILITY. USA+45 USA-45 INT/ORG PROB/SOLV BUDGET INT/TRADE PRICE...STAT CHARTS 19/20 GOLD/STAND. PAGE 145 A2963 — FINAN ECO/DEV ECO/TAC BAL/PAY

B61
US HOUSE COMM FOREIGN AFFAIRS,THE INTERNATIONAL DEVELOPMENT AND SECURITY ACT: HEARINGS BEFORE COMMITTEE ON FOREIGN AFFAIRS, HOUSE OF REP: HR7372. USA+45 AGRI INT/ORG NAT/G CONSULT DELIB/GP DIPLOM ECO/TAC INT/TRADE LOBBY REPRESENT 20 MCNAMARA/R DILLON/D RUSK/D CONGRESS. PAGE 153 A3128 — FOR/AID CONFER LEGIS ECO/UNDEV

B61
US SENATE COMM ON FOREIGN RELS,INTERNATIONAL DEVELOPMENT AND SECURITY: HEARINGS ON BILL (2 VOLS.). ECO/UNDEV FINAN FORCES REV COST WEALTH ...CHARTS 20 AID PRESIDENT. PAGE 157 A3191 — FOR/AID CIVMIL/REL ORD/FREE ECO/TAC

B61
WARD B.J.,INDIA AND THE WEST. INDIA UK USA+45 INT/TRADE GIVE COLONIAL ATTIT MARXISM 19/20. PAGE 161 A3279 — PLAN ECO/UNDEV ECO/TAC FOR/AID

B61
WILLOUGHBY W.R.,THE ST LAWRENCE WATERWAY: A STUDY IN POLITICS AND DIPLOMACY. USA+45 ECO/DEV COM/IND INT/ORG CONSULT DELIB/GP ACT/RES TEC/DEV DIPLOM ECO/TAC ROUTINE...TIME/SEQ 20. PAGE 165 A3357 — LEGIS INT/TRADE CANADA DIST/IND

L61
HOYT E.C.,"UNITED STATES REACTION TO THE KOREAN ATTACK." COM KOREA USA+45 CONSTN DELIB/GP FORCES PLAN ECO/TAC DOMIN EDU/PROP LEGIT ROUTINE COERCE WAR ATTIT DISPL RIGID/FLEX ORD/FREE PWR...POLICY INT/LAW TREND UN 20. PAGE 68 A1402 — ASIA INT/ORG BAL/PWR DIPLOM

S61
ASHFORD D.E.,"A CASE STUDY IN THE DIPLOMACY OF SOCIAL REVOLUTION." USA+45 WOR+45 DIPLOM ECO/TAC FOR/AID REV ALL/VALS VAL/FREE 20. PAGE 9 A0187 — ECO/UNDEV PLAN

S61
BALL M.M.,"ISSUES FOR THE AMERICAS: NON-INTERVENTION VS HUMAN RIGHTS AND THE PRESERVATION OF DEMOCRATIC INSTITUTIONS." USA+45 INTELL INT/ORG NAT/G DIPLOM ECO/TAC LEGIT...TREND OAS TOT/POP 20. PAGE 11 A0213 — L/A+17C MORAL

S61
BARALL M.,"THE UNITED STATES GOVERNMENT RESPONDS." L/A+17C USA+45 SOCIETY NAT/G CREATE PLAN DIPLOM ECO/TAC ATTIT DRIVE RIGID/FLEX KNOWL SKILL WEALTH ...METH/CNCPT TIME/SEQ GEN/METH 20. PAGE 11 A0217 — ECO/UNDEV ACT/RES FOR/AID

S61
GALBRAITH J.K.,"A POSITIVE APPROACH TO ECONOMIC AID." FUT USA+45 INTELL NAT/G CONSULT ACT/RES DIPLOM ECO/TAC EDU/PROP ATTIT KNOWL PWR WEALTH ...SOC STERTYP 20. PAGE 50 A1030 — ECO/UNDEV ROUTINE FOR/AID

S61
HEILBRONER R.L.,"DYNAMICS OF FOREIGN AID: PROBLEMS OF UNDERDEVELOPED NATIONS PLAGUE ASSISTANCE PROGRAM." FUT USA+45 WOR+45 STRATA NAT/G PLAN TEC/DEV ATTIT DRIVE WEALTH WORK 20. PAGE 64 A1307 — ECO/UNDEV ECO/TAC FOR/AID

S61
LANFALUSSY A.,"EUROPE'S PROGRESS: DUE TO COMMON MARKET." EUR+WWI ECO/DEV DELIB/GP PLAN ECO/TAC ROUTINE WEALTH...GEOG TREND EEC 20. PAGE 84 A1721 — INT/ORG MARKET

S61
OCHENG D.,"ECONOMIC FORCES AND UGANDA'S FOREIGN POLICY." AFR UGANDA INT/TRADE TARIFFS INCOME SOVEREIGN WEALTH 20 EACM EEC TANGANYIKA. PAGE 111 A2274 — ECO/TAC DIPLOM ECO/UNDEV INT/ORG

S61
OCHENG D.,"AN ECONOMIST LOOKS AT UGANDA'S FUTURE." FUT UGANDA AGRI INDUS PLAN PROB/SOLV INT/TRADE SOVEREIGN 20. PAGE 111 A2275 — ECO/UNDEV INCOME ECO/TAC OWN

S61
RAY J.,"THE EUROPEAN FREE-TRADE ASSOCIATION AND ITS IMPACT ON INDIA'S TRADE." EUR+WWI FRANCE GERMANY INDIA S/ASIA UK NAT/G VOL/ASSN PLAN INT/TRADE ROUTINE WEALTH...STAT CHARTS CMN/WLTH EEC OEEC 20 EFTA. PAGE 120 A2453 — ECO/DEV ECO/TAC

S61
ROSTOW W.W.,"THE FUTURE OF FOREIGN AID." COM FUT WOR+45 ECO/DEV INDUS INT/ORG NAT/G CONSULT ACT/RES PLAN DOMIN LEGIT CHOOSE RIGID/FLEX ALL/VALS ...MAJORIT CONCPT TREND TOT/POP 20. PAGE 124 A2544 — ECO/UNDEV ECO/TAC FOR/AID

S61
TRAMPE G.,"DIE FORM DER DIPLOMATIC ALS POLITSCHE WAFFE." WOR+45 WOR-45 SOCIETY STRATA INT/ORG NAT/G ACT/RES PLAN ECO/TAC EDU/PROP COERCE WAR ATTIT RIGID/FLEX...DECISION CONCPT TREND. PAGE 145 A2959 — CONSULT PWR DIPLOM

S61
VINER J.,"ECONOMIC FOREIGN POLICY ON THE NEW FRONTIER." USA+45 ECO/UNDEV AGRI FINAN INDUS MARKET INT/ORG NAT/G FOR/AID INT/TRADE ADMIN ATTIT PWR 20 KENNEDY/JF. PAGE 159 A3239 — TOP/EX ECO/TAC BAL/PAY TARIFFS

S61
ZAGORIA D.S.,"SINO-SOVIET FRICTION IN UNDERDEVELOPED AREAS." ASIA CHINA/COM COM ACT/RES PLAN ATTIT ORD/FREE PWR COLD/WAR 20. PAGE 169 A3443 — ECO/UNDEV ECO/TAC INT/TRADE USSR

B62
ARNOLD H.J.P.,AID FOR DEVELOPING COUNTRIES. COM EUR+WWI USA+45 USSR WOR+45 EDU/PROP ATTIT DRIVE PWR WEALTH...TREND CHARTS STERTYP NAT/ 20. PAGE 9 A0177 — ECO/UNDEV ECO/TAC FOR/AID

B62
BEATON L.,THE SPREAD OF NUCLEAR WEAPONS. WOR+45 NAT/G PLAN PROB/SOLV DIPLOM ECO/TAC DETER...POLICY 20 COLD/WAR. PAGE 12 A0242 — ARMS/CONT NUC/PWR TEC/DEV FUT

B62
BURTON J.W.,PEACE THEORY: PRECONDITIONS OF DISARMAMENT. COM EUR+WWI USA+45 NAT/G FORCES BAL/PWR DIPLOM ECO/TAC EDU/PROP REGION COERCE DETER PEACE ATTIT PWR TOT/POP COLD/WAR 20. PAGE 22 A0446 — INT/ORG PLAN ARMS/CONT

B62
CALVOCORESSI P.,WORLD ORDER AND NEW STATES: PROBLEMS OF KEEPING THE PEACE. AFR EUR+WWI S/ASIA ELITES NAT/G ECO/TAC FOR/AID EDU/PROP COERCE ATTIT DRIVE ALL/VALS...GEN/LAWS COLD/WAR 20 UN. PAGE 23 A0471 — INT/ORG PEACE

B62
CARLSTON K.S.,LAW AND ORGANIZATION IN WORLD SOCIETY. WOR+45 FINAN ECO/TAC DOMIN LEGIT CT/SYS ROUTINE COERCE ORD/FREE PWR WEALTH...PLURIST DECISION JURID MGT METH/CNCPT GEN/LAWS 20. PAGE 24 A0487 — INT/ORG LAW

B62
CLUBB O.E. JR.,THE UNITED STATES AND THE SINO-SOVIET BLOC IN SOUTHEAST ASIA. ASIA CHINA/COM COM USA+45 USSR ECO/UNDEV INT/ORG NAT/G FORCES TOP/EX PLAN ECO/TAC DOMIN COERCE GUERRILLA ATTIT RIGID/FLEX...POLICY OBS TREND 20. PAGE 27 A0553 — S/ASIA PWR BAL/PWR DIPLOM

B62
COUNCIL ON WORLD TENSIONS,A STUDY OF WORLD TENSIONS AND DEVELOPMENT. WOR+45 ECO/DEV ECO/UNDEV INT/ORG PLAN DIPLOM ECO/TAC EDU/PROP ATTIT KNOWL ORD/FREE PWR WEALTH...CONCPT TREND CHARTS STERTYP COLD/WAR TOT/POP 20. PAGE 31 A0640 — TEC/DEV SOC

B62
COUNCIL ON WORLD TENSIONS,RESTLESS NATIONS. WOR+45 STRUCT INT/ORG NAT/G PLAN ECO/TAC...NAT/COMP ANTHOL 20. PAGE 32 A0641 — ECO/UNDEV POLICY DIPLOM TASK

B62
DREIER J.C.,THE ORGANIZATION OF AMERICAN STATES AND THE HEMISPHERE CRISIS. CUBA USA+45 CULTURE STRATA — L/A+17C CONCPT

NAT/G VOL/ASSN CONSULT FORCES ACT/RES CREATE DIPLOM ECO/TAC FOR/AID ALL/VALS...POLICY OBS OAS 20. PAGE 38 A0786

B62
DREIER J.C.,THE ALLIANCE FOR PROGRESS. L/A+17C USA+45 CULTURE ECO/DEV ECO/UNDEV NAT/G PLAN DIPLOM PWR 20 OAS. PAGE 39 A0787
FOR/AID INT/ORG ECO/TAC POLICY

B62
DUROSELLE J.B.,LES NOUVEAUX ETATS DANS LES RELATIONS INTERNATIONALES. AFR CHINA/COM FRANCE MOROCCO S/ASIA USSR ECO/UNDEV INT/ORG PLAN ECO/TAC EDU/PROP ATTIT DRIVE...TREND TOT/POP TUNIS 20. PAGE 39 A0806
NAT/G CONSTN DIPLOM

B62
EBENSTEIN W.,TWO WAYS OF LIFE. USA+45 CULTURE ECO/DEV PLAN EDU/PROP CONTROL ORD/FREE...GOV/COMP IDEA/COMP T 20 MARX/KARL ENGELS/F LENIN/VI LOCKE/JOHN MILL/JS. PAGE 40 A0819
MARXISM POPULISM ECO/TAC DIPLOM

B62
EVANS M.S.,THE FRINGE ON TOP. USSR EX/STRUC FORCES DIPLOM ECO/TAC PEACE CONSERVE SOCISM...TREND 20 KENNEDY/JF. PAGE 43 A0877
NAT/G PWR CENTRAL POLICY

B62
FAO,FOOD AND AGRICULTURE ORGANIZATION AFRICAN SURVEY. AFR CONGO/BRAZ GHANA STRATA AGRI INT/ORG TEC/DEV FOR/AID INT/TRADE RACE/REL DEMAND EFFICIENCY PRODUC...GEOG 20 UN CONGO/LEOP. PAGE 44 A0898
ECO/TAC WEALTH EXTR/IND ECO/UNDEV

B62
FORD A.G.,THE GOLD STANDARD 1880-1914: BRITAIN AND ARGENTINA. UK ECO/UNDEV INT/TRADE ADMIN GOV/REL DEMAND EFFICIENCY...STAT CHARTS 19/20 ARGEN GOLD/STAND. PAGE 47 A0960
FINAN ECO/TAC BUDGET BAL/PAY

B62
FRIEDMANN W.,METHODS AND POLICIES OF PRINCIPAL DONOR COUNTRIES IN PUBLIC INTERNATIONAL DEVELOPMENT FINANCING: PRELIMINARY APPRAISAL. FRANCE GERMANY/W UK USA+45 USSR WOR+45 FINAN TEC/DEV CAP/ISM DIPLOM ECO/TAC ATTIT 20 EEC. PAGE 49 A1002
INT/ORG FOR/AID NAT/COMP ADMIN

B62
FRIEDRICH-EBERT-STIFTUNG,THE SOVIET BLOC AND DEVELOPING COUNTRIES. CHINA/COM COM GERMANY/E USSR WOR+45 ECO/UNDEV INT/ORG NAT/G TEC/DEV NEUTRAL PWR ...POLICY 20. PAGE 49 A1008
MARXISM DIPLOM ECO/TAC FOR/AID

B62
GRAEBNER N.,COLD WAR DIPLOMACY 1945-1960. WOR+45 INT/ORG ECO/TAC EDU/PROP COERCE ORD/FREE PWR WEALTH ...HIST/WRIT TOT/POP VAL/FREE COLD/WAR 20. PAGE 55 A1122
USA+45 DIPLOM

B62
GUTTMAN A.,THE WOUND IN THE HEART: AMERICA AND THE SPANISH CIVIL WAR. SPAIN USA-45 POL/PAR LEGIS ECO/TAC CHOOSE ANOMIE ATTIT MARXISM...POLICY ANARCH BIBLIOG 20 ROOSEVLT/F. PAGE 58 A1198
ALL/IDEOS WAR DIPLOM CATHISM

B62
HIGGANS B.,UNITED NATIONS AND U.S. FOREIGN ECONOMIC POLICY. FUT USA+45 WOR+45 ECO/DEV ECO/UNDEV NAT/G ECO/TAC WEALTH...TIME/SEQ TOT/POP UN 20. PAGE 65 A1328
INT/ORG ACT/RES FOR/AID DIPLOM

B62
HOLMAN A.G.,SOME MEASURES AND INTERPRETATIONS OF EFFECTS OF US FOREIGN ENTERPRISES ON US BALANCE OF PAYMENTS. USA+45 COST INCOME WEALTH...MATH CHARTS 20. PAGE 67 A1371
BAL/PAY INT/TRADE FINAN ECO/TAC

B62
HUMPHREY D.D.,THE UNITED STATES AND THE COMMON MARKET. USA+45 INDUS MARKET INT/ORG PLAN EDU/PROP BAL/PAY DRIVE PWR WEALTH...TREND STERTYP EEC 20. PAGE 69 A1415
ATTIT ECO/TAC

B62
JORDAN A.A. JR.,FOREIGN AID AND THE DEFENSE OF SOUTHEAST ASIA. PAKISTAN VIETNAM/S FINAN PLAN BUDGET ECO/TAC DETER WAR ORD/FREE...POLICY DECISION CENSUS CHARTS BIBLIOG 20. PAGE 75 A1535
FOR/AID S/ASIA FORCES ECO/UNDEV

B62
KINDLEBERGER C.P.,FOREIGN TRADE AND THE NATIONAL ECONOMY. WOR+45 ECO/DEV ECO/UNDEV ECO/TAC COST DEMAND 20. PAGE 79 A1622
INT/TRADE GOV/COMP BAL/PAY POLICY

B62
KING-HALL S.,POWER POLITICS IN THE NUCLEAR AGE: A POLICY FOR BRITAIN. UK WOR+45 PLAN ECO/TAC CONTROL RISK ARMS/CONT MORAL PWR RESPECT...OLD/LIB 20. PAGE 79 A1625
BAL/PWR NUC/PWR POLICY DIPLOM

B62
KRAFT J.,THE GRAND DESIGN. EUR+WWI USA+45 AGRI FINAN INDUS MARKET INT/ORG NAT/G PLAN ECO/TAC TARIFFS REGION DRIVE ORD/FREE WEALTH...POLICY OBS TREND EEC 20. PAGE 82 A1674
VOL/ASSN ECO/DEV INT/TRADE

B62
LAQUEUR W.,POLYCENTRISM. CHINA/COM COM USSR WOR+45 INT/ORG NAT/G ECO/TAC DOMIN LEAD ATTIT PWR SOVEREIGN...ANTHOL 20. PAGE 85 A1732
MARXISM DIPLOM BAL/PWR POLICY

B62
LEWIS J.P.,QUIET CRISIS IN INDIA. INDIA USA+45 CULTURE ECO/UNDEV AGRI INDUS PROC/MFG NAT/G PLAN TEC/DEV DRIVE PWR SKILL WEALTH...MYTH 20. PAGE 88 A1801
S/ASIA ECO/TAC FOR/AID

B62
LUTZ F.A.,GELD UND WAHRUNG. MARKET LABOR BUDGET 20 GOLD/STAND EUROPE. PAGE 92 A1875
ECO/TAC FINAN DIPLOM POLICY

B62
MEADE J.E.,CASE STUDIES IN EUROPEAN ECONOMIC UNION. BELGIUM EUR+WWI LUXEMBOURG NAT/G INT/TRADE REGION ROUTINE WEALTH...METH/CNCPT STAT CHARTS ECSC TOT/POP OEEC EEC 20. PAGE 99 A2028
INT/ORG ECO/TAC

B62
MODELSKI G.,SEATO-SIX STUDIES. ASIA CHINA/COM INDIA S/ASIA INT/ORG NAT/G ECO/TAC DETER ATTIT ORD/FREE PWR...TIME/SEQ COLD/WAR TOT/POP 20 SEATO. PAGE 102 A2098
MARKET ECO/UNDEV INT/TRADE

B62
MORRAY J.P.,THE SECOND REVOLUTION IN CUBA. CUBA AGRI LABOR POL/PAR DIPLOM FOR/AID GUERRILLA TOTALISM MARXISM 20. PAGE 104 A2146
REV MARXIST ECO/TAC NAT/LISM

B62
PAKISTAN MINISTRY OF FINANCE,FOREIGN ECONOMIC AID: A REVIEW OF FOREIGN ECONOMIC AID TO PAKISTAN. EUR+WWI PAKISTAN UK USA+45 USSR ECO/UNDEV INT/ORG DELIB/GP DIPLOM ECO/TAC...CHARTS CMN/WLTH CHINJAP. PAGE 113 A2318
FOR/AID RECEIVE WEALTH FINAN

B62
POSTON R.W.,DEMOCRACY SPEAKS MANY TONGUES. L/A+17C USA+45 ECO/UNDEV ACT/RES ECO/TAC ADMIN ORD/FREE ...METH/COMP 20. PAGE 117 A2397
FOR/AID DIPLOM CAP/ISM MARXISM

B62
RIVKIN A.,AFRICA AND THE WEST. AFR EUR+WWI FUT ISLAM ISRAEL USA+45 SOCIETY INT/ORG FORCES CREATE PLAN FOR/AID EDU/PROP ATTIT...CONCPT TREND EEC 20 CONGRESS UN. PAGE 121 A2488
ECO/UNDEV ECO/TAC

B62
ROBERTSON B.C.,REGIONAL DEVELOPMENT IN THE EUROPEAN ECONOMIC COMMUNITY. EUR+WWI FRANCE FUT ITALY UK ECO/UNDEV WORKER ACT/RES PROB/SOLV TEC/DEV ECO/TAC INT/TRADE EEC. PAGE 122 A2499
PLAN ECO/DEV INT/ORG REGION

B62
ROY P.A.,SOUTH WIND RED. L/A+17C USA+45 ECO/UNDEV NAT/G CAP/ISM MARXISM SOCISM...OLD/LIB GEOG RECORD INT CENSUS 20 COLD/WAR. PAGE 125 A2554
DIPLOM INDUS POLICY ECO/TAC

B62
SCHRODER P.M.,METTERNICH'S DIPLOMACY AT ITS ZENITH, 1820-1823. MOD/EUR ELITES INT/ORG VOL/ASSN DELIB/GP ECO/TAC EDU/PROP DISPL PWR SOVEREIGN...POLICY CONCPT GEN/LAWS 19 METTRNCH/K. PAGE 129 A2647
ORD/FREE BIOG BAL/PWR DIPLOM

B62
SHAW C.,LEGAL PROBLEMS IN INTERNATIONAL TRADE AND INVESTMENT. WOR+45 ECO/DEV ECO/UNDEV MARKET DIPLOM TAX INCOME ROLE...ANTHOL BIBLIOG 20 TREATY UN IMF GATT. PAGE 132 A2698
INT/LAW INT/TRADE FINAN ECO/TAC

B62
THANT U.,THE UNITED NATIONS' DEVELOPMENT DECADE: PROPOSALS FOR ACTION. WOR+45 SOCIETY ECO/UNDEV AGRI COM/IND FINAN R+D MUNIC SCHOOL VOL/ASSN CONSULT PLAN TEC/DEV ECO/TAC EDU/PROP ADMIN ROUTINE RIGID/FLEX...MGT SOC CONCPT UNESCO UN TOT/POP VAL/FREE. PAGE 142 A2906
INT/ORG ALL/VALS

B62
US CONGRESS JOINT ECO COMM,FACTORS AFFECTING THE UNITED STATES BALANCE OF PAYMENTS. USA+45 DELIB/GP PLAN DIPLOM FOR/AID PRODUC WEALTH...CHARTS 20 CONGRESS OEEC. PAGE 150 A3064
BAL/PAY INT/TRADE ECO/TAC FINAN

B62
WILLIAMS W.A.,THE UNITED STATES, CUBA, AND CASTRO: AN ESSAY ON THE DYNAMICS OF REVOLUTION AND THE DISSOLUTION OF EMPIRE. CUBA USA+45 AGRI VOL/ASSN DIPLOM ECO/TAC DOMIN COERCE...POLICY 20 EISNHWR/DD CIA KENNEDY/JF CASTRO/F. PAGE 165 A3354
REV CONSTN COM LEAD

B62
ZOOK P.D.,FOREIGN TRADE AND HUMAN CAPITAL. L/A+17C USA+45 FINAN DIPLOM ECO/TAC PRODUC...POLICY 20. PAGE 170 A3458
INT/TRADE ECO/UNDEV FOR/AID BAL/PAY

L62
MALINOWSKI W.R.,"CENTRALIZATION AND DE-CENTRALIZATION IN THE UNITED NATIONS' ECONOMIC AND SOCIAL ACTIVITIES." WOR+45 CONSTN ECO/UNDEV INT/ORG VOL/ASSN DELIB/GP ECO/TAC EDU/PROP ADMIN RIGID/FLEX ...OBS CHARTS UNESCO UN EEC OAS OEEC 20. PAGE 93 A1913
CREATE GEN/LAWS

L62
MURACCIOLE L.,"LA BANQUE CENTRALE DES ETATS DE L'AFRIQUE DE L'OUEST." AFR LAW ECO/UNDEV INT/ORG NAT/G CONSULT ECO/TAC ROUTINE...CHARTS 20. PAGE 106 A2175
ISLAM FINAN INT/TRADE

L62
NIZARD L.,"CUBAN QUESTION AND SECURITY COUNCIL." L/A+17C USA+45 ECO/UNDEV NAT/G POL/PAR DELIB/GP ECO/TAC PWR...RELATIV OBS TIME/SEQ TREND GEN/LAWS UN 20 UN. PAGE 109 A2242
INT/ORG JURID DIPLOM CUBA

S62
ALBONETTI A.,"IL SECONDO PROGRAMMA QUINQUENNALE 1963-67 ED IL BILANCIO RICERCHE ED INVESTIMENTI PER IL 1963 DELL'ERATOM." EUR+WWI FUT ITALY WOR+45 ECO/DEV SERV/IND INT/ORG TEC/DEV ECO/TAC ATTIT SKILL WEALTH...MGT TIME/SEQ OEEC 20. PAGE 5 A0108
R+D PLAN NUC/PWR

S62
BELSHAW C.,"TRAINING AND RECRUITMENT: SOME PRINCIPLES OF INTERNATIONAL AID." FUT WOR+45 SOCIETY INT/ORG NAT/G CREATE PLAN TEC/DEV ECO/TAC FOR/AID EDU/PROP ATTIT PERCEPT...HUM UN FAO ILO UNESCO 20. PAGE 13 A0263
VOL/ASSN ECO/UNDEV

S62
BRZEZINSKI Z.K.,"PEACEFUL ENGAGEMENT IN COMMUNIST DISUNITY." ASIA CHINA/COM USA+45 USSR NAT/G TOP/EX CREATE ECO/TAC FOR/AID DOMIN ATTIT PERCEPT RIGID/FLEX PWR...PSY 20. PAGE 20 A0417
COM DIPLOM TOTALISM

S62
DEUTSCH K.W.,"TOWARDS WESTERN EUROPEAN INTEGRATION: AN INTERIM ASSESSMENT." EUR+WWI STRUCT ECO/DEV INT/ORG ECO/TAC INT/TRADE EDU/PROP PEACE ATTIT DRIVE PWR SOVEREIGN...PSY SOC TIME/SEQ CHARTS STERTYP 20. PAGE 36 A0741
VOL/ASSN RIGID/FLEX REGION

S62
DRACHKOVITCH M.M.,"THE EMERGING PATTERN OF YUGOSLAV-SOVIET RELATIONS." COM FUT USSR WOR+45 INT/ORG ECO/TAC FOR/AID DOMIN COERCE ATTIT PERSON ORD/FREE PWR...TIME/SEQ 20 TITO/MARSH KHRUSH/N STALIN/J. PAGE 38 A0783
TOP/EX DIPLOM YUGOSLAVIA

S62
FENWICK C.G.,"ISSUES AT PUNTA DEL ESTE: NON-INTERVENTION VS COLLECTIVE SECURITY." L/A+17C USA+45 VOL/ASSN DELIB/GP ECO/TAC LEGIT ADJUD REGION ORD/FREE OAS COLD/WAR 20. PAGE 45 A0917
INT/ORG CUBA

S62
JACOBSON H.K.,"THE UNITED NATIONS AND COLONIALISM: A TENTATIVE APPRAISAL." AFR FUT S/ASIA USA+45 USSR WOR+45 NAT/G DELIB/GP PLAN DIPLOM ECO/TAC DOMIN ADMIN ROUTINE COERCE ATTIT RIGID/FLEX ORD/FREE PWR ...OBS STERTYP UN 20. PAGE 73 A1486
INT/ORG CONCPT COLONIAL

S62
MILLIKEN M.,"NEW AND OLD CRITERIA FOR AID." WOR+45 ECO/DEV ECO/UNDEV ACT/RES PLAN ATTIT KNOWL...TREND CON/ANAL SIMUL GEN/METH 20. PAGE 102 A2083
USA+45 ECO/TAC FOR/AID

S62
MORGENTHAU H.J.,"A POLITICAL THEORY OF FOREIGN AID." ECO/UNDEV NAT/G DELIB/GP PLAN ECO/TAC EDU/PROP EXEC ORD/FREE RESPECT WEALTH...METH/CNCPT TREND 20. PAGE 104 A2140
USA+45 PHIL/SCI FOR/AID

S62
PIQUEMAL M.,"LA COOPERATION FINANCIERE ENTRE LA FRANCE ET LES ETATS AFRICAINS ET MALGACHE." ISLAM INT/ORG TOP/EX ECO/TAC...JURID CHARTS 20. PAGE 116 A2383
AFR FINAN FRANCE MADAGASCAR

S62
PYE L.W.,"THE POLITICAL IMPULSES AND FANTASIES BEHIND FOREIGN AID." FUT USA+45 ECO/UNDEV DIPLOM ECO/TAC ROUTINE DRIVE KNOWL...SOC METH/CNCPT NEW/IDEA TREND HYPO/EXP STERTYP GEN/METH 20. PAGE 118 A2420
ACT/RES ATTIT FOR/AID

S62
RAZAFIMBAHINY J.,"L'ORGANISATION AFRICAINE ET MALGACHE DE COOPERATION ECONOMIQUE." AFR ISLAM MADAGASCAR NAT/G ACT/RES ECO/TAC ALL/VALS ...TIME/SEQ 20. PAGE 120 A2454
INT/ORG ECO/UNDEV

S62
RUBINSTEIN A.Z.,"RUSSIA AND THE UNCOMMITTED NATIONS." AFR INDIA ISLAM L/A+17C LAOS S/ASIA ELITES ECO/UNDEV INT/ORG KIN CREATE PLAN TEC/DEV NAT/LISM RIGID/FLEX PWR WEALTH...METH/CNCPT TIME/SEQ GEN/LAWS WORK. PAGE 125 A2562
ECO/TAC TREND COLONIAL USSR

S62
SCOTT J.B.,"ANGLO-SOVIET TRADE AND ITS EFFECTS ON THE COMMONWEALTH." COM FUT UK USSR WOR+45 ECO/DEV MARKET INT/ORG CONSULT WEALTH...POLICY TREND CMN/WLTH 20. PAGE 130 A2673
NAT/G ECO/TAC

S62
SPENSER J.H.,"AFRICA AT THE UNITED NATIONS: SOME OBSERVATIONS." FUT ECO/UNDEV NAT/G CONSULT DELIB/GP PLAN BAL/PWR ECO/TAC EDU/PROP ATTIT RIGID/FLEX HEALTH ORD/FREE PWR WEALTH...POLICY CONCPT OBS TREND STERTYP GEN/METH UN VAL/FREE. PAGE 136 A2786
AFR INT/ORG REGION

S62
TOWSTER J.,"THE USSR AND THE USA: CHALLENGE AND RESPONSE." COM GERMANY USA+45 USSR WOR+45 ECO/UNDEV INT/ORG VOL/ASSN EX/STRUC FORCES TOP/EX CREATE PLAN TEC/DEV DIPLOM ECO/TAC EDU/PROP COLONIAL COERCE PWR ...GEN/METH COLD/WAR 20 KENNEDY/JF. PAGE 145 A2956
ACT/RES GEN/LAWS

S62
TRUMAN D.,"THE DOMESTIC POLITICS OF FOREIGN AID." USA+45 WOR+45 NAT/G POL/PAR LEGIS DIPLOM ECO/TAC EDU/PROP ADMIN CHOOSE ATTIT PWR CONGRESS 20 CONGRESS. PAGE 145 A2970
ROUTINE FOR/AID

B63
ABSHIRE D.M.,NATIONAL SECURITY: POLITICAL, MILITARY, AND ECONOMIC STRATEGIES IN THE DECADE AHEAD. ASIA COM USA+45 WOR+45 ECO/DEV ECO/UNDEV INT/ORG DELIB/GP FORCES ECO/TAC COERCE ATTIT RIGID/FLEX HEALTH ORD/FREE PWR WEALTH...POLICY STAT CHARTS ANTHOL COLD/WAR VAL/FREE. PAGE 4 A0083
FUT ACT/RES BAL/PWR

B63
BRZEZINSKI Z.K.,AFRICA AND THE COMMUNIST WORLD. AFR ASIA COM CULTURE SOCIETY INT/ORG DELIB/GP ACT/RES ECO/TAC COERCE ORD/FREE PWR WEALTH...STAT TOT/POP VAL/FREE 20. PAGE 21 A0418
ATTIT EDU/PROP DIPLOM USSR

B63
CANELAS O.A.,RADIOGRAFIA DE LA ALIANZA PARA EL ATRASO. L/A+17C USA+45 ECO/TAC DOMIN COLONIAL NAT/LISM...SOCIALIST NAT/COMP 20. PAGE 23 A0476
REV DIPLOM ECO/UNDEV REGION

B63
CENTRO PARA EL DESARROLLO,LA ALIANZA PARA EL PROGRESO Y EL DESARROLLO SOCIAL DE AMERICA LATINA. L/A+17C INT/ORG DIPLOM ECO/TAC INT/TRADE ATTIT 20. PAGE 25 A0512
ECO/UNDEV FOR/AID PLAN REGION

B63
CERAMI C.A.,ALLIANCE BORN OF DANGER. EUR+WWI USA+45 USSR ECO/DEV INDUS VOL/ASSN ECO/TAC REGION ATTIT MARXISM ATLAN/ALL 20 NATO EEC. PAGE 25 A0514
DIPLOM INT/ORG NAT/G POLICY

B63
DUNN F.S.,PEACE-MAKING AND THE SETTLEMENT WITH JAPAN. ASIA USA+45 USA-45 FORCES BAL/PWR ECO/TAC CONFER WAR PWR SOVEREIGN 20 CHINJAP COLD/WAR TREATY. PAGE 39 A0802
POLICY PEACE PLAN DIPLOM

B63
FIFIELD R.H.,SOUTHEAST ASIA IN UNITED STATES POLICY. S/ASIA USA+45 ECO/UNDEV NAT/G DIPLOM ECO/TAC DOMIN COERCE ORD/FREE...POLICY MAJORIT 20. PAGE 45 A0928
INT/ORG PWR

B63
FISCHER-GALATI S.,EASTERN EUROPE IN THE SIXTIES. ALBANIA USSR YUGOSLAVIA ECO/UNDEV AGRI MARKET LABOR WORKER DIPLOM INT/TRADE EDU/PROP GOV/REL PRODUC UTOPIA SOCISM 20. PAGE 46 A0939
MARXISM TEC/DEV BAL/PWR ECO/TAC

B63
FLORES E.,LAND REFORM AND THE ALLIANCE FOR PROGRESS (PAMPHLET). L/A+17C USA+45 STRUCT ECO/UNDEV NAT/G WORKER CREATE PLAN ECO/TAC COERCE REV 20. PAGE 47 A0953
AGRI INT/ORG DIPLOM POLICY

B63
GILBERT M.,THE APPEASERS. COM GERMANY UK PLAN ECO/TAC COLONIAL CONTROL EXEC ORD/FREE PWR FASCISM 20 PARLIAMENT. PAGE 52 A1068
DIPLOM WAR POLICY DECISION

B63
GOLDSCHMIDT W.,THE UNITED STATES AND AFRICA. USA+45 CULTURE ECO/TAC INT/TRADE GOV/REL...SOC ANTHOL 20 INTERVENT. PAGE 53 A1091
AFR ECO/UNDEV DIPLOM

B63
GOLDWIN R.A.,FOREIGN AND MILITARY POLICY. COM USSR WOR+45 ECO/DEV INT/ORG FORCES PLAN ECO/TAC REGION ARMS/CONT MARXISM 20 UN. PAGE 54 A1097
DIPLOM POLICY PWR NAT/G

B63
GONZALEZ PEDRERO E.,ANATOMIA DE UN CONFLICTO. WOR+45 ECO/DEV ECO/UNDEV ECO/TAC FOR/AID CONTROL ARMS/CONT GOV/REL...NAT/COMP 20 COLD/WAR. PAGE 54 A1099
DIPLOM DETER BAL/PWR

B63
GORDON L.,A NEW DEAL FOR LATIN AMERICA. L/A+17C USA+45 CULTURE NAT/G TEC/DEV DIPLOM FOR/AID REGION TASK...POLICY 20 DEPT/STATE. PAGE 54 A1115
ECO/UNDEV ECO/TAC INT/ORG PLAN

B63
HAMM H.,ALBANIA - CHINA'S BEACHHEAD IN EUROPE. ALBANIA CHINA/COM USSR YUGOSLAVIA ELITES SOCIETY POL/PAR DELIB/GP FORCES ECO/TAC COERCE ISOLAT PEACE MARXISM...IDEA/COMP 20 MAO. PAGE 61 A1248
DIPLOM REV NAT/G POLICY

B63
HENDERSON W.,SOUTHEAST ASIA: PROBLEMS OF UNITED STATES POLICY. COM S/ASIA CULTURE STRATA ECO/UNDEV INT/ORG DELIB/GP ACT/RES ECO/TAC DOMIN EDU/PROP LEGIT COERCE ATTIT ALL/VALS...STAT TIME/SEQ ANTHOL VAL/FREE 20. PAGE 64 A1313
ASIA USA+45 DIPLOM

B63
HONEY P.J.,COMMUNISM IN NORTH VIETNAM: ITS ROLE IN THE SINO-SOVIET DISPUTE. CHINA/COM INDIA USSR VIETNAM/N AGRI POL/PAR LEGIS ECO/TAC WAR PEACE ATTIT...GEOG IDEA/COMP 20. PAGE 67 A1378
POLICY MARXISM CHIEF DIPLOM

B63
HYDE D.,THE PEACEFUL ASSAULT. COM UAR USSR ECO/DEV ECO/UNDEV NAT/G POL/PAR CAP/ISM PWR 20. PAGE 69 A1427
MARXISM CONTROL ECO/TAC DIPLOM

B63
INTERAMERICAN ECO AND SOC COUN,THE ALLIANCE FOR
INT/ORG

PROGRESS: ITS FIRST YEAR: 1961-1962. AGRI SCHOOL PLAN TEC/DEV INT/TRADE TAX GIVE ADMIN WEALTH...SOC 20 SOUTH/AMER. PAGE 71 A1449 PROB/SOLV ECO/TAC L/A+17C

INTERNATIONAL BANK RECONST DEV,THE WORLD BANK GROUP IN ASIA. ASIA S/ASIA INDUS TEC/DEV ECO/TAC...RECORD 20 IBRD WORLD/BANK. PAGE 71 A1451 B63 INT/ORG DIPLOM ECO/UNDEV FINAN

JACOBSON H.K.,THE USSR AND THE UN'S ECONOMIC AND SOCIAL ACTIVITIES. COM WOR+45 DELIB/GP ACT/RES ECO/TAC EDU/PROP RIGID/FLEX SUPEGO HEALTH PWR SKILL ...POLICY CHARTS GEN/METH VAL/FREE UNESCO 20 UN. PAGE 73 A1487 B63 INT/ORG ATTIT USSR

KRAVIS I.B.,DOMESTIC INTERESTS AND INTERNATIONAL OBLIGATIONS: SAFEGUARDS IN INTERNATIONAL TRADE ORGANIZATIONS. EUR+WWI USA+45 WOR+45 FINAN DELIB/GP ATTIT RIGID/FLEX WEALTH...STAT EEC VAL/FREE OEEC ECSC 20. PAGE 82 A1680 B63 INT/ORG ECO/TAC INT/TRADE

LERCHE C.O. JR.,CONCEPTS OF INTERNATIONAL POLITICS. WOR+45 WOR-45 LAW DELIB/GP EX/STRUC TEC/DEV ECO/TAC INT/TRADE LEGIT ROUTINE COERCE ATTIT ORD/FREE PWR RESPECT...STERTYP GEN/LAWS VAL/FREE. PAGE 87 A1782 B63 INT/ORG WAR

LERCHE C.O. JR.,AMERICA IN WORLD AFFAIRS. COM UK USA+45 INT/ORG FORCES ECO/TAC INT/TRADE EDU/PROP WAR NAT/LISM PEACE...BIBLIOG 18/20 UN CONGRESS PRESIDENT COLD/WAR. PAGE 87 A1783 B63 NAT/G DIPLOM PLAN

LINDBERG L.,POLITICAL DYNAMICS OF EUROPEAN ECONOMIC INTEGRATION. EUR+WWI ECO/DEV INT/ORG VOL/ASSN DELIB/GP ADMIN WEALTH...DECISION EEC 20. PAGE 89 A1820 B63 MARKET ECO/TAC

LUNDBERG F.,THE COMING WORLD TRANSFORMATION. CULTURE SOCIETY ECO/DEV INT/ORG NAT/G DIPLOM ECO/TAC EDU/PROP 15/21. PAGE 91 A1873 B63 PREDICT FUT WOR+45 TEC/DEV

MANGER W.,THE ALLIANCE FOR PROGRESS: A CRITICAL APPRAISAL. FUT L/A+17C USA+45 CULTURE ECO/UNDEV ACADEM NAT/G SCHOOL PLAN FOR/AID...POLICY OAS. PAGE 94 A1918 B63 DIPLOM INT/ORG ECO/TAC REGION

MANSERGH N.,DOCUMENTS AND SPEECHES ON COMMONWEALTH AFFAIRS 1952-1962. CANADA INDIA PAKISTAN UK CONSTN FORCES ECO/TAC EDU/PROP COLONIAL DETER WAR ORD/FREE SOVEREIGN...POLICY 20 AUSTRAL. PAGE 94 A1932 B63 BIBLIOG/A FEDERAL INT/TRADE DIPLOM

MARITANO N.,AN ALLIANCE FOR PROGRESS. FUT L/A+17C USA+45 CULTURE ECO/UNDEV NAT/G PLAN CONTROL POLICY. PAGE 95 A1941 B63 DIPLOM INT/ORG ECO/TAC FOR/AID

MAYNE R.,THE COMMUNITY OF EUROPE. UK CONSTN NAT/G CONSULT DELIB/GP CREATE PLAN ECO/TAC LEGIT ADMIN ROUTINE ORD/FREE PWR WEALTH...CONCPT TIME/SEQ EEC EURATOM 20. PAGE 97 A1985 B63 EUR+WWI INT/ORG REGION

MULLENBACH P.,CIVILIAN NUCLEAR POWER: ECONOMIC ISSUES AND POLICY FORMATION. FINAN INT/ORG DELIB/GP ACT/RES ECO/TAC ATTIT SUPEGO HEALTH ORD/FREE PWR ...POLICY CONCPT MATH STAT CHARTS VAL/FREE 20 COLD/WAR. PAGE 105 A2166 B63 USA+45 ECO/DEV NUC/PWR

MYRDAL G.,CHALLENGE TO AFFLUENCE. USA+45 WOR+45 FINAN INT/ORG NAT/G PLAN ECO/TAC INT/TRADE BAL/PAY ORD/FREE 20 EUROPE/W. PAGE 107 A2189 B63 ECO/DEV WEALTH DIPLOM PRODUC

RAO V.K.R.,FOREIGN AID AND INDIA'S ECONOMIC DEVELOPMENT. INDIA INT/ORG PROB/SOLV TEC/DEV ECO/TAC CONTROL WEALTH...TREND 20. PAGE 119 A2445 B63 FOR/AID ECO/UNDEV RECEIVE DIPLOM

RIUKIN A.,THE AFRICAN PRESENCE IN WORLD AFFAIRS. AFR WOR+45 ECO/UNDEV AGRI INT/ORG BAL/PWR ECO/TAC COLONIAL NEUTRAL NAT/LISM PEACE SOVEREIGN 20 UN. PAGE 121 A2486 B63 DIPLOM NAT/G POLICY PWR

ROBOCK S.H.,OVERVIEW OF TOTAL BRAZILIAN SETTING, NEWER REGIONAL PATTERNS NING AND FOREIGN AID. BRAZIL ECO/UNDEV AGRI FINAN INDUS INT/ORG INCOME UTIL...CHARTS 20. PAGE 122 A2507 B63 ECO/TAC REGION PLAN FOR/AID

ROSECRANCE R.N.,ACTION AND REACTION IN WORLD POLITICS. FUT WOR-45 SOCIETY DELIB/GP ACT/RES CREATE DIPLOM ECO/TAC DOMIN EDU/PROP COERCE ATTIT PERSON SUPEGO ORD/FREE PWR...CHARTS SIMUL LEAGUE/NAT VAL/FREE UN 19/20. PAGE 123 A2529 B63 WOR+45 INT/ORG BAL/PWR

ROSS H.,THE COLD WAR: CONTAINMENT AND ITS CRITICSS. WOR+45 POL/PAR BAL/PWR ECO/TAC PEACE ORD/FREE ...POLICY IDEA/COMP ANTHOL T 20 COLD/WAR DULLES/JF TRUMAN/HS EISNHWR/DD. PAGE 124 A2541 B63 MARXISM ARMS/CONT DIPLOM

SCHMELTZ G.W.,LA POLITIQUE MONDIALE CONTEMPORAINE. SOCIETY ECO/UNDEV INDUS INT/ORG NAT/G POL/PAR CONSULT DELIB/GP PLAN TEC/DEV ECO/TAC DOMIN EDU/PROP ROUTINE COERCE PERCEPT PERSON LOVE SKILL ...SOC RECORD TOT/POP. PAGE 128 A2629 B63 WOR+45 COLONIAL

SMITH J.E.,THE DEFENSE OF BERLIN. COM GUATEMALA WOR+45 ECO/TAC ADMIN NEUTRAL ATTIT ORD/FREE SOVEREIGN...DECISION 20 DEPT/STATE. PAGE 134 A2747 B63 DIPLOM FORCES BAL/PWR PLAN

THEOBALD R.,FREE MEN AND FREE MARKETS. USA+45 USA-45 ECO/DEV NAT/G TEC/DEV DIPLOM INT/TRADE INCOME ORD/FREE WEALTH...TREND 19/20 KEYNES/JM. PAGE 143 A2915 B63 CONCPT ECO/TAC CAP/ISM MARKET

TUCKER R.C.,THE SOVIET POLITICAL MIND. WOR+45 ELITES INT/ORG NAT/G POL/PAR PLAN DIPLOM ECO/TAC DOMIN ADMIN NUC/PWR REV DRIVE PERSON SUPEGO PWR WEALTH...POLICY MGT PSY CONCPT OBS BIOG TREND COLD/WAR MARX/KARL 20. PAGE 145 A2972 B63 COM TOP/EX USSR

UN SECRETARY GENERAL,PLANNING FOR ECONOMIC DEVELOPMENT. ECO/UNDEV FINAN BUDGET INT/TRADE TARIFFS TAX ADMIN 20 UN. PAGE 147 A3005 B63 PLAN ECO/TAC MGT NAT/COMP

UNITED STATES GOVERNMENT,REPORT TO THE INTER-AMERICAN ECONOMIC AND SOCIAL COUNCIL. L/A+17C INDUS PLAN INT/TRADE TARIFFS CONFER...CHARTS 20 LAFTA. PAGE 149 A3038 B63 FOR/AID ECO/TAC ECO/UNDEV DIPLOM

US CONGRESS JOINT ECO COMM,THE UNITED STATES BALANCE OF PAYMENTS. USA+45 DELIB/GP BUDGET PRICE PRODUC 20 CONGRESS GOLD/STAND MONEY. PAGE 150 A3067 B63 BAL/PAY INT/TRADE FINAN ECO/TAC

US CONGRESS JOINT ECO COMM,THE UNITED STATES BALANCE OF PAYMENTS. USA+45 DELIB/GP CONFER...MATH PREDICT CHARTS 20 CONGRESS. PAGE 150 A3068 B63 BAL/PAY ECO/TAC INT/TRADE CONSULT

US GOVERNMENT,REPORT TO INTER-AMERICAN ECONOMIC AND SOCIAL COUNCIL AT SECOND ANNUAL MEETING. L/A+17C USA+45 VOL/ASSN TEC/DEV DIPLOM TAX EATING EFFICIENCY HEALTH...STAT CHARTS 20 AID. PAGE 153 A3116 B63 ECO/TAC FOR/AID FINAN PLAN

US HOUSE COMM BANKING-CURR,RECENT CHANGES IN MONETARY POLICY AND BALANCE OF PAYMENTS PROBLEMS. USA+45 DELIB/GP PLAN DIPLOM...CHARTS 20 CONGRESS. PAGE 153 A3121 B63 BAL/PAY FINAN ECO/TAC POLICY

US SENATE COMM GOVT OPERATIONS,REPORT OF A STUDY OF US FOREIGN AID IN TEN MIDDLE EASTERN AND AFRICAN COUNTRIES. AFR ISLAM USA+45 FORCES PLAN BUDGET DIPLOM TAX DETER WEALTH...STAT CHARTS 20 CONGRESS AID MID/EAST. PAGE 156 A3174 B63 FOR/AID EFFICIENCY ECO/TAC FINAN

WELLESLEY COLLEGE,SYMPOSIUM ON LATIN AMERICA. FUT L/A+17C USA+45 INT/ORG ECO/TAC PARL/PROC REGION ANTHOL. PAGE 163 A3316 B63 ECO/UNDEV CULTURE ORD/FREE DIPLOM

YOUNG A.N.,CHINA AND THE HELPING HAND. ASIA USA+45 FINAN INDUS ECO/TAC GIVE WEALTH...METH/COMP 20 LEND/LEASE GOLD/STAND. PAGE 169 A3434 B63 FOR/AID DIPLOM WAR

LISSITZYN O.J.,"INTERNATIONAL LAW IN A DIVIDED WORLD." FUT WOR+45 CONSTN CULTURE ECO/DEV ECO/UNDEV DIST/IND NAT/G FORCES ECO/TAC LEGIT ADJUD ADMIN COERCE ATTIT HEALTH MORAL ORD/FREE PWR RESPECT WEALTH VAL/FREE. PAGE 90 A1841 L63 INT/ORG LAW

PADELFORD N.J.,"FINANCIAL CRISIS AND THE UNITED NATIONS." FUT USSR WOR+45 LAW CONSTN FINAN INT/ORG DELIB/GP FORCES PLAN BUDGET DIPLOM COST WEALTH ...STAT CHARTS UN CONGO 20. PAGE 113 A2311 L63 CREATE ECO/TAC

PRINCETON UNIV. CONFERENCE,"ARAB DEVELOPMENT IN THE EMERGING INTERNATIONAL ECONOMY." FUT USA+45 DIST/IND FINAN DELIB/GP PLAN ECO/TAC WEALTH VAL/FREE 20. PAGE 118 A2413 L63 ISLAM ECO/UNDEV FOR/AID INT/TRADE

SINGER J.D.,"WEAPONS MANAGEMENT IN WORLD POLITICS: PROCEEDINGS OF THE INTERNATIONAL ARMS CONTROL SYMPOSIUM, DECEMBER, 1962." FUT WOR+45 SOCIETY ECO/DEV INDUS INT/ORG DELIB/GP FORCES ACT/RES ECO/TAC EDU/PROP ARMS/CONT SUPEGO HEALTH ORD/FREE PWR SKILL...POLICY CHARTS SIMUL ANTHOL VAL/FREE 20. PAGE 133 A2729 L63 CONSULT ATTIT DIPLOM NUC/PWR

SZASZY E.,"L'EVOLUTION DES PRINCIPES GENERAUX DU DROIT INTERNATIONAL PRIVE DANS LES PAYS DE L63 DIPLOM TOTALISM

DEMOCRATIE POPULAIRE." COM FUT WOR+45 LAW ECO/DEV PERF/ART POL/PAR PROF/ORG ECO/TAC INT/TRADE EDU/PROP ATTIT RIGID/FLEX ALL/VALS SOCISM...JURID TREND GEN/LAWS WORK 20. PAGE 141 A2876 INT/LAW INT/ORG

L63
WILCOX F.O.,"THE ATLANTIC COMMUNITY: PROGRESS AND PROSPECTS." EUR+WWI FUT USA+45 WOR+45 SOCIETY CREATE ECO/TAC EDU/PROP LEGIT REGION ATTIT ALL/VALS ...POLICY ANTHOL VAL/FREE 20. PAGE 164 A3346 INT/ORG ACT/RES

S63
ALPHAND H.,"FRANCE AND HER ALLIES." EUR+WWI UK USA+45 ECO/DEV INT/ORG NAT/G VOL/ASSN FORCES TOP/EX DIPLOM ECO/TAC LEGIT ATTIT DRIVE ORD/FREE PWR WEALTH...STAT EEC TOT/POP 20. PAGE 6 A0130 ACT/RES FRANCE

S63
ANGUILE G.,"CIVILISATION DU PLAN DANS L'EUROPE ET L'AFRIQUE DE DEMAIN." AFR EUR+WWI GABON ECO/DEV FINAN MARKET DELIB/GP ECO/TAC WEALTH...TREND 20. PAGE 8 A0163 ECO/UNDEV PLAN INT/TRADE

S63
BANFIELD J.,"FEDERATION IN EAST-AFRICA." AFR UGANDA ELITES INT/ORG NAT/G VOL/ASSN LEGIS ECO/TAC FEDERAL ATTIT SOVEREIGN TOT/POP 20 TANGANYIKA. PAGE 11 A0216 EX/STRUC PWR REGION

S63
COSER L.,"AMERICA AND THE WORLD REVOLUTION." COM FUT USA+45 WOR+45 INTELL SOCIETY NAT/G ECO/TAC EDU/PROP ALL/VALS SOCISM...PSY GEN/LAWS TOT/POP 20 COLD/WAR. PAGE 31 A0629 ECO/UNDEV PLAN FOR/AID DIPLOM

S63
DARLING F.C.,"THE GEOPOLITICS OF AMERICAN FOREIGN POLITICS IN ASIA." COM S/ASIA USA+45 USSR ECO/UNDEV NAT/G VOL/ASSN CONSULT PLAN GUERRILLA...STAT TOT/POP 20. PAGE 34 A0682 FORCES ECO/TAC FOR/AID DIPLOM

S63
DIEBOLD W. JR.,"THE NEW SITUATION OF INTERNATIONAL TRADE POLICY." EUR+WWI FRANCE FUT UK USA+45 WOR+45 DIST/IND PLAN INT/TRADE EDU/PROP PWR WEALTH ...RECORD TREND GEN/LAWS EEC VAL/FREE 20. PAGE 37 A0760 MARKET ECO/TAC

S63
EMERSON R.,"THE ATLANTIC COMMUNITY AND THE EMERGING COUNTRIES." FUT WOR+45 ECO/DEV ECO/UNDEV R+D NAT/G DELIB/GP BAL/PWR ECO/TAC EDU/PROP ROUTINE ORD/FREE PWR WEALTH...POLICY CONCPT TREND GEN/METH EEC 20 NATO. PAGE 42 A0848 ATTIT INT/TRADE

S63
ETIENNE G.,"'LOIS OBJECTIVES' ET PROBLEMES DE DEVELOPPEMENT DANS LE CONTEXTE CHINE-URSS." ASIA CHINA/COM COM FUT STRUCT INT/ORG VOL/ASSN TOP/EX TEC/DEV ECO/TAC ATTIT RIGID/FLEX...GEOG MGT TIME/SEQ TOT/POP 20. PAGE 42 A0866 TOTALISM USSR

S63
ETZIONI A.,"EUROPEAN UNIFICATION: A STRATEGY OF CHANGE." EUR+WWI CULTURE ECO/DEV DELIB/GP ACT/RES ECO/TAC EDU/PROP ATTIT ORD/FREE PWR SKILL WEALTH ...STAT TIME/SEQ EEC TOT/POP VAL/FREE 20. PAGE 42 A0869 INT/ORG RIGID/FLEX

S63
ETZIONI A.,"EUROPEAN UNIFICATION AND PERSPECTIVES ON SOVEREIGNTY." EUR+WWI FUT DELIB/GP TEC/DEV ECO/TAC EDU/PROP DETER NUC/PWR ATTIT DRIVE ORD/FREE PWR WEALTH...CONCPT RECORD TIME/SEQ EEC VAL/FREE 20. PAGE 43 A0870 INT/ORG ECO/DEV SOVEREIGN

S63
GANDOLFI A.,"LES ACCORDS DE COOPERATION EN MATIERE DE POLITIQUE ETRANGERE ENTRE LA FRANCE ET LES NOUVEAUX ETATS AFRICAINS ET." AFR ISLAM MADAGASCAR WOR+45 ECO/DEV INT/ORG NAT/G DELIB/GP ECO/TAC ALL/VALS...CON/ANAL 20. PAGE 51 A1038 VOL/ASSN ECO/UNDEV DIPLOM FRANCE

S63
GORDON B.,"ECONOMIC IMPEDIMENTS TO REGIONALISM IN SOUTH EAST ASIA." BURMA FUT S/ASIA THAILAND USA+45 AGRI INDUS R+D NAT/G PLAN ECO/TAC WEALTH...STAT CONT/OBS 20. PAGE 54 A1110 VOL/ASSN ECO/UNDEV INT/TRADE REGION

S63
HALLSTEIN W.,"THE EUROPEAN COMMUNITY AND ATLANTIC PARTNERSHIP." EUR+WWI USA+45 MARKET NAT/G VOL/ASSN DELIB/GP ARMS/CONT NUC/PWR ATTIT PWR...CONCPT STAT TIME/SEQ TREND OEEC 20 EEC. PAGE 60 A1235 INT/ORG ECO/TAC UK

S63
HARNETTY P.,"CANADA, SOUTH AFRICA AND THE COMMONWEALTH." CANADA SOUTH/AFR LAW INT/ORG VOL/ASSN DELIB/GP LEGIS TOP/EX ECO/TAC LEGIT DRIVE MORAL...CONCPT CMN/WLTH 20. PAGE 62 A1263 AFR ATTIT

S63
HAVILAND H.F.,"BUILDING A POLITICAL COMMUNITY." EUR+WWI FUT UK USA+45 ECO/DEV ECO/UNDEV INT/ORG NAT/G DELIB/GP BAL/PWR ECO/TAC NEUTRAL ROUTINE ATTIT PWR WEALTH...CONCPT COLD/WAR TOT/POP 20. PAGE 63 A1293 VOL/ASSN DIPLOM

S63
HINDLEY D.,"FOREIGN AID TO INDONESIA AND ITS POLITICAL IMPLICATIONS." INDONESIA POL/PAR ATTIT SOVEREIGN...CHARTS 20. PAGE 65 A1336 FOR/AID NAT/G WEALTH ECO/TAC

S63
HOLBO P.S.,"COLD WAR DRIFT IN LATIN AMERICA." CUBA L/A+17C USA+45 USA-45 INT/ORG NAT/G NEIGH VOL/ASSN ACT/RES PLAN ECO/TAC ATTIT RIGID/FLEX ALL/VALS ...RECORD TIME/SEQ OAS LAFTA 20 COLD/WAR. PAGE 66 A1363 DELIB/GP CREATE FOR/AID

S63
HORVATH J.,"MOSCOW'S AID PROGRAM: THE PERFORMANCE SO FAR." COM FUT USSR WOR+45 ECO/DEV FINAN PLAN TEC/DEV FOR/AID EDU/PROP ATTIT ORD/FREE PWR WEALTH ...POLICY STAT CHARTS VAL/FREE 20. PAGE 68 A1389 ECO/UNDEV ECO/TAC

S63
KRAVIS I.B.,"THE POLITICAL ARITHMETIC OF INTERNATIONAL BURDENSHARING." FUT USA+45 WOR+45 FINAN DELIB/GP ACT/RES CREATE TEC/DEV ATTIT PWR WEALTH...POLICY MATH STAT VAL/FREE 20. PAGE 82 A1681 INT/ORG ECO/TAC

S63
LEDUC G.,"L'AIDE INTERNATIONALE AU DEVELOPPEMENT." FUT WOR+45 ECO/DEV ECO/UNDEV R+D PROF/ORG TEC/DEV ECO/TAC ROUTINE ATTIT ALL/VALS...MGT TIME/SEQ TOT/POP 20. PAGE 86 A1758 FINAN PLAN FOR/AID

S63
MANGONE G.,"THE UNITED NATIONS AND UNITED STATES FOREIGN POLICY." USA+45 WOR+45 ECO/UNDEV NAT/G DIPLOM LEGIT ROUTINE ATTIT DRIVE...TIME/SEQ UN COLD/WAR 20. PAGE 94 A1922 INT/ORG ECO/TAC FOR/AID

S63
MATHUR P.N.,"GAINS IN ECONOMIC GROWTH FROM INTERNATIONAL TRADE." USA-45 ECO/DEV FINAN INDUS ATTIT WEALTH...MATH QUANT STAT BIOG TREND GEN/LAWS WORK 20. PAGE 96 A1966 MARKET ECO/TAC CAP/ISM INT/TRADE

S63
NADLER E.B.,"SOME ECONOMIC DISADVANTAGES OF THE ARMS RACE." USA+45 INDUS R+D FORCES PLAN TEC/DEV ECO/TAC FOR/AID EDU/PROP PWR WEALTH...TREND COLD/WAR 20. PAGE 107 A2190 ECO/DEV MGT BAL/PAY

S63
NYE J.S. JR.,"EAST AFRICAN ECONOMIC INTEGRATION." AFR UGANDA PROVS DELIB/GP PLAN ECO/TAC INT/TRADE ADMIN ROUTINE ORD/FREE PWR WEALTH...OBS TIME/SEQ VAL/FREE 20. PAGE 110 A2264 ECO/UNDEV INT/ORG

S63
PINCUS J.,"THE COST OF FOREIGN AID." WOR+45 ECO/DEV FINAN NAT/G VOL/ASSN CREATE ECO/TAC EDU/PROP WEALTH ...METH/CNCPT STAT CHARTS HYPO/EXP TOT/POP VAL/FREE 20. PAGE 116 A2380 USA+45 ECO/UNDEV FOR/AID

S63
RAMERIE L.,"TENSION AU SEIN DU COMECON: LE CAS ROUMAIN." COM EUR+WWI USSR WOR+45 ECO/DEV DIST/IND NAT/G POL/PAR VOL/ASSN EDU/PROP TOTALISM ATTIT WEALTH...TIME/SEQ 20 COMECON. PAGE 119 A2438 INT/ORG ECO/TAC INT/TRADE ROMANIA

S63
SCHMIDT W.E.,"THE CASE AGAINST COMMODITY AGREEMENTS." FUT L/A+17C STRATA CONSULT PLAN ECO/TAC EDU/PROP ATTIT DRIVE RIGID/FLEX WEALTH ...MYTH 20. PAGE 128 A2631 ECO/UNDEV ACT/RES INT/TRADE

S63
SCHOFLING J.A.,"EFTA: THE OTHER EUROPE." ECO/DEV MARKET CONSULT ECO/TAC WEALTH...TIME/SEQ EEC OEEC 20 EFTA. PAGE 129 A2642 EUR+WWI INT/ORG REGION

S63
SHONFIELD A.,"AFTER BRUSSELS." EUR+WWI FRANCE GERMANY UK ECO/DEV DIST/IND MARKET VOL/ASSN DELIB/GP CREATE INT/TRADE ATTIT RIGID/FLEX...RECORD TREND GEN/LAWS EEC CMN/WLTH 20. PAGE 132 A2705 PLAN ECO/TAC

S63
SHWADRAN B.,"MIDDLE EAST OIL, 1962." ISLAM USSR ECO/DEV DIST/IND INDUS PLAN BAL/PWR DISPL DRIVE ...POLICY STAT TREND GEN/LAWS EEC OEEC 20 OIL. PAGE 132 A2712 MARKET ECO/TAC INT/TRADE

S63
SINGER M.R.,"ELECTIONS WITHIN THE UNITED NATIONS: AN EXPERIMENTAL STUDY UTILIZING STATISTICAL ANALYSIS." USA+45 WOR+45 DIPLOM ECO/TAC COERCE PWR WEALTH...STAT CHARTS SIMUL GEN/LAWS COLD/WAR VAL/FREE UN 20. PAGE 133 A2732 INT/ORG CHOOSE

S63
SONNENFELDT H.,"FOREIGN POLICY FROM MALENKOV TO KHRUSHCHEV." WOR+45 NAT/G FORCES BAL/PWR DIPLOM ECO/TAC COERCE ATTIT PWR...CONCPT HIST/WRIT COLD/WAR 20. PAGE 135 A2768 COM DOMIN FOR/AID USSR

S63
VINER J.,"REPORT OF THE CLAY COMMITTEE ON FOREIGN AID: A SYMPOSIUM." USA+45 WOR+45 NAT/G CONSULT PLAN BAL/PWR ATTIT WEALTH...MGT CONCPT TOT/POP 20. PAGE 159 A3240 ACT/RES ECO/TAC FOR/AID

S63
WALKER H.,"THE INTERNATIONAL LAW OF COMMODITY AGREEMENTS." FUT WOR+45 ECO/DEV ECO/UNDEV FINAN INT/ORG NAT/G CONSULT CREATE PLAN ECO/TAC ATTIT PERCEPT...CONCPT GEN/LAWS TOT/POP GATT 20. PAGE 160 A3265 MARKET VOL/ASSN INT/LAW INT/TRADE

S63
WELLS H.,"THE OAS AND THE DOMINICAN ELECTIONS." L/A+17C INT/ORG NAT/G POL/PAR TEC/DEV ECO/TAC CONSULT CHOOSE

EDU/PROP PERCEPT...TIME/SEQ OAS TOT/POP 20. PAGE 163 A3317 DOMIN/REP

S63
WOLF C.,"SOME ASPECTS OF THE 'VALUE' OF LESS-DEVELOPED COUNTRIES TO THE UNITED STATES." ASIA CHINA/COM COM USA+45 USSR ECO/UNDEV BAL/PWR ECO/TAC FOR/AID DOMIN EDU/PROP ATTIT PWR...POLICY METH/CNCPT CONT/OBS TREND CHARTS 20. PAGE 166 A3379 CONCPT GEN/LAWS DIPLOM

S63
WOLFERS A.,"INTEGRATION IN THE WEST: THE CONFLICT OF PERSPECTIVES." EUR+WWI USA+45 ECO/DEV INT/ORG DELIB/GP CREATE TEC/DEV DIPLOM ATTIT PWR...CONCPT HIST/WRIT TREND GEN/LAWS COLD/WAR EEC 20. PAGE 166 A3386 RIGID/FLEX ECO/TAC

B64
BARKER A.J.,SUEZ: THE SEVEN DAY WAR. EUR+WWI ISLAM UAR INT/ORG NAT/G PLAN DIPLOM ECO/TAC DOMIN NAT/LISM DRIVE RIGID/FLEX PWR SOVEREIGN...POLICY JURID TREND CHARTS SUEZ UN 20. PAGE 11 A0221 FORCES COERCE UK

B64
CALDER R.,TWO-WAY PASSAGE. INT/ORG TEC/DEV WAR PERSON ORD/FREE 20. PAGE 23 A0467 FOR/AID ECO/UNDEV ECO/TAC DIPLOM

B64
COLUMBIA U SCHOOL OF LAW,PUBLIC INTERNATIONAL DEVELOPMENT FINANCING IN INDIA. GERMANY/W INDIA UK USA+45 INDUS PLAN TEC/DEV DIPLOM ECO/TAC GIVE ADMIN UTIL ATTIT 20. PAGE 28 A0572 ECO/UNDEV FINAN FOR/AID INT/ORG

B64
DAVIES U.P. JR.,FOREIGN AND OTHER AFFAIRS. EUR+WWI L/A+17C S/ASIA USA+45 ECO/UNDEV CHIEF PLAN ECO/TAC PWR MARXISM 20 KENNEDY/JF UN. PAGE 34 A0688 DIPLOM NAT/G POLICY FOR/AID

B64
DUROSELLE J.B.,POLITIQUES NATIONALES ENVERS LES JEUNES ETATS. FRANCE ISRAEL ITALY UK USA+45 USSR YUGOSLAVIA ECO/DEV FINAN ECO/TAC INT/TRADE ADMIN PWR 20. PAGE 40 A0809 DIPLOM ECO/UNDEV COLONIAL DOMIN

B64
ETZIONI A.,WINNING WITHOUT WAR. FUT MOD/EUR USA+45 WOR+45 ECO/DEV ECO/UNDEV INT/ORG NAT/G FORCES TOP/EX PLAN TEC/DEV ECO/TAC DOMIN EDU/PROP LEGIT COERCE CHOOSE ATTIT MORAL ORD/FREE RESPECT WEALTH MAJORIT. PAGE 43 A0871 PWR TREND DIPLOM USSR

B64
FALL B.,STREET WITHOUT JOY. FRANCE USA+45 DIPLOM ECO/TAC FOR/AID GUERRILLA REV WEAPON...TREND 20. PAGE 44 A0894 WAR S/ASIA FORCES COERCE

B64
FATOUROS A.A.,CANADA'S OVERSEAS AID. CANADA WOR+45 ECO/DEV FINAN NAT/G BUDGET ECO/TAC CONFER ADMIN 20. PAGE 44 A0904 FOR/AID DIPLOM ECO/UNDEV POLICY

B64
FEIS H.,FOREIGN AID AND FOREIGN POLICY. USA+45 WOR+45 NAT/G VOL/ASSN ACT/RES TEC/DEV ATTIT HEALTH WEALTH...SOC GEN/LAWS 20. PAGE 45 A0912 ECO/UNDEV ECO/TAC FOR/AID DIPLOM

B64
FISHER R.,INTERNATIONAL CONFLICT AND BEHAVIORAL SCIENCE: THE CRAIGVILLE PAPERS. COM FUT USA+45 WOR+45 NAT/G DELIB/GP EX/STRUC FORCES ECO/TAC DOMIN EDU/PROP LEGIT COERCE ATTIT PERCEPT ORD/FREE PWR RESPECT...PSY SOC VAL/FREE. PAGE 46 A0940 INT/ORG PLAN DIPLOM

B64
FREUD A.,OF HUMAN SOVEREIGNTY. WOR+45 INDUS SECT ECO/TAC CRIME CHOOSE ATTIT MORAL MARXISM...POLICY BIBLIOG 20. PAGE 49 A0998 NAT/LISM DIPLOM WAR PEACE

B64
FREYMOND J.,WESTERN EUROPE SINCE THE WAR. COM EUR+WWI USA+45 DIPLOM...BIBLIOG 20 NATO UN EEC. PAGE 49 A1001 INT/ORG POLICY ECO/DEV ECO/TAC

B64
GARDNER L.C.,ECONOMIC ASPECTS OF NEW DEAL DIPLOMACY. USA-45 WOR-45 LAW ECO/DEV INT/ORG NAT/G VOL/ASSN LEGIS TOP/EX EDU/PROP ORD/FREE PWR WEALTH ...POLICY TIME/SEQ VAL/FREE 20 ROOSEVLT/F. PAGE 51 A1043 ECO/TAC DIPLOM

B64
HALPERIN S.W.,MUSSOLINI AND ITALIAN FASCISM. ITALY NAT/G POL/PAR SECT ECO/TAC LEAD PWR SOCISM...POLICY 20 MUSSOLIN/B. PAGE 60 A1241 FASCISM NAT/LISM EDU/PROP CHIEF

B64
HAMBRIDGE G.,DYNAMICS OF DEVELOPMENT. AGRI FINAN INDUS LABOR INT/TRADE EDU/PROP ADMIN LEAD OWN HEALTH...ANTHOL BIBLIOG 20. PAGE 61 A1245 ECO/UNDEV ECO/TAC OP/RES ACT/RES

B64
HANSEN B.,INTERNATIONAL LIQUIDITY. USA+45 INT/ORG ECO/TAC PRICE CONTROL WEALTH...POLICY 20. PAGE 61 A1254 BAL/PAY INT/TRADE DIPLOM

FINAN

B64
HINSHAW R.,THE EUROPEAN COMMUNITY AND AMERICAN TRADE: A STUDY IN ATLANTIC ECONOMICS AND POLICY. EUR+WWI UK USA+45 ECO/DEV ECO/UNDEV AGRI INDUS INT/ORG NAT/G ECO/TAC TARIFFS REGION...STAT CHARTS EEC 20. PAGE 65 A1337 MARKET TREND INT/TRADE

B64
INTL INF CTR LOCAL CREDIT,GOVERNMENT MEASURES FOR THE PROMOTION OF REGIONAL ECONOMIC DEVELOPMENT. WOR+45 ECO/UNDEV FINAN INT/ORG DIPLOM ORD/FREE ...POLICY GEOG 20. PAGE 71 A1464 FOR/AID PLAN ECO/TAC REGION

B64
JANOWITZ M.,THE MILITARY IN THE POLITICAL DEVELOPMENT OF NEW NATIONS: AN ESSAY IN COMPARATIVE ANALYSIS. AFR ASIA ISLAM L/A+17C S/ASIA USA+45 ECO/UNDEV INT/ORG NAT/G POL/PAR DELIB/GP PLAN ECO/TAC DOMIN LEGIT COERCE ATTIT DRIVE RESPECT ...SOC CONCPT CENSUS VAL/FREE. PAGE 73 A1495 FORCES PWR

B64
KENNEDY J.F.,THE BURDEN AND THE GLORY. FUT USA+45 TEC/DEV ECO/TAC EDU/PROP ARMS/CONT MURDER RACE/REL PEACE...ANTHOL 20 KENNEDY/JF COLD/WAR NATO PRESIDENT. PAGE 78 A1593 ADMIN POLICY GOV/REL DIPLOM

B64
LATOURETTE K.S.,CHINA. ASIA CHINA/COM FUT USSR ECO/UNDEV ECO/TAC WAR 19/20. PAGE 85 A1744 MARXISM NAT/G POLICY DIPLOM

B64
LITTLE I.M.D.,AID TO AFRICA. AFR UK TEC/DEV DIPLOM ECO/TAC INCOME WEALTH 20. PAGE 90 A1844 FOR/AID ECO/UNDEV ADMIN POLICY

B64
MARKHAM J.W.,THE COMMON MARKET: FRIEND OR COMPETITOR. EUR+WWI FUT USA+45 INT/ORG LG/CO NAT/G VOL/ASSN DELIB/GP EX/STRUC PLAN TARIFFS ORD/FREE PWR WEALTH...POLICY STAT TREND EEC VAL/FREE 20. PAGE 95 A1943 ECO/DEV ECO/TAC

B64
MASON E.S.,FOREIGN AID AND FOREIGN POLICY. USA+45 AGRI INDUS NAT/G EX/STRUC ACT/RES RIGID/FLEX ALL/VALS...POLICY GEN/LAWS MARSHL/PLN CONGRESS 20. PAGE 95 A1956 ECO/UNDEV ECO/TAC FOR/AID DIPLOM

B64
MAUD J.,AID FOR DEVELOPING COUNTRIES. COM EUR+WWI UK INT/TRADE ORD/FREE...GOV/COMP 20. PAGE 96 A1979 FOR/AID DIPLOM ECO/TAC ECO/UNDEV

B64
OWEN W.,STRATEGY FOR MOBILITY. FUT WOR+45 WOR-45 DIST/IND INT/ORG NAT/G DELIB/GP PLAN TEC/DEV ECO/TAC ORD/FREE PWR WEALTH...STAT TIME/SEQ VAL/FREE 20. PAGE 112 A2304 COM/IND ECO/UNDEV

B64
PENNOCK J.R.,SELF-GOVERNMENT IN MODERNIZING NATIONS. AFR COM USA+45 ECO/DEV POL/PAR PROB/SOLV DIPLOM ECO/TAC COLONIAL REV POPULISM SOCISM 20. PAGE 114 A2350 ECO/UNDEV POLICY SOVEREIGN NAT/G

B64
PERKINS D.,THE AMERICAN DEMOCRACY: ITS RISE TO POWER. ASIA USSR LAW CULTURE FINAN EDU/PROP COLONIAL CHOOSE...POLICY CHARTS BIBLIOG WORSHIP PRESIDENT 15/20 NEGRO. PAGE 115 A2362 LOC/G ECO/TAC WAR DIPLOM

B64
PLISCHKE E.,SYSTEMS OF INTEGRATING THE INTERNATIONAL COMMUNITY. WOR+45 NAT/G VOL/ASSN ECO/TAC LEGIT PWR WEALTH...TIME/SEQ ANTHOL UN TOT/POP 20. PAGE 116 A2391 INT/ORG EX/STRUC REGION

B64
RAMAZANI R.K.,THE MIDDLE EAST AND THE EUROPEAN COMMON MARKET. EUR+WWI ISLAM ECO/DEV EXTR/IND MARKET PROC/MFG INT/ORG NAT/G TEC/DEV ECO/TAC REGION DRIVE WEALTH...STAT CHARTS EEC TOT/POP 20. PAGE 119 A2437 ECO/UNDEV ATTIT INT/TRADE

B64
RANIS G.,THE UNITED STATES AND THE DEVELOPING ECONOMIES. COM USA+45 AGRI FINAN TEC/DEV CAP/ISM ECO/TAC INT/TRADE...POLICY METH/COMP ANTHOL 20 AID. PAGE 119 A2441 ECO/UNDEV DIPLOM FOR/AID

B64
REUSS H.S.,THE CRITICAL DECADE - AN ECONOMIC POLICY FOR AMERICA AND THE FREE WORLD. USA+45 FINAN POL/PAR WORKER PLAN DIPLOM ECO/TAC TARIFFS BAL/PAY ...POLICY 20 CONGRESS GOLD/STAND. PAGE 120 A2468 FOR/AID INT/TRADE LABOR LEGIS

B64
RIVKIN A.,AFRICA AND THE EUROPEAN COMMON MARKET (PAMPHLET). AFR MOD/EUR WOR+45 TEC/DEV FOR/AID TARIFFS BAL/PAY...POLICY 20 EEC. PAGE 121 A2490 INT/ORG INT/TRADE ECO/TAC ECO/UNDEV

B64
RUBIN J.A.,YOUR HUNDRED BILLION DOLLARS. USA+45 USSR INDUS INT/ORG TEC/DEV ECO/TAC...METH/COMP 20 PEACE/CORP. PAGE 125 A2559 FOR/AID DIPLOM ECO/UNDEV

B64
RUBINSTEIN A.Z.,THE SOVIETS IN INTERNATIONAL ORGANIZATIONS: CHANGING POLICY TOWARD DEVELOPING COUNTRIES, 1953-1963. COM DELIB/GP ACT/RES ECO/TAC EDU/PROP ADMIN ATTIT ORD/FREE PWR...INT VAL/FREE UN 20. PAGE 125 A2563
ECO/UNDEV INT/ORG USSR

B64
SEGAL R.,SANCTIONS AGAINST SOUTH AFRICA. AFR SOUTH/AFR NAT/G INT/TRADE RACE/REL PEACE PWR ...INT/LAW ANTHOL 20 UN. PAGE 131 A2681
SANCTION DISCRIM ECO/TAC POLICY

B64
SINGER H.W.,INTERNATIONAL DEVELOPMENT: GROWTH AND CHANGE. AFR BRAZIL L/A+17C WOR+45 CULTURE AGRI INDUS NAT/G ACT/RES ECO/TAC EDU/PROP WEALTH...GEOG CONCPT METH/CNCPT STAT HYPO/EXP WORK TOT/POP 20. PAGE 133 A2723
FINAN ECO/UNDEV FOR/AID INT/TRADE

B64
STEWART C.F.,A BIBLIOGRAPHY OF INTERNATIONAL BUSINESS. WOR+45 FINAN LG/CO NAT/G PLAN ECO/TAC TARIFFS...DECISION MGT GP/COMP NAT/COMP 20 EEC. PAGE 138 A2824
BIBLIOG INT/ORG OP/RES INT/TRADE

B64
STOESSINGER J.G.,FINANCING THE UNITED NATIONS SYSTEM. FUT WOR+45 CONSTN NAT/G VOL/ASSN DELIB/GP EX/STRUC ECO/TAC LEGIT CT/SYS PWR WEALTH...STAT TIME/SEQ TREND CHARTS VAL/FREE. PAGE 138 A2830
FINAN INT/ORG

B64
TEPASKE J.J.,EXPLOSIVE FORCES IN LATIN AMERICA. CULTURE INTELL ECO/UNDEV INT/ORG NAT/G SECT FORCES ECO/TAC EDU/PROP PWR WEALTH SOC. PAGE 142 A2903
L/A+17C RIGID/FLEX FOR/AID USSR

B64
TONG T.,UNITED STATES DIPLOMACY IN CHINA, 1844-1860. ASIA USA-45 ECO/UNDEV ECO/TAC COERCE GP/REL...INT/LAW 19 TREATY. PAGE 144 A2949
DIPLOM INT/TRADE COLONIAL

B64
UN PUB. INFORM. ORGAN.,EVERY MAN'S UNITED NATIONS. UNIV WOR+45 CONSTN CULTURE SOCIETY ECO/DEV ECO/UNDEV NAT/G ACT/RES PLAN ECO/TAC INT/TRADE EDU/PROP LEGIT PEACE ATTIT ALL/VALS...POLICY HUM INT/LAW CONCPT CHARTS UN TOT/POP 20. PAGE 147 A3004
INT/ORG ROUTINE

B64
US HOUSE COMM FOREIGN AFFAIRS,HEARINGS ON H.R. 10502 TO AMEND FURTHER THE FOREIGN ASSISTANCE ACT OF 1961. AFR ASIA L/A+17C INT/ORG CONSULT DELIB/GP TEC/DEV ECO/TAC EDU/PROP CONFER 20 UN NATO CONGRESS AID. PAGE 153 A3130
FOR/AID DIPLOM ORD/FREE ECO/UNDEV

B64
US HOUSE COMM GOVT OPERATIONS,US OWNED FOREIGN CURRENCIES: HEARINGS (COMMITTEE ON GOVERNMENT OPERATIONS). INDIA ECO/DEV PLAN BUDGET TAX DEMAND EFFICIENCY 20 AID CONGRESS. PAGE 154 A3138
FINAN ECO/TAC FOR/AID OWN

B64
WOODHOUSE C.M.,THE NEW CONCERT OF NATIONS. WOR+45 ECO/DEV ECO/UNDEV NAT/G BAL/PWR ECO/TAC NAT/LISM PWR SOVEREIGN ALL/IDEOS 20 UN COLD/WAR. PAGE 166 A3391
DIPLOM MORAL FOR/AID COLONIAL

B64
WYTHE G.,THE UNITED STATES AND INTER-AMERICAN RELATIONS: A CONTEMPORARY APPRAISAL. L/A+17C USA+45 ECO/UNDEV INT/ORG NAT/G VOL/ASSN INT/TRADE EDU/PROP DRIVE...SOC TREND OAS UN 20. PAGE 168 A3425
ATTIT ECO/TAC FOR/AID

L64
ARMENGALD A.,"ECONOMIE ET COEXISTENCE." COM EUR+WWI FUT USA+45 WOR+45 ECO/DEV ECO/UNDEV FINAN INT/ORG NAT/G EXEC CHOOSE ATTIT ALL/VALS...POLICY RELATIV DECISION TREND SOC/EXP COLD/WAR WORK 20. PAGE 9 A0173
MARKET ECO/TAC CAP/ISM

L64
BARROS J.,"THE GREEK-BULGARIAN INCIDENT OF 1925: THE LEAGUE OF NATIONS AND THE GREAT POWERS." BULGARIA EUR+WWI NAT/G FORCES ECO/TAC EDU/PROP LEGIT ROUTINE COERCE WAR PEACE DRIVE PWR...JURID CONCPT METH/CNCPT GEN/LAWS GEN/METH LEAGUE/NAT TOT/POP 20. PAGE 11 A0228
INT/ORG ORD/FREE DIPLOM

L64
CAMPBELL J.C.,"THE MIDDLE EAST IN THE MUTED COLD WAR." COM EUR+WWI UAR USA+45 USSR STRUCT ECO/UNDEV NAT/G VOL/ASSN EX/STRUC TOP/EX DIPLOM ECO/TAC EDU/PROP...TIME/SEQ COLD/WAR 20. PAGE 23 A0475
ISLAM FOR/AID NAT/LISM

L64
CARNEGIE ENDOWMENT INT. PEACE,"ECONOMIC AND SOCIAL QUESTION (ISSUES BEFORE THE NINETEENTH GENERAL ASSEMBLY)." WOR+45 ECO/DEV ECO/UNDEV INDUS R+D DELIB/GP CREATE PLAN TEC/DEV ECO/TAC FOR/AID BAL/PAY...RECORD UN 20. PAGE 24 A0493
INT/ORG INT/TRADE

L64
HAAS E.B.,"ECONOMICS AND DIFFERENTIAL PATTERNS OF POLITICAL INTEGRATION: PROJECTIONS ABOUT UNITY IN LATIN AMERICA." SOCIETY NAT/G DELIB/GP ACT/RES CREATE PLAN ECO/TAC REGION ROUTINE ATTIT DRIVE PWR WEALTH...CONCPT TREND CHARTS LAFTA 20. PAGE 59 A1208
L/A+17C INT/ORG MARKET

L64
KORBONSKI A.,"COMECON." ASIA ECO/DEV ECO/UNDEV ECO/TAC BAL/PAY NAT/LISM 20 COMECON. PAGE 81 A1671
COM INT/ORG INT/TRADE

L64
WORLD PEACE FOUNDATION,"INTERNATIONAL ORGANIZATIONS: SUMMARY OF ACTIVITIES." INDIA PAKISTAN TURKEY WOR+45 CONSTN CONSULT EX/STRUC ECO/TAC EDU/PROP LEGIT ORD/FREE...JURID SOC UN 20 CYPRESS. PAGE 167 A3397
INT/ORG ROUTINE

S64
ASHRAF S.,"INDIA AND WORLD AFFAIRS: AN ANNUAL BIBLIOGRAPHY, 1962." WOR+45 LAW ECO/UNDEV INT/ORG FORCES PLAN ECO/TAC COERCE ORD/FREE PWR WEALTH ...HIST/WRIT VAL/FREE. PAGE 9 A0188
S/ASIA NAT/G

S64
BEIM D.,"THE COMMUNIST BLOC AND THE FOREIGN-AID GAME." WOR+45 NAT/G PLAN ROUTINE ATTIT KNOWL ORD/FREE...DECISION QUANT CONT/OBS TIME/SEQ CHARTS GAME SIMUL COLD/WAR 20. PAGE 12 A0252
COM ECO/UNDEV ECO/TAC FOR/AID

S64
CARNEGIE ENDOWMENT INT. PEACE,"COLONIAL COUNTRIES AND PEOPLES (ISSUES BEFORE THE NINETEENTH GENERAL ASSEMBLY)." AFR ISLAM L/A+17C WOR+45 DELIB/GP LEGIS ECO/TAC EDU/PROP NAT/LISM PEACE ALL/VALS...RECORD UN CMN/WLTH 20. PAGE 24 A0491
INT/ORG ECO/UNDEV COLONIAL

S64
CARNEGIE ENDOWMENT INT. PEACE,"ADMINISTRATION AND BUDGET (ISSUES BEFORE THE NINETEENTH GENERAL ASSEMBLY)." WOR+45 FINAN BUDGET ECO/TAC ROUTINE COST...STAT RECORD UN. PAGE 24 A0495
INT/ORG ADMIN

S64
COCHRANE J.D.,"US ATTITUDES TOWARD CENTRAL-AMERICAN INTEGRATION." L/A+17C USA+45 ECO/UNDEV FACE/GP VOL/ASSN DELIB/GP ECO/TAC INT/TRADE EDU/PROP RIGID/FLEX ORD/FREE WEALTH...TIME/SEQ TOT/POP 20. PAGE 27 A0555
NAT/G ATTIT REGION

S64
DE GAULLE C.,"FRENCH WORLD VIEW." AFR ASIA CHINA/COM EUR+WWI ISLAM ECO/UNDEV INT/ORG NAT/G VOL/ASSN ACT/RES DIPLOM ECO/TAC EDU/PROP ATTIT DRIVE WEALTH 20. PAGE 35 A0702
TOP/EX PWR FOR/AID FRANCE

S64
DERWINSKI E.J.,"THE COST OF THE INTERNATIONAL COFFEE AGREEMENT." L/A+17C USA+45 WOR+45 ECO/UNDEV NAT/G VOL/ASSN LEGIS DIPLOM ECO/TAC FOR/AID LEGIT ATTIT...TIME/SEQ CONGRESS 20 TREATY. PAGE 36 A0732
MARKET DELIB/GP INT/TRADE

S64
DEVILLERS P.H.,"L'URSS, LA CHINE ET LES ORIGINES DE LA GUERRE DE COREE." ASIA CHINA/COM USSR INT/ORG ECO/TAC EDU/PROP ATTIT RIGID/FLEX PWR...STAND/INT HIST/WRIT COLD/WAR 20. PAGE 37 A0751
WOR+45 KOREA

S64
GARDNER R.N.,"THE SOVIET UNION AND THE UNITED NATIONS." WOR+45 FINAN POL/PAR VOL/ASSN FORCES ECO/TAC DOMIN EDU/PROP LEGIT ADJUD ADMIN ARMS/CONT COERCE ATTIT ALL/VALS...POLICY MAJORIT CONCPT OBS TIME/SEQ TREND STERTYP UN. PAGE 51 A1046
COM INT/ORG USSR

S64
GARDNER R.N.,"GATT AND THE UNITED NATIONS CONFERENCE ON TRADE AND DEVELOPMENT." USA+45 WOR+45 SOCIETY ECO/UNDEV MARKET NAT/G DELIB/GP ACT/RES PLAN ECO/TAC TARIFFS EDU/PROP ROUTINE DRIVE RIGID/FLEX WEALTH...DECISION MGT TREND UN TOT/POP 20 GATT. PAGE 51 A1047
INT/ORG INT/TRADE

S64
GARMARNIKOW M.,"INFLUENCE-BUYING IN WEST AFRICA." COM FUT USSR INTELL NAT/G PLAN TEC/DEV ECO/TAC DOMIN EDU/PROP REGION NAT/LISM ATTIT DRIVE ALL/VALS SOVEREIGN...POLICY PSY SOC CONCPT TREND STERTYP WORK COLD/WAR 20. PAGE 51 A1049
AFR ECO/UNDEV FOR/AID SOCISM

S64
HUELIN D.,"ECONOMIC INTEGRATION IN LATIN AMERICAN: PROGRESS AND PROBLEMS." L/A+17C ECO/DEV AGRI DIST/IND FINAN INDUS NAT/G VOL/ASSN CONSULT DELIB/GP EX/STRUC ACT/RES PLAN TEC/DEV ECO/TAC ROUTINE BAL/PAY WEALTH WORK 20. PAGE 69 A1411
MARKET ECO/UNDEV INT/TRADE

S64
HUTCHINSON E.C.,"AMERICAN AID TO AFRICA." FUT USA+45 MARKET INT/ORG LOC/G NAT/G PUB/INST PLAN ECO/TAC ATTIT RIGID/FLEX...POLICY CONCPT TREND 20. PAGE 69 A1423
AFR ECO/UNDEV FOR/AID

S64
KOJIMA K.,"THE PATTERN OF INTERNATIONAL TRADE AMONG ADVANCED COUNTRIES." EUR+WWI UK USA+45 WOR+45 MARKET NAT/G ECO/TAC WEALTH...MATH STAT CON/ANAL CHARTS EEC CHINJAP 20 CHINJAP. PAGE 81 A1665
ECO/DEV TREND INT/TRADE

S64
MARTELLI G.,"PORTUGAL AND THE UNITED NATIONS." AFR EUR+WWI ELITES INT/ORG NAT/G PROVS PLAN DIPLOM ECO/TAC DOMIN COLONIAL RIGID/FLEX MORAL ORD/FREE PWR WEALTH...MYTH UN 20. PAGE 95 A1947
ATTIT PORTUGAL

S64
MAZRUI A.A.,"THE UNITED NATIONS AND SOME AFRICAN POLITICAL ATTITUDES." ECO/TAC FOR/AID DOMIN ROUTINE CHOOSE ATTIT DRIVE MORAL PWR RESPECT WEALTH...PSY CONCPT OBS TREND UN VAL/FREE 20. PAGE 97 A1987
AFR INT/ORG SOVEREIGN

S64
MOWER A.G.,"THE OFFICIAL PRESSURE GROUP OF THE COUNCIL OF EUROPE'S CONSULATIVE ASSEMBLY." EUR+WWI SOCIETY STRUCT FINAN CONSULT ECO/TAC ADMIN ROUTINE ATTIT PWR WEALTH...STAT CHARTS 20 COUNCL/EUR. PAGE 105 A2160
INT/ORG EDU/PROP

S64
NEISSER H.,"THE EXTERNAL EQUILIBRIUM OF THE UNITED STATES ECONOMY." FUT USA+45 NAT/G ACT/RES PLAN ECO/TAC ATTIT WEALTH...METH/CNCPT GEN/METH VAL/FREE 20. PAGE 108 A2216
FINAN ECO/DEV BAL/PAY INT/TRADE

S64
PADELFORD N.J.,"THE ORGANIZATION OF AFRICAN UNITY." ECO/UNDEV INT/ORG PLAN BAL/PWR DIPLOM ECO/TAC NAT/LISM ORD/FREE PWR WEALTH...CONCPT TREND STERTYP VAL/FREE COLD/WAR 20. PAGE 113 A2313
AFR VOL/ASSN REGION

S64
PALMER N.D.,"INDIA AS A FACTOR IN UNITED STATES FOREIGN POLICY." INDIA USA+45 USA-45 ECO/UNDEV NAT/G TOP/EX ECO/TAC EDU/PROP...METH/CNCPT TIME/SEQ 20. PAGE 113 A2323
S/ASIA ATTIT FOR/AID DIPLOM

S64
PESELT B.M.,"COMMUNIST ECONOMIC OFFENSIVE." WOR+45 SOCIETY INT/ORG PLAN ECO/TAC DOMIN EDU/PROP ATTIT PERSON PWR WEALTH...TREND CHARTS 20. PAGE 115 A2366
COM ECO/UNDEV FOR/AID USSR

S64
ROTHCHILD D.,"EAST AFRICAN FEDERATION." AFR TANZANIA UGANDA INDUS REGION 20. PAGE 124 A2547
INT/ORG DIPLOM ECO/UNDEV ECO/TAC

S64
SAAB H.,"THE ARAB SEARCH FOR A FEDERAL UNION." SOCIETY INT/ORG NAT/G DELIB/GP FORCES ACT/RES TEC/DEV ECO/TAC DOMIN LEGIT REGION ROUTINE ATTIT DRIVE RIGID/FLEX ALL/VALS...SOC CONCPT NEW/IDEA TIME/SEQ TREND. PAGE 126 A2580
ISLAM PLAN

S64
SALVADORI M.,"EL CAPITALISMO EN LA EUROPA DE LA POSGUERRA." INT/ORG NAT/G POL/PAR PLAN ECO/TAC ATTIT ORD/FREE WEALTH...HIST/WRIT COLD/WAR EEC 20. PAGE 127 A2596
EUR+WWI ECO/DEV CAP/ISM

S64
TAUBENFELD R.K.,"INDEPENDENT REVENUE FOR THE UNITED NATIONS." WOR+45 SOCIETY STRUCT INDUS NAT/G CONSULT ACT/RES PLAN ECO/TAC LEGIT WEALTH...DECISION CON/ANAL GEN/METH UN 20. PAGE 142 A2896
INT/ORG FINAN

S64
TRISKA J.F.,"SOVIET TREATY LAW: A QUANTITATIVE ANALYSIS." WOR+45 LAW ECO/UNDEV AGRI COM/IND INDUS CREATE TEC/DEV DIPLOM ATTIT PWR WEALTH...JURID SAMP TIME/SEQ TREND CHARTS VAL/FREE 20 TREATY. PAGE 145 A2967
COM ECO/TAC INT/LAW USSR

S64
ZARTMAN I.W.,"LES RELATIONS ENTRE LA FRANCE ET L'ALGERIA DEPUIS LES ACCORDS D'EVIAN." EUR+WWI FUT ISLAM CULTURE AGRI EXTR/IND FINAN INDUS POL/PAR DIPLOM ECO/TAC FOR/AID PEACE ATTIT DRIVE ALL/VALS ...TIME/SEQ VAL/FREE 20. PAGE 169 A3446
ECO/UNDEV ALGERIA FRANCE

B65
ANALYSIS AND ASSESSMENT OF THE ECONOMIC EFFECTS: PUBLIC LAW 480 TITLE I PROGRAM TURKEY. INDIA TURKEY USA+45 AGRI NAT/G PLAN BUDGET DIPLOM COST EFFICIENCY...CHARTS 20. PAGE 3 A0070
ECO/TAC FOR/AID FINAN ECO/UNDEV

B65
ADENAUER K.,MEMOIRS 1945-53. EUR+WWI GERMANY/W ECO/DEV CHIEF FORCES ECO/TAC WAR GOV/REL PWR SOVEREIGN 20 NATO ADENAUER/K. PAGE 4 A0088
BIOG DIPLOM NAT/G PERS/REL

B65
AMERICAN ECONOMIC ASSOCIATION,INDEX OF ECONOMIC JOURNALS 1886-1965 (7 VOLS.). UK USA+45 USA-45 AGRI FINAN PLAN ECO/TAC INT/TRADE ADMIN...STAT CENSUS 19/20. PAGE 7 A0145
BIBLIOG WRITING INDUS

B65
BROOKINGS INSTITUTION,BROOKINGS PAPERS ON PUBLIC POLICY. USA+45 ECO/UNDEV LEGIS CAP/ISM ECO/TAC TAX EDU/PROP CONTROL APPORT 20. PAGE 19 A0395
DIPLOM FOR/AID POLICY FINAN

B65
CASSELL F.,GOLD OR CREDIT? THE ECONOMICS AND POLITICS OF INTERNATIONAL MONEY. WOR+45 PLAN PROB/SOLV BAL/PAY SOVEREIGN WEALTH 20 OEEC GOLD/STAND. PAGE 25 A0506
FINAN INT/ORG DIPLOM ECO/TAC

B65
CORDIER A.W.,THE QUEST FOR PEACE. WOR+45 NAT/G PLAN BAL/PWR ECO/TAC ARMS/CONT NUC/PWR PWR...ANTHOL UN COLD/WAR. PAGE 30 A0617
PEACE DIPLOM POLICY INT/ORG

B65
COWEN Z.,THE BRITISH COMMONWEALTH OF NATIONS IN A CHANGING WORLD. UK ECO/UNDEV INT/ORG ECO/TAC INT/TRADE COLONIAL WAR GP/REL RACE/REL SOVEREIGN SOC/INTEG 20 TREATY EEC COMMONWLTH. PAGE 32 A0644
JURID DIPLOM PARL/PROC NAT/LISM

B65
FAGG J.E.,CUBA, HAITI, AND THE DOMINICAN REPUBLIC. CUBA DOMIN/REP HAITI L/A+17C NAT/G DIPLOM ECO/TAC DOMIN CHOOSE AUTHORIT ROLE SOVEREIGN POPULISM 17/20. PAGE 43 A0883
COLONIAL ECO/UNDEV REV GOV/COMP

B65
HOSELITZ B.F.,ECONOMICS AND THE IDEA OF MANKIND. UNIV ECO/DEV ECO/UNDEV DIST/IND INDUS INT/ORG NAT/G ACT/RES ECO/TAC WEALTH...CONCPT STAT. PAGE 68 A1392
CREATE INT/TRADE

B65
JALEE P.,THE PILLAGE OF THE THIRD WORLD (TRANS. BY MARY KLOPPER). WOR+45 AGRI INDUS ECO/TAC FOR/AID COLONIAL CONTROL PRODUC PWR WEALTH...STAT CHARTS 20 RESOURCE/N. PAGE 73 A1493
ECO/UNDEV DOMIN INT/TRADE DIPLOM

B65
JOHNSTONE A.,UNITED STATES DIRECT INVESTMENT IN FRANCE: AN INVESTIGATION OF THE FRENCH CHARGES. FRANCE USA+45 ECO/DEV INDUS LG/CO NAT/G ECO/TAC CONTROL WEALTH...BIBLIOG 20 INTERVENT. PAGE 75 A1529
FINAN DIPLOM POLICY SOVEREIGN

B65
KIRKWOOD K.,BRITAIN AND AFRICA. AFR UK ECO/UNDEV ECO/TAC WAR NAT/LISM SOVEREIGN 19/20. PAGE 80 A1636
NAT/G DIPLOM POLICY COLONIAL

B65
LEISS A.C.,APARTHEID AND UNITED NATIONS COLLECTIVE MEASURES. SOUTH/AFR ECO/UNDEV EXTR/IND FORCES WORKER ECO/TAC FOR/AID INT/TRADE WEALTH...TREND CHARTS 20 UN NEGRO. PAGE 86 A1770
DISCRIM RACE/REL STRATA DIPLOM

B65
LIEUWEN E.,U.S. POLICY IN LATIN AMERICA: A SHORT HISTORY. L/A+17C USA+45 USA-45 DELIB/GP ECO/TAC 19/20 COLD/WAR MONROE/DOC. PAGE 89 A1812
DIPLOM COLONIAL NAT/G FOR/AID

B65
MACDONALD R.W.,THE LEAGUE OF ARAB STATES: A STUDY IN THE DYNAMICS OF REGIONAL ORGANIZATION. ISRAEL UAR USSR FINAN INT/ORG DELIB/GP ECO/TAC AGREE NEUTRAL ORD/FREE PWR...DECISION BIBLIOG 20 TREATY UN. PAGE 92 A1888
ISLAM REGION DIPLOM ADMIN

B65
MANSFIELD P.,NASSER'S EGYPT. AFR ISLAM UAR ECO/UNDEV AGRI COLONIAL SOVEREIGN...CHARTS 20 NASSER/G MID/EAST. PAGE 94 A1934
CHIEF ECO/TAC DIPLOM POLICY

B65
MIDDLETON D.,CRISIS IN THE WEST. EUR+WWI FUT WOR+45 CHIEF PLAN ECO/TAC LEAD REGION NUC/PWR NAT/LISM MARXISM 20 COLD/WAR NATO EEC. PAGE 101 A2068
INT/ORG DIPLOM NAT/G POLICY

B65
MONCRIEFF A.,SECOND THOUGHTS ON AID. WOR+45 ECO/UNDEV AGRI FINAN VOL/ASSN PLAN TEC/DEV GIVE EDU/PROP ROLE WEALTH 20. PAGE 102 A2105
FOR/AID ECO/TAC INT/ORG IDEA/COMP

B65
MURUMBI J.,PROBLEMS OF ECONOMIC DEVELOPMENT IN EAST AFRICA. FINAN INDUS WORKER TEC/DEV INT/TRADE TAX DEMAND EFFICIENCY PRODUC SOCISM...TREND CHARTS 20 AFRICA/E. PAGE 106 A2184
AGRI ECO/TAC ECO/UNDEV PROC/MFG

B65
NKRUMAH K.,NEO-COLONIALISM: THE LAST STAGE OF IMPERIALISM. AFR INT/ORG WORKER FOR/AID INT/TRADE EDU/PROP GOV/REL NAT/LISM SOVEREIGN POPULISM SOCISM ...SOCIALIST 20 THIRD/WRLD INTRVN/ECO. PAGE 109 A2243
COLONIAL DIPLOM ECO/UNDEV ECO/TAC

B65
RAPPAPORT A.,ISSUES IN AMERICAN DIPLOMACY: WORLD POWER AND LEADERSHIP SINCE 1895 (VOL. II). CHINA/COM EUR+WWI L/A+17C USA+45 USA-45 NAT/G ECO/TAC DOMIN CONFER LEAD NUC/PWR WEAPON...DECISION 19/20 WILSON/W ROOSEVLT/F CHINJAP. PAGE 119 A2447
WAR POLICY DIPLOM

B65
ROLFE S.E.,GOLD AND WORLD POWER. UK USA+45 WOR-45 INDUS WORKER INT/TRADE DEMAND...MGT CHARTS 20 GOLD/STAND. PAGE 123 A2517
BAL/PAY EQUILIB ECO/TAC DIPLOM

B65
SABLE M.H.,PERIODICALS FOR LATIN AMERICAN ECONOMIC DEVELOPMENT, TRADE, AND FINANCE: AN ANNOTATED BIBLIOGRAPHY (A PAMPHLET). ECO/TAC PRODUC PROFIT ...STAT NAT/COMP 20 OAS. PAGE 126 A2583
BIBLIOG/A L/A+17C ECO/UNDEV INT/TRADE

B65
SCOTT A.M.,THE REVOLUTION IN STATECRAFT: INFORMAL PENETRATION. WOR+45 WOR-45 CULTURE INT/ORG FORCES ECO/TAC ROUTINE...BIBLIOG 20. PAGE 130 A2670
DIPLOM EDU/PROP FOR/AID

B65
TREFOUSSE H.L.,THE COLD WAR: A BOOK OF DOCUMENTS. ASIA L/A+17C USSR WOR+45 WOR-45 ECO/TAC FOR/AID ARMS/CONT NUC/PWR PEACE ORD/FREE...ANTHOL 20 COLD/WAR KENNEDY/JF EISNHWR/DD. PAGE 145 A2961
BAL/PWR DIPLOM MARXISM

B65
US HOUSE COMM FOREIGN AFFAIRS,HEARINGS ON DRAFT BILL TO AMEND FURTHER THE FOREIGN ASSISTANCE ACT OF 1961. AFR ASIA L/A+17C USA+45 INT/ORG DELIB/GP TEC/DEV ECO/TAC CONFER TOTALISM 20 CONGRESS AID. PAGE 153 A3131
FOR/AID ECO/UNDEV DIPLOM ORD/FREE

B65
US SENATE COMM BANKING CURR,BALANCE OF PAYMENTS - 1965. USA+45 ECO/TAC PRICE WEALTH...CHARTS 20 CONGRESS GOLD/STAND. PAGE 156 A3171
BAL/PAY FINAN DIPLOM INT/TRADE

B65
US SENATE COMM ON JUDICIARY,ANTITRUST EXEMPTIONS FOR AGREEMENTS RELATING TO BALANCE OF PAYMENTS. FINAN ECO/TAC CONTROL WEALTH...POLICY 20 CONGRESS. PAGE 157 A3195
BAL/PAY ADJUD MARKET INT/TRADE

B65
WHITE J.,GERMAN AID. GERMANY/W FINAN PLAN TEC/DEV INT/TRADE ADMIN ATTIT...POLICY 20. PAGE 164 A3335
FOR/AID ECO/UNDEV DIPLOM ECO/TAC

L65
KAPLAN M.A.,"OLD REALITIES AND NEW MYTHS." USA+45 WOR+45 INT/ORG NAT/G TOP/EX ACT/RES BAL/PWR ECO/TAC EDU/PROP LEGIT RIGID/FLEX ALL/VALS...RECORD COLD/WAR 20. PAGE 76 A1564
ATTIT MYTH DIPLOM

L65
WIONCZEK M.,"LATIN AMERICA FREE TRADE ASSOCIATION." AGRI DIST/IND FINAN INDUS INT/ORG LABOR NAT/G TEC/DEV ECO/TAC HEALTH SKILL WEALTH...POLICY RELATIV MGT LAFTA 20. PAGE 165 A3369
L/A+17C MARKET REGION

S65
FLEMING D.F.,"CAN PAX AMERICANA SUCCEED?" ASIA CHINA/COM EUR+WWI USSR VIETNAM BAL/PWR DIPLOM DOMIN COERCE GOV/REL 20. PAGE 46 A0948
DECISION ATTIT ECO/TAC

S65
KHOURI F.J.,"THE JORDON RIVER CONTROVERSY." LAW SOCIETY ECO/UNDEV AGRI FINAN INDUS SECT FORCES ACT/RES PLAN TEC/DEV ECO/TAC EDU/PROP COERCE ATTIT DRIVE PERCEPT RIGID/FLEX ALL/VALS...GEOG SOC MYTH WORK. PAGE 78 A1610
ISLAM INT/ORG ISRAEL JORDAN

S65
KORBONSKI A.,"USA POLICY IN EAST EUROPE." COM EUR+WWI GERMANY USA+45 CULTURE ECO/UNDEV EDU/PROP RIGID/FLEX WEALTH 20. PAGE 82 A1672
ACT/RES ECO/TAC FOR/AID

S65
QUADE Q.L.,"THE TRUMAN ADMINISTRATION AND THE SEPARATION OF POWERS: THE CASE OF THE MARSHALL PLAN." SOCIETY INT/ORG NAT/G CONSULT DELIB/GP LEGIS PLAN ECO/TAC ROUTINE DRIVE PERCEPT RIGID/FLEX ORD/FREE PWR WEALTH...DECISION GEOG NEW/IDEA TREND 20 TRUMAN/HS. PAGE 118 A2422
USA+45 ECO/UNDEV DIPLOM

S65
RODNEY W.,"THE ENTENTE STATES OF WEST AFRICA." AFR FRANCE USA+45 POL/PAR SCHOOL FORCES ECO/TAC COLONIAL PWR 20 AFRICA/W. PAGE 123 A2512
DIPLOM POLICY NAT/G ECO/UNDEV

B66
AMERICAN ASSEMBLY COLUMBIA U,A WORLD OF NUCLEAR POWERS? FUT WOR+45 ECO/DEV BAL/PWR ECO/TAC CONTROL RISK EFFICIENCY ATTIT PWR...METH/COMP ANTHOL 20. PAGE 7 A0137
NUC/PWR DIPLOM TEC/DEV ARMS/CONT

B66
BALDWIN D.A.,ECONOMIC DEVELOPMENT AND AMERICAN FOREIGN POLICY. USA+45 FINAN LG/CO LEGIS DIPLOM GIVE 20. PAGE 10 A0210
ECO/TAC FOR/AID ECO/UNDEV POLICY

B66
ENTWICKLUNGSPOLITIK - HANDBUCH UND LEXIKON. MARKET SECT DIPLOM INT/TRADE EDU/PROP CATHISM 20. PAGE 14 A0283
ECO/UNDEV FOR/AID ECO/TAC PLAN

B66
COLE A.B.,SOCIALIST PARTIES IN POSTWAR JAPAN. STRATA AGRI LABOR PLAN DIPLOM ECO/TAC AGREE LEAD CHOOSE ATTIT...CHARTS 20 CHINJAP SOC/DEMPAR. PAGE 28 A0566
POL/PAR POLICY SOCISM NAT/G

B66
DYCK H.V.,WEIMAR GERMANY AND SOVIET RUSSIA 1926-1933. EUR+WWI GERMANY UK USSR ECO/TAC INT/TRADE NEUTRAL WAR ATTIT 20 WEIMAR/REP TREATY. PAGE 40 A0814
DIPLOM GOV/REL POLICY

B66
EDWARDS C.D.,TRADE REGULATIONS OVERSEAS. IRELAND NEW/ZEALND SOUTH/AFR NAT/G CAP/ISM TARIFFS CONTROL ...POLICY JURID 20 EEC CHINJAP. PAGE 40 A0823
INT/TRADE DIPLOM INT/LAW ECO/TAC

B66
EWING L.L.,THE REFERENCE HANDBOOK OF THE ARMED FORCES OF THE WORLD. WOR+45 ECO/TAC FOR/AID COERCE WAR PWR 20. PAGE 43 A0879
FORCES STAT DIPLOM PLAN

B66
FINKLE J.L.,POLITICAL DEVELOPMENT AND SOCIAL CHANGE. WOR+45 CULTURE NAT/G OP/RES PROB/SOLV DIPLOM ECO/TAC INGP/REL...METH/COMP ANTHOL 20. PAGE 46 A0934
ECO/UNDEV SOCIETY CREATE

B66
FITZGERALD C.P.,THE BIRTH OF COMMUNIST CHINA (2ND ED.). ASIA CHINA/COM STRUCT BAL/PWR DIPLOM ECO/TAC INT/TRADE WEALTH 20. PAGE 46 A0942
REV MARXISM ECO/UNDEV

B66
FREIDEL F.,AMERICAN ISSUES IN THE TWENTIETH CENTURY. SOCIETY FINAN ECO/TAC FOR/AID CONTROL NUC/PWR WAR RACE/REL PEACE ATTIT...ANTHOL T 20 WILSON/W ROOSEVLT/F KENNEDY/JF TRUMAN/HS. PAGE 49 A0995
DIPLOM POLICY NAT/G ORD/FREE

B66
HALLET R.,PEOPLE AND PROGRESS IN WEST AFRICA: AN INTRODUCTION TO THE PROBLEMS OF DEVELOPMENT. COM/IND INDUS KIN DIPLOM FOR/AID INT/TRADE HEALTH ...GEOG TREND CHARTS BIBLIOG/A 20 AFRICA/W. PAGE 60 A1233
AFR SOCIETY ECO/UNDEV ECO/TAC

B66
HOLT R.T.,THE POLITICAL BASIS OF ECONOMIC DEVELOPMENT. STRATA STRUCT NAT/G DIPLOM ADMIN...SOC NAT/COMP BIBLIOG 20. PAGE 67 A1376
ECO/TAC GOV/COMP CONSTN EX/STRUC

B66
HOROWITZ D.,HEMISPHERES NORTH AND SOUTH: ECONOMIC DISPARITY AMONG NATIONS. WOR+45 ECO/DEV ECO/UNDEV INT/ORG PLAN DIPLOM INT/TRADE GIVE PARTIC GP/REL ...WELF/ST 20. PAGE 67 A1387
ECO/TAC FOR/AID STRATA WEALTH

B66
INTERNATIONAL ECO POLICY ASSN,THE UNITED STATES BALANCE OF PAYMENTS. INT/ORG NAT/G PROB/SOLV BUDGET DIPLOM INT/TRADE WEALTH 20. PAGE 71 A1454
BAL/PAY ECO/TAC POLICY FINAN

B66
INTL CONF ON WORLD POLITICS-5,EASTERN EUROPE IN TRANSITION. EUR+WWI USSR ECO/TAC NAT/LISM ATTIT SOVEREIGN...CHARTS ANTHOL 20 TREATY WARSAW/P. PAGE 71 A1463
COM NAT/COMP MARXISM DIPLOM

B66
KANET R.E.,THE SOVIET UNION AND SUB-SAHARAN AFRICA: COMMUNIST POLICY TOWARD AFRICA, 1917-1965. AFR USSR ECO/UNDEV TEC/DEV EDU/PROP TASK DISCRIM PEACE WEALTH ALL/IDEOS...CHARTS BIBLIOG SOC/INTEG 19/20 NEGRO UN INTERVENT. PAGE 76 A1555
DIPLOM ECO/TAC MARXISM

B66
LALL A.,MODERN INTERNATIONAL NEGOTIATION: PRINCIPLES AND PRACTICE. WOR+45 INT/ORG DELIB/GP PROB/SOLV DETER...INT/LAW TREATY. PAGE 84 A1712
DIPLOM ECO/TAC ATTIT

B66
LAMBERG R.F.,PRAG UND DIE DRITTE WELT. AFR ASIA CZECHOSLVK L/A+17C MARKET TEC/DEV ECO/TAC REV ATTIT 20 TREATY. PAGE 84 A1713
DIPLOM ECO/UNDEV INT/TRADE FOR/AID

B66
MEERHAEGHE M.,INTERNATIONAL ECONOMIC INSTITUTIONS. EUR+WWI FINAN INDUS MARKET PLAN TARIFFS BAL/PAY EQUILIB...POLICY BIBLIOG/A 20 GATT OEEC EEC IBRD EURCOALSTL. PAGE 99 A2032
ECO/TAC ECO/DEV INT/TRADE INT/ORG

B66
MONTGOMERY J.D.,APPROACHES TO DEVELOPMENT: POLITICS, ADMINISTRATION AND CHANGE. USA+45 AGRI FOR/AID ORD/FREE...CONCPT IDEA/COMP METH/COMP ANTHOL. PAGE 103 A2116
ECO/UNDEV ADMIN POLICY ECO/TAC

B66
MOOMAW I.W.,THE CHALLENGE OF HUNGER. USA+45 PLAN ADMIN EATING 20. PAGE 103 A2118
FOR/AID DIPLOM ECO/UNDEV ECO/TAC

B66
MURPHY G.G.,SOVIET MONGOLIA: A STUDY OF THE OLDEST POLITICAL SATELLITE. USSR STRATA STRUCT COST INCOME ATTIT SOCISM 20. PAGE 106 A2177
DIPLOM ECO/TAC PLAN DOMIN

B66
PAN S.,VIETNAM CRISIS. ASIA FRANCE USA+45 USA-45 VIETNAM CULTURE SOCIETY INT/ORG ECO/TAC AGREE CONTROL WAR MARXISM 20. PAGE 113 A2325
ECO/UNDEV POLICY DIPLOM NAT/COMP

B66
PASSIN H.,THE UNITED STATES AND JAPAN. USA+45 INDUS CAP/ISM...TREND 20 CHINJAP TREATY. PAGE 114 A2337
DIPLOM INT/TRADE ECO/DEV ECO/TAC

B66
PIQUET H.S.,THE US BALANCE OF PAYMENTS AND INTERNATIONAL MONETARY RESERVES. USA+45 PROB/SOLV INT/TRADE GOV/REL EQUILIB...POLICY STAT CHARTS 20 GOLD/STAND. PAGE 116 A2384
BAL/PAY DIPLOM FINAN ECO/TAC

B66
SALTER L.M.,RESOLUTION OF INTERNATIONAL CONFLICT. USA+45 INT/ORG SECT DIPLOM ECO/TAC FOR/AID DETER NUC/PWR WAR 20. PAGE 127 A2595
PROB/SOLV PEACE INT/LAW POLICY

B66
SAPIN B.M.,THE MAKING OF UNITED STATES FOREIGN POLICY. USA+45 INT/ORG DELIB/GP FORCES PLAN ECO/TAC CIVMIL/REL PRESIDENT. PAGE 127 A2603
DIPLOM EX/STRUC DECISION NAT/G

B66
SCHATTEN F.,COMMUNISM IN AFRICA. AFR GHANA GUINEA MALI CULTURE ECO/UNDEV LABOR SECT ECO/TAC EDU/PROP REV 20. PAGE 128 A2619
COLONIAL NAT/LISM MARXISM

DIPLOM

B66
SINGH L.P.,THE POLITICS OF ECONOMIC COOPERATION IN ASIA; A STUDY OF ASIAN INTERNATIONAL ORGANIZATIONS. ASIA INT/ORG ACT/RES PLAN GP/REL...POLICY GP/COMP BIBLIOG 20 UN SEATO. PAGE 133 A2733
ECO/UNDEV ECO/TAC REGION DIPLOM

B66
SKILLING H.G.,THE GOVERNMENTS OF COMMUNIST EAST EUROPE. COM EUR+WWI ELITES FORCES DIPLOM ECO/TAC CONTROL HABITAT SOCISM...DECISION BIBLIOG 20 EUROPE/E COM/PARTY. PAGE 134 A2738
MARXISM NAT/COMP GP/COMP DOMIN

B66
SPINELLI A.,THE EUROCRATS; CONFLICT AND CRISIS IN THE EUROPEAN COMMUNITY (TRANS. BY C. GROVE HAINES). EUR+WWI MARKET POL/PAR ECO/TAC PARL/PROC EEC OEEC ECSC EURATOM. PAGE 136 A2789
INT/ORG INGP/REL CONSTN ADMIN

B66
TRIFFIN R.,THE WORLD MONEY MAZE. INT/ORG ECO/TAC PRICE OPTIMAL WEALTH...METH/COMP 20 EEC OEEC GOLD/STAND SILVER. PAGE 145 A2964
BAL/PAY FINAN INT/TRADE DIPLOM

B66
TRIFFIN R.,THE BALANCE OF PAYMENTS AND THE FOREIGN INVESTMENT POSITION OF THE UNITED STATES. USA+45 INT/ORG INT/TRADE PRICE CONTROL...POLICY 20 GOLD/STAND. PAGE 145 A2965
BAL/PAY DIPLOM FINAN ECO/TAC

B66
US CONGRESS JOINT ECO COMM,NEW APPROACH TO UNITED STATES INTERNATIONAL ECONOMIC POLICY. USA+45 WOR+45 CHIEF DELIB/GP CONFER...CHARTS 20 CONGRESS MONEY. PAGE 150 A3070
DIPLOM ECO/TAC BAL/PAY FINAN

B66
US HOUSE COMM FOREIGN AFFAIRS,HEARINGS ON HR 12449 A BILL TO AMEND FURTHER THE FOREIGN ASSISTANCE ACT OF 1961. AFR ASIA L/A+17C USA+45 VIETNAM INT/ORG TEC/DEV INT/TRADE ATTIT ORD/FREE 20 UN NATO CONGRESS AID. PAGE 154 A3132
FOR/AID ECO/TAC ECO/UNDEV DIPLOM

B66
WARBURG J.P.,THE UNITED STATES IN THE POSTWAR WORLD. USA+45 ECO/TAC...POLICY 20 COLD/WAR. PAGE 161 A3277
FOR/AID DIPLOM PLAN ADMIN

B66
WESTIN A.F.,VIEWS OF AMERICA. COM USA+45 USSR SOCIETY ECO/UNDEV POL/PAR ECO/TAC GP/REL STRANGE MARXISM...MARXIST 20. PAGE 163 A3323
CONCPT ATTIT DIPLOM IDEA/COMP

B66
WESTWOOD A.F.,FOREIGN AID IN A FOREIGN POLICY FRAMEWORK. AFR ASIA INDIA IRAN L/A+17C USA+45 USSR ECO/UNDEV AGRI FORCES LEGIS PLAN PROB/SOLV ...DECISION 20 COLD/WAR. PAGE 163 A3324
FOR/AID DIPLOM POLICY ECO/TAC

B66
WILLIAMS P.,AID IN UGANDA - EDUCATION. UGANDA UK FINAN ACADEM INT/ORG SCHOOL PROB/SOLV ECO/TAC UTIL ...STAT CHARTS 20. PAGE 165 A3352
PLAN EDU/PROP FOR/AID ECO/UNDEV

B66
YEAGER L.B.,INTERNATIONAL MONETARY RELATIONS: THEORY, HISTORY, AND POLICY. WOR+45 WOR-45 INT/TRADE BAL/PAY...NAT/COMP 18/20 MONEY. PAGE 169 A3432
FINAN DIPLOM ECO/TAC IDEA/COMP

B66
ZISCHKA A.,WAR ES EIN WUNDER? GERMANY/W ECO/DEV FINAN LG/CO BARGAIN CAP/ISM FOR/AID RATION 20 MARSHL/PLN. PAGE 170 A3456
ECO/TAC INT/TRADE INDUS WAR

S66
GAMER R.E.,"URGENT SINGAPORE, PATIENT MALAYSIA." MALAYSIA S/ASIA ECO/UNDEV POL/PAR CHIEF TARIFFS TAX CONTROL LEAD REGION PWR 20 SINGAPORE. PAGE 51 A1036
DIPLOM NAT/G POLICY ECO/TAC

S66
JAVITS J.K.,"POLITICAL ACTION VITAL FOR LATIN AMERICAN INTEGRATION." ECO/UNDEV INT/ORG POL/PAR VOL/ASSN PLAN PROB/SOLV INT/TRADE EFFICIENCY 20 OAS LAFTA. PAGE 73 A1500
L/A+17C ECO/TAC REGION

S66
SKILLING H.G.,"THE RUMANIAN NATIONAL COURSE." COM EUR+WWI ROMANIA NAT/G ECO/TAC PWR 20. PAGE 134 A2739
NAT/LISM POLICY DIPLOM MARXISM

N66
EOMMITTEE ECONOMIC DEVELOPMENT,THE DOLLAR AND THE WORLD MONETARY SYSTEM: A STATEMENT ON NATIONAL POLICY (PAMPHLET). USA+45 NAT/G PLAN PROB/SOLV BUDGET ECO/TAC FOR/AID INCOME...POLICY 20 GOLD/STAND EUROPE. PAGE 42 A0854
FINAN BAL/PAY DIPLOM ECO/DEV

B67
AUBREY H.G.,ATLANTIC ECONOMIC COOPERATION. ECO/DEV INDUS VOL/ASSN PROB/SOLV DIPLOM INT/TRADE TARIFFS CONFER 20. PAGE 10 A0197
INT/ORG ECO/TAC TEC/DEV CAP/ISM

B67
CLARK S.V.O.,CENTRAL BANK COOPERATION: 1924-31. WOR-45 PROB/SOLV ECO/TAC ADJUST BAL/PAY...TREND CHARTS METH/COMP 20. PAGE 27 A0542
FINAN EQUILIB DIPLOM POLICY

B67
HIRSCHMAN A.O.,DEVELOPMENT PROJECTS OBSERVED. INDUS INT/ORG CONSULT EX/STRUC CREATE OP/RES ECO/TAC DEMAND...POLICY MGT METH/COMP 20 WORLD/BANK. PAGE 65 A1339
ECO/UNDEV R+D FINAN PLAN

B67
HOLLERMAN L.,JAPAN'S DEPENDENCE ON THE WORLD ECONOMY. INDUS MARKET LABOR NAT/G DIPLOM 20 CHINJAP. PAGE 67 A1369
PLAN ECO/DEV ECO/TAC INT/TRADE

B67
POGANY A.H.,POLITICAL SCIENCE AND INTERNATIONAL RELATIONS, BOOKS RECOMMENDED FOR AMERICAN CATHOLIC COLLEGE LIBRARIES. INT/ORG LOC/G NAT/G FORCES BAL/PWR ECO/TAC NUC/PWR...CATH INT/LAW TREATY 20. PAGE 117 A2393
BIBLIOG DIPLOM

B67
ROACH J.R.,THE UNITED STATES AND THE ATLANTIC COMMUNITY; ISSUES AND PROSPECTS. WOR+45 TEC/DEV ECO/TAC COLONIAL REGION PEACE ROLE...ANTHOL NATO COLD/WAR EEC. PAGE 121 A2491
INT/ORG POLICY ADJUST DIPLOM

B67
RUEFF J.,BALANCE OF PAYMENTS. WOR+45 FINAN TEC/DEV DIPLOM TARIFFS PRICE CONTROL...POLICY CONCPT IDEA/COMP. PAGE 125 A2567
INT/TRADE BAL/PAY ECO/TAC NAT/COMP

B67
SHAFFER H.G.,THE COMMUNIST WORLD: MARXIST AND NON-MARXIST VIEWS. WOR+45 SOCIETY DIPLOM ECO/TAC CONTROL SOCISM...MARXIST ANTHOL BIBLIOG/A 20. PAGE 131 A2691
MARXISM NAT/COMP IDEA/COMP COM

B67
UNIVERSAL REFERENCE SYSTEM,ECONOMIC REGULATION, BUSINESS, AND GOVERNMENT (VOLUME VIII). WOR+45 WOR-45 ECO/DEV ECO/UNDEV FINAN LABOR TEC/DEV ECO/TAC INT/TRADE GOV/REL...POLICY COMPUT/IR. PAGE 149 A3043
BIBLIOG/A CONTROL NAT/G

B67
US AGENCY INTERNATIONAL DEV,PROPOSED FOREIGN AID PROGRAM FOR 1968: SUMMARY PRESENTATION TO THE CONGRESS. AFR S/ASIA USA+45 AGRI TEC/DEV DIPLOM ECO/TAC BAL/PAY COST HEALTH KNOWL SKILL 20 AID CONGRESS. PAGE 149 A3053
ECO/UNDEV BUDGET FOR/AID STAT

B67
US DEPARTMENT OF STATE,THE COUNTRY TEAM - AN ILLUSTRATED PROFILE OF OUR AMERICAN MISSIONS ABROAD. ECO/TAC FOR/AID EDU/PROP TASK PERS/REL ATTIT 20. PAGE 152 A3099
DIPLOM NAT/G VOL/ASSN GOV/REL

L67
DEVADHAR Y.C.,"THE ROLE OF FOREIGN PRIVATE CAPITAL IN INDIA'S ECONOMIC DEVELOPMENT* ASSESSMENT OF POLICY AND PERFORMANCE." INDIA INDUS PLAN TEC/DEV BUDGET DIPLOM ECO/TAC BAL/PAY PRODUC WEALTH ...CHARTS 20. PAGE 37 A0750
CAP/ISM FOR/AID POLICY ACT/RES

L67
GALTUNG J.,"ON THE EFFECTS OF INTERNATIONAL ECONOMIC SANCTIONS, WITH EXAMPLES FROM THE CASE OF RHODESIA." NAT/G DIPLOM EDU/PROP ADJUST EFFICIENCY ATTIT MORAL...OBS CHARTS 20. PAGE 51 A1035
SANCTION ECO/TAC INT/TRADE ECO/UNDEV

L67
MACDONALD R.S.J.,"THE RESORT TO ECONOMIC COERCION BY INTERNATIONAL POLITICAL ORGANIZATIONS." CUBA ETHIOPIA RHODESIA SOUTH/AFR NAT/G FOR/AID INT/TRADE DOMIN CONTROL SANCTION...DECISION LEAGUE/NAT UN OAS 20. PAGE 92 A1887
INT/ORG COERCE ECO/TAC DIPLOM

S67
APEL H.,"LES NOUVEAUX ASPECTS DE LA POLITIQUE ETRANGERE ALLEMANDE." EUR+WWI GERMANY POL/PAR BAL/PWR ECO/TAC INT/TRADE NUC/PWR NAT/LISM PEACE ...POLICY 20 EEC COLD/WAR. PAGE 8 A0168
DIPLOM INT/ORG FEDERAL

S67
BUTT R.,"THE COMMON MARKET AND CONSERVATIVE POLITICS, 1961-2." UK CHIEF DIPLOM ECO/TAC INT/TRADE CONFER DEBATE REGION ATTIT...POLICY 20 EEC. PAGE 22 A0454
EUR+WWI INT/ORG POL/PAR

S67
CHAND A.,"INDIA AND TANZANIA." INDIA TANZANIA TEC/DEV ECO/TAC FOR/AID COLONIAL PEACE UTIL WEALTH ...GOV/COMP 20. PAGE 25 A0518
ECO/UNDEV NEUTRAL DIPLOM PLAN

S67
COSGROVE C.A.,"AGRICULTURE, FINANCE AND POLITICS IN THE EUROPEAN COMMUNITY." EUR+WWI DIST/IND MARKET INT/ORG VOL/ASSN DELIB/GP TEC/DEV BAL/PWR BARGAIN ECO/TAC RATION CONFER 20 EEC. PAGE 31 A0630
ECO/DEV DIPLOM AGRI INT/TRADE

S67
DE ROUGEMENT D.,"THE CAMPAIGN OF THE EUROPEAN CONGRESSES." ELITES INTELL DIPLOM ECO/TAC CONFER PEACE...POLICY PREDICT. PAGE 35 A0710
EUR+WWI REGION FEDERAL INT/ORG

S67
FELDMAN H.,"AID AS IMPERIALISM?" INDIA PAKISTAN UK USA+45 BAL/PWR CAP/ISM DIPLOM ECO/TAC DOMIN BAL/PAY WEALTH...POLICY 20. PAGE 45 A0914
COLONIAL FOR/AID S/ASIA

ECO/UNDEV
S67
FRANK I.,"NEW PERSPECTIVES ON TRADE AND DEVELOPMENT." PROB/SOLV BARGAIN DIPLOM FOR/AID CONFER GP/REL WEALTH 20 UN GATT. PAGE 48 A0980 ECO/UNDEV INT/ORG INT/TRADE ECO/TAC
S67
FRANKLIN W.O.,"CLAUSEWITZ ON LIMITED WAR." VIETNAM WOR+45 WOR-45 PROB/SOLV DIPLOM ECO/TAC DOMIN COLONIAL...METH/COMP 19/20. PAGE 48 A0986 COERCE WAR PLAN GUERRILLA
S67
FRENCH D.S.,"DOES THE U.S. EXPLOIT THE DEVELOPING NATIONS?" INT/ORG NAT/G CAP/ISM BAL/PAY WEALTH POLICY. PAGE 49 A0997 ECO/UNDEV INT/TRADE ECO/TAC COLONIAL
S67
GOLDMAN M.I.,"SOVIET ECONOMIC GROWTH SINCE THE REVOLUTION." USSR WORKER INT/TRADE PRODUC MARXISM ...POLICY TIME/SEQ 20. PAGE 53 A1090 ECO/DEV AGRI ECO/TAC INDUS
S67
HALL M.,"GERMANY, EAST AND WEST* DANGER AT THE CROSSROADS." GERMANY ELITES CHIEF FORCES DIPLOM ECO/TAC REPAR ARMS/CONT...SOCIALIST 20. PAGE 60 A1227 NAT/LISM ATTIT FASCISM WEAPON
S67
HEATH D.B.,"BOLIVIA UNDER BARRIENTOS." L/A+17C NAT/G CHIEF DIPLOM ECO/TAC...POLICY 20 BOLIV. PAGE 64 A1306 ECO/UNDEV POL/PAR REV CONSTN
S67
HULL E.W.S.,"THE POLITICAL OCEAN." FUT UNIV WOR+45 EXTR/IND R+D VOL/ASSN PLAN BAL/PWR ECO/TAC PEACE WEALTH 20 UN. PAGE 69 A1414 DIPLOM ECO/UNDEV INT/ORG INT/LAW
S67
JAVITS J.K.,"LAST CHANCE FOR A COMMON MARKET." L/A+17C INT/ORG 20 EEC LAFTA. PAGE 73 A1501 FOR/AID ECO/UNDEV INT/TRADE ECO/TAC
S67
JOHNSON J.,"THE UNITED STATES AND THE LATIN AMERICAN LEFT WINGS." L/A+17C STRATA POL/PAR INT/TRADE 20. PAGE 74 A1524 ECO/UNDEV WORKER ECO/TAC REGION
S67
KAISER R.G.,"THE TRUMAN DOCTRINE* HOW IT ALL BEGAN." COM EUR+WWI USA+45 R+D INT/ORG BAL/PWR ECO/TAC PEACE TRUMAN/DOC. PAGE 76 A1550 DIPLOM ECO/UNDEV FOR/AID
S67
KRAUS J.,"A MARXIST IN GHANA." GHANA ELITES CHIEF PROB/SOLV TEC/DEV DIPLOM ECO/TAC COLONIAL PARTIC PWR 20 NKRUMAH/K. PAGE 82 A1676 MARXISM PLAN ATTIT CREATE
S67
LEFF N.H.,"EXPORT STAGNATION AND AUTARKIC DEVELOPMENT IN BRAZIL, 19471962." BRAZIL ECO/TAC TARIFFS 20. PAGE 86 A1764 BAL/PAY INT/TRADE WEALTH DIPLOM
S67
PAUKER G.J.,"TOWARD A NEW ORDER IN INDONESIA." COM INDONESIA S/ASIA ECO/UNDEV POL/PAR EX/STRUC TOP/EX BAL/PWR ECO/TAC FOR/AID DOMIN NAT/LISM AUTHORIT ORD/FREE PWR 20. PAGE 114 A2342 REV NAT/G DIPLOM CIVMIL/REL
S67
PERLO V.,"NEW DIMENSIONS IN EAST-WEST TRADE." UK USA+45 USSR WOR+45 ECO/DEV NAT/G CAP/ISM PEACE WEALTH LAISSEZ...SOCIALIST MGT 20. PAGE 115 A2364 BAL/PWR ECO/TAC INT/TRADE
S67
PEUKERT W.,"WEST GERMANY'S 'RED TRADE'." COM GERMANY INDUS CAP/ISM DOMIN SANCTION DEMAND PEACE UTIL...MARXIST 20 COLD/WAR. PAGE 115 A2371 DIPLOM ECO/TAC INT/TRADE
S67
ROCKE J.R.M.,"THE BRITISH EXPORT BATTLE FOR THE CARIBBEAN" GP/REL...POLICY 20 CMN/WLTH. PAGE 122 A2510 INT/TRADE DIPLOM MARKET ECO/TAC
S67
SHERSHNEV Y.,"THE KENNEDY ROUND* PLANS AND REALITY." EUR+WWI USA+45 INT/ORG DIPLOM TARIFFS DOMIN CONFER PWR...MARXIST PREDICT. PAGE 132 A2701 ECO/TAC ECO/DEV INT/TRADE BAL/PWR
S67
STEEL R.,"WHAT CAN THE UN DO?" RHODESIA ECO/UNDEV DIPLOM ECO/TAC SANCTION...INT/LAW UN. PAGE 137 A2810 INT/ORG BAL/PWR PEACE FOR/AID
S67
WEIL G.L.,"THE MERGER OF THE INSTITUTIONS OF THE EUROPEAN COMMUNITIES" EUR+WWI ECO/DEV INT/TRADE CONSEN PLURISM...DECISION MGT 20 EEC EURATOM ECSC TREATY. PAGE 162 A3300 ECO/TAC INT/ORG CENTRAL INT/LAW
N67
US GOVERNMENT,TREATIES IN FORCE. NAT/G ECO/TAC FOR/AID INT/TRADE NUC/PWR 20. PAGE 153 A3117 DIPLOM INT/ORG

BAL/PWR
C83
BURKE E.,"RESOLUTIONS FOR CONCILIATION WITH AMERICA" (1775), IN E. BURKE, COLLECTED WORKS, VOL. 2." UK USA-45 FORCES INT/TRADE TARIFFS TAX SANCTION PEACE...POLICY 18 PRE/US/AM. PAGE 21 A0436 COLONIAL WAR SOVEREIGN ECO/TAC

ECO/UNDEV....ECONOMIC SYSTEM IN DEVELOPING COUNTRIES

N
INDIAN COUNCIL WORLD AFFAIRS,SELECT ARTICLES ON CURRENT AFFAIRS (BIBLIOGRAPHICAL SERIES: 7). AFR ASIA COM EUR+WWI S/ASIA UK COLONIAL NUC/PWR PEACE ATTIT...INT/LAW SOC 20. PAGE 70 A1437 BIBLIOG DIPLOM INT/ORG ECO/UNDEV
N
UNIVERSITY OF FLORIDA LIBRARY,DOORS TO LATIN AMERICA; RECENT BOOKS AND PAMPHLETS. CONSTN CULTURE SOCIETY ECO/UNDEV COLONIAL LEAD GOV/REL NAT/LISM ATTIT...HUM SOC 20. PAGE 149 A3047 BIBLIOG/A L/A+17C DIPLOM NAT/G
N
AFRICANA NEWSLETTER. ECO/UNDEV ACADEM SECT DIPLOM PRESS COLONIAL NAT/LISM 20. PAGE 1 A0001 BIBLIOG/A AFR NAT/G
N
BULLETIN ANALYTIQUE DE DOCUMENTATION POLITIQUE, ECONOMIQUE, ET SOCIAL CONTEMPORAIRE. FRANCE WOR+45 SOCIETY ECO/DEV ECO/UNDEV INT/ORG LOC/G PROB/SOLV FOR/AID LEAD REGION SOC. PAGE 1 A0006 BIBLIOG/A DIPLOM NAT/COMP NAT/G
N
INTERNATIONAL AFFAIRS. WOR+45 WOR-45 ECO/UNDEV INT/ORG NAT/G PROB/SOLV FOR/AID WAR...POLICY 20. PAGE 1 A0009 BIBLIOG/A DIPLOM INT/LAW INT/TRADE
N
INTERNATIONAL BOOK NEWS, 1928-1934. ECO/UNDEV FINAN INDUS LABOR INT/TRADE CONFER ADJUD COLONIAL...HEAL SOC/WK CHARTS 20 LEAGUE/NAT. PAGE 1 A0010 BIBLIOG/A DIPLOM INT/LAW INT/ORG
N
INTERNATIONAL REVIEW OF ADMINISTRATIVE SCIENCES. WOR+45 WOR-45 STRATA ECO/DEV ECO/UNDEV CREATE PLAN PROB/SOLV DIPLOM CONTROL REPRESENT...MGT 20. PAGE 1 A0011 BIBLIOG/A ADMIN INT/ORG NAT/G
N
INTERNATIONAL STUDIES. ASIA S/ASIA WOR+45 ECO/UNDEV INT/ORG NAT/G LEAD ATTIT WEALTH...SOC 20. PAGE 1 A0012 BIBLIOG/A DIPLOM INT/LAW INT/TRADE
N
JOURNAL OF INTERNATIONAL AFFAIRS. WOR+45 ECO/UNDEV POL/PAR ECO/TAC WAR PEACE PERSON ALL/IDEOS ...INT/LAW TREND. PAGE 1 A0015 BIBLIOG DIPLOM INT/ORG NAT/G
N
MIDDLE EAST JOURNAL. CULTURE SECT DIPLOM LEAD GOV/REL ATTIT...POLICY PHIL/SCI SOC LING BIOG 20. PAGE 1 A0019 BIBLIOG ISLAM NAT/G ECO/UNDEV
N
NEUE POLITISCHE LITERATUR. AFR ASIA EUR+WWI GERMANY RUSSIA SOCIETY ECO/DEV ECO/UNDEV PLAN PROB/SOLV LEAD MARXISM...PHIL/SCI CONCPT 20. PAGE 1 A0021 BIBLIOG DIPLOM COM NAT/G
N
BIBLIOGRAPHIE DER SOZIALWISSENSCHAFTEN. WOR-45 CONSTN SOCIETY ECO/DEV ECO/UNDEV DIPLOM LEAD WAR PEACE...PHIL/SCI SOC 19/20. PAGE 2 A0030 BIBLIOG LAW CONCPT NAT/G
N
FOREIGN AFFAIRS. SPACE WOR+45 WOR-45 CULTURE ECO/UNDEV FINAN NAT/G TEC/DEV INT/TRADE ARMS/CONT NUC/PWR...POLICY 20 UN EURATOM ECSC EEC. PAGE 2 A0034 BIBLIOG DIPLOM INT/ORG INT/LAW
N
HANDBOOK OF LATIN AMERICAN STUDIES. LAW CULTURE ECO/UNDEV POL/PAR ADMIN LEAD...SOC 20. PAGE 2 A0035 BIBLIOG/A L/A+17C NAT/G DIPLOM
N
LATIN AMERICA IN PERIODICAL LITERATURE. LAW TEC/DEV DIPLOM RECEIVE EDU/PROP...GEOG HUM MGT 20. PAGE 2 A0037 BIBLIOG/A L/A+17C SOCIETY ECO/UNDEV
N
SEMINAR: THE MONTHLY SYMPOSIUM. INDIA ACT/RES TEC/DEV DIPLOM ATTIT...BIBLIOG 20. PAGE 2 A0041 NAT/G ECO/UNDEV SOVEREIGN POLICY
N
THE MIDDLE EAST AND NORTH AFRICA. AFR ISLAM CULTURE ECO/UNDEV AGRI NAT/G TEC/DEV FOR/AID INT/TRADE EDU/PROP...CHARTS 20. PAGE 2 A0043 INDEX INDUS FINAN STAT
N
AFRICAN BIBLIOGRAPHIC CENTER,A CURRENT BIBLIOGRAPHY ON AFRICAN AFFAIRS. LAW CULTURE ECO/UNDEV LABOR BIBLIOG/A AFR

SECT DIPLOM FOR/AID COLONIAL NAT/LISM...LING 20. PAGE 5 A0094
NAT/G REGION

N
AMERICAN ECONOMIC ASSOCIATION,THE JOURNAL OF ECONOMIC ABSTRACTS. ECO/UNDEV MARKET LABOR DIPLOM ...MGT CONCPT METH 20. PAGE 7 A0144
BIBLIOG/A R+D FINAN

N
ASIA FOUNDATION,LIBRARY NOTES. LAW CONSTN CULTURE SOCIETY ECO/UNDEV INT/ORG NAT/G COLONIAL LEAD REGION NAT/LISM ATTIT 20 UN. PAGE 9 A0189
BIBLIOG/A ASIA S/ASIA DIPLOM

N
CARIBBEAN COMMISSION,CURRENT CARIBBEAN BIBLIOGRAPHY. FRANCE NETHERLAND UK CULTURE ECO/UNDEV PRESS LEAD ATTIT...GEOG SOC 20. PAGE 24 A0482
BIBLIOG NAT/G L/A+17C DIPLOM

N
CORNELL UNIVERSITY LIBRARY,SOUTHEAST ASIA ACCESSIONS LIST. LAW SOCIETY STRUCT ECO/UNDEV POL/PAR TEC/DEV DIPLOM LEAD REGION. PAGE 31 A0626
BIBLIOG S/ASIA NAT/G CULTURE

N
DOHERTY D.K.,PRELIMINARY BIBLIOGRAPHY OF COLONIZATION AND SETTLEMENT IN LATIN AMERICA AND ANGLO-AMERICA. L/A+17C PRE/AMER USA-45 ECO/UNDEV NAT/G 15/20. PAGE 38 A0768
BIBLIOG COLONIAL ADMIN DIPLOM

N
FOREIGN TRADE LIBRARY,NEW TITLES RECEIVED IN THE LIBRARY. WOR+45 ECO/UNDEV FINAN NAT/G PLAN TEC/DEV BUDGET ECO/TAC TARIFFS GOV/REL STAT. PAGE 47 A0964
BIBLIOG/A INT/TRADE INDUS ECO/DEV

N
HOOVER INSTITUTION,UNITED STATES AND CANADIAN PUBLICATIONS ON AFRICA. CULTURE ECO/UNDEV AGRI TEC/DEV EDU/PROP COLONIAL RACE/REL NAT/LISM ATTIT HEALTH...SOC SOC/WK 20. PAGE 67 A1381
BIBLIOG DIPLOM NAT/G AFR

N
IMF AND IBRD, JOINT LIBRARY,LIST OF RECENT ADDITIONS. WOR+45 ECO/DEV ECO/UNDEV BUDGET FOR/AID RATION...CONCPT IDEA/COMP. PAGE 70 A1434
BIBLIOG INT/ORG INT/TRADE FINAN

N
IMF AND IBRD, JOINT LIBRARY,LIST OF RECENT PERIODICAL ARTICLES. WOR+45 ECO/DEV ECO/UNDEV BUDGET FOR/AID RATION...CONCPT IDEA/COMP. PAGE 70 A1435
BIBLIOG INT/ORG INT/TRADE FINAN

N
INSTITUTE OF HISPANIC STUDIES,HISPANIC AMERICAN REPORT. EUR+WWI SPAIN LAW CONSTN ECO/UNDEV POL/PAR EX/STRUC LEGIS LEAD...HUM SOC 20. PAGE 70 A1445
BIBLIOG/A L/A+17C NAT/G DIPLOM

N
JOHNS HOPKINS UNIVERSITY LIB,RECENT ADDITIONS. WOR+45 ECO/UNDEV NAT/G POL/PAR FOR/AID INT/TRADE LEAD REGION ATTIT ALL/IDEOS TREND. PAGE 74 A1518
BIBLIOG DIPLOM INT/LAW INT/ORG

N
KYRIAK T.E.,ASIAN DEVELOPMENTS: A BIBLIOGRAPHY. INDONESIA KOREA/N VIETNAM/N CULTURE SOCIETY ECO/UNDEV NAT/G DIPLOM...SOC TREND 20 MONGOLIA. PAGE 83 A1699
BIBLIOG/A ALL/IDEOS S/ASIA ASIA

N
UNITED NATIONS,UNITED NATIONS PUBLICATIONS. WOR+45 ECO/UNDEV AGRI FINAN FORCES ADMIN LEAD WAR PEACE ...POLICY INT/LAW 20 UN. PAGE 148 A3034
BIBLIOG INT/ORG DIPLOM

N
UNIVERSITY OF CALIFORNIA,STATISTICAL ABSTRACT OF LATIN AMERICA. L/A+17C DIPLOM 20. PAGE 149 A3046
BIBLIOG NAT/G ECO/UNDEV STAT

N
US CONSOLATE GENERAL HONG KONG,REVIEW OF THE HONG KONG CHINESE PRESS. ECO/UNDEV LOC/G NAT/G PLAN DIPLOM EDU/PROP LEAD GP/REL MARXISM...POLICY INDEX 20. PAGE 150 A3073
BIBLIOG/A ASIA PRESS ATTIT

N
US CONSULATE GENERAL HONG KONG,CURRENT BACKGROUND. CHINA/COM ECO/UNDEV LOC/G NAT/G PLAN DIPLOM EDU/PROP LEAD REV ATTIT...POLICY INDEX 20. PAGE 151 A3074
BIBLIOG/A MARXIST ASIA PRESS

N
US CONSULATE GENERAL HONG KONG,SURVEY OF CHINA MAINLAND PRESS. CHINA/COM ECO/UNDEV LOC/G NAT/G PLAN DIPLOM EDU/PROP LEAD REV ATTIT...POLICY INDEX 20. PAGE 151 A3075
BIBLIOG/A MARXIST ASIA PRESS

N
US CONSULATE GENERAL HONG KONG,US CONSULATE GENERAL, HONG KONG, PRESS SUMMARIES. CHINA/COM ECO/UNDEV LOC/G NAT/G PLAN DIPLOM EDU/PROP LEAD REV ATTIT...POLICY INDEX 20. PAGE 151 A3076
BIBLIOG/A MARXIST ASIA PRESS

N
US LIBRARY OF CONGRESS,ACCESSIONS LIST - INDIA. INDIA CULTURE AGRI LOC/G POL/PAR PLAN PROB/SOLV TEC/DEV DIPLOM EDU/PROP LEAD GP/REL ATTIT 20. PAGE 154 A3142
BIBLIOG S/ASIA ECO/UNDEV NAT/G

N
US LIBRARY OF CONGRESS,ACCESSIONS LIST -- ISRAEL. ISRAEL CULTURE ECO/UNDEV POL/PAR PLAN PROB/SOLV TEC/DEV DIPLOM EDU/PROP LEAD WAR ATTIT 20 JEWS. PAGE 154 A3143
BIBLIOG ISLAM NAT/G GP/REL

N
US SUPERINTENDENT OF DOCUMENTS,FOREIGN RELATIONS OF THE UNITED STATES; PUBLICATIONS RELATING TO FOREIGN COUNTRIES (PRICE LIST 65). UAR USA+45 VIETNAM ECO/UNDEV VOL/ASSN FOR/AID EDU/PROP ARMS/CONT HEALTH MARXISM...POLICY INT/LAW UN NATO. PAGE 157 A3201
BIBLIOG/A DIPLOM INT/ORG NAT/G

N/R
FULBRIGHT J.W.,THE ARROGANCE OF POWER. USA+45 WOR+45 ECO/UNDEV ACADEM LEGIS ECO/TAC FOR/AID PEACE ROLE ORD/FREE PWR 20 COLD/WAR CONGRESS. PAGE 50 A1014
DIPLOM POLICY REV

NCO
CARRINGTON C.E.,THE COMMONWEALTH IN AFRICA (PAMPHLET). UK STRUCT NAT/G COLONIAL REPRESENT GOV/REL RACE/REL NAT/LISM...MAJORIT 20 EEC NEGRO COLD/WAR. PAGE 25 A0500
ECO/UNDEV AFR DIPLOM PLAN

B00
MORRIS H.C.,THE HISTORY OF COLONIZATION. WOR+45 WOR-45 ECO/DEV ECO/UNDEV INT/ORG ACT/RES PLAN ECO/TAC LEGIT ROUTINE COERCE ATTIT DRIVE ALL/VALS ...GEOG TREND 19. PAGE 105 A2148
DOMIN SOVEREIGN COLONIAL

B00
VOLPICELLI Z.,RUSSIA ON THE PACIFIC AND THE SIBERIAN RAILWAY. MOD/EUR ECO/UNDEV INT/ORG FORCES PLAN DOMIN COLONIAL ROUTINE ATTIT ALL/VALS...OBS HIST/WRIT TIME/SEQ TREND CON/ANAL AUD/VIS CHARTS 18/19. PAGE 159 A3248
NAT/G ACT/RES RUSSIA

B01
GRIFFIN A.P.C.,LIST OF BOOKS ON SAMOA (PAMPHLET). GERMANY S/ASIA UK USA-45 WOR-45 ECO/UNDEV REGION ALL/VALS ORD/FREE ALL/IDEOS...GEOG INT/LAW 19 SAMOA GUAM. PAGE 56 A1150
BIBLIOG/A COLONIAL DIPLOM

B14
HARRIS N.D.,INTERVENTION AND COLONIZATION IN AFRICA. BELGIUM FRANCE GERMANY MOD/EUR PORTUGAL UK ECO/UNDEV BAL/PWR DOMIN CONTROL PWR...GEOG 19/20. PAGE 62 A1267
AFR COLONIAL DIPLOM

N19
ASIAN-AFRICAN CONFERENCE,SELECTED DOCUMENTS OF THE BANDUNG CONFERENCE (PAMPHLET). S/ASIA PLAN ECO/TAC CONFER REGION REV NAT/LISM 20. PAGE 9 A0191
NEUTRAL ECO/UNDEV COLONIAL DIPLOM

N19
BASCH A.,THE FUTURE OF FOREIGN LENDING FOR DEVELOPMENT (PAMPHLET). WOR+45 ECO/UNDEV FINAN INT/ORG ECO/TAC ATTIT...PREDICT 20. PAGE 11 A0232
FOR/AID ECO/DEV DIPLOM GIVE

N19
FANI-KAYODE R.,BLACKISM (PAMPHLET). AFR WOR+45 INT/ORG BAL/PWR CONTROL CENTRAL...DECISION 20 UN. PAGE 44 A0896
RACE/REL ECO/UNDEV REGION DIPLOM

N19
FRANCK P.G.,AFGHANISTAN BETWEEN EAST AND WEST: THE ECONOMICS OF COMPETITIVE COEXISTENCE (PAMPHLET). AFGHANISTN USA+45 USA-45 USSR INDUS ECO/TAC INT/TRADE CONTROL NEUTRAL ORD/FREE MARXISM...GEOG 20 UN. PAGE 48 A0977
FOR/AID PLAN DIPLOM ECO/UNDEV

N19
HANNA A.J.,EUROPEAN RULE IN AFRICA (PAMPHLET). BELGIUM FRANCE MOD/EUR UK WOR+45 WOR-45 ECO/UNDEV NAT/G PARTIC SOVEREIGN...NAT/COMP 19/20. PAGE 61 A1252
DIPLOM COLONIAL AFR NAT/LISM

N19
HAUSER P.M.,WORLD POPULATION PROBLEMS (PAMPHLET). USA+45 WOR+45 ECO/DEV ECO/UNDEV FAM ACT/RES PLAN PROB/SOLV FOR/AID GIVE EATING...CHARTS 20 BIRTH/CON RESOURCE/N. PAGE 63 A1289
CONTROL CENSUS ATTIT PREDICT

N19
JACKSON R.G.A.,THE CASE FOR AN INTERNATIONAL DEVELOPMENT AUTHORITY (PAMPHLET). WOR+45 ECO/DEV DIPLOM GIVE CONTROL GP/REL EFFICIENCY NAT/LISM SOVEREIGN 20. PAGE 72 A1478
FOR/AID INT/ORG ECO/UNDEV ADMIN

N19
KUWAIT ARABIA,KUWAIT FUND FOR ARAB ECONOMIC DEVELOPMENT (PAMPHLET). ISLAM KUWAIT UAR ECO/UNDEV LEGIS ECO/TAC WEALTH 20. PAGE 83 A1697
FOR/AID DIPLOM FINAN ADMIN

N19
LANGE O.R.,"DISARMAMENT ECONOMIC GROWTH AND INTERNATIONAL CO-OPERATION" (PAMPHLET). WOR+45 DIST/IND PLAN INT/TRADE GIVE TASK DETER WEALTH SOCISM 18/19 BOLIVAR/S. PAGE 84 A1723
ARMS/CONT DIPLOM ECO/DEV ECO/UNDEV

N19
LISKA G.,THE GREATER MAGHREB: FROM INDEPENDENCE TO UNITY? (PAMPHLET). ALGERIA ISLAM MOROCCO PROB/SOLV BAL/PWR CONFER COLONIAL REPRESENT NAT/LISM 20 TUNIS. PAGE 90 A1835
ECO/UNDEV REGION DIPLOM DOMIN

N19
MARCUS W.,US PRIVATE INVESTMENT AND ECONOMIC AID IN
FOR/AID

UNDERDEVELOPED COUNTRIES (PAMPHLET). USA+45 LG/CO NAT/G CAP/ISM EDU/PROP 20. PAGE 94 A1937 ECO/UNDEV FINAN PLAN

N19
MASON E.S.,THE DIPLOMACY OF ECONOMIC ASSISTANCE (PAMPHLET). INDIA PAKISTAN USA+45 ECO/UNDEV NAT/G BUDGET ATTIT...POLICY 20. PAGE 95 A1955 FOR/AID DIPLOM FINAN

N19
NATIONAL ACADEMY OF SCIENCES,THE GROWTH OF WORLD POPULATION: ANALYSIS OF THE PROBLEMS AND RECOMMENDATIONS FOR RESEARCH AND TRAINING (PAMPHLET). WOR+45 CULTURE ECO/UNDEV EDU/PROP MARRIAGE AGE HEALTH...ANTHOL 20 BIRTH/CON. PAGE 107 A2199 CENSUS PLAN FAM INT/ORG

N19
PROVISIONS SECTION OAU,ORGANIZATION OF AFRICAN UNITY: BASIC DOCUMENTS AND RESOLUTIONS (PAMPHLET). AFR CULTURE ECO/UNDEV DIPLOM ECO/TAC EDU/PROP COLONIAL ARMS/CONT NUC/PWR RACE/REL DISCRIM NAT/LISM 20 UN OAU. PAGE 118 A2415 CONSTN EX/STRUC SOVEREIGN INT/ORG

N19
SALKEVER L.R.,SUB-SAHARA AFRICA (PAMPHLET). AFR USSR EXTR/IND NAT/G SCHOOL DIPLOM COLONIAL WEALTH ...GEOG CHARTS 16/20. PAGE 127 A2594 ECO/UNDEV TEC/DEV TASK INT/TRADE

N19
STEUBER F.A.,THE CONTRIBUTION OF SWITZERLAND TO THE ECONOMIC AND SOCIAL DEVELOPMENT OF LOW-INCOME COUNTRIES (PAMPHLET). SWITZERLND FINAN NAT/G VOL/ASSN INT/TRADE DRIVE...CHARTS 20. PAGE 138 A2820 FOR/AID ECO/UNDEV PLAN DIPLOM

N19
VELYAMINOV G.,AFRICA AND THE COMMON MARKET (PAMPHLET). AFR MARKET VOL/ASSN ECO/TAC COLONIAL ORD/FREE...SOCIALIST 20 THIRD/WRLD. PAGE 158 A3227 INT/ORG INT/TRADE SOVEREIGN ECO/UNDEV

B20
BURNS C.D.,INTERNATIONAL POLITICS. WOR-45 CULTURE SOCIETY ECO/UNDEV NAT/G VOL/ASSN DELIB/GP ACT/RES CREATE DOMIN EDU/PROP LEGIT ATTIT DRIVE RIGID/FLEX ALL/VALS...PLURIST PSY CONCPT TREND. PAGE 22 A0442 INT/ORG PEACE SOVEREIGN

B27
HARRIS N.D.,EUROPE AND AFRICA. BELGIUM FRANCE GERMANY MOD/EUR PORTUGAL UK ECO/UNDEV BAL/PWR PWR ...GEOG 19/20. PAGE 62 A1268 AFR COLONIAL DIPLOM

B28
HALL W.P.,EMPIRE TO COMMONWEALTH. FUT WOR-45 CONSTN ECO/DEV ECO/UNDEV INT/ORG PROVS PLAN DIPLOM EDU/PROP ADMIN COLONIAL PEACE PERSON ALL/VALS ...POLICY GEOG SOC OBS RECORD TREND CMN/WLTH PARLIAMENT 19/20. PAGE 60 A1229 VOL/ASSN NAT/G UK

B28
STUART G.H.,LATIN AMERICA AND THE UNITED STATES. USA-45 ECO/UNDEV INT/ORG NAT/G POL/PAR PLAN DOMIN EDU/PROP COLONIAL REGION COERCE ATTIT ALL/VALS ...POLICY GEOG TREND 19/20. PAGE 139 A2853 L/A+17C DIPLOM

B29
PRATT I.A.,MODERN EGYPT: A LIST OF REFERENCES TO MATERIAL IN THE NEW YORK PUBLIC LIBRARY. UAR ECO/UNDEV...GEOG JURID SOC LING 20. PAGE 117 A2407 BIBLIOG ISLAM DIPLOM NAT/G

B30
SMUTS J.C.,AFRICA AND SOME WORLD PROBLEMS. RHODESIA SOUTH/AFR CULTURE ECO/UNDEV INDUS INT/ORG SECT PROB/SOLV REGION GOV/REL DISCRIM ATTIT 19/20 LEAGUE/NAT LIVNGSTN/D NEGRO. PAGE 134 A2748 LEGIS AFR COLONIAL RACE/REL

B30
WRIGHT Q.,MANDATES UNDER THE LEAGUE OF NATIONS. WOR-45 CONSTN ECO/DEV ECO/UNDEV NAT/G DELIB/GP TOP/EX LEGIT ALL/VALS...JURID CONCPT LEAGUE/NAT 20. PAGE 167 A3403 INT/ORG LAW INT/LAW

B31
HODGES C.,THE BACKGROUND OF INTERNATIONAL RELATIONS. WOR-45 SOCIETY ECO/DEV ECO/UNDEV INT/ORG DIPLOM DOMIN EDU/PROP LEGIT WAR ATTIT DRIVE PERSON ALL/VALS...CONCPT METH/CNCPT TIME/SEQ CHARTS WORK LEAGUE/NAT 19/20. PAGE 66 A1350 NAT/G BAL/PWR

B35
BUREAU ECONOMIC RES LAT AM,THE ECONOMIC LITERATURE OF LATIN AMERICA (2 VOLS.). CHRIST-17C AGRI DIST/IND EXTR/IND INDUS WORKER INT/TRADE...GEOG 16/20. PAGE 21 A0433 BIBLIOG L/A+17C ECO/UNDEV FINAN

B36
HARVARD BUREAU ECO RES LAT AM,THE ECONOMIC LITERATURE OF LATIN AMERICA: A TENTATIVE BIBLIOGRAPHY. NAT/G TARIFFS CENTRAL COST DEMAND 20. PAGE 62 A1277 BIBLIOG ECO/UNDEV L/A+17C INT/TRADE

B36
ROBINSON H.,DEVELOPMENT OF THE BRITISH EMPIRE. WOR-45 CULTURE SOCIETY STRUCT ECO/DEV ECO/UNDEV INT/ORG VOL/ASSN FORCES CREATE PLAN DOMIN EDU/PROP ADMIN COLONIAL PWR WEALTH...POLICY GEOG CHARTS CMN/WLTH 16/20. PAGE 122 A2503 NAT/G HIST/WRIT UK

B37
ROYAL INST. INT. AFF.,THE COLONIAL PROBLEM. WOR-45 LAW ECO/DEV ECO/UNDEV NAT/G PLAN ECO/TAC EDU/PROP ADMIN ATTIT ALL/VALS...CONCPT 20. PAGE 125 A2556 INT/ORG ACT/RES SOVEREIGN COLONIAL

B38
COLBY C.C.,GEOGRAPHICAL ASPECTS OF INTERNATIONAL RELATIONS. WOR-45 ECO/DEV ECO/UNDEV AGRI EXTR/IND INDUS MARKET R+D INT/ORG NAT/G TEC/DEV ECO/TAC INT/TRADE NAT/LISM WEALTH...METH/CNCPT CHARTS GEN/LAWS 20. PAGE 28 A0565 PLAN GEOG DIPLOM

B38
FRANKEL S.H.,CAPITAL INVESTMENT IN AFRICA. AFR EUR+WWI RHODESIA SOUTH/AFR UK FINAN FOR/AID COLONIAL DEMAND UTIL WEALTH...METH/CNCPT CHARTS 20 CONGO/LEOP. PAGE 48 A0983 ECO/UNDEV EXTR/IND DIPLOM PRODUC

B38
HOBSON J.A.,IMPERIALISM. MOD/EUR UK WOR-45 CULTURE ECO/UNDEV NAT/G VOL/ASSN PLAN EDU/PROP LEGIT REGION COERCE ATTIT PWR...POLICY PLURIST TIME/SEQ GEN/LAWS 19/20. PAGE 66 A1348 DOMIN ECO/TAC BAL/PWR COLONIAL

B39
FURNIVALL J.S.,NETHERLANDS INDIA. INDIA NETHERLAND CULTURE INDUS NAT/G DIPLOM ADMIN WEALTH...POLICY CHARTS 17/20. PAGE 50 A1029 COLONIAL ECO/UNDEV SOVEREIGN PLURISM

B39
ROBBINS L.,ECONOMIC CAUSES OF WAR. WOR-45 ECO/DEV ECO/UNDEV INT/ORG NAT/G TEC/DEV DIPLOM DOMIN COLONIAL ATTIT DRIVE PWR WEALTH...POLICY CONCPT OBS SAMP TREND CON/ANAL GEN/LAWS MARX/KARL 20. PAGE 122 A2493 COERCE ECO/TAC WAR

B39
ZIMMERN A.,MODERN POLITICAL DOCTRINE. WOR-45 CULTURE SOCIETY ECO/UNDEV DELIB/GP EX/STRUC CREATE DOMIN COERCE NAT/LISM ATTIT RIGID/FLEX ORD/FREE PWR WEALTH...POLICY CONCPT OBS TIME/SEQ TREND TOT/POP LEAGUE/NAT 20. PAGE 170 A3454 NAT/G ECO/TAC BAL/PWR INT/TRADE

B40
BROWN A.D.,PANAMA CANAL AND PANAMA CANAL ZONE: A SELECTED LIST OF REFERENCES. PANAMA NAT/G SCHOOL DIPLOM HEALTH...GEOG SOC 20 CANAL/ZONE. PAGE 19 A0397 BIBLIOG/A ECO/UNDEV

B41
GRISMER R.,A NEW BIBLIOGRAPHY OF THE LITERATURES OF SPAIN AND SPANISH AMERICA. CHRIST-17C MOD/EUR PRE/AMER SPAIN CULTURE DIPLOM EDU/PROP...ART/METH GEOG HUM PHIL/SCI 20. PAGE 57 A1165 BIBLIOG LAW NAT/G ECO/UNDEV

B41
KEESING F.M.,THE SOUTH SEAS IN THE MODERN WORLD. INDONESIA STRUCT FAM SECT EDU/PROP LEAD INCOME WEALTH...HEAL SOC 20. PAGE 77 A1577 CULTURE ECO/UNDEV GOV/COMP DIPLOM

B41
PERHAM M.,AFRICANS AND BRITISH RULE. AFR UK ECO/TAC CONTROL GP/REL ATTIT 20. PAGE 115 A2355 DIPLOM COLONIAL ADMIN ECO/UNDEV

B42
CONOVER H.F.,FRENCH COLONIES IN AFRICA: A LIST OF REFERENCES. ALGERIA FRANCE MOROCCO SOMALIA SUDAN CULTURE AGRI LOC/G SECT FORCES DIPLOM INT/TRADE NAT/LISM HEALTH...CON/ANAL 20. PAGE 29 A0594 BIBLIOG AFR ECO/UNDEV COLONIAL

B42
CONOVER H.F.,NEW ZEALAND: A SELECTED LIST OF REFERENCES (PAMPHLET). NEW/ZEALND ECO/UNDEV AGRI INDUS LABOR NAT/G SCHOOL FORCES DIPLOM COLONIAL WAR ...HUM 20. PAGE 29 A0595 BIBLIOG/A S/ASIA CULTURE

B42
CORBETT P.E.,POST WAR WORLDS. ASIA EUR+WWI FUT S/ASIA USA-45 ECO/DEV ECO/UNDEV NAT/G DELIB/GP FORCES PLAN ROUTINE ATTIT PWR 20. PAGE 30 A0613 WOR-45 INT/ORG

B42
JOSHI P.S.,THE TYRANNY OF COLOUR. INDIA SOUTH/AFR UK ECO/UNDEV NAT/G POL/PAR DIPLOM ECO/TAC WAR ...POLICY 19/20. PAGE 75 A1538 COLONIAL DISCRIM RACE/REL

L42
SHOTWELL J.,"LESSON OF THE LAST WORLD WAR." EUR+WWI MOD/EUR USA-45 SOCIETY ECO/UNDEV INDUS VOL/ASSN CONSULT ACT/RES CREATE CAP/ISM INT/TRADE DRIVE ALL/VALS...CONCPT NEW/IDEA SELF/OBS GEN/LAWS LEAGUE/NAT NAZI 20. PAGE 132 A2708 INT/ORG ORD/FREE

B43
BROWN A.D.,BRITISH POSSESSIONS IN THE CARIBBEAN AREA: A SELECTED LIST OF REFERENCES. UK NAT/G DIPLOM...GEOG 20 CARIBBEAN. PAGE 20 A0398 BIBLIOG COLONIAL ECO/UNDEV L/A+17C

B43
BROWN A.D.,GREECE: SELECTED LIST OF REFERENCES. GREECE ECO/UNDEV AGRI FINAN INDUS LABOR SECT TEC/DEV INT/TRADE LEAD...SOC 20. PAGE 20 A0399 BIBLIOG/A WAR DIPLOM NAT/G

B43
CARLO A.M.,ENSAYO DE UNA BIBLIOGRAFIA DE BIBLIOGRAFIAS MEXICANAS. ECO/UNDEV LOC/G ADMIN LEAD 20 MEXIC/AMER. PAGE 24 A0485 BIBLIOG L/A+17C NAT/G DIPLOM

B43
LEWIN E.,ROYAL EMPIRE SOCIETY BIBLIOGRAPHIES NO. 9: BIBLIOG

SUB-SAHARA AFRICA. ECO/UNDEV TEC/DEV DIPLOM ADMIN COLONIAL LEAD 20. PAGE 88 A1800 — AFR NAT/G SOCIETY

B44
FULLER G.H.,TURKEY: A SELECTED LIST OF REFERENCES. ISLAM TURKEY CULTURE ECO/UNDEV AGRI DIPLOM NAT/LISM CONSERVE...GEOG HUM INT/LAW SOC 7/20 MAPS. PAGE 50 A1024 — BIBLIOG/A ALL/VALS

B44
RAGATZ L.J.,LITERATURE OF EUROPEAN IMPERIALISM. ECO/TAC INT/TRADE DOMIN GOV/REL DEMAND NAT/LISM PWR WEALTH 19/20. PAGE 119 A2432 — BIBLIOG COLONIAL INT/ORG ECO/UNDEV

B44
SHELBY C.,LATIN AMERICAN PERIODICALS CURRENTLY RECEIVED IN THE LIBRARY OF CONGRESS AND IN LIBRARY OF DEPARTMENT OF AGRICULTURE. SOCIETY AGRI INDUS LABOR POL/PAR INT/TRADE...GEOG SOC 20. PAGE 132 A2699 — BIBLIOG ECO/UNDEV CULTURE L/A+17C

L44
HAILEY,"THE FUTURE OF COLONIAL PEOPLES." WOR-45 CONSTN CULTURE ECO/UNDEV AGRI MARKET INT/ORG NAT/G SECT CONSULT ECO/TAC LEGIT ADMIN NAT/LISM ALL/VALS ...SOC OBS TREND STERTYP CMN/WLTH LEAGUE/NAT PARLIAMENT 20. PAGE 59 A1218 — PLAN CONCPT DIPLOM UK

N45
INDIA QUARTERLY, A JOURNAL OF INTERNATIONAL AFFAIRS. INDIA LAW CONSTN ECO/UNDEV INT/ORG POL/PAR COLONIAL LEAD PARL/PROC WAR ATTIT...SOC 20 CMN/WLTH. PAGE 3 A0053 — BIBLIOG/A S/ASIA DIPLOM NAT/G

B45
CLAGETT H.L.,COMMUNIST CHINA: RUTHLESS ENEMY OR PAPER TIGER (PAMPHLET). CHINA/COM ECO/UNDEV AGRI INDUS NAT/G POL/PAR ECO/TAC INT/TRADE GUERRILLA ATTIT...CHARTS NAT/COMP ORG/CHARTS 20. PAGE 26 A0540 — BIBLIOG/A MARXISM DIPLOM COERCE

B45
PERAZA SARAUSA F.,BIBLIOGRAFIAS CUBANAS. CUBA CULTURE ECO/UNDEV AGRI EDU/PROP PRESS CIVMIL/REL ...POLICY GEOG PHIL/SCI BIOG 19/20. PAGE 115 A2353 — BIBLIOG/A L/A+17C NAT/G DIPLOM

S46
SILBERNER E.,"THE PROBLEM OF WAR IN NINETEENTH CENTURY ECONOMIC THOUGHT." EUR+WWI MOD/EUR UNIV LAW ECO/DEV ECO/UNDEV FINAN INDUS MARKET INT/ORG NAT/G CONSULT FORCES...CONCPT GEN/LAWS GEN/METH 19. PAGE 133 A2715 — ATTIT ECO/TAC WAR

B47
BROOKINGS INST.,MAJOR PROBLEMS OF UNITED STATES FOREIGN POLICY. USA+45 WOR+45 STRUCT ECO/DEV ECO/UNDEV INT/ORG NAT/G POL/PAR VOL/ASSN DELIB/GP FORCES ECO/TAC LEGIT COERCE ORD/FREE PWR WEALTH ...POLICY STAT TREND CHARTS TOT/POP. PAGE 19 A0392 — ACT/RES DIPLOM

B47
CONOVER H.F.,NON-SELF-GOVERNING AREAS. BELGIUM FRANCE ITALY UK WOR+45 CULTURE ECO/UNDEV INT/ORG LOC/G NAT/G ECO/TAC INT/TRADE ADMIN HEALTH...SOC UN. PAGE 30 A0601 — BIBLIOG/A COLONIAL DIPLOM

B47
PERKINS D.,THE UNITED STATES AND THE CARIBBEAN. CUBA DOMIN/REP GUATEMALA HAITI PANAMA CULTURE ECO/UNDEV FOR/AID ADMIN COERCE HABITAT...POLICY 19/20. PAGE 115 A2359 — DIPLOM L/A+17C USA-45

B48
GUIDE TO THE RECORDS IN THE NATIONAL ARCHIVES. ECO/UNDEV ADMIN COLONIAL 16/20. PAGE 3 A0055 — BIBLIOG NAT/G L/A+17C DIPLOM

B48
MINISTERE FINANCES ET ECO,BULLETIN BIBLIOGRAPHIQUE. AFR EUR+WWI FRANCE CULTURE STRUCT FINAN NAT/G ACT/RES INT/TRADE ADMIN REGION PRODUC STAT. PAGE 102 A2088 — BIBLIOG/A ECO/UNDEV TEC/DEV COLONIAL

B48
PELCOVITS N.A.,OLD CHINA HANDS AND THE FOREIGN OFFICE. ASIA BURMA UK ECO/UNDEV NAT/G ECO/TAC FOR/AID TARIFFS DOMIN COLONIAL GOV/REL SOVEREIGN 19 HONG/KONG TREATY. PAGE 114 A2348 — INT/TRADE ATTIT DIPLOM

B49
BEHRENDT R.F.,MODERN LATIN AMERICA IN SOCIAL SCIENCE LITERATURE. STRUCT ECO/UNDEV SCHOOL DIPLOM INT/TRADE EDU/PROP...GEOG 20. PAGE 12 A0250 — BIBLIOG/A SOC L/A+17C

B49
BORBA DE MORAES R.,MANUAL BIBLIOGRAFICO DE ESTUDOS BRASILEIROS. BRAZIL DIPLOM ADMIN LEAD...SOC 20. PAGE 17 A0336 — BIBLIOG L/A+17C NAT/G ECO/UNDEV

B49
MARITAIN J.,HUMAN RIGHTS: COMMENTS AND INTERPRETATIONS. COM UNIV WOR+45 LAW CONSTN CULTURE SOCIETY ECO/DEV ECO/UNDEV SCHOOL DELIB/GP EDU/PROP ATTIT PERCEPT ALL/VALS...HUM SOC TREND UNESCO 20. PAGE 95 A1939 — INT/ORG CONCPT

B50
BEHRENDT R.F.,MODERN LATIN AMERICA IN SOCIAL SCIENCE LITERATURE (SUPPLEMENTS I AND II). STRUCT ECO/UNDEV SCHOOL DIPLOM INT/TRADE...GEOG 20. PAGE 12 A0251 — BIBLIOG/A SOC L/A+17C

B50
CHUKWUEMEKA N.,AFRICAN DEPENDENCIES: A CHALLENGE TO WESTERN DEMOCRACY. NIGERIA ECO/DEV INDUS FOR/AID INT/TRADE DOMIN 20. PAGE 26 A0536 — DIPLOM ECO/UNDEV COLONIAL AFR

B50
CORNELL U DEPT ASIAN STUDIES,SOUTHEAST ASIA PROGRAM DATA PAPER. BURMA CAMBODIA INDONESIA MALAYSIA VIETNAM SOCIETY STRUCT NAT/G SECT DIPLOM FOR/AID PWR WEALTH...SOC 20. PAGE 31 A0625 — BIBLIOG/A CULTURE S/ASIA ECO/UNDEV

B50
MOCKFORD J.,SOUTH-WEST AFRICA AND THE INTERNATIONAL COURT (PAMPHLET). AFR GERMANY SOUTH/AFR UK ECO/UNDEV DIPLOM CONTROL DISCRIM...DECISION JURID 20 AFRICA/SW. PAGE 102 A2094 — COLONIAL SOVEREIGN INT/LAW DOMIN

B50
NORTHROP F.S.C.,THE TAMING OF THE NATIONS. KOREA USA+45 USSR WOR+45 STRUCT ECO/UNDEV INT/ORG NAT/G TOP/EX NUC/PWR ATTIT ALL/VALS...TIME/SEQ 20 HIROSHIMA. PAGE 110 A2255 — CONCPT BAL/PWR

B50
PERHAM M.,COLONIAL GOVERNMENT: ANNOTATED READING LIST ON BRITISH COLONIAL GOVERNMENT. UK WOR+45 WOR-45 ECO/UNDEV INT/ORG LEGIS FOR/AID INT/TRADE DOMIN ADMIN REV 20. PAGE 115 A2356 — BIBLIOG/A COLONIAL GOV/REL NAT/G

B50
STONE J.,THE PROVINCE AND FUNCTION OF LAW. UNIV WOR+45 WOR-45 CULTURE INTELL SOCIETY ECO/DEV ECO/UNDEV NAT/G LEGIT ROUTINE ATTIT PERCEPT PERSON ...JURID CONCPT GEN/LAWS GEN/METH 20. PAGE 138 A2833 — INT/ORG LAW

B50
US DEPARTMENT OF STATE,POINT FOUR: COOPERATIVE PROGRAM FOR AID IN THE DEVELOPMENT OF ECONOMICALLY UNDERDEVELOPED AREAS. WOR+45 AGRI INDUS INT/ORG PLAN TEC/DEV DIPLOM EDU/PROP ADMIN PEACE PRODUC WEALTH 20 CONGRESS UN. PAGE 151 A3085 — ECO/UNDEV FOR/AID FINAN INT/TRADE

L50
US SENATE COMM. GOVT. OPER.,"REVISION OF THE UN CHARTER." FUT USA+45 WOR+45 CONSTN ECO/DEV ECO/UNDEV NAT/G DELIB/GP ACT/RES CREATE PLAN EXEC ROUTINE CHOOSE ALL/VALS...POLICY CONCPT CONGRESS UN TOT/POP 20 COLD/WAR. PAGE 157 A3196 — INT/ORG LEGIS PEACE

C50
ELLSWORTH P.T.,"INTERNATIONAL ECONOMY." ECO/DEV ECO/UNDEV FINAN LABOR DIPLOM FOR/AID TARIFFS BAL/PAY EQUILIB NAT/LISM OPTIMAL...INT/LAW 20 ILO GATT. PAGE 41 A0843 — BIBLIOG INT/TRADE ECO/TAC INT/ORG

B51
CHRISTENSEN A.N.,THE EVOLUTION OF LATIN AMERICAN GOVERNMENT: A BOOK OF READINGS. ECO/UNDEV INDUS LOC/G POL/PAR EX/STRUC LEGIS FOR/AID CT/SYS ...SOC/WK 20 SOUTH/AMER. PAGE 26 A0535 — NAT/G CONSTN DIPLOM L/A+17C

B51
US HOUSE COMM APPROPRIATIONS,MUTUAL SECURITY PROGRAM APPROPRIATIONS FOR 1952: HEARINGS BEFORE A SUBCOMMITTEE OF THE COMMITTEE ON APPROPRIATIONS. KOREA L/A+17C ECO/DEV ECO/UNDEV INT/ORG INSPECT BAL/PWR DIPLOM DEBATE WAR...POLICY STAT ASIA/S 20 CONGRESS NATO COLD/WAR MID/EAST. PAGE 153 A3118 — LEGIS FORCES BUDGET FOR/AID

B51
YOUNG T.C.,NEAR EASTERN CULTURE AND SOCIETY. ISLAM ECO/UNDEV SECT WRITING ATTIT HABITAT ORD/FREE 20. PAGE 169 A3438 — CULTURE STRUCT REGION DIPLOM

B52
ALEXANDROWICZ C.H.,INTERNATIONAL ECONOMIC ORGANIZATION. WOR+45 ECO/DEV ECO/UNDEV DIST/IND FINAN MARKET PLAN ECO/TAC LEGIT DRIVE WEALTH ...POLICY CONCPT QUANT OBS TIME/SEQ GEN/LAWS WORK EEC ILO OEEC UNESCO 20. PAGE 6 A0114 — INT/ORG INT/TRADE

B52
HOSELITZ B.F.,THE PROGRESS OF UNDERDEVELOPED AREAS. FUT WOR+45 WOR-45 ECO/DEV ECO/TAC INT/TRADE WEALTH ...SOC TREND GEN/LAWS TOT/POP VAL/FREE COLD/WAR 20. PAGE 68 A1391 — ECO/UNDEV PLAN FOR/AID

B52
US MUTUAL SECURITY AGENCY,U. S. TECHNICAL AND ECONOMIC ASSISTANCE IN THE FAR EAST (PAMPHLET). ASIA BURMA INDONESIA PHILIPPINE TAIWAN THAILAND USA+45 AGRI INDUS PLAN EDU/PROP ADMIN HEALTH. PAGE 155 A3161 — FOR/AID TEC/DEV ECO/UNDEV BUDGET

B53
MCNEILL W.H.,AMERICA, BRITAIN, AND RUSSIA; THEIR COOPERATION AND CONFLICT. UK USA-45 USSR ECO/DEV ECO/UNDEV FORCES PLAN ADMIN AGREE PERS/REL ...DECISION 20 TREATY. PAGE 98 A2021 — WAR DIPLOM DOMIN

B53
SHIRATO I.,JAPANESE SOURCES ON THE HISTORY OF THE CHINESE COMMUNIST MOVEMENT (PAMPHLET). CHINA/COM USSR CONSTRUC NAT/G POL/PAR FORCES DIPLOM DOMIN EDU/PROP CONTROL WAR TOTALISM SOCISM 20. PAGE 132 A2702 — BIBLIOG/A MARXISM ECO/UNDEV

B53
THAYER P.W.,SOUTHEAST ASIA IN THE COMING WORLD. ASIA S/ASIA USA+45 USA-45 SOCIETY INT/ORG ACT/RES ECO/TAC EDU/PROP COERCE TOTALISM ALL/VALS...JURID 20. PAGE 142 A2909 — ECO/UNDEV ATTIT FOR/AID DIPLOM

B54
BINANI G.D.,INDIA AT A GLANCE (REV. ED.). INDIA COM/IND FINAN INDUS LABOR PROVS SCHOOL PLAN DIPLOM INT/TRADE ADMIN...JURID 20. PAGE 14 A0288 — INDEX CON/ANAL NAT/G ECO/UNDEV

B54
COOKSON J.,BEFORE THE AFRICAN STORM. BELGIUM CENTRL/AFR FRANCE UK ECO/UNDEV POL/PAR CREATE BAL/PWR RACE/REL NAT/LISM ORD/FREE CONSERVE MARXISM SOC/INTEG 20 CONGO/LEOP. PAGE 30 A0607 — COLONIAL REV DISCRIM DIPLOM

B54
KENWORTHY L.S.,FREE AND INEXPENSIVE MATERIALS ON WORLD AFFAIRS (PAMPHLET). WOR+45 CULTURE ECO/UNDEV INT/TRADE ARMS/CONT NUC/PWR UN. PAGE 78 A1597 — BIBLIOG/A NAT/G INT/ORG DIPLOM

B54
NATION ASSOCIATES,SECURITY AND THE MIDDLE EAST - THE PROBLEM AND ITS SOLUTION. ISRAEL JORDAN LEBANON SYRIA UAR FORCES FOR/AID GP/REL NAT/LISM PEACE TOTALISM...POLICY 20. PAGE 107 A2198 — DIPLOM ECO/UNDEV WAR PLAN

B54
STALEY E.,THE FUTURE OF UNDERDEVELOPED COUNTRIES: POLITICAL IMPLICATIONS OF ECONOMIC DEVELOPMENT. COM FUT USA+45 SOCIETY ECO/UNDEV CREATE PLAN CAP/ISM ATTIT DRIVE MARXISM SOCISM...POLICY CONCPT CHARTS COLD/WAR 20. PAGE 137 A2801 — EDU/PROP ECO/TAC FOR/AID

B54
TINBERGEN J.,INTERNATIONAL ECONOMIC INTEGRATION. WOR+45 WOR-45 ECO/UNDEV NAT/G ECO/TAC BAL/PAY ...METH/CNCPT STAT TIME/SEQ GEN/METH OEEC 20. PAGE 144 A2941 — INT/ORG ECO/DEV INT/TRADE

L54
CHARLESWORTH J.C.,"AMERICA AND A NEW ASIA." ASIA INDIA ISLAM S/ASIA USA+45 USA-45 ECO/UNDEV NAT/G POL/PAR FORCES FOR/AID DOMIN EDU/PROP COERCE DRIVE ALL/VALS MARXISM SOCISM TOT/POP 20. PAGE 26 A0522 — ECO/TAC DIPLOM NAT/LISM

S54
DODD S.C.,"THE SCIENTIFIC MEASUREMENT OF FITNESS FOR SELF-GOVERNMENT." FUT CONSTN ECO/UNDEV INT/ORG PLAN PWR...CONCPT QUANT CON/ANAL SOC/EXP UN LEAGUE/NAT 20. PAGE 38 A0767 — NAT/G STAT SOVEREIGN

B55
CHOWDHURI R.N.,INTERNATIONAL MANDATES AND TRUSTEESHIP SYSTEMS. WOR+45 STRUCT ECO/UNDEV INT/ORG LEGIS DOMIN EDU/PROP LEGIT ADJUD EXEC PWR ...CONCPT TIME/SEQ UN 20. PAGE 26 A0534 — DELIB/GP PLAN SOVEREIGN

B55
COMM. STUDY ORGAN. PEACE,REPORTS. WOR-45 ECO/DEV ECO/UNDEV VOL/ASSN CONSULT FORCES PLAN TEC/DEV DOMIN EDU/PROP NUC/PWR ATTIT PWR WEALTH...JURID STERTYP FAO ILO 20 UN. PAGE 28 A0579 — WOR+45 INT/ORG ARMS/CONT

B55
COTTRELL W.F.,ENERGY AND SOCIETY. FUT WOR+45 WOR-45 ECO/DEV ECO/UNDEV INT/ORG NAT/G DETER ORD/FREE PWR SKILL WEALTH...SOC TIME/SEQ TOT/POP VAL/FREE 20. PAGE 31 A0634 — TEC/DEV BAL/PWR PEACE

B55
JOY C.T.,HOW COMMUNISTS NEGOTIATE. COM USA+45 CONSTN CULTURE ECO/UNDEV NAT/G CONSULT DELIB/GP FORCES PLAN ECO/TAC DOMIN EDU/PROP LEGIT EXEC ROUTINE COERCE WAR CHOOSE PEACE ATTIT RIGID/FLEX ORD/FREE PWR...POLICY 20. PAGE 75 A1539 — ASIA INT/ORG DIPLOM

B55
OECD,MARSHALL PLAN IN TURKEY. TURKEY USA+45 COM/IND CONSTRUC SERV/IND FORCES BUDGET...STAT 20 MARSHL/PLN. PAGE 111 A2277 — FOR/AID ECO/UNDEV AGRI INDUS

B55
PANT Y.P.,PLANNING IN UNDERDEVELOPED ECONOMIES. INDIA NEPAL INT/TRADE COLONIAL SOVEREIGN ALL/IDEOS ...TIME/SEQ METH/COMP 20. PAGE 114 A2334 — ECO/UNDEV PLAN ECO/TAC DIPLOM

B55
QUAN K.L.,INTRODUCTION TO ASIA: A SELECTIVE GUIDE TO BACKGROUND READING. ECO/UNDEV NAT/G PROB/SOLV DIPLOM ATTIT 20. PAGE 118 A2424 — BIBLIOG/A S/ASIA CULTURE ASIA

B55
STILLMAN C.W.,AFRICA IN THE MODERN WORLD. AFR USA+45 WOR+45 INT/TRADE COLONIAL PARTIC REGION GOV/REL RACE/REL 20. PAGE 138 A2826 — ECO/UNDEV DIPLOM POLICY STRUCT

L55
KISER M.,"ORGANIZATION OF AMERICAN STATES." L/A+17C USA+45 ECO/UNDEV INT/ORG NAT/G PLAN TEC/DEV DIPLOM ECO/TAC INT/TRADE EDU/PROP ADMIN ALL/VALS...POLICY MGT RECORD ORG/CHARTS OAS 20. PAGE 80 A1639 — VOL/ASSN ECO/DEV REGION

B56
BALL W.M.,NATIONALISM AND COMMUNISM IN EAST ASIA. ASIA BURMA EUR+WWI KOREA USA+45 ECO/UNDEV NAT/G POL/PAR DIPLOM ECO/TAC FOR/AID EDU/PROP COERCE RACE/REL NAT/LISM DRIVE SOVEREIGN...TREND 20 CHINJAP. PAGE 11 A0214 — S/ASIA ATTIT

B56
BOWLES C.,AFRICA'S CHALLENGE TO AMERICA. USA+45 ECO/UNDEV NAT/G LEGIS COLONIAL CONTROL REV ORD/FREE SOVEREIGN 20 COLD/WAR. PAGE 18 A0358 — AFR DIPLOM POLICY FOR/AID

B56
BROOK D.,THE UNITED NATIONS AND CHINA DILEMMA. CHINA/COM FUT WOR+45 ECO/UNDEV NAT/G DELIB/GP ACT/RES DIPLOM ROUTINE NAT/LISM TOTALISM ATTIT DRIVE...CONCPT OBS TIME/SEQ UN TOT/POP TIME UN 20. PAGE 19 A0390 — ASIA INT/ORG BAL/PWR

B56
KIRK G.,THE CHANGING ENVIRONMENT OF INTERNATIONAL RELATIONS. ASIA S/ASIA USA+45 WOR+45 ECO/UNDEV INT/ORG NAT/G FOR/AID EDU/PROP PEACE KNOWL ...PLURIST COLD/WAR TOT/POP 20. PAGE 80 A1634 — FUT EXEC DIPLOM

B56
KNORR K.E.,RUBLE DIPLOMACY: CHALLENGE TO AMERICAN FOREIGN AID(PAMPHLET). CHINA/COM USA+45 USSR PLAN TEC/DEV CAP/ISM INT/TRADE DOMIN EDU/PROP CONTROL LEAD 20 COLD/WAR. PAGE 81 A1654 — ECO/UNDEV COM DIPLOM FOR/AID

B56
PHILIPPINE STUDIES PROGRAM,SELECTED BIBLIOGRAPHY ON THE PHILIPPINES, TOPICALLY ARRANGED AND ANNOTATED. PHILIPPINE SECT DIPLOM COLONIAL LEAD...SOC 18/20. PAGE 116 A2375 — BIBLIOG/A S/ASIA NAT/G ECO/UNDEV

B56
UN HEADQUARTERS LIBRARY,BIBLIOGRAPHY OF INDUSTRIALIZATION IN UNDERDEVELOPED COUNTRIES (BIBLIOGRAPHICAL SERIES NO. 6). WOR+45 R+D ACADEM INT/ORG NAT/G. PAGE 147 A3002 — BIBLIOG ECO/UNDEV TEC/DEV

B56
UNITED NATIONS,BIBLIOGRAPHY ON INDUSTRIALIZATION IN UNDER-DEVELOPED COUNTRIES. WOR+45 R+D INT/ORG NAT/G FOR/AID ADMIN LEAD 20 UN. PAGE 149 A3036 — BIBLIOG ECO/UNDEV INDUS TEC/DEV

B56
US DEPARTMENT OF STATE,ECONOMIC PROBLEMS OF UNDERDEVELOPED AREAS (PAMPHLET). AFR ASIA ISLAM L/A+17C AGRI FINAN INDUS INT/ORG LABOR INT/TRADE ...PSY SOC 20. PAGE 151 A3090 — BIBLIOG ECO/UNDEV TEC/DEV R+D

B56
US LIBRARY OF CONGRESS,UNITED STATES DIRECT ECONOMIC AID TO FOREIGN COUNTRIES: A COLLECTION OF EXCERPTS AND A BIBLIOGRAPHY (PAMPHLET). USA+45 PRESS DEBATE...ANTHOL BIBLIOG/A CONGRESS. PAGE 155 A3154 — FOR/AID POLICY DIPLOM ECO/UNDEV

B57
ASHER R.E.,THE UNITED NATIONS AND THE PROMOTION OF THE GENERAL WELFARE. WOR+45 WOR-45 ECO/UNDEV EX/STRUC ACT/RES PLAN EDU/PROP ROUTINE HEALTH...HUM CONCPT CHARTS UNESCO UN ILO 20. PAGE 9 A0185 — INT/ORG CONSULT

B57
ASHER R.E.,THE UNITED NATIONS AND ECONOMIC AND SOCIAL COOPERATION. ECO/UNDEV COM/IND DIST/IND FINAN PLAN PROB/SOLV INT/TRADE TASK WEALTH...SOC 20 UN. PAGE 9 A0186 — INT/ORG DIPLOM FOR/AID

B57
BURNS A.,IN DEFENCE OF COLONIES; BRITISH COLONIAL TERRITORIES IN INTERNATIONAL AFFAIRS. UK ECO/UNDEV PLAN DOMIN SOVEREIGN...MAJORIT 18/20 CMN/WLTH INTERVENT. PAGE 22 A0439 — COLONIAL POLICY ATTIT DIPLOM

B57
CARIBBEAN COMMISSION,A CATALOGUE OF CARIBBEAN COMMISSION PUBLICATIONS (PAMPHLET). WEST/IND CULTURE ECO/UNDEV LOC/G DIPLOM SOC. PAGE 24 A0483 — BIBLIOG L/A+17C INT/ORG NAT/G

B57
CASTLE E.W.,THE GREAT GIVEAWAY: THE REALITIES OF FOREIGN AID. USA+45 DIPLOM EDU/PROP NEUTRAL ...DECISION 20. PAGE 25 A0508 — FOR/AID GIVE ECO/UNDEV PROB/SOLV

B57
CONOVER H.F.,NORTH AND NORTHEAST AFRICA; A SELECTED ANNOTATED LIST OF WRITINGS. ALGERIA MOROCCO SUDAN UAR CULTURE INT/ORG PROB/SOLV ADJUD NAT/LISM PWR WEALTH...SOC 20 UN. PAGE 30 A0603 — BIBLIOG/A DIPLOM AFR ECO/UNDEV

B57
DEAN V.M.,THE NATURE OF THE NON-WESTERN WORLD. AFR ASIA L/A+17C S/ASIA CULTURE SOCIETY STRATA ECO/DEV DIPLOM ECO/TAC FOR/AID ATTIT DRIVE ALL/VALS ...RELATIV SOC CONCPT TIME/SEQ TREND TOT/POP 20. PAGE 35 A0718 — ECO/UNDEV STERTYP NAT/LISM

B57
HALD M.,A SELECTED BIBLIOGRAPHY ON ECONOMIC DEVELOPMENT AND FOREIGN AID. INT/ORG PROB/SOLV ...SOC 20. PAGE 59 A1222 — BIBLIOG ECO/UNDEV TEC/DEV FOR/AID

B57
MCNEILL W.H.,GREECE: AMERICAN AID IN ACTION. GREECE UK USA+45 FINAN CAP/ISM INT/TRADE BAL/PAY PRODUC WEALTH...POLICY METH/COMP 20. PAGE 99 A2022 — FOR/AID DIPLOM ECO/UNDEV

B57
MILLIKAN M.F.,A PROPOSAL: KEY TO AN EFFECTIVE — FOR/AID

FOREIGN POLICY. USA+45 AGRI FINAN DELIB/GP DIPLOM REPRESENT MAJORITY...NEW/IDEA CHARTS. PAGE 101 A2081
GIVE ECO/UNDEV PLAN

B57
MOYER K.E.,FROM IRAN TO MORROCCO; FROM TURKEY TO THE SUDAN: A SELECTED AND ANNOTATED BIBLIOGRAPHY OF NORTH AFRICA AND NEAR EAST... ISLAM DIPLOM EDU/PROP 20. PAGE 105 A2162
BIBLIOG/A ECO/UNDEV SECT NAT/G

B57
US SENATE SPEC COMM FOR AID,COMPILATION OF STUDIES AND SURVEYS. AFR ASIA L/A+17C USA+45 ECO/UNDEV AGRI INT/ORG CONSULT TEC/DEV CONFER TOTALISM...NAT/COMP 20 CONGRESS. PAGE 157 A3197
FOR/AID DIPLOM ORD/FREE DELIB/GP

B57
US SENATE SPEC COMM FOR AID,HEARINGS BEFORE THE SPECIAL COMMITTEE TO STUDY THE FOREIGN AID PROGRAM. USA+45 USSR ECO/UNDEV INT/ORG FORCES WEAPON TOTALISM ATTIT SUPEGO...NAT/COMP CONGRESS. PAGE 157 A3198
FOR/AID DIPLOM ORD/FREE TEC/DEV

B57
WILSON P.,SOUTH ASIA; A SELECTED BIBLIOGRAPHY ON INDIA, PAKISTAN, CEYLON (PAMPHLET). CEYLON INDIA PAKISTAN LAW ECO/UNDEV PLAN DIPLOM 20. PAGE 165 A3362
BIBLIOG S/ASIA CULTURE NAT/G

L57
FURNISS E.S.,"SOME PERSPECTIVES ON AMERICAN MILITARY ASSISTANCE." USA+45 WOR+45 ECO/UNDEV INT/ORG ECO/TAC ORD/FREE...GEOG TIME/SEQ TREND COLD/WAR 20. PAGE 50 A1028
FORCES FOR/AID WEAPON

L57
WARREN S.,"FOREIGN AID AND FOREIGN POLICY." USA+45 WOR+45 WOR-45 DIST/IND INDUS MARKET CONSULT CREATE DIPLOM EDU/PROP LEGIT ATTIT RIGID/FLEX...TIME/SEQ GEN/LAWS WORK 20. PAGE 161 A3285
ECO/UNDEV ALL/VALS ECO/TAC FOR/AID

S57
ALLEN R.L.,"UNITED NATIONS TECHNICAL ASSISTANCE: SOVIET AND EAST-EUROPEAN PARTICIPATION." COM WOR+45 AGRI INDUS INT/ORG NAT/G FOR/AID SKILL UN 20. PAGE 6 A0124
ECO/UNDEV TEC/DEV USSR

S57
HOAG M.W.,"ECONOMIC PROBLEMS OF ALLIANCE." COM EUR+WWI WOR+45 ECO/DEV ECO/UNDEV NAT/G VOL/ASSN FORCES PLAN TEC/DEV DIPLOM COERCE ORD/FREE PWR WEALTH...DECISION GEN/LAWS NATO COLD/WAR. PAGE 65 A1345
INT/ORG ECO/TAC

N57
US SENATE SPECIAL COMM FOR AFF,REPORT OF THE SPECIAL COMMITTEE TO STUDY THE FOREIGN AID PROGRAM (PAMPHLET). USA+45 CONSULT DELIB/GP LEGIS PLAN TEC/DEV CONFER SUPEGO CONGRESS. PAGE 157 A3199
FOR/AID ORD/FREE ECO/UNDEV DIPLOM

B58
ALMEYDA M.C.,REFLEXIONES POLITICAS. CHILE L/A+17C USA+45 INT/ORG POL/PAR ECO/TAC PARTIC ATTIT 20. PAGE 6 A0128
ECO/UNDEV REGION DIPLOM INT/TRADE

B58
APPADORAI A.,THE USE OF FORCE IN INTERNATIONAL RELATIONS. WOR+45 CULTURE ECO/UNDEV CAP/ISM ARMS/CONT REV WAR ATTIT PERSON SOVEREIGN MARXISM ...INT/LAW PACIFIST 20 UN INTERVENT THIRD/WRLD COLD/WAR. PAGE 8 A0169
PEACE FEDERAL INT/ORG

B58
BERLINER J.S.,SOVIET ECONOMIC AID: THE AID AND TRADE POLICY IN UNDERDEVELOPED COUNTRIES. AFR COM ISLAM L/A+17C S/ASIA USSR ECO/DEV DIST/IND FINAN MARKET INT/ORG ACT/RES PLAN BAL/PWR WEAPON PWR WEALTH...CHARTS 20. PAGE 14 A0277
ECO/UNDEV ECO/TAC FOR/AID

B58
BOWLES C.,IDEAS, PEOPLE AND PEACE. ASIA CHINA/COM FUT INDIA USA+45 USSR ECO/UNDEV INT/ORG LEAD TASK MARXISM 20 NATO UN COLD/WAR. PAGE 18 A0359
PEACE POLICY NAT/G DIPLOM

B58
HAUSER P.H.,POPULATION AND WORLD POLITICS. FUT WOR+45 WOR-45 AGRI DIST/IND INDUS INT/ORG PLAN ECO/TAC DISPL HEALTH COLD/WAR 20. PAGE 63 A1288
NAT/G ECO/UNDEV FOR/AID

B58
INDIAN COUNCIL WORLD AFFAIRS,DEFENCE AND SECURITY IN THE INDIAN OCEAN AREA. INDIA S/ASIA CULTURE CONSULT DELIB/GP FORCES PROB/SOLV DIPLOM INT/TRADE 20 CMN/WLTH. PAGE 70 A1438
GEOG HABITAT ECO/UNDEV ORD/FREE

B58
JENNINGS I.,PROBLEMS OF THE NEW COMMONWEALTH. CEYLON INDIA PAKISTAN S/ASIA ECO/UNDEV INT/ORG LOC/G DIPLOM ECO/TAC INT/TRADE COLONIAL RACE/REL DISCRIM 20 COMMONWLTH PARLIAMENT. PAGE 74 A1508
NAT/LISM NEUTRAL FOR/AID POL/PAR

B58
JENNINGS W.I.,PROBLEMS OF THE NEW COMMONWEALTH. CEYLON INDIA MALAYSIA PAKISTAN ECO/UNDEV VOL/ASSN RACE/REL NAT/LISM ROLE 20 CMN/WLTH. PAGE 74 A1511
GP/REL INGP/REL COLONIAL INT/ORG

B58
KINDLEBERGER C.P.,INTERNATIONAL ECONOMICS. WOR+45 WOR-45 ECO/DEV ECO/UNDEV FINAN VOL/ASSN ACT/RES DIPLOM ECO/TAC LEGIT REGION ATTIT DRIVE ORD/FREE WEALTH...POLICY STAT TREND GEN/LAWS EEC ECSC OEEC 20. PAGE 79 A1620
INT/ORG BAL/PWR TARIFFS

B58
MASON J.B.,THAILAND BIBLIOGRAPHY. S/ASIA THAILAND CULTURE EDU/PROP ADMIN...GEOG SOC LING 20. PAGE 95 A1958
BIBLIOG/A ECO/UNDEV DIPLOM NAT/G

B58
NEHRU J.,SPEECHES. INDIA ECO/UNDEV AGRI INDUS INT/ORG POL/PAR DIPLOM FOR/AID NAT/LISM...ANTHOL 20. PAGE 108 A2213
PLAN CHIEF COLONIAL NEUTRAL

B58
PALMER E.E.,AMERICAN FOREIGN POLICY. USA+45 CULTURE ECO/UNDEV NAT/G PLAN GIVE BAL/PAY ORD/FREE WEALTH POPULISM...DECISION ANTHOL 20. PAGE 113 A2319
DIPLOM ECO/TAC POLICY

B58
PALMER E.E.,THE COMMUNIST CHALLENGE. COM USA+45 USA-45 ECO/DEV ECO/UNDEV NEUTRAL ORD/FREE POPULISM ...CONCPT NAT/COMP ANTHOL 19/20 LENIN/VI STALIN/J MAO MARX/KARL COM/PARTY. PAGE 113 A2320
MARXISM DIPLOM IDEA/COMP POLICY

B58
PAN AMERICAN UNION,REPERTORIO DE PUBLICACIONES PERIODICAS ACTUALES LATINO-AMERICANAS. CULTURE ECO/UNDEV ADMIN LEAD GOV/REL 20 OAS. PAGE 113 A2326
BIBLIOG L/A+17C NAT/G DIPLOM

B58
TILLION G.,ALGERIA: THE REALITIES. ALGERIA FRANCE ISLAM CULTURE STRATA PROB/SOLV DOMIN REV NAT/LISM WEALTH MARXISM...GEOG 20. PAGE 144 A2940
ECO/UNDEV SOC COLONIAL DIPLOM

B58
US HOUSE COMM GOVT OPERATIONS,HEARINGS BEFORE A SUBCOMMITTEE OF THE COMMITTEE ON GOVERNMENT OPERATIONS. CAMBODIA PHILIPPINE USA+45 CONSTRUC TEC/DEV ADMIN CONTROL WEAPON EFFICIENCY HOUSE/REP. PAGE 154 A3135
FOR/AID DIPLOM ORD/FREE ECO/UNDEV

B58
US OPERATIONS MISSION TO VIET,BUILDING ECONOMIC STRENGTH (PAMPHLET). USA+45 VIETNAM/S INDUS TEC/DEV BUDGET ADMIN EATING HEALTH...STAT 20. PAGE 155 A3162
FOR/AID ECO/UNDEV AGRI EDU/PROP

B58
VARG P.A.,MISSIONARIES, CHINESE, AND DIPLOMATS: THE AMERICAN PROTESTANT MISSIONARY MOVEMENT IN CHINA, 1890-1952. ASIA ECO/UNDEV NAT/G PROB/SOLV CAP/ISM EDU/PROP COLONIAL NAT/LISM ATTIT MARXISM...NAT/COMP STERTYP 20 CHINJAP PROTESTANT MISSION. PAGE 158 A3221
CULTURE DIPLOM SECT

B58
WIGGINS J.W.,FOREIGN AID REEXAMINED: A CRITICAL APPRAISAL. CHINA/COM INDONESIA USA+45 FINAN INT/TRADE REGION NAT/LISM ATTIT...CENSUS 20. PAGE 164 A3342
FOR/AID DIPLOM ECO/UNDEV SOVEREIGN

L58
TRAGER F.N.,"A SELECTED AND ANNOTATED BIBLIOGRAPHY ON ECONOMIC DEVELOPMENT, 1953-1957." WOR+45 AGRI FINAN INDUS MARKET LABOR MUNIC WORKER PLAN INT/TRADE PRODUC CENSUS. PAGE 145 A2958
BIBLIOG/A ECO/UNDEV ECO/DEV

S58
JORDAN A.,"MILITARY ASSISTANCE AND NATIONAL POLICY." ASIA FUT USA+45 WOR+45 ECO/DEV ECO/UNDEV INT/ORG NAT/G PLAN ECO/TAC ROUTINE WEAPON ATTIT RIGID/FLEX PWR...CONCPT TREND 20. PAGE 75 A1533
FORCES POLICY FOR/AID DIPLOM

C58
BLANCHARD W.,"THAILAND." THAILAND CULTURE AGRI FINAN INDUS FAM LABOR INT/TRADE ATTIT...GEOG HEAL SOC BIBLIOG 20. PAGE 15 A0307
NAT/G DIPLOM ECO/UNDEV S/ASIA

N58
INVESTMENT FUND ECO SOC DEV,FRENCH AFRICA: A DECADE OF PROGRESS 1948-1958 (PAMPHLET). AFR FRANCE EXTR/IND INDUS EDU/PROP HEALTH 20. PAGE 71 A1465
FOR/AID DIPLOM ECO/UNDEV AGRI

N58
US HOUSE COMM FOREIGN AFFAIRS,HEARINGS ON REVIEW OF THE MUTUAL SECURITY PROGRAMS; EXAMINATION OF SELECTED PROJECTS IN FORMOSA AND PAKISTAN (PAMPHLET). ASIA PAKISTAN TAIWAN INDUS CONSULT DELIB/GP LEGIS BUDGET CONFER DEBATE 20. PAGE 153 A3125
FOR/AID ECO/UNDEV DIPLOM ECO/TAC

B59
AIR FORCE ACADEMY ASSEMBLY '59,INTERNATIONAL STABILITY AND PROGRESS (PAMPHLET). USA+45 USSR ECO/UNDEV PROB/SOLV BUDGET DIPLOM ADMIN DETER COST ATTIT...TREND 20. PAGE 5 A0103
FOR/AID FORCES WAR PLAN

B59
ALLEN R.L.,SOVIET INFLUENCE IN LATIN AMERICA. ECO/UNDEV FINAN PROC/MFG NAT/G TEC/DEV EDU/PROP EXEC ROUTINE ATTIT DRIVE PERSON ALL/VALS PWR...STAT CHARTS WORK 20. PAGE 6 A0125
L/A+17C ECO/TAC INT/TRADE USSR

B59
AMERICAN FRIENDS OF VIETNAM,AID TO VIETNAM: AN AMERICAN SUCCESS STORY (PAMPHLET). ASIA FUT USA+45 VIETNAM ECO/UNDEV WAR CIVMIL/REL GOV/REL...ANTHOL 20. PAGE 7 A0148
DIPLOM NAT/G FOR/AID FORCES

B59
ARON R.,IMPERIALISM AND COLONIALISM (PAMPHLET). WOR+45 WOR-45 ECO/TAC CONTROL REV ORD/FREE 19/20. PAGE 9 A0183
COLONIAL DOMIN ECO/UNDEV DIPLOM

B59
GOLDWIN R.A.,READINGS IN AMERICAN FOREIGN POLICY. USA+45 USA-45 ARMS/CONT NUC/PWR...INT/LAW 18/20. PAGE 53 A1094
ANTHOL DIPLOM INT/ORG ECO/UNDEV

B59
HAZLEWOOD A.,THE ECONOMICS OF "UNDER-DEVELOPED" AREAS. WOR+45 DIST/IND EXTR/IND FINAN INDUS MARKET PLAN FOR/AID...GEOG 20. PAGE 63 A1302
BIBLIOG/A ECO/UNDEV AGRI INT/TRADE

B59
JACKSON B.W.,FIVE IDEAS THAT CHANGE THE WORLD. FUT WOR+45 WOR-45 ECO/UNDEV INDUS DIPLOM DOMIN CONTROL ...IDEA/COMP 20. PAGE 72 A1473
MARXISM NAT/LISM COLONIAL ECO/TAC

B59
JOSEPH F.M.,AS OTHERS SEE US: THE UNITED STATES THROUGH FOREIGN EYES. AFR EUR+WWI ISLAM L/A+17C S/ASIA USA+45 CULTURE SOCIETY ECO/DEV ECO/UNDEV INT/ORG NAT/G DIPLOM ECO/TAC REV ATTIT RIGID/FLEX HEALTH ORD/FREE WEALTH 20. PAGE 75 A1537
RESPECT DOMIN NAT/LISM SOVEREIGN

B59
KARUNAKARAN K.P.,INDIA IN WORLD AFFAIRS, 1952-1958 (VOL. II). INDIA ECO/UNDEV SECT FOR/AID INT/TRADE ADJUD NEUTRAL REV WAR DISCRIM ORD/FREE MARXISM ...BIBLIOG 20. PAGE 77 A1569
DIPLOM INT/ORG S/ASIA COLONIAL

B59
KULSKI W.W.,PEACEFUL CO-EXISTENCE: AN ANALYSIS OF SOVIET FOREIGN POLICY. WOR+45 INTELL SOCIETY ECO/UNDEV POL/PAR EDU/PROP COERCE DRIVE RIGID/FLEX PWR SKILL...PSY CONCPT HIST/WRIT CON/ANAL GEN/METH WORK VAL/FREE 20. PAGE 83 A1691
PLAN DIPLOM USSR

B59
LAQUER W.Z.,THE SOVIET UNION AND THE MIDDLE EAST. COM UAR USSR ECO/UNDEV NAT/G VOL/ASSN ECO/TAC EDU/PROP COLONIAL EXEC PWR...TIME/SEQ TREND COLD/WAR 20. PAGE 85 A1730
ISLAM DRIVE FOR/AID NAT/LISM

B59
MEZERK A.G.,FINANCIAL ASSISTANCE FOR ECONOMIC DEVELOPMENT. WOR+45 INDUS DIPLOM INT/TRADE...CHARTS GOV/COMP UN. PAGE 101 A2064
FOR/AID FINAN ECO/TAC ECO/UNDEV

B59
NUNEZ JIMENEZ A.,LA LIBERACION DE LAS ISLAS. CUBA L/A+17C USA+45 LAW CHIEF PLAN DIPLOM FOR/AID OWN WEALTH 20 CASTRO/F. PAGE 110 A2261
AGRI REV ECO/UNDEV NAT/G

B59
OKINSHEVICH L.A.,LATIN AMERICA IN SOVIET WRITINGS, 1945-1958: A BIBLIOGRAPHY. USSR LAW ECO/UNDEV LABOR DIPLOM EDU/PROP REV...GEOG SOC 20. PAGE 111 A2287
BIBLIOG WRITING COM L/A+17C

B59
ROBINSON J.A.,THE MONRONEY RESOULUTION: CONGRESSIONAL INITIATIVE IN FOREIGN POLICY MAKING. USA+45 POL/PAR TOP/EX DIPLOM INT/TRADE 20 CONGRESS WORLD/BANK INTL/DEV. PAGE 122 A2504
LEGIS FINAN ECO/UNDEV CHIEF

B59
ROPKE W.,INTERNATIONAL ORDER AND ECONOMIC INTEGRATION. ECO/DEV ECO/UNDEV AGRI FINAN INDUS INT/ORG WAR PEACE ORD/FREE...SOC METH/COMP 20 EEC. PAGE 123 A2524
INT/TRADE DIPLOM BAL/PAY ALL/IDEOS

B59
US GENERAL ACCOUNTING OFFICE,EXAM OF ECONOMIC AND TECHNICAL ASSISTANCE PROGRAM FOR INDIA INT'NAT'L COOP ADMIN REPORT TO CONGRESS 1955-1958. INDIA USA+45 ECO/UNDEV FINAN PLAN DIPLOM COST UTIL WEALTH ...CHARTS 20 CONGRESS AID. PAGE 153 A3114
FOR/AID EFFICIENCY ECO/TAC TEC/DEV

B59
US HOUSE COMM GOVT OPERATIONS,UNITED STATES AID OPERATIONS IN LAOS. LAOS USA+45 PLAN INSPECT HOUSE/REP. PAGE 154 A3136
FOR/AID ADMIN FORCES ECO/UNDEV

B59
US PRES COMM STUDY MIL ASSIST,COMPOSITE REPORT. USA+45 ECO/UNDEV PLAN BUDGET DIPLOM EFFICIENCY ...POLICY MGT 20. PAGE 155 A3164
FOR/AID FORCES WEAPON ORD/FREE

B59
VINACKE H.M.,A HISTORY OF THE FAR EAST IN MODERN TIMES (6TH ED.). KOREA S/ASIA USSR CONSTN CULTURE STRATA ECO/UNDEV NAT/G CHIEF FOR/AID INT/TRADE GP/REL...SOC NAT/COMP 19/20 CHINJAP. PAGE 159 A3235
STRUCT ASIA

B59
WARD B.,5 IDEAS THAT CHANGE THE WORLD. WOR+45 WOR-45 SOCIETY STRUCT AGRI INDUS INT/ORG NAT/G FORCES ACT/RES ARMS/CONT TOTALISM ATTIT DRIVE GEN/LAWS. PAGE 161 A3278
ECO/UNDEV ALL/VALS NAT/LISM COLONIAL

B59
YRARRAZAVAL E.,AMERICA LATINE EN LA GUERRA FRIA. EUR+WWI L/A+17C USA+45 USSR WOR+45 INDUS INT/ORG NAT/LISM...POLICY COLD/WAR. PAGE 169 A3439
REGION DIPLOM ECO/UNDEV INT/TRADE

L59
BEGUIN B.,"ILO AND THE TRIPARTITE SYSTEM." EUR+WWI WOR+45 WOR-45 CONSTN ECO/DEV ECO/UNDEV INDUS INT/ORG NAT/G VOL/ASSN DELIB/GP PLAN TEC/DEV LEGIT ORD/FREE WEALTH...CONCPT TIME/SEQ WORK ILO 20. PAGE 12 A0249
LABOR

L59
GARDNER R.N.,"NEW DIRECTIONS IN UNITED STATES FOREIGN ECONOMIC POLICY." USA+45 CONSULT...GEN/LAWS GEN/METH COLD/WAR 20. PAGE 51 A1044
ECO/UNDEV ECO/TAC FOR/AID DIPLOM

L59
WURFEL D.,"FOREIGN AID AND SOCIAL REFORM IN POLITICAL DEVELOPMENT" (BMR)" PHILIPPINE USA+45 WOR+45 SOCIETY POL/PAR ACT/RES TEC/DEV DIPLOM 20. PAGE 168 A3424
FOR/AID PROB/SOLV ECO/TAC ECO/UNDEV

S59
KOHN L.Y.,"ISRAEL AND NEW NATION STATES OF ASIA AND AFRICA." AFR ASIA FUT S/ASIA VOL/ASSN TEC/DEV NAT/LISM RIGID/FLEX SKILL WEALTH...RELATIV OBS TREND CON/ANAL 20. PAGE 81 A1663
ECO/UNDEV ECO/TAC FOR/AID ISRAEL

S59
PADELFORD N.J.,"REGIONAL COOPERATION IN THE SOUTH PACIFIC: THE SOUTH PACIFIC COMMISSION." FUT NEW/ZEALND UK WOR+45 CULTURE ECO/UNDEV LOC/G VOL/ASSN...OBS CON/ANAL UNESCO VAL/FREE AUSTRAL 20. PAGE 112 A2308
INT/ORG ADMIN

S59
REUBENS E.D.,"THE BASIS FOR REORIENATION OF AMERICAN FOREIGN AID POLICY." USA+45 USSR STRUCT INT/ORG CONSULT ECO/TAC ADMIN DRIVE MORAL ORD/FREE PWR WEALTH...RELATIV MATH STAT TREND GEN/LAWS VAL/FREE 20. PAGE 120 A2467
ECO/UNDEV PLAN FOR/AID DIPLOM

S59
SAYEGH F.,"ARAB NATIONALISM AND SOVIET-AMERICAN RELATIONS." ISLAM USA+45 ECO/UNDEV PLAN ECO/TAC LEGIT NAT/LISM DRIVE PERCEPT KNOWL PWR...DECISION CONCPT STAT RECORD TREND CON/ANAL VAL/FREE 20 COLD/WAR. PAGE 127 A2610
DIPLOM USSR

S59
TIPTON J.B.,"PARTICIPATION OF THE UNITED STATES IN THE INTERNATIONAL LABOR ORGANIZATION." USA+45 LAW STRUCT ECO/DEV ECO/UNDEV INDUS TEC/DEV ECO/TAC ADMIN PERCEPT ORD/FREE SKILL...STAT HIST/WRIT GEN/METH ILO WORK 20. PAGE 144 A2946
LABOR INT/ORG

C59
KULSKI W.W.,"PEACEFUL COEXISTENCE." USSR ECO/UNDEV INT/ORG POL/PAR EDU/PROP COLONIAL CONTROL REV NAT/LISM PEACE PWR MARXISM...BIBLIOG 20. PAGE 83 A1692
COM DIPLOM DOMIN

B60
ASPREMONT-LYNDEN H.,RAPPORT SUR L'ADMINISTRATION BELGE DU RUANDA-URUNDI PENDANT L'ANNEE 1959. BELGIUM RWANDA AGRI INDUS DIPLOM ECO/TAC INT/TRADE DOMIN ADMIN RACE/REL...GEOG CENSUS 20 UN. PAGE 9 A0192
AFR COLONIAL ECO/UNDEV INT/ORG

B60
BILLERBECK K.,SOVIET BLOC FOREIGN AID TO UNDERDEVELOPED COUNTRIES. COM FUT USSR FINAN FORCES TEC/DEV DIPLOM INT/TRADE EDU/PROP NUC/PWR...TREND 20. PAGE 14 A0287
FOR/AID ECO/UNDEV ECO/TAC MARXISM

B60
BLACK E.R.,THE DIPLOMACY OF ECONOMIC DEVELOPMENT. WOR+45 CONSULT PLAN TEC/DEV DIPLOM ECO/TAC FOR/AID ...CONCPT TREND 20. PAGE 15 A0297
ECO/UNDEV ACT/RES

B60
CAMPAIGNE J.G.,AMERICAN MIGHT AND SOVIET MYTH. COM EUR+WWI ECO/DEV ECO/UNDEV INT/ORG NAT/G CAP/ISM ECO/TAC FOR/AID EDU/PROP ATTIT PWR WEALTH...POLICY CONCPT MYTH TREND STERTYP GEN/LAWS COLD/WAR. PAGE 23 A0473
USA+45 DOMIN DIPLOM USSR

B60
ENGEL J.,THE SECURITY OF THE FREE WORLD. USSR WOR+45 STRATA STRUCT ECO/DEV ECO/UNDEV INT/ORG DELIB/GP FORCES DOMIN LEGIT ADJUD EXEC ARMS/CONT COERCE...POLICY CONCPT NEW/IDEA TIME/SEQ GEN/LAWS COLD/WAR WORK UN 20 NATO. PAGE 42 A0851
COM TREND DIPLOM

B60
FISCHER L.,RUSSIA, AMERICA, AND THE WORLD. FUT USA+45 USSR WOR+45 FORCES PLAN BAL/PWR ECO/TAC FOR/AID NEUTRAL TASK NUC/PWR PWR 20 COLD/WAR. PAGE 46 A0937
DIPLOM POLICY MARXISM ECO/UNDEV

B60
FOREIGN POLICY CLEARING HOUSE,STRATEGY FOR THE 60'S. FUT USA+45 WOR+45 ECO/UNDEV FORCES BAL/PWR TASK ARMS/CONT DETER PWR MARXISM 20 SENATE. PAGE 47 A0963
DIPLOM NAT/G POLICY ACT/RES

B60
FRANCK P.G.,AFGHANISTAN: BETWEEN EAST AND WEST. AFGHANISTN USA+45 USSR ECO/UNDEV PLAN ADMIN ROUTINE ATTIT PWR...STAT OBS CHARTS TOT/POP COLD/WAR 20. PAGE 48 A0978
ECO/TAC TREND FOR/AID

B60
HEYSE T.,PROBLEMS FONCIERS ET REGIME DES TERRES
BIBLIOG

(ASPECTS ECONOMIQUES, JURIDIQUES ET SOCIAUX). AFR CONGO/BRAZ INT/ORG DIPLOM SOVEREIGN...GEOG TREATY 20. PAGE 64 A1325
AGRI ECO/UNDEV LEGIS

B60
HOFFMANN P.G.,ONE HUNDRED COUNTRIES, ONE AND ONE QUARTER BILLION PEOPLE. MARKET INT/ORG TEC/DEV CAP/ISM...GEOG CHARTS METH/COMP 20 UN. PAGE 66 A1354
FOR/AID ECO/TAC ECO/UNDEV INT/TRADE

B60
HYDE L.K.G.,THE US AND THE UN. WOR+45 STRUCT ECO/DEV ECO/UNDEV NAT/G ACT/RES PLAN DIPLOM EDU/PROP ADMIN ALL/VALS...CONCPT TIME/SEQ GEN/LAWS UN VAL/FREE 20. PAGE 70 A1428
USA+45 INT/ORG FOR/AID

B60
JACOBSON H.K.,AMERICAN FOREIGN POLICY. COM EUR+WWI USA+45 USA-45 ECO/DEV ECO/UNDEV INT/ORG NAT/G INT/TRADE EDU/PROP COLONIAL CHOOSE MARXISM 20 NATO. PAGE 72 A1485
POL/PAR PWR DIPLOM

B60
KENEN P.B.,GIANT AMONG NATIONS: PROBLEMS IN UNITED STATES FOREIGN ECONOMIC POLICY. USA+45 FINAN DIPLOM TARIFFS BAL/PAY WEALTH 20 COLD/WAR. PAGE 77 A1584
FOR/AID ECO/UNDEV INT/TRADE PLAN

B60
KRISTENSEN T.,THE ECONOMIC WORLD BALANCE. FUT WOR+45 CULTURE ECO/DEV BAL/PWR INT/TRADE REGION PWR WEALTH...STAT TREND CHARTS 20. PAGE 82 A1685
ECO/UNDEV ECO/TAC FOR/AID

B60
LATIFI D.,INDIA AND UNITED STATES AID. ASIA INDIA UK USA+45 AGRI FINAN INDUS COLONIAL ORD/FREE SOVEREIGN WEALTH...METH/COMP 20. PAGE 85 A1743
FOR/AID DIPLOM ECO/UNDEV

B60
LERNER A.P.,THE ECONOMICS OF CONTROL. USA+45 ECO/UNDEV INT/ORG ACT/RES PLAN CAP/ISM INT/TRADE ATTIT WEALTH...SOC MATH STAT GEN/LAWS INDEX 20. PAGE 87 A1785
ECO/DEV ROUTINE ECO/TAC SOCISM

B60
LEVIN J.V.,THE EXPORT ECONOMIES: THEIR PATTERN OF DEVELOPMENT IN HISTORICAL PERSPECTIVE. BURMA PERU AGRI WORKER COLONIAL COST DEMAND INCOME 20. PAGE 88 A1795
INT/TRADE ECO/UNDEV BAL/PAY EXTR/IND

B60
LIEUWEN E.,ARMS AND POLITICS IN LATIN AMERICA. FUT USA+45 USA-45 ECO/UNDEV INT/ORG NAT/G FORCES DIPLOM COERCE ATTIT ALL/VALS VAL/FREE OAS 20. PAGE 88 A1811
L/A+17C FOR/AID

B60
MC CLELLAN G.S.,INDIA. CHINA/COM INDIA CONSTN ELITES STRATA AGRI POL/PAR FOR/AID ARMS/CONT REV MARXISM...CENSUS BIBLIOG 20 COLD/WAR GANDHI/M NEHRU/J. PAGE 97 A1990
DIPLOM NAT/G SOCIETY ECO/UNDEV

B60
MCKINNEY R.,REVIEW OF THE INTERNATIONAL ATOMIC POLICIES AND PROGRAMS OF THE UNITED STATES (5 VOLS.). COM FUT USA+45 ECO/DEV ECO/UNDEV INT/ORG DELIB/GP PLAN ADMIN 20 THIRD/WRLD. PAGE 98 A2016
NUC/PWR PEACE DIPLOM POLICY

B60
MENEZES A.J.,O BRASIL E O MUNDO ASIO-AFRICANO (REV. ED.). AFR ASIA BRAZIL WOR+45 INT/TRADE ORD/FREE PWR SOVEREIGN...POLICY 20. PAGE 99 A2040
DIPLOM BAL/PWR LEAD ECO/UNDEV

B60
NEALE A.D.,THE FLOW OF RESOURCES FROM RICH TO POOR. WOR+45 ECO/DEV ECO/UNDEV FINAN INDUS NAT/G PLAN EFFICIENCY WEALTH...POLICY NAT/COMP 20 RESOURCE/N. PAGE 108 A2209
FOR/AID DIPLOM METH/CNCPT

B60
PAN AMERICAN UNION,FIFTH MEETING OF CONSULTATION OF MINISTERS OF FOREIGN AFFAIRS OF AMERICAN STATES. L/A+17C FORCES PLAN PROB/SOLV ADJUD PEACE...POLICY INT/LAW 20 OAS. PAGE 113 A2327
INT/ORG DIPLOM DELIB/GP ECO/UNDEV

B60
PENTONY D.E.,THE UNDERDEVELOPED LANDS. FUT WOR+45 CULTURE AGRI FINAN INDUS MARKET INT/ORG LABOR NAT/G VOL/ASSN CONSULT TEC/DEV ECO/TAC EDU/PROP COLONIAL ATTIT WEALTH...OBS RECORD SAMP TREND GEN/METH WORK UN 20. PAGE 115 A2351
ECO/UNDEV POLICY FOR/AID INT/TRADE

B60
PENTONY D.E.,UNITED STATES FOREIGN AID. INDIA LAOS USA+45 ECO/UNDEV INT/TRADE ADMIN PEACE ATTIT ...POLICY METH/COMP ANTHOL 20. PAGE 115 A2352
FOR/AID DIPLOM ECO/TAC

B60
PHILLIPS J.F.V.,KWAME NKRUMAH AND THE FUTURE OF AFRICA. FUT GHANA ISLAM ECO/UNDEV CHIEF DIPLOM COLONIAL RACE/REL NAT/LISM...TREND IDEA/COMP BIBLIOG 20 NKRUMAH/K. PAGE 116 A2376
BIOG LEAD SOVEREIGN AFR

B60
PLAMENATZ J.,ON ALIEN RULE AND SELF-GOVERNMENT. AFR FUT S/ASIA WOR+45 CULTURE SOCIETY ECO/UNDEV INT/ORG DOMIN EDU/PROP ATTIT RIGID/FLEX ALL/VALS...POLICY CONCPT OBS TREND CON/ANAL GEN/LAWS TOT/POP VAL/FREE. PAGE 116 A2386
NAT/G CONSTN NAT/LISM SOVEREIGN

B60
PRINCETON U CONFERENCE,CURRENT PROBLEMS IN NORTH AFRICA. ALGERIA LIBYA MOROCCO USA+45 EXTR/IND POL/PAR PROB/SOLV DIPLOM ECO/TAC WAR...ANTHOL 20 TUNIS. PAGE 118 A2412
POLICY ECO/UNDEV NAT/G

B60
RAO V.K.R.,INTERNATIONAL AID FOR ECONOMIC DEVELOPMENT - POSSIBILITIES AND LIMITATIONS. FINAN PLAN TEC/DEV ADMIN TASK EFFICIENCY...POLICY SOC METH/CNCPT CHARTS 20 UN. PAGE 119 A2444
FOR/AID DIPLOM INT/ORG ECO/UNDEV

B60
RITNER P.,THE DEATH OF AFRICA. USA+45 ECO/UNDEV DIPLOM ECO/TAC REGION RACE/REL NAT/LISM ORD/FREE ...POLICY 20 NEGRO. PAGE 121 A2485
AFR SOCIETY FUT TASK

B60
SCHLESINGER J.R.,THE POLITICAL ECONOMY OF NATIONAL SECURITY. USA+45 USSR WOR+45 ECO/DEV ECO/UNDEV NAT/G DELIB/GP TOP/EX BAL/PWR DIPLOM INT/TRADE ATTIT PWR...STERTYP TOT/POP 20. PAGE 128 A2628
PLAN ECO/TAC

B60
SHONFIELD A.,THE ATTACK ON WORLD POVERTY. WOR+45 ECO/DEV ECO/UNDEV FINAN VOL/ASSN PLAN EDU/PROP DRIVE KNOWL WEALTH...CONT/OBS STAND/INT ORG/CHARTS TOT/POP UNESCO 20. PAGE 132 A2704
INT/ORG ECO/TAC FOR/AID INT/TRADE

B60
STEVENSON A.E.,PUTTING FIRST THINGS FIRST. USA+45 INT/ORG NEIGH FOR/AID DISCRIM...ANTHOL 20. PAGE 138 A2822
DIPLOM ECO/UNDEV ORD/FREE EDU/PROP

B60
THEOBALD R.,THE RICH AND THE POOR: A STUDY OF THE ECONOMICS OF RISING EXPECTATIONS. WOR+45 CONSTN ECO/DEV ECO/UNDEV INT/ORG NAT/G PLAN FOR/AID ROUTINE BAL/PAY ORD/FREE PWR WEALTH...GEOG TREND WORK 20. PAGE 142 A2912
ECO/TAC INT/TRADE

B60
THEOBOLD R.,THE NEW NATIONS OF WEST AFRICA. GHANA NIGERIA CULTURE INT/ORG ECO/TAC FOR/AID COLONIAL RACE/REL POPULISM...ANTHOL BIBLIOG 20 UN. PAGE 143 A2916
AFR SOVEREIGN ECO/UNDEV DIPLOM

B60
UNITED WORLD FEDERALISTS,UNITED WORLD FEDERALISTS; PANORAMA OF RECENT BOOKS, FILMS, AND JOURNALS ON WORLD FEDERATION, THE UN, AND WORLD PEACE. CULTURE ECO/UNDEV PROB/SOLV FOR/AID ARMS/CONT NUC/PWR ...INT/LAW PHIL/SCI 20 UN. PAGE 149 A3039
BIBLIOG/A DIPLOM INT/ORG PEACE

B60
VOGT W.,PEOPLE: CHALLENGE TO SURVIVAL. WOR+45 ECO/DEV ECO/UNDEV FAM INT/ORG NAT/G PLAN PROB/SOLV FOR/AID GIVE EATING 20 BIRTH/CON. PAGE 159 A3247
CENSUS CONTROL ATTIT TEC/DEV

B60
WHITING A.S.,CHINA CROSSES THE YALU: THE DECISION TO ENTER THE KOREAN WAR. ASIA CHINA/COM KOREA ECO/UNDEV R+D INT/ORG TOP/EX ACT/RES BAL/PWR ATTIT PWR...GEN/METH 20. PAGE 164 A3338
PLAN COERCE WAR

B60
WODDIS J.,AFRICA: THE ROOTS OF REVOLT. SOUTH/AFR WORKER INT/TRADE RACE/REL DISCRIM ORD/FREE 20. PAGE 166 A3374
COLONIAL SOVEREIGN WAR ECO/UNDEV

B60
WOLF C.,FOREIGN AID: THEORY AND PRACTICE IN SOUTHERN ASIA. CEYLON INDONESIA PHILIPPINE S/ASIA CULTURE STRATA ECO/UNDEV PLAN EDU/PROP ATTIT ...METH/CNCPT MATH QUANT STAT CONT/OBS TIME/SEQ SIMUL TOT/POP 20. PAGE 166 A3378
ACT/RES ECO/TAC FOR/AID

S60
"THE EMERGING COMMON MARKETS IN LATIN AMERICA." FUT L/A+17C STRATA DIST/IND INDUS LABOR NAT/G LEGIS ECO/TAC ADMIN RIGID/FLEX HEALTH...NEW/IDEA TIME/SEQ OAS 20. PAGE 3 A0059
FINAN ECO/UNDEV INT/TRADE

S60
CLARK W.,"NEW FORCES IN THE UN." FUT UK WOR+45 CONSTN BAL/PWR DIPLOM DRIVE PWR SKILL...CONCPT TREND UN TOT/POP 20. PAGE 27 A0543
INT/ORG ECO/UNDEV SOVEREIGN

S60
COHEN A.,"THE NEW AFRICA AND THE UN." FUT ECO/UNDEV NAT/G ECO/TAC INT/TRADE CHOOSE ATTIT ORD/FREE PWR ...POLICY METH/CNCPT OBS TREND CON/ANAL GEN/LAWS TOT/POP VAL/FREE UN 20. PAGE 27 A0558
AFR INT/ORG BAL/PWR FOR/AID

S60
FITZGIBBON R.H.,"DICTATORSHIP AND DEMOCRACY IN LATIN AMERICA." FUT ECO/DEV ECO/UNDEV INT/ORG LOC/G NAT/G TOP/EX PLAN TEC/DEV ECO/TAC CHOOSE ATTIT DRIVE PERSON ALL/VALS OAS TOT/POP 20. PAGE 46 A0943
L/A+17C ACT/RES INT/TRADE

S60
FRANKEL S.H.,"ECONOMIC ASPECTS OF POLITICAL INDEPENDENCE IN AFRICA." AFR FUT SOCIETY ECO/UNDEV COM/IND FINAN LEGIS PLAN TEC/DEV CAP/ISM ECO/TAC INT/TRADE ADMIN ATTIT DRIVE RIGID/FLEX PWR WEALTH ...MGT NEW/IDEA MATH TIME/SEQ VAL/FREE 20. PAGE 48 A0984
NAT/G FOR/AID

S60
HAVILAND H.F.,"PROBLEMS OF AMERICAN FOREIGN POLICY." ASIA COM USA+45 WOR+45 INT/ORG NAT/G CONSULT ECO/TAC FOR/AID DOMIN COERCE NUC/PWR ATTIT DRIVE ORD/FREE PWR RESPECT SKILL...POLICY GEOG OBS SAMP TREND GEN/METH METH COLD/WAR UN 20. PAGE 63
ECO/UNDEV FORCES DIPLOM

A1292

S60
JACOBSON H.K.,"THE USSR AND ILO." COM STRUCT ECO/DEV ECO/UNDEV CONSULT DELIB/GP ECO/TAC ILO WORK COLD/WAR 20. PAGE 72 A1484
INT/ORG LABOR USSR

S60
MIKESELL R.F.,"AMERICA'S ECONOMIC RESPONSIBILITY AS A GREAT POWER." COM FUT USA+45 USSR WOR+45 INT/ORG PLAN ECO/TAC FOR/AID EDU/PROP CHOOSE WEALTH ...POLICY 20. PAGE 101 A2069
ECO/UNDEV BAL/PWR CAP/ISM

S60
MORA J.A.,"THE ORGANIZATION OF AMERICAN STATES." USA+45 LAW ECO/UNDEV VOL/ASSN DELIB/GP PLAN BAL/PWR EDU/PROP ADMIN DRIVE RIGID/FLEX ORD/FREE WEALTH ...TIME/SEQ GEN/LAWS OAS 20. PAGE 103 A2126
L/A+17C INT/ORG REGION

S60
MORALES C.J.,"TRADE AND ECONOMIC INTEGRATION IN LATIN AMERICA." FUT L/A+17C LAW STRATA ECO/UNDEV DIST/IND INDUS LABOR NAT/G LEGIS ECO/TAC ADMIN RIGID/FLEX WEALTH...CONCPT NEW/IDEA CONT/OBS TIME/SEQ WORK 20. PAGE 104 A2128
FINAN INT/TRADE REGION

S60
MURPHY J.C.,"INTERNATIONAL INVESTMENT AND THE NATIONAL INTEREST." WOR+45 WOR-45 ECO/DEV ECO/UNDEV NAT/G ACT/RES...CHARTS TOT/POP COLD/WAR 20. PAGE 106 A2179
FINAN WEALTH FOR/AID

S60
NANES A.,"THE EUROPEAN COMMUNITY AND THE UNITED STATES: EVOLVING RELATIONS." EUR+WWI USA+45 WOR+45 ECO/UNDEV MARKET NAT/G DELIB/GP PLAN LEGIT ATTIT PWR WEALTH...CONCPT STAT TIME/SEQ CON/ANAL EEC OEEC 20 EURATOM. PAGE 107 A2194
INT/ORG REGION

S60
OWEN C.F.,"US AND SOVIET RELATIONS WITH UNDERDEVELOPED COUNTRIES: LATIN AMERICA-A CASE STUDY." AFR COM L/A+17C USA+45 USSR EXTR/IND MARKET TEC/DEV DIPLOM ECO/TAC NAT/LISM ORD/FREE PWR ...TREND WORK 20. PAGE 112 A2303
ECO/UNDEV DRIVE INT/TRADE

S60
PYE L.W.,"SOVIET AND AMERICAN STYLES IN FOREIGN AID." COM USA+45 USSR WOR+45 NAT/G PLAN ECO/TAC ROUTINE RIGID/FLEX...POLICY CONCPT TREND GEN/LAWS TOT/POP 20. PAGE 118 A2419
ECO/UNDEV ATTIT FOR/AID

S60
RIVKIN A.,"AFRICAN ECONOMIC DEVELOPMENT: ADVANCED TECHNOLOGY AND THE STAGES OF GROWTH." CULTURE ECO/UNDEV AGRI COM/IND EXTR/IND PLAN ECO/TAC ATTIT DRIVE RIGID/FLEX SKILL WEALTH...MGT SOC GEN/LAWS WORK TOT/POP 20. PAGE 121 A2487
AFR TEC/DEV FOR/AID

C60
WRIGGINS W.H.,"CEYLON: DILEMMAS OF A NEW NATION." ASIA CEYLON CONSTN STRUCT POL/PAR SECT FORCES DIPLOM GOV/REL NAT/LISM...CHARTS BIBLIOG 20. PAGE 167 A3399
PROB/SOLV NAT/G ECO/UNDEV

N60
INTERNATIONAL FEDN DOCUMENTTN,BIBLIOGRAPHY OF DIRECTORIES OF SOURCES OF INFORMATION (PAMPHLET). WOR+45 R+D INT/ORG NAT/G TEC/DEV DIPLOM. PAGE 71 A1456
BIBLIOG/A ECO/DEV ECO/UNDEV

B61
AUBREY H.G.,COEXISTENCE: ECONOMIC CHALLENGE AND RESPONSE. USSR WOR+45 ACT/RES BAL/PWR CAP/ISM DIPLOM ECO/TAC FOR/AID INT/TRADE PEACE SOCISM ...METH/COMP NAT/COMP COLD/WAR. PAGE 10 A0196
POLICY ECO/UNDEV PLAN COM

B61
BAGU S.,ARGENTINA EN EL MUNDO. L/A+17C INDUS INT/TRADE WAR ATTIT ROLE...TREND 19/20 ARGEN OAS. PAGE 10 A0202
DIPLOM INT/ORG REGION ECO/UNDEV

B61
BONNEFOUS M.,EUROPE ET TIERS MONDE. EUR+WWI SOCIETY INT/ORG NAT/G VOL/ASSN ACT/RES TEC/DEV CAP/ISM ECO/TAC ATTIT ORD/FREE SOVEREIGN...POLICY CONCPT TREND 20. PAGE 16 A0334
AFR ECO/UNDEV FOR/AID INT/TRADE

B61
CAMERON J.,THE AFRICAN REVOLUTION. AFR UK ECO/UNDEV POL/PAR REGION RACE/REL DISCRIM PWR CONSERVE ...CONCPT SOC/INTEG 20 NEGRO. PAGE 23 A0472
REV COLONIAL ORD/FREE DIPLOM

B61
CHIDZERO B.T.G.,TANGANYIKA AND INTERNATIONAL TRUSTEESHIP. AFR WOR+45 WOR-45 ECO/DEV INT/ORG ECO/TAC DOMIN COLONIAL...RECORD CHARTS 20 TANGANYIKA CMN/WLTH. PAGE 26 A0528
ECO/UNDEV CONSTN

B61
CONOVER H.F.,SERIALS FOR AFRICAN STUDIES. ECO/UNDEV DIPLOM LEAD NAT/LISM ATTIT...SOC 20. PAGE 30 A0604
BIBLIOG AFR NAT/G

B61
DEAN V.M.,BUILDERS OF EMERGING NATIONS. WOR+45 ECO/UNDEV ECO/TAC NEUTRAL TOTALISM ORD/FREE PWR ...BIOG AUD/VIS IDEA/COMP BIBLIOG 20 COLD/WAR. PAGE 35 A0719
NAT/G CHIEF POLICY DIPLOM

B61
DETHINE P.,BIBLIOGRAPHIE DES ASPECTS ECONOMIQUES ET SOCIAUX DE L'INDUSTRIALISATION EN AFRIQUE. AFR FINAN LABOR FOR/AID...SOC 20. PAGE 36 A0734
BIBLIOG/A ECO/UNDEV INDUS TEC/DEV

B61
DIA M.,THE AFRICAN NATIONS AND WORLD SOLIDARITY. ISLAM CULTURE ELITES ECO/DEV ECO/UNDEV INT/ORG NAT/G PLAN ECO/TAC INT/TRADE EDU/PROP NAT/LISM ATTIT DRIVE ORD/FREE WEALTH...SOCIALIST CONCPT CON/ANAL GEN/LAWS TOT/POP 20. PAGE 37 A0753
AFR REGION SOCISM

B61
FRIEDMANN W.G.,JOINT INTERNATIONAL BUSINESS VENTURES. ASIA ISLAM L/A+17C ECO/DEV DIST/IND FINAN PROC/MFG FACE/GP LG/CO NAT/G VOL/ASSN CONSULT EX/STRUC PLAN ADMIN ROUTINE WEALTH...OLD/LIB WORK 20. PAGE 49 A1004
ECO/UNDEV INT/TRADE

B61
GANGULI B.N.,ECONOMIC INTEGRATION. FINAN LABOR CAP/ISM DIPLOM WEALTH...NAT/COMP 20. PAGE 51 A1041
ECO/TAC METH/CNCPT EQUILIB ECO/UNDEV

B61
GURTOO D.H.N.,INDIA'S BALANCE OF PAYMENTS (1920-1960). INDIA FINAN DIPLOM FOR/AID INT/TRADE PRICE COLONIAL...CHARTS BIBLIOG 20. PAGE 58 A1197
BAL/PAY STAT ECO/TAC ECO/UNDEV

B61
HADDAD J.A.,REVOLUCAO CUBANA E REVOLUCAO BRASILEIRA. BRAZIL CUBA L/A+17C STRATA AGRI WORKER EDU/PROP REGION...POLICY NAT/COMP 20. PAGE 59 A1210
REV ORD/FREE DIPLOM ECO/UNDEV

B61
HARRISON J.P.,GUIDE TO MATERIALS ON LATIN AMERICA IN THE NATIONAL ARCHIVES (2 VOLS.). USA+45 ECO/UNDEV FINAN LOC/G FORCES 20. PAGE 62 A1271
BIBLIOG L/A+17C NAT/G DIPLOM

B61
HARRISON S.,INDIA AND THE UNITED STATES. FUT S/ASIA USA+45 WOR+45 INTELL ECO/DEV ECO/UNDEV AGRI INDUS INT/ORG NAT/G CONSULT EX/STRUC TOP/EX PLAN ECO/TAC NEUTRAL ALL/VALS...MGT TOT/POP 20. PAGE 62 A1272
DELIB/GP ACT/RES FOR/AID INDIA

B61
HASAN H.S.,PAKISTAN AND THE UN. ISLAM WOR+45 ECO/DEV ECO/UNDEV NAT/G TOP/EX ECO/TAC FOR/AID EDU/PROP ADMIN DRIVE PERCEPT...OBS TIME/SEQ UN 20. PAGE 62 A1284
INT/ORG ATTIT PAKISTAN

B61
INTERNATIONAL BANK RECONST DEV,THE WORLD BANK IN AFRICA: SUMMARY OF ACTIVITIES. AGRI COM/IND DIST/IND EXTR/IND INDUS TAX COST...CHARTS 20. PAGE 71 A1450
FINAN ECO/UNDEV INT/ORG AFR

B61
JAVITS B.A.,THE PEACE BY INVESTMENT CORPORATION. WOR+45 NAT/G LEGIS PROB/SOLV PERS/REL WEALTH ...POLICY 20. PAGE 73 A1499
ECO/UNDEV DIPLOM FOR/AID PEACE

B61
KISSINGER H.A.,THE NECESSITY FOR CHOICE. FUT USA+45 ECO/UNDEV NAT/G PLAN BAL/PWR ECO/TAC ARMS/CONT DETER NUC/PWR ATTIT...POLICY CONCPT RECORD GEN/LAWS COLD/WAR 20. PAGE 80 A1642
TOP/EX TREND DIPLOM

B61
KNORR K.E.,THE INTERNATIONAL SYSTEM. FUT SOCIETY INT/ORG NAT/G PLAN BAL/PWR DIPLOM WAR PWR ...DECISION METH/CNCPT CONT/OBS GAME METH UN 20. PAGE 81 A1655
ACT/RES SIMUL ECO/UNDEV

B61
LANDSKROY W.A.,OFFICIAL SERIAL PUBLICATIONS RELATING TO ECONOMIC DEVELOPMENT IN AFRICA SOUTH OF THE SAHARA (PAMPHLET). AFR UK R+D ACT/RES 20 UN. PAGE 84 A1720
BIBLIOG ECO/UNDEV COLONIAL INT/ORG

B61
LETHBRIDGE H.J.,CHINA'S URBAN COMMUNES. CHINA/COM FUT ECO/UNDEV DIPLOM EDU/PROP DEMAND INCOME MARXISM ...POLICY 20. PAGE 87 A1790
MUNIC CONTROL ECO/TAC NAT/G

B61
MEZERIK A.G.,ECONOMIC DEVELOPMENT AIDS FOR UNDERDEVELOPED COUNTRIES. WOR+45 FINAN LEGIS PROB/SOLV TEC/DEV DIPLOM FOR/AID GIVE TASK WAR 20 UN. PAGE 101 A2062
ECO/UNDEV INT/ORG WEALTH PLAN

B61
MILLIKAW M.F.,THE EMERGING NATIONS: THEIR GROWTH AND UNITED STATES POLICY. FUT USA+45 WOR+45 WOR-45 NAT/G PLAN TEC/DEV BAL/PWR GOV/REL PEACE ORD/FREE 20. PAGE 101 A2082
ECO/UNDEV POLICY DIPLOM FOR/AID

B61
MORLEY L.,THE PATCHWORK HISTORY OF FOREIGN AID. KOREA/S USA+45 USSR LAW FINAN INT/ORG TEC/DEV BAL/PWR GIVE 20 COLD/WAR NATO. PAGE 104 A2144
FOR/AID ECO/UNDEV FORCES DIPLOM

B61
NATIONAL BANK OF LIBYA,INFLATION IN LIBYA (PAMPHLET). LIBYA SOCIETY NAT/G PLAN INT/TRADE ...STAT CHARTS 20 GOLD/STAND. PAGE 107 A2200
ECO/TAC ECO/UNDEV FINAN BUDGET

B61
OAKES J.B.,THE EDGE OF FREEDOM. EUR+WWI USA+45 USSR AFR

ECO/UNDEV BAL/PWR DIPLOM DOMIN COLONIAL PWR MARXISM POPULISM...IDEA/COMP 20 COLD/WAR. PAGE 111 A2271
ORD/FREE SOVEREIGN NEUTRAL

B61
PALMER N.D.,THE INDIAN POLITICAL SYSTEM. INDIA ECO/UNDEV SECT CHIEF COLONIAL CHOOSE ALL/IDEOS SOCISM...CHARTS BIBLIOG/A 20. PAGE 113 A2322
NAT/LISM POL/PAR NAT/G DIPLOM

B61
PANIKKAR K.M.,REVOLUTION IN AFRICA. AFR GUINEA ECO/UNDEV POL/PAR DIPLOM COLONIAL EXEC LEAD SOVEREIGN...CHARTS 20. PAGE 114 A2332
NAT/LISM NAT/G CHIEF

B61
PECKERT J.,DIE GROSSEN UND DIE KLEINEN MAECHTE. COM GERMANY/W ECO/DEV ECO/UNDEV NAT/G WAR RACE/REL PEACE...POLICY GP/COMP GOV/COMP 20 COLD/WAR. PAGE 114 A2346
DIPLOM ECO/TAC BAL/PWR

B61
ROBINS D.B.,EVOLVING UNITED STATES POLICIES TOWARD THE EMERGING NATIONS OF ASIA AND AFRICA (PAMPHLET). ISLAM ECO/UNDEV INT/ORG CONSULT CREATE PLAN TEC/DEV FOR/AID CONFER ALL/VALS 20 KENNEDY/JF EISNHWR/DD UN AID. PAGE 122 A2501
AFR S/ASIA DIPLOM BIBLIOG

B61
SHARP W.R.,FIELD ADMINISTRATION IN THE UNITED NATION SYSTEM: THE CONDUCT OF INTERNATIONAL ECONOMIC AND SOCIAL PROGRAMS. FUT WOR+45 CONSTN SOCIETY ECO/UNDEV R+D DELIB/GP ACT/RES PLAN TEC/DEV EDU/PROP EXEC ROUTINE HEALTH WEALTH...HUM CONCPT CHARTS METH ILO UNESCO VAL/FREE UN 20. PAGE 132 A2697
INT/ORG CONSULT

B61
SSU-YU T.,JAPANESE STUDIES ON JAPAN AND THE FAR EAST: A SHORT BIOGRAPHICAL AND BIBLIOGRAPHICAL INTRODUCTION. ASIA CULTURE ECO/UNDEV NAT/G DIPLOM 20 CHINJAP. PAGE 136 A2795
BIBLIOG SOC

B61
STARK H.,SOCIAL AND ECONOMIC FRONTIERS IN LATIN AMERICA (2ND ED.). CUBA FUT CULTURE AGRI INDUS ECO/TAC PRODUC ATTIT MARXISM...NAT/COMP BIBLIOG T 20. PAGE 137 A2807
L/A+17C SOCIETY DIPLOM ECO/UNDEV

B61
STILLMAN E.,THE NEW POLITICS: AMERICA AND THE END OF THE POSTWAR WORLD. FUT WOR+45 CULTURE SOCIETY ECO/UNDEV INT/ORG NAT/G FORCES TOP/EX ACT/RES DIPLOM EDU/PROP LEGIT ROUTINE DETER ATTIT ORD/FREE PWR...OBS STERTYP COLD/WAR TOT/POP VAL/FREE. PAGE 138 A2827
USA+45 PLAN

B61
SYATAUW J.J.G.,SOME NEWLY ESTABLISHED ASIAN STATES AND THE DEVELOPMENT OF INTERNATIONAL LAW. BURMA CEYLON INDIA INDONESIA ECO/UNDEV COLONIAL NEUTRAL WAR PEACE SOVEREIGN...CHARTS 19/20. PAGE 140 A2873
INT/LAW ADJUST SOCIETY S/ASIA

B61
THEOBALD R.,THE CHALLENGE OF ABUNDANCE. USA+45 WOR+45 MARKET DIPLOM FOR/AID REV PRODUC UTOPIA SUPEGO...POLICY TREND BIBLIOG/A 20. PAGE 142 A2913
WELF/ST ECO/UNDEV PROB/SOLV ECO/TAC

B61
US GENERAL ACCOUNTING OFFICE,EXAMINATION OF ECONOMIC AND TECHNICAL ASSISTANCE PROGRAM FOR IRAN. IRAN USA+45 AGRI INDUS DIPLOM CONTROL COST 20. PAGE 153 A3115
FOR/AID ADMIN TEC/DEV ECO/UNDEV

B61
US HOUSE COMM APPROPRIATIONS,INTER-AMERICAN PROGRAMS FOR 1961: DENIAL OF 1962 BUDGET INFORMATION. CHILE L/A+17C USA+45 FINAN CONSULT BUDGET ADJUD COST EFFICIENCY WEALTH...POLICY CHARTS 20 CONGRESS. PAGE 153 A3119
LEGIS FOR/AID DELIB/GP ECO/UNDEV

B61
US HOUSE COMM FOREIGN AFFAIRS,THE INTERNATIONAL DEVELOPMENT AND SECURITY ACT: HEARINGS BEFORE COMMITTEE ON FOREIGN AFFAIRS, HOUSE OF REP: HR7372. USA+45 AGRI INT/ORG NAT/G CONSULT DELIB/GP DIPLOM ECO/TAC INT/TRADE LOBBY REPRESENT 20 MCNAMARA/R DILLON/D RUSK/D CONGRESS. PAGE 153 A3128
FOR/AID CONFER LEGIS ECO/UNDEV

B61
US SENATE COMM ON FOREIGN RELS,INTERNATIONAL DEVELOPMENT AND SECURITY: HEARINGS ON BILL (2 VOLS.). ECO/UNDEV FINAN FORCES REV COST WEALTH ...CHARTS 20 AID PRESIDENT. PAGE 157 A3191
FOR/AID CIVMIL/REL ORD/FREE ECO/TAC

B61
WALLERSTEIN I.M.,AFRICA; THE POLITICS OF INDEPENDENCE. AFR SOCIETY STRUCT LEAD PARL/PROC PARTIC GP/REL...POLICY 20. PAGE 160 A3269
ECO/UNDEV DIPLOM COLONIAL ORD/FREE

B61
WARD B.J.,INDIA AND THE WEST. INDIA UK USA+45 INT/TRADE GIVE COLONIAL ATTIT MARXISM 19/20. PAGE 161 A3279
PLAN ECO/UNDEV ECO/TAC FOR/AID

B61
WINTER R.C.,BLUEPRINTS FOR INDEPENDENCE. WOR+45 INT/ORG DIPLOM COLONIAL CONTROL REV WAR PWR ...BIBLIOG 20 UN. PAGE 165 A3367
NAT/G ECO/UNDEV SOVEREIGN CONSTN

B61
YUAN TUNG-LI,A GUIDE TO DOCTORAL DISSERTATIONS BY CHINESE STUDENTS IN AMERICA, 1905-1960. ASIA CULTURE SOCIETY ECO/UNDEV NAT/G PROB/SOLV DIPLOM LEAD ATTIT...HUM SOC STAT 20. PAGE 169 A3441
BIBLIOG ACADEM ACT/RES OP/RES

L61
HILSMAN R. JR.,"THE NEW COMMUNIST TACTIC: PRECIS-INTERNAL WAR." COM FUT USA+45 ECO/UNDEV POL/PAR FOR/AID RIGID/FLEX ALL/VALS...TREND COLD/WAR 20. PAGE 65 A1334
FORCES COERCE USSR GUERRILLA

S61
"CRITERIA FOR ALLOCATING INVESTMENT RESOURCES AMONG VARIOUS FIELDS OF DEVELOPMENT IN UNDERDEVELOPED ECONOMIES." ASIA AGRI INT/ORG CAP/ISM BAL/PAY EFFICIENCY PROFIT WEALTH...STAT 20 UN. PAGE 3 A0061
BIBLIOG/A ECO/UNDEV PLAN TEC/DEV

S61
ASHFORD D.E.,"A CASE STUDY IN THE DIPLOMACY OF SOCIAL REVOLUTION." USA+45 WOR+45 DIPLOM ECO/TAC FOR/AID REV ALL/VALS VAL/FREE 20. PAGE 9 A0187
ECO/UNDEV PLAN

S61
BARALL M.,"THE UNITED STATES GOVERNMENT RESPONDS." L/A+17C USA+45 SOCIETY NAT/G CREATE PLAN DIPLOM ECO/TAC ATTIT DRIVE RIGID/FLEX KNOWL SKILL WEALTH ...METH/CNCPT TIME/SEQ GEN/METH 20. PAGE 11 A0217
ECO/UNDEV ACT/RES FOR/AID

S61
CARLETON W.G.,"AMERICAN FOREIGN POLICY: MYTHS AND REALITIES." FUT USA+45 WOR+45 ECO/UNDEV INT/ORG EX/STRUC ARMS/CONT NUC/PWR WAR ATTIT...POLICY CONCPT CONT/OBS GEN/METH COLD/WAR TOT/POP 20. PAGE 24 A0484
PLAN MYTH DIPLOM

S61
CASTANEDA J.,"THE UNDERDEVELOPED NATIONS AND THE DEVELOPMENT OF INTERNATIONAL LAW." FUT UNIV LAW ACT/RES FOR/AID LEGIT PERCEPT SKILL...JURID METH/CNCPT TIME/SEQ TOT/POP 20 UN. PAGE 25 A0507
INT/ORG ECO/UNDEV PEACE INT/LAW

S61
GALBRAITH J.K.,"A POSITIVE APPROACH TO ECONOMIC AID." FUT USA+45 INTELL NAT/G CONSULT ACT/RES DIPLOM ECO/TAC EDU/PROP ATTIT KNOWL PWR WEALTH ...SOC STERTYP 20. PAGE 50 A1030
ECO/UNDEV ROUTINE FOR/AID

S61
GOODWIN G.L.,"THE EXPANDING UNITED NATIONS: 2-DIPLOMATIC PRESSURES AND TECHNIQUES." COM ECO/UNDEV TOP/EX BAL/PWR DIPLOM DOMIN...POLICY CONCPT UN COLD/WAR 20. PAGE 54 A1108
INT/ORG PWR

S61
HEILBRONER R.L.,"DYNAMICS OF FOREIGN AID: PROBLEMS OF UNDERDEVELOPED NATIONS PLAGUE ASSISTANCE PROGRAM." FUT USA+45 WOR+45 STRATA NAT/G PLAN TEC/DEV ATTIT DRIVE WEALTH WORK 20. PAGE 64 A1307
ECO/UNDEV ECO/TAC FOR/AID

S61
NOVE A.,"THE SOVIET MODEL AND UNDERDEVELOPED COUNTRIES." COM FUT USSR WOR+45 CULTURE ECO/DEV POL/PAR FOR/AID EDU/PROP ADMIN MORAL WEALTH ...POLICY RECORD HIST/WRIT 20. PAGE 110 A2258
ECO/UNDEV PLAN

S61
OCHENG D.,"ECONOMIC FORCES AND UGANDA'S FOREIGN POLICY." AFR UGANDA INT/TRADE TARIFFS INCOME SOVEREIGN WEALTH 20 EACM EEC TANGANYIKA. PAGE 111 A2274
ECO/TAC DIPLOM ECO/UNDEV INT/ORG

S61
OCHENG D.,"AN ECONOMIST LOOKS AT UGANDA'S FUTURE." FUT UGANDA AGRI INDUS PLAN PROB/SOLV INT/TRADE SOVEREIGN 20. PAGE 111 A2275
ECO/UNDEV INCOME ECO/TAC OWN

S61
PADELFORD N.J.,"POLITICS AND THE FUTURE OF ECOSOC." AFR S/ASIA ECO/UNDEV INDUS NAT/G DELIB/GP ACT/RES ORD/FREE WEALTH...CONCPT CHARTS UN 20 ECOSOC. PAGE 113 A2310
INT/ORG TEC/DEV

S61
ROSTOW W.W.,"THE FUTURE OF FOREIGN AID." COM FUT WOR+45 ECO/DEV INDUS INT/ORG NAT/G CONSULT ACT/RES PLAN DOMIN LEGIT CHOOSE RIGID/FLEX ALL/VALS ...MAJORIT CONCPT TREND TOT/POP 20. PAGE 124 A2544
ECO/UNDEV ECO/TAC FOR/AID

S61
VERNON R.,"A TRADE POLICY FOR THE 1960'S." COM FUT USA+45 WOR+45 ECO/DEV ECO/UNDEV FINAN TOP/EX ACT/RES...WELF/ST METH/CNCPT CONT/OBS TOT/POP 20. PAGE 159 A3229
PLAN INT/TRADE

S61
VINER J.,"ECONOMIC FOREIGN POLICY ON THE NEW FRONTIER." USA+45 ECO/UNDEV AGRI FINAN INDUS MARKET INT/ORG NAT/G FOR/AID INT/TRADE ADMIN ATTIT PWR 20 KENNEDY/JF. PAGE 159 A3239
TOP/EX ECO/TAC BAL/PAY TARIFFS

S61
WEST F.J.,"THE NEW GUINEA QUESTION: AN AUSTRALIAN VIEW." WOR+45 INT/ORG VOL/ASSN LEGIT PERCEPT ...POLICY TIME/SEQ AUSTRAL VAL/FREE 20 CMN/WLTH. PAGE 163 A3320
S/ASIA ECO/UNDEV

S61
ZAGORIA D.S.,"SINO-SOVIET FRICTION IN UNDERDEVELOPED AREAS." ASIA CHINA/COM COM ACT/RES PLAN ATTIT ORD/FREE PWR COLD/WAR 20. PAGE 169 A3443
ECO/UNDEV ECO/TAC INT/TRADE USSR

B62
ROUND TABLE ON EUROPE'S ROLE IN LATIN AMERICAN DEVELOPMENT. EUR+WWI L/A+17C PLAN BAL/PAY UTIL ROLE WEALTH...CHARTS ANTHOL 20 UN INT/AM/DEV. PAGE 3 A0063
ECO/UNDEV FINAN TEC/DEV FOR/AID

B62
ARNOLD H.J.P.,AID FOR DEVELOPING COUNTRIES. COM EUR+WWI USA+45 USSR WOR+45 EDU/PROP ATTIT DRIVE PWR WEALTH...TREND CHARTS STERTYP NAT/ 20. PAGE 9 A0177
ECO/UNDEV ECO/TAC FOR/AID

B62
BRIMMER B.,A GUIDE TO THE USE OF UNITED NATIONS DOCUMENTS. WOR+45 ECO/UNDEV AGRI EX/STRUC FORCES PROB/SOLV ADMIN WAR PEACE WEALTH...POLICY UN. PAGE 19 A0378
BIBLIOG/A INT/ORG DIPLOM

B62
CALDER R.,COMMON SENSE ABOUT A STARVING WORLD. WOR+45 STRATA ECO/DEV PLAN GP/REL BIO/SOC HABITAT ...POLICY GEOG STAT RECORD 20 UN BIRTH/CON. PAGE 23 A0466
FOR/AID CENSUS ECO/UNDEV AGRI

B62
CLUBB O.E. JR.,THE UNITED STATES AND THE SINO-SOVIET BLOC IN SOUTHEAST ASIA. ASIA CHINA/COM COM USA+45 USSR ECO/UNDEV INT/ORG NAT/G FORCES TOP/EX PLAN ECO/TAC DOMIN COERCE GUERRILLA ATTIT RIGID/FLEX...POLICY OBS TREND 20. PAGE 27 A0553
S/ASIA PWR BAL/PWR DIPLOM

B62
COSTA RICA UNIVERSIDAD BIBL,LISTA DE TESIS DE GRADO DE LA UNIVERSIDAD DE COSTA RICA. COSTA/RICA LAW LOC/G ADMIN LEAD...SOC 20. PAGE 31 A0631
BIBLIOG/A NAT/G DIPLOM ECO/UNDEV

B62
COUNCIL ON WORLD TENSIONS,A STUDY OF WORLD TENSIONS AND DEVELOPMENT. WOR+45 ECO/DEV ECO/UNDEV INT/ORG PLAN DIPLOM ECO/TAC EDU/PROP ATTIT KNOWL ORD/FREE PWR WEALTH...CONCPT TREND CHARTS STERTYP COLD/WAR TOT/POP 20. PAGE 31 A0640
TEC/DEV SOC

B62
COUNCIL ON WORLD TENSIONS,RESTLESS NATIONS. WOR+45 STRUCT INT/ORG NAT/G PLAN ECO/TAC...NAT/COMP ANTHOL 20. PAGE 32 A0641
ECO/UNDEV POLICY DIPLOM TASK

B62
DIAZ J.S.,MANUAL DE BIBLIOGRAFIA DE LA LITERATURA ESPANOLA. PRE/AMER SPAIN ECO/UNDEV DIPLOM LEAD ATTIT...SOC 15/20. PAGE 37 A0755
BIBLIOG L/A+17C NAT/G COLONIAL

B62
DOUGLAS W.O.,DEMOCRACY'S MANIFESTO. COM USA+45 ECO/UNDEV INT/ORG FORCES PLAN NEUTRAL TASK MARXISM ...JURID 20 NATO SEATO. PAGE 38 A0779
DIPLOM POLICY NAT/G ORD/FREE

B62
DREIER J.C.,THE ALLIANCE FOR PROGRESS. L/A+17C USA+45 CULTURE ECO/DEV ECO/UNDEV NAT/G PLAN DIPLOM PWR 20 OAS. PAGE 39 A0787
FOR/AID INT/ORG ECO/TAC POLICY

B62
DUROSELLE J.B.,LES NOUVEAUX ETATS DANS LES RELATIONS INTERNATIONALES. AFR CHINA/COM FRANCE MOROCCO S/ASIA USSR ECO/UNDEV INT/ORG PLAN ECO/TAC EDU/PROP ATTIT DRIVE...TREND TOT/POP TUNIS 20. PAGE 39 A0806
NAT/G CONSTN DIPLOM

B62
ELLIOTT J.R.,THE APPEAL OF COMMUNISM IN THE UNDERDEVELOPED NATIONS. USSR WOR+45 INT/ORG NAT/G DIPLOM DOMIN EDU/PROP ROUTINE ATTIT RIGID/FLEX ORD/FREE PWR WEALTH MARXISM...POLICY SOC METH/CNCPT MYTH TOT/POP COLD/WAR 20. PAGE 41 A0842
COM ECO/UNDEV

B62
FAO,FOOD AND AGRICULTURE ORGANIZATION AFRICAN SURVEY. AFR CONGO/BRAZ GHANA STRATA AGRI INT/ORG TEC/DEV FOR/AID INT/TRADE RACE/REL DEMAND EFFICIENCY PRODUC...GEOG 20 UN CONGO/LEOP. PAGE 44 A0898
ECO/TAC WEALTH EXTR/IND ECO/UNDEV

B62
FATOUROS A.A.,GOVERNMENT GUARANTEES TO FOREIGN INVESTORS. WOR+45 ECO/UNDEV INDUS WORKER ADJUD ...NAT/COMP BIBLIOG TREATY. PAGE 44 A0903
NAT/G FINAN INT/TRADE ECO/DEV

B62
FORD A.G.,THE GOLD STANDARD 1880-1914: BRITAIN AND ARGENTINA. UK ECO/UNDEV INT/TRADE ADMIN GOV/REL DEMAND EFFICIENCY...STAT CHARTS 19/20 ARGEN GOLD/STAND. PAGE 47 A0960
FINAN ECO/TAC BUDGET BAL/PAY

B62
FRIEDRICH-EBERT-STIFTUNG,THE SOVIET BLOC AND DEVELOPING COUNTRIES. CHINA/COM COM GERMANY/E USSR WOR+45 ECO/UNDEV INT/ORG NAT/G TEC/DEV NEUTRAL PWR ...POLICY 20. PAGE 49 A1008
MARXISM DIPLOM ECO/TAC FOR/AID

B62
GOLDWIN R.A.,WHY FOREIGN AID? - TWO MESSAGES BY PRESIDENT KENNEDY AND ESSAYS. S/ASIA USA+45 ECO/UNDEV 20 KENNEDY/JF THIRD/WRLD. PAGE 54 A1096
DIPLOM FOR/AID POLICY

B62
GUENA Y.,HISTORIQUE DE LA COMMUNAUTE. FUT ECO/UNDEV NAT/G PLAN EDU/PROP COLONIAL REGION NAT/LISM ALL/VALS SOVEREIGN...CONCPT OBS CHARTS 20. PAGE 58 A1186
AFR VOL/ASSN FOR/AID FRANCE

B62
HARARI M.,GOVERNMENT AND POLITICS OF THE MIDDLE EAST. ISLAM USA+45 NAT/G SECT CHIEF ADMIN ORD/FREE 20. PAGE 61 A1257
DIPLOM ECO/UNDEV TEC/DEV POLICY

B62
HATCH J.,AFRICA TODAY-AND TOMORROW: AN OUTLINE OF BASIC FACTS AND MAJOR PROBLEMS. AFR FUT ISLAM STRATA ECO/UNDEV INT/ORG NAT/G POL/PAR DELIB/GP TOP/EX EDU/PROP LEGIT CHOOSE ATTIT...TIME/SEQ TOT/POP COLD/WAR 20. PAGE 63 A1287
PLAN CONSTN NAT/LISM

B62
HIGGANS B.,UNITED NATIONS AND U.S. FOREIGN ECONOMIC POLICY. FUT USA+45 WOR+45 ECO/DEV ECO/UNDEV NAT/G ECO/TAC WEALTH...TIME/SEQ TOT/POP UN 20. PAGE 65 A1328
INT/ORG ACT/RES FOR/AID DIPLOM

B62
HOFFMAN P.,WORLD WITHOUT WANT. FUT WOR+45 ECO/UNDEV INT/ORG HEALTH KNOWL...TREND TOT/POP FAO 20. PAGE 66 A1353
CONCPT POLICY FOR/AID

B62
JORDAN A.A. JR.,FOREIGN AID AND THE DEFENSE OF SOUTHEAST ASIA. PAKISTAN VIETNAM/S FINAN PLAN BUDGET ECO/TAC DETER WAR ORD/FREE...POLICY DECISION CENSUS CHARTS BIBLIOG 20. PAGE 75 A1535
FOR/AID S/ASIA FORCES ECO/UNDEV

B62
KINDLEBERGER C.P.,FOREIGN TRADE AND THE NATIONAL ECONOMY. WOR+45 ECO/DEV ECO/UNDEV ECO/TAC COST DEMAND 20. PAGE 79 A1622
INT/TRADE GOV/COMP BAL/PAY POLICY

B62
LAUERHAUSS L.,COMMUNISM IN LATIN AMERICA: THE POST-WAR YEARS (1945 -1960) (PAPER). INTELL STRATA ECO/UNDEV AGRI WORKER FOR/AID INT/TRADE COLONIAL GUERRILLA 20. PAGE 85 A1745
BIBLIOG L/A+17C MARXISM REV

B62
LERNER M.,THE AGE OF OVERKILL: A PREFACE TO WORLD POLITICS. USA+45 USSR WOR+45 SOCIETY ECO/UNDEV BAL/PWR NEUTRAL PARTIC REV ALL/IDEOS MARXISM ...BIBLIOG/A 20. PAGE 87 A1787
DIPLOM NUC/PWR PWR DEATH

B62
LESSING P.,AFRICA'S RED HARVEST. AFR CHINA/COM COM USSR ECO/UNDEV BAL/PWR DIPLOM CONTROL PWR 20 COLD/WAR INTERVENT. PAGE 87 A1789
NAT/LISM MARXISM FOR/AID EDU/PROP

B62
LEWIS J.P.,QUIET CRISIS IN INDIA. INDIA USA+45 CULTURE ECO/UNDEV AGRI INDUS PROC/MFG NAT/G PLAN TEC/DEV DRIVE PWR SKILL WEALTH...MYTH 20. PAGE 88 A1801
S/ASIA ECO/TAC FOR/AID

B62
MODELSKI G.,SEATO-SIX STUDIES. ASIA CHINA/COM INDIA S/ASIA INT/ORG NAT/G ECO/TAC DETER ATTIT ORD/FREE PWR...TIME/SEQ COLD/WAR TOT/POP 20 SEATO. PAGE 102 A2098
MARKET ECO/UNDEV INT/TRADE

B62
MOUSSA P.,THE UNDERPRIVILEGED NATIONS. FINAN INT/ORG PLAN PROB/SOLV CAP/ISM GIVE TASK WEALTH ...POLICY SOC 20. PAGE 105 A2159
ECO/UNDEV NAT/G DIPLOM FOR/AID

B62
PAKISTAN MINISTRY OF FINANCE,FOREIGN ECONOMIC AID: A REVIEW OF FOREIGN ECONOMIC AID TO PAKISTAN. EUR+WWI PAKISTAN UK USA+45 USSR ECO/UNDEV INT/ORG DELIB/GP DIPLOM ECO/TAC...CHARTS CMN/WLTH CHINJAP. PAGE 113 A2318
FOR/AID RECEIVE WEALTH FINAN

B62
POSTON R.W.,DEMOCRACY SPEAKS MANY TONGUES. L/A+17C USA+45 ECO/UNDEV ACT/RES ECO/TAC ADMIN ORD/FREE ...METH/COMP 20. PAGE 117 A2397
FOR/AID DIPLOM CAP/ISM MARXISM

B62
RIMALOV V.V.,ECONOMIC COOPERATION BETWEEN USSR AND UNDERDEVELOPED COUNTRIES. USSR FINAN TEC/DEV INT/TRADE DOMIN EDU/PROP COLONIAL NAT/LISM DRIVE SOVEREIGN...AUD/VIS 20. PAGE 121 A2482
FOR/AID PLAN ECO/UNDEV DIPLOM

B62
RIVKIN A.,AFRICA AND THE WEST. AFR EUR+WWI FUT ISLAM ISRAEL USA+45 SOCIETY INT/ORG FORCES CREATE PLAN FOR/AID EDU/PROP ATTIT...CONCPT TREND EEC 20 CONGRESS UN. PAGE 121 A2488
ECO/UNDEV ECO/TAC

B62
ROBERTSON B.C.,REGIONAL DEVELOPMENT IN THE EUROPEAN ECONOMIC COMMUNITY. EUR+WWI FRANCE FUT ITALY UK ECO/UNDEV WORKER ACT/RES PROB/SOLV TEC/DEV ECO/TAC INT/TRADE EEC. PAGE 122 A2499
PLAN ECO/DEV INT/ORG REGION

B62
ROY P.A.,SOUTH WIND RED. L/A+17C USA+45 ECO/UNDEV NAT/G CAP/ISM MARXISM SOCISM...OLD/LIB GEOG RECORD INT CENSUS 20 COLD/WAR. PAGE 125 A2554
DIPLOM INDUS POLICY ECO/TAC

B62
SELOSOEMARDJAN O.,SOCIAL CHANGES IN JOGJAKARTA. INDONESIA NETHERLAND ELITES STRATA STRUCT FAM
ECO/UNDEV CULTURE

POL/PAR CREATE DIPLOM INT/TRADE EDU/PROP ADMIN GOV/REL...SOC 20 JAVA CHINJAP. PAGE 131 A2683
REV COLONIAL

B62
SHAW C.,LEGAL PROBLEMS IN INTERNATIONAL TRADE AND INVESTMENT. WOR+45 ECO/DEV ECO/UNDEV MARKET DIPLOM TAX INCOME ROLE...ANTHOL BIBLIOG 20 TREATY UN IMF GATT. PAGE 132 A2698
INT/LAW INT/TRADE FINAN ECO/TAC

B62
TAYLOR D.,THE BRITISH IN AFRICA. UK CULTURE ECO/UNDEV INDUS DIPLOM INT/TRADE ADMIN WAR RACE/REL ORD/FREE SOVEREIGN...POLICY BIBLIOG 15/20 CMN/WLTH. PAGE 142 A2898
AFR COLONIAL DOMIN

B62
THANT U.,THE UNITED NATIONS' DEVELOPMENT DECADE: PROPOSALS FOR ACTION. WOR+45 SOCIETY ECO/UNDEV AGRI COM/IND FINAN R+D MUNIC SCHOOL VOL/ASSN CONSULT PLAN TEC/DEV ECO/TAC EDU/PROP ADMIN ROUTINE RIGID/FLEX...MGT SOC CONCPT UNESCO UN TOT/POP VAL/FREE. PAGE 142 A2906
INT/ORG ALL/VALS

B62
THEOBALD R.,NATIONAL DEVELOPMENT EFFORTS (PAMPHLET). WOR+45 AGRI BUDGET FOR/AID INT/TRADE TAX 20. PAGE 142 A2914
ECO/UNDEV PLAN BAL/PAY WEALTH

B62
UNECA LIBRARY,BOOKS ON AFRICA IN THE UNECA LIBRARY. WOR+45 AGRI INT/ORG NAT/G PLAN WRITING REGION...SOC STAT UN. PAGE 147 A3008
BIBLIOG AFR ECO/UNDEV TEC/DEV

B62
UNECA LIBRARY,NEW ACQUISITIONS IN THE UNECA LIBRARY. LAW NAT/G PLAN PROB/SOLV TEC/DEV ADMIN REGION...GEOG SOC 20 UN. PAGE 147 A3009
BIBLIOG AFR ECO/UNDEV INT/ORG

B62
UNESCO,GENERAL CATALOGUE OF UNESCO PUBLICATIONS AND UNESCO SPONSORED PUBLICATIONS, 1946-1959. WOR+45 ...POLICY ART/METH HUM PHIL/SCI UN. PAGE 148 A3022
BIBLIOG INT/ORG ECO/UNDEV SOC

B62
US CONGRESS JOINT ECO COMM,ECONOMIC DEVELOPMENTS IN SOUTH AMERICA. USA+45 SOCIETY FINAN NAT/G PROB/SOLV TEC/DEV INT/TRADE TAX EFFICIENCY PRODUC ATTIT ...POLICY 20 CONGRESS SOUTH/AMER. PAGE 150 A3065
L/A+17C ECO/UNDEV FOR/AID DIPLOM

B62
VIET J.,INTERNATIONAL COOPERATION AND PROGRAMMES OF ECONOMIC AND SOCIAL DEVELOPMENT. TEC/DEV FOR/AID DOMIN COLONIAL PEACE WEALTH 20 UNESCO. PAGE 159 A3232
BIBLIOG/A INT/ORG DIPLOM ECO/UNDEV

B62
ZOOK P.D.,FOREIGN TRADE AND HUMAN CAPITAL. L/A+17C USA+45 FINAN DIPLOM ECO/TAC PRODUC...POLICY 20. PAGE 170 A3458
INT/TRADE ECO/UNDEV FOR/AID BAL/PAY

L62
"HIGHER EDUCATION AND ECONOMIC AND SOCIAL DEVELOPMENT IN LATIN AMERICA: A BIBLIOGRAPHY." L/A+17C SOCIETY ECO/UNDEV PROF/ORG DIPLOM CONFER ...SOC 20. PAGE 3 A0062
BIBLIOG/A ACADEM INTELL EDU/PROP

L62
MALINOWSKI W.R.,"CENTRALIZATION AND DE-CENTRALIZATION IN THE UNITED NATIONS' ECONOMIC AND SOCIAL ACTIVITIES." WOR+45 CONSTN ECO/UNDEV INT/ORG VOL/ASSN DELIB/GP ECO/TAC EDU/PROP ADMIN RIGID/FLEX ...OBS CHARTS UNESCO UN EEC OAS OEEC 20. PAGE 93 A1913
CREATE GEN/LAWS

L62
MURACCIOLE L.,"LA LOI FONDAMENTALE DE LA REPUBLIQUE DU CONGO." WOR+45 SOCIETY ECO/UNDEV INT/ORG NAT/G LEGIS PLAN LEGIT ADJUD COLONIAL ROUTINE ATTIT SOVEREIGN 20 CONGO. PAGE 106 A2174
AFR CONSTN

L62
MURACCIOLE L.,"LA BANQUE CENTRALE DES ETATS DE L'AFRIQUE DE L'OUEST." AFR LAW ECO/UNDEV INT/ORG NAT/G CONSULT ECO/TAC ROUTINE...CHARTS 20. PAGE 106 A2175
ISLAM FINAN INT/TRADE

L62
NIZARD L.,"CUBAN QUESTION AND SECURITY COUNCIL." L/A+17C USA+45 ECO/UNDEV NAT/G POL/PAR DELIB/GP ECO/TAC PWR...RELATIV OBS TIME/SEQ TREND GEN/LAWS UN 20 UN. PAGE 109 A2242
INT/ORG JURID DIPLOM CUBA

L62
WILCOX F.O.,"THE UN AND THE NON-ALIGNED NATIONS." AFR S/ASIA USA+45 ECO/UNDEV INT/ORG TEC/DEV EDU/PROP RIGID/FLEX ORD/FREE PWR...POLICY HUM CONCPT STAT OBS TIME/SEQ STERTYP GEN/METH UN 20. PAGE 164 A3345
ATTIT TREND

S62
BELSHAW C.,"TRAINING AND RECRUITMENT: SOME PRINCIPLES OF INTERNATIONAL AID." FUT WOR+45 SOCIETY INT/ORG NAT/G CREATE PLAN TEC/DEV ECO/TAC FOR/AID EDU/PROP ATTIT PERCEPT...HUM UN FAO ILO UNESCO 20. PAGE 13 A0263
VOL/ASSN ECO/UNDEV

S62
BLOOMFIELD L.P.,"THE UNITED NATIONS IN CRISIS: THE ROLE OF THE UN IN USA FOREIGN POLICY." FUT USA+45 WOR+45 ECO/UNDEV DIPLOM ATTIT ORD/FREE...CONCPT UN. PAGE 16 A0317
INT/ORG TREND REV

S62
CLEVELAND H.,"THE FUTURE ROLE OF THE UNITED STATES IN THE UNITED NATIONS." USA+45 ECO/UNDEV INT/ORG EX/STRUC DIPLOM FOR/AID ROUTINE SKILL SOVEREIGN WEALTH UN 20. PAGE 27 A0550
FUT ATTIT

S62
CORET A.,"LE STATUT DE L'ILE CHRISTMAS DE L'OCEAN INDIEN." FUT S/ASIA ECO/DEV ECO/UNDEV VOL/ASSN DELIB/GP PLAN...RELATIV OBS TIME/SEQ TREND AUSTRAL 20. PAGE 30 A0619
NAT/G INT/ORG NEW/ZEALND

S62
CORET A.,"LA DECLARATION DE L'ASSEMBLEE GENERAL DE L'ONU SUR L'OCTROI DE L'INDEPENDENCE AUX PAYS ET AUX PEUPLES." AFR ASIA ISLAM NIGERIA S/ASIA USSR WOR+45 ECO/UNDEV NAT/G DELIB/GP COLONIAL ALL/VALS ...CONCPT TIME/SEQ TREND UN TOT/POP 20 MEXIC/AMER. PAGE 31 A0621
INT/ORG STRUCT SOVEREIGN

S62
FISCHER G.,"UNE NOUVELLE ORGANIZATION REGIONALE: L'ASA." S/ASIA WOR+45 ECO/UNDEV VOL/ASSN PERCEPT RIGID/FLEX...TIME/SEQ 20 ASA. PAGE 46 A0935
INT/ORG DRIVE REGION

S62
GAREAU F.H.,"BLOC POLITICS IN WEST AFRICA." AFR CONGO/BRAZ GHANA GUINEA MALI WOR+45 STRUCT ECO/UNDEV INT/ORG VOL/ASSN CHOOSE ORD/FREE PWR UN 20. PAGE 51 A1048
NAT/G NAT/LISM

S62
MANGIN G.,"LES ACCORDS DE COOPERATION EN MATIERE DE JUSTICE ENTRE LA FRANCE ET LES ETATS AFRICAINS ET MALGACHE." AFR ISLAM WOR+45 STRUCT ECO/UNDEV NAT/G DELIB/GP PERCEPT ALL/VALS...JURID MGT TIME/SEQ 20. PAGE 94 A1919
INT/ORG LAW FRANCE

S62
MILLIKEN M.,"NEW AND OLD CRITERIA FOR AID." WOR+45 ECO/DEV ECO/UNDEV ACT/RES PLAN ATTIT KNOWL...TREND CON/ANAL SIMUL GEN/METH 20. PAGE 102 A2083
USA+45 ECO/TAC FOR/AID

S62
MORGENTHAU H.J.,"A POLITICAL THEORY OF FOREIGN AID." ECO/UNDEV NAT/G DELIB/GP PLAN ECO/TAC EDU/PROP EXEC ORD/FREE RESPECT WEALTH...METH/CNCPT TREND 20. PAGE 104 A2140
USA+45 PHIL/SCI FOR/AID

S62
PIQUEMAL M.,"LES PROBLEMES DES UNIONS D'ETATS EN AFRIQUE NOIRE." FRANCE SOCIETY INT/ORG NAT/G DELIB/GP PLAN LEGIT ADMIN COLONIAL ROUTINE ATTIT ORD/FREE PWR...GEOG METH/CNCPT 20. PAGE 116 A2382
AFR ECO/UNDEV REGION

S62
PYE L.W.,"THE POLITICAL IMPULSES AND FANTASIES BEHIND FOREIGN AID." FUT USA+45 ECO/UNDEV DIPLOM ECO/TAC ROUTINE DRIVE KNOWL...SOC METH/CNCPT NEW/IDEA TREND HYPO/EXP STERTYP GEN/METH 20. PAGE 118 A2420
ACT/RES ATTIT FOR/AID

S62
RAZAFIMBAHINY J.,"L'ORGANISATION AFRICAINE ET MALGACHE DE COOPERATION ECONOMIQUE." AFR ISLAM MADAGASCAR NAT/G ACT/RES ECO/TAC ALL/VALS ...TIME/SEQ 20. PAGE 120 A2454
INT/ORG ECO/UNDEV

S62
RUBINSTEIN A.Z.,"RUSSIA AND THE UNCOMMITTED NATIONS." AFR INDIA ISLAM L/A+17C LAOS S/ASIA ELITES ECO/UNDEV INT/ORG KIN CREATE PLAN TEC/DEV NAT/LISM RIGID/FLEX PWR WEALTH...METH/CNCPT TIME/SEQ GEN/LAWS WORK. PAGE 125 A2562
ECO/TAC TREND COLONIAL USSR

S62
SPECTOR I.,"SOVIET POLICY IN ASIA: A REAPPRAISAL." ASIA CHINA/COM COM INDIA INDONESIA ECO/UNDEV INT/ORG DOMIN EDU/PROP REGION RESPECT...CONCPT TREND TOT/POP COLD/WAR 20 CHINJAP. PAGE 135 A2774
S/ASIA PWR FOR/AID USSR

S62
SPENSER J.H.,"AFRICA AT THE UNITED NATIONS: SOME OBSERVATIONS." FUT ECO/UNDEV NAT/G CONSULT DELIB/GP PLAN BAL/PWR ECO/TAC EDU/PROP ATTIT RIGID/FLEX HEALTH ORD/FREE PWR WEALTH...POLICY CONCPT OBS TREND STERTYP GEN/METH UN VAL/FREE. PAGE 136 A2786
AFR INT/ORG REGION

S62
SPRINGER H.W.,"FEDERATION IN THE CARIBBEAN: AN ATTEMPT THAT FAILED." L/A+17C ECO/UNDEV INT/ORG POL/PAR PROVS LEGIS CREATE PLAN LEGIT ADMIN FEDERAL ATTIT DRIVE PERSON ORD/FREE PWR...POLICY GEOG PSY CONCPT OBS CARIBBEAN CMN/WLTH 20. PAGE 136 A2791
VOL/ASSN NAT/G REGION

S62
TOWSTER J.,"THE USSR AND THE USA: CHALLENGE AND RESPONSE." COM GERMANY USA+45 USSR WOR+45 ECO/UNDEV INT/ORG VOL/ASSN EX/STRUC FORCES TOP/EX CREATE PLAN TEC/DEV DIPLOM ECO/TAC EDU/PROP COLONIAL COERCE PWR ...GEN/METH COLD/WAR 20 KENNEDY/JF. PAGE 145 A2956
ACT/RES GEN/LAWS

S62
VASAK K.,"DE LA CONVENTION EUROPEENNE A LA CONVENTION AFRICAINE DES DROITS DE L'HOMME." AFR ISLAM WOR+45 LAW CONSTN ECO/UNDEV INT/ORG PERCEPT ALL/VALS 20. PAGE 158 A3223
DELIB/GP CONCPT COLONIAL

C62
DUFFY J.,"PORTUGAL IN AFRICA." PORTUGAL SIER/LEONE INDUS WORKER INT/TRADE WAR CONSERVE...CATH GEOG
BIBLIOG RACE/REL

TREND 16/20. PAGE 39 A0795 ECO/UNDEV COLONIAL

B63
BRITISH AID. UK AGRI DIST/IND INDUS SCHOOL TEC/DEV INT/TRADE COLONIAL DEMAND...TREND CHARTS 20. PAGE 3 A0064 FOR/AID ECO/UNDEV NAT/G FINAN

B63
ABSHIRE D.M.,NATIONAL SECURITY: POLITICAL, MILITARY, AND ECONOMIC STRATEGIES IN THE DECADE AHEAD. ASIA COM USA+45 WOR+45 ECO/DEV ECO/UNDEV INT/ORG DELIB/GP FORCES ECO/TAC COERCE ATTIT RIGID/FLEX HEALTH ORD/FREE PWR WEALTH...POLICY STAT CHARTS ANTHOL COLD/WAR VAL/FREE. PAGE 4 A0083 FUT ACT/RES BAL/PWR

B63
AFRICAN BIBLIOGRAPHIC CENTER,THE SCENE IS GUINEA AND THE PERSONAGE IS SEKOU TOURE: A SELECTED CURRENT READING LIST, 1959-1962 (PAMPHLET). GUINEA ECO/UNDEV CHIEF FOR/AID COLONIAL...BIOG 20. PAGE 5 A0095 BIBLIOG AFR POL/PAR COM

B63
AFRICAN BIBLIOGRAPHIC CENTER,THE SCENE IS KENYA AND THE PERSONAGE IS TOM MBOYA: A SELECTED CURRENT READING LIST FROM 1956-1962 (PAMPHLET). ECO/UNDEV LABOR POL/PAR CHIEF COLONIAL CHOOSE NAT/LISM ORD/FREE 20. PAGE 5 A0096 BIBLIOG DIPLOM AFR NAT/G

B63
BRECHER M.,THE NEW STATES OF ASIA. ASIA S/ASIA INT/ORG BAL/PWR COLONIAL NEUTRAL ORD/FREE PWR 20 UN. PAGE 18 A0369 NAT/G ECO/UNDEV DIPLOM POLICY

B63
BROEKMEIJER M.W.,DEVELOPING COUNTRIES AND NATO. USSR FORCES DIPLOM NUC/PWR WAR PEACE TOTALISM 20 NATO. PAGE 19 A0384 ECO/UNDEV FOR/AID ORD/FREE NAT/G

B63
BROWN W.N.,THE UNITED STATES AND INDIA AND PAKISTAN (REV. ED.). INDIA PAKISTAN S/ASIA WOR+45 POL/PAR SECT INT/TRADE COLONIAL COERCE DISCRIM. PAGE 20 A0408 DIPLOM ECO/UNDEV SOVEREIGN STRUCT

B63
BUTTS R.F.,AMERICAN EDUCATION IN INTERNATIONAL DEVELOPMENT. USA+45 WOR+45 INTELL SCHOOL DIPLOM EDU/PROP...BIBLIOG 20. PAGE 23 A0457 ACADEM FOR/AID CONSULT ECO/UNDEV

B63
CANELAS O.A.,RADIOGRAFIA DE LA ALIANZA PARA EL ATRASO. L/A+17C USA+45 ECO/TAC DOMIN COLONIAL NAT/LISM...SOCIALIST NAT/COMP 20. PAGE 23 A0476 REV DIPLOM ECO/UNDEV REGION

B63
CENTRO PARA EL DESARROLLO,LA ALIANZA PARA EL PROGRESO Y EL DESARROLLO SOCIAL DE AMERICA LATINA. L/A+17C INT/ORG DIPLOM ECO/TAC INT/TRADE ATTIT 20. PAGE 25 A0512 ECO/UNDEV FOR/AID PLAN REGION

B63
COLUMBIA U SCHOOL OF LAW,PUBLIC INTERNATIONAL DEVELOPMENT FINANCING IN SENEGAL. SENEGAL FINAN DELIB/GP GIVE EFFICIENCY...CHARTS GOV/COMP ANTHOL 20. PAGE 28 A0571 FOR/AID PLAN RECEIVE ECO/UNDEV

B63
COMISION DE HISTORIO,GUIA DE LOS DOCUMENTOS MICROFOTOGRAFIADOS POR LA UNIDAD MOVIL DE LA UNESCO. SOCIETY ECO/UNDEV INT/ORG ADMIN...SOC 20 UNESCO. PAGE 28 A0573 BIBLIOG NAT/G L/A+17C DIPLOM

B63
CONF ON FUTURE OF COMMONWEALTH,THE FUTURE OF THE COMMONWEALTH. UK ECO/UNDEV AGRI EDU/PROP ADMIN SOC/INTEG 20 COMMONWLTH. PAGE 29 A0583 DIPLOM RACE/REL ORD/FREE TEC/DEV

B63
EL-NAGGAR S.,FOREIGN AID TO UNITED ARAB REPUBLIC. UAR USA+45 USSR AGRI FINAN INDUS FORCES EATING DEMAND...CHARTS METH/COMP 20 RESOURCE/N AID. PAGE 41 A0838 FOR/AID ECO/UNDEV RECEIVE PLAN

B63
ELLENDER A.J.,A REPORT ON UNITED STATES FOREIGN OPERATIONS IN AFRICA. SOUTH/AFR USA+45 STRATA EXTR/IND FORCES RACE/REL ISOLAT SOVEREIGN...CHARTS 20 NEGRO. PAGE 41 A0840 FOR/AID DIPLOM WEALTH ECO/UNDEV

B63
FIFIELD R.H.,SOUTHEAST ASIA IN UNITED STATES POLICY. S/ASIA USA+45 ECO/UNDEV NAT/G DIPLOM ECO/TAC ADMIN COERCE ORD/FREE...POLICY MAJORIT 20. PAGE 45 A0928 INT/ORG PWR

B63
FISCHER-GALATI S.,EASTERN EUROPE IN THE SIXTIES. ALBANIA USSR YUGOSLAVIA ECO/UNDEV AGRI MARKET LABOR WORKER DIPLOM INT/TRADE EDU/PROP GOV/REL PRODUC UTOPIA SOCISM 20. PAGE 46 A0939 MARXISM TEC/DEV BAL/PWR ECO/TAC

B63
FLORES E.,LAND REFORM AND THE ALLIANCE FOR PROGRESS (PAMPHLET). L/A+17C USA+45 STRUCT ECO/UNDEV NAT/G WORKER CREATE PLAN ECO/TAC COERCE REV 20. PAGE 47 A0953 AGRI INT/ORG DIPLOM POLICY

B63
GOLDSCHMIDT W.,THE UNITED STATES AND AFRICA. USA+45 CULTURE ECO/TAC INT/TRADE GOV/REL...SOC ANTHOL 20 INTERVENT. PAGE 53 A1091 AFR ECO/UNDEV DIPLOM

B63
GONZALEZ PEDRERO E.,ANATOMIA DE UN CONFLICTO. WOR+45 ECO/DEV ECO/UNDEV ECO/TAC FOR/AID CONTROL ARMS/CONT GOV/REL...NAT/COMP 20 COLD/WAR. PAGE 54 A1099 DIPLOM DETER BAL/PWR

B63
GORDON L.,A NEW DEAL FOR LATIN AMERICA. L/A+17C USA+45 CULTURE NAT/G TEC/DEV DIPLOM FOR/AID REGION TASK...POLICY 20 DEPT/STATE. PAGE 54 A1115 ECO/UNDEV ECO/TAC INT/ORG PLAN

B63
GUIMARAES A.P.,INFLACAO E MONOPOLIO NO BRASIL. BRAZIL FINAN NAT/G PLAN PAY...METH/COMP 20. PAGE 58 A1189 ECO/UNDEV PRICE INT/TRADE BAL/PAY

B63
HENDERSON W.,SOUTHEAST ASIA: PROBLEMS OF UNITED STATES POLICY. COM S/ASIA CULTURE STRATA ECO/UNDEV INT/ORG DELIB/GP ACT/RES ECO/TAC DOMIN EDU/PROP LEGIT COERCE ATTIT ALL/VALS...STAT TIME/SEQ ANTHOL VAL/FREE 20. PAGE 64 A1313 ASIA USA+45 DIPLOM

B63
HUSSEY W.D.,THE BRITISH EMPIRE AND COMMONWEALTH 1500 TO 1961. UK USA-45 SOCIETY ECO/UNDEV NAT/G VOL/ASSN INT/TRADE DOMIN CONTROL WAR PWR ...DICTIONARY 16/20 COMMONWLTH TRUST/TERR. PAGE 69 A1422 COLONIAL SOVEREIGN INT/ORG

B63
HYDE D.,THE PEACEFUL ASSAULT. COM UAR USSR ECO/DEV ECO/UNDEV NAT/G POL/PAR CAP/ISM PWR 20. PAGE 69 A1427 MARXISM CONTROL ECO/TAC DIPLOM

B63
INTERNATIONAL BANK RECONST DEV,THE WORLD BANK GROUP IN ASIA. ASIA S/ASIA INDUS TEC/DEV ECO/TAC...RECORD 20 IBRD WORLD/BANK. PAGE 71 A1451 INT/ORG DIPLOM ECO/UNDEV FINAN

B63
INTERNATIONAL MONETARY FUND,COMPENSATORY FINANCING OF EXPORT FLUCTUATIONS (PAMPHLET). WOR+45 ECO/DEV ECO/UNDEV INT/ORG WEALTH...TREND 20 IMF MONEY. PAGE 71 A1459 BAL/PAY FINAN BUDGET INT/TRADE

B63
JENNINGS W.I.,DEMOCRACY IN AFRICA. UK CULTURE STRUCT ECO/UNDEV DIPLOM COLONIAL GP/REL ADJUST NAT/LISM ORD/FREE...GOV/COMP 20 THIRD/WRLD. PAGE 74 A1512 PROB/SOLV AFR CONSTN POPULISM

B63
KATZ S.M.,A SELECTED LIST OF US READINGS ON DEVELOPMENT. AGRI COM/IND DIST/IND INDUS LABOR PLAN FOR/AID EDU/PROP HEALTH...POLICY SOC/WK 20. PAGE 77 A1571 BIBLIOG/A ECO/UNDEV TEC/DEV ACT/RES

B63
LANGE O.,ECONOMIC DEVELOPMENT, PLANNING, AND INTERNATIONAL COOPERATION. UAR WOR+45 FINAN CAP/ISM PERS/REL 20. PAGE 84 A1722 ECO/UNDEV DIPLOM INT/TRADE PLAN

B63
LYON P.,NEUTRALISM. ECO/UNDEV EDU/PROP COLONIAL ALL/IDEOS...IDEA/COMP 20 COLD/WAR UN. PAGE 92 A1879 NAT/COMP NAT/LISM DIPLOM NEUTRAL

B63
MANGER W.,THE ALLIANCE FOR PROGRESS: A CRITICAL APPRAISAL. FUT L/A+17C USA+45 CULTURE ECO/UNDEV ACADEM NAT/G SCHOOL PLAN FOR/AID...POLICY OAS. PAGE 94 A1918 DIPLOM INT/ORG ECO/TAC REGION

B63
MARITANO N.,AN ALLIANCE FOR PROGRESS. FUT L/A+17C USA+45 CULTURE ECO/UNDEV NAT/G PLAN CONTROL POLICY. PAGE 95 A1941 DIPLOM INT/ORG ECO/TAC FOR/AID

B63
MBOYA T.,FREEDOM AND AFTER. AFR LABOR POL/PAR DIPLOM EDU/PROP COERCE SOCISM 20. PAGE 97 A1989 COLONIAL ECO/UNDEV NAT/LISM INT/ORG

B63
MENDES C.,NACIONALISMO E DESENVOLVIMENTO. AFR ASIA L/A+17C STRATA INT/TRADE COLONIAL. PAGE 99 A2039 NAT/LISM ECO/UNDEV DIPLOM REV

B63
MENEZES A.J.,SUBDESENVOLVIMENTO E POLITICA INTERNACIONAL. BRAZIL WOR+45 PLAN CONTROL LEAD NAT/LISM ORD/FREE 20 THIRD/WRLD. PAGE 99 A2041 ECO/UNDEV DIPLOM POLICY BAL/PWR

B63
PIKE F.B.,CHILE AND THE UNITED STATES 1880-1962: THE EMERGENCE OF CHILE'S CRISIS AND THE CHALLENGE TO US DIPLOMACY. CHILE COM USA+45 USA-45 SOCIETY STRATA ECO/UNDEV...MYTH 19/20. PAGE 116 A2378 FOR/AID DIPLOM ATTIT STRUCT

B63
RAO V.K.R.,FOREIGN AID AND INDIA'S ECONOMIC DEVELOPMENT. INDIA INT/ORG PROB/SOLV TEC/DEV ECO/TAC CONTROL WEALTH...TREND 20. PAGE 119 A2445 FOR/AID ECO/UNDEV RECEIVE DIPLOM

B63
RIUKIN A.,THE AFRICAN PRESENCE IN WORLD AFFAIRS. AFR WOR+45 ECO/UNDEV AGRI INT/ORG BAL/PWR ECO/TAC COLONIAL NEUTRAL NAT/LISM PEACE SOVEREIGN 20 UN. PAGE 121 A2486 DIPLOM NAT/G POLICY PWR

B63
RIVKIN A.,THE AFRICAN PRESENCE IN WORLD AFFAIRS. ECO/UNDEV AGRI INT/ORG LOC/G NAT/LISM...OBS PREDICT GOV/COMP 20. PAGE 121 A2489 AFR NAT/G DIPLOM BAL/PWR

B63
ROBOCK S.H.,OVERVIEW OF TOTAL BRAZILIAN SETTING, NEWER REGIONAL PATTERNS NING AND FOREIGN AID. BRAZIL ECO/UNDEV AGRI FINAN INDUS INT/ORG INCOME UTIL...CHARTS 20. PAGE 122 A2507 ECO/TAC REGION PLAN FOR/AID

B63
ROSSI M.,THE THIRD WORLD. FUT WOR+45 INT/ORG NAT/G CAP/ISM COLONIAL PEACE PWR MARXISM 20 UN THIRD/WRLD. PAGE 124 A2542 ECO/UNDEV DIPLOM BAL/PWR NEUTRAL

B63
SCHMELTZ G.W.,LA POLITIQUE MONDIALE CONTEMPORAINE. SOCIETY ECO/UNDEV INDUS INT/ORG NAT/G POL/PAR CONSULT DELIB/GP PLAN TEC/DEV ECO/TAC DOMIN EDU/PROP ROUTINE COERCE PERCEPT PERSON LOVE SKILL ...SOC RECORD TOT/POP. PAGE 128 A2629 WOR+45 COLONIAL

B63
SCHRADER R.,SCIENCE AND POLICY. WOR+45 ECO/DEV ECO/UNDEV R+D FORCES PLAN DIPLOM GOV/REL TECHRACY BIBLIOG. PAGE 129 A2644 TEC/DEV NAT/G POLICY ADMIN

B63
SZULC T.,THE WINDS OF REVOLUTION; LATIN AMERICA TODAY - AND TOMORROW. L/A+17C ORD/FREE SOCISM ...PREDICT TREND 20. PAGE 141 A2880 REV INT/ORG MARXISM ECO/UNDEV

B63
UN SECRETARY GENERAL,PLANNING FOR ECONOMIC DEVELOPMENT. ECO/UNDEV FINAN BUDGET INT/TRADE TARIFFS TAX ADMIN 20 UN. PAGE 147 A3005 PLAN ECO/TAC MGT NAT/COMP

B63
UNITED STATES GOVERNMENT,REPORT TO THE INTER-AMERICAN ECONOMIC AND SOCIAL COUNCIL. L/A+17C INDUS PLAN INT/TRADE TARIFFS CONFER...CHARTS 20 LAFTA. PAGE 149 A3038 FOR/AID ECO/TAC ECO/UNDEV DIPLOM

B63
US AGENCY INTERNATIONAL DEV,US FOREIGN ASSISTANCE AND ASSISTANCE FROM INTERNATIONAL ORGANIZATIONS. USA+45 WOR+45 ECO/UNDEV AGRI NAT/G TEC/DEV BUDGET. PAGE 149 A3050 FOR/AID INT/ORG CHARTS STAT

B63
US ECON SURVEY TEAM INDONESIA,INDONESIA - PERSPECTIVE AND PROPOSALS FOR UNITED STATES ECONOMIC AID. INDONESIA AGRI MARKET TEC/DEV DIPLOM INT/TRADE EDU/PROP 20. PAGE 153 A3113 FOR/AID ECO/UNDEV PLAN INDUS

B63
US SENATE COMM ON FOREIGN REL,HEARINGS ON S 1276 A BILL TO AMEND FURTHER THE FOREIGN ASSISTANCE ACT OF 1961. USA+45 WOR+45 INDUS INT/ORG FORCES TAX WEAPON SUPEGO...NAT/COMP 20 UN CONGRESS PRESIDENT. PAGE 156 A3182 FOR/AID DIPLOM ECO/UNDEV ORD/FREE

B63
VON HALLER A.,DIE LETZTEN WOLLEN DIE ERSTEN SEIN. AFR S/ASIA INT/TRADE REV ORD/FREE SOVEREIGN 20. PAGE 160 A3251 FOR/AID ECO/UNDEV MARXISM CAP/ISM

B63
WELLESLEY COLLEGE,SYMPOSIUM ON LATIN AMERICA. FUT L/A+17C USA+45 INT/ORG ECO/TAC PARL/PROC REGION ANTHOL. PAGE 163 A3316 ECO/UNDEV CULTURE ORD/FREE DIPLOM

B63
WILCOX W.A.,PAKISTAN; THE CONSOLIDATION OF A NATION. INDIA PAKISTAN CONSTN SECT PROB/SOLV COLONIAL PARTIC GP/REL FEDERAL...POLICY 19/20. PAGE 164 A3348 NAT/LISM ECO/UNDEV DIPLOM STRUCT

L63
LISSITZYN O.J.,"INTERNATIONAL LAW IN A DIVIDED WORLD." FUT WOR+45 CONSTN CULTURE ECO/DEV ECO/UNDEV DIST/IND NAT/G FORCES ECO/TAC LEGIT ADJUD ADMIN COERCE ATTIT HEALTH MORAL ORD/FREE PWR RESPECT WEALTH VAL/FREE. PAGE 90 A1841 INT/ORG LAW

L63
MOUSKHELY M.,"LE BLOC COMMUNISTE ET LA COMMUNAUTE ECONOMIQUE EUROPEENNE." AFR COM EUR+WWI FUT USSR WOR+45 INTELL ECO/UNDEV LABOR POL/PAR NUC/PWR RIGID/FLEX...TIME/SEQ ORG/CHARTS EEC TOT/POP 20. PAGE 105 A2158 INT/ORG ECO/DEV

L63
PRINCETON UNIV. CONFERENCE,"ARAB DEVELOPMENT IN THE EMERGING INTERNATIONAL ECONOMY." FUT USA+45 DIST/IND FINAN DELIB/GP PLAN ECO/TAC WEALTH VAL/FREE 20. PAGE 118 A2413 ISLAM ECO/UNDEV FOR/AID INT/TRADE

S63
ALEXANDER R.,"LATIN AMERICA AND THE COMMUNIST BLOC." ASIA COM CUBA L/A+17C USA+45 USSR NAT/G VOL/ASSN TEC/DEV FOR/AID LEGIT PWR WEALTH COLD/WAR 20. PAGE 6 A0112 ECO/UNDEV RECORD

S63
ANGUILE G.,"CIVILISATION DU PLAN DANS L'EUROPE ET L'AFRIQUE DE DEMAIN." AFR EUR+WWI GABON ECO/DEV FINAN MARKET DELIB/GP ECO/TAC WEALTH...TREND 20. PAGE 8 A0163 ECO/UNDEV PLAN INT/TRADE

S63
CHAKRAVARTI P.C.,"INDIAN NON-ALIGNMENT AND UNITED STATES POLICY." ASIA INDIA S/ASIA USA+45 CULTURE ECO/UNDEV NAT/G VOL/ASSN DELIB/GP TOP/EX FOR/AID NEUTRAL...POLICY HUM CONCPT RECORD GEN/LAWS 20. PAGE 25 A0515 ATTIT ALL/VALS COLONIAL DIPLOM

S63
COSER L.,"AMERICA AND THE WORLD REVOLUTION." COM FUT USA+45 WOR+45 INTELL SOCIETY NAT/G ECO/TAC EDU/PROP ALL/VALS SOCISM...PSY GEN/LAWS TOT/POP 20 COLD/WAR. PAGE 31 A0629 ECO/UNDEV PLAN FOR/AID DIPLOM

S63
COUTY P.,"L'ASSISTANCE POUR LE DEVELOPPEMENT: POINT DE VUE SCANDINAVES." EUR+WWI FINLAND FUT SWEDEN WOR+45 ECO/DEV ECO/UNDEV COM/IND LABOR NAT/G PROF/ORG ACT/RES SKILL WEALTH TOT/POP 20. PAGE 32 A0643 FINAN ROUTINE FOR/AID

S63
DARLING F.C.,"THE GEOPOLITICS OF AMERICAN FOREIGN POLITICS IN ASIA." COM S/ASIA USA+45 USSR ECO/UNDEV NAT/G VOL/ASSN CONSULT PLAN GUERRILLA...STAT TOT/POP 20. PAGE 34 A0682 FORCES ECO/TAC FOR/AID DIPLOM

S63
EMERSON R.,"THE ATLANTIC COMMUNITY AND THE EMERGING COUNTRIES." FUT WOR+45 ECO/DEV ECO/UNDEV R+D NAT/G DELIB/GP BAL/PWR ECO/TAC EDU/PROP ROUTINE ORD/FREE PWR WEALTH...POLICY CONCPT TREND GEN/METH EEC 20 NATO. PAGE 42 A0848 ATTIT INT/TRADE

S63
GANDILHON J.,"LA SCIENCE ET LA TECHNIQUE A L'AIDE DES REGIONS PEU DEVELOPPEES." FRANCE FUT WOR+45 ECO/DEV R+D PROF/ORG ACT/RES PLAN...MGT TOT/POP VAL/FREE 20 UN. PAGE 51 A1037 ECO/UNDEV TEC/DEV FOR/AID

S63
GANDOLFI A.,"LES ACCORDS DE COOPERATION EN MATIERE DE POLITIQUE ETRANGERE ENTRE LA FRANCE ET LES NOUVEAUX ETATS AFRICAINS ET." AFR ISLAM MADAGASCAR WOR+45 ECO/DEV INT/ORG NAT/G DELIB/GP ECO/TAC ALL/VALS...CON/ANAL 20. PAGE 51 A1038 VOL/ASSN ECO/UNDEV DIPLOM FRANCE

S63
GORDON B.,"ECONOMIC IMPEDIMENTS TO REGIONALISM IN SOUTH EAST ASIA." BURMA FUT S/ASIA THAILAND USA+45 AGRI INDUS R+D NAT/G PLAN ECO/TAC WEALTH...STAT CONT/OBS 20. PAGE 54 A1110 VOL/ASSN ECO/UNDEV INT/TRADE REGION

S63
HAVILAND H.F.,"BUILDING A POLITICAL COMMUNITY." EUR+WWI FUT UK USA+45 ECO/DEV ECO/UNDEV INT/ORG NAT/G DELIB/GP BAL/PWR ECO/TAC NEUTRAL ROUTINE ATTIT PWR WEALTH...CONCPT COLD/WAR TOT/POP 20. PAGE 63 A1293 VOL/ASSN DIPLOM

S63
HORVATH J.,"MOSCOW'S AID PROGRAM: THE PERFORMANCE SO FAR." COM FUT USSR WOR+45 ECO/DEV FINAN PLAN TEC/DEV FOR/AID EDU/PROP ATTIT ORD/FREE PWR WEALTH ...POLICY STAT CHARTS VAL/FREE 20. PAGE 68 A1389 ECO/UNDEV ECO/TAC

S63
LEDUC G.,"L'AIDE INTERNATIONALE AU DEVELOPPEMENT." FUT WOR+45 ECO/DEV ECO/UNDEV R+D PROF/ORG TEC/DEV ECO/TAC ROUTINE ATTIT ALL/VALS...MGT TIME/SEQ TOT/POP 20. PAGE 86 A1758 FINAN PLAN FOR/AID

S63
LIGOT M.,"LA COOPERATION MILITAIRE DANS LES ACCORDS, PASSES ENTRE LA FRANCE ET LES ETATS AFRICAINS ET MALGACHE D'EXPRESSION." ECO/UNDEV INT/ORG NAT/G VOL/ASSN...CONCPT TIME/SEQ 20. PAGE 89 A1814 AFR FORCES FOR/AID FRANCE

S63
MANGONE G.,"THE UNITED NATIONS AND UNITED STATES FOREIGN POLICY." USA+45 WOR+45 ECO/UNDEV NAT/G DIPLOM LEGIT ROUTINE ATTIT DRIVE...TIME/SEQ UN COLD/WAR 20. PAGE 94 A1922 INT/ORG ECO/TAC FOR/AID

S63
NYE J.S. JR.,"EAST AFRICAN ECONOMIC INTEGRATION." AFR UGANDA PROVS DELIB/GP PLAN ECO/TAC INT/TRADE ADMIN ROUTINE ORD/FREE PWR WEALTH...OBS TIME/SEQ VAL/FREE 20. PAGE 110 A2264 ECO/UNDEV INT/ORG

S63
PINCUS J.,"THE COST OF FOREIGN AID." WOR+45 ECO/DEV FINAN NAT/G VOL/ASSN CREATE ECO/TAC EDU/PROP WEALTH ...METH/CNCPT STAT CHARTS HYPO/EXP TOT/POP VAL/FREE 20. PAGE 116 A2380 USA+45 ECO/UNDEV FOR/AID

S63
ROUGEMONT D.,"LES NOUVELLES CHANCES DE L'EUROPE." ECO/UNDEV

EUR+WWI FUT ECO/DEV INT/ORG NAT/G ACT/RES PLAN TEC/DEV EDU/PROP ADMIN COLONIAL FEDERAL ATTIT PWR SKILL...TREND 20. PAGE 124 A2549
PERCEPT

S63
SCHMIDT W.E.,"THE CASE AGAINST COMMODITY AGREEMENTS." FUT L/A+17C STRATA CONSULT PLAN ECO/TAC EDU/PROP ATTIT DRIVE RIGID/FLEX WEALTH ...MYTH 20. PAGE 128 A2631
ECO/UNDEV ACT/RES INT/TRADE

S63
WALKER H.,"THE INTERNATIONAL LAW OF COMMODITY AGREEMENTS." FUT WOR+45 ECO/DEV ECO/UNDEV FINAN INT/ORG NAT/G CONSULT CREATE PLAN ECO/TAC ATTIT PERCEPT...CONCPT GEN/LAWS TOT/POP GATT 20. PAGE 160 A3265
MARKET VOL/ASSN INT/LAW INT/TRADE

S63
WEILLER J.,"UNIONS MONETAIRES ET RAPPORTS DE COOPERATION INTERNATIONALE DANS UN MONDE EN TRANSITION: L'EXAMPLE." AFR FUT UNIV WOR+45 SOCIETY ECO/UNDEV MARKET R+D NAT/G FOR/AID PERCEPT RIGID/FLEX...NEW/IDEA 20. PAGE 162 A3303
FINAN INT/ORG

S63
WOLF C.,"SOME ASPECTS OF THE 'VALUE' OF LESS-DEVELOPED COUNTRIES TO THE UNITED STATES." ASIA CHINA/COM COM USA+45 USSR ECO/UNDEV BAL/PWR ECO/TAC FOR/AID DOMIN EDU/PROP ATTIT PWR...POLICY METH/CNCPT CONT/OBS TREND CHARTS 20. PAGE 166 A3379
CONCPT GEN/LAWS DIPLOM

N63
LIBRARY HUNGARIAN ACADEMY SCI,HUNGARIAN PUBLICATIONS ON ASIA AND AFRICA, 1950-1962: A SELECTED BIBLIOGRAPHY (PAMPHLET). AFR ASIA HUNGARY S/ASIA ECO/UNDEV NAT/G EDU/PROP ATTIT 20 UNESCO. PAGE 88 A1807
BIBLIOG REGION DIPLOM WRITING

N63
US AGENCY INTERNATIONAL DEV,PRINCIPLES OF FOREIGN ECONOMIC ASSISTANCE (PAMPHLET). USA+45 FINAN GP/REL BAL/PAY EFFICIENCY 20 AID. PAGE 149 A3051
FOR/AID PLAN ECO/UNDEV ATTIT

B64
THE SPECIAL COMMONWEALTH AFRICAN ASSISTANCE PLAN. AFR CANADA INDIA NIGERIA UK FINAN SCHOOL...CHARTS 20 COMMONWLTH. PAGE 3 A0065
ECO/UNDEV TREND FOR/AID ADMIN

B64
AFRO ASIAN SOLIDARITY AGAINST IMPERIALISM. AFR ISLAM S/ASIA ECO/UNDEV NAT/G POL/PAR TOP/EX PRESS ...INT ANTHOL 20 CHOU/ENLAI. PAGE 3 A0066
MARXISM DIPLOM EDU/PROP CHIEF

B64
ALVIM J.C.,A REVOLUCAO SEM RUMO. BRAZIL NAT/G BAL/PWR DIPLOM INT/TRADE PARTIC WEALTH...POLICY SOC SOC/INTEG 20. PAGE 6 A0132
REV CIVMIL/REL ECO/UNDEV ORD/FREE

B64
AMERICAN ASSEMBLY,THE UNITED STATES AND THE MIDDLE EAST. ISRAEL USA+45 STRUCT ECO/DEV ECO/UNDEV INT/ORG NAT/G SCHOOL SECT VOL/ASSN EX/STRUC TEC/DEV NAT/LISM...SOC 20. PAGE 7 A0135
ISLAM DRIVE REGION

B64
BUTWELL R.,SOUTHEAST ASIA TODAY - AND TOMORROW. NAT/G COLONIAL LEAD REGION WAR CHOOSE WEALTH MARXISM 20. PAGE 23 A0458
S/ASIA DIPLOM ECO/UNDEV NAT/LISM

B64
CALDER R.,TWO-WAY PASSAGE. INT/ORG TEC/DEV WAR PERSON ORD/FREE 20. PAGE 23 A0467
FOR/AID ECO/UNDEV ECO/TAC DIPLOM

B64
CASEY R.G.,THE FUTURE OF THE COMMONWEALTH. INDIA PAKISTAN UK ECO/UNDEV INT/ORG TEC/DEV COLONIAL SUPEGO 20 EEC AUSTRAL. PAGE 25 A0505
DIPLOM SOVEREIGN NAT/LISM FOR/AID

B64
CEPEDE M.,POPULATION AND FOOD. USA+45 STRUCT ECO/UNDEV FAM PLAN TEC/DEV FOR/AID CONTROL...CATH SOC TREND 19/20. PAGE 25 A0513
FUT GEOG AGRI CENSUS

B64
COFFIN F.M.,WITNESS FOR AID. COM EUR+WWI USA+45 DIPLOM GP/REL CONSEN ORD/FREE MARXISM...NEW/IDEA 20 CONGRESS AID. PAGE 27 A0557
FOR/AID ECO/UNDEV DELIB/GP PLAN

B64
COLUMBIA U SCHOOL OF LAW,PUBLIC INTERNATIONAL DEVELOPMENT FINANCING IN INDIA. GERMANY/W INDIA UK USA+45 INDUS PLAN TEC/DEV DIPLOM ECO/TAC GIVE ADMIN UTIL ATTIT 20. PAGE 28 A0572
ECO/UNDEV FINAN FOR/AID INT/ORG

B64
CURRIE D.P.,FEDERALISM AND THE NEW NATIONS OF AFRICA. CANADA USA+45 INT/TRADE TAX GP/REL ...NAT/COMP SOC/INTEG 20. PAGE 33 A0667
FEDERAL AFR ECO/UNDEV INT/LAW

B64
DAVIES U.P. JR.,FOREIGN AND OTHER AFFAIRS. EUR+WWI L/A+17C S/ASIA USA+45 ECO/UNDEV CHIEF PLAN ECO/TAC PWR MARXISM 20 KENNEDY/JF UN. PAGE 34 A0688
DIPLOM NAT/G POLICY FOR/AID

B64
DESHMUKH C.D.,THE COMMONWEALTH AS INDIA SEES IT. INDIA UK ECO/UNDEV TEC/DEV INT/TRADE GP/REL RACE/REL SOVEREIGN SOC/INTEG 19/20 COMMONWLTH. PAGE 36 A0733
DIPLOM COLONIAL NAT/LISM ATTIT

B64
DUROSELLE J.B.,LA COMMUNAUTE INTERNATIONALE FACE AUX JEUNES ETATS. CHINA/COM COM S/ASIA USSR INT/ORG ROLE...ANTHOL 20 UN SEATO THIRD/WRLD. PAGE 40 A0808
DIPLOM COLONIAL ECO/UNDEV SOVEREIGN

B64
DUROSELLE J.B.,POLITIQUES NATIONALES ENVERS LES JFUNES ETATS. FRANCE ISRAEL ITALY UK USA+45 USSR YUGOSLAVIA ECO/DEV FINAN ECO/TAC INT/TRADE ADMIN PWR 20. PAGE 40 A0809
DIPLOM ECO/UNDEV COLONIAL DOMIN

B64
EMBREE A.T.,A GUIDE TO PAPERBACKS ON ASIA; SELECTED AND ANNOTATED (PAMPHLET). CULTURE SOCIETY ECO/UNDEV SECT DIPLOM COLONIAL MARXISM...SOC 20. PAGE 41 A0845
BIBLIOG/A ASIA S/ASIA NAT/G

B64
ETZIONI A.,WINNING WITHOUT WAR. FUT MOD/EUR USA+45 WOR+45 ECO/DEV ECO/UNDEV INT/ORG NAT/G FORCES TOP/EX PLAN TEC/DEV ECO/TAC DOMIN EDU/PROP LEGIT COERCE CHOOSE ATTIT MORAL ORD/FREE RESPECT WEALTH MAJORIT. PAGE 43 A0871
PWR TREND DIPLOM USSR

B64
FATOUROS A.A.,CANADA'S OVERSEAS AID. CANADA WOR+45 ECO/DEV FINAN NAT/G BUDGET ECO/TAC CONFER ADMIN 20. PAGE 44 A0904
FOR/AID DIPLOM ECO/UNDEV POLICY

B64
FEIS H.,FOREIGN AID AND FOREIGN POLICY. USA+45 WOR+45 NAT/G VOL/ASSN ACT/RES TEC/DEV ATTIT HEALTH WEALTH...SOC GEN/LAWS 20. PAGE 45 A0912
ECO/UNDEV ECO/TAC FOR/AID DIPLOM

B64
FREE L.A.,THE ATTITUDES, HOPES AND FEARS OF NIGERIANS. AFR NIGERIA ECO/UNDEV AGRI ACADEM PLAN TASK...GEOG CHARTS METH 20. PAGE 49 A0993
NAT/LISM SYS/QU DIPLOM

B64
GIBSON J.S.,IDEOLOGY AND WORLD AFFAIRS. FUT WOR+45 ECO/UNDEV NAT/G CAP/ISM TOTALISM ORD/FREE FASCISM MARXISM 20. PAGE 52 A1067
ALL/IDEOS DIPLOM POLICY IDEA/COMP

B64
HAMBRIDGE G.,DYNAMICS OF DEVELOPMENT. AGRI FINAN INDUS LABOR INT/TRADE EDU/PROP ADMIN LEAD OWN HEALTH...ANTHOL BIBLIOG 20. PAGE 61 A1245
ECO/UNDEV ECO/TAC OP/RES ACT/RES

B64
HAMRELL S.,THE SOVIET BLOC, CHINA, AND AFRICA. AFR CHINA/COM COM USSR ECO/UNDEV EDU/PROP 20. PAGE 61 A1249
MARXISM DIPLOM CONTROL FOR/AID

B64
HAZLEWOOD A.,THE ECONOMICS OF DEVELOPMENT: AN ANNOTATED LIST OF BOOKS AND ARTICLES PUBLISHED 1958-1962. AGRI FINAN INDUS LABOR NAT/G DIPLOM INT/TRADE INCOME...MGT 20. PAGE 63 A1303
BIBLIOG/A ECO/UNDEV TEC/DEV

B64
HEKHUIS D.J.,INTERNATIONAL STABILITY: MILITARY, ECONOMIC AND POLITICAL DIMENSIONS. FUT WOR+45 LAW ECO/UNDEV INT/ORG NAT/G VOL/ASSN FORCES ACT/RES BAL/PWR PWR WEALTH...STAT UN 20. PAGE 64 A1310
TEC/DEV DETER REGION

B64
HINSHAW R.,THE EUROPEAN COMMUNITY AND AMERICAN TRADE: A STUDY IN ATLANTIC ECONOMICS AND POLICY. EUR+WWI UK USA+45 ECO/DEV ECO/UNDEV AGRI INDUS INT/ORG NAT/G ECO/TAC TARIFFS REGION...STAT CHARTS EEC 20. PAGE 65 A1337
MARKET TREND INT/TRADE

B64
HOROWITZ I.L.,REVOLUTION IN BRAZIL. BRAZIL L/A+17C ELITES STRATA NAT/G BAL/PWR PARTIC ATTIT 20. PAGE 68 A1388
ECO/UNDEV DIPLOM POLICY ORD/FREE

B64
INTL INF CTR LOCAL CREDIT,GOVERNMENT MEASURES FOR THE PROMOTION OF REGIONAL ECONOMIC DEVELOPMENT. WOR+45 ECO/UNDEV FINAN INT/ORG DIPLOM ORD/FREE ...POLICY GEOG 20. PAGE 71 A1464
FOR/AID PLAN ECO/TAC REGION

B64
IRISH M.D.,WORLD PRESSURES ON AMERICAN FOREIGN POLICY. ASIA COM L/A+17C SOUTH/AFR UK WOR+45 ECO/DEV ECO/UNDEV COLONIAL SANCTION COERCE REV TOTALISM...ANTHOL 20 COLD/WAR EUROPE/W INTERVENT. PAGE 72 A1467
DIPLOM POLICY

B64
JANOWITZ M.,THE MILITARY IN THE POLITICAL DEVELOPMENT OF NEW NATIONS: AN ESSAY IN COMPARATIVE ANALYSIS. AFR ASIA ISLAM L/A+17C S/ASIA USA+45 ECO/UNDEV INT/ORG NAT/G POL/PAR DELIB/GP PLAN ECO/TAC DOMIN LEGIT COERCE ATTIT DRIVE RESPECT ...SOC CONCPT CENSUS VAL/FREE. PAGE 73 A1495
FORCES PWR

B64
KALDOR N.,ESSAYS ON ECONOMIC POLICY (VOL. II). CHILE GERMANY INDIA FINAN...GOV/COMP METH/COMP 20 KEYNES/JM. PAGE 76 A1551
BAL/PAY
INT/TRADE
METH/CNCPT
ECO/UNDEV

B64
KITCHEN H.,A HANDBOOK OF AFRICAN AFFAIRS. ECO/UNDEV CREATE DIPLOM COLONIAL RACE/REL...ART/METH GEOG CHARTS 20. PAGE 80 A1646
AFR
NAT/G
INT/ORG
FORCES

B64
KNIGHT R.,BIBLIOGRAPHY ON INCOME AND WEALTH, 1957-1960 (VOL VIII). WOR+45 ECO/DEV FINAN INT/TRADE...GOV/COMP METH/COMP. PAGE 80 A1652
BIBLIOG/A
ECO/UNDEV
WEALTH
INCOME

B64
KRETZSCHMAR W.W.,AUSLANDSHILFE ALS MITTEL DER AUSSENWIRTSCHAFTS- UND AUSSENPOLITIK. ASIA GERMANY/W UK USA+45 SOCIETY STRUCT ECO/UNDEV LOBBY EFFICIENCY 20. PAGE 82 A1683
FOR/AID
DIPLOM
AGRI
DIST/IND

B64
LATOURETTE K.S.,CHINA. ASIA CHINA/COM FUT USSR ECO/UNDEV ECO/TAC WAR 19/20. PAGE 85 A1744
MARXISM
NAT/G
POLICY
DIPLOM

B64
LEGGE J.D.,INDONESIA. INDONESIA ELITES ECO/UNDEV POL/PAR CHIEF FORCES INT/TRADE COERCE CHOOSE ORD/FREE...SOC CHARTS BIBLIOG 16/20 CHINJAP. PAGE 86 A1765
S/ASIA
DOMIN
NAT/LISM
POLICY

B64
LITTLE I.M.D.,AID TO AFRICA. AFR UK TEC/DEV DIPLOM ECO/TAC INCOME WEALTH 20. PAGE 90 A1844
FOR/AID
ECO/UNDEV
ADMIN
POLICY

B64
LUTHULI A.,AFRICA'S FREEDOM. KIN LABOR POL/PAR SCHOOL DIPLOM NEUTRAL REGION REV NAT/LISM PWR WEALTH SOCISM SOC/INTEG 20. PAGE 92 A1874
AFR
ECO/UNDEV
COLONIAL

B64
MAHAR J.M.,INDIA: A CRITICAL BIBLIOGRAPHY. INDIA PAKISTAN CULTURE ECO/UNDEV LOC/G POL/PAR SECT PROB/SOLV DIPLOM ADMIN COLONIAL PARL/PROC ATTIT 20. PAGE 93 A1906
BIBLIOG/A
S/ASIA
NAT/G
LEAD

B64
MASON E.S.,FOREIGN AID AND FOREIGN POLICY. USA+45 AGRI INDUS NAT/G EX/STRUC ACT/RES RIGID/FLEX ALL/VALS...POLICY GEN/LAWS MARSHL/PLN CONGRESS 20. PAGE 95 A1956
ECO/UNDEV
ECO/TAC
FOR/AID
DIPLOM

B64
MATTHEWS D.G.,A CURRENT VIEW OF AFRICANA (PAMPHLET). CULTURE ECO/UNDEV DIPLOM RACE/REL ATTIT 20. PAGE 96 A1968
BIBLIOG/A
AFR
NAT/G
NAT/LISM

B64
MAUD J.,AID FOR DEVELOPING COUNTRIES. COM EUR+WWI UK INT/TRADE ORD/FREE...GOV/COMP 20. PAGE 96 A1979
FOR/AID
DIPLOM
ECO/TAC
ECO/UNDEV

B64
MYINT H.,THE ECONOMICS OF THE DEVELOPING COUNTRIES. WOR+45 AGRI PLAN COST...POLICY GEOG 20 MONEY. PAGE 107 A2187
ECO/UNDEV
INT/TRADE
EXTR/IND
FINAN

B64
NEHEMKIS P.,LATIN AMERICA: MYTH AND REALITY. INDUS INT/ORG MUNIC PROB/SOLV CAP/ISM DIPLOM REV...SOC 20. PAGE 108 A2211
REGION
MYTH
L/A+17C
ECO/UNDEV

B64
NEWBURY C.W.,THE WEST AFRICAN COMMONWEALTH. CONSTN INTELL ECO/UNDEV VOL/ASSN CHIEF DELIB/GP LEGIS INT/TRADE COLONIAL FEDERAL ATTIT 20 COMMONWLTH AFRICA/W. PAGE 108 A2223
INT/ORG
SOVEREIGN
GOV/REL
AFR

B64
NEWCOMER H.A.,INTERNATIONAL AIDS TO OVERSEAS INVESTMENTS AND TRADE. ECO/UNDEV TARIFFS PROFIT ...BIBLIOG 20 GATT UN. PAGE 108 A2225
INT/TRADE
FINAN
DIPLOM
FOR/AID

B64
OECD,DEVELOPMENT ASSISTANCE EFFORTS - POLICIES OF THE MEMBERS. AGRI INDUS BUDGET...GEOG NAT/COMP 20 OECD. PAGE 111 A2280
INT/ORG
FOR/AID
ECO/UNDEV
TEC/DEV

B64
OECD,THE FLOW OF FINANCIAL RESOURCES TO LESS DEVELOPED COUNTRIES 1956-1963. WOR+45 FINAN CAP/ISM ...POLICY STAT 20. PAGE 111 A2281
FOR/AID
BUDGET
INT/ORG
ECO/UNDEV

B64
OWEN W.,STRATEGY FOR MOBILITY. FUT WOR+45 WOR-45 DIST/IND INT/ORG NAT/G DELIB/GP PLAN TEC/DEV ECO/TAC ORD/FREE PWR WEALTH...STAT TIME/SEQ VAL/FREE 20. PAGE 112 A2304
COM/IND
ECO/UNDEV

B64
PENNOCK J.R.,SELF-GOVERNMENT IN MODERNIZING NATIONS. AFR COM USA+45 ECO/DEV POL/PAR PROB/SOLV DIPLOM ECO/TAC COLONIAL REV POPULISM SOCISM 20. PAGE 114 A2350
ECO/UNDEV
POLICY
SOVEREIGN
NAT/G

B64
RAMAZANI R.K.,THE MIDDLE EAST AND THE EUROPEAN COMMON MARKET. EUR+WWI ISLAM ECO/DEV EXTR/IND MARKET PROC/MFG INT/ORG NAT/G TEC/DEV ECO/TAC REGION DRIVE WEALTH...STAT CHARTS EEC TOT/POP 20. PAGE 119 A2437
ECO/UNDEV
ATTIT
INT/TRADE

B64
RANIS G.,THE UNITED STATES AND THE DEVELOPING ECONOMIES. COM USA+45 AGRI FINAN TEC/DEV CAP/ISM ECO/TAC INT/TRADE...POLICY METH/COMP ANTHOL 20 AID. PAGE 119 A2441
ECO/UNDEV
DIPLOM
FOR/AID

B64
REGALA R.,WORLD PEACE THROUGH DIPLOMACY AND LAW. S/ASIA WOR+45 ECO/UNDEV INT/ORG FORCES PLAN PROB/SOLV FOR/AID NUC/PWR WAR...POLICY INT/LAW 20. PAGE 120 A2456
DIPLOM
PEACE
ADJUD

B64
RIVKIN A.,AFRICA AND THE EUROPEAN COMMON MARKET (PAMPHLET). AFR MOD/EUR WOR+45 TEC/DEV FOR/AID TARIFFS BAL/PAY...POLICY 20 EEC. PAGE 121 A2490
INT/ORG
INT/TRADE
ECO/TAC
ECO/UNDEV

B64
RUBIN J.A.,YOUR HUNDRED BILLION DOLLARS. USA+45 USSR INDUS INT/ORG TEC/DEV ECO/TAC...METH/COMP 20 PEACE/CORP. PAGE 125 A2559
FOR/AID
DIPLOM
ECO/UNDEV

B64
RUBINSTEIN A.Z.,THE SOVIETS IN INTERNATIONAL ORGANIZATIONS: CHANGING POLICY TOWARD DEVELOPING COUNTRIES, 1953-1963. COM DELIB/GP ACT/RES ECO/TAC EDU/PROP ADMIN ATTIT ORD/FREE PWR...INT VAL/FREE UN 20. PAGE 125 A2563
ECO/UNDEV
INT/ORG
USSR

B64
SAKAI R.K.,STUDIES ON ASIA, 1964. ASIA CHINA/COM ISRAEL MALAYSIA S/ASIA USA+45 USSR ECO/UNDEV FAM POL/PAR SECT CONSULT NAT/LISM...POLICY SOC 20 CHINJAP. PAGE 126 A2588
PWR
DIPLOM

B64
SINGER H.W.,INTERNATIONAL DEVELOPMENT: GROWTH AND CHANGE. AFR BRAZIL L/A+17C WOR+45 CULTURE AGRI INDUS NAT/G ACT/RES ECO/TAC EDU/PROP WEALTH...GEOG CONCPT METH/CNCPT STAT HYPO/EXP WORK TOT/POP 20. PAGE 133 A2723
FINAN
ECO/UNDEV
FOR/AID
INT/TRADE

B64
STILLMAN E.O.,THE POLITICS OF HYSTERIA: THE SOURCES OF TWENTIETH-CENTURY CONFLICT. WOR+45 WOR-45 CULTURE ECO/UNDEV PLAN CAP/ISM WAR MARXISM ...PREDICT BIBLIOG 20 COLD/WAR. PAGE 138 A2828
DIPLOM
IDEA/COMP
COLONIAL
CONTROL

B64
SULLIVAN G.,THE STORY OF THE PEACE CORPS. USA+45 WOR+45 INTELL FACE/GP NAT/G SCHOOL VOL/ASSN CONSULT EX/STRUC PLAN EDU/PROP ADMIN ATTIT DRIVE ALL/VALS ...POLICY HEAL SOC CONCPT INT QU BIOG TREND SOC/EXP WORK. PAGE 140 A2861
INT/ORG
ECO/UNDEV
FOR/AID
PEACE

B64
TEPASKE J.J.,EXPLOSIVE FORCES IN LATIN AMERICA. CULTURE INTELL ECO/UNDEV INT/ORG NAT/G SECT FORCES ECO/TAC EDU/PROP PWR WEALTH SOC. PAGE 142 A2903
L/A+17C
RIGID/FLEX
FOR/AID
USSR

B64
TONG T.,UNITED STATES DIPLOMACY IN CHINA, 1844-1860. ASIA USA-45 ECO/UNDEV ECO/TAC COERCE GP/REL...INT/LAW 19 TREATY. PAGE 144 A2949
DIPLOM
INT/TRADE
COLONIAL

B64
TULLY A.,WHERE DID YOUR MONEY GO. USA+45 USSR ECO/UNDEV ADMIN EFFICIENCY WEALTH...METH/COMP 20. PAGE 146 A2976
FOR/AID
DIPLOM
CONTROL

B64
UN PUB. INFORM. ORGAN.,EVERY MAN'S UNITED NATIONS. UNIV WOR+45 CONSTN CULTURE SOCIETY ECO/DEV ECO/UNDEV NAT/G ACT/RES PLAN ECO/TAC INT/TRADE EDU/PROP LEGIT PEACE ATTIT ALL/VALS...POLICY HUM INT/LAW CONCPT CHARTS UN TOT/POP 20. PAGE 147 A3004
INT/ORG
ROUTINE

B64
US AGENCY INTERNATIONAL DEV,REPORT TO CONGRESS ON THE FOREIGN ASSISTANCE PROGRAM. AFR ASIA L/A+17C USA+45 INT/ORG VOL/ASSN FORCES CAP/ISM ADMIN WEAPON. PAGE 149 A3052
FOR/AID
ECO/UNDEV
TEC/DEV
BUDGET

B64
US HOUSE COMM FOREIGN AFFAIRS,HEARINGS ON H.R. 10502 TO AMEND FURTHER THE FOREIGN ASSISTANCE ACT OF 1961. AFR ASIA L/A+17C INT/ORG CONSULT DELIB/GP TEC/DEV ECO/TAC EDU/PROP CONFER 20 UN NATO CONGRESS AID. PAGE 153 A3130
FOR/AID
DIPLOM
ORD/FREE
ECO/UNDEV

B64
VOELKMANN K.,HERRSCHER VON MORGEN? BAL/PWR COLONIAL NEUTRAL REGION RACE/REL ALL/VALS SOVEREIGN...RECORD 20 COLD/WAR THIRD/WRLD. PAGE 159 A3246
DIPLOM
ECO/UNDEV
CONTROL
NAT/COMP

B64
WALLBANK T.W.,DOCUMENTS ON MODERN AFRICA. NAT/G COLONIAL GP/REL ATTIT PWR...BIBLIOG 19/20. PAGE 160 A3267
AFR
NAT/LISM
ECO/UNDEV
DIPLOM

B64
WITHERELL J.W.,OFFICIAL PUBLICATIONS OF FRENCH EQUATORIAL AFRICA, FRENCH CAMEROONS, AND TOGO, 1946-1958 (PAMPHLET). CAMEROON CHAD FRANCE GABON TOGO LAW ECO/UNDEV EXTR/IND INT/TRADE...GEOG HEAL 20. PAGE 165 A3370
BIBLIOG/A AFR NAT/G ADMIN

B64
WITHERS W.,THE ECONOMIC CRISIS IN LATIN AMERICA. BRAZIL CHILE STRATA AGRI DIPLOM FOR/AID PWR SOCISM ...POLICY 20 MEXIC/AMER ARGEN. PAGE 166 A3372
L/A+17C ECO/UNDEV CAP/ISM ALL/IDEOS

B64
WOODHOUSE C.M.,THE NEW CONCERT OF NATIONS. WOR+45 ECO/DEV ECO/UNDEV NAT/G BAL/PWR ECO/TAC NAT/LISM PWR SOVEREIGN ALL/IDEOS 20 UN COLD/WAR. PAGE 166 A3391
DIPLOM MORAL FOR/AID COLONIAL

B64
WYTHE G.,THE UNITED STATES AND INTER-AMERICAN RELATIONS: A CONTEMPORARY APPRAISAL. L/A+17C USA+45 ECO/UNDEV INT/ORG NAT/G VOL/ASSN INT/TRADE EDU/PROP DRIVE...SOC TREND OAS UN 20. PAGE 168 A3425
ATTIT ECO/TAC FOR/AID

L64
ARMENGALD A.,"ECONOMIE ET COEXISTENCE." COM EUR+WWI FUT USA+45 WOR+45 ECO/DEV ECO/UNDEV FINAN INT/ORG NAT/G EXEC CHOOSE ATTIT ALL/VALS...POLICY RELATIV DECISION TREND SOC/EXP COLD/WAR WORK 20. PAGE 9 A0173
MARKET ECO/TAC CAP/ISM

L64
CAMPBELL J.C.,"THE MIDDLE EAST IN THE MUTED COLD WAR." COM EUR+WWI UAR USA+45 USSR STRUCT ECO/UNDEV NAT/G VOL/ASSN EX/STRUC TOP/EX DIPLOM ECO/TAC EDU/PROP...TIME/SEQ COLD/WAR 20. PAGE 23 A0475
ISLAM FOR/AID NAT/LISM

L64
CARNEGIE ENDOWMENT INT. PEACE,"ECONOMIC AND SOCIAL QUESTION (ISSUES BEFORE THE NINETEENTH GENERAL ASSEMBLY)." WOR+45 ECO/DEV ECO/UNDEV INDUS R+D DELIB/GP CREATE PLAN TEC/DEV ECO/TAC FOR/AID BAL/PAY...RECORD UN 20. PAGE 24 A0493
INT/ORG INT/TRADE

L64
KORBONSKI A.,"COMECON." ASIA ECO/DEV ECO/UNDEV ECO/TAC BAL/PAY NAT/LISM 20 COMECON. PAGE 81 A1671
COM INT/ORG INT/TRADE

L64
MANZER R.A.,"THE UNITED NATIONS SPECIAL FUND." WOR+45 CONSTN ECO/UNDEV NAT/G TOP/EX LEGIT WEALTH ...CHARTS UN 20. PAGE 94 A1936
FINAN INT/ORG

L64
POUNDS N.J.G.,"THE POLITICS OF PARTITION." AFR ASIA COM EUR+WWI FUT ISLAM S/ASIA USA-45 LAW ECO/DEV ECO/UNDEV AGRI INDUS INT/ORG POL/PAR PROVS SECT FORCES TOP/EX EDU/PROP LEGIT ATTIT MORAL ORD/FREE PWR RESPECT WEALTH. PAGE 117 A2402
NAT/G NAT/LISM

S64
ASHRAF S.,"INDIA AND WORLD AFFAIRS: AN ANNUAL BIBLIOGRAPHY, 1962." WOR+45 LAW ECO/UNDEV INT/ORG FORCES PLAN ECO/TAC COERCE ORD/FREE PWR WEALTH ...HIST/WRIT VAL/FREE. PAGE 9 A0188
S/ASIA NAT/G

S64
BEIM D.,"THE COMMUNIST BLOC AND THE FOREIGN-AID GAME." WOR+45 NAT/G PLAN ROUTINE ATTIT KNOWL ORD/FREE...DECISION QUANT CONT/OBS TIME/SEQ CHARTS GAME SIMUL COLD/WAR 20. PAGE 12 A0252
COM ECO/UNDEV ECO/TAC FOR/AID

S64
CARNEGIE ENDOWMENT INT. PEACE,"COLONIAL COUNTRIES AND PEOPLES (ISSUES BEFORE THE NINETEENTH GENERAL ASSEMBLY)." AFR ISLAM L/A+17C WOR+45 DELIB/GP LEGIS ECO/TAC EDU/PROP NAT/LISM PEACE ALL/VALS...RECORD UN CMN/WLTH 20. PAGE 24 A0491
INT/ORG ECO/UNDEV COLONIAL

S64
COCHRANE J.D.,"US ATTITUDES TOWARD CENTRAL-AMERICAN INTEGRATION." L/A+17C USA+45 ECO/UNDEV FACE/GP VOL/ASSN DELIB/GP ECO/TAC INT/TRADE EDU/PROP RIGID/FLEX ORD/FREE WEALTH...TIME/SEQ TOT/POP 20. PAGE 27 A0555
NAT/G ATTIT REGION

S64
DE GAULLE C.,"FRENCH WORLD VIEW." AFR ASIA CHINA/COM EUR+WWI ISLAM ECO/UNDEV INT/ORG NAT/G VOL/ASSN ACT/RES DIPLOM ECO/TAC EDU/PROP ATTIT DRIVE WEALTH 20. PAGE 35 A0702
TOP/EX PWR FOR/AID FRANCE

S64
DERWINSKI E.J.,"THE COST OF THE INTERNATIONAL COFFEE AGREEMENT." L/A+17C USA+45 WOR+45 ECO/UNDEV NAT/G VOL/ASSN LEGIS DIPLOM ECO/TAC FOR/AID LEGIT ATTIT...TIME/SEQ CONGRESS 20 TREATY. PAGE 36 A0732
MARKET DELIB/GP INT/TRADE

S64
DRAKE S.T.C.,"DEMOCRACY ON TRIAL IN AFRICA." EUR+WWI FUT USA+45 ECO/UNDEV INT/ORG NAT/G POL/PAR TOP/EX EDU/PROP LEGIT ATTIT ALL/VALS...POLICY TREND GEN/LAWS VAL/FREE 20. PAGE 38 A0785
AFR STERTYP

S64
GARDNER R.N.,"GATT AND THE UNITED NATIONS CONFERENCE ON TRADE AND DEVELOPMENT." USA+45 WOR+45 SOCIETY ECO/UNDEV MARKET NAT/G DELIB/GP ACT/RES PLAN ECO/TAC TARIFFS EDU/PROP ROUTINE DRIVE RIGID/FLEX WEALTH...DECISION MGT TREND UN TOT/POP 20 GATT. PAGE 51 A1047
INT/ORG INT/TRADE

S64
GARMARNIKOW M.,"INFLUENCE-BUYING IN WEST AFRICA." COM FUT USSR INTELL NAT/G PLAN TEC/DEV ECO/TAC DOMIN EDU/PROP REGION NAT/LISM ATTIT DRIVE ALL/VALS SOVEREIGN...POLICY PSY SOC CONCPT TREND STERTYP WORK COLD/WAR 20. PAGE 51 A1049
AFR ECO/UNDEV FOR/AID SOCISM

S64
HABERLER G.,"INTEGRATION AND GROWTH OF THE WORLD ECONOMY IN HISTORICAL PERSPECTIVE." FUT WOR+45 WOR-45 ECO/DEV ECO/UNDEV...TIME/SEQ TREND VAL/FREE 20. PAGE 59 A1209
WEALTH INT/TRADE

S64
HUELIN D.,"ECONOMIC INTEGRATION IN LATIN AMERICAN: PROGRESS AND PROBLEMS." L/A+17C ECO/DEV AGRI DIST/IND FINAN INDUS NAT/G VOL/ASSN CONSULT DELIB/GP EX/STRUC ACT/RES PLAN TEC/DEV ECO/TAC ROUTINE BAL/PAY WEALTH WORK 20. PAGE 69 A1411
MARKET ECO/UNDEV INT/TRADE

S64
HUTCHINSON E.C.,"AMERICAN AID TO AFRICA." FUT USA+45 MARKET INT/ORG LOC/G NAT/G PUB/INST PLAN ECO/TAC ATTIT RIGID/FLEX...POLICY CONCPT TREND 20. PAGE 69 A1423
AFR ECO/UNDEV FOR/AID

S64
MOORE W.E.,"PREDICTING DISCONTINUITIES IN SOCIAL CHANGE." UNIV WOR+45 ECO/DEV ECO/UNDEV INT/ORG NAT/G COERCE ALL/VALS...METH/CNCPT TIME/SEQ TREND TOT/POP VAL/FREE 20. PAGE 103 A2125
SOCIETY GEN/LAWS REV

S64
PADELFORD N.J.,"THE ORGANIZATION OF AFRICAN UNITY." ECO/UNDEV INT/ORG PLAN BAL/PWR DIPLOM ECO/TAC NAT/LISM ORD/FREE PWR WEALTH...CONCPT TREND STERTYP VAL/FREE COLD/WAR 20. PAGE 113 A2313
AFR VOL/ASSN REGION

S64
PALMER N.D.,"INDIA AS A FACTOR IN UNITED STATES FOREIGN POLICY." INDIA USA+45 USA-45 ECO/UNDEV NAT/G TOP/EX ECO/TAC EDU/PROP...METH/CNCPT TIME/SEQ 20. PAGE 113 A2323
S/ASIA ATTIT FOR/AID DIPLOM

S64
PESELT B.M.,"COMMUNIST ECONOMIC OFFENSIVE." WOR+45 SOCIETY INT/ORG PLAN ECO/TAC DOMIN EDU/PROP ATTIT PERSON PWR WEALTH...TREND CHARTS 20. PAGE 115 A2366
COM ECO/UNDEV FOR/AID USSR

S64
ROTHCHILD D.,"EAST AFRICAN FEDERATION." AFR TANZANIA UGANDA INDUS REGION 20. PAGE 124 A2547
INT/ORG DIPLOM ECO/UNDEV ECO/TAC

S64
TOUVAL S.,"THE SOMALI REPUBLIC." AFR ISLAM SOMALIA FAM KIN NAT/G CREATE FOR/AID LEGIT ATTIT ALL/VALS ...RECORD TREND 20. PAGE 144 A2954
ECO/UNDEV RIGID/FLEX

S64
TRISKA J.F.,"SOVIET TREATY LAW: A QUANTITATIVE ANALYSIS." WOR+45 LAW ECO/UNDEV AGRI COM/IND INDUS CREATE TEC/DEV DIPLOM ATTIT PWR WEALTH...JURID SAMP TIME/SEQ TREND CHARTS VAL/FREE 20 TREATY. PAGE 145 A2967
COM ECO/TAC INT/LAW USSR

S64
WOOD H.B.,"STRETCHING YOUR FOREIGN-AID DOLLAR." USA+45 WOR+45 CONSULT EDU/PROP ATTIT WEALTH...OBS TOT/POP CONGRESS 20. PAGE 166 A3390
ECO/UNDEV MGT FOR/AID

S64
ZARTMAN I.W.,"LES RELATIONS ENTRE LA FRANCE ET L'ALGERIA DEPUIS LES ACCORDS D'EVIAN." EUR+WWI FUT ISLAM CULTURE AGRI EXTR/IND FINAN INDUS POL/PAR DIPLOM ECO/TAC FOR/AID PEACE ATTIT DRIVE ALL/VALS ...TIME/SEQ VAL/FREE 20. PAGE 169 A3446
ECO/UNDEV ALGERIA FRANCE

C64
EASTON S.C.,"THE RISE AND FALL OF WESTERN COLONIALISM." AFR ISLAM L/A+17C ECO/UNDEV REV NAT/LISM...CHARTS BIBLIOG 15/20. PAGE 40 A0817
COLONIAL DIPLOM ORD/FREE WAR

C64
SCHRAMM W.,"MASS MEDIA AND NATIONAL DEVELOPMENT: THE ROLE OF INFORMATION IN DEVELOPING COUNTRIES." FINAN R+D ACT/RES PLAN TEC/DEV DIPLOM CHOOSE SUPEGO ORD/FREE...BIBLIOG 20. PAGE 129 A2645
ECO/UNDEV COM/IND EDU/PROP MAJORIT

N64
GREAT BRITAIN CENTRAL OFF INF,THE COLOMBO PLAN (PAMPHLET). ASIA S/ASIA USA+45 VOL/ASSN...CHARTS 20 COMMONWLTH RESOURCE/N. PAGE 55 A1134
FOR/AID PLAN INT/ORG ECO/UNDEV

B65
ANALYSIS AND ASSESSMENT OF THE ECONOMIC EFFECTS: PUBLIC LAW 480 TITLE I PROGRAM TURKEY. INDIA TURKEY USA+45 AGRI NAT/G PLAN BUDGET DIPLOM COST EFFICIENCY...CHARTS 20. PAGE 3 A0070
ECO/TAC FOR/AID FINAN ECO/UNDEV

B65
AIR UNIVERSITY LIBRARY,LATIN AMERICA, SELECTED REFERENCES. ECO/UNDEV FORCES EDU/PROP MARXISM 20 OAS. PAGE 5 A0106
BIBLIOG L/A+17C NAT/G DIPLOM

B65
BROOKINGS INSTITUTION,BROOKINGS PAPERS ON PUBLIC POLICY. USA+45 ECO/UNDEV LEGIS CAP/ISM ECO/TAC TAX EDU/PROP CONTROL APPORT 20. PAGE 19 A0395
DIPLOM FOR/AID POLICY

FINAN

B65
COOMBS P.H.,EDUCATION AND FOREIGN AID. AFR USA+45 DIPLOM EFFICIENCY KNOWL ORD/FREE...ANTHOL 20 AID. PAGE 30 A0608
EDU/PROP FOR/AID SCHOOL ECO/UNDEV

B65
COWEN Z.,THE BRITISH COMMONWEALTH OF NATIONS IN A CHANGING WORLD. UK ECO/UNDEV INT/ORG ECO/TAC INT/TRADE COLONIAL WAR GP/REL RACE/REL SOVEREIGN SOC/INTEG 20 TREATY EEC COMMONWLTH. PAGE 32 A0644
JURID DIPLOM PARL/PROC NAT/LISM

B65
DAVISON W.P.,INTERNATIONAL POLITICAL COMMUNICATION. COM USA+45 WOR+45 CULTURE ECO/UNDEV NAT/G PROB/SOLV PRESS TV ADMIN 20 FILM. PAGE 34 A0693
EDU/PROP DIPLOM PERS/REL COM/IND

B65
DEMAS W.G.,THE ECONOMICS OF DEVELOPMENT IN SMALL COUNTRIES WITH SPECIAL REFERENCE TO THE CARIBBEAN. WOR+45 BAL/PAY DEMAND EFFICIENCY PRODUC...GEOG CARIBBEAN. PAGE 36 A0731
ECO/UNDEV PLAN WEALTH INT/TRADE

B65
EMERSON R.,THE POLITICAL AWAKENING OF AFRICA. ECO/UNDEV INT/ORG COLONIAL RACE/REL ORD/FREE MARXISM...TREND ANTHOL 20. PAGE 42 A0849
AFR NAT/LISM DIPLOM POL/PAR

B65
FAGG J.E.,CUBA, HAITI, AND THE DOMINICAN REPUBLIC. CUBA DOMIN/REP HAITI L/A+17C NAT/G DIPLOM ECO/TAC DOMIN CHOOSE AUTHORIT ROLE SOVEREIGN POPULISM 17/20. PAGE 43 A0883
COLONIAL ECO/UNDEV REV GOV/COMP

B65
FORM W.H.,INDUSTRIAL RELATIONS AND SOCIAL CHANGE IN LATIN AMERICA. L/A+17C AGRI LABOR NAT/G PLAN PROB/SOLV DIPLOM...MGT SOC ANTHOL BIBLIOG/A METH 20. PAGE 47 A0966
INDUS GP/REL NAT/COMP ECO/UNDEV

B65
FRIEDMANN W.,AN INTRODUCTION TO WORLD POLITICS (5TH ED.). WOR+45 ECO/UNDEV BAL/PWR FOR/AID INT/TRADE PEACE...STAT CENSUS CHARTS BIBLIOG T 20 COLD/WAR UN THIRD/WRLD. PAGE 49 A1003
DIPLOM INT/ORG PROB/SOLV

B65
HOSELITZ B.F.,ECONOMICS AND THE IDEA OF MANKIND. UNIV ECO/DEV ECO/UNDEV DIST/IND INDUS INT/ORG NAT/G ACT/RES ECO/TAC WEALTH...CONCPT STAT. PAGE 68 A1392
CREATE INT/TRADE

B65
INGRAM D.,COMMONWEALTH FOR A COLOUR-BLIND WORLD. AFR INDIA UK STRATA ECO/UNDEV VOL/ASSN CREATE PLAN CONFER COLONIAL ORD/FREE SOC/INTEG 20 COMMONWLTH. PAGE 70 A1441
RACE/REL INT/ORG INGP/REL PROB/SOLV

B65
JALEE P.,THE PILLAGE OF THE THIRD WORLD (TRANS. BY MARY KLOPPER). WOR+45 AGRI INDUS ECO/TAC FOR/AID COLONIAL CONTROL PRODUC PWR WEALTH...STAT CHARTS 20 RESOURCE/N. PAGE 73 A1493
ECO/UNDEV DOMIN INT/TRADE DIPLOM

B65
JOHNSON H.G.,THE WORLD ECONOMY AT THE CROSSROADS. COM WOR-45 ECO/DEV AGRI INDUS INT/TRADE REGION NAT/LISM 20. PAGE 74 A1523
FINAN DIPLOM INT/ORG ECO/UNDEV

B65
KIRKWOOD K.,BRITAIN AND AFRICA. AFR UK ECO/UNDEV ECO/TAC WAR NAT/LISM SOVEREIGN 19/20. PAGE 80 A1636
NAT/G DIPLOM POLICY COLONIAL

B65
KRAUSE W.,ECONOMIC DEVELOPMENT: THE UNDERDEVELOPED WORLD AND THE AMERICAN INTEREST. USA+45 AGRI PLAN MARXISM...CHARTS 20. PAGE 82 A1679
FOR/AID ECO/UNDEV FINAN PROB/SOLV

B65
LACOUTRE J.,VIETNAM: BETWEEN TWO TRUCES. USA+45 VIETNAM NAT/G REV 20. PAGE 83 A1707
WAR ECO/UNDEV DIPLOM POLICY

B65
LASKY V.,THE UGLY RUSSIAN. AFR ASIA USSR ECO/UNDEV NAT/LISM TOTALISM PERSON 20. PAGE 85 A1738
FOR/AID ATTIT DIPLOM

B65
LEE M.,THE UNITED NATIONS AND WORLD REALITIES. ECO/UNDEV FORCES WAR PEACE ATTIT ROLE WEALTH 20 UN. PAGE 86 A1761
INT/ORG COLONIAL ARMS/CONT DIPLOM

B65
LEISS A.C.,APARTHEID AND UNITED NATIONS COLLECTIVE MEASURES. SOUTH/AFR ECO/UNDEV EXTR/IND FORCES WORKER ECO/TAC FOR/AID INT/TRADE WEALTH...TREND CHARTS 20 UN NEGRO. PAGE 86 A1770
DISCRIM RACE/REL STRATA DIPLOM

B65
LEWIS W.A.,POLITICS IN WEST AFRICA. AFR BAL/PWR DIPLOM REPRESENT...POLICY 20. PAGE 88 A1804
POL/PAR ELITES NAT/G ECO/UNDEV

B65
MANSFIELD P.,NASSER'S EGYPT. AFR ISLAM UAR ECO/UNDEV AGRI COLONIAL SOVEREIGN...CHARTS 20 NASSER/G MID/EAST. PAGE 94 A1934
CHIEF ECO/TAC DIPLOM POLICY

B65
MEAGHER R.F.,PUBLIC INTERNATIONAL DEVELOPMENT FINANCING IN SUDAN. SUDAN FINAN DELIB/GP GIVE ...CHARTS GOV/COMP 20. PAGE 99 A2029
FOR/AID PLAN RECEIVE ECO/UNDEV

B65
MEDIVA J.T.,LA IMPRENTA EN MEXICO, 1539-1821 (8 VOLS.). SOCIETY ECO/UNDEV DIPLOM COLONIAL GP/REL 16/19 MEXIC/AMER. PAGE 99 A2031
BIBLIOG WRITING NAT/G L/A+17C

B65
MOLNAR T.,AFRICA: A POLITICAL TRAVELOGUE. STRUCT ECO/UNDEV DIPLOM EDU/PROP LEAD RACE/REL MARXISM 20 INTERVENT EUROPE. PAGE 102 A2101
COLONIAL AFR ORD/FREE

B65
MONCRIEFF A.,SECOND THOUGHTS ON AID. WOR+45 ECO/UNDEV AGRI FINAN VOL/ASSN PLAN TEC/DEV GIVE EDU/PROP ROLE WEALTH 20. PAGE 102 A2105
FOR/AID ECO/TAC INT/ORG IDEA/COMP

B65
MURUMBI J.,PROBLEMS OF ECONOMIC DEVELOPMENT IN EAST AFRICA. FINAN INDUS WORKER TEC/DEV INT/TRADE TAX DEMAND EFFICIENCY PRODUC SOCISM...TREND CHARTS 20 AFRICA/E. PAGE 106 A2184
AGRI ECO/TAC ECO/UNDEV PROC/MFG

B65
NATIONAL CENTRAL LIBRARY,LATIN AMERICAN ECONOMIC AND SOCIAL SERIALS. UK SOCIETY NAT/G PLAN PROB/SOLV ...SOC 20. PAGE 107 A2202
BIBLIOG INT/TRADE ECO/UNDEV L/A+17C

B65
NKRUMAH K.,NEO-COLONIALISM: THE LAST STAGE OF IMPERIALISM. AFR INT/ORG WORKER FOR/AID INT/TRADE EDU/PROP GOV/REL NAT/LISM SOVEREIGN POPULISM SOCISM ...SOCIALIST 20 THIRD/WRLD INTRVN/ECO. PAGE 109 A2243
COLONIAL DIPLOM ECO/UNDEV ECO/TAC

B65
PANJAB U EXTENSION LIBRARY,INDIAN NEWS INDEX. INDIA ECO/UNDEV INDUS INT/ORG SCHOOL FORCES ADJUD WAR ATTIT WEALTH 20. PAGE 114 A2333
BIBLIOG PRESS WRITING DIPLOM

B65
REQUA E.G.,THE DEVELOPING NATIONS: A GUIDE TO INFORMATION SOURCES CONCERNING THEIR ECON, POLIT, TECHNICAL, AND SOCIAL PROBLEMS. AFR ASIA ISLAM L/A+17C INDUS INT/ORG CONSULT PLAN PROB/SOLV...SOC 20 UN. PAGE 120 A2466
BIBLIOG/A ECO/UNDEV FOR/AID TEC/DEV

B65
RODRIGUES J.H.,BRAZIL AND AFRICA. AFR BRAZIL PORTUGAL UK USA+45 USA-45 CULTURE ECO/UNDEV INT/ORG INT/TRADE RACE/REL ORD/FREE 15/20 UN MISCEGEN. PAGE 123 A2513
DIPLOM COLONIAL POLICY ATTIT

B65
SABLE M.H.,PERIODICALS FOR LATIN AMERICAN ECONOMIC DEVELOPMENT, TRADE, AND FINANCE: AN ANNOTATED BIBLIOGRAPHY. ECO/TAC PRODUC PROFIT ...STAT NAT/COMP 20 OAS. PAGE 126 A2583
BIBLIOG/A L/A+17C ECO/UNDEV INT/TRADE

B65
SILVA SOLAR J.,EL DESARROLLO DE LA NUEVA SOCIEDAD EN AMERICA. L/A+17C SOCIETY AGRI PROB/SOLV DIPLOM PARTIC GP/REL OWN...POLICY SOC 20 REFORMERS. PAGE 133 A2716
STRUCT ECO/UNDEV REGION CONTROL

B65
STEWART I.G.,AFRICAN PRIMARY PRODUCTS AND INTERNATIONAL TRADE. ECO/UNDEV AGRI FINAN DIPLOM CONTROL 20. PAGE 138 A2825
AFR INT/TRADE INT/ORG

B65
SULZBERGER C.L.,UNFINISHED REVOLUTION. USA+45 WOR+45 INT/ORG TEC/DEV BAL/PWR FOR/AID COLONIAL NEUTRAL PWR SOVEREIGN MARXISM 20. PAGE 140 A2863
DIPLOM ECO/UNDEV POLICY NAT/G

B65
US BUREAU EDUC CULTURAL AFF,RESOURCES SURVEY FOR LATIN AMERICAN COUNTRIES. L/A+17C USA+45 CULTURE INDUS INT/ORG SECT PLAN EDU/PROP POLICY. PAGE 150 A3056
NAT/G ECO/UNDEV FOR/AID DIPLOM

B65
US HOUSE COMM FOREIGN AFFAIRS,HEARINGS ON DRAFT BILL TO AMEND FURTHER THE FOREIGN ASSISTANCE ACT OF 1961. AFR ASIA L/A+17C USA+45 INT/ORG DELIB/GP TEC/DEV ECO/TAC CONFER TOTALISM 20 CONGRESS AID. PAGE 153 A3131
FOR/AID ECO/UNDEV DIPLOM ORD/FREE

B65
US SENATE COMM ON FOREIGN REL,HEARINGS ON THE FOREIGN ASSISTANCE PROGRAM. AFR ASIA L/A+17C USA+45 WOR+45 FORCES TEC/DEV BUDGET CONTROL WEAPON ORD/FREE 20 UN CONGRESS SEC/STATE. PAGE 156 A3183
FOR/AID DIPLOM INT/ORG ECO/UNDEV

B65
VAN DEN BERGHE P.L.,AFRICA: SOCIAL PROBLEMS OF CHANGE AND CONFLICT. ELITES STRATA ECO/UNDEV KIN MUNIC DIPLOM GP/REL RACE/REL NAT/LISM...ANTHOL BIBLIOG 20. PAGE 158 A3210
SOC CULTURE AFR STRUCT

B65
WEAVER J.N.,THE INTERNATIONAL DEVELOPMENT
FOR/AID

ASSOCIATION: A NEW APPROACH TO FOREIGN AID. USA+45 NAT/G OP/RES PLAN PROB/SOLV WEALTH...CHARTS BIBLIOG 20 UN. PAGE 162 A3295 — INT/ORG ECO/UNDEV FINAN

B65
WHITE J.,GERMAN AID. GERMANY/W FINAN PLAN TEC/DEV INT/TRADE ADMIN ATTIT...POLICY 20. PAGE 164 A3335 — FOR/AID ECO/UNDEV DIPLOM ECO/TAC

L65
MATTHEWS D.G.,"A CURRENT BIBLIOGRAPHY ON ETHIOPIAN AFFAIRS: A SELECT BIBLIOGRAPHY FROM 1950-1964." ETHIOPIA LAW CULTURE ECO/UNDEV INDUS LABOR SECT FORCES DIPLOM CIVMIL/REL RACE/REL...LING STAT 20. PAGE 96 A1969 — BIBLIOG/A ADMIN POL/PAR NAT/G

L65
MATTHEWS D.G.,"A CURRENT BIBLIOGRAPHY ON SUDANESE AFFAIRS; A SELECT BIBLIOGRAPHY FROM 1960-1964." SUDAN LAW CULTURE AGRI FINAN INDUS LABOR POL/PAR TEC/DEV FOR/AID RACE/REL LITERACY...LING 20. PAGE 96 A1970 — BIBLIOG ECO/UNDEV NAT/G DIPLOM

L65
MATTHEWS D.G.,"LE TIERS MONDE: A SELECT AND PRELIMINARY BIBLIOGRAPHIC SURVEY OF MANPOWER IN DEVELOPING COUNTRIES, 1960-1964." AFR ISLAM L/A+17C INDUS PLAN PROB/SOLV TEC/DEV INT/TRADE EFFICIENCY WEALTH...STAT 20. PAGE 96 A1971 — BIBLIOG/A ECO/UNDEV LABOR WORKER

S65
KHOURI F.J.,"THE JORDON RIVER CONTROVERSY." LAW SOCIETY ECO/UNDEV AGRI FINAN INDUS SECT FORCES ACT/RES PLAN TEC/DEV ECO/TAC EDU/PROP COERCE ATTIT DRIVE PERCEPT RIGID/FLEX ALL/VALS...GEOG SOC MYTH WORK. PAGE 78 A1610 — ISLAM INT/ORG ISRAEL JORDAN

S65
KORBONSKI A.,"USA POLICY IN EAST EUROPE." COM EUR+WWI GERMANY USA+45 CULTURE ECO/UNDEV EDU/PROP RIGID/FLEX WEALTH 20. PAGE 82 A1672 — ACT/RES ECO/TAC FOR/AID

S65
QUADE Q.L.,"THE TRUMAN ADMINISTRATION AND THE SEPARATION OF POWERS: THE CASE OF THE MARSHALL PLAN." SOCIETY INT/ORG NAT/G CONSULT DELIB/GP LEGIS PLAN ECO/TAC ROUTINE DRIVE PERCEPT RIGID/FLEX ORD/FREE PWR WEALTH...DECISION GEOG NEW/IDEA TREND 20 TRUMAN/HS. PAGE 118 A2422 — USA+45 ECO/UNDEV DIPLOM

S65
RODNEY W.,"THE ENTENTE STATES OF WEST AFRICA." AFR FRANCE USA+45 POL/PAR SCHOOL FORCES ECO/TAC COLONIAL PWR 20 AFRICA/W. PAGE 123 A2512 — DIPLOM POLICY NAT/G ECO/UNDEV

S65
SCHNEIDER R.M.,"THE US IN LATIN AMERICA." L/A+17C USA+45 NAT/G POL/PAR PLAN RIGID/FLEX ALL/VALS OAS 20. PAGE 129 A2640 — VOL/ASSN ECO/UNDEV FOR/AID

C65
MARK M.,"BEYOND SOVEREIGNTY." WOR+45 WOR-45 ECO/UNDEV BAL/PWR INT/TRADE NUC/PWR REV WAR MARXISM NEW/LIB BIBLIOG. PAGE 95 A1942 — NAT/LISM NAT/G DIPLOM INTELL

B66
BALDWIN D.A.,ECONOMIC DEVELOPMENT AND AMERICAN FOREIGN POLICY. USA+45 FINAN LG/CO LEGIS DIPLOM GIVE 20. PAGE 10 A0210 — ECO/TAC FOR/AID ECO/UNDEV POLICY

B66
ENTWICKLUNGSPOLITIK - HANDBUCH UND LEXIKON. MARKET SECT DIPLOM INT/TRADE EDU/PROP CATHISM 20. PAGE 14 A0283 — ECO/UNDEV FOR/AID ECO/TAC PLAN

B66
BIRMINGHAM D.,TRADE AND CONFLICT IN ANGOLA. PORTUGAL CULTURE FORCES DIPLOM GP/REL PROFIT HABITAT NAT/COMP. PAGE 14 A0291 — WAR INT/TRADE ECO/UNDEV COLONIAL

B66
BLACK C.E.,THE DYNAMICS OF MODERNIZATION: A STUDY IN COMPARATIVE HISTORY. STRUCT ECO/DEV ECO/UNDEV NAT/G DIPLOM LEAD REV...PREDICT TIME/SEQ TREND SOC/INTEG 17/20. PAGE 15 A0296 — SOCIETY SOC NAT/COMP

B66
BRACKMAN A.C.,SOUTHEAST ASIA'S SECOND FRONT: THE POWER STRUGGLE IN THE MALAY ARCHIPELAGO. CHINA/COM INDONESIA MALAYSIA ECO/UNDEV INT/ORG NAT/G FORCES DIPLOM EDU/PROP REGION COERCE GUERRILLA AUTHORIT POPULISM...MAJORIT 20 KENNEDY/JF SEATO. PAGE 18 A0367 — S/ASIA MARXISM REV

B66
BROEKMEIJER M.W.J.,FICTION AND TRUTH ABOUT THE "DECADE OF DEVELOPMENT" WOR+45 AGRI FINAN INDUS NAT/G TEC/DEV DIPLOM EDU/PROP LEAD SKILL 20 THIRD/WRLD. PAGE 19 A0385 — FOR/AID POLICY ECO/UNDEV PLAN

B66
BROWN J.F.,THE NEW EASTERN EUROPE. ALBANIA BULGARIA HUNGARY POLAND ROMANIA CULTURE AGRI POL/PAR WAR NAT/LISM MARXISM...CHARTS BIBLIOG 20. PAGE 20 A0404 — DIPLOM COM NAT/G ECO/UNDEV

B66
BROWN L.C.,STATE AND SOCIETY IN INDEPENDENT NORTH AFRICA. ALGERIA LIBYA MOROCCO AGRI INDUS INT/ORG POL/PAR SECT PLAN DIPLOM COLONIAL...LING NAT/COMP ANTHOL BIBLIOG 20 TUNIS MUSLIM. PAGE 20 A0406 — NAT/G SOCIETY CULTURE ECO/UNDEV

B66
BRYNES A.,WE GIVE TO CONQUER. USA+45 USSR STRATA ECO/UNDEV INT/ORG NAT/G DIPLOM DRIVE...TREND IDEA/COMP 20. PAGE 20 A0414 — FOR/AID CONTROL GIVE WAR

B66
CLENDENON C.,AMERICANS IN AFRICA 1865-1900. AFR USA-45 ECO/UNDEV SECT REV RACE/REL CONSERVE ...TRADIT GEOG BIBLIOG 16/18. PAGE 27 A0549 — DIPLOM COLONIAL INT/TRADE

B66
COPLIN W.D.,THE FUNCTIONS OF INTERNATIONAL LAW. WOR+45 ECO/DEV ECO/UNDEV ADJUD COLONIAL WAR OWN SOVEREIGN...POLICY GEN/LAWS 20. PAGE 30 A0611 — INT/LAW DIPLOM INT/ORG

B66
COYLE D.C.,THE UNITED NATIONS AND HOW IT WORKS. ECO/UNDEV DELIB/GP BAL/PWR EDU/PROP ARMS/CONT NUC/PWR WAR 20 UN. PAGE 32 A0648 — INT/ORG PEACE DIPLOM INT/TRADE

B66
CURRIE L.,ACCELERATING DEVELOPMENT: THE NECESSITY AND MEANS. COLOMBIA USA+45 INDUS DIPLOM EFFICIENCY WEALTH...METH/CNCPT NEW/IDEA 20. PAGE 33 A0668 — PLAN ECO/UNDEV FOR/AID TEC/DEV

B66
EMBREE A.T.,ASIA: A GUIDE TO BASIC BOOKS (PAMPHLET). ECO/UNDEV SECT FORCES DIPLOM ALL/IDEOS ...SOC 20. PAGE 41 A0846 — BIBLIOG/A ASIA S/ASIA NAT/G

B66
FERKISS V.C.,AFRICA'S SEARCH FOR IDENTITY. AFR USA+45 CULTURE ECO/UNDEV INT/ORG NAT/G COLONIAL MARXISM 20. PAGE 45 A0918 — NAT/LISM SOVEREIGN DIPLOM ROLE

B66
FINKLE J.L.,POLITICAL DEVELOPMENT AND SOCIAL CHANGE. WOR+45 CULTURE NAT/G OP/RES PROB/SOLV DIPLOM ECO/TAC INGP/REL...METH/COMP ANTHOL 20. PAGE 46 A0934 — ECO/UNDEV SOCIETY CREATE

B66
FITZGERALD C.P.,THE BIRTH OF COMMUNIST CHINA (2ND ED.). ASIA CHINA/COM STRUCT BAL/PWR DIPLOM ECO/TAC INT/TRADE WEALTH 20. PAGE 46 A0942 — REV MARXISM ECO/UNDEV

B66
HALLET R.,PEOPLE AND PROGRESS IN WEST AFRICA: AN INTRODUCTION TO THE PROBLEMS OF DEVELOPMENT. COM/IND INDUS KIN DIPLOM FOR/AID INT/TRADE HEALTH ...GEOG TREND CHARTS BIBLIOG/A 20 AFRICA/W. PAGE 60 A1233 — AFR SOCIETY ECO/UNDEV ECO/TAC

B66
HANSON J.W.,EDUCATION AND THE DEVELOPMENT OF NATIONS. DIPLOM TASK ADJUST EFFICIENCY...POLICY ANTHOL 20. PAGE 61 A1256 — ECO/UNDEV EDU/PROP NAT/G PLAN

B66
HAYER T.,FRENCH AID. AFR FRANCE AGRI FINAN BUDGET ADMIN WAR PRODUC...CHARTS 18/20 THIRD/WRLD OVRSEA/DEV. PAGE 63 A1295 — TEC/DEV COLONIAL FOR/AID ECO/UNDEV

B66
HOROWITZ D.,HEMISPHERES NORTH AND SOUTH: ECONOMIC DISPARITY AMONG NATIONS. WOR+45 ECO/DEV ECO/UNDEV INT/ORG PLAN DIPLOM INT/TRADE GIVE PARTIC GP/REL ...WELF/ST 20. PAGE 67 A1387 — ECO/TAC FOR/AID STRATA WEALTH

B66
INTERNATIONAL ECONOMIC ASSN,STABILITY AND PROGRESS IN THE WORLD ECONOMY: THE FIRST CONGRESS OF THE INTERNATIONAL ECONOMIC ASSOCIATION. WOR+45 ECO/DEV ECO/UNDEV DELIB/GP FOR/AID BAL/PAY...TREND CMN/WLTH 20. PAGE 71 A1455 — INT/TRADE

B66
KANET R.E.,THE SOVIET UNION AND SUB-SAHARAN AFRICA: COMMUNIST POLICY TOWARD AFRICA, 1917-1965. AFR USSR ECO/UNDEV TEC/DEV EDU/PROP TASK DISCRIM PEACE WEALTH ALL/IDEOS...CHARTS BIBLIOG SOC/INTEG 19/20 NEGRO UN INTERVENT. PAGE 76 A1555 — DIPLOM ECO/TAC MARXISM

B66
KAREFA-SMART J.,AFRICA: PROGRESS THROUGH COOPERATION. AFR FINAN TEC/DEV DIPLOM FOR/AID EDU/PROP CONFER REGION GP/REL WEALTH...HEAL SOC/INTEG 20. PAGE 76 A1566 — ORD/FREE ECO/UNDEV VOL/ASSN PLAN

B66
KEENLEYSIDE H.L.,INTERNATIONAL AID: A SUMMARY. AFR INDIA S/ASIA UK STRATA EXTR/IND TEC/DEV ADMIN RACE/REL DEMAND NAT/LISM WEALTH...TREND CHINJAP. PAGE 77 A1575 — ECO/UNDEV FOR/AID DIPLOM TASK

B66
KEYES J.G.,A BIBLIOGRAPHY OF WESTERN LANGUAGE PUBLICATIONS CONCERNING NORTH VIETNAM IN THE CORNELL LIBRARY. VIETNAM/N NAT/G FORCES TEC/DEV DIPLOM LEAD RACE/REL...GEOG SOC 20. PAGE 78 A1603 — BIBLIOG/A CULTURE ECO/UNDEV S/ASIA

B66
KIM Y.K.,PATTERNS OF COMPETITIVE COEXISTENCE: USA VS. USSR. USA+45 USSR ECO/DEV ECO/UNDEV INT/ORG — DIPLOM PEACE

FOR/AID INT/TRADE ARMS/CONT...BIBLIOG 20 COLD/WAR. PAGE 79 A1618
BAL/PWR DETER

B66
KIRDAR U.,THE STRUCTURE OF UNITED NATIONS ECONOMIC AID TO UNDERDEVELOPED COUNTRIES. AGRI FINAN INDUS NAT/G EX/STRUC PLAN GIVE TASK...POLICY 20 UN. PAGE 79 A1631
INT/ORG FOR/AID ECO/UNDEV ADMIN

B66
KOH S.J.,STAGES OF INDUSTRIAL DEVELOPMENT IN ASIA. ASIA INDIA KOREA STRATA STRUCT NAT/G INT/TRADE ...CHARTS 19/20 CHINJAP. PAGE 81 A1659
INDUS ECO/UNDEV ECO/DEV LABOR

B66
LAMBERG R.F.,PRAG UND DIE DRITTE WELT. AFR ASIA CZECHOSLVK L/A+17C MARKET TEC/DEV ECO/TAC REV ATTIT 20 TREATY. PAGE 84 A1713
DIPLOM ECO/UNDEV INT/TRADE FOR/AID

B66
LEAGUE OF WOMEN VOTERS OF US,FOREIGN AID AT THE CROSSROADS. USA+45 WOR+45 DELIB/GP PROB/SOLV DIPLOM INT/TRADE RECEIVE BAL/PAY...CHARTS 20 UN. PAGE 86 A1756
FOR/AID GIVE ECO/UNDEV PLAN

B66
LENGYEL E.,AFRICA: PAST, PRESENT, AND FUTURE. FUT SOUTH/AFR COLONIAL RACE/REL SOVEREIGN...GEOG AUD/VIS CHARTS T 20 CONGO/LEOP NEGRO. PAGE 87 A1771
AFR CONSTN ECO/UNDEV

B66
LENT H.B.,THE PEACE CORPS: AMBASSADORS OF GOOD WILL. USA+45 ECO/UNDEV...INT TESTS BIOG AUD/VIS SOC/INTEG 20 PEACE/CORP. PAGE 87 A1776
VOL/ASSN FOR/AID DIPLOM CONSULT

B66
MCKAY V.,AFRICAN DIPLOMACY STUDIES IN THE DETERMINANTS OF FOREIGN POLICY. AFR SOUTH/AFR CULTURE NEUTRAL REGION SOVEREIGN...INT/LAW GOV/COMP ANTHOL 20. PAGE 98 A2013
ECO/UNDEV RACE/REL CIVMIL/REL DIPLOM

B66
MIKESELL R.F.,PUBLIC INTERNATIONAL LENDING FOR DEVELOPMENT. WOR+45 WOR-45 DELIB/GP...TIME/SEQ CHARTS BIBLIOG 20. PAGE 101 A2070
INT/ORG FOR/AID ECO/UNDEV FINAN

B66
MONTGOMERY J.D.,APPROACHES TO DEVELOPMENT: POLITICS, ADMINISTRATION AND CHANGE. USA+45 AGRI FOR/AID ORD/FREE...CONCPT IDEA/COMP METH/COMP ANTHOL. PAGE 103 A2116
ECO/UNDEV ADMIN POLICY ECO/TAC

B66
MOOMAW I.W.,THE CHALLENGE OF HUNGER. USA+45 PLAN ADMIN EATING 20. PAGE 103 A2118
FOR/AID DIPLOM ECO/UNDEV ECO/TAC

B66
NATIONAL COUN APPLIED ECO RES,DEVELOPMENT WITHOUT AID. INDIA FINAN TEC/DEV EFFICIENCY...ANTHOL 20. PAGE 107 A2203
FOR/AID PLAN SOVEREIGN ECO/UNDEV

B66
O'CONNER A.M.,AN ECONOMIC GEOGRAPHY OF EAST AFRICA. AFR TANZANIA UGANDA AGRI WORKER INT/TRADE COLONIAL GOV/REL...CHARTS METH/COMP 20 AFRICA/E. PAGE 111 A2269
ECO/UNDEV EXTR/IND GEOG HABITAT

B66
OHLIN G.,FOREIGN AID POLICIES RECONSIDERED. ECO/DEV ECO/UNDEV VOL/ASSN CONSULT PLAN CONTROL ATTIT ...CONCPT CHARTS BIBLIOG 20. PAGE 111 A2286
FOR/AID DIPLOM GIVE

B66
PAN S.,VIETNAM CRISIS. ASIA FRANCE USA+45 USA-45 VIETNAM CULTURE SOCIETY INT/ORG ECO/TAC AGREE CONTROL WAR MARXISM 20. PAGE 113 A2325
ECO/UNDEV POLICY DIPLOM NAT/COMP

B66
ROBOCK S.H.,INTERNATIONAL DEVELOPMENT 1965. AGRI INDUS VOL/ASSN PLAN TEC/DEV EDU/PROP HEALTH...JURID 20 UN PEACE/CORP. PAGE 122 A2508
FOR/AID INT/ORG GEOG ECO/UNDEV

B66
SCHATTEN F.,COMMUNISM IN AFRICA. AFR GHANA GUINEA MALI CULTURE ECO/UNDEV LABOR SECT ECO/TAC EDU/PROP REV 20. PAGE 128 A2619
COLONIAL NAT/LISM MARXISM DIPLOM

B66
SINGH L.P.,THE POLITICS OF ECONOMIC COOPERATION IN ASIA; A STUDY OF ASIAN INTERNATIONAL ORGANIZATIONS. ASIA INT/ORG ACT/RES PLAN GP/REL...POLICY GP/COMP BIBLIOG 20 UN SEATO. PAGE 133 A2733
ECO/UNDEV ECO/TAC REGION DIPLOM

B66
SPULBER N.,THE STATE AND ECONOMIC DEVELOPMENT IN EASTERN EUROPE. BULGARIA COM CZECHOSLVK HUNGARY POLAND YUGOSLAVIA CULTURE PLAN CAP/ISM INT/TRADE CONTROL...POLICY CHARTS METH/COMP BIBLIOG/A 19/20. PAGE 136 A2793
ECO/DEV ECO/UNDEV NAT/G TOTALISM

B66
THOMPSON J.H.,MODERNIZATION OF THE ARAB WORLD. FUT ISRAEL STRUCT ECO/UNDEV DIPLOM INGP/REL ATTIT ...CENSUS ANTHOL 20 ARABS. PAGE 143 A2926
ADJUST ISLAM PROB/SOLV NAT/COMP

B66
TINKER H.,SOUTH ASIA. UK LAW ECO/UNDEV AGRI ACADEM SECT DIPLOM EDU/PROP REV WEALTH ALL/IDEOS...CHARTS BIBLIOG GANDHI/M NEHRU/J. PAGE 144 A2945
S/ASIA COLONIAL TREND

B66
TYSON G.,NEHRU: THE YEARS OF POWER. INDIA UK STRATA ECO/UNDEV FINAN SECT TASK WAR ORD/FREE MARXISM ...POLICY BIBLIOG 20 NEHRU/J. PAGE 146 A2985
CHIEF PWR DIPLOM NAT/G

B66
US DEPARTMENT OF STATE,RESEARCH ON AFRICA (EXTERNAL RESEARCH LIST NO 5-25). LAW CULTURE ECO/UNDEV POL/PAR DIPLOM EDU/PROP LEAD REGION MARXISM...GEOG LING WORSHIP 20. PAGE 152 A3094
BIBLIOG/A ASIA S/ASIA NAT/G

B66
US DEPARTMENT OF THE ARMY,SOUTH ASIA: A STRATEGIC SURVEY (PAMPHLET NO. 550-3). AFGHANISTN INDIA NEPAL PAKISTAN ECO/UNDEV INT/ORG POL/PAR FORCES FOR/AID INT/TRADE LEAD WAR...POLICY SOC TREND 20. PAGE 152 A3110
BIBLIOG/A S/ASIA DIPLOM NAT/G

B66
US HOUSE COMM APPROPRIATIONS,HEARINGS ON FOREIGN OPERATIONS AND RELATED AGENCIES APPROPRIATIONS. CUBA USA+45 VOL/ASSN DELIB/GP DIPLOM CONFER ORD/FREE 20 CONGRESS MIGRATION INT/AM/DEV PEACE/CORP. PAGE 153 A3120
FOR/AID BUDGET ECO/UNDEV FORCES

B66
US HOUSE COMM FOREIGN AFFAIRS,HEARINGS ON HR 12449 A BILL TO AMEND FURTHER THE FOREIGN ASSISTANCE ACT OF 1961. AFR ASIA L/A+17C USA+45 VIETNAM INT/ORG TEC/DEV INT/TRADE ATTIT ORD/FREE 20 UN NATO CONGRESS AID. PAGE 154 A3132
FOR/AID ECO/TAC ECO/UNDEV DIPLOM

B66
US HOUSE COMM GOVT OPERATIONS,AN INVESTIGATION OF THE US ECONOMIC AND MILITARY ASSISTANCE PROGRAMS IN VIETNAM. USA+45 VIETNAM/S SOCIETY CONSTRUC FINAN FORCES BUDGET INT/TRADE PEACE HEALTH...MGT HOUSE/REP AID. PAGE 154 A3139
FOR/AID ECO/UNDEV WAR INSPECT

B66
US SENATE COMM GOVT OPERATIONS,POPULATION CRISIS. USA+45 ECO/DEV ECO/UNDEV AGRI SECT DELIB/GP PROB/SOLV FOR/AID REPRESENT ATTIT...GEOG CHARTS 20 CONGRESS DEPT/STATE DEPT/HEW BIRTH/CON. PAGE 156 A3178
CENSUS CONTROL LEGIS CONSULT

B66
US SENATE COMM ON FOREIGN REL,HEARINGS ON S 2859 AND S 2861. USA+45 WOR+45 FORCES BUDGET CAP/ISM ADMIN DETER WEAPON TOTALISM...NAT/COMP 20 UN CONGRESS. PAGE 156 A3185
FOR/AID DIPLOM ORD/FREE ECO/UNDEV

B66
US SENATE COMM ON FOREIGN REL,ASIAN DEVELOPMENT BANK ACT. USA+45 LAW DIPLOM...CHARTS 20 BLACK/EUG S/EASTASIA. PAGE 156 A3186
FOR/AID FINAN ECO/UNDEV S/ASIA

B66
VAN DYKE V.,INTERNATIONAL POLITICS. WOR+45 ECO/DEV ECO/UNDEV INT/ORG BAL/PWR AGREE ARMS/CONT NAT/LISM PEACE PWR...INT/LAW 20 TREATY UN. PAGE 158 A3212
DIPLOM NAT/G WAR SOVEREIGN

B66
VYAS R.,DAWNING ON THE CAPITOL: US CONGRESS AND INDIA. INDIA S/ASIA USA+45 ELITES ECO/DEV ECO/UNDEV PLAN FOR/AID...BIBLIOG 20 CONGRESS. PAGE 160 A3256
POLICY LEGIS NAT/G DIPLOM

B66
WELCH C.E.,DREAM OF UNITY; PAN-AFRICANISM AND POLITICAL UNIFICATION IN WEST AFRICA. AFR ECO/UNDEV CONFER COLONIAL LEAD...INT/LAW 20. PAGE 163 A3312
INT/ORG REGION NAT/LISM DIPLOM

B66
WESTIN A.F.,VIEWS OF AMERICA. COM USA+45 USSR SOCIETY ECO/UNDEV POL/PAR ECO/TAC GP/REL STRANGE MARXISM...MARXIST 20. PAGE 163 A3323
CONCPT ATTIT DIPLOM IDEA/COMP

B66
WESTWOOD A.F.,FOREIGN AID IN A FOREIGN POLICY FRAMEWORK. AFR ASIA INDIA IRAN L/A+17C USA+45 USSR ECO/UNDEV AGRI FORCES LEGIS PLAN PROB/SOLV ...DECISION 20 COLD/WAR. PAGE 163 A3324
FOR/AID DIPLOM POLICY ECO/TAC

B66
WHITAKER A.P.,NATIONALISM IN CONTEMPORARY LATIN AMERICA. AGRI NAT/G WEALTH...POLICY SOC CONCPT OBS TREND 20. PAGE 164 A3333
NAT/LISM L/A+17C DIPLOM ECO/UNDEV

B66
WILLIAMS P.,AID IN UGANDA - EDUCATION. UGANDA UK FINAN ACADEM INT/ORG SCHOOL PROB/SOLV ECO/TAC UTIL ...STAT CHARTS 20. PAGE 165 A3352
PLAN EDU/PROP FOR/AID ECO/UNDEV

L66
CHENERY H.B.,"FOREIGN ASSISTANCE AND ECONOMIC DEVELOPMENT" FUT WOR+45 NAT/G DIPLOM GIVE PRODUC ...METH/CNCPT CHARTS 20. PAGE 26 A0526
FOR/AID EFFICIENCY ECO/UNDEV TEC/DEV

S66
ERB GF,"THE UNITED NATIONS CONFERENCE ON TRADE AND
BIBLIOG/A

DEVELOPMENT (UNCTAD): A SELECTED CURRENT READING LIST." FINAN FOR/AID CONFER 20 UN. PAGE 42 A0858 — INT/TRADE ECO/UNDEV INT/ORG

S66
GAMER R.E.,"URGENT SINGAPORE, PATIENT MALAYSIA." MALAYSIA S/ASIA ECO/UNDEV POL/PAR CHIEF TARIFFS TAX CONTROL LEAD REGION PWR 20 SINGAPORE. PAGE 51 A1036 — DIPLOM NAT/G POLICY ECO/TAC

S66
JAVITS J.K.,"POLITICAL ACTION VITAL FOR LATIN AMERICAN INTEGRATION." ECO/UNDEV INT/ORG POL/PAR VOL/ASSN PLAN PROB/SOLV INT/TRADE EFFICIENCY 20 OAS LAFTA. PAGE 73 A1500 — L/A+17C ECO/TAC REGION

S66
MATTHEWS D.G.,"ETHIOPIAN OUTLINE: A BIBLIOGRAPHIC RESEARCH GUIDE." ETHIOPIA LAW STRUCT ECO/UNDEV AGRI LABOR SECT CHIEF DELIB/GP EX/STRUC ADMIN...LING ORG/CHARTS 20. PAGE 96 A1972 — BIBLIOG NAT/G DIPLOM POL/PAR

C66
KULSKI W.W.,"DEGAULLE AND THE WORLD: THE FOREIGN POLICY OF THE FIFTH FRENCH REPUBLIC." FRANCE ECO/UNDEV POL/PAR BAL/PWR DETER NUC/PWR ATTIT PWR ...RECORD BIBLIOG DEGAULLE NATO EEC. PAGE 83 A1694 — POLICY SOVEREIGN PERSON DIPLOM

C66
TARLING N.,"A CONCISE HISTORY OF SOUTHEAST ASIA." BURMA CAMBODIA LAOS S/ASIA THAILAND VIETNAM ECO/UNDEV POL/PAR FORCES ADMIN REV WAR CIVMIL/REL ORD/FREE MARXISM SOCISM 13/20. PAGE 141 A2890 — COLONIAL DOMIN INT/TRADE NAT/LISM

C66
WINT G.,"ASIA: A HANDBOOK." ASIA S/ASIA INDUS LABOR SECT PRESS RACE/REL MARXISM...STAT CHARTS BIBLIOG 20. PAGE 165 A3366 — ECO/UNDEV DIPLOM NAT/G SOCIETY

B67
BARANSON J.,TECHNOLOGY FOR UNDERDEVELOPED AREAS: AN ANNOTATED BIBLIOGRAPHY. FUT WOR+45 CULTURE INDUS INT/ORG CREATE PROB/SOLV INT/TRADE EDU/PROP AUTOMAT ...CONCPT METH. PAGE 11 A0218 — BIBLIOG/A ECO/UNDEV TEC/DEV R+D

B67
BELL W.,THE DEMOCRATIC REVOLUTION IN THE WEST INDIES. WEST/IND WOR+45 DIPLOM RACE/REL NAT/LISM ...INT QU ANTHOL 20. PAGE 13 A0257 — REGION ATTIT ORD/FREE ECO/UNDEV

B67
DILLARD D.,ECONOMIC DEVELOPMENT OF THE NORTH ATLANTIC COMMUNITY. EUR+WWI MOD/EUR USA+45 USA-45 ECO/UNDEV LABOR CAP/ISM WAR BAL/PAY...NAT/COMP 15/20. PAGE 37 A0763 — ECO/DEV INT/TRADE INDUS DIPLOM

B67
HIRSCHMAN A.O.,DEVELOPMENT PROJECTS OBSERVED. INDUS INT/ORG CONSULT EX/STRUC CREATE OP/RES ECO/TAC DEMAND...POLICY MGT METH/COMP 20 WORLD/BANK. PAGE 65 A1339 — ECO/UNDEV R+D FINAN PLAN

B67
JAGAN C.,THE WEST ON TRIAL. GUYANA CONSTN ECO/UNDEV DIPLOM COERCE PWR SOVEREIGN...BIOG 20. PAGE 73 A1490 — SOCISM CREATE PLAN COLONIAL

B67
JOHNSON A.M.,BOSTON CAPITALISTS AND WESTERN RAILROADS: A STUDY IN THE NINETEENTH CENTURY RAILROAD INVESTMENT PROCESS. CREATE BARGAIN INT/TRADE GAMBLE KNOWL 19 BOSTON. PAGE 74 A1519 — FINAN DIST/IND CAP/ISM ECO/UNDEV

B67
JOHNSON D.G.,THE STRUGGLE AGAINST WORLD HUNGER (HEADLINE SERIES, NO. 184) (PAMPHLET). PLAN TEC/DEV FOR/AID...CHARTS 20 FAO MEXIC/AMER. PAGE 74 A1520 — AGRI PROB/SOLV ECO/UNDEV HEALTH

B67
LANDEN R.G.,OMAN SINCE 1856: DISRUPTIVE MODERNIZATION IN A TRADITIONAL ARAB SOCIETY. UK DIST/IND EXTR/IND SECT DIPLOM INT/TRADE...SOC LING CHARTS BIBLIOG 19/20. PAGE 84 A1714 — ISLAM CULTURE ECO/UNDEV NAT/G

B67
MAZRUI A.A.,TOWARDS A PAX AFRICANA. AFR STRUCT ECO/UNDEV NAT/G DIPLOM COLONIAL REGION WAR ATTIT 20. PAGE 97 A1988 — PEACE FORCES PROB/SOLV SOVEREIGN

B67
NYERERE J.K.,FREEDOM AND UNITY/UHURU NA UMOJA: A SELECTION FROM WRITINGS AND SPEECHES, 1952-65. TANZANIA ELITES ECO/UNDEV INT/ORG NAT/G CREATE DIPLOM COLONIAL REGION RACE/REL...ANTHOL 20. PAGE 110 A2265 — SOVEREIGN AFR TREND ORD/FREE

B67
PIKE F.B.,FREEDOM AND REFORM IN LATIN AMERICA. BRAZIL URUGUAY CONSTN CULTURE SECT DIPLOM EDU/PROP PARTIC DRIVE ALL/VALS CATHISM...GEOG ANTHOL BIBLIOG REFORMERS BOLIV. PAGE 116 A2379 — L/A+17C ORD/FREE ECO/UNDEV REV

B67
SACHS M.Y.,THE WORLDMARK ENCYCLOPEDIA OF THE NATIONS (5 VOLS.). ELITES SOCIETY STRATA ECO/DEV ECO/UNDEV AGRI EXTR/IND FINAN LABOR LOC/G NAT/G POL/PAR SECT INT/TRADE SOVEREIGN...SOC 20. PAGE 126 A2585 — WOR+45 INT/ORG BAL/PWR

B67
UNESCO,PRINCIPLES AND PROBLEMS OF NATIONAL SCIENCE POLICIES. WOR+45 ECO/DEV ECO/UNDEV R+D INT/ORG PROB/SOLV CONFER...PHIL/SCI CHARTS 20 UNESCO UN. PAGE 148 A3026 — NAT/COMP POLICY TEC/DEV CREATE

B67
UNIVERSAL REFERENCE SYSTEM,ECONOMIC REGULATION, BUSINESS, AND GOVERNMENT (VOLUME VIII). WOR+45 WOR-45 ECO/DEV ECO/UNDEV FINAN LABOR TEC/DEV ECO/TAC INT/TRADE GOV/REL...POLICY COMPUT/IR. PAGE 149 A3043 — BIBLIOG/A CONTROL NAT/G

B67
US AGENCY INTERNATIONAL DEV,PROPOSED FOREIGN AID PROGRAM FOR 1968: SUMMARY PRESENTATION TO THE CONGRESS. AFR S/ASIA USA+45 AGRI TEC/DEV DIPLOM ECO/TAC BAL/PAY COST HEALTH KNOWL SKILL 20 AID CONGRESS. PAGE 149 A3053 — ECO/UNDEV BUDGET FOR/AID STAT

L67
GALTUNG J.,"ON THE EFFECTS OF INTERNATIONAL ECONOMIC SANCTIONS, WITH EXAMPLES FROM THE CASE OF RHODESIA." NAT/G DIPLOM EDU/PROP ADJUST EFFICIENCY ATTIT MORAL...OBS CHARTS 20. PAGE 51 A1035 — SANCTION ECO/TAC INT/TRADE ECO/UNDEV

L67
SEGAL A.,"THE INTEGRATION OF DEVELOPING COUNTRIES: SOME THOUGHTS ON EAST AFRICA AND CENTRAL AMERICA." AFR L/A+17C INT/ORG NAT/G VOL/ASSN FOR/AID INT/TRADE EQUILIB NAT/LISM PWR 20. PAGE 131 A2680 — ECO/UNDEV DIPLOM REGION

S67
BUTTINGER J.,"VIETNAM* FRAUD OF THE 'OTHER WAR'." VIETNAM/S ELITES STRUCT AGRI NAT/G FOR/AID RENT TREND. PAGE 22 A0456 — PLAN WEALTH REV ECO/UNDEV

S67
CHAND A.,"INDIA AND TANZANIA." INDIA TANZANIA TEC/DEV ECO/TAC FOR/AID COLONIAL PEACE UTIL WEALTH ...GOV/COMP 20. PAGE 25 A0518 — ECO/UNDEV NEUTRAL DIPLOM PLAN

S67
FALKOWSKI M.,"SOCIALIST ECONOMISTS AND THE DEVELOPING COUNTRIES." COM PLAN TEC/DEV ROUTINE DEMAND EFFICIENCY PRODUC WEALTH...MARXIST TREND GEN/METH. PAGE 44 A0893 — DIPLOM SOCISM ECO/UNDEV INDUS

S67
FELDMAN H.,"AID AS IMPERIALISM?" INDIA PAKISTAN UK USA+45 BAL/PWR CAP/ISM DIPLOM ECO/TAC DOMIN BAL/PAY WEALTH...POLICY 20. PAGE 45 A0914 — COLONIAL FOR/AID S/ASIA ECO/UNDEV

S67
FRANK I.,"NEW PERSPECTIVES ON TRADE AND DEVELOPMENT." PROB/SOLV BARGAIN DIPLOM FOR/AID CONFER GP/REL WEALTH 20 UN GATT. PAGE 48 A0980 — ECO/UNDEV INT/ORG INT/TRADE ECO/TAC

S67
FRANKEL M.,"THE WAR IN VIETNAM." VIETNAM ECO/UNDEV DIPLOM CONFER INGP/REL PEACE PWR...POLICY PREDICT 20. PAGE 48 A0982 — WAR COERCE PLAN GUERRILLA

S67
FRENCH D.S.,"DOES THE U.S. EXPLOIT THE DEVELOPING NATIONS?" INT/ORG NAT/G CAP/ISM BAL/PAY WEALTH POLICY. PAGE 49 A0997 — ECO/UNDEV INT/TRADE ECO/TAC COLONIAL

S67
GLOBERSON A.,"SOCIAL GROWTH IN THE DEVELOPING COUNTRIES." CULTURE SOCIETY CONSULT PROB/SOLV SOC. PAGE 53 A1082 — ECO/UNDEV FOR/AID EDU/PROP PLAN

S67
GODUNSKY Y.,"'APOSTLES OF PEACE' IN LATIN AMERICA." L/A+17C USA+45 BAL/PWR DIPLOM FOR/AID DOMIN COLONIAL CIVMIL/REL MARXIST. PAGE 53 A1086 — ECO/UNDEV REV VOL/ASSN EDU/PROP

S67
GRUNDY K.W.,"AFRICA IN THE WORLD ARENA." ECO/UNDEV BAL/PWR FOR/AID NEUTRAL REV NAT/LISM GOV/COMP. PAGE 58 A1183 — AFR DIPLOM INT/ORG COLONIAL

S67
HEATH D.B.,"BOLIVIA UNDER BARRIENTOS." L/A+17C NAT/G CHIEF DIPLOM ECO/TAC...POLICY 20 BOLIV. PAGE 64 A1306 — ECO/UNDEV POL/PAR REV CONSTN

S67
HIBBERT R.A.,"THE MONGOLIAN PEOPLE'S REPUBLIC IN THE 1960'S." INT/ORG PLAN FOR/AID 20. PAGE 64 A1326 — ASIA ECO/UNDEV PROB/SOLV DIPLOM

S67
HULL E.W.S.,"THE POLITICAL OCEAN." FUT UNIV WOR+45 EXTR/IND R+D VOL/ASSN PLAN BAL/PWR ECO/TAC PEACE WEALTH 20 UN. PAGE 69 A1414 — DIPLOM ECO/UNDEV INT/ORG INT/LAW

S67
JAVITS J.K.,"LAST CHANCE FOR A COMMON MARKET." L/A+17C INT/ORG 20 EEC LAFTA. PAGE 73 A1501 — FOR/AID ECO/UNDEV INT/TRADE

ECO/TAC

S67
JOHNSON J.,"THE UNITED STATES AND THE LATIN AMERICAN LEFT WINGS." L/A+17C STRATA POL/PAR INT/TRADE 20. PAGE 74 A1524
ECO/UNDEV WORKER ECO/TAC REGION

S67
KAISER R.G.,"THE TRUMAN DOCTRINE* HOW IT ALL BEGAN." COM EUR+WWI USA+45 R+D INT/ORG BAL/PWR ECO/TAC PEACE TRUMAN/DOC. PAGE 76 A1550
DIPLOM ECO/UNDEV FOR/AID

S67
KIERNAN V.G.,"INDIA AND THE LABOUR PARTY." INDIA UK CAP/ISM GP/REL EFFICIENCY NAT/LISM PWR SOCISM ...SOCIALIST TIME/SEQ 20. PAGE 79 A1616
COLONIAL DIPLOM POL/PAR ECO/UNDEV

S67
KINGSLEY R.E.,"THE US BUSINESS IMAGE IN LATIN AMERICA." L/A+17C USA+45 NAT/G TEC/DEV CAP/ISM FOR/AID DOMIN EDU/PROP...CONCPT LING IDEA/COMP 20. PAGE 79 A1626
ATTIT LOVE DIPLOM ECO/UNDEV

S67
KRISTENSEN T.,"THE SOUTH AS AN INDUSTRIAL POWER." FUT WOR+45 ECO/DEV AGRI INDUS TEC/DEV...CENSUS TREND CHARTS 20. PAGE 82 A1686
DIPLOM ECO/UNDEV PREDICT PRODUC

S67
LOSMAN D.L.,"FOREIGN AID, SOCIALISM AND THE EMERGING COUNTRIES" WOR+45 ADMIN CONTROL PWR 20. PAGE 91 A1864
ECO/UNDEV FOR/AID SOC

S67
MCCORD W.,"ARMIES AND POLITICS; A PROBLEM IN THE THIRD WORLD." AFR ISLAM USA+45 ECO/UNDEV TOTALISM 20. PAGE 98 A2002
FOR/AID POLICY NAT/G FORCES

S67
MONTALVA E.F.,"THE ALLIANCE THAT LOST ITS WAY." L/A+17C USA+45 R+D BAL/PWR INT/TRADE RECEIVE REV PEACE...POLICY 20. PAGE 103 A2111
ECO/UNDEV DIPLOM FOR/AID INT/ORG

S67
MOSELY P.E.,"EASTERN EUROPE IN WORLD POWER POLITICS: WHERE DE-STALINIZATION HAS LED." ECO/UNDEV NAT/LISM 20. PAGE 105 A2153
COM NAT/G DIPLOM MARXISM

S67
NEUCHTERLEIN D.E.,"THAILAND* ANOTHER VIETNAM?" THAILAND ECO/UNDEV DIPLOM ADMIN REGION CENTRAL NAT/LISM...POLICY 20. PAGE 108 A2220
WAR GUERRILLA S/ASIA NAT/G

S67
PAUKER G.J.,"TOWARD A NEW ORDER IN INDONESIA." COM INDONESIA S/ASIA ECO/UNDEV POL/PAR EX/STRUC TOP/EX BAL/PWR ECO/TAC FOR/AID DOMIN NAT/LISM AUTHORIT ORD/FREE PWR 20. PAGE 114 A2342
REV NAT/G DIPLOM CIVMIL/REL

S67
ROSE S.,"ASIAN NATIONALISM* THE SECOND STAGE." ASIA COM ECO/UNDEV NAT/G PROB/SOLV DIPLOM FOR/AID DOMIN NEUTRAL REGION TASK...METH/COMP 20. PAGE 123 A2528
NAT/LISM S/ASIA BAL/PWR COLONIAL

S67
SAPP B.B.,"TRIBAL CULTURES AND COMMUNISM." AFR USA+45 STRATA DIPLOM FOR/AID REGION CENTRAL ATTIT AUTHORIT RIGID/FLEX KNOWL. PAGE 127 A2604
KIN MARXISM ECO/UNDEV STRUCT

S67
SARBADHIKARI P.,"A NOTE ON THE DOMESTIC CRISIS OF NON-ALIGNMENT." ELITES INTELL ECO/UNDEV FOR/AID DOMIN. PAGE 127 A2605
NEUTRAL WEALTH TOTALISM BAL/PWR

S67
STEEL R.,"WHAT CAN THE UN DO?" RHODESIA ECO/UNDEV DIPLOM ECO/TAC SANCTION...INT/LAW UN. PAGE 137 A2810
INT/ORG BAL/PWR PEACE FOR/AID

S67
STEEL R.,"BEYOND THE POWER BLOCS." USA+45 USSR ECO/UNDEV NEUTRAL NUC/PWR NAT/LISM ATTIT...GEOG NATO WARSAW/P COLD/WAR. PAGE 137 A2811
DIPLOM TREND BAL/PWR PLAN

S67
STEGER H.S.,"RESEARCH ON LATIN AMERICA IN THE FEDERAL REPUBLIC OF GERMANY AND WEST BERLIN." FINAN DIPLOM INT/TRADE EDU/PROP...GEOG JURID CHARTS 19/20. PAGE 137 A2813
SOCIETY ECO/UNDEV ACADEM L/A+17C

S67
WALKER R.L.,"THE WEST AND THE 'NEW ASIA'." CHINA/COM ECO/UNDEV DIPLOM...PREDICT 20. PAGE 160 A3266
ASIA INT/TRADE COLONIAL REGION

C67
SPANIER J.W.,"WORLD POLITICS IN AN AGE OF REVOLUTION." COM WOR+45 FORCES COERCE WAR NAT/LISM SOVEREIGN...POLICY BIBLIOG 20. PAGE 135 A2772
DIPLOM TEC/DEV REV ECO/UNDEV

B68
ANTWERP-INST UNIVERSITAIRE,BIBLIOGRAPHIC COMPENDIUM: DEVELOPING COUNTRIES (ANTWERP-INST UNIVERSITAIRE DES TERRITOIRES D'OUTRE-MER). AFR EUR+WWI SOCIETY AGRI FINAN NEIGH VOL/ASSN PROB/SOLV TEC/DEV FOR/AID INT/TRADE 20. PAGE 8 A0166
BIBLIOG ECO/UNDEV DIPLOM PLAN

ECOLOGY....SEE HABITAT

ECOMETRIC....MATHEMATICAL ECONOMICS, ECONOMETRICS

B65
UNIVERSAL REFERENCE SYSTEM,INTERNATIONAL AFFAIRS: VOLUME I IN THE POLITICAL SCIENCE, GOVERNMENT, AND PUBLIC POLICY SERIES....DECISION ECOMETRIC GEOG INT/LAW JURID MGT PHIL/SCI PSY SOC. PAGE 149 A3041
BIBLIOG/A GEN/METH COMPUT/IR DIPLOM

B66
WOOLLEY H.B.,MEASURING TRANSACTIONS BETWEEN WORLD AREAS. WOR+45 FINAN...STAT NET/THEORY CHARTS DICTIONARY 20 GOLD/STAND. PAGE 167 A3395
INT/TRADE BAL/PAY DIPLOM ECOMETRIC

ECONOMIC DETERMINISM....SEE GEN/LAWS

ECONOMIC WARFARE....SEE ECO/TAC

ECONOMIDES C.P. A0821

ECOSOC....UNITED NATIONS ECONOMIC AND SOCIAL COUNCIL

S61
PADELFORD N.J.,"POLITICS AND THE FUTURE OF ECOSOC." AFR S/ASIA ECO/UNDEV INDUS NAT/G DELIB/GP ACT/RES ORD/FREE WEALTH...CONCPT CHARTS UN 20 ECOSOC. PAGE 113 A2310
INT/ORG TEC/DEV

ECSC....EUROPEAN COAL AND STEEL COMMUNITY, SEE ALSO VOL/ASSN

N
FOREIGN AFFAIRS. SPACE WOR+45 WOR-45 CULTURE ECO/UNDEV FINAN NAT/G TEC/DEV INT/TRADE ARMS/CONT NUC/PWR...POLICY 20 UN EURATOM ECSC EEC. PAGE 2 A0034
BIBLIOG DIPLOM INT/ORG INT/LAW

B57
TRIFFIN R.,EUROPE AND THE MONEY MUDDLE. USA+45 INT/ORG NAT/G CONSULT PLAN ECO/TAC EXEC ROUTINE BAL/PAY WEALTH...METH/CNCPT OBS TREND CHARTS STERTYP GEN/METH EEC VAL/FREE ECSC. PAGE 145 A2962
EUR+WWI ECO/DEV REGION

B58
HAAS E.B.,THE UNITING OF EUROPE. EUR+WWI INT/ORG NAT/G POL/PAR TOP/EX ECO/TAC EDU/PROP LEGIT FEDERAL NAT/LISM DRIVE RIGID/FLEX ORD/FREE PWR PLURISM ...POLICY CONCPT INT GEN/LAWS ECSC EEC 20. PAGE 59 A1204
VOL/ASSN ECO/DEV

B58
KINDLEBERGER C.P.,INTERNATIONAL ECONOMICS. WOR+45 WOR-45 ECO/DEV ECO/UNDEV FINAN VOL/ASSN ACT/RES DIPLOM ECO/TAC LEGIT REGION ATTIT DRIVE ORD/FREE WEALTH...POLICY STAT TREND GEN/LAWS EEC ECSC OEEC 20. PAGE 79 A1620
INT/ORG BAL/PWR TARIFFS

B58
SCITOUSKY T.,ECONOMIC THEORY AND WESTERN EUROPEAN INTEGRATION. EUR+WWI INT/ORG ACT/RES INT/TRADE REGION BAL/PAY WEALTH...METH/CNCPT STAT CHARTS GEN/METH ECSC TOT/POP EEC OEEC 20. PAGE 130 A2668
ECO/TAC

B59
DIEBOLD W. JR.,THE SCHUMAN PLAN: A STUDY IN ECONOMIC COOPERATION, 1950-1959. EUR+WWI FRANCE GERMANY USA+45 EXTR/IND CONSULT DELIB/GP PLAN DIPLOM ECO/TAC INT/TRADE ROUTINE ORD/FREE WEALTH ...METH/CNCPT STAT CONT/OBS INT TIME/SEQ ECSC 20. PAGE 37 A0759
INT/ORG REGION

B59
ROBERTSON A.H.,EUROPEAN INSTITUTIONS: COOPERATION, INTEGRATION, UNIFICATION. EUR+WWI FINAN INT/ORG FORCES INT/TRADE TARIFFS 20 EEC EURATOM ECSC NATO TREATY. PAGE 122 A2496
ECO/DEV DIPLOM INDUS ECO/TAC

B60
LISTER L.,EUROPE'S COAL AND STEEL COMMUNITY. FRANCE GERMANY STRUCT ECO/DEV EXTR/IND INDUS MARKET NAT/G DELIB/GP ECO/TAC INT/TRADE EDU/PROP ATTIT RIGID/FLEX ORD/FREE PWR WEALTH...CONCPT STAT TIME/SEQ CHARTS ECSC 20. PAGE 90 A1843
EUR+WWI INT/ORG REGION

B61
PEASLEE A.J.,INTERNATIONAL GOVERNMENTAL ORGANIZATIONS (2 VOLS.). CONSTN VOL/ASSN DIPLOM ...GP/COMP 20 UN OAS EEC EFTA ECSC. PAGE 114 A2345
BIBLIOG INT/ORG INDEX LAW

B62
ALEXANDROWICZ C.H.,WORLD ECONOMIC AGENCIES: LAW AND PRACTICE. WOR+45 DIST/IND FINAN LABOR CONSULT INT/TRADE TARIFFS REPRESENT HEALTH...JURID 20 UN GATT EEC OAS ECSC. PAGE 6 A0115
INT/LAW INT/ORG DIPLOM ADJUD

B62
GYORGY A.,PROBLEMS IN INTERNATIONAL RELATIONS. COM CT/SYS NUC/PWR ALL/IDEOS 20 UN EEC ECSC. PAGE 58 A1199
DIPLOM NEUTRAL BAL/PWR REV

B62
MEADE J.E.,CASE STUDIES IN EUROPEAN ECONOMIC UNION. BELGIUM EUR+WWI LUXEMBOURG NAT/G INT/TRADE REGION ROUTINE WEALTH...METH/CNCPT STAT CHARTS ECSC TOT/POP OEEC EEC 20. PAGE 99 A2028
INT/ORG ECO/TAC

B63
KRAVIS I.B.,DOMESTIC INTERESTS AND INTERNATIONAL OBLIGATIONS: SAFEGUARDS IN INTERNATIONAL TRADE ORGANIZATIONS. EUR+WWI USA+45 WOR+45 FINAN DELIB/GP ATTIT RIGID/FLEX HEALTH...STAT EEC VAL/FREE OEEC ECSC 20. PAGE 82 A1680
INT/ORG ECO/TAC INT/TRADE

C65
SCHEINGOLD S.A.,"THE RULE OF LAW IN EUROPEAN INTEGRATION: THE PATH OF THE SCHUMAN PLAN." EUR+WWI JUDGE ADJUD FEDERAL ATTIT PWR...RECORD INT BIBLIOG EEC ECSC. PAGE 128 A2621
INT/LAW CT/SYS REGION CENTRAL

B66
NIJHOFF M.,ANNUAIRE EUROPEEN (VOL. XII). INT/TRADE REGION PEACE 20 EFTA EEC ECSC EURATOM. PAGE 109 A2241
BIBLIOG INT/ORG EUR+WWI DIPLOM

B66
SPINELLI A.,THE EUROCRATS; CONFLICT AND CRISIS IN THE EUROPEAN COMMUNITY (TRANS. BY C. GROVE HAINES). EUR+WWI MARKET POL/PAR ECO/TAC PARL/PROC EEC OEEC ECSC EURATOM. PAGE 136 A2789
INT/ORG INGP/REL CONSTN ADMIN

L67
CAHIERS P.,"LE RECOURS EN CONSTATATION DE MANQUEMENTS DES ETATS MEMBRES DEVANT LA COUR DES COMMUNAUTES EUROPEENNES." LAW PROB/SOLV DIPLOM ADMIN CT/SYS SANCTION ATTIT...POLICY DECISION JURID ECSC EEC. PAGE 23 A0465
INT/ORG CONSTN ROUTINE ADJUD

S67
OLIVIER G.,"ASPECTS JURIDIQUES DE L'ADOPTION DU TRAITE CECA A LA CRISE CHARBONNIERE (SUITE ET FIN)" LAW DIST/IND PLAN DIPLOM RATION PRICE ADMIN COST DEMAND...POLICY CON/ANAL ECSC TREATY. PAGE 112 A2288
INT/TRADE INT/ORG EXTR/IND CONSTN

S67
WEIL G.L.,"THE MERGER OF THE INSTITUTIONS OF THE EUROPEAN COMMUNITIES" EUR+WWI ECO/DEV INT/TRADE CONSEN PLURISM...DECISION MGT 20 EEC EURATOM ECSC TREATY. PAGE 162 A3300
ECO/TAC INT/ORG CENTRAL INT/LAW

ECUADOR....SEE ALSO L/A+17C

ECUMENIC....ECUMENICAL MOVEMENT OF CHURCHES

EDEN/A....ANTHONY EDEN

B61
ACHESON D.,SKETCHES FROM LIFE. WOR+45 20 CHURCHLL/W EDEN/A ADENAUER/K SALAZAR/A. PAGE 4 A0085
BIOG LEAD CHIEF DIPLOM

EDGELL A.G. A0241

EDSEL....EDSEL (AUTOMOBILE)

EDU/PROP....EDUCATION, PROPAGANDA, PERSUASION

N
AMERICAN DOCUMENTATION INST,DOCUMENTATION ABSTRACTS. WOR+45 NAT/G COMPUTER CREATE TEC/DEV DIPLOM EDU/PROP REGION KNOWL...PHIL/SCI CLASSIF LING. PAGE 7 A0143
BIBLIOG/A AUTOMAT COMPUT/IR R+D

N
SABIN J.,BIBLIOTHECA AMERICANA: A DICTIONARY OF BOOKS RELATING TO AMERICA, FROM ITS DISCOVERY TO THE PRESENT TIME(29 VOLS.). CONSTN CULTURE SOCIETY ECO/DEV LOC/G EDU/PROP NAT/LISM...POLICY GEOG SOC 19. PAGE 126 A2581
BIBLIOG L/A+17C DIPLOM NAT/G

N
BACKGROUND; JOURNAL OF INTERNATIONAL STUDIES ASSOCIATION. INT/ORG FORCES ACT/RES EDU/PROP COERCE NAT/LISM PEACE ATTIT...INT/LAW CONCPT 20. PAGE 1 A0005
BIBLIOG DIPLOM POLICY

N
JOURNAL OF ASIAN STUDIES. CULTURE ECO/DEV SECT DIPLOM EDU/PROP WAR NAT/LISM...PHIL/SCI SOC 20. PAGE 1 A0013
BIBLIOG ASIA S/ASIA NAT/G

N
PEKING REVIEW. CHINA/COM CULTURE AGRI INDUS DIPLOM EDU/PROP GUERRILLA ATTIT MARXISM...BIBLIOG 20. PAGE 1 A0022
MARXIST NAT/G POL/PAR PRESS

N
INDIA: A REFERENCE ANNUAL. INDIA CULTURE COM/IND R+D FORCES PLAN RECEIVE EDU/PROP HEALTH...STAT CHARTS BIBLIOG 20. PAGE 2 A0036
CONSTN LABOR INT/ORG

N
LATIN AMERICA IN PERIODICAL LITERATURE. LAW TEC/DEV DIPLOM RECEIVE EDU/PROP...GEOG HUM MGT 20. PAGE 2 A0037
BIBLIOG/A L/A+17C SOCIETY ECO/UNDEV

N
THE MIDDLE EAST AND NORTH AFRICA. AFR ISLAM CULTURE ECO/UNDEV AGRI NAT/G TEC/DEV FOR/AID INT/TRADE EDU/PROP...CHARTS 20. PAGE 2 A0043
INDEX INDUS FINAN STAT

N
THE WORLD OF LEARNING. INTELL ACT/RES EDU/PROP 20 UNESCO. PAGE 2 A0045
BIBLIOG/A ACADEM R+D INT/ORG

N
HOOVER INSTITUTION,UNITED STATES AND CANADIAN PUBLICATIONS ON AFRICA. CULTURE ECO/UNDEV AGRI TEC/DEV EDU/PROP COLONIAL RACE/REL NAT/LISM ATTIT HEALTH...SOC SOC/WK 20. PAGE 67 A1381
BIBLIOG DIPLOM NAT/G AFR

N
US BUREAU OF THE CENSUS,BIBLIOGRAPHY OF SOCIAL SCIENCE PERIODICALS AND MONOGRAPH SERIES. WOR+45 LAW DIPLOM EDU/PROP HEALTH...PSY SOC LING STAT. PAGE 150 A3058
BIBLIOG/A CULTURE NAT/G SOCIETY

N
US CONSOLATE GENERAL HONG KONG,REVIEW OF THE HONG KONG CHINESE PRESS. ECO/UNDEV LOC/G NAT/G PLAN DIPLOM EDU/PROP LEAD GP/REL MARXISM...POLICY INDEX 20. PAGE 150 A3073
BIBLIOG/A ASIA PRESS ATTIT

N
US CONSULATE GENERAL HONG KONG,CURRENT BACKGROUND. CHINA/COM ECO/UNDEV LOC/G NAT/G PLAN DIPLOM EDU/PROP LEAD REV ATTIT...POLICY INDEX 20. PAGE 151 A3074
BIBLIOG/A MARXIST ASIA PRESS

N
US CONSULATE GENERAL HONG KONG,SURVEY OF CHINA MAINLAND PRESS. CHINA/COM ECO/UNDEV LOC/G NAT/G PLAN DIPLOM EDU/PROP LEAD REV ATTIT...POLICY INDEX 20. PAGE 151 A3075
BIBLIOG/A MARXIST ASIA PRESS

N
US CONSULATE GENERAL HONG KONG,US CONSULATE GENERAL, HONG KONG, PRESS SUMMARIES. CHINA/COM ECO/UNDEV LOC/G NAT/G PLAN DIPLOM EDU/PROP LEAD REV ATTIT...POLICY INDEX 20. PAGE 151 A3076
BIBLIOG/A MARXIST ASIA PRESS

N
US DEPARTMENT OF STATE,BIBLIOGRAPHY (PAMPHLETS). AGRI INDUS INT/ORG FOR/AID EDU/PROP WAR MARXISM ...SOC GOV/COMP METH/COMP 20. PAGE 151 A3079
BIBLIOG DIPLOM ECO/DEV NAT/G

N
US LIBRARY OF CONGRESS,ACCESSIONS LIST - INDIA. INDIA CULTURE AGRI LOC/G POL/PAR PLAN PROB/SOLV TEC/DEV DIPLOM EDU/PROP LEAD GP/REL ATTIT 20. PAGE 154 A3142
BIBLIOG S/ASIA ECO/UNDEV NAT/G

N
US LIBRARY OF CONGRESS,ACCESSIONS LIST -- ISRAEL. ISRAEL CULTURE ECO/UNDEV POL/PAR PLAN PROB/SOLV TEC/DEV DIPLOM EDU/PROP LEAD WAR ATTIT 20 JEWS. PAGE 154 A3143
BIBLIOG ISLAM NAT/G GP/REL

N
US SUPERINTENDENT OF DOCUMENTS,FOREIGN RELATIONS OF THE UNITED STATES; PUBLICATIONS RELATING TO FOREIGN COUNTRIES (PRICE LIST 65). UAR USA+45 VIETNAM ECO/UNDEV VOL/ASSN FOR/AID EDU/PROP ARMS/CONT HEALTH MARXISM...POLICY INT/LAW UN NATO. PAGE 157 A3201
BIBLIOG/A DIPLOM INT/ORG NAT/G

N
US SUPERINTENDENT OF DOCUMENTS,MONTHLY CATALOG OF UNITED STATES GOVERNMENT PUBLICATIONS. USA+45 USA-45 AGRI LABOR FORCES INT/TRADE TARIFFS TAX EDU/PROP CT/SYS ARMS/CONT RACE/REL 19/20 CONGRESS PRESIDENT. PAGE 157 A3203
BIBLIOG NAT/G VOL/ASSN POLICY

B02
SEELEY J.R.,THE EXPANSION OF ENGLAND. MOD/EUR S/ASIA UK CULTURE NAT/G FORCES PLAN DOMIN EDU/PROP COLONIAL ROUTINE ATTIT ALL/VALS SOVEREIGN...CONCPT HIST/WRIT PARLIAMENT 18 CMN/WLTH. PAGE 131 A2679
INT/ORG ACT/RES CAP/ISM INDIA

B04
CRANDALL S.B.,TREATIES: THEIR MAKING AND ENFORCEMENT. MOD/EUR USA-45 CONSTN INT/ORG NAT/G LEGIS EDU/PROP LEGIT EXEC PEACE KNOWL MORAL...JURID CONGRESS 19/20 TREATY. PAGE 32 A0655
LAW

B15
FARIES J.C.,THE RISE OF INTERNATIONALISM. ASIA MOD/EUR NAT/G VOL/ASSN DELIB/GP BAL/PWR EDU/PROP ARMS/CONT RIGID/FLEX TREND. PAGE 44 A0899
INT/ORG DIPLOM PEACE

B15
HOBSON J.A.,TOWARDS INTERNATIONAL GOVERNMENT. MOD/EUR STRUCT ECO/TAC EDU/PROP ADJUD ALL/VALS ...SOCIALIST CONCPT GEN/LAWS TOT/POP 20. PAGE 65 A1347
FUT INT/ORG CENTRAL

B16
ROOT E.,THE MILITARY AND COLONIAL POLICY OF THE US. L/A+17C USA-45 LAW SOCIETY STRATA STRUCT INT/ORG NAT/G SCHOOL FORCES EDU/PROP ALL/VALS...OBS VAL/FREE 19/20. PAGE 123 A2522
ACT/RES PLAN DIPLOM WAR

B17
VEBLEN T.B.,AN INQUIRY INTO THE NATURE OF PEACE AND THE TERMS OF ITS PERPETUATION. UNIV STRATA FINAN EDU/PROP PRICE COST DISCRIM NAT/LISM MORAL ORD/FREE PACIFIST 20 WORLDUNITY. PAGE 158 A3224
PEACE DIPLOM WAR NAT/G

S17
ROOT E.,"THE EFFECT OF DEMOCRACY ON INTERNATIONAL LAW." USA-45 WOR-45 INTELL SOCIETY INT/ORG NAT/G CONSULT ACT/RES CREATE PLAN EDU/PROP PEACE SKILL ...CONCPT METH/CNCPT OBS 20. PAGE 123 A2523
LEGIS JURID INT/LAW

N19
GRANT N.,COMMUNIST PSYCHOLOGICAL OFFENSIVE: DISTORTION IN THE TRANSLATION OF OFFICIAL DOCUMENTS (PAMPHLET). USSR POL/PAR CHIEF FOR/AID PRESS WRITING COLONIAL LEAD WAR PEACE 20 KHRUSH/N. PAGE 55 A1129
MARXISM DIPLOM EDU/PROP

N19
HAJDA J.,THE COLD WAR VIEWED AS A SOCIOLOGICAL PROBLEM (PAMPHLET). COM CZECHOSLVK EUR+WWI SOCIETY PLAN EDU/PROP CONTROL TASK ATTIT MARXISM...POLICY 20 COLD/WAR MIGRATION. PAGE 59 A1220
DIPLOM LEAD PWR NAT/G

N19
MARCUS W.,US PRIVATE INVESTMENT AND ECONOMIC AID IN UNDERDEVELOPED COUNTRIES (PAMPHLET). USA+45 LG/CO NAT/G CAP/ISM EDU/PROP 20. PAGE 94 A1937
FOR/AID ECO/UNDEV FINAN PLAN

N19
MEZERIK A.G.,U-2 AND OPEN SKIES (PAMPHLET). USA+45 USSR INT/ORG CHIEF FORCES PLAN EDU/PROP CONTROL SANCTION ARMS/CONT 20 UN EISNHWR/DD. PAGE 100 A2060
DIPLOM RISK DEBATE

N19
NATIONAL ACADEMY OF SCIENCES,THE GROWTH OF WORLD POPULATION: ANALYSIS OF THE PROBLEMS AND RECOMMENDATIONS FOR RESEARCH AND TRAINING (PAMPHLET). WOR+45 CULTURE ECO/UNDEV EDU/PROP MARRIAGE AGE HEALTH...ANTHOL 20 BIRTH/CON. PAGE 107 A2199
CENSUS PLAN FAM INT/ORG

N19
PROVISIONS SECTION OAU,ORGANIZATION OF AFRICAN UNITY: BASIC DOCUMENTS AND RESOLUTIONS (PAMPHLET). AFR CULTURE ECO/UNDEV DIPLOM ECO/TAC EDU/PROP COLONIAL ARMS/CONT NUC/PWR RACE/REL DISCRIM NAT/LISM 20 UN OAU. PAGE 118 A2415
CONSTN EX/STRUC SOVEREIGN INT/ORG

N19
UNITED ARAB REPUBLIC,THE PROBLEM OF THE PALESTINIAN REFUGEES (PAMPHLET). ISRAEL UAR LAW PROB/SOLV EDU/PROP CONFER ADJUD CONTROL NAT/LISM HEALTH 20 JEWS UN MIGRATION. PAGE 148 A3029
STRANGE GP/REL INGP/REL DIPLOM

B20
BURNS C.D.,INTERNATIONAL POLITICS. WOR-45 CULTURE SOCIETY ECO/UNDEV NAT/G VOL/ASSN DELIB/GP ACT/RES CREATE DOMIN EDU/PROP LEGIT ATTIT DRIVE RIGID/FLEX ALL/VALS...PLURIST PSY CONCPT TREND. PAGE 22 A0442
INT/ORG PEACE SOVEREIGN

B20
DICKINSON E.,THE EQUALITY OF STATES IN INTERNATIONAL LAW. WOR-45 INT/ORG NAT/G DIPLOM EDU/PROP LEGIT PEACE ATTIT ALL/VALS...JURID TIME/SEQ LEAGUE/NAT. PAGE 37 A0757
LAW CONCPT SOVEREIGN

B20
HALDANE R.B.,BEFORE THE WAR. MOD/EUR SOCIETY INT/ORG NAT/G DELIB/GP PLAN DOMIN EDU/PROP LEGIT ADMIN COERCE ATTIT DRIVE MORAL ORD/FREE PWR...SOC CONCPT SELF/OBS RECORD BIOG TIME/SEQ. PAGE 60 A1223
POLICY DIPLOM UK

B21
STUART G.H.,FRENCH FOREIGN POLICY. CONSTN INT/ORG NAT/G POL/PAR EX/STRUC FORCES PLAN ECO/TAC DOMIN EDU/PROP ADJUD COERCE ATTIT DRIVE RIGID/FLEX ALL/VALS...POLICY OBS RECORD BIOG TIME/SEQ TREND. PAGE 139 A2852
MOD/EUR DIPLOM FRANCE

B22
FICHTE J.G.,ADDRESSES TO THE GERMAN NATION. GERMANY PRUSSIA ELITES NAT/G SECT CREATE INT/TRADE HEREDITY ...ART/METH LING 19 FRANK/PARL. PAGE 45 A0923
NAT/LISM CULTURE EDU/PROP REGION

B22
POTTER P.B.,AN INTRODUCTION TO THE STUDY OF INTERNATIONAL ORGANIZATION. WOR-45 ACT/RES CREATE EDU/PROP ROUTINE PERCEPT KNOWL...CONT/OBS RECORD GEN/LAWS TOT/POP VAL/FREE 20. PAGE 117 A2398
INT/ORG CONCPT

B22
REINSCH P.,SECRET DIPLOMACY: HOW FAR CAN IT BE ELIMINATED. FUT WOR-45 CULTURE INT/ORG NAT/G EDU/PROP WAR...MYTH HIST/WRIT CON/ANAL 20. PAGE 120 A2460
RIGID/FLEX PWR DIPLOM

B23
KADEN E.H.,DER POLITISCHE CHARAKTER DER FRANZOSISCHEN KULTURPROPAGANDA AM RHEIN. FRANCE MOD/EUR DOMIN PRESS...GEOG METH/COMP 20. PAGE 75 A1544
EDU/PROP ATTIT DIPLOM NAT/G

B24
POOLE D.C.,THE CONDUCT OF FOREIGN RELATIONS UNDER MODERN DEMOCRATIC CONDITIONS. EUR+WWI USA-45 INT/ORG PLAN LEGIT ADMIN KNOWL PWR...MAJORIT OBS/ENVIR HIST/WRIT GEN/LAWS 20. PAGE 117 A2395
NAT/G EDU/PROP DIPLOM

B25
GODET M.,INDEX BIBLIOGRAPHICUS: INTERNATIONAL CATALOGUE OF SOURCES OF CURRENT BIBLIOGRAPHIC INFORMATION. EUR+WWI MOD/EUR SOCIETY SECT TAX ...JURID PHIL/SCI SOC MATH. PAGE 53 A1085
BIBLIOG/A DIPLOM EDU/PROP LAW

B28
HALL W.P.,EMPIRE TO COMMONWEALTH. FUT WOR-45 CONSTN ECO/DEV ECO/UNDEV INT/ORG PROVS PLAN DIPLOM EDU/PROP ADMIN COLONIAL PEACE PERSON ALL/VALS ...POLICY GEOG SOC OBS RECORD TREND CMN/WLTH PARLIAMENT 19/20. PAGE 60 A1229
VOL/ASSN NAT/G UK

B28
HUBER G.,DIE FRANZOSISCHE PROPAGANDA IM WELTKRIEG GEGEN DEUTSCHLAND 1914 BIS 1918. FRANCE GERMANY MOD/EUR DIPLOM WAR...EXHIBIT 20 WWI. PAGE 68 A1403
EDU/PROP ATTIT DOMIN PRESS

B28
PLAYNE C.E.,THE PRE-WAR MIND IN BRITAIN. GERMANY MOD/EUR UK STRATA SECT DIPLOM EDU/PROP CROWD SUFF ...POLICY ANARCH PSY SOC IDEA/COMP 20 WWI. PAGE 116 A2388
PRESS WAR DOMIN ATTIT

B28
STUART G.H.,LATIN AMERICA AND THE UNITED STATES. USA-45 ECO/UNDEV INT/ORG NAT/G POL/PAR PLAN DOMIN EDU/PROP COLONIAL REGION COERCE ATTIT ALL/VALS ...POLICY GEOG TREND 19/20. PAGE 139 A2853
L/A+17C DIPLOM

B29
CONWELL-EVANS T.P.,THE LEAGUE COUNCIL IN ACTION. EUR+WWI TURKEY UK USSR WOR-45 INT/ORG FORCES JUDGE ECO/TAC EDU/PROP LEGIT ROUTINE ARMS/CONT COERCE ATTIT PWR...MAJORIT GEOG JURID CONCPT LEAGUE/NAT TOT/POP VAL/FREE TUNIS 20. PAGE 30 A0605
DELIB/GP INT/LAW

B31
BEALES A.C.,THE HISTORY OF PEACE. WOR-45 VOL/ASSN DELIB/GP CREATE PLAN EDU/PROP ATTIT MORAL ...TIME/SEQ VAL/FREE 19/20. PAGE 12 A0239
INT/ORG ARMS/CONT PEACE

B31
GREAVES H.R.G.,THE LEAGUE COMMITTEES AND WORLD ORDER. WOR-45 DELIB/GP EX/STRUC EDU/PROP ALL/VALS LEAGUE/NAT VAL/FREE 20. PAGE 55 A1136
INT/ORG DIPLOM ROUTINE

B31
HILL N.,INTERNATIONAL ADMINISTRATION. WOR-45 DELIB/GP DIPLOM EDU/PROP ALL/VALS...MGT TIME/SEQ LEAGUE/NAT TOT/POP VAL/FREE 20. PAGE 65 A1331
INT/ORG ADMIN

B31
HODGES C.,THE BACKGROUND OF INTERNATIONAL RELATIONS. WOR-45 SOCIETY ECO/DEV ECO/UNDEV INT/ORG DIPLOM DOMIN EDU/PROP LEGIT WAR ATTIT DRIVE PERSON ALL/VALS...CONCPT METH/CNCPT TIME/SEQ CHARTS WORK LEAGUE/NAT 19/20. PAGE 66 A1350
NAT/G BAL/PWR

B31
STOWELL E.C.,INTERNATIONAL LAW. FUT UNIV WOR-45 SOCIETY CONSULT EX/STRUC FORCES ACT/RES PLAN DIPLOM EDU/PROP LEGIT DISPL PWR SKILL...POLICY CONCPT OBS TREND TOT/POP 20. PAGE 139 A2839
INT/ORG ROUTINE INT/LAW

B32
EAGLETON C.,INTERNATIONAL GOVERNMENT. BRAZIL FRANCE GERMANY ITALY UK USSR WOR-45 DELIB/GP TOP/EX PLAN ECO/TAC EDU/PROP LEGIT ADJUD REGION ARMS/CONT COERCE ATTIT PWR...GEOG MGT VAL/FREE LEAGUE/NAT 20. PAGE 40 A0816
INT/ORG JURID DIPLOM INT/LAW

B32
FLEMMING D.,THE UNITED STATES AND THE LEAGUE OF NATIONS, 1918-1920. FUT USA-45 NAT/G LEGIS TOP/EX DEBATE CHOOSE PEACE ATTIT SOVEREIGN...TIME/SEQ CON/ANAL CONGRESS LEAGUE/NAT 20 TREATY. PAGE 46 A0950
INT/ORG EDU/PROP

B32
HANSEN A.H.,ECONOMIC STABILIZATION IN AN UNBALANCED WORLD. COM EUR+WWI USA-45 WOR-45 AGRI FINAN INDUS MARKET INT/ORG LABOR VOL/ASSN EDU/PROP ATTIT HEALTH KNOWL WEALTH...HIST/WRIT TREND VAL/FREE 20. PAGE 61 A1253
NAT/G ECO/DEV CAP/ISM SOCISM

B32
MORLEY F.,THE SOCIETY OF NATIONS. EUR+WWI UNIV WOR-45 LAW CONSTN ACT/RES PLAN EDU/PROP LEGIT ROUTINE...POLICY TIME/SEQ LEAGUE/NAT TOT/POP 20. PAGE 104 A2143
INT/ORG CONCPT

B33
DAHLIN E.,FRENCH AND GERMAN PUBLIC OPINION ON DECLARED WAR AIMS 1914-1918. BELGIUM FRANCE GERMANY NAT/G POL/PAR DIPLOM COERCE REV WAR PEACE 20 WWI WILSON/W. PAGE 33 A0674
ATTIT EDU/PROP DOMIN NAT/COMP

B33
LANGER W.L.,FOREIGN AFFAIRS BIBLIOGRAPHY. WOR-45 INT/ORG CONSULT EDU/PROP ROUTINE NAT/LISM ATTIT SOVEREIGN...STAT RECORD GEN/METH LEAGUE/NAT TOT/POP. PAGE 84 A1725
KNOWL

B33
PUBLIC OPINION AND WORLD POLITICS. UNIV LAW CULTURE NAT/G PRESS REV GP/REL...MAJORIT METH/COMP ANTHOL 20. PAGE 167 A3400
DIPLOM EDU/PROP ATTIT MAJORITY

B34
EINSTEIN A.,THE WORLD AS I SEE IT. WOR-45 INTELL R+D INT/ORG NAT/G SECT VOL/ASSN FORCES CREATE EDU/PROP LEGIT ARMS/CONT WAR WEAPON NAT/LISM ALL/VALS...POLICY CONCPT 20. PAGE 41 A0828
SOCIETY PHIL/SCI DIPLOM PACIFISM

B35
HUDSON M.,BY PACIFIC MEANS. WOR-45 EDU/PROP ORD/FREE...CONCPT TIME/SEQ GEN/LAWS LEAGUE/NAT TOT/POP 20 TREATY. PAGE 68 A1407
INT/ORG CT/SYS PEACE

B36
HUGENDUBEL P.,DIE KRIEGSMACHE DER FRANZOSISCHEN PRESSE. FRANCE GERMANY MOD/EUR COM/IND NAT/G DIPLOM DOMIN PWR 20. PAGE 69 A1412
PRESS EDU/PROP WAR ATTIT

B36
METZ I.,DIE DEUTSCHF FLOTTE IN DER ENGLISCHEN PRESSE, DER NAVY SCARE VOM WINTER 1904/05. GERMANY UK FORCES DIPLOM WAR 20 NAVY. PAGE 100 A2047
EDU/PROP ATTIT DOMIN PRESS

B36
ROBINSON H.,DEVELOPMENT OF THE BRITISH EMPIRE. WOR-45 CULTURE SOCIETY STRUCT ECO/DEV ECO/UNDEV INT/ORG VOL/ASSN FORCES CREATE PLAN DOMIN EDU/PROP ADMIN COLONIAL PWR WEALTH...POLICY GEOG CHARTS CMN/WLTH 16/20. PAGE 122 A2503
NAT/G HIST/WRIT UK

B36
SHOTWELL J.,ON THE RIM OF THE ABYSS. EUR+WWI USA-45 STRUCT INT/ORG ACT/RES PLAN EDU/PROP EXEC ATTIT ALL/VALS...TIME/SEQ LEAGUE/NAT TOT/POP 20. PAGE 132 A2706
NAT/G BAL/PWR

B37
ROYAL INST. INT. AFF.,THE COLONIAL PROBLEM. WOR-45 LAW ECO/DEV ECO/UNDEV NAT/G PLAN ECO/TAC EDU/PROP ADMIN ATTIT ALL/VALS...CONCPT 20. PAGE 125 A2556
INT/ORG ACT/RES SOVEREIGN COLONIAL

B37
UNION OF SOUTH AFRICA,REPORT CONCERNING ADMINISTRATION OF SOUTH WEST AFRICA (6 VOLS.). SOUTH/AFR INDUS PUB/INST FORCES LEGIS BUDGET DIPLOM EDU/PROP ADJUD CT/SYS...GEOG CHARTS 20 AFRICA/SW LEAGUE/NAT. PAGE 148 A3028
NAT/G ADMIN COLONIAL CONSTN

B38
DE MADARIAGA S.,THE WORLD'S DESIGN. WOR-45 SOCIETY STRUCT EDU/PROP PEACE ATTIT PERSON ALL/VALS ...SOCIALIST CONCPT TIME/SEQ TREND GEN/LAWS LEAGUE/NAT. PAGE 35 A0706
FUT INT/ORG DIPLOM

B38
FLEMMING D.,THE UNITED STATES AND WORLD ORGANIZATION, 1920-1933. ASIA FUT WOR-45 NAT/G TOP/EX DIPLOM ECO/TAC EDU/PROP LEGIT COERCE WAR ...TIME/SEQ LEAGUE/NAT 20 CHINJAP. PAGE 47 A0951
USA-45 INT/ORG PEACE

B38
HOBSON J.A.,IMPERIALISM. MOD/EUR UK WOR-45 CULTURE ECO/UNDEV NAT/G VOL/ASSN PLAN EDU/PROP LEGIT REGION COERCE ATTIT PWR...POLICY PLURIST TIME/SEQ GEN/LAWS 19/20. PAGE 66 A1348
DOMIN ECO/TAC BAL/PWR COLONIAL

B38
PETTEE G.S.,THE PROCESS OF REVOLUTION. COM FRANCE ITALY MOD/EUR RUSSIA SPAIN WOR-45 ELITES INTELL SOCIETY STRATA STRUCT INT/ORG NAT/G POL/PAR ACT/RES PLAN EDU/PROP LEGIT EXEC...SOC MYTH TIME/SEQ TOT/POP 18/20. PAGE 115 A2370
COERCE CONCPT REV

B38
RAPPARD W.E.,THE CRISIS OF DEMOCRACY. EUR+WWI UNIV WOR-45 CULTURE SOCIETY ECO/DEV INT/ORG POL/PAR ACT/RES EDU/PROP EXEC CHOOSE ATTIT ALL/VALS...SOC OBS HIST/WRIT TIME/SEQ LEAGUE/NAT NAZI TOT/POP 20. PAGE 119 A2449
NAT/G CONCPT

B38
WARE E.E.,THE STUDY OF INTERNATIONAL RELATIONS IN THE UNITED STATES. USA+45 USA-45 WOR-45 INTELL SERV/IND INT/ORG NAT/G PROF/ORG SECT CONSULT INT/TRADE EDU/PROP ARMS/CONT...CONCPT 20. PAGE 161 A3283
KNOWL DIPLOM

B39
BROWN J.F.,CONTEMPORARY WORLD POLITICS. WOR-45 NAT/G PLAN BAL/PWR EDU/PROP LEGIT REGION NAT/LISM ORD/FREE PWR SOVEREIGN...POLICY CONCPT HIST/WRIT TIME/SEQ GEN/LAWS LEAGUE/NAT. PAGE 20 A0403
INT/ORG DIPLOM PEACE

B39
CARR E.H.,PROPAGANDA IN INTERNATIONAL POLITICS (PAMPHLET). EUR+WWI GERMANY MOD/EUR NAT/G AGREE WAR MORAL...POLICY 20 TREATY. PAGE 24 A0497
DIPLOM EDU/PROP CONTROL ATTIT

B39
DULLES J.,WAR, PEACE AND CHANGE. FRANCE ITALY UK USA-45 WOR-45 LAW INT/ORG NAT/G SECT VOL/ASSN FORCES TOP/EX DOMIN ARMS/CONT COERCE ATTIT PERSON RIGID/FLEX MORAL PWR...JURID STERTYP TOT/POP LEAGUE/NAT 20. PAGE 39 A0796
EDU/PROP TOTALISM WAR

B39
SPEIER H.,WAR IN OUR TIME. WOR-45 AGRI FINAN FORCES TEC/DEV BAL/PWR EDU/PROP WEAPON PEACE PWR...ANTHOL 20. PAGE 136 A2779
FASCISM WAR DIPLOM NAT/G

B40
FULLER G.H.,A LIST OF BIBLIOGRAPHIES ON PROPAGANDA (PAMPHLET). MOD/EUR USA-45 CONSULT ACT/RES PRESS FEEDBACK TASK WAR ATTIT PWR...CON/ANAL METH/COMP 20. PAGE 50 A1020
BIBLIOG/A EDU/PROP DOMIN DIPLOM

B40
MIDDLEBUSH F.,ELEMENTS OF INTERNATIONAL RELATIONS. WOR-45 PROVS CONSULT EDU/PROP LEGIT WAR NAT/LISM ATTIT KNOWL MORAL ORD/FREE PWR...JURID LEAGUE/NAT TOT/POP VAL/FREE. PAGE 101 A2067
NAT/G INT/ORG PEACE DIPLOM

B40
MILLER E.,THE NEUROSES OF WAR. UNIV INTELL SOCIETY INT/ORG NAT/G EDU/PROP DISPL DRIVE PERCEPT PERSON RIGID/FLEX...SOC TIME/SEQ 20. PAGE 101 A2075
HEALTH PSY WAR

B40
NAFZIGER R.O.,INTERNATIONAL NEWS AND THE PRESS: COMMUNICATIONS, ORGANIZATION OF NEWS-GATHERING INTERNATIONAL AFFAIRS AND FOREIGN... COM/IND FORCES WAR ATTIT...POLICY 20. PAGE 107 A2191
BIBLIOG/A PRESS DIPLOM EDU/PROP

B40
WANDERSCHECK H.,FRANKREICHS PROPAGANDA GEGEN DEUTSCHLAND. FRANCE GERMANY MOD/EUR UK NAT/G DIPLOM WAR 20 JEWS. PAGE 161 A3273
EDU/PROP ATTIT DOMIN PRESS

S40
FLORIN J.,"BOLSHEVIST AND NATIONAL SOCIALIST DOCTRINES OF INTERNATIONAL LAW." EUR+WWI GERMANY USSR R+D INT/ORG NAT/G DIPLOM DOMIN EDU/PROP SOCISM ...CONCPT TIME/SEQ 20. PAGE 47 A0955
LAW ATTIT TOTALISM INT/LAW

C40
FAHS C.B.,"GOVERNMENT IN JAPAN." FINAN FORCES LEGIS TOP/EX BUDGET INT/TRADE EDU/PROP SOVEREIGN ...CON/ANAL BIBLIOG/A 20 CHINJAP. PAGE 43 A0884
ASIA DIPLOM NAT/G ADMIN

B41
BAUMANN G.,GRUNDLAGEN UND PRAXIS DER INTERNATIONALEN PROPAGANDA. FRANCE GERMANY UK CULTURE COM/IND PRESS PWR...PSY METH/COMP 20. PAGE 12 A0236
EDU/PROP DOMIN ATTIT DIPLOM

B41
GRISMER R.,A NEW BIBLIOGRAPHY OF THE LITERATURES OF SPAIN AND SPANISH AMERICA. CHRIST-17C MOD/EUR PRE/AMER SPAIN CULTURE DIPLOM EDU/PROP...ART/METH GEOG HUM PHIL/SCI 20. PAGE 57 A1165
BIBLIOG LAW NAT/G ECO/UNDEV

B41
KEESING F.M.,THE SOUTH SEAS IN THE MODERN WORLD. INDONESIA STRUCT FAM SECT EDU/PROP LEAD INCOME WEALTH...HEAL SOC 20. PAGE 77 A1577
CULTURE ECO/UNDEV GOV/COMP DIPLOM

L41
COMM. STUDY ORGAN. PEACE,"ORGANIZATION OF PEACE." USA-45 WOR-45 STRATA NAT/G ACT/RES DIPLOM ECO/TAC EDU/PROP ADJUD ATTIT ORD/FREE PWR...SOC CONCPT ANTHOL LEAGUE/NAT 20. PAGE 28 A0575
INT/ORG PLAN PEACE

S41
LASSWELL H.D.,"THE GARRISON STATE" (BMR)" FUT WOR+45 ELITES INTELL FORCES ECO/TAC DOMIN EDU/PROP COERCE INGP/REL 20. PAGE 85 A1739
NAT/G DIPLOM PWR CIVMIL/REL

S41
WRIGHT Q.,"FUNDAMENTAL PROBLEMS OF INTERNATIONAL ORGANIZATION." UNIV WOR-45 STRUCT FORCES ACT/RES CREATE DOMIN EDU/PROP LEGIT REGION NAT/LISM ORD/FREE PWR RESPECT SOVEREIGN...JURID SOC CONCPT METH/CNCPT TIME/SEQ 20. PAGE 167 A3405
INT/ORG ATTIT PEACE

B42
BORNSTEIN J.,ACTION AGAINST THE ENEMY'S MIND. EUR+WWI GERMANY USA-45 DIPLOM DOMIN PRESS LEAD GP/REL DISCRIM PERCEPT FASCISM MARXISM 20 JEWS NAZI ANTI/SEMIT. PAGE 17 A0343
EDU/PROP PSY WAR CONTROL

B42
HAMBRO C.J.,HOW TO WIN THE PEACE. ECO/TAC EDU/PROP ADJUD PERSON ALL/VALS...SOCIALIST TREND GEN/LAWS 20. PAGE 61 A1246
FUT INT/ORG PEACE

S42
TURNER F.J.,"AMERICAN SECTIONALISM AND WORLD ORGANIZATION." EUR+WWI UNIV USA-45 WOR-45 INTELL ECO/DEV TOP/EX ACT/RES PLAN EDU/PROP LEGIT ALL/VALS ...CONCPT NEW/IDEA OBS TREND LEAGUE/NAT TOT/POP 20. PAGE 146 A2981
INT/ORG DRIVE BAL/PWR

B43
HEMLEBEN S.J.,PLANS FOR WORLD PEACE THROUGH SIX CENTURIES. WOR-45 EDU/PROP DRIVE PWR...CONCPT TIME/SEQ GEN/LAWS TOT/POP LEAGUE/NAT 14/20. PAGE 64 A1312
INT/ORG PEACE

B43
LIPPMANN W.,US FOREIGN POLICY: SHIELD OF THE REPUBLIC. USA-45 WOR-45 CULTURE INT/ORG POL/PAR CREATE BAL/PWR DOMIN EDU/PROP WAR ORD/FREE PWR ...PLURIST CONCPT TREND CON/ANAL 20. PAGE 89 A1827
NAT/G DIPLOM PEACE

B43
US LIBRARY OF CONGRESS,POLITICAL DEVELOPMENTS AND THE WAR: APRIL-DECEMBER 1942 (SUPPLEMENT 1). WOR-45 CONSTN NAT/G POL/PAR CREATE RECEIVE EDU/PROP ATTIT 20. PAGE 154 A3148
BIBLIOG/A WAR DIPLOM

B44
BARTLETT R.J.,THE LEAGUE TO ENFORCE PEACE. FUT USA-45 NAT/G POL/PAR CREATE EDU/PROP ADMIN RIGID/FLEX PWR...CONCPT TREND GEN/METH LEAGUE/NAT 20. PAGE 11 A0231
INT/ORG ORD/FREE DIPLOM

B44
COMM. STUDY ORGAN. PEACE,UNITED NATIONS GUARDS AND TECHNICAL FIELD SERVICES. WOR+45 DELIB/GP EDU/PROP DRIVE PWR SKILL...CONCPT GEN/LAWS UN TOT/POP 20. PAGE 28 A0576
INT/ORG FORCES PEACE

B44
DAVIS H.E.,PIONEERS IN WORLD ORDER. WOR-45 CONSTN ECO/TAC DOMIN EDU/PROP LEGIT ADJUD ADMIN ARMS/CONT CHOOSE KNOWL ORD/FREE...POLICY JURID SOC STAT OBS CENSUS TIME/SEQ ANTHOL LEAGUE/NAT 20. PAGE 34 A0691
INT/ORG ROUTINE

B44
HUDSON M.,INTERNATIONAL TRIBUNALS PAST AND FUTURE. FUT WOR-45 LAW EDU/PROP ADJUD ORD/FREE...CONCPT TIME/SEQ TREND GEN/LAWS TOT/POP VAL/FREE 18/20. PAGE 69 A1408
INT/ORG STRUCT INT/LAW

B44
MACIVER R.M.,TOWARDS AN ABIDING PEACE. USA-45 ECO/TAC EDU/PROP DRIVE ORD/FREE PWR WEALTH...CONCPT TIME/SEQ GEN/METH TOT/POP 20. PAGE 92 A1890
INT/ORG PEACE INT/LAW

B45
CONOVER H.F.,THE NAZI STATE: WAR CRIMES AND WAR CRIMINALS. GERMANY CULTURE NAT/G SECT FORCES DIPLOM INT/TRADE EDU/PROP...INT/LAW BIOG HIST/WRIT TIME/SEQ 20. PAGE 30 A0600
BIBLIOG WAR CRIME

B45
GALLOWAY E.,ABSTRACTS OF POSTWAR LITERATURE (VOL. IV) JAN.-JULY, 1945 NOS. 901-1074. POLAND USA+45 USSR WOR+45 INDUS LABOR PLAN ECO/TAC INT/TRADE TAX EDU/PROP ADMIN COLONIAL INT/LAW. PAGE 51 A1033
BIBLIOG/A NUC/PWR NAT/G DIPLOM

B45
HILL N.,CLAIMS TO TERRITORY IN INTERNATIONAL LAW AND RELATIONS. WOR-45 NAT/G DOMIN EDU/PROP LEGIT REGION ROUTINE ORD/FREE PWR WEALTH...GEOG INT/LAW JURID 20. PAGE 65 A1332
INT/ORG ADJUD SOVEREIGN

B45
KANDELL I.L.,UNITED STATES ACTIVITIES IN INTERNATIONAL CULTURAL RELATIONS. INT/ORG NAT/G VOL/ASSN CREATE DIPLOM EDU/PROP ATTIT RIGID/FLEX KNOWL...PLURIST CONCPT OBS TREND GEN/LAWS TOT/POP UNESCO 20. PAGE 76 A1554
USA-45 CULTURE

B45
PERAZA SARAUSA F.,BIBLIOGRAFIAS CUBANAS. CUBA CULTURE ECO/UNDEV AGRI EDU/PROP PRESS CIVMIL/REL ...POLICY GEOG PHIL/SCI BIOG 19/20. PAGE 115 A2353
BIBLIOG/A L/A+17C NAT/G DIPLOM

B46
LOWENSTEIN R.,POLITICAL RECONSTRUCTION. WOR+45 EX/STRUC EDU/PROP NAT/LISM ATTIT KNOWL ORD/FREE PWR ...SOCIALIST CONCPT GEN/LAWS TOT/POP 20. PAGE 91 A1869
FUT INT/ORG DIPLOM

L46
MASTERS D.,"ONE WORLD OR NONE." FUT WOR+45 INTELL INT/ORG ACT/RES EDU/PROP DETER ATTIT RIGID/FLEX SUPEGO KNOWL...STAT TREND ORG/CHARTS 20. PAGE 96 A1960
POLICY PHIL/SCI ARMS/CONT NUC/PWR

S46
DOUGLAS W.O.,"SYMPOSIUM ON WORLD ORGANIZATION." FUT USA+45 WOR+45 CONSTN SOCIETY NAT/G PLAN EDU/PROP LEGIT RIGID/FLEX KNOWL...INT/LAW JURID STERTYP TOT/POP 20. PAGE 38 A0778
INT/ORG LAW

B47
KIRK G.,THE STUDY OF INTERNATIONAL RELATIONS. FUT USA-45 R+D ACADEM INT/ORG CONSULT DELIB/GP INT/TRADE EDU/PROP PEACE RIGID/FLEX KNOWL VAL/FREE 20. PAGE 80 A1632
USA+45 DIPLOM

B47
MANDER L.,FOUNDATIONS OF MODERN WORLD SOCIETY. WOR+45 DELIB/GP ECO/TAC INT/TRADE EDU/PROP ALL/VALS ...TIME/SEQ GEN/LAWS TOT/POP VAL/FREE ILO 20. PAGE 94 A1917
INT/ORG EX/STRUC DIPLOM

B48
CHAMBERLAIN L.H.,AMERICAN FOREIGN POLICY. FUT USA+45 USA-45 WOR+45 WOR-45 NAT/G LEGIS TOP/EX ECO/TAC FOR/AID EDU/PROP EXEC ATTIT ORD/FREE ...JURID TREND TOT/POP 20. PAGE 25 A0517
CONSTN DIPLOM

B48
COTTRELL L.S. JR.,AMERICAN PUBLIC OPINION ON WORLD AFFAIRS IN THE ATOMIC AGE. USA+45 CULTURE INT/ORG NAT/G DIPLOM EDU/PROP PEACE RIGID/FLEX ORD/FREE ...POLICY SOC CONCPT STAND/INT TOT/POP 20. PAGE 31 A0633
SOCIETY ATTIT ARMS/CONT NUC/PWR

B48
FLOREN LOZANO L.,BIBLIOGRAFIA DE LA BIBLIOGRAFIA DOMINICANA. DOMIN/REP NAT/G DIPLOM EDU/PROP CIVMIL/REL...POLICY ART/METH GEOG PHIL/SCI HIST/WRIT 20. PAGE 47 A0952
BIBLIOG/A BIOG L/A+17C CULTURE

B48
JESSUP P.C.,A MODERN LAW OF NATIONS. FUT WOR+45 WOR-45 SOCIETY NAT/G DELIB/GP LEGIS BAL/PWR EDU/PROP LEGIT PWR...INT/LAW JURID TIME/SEQ LEAGUE/NAT 20. PAGE 74 A1514
INT/ORG ADJUD

B48
JONES H.D.,UNESCO: A SELECTED LIST OF REFERENCES. CULTURE CREATE PEACE ATTIT DRIVE 20 UNESCO UN. PAGE 75 A1531
BIBLIOG/A INT/ORG DIPLOM EDU/PROP

B48
LINEBARGER P.,PSYCHOLOGICAL WARFARE. NAT/G PLAN DIPLOM DOMIN ATTIT...POLICY CONCPT EXHIBIT 20 WWI. PAGE 89 A1824
EDU/PROP PSY WAR COM/IND

B49
THE CURRENT DIGEST OF THE SOVIET PRESS. USSR WOR+45 LOC/G NAT/G DIPLOM EDU/PROP...MARXIST 20. PAGE 3 A0056
BIBLIOG/A COM ATTIT PRESS

B49
BEHRENDT R.F.,MODERN LATIN AMERICA IN SOCIAL SCIENCE LITERATURE. STRUCT ECO/UNDEV SCHOOL DIPLOM INT/TRADE EDU/PROP...GEOG 20. PAGE 12 A0250
BIBLIOG/A SOC L/A+17C

B49
FORD FOUNDATION,REPORT OF THE STUDY FOR THE FORD FOUNDATION ON POLICY AND PROGRAM. SOCIETY R+D ACT/RES CAP/ISM FOR/AID EDU/PROP ADMIN KNOWL ...POLICY PSY SOC 20. PAGE 47 A0961
WEALTH GEN/LAWS

B49
MARITAIN J.,HUMAN RIGHTS: COMMENTS AND INTERPRETATIONS. COM UNIV WOR+45 LAW CONSTN CULTURE SOCIETY ECO/DEV ECO/UNDEV SCHOOL DELIB/GP EDU/PROP ATTIT PERCEPT ALL/VALS...HUM SOC TREND UNESCO 20. PAGE 95 A1939
INT/ORG CONCPT

B49
OGBURN W.,TECHNOLOGY AND INTERNATIONAL RELATIONS. WOR+45 WOR-45 ECO/DEV CREATE PLAN ECO/TAC EDU/PROP COERCE PWR SKILL WEALTH...TECHNIC PSY SOC NEW/IDEA CHARTS TOT/POP 20. PAGE 111 A2283
TEC/DEV DIPLOM INT/ORG

B49
ROSENHAUPT H.W.,HOW TO WAGE PEACE. USA+45 SOCIETY STRATA STRUCT R+D INT/ORG POL/PAR LEGIS ACT/RES CREATE PLAN EDU/PROP ADMIN EXEC ATTIT ALL/VALS ...TIME/SEQ TREND COLD/WAR 20. PAGE 124 A2536
INTELL CONCPT DIPLOM

B49
STETTINIUS E.R.,ROOSEVELT AND THE RUSSIANS: THE YALTA CONFERENCE. UK USSR WOR+45 WOR-45 INT/ORG VOL/ASSN TOP/EX ACT/RES EDU/PROP PEACE ATTIT DRIVE PERSON SUPEGO PWR...POLICY CONCPT MYTH OBS TIME/SEQ AUD/VIS COLD/WAR 20 CHURCHLL/W YALTA ROOSEVLT/F. PAGE 138 A2819
DIPLOM DELIB/GP BIOG

B49
US DEPARTMENT OF STATE,SOVIET BIBLIOGRAPHY (PAMPHLET). CHINA/COM COM USSR LAW AGRI INT/ORG ECO/TAC EDU/PROP...POLICY GEOG 20. PAGE 151 A3084
BIBLIOG/A MARXISM CULTURE DIPLOM

L49
UNESCO,"SOME SUGGESTIONS ON TEACHING ABOUT THE UN AND ITS SPECIALIZED AGENCIES." UNIV WOR+45 SOCIETY STRATA SCHOOL WAR ALL/VALS KNOWL...SOC CONCPT UNESCO 20 UN. PAGE 147 A3011
INT/ORG EDU/PROP

S49
KIRK G.,"MATTERIALS FOR THE STUDY OF INTERNATIONAL RELATIONS." FUT UNIV WOR+45 INTELL EDU/PROP ROUTINE PEACE ATTIT...INT/LAW JURID CONCPT OBS. PAGE 80 A1633
INT/ORG ACT/RES DIPLOM

B50
BARGHOORN F.C.,THE SOVIET IMAGE OF THE UNITED STATES: A STUDY IN DISTORTION. COM USSR DOMIN WAR NAT/LISM TOTALISM SOCISM...PSY 20. PAGE 11 A0220
PROB/SOLV EDU/PROP DIPLOM ATTIT

B50
BERLE A.A.,NATURAL SELECTION OF POLITICAL FORCES. FUT WOR+45 WOR-45 CULTURE SOCIETY INT/ORG NAT/G FORCES EDU/PROP LEGIT COERCE...CONCPT HIST/WRIT TREND 20. PAGE 13 A0274
POL/PAR BAL/PWR DIPLOM

B50
LAUTERPACHT H.,INTERNATIONAL LAW AND HUMAN RIGHTS. USA+45 CONSTN STRUCT INT/ORG ACT/RES EDU/PROP PEACE PERSON ALL/VALS...CONCPT CON/ANAL GEN/LAWS UN 20. PAGE 86 A1750
DELIB/GP LAW INT/LAW

B50
LINCOLN G.,ECONOMICS OF NATIONAL SECURITY. USA+45 ELITES COM/IND DIST/IND INDUS NAT/G VOL/ASSN DELIB/GP EX/STRUC FOR/AID EDU/PROP COERCE NUC/PWR WAR ATTIT KNOWL ORD/FREE PWR COLD/WAR TOT/POP VAL/FREE 20. PAGE 89 A1818
FORCES ECO/TAC

B50
MCCAMY J.,THE ADMINISTRATION OF AMERICAN FOREIGN AFFAIRS. USA+45 SOCIETY INT/ORG NAT/G ACT/RES PLAN INT/TRADE EDU/PROP ADJUD ALL/VALS...METH/CNCPT TIME/SEQ CONGRESS 20. PAGE 97 A1996
EXEC STRUCT DIPLOM

B50
US DEPARTMENT OF STATE,POINT FOUR: COOPERATIVE PROGRAM FOR AID IN THE DEVELOPMENT OF ECONOMICALLY UNDERDEVELOPED AREAS. WOR+45 AGRI INDUS INT/ORG PLAN TEC/DEV DIPLOM EDU/PROP ADMIN PEACE PRODUC WEALTH 20 CONGRESS UN. PAGE 151 A3085
ECO/UNDEV FOR/AID FINAN INT/TRADE

S50
CORBETT P.E.,"OBJECTIVITY IN THE STUDY OF
INT/ORG

INTERNATIONAL AFFAIRS." WOR+45 SOCIETY ACT/RES EDU/PROP PERSON RIGID/FLEX KNOWL TOT/POP 20. PAGE 30 A0614
DIPLOM

S50
UNESCO,"MEETING ON UNIVERSITY TEACHING OF INTERNATIONAL RELATIONS." FUT WOR+45 R+D VOL/ASSN CONSULT PLAN EDU/PROP ATTIT...CONCPT TREND 20. PAGE 147 A3012
INT/ORG
KNOWL
DIPLOM

S50
WITTFOGEL K.A.,"RUSSIA AND ASIA: PROBLEMS OF CONTEMPORARY AREA STUDIES AND INTERNATIONAL RELATIONS." ASIA COM USA+45 SOCIETY NAT/G DIPLOM ECO/TAC FOR/AID EDU/PROP KNOWL...HIST/WRIT TOT/POP 20. PAGE 166 A3373
ECO/DEV
ADMIN
RUSSIA
USSR

B51
BLANSHARD P.,COMMUNISM, DEMOCRACY AND CATHOLIC POWER. USSR VATICAN WOR+45 WOR-45 CULTURE ELITES INTELL SOCIETY STRUCT INT/ORG POL/PAR EDU/PROP COERCE ATTIT KNOWL PWR MARXISM...CONCPT COLD/WAR 20. PAGE 15 A0308
COM
SECT
TOTALISM

B51
HAVILAND H.F.,THE POLITICAL ROLE OF THE GENERAL ASSEMBLY. WOR+45 DELIB/GP EDU/PROP PEACE RIGID/FLEX PWR...CONCPT TIME/SEQ GEN/LAWS UN VAL/FREE 20. PAGE 63 A1290
INT/ORG
ORD/FREE
DIPLOM

B51
JENNINGS S.I.,THE COMMONWEALTH IN ASIA. CEYLON INDIA PAKISTAN S/ASIA UK CONSTN CULTURE SOCIETY STRATA STRUCT NAT/G POL/PAR EDU/PROP LEAD WAR 20 CMN/WLTH. PAGE 74 A1510
NAT/LISM
REGION
COLONIAL
DIPLOM

B51
MACLAURIN J.,THE UNITED NATIONS AND POWER POLITICS. WOR+45 CONSULT EDU/PROP LEGIT ADJUD EXEC MORAL ORD/FREE...HUM JURID CONCPT RECORD TIME/SEQ UN COLD/WAR 20. PAGE 93 A1896
INT/ORG
ROUTINE

B51
MCKEON R.,DEMOCRACY IN A WORLD OF TENSION. UNIV LAW INTELL STRUCT R+D INT/ORG SCHOOL EDU/PROP LEGIT ATTIT DRIVE PERCEPT PERSON...POLICY JURID PSY SOC CONCPT METH/CNCPT OBS UNESCO TOT/POP VAL/FREE. PAGE 98 A2015
SOCIETY
ALL/VALS
ORD/FREE

B51
STANTON A.H.,PERSONALITY AND POLITICAL CRISIS. WOR+45 WOR-45 STRUCT DIPLOM INGP/REL TOTALISM MORAL ...ANTHOL 20 LASSWELL/H PARSONS/T RIESMAN/D. PAGE 137 A2806
EDU/PROP
WAR
PERSON
PSY

B51
UNESCO,FREEDOM AND CULTURE. FUT WOR+45 CONSTN CULTURE PERF/ART VOL/ASSN EDU/PROP PEACE ATTIT ALL/VALS SOVEREIGN...POLICY MAJORIT CONCPT TREND STERTYP GEN/LAWS UN TOT/POP 20. PAGE 147 A3013
INT/ORG
SOCIETY

B51
US DEPARTMENT OF STATE,LIVRES AMERICAINS TRADUITS EN FRANCAIS ET LIVRES FRANCAIS SUR LES ETATS-UNIS D'AMERIQUE (2ND ED.). FRANCE USA+45 SECT DIPLOM EDU/PROP LEISURE...ART/METH GEOG HUM 20. PAGE 151 A3086
BIBLIOG/A
SOC

B51
WELLES S.,SEVEN DECISIONS THAT SHAPED HISTORY. ASIA FRANCE FUT USA+45 WOR+45 WOR-45 CONSTN STRUCT INT/ORG NAT/G ACT/RES EDU/PROP DRIVE...POLICY CONCPT TIME/SEQ TREND TOT/POP UN 20 CHINJAP. PAGE 163 A3315
USA-45
DIPLOM
WAR

S51
CONNERY R.H.,"THE MUTUAL DEFENSE ASSISTANCE PROGRAM." COM EUR+WWI KOREA USA+45 NAT/G VOL/ASSN CREATE PLAN BAL/PWR EDU/PROP PERCEPT...POLICY DECISION CONCPT NATO 20. PAGE 29 A0587
INT/ORG
FORCES
FOR/AID

B52
DILLON D.R.,LATIN AMERICA, 1935-1949; A SELECTED BIBLIOGRAPHY. LAW EDU/PROP...SOC 20. PAGE 37 A0764
BIBLIOG
L/A+17C
NAT/G
DIPLOM

B52
JACKSON E.,MEETING OF THE MINDS: A WAY TO PEACE THROUGH MEDIATION. WOR+45 INDUS INT/ORG NAT/G DELIB/GP DIPLOM EDU/PROP LEGIT ORD/FREE...NEW/IDEA SELF/OBS TIME/SEQ CHARTS GEN/LAWS TOT/POP 20 UN TREATY. PAGE 72 A1474
LABOR
JUDGE

B52
SHULIM J.I.,THE OLD DOMINION AND NAPOLEON BONAPARTE. POL/PAR DOMIN PRESS REV WAR 18/19 VIRGINIA. PAGE 132 A2710
ATTIT
PROVS
EDU/PROP
DIPLOM

B52
SKALWEIT S.,FRANKREICH UND FRIEDRICH DER GROSSE. FRANCE GERMANY PRUSSIA NAT/G DOMIN WAR 18 FREDERICK. PAGE 134 A2737
ATTIT
EDU/PROP
DIPLOM
SOC

B52
SMITH C.M.,INTERNATIONAL COMMUNICATION AND POLITICAL WARFARE: AN ANNOTATED BIBLIOGRAPHY (A PAPER). WOR+45 INTELL R+D NAT/G FORCES ACT/RES DIPLOM COERCE ALL/IDEOS. PAGE 134 A2745
BIBLIOG/A
EDU/PROP
WAR
COM/IND

B52
UNESCO,THESES DE SCIENCES SOCIALES: CATALOGUE ANALYTIQUE INTERNATIONAL DE THESES INEDITES DE DOCTORAT, 1940-1950. INT/ORG DIPLOM EDU/PROP...GEOG INT/LAW MGT PSY SOC 20. PAGE 147 A3015
BIBLIOG
ACADEM
WRITING

B52
US MUTUAL SECURITY AGENCY,U. S. TECHNICAL AND ECONOMIC ASSISTANCE IN THE FAR EAST (PAMPHLET). ASIA BURMA INDONESIA PHILIPPINE TAIWAN THAILAND USA+45 AGRI INDUS PLAN EDU/PROP ADMIN HEALTH. PAGE 155 A3161
FOR/AID
TEC/DEV
ECO/UNDEV
BUDGET

B52
VANDENBOSCH A.,THE UN: BACKGROUND, ORGANIZATION, FUNCTIONS, ACTIVITIES. WOR+45 LAW CONSTN STRUCT INT/ORG CONSULT BAL/PWR EDU/PROP EXEC ALL/VALS ...POLICY CONCPT UN 20. PAGE 158 A3218
DELIB/GP
TIME/SEQ
PEACE

B52
WALTERS F.P.,A HISTORY OF THE LEAGUE OF NATIONS. EUR+WWI CONSTN NAT/G LEGIS TOP/EX ACT/RES PLAN EDU/PROP LEGIT ROUTINE ATTIT...TREND LEAGUE/NAT 20 CHINJAP. PAGE 161 A3271
INT/ORG
TIME/SEQ
NAT/LISM

L52
HILSMAN R. JR.,"INTELLIGENCE AND POLICY MAKING IN FOREIGN AFFAIRS." USA+45 CONSULT ACT/RES DIPLOM EDU/PROP ROUTINE PEACE PERCEPT PWR SKILL...POLICY MGT HYPO/EXP CONGRESS 20 CIA. PAGE 65 A1333
PROF/ORG
SIMUL
WAR

B53
BARBER H.W.,FOREIGN POLICIES OF THE UNITED STATES. USA+45 USA-45 WOR+45 INT/ORG NAT/G EX/STRUC ECO/TAC DOMIN EDU/PROP LEGIT COERCE KNOWL PWR COLD/WAR COLD/WAR 20. PAGE 11 A0219
CONCPT
DIPLOM

B53
COHEN B.C.,CITIZEN EDUCATION IN WORLD AFFAIRS. USA+45 INT/ORG VOL/ASSN CONSULT ATTIT PWR...INT TIME/SEQ 20. PAGE 27 A0559
KNOWL
EDU/PROP
DIPLOM

B53
COUSINS N.,WHO SPEAKS FOR MAN. GERMANY KOREA WOR+45 SOCIETY INT/ORG NAT/G CREATE EDU/PROP HEALTH KNOWL LOVE MORAL...OBS SELF/OBS BIOG HYPO/EXP TOT/POP 20 CHINJAP. PAGE 32 A0642
ATTIT
WAR
PEACE

B53
MENDE T.,WORLD POWER IN THE BALANCE. FUT USA+45 USSR WOR-45 ECO/DEV ECO/TAC INT/TRADE EDU/PROP UTOPIA ATTIT...HUM CONCPT TREND COLD/WAR TOT/POP 20. PAGE 99 A2036
WOR+45
PWR
BAL/PWR

B53
MURPHY G.,IN THE MINDS OF MEN: THE STUDY OF HUMAN BEHAVIOR AND SOCIAL TENSIONS IN INDIA. FUT S/ASIA FAM INT/ORG NAT/G DIPLOM EDU/PROP GP/REL ATTIT RIGID/FLEX ALL/VALS...SOC QU UNESCO 20. PAGE 106 A2176
SECT
STRATA
INDIA

B53
SHIRATO I.,JAPANESE SOURCES ON THE HISTORY OF THE CHINESE COMMUNIST MOVEMENT (PAMPHLET). CHINA/COM USSR CONSTRUC NAT/G POL/PAR FORCES DIPLOM DOMIN EDU/PROP CONTROL WAR TOTALISM SOCISM 20. PAGE 132 A2702
BIBLIOG/A
MARXISM
ECO/UNDEV

B53
SQUIRES J.D.,BRITISH PROPAGANDA AT HOME AND IN THE UNITED STATES FROM 1914 TO 1917. UK NAT/G PROB/SOLV DOMIN PRESS EFFICIENCY...PSY PREDICT 20 WWI INTERVENT PSY/WAR. PAGE 136 A2794
EDU/PROP
CONTROL
WAR
DIPLOM

B53
THAYER P.W.,SOUTHEAST ASIA IN THE COMING WORLD. ASIA S/ASIA USA+45 USA-45 SOCIETY INT/ORG ACT/RES ECO/TAC EDU/PROP COERCE TOTALISM ALL/VALS...JURID 20. PAGE 142 A2909
ECO/UNDEV
ATTIT
FOR/AID
DIPLOM

B53
ZIMMERN A.,THE AMERICAN ROAD TO PEACE. USA+45 LAW INT/ORG NAT/G EX/STRUC TOP/EX EDU/PROP LEGIT COERCE PEACE ATTIT ORD/FREE PWR...CONCPT TIME/SEQ LEAGUE/NAT TOT/POP VAL/FREE 20 UN. PAGE 170 A3455
USA-45
DIPLOM

L53
UNESCO,"THE TECHNIQUE OF INTERNATIONAL CONFERENCES." WOR+45 INT/ORG VOL/ASSN EDU/PROP ROUTINE ATTIT DRIVE KNOWL ORD/FREE...SOC UNESCO 20. PAGE 148 A3016
DELIB/GP
ACT/RES

S53
CORY R.H. JR.,"FORGING A PUBLIC INFORMATION POLICY FOR THE UNITED NATIONS." FUT WOR+45 SOCIETY ADMIN PEACE ATTIT PERSON SKILL...CONCPT 20 UN. PAGE 31 A0628
INT/ORG
EDU/PROP
BAL/PWR

S53
LINCOLN G.,"FACTORS DETERMINING ARMS AID." COM FUT USA+45 USSR WOR+45 ECO/DEV NAT/G CONSULT PLAN TEC/DEV DIPLOM DOMIN EDU/PROP PERCEPT PWR ...DECISION CONCPT TREND MARX/KARL 20. PAGE 89 A1819
FORCES
POLICY
BAL/PWR
FOR/AID

S53
MANNING C.A.W.,"THE PRETENTIONS OF INTERNATIONAL RELATIONS." WOR+45 SOCIETY CREATE EDU/PROP ATTIT PERSON KNOWL...GEN/LAWS TOT/POP VAL/FREE 20. PAGE 94 A1924
INT/ORG
DIPLOM
UK

B54
ARON R.,CENTURY OF TOTAL WAR. FUT WOR+45 WOR-45 SOCIETY INT/ORG NAT/G FORCES TOP/EX CREATE BAL/PWR DOMIN EDU/PROP COERCE DETER PEACE TOTALISM PWR ...TIME/SEQ TREND COLD/WAR TOT/POP VAL/FREE
ATTIT
WAR

LEAGUE/NAT 20. PAGE 9 A0179

B54
COOK T.,POWER THROUGH PURPOSE. USA+45 WOR+45 WOR-45 INT/ORG VOL/ASSN BAL/PWR DIPLOM EDU/PROP LEGIT PERSON...GEN/LAWS LEAGUE/NAT 20. PAGE 30 A0606 ATTIT CONCPT

B54
COUDENHOVE-KALERGI,AN IDEA CONQUERS THE WORLD. EUR+WWI MOD/EUR USA-45 CONSTN FAM CREATE EDU/PROP ATTIT PERSON KNOWL...CONCPT SELF/OBS TIME/SEQ. PAGE 31 A0635 INT/ORG BIOG DIPLOM

B54
GROSS F.,FOREIGN POLICY ANALYSIS. USA+45 TOP/EX PLAN INGP/REL ATTIT TECHRACY...CONCPT 20. PAGE 57 A1171 POLICY DIPLOM DECISION EDU/PROP

B54
MANNING C.A.W.,THE UNIVERSITY TEACHING OF SOCIAL SCIENCES: INTERNATIONAL RELATIONS. WOR+45 INTELL STRATA R+D ACADEM INT/ORG NAT/G CONSULT DELIB/GP ACT/RES EDU/PROP NAT/LISM ATTIT...POLICY CONT/OBS HYPO/EXP VAL/FREE LEAGUE/NAT UNESCO 20. PAGE 94 A1925 KNOWL PHIL/SCI DIPLOM

B54
NORTHROP F.S.C.,EUROPEAN UNION AND UNITED STATES FOREIGN POLICY: A STUDY IN SOCIOLOGICAL JURISPRUDENCE. EUR+WWI MOD/EUR USA+45 SOCIETY STRUCT NAT/G CREATE ECO/TAC DOMIN EDU/PROP REGION ATTIT RIGID/FLEX HEALTH ORD/FREE WEALTH ...METH/CNCPT TIME/SEQ TREND. PAGE 110 A2256 INT/ORG SOC DIPLOM

B54
SALVEMINI G.,PRELUDE TO WORLD WAR II. ITALY MOD/EUR INT/ORG BAL/PWR EDU/PROP CONTROL TOTALISM...TREND NAT/COMP BIBLIOG 19 HITLER/A LEAGUE/NAT MUSSOLIN/B. PAGE 127 A2597 WAR FASCISM LEAD PWR

B54
SCHIFFER W.,THE LEGAL COMMUNITY OF MANKIND. UNIV WOR+45 WOR-45 SOCIETY NAT/G EDU/PROP LEGIT ATTIT PERSON ORD/FREE PWR...CONCPT HIST/WRIT TREND LEAGUE/NAT UN 20. PAGE 128 A2626 INT/ORG PHIL/SCI

B54
STALEY E.,THE FUTURE OF UNDERDEVELOPED COUNTRIES: POLITICAL IMPLICATIONS OF ECONOMIC DEVELOPMENT. COM FUT USA+45 SOCIETY ECO/UNDEV CREATE PLAN CAP/ISM ATTIT DRIVE MARXISM SOCISM...POLICY CONCPT CHARTS COLD/WAR 20. PAGE 137 A2801 EDU/PROP ECO/TAC FOR/AID

B54
STRAUSZ-HUPE R.,INTERNATIONAL RELATIONS IN THE AGE OF THE CONFLICT BETWEEN DEMOCRACY AND DICTATORSHIP (2ND ED.). INT/ORG BAL/PWR EDU/PROP ADMIN WAR PEACE PWR...CONCPT CHARTS BIBLIOG 20 COLD/WAR UN LEAGUE/NAT. PAGE 139 A2846 DIPLOM POPULISM MARXISM

B54
US DEPARTMENT OF STATE,PUBLICATIONS OF THE DEPARTMENT OF STATE, OCTOBER 1,1929 TO JANUARY 1, 1953. AGRI INT/ORG FORCES FOR/AID EDU/PROP ARMS/CONT NUC/PWR ATTIT 20 DEPT/STATE OAS UN NATO. PAGE 151 A3089 BIBLIOG DIPLOM

B54
WRIGHT Q.,PROBLEMS OF STABILITY AND PROGRESS IN INTERNATIONAL RELATIONSHIPS. FUT WOR+45 WOR-45 SOCIETY LEGIS CREATE TEC/DEV ECO/TAC EDU/PROP ADJUD WAR PEACE ORD/FREE PWR...KNO/TEST TREND GEN/LAWS 20. PAGE 167 A3409 INT/ORG CONCPT DIPLOM

L54
CHARLESWORTH J.C.,"AMERICA AND A NEW ASIA." ASIA INDIA ISLAM S/ASIA USA+45 USA-45 ECO/UNDEV NAT/G POL/PAR FORCES FOR/AID DOMIN EDU/PROP COERCE DRIVE ALL/VALS MARXISM SOCISM TOT/POP 20. PAGE 26 A0522 ECO/TAC DIPLOM NAT/LISM

L54
OPLER M.E.,"SOCIAL ASPECTS OF TECHNICAL ASSISTANCE IN OPERATION." WOR+45 VOL/ASSN CREATE PLAN TEC/DEV EDU/PROP ALL/VALS...METH/CNCPT OBS RECORD TREND UN 20. PAGE 112 A2292 INT/ORG CONSULT FOR/AID

S54
FOX W.T.R.,"CIVIL-MILITARY RELATIONS." USA+45 USA-45 R+D ACT/RES DIPLOM INT/TRADE EDU/PROP DETER DISPL DRIVE ORD/FREE...METH/CNCPT TREND COLD/WAR 20. PAGE 48 A0974 POLICY FORCES PLAN SOCIETY

B55
CHOWDHURI R.N.,INTERNATIONAL MANDATES AND TRUSTEESHIP SYSTEMS. WOR+45 STRUCT ECO/UNDEV INT/ORG LEGIS DOMIN EDU/PROP LEGIT ADJUD EXEC PWR ...CONCPT TIME/SEQ UN 20. PAGE 26 A0534 DELIB/GP PLAN SOVEREIGN

B55
COMM. STUDY ORGAN. PEACE,REPORTS. WOR-45 ECO/DEV ECO/UNDEV VOL/ASSN CONSULT FORCES PLAN TEC/DEV DOMIN EDU/PROP NUC/PWR ATTIT PWR WEALTH...JURID STERTYP FAO ILO 20 UN. PAGE 28 A0579 WOR+45 INT/ORG ARMS/CONT

B55
JOY C.T.,HOW COMMUNISTS NEGOTIATE. COM USA+45 CONSTN CULTURE ECO/UNDEV NAT/G CONSULT DELIB/GP FORCES PLAN ECO/TAC DOMIN EDU/PROP LEGIT EXEC ROUTINE COERCE WAR CHOOSE PEACE ATTIT RIGID/FLEX ORD/FREE PWR...POLICY 20. PAGE 75 A1539 ASIA INT/ORG DIPLOM

B55
MOCH J.,HUMAN FOLLY: DISARM OR PERISH. USA+45 WOR+45 SOCIETY INT/ORG NAT/G ACT/RES EDU/PROP ATTIT PERSON KNOWL ORD/FREE PWR...MAJORIT TOT/POP COLD/WAR 20. PAGE 102 A2093 FUT DELIB/GP ARMS/CONT NUC/PWR

B55
MYRDAL A.R.,AMERICA'S ROLE IN INTERNATIONATIONAL SOCIAL WELFARE. FUT WOR+45 SOCIETY R+D VOL/ASSN ECO/TAC EDU/PROP HEALTH KNOWL WEALTH...SOC CHARTS ORG/CHARTS TOT/POP 20. PAGE 107 A2188 PLAN SKILL FOR/AID

B55
SNYDER R.C.,AMERICAN FOREIGN POLICY. USA+45 USA-45 WOR+45 WOR-45 CONSTN INT/ORG POL/PAR VOL/ASSN DELIB/GP LEGIS CREATE DOMIN EDU/PROP EXEC COERCE ATTIT DRIVE ORD/FREE PWR...MGT OBS RECORD TIME/SEQ TREND. PAGE 134 A2752 NAT/G DIPLOM

B55
STEPHENS O.,FACTS TO A CANDID WORLD. USA+45 WOR+45 COM/IND EX/STRUC PRESS ROUTINE EFFICIENCY ATTIT ...PSY 20. PAGE 138 A2817 EDU/PROP PHIL/SCI NAT/G DIPLOM

B55
THOMPSON V.,MINORITY PROBLEMS IN SOUTHEAST ASIA. CAMBODIA CHINA/COM LAOS S/ASIA KIN NAT/G SECT PROB/SOLV EDU/PROP REGION GP/REL RACE/REL MARXISM ...SOC 20 BUDDHISM UN. PAGE 143 A2933 INGP/REL GEOG DIPLOM STRUCT

B55
UN ECONOMIC AND SOCIAL COUNCIL,BIBLIOGRAPHY OF PUBLICATIONS OF THE UN AND SPECIALIZED AGENCIES IN THE SOCIAL WELFARE FIELD, 1946-1952. WOR+45 FAM INT/ORG MUNIC ACT/RES PLAN PROB/SOLV EDU/PROP AGE/C AGE/Y HABITAT...HEAL UN. PAGE 147 A3000 BIBLIOG/A SOC/WK ADMIN WEALTH

B55
WRIGHT Q.,THE STUDY OF INTERNATIONAL RELATIONS. WOR+45 WOR-45 SOCIETY ECO/TAC INT/TRADE EDU/PROP ALL/VALS...CONCPT GEN/METH 20. PAGE 167 A3410 INT/ORG DIPLOM

L55
KISER M.,"ORGANIZATION OF AMERICAN STATES." L/A+17C USA+45 ECO/UNDEV INT/ORG NAT/G PLAN TEC/DEV DIPLOM ECO/TAC INT/TRADE EDU/PROP ADMIN ALL/VALS...POLICY MGT RECORD ORG/CHARTS OAS 20. PAGE 80 A1639 VOL/ASSN ECO/DEV REGION

S55
TORRE M.,"PSYCHIATRIC OBSERVATIONS OF INTERNATIONAL CONFERENCES." WOR+45 INT/ORG PROF/ORG VOL/ASSN CONSULT EDU/PROP ROUTINE ATTIT DRIVE KNOWL...PSY METH/CNCPT OBS/ENVIR STERTYP 20. PAGE 144 A2950 DELIB/GP OBS DIPLOM

S55
WRIGHT Q.,"THE PEACEFUL ADJUSTMENT OF INTERNATIONAL RELATIONS: PROBLEMS AND RESEARCH APPROACHES." UNIV INTELL EDU/PROP ADJUD ROUTINE KNOWL SKILL...INT/LAW JURID PHIL/SCI CLASSIF 20. PAGE 167 A3411 R+D METH/CNCPT PEACE

B56
BALL W.M.,NATIONALISM AND COMMUNISM IN EAST ASIA. ASIA BURMA EUR+WWI KOREA USA+45 ECO/UNDEV NAT/G POL/PAR DIPLOM ECO/TAC FOR/AID EDU/PROP COERCE RACE/REL NAT/LISM DRIVE SOVEREIGN...TREND 20 CHINJAP. PAGE 11 A0214 S/ASIA ATTIT

B56
CHANG C.J.,THE MINORITY GROUPS OF YUNN AN AND CHINESE POLITICAL EXPANSION INTO SOUTHEAST ASIA (DOCTORAL THESIS). ASIA CHINA/COM S/ASIA FORCES TEC/DEV DIPLOM EDU/PROP...GEOG BIBLIOG 20. PAGE 26 A0520 GP/REL REGION DOMIN MARXISM

B56
ESTEP R.,AN AIR POWER BIBLIOGRAPHY. USA+45 TEC/DEV BUDGET DIPLOM EDU/PROP DETER CIVMIL/REL...DECISION INT/LAW 20. PAGE 42 A0862 BIBLIOG/A FORCES WEAPON PLAN

B56
KIRK G.,THE CHANGING ENVIRONMENT OF INTERNATIONAL RELATIONS. ASIA S/ASIA USA+45 WOR+45 ECO/UNDEV INT/ORG NAT/G FOR/AID EDU/PROP PEACE KNOWL ...PLURIST COLD/WAR TOT/POP 20. PAGE 80 A1634 FUT EXEC DIPLOM

B56
KNORR K.E.,RUBLE DIPLOMACY: CHALLENGE TO AMERICAN FOREIGN AID(PAMPHLET). CHINA/COM USA+45 USSR PLAN TEC/DEV CAP/ISM INT/TRADE DOMIN EDU/PROP CONTROL LEAD 20 COLD/WAR. PAGE 81 A1654 ECO/UNDEV COM DIPLOM FOR/AID

B56
REITZEL W.,UNITED STATES FOREIGN POLICY, 1945-1955. USA+45 WOR+45 CONSTN INT/ORG EDU/PROP LEGIT EXEC COERCE NUC/PWR PEACE ATTIT ORD/FREE PWR...DECISION CONCPT OBS RECORD TIME/SEQ TREND COLD/WAR UN CONGRESS. PAGE 120 A2464 NAT/G POLICY DIPLOM

B56
WEIS P.,NATIONALITY AND STATELESSNESS IN INTERNATIONAL LAW. UK WOR+45 WOR-45 LAW CONSTN NAT/G DIPLOM EDU/PROP LEGIT ROUTINE RIGID/FLEX ...JURID RECORD CMN/WLTH 20. PAGE 162 A3309 INT/ORG SOVEREIGN INT/LAW

B56
WOLFERS A.,THE ANGLO-AMERICAN TRADITION IN FOREIGN AFFAIRS. UK USA+45 WOR-45 CULTURE SOCIETY ECO/DEV INT/ORG NAT/G CREATE PLAN BAL/PWR ECO/TAC EDU/PROP PEACE DISPL DRIVE...TREND GEN/LAWS 20. PAGE 166 A3382 ATTIT CONCPT DIPLOM

B56
WOLFF R.L.,THE BALKANS IN OUR TIME. ALBANIA FUT MOD/EUR USSR YUGOSLAVIA CULTURE INT/ORG SECT DIPLOM GEOG COM

EDU/PROP COERCE WAR ORD/FREE...CHARTS 4/20 BALKANS COMINFORM. PAGE 166 A3388

S56

GORDON L.,"THE ORGANIZATION FOR EUROPEAN ECONOMIC COOPERATION." EUR+WWI INDUS INT/ORG NAT/G CONSULT DELIB/GP ACT/RES CREATE PLAN TEC/DEV EDU/PROP LEGIT WEALTH OEEC 20. PAGE 54 A1114 VOL/ASSN ECO/DEV

B57

ARON R.,FRANCE DEFEATS EDC. EUR+WWI GERMANY LEGIS DIPLOM DOMIN EDU/PROP ADMIN...HIST/WRIT 20. PAGE 9 A0180 INT/ORG FORCES DETER FRANCE

B57

ASHER R.E.,THE UNITED NATIONS AND THE PROMOTION OF THE GENERAL WELFARE. WOR+45 WOR-45 ECO/UNDEV EX/STRUC ACT/RES PLAN EDU/PROP ROUTINE HEALTH...HUM CONCPT CHARTS UNESCO UN ILO 20. PAGE 9 A0185 INT/ORG CONSULT

B57

BUCK P.W.,CONTOL OF FOREIGN RELATIONS IN MODERN NATIONS. FRANCE L/A+17C NETHERLAND USSR WOR+45 INT/ORG TOP/EX BAL/PWR DOMIN EDU/PROP COERCE PEACE ATTIT...CONCPT TREND 20 CMN/WLTH. PAGE 21 A0427 NAT/G PWR DIPLOM

B57

BYRNES R.F.,BIBLIOGRAPHY OF AMERICAN PUBLICATIONS ON EAST CENTRAL EUROPE, 1945-1957 (VOL. XXII). SECT DIPLOM EDU/PROP RACE/REL...ART/METH GEOG JURID SOC LING 20 JEWS. PAGE 23 A0462 BIBLIOG/A COM MARXISM NAT/G

B57

CASTLE E.W.,THE GREAT GIVEAWAY: THE REALITIES OF FOREIGN AID. USA+45 DIPLOM EDU/PROP NEUTRAL ...DECISION 20. PAGE 25 A0508 FOR/AID GIVE ECO/UNDEV PROB/SOLV

B57

DEUTSCH K.W.,POLITICAL COMMUNITY AND THE NORTH ATLANTIC AREA: INTERNATIONAL ORGANIZATION IN THE LIGHT OF HISTORICAL EXPERIENCE. MOD/EUR USA+45 USA-45 SOCIETY FORCES TOP/EX CREATE PLAN DIPLOM DOMIN EDU/PROP LEGIT ATTIT ORD/FREE PWR...SAMP/SIZ TIME/SEQ CHARTS TOT/POP. PAGE 36 A0736 EUR+WWI INT/ORG PEACE REGION

B57

FRASER L.,PROPAGANDA. GERMANY USSR WOR+45 WOR-45 NAT/G POL/PAR CONTROL FEEDBACK LOBBY CROWD WAR CONSEN NAT/LISM 20. PAGE 48 A0988 EDU/PROP FASCISM MARXISM DIPLOM

B57

HOLCOMBE A.N.,STRENGTHENING THE UNITED NATIONS. USA+45 ACT/RES CREATE PLAN EDU/PROP ATTIT PERCEPT PWR...METH/CNCPT CONT/OBS RECORD UN COLD/WAR 20. PAGE 66 A1365 INT/ORG ROUTINE

B57

KENNAN G.F.,RUSSIA, THE ATOM AND THE WEST. COM EUR+WWI FUT WOR+45 SOCIETY ECO/DEV FORCES DIPLOM ECO/TAC DOMIN EDU/PROP COERCE NUC/PWR ATTIT DRIVE ORD/FREE PWR...POLICY OBS TIME/SEQ TREND COLD/WAR NATO 20. PAGE 77 A1574 NAT/G INT/ORG USSR

B57

LAVES W.H.C.,UNESCO. FUT WOR+45 NAT/G CONSULT DELIB/GP TEC/DEV ECO/TAC EDU/PROP PEACE ORD/FREE ...CONCPT TIME/SEQ TREND UNESCO VAL/FREE 20. PAGE 86 A1751 INT/ORG KNOWL

B57

LEFEVER E.W.,ETHICS AND UNITED STATUS FOREIGN POLICY. SOCIETY INT/ORG NAT/G ACT/RES DIPLOM EDU/PROP COERCE ATTIT MORAL...TREND GEN/LAWS COLD/WAR 20. PAGE 86 A1762 USA+45 CULTURE CONCPT POLICY

B57

MOYER K.E.,FROM IRAN TO MORROCCO; FROM TURKEY TO THE SUDAN: A SELECTED AND ANNOTATED BIBLIOGRAPHY OF NORTH AFRICA AND NEAR EAST... ISLAM DIPLOM EDU/PROP 20. PAGE 105 A2162 BIBLIOG/A ECO/UNDEV SECT NAT/G

B57

MURRAY J.N.,THE UNITED NATIONS TRUSTEESHIP SYSTEM. AFR WOR+45 CONSTN CONSULT LEGIS EDU/PROP LEGIT EXEC ROUTINE...INT TIME/SEQ SOMALI UN 20. PAGE 106 A2181 INT/ORG DELIB/GP

B57

PALMER N.D.,INTERNATIONAL RELATIONS. WOR+45 INT/ORG NAT/G ECO/TAC EDU/PROP COLONIAL WAR PWR SOVEREIGN ...POLICY T 20 TREATY. PAGE 113 A2321 DIPLOM BAL/PWR NAT/COMP

B57

PETERSON H.C.,OPPONENTS OF WAR 1917-1918. USA-45 POL/PAR DOMIN ORD/FREE PWR PACIFISM SOCISM 20 IWW CONSCN/OBJ. PAGE 115 A2368 WAR PEACE ATTIT EDU/PROP

B57

US COMMISSION GOVT SECURITY,RECOMMENDATIONS; AREA: IMMIGRANT PROGRAM. USA+45 LAW WORKER DIPLOM EDU/PROP WRITING ADMIN PEACE ATTIT...CONCPT ANTHOL 20 MIGRATION SUBVERT. PAGE 150 A3060 POLICY CONTROL PLAN NAT/G

L57

HAAS E.B.,"REGIONAL INTEGRATION AND NATIONAL POLICY." WOR+45 VOL/ASSN DELIB/GP EX/STRUC ECO/TAC DOMIN EDU/PROP LEGIT COERCE ATTIT PERCEPT KNOWL ...TIME/SEQ COLD/WAR 20 UN. PAGE 59 A1203 INT/ORG ORD/FREE REGION

L57

WARREN S.,"FOREIGN AID AND FOREIGN POLICY." USA+45 WOR+45 WOR-45 DIST/IND INDUS MARKET CONSULT CREATE ECO/UNDEV ALL/VALS

DIPLOM EDU/PROP LEGIT ATTIT RIGID/FLEX...TIME/SEQ GEN/LAWS WORK 20. PAGE 161 A3285 ECO/TAC FOR/AID

S57

DEUTSCH K.W.,"MASS COMMUNICATIONS AND THE LOSS OF FREEDOM IN NATIONAL DECISION MAKING." FUT WOR+45 SOCIETY COM/IND INT/ORG NAT/G ACT/RES CREATE TEC/DEV EDU/PROP MAJORITY PERCEPT...METH/CNCPT 20. PAGE 36 A0737 COERCE DECISION WAR

S57

ELDER R.E.,"THE PUBLIC STUDIES DIVISION OF THE DEPARTMENT OF STATE: PUBLIC OPINION ANALYSTS IN THE FORMULATION AND CONDUCT OF." INT/ORG CONSULT DOMIN EDU/PROP ADMIN ATTIT PWR...CONCPT OBS TIME/SEQ VAL/FREE 20. PAGE 41 A0836 USA+45 NAT/G DIPLOM

C57

TANG P.S.H.,"COMMUNIST CHINA TODAY: DOMESTIC AND FOREIGN POLICIES." CHINA/COM COM S/ASIA USSR STRATA FORCES DIPLOM EDU/PROP COERCE GOV/REL...POLICY MAJORIT BIBLIOG 20. PAGE 141 A2886 POL/PAR LEAD ADMIN CONSTN

B58

ANGELL N.,DEFENCE AND THE ENGLISH-SPEAKING ROLE. CHINA/COM UK USSR INT/ORG FORCES EDU/PROP NEUTRAL NUC/PWR NAT/LISM PEACE TOTALISM 20 COLD/WAR COEXIST. PAGE 8 A0161 DIPLOM WAR MARXISM ORD/FREE

B58

CAMPBELL J.C.,DEFENSE OF THE MIDDLE EAST: PROBLEMS OF AMERICAN POLICY. ISLAM USA+45 INT/ORG NAT/G EX/STRUC FORCES ECO/TAC DOMIN EDU/PROP LEGIT REGION COERCE...METH/CNCPT COLD/WAR TOT/POP 20. PAGE 23 A0474 TOP/EX ORD/FREE DIPLOM

B58

DUCLOUX L.,FROM BLACKMAIL TO TREASON. FRANCE PLAN DIPLOM EDU/PROP PRESS RUMOR NAT/LISM...CRIMLGY 20. PAGE 39 A0793 COERCE CRIME NAT/G PWR

B58

HAAS E.B.,THE UNITING OF EUROPE. EUR+WWI INT/ORG NAT/G POL/PAR TOP/EX ECO/TAC EDU/PROP LEGIT FEDERAL NAT/LISM DRIVE RIGID/FLEX ORD/FREE PWR PLURISM ...POLICY CONCPT INT GEN/LAWS ECSC EEC 20. PAGE 59 A1204 VOL/ASSN ECO/DEV

B58

HENKIN L.,ARMS CONTROL AND INSPECTION IN AMERICAN LAW. LAW CONSTN INT/ORG LOC/G MUNIC NAT/G PROVS EDU/PROP LEGIT EXEC NUC/PWR KNOWL ORD/FREE...OBS TOT/POP CONGRESS 20. PAGE 64 A1315 USA+45 JURID ARMS/CONT

B58

HOLT R.T.,RADIO FREE EUROPE. FUT USA+45 CULTURE ECO/DEV INT/ORG KIN POL/PAR SECT FORCES ACT/RES DIPLOM COERCE REV CHOOSE PEACE ATTIT PWR...MAJORIT CONCPT COLD/WAR WORK 20 RFE. PAGE 67 A1374 COM EDU/PROP COM/IND

B58

MARTIN L.J.,INTERNATIONAL PROPAGANDA: ITS LEGAL AND DIPLOMATIC CONTROL. UK USA+45 USSR CONSULT DELIB/GP DOMIN CONTROL 20. PAGE 95 A1951 EDU/PROP DIPLOM INT/LAW ATTIT

B58

MASON J.B.,THAILAND BIBLIOGRAPHY. S/ASIA THAILAND CULTURE EDU/PROP ADMIN...GEOG SOC LING 20. PAGE 95 A1958 BIBLIOG/A ECO/UNDEV DIPLOM NAT/G

B58

MELMAN S.,INSPECTION FOR DISARMAMENT. USA+45 WOR+45 SOCIETY INT/ORG NAT/G CONSULT ACT/RES PLAN EDU/PROP CONTROL DETER PEACE ATTIT PERSON KNOWL...PSY STAT OBS CHARTS TOT/POP VAL/FREE 20. PAGE 99 A2035 FUT ORD/FREE ARMS/CONT NUC/PWR

B58

MILLIS W.,FOREIGN POLICY AND THE FREE SOCIETY. USA+45 WOR+45 SOCIETY NAT/G FORCES BAL/PWR FOR/AID EDU/PROP DETER ATTIT PWR 20 COLD/WAR. PAGE 102 A2084 DIPLOM POLICY ORD/FREE CONSULT

B58

NOEL-BAKER D.,THE ARMS RACE. WOR+45 NAT/G DELIB/GP ACT/RES TEC/DEV EDU/PROP NUC/PWR ATTIT KNOWL PWR ...CONCPT OBS LEAGUE/NAT 20 COLD/WAR. PAGE 109 A2245 FUT INT/ORG ARMS/CONT PEACE

B58

RIGGS R.,POLITICS IN THE UNITED NATIONS: A STUDY OF UNITED STATES INFLUENCE IN THE GENERAL ASSEMBLY. USA+45 WOR+45 LEGIS TOP/EX CREATE BAL/PWR DIPLOM DOMIN EDU/PROP COLONIAL ROUTINE ATTIT RIGID/FLEX PWR...CONCPT OBS HIST/WRIT CHARTS STERTYP GEN/LAWS UN COLD/WAR 20. PAGE 121 A2480 INT/ORG

B58

SCOTT W.A.,THE UNITED STATES AND THE UNITED NATIONS: THE PUBLIC VIEW 1945-1955. USA+45 EDU/PROP ...INT QU KNO/TEST SAMP GP/COMP 20 UN. PAGE 130 A2674 ATTIT DIPLOM INT/ORG

B58

SLICK T.,PERMANENT PEACE: A CHECK AND BALANCE PLAN. FUT WOR+45 NAT/G FORCES CREATE PLAN EDU/PROP LEGIT ADJUD COERCE NAT/LISM RIGID/FLEX MORAL...HUM CONCPT METH/CNCPT NEW/IDEA TREND CHARTS TOT/POP 20. PAGE 134 A2742 INT/ORG ORD/FREE PEACE ARMS/CONT

B58

UN INTL CONF ON PEACEFUL USE,PROGRESS IN ATOMIC NUC/PWR

ENERGY (VOL. I). WOR+45 R+D PLAN TEC/DEV CONFER CONTROL PEACE SKILL...CHARTS ANTHOL 20 UN BAGHDAD. PAGE 147 A3003 — DIPLOM WORKER EDU/PROP

B58
US DEPARTMENT OF STATE,PUBLICATIONS OF THE DEPARTMENT OF STATE, JANUARY 1,1953 TO DECEMBER 31, 1957. AGRI INT/ORG FORCES FOR/AID EDU/PROP ARMS/CONT NUC/PWR ATTIT 20 DEPT/STATE OAS UN NATO. PAGE 151 A3092 — BIBLIOG DIPLOM

B58
US OPERATIONS MISSION TO VIET,BUILDING ECONOMIC STRENGTH (PAMPHLET). USA+45 VIETNAM/S INDUS TEC/DEV BUDGET ADMIN EATING HEALTH...STAT 20. PAGE 155 A3162 — FOR/AID ECO/UNDEV AGRI EDU/PROP

B58
VARG P.A.,MISSIONARIES, CHINESE, AND DIPLOMATS: THE AMERICAN PROTESTANT MISSIONARY MOVEMENT IN CHINA, 1890-1952. ASIA ECO/UNDEV NAT/G PROB/SOLV CAP/ISM EDU/PROP COLONIAL NAT/LISM ATTIT MARXISM...NAT/COMP STERTYP 20 CHINJAP PROTESTANT MISSION. PAGE 158 A3221 — CULTURE DIPLOM SECT

L58
INT. SOC. SCI. BULL.,"TECHNIQUES OF MEDIATION AND CONCILIATION." EUR+WWI USA+45 SOCIETY INDUS INT/ORG LABOR NAT/G LEGIS DIPLOM EDU/PROP CHOOSE ATTIT RIGID/FLEX...JURID CONCPT GEN/LAWS 20. PAGE 70 A1447 — VOL/ASSN DELIB/GP INT/LAW

S58
BLAISDELL D.C.,"PRESSURE GROUPS, FOREIGN POLICIES, AND INTERNATIONAL POLITICS." USA+45 WOR+45 INT/ORG PLAN DOMIN EDU/PROP LEGIT ADMIN ROUTINE CHOOSE ...DECISION MGT METH/CNCPT CON/ANAL 20. PAGE 15 A0303 — PROF/ORG PWR

S58
BOGART L.,"MEASURING THE EFFECTIVENESS OF AN OVERSEAS INFORMATION CAMPAIGN." EUR+WWI GREECE USA+45 INT/ORG MUNIC PLAN DIPLOM PEACE PERCEPT RIGID/FLEX KNOWL...TECHNIC PSY SOC NEW/IDEA CONT/OBS REC/INT STAND/INT SAMP/SIZ COLD/WAR 20. PAGE 16 A0328 — ATTIT EDU/PROP

S58
LASSWELL H.D.,"THE SCIENTIFIC STUDY OF INTERNATIONAL RELATIONS." USA+45 INT/ORG CREATE EDU/PROP DETER ATTIT PERCEPT PWR...DECISION CONCPT METH/CNCPT STYLE CON/ANAL 20. PAGE 85 A1740 — PHIL/SCI GEN/METH DIPLOM

S58
STAAR R.F.,"ELECTIONS IN COMMUNIST POLAND." EUR+WWI SOCIETY INT/ORG NAT/G POL/PAR LEGIS ACT/RES ECO/TAC EDU/PROP ADJUD ADMIN ROUTINE COERCE TOTALISM ATTIT ORD/FREE PWR 20. PAGE 137 A2797 — COM CHOOSE POLAND

S58
THOMPSON K.W.,"NATIONAL SECURITY IN A NUCLEAR AGE." USA+45 WOR+45 SOCIETY INT/ORG NAT/G TOP/EX DIPLOM DOMIN EDU/PROP LEGIT ARMS/CONT COERCE ORD/FREE ...TREND STERTYP TOT/POP VAL/FREE COLD/WAR 20. PAGE 143 A2929 — FORCES PWR BAL/PWR

C58
CARTER G.M.,"THE POLITICS OF INEQUALITY: SOUTH AFRICA SINCE 1948." SOUTH/AFR CONSTN DIPLOM EDU/PROP REPRESENT DISCRIM ATTIT...POLICY PREDICT CHARTS BIBLIOG 20. PAGE 25 A0504 — RACE/REL POL/PAR CHOOSE DOMIN

N58
INVESTMENT FUND ECO SOC DEV,FRENCH AFRICA: A DECADE OF PROGRESS 1948-1958 (PAMPHLET). AFR FRANCE EXTR/IND INDUS EDU/PROP HEALTH 20. PAGE 71 A1465 — FOR/AID DIPLOM ECO/UNDEV AGRI

B59
ALLEN R.L.,SOVIET INFLUENCE IN LATIN AMERICA. ECO/UNDEV FINAN PROC/MFG NAT/G TEC/DEV EDU/PROP EXEC ROUTINE ATTIT DRIVE PERSON ALL/VALS PWR...STAT CHARTS WORK 20. PAGE 6 A0125 — L/A+17C ECO/TAC INT/TRADE USSR

B59
BALL M.M.,NATO AND THE EUROPEAN MOVEMENT. EUR+WWI USA+45 INT/ORG FORCES BAL/PWR EDU/PROP LEGIT REGION ATTIT ORD/FREE PWR...STAT OBS TIME/SEQ TREND CHARTS ORG/CHARTS STERTYP COLD/WAR EEC OEEC 20 NATO. PAGE 10 A0212 — DELIB/GP STRUCT

B59
CHANDLER E.H.S.,THE HIGH TOWER OF REFUGE: THE INSPIRING STORY OF REFUGEE RELIEF THROUGHOUT THE WORLD. WOR+45 NEIGH SECT WORKER PROB/SOLV DIPLOM ECO/TAC EDU/PROP COST HABITAT. PAGE 25 A0519 — GIVE WEALTH STRANGE INT/ORG

B59
CHINA INSTITUTE OF AMERICA.,CHINA AND THE UNITED NATIONS. CHINA/COM FUT STRUCT EDU/PROP LEGIT ADMIN ATTIT KNOWL ORD/FREE PWR...OBS RECORD STAND/INT TIME/SEQ UN LEAGUE/NAT UNESCO 20. PAGE 26 A0531 — ASIA INT/ORG

B59
FOX W.T.R.,THEORETICAL ASPECTS OF INTERNATIONAL RELATIONS. WOR+45 INT/ORG NAT/G POL/PAR CONSULT PLAN ECO/TAC DOMIN EDU/PROP LEGIT EXEC COERCE PWR WEALTH...RELATIV CONCPT 20. PAGE 48 A0975 — DELIB/GP ANTHOL

B59
JONES A.C.,NEW FABIAN COLONIAL ESSAYS. UK SOCIETY POL/PAR EDU/PROP ADMIN ORD/FREE SOVEREIGN SOCISM ...ANTHOL 20 CMN/WLTH LABOR/PAR. PAGE 75 A1530 — COLONIAL INT/ORG INGP/REL

DOMIN

B59
KULSKI W.W.,PEACEFUL CO-EXISTENCE: AN ANALYSIS OF SOVIET FOREIGN POLICY. WOR+45 INTELL SOCIETY ECO/UNDEV POL/PAR EDU/PROP COERCE DRIVE RIGID/FLEX PWR SKILL...PSY CONCPT HIST/WRIT CON/ANAL GEN/METH WORK VAL/FREE 20. PAGE 83 A1691 — PLAN DIPLOM USSR

B59
LAQUER W.Z.,THE SOVIET UNION AND THE MIDDLE EAST. COM UAR USSR ECO/UNDEV NAT/G VOL/ASSN ECO/TAC EDU/PROP COLONIAL EXEC PWR...TIME/SEQ TREND COLD/WAR 20. PAGE 85 A1730 — ISLAM DRIVE FOR/AID NAT/LISM

B59
OKINSHEVICH L.A.,LATIN AMERICA IN SOVIET WRITINGS, 1945-1958: A BIBLIOGRAPHY. USSR LAW ECO/UNDEV LABOR DIPLOM EDU/PROP REV...GEOG SOC 20. PAGE 111 A2287 — BIBLIOG WRITING COM L/A+17C

B59
PAGAN B.,HISTORIA DE LOS PARTIDOS POLITICOS PUERTORRIQUENOS 1898-1956. PUERT/RICO PROVS DIPLOM DOMIN EDU/PROP PARTIC 20. PAGE 113 A2316 — POL/PAR CHOOSE COLONIAL PWR

B59
SCHURZ W.L.,AMERICAN FOREIGN AFFAIRS: A GUIDE TO INTERNATIONAL AFFAIRS. USA+45 WOR+45 WOR-45 NAT/G FORCES LEGIS TOP/EX PLAN EDU/PROP LEGIT ADMIN ROUTINE ATTIT ORD/FREE PWR...SOC CONCPT STAT SAMP/SIZ CHARTS STERTYP 20. PAGE 129 A2653 — INT/ORG SOCIETY DIPLOM

B59
SHANNON D.A.,THE DECLINE OF AMERICAN COMMUNISM; A HISTORY OF THE COMMUNIST PARTY OF THE UNITED STATES SINCE 1945. USA+45 LAW SOCIETY LABOR NAT/G WORKER DIPLOM EDU/PROP LEAD...POLICY BIBLIOG 20 KHRUSH/N NEGRO AFL/CIO COLD/WAR COM/PARTY. PAGE 131 A2692 — MARXISM POL/PAR ATTIT POPULISM

B59
SWIFT R.W.,WORLD AFFAIRS AND THE COLLEGE CURRICULUM. USA+45 PLAN EFFICIENCY PERCEPT...HUM METH/CNCPT. PAGE 140 A2871 — ACADEM DIPLOM METH/COMP EDU/PROP

B59
THOMAS N.,THE PREREQUISITES FOR PEACE. ASIA EUR+WWI FUT ISLAM S/ASIA WOR+45 FORCES PLAN BAL/PWR EDU/PROP LEGIT ATTIT PWR...SOCIALIST CONCPT COLD/WAR 20 UN. PAGE 143 A2924 — INT/ORG ORD/FREE ARMS/CONT PEACE

B59
VORSPAN A.,JUSTICE AND JUDAISM. FAM DIPLOM ECO/TAC EDU/PROP CRIME RACE/REL MARRIAGE ANOMIE ATTIT ORD/FREE...POLICY 20 UN. PAGE 160 A3254 — SECT CULTURE ACT/RES GP/REL

B59
YOUNG J.,CHECKLIST OF MICROFILM REPRODUCTIONS OF SELECTED ARCHIVES OF THE JAPANESE ARMY, NAVY, AND OTHER GOVT AGENCIES, 1868-1945. DELIB/GP LEGIS DIPLOM EDU/PROP CIVMIL/REL 19/20 CHINJAP. PAGE 169 A3436 — BIBLIOG ASIA FORCES WAR

L59
GRANDIN T.,"THE POLITICAL USE OF THE RADIO." EUR+WWI SOCIETY INT/ORG DIPLOM CONTROL ATTIT ORD/FREE...CONCPT STAT RECORD SAMP GEN/LAWS TOT/POP 20. PAGE 55 A1128 — COM/IND EDU/PROP NAT/LISM

L59
KAPLAN M.A.,"SOME PROBLEMS IN THE STRATEGIC ANALYSIS OF INTERNATIONAL POLITICS." UNIV R+D INT/ORG CREATE PLAN DIPLOM EDU/PROP COERCE DISPL PWR...METH/CNCPT NEW/IDEA HYPO/EXP TOT/POP 20. PAGE 76 A1561 — DECISION BAL/PWR

L59
MCDOUGAL M.S.,"THE IDENTIFICATION AND APPRAISAL OF DIVERSE SYSTEMS OF PUBLIC ORDER (BMR)" WOR+45 NAT/G CONSULT EDU/PROP POLICY. PAGE 98 A2005 — INT/LAW DIPLOM ALL/IDEOS

S59
BROMKE A.,"DISENGAGEMENT IN EAST EUROPE." COM USSR INT/ORG DIPLOM EDU/PROP NEUTRAL NUC/PWR DRIVE RIGID/FLEX PWR...PSY CONCPT CON/ANAL GEN/METH VAL/FREE 20. PAGE 19 A0388 — BAL/PWR

S59
HOFFMANN S.,"IMPLEMENTATION OF INTERNATIONAL INSTRUMENTS ON HUMAN RIGHTS." WOR+45 VOL/ASSN DELIB/GP JUDGE EDU/PROP LEGIT ROUTINE PEACE COLD/WAR 20. PAGE 66 A1355 — INT/ORG MORAL

S59
LASSWELL H.D.,"UNIVERSALITY IN PERSPECTIVE." FUT UNIV SOCIETY CONSULT TOP/EX PLAN EDU/PROP ADJUD ROUTINE ARMS/CONT COERCE PEACE ATTIT PERSON ALL/VALS. PAGE 85 A1741 — INT/ORG JURID TOTALISM

S59
PUGWASH CONFERENCE,"ON BIOLOGICAL AND CHEMICAL WARFARE." WOR+45 SOCIETY PROC/MFG INT/ORG FORCES EDU/PROP ADJUD RIGID/FLEX ORD/FREE PWR...DECISION PSY NEW/IDEA MATH VAL/FREE 20. PAGE 118 A2417 — ACT/RES BIO/SOC WAR WEAPON

C59
KULSKI W.W.,"PEACEFUL COEXISTENCE." USSR ECO/UNDEV INT/ORG POL/PAR EDU/PROP COLONIAL CONTROL REV NAT/LISM PEACE PWR MARXISM...BIBLIOG 20. PAGE 83 A1692 — COM DIPLOM DOMIN

B60

ARMS CONTROL. FUT UNIV WOR+45 INTELL R+D INT/ORG NAT/G VOL/ASSN CONSULT CREATE EDU/PROP PEACE...HUM GEN/LAWS TOT/POP 20. PAGE 3 A0060

DELIB/GP ORD/FREE ARMS/CONT NUC/PWR

B60

BAILEY S.D.,THE GENERAL ASSEMBLY OF THE UNITED NATIONS. FUT WOR+45 STRUCT LEGIS ACT/RES PLAN EDU/PROP LEGIT ADMIN EXEC PEACE ATTIT HEALTH PWR ...CONCPT TREND CHARTS GEN/LAWS UN TOT/POP VAL/FREE COLD/WAR 20. PAGE 10 A0204

INT/ORG DELIB/GP DIPLOM

B60

BARNET R.,WHO WANTS DISARMAMENT. COM EUR+WWI USA+45 USSR INT/ORG NAT/G BAL/PWR DIPLOM EDU/PROP COERCE DETER NUC/PWR WAR WEAPON ATTIT PWR...TIME/SEQ COLD/WAR CONGRESS 20. PAGE 11 A0225

PLAN FORCES ARMS/CONT

B60

BILLERBECK K.,SOVIET BLOC FOREIGN AID TO UNDERDEVELOPED COUNTRIES. COM FUT USSR FINAN FORCES TEC/DEV DIPLOM INT/TRADE EDU/PROP NUC/PWR...TREND 20. PAGE 14 A0287

FOR/AID ECO/UNDEV ECO/TAC MARXISM

B60

BROOKINGS INSTITUTION,UNITED STATES FOREIGN POLICY: STUDY NO 9: THE FORMULATION AND ADMINISTRATION OF UNITED STATES FOREIGN POLICY. USA+45 WOR+45 EX/STRUC LEGIS BAL/PWR FOR/AID EDU/PROP CIVMIL/REL GOV/REL...INT COLD/WAR. PAGE 19 A0394

DIPLOM INT/ORG CREATE

B60

CAMPAIGNE J.G.,AMERICAN MIGHT AND SOVIET MYTH. COM EUR+WWI ECO/DEV ECO/UNDEV INT/ORG NAT/G CAP/ISM ECO/TAC FOR/AID EDU/PROP ATTIT PWR WEALTH...POLICY CONCPT MYTH TREND STERTYP GEN/LAWS COLD/WAR. PAGE 23 A0473

USA+45 DOMIN DIPLOM USSR

B60

CARNEGIE ENDOWMENT INT. PEACE,PERSPECTIVES ON PEACE - 1910-1960. WOR+45 WOR-45 INTELL INT/ORG CONSULT ACT/RES EDU/PROP ATTIT KNOWL ORD/FREE...TIME/SEQ TREND EEC OAS UNESCO NAZI 20. PAGE 24 A0489

FUT CONCPT ARMS/CONT PEACE

B60

DAVIDS J.,AMERICA AND THE WORLD OF OUR TIME: UNITED STATES DIPLOMACY IN THE TWENTIETH CENTURY. USA-45 SOCIETY ECO/DEV INT/ORG NAT/G POL/PAR FORCES ECO/TAC DOMIN EDU/PROP EXEC COERCE WAR CHOOSE ATTIT PERSON ORD/FREE...CONCPT TIME/SEQ TOT/POP 20. PAGE 34 A0686

USA+45 PWR DIPLOM

B60

HOLT R.T.,STRATEGIC PSYCHOLOGICAL OPERATIONS AND AMERICAN FOREIGN POLICY. ITALY USA+45 FOR/AID DOMIN RUMOR ADMIN TASK WAR CHOOSE ATTIT ALL/IDEOS...PSY COLD/WAR. PAGE 67 A1375

EDU/PROP ACT/RES DIPLOM POLICY

B60

HYDE L.K.G.,THE US AND THE UN. WOR+45 STRUCT ECO/DEV ECO/UNDEV NAT/G ACT/RES PLAN DIPLOM EDU/PROP ADMIN ALL/VALS...CONCPT TIME/SEQ GEN/LAWS UN VAL/FREE 20. PAGE 70 A1428

USA+45 INT/ORG FOR/AID

B60

JACOBSON H.K.,AMERICAN FOREIGN POLICY. COM EUR+WWI USA+45 USA-45 ECO/DEV ECO/UNDEV INT/ORG NAT/G INT/TRADE EDU/PROP COLONIAL CHOOSE MARXISM 20 NATO. PAGE 72 A1485

POL/PAR PWR DIPLOM

B60

JENNINGS R.,PROGRESS OF INTERNATIONAL LAW. FUT WOR+45 WOR-45 SOCIETY NAT/G VOL/ASSN DELIB/GP DIPLOM EDU/PROP LEGIT COERCE ATTIT DRIVE MORAL ORD/FREE...JURID CONCPT OBS TIME/SEQ TREND GEN/LAWS. PAGE 74 A1509

INT/ORG LAW INT/LAW

B60

KARDELJE,SOCIALISM AND WAR. CHINA/COM WOR+45 YUGOSLAVIA DIPLOM EDU/PROP ATTIT...POLICY CONCPT IDEA/COMP COLD/WAR. PAGE 76 A1565

MARXIST WAR MARXISM BAL/PWR

B60

KHRUSHCHEV N.S.,KHRUSHCHEV IN AMERICA. USA+45 USSR INT/TRADE EDU/PROP PRESS PEACE...MARXIST RECORD INT 20 COLD/WAR KHRUSH/N. PAGE 79 A1613

MARXISM CHIEF DIPLOM

B60

LISTER L.,EUROPE'S COAL AND STEEL COMMUNITY. FRANCE GERMANY STRUCT ECO/DEV EXTR/IND INDUS MARKET NAT/G DELIB/GP ECO/TAC INT/TRADE EDU/PROP ATTIT RIGID/FLEX ORD/FREE PWR WEALTH...CONCPT STAT TIME/SEQ CHARTS ECSC 20. PAGE 90 A1843

EUR+WWI INT/ORG REGION

B60

MUNRO L.,UNITED NATIONS, HOPE FOR A DIVIDED WORLD. FUT WOR+45 CONSTN DELIB/GP CREATE TEC/DEV DIPLOM EDU/PROP LEGIT PEACE ATTIT HEALTH ORD/FREE PWR ...CONCPT TREND UN VAL/FREE 20. PAGE 106 A2172

INT/ORG ROUTINE

B60

PENTONY D.E.,THE UNDERDEVELOPED LANDS. FUT WOR+45 CULTURE AGRI FINAN INDUS MARKET INT/ORG LABOR NAT/G VOL/ASSN CONSULT TEC/DEV ECO/TAC EDU/PROP COLONIAL ATTIT WEALTH...OBS RECORD SAMP TREND GEN/METH WORK UN 20. PAGE 115 A2351

ECO/UNDEV POLICY FOR/AID INT/TRADE

B60

PLAMENATZ J.,ON ALIEN RULE AND SELF-GOVERNMENT. AFR FUT S/ASIA WOR+45 CULTURE SOCIETY ECO/UNDEV INT/ORG DOMIN EDU/PROP ATTIT RIGID/FLEX ALL/VALS...POLICY CONCPT OBS TREND CON/ANAL GEN/LAWS TOT/POP VAL/FREE. PAGE 116 A2386

NAT/G CONSTN NAT/LISM SOVEREIGN

B60

SCANLON D.G.,INTERNATIONAL EDUCATION: A DOCUMENTARY HISTORY. ADMIN CONTROL ATTIT PERCEPT...BIOG ANTHOL METH 20. PAGE 127 A2612

EDU/PROP INT/ORG NAT/COMP DIPLOM

B60

SETON-WATSON H.,NEITHER WAR NOR PEACE. ASIA USSR WOR+45 ELITES INT/ORG NAT/G EX/STRUC FORCES BAL/PWR ECO/TAC EDU/PROP COERCE NAT/LISM ORD/FREE WEALTH TOT/POP 20. PAGE 131 A2688

ATTIT PWR DIPLOM TOTALISM

B60

SHONFIELD A.,THE ATTACK ON WORLD POVERTY. WOR+45 ECO/DEV ECO/UNDEV FINAN VOL/ASSN PLAN EDU/PROP DRIVE KNOWL WEALTH...CONT/OBS STAND/INT ORG/CHARTS TOT/POP UNESCO 20. PAGE 132 A2704

INT/ORG ECO/TAC FOR/AID INT/TRADE

B60

SPEIER H.,DIVIDED BERLIN: THE ANATOMY OF SOVIET POLITICAL BLACKMAIL. COM GERMANY USA+45 USSR WOR+45 NAT/G TOP/EX DOMIN EDU/PROP ALL/VALS...POLICY CONCPT COLD/WAR 20 U-2. PAGE 136 A2782

INT/ORG ACT/RES DIPLOM

B60

STEVENSON A.E.,PUTTING FIRST THINGS FIRST. USA+45 INT/ORG NEIGH FOR/AID DISCRIM...ANTHOL 20. PAGE 138 A2822

DIPLOM ECO/UNDEV ORD/FREE EDU/PROP

B60

WOLF C.,FOREIGN AID: THEORY AND PRACTICE IN SOUTHERN ASIA. CEYLON INDONESIA PHILIPPINE S/ASIA CULTURE STRATA ECO/UNDEV PLAN EDU/PROP ATTIT ...METH/CNCPT MATH QUANT STAT CONT/OBS TIME/SEQ SIMUL TOT/POP 20. PAGE 166 A3378

ACT/RES ECO/TAC FOR/AID

L60

DEUTSCH K.W.,"TOWARD AN INVENTORY OF BASIC TRENDS AND PATTERNS IN COMPARATIVE AND INTERNATIONAL POLITICS." UNIV WOR+45 SOCIETY STRUCT INT/ORG NAT/G CREATE PLAN EDU/PROP KNOWL...PHIL/SCI METH/CNCPT STAT SELF/OBS OBS/ENVIR SAMP TREND CON/ANAL CHARTS SOC/EXP GEN/METH 20. PAGE 36 A0739

R+D PERCEPT

L60

FERNBACH A.P.,"SOVIET COEXISTENCE STRATEGY." WOR+45 PROF/ORG VOL/ASSN DIPLOM DOMIN EDU/PROP ATTIT DRIVE PERSON PWR SKILL WEALTH...POLICY OBS SAMP TREND STERTYP ILO WORK COLD/WAR 420. PAGE 45 A0919

LABOR INT/ORG USSR

L60

HOLTON G.,"ARMS CONTROL." FUT WOR+45 CULTURE INT/ORG NAT/G FORCES TOP/EX PLAN EDU/PROP COERCE ATTIT RIGID/FLEX ORD/FREE...POLICY PHIL/SCI SOC TREND COLD/WAR. PAGE 67 A1377

ACT/RES CONSULT ARMS/CONT NUC/PWR

L60

JACOB P.E.,"THE DISARMAMENT CONSENSUS." USA+45 USSR WOR+45 INT/ORG NAT/G ACT/RES TEC/DEV BAL/PWR EDU/PROP ADMIN COERCE DETER NUC/PWR CONSEN RIGID/FLEX PWR...CONCPT RECORD CHARTS COLD/WAR 20. PAGE 72 A1482

DELIB/GP ATTIT ARMS/CONT

L60

MCCLELLAND C.A.,"THE FUNCTION OF THEORY IN INTERNATIONAL RELATIONS." WOR+45 PLAN EDU/PROP ROUTINE ORD/FREE...PHIL/SCI PSY SOC METH/CNCPT NEW/IDEA OBS TREND GEN/METH 20. PAGE 97 A1997

INT/ORG CONCPT DIPLOM

L60

NOGEE J.L.,"THE DIPLOMACY OF DISARMAMENT." WOR+45 INT/ORG NAT/G CONSULT DELIB/GP TOP/EX BAL/PWR DIPLOM EDU/PROP COERCE DETER WEAPON PEACE ATTIT ...RECORD TIME/SEQ TOT/POP VAL/FREE COLD/WAR 20. PAGE 109 A2246

PWR ORD/FREE ARMS/CONT NUC/PWR

L60

RIGGS R.,"OVER-SELLING THE U.N. CHARTER, FACT AND MYTH." USA+45 SOCIETY NAT/G TOP/EX PLAN DIPLOM EDU/PROP PEACE ATTIT PERCEPT MORAL...POLICY SAMP UN 20. PAGE 121 A2481

INT/ORG MYTH

S60

BOGARDUS E.S.,"THE SOCIOLOGY OF A STRUCTURED PEACE." FUT SOCIETY CREATE DIPLOM EDU/PROP ADJUD ROUTINE ATTIT RIGID/FLEX KNOWL ORD/FREE RESPECT ...POLICY INT/LAW JURID NEW/IDEA SELF/OBS TOT/POP 20 UN. PAGE 16 A0327

INT/ORG SOC NAT/LISM PEACE

S60

DOUGHERTY J.E.,"KEY TO SECURITY: DISARMAMENT OR ARMS STABILITY." COM USA+45 USSR INT/ORG NAT/G CREATE EDU/PROP COERCE DETER ATTIT PWR...DECISION CONCPT MYTH NEW/IDEA TREND 20 COLD/WAR. PAGE 38 A0777

FORCES ORD/FREE ARMS/CONT NUC/PWR

S60

GINSBURGS G.,"PEKING-LHASA-NEW DELHI." CHINA/COM FUT INDIA S/ASIA KIN NAT/G PROVS SECT FORCES BAL/PWR ECO/TAC DOMIN EDU/PROP LEGIT ADMIN REGION GUERRILLA PWR...TREND TIBET 20. PAGE 52 A1074

ASIA COERCE DIPLOM

S60

GOODMAN E.,"THE CRY OF NATIONAL LIBERATION: RECENT SOVIET ATTITUDES TOWARDS NATIONAL SELF-DETERMINATION." COM INT/ORG LEGIS ROUTINE PWR ...TIME/SEQ CON/ANAL STERTYP GEN/LAWS 20 UN. PAGE 54 A1101

ATTIT EDU/PROP SOVEREIGN USSR

S60
GOODRICH L.,"GEOGRAPHICAL DISTRIBUTION OF THE STAFF OF THE UN SECRETARIAT." FUT WOR+45 CONSTN BAL/PWR DIPLOM EDU/PROP LEGIT ROUTINE RIGID/FLEX...CHARTS UN 20. PAGE 54 A1105
INT/ORG EX/STRUC

S60
IKLE F.C.,"NTH COUNTRIES AND DISARMAMENT." WOR+45 DELIB/GP ECO/TAC DOMIN EDU/PROP LEGIT ROUTINE COERCE RIGID/FLEX ORD/FREE...MARXIST TREND 20. PAGE 70 A1432
FUT INT/ORG ARMS/CONT NUC/PWR

S60
KALUODA J.,"COMMUNIST STRATEGY IN LATIN AMERICA." L/A+17C USA+45 INT/ORG NAT/G POL/PAR DIPLOM ECO/TAC EDU/PROP COERCE WEALTH...CONCPT OAS COLD/WAR 20. PAGE 76 A1553
COM PWR CUBA

S60
KISTIAKOWSKY G.B.,"SCIENCE AND FOREIGN AFFAIRS." FUT WOR+45 NAT/G PROF/ORG PLAN ECO/TAC EDU/PROP NUC/PWR...TREND COLD/WAR 20. PAGE 80 A1645
CONSULT TEC/DEV FOR/AID DIPLOM

S60
LEAR J.,"PEACE: SCIENCE'S NEXT GREAT EXPLORATION." USA+45 INT/ORG TOP/EX TEC/DEV EDU/PROP ROUTINE PEACE KNOWL SKILL 20. PAGE 86 A1757
EX/STRUC ARMS/CONT NUC/PWR

S60
MIKESELL R.F.,"AMERICA'S ECONOMIC RESPONSIBILITY AS A GREAT POWER." COM FUT USA+45 USSR WOR+45 INT/ORG PLAN ECO/TAC FOR/AID EDU/PROP CHOOSE WEALTH ...POLICY 20. PAGE 101 A2069
ECO/UNDEV BAL/PWR CAP/ISM

S60
MORA J.A.,"THE ORGANIZATION OF AMERICAN STATES." USA+45 LAW ECO/UNDEV VOL/ASSN DELIB/GP PLAN BAL/PWR EDU/PROP ADMIN DRIVE RIGID/FLEX ORD/FREE WEALTH ...TIME/SEQ GEN/LAWS OAS 20. PAGE 103 A2126
L/A+17C INT/ORG REGION

S60
PETERSON E.N.,"HISTORICAL SCHOLARSHIP AND WORLD UNITY." FUT UNIV WOR-45 CULTURE INTELL INT/ORG NAT/G ACT/RES EDU/PROP ATTIT PERCEPT RIGID/FLEX ...NEW/IDEA OBS HIST/WRIT TREND COLD/WAR TOT/POP 20. PAGE 115 A2367
PLAN KNOWL NAT/LISM

S60
RHYNE C.S.,"LAW AS AN INSTRUMENT FOR PEACE." FUT WOR+45 PLAN LEGIT ROUTINE ARMS/CONT NUC/PWR ATTIT ORD/FREE...JURID METH/CNCPT TREND CON/ANAL HYPO/EXP COLD/WAR 20. PAGE 120 A2471
ADJUD EDU/PROP INT/LAW PEACE

S60
RUSSEL R.W.,"ROLES FOR PSYCHOLOGISTS IN THE MAINTENANCE OF PEACE." FUT USA+45 CULTURE INT/ORG DIPLOM FOR/AID EDU/PROP ATTIT KNOWL MORAL PWR ...POLICY SOC COLD/WAR 20. PAGE 125 A2572
PSY GEN/METH

S60
SWIFT R.,"THE UNITED NATIONS AND ITS PUBLIC." WOR+45 CONSTN FINAN CONSULT DELIB/GP ACT/RES ADMIN ROUTINE RIGID/FLEX SKILL UN 20. PAGE 140 A2870
INT/ORG EDU/PROP

C60
FITZSIMMONS T.,"USSR: ITS PEOPLE, ITS SOCIETY, ITS CULTURE." USSR FAM SECT DIPLOM EDU/PROP ADMIN RACE/REL ATTIT...POLICY CHARTS BIBLIOG 20. PAGE 46 A0944
CULTURE STRUCT SOCIETY COM

B61
AMORY J.F.,AROUND THE EDGE OF WAR: A NEW APPROACH TO THE PROBLEMS OF AMERICAN FOREIGN POLICY. COM L/A+17C USA+45 USSR FOR/AID EDU/PROP AGREE CONTROL ARMS/CONT NUC/PWR WAR PWR...IDEA/COMP 20 TREATY ESPIONAGE. PAGE 8 A0154
NAT/G DIPLOM POLICY

B61
ASIA SOCIETY,AMERICAN INSTITUTIONS ANS ORGANIZATIONS INTERESTED IN ASIA; A REFERENCE DIRECTORY (2ND ED.). ASIA USA+45 CULTURE SECT DIPLOM EDU/PROP...INDEX 20. PAGE 9 A0190
VOL/ASSN ACADEM PROF/ORG

B61
BARNES W.,THE FOREIGN SERVICE OF THE UNITED STATES. USA+45 USA-45 CONSTN INT/ORG POL/PAR CONSULT DELIB/GP LEGIS DOMIN EDU/PROP EXEC ATTIT RIGID/FLEX ORD/FREE PWR...POLICY CONCPT STAT OBS RECORD BIOG TIME/SEQ TREND. PAGE 11 A0224
NAT/G MGT DIPLOM

B61
BECHHOEFER B.G.,POSTWAR NEGOTIATIONS FOR ARMS CONTROL. COM EUR+WWI USSR INT/ORG NAT/G ACT/RES BAL/PWR DIPLOM ECO/TAC EDU/PROP ADMIN REGION DETER NUC/PWR WAR WEAPON PEACE ATTIT PWR...POLICY TIME/SEQ COLD/WAR CONGRESS 20. PAGE 12 A0244
USA+45 ARMS/CONT

B61
BISHOP D.G.,THE ADMINISTRATION OF BRITISH FOREIGN RELATIONS. EUR+WWI MOD/EUR INT/ORG NAT/G POL/PAR DELIB/GP LEGIS TOP/EX ECO/TAC DOMIN EDU/PROP ADMIN COERCE 20. PAGE 14 A0292
ROUTINE PWR DIPLOM UK

B61
BURDETTE F.L.,POLITICAL SCIENCE: A SELECTED BIBLIOGRAPHY OF BOOKS IN PRINT, WITH ANNOTATIONS (PAMPHLET). LAW LOC/G NAT/G POL/PAR PROVS DIPLOM EDU/PROP ADMIN CHOOSE ATTIT 20. PAGE 21 A0432
BIBLIOG/A GOV/COMP CONCPT ROUTINE

B61
COLLISON R.L.,BIBLIOGRAPHICAL SERVICES THROUGHOUT THE WORLD: 1950-59 (VOL. 9). WOR+45 INT/ORG EDU/PROP PRESS WRITING ADMIN CENTRAL 20 UNESCO. PAGE 28 A0568
BIBLIOG COM/IND DIPLOM

B61
DALLIN D.J.,SOVIET FOREIGN POLICY AFTER STALIN. ASIA CHINA/COM EUR+WWI GERMANY IRAN UK YUGOSLAVIA INT/ORG NAT/G VOL/ASSN FORCES TOP/EX BAL/PWR DOMIN EDU/PROP COERCE ATTIT PWR 20. PAGE 33 A0679
COM DIPLOM USSR

B61
DIA M.,THE AFRICAN NATIONS AND WORLD SOLIDARITY. ISLAM CULTURE ELITES ECO/DEV ECO/UNDEV INT/ORG NAT/G PLAN ECO/TAC INT/TRADE EDU/PROP NAT/LISM ATTIT DRIVE ORD/FREE WEALTH...SOCIALIST CONCPT CON/ANAL GEN/LAWS TOT/POP 20. PAGE 37 A0753
AFR REGION SOCISM

B61
EISENHOWER D.D.,PEACE WITH JUSTICE: SELECTED ADDRESSES. USSR PARTIC ARMS/CONT MORAL...TRADIT CONCPT GEN/LAWS ANTHOL 20 PRESIDENT COLD/WAR. PAGE 41 A0832
PEACE DIPLOM EDU/PROP POLICY

B61
GRAEBNER N.,THE NEW ISOLATIONISM: A STUDY IN POLITICS AND FOREIGN POLICY SINCE 1960. USA+45 INT/ORG LOC/G NAT/G POL/PAR LEGIS BAL/PWR EDU/PROP CHOOSE ATTIT PERSON ORD/FREE 20 TRUMAN/HS EISNHWR/DD. PAGE 55 A1120
EXEC PWR DIPLOM

B61
HADDAD J.A.,REVOLUCAO CUBANA E REVOLUCAO BRASILEIRA. BRAZIL CUBA L/A+17C STRATA AGRI WORKER EDU/PROP REGION...POLICY NAT/COMP 20. PAGE 59 A1210
REV ORD/FREE DIPLOM ECO/UNDEV

B61
HASAN H.S.,PAKISTAN AND THE UN. ISLAM WOR+45 ECO/DEV ECO/UNDEV NAT/G TOP/EX ECO/TAC FOR/AID EDU/PROP ADMIN DRIVE PERCEPT...OBS TIME/SEQ UN 20. PAGE 62 A1284
INT/ORG ATTIT PAKISTAN

B61
HENKIN L.,ARMS CONTROL: ISSUES FOR THE PUBLIC. EUR+WWI FUT USA+45 USSR INT/ORG NAT/G DIPLOM EDU/PROP DETER NUC/PWR ATTIT PWR...CONCPT RECORD HIST/WRIT TIME/SEQ TOT/POP COLD/WAR 20. PAGE 64 A1316
WOR+45 DELIB/GP ARMS/CONT

B61
HISTORICAL RESEARCH INSTITUTE,A SHORT BIBLIOGRAPHY OF INDO-MUSLIM HISTORY. INDIA S/ASIA DIPLOM EDU/PROP COLONIAL LEAD NAT/LISM ATTIT...BIOG 19/20. PAGE 65 A1343
BIBLIOG NAT/G SECT POL/PAR

B61
JENKS C.W.,INTERNATIONAL IMMUNITIES. PLAN EDU/PROP ADMIN PERCEPT...OLD/LIB JURID CONCPT TREND TOT/POP. PAGE 74 A1506
INT/ORG DIPLOM

B61
LERCHE C.O. JR.,FOREIGN POLICY OF THE AMERICAN PEOPLE (REV. ED.). USA+45 USSR FORCES TEC/DEV EDU/PROP WAR PRODUC ORD/FREE MARXISM...POLICY TREND BIBLIOG 20 COLD/WAR. PAGE 87 A1781
DECISION PLAN PEACE DIPLOM

B61
LETHBRIDGE H.J.,CHINA'S URBAN COMMUNES. CHINA/COM FUT ECO/UNDEV DIPLOM EDU/PROP DEMAND INCOME MARXISM ...POLICY 20. PAGE 87 A1790
MUNIC CONTROL ECO/TAC NAT/G

B61
LUKACS J.,A HISTORY OF THE COLD WAR. ASIA COM EUR+WWI USA+45 USA-45 INT/ORG NAT/G DELIB/GP ACT/RES BAL/PWR DIPLOM DOMIN EDU/PROP LEGIT DRIVE ORD/FREE...TREND COLD/WAR 20. PAGE 91 A1872
PWR TIME/SEQ USSR

B61
MCDOUGAL M.S.,LAW AND MINIMUM WORLD PUBLIC ORDER. WOR+45 SOCIETY NAT/G DELIB/GP EDU/PROP LEGIT ADJUD COERCE ATTIT PERSON...JURID CONCPT RECORD TREND TOT/POP 20. PAGE 98 A2006
INT/ORG ORD/FREE INT/LAW

B61
NOGEE J.L.,SOVIET POLICY TOWARD INTERNATIONAL CONTROL OF ATOMIC ENERGY. COM USA+45 WOR+45 INTELL NAT/G ACT/RES DIPLOM EDU/PROP NUC/PWR TOTALISM PERCEPT KNOWL PWR...TIME/SEQ COLD/WAR 20. PAGE 109 A2247
INT/ORG ATTIT ARMS/CONT USSR

B61
OVERSTREET H.,THE WAR CALLED PEACE. USSR WOR+45 COM/IND INT/ORG POL/PAR BAL/PWR EDU/PROP PEACE ATTIT...CONCPT 20 KHRUSH/N. PAGE 112 A2302
DIPLOM COM POLICY LEAD

B61
SOCIAL SCIENCE SERIALS IN SPECIAL LIBRARIES IN THE NEW YORK AREA; A SELECTED LIST. R+D ACADEM EDU/PROP WRITING...PSY 20. PAGE 119 A2448
BIBLIOG DIPLOM SOC

B61
RIENOW R.,CONTEMPORARY INTERNATIONAL POLITICS. WOR+45 INT/ORG BAL/PWR EDU/PROP COLONIAL NEUTRAL REGION WAR PEACE...INT/LAW 20 COLD/WAR UN. PAGE 121 A2476
DIPLOM PWR POLICY NAT/G

B61
ROBINSON M.E.,EDUCATION FOR SOCIAL CHANGE: ESTABLISHING INSTITUTES OF PUBLIC AND BUSINESS ADMINISTRATION ABROAD (PAMPHLET). WOR+45 SOCIETY ACADEM CONFER INGP/REL ROLE...SOC CHARTS BIBLIOG 20 ICA. PAGE 122 A2506
FOR/AID EDU/PROP MGT ADJUST

B61
ROSENAU J.N.,PUBLIC OPINION AND FOREIGN POLICY; AN
ATTIT

OPERATIONAL FORMULA. USA+45 COM/IND OP/RES EDU/PROP LOBBY CROWD...CON/ANAL BIBLIOG 20. PAGE 124 A2532
PRESS DIPLOM

B61
SHARP W.R.,FIELD ADMINISTRATION IN THE UNITED NATION SYSTEM: THE CONDUCT OF INTERNATIONAL ECONOMIC AND SOCIAL PROGRAMS. FUT WOR+45 CONSTN SOCIETY ECO/UNDEV R+D DELIB/GP ACT/RES PLAN TEC/DEV EDU/PROP EXEC ROUTINE HEALTH WEALTH...HUM CONCPT CHARTS METH ILO UNESCO VAL/FREE UN 20. PAGE 132 A2697
INT/ORG CONSULT

B61
STILLMAN E.,THE NEW POLITICS: AMERICA AND THE END OF THE POSTWAR WORLD. FUT WOR+45 CULTURE SOCIETY ECO/UNDEV INT/ORG NAT/G FORCES TOP/EX ACT/RES DIPLOM EDU/PROP LEGIT ROUTINE DETER ATTIT ORD/FREE PWR...OBS STERTYP COLD/WAR TOT/POP VAL/FREE. PAGE 138 A2827
USA+45 PLAN

B61
STRAUSZ-HUPE R.,A FORWARD STRATEGY FOR AMERICA. FUT WOR+45 ECO/DEV INT/ORG NAT/G POL/PAR DELIB/GP FORCES ACT/RES CREATE ECO/TAC DOMIN EDU/PROP ATTIT DRIVE PWR...MAJORIT CONCPT STAT OBS TIME/SEQ TREND COLD/WAR TOT/POP. PAGE 139 A2848
USA+45 PLAN DIPLOM

B61
UAR MINISTRY OF CULTURE,A BIBLIOGRAPHICAL LIST OF TUNISIA. ISLAM CULTURE NAT/G EDU/PROP COLONIAL ...GEOG 19/20 TUNIS. PAGE 146 A2989
BIBLIOG DIPLOM SECT

B61
US LIBRARY OF CONGRESS,WORLD COMMUNIST MOVEMENT. USA+45 USSR WOR+45 INT/ORG DIPLOM REV ATTIT 19/20. PAGE 155 A3155
BIBLIOG/A EDU/PROP MARXISM POL/PAR

B61
ZIMMERMAN I.,A GUIDE TO CURRENT LATIN AMERICAN PERIODICALS: HUMANITIES AND SOCIAL SCIENCES. LABOR SECT EDU/PROP...GEOG HUM SOC LING STAT NAT/COMP 20. PAGE 170 A3452
BIBLIOG/A DIPLOM L/A+17C PHIL/SCI

L61
CLAUDE I.,"THE UNITED NATIONS AND THE USE OF FORCE." FUT WOR+45 SOCIETY DIPLOM EDU/PROP LEGIT ADMIN ROUTINE COERCE WAR PEACE ORD/FREE...CONCPT TREND UN 20. PAGE 27 A0545
INT/ORG FORCES

L61
HOYT E.C.,"UNITED STATES REACTION TO THE KOREAN ATTACK." COM KOREA USA+45 CONSTN DELIB/GP FORCES PLAN ECO/TAC DOMIN EDU/PROP LEGIT ROUTINE COERCE WAR ATTIT DISPL RIGID/FLEX ORD/FREE PWR...POLICY INT/LAW TREND UN 20. PAGE 68 A1402
ASIA INT/ORG BAL/PWR DIPLOM

S61
ALGER C.F.,"NON-RESOLUTION CONSEQUENCES OF THE UNITED NATIONS AND THEIR EFFECT ON INTERNATIONAL CONFLICT." WOR+45 CONSTN ECO/DEV NAT/G CONSULT DELIB/GP TOP/EX ACT/RES PLAN DIPLOM EDU/PROP ROUTINE ATTIT ALL/VALS...INT/LAW TOT/POP UN 20. PAGE 6 A0117
INT/ORG DRIVE BAL/PWR

S61
BRZEZINSKI Z.K.,"THE ORGANIZATION OF THE COMMUNIST CAMP." COM CZECHOSLVK COM/IND NAT/G DELIB/GP INT/TRADE DOMIN EDU/PROP EXEC ROUTINE COERCE ATTIT PWR...MGT CONCPT TIME/SEQ CHARTS VAL/FREE 20 TREATY. PAGE 20 A0416
VOL/ASSN DIPLOM USSR

S61
DEUTSCH K.W.,"NATIONAL INDUSTRIALIZATION AND THE DECLINING SHARE OF THE INTERNATIONAL ECONOMIC SECTOR." EUR+WWI FUT WOR+45 WOR-45 MARKET PLAN EDU/PROP WEALTH...WELF/ST OBS TESTS 20. PAGE 36 A0740
DIST/IND ECO/DEV INT/TRADE

S61
GALBRAITH J.K.,"A POSITIVE APPROACH TO ECONOMIC AID." FUT USA+45 INTELL NAT/G CONSULT ACT/RES DIPLOM ECO/TAC EDU/PROP ATTIT KNOWL PWR WEALTH ...SOC STERTYP 20. PAGE 50 A1030
ECO/UNDEV ROUTINE FOR/AID

S61
KRANNHALS H.V.,"COMMAND INTEGRATION WITHIN THE WARSAW PACT." COM USSR WOR+45 DELIB/GP EDU/PROP ...CONCPT AUD/VIS CHARTS COLD/WAR TOT/POP VAL/FREE 20 TREATY WARSAW/P. PAGE 82 A1675
INT/ORG FORCES TOTALISM

S61
MACHOWSKI K.,"SELECTED PROBLEMS OF NATIONAL SOVEREIGNTY WITH REFERENCE TO THE LAW OF OUTER SPACE." FUT WOR+45 AIR LAW INTELL SOCIETY ECO/DEV PLAN EDU/PROP DETER DRIVE PERCEPT SOVEREIGN ...POLICY INT/LAW OBS TREND TOT/POP 20. PAGE 92 A1889
UNIV ACT/RES NUC/PWR SPACE

S61
NOVE A.,"THE SOVIET MODEL AND UNDERDEVELOPED COUNTRIES." COM FUT USSR WOR+45 CULTURE ECO/DEV POL/PAR FOR/AID EDU/PROP ADMIN MORAL WEALTH ...POLICY RECORD HIST/WRIT 20. PAGE 110 A2258
ECO/UNDEV PLAN

S61
RALEIGH J.S.,"THE MIDDLE EAST IN 1960: A POLITICAL SURVEY." FUT ISLAM INTELL KIN BAL/PWR EDU/PROP NAT/LISM...TREND VAL/FREE 20. PAGE 119 A2435
INT/ORG EX/STRUC

S61
SINGER J.D.,"THE LEVEL OF ANALYSIS: PROBLEMS IN INTERNATIONAL RELATIONS." FUT INTELL R+D INT/ORG CREATE EDU/PROP...METH/CNCPT HYPO/EXP GEN/METH METH VAL/FREE. PAGE 133 A2725
SOCIETY SOC DIPLOM

S61
TRAMPE G.,"DIE FORM DER DIPLOMATIC ALS POLITSCHE WAFFE." WOR+45 WOR-45 SOCIETY STRATA INT/ORG NAT/G ACT/RES PLAN ECO/TAC EDU/PROP COERCE WAR ATTIT RIGID/FLEX...DECISION CONCPT TREND. PAGE 145 A2959
CONSULT PWR DIPLOM

B62
ARNOLD H.J.P.,AID FOR DEVELOPING COUNTRIES. COM EUR+WWI USA+45 USSR WOR+45 EDU/PROP ATTIT DRIVE PWR WEALTH...TREND CHARTS STERTYP NAT/ 20. PAGE 9 A0177
ECO/UNDEV ECO/TAC FOR/AID

B62
BAILEY S.D.,THE SECRETARIAT OF THE UNITED NATIONS. FUT WOR+45 DELIB/GP PLAN BAL/PWR DOMIN EDU/PROP ADMIN PEACE ATTIT PWR...DECISION CONCPT TREND CON/ANAL CHARTS UN VAL/FREE COLD/WAR 20. PAGE 10 A0205
INT/ORG EXEC DIPLOM

B62
BLANSHARD P.,FREEDOM AND CATHOLIC POWER IN SPAIN AND PORTUGAL: AN AMERICAN INTERPRETATION. AFR PORTUGAL SPAIN USA+45 LAW LABOR DIPLOM EDU/PROP DISCRIM ISOLAT TOTALISM 20 CHURCH/STA. PAGE 15 A0309
GP/REL FASCISM CATHISM PWR

B62
BOUSCAREN A.T.,SOVIET FOREIGN POLICY: A PATTERN OF PERSISTANCE. WOR+45 WOR-45 SOCIETY STRUCT INT/ORG POL/PAR CREATE PLAN EDU/PROP ROUTINE ATTIT RIGID/FLEX...POLICY CONCPT RECORD HIST/WRIT TIME/SEQ MARX/KARL 20. PAGE 17 A0352
COM NAT/G DIPLOM USSR

B62
BURTON J.W.,PEACE THEORY: PRECONDITIONS OF DISARMAMENT. COM EUR+WWI USA+45 NAT/G FORCES BAL/PWR DIPLOM ECO/TAC EDU/PROP REGION COERCE DETER PEACE ATTIT PWR TOT/POP COLD/WAR 20. PAGE 22 A0446
INT/ORG PLAN ARMS/CONT

B62
CADWELL R.,COMMUNISM IN THE MODERN WORLD. USSR WOR+45 SOCIETY AGRI INDUS INT/ORG SECT EDU/PROP COLONIAL PEACE...SOC 20. PAGE 23 A0463
COM DIPLOM POLICY CONCPT

B62
CALVOCORESSI P.,WORLD ORDER AND NEW STATES: PROBLEMS OF KEEPING THE PEACE. AFR EUR+WWI S/ASIA ELITES NAT/G ECO/TAC FOR/AID EDU/PROP COERCE ATTIT DRIVE ALL/VALS...GEN/LAWS COLD/WAR 20 UN. PAGE 23 A0471
INT/ORG PEACE

B62
CARDOZA M.H.,DIPLOMATS IN INTERNATIONAL COOPERATION: STEPCHILDREN OF THE FOREIGN SERVICE. EUR+WWI USA+45 NAT/G CONSULT ACT/RES EDU/PROP ROUTINE RIGID/FLEX KNOWL SKILL...SOC OBS TIME/SEQ EEC OEEC NATO 20. PAGE 24 A0480
INT/ORG METH/CNCPT DIPLOM

B62
COUNCIL ON WORLD TENSIONS,A STUDY OF WORLD TENSIONS AND DEVELOPMENT. WOR+45 ECO/DEV ECO/UNDEV INT/ORG PLAN DIPLOM ECO/TAC EDU/PROP ATTIT KNOWL ORD/FREE PWR WEALTH...CONCPT TREND CHARTS STERTYP COLD/WAR TOT/POP 20. PAGE 31 A0640
TEC/DEV SOC

B62
DALLIN A.,THE SOVIET UNION AT THE UNITED NATIONS: AN INQUIRY INTO SOVIET MOTIVES AND OBJECTIVES. ACT/RES EDU/PROP LEGIT ATTIT KNOWL PWR...POLICY RECORD HIST/WRIT TIME/SEQ TREND ORG/CHARTS GEN/METH COLD/WAR FAO 20 UN. PAGE 33 A0675
COM INT/ORG USSR

B62
DELANEY R.F.,THE LITERATURE OF COMMUNISM IN AMERICA. COM USA+45 USA-45 INT/ORG LABOR NAT/G POL/PAR INGP/REL...MAJORIT 20. PAGE 36 A0727
BIBLIOG/A MARXISM EDU/PROP IDEA/COMP

B62
DUROSELLE J.B.,LES NOUVEAUX ETATS DANS LES RELATIONS INTERNATIONALES. AFR CHINA/COM FRANCE MOROCCO S/ASIA USSR ECO/UNDEV INT/ORG PLAN ECO/TAC EDU/PROP ATTIT DRIVE...TREND TOT/POP TUNIS 20. PAGE 39 A0806
NAT/G CONSTN DIPLOM

B62
EBENSTEIN W.,TWO WAYS OF LIFE. USA+45 CULTURE ECO/DEV PLAN EDU/PROP CONTROL ORD/FREE...GOV/COMP IDEA/COMP T 20 MARX/KARL ENGELS/F LENIN/VI LOCKE/JOHN MILL/JS. PAGE 40 A0819
MARXISM POPULISM ECO/TAC DIPLOM

B62
ELLIOTT J.R.,THE APPEAL OF COMMUNISM IN THE UNDERDEVELOPED NATIONS. USSR WOR+45 INT/ORG NAT/G DIPLOM DOMIN EDU/PROP ROUTINE ATTIT RIGID/FLEX ORD/FREE PWR WEALTH MARXISM...POLICY SOC METH/CNCPT MYTH TOT/POP COLD/WAR 20. PAGE 41 A0842
COM ECO/UNDEV

B62
GILPIN R.,AMERICAN SCIENTISTS AND NUCLEAR WEAPONS POLICY. COM FUT USA+45 WOR+45 INT/ORG NAT/G PROF/ORG CONSULT FORCES CREATE TEC/DEV BAL/PWR EDU/PROP ARMS/CONT WAR PERCEPT KNOWL MORAL PWR ...PHIL/SCI SOC CONCPT GEN/LAWS 20. PAGE 52 A1073
INTELL ATTIT DETER NUC/PWR

B62
GRAEBNER N.,COLD WAR DIPLOMACY 1945-1960. WOR+45 INT/ORG ECO/TAC EDU/PROP COERCE ORD/FREE PWR WEALTH ...HIST/WRIT TOT/POP VAL/FREE COLD/WAR 20. PAGE 55 A1122
USA+45 DIPLOM

B62
GUENA Y.,HISTORIQUE DE LA COMMUNAUTE. FUT ECO/UNDEV NAT/G PLAN EDU/PROP COLONIAL REGION NAT/LISM ALL/VALS SOVEREIGN...CONCPT OBS CHARTS 20. PAGE 58 A1186
AFR VOL/ASSN FOR/AID FRANCE

B62
HADWEN J.G.,HOW UNITED NATIONS DECISIONS ARE MADE. WOR+45 LAW EDU/PROP LEGIT ADMIN PWR...DECISION SELF/OBS GEN/LAWS UN 20. PAGE 59 A1212
INT/ORG ROUTINE

B62
HATCH J.,AFRICA TODAY-AND TOMORROW: AN OUTLINE OF BASIC FACTS AND MAJOR PROBLEMS. AFR FUT ISLAM STRATA ECO/UNDEV INT/ORG NAT/G POL/PAR DELIB/GP TOP/EX EDU/PROP LEGIT CHOOSE ATTIT...TIME/SEQ TOT/POP COLD/WAR 20. PAGE 63 A1287
PLAN CONSTN NAT/LISM

B62
HENDRICKS D.,PAMPHLETS ON THE FIRST WORLD WAR: AN ANNOTATED BIBLIOGRAPHY (OCCASIONAL PAPER NO. 79). GERMANY WOR-45 EDU/PROP NAT/LISM ATTIT PWR ALL/IDEOS 20. PAGE 64 A1314
BIBLIOG/A WAR DIPLOM NAT/G

B62
HETHERINGTON H.,SOME ASPECTS OF THE BRITISH EXPERIMENT IN DEMOCRACY. UK DIPLOM COLONIAL ...CONCPT 20 CMN/WLTH. PAGE 64 A1322
EDU/PROP AFR POPULISM SOC/EXP

B62
HUMPHREY D.D.,THE UNITED STATES AND THE COMMON MARKET. USA+45 INDUS MARKET INT/ORG PLAN EDU/PROP BAL/PAY DRIVE PWR WEALTH...TREND STERTYP EEC 20. PAGE 69 A1415
ATTIT ECO/TAC

B62
HUNTINGTON S.P.,CHANGING PATTERNS OF MILITARY POLITICS. EUR+WWI L/A+17C S/ASIA USA+45 WOR+45 CULTURE INT/ORG NAT/G CONSULT PLAN DOMIN EDU/PROP LEGIT DETER WAR ATTIT PERSON PWR...DECISION CONCPT SIMUL GEN/LAWS ANTHOL COLD/WAR 20. PAGE 69 A1419
FORCES RIGID/FLEX

B62
JEWELL M.E.,SENATORIAL POLITICS AND FOREIGN POLICY. NAT/G POL/PAR CHIEF DELIB/GP TOP/EX FOR/AID EDU/PROP ROUTINE ATTIT PWR SKILL...MAJORIT METH/CNCPT TIME/SEQ CONGRESS 20 PRESIDENT. PAGE 74 A1516
USA+45 LEGIS DIPLOM

B62
KAHN H.,THINKING ABOUT THE UNTHINKABLE. FUT USA+45 LAW NAT/G CONSULT FORCES ACT/RES CREATE PLAN TEC/DEV BAL/PWR DIPLOM EDU/PROP ARMS/CONT DETER ATTIT...CONCPT OBS TREND COLD/WAR 20. PAGE 76 A1547
INT/ORG ORD/FREE NUC/PWR PEACE

B62
LAWSON R.,INTERNATIONAL REGIONAL ORGANIZATIONS. WOR+45 NAT/G VOL/ASSN CONSULT LEGIS EDU/PROP LEGIT ADMIN EXEC ROUTINE HEALTH PWR WEALTH...JURID EEC COLD/WAR 20 UN. PAGE 86 A1752
INT/ORG DELIB/GP REGION

B62
LESSING P.,AFRICA'S RED HARVEST. AFR CHINA/COM COM USSR ECO/UNDEV BAL/PWR DIPLOM CONTROL PWR 20 COLD/WAR INTERVENT. PAGE 87 A1789
NAT/LISM MARXISM FOR/AID EDU/PROP

B62
MORGENTHAU H.J.,POLITICS IN THE TWENTIETH CENTURY: IMPASSE OF AMERICAN FOREIGN POLICY. FUT GERMANY USA+45 USSR WOR+45 INT/ORG NAT/G ACT/RES PLAN FOR/AID EDU/PROP LEGIT COERCE WAR PWR...TIME/SEQ TREND COLD/WAR 20. PAGE 104 A2138
SKILL DIPLOM

B62
MORGENTHAU H.J.,POLITICS IN THE 20TH CENTURY: RESTORATION OF AMERICAN POLITICS. ASIA GERMANY USA+45 USSR WOR+45 NAT/G PLAN EDU/PROP LEGIT NUC/PWR ATTIT PWR SKILL...CONCPT TREND COLD/WAR 20. PAGE 104 A2139
INT/ORG DIPLOM

B62
NEAL F.W.,WAR AND PEACE AND GERMANY. EUR+WWI USSR STRUCT INT/ORG NAT/G FORCES DOMIN EDU/PROP LEGIT EXEC COERCE ORD/FREE...HUM SOC NEW/IDEA OBS TIME/SEQ TOT/POP COLD/WAR 20 BERLIN. PAGE 108 A2208
USA+45 POLICY DIPLOM GERMANY

B62
NOBECOURT R.G.,LES SECRETS DE LA PROPAGANDE EN FRANCE OCCUPEE. FRANCE ELITES NAT/G DIPLOM GP/REL NAT/LISM TOTALISM ORD/FREE 20 VICHY VICHY. PAGE 109 A2244
METH/COMP EDU/PROP WAR CONTROL

B62
OSGOOD C.E.,AN ALTERNATIVE TO WAR OR SURRENDER. FUT UNIV CULTURE INTELL SOCIETY R+D INT/ORG CONSULT DELIB/GP ACT/RES PLAN CHOOSE ATTIT PERCEPT KNOWL ...PHIL/SCI PSY SOC TREND GEN/LAWS 20. PAGE 112 A2300
ORD/FREE EDU/PROP PEACE WAR

B62
RIMALOV V.V.,ECONOMIC COOPERATION BETWEEN USSR AND UNDERDEVELOPED COUNTRIES. USSR FINAN TEC/DEV INT/TRADE DOMIN EDU/PROP COLONIAL NAT/LISM DRIVE SOVEREIGN...AUD/VIS 20. PAGE 121 A2482
FOR/AID PLAN ECO/UNDEV DIPLOM

B62
RIVKIN A.,AFRICA AND THE WEST. AFR EUR+WWI FUT ISLAM ISRAEL USA+45 SOCIETY INT/ORG FORCES CREATE PLAN FOR/AID EDU/PROP ATTIT...CONCPT TREND EEC 20 CONGRESS UN. PAGE 121 A2488
ECO/UNDEV ECO/TAC

B62
ROBINSON A.D.,DUTCH ORGANIZED AGRICULTURE IN INTERNATIONAL POLITICS, 1945-1960. EUR+WWI NETHERLAND STRUCT ECO/DEV NAT/G VOL/ASSN CONSULT DELIB/GP PLAN TEC/DEV INT/TRADE EDU/PROP ATTIT RIGID/FLEX ALL/VALS...NEW/IDEA TREND EEC 20. PAGE 122 A2502
AGRI INT/ORG

B62
ROSAMOND R.,CRUSADE FOR PEACE: EISENHOWER'S PRESIDENTIAL LEGACY WITH THE PROGRAM FOR ACTION. USA+45 PARTIC ARMS/CONT MORAL MARXISM...TRADIT CONCPT CHARTS GEN/LAWS ANTHOL 20 PRESIDENT EISNHWR/DD. PAGE 123 A2526
PEACE DIPLOM EDU/PROP POLICY

B62
ROSENNE S.,THE WORLD COURT: WHAT IT IS AND HOW IT WORKS. WOR+45 WOR-45 LAW CONSTN JUDGE EDU/PROP LEGIT ROUTINE CHOOSE PEACE ORD/FREE...JURID OBS TIME/SEQ CHARTS UN TOT/POP VAL/FREE 20. PAGE 124 A2538
INT/ORG ADJUD INT/LAW

B62
SAVORD R.,AMERICAN AGENCIES INTERESTED IN INTERNATIONAL AFFAIRS. USA-45 R+D NAT/G VOL/ASSN ACT/RES EDU/PROP KNOWL...CONCPT 20. PAGE 127 A2608
INT/ORG CONSULT DIPLOM

B62
SCHRODER P.M.,METTERNICH'S DIPLOMACY AT ITS ZENITH, 1820-1823. MOD/EUR ELITES INT/ORG VOL/ASSN DELIB/GP ECO/TAC EDU/PROP DISPL PWR SOVEREIGN...POLICY CONCPT GEN/LAWS 19 METTRNCH/K. PAGE 129 A2647
ORD/FREE BIOG BAL/PWR DIPLOM

B62
SCHUMAN F.L.,THE COLD WAR: RETROSPECT AND PROSPECT. FUT USA+45 USSR WOR+45 BAL/PWR EDU/PROP ARMS/CONT ATTIT...MAJORIT IDEA/COMP ANTHOL BIBLIOG 20 COLD/WAR. PAGE 129 A2651
MARXISM TEC/DEV DIPLOM NUC/PWR

B62
SELOSOEMARDJAN O.,SOCIAL CHANGES IN JOGJAKARTA. INDONESIA NETHERLAND ELITES STRATA STRUCT FAM POL/PAR CREATE DIPLOM INT/TRADE EDU/PROP ADMIN GOV/REL...SOC 20 JAVA CHINJAP. PAGE 131 A2683
ECO/UNDEV CULTURE REV COLONIAL

B62
SHAPIRO D.,A SELECT BIBLIOGRAPHY OF WORKS IN ENGLISH ON RUSSIAN HISTORY, 1801-1917. COM USSR STRATA FORCES EDU/PROP ADMIN REV RACE/REL ATTIT 19/20. PAGE 131 A2693
BIBLIOG DIPLOM COLONIAL

B62
SPANIER J.W.,THE POLITICS OF DISARMAMENT. COM USA+45 USSR EDU/PROP ATTIT ORD/FREE PWR RESPECT ...MYTH RECORD 20 COLD/WAR. PAGE 135 A2771
INT/ORG DELIB/GP ARMS/CONT

B62
STARR R.E.,POLAND 1944-1962: THE SOVIETIZATION OF A CAPTIVE PEOPLE. COM POLAND USSR POL/PAR SECT LEGIS DIPLOM DOMIN EDU/PROP CHOOSE ORD/FREE...POLICY CHARTS BIBLIOG 20. PAGE 137 A2808
MARXISM NAT/G TOTALISM NAT/COMP

B62
STRACHEY J.,ON THE PREVENTION OF WAR. FUT WOR+45 INT/ORG NAT/G ACT/RES PLAN BAL/PWR DOMIN EDU/PROP PEACE ATTIT...POLICY TREND TOT/POP COLD/WAR 20 UN. PAGE 139 A2842
FORCES ORD/FREE ARMS/CONT NUC/PWR

B62
THANT U.,THE UNITED NATIONS' DEVELOPMENT DECADE: PROPOSALS FOR ACTION. WOR+45 SOCIETY ECO/UNDEV AGRI COM/IND FINAN R+D MUNIC SCHOOL VOL/ASSN CONSULT PLAN TEC/DEV ECO/TAC EDU/PROP ADMIN ROUTINE RIGID/FLEX...MGT SOC CONCPT UNESCO UN TOT/POP VAL/FREE. PAGE 142 A2906
INT/ORG ALL/VALS

B62
US LIBRARY OF CONGRESS,A LIST OF AMERICAN DOCTORAL DISSERTATIONS ON AFRICA. SOCIETY SECT DIPLOM EDU/PROP ADMIN...GEOG 19/20. PAGE 155 A3157
BIBLIOG AFR ACADEM CULTURE

B62
WEIDNER E.W.,THE WORLD ROLE OF UNIVERSITIES. USA+45 WOR+45 SECT ACT/RES PROB/SOLV GIVE EFFICIENCY KNOWL ...LING CHARTS BIBLIOG 20. PAGE 162 A3297
ACADEM EDU/PROP DIPLOM POLICY

B62
WELLEQUET J.,LE CONGO BELGE ET LA WELTPOLITIK (1894-1914. GERMANY DOMIN EDU/PROP WAR ATTIT ...BIBLIOG T CONGO/LEOP. PAGE 163 A3314
ADMIN DIPLOM GP/REL COLONIAL

L62
"HIGHER EDUCATION AND ECONOMIC AND SOCIAL DEVELOPMENT IN LATIN AMERICA: A BIBLIOGRAPHY." L/A+17C SOCIETY ECO/UNDEV PROF/ORG DIPLOM CONFER ...SOC 20. PAGE 3 A0062
BIBLIOG/A ACADEM INTELL EDU/PROP

L62
GROSS L.,"IMMUNITIES AND PRIVILEGES OF DELIGATIONS TO THE UNITED NATIONS." USA+45 WOR+45 STRATA NAT/G VOL/ASSN CONSULT DIPLOM EDU/PROP ROUTINE RESPECT ...POLICY INT/LAW CONCPT UN 20. PAGE 57 A1176
INT/ORG LAW ELITES

L62
MALINOWSKI W.R.,"CENTRALIZATION AND DE-CENTRALIZATION IN THE UNITED NATIONS' ECONOMIC AND SOCIAL ACTIVITIES." WOR+45 CONSTN ECO/UNDEV INT/ORG VOL/ASSN DELIB/GP ECO/TAC EDU/PROP ADMIN RIGID/FLEX ...OBS CHARTS UNESCO UN EEC OAS OEEC 20. PAGE 93 A1913
CREATE GEN/LAWS

L62
ULYSSES,"THE INTERNATIONAL AIMS AND POLICIES OF THE SOVIET UNION: THE NEW CONCEPTS AND STRATEGY OF KHRUSHCHEV." FUT USSR WOR+45 SOCIETY INT/ORG NAT/G POL/PAR FORCES TOP/EX PLAN DOMIN EDU/PROP COERCE ATTIT PERSON PWR...TREND COLD/WAR 20 KHRUSH/N. PAGE 146 A2994
COM POLICY BAL/PWR DIPLOM

L62
WILCOX F.O.,"THE UN AND THE NON-ALIGNED NATIONS." AFR S/ASIA USA+45 ECO/UNDEV INT/ORG TEC/DEV EDU/PROP RIGID/FLEX ORD/FREE PWR...POLICY HUM CONCPT STAT OBS TIME/SEQ STERTYP GEN/METH UN 20. PAGE 164 A3345
ATTIT TREND

S62
BELSHAW C.,"TRAINING AND RECRUITMENT: SOME PRINCIPLES OF INTERNATIONAL AID." FUT WOR+45 SOCIETY INT/ORG NAT/G CREATE PLAN TEC/DEV ECO/TAC FOR/AID EDU/PROP ATTIT PERCEPT...HUM UN FAO ILO UNESCO 20. PAGE 13 A0263
VOL/ASSN ECO/UNDEV

S62
BIERZANECK R.,"LA NON-RECONAISSANCE ET LE DROIT INTERNATIONAL CONTEMPORAIN." EUR+WWI FUT WOR+45 LAW ECO/DEV ATTIT RIGID/FLEX...CONCPT TIME/SEQ TOT/POP 20. PAGE 14 A0286
EDU/PROP JURID DIPLOM INT/LAW

S62
BOKOR-SZEGO H.,"LA CONVENTION DE BELGRADE ET LE REGIME DU DANUBE." COM EUR+WWI WOR+45 STRUCT POL/PAR VOL/ASSN PLAN EDU/PROP WEALTH...TIME/SEQ 20. PAGE 16 A0333
INT/ORG TOTALISM YUGOSLAVIA

S62
CROAN M.,"POLYCENTRISM: COMMUNIST INTERNATIONAL RELATIONS." ASIA STRUCT INT/ORG NAT/G POL/PAR CONSULT PLAN DOMIN EDU/PROP COERCE ATTIT RIGID/FLEX SOCISM...POLICY CONCPT TREND CON/ANAL GEN/LAWS MARX/KARL. PAGE 33 A0663
COM CREATE DIPLOM NAT/LISM

S62
DALLIN A.,"THE SOVIET VIEW OF THE UNITED NATIONS." WOR+45 VOL/ASSN TOP/EX DIPLOM DOMIN EDU/PROP LEGIT ATTIT RIGID/FLEX PWR...CONCPT OBS HIST/WRIT TIME/SEQ STERTYP GEN/LAWS COLD/WAR UN 20. PAGE 33 A0676
COM INT/ORG USSR

S62
DEUTSCH K.W.,"TOWARDS WESTERN EUROPEAN INTEGRATION: AN INTERIM ASSESSMENT." EUR+WWI STRUCT ECO/DEV INT/ORG ECO/TAC INT/TRADE EDU/PROP PEACE ATTIT DRIVE PWR SOVEREIGN...PSY SOC TIME/SEQ CHARTS STERTYP 20. PAGE 36 A0741
VOL/ASSN RIGID/FLEX REGION

S62
FINKELSTEIN L.S.,"THE UNITED NATIONS AND ORGANIZATIONS FOR CONTROL OF ARMAMENT." FUT WOR+45 VOL/ASSN DELIB/GP TOP/EX CREATE EDU/PROP LEGIT ADJUD NUC/PWR ATTIT RIGID/FLEX ORD/FREE...POLICY DECISION CONCPT OBS TREND GEN/LAWS TOT/POP COLD/WAR. PAGE 46 A0933
INT/ORG PWR ARMS/CONT

S62
FOCSANEANU L.,"LES GRANDS TRAITES DE LA REPUBLIQUE POPULAIRE DE CHINE." ASIA CHINA/COM COM USSR WOR+45 INT/ORG NAT/G POL/PAR ACT/RES PLAN DIPLOM EDU/PROP ...CONCPT TIME/SEQ 20 TREATY. PAGE 47 A0957
VOL/ASSN TOTALISM

S62
FOSTER W.C.,"ARMS CONTROL AND DISARMAMENT IN A DIVIDED WORLD." COM FUT USA+45 USSR WOR+45 INTELL INT/ORG NAT/G VOL/ASSN CONSULT CREATE PLAN TEC/DEV EDU/PROP LEGIT NUC/PWR ATTIT RIGID/FLEX...CONCPT TREND TOT/POP 20 UN. PAGE 47 A0971
DELIB/GP POLICY ARMS/CONT DIPLOM

S62
GUETZKOW H.,"THE POTENTIAL OF CASE STUDY IN ANALYZING INTERNATIONAL CONFLICT." EUR+WWI FUT GERMANY INTELL SOCIETY STRUCT INT/ORG LOC/G NAT/G CONSULT CREATE PLAN CHOOSE ATTIT RIGID/FLEX ...POLICY SAAR 20. PAGE 58 A1188
EDU/PROP METH/CNCPT COERCE FRANCE

S62
JOHNSON O.H.,"THE ENGLISH TRADITION IN INTERNATIONAL LAW." CHRIST-17C MOD/EUR EDU/PROP LEGIT CT/SYS ORD/FREE...JURID CONCPT TIME/SEQ. PAGE 75 A1526
LAW INT/LAW UK

S62
KOLARZ W.,"THE IMPACT OF COMMUNISM ON WEST AFRICA." AFR FUT SOCIETY INT/ORG NAT/G CREATE PLAN DOMIN EDU/PROP COERCE NAT/LISM ATTIT RIGID/FLEX SOCISM ...POLICY CONCPT TREND MARX/KARL 20. PAGE 81 A1666
COM POL/PAR COLONIAL

S62
MILLAR T.B.,"THE COMMONWEALTH AND THE UNITED NATIONS." FUT WOR+45 STRUCT NAT/G VOL/ASSN CONSULT DELIB/GP EDU/PROP LEGIT ATTIT...POLICY CONCPT TREND CMN/WLTH UN 20. PAGE 101 A2072
INT/ORG

S62
MORGENTHAU H.J.,"A POLITICAL THEORY OF FOREIGN AID." ECO/UNDEV NAT/G DELIB/GP PLAN ECO/TAC EDU/PROP EXEC ORD/FREE RESPECT WEALTH...METH/CNCPT TREND 20. PAGE 104 A2140
USA+45 PHIL/SCI FOR/AID

S62
RUSSETT B.M.,"CAUSE, SURPRISE, AND NO ESCAPE." FUT WOR-45 CULTURE SOCIETY INT/ORG FORCES TEC/DEV BAL/PWR EDU/PROP ARMS/CONT NUC/PWR WAR WEAPON PEACE KNOWL ORD/FREE PWR...POLICY CONCPT RECORD TIME/SEQ TREND GEN/LAWS 20 WWI. PAGE 126 A2578
COERCE DIPLOM

S62
SPECTOR I.,"SOVIET POLICY IN ASIA: A REAPPRAISAL." ASIA CHINA/COM COM INDIA INDONESIA ECO/UNDEV INT/ORG DOMIN EDU/PROP REGION RESPECT...CONCPT TREND TOT/POP COLD/WAR 20 CHINJAP. PAGE 135 A2774
S/ASIA PWR FOR/AID USSR

S62
SPENSER J.H.,"AFRICA AT THE UNITED NATIONS: SOME OBSERVATIONS." FUT ECO/UNDEV NAT/G CONSULT DELIB/GP PLAN BAL/PWR ECO/TAC EDU/PROP ATTIT RIGID/FLEX HEALTH ORD/FREE PWR WEALTH...POLICY CONCPT OBS TREND STERTYP GEN/METH UN VAL/FREE. PAGE 136 A2786
AFR INT/ORG REGION

S62
STRACHEY J.,"COMMUNIST INTENTIONS." ASIA USSR YUGOSLAVIA INT/ORG NAT/G FORCES DOMIN EDU/PROP COERCE NUC/PWR NAT/LISM PEACE RIGID/FLEX PWR MARXISM...CONCPT MYTH OBS TIME/SEQ TREND COLD/WAR TOT/POP 20. PAGE 139 A2843
COM ATTIT WAR

S62
TOWSTER J.,"THE USSR AND THE USA: CHALLENGE AND RESPONSE." COM GERMANY USA+45 USSR WOR+45 ECO/UNDEV INT/ORG VOL/ASSN EX/STRUC FORCES TOP/EX CREATE PLAN TEC/DEV DIPLOM ECO/TAC EDU/PROP COLONIAL COERCE PWR ...GEN/METH COLD/WAR 20 KENNEDY/JF. PAGE 145 A2956
ACT/RES GEN/LAWS

S62
TRUMAN D.,"THE DOMESTIC POLITICS OF FOREIGN AID." USA+45 WOR+45 NAT/G POL/PAR LEGIS DIPLOM ECO/TAC EDU/PROP ADMIN CHOOSE ATTIT PWR CONGRESS 20 CONGRESS. PAGE 145 A2970
ROUTINE FOR/AID

C62
BACON F.,"OF THE TRUE GREATNESS OF KINGDOMS AND ESTATES" (1612) IN F. BACON, ESSAYS." ELITES FORCES DOMIN EDU/PROP LEGIT...POLICY GEN/LAWS 16/17 TREATY. PAGE 10 A0200
WAR PWR DIPLOM CONSTN

B63
BOISSIER P.,HISTORIE DU COMITE INTERNATIONAL DE LA CROIX ROUGE. MOD/EUR WOR-45 CONSULT FORCES PLAN DIPLOM EDU/PROP ADMIN MORAL ORD/FREE...SOC CONCPT RECORD TIME/SEQ GEN/LAWS TOT/POP VAL/FREE 19/20. PAGE 16 A0332
INT/ORG HEALTH ARMS/CONT WAR

B63
BOWETT D.W.,THE LAW OF INTERNATIONAL INSTITUTIONS. WOR+45 WOR-45 CONSTN DELIB/GP EX/STRUC JUDGE EDU/PROP LEGIT CT/SYS EXEC ROUTINE RIGID/FLEX ORD/FREE PWR...JURID CONCPT ORG/CHARTS GEN/METH LEAGUE/NAT OAS OEEC 20 UN. PAGE 17 A0354
INT/ORG ADJUD DIPLOM

B63
BRZEZINSKI Z.K.,AFRICA AND THE COMMUNIST WORLD. AFR ASIA COM CULTURE SOCIETY INT/ORG DELIB/GP ACT/RES ECO/TAC COERCE ORD/FREE PWR WEALTH...STAT TOT/POP VAL/FREE 20. PAGE 21 A0418
ATTIT EDU/PROP DIPLOM USSR

B63
BUTTS R.F.,AMERICAN EDUCATION IN INTERNATIONAL DEVELOPMENT. USA+45 WOR+45 INTELL SCHOOL DIPLOM EDU/PROP...BIBLIOG 20. PAGE 23 A0457
ACADEM FOR/AID CONSULT ECO/UNDEV

B63
CONF ON FUTURE OF COMMONWEALTH,THE FUTURE OF THE COMMONWEALTH. UK ECO/UNDEV AGRI EDU/PROP ADMIN SOC/INTEG 20 COMMONWLTH. PAGE 29 A0583
DIPLOM RACE/REL ORD/FREE TEC/DEV

B63
CREMEANS C.,THE ARABS AND THE WORLD: NASSER'S ARAB NATIONALIST POLICY. FUT ISLAM UAR USA+45 SOCIETY STRATA NAT/G POL/PAR PLAN DIPLOM EDU/PROP LEGIT DRIVE ALL/VALS...INT TIME/SEQ CHARTS 20 NASSER/G. PAGE 33 A0662
TOP/EX ATTIT REGION NAT/LISM

B63
FABER K.,DIE NATIONALISTISCHE PUBLIZISTIK DEUTSCHLANDS VON 1866 BIS 1871 (2 VOLS.). EUR+WWI GERMANY DIPLOM EDU/PROP 19. PAGE 43 A0881
BIBLIOG/A NAT/G NAT/LISM POL/PAR

B63
FALK R.A.,LAW, MORALITY, AND WAR IN THE CONTEMPORARY WORLD. WOR+45 LAW INT/ORG EX/STRUC FORCES EDU/PROP LEGIT DETER NUC/PWR MORAL ORD/FREE ...JURID TOT/POP 20. PAGE 43 A0888
ADJUD ARMS/CONT PEACE INT/LAW

B63
FISCHER-GALATI S.,EASTERN EUROPE IN THE SIXTIES. ALBANIA USSR YUGOSLAVIA ECO/UNDEV AGRI MARKET LABOR WORKER DIPLOM INT/TRADE EDU/PROP GOV/REL PRODUC UTOPIA SOCISM 20. PAGE 46 A0939
MARXISM TEC/DEV BAL/PWR ECO/TAC

B63
GALLAGHER M.P.,THE SOVIET HISTORY OF WORLD WAR II. EUR+WWI USSR DIPLOM DOMIN WRITING CONTROL WAR MARXISM...PSY TIME/SEQ 20 STALIN/J. PAGE 50 A1031
CIVMIL/REL EDU/PROP HIST/WRIT PRESS

B63
GORDON G.N.,THE IDEA INVADERS. USA+45 USSR CULTURE COM/IND DIPLOM PRESS TV TOTALISM MARXISM 20. PAGE 54 A1113
EDU/PROP ATTIT ORD/FREE CONTROL

B63
GRAEBNER N.A.,THE COLD WAR: IDEOLOGICAL CONFLICT OR POWER STRUGGLE? USSR WOR+45 WOR-45 PROB/SOLV EDU/PROP ARMS/CONT REV NAT/LISM PEACE ORD/FREE
DIPLOM BAL/PWR MARXISM

...IDEA/COMP ANTHOL BIBLIOG/A 20 COLD/WAR. PAGE 55 A1123

B63
GREAT BRITAIN CENTRAL OFF INF,CONSULTATION AND CO-OPERATION IN THE COMMONWEALTH. LAW R+D FORCES PLAN EDU/PROP CONFER INGP/REL...GEOG CENSUS 19/20 CMN/WLTH. PAGE 55 A1133
DIPLOM DELIB/GP VOL/ASSN REGION

B63
GRIFFITH W.E.,ALBANIA AND THE SINO-SOVIET RIFT. ALBANIA CHINA/COM USSR POL/PAR CHIEF LEGIS DIPLOM DOMIN ATTIT PWR...POLICY 20 KHRUSH/N MAO. PAGE 57 A1161
EDU/PROP MARXISM NAT/LISM GOV/REL

B63
HENDERSON W.,SOUTHEAST ASIA: PROBLEMS OF UNITED STATES POLICY. COM S/ASIA CULTURE STRATA ECO/UNDEV INT/ORG DELIB/GP ACT/RES ECO/TAC DOMIN EDU/PROP LEGIT COERCE ATTIT ALL/VALS...STAT TIME/SEQ ANTHOL VAL/FREE 20. PAGE 64 A1313
ASIA USA+45 DIPLOM

B63
HOVET T. JR.,AFRICA IN THE UNITED NATIONS. AFR DELIB/GP EDU/PROP LOBBY CHOOSE ORD/FREE PWR RESPECT SKILL...STAT TIME/SEQ CON/ANAL CHARTS STERTYP VAL/FREE 20 UN. PAGE 68 A1397
INT/ORG USSR

B63
JACOBSON H.K.,THE USSR AND THE UN'S ECONOMIC AND SOCIAL ACTIVITIES. COM WOR+45 DELIB/GP ACT/RES ECO/TAC EDU/PROP RIGID/FLEX SUPEGO HEALTH PWR SKILL ...POLICY CHARTS GEN/METH VAL/FREE UNESCO 20 UN. PAGE 73 A1487
INT/ORG ATTIT USSR

B63
JAIRAZBHOY R.A.,FOREIGN INFLUENCE IN ANCIENT INDIA. INDIA ELITES SECT DIPLOM EDU/PROP COLONIAL REGION GP/REL...ART/METH LING WORSHIP +/14 GRECO/ROMN MESOPOTAM PERSIA PARTH/SASS. PAGE 73 A1491
CULTURE SOCIETY COERCE DOMIN

B63
JOYCE W.,THE PROPAGANDA GAP. USA+45 COM/IND ACADEM DOMIN FEEDBACK REV CIVMIL/REL...REALPOL COLD/WAR. PAGE 75 A1540
EDU/PROP PERCEPT BAL/PWR DIPLOM

B63
KATZ S.M.,A SELECTED LIST OF US READINGS ON DEVELOPMENT. AGRI COM/IND DIST/IND INDUS LABOR PLAN FOR/AID EDU/PROP HEALTH...POLICY SOC/WK 20. PAGE 77 A1571
BIBLIOG/A ECO/UNDEV TEC/DEV ACT/RES

B63
KHADDURI M.,MODERN LIBYA: A STUDY IN POLITICAL DEVELOPMENT. EUR+WWI ISLAM LIBYA ELITES INT/ORG POL/PAR FORCES DIPLOM FOR/AID DOMIN EDU/PROP LEGIT NAT/LISM DRIVE RIGID/FLEX SKILL...CONCPT TIME/SEQ TREND 20. PAGE 78 A1606
NAT/G STRUCT

B63
LERCHE C.O. JR.,AMERICA IN WORLD AFFAIRS. COM UK USA+45 INT/ORG FORCES ECO/TAC INT/TRADE EDU/PROP WAR NAT/LISM PEACE...BIBLIOG 18/20 UN CONGRESS PRESIDENT COLD/WAR. PAGE 87 A1783
NAT/G DIPLOM PLAN

B63
LUNDBERG F.,THE COMING WORLD TRANSFORMATION. CULTURE SOCIETY ECO/DEV INT/ORG NAT/G DIPLOM ECO/TAC EDU/PROP 15/21. PAGE 91 A1873
PREDICT FUT WOR+45 TEC/DEV

B63
LYON P.,NEUTRALISM. ECO/UNDEV EDU/PROP COLONIAL ALL/IDEOS...IDEA/COMP 20 COLD/WAR UN. PAGE 92 A1879
NAT/COMP NAT/LISM DIPLOM NEUTRAL

B63
MALIK C.,MAN IN THE STRUGGLE FOR PEACE. USSR WOR+45 CHIEF PLAN PROB/SOLV PARTIC NUC/PWR REV ORD/FREE ...IDEA/COMP METH/COMP 20 UN COLD/WAR. PAGE 93 A1912
PEACE MARXISM DIPLOM EDU/PROP

B63
MANSERGH N.,DOCUMENTS AND SPEECHES ON COMMONWEALTH AFFAIRS 1952-1962. CANADA INDIA PAKISTAN UK CONSTN FORCES ECO/TAC EDU/PROP COLONIAL DETER WAR ORD/FREE SOVEREIGN...POLICY 20 AUSTRAL. PAGE 94 A1932
BIBLIOG/A FEDERAL INT/TRADE DIPLOM

B63
MBOYA T.,FREEDOM AND AFTER. AFR LABOR POL/PAR DIPLOM EDU/PROP COERCE SOCISM 20. PAGE 97 A1989
COLONIAL ECO/UNDEV NAT/LISM INT/ORG

B63
NORTH R.C.,CONTENT ANALYSIS: A HANDBOOK WITH APPLICATIONS FOR THE STUDY OF INTERNATIONAL CRISIS. ASIA COM EUR+WWI MOD/EUR INT/ORG TEC/DEV DOMIN EDU/PROP ROUTINE COERCE PERCEPT RIGID/FLEX ALL/VALS ...QUANT TESTS CON/ANAL SIMUL GEN/LAWS VAL/FREE. PAGE 110 A2252
METH/CNCPT COMPUT/IR USSR

B63
OECD,SCIENCE AND THE POLICIES OF GOVERNMENTS: THE IMPLICATIONS OF SCIENCE AND TECHNOLOGY FOR NATL AND INTL AFFAIRS. WOR+45 INT/ORG EDU/PROP AUTOMAT ...POLICY PHIL/SCI 20. PAGE 111 A2279
CREATE TEC/DEV DIPLOM NAT/G

B63
PANAMERICAN UNION,DOCUMENTOS OFICIALES DE LA ORGANIZACION DE LOS ESTADOS AMERICANOS, INDICE Y LISTA (VOL. III, 1962). L/A+17C DELIB/GP INT/TRADE EDU/PROP REGION NUC/PWR...HEAL INT/LAW SOC/WK 20 OAS. PAGE 113 A2329
BIBLIOG INT/ORG DIPLOM

B63
QUAISON-SACKEY A.,AFRICA UNBOUND: REFLECTIONS OF AN AFRICAN STATESMAN. ISLAM CULTURE INTELL INT/ORG POL/PAR TOP/EX DOMIN EDU/PROP LEGIT ATTIT PERSON ...CONCPT OBS TIME/SEQ CHARTS STERTYP 20 UN. PAGE 118 A2423
AFR BIOG

B63
RAVENS J.P.,STAAT UND KATHOLISCHE KIRCHE IN PREUSSENS POLNISCHEN TEILUNGSGEBIETEN. GERMANY POLAND PRUSSIA PROVS DIPLOM EDU/PROP DEBATE NAT/LISM...JURID 18 CHURCH/STA. PAGE 119 A2451
GP/REL CATHISM SECT NAT/G

B63
ROSECRANCE R.N.,ACTION AND REACTION IN WORLD POLITICS. FUT WOR-45 SOCIETY DELIB/GP ACT/RES CREATE DIPLOM ECO/TAC DOMIN EDU/PROP COERCE ATTIT PERSON SUPEGO ORD/FREE PWR...CHARTS SIMUL LEAGUE/NAT VAL/FREE UN 19/20. PAGE 123 A2529
WOR+45 INT/ORG BAL/PWR

B63
SCHMELTZ G.W.,LA POLITIQUE MONDIALE CONTEMPORAINE. SOCIETY ECO/UNDEV INDUS INT/ORG NAT/G POL/PAR CONSULT DELIB/GP PLAN TEC/DEV ECO/TAC DOMIN EDU/PROP ROUTINE COERCE PERCEPT PERSON LOVE SKILL ...SOC RECORD TOT/POP. PAGE 128 A2629
WOR+45 COLONIAL

B63
THORELLI H.B.,INTOP: INTERNATIONAL OPERATIONS SIMULATION: PLAYER'S MANUAL. BRAZIL FINAN OP/RES ADMIN GP/REL INGP/REL PRODUC PERCEPT...DECISION MGT EEC. PAGE 144 A2935
GAME INT/TRADE EDU/PROP LG/CO

B63
US DEPARTMENT OF THE ARMY,SOVIET RUSSIA: STRATEGIC SURVEY (PAMPHLET). USSR POL/PAR PLAN DOMIN EDU/PROP ARMS/CONT GUERRILLA WAR WEAPON...TREND CHARTS ORG/CHARTS 20. PAGE 152 A3106
BIBLIOG/A MARXISM DIPLOM COERCE

B63
US ECON SURVEY TEAM INDONESIA,INDONESIA - PERSPECTIVE AND PROPOSALS FOR UNITED STATES ECONOMIC AID. INDONESIA AGRI MARKET TEC/DEV DIPLOM INT/TRADE EDU/PROP 20. PAGE 153 A3113
FOR/AID ECO/UNDEV PLAN INDUS

B63
VOSS E.H.,NUCLEAR AMBUSH: THE TEST-BAN TRAP. WOR+45 COM/IND INT/ORG NAT/G DELIB/GP FORCES LEGIS TOP/EX ACT/RES DOMIN EDU/PROP LEGIT ROUTINE COERCE ATTIT PERCEPT RIGID/FLEX HEALTH MORAL ORD/FREE PWR. PAGE 160 A3255
TEC/DEV HIST/WRIT ARMS/CONT NUC/PWR

B63
WATKINS K.W.,BRITAIN DIVIDED; THE EFFECT OF THE SPANISH CIVIL WAR ON BRITISH POLITICAL OPINION. SPAIN UK POL/PAR BAL/PWR LOBBY NEUTRAL 20. PAGE 162 A3293
EDU/PROP WAR POLICY DIPLOM

B63
WESTERFIELD H.,THE INSTRUMENTS OF AMERICA'S FOREIGN POLICY. WOR+45 ECO/DEV NAT/G CONSULT EX/STRUC LEGIS BAL/PWR FOR/AID INT/TRADE DOMIN EDU/PROP LEGIT ATTIT KNOWL ORD/FREE PWR WEALTH...OBS COLD/WAR TOT/POP VAL/FREE. PAGE 163 A3322
USA+45 INT/ORG DIPLOM

B63
WHITTON J.B.,PROPAGANDA AND THE COLD WAR. USA+45 USSR INDUS NAT/G PLAN WRITING EFFICIENCY...POLICY 20 COLD/WAR. PAGE 164 A3341
ATTIT EDU/PROP COM/IND DIPLOM

L63
PHELPS J.,"STUDIES IN DETERRENCE VIII: MILITARY STABILITARY AND ARMS CONTROL: A CRITICAL SURVEY." FUT WOR+45 INT/ORG ACT/RES EDU/PROP COERCE NUC/PWR WAR HEALTH PWR...POLICY TECHNIC TREND SIMUL TOT/POP 20. PAGE 116 A2373
FORCES ORD/FREE ARMS/CONT DETER

L63
RUSSETT B.M.,"TOWARD A MODEL OF COMPETITIVE INTERNATIONAL POLITICS." USA+45 WOR+45 INT/ORG NAT/G POL/PAR VOL/ASSN LEGIS BAL/PWR DIPLOM LEGIT PWR...CONCPT CONT/OBS STERTYP GEN/LAWS TOT/POP COLD/WAR 20 UN. PAGE 126 A2579
ATTIT EDU/PROP

L63
SINGER J.D.,"WEAPONS MANAGEMENT IN WORLD POLITICS: PROCEEDINGS OF THE INTERNATIONAL ARMS CONTROL SYMPOSIUM, DECEMBER, 1962." FUT WOR+45 SOCIETY ECO/DEV INDUS INT/ORG DELIB/GP FORCES ACT/RES ECO/TAC EDU/PROP ARMS/CONT SUPEGO HEALTH ORD/FREE PWR SKILL...POLICY CHARTS SIMUL ANTHOL VAL/FREE 20. PAGE 133 A2729
CONSULT ATTIT DIPLOM NUC/PWR

L63
SZASZY E.,"L'EVOLUTION DES PRINCIPES GENERAUX DU DROIT INTERNATIONAL PRIVE DANS LES PAYS DE DEMOCRATIE POPULAIRE." COM FUT WOR+45 LAW ECO/DEV PERF/ART POL/PAR PROF/ORG ECO/TAC INT/TRADE EDU/PROP ATTIT RIGID/FLEX ALL/VALS SOCISM...JURID TREND GEN/LAWS WORK 20. PAGE 141 A2876
DIPLOM TOTALISM INT/LAW INT/ORG

L63
WILCOX F.O.,"THE ATLANTIC COMMUNITY: PROGRESS AND PROSPECTS." EUR+WWI FUT USA+45 WOR+45 SOCIETY CREATE ECO/TAC EDU/PROP LEGIT REGION ATTIT ALL/VALS ...POLICY ANTHOL VAL/FREE 20. PAGE 164 A3346
INT/ORG ACT/RES

L63
ZARTMAN I.W.,"THE SAHARA--BRIDGE OR BARRIER." ISLAM
INT/ORG

CULTURE SOCIETY NAT/G DELIB/GP DOMIN EDU/PROP LEGIT PWR
ATTIT...HIST/WRIT TIME/SEQ CHARTS TOT/POP VAL/FREE NAT/LISM
20. PAGE 169 A3445

S63
BECHHOEFER B.G.,"UNITED NATIONS PROCEDURES IN CASE INT/ORG
OF VIOLATIONS OF DISARMAMENT AGREEMENTS." COM DELIB/GP
USA+45 USSR LAW CONSTN NAT/G EX/STRUC FORCES LEGIS
BAL/PWR EDU/PROP CT/SYS ARMS/CONT ORD/FREE PWR
...POLICY STERTYP UN VAL/FREE 20. PAGE 12 A0245

S63
COSER L.,"AMERICA AND THE WORLD REVOLUTION." COM ECO/UNDEV
FUT USA+45 WOR+45 INTELL SOCIETY NAT/G ECO/TAC PLAN
EDU/PROP ALL/VALS SOCISM...PSY GEN/LAWS TOT/POP 20 FOR/AID
COLD/WAR. PAGE 31 A0629 DIPLOM

S63
DIEBOLD W. JR.,"THE NEW SITUATION OF INTERNATIONAL MARKET
TRADE POLICY." EUR+WWI FRANCE FUT UK USA+45 WOR+45 ECO/TAC
DIST/IND PLAN INT/TRADE EDU/PROP PWR WEALTH
...RECORD TREND GEN/LAWS EEC VAL/FREE 20. PAGE 37
A0760

S63
EMERSON R.,"THE ATLANTIC COMMUNITY AND THE EMERGING ATTIT
COUNTRIES." FUT WOR+45 ECO/DEV ECO/UNDEV R+D NAT/G INT/TRADE
DELIB/GP BAL/PWR ECO/TAC EDU/PROP ROUTINE ORD/FREE
PWR WEALTH...POLICY CONCPT TREND GEN/METH EEC 20
NATO. PAGE 42 A0848

S63
ETZIONI A.,"EUROPEAN UNIFICATION: A STRATEGY OF INT/ORG
CHANGE." EUR+WWI CULTURE ECO/DEV DELIB/GP ACT/RES RIGID/FLEX
ECO/TAC EDU/PROP ATTIT ORD/FREE PWR SKILL WEALTH
...STAT TIME/SEQ EEC TOT/POP VAL/FREE 20. PAGE 42
A0869

S63
ETZIONI A.,"EUROPEAN UNIFICATION AND PERSPECTIVES INT/ORG
ON SOVEREIGNTY." EUR+WWI FUT DELIB/GP TEC/DEV ECO/DEV
ECO/TAC EDU/PROP DETER NUC/PWR ATTIT DRIVE ORD/FREE SOVEREIGN
PWR WEALTH...CONCPT RECORD TIME/SEQ EEC VAL/FREE
20. PAGE 43 A0870

S63
GUPTA S.C.,"INDIA AND THE SOVIET UNION." CHINA/COM DISPL
COM INDIA S/ASIA VOL/ASSN TOP/EX FOR/AID EDU/PROP MYTH
PEACE PWR...RECORD COLD/WAR 20. PAGE 58 A1195 USSR

S63
HORVATH J.,"MOSCOW'S AID PROGRAM: THE PERFORMANCE ECO/UNDEV
SO FAR." COM FUT USSR WOR+45 ECO/DEV FINAN PLAN ECO/TAC
TEC/DEV FOR/AID EDU/PROP ATTIT ORD/FREE PWR WEALTH
...POLICY STAT CHARTS VAL/FREE 20. PAGE 68 A1389

S63
KISSINGER H.A.,"STRAINS ON THE ALLIANCE." EUR+WWI VOL/ASSN
FRANCE GERMANY GERMANY/W USA+45 ECO/DEV INT/ORG DRIVE
NAT/G TOP/EX EDU/PROP NUC/PWR ATTIT PWR...PSY TREND DIPLOM
20. PAGE 80 A1643

S63
LOPEZIBOR J.,"L'EUROPE, FORME DE VIE." CHRIST-17C NAT/G
EUR+WWI FUT MOD/EUR SOCIETY INT/ORG SECT EDU/PROP CULTURE
ATTIT RIGID/FLEX ALL/VALS...POLICY HUM SOC TIME/SEQ
TREND GEN/LAWS. PAGE 91 A1862

S63
MAZRUI A.A.,"ON THE CONCEPT 'WE ARE ALL AFRICANS'." PROVS
AFR CULTURE KIN LOC/G NAT/G DOMIN EDU/PROP LEGIT INT/ORG
ATTIT PERCEPT PERSON KNOWL ORD/FREE...TIME/SEQ NAT/LISM
TOT/POP 20. PAGE 97 A1986

S63
NADLER E.B.,"SOME ECONOMIC DISADVANTAGES OF THE ECO/DEV
ARMS RACE." USA+45 INDUS R+D FORCES PLAN TEC/DEV MGT
ECO/TAC FOR/AID EDU/PROP PWR WEALTH...TREND BAL/PAY
COLD/WAR 20. PAGE 107 A2190

S63
NEIDLE A.F.,"PEACE KEEPING AND DISARMAMENT." COM DELIB/GP
USA+45 USSR WOR+45 INT/ORG NAT/G BAL/PWR EDU/PROP ACT/RES
LEGIT ATTIT PWR 20. PAGE 108 A2214 ARMS/CONT
PEACE

S63
NOGEE J.L.,"PROPOGANDA AND NEGOTIATION: THE CASE OF INT/ORG
THE TEN NATION DISARMAMENT COMMITTEE." COM EUR+WWI EDU/PROP
USA+45 VOL/ASSN DELIB/GP FORCES DIPLOM DOMIN LEGIT ARMS/CONT
PWR...METH/CNCPT STERTYP COLD/WAR VAL/FREE 20.
PAGE 110 A2248

S63
PINCUS J.,"THE COST OF FOREIGN AID." WOR+45 ECO/DEV USA+45
FINAN NAT/G VOL/ASSN CREATE ECO/TAC EDU/PROP WEALTH ECO/UNDEV
...METH/CNCPT STAT CHARTS HYPO/EXP TOT/POP VAL/FREE FOR/AID
20. PAGE 116 A2380

S63
RAMERIE L.,"TENSION AU SEIN DU COMECON: LE CAS INT/ORG
ROUMAIN." COM EUR+WWI USSR WOR+45 ECO/DEV DIST/IND ECO/TAC
NAT/G POL/PAR VOL/ASSN EDU/PROP TOTALISM ATTIT INT/TRADE
WEALTH...TIME/SEQ 20 COMECON. PAGE 119 A2438 ROMANIA

S63
ROUGEMONT D.,"LES NOUVELLES CHANCES DE L'EUROPE." ECO/UNDEV
EUR+WWI FUT ECO/DEV INT/ORG NAT/G ACT/RES PLAN PERCEPT
TEC/DEV EDU/PROP ADMIN COLONIAL FEDERAL ATTIT PWR
SKILL...TREND 20. PAGE 124 A2549

S63
SCHMIDT W.E.,"THE CASE AGAINST COMMODITY ECO/UNDEV
AGREEMENTS." FUT L/A+17C STRATA CONSULT PLAN ACT/RES
ECO/TAC EDU/PROP ATTIT DRIVE RIGID/FLEX WEALTH INT/TRADE
...MYTH 20. PAGE 128 A2631

S63
WELLS H.,"THE OAS AND THE DOMINICAN ELECTIONS." CONSULT
L/A+17C INT/ORG NAT/G POL/PAR TEC/DEV ECO/TAC CHOOSE
EDU/PROP PERCEPT...TIME/SEQ OAS TOT/POP 20. DOMIN/REP
PAGE 163 A3317

S63
WOLF C.,"SOME ASPECTS OF THE 'VALUE' OF LESS- CONCPT
DEVELOPED COUNTRIES TO THE UNITED STATES." ASIA GEN/LAWS
CHINA/COM COM USA+45 USSR ECO/UNDEV BAL/PWR ECO/TAC DIPLOM
FOR/AID DOMIN EDU/PROP ATTIT PWR...POLICY
METH/CNCPT CONT/OBS TREND CHARTS 20. PAGE 166 A3379

S63
WRIGHT Q.,"PROJECTED EUROPEAN UNION AND AMERICAN FUT
INTERNATIONAL PRESTIGE." EUR+WWI FRANCE GERMANY UK ORD/FREE
USA+45 INT/ORG NAT/G EDU/PROP ATTIT PERCEPT PWR REGION
...CONCPT OBS EEC 20 UN. PAGE 168 A3417

N63
LIBRARY HUNGARIAN ACADEMY SCI,HUNGARIAN BIBLIOG
PUBLICATIONS ON ASIA AND AFRICA, 1950-1962: A REGION
SELECTED BIBLIOGRAPHY (PAMPHLET). AFR ASIA HUNGARY DIPLOM
S/ASIA ECO/UNDEV NAT/G EDU/PROP ATTIT 20 UNESCO. WRITING
PAGE 88 A1807

B64
AFRO ASIAN SOLIDARITY AGAINST IMPERIALISM. AFR MARXISM
ISLAM S/ASIA ECO/UNDEV NAT/G POL/PAR TOP/EX PRESS DIPLOM
...INT ANTHOL 20 CHOU/ENLAI. PAGE 3 A0066 EDU/PROP
CHIEF

B64
ANDREWS D.H.,LATIN AMERICA: A BIBLIOGRAPHY OF BIBLIOG
PAPERBACK BOOKS. SECT INT/TRADE EDU/PROP WAR L/A+17C
GOV/REL ADJUST NAT/LISM ATTIT...ART/METH LING BIOG CULTURE
20. PAGE 8 A0160 NAT/G

B64
APTER D.E.,IDEOLOGY AND DISCONTENT. FUT WOR+45 ACT/RES
CONSTN CULTURE INTELL SOCIETY STRUCT INT/ORG NAT/G ATTIT
DELIB/GP LEGIS CREATE PLAN TEC/DEV EDU/PROP EXEC
PERCEPT PERSON RIGID/FLEX ALL/VALS...POLICY
TOT/POP. PAGE 8 A0171

B64
BLACKSTOCK P.W.,THE STRATEGY OF SUBVERSION. USA+45 ORD/FREE
FORCES EDU/PROP ADMIN COERCE GOV/REL...DECISION MGT DIPLOM
20 DEPT/DEFEN CIA DEPT/STATE. PAGE 15 A0301 CONTROL

B64
DUBOIS J.,DANGER OVER PANAMA. FUT PANAMA SCHOOL DIPLOM
PROB/SOLV EDU/PROP MARXISM...POLICY 19/20 TREATY COERCE
INTERVENT CANAL/ZONE. PAGE 39 A0790

B64
ETZIONI A.,WINNING WITHOUT WAR. FUT MOD/EUR USA+45 PWR
WOR+45 ECO/DEV ECO/UNDEV INT/ORG NAT/G FORCES TREND
TOP/EX PLAN TEC/DEV ECO/TAC DOMIN EDU/PROP LEGIT DIPLOM
COERCE CHOOSE ATTIT MORAL ORD/FREE RESPECT WEALTH USSR
MAJORIT. PAGE 43 A0871

B64
FALK R.A.,THE ROLE OF DOMESTIC COURTS IN THE LAW
INTERNATIONAL LEGAL ORDER. FUT WOR+45 INT/ORG NAT/G INT/LAW
JUDGE EDU/PROP LEGIT CT/SYS...POLICY RELATIV JURID
CONCPT GEN/LAWS 20. PAGE 43 A0889

B64
FISHER R.,INTERNATIONAL CONFLICT AND BEHAVIORAL INT/ORG
SCIENCE: THE CRAIGVILLE PAPERS. COM FUT USA+45 PLAN
WOR+45 NAT/G DELIB/GP EX/STRUC FORCES ECO/TAC DOMIN DIPLOM
EDU/PROP LEGIT COERCE ATTIT PERCEPT ORD/FREE PWR
RESPECT...PSY SOC VAL/FREE. PAGE 46 A0940

B64
GARDNER L.C.,ECONOMIC ASPECTS OF NEW DEAL ECO/TAC
DIPLOMACY. USA-45 WOR-45 LAW ECO/DEV INT/ORG NAT/G DIPLOM
VOL/ASSN LEGIS TOP/EX EDU/PROP ORD/FREE PWR WEALTH
...POLICY TIME/SEQ VAL/FREE 20 ROOSEVLT/F. PAGE 51
A1043

B64
GRODZINS M.,THE ATOMIC AGE: FORTY-FIVE SCIENTISTS INTELL
AND SCHOLARS SPEAK ON NATIONAL AND WORLD AFFAIRS. ARMS/CONT
FUT USA+45 WOR+45 R+D INT/ORG NAT/G CONSULT TEC/DEV NUC/PWR
EDU/PROP ATTIT PERSON ORD/FREE...HUM CONCPT
TIME/SEQ CON/ANAL. PAGE 57 A1169

B64
HALPERIN S.W.,MUSSOLINI AND ITALIAN FASCISM. ITALY FASCISM
NAT/G POL/PAR SECT ECO/TAC LEAD PWR SOCISM...POLICY NAT/LISM
20 MUSSOLIN/B. PAGE 60 A1241 EDU/PROP
CHIEF

B64
HAMBRIDGE G.,DYNAMICS OF DEVELOPMENT. AGRI FINAN ECO/UNDEV
INDUS LABOR INT/TRADE EDU/PROP ADMIN LEAD OWN ECO/TAC
HEALTH...ANTHOL BIBLIOG 20. PAGE 61 A1245 OP/RES
ACT/RES

B64
HAMRELL S.,THE SOVIET BLOC, CHINA, AND AFRICA. AFR MARXISM
CHINA/COM COM USSR ECO/UNDEV EDU/PROP 20. PAGE 61 DIPLOM
A1249 CONTROL
FOR/AID

B64
IKLE F.C.,HOW NATIONS NEGOTIATE. COM EUR+WWI USA+45 NAT/G
INTELL INT/ORG VOL/ASSN DELIB/GP ACT/RES CREATE PWR
DOMIN EDU/PROP ADJUD ROUTINE ATTIT PERSON ORD/FREE POLICY

RESPECT SKILL...PSY SOC OBS VAL/FREE. PAGE 70 A1433

B64
KENNEDY J.F.,THE BURDEN AND THE GLORY. FUT USA+45 TEC/DEV ECO/TAC EDU/PROP ARMS/CONT MURDER RACE/REL PEACE...ANTHOL 20 KENNEDY/JF COLD/WAR NATO PRESIDENT. PAGE 78 A1593
ADMIN POLICY GOV/REL DIPLOM

B64
KOLARZ W.,COMMUNISM AND COLONIALISM. AFR ASIA USSR DISCRIM ATTIT ORD/FREE SOVEREIGN SOC/INTEG 20. PAGE 81 A1668
EDU/PROP DIPLOM TOTALISM COLONIAL

B64
MEYER F.S.,WHAT IS CONSERVATISM? USA+45 NAT/G FORCES DIPLOM ORD/FREE IDEA/COMP. PAGE 100 A2048
CONSERVE CONCPT EDU/PROP CAP/ISM

B64
PERKINS D.,THE AMERICAN DEMOCRACY: ITS RISE TO POWER. ASIA USSR LAW CULTURE FINAN EDU/PROP COLONIAL CHOOSE...POLICY CHARTS BIBLIOG WORSHIP PRESIDENT 15/20 NEGRO. PAGE 115 A2362
LOC/G ECO/TAC WAR DIPLOM

B64
ROSENAU J.N.,INTERNATIONAL ASPECTS OF CIVIL STRIFE. CHINA/COM CUBA EUR+WWI USA+45 USSR BAL/PWR EDU/PROP NEUTRAL COERCE MORAL...NAT/COMP 20 COLD/WAR UN. PAGE 124 A2533
POLICY DIPLOM REV WAR

B64
RUBINSTEIN A.Z.,THE SOVIETS IN INTERNATIONAL ORGANIZATIONS: CHANGING POLICY TOWARD DEVELOPING COUNTRIES, 1953-1963. COM DELIB/GP ACT/RES ECO/TAC EDU/PROP ADMIN ATTIT ORD/FREE PWR...INT VAL/FREE UN 20. PAGE 125 A2563
ECO/UNDEV INT/ORG USSR

B64
SINGER H.W.,INTERNATIONAL DEVELOPMENT: GROWTH AND CHANGE. AFR BRAZIL L/A+17C WOR+45 CULTURE AGRI INDUS NAT/G ACT/RES ECO/TAC EDU/PROP WEALTH...GEOG CONCPT METH/CNCPT STAT HYPO/EXP WORK TOT/POP 20. PAGE 133 A2723
FINAN ECO/UNDEV FOR/AID INT/TRADE

B64
SPECTOR S.D.,A CHECKLIST OF PAPERBOUND BOOKS ON RUSSIA. USSR SECT DIPLOM EDU/PROP HEALTH...PHIL/SCI PSY SOC SOC/WK WORSHIP 20. PAGE 135 A2775
BIBLIOG COM PERF/ART

B64
SULLIVAN G.,THE STORY OF THE PEACE CORPS. USA+45 WOR+45 INTELL FACE/GP NAT/G SCHOOL VOL/ASSN CONSULT EX/STRUC PLAN EDU/PROP ADMIN ATTIT DRIVE ALL/VALS ...POLICY HEAL SOC CONCPT INT QU BIOG TREND SOC/EXP WORK. PAGE 140 A2861
INT/ORG ECO/UNDEV FOR/AID PEACE

B64
TEPASKE J.J.,EXPLOSIVE FORCES IN LATIN AMERICA. CULTURE INTELL ECO/UNDEV INT/ORG NAT/G SECT FORCES ECO/TAC EDU/PROP PWR WEALTH SOC. PAGE 142 A2903
L/A+17C RIGID/FLEX FOR/AID USSR

B64
THANT U.,TOWARD WORLD PEACE. DELIB/GP TEC/DEV EDU/PROP WAR SOVEREIGN...INT/LAW 20 UN MID/EAST. PAGE 142 A2907
DIPLOM BIOG PEACE COERCE

B64
UN PUB. INFORM. ORGAN.,EVERY MAN'S UNITED NATIONS. UNIV WOR+45 CONSTN CULTURE SOCIETY ECO/DEV ECO/UNDEV NAT/G ACT/RES PLAN ECO/TAC INT/TRADE EDU/PROP LEGIT PEACE ATTIT ALL/VALS...POLICY HUM INT/LAW CONCPT CHARTS UN TOT/POP 20. PAGE 147 A3004
INT/ORG ROUTINE

B64
UNESCO,WORLD COMMUNICATIONS: PRESS, RADIO, TELEVISION, FILM (4TH ED.). WOR+45 DIPLOM TV PEACE ...NAT/COMP SOC/INTEG 20 FILM. PAGE 148 A3023
COM/IND EDU/PROP PRESS TEC/DEV

B64
US HOUSE COMM FOREIGN AFFAIRS,HEARINGS ON H.R. 10502 TO AMEND FURTHER THE FOREIGN ASSISTANCE ACT OF 1961. AFR ASIA L/A+17C INT/ORG CONSULT DELIB/GP TEC/DEV ECO/TAC EDU/PROP CONFER 20 UN NATO CONGRESS AID. PAGE 153 A3130
FOR/AID DIPLOM ORD/FREE ECO/UNDEV

B64
WEINTRAUB S.,THE WAR IN THE WARDS. KOREA/N WOR+45 DIPLOM COERCE ORD/FREE SKILL 20 TREATY. PAGE 162 A3308
EDU/PROP PEACE CROWD PUB/INST

B64
WYTHE G.,THE UNITED STATES AND INTER-AMERICAN RELATIONS: A CONTEMPORARY APPRAISAL. L/A+17C USA+45 ECO/UNDEV INT/ORG NAT/G VOL/ASSN INT/TRADE EDU/PROP DRIVE...SOC TREND OAS UN 20. PAGE 168 A3425
ATTIT ECO/TAC FOR/AID

L64
BARROS J.,"THE GREEK-BULGARIAN INCIDENT OF 1925: THE LEAGUE OF NATIONS AND THE GREAT POWERS." BULGARIA EUR+WWI NAT/G FORCES ECO/TAC EDU/PROP LEGIT ROUTINE COERCE WAR PEACE DRIVE PWR...JURID CONCPT METH/CNCPT GEN/LAWS GEN/METH LEAGUE/NAT TOT/POP 20. PAGE 11 A0228
INT/ORG ORD/FREE DIPLOM

L64
CAMPBELL J.C.,"THE MIDDLE EAST IN THE MUTED COLD WAR." COM EUR+WWI UAR USA+45 USSR STRUCT ECO/UNDEV NAT/G VOL/ASSN EX/STRUC TOP/EX DIPLOM ECO/TAC EDU/PROP...TIME/SEQ COLD/WAR 20. PAGE 23 A0475
ISLAM FOR/AID NAT/LISM

L64
CARNEGIE ENDOWMENT INT. PEACE,"POLITICAL QUESTIONS (ISSUES BEFORE THE NINETEENTH GENERAL ASSEMBLY)." SPACE WOR+45 CONSTN FINAN NAT/G CONSULT DELIB/GP FORCES LEGIS TEC/DEV EDU/PROP LEGIT ARMS/CONT COERCE NUC/PWR ATTIT ALL/VALS...CONCPT OBS UN COLD/WAR 20. PAGE 24 A0490
INT/ORG PEACE

L64
CLAUDE I.,"THE OAS, THE UN, AND THE UNITED STATES." L/A+17C USA+45 CONSTN NAT/G DELIB/GP DOMIN EDU/PROP LEGIT REGION COERCE ORD/FREE PWR...TIME/SEQ TREND STERTYP OAS UN 20. PAGE 27 A0546
INT/ORG POLICY

L64
POUNDS N.J.G.,"THE POLITICS OF PARTITION." AFR ASIA COM EUR+WWI FUT ISLAM S/ASIA USA-45 LAW ECO/DEV ECO/UNDEV AGRI INDUS INT/ORG POL/PAR PROVS SECT FORCES TOP/EX EDU/PROP LEGIT ATTIT MORAL ORD/FREE PWR RESPECT WEALTH. PAGE 117 A2402
NAT/G NAT/LISM

L64
SYMONDS R.,"REFLECTIONS IN LOCALISATION." AFR S/ASIA UK STRATA INT/ORG NAT/G SCHOOL EDU/PROP LEGIT KNOWL ORD/FREE PWR RESPECT CMN/WLTH 20. PAGE 140 A2874
ADMIN MGT COLONIAL

L64
WORLD PEACE FOUNDATION,"INTERNATIONAL ORGANIZATIONS: SUMMARY OF ACTIVITIES." INDIA PAKISTAN TURKEY WOR+45 CONSTN CONSULT EX/STRUC ECO/TAC EDU/PROP LEGIT ORD/FREE...JURID SOC UN 20 CYPRESS. PAGE 167 A3397
INT/ORG ROUTINE

S64
CARNEGIE ENDOWMENT INT. PEACE,"COLONIAL COUNTRIES AND PEOPLES (ISSUES BEFORE THE NINETEENTH GENERAL ASSEMBLY)." AFR ISLAM L/A+17C WOR+45 DELIB/GP LEGIS ECO/TAC EDU/PROP NAT/LISM PEACE ALL/VALS...RECORD UN CMN/WLTH 20. PAGE 24 A0491
INT/ORG ECO/UNDEV COLONIAL

S64
CARNEGIE ENDOWMENT INT. PEACE,"HUMAN RIGHTS (ISSUES BEFORE THE NINETEENTH GENERAL ASSEMBLY)." AFR WOR+45 LAW CONSTN NAT/G EDU/PROP GP/REL DISCRIM PEACE ATTIT MORAL ORD/FREE...INT/LAW PSY CONCPT RECORD UN 20. PAGE 24 A0492
INT/ORG PERSON RACE/REL

S64
COCHRANE J.D.,"US ATTITUDES TOWARD CENTRAL-AMERICAN INTEGRATION." L/A+17C USA+45 ECO/UNDEV FACE/GP VOL/ASSN DELIB/GP ECO/TAC INT/TRADE EDU/PROP RIGID/FLEX ORD/FREE WEALTH...TIME/SEQ TOT/POP 20. PAGE 27 A0555
NAT/G ATTIT REGION

S64
COFFEY J.,"THE SOVIET VIEW OF A DISARMED WORLD." COM USA+45 INT/ORG NAT/G EX/STRUC EDU/PROP COERCE PERCEPT ORD/FREE PWR...TREND STERTYP VAL/FREE 20 UN. PAGE 27 A0556
FORCES ATTIT ARMS/CONT USSR

S64
DE GAULLE C.,"FRENCH WORLD VIEW." AFR ASIA CHINA/COM EUR+WWI ISLAM ECO/UNDEV INT/ORG NAT/G VOL/ASSN ACT/RES DIPLOM ECO/TAC EDU/PROP ATTIT DRIVE WEALTH 20. PAGE 35 A0702
TOP/EX PWR FOR/AID FRANCE

S64
DELGADO J.,"EL MOMENTO POLITICO HISPANOAMERICA." CHINA/COM FUT PANAMA USA+45 USSR INT/ORG NAT/G POL/PAR FORCES DOMIN REGION COERCE ATTIT ALL/VALS ...TRADIT CONCPT COLD/WAR 20. PAGE 36 A0728
L/A+17C EDU/PROP NAT/LISM

S64
DEVILLERS P.H.,"L'URSS, LA CHINE ET LES ORIGINES DE LA GUERRE DE COREE." ASIA CHINA/COM USSR INT/ORG ECO/TAC EDU/PROP ATTIT RIGID/FLEX PWR...STAND/INT HIST/WRIT COLD/WAR 20. PAGE 37 A0751
WOR+45 KOREA

S64
DRAKE S.T.C.,"DEMOCRACY ON TRIAL IN AFRICA." EUR+WWI FUT USA+45 ECO/UNDEV INT/ORG NAT/G POL/PAR TOP/EX EDU/PROP LEGIT ATTIT ALL/VALS...POLICY TREND GEN/LAWS VAL/FREE 20. PAGE 38 A0785
AFR STERTYP

S64
GARDNER R.N.,"THE SOVIET UNION AND THE UNITED NATIONS." WOR+45 FINAN POL/PAR VOL/ASSN FORCES ECO/TAC DOMIN EDU/PROP LEGIT ADJUD ADMIN ARMS/CONT COERCE ATTIT ALL/VALS...POLICY MAJORIT CONCPT OBS TIME/SEQ TREND STERTYP UN. PAGE 51 A1046
COM INT/ORG USSR

S64
GARDNER R.N.,"GATT AND THE UNITED NATIONS CONFERENCE ON TRADE AND DEVELOPMENT." USA+45 WOR+45 SOCIETY ECO/UNDEV MARKET NAT/G DELIB/GP ACT/RES PLAN ECO/TAC TARIFFS EDU/PROP ROUTINE DRIVE RIGID/FLEX WEALTH...DECISION MGT TREND UN TOT/POP 20 GATT. PAGE 51 A1047
INT/ORG INT/TRADE

S64
GARMARNIKOW M.,"INFLUENCE-BUYING IN WEST AFRICA." COM FUT USSR INTELL NAT/G PLAN TEC/DEV ECO/TAC DOMIN EDU/PROP REGION NAT/LISM ATTIT DRIVE ALL/VALS SOVEREIGN...POLICY PSY SOC CONCPT TREND STERTYP WORK COLD/WAR 20. PAGE 51 A1049
AFR ECO/UNDEV FOR/AID SOCISM

S64
GERBET P.,"LA MISE EN OEUVRE DU MARCHE COMMUN AGRICOLE." ECO/DEV MARKET INT/ORG NAT/G PLAN EDU/PROP NAT/LISM WEALTH...OBS EEC VAL/FREE 20.
EUR+WWI AGRI REGION

PAGE 52 A1064

S64
GREENBERG S.,"JUDAISM AND WORLD JUSTICE." MEDIT-7 WOR+45 LAW CULTURE SOCIETY INT/ORG NAT/G FORCES EDU/PROP ATTIT DRIVE PERSON SUPEGO ALL/VALS ...POLICY PSY CONCPT GEN/LAWS JEWS. PAGE 55 A1140 SECT JURID PEACE

S64
GROSSER A.,"Y A-T-IL UN CONFLIT FRANCO-AMERICAIN." EUR+WWI USA+45 INT/ORG NAT/G PLAN BAL/PWR DIPLOM EDU/PROP NUC/PWR ATTIT DRIVE ORD/FREE PWR...CONCPT OBS TIME/SEQ TREND STERTYP VAL/FREE COLD/WAR. PAGE 57 A1179 VOL/ASSN NAT/LISM FRANCE

S64
GRZYBOWSKI K.,"INTERNATIONAL ORGANIZATIONS FROM THE SOVIET POINT OF VIEW." WOR+45 WOR-45 CULTURE ECO/DEV VOL/ASSN EDU/PROP ATTIT RIGID/FLEX KNOWL ...SOC OBS TIME/SEQ TREND GEN/LAWS VAL/FREE ILO UN 20. PAGE 58 A1184 COM INT/ORG DIPLOM USSR

S64
HOFFMANN S.,"CE QU'EN PENSENT LES AMERICAINS." EUR+WWI INT/ORG VOL/ASSN PLAN BAL/PWR DIPLOM DOMIN EDU/PROP REGION ARMS/CONT DRIVE ORD/FREE PWR ...POLICY CONCPT OBS TREND STERTYP COLD/WAR VAL/FREE 20. PAGE 66 A1357 USA+45 ATTIT FRANCE

S64
HOSCH L.G.,"PUBLIC ADMINISTRATION ON THE INTERNATIONAL FRONTIER." WOR+45 R+D NAT/G EDU/PROP EXEC KNOWL ORD/FREE VAL/FREE 20 UN. PAGE 68 A1390 INT/ORG MGT

S64
HOSKYNS C.,"THE AFRICAN STATES AND THE UNITED NATIONS: 1958-1964." SOUTH/AFR NAT/G VOL/ASSN CONSULT BAL/PWR EDU/PROP MORAL ORD/FREE PWR ...CONCPT TREND UN 20. PAGE 68 A1393 AFR INT/ORG DIPLOM

S64
HOVET T. JR.,"THE ROLE OF AFRICA IN THE UNITED NATIONS." FUT WOR+45 NAT/G DELIB/GP DOMIN EDU/PROP LEGIT ORD/FREE PWR RESPECT SKILL...OBS TIME/SEQ TREND VAL/FREE UN 20. PAGE 68 A1398 AFR INT/ORG DIPLOM

S64
JACK H.,"NONALIGNMENT AND A TEST BAN AGREEMENT: THE ROLE OF THE NON-ALIGNED STATES." WOR+45 INT/ORG CONSULT DOMIN EDU/PROP LEGIT CHOOSE PEACE ATTIT DRIVE KNOWL ORD/FREE...TREND CHARTS GEN/LAWS UN VAL/FREE 20. PAGE 72 A1471 PWR CONCPT NUC/PWR

S64
JORDAN A.,"POLITICAL COMMUNICATION: THE THIRD DIMENSION OF STRATEGY." USA+45 WOR+45 INT/ORG NAT/G CONSULT FORCES PLAN LEGIT EXEC PERCEPT ALL/VALS ...POLICY RELATIV PSY NEW/IDEA AUD/VIS EXHIBIT TOT/POP 20. PAGE 75 A1534 EDU/PROP RIGID/FLEX ATTIT

S64
KHAN M.Z.,"ISLAM AND INTERNATIONAL RELATIONS." FUT WOR+45 LAW CULTURE SOCIETY NAT/G SECT DELIB/GP FORCES EDU/PROP ATTIT PERSON SUPEGO ALL/VALS ...POLICY PSY CONCPT MYTH HIST/WRIT GEN/LAWS. PAGE 78 A1608 ISLAM INT/ORG DIPLOM

S64
KHAN M.Z.,"THE PRESIDENT OF THE GENERAL ASSEMBLY." WOR+45 CONSTN DELIB/GP EDU/PROP LEGIT ROUTINE PWR RESPECT SKILL...DECISION SOC BIOG TREND UN 20. PAGE 78 A1609 INT/ORG TOP/EX

S64
KOTANI H.,"PEACE-KEEPING: PROBLEMS FOR SMALLER COUNTRIES." FUT WOR+45 NAT/G ACT/RES PLAN DOMIN EDU/PROP COERCE ALL/VALS...POLICY UN TOT/POP 20. PAGE 82 A1673 INT/ORG FORCES

S64
LERNER W.,"THE HISTORICAL ORIGINS OF THE SOVIET DOCTRINE OF PEACEFUL COEXISTENCE." COM USSR INT/ORG NAT/G VOL/ASSN PLAN PEACE ATTIT RIGID/FLEX PWR MARXISM...TIME/SEQ COLD/WAR 20. PAGE 87 A1788 EDU/PROP DIPLOM

S64
LEVI W.,"CHINA AND THE UNITED NATIONS." ASIA CHINA CHINA/COM WOR+45 WOR-45 CONSTN NAT/G DELIB/GP EX/STRUC FORCES ACT/RES EDU/PROP PWR...POLICY RECORD TIME/SEQ GEN/LAWS UN COLD/WAR 20. PAGE 88 A1794 INT/ORG ATTIT NAT/LISM

S64
MOWER A.G.,"THE OFFICIAL PRESSURE GROUP OF THE COUNCIL OF EUROPE'S CONSULATIVE ASSEMBLY." EUR+WWI SOCIETY STRUCT FINAN CONSULT ECO/TAC ADMIN ROUTINE ATTIT PWR WEALTH...STAT CHARTS 20 COUNCL/EUR. PAGE 105 A2160 INT/ORG EDU/PROP

S64
PALMER N.D.,"INDIA AS A FACTOR IN UNITED STATES FOREIGN POLICY." INDIA USA+45 USA-45 ECO/UNDEV NAT/G TOP/EX ECO/TAC EDU/PROP...METH/CNCPT TIME/SEQ 20. PAGE 113 A2323 S/ASIA ATTIT FOR/AID DIPLOM

S64
PESELT B.M.,"COMMUNIST ECONOMIC OFFENSIVE." WOR+45 SOCIETY INT/ORG PLAN ECO/TAC DOMIN EDU/PROP ATTIT PERSON PWR WEALTH...TREND CHARTS 20. PAGE 115 A2366 COM ECO/UNDEV FOR/AID USSR

S64
RUBIN R.,"THE UN CORRESPONDENT." WOR+45 FACE/GP PROF/ORG EDU/PROP ROUTINE PERCEPT KNOWL...RECORD STAND/INT QU UN WORK TOT/POP VAL/FREE 20. PAGE 125 A2560 INT/ORG ATTIT DIPLOM

S64
RUBINSTEIN A.Z.,"THE SOVIET IMAGE OF WESTERN EUROPE." COM EUR+WWI FRANCE GERMANY GERMANY/W USA+45 USSR INT/ORG NAT/G VOL/ASSN FORCES TOP/EX BAL/PWR EDU/PROP ORD/FREE PWR...MYTH RECORD NATO EEC 20. PAGE 125 A2564 RIGID/FLEX ATTIT

S64
SCHWELB E.,"OPERATION OF THE EUROPEAN CONVENTION ON HUMAN RIGHTS." EUR+WWI LAW SOCIETY CREATE EDU/PROP ADJUD ADMIN PEACE ATTIT ORD/FREE PWR...POLICY INT/LAW CONCPT OBS GEN/LAWS UN VAL/FREE ILO 20 ECHR. PAGE 130 A2665 INT/ORG MORAL

S64
SINGH N.,"THE CONTEMPORARY PRACTICE OF INDIA IN THE FIELD OF INTERNATIONAL LAW." INDIA S/ASIA INT/ORG NAT/G DOMIN EDU/PROP LEGIT KNOWL...CONCPT TOT/POP 20. PAGE 133 A2734 LAW ATTIT DIPLOM INT/LAW

S64
WOOD H.B.,"STRETCHING YOUR FOREIGN-AID DOLLAR." USA+45 WOR+45 CONSULT EDU/PROP ATTIT WEALTH...OBS TOT/POP CONGRESS 20. PAGE 166 A3390 ECO/UNDEV MGT FOR/AID

C64
SCHRAMM W.,"MASS MEDIA AND NATIONAL DEVELOPMENT: THE ROLE OF INFORMATION IN DEVELOPING COUNTRIES." FINAN R+D ACT/RES PLAN TEC/DEV DIPLOM CHOOSE SUPEGO ORD/FREE...BIBLIOG 20. PAGE 129 A2645 ECO/UNDEV COM/IND EDU/PROP MAJORIT

B65
AIR UNIVERSITY LIBRARY,LATIN AMERICA, SELECTED REFERENCES. ECO/UNDEV FORCES EDU/PROP MARXISM 20 OAS. PAGE 5 A0106 BIBLIOG L/A+17C NAT/G DIPLOM

B65
BRACKETT R.D.,PATHWAYS TO PEACE. SECT VOL/ASSN GP/REL PERS/REL DISCRIM...LING 20 UN PEACE/CORP. PAGE 18 A0366 PEACE INT/ORG EDU/PROP PARTIC

B65
BRIDGMAN J.,GERMAN AFRICA: A SELECT ANNOTATED BIBLIOGRAPHY. AFR AGRI DIPLOM REPAR WAR FASCISM 20. PAGE 18 A0374 BIBLIOG/A COLONIAL NAT/G EDU/PROP

B65
BROOKINGS INSTITUTION,BROOKINGS PAPERS ON PUBLIC POLICY. USA+45 ECO/UNDEV LEGIS CAP/ISM ECO/TAC TAX EDU/PROP CONTROL APPORT 20. PAGE 19 A0395 DIPLOM FOR/AID POLICY FINAN

B65
COOMBS P.H.,EDUCATION AND FOREIGN AID. AFR USA+45 DIPLOM EFFICIENCY KNOWL ORD/FREE...ANTHOL 20 AID. PAGE 30 A0608 EDU/PROP FOR/AID SCHOOL ECO/UNDEV

B65
COOPER S.,BEHIND THE GOLDEN CURTAIN: A VIEW OF THE USA. UK USA+45 SECT EDU/PROP COERCE LEISURE ORD/FREE WEALTH 20. PAGE 30 A0609 SOCIETY DIPLOM ATTIT ACT/RES

B65
DAVISON W.P.,INTERNATIONAL POLITICAL COMMUNICATION. COM USA+45 WOR+45 CULTURE ECO/UNDEV NAT/G PROB/SOLV PRESS TV ADMIN 20 FILM. PAGE 34 A0693 EDU/PROP DIPLOM PERS/REL COM/IND

B65
DOMENACH J.M.,LA PROPAGANDE POLITIQUE. COM/IND INT/ORG POL/PAR DOMIN RIGID/FLEX FASCISM MARXISM ...PSY 20. PAGE 38 A0770 ATTIT EDU/PROP TEC/DEV MYTH

B65
EDUCATION AND WORLD AFFAIRS,THE UNIVERSITY LOOKS ABROAD: APPROACHES TO WORLD AFFAIRS AT SIX AMERICAN UNIVERSITIES. USA+45 CREATE EDU/PROP CONFER LEAD KNOWL 20 CORNELL/U MICH/STA/U STANFORD/U TULANE/U WISCONSN/U. PAGE 40 A0822 ACADEM DIPLOM ATTIT GP/COMP

B65
FLYNN A.H.,WORLD UNDERSTANDING: A SELECTED BIBLIOGRAPHY. WOR+45 PROB/SOLV BAL/PWR DIPLOM EFFICIENCY PEACE UN. PAGE 47 A0956 BIBLIOG/A INT/ORG EDU/PROP ROUTINE

B65
FRASER S.,GOVERNMENTAL POLICY AND INTERNATIONAL EDUCATION. CHINA/COM COM USA+45 WOR+45 CONTROL MARXISM...ANTHOL BIBLIOG/A 20 UN. PAGE 48 A0989 EDU/PROP DIPLOM POLICY NAT/G

B65
HALLE L.J.,THE SOCIETY OF MAN. WOR+45 WOR-45 EDU/PROP NAT/LISM MARXISM CONCPT. PAGE 60 A1231 DIPLOM PHIL/SCI CREATE SOCIETY

B65
HALPERIN E.,NATIONALISM AND COMMUNISM. CHILE L/A+17C CAP/ISM EDU/PROP CHOOSE DISCRIM SOCISM ...BIBLIOG 20 COM/PARTY. PAGE 60 A1236 NAT/LISM MARXISM POL/PAR REV

B65
HUSS P.J.,RED SPIES IN THE UN. CZECHOSLVK USA+45 PEACE

USSR COM/IND FORCES EDU/PROP NUC/PWR MARXISM 20 UN COLD/WAR. PAGE 69 A1421 — INT/ORG BAL/PWR DIPLOM

B65
LAFAVE W.R.,LAW AND SOVIET SOCIETY. EX/STRUC DIPLOM DOMIN EDU/PROP PRESS ADMIN CRIME OWN MARXISM 20 KHRUSH/N. PAGE 84 A1710 — JURID CT/SYS ADJUD GOV/REL

B65
MEYERHOFF A.E.,THE STRATEGY OF PERSUASION: THE USE OF ADVERTISING SKILLS IN FIGHTING THE COLD WAR. USA+45 USSR PLAN ATTIT DRIVE...BIBLIOG 20 COLD/WAR. PAGE 100 A2054 — EDU/PROP SERV/IND METH/COMP DIPLOM

B65
MOLNAR T.,AFRICA: A POLITICAL TRAVELOGUE. STRUCT ECO/UNDEV DIPLOM EDU/PROP LEAD RACE/REL MARXISM 20 INTERVENT EUROPE. PAGE 102 A2101 — COLONIAL AFR ORD/FREE

B65
MONCRIEFF A.,SECOND THOUGHTS ON AID. WOR+45 ECO/UNDEV AGRI FINAN VOL/ASSN PLAN TEC/DEV GIVE EDU/PROP ROLE WEALTH 20. PAGE 102 A2105 — FOR/AID ECO/TAC INT/ORG IDEA/COMP

B65
NKRUMAH K.,NEO-COLONIALISM: THE LAST STAGE OF IMPERIALISM. AFR INT/ORG WORKER FOR/AID INT/TRADE EDU/PROP GOV/REL NAT/LISM SOVEREIGN POPULISM SOCISM ...SOCIALIST 20 THIRD/WRLD INTRVN/ECO. PAGE 109 A2243 — COLONIAL DIPLOM ECO/UNDEV ECO/TAC

B65
OGILVY-WEBB M.,THE GOVERNMENT EXPLAINS: A STUDY OF THE INFORMATION SERVICES. UK DELIB/GP LEGIS WORKER BUDGET DIPLOM 20. PAGE 111 A2284 — EDU/PROP ATTIT NAT/G ADMIN

B65
QURESHI I.H.,THE STRUGGLE FOR PAKISTAN. INDIA PAKISTAN UK CULTURE LEGIS DIPLOM EDU/PROP COLONIAL ATTIT SOVEREIGN 19/20 MUSLIM. PAGE 118 A2429 — GP/REL RACE/REL WAR SECT

B65
RANSOM H.H.,AN AMERICAN FOREIGN POLICY READER. USA+45 FORCES EDU/PROP COERCE NUC/PWR WAR PEACE ...DECISION 20. PAGE 119 A2443 — NAT/G DIPLOM POLICY

B65
ROSENBERG A.,DEMOCRACY AND SOCIALISM. COM EUR+WWI FRANCE MOD/EUR STRUCT INT/ORG NAT/G POL/PAR TOP/EX EDU/PROP COERCE PERSON PWR FASCISM MARXISM...CONCPT TIME/SEQ MARX/KARL 19/20. PAGE 124 A2535 — ATTIT

B65
SABLE M.H.,MASTER DIRECTORY FOR LATIN AMERICA. AGRI COM/IND FINAN R+D ACADEM LABOR NAT/G POL/PAR VOL/ASSN INT/TRADE EDU/PROP 20. PAGE 126 A2582 — INDEX L/A+17C INT/ORG DIPLOM

B65
SCOTT A.M.,THE REVOLUTION IN STATECRAFT: INFORMAL PENETRATION. WOR+45 WOR-45 CULTURE INT/ORG FORCES ECO/TAC ROUTINE...BIBLIOG 20. PAGE 130 A2670 — DIPLOM EDU/PROP FOR/AID

B65
UNESCO,HANDBOOK OF INTERNATIONAL EXCHANGES. COM/IND R+D ACADEM PROF/ORG VOL/ASSN CREATE TEC/DEV EDU/PROP AGREE 20 TREATY. PAGE 148 A3025 — INDEX INT/ORG DIPLOM PRESS

B65
US BUREAU EDUC CULTURAL AFF,RESOURCES SURVEY FOR LATIN AMERICAN COUNTRIES. L/A+17C USA+45 CULTURE INDUS INT/ORG SECT PLAN EDU/PROP POLICY. PAGE 150 A3056 — NAT/G ECO/UNDEV FOR/AID DIPLOM

B65
US DEPARTMENT OF DEFENSE,US SECURITY ARMS CONTROL, AND DISARMAMENT 1961-1965 (PAMPHLET). CHINA/COM COM GERMANY/W ISRAEL SPACE USA+45 USSR WOR+45 FORCES EDU/PROP DETER EQUILIB PEACE ALL/VALS...GOV/COMP 20 NATO. PAGE 151 A3077 — BIBLIOG/A ARMS/CONT NUC/PWR DIPLOM

B65
WARBEY W.,VIETNAM: THE TRUTH. FRANCE S/ASIA USA+45 VIETNAM CULTURE INT/ORG NAT/G DIPLOM FOR/AID EDU/PROP ARMS/CONT PEACE 20 TREATY NLF UN. PAGE 161 A3274 — WAR AGREE

B65
WRESZIN M.,OSWALD GARRISON VILLARD: PACIFIST AT WAR. EDU/PROP MORAL ORD/FREE. PAGE 167 A3398 — USA-45 NAT/G INT/ORG INTELL

L65
KAPLAN M.A.,"OLD REALITIES AND NEW MYTHS." USA+45 WOR+45 INT/ORG NAT/G TOP/EX ACT/RES BAL/PWR ECO/TAC EDU/PROP LEGIT RIGID/FLEX ALL/VALS...RECORD COLD/WAR 20. PAGE 76 A1564 — ATTIT MYTH DIPLOM

S65
DOSSICK J.J.,"DOCTORAL DISSERTATIONS ON RUSSIA, THE SOVIET UNION, AND EASTERN EUROPE." USSR ACADEM DIPLOM EDU/PROP MARXISM 19/20 COLD/WAR. PAGE 38 A0775 — BIBLIOG HUM SOC

S65
KHOURI F.J.,"THE JORDON RIVER CONTROVERSY." LAW SOCIETY ECO/UNDEV AGRI FINAN INDUS SECT FORCES ACT/RES PLAN TEC/DEV ECO/TAC EDU/PROP COERCE ATTIT DRIVE PERCEPT RIGID/FLEX ALL/VALS...GEOG SOC MYTH WORK. PAGE 78 A1610 — ISLAM INT/ORG ISRAEL JORDAN

S65
KORBONSKI A.,"USA POLICY IN EAST EUROPE." COM EUR+WWI GERMANY USA+45 CULTURE ECO/UNDEV EDU/PROP RIGID/FLEX WEALTH 20. PAGE 82 A1672 — ACT/RES ECO/TAC FOR/AID

S65
MERRITT R.L.,"WOODROW WILSON AND THE 'GREAT AND SOLEMN REFERENDUM,' 1920." USA-45 SOCIETY NAT/G CONSULT LEGIS ACT/RES PLAN DOMIN EDU/PROP ROUTINE ATTIT DISPL DRIVE PERSON RIGID/FLEX MORAL ORD/FREE ...PSY SOC CONCPT MYTH LEAGUE/NAT. PAGE 100 A2044 — INT/ORG TOP/EX DIPLOM

S65
RAY H.,"THE POLICY OF RUSSIA TOWARDS SINO-INDIAN CONFLICT." ASIA CHINA/COM COM INDIA USSR NAT/G TOP/EX FOR/AID EDU/PROP NEUTRAL COERCE PEACE RIGID/FLEX PWR...METH/CNCPT TIME/SEQ VAL/FREE 20. PAGE 120 A2452 — S/ASIA ATTIT DIPLOM WAR

S65
ROGGER H.,"EAST GERMANY: STABLE OR IMMOBILE." COM EUR+WWI GERMANY/E NAT/G INT/TRADE DOMIN EDU/PROP COERCE TOTALISM COLD/WAR 20. PAGE 123 A2516 — TOP/EX RIGID/FLEX GERMANY

S65
SPAAK P.H.,"THE SEARCH FOR CONSENSUS: A NEW EFFORT TO BUILD EUROPE." FRANCE GERMANY ECO/DEV NAT/G CONSULT FORCES PLAN EDU/PROP REGION CONSEN ATTIT ...SOC METH/CNCPT OBS TREND EEC NATO WORK 20. PAGE 135 A2770 — EUR+WWI INT/ORG

S65
TURNER F.C.,"THE IMPLICATIONS OF DEMOGRAPHIC CHANGE FOR NATIONALISM AND INTERNATIONALISM." FUT WOR+45 NAT/LISM AGE SEX CONCPT. PAGE 146 A2980 — SOCIETY EDU/PROP DIPLOM ORD/FREE

B66
ENTWICKLUNGSPOLITIK - HANDBUCH UND LEXIKON. MARKET SECT DIPLOM INT/TRADE EDU/PROP CATHISM 20. PAGE 14 A0283 — ECO/UNDEV FOR/AID ECO/TAC PLAN

B66
BLACKSTOCK P.W.,AGENTS OF DECEIT: FRAUDS, FORGERIES AND POLITICAL INTRIGUES AMONG NATIONS. USSR EDU/PROP WRITING KNOWL 18/20 COLD/WAR KENNAN/G. PAGE 15 A0302 — CON/ANAL DIPLOM HIST/WRIT

B66
BLOOMFIELD L.P.,KHRUSHCHEV AND THE ARMS RACE. USA+45 USSR ECO/DEV BAL/PWR EDU/PROP CONFER NUC/PWR ATTIT...CHARTS 20 KHRUSH/N. PAGE 16 A0321 — ARMS/CONT COM POLICY DIPLOM

B66
BRACKMAN A.C.,SOUTHEAST ASIA'S SECOND FRONT: THE POWER STRUGGLE IN THE MALAY ARCHIPELAGO. CHINA/COM INDONESIA MALAYSIA ECO/UNDEV INT/ORG NAT/G FORCES DIPLOM EDU/PROP REGION COERCE GUERRILLA AUTHORIT POPULISM...MAJORIT 20 KENNEDY/JF SEATO. PAGE 18 A0367 — S/ASIA MARXISM REV

B66
BROEKMEIJER M.W.J.,FICTION AND TRUTH ABOUT THE "DECADE OF DEVELOPMENT" WOR+45 AGRI FINAN INDUS NAT/G TEC/DEV DIPLOM EDU/PROP LEAD SKILL 20 THIRD/WRLD. PAGE 19 A0385 — FOR/AID POLICY ECO/UNDEV PLAN

B66
CLAUSEWITZ C.V.,ON WAR (VOL. III). UNIV EDU/PROP ...POLICY DECISION METH 18/20. PAGE 27 A0548 — WAR FORCES PLAN CIVMIL/REL

B66
COYLE D.C.,THE UNITED NATIONS AND HOW IT WORKS. ECO/UNDEV DELIB/GP BAL/PWR EDU/PROP ARMS/CONT NUC/PWR WAR 20 UN. PAGE 32 A0648 — INT/ORG PEACE DIPLOM INT/TRADE

B66
FREUND L.,POLITISCHE WAFFEN. EUR+WWI GERMANY CONSULT FORCES CONFER NUC/PWR 20. PAGE 49 A1000 — EDU/PROP DIPLOM ATTIT

B66
HANSON J.W.,EDUCATION AND THE DEVELOPMENT OF NATIONS. DIPLOM TASK ADJUST EFFICIENCY...POLICY ANTHOL 20. PAGE 61 A1256 — ECO/UNDEV EDU/PROP NAT/G PLAN

B66
HORMANN K.,PEACE AND MODERN WAR IN THE JUDGEMENT OF THE CHURCH. INT/ORG FORCES EDU/PROP ATTIT 20. PAGE 67 A1384 — PEACE WAR CATH MORAL

B66
KANET R.E.,THE SOVIET UNION AND SUB-SAHARAN AFRICA: COMMUNIST POLICY TOWARD AFRICA, 1917-1965. AFR USSR ECO/UNDEV TEC/DEV EDU/PROP TASK DISCRIM PEACE WEALTH ALL/IDEOS...CHARTS BIBLIOG SOC/INTEG 19/20 NEGRO UN INTERVENT. PAGE 76 A1555 — DIPLOM ECO/TAC MARXISM

B66
KAREFA-SMART J.,AFRICA: PROGRESS THROUGH COOPERATION. AFR FINAN TEC/DEV DIPLOM FOR/AID EDU/PROP CONFER REGION GP/REL WEALTH...HEAL SOC/INTEG 20. PAGE 76 A1566 — ORD/FREE ECO/UNDEV VOL/ASSN PLAN

B66
LEWIS S.,TOWARDS INTERNATIONAL CO-OPERATION (1ST ED.). WOR+45 AGRI INDUS EDU/PROP RACE/REL ISOLAT NAT/LISM ATTIT HEALTH WEALTH...CHARTS WORSHIP 20 UN. PAGE 88 A1803
DIPLOM ANOMIE PROB/SOLV INT/ORG

B66
MC CLELLAND C.A.,THEORY AND THE INTERNATIONAL SYSTEM. EDU/PROP PWR...DECISION SOC METH. PAGE 97 A1991
DIPLOM METH/CNCPT ACT/RES R+D

B66
RIESELBACH L.N.,THE ROOTS OF ISOLATIONISM* CONGRESSIONAL VOTING AND PRESIDENTIAL LEADERSHIP IN FOREIGN POLICY. POL/PAR LEGIS DIPLOM EDU/PROP LEAD REGION REPRESENT...SOC STAT IDEA/COMP HYPO/EXP BIBLIOG 19/20 CONGRESS. PAGE 121 A2477
ISOLAT CHOOSE CHIEF POLICY

B66
ROBOCK S.H.,INTERNATIONAL DEVELOPMENT 1965. AGRI INDUS VOL/ASSN PLAN TEC/DEV EDU/PROP HEALTH...JURID 20 UN PEACE/CORP. PAGE 122 A2508
FOR/AID INT/ORG GEOG ECO/UNDEV

B66
SAGER P.,MOSKAUS HAND IN INDIEN. INDIA USSR DIPLOM DOMIN...PSY CONCPT 20 COM/PARTY. PAGE 126 A2586
PRESS EDU/PROP METH POL/PAR

B66
SCHATTEN F.,COMMUNISM IN AFRICA. AFR GHANA GUINEA MALI CULTURE ECO/UNDEV LABOR SECT ECO/TAC EDU/PROP REV 20. PAGE 128 A2619
COLONIAL NAT/LISM MARXISM DIPLOM

B66
SMITH D.M.,AMERICAN INTERVENTION, 1917. GERMANY UK USA-45 SEA FORCES DIPLOM INT/TRADE EDU/PROP COERCE WEAPON PEACE 20 WILSON/W WWI. PAGE 134 A2746
WAR ATTIT POLICY NEUTRAL

B66
TINKER H.,SOUTH ASIA. UK LAW ECO/UNDEV AGRI ACADEM SECT DIPLOM EDU/PROP REV WEALTH ALL/IDEOS...CHARTS BIBLIOG GANDHI/M NEHRU/J. PAGE 144 A2945
S/ASIA COLONIAL TREND

B66
UN ECAFE,ADMINISTRATIVE ASPECTS OF FAMILY PLANNING PROGRAMMES (PAMPHLET). ASIA THAILAND WOR+45 VOL/ASSN PROB/SOLV BUDGET FOR/AID EDU/PROP CONFER CONTROL GOV/REL TIME 20 UN BIRTH/CON. PAGE 147 A2999
PLAN CENSUS FAM ADMIN

B66
US DEPARTMENT OF STATE,RESEARCH ON AFRICA (EXTERNAL RESEARCH LIST NO 5-25). LAW CULTURE ECO/UNDEV POL/PAR DIPLOM EDU/PROP LEAD REGION MARXISM...GEOG LING WORSHIP 20. PAGE 152 A3094
BIBLIOG/A ASIA S/ASIA NAT/G

B66
US DEPARTMENT OF STATE,RESEARCH ON THE AMERICAN REPUBLICS (EXTERNAL RESEARCH LIST NO 6-25). CULTURE SOCIETY POL/PAR DIPLOM EDU/PROP MARXISM WORSHIP 20 OAS. PAGE 152 A3095
BIBLIOG/A L/A+17C REGION NAT/G

B66
US DEPARTMENT OF STATE,RESEARCH ON THE MIDDLE EAST (EXTERNAL RESEARCH LIST NO 4-25). GREECE ISRAEL SYRIA UAR YEMEN CULTURE SOCIETY POL/PAR SECT DIPLOM EDU/PROP WAR NAT/LISM...GEOG GOV/COMP 20. PAGE 152 A3096
BIBLIOG/A ISLAM NAT/G REGION

B66
US DEPARTMENT OF STATE,RESEARCH ON THE USSR AND EASTERN EUROPE (EXTERNAL RESEARCH LIST NO 1-25). USSR LAW CULTURE SOCIETY NAT/G TEC/DEV DIPLOM EDU/PROP REGION...GEOG LING. PAGE 152 A3097
BIBLIOG/A EUR+WWI COM MARXISM

B66
US DEPARTMENT OF STATE,RESEARCH ON WESTERN EUROPE, GREAT BRITAIN, AND CANADA (EXTERNAL RESEARCH LIST NO 3-25). CANADA GERMANY/W UK LAW CULTURE NAT/G POL/PAR FORCES EDU/PROP REGION MARXISM...GEOG SOC WORSHIP 20 CMN/WLTH. PAGE 152 A3098
BIBLIOG/A EUR+WWI DIPLOM

B66
US SENATE COMM AERO SPACE SCI,SOVIET SPACE PROGRAMS, 1962-65; GOALS AND PURPOSES, ACHIEVEMENTS, PLANS, AND INTERNATIONAL IMPLICATIONS. USA+45 USSR R+D FORCES PLAN EDU/PROP PRESS ADJUD ARMS/CONT ATTIT MARXISM. PAGE 155 A3168
CONSULT SPACE FUT DIPLOM

B66
WILLIAMS P.,AID IN UGANDA - EDUCATION. UGANDA UK FINAN ACADEM INT/ORG SCHOOL PROB/SOLV ECO/TAC UTIL ...STAT CHARTS 20. PAGE 165 A3352
PLAN EDU/PROP FOR/AID ECO/UNDEV

S66
KLEIN S.,"A SURVEY OF SINO-JAPANESE TRADE, 1950-1966" TAIWAN EDU/PROP 20 CHINJAP. PAGE 80 A1649
INT/TRADE DIPLOM MARXISM

B67
BARANSON J.,TECHNOLOGY FOR UNDERDEVELOPED AREAS: AN ANNOTATED BIBLIOGRAPHY. FUT WOR+45 CULTURE INDUS INT/ORG CREATE PROB/SOLV INT/TRADE EDU/PROP AUTOMAT ...CONCPT METH. PAGE 11 A0218
BIBLIOG/A ECO/UNDEV TEC/DEV R+D

B67
CRABBS R.F.,UNITED STATES HIGHER EDUCATION AND WORLD AFFAIRS. WOR+45 R+D ACADEM...POLICY 20. PAGE 32 A0650
BIBLIOG/A NAT/G EDU/PROP DIPLOM

B67
DE BLIJ H.J.,SYSTEMATIC POLITICAL GEOGRAPHY. WOR+45 STRUCT INT/ORG NAT/G EDU/PROP ADMIN COLONIAL ROUTINE ORD/FREE PWR...IDEA/COMP T 20. PAGE 34 A0697
GEOG CONCPT METH

B67
FILENE P.G.,AMERICANS AND THE SOVIET EXPERIMENT, 1917-1933. USA-45 USSR INTELL NAT/G CAP/ISM DIPLOM EDU/PROP PRESS REV SOCISM...PSY 20. PAGE 45 A0930
ATTIT RIGID/FLEX MARXISM SOCIETY

B67
HOLSTI K.J.,INTERNATIONAL POLITICS* A FRAMEWORK FOR ANALYSIS. WOR+45 WOR-45 NAT/G EDU/PROP DETER WAR WEAPON PWR BIBLIOG. PAGE 67 A1372
DIPLOM BARGAIN POLICY INT/LAW

B67
KAROL K.S.,CHINA, THE OTHER COMMUNISM (TRANS. BY TOM BAISTOW). CHINA/COM CULTURE INDUS FORCES DIPLOM EDU/PROP CONTROL EXEC NUC/PWR ATTIT...SOC CHARTS 20. PAGE 77 A1567
NAT/G POL/PAR MARXISM INGP/REL

B67
MEHDI M.T.,PEACE IN THE MIDDLE EAST. ISRAEL SOCIETY NAT/G PLAN EDU/PROP NAT/LISM DRIVE...IDEA/COMP 20 JEWS. PAGE 99 A2033
ISLAM DIPLOM GP/REL COERCE

B67
MURTY B.S.,PROPAGANDA AND WORLD PUBLIC ORDER. FUT WOR+45 COM/IND INT/ORG PROB/SOLV ATTIT KNOWL ORD/FREE...POLICY UN. PAGE 106 A2183
EDU/PROP DIPLOM CONTROL JURID

B67
O'LEARY M.K.,THE POLITICS OF AMERICAN FOREIGN AID. USA+45 POL/PAR CHIEF BUDGET EDU/PROP LOBBY CONGRESS. PAGE 111 A2270
FOR/AID DIPLOM PARL/PROC ATTIT

B67
PIKE F.B.,FREEDOM AND REFORM IN LATIN AMERICA. BRAZIL URUGUAY CONSTN CULTURE SECT DIPLOM EDU/PROP PARTIC DRIVE ALL/VALS CATHISM...GEOG ANTHOL BIBLIOG REFORMERS BOLIV. PAGE 116 A2379
L/A+17C ORD/FREE ECO/UNDEV REV

B67
SALISBURY H.E.,ORBIT OF CHINA. ASIA CHINA/COM DIPLOM PEACE PWR 20. PAGE 126 A2593
EDU/PROP OBS INT ARMS/CONT

B67
US DEPARTMENT OF STATE,THE COUNTRY TEAM - AN ILLUSTRATED PROFILE OF OUR AMERICAN MISSIONS ABROAD. ECO/TAC FOR/AID EDU/PROP TASK PERS/REL ATTIT 20. PAGE 152 A3099
DIPLOM NAT/G VOL/ASSN GOV/REL

L67
GALTUNG J.,"ON THE EFFECTS OF INTERNATIONAL ECONOMIC SANCTIONS, WITH EXAMPLES FROM THE CASE OF RHODESIA." NAT/G DIPLOM EDU/PROP ADJUST EFFICIENCY ATTIT MORAL...OBS CHARTS 20. PAGE 51 A1035
SANCTION ECO/TAC INT/TRADE ECO/UNDEV

L67
GRAUBARD S.R.,"TOWARD THE YEAR 2000: WORK IN PROGRESS." FUT ACADEM SECT DELIB/GP DIPLOM EDU/PROP AGE/Y PERSON ROLE...PSY ANTHOL. PAGE 55 A1131
PREDICT PROB/SOLV SOCIETY CULTURE

S67
GLOBERSON A.,"SOCIAL GROWTH IN THE DEVELOPING COUNTRIES." CULTURE SOCIETY CONSULT PROB/SOLV SOC. PAGE 53 A1082
ECO/UNDEV FOR/AID EDU/PROP PLAN

S67
GODUNSKY Y.,"'APOSTLES OF PEACE' IN LATIN AMERICA." L/A+17C USA+45 BAL/PWR DIPLOM FOR/AID DOMIN COLONIAL CIVMIL/REL MARXIST. PAGE 53 A1086
ECO/UNDEV REV VOL/ASSN EDU/PROP

S67
KINGSLEY R.E.,"THE US BUSINESS IMAGE IN LATIN AMERICA." L/A+17C USA+45 NAT/G TEC/DEV CAP/ISM FOR/AID DOMIN EDU/PROP...CONCPT LING IDEA/COMP 20. PAGE 79 A1626
ATTIT LOVE DIPLOM ECO/UNDEV

S67
ROGERS W.C.,"A COMPARISON OF INFORMED AND GENERAL PUBLIC OPINION ON US FOREIGN POLICY." USA+45 DIPLOM EDU/PROP ORD/FREE...POLICY SAMP IDEA/COMP 20. PAGE 123 A2515
KNOWL ATTIT GP/COMP ELITES

S67
ROMANOVSKY S.,"MISUSE OF CULTURAL COOPERATION." USA+45 INTELL DIPLOM DOMIN ATTIT COLD/WAR. PAGE 123 A2518
EDU/PROP POLICY MARXISM CAP/ISM

S67
SENCOURT R.,"FOREIGN POLICY* AN HISTORIC RECTIFICATION." EUR+WWI UK DIPLOM EDU/PROP LEAD WAR CHOOSE PERS/REL...METH/COMP PARLIAMENT. PAGE 131 A2685
POLICY POL/PAR NAT/G

S67
SHOEMAKER R.L.,"JAPANESE ARMY AND THE WEST." ASIA ELITES EX/STRUC DIPLOM DOMIN EDU/PROP COERCE ATTIT AUTHORIT PWR 1/20 CHINJAP. PAGE 132 A2703
FORCES TEC/DEV WAR

PAGES:

Checked against order trays by ______

Checked against Card Catalog by ______

Completed to page

Please check:

LIBRARIANS:

Initial whem completed

320 ______________

330 ______________

340 ______________

390 ______________

BIOG. ______________

930 ______________

970 ______________

Typist: Completed to page ______________

Completed by Initial ______________

TOTALISM

S67
STEELE R.,"A TASTE FOR INTERVENTION." USA+45 FOR/AID INT/TRADE EDU/PROP COLONIAL WAR PWR...TREND 20 COLD/WAR. PAGE 137 A2812
POLICY DIPLOM DOMIN ATTIT

S67
STEGER H.S.,"RESEARCH ON LATIN AMERICA IN THE FEDERAL REPUBLIC OF GERMANY AND WEST BERLIN." FINAN DIPLOM INT/TRADE EDU/PROP...GEOG JURID CHARTS 19/20. PAGE 137 A2813
SOCIETY ECO/UNDEV ACADEM L/A+17C

S67
TERRILL R.,"THE SIEGE MENTALITY." CHINA/COM NAT/G FORCES DIPLOM REV EFFICIENCY NAT/LISM MARXISM ...TREND 20. PAGE 142 A2904
EDU/PROP WAR DOMIN

S67
WILLIAMS B.H.,"FREEDOM AS A SLOGAN IN INTERNATIONAL CONFLICT." VIETNAM DIPLOM COLONIAL. PAGE 164 A3351
EDU/PROP ORD/FREE WAR PWR

C67
GEHLEN M.P.,"THE POLITICS OF COEXISTENCE: SOVIET METHODS AND MOTIVES." COM USSR NAT/G INT/TRADE EDU/PROP ARMS/CONT DETER KNOWL...CHARTS IDEA/COMP 20 COLD/WAR. PAGE 52 A1056
BIBLIOG PEACE DIPLOM MARXISM

N67
US SUPERINTENDENT OF DOCUMENTS,SPACE: MISSILES, THE MOON, NASA, AND SATELLITES (PRICE LIST 79A). USA+45 COM/IND R+D NAT/G DIPLOM EDU/PROP ADMIN CONTROL HEALTH...POLICY SIMUL NASA CONGRESS. PAGE 157 A3206
BIBLIOG/A SPACE TEC/DEV PEACE

EDUCATION AND WORLD AFFAIRS A0822

EDUCATION....SEE EDU/PROP

EDUCATIONAL INSTITUTIONS....SEE ACADEM, SCHOOL

EDWARDS C.D. A0823

EEC....EUROPEAN ECONOMIC COMMUNITY; SEE ALSO VOL/ASSN

N
MONPIED E.,BIBLIOGRAPHIE FEDERALISTE: ARTICLES ET DOCUMENTS PUBLIES DANS LES PERIODIQUES PARUS EN FRANCE NOV. 1945-OCT. 1950. EUR+WWI WOR+45 ADMIN REGION ATTIT MARXISM PACIFISM 20 EEC. PAGE 103 A2108
BIBLIOG/A FEDERAL CENTRAL INT/ORG

N
FOREIGN AFFAIRS. SPACE WOR+45 WOR-45 CULTURE ECO/UNDEV FINAN NAT/G TEC/DEV INT/TRADE ARMS/CONT NUC/PWR...POLICY 20 UN EURATOM ECSC EEC. PAGE 2 A0034
BIBLIOG DIPLOM INT/ORG INT/LAW

NCO
CARRINGTON C.E.,THE COMMONWEALTH IN AFRICA (PAMPHLET). UK STRUCT NAT/G COLONIAL REPRESENT GOV/REL RACE/REL NAT/LISM...MAJORIT 20 EEC NEGRO COLD/WAR. PAGE 25 A0500
ECO/UNDEV AFR DIPLOM PLAN

B51
WHITE L.C.,INTERNATIONAL NON-GOVERNMENTAL ORGANIZATIONS. AFR ASIA COM EUR+WWI USA+45 WOR+45 INT/ORG DIPLOM INT/TRADE ALL/VALS...HUM FAO ILO EEC 20. PAGE 164 A3337
VOL/ASSN CONSULT

B52
ALEXANDROWICZ C.H.,INTERNATIONAL ECONOMIC ORGANIZATION. WOR+45 ECO/DEV ECO/UNDEV DIST/IND FINAN MARKET PLAN ECO/TAC LEGIT DRIVE WEALTH ...POLICY CONCPT QUANT OBS TIME/SEQ GEN/LAWS WORK EEC ILO OEEC UNESCO 20. PAGE 6 A0114
INT/ORG INT/TRADE

C54
BOWIE R.R.,"STUDIES IN FEDERALISM." AGRI FINAN LABOR EX/STRUC FORCES LEGIS DIPLOM INT/TRADE ADJUD ...BIBLIOG 20 EEC. PAGE 17 A0357
FEDERAL EUR+WWI INT/ORG CONSTN

B55
LANDHEER B.,EUROPEAN YEARBOOK, 1955. CONSTN ECO/DEV DIST/IND FINAN DELIB/GP ECO/TAC DETER NUC/PWR ...BIBLIOG 20 EEC. PAGE 84 A1717
EUR+WWI INT/ORG GOV/REL INT/TRADE

B57
ARON R.,L'UNIFICATION ECONOMIQUE DE L'EUROPE. EUR+WWI SWITZERLND UK INT/ORG NAT/G REGION NAT/LISM ORD/FREE PWR...CONCPT METH/CNCPT OBS TREND STERTYP GEN/LAWS EEC 20. PAGE 9 A0181
VOL/ASSN ECO/TAC

B57
TRIFFIN R.,EUROPE AND THE MONEY MUDDLE. USA+45 INT/ORG NAT/G CONSULT PLAN ECO/TAC EXEC ROUTINE BAL/PAY WEALTH...METH/CNCPT OBS TREND CHARTS STERTYP GEN/METH EEC VAL/FREE ECSC. PAGE 145 A2962
EUR+WWI ECO/DEV REGION

B58
HAAS E.B.,THE UNITING OF EUROPE. EUR+WWI INT/ORG NAT/G POL/PAR TOP/EX ECO/TAC EDU/PROP LEGIT FEDERAL NAT/LISM DRIVE RIGID/FLEX ORD/FREE PWR PLURISM ...POLICY CONCPT INT GEN/LAWS ECSC EEC 20. PAGE 59 A1204
VOL/ASSN ECO/DEV

B58
KINDLEBERGER C.P.,INTERNATIONAL ECONOMICS. WOR+45 WOR-45 ECO/DEV ECO/UNDEV FINAN VOL/ASSN ACT/RES DIPLOM ECO/TAC LEGIT REGION ATTIT DRIVE ORD/FREE WEALTH...POLICY STAT TREND GEN/LAWS EEC ECSC OEEC 20. PAGE 79 A1620
INT/ORG BAL/PWR TARIFFS

B58
SCITOUSKY T.,ECONOMIC THEORY AND WESTERN EUROPEAN INTEGRATION. EUR+WWI INT/ORG ACT/RES INT/TRADE REGION BAL/PAY WEALTH...METH/CNCPT STAT CHARTS GEN/METH ECSC TOT/POP EEC OEEC 20. PAGE 130 A2668
ECO/TAC

B59
BALL M.M.,NATO AND THE EUROPEAN MOVEMENT. EUR+WWI USA+45 INT/ORG FORCES BAL/PWR EDU/PROP LEGIT REGION ATTIT ORD/FREE PWR...STAT OBS TIME/SEQ TREND CHARTS ORG/CHARTS STERTYP COLD/WAR EEC OEEC 20 NATO. PAGE 10 A0212
DELIB/GP STRUCT

B59
ROBERTSON A.H.,EUROPEAN INSTITUTIONS: COOPERATION, INTEGRATION, UNIFICATION. EUR+WWI FINAN INT/ORG FORCES INT/TRADE TARIFFS 20 EEC EURATOM ECSC NATO TREATY. PAGE 122 A2496
ECO/DEV DIPLOM INDUS ECO/TAC

B59
ROPKE W.,INTERNATIONAL ORDER AND ECONOMIC INTEGRATION. ECO/DEV ECO/UNDEV AGRI FINAN INDUS INT/ORG WAR PEACE ORD/FREE...SOC METH/COMP 20 EEC. PAGE 123 A2524
INT/TRADE DIPLOM BAL/PAY ALL/IDEOS

B59
SANNWALD R.E.,ECONOMIC INTEGRATION: THEORETICAL ASSUMPTIONS AND CONSEQUENCES OF EUROPEAN UNIFICATION. EUR+WWI FUT FINAN INDUS VOL/ASSN ACT/RES ECO/TAC...PLURIST EEC OEEC 20. PAGE 127 A2601
INT/ORG ECO/DEV INT/TRADE

B59
WENTHOLT W.,SOME COMMENTS ON THE LIQUIDATION OF THE EUROPEAN PAYMENT UNION AND RELATED PROBLEMS (PAMPHLET). WOR+45 PLAN BUDGET PRICE CONTROL 20 EEC GOLD/STAND. PAGE 163 A3319
FINAN ECO/DEV INT/ORG ECO/TAC

L59
MURPHY J.C.,"SOME IMPLICATIONS OF EUROPE'S COMMON MARKET. IN (COOK P. ECONOMIC DEVELOPMENT AND INTERNATIONAL TRADE,." EUR+WWI ECO/DEV DIST/IND INDUS NAT/G PLAN ECO/TAC INT/TRADE WEALTH...STAT TREND OEEC TOT/POP 20 EEC. PAGE 106 A2178
MARKET INT/ORG REGION

S59
BELOFF M.,"NATIONAL GOVERNMENT AND INTERNATIONAL GOVERNMENT." WOR+45 R+D DELIB/GP ACT/RES PLAN PWR ...GEN/METH VAL/FREE EEC OEEC 20. PAGE 13 A0259
NAT/G INT/ORG DIPLOM

S59
SOLDATI A.,"EOCNOMIC DISINTEGRATION IN EUROPE." EUR+WWI FUT WOR+45 INDUS INT/ORG NAT/G CAP/ISM WEALTH...NEW/IDEA OBS TREND CHARTS EEC 20. PAGE 135 A2764
FINAN ECO/TAC

B60
CARNEGIE ENDOWMENT INT. PEACE,PERSPECTIVES ON PEACE - 1910-1960. WOR+45 WOR-45 INTELL INT/ORG CONSULT ACT/RES EDU/PROP ATTIT KNOWL ORD/FREE...TIME/SEQ TREND EEC OAS UNESCO NAZI 20. PAGE 24 A0489
FUT CONCPT ARMS/CONT PEACE

B60
ROPKE W.,A HUMANE ECONOMY. CULTURE ECO/DEV FINAN INDUS GP/REL CENTRAL WEALTH...GEOG SOC IDEA/COMP 20 EEC. PAGE 123 A2525
ECO/TAC INT/ORG DIPLOM ORD/FREE

B60
STEIN E.,AMERICAN ENTERPRISE IN THE EUROPEAN COMMON MARKET: A LEGAL PROFILE. EUR+WWI FUT USA+45 SOCIETY STRUCT ECO/DEV NAT/G VOL/ASSN CONSULT PLAN TEC/DEV ECO/TAC INT/TRADE ADMIN ATTIT RIGID/FLEX PWR...MGT NEW/IDEA STAT TREND COMPUT/IR SIMUL EEC 20. PAGE 137 A2814
MARKET ADJUD INT/LAW

B60
THE ECONOMIST (LONDON),THE COMMONWEALTH AND EUROPE. EUR+WWI WOR+45 AGRI FINAN INCOME...STAT CENSUS CHARTS CMN/WLTH EEC. PAGE 142 A2911
INT/TRADE INDUS INT/ORG NAT/COMP

S60
KREININ M.E.,"THE 'OUTER-SEVEN' AND EUROPEAN INTEGRATION." EUR+WWI FRANCE GERMANY ITALY UK ECO/DEV DIST/IND INT/TRADE DRIVE WEALTH...MYTH CHARTS EEC OEEC 20. PAGE 82 A1682
ECO/TAC GEN/LAWS

S60
NANES A.,"THE EUROPEAN COMMUNITY AND THE UNITED STATES: EVOLVING RELATIONS." EUR+WWI USA+45 WOR+45 ECO/UNDEV MARKET NAT/G DELIB/GP PLAN LEGIT ATTIT PWR WEALTH...CONCPT STAT TIME/SEQ CON/ANAL EEC OEEC 20 EURATOM. PAGE 107 A2194
INT/ORG REGION

N60
ERDMAN P.E.,COMMON MARKETS AND FREE TRADE AREAS (PAMPHLET). USA+45 MARKET INT/ORG TEC/DEV DIPLOM UTIL...CON/ANAL CHARTS BIBLIOG 20 EEC OEEC. PAGE 42 A0859
TREND PROB/SOLV INT/TRADE ECO/DEV

B61
BELOFF M.,NEW DIMENSIONS IN FOREIGN POLICY: A STUDY IN BRITISH ADMINISTRATION. UK NAT/G ATTIT RIGID/FLEX ORD/FREE...GEN/LAWS EUR+WWI CMN/WLTH EEC 20. PAGE 13 A0260
INT/ORG DIPLOM

B61
KITZINGER V.W.,THE CHALLENGE OF THE COMMON MARKET. EUR+WWI ECO/DEV DIST/IND PLAN ECO/TAC INT/TRADE LEGIT ATTIT PWR WEALTH...TIME/SEQ TREND CHARTS EEC 20. PAGE 80 A1647
MARKET INT/ORG UK

B61
PEASLEE A.J.,INTERNATIONAL GOVERNMENTAL ORGANIZATIONS (2 VOLS.). CONSTN VOL/ASSN DIPLOM ...GP/COMP 20 UN OAS EEC EFTA ECSC. PAGE 114 A2345
BIBLIOG INT/ORG INDEX LAW

S61
LANFALUSSY A.,"EUROPE'S PROGRESS: DUE TO COMMON MARKET." EUR+WWI ECO/DEV DELIB/GP PLAN ECO/TAC ROUTINE WEALTH...GEOG TREND EEC 20. PAGE 84 A1721
INT/ORG MARKET

S61
OCHENG D.,"ECONOMIC FORCES AND UGANDA'S FOREIGN POLICY." AFR UGANDA INT/TRADE TARIFFS INCOME SOVEREIGN WEALTH 20 EACM EEC TANGANYIKA. PAGE 111 A2274
ECO/TAC DIPLOM ECO/UNDEV INT/ORG

S61
RAY J.,"THE EUROPEAN FREE-TRADE ASSOCIATION AND ITS IMPACT ON INDIA'S TRADE." EUR+WWI FRANCE GERMANY INDIA S/ASIA UK NAT/G VOL/ASSN PLAN INT/TRADE ROUTINE WEALTH...STAT CHARTS CMN/WLTH EEC OEEC 20 EFTA. PAGE 120 A2453
ECO/DEV ECO/TAC

B62
ALEXANDROWICZ C.H.,WORLD ECONOMIC AGENCIES: LAW AND PRACTICE. WOR+45 DIST/IND FINAN LABOR CONSULT INT/TRADE TARIFFS REPRESENT HEALTH...JURID 20 UN GATT EEC OAS ECSC. PAGE 6 A0115
INT/LAW INT/ORG DIPLOM ADJUD

B62
BRYANT A.,A CHOICE FOR DESTINY: COMMONWEALTH AND THE COMMON MARKET. EUR+WWI FUT UK INT/TRADE COLONIAL ATTIT SOVEREIGN 20 CMN/WLTH EEC. PAGE 20 A0411
INT/ORG VOL/ASSN DIPLOM CHOOSE

B62
CARDOZA M.H.,DIPLOMATS IN INTERNATIONAL COOPERATION: STEPCHILDREN OF THE FOREIGN SERVICE. EUR+WWI USA+45 NAT/G CONSULT ACT/RES EDU/PROP ROUTINE RIGID/FLEX KNOWL SKILL...SOC OBS TIME/SEQ EEC OEEC NATO 20. PAGE 24 A0480
INT/ORG METH/CNCPT DIPLOM

B62
FRIEDMANN W.,METHODS AND POLICIES OF PRINCIPAL DONOR COUNTRIES IN PUBLIC INTERNATIONAL DEVELOPMENT FINANCING: PRELIMINARY APPRAISAL. FRANCE GERMANY/W UK USA+45 USSR WOR+45 FINAN TEC/DEV CAP/ISM DIPLOM ECO/TAC ATTIT 20 EEC. PAGE 49 A1002
INT/ORG FOR/AID NAT/COMP ADMIN

B62
GYORGY A.,PROBLEMS IN INTERNATIONAL RELATIONS. COM CT/SYS NUC/PWR ALL/IDEOS 20 UN EEC ECSC. PAGE 58 A1199
DIPLOM NEUTRAL BAL/PWR REV

B62
HUMPHREY D.D.,THE UNITED STATES AND THE COMMON MARKET. USA+45 INDUS MARKET INT/ORG PLAN EDU/PROP BAL/PAY DRIVE PWR WEALTH...TREND STERTYP EEC 20. PAGE 69 A1415
ATTIT ECO/TAC

B62
KRAFT J.,THE GRAND DESIGN. EUR+WWI USA+45 AGRI FINAN INDUS MARKET INT/ORG NAT/G PLAN ECO/TAC TARIFFS REGION DRIVE ORD/FREE WEALTH...POLICY OBS TREND EEC 20. PAGE 82 A1674
VOL/ASSN ECO/DEV INT/TRADE

B62
LAWSON R.,INTERNATIONAL REGIONAL ORGANIZATIONS. WOR+45 NAT/G VOL/ASSN CONSULT LEGIS EDU/PROP LEGIT ADMIN EXEC ROUTINE HEALTH PWR WEALTH...JURID EEC COLD/WAR 20 UN. PAGE 86 A1752
INT/ORG DELIB/GP REGION

B62
LIPPMANN W.,WESTERN UNITY AND THE COMMON MARKET. EUR+WWI FRANCE GERMANY/W UK USA+45 ECO/DEV AGRI FINAN MARKET INT/ORG NAT/G FOR/AID AGREE WEALTH 20 EEC. PAGE 89 A1831
DIPLOM INT/TRADE VOL/ASSN

B62
MEADE J.E.,CASE STUDIES IN EUROPEAN ECONOMIC UNION. BELGIUM EUR+WWI LUXEMBOURG NAT/G INT/TRADE REGION ROUTINE WEALTH...METH/CNCPT STAT CHARTS ECSC TOT/POP OEEC EEC 20. PAGE 99 A2028
INT/ORG ECO/TAC

B62
RIVKIN A.,AFRICA AND THE WEST. AFR EUR+WWI FUT ISLAM ISRAEL USA+45 SOCIETY INT/ORG FORCES CREATE PLAN FOR/AID EDU/PROP ATTIT...CONCPT TREND EEC 20 CONGRESS UN. PAGE 121 A2488
ECO/UNDEV ECO/TAC

B62
ROBERTSON B.C.,REGIONAL DEVELOPMENT IN THE EUROPEAN ECONOMIC COMMUNITY. EUR+WWI FRANCE FUT ITALY UK ECO/UNDEV WORKER ACT/RES PROB/SOLV TEC/DEV ECO/TAC INT/TRADE EEC. PAGE 122 A2499
PLAN ECO/DEV INT/ORG REGION

B62
ROBINSON A.D.,DUTCH ORGANIZED AGRICULTURE IN INTERNATIONAL POLITICS, 1945-1960. EUR+WWI NETHERLAND STRUCT ECO/DEV NAT/G VOL/ASSN CONSULT DELIB/GP PLAN TEC/DEV INT/TRADE EDU/PROP ATTIT RIGID/FLEX ALL/VALS...NEW/IDEA TREND EEC 20. PAGE 122 A2502
AGRI INT/ORG

B62
SCHMITT H.A.,THE PATH TO EUROPEAN UNITY. EUR+WWI USA+45 PLAN TEC/DEV DIPLOM FOR/AID CONFER...INT/LAW 20 EEC EURCOALSTL MARSHL/PLN UNIFICA. PAGE 128 A2634
INT/ORG INT/TRADE REGION ECO/DEV

L62
MALINOWSKI W.R.,"CENTRALIZATION AND DE-CENTRALIZATION IN THE UNITED NATIONS' ECONOMIC AND SOCIAL ACTIVITIES." WOR+45 CONSTN ECO/UNDEV INT/ORG VOL/ASSN DELIB/GP ECO/TAC EDU/PROP ADMIN RIGID/FLEX ...OBS CHARTS UNESCO UN EEC OAS OEEC 20. PAGE 93 A1913
CREATE GEN/LAWS

S62
THOMPSON D.,"THE UNITED KINGDOM AND THE TREATY OF ROME." EUR+WWI INT/ORG NAT/G DELIB/GP LEGIS INT/TRADE RIGID/FLEX...CONCPT EEC PARLIAMENT CMN/WLTH 20. PAGE 143 A2925
ADJUD JURID

B63
BELOFF M.,THE UNITED STATES AND THE UNITY OF EUROPE. EUR+WWI UK USA+45 WOR+45 VOL/ASSN DIPLOM REGION ATTIT PWR...CONCPT EEC OEEC 20 NATO. PAGE 13 A0261
ECO/DEV INT/ORG

B63
CERAMI C.A.,ALLIANCE BORN OF DANGER. EUR+WWI USA+45 USSR ECO/DEV INDUS VOL/ASSN ECO/TAC REGION ATTIT MARXISM ATLAN/ALL 20 NATO EEC. PAGE 25 A0514
DIPLOM INT/ORG NAT/G POLICY

B63
FATEMI N.S.,THE DOLLAR CRISIS. USA+45 INDUS NAT/G LEGIS BUDGET TAX COST...CHARTS METH/COMP 20 EEC. PAGE 44 A0902
PROB/SOLV BAL/PAY FOR/AID PLAN

B63
KLEIMAN R.,ATLANTIC CRISIS; AMERICAN DIPLOMACY CONFRONTS A RESURGENT EUROPE. EUR+WWI USA+45 ECO/DEV AGRI NAT/G CHIEF FORCES PLAN LEAD ATTIT ...CONCPT 20 NATO KENNEDY/JF DEGAULLE/C EEC JOHNSON/LB. PAGE 80 A1648
DIPLOM REGION POLICY

B63
KRAVIS I.B.,DOMESTIC INTERESTS AND INTERNATIONAL OBLIGATIONS: SAFEGUARDS IN INTERNATIONAL TRADE ORGANIZATIONS. EUR+WWI USA+45 WOR+45 FINAN DELIB/GP ATTIT RIGID/FLEX HEALTH...STAT EEC VAL/FREE OEEC ECSC 20. PAGE 82 A1680
INT/ORG ECO/TAC INT/TRADE

B63
LICHTHEIM G.,THE NEW EUROPE: TODAY AND TOMORROW. EUR+WWI FINAN 20 EEC EUROPE/W. PAGE 88 A1809
DIPLOM ECO/DEV INT/ORG INT/TRADE

B63
LINDBERG L.,POLITICAL DYNAMICS OF EUROPEAN ECONOMIC INTEGRATION. EUR+WWI ECO/DEV INT/ORG VOL/ASSN DELIB/GP ADMIN WEALTH...DECISION EEC 20. PAGE 89 A1820
MARKET ECO/TAC

B63
MAYNE R.,THE COMMUNITY OF EUROPE. UK CONSTN NAT/G CONSULT DELIB/GP CREATE PLAN ECO/TAC LEGIT ADMIN ROUTINE ORD/FREE PWR WEALTH...CONCPT TIME/SEQ EEC EURATOM 20. PAGE 97 A1985
EUR+WWI INT/ORG REGION

B63
SALENT W.S.,THE UNITED STATES BALANCE OF PAYMENTS IN 1968. EUR+WWI UK USA+45 AGRI R+D LABOR FORCES PRODUC...GEOG CONCPT CHARTS 20 CHINJAP EEC. PAGE 126 A2589
BAL/PAY DEMAND FINAN INT/TRADE

B63
THORELLI H.B.,INTOP: INTERNATIONAL OPERATIONS SIMULATION: PLAYER'S MANUAL. BRAZIL FINAN OP/RES ADMIN GP/REL INGP/REL PRODUC PERCEPT...DECISION MGT EEC. PAGE 144 A2935
GAME INT/TRADE EDU/PROP LG/CO

L63
MOUSKHELY M.,"LE BLOC COMMUNISTE ET LA COMMUNAUTE ECONOMIQUE EUROPEENNE." AFR COM EUR+WWI FUT USSR WOR+45 INTELL ECO/UNDEV LABOR POL/PAR NUC/PWR RIGID/FLEX...TIME/SEQ ORG/CHARTS EEC TOT/POP 20. PAGE 105 A2158
INT/ORG ECO/DEV

S63
ALPHAND H.,"FRANCE AND HER ALLIES." EUR+WWI UK USA+45 ECO/DEV INT/ORG NAT/G VOL/ASSN FORCES TOP/EX DIPLOM ECO/TAC LEGIT ATTIT DRIVE ORD/FREE PWR WEALTH...STAT EEC TOT/POP 20. PAGE 6 A0130
ACT/RES FRANCE

S63
BALOGH T.,"L'INFLUENCE DES INSTITUTIONS MONETAIRES ET COMMERCIALES SUR LA STRUCTURE ECONOMIQUE AFRICAIN." AFR EUR+WWI FUT USA+45 USA-45 WOR+45 SERV/IND INT/ORG NAT/G TOP/EX ROUTINE...INDEX EEC 20. PAGE 11 A0215
FINAN

S63
BELOFF M.,"BRITAIN, EUROPE AND THE ATLANTIC COMMUNITY." EUR+WWI ELITES NAT/G VOL/ASSN TOP/EX ATTIT ORD/FREE PWR SOVEREIGN WEALTH EEC TOT/POP VAL/FREE CMN/WLTH 20. PAGE 13 A0262
INT/ORG ECO/DEV UK

S63
DIEBOLD W. JR.,"THE NEW SITUATION OF INTERNATIONAL TRADE POLICY." EUR+WWI FRANCE FUT UK USA+45 WOR+45 DIST/IND PLAN INT/TRADE EDU/PROP PWR WEALTH ...RECORD TREND GEN/LAWS EEC VAL/FREE 20. PAGE 37 A0760
MARKET ECO/TAC

S63
EMERSON R.,"THE ATLANTIC COMMUNITY AND THE EMERGING COUNTRIES." FUT WOR+45 ECO/DEV ECO/UNDEV R+D NAT/G DELIB/GP BAL/PWR ECO/TAC EDU/PROP ROUTINE ORD/FREE PWR WEALTH...POLICY CONCPT TREND GEN/METH EEC 20 NATO. PAGE 42 A0848
ATTIT INT/TRADE

S63
ETZIONI A.,"EUROPEAN UNIFICATION: A STRATEGY OF CHANGE." EUR+WWI CULTURE ECO/DEV DELIB/GP ACT/RES ECO/TAC EDU/PROP ATTIT ORD/FREE PWR SKILL WEALTH ...STAT TIME/SEQ EEC TOT/POP VAL/FREE 20. PAGE 42 A0869
INT/ORG RIGID/FLEX

S63
ETZIONI A.,"EUROPEAN UNIFICATION AND PERSPECTIVES ON SOVEREIGNTY." EUR+WWI FUT DELIB/GP TEC/DEV ECO/TAC EDU/PROP DETER NUC/PWR ATTIT DRIVE ORD/FREE PWR WEALTH...CONCPT RECORD TIME/SEQ EEC VAL/FREE 20. PAGE 43 A0870
INT/ORG ECO/DEV SOVEREIGN

S63
HALLSTEIN W.,"THE EUROPEAN COMMUNITY AND ATLANTIC PARTNERSHIP." EUR+WWI USA+45 MARKET NAT/G VOL/ASSN DELIB/GP ARMS/CONT NUC/PWR ATTIT PWR...CONCPT STAT TIME/SEQ TREND OEEC 20 EEC. PAGE 60 A1235
INT/ORG ECO/TAC UK

S63
SCHOFLING J.A.,"EFTA: THE OTHER EUROPE." ECO/DEV MARKET CONSULT ECO/TAC WEALTH...TIME/SEQ EEC OEEC 20 EFTA. PAGE 129 A2642
EUR+WWI INT/ORG REGION

S63
SHONFIELD A.,"AFTER BRUSSELS." EUR+WWI FRANCE GERMANY UK ECO/DEV DIST/IND MARKET VOL/ASSN DELIB/GP CREATE INT/TRADE ATTIT RIGID/FLEX...RECORD TREND GEN/LAWS EEC CMN/WLTH 20. PAGE 132 A2705
PLAN ECO/TAC

S63
SHWADRAN B.,"MIDDLE EAST OIL, 1962." ISLAM USSR ECO/DEV DIST/IND INDUS PLAN BAL/PWR DISPL DRIVE ...POLICY STAT TREND GEN/LAWS EEC OEEC 20 OIL. PAGE 132 A2712
MARKET ECO/TAC INT/TRADE

S63
WOLFERS A.,"INTEGRATION IN THE WEST: THE CONFLICT OF PERSPECTIVES." EUR+WWI USA+45 ECO/DEV INT/ORG DELIB/GP CREATE TEC/DEV DIPLOM ATTIT PWR...CONCPT HIST/WRIT TREND GEN/LAWS COLD/WAR EEC 20. PAGE 166 A3386
RIGID/FLEX ECO/TAC

S63
WRIGHT Q.,"PROJECTED EUROPEAN UNION AND AMERICAN INTERNATIONAL PRESTIGE." EUR+WWI FRANCE GERMANY UK USA+45 INT/ORG NAT/G EDU/PROP ATTIT PERCEPT PWR ...CONCPT OBS EEC 20 UN. PAGE 168 A3417
FUT ORD/FREE REGION

B64
CASEY R.G.,THE FUTURE OF THE COMMONWEALTH. INDIA PAKISTAN UK ECO/UNDEV INT/ORG TEC/DEV COLONIAL SUPEGO 20 EEC AUSTRAL. PAGE 25 A0505
DIPLOM SOVEREIGN NAT/LISM FOR/AID

B64
ECONOMIDES C.P.,LE POUVOIR DE DECISION DES ORGANISATIONS INTERNATIONALES EUROPEENNES. DIPLOM DOMIN INGP/REL EFFICIENCY...INT/LAW JURID 20 NATO OEEC EEC COUNCL/EUR EURATOM. PAGE 40 A0821
INT/ORG PWR DECISION GP/COMP

B64
FREYMOND J.,WESTERN EUROPE SINCE THE WAR. COM EUR+WWI USA+45 DIPLOM...BIBLIOG 20 NATO UN EEC. PAGE 49 A1001
INT/ORG POLICY ECO/DEV ECO/TAC

B64
HINSHAW R.,THE EUROPEAN COMMUNITY AND AMERICAN TRADE: A STUDY IN ATLANTIC ECONOMICS AND POLICY. EUR+WWI UK USA+45 ECO/DEV ECO/UNDEV AGRI INDUS INT/ORG NAT/G ECO/TAC TARIFFS REGION...STAT CHARTS EEC 20. PAGE 65 A1337
MARKET TREND INT/TRADE

B64
KRAUSE L.B.,THE COMMON MARKET: PROGRESS AND CONTROVERSY. EUR+WWI UK ECO/DEV REGION...ANTHOL NATO EEC. PAGE 82 A1678
DIPLOM MARKET INT/TRADE INT/ORG

B64
LISKA G.,EUROPE ASCENDANT. EUR+WWI ECO/DEV FORCES INT/TRADE MARXISM 20 EEC. PAGE 90 A1838
DIPLOM BAL/PWR TARIFFS CENTRAL

B64
MARKHAM J.W.,THE COMMON MARKET: FRIEND OR COMPETITOR. EUR+WWI FUT USA+45 INT/ORG LG/CO NAT/G VOL/ASSN DELIB/GP EX/STRUC PLAN TARIFFS ORD/FREE PWR WEALTH...POLICY STAT TREND EEC VAL/FREE 20. PAGE 95 A1943
ECO/DEV ECO/TAC

B64
RAMAZANI R.K.,THE MIDDLE EAST AND THE EUROPEAN COMMON MARKET. EUR+WWI ISLAM ECO/DEV EXTR/IND MARKET PROC/MFG INT/ORG NAT/G TEC/DEV ECO/TAC REGION DRIVE WEALTH...STAT CHARTS EEC TOT/POP 20. PAGE 119 A2437
ECO/UNDEV ATTIT INT/TRADE

B64
RIVKIN A.,AFRICA AND THE EUROPEAN COMMON MARKET (PAMPHLET). AFR MOD/EUR WOR+45 TEC/DEV FOR/AID TARIFFS BAL/PAY...POLICY 20 EEC. PAGE 121 A2490
INT/ORG INT/TRADE ECO/TAC ECO/UNDEV

B64
STEWART C.F.,A BIBLIOGRAPHY OF INTERNATIONAL BUSINESS. WOR+45 FINAN LG/CO NAT/G PLAN ECO/TAC TARIFFS...DECISION MGT GP/COMP NAT/COMP 20 EEC. PAGE 138 A2824
BIBLIOG INT/ORG OP/RES INT/TRADE

S64
GERBET P.,"LA MISE EN OEUVRE DU MARCHE COMMUN AGRICOLE." ECO/DEV MARKET INT/ORG NAT/G PLAN EDU/PROP NAT/LISM WEALTH...OBS EEC VAL/FREE 20. PAGE 52 A1064
EUR+WWI AGRI REGION

S64
KOJIMA K.,"THE PATTERN OF INTERNATIONAL TRADE AMONG ADVANCED COUNTRIES." EUR+WWI UK USA+45 WOR+45 MARKET NAT/G ECO/TAC WEALTH...MATH STAT CON/ANAL CHARTS EEC CHINJAP 20 CHINJAP. PAGE 81 A1665
ECO/DEV TREND INT/TRADE

S64
RUBINSTEIN A.Z.,"THE SOVIET IMAGE OF WESTERN EUROPE." COM EUR+WWI FRANCE GERMANY GERMANY/W USA+45 USSR INT/ORG NAT/G VOL/ASSN FORCES TOP/EX BAL/PWR EDU/PROP ORD/FREE PWR...MYTH RECORD NATO EEC 20. PAGE 125 A2564
RIGID/FLEX ATTIT

S64
SALVADORI M.,"EL CAPITALISMO EN LA EUROPA DE LA POSGUERRA." INT/ORG NAT/G POL/PAR PLAN ECO/TAC ATTIT ORD/FREE WEALTH...HIST/WRIT COLD/WAR EEC 20. PAGE 127 A2596
EUR+WWI ECO/DEV CAP/ISM

B65
CALLEO D.P.,EUROPE'S FUTURE: THE GRAND ALTERNATIVES. UK INT/ORG DIPLOM PWR SOVEREIGN ...CONCPT IDEA/COMP NAT/COMP BIBLIOG 20 EEC EUROPE DEGAULLE/C NATO. PAGE 23 A0468
FUT EUR+WWI FEDERAL NAT/LISM

B65
COWEN Z.,THE BRITISH COMMONWEALTH OF NATIONS IN A CHANGING WORLD. UK ECO/UNDEV INT/ORG ECO/TAC INT/TRADE COLONIAL WAR GP/REL RACE/REL SOVEREIGN SOC/INTEG 20 TREATY EEC COMMONWLTH. PAGE 32 A0644
JURID DIPLOM PARL/PROC NAT/LISM

B65
LYONS G.M.,AMERICA: PURPOSE AND POWER. UK USA+45 FINAN INDUS MARKET WORKER TEC/DEV DIPLOM AUTOMAT NUC/PWR WAR RACE/REL ORD/FREE 20 EEC CONGRESS SUPREME/CT CIV/RIGHTS. PAGE 92 A1881
PWR PROB/SOLV ECO/DEV TASK

B65
MIDDLETON D.,CRISIS IN THE WEST. EUR+WWI FUT WOR+45 CHIEF PLAN ECO/TAC LEAD REGION NUC/PWR NAT/LISM MARXISM 20 COLD/WAR NATO EEC. PAGE 101 A2068
INT/ORG DIPLOM NAT/G POLICY

B65
WEIL G.L.,A HANDBOOK ON THE EUROPEAN ECONOMIC COMMUNITY. BELGIUM EUR+WWI FRANCE GERMANY/W ITALY CONSTN ECO/DEV CREATE PARTIC GP/REL...DECISION MGT CHARTS 20 EEC. PAGE 162 A3299
INT/TRADE INT/ORG TEC/DEV INT/LAW

S65
BROWN S.,"AN ALTERNATIVE TO THE GRAND DESIGN." EUR+WWI FUT USA+45 INT/ORG NAT/G EX/STRUC FORCES CREATE BAL/PWR DOMIN RIGID/FLEX ORD/FREE PWR ...NEW/IDEA RECORD EEC NATO 20. PAGE 20 A0407
VOL/ASSN CONCPT DIPLOM

S65
SPAAK P.H.,"THE SEARCH FOR CONSENSUS: A NEW EFFORT TO BUILD EUROPE." FRANCE GERMANY ECO/DEV NAT/G CONSULT FORCES PLAN EDU/PROP REGION CONSEN ATTIT ...SOC METH/CNCPT OBS TREND EEC NATO WORK 20. PAGE 135 A2770
EUR+WWI INT/ORG

C65
SCHEINGOLD S.A.,"THE RULE OF LAW IN EUROPEAN INTEGRATION: THE PATH OF THE SCHUMAN PLAN." EUR+WWI JUDGE ADJUD FEDERAL ATTIT PWR...RECORD INT BIBLIOG EEC ECSC. PAGE 128 A2621
INT/LAW CT/SYS REGION CENTRAL

B66
EDWARDS C.D.,TRADE REGULATIONS OVERSEAS. IRELAND NEW/ZEALND SOUTH/AFR NAT/G CAP/ISM TARIFFS CONTROL ...POLICY JURID 20 EEC CHINJAP. PAGE 40 A0823
INT/TRADE DIPLOM INT/LAW ECO/TAC

B66
HAY P.,FEDERALISM AND SUPRANATIONAL ORGANIZATIONS: PATTERNS FOR NEW LEGAL STRUCTURES. EUR+WWI LAW NAT/G VOL/ASSN DIPLOM PWR...NAT/COMP TREATY EEC. PAGE 63 A1294
SOVEREIGN FEDERAL INT/ORG INT/LAW

B66
LUARD E.,THE EVOLUTION OF INTERNATIONAL ORGANIZATIONS. UK WOR+45 BUDGET INT/TRADE WAR BAL/PAY PEACE ORD/FREE...POLICY 19/20 EEC ILO LEAGUE/NAT UN. PAGE 91 A1871
INT/ORG EFFICIENCY CREATE TREND

B66
MEERHAEGHE M.,INTERNATIONAL ECONOMIC INSTITUTIONS. EUR+WWI FINAN INDUS MARKET PLAN TARIFFS BAL/PAY EQUILIB...POLICY BIBLIOG/A 20 GATT OEEC EEC IBRD EURCOALSTL. PAGE 99 A2032
ECO/TAC ECO/DEV INT/TRADE INT/ORG

B66
NIJHOFF M.,ANNUAIRE EUROPEEN (VOL. XII). INT/TRADE REGION PEACE 20 EFTA EEC ECSC EURATOM. PAGE 109 A2241
BIBLIOG INT/ORG EUR+WWI DIPLOM

B66
SPINELLI A.,THE EUROCRATS; CONFLICT AND CRISIS IN THE EUROPEAN COMMUNITY (TRANS. BY C. GROVE HAINES). EUR+WWI MARKET POL/PAR ECO/TAC PARL/PROC EEC OEEC
INT/ORG INGP/REL CONSTN

ECSC EURATOM. PAGE 136 A2789 — ADMIN

B66
TRIFFIN R.,THE WORLD MONEY MAZE. INT/ORG ECO/TAC PRICE OPTIMAL WEALTH...METH/COMP 20 EEC OEEC GOLD/STAND SILVER. PAGE 145 A2964 — BAL/PAY FINAN INT/TRADE DIPLOM

C66
KULSKI W.W.,"DEGAULLE AND THE WORLD: THE FOREIGN POLICY OF THE FIFTH FRENCH REPUBLIC." FRANCE ECO/UNDEV POL/PAR BAL/PWR DETER NUC/PWR ATTIT PWR ...RECORD BIBLIOG DEGAULLE NATO EEC. PAGE 83 A1694 — POLICY SOVEREIGN PERSON DIPLOM

B67
ISENBERG I.,FRANCE UNDER DE GAULLE (THE REFERENCE SHELF VOL. 39 NO. 1). EUR+WWI FRANCE ECO/DEV ...BIBLIOG 20 DEGAULLE/C NATO EEC. PAGE 72 A1469 — ATTIT DIPLOM POLICY CHIEF

B67
ROACH J.R.,THE UNITED STATES AND THE ATLANTIC COMMUNITY; ISSUES AND PROSPECTS. WOR+45 TEC/DEV ECO/TAC COLONIAL REGION PEACE ROLE...ANTHOL NATO COLD/WAR EEC. PAGE 121 A2491 — INT/ORG POLICY ADJUST DIPLOM

L67
BODENHEIMER S.J.,"THE 'POLITICAL UNION' DEBATE IN EUROPE* A CASE STUDY IN INTERGOVERNMENTAL DIPLOMACY." EUR+WWI FUT NAT/G FORCES PLAN DEBATE SOVEREIGN...CONCPT PREDICT EEC NATO. PAGE 16 A0326 — DIPLOM REGION INT/ORG

L67
CAHIERS P.,"LE RECOURS EN CONSTATATION DE MANQUEMENTS DES ETATS MEMBRES DEVANT LA COUR DES COMMUNAUTES EUROPEENNES." LAW PROB/SOLV DIPLOM ADMIN CT/SYS SANCTION ATTIT...POLICY DECISION JURID ECSC EEC. PAGE 23 A0465 — INT/ORG CONSTN ROUTINE ADJUD

S67
APEL H.,"LES NOUVEAUX ASPECTS DE LA POLITIQUE ETRANGERE ALLEMANDE." EUR+WWI GERMANY POL/PAR BAL/PWR ECO/TAC INT/TRADE NUC/PWR NAT/LISM PEACE ...POLICY 20 EEC COLD/WAR. PAGE 8 A0168 — DIPLOM INT/ORG FEDERAL

S67
BUTT R.,"THE COMMON MARKET AND CONSERVATIVE POLITICS, 1961-2." UK CHIEF DIPLOM ECO/TAC INT/TRADE CONFER DEBATE REGION ATTIT...POLICY 20 EEC. PAGE 22 A0454 — EUR+WWI INT/ORG POL/PAR

S67
COSGROVE C.A.,"AGRICULTURE, FINANCE AND POLITICS IN THE EUROPEAN COMMUNITY." EUR+WWI DIST/IND MARKET INT/ORG VOL/ASSN DELIB/GP TEC/DEV BAL/PWR BARGAIN ECO/TAC RATION CONFER 20 EEC. PAGE 31 A0630 — ECO/DEV DIPLOM AGRI INT/TRADE

S67
DEUTSCH K.W.,"ARMS CONTROL AND EUROPEAN UNITY* THE NEXT TEN YEARS." USA+45 ELITES NAT/G BAL/PWR DIPLOM NUC/PWR...INT KNO/TEST NATO EEC. PAGE 36 A0742 — ARMS/CONT PEACE REGION PLAN

S67
JAVITS J.K.,"LAST CHANCE FOR A COMMON MARKET." L/A+17C INT/ORG 20 EEC LAFTA. PAGE 73 A1501 — FOR/AID ECO/UNDEV INT/TRADE ECO/TAC

S67
LEVI M.,"LES DIFFICULTES ECONOMIQUES DE LA GRANDE-BRETAGNE." UK INT/ORG TEC/DEV BARGAIN DIPLOM DOMIN REPRESENT DEMAND WEALTH...POLICY 20 EEC. PAGE 88 A1792 — BAL/PAY INT/TRADE PRODUC

S67
WEIL G.L.,"THE MERGER OF THE INSTITUTIONS OF THE EUROPEAN COMMUNITIES" EUR+WWI ECO/DEV INT/TRADE CONSEN PLURISM...DECISION MGT 20 EEC EURATOM ECSC TREATY. PAGE 162 A3300 — ECO/TAC INT/ORG CENTRAL INT/LAW

S67
WEIL G.L.,"THE EUROPEAN COMMUNITY* WHAT LIES BEYOND THE POINT OF NO RETURN?" VOL/ASSN PROB/SOLV DIPLOM REGION INGP/REL CENTRAL PWR 20 EEC. PAGE 162 A3301 — INT/ORG ECO/DEV INT/TRADE PREDICT

EFFECTIVENESS....SEE EFFICIENCY, PRODUC

EFFICIENCY....EFFECTIVENESS

N19
JACKSON R.G.A.,THE CASE FOR AN INTERNATIONAL DEVELOPMENT AUTHORITY (PAMPHLET). WOR+45 ECO/DEV DIPLOM GIVE CONTROL GP/REL EFFICIENCY NAT/LISM SOVEREIGN 20. PAGE 72 A1478 — FOR/AID INT/ORG ECO/UNDEV ADMIN

N19
MEZERIK A.G.,COLONIALISM AND THE UNITED NATIONS (PAMPHLET). WOR+45 NAT/G ADMIN LEAD WAR CHOOSE EFFICIENCY PEACE ATTIT ORD/FREE...POLICY CHARTS UN COLD/WAR. PAGE 100 A2061 — COLONIAL DIPLOM BAL/PWR INT/ORG

N19
MORGENSTERN O.,THE COMMAND AND CONTROL STRUCTURE (PAMPHLET). USSR COM/IND INT/ORG WEAPON PEACE UTIL ...TREND 20 NATO. PAGE 104 A2132 — CONTROL FORCES EFFICIENCY PLAN

B43
CONOVER H.F.,SOVIET RUSSIA: SELECTED LIST OF REFERENCES. USSR CULTURE INDUS NAT/G TOP/EX TEC/DEV BUDGET WAR CIVMIL/REL EFFICIENCY MARXISM 20. PAGE 29 A0597 — BIBLIOG ECO/DEV COM DIPLOM

B45
CONOVER H.F.,ITALY: ECONOMICS, POLITICS AND MILITARY AFFAIRS, 1940-1945. ITALY ELITES NAT/G POL/PAR EX/STRUC TOP/EX DIPLOM DOMIN CONTROL COERCE WAR CIVMIL/REL EFFICIENCY 20. PAGE 29 A0599 — BIBLIOG TOTALISM FORCES

B47
DE HUSZAR G.B.,PERSISTENT INTERNATIONAL ISSUES. WOR+45 WOR-45 AGRI INDUS INT/ORG PROB/SOLV EFFICIENCY WEALTH...CON/ANAL ANTHOL UN. PAGE 35 A0704 — DIPLOM PEACE ECO/TAC FOR/AID

B53
SQUIRES J.D.,BRITISH PROPAGANDA AT HOME AND IN THE UNITED STATES FROM 1914 TO 1917. UK NAT/G PROB/SOLV DOMIN PRESS EFFICIENCY...PSY PREDICT 20 WWI INTERVENT PSY/WAR. PAGE 136 A2794 — EDU/PROP CONTROL WAR DIPLOM

B54
BUTZ O.,GERMANY: DILEMMA FOR AMERICAN POLICY. GERMANY USA+45 USA-45 USSR WOR+45 INT/ORG FORCES NUC/PWR EFFICIENCY PEACE PWR...GOV/COMP 20 COLD/WAR. PAGE 23 A0459 — DIPLOM NAT/G WAR POLICY

B55
STEPHENS O.,FACTS TO A CANDID WORLD. USA+45 WOR+45 COM/IND EX/STRUC PRESS ROUTINE EFFICIENCY ATTIT ...PSY 20. PAGE 138 A2817 — EDU/PROP PHIL/SCI NAT/G DIPLOM

B58
US HOUSE COMM GOVT OPERATIONS,HEARINGS BEFORE A SUBCOMMITTEE OF THE COMMITTEE ON GOVERNMENT OPERATIONS. CAMBODIA PHILIPPINE USA+45 CONSTRUC TEC/DEV ADMIN CONTROL WEAPON EFFICIENCY HOUSE/REP. PAGE 154 A3135 — FOR/AID DIPLOM ORD/FREE ECO/UNDEV

B59
KAPLAN D.,THE ARAB REFUGEES: AN ABNORMAL PROBLEM. UAR WOR+45 PROB/SOLV DIPLOM GOV/REL ADJUST EFFICIENCY...POLICY GEOG INT/LAW 20 UN JEWS MIGRATION. PAGE 76 A1557 — STRANGE HABITAT GP/REL INGP/REL

B59
NOVE A.,COMMUNIST ECONOMIC STRATEGY: SOVIET GROWTH AND CAPABILITIES. USSR AGRI LABOR PLAN TEC/DEV CAP/ISM INT/TRADE EFFICIENCY MARXISM 20 THIRD/WRLD. PAGE 110 A2257 — FOR/AID ECO/TAC DIPLOM INDUS

B59
SWIFT R.W.,WORLD AFFAIRS AND THE COLLEGE CURRICULUM. USA+45 PLAN EFFICIENCY PERCEPT...HUM METH/CNCPT. PAGE 140 A2871 — ACADEM DIPLOM METH/COMP EDU/PROP

B59
US GENERAL ACCOUNTING OFFICE,EXAM OF ECONOMIC AND TECHNICAL ASSISTANCE PROGRAM FOR INDIA INT'NAT'L COOP ADMIN REPORT TO CONGRESS 1955-1958. INDIA USA+45 ECO/UNDEV FINAN PLAN DIPLOM COST UTIL WEALTH ...CHARTS 20 CONGRESS AID. PAGE 153 A3114 — FOR/AID EFFICIENCY ECO/TAC TEC/DEV

B59
US PRES COMM STUDY MIL ASSIST,COMPOSITE REPORT. USA+45 ECO/UNDEV PLAN BUDGET DIPLOM EFFICIENCY ...POLICY MGT 20. PAGE 155 A3164 — FOR/AID FORCES WEAPON ORD/FREE

B59
VAN WAGENEN R.W.,SOME VIEWS OF AMERICAN DEFENSE OFFICIALS ABOUT THE UNITED NATIONS (PAPER). FUT USA+45 NAT/G DIPLOM WAR EFFICIENCY PEACE...POLICY INT 20 UN DEPT/DEFEN. PAGE 158 A3216 — INT/ORG LEAD ATTIT FORCES

B60
MONTGOMERY B.L.,AN APPROACH TO SANITY; A STUDY OF EAST-WEST RELATIONS. CONFER WAR EFFICIENCY ATTIT ...POLICY 20 NATO COLD/WAR KHRUSH/N. PAGE 103 A2113 — DIPLOM INT/ORG BAL/PWR DETER

B60
NEALE A.D.,THE FLOW OF RESOURCES FROM RICH TO POOR. WOR+45 ECO/DEV ECO/UNDEV FINAN INDUS NAT/G PLAN EFFICIENCY WEALTH...POLICY NAT/COMP 20 RESOURCE/N. PAGE 108 A2209 — FOR/AID DIPLOM METH/CNCPT

B60
RAO V.K.R.,INTERNATIONAL AID FOR ECONOMIC DEVELOPMENT - POSSIBILITIES AND LIMITATIONS. FINAN PLAN TEC/DEV ADMIN TASK EFFICIENCY...POLICY SOC METH/CNCPT CHARTS 20 UN. PAGE 119 A2444 — FOR/AID DIPLOM INT/ORG ECO/UNDEV

B60
US HOUSE COMM GOVT OPERATIONS,OPERATIONS OF THE DEVELOPMENT LOAN FUND: HEARINGS (COMMITTEE ON GOVERNMENT OPERATIONS). USA+45 PLAN BUDGET DIPLOM GOV/REL COST...CHARTS 20 CONGRESS DEPT/STATE AID. PAGE 154 A3137 — FINAN FOR/AID ECO/TAC EFFICIENCY

B60
US SENATE COMM ON FOREIGN REL,SITUATION IN VIETNAM (2 VOLS.). USA+45 VIETNAM ECO/TAC COST SENATE DEPT/STATE. PAGE 156 A3181 — FOR/AID PLAN EFFICIENCY INSPECT

B61
SHAPP W.R.,FIELD ADMINISTRATION IN THE UNITED NATIONS SYSTEM. FINAN PROB/SOLV INSPECT DIPLOM EXEC REGION ROUTINE EFFICIENCY ROLE...INT CHARTS 20 UN. PAGE 131 A2694 — INT/ORG ADMIN GP/REL FOR/AID

B61
US HOUSE COMM APPROPRIATIONS,INTER-AMERICAN — LEGIS

PROGRAMS FOR 1961: DENIAL OF 1962 BUDGET INFORMATION. CHILE L/A+17C USA+45 FINAN CONSULT BUDGET ADJUD COST EFFICIENCY WEALTH...POLICY CHARTS 20 CONGRESS. PAGE 153 A3119
FOR/AID DELIB/GP ECO/UNDEV

S61
"CRITERIA FOR ALLOCATING INVESTMENT RESOURCES AMONG VARIOUS FIELDS OF DEVELOPMENT IN UNDERDEVELOPED ECONOMIES." ASIA AGRI INT/ORG CAP/ISM BAL/PAY EFFICIENCY PROFIT WEALTH...STAT 20 UN. PAGE 3 A0061
BIBLIOG/A ECO/UNDEV PLAN TEC/DEV

B62
FAO,FOOD AND AGRICULTURE ORGANIZATION AFRICAN SURVEY. AFR CONGO/BRAZ GHANA STRATA AGRI INT/ORG TEC/DEV FOR/AID INT/TRADE RACE/REL DEMAND EFFICIENCY PRODUC...GEOG 20 UN CONGO/LEOP. PAGE 44 A0898
ECO/TAC WEALTH EXTR/IND ECO/UNDEV

B62
FORD A.G.,THE GOLD STANDARD 1880-1914: BRITAIN AND ARGENTINA. UK ECO/UNDEV INT/TRADE ADMIN GOV/REL DEMAND EFFICIENCY...STAT CHARTS 19/20 ARGEN GOLD/STAND. PAGE 47 A0960
FINAN ECO/TAC BUDGET BAL/PAY

B62
US CONGRESS JOINT ECO COMM,ECONOMIC DEVELOPMENTS IN SOUTH AMERICA. USA+45 SOCIETY FINAN NAT/G PROB/SOLV TEC/DEV INT/TRADE TAX EFFICIENCY PRODUC ATTIT ...POLICY 20 CONGRESS SOUTH/AMER. PAGE 150 A3065
L/A+17C ECO/UNDEV FOR/AID DIPLOM

B62
WEIDNER E.W.,THE WORLD ROLE OF UNIVERSITIES. USA+45 WOR+45 SECT ACT/RES PROB/SOLV GIVE EFFICIENCY KNOWL ...LING CHARTS BIBLIOG 20. PAGE 162 A3297
ACADEM EDU/PROP DIPLOM POLICY

B63
COLUMBIA U SCHOOL OF LAW,PUBLIC INTERNATIONAL DEVELOPMENT FINANCING IN SENEGAL. SENEGAL FINAN DELIB/GP GIVE EFFICIENCY...CHARTS GOV/COMP ANTHOL 20. PAGE 28 A0571
FOR/AID PLAN RECEIVE ECO/UNDEV

B63
US GOVERNMENT,REPORT TO INTER-AMERICAN ECONOMIC AND SOCIAL COUNCIL AT SECOND ANNUAL MEETING. L/A+17C USA+45 VOL/ASSN TEC/DEV DIPLOM TAX EATING EFFICIENCY HEALTH...STAT CHARTS 20 AID. PAGE 153 A3116
ECO/TAC FOR/AID FINAN PLAN

B63
US SENATE COMM APPROPRIATIONS,PERSONNEL ADMINISTRATION AND OPERATIONS OF AGENCY FOR INTERNATIONAL DEVELOPMENT: SPECIAL HEARING. FINAN LEAD COST UTIL SKILL...CHARTS 20 CONGRESS AID CIVIL/SERV. PAGE 155 A3170
ADMIN FOR/AID EFFICIENCY DIPLOM

B63
US SENATE COMM GOVT OPERATIONS,REPORT OF A STUDY OF US FOREIGN AID IN TEN MIDDLE EASTERN AND AFRICAN COUNTRIES. AFR ISLAM USA+45 FORCES PLAN BUDGET DIPLOM TAX DETER WEALTH...STAT CHARTS 20 CONGRESS AID MID/EAST. PAGE 156 A3174
FOR/AID EFFICIENCY ECO/TAC FINAN

B63
WHITTON J.B.,PROPAGANDA AND THE COLD WAR. USA+45 USSR INDUS NAT/G PLAN WRITING EFFICIENCY...POLICY 20 COLD/WAR. PAGE 164 A3341
ATTIT EDU/PROP COM/IND DIPLOM

N63
US AGENCY INTERNATIONAL DEV,PRINCIPLES OF FOREIGN ECONOMIC ASSISTANCE (PAMPHLET). USA+45 FINAN GP/REL BAL/PAY EFFICIENCY 20 AID. PAGE 149 A3051
FOR/AID PLAN ECO/UNDEV ATTIT

B64
ECONOMIDES C.P.,LE POUVOIR DE DECISION DES ORGANISATIONS INTERNATIONALES EUROPEENNES. DIPLOM DOMIN INGP/REL EFFICIENCY...INT/LAW JURID 20 NATO OEEC EEC COUNCL/EUR EURATOM. PAGE 40 A0821
INT/ORG PWR DECISION GP/COMP

B64
KRETZSCHMAR W.W.,AUSLANDSHILFE ALS MITTEL DER AUSSENWIRTSCHAFTS- UND AUSSENPOLITIK. ASIA GERMANY/W UK USA+45 SOCIETY STRUCT ECO/UNDEV LOBBY EFFICIENCY 20. PAGE 82 A1683
FOR/AID DIPLOM AGRI DIST/IND

B64
RUSSELL R.B.,UNITED NATIONS EXPERIENCE WITH MILITARY FORCES: POLITICAL AND LEGAL ASPECTS. AFR KOREA WOR+45 LEGIS PROB/SOLV ADMIN CONTROL EFFICIENCY PEACE...POLICY INT/LAW BIBLIOG UN. PAGE 126 A2576
FORCES DIPLOM SANCTION ORD/FREE

B64
TULLY A.,WHERE DID YOUR MONEY GO. USA+45 USSR ECO/UNDEV ADMIN EFFICIENCY WEALTH...METH/COMP 20. PAGE 146 A2976
FOR/AID DIPLOM CONTROL

B64
US HOUSE COMM GOVT OPERATIONS,US OWNED FOREIGN CURRENCIES: HEARINGS (COMMITTEE ON GOVERNMENT OPERATIONS). INDIA ECO/DEV PLAN BUDGET TAX DEMAND EFFICIENCY 20 AID CONGRESS. PAGE 154 A3138
FINAN ECO/TAC FOR/AID OWN

B65
ANALYSIS AND ASSESSMENT OF THE ECONOMIC EFFECTS: PUBLIC LAW 480 TITLE I PROGRAM TURKEY. INDIA TURKEY USA+45 AGRI NAT/G PLAN BUDGET DIPLOM COST EFFICIENCY...CHARTS 20. PAGE 3 A0070
ECO/TAC FOR/AID FINAN ECO/UNDEV

B65
COOMBS P.H.,EDUCATION AND FOREIGN AID. AFR USA+45 DIPLOM EFFICIENCY KNOWL ORD/FREE...ANTHOL 20 AID. PAGE 30 A0608
EDU/PROP FOR/AID SCHOOL ECO/UNDEV

B65
DEMAS W.G.,THE ECONOMICS OF DEVELOPMENT IN SMALL COUNTRIES WITH SPECIAL REFERENCE TO THE CARIBBEAN. WOR+45 BAL/PAY DEMAND EFFICIENCY PRODUC...GEOG CARIBBEAN. PAGE 36 A0731
ECO/UNDEV PLAN WEALTH INT/TRADE

B65
FLYNN A.H.,WORLD UNDERSTANDING: A SELECTED BIBLIOGRAPHY. WOR+45 PROB/SOLV BAL/PWR DIPLOM EFFICIENCY PEACE UN. PAGE 47 A0956
BIBLIOG/A INT/ORG EDU/PROP ROUTINE

B65
MURUMBI J.,PROBLEMS OF ECONOMIC DEVELOPMENT IN EAST AFRICA. FINAN INDUS WORKER TEC/DEV INT/TRADE TAX DEMAND EFFICIENCY PRODUC SOCISM...TREND CHARTS 20 AFRICA/E. PAGE 106 A2184
AGRI ECO/TAC ECO/UNDEV PROC/MFG

B65
THAYER F.C. JR.,AIR TRANSPORT POLICY AND NATIONAL SECURITY: A POLITICAL, ECONOMIC, AND MILITARY ANALYSIS. DIST/IND OP/RES PLAN TEC/DEV DIPLOM DETER WAR COST EFFICIENCY...POLICY BIBLIOG 20 DEPT/DEFEN FAA CAB. PAGE 142 A2908
AIR FORCES CIVMIL/REL ORD/FREE

B65
UN,SPACE ACTIVITIES AND RESOURCES: REVIEW OF UNITED NATION'S NATIONAL AND INTERNATIONAL PROGRAMS. INT/ORG LABOR PLAN TEC/DEV DIPLOM EFFICIENCY HEALTH ...GOV/COMP 20 UN. PAGE 146 A2995
SPACE NUC/PWR FOR/AID PEACE

B65
US SENATE COMM ON JUDICIARY,REFUGEE PROBLEMS IN SOUTH VIETNAM AND LAOS: HEARINGS BEFORE SUBCOMMITTEE TO INVESTIGATE PROBLEMS OF REFUGEES, ESCAPEES. CHINA/COM LAOS USA+45 VIETNAM/S PROB/SOLV DIPLOM GOV/REL GP/REL EFFICIENCY ORD/FREE...POLICY GEOG 20 CONGRESS MIGRATION. PAGE 157 A3194
STRANGE HABITAT FOR/AID CIVMIL/REL

L65
MATTHEWS D.G.,"LE TIERS MONDE: A SELECT AND PRELIMINARY BIBLIOGRAPHIC SURVEY OF MANPOWER IN DEVELOPING COUNTRIES, 1960-1964." AFR ISLAM L/A+17C INDUS PLAN PROB/SOLV TEC/DEV INT/TRADE EFFICIENCY WEALTH...STAT 20. PAGE 96 A1971
BIBLIOG/A ECO/UNDEV LABOR WORKER

B66
AMERICAN ASSEMBLY COLUMBIA U,A WORLD OF NUCLEAR POWERS? FUT WOR+45 ECO/DEV BAL/PWR ECO/TAC CONTROL RISK EFFICIENCY ATTIT PWR...METH/COMP ANTHOL 20. PAGE 7 A0137
NUC/PWR DIPLOM TEC/DEV ARMS/CONT

B66
CURRIE L.,ACCELERATING DEVELOPMENT: THE NECESSITY AND MEANS. COLOMBIA USA+45 INDUS DIPLOM EFFICIENCY WEALTH...METH/CNCPT NEW/IDEA 20. PAGE 33 A0668
PLAN ECO/UNDEV FOR/AID TEC/DEV

B66
DONALD A.D.,JOHN F. KENNEDY AND THE NEW FRONTIER. LEGIS DIPLOM DISCRIM PEACE PWR 20. PAGE 38 A0771
LEAD CHIEF BIOG EFFICIENCY

B66
FEHRENBACH T.R.,THIS KIND OF PEACE. WOR+45 LEAD PARTIC WAR EFFICIENCY ATTIT UN. PAGE 44 A0906
PEACE DIPLOM INT/ORG BAL/PWR

B66
FRANK E.,LAWMAKERS IN A CHANGING WORLD. FRANCE UK USSR WOR+45 PARTIC EFFICIENCY ROLE ALL/IDEOS ...CHARTS ANTHOL PARLIAMENT 20 UN COLD/WAR. PAGE 48 A0979
GOV/COMP LEGIS NAT/G DIPLOM

B66
HANSON J.W.,EDUCATION AND THE DEVELOPMENT OF NATIONS. DIPLOM TASK ADJUST EFFICIENCY...POLICY ANTHOL 20. PAGE 61 A1256
ECO/UNDEV EDU/PROP NAT/G PLAN

B66
LUARD E.,THE EVOLUTION OF INTERNATIONAL ORGANIZATIONS. UK WOR+45 BUDGET INT/TRADE WAR BAL/PAY PEACE ORD/FREE...POLICY 19/20 EEC ILO LEAGUE/NAT UN. PAGE 91 A1871
INT/ORG EFFICIENCY CREATE TREND

B66
NATIONAL COUN APPLIED ECO RES,DEVELOPMENT WITHOUT AID. INDIA FINAN TEC/DEV EFFICIENCY...ANTHOL 20. PAGE 107 A2203
FOR/AID PLAN SOVEREIGN ECO/UNDEV

L66
CHENERY H.B.,"FOREIGN ASSISTANCE AND ECONOMIC DEVELOPMENT" FUT WOR+45 NAT/G DIPLOM GIVE PRODUC ...METH/CNCPT CHARTS 20. PAGE 26 A0526
FOR/AID EFFICIENCY ECO/UNDEV TEC/DEV

S66
JAVITS J.K.,"POLITICAL ACTION VITAL FOR LATIN AMERICAN INTEGRATION." ECO/UNDEV INT/ORG POL/PAR VOL/ASSN PLAN PROB/SOLV INT/TRADE EFFICIENCY 20 OAS LAFTA. PAGE 73 A1500
L/A+17C ECO/TAC REGION

C66
BLAISDELL D.C.,"INTERNATIONAL ORGANIZATION." FUT WOR+45 ECO/DEV DELIB/GP FORCES EFFICIENCY PEACE ORD/FREE...INT/LAW 20 UN LEAGUE/NAT NATO. PAGE 15 A0304
BIBLIOG INT/ORG DIPLOM ARMS/CONT

B67
HOHENBERG J.,BETWEEN TWO WORLDS. ASIA S/ASIA USA+45 PRESS TV PERS/REL ISOLAT...INT CHARTS METH/COMP 20. PAGE 66 A1362
COM/IND DIPLOM EFFICIENCY KNOWL

B67
ZUCKERMAN S.,SCIENTISTS AND WAR. ELITES INDUS DIPLOM CENTRAL EFFICIENCY KNOWL 20. PAGE 170 A3459
R+D CONSULT ACT/RES GP/REL

L67
GALTUNG J.,"ON THE EFFECTS OF INTERNATIONAL ECONOMIC SANCTIONS, WITH EXAMPLES FROM THE CASE OF RHODESIA." NAT/G DIPLOM EDU/PROP ADJUST EFFICIENCY ATTIT MORAL...OBS CHARTS 20. PAGE 51 A1035
SANCTION ECO/TAC INT/TRADE ECO/UNDEV

S67
FALKOWSKI M.,"SOCIALIST ECONOMISTS AND THE DEVELOPING COUNTRIES." COM PLAN TEC/DEV ROUTINE DEMAND EFFICIENCY PRODUC WEALTH...MARXIST TREND GEN/METH. PAGE 44 A0893
DIPLOM SOCISM ECO/UNDEV INDUS

S67
HODGE G.,"THE RISE AND DEMISE OF THE UN TECHNICAL ASSISTANCE ADMINISTRATION." RISK TASK INGP/REL CONSEN EFFICIENCY 20 UN. PAGE 66 A1349
ADMIN TEC/DEV EX/STRUC INT/ORG

S67
KIERNAN V.G.,"INDIA AND THE LABOUR PARTY." INDIA UK CAP/ISM GP/REL EFFICIENCY NAT/LISM PWR SOCISM ...SOCIALIST TIME/SEQ 20. PAGE 79 A1616
COLONIAL DIPLOM POL/PAR ECO/UNDEV

S67
TERRILL R.,"THE SIEGE MENTALITY." CHINA/COM NAT/G FORCES DIPLOM REV EFFICIENCY NAT/LISM MARXISM ...TREND 20. PAGE 142 A2904
EDU/PROP WAR DOMIN

S67
YOUNG K.T.,"UNITED STATES POLICY AND VIETNAMESE POLITICAL VIABILITY 1954-1967." VIETNAM/S LOC/G MUNIC FOR/AID ORD/FREE...POLICY 20. PAGE 169 A3437
LEAD ADMIN GP/REL EFFICIENCY

EFIMENCO N.M. A0824

EFRON R. A2194

EFTA....EUROPEAN FREE TRADE ASSOCIATION

B61
PEASLEE A.J.,INTERNATIONAL GOVERNMENTAL ORGANIZATIONS (2 VOLS.). CONSTN VOL/ASSN DIPLOM ...GP/COMP 20 UN OAS EEC EFTA ECSC. PAGE 114 A2345
BIBLIOG INT/ORG INDEX LAW

S61
RAY J.,"THE EUROPEAN FREE-TRADE ASSOCIATION AND ITS IMPACT ON INDIA'S TRADE." EUR+WWI FRANCE GERMANY INDIA S/ASIA UK NAT/G VOL/ASSN PLAN INT/TRADE ROUTINE WEALTH...STAT CHARTS CMN/WLTH EEC OEEC 20 EFTA. PAGE 120 A2453
ECO/DEV ECO/TAC

S63
SCHOFLING J.A.,"EFTA: THE OTHER EUROPE." ECO/DEV MARKET CONSULT ECO/TAC WEALTH...TIME/SEQ EEC OEEC 20 EFTA. PAGE 129 A2642
EUR+WWI INT/ORG REGION

B66
NIJHOFF M.,ANNUAIRE EUROPEEN (VOL. XII). INT/TRADE REGION PEACE 20 EFTA EEC ECSC EURATOM. PAGE 109 A2241
BIBLIOG INT/ORG EUR+WWI DIPLOM

EGBERT D.D. A0825

EGYPT....SEE ALSO ISLAM, UAR, EGYPT/ANC

EGYPT/ANC....ANCIENT EGYPT

EGYPTIAN SOCIETY OF INT LAW A0826

EHRENBURG I. A0827

EIB....EUROPEAN INVESTMENT BANK

EICHMANN/A....ADOLF EICHMANN

EINSTEIN A. A0828,A0829

EINSTEIN/A....ALBERT EINSTEIN

EINZIG P. A0830

EISENDRATH C. A0831

EISENHOWER D.D. A0832,A0833

EISNHWR/DD....PRESIDENT DWIGHT DAVID EISENHOWER

N19
MEZERIK A.G.,U-2 AND OPEN SKIES (PAMPHLET). USA+45 USSR INT/ORG CHIEF FORCES PLAN EDU/PROP CONTROL SANCTION ARMS/CONT 20 UN EISNHWR/DD. PAGE 100 A2060
DIPLOM RISK DEBATE

S56
CUTLER R.,"THE DEVELOPMENT OF THE NATIONAL SECURITY COUNCIL." USA+45 INTELL CONSULT EX/STRUC DIPLOM LEAD 20 TRUMAN/HS EISNHWR/DD NSC. PAGE 33 A0670
ORD/FREE DELIB/GP PROB/SOLV NAT/G

B58
HUNT B.I.,BIPARTISANSHIP: A CASE STUDY OF THE FOREIGN ASSISTANCE PROGRAM, 1947-56 (DOCTORAL THESIS). USA+45 INT/ORG CONSULT LEGIS TEC/DEV ...BIBLIOG PRESIDENT TREATY NATO TRUMAN/HS EISNHWR/DD CONGRESS. PAGE 69 A1418
FOR/AID POL/PAR GP/REL DIPLOM

B59
FERRELL R.H.,AMERICAN DIPLOMACY: A HISTORY. USA+45 USA-45 PLAN ROUTINE REV WAR PWR...T 18/20 EISNHWR/DD WWI. PAGE 45 A0921
DIPLOM NAT/G POLICY

B61
FLEMING D.F.,THE COLD WAR AND ITS ORIGINS: 1950-1960 (VOL. II). ASIA FUT HUNGARY POLAND WOR+45 TEC/DEV DOMIN NUC/PWR REV PEACE...T 20 COLD/WAR EISNHWR/DD SUEZ. PAGE 46 A0946
MARXISM DIPLOM BAL/PWR

B61
GRAEBNER N.,THE NEW ISOLATIONISM: A STUDY IN POLITICS AND FOREIGN POLICY SINCE 1960. USA+45 INT/ORG LOC/G NAT/G POL/PAR LEGIS BAL/PWR EDU/PROP CHOOSE ATTIT PERSON ORD/FREE 20 TRUMAN/HS EISNHWR/DD. PAGE 55 A1120
EXEC PWR DIPLOM

B61
ROBINS D.B.,EVOLVING UNITED STATES POLICIES TOWARD THE EMERGING NATIONS OF ASIA AND AFRICA (PAMPHLET). ISLAM ECO/UNDEV INT/ORG CONSULT CREATE PLAN TEC/DEV FOR/AID CONFER ALL/VALS 20 KENNEDY/JF EISNHWR/DD UN AID. PAGE 122 A2501
AFR S/ASIA DIPLOM BIBLIOG

B62
ROSAMOND R.,CRUSADE FOR PEACE: EISENHOWER'S PRESIDENTIAL LEGACY WITH THE PROGRAM FOR ACTION. USA+45 PARTIC ARMS/CONT MORAL MARXISM...TRADIT CONCPT CHARTS GEN/LAWS ANTHOL 20 PRESIDENT EISNHWR/DD. PAGE 123 A2526
PEACE DIPLOM EDU/PROP POLICY

B62
WILLIAMS W.A.,THE UNITED STATES, CUBA, AND CASTRO: AN ESSAY ON THE DYNAMICS OF REVOLUTION AND THE DISSOLUTION OF EMPIRE. CUBA USA+45 AGRI VOL/ASSN DIPLOM ECO/TAC DOMIN COERCE...POLICY 20 EISNHWR/DD CIA KENNEDY/JF CASTRO/F. PAGE 165 A3354
REV CONSTN COM LEAD

B63
ROSS H.,THE COLD WAR: CONTAINMENT AND ITS CRITICSS. WOR+45 POL/PAR BAL/PWR ECO/TAC PEACE ORD/FREE ...POLICY IDEA/COMP ANTHOL T 20 COLD/WAR DULLES/JF TRUMAN/HS EISNHWR/DD. PAGE 124 A2541
MARXISM ARMS/CONT DIPLOM

B64
WARREN S.,THE PRESIDENT AS WORLD LEADER. USA+45 WOR+45 ELITES COM/IND INT/ORG NAT/G VOL/ASSN CHIEF EX/STRUC LEGIT COERCE ATTIT PERSON RIGID/FLEX...INT TIME/SEQ COLD/WAR 20 ROOSEVLT/F TRUMAN/HS EISNHWR/DD KENNEDY/JF. PAGE 161 A3286
TOP/EX PWR DIPLOM

B65
EISENHOWER D.D.,WAGING PEACE 1956-61: THE WHITE HOUSE YEARS. USA+45 DIPLOM LEAD INGP/REL RACE/REL PEACE ATTIT...TRADIT TIME/SEQ 20 EISNHWR/DD PRESIDENT COLD/WAR CIV/RIGHTS BERLIN. PAGE 41 A0833
TOP/EX BIOG ORD/FREE POLICY

B65
TREFOUSSE H.L.,THE COLD WAR: A BOOK OF DOCUMENTS. ASIA L/A+17C USSR WOR+45 WOR-45 ECO/TAC FOR/AID ARMS/CONT NUC/PWR PEACE ORD/FREE...ANTHOL 20 COLD/WAR KENNEDY/JF EISNHWR/DD. PAGE 145 A2961
BAL/PWR DIPLOM MARXISM

B66
MAY E.R.,ANXIETY AND AFFLUENCE: 1945-1965. USA+45 DIPLOM FOR/AID ARMS/CONT RACE/REL CONSEN...ANTHOL 20 COLD/WAR KENNEDY/JF EISNHWR/DD TRUMAN/HS BERLIN/BLO. PAGE 97 A1982
ANOMIE ECO/DEV NUC/PWR WEALTH

EKIRCH A.A. A0834

EL/SALVADR....EL SALVADOR; SEE ALSO L/A+17C

B60
FLORES R.H.,CATALOGO DE TESIS DOCTORALES DE LAS FACULTADES DE LA UNIVERSIDAD DE EL SALVADOR. EL/SALVADR LAW DIPLOM ADMIN LEAD GOV/REL...SOC 19/20. PAGE 47 A0954
BIBLIOG ACADEM L/A+17C NAT/G

ELAHI K.N. A0835

ELDER R.E. A0836

ELECT/COLL....ELECTORAL COLLEGE

ELECTIONS....SEE CHOOSE

ELECTORAL COLLEGE....SEE ELECT/COLL

ELIAS T.O. A0837

ELITES....POWER-DOMINANT GROUPINGS OF A SOCIETY

B03
GRIFFIN A.P.C.,LISTS PUBLISHED 1902-03: ANGLO-SAXON INTERESTS (PAMPHLET). UK USA-45 ELITES SOCIETY DIPLOM ISOLAT 19/20. PAGE 56 A1152
BIBLIOG COLONIAL RACE/REL DOMIN

B22
FICHTE J.G.,ADDRESSES TO THE GERMAN NATION. GERMANY PRUSSIA ELITES NAT/G SECT CREATE INT/TRADE HEREDITY ...ART/METH LING 19 FRANK/PARL. PAGE 45 A0923
NAT/LISM CULTURE EDU/PROP REGION

B30
BYNKERSHOEK C.,QUAESTIONUM JURIS PUBLICI LIBRI DUO. CHRIST-17C MOD/EUR CONSTN ELITES SOCIETY NAT/G PROVS EX/STRUC FORCES TOP/EX BAL/PWR DIPLOM ATTIT MORAL...TRADIT CONCPT. PAGE 23 A0460
INT/ORG LAW NAT/LISM INT/LAW

B38
PETTEE G.S.,THE PROCESS OF REVOLUTION. COM FRANCE ITALY MOD/EUR RUSSIA SPAIN WOR-45 ELITES INTELL SOCIETY STRATA STRUCT INT/ORG NAT/G POL/PAR ACT/RES PLAN EDU/PROP LEGIT EXEC...SOC MYTH TIME/SEQ TOT/POP 18/20. PAGE 115 A2370
COERCE CONCPT REV

S41
LASSWELL H.D.,"THE GARRISON STATE" (BMR)" FUT WOR+45 ELITES INTELL FORCES ECO/TAC DOMIN EDU/PROP COERCE INGP/REL 20. PAGE 85 A1739
NAT/G DIPLOM PWR CIVMIL/REL

B42
CROWE S.E.,THE BERLIN WEST AFRICA CONFERENCE, 1884-85. GERMANY ELITES MARKET INT/ORG DELIB/GP FORCES PROB/SOLV BAL/PWR CAP/ISM DOMIN COLONIAL ...INT/LAW 19. PAGE 33 A0664
AFR CONFER INT/TRADE DIPLOM

B43
GRIERSON P.,BOOKS ON SOVIET RUSSIA 1917-42: A BIBLIOGRAPHY AND A GUIDE TO READING. USSR CULTURE ELITES NAT/G PLAN DIPLOM REV...GEOG 20. PAGE 56 A1148
BIBLIOG/A COM MARXISM LEAD

B45
CONOVER H.F.,ITALY: ECONOMICS, POLITICS AND MILITARY AFFAIRS, 1940-1945. ITALY ELITES NAT/G POL/PAR EX/STRUC TOP/EX DIPLOM DOMIN CONTROL COERCE WAR CIVMIL/REL EFFICIENCY 20. PAGE 29 A0599
BIBLIOG TOTALISM FORCES

B50
ALMOND G.A.,THE AMERICAN PEOPLE AND FOREIGN POLICY. USA+45 USA-45 CULTURE SOCIETY STRUCT CONSEN PERSON PWR POPULISM...TIME/SEQ TREND 20 COLD/WAR. PAGE 6 A0129
ATTIT DIPLOM DECISION ELITES

B50
LINCOLN G.,ECONOMICS OF NATIONAL SECURITY. USA+45 ELITES COM/IND DIST/IND INDUS NAT/G VOL/ASSN DELIB/GP EX/STRUC FOR/AID EDU/PROP COERCE NUC/PWR WAR ATTIT KNOWL ORD/FREE PWR COLD/WAR TOT/POP VAL/FREE 20. PAGE 89 A1818
FORCES ECO/TAC

B51
BISSAINTHE M.,DICTIONNAIRE DE BIBLIOGRAPHIE HAITIENNE. HAITI ELITES AGRI LEGIS DIPLOM INT/TRADE WRITING ORD/FREE CATHISM...ART/METH GEOG 19/20 NEGRO TREATY. PAGE 15 A0295
BIBLIOG L/A+17C SOCIETY NAT/G

B51
BLANSHARD P.,COMMUNISM, DEMOCRACY AND CATHOLIC POWER. USSR VATICAN WOR+45 WOR-45 CULTURE ELITES INTELL SOCIETY STRUCT INT/ORG POL/PAR EDU/PROP COERCE ATTIT KNOWL PWR MARXISM...CONCPT COLD/WAR 20. PAGE 15 A0308
COM SECT TOTALISM

B52
GURLAND A.R.L.,POLITICAL SCIENCE IN WESTERN GERMANY: THOUGHTS AND WRITINGS, 1950-1952 (PAMPHLET). EUR+WWI GERMANY/W ELITES SOCIETY NAT/G NAT/LISM TOTALISM 20. PAGE 58 A1196
BIBLIOG/A DIPLOM CIVMIL/REL FASCISM

B52
SCHUMAN F.,THE COMMONWEALTH OF MAN. WOR+45 WOR-45 LAW CULTURE ELITES SOCIETY FAM INT/ORG NAT/G VOL/ASSN TOP/EX PLAN BAL/PWR LEGIT ATTIT DISPL DRIVE...POLICY MYTH TREND TOT/POP ILO OEEC 20. PAGE 129 A2649
CONCPT GEN/LAWS

B52
THOM J.M.,GUIDE TO RESEARCH MATERIAL IN POLITICAL SCIENCE (PAMPHLET). ELITES LOC/G MUNIC NAT/G LEGIS DIPLOM ADJUD CIVMIL/REL GOV/REL PWR MGT. PAGE 143 A2919
BIBLIOG/A KNOWL

B53
CRAIG G.A.,THE DIPLOMATS 1919-1939. WAR PEACE ATTIT ...POLICY BIOG 20. PAGE 32 A0651
DIPLOM ELITES FASCISM

B54
BUTOW R.J.C.,JAPAN'S DECISION TO SURRENDER. USA-45 USSR CHIEF FORCES DOMIN NUC/PWR...BIBLIOG 20 TREATY CHINJAP. PAGE 22 A0453
ELITES DIPLOM WAR PEACE

B55
TAN C.C.,THE BOXER CATASTROPHE. ASIA UK USSR ELITES POL/PAR VOL/ASSN FORCES PROB/SOLV DIPLOM ADMIN COLONIAL NAT/LISM PEACE TREATY 19/20 BOXER/REBL. PAGE 141 A2885
REV NAT/G WAR

B56
HAAS E.B.,DYNAMICS OF INTERNATIONAL RELATIONS. WOR-45 ELITES INT/ORG VOL/ASSN EX/STRUC FORCES ECO/TAC DOMIN LEGIT COERCE ATTIT PERSON PWR ...CONCPT TIME/SEQ CHARTS COLD/WAR 20. PAGE 58 A1202
WOR+45 NAT/G DIPLOM

B58
GROBLER J.H.,AFRICA'S DESTINY. AFR EUR+WWI SOUTH/AFR UK USA+45 ELITES KIN LOC/G DIPLOM DISCRIM ATTIT CONSERVE MARXISM 20 ROOSEVLT/T NEGRO. PAGE 57 A1168
POLICY ORD/FREE COLONIAL CONSTN

B58
KENNAN G.F.,THE DECISION TO INTERVENE: SOVIET-AMERICAN RELATIONS, 1917-1920 (VOL. II). CZECHOSLVK EUR+WWI USA-45 USSR ELITES NAT/G FORCES PROB/SOLV REV WAR TOTALISM PWR...CHARTS BIBLIOG 20 TREATY PRESIDENT CHINJAP. PAGE 78 A1588
DIPLOM POLICY ATTIT

S58
SINGER J.D.,"THREAT PERCEPTION AND THE ARMAMENT TENSION DILEMMA." WOR+45 WOR-45 ELITES INT/ORG NAT/G DELIB/GP PLAN LEGIT COERCE DETER ATTIT RIGID/FLEX PWR...DECISION PSY 20. PAGE 133 A2724
PERCEPT ARMS/CONT BAL/PWR

B59
GOLDWIN R.A.,READINGS IN RUSSIAN FOREIGN POLICY. HUNGARY USSR YUGOSLAVIA ELITES INT/ORG NAT/G REV WAR NAT/LISM PERSON SOCISM...CHARTS 20 MAPS BOLSHEVISM. PAGE 53 A1095
COM MARXISM DIPLOM POLICY

B59
COLUMBIA U BUR APPL SOC RES,ATTITUDES OF PROMINENT AMERICANS TOWARD "WORLD PEACE THROUGH WORLD LAW" (SUPRA-NATL ORGANIZATION FOR WAR PREVENTION). USA+45 USSR ELITES FORCES PLAN PROB/SOLV CONTROL WAR PWR...POLICY SOC QU IDEA/COMP 20 UN. PAGE 117 A2403
ATTIT ACT/RES INT/LAW STAT

B59
THOMAS D.H.,GUIDE TO THE DIPLOMATIC ARCHIVES OF WESTERN EUROPE. EUR+WWI ELITES INT/ORG NAT/G BAL/PWR INT/TRADE PEACE. PAGE 143 A2921
BIBLIOG DIPLOM CONFER

B60
AMERICAN ASSEMBLY COLUMBIA U,THE SECRETARY OF STATE. USA+45 ELITES NAT/G PLAN ADMIN GOV/REL CENTRAL ATTIT...POLICY MGT 20 SEC/STATE CONGRESS PRESIDENT. PAGE 7 A0136
DELIB/GP EX/STRUC GP/REL DIPLOM

B60
DE GAULLE C.,THE EDGE OF THE SWORD. EUR+WWI FRANCE ELITES CHIEF DIPLOM ROLE...REALPOL TRADIT. PAGE 34 A0701
FORCES SUPEGO LEAD WAR

B60
FURNIA A.H.,THE DIPLOMACY OF APPEASEMENT: ANGLO-FRENCH RELATIONS AND THE PRELUDE TO WORLD WAR II 1931-1938. FRANCE GERMANY UK ELITES NAT/G DELIB/GP FORCES WAR PEACE RIGID/FLEX 20. PAGE 50 A1026
DIPLOM BAL/PWR COERCE

B60
MC CLELLAN G.S.,INDIA. CHINA/COM INDIA CONSTN ELITES STRATA AGRI POL/PAR FOR/AID ARMS/CONT REV MARXISM...CENSUS BIBLIOG 20 COLD/WAR GANDHI/M NEHRU/J. PAGE 97 A1990
DIPLOM NAT/G SOCIETY ECO/UNDEV

B60
PRICE D.,THE SECRETARY OF STATE. USA+45 CONSTN ELITES INTELL CHIEF EX/STRUC TOP/EX LEGIT ATTIT PWR SKILL...DECISION 20 CONGRESS. PAGE 117 A2410
CONSULT DIPLOM INT/LAW

B60
SETON-WATSON H.,NEITHER WAR NOR PEACE. ASIA USSR WOR+45 ELITES INT/ORG NAT/G EX/STRUC FORCES BAL/PWR ECO/TAC EDU/PROP COERCE NAT/LISM ORD/FREE WEALTH TOT/POP 20. PAGE 131 A2688
ATTIT PWR DIPLOM TOTALISM

B61
CARNELL F.,THE POLITICS OF THE NEW STATES: A SELECT ANNOTATED BIBLIOGRAPHY WITH SPECIAL REFERENCE TO THE COMMONWEALTH. CONSTN ELITES LABOR NAT/G POL/PAR EX/STRUC DIPLOM ADJUD ADMIN...GOV/COMP 20 COMMONWLTH. PAGE 24 A0496
BIBLIOG/A AFR ASIA COLONIAL

B61
DIA M.,THE AFRICAN NATIONS AND WORLD SOLIDARITY. ISLAM CULTURE ELITES ECO/DEV ECO/UNDEV INT/ORG NAT/G PLAN ECO/TAC INT/TRADE EDU/PROP NAT/LISM ATTIT DRIVE ORD/FREE WEALTH...SOCIALIST CONCPT CON/ANAL GEN/LAWS TOT/POP 20. PAGE 37 A0753
AFR REGION SOCISM

B61
ROSENAU J.N.,INTERNATIONAL POLITICS AND FOREIGN POLICY: A READER IN RESEARCH AND THEORY. ELITES ATTIT SOVEREIGN...DECISION CHARTS HYPO/EXP GAME SIMUL ANTHOL BIBLIOG METH 20. PAGE 124 A2531
ACT/RES DIPLOM CONCPT POLICY

B61
SCHWARTZ H.,THE RED PHOENIX: RUSSIA SINCE WORLD WAR II. USA+45 WOR+45 ELITES POL/PAR TEC/DEV ECO/TAC MARXISM. PAGE 130 A2655
DIPLOM NAT/G ECO/DEV

B62
ALTHING F.A.M.,EUROPEAN ORGANIZATIONS AND FOREIGN RELATIONS OF STATES: A COMPARATIVE ANALYSIS OF DECISION-MAKING. EUR+WWI CONSTN ELITES BAL/PWR INT/TRADE SOVEREIGN TREATY. PAGE 6 A0131
DELIB/GP INT/ORG DECISION DIPLOM

B62
CALVOCORESSI P.,WORLD ORDER AND NEW STATES: PROBLEMS OF KEEPING THE PEACE. AFR EUR+WWI S/ASIA ELITES NAT/G ECO/TAC FOR/AID EDU/PROP COERCE ATTIT DRIVE ALL/VALS...GEN/LAWS COLD/WAR 20 UN. PAGE 23 A0471
INT/ORG PEACE

B62
DAVAR F.C.,IRAN AND INDIA THROUGH THE AGES. INDIA IRAN ELITES SECT CREATE ORD/FREE...LING BIBLIOG. PAGE 34 A0683
NAT/COMP DIPLOM CULTURE

B62
NOBECOURT R.G.,LES SECRETS DE LA PROPAGANDE EN FRANCE OCCUPEE. FRANCE ELITES NAT/G DIPLOM GP/REL NAT/LISM TOTALISM ORD/FREE 20 VICHY VICHY. PAGE 109 A2244
METH/COMP EDU/PROP WAR CONTROL

B62
SCHRODER P.M.,METTERNICH'S DIPLOMACY AT ITS ZENITH, 1820-1823. MOD/EUR ELITES INT/ORG VOL/ASSN DELIB/GP ECO/TAC EDU/PROP DISPL PWR SOVEREIGN...POLICY CONCPT GEN/LAWS 19 METTRNCH/K. PAGE 129 A2647
ORD/FREE BIOG BAL/PWR DIPLOM

B62
SELOSOEMARDJAN O.,SOCIAL CHANGES IN JOGJAKARTA. INDONESIA NETHERLAND ELITES STRATA STRUCT FAM POL/PAR CREATE DIPLOM INT/TRADE EDU/PROP ADMIN GOV/REL...SOC 20 JAVA CHINJAP. PAGE 131 A2683
ECO/UNDEV CULTURE REV COLONIAL

L62
GROSS L.,"IMMUNITIES AND PRIVILEGES OF DELIGATIONS TO THE UNITED NATIONS." USA+45 WOR+45 STRATA NAT/G VOL/ASSN CONSULT DIPLOM EDU/PROP ROUTINE RESPECT ...POLICY INT/LAW CONCPT UN 20. PAGE 57 A1176
INT/ORG LAW ELITES

S62
RUBINSTEIN A.Z.,"RUSSIA AND THE UNCOMMITTED NATIONS." AFR INDIA ISLAM L/A+17C LAOS S/ASIA ELITES ECO/UNDEV INT/ORG KIN CREATE PLAN TEC/DEV NAT/LISM RIGID/FLEX PWR WEALTH...METH/CNCPT TIME/SEQ GEN/LAWS WORK. PAGE 125 A2562
ECO/TAC TREND COLONIAL USSR

C62
BACON F.,"OF THE TRUE GREATNESS OF KINGDOMS AND ESTATES" (1612) IN F. BACON, ESSAYS." ELITES FORCES DOMIN EDU/PROP LEGIT...POLICY GEN/LAWS 16/17 TREATY. PAGE 10 A0200
WAR PWR DIPLOM CONSTN

C62
BACON F.,"OF EMPIRE" (1612) IN F. BACON, ESSAYS." ELITES NAT/G PROB/SOLV DIPLOM ADMIN CONTROL WEALTH 16/17 KING. PAGE 10 A0201
PWR CHIEF DOMIN GEN/LAWS

B63
FRANKEL J.,THE MAKING OF FOREIGN POLICY: AN ANALYSIS OF DECISION-MAKING. CHINA/COM EUR+WWI USA+45 ELITES INTELL FORCES LEGIS PLAN ATTIT ALL/VALS MORAL CONSERVE...GOV/COMP 20 PRESIDENT UN TREATY. PAGE 48 A0981
POLICY DECISION PROB/SOLV DIPLOM

B63
HAMM H.,ALBANIA - CHINA'S BEACHHEAD IN EUROPE. ALBANIA CHINA/COM USSR YUGOSLAVIA ELITES SOCIETY POL/PAR DELIB/GP FORCES ECO/TAC COERCE ISOLAT PEACE MARXISM...IDEA/COMP 20 MAO. PAGE 61 A1248
DIPLOM REV NAT/G POLICY

B63
HARTLEY A.,A STATE OF ENGLAND. UK ELITES SOCIETY ACADEM NAT/G SCHOOL INGP/REL CONSEN ORD/FREE NEW/LIB...POLICY 20. PAGE 62 A1275
DIPLOM ATTIT INTELL ECO/DEV

B63
JAIRAZBHOY R.A.,FOREIGN INFLUENCE IN ANCIENT INDIA. INDIA ELITES SECT DIPLOM EDU/PROP COLONIAL REGION GP/REL...ART/METH LING WORSHIP +/14 GRECO/ROMN MESOPOTAM PERSIA PARTH/SASS. PAGE 73 A1491
CULTURE SOCIETY COERCE DOMIN

B63
KAHIN G.M.,MAJOR GOVERNMENTS OF ASIA (2ND ED.). ASIA INDIA INDONESIA PAKISTAN S/ASIA DIPLOM...SOC 20 CHINJAP. PAGE 75 A1546
GOV/COMP POL/PAR ELITES

B63
KHADDURI M.,MODERN LIBYA: A STUDY IN POLITICAL DEVELOPMENT. EUR+WWI ISLAM LIBYA ELITES INT/ORG POL/PAR FORCES DIPLOM FOR/AID DOMIN EDU/PROP LEGIT NAT/LISM DRIVE RIGID/FLEX SKILL...CONCPT TIME/SEQ TREND 20. PAGE 78 A1606
NAT/G STRUCT

B63
TUCKER R.C.,THE SOVIET POLITICAL MIND. WOR+45 ELITES INT/ORG NAT/G POL/PAR PLAN DIPLOM ECO/TAC DOMIN ADMIN NUC/PWR REV DRIVE PERSON SUPEGO PWR WEALTH...POLICY MGT PSY CONCPT OBS BIOG TREND COLD/WAR MARX/KARL 20. PAGE 145 A2972
COM TOP/EX USSR

S63
BANFIELD J.,"FEDERATION IN EAST-AFRICA." AFR UGANDA ELITES INT/ORG NAT/G VOL/ASSN LEGIS ECO/TAC FEDERAL ATTIT SOVEREIGN TOT/POP 20 TANGANYIKA. PAGE 11 A0216
EX/STRUC PWR REGION

S63
BELOFF M.,"BRITAIN, EUROPE AND THE ATLANTIC COMMUNITY." EUR+WWI ELITES NAT/G VOL/ASSN TOP/EX ATTIT ORD/FREE PWR SOVEREIGN WEALTH EEC TOT/POP VAL/FREE CMN/WLTH 20. PAGE 13 A0262
INT/ORG ECO/DEV UK

S63
LERNER D.,"FRENCH ELITE PERSPECTIVES ON THE UNITED NATIONS." EUR+WWI INT/ORG HEALTH ORD/FREE PWR RESPECT...STAT INT SAMP/SIZ VAL/FREE UN 20. PAGE 87 A1786
ATTIT STERTYP ELITES FRANCE

S63
STANLEY T.W.,"DECENTRALIZING NUCLEAR CONTROL IN NATO." EUR+WWI USA+45 ELITES FORCES ACT/RES ATTIT ORD/FREE PWR...NEW/IDEA HYPO/EXP TOT/POP 20 NATO. PAGE 137 A2805
INT/ORG EX/STRUC NUC/PWR

B64
HARPER F.,OUT OF CHINA. CHINA/COM ELITES STRATA ATTIT PERSON...BIOG 20 MAO HONG/KONG MIGRATION. PAGE 62 A1264
HABITAT DEEP/INT DIPLOM MARXISM

B64
HOROWITZ I.L.,REVOLUTION IN BRAZIL. BRAZIL L/A+17C ELITES STRATA NAT/G BAL/PWR PARTIC ATTIT 20. PAGE 68 A1388
ECO/UNDEV DIPLOM POLICY ORD/FREE

B64
LEGGE J.D.,INDONESIA. INDONESIA ELITES ECO/UNDEV POL/PAR CHIEF FORCES INT/TRADE COERCE CHOOSE ORD/FREE...SOC CHARTS BIBLIOG 16/20 CHINJAP. PAGE 86 A1765
S/ASIA DOMIN NAT/LISM POLICY

B64
LENSEN G.A.,REVELATIONS OF A RUSSIAN DIPLOMAT: THE MEMOIRS OF DMITRII I. ABRIKOSSOV. ASIA MOD/EUR RUSSIA USA-45 ELITES ACADEM CHIEF FORCES REV WAR PWR CONSERVE MARXISM 19/20 ABRIKSSV/D CHINJAP BOLSHEVISM. PAGE 87 A1775
DIPLOM POLICY OBS

B64
REMAK J.,THE GENTLE CRITIC: THEODOR FONTANE AND GERMAN POLITICS, 1848-1898. GERMANY PRUSSIA CULTURE ELITES BAL/PWR DIPLOM WRITING GOV/REL...HUM BIOG 19 BISMARCK/O JUNKER FONTANE/T. PAGE 120 A2465
PERSON SOCIETY WORKER CHIEF

B64
WARREN S.,THE PRESIDENT AS WORLD LEADER. USA+45 WOR+45 ELITES COM/IND INT/ORG NAT/G VOL/ASSN CHIEF EX/STRUC LEGIT COERCE ATTIT PERSON RIGID/FLEX...INT TIME/SEQ COLD/WAR 20 ROOSEVLT/F TRUMAN/HS EISNHWR/DD KENNEDY/JF. PAGE 161 A3286
TOP/EX PWR DIPLOM

S64
MARTELLI G.,"PORTUGAL AND THE UNITED NATIONS." AFR EUR+WWI ELITES INT/ORG NAT/G PROVS PLAN DIPLOM ECO/TAC DOMIN COLONIAL RIGID/FLEX MORAL ORD/FREE PWR WEALTH...MYTH UN 20. PAGE 95 A1947
ATTIT PORTUGAL

B65
GERASSI J.,THE GREAT FEAR IN LATIN AMERICA. L/A+17C USA+45 ELITES STRUCT INT/ORG REV ORD/FREE WEALTH 20 LAFTA. PAGE 52 A1063
SOCIETY FOR/AID DIPLOM

B65
LEWIS W.A.,POLITICS IN WEST AFRICA. AFR BAL/PWR DIPLOM REPRESENT...POLICY 20. PAGE 88 A1804
POL/PAR ELITES NAT/G ECO/UNDEV

B65
RUBINSTEIN A.Z.,THE CHALLENGE OF POLITICS: IDEAS AND ISSUES (2ND ED.). UNIV ELITES SOCIETY EX/STRUC BAL/PWR PARL/PROC AUTHORIT...DECISION ANTHOL 20. PAGE 125 A2565
NAT/G DIPLOM GP/REL ORD/FREE

B65
VAN DEN BERGHE P.L.,AFRICA: SOCIAL PROBLEMS OF CHANGE AND CONFLICT. ELITES STRATA ECO/UNDEV KIN MUNIC DIPLOM GP/REL RACE/REL NAT/LISM...ANTHOL BIBLIOG 20. PAGE 158 A3210
SOC CULTURE AFR STRUCT

B66
GRENVILLE J.A.S.,POLITICS, STRATEGY, AND AMERICAN DEMOCRACY: STUDIES IN FOREIGN POLICY, 1873-1917. CUBA PHILIPPINE SPAIN USA-45 VENEZUELA ELITES NAT/G CREATE PARTIC WAR RIGID/FLEX ORD/FREE...DECISION TREND 19/20 HAWAII. PAGE 56 A1146
DIPLOM COLONIAL POLICY

B66
HAMILTON W.B.,A DECADE OF THE COMMONWEALTH, 1955-1964. UK LAW ELITES FINAN FOR/AID CONFER COLONIAL PWR...GEOG CHARTS ANTHOL 20 CMN/WLTH UN. PAGE 61 A1247
INT/ORG INGP/REL DIPLOM NAT/G

B66
SKILLING H.G.,THE GOVERNMENTS OF COMMUNIST EAST EUROPE. COM EUR+WWI ELITES FORCES DIPLOM ECO/TAC CONTROL HABITAT SOCISM...DECISION BIBLIOG 20 EUROPE/E COM/PARTY. PAGE 134 A2738
MARXISM NAT/COMP GP/COMP DOMIN

B66
VYAS R.,DAWNING ON THE CAPITOL: US CONGRESS AND INDIA. INDIA S/ASIA USA+45 ELITES ECO/DEV ECO/UNDEV PLAN FOR/AID...BIBLIOG 20 CONGRESS. PAGE 160 A3256
POLICY LEGIS NAT/G DIPLOM

B66
WILSON H.A.,THE IMPERIAL POLICY OF SIR ROBERT BORDEN. CANADA UK ELITES INT/ORG VOL/ASSN CONTROL LEAD WAR ROLE 20 CMN/WLTH BORDEN/R. PAGE 165 A3360
INGP/REL COLONIAL CONSTN CHIEF

S66
"RESEARCH WORK 1965-1966." NEW/ZEALND ELITES ACADEM LOC/G MUNIC POL/PAR PROVS DIPLOM COLONIAL...SOC 20 AUSTRAL. PAGE 4 A0073
BIBLIOG NAT/G CULTURE S/ASIA

S66
MERRITT R.L.,"SELECTED ARTICLES AND DOCUMENTS ON COMPARATIVE GOVERNMENT AND CROSS-NATIONAL RESEARCH." AFR ASIA EUR+WWI L/A+17C MOD/EUR ELITES R+D ACT/RES DIPLOM PWR...SOC CONCPT 18/20. PAGE 100 A2046
BIBLIOG GOV/COMP NAT/G GOV/REL

C66
DUROSELLE J.B.,"LE CONFLIT DE TRIESTE 1943-1954:
BIBLIOG

ETUDES DE CAS DE CONFLITS INTERNATIONAUX III." ITALY USA+45 YUGOSLAVIA ELITES DELIB/GP PLAN ADJUST ...POLICY GEOG CHARTS IDEA/COMP TIME 20 TREATY UN COLD/WAR. PAGE 40 A0810 — WAR DIPLOM GEN/LAWS

B67
NYERERE J.K.,FREEDOM AND UNITY/UHURU NA UMOJA: A SELECTION FROM WRITINGS AND SPEECHES, 1952-65. TANZANIA ELITES ECO/UNDEV INT/ORG NAT/G CREATE DIPLOM COLONIAL REGION RACE/REL...ANTHOL 20. PAGE 110 A2265 — SOVEREIGN AFR TREND ORD/FREE

B67
SACHS M.Y.,THE WORLDMARK ENCYCLOPEDIA OF THE NATIONS (5 VOLS.). ELITES SOCIETY STRATA ECO/DEV ECO/UNDEV AGRI EXTR/IND FINAN LABOR LOC/G NAT/G POL/PAR SECT INT/TRADE SOVEREIGN...SOC 20. PAGE 126 A2585 — WOR+45 INT/ORG BAL/PWR

B67
THORNE C.,THE APPROACH OF WAR, 1938-1939. EUR+WWI POL/PAR CHIEF FORCES LEAD DRIVE PWR FASCISM ...BIBLIOG/A 20 HITLER/A. PAGE 144 A2936 — DIPLOM WAR ELITES

B67
ZUCKERMAN S.,SCIENTISTS AND WAR. ELITES INDUS DIPLOM CENTRAL EFFICIENCY KNOWL 20. PAGE 170 A3459 — R+D CONSULT ACT/RES GP/REL

S67
BREGMAN A.,"WHITHER RUSSIA?" COM RUSSIA INTELL POL/PAR DIPLOM PARTIC NAT/LISM TOTALISM ATTIT ORD/FREE 20. PAGE 18 A0370 — MARXISM ELITES ADMIN CREATE

S67
BUTTINGER J.,"VIETNAM* FRAUD OF THE 'OTHER WAR'." VIETNAM/S ELITES STRUCT AGRI NAT/G FOR/AID RENT TREND. PAGE 22 A0456 — PLAN WEALTH REV ECO/UNDEV

S67
DE ROUGEMENT D.,"THE CAMPAIGN OF THE EUROPEAN CONGRESSES." ELITES INTELL DIPLOM ECO/TAC CONFER PEACE...POLICY PREDICT. PAGE 35 A0710 — EUR+WWI REGION FEDERAL INT/ORG

S67
DEUTSCH K.W.,"ARMS CONTROL AND EUROPEAN UNITY* THE NEXT TEN YEARS." USA+45 ELITES NAT/G BAL/PWR DIPLOM NUC/PWR...INT KNO/TEST NATO EEC. PAGE 36 A0742 — ARMS/CONT PEACE REGION PLAN

S67
HALL M.,"GERMANY, EAST AND WEST* DANGER AT THE CROSSROADS." GERMANY ELITES CHIEF FORCES DIPLOM ECO/TAC REPAR ARMS/CONT...SOCIALIST 20. PAGE 60 A1227 — NAT/LISM ATTIT FASCISM WEAPON

S67
KRAUS J.,"A MARXIST IN GHANA." GHANA ELITES CHIEF PROB/SOLV TEC/DEV DIPLOM ECO/TAC COLONIAL PARTIC PWR 20 NKRUMAH/K. PAGE 82 A1676 — MARXISM PLAN ATTIT CREATE

S67
ROGERS W.C.,"A COMPARISON OF INFORMED AND GENERAL PUBLIC OPINION ON US FOREIGN POLICY." USA+45 DIPLOM EDU/PROP ORD/FREE...POLICY SAMP IDEA/COMP 20. PAGE 123 A2515 — KNOWL ATTIT GP/COMP ELITES

S67
SARBADHIKARI P.,"A NOTE ON THE DOMESTIC CRISIS OF NON-ALIGNMENT." ELITES INTELL ECO/UNDEV FOR/AID DOMIN. PAGE 127 A2605 — NEUTRAL WEALTH TOTALISM BAL/PWR

S67
SHOEMAKER R.L.,"JAPANESE ARMY AND THE WEST." ASIA ELITES EX/STRUC DIPLOM DOMIN EDU/PROP COERCE ATTIT AUTHORIT PWR 1/20 CHINJAP. PAGE 132 A2703 — FORCES TEC/DEV WAR TOTALISM

S67
THIEN T.T.,"VIETNAM: A CASE OF SOCIAL ALIENATION." VIETNAM AGRI FORCES FOR/AID ADMIN REPRESENT INGP/REL PWR 19/20. PAGE 143 A2918 — NAT/G ELITES WORKER STRANGE

B96
LOWELL A.L.,GOVERNMENTS AND PARTIES IN CONTINENTAL EUROPE, VOL. II. AUSTRIA GERMANY HUNGARY MOD/EUR SWITZERLND SOCIETY EX/STRUC LEGIS DIPLOM AGREE LEAD PARL/PROC PWR...POLICY 19. PAGE 91 A1867 — POL/PAR NAT/G GOV/REL ELITES

ELIZABTH/I....ELIZABETH I OF ENGLAND

EL-NAGGAR S. A0838

ELKIN A.B. A0839

ELKIN/AP....A.P. ELKIN

ELLENDER A.J. A0840

ELLERT R.B. A0841

ELLIOTT J.R. A0842

ELLSWORTH P.T. A0843

ELTON G.E. A0844

EMBREE A.T. A0845,A0846

EMENY B. A2718

EMERGENCY....SEE DECISION

EMERSON R. A0847,A0848,A0849,A2312

EMME E.M. A0850

EMPLOYMENT....SEE WORKER

ENG/CIV/WR....ENGLISH CIVIL WAR

ENGEL J. A0851

ENGELENBURG F.V. A0396

ENGEL-JANOSI F. A0852

ENGELMAN F.L. A0853

ENGELS/F....FRIEDRICH ENGELS

B62
EBENSTEIN W.,TWO WAYS OF LIFE. USA+45 CULTURE ECO/DEV PLAN EDU/PROP CONTROL ORD/FREE...GOV/COMP IDEA/COMP T 20 MARX/KARL ENGELS/F LENIN/VI LOCKE/JOHN MILL/JS. PAGE 40 A0819 — MARXISM POPULISM ECO/TAC DIPLOM

ENGLAND....SEE UK, ALSO APPROPRIATE TIME/SPACE/CULTURE INDEX

ENGLISH CIVIL WAR....SEE ENG/CIV/WR

ENGLSH/LAW....ENGLISH LAW

B66
MCNAIR A.D.,THE LEGAL EFFECTS OF WAR. UK FINAN DIPLOM ORD/FREE 20 ENGLSH/LAW. PAGE 98 A2019 — JURID WAR INT/TRADE LABOR

ENLIGHTNMT....THE ENLIGHTENMENT

ENTREPRENEURSHIP....SEE OWN, INDUS, CAP/ISM

ENVY....SEE WEALTH, LOVE, AND VALUES INDEX

EPIST....EPISTEMOLOGY, SOCIOLOGY OF KNOWLEDGE

N
AMERICAN BIBLIOGRAPHIC SERVICE,INTERNATIONAL GUIDE TO INDIC STUDIES - A QUARTERLY INDEX TO PERIODICAL LITERATURE. INDIA CULTURE NAT/G DIPLOM...EPIST SOC BIOG 20. PAGE 7 A0140 — BIBLIOG S/ASIA CON/ANAL

B45
MACMINN N.,BIBLIOGRAPHY OF THE PUBLISHED WRITINGS OF JOHN STUART MILL. MOD/EUR UK CAP/ISM DIPLOM KNOWL...EPIST CONCPT 19 MILL/JS. PAGE 93 A1901 — BIBLIOG/A SOCIETY INGP/REL LAISSEZ

B57
YAMADA H.,ANNALS OF THE SOCIAL SCIENCES. WOR+45 WOR-45 LAW CULTURE SOCIETY STRUCT DIPLOM...EPIST PSY CONCPT 15/20. PAGE 168 A3428 — BIBLIOG/A TREND IDEA/COMP SOC

EPISTEMOLOGY....SEE EPIST

EPSTEIN F.T. A0855

EPSTEIN H.M. A0856

EPSTEIN L.D. A0857

EPTA....EXPANDED PROGRAM OF TECHNICAL ASSISTANCE

EQUILIB....EQUILIBRIUM; SEE ALSO BAL/PWR

B08
GRIFFIN A.P.C.,LIST OF REFERENCES ON INTERNATIONAL ARBITRATION. FRANCE L/A+17C USA-45 WOR-45 DIPLOM CONFER COLONIAL ARMS/CONT BAL/PAY EQUILIB SOVEREIGN ...DECISION 19/20 MEXIC/AMER. PAGE 56 A1156 — BIBLIOG/A INT/ORG INT/LAW DELIB/GP

B39
FULLER G.H.,A SELECTED LIST OF REFERENCES ON THE EXPANSION OF THE US NAVY, 1933-1939 (PAMPHLET). MOD/EUR USA-45 NAT/G PLAN DIPLOM DOMIN RISK ARMS/CONT EQUILIB PWR 20 NAVY. PAGE 50 A1019 — BIBLIOG FORCES WEAPON WAR

B50
DE RUSETT A.,STRENGTHENING THE FRAMEWORK OF PEACE. WOR+45 VOL/ASSN FORCES CREATE INSPECT ADJUD CONTROL WAR EQUILIB FEDERAL ORD/FREE 20 UN EUROPE. PAGE 35 A0711
INT/ORG DIPLOM PEACE METH/COMP

C50
ELLSWORTH P.T.,"INTERNATIONAL ECONOMY." ECO/DEV ECO/UNDEV FINAN LABOR DIPLOM FOR/AID TARIFFS BAL/PAY EQUILIB NAT/LISM OPTIMAL...INT/LAW 20 ILO GATT. PAGE 41 A0843
BIBLIOG INT/TRADE ECO/TAC INT/ORG

B53
NEISSER H.,NATIONAL INCOMES AND INTERNATIONAL TRADE. FRANCE GERMANY SWEDEN UK USA-45 EXTR/IND FINAN INDUS TEC/DEV PRICE BAL/PAY EQUILIB INCOME WEALTH...CHARTS METH 19 CHINJAP. PAGE 108 A2215
INT/TRADE PRODUC MARKET CON/ANAL

B59
ALLEN W.R.,FOREIGN TRADE AND FINANCE. ECO/DEV DIPLOM BAL/PAY...POLICY CONCPT ANTHOL 20. PAGE 6 A0127
INT/TRADE EQUILIB FINAN

B59
LINK R.G.,ENGLISH THEORIES OF ECONOMIC FLUCTUATIONS: 1815-1848. FRANCE UK AGRI WORKER DIPLOM PRICE TASK WAR DEMAND PRODUC...POLICY BIBLIOG 18 MALTHUS MILL/JS WILSON/J. PAGE 89 A1826
IDEA/COMP ECO/DEV WEALTH EQUILIB

B61
BUSSCHAU W.J.,GOLD AND INTERNATIONAL LIQUIDITY. WOR+45 PRICE EQUILIB WEALTH...CHARTS 20 GOLD/STAND. PAGE 22 A0450
FINAN DIPLOM PROB/SOLV

B61
GANGULI B.N.,ECONOMIC INTEGRATION. FINAN LABOR CAP/ISM DIPLOM WEALTH...NAT/COMP 20. PAGE 51 A1041
ECO/TAC METH/CNCPT EQUILIB ECO/UNDEV

B62
LUTZ F.A.,THE PROBLEM OF INTERNATIONAL ECONOMIC EQUILIBRIUM. FINAN PRODUC WEALTH 20 MONEY. PAGE 92 A1876
DIPLOM EQUILIB BAL/PAY PROB/SOLV

B64
ZEBOT C.A.,THE ECONOMICS OF COMPETITIVE COEXISTENCE. CHINA/COM USSR WOR+45 FINAN MARKET FOR/AID PRICE DEMAND EQUILIB WEALTH ALL/IDEOS 20. PAGE 169 A3450
TEC/DEV DIPLOM METH/COMP

B65
MCCOLL G.D.,THE AUSTRALIAN BALANCE OF PAYMENTS. UK USA+45 AGRI WORKER DIPLOM EQUILIB PRODUC...STAT TREND CHARTS BIBLIOG/A 20 AUSTRAL. PAGE 97 A2001
ECO/DEV BAL/PAY INT/TRADE COST

B65
ROLFE S.E.,GOLD AND WORLD POWER. UK USA+45 WOR-45 INDUS WORKER INT/TRADE DEMAND...MGT CHARTS 20 GOLD/STAND. PAGE 123 A2517
BAL/PAY EQUILIB ECO/TAC DIPLOM

B65
US DEPARTMENT OF DEFENSE,US SECURITY ARMS CONTROL, AND DISARMAMENT 1961-1965 (PAMPHLET). CHINA/COM COM GERMANY/W ISRAEL SPACE USA+45 USSR WOR+45 FORCES EDU/PROP DETER EQUILIB PEACE ALL/VALS...GOV/COMP 20 NATO. PAGE 151 A3077
BIBLIOG/A ARMS/CONT NUC/PWR DIPLOM

B66
MEERHAEGHE M.,INTERNATIONAL ECONOMIC INSTITUTIONS. EUR+WWI FINAN INDUS MARKET PLAN TARIFFS BAL/PAY EQUILIB...POLICY BIBLIOG/A 20 GATT OEEC EEC IBRD EURCOALSTL. PAGE 99 A2032
ECO/TAC ECO/DEV INT/TRADE INT/ORG

B66
PIQUET H.S.,THE US BALANCE OF PAYMENTS AND INTERNATIONAL MONETARY RESERVES. USA+45 PROB/SOLV INT/TRADE GOV/REL EQUILIB...POLICY STAT CHARTS 20 GOLD/STAND. PAGE 116 A2384
BAL/PAY DIPLOM FINAN ECO/TAC

B67
CLARK S.V.O.,CENTRAL BANK COOPERATION: 1924-31. WOR-45 PROB/SOLV ECO/TAC ADJUST BAL/PAY...TREND CHARTS METH/COMP 20. PAGE 27 A0542
FINAN EQUILIB DIPLOM POLICY

B67
SCOTT A.M.,THE FUNCTIONING OF THE INTERNATIONAL POLITICAL SYSTEM. INT/ORG OP/RES PROB/SOLV COERCE WAR EQUILIB...METH/CNCPT BIBLIOG. PAGE 130 A2671
DIPLOM DECISION BAL/PWR

L67
SEGAL A.,"THE INTEGRATION OF DEVELOPING COUNTRIES: SOME THOUGHTS ON EAST AFRICA AND CENTRAL AMERICA." AFR L/A+17C INT/ORG NAT/G VOL/ASSN FOR/AID INT/TRADE EQUILIB NAT/LISM PWR 20. PAGE 131 A2680
ECO/UNDEV DIPLOM REGION

S67
D'AMATO D.,"LEGAL ASPECTS OF THE FRENCH NUCLEAR TESTS." FRANCE WOR+45 ACT/RES COLONIAL RISK GOV/REL EQUILIB ORD/FREE PWR DECISION. PAGE 33 A0672
INT/LAW DIPLOM NUC/PWR ADJUD

S67
HAZARD J.N.,"POST-DISARMAMENT INTERNATIONAL LAW." FUT USSR WOR+45 INT/ORG DELIB/GP FORCES DETER EQUILIB SOVEREIGN MARXISM 20 UN. PAGE 63 A1301
INT/LAW ARMS/CONT PWR PLAN

ERASMUS/D

B49
BOYD A.,WESTERN UNION: A STUDY OF THE TREND TOWARD EUROPEAN UNITY. FUT REGION NAT/LISM...POLICY IDEA/COMP BIBLIOG 14/20 OEEC ERASMUS/D COUNCL/EUR FULBRGHT/J NATO. PAGE 18 A0363
DIPLOM AGREE TREND INT/ORG

ERB G.F. A0858

ERDEMLI....ERDEMLI, TURKEY

ERDMAN P.E. A0859

ERHARD L. A0860

ERICKSON J. A0861

ESPIONAGE....ESPIONAGE

B37
THOMPSON J.W.,SECRET DIPLOMACY: A RECORD OF ESPIONAGE AND DOUBLE-DEALING: 1500-1815. CHRIST-17C MOD/EUR NAT/G WRITING RISK MORAL...ANTHOL BIBLIOG 16/19 ESPIONAGE. PAGE 143 A2927
DIPLOM CRIME

B61
AMORY J.F.,AROUND THE EDGE OF WAR: A NEW APPROACH TO THE PROBLEMS OF AMERICAN FOREIGN POLICY. COM L/A+17C USA+45 USSR FOR/AID EDU/PROP AGREE CONTROL ARMS/CONT NUC/PWR WAR PWR...IDEA/COMP 20 TREATY ESPIONAGE. PAGE 8 A0154
NAT/G DIPLOM POLICY

B63
WHITNEY T.P.,KHRUSHCHEV SPEAKS. USSR AGRI LEAD ...BIOG ANTHOL 20 KHRUSH/N STALIN/J ESPIONAGE. PAGE 164 A3339
DIPLOM MARXISM CHIEF

ESTEP R. A0862

ESTHUS R.A. A0863,A0864

ESTIMATION....SEE COST

ESTONIA....SEE ALSO USSR

ESTRANGEMENT....SEE STRANGE

ETHIC....PERSONAL ETHICS

ETHIOPIA....SEE ALSO AFR

B36
THWAITE D.,THE SEETHING AFRICAN POT: A STUDY OF BLACK NATIONALISM 1882-1935. ETHIOPIA SECT VOL/ASSN COERCE GUERRILLA MURDER DISCRIM MARXISM...PSY TIME/SEQ 18/20 NEGRO. PAGE 144 A2939
NAT/LISM AFR RACE/REL DIPLOM

B36
VARLEY D.H.,A BIBLIOGRAPHY OF ITALIAN COLONISATION IN AFRICA WITH A SECTION ON ABYSSINIA. AFR ETHIOPIA ITALY LIBYA SOMALIA AGRI FINAN LABOR TEC/DEV DIPLOM INT/TRADE RACE/REL DISCRIM 19/20. PAGE 158 A3222
BIBLIOG COLONIAL ADMIN LAW

B63
ETHIOPIAN MINISTRY INFORMATION,AFRICAN SUMMIT CONFERENCE ADDIS ABABA, ETHIOPIA, 1963. ETHIOPIA DELIB/GP COLONIAL NAT/LISM...POLICY DECISION 20. PAGE 42 A0865
AFR CONFER REGION DIPLOM

L65
MATTHEWS D.G.,"A CURRENT BIBLIOGRAPHY ON ETHIOPIAN AFFAIRS: A SELECT BIBLIOGRAPHY FROM 1950-1964." ETHIOPIA LAW CULTURE ECO/UNDEV INDUS LABOR SECT FORCES DIPLOM CIVMIL/REL RACE/REL...LING STAT 20. PAGE 96 A1969
BIBLIOG/A ADMIN POL/PAR NAT/G

S66
MATTHEWS D.G.,"ETHIOPIAN OUTLINE: A BIBLIOGRAPHIC RESEARCH GUIDE." ETHIOPIA LAW STRUCT ECO/UNDEV AGRI LABOR SECT CHIEF DELIB/GP EX/STRUC ADMIN...LING ORG/CHARTS 20. PAGE 96 A1972
BIBLIOG NAT/G DIPLOM POL/PAR

L67
LANDIS E.S.,"THE SOUTH WEST AFRICA CASES* REMAND TO THE UNITED NATIONS." ETHIOPIA LIBERIA SOUTH/AFR BAL/PWR 20 UN. PAGE 84 A1719
INT/LAW INT/ORG DIPLOM ADJUD

L67
MACDONALD R.S.J.,"THE RESORT TO ECONOMIC COERCION BY INTERNATIONAL POLITICAL ORGANIZATIONS." CUBA ETHIOPIA RHODESIA SOUTH/AFR NAT/G FOR/AID INT/TRADE DOMIN CONTROL SANCTION...DECISION LEAGUE/NAT UN OAS 20. PAGE 92 A1887
INT/ORG COERCE ECO/TAC DIPLOM

S67
JOHNSON D.H.N.,"THE SOUTH-WEST AFRICA CASES." AFR ETHIOPIA LIBERIA SOUTH/AFR CONSULT JUDGE BAL/PWR 20. PAGE 74 A1521
INT/LAW DIPLOM INT/ORG ADJUD

ETHIOPIAN MINISTRY INFORMATION A0865

ETHNICITY....SEE RACE/REL

ETIENNE G. A0866

ETIQUET....ETIQUETTE, STYLING, FASHION, MANNERS

B58
SALETORE B.A.,INDIA'S DIPLOMATIC RELATIONS WITH THE WEST. GREECE INDIA CULTURE ETIQUET...IDEA/COMP 3 ROM/EMP PERSIA. PAGE 126 A2590 — DIPLOM CONCPT INT/TRADE

B60
SALETORE B.A.,INDIA'S DIPLOMATIC RELATIONS WITH THE EAST. ASIA CEYLON INDIA NEPAL S/ASIA CULTURE 7/14 PERSIA. PAGE 126 A2591 — DIPLOM NAT/COMP ETIQUET

B65
FORGAC A.A.,NEW DIPLOMACY AND THE UNITED NATIONS. FRANCE GERMANY UK USSR INT/ORG DELIB/GP EX/STRUC PEACE...INT/LAW CONCPT UN. PAGE 47 A0965 — DIPLOM ETIQUET NAT/G

ETSCHMANN R. A0867

ETZIONI A. A0868,A0869,A0870,A0871

EUBANK K. A0872

EUDIN X.J. A0873,A2253

EUGENICS....SEE BIO/SOC+GEOG

EUGENIE....EMPRESS EUGENIE (FRANCE)

EUR+WWI....EUROPE SINCE WORLD WAR I

EURATOM....EUROPEAN ATOMIC ENERGY COMMUNITY

N
FOREIGN AFFAIRS. SPACE WOR+45 WOR-45 CULTURE ECO/UNDEV FINAN NAT/G TEC/DEV INT/TRADE ARMS/CONT NUC/PWR...POLICY 20 UN EURATOM ECSC EEC. PAGE 2 A0034 — BIBLIOG DIPLOM INT/ORG INT/LAW

B59
ROBERTSON A.H.,EUROPEAN INSTITUTIONS: COOPERATION, INTEGRATION, UNIFICATION. EUR+WWI FINAN INT/ORG FORCES INT/TRADE TARIFFS 20 EEC EURATOM ECSC NATO TREATY. PAGE 122 A2496 — ECO/DEV DIPLOM INDUS ECO/TAC

S60
NANES A.,"THE EUROPEAN COMMUNITY AND THE UNITED STATES: EVOLVING RELATIONS." EUR+WWI USA+45 WOR+45 ECO/UNDEV MARKET NAT/G DELIB/GP PLAN LEGIT ATTIT PWR WEALTH...CONCPT STAT TIME/SEQ CON/ANAL EEC OEEC 20 EURATOM. PAGE 107 A2194 — INT/ORG REGION

B63
MAYNE R.,THE COMMUNITY OF EUROPE. UK CONSTN NAT/G CONSULT DELIB/GP CREATE PLAN ECO/TAC LEGIT ADMIN ROUTINE ORD/FREE PWR WEALTH...CONCPT TIME/SEQ EEC EURATOM 20. PAGE 97 A1985 — EUR+WWI INT/ORG REGION

B64
ECONOMIDES C.P.,LE POUVOIR DE DECISION DES ORGANISATIONS INTERNATIONALES EUROPEENNES. DIPLOM DOMIN INGP/REL EFFICIENCY...INT/LAW JURID 20 NATO OEEC EEC COUNCL/EUR EURATOM. PAGE 40 A0821 — INT/ORG PWR DECISION GP/COMP

B65
HASSON J.A.,THE ECONOMICS OF NUCLEAR POWER. INDIA UK USA+45 WOR+45 INT/ORG TEC/DEV COST...SOC STAT CHARTS 20 EURATOM. PAGE 63 A1286 — NUC/PWR INDUS ECO/DEV METH

B65
US CONGRESS JT ATOM ENRGY COMM,ATOMIC ENERGY LEGISLATION THROUGH 89TH CONGRESS, 1ST SESSION. USA+45 LAW INT/ORG DELIB/GP BUDGET DIPLOM 20 AEC CONGRESS CASEBOOK EURATOM IAEA. PAGE 150 A3071 — NUC/PWR FORCES PEACE LEGIS

B66
NIJHOFF M.,ANNUAIRE EUROPEEN (VOL. XII). INT/TRADE REGION PEACE 20 EFTA EEC ECSC EURATOM. PAGE 109 A2241 — BIBLIOG INT/ORG EUR+WWI DIPLOM

B66
SPINELLI A.,THE EUROCRATS; CONFLICT AND CRISIS IN THE EUROPEAN COMMUNITY (TRANS. BY C. GROVE HAINES). EUR+WWI MARKET POL/PAR ECO/TAC PARL/PROC EEC OEEC ECSC EURATOM. PAGE 136 A2789 — INT/ORG INGP/REL CONSTN ADMIN

S67
WEIL G.L.,"THE MERGER OF THE INSTITUTIONS OF THE EUROPEAN COMMUNITIES" EUR+WWI ECO/DEV INT/TRADE CONSEN PLURISM...DECISION MGT 20 EEC EURATOM ECSC TREATY. PAGE 162 A3300 — ECO/TAC INT/ORG CENTRAL INT/LAW

EURCOALSTL....EUROPEAN COAL AND STEEL COMMUNITY; SEE ALSO VOL/ASSN, INT/ORG

B62
SCHMITT H.A.,THE PATH TO EUROPEAN UNITY. EUR+WWI USA+45 PLAN TEC/DEV DIPLOM FOR/AID CONFER...INT/LAW 20 EEC EURCOALSTL MARSHL/PLN UNIFICA. PAGE 128 A2634 — INT/ORG INT/TRADE REGION ECO/DEV

B66
MEERHAEGHE M.,INTERNATIONAL ECONOMIC INSTITUTIONS. EUR+WWI FINAN INDUS MARKET PLAN TARIFFS BAL/PAY EQUILIB...POLICY BIBLIOG/A 20 GATT OEEC EEC IBRD EURCOALSTL. PAGE 99 A2032 — ECO/TAC ECO/DEV INT/TRADE INT/ORG

EURCT/JUST....EUROPEAN COURT OF JUSTICE

B64
SCHECHTER A.H.,INTERPRETATION OF AMBIGUOUS DOCUMENTS BY INTERNATIONAL ADMINISTRATIVE TRIBUNALS. WOR+45 EX/STRUC INT/TRADE CT/SYS SOVEREIGN 20 UN ILO EURCT/JUST. PAGE 128 A2620 — INT/LAW DIPLOM INT/ORG ADJUD

B66
AMERICAN JOURNAL COMP LAW,THE AMERICAN JOURNAL OF COMPARATIVE LAW READER. EUR+WWI USA+45 USA-45 LAW CONSTN LOC/G MUNIC NAT/G DIPLOM...ANTHOL 20 SUPREME/CT EURCT/JUST. PAGE 7 A0151 — IDEA/COMP JURID INT/LAW CT/SYS

EUROPA PUBLICATIONS LIMITED A0874

EUROPA-ARCHIV A0875

EUROPE....SEE EUR+WWI, MOD/EUR

B50
DE RUSETT A.,STRENGTHENING THE FRAMEWORK OF PEACE. WOR+45 VOL/ASSN FORCES CREATE INSPECT ADJUD CONTROL WAR EQUILIB FEDERAL ORD/FREE 20 UN EUROPE. PAGE 35 A0711 — INT/ORG DIPLOM PEACE METH/COMP

B50
DUCLOS P.,L'EVOLUTION DES RAPPORTS POLITIQUES DEPUIS 1750 (LIBERTE, INTEGRATION, UNITE). LAW INT/ORG FEDERAL TOTALISM ATTIT PWR...MAJORIT BIBLIOG 18/20 PARLIAMENT EUROPE. PAGE 39 A0792 — ORD/FREE DIPLOM NAT/G GOV/COMP

B52
MACARTHUR D.,REVITALIZING A NATION. ASIA COM FUT KOREA WOR+45 NAT/G FOR/AID TAX GIVE WAR ATTIT SOCISM 20 CHINJAP EUROPE. PAGE 92 A1885 — LEAD FORCES TOP/EX POLICY

B53
LANGER W.L.,THE UNDECLARED WAR, 1940-1941. EUR+WWI GERMANY USA-45 USSR AIR FORCES TEC/DEV CONFER CONTROL COERCE PERCEPT ORD/FREE PWR 20 CHINJAP EUROPE. PAGE 84 A1727 — WAR POLICY DIPLOM

B54
TAYLOR A.J.P.,THE STRUGGLE FOR MASTERY IN EUROPE 1848-1918. MOD/EUR VOL/ASSN FORCES BAL/PWR DOMIN CONTROL PEACE MORAL 19/20 TREATY EUROPE WWI. PAGE 142 A2897 — DIPLOM WAR PWR

B55
ARNOLD G.L.,THE PATTERN OF WORLD CONFLICT. USA+45 INT/ORG ECO/TAC INT/TRADE PEACE 20 EUROPE. PAGE 9 A0176 — DIPLOM BAL/PWR NAT/LISM PLAN

B57
WARBURG J.P.,AGENDA FOR ACTION. ISLAM ISRAEL USA+45 FOR/AID INT/TRADE WAR NAT/LISM 20 MID/EAST EUROPE ARABS. PAGE 161 A3275 — DIPLOM POLICY INT/ORG BAL/PWR

B58
PALYI M.,MANAGED MONEY AT THE CROSSROADS: THE EUROPEAN EXPERIENCE. WOR+45 WOR-45 TEC/DEV DIPLOM INT/TRADE DEMAND WEALTH...CHARTS BIBLIOG 19/20 EUROPE GOLD/STAND SILVER. PAGE 113 A2324 — FINAN ECO/TAC ECO/DEV PRODUC

B59
EMME E.M.,THE IMPACT OF AIR POWER - NATIONAL SECURITY AND WORLD POLITICS. USA+45 USSR FORCES DIPLOM WEAPON PEACE TOTALISM...POLICY NAT/COMP 20 EUROPE. PAGE 42 A0850 — DETER AIR WAR ORD/FREE

B60
ALBRECHT-CARRIE R.,FRANCE, EUROPE AND THE TWO WORLD WARS. EUR+WWI FRANCE GERMANY MOD/EUR UK ECO/DEV NAT/G FORCES BAL/PWR DOMIN ARMS/CONT PEACE PWR 20 TREATY EUROPE. PAGE 5 A0109 — DIPLOM WAR

B62
LUTZ F.A.,GELD UND WAHRUNG. MARKET LABOR BUDGET 20 GOLD/STAND EUROPE. PAGE 92 A1875 — ECO/TAC FINAN DIPLOM POLICY

S63
BRZEZINSKI Z.,"SOVIET QUIESCENCE." EUR+WWI USA+45 USSR FORCES CREATE PLAN COERCE DETER WAR ATTIT 20 TREATY EUROPE. PAGE 20 A0415 — DIPLOM ARMS/CONT NUC/PWR AGREE

B65
CALLEO D.P.,EUROPE'S FUTURE: THE GRAND ALTERNATIVES. UK INT/ORG DIPLOM PWR SOVEREIGN ...CONCPT IDEA/COMP NAT/COMP BIBLIOG 20 EEC EUROPE — FUT EUR+WWI FEDERAL

DEGAULLE/C NATO. PAGE 23 A0468 — NAT/LISM

B65
MOLNAR T.,AFRICA: A POLITICAL TRAVELOGUE. STRUCT ECO/UNDEV DIPLOM EDU/PROP LEAD RACE/REL MARXISM 20 INTERVENT EUROPE. PAGE 102 A2101 — COLONIAL AFR ORD/FREE

B66
BEAUFRE A.,NATO AND EUROPE. WOR+45 PLAN CONFER EXEC NUC/PWR ATTIT...POLICY 20 NATO EUROPE. PAGE 12 A0243 — INT/ORG DETER DIPLOM ADMIN

N66
EOMMITTEE ECONOMIC DEVELOPMENT,THE DOLLAR AND THE WORLD MONETARY SYSTEM: A STATEMENT ON NATIONAL POLICY (PAMPHLET). USA+45 NAT/G PLAN PROB/SOLV BUDGET ECO/TAC FOR/AID INCOME...POLICY 20 GOLD/STAND EUROPE. PAGE 42 A0854 — FINAN BAL/PAY DIPLOM ECO/DEV

EUROPE/E....EASTERN EUROPE (ALL EUROPEAN COMMUNIST NATIONS)

B60
MOSELY P.E.,THE KREMLIN AND WORLD POLITICS. EUR+WWI GERMANY USA+45 USSR CHIEF TOP/EX BAL/PWR DOMIN PEACE PWR...METH 20 COLD/WAR STALIN/J EUROPE/E. PAGE 105 A2151 — COM DIPLOM POLICY WAR

B62
KLUCKHOHN F.L.,THE NAKED RISE OF COMMUNISM. CHINA/COM COM USSR WOR+45 CONSTN POL/PAR PLAN CONTROL LEAD NEUTRAL CONSERVE 20 STALIN/J EUROPE/E COM/PARTY. PAGE 80 A1650 — MARXISM IDEA/COMP DIPLOM DOMIN

B64
GRIFFITH W.E.,COMMUNISM IN EUROPE (2 VOLS.). CZECHOSLVK USSR WOR+45 WOR-45 YUGOSLAVIA INGP/REL MARXISM SOCISM...ANTHOL 20 EUROPE/E. PAGE 57 A1162 — COM POL/PAR DIPLOM GOV/COMP

B64
KIS T.I.,LES PAYS DE L'EUROPE DE L'EST: LEURS RAPPORTS MUTUELS ET LE PROBLEME DE LEUR INTEGRATION DANS L'ORBITE DE L'USSR. EUR+WWI RUSSIA USSR INT/ORG NAT/G REV ATTIT...JURID SOC BIBLIOG WARSAW/P COMECON EUROPE/E. PAGE 80 A1638 — DIPLOM COM MARXISM REGION

B66
SKILLING H.G.,THE GOVERNMENTS OF COMMUNIST EAST EUROPE. COM EUR+WWI ELITES FORCES DIPLOM ECO/TAC CONTROL HABITAT SOCISM...DECISION BIBLIOG 20 EUROPE/E COM/PARTY. PAGE 134 A2738 — MARXISM NAT/COMP GP/COMP DOMIN

EUROPE/W....WESTERN EUROPE (NON-COMMUNIST EUROPE, EXCLUDING GREECE, TURKEY, SCANDINAVIA, AND THE BRITISH ISLES)

B45
STRAUSZ-HUPE R.,THE BALANCE OF TOMORROW: POWER AND FOREIGN POLICY IN THE UNITED STATES. FUT USA+45 ECO/DEV EXTR/IND INT/ORG FORCES BAL/PWR REGION NUC/PWR...GEOG CHARTS 20 COLD/WAR EUROPE/W. PAGE 139 A2845 — DIPLOM PWR POLICY WAR

N47
FOX W.T.R.,UNITED STATES POLICY IN A TWO POWER WORLD. COM USA+45 USSR FORCES DOMIN AGREE NEUTRAL NUC/PWR ORD/FREE SOVEREIGN 20 COLD/WAR TREATY EUROPE/W INTERVENT. PAGE 48 A0972 — DIPLOM FOR/AID POLICY

B56
FOSTER J.G.,BRITAIN IN WESTERN EUROPE: WEU AND THE ATLANTIC ALLIANCE. EUR+WWI FRANCE GERMANY GERMANY/W ITALY UK STRATA NAT/G DELIB/GP ECO/TAC ORD/FREE PWR ...TRADIT TIME/SEQ TREND OEEC PARLIAMENT 20 EUROPE/W. PAGE 47 A0969 — INT/ORG FORCES WEAPON

B59
BLOOMFIELD L.P.,WESTERN EUROPE AND THE UN - TRENDS AND PROSPECTS. EUR+WWI BAL/PWR DIPLOM ECO/TAC COLONIAL ATTIT PWR...POLICY 20 UN EUROPE/W. PAGE 16 A0316 — INT/ORG TREND FUT NAT/G

B63
LICHTHEIM G.,THE NEW EUROPE: TODAY AND TOMORROW. EUR+WWI FINAN 20 EEC EUROPE/W. PAGE 88 A1809 — DIPLOM ECO/DEV INT/ORG INT/TRADE

B63
MYRDAL G.,CHALLENGE TO AFFLUENCE. USA+45 WOR+45 FINAN INT/ORG NAT/G PLAN ECO/TAC INT/TRADE BAL/PAY ORD/FREE 20 EUROPE/W. PAGE 107 A2189 — ECO/DEV WEALTH DIPLOM PRODUC

B64
IRISH M.D.,WORLD PRESSURES ON AMERICAN FOREIGN POLICY. ASIA COM L/A+17C SOUTH/AFR UK WOR+45 ECO/DEV ECO/UNDEV COLONIAL SANCTION COERCE REV TOTALISM...ANTHOL 20 COLD/WAR EUROPE/W INTERVENT. PAGE 72 A1467 — DIPLOM POLICY

B66
MARTIN L.W.,DIPLOMACY IN MODERN EUROPEAN HISTORY. EUR+WWI MOD/EUR INT/ORG NAT/G EX/STRUC ROUTINE WAR PEACE TOTALISM PWR 15/20 COLD/WAR EUROPE/W. PAGE 95 A1953 — DIPLOM POLICY

EUROPEAN ATOMIC ENERGY COMMUNITY....SEE EURATOM

EUROPEAN COAL AND STEEL COMMUNITY....SEE EURCOALSTL

EUROPEAN CONVENTION ON HUMAN RIGHTS....SEE ECHR

EUROPEAN COURT OF JUSTICE....SEE EURCT/JUST

EUROPEAN ECONOMIC COMMUNITY....SEE EEC

EUROPEAN FREE TRADE ASSOCIATION....SEE EFTA

EUROPEAN INVESTMENT BANK....SEE EIB

EVANS C. A0876

EVANS M.S. A0877

EVERS/MED....MEDGAR EVERS

EWING B.G. A0878

EWING L.L. A0879

EX POST FACTO LAWS....SEE EXPOSTFACT

EX/IM/BANK....EXPORT-IMPORT BANK

EX/STRUC....EXECUTIVE ESTABLISHMENTS

N
JOURNAL OF POLITICS. USA+45 USA-45 CONSTN POL/PAR EX/STRUC LEGIS PROB/SOLV DIPLOM CT/SYS CHOOSE RACE/REL 20. PAGE 1 A0017 — BIBLIOG/A NAT/G LAW LOC/G

N
INSTITUTE OF HISPANIC STUDIES,HISPANIC AMERICAN REPORT. EUR+WWI SPAIN LAW CONSTN ECO/UNDEV POL/PAR EX/STRUC LEGIS LEAD...HUM SOC 20. PAGE 70 A1445 — BIBLIOG/A L/A+17C NAT/G DIPLOM

N
UNESCO,INTERNATIONAL BIBLIOGRAPHY OF POLITICAL SCIENCE (VOLUMES 1-8). WOR+45 LAW NAT/G EX/STRUC LEGIS PROB/SOLV DIPLOM ADMIN GOV/REL 20 UNESCO. PAGE 147 A3010 — BIBLIOG CONCPT IDEA/COMP

B06
FOSTER J.W.,THE PRACTICE OF DIPLOMACY AS ILLUSTRATED IN THE FOREIGN RELATIONS OF THE UNITED STATES. MOD/EUR USA-45 NAT/G EX/STRUC ADMIN ...POLICY INT/LAW BIBLIOG 19/20. PAGE 47 A0970 — DIPLOM ROUTINE PHIL/SCI

B18
US LIBRARY OF CONGRESS,LIST OF REFERENCES ON A LEAGUE OF NATIONS. DIPLOM WAR PEACE 20 LEAGUE/NAT. PAGE 154 A3145 — BIBLIOG INT/ORG ADMIN EX/STRUC

N19
PROVISIONS SECTION OAU,ORGANIZATION OF AFRICAN UNITY: BASIC DOCUMENTS AND RESOLUTIONS (PAMPHLET). AFR CULTURE ECO/UNDEV DIPLOM ECO/TAC EDU/PROP COLONIAL ARMS/CONT NUC/PWR RACE/REL DISCRIM NAT/LISM 20 UN OAU. PAGE 118 A2415 — CONSTN EX/STRUC SOVEREIGN INT/ORG

B21
STUART G.H.,FRENCH FOREIGN POLICY. CONSTN INT/ORG NAT/G POL/PAR EX/STRUC FORCES PLAN ECO/TAC DOMIN EDU/PROP ADJUD COERCE ATTIT DRIVE RIGID/FLEX ALL/VALS...POLICY OBS RECORD BIOG TIME/SEQ TREND. PAGE 139 A2852 — MOD/EUR DIPLOM FRANCE

B26
INTERNATIONAL BIBLIOGRAPHY OF POLITICAL SCIENCE. WOR+45 NAT/G POL/PAR EX/STRUC LEGIS CT/SYS LEAD CHOOSE GOV/REL ATTIT...PHIL/SCI 20. PAGE 3 A0049 — BIBLIOG DIPLOM CONCPT ADMIN

B26
LEWIN E.,RECENT PUBLICATIONS IN THE LIBRARY OF THE ROYAL COLONIAL INSTITUTE (PAMPHLET). CANADA UK EX/STRUC PARL/PROC NAT/LISM SOVEREIGN 20 CMN/WLTH PARLIAMENT. PAGE 88 A1799 — BIBLIOG COLONIAL CONSTN DIPLOM

B27
GOOCH G.P.,ENGLISH DEMOCRATIC IDEAS IN THE SEVENTEENTH CENTURY (2ND ED.). UK LAW SECT FORCES DIPLOM LEAD PARL/PROC REV ATTIT AUTHORIT...ANARCH CONCPT 17 PARLIAMENT CMN/WLTH REFORMERS. PAGE 54 A1100 — IDEA/COMP MAJORIT EX/STRUC CONSERVE

B30
BYNKERSHOEK C.,QUAESTIONUM JURIS PUBLICI LIBRI DUO. CHRIST-17C MOD/EUR CONSTN ELITES SOCIETY NAT/G PROVS EX/STRUC FORCES TOP/EX BAL/PWR DIPLOM ATTIT MORAL...TRADIT CONCPT. PAGE 23 A0460 — INT/ORG LAW NAT/LISM INT/LAW

B31
GREAVES H.R.G.,THE LEAGUE COMMITTEES AND WORLD ORDER. WOR-45 DELIB/GP EX/STRUC EDU/PROP ALL/VALS LEAGUE/NAT VAL/FREE 20. PAGE 55 A1136 — INT/ORG DIPLOM ROUTINE

B31
STOWELL E.C.,INTERNATIONAL LAW. FUT UNIV WOR-45 SOCIETY CONSULT EX/STRUC FORCES ACT/RES PLAN DIPLOM EDU/PROP LEGIT DISPL PWR SKILL...POLICY CONCPT OBS TREND TOT/POP 20. PAGE 139 A2839 — INT/ORG ROUTINE INT/LAW

B32
CARDINALL AW,A BIBLIOGRAPHY OF THE GOLD COAST. AFR UK NAT/G EX/STRUC ATTIT...POLICY 19/20. PAGE 24 — BIBLIOG ADMIN

A0479 COLONIAL DIPLOM

B39
ZIMMERN A.,THE LEAGUE OF NATIONS AND THE RULE OF LAW. WOR-45 STRUCT NAT/G DELIB/GP EX/STRUC BAL/PWR DOMIN LEGIT COERCE ORD/FREE PWR...POLICY RECORD LEAGUE/NAT TOT/POP VAL/FREE 20 LEAGUE/NAT. PAGE 170 A3453 INT/ORG LAW DIPLOM

B39
ZIMMERN A.,MODERN POLITICAL DOCTRINE. WOR-45 CULTURE SOCIETY ECO/UNDEV DELIB/GP EX/STRUC CREATE DOMIN COERCE NAT/LISM ATTIT RIGID/FLEX ORD/FREE PWR WEALTH...POLICY CONCPT OBS TIME/SEQ TREND TOT/POP LEAGUE/NAT 20. PAGE 170 A3454 NAT/G ECO/TAC BAL/PWR INT/TRADE

L39
NEARING S.,"A WARLESS WORLD." FUT WOR-45 SOCIETY INT/ORG NAT/G EX/STRUC PLAN DOMIN WAR ATTIT DRIVE PWR...POLICY PSY CONCPT OBS TREND HYPO/EXP MARX/KARL 20 MARX/KARL LENIN/VI. PAGE 108 A2210 COERCE PEACE

B41
BURTON M.E.,THE ASSEMBLY OF THE LEAGUE OF NATIONS. WOR-45 CONSTN SOCIETY STRUCT INT/ORG NAT/G CREATE ATTIT RIGID/FLEX PWR...POLICY TIME/SEQ LEAGUE/NAT 20. PAGE 22 A0448 DELIB/GP EX/STRUC DIPLOM

B44
ADLER M.J.,HOW TO THINK ABOUT WAR AND PEACE. WOR-45 LAW SOCIETY EX/STRUC DIPLOM KNOWL ORD/FREE...POLICY TREND GEN/LAWS 20. PAGE 4 A0092 INT/ORG CREATE ARMS/CONT PEACE

L44
CORWIN E.S.,"THE CONSTITUTION AND WORLD ORGANIZATION." FUT USA+45 USA-45 NAT/G EX/STRUC LEGIS PEACE KNOWL...CON/ANAL UN 20. PAGE 31 A0627 INT/ORG CONSTN SOVEREIGN

L44
WRIGHT Q.,"THE US AND INTERNATIONAL AGREEMENTS." FUT USA-45 CONSTN INTELL INT/ORG LOC/G NAT/G CHIEF CONSULT EX/STRUC DIPLOM LEGIT DRIVE PERCEPT PWR ...CONCPT CONGRESS 20. PAGE 167 A3407 DELIB/GP TOP/EX PEACE

S44
WRIGHT Q.,"CONSTITUTIONAL PROCEDURES OF THE US FOR CARRYING OUT OBLIGATIONS FOR MILITARY SANCTIONS." EUR+WWI FUT USA-45 WOR-45 CONSTN INTELL NAT/G CONSULT EX/STRUC LEGIS ROUTINE DRIVE...POLICY JURID CONCPT OBS TREND TOT/POP 20. PAGE 167 A3406 TOP/EX FORCES INT/LAW WAR

B45
CARR E.H.,NATIONALISM AND AFTER. FUT WOR-45 NAT/G VOL/ASSN EX/STRUC PLAN ROUTINE TOTALISM ATTIT HEALTH ORD/FREE PWR...CONCPT 20. PAGE 25 A0499 INT/ORG TREND NAT/LISM REGION

B45
CONOVER H.F.,THE GOVERNMENTS OF THE MAJOR FOREIGN POWERS: A BIBLIOGRAPHY. FRANCE GERMANY ITALY UK USSR CONSTN LOC/G POL/PAR EX/STRUC FORCES ADMIN CT/SYS CIVMIL/REL TOTALISM...POLICY 19/20. PAGE 29 A0598 BIBLIOG NAT/G DIPLOM

B45
CONOVER H.F.,ITALY: ECONOMICS, POLITICS AND MILITARY AFFAIRS, 1940-1945. ITALY ELITES NAT/G POL/PAR EX/STRUC TOP/EX DIPLOM DOMIN CONTROL COERCE WAR CIVMIL/REL EFFICIENCY 20. PAGE 29 A0599 BIBLIOG TOTALISM FORCES

B46
LOWENSTEIN R.,POLITICAL RECONSTRUCTION. WOR+45 EX/STRUC EDU/PROP NAT/LISM ATTIT KNOWL ORD/FREE PWR ...SOCIALIST CONCPT GEN/LAWS TOT/POP 20. PAGE 91 A1869 FUT INT/ORG DIPLOM

C46
GOODRICH L.M.,"CHARTER OF THE UNITED NATIONS: COMMENTARY AND DOCUMENTS." EX/STRUC ADMIN...INT/LAW CON/ANAL BIBLIOG 20 UN. PAGE 54 A1106 CONSTN INT/ORG DIPLOM

B47
MANDER L.,FOUNDATIONS OF MODERN WORLD SOCIETY. WOR+45 DELIB/GP ECO/TAC INT/TRADE EDU/PROP ALL/VALS ...TIME/SEQ GEN/LAWS TOT/POP VAL/FREE ILO 20. PAGE 94 A1917 INT/ORG EX/STRUC DIPLOM

L47
HISS D.,"UNITED STATES PARTICIPATION IN THE UNITED NATIONS." USA+45 EX/STRUC PLAN DIPLOM ROUTINE CHOOSE...PLURIST UN 20. PAGE 65 A1342 INT/ORG PWR

N49
UN DEPARTMENT PUBLIC INF,SELECTED BIBLIOGRAPHY OF THE SPECIALIZED AGENCIES RELATED TO THE UNITED NATIONS (PAMPHLET). USA+45 ROLE 20 UN. PAGE 146 A2996 BIBLIOG INT/ORG EX/STRUC ADMIN

B50
LINCOLN G.,ECONOMICS OF NATIONAL SECURITY. USA+45 ELITES COM/IND DIST/IND INDUS NAT/G VOL/ASSN DELIB/GP EX/STRUC FOR/AID EDU/PROP COERCE NUC/PWR WAR ATTIT KNOWL ORD/FREE PWR COLD/WAR TOT/POP VAL/FREE 20. PAGE 89 A1818 FORCES ECO/TAC

B51
CHRISTENSEN A.N.,THE EVOLUTION OF LATIN AMERICAN GOVERNMENT: A BOOK OF READINGS. ECO/UNDEV INDUS LOC/G POL/PAR EX/STRUC LEGIS FOR/AID CT/SYS ...SOC/WK 20 SOUTH/AMER. PAGE 26 A0535 NAT/G CONSTN DIPLOM L/A+17C

B51
CORMACK M.,SELECTED PAMPHLETS ON THE UNITED NATIONS AND INTERNATIONAL RELATIONS (PAMPHLET). USA+45 R+D EX/STRUC PROB/SOLV ROUTINE...POLICY CON/ANAL 20 UN NATO. PAGE 31 A0624 BIBLIOG/A NAT/G INT/ORG DIPLOM

B51
LEONARD L.L.,INTERNATIONAL ORGANIZATION. WOR+45 WOR-45 EX/STRUC FORCES LEGIS ECO/TAC INT/TRADE COLONIAL ARMS/CONT...SOC/WK GOV/COMP BIBLIOG. PAGE 87 A1778 NAT/G DIPLOM INT/ORG DELIB/GP

B52
FLECHTHEIM O.K.,FUNDAMENTALS OF POLITICAL SCIENCE. WOR+45 WOR-45 LAW POL/PAR EX/STRUC LEGIS ADJUD ATTIT PWR...INT/LAW. PAGE 46 A0945 NAT/G DIPLOM IDEA/COMP CONSTN

L52
WRIGHT Q.,"CONGRESS AND THE TREATY-MAKING POWER." USA+45 WOR+45 CONSTN INTELL NAT/G CHIEF CONSULT EX/STRUC LEGIS TOP/EX CREATE GOV/REL DISPL DRIVE RIGID/FLEX...TREND TOT/POP CONGRESS CONGRESS 20 TREATY. PAGE 167 A3408 ROUTINE DIPLOM INT/LAW DELIB/GP

B53
BARBER H.W.,FOREIGN POLICIES OF THE UNITED STATES. USA+45 USA-45 WOR+45 INT/ORG NAT/G EX/STRUC ECO/TAC DOMIN EDU/PROP LEGIT COERCE KNOWL PWR COLD/WAR COLD/WAR 20. PAGE 11 A0219 CONCPT DIPLOM

B53
MACK R.T.,RAISING THE WORLDS STANDARD OF LIVING. IRAN INT/ORG VOL/ASSN EX/STRUC ECO/TAC WEALTH...MGT METH/CNCPT STAT CONT/OBS INT TOT/POP VAL/FREE 20 UN. PAGE 92 A1893 WOR+45 FOR/AID INT/TRADE

B53
ZIMMERN A.,THE AMERICAN ROAD TO PEACE. USA+45 LAW INT/ORG NAT/G EX/STRUC TOP/EX EDU/PROP LEGIT COERCE PEACE ATTIT ORD/FREE PWR...CONCPT TIME/SEQ LEAGUE/NAT TOT/POP VAL/FREE 20 UN. PAGE 170 A3455 USA-45 DIPLOM

C54
BOWIE R.R.,"STUDIES IN FEDERALISM." AGRI FINAN LABOR EX/STRUC FORCES LEGIS DIPLOM INT/TRADE ADJUD ...BIBLIOG 20 EEC. PAGE 17 A0357 FEDERAL EUR+WWI INT/ORG CONSTN

B55
HOGAN W.N.,INTERNATIONAL CONFLICT AND COLLECTIVE SECURITY: THE PRINCIPLE OF CONCERN IN INTERNATIONAL ORGANIZATION. CONSTN EX/STRUC BAL/PWR DIPLOM ADJUD CONTROL CENTRAL CONSEN PEACE...INT/LAW CONCPT METH/COMP 20 UN LEAGUE/NAT. PAGE 66 A1361 INT/ORG WAR ORD/FREE FORCES

B55
STEPHENS O.,FACTS TO A CANDID WORLD. USA+45 WOR+45 COM/IND EX/STRUC PRESS ROUTINE EFFICIENCY ATTIT ...PSY 20. PAGE 138 A2817 EDU/PROP PHIL/SCI NAT/G DIPLOM

B56
DEGRAS J.,THE COMMUNIST INTERNATIONAL, 1919-1943: DOCUMENTS (3 VOLS.). EX/STRUC...ANTHOL BIBLIOG 20. PAGE 36 A0723 COM DIPLOM POLICY POL/PAR

B56
HAAS E.B.,DYNAMICS OF INTERNATIONAL RELATIONS. WOR-45 ELITES INT/ORG VOL/ASSN EX/STRUC FORCES ECO/TAC DOMIN LEGIT COERCE ATTIT PERSON PWR ...CONCPT TIME/SEQ CHARTS COLD/WAR 20. PAGE 58 A1202 WOR+45 NAT/G DIPLOM

B56
KOENIG L.W.,THE TRUMAN ADMINISTRATION: ITS PRINCIPLES AND PRACTICE. USA+45 POL/PAR CHIEF LEGIS DIPLOM DEATH NUC/PWR WAR CIVMIL/REL PEACE ...DECISION 20 TRUMAN/HS PRESIDENT TREATY. PAGE 81 A1658 ADMIN POLICY EX/STRUC GOV/REL

S56
CUTLER R.,"THE DEVELOPMENT OF THE NATIONAL SECURITY COUNCIL." USA+45 INTELL CONSULT EX/STRUC DIPLOM LEAD 20 TRUMAN/HS EISNHWR/DD NSC. PAGE 33 A0670 ORD/FREE DELIB/GP PROB/SOLV NAT/G

B57
ASHER R.E.,THE UNITED NATIONS AND THE PROMOTION OF THE GENERAL WELFARE. WOR+45 WOR-45 ECO/UNDEV EX/STRUC ACT/RES PLAN EDU/PROP ROUTINE HEALTH...HUM CONCPT CHARTS UNESCO UN ILO 20. PAGE 9 A0185 INT/ORG CONSULT

B57
BEAL J.R.,JOHN FOSTER DULLES, A BIOGRAPHY. USA+45 USSR WOR+45 CONSTN INT/ORG NAT/G EX/STRUC LEGIT ADMIN NUC/PWR DISPL PERSON ORD/FREE PWR SKILL ...POLICY PSY OBS RECORD COLD/WAR UN 20 DULLES/JF. PAGE 12 A0237 BIOG DIPLOM

L57
HAAS E.B.,"REGIONAL INTEGRATION AND NATIONAL POLICY." WOR+45 VOL/ASSN DELIB/GP EX/STRUC ECO/TAC DOMIN EDU/PROP LEGIT COERCE ATTIT PERCEPT KNOWL ...TIME/SEQ COLD/WAR 20 UN. PAGE 59 A1203 INT/ORG ORD/FREE REGION

B58
CAMPBELL J.C.,DEFENSE OF THE MIDDLE EAST: PROBLEMS OF AMERICAN POLICY. ISLAM USA+45 INT/ORG NAT/G EX/STRUC FORCES ECO/TAC DOMIN EDU/PROP LEGIT REGION COERCE...METH/CNCPT COLD/WAR TOT/POP 20. PAGE 23 A0474 TOP/EX ORD/FREE DIPLOM

S58
ELKIN A.B.,"OEEC-ITS STRUCTURE AND POWERS." EUR+WWI ECO/DEV

CONSTN INDUS INT/ORG NAT/G VOL/ASSN DELIB/GP ACT/RES PLAN ORD/FREE WEALTH...CHARTS ORG/CHARTS OEEC 20. PAGE 41 A0839 EX/STRUC

C58

GOLAY J.F.,"THE FOUNDING OF THE FEDERAL REPUBLIC OF GERMANY." GERMANY/W CONSTN EX/STRUC DIPLOM ADMIN CHOOSE...DECISION BIBLIOG 20. PAGE 53 A1088 FEDERAL NAT/G PARL/PROC POL/PAR

B59

BOWLES C.,THE COMING POLITICAL BREAKTHROUGH. USA+45 ECO/DEV EX/STRUC ATTIT...CONCPT OBS 20. PAGE 18 A0360 DIPLOM CHOOSE PREDICT POL/PAR

B59

DAWSON R.H.,THE DECISION TO AID RUSSIA* FOREIGN POLICY AND DOMESTIC POLITICS. GERMANY USSR CHIEF EX/STRUC LEGIS TOP/EX PROB/SOLV WAR ATTIT...POLICY CONGRESS. PAGE 34 A0695 DECISION DELIB/GP DIPLOM FOR/AID

B60

AMERICAN ASSEMBLY COLUMBIA U,THE SECRETARY OF STATE. USA+45 ELITES NAT/G PLAN ADMIN GOV/REL CENTRAL ATTIT...POLICY MGT 20 SEC/STATE CONGRESS PRESIDENT. PAGE 7 A0136 DELIB/GP EX/STRUC GP/REL DIPLOM

B60

BROOKINGS INSTITUTION,UNITED STATES FOREIGN POLICY: STUDY NO 9: THE FORMULATION AND ADMINISTRATION OF UNITED STATES FOREIGN POLICY. USA+45 WOR+45 EX/STRUC LEGIS BAL/PWR FOR/AID EDU/PROP CIVMIL/REL GOV/REL...INT COLD/WAR. PAGE 19 A0394 DIPLOM INT/ORG CREATE

B60

BYRD E.M. JR.,TREATIES AND EXECUTIVE AGREEMENTS IN THE UNITED STATES: THEIR SEPARATE ROLES AND LIMITATIONS. USA+45 USA-45 EX/STRUC TARIFFS CT/SYS GOV/REL FEDERAL...IDEA/COMP BIBLIOG SUPREME/CT SENATE CONGRESS. PAGE 23 A0461 CHIEF INT/LAW DIPLOM

B60

MORISON E.E.,TURMOIL AND TRADITION: A STUDY OF THE LIFE AND TIMES OF HENRY L. STIMSON. USA+45 USA-45 POL/PAR CHIEF DELIB/GP FORCES BAL/PWR DIPLOM ARMS/CONT WAR PEACE 19/20 STIMSON/HL ROOSEVLT/F TAFT/WH HOOVER/H REPUBLICAN. PAGE 104 A2142 BIOG NAT/G EX/STRUC

B60

PRICE D.,THE SECRETARY OF STATE. USA+45 CONSTN ELITES INTELL CHIEF EX/STRUC TOP/EX LEGIT ATTIT PWR SKILL...DECISION 20 CONGRESS. PAGE 117 A2410 CONSULT DIPLOM INT/LAW

B60

SETON-WATSON H.,NEITHER WAR NOR PEACE. ASIA USSR WOR+45 ELITES INT/ORG NAT/G EX/STRUC FORCES BAL/PWR ECO/TAC EDU/PROP COERCE NAT/LISM ORD/FREE WEALTH TOT/POP 20. PAGE 131 A2688 ATTIT PWR DIPLOM TOTALISM

B60

WHEARE K.C.,THE CONSTITUTIONAL STRUCTURE OF THE COMMONWEALTH. UK EX/STRUC DIPLOM DOMIN ADMIN COLONIAL CONTROL LEAD INGP/REL SUPEGO 20 CMN/WLTH. PAGE 163 A3325 CONSTN INT/ORG VOL/ASSN SOVEREIGN

S60

GOODRICH L.,"GEOGRAPHICAL DISTRIBUTION OF THE STAFF OF THE UN SECRETARIAT." FUT WOR+45 CONSTN BAL/PWR DIPLOM EDU/PROP LEGIT ROUTINE RIGID/FLEX...CHARTS UN 20. PAGE 54 A1105 INT/ORG EX/STRUC

S60

HAYTON R.D.,"THE ANTARCTIC SETTLEMENT OF 1959." FUT USA+45 WOR+45 WOR-45 STRUCT R+D INT/ORG EX/STRUC CREATE TEC/DEV LEGIT PEACE ATTIT SOVEREIGN ...TIME/SEQ 20 TREATY IGY. PAGE 63 A1297 DELIB/GP JURID DIPLOM REGION

S60

LEAR J.,"PEACE: SCIENCE'S NEXT GREAT EXPLORATION." USA+45 INT/ORG TOP/EX TEC/DEV EDU/PROP ROUTINE PEACE KNOWL SKILL 20. PAGE 86 A1757 EX/STRUC ARMS/CONT NUC/PWR

S60

PADELFORD N.J.,"POLITICS AND CHANGE IN THE SECURITY COUNCIL." FUT WOR+45 CONSTN NAT/G EX/STRUC LEGIS ORD/FREE...CONCPT CHARTS UN 20. PAGE 113 A2309 INT/ORG DELIB/GP

B61

CARNELL F.,THE POLITICS OF THE NEW STATES: A SELECT ANNOTATED BIBLIOGRAPHY WITH SPECIAL REFERENCE TO THE COMMONWEALTH. CONSTN ELITES LABOR NAT/G POL/PAR EX/STRUC DIPLOM ADJUD ADMIN...GOV/COMP 20 COMMONWLTH. PAGE 24 A0496 BIBLIOG/A AFR ASIA COLONIAL

B61

FRIEDMANN W.G.,JOINT INTERNATIONAL BUSINESS VENTURES. ASIA ISLAM L/A+17C ECO/DEV DIST/IND FINAN PROC/MFG FACE/GP LG/CO NAT/G VOL/ASSN CONSULT EX/STRUC PLAN ADMIN ROUTINE WEALTH...OLD/LIB WORK 20. PAGE 49 A1004 ECO/UNDEV INT/TRADE

B61

HARRISON S.,INDIA AND THE UNITED STATES. FUT S/ASIA USA+45 WOR+45 INTELL ECO/DEV ECO/UNDEV AGRI INDUS INT/ORG NAT/G CONSULT EX/STRUC TOP/EX PLAN ECO/TAC NEUTRAL ALL/VALS...MGT TOT/POP 20. PAGE 62 A1272 DELIB/GP ACT/RES FOR/AID INDIA

B61

HAYTER W.,THE DIPLOMACY OF THE GREAT POWERS. FRANCE UK USSR WOR+45 EX/STRUC TOP/EX NUC/PWR PEACE...OBS 20. PAGE 63 A1296 DIPLOM POLICY NAT/G

B61

PEASLEE A.J.,INTERNATIONAL GOVERNMENT ORGANIZATIONS, CONSTITUTIONAL DOCUMENTS. WOR+45 WOR-45 CONSTN VOL/ASSN DELIB/GP EX/STRUC ROUTINE KNOWL TOT/POP 20. PAGE 114 A2344 INT/ORG STRUCT

B61

WECHSLER H.,PRINCIPLES, POLITICS AND FUNDAMENTAL LAW: SELECTED ESSAYS. USA+45 USA-45 LAW SOCIETY NAT/G PROVS DELIB/GP EX/STRUC ACT/RES LEGIT PERSON KNOWL PWR...JURID 20 NUREMBERG. PAGE 162 A3296 CT/SYS CONSTN INT/LAW

L61

SAND P.T.,"AN HISTORICAL SURVEY OF INTERNATIONAL AIR LAW SINCE 1944." USA+45 USA-45 WOR+45 WOR-45 SOCIETY ECO/DEV NAT/G CONSULT EX/STRUC ACT/RES PLAN LEGIT ROUTINE...JURID CONCPT METH/CNCPT TREND 20. PAGE 127 A2598 INT/ORG LAW INT/LAW SPACE

S61

ANGLIN D.,"UNITED STATES OPPOSITION TO CANADIAN MEMBERSHIP IN THE PAN AMERICAN UNION: A CANADIAN VIEW." L/A+17C UK USA+45 VOL/ASSN DELIB/GP EX/STRUC PLAN DIPLOM DOMIN REGION ATTIT RIGID/FLEX PWR ...RELATIV CONCPT STERTYP CMN/WLTH OAS 20. PAGE 8 A0162 INT/ORG CANADA

S61

CARLETON W.G.,"AMERICAN FOREIGN POLICY: MYTHS AND REALITIES." FUT USA+45 WOR+45 ECO/UNDEV INT/ORG EX/STRUC ARMS/CONT NUC/PWR WAR ATTIT...POLICY CONCPT CONT/OBS GEN/METH COLD/WAR TOT/POP 20. PAGE 24 A0484 PLAN MYTH DIPLOM

S61

HAAS E.B.,"INTERNATIONAL INTEGRATION: THE EUROPEAN AND THE UNIVERSAL PROCESS." EUR+WWI FUT WOR+45 NAT/G EX/STRUC ATTIT DRIVE ORD/FREE PWR...CONCPT GEN/LAWS OEEC 20 NATO COUNCL/EUR. PAGE 59 A1207 INT/ORG TREND REGION

S61

RALEIGH J.S.,"THE MIDDLE EAST IN 1960: A POLITICAL SURVEY." FUT ISLAM INTELL KIN BAL/PWR EDU/PROP NAT/LISM...TREND VAL/FREE 20. PAGE 119 A2435 INT/ORG EX/STRUC

B62

BRIMMER B.,A GUIDE TO THE USE OF UNITED NATIONS DOCUMENTS. WOR+45 ECO/UNDEV AGRI EX/STRUC FORCES PROB/SOLV ADMIN WAR PEACE WEALTH...POLICY UN. PAGE 19 A0378 BIBLIOG/A INT/ORG DIPLOM

B62

BROWN L.C.,LATIN AMERICA, A BIBLIOGRAPHY. EX/STRUC ADMIN LEAD ATTIT...POLICY 20. PAGE 20 A0405 BIBLIOG L/A+17C DIPLOM NAT/G

B62

EVANS M.S.,THE FRINGE ON TOP. USSR EX/STRUC FORCES DIPLOM ECO/TAC PEACE CONSERVE SOCISM...TREND 20 KENNEDY/JF. PAGE 43 A0877 NAT/G PWR CENTRAL POLICY

B62

LEOPOLD R.W.,THE GROWTH OF AMERICAN FOREIGN POLICY: A HISTORY. USA+45 USA-45 EX/STRUC LEGIS INT/TRADE WAR...CHARTS BIBLIOG/A T 18/20. PAGE 87 A1780 NAT/G DIPLOM POLICY

B62

MULLEY F.W.,THE POLITICS OF WESTERN DEFENSE. EUR+WWI USA-45 WOR+45 VOL/ASSN EX/STRUC FORCES COERCE DETER PEACE ATTIT ORD/FREE PWR...RECORD TIME/SEQ CHARTS COLD/WAR 20 NATO. PAGE 106 A2168 INT/ORG DELIB/GP NUC/PWR

B62

NICHOLAS H.G.,THE UNITED NATIONS AS A POLITICAL INSTITUTION. WOR+45 CONSTN EX/STRUC ACT/RES LEGIT PERCEPT KNOWL PWR...CONCPT TIME/SEQ CON/ANAL ORG/CHARTS UN 20. PAGE 109 A2228 INT/ORG ROUTINE

S62

ALGER C.F.,"THE EXTERNAL BUREAUCRACY IN UNITED STATES FOREIGN AFFAIRS." USA+45 WOR+45 SOCIETY COM/IND INT/ORG NAT/G CONSULT EX/STRUC ACT/RES ...MGT SOC CONCPT TREND 20. PAGE 6 A0118 ADMIN ATTIT DIPLOM

S62

CLEVELAND H.,"THE FUTURE ROLE OF THE UNITED STATES IN THE UNITED NATIONS." USA+45 ECO/UNDEV INT/ORG EX/STRUC DIPLOM FOR/AID ROUTINE SKILL SOVEREIGN WEALTH UN 20. PAGE 27 A0550 FUT ATTIT

S62

TOWSTER J.,"THE USSR AND THE USA: CHALLENGE AND RESPONSE." COM GERMANY USA+45 USSR WOR+45 ECO/UNDEV INT/ORG VOL/ASSN EX/STRUC FORCES TOP/EX CREATE PLAN TEC/DEV DIPLOM ECO/TAC EDU/PROP COLONIAL COERCE PWR ...GEN/METH COLD/WAR 20 KENNEDY/JF. PAGE 145 A2956 ACT/RES GEN/LAWS

B63

BOWETT D.W.,THE LAW OF INTERNATIONAL INSTITUTIONS. WOR+45 WOR-45 CONSTN DELIB/GP EX/STRUC JUDGE EDU/PROP LEGIT CT/SYS EXEC ROUTINE RIGID/FLEX ORD/FREE PWR...JURID CONCPT ORG/CHARTS GEN/METH LEAGUE/NAT OAS OEEC 20 UN. PAGE 17 A0354 INT/ORG ADJUD DIPLOM

B63

CROZIER B.,THE MORNING AFTER; A STUDY OF INDEPENDENCE. WOR+45 EX/STRUC PLAN BAL/PWR COLONIAL GP/REL 20 COLD/WAR. PAGE 33 A0666 SOVEREIGN NAT/LISM NAT/G DIPLOM

B63

FALK R.A.,LAW, MORALITY, AND WAR IN THE CONTEMPORARY WORLD. WOR+45 LAW INT/ORG EX/STRUC FORCES EDU/PROP LEGIT DETER NUC/PWR MORAL ORD/FREE ADJUD ARMS/CONT PEACE

...JURID TOT/POP 20. PAGE 43 A0888 INT/LAW

B63
LERCHE C.O. JR.,CONCEPTS OF INTERNATIONAL POLITICS. WOR+45 WOR-45 LAW DELIB/GP EX/STRUC TEC/DEV ECO/TAC INT/TRADE LEGIT ROUTINE COERCE ATTIT ORD/FREE PWR RESPECT...STERTYP GEN/LAWS VAL/FREE. PAGE 87 A1782
INT/ORG WAR

B63
MILLER W.J.,THE MEANING OF COMMUNISM. USSR SOCIETY ECO/DEV EX/STRUC WORKER TEC/DEV ADMIN TOTALISM ...POLICY CONCPT CHARTS BIBLIOG T 20 COLD/WAR LENIN/VI STALIN/J. PAGE 101 A2080
MARXISM TRADIT DIPLOM NAT/G

B63
STEVENSON A.E.,LOOKING OUTWARD: YEARS OF CRISIS AT THE UNITED NATIONS. COM CUBA USA+45 WOR+45 SOCIETY NAT/G EX/STRUC ACT/RES LEGIT COLONIAL ATTIT PERSON SUPEGO ALL/VALS...POLICY HUM UN COLD/WAR CONGO 20. PAGE 138 A2823
INT/ORG CONCPT ARMS/CONT

B63
STROMBERG R.N.,COLLECTIVE SECURITY AND AMERICAN FOREIGN POLICY FROM THE LEAGUE OF NATIONS TO NATO. USA+45 USA-45 WOR-45 INT/ORG VOL/ASSN EX/STRUC FORCES LEGIT ROUTINE DRIVE...CONCPT TREND UN LEAGUE/NAT 20 NATO. PAGE 139 A2851
ORD/FREE TIME/SEQ DIPLOM

B63
WESTERFIELD H.,THE INSTRUMENTS OF AMERICA'S FOREIGN POLICY. WOR+45 ECO/DEV NAT/G CONSULT EX/STRUC LEGIS BAL/PWR FOR/AID INT/TRADE DOMIN EDU/PROP LEGIT ATTIT KNOWL ORD/FREE PWR WEALTH...OBS COLD/WAR TOT/POP VAL/FREE. PAGE 163 A3322
USA+45 INT/ORG DIPLOM

S63
BANFIELD J.,"FEDERATION IN EAST-AFRICA." AFR UGANDA ELITES INT/ORG NAT/G VOL/ASSN LEGIS ECO/TAC FEDERAL ATTIT SOVEREIGN TOT/POP 20 TANGANYIKA. PAGE 11 A0216
EX/STRUC PWR REGION

S63
BECHHOEFER B.G.,"UNITED NATIONS PROCEDURES IN CASE OF VIOLATIONS OF DISARMAMENT AGREEMENTS." COM USA+45 USSR LAW CONSTN NAT/G EX/STRUC FORCES LEGIS BAL/PWR EDU/PROP CT/SYS ARMS/CONT ORD/FREE PWR ...POLICY STERTYP UN VAL/FREE 20. PAGE 12 A0245
INT/ORG DELIB/GP

S63
MULLEY F.W.,"NUCLEAR WEAPONS: CHALLENGE TO NATIONAL SOVEREIGNTY." EUR+WWI FRANCE UK USA+45 VOL/ASSN EX/STRUC FORCES TOP/EX ACT/RES REGION DRIVE PWR 20 NATO DEGAULLE/C. PAGE 106 A2169
INT/ORG ATTIT DIPLOM NUC/PWR

S63
STANLEY T.W.,"DECENTRALIZING NUCLEAR CONTROL IN NATO." EUR+WWI USA+45 ELITES FORCES ACT/RES ATTIT ORD/FREE PWR...NEW/IDEA HYPO/EXP TOT/POP 20 NATO. PAGE 137 A2805
INT/ORG EX/STRUC NUC/PWR

B64
ADAMS V.,THE PEACE CORPS IN ACTION. USA+45 VOL/ASSN EX/STRUC GOV/REL PERCEPT ORD/FREE...OBS 20 KENNEDY/JF PEACE/CORP. PAGE 4 A0087
DIPLOM FOR/AID PERSON DRIVE

B64
AMERICAN ASSEMBLY,THE UNITED STATES AND THE MIDDLE EAST. ISRAEL USA+45 STRUCT ECO/DEV ECO/UNDEV INT/ORG NAT/G SCHOOL SECT VOL/ASSN EX/STRUC TEC/DEV NAT/LISM...SOC 20. PAGE 7 A0135
ISLAM DRIVE REGION

B64
BINDER L.,THE IDEOLOGICAL REVOLUTION IN THE MIDDLE EAST. ISLAM STRUCT INT/ORG KIN SECT EX/STRUC TOP/EX PLAN ATTIT DRIVE RIGID/FLEX PWR...MYTH TOT/POP 20. PAGE 14 A0289
POL/PAR NAT/G NAT/LISM

B64
CLAUDE I.,SWORDS INTO PLOWSHARES. FUT WOR+45 WOR-45 DELIB/GP EX/STRUC LEGIT ATTIT ORD/FREE...CONCPT TIME/SEQ TREND UN TOT/POP 20. PAGE 27 A0547
INT/ORG STRUCT

B64
COTTRELL A.J.,THE POLITICS OF THE ATLANTIC ALLIANCE. EUR+WWI USA+45 INT/ORG NAT/G DELIB/GP EX/STRUC BAL/PWR DIPLOM REGION DETER ATTIT ORD/FREE ...CONCPT RECORD GEN/LAWS GEN/METH NATO 20. PAGE 31 A0632
VOL/ASSN FORCES

B64
DALLIN A.,THE SOVIET UNION, ARMS CONTROL AND DISARMAMENT. COM INT/ORG VOL/ASSN EX/STRUC DIPLOM NUC/PWR ATTIT PWR TOT/POP COLD/WAR 20. PAGE 33 A0678
ORD/FREE ARMS/CONT USSR

B64
DE SMITH S.A.,THE NEW COMMONWEALTH AND ITS CONSTITUTIONS. AFR CYPRUS PAKISTAN S/ASIA INT/ORG NAT/G LEGIS LEGIT RIGID/FLEX PWR...CONCPT TIME/SEQ CMN/WLTH 20. PAGE 35 A0713
EX/STRUC CONSTN SOVEREIGN

B64
FISHER R.,INTERNATIONAL CONFLICT AND BEHAVIORAL SCIENCE: THE CRAIGVILLE PAPERS. COM FUT USA+45 WOR+45 NAT/G DELIB/GP EX/STRUC FORCES ECO/TAC DOMIN EDU/PROP LEGIT COERCE ATTIT PERCEPT ORD/FREE PWR RESPECT...PSY SOC VAL/FREE. PAGE 46 A0940
INT/ORG PLAN DIPLOM

B64
MARKHAM J.W.,THE COMMON MARKET: FRIEND OR COMPETITOR. EUR+WWI FUT USA+45 INT/ORG LG/CO NAT/G VOL/ASSN DELIB/GP EX/STRUC PLAN TARIFFS ORD/FREE PWR WEALTH...POLICY STAT TREND EEC VAL/FREE 20. PAGE 95 A1943
ECO/DEV ECO/TAC

B64
MASON E.S.,FOREIGN AID AND FOREIGN POLICY. USA+45 AGRI INDUS NAT/G EX/STRUC ACT/RES RIGID/FLEX ALL/VALS...POLICY GEN/LAWS MARSHL/PLN CONGRESS 20. PAGE 95 A1956
ECO/UNDEV ECO/TAC FOR/AID DIPLOM

B64
PLISCHKE E.,SYSTEMS OF INTEGRATING THE INTERNATIONAL COMMUNITY. WOR+45 NAT/G VOL/ASSN ECO/TAC LEGIT PWR WEALTH...TIME/SEQ ANTHOL UN TOT/POP 20. PAGE 116 A2391
INT/ORG EX/STRUC REGION

B64
SARROS P.P.,CONGRESS AND THE NEW DIPLOMACY: THE FORMULATION OF MUTUAL SECURITY POLICY: 1953-60 (THESIS). USA+45 CHIEF EX/STRUC REGION ROUTINE CHOOSE GOV/REL PEACE ROLE...POLICY 20 PRESIDENT CONGRESS. PAGE 127 A2606
DIPLOM POL/PAR NAT/G

B64
SCHECHTER A.H.,INTERPRETATION OF AMBIGUOUS DOCUMENTS BY INTERNATIONAL ADMINISTRATIVE TRIBUNALS. WOR+45 EX/STRUC INT/TRADE CT/SYS SOVEREIGN 20 UN ILO EURCT/JUST. PAGE 128 A2620
INT/LAW DIPLOM INT/ORG ADJUD

B64
SEGUNDO-SANCHEZ M.,OBRAS (2 VOLS.). VENEZUELA EX/STRUC DIPLOM ADMIN 19/20. PAGE 131 A2682
BIBLIOG LEAD NAT/G L/A+17C

B64
STOESSINGER J.G.,FINANCING THE UNITED NATIONS SYSTEM. FUT WOR+45 CONSTN NAT/G VOL/ASSN DELIB/GP EX/STRUC ECO/TAC LEGIT CT/SYS PWR WEALTH...STAT TIME/SEQ TREND CHARTS VAL/FREE. PAGE 138 A2830
FINAN INT/ORG

B64
SULLIVAN G.,THE STORY OF THE PEACE CORPS. USA+45 WOR+45 INTELL FACE/GP NAT/G SCHOOL VOL/ASSN CONSULT EX/STRUC PLAN EDU/PROP ADMIN ATTIT DRIVE ALL/VALS ...POLICY HEAL SOC CONCPT INT QU BIOG TREND SOC/EXP WORK. PAGE 140 A2861
INT/ORG ECO/UNDEV FOR/AID PEACE

B64
US SENATE COMM GOVT OPERATIONS,THE SECRETARY OF STATE AND THE AMBASSADOR. USA+45 CHIEF CONSULT EX/STRUC FORCES PLAN ADMIN EXEC INGP/REL ROLE ...ANTHOL 20 PRESIDENT DEPT/STATE. PAGE 156 A3175
DIPLOM DELIB/GP NAT/G

B64
VECCHIO G.D.,L'ETAT ET LE DROIT. ITALY CONSTN EX/STRUC LEGIS DIPLOM CT/SYS...JURID 20 UN. PAGE 158 A3225
NAT/G SOVEREIGN CONCPT INT/LAW

B64
WARREN S.,THE PRESIDENT AS WORLD LEADER. USA+45 WOR+45 ELITES COM/IND INT/ORG NAT/G VOL/ASSN CHIEF EX/STRUC LEGIT COERCE ATTIT PERSON RIGID/FLEX...INT TIME/SEQ COLD/WAR 20 ROOSEVLT/F TRUMAN/HS EISNHWR/DD KENNEDY/JF. PAGE 161 A3286
TOP/EX PWR DIPLOM

L64
CAMPBELL J.C.,"THE MIDDLE EAST IN THE MUTED COLD WAR." COM EUR+WWI UAR USA+45 USSR STRUCT ECO/UNDEV NAT/G VOL/ASSN EX/STRUC TOP/EX DIPLOM ECO/TAC EDU/PROP...TIME/SEQ COLD/WAR 20. PAGE 23 A0475
ISLAM FOR/AID NAT/LISM

L64
MILLIS W.,"THE DEMILITARIZED WORLD." COM USA+45 USSR WOR+45 CONSTN NAT/G EX/STRUC PLAN LEGIT ATTIT DRIVE...CONCPT TIME/SEQ STERTYP TOT/POP COLD/WAR 20. PAGE 102 A2085
FUT INT/ORG BAL/PWR PEACE

L64
WORLD PEACE FOUNDATION,"INTERNATIONAL ORGANIZATIONS: SUMMARY OF ACTIVITIES." INDIA PAKISTAN TURKEY WOR+45 CONSTN CONSULT EX/STRUC ECO/TAC EDU/PROP LEGIT ORD/FREE...JURID SOC UN 20 CYPRESS. PAGE 167 A3397
INT/ORG ROUTINE

S64
COFFEY J.,"THE SOVIET VIEW OF A DISARMED WORLD." COM USA+45 INT/ORG NAT/G EX/STRUC EDU/PROP COERCE PERCEPT ORD/FREE PWR...TREND STERTYP VAL/FREE 20 UN. PAGE 27 A0556
FORCES ATTIT ARMS/CONT USSR

S64
GROSS J.A.,"WHITEHALL AND THE COMMONWEALTH." EUR+WWI MOD/EUR INT/ORG NAT/G CONSULT DELIB/GP LEGIS DOMIN ADMIN COLONIAL ROUTINE PWR CMN/WLTH 19/20. PAGE 57 A1174
EX/STRUC ATTIT TREND

S64
HUELIN D.,"ECONOMIC INTEGRATION IN LATIN AMERICAN: PROGRESS AND PROBLEMS." L/A+17C ECO/DEV AGRI DIST/IND FINAN INDUS NAT/G VOL/ASSN CONSULT DELIB/GP EX/STRUC ACT/RES PLAN TEC/DEV ECO/TAC ROUTINE BAL/PAY WEALTH WORK 20. PAGE 69 A1411
MARKET ECO/UNDEV INT/TRADE

S64
LEVI W.,"CHINA AND THE UNITED NATIONS." ASIA CHINA CHINA/COM WOR+45 WOR-45 CONSTN NAT/G DELIB/GP EX/STRUC FORCES ACT/RES EDU/PROP PWR...POLICY RECORD TIME/SEQ GEN/LAWS UN COLD/WAR 20. PAGE 88 A1794
INT/ORG ATTIT NAT/LISM

B65
FORGAC A.A.,NEW DIPLOMACY AND THE UNITED NATIONS. FRANCE GERMANY UK USSR INT/ORG DELIB/GP EX/STRUC PEACE...INT/LAW CONCPT UN. PAGE 47 A0965
DIPLOM ETIQUET NAT/G

B65
HAIGHT D.E.,THE PRESIDENT; ROLES AND POWERS. USA+45 USA-45 POL/PAR PLAN DIPLOM CHOOSE PERS/REL PWR 18/20 PRESIDENT CONGRESS. PAGE 59 A1217
CHIEF LEGIS TOP/EX EX/STRUC

B65
LAFAVE W.R.,LAW AND SOVIET SOCIETY. EX/STRUC DIPLOM DOMIN EDU/PROP PRESS ADMIN CRIME OWN MARXISM 20 KHRUSH/N. PAGE 84 A1710
JURID CT/SYS ADJUD GOV/REL

B65
MCSHERRY J.E.,RUSSIA AND THE UNITED STATES UNDER EISENHOWER, KHRUSHCHEV, AND KENNEDY. USSR EX/STRUC TOP/EX PRESS WAR...POLICY TREND 20. PAGE 99 A2024
DIPLOM CHIEF NAT/G PEACE

B65
MORGENTHAU H.,MORGENTHAU DIARY (CHINA) (2 VOLS.). ASIA USA+45 USA-45 LAW DELIB/GP EX/STRUC PLAN FOR/AID INT/TRADE CONFER WAR MARXISM 20 CHINJAP. PAGE 104 A2136
DIPLOM ADMIN

B65
ROTBERG R.I.,A POLITICAL HISTORY OF TROPICAL AFRICA. EX/STRUC DIPLOM INT/TRADE DOMIN ADMIN RACE/REL NAT/LISM PWR SOVEREIGN...GEOG TIME/SEQ BIBLIOG 1/20. PAGE 124 A2545
AFR CULTURE COLONIAL

B65
RUBINSTEIN A.Z.,THE CHALLENGE OF POLITICS: IDEAS AND ISSUES (2ND ED.). UNIV ELITES SOCIETY EX/STRUC BAL/PWR PARL/PROC AUTHORIT...DECISION ANTHOL 20. PAGE 125 A2565
NAT/G DIPLOM GP/REL ORD/FREE

B65
SPEECKAERT G.P.,SELECT BIBLIOGRAPHY ON INTERNATIONAL ORGANIZATION, 1885-1964. WOR+45 WOR-45 EX/STRUC DIPLOM ADMIN REGION 19/20 UN. PAGE 136 A2777
BIBLIOG INT/ORG GEN/LAWS STRATA

B65
STOETZER O.C.,THE ORGANIZATION OF AMERICAN STATES. L/A+17C EX/STRUC FOR/AID CONFER PARL/PROC ORD/FREE SOVEREIGN...POLICY INT/LAW 20 OAS. PAGE 138 A2831
INT/ORG REGION DIPLOM BAL/PWR

L65
RUBIN A.P.,"UNITED STATES CONTEMPORARY PRACTICE RELATING TO INTERNATIONAL LAW." USA+45 WOR+45 CONSTN INT/ORG NAT/G DELIB/GP EX/STRUC DIPLOM DOMIN CT/SYS ROUTINE ORD/FREE...CONCPT COLD/WAR 20. PAGE 125 A2558
LAW LEGIT INT/LAW

S65
BROWN S.,"AN ALTERNATIVE TO THE GRAND DESIGN." EUR+WWI FUT USA+45 INT/ORG NAT/G EX/STRUC FORCES CREATE BAL/PWR DOMIN RIGID/FLEX ORD/FREE PWR ...NEW/IDEA RECORD EEC NATO 20. PAGE 20 A0407
VOL/ASSN CONCPT DIPLOM

B66
DRACHOVITCH M.M.,THE COMINTERN HISTORICAL HIGHLIGHTS. USSR INT/ORG EX/STRUC LEGIT LEAD GUERRILLA...ANTHOL 20 COMINTERN LENIN/VI. PAGE 38 A0784
DIPLOM REV MARXISM PERSON

B66
HOLT R.T.,THE POLITICAL BASIS OF ECONOMIC DEVELOPMENT. STRATA STRUCT NAT/G DIPLOM ADMIN...SOC NAT/COMP BIBLIOG 20. PAGE 67 A1376
ECO/TAC GOV/COMP CONSTN EX/STRUC

B66
KIRDAR U.,THE STRUCTURE OF UNITED NATIONS ECONOMIC AID TO UNDERDEVELOPED COUNTRIES. AGRI FINAN INDUS NAT/G EX/STRUC PLAN GIVE TASK...POLICY 20 UN. PAGE 79 A1631
INT/ORG FOR/AID ECO/UNDEV ADMIN

B66
LATHAM E.,THE COMMUNIST CONTROVERSY IN WASHINGTON. USA+45 USA-45 DELIB/GP EX/STRUC LEGIS DIPLOM NAT/LISM MARXISM 20. PAGE 85 A1742
POL/PAR TOTALISM ORD/FREE NAT/G

B66
MARTIN L.W.,DIPLOMACY IN MODERN EUROPEAN HISTORY. EUR+WWI MOD/EUR INT/ORG NAT/G EX/STRUC ROUTINE WAR PEACE TOTALISM PWR 15/20 COLD/WAR EUROPE/W. PAGE 95 A1953
DIPLOM POLICY

B66
NEUMANN R.G.,THE GOVERNMENT OF THE GERMAN FEDERAL REPUBLIC. EUR+WWI GERMANY/W LOC/G EX/STRUC LEGIS CT/SYS INGP/REL PWR...BIBLIOG 20 ADENAUER/K. PAGE 108 A2222
NAT/G POL/PAR DIPLOM CONSTN

B66
SAPIN B.M.,THE MAKING OF UNITED STATES FOREIGN POLICY. USA+45 INT/ORG DELIB/GP FORCES PLAN ECO/TAC CIVMIL/REL PRESIDENT. PAGE 127 A2603
DIPLOM EX/STRUC DECISION NAT/G

B66
US DEPARTMENT OF THE ARMY,COMMUNIST CHINA: A STRATEGIC SURVEY: A BIBLIOGRAPHY (PAMPHLET NO. 20-67). CHINA/COM COM INDIA USSR NAT/G POL/PAR EX/STRUC FORCES NUC/PWR REV ATTIT...POLICY GEOG CHARTS. PAGE 152 A3109
BIBLIOG/A MARXISM S/ASIA DIPLOM

S66
MATTHEWS D.G.,"ETHIOPIAN OUTLINE: A BIBLIOGRAPHIC RESEARCH GUIDE." ETHIOPIA LAW STRUCT ECO/UNDEV AGRI LABOR SECT CHIEF DELIB/GP EX/STRUC ADMIN...LING ORG/CHARTS 20. PAGE 96 A1972
BIBLIOG NAT/G DIPLOM POL/PAR

B67
BRZEZINSKI Z.K.,IDEOLOGY AND POWER IN SOVIET POLITICS. USSR NAT/G POL/PAR PWR...GEN/LAWS 19/20. PAGE 21 A0419
DIPLOM EX/STRUC MARXISM

B67
BRZEZINSKI Z.K.,THE SOVIET BLOC: UNITY AND CONFLICT (2ND ED., REV., ENLARGED). COM POLAND USSR INTELL CHIEF EX/STRUC CONTROL EXEC GOV/REL PWR MARXISM ...TREND IDEA/COMP 20 LENIN/VI MARX/KARL STALIN/J. PAGE 21 A0420
NAT/G DIPLOM

B67
HIRSCHMAN A.O.,DEVELOPMENT PROJECTS OBSERVED. INDUS INT/ORG CONSULT EX/STRUC CREATE OP/RES ECO/TAC DEMAND...POLICY MGT METH/COMP 20 WORLD/BANK. PAGE 65 A1339
ECO/UNDEV R+D FINAN PLAN

B67
MACRIDIS R.C.,FOREIGN POLICY IN WORLD POLITICS (3RD ED.). EX/STRUC BAL/PWR COLONIAL NAT/LISM SKILL SOVEREIGN WEALTH...CONCPT TIME/SEQ ANTHOL 20 COLD/WAR. PAGE 93 A1902
DIPLOM POLICY NAT/G IDEA/COMP

B67
RALSTON D.B.,THE ARMY OF THE REPUBLIC; THE PLACE OF THE MILITARY IN THE POLITICAL EVOLUTION OF FRANCE 1871-1914. FRANCE MOD/EUR EX/STRUC LEGIS TOP/EX DIPLOM ADMIN WAR GP/REL ROLE...BIBLIOG 19/20. PAGE 119 A2436
FORCES NAT/G CIVMIL/REL POLICY

B67
WATERS M.,THE UNITED NATIONS* INTERNATIONAL ORGANIZATION AND ADMINISTRATION. WOR+45 EX/STRUC FORCES DIPLOM LEAD REGION ARMS/CONT REPRESENT INGP/REL ROLE...METH/COMP ANTHOL 20 UN LEAGUE/NAT. PAGE 162 A3291
CONSTN INT/ORG ADMIN ADJUD

L67
"RESTRICTIVE SOVEREIGN IMMUNITY, THE STATE DEPARTMENT, AND THE COURTS." USA+45 USA-45 EX/STRUC DIPLOM ADJUD CONTROL GOV/REL 19/20 DEPT/STATE SUPREME/CT. PAGE 4 A0080
SOVEREIGN ORD/FREE PRIVIL CT/SYS

S67
FABREGA J.,"ANTECEDENTES EXTRANJEROS EN LA CONSTITUCION PANAMENA." CUBA L/A+17C PANAMA URUGUAY EX/STRUC LEGIS DIPLOM ORD/FREE 19/20 COLOMB MEXIC/AMER. PAGE 43 A0882
CONSTN JURID NAT/G PARL/PROC

S67
HODGE G.,"THE RISE AND DEMISE OF THE UN TECHNICAL ASSISTANCE ADMINISTRATION." RISK TASK INGP/REL CONSEN EFFICIENCY 20 UN. PAGE 66 A1349
ADMIN TEC/DEV EX/STRUC INT/ORG

S67
PAUKER G.J.,"TOWARD A NEW ORDER IN INDONESIA." COM INDONESIA S/ASIA ECO/UNDEV POL/PAR EX/STRUC TOP/EX BAL/PWR ECO/TAC FOR/AID DOMIN NAT/LISM AUTHORIT ORD/FREE PWR 20. PAGE 114 A2342
REV NAT/G DIPLOM CIVMIL/REL

S67
ROTBERG R.I.,"COLONIALISM AND AFTER: THE POLITICAL LITERATURE OF CENTRAL AFRICA - A BIBLIOGRAPHIC ESSAY." AFR CHIEF EX/STRUC REV INGP/REL RACE/REL SOVEREIGN 20. PAGE 124 A2546
BIBLIOG/A COLONIAL DIPLOM NAT/G

S67
SHOEMAKER R.L.,"JAPANESE ARMY AND THE WEST." ASIA ELITES EX/STRUC DIPLOM DOMIN EDU/PROP COERCE ATTIT AUTHORIT PWR 1/20 CHINJAP. PAGE 132 A2703
FORCES TEC/DEV WAR TOTALISM

B90
HOSMAR J.K.,A SHORT HISTORY OF ANGLO-SAXON FREEDOM. UK USA-45 ROMAN/EMP NAT/G EX/STRUC LEGIS COLONIAL REV NAT/LISM POPULISM PARLIAMENT ANGLO/SAX MAGNA/CART. PAGE 68 A1394
CONSTN ORD/FREE DIPLOM PARL/PROC

B96
LOWELL A.L.,GOVERNMENTS AND PARTIES IN CONTINENTAL EUROPE, VOL. II. AUSTRIA GERMANY HUNGARY MOD/EUR SWITZERLND SOCIETY EX/STRUC LEGIS DIPLOM AGREE LEAD PARL/PROC PWR...POLICY 19. PAGE 91 A1867
POL/PAR NAT/G GOV/REL ELITES

EXEC....EXECUTIVE PROCESS

B00
MAINE H.S.,INTERNATIONAL LAW. MOD/EUR UNIV SOCIETY STRUCT ACT/RES EXEC WAR ATTIT PERSON ALL/VALS ...POLICY JURID CONCPT OBS TIME/SEQ TOT/POP. PAGE 93 A1908
INT/ORG LAW PEACE INT/LAW

B04
CRANDALL S.B.,TREATIES: THEIR MAKING AND ENFORCEMENT. MOD/EUR USA-45 CONSTN INT/ORG NAT/G LEGIS EDU/PROP LEGIT EXEC PEACE KNOWL MORAL...JURID CONGRESS 19/20 TREATY. PAGE 32 A0655
LAW

B11
PHILLIPSON C.,THE INTERNATIONAL LAW AND CUSTOM OF ANCIENT GREECE AND ROME. MEDIT-7 UNIV INTELL SOCIETY STRUCT NAT/G LEGIS EXEC PERSON...CONCPT OBS CON/ANAL ROM/EMP. PAGE 116 A2377
INT/ORG LAW INT/LAW

B16
ROOT E.,ADDRESSES ON INTERNATIONAL SUBJECTS. MOD/EUR UNIV USA-45 LAW SOCIETY EXEC ATTIT ALL/VALS ...POLICY JURID CONCPT 20 CHINJAP. PAGE 123 A2521
INT/ORG ACT/RES PEACE INT/LAW

B17
UPTON E.,THE MILITARY POLICY OF THE US. USA-45 STRUCT INT/ORG EXEC ATTIT PERCEPT...MGT CONCPT OBS HIST/WRIT CHARTS CONGRESS 18/20. PAGE 149 A3049
FORCES SKILL WAR

B19
SUTHERLAND G.,CONSTITUTIONAL POWER AND WORLD AFFAIRS. CONSTN STRUCT INT/ORG NAT/G CHIEF LEGIS ACT/RES PLAN GOV/REL ALL/VALS...OBS TIME/SEQ CONGRESS VAL/FREE 20 PRESIDENT. PAGE 140 A2866
USA-45 EXEC DIPLOM

B22
WRIGHT Q.,THE CONTROL OF AMERICAN FOREIGN RELATIONS. USA-45 WOR-45 CONSTN INT/ORG CONSULT LEGIS LEGIT ROUTINE ORD/FREE PWR...POLICY JURID CONCPT METH/CNCPT RECORD LEAGUE/NAT 20. PAGE 167 A3402
NAT/G EXEC DIPLOM

B29
DUNN F.,THE PRACTICE AND PROCEDURE OF INTERNATIONAL CONFERENCES. WOR-45 NAT/G DELIB/GP BAL/PWR LEGIT EXEC ROUTINE PEACE ORD/FREE RESPECT...JURID CONCPT METH/CNCPT OBS RECORD TIME/SEQ 20. PAGE 39 A0799
INT/ORG DIPLOM

B32
MASTERS R.D.,INTERNATIONAL LAW IN INTERNATIONAL COURTS. BELGIUM EUR+WWI FRANCE GERMANY MOD/EUR SWITZERLND WOR-45 SOCIETY STRATA STRUCT LEGIT EXEC ALL/VALS...JURID HIST/WRIT TIME/SEQ TREND GEN/LAWS 20. PAGE 96 A1961
INT/ORG LAW INT/LAW

B35
KENNEDY W.P.,THE LAW AND CUSTOM OF THE SOUTH AFRICAN CONSTITUTION. AFR SOUTH/AFR KIN LOC/G PROVS DIPLOM ADJUD ADMIN EXEC 20. PAGE 78 A1594
CT/SYS CONSTN JURID PARL/PROC

B36
SHOTWELL J.,ON THE RIM OF THE ABYSS. EUR+WWI USA-45 STRUCT INT/ORG ACT/RES PLAN EDU/PROP EXEC ATTIT ALL/VALS...TIME/SEQ LEAGUE/NAT TOT/POP 20. PAGE 132 A2706
NAT/G BAL/PWR

B38
PETTEE G.S.,THE PROCESS OF REVOLUTION. COM FRANCE ITALY MOD/EUR RUSSIA SPAIN WOR-45 ELITES INTELL SOCIETY STRATA STRUCT INT/ORG NAT/G POL/PAR ACT/RES PLAN EDU/PROP LEGIT EXEC...SOC MYTH TIME/SEQ TOT/POP 18/20. PAGE 115 A2370
COERCE CONCPT REV

B38
RAPPARD W.E.,THE CRISIS OF DEMOCRACY. EUR+WWI UNIV WOR-45 CULTURE SOCIETY ECO/DEV INT/ORG POL/PAR ACT/RES EDU/PROP EXEC CHOOSE ATTIT ALL/VALS...SOC OBS HIST/WRIT TIME/SEQ LEAGUE/NAT NAZI TOT/POP 20. PAGE 119 A2449
NAT/G CONCPT

C39
REISCHAUER R.,"JAPAN'S GOVERNMENT--POLITICS." CONSTN STRATA POL/PAR FORCES LEGIS DIPLOM ADMIN EXEC CENTRAL...POLICY BIBLIOG 20 CHINJAP. PAGE 120 A2462
NAT/G S/ASIA CONCPT ROUTINE

B40
RAPPARD W.E.,THE QUEST FOR PEACE. UNIV USA-45 WOR-45 SOCIETY INT/ORG NAT/G PLAN EXEC ROUTINE WAR ATTIT DRIVE ALL/VALS...POLICY CONCPT OBS TIME/SEQ LEAGUE/NAT TOT/POP 20. PAGE 119 A2450
EUR+WWI ACT/RES PEACE

B41
YOUNG G.,FEDERALISM AND FREEDOM. EUR+WWI MOD/EUR RUSSIA USA-45 WOR-45 SOCIETY STRUCT ECO/DEV INT/ORG EXEC FEDERAL ATTIT PERSON ALL/VALS...OLD/LIB CONCPT OBS TREND LEAGUE/NAT TOT/POP. PAGE 169 A3435
NAT/G WAR

B44
WHITTON J.B.,THE SECOND CHANCE: AMERICA AND THE PEACE. EUR+WWI USA-45 SOCIETY STRUCT INT/ORG NAT/G LEGIT EXEC WAR ALL/VALS...SOC CONCPT TIME/SEQ TREND CONGRESS 20. PAGE 164 A3340
LEGIS PEACE

B45
RANSHOFFEN-WERTHEIMER EF,THE INTERNATIONAL SECRETARIAT: A GREAT EXPERIMENT IN INTERNATIONAL ADMINISTRATION. EUR+WWI FUT CONSTN FACE/GP CONSULT DELIB/GP ACT/RES ADMIN ROUTINE PEACE ORD/FREE...MGT RECORD ORG/CHARTS LEAGUE/NAT WORK 20. PAGE 119 A2442
INT/ORG EXEC

B47
BORGESE G.,COMMON CAUSE. LAW CONSTN SOCIETY STRATA ECO/DEV INT/ORG POL/PAR FORCES LEGIS TOP/EX CAP/ISM DIPLOM ADMIN EXEC ATTIT PWR 20. PAGE 17 A0339
WOR+45 NAT/G SOVEREIGN REGION

B47
FEIS H.,SEEN FROM E A, THREE INTERNATIONAL EPISODES. EUR+WWI ITALY USA-45 WOR-45 AGRI INT/ORG NAT/G INT/TRADE LEGIT EXEC ATTIT ORD/FREE...POLICY LEAGUE/NAT TOT/POP 20 OIL. PAGE 44 A0908
EXTR/IND ECO/TAC DIPLOM

B48
CHAMBERLAIN L.H.,AMERICAN FOREIGN POLICY. FUT USA+45 USA-45 WOR+45 WOR-45 NAT/G LEGIS TOP/EX ECO/TAC FOR/AID EDU/PROP EXEC ATTIT ORD/FREE ...JURID TREND TOT/POP 20. PAGE 25 A0517
CONSTN DIPLOM

B49
ROSENHAUPT H.W.,HOW TO WAGE PEACE. USA+45 SOCIETY STRATA STRUCT R+D INT/ORG POL/PAR LEGIS ACT/RES CREATE PLAN EDU/PROP ADMIN EXEC ATTIT ALL/VALS ...TIME/SEQ TREND COLD/WAR 20. PAGE 124 A2536
INTELL CONCPT DIPLOM

B49
STREIT C.,UNION NOW. UNIV USA-45 WOR-45 INTELL STRUCT INT/ORG NAT/G PLAN DIPLOM EXEC ATTIT ...CONCPT TIME/SEQ. PAGE 139 A2849
SOCIETY ACT/RES WAR

B50
MCCAMY J.,THE ADMINISTRATION OF AMERICAN FOREIGN AFFAIRS. USA+45 SOCIETY INT/ORG NAT/G ACT/RES PLAN INT/TRADE EDU/PROP ADJUD ALL/VALS...METH/CNCPT TIME/SEQ CONGRESS 20. PAGE 97 A1996
EXEC STRUCT DIPLOM

L50
US SENATE COMM. GOVT. OPER.,"REVISION OF THE UN CHARTER." FUT USA+45 WOR+45 CONSTN ECO/DEV ECO/UNDEV NAT/G DELIB/GP ACT/RES CREATE PLAN EXEC ROUTINE CHOOSE ALL/VALS...POLICY CONCPT CONGRESS UN TOT/POP 20 COLD/WAR. PAGE 157 A3196
INT/ORG LEGIS PEACE

B51
MACLAURIN J.,THE UNITED NATIONS AND POWER POLITICS. WOR+45 CONSULT EDU/PROP LEGIT ADJUD EXEC MORAL ORD/FREE...HUM JURID CONCPT RECORD TIME/SEQ UN COLD/WAR 20. PAGE 93 A1896
INT/ORG ROUTINE

B52
ULAM A.B.,TITOISM AND THE COMINFORM. USSR WOR+45 STRUCT INT/ORG NAT/G ACT/RES PLAN EXEC ATTIT DRIVE ALL/VALS...CONCPT OBS VAL/FREE 20 COMINTERN TITO/MARSH. PAGE 146 A2993
COM POL/PAR TOTALISM YUGOSLAVIA

B52
VANDENBOSCH A.,THE UN: BACKGROUND, ORGANIZATION, FUNCTIONS, ACTIVITIES. WOR+45 LAW CONSTN STRUCT INT/ORG CONSULT BAL/PWR EDU/PROP EXEC ALL/VALS ...POLICY CONCPT UN 20. PAGE 158 A3218
DELIB/GP TIME/SEQ PEACE

B53
MACMAHON A.W.,ADMINISTRATION IN FOREIGN AFFAIRS. NAT/G CONSULT DELIB/GP LEGIS ACT/RES CREATE ADMIN EXEC RIGID/FLEX PWR...METH/CNCPT TIME/SEQ TOT/POP VAL/FREE 20. PAGE 93 A1899
USA+45 ROUTINE FOR/AID DIPLOM

B53
MATLOFF M.,STRATEGIC PLANNING FOR COALITION WARFARE. UK USA-45 CHIEF DIPLOM EXEC GOV/REL ...METH/COMP 20. PAGE 96 A1967
WAR PLAN DECISION FORCES

B54
NUSSBAUM D.,A CONCISE HISTORY OF THE LAW OF NATIONS. ASIA CHRIST-17C EUR+WWI ISLAM MEDIT-7 MOD/EUR S/ASIA UNIV WOR+45 WOR-45 SOCIETY STRUCT EXEC ATTIT ALL/VALS...CONCPT HIST/WRIT TIME/SEQ. PAGE 110 A2263
INT/ORG LAW PEACE INT/LAW

B55
ALFIERI D.,DICTATORS FACE TO FACE. NAT/G TOP/EX DIPLOM EXEC COERCE ORD/FREE FASCISM...POLICY OBS 20 HITLER/A MUSSOLIN/B. PAGE 6 A0116
WAR CHIEF TOTALISM PERS/REL

B55
CHOWDHURI R.N.,INTERNATIONAL MANDATES AND TRUSTEESHIP SYSTEMS. WOR+45 STRUCT ECO/UNDEV INT/ORG LEGIS DOMIN EDU/PROP LEGIT ADJUD EXEC PWR ...CONCPT TIME/SEQ UN 20. PAGE 26 A0534
DELIB/GP PLAN SOVEREIGN

B55
JOY C.T.,HOW COMMUNISTS NEGOTIATE. COM USA+45 CONSTN CULTURE ECO/UNDEV NAT/G CONSULT DELIB/GP FORCES PLAN ECO/TAC DOMIN EDU/PROP LEGIT EXEC ROUTINE COERCE WAR CHOOSE PEACE ATTIT RIGID/FLEX ORD/FREE PWR...POLICY 20. PAGE 75 A1539
ASIA INT/ORG DIPLOM

B55
PLISCHKE E.,AMERICAN FOREIGN RELATIONS: A BIBLIOGRAPHY OF OFFICIAL SOURCES. USA+45 USA-45 INT/ORG FORCES PRESS WRITING DEBATE EXEC...POLICY INT/LAW 18/20 CONGRESS. PAGE 116 A2390
BIBLIOG/A DIPLOM NAT/G

B55
SNYDER R.C.,AMERICAN FOREIGN POLICY. USA+45 USA-45 WOR+45 WOR-45 CONSTN INT/ORG POL/PAR VOL/ASSN DELIB/GP LEGIS CREATE DOMIN EDU/PROP EXEC COERCE ATTIT DRIVE ORD/FREE PWR...MGT OBS RECORD TIME/SEQ TREND. PAGE 134 A2752
NAT/G DIPLOM

B56
GEORGE A.L.,WOODROW WILSON AND COLONEL HOUSE. WOR-45 CONSTN FACE/GP INT/ORG NAT/G POL/PAR CONSULT LEGIT EXEC COERCE CHOOSE ATTIT DRIVE PERSON MORAL ORD/FREE PWR RESPECT...POLICY MGT PSY OBS RECORD INT LEAGUE/NAT. PAGE 52 A1060
USA-45 BIOG DIPLOM

B56
KIRK G.,THE CHANGING ENVIRONMENT OF INTERNATIONAL RELATIONS. ASIA S/ASIA USA+45 WOR+45 ECO/UNDEV INT/ORG NAT/G FOR/AID EDU/PROP PEACE KNOWL ...PLURIST COLD/WAR TOT/POP 20. PAGE 80 A1634
FUT EXEC DIPLOM

B56
LOVEDAY A.,REFLECTIONS ON INTERNATIONAL ADMINISTRATION. WOR+45 WOR-45 DELIB/GP ACT/RES ADMIN EXEC ROUTINE DRIVE...METH/CNCPT TIME/SEQ CON/ANAL SIMUL TOT/POP 20. PAGE 91 A1865
INT/ORG MGT

B56
REITZEL W.,UNITED STATES FOREIGN POLICY, 1945-1955. USA+45 WOR+45 CONSTN INT/ORG EDU/PROP LEGIT EXEC COERCE NUC/PWR PEACE ATTIT ORD/FREE PWR...DECISION CONCPT OBS RECORD TIME/SEQ TREND COLD/WAR UN CONGRESS. PAGE 120 A2464
NAT/G POLICY DIPLOM

B56
SOHN L.B.,BASIC DOCUMENTS OF THE UNITED NATIONS. WOR+45 LAW INT/ORG LEGIT EXEC ROUTINE CHOOSE PWR ...JURID CONCPT GEN/LAWS ANTHOL UN TOT/POP OAS FAO ILO 20. PAGE 135 A2761
DELIB/GP CONSTN

B57
MURRAY J.N.,THE UNITED NATIONS TRUSTEESHIP SYSTEM. AFR WOR+45 CONSTN CONSULT LEGIS EDU/PROP LEGIT EXEC ROUTINE...INT TIME/SEQ SOMALI UN 20. PAGE 106 A2181
INT/ORG DELIB/GP

B57
TRIFFIN R.,EUROPE AND THE MONEY MUDDLE. USA+45 INT/ORG NAT/G CONSULT PLAN ECO/TAC EXEC ROUTINE BAL/PAY WEALTH...METH/CNCPT OBS TREND CHARTS STERTYP GEN/METH EEC VAL/FREE ECSC. PAGE 145 A2962
EUR+WWI ECO/DEV REGION

B58
GANGE J.,UNIVERSITY RESEARCH ON INTERNATIONAL AFFAIRS. USA+45 ACADEM INT/ORG CONSULT CREATE EXEC ROUTINE...QUANT STAT INT STERTYP GEN/METH TOT/POP VAL/FREE 20. PAGE 51 A1040
R+D MGT DIPLOM

B58
HENKIN L.,ARMS CONTROL AND INSPECTION IN AMERICAN LAW. LAW CONSTN INT/ORG LOC/G MUNIC NAT/G PROVS EDU/PROP LEGIT EXEC NUC/PWR KNOWL ORD/FREE...OBS TOT/POP CONGRESS 20. PAGE 64 A1315
USA+45 JURID ARMS/CONT

B58
ISLAM R.,INTERNATIONAL ECONOMIC COOPERATION AND THE UNITED NATIONS. FINAN PLAN EXEC TASK WAR PEACE ...SOC METH/CNCPT 20 UN LEAGUE/NAT. PAGE 72 A1470
INT/ORG DIPLOM ADMIN

L58
HAVILAND H.F.,"FOREIGN AID AND THE POLICY PROCESS: 1957." USA+45 FACE/GP POL/PAR VOL/ASSN CHIEF DELIB/GP ACT/RES LEGIT EXEC GOV/REL ATTIT DRIVE PWR ...POLICY TESTS CONGRESS 20. PAGE 63 A1291
LEGIS PLAN FOR/AID

B59
ALLEN R.L.,SOVIET INFLUENCE IN LATIN AMERICA. ECO/UNDEV FINAN PROC/MFG NAT/G TEC/DEV EDU/PROP EXEC ROUTINE ATTIT DRIVE PERSON ALL/VALS PWR...STAT CHARTS WORK 20. PAGE 6 A0125
L/A+17C ECO/TAC INT/TRADE USSR

B59
FOX W.T.R.,THEORETICAL ASPECTS OF INTERNATIONAL RELATIONS. WOR+45 INT/ORG NAT/G POL/PAR CONSULT PLAN ECO/TAC DOMIN EDU/PROP LEGIT EXEC COERCE PWR WEALTH...RELATIV CONCPT 20. PAGE 48 A0975
DELIB/GP ANTHOL

B59
LAQUER W.Z.,THE SOVIET UNION AND THE MIDDLE EAST. COM UAR USSR ECO/UNDEV NAT/G VOL/ASSN ECO/TAC EDU/PROP COLONIAL EXEC PWR...TIME/SEQ TREND COLD/WAR 20. PAGE 85 A1730
ISLAM DRIVE FOR/AID NAT/LISM

S59
SUTTON F.X.,"REPRESENTATION AND THE NATURE OF POLITICAL SYSTEMS." UNIV WOR-45 CULTURE SOCIETY STRATA INT/ORG FORCES JUDGE DOMIN LEGIT EXEC REGION REPRESENT ATTIT ORD/FREE RESPECT...SOC HIST/WRIT TIME/SEQ. PAGE 140 A2867
NAT/G CONCPT

B60
BAILEY S.D.,THE GENERAL ASSEMBLY OF THE UNITED NATIONS. FUT WOR+45 STRUCT LEGIS ACT/RES PLAN EDU/PROP LEGIT ADMIN EXEC PEACE ATTIT HEALTH PWR ...CONCPT TREND CHARTS GEN/LAWS UN TOT/POP VAL/FREE COLD/WAR 20. PAGE 10 A0204
INT/ORG DELIB/GP DIPLOM

B60
DAVIDS J.,AMERICA AND THE WORLD OF OUR TIME: UNITED STATES DIPLOMACY IN THE TWENTIETH CENTURY. USA-45 SOCIETY ECO/DEV INT/ORG NAT/G POL/PAR FORCES ECO/TAC DOMIN EDU/PROP EXEC COERCE WAR CHOOSE ATTIT PERSON ORD/FREE...CONCPT TIME/SEQ TOT/POP 20. PAGE 34 A0686
USA+45 PWR DIPLOM

B60
ENGEL J.,THE SECURITY OF THE FREE WORLD. USSR WOR+45 STRATA STRUCT ECO/DEV ECO/UNDEV INT/ORG DELIB/GP FORCES DOMIN LEGIT ADJUD EXEC ARMS/CONT COERCE...POLICY CONCPT NEW/IDEA TIME/SEQ GEN/LAWS COLD/WAR WORK UN 20 NATO. PAGE 42 A0851
COM TREND DIPLOM

B60
KENNAN G.F.,RUSSIA AND THE WEST. ASIA COM EUR+WWI GERMANY UK USA+45 USA-45 USSR INT/ORG NAT/G VOL/ASSN DOMIN REV WAR PWR...TIME/SEQ 20. PAGE 78 A1590
EXEC DIPLOM

S60
BOWIE R.,"POLICY FORMATION IN AMERICAN FOREIGN POLICY." FUT USA+45 WOR+45 STRUCT ECO/DEV INT/ORG POL/PAR LEGIS ACT/RES EXEC ALL/VALS...POLICY OBS VAL/FREE 20. PAGE 17 A0355
PLAN DRIVE DIPLOM

B61
BARNES W.,THE FOREIGN SERVICE OF THE UNITED STATES. USA+45 USA-45 CONSTN INT/ORG POL/PAR CONSULT DELIB/GP LEGIS DOMIN EDU/PROP EXEC ATTIT RIGID/FLEX ORD/FREE PWR...POLICY CONCPT STAT OBS RECORD BIOG TIME/SEQ TREND. PAGE 11 A0224
NAT/G MGT DIPLOM

B61
GRAEBNER N.,THE NEW ISOLATIONISM: A STUDY IN POLITICS AND FOREIGN POLICY SINCE 1960. USA+45 INT/ORG LOC/G NAT/G POL/PAR LEGIS BAL/PWR EDU/PROP CHOOSE ATTIT PERSON ORD/FREE 20 TRUMAN/HS EISNHWR/DD. PAGE 55 A1120
EXEC PWR DIPLOM

B61
NOLLAU G.,INTERNATIONAL COMMUNISM AND WORLD REVOLUTION: HISTORY AND METHODS. RUSSIA USSR INT/ORG NAT/G POL/PAR VOL/ASSN FORCES BAL/PWR DIPLOM EXEC REGION WAR ATTIT PWR MARXISM...CONCPT TIME/SEQ COLD/WAR 19/20. PAGE 102 A2100
COM REV

B61
PANIKKAR K.M.,REVOLUTION IN AFRICA. AFR GUINEA ECO/UNDEV POL/PAR DIPLOM COLONIAL EXEC LEAD SOVEREIGN...CHARTS 20. PAGE 114 A2332
NAT/LISM NAT/G CHIEF

B61
SHAPP W.R.,FIELD ADMINISTRATION IN THE UNITED NATIONS SYSTEM. FINAN PROB/SOLV INSPECT DIPLOM EXEC REGION ROUTINE EFFICIENCY ROLE...INT CHARTS 20 UN. PAGE 131 A2694
INT/ORG ADMIN GP/REL FOR/AID

B61
SHARP W.R.,FIELD ADMINISTRATION IN THE UNITED NATION SYSTEM: THE CONDUCT OF INTERNATIONAL ECONOMIC AND SOCIAL PROGRAMS. FUT WOR+45 CONSTN SOCIETY ECO/UNDEV R+D DELIB/GP ACT/RES PLAN TEC/DEV EDU/PROP EXEC ROUTINE HEALTH WEALTH...HUM CONCPT CHARTS METH ILO UNESCO VAL/FREE UN 20. PAGE 132 A2697
INT/ORG CONSULT

S61
BRZEZINSKI Z.K.,"THE ORGANIZATION OF THE COMMUNIST CAMP." COM CZECHOSLVK COM/IND NAT/G DELIB/GP INT/TRADE DOMIN EDU/PROP EXEC ROUTINE COERCE ATTIT PWR...MGT CONCPT TIME/SEQ CHARTS VAL/FREE 20 TREATY. PAGE 20 A0416
VOL/ASSN DIPLOM USSR

S61
JACKSON E.,"CONSTITUTIONAL DEVELOPMENTS OF THE UNITED NATIONS: THE GROWTH OF ITS EXECUTIVE CAPACITY." FUT WOR+45 CONSTN STRUCT ACT/RES PLAN ALL/VALS...NEW/IDEA OBS COLD/WAR UN 20. PAGE 72 A1475
INT/ORG EXEC

B62
AMERICAN LAW INSTITUTE,FOREIGN RELATIONS LAW OF THE UNITED STATES: RESTATEMENT, SECOND. USA+45 NAT/G LEGIS ADJUD EXEC ROUTINE GOV/REL...INT/LAW JURID CONCPT 20 TREATY. PAGE 7 A0152
PROF/ORG LAW DIPLOM ORD/FREE

B62
BAILEY S.D.,THE SECRETARIAT OF THE UNITED NATIONS. FUT WOR+45 DELIB/GP PLAN BAL/PWR DOMIN EDU/PROP ADMIN PEACE ATTIT PWR...DECISION CONCPT TREND CON/ANAL CHARTS UN VAL/FREE COLD/WAR 20. PAGE 10 A0205
INT/ORG EXEC DIPLOM

B62
LAWSON R.,INTERNATIONAL REGIONAL ORGANIZATIONS. WOR+45 NAT/G VOL/ASSN CONSULT LEGIS EDU/PROP LEGIT ADMIN EXEC ROUTINE HEALTH PWR WEALTH...JURID EEC COLD/WAR 20 UN. PAGE 86 A1752
INT/ORG DELIB/GP REGION

B62
MORTON L.,STRATEGY AND COMMAND: THE FIRST TWO YEARS. USA-45 NAT/G CONTROL EXEC LEAD WEAPON CIVMIL/REL PWR...POLICY AUD/VIS CHARTS 20 CHINJAP. PAGE 105 A2150
WAR FORCES PLAN DIPLOM

B62
NEAL F.W.,WAR AND PEACE AND GERMANY. EUR+WWI USSR STRUCT INT/ORG NAT/G FORCES DOMIN EDU/PROP LEGIT EXEC COERCE ORD/FREE...HUM SOC NEW/IDEA OBS TIME/SEQ TOT/POP COLD/WAR 20 BERLIN. PAGE 108 A2208
USA+45 POLICY DIPLOM GERMANY

L62
BAILEY S.D.,"THE TROIKA AND THE FUTURE OF THE UN." CONSTN CREATE LEGIT EXEC CHOOSE ORD/FREE PWR ...CONCPT NEW/IDEA UN COLD/WAR 20. PAGE 10 A0206
FUT INT/ORG USSR

L62
CORET A.,"L'INDEPENDANCE DU SAMOA OCCIDENTAL." S/ASIA LAW INT/ORG EXEC ALL/VALS SAMOA UN 20. PAGE 31 A0622
NAT/G STRUCT SOVEREIGN

S62
MORGENTHAU H.J.,"A POLITICAL THEORY OF FOREIGN AID." ECO/UNDEV NAT/G DELIB/GP PLAN ECO/TAC EDU/PROP EXEC ORD/FREE RESPECT WEALTH...METH/CNCPT TREND 20. PAGE 104 A2140
USA+45 PHIL/SCI FOR/AID

C62
ROBINSON J.A.,"CONGRESS AND FOREIGN POLICY-MAKING: A STUDY IN LEGISLATIVE INFLUENCE AND INITIATIVE." USA+45 CHIEF DELIB/GP CREATE CONTROL EXEC GOV/REL PERCEPT...TREND BIBLIOG 20 CONGRESS. PAGE 122 A2505
LEGIS DIPLOM POLICY DECISION

B63
BOWETT D.W.,THE LAW OF INTERNATIONAL INSTITUTIONS. WOR+45 WOR-45 CONSTN DELIB/GP EX/STRUC JUDGE EDU/PROP LEGIT CT/SYS EXEC ROUTINE RIGID/FLEX ORD/FREE PWR...JURID CONCPT ORG/CHARTS GEN/METH LEAGUE/NAT OAS OEEC 20 UN. PAGE 17 A0354
INT/ORG ADJUD DIPLOM

B63
BURNS A.L.,PEACE-KEEPING BY U.N.FORCES - FROM SUEZ TO THE CONGO. AFR FUT ISLAM ISRAEL USSR WOR+45 NAT/G DELIB/GP BAL/PWR DOMIN LEGIT EXEC COERCE PEACE ATTIT PWR RESPECT SOVEREIGN...CONCPT UN 20. PAGE 22 A0441
INT/ORG FORCES ORD/FREE

B63
DRACHKOVITCH,UNITED STATES AID TO YUGOSLAVIA AND POLAND. POLAND USA+45 YUGOSLAVIA LEGIS EXEC TOTALISM MARXISM 20 CONGRESS. PAGE 38 A0782
FOR/AID POLICY DIPLOM ATTIT

B63
GILBERT M.,THE APPEASERS. COM GERMANY UK PLAN ECO/TAC COLONIAL CONTROL EXEC ORD/FREE PWR FASCISM 20 PARLIAMENT. PAGE 52 A1068 — DIPLOM WAR POLICY DECISION

C63
SCHMITT K.M.,"EVOLUTION OR CHAOS: DYNAMICS OF LATIN AMERICAN GOVERNMENT AND POLITICS." L/A+17C AGRI FINAN CAP/ISM EXEC LEAD BAL/PAY TOTALISM ATTIT ...TREND BIBLIOG 20. PAGE 129 A2635 — DIPLOM POLICY POL/PAR LOBBY

B64
APTER D.E.,IDEOLOGY AND DISCONTENT. FUT WOR+45 CONSTN CULTURE INTELL SOCIETY STRUCT INT/ORG NAT/G DELIB/GP LEGIS CREATE PLAN TEC/DEV EDU/PROP EXEC PERCEPT PERSON RIGID/FLEX ALL/VALS...POLICY TOT/POP. PAGE 8 A0171 — ACT/RES ATTIT

B64
US SENATE COMM GOVT OPERATIONS,THE SECRETARY OF STATE AND THE AMBASSADOR. USA+45 CHIEF CONSULT EX/STRUC FORCES PLAN ADMIN EXEC INGP/REL ROLE ...ANTHOL 20 PRESIDENT DEPT/STATE. PAGE 156 A3175 — DIPLOM DELIB/GP NAT/G

L64
ARMENGALD A.,"ECONOMIE ET COEXISTENCE." COM EUR+WWI FUT USA+45 WOR+45 ECO/DEV ECO/UNDEV FINAN INT/ORG NAT/G EXEC CHOOSE ATTIT ALL/VALS...POLICY RELATIV DECISION TREND SOC/EXP COLD/WAR WORK 20. PAGE 9 A0173 — MARKET ECO/TAC CAP/ISM

L64
BERKS R.N.,"THE US AND WEAPONS CONTROL." WOR+45 LAW INT/ORG NAT/G LEGIS EXEC COERCE PEACE ATTIT RIGID/FLEX ALL/VALS PWR...POLICY TOT/POP 20. PAGE 13 A0273 — USA+45 PLAN ARMS/CONT

L64
RIPLEY R.B.,"INTERAGENCY COMMITTEES AND INCREMENTALISM: THE CASE OF AID TO INDIA." INDIA USA+45 INTELL NAT/G DELIB/GP ACT/RES DIPLOM ROUTINE NAT/LISM ATTIT PWR...SOC CONCPT NEW/IDEA TIME/SEQ CON/ANAL VAL/FREE 20. PAGE 121 A2483 — EXEC MGT FOR/AID

L64
WARD C.,"THE 'NEW MYTHS' AND 'OLD REALITIES' OF NUCLEAR WAR." COM FUT USA+45 USSR WOR+45 INT/ORG NAT/G DOMIN LEGIT EXEC ATTIT PERCEPT ALL/VALS ...POLICY RELATIV PSY MYTH TREND 20. PAGE 161 A3280 — FORCES COERCE ARMS/CONT NUC/PWR

S64
HOSCH L.G.,"PUBLIC ADMINISTRATION ON THE INTERNATIONAL FRONTIER." WOR+45 R+D NAT/G EDU/PROP EXEC KNOWL ORD/FREE VAL/FREE 20 UN. PAGE 68 A1390 — INT/ORG MGT

S64
JORDAN A.,"POLITICAL COMMUNICATION: THE THIRD DIMENSION OF STRATEGY." USA+45 WOR+45 INT/ORG NAT/G CONSULT FORCES PLAN LEGIT EXEC PERCEPT ALL/VALS ...POLICY RELATIV PSY NEW/IDEA AUD/VIS EXHIBIT TOT/POP 20. PAGE 75 A1534 — EDU/PROP RIGID/FLEX ATTIT

S64
WASKOW A.I.,"NEW ROADS TO A WORLD WITHOUT WAR." FUT WOR+45 CULTURE INTELL SOCIETY NAT/G DOMIN LEGIT EXEC COERCE PEACE ATTIT DISPL PERCEPT RIGID/FLEX ALL/VALS...POLICY RELATIV SOC NEW/IDEA 20. PAGE 161 A3288 — INT/ORG FORCES

B65
VONGLAHN G.,LAW AMONG NATIONS: AN INTRODUCTION TO PUBLIC INTERNATIONAL LAW. UNIV WOR+45 LAW INT/ORG NAT/G LEGIT EXEC RIGID/FLEX...CONCPT TIME/SEQ GEN/LAWS UN TOT/POP 20. PAGE 160 A3253 — CONSTN JURID INT/LAW

B66
BEAUFRE A.,NATO AND EUROPE. WOR+45 PLAN CONFER EXEC NUC/PWR ATTIT...POLICY 20 NATO EUROPE. PAGE 12 A0243 — INT/ORG DETER DIPLOM ADMIN

S66
CRANMER-BYNG J.L.,"THE CHINESE ATTITUDE TOWARDS EXTERNAL RELATIONS." ASIA CHINA/COM EXEC NAT/LISM MARXISM...POLICY 20. PAGE 32 A0660 — ATTIT DIPLOM NAT/G

B67
BRZEZINSKI Z.K.,THE SOVIET BLOC: UNITY AND CONFLICT (2ND ED., REV., ENLARGED). COM POLAND USSR INTELL CHIEF EX/STRUC CONTROL EXEC GOV/REL PWR MARXISM ...TREND IDEA/COMP 20 LENIN/VI MARX/KARL STALIN/J. PAGE 21 A0420 — NAT/G DIPLOM

B67
KAROL K.S.,CHINA, THE OTHER COMMUNISM (TRANS. BY TOM BAISTOW). CHINA/COM CULTURE INDUS FORCES DIPLOM EDU/PROP CONTROL EXEC NUC/PWR ATTIT...SOC CHARTS 20. PAGE 77 A1567 — NAT/G POL/PAR MARXISM INGP/REL

B91
SIDGWICK H.,THE ELEMENTS OF POLITICS. LOC/G NAT/G LEGIS DIPLOM ADJUD CONTROL EXEC PARL/PROC REPRESENT GOV/REL SOVEREIGN ALL/IDEOS 19 MILL/JS BENTHAM/J. PAGE 132 A2713 — POLICY LAW CONCPT

EXECUTIVE....SEE TOP/EX

EXECUTIVE ESTABLISHMENTS....SEE EX/STRUC

EXECUTIVE PROCESS....SEE EXEC

EXHIBIT....DISPLAY

EXPECTATIONS....SEE PROBABIL, SUPEGO, PREDICT

EXPERIMENTATION....SEE EXPERIMENTATION INDEX, P. XIV

EXPOSTFACT....EX POST FACTO LAWS

EXPROPRIAT....EXPROPRIATION

B65
FALK R.A.,THE AFTERMATH OF SABBATINO: BACKGROUND PAPERS AND PROCEEDINGS OF SEVENTH HAMMARSKJOLD FORUM. USA+45 LAW ACT/RES ADJUD ROLE...BIBLIOG 20 EXPROPRIAT SABBATINO HARLAN/JM. PAGE 44 A0891 — SOVEREIGN CT/SYS INT/LAW OWN

EXTR/IND....EXTRACTIVE INDUSTRY (FISHING, LUMBERING, ETC.)

N
KYRIAK T.E.,EAST EUROPE: BIBLIOGRAPHY--INDEX TO US JPRS RESEARCH TRANSLATIONS. ALBANIA BULGARIA COM CZECHOSLVK HUNGARY POLAND ROMANIA AGRI EXTR/IND FINAN SERV/IND INT/TRADE WEAPON...GEOG MGT SOC 20. PAGE 83 A1701 — BIBLIOG/A PRESS MARXISM INDUS

N
KYRIAK T.E.,SOVIET UNION: BIBLIOGRAPHY INDEX TO US JPRS RESEARCH TRANSLATIONS. USSR ECO/DEV AGRI COM/IND CONSTRUC DIST/IND EXTR/IND PROC/MFG R+D INT/TRADE...SOC 20. PAGE 83 A1703 — BIBLIOG/A INDUS MARXISM PRESS

B10
MENDELSSOHN S.,SOUTH AFRICAN BIBLIOGRAPHY (2 VOLS.). SOUTH/AFR EXTR/IND LABOR SECT DIPLOM INT/TRADE COLONIAL RACE/REL DISCRIM...GEOG 20. PAGE 99 A2038 — BIBLIOG/A AFR NAT/G NAT/LISM

N19
SALKEVER L.R.,SUB-SAHARA AFRICA (PAMPHLET). AFR USSR EXTR/IND NAT/G SCHOOL DIPLOM COLONIAL WEALTH ...GEOG CHARTS 16/20. PAGE 127 A2594 — ECO/UNDEV TEC/DEV TASK INT/TRADE

B35
BUREAU ECONOMIC RES LAT AM,THE ECONOMIC LITERATURE OF LATIN AMERICA (2 VOLS.). CHRIST-17C AGRI DIST/IND EXTR/IND INDUS WORKER INT/TRADE...GEOG 16/20. PAGE 21 A0433 — BIBLIOG L/A+17C ECO/UNDEV FINAN

B38
COLBY C.C.,GEOGRAPHICAL ASPECTS OF INTERNATIONAL RELATIONS. WOR-45 ECO/DEV ECO/UNDEV AGRI EXTR/IND INDUS MARKET R+D INT/ORG NAT/G TEC/DEV ECO/TAC INT/TRADE NAT/LISM WEALTH...METH/CNCPT CHARTS GEN/LAWS 20. PAGE 28 A0565 — PLAN GEOG DIPLOM

B38
FRANKEL S.H.,CAPITAL INVESTMENT IN AFRICA. AFR EUR+WWI RHODESIA SOUTH/AFR UK FINAN FOR/AID COLONIAL DEMAND UTIL WEALTH...METH/CNCPT CHARTS 20 CONGO/LEOP. PAGE 48 A0983 — ECO/UNDEV EXTR/IND DIPLOM PRODUC

B45
STRAUSZ-HUPE R.,THE BALANCE OF TOMORROW: POWER AND FOREIGN POLICY IN THE UNITED STATES. FUT USA+45 ECO/DEV EXTR/IND INT/ORG FORCES BAL/PWR REGION NUC/PWR...GEOG CHARTS 20 COLD/WAR EUROPE/W. PAGE 139 A2845 — DIPLOM PWR POLICY WAR

B47
FEIS H.,SEEN FROM E A, THREE INTERNATIONAL EPISODES. EUR+WWI ITALY USA-45 WOR-45 AGRI INT/ORG NAT/G INT/TRADE LEGIT EXEC ATTIT ORD/FREE...POLICY LEAGUE/NAT TOT/POP 20 OIL. PAGE 44 A0908 — EXTR/IND ECO/TAC DIPLOM

B51
US TARIFF COMMISSION,LIST OF PUBLICATIONS OF THE TARIFF COMMISSION (PAMPHLET). USA+45 USA-45 AGRI EXTR/IND INDUS INT/TRADE...STAT 20. PAGE 157 A3207 — BIBLIOG TARIFFS NAT/G ADMIN

B52
UN DEPT. SOC. AFF.,PRELIMINARY REPORT ON THE WORLD SOCIAL SITUATION. ISLAM L/A+17C WOR+45 STRATA AGRI EXTR/IND INDUS INT/ORG SCHOOL ADMIN...GEOG SOC TREND UNESCO WORK FAO 20. PAGE 147 A2998 — R+D HEALTH FOR/AID

B53
NEISSER H.,NATIONAL INCOMES AND INTERNATIONAL TRADE. FRANCE GERMANY SWEDEN UK USA-45 EXTR/IND FINAN INDUS TEC/DEV PRICE BAL/PAY EQUILIB INCOME WEALTH...CHARTS METH 19 CHINJAP. PAGE 108 A2215 — INT/TRADE PRODUC MARKET CON/ANAL

N58
INVESTMENT FUND ECO SOC DEV,FRENCH AFRICA: A DECADE OF PROGRESS 1948-1958 (PAMPHLET). AFR FRANCE EXTR/IND INDUS EDU/PROP HEALTH 20. PAGE 71 A1465 — FOR/AID DIPLOM ECO/UNDEV AGRI

B59
DIEBOLD W. JR.,THE SCHUMAN PLAN: A STUDY IN ECONOMIC COOPERATION, 1950-1959. EUR+WWI FRANCE GERMANY USA+45 EXTR/IND CONSULT DELIB/GP PLAN DIPLOM ECO/TAC INT/TRADE ROUTINE ORD/FREE WEALTH ...METH/CNCPT STAT CONT/OBS INT TIME/SEQ ECSC 20. PAGE 37 A0759 — INT/ORG REGION

B59
HAZLEWOOD A.,THE ECONOMICS OF "UNDER-DEVELOPED" AREAS. WOR+45 DIST/IND EXTR/IND FINAN INDUS MARKET — BIBLIOG/A ECO/UNDEV

PLAN FOR/AID...GEOG 20. PAGE 63 A1302 AGRI INT/TRADE

B60
LEVIN J.V.,THE EXPORT ECONOMIES: THEIR PATTERN OF DEVELOPMENT IN HISTORICAL PERSPECTIVE. BURMA PERU AGRI WORKER COLONIAL COST DEMAND INCOME 20. PAGE 88 A1795 INT/TRADE ECO/UNDEV BAL/PAY EXTR/IND

B60
LISTER L.,EUROPE'S COAL AND STEEL COMMUNITY. FRANCE GERMANY STRUCT ECO/DEV EXTR/IND INDUS MARKET NAT/G DELIB/GP ECO/TAC INT/TRADE EDU/PROP ATTIT RIGID/FLEX ORD/FREE PWR WEALTH...CONCPT STAT TIME/SEQ CHARTS ECSC 20. PAGE 90 A1843 EUR+WWI INT/ORG REGION

B60
PRINCETON U CONFERENCE,CURRENT PROBLEMS IN NORTH AFRICA. ALGERIA LIBYA MOROCCO USA+45 EXTR/IND POL/PAR PROB/SOLV DIPLOM ECO/TAC WAR...ANTHOL 20 TUNIS. PAGE 118 A2412 POLICY ECO/UNDEV NAT/G

B60
US HOUSE COMM. SCI. ASTRONAUT.,OCEAN SCIENCES AND NATIONAL SECURITY. FUT SEA ECO/DEV EXTR/IND INT/ORG NAT/G FORCES ACT/RES TEC/DEV ECO/TAC COERCE WAR BIO/SOC KNOWL PWR...CONCPT RECORD LAB/EXP 20. PAGE 154 A3141 R+D ORD/FREE

S60
OWEN C.F.,"US AND SOVIET RELATIONS WITH UNDERDEVELOPED COUNTRIES: LATIN AMERICA-A CASE STUDY." AFR COM L/A+17C USA+45 USSR EXTR/IND MARKET TEC/DEV DIPLOM ECO/TAC NAT/LISM ORD/FREE PWR ...TREND WORK 20. PAGE 112 A2303 ECO/UNDEV DRIVE INT/TRADE

S60
RIVKIN A.,"AFRICAN ECONOMIC DEVELOPMENT: ADVANCED TECHNOLOGY AND THE STAGES OF GROWTH." CULTURE ECO/UNDEV AGRI COM/IND EXTR/IND PLAN ECO/TAC ATTIT DRIVE RIGID/FLEX SKILL WEALTH...MGT SOC GEN/LAWS WORK TOT/POP 20. PAGE 121 A2487 AFR TEC/DEV FOR/AID

B61
INTERNATIONAL BANK RECONST DEV,THE WORLD BANK IN AFRICA: SUMMARY OF ACTIVITIES. AGRI COM/IND DIST/IND EXTR/IND INDUS TAX COST...CHARTS 20. PAGE 71 A1450 FINAN ECO/UNDEV INT/ORG AFR

B61
SCHNAPPER B.,LA POLITIQUE ET LE COMMERCE FRANCAIS DANS LE GOLFE DE GUINEE DE 1838 A 1871. FRANCE GUINEA UK SEA EXTR/IND NAT/G DELIB/GP LEGIS ADMIN ORD/FREE...POLICY GEOG CENSUS CHARTS BIBLIOG 19. PAGE 129 A2636 COLONIAL INT/TRADE DOMIN AFR

B62
COLOMBOS C.J.,THE INTERNATIONAL LAW OF THE SEA. WOR+45 EXTR/IND DIPLOM INT/TRADE TARIFFS AGREE WAR ...TIME/SEQ 20 TREATY. PAGE 28 A0570 INT/LAW SEA JURID ADJUD

B62
FAO,FOOD AND AGRICULTURE ORGANIZATION AFRICAN SURVEY. AFR CONGO/BRAZ GHANA STRATA AGRI INT/ORG TEC/DEV FOR/AID INT/TRADE RACE/REL DEMAND EFFICIENCY PRODUC...GEOG 20 UN CONGO/LEOP. PAGE 44 A0898 ECO/TAC WEALTH EXTR/IND ECO/UNDEV

B63
ELLENDER A.J.,A REPORT ON UNITED STATES FOREIGN OPERATIONS IN AFRICA. SOUTH/AFR USA+45 STRATA EXTR/IND FORCES RACE/REL ISOLAT SOVEREIGN...CHARTS 20 NEGRO. PAGE 41 A0840 FOR/AID DIPLOM WEALTH ECO/UNDEV

B64
MYINT H.,THE ECONOMICS OF THE DEVELOPING COUNTRIES. WOR+45 AGRI PLAN COST...POLICY GEOG 20 MONEY. PAGE 107 A2187 ECO/UNDEV INT/TRADE EXTR/IND FINAN

B64
RAMAZANI R.K.,THE MIDDLE EAST AND THE EUROPEAN COMMON MARKET. EUR+WWI ISLAM ECO/DEV EXTR/IND MARKET PROC/MFG INT/ORG NAT/G TEC/DEV ECO/TAC REGION DRIVE WEALTH...STAT CHARTS EEC TOT/POP 20. PAGE 119 A2437 ECO/UNDEV ATTIT INT/TRADE

B64
WITHERELL J.W.,OFFICIAL PUBLICATIONS OF FRENCH EQUATORIAL AFRICA, FRENCH CAMEROONS, AND TOGO, 1946-1958 (PAMPHLET). CAMEROON CHAD FRANCE GABON TOGO LAW ECO/UNDEV EXTR/IND INT/TRADE...GEOG HEAL 20. PAGE 165 A3370 BIBLIOG/A AFR NAT/G ADMIN

S64
ZARTMAN I.W.,"LES RELATIONS ENTRE LA FRANCE ET L'ALGERIA DEPUIS LES ACCORDS D'EVIAN." EUR+WWI FUT ISLAM CULTURE AGRI EXTR/IND FINAN INDUS POL/PAR DIPLOM ECO/TAC FOR/AID PEACE ATTIT DRIVE ALL/VALS ...TIME/SEQ VAL/FREE 20. PAGE 169 A3446 ECO/UNDEV ALGERIA FRANCE

B65
WHITE HOUSE CONFERENCE ON INTERNATIONAL COOPERATION(VOL.II). SPACE WOR+45 EXTR/IND INT/ORG LABOR WORKER NUC/PWR PEACE AGE/Y...CENSUS ANTHOL 20 RESOURCE/N URBAN/RNWL PUB/TRANS. PAGE 3 A0071 R+D CONFER TEC/DEV DIPLOM

B65
JOHNSTON D.M.,THE INTERNATIONAL LAW OF FISHERIES: A FRAMEWORK FOR POLICYORIENTED INQUIRIES. WOR+45 ACT/RES PLAN PROB/SOLV CONTROL SOVEREIGN. PAGE 75 A1527 CONCPT EXTR/IND JURID DIPLOM

B65
LEISS A.C.,APARTHEID AND UNITED NATIONS COLLECTIVE MEASURES. SOUTH/AFR ECO/UNDEV EXTR/IND FORCES WORKER ECO/TAC FOR/AID INT/TRADE WEALTH...TREND CHARTS 20 UN NEGRO. PAGE 86 A1770 DISCRIM RACE/REL STRATA DIPLOM

B66
SUPPLEMENTAL FOREIGN ASSISTANCE FISCAL YEAR 1966: VIETNAM. CHINA/COM COM S/ASIA USA+45 VIETNAM EXTR/IND FINAN DIPLOM TAX GUERRILLA HABITAT ORD/FREE...STAT CHARTS 20 SENATE PRESIDENT. PAGE 4 A0077 CONFER LEGIS WAR FOR/AID

B66
KEENLEYSIDE H.L.,INTERNATIONAL AID: A SUMMARY. AFR INDIA S/ASIA UK STRATA EXTR/IND TEC/DEV ADMIN RACE/REL DEMAND NAT/LISM WEALTH...TREND CHINJAP. PAGE 77 A1575 ECO/UNDEV FOR/AID DIPLOM TASK

B66
O'CONNER A.M.,AN ECONOMIC GEOGRAPHY OF EAST AFRICA. AFR TANZANIA UGANDA AGRI WORKER INT/TRADE COLONIAL GOV/REL...CHARTS METH/COMP 20 AFRICA/E. PAGE 111 A2269 ECO/UNDEV EXTR/IND GEOG HABITAT

B67
LANDEN R.G.,OMAN SINCE 1856: DISRUPTIVE MODERNIZATION IN A TRADITIONAL ARAB SOCIETY. UK DIST/IND EXTR/IND SECT DIPLOM INT/TRADE...SOC LING CHARTS BIBLIOG 19/20. PAGE 84 A1714 ISLAM CULTURE ECO/UNDEV NAT/G

B67
PIPER D.C.,THE INTERNATIONAL LAW OF THE GREAT LAKES. CANADA EXTR/IND MUNIC LICENSE ARMS/CONT CRIME...GEOG 19/20. PAGE 116 A2381 CONCPT DIPLOM INT/LAW

B67
SACHS M.Y.,THE WORLDMARK ENCYCLOPEDIA OF THE NATIONS (5 VOLS.). ELITES SOCIETY STRATA ECO/DEV ECO/UNDEV AGRI EXTR/IND FINAN LABOR LOC/G NAT/G POL/PAR SECT INT/TRADE SOVEREIGN...SOC 20. PAGE 126 A2585 WOR+45 INT/ORG BAL/PWR

S67
HULL E.W.S.,"THE POLITICAL OCEAN." FUT UNIV WOR+45 EXTR/IND R+D VOL/ASSN PLAN BAL/PWR ECO/TAC PEACE WEALTH 20 UN. PAGE 69 A1414 DIPLOM ECO/UNDEV INT/ORG INT/LAW

S67
OLIVIER G.,"ASPECTS JURIDIQUES DE L'ADOPTION DU TRAITE CECA A LA CRISE CHARBONNIERE (SUITE ET FIN)" LAW DIST/IND PLAN DIPLOM RATION PRICE ADMIN COST DEMAND...POLICY CON/ANAL ECSC TREATY. PAGE 112 A2288 INT/TRADE INT/ORG EXTR/IND CONSTN

EXTRACTIVE INDUSTRY....SEE EXTR/IND

F

FAA....U.S. FEDERAL AVIATION AGENCY

B65
THAYER F.C. JR.,AIR TRANSPORT POLICY AND NATIONAL SECURITY: A POLITICAL, ECONOMIC, AND MILITARY ANALYSIS. DIST/IND OP/RES PLAN TEC/DEV DIPLOM DETER WAR COST EFFICIENCY...POLICY BIBLIOG 20 DEPT/DEFEN FAA CAB. PAGE 142 A2908 AIR FORCES CIVMIL/REL ORD/FREE

FABAR R. A0880

FABER K. A0881

FABIAN....FABIANS: MEMBERS AND/OR SUPPORTERS OF FABIAN SOCIETY

FABREGA J. A0882

FACE/GP....ACQUAINTANCE GROUP

B20
VINOGRADOFF P.,OUTLINES OF HISTORICAL JURISPRUDENCE (2 VOLS.). GREECE MEDIT-7 LAW CONSTN FACE/GP FAM KIN MUNIC CRIME OWN...INT/LAW IDEA/COMP BIBLIOG. PAGE 159 A3241 JURID METH

B45
RANSHOFFEN-WERTHEIMER EF,THE INTERNATIONAL SECRETARIAT: A GREAT EXPERIMENT IN INTERNATIONAL ADMINISTRATION. EUR+WWI FUT CONSTN FACE/GP CONSULT DELIB/GP ACT/RES ADMIN ROUTINE PEACE ORD/FREE...MGT RECORD ORG/CHARTS LEAGUE/NAT WORK 20. PAGE 119 A2442 INT/ORG EXEC

S51
ICHHEISER G.,"MISUNDERSTANDING IN INTERNATIONAL RELATIONS." UNIV SOCIETY FACE/GP INT/ORG SECT ATTIT PERSON RIGID/FLEX LOVE RESPECT...RELATIV PSY SOC CONCPT MYTH SOC/EXP GEN/LAWS. PAGE 70 A1431 PERCEPT STERTYP NAT/LISM DIPLOM

B56
GEORGE A.L.,WOODROW WILSON AND COLONEL HOUSE. WOR-45 CONSTN FACE/GP INT/ORG NAT/G POL/PAR CONSULT LEGIT EXEC COERCE CHOOSE ATTIT DRIVE PERSON MORAL ORD/FREE PWR RESPECT...POLICY MGT PSY OBS RECORD INT LEAGUE/NAT. PAGE 52 A1060 USA-45 BIOG DIPLOM

S57
SCHELLING T.C.,"BARGAINING COMMUNICATION, AND LIMITED WAR." UNIV WOR+45 FACE/GP INT/ORG NAT/G ROUTINE DECISION

FORCES ACT/RES WAR PERCEPT ALL/VALS...PSY OBS PROJ/TEST CHARTS HYPO/EXP GEN/LAWS TOT/POP 20. PAGE 128 A2622

L58
HAVILAND H.F.,"FOREIGN AID AND THE POLICY PROCESS: 1957." USA+45 FACE/GP POL/PAR VOL/ASSN CHIEF DELIB/GP ACT/RES LEGIT EXEC GOV/REL ATTIT DRIVE PWR ...POLICY TESTS CONGRESS 20. PAGE 63 A1291
LEGIS PLAN FOR/AID

B61
FRIEDMANN W.G.,JOINT INTERNATIONAL BUSINESS VENTURES. ASIA ISLAM L/A+17C ECO/DEV DIST/IND FINAN PROC/MFG FACE/GP LG/CO NAT/G VOL/ASSN CONSULT EX/STRUC PLAN ADMIN ROUTINE WEALTH...OLD/LIB WORK 20. PAGE 49 A1004
ECO/UNDEV INT/TRADE

B62
BELL C.,NEGOTIATION FROM STRENGTH. WOR+45 FACE/GP INT/ORG DELIB/GP FORCES PLAN DOMIN COERCE NUC/PWR PEACE DRIVE PWR...POLICY LOG OBS RECORD INT SAMP TREND COLD/WAR 20. PAGE 13 A0255
NAT/G CONCPT DIPLOM

B64
CZERNIN F.,VERSAILLES - 1919. EUR+WWI USA-45 FACE/GP POL/PAR VOL/ASSN DELIB/GP TOP/EX CREATE BAL/PWR DIPLOM LEGIT NAT/LISM PEACE ATTIT RIGID/FLEX ORD/FREE PWR...CON/ANAL LEAGUE/NAT 20 VERSAILLES. PAGE 33 A0671
INT/ORG STRUCT

B64
SULLIVAN G.,THE STORY OF THE PEACE CORPS. USA+45 WOR+45 INTELL FACE/GP NAT/G SCHOOL VOL/ASSN CONSULT EX/STRUC PLAN EDU/PROP ADMIN ATTIT DRIVE ALL/VALS ...POLICY HEAL SOC CONCPT INT QU BIOG TREND SOC/EXP WORK. PAGE 140 A2861
INT/ORG ECO/UNDEV FOR/AID PEACE

S64
COCHRANE J.D.,"US ATTITUDES TOWARD CENTRAL-AMERICAN INTEGRATION." L/A+17C USA+45 ECO/UNDEV FACE/GP VOL/ASSN DELIB/GP ECO/TAC INT/TRADE EDU/PROP RIGID/FLEX ORD/FREE WEALTH...TIME/SEQ TOT/POP 20. PAGE 27 A0555
NAT/G ATTIT REGION

S64
RUBIN R.,"THE UN CORRESPONDENT." WOR+45 FACE/GP PROF/ORG EDU/PROP ROUTINE PERCEPT KNOWL...RECORD STAND/INT QU UN WORK TOT/POP VAL/FREE 20. PAGE 125 A2560
INT/ORG ATTIT DIPLOM

S65
FALK R.A.,"INTERNATIONAL LEGAL ORDER." USA+45 INTELL FACE/GP INT/ORG LEGIT KNOWL...CONCPT METH/CNCPT STYLE RECORD GEN/METH 20. PAGE 44 A0890
ATTIT GEN/LAWS INT/LAW

FACTION....FACTION

FACTOR ANALYSIS....SEE CON/ANAL

FAGG J.E. A0883

FAHS C.B. A0884

FAIR/LABOR....FAIR LABOR STANDARD ACT

FAIRBANKS J. A0356,A0886

FAIRCHILD B. A0585

FAIRNESS, JUSTICE....SEE VALUES INDEX

FALANGE....FALANGE PARTY (SPAIN)

FALK I. A1113

FALK R.A. A0887,A0888,A0889,A0890,A0891

FALK S.L. A0892

FALKLAND/I....FALKLAND ISLANDS

FALKOWSKI M. A0893

FALL B.B. A0894,A0895

FAM....FAMILY

B02
MOREL E.D.,AFFAIRS OF WEST AFRICA. UK FINAN INDUS FAM KIN SECT CHIEF WORKER DIPLOM RACE/REL LITERACY HEALTH...CHARTS 18/20 AFRICA/W NEGRO. PAGE 104 A2129
COLONIAL ADMIN AFR

N19
HAUSER P.M.,WORLD POPULATION PROBLEMS (PAMPHLET). USA+45 WOR+45 ECO/DEV ECO/UNDEV FAM ACT/RES PLAN PROB/SOLV FOR/AID GIVE EATING...CHARTS 20 BIRTH/CON RESOURCE/N. PAGE 63 A1289
CONTROL CENSUS ATTIT PREDICT

N19
NATIONAL ACADEMY OF SCIENCES,THE GROWTH OF WORLD POPULATION: ANALYSIS OF THE PROBLEMS AND RECOMMENDATIONS FOR RESEARCH AND TRAINING (PAMPHLET). WOR+45 CULTURE ECO/UNDEV EDU/PROP MARRIAGE AGE HEALTH...ANTHOL 20 BIRTH/CON. PAGE 107 A2199
CENSUS PLAN FAM INT/ORG

B20
VINOGRADOFF P.,OUTLINES OF HISTORICAL JURISPRUDENCE (2 VOLS.). GREECE MEDIT-7 LAW CONSTN FACE/GP FAM KIN MUNIC CRIME OWN...INT/LAW IDEA/COMP BIBLIOG. PAGE 159 A3241
JURID METH

B24
NAVILLE A.,LIBERTE, EGALITE, SOLIDARITE: ESSAIS D'ANALYSE. STRATA FAM VOL/ASSN INT/TRADE GP/REL MORAL MARXISM SOCISM...PSY TREATY. PAGE 107 A2205
ORD/FREE SOC IDEA/COMP DIPLOM

B41
KEESING F.M.,THE SOUTH SEAS IN THE MODERN WORLD. INDONESIA STRUCT FAM SECT EDU/PROP LEAD INCOME WEALTH...HEAL SOC 20. PAGE 77 A1577
CULTURE ECO/UNDEV GOV/COMP DIPLOM

B52
SCHUMAN F.,THE COMMONWEALTH OF MAN. WOR+45 WOR-45 LAW CULTURE ELITES SOCIETY FAM INT/ORG NAT/G VOL/ASSN TOP/EX PLAN BAL/PWR LEGIT ATTIT DISPL DRIVE...POLICY MYTH TREND TOT/POP ILO OEEC 20. PAGE 129 A2649
CONCPT GEN/LAWS

B53
MURPHY G.,IN THE MINDS OF MEN: THE STUDY OF HUMAN BEHAVIOR AND SOCIAL TENSIONS IN INDIA. FUT S/ASIA FAM INT/ORG NAT/G DIPLOM EDU/PROP GP/REL ATTIT RIGID/FLEX ALL/VALS...SOC QU UNESCO 20. PAGE 106 A2176
SECT STRATA INDIA

B54
COUDENHOVE-KALERGI,AN IDEA CONQUERS THE WORLD. EUR+WWI MOD/EUR USA-45 CONSTN FAM CREATE EDU/PROP ATTIT PERSON KNOWL...CONCPT SELF/OBS TIME/SEQ. PAGE 31 A0635
INT/ORG BIOG DIPLOM

B55
UN ECONOMIC AND SOCIAL COUNCIL,BIBLIOGRAPHY OF PUBLICATIONS OF THE UN AND SPECIALIZED AGENCIES IN THE SOCIAL WELFARE FIELD, 1946-1952. WOR+45 FAM INT/ORG MUNIC ACT/RES PLAN PROB/SOLV EDU/PROP AGE/C AGE/Y HABITAT...HEAL UN. PAGE 147 A3000
BIBLIOG/A SOC/WK ADMIN WEALTH

C58
BLANCHARD W.,"THAILAND." THAILAND CULTURE AGRI FINAN INDUS FAM LABOR INT/TRADE ATTIT...GEOG HEAL SOC BIBLIOG 20. PAGE 15 A0307
NAT/G DIPLOM ECO/UNDEV S/ASIA

B59
VORSPAN A.,JUSTICE AND JUDAISM. FAM DIPLOM ECO/TAC EDU/PROP CRIME RACE/REL MARRIAGE ANOMIE ATTIT ORD/FREE...POLICY 20 UN. PAGE 160 A3254
SECT CULTURE ACT/RES GP/REL

B60
HAMADY S.,TEMPERAMENT AND CHARACTER OF THE ARABS. FAM NAT/G SECT DIPLOM NAT/LISM...POLICY 20 ARABS. PAGE 61 A1244
NAT/COMP PERSON CULTURE ISLAM

B60
VOGT W.,PEOPLE: CHALLENGE TO SURVIVAL. WOR+45 ECO/DEV ECO/UNDEV FAM INT/ORG NAT/G PLAN PROB/SOLV FOR/AID GIVE EATING 20 BIRTH/CON. PAGE 159 A3247
CENSUS CONTROL ATTIT TEC/DEV

C60
FITZSIMMONS T.,"USSR: ITS PEOPLE, ITS SOCIETY, ITS CULTURE." USSR FAM SECT DIPLOM EDU/PROP ADMIN RACE/REL ATTIT...POLICY CHARTS BIBLIOG 20. PAGE 46 A0944
CULTURE STRUCT SOCIETY COM

L61
LEVINE R.A.,"THE ANTHROPOLOGY OF CONFLICT." FUT CULTURE INTELL FAM INT/ORG LG/CO SML/CO ATTIT KNOWL ...METH/CNCPT VAL/FREE 20. PAGE 88 A1796
SOCIETY ACT/RES

B62
SELOSOEMARDJAN O.,SOCIAL CHANGES IN JOGJAKARTA. INDONESIA NETHERLAND ELITES STRATA STRUCT FAM POL/PAR CREATE DIPLOM INT/TRADE EDU/PROP ADMIN GOV/REL...SOC 20 JAVA CHINJAP. PAGE 131 A2683
ECO/UNDEV CULTURE REV COLONIAL

B64
BLANCHARD C.H.,KOREAN WAR BIBLIOGRAPHY. KOREA FAM BAL/PWR RATION MURDER WEAPON MARXISM...CHARTS 20. PAGE 15 A0306
BIBLIOG/A WAR DIPLOM FORCES

B64
CEPEDE M.,POPULATION AND FOOD. USA+45 STRUCT ECO/UNDEV FAM PLAN TEC/DEV FOR/AID CONTROL...CATH SOC TREND 19/20. PAGE 25 A0513
FUT GEOG AGRI CENSUS

B64
HALPERN J.M.,GOVERNMENT, POLITICS, AND SOCIAL STRUCTURE IN LAOS. LAOS CULTURE SOCIETY STRATA STRUCT FAM DIPLOM DOMIN MARXISM...INT GOV/COMP WORSHIP SOC/INTEG 20. PAGE 60 A1242
NAT/G SOC LOC/G

B64
SAKAI R.K.,STUDIES ON ASIA, 1964. ASIA CHINA/COM ISRAEL MALAYSIA S/ASIA USA+45 USSR ECO/UNDEV FAM POL/PAR SECT CONSULT NAT/LISM...POLICY SOC 20 CHINJAP. PAGE 126 A2588
PWR DIPLOM

S64
TOUVAL S.,"THE SOMALI REPUBLIC." AFR ISLAM SOMALIA FAM KIN NAT/G CREATE FOR/AID LEGIT ATTIT ALL/VALS ...RECORD TREND 20. PAGE 144 A2954 — ECO/UNDEV RIGID/FLEX

B65
FANON F.,STUDIES IN A DYING COLONIALISM. ALGERIA FRANCE STRATA FAM DIPLOM DOMIN WAR RACE/REL DISCRIM HEALTH 20. PAGE 44 A0897 — NAT/LISM COLONIAL REV SOVEREIGN

B66
SZLADITS C.,A BIBLIOGRAPHY ON FOREIGN AND COMPARATIVE LAW (SUPPLEMENT 1964). FINAN FAM LABOR LG/CO LEGIS JUDGE ADMIN CRIME...CRIMLGY 20. PAGE 141 A2878 — BIBLIOG/A CT/SYS INT/LAW

B66
UN ECAFE,ADMINISTRATIVE ASPECTS OF FAMILY PLANNING PROGRAMMES (PAMPHLET). ASIA THAILAND WOR+45 VOL/ASSN PROB/SOLV BUDGET FOR/AID EDU/PROP CONFER CONTROL GOV/REL TIME 20 UN BIRTH/CON. PAGE 147 A2999 — PLAN CENSUS FAM ADMIN

B96
SMITH A.,LECTURES ON JUSTICE, POLICE, REVENUE AND ARMS (1763). UK LAW FAM FORCES TARIFFS AGREE COERCE INCOME OWN WEALTH LAISSEZ...GEN/LAWS 17/18. PAGE 134 A2743 — DIPLOM JURID OLD/LIB TAX

FAMILY....SEE FAM

FAMINE....SEE AGRI, HEALTH

FANI-KAYODE R. A0896

FANON F. A0897

FAO A0898

FAO....FOOD AND AGRICULTURE ORGANIZATION; SEE ALSO UN, INT/ORG

S42
SHOTWELL J.,"AFTER THE WAR." COM EUR+WWI USA+45 USA-45 NAT/G DIPLOM INT/TRADE ARMS/CONT SOVEREIGN ...CONCPT LEAGUE/NAT TOT/POP FAO 20. PAGE 132 A2707 — FUT INT/ORG PEACE

B51
WHITE L.C.,INTERNATIONAL NON-GOVERNMENTAL ORGANIZATIONS. AFR ASIA COM EUR+WWI USA+45 WOR+45 INT/ORG DIPLOM INT/TRADE ALL/VALS...HUM FAO ILO EEC 20. PAGE 164 A3337 — VOL/ASSN CONSULT

B52
UN DEPT. SOC. AFF.,PRELIMINARY REPORT ON THE WORLD SOCIAL SITUATION. ISLAM L/A+17C WOR+45 STRATA AGRI EXTR/IND INDUS INT/ORG SCHOOL ADMIN...GEOG SOC TREND UNESCO WORK FAO 20. PAGE 147 A2998 — R+D HEALTH FOR/AID

B55
COMM. STUDY ORGAN. PEACE,REPORTS. WOR-45 ECO/DEV ECO/UNDEV VOL/ASSN CONSULT FORCES PLAN TEC/DEV DOMIN EDU/PROP NUC/PWR ATTIT PWR WEALTH...JURID STERTYP FAO ILO 20 UN. PAGE 28 A0579 — WOR+45 INT/ORG ARMS/CONT

B56
SOHN L.B.,BASIC DOCUMENTS OF THE UNITED NATIONS. WOR+45 LAW INT/ORG LEGIT EXEC ROUTINE CHOOSE PWR ...JURID CONCPT GEN/LAWS ANTHOL UN TOT/POP OAS FAO ILO 20. PAGE 135 A2761 — DELIB/GP CONSTN

S59
HARVEY M.F.,"THE PALESTINE REFUGEE PROBLEM: ELEMENTS OF A SOLUTION." ISLAM LAW INT/ORG DELIB/GP TOP/EX ECO/TAC ROUTINE DRIVE HEALTH LOVE ORD/FREE PWR WEALTH...MAJORIT FAO 20. PAGE 62 A1283 — ACT/RES LEGIT PEACE ISRAEL

B62
DALLIN A.,THE SOVIET UNION AT THE UNITED NATIONS: AN INQUIRY INTO SOVIET MOTIVES AND OBJECTIVES. ACT/RES EDU/PROP LEGIT ATTIT KNOWL PWR...POLICY RECORD HIST/WRIT TIME/SEQ TREND ORG/CHARTS GEN/METH COLD/WAR FAO 20 UN. PAGE 33 A0675 — COM INT/ORG USSR

B62
HOFFMAN P.,WORLD WITHOUT WANT. FUT WOR+45 ECO/UNDEV INT/ORG HEALTH KNOWL...TREND TOT/POP FAO 20. PAGE 66 A1353 — CONCPT POLICY FOR/AID

S62
BELSHAW C.,"TRAINING AND RECRUITMENT: SOME PRINCIPLES OF INTERNATIONAL AID." FUT WOR+45 SOCIETY INT/ORG NAT/G CREATE PLAN TEC/DEV ECO/TAC FOR/AID EDU/PROP ATTIT PERCEPT...HUM UN FAO ILO UNESCO 20. PAGE 13 A0263 — VOL/ASSN ECO/UNDEV

B67
JOHNSON D.G.,THE STRUGGLE AGAINST WORLD HUNGER (HEADLINE SERIES, NO. 184) (PAMPHLET). PLAN TEC/DEV FOR/AID...CHARTS 20 FAO MEXIC/AMER. PAGE 74 A1520 — AGRI PROB/SOLV ECO/UNDEV HEALTH

FARIES J.C. A0899

FARM/BUR....FARM BUREAU

FARMING....SEE AGRI

FARQUHAR D.M. A0900

FARWELL G. A0901

FASCISM....FASCISM; SEE ALSO TOTALISM, FASCIST

C28
SCHNEIDER H.W.,"MAKING THE FASCIST STATE." ITALY CULTURE LABOR DIPLOM REV WAR NAT/LISM TOTALISM ATTIT DRIVE SOCISM...BIBLIOG PARLIAMENT 20. PAGE 129 A2638 — FASCISM POLICY POL/PAR

B35
SIMONDS F.H.,THE GREAT POWERS IN WORLD POLITICS. FRANCE GERMANY UK WOR-45 INT/ORG NAT/G ARMS/CONT PEACE FASCISM...POLICY GEOG 20 DEPRESSION NAZI. PAGE 133 A2718 — DIPLOM WEALTH WAR

B37
BORGESE G.A.,GOLIATH: THE MARCH OF FASCISM. GERMANY ITALY LAW POL/PAR SECT DIPLOM SOCISM...JURID MYTH 20 DANTE MACHIAVELL MUSSOLIN/B. PAGE 17 A0341 — POLICY NAT/LISM FASCISM NAT/G

B37
KOHN H.,FORCE OR REASON; ISSUES OF THE TWENTIETH CENTURY. WOR+45 NAT/G DIPLOM WAR DRIVE ORD/FREE ALL/IDEOS FASCISM PLURISM...POLICY IDEA/COMP 20. PAGE 81 A1660 — COERCE DOMIN RATIONAL COLONIAL

B39
KOHN H.,REVOLUTIONS AND DICTATORSHIPS. COM EUR+WWI ISLAM MOD/EUR NAT/G CHIEF FORCES WAR CIVMIL/REL PWR MARXISM 18/20. PAGE 81 A1661 — NAT/LISM TOTALISM REV FASCISM

B39
SPEIER H.,WAR IN OUR TIME. WOR-45 AGRI FINAN FORCES TEC/DEV BAL/PWR EDU/PROP WEAPON PEACE PWR...ANTHOL 20. PAGE 136 A2779 — FASCISM WAR DIPLOM NAT/G

B42
BORNSTEIN J.,ACTION AGAINST THE ENEMY'S MIND. EUR+WWI GERMANY USA-45 DIPLOM DOMIN PRESS LEAD GP/REL DISCRIM PERCEPT FASCISM MARXISM 20 JEWS NAZI ANTI/SEMIT. PAGE 17 A0343 — EDU/PROP PSY WAR CONTROL

B43
SERENI A.P.,THE ITALIAN CONCEPTION OF INTERNATIONAL LAW. EUR+WWI MOD/EUR INT/ORG NAT/G DOMIN COERCE ORD/FREE FASCISM...OBS/ENVIR TREND 20. PAGE 131 A2686 — LAW TIME/SEQ INT/LAW ITALY

B43
SULZBACH W.,NATIONAL CONSCIOUSNESS. FUT WOR-45 INT/ORG PEACE MORAL FASCISM MARXISM...MAJORIT TREND WORSHIP 19/20 LEAGUE/NAT INTERVENT WWI. PAGE 140 A2862 — NAT/LISM NAT/G DIPLOM WAR

B43
US DEPARTMENT OF STATE,NATIONAL SOCIALISM; BASIC PRINCIPLES, THEIR APPLICATION BY THE NAZI PARTY'S FOREIGN ORGANIZATION... GERMANY WOR-45 ECO/DEV LOC/G POL/PAR FORCES DIPLOM DOMIN COLONIAL ARMS/CONT COERCE NAT/LISM PWR 20 NAZI. PAGE 151 A3081 — FASCISM SOCISM NAT/G TOTALISM

B46
BLUM L.,FOR ALL MANKIND (TRANS. BY W. PICKLES). FRANCE GERMANY USSR LAW SOCIETY STRUCT POL/PAR WORKER DIPLOM DOMIN CHOOSE ORD/FREE FASCISM 20. PAGE 16 A0323 — POPULISM SOCIALIST NAT/G WAR

B46
STURZO D.L.,NATIONALISM AND INTERNATIONALISM. WOR-45 INT/ORG LABOR NAT/G POL/PAR TOTALISM MORAL ORD/FREE FASCISM...MAJORIT 19/20 UN LEAGUE/NAT MUSSOLIN/B. PAGE 140 A2857 — NAT/LISM DIPLOM WAR PEACE

B52
GURLAND A.R.L.,POLITICAL SCIENCE IN WESTERN GERMANY: THOUGHTS AND WRITINGS, 1950-1952 (PAMPHLET). EUR+WWI GERMANY/W ELITES SOCIETY NAT/G NAT/LISM TOTALISM 20. PAGE 58 A1196 — BIBLIOG/A DIPLOM CIVMIL/REL FASCISM

B53
CRAIG G.A.,THE DIPLOMATS 1919-1939. WAR PEACE ATTIT ...POLICY BIOG 20. PAGE 32 A0651 — DIPLOM ELITES FASCISM

B54
SALVEMINI G.,PRELUDE TO WORLD WAR II. ITALY MOD/EUR INT/ORG BAL/PWR EDU/PROP CONTROL TOTALISM...TREND NAT/COMP BIBLIOG 19 HITLER/A LEAGUE/NAT MUSSOLIN/B. PAGE 127 A2597 — WAR FASCISM LEAD PWR

B55
ALFIERI D.,DICTATORS FACE TO FACE. NAT/G TOP/EX DIPLOM EXEC COERCE ORD/FREE FASCISM...POLICY OBS 20 HITLER/A MUSSOLIN/B. PAGE 6 A0116 — WAR CHIEF TOTALISM PERS/REL

B55
KOHN H.,NATIONALISM: ITS MEANING AND HISTORY. GP/REL INGP/REL ATTIT...CONCPT NAT/COMP 16/20 MACHIAVELL. PAGE 81 A1662 — NAT/LISM DIPLOM FASCISM REV

B55
SEMJONOW J.M.,DIE FASCHISTISCHE GEOPOLITIK IM DIENSTE DES AMERIKANISCHEN IMPERIALISMUS. USA+45 USA-45 CAP/ISM PEACE ORD/FREE MARXISM SOCISM — DIPLOM COERCE FASCISM

...POLICY GEOG 20. PAGE 131 A2684
WAR

B57
FRASER L.,PROPAGANDA. GERMANY USSR WOR+45 WOR-45 NAT/G POL/PAR CONTROL FEEDBACK LOBBY CROWD WAR CONSEN NAT/LISM 20. PAGE 48 A0988
EDU/PROP FASCISM MARXISM DIPLOM

S58
ROTHFELS H.,"THE GERMAN RESISTANCE IN ITS INTERNATIONAL ASPECTS" (BMR)" EUR+WWI GERMANY UNIV CHIEF DIPLOM WAR NAT/LISM ATTIT...POLICY 20 HITLER/A NAZI. PAGE 124 A2548
VOL/ASSN MORAL FASCISM CIVMIL/REL

B61
DELZELL C.F.,MUSSOLINI'S ENEMIES - THE ITALIAN ANTI-FASCIST RESISTANCE. ITALY DIPLOM PRESS DETER WAR TOTALISM ORD/FREE MARXISM 20. PAGE 36 A0730
FASCISM GP/REL POL/PAR REV

B61
FLEMING D.F.,THE COLD WAR AND ITS ORIGINS: 1917-1950 (VOL. I). ASIA USSR WOR+45 WOR-45 TEC/DEV FOR/AID NUC/PWR REV WAR PEACE FASCISM...T 20 COLD/WAR NATO BERLIN/BLO. PAGE 46 A0947
DIPLOM MARXISM BAL/PWR

B61
FUCHS G.,GEGEN HITLER UND HENLEIN. CZECHOSLVK GERMANY DIPLOM CHOOSE GP/REL TOTALISM SOVEREIGN 20 HITLER/A. PAGE 50 A1013
FASCISM WORKER POL/PAR NAT/LISM

B61
SCHONBRUNN G.,WELTKRIEGE UND REVOLUTIONEN 1914-1945. USSR DIPLOM TOTALISM ORD/FREE 20 TREATY WWI NAZI. PAGE 129 A2643
WAR REV FASCISM SOCISM

B61
TETENS T.H.,THE NEW GERMANY AND THE OLD NAZIS. EUR+WWI GERMANY/W USA+45 NAT/G CRIME CHOOSE RACE/REL TOTALISM AGE/Y ATTIT 20 JEWS NAZI ADENAUER/K. PAGE 142 A2905
FASCISM DIPLOM FOR/AID POL/PAR

B62
BLANSHARD P.,FREEDOM AND CATHOLIC POWER IN SPAIN AND PORTUGAL: AN AMERICAN INTERPRETATION. AFR PORTUGAL SPAIN USA+45 LAW LABOR DIPLOM EDU/PROP DISCRIM ISOLAT TOTALISM 20 CHURCH/STA. PAGE 15 A0309
GP/REL FASCISM CATHISM PWR

B62
KENT G.O.,A CATALOG OF FILES AND MICROFILMS OF THE GERMAN FOREIGN MINISTRY ARCHIVES, 1920-1945 (3 VOLS.). GERMANY WOR-45 WRITING WAR 20. PAGE 78 A1595
BIBLIOG NAT/G DIPLOM FASCISM

B62
SCOTT W.E.,ALLIANCE AGAINST HITLER. EUR+WWI FRANCE GERMANY USSR BAL/PWR LEAD TOTALISM PWR FASCISM MARXISM...POLICY BIBLIOG 20 HITLER/A. PAGE 131 A2675
WAR DIPLOM FORCES

B63
GILBERT M.,THE APPEASERS. COM GERMANY UK PLAN ECO/TAC COLONIAL CONTROL EXEC ORD/FREE PWR FASCISM 20 PARLIAMENT. PAGE 52 A1068
DIPLOM WAR POLICY DECISION

B64
GIBSON J.S.,IDEOLOGY AND WORLD AFFAIRS. FUT WOR+45 ECO/UNDEV NAT/G CAP/ISM TOTALISM ORD/FREE FASCISM MARXISM 20. PAGE 52 A1067
ALL/IDEOS DIPLOM POLICY IDEA/COMP

B64
HALPERIN S.W.,MUSSOLINI AND ITALIAN FASCISM. ITALY NAT/G POL/PAR SECT ECO/TAC LEAD PWR SOCISM...POLICY 20 MUSSOLIN/B. PAGE 60 A1241
FASCISM NAT/LISM EDU/PROP CHIEF

B65
BRIDGMAN J.,GERMAN AFRICA: A SELECT ANNOTATED BIBLIOGRAPHY. AFR AGRI DIPLOM REPAR WAR FASCISM 20. PAGE 18 A0374
BIBLIOG/A COLONIAL NAT/G EDU/PROP

B65
COX R.H.,THE STATE IN INTERNATIONAL RELATIONS. INT/ORG DIPLOM REV WAR PEACE MARXISM...CONCPT GOV/COMP. PAGE 32 A0647
SOVEREIGN NAT/G FASCISM ORD/FREE

B65
DOMENACH J.M.,LA PROPAGANDE POLITIQUE. COM/IND INT/ORG POL/PAR DOMIN RIGID/FLEX FASCISM MARXISM ...PSY 20. PAGE 38 A0770
ATTIT EDU/PROP TEC/DEV MYTH

B65
GILBERT M.,THE EUROPEAN POWERS 1900-45. EUR+WWI ITALY MOD/EUR USSR REV WAR PWR ALL/IDEOS FASCISM ...AUD/VIS CHARTS BIBLIOG 20. PAGE 52 A1069
DIPLOM NAT/G POLICY BAL/PWR

B65
HART B.H.L.,THE MEMOIRS OF CAPTAIN LIDDELL HART (VOL. I). UK NAT/G PLAN TEC/DEV DIPLOM ADMIN WEAPON GOV/REL PERS/REL ATTIT PWR FASCISM...POLICY 20. PAGE 62 A1274
FORCES BIOG LEAD WAR

B65
ROSENBERG A.,DEMOCRACY AND SOCIALISM. COM EUR+WWI FRANCE MOD/EUR STRUCT INT/ORG NAT/G POL/PAR TOP/EX EDU/PROP COERCE PERSON PWR FASCISM MARXISM...CONCPT TIME/SEQ MARX/KARL 19/20. PAGE 124 A2535
ATTIT

B65
SMITH A.L. JR.,THE DEUTSCHTUM OF NAZI GERMANY AND THE UNITED STATES. GERMANY USA-45 DIPLOM ATTIT FASCISM...BIBLIOG 20 MIGRATION NAZI. PAGE 134 A2744
INGP/REL NAT/LISM STRANGE DELIB/GP

B66
GILBERT M.,THE ROOTS OF APPEASEMENT. EUR+WWI GERMANY UK MUNIC BAL/PWR FASCISM...NEW/IDEA 20. PAGE 52 A1070
DIPLOM REPAR PROB/SOLV POLICY

B66
RISTIC D.N.,YUGOSLAVIA'S REVOLUTION OF 1941. EUR+WWI YUGOSLAVIA NAT/G WAR ORD/FREE...RECORD BIBLIOG 20 HITLER/A TREATY. PAGE 121 A2484
REV ATTIT FASCISM DIPLOM

B66
SANDERS R.E.,SPAIN AND THE UNITED NATIONS 1945-1950. SPAIN CHIEF DIPLOM CONFER SANCTION ATTIT ...POLICY 20 UN COLD/WAR. PAGE 127 A2599
INT/ORG FASCISM GP/REL STRANGE

B66
WELCH R.H.W.,THE NEW AMERICANISM, AND OTHER SPEECHES AND ESSAYS. USA+45 ACADEM POL/PAR SCHOOL VOL/ASSN FORCES CAP/ISM TAX REV DISCRIM 20 CIV/RIGHTS COLD/WAR BIRCH/SOC. PAGE 163 A3313
DIPLOM FASCISM MARXISM RACE/REL

B67
THORNE C.,THE APPROACH OF WAR, 1938-1939. EUR+WWI POL/PAR CHIEF FORCES LEAD DRIVE PWR FASCISM ...BIBLIOG/A 20 HITLER/A. PAGE 144 A2936
DIPLOM WAR ELITES

S67
HALL M.,"GERMANY, EAST AND WEST* DANGER AT THE CROSSROADS." GERMANY ELITES CHIEF FORCES DIPLOM ECO/TAC REPAR ARMS/CONT...SOCIALIST 20. PAGE 60 A1227
NAT/LISM ATTIT FASCISM WEAPON

FASCIST....FASCIST

B40
ITALIAN LIBRARY OF INFORMATION: OUTLINE STUDIES (VOL. V). ITALY LIBYA CONTROL...FASCIST 20. PAGE 3 A0052
COLONIAL DIPLOM ECO/TAC POLICY

B43
MICAUD C.A.,THE FRENCH RIGHT AND NAZI GERMANY 1933-1939: A STUDY OF PUBLIC OPINION. GERMANY UK USSR POL/PAR ARMS/CONT COERCE DETER PEACE RIGID/FLEX PWR MARXISM...FASCIST TREND 20 LEAGUE/NAT TREATY. PAGE 101 A2065
DIPLOM AGREE

B54
GERMANY FOREIGN MINISTRY,DOCUMENTS ON GERMAN FOREIGN POLICY 1918-1945, SERIES C (1933-1937) VOLS. I-V. GERMANY MOD/EUR FORCES PLAN ECO/TAC ...FASCIST CHARTS ANTHOL 20. PAGE 52 A1065
NAT/G DIPLOM POLICY

FASHION....SEE ETIQUET

FATEMI N.S. A0902

FATHER/DIV....FATHER DIVINE AND HIS FOLLOWERS

FATOUROS A.A. A0903,A0904

FAWCETT J.E.S. A0905

FBI....U.S. FEDERAL BUREAU OF INVESTIGATION

B66
HOEVELER H.J.,INTERNATIONALE BEKAMPFUNG DES VERBRECHENS. AUSTRIA SWITZERLND WOR+45 INT/ORG CONTROL BIO/SOC...METH/COMP NAT/COMP 20 MAFIA SCOT/YARD FBI. PAGE 66 A1352
CRIMLGY CRIME DIPLOM INT/LAW

FCC....U.S. FEDERAL COMMUNICATIONS COMMISSION

FDA....U.S. FOOD AND DRUG ADMINISTRATION

FDR....FRANKLIN D. ROOSEVELT

FEARS....SEE ANOMIE

FECHNER/GT....GUSTAV THEODOR FECHNER

FED/OPNMKT....FEDERAL OPEN MARKET COMMITTEE

FED/RESERV....U.S. FEDERAL RESERVE SYSTEM (INCLUDES FEDERAL RESERVE BANK)

FEDERAL AVIATION AGENCY....SEE FAA

FEDERAL BUREAU OF INVESTIGATION....SEE FBI

FEDERAL COMMUNICATIONS COMMISSION....SEE FCC

FEDERAL COUNCIL FOR SCIENCE + TECHNOLOGY....SEE FEDSCI/TEC

FEDERAL RESERVE SYSTEM....SEE FED/RESERV

FEDERAL....FEDERALISM

N
MONPIED E.,BIBLIOGRAPHIE FEDERALISTE: ARTICLES ET DOCUMENTS PUBLIES DANS LES PERIODIQUES PARUS EN FRANCE NOV. 1945-OCT. 1950. EUR+WWI WOR+45 ADMIN REGION ATTIT MARXISM PACIFISM 20 EEC. PAGE 103 A2108 — BIBLIOG/A FEDERAL CENTRAL INT/ORG

N19
FREEMAN H.A.,COERCION OF STATES IN FEDERAL UNIONS (PAMPHLET). WOR-45 DIPLOM CONTROL COERCE PEACE ORD/FREE...GOV/COMP METH/COMP NAT/COMP PACIFIST 20. PAGE 49 A0994 — FEDERAL WAR INT/ORG PACIFISM

B38
MATTHEWS M.A.,FEDERALISM: SELECT LIST OF REFERENCES ON FEDERAL GOVERNMENT REGIONALISM...EXAMPLES OF FEDERATIONS (PAMPHLET). WOR-45 CONSTN INT/ORG NAT/G 19/20 OAS LEAGUE/NAT. PAGE 96 A1976 — BIBLIOG/A FEDERAL REGION DIPLOM

B41
SCHWARZENBERGER G.,POWER POLITICS: AN INTRODUCTION TO THE STUDY OF INTERNATIONAL RELATIONS AND POST-WAR PLANNING. INT/ORG FORCES COERCE WAR FEDERAL PEACE MORAL...POLICY CONCPT CON/ANAL BIBLIOG 20. PAGE 130 A2660 — DIPLOM UTOPIA PWR

B41
YOUNG G.,FEDERALISM AND FREEDOM. EUR+WWI MOD/EUR RUSSIA USA-45 WOR-45 SOCIETY STRUCT ECO/DEV INT/ORG EXEC FEDERAL ATTIT PERSON ALL/VALS...OLD/LIB CONCPT OBS TREND LEAGUE/NAT TOT/POP. PAGE 169 A3435 — NAT/G WAR

S48
GROSS L.,"THE PEACE OF WESTPHALIA, 1648-1948." WOR+45 WOR-45 CONSTN BAL/PWR FEDERAL 17/20 TREATY WESTPHALIA. PAGE 57 A1175 — INT/LAW AGREE CONCPT DIPLOM

B50
DE RUSETT A.,STRENGTHENING THE FRAMEWORK OF PEACE. WOR+45 VOL/ASSN FORCES CREATE INSPECT ADJUD CONTROL WAR EQUILIB FEDERAL ORD/FREE 20 UN EUROPE. PAGE 35 A0711 — INT/ORG DIPLOM PEACE METH/COMP

B50
DUCLOS P.,L'EVOLUTION DES RAPPORTS POLITIQUES DEPUIS 1750 (LIBERTE, INTEGRATION, UNITE). LAW INT/ORG FEDERAL TOTALISM ATTIT PWR...MAJORIT BIBLIOG 18/20 PARLIAMENT EUROPE. PAGE 39 A0792 — ORD/FREE DIPLOM NAT/G GOV/COMP

B50
MONPIED E.,BIBLIOGRAPHIE FEDERALISTE: OUVRAGES CHOISIS (VOL. I, MIMEOGRAPHED PAPER). EUR+WWI DIPLOM ADMIN REGION ATTIT PACIFISM SOCISM...INT/LAW 19/20. PAGE 103 A2109 — BIBLIOG/A FEDERAL CENTRAL INT/ORG

N51
MONPIED E.,FEDERALIST BIBLIOGRAPHY: ARTICLES AND DOCUMENTS PUBLISHED IN BRITISH PERIODICALS 1945-1951 (MIMEOGRAPHED). EUR+WWI UK WOR+45 DIPLOM REGION ATTIT SOCISM...INT/LAW 20. PAGE 103 A2110 — BIBLIOG/A INT/ORG FEDERAL CENTRAL

B54
MILLARD E.L.,FREEDOM IN A FEDERAL WORLD. FUT WOR+45 VOL/ASSN TOP/EX LEGIT ROUTINE FEDERAL PEACE ATTIT DISPL ORD/FREE PWR...MAJORIT INT/LAW JURID TREND COLD/WAR 20. PAGE 101 A2073 — INT/ORG CREATE ADJUD BAL/PWR

C54
BOWIE R.R.,"STUDIES IN FEDERALISM." AGRI FINAN LABOR EX/STRUC FORCES LEGIS DIPLOM INT/TRADE ADJUD ...BIBLIOG 20 EEC. PAGE 17 A0357 — FEDERAL EUR+WWI INT/ORG CONSTN

B55
MACMAHON A.W.,FEDERALISM: MATURE AND EMERGENT. EUR+WWI FUT WOR+45 WOR-45 INT/ORG NAT/G REPRESENT FEDERAL...POLICY MGT RECORD TREND GEN/LAWS 20. PAGE 93 A1900 — STRUCT CONCPT

B56
JAMESON J.F.,THE AMERICAN REVOLUTION CONSIDERED AS A SOCIAL MOVEMENT. USA-45 AGRI FINAN SECT INT/TRADE REPRESENT SUFF INGP/REL RACE/REL DISCRIM...MAJORIT 18/19 CHURCH/STA. PAGE 73 A1494 — ORD/FREE REV FEDERAL CONSTN

B58
APPADORAI A.,THE USE OF FORCE IN INTERNATIONAL RELATIONS. WOR+45 CULTURE ECO/UNDEV CAP/ISM ARMS/CONT REV WAR ATTIT PERSON SOVEREIGN MARXISM ...INT/LAW PACIFIST 20 UN INTERVENT THIRD/WRLD COLD/WAR. PAGE 8 A0169 — PEACE FEDERAL INT/ORG

B58
HAAS E.B.,THE UNITING OF EUROPE. EUR+WWI INT/ORG NAT/G POL/PAR TOP/EX ECO/TAC EDU/PROP LEGIT FEDERAL NAT/LISM DRIVE RIGID/FLEX ORD/FREE PWR PLURISM ...POLICY CONCPT INT GEN/LAWS ECSC EEC 20. PAGE 59 A1204 — VOL/ASSN ECO/DEV

C58
GOLAY J.F.,"THE FOUNDING OF THE FEDERAL REPUBLIC OF GERMANY." GERMANY/W CONSTN EX/STRUC DIPLOM ADMIN CHOOSE...DECISION BIBLIOG 20. PAGE 53 A1088 — FEDERAL NAT/G PARL/PROC POL/PAR

B59
BROOKES E.H.,THE COMMONWEALTH TODAY. UK ROMAN/EMP INT/ORG RACE/REL NAT/LISM SOVEREIGN...TREND SOC/INTEG 20. PAGE 19 A0391 — FEDERAL DIPLOM JURID IDEA/COMP

N59
BRITISH COMMONWEALTH REL CONF,EXTRACTS FROM THE PROCEEDINGS OF THE SIXTH UNOFFICIAL CONFERENCE (PAMPHLET). GHANA INDIA RHODESIA UK FINAN FORCES DETER FEDERAL...LING 20 PARLIAMENT. PAGE 19 A0379 — DIPLOM PARL/PROC INT/TRADE ORD/FREE

B60
BYRD E.M. JR.,TREATIES AND EXECUTIVE AGREEMENTS IN THE UNITED STATES: THEIR SEPARATE ROLES AND LIMITATIONS. USA+45 USA-45 EX/STRUC TARIFFS CT/SYS GOV/REL FEDERAL...IDEA/COMP BIBLIOG SUPREME/CT SENATE CONGRESS. PAGE 23 A0461 — CHIEF INT/LAW DIPLOM

B60
QUBAIN F.I.,INSIDE THE ARAB MIND: A BIBLIOGRAPHIC SURVEY OF LITERATURE IN ARABIC ON ARAB NATIONALISM AND UNITY. ISLAM POL/PAR SECT LEAD SOVEREIGN MARXISM SOCISM. PAGE 118 A2425 — BIBLIOG/A FEDERAL DIPLOM NAT/LISM

B61
SCOTT A.M.,POLITICS, USA; CASES ON THE AMERICAN DEMOCRATIC PROCESS. USA+45 CHIEF FORCES DIPLOM LOBBY CHOOSE RACE/REL FEDERAL ATTIT...JURID ANTHOL T 20 PRESIDENT CONGRESS CIVIL/LIB. PAGE 130 A2669 — CT/SYS CONSTN NAT/G PLAN

B62
SPIRO H.J.,POLITICS IN AFRICA: PROSPECTS SOUTH OF THE SAHARA. INT/ORG KIN FORCES LEGIS PROB/SOLV COERCE RACE/REL FEDERAL...TREND CHARTS BIBLIOG 20. PAGE 136 A2790 — AFR NAT/LISM DIPLOM

B62
US DEPARTMENT OF THE ARMY,AFRICA: ITS PROBLEMS AND PROSPECTS. CHINA/COM USSR INT/ORG FOR/AID COLONIAL LEAD FEDERAL DRIVE SOVEREIGN MARXISM...GEOG 20 COLD/WAR. PAGE 152 A3104 — BIBLIOG/A AFR NAT/LISM DIPLOM

S62
DE MADARIAGA S.,"TOWARD THE UNITED STATES OF EUROPE." EUR+WWI PLAN DOMIN FEDERAL ATTIT PWR SOVEREIGN...GEOG TOT/POP 20. PAGE 35 A0707 — FUT INT/ORG

S62
ORBAN M.,"L'EUROPE EN FORMATION ET SES PROBLEMES." EUR+WWI FUT WOR+45 WOR-45 INTELL STRUCT DELIB/GP ACT/RES FEDERAL RIGID/FLEX WEALTH...CONCPT TIME/SEQ OEEC 20. PAGE 112 A2295 — INT/ORG PLAN REGION

S62
SPRINGER H.W.,"FEDERATION IN THE CARIBBEAN: AN ATTEMPT THAT FAILED." L/A+17C ECO/UNDEV INT/ORG POL/PAR PROVS LEGIS CREATE PLAN LEGIT ADMIN FEDERAL ATTIT DRIVE PERSON ORD/FREE PWR...POLICY GEOG PSY CONCPT OBS CARIBBEAN CMN/WLTH 20. PAGE 136 A2791 — VOL/ASSN NAT/G REGION

B63
MANSERGH N.,DOCUMENTS AND SPEECHES ON COMMONWEALTH AFFAIRS 1952-1962. CANADA INDIA PAKISTAN UK CONSTN FORCES ECO/TAC EDU/PROP COLONIAL DETER WAR ORD/FREE SOVEREIGN...POLICY 20 AUSTRAL. PAGE 94 A1932 — BIBLIOG/A FEDERAL INT/TRADE DIPLOM

B63
WILCOX W.A.,PAKISTAN; THE CONSOLIDATION OF A NATION. INDIA PAKISTAN CONSTN SECT PROB/SOLV COLONIAL PARTIC GP/REL FEDERAL...POLICY 19/20. PAGE 164 A3348 — NAT/LISM ECO/UNDEV DIPLOM STRUCT

S63
BANFIELD J.,"FEDERATION IN EAST-AFRICA." AFR UGANDA ELITES INT/ORG NAT/G VOL/ASSN LEGIS ECO/TAC FEDERAL ATTIT SOVEREIGN TOT/POP 20 TANGANYIKA. PAGE 11 A0216 — EX/STRUC PWR REGION

S63
KAWALKOWSKI A.,"POUR UNE EUROPE INDEPENDENTE ET REUNIFIEE." EUR+WWI FUT USA+45 USSR WOR+45 ECO/DEV PROC/MFG INT/ORG NAT/G ACT/RES TEC/DEV FEDERAL RIGID/FLEX...CONCPT METH/CNCPT OEEC TOT/POP 20 DEGAULLE/C. PAGE 77 A1573 — R+D PLAN NUC/PWR

S63
ROUGEMONT D.,"LES NOUVELLES CHANCES DE L'EUROPE." EUR+WWI FUT ECO/DEV INT/ORG NAT/G ACT/RES PLAN TEC/DEV EDU/PROP ADMIN COLONIAL FEDERAL ATTIT PWR SKILL...TREND 20. PAGE 124 A2549 — ECO/UNDEV PERCEPT

B64
CURRIE D.P.,FEDERALISM AND THE NEW NATIONS OF AFRICA. CANADA USA+45 INT/TRADE TAX GP/REL ...NAT/COMP SOC/INTEG 20. PAGE 33 A0667 — FEDERAL AFR ECO/UNDEV INT/LAW

B64
NEWBURY C.W.,THE WEST AFRICAN COMMONWEALTH. CONSTN INTELL ECO/UNDEV VOL/ASSN CHIEF DELIB/GP LEGIS INT/TRADE COLONIAL FEDERAL ATTIT 20 COMMONWLTH AFRICA/W. PAGE 108 A2223 — INT/ORG SOVEREIGN GOV/REL AFR

S64
BARKUN M.,"CONFLICT RESOLUTION THROUGH IMPLICIT MEDIATION." UNIV BARGAIN CONSEN FEDERAL JURID. PAGE 11 A0222 — CONSULT CENTRAL INT/LAW IDEA/COMP

B65
CALLEO D.P.,EUROPE'S FUTURE: THE GRAND ALTERNATIVES. UK INT/ORG DIPLOM PWR SOVEREIGN ...CONCPT IDEA/COMP NAT/COMP BIBLIOG 20 EEC EUROPE DEGAULLE/C NATO. PAGE 23 A0468 — FUT EUR+WWI FEDERAL NAT/LISM

B65
MERKL P.H.,GERMANY: YESTERDAY AND TOMORROW. GERMANY POL/PAR PLAN DIPLOM LEAD FEDERAL 19/20. PAGE 100 A2043 — NAT/G FUT

C65
SCHEINGOLD S.A.,"THE RULE OF LAW IN EUROPEAN INTEGRATION: THE PATH OF THE SCHUMAN PLAN." EUR+WWI JUDGE ADJUD FEDERAL ATTIT PWR...RECORD INT BIBLIOG EEC ECSC. PAGE 128 A2621 — INT/LAW CT/SYS REGION CENTRAL

B66
HAY P.,FEDERALISM AND SUPRANATIONAL ORGANIZATIONS: PATTERNS FOR NEW LEGAL STRUCTURES. EUR+WWI LAW NAT/G VOL/ASSN DIPLOM PWR...NAT/COMP TREATY EEC. PAGE 63 A1294 — SOVEREIGN FEDERAL INT/ORG INT/LAW

S67
APEL H.,"LES NOUVEAUX ASPECTS DE LA POLITIQUE ETRANGERE ALLEMANDE." EUR+WWI GERMANY POL/PAR BAL/PWR ECO/TAC INT/TRADE NUC/PWR NAT/LISM PEACE ...POLICY 20 EEC COLD/WAR. PAGE 8 A0168 — DIPLOM INT/ORG FEDERAL

S67
DAVIS H.B.,"LENIN AND NATIONALISM: THE REDIRECTION OF THE MARXIST THEORY OF NATIONALISM." COM MOD/EUR USSR STRATA INT/ORG PLAN DOMIN COLONIAL FEDERAL ...TREND 20. PAGE 34 A0690 — NAT/LISM MARXISM ATTIT CENTRAL

S67
DE ROUGEMENT D.,"THE CAMPAIGN OF THE EUROPEAN CONGRESSES." ELITES INTELL DIPLOM ECO/TAC CONFER PEACE...POLICY PREDICT. PAGE 35 A0710 — EUR+WWI REGION FEDERAL INT/ORG

S67
LIVNEH E.,"A NEW BEGINNING." ISRAEL USSR WOR+45 NAT/G DIPLOM INGP/REL FEDERAL HABITAT PWR...GEOG PSY JEWS. PAGE 90 A1847 — WAR PERSON PEACE PLAN

S67
RABIER J.-R.,"THE EUROPEAN IDEA AND NATIONAL PUBLIC OPINIONS." ACT/RES PLAN DIPLOM PARTIC CONSEN ATTIT PERCEPT...DECISION CHARTS. PAGE 118 A2430 — POLICY FEDERAL EUR+WWI PROB/SOLV

FEDERALIST....FEDERALIST PARTY (ALL NATIONS)

B01
HART A.B.,AMERICAN HISTORY TOLD BY CONTEMPORARIES. UK CULTURE FINAN SECT FORCES DIPLOM TAX RUMOR CT/SYS REV GOV/REL GP/REL...ANTHOL 17/18 PRE/US/AM FEDERALIST. PAGE 62 A1273 — USA-45 COLONIAL SOVEREIGN

FEDSCI/TEC....FEDERAL COUNCIL FOR SCIENCE AND TECHNOLOGY

FEEDBACK....FEEDBACK PHENOMENA

B05
GRIFFIN A.P.C.,LIST OF REFERENCES ON THE US CONSULAR SERVICE (PAMPHLET). FRANCE GERMANY SPAIN UK USA-45 WOR-45 OP/RES DOMIN ADMIN FEEDBACK ROUTINE GOV/REL...DECISION 19. PAGE 56 A1153 — BIBLIOG/A NAT/G DIPLOM CONSULT

B27
PARRINGTON V.L.,MAIN CURRENTS IN AMERICAN THOUGHT (VOL.I). USA-45 AGRI POL/PAR DIPLOM TAX REGION REV 17/18 FRANKLIN/B JEFFERSN/T. PAGE 114 A2336 — COLONIAL SECT FEEDBACK ALL/IDEOS

B40
FULLER G.H.,A LIST OF BIBLIOGRAPHIES ON PROPAGANDA (PAMPHLET). MOD/EUR USA-45 CONSULT ACT/RES PRESS FEEDBACK TASK WAR ATTIT PWR...CON/ANAL METH/COMP 20. PAGE 50 A1020 — BIBLIOG/A EDU/PROP DOMIN DIPLOM

B57
FRASER L.,PROPAGANDA. GERMANY USSR WOR+45 WOR-45 NAT/G POL/PAR CONTROL FEEDBACK LOBBY CROWD WAR CONSEN NAT/LISM 20. PAGE 48 A0988 — EDU/PROP FASCISM MARXISM DIPLOM

B63
JOYCE W.,THE PROPAGANDA GAP. USA+45 COM/IND ACADEM DOMIN FEEDBACK REV CIVMIL/REL...REALPOL COLD/WAR. PAGE 75 A1540 — EDU/PROP PERCEPT BAL/PWR DIPLOM

FEHRENBACH T.R. A0906

FEILCHENFELD E.H. A0907

FEIS H. A0908,A0909,A0910,A0911,A0912

FELD B.T. A0913

FELDMAN H. A0914

FELICIANO F.P. A2006

FELKER J.L. A0915

FEMALE/SEX....FEMALE SEX

FENWICK C.G. A0916,A0917

FEPC....FAIR EMPLOYMENT PRACTICES COMMISSION

FERKISS V.C. A0918

FERNBACH A.P. A0919

FERRELL R.H. A0920,A0921

FERRERO G. A0922

FEUDALISM....FEUDALISM

FHA....U.S. FEDERAL HOUSING ADMINISTRATION

FICHTE J.G. A0923

FICHTE/JG....JOHANN GOTTLIEB FICHTE

FICTIONS....SEE MYTH

FIELD G.C. A0924

FIELD/S....STEVEN FIELD

FIFIELD R.H. A0925,A0926,A0927,A0928

FIGANIERE J.C. A0929

FILENE P.G. A0930

FILLMORE/M....PRESIDENT MILLARD FILLMORE

FILM....FILM AND CINEMA

B64
UNESCO,WORLD COMMUNICATIONS: PRESS, RADIO, TELEVISION, FILM (4TH ED.). WOR+45 DIPLOM TV PEACE ...NAT/COMP SOC/INTEG 20 FILM. PAGE 148 A3023 — COM/IND EDU/PROP PRESS TEC/DEV

B65
DAVISON W.P.,INTERNATIONAL POLITICAL COMMUNICATION. COM USA+45 WOR+45 CULTURE ECO/UNDEV NAT/G PROB/SOLV PRESS TV ADMIN 20 FILM. PAGE 34 A0693 — EDU/PROP DIPLOM PERS/REL COM/IND

FINAN....FINANCIAL SERVICE, BANKS, INSURANCE SYSTEMS, SECURITIES, EXCHANGES

N
LONDON INSTITUTE WORLD AFFAIRS,THE YEAR BOOK OF WORLD AFFAIRS. FINAN BAL/PWR ARMS/CONT WAR ...INT/LAW BIBLIOG 20. PAGE 91 A1856 — DIPLOM FOR/AID INT/ORG

N
CANADIAN GOVERNMENT PUBLICATIONS (1955-). CANADA AGRI FINAN LABOR FORCES INT/TRADE HEALTH...JURID 20 PARLIAMENT. PAGE 1 A0007 — BIBLIOG/A NAT/G DIPLOM INT/ORG

N
INTERNATIONAL BOOK NEWS, 1928-1934. ECO/UNDEV FINAN INDUS LABOR INT/TRADE CONFER ADJUD COLONIAL...HEAL SOC/WK CHARTS 20 LEAGUE/NAT. PAGE 1 A0010 — BIBLIOG/A DIPLOM INT/LAW INT/ORG

N
DOCUMENTATION ECONOMIQUE: REVUE BIBLIOGRAPHIQUE DE SYNTHESE. WOR+45 COM/IND FINAN BUDGET DIPLOM...GEOG 20. PAGE 2 A0033 — BIBLIOG/A SOC

N
FOREIGN AFFAIRS. SPACE WOR+45 WOR-45 CULTURE ECO/UNDEV FINAN NAT/G TEC/DEV INT/TRADE ARMS/CONT NUC/PWR...POLICY 20 UN EURATOM ECSC EEC. PAGE 2 A0034 — BIBLIOG DIPLOM INT/ORG INT/LAW

N
THE MIDDLE EAST AND NORTH AFRICA. AFR ISLAM CULTURE ECO/UNDEV AGRI NAT/G TEC/DEV FOR/AID INT/TRADE EDU/PROP...CHARTS 20. PAGE 2 A0043 — INDEX INDUS FINAN STAT

N
AMERICAN ECONOMIC ASSOCIATION,THE JOURNAL OF ECONOMIC ABSTRACTS. ECO/UNDEV MARKET LABOR DIPLOM ...MGT CONCPT METH 20. PAGE 7 A0144 — BIBLIOG/A R+D FINAN

N
EUROPA PUBLICATIONS LIMITED,THE EUROPA YEAR BOOK. CONSTN FINAN INDUS POL/PAR DIPLOM TV CT/SYS...STAT BIOG CHARTS WORSHIP 20. PAGE 43 A0874 — BIBLIOG NAT/G PRESS INT/ORG

N
FOREIGN TRADE LIBRARY,NEW TITLES RECEIVED IN THE LIBRARY. WOR+45 ECO/UNDEV FINAN NAT/G PLAN TEC/DEV BUDGET ECO/TAC TARIFFS GOV/REL STAT. PAGE 47 A0964 — BIBLIOG/A INT/TRADE INDUS ECO/DEV

N
IMF AND IBRD, JOINT LIBRARY,LIST OF RECENT — BIBLIOG

ADDITIONS. WOR+45 ECO/DEV ECO/UNDEV BUDGET FOR/AID INT/ORG
RATION...CONCPT IDEA/COMP. PAGE 70 A1434 INT/TRADE
FINAN
N

IMF AND IBRD, JOINT LIBRARY,LIST OF RECENT BIBLIOG
PERIODICAL ARTICLES. WOR+45 ECO/DEV ECO/UNDEV INT/ORG
BUDGET FOR/AID RATION...CONCPT IDEA/COMP. PAGE 70 INT/TRADE
A1435 FINAN
N

KAPLAN L.,REVIEW INDEX. USA+45 USA-45 FINAN INDUS BIBLIOG
LABOR RACE/REL...GEOG PSY SOC 20. PAGE 76 A1558 PROF/ORG
ECO/DEV
DIPLOM
N

KYRIAK T.E.,CHINA: A BIBLIOGRAPHY. ASIA CHINA/COM BIBLIOG/A
AGRI FINAN INDUS NAT/G INT/TRADE PRESS...SOC 20. MARXISM
PAGE 83 A1700 TOP/EX
POL/PAR
N

KYRIAK T.E.,EAST EUROPE: BIBLIOGRAPHY--INDEX TO US BIBLIOG/A
JPRS RESEARCH TRANSLATIONS. ALBANIA BULGARIA COM PRESS
CZECHOSLVK HUNGARY POLAND ROMANIA AGRI EXTR/IND MARXISM
FINAN SERV/IND INT/TRADE WEAPON...GEOG MGT SOC 20. INDUS
PAGE 83 A1701
N

MCSPADDEN J.W.,THE AMERICAN STATESMAN'S YEARBOOK. DIPLOM
WOR-45 LAW CONSTN AGRI FINAN DEBATE ADMIN PARL/PROC NAT/G
...CHARTS BIBLIOG/A 20. PAGE 99 A2025 PROVS
LEGIS
N

MURRA R.O.,POST-WAR PROBLEMS: A CURRENT LIST OF BIBLIOG/A
UNITED STATES GOVERNMENT PUBLICATIONS (PAMPHLET). ADJUST
WOR+45 SOCIETY FINAN INT/ORG SCHOOL WORKER TEC/DEV AGRI
ECO/TAC...SOC 20. PAGE 106 A2180 INDUS
N

UNITED NATIONS,UNITED NATIONS PUBLICATIONS. WOR+45 BIBLIOG
ECO/UNDEV AGRI FINAN FORCES ADMIN LEAD WAR PEACE INT/ORG
...POLICY INT/LAW 20 UN. PAGE 148 A3034 DIPLOM
N

WORLD PEACE FOUNDATION,DOCUMENTS OF INTERNATIONAL BIBLIOG
ORGANIZATIONS: A SELECTED BIBLIOGRAPHY. WOR+45 DIPLOM
WOR-45 AGRI FINAN ACT/RES OP/RES INT/TRADE ADMIN INT/ORG
...CON/ANAL 20 UN UNESCO LEAGUE/NAT. PAGE 167 A3396 REGION
B01

HART A.B.,AMERICAN HISTORY TOLD BY CONTEMPORARIES. USA-45
UK CULTURE FINAN SECT FORCES DIPLOM TAX RUMOR COLONIAL
CT/SYS REV GOV/REL GP/REL...ANTHOL 17/18 PRE/US/AM SOVEREIGN
FEDERALIST. PAGE 62 A1273
B02

MOREL E.D.,AFFAIRS OF WEST AFRICA. UK FINAN INDUS COLONIAL
FAM KIN SECT CHIEF WORKER DIPLOM RACE/REL LITERACY ADMIN
HEALTH...CHARTS 18/20 AFRICA/W NEGRO. PAGE 104 AFR
A2129
B03

FORTESCUE G.K.,SUBJECT INDEX OF THE MODERN WORKS BIBLIOG
ADDED TO THE LIBRARY OF THE BRITISH MUSEUM IN THE INDEX
YEARS 1881-1900 (3 VOLS.). UK LAW CONSTN FINAN WRITING
NAT/G FORCES INT/TRADE COLONIAL 19. PAGE 47 A0968
B17

MEYER H.H.B.,THE UNITED STATES AT WAR, BIBLIOG/A
ORGANIZATIONS AND LITERATURE. USA-45 AGRI FINAN WAR
INDUS CHIEF FORCES DIPLOM FOR/AID INT/TRADE...SOC NAT/G
20 PRESIDENT. PAGE 100 A2050 VOL/ASSN
B17

VEBLEN T.B.,AN INQUIRY INTO THE NATURE OF PEACE AND PEACE
THE TERMS OF ITS PERPETUATION. UNIV STRATA FINAN DIPLOM
EDU/PROP PRICE COST DISCRIM NAT/LISM MORAL ORD/FREE WAR
PACIFIST 20 WORLDUNITY. PAGE 158 A3224 NAT/G
B19

KEYNES J.M.,THE ECONOMIC CONSEQUENCES OF THE PEACE. EUR+WWI
FUT GERMANY MOD/EUR RUSSIA UK USA-45 CULTURE SOCIETY
ECO/DEV FINAN INDUS INT/ORG TOP/EX ECO/TAC ROUTINE PEACE
WAR ATTIT PERCEPT ALL/VALS...OLD/LIB MYTH OBS
TIME/SEQ TREND 20 TREATY. PAGE 78 A1605
N19

BASCH A.,THE FUTURE OF FOREIGN LENDING FOR FOR/AID
DEVELOPMENT (PAMPHLET). WOR+45 ECO/UNDEV FINAN ECO/DEV
INT/ORG ECO/TAC ATTIT...PREDICT 20. PAGE 11 A0232 DIPLOM
GIVE
N19

KUWAIT ARABIA,KUWAIT FUND FOR ARAB ECONOMIC FOR/AID
DEVELOPMENT (PAMPHLET). ISLAM KUWAIT UAR ECO/UNDEV DIPLOM
LEGIS ECO/TAC WEALTH 20. PAGE 83 A1697 FINAN
ADMIN
N19

MARCUS W.,US PRIVATE INVESTMENT AND ECONOMIC AID IN FOR/AID
UNDERDEVELOPED COUNTRIES (PAMPHLET). USA+45 LG/CO ECO/UNDEV
NAT/G CAP/ISM EDU/PROP 20. PAGE 94 A1937 FINAN
PLAN
N19

MASON E.S.,THE DIPLOMACY OF ECONOMIC ASSISTANCE FOR/AID
(PAMPHLET). INDIA PAKISTAN USA+45 ECO/UNDEV NAT/G DIPLOM
BUDGET ATTIT...POLICY 20. PAGE 95 A1955 FINAN
N19

STEUBER F.A.,THE CONTRIBUTION OF SWITZERLAND TO THE FOR/AID
ECONOMIC AND SOCIAL DEVELOPMENT OF LOW-INCOME ECO/UNDEV
COUNTRIES (PAMPHLET). SWITZERLND FINAN NAT/G PLAN
VOL/ASSN INT/TRADE DRIVE...CHARTS 20. PAGE 138 DIPLOM
A2820
B20

WOOLF L.,EMPIRE AND COMMERCE IN AFRICA. EUR+WWI AFR
MOD/EUR FINAN INDUS MARKET INT/ORG PLAN COERCE DOMIN
ATTIT DRIVE PWR WEALTH...CONCPT TIME/SEQ TREND COLONIAL
CHARTS 20. PAGE 167 A3394 SOVEREIGN
B31

BORCHARD E.H.,GUIDE TO THE LAW AND LEGAL LITERATURE BIBLIOG/A
OF FRANCE. FRANCE FINAN INDUS LABOR SECT LEGIS LAW
ADMIN COLONIAL CRIME OWN...INT/LAW 20. PAGE 17 CONSTN
A0337 METH
B32

HANSEN A.H.,ECONOMIC STABILIZATION IN AN UNBALANCED NAT/G
WORLD. COM EUR+WWI USA-45 WOR-45 AGRI FINAN INDUS ECO/DEV
MARKET INT/ORG LABOR VOL/ASSN EDU/PROP ATTIT HEALTH CAP/ISM
KNOWL WEALTH...HIST/WRIT TREND VAL/FREE 20. PAGE 61 SOCISM
A1253
B32

WRIGHT Q.,GOLD AND MONETARY STABILIZATION. FUT FINAN
USA-45 WOR-45 INTELL ECO/DEV INT/ORG NAT/G CONSULT POLICY
PLAN ECO/TAC ADMIN ATTIT WEALTH...CONCPT TREND 20.
PAGE 167 A3404
B33

AMERICAN FOREIGN LAW ASSN,BIOGRAPHICAL NOTES ON THE BIBLIOG/A
LAWS AND LEGAL LITERATURE OF URUGUAY AND CURACAO. LAW
URUGUAY CONSTN FINAN SECT FORCES JUDGE DIPLOM JURID
INT/TRADE ADJUD CT/SYS CRIME 20. PAGE 7 A0147 ADMIN
B33

FERRERO G.,PEACE AND WAR (TRANS. BY BERTHA WAR
PRITCHARD). CULTURE FINAN SECT ATTIT SUPEGO MORAL PEACE
ORD/FREE CONSERVE POPULISM SOCISM POLICY. PAGE 45 DIPLOM
A0922 PROB/SOLV
B33

OHLIN B.,INTERREGIONAL AND INTERNATIONAL TRADE. INT/ORG
USA-45 WOR-45 CULTURE FINAN MARKET CONSULT PLAN ECO/DEV
ECO/TAC ATTIT WEALTH...CONCPT MATH TOT/POP 20. INT/TRADE
PAGE 111 A2285 REGION
B35

BUREAU ECONOMIC RES LAT AM,THE ECONOMIC LITERATURE BIBLIOG
OF LATIN AMERICA (2 VOLS.). CHRIST-17C AGRI L/A+17C
DIST/IND EXTR/IND INDUS WORKER INT/TRADE...GEOG ECO/UNDEV
16/20. PAGE 21 A0433 FINAN
B35

STALEY E.,WAR AND THE PRIVATE INVESTOR. UNIV WOR-45 FINAN
INTELL SOCIETY INT/ORG NAT/G TOP/EX CAP/ISM ECO/TAC INT/TRADE
WAR ATTIT ALL/VALS...INT TIME/SEQ TREND CON/ANAL DIPLOM
WORK TOT/POP 20. PAGE 137 A2799
B36

HUDSON M.O.,INTERNATIONAL LEGISLATION: 1929-1931. INT/LAW
WOR-45 SEA AIR AGRI FINAN LABOR DIPLOM ECO/TAC PARL/PROC
REPAR CT/SYS ARMS/CONT WAR WEAPON...JURID 20 TREATY ADJUD
LEAGUE/NAT. PAGE 69 A1409 LAW
B36

VARLEY D.H.,A BIBLIOGRAPHY OF ITALIAN COLONISATION BIBLIOG
IN AFRICA WITH A SECTION ON ABYSSINIA. AFR ETHIOPIA COLONIAL
ITALY LIBYA SOMALIA AGRI FINAN LABOR TEC/DEV DIPLOM ADMIN
INT/TRADE RACE/REL DISCRIM 19/20. PAGE 158 A3222 LAW
B37

ROBBINS L.,ECONOMIC PLANNING AND INTERNATIONAL INT/ORG
ORDER. WOR-45 SOCIETY FINAN INDUS NAT/G ECO/TAC PLAN
ROUTINE WEALTH...SOC TIME/SEQ GEN/METH WORK 20 INT/TRADE
KEYNES/JM. PAGE 122 A2492
B38

FRANKEL S.H.,CAPITAL INVESTMENT IN AFRICA. AFR ECO/UNDEV
EUR+WWI RHODESIA SOUTH/AFR UK FINAN FOR/AID EXTR/IND
COLONIAL DEMAND UTIL WEALTH...METH/CNCPT CHARTS 20 DIPLOM
CONGO/LEOP. PAGE 48 A0983 PRODUC
B39

SPEIER H.,WAR IN OUR TIME. WOR-45 AGRI FINAN FORCES FASCISM
TEC/DEV BAL/PWR EDU/PROP WEAPON PEACE PWR...ANTHOL WAR
20. PAGE 136 A2779 DIPLOM
NAT/G
B39

THOMAS J.A.,THE HOUSE OF COMMONS, 1832-1901; A PARL/PROC
STUDY OF ITS ECONOMIC AND FUNCTIONAL CHARACTER. UK LEGIS
LAW STRATA FINAN DIPLOM CONTROL LEAD LOBBY POL/PAR
REPRESENT WEALTH...POLICY STAT BIBLIOG 19/20 ECO/DEV
PARLIAMENT. PAGE 143 A2922
B40

CONOVER H.F.,JAPAN-ECONOMIC DEVELOPMENT AND FOREIGN BIBLIOG
POLICY, A SELECTED LIST OF REFERENCES (PAMPHLET). ASIA
CULTURE FINAN INDUS NAT/G FORCES INT/TRADE WAR ECO/DEV
...SOC TREND 20 CHINJAP. PAGE 29 A0593 DIPLOM
C40

FAHS C.B.,"GOVERNMENT IN JAPAN." FINAN FORCES LEGIS ASIA
TOP/EX BUDGET INT/TRADE EDU/PROP SOVEREIGN DIPLOM
...CON/ANAL BIBLIOG/A 20 CHINJAP. PAGE 43 A0884 NAT/G
ADMIN
B42

FULLER G.H.,DEFENSE FINANCING: A SUPPLEMENTARY LIST BIBLIOG/A
OF REFERENCES (PAMPHLET). CANADA UK USA-45 ECO/DEV FINAN
NAT/G DELIB/GP BUDGET ADJUD ARMS/CONT WEAPON COST FORCES
PEACE PWR 20 AUSTRAL CHINJAP CONGRESS. PAGE 50 DIPLOM
A1021

B42
US LIBRARY OF CONGRESS,ECONOMICS OF WAR (APRIL 1941-MARCH 1942). WOR-45 FINAN INDUS LOC/G NAT/G PLAN BUDGET RATION COST DEMAND...POLICY 20. PAGE 154 A3146
BIBLIOG/A INT/TRADE ECO/TAC WAR

B43
BROWN A.D.,GREECE: SELECTED LIST OF REFERENCES. GREECE ECO/UNDEV AGRI FINAN INDUS LABOR SECT TEC/DEV INT/TRADE LEAD...SOC 20. PAGE 20 A0399
BIBLIOG/A WAR DIPLOM NAT/G

B45
VANCE H.L.,GUIDE TO THE LAW AND LEGAL LITERATURE OF MEXICO. LAW CONSTN FINAN LABOR FORCES ADJUD ADMIN ...CRIMLGY PHIL/SCI CON/ANAL 20 MEXIC/AMER. PAGE 158 A3217
BIBLIOG/A INT/LAW JURID CT/SYS

S46
SILBERNER E.,"THE PROBLEM OF WAR IN NINETEENTH CENTURY ECONOMIC THOUGHT." EUR+WWI MOD/EUR UNIV LAW ECO/DEV ECO/UNDEV FINAN INDUS MARKET INT/ORG NAT/G CONSULT FORCES...CONCPT GEN/LAWS GEN/METH 19. PAGE 133 A2715
ATTIT ECO/TAC WAR

B47
GORDON D.L.,THE HIDDEN WEAPON: THE STORY OF ECONOMIC WARFARE. EUR+WWI USA-45 LAW FINAN INDUS NAT/G CONSULT FORCES PLAN DOMIN PWR WEALTH ...INT/LAW CONCPT OBS TOT/POP NAZI 20. PAGE 54 A1112
INT/ORG ECO/TAC INT/TRADE WAR

B47
TOWLE L.W.,INTERNATIONAL TRADE AND COMMERCIAL POLICY. WOR+45 LAW ECO/DEV FINAN INDUS NAT/G ECO/TAC WEALTH...TIME/SEQ ILO 20. PAGE 144 A2955
MARKET INT/ORG INT/TRADE

B48
GRAHAM F.D.,THE THEORY OF INTERNATIONAL VALUES. FUT WOR+45 WOR-45 ECO/DEV FINAN INT/ORG PLAN TEC/DEV CAP/ISM DIPLOM ECO/TAC TARIFFS ROUTINE BAL/PAY DRIVE PWR WEALTH SOCISM...POLICY STAT HYPO/EXP GEN/LAWS 20. PAGE 55 A1125
NEW/IDEA INT/TRADE

B48
MINISTERE FINANCES ET ECO,BULLETIN BIBLIOGRAPHIQUE. AFR EUR+WWI FRANCE CULTURE STRUCT FINAN NAT/G ACT/RES INT/TRADE ADMIN REGION PRODUC STAT. PAGE 102 A2088
BIBLIOG/A ECO/UNDEV TEC/DEV COLONIAL

B48
NEUBURGER O.,GUIDE TO OFFICIAL PUBLICATIONS OF THE OTHER AMERICAN REPUBLICS: VENEZUELA (VOL. XIX). VENEZUELA FINAN LEGIS PLAN BUDGET DIPLOM CT/SYS PARL/PROC 19/20. PAGE 108 A2219
BIBLIOG/A NAT/G CONSTN LAW

B50
DAVIS E.P.,PERIODICALS OF INTERNATIONAL ORGANIZATIONS; PART I, THE UN AND SPECIALIZED AGENCIES; PART II, INTER-AMERICAN ORGS. CULTURE AGRI FINAN INDUS LABOR INT/TRADE...GEOG HEAL STAT 20 UN OAS UNESCO. PAGE 34 A0689
BIBLIOG/A INT/ORG DIPLOM L/A+17C

B50
US DEPARTMENT OF STATE,POINT FOUR: COOPERATIVE PROGRAM FOR AID IN THE DEVELOPMENT OF ECONOMICALLY UNDERDEVELOPED AREAS. WOR+45 AGRI INDUS INT/ORG PLAN TEC/DEV DIPLOM EDU/PROP ADMIN PEACE PRODUC WEALTH 20 CONGRESS UN. PAGE 151 A3085
ECO/UNDEV FOR/AID FINAN INT/TRADE

C50
ELLSWORTH P.T.,"INTERNATIONAL ECONOMY." ECO/DEV ECO/UNDEV FINAN LABOR DIPLOM FOR/AID TARIFFS BAL/PAY EQUILIB NAT/LISM OPTIMAL...INT/LAW 20 ILO GATT. PAGE 41 A0843
BIBLIOG INT/TRADE ECO/TAC INT/ORG

B51
US DEPARTMENT OF STATE,POINT FOUR, NEAR EAST AND AFRICA, A SELECTED BIBLIOGRAPHY OF STUDIES ON ECONOMICALLY UNDERDEVELOPED COUNTRIES. AGRI COM/IND FINAN INDUS PLAN INT/TRADE...SOC TREND 20. PAGE 151 A3087
BIBLIOG/A AFR S/ASIA ISLAM

B51
VINER J.,INTERNATIONAL ECONOMICS. USA-45 WOR-45 ECO/DEV INDUS NAT/G ECO/TAC ALL/VALS...TIME/SEQ 20. PAGE 159 A3238
FINAN INT/ORG WAR INT/TRADE

C51
LEONARD L.L.,"INTERNATIONAL ORGANIZATION (1ST ED.)" WOR+45 FINAN DELIB/GP ECO/TAC GIVE DOMIN SANCTION PEACE BIO/SOC ORD/FREE...INT/LAW 20 UN LEAGUE/NAT. PAGE 87 A1779
BIBLIOG POLICY DIPLOM INT/ORG

B52
ALEXANDROWICZ C.H.,INTERNATIONAL ECONOMIC ORGANIZATION. WOR+45 ECO/DEV ECO/UNDEV DIST/IND FINAN MARKET PLAN ECO/TAC LEGIT DRIVE WEALTH ...POLICY CONCPT QUANT OBS TIME/SEQ GEN/LAWS WORK EEC ILO OEEC UNESCO 20. PAGE 6 A0114
INT/ORG INT/TRADE

B52
MANTOUX E.,THE CARTHAGINIAN PEACE. GERMANY WOR-45 SOCIETY FINAN INT/ORG DELIB/GP FORCES PLAN LEGIT ...CONCPT TIME/SEQ 20 KEYNES/JM HITLER/A. PAGE 94 A1935
ECO/DEV INT/TRADE WAR

B52
RIGGS F.W.,FORMOSA UNDER CHINESE NATIONALIST RULE. CHINA/COM USA+45 CONSTN AGRI FINAN LABOR LOC/G NAT/G POL/PAR FORCES HEALTH KNOWL...STAT WORK VAL/FREE 20. PAGE 121 A2479
ASIA FOR/AID DIPLOM

B52
SURANYI-UNGER T.,COMPARATIVE ECONOMIC SYSTEMS. FINAN MARKET DIPLOM PRICE WEALTH...GEOG SOC BIBLIOG METH T 20. PAGE 140 A2865
LAISSEZ PLAN ECO/DEV IDEA/COMP

B53
NEISSER H.,NATIONAL INCOMES AND INTERNATIONAL TRADE. FRANCE GERMANY SWEDEN UK USA-45 EXTR/IND FINAN INDUS TEC/DEV PRICE BAL/PAY EQUILIB INCOME WEALTH...CHARTS METH 19 CHINJAP. PAGE 108 A2215
INT/TRADE PRODUC MARKET CON/ANAL

B53
STOUT H.M.,BRITISH GOVERNMENT. UK FINAN LOC/G POL/PAR DELIB/GP DIPLOM ADMIN COLONIAL CHOOSE ORD/FREE...JURID BIBLIOG 20 COMMONWLTH. PAGE 139 A2837
NAT/G PARL/PROC CONSTN NEW/LIB

B54
BINANI G.D.,INDIA AT A GLANCE (REV. ED.). INDIA COM/IND FINAN INDUS LABOR PROVS SCHOOL PLAN DIPLOM INT/TRADE ADMIN...JURID 20. PAGE 14 A0288
INDEX CON/ANAL NAT/G ECO/UNDEV

C54
BOWIE R.R.,"STUDIES IN FEDERALISM." AGRI FINAN LABOR EX/STRUC FORCES LEGIS DIPLOM INT/TRADE ADJUD ...BIBLIOG 20 EEC. PAGE 17 A0357
FEDERAL EUR+WWI INT/ORG CONSTN

B55
LANDHEER B.,EUROPEAN YEARBOOK, 1955. CONSTN ECO/DEV DIST/IND FINAN DELIB/GP ECO/TAC DETER NUC/PWR ...BIBLIOG 20 EEC. PAGE 84 A1717
EUR+WWI INT/ORG GOV/REL INT/TRADE

B55
O3HEVSS E.,WIRTSCHAFTSSYSTEME UND INTERNATIONALER HANDEL. ECO/DEV FINAN MARKET DIPLOM ECO/TAC COST ...METH/COMP NAT/COMP 20. PAGE 112 A2306
CAP/ISM SOCISM INT/TRADE IDEA/COMP

B56
JAMESON J.F.,THE AMERICAN REVOLUTION CONSIDERED AS A SOCIAL MOVEMENT. USA-45 AGRI FINAN SECT INT/TRADE REPRESENT SUFF INGP/REL RACE/REL DISCRIM...MAJORIT 18/19 CHURCH/STA. PAGE 73 A1494
ORD/FREE REV FEDERAL CONSTN

B56
JUAN T.L.,ECONOMIC AND SOCIAL DEVELOPMENT OF MODERN CHINA: A BIBLIOGRAPHICAL GUIDE. ASIA AGRI COM/IND DIST/IND FINAN INDUS DIPLOM...STAT 20. PAGE 75 A1541
BIBLIOG SOC

B56
US DEPARTMENT OF STATE,ECONOMIC PROBLEMS OF UNDERDEVELOPED AREAS (PAMPHLET). AFR ASIA ISLAM L/A+17C AGRI FINAN INDUS INT/ORG LABOR INT/TRADE ...PSY SOC 20. PAGE 151 A3090
BIBLIOG ECO/UNDEV TEC/DEV R+D

B57
ASHER R.E.,THE UNITED NATIONS AND ECONOMIC AND SOCIAL COOPERATION. ECO/UNDEV COM/IND DIST/IND FINAN PLAN PROB/SOLV INT/TRADE TASK WEALTH...SOC 20 UN. PAGE 9 A0186
INT/ORG DIPLOM FOR/AID

B57
MATECKI B.,ESTABLISHMENT OF THE INTERNATIONAL FINANCE CORPORATION AND UNITED STATES POLICY. USA+45 WOR+45 CONSTN NAT/G CREATE RIGID/FLEX KNOWL ...METH/CNCPT TIME/SEQ SIMUL TOT/POP 20 INTL/FINAN. PAGE 96 A1964
FINAN INT/ORG DIPLOM

B57
MCNEILL W.H.,GREECE: AMERICAN AID IN ACTION. GREECE UK USA+45 FINAN CAP/ISM INT/TRADE BAL/PAY PRODUC WEALTH...POLICY METH/COMP 20. PAGE 99 A2022
FOR/AID DIPLOM ECO/UNDEV

B57
MILLIKAN M.F.,A PROPOSAL: KEY TO AN EFFECTIVE FOREIGN POLICY. USA+45 AGRI FINAN DELIB/GP DIPLOM REPRESENT MAJORITY...NEW/IDEA CHARTS. PAGE 101 A2081
FOR/AID GIVE ECO/UNDEV PLAN

B57
US PRES CITIZEN ADVISERS,REPORT TO THE PRESIDENT ON THE MUTUAL SECURITY PROGRAM. COM USA+45 WOR+45 FINAN INDUS PLAN BUDGET CAP/ISM DIPLOM FOR/AID INT/TRADE REGION 20 SECUR/PROG. PAGE 155 A3163
BAL/PWR FORCES INT/ORG ECO/TAC

B58
AVRAMOVIC D.,POSTWAR GROWTH IN INTERNATIONAL INDEBTEDNESS. WOR+45 AGRI INDUS CAP/ISM PRICE INCOME...NAT/COMP 20 GOLD/STAND SILVER. PAGE 10 A0199
INT/TRADE FINAN COST BAL/PAY

B58
BERLINER J.S.,SOVIET ECONOMIC AID: THE AID AND TRADE POLICY IN UNDERDEVELOPED COUNTRIES. AFR COM ISLAM L/A+17C S/ASIA USSR ECO/DEV DIST/IND FINAN MARKET INT/ORG ACT/RES PLAN BAL/PWR WEAPON PWR WEALTH...CHARTS 20. PAGE 14 A0277
ECO/UNDEV ECO/TAC FOR/AID

B58
ISLAM R.,INTERNATIONAL ECONOMIC COOPERATION AND THE UNITED NATIONS. FINAN PLAN EXEC TASK WAR PEACE ...SOC METH/CNCPT 20 UN LEAGUE/NAT. PAGE 72 A1470
INT/ORG DIPLOM ADMIN

B58
KINDLEBERGER C.P.,INTERNATIONAL ECONOMICS. WOR+45 WOR-45 ECO/DEV ECO/UNDEV FINAN VOL/ASSN ACT/RES DIPLOM ECO/TAC LEGIT REGION ATTIT DRIVE ORD/FREE WEALTH...POLICY STAT TREND GEN/LAWS EEC ECSC OEEC 20. PAGE 79 A1620
INT/ORG BAL/PWR TARIFFS

B58
MUNKMAN C.A.,AMERICAN AID TO GREECE. GREECE USA+45 AGRI FINAN PROB/SOLV WAR PWR...CHARTS 20 UN. PAGE 106 A2171
FOR/AID PLAN ECO/DEV INT/TRADE

B58
PALYI M.,MANAGED MONEY AT THE CROSSROADS: THE EUROPEAN EXPERIENCE. WOR+45 WOR-45 TEC/DEV DIPLOM INT/TRADE DEMAND WEALTH...CHARTS BIBLIOG 19/20 EUROPE GOLD/STAND SILVER. PAGE 113 A2324
FINAN ECO/TAC ECO/DEV PRODUC

B58
WIGGINS J.W.,FOREIGN AID REEXAMINED: A CRITICAL APPRAISAL. CHINA/COM INDONESIA USA+45 FINAN INT/TRADE REGION NAT/LISM ATTIT...CENSUS 20. PAGE 164 A3342
FOR/AID DIPLOM ECO/UNDEV SOVEREIGN

L58
TRAGER F.N.,"A SELECTED AND ANNOTATED BIBLIOGRAPHY ON ECONOMIC DEVELOPMENT, 1953-1957." WOR+45 AGRI FINAN INDUS MARKET LABOR MUNIC WORKER PLAN INT/TRADE PRODUC CENSUS. PAGE 145 A2958
BIBLIOG/A ECO/UNDEV ECO/DEV

C58
BLANCHARD W.,"THAILAND." THAILAND CULTURE AGRI FINAN INDUS FAM LABOR INT/TRADE ATTIT...GEOG HEAL SOC BIBLIOG 20. PAGE 15 A0307
NAT/G DIPLOM ECO/UNDEV S/ASIA

B59
ALLEN R.L.,SOVIET INFLUENCE IN LATIN AMERICA. ECO/UNDEV FINAN PROC/MFG NAT/G TEC/DEV EDU/PROP EXEC ROUTINE ATTIT DRIVE PERSON ALL/VALS PWR...STAT CHARTS WORK 20. PAGE 6 A0125
L/A+17C ECO/TAC INT/TRADE USSR

B59
ALLEN W.R.,FOREIGN TRADE AND FINANCE. ECO/DEV DIPLOM BAL/PAY...POLICY CONCPT ANTHOL 20. PAGE 6 A0127
INT/TRADE EQUILIB FINAN

B59
ETSCHMANN R.,DIE WAHRUNGS- UND DEVISENPOLITIK DES OSTBLOCKS UND IHRE AUSWIRKUNGEN AUF DIE WIRTSCHAFTSBEZIEHUNGEN ZWISCHEN OST U WEST. BULGARIA CZECHOSLVK HUNGARY POLAND USSR MARKET NAT/G PLAN DIPLOM...NAT/COMP 20. PAGE 42 A0867
ECO/TAC FINAN POLICY INT/TRADE

B59
HARVARD UNIVERSITY LAW SCHOOL,INTERNATIONAL PROBLEMS OF FINANCIAL PROTECTION AGAINST NUCLEAR RISK. WOR+45 NAT/G DELIB/GP PROB/SOLV DIPLOM CONTROL ATTIT...POLICY INT/LAW MATH 20. PAGE 62 A1281
NUC/PWR ADJUD INDUS FINAN

B59
HAZLEWOOD A.,THE ECONOMICS OF "UNDER-DEVELOPED" AREAS. WOR+45 DIST/IND EXTR/IND FINAN INDUS MARKET PLAN FOR/AID...GEOG 20. PAGE 63 A1302
BIBLIOG/A ECO/UNDEV AGRI INT/TRADE

B59
MEZERK A.G.,FINANCIAL ASSISTANCE FOR ECONOMIC DEVELOPMENT. WOR+45 INDUS DIPLOM INT/TRADE...CHARTS GOV/COMP UN. PAGE 101 A2064
FOR/AID FINAN ECO/TAC ECO/UNDEV

B59
ROBERTSON A.H.,EUROPEAN INSTITUTIONS: COOPERATION, INTEGRATION, UNIFICATION. EUR+WWI FINAN INT/ORG FORCES INT/TRADE TARIFFS 20 EEC EURATOM ECSC NATO TREATY. PAGE 122 A2496
ECO/DEV DIPLOM INDUS ECO/TAC

B59
ROBINSON J.A.,THE MONRONEY RESOULUTION: CONGRESSIONAL INITIATIVE IN FOREIGN POLICY MAKING. USA+45 POL/PAR TOP/EX DIPLOM INT/TRADE 20 CONGRESS WORLD/BANK INTL/DEV. PAGE 122 A2504
LEGIS FINAN ECO/UNDEV CHIEF

B59
ROPKE W.,INTERNATIONAL ORDER AND ECONOMIC INTEGRATION. ECO/DEV ECO/UNDEV AGRI FINAN INDUS INT/ORG WAR PEACE ORD/FREE...SOC METH/COMP 20 EEC. PAGE 123 A2524
INT/TRADE DIPLOM BAL/PAY ALL/IDEOS

B59
SANNWALD R.E.,ECONOMIC INTEGRATION: THEORETICAL ASSUMPTIONS AND CONSEQUENCES OF EUROPEAN UNIFICATION. EUR+WWI FUT FINAN INDUS VOL/ASSN ACT/RES ECO/TAC...PLURIST EEC OEEC 20. PAGE 127 A2601
INT/ORG ECO/DEV INT/TRADE

B59
STOVEL J.A.,CANADA IN THE WORLD ECONOMY. CANADA PRICE DEMAND...STAT CHARTS BIBLIOG 20 VINER/J. PAGE 139 A2838
INT/TRADE BAL/PAY FINAN ECO/TAC

B59
US GENERAL ACCOUNTING OFFICE,EXAM OF ECONOMIC AND TECHNICAL ASSISTANCE PROGRAM FOR INDIA INT'NAT'L COOP ADMIN REPORT TO CONGRESS 1955-1958. INDIA USA+45 ECO/UNDEV FINAN PLAN DIPLOM COST UTIL WEALTH ...CHARTS 20 CONGRESS AID. PAGE 153 A3114
FOR/AID EFFICIENCY ECO/TAC TEC/DEV

B59
WENTHOLT W.,SOME COMMENTS ON THE LIQUIDATION OF THE EUROPEAN PAYMENT UNION AND RELATED PROBLEMS (PAMPHLET). WOR+45 PLAN BUDGET PRICE CONTROL 20 EEC GOLD/STAND. PAGE 163 A3319
FINAN ECO/DEV INT/ORG ECO/TAC

S59
KINDLEBERGER C.P.,"UNITED STATES ECONOMIC FOREIGN POLICY: RESEARCH REQUIREMENTS FOR 1965." FUT USA+45 WOR+45 DIST/IND MARKET INT/ORG ECO/TAC INT/TRADE WEALTH...OBS TREND CON/ANAL GEN/LAWS VAL/FREE 20. PAGE 79 A1621
FINAN ECO/DEV FOR/AID

S59
SOLDATI A.,"EOCNOMIC DISINTEGRATION IN EUROPE." EUR+WWI FUT WOR+45 INDUS INT/ORG NAT/G CAP/ISM WEALTH...NEW/IDEA OBS TREND CHARTS EEC 20. PAGE 135 A2764
FINAN ECO/TAC

N59
BRITISH COMMONWEALTH REL CONF,EXTRACTS FROM THE PROCEEDINGS OF THE SIXTH UNOFFICIAL CONFERENCE (PAMPHLET). GHANA INDIA RHODESIA UK FINAN FORCES DETER FEDERAL...LING 20 PARLIAMENT. PAGE 19 A0379
DIPLOM PARL/PROC INT/TRADE ORD/FREE

B60
ALLEN R.L.,SOVIET ECONOMIC WARFARE. USSR FINAN INDUS NAT/G PLAN TEC/DEV FOR/AID DETER WEALTH ...TREND GEN/LAWS 20. PAGE 6 A0126
COM ECO/TAC

B60
APTHEKER H.,DISARMAMENT AND THE AMERICAN ECONOMY: A SYMPOSIUM. FUT USA+45 ECO/DEV DIST/IND FINAN INDUS PROC/MFG LABOR NAT/G POL/PAR CONSULT PLAN CAP/ISM INT/TRADE PEACE ATTIT MORAL WEALTH...TREND GEN/LAWS TOT/POP 20. PAGE 9 A0172
MARXIST ARMS/CONT

B60
BILLERBECK K.,SOVIET BLOC FOREIGN AID TO UNDERDEVELOPED COUNTRIES. COM FUT USSR FINAN FORCES TEC/DEV DIPLOM INT/TRADE EDU/PROP NUC/PWR...TREND 20. PAGE 14 A0287
FOR/AID ECO/UNDEV ECO/TAC MARXISM

B60
KENEN P.B.,GIANT AMONG NATIONS: PROBLEMS IN UNITED STATES FOREIGN ECONOMIC POLICY. USA+45 FINAN DIPLOM TARIFFS BAL/PAY WEALTH 20 COLD/WAR. PAGE 77 A1584
FOR/AID ECO/UNDEV INT/TRADE PLAN

B60
KENEN P.B.,BRITISH MONETARY POLICY AND THE BALANCE OF PAYMENTS 1951-57. UK PLAN BUDGET ECO/TAC INT/TRADE PAY PRICE COST ATTIT 20. PAGE 77 A1585
BAL/PAY PROB/SOLV FINAN NAT/G

B60
LATIFI D.,INDIA AND UNITED STATES AID. ASIA INDIA UK USA+45 AGRI FINAN INDUS COLONIAL ORD/FREE SOVEREIGN WEALTH...METH/COMP 20. PAGE 85 A1743
FOR/AID DIPLOM ECO/UNDEV

B60
NEALE A.D.,THE FLOW OF RESOURCES FROM RICH TO POOR. WOR+45 ECO/DEV ECO/UNDEV FINAN INDUS NAT/G PLAN EFFICIENCY WEALTH...POLICY NAT/COMP 20 RESOURCE/N. PAGE 108 A2209
FOR/AID DIPLOM METH/CNCPT

B60
PENTONY D.E.,THE UNDERDEVELOPED LANDS. FUT WOR+45 CULTURE AGRI FINAN INDUS MARKET INT/ORG LABOR NAT/G VOL/ASSN CONSULT TEC/DEV ECO/TAC EDU/PROP COLONIAL ATTIT WEALTH...OBS RECORD SAMP TREND GEN/METH WORK UN 20. PAGE 115 A2351
ECO/UNDEV POLICY FOR/AID INT/TRADE

B60
RAO V.K.R.,INTERNATIONAL AID FOR ECONOMIC DEVELOPMENT - POSSIBILITIES AND LIMITATIONS. FINAN PLAN TEC/DEV ADMIN TASK EFFICIENCY...POLICY SOC METH/CNCPT CHARTS 20 UN. PAGE 119 A2444
FOR/AID DIPLOM INT/ORG ECO/UNDEV

B60
ROPKE W.,A HUMANE ECONOMY. CULTURE ECO/DEV FINAN INDUS GP/REL CENTRAL WEALTH...GEOG SOC IDEA/COMP 20 EEC. PAGE 123 A2525
ECO/TAC INT/ORG DIPLOM ORD/FREE

B60
SHONFIELD A.,THE ATTACK ON WORLD POVERTY. WOR+45 ECO/DEV ECO/UNDEV FINAN VOL/ASSN PLAN EDU/PROP DRIVE KNOWL WEALTH...CONT/OBS STAND/INT ORG/CHARTS TOT/POP UNESCO 20. PAGE 132 A2704
INT/ORG ECO/TAC FOR/AID INT/TRADE

B60
STOLPER W.F.,GERMANY BETWEEN EAST AND WEST: THE ECONOMICS OF COMPETITIVE COEXISTENCE. FUT GERMANY/E GERMANY/W WOR+45 FINAN POL/PAR BUDGET ECO/TAC FOR/AID INT/TRADE...STAT CHARTS METH/COMP 20 COLD/WAR. PAGE 138 A2832
ECO/DEV DIPLOM GOV/COMP BAL/PWR

B60
THE ECONOMIST (LONDON),THE COMMONWEALTH AND EUROPE. EUR+WWI WOR+45 AGRI FINAN INCOME...STAT CENSUS CHARTS CMN/WLTH EEC. PAGE 142 A2911
INT/TRADE INDUS INT/ORG NAT/COMP

B60
US HOUSE COMM GOVT OPERATIONS,OPERATIONS OF THE DEVELOPMENT LOAN FUND: HEARINGS (COMMITTEE ON GOVERNMENT OPERATIONS). USA+45 PLAN BUDGET DIPLOM GOV/REL COST...CHARTS 20 CONGRESS DEPT/STATE AID. PAGE 154 A3137
FINAN FOR/AID ECO/TAC EFFICIENCY

S60
"THE EMERGING COMMON MARKETS IN LATIN AMERICA." FUT L/A+17C STRATA DIST/IND INDUS LABOR NAT/G LEGIS ECO/TAC ADMIN RIGID/FLEX HEALTH...NEW/IDEA TIME/SEQ OAS 20. PAGE 3 A0059
FINAN ECO/UNDEV INT/TRADE

S60
FRANKEL S.H.,"ECONOMIC ASPECTS OF POLITICAL INDEPENDENCE IN AFRICA." AFR FUT SOCIETY ECO/UNDEV COM/IND FINAN LEGIS PLAN TEC/DEV CAP/ISM ECO/TAC INT/TRADE ADMIN ATTIT DRIVE RIGID/FLEX PWR WEALTH ...MGT NEW/IDEA MATH TIME/SEQ VAL/FREE 20. PAGE 48
NAT/G FOR/AID

A0984

S60
LINDHOLM R.W.,"ACCELERATED DEVELOPMENT WITH A MINIMUM OF FOREIGN AID AND ECONOMIC CONTROLS." SOCIETY INDUS ECO/TAC WEALTH...CONCPT 20. PAGE 89 A1822
ECO/DEV FINAN FOR/AID

S60
MORALES C.J.,"TRADE AND ECONOMIC INTEGRATION IN LATIN AMERICA." FUT L/A+17C LAW STRATA ECO/UNDEV DIST/IND INDUS LABOR NAT/G LEGIS ECO/TAC ADMIN RIGID/FLEX WEALTH...CONCPT NEW/IDEA CONT/OBS TIME/SEQ WORK 20. PAGE 104 A2128
FINAN INT/TRADE REGION

S60
MURPHY J.C.,"INTERNATIONAL INVESTMENT AND THE NATIONAL INTEREST." WOR+45 WOR-45 ECO/DEV ECO/UNDEV NAT/G ACT/RES...CHARTS TOT/POP COLD/WAR 20. PAGE 106 A2179
FINAN WEALTH FOR/AID

S60
SWIFT R.,"THE UNITED NATIONS AND ITS PUBLIC." WOR+45 CONSTN FINAN CONSULT DELIB/GP ACT/RES ADMIN ROUTINE RIGID/FLEX SKILL UN 20. PAGE 140 A2870
INT/ORG EDU/PROP

B61
BUSSCHAU W.J.,GOLD AND INTERNATIONAL LIQUIDITY. WOR+45 PRICE EQUILIB WEALTH...CHARTS 20 GOLD/STAND. PAGE 22 A0450
FINAN DIPLOM PROB/SOLV

B61
DETHINE P.,BIBLIOGRAPHIE DES ASPECTS ECONOMIQUES ET SOCIAUX DE L'INDUSTRIALISATION EN AFRIQUE. AFR FINAN LABOR FOR/AID...SOC 20. PAGE 36 A0734
BIBLIOG/A ECO/UNDEV INDUS TEC/DEV

B61
DIMOCK M.E.,BUSINESS AND GOVERNMENT (4TH ED.). AGRI FINAN OP/RES PLAN BUDGET DIPLOM LOBBY NUC/PWR NEW/LIB SOCISM...POLICY BIBLIOG 20. PAGE 37 A0765
NAT/G INDUS LABOR ECO/TAC

B61
EINZIG P.,A DYNAMIC THEORY OF FORWARD EXCHANGE. FUT WOR+45 WOR-45 INT/TRADE BAL/PAY WEALTH...OLD/LIB NEW/IDEA OBS TREND 20. PAGE 41 A0830
FINAN ECO/TAC

B61
FRIEDMANN W.G.,JOINT INTERNATIONAL BUSINESS VENTURES. ASIA ISLAM L/A+17C ECO/DEV DIST/IND FINAN PROC/MFG FACE/GP LG/CO NAT/G VOL/ASSN CONSULT EX/STRUC PLAN ADMIN ROUTINE WEALTH...OLD/LIB WORK 20. PAGE 49 A1004
ECO/UNDEV INT/TRADE

B61
GANGULI B.N.,ECONOMIC INTEGRATION. FINAN LABOR CAP/ISM DIPLOM WEALTH...NAT/COMP 20. PAGE 51 A1041
ECO/TAC METH/CNCPT EQUILIB ECO/UNDEV

B61
GURTOO D.H.N.,INDIA'S BALANCE OF PAYMENTS (1920-1960). INDIA FINAN DIPLOM FOR/AID INT/TRADE PRICE COLONIAL...CHARTS BIBLIOG 20. PAGE 58 A1197
BAL/PAY STAT ECO/TAC ECO/UNDEV

B61
HARRIS S.E.,THE DOLLAR IN CRISIS. USA+45 MARKET INT/ORG ECO/TAC PRICE CONTROL WEALTH...METH/COMP ANTHOL 20 GOLD/STAND. PAGE 62 A1269
BAL/PAY DIPLOM FINAN INT/TRADE

B61
HARRISON J.P.,GUIDE TO MATERIALS ON LATIN AMERICA IN THE NATIONAL ARCHIVES (2 VOLS.). USA+45 ECO/UNDEV FINAN LOC/G FORCES 20. PAGE 62 A1271
BIBLIOG L/A+17C NAT/G DIPLOM

B61
INTERNATIONAL BANK RECONST DEV,THE WORLD BANK IN AFRICA: SUMMARY OF ACTIVITIES. AGRI COM/IND DIST/IND EXTR/IND INDUS TAX COST...CHARTS 20. PAGE 71 A1450
FINAN ECO/UNDEV INT/ORG AFR

B61
MEZERIK A.G.,ECONOMIC DEVELOPMENT AIDS FOR UNDERDEVELOPED COUNTRIES. WOR+45 FINAN LEGIS PROB/SOLV TEC/DEV DIPLOM FOR/AID GIVE TASK WAR 20 UN. PAGE 101 A2062
ECO/UNDEV INT/ORG WEALTH PLAN

B61
MORLEY L.,THE PATCHWORK HISTORY OF FOREIGN AID. KOREA/S USA+45 USSR LAW FINAN INT/ORG TEC/DEV BAL/PWR GIVE 20 COLD/WAR NATO. PAGE 104 A2144
FOR/AID ECO/UNDEV FORCES DIPLOM

B61
NATIONAL BANK OF LIBYA,INFLATION IN LIBYA (PAMPHLET). LIBYA SOCIETY NAT/G PLAN INT/TRADE ...STAT CHARTS 20 GOLD/STAND. PAGE 107 A2200
ECO/TAC ECO/UNDEV FINAN BUDGET

B61
OECD,STATISTICS OF BALANCE OF PAYMENTS 1950-61. WOR+45 FINAN ECO/TAC INT/TRADE DEMAND WEALTH...STAT NAT/COMP 20 OEEC OECD. PAGE 111 A2278
BAL/PAY ECO/DEV INT/ORG CHARTS

B61
OEEC,LIBERALISATION OF CURRENT INVISIBLES AND CAPITAL MOVEMENTS BY THE OEEC (PAMPHLET). WOR+45 ECO/DEV BUDGET ECO/TAC ORD/FREE 20. PAGE 111 A2282
FINAN INT/ORG INT/TRADE BAL/PAY

B61
PANIKKAR K.M.,THE VOICE OF FREEDOM: SELECTED SPEECHES OF PANDIT MOTILAL NEHRU. INDIA UK CONSTN FINAN FORCES LEGIS DIPLOM TAX COLONIAL...POLICY MAJORIT ANTHOL 20 NEHRU/PM. PAGE 114 A2331
NAT/LISM ORD/FREE CHIEF NAT/G

B61
PERLO V.,EL IMPERIALISMO NORTHEAMERICANO. USA+45 USA-45 FINAN CAP/ISM DIPLOM DOMIN CONTROL DISCRIM 19/20. PAGE 115 A2363
SOCIALIST ECO/DEV INT/TRADE ECO/TAC

B61
SCAMMEL W.M.,INTERNATIONAL MONETARY POLICY. WOR+45 WOR-45 ACT/RES ECO/TAC LEGIT WEALTH...GEN/METH UN 20. PAGE 127 A2611
INT/ORG FINAN BAL/PAY

B61
SHAPP W.R.,FIELD ADMINISTRATION IN THE UNITED NATIONS SYSTEM. FINAN PROB/SOLV INSPECT DIPLOM EXEC REGION ROUTINE EFFICIENCY ROLE...INT CHARTS 20 UN. PAGE 131 A2694
INT/ORG ADMIN GP/REL FOR/AID

B61
SINGER J.D.,FINANCING INTERNATIONAL ORGANIZATION: THE UNITED NATIONS BUDGET PROCESS. WOR+45 FINAN ACT/RES CREATE PLAN BUDGET ECO/TAC ADMIN ROUTINE ATTIT KNOWL...DECISION METH/CNCPT TIME/SEQ UN 20. PAGE 133 A2726
INT/ORG MGT

B61
TRIFFIN R.,GOLD AND THE DOLLAR CRISIS: THE FUTURE OF CONVERTIBILITY. USA+45 USA-45 INT/ORG PROB/SOLV BUDGET INT/TRADE PRICE...STAT CHARTS 19/20 GOLD/STAND. PAGE 145 A2963
FINAN ECO/DEV ECO/TAC BAL/PAY

B61
US CONGRESS JOINT ECO COMM,INTERNATIONAL PAYMENTS IMBALANCES AND NEED FOR STRENGTHENING INTERNATIONAL FINANCIAL ARRANGEMENTS. USA+45 WOR+45 DELIB/GP DIPLOM INT/TRADE...CHARTS 20 CONGRESS OEEC. PAGE 150 A3063
BAL/PAY INT/ORG FINAN PROB/SOLV

B61
US HOUSE COMM APPROPRIATIONS,INTER-AMERICAN PROGRAMS FOR 1961: DENIAL OF 1962 BUDGET INFORMATION. CHILE L/A+17C USA+45 FINAN CONSULT BUDGET ADJUD COST EFFICIENCY WEALTH...POLICY CHARTS 20 CONGRESS. PAGE 153 A3119
LEGIS FOR/AID DELIB/GP ECO/UNDEV

B61
US SENATE COMM ON FOREIGN RELS,INTERNATIONAL DEVELOPMENT AND SECURITY: HEARINGS ON BILL (2 VOLS.). ECO/UNDEV FINAN FORCES REV COST WEALTH ...CHARTS 20 AID PRESIDENT. PAGE 157 A3191
FOR/AID CIVMIL/REL ORD/FREE ECO/TAC

S61
JACKSON E.,"THE FUTURE DEVELOPMENT OF THE UNITED NATIONS: SOME SUGGESTIONS FOR RESEARCH." FUT LAW CONSTN ECO/DEV FINAN PEACE WEALTH...WELF/ST CONCPT UN 20. PAGE 72 A1476
INT/ORG PWR

S61
VERNON R.,"A TRADE POLICY FOR THE 1960'S." COM FUT USA+45 WOR+45 ECO/DEV ECO/UNDEV FINAN TOP/EX ACT/RES...WELF/ST METH/CNCPT CONT/OBS TOT/POP 20. PAGE 159 A3229
PLAN INT/TRADE

S61
VINER J.,"ECONOMIC FOREIGN POLICY ON THE NEW FRONTIER." USA+45 ECO/UNDEV AGRI FINAN INDUS MARKET INT/ORG NAT/G FOR/AID INT/TRADE ADMIN ATTIT PWR 20 KENNEDY/JF. PAGE 159 A3239
TOP/EX ECO/TAC BAL/PAY TARIFFS

B62
ROUND TABLE ON EUROPE'S ROLE IN LATIN AMERICAN DEVELOPMENT. EUR+WWI L/A+17C PLAN BAL/PAY UTIL ROLE WEALTH...CHARTS ANTHOL 20 UN INT/AM/DEV. PAGE 3 A0063
ECO/UNDEV FINAN TEC/DEV FOR/AID

B62
ALEXANDROWICZ C.H.,WORLD ECONOMIC AGENCIES: LAW AND PRACTICE. WOR+45 DIST/IND FINAN LABOR CONSULT INT/TRADE TARIFFS REPRESENT HEALTH...JURID 20 UN GATT EEC OAS ECSC. PAGE 6 A0115
INT/LAW INT/ORG DIPLOM ADJUD

B62
CARLSTON K.S.,LAW AND ORGANIZATION IN WORLD SOCIETY. WOR+45 FINAN ECO/TAC DOMIN LEGIT CT/SYS ROUTINE COERCE ORD/FREE PWR WEALTH...PLURIST DECISION JURID MGT METH/CNCPT GEN/LAWS 20. PAGE 24 A0487
INT/ORG LAW

B62
FATOUROS A.A.,GOVERNMENT GUARANTEES TO FOREIGN INVESTORS. WOR+45 ECO/UNDEV INDUS WORKER ADJUD ...NAT/COMP BIBLIOG TREATY. PAGE 44 A0903
NAT/G FINAN INT/TRADE ECO/DEV

B62
FORD A.G.,THE GOLD STANDARD 1880-1914: BRITAIN AND ARGENTINA. UK ECO/UNDEV INT/TRADE ADMIN GOV/REL DEMAND EFFICIENCY...STAT CHARTS 19/20 ARGEN GOLD/STAND. PAGE 47 A0960
FINAN ECO/TAC BUDGET BAL/PAY

B62
FRIEDMANN W.,METHODS AND POLICIES OF PRINCIPAL DONOR COUNTRIES IN PUBLIC INTERNATIONAL DEVELOPMENT FINANCING: PRELIMINARY APPRAISAL. FRANCE GERMANY/W UK USA+45 USSR WOR+45 FINAN TEC/DEV CAP/ISM DIPLOM ECO/TAC ATTIT 20 EEC. PAGE 49 A1002
INT/ORG FOR/AID NAT/COMP ADMIN

B62
HOLMAN A.G.,SOME MEASURES AND INTERPRETATIONS OF
BAL/PAY

EFFECTS OF US FOREIGN ENTERPRISES ON US BALANCE OF PAYMENTS. USA+45 COST INCOME WEALTH...MATH CHARTS 20. PAGE 67 A1371
INT/TRADE FINAN ECO/TAC

B62
JORDAN A.A. JR.,FOREIGN AID AND THE DEFENSE OF SOUTHEAST ASIA. PAKISTAN VIETNAM/S FINAN PLAN BUDGET ECO/TAC DETER WAR ORD/FREE...POLICY DECISION CENSUS CHARTS BIBLIOG 20. PAGE 75 A1535
FOR/AID S/ASIA FORCES ECO/UNDEV

B62
KRAFT J.,THE GRAND DESIGN. EUR+WWI USA+45 AGRI FINAN INDUS MARKET INT/ORG NAT/G PLAN ECO/TAC TARIFFS REGION DRIVE ORD/FREE WEALTH...POLICY OBS TREND EEC 20. PAGE 82 A1674
VOL/ASSN ECO/DEV INT/TRADE

B62
LIPPMANN W.,WESTERN UNITY AND THE COMMON MARKET. EUR+WWI FRANCE GERMANY/W UK USA+45 ECO/DEV AGRI FINAN MARKET INT/ORG NAT/G FOR/AID AGREE WEALTH 20 EEC. PAGE 89 A1831
DIPLOM INT/TRADE VOL/ASSN

B62
LUTZ F.A.,GELD UND WAHRUNG. MARKET LABOR BUDGET 20 GOLD/STAND EUROPE. PAGE 92 A1875
ECO/TAC FINAN DIPLOM POLICY

B62
LUTZ F.A.,THE PROBLEM OF INTERNATIONAL ECONOMIC EQUILIBRIUM. FINAN PRODUC WEALTH 20 MONEY. PAGE 92 A1876
DIPLOM EQUILIB BAL/PAY PROB/SOLV

B62
MOUSSA P.,THE UNDERPRIVILEGED NATIONS. FINAN INT/ORG PLAN PROB/SOLV CAP/ISM GIVE TASK WEALTH ...POLICY SOC 20. PAGE 105 A2159
ECO/UNDEV NAT/G DIPLOM FOR/AID

B62
PAKISTAN MINISTRY OF FINANCE,FOREIGN ECONOMIC AID: A REVIEW OF FOREIGN ECONOMIC AID TO PAKISTAN. EUR+WWI PAKISTAN UK USA+45 USSR ECO/UNDEV INT/ORG DELIB/GP DIPLOM ECO/TAC...CHARTS CMN/WLTH CHINJAP. PAGE 113 A2318
FOR/AID RECEIVE WEALTH FINAN

B62
RIMALOV V.V.,ECONOMIC COOPERATION BETWEEN USSR AND UNDERDEVELOPED COUNTRIES. USSR FINAN TEC/DEV INT/TRADE DOMIN EDU/PROP COLONIAL NAT/LISM DRIVE SOVEREIGN...AUD/VIS 20. PAGE 121 A2482
FOR/AID PLAN ECO/UNDEV DIPLOM

B62
SHAW C.,LEGAL PROBLEMS IN INTERNATIONAL TRADE AND INVESTMENT. WOR+45 ECO/DEV ECO/UNDEV MARKET DIPLOM TAX INCOME ROLE...ANTHOL BIBLIOG 20 TREATY UN IMF GATT. PAGE 132 A2698
INT/LAW INT/TRADE FINAN ECO/TAC

B62
SNOW J.H.,GOVERNMENT BY TREASON. USA+45 USA-45 LEGIS DIPLOM FOR/AID GIVE CONTROL WEALTH MARXISM ...MAJORIT 20 CONGRESS COLD/WAR. PAGE 134 A2750
FINAN TAX PWR POLICY

B62
THANT U.,THE UNITED NATIONS' DEVELOPMENT DECADE: PROPOSALS FOR ACTION. WOR+45 SOCIETY ECO/UNDEV AGRI COM/IND FINAN R+D MUNIC SCHOOL VOL/ASSN CONSULT PLAN TEC/DEV ECO/TAC EDU/PROP ADMIN ROUTINE RIGID/FLEX...MGT SOC CONCPT UNESCO UN TOT/POP VAL/FREE. PAGE 142 A2906
INT/ORG ALL/VALS

B62
US CONGRESS JOINT ECO COMM,FACTORS AFFECTING THE UNITED STATES BALANCE OF PAYMENTS. USA+45 DELIB/GP PLAN DIPLOM FOR/AID PRODUC WEALTH...CHARTS 20 CONGRESS OEEC. PAGE 150 A3064
BAL/PAY INT/TRADE ECO/TAC FINAN

B62
US CONGRESS JOINT ECO COMM,ECONOMIC DEVELOPMENTS IN SOUTH AMERICA. USA+45 SOCIETY FINAN NAT/G PROB/SOLV TEC/DEV INT/TRADE TAX EFFICIENCY PRODUC ATTIT ...POLICY 20 CONGRESS SOUTH/AMER. PAGE 150 A3065
L/A+17C ECO/UNDEV FOR/AID DIPLOM

B62
ZOOK P.D.,FOREIGN TRADE AND HUMAN CAPITAL. L/A+17C USA+45 FINAN DIPLOM ECO/TAC PRODUC...POLICY 20. PAGE 170 A3458
INT/TRADE ECO/UNDEV FOR/AID BAL/PAY

L62
MURACCIOLE L.,"LA BANQUE CENTRALE DES ETATS DE L'AFRIQUE DE L'OUEST." AFR LAW ECO/UNDEV INT/ORG NAT/G CONSULT ECO/TAC ROUTINE...CHARTS 20. PAGE 106 A2175
ISLAM FINAN INT/TRADE

S62
PIQUEMAL M.,"LA COOPERATION FINANCIERE ENTRE LA FRANCE ET LES ETATS AFRICAINS ET MALGACHE." ISLAM INT/ORG TOP/EX ECO/TAC...JURID CHARTS 20. PAGE 116 A2383
AFR FINAN FRANCE MADAGASCAR

B63
BRITISH AID. UK AGRI DIST/IND INDUS SCHOOL TEC/DEV INT/TRADE COLONIAL DEMAND...TREND CHARTS 20. PAGE 3 A0064
FOR/AID ECO/UNDEV NAT/G FINAN

B63
COLUMBIA U SCHOOL OF LAW,PUBLIC INTERNATIONAL DEVELOPMENT FINANCING IN SENEGAL. SENEGAL FINAN DELIB/GP GIVE EFFICIENCY...CHARTS GOV/COMP ANTHOL 20. PAGE 28 A0571
FOR/AID PLAN RECEIVE ECO/UNDEV

B63
EL-NAGGAR S.,FOREIGN AID TO UNITED ARAB REPUBLIC. UAR USA+45 USSR AGRI FINAN INDUS FORCES EATING DEMAND...CHARTS METH/COMP 20 RESOURCE/N AID. PAGE 41 A0838
FOR/AID ECO/UNDEV RECEIVE PLAN

B63
GUIMARAES A.P.,INFLACAO E MONOPOLIO NO BRASIL. BRAZIL FINAN NAT/G PLAN PAY...METH/COMP 20. PAGE 58 A1189
ECO/UNDEV PRICE INT/TRADE BAL/PAY

B63
INTERNATIONAL BANK RECONST DEV,THE WORLD BANK GROUP IN ASIA. ASIA S/ASIA INDUS TEC/DEV ECO/TAC...RECORD 20 IBRD WORLD/BANK. PAGE 71 A1451
INT/ORG DIPLOM ECO/UNDEV FINAN

B63
INTERNATIONAL MONETARY FUND,COMPENSATORY FINANCING OF EXPORT FLUCTUATIONS (PAMPHLET). WOR+45 ECO/DEV ECO/UNDEV INT/ORG WEALTH...TREND 20 IMF MONEY. PAGE 71 A1459
BAL/PAY FINAN BUDGET INT/TRADE

B63
KRAVIS I.B.,DOMESTIC INTERESTS AND INTERNATIONAL OBLIGATIONS: SAFEGUARDS IN INTERNATIONAL TRADE ORGANIZATIONS. EUR+WWI USA+45 WOR+45 FINAN DELIB/GP ATTIT RIGID/FLEX HEALTH...STAT EEC VAL/FREE OEEC ECSC 20. PAGE 82 A1680
INT/ORG ECO/TAC INT/TRADE

B63
LANGE O.,ECONOMIC DEVELOPMENT, PLANNING, AND INTERNATIONAL COOPERATION. UAR WOR+45 FINAN CAP/ISM PERS/REL 20. PAGE 84 A1722
ECO/UNDEV DIPLOM INT/TRADE PLAN

B63
LARY M.B.,PROBLEMS OF THE UNITED STATES AS WORLD TRADER AND BANKER. USA+45 NAT/G PLAN DIPLOM FOR/AID ...TREND CHARTS. PAGE 85 A1737
ECO/DEV FINAN BAL/PAY INT/TRADE

B63
LICHTHEIM G.,THE NEW EUROPE: TODAY AND TOMORROW. EUR+WWI FINAN 20 EEC EUROPE/W. PAGE 88 A1809
DIPLOM ECO/DEV INT/ORG INT/TRADE

B63
MONTER W.,THE GOVERNMENT OF GENEVA, 1536-1605 (DOCTORAL THESIS). SWITZERLND DIPLOM LEAD ORD/FREE SOVEREIGN 16/17 CALVIN/J ROME. PAGE 103 A2112
SECT FINAN LOC/G ADMIN

B63
MULLENBACH P.,CIVILIAN NUCLEAR POWER: ECONOMIC ISSUES AND POLICY FORMATION. FINAN INT/ORG DELIB/GP ACT/RES ECO/TAC ATTIT SUPEGO HEALTH ORD/FREE PWR ...POLICY CONCPT MATH STAT CHARTS VAL/FREE 20 COLD/WAR. PAGE 105 A2166
USA+45 ECO/DEV NUC/PWR

B63
MYRDAL G.,CHALLENGE TO AFFLUENCE. USA+45 WOR+45 FINAN INT/ORG NAT/G PLAN ECO/TAC INT/TRADE BAL/PAY ORD/FREE 20 EUROPE/W. PAGE 107 A2189
ECO/DEV WEALTH DIPLOM PRODUC

B63
PAENSON I.,SYSTEMATIC GLOSSARY ENGLISH, FRENCH, SPANISH, RUSSIAN OF SELECTED ECONOMIC AND SOCIAL TERMS. WOR+45 FINAN LABOR INT/TRADE DEMAND PRODUC 20. PAGE 113 A2315
DICTIONARY SOC LING

B63
ROBOCK S.H.,OVERVIEW OF TOTAL BRAZILIAN SETTING, NEWER REGIONAL PATTERNS NING AND FOREIGN AID. BRAZIL ECO/UNDEV AGRI FINAN INDUS INT/ORG INCOME UTIL...CHARTS 20. PAGE 122 A2507
ECO/TAC REGION PLAN FOR/AID

B63
SALENT W.S.,THE UNITED STATES BALANCE OF PAYMENTS IN 1968. EUR+WWI UK USA+45 AGRI R+D LABOR FORCES PRODUC...GEOG CONCPT CHARTS 20 CHINJAP EEC. PAGE 126 A2589
BAL/PAY DEMAND FINAN INT/TRADE

B63
THORELLI H.B.,INTOP: INTERNATIONAL OPERATIONS SIMULATION: PLAYER'S MANUAL. BRAZIL FINAN OP/RES ADMIN GP/REL INGP/REL PRODUC PERCEPT...DECISION MGT EEC. PAGE 144 A2935
GAME INT/TRADE EDU/PROP LG/CO

B63
UAR MINISTRY OF CULTURE,A BIBLIOGRAPHICAL LIST OF ARABIAN PENINSULA. ISLAM SAUDI/ARAB YEMEN FINAN NAT/G DIPLOM 19/20. PAGE 146 A2990
BIBLIOG GEOG INDUS SECT

B63
UN SECRETARY GENERAL,PLANNING FOR ECONOMIC DEVELOPMENT. ECO/UNDEV FINAN BUDGET INT/TRADE TARIFFS TAX ADMIN 20 UN. PAGE 147 A3005
PLAN ECO/TAC MGT NAT/COMP

B63
US CONGRESS JOINT ECO COMM,THE UNITED STATES BALANCE OF PAYMENTS. USA+45 DELIB/GP BUDGET PRICE PRODUC 20 CONGRESS GOLD/STAND MONEY. PAGE 150 A3067
BAL/PAY INT/TRADE FINAN ECO/TAC

B63
US GOVERNMENT,REPORT TO INTER-AMERICAN ECONOMIC AND SOCIAL COUNCIL AT SECOND ANNUAL MEETING. L/A+17C USA+45 VOL/ASSN TEC/DEV DIPLOM TAX EATING
ECO/TAC FOR/AID FINAN

EFFICIENCY HEALTH...STAT CHARTS 20 AID. PAGE 153 A3116 PLAN

B63
US HOUSE COMM BANKING-CURR,RECENT CHANGES IN MONETARY POLICY AND BALANCE OF PAYMENTS PROBLEMS. USA+45 DELIB/GP PLAN DIPLOM...CHARTS 20 CONGRESS. PAGE 153 A3121 BAL/PAY FINAN ECO/TAC POLICY

B63
US SENATE COMM APPROPRIATIONS,PERSONNEL ADMINISTRATION AND OPERATIONS OF AGENCY FOR INTERNATIONAL DEVELOPMENT: SPECIAL HEARING. FINAN LEAD COST UTIL SKILL...CHARTS 20 CONGRESS AID CIVIL/SERV. PAGE 155 A3170 ADMIN FOR/AID EFFICIENCY DIPLOM

B63
US SENATE COMM GOVT OPERATIONS,REPORT OF A STUDY OF US FOREIGN AID IN TEN MIDDLE EASTERN AND AFRICAN COUNTRIES. AFR ISLAM USA+45 FORCES PLAN BUDGET DIPLOM TAX DETER WEALTH...STAT CHARTS 20 CONGRESS AID MID/EAST. PAGE 156 A3174 FOR/AID EFFICIENCY ECO/TAC FINAN

B63
VAN SLYCK P.,PEACE: THE CONTROL OF NATIONAL POWER. CUBA WOR+45 FINAN NAT/G FORCES PROB/SOLV TEC/DEV BAL/PWR ADMIN CONTROL ORD/FREE...POLICY INT/LAW UN COLD/WAR TREATY. PAGE 158 A3214 ARMS/CONT PEACE INT/ORG DIPLOM

B63
YOUNG A.N.,CHINA AND THE HELPING HAND. ASIA USA+45 FINAN INDUS ECO/TAC GIVE WEALTH...METH/COMP 20 LEND/LEASE GOLD/STAND. PAGE 169 A3434 FOR/AID DIPLOM WAR

L63
PADELFORD N.J.,"FINANCIAL CRISIS AND THE UNITED NATIONS." FUT USSR WOR+45 LAW CONSTN FINAN INT/ORG DELIB/GP FORCES PLAN BUDGET DIPLOM COST WEALTH ...STAT CHARTS UN CONGO 20. PAGE 113 A2311 CREATE ECO/TAC

L63
PRINCETON UNIV. CONFERENCE,"ARAB DEVELOPMENT IN THE EMERGING INTERNATIONAL ECONOMY." FUT USA+45 DIST/IND FINAN DELIB/GP PLAN ECO/TAC WEALTH VAL/FREE 20. PAGE 118 A2413 ISLAM ECO/UNDEV FOR/AID INT/TRADE

S63
ANGUILE G.,"CIVILISATION DU PLAN DANS L'EUROPE ET L'AFRIQUE DE DEMAIN." AFR EUR+WWI GABON ECO/DEV FINAN MARKET DELIB/GP ECO/TAC WEALTH...TREND 20. PAGE 8 A0163 ECO/UNDEV PLAN INT/TRADE

S63
BALOGH T.,"L'INFLUENCE DES INSTITUTIONS MONETAIRES ET COMMERCIALES SUR LA STRUCTURE ECONOMIQUE AFRICAIN." AFR EUR+WWI FUT USA+45 USA-45 WOR+45 SERV/IND INT/ORG NAT/G TOP/EX ROUTINE...INDEX EEC 20. PAGE 11 A0215 FINAN

S63
BARTHELEMY G.,"LE NOUVEAU FRANC (CFA) ET LA BANQUE CENTRALE DES ETATS DE L'AFRIQUE DE L'OUEST." FUT STRUCT INT/ORG PLAN ATTIT ALL/VALS 20. PAGE 11 A0230 AFR FINAN

S63
COUTY P.,"L'ASSISTANCE POUR LE DEVELOPPEMENT: POINT DE VUE SCANDINAVES." EUR+WWI FINLAND FUT SWEDEN WOR+45 ECO/DEV ECO/UNDEV COM/IND LABOR NAT/G PROF/ORG ACT/RES SKILL WEALTH TOT/POP 20. PAGE 32 A0643 FINAN ROUTINE FOR/AID

S63
DAVEE R.,"POUR UN FONDS DE DEVELOPPEMENT SOCIAL." FUT WOR+45 INTELL SOCIETY ECO/DEV FINAN TEC/DEV ROUTINE WEALTH...TREND TOT/POP VAL/FREE UN 20. PAGE 34 A0684 INT/ORG SOC FOR/AID

S63
HORVATH J.,"MOSCOW'S AID PROGRAM: THE PERFORMANCE SO FAR." COM FUT USSR WOR+45 ECO/DEV FINAN PLAN TEC/DEV FOR/AID EDU/PROP ATTIT ORD/FREE PWR WEALTH ...POLICY STAT CHARTS VAL/FREE 20. PAGE 68 A1389 ECO/UNDEV ECO/TAC

S63
KRAVIS I.B.,"THE POLITICAL ARITHMETIC OF INTERNATIONAL BURDENSHARING." FUT USA+45 WOR+45 FINAN DELIB/GP ACT/RES CREATE TEC/DEV ATTIT PWR WEALTH...POLICY MATH STAT VAL/FREE 20. PAGE 82 A1681 INT/ORG ECO/TAC

S63
LEDUC G.,"L'AIDE INTERNATIONALE AU DEVELOPPEMENT." FUT WOR+45 ECO/DEV ECO/UNDEV R+D PROF/ORG TEC/DEV ECO/TAC ROUTINE ATTIT ALL/VALS...MGT TIME/SEQ TOT/POP 20. PAGE 86 A1758 FINAN PLAN FOR/AID

S63
MANOLIU F.,"PERSPECTIVES D'UNE INTEGRATION ECONOMIQUE LATINOAMERICAINE." FUT L/A+17C STRUCT MARKET LABOR POL/PAR VOL/ASSN PLAN RIGID/FLEX PWR ...METH/CNCPT OAS TOT/POP 20. PAGE 94 A1927 FINAN INT/ORG PEACE

S63
MATHUR P.N.,"GAINS IN ECONOMIC GROWTH FROM INTERNATIONAL TRADE." USA-45 ECO/DEV FINAN INDUS ATTIT WEALTH...MATH QUANT STAT BIOG TREND GEN/LAWS WORK 20. PAGE 96 A1966 MARKET ECO/TAC CAP/ISM INT/TRADE

S63
PINCUS J.,"THE COST OF FOREIGN AID." WOR+45 ECO/DEV FINAN NAT/G VOL/ASSN CREATE ECO/TAC EDU/PROP WEALTH ...METH/CNCPT STAT CHARTS HYPO/EXP TOT/POP VAL/FREE 20. PAGE 116 A2380 USA+45 ECO/UNDEV FOR/AID

S63
WALKER H.,"THE INTERNATIONAL LAW OF COMMODITY AGREEMENTS." FUT WOR+45 ECO/DEV ECO/UNDEV FINAN INT/ORG NAT/G CONSULT CREATE PLAN ECO/TAC ATTIT PERCEPT...CONCPT GEN/LAWS TOT/POP GATT 20. PAGE 160 A3265 MARKET VOL/ASSN INT/LAW INT/TRADE

S63
WEILLER J.,"UNIONS MONETAIRES ET RAPPORTS DE COOPERATION INTERNATIONALE DANS UN MONDE EN TRANSITION: L'EXAMPLE." AFR FUT UNIV WOR+45 SOCIETY ECO/UNDEV MARKET R+D NAT/G FOR/AID PERCEPT RIGID/FLEX...NEW/IDEA 20. PAGE 162 A3303 FINAN INT/ORG

S63
WYZNER E.,"NIEKTORE ASPEKTY PRAWNE FINANSOWANIA OPERACJI ONZ W KONGO I NA BEIZKIM WSCHODZIE." S/ASIA CONSTN FINAN INT/ORG TOP/EX...TIME/SEQ UN 20 CONGRESS. PAGE 168 A3426 FORCES JURID DIPLOM

C63
SCHMITT K.M.,"EVOLUTION OR CHAOS: DYNAMICS OF LATIN AMERICAN GOVERNMENT AND POLITICS." L/A+17C AGRI FINAN CAP/ISM EXEC LEAD BAL/PAY TOTALISM ATTIT ...TREND BIBLIOG 20. PAGE 129 A2635 DIPLOM POLICY POL/PAR LOBBY

N63
US AGENCY INTERNATIONAL DEV,PRINCIPLES OF FOREIGN ECONOMIC ASSISTANCE (PAMPHLET). USA+45 FINAN GP/REL BAL/PAY EFFICIENCY 20 AID. PAGE 149 A3051 FOR/AID PLAN ECO/UNDEV ATTIT

B64
THE SPECIAL COMMONWEALTH AFRICAN ASSISTANCE PLAN. AFR CANADA INDIA NIGERIA UK FINAN SCHOOL...CHARTS 20 COMMONWLTH. PAGE 3 A0065 ECO/UNDEV TREND FOR/AID ADMIN

B64
CHENG C.,ECONOMIC RELATIONS BETWEEN PEKING AND MOSCOW: 1949-63. ASIA CHINA/COM COM USSR FINAN INDUS CONSULT TEC/DEV INT/TRADE...PREDICT CHARTS BIBLIOG 20. PAGE 26 A0527 DIPLOM FOR/AID MARXISM

B64
COLUMBIA U SCHOOL OF LAW,PUBLIC INTERNATIONAL DEVELOPMENT FINANCING IN INDIA. GERMANY/W INDIA UK USA+45 INDUS PLAN TEC/DEV DIPLOM ECO/TAC GIVE ADMIN UTIL ATTIT 20. PAGE 28 A0572 ECO/UNDEV FINAN FOR/AID INT/ORG

B64
DUROSELLE J.B.,POLITIQUES NATIONALES ENVERS LES JEUNES ETATS. FRANCE ISRAEL ITALY UK USA+45 USSR YUGOSLAVIA ECO/DEV FINAN ECO/TAC INT/TRADE ADMIN PWR 20. PAGE 40 A0809 DIPLOM ECO/UNDEV COLONIAL DOMIN

B64
FATOUROS A.A.,CANADA'S OVERSEAS AID. CANADA WOR+45 ECO/DEV FINAN NAT/G BUDGET ECO/TAC CONFER ADMIN 20. PAGE 44 A0904 FOR/AID DIPLOM ECO/UNDEV POLICY

B64
GESELLSCHAFT RECHTSVERGLEICH,BIBLIOGRAPHIE DES DEUTSCHEN RECHTS (BIBLIOGRAPHY OF GERMAN LAW, TRANS. BY COURTLAND PETERSON). GERMANY FINAN INDUS LABOR SECT FORCES CT/SYS PARL/PROC CRIME...INT/LAW SOC NAT/COMP 20. PAGE 52 A1066 BIBLIOG/A JURID CONSTN ADMIN

B64
HAMBRIDGE G.,DYNAMICS OF DEVELOPMENT. AGRI FINAN INDUS LABOR INT/TRADE EDU/PROP ADMIN LEAD OWN HEALTH...ANTHOL BIBLIOG 20. PAGE 61 A1245 ECO/UNDEV ECO/TAC OP/RES ACT/RES

B64
HANSEN B.,INTERNATIONAL LIQUIDITY. USA+45 INT/ORG ECO/TAC PRICE CONTROL WEALTH...POLICY 20. PAGE 61 A1254 BAL/PAY INT/TRADE DIPLOM FINAN

B64
HAZLEWOOD A.,THE ECONOMICS OF DEVELOPMENT: AN ANNOTATED LIST OF BOOKS AND ARTICLES PUBLISHED 1958-1962. AGRI FINAN INDUS LABOR NAT/G DIPLOM INT/TRADE INCOME...MGT 20. PAGE 63 A1303 BIBLIOG/A ECO/UNDEV TEC/DEV

B64
INTL INF CTR LOCAL CREDIT,GOVERNMENT MEASURES FOR THE PROMOTION OF REGIONAL ECONOMIC DEVELOPMENT. WOR+45 ECO/UNDEV FINAN INT/ORG DIPLOM ORD/FREE ...POLICY GEOG 20. PAGE 71 A1464 FOR/AID PLAN ECO/TAC REGION

B64
KALDOR N.,ESSAYS ON ECONOMIC POLICY (VOL. II). CHILE GERMANY INDIA FINAN...GOV/COMP METH/COMP 20 KEYNES/JM. PAGE 76 A1551 BAL/PAY INT/TRADE METH/CNCPT ECO/UNDEV

B64
KNIGHT R.,BIBLIOGRAPHY ON INCOME AND WEALTH, 1957-1960 (VOL VIII). WOR+45 ECO/DEV FINAN INT/TRADE...GOV/COMP METH/COMP. PAGE 80 A1652 BIBLIOG/A ECO/UNDEV WEALTH INCOME

B64
KNOX V.H.,PUBLIC FINANCE: INFORMATION SOURCES. USA+45 DIPLOM ADMIN GOV/REL COST...POLICY 20. PAGE 81 A1657 BIBLIOG/A FINAN TAX BUDGET

B64
MYINT H.,THE ECONOMICS OF THE DEVELOPING COUNTRIES. WOR+45 AGRI PLAN COST...POLICY GEOG 20 MONEY. ECO/UNDEV INT/TRADE

PAGE 107 A2187 EXTR/IND FINAN

B64
NEWCOMER H.A.,INTERNATIONAL AIDS TO OVERSEAS INVESTMENTS AND TRADE. ECO/UNDEV TARIFFS PROFIT ...BIBLIOG 20 GATT UN. PAGE 108 A2225 INT/TRADE FINAN DIPLOM FOR/AID

B64
OECD,THE FLOW OF FINANCIAL RESOURCES TO LESS DEVELOPED COUNTRIES 1956-1963. WOR+45 FINAN CAP/ISM ...POLICY STAT 20. PAGE 111 A2281 FOR/AID BUDGET INT/ORG ECO/UNDEV

B64
PERKINS D.,THE AMERICAN DEMOCRACY: ITS RISE TO POWER. ASIA USSR LAW CULTURE FINAN EDU/PROP COLONIAL CHOOSE...POLICY CHARTS BIBLIOG WORSHIP PRESIDENT 15/20 NEGRO. PAGE 115 A2362 LOC/G ECO/TAC WAR DIPLOM

B64
RANIS G.,THE UNITED STATES AND THE DEVELOPING ECONOMIES. COM USA+45 AGRI FINAN TEC/DEV CAP/ISM ECO/TAC INT/TRADE...POLICY METH/COMP ANTHOL 20 AID. PAGE 119 A2441 ECO/UNDEV DIPLOM FOR/AID

B64
REUSS H.S.,THE CRITICAL DECADE - AN ECONOMIC POLICY FOR AMERICA AND THE FREE WORLD. USA+45 FINAN POL/PAR WORKER PLAN DIPLOM ECO/TAC TARIFFS BAL/PAY ...POLICY 20 CONGRESS GOLD/STAND. PAGE 120 A2468 FOR/AID INT/TRADE LABOR LEGIS

B64
RICHARDSON I.L.,BIBLIOGRAFIA BRASILEIRA DE ADMINISTRACAO PUBLICA E ASSUNTOS CORRELATOS. BRAZIL CONSTN FINAN LOC/G NAT/G POL/PAR PLAN DIPLOM RECEIVE ATTIT...METH 20. PAGE 121 A2474 BIBLIOG MGT ADMIN LAW

B64
SINGER H.W.,INTERNATIONAL DEVELOPMENT: GROWTH AND CHANGE. AFR BRAZIL L/A+17C WOR+45 CULTURE AGRI INDUS NAT/G ACT/RES ECO/TAC EDU/PROP WEALTH...GEOG CONCPT METH/CNCPT STAT HYPO/EXP WORK TOT/POP 20. PAGE 133 A2723 FINAN ECO/UNDEV FOR/AID INT/TRADE

B64
STEWART C.F.,A BIBLIOGRAPHY OF INTERNATIONAL BUSINESS. WOR+45 FINAN LG/CO NAT/G PLAN ECO/TAC TARIFFS...DECISION MGT GP/COMP NAT/COMP 20 EEC. PAGE 138 A2824 BIBLIOG INT/ORG OP/RES INT/TRADE

B64
STOESSINGER J.G.,FINANCING THE UNITED NATIONS SYSTEM. FUT WOR+45 CONSTN NAT/G VOL/ASSN DELIB/GP EX/STRUC ECO/TAC LEGIT CT/SYS PWR WEALTH...STAT TIME/SEQ TREND CHARTS VAL/FREE. PAGE 138 A2830 FINAN INT/ORG

B64
SZLADITS C.,BIBLIOGRAPHY ON FOREIGN AND COMPARATIVE LAW: BOOKS AND ARTICLES IN ENGLISH (SUPPLEMENT 1962). FINAN INDUS JUDGE LICENSE ADMIN CT/SYS PARL/PROC OWN...INT/LAW CLASSIF METH/COMP NAT/COMP 20. PAGE 141 A2877 BIBLIOG/A JURID ADJUD LAW

B64
US HOUSE COMM GOVT OPERATIONS,US OWNED FOREIGN CURRENCIES: HEARINGS (COMMITTEE ON GOVERNMENT OPERATIONS). INDIA ECO/DEV PLAN BUDGET TAX DEMAND EFFICIENCY 20 AID CONGRESS. PAGE 154 A3138 FINAN ECO/TAC FOR/AID OWN

B64
ZEBOT C.A.,THE ECONOMICS OF COMPETITIVE COEXISTENCE. CHINA/COM USSR WOR+45 FINAN MARKET FOR/AID PRICE DEMAND EQUILIB WEALTH ALL/IDEOS 20. PAGE 169 A3450 TEC/DEV DIPLOM METH/COMP

L64
ARMENGALD A.,"ECONOMIE ET COEXISTENCE." COM EUR+WWI FUT USA+45 WOR+45 ECO/DEV ECO/UNDEV FINAN INT/ORG NAT/G EXEC CHOOSE ATTIT ALL/VALS...POLICY RELATIV DECISION TREND SOC/EXP COLD/WAR WORK 20. PAGE 9 A0173 MARKET ECO/TAC CAP/ISM

L64
CARNEGIE ENDOWMENT INT. PEACE,"POLITICAL QUESTIONS (ISSUES BEFORE THE NINETEENTH GENERAL ASSEMBLY)." SPACE WOR+45 CONSTN FINAN NAT/G CONSULT DELIB/GP FORCES LEGIS TEC/DEV EDU/PROP LEGIT ARMS/CONT COERCE NUC/PWR ATTIT ALL/VALS...CONCPT OBS UN COLD/WAR 20. PAGE 24 A0490 INT/ORG PEACE

L64
MANZER R.A.,"THE UNITED NATIONS SPECIAL FUND." WOR+45 CONSTN ECO/UNDEV NAT/G TOP/EX LEGIT WEALTH ...CHARTS UN 20. PAGE 94 A1936 FINAN INT/ORG

S64
CARNEGIE ENDOWMENT INT. PEACE,"ADMINISTRATION AND BUDGET (ISSUES BEFORE THE NINETEENTH GENERAL ASSEMBLY)." WOR+45 FINAN BUDGET ECO/TAC ROUTINE COST...STAT RECORD UN. PAGE 24 A0495 INT/ORG ADMIN

S64
GARDNER R.N.,"THE SOVIET UNION AND THE UNITED NATIONS." WOR+45 FINAN POL/PAR VOL/ASSN FORCES ECO/TAC DOMIN EDU/PROP LEGIT ADJUD ADMIN ARMS/CONT COERCE ATTIT ALL/VALS...POLICY MAJORIT CONCPT OBS TIME/SEQ TREND STERTYP UN. PAGE 51 A1046 COM INT/ORG USSR

S64
HUELIN D.,"ECONOMIC INTEGRATION IN LATIN AMERICAN: PROGRESS AND PROBLEMS." L/A+17C ECO/DEV AGRI DIST/IND FINAN INDUS NAT/G VOL/ASSN CONSULT DELIB/GP EX/STRUC ACT/RES PLAN TEC/DEV ECO/TAC ROUTINE BAL/PAY WEALTH WORK 20. PAGE 69 A1411 MARKET ECO/UNDEV INT/TRADE

S64
MOWER A.G.,"THE OFFICIAL PRESSURE GROUP OF THE COUNCIL OF EUROPE'S CONSULATIVE ASSEMBLY." EUR+WWI SOCIETY STRUCT FINAN CONSULT ECO/TAC ADMIN ROUTINE ATTIT PWR WEALTH...STAT CHARTS 20 COUNCL/EUR. PAGE 105 A2160 INT/ORG EDU/PROP

S64
NEISSER H.,"THE EXTERNAL EQUILIBRIUM OF THE UNITED STATES ECONOMY." FUT USA+45 NAT/G ACT/RES PLAN ECO/TAC ATTIT WEALTH...METH/CNCPT GEN/METH VAL/FREE 20. PAGE 108 A2216 FINAN ECO/DEV BAL/PAY INT/TRADE

S64
TAUBENFELD R.K.,"INDEPENDENT REVENUE FOR THE UNITED NATIONS." WOR+45 SOCIETY STRUCT INDUS NAT/G CONSULT ACT/RES PLAN ECO/TAC LEGIT WEALTH...DECISION CON/ANAL GEN/METH UN 20. PAGE 142 A2896 INT/ORG FINAN

S64
ZARTMAN I.W.,"LES RELATIONS ENTRE LA FRANCE ET L'ALGERIA DEPUIS LES ACCORDS D'EVIAN." EUR+WWI FUT ISLAM CULTURE AGRI EXTR/IND FINAN INDUS POL/PAR DIPLOM ECO/TAC FOR/AID PEACE ATTIT DRIVE ALL/VALS ...TIME/SEQ VAL/FREE 20. PAGE 169 A3446 ECO/UNDEV ALGERIA FRANCE

C64
SCHRAMM W.,"MASS MEDIA AND NATIONAL DEVELOPMENT: THE ROLE OF INFORMATION IN DEVELOPING COUNTRIES." FINAN R+D ACT/RES PLAN TEC/DEV DIPLOM CHOOSE SUPEGO ORD/FREE...BIBLIOG 20. PAGE 129 A2645 ECO/UNDEV COM/IND EDU/PROP MAJORIT

B65
ANALYSIS AND ASSESSMENT OF THE ECONOMIC EFFECTS: PUBLIC LAW 480 TITLE I PROGRAM TURKEY. INDIA TURKEY USA+45 AGRI NAT/G PLAN BUDGET DIPLOM COST EFFICIENCY...CHARTS 20. PAGE 3 A0070 ECO/TAC FOR/AID FINAN ECO/UNDEV

B65
AMERICAN ECONOMIC ASSOCIATION,INDEX OF ECONOMIC JOURNALS 1886-1965 (7 VOLS.). UK USA+45 USA-45 AGRI FINAN PLAN ECO/TAC INT/TRADE ADMIN...STAT CENSUS 19/20. PAGE 7 A0145 BIBLIOG WRITING INDUS

B65
BROOKINGS INSTITUTION,BROOKINGS PAPERS ON PUBLIC POLICY. USA+45 ECO/UNDEV LEGIS CAP/ISM ECO/TAC TAX EDU/PROP CONTROL APPORT 20. PAGE 19 A0395 DIPLOM FOR/AID POLICY FINAN

B65
CASSELL F.,GOLD OR CREDIT? THE ECONOMICS AND POLITICS OF INTERNATIONAL MONEY. WOR+45 PLAN PROB/SOLV BAL/PAY SOVEREIGN WEALTH 20 OEEC GOLD/STAND. PAGE 25 A0506 FINAN INT/ORG DIPLOM ECO/TAC

B65
FRUTKIN A.W.,SPACE AND THE INTERNATIONAL COOPERATION YEAR: A NATIONAL CHALLENGE (PAMPHLET). EUR+WWI USA+45 FINAN TEC/DEV BUDGET...MGT 20 NASA. PAGE 49 A1011 SPACE INDUS NAT/G DIPLOM

B65
INTERNATIONAL SOCIAL SCI COUN,SOCIAL SCIENCES IN THE USSR. USSR ECO/DEV AGRI FINAN INDUS PLAN CAP/ISM...INT/LAW PHIL/SCI PSY SOC 20. PAGE 71 A1460 BIBLIOG/A ACT/RES MARXISM JURID

B65
JOHNSON H.G.,THE WORLD ECONOMY AT THE CROSSROADS. COM WOR-45 ECO/DEV AGRI INDUS INT/TRADE REGION NAT/LISM 20. PAGE 74 A1523 FINAN DIPLOM INT/ORG ECO/UNDEV

B65
JOHNSTONE A.,UNITED STATES DIRECT INVESTMENT IN FRANCE: AN INVESTIGATION OF THE FRENCH CHARGES. FRANCE USA+45 ECO/DEV INDUS LG/CO NAT/G ECO/TAC CONTROL WEALTH...BIBLIOG 20 INTERVENT. PAGE 75 A1529 FINAN DIPLOM POLICY SOVEREIGN

B65
KRAUSE W.,ECONOMIC DEVELOPMENT: THE UNDERDEVELOPED WORLD AND THE AMERICAN INTEREST. USA+45 AGRI PLAN MARXISM...CHARTS 20. PAGE 82 A1679 FOR/AID ECO/UNDEV FINAN PROB/SOLV

B65
LYONS G.M.,AMERICA: PURPOSE AND POWER. UK USA+45 FINAN INDUS MARKET WORKER TEC/DEV DIPLOM AUTOMAT NUC/PWR WAR RACE/REL ORD/FREE 20 EEC CONGRESS SUPREME/CT CIV/RIGHTS. PAGE 92 A1881 PWR PROB/SOLV ECO/DEV TASK

B65
MACDONALD R.W.,THE LEAGUE OF ARAB STATES: A STUDY IN THE DYNAMICS OF REGIONAL ORGANIZATION. ISRAEL UAR USSR FINAN INT/ORG DELIB/GP ECO/TAC AGREE NEUTRAL ORD/FREE PWR...DECISION BIBLIOG 20 TREATY UN. PAGE 92 A1888 ISLAM REGION DIPLOM ADMIN

B65
MEAGHER R.F.,PUBLIC INTERNATIONAL DEVELOPMENT FINANCING IN SUDAN. SUDAN FINAN DELIB/GP GIVE ...CHARTS GOV/COMP 20. PAGE 99 A2029 FOR/AID PLAN RECEIVE ECO/UNDEV

B65
MONCRIEFF A.,SECOND THOUGHTS ON AID. WOR+45 ECO/UNDEV AGRI FINAN VOL/ASSN PLAN TEC/DEV GIVE EDU/PROP ROLE WEALTH 20. PAGE 102 A2105 FOR/AID ECO/TAC INT/ORG IDEA/COMP

B65
MURUMBI J.,PROBLEMS OF ECONOMIC DEVELOPMENT IN EAST AFRICA. FINAN INDUS WORKER TEC/DEV INT/TRADE TAX DEMAND EFFICIENCY PRODUC SOCISM...TREND CHARTS 20 AFRICA/E. PAGE 106 A2184
AGRI ECO/TAC ECO/UNDEV PROC/MFG

B65
SABLE M.H.,MASTER DIRECTORY FOR LATIN AMERICA. AGRI COM/IND FINAN R+D ACADEM LABOR NAT/G POL/PAR VOL/ASSN INT/TRADE EDU/PROP 20. PAGE 126 A2582
INDEX L/A+17C INT/ORG DIPLOM

B65
STEWART I.G.,AFRICAN PRIMARY PRODUCTS AND INTERNATIONAL TRADE. ECO/UNDEV AGRI FINAN DIPLOM CONTROL 20. PAGE 138 A2825
AFR INT/TRADE INT/ORG

B65
US BUREAU OF THE BUDGET,THE BALANCE OF PAYMENTS STATISTICS OF THE UNITED STATES: A REVIEW AND APPRAISAL. USA+45 FINAN NAT/G PROB/SOLV DIPLOM. PAGE 150 A3057
BAL/PAY STAT METH/COMP BUDGET

B65
US CONGRESS JOINT ECO COMM,GUIDELINES FOR INTERNATIONAL MONETARY REFORM. USA+45 WOR+45 DELIB/GP BAL/PAY 20 CONGRESS IMF MONEY. PAGE 150 A3069
DIPLOM FINAN PLAN INT/ORG

B65
US SENATE COMM BANKING CURR,BALANCE OF PAYMENTS - 1965. USA+45 ECO/TAC PRICE WEALTH...CHARTS 20 CONGRESS GOLD/STAND. PAGE 156 A3171
BAL/PAY FINAN DIPLOM INT/TRADE

B65
US SENATE COMM ON JUDICIARY,ANTITRUST EXEMPTIONS FOR AGREEMENTS RELATING TO BALANCE OF PAYMENTS. FINAN ECO/TAC CONTROL WEALTH...POLICY 20 CONGRESS. PAGE 157 A3195
BAL/PAY ADJUD MARKET INT/TRADE

B65
WEAVER J.N.,THE INTERNATIONAL DEVELOPMENT ASSOCIATION: A NEW APPROACH TO FOREIGN AID. USA+45 NAT/G OP/RES PLAN PROB/SOLV WEALTH...CHARTS BIBLIOG 20 UN. PAGE 162 A3295
FOR/AID INT/ORG ECO/UNDEV FINAN

B65
WEILER J.,L'ECONOMIE INTERNATIONALE DEPUIS 1950. WOR+45 DIPLOM TARIFFS CONFER...POLICY TREATY. PAGE 162 A3302
FINAN INT/TRADE REGION FOR/AID

B65
WHITE J.,GERMAN AID. GERMANY/W FINAN PLAN TEC/DEV INT/TRADE ADMIN ATTIT...POLICY 20. PAGE 164 A3335
FOR/AID ECO/UNDEV DIPLOM ECO/TAC

L65
LOFTUS M.L.,"INTERNATIONAL MONETARY FUND, 1962-1965: A SELECTED BIBLIOGRAPHY." WOR+45 PLAN BUDGET INCOME PROFIT WEALTH. PAGE 90 A1852
BIBLIOG FINAN INT/TRADE INT/ORG

L65
MATTHEWS D.G.,"A CURRENT BIBLIOGRAPHY ON SUDANESE AFFAIRS; A SELECT BIBLIOGRAPHY FROM 1960-1964." SUDAN LAW CULTURE AGRI FINAN INDUS LABOR POL/PAR TEC/DEV FOR/AID RACE/REL LITERACY...LING 20. PAGE 96 A1970
BIBLIOG ECO/UNDEV NAT/G DIPLOM

L65
WIONCZEK M.,"LATIN AMERICA FREE TRADE ASSOCIATION." AGRI DIST/IND FINAN INDUS INT/ORG LABOR NAT/G TEC/DEV ECO/TAC HEALTH SKILL WEALTH...POLICY RELATIV MGT LAFTA 20. PAGE 165 A3369
L/A+17C MARKET REGION

S65
AFRICAN BIBLIOGRAPHIC CENTER,"US TREATIES AND AGREEMENTS WITH COUNTRIES IN AFRICA, 1957 TO MID-1963." AFR USA+45 AGRI FINAN FORCES TEC/DEV CAP/ISM FOR/AID 20. PAGE 5 A0097
BIBLIOG DIPLOM INT/ORG INT/TRADE

S65
KHOURI F.J.,"THE JORDON RIVER CONTROVERSY." LAW SOCIETY ECO/UNDEV AGRI FINAN INDUS SECT FORCES ACT/RES PLAN TEC/DEV ECO/TAC EDU/PROP COERCE ATTIT DRIVE PERCEPT RIGID/FLEX ALL/VALS...GEOG SOC MYTH WORK. PAGE 78 A1610
ISLAM INT/ORG ISRAEL JORDAN

B66
SUPPLEMENTAL FOREIGN ASSISTANCE FISCAL YEAR 1966: VIETNAM. CHINA/COM COM S/ASIA USA+45 VIETNAM EXTR/IND FINAN DIPLOM TAX GUERRILLA HABITAT ORD/FREE...STAT CHARTS 20 SENATE PRESIDENT. PAGE 4 A0077
CONFER LEGIS WAR FOR/AID

B66
BALDWIN D.A.,ECONOMIC DEVELOPMENT AND AMERICAN FOREIGN POLICY. USA+45 FINAN LG/CO LEGIS DIPLOM GIVE 20. PAGE 10 A0210
ECO/TAC FOR/AID ECO/UNDEV POLICY

B66
BROEKMEIJER M.W.J.,FICTION AND TRUTH ABOUT THE "DECADE OF DEVELOPMENT" WOR+45 AGRI FINAN INDUS NAT/G TEC/DEV DIPLOM EDU/PROP LEAD SKILL 20 THIRD/WRLD. PAGE 19 A0385
FOR/AID POLICY ECO/UNDEV PLAN

B66
FREIDEL F.,AMERICAN ISSUES IN THE TWENTIETH CENTURY. SOCIETY FINAN ECO/TAC FOR/AID CONTROL NUC/PWR WAR RACE/REL PEACE ATTIT...ANTHOL T 20 WILSON/W ROOSEVLT/F KENNEDY/JF TRUMAN/HS. PAGE 49 A0995
DIPLOM POLICY NAT/G ORD/FREE

B66
HAMILTON W.B.,A DECADE OF THE COMMONWEALTH, 1955-1964. UK LAW ELITES FINAN FOR/AID CONFER COLONIAL PWR...GEOG CHARTS ANTHOL 20 CMN/WLTH UN. PAGE 61 A1247
INT/ORG INGP/REL DIPLOM NAT/G

B66
HAYER T.,FRENCH AID. AFR FRANCE AGRI FINAN BUDGET ADMIN WAR PRODUC...CHARTS 18/20 THIRD/WRLD OVRSEA/DEV. PAGE 63 A1295
TEC/DEV COLONIAL FOR/AID ECO/UNDEV

B66
INTERNATIONAL ECO POLICY ASSN,THE UNITED STATES BALANCE OF PAYMENTS. INT/ORG NAT/G PROB/SOLV BUDGET DIPLOM INT/TRADE WEALTH 20. PAGE 71 A1454
BAL/PAY ECO/TAC POLICY FINAN

B66
KAREFA-SMART J.,AFRICA: PROGRESS THROUGH COOPERATION. AFR FINAN TEC/DEV DIPLOM FOR/AID EDU/PROP CONFER REGION GP/REL WEALTH...HEAL SOC/INTEG 20. PAGE 76 A1566
ORD/FREE ECO/UNDEV VOL/ASSN PLAN

B66
KINDLEBERGER C.P.,EUROPE AND THE DOLLAR. EUR+WWI FRANCE GERMANY/W USA+45 CONSTN INT/ORG DIPLOM INT/TRADE...ANTHOL 20 GOLD/STAND. PAGE 79 A1623
BAL/PAY BUDGET FINAN ECO/DEV

B66
KIRDAR U.,THE STRUCTURE OF UNITED NATIONS ECONOMIC AID TO UNDERDEVELOPED COUNTRIES. AGRI FINAN INDUS NAT/G EX/STRUC PLAN GIVE TASK...POLICY 20 UN. PAGE 79 A1631
INT/ORG FOR/AID ECO/UNDEV ADMIN

B66
MCNAIR A.D.,THE LEGAL EFFECTS OF WAR. UK FINAN DIPLOM ORD/FREE 20 ENGLSH/LAW. PAGE 98 A2019
JURID WAR INT/TRADE LABOR

B66
MEERHAEGHE M.,INTERNATIONAL ECONOMIC INSTITUTIONS. EUR+WWI FINAN INDUS MARKET PLAN TARIFFS BAL/PAY EQUILIB...POLICY BIBLIOG/A 20 GATT OEEC EEC IBRD EURCOALSTL. PAGE 99 A2032
ECO/TAC ECO/DEV INT/TRADE INT/ORG

B66
MIKESELL R.F.,PUBLIC INTERNATIONAL LENDING FOR DEVELOPMENT. WOR+45 WOR-45 DELIB/GP...TIME/SEQ CHARTS BIBLIOG 20. PAGE 101 A2070
INT/ORG FOR/AID ECO/UNDEV FINAN

B66
NATIONAL COUN APPLIED ECO RES,DEVELOPMENT WITHOUT AID. INDIA FINAN TEC/DEV EFFICIENCY...ANTHOL 20. PAGE 107 A2203
FOR/AID PLAN SOVEREIGN ECO/UNDEV

B66
PIQUET H.S.,THE US BALANCE OF PAYMENTS AND INTERNATIONAL MONETARY RESERVES. USA+45 PROB/SOLV INT/TRADE GOV/REL EQUILIB...POLICY STAT CHARTS 20 GOLD/STAND. PAGE 116 A2384
BAL/PAY DIPLOM FINAN ECO/TAC

B66
ROBERTSON D.J.,THE BRITISH BALANCE OF PAYMENTS. UK WOR+45 INDUS BUDGET TAX ADJUST...CHARTS ANTHOL 20. PAGE 122 A2500
FINAN BAL/PAY ECO/DEV INT/TRADE

B66
SPICER K.,A SAMARITAN STATE? AFR CANADA INDIA PAKISTAN UK USA+45 FINAN INDUS PRODUC...CHARTS 20 NATO. PAGE 136 A2787
DIPLOM FOR/AID ECO/DEV ADMIN

B66
SZLADITS C.,A BIBLIOGRAPHY ON FOREIGN AND COMPARATIVE LAW (SUPPLEMENT 1964). FINAN FAM LABOR LG/CO LEGIS JUDGE ADMIN CRIME...CRIMLGY 20. PAGE 141 A2878
BIBLIOG/A CT/SYS INT/LAW

B66
TRIFFIN R.,THE WORLD MONEY MAZE. INT/ORG ECO/TAC PRICE OPTIMAL WEALTH...METH/COMP 20 EEC OEEC GOLD/STAND SILVER. PAGE 145 A2964
BAL/PAY FINAN INT/TRADE DIPLOM

B66
TRIFFIN R.,THE BALANCE OF PAYMENTS AND THE FOREIGN INVESTMENT POSITION OF THE UNITED STATES. USA+45 INT/ORG INT/TRADE PRICE CONTROL...POLICY 20 GOLD/STAND. PAGE 145 A2965
BAL/PAY DIPLOM FINAN ECO/TAC

B66
TYSON G.,NEHRU: THE YEARS OF POWER. INDIA UK STRATA ECO/UNDEV FINAN SECT TASK WAR ORD/FREE MARXISM ...POLICY BIBLIOG 20 NEHRU/J. PAGE 146 A2985
CHIEF PWR DIPLOM NAT/G

B66
US CONGRESS JOINT ECO COMM,NEW APPROACH TO UNITED STATES INTERNATIONAL ECONOMIC POLICY. USA+45 WOR+45 CHIEF DELIB/GP CONFER...CHARTS 20 CONGRESS MONEY. PAGE 150 A3070
DIPLOM ECO/TAC BAL/PAY FINAN

B66
US HOUSE COMM GOVT OPERATIONS,AN INVESTIGATION OF THE US ECONOMIC AND MILITARY ASSISTANCE PROGRAMS IN VIETNAM. USA+45 VIETNAM/S SOCIETY CONSTRUC FINAN
FOR/AID ECO/UNDEV WAR

FORCES BUDGET INT/TRADE PEACE HEALTH...MGT HOUSE/REP AID. PAGE 154 A3139 — INSPECT

B66
US SENATE COMM ON FOREIGN REL,ASIAN DEVELOPMENT BANK ACT. USA+45 LAW DIPLOM...CHARTS 20 BLACK/EUG S/EASTASIA. PAGE 156 A3186 — FOR/AID FINAN ECO/UNDEV S/ASIA

B66
WILLIAMS P.,AID IN UGANDA - EDUCATION. UGANDA UK FINAN ACADEM INT/ORG SCHOOL PROB/SOLV ECO/TAC UTIL ...STAT CHARTS 20. PAGE 165 A3352 — PLAN EDU/PROP FOR/AID ECO/UNDEV

B66
WOOLLEY H.B.,MEASURING TRANSACTIONS BETWEEN WORLD AREAS. WOR+45 FINAN...STAT NET/THEORY CHARTS DICTIONARY 20 GOLD/STAND. PAGE 167 A3395 — INT/TRADE BAL/PAY DIPLOM ECOMETRIC

B66
YEAGER L.B.,INTERNATIONAL MONETARY RELATIONS: THEORY, HISTORY, AND POLICY. WOR+45 WOR-45 INT/TRADE BAL/PAY...NAT/COMP 18/20 MONEY. PAGE 169 A3432 — FINAN DIPLOM ECO/TAC IDEA/COMP

B66
ZISCHKA A.,WAR ES EIN WUNDER? GERMANY/W ECO/DEV FINAN LG/CO BARGAIN CAP/ISM FOR/AID RATION 20 MARSHL/PLN. PAGE 170 A3456 — ECO/TAC INT/TRADE INDUS WAR

L66
AMERICAN ECONOMIC REVIEW,"SIXTY-THIRD LIST OF DOCTORAL DISSERTATIONS IN POLITICAL ECONOMY IN AMERICAN UNIVERSITIES AND COLLEGES." ECO/DEV AGRI FINAN LABOR WORKER PLAN BUDGET INT/TRADE ADMIN DEMAND...MGT STAT 20. PAGE 7 A0146 — BIBLIOG/A CONCPT ACADEM

S66
"WORLD BANK CONVENTION ON INVESTMENT DISPUTES: A BIBLIOGRAPH ICAL NOTE." VOL/ASSN CONSULT CAP/ISM DIPLOM INT/TRADE 20 SENATE PRESIDENT. PAGE 4 A0074 — BIBLIOG ADJUD FINAN INT/ORG

S66
ERB GF,"THE UNITED NATIONS CONFERENCE ON TRADE AND DEVELOPMENT (UNCTAD): A SELECTED CURRENT READING LIST." FINAN FOR/AID CONFER 20 UN. PAGE 42 A0858 — BIBLIOG/A INT/TRADE ECO/UNDEV INT/ORG

N66
EOMMITTEE ECONOMIC DEVELOPMENT,THE DOLLAR AND THE WORLD MONETARY SYSTEM: A STATEMENT ON NATIONAL POLICY (PAMPHLET). USA+45 NAT/G PLAN PROB/SOLV BUDGET ECO/TAC FOR/AID INCOME...POLICY 20 GOLD/STAND EUROPE. PAGE 42 A0854 — FINAN BAL/PAY DIPLOM ECO/DEV

B67
CLARK S.V.O.,CENTRAL BANK COOPERATION: 1924-31. WOR-45 PROB/SOLV ECO/TAC ADJUST BAL/PAY...TREND CHARTS METH/COMP 20. PAGE 27 A0542 — FINAN EQUILIB DIPLOM POLICY

B67
HIRSCHMAN A.O.,DEVELOPMENT PROJECTS OBSERVED. INDUS INT/ORG CONSULT EX/STRUC CREATE OP/RES ECO/TAC DEMAND...POLICY MGT METH/COMP 20 WORLD/BANK. PAGE 65 A1339 — ECO/UNDEV R+D FINAN PLAN

B67
JOHNSON A.M.,BOSTON CAPITALISTS AND WESTERN RAILROADS: A STUDY IN THE NINETEENTH CENTURY RAILROAD INVESTMENT PROCESS. CREATE BARGAIN INT/TRADE GAMBLE KNOWL 19 BOSTON. PAGE 74 A1519 — FINAN DIST/IND CAP/ISM ECO/UNDEV

B67
ROBINSON R.D.,INTERNATIONAL MANAGEMENT. USA+45 FINAN R+D PLAN PRODUC...DECISION T. PAGE 92 A1882 — INT/TRADE MGT INT/LAW MARKET

B67
ROYAL INSTITUTE INTL AFFAIRS,SURVEY OF INTERNATIONAL AFFAIRS. WOR+45 WOR-45 FINAN INT/TRADE PWR...CHARTS 20. PAGE 125 A2557 — DIPLOM BAL/PWR INT/ORG

B67
RUEFF J.,BALANCE OF PAYMENTS. WOR+45 FINAN TEC/DEV DIPLOM TARIFFS PRICE CONTROL...POLICY CONCPT IDEA/COMP. PAGE 125 A2567 — INT/TRADE BAL/PAY ECO/TAC NAT/COMP

B67
SABLE M.H.,A GUIDE TO LATIN AMERICAN STUDIES (2 VOLS). CONSTN FINAN INT/ORG LABOR MUNIC POL/PAR FORCES CAP/ISM FOR/AID ADMIN MARXISM SOCISM OAS. PAGE 126 A2584 — BIBLIOG/A L/A+17C DIPLOM NAT/LISM

B67
SACHS M.Y.,THE WORLDMARK ENCYCLOPEDIA OF THE NATIONS (5 VOLS.). ELITES SOCIETY STRATA ECO/DEV ECO/UNDEV AGRI EXTR/IND FINAN LABOR LOC/G NAT/G POL/PAR SECT INT/TRADE SOVEREIGN...SOC 20. PAGE 126 A2585 — WOR+45 INT/ORG BAL/PWR

B67
UNIVERSAL REFERENCE SYSTEM,ECONOMIC REGULATION, BUSINESS, AND GOVERNMENT (VOLUME VIII). WOR+45 WOR-45 ECO/DEV ECO/UNDEV FINAN LABOR TEC/DEV ECO/TAC INT/TRADE GOV/REL...POLICY COMPUT/IR. PAGE 149 A3043 — BIBLIOG/A CONTROL NAT/G

B67
US CONGRESS SENATE,SURVEY OF THE ALLIANCE FOR PROGRESS: INFLATION IN LATIN AMERICA (PAMPHLET). USA+45 MARKET INT/ORG DIPLOM INT/TRADE BAL/PAY SENATE. PAGE 150 A3072 — L/A+17C FINAN POLICY FOR/AID

B67
YAMAMURA K.,ECONOMIC POLICY IN POSTWAR JAPAN. ASIA FINAN POL/PAR DIPLOM LEAD NAT/LISM ATTIT NEW/LIB POPULISM 20 CHINJAP. PAGE 168 A3429 — ECO/DEV POLICY NAT/G TEC/DEV

S67
HERRERA F.,"EUROPEAN PARTICIPATION IN THE LATIN AMERICAN REGIONAL INTEGRATION" EUR+WWI L/A+17C GP/REL INGP/REL 20. PAGE 64 A1318 — DIPLOM REGION INT/ORG FINAN

S67
MOBERG E.,"THE EFFECT OF SECURITY POLICY MEASURES: DISCUSSION RELATED TO SWEDEN'S SECURITY POLICY." SWEDEN PLAN PROB/SOLV DIPLOM GOV/REL MORAL...CHARTS 20. PAGE 102 A2092 — POLICY ORD/FREE BUDGET FINAN

S67
STEGER H.S.,"RESEARCH ON LATIN AMERICA IN THE FEDERAL REPUBLIC OF GERMANY AND WEST BERLIN." FINAN DIPLOM INT/TRADE EDU/PROP...GEOG JURID CHARTS 19/20. PAGE 137 A2813 — SOCIETY ECO/UNDEV ACADEM L/A+17C

N67
US SENATE COMM ON FOREIGN REL,ARMS SALES AND FOREIGN POLICY (PAMPHLET). FINAN FOR/AID CONTROL 20. PAGE 156 A3187 — ARMS/CONT ADMIN OP/RES DIPLOM

B68
ANTWERP-INST UNIVERSITAIRE,BIBLIOGRAPHIC COMPENDIUM: DEVELOPING COUNTRIES (ANTWERP-INST UNIVERSITAIRE DES TERRITOIRES D'OUTRE-MER). AFR EUR+WWI SOCIETY AGRI FINAN NEIGH VOL/ASSN PROB/SOLV TEC/DEV FOR/AID INT/TRADE 20. PAGE 8 A0166 — BIBLIOG ECO/UNDEV DIPLOM PLAN

B96
DE VATTEL E.,THE LAW OF NATIONS. AGRI FINAN CHIEF DIPLOM INT/TRADE AGREE OWN ALL/VALS MORAL ORD/FREE SOVEREIGN...GEN/LAWS 18 NATURL/LAW WOLFF/C. PAGE 35 A0714 — LAW CONCPT NAT/G INT/LAW

FINANCE....SEE FINAN

FINCH/D....DANIEL FINCH

FINCH/ER....E.R. FINCH

FINE S. A0931

FINE ARTS....SEE ART/METH

FINER H. A0932

FINKELSTEIN L.S. A0933

FINKLE J.L. A0934

FINLAND....SEE ALSO APPROPRIATE TIME/SPACE/CULTURE INDEX

B56
VON HARPE W.,DIE SOWJETUNION FINNLAND UND SKANDANAVIEN, 1945-1955. EUR+WWI FINLAND GERMANY USSR WAR INGP/REL ORD/FREE SOVEREIGN MARXISM ...POLICY GOV/COMP BIBLIOG 20 STALIN/J. PAGE 160 A3252 — DIPLOM COM NEUTRAL BAL/PWR

B60
SOBEL R.,THE ORIGINS OF INTERVENTIONISM: THE UNITED STATES AND THE RUSSO-FINNISH WAR. FINLAND USA-45 USSR LEGIS ATTIT RIGID/FLEX...BIBLIOG 20 INTERVENT. PAGE 135 A2755 — DIPLOM WAR PROB/SOLV NEUTRAL

B61
JAKOBSON M.,THE DIPLOMACY OF THE WINTER WAR. EUR+WWI FINLAND GERMANY USSR INT/ORG NAT/G PEACE TOTALISM PWR...POLICY CONCPT 20 TREATY. PAGE 73 A1492 — WAR ORD/FREE DIPLOM

S63
COUTY P.,"L'ASSISTANCE POUR LE DEVELOPPEMENT: POINT DE VUE SCANDINAVES." EUR+WWI FINLAND FUT SWEDEN WOR+45 ECO/DEV ECO/UNDEV COM/IND LABOR NAT/G PROF/ORG ACT/RES SKILL WEALTH TOT/POP 20. PAGE 32 A0643 — FINAN ROUTINE FOR/AID

C65
WUORINEN J.H.,"SCANDINAVIA." DENMARK FINLAND ICELAND NORWAY SWEDEN SOCIETY AGRI POL/PAR DELIB/GP DIPLOM INT/TRADE NEUTRAL WAR...CHARTS TREATY 20. PAGE 168 A3423 — BIBLIOG NAT/G POLICY

FIRM....SEE INDUS

FISCAL POLICY....SEE BUDGET

FISCHER G. A0935

FISCHER L. A0936,A0937,A0938

N19
STEUBER F.A.,THE CONTRIBUTION OF SWITZERLAND TO THE ECONOMIC AND SOCIAL DEVELOPMENT OF LOW-INCOME COUNTRIES (PAMPHLET). SWITZERLND FINAN NAT/G VOL/ASSN INT/TRADE DRIVE...CHARTS 20. PAGE 138 A2820
FOR/AID ECO/UNDEV PLAN DIPLOM

B38
FRANKEL S.H.,CAPITAL INVESTMENT IN AFRICA. AFR EUR+WWI RHODESIA SOUTH/AFR UK FINAN FOR/AID COLONIAL DEMAND UTIL WEALTH...METH/CNCPT CHARTS 20 CONGO/LEOP. PAGE 48 A0983
ECO/UNDEV EXTR/IND DIPLOM PRODUC

B43
FULLER G.F.,FOREIGN RELIEF AND REHABILITATION (PAMPHLET). FUT GERMANY UK USA-45 INT/ORG PROB/SOLV DIPLOM FOR/AID ADMIN ADJUST PEACE ALL/VALS...SOC/WK 20 UN JEWS. PAGE 50 A1018
BIBLIOG/A PLAN GIVE WAR

B47
DE HUSZAR G.B.,PERSISTENT INTERNATIONAL ISSUES. WOR+45 WOR-45 AGRI INDUS INT/ORG PROB/SOLV EFFICIENCY WEALTH...CON/ANAL ANTHOL UN. PAGE 35 A0704
DIPLOM PEACE ECO/TAC FOR/AID

B47
PERKINS D.,THE UNITED STATES AND THE CARIBBEAN. CUBA DOMIN/REP GUATEMALA HAITI PANAMA CULTURE ECO/UNDEV FOR/AID ADMIN COERCE HABITAT...POLICY 19/20. PAGE 115 A2359
DIPLOM L/A+17C USA-45

N47
FOX W.T.R.,UNITED STATES POLICY IN A TWO POWER WORLD. COM USA+45 USSR FORCES DOMIN AGREE NEUTRAL NUC/PWR ORD/FREE SOVEREIGN 20 COLD/WAR TREATY EUROPE/W INTERVENT. PAGE 48 A0972
DIPLOM FOR/AID POLICY

B48
CHAMBERLAIN L.H.,AMERICAN FOREIGN POLICY. FUT USA+45 USA-45 WOR+45 WOR-45 NAT/G LEGIS TOP/EX ECO/TAC FOR/AID EDU/PROP EXEC ATTIT ORD/FREE ...JURID TREND TOT/POP 20. PAGE 25 A0517
CONSTN DIPLOM

B48
PELCOVITS N.A.,OLD CHINA HANDS AND THE FOREIGN OFFICE. ASIA BURMA UK ECO/UNDEV NAT/G ECO/TAC FOR/AID TARIFFS DOMIN COLONIAL GOV/REL SOVEREIGN 19 HONG/KONG TREATY. PAGE 114 A2348
INT/TRADE ATTIT DIPLOM

B48
VISSON A.,AS OTHERS SEE US. EUR+WWI FRANCE UK USA+45 CULTURE INTELL SOCIETY STRATA NAT/G POL/PAR FOR/AID ATTIT DRIVE LOVE ORD/FREE RESPECT WEALTH ...PLURIST SOC OBS TOT/POP 20. PAGE 159 A3244
USA-45 PERCEPT

B49
FORD FOUNDATION,REPORT OF THE STUDY FOR THE FORD FOUNDATION ON POLICY AND PROGRAM. SOCIETY R+D ACT/RES CAP/ISM FOR/AID EDU/PROP ADMIN KNOWL ...POLICY PSY SOC 20. PAGE 47 A0961
WEALTH GEN/LAWS

B50
BROOKINGS INSTITUTION,MAJOR PROBLEMS OF UNITED STATES FOREIGN POLICY. AFR ASIA INDIA UK USA+45 USSR BAL/PWR FOR/AID WAR PEACE TOTALISM MARXISM SOCISM 20 CHINJAP COLD/WAR. PAGE 19 A0393
DIPLOM POLICY ORD/FREE

B50
CHUKWUEMEKA N.,AFRICAN DEPENDENCIES: A CHALLENGE TO WESTERN DEMOCRACY. NIGERIA ECO/DEV INDUS FOR/AID INT/TRADE DOMIN 20. PAGE 26 A0536
DIPLOM ECO/UNDEV COLONIAL AFR

B50
CORNELL U DEPT ASIAN STUDIES,SOUTHEAST ASIA PROGRAM DATA PAPER. BURMA CAMBODIA INDONESIA MALAYSIA VIETNAM SOCIETY STRUCT NAT/G SECT DIPLOM FOR/AID PWR WEALTH...SOC 20. PAGE 31 A0625
BIBLIOG/A CULTURE S/ASIA ECO/UNDEV

B50
GUERRANT E.O.,ROOSEVELT'S GOOD NEIGHBOR POLICY. L/A+17C USA+45 USA-45 FOR/AID...IDEA/COMP 20 ROOSEVLT/F TRUMAN/HS. PAGE 58 A1187
DIPLOM NAT/G CHIEF POLICY

B50
LINCOLN G.,ECONOMICS OF NATIONAL SECURITY. USA+45 ELITES COM/IND DIST/IND INDUS NAT/G VOL/ASSN DELIB/GP EX/STRUC FOR/AID EDU/PROP COERCE NUC/PWR WAR ATTIT KNOWL ORD/FREE PWR COLD/WAR TOT/POP VAL/FREE 20. PAGE 89 A1818
FORCES ECO/TAC

B50
PERHAM M.,COLONIAL GOVERNMENT: ANNOTATED READING LIST ON BRITISH COLONIAL GOVERNMENT. UK WOR+45 WOR-45 ECO/UNDEV INT/ORG LEGIS FOR/AID INT/TRADE DOMIN ADMIN REV 20. PAGE 115 A2356
BIBLIOG/A COLONIAL GOV/REL NAT/G

B50
US DEPARTMENT OF STATE,POINT FOUR: COOPERATIVE PROGRAM FOR AID IN THE DEVELOPMENT OF ECONOMICALLY UNDERDEVELOPED AREAS. WOR+45 AGRI INDUS INT/ORG PLAN TEC/DEV DIPLOM EDU/PROP ADMIN PEACE PRODUC WEALTH 20 CONGRESS UN. PAGE 151 A3085
ECO/UNDEV FOR/AID FINAN INT/TRADE

S50
WITTFOGEL K.A.,"RUSSIA AND ASIA: PROBLEMS OF CONTEMPORARY AREA STUDIES AND INTERNATIONAL RELATIONS." ASIA COM USA+45 SOCIETY NAT/G DIPLOM ECO/TAC FOR/AID EDU/PROP KNOWL...HIST/WRIT TOT/POP 20. PAGE 166 A3373
ECO/DEV ADMIN RUSSIA USSR

C50
ELLSWORTH P.T.,"INTERNATIONAL ECONOMY." ECO/DEV ECO/UNDEV FINAN LABOR DIPLOM FOR/AID TARIFFS BAL/PAY EQUILIB NAT/LISM OPTIMAL...INT/LAW 20 ILO GATT. PAGE 41 A0843
BIBLIOG INT/TRADE ECO/TAC INT/ORG

B51
CHRISTENSEN A.N.,THE EVOLUTION OF LATIN AMERICAN GOVERNMENT: A BOOK OF READINGS. ECO/UNDEV INDUS LOC/G POL/PAR EX/STRUC LEGIS FOR/AID CT/SYS ...SOC/WK 20 SOUTH/AMER. PAGE 26 A0535
NAT/G CONSTN DIPLOM L/A+17C

B51
US HOUSE COMM APPROPRIATIONS,MUTUAL SECURITY PROGRAM APPROPRIATIONS FOR 1952: HEARINGS BEFORE A SUBCOMMITTEE OF THE COMMITTEE ON APPROPRIATIONS. KOREA L/A+17C ECO/DEV ECO/UNDEV INT/ORG INSPECT BAL/PWR DIPLOM DEBATE WAR...POLICY STAT ASIA/S 20 CONGRESS NATO COLD/WAR MID/EAST. PAGE 153 A3118
LEGIS FORCES BUDGET FOR/AID

S51
CONNERY R.H.,"THE MUTUAL DEFENSE ASSISTANCE PROGRAM." COM EUR+WWI KOREA USA+45 NAT/G VOL/ASSN CREATE PLAN BAL/PWR EDU/PROP PERCEPT...POLICY DECISION CONCPT NATO 20. PAGE 29 A0587
INT/ORG FORCES FOR/AID

B52
HOSELITZ B.F.,THE PROGRESS OF UNDERDEVELOPED AREAS. FUT WOR+45 WOR-45 ECO/DEV ECO/TAC INT/TRADE WEALTH ...SOC TREND GEN/LAWS TOT/POP VAL/FREE COLD/WAR 20. PAGE 68 A1391
ECO/UNDEV PLAN FOR/AID

B52
MACARTHUR D.,REVITALIZING A NATION. ASIA COM FUT KOREA WOR+45 NAT/G FOR/AID TAX GIVE WAR ATTIT SOCISM 20 CHINJAP EUROPE. PAGE 92 A1885
LEAD FORCES TOP/EX POLICY

B52
RIGGS F.W.,FORMOSA UNDER CHINESE NATIONALIST RULE. CHINA/COM USA+45 CONSTN AGRI FINAN LABOR LOC/G NAT/G POL/PAR FORCES HEALTH KNOWL...STAT WORK VAL/FREE 20. PAGE 121 A2479
ASIA FOR/AID DIPLOM

B52
U OF MICH SURVEY RESEARCH CTR,AMERICA'S ROLE IN WORLD AFFAIRS. ASIA COM EUR+WWI USA+45 USSR FOR/AID WAR AUTHORIT ORD/FREE...DEEP/QU 20. PAGE 146 A2986
DIPLOM NAT/G ROLE POLICY

B52
UN DEPT. SOC. AFF.,PRELIMINARY REPORT ON THE WORLD SOCIAL SITUATION. ISLAM L/A+17C WOR+45 STRATA AGRI EXTR/IND INDUS INT/ORG SCHOOL ADMIN...GEOG SOC TREND UNESCO WORK FAO 20. PAGE 147 A2998
R+D HEALTH FOR/AID

B52
US MUTUAL SECURITY AGENCY,U. S. TECHNICAL AND ECONOMIC ASSISTANCE IN THE FAR EAST (PAMPHLET). ASIA BURMA INDONESIA PHILIPPINE TAIWAN THAILAND USA+45 AGRI INDUS PLAN EDU/PROP ADMIN HEALTH. PAGE 155 A3161
FOR/AID TEC/DEV ECO/UNDEV BUDGET

B53
FEIS H.,THE CHINA TANGLE. ASIA COM USA+45 USA-45 FORCES ECO/TAC REV ATTIT 20 INTERVENT. PAGE 45 A0910
POLICY DIPLOM WAR FOR/AID

B53
MACK R.T.,RAISING THE WORLDS STANDARD OF LIVING. IRAN INT/ORG VOL/ASSN EX/STRUC ECO/TAC WEALTH...MGT METH/CNCPT STAT CONT/OBS INT TOT/POP VAL/FREE 20 UN. PAGE 92 A1893
WOR+45 FOR/AID INT/TRADE

B53
MACMAHON A.W.,ADMINISTRATION IN FOREIGN AFFAIRS. NAT/G CONSULT DELIB/GP LEGIS ACT/RES CREATE ADMIN EXEC RIGID/FLEX PWR...METH/CNCPT TIME/SEQ TOT/POP VAL/FREE 20. PAGE 93 A1899
USA+45 ROUTINE FOR/AID DIPLOM

B53
THAYER P.W.,SOUTHEAST ASIA IN THE COMING WORLD. ASIA S/ASIA USA+45 USA-45 SOCIETY INT/ORG ACT/RES ECO/TAC EDU/PROP COERCE TOTALISM ALL/VALS...JURID 20. PAGE 142 A2909
ECO/UNDEV ATTIT FOR/AID DIPLOM

S53
BOULDING K.E.,"ECONOMIC ISSUES IN INTERNATIONAL CONFLICT." WOR+45 ECO/DEV NAT/G TOP/EX DIPLOM ECO/TAC DOMIN ATTIT WEALTH...MAJORIT OBS/ENVIR TREND GEN/LAWS COLD/WAR TOT/POP 20. PAGE 17 A0345
PWR FOR/AID

S53
LINCOLN G.,"FACTORS DETERMINING ARMS AID." COM FUT USA+45 USSR WOR+45 ECO/DEV NAT/G CONSULT PLAN TEC/DEV DIPLOM DOMIN EDU/PROP PERCEPT PWR ...DECISION CONCPT TREND MARX/KARL 20. PAGE 89 A1819
FORCES POLICY BAL/PWR FOR/AID

B54
EPSTEIN L.D.,BRITAIN - UNEASY ALLY. KOREA UK USA+45 NAT/G POL/PAR ECO/TAC FOR/AID INT/TRADE WAR LABOR/PAR CONSRV/PAR. PAGE 42 A0857
DIPLOM ATTIT POLICY NAT/COMP

B54
NATION ASSOCIATES,SECURITY AND THE MIDDLE EAST - THE PROBLEM AND ITS SOLUTION. ISRAEL JORDAN LEBANON SYRIA UAR FORCES FOR/AID GP/REL NAT/LISM PEACE TOTALISM...POLICY 20. PAGE 107 A2198
DIPLOM ECO/UNDEV WAR PLAN

B54
STALEY E.,THE FUTURE OF UNDERDEVELOPED COUNTRIES: POLITICAL IMPLICATIONS OF ECONOMIC DEVELOPMENT. COM FUT USA+45 SOCIETY ECO/UNDEV CREATE PLAN CAP/ISM
EDU/PROP ECO/TAC FOR/AID

ATTIT DRIVE MARXISM SOCISM...POLICY CONCPT CHARTS COLD/WAR 20. PAGE 137 A2801

B54
US DEPARTMENT OF STATE,PUBLICATIONS OF THE DEPARTMENT OF STATE, OCTOBER 1,1929 TO JANUARY 1, 1953. AGRI INT/ORG FORCES FOR/AID EDU/PROP ARMS/CONT NUC/PWR ATTIT 20 DEPT/STATE OAS UN NATO. PAGE 151 A3089
BIBLIOG DIPLOM

L54
CHARLESWORTH J.C.,"AMERICA AND A NEW ASIA." ASIA INDIA ISLAM S/ASIA USA+45 USA-45 ECO/UNDEV NAT/G POL/PAR FORCES FOR/AID DOMIN EDU/PROP COERCE DRIVE ALL/VALS MARXISM SOCISM TOT/POP 20. PAGE 26 A0522
ECO/TAC DIPLOM NAT/LISM

L54
OPLER M.E.,"SOCIAL ASPECTS OF TECHNICAL ASSISTANCE IN OPERATION." WOR+45 VOL/ASSN CREATE PLAN TEC/DEV EDU/PROP ALL/VALS...METH/CNCPT OBS RECORD TREND UN 20. PAGE 112 A2292
INT/ORG CONSULT FOR/AID

B55
JONES J.M.,THE FIFTEEN WEEKS (FEBRUARY 21-JUNE 5, 1947). EUR+WWI USA+45 PROB/SOLV BAL/PWR...POLICY TIME/SEQ 20 COLD/WAR MARSHL/PLN TRUMAN/HS WASHING/DC. PAGE 75 A1532
DIPLOM ECO/TAC FOR/AID

B55
MYRDAL A.R.,AMERICA'S ROLE IN INTERNATIONATIONAL SOCIAL WELFARE. FUT WOR+45 SOCIETY R+D VOL/ASSN ECO/TAC EDU/PROP HEALTH KNOWL WEALTH...SOC CHARTS ORG/CHARTS TOT/POP 20. PAGE 107 A2188
PLAN SKILL FOR/AID

B55
OECD,MARSHALL PLAN IN TURKEY. TURKEY USA+45 COM/IND CONSTRUC SERV/IND FORCES BUDGET...STAT 20 MARSHL/PLN. PAGE 111 A2277
FOR/AID ECO/UNDEV AGRI INDUS

B56
BALL W.M.,NATIONALISM AND COMMUNISM IN EAST ASIA. ASIA BURMA EUR+WWI KOREA USA+45 ECO/UNDEV NAT/G POL/PAR DIPLOM ECO/TAC FOR/AID EDU/PROP COERCE RACE/REL NAT/LISM DRIVE SOVEREIGN...TREND 20 CHINJAP. PAGE 11 A0214
S/ASIA ATTIT

B56
BOWLES C.,AFRICA'S CHALLENGE TO AMERICA. USA+45 ECO/UNDEV NAT/G LEGIS COLONIAL CONTROL REV ORD/FREE SOVEREIGN 20 COLD/WAR. PAGE 18 A0358
AFR DIPLOM POLICY FOR/AID

B56
BUREAU OF PUBLIC AFFAIRS,AMERICAN FOREIGN POLICY: CURRENT DOCUMENTS. COM USA+45 USSR WOR+45 DELIB/GP FOR/AID INT/TRADE ARMS/CONT NUC/PWR ALL/VALS ALL/IDEOS...DECISION 20 NATO. PAGE 21 A0434
BIBLIOG/A DIPLOM POLICY

B56
KIRK G.,THE CHANGING ENVIRONMENT OF INTERNATIONAL RELATIONS. ASIA S/ASIA USA+45 WOR+45 ECO/UNDEV INT/ORG NAT/G FOR/AID EDU/PROP PEACE KNOWL ...PLURIST COLD/WAR TOT/POP 20. PAGE 80 A1634
FUT EXEC DIPLOM

B56
KNORR K.E.,RUBLE DIPLOMACY: CHALLENGE TO AMERICAN FOREIGN AID(PAMPHLET). CHINA/COM USA+45 USSR PLAN TEC/DEV CAP/ISM INT/TRADE DOMIN EDU/PROP CONTROL LEAD 20 COLD/WAR. PAGE 81 A1654
ECO/UNDEV COM DIPLOM FOR/AID

B56
ROBERTS H.L.,RUSSIA AND AMERICA. CHINA/COM S/ASIA USSR FORCES TEC/DEV FOR/AID NUC/PWR ALL/IDEOS ...MAJORIT TREND NAT/COMP 20 COLD/WAR UN NATO. PAGE 122 A2494
DIPLOM INT/ORG BAL/PWR TOTALISM

B56
UNITED NATIONS,BIBLIOGRAPHY ON INDUSTRIALIZATION IN UNDER-DEVELOPED COUNTRIES. WOR+45 R+D INT/ORG NAT/G FOR/AID ADMIN LEAD 20 UN. PAGE 149 A3036
BIBLIOG ECO/UNDEV INDUS TEC/DEV

B56
US LIBRARY OF CONGRESS,UNITED STATES DIRECT ECONOMIC AID TO FOREIGN COUNTRIES: A COLLECTION OF EXCERPTS AND A BIBLIOGRAPHY (PAMPHLET). USA+45 PRESS DEBATE...ANTHOL BIBLIOG/A CONGRESS. PAGE 155 A3154
FOR/AID POLICY DIPLOM ECO/UNDEV

B57
ASHER R.E.,THE UNITED NATIONS AND ECONOMIC AND SOCIAL COOPERATION. ECO/UNDEV COM/IND DIST/IND FINAN PLAN PROB/SOLV INT/TRADE TASK WEALTH...SOC 20 UN. PAGE 9 A0186
INT/ORG DIPLOM FOR/AID

B57
CASTLE E.W.,THE GREAT GIVEAWAY: THE REALITIES OF FOREIGN AID. USA+45 DIPLOM EDU/PROP NEUTRAL ...DECISION 20. PAGE 25 A0508
FOR/AID GIVE ECO/UNDEV PROB/SOLV

B57
DEAN V.M.,THE NATURE OF THE NON-WESTERN WORLD. AFR ASIA L/A+17C S/ASIA CULTURE SOCIETY STRATA ECO/DEV DIPLOM ECO/TAC FOR/AID ATTIT DRIVE ALL/VALS ...RELATIV SOC CONCPT TIME/SEQ TREND TOT/POP 20. PAGE 35 A0718
ECO/UNDEV STERTYP NAT/LISM

B57
DRUCKER P.F.,AMERICA'S NEXT TWENTY YEARS. USA+45 DIST/IND ACADEM MUNIC SCHOOL DIPLOM ECO/TAC AUTOMAT HABITAT HEALTH...SOC/WK TREND 20 URBAN/RNWL PUB/TRANS. PAGE 39 A0788
WORKER FOR/AID CENSUS GEOG

B57
HALD M.,A SELECTED BIBLIOGRAPHY ON ECONOMIC DEVELOPMENT AND FOREIGN AID. INT/ORG PROB/SOLV ...SOC 20. PAGE 59 A1222
BIBLIOG ECO/UNDEV TEC/DEV FOR/AID

B57
MCNEILL W.H.,GREECE: AMERICAN AID IN ACTION. GREECE UK USA+45 FINAN CAP/ISM INT/TRADE BAL/PAY PRODUC WEALTH...POLICY METH/COMP 20. PAGE 99 A2022
FOR/AID DIPLOM ECO/UNDEV

B57
MILLIKAN M.F.,A PROPOSAL: KEY TO AN EFFECTIVE FOREIGN POLICY. USA+45 AGRI FINAN DELIB/GP DIPLOM REPRESENT MAJORITY...NEW/IDEA CHARTS. PAGE 101 A2081
FOR/AID GIVE ECO/UNDEV PLAN

B57
US PRES CITIZEN ADVISERS,REPORT TO THE PRESIDENT ON THE MUTUAL SECURITY PROGRAM. COM USA+45 WOR+45 FINAN INDUS PLAN BUDGET CAP/ISM DIPLOM FOR/AID INT/TRADE REGION 20 SECUR/PROG. PAGE 155 A3163
BAL/PWR FORCES INT/ORG ECO/TAC

B57
US SENATE SPEC COMM FOR AID,COMPILATION OF STUDIES AND SURVEYS. AFR ASIA L/A+17C USA+45 ECO/UNDEV AGRI INT/ORG CONSULT TEC/DEV CONFER TOTALISM...NAT/COMP 20 CONGRESS. PAGE 157 A3197
FOR/AID DIPLOM ORD/FREE DELIB/GP

B57
US SENATE SPEC COMM FOR AID,HEARINGS BEFORE THE SPECIAL COMMITTEE TO STUDY THE FOREIGN AID PROGRAM. USA+45 USSR ECO/UNDEV INT/ORG FORCES WEAPON TOTALISM ATTIT SUPEGO...NAT/COMP CONGRESS. PAGE 157 A3198
FOR/AID DIPLOM ORD/FREE TEC/DEV

B57
WARBURG J.P.,AGENDA FOR ACTION. ISLAM ISRAEL USA+45 FOR/AID INT/TRADE WAR NAT/LISM 20 MID/EAST EUROPE ARABS. PAGE 161 A3275
DIPLOM POLICY INT/ORG BAL/PWR

L57
FURNISS E.S.,"SOME PERSPECTIVES ON AMERICAN MILITARY ASSISTANCE." USA+45 WOR+45 ECO/UNDEV INT/ORG ECO/TAC ORD/FREE...GEOG TIME/SEQ TREND COLD/WAR 20. PAGE 50 A1028
FORCES FOR/AID WEAPON

L57
WARREN S.,"FOREIGN AID AND FOREIGN POLICY." USA+45 WOR+45 WOR-45 DIST/IND INDUS MARKET CONSULT CREATE DIPLOM EDU/PROP LEGIT ATTIT RIGID/FLEX...TIME/SEQ GEN/LAWS WORK 20. PAGE 161 A3285
ECO/UNDEV ALL/VALS ECO/TAC FOR/AID

S57
ALLEN R.L.,"UNITED NATIONS TECHNICAL ASSISTANCE: SOVIET AND EAST-EUROPEAN PARTICIPATION." COM WOR+45 AGRI INDUS INT/ORG NAT/G FOR/AID SKILL UN 20. PAGE 6 A0124
ECO/UNDEV TEC/DEV USSR

N57
US SENATE SPECIAL COMM FOR AFF,REPORT OF THE SPECIAL COMMITTEE TO STUDY THE FOREIGN AID PROGRAM (PAMPHLET). USA+45 CONSULT DELIB/GP LEGIS PLAN TEC/DEV CONFER SUPEGO CONGRESS. PAGE 157 A3199
FOR/AID ORD/FREE ECO/UNDEV DIPLOM

B58
BERLINER J.S.,SOVIET ECONOMIC AID: THE AID AND TRADE POLICY IN UNDERDEVELOPED COUNTRIES. AFR COM ISLAM L/A+17C S/ASIA USSR ECO/DEV DIST/IND FINAN MARKET INT/ORG ACT/RES PLAN BAL/PWR WEAPON PWR WEALTH...CHARTS 20. PAGE 14 A0277
ECO/UNDEV ECO/TAC FOR/AID

B58
CARROLL H.N.,THE HOUSE OF REPRESENTATIVES AND FOREIGN AFFAIRS. USA+45 USA-45 NAT/G POL/PAR DIPLOM FOR/AID LEGIT ROUTINE PWR...TIME/SEQ CONGRESS. PAGE 25 A0502
DELIB/GP LEGIS

B58
HAUSER P.H.,POPULATION AND WORLD POLITICS. FUT WOR+45 WOR-45 AGRI DIST/IND INDUS INT/ORG PLAN ECO/TAC DISPL HEALTH COLD/WAR 20. PAGE 63 A1288
NAT/G ECO/UNDEV FOR/AID

B58
HUNT B.I.,BIPARTISANSHIP: A CASE STUDY OF THE FOREIGN ASSISTANCE PROGRAM, 1947-56 (DOCTORAL THESIS). USA+45 INT/ORG CONSULT LEGIS TEC/DEV ...BIBLIOG PRESIDENT TREATY NATO TRUMAN/HS EISNHWR/DD CONGRESS. PAGE 69 A1418
FOR/AID POL/PAR GP/REL DIPLOM

B58
JENNINGS I.,PROBLEMS OF THE NEW COMMONWEALTH. CEYLON INDIA PAKISTAN S/ASIA ECO/UNDEV INT/ORG LOC/G DIPLOM ECO/TAC INT/TRADE COLONIAL RACE/REL DISCRIM 20 COMMONWLTH PARLIAMENT. PAGE 74 A1508
NAT/LISM NEUTRAL FOR/AID POL/PAR

B58
MILLIS W.,FOREIGN POLICY AND THE FREE SOCIETY. USA+45 WOR+45 SOCIETY NAT/G FORCES BAL/PWR FOR/AID EDU/PROP DETER ATTIT PWR 20 COLD/WAR. PAGE 102 A2084
DIPLOM POLICY ORD/FREE CONSULT

B58
MUNKMAN C.A.,AMERICAN AID TO GREECE. GREECE USA+45 AGRI FINAN PROB/SOLV WAR PWR...CHARTS 20 UN. PAGE 106 A2171
FOR/AID PLAN ECO/DEV INT/TRADE

B58
NEHRU J.,SPEECHES. INDIA ECO/UNDEV AGRI INDUS INT/ORG POL/PAR DIPLOM FOR/AID NAT/LISM...ANTHOL 20. PAGE 108 A2213
PLAN CHIEF COLONIAL NEUTRAL

B58
US DEPARTMENT OF STATE,PUBLICATIONS OF THE DEPARTMENT OF STATE, JANUARY 1,1953 TO DECEMBER 31, 1957. AGRI INT/ORG FORCES FOR/AID EDU/PROP ARMS/CONT NUC/PWR ATTIT 20 DEPT/STATE OAS UN NATO. PAGE 151 A3092 BIBLIOG DIPLOM

B58
US HOUSE COMM GOVT OPERATIONS,HEARINGS BEFORE A SUBCOMMITTEE OF THE COMMITTEE ON GOVERNMENT OPERATIONS. CAMBODIA PHILIPPINE USA+45 CONSTRUC TEC/DEV ADMIN CONTROL WEAPON EFFICIENCY HOUSE/REP. PAGE 154 A3135 FOR/AID DIPLOM ORD/FREE ECO/UNDEV

B58
US OPERATIONS MISSION TO VIET,BUILDING ECONOMIC STRENGTH (PAMPHLET). USA+45 VIETNAM/S INDUS TEC/DEV BUDGET ADMIN EATING HEALTH...STAT 20. PAGE 155 A3162 FOR/AID ECO/UNDEV AGRI EDU/PROP

B58
WIGGINS J.W.,FOREIGN AID REEXAMINED: A CRITICAL APPRAISAL. CHINA/COM INDONESIA USA+45 FINAN INT/TRADE REGION NAT/LISM ATTIT...CENSUS 20. PAGE 164 A3342 FOR/AID DIPLOM ECO/UNDEV SOVEREIGN

L58
HAVILAND H.F.,"FOREIGN AID AND THE POLICY PROCESS: 1957." USA+45 FACE/GP POL/PAR VOL/ASSN CHIEF DELIB/GP ACT/RES LEGIT EXEC GOV/REL ATTIT DRIVE PWR ...POLICY TESTS CONGRESS 20. PAGE 63 A1291 LEGIS PLAN FOR/AID

S58
DAVENPORT J.,"ARMS AND THE WELFARE STATE." INTELL STRUCT FORCES CREATE ECO/TAC FOR/AID DOMIN LEGIT ADMIN WAR ORD/FREE PWR...POLICY SOC CONCPT MYTH OBS TREND COLD/WAR TOT/POP 20. PAGE 34 A0685 USA+45 NAT/G USSR

S58
JORDAN A.,"MILITARY ASSISTANCE AND NATIONAL POLICY." ASIA FUT USA+45 WOR+45 ECO/DEV ECO/UNDEV INT/ORG NAT/G PLAN ECO/TAC ROUTINE WEAPON ATTIT RIGID/FLEX PWR...CONCPT TREND 20. PAGE 75 A1533 FORCES POLICY FOR/AID DIPLOM

N58
INVESTMENT FUND ECO SOC DEV,FRENCH AFRICA: A DECADE OF PROGRESS 1948-1958 (PAMPHLET). AFR FRANCE EXTR/IND INDUS EDU/PROP HEALTH 20. PAGE 71 A1465 FOR/AID DIPLOM ECO/UNDEV AGRI

N58
US HOUSE COMM FOREIGN AFFAIRS,HEARINGS ON THE FAR EAST AND THE PACIFIC (PAMPHLET). LAOS USA+45 NAT/G CONSULT FORCES CONFER DEBATE ORD/FREE 20. PAGE 153 A3124 FOR/AID DIPLOM DELIB/GP LEGIS

N58
US HOUSE COMM FOREIGN AFFAIRS,HEARINGS ON REVIEW OF THE MUTUAL SECURITY PROGRAMS; EXAMINATION OF SELECTED PROJECTS IN FORMOSA AND PAKISTAN (PAMPHLET). ASIA PAKISTAN TAIWAN INDUS CONSULT DELIB/GP LEGIS BUDGET CONFER DEBATE 20. PAGE 153 A3125 FOR/AID ECO/UNDEV DIPLOM ECO/TAC

B59
AIR FORCE ACADEMY ASSEMBLY '59,INTERNATIONAL STABILITY AND PROGRESS (PAMPHLET). USA+45 USSR ECO/UNDEV PROB/SOLV BUDGET DIPLOM ADMIN DETER COST ATTIT...TREND 20. PAGE 5 A0103 FOR/AID FORCES WAR PLAN

B59
AMERICAN FRIENDS OF VIETNAM,AID TO VIETNAM: AN AMERICAN SUCCESS STORY (PAMPHLET). ASIA FUT USA+45 VIETNAM ECO/UNDEV WAR CIVMIL/REL GOV/REL...ANTHOL 20. PAGE 7 A0148 DIPLOM NAT/G FOR/AID FORCES

B59
DAWSON R.H.,THE DECISION TO AID RUSSIA* FOREIGN POLICY AND DOMESTIC POLITICS. GERMANY USSR CHIEF EX/STRUC LEGIS TOP/EX PROB/SOLV WAR ATTIT...POLICY CONGRESS. PAGE 34 A0695 DECISION DELIB/GP DIPLOM FOR/AID

B59
HAZLEWOOD A.,THE ECONOMICS OF "UNDER-DEVELOPED" AREAS. WOR+45 DIST/IND EXTR/IND FINAN INDUS MARKET PLAN FOR/AID...GEOG 20. PAGE 63 A1302 BIBLIOG/A ECO/UNDEV AGRI INT/TRADE

B59
HUGHES E.M.,AMERICA THE VINCIBLE. USA+45 FOR/AID ARMS/CONT NUC/PWR PERS/REL RATIONAL ATTIT ALL/VALS 20 COLD/WAR. PAGE 69 A1413 ORD/FREE DIPLOM WAR

B59
KARUNAKARAN K.P.,INDIA IN WORLD AFFAIRS, 1952-1958 (VOL. II). INDIA ECO/UNDEV SECT FOR/AID INT/TRADE ADJUD NEUTRAL REV WAR DISCRIM ORD/FREE MARXISM ...BIBLIOG 20. PAGE 77 A1569 DIPLOM INT/ORG S/ASIA COLONIAL

B59
LAQUER W.Z.,THE SOVIET UNION AND THE MIDDLE EAST. COM UAR USSR ECO/UNDEV NAT/G VOL/ASSN ECO/TAC EDU/PROP COLONIAL EXEC PWR...TIME/SEQ TREND COLD/WAR 20. PAGE 85 A1730 ISLAM DRIVE FOR/AID NAT/LISM

B59
MEZERK A.G.,FINANCIAL ASSISTANCE FOR ECONOMIC DEVELOPMENT. WOR+45 INDUS DIPLOM INT/TRADE...CHARTS GOV/COMP UN. PAGE 101 A2064 FOR/AID FINAN ECO/TAC ECO/UNDEV

B59
NOVE A.,COMMUNIST ECONOMIC STRATEGY: SOVIET GROWTH AND CAPABILITIES. USSR AGRI LABOR PLAN TEC/DEV CAP/ISM INT/TRADE EFFICIENCY MARXISM 20 THIRD/WRLD. PAGE 110 A2257 FOR/AID ECO/TAC DIPLOM INDUS

B59
NUNEZ JIMENEZ A.,LA LIBERACION DE LAS ISLAS. CUBA L/A+17C USA+45 LAW CHIEF PLAN DIPLOM FOR/AID OWN WEALTH 20 CASTRO/F. PAGE 110 A2261 AGRI REV ECO/UNDEV NAT/G

B59
US GENERAL ACCOUNTING OFFICE,EXAM OF ECONOMIC AND TECHNICAL ASSISTANCE PROGRAM FOR INDIA INT'NAT'L COOP ADMIN REPORT TO CONGRESS 1955-1958. INDIA USA+45 ECO/UNDEV FINAN PLAN DIPLOM COST UTIL WEALTH ...CHARTS 20 CONGRESS AID. PAGE 153 A3114 FOR/AID EFFICIENCY ECO/TAC TEC/DEV

B59
US HOUSE COMM GOVT OPERATIONS,UNITED STATES AID OPERATIONS IN LAOS. LAOS USA+45 PLAN INSPECT HOUSE/REP. PAGE 154 A3136 FOR/AID ADMIN FORCES ECO/UNDEV

B59
US PRES COMM STUDY MIL ASSIST,COMPOSITE REPORT. USA+45 ECO/UNDEV PLAN BUDGET DIPLOM EFFICIENCY ...POLICY MGT 20. PAGE 155 A3164 FOR/AID FORCES WEAPON ORD/FREE

B59
VINACKE H.M.,A HISTORY OF THE FAR EAST IN MODERN TIMES (6TH ED.). KOREA S/ASIA USSR CONSTN CULTURE STRATA ECO/UNDEV NAT/G CHIEF FOR/AID INT/TRADE GP/REL...SOC NAT/COMP 19/20 CHINJAP. PAGE 159 A3235 STRUCT ASIA

L59
GARDNER R.N.,"NEW DIRECTIONS IN UNITED STATES FOREIGN ECONOMIC POLICY." USA+45 CONSULT...GEN/LAWS GEN/METH COLD/WAR 20. PAGE 51 A1044 ECO/UNDEV ECO/TAC FOR/AID DIPLOM

L59
WURFEL D.,"FOREIGN AID AND SOCIAL REFORM IN POLITICAL DEVELOPMENT" (BMR)" PHILIPPINE USA+45 WOR+45 SOCIETY POL/PAR ACT/RES TEC/DEV DIPLOM 20. PAGE 168 A3424 FOR/AID PROB/SOLV ECO/TAC ECO/UNDEV

S59
KINDLEBERGER C.P.,"UNITED STATES ECONOMIC FOREIGN POLICY: RESEARCH REQUIREMENTS FOR 1965." FUT USA+45 WOR+45 DIST/IND MARKET INT/ORG ECO/TAC INT/TRADE WEALTH...OBS TREND CON/ANAL GEN/LAWS VAL/FREE 20. PAGE 79 A1621 FINAN ECO/DEV FOR/AID

S59
KOHN L.Y.,"ISRAEL AND NEW NATION STATES OF ASIA AND AFRICA." AFR ASIA FUT S/ASIA VOL/ASSN TEC/DEV NAT/LISM RIGID/FLEX SKILL WEALTH...RELATIV OBS TREND CON/ANAL 20. PAGE 81 A1663 ECO/UNDEV ECO/TAC FOR/AID ISRAEL

S59
KRIPALANI A.J.B.,"FOR PRINCIPLED NEUTRALITY." CHINA/COM INDIA S/ASIA PLAN ECO/TAC RIGID/FLEX MORAL PWR...MYSTIC SOC RECORD 20 GANDHI/M. PAGE 82 A1684 ATTIT FOR/AID DIPLOM

S59
REUBENS E.D.,"THE BASIS FOR REORIENATION OF AMERICAN FOREIGN AID POLICY." USA+45 USSR STRUCT INT/ORG CONSULT ECO/TAC ADMIN DRIVE MORAL ORD/FREE PWR WEALTH...RELATIV MATH STAT TREND GEN/LAWS VAL/FREE 20. PAGE 120 A2467 ECO/UNDEV PLAN FOR/AID DIPLOM

S59
STOESSINGER J.G.,"THE INTERNATIONAL ATOMIC ENERGY AGENCY: THE FIRST PHASE." FUT WOR+45 NAT/G VOL/ASSN DELIB/GP BAL/PWR LEGIT ADMIN ROUTINE PWR...OBS CON/ANAL GEN/LAWS VAL/FREE 20 IAEA. PAGE 138 A2829 INT/ORG ECO/DEV FOR/AID NUC/PWR

N59
US HOUSE COMM FOREIGN AFFAIRS,HEARINGS ON DRAFT LEGISLATION TO AMEND FURTHER THE MUTUAL SECURITY ACT OF 1954 (PAMPHLET). USA+45 USSR CONSULT DELIB/GP FORCES ECO/TAC CONFER...POLICY 20 CONGRESS. PAGE 153 A3126 DIPLOM FOR/AID ORD/FREE LEGIS

B60
ALLEN R.L.,SOVIET ECONOMIC WARFARE. USSR FINAN INDUS NAT/G PLAN TEC/DEV FOR/AID DETER WEALTH ...TREND GEN/LAWS 20. PAGE 6 A0126 COM ECO/TAC

B60
BILLERBECK K.,SOVIET BLOC FOREIGN AID TO UNDERDEVELOPED COUNTRIES. COM FUT USSR FINAN FORCES TEC/DEV DIPLOM INT/TRADE EDU/PROP NUC/PWR...TREND 20. PAGE 14 A0287 FOR/AID ECO/UNDEV ECO/TAC MARXISM

B60
BLACK E.R.,THE DIPLOMACY OF ECONOMIC DEVELOPMENT. WOR+45 CONSULT PLAN TEC/DEV DIPLOM ECO/TAC FOR/AID ...CONCPT TREND 20. PAGE 15 A0297 ECO/UNDEV ACT/RES

B60
BROOKINGS INSTITUTION,UNITED STATES FOREIGN POLICY: STUDY NO 9: THE FORMULATION AND ADMINISTRATION OF UNITED STATES FOREIGN POLICY. USA+45 WOR+45 EX/STRUC LEGIS BAL/PWR FOR/AID EDU/PROP CIVMIL/REL GOV/REL...INT COLD/WAR. PAGE 19 A0394 DIPLOM INT/ORG CREATE

B60
CAMPAIGNE J.G.,AMERICAN MIGHT AND SOVIET MYTH. COM EUR+WWI ECO/DEV ECO/UNDEV INT/ORG NAT/G CAP/ISM ECO/TAC FOR/AID EDU/PROP ATTIT PWR WEALTH...POLICY CONCPT MYTH TREND STERTYP GEN/LAWS COLD/WAR. PAGE 23 A0473 USA+45 DOMIN DIPLOM USSR

B60
FISCHER L.,RUSSIA, AMERICA, AND THE WORLD. FUT USA+45 USSR WOR+45 FORCES PLAN BAL/PWR ECO/TAC FOR/AID NEUTRAL TASK NUC/PWR PWR 20 COLD/WAR. PAGE 46 A0937
DIPLOM POLICY MARXISM ECO/UNDEV

B60
FRANCK P.G.,AFGHANISTAN: BETWEEN EAST AND WEST. AFGHANISTN USA+45 USSR ECO/UNDEV PLAN ADMIN ROUTINE ATTIT PWR...STAT OBS CHARTS TOT/POP COLD/WAR 20. PAGE 48 A0978
ECO/TAC TREND FOR/AID

B60
HAHN W.F.,AMERICAN STRATEGY FOR THE NUCLEAR AGE. USA+45 NAT/G TEC/DEV ECO/TAC FOR/AID ARMS/CONT NUC/PWR ORD/FREE MARXISM...ANTHOL 20. PAGE 59 A1216
DIPLOM PLAN PEACE

B60
HOFFMANN P.G.,ONE HUNDRED COUNTRIES, ONE AND ONE QUARTER BILLION PEOPLE. MARKET INT/ORG TEC/DEV CAP/ISM...GEOG CHARTS METH/COMP 20 UN. PAGE 66 A1354
FOR/AID ECO/TAC ECO/UNDEV INT/TRADE

B60
HOLT R.T.,STRATEGIC PSYCHOLOGICAL OPERATIONS AND AMERICAN FOREIGN POLICY. ITALY USA+45 FOR/AID DOMIN RUMOR ADMIN TASK WAR CHOOSE ATTIT ALL/IDEOS...PSY COLD/WAR. PAGE 67 A1375
EDU/PROP ACT/RES DIPLOM POLICY

B60
HYDE L.K.G.,THE US AND THE UN. WOR+45 STRUCT ECO/DEV ECO/UNDEV NAT/G ACT/RES PLAN DIPLOM EDU/PROP ADMIN ALL/VALS...CONCPT TIME/SEQ GEN/LAWS UN VAL/FREE 20. PAGE 70 A1428
USA+45 INT/ORG FOR/AID

B60
KENEN P.B.,GIANT AMONG NATIONS: PROBLEMS IN UNITED STATES FOREIGN ECONOMIC POLICY. USA+45 FINAN DIPLOM TARIFFS BAL/PAY WEALTH 20 COLD/WAR. PAGE 77 A1584
FOR/AID ECO/UNDEV INT/TRADE PLAN

B60
KRISTENSEN T.,THE ECONOMIC WORLD BALANCE. FUT WOR+45 CULTURE ECO/DEV BAL/PWR INT/TRADE REGION PWR WEALTH...STAT TREND CHARTS 20. PAGE 82 A1685
ECO/UNDEV ECO/TAC FOR/AID

B60
LATIFI D.,INDIA AND UNITED STATES AID. ASIA INDIA UK USA+45 AGRI FINAN INDUS COLONIAL ORD/FREE SOVEREIGN WEALTH...METH/COMP 20. PAGE 85 A1743
FOR/AID DIPLOM ECO/UNDEV

B60
LIEUWEN E.,ARMS AND POLITICS IN LATIN AMERICA. FUT USA+45 USA-45 ECO/UNDEV INT/ORG NAT/G FORCES DIPLOM COERCE ATTIT ALL/VALS VAL/FREE OAS 20. PAGE 88 A1811
L/A+17C FOR/AID

B60
LISKA G.,THE NEW STATECRAFT. WOR+45 WOR-45 LEGIS DIPLOM ADMIN ATTIT PWR WEALTH...HIST/WRIT TREND COLD/WAR 20. PAGE 90 A1837
ECO/TAC CONCPT FOR/AID

B60
MC CLELLAN G.S.,INDIA. CHINA/COM INDIA CONSTN ELITES STRATA AGRI POL/PAR FOR/AID ARMS/CONT REV MARXISM...CENSUS BIBLIOG 20 COLD/WAR GANDHI/M NEHRU/J. PAGE 97 A1990
DIPLOM NAT/G SOCIETY ECO/UNDEV

B60
NEALE A.D.,THE FLOW OF RESOURCES FROM RICH TO POOR. WOR+45 ECO/DEV ECO/UNDEV FINAN INDUS NAT/G PLAN EFFICIENCY WEALTH...POLICY NAT/COMP 20 RESOURCE/N. PAGE 108 A2209
FOR/AID DIPLOM METH/CNCPT

B60
PENTONY D.E.,THE UNDERDEVELOPED LANDS. FUT WOR+45 CULTURE AGRI FINAN INDUS MARKET INT/ORG LABOR NAT/G VOL/ASSN CONSULT TEC/DEV ECO/TAC EDU/PROP COLONIAL ATTIT WEALTH...OBS RECORD SAMP TREND GEN/METH WORK UN 20. PAGE 115 A2351
ECO/UNDEV POLICY FOR/AID INT/TRADE

B60
PENTONY D.E.,UNITED STATES FOREIGN AID. INDIA LAOS USA+45 ECO/UNDEV INT/TRADE ADMIN PEACE ATTIT ...POLICY METH/COMP ANTHOL 20. PAGE 115 A2352
FOR/AID DIPLOM ECO/TAC

B60
RAO V.K.R.,INTERNATIONAL AID FOR ECONOMIC DEVELOPMENT - POSSIBILITIES AND LIMITATIONS. FINAN PLAN TEC/DEV ADMIN TASK EFFICIENCY...POLICY SOC METH/CNCPT CHARTS 20 UN. PAGE 119 A2444
FOR/AID DIPLOM INT/ORG ECO/UNDEV

B60
SHONFIELD A.,THE ATTACK ON WORLD POVERTY. WOR+45 ECO/DEV ECO/UNDEV FINAN VOL/ASSN PLAN EDU/PROP DRIVE KNOWL WEALTH...CONT/OBS STAND/INT ORG/CHARTS TOT/POP UNESCO 20. PAGE 132 A2704
INT/ORG ECO/TAC FOR/AID INT/TRADE

B60
STEVENSON A.E.,PUTTING FIRST THINGS FIRST. USA+45 INT/ORG NEIGH FOR/AID DISCRIM...ANTHOL 20. PAGE 138 A2822
DIPLOM ECO/UNDEV ORD/FREE EDU/PROP

B60
STOLPER W.F.,GERMANY BETWEEN EAST AND WEST: THE ECONOMICS OF COMPETITIVE COEXISTENCE. FUT GERMANY/E GERMANY/W WOR+45 FINAN POL/PAR BUDGET ECO/TAC FOR/AID INT/TRADE...STAT CHARTS METH/COMP 20 COLD/WAR. PAGE 138 A2832
ECO/DEV DIPLOM GOV/COMP BAL/PWR

B60
THEOBALD R.,THE RICH AND THE POOR: A STUDY OF THE ECONOMICS OF RISING EXPECTATIONS. WOR+45 CONSTN ECO/DEV ECO/UNDEV INT/ORG NAT/G PLAN FOR/AID ROUTINE BAL/PAY ORD/FREE PWR WEALTH...GEOG TREND WORK 20. PAGE 142 A2912
ECO/TAC INT/TRADE

B60
THEOBOLD R.,THE NEW NATIONS OF WEST AFRICA. GHANA NIGERIA CULTURE INT/ORG ECO/TAC FOR/AID COLONIAL RACE/REL POPULISM...ANTHOL BIBLIOG 20 UN. PAGE 143 A2916
AFR SOVEREIGN ECO/UNDEV DIPLOM

B60
UNITED WORLD FEDERALISTS,UNITED WORLD FEDERALISTS; PANORAMA OF RECENT BOOKS, FILMS, AND JOURNALS ON WORLD FEDERATION, THE UN, AND WORLD PEACE. CULTURE ECO/UNDEV PROB/SOLV FOR/AID ARMS/CONT NUC/PWR ...INT/LAW PHIL/SCI 20 UN. PAGE 149 A3039
BIBLIOG/A DIPLOM INT/ORG PEACE

B60
US HOUSE COMM FOREIGN AFFAIRS,HEARINGS ON A BILL TO AMEND FURTHER THE MUTUAL SECURITY ACT OF 1954. USA+45 CONSULT FORCES BUDGET FOR/AID CONFER DETER ...CHARTS 20 DEPT/DEFEN DEPT/STATE UNEF. PAGE 153 A3127
DIPLOM ORD/FREE DELIB/GP LEGIS

B60
US HOUSE COMM GOVT OPERATIONS,OPERATIONS OF THE DEVELOPMENT LOAN FUND: HEARINGS (COMMITTEE ON GOVERNMENT OPERATIONS). USA+45 PLAN BUDGET DIPLOM GOV/REL COST...CHARTS 20 CONGRESS DEPT/STATE AID. PAGE 154 A3137
FINAN FOR/AID ECO/TAC EFFICIENCY

B60
US SENATE COMM ON FOREIGN REL,SITUATION IN VIETNAM (2 VOLS.). USA+45 VIETNAM ECO/TAC COST SENATE DEPT/STATE. PAGE 156 A3181
FOR/AID PLAN EFFICIENCY INSPECT

B60
VAN HOOGSTRATE D.J.,AMERICAN FOREIGN POLICY: REALISTS AND IDEALISTS: A CATHOLIC INTERPRETATION. BAL/PWR FOR/AID ARMS/CONT GOV/REL PEACE LOVE MORAL SOVEREIGN CATHISM...BIBLIOG 20. PAGE 158 A3213
CATH DIPLOM POLICY IDEA/COMP

B60
VOGT W.,PEOPLE: CHALLENGE TO SURVIVAL. WOR+45 ECO/DEV ECO/UNDEV FAM INT/ORG NAT/G PLAN PROB/SOLV FOR/AID GIVE EATING 20 BIRTH/CON. PAGE 159 A3247
CENSUS CONTROL ATTIT TEC/DEV

B60
WOLF C.,FOREIGN AID: THEORY AND PRACTICE IN SOUTHERN ASIA. CEYLON INDONESIA PHILIPPINE S/ASIA CULTURE STRATA ECO/UNDEV PLAN EDU/PROP ATTIT ...METH/CNCPT MATH QUANT STAT CONT/OBS TIME/SEQ SIMUL TOT/POP 20. PAGE 166 A3378
ACT/RES ECO/TAC FOR/AID

S60
COHEN A.,"THE NEW AFRICA AND THE UN." FUT ECO/UNDEV NAT/G ECO/TAC INT/TRADE CHOOSE ATTIT ORD/FREE PWR ...POLICY METH/CNCPT OBS TREND CON/ANAL GEN/LAWS TOT/POP VAL/FREE UN 20. PAGE 27 A0558
AFR INT/ORG BAL/PWR FOR/AID

S60
FRANKEL S.H.,"ECONOMIC ASPECTS OF POLITICAL INDEPENDENCE IN AFRICA." AFR FUT SOCIETY ECO/UNDEV COM/IND FINAN LEGIS PLAN TEC/DEV CAP/ISM ECO/TAC INT/TRADE ADMIN ATTIT DRIVE RIGID/FLEX PWR WEALTH ...MGT NEW/IDEA MATH TIME/SEQ VAL/FREE 20. PAGE 48 A0984
NAT/G FOR/AID

S60
HAVILAND H.F.,"PROBLEMS OF AMERICAN FOREIGN POLICY." ASIA COM USA+45 WOR+45 INT/ORG NAT/G CONSULT ECO/TAC FOR/AID DOMIN COERCE NUC/PWR ATTIT DRIVE ORD/FREE PWR RESPECT SKILL...POLICY GEOG OBS SAMP TREND GEN/METH METH COLD/WAR UN 20. PAGE 63 A1292
ECO/UNDEV FORCES DIPLOM

S60
KEYFITZ N.,"WESTERN PERSPECTIVES AND ASIAN PROBLEMS." ASIA EUR+WWI S/ASIA SOCIETY FOR/AID ...POLICY SOC CONCPT STERTYP WORK TOT/POP 20. PAGE 78 A1604
CULTURE ATTIT

S60
KISTIAKOWSKY G.B.,"SCIENCE AND FOREIGN AFFAIRS." FUT WOR+45 NAT/G PROF/ORG PLAN ECO/TAC EDU/PROP NUC/PWR...TREND COLD/WAR 20. PAGE 80 A1645
CONSULT TEC/DEV FOR/AID DIPLOM

S60
LINDHOLM R.W.,"ACCELERATED DEVELOPMENT WITH A MINIMUM OF FOREIGN AID AND ECONOMIC CONTROLS." SOCIETY INDUS ECO/TAC WEALTH...CONCPT 20. PAGE 89 A1822
ECO/DEV FINAN FOR/AID

S60
MARTIN E.M.,"NEW TRENDS IN UNITED STATES ECONOMIC FOREIGN POLICY." USA+45 INTELL DELIB/GP FOR/AID INT/TRADE ROUTINE BAL/PAY...RELATIV 20. PAGE 95 A1949
NAT/G PLAN DIPLOM

S60
MIKESELL R.F.,"AMERICA'S ECONOMIC RESPONSIBILITY AS A GREAT POWER." COM FUT USA+45 USSR WOR+45 INT/ORG PLAN ECO/TAC FOR/AID EDU/PROP CHOOSE WEALTH ...POLICY 20. PAGE 101 A2069
ECO/UNDEV BAL/PWR CAP/ISM

S60
MURPHY J.C.,"INTERNATIONAL INVESTMENT AND THE NATIONAL INTEREST." WOR+45 WOR-45 ECO/DEV ECO/UNDEV NAT/G ACT/RES...CHARTS TOT/POP COLD/WAR 20. PAGE 106 A2179
FINAN WEALTH FOR/AID

S60
PYE L.W.,"SOVIET AND AMERICAN STYLES IN FOREIGN AID." COM USA+45 USSR WOR+45 NAT/G PLAN ECO/TAC ROUTINE RIGID/FLEX...POLICY CONCPT TREND GEN/LAWS TOT/POP 20. PAGE 118 A2419
ECO/UNDEV ATTIT FOR/AID

S60
RIESELBACH Z.N.,"QUANTITATIVE TECHNIQUES FOR STUDYING VOTING BEHAVIOR IN THE UNITED NATIONS GENERAL ASSEMBLY." FUT S/ASIA USA+45 INT/ORG BAL/PWR DIPLOM ECO/TAC FOR/AID ADMIN PWR...POLICY METH/CNCPT METH UN 20. PAGE 121 A2478
QUANT CHOOSE

S60
RIVKIN A.,"AFRICAN ECONOMIC DEVELOPMENT: ADVANCED TECHNOLOGY AND THE STAGES OF GROWTH." CULTURE ECO/UNDEV AGRI COM/IND EXTR/IND PLAN ECO/TAC ATTIT DRIVE RIGID/FLEX SKILL WEALTH...MGT SOC GEN/LAWS WORK TOT/POP 20. PAGE 121 A2487
AFR TEC/DEV FOR/AID

S60
RUSSEL R.W.,"ROLES FOR PSYCHOLOGISTS IN THE MAINTENANCE OF PEACE." FUT USA+45 CULTURE INT/ORG DIPLOM FOR/AID EDU/PROP ATTIT KNOWL MORAL PWR ...POLICY SOC COLD/WAR 20. PAGE 125 A2572
PSY GEN/METH

B61
AMORY J.F.,AROUND THE EDGE OF WAR: A NEW APPROACH TO THE PROBLEMS OF AMERICAN FOREIGN POLICY. COM L/A+17C USA+45 USSR FOR/AID EDU/PROP AGREE CONTROL ARMS/CONT NUC/PWR WAR PWR...IDEA/COMP 20 TREATY ESPIONAGE. PAGE 8 A0154
NAT/G DIPLOM POLICY

B61
AUBREY H.G.,COEXISTENCE: ECONOMIC CHALLENGE AND RESPONSE. USSR WOR+45 ACT/RES BAL/PWR CAP/ISM DIPLOM ECO/TAC FOR/AID INT/TRADE PEACE SOCISM ...METH/COMP NAT/COMP COLD/WAR. PAGE 10 A0196
POLICY ECO/UNDEV PLAN COM

B61
BONNEFOUS M.,EUROPE ET TIERS MONDE. EUR+WWI SOCIETY INT/ORG NAT/G VOL/ASSN ACT/RES TEC/DEV CAP/ISM ECO/TAC ATTIT ORD/FREE SOVEREIGN...POLICY CONCPT TREND 20. PAGE 16 A0334
AFR ECO/UNDEV FOR/AID INT/TRADE

B61
DETHINE P.,BIBLIOGRAPHIE DES ASPECTS ECONOMIQUES ET SOCIAUX DE L'INDUSTRIALISATION EN AFRIQUE. AFR FINAN LABOR FOR/AID...SOC 20. PAGE 36 A0734
BIBLIOG/A ECO/UNDEV INDUS TEC/DEV

B61
FLEMING D.F.,THE COLD WAR AND ITS ORIGINS: 1917-1950 (VOL. I). ASIA USSR WOR+45 WOR-45 TEC/DEV FOR/AID NUC/PWR REV WAR PEACE FASCISM...T 20 COLD/WAR NATO BERLIN/BLO. PAGE 46 A0947
DIPLOM MARXISM BAL/PWR

B61
GURTOO D.H.N.,INDIA'S BALANCE OF PAYMENTS (1920-1960). INDIA FINAN DIPLOM FOR/AID INT/TRADE PRICE COLONIAL...CHARTS BIBLIOG 20. PAGE 58 A1197
BAL/PAY STAT ECO/TAC ECO/UNDEV

B61
HARRISON S.,INDIA AND THE UNITED STATES. FUT S/ASIA USA+45 WOR+45 INTELL ECO/DEV ECO/UNDEV AGRI INDUS INT/ORG NAT/G CONSULT EX/STRUC TOP/EX PLAN ECO/TAC NEUTRAL ALL/VALS...MGT TOT/POP 20. PAGE 62 A1272
DELIB/GP ACT/RES FOR/AID INDIA

B61
HASAN H.S.,PAKISTAN AND THE UN. ISLAM WOR+45 ECO/DEV ECO/UNDEV NAT/G TOP/EX ECO/TAC FOR/AID EDU/PROP ADMIN DRIVE PERCEPT...OBS TIME/SEQ UN 20. PAGE 62 A1284
INT/ORG ATTIT PAKISTAN

B61
JAVITS B.A.,THE PEACE BY INVESTMENT CORPORATION. WOR+45 NAT/G LEGIS PROB/SOLV PERS/REL WEALTH ...POLICY 20. PAGE 73 A1499
ECO/UNDEV DIPLOM FOR/AID PEACE

B61
MEZERIK A.G.,ECONOMIC DEVELOPMENT AIDS FOR UNDERDEVELOPED COUNTRIES. WOR+45 FINAN LEGIS PROB/SOLV TEC/DEV DIPLOM FOR/AID GIVE TASK WAR 20 UN. PAGE 101 A2062
ECO/UNDEV INT/ORG WEALTH PLAN

B61
MILLIKAW M.F.,THE EMERGING NATIONS: THEIR GROWTH AND UNITED STATES POLICY. FUT USA+45 WOR+45 WOR-45 NAT/G PLAN TEC/DEV BAL/PWR GOV/REL PEACE ORD/FREE 20. PAGE 101 A2082
ECO/UNDEV POLICY DIPLOM FOR/AID

B61
MORLEY L.,THE PATCHWORK HISTORY OF FOREIGN AID. KOREA/S USA+45 USSR LAW FINAN INT/ORG TEC/DEV BAL/PWR GIVE 20 COLD/WAR NATO. PAGE 104 A2144
FOR/AID ECO/UNDEV FORCES DIPLOM

B61
MORRAY J.P.,FROM YALTA TO DISARMAMENT: COLD WAR DEBATE. USA+45 CAP/ISM FOR/AID CONTROL NUC/PWR 20 UN COLD/WAR CHURCHLL/W. PAGE 104 A2145
MARXIST ARMS/CONT DIPLOM BAL/PWR

B61
ROBINS D.B.,EVOLVING UNITED STATES POLICIES TOWARD THE EMERGING NATIONS OF ASIA AND AFRICA (PAMPHLET). ISLAM ECO/UNDEV INT/ORG CONSULT CREATE PLAN TEC/DEV FOR/AID CONFER ALL/VALS 20 KENNEDY/JF EISNHWR/DD UN AID. PAGE 122 A2501
AFR S/ASIA DIPLOM BIBLIOG

B61
ROBINSON M.E.,EDUCATION FOR SOCIAL CHANGE: ESTABLISHING INSTITUTES OF PUBLIC AND BUSINESS ADMINISTRATION ABROAD (PAMPHLET). WOR+45 SOCIETY ACADEM CONFER INGP/REL ROLE...SOC CHARTS BIBLIOG 20 ICA. PAGE 122 A2506
FOR/AID EDU/PROP MGT ADJUST

B61
SHAPP W.R.,FIELD ADMINISTRATION IN THE UNITED NATIONS SYSTEM. FINAN PROB/SOLV INSPECT DIPLOM EXEC REGION ROUTINE EFFICIENCY ROLE...INT CHARTS 20 UN. PAGE 131 A2694
INT/ORG ADMIN GP/REL FOR/AID

B61
TETENS T.H.,THE NEW GERMANY AND THE OLD NAZIS. EUR+WWI GERMANY/W USA+45 NAT/G CRIME CHOOSE RACE/REL TOTALISM AGE/Y ATTIT 20 JEWS NAZI ADENAUER/K. PAGE 142 A2905
FASCISM DIPLOM FOR/AID POL/PAR

B61
THEOBALD R.,THE CHALLENGE OF ABUNDANCE. USA+45 WOR+45 MARKET DIPLOM FOR/AID REV PRODUC UTOPIA SUPEGO...POLICY TREND BIBLIOG/A 20. PAGE 142 A2913
WELF/ST ECO/UNDEV PROB/SOLV ECO/TAC

B61
US GENERAL ACCOUNTING OFFICE,EXAMINATION OF ECONOMIC AND TECHNICAL ASSISTANCE PROGRAM FOR IRAN. IRAN USA+45 AGRI INDUS DIPLOM CONTROL COST 20. PAGE 153 A3115
FOR/AID ADMIN TEC/DEV ECO/UNDEV

B61
US HOUSE COMM APPROPRIATIONS,INTER-AMERICAN PROGRAMS FOR 1961: DENIAL OF 1962 BUDGET INFORMATION. CHILE L/A+17C USA+45 FINAN CONSULT BUDGET ADJUD COST EFFICIENCY WEALTH...POLICY CHARTS 20 CONGRESS. PAGE 153 A3119
LEGIS FOR/AID DELIB/GP ECO/UNDEV

B61
US HOUSE COMM FOREIGN AFFAIRS,THE INTERNATIONAL DEVELOPMENT AND SECURITY ACT: HEARINGS BEFORE COMMITTEE ON FOREIGN AFFAIRS, HOUSE OF REP: HR7372. USA+45 AGRI INT/ORG NAT/G CONSULT DELIB/GP DIPLOM ECO/TAC INT/TRADE LOBBY REPRESENT 20 MCNAMARA/R DILLON/D RUSK/D CONGRESS. PAGE 153 A3128
FOR/AID CONFER LEGIS ECO/UNDEV

B61
US SENATE COMM ON FOREIGN RELS,INTERNATIONAL DEVELOPMENT AND SECURITY: HEARINGS ON BILL (2 VOLS.). ECO/UNDEV FINAN FORCES REV COST WEALTH ...CHARTS 20 AID PRESIDENT. PAGE 157 A3191
FOR/AID CIVMIL/REL ORD/FREE ECO/TAC

B61
WARD B.J.,INDIA AND THE WEST. INDIA UK USA+45 INT/TRADE GIVE COLONIAL ATTIT MARXISM 19/20. PAGE 161 A3279
PLAN ECO/UNDEV ECO/TAC FOR/AID

B61
WARNER D.,HURRICANE FROM CHINA. ASIA CHINA/COM FUT L/A+17C USA+45 CULTURE NAT/G FORCES TOP/EX FOR/AID DRIVE PWR...CONCPT TIME/SEQ SEATO WORK 20. PAGE 161 A3284
ATTIT TREND REV

L61
HILSMAN R. JR.,"THE NEW COMMUNIST TACTIC: PRECIS- INTERNAL WAR." COM FUT USA+45 ECO/UNDEV POL/PAR FOR/AID RIGID/FLEX ALL/VALS...TREND COLD/WAR 20. PAGE 65 A1334
FORCES COERCE USSR GUERRILLA

S61
ASHFORD D.E.,"A CASE STUDY IN THE DIPLOMACY OF SOCIAL REVOLUTION." USA+45 WOR+45 DIPLOM ECO/TAC FOR/AID REV ALL/VALS VAL/FREE 20. PAGE 9 A0187
ECO/UNDEV PLAN

S61
BARALL M.,"THE UNITED STATES GOVERNMENT RESPONDS." L/A+17C USA+45 SOCIETY NAT/G CREATE PLAN DIPLOM ECO/TAC ATTIT DRIVE RIGID/FLEX KNOWL SKILL WEALTH ...METH/CNCPT TIME/SEQ GEN/METH 20. PAGE 11 A0217
ECO/UNDEV ACT/RES FOR/AID

S61
CASTANEDA J.,"THE UNDERDEVELOPED NATIONS AND THE DEVELOPMENT OF INTERNATIONAL LAW." FUT UNIV LAW ACT/RES FOR/AID LEGIT PERCEPT SKILL...JURID METH/CNCPT TIME/SEQ TOT/POP 20 UN. PAGE 25 A0507
INT/ORG ECO/UNDEV PEACE INT/LAW

S61
DELLA PORT G.,"PROBLEMI E PROSPETTIVE DI COESISTENZA FRA ORIENTE ED OCCIDENTE, (PART 3)." COM FUT WOR+45 NAT/G BAL/PWR FOR/AID BAL/PAY PWR WEALTH...SOC CONCPT GEN/LAWS COLD/WAR 20. PAGE 36 A0729
INT/TRADE

S61
GALBRAITH J.K.,"A POSITIVE APPROACH TO ECONOMIC AID." FUT USA+45 INTELL NAT/G CONSULT ACT/RES DIPLOM ECO/TAC EDU/PROP ATTIT KNOWL PWR WEALTH ...SOC STERTYP 20. PAGE 50 A1030
ECO/UNDEV ROUTINE FOR/AID

S61
HEILBRONER R.L.,"DYNAMICS OF FOREIGN AID: PROBLEMS OF UNDERDEVELOPED NATIONS PLAGUE ASSISTANCE PROGRAM." FUT USA+45 WOR+45 STRATA NAT/G PLAN TEC/DEV ATTIT DRIVE WEALTH WORK 20. PAGE 64 A1307
ECO/UNDEV ECO/TAC FOR/AID

S61
NOVE A.,"THE SOVIET MODEL AND UNDERDEVELOPED COUNTRIES." COM FUT USSR WOR+45 CULTURE ECO/DEV POL/PAR FOR/AID EDU/PROP ADMIN MORAL WEALTH ...POLICY RECORD HIST/WRIT 20. PAGE 110 A2258
ECO/UNDEV PLAN

S61
ROSTOW W.W.,"THE FUTURE OF FOREIGN AID." COM FUT WOR+45 ECO/DEV INDUS INT/ORG NAT/G CONSULT ACT/RES PLAN DOMIN LEGIT CHOOSE RIGID/FLEX ALL/VALS
ECO/UNDEV ECO/TAC FOR/AID

...MAJORIT CONCPT TREND TOT/POP 20. PAGE 124 A2544

S61
TANNENBAUM F.,"THE UNITED STATES AND LATIN AMERICA." FUT USA+45 NAT/G FOR/AID CHOOSE ATTIT ALL/VALS VAL/FREE 20. PAGE 141 A2888 L/A+17C ECO/DEV DIPLOM

S61
VINER J.,"ECONOMIC FOREIGN POLICY ON THE NEW FRONTIER." USA+45 ECO/UNDEV AGRI FINAN INDUS MARKET INT/ORG NAT/G FOR/AID INT/TRADE ADMIN ATTIT PWR 20 KENNEDY/JF. PAGE 159 A3239 TOP/EX ECO/TAC BAL/PAY TARIFFS

B62
ROUND TABLE ON EUROPE'S ROLE IN LATIN AMERICAN DEVELOPMENT. EUR+WWI L/A+17C PLAN BAL/PAY UTIL ROLE WEALTH...CHARTS ANTHOL 20 UN INT/AM/DEV. PAGE 3 A0063 ECO/UNDEV FINAN TEC/DEV FOR/AID

B62
AIR FORCE ACADEMY LIBRARY,INTERNATIONAL ORGANIZATIONS AND MILITARY SECURITY SYSTEMS (PAMPHLET) (SPECIAL BIBLIOGRAPHY SERIES, NUMBER 25). DIPLOM FOR/AID INT/TRADE NUC/PWR PEACE 20 UN NATO OAS SEATO LEAGUE/NAT. PAGE 5 A0104 BIBLIOG INT/ORG FORCES DETER

B62
ARNOLD H.J.P.,AID FOR DEVELOPING COUNTRIES. COM EUR+WWI USA+45 USSR WOR+45 EDU/PROP ATTIT DRIVE PWR WEALTH...TREND CHARTS STERTYP NAT/ 20. PAGE 9 A0177 ECO/UNDEV ECO/TAC FOR/AID

B62
CALDER R.,COMMON SENSE ABOUT A STARVING WORLD. WOR+45 STRATA ECO/DEV PLAN GP/REL BIO/SOC HABITAT ...POLICY GEOG STAT RECORD 20 UN BIRTH/CON. PAGE 23 A0466 FOR/AID CENSUS ECO/UNDEV AGRI

B62
CALVOCORESSI P.,WORLD ORDER AND NEW STATES: PROBLEMS OF KEEPING THE PEACE. AFR EUR+WWI S/ASIA ELITES NAT/G ECO/TAC FOR/AID EDU/PROP COERCE ATTIT DRIVE ALL/VALS...GEN/LAWS COLD/WAR 20 UN. PAGE 23 A0471 INT/ORG PEACE

B62
DREIER J.C.,THE ORGANIZATION OF AMERICAN STATES AND THE HEMISPHERE CRISIS. CUBA USA+45 CULTURE STRATA NAT/G VOL/ASSN CONSULT FORCES ACT/RES CREATE DIPLOM ECO/TAC FOR/AID ALL/VALS...POLICY OBS OAS 20. PAGE 38 A0786 L/A+17C CONCPT

B62
DREIER J.C.,THE ALLIANCE FOR PROGRESS. L/A+17C USA+45 CULTURE ECO/DEV ECO/UNDEV NAT/G PLAN DIPLOM PWR 20 OAS. PAGE 39 A0787 FOR/AID INT/ORG ECO/TAC POLICY

B62
FAO,FOOD AND AGRICULTURE ORGANIZATION AFRICAN SURVEY. AFR CONGO/BRAZ GHANA STRATA AGRI INT/ORG TEC/DEV FOR/AID INT/TRADE RACE/REL DEMAND EFFICIENCY PRODUC...GEOG 20 UN CONGO/LEOP. PAGE 44 A0898 ECO/TAC WEALTH EXTR/IND ECO/UNDEV

B62
FRIEDMANN W.,METHODS AND POLICIES OF PRINCIPAL DONOR COUNTRIES IN PUBLIC INTERNATIONAL DEVELOPMENT FINANCING: PRELIMINARY APPRAISAL. FRANCE GERMANY/W UK USA+45 USSR WOR+45 FINAN TEC/DEV CAP/ISM DIPLOM ECO/TAC ATTIT 20 EEC. PAGE 49 A1002 INT/ORG FOR/AID NAT/COMP ADMIN

B62
FRIEDRICH-EBERT-STIFTUNG,THE SOVIET BLOC AND DEVELOPING COUNTRIES. CHINA/COM COM GERMANY/E USSR WOR+45 ECO/UNDEV INT/ORG NAT/G TEC/DEV NEUTRAL PWR ...POLICY 20. PAGE 49 A1008 MARXISM DIPLOM ECO/TAC FOR/AID

B62
GOLDWATER B.M.,WHY NOT VICTORY? A FRESH LOOK AT AMERICAN FOREIGN POLICY. USA+45 WOR+45 FOR/AID LEAD ARMS/CONT WAR PEACE ATTIT ORD/FREE PWR MARXISM ...INT/LAW 20 TREATY ECHR COUNCL/EUR. PAGE 53 A1092 DIPLOM POLICY CONSERVE NAT/LISM

B62
GOLDWIN R.A.,WHY FOREIGN AID? - TWO MESSAGES BY PRESIDENT KENNEDY AND ESSAYS. S/ASIA USA+45 ECO/UNDEV 20 KENNEDY/JF THIRD/WRLD. PAGE 54 A1096 DIPLOM FOR/AID POLICY

B62
GUENA Y.,HISTORIQUE DE LA COMMUNAUTE. FUT ECO/UNDEV NAT/G PLAN EDU/PROP COLONIAL REGION NAT/LISM ALL/VALS SOVEREIGN...CONCPT OBS CHARTS 20. PAGE 58 A1186 AFR VOL/ASSN FOR/AID FRANCE

B62
HIGGANS B.,UNITED NATIONS AND U.S. FOREIGN ECONOMIC POLICY. FUT USA+45 WOR+45 ECO/DEV ECO/UNDEV NAT/G ECO/TAC WEALTH...TIME/SEQ TOT/POP UN 20. PAGE 65 A1328 INT/ORG ACT/RES FOR/AID DIPLOM

B62
HOFFMAN P.,WORLD WITHOUT WANT. FUT WOR+45 ECO/UNDEV INT/ORG HEALTH KNOWL...TREND TOT/POP FAO 20. PAGE 66 A1353 CONCPT POLICY FOR/AID

B62
JEWELL M.E.,SENATORIAL POLITICS AND FOREIGN POLICY. NAT/G POL/PAR CHIEF DELIB/GP TOP/EX FOR/AID EDU/PROP ROUTINE ATTIT PWR SKILL...MAJORIT METH/CNCPT TIME/SEQ CONGRESS 20 PRESIDENT. PAGE 74 A1516 USA+45 LEGIS DIPLOM

B62
JORDAN A.A. JR.,FOREIGN AID AND THE DEFENSE OF SOUTHEAST ASIA. PAKISTAN VIETNAM/S FINAN PLAN BUDGET ECO/TAC DETER WAR ORD/FREE...POLICY DECISION CENSUS CHARTS BIBLIOG 20. PAGE 75 A1535 FOR/AID S/ASIA FORCES ECO/UNDEV

B62
LAUERHAUSS L.,COMMUNISM IN LATIN AMERICA: THE POST-WAR YEARS (1945 -1960) (PAPER). INTELL STRATA ECO/UNDEV AGRI WORKER FOR/AID INT/TRADE COLONIAL GUERRILLA 20. PAGE 85 A1745 BIBLIOG L/A+17C MARXISM REV

B62
LESSING P.,AFRICA'S RED HARVEST. AFR CHINA/COM COM USSR ECO/UNDEV BAL/PWR DIPLOM CONTROL PWR 20 COLD/WAR INTERVENT. PAGE 87 A1789 NAT/LISM MARXISM FOR/AID EDU/PROP

B62
LEWIS J.P.,QUIET CRISIS IN INDIA. INDIA USA+45 CULTURE ECO/UNDEV AGRI INDUS PROC/MFG NAT/G PLAN TEC/DEV DRIVE PWR SKILL WEALTH...MYTH 20. PAGE 88 A1801 S/ASIA ECO/TAC FOR/AID

B62
LIPPMANN W.,WESTERN UNITY AND THE COMMON MARKET. EUR+WWI FRANCE GERMANY/W UK USA+45 ECO/DEV AGRI FINAN MARKET INT/ORG NAT/G FOR/AID AGREE WEALTH 20 EEC. PAGE 89 A1831 DIPLOM INT/TRADE VOL/ASSN

B62
MANDER J.,BERLIN: HOSTAGE FOR THE WEST. FUT GERMANY WOR+45 FOR/AID RISK ATTIT ORD/FREE 20 BERLIN COLD/WAR. PAGE 93 A1916 DIPLOM BAL/PWR DOMIN DETER

B62
MONTGOMERY J.D.,THE POLITICS OF FOREIGN AID: AMERICAN EXPERIENCE IN SOUTHEAST ASIA. S/ASIA USA+45 NAT/G PROB/SOLV COLONIAL 20. PAGE 103 A2115 FOR/AID DIPLOM GOV/REL GIVE

B62
MORGENTHAU H.J.,POLITICS IN THE TWENTIETH CENTURY: IMPASSE OF AMERICAN FOREIGN POLICY. FUT GERMANY USA+45 USSR WOR+45 INT/ORG NAT/G ACT/RES PLAN FOR/AID EDU/PROP LEGIT COERCE WAR PWR...TIME/SEQ TREND COLD/WAR 20. PAGE 104 A2138 SKILL DIPLOM

B62
MORRAY J.P.,THE SECOND REVOLUTION IN CUBA. CUBA AGRI LABOR POL/PAR DIPLOM FOR/AID GUERRILLA TOTALISM MARXISM 20. PAGE 104 A2146 REV MARXIST ECO/TAC NAT/LISM

B62
MOUSSA P.,THE UNDERPRIVILEGED NATIONS. FINAN INT/ORG PLAN PROB/SOLV CAP/ISM GIVE TASK WEALTH ...POLICY SOC 20. PAGE 105 A2159 ECO/UNDEV NAT/G DIPLOM FOR/AID

B62
PAKISTAN MINISTRY OF FINANCE,FOREIGN ECONOMIC AID: A REVIEW OF FOREIGN ECONOMIC AID TO PAKISTAN. EUR+WWI PAKISTAN UK USA+45 USSR ECO/UNDEV INT/ORG DELIB/GP DIPLOM ECO/TAC...CHARTS CMN/WLTH CHINJAP. PAGE 113 A2318 FOR/AID RECEIVE WEALTH FINAN

B62
POSTON R.W.,DEMOCRACY SPEAKS MANY TONGUES. L/A+17C USA+45 ECO/UNDEV ACT/RES ECO/TAC ADMIN ORD/FREE ...METH/COMP 20. PAGE 117 A2397 FOR/AID DIPLOM CAP/ISM MARXISM

B62
RIMALOV V.V.,ECONOMIC COOPERATION BETWEEN USSR AND UNDERDEVELOPED COUNTRIES. USSR FINAN TEC/DEV INT/TRADE DOMIN EDU/PROP COLONIAL NAT/LISM DRIVE SOVEREIGN...AUD/VIS 20. PAGE 121 A2482 FOR/AID PLAN ECO/UNDEV DIPLOM

B62
RIVKIN A.,AFRICA AND THE WEST. AFR EUR+WWI FUT ISLAM ISRAEL USA+45 SOCIETY INT/ORG FORCES CREATE PLAN FOR/AID EDU/PROP ATTIT...CONCPT TREND EEC 20 CONGRESS UN. PAGE 121 A2488 ECO/UNDEV ECO/TAC

B62
SCHMITT H.A.,THE PATH TO EUROPEAN UNITY. EUR+WWI USA+45 PLAN TEC/DEV DIPLOM FOR/AID CONFER...INT/LAW 20 EEC EURCOALSTL MARSHL/PLN UNIFICA. PAGE 128 A2634 INT/ORG INT/TRADE REGION ECO/DEV

B62
SNOW J.H.,GOVERNMENT BY TREASON. USA+45 USA-45 LEGIS DIPLOM FOR/AID GIVE CONTROL WEALTH MARXISM ...MAJORIT 20 CONGRESS COLD/WAR. PAGE 134 A2750 FINAN TAX PWR POLICY

B62
STEEL R.,THE END OF THE ALLIANCE. FRANCE FUT GERMANY/E GERMANY/W UK USA+45 NAT/G FORCES FOR/AID 20 NATO. PAGE 137 A2809 EUR+WWI POLICY DIPLOM INT/ORG

B62
THEOBALD R.,NATIONAL DEVELOPMENT EFFORTS (PAMPHLET). WOR+45 AGRI BUDGET FOR/AID INT/TRADE TAX 20. PAGE 142 A2914 ECO/UNDEV PLAN BAL/PAY WEALTH

B62
UNIVERSITY OF TENNESSEE,GOVERNMENT AND WORLD CRISIS. USA+45 FOR/AID ORD/FREE...ANTHOL 20 UN. PAGE 149 A3048 ECO/DEV DIPLOM NAT/G INT/ORG

B62
US CONGRESS JOINT ECO COMM,FACTORS AFFECTING THE BAL/PAY

UNITED STATES BALANCE OF PAYMENTS. USA+45 DELIB/GP PLAN DIPLOM FOR/AID PRODUC WEALTH...CHARTS 20 CONGRESS OEEC. PAGE 150 A3064 INT/TRADE ECO/TAC FINAN

B62

US CONGRESS JOINT ECO COMM,ECONOMIC DEVELOPMENTS IN SOUTH AMERICA. USA+45 SOCIETY FINAN NAT/G PROB/SOLV TEC/DEV INT/TRADE TAX EFFICIENCY PRODUC ATTIT ...POLICY 20 CONGRESS SOUTH/AMER. PAGE 150 A3065 L/A+17C ECO/UNDEV FOR/AID DIPLOM

B62

US DEPARTMENT OF THE ARMY,AFRICA: ITS PROBLEMS AND PROSPECTS. CHINA/COM USSR INT/ORG FOR/AID COLONIAL LEAD FEDERAL DRIVE SOVEREIGN MARXISM...GEOG 20 COLD/WAR. PAGE 152 A3104 BIBLIOG/A AFR NAT/LISM DIPLOM

B62

US LIBRARY OF CONGRESS,UNITED STATES AND CANADIAN PUBLICATIONS ON AFRICA IN 1960. CANADA USA+45 CULTURE TEC/DEV DIPLOM FOR/AID RACE/REL...GEOG HUM SOC SOC/WK LING 20. PAGE 155 A3156 BIBLIOG/A AFR

B62

VIET J.,INTERNATIONAL COOPERATION AND PROGRAMMES OF ECONOMIC AND SOCIAL DEVELOPMENT. TEC/DEV FOR/AID DOMIN COLONIAL PEACE WEALTH 20 UNESCO. PAGE 159 A3232 BIBLIOG/A INT/ORG DIPLOM ECO/UNDEV

B62

ZOOK P.D.,FOREIGN TRADE AND HUMAN CAPITAL. L/A+17C USA+45 FINAN DIPLOM ECO/TAC PRODUC...POLICY 20. PAGE 170 A3458 INT/TRADE ECO/UNDEV FOR/AID BAL/PAY

S62

BELSHAW C.,"TRAINING AND RECRUITMENT: SOME PRINCIPLES OF INTERNATIONAL AID." FUT WOR+45 SOCIETY INT/ORG NAT/G CREATE PLAN TEC/DEV ECO/TAC FOR/AID EDU/PROP ATTIT PERCEPT...HUM UN FAO ILO UNESCO 20. PAGE 13 A0263 VOL/ASSN ECO/UNDEV

S62

BRZEZINSKI Z.K.,"PEACEFUL ENGAGEMENT IN COMMUNIST DISUNITY." ASIA CHINA/COM USA+45 USSR NAT/G TOP/EX CREATE ECO/TAC FOR/AID DOMIN ATTIT PERCEPT RIGID/FLEX PWR...PSY 20. PAGE 20 A0417 COM DIPLOM TOTALISM

S62

CLEVELAND H.,"THE FUTURE ROLE OF THE UNITED STATES IN THE UNITED NATIONS." USA+45 ECO/UNDEV INT/ORG EX/STRUC DIPLOM FOR/AID ROUTINE SKILL SOVEREIGN WEALTH UN 20. PAGE 27 A0550 FUT ATTIT

S62

DRACHKOVITCH M.M.,"THE EMERGING PATTERN OF YUGOSLAV-SOVIET RELATIONS." COM FUT USSR WOR+45 INT/ORG ECO/TAC FOR/AID DOMIN COERCE ATTIT PERSON ORD/FREE PWR...TIME/SEQ 20 TITO/MARSH KHRUSH/N STALIN/J. PAGE 38 A0783 TOP/EX DIPLOM YUGOSLAVIA

S62

MILLIKEN M.,"NEW AND OLD CRITERIA FOR AID." WOR+45 ECO/DEV ECO/UNDEV ACT/RES PLAN ATTIT KNOWL...TREND CON/ANAL SIMUL GEN/METH 20. PAGE 102 A2083 USA+45 ECO/TAC FOR/AID

S62

MORGENTHAU H.J.,"A POLITICAL THEORY OF FOREIGN AID." ECO/UNDEV NAT/G DELIB/GP PLAN ECO/TAC EDU/PROP EXEC ORD/FREE RESPECT WEALTH...METH/CNCPT TREND 20. PAGE 104 A2140 USA+45 PHIL/SCI FOR/AID

S62

PYE L.W.,"THE POLITICAL IMPULSES AND FANTASIES BEHIND FOREIGN AID." FUT USA+45 ECO/UNDEV DIPLOM ECO/TAC ROUTINE DRIVE KNOWL...SOC METH/CNCPT NEW/IDEA TREND HYPO/EXP STERTYP GEN/METH 20. PAGE 118 A2420 ACT/RES ATTIT FOR/AID

S62

SPECTOR I.,"SOVIET POLICY IN ASIA: A REAPPRAISAL." ASIA CHINA/COM COM INDIA INDONESIA ECO/UNDEV INT/ORG DOMIN EDU/PROP REGION RESPECT...CONCPT TREND TOT/POP COLD/WAR 20 CHINJAP. PAGE 135 A2774 S/ASIA PWR FOR/AID USSR

S62

TRUMAN D.,"THE DOMESTIC POLITICS OF FOREIGN AID." USA+45 WOR+45 NAT/G POL/PAR LEGIS DIPLOM ECO/TAC EDU/PROP ADMIN CHOOSE ATTIT PWR CONGRESS 20 CONGRESS. PAGE 145 A2970 ROUTINE FOR/AID

B63

BRITISH AID. UK AGRI DIST/IND INDUS SCHOOL TEC/DEV INT/TRADE COLONIAL DEMAND...TREND CHARTS 20. PAGE 3 A0064 FOR/AID ECO/UNDEV NAT/G FINAN

B63

AFRICAN BIBLIOGRAPHIC CENTER,THE SCENE IS GUINEA AND THE PERSONAGE IS SEKOU TOURE: A SELECTED CURRENT READING LIST, 1959-1962 (PAMPHLET). GUINEA ECO/UNDEV CHIEF FOR/AID COLONIAL...BIOG 20. PAGE 5 A0095 BIBLIOG AFR POL/PAR COM

B63

BLOCH-MORHANGE J.,VINGT ANNEES D'HISTOIRE CONTEMPORAINE. FORCES FOR/AID CONFER LEAD 20 COLD/WAR. PAGE 15 A0311 WAR DIPLOM INT/ORG CHIEF

B63

BROEKMEIJER M.W.,DEVELOPING COUNTRIES AND NATO. USSR FORCES DIPLOM NUC/PWR WAR PEACE TOTALISM 20 NATO. PAGE 19 A0384 ECO/UNDEV FOR/AID ORD/FREE NAT/G

B63

BUTTS R.F.,AMERICAN EDUCATION IN INTERNATIONAL DEVELOPMENT. USA+45 WOR+45 INTELL SCHOOL DIPLOM EDU/PROP...BIBLIOG 20. PAGE 23 A0457 ACADEM FOR/AID CONSULT ECO/UNDEV

B63

CENTRO PARA EL DESARROLLO,LA ALIANZA PARA EL PROGRESO Y EL DESARROLLO SOCIAL DE AMERICA LATINA. L/A+17C INT/ORG DIPLOM ECO/TAC INT/TRADE ATTIT 20. PAGE 25 A0512 ECO/UNDEV FOR/AID PLAN REGION

B63

COLUMBIA U SCHOOL OF LAW,PUBLIC INTERNATIONAL DEVELOPMENT FINANCING IN SENEGAL. SENEGAL FINAN DELIB/GP GIVE EFFICIENCY...CHARTS GOV/COMP ANTHOL 20. PAGE 28 A0571 FOR/AID PLAN RECEIVE ECO/UNDEV

B63

DRACHKOVITCH,UNITED STATES AID TO YUGOSLAVIA AND POLAND. POLAND USA+45 YUGOSLAVIA LEGIS EXEC TOTALISM MARXISM 20 CONGRESS. PAGE 38 A0782 FOR/AID POLICY DIPLOM ATTIT

B63

EL-NAGGAR S.,FOREIGN AID TO UNITED ARAB REPUBLIC. UAR USA+45 USSR AGRI FINAN INDUS FORCES EATING DEMAND...CHARTS METH/COMP 20 RESOURCE/N AID. PAGE 41 A0838 FOR/AID ECO/UNDEV RECEIVE PLAN

B63

ELLENDER A.J.,A REPORT ON UNITED STATES FOREIGN OPERATIONS IN AFRICA. SOUTH/AFR USA+45 STRATA EXTR/IND FORCES RACE/REL ISOLAT SOVEREIGN...CHARTS 20 NEGRO. PAGE 41 A0840 FOR/AID DIPLOM WEALTH ECO/UNDEV

B63

FATEMI N.S.,THE DOLLAR CRISIS. USA+45 INDUS NAT/G LEGIS BUDGET TAX COST...CHARTS METH/COMP 20 EEC. PAGE 44 A0902 PROB/SOLV BAL/PAY FOR/AID PLAN

B63

GONZALEZ PEDRERO E.,ANATOMIA DE UN CONFLICTO. WOR+45 ECO/DEV ECO/UNDEV ECO/TAC FOR/AID CONTROL ARMS/CONT GOV/REL...NAT/COMP 20 COLD/WAR. PAGE 54 A1099 DIPLOM DETER BAL/PWR

B63

GORDON L.,A NEW DEAL FOR LATIN AMERICA. L/A+17C USA+45 CULTURE NAT/G TEC/DEV DIPLOM FOR/AID REGION TASK...POLICY 20 DEPT/STATE. PAGE 54 A1115 ECO/UNDEV ECO/TAC INT/ORG PLAN

B63

KATZ S.M.,A SELECTED LIST OF US READINGS ON DEVELOPMENT. AGRI COM/IND DIST/IND INDUS LABOR PLAN FOR/AID EDU/PROP HEALTH...POLICY SOC/WK 20. PAGE 77 A1571 BIBLIOG/A ECO/UNDEV TEC/DEV ACT/RES

B63

KHADDURI M.,MODERN LIBYA: A STUDY IN POLITICAL DEVELOPMENT. EUR+WWI ISLAM LIBYA ELITES INT/ORG POL/PAR FORCES DIPLOM FOR/AID DOMIN EDU/PROP LEGIT NAT/LISM DRIVE RIGID/FLEX SKILL...CONCPT TIME/SEQ TREND 20. PAGE 78 A1606 NAT/G STRUCT

B63

LARY M.B.,PROBLEMS OF THE UNITED STATES AS WORLD TRADER AND BANKER. USA+45 NAT/G PLAN DIPLOM FOR/AID ...TREND CHARTS. PAGE 85 A1737 ECO/DEV FINAN BAL/PAY INT/TRADE

B63

MANGER W.,THE ALLIANCE FOR PROGRESS: A CRITICAL APPRAISAL. FUT L/A+17C USA+45 CULTURE ECO/UNDEV ACADEM NAT/G SCHOOL PLAN FOR/AID...POLICY OAS. PAGE 94 A1918 DIPLOM INT/ORG ECO/TAC REGION

B63

MARITANO N.,AN ALLIANCE FOR PROGRESS. FUT L/A+17C USA+45 CULTURE ECO/UNDEV NAT/G PLAN CONTROL POLICY. PAGE 95 A1941 DIPLOM INT/ORG ECO/TAC FOR/AID

B63

PIKE F.B.,CHILE AND THE UNITED STATES 1880-1962: THE EMERGENCE OF CHILE'S CRISIS AND THE CHALLENGE TO US DIPLOMACY. CHILE COM USA+45 USA-45 SOCIETY STRATA ECO/UNDEV...MYTH 19/20. PAGE 116 A2378 FOR/AID DIPLOM ATTIT STRUCT

B63

RAO V.K.R.,FOREIGN AID AND INDIA'S ECONOMIC DEVELOPMENT. INDIA INT/ORG PROB/SOLV TEC/DEV ECO/TAC CONTROL WEALTH...TREND 20. PAGE 119 A2445 FOR/AID ECO/UNDEV RECEIVE DIPLOM

B63

ROBOCK S.H.,OVERVIEW OF TOTAL BRAZILIAN SETTING, NEWER REGIONAL PATTERNS NING AND FOREIGN AID. BRAZIL ECO/UNDEV AGRI FINAN INDUS INT/ORG INCOME UTIL...CHARTS 20. PAGE 122 A2507 ECO/TAC REGION PLAN FOR/AID

B63

RUSK D.,THE WINDS OF FREEDOM. S/ASIA SOUTH/AFR INT/ORG FORCES NUC/PWR PEACE ORD/FREE 20 UN COLD/WAR. PAGE 125 A2569 DIPLOM FOR/AID INT/TRADE

B63

THIEN T.T.,INDIA AND SOUTHEAST ASIA 1947-1960. COM INDIA S/ASIA SECT DELIB/GP FOR/AID RACE/REL NAT/LISM SOCISM...CHARTS BIBLIOG 20 UN NEHRU/J TREATY. PAGE 143 A2917 DRIVE DIPLOM POLICY

B63
UNITED STATES GOVERNMENT,REPORT TO THE INTER-AMERICAN ECONOMIC AND SOCIAL COUNCIL. L/A+17C INDUS PLAN INT/TRADE TARIFFS CONFER...CHARTS 20 LAFTA. PAGE 149 A3038 FOR/AID ECO/TAC ECO/UNDEV DIPLOM

B63
US AGENCY INTERNATIONAL DEV,US FOREIGN ASSISTANCE AND ASSISTANCE FROM INTERNATIONAL ORGANIZATIONS. USA+45 WOR+45 ECO/UNDEV AGRI NAT/G TEC/DEV BUDGET. PAGE 149 A3050 FOR/AID INT/ORG CHARTS STAT

B63
US ECON SURVEY TEAM INDONESIA,INDONESIA - PERSPECTIVE AND PROPOSALS FOR UNITED STATES ECONOMIC AID. INDONESIA AGRI MARKET TEC/DEV DIPLOM INT/TRADE EDU/PROP 20. PAGE 153 A3113 FOR/AID ECO/UNDEV PLAN INDUS

B63
US GOVERNMENT,REPORT TO INTER-AMERICAN ECONOMIC AND SOCIAL COUNCIL AT SECOND ANNUAL MEETING. L/A+17C USA+45 VOL/ASSN TEC/DEV DIPLOM TAX EATING EFFICIENCY HEALTH...STAT CHARTS 20 AID. PAGE 153 A3116 ECO/TAC FOR/AID FINAN PLAN

B63
US HOUSE COMM FOREIGN AFFAIRS,HEARINGS ON H.R. 5490 TO AMEND FURTHER THE FOREIGN ASSISTANCE ACT OF 1961. CUBA EUR+WWI INDIA INT/ORG DELIB/GP LEGIS DIPLOM CONFER ORD/FREE 20 DEPT/STATE DEPT/DEFEN UN. PAGE 153 A3129 FOR/AID INT/TRADE FORCES WEAPON

B63
US SENATE COMM APPROPRIATIONS,PERSONNEL ADMINISTRATION AND OPERATIONS OF AGENCY FOR INTERNATIONAL DEVELOPMENT: SPECIAL HEARING. FINAN LEAD COST UTIL SKILL...CHARTS 20 CONGRESS AID CIVIL/SERV. PAGE 155 A3170 ADMIN FOR/AID EFFICIENCY DIPLOM

B63
US SENATE COMM GOVT OPERATIONS,REPORT OF A STUDY OF US FOREIGN AID IN TEN MIDDLE EASTERN AND AFRICAN COUNTRIES. AFR ISLAM USA+45 FORCES PLAN BUDGET DIPLOM TAX DETER WEALTH...STAT CHARTS 20 CONGRESS AID MID/EAST. PAGE 156 A3174 FOR/AID EFFICIENCY ECO/TAC FINAN

B63
US SENATE COMM ON FOREIGN REL,HEARINGS ON S 1276 A BILL TO AMEND FURTHER THE FOREIGN ASSISTANCE ACT OF 1961. USA+45 WOR+45 INDUS INT/ORG FORCES TAX WEAPON SUPEGO...NAT/COMP 20 UN CONGRESS PRESIDENT. PAGE 156 A3182 FOR/AID DIPLOM ECO/UNDEV ORD/FREE

B63
VON HALLER A.,DIE LETZTEN WOLLEN DIE ERSTEN SEIN. AFR S/ASIA INT/TRADE REV ORD/FREE SOVEREIGN 20. PAGE 160 A3251 FOR/AID ECO/UNDEV MARXISM CAP/ISM

B63
WESTERFIELD H.,THE INSTRUMENTS OF AMERICA'S FOREIGN POLICY. WOR+45 ECO/DEV NAT/G CONSULT EX/STRUC LEGIS BAL/PWR FOR/AID INT/TRADE DOMIN EDU/PROP LEGIT ATTIT KNOWL ORD/FREE PWR WEALTH...OBS COLD/WAR TOT/POP VAL/FREE. PAGE 163 A3322 USA+45 INT/ORG DIPLOM

B63
YOUNG A.N.,CHINA AND THE HELPING HAND. ASIA USA+45 FINAN INDUS ECO/TAC GIVE WEALTH...METH/COMP 20 LEND/LEASE GOLD/STAND. PAGE 169 A3434 FOR/AID DIPLOM WAR

L63
PRINCETON UNIV. CONFERENCE,"ARAB DEVELOPMENT IN THE EMERGING INTERNATIONAL ECONOMY." FUT USA+45 DIST/IND FINAN DELIB/GP PLAN ECO/TAC WEALTH VAL/FREE 20. PAGE 118 A2413 ISLAM ECO/UNDEV FOR/AID INT/TRADE

S63
ALEXANDER R.,"LATIN AMERICA AND THE COMMUNIST BLOC." ASIA COM CUBA L/A+17C USA+45 USSR NAT/G VOL/ASSN TEC/DEV FOR/AID LEGIT PWR WEALTH COLD/WAR 20. PAGE 6 A0112 ECO/UNDEV RECORD

S63
CHAKRAVARTI P.C.,"INDIAN NON-ALIGNMENT AND UNITED STATES POLICY." ASIA INDIA S/ASIA USA+45 CULTURE ECO/UNDEV NAT/G VOL/ASSN DELIB/GP TOP/EX FOR/AID NEUTRAL...POLICY HUM CONCPT RECORD GEN/LAWS 20. PAGE 25 A0515 ATTIT ALL/VALS COLONIAL DIPLOM

S63
COSER L.,"AMERICA AND THE WORLD REVOLUTION." COM FUT USA+45 WOR+45 INTELL SOCIETY NAT/G ECO/TAC EDU/PROP ALL/VALS SOCISM...PSY GEN/LAWS TOT/POP 20 COLD/WAR. PAGE 31 A0629 ECO/UNDEV PLAN FOR/AID DIPLOM

S63
COUTY P.,"L'ASSISTANCE POUR LE DEVELOPPEMENT: POINT DE VUE SCANDINAVES." EUR+WWI FINLAND FUT SWEDEN WOR+45 ECO/DEV ECO/UNDEV COM/IND LABOR NAT/G PROF/ORG ACT/RES SKILL WEALTH TOT/POP 20. PAGE 32 A0643 FINAN ROUTINE FOR/AID

S63
DARLING F.C.,"THE GEOPOLITICS OF AMERICAN FOREIGN POLITICS IN ASIA." COM S/ASIA USA+45 USSR ECO/UNDEV NAT/G VOL/ASSN CONSULT PLAN GUERRILLA...STAT TOT/POP 20. PAGE 34 A0682 FORCES ECO/TAC FOR/AID DIPLOM

S63
DAVEE R.,"POUR UN FONDS DE DEVELOPPEMENT SOCIAL." FUT WOR+45 INTELL SOCIETY ECO/DEV FINAN TEC/DEV ROUTINE WEALTH...TREND TOT/POP VAL/FREE UN 20. PAGE 34 A0684 INT/ORG SOC FOR/AID

S63
GANDILHON J.,"LA SCIENCE ET LA TECHNIQUE A L'AIDE DES REGIONS PEU DEVELOPPEES." FRANCE FUT WOR+45 ECO/DEV R+D PROF/ORG ACT/RES PLAN...MGT TOT/POP VAL/FREE 20 UN. PAGE 51 A1037 ECO/UNDEV TEC/DEV FOR/AID

S63
GUPTA S.C.,"INDIA AND THE SOVIET UNION." CHINA/COM COM INDIA S/ASIA VOL/ASSN TOP/EX FOR/AID EDU/PROP PEACE PWR...RECORD COLD/WAR 20. PAGE 58 A1195 DISPL MYTH USSR

S63
HINDLEY D.,"FOREIGN AID TO INDONESIA AND ITS POLITICAL IMPLICATIONS." INDONESIA POL/PAR ATTIT SOVEREIGN...CHARTS 20. PAGE 65 A1336 FOR/AID NAT/G WEALTH ECO/TAC

S63
HOLBO P.S.,"COLD WAR DRIFT IN LATIN AMERICA." CUBA L/A+17C USA+45 USA-45 INT/ORG NAT/G NEIGH VOL/ASSN ACT/RES PLAN ECO/TAC ATTIT RIGID/FLEX ALL/VALS ...RECORD TIME/SEQ OAS LAFTA 20 COLD/WAR. PAGE 66 A1363 DELIB/GP CREATE FOR/AID

S63
HORVATH J.,"MOSCOW'S AID PROGRAM: THE PERFORMANCE SO FAR." COM FUT USSR WOR+45 ECO/DEV FINAN PLAN TEC/DEV FOR/AID EDU/PROP ATTIT ORD/FREE PWR WEALTH ...POLICY STAT CHARTS VAL/FREE 20. PAGE 68 A1389 ECO/UNDEV ECO/TAC

S63
LEDUC G.,"L'AIDE INTERNATIONALE AU DEVELOPPEMENT." FUT WOR+45 ECO/DEV ECO/UNDEV R+D PROF/ORG TEC/DEV ECO/TAC ROUTINE ATTIT ALL/VALS...MGT TIME/SEQ TOT/POP 20. PAGE 86 A1758 FINAN PLAN FOR/AID

S63
LIGOT M.,"LA COOPERATION MILITAIRE DANS LES ACCORDS, PASSES ENTRE LA FRANCE ET LES ETATS AFRICAINS ET MALGACHE D'EXPRESSION." ECO/UNDEV INT/ORG NAT/G VOL/ASSN...CONCPT TIME/SEQ 20. PAGE 89 A1814 AFR FORCES FOR/AID FRANCE

S63
MANGONE G.,"THE UNITED NATIONS AND UNITED STATES FOREIGN POLICY." USA+45 WOR+45 ECO/UNDEV NAT/G DIPLOM LEGIT ROUTINE ATTIT DRIVE...TIME/SEQ UN COLD/WAR 20. PAGE 94 A1922 INT/ORG ECO/TAC FOR/AID

S63
MARTHELOT P.,"PROGRES DE LA REFORME AGRAIRE." INTELL ECO/DEV R+D FOR/AID ADMIN KNOWL...OBS VAL/FREE UN 20. PAGE 95 A1948 AGRI INT/ORG

S63
NADLER E.B.,"SOME ECONOMIC DISADVANTAGES OF THE ARMS RACE." USA+45 INDUS R+D FORCES PLAN TEC/DEV ECO/TAC FOR/AID EDU/PROP PWR WEALTH...TREND COLD/WAR 20. PAGE 107 A2190 ECO/DEV MGT BAL/PAY

S63
PINCUS J.,"THE COST OF FOREIGN AID." WOR+45 ECO/DEV FINAN NAT/G VOL/ASSN CREATE ECO/TAC EDU/PROP WEALTH ...METH/CNCPT STAT CHARTS HYPO/EXP TOT/POP VAL/FREE 20. PAGE 116 A2380 USA+45 ECO/UNDEV FOR/AID

S63
SONNENFELDT H.,"FOREIGN POLICY FROM MALENKOV TO KHRUSHCHEV." WOR+45 NAT/G FORCES BAL/PWR DIPLOM ECO/TAC COERCE ATTIT PWR...CONCPT HIST/WRIT COLD/WAR 20. PAGE 135 A2768 COM DOMIN FOR/AID USSR

S63
VEROFF J.,"AFRICAN STUDENTS IN THE UNITED STATES." AFR USA+45 CULTURE ACT/RES FOR/AID PEACE ATTIT KNOWL...SOC RECORD DEEP/QU SYS/QU CHARTS STERTYP TOT/POP 20. PAGE 159 A3230 PERCEPT RIGID/FLEX RACE/REL

S63
VINER J.,"REPORT OF THE CLAY COMMITTEE ON FOREIGN AID: A SYMPOSIUM." USA+45 WOR+45 NAT/G CONSULT PLAN BAL/PWR ATTIT WEALTH...MGT CONCPT TOT/POP 20. PAGE 159 A3240 ACT/RES ECO/TAC FOR/AID

S63
WEILLER J.,"UNIONS MONETAIRES ET RAPPORTS DE COOPERATION INTERNATIONALE DANS UN MONDE EN TRANSITION: L'EXAMPLE." AFR FUT UNIV WOR+45 SOCIETY ECO/UNDEV MARKET R+D NAT/G FOR/AID PERCEPT RIGID/FLEX...NEW/IDEA 20. PAGE 162 A3303 FINAN INT/ORG

S63
WOLF C.,"SOME ASPECTS OF THE 'VALUE' OF LESS-DEVELOPED COUNTRIES TO THE UNITED STATES." ASIA CHINA/COM COM USA+45 USSR ECO/UNDEV BAL/PWR ECO/TAC FOR/AID DOMIN EDU/PROP ATTIT PWR...POLICY METH/CNCPT CONT/OBS TREND CHARTS 20. PAGE 166 A3379 CONCPT GEN/LAWS DIPLOM

C63
CHARLETON W.G.,"THE REVOLUTION IN AMERICAN FOREIGN POLICY." COM PROB/SOLV FOR/AID DOMIN COLONIAL NEUTRAL DETER WAR ISOLAT NAT/LISM...BIBLIOG 19/20 UN COLD/WAR NATO. PAGE 26 A0523 DIPLOM INT/ORG BAL/PWR

N63
US AGENCY INTERNATIONAL DEV,PRINCIPLES OF FOREIGN ECONOMIC ASSISTANCE (PAMPHLET). USA+45 FINAN GP/REL BAL/PAY EFFICIENCY 20 AID. PAGE 149 A3051 FOR/AID PLAN ECO/UNDEV ATTIT

N63
US COMM STRENG SEC FREE WORLD,THE SCOPE AND DISTRIBUTION OF UNITED STATES MILITARY AND ECONOMIC DELIB/GP POLICY

ASSISTANCE PROGRAMS (PAMPHLET). USA+45 PLAN BAL/PWR BUDGET DIPLOM CONTROL CIVMIL/REL ATTIT. PAGE 150 A3059 FOR/AID ORD/FREE B64

THE SPECIAL COMMONWEALTH AFRICAN ASSISTANCE PLAN. AFR CANADA INDIA NIGERIA UK FINAN SCHOOL...CHARTS 20 COMMONWLTH. PAGE 3 A0065 ECO/UNDEV TREND FOR/AID ADMIN B64

ADAMS V.,THE PEACE CORPS IN ACTION. USA+45 VOL/ASSN EX/STRUC GOV/REL PERCEPT ORD/FREE...OBS 20 KENNEDY/JF PEACE/CORP. PAGE 4 A0087 DIPLOM FOR/AID PERSON DRIVE B64

ARNOLD G.,TOWARDS PEACE AND A MULTIRACIAL COMMONWEALTH. UK TEC/DEV BAL/PWR COLONIAL GP/REL NAT/LISM PEACE SOVEREIGN...POLICY SOC/INTEG 20 CMN/WLTH. PAGE 9 A0175 DIPLOM INT/TRADE FOR/AID ORD/FREE B64

BAILEY T.A.,A DIPLOMATIC HISTORY OF THE AMERICAN PEOPLE (7TH ED.). USA+45 USA-45 FOR/AID COLONIAL PARL/PROC WAR...CHARTS BIBLIOG/A T 18/20. PAGE 10 A0208 DIPLOM NAT/G B64

CALDER R.,TWO-WAY PASSAGE. INT/ORG TEC/DEV WAR PERSON ORD/FREE 20. PAGE 23 A0467 FOR/AID ECO/UNDEV ECO/TAC DIPLOM B64

CASEY R.G.,THE FUTURE OF THE COMMONWEALTH. INDIA PAKISTAN UK ECO/UNDEV INT/ORG TEC/DEV COLONIAL SUPEGO 20 EEC AUSTRAL. PAGE 25 A0505 DIPLOM SOVEREIGN NAT/LISM FOR/AID B64

CEPEDE M.,POPULATION AND FOOD. USA+45 STRUCT ECO/UNDEV FAM PLAN TEC/DEV FOR/AID CONTROL...CATH SOC TREND 19/20. PAGE 25 A0513 FUT GEOG AGRI CENSUS B64

CHENG C.,ECONOMIC RELATIONS BETWEEN PEKING AND MOSCOW: 1949-63. ASIA CHINA/COM COM USSR FINAN INDUS CONSULT TEC/DEV INT/TRADE...PREDICT CHARTS BIBLIOG 20. PAGE 26 A0527 DIPLOM FOR/AID MARXISM B64

COFFIN F.M.,WITNESS FOR AID. COM EUR+WWI USA+45 DIPLOM GP/REL CONSEN ORD/FREE MARXISM...NEW/IDEA 20 CONGRESS AID. PAGE 27 A0557 FOR/AID ECO/UNDEV DELIB/GP PLAN B64

COLUMBIA U SCHOOL OF LAW,PUBLIC INTERNATIONAL DEVELOPMENT FINANCING IN INDIA. GERMANY/W INDIA UK USA+45 INDUS PLAN TEC/DEV DIPLOM ECO/TAC GIVE ADMIN UTIL ATTIT 20. PAGE 28 A0572 ECO/UNDEV FINAN FOR/AID INT/ORG B64

DAVIES U.P. JR.,FOREIGN AND OTHER AFFAIRS. EUR+WWI L/A+17C S/ASIA USA+45 ECO/UNDEV CHIEF PLAN ECO/TAC PWR MARXISM 20 KENNEDY/JF UN. PAGE 34 A0688 DIPLOM NAT/G POLICY FOR/AID B64

ESTHUS R.A.,FROM ENMITY TO ALLIANCE: US AUSTRALIAN RELATIONS. S/ASIA DIST/IND VOL/ASSN FORCES ATTIT 20 AUSTRAL TREATY CMN/WLTH. PAGE 42 A0863 DIPLOM WAR INT/TRADE FOR/AID B64

FALL B.,STREET WITHOUT JOY. FRANCE USA+45 DIPLOM ECO/TAC FOR/AID GUERRILLA REV WEAPON...TREND 20. PAGE 44 A0894 WAR S/ASIA FORCES COERCE B64

FATOUROS A.A.,CANADA'S OVERSEAS AID. CANADA WOR+45 ECO/DEV FINAN NAT/G BUDGET ECO/TAC CONFER ADMIN 20. PAGE 44 A0904 FOR/AID DIPLOM ECO/UNDEV POLICY B64

FEIS H.,FOREIGN AID AND FOREIGN POLICY. USA+45 WOR+45 NAT/G VOL/ASSN ACT/RES TEC/DEV ATTIT HEALTH WEALTH...SOC GEN/LAWS 20. PAGE 45 A0912 ECO/UNDEV ECO/TAC FOR/AID DIPLOM B64

HAMRELL S.,THE SOVIET BLOC, CHINA, AND AFRICA. AFR CHINA/COM COM USSR ECO/UNDEV EDU/PROP 20. PAGE 61 A1249 MARXISM DIPLOM CONTROL FOR/AID B64

INTL INF CTR LOCAL CREDIT,GOVERNMENT MEASURES FOR THE PROMOTION OF REGIONAL ECONOMIC DEVELOPMENT. WOR+45 ECO/UNDEV FINAN INT/ORG DIPLOM ORD/FREE ...POLICY GEOG 20. PAGE 71 A1464 FOR/AID PLAN ECO/TAC REGION B64

KRETZSCHMAR W.W.,AUSLANDSHILFE ALS MITTEL DER AUSSENWIRTSCHAFTS- UND AUSSENPOLITIK. ASIA GERMANY/W UK USA+45 SOCIETY STRUCT ECO/UNDEV LOBBY EFFICIENCY 20. PAGE 82 A1683 FOR/AID DIPLOM AGRI DIST/IND B64

LIEVWEN E.,GENERALS VS PRESIDENTS: WEOMILITARISM IN LATIN AMERICA. L/A+17C FORCES DIPLOM FOR/AID LEAD ...NAT/COMP 20 PRESIDENT. PAGE 89 A1813 CIVMIL/REL REV CONSERVE ORD/FREE B64

LITTLE I.M.D.,AID TO AFRICA. AFR UK TEC/DEV DIPLOM ECO/TAC INCOME WEALTH 20. PAGE 90 A1844 FOR/AID ECO/UNDEV ADMIN POLICY B64

MAIER J.,POLITICS OF CHANGE IN LATIN AMERICA. BRAZIL L/A+17C STRATA INT/ORG NAT/G POL/PAR FOR/AID REV 20. PAGE 93 A1907 SOCIETY NAT/LISM DIPLOM REGION B64

MASON E.S.,FOREIGN AID AND FOREIGN POLICY. USA+45 AGRI INDUS NAT/G EX/STRUC ACT/RES RIGID/FLEX ALL/VALS...POLICY GEN/LAWS MARSHL/PLN CONGRESS 20. PAGE 95 A1956 ECO/UNDEV ECO/TAC FOR/AID DIPLOM B64

MAUD J.,AID FOR DEVELOPING COUNTRIES. COM EUR+WWI UK INT/TRADE ORD/FREE...GOV/COMP 20. PAGE 96 A1979 FOR/AID DIPLOM ECO/TAC ECO/UNDEV B64

MC GOVERN G.S.,WAR AGAINST WANT. USA+45 AGRI DIPLOM INT/TRADE GIVE RECEIVE DEMAND HEALTH 20 KENNEDY/JF FOOD/PEACE. PAGE 97 A1993 FOR/AID ECO/DEV POLICY EATING B64

NEWCOMER H.A.,INTERNATIONAL AIDS TO OVERSEAS INVESTMENTS AND TRADE. ECO/UNDEV TARIFFS PROFIT ...BIBLIOG 20 GATT UN. PAGE 108 A2225 INT/TRADE FINAN DIPLOM FOR/AID B64

OECD,DEVELOPMENT ASSISTANCE EFFORTS - POLICIES OF THE MEMBERS. AGRI INDUS BUDGET...GEOG NAT/COMP 20 OECD. PAGE 111 A2280 INT/ORG FOR/AID ECO/UNDEV TEC/DEV B64

OECD,THE FLOW OF FINANCIAL RESOURCES TO LESS DEVELOPED COUNTRIES 1956-1963. WOR+45 FINAN CAP/ISM ...POLICY STAT 20. PAGE 111 A2281 FOR/AID BUDGET INT/ORG ECO/UNDEV B64

RANIS G.,THE UNITED STATES AND THE DEVELOPING ECONOMIES. COM USA+45 AGRI FINAN TEC/DEV CAP/ISM ECO/TAC INT/TRADE...POLICY METH/COMP ANTHOL 20 AID. PAGE 119 A2441 ECO/UNDEV DIPLOM FOR/AID B64

REGALA R.,WORLD PEACE THROUGH DIPLOMACY AND LAW. S/ASIA WOR+45 ECO/UNDEV INT/ORG FORCES PLAN PROB/SOLV FOR/AID NUC/PWR WAR...POLICY INT/LAW 20. PAGE 120 A2456 DIPLOM PEACE ADJUD B64

REUSS H.S.,THE CRITICAL DECADE - AN ECONOMIC POLICY FOR AMERICA AND THE FREE WORLD. USA+45 FINAN POL/PAR WORKER PLAN DIPLOM ECO/TAC TARIFFS BAL/PAY ...POLICY 20 CONGRESS GOLD/STAND. PAGE 120 A2468 FOR/AID INT/TRADE LABOR LEGIS B64

RIVKIN A.,AFRICA AND THE EUROPEAN COMMON MARKET (PAMPHLET). AFR MOD/EUR WOR+45 TEC/DEV FOR/AID TARIFFS BAL/PAY...POLICY 20 EEC. PAGE 121 A2490 INT/ORG INT/TRADE ECO/TAC ECO/UNDEV B64

ROBERTS HL,FOREIGN AFFAIRS BIBLIOGRAPHY, 1952-1962. ECO/DEV SECT PLAN FOR/AID INT/TRADE ARMS/CONT NAT/LISM ATTIT...INT/LAW GOV/COMP IDEA/COMP 20. PAGE 122 A2495 BIBLIOG/A DIPLOM INT/ORG WAR B64

RUBIN J.A.,YOUR HUNDRED BILLION DOLLARS. USA+45 USSR INDUS INT/ORG TEC/DEV ECO/TAC...METH/COMP 20 PEACE/CORP. PAGE 125 A2559 FOR/AID DIPLOM ECO/UNDEV B64

SINGER H.W.,INTERNATIONAL DEVELOPMENT: GROWTH AND CHANGE. AFR BRAZIL L/A+17C WOR+45 CULTURE AGRI INDUS NAT/G ACT/RES ECO/TAC EDU/PROP WEALTH...GEOG CONCPT METH/CNCPT STAT HYPO/EXP WORK TOT/POP 20. PAGE 133 A2723 FINAN ECO/UNDEV FOR/AID INT/TRADE B64

SULLIVAN G.,THE STORY OF THE PEACE CORPS. USA+45 WOR+45 INTELL FACE/GP NAT/G SCHOOL VOL/ASSN CONSULT EX/STRUC PLAN EDU/PROP ADMIN ATTIT DRIVE ALL/VALS ...POLICY HEAL SOC CONCPT INT QU BIOG TREND SOC/EXP WORK. PAGE 140 A2861 INT/ORG ECO/UNDEV FOR/AID PEACE B64

TEPASKE J.J.,EXPLOSIVE FORCES IN LATIN AMERICA. CULTURE INTELL ECO/UNDEV INT/ORG NAT/G SECT FORCES ECO/TAC EDU/PROP PWR WEALTH SOC. PAGE 142 A2903 L/A+17C RIGID/FLEX FOR/AID USSR B64

TULLY A.,WHERE DID YOUR MONEY GO. USA+45 USSR ECO/UNDEV ADMIN EFFICIENCY WEALTH...METH/COMP 20. PAGE 146 A2976 FOR/AID DIPLOM CONTROL B64

US AGENCY INTERNATIONAL DEV,REPORT TO CONGRESS ON THE FOREIGN ASSISTANCE PROGRAM. AFR ASIA L/A+17C USA+45 INT/ORG VOL/ASSN FORCES CAP/ISM ADMIN FOR/AID ECO/UNDEV TEC/DEV

WEAPON. PAGE 149 A3052 — BUDGET

B64
US HOUSE COMM FOREIGN AFFAIRS,HEARINGS ON H.R. 10502 TO AMEND FURTHER THE FOREIGN ASSISTANCE ACT OF 1961. AFR ASIA L/A+17C INT/ORG CONSULT DELIB/GP TEC/DEV ECO/TAC EDU/PROP CONFER 20 UN NATO CONGRESS AID. PAGE 153 A3130 — FOR/AID DIPLOM ORD/FREE ECO/UNDEV

B64
US HOUSE COMM GOVT OPERATIONS,US OWNED FOREIGN CURRENCIES: HEARINGS (COMMITTEE ON GOVERNMENT OPERATIONS). INDIA ECO/DEV PLAN BUDGET TAX DEMAND EFFICIENCY 20 AID CONGRESS. PAGE 154 A3138 — FINAN ECO/TAC FOR/AID OWN

B64
WITHERS W.,THE ECONOMIC CRISIS IN LATIN AMERICA. BRAZIL CHILE STRATA AGRI DIPLOM FOR/AID PWR SOCISM ...POLICY 20 MEXIC/AMER ARGEN. PAGE 166 A3372 — L/A+17C ECO/UNDEV CAP/ISM ALL/IDEOS

B64
WOODHOUSE C.M.,THE NEW CONCERT OF NATIONS. WOR+45 ECO/DEV ECO/UNDEV NAT/G BAL/PWR ECO/TAC NAT/LISM PWR SOVEREIGN ALL/IDEOS 20 UN COLD/WAR. PAGE 166 A3391 — DIPLOM MORAL FOR/AID COLONIAL

B64
WYTHE G.,THE UNITED STATES AND INTER-AMERICAN RELATIONS: A CONTEMPORARY APPRAISAL. L/A+17C USA+45 ECO/UNDEV INT/ORG NAT/G VOL/ASSN INT/TRADE EDU/PROP DRIVE...SOC TREND OAS UN 20. PAGE 168 A3425 — ATTIT ECO/TAC FOR/AID

B64
ZEBOT C.A.,THE ECONOMICS OF COMPETITIVE COEXISTENCE. CHINA/COM USSR WOR+45 FINAN MARKET FOR/AID PRICE DEMAND EQUILIB WEALTH ALL/IDEOS 20. PAGE 169 A3450 — TEC/DEV DIPLOM METH/COMP

L64
CAMPBELL J.C.,"THE MIDDLE EAST IN THE MUTED COLD WAR." COM EUR+WWI UAR USA+45 USSR STRUCT ECO/UNDEV NAT/G VOL/ASSN EX/STRUC TOP/EX DIPLOM ECO/TAC EDU/PROP...TIME/SEQ COLD/WAR 20. PAGE 23 A0475 — ISLAM FOR/AID NAT/LISM

L64
CARNEGIE ENDOWMENT INT. PEACE,"ECONOMIC AND SOCIAL QUESTION (ISSUES BEFORE THE NINETEENTH GENERAL ASSEMBLY)." WOR+45 ECO/DEV ECO/UNDEV INDUS R+D DELIB/GP CREATE PLAN TEC/DEV ECO/TAC FOR/AID BAL/PAY...RECORD UN 20. PAGE 24 A0493 — INT/ORG INT/TRADE

L64
RIPLEY R.B.,"INTERAGENCY COMMITTEES AND INCREMENTALISM: THE CASE OF AID TO INDIA." INDIA USA+45 INTELL NAT/G DELIB/GP ACT/RES DIPLOM ROUTINE NAT/LISM ATTIT PWR...SOC CONCPT NEW/IDEA TIME/SEQ CON/ANAL VAL/FREE 20. PAGE 121 A2483 — EXEC MGT FOR/AID

S64
BEIM D.,"THE COMMUNIST BLOC AND THE FOREIGN-AID GAME." WOR+45 NAT/G PLAN ROUTINE ATTIT KNOWL ORD/FREE...DECISION QUANT CONT/OBS TIME/SEQ CHARTS GAME SIMUL COLD/WAR 20. PAGE 12 A0252 — COM ECO/UNDEV ECO/TAC FOR/AID

S64
DE GAULLE C.,"FRENCH WORLD VIEW." AFR ASIA CHINA/COM EUR+WWI ISLAM ECO/UNDEV INT/ORG NAT/G VOL/ASSN ACT/RES DIPLOM ECO/TAC EDU/PROP ATTIT DRIVE WEALTH 20. PAGE 35 A0702 — TOP/EX PWR FOR/AID FRANCE

S64
DERWINSKI E.J.,"THE COST OF THE INTERNATIONAL COFFEE AGREEMENT." L/A+17C USA+45 WOR+45 ECO/UNDEV NAT/G VOL/ASSN LEGIS DIPLOM ECO/TAC FOR/AID LEGIT ATTIT...TIME/SEQ CONGRESS 20 TREATY. PAGE 36 A0732 — MARKET DELIB/GP INT/TRADE

S64
GARMARNIKOW M.,"INFLUENCE-BUYING IN WEST AFRICA." COM FUT USSR INTELL NAT/G PLAN TEC/DEV ECO/TAC DOMIN EDU/PROP REGION NAT/LISM ATTIT DRIVE ALL/VALS SOVEREIGN...POLICY PSY SOC CONCPT TREND STERTYP WORK COLD/WAR 20. PAGE 51 A1049 — AFR ECO/UNDEV FOR/AID SOCISM

S64
HUTCHINSON E.C.,"AMERICAN AID TO AFRICA." FUT USA+45 MARKET INT/ORG LOC/G NAT/G PUB/INST PLAN ECO/TAC ATTIT RIGID/FLEX...POLICY CONCPT TREND 20. PAGE 69 A1423 — AFR ECO/UNDEV FOR/AID

S64
MAZRUI A.A.,"THE UNITED NATIONS AND SOME AFRICAN POLITICAL ATTITUDES." ECO/TAC FOR/AID DOMIN ROUTINE CHOOSE ATTIT DRIVE MORAL PWR RESPECT WEALTH...PSY CONCPT OBS TREND UN VAL/FREE 20. PAGE 97 A1987 — AFR INT/ORG SOVEREIGN

S64
PALMER N.D.,"INDIA AS A FACTOR IN UNITED STATES FOREIGN POLICY." INDIA USA+45 USA-45 ECO/UNDEV NAT/G TOP/EX ECO/TAC EDU/PROP...METH/CNCPT TIME/SEQ 20. PAGE 113 A2323 — S/ASIA ATTIT FOR/AID DIPLOM

S64
PESELT B.M.,"COMMUNIST ECONOMIC OFFENSIVE." WOR+45 SOCIETY INT/ORG PLAN ECO/TAC DOMIN EDU/PROP ATTIT PERSON PWR WEALTH...TREND CHARTS 20. PAGE 115 A2366 — COM ECO/UNDEV FOR/AID USSR

S64
TOUVAL S.,"THE SOMALI REPUBLIC." AFR ISLAM SOMALIA FAM KIN NAT/G CREATE FOR/AID LEGIT ATTIT ALL/VALS ...RECORD TREND 20. PAGE 144 A2954 — ECO/UNDEV RIGID/FLEX

S64
WOOD H.B.,"STRETCHING YOUR FOREIGN-AID DOLLAR." USA+45 WOR+45 CONSULT EDU/PROP ATTIT WEALTH...OBS TOT/POP CONGRESS 20. PAGE 166 A3390 — ECO/UNDEV MGT FOR/AID

S64
ZARTMAN I.W.,"LES RELATIONS ENTRE LA FRANCE ET L'ALGERIA DEPUIS LES ACCORDS D'EVIAN." EUR+WWI FUT ISLAM CULTURE AGRI EXTR/IND FINAN INDUS POL/PAR DIPLOM ECO/TAC FOR/AID PEACE ATTIT DRIVE ALL/VALS ...TIME/SEQ VAL/FREE 20. PAGE 169 A3446 — ECO/UNDEV ALGERIA FRANCE

N64
GREAT BRITAIN CENTRAL OFF INF,THE COLOMBO PLAN (PAMPHLET). ASIA S/ASIA USA+45 VOL/ASSN...CHARTS 20 COMMONWLTH RESOURCE/N. PAGE 55 A1134 — FOR/AID PLAN INT/ORG ECO/UNDEV

B65
ANALYSIS AND ASSESSMENT OF THE ECONOMIC EFFECTS: PUBLIC LAW 480 TITLE I PROGRAM TURKEY. INDIA TURKEY USA+45 AGRI NAT/G PLAN BUDGET DIPLOM COST EFFICIENCY...CHARTS 20. PAGE 3 A0070 — ECO/TAC FOR/AID FINAN ECO/UNDEV

B65
PEACE RESEARCH ABSTRACTS. FUT WOR+45 R+D INT/ORG NAT/G PLAN TEC/DEV BAL/PWR DIPLOM FOR/AID NUC/PWR HEALTH. PAGE 4 A0072 — BIBLIOG/A PEACE ARMS/CONT WAR

B65
BROOKINGS INSTITUTION,BROOKINGS PAPERS ON PUBLIC POLICY. USA+45 ECO/UNDEV LEGIS CAP/ISM ECO/TAC TAX EDU/PROP CONTROL APPORT 20. PAGE 19 A0395 — DIPLOM FOR/AID POLICY FINAN

B65
COOMBS P.H.,EDUCATION AND FOREIGN AID. AFR USA+45 DIPLOM EFFICIENCY KNOWL ORD/FREE...ANTHOL 20 AID. PAGE 30 A0608 — EDU/PROP FOR/AID SCHOOL ECO/UNDEV

B65
FRIEDMANN W.,AN INTRODUCTION TO WORLD POLITICS (5TH ED.). WOR+45 ECO/UNDEV BAL/PWR FOR/AID INT/TRADE PEACE...STAT CENSUS CHARTS BIBLIOG T 20 COLD/WAR UN THIRD/WRLD. PAGE 49 A1003 — DIPLOM INT/ORG PROB/SOLV

B65
GERASSI J.,THE GREAT FEAR IN LATIN AMERICA. L/A+17C USA+45 ELITES STRUCT INT/ORG REV ORD/FREE WEALTH 20 LAFTA. PAGE 52 A1063 — SOCIETY FOR/AID DIPLOM

B65
HAGRAS K.M.,UNITED NATIONS CONFERENCE ON TRADE AND DEVELOPMENT: A CASE STUDY OF UN DIPLOMACY. CONSULT ACT/RES TEC/DEV FOR/AID INT/TRADE...BIBLIOG 20 UN LEAGUE/NAT UNCTAD. PAGE 59 A1213 — INT/ORG ADMIN DELIB/GP DIPLOM

B65
JALEE P.,THE PILLAGE OF THE THIRD WORLD (TRANS. BY MARY KLOPPER). WOR+45 AGRI INDUS ECO/TAC FOR/AID COLONIAL CONTROL PRODUC PWR WEALTH...STAT CHARTS 20 RESOURCE/N. PAGE 73 A1493 — ECO/UNDEV DOMIN INT/TRADE DIPLOM

B65
KRAUSE W.,ECONOMIC DEVELOPMENT: THE UNDERDEVELOPED WORLD AND THE AMERICAN INTEREST. USA+45 AGRI PLAN MARXISM...CHARTS 20. PAGE 82 A1679 — FOR/AID ECO/UNDEV FINAN PROB/SOLV

B65
LASKY V.,THE UGLY RUSSIAN. AFR ASIA USSR ECO/UNDEV NAT/LISM TOTALISM PERSON 20. PAGE 85 A1738 — FOR/AID ATTIT DIPLOM

B65
LEISS A.C.,APARTHEID AND UNITED NATIONS COLLECTIVE MEASURES. SOUTH/AFR ECO/UNDEV EXTR/IND FORCES WORKER ECO/TAC FOR/AID INT/TRADE WEALTH...TREND CHARTS 20 UN NEGRO. PAGE 86 A1770 — DISCRIM RACE/REL STRATA DIPLOM

B65
LIEUWEN E.,U.S. POLICY IN LATIN AMERICA: A SHORT HISTORY. L/A+17C USA+45 USA-45 DELIB/GP ECO/TAC 19/20 COLD/WAR MONROE/DOC. PAGE 89 A1812 — DIPLOM COLONIAL NAT/G FOR/AID

B65
MEAGHER R.F.,PUBLIC INTERNATIONAL DEVELOPMENT FINANCING IN SUDAN. SUDAN FINAN DELIB/GP GIVE ...CHARTS GOV/COMP 20. PAGE 99 A2029 — FOR/AID PLAN RECEIVE ECO/UNDEV

B65
MONCRIEFF A.,SECOND THOUGHTS ON AID. WOR+45 ECO/UNDEV AGRI FINAN VOL/ASSN PLAN TEC/DEV GIVE EDU/PROP ROLE WEALTH 20. PAGE 102 A2105 — FOR/AID ECO/TAC INT/ORG IDEA/COMP

B65
MORGENTHAU H.,MORGENTHAU DIARY (CHINA) (2 VOLS.). ASIA USA+45 USA-45 LAW DELIB/GP EX/STRUC PLAN FOR/AID INT/TRADE CONFER WAR MARXISM 20 CHINJAP. PAGE 104 A2136 — DIPLOM ADMIN

B65
MOWRY G.E.,THE URBAN NATION 1920-1960. USA+45 USA-45 SOCIETY ECO/DEV MUNIC FOR/AID INT/TRADE AUTOMAT...BIBLIOG/A 20. PAGE 105 A2161 — TEC/DEV NAT/G TOTALISM DIPLOM

B65
NKRUMAH K.,NEO-COLONIALISM: THE LAST STAGE OF IMPERIALISM. AFR INT/ORG WORKER FOR/AID INT/TRADE EDU/PROP GOV/REL NAT/LISM SOVEREIGN POPULISM SOCISM ...SOCIALIST 20 THIRD/WRLD INTRVN/ECO. PAGE 109 — COLONIAL DIPLOM ECO/UNDEV ECO/TAC

A2243

B65
REQUA E.G.,THE DEVELOPING NATIONS: A GUIDE TO INFORMATION SOURCES CONCERNING THEIR ECON. POLIT. TECHNICAL, AND SOCIAL PROBLEMS. AFR ASIA ISLAM L/A+17C INDUS INT/ORG CONSULT PLAN PROB/SOLV...SOC 20 UN. PAGE 120 A2466 BIBLIOG/A ECO/UNDEV FOR/AID TEC/DEV

B65
SCOTT A.M.,THE REVOLUTION IN STATECRAFT: INFORMAL PENETRATION. WOR+45 WOR-45 CULTURE INT/ORG FORCES ECO/TAC ROUTINE...BIBLIOG 20. PAGE 130 A2670 DIPLOM EDU/PROP FOR/AID

B65
STOETZER O.C.,THE ORGANIZATION OF AMERICAN STATES. L/A+17C EX/STRUC FOR/AID CONFER PARL/PROC ORD/FREE SOVEREIGN...POLICY INT/LAW 20 OAS. PAGE 138 A2831 INT/ORG REGION DIPLOM BAL/PWR

B65
SULZBERGER C.L.,UNFINISHED REVOLUTION. USA+45 WOR+45 INT/ORG TEC/DEV BAL/PWR FOR/AID COLONIAL NEUTRAL PWR SOVEREIGN MARXISM 20. PAGE 140 A2863 DIPLOM ECO/UNDEV POLICY NAT/G

B65
TREFOUSSE H.L.,THE COLD WAR: A BOOK OF DOCUMENTS. ASIA L/A+17C USSR WOR+45 WOR-45 ECO/TAC FOR/AID ARMS/CONT NUC/PWR PEACE ORD/FREE...ANTHOL 20 COLD/WAR KENNEDY/JF EISNHWR/DD. PAGE 145 A2961 BAL/PWR DIPLOM MARXISM

B65
UN,SPACE ACTIVITIES AND RESOURCES: REVIEW OF UNITED NATION'S NATIONAL AND INTERNATIONAL PROGRAMS. INT/ORG LABOR PLAN TEC/DEV DIPLOM EFFICIENCY HEALTH ...GOV/COMP 20 UN. PAGE 146 A2995 SPACE NUC/PWR FOR/AID PEACE

B65
US BUREAU EDUC CULTURAL AFF,RESOURCES SURVEY FOR LATIN AMERICAN COUNTRIES. L/A+17C USA+45 CULTURE INDUS INT/ORG SECT PLAN EDU/PROP POLICY. PAGE 150 A3056 NAT/G ECO/UNDEV FOR/AID DIPLOM

B65
US HOUSE COMM FOREIGN AFFAIRS,HEARINGS ON DRAFT BILL TO AMEND FURTHER THE FOREIGN ASSISTANCE ACT OF 1961. AFR ASIA L/A+17C USA+45 INT/ORG DELIB/GP TEC/DEV ECO/TAC CONFER TOTALISM 20 CONGRESS AID. PAGE 153 A3131 FOR/AID ECO/UNDEV DIPLOM ORD/FREE

B65
US SENATE COMM ON FOREIGN REL,HEARINGS ON THE FOREIGN ASSISTANCE PROGRAM. AFR ASIA L/A+17C USA+45 WOR+45 FORCES TEC/DEV BUDGET CONTROL WEAPON ORD/FREE 20 UN CONGRESS SEC/STATE. PAGE 156 A3183 FOR/AID DIPLOM INT/ORG ECO/UNDEV

B65
US SENATE COMM ON JUDICIARY,REFUGEE PROBLEMS IN SOUTH VIETNAM AND LAOS: HEARINGS BEFORE SUBCOMMITTEE TO INVESTIGATE PROBLEMS OF REFUGEES, ESCAPEES. CHINA/COM LAOS USA+45 VIETNAM/S PROB/SOLV DIPLOM GOV/REL GP/REL EFFICIENCY ORD/FREE...POLICY GEOG 20 CONGRESS MIGRATION. PAGE 157 A3194 STRANGE HABITAT FOR/AID CIVMIL/REL

B65
WARBEY W.,VIETNAM: THE TRUTH. FRANCE S/ASIA USA+45 VIETNAM CULTURE INT/ORG NAT/G DIPLOM FOR/AID EDU/PROP ARMS/CONT PEACE 20 TREATY NLF UN. PAGE 161 A3274 WAR AGREE

B65
WEAVER J.N.,THE INTERNATIONAL DEVELOPMENT ASSOCIATION: A NEW APPROACH TO FOREIGN AID. USA+45 NAT/G OP/RES PLAN PROB/SOLV WEALTH...CHARTS BIBLIOG 20 UN. PAGE 162 A3295 FOR/AID INT/ORG ECO/UNDEV FINAN

B65
WEILER J.,L'ECONOMIE INTERNATIONALE DEPUIS 1950. WOR+45 DIPLOM TARIFFS CONFER...POLICY TREATY. PAGE 162 A3302 FINAN INT/TRADE REGION FOR/AID

B65
WEISNER J.B.,WHERE SCIENCE AND POLITICS MEET. USA+45 ECO/DEV R+D FORCES PROB/SOLV DIPLOM FOR/AID CONTROL...PHIL/SCI PRESIDENT KENNEDY/JF JOHNSON/LB. PAGE 163 A3310 CHIEF NAT/G POLICY TEC/DEV

B65
WHITE J.,GERMAN AID. GERMANY/W FINAN PLAN TEC/DEV INT/TRADE ADMIN ATTIT...POLICY 20. PAGE 164 A3335 FOR/AID ECO/UNDEV DIPLOM ECO/TAC

L65
MATTHEWS D.G.,"A CURRENT BIBLIOGRAPHY ON SUDANESE AFFAIRS; A SELECT BIBLIOGRAPHY FROM 1960-1964." SUDAN LAW CULTURE AGRI FINAN INDUS LABOR POL/PAR TEC/DEV FOR/AID RACE/REL LITERACY...LING 20. PAGE 96 A1970 BIBLIOG ECO/UNDEV NAT/G DIPLOM

S65
AFRICAN BIBLIOGRAPHIC CENTER,"US TREATIES AND AGREEMENTS WITH COUNTRIES IN AFRICA, 1957 TO MID-1963." AFR USA+45 AGRI FINAN FORCES TEC/DEV CAP/ISM FOR/AID 20. PAGE 5 A0097 BIBLIOG DIPLOM INT/ORG INT/TRADE

S65
KORBONSKI A.,"USA POLICY IN EAST EUROPE." COM EUR+WWI GERMANY USA+45 CULTURE ECO/UNDEV EDU/PROP RIGID/FLEX WEALTH 20. PAGE 82 A1672 ACT/RES ECO/TAC FOR/AID

S65
RAY H.,"THE POLICY OF RUSSIA TOWARDS SINO-INDIAN CONFLICT." ASIA CHINA/COM COM INDIA USSR NAT/G TOP/EX FOR/AID EDU/PROP NEUTRAL COERCE PEACE RIGID/FLEX PWR...METH/CNCPT TIME/SEQ VAL/FREE 20. PAGE 120 A2452 S/ASIA ATTIT DIPLOM WAR

S65
SCHNEIDER R.M.,"THE US IN LATIN AMERICA." L/A+17C USA+45 NAT/G POL/PAR PLAN RIGID/FLEX ALL/VALS OAS 20. PAGE 129 A2640 VOL/ASSN ECO/UNDEV FOR/AID

C65
US AIR FORCE ACADEMY,"AMERICAN DEFENSE POLICY." COM INT/ORG TEC/DEV FOR/AID ARMS/CONT DETER NUC/PWR ...POLICY DECISION CONCPT ANTHOL BIBLIOG/A 20 COLD/WAR NATO. PAGE 149 A3054 PLAN FORCES WAR COERCE

B66
SUPPLEMENTAL FOREIGN ASSISTANCE FISCAL YEAR 1966: VIETNAM. CHINA/COM COM S/ASIA USA+45 VIETNAM EXTR/IND FINAN DIPLOM TAX GUERRILLA HABITAT ORD/FREE...STAT CHARTS 20 SENATE PRESIDENT. PAGE 4 A0077 CONFER LEGIS WAR FOR/AID

B66
BALDWIN D.A.,ECONOMIC DEVELOPMENT AND AMERICAN FOREIGN POLICY. USA+45 FINAN LG/CO LEGIS DIPLOM GIVE 20. PAGE 10 A0210 ECO/TAC FOR/AID ECO/UNDEV POLICY

B66
ENTWICKLUNGSPOLITIK - HANDBUCH UND LEXIKON. MARKET SECT DIPLOM INT/TRADE EDU/PROP CATHISM 20. PAGE 14 A0283 ECO/UNDEV FOR/AID ECO/TAC PLAN

B66
BROEKMEIJER M.W.J.,FICTION AND TRUTH ABOUT THE "DECADE OF DEVELOPMENT" WOR+45 AGRI FINAN INDUS NAT/G TEC/DEV DIPLOM EDU/PROP LEAD SKILL 20 THIRD/WRLD. PAGE 19 A0385 FOR/AID POLICY ECO/UNDEV PLAN

B66
BRYNES A.,WE GIVE TO CONQUER. USA+45 USSR STRATA ECO/UNDEV INT/ORG NAT/G DIPLOM DRIVE...TREND IDEA/COMP 20. PAGE 20 A0414 FOR/AID CONTROL GIVE WAR

B66
CONNEL-SMITH G.,THE INTERAMERICAN SYSTEM. CUBA L/A+17C DELIB/GP FOR/AID COLONIAL PEACE PWR MARXISM ...BIBLIOG 19/20 OAS. PAGE 29 A0586 DIPLOM INT/TRADE REGION INT/ORG

B66
CURRIE L.,ACCELERATING DEVELOPMENT: THE NECESSITY AND MEANS. COLOMBIA USA+45 INDUS DIPLOM EFFICIENCY WEALTH...METH/CNCPT NEW/IDEA 20. PAGE 33 A0668 PLAN ECO/UNDEV FOR/AID TEC/DEV

B66
EWING L.L.,THE REFERENCE HANDBOOK OF THE ARMED FORCES OF THE WORLD. WOR+45 ECO/TAC FOR/AID COERCE WAR PWR 20. PAGE 43 A0879 FORCES STAT DIPLOM PLAN

B66
FISHER S.N.,NEW HORIZONS FOR THE UNITED STATES IN WORLD AFFAIRS. USA+45 FOR/AID...ANTHOL 20 UN. PAGE 46 A0941 DIPLOM PLAN INT/ORG

B66
FREIDEL F.,AMERICAN ISSUES IN THE TWENTIETH CENTURY. SOCIETY FINAN ECO/TAC FOR/AID CONTROL NUC/PWR WAR RACE/REL PEACE ATTIT...ANTHOL T 20 WILSON/W ROOSEVLT/F KENNEDY/JF TRUMAN/HS. PAGE 49 A0995 DIPLOM POLICY NAT/G ORD/FREE

B66
HALLET R.,PEOPLE AND PROGRESS IN WEST AFRICA: AN INTRODUCTION TO THE PROBLEMS OF DEVELOPMENT. COM/IND INDUS KIN DIPLOM FOR/AID INT/TRADE HEALTH ...GEOG TREND CHARTS BIBLIOG/A 20 AFRICA/W. PAGE 60 A1233 AFR SOCIETY ECO/UNDEV ECO/TAC

B66
HAMILTON W.B.,A DECADE OF THE COMMONWEALTH, 1955-1964. UK LAW ELITES FINAN FOR/AID CONFER COLONIAL PWR...GEOG CHARTS ANTHOL 20 CMN/WLTH UN. PAGE 61 A1247 INT/ORG INGP/REL DIPLOM NAT/G

B66
HAYER T.,FRENCH AID. AFR FRANCE AGRI FINAN BUDGET ADMIN WAR PRODUC...CHARTS 18/20 THIRD/WRLD OVRSEA/DEV. PAGE 63 A1295 TEC/DEV COLONIAL FOR/AID ECO/UNDEV

B66
HERZ M.F.,BEGINNINGS OF THE COLD WAR. COM POLAND USA+45 USSR INT/ORG NAT/G CHIEF FOR/AID DOMIN CONFER AGREE WAR PEACE 20 STALIN/J COLD/WAR UN. PAGE 64 A1321 DIPLOM

B66
HOROWITZ D.,HEMISPHERES NORTH AND SOUTH: ECONOMIC DISPARITY AMONG NATIONS. WOR+45 ECO/DEV ECO/UNDEV INT/ORG PLAN DIPLOM INT/TRADE GIVE PARTIC GP/REL ...WELF/ST 20. PAGE 67 A1387 ECO/TAC FOR/AID STRATA WEALTH

B66
INTERNATIONAL ECONOMIC ASSN,STABILITY AND PROGRESS IN THE WORLD ECONOMY: THE FIRST CONGRESS OF THE INTERNATIONAL ECONOMIC ASSOCIATION. WOR+45 ECO/DEV ECO/UNDEV DELIB/GP FOR/AID BAL/PAY...TREND CMN/WLTH 20. PAGE 71 A1455 INT/TRADE

B66
JACK H.A.,RELIGION AND PEACE: PAPERS FROM THE NATIONAL INTER-RELIGIOUS CONFERENCE ON PEACE, WASHINGTON, 1966. CHINA/COM USA+45 VIETNAM WOR+45 FORCES FOR/AID LEAD PERS/REL. PAGE 72 A1472 PEACE SECT SUPEGO DIPLOM

B66
KAREFA-SMART J.,AFRICA: PROGRESS THROUGH COOPERATION. AFR FINAN TEC/DEV DIPLOM FOR/AID EDU/PROP CONFER REGION GP/REL WEALTH...HEAL SOC/INTEG 20. PAGE 76 A1566 ORD/FREE ECO/UNDEV VOL/ASSN PLAN

B66
KEENLEYSIDE H.L.,INTERNATIONAL AID: A SUMMARY. AFR INDIA S/ASIA UK STRATA EXTR/IND TEC/DEV ADMIN RACE/REL DEMAND NAT/LISM WEALTH...TREND CHINJAP. PAGE 77 A1575 ECO/UNDEV FOR/AID DIPLOM TASK

B66
KIM Y.K.,PATTERNS OF COMPETITIVE COEXISTENCE: USA VS. USSR. USA+45 USSR ECO/DEV ECO/UNDEV INT/ORG FOR/AID INT/TRADE ARMS/CONT...BIBLIOG 20 COLD/WAR. PAGE 79 A1618 DIPLOM PEACE BAL/PWR DETER

B66
KIRDAR U.,THE STRUCTURE OF UNITED NATIONS ECONOMIC AID TO UNDERDEVELOPED COUNTRIES. AGRI FINAN INDUS NAT/G EX/STRUC PLAN GIVE TASK...POLICY 20 UN. PAGE 79 A1631 INT/ORG FOR/AID ECO/UNDEV ADMIN

B66
LAMBERG R.F.,PRAG UND DIE DRITTE WELT. AFR ASIA CZECHOSLVK L/A+17C MARKET TEC/DEV ECO/TAC REV ATTIT 20 TREATY. PAGE 84 A1713 DIPLOM ECO/UNDEV INT/TRADE FOR/AID

B66
LEAGUE OF WOMEN VOTERS OF US,FOREIGN AID AT THE CROSSROADS. USA+45 WOR+45 DELIB/GP PROB/SOLV DIPLOM INT/TRADE RECEIVE BAL/PAY...CHARTS 20 UN. PAGE 86 A1756 FOR/AID GIVE ECO/UNDEV PLAN

B66
LENT H.B.,THE PEACE CORPS: AMBASSADORS OF GOOD WILL. USA+45 ECO/UNDEV...INT TESTS BIOG AUD/VIS SOC/INTEG 20 PEACE/CORP. PAGE 87 A1776 VOL/ASSN FOR/AID DIPLOM CONSULT

B66
LONG B.,THE WAR DIARY OF BRECKINRIDGE LONG: SELECTIONS FROM THE YEARS 1939-1944. USA-45 INT/ORG FORCES FOR/AID CHOOSE 20. PAGE 91 A1859 DIPLOM WAR DELIB/GP

B66
MAY E.R.,ANXIETY AND AFFLUENCE: 1945-1965. USA+45 DIPLOM FOR/AID ARMS/CONT RACE/REL CONSEN...ANTHOL 20 COLD/WAR KENNEDY/JF EISNHWR/DD TRUMAN/HS BERLIN/BLO. PAGE 97 A1982 ANOMIE ECO/DEV NUC/PWR WEALTH

B66
MIKESELL R.F.,PUBLIC INTERNATIONAL LENDING FOR DEVELOPMENT. WOR+45 WOR-45 DELIB/GP...TIME/SEQ CHARTS BIBLIOG 20. PAGE 101 A2070 INT/ORG FOR/AID ECO/UNDEV FINAN

B66
MONTGOMERY J.D.,APPROACHES TO DEVELOPMENT: POLITICS, ADMINISTRATION AND CHANGE. USA+45 AGRI FOR/AID ORD/FREE...CONCPT IDEA/COMP METH/COMP ANTHOL. PAGE 103 A2116 ECO/UNDEV ADMIN POLICY ECO/TAC

B66
MOOMAW I.W.,THE CHALLENGE OF HUNGER. USA+45 PLAN ADMIN EATING 20. PAGE 103 A2118 FOR/AID DIPLOM ECO/UNDEV ECO/TAC

B66
NATIONAL COUN APPLIED ECO RES,DEVELOPMENT WITHOUT AID. INDIA FINAN TEC/DEV EFFICIENCY...ANTHOL 20. PAGE 107 A2203 FOR/AID PLAN SOVEREIGN ECO/UNDEV

B66
OHLIN G.,FOREIGN AID POLICIES RECONSIDERED. ECO/DEV ECO/UNDEV VOL/ASSN CONSULT PLAN CONTROL ATTIT ...CONCPT CHARTS BIBLIOG 20. PAGE 111 A2286 FOR/AID DIPLOM GIVE

B66
ROBOCK S.H.,INTERNATIONAL DEVELOPMENT 1965. AGRI INDUS VOL/ASSN PLAN TEC/DEV EDU/PROP HEALTH...JURID 20 UN PEACE/CORP. PAGE 122 A2508 FOR/AID INT/ORG GEOG ECO/UNDEV

B66
SALTER L.M.,RESOLUTION OF INTERNATIONAL CONFLICT. USA+45 INT/ORG SECT DIPLOM ECO/TAC FOR/AID DETER NUC/PWR WAR 20. PAGE 127 A2595 PROB/SOLV PEACE INT/LAW POLICY

B66
SOBEL L.A.,SOUTH VIETNAM: US-COMMUNIST CONFRONTATION IN SOUTHEAST ASIA 1961-65. VIETNAM FOR/AID CROWD DETER REV PEACE...GEOG 20 INTERVENT DIEM COLD/WAR. PAGE 134 A2754 WAR TIME/SEQ FORCES NAT/G

B66
SPICER K.,A SAMARITAN STATE? AFR CANADA INDIA PAKISTAN UK USA+45 FINAN INDUS PRODUC...CHARTS 20 NATO. PAGE 136 A2787 DIPLOM FOR/AID ECO/DEV ADMIN

B66
UN ECAFE,ADMINISTRATIVE ASPECTS OF FAMILY PLANNING PROGRAMMES (PAMPHLET). ASIA THAILAND WOR+45 VOL/ASSN PROB/SOLV BUDGET FOR/AID EDU/PROP CONFER CONTROL GOV/REL TIME 20 UN BIRTH/CON. PAGE 147 A2999 PLAN CENSUS FAM ADMIN

B66
US DEPARTMENT OF THE ARMY,SOUTH ASIA: A STRATEGIC SURVEY (PAMPHLET NO. 550-3). AFGHANISTN INDIA NEPAL PAKISTAN ECO/UNDEV INT/ORG POL/PAR FORCES FOR/AID INT/TRADE LEAD WAR...POLICY SOC TREND 20. PAGE 152 A3110 BIBLIOG/A S/ASIA DIPLOM NAT/G

B66
US HOUSE COMM APPROPRIATIONS,HEARINGS ON FOREIGN OPERATIONS AND RELATED AGENCIES APPROPRIATIONS. CUBA USA+45 VOL/ASSN DELIB/GP DIPLOM CONFER ORD/FREE 20 CONGRESS MIGRATION INT/AM/DEV PEACE/CORP. PAGE 153 A3120 FOR/AID BUDGET ECO/UNDEV FORCES

B66
US HOUSE COMM FOREIGN AFFAIRS,HEARINGS ON HR 12449 A BILL TO AMEND FURTHER THE FOREIGN ASSISTANCE ACT OF 1961. AFR ASIA L/A+17C USA+45 VIETNAM INT/ORG TEC/DEV INT/TRADE ATTIT ORD/FREE 20 UN NATO CONGRESS AID. PAGE 154 A3132 FOR/AID ECO/TAC ECO/UNDEV DIPLOM

B66
US HOUSE COMM GOVT OPERATIONS,AN INVESTIGATION OF THE US ECONOMIC AND MILITARY ASSISTANCE PROGRAMS IN VIETNAM. USA+45 VIETNAM/S SOCIETY CONSTRUC FINAN FORCES BUDGET INT/TRADE PEACE HEALTH...MGT HOUSE/REP AID. PAGE 154 A3139 FOR/AID ECO/UNDEV WAR INSPECT

B66
US SENATE COMM GOVT OPERATIONS,POPULATION CRISIS. USA+45 ECO/DEV ECO/UNDEV AGRI SECT DELIB/GP PROB/SOLV FOR/AID REPRESENT ATTIT...GEOG CHARTS 20 CONGRESS DEPT/STATE DEPT/HEW BIRTH/CON. PAGE 156 A3178 CENSUS CONTROL LEGIS CONSULT

B66
US SENATE COMM ON FOREIGN REL,HEARINGS ON S 2859 AND S 2861. USA+45 WOR+45 FORCES BUDGET CAP/ISM ADMIN DETER WEAPON TOTALISM...NAT/COMP 20 UN CONGRESS. PAGE 156 A3185 FOR/AID DIPLOM ORD/FREE ECO/UNDEV

B66
US SENATE COMM ON FOREIGN REL,ASIAN DEVELOPMENT BANK ACT. USA+45 LAW DIPLOM...CHARTS 20 BLACK/EUG S/EASTASIA. PAGE 156 A3186 FOR/AID FINAN ECO/UNDEV S/ASIA

B66
VYAS R.,DAWNING ON THE CAPITOL: US CONGRESS AND INDIA. INDIA S/ASIA USA+45 ELITES ECO/DEV ECO/UNDEV PLAN FOR/AID...BIBLIOG 20 CONGRESS. PAGE 160 A3256 POLICY LEGIS NAT/G DIPLOM

B66
WARBURG J.P.,THE UNITED STATES IN THE POSTWAR WORLD. USA+45 ECO/TAC...POLICY 20 COLD/WAR. PAGE 161 A3277 FOR/AID DIPLOM PLAN ADMIN

B66
WESTWOOD A.F.,FOREIGN AID IN A FOREIGN POLICY FRAMEWORK. AFR ASIA INDIA IRAN L/A+17C USA+45 USSR ECO/UNDEV AGRI FORCES LEGIS PLAN PROB/SOLV ...DECISION 20 COLD/WAR. PAGE 163 A3324 FOR/AID DIPLOM POLICY ECO/TAC

B66
WILLIAMS P.,AID IN UGANDA - EDUCATION. UGANDA UK FINAN ACADEM INT/ORG SCHOOL PROB/SOLV ECO/TAC UTIL ...STAT CHARTS 20. PAGE 165 A3352 PLAN EDU/PROP FOR/AID ECO/UNDEV

B66
ZISCHKA A.,WAR ES EIN WUNDER? GERMANY/W ECO/DEV FINAN LG/CO BARGAIN CAP/ISM FOR/AID RATION 20 MARSHL/PLN. PAGE 170 A3456 ECO/TAC INT/TRADE INDUS WAR

L66
CHENERY H.B.,"FOREIGN ASSISTANCE AND ECONOMIC DEVELOPMENT" FUT WOR+45 NAT/G DIPLOM GIVE PRODUC ...METH/CNCPT CHARTS 20. PAGE 26 A0526 FOR/AID EFFICIENCY ECO/UNDEV TEC/DEV

S66
AFRICAN BIBLIOGRAPHIC CENTER,"A CURRENT VIEW OF AFRICANA: A SELECT AND ANNOTATED BIBLIOGRAPHICAL PUBLISHING GUIDE, 1965-1966." AFR CULTURE INDUS LABOR SECT FOR/AID ADMIN COLONIAL REV RACE/REL SOCISM...LING 20. PAGE 5 A0098 BIBLIOG/A NAT/G TEC/DEV POL/PAR

S66
AFRICAN BIBLIOGRAPHIC CENTER,"THE NEW AFRO-ASIAN STATES IN PERSPECTIVE, 1960-1963: A SELECT BIBLIOGRAPHY." AFR ASIA CULTURE SOCIETY INT/ORG LABOR TEC/DEV LITERACY 20 UN. PAGE 5 A0100 BIBLIOG DIPLOM FOR/AID INT/TRADE

S66
ERB GF,"THE UNITED NATIONS CONFERENCE ON TRADE AND DEVELOPMENT (UNCTAD): A SELECTED CURRENT READING LIST." FINAN FOR/AID CONFER 20 UN. PAGE 42 A0858 BIBLIOG/A INT/TRADE ECO/UNDEV INT/ORG

S66
FRIEND A.,"THE MIDDLE EAST CRISIS" COM ISLAM ISRAEL SYRIA UAR USA+45 USSR FORCES PLAN FOR/AID CONTROL ORD/FREE PWR...SOCIALIST TIME/SEQ 20 NASSER/G. PAGE 49 A1009 WAR INT/ORG DIPLOM PEACE

N66
BRITISH DEVELOPMENT POLICIES: 1966 (PAMPHLET). UK WEALTH

AGRI TARIFFS BAL/PAY...TREND CHARTS 20 OVRSEA/DEV. PAGE 4 A0076 — DIPLOM INT/TRADE FOR/AID

N66
EOMMITTEE ECONOMIC DEVELOPMENT,THE DOLLAR AND THE WORLD MONETARY SYSTEM: A STATEMENT ON NATIONAL POLICY (PAMPHLET). USA+45 NAT/G PLAN PROB/SOLV BUDGET ECO/TAC FOR/AID INCOME...POLICY 20 GOLD/STAND EUROPE. PAGE 42 A0854 — FINAN BAL/PAY DIPLOM ECO/DEV

B67
CHO S.S.,KOREA IN WORLD POLITICS 1940-1950; AN EVALUATION OF AMERICAN RESPONSIBILITY. KOREA USA+45 USSR CONSTN INT/ORG NAT/G FORCES FOR/AID ANOMIE SUPEGO MARXISM...DECISION BIBLIOG 20. PAGE 26 A0533 — POLICY DIPLOM PROB/SOLV WAR

B67
FRASER-TYTLER W.K.,AFGHANISTAN: A STUDY OF POLITICAL DEVELOPMENTS IN CENTRAL AND SOUTHERN ASIA (3RD ED.). AFGHANISTN INDIA KIN FOR/AID PWR ...BIBLIOG. PAGE 48 A0990 — DIPLOM NAT/G CONSTN GEOG

B67
JOHNSON D.G.,THE STRUGGLE AGAINST WORLD HUNGER (HEADLINE SERIES, NO. 184) (PAMPHLET). PLAN TEC/DEV FOR/AID...CHARTS 20 FAO MEXIC/AMER. PAGE 74 A1520 — AGRI PROB/SOLV ECO/UNDEV HEALTH

B67
MAW B.,BREAKTHROUGH IN BURMA: MEMOIRS OF A REVOLUTION, 1939-1946. BURMA UK FORCES PROB/SOLV DIPLOM FOR/AID DOMIN LEAD...BIOG 20. PAGE 97 A1980 — REV ORD/FREE NAT/LISM COLONIAL

B67
O'LEARY M.K.,THE POLITICS OF AMERICAN FOREIGN AID. USA+45 POL/PAR CHIEF BUDGET EDU/PROP LOBBY CONGRESS. PAGE 111 A2270 — FOR/AID DIPLOM PARL/PROC ATTIT

B67
SABLE M.H.,A GUIDE TO LATIN AMERICAN STUDIES (2 VOLS). CONSTN FINAN INT/ORG LABOR MUNIC POL/PAR FORCES CAP/ISM FOR/AID ADMIN MARXISM SOCISM OAS. PAGE 126 A2584 — BIBLIOG/A L/A+17C DIPLOM NAT/LISM

B67
US AGENCY INTERNATIONAL DEV,PROPOSED FOREIGN AID PROGRAM FOR 1968: SUMMARY PRESENTATION TO THE CONGRESS. AFR S/ASIA USA+45 AGRI TEC/DEV DIPLOM ECO/TAC BAL/PAY COST HEALTH KNOWL SKILL 20 AID CONGRESS. PAGE 149 A3053 — ECO/UNDEV BUDGET FOR/AID STAT

B67
US CONGRESS SENATE,SURVEY OF THE ALLIANCE FOR PROGRESS; INFLATION IN LATIN AMERICA (PAMPHLET). USA+45 MARKET INT/ORG DIPLOM INT/TRADE BAL/PAY SENATE. PAGE 150 A3072 — L/A+17C FINAN POLICY FOR/AID

B67
US DEPARTMENT OF STATE,THE COUNTRY TEAM - AN ILLUSTRATED PROFILE OF OUR AMERICAN MISSIONS ABROAD. ECO/TAC FOR/AID EDU/PROP TASK PERS/REL ATTIT 20. PAGE 152 A3099 — DIPLOM NAT/G VOL/ASSN GOV/REL

B67
US SENATE COMM ON FOREIGN REL,BACKGROUND INFORMATION RELATING TO SOUTHEAST ASIA AND VIETNAM (3RD REV. ED.). USA+45 VIETNAM/S VIETNAM/N...CHARTS 20 SENATE UN. PAGE 156 A3188 — DIPLOM WAR FOR/AID

B67
US SENATE COMM ON FOREIGN REL,UNITED STATES ARMAMENT AND DISARMAMENT PROBLEMS. USA+45 AIR BAL/PWR DIPLOM FOR/AID NUC/PWR ORD/FREE SENATE TREATY. PAGE 156 A3190 — ARMS/CONT WEAPON FORCES PROB/SOLV

L67
DEVADHAR Y.C.,"THE ROLE OF FOREIGN PRIVATE CAPITAL IN INDIA'S ECONOMIC DEVELOPMENT* ASSESSMENT OF POLICY AND PERFORMANCE." INDIA INDUS PLAN TEC/DEV BUDGET DIPLOM ECO/TAC BAL/PAY PRODUC WEALTH ...CHARTS 20. PAGE 37 A0750 — CAP/ISM FOR/AID POLICY ACT/RES

L67
MACDONALD R.S.J.,"THE RESORT TO ECONOMIC COERCION BY INTERNATIONAL POLITICAL ORGANIZATIONS." CUBA ETHIOPIA RHODESIA SOUTH/AFR NAT/G FORCES FOR/AID INT/TRADE DOMIN CONTROL SANCTION...DECISION LEAGUE/NAT UN OAS 20. PAGE 92 A1887 — INT/ORG COERCE ECO/TAC DIPLOM

L67
MOORE N.,"THE LAWFULNESS OF MILITARY ASSISTANCE TO THE REPUBLIC OF VIET NAM." USA+45 VIETNAM WOR+45 FOR/AID DOMIN DETER WAR WEAPON...DECISION INT/LAW 20 UN. PAGE 103 A2123 — PWR DIPLOM FORCES GOV/REL

L67
SEGAL A.,"THE INTEGRATION OF DEVELOPING COUNTRIES: SOME THOUGHTS ON EAST AFRICA AND CENTRAL AMERICA." AFR L/A+17C INT/ORG NAT/G VOL/ASSN FOR/AID INT/TRADE EQUILIB NAT/LISM PWR 20. PAGE 131 A2680 — ECO/UNDEV DIPLOM REGION

S67
AFRICAN BIBLIOGRAPHIC CENTER,"THE SWORD AND GOVERNMENT: A PRELIMINARY AND SELECTED BIBLIOGRAPHICAL GUIDE TO AFRICAN MILITARY AFFAIRS; PART I." AFR USA+45 USSR INT/ORG POL/PAR FOR/AID COLONIAL ARMS/CONT PWR 20 UN. PAGE 5 A0101 — BIBLIOG/A FORCES CIVMIL/REL DIPLOM

S67
BUTTINGER J.,"VIETNAM* FRAUD OF THE 'OTHER WAR'." VIETNAM/S ELITES STRUCT AGRI NAT/G FOR/AID RENT TREND. PAGE 22 A0456 — PLAN WEALTH REV ECO/UNDEV

S67
CHAND A.,"INDIA AND TANZANIA." INDIA TANZANIA TEC/DEV ECO/TAC FOR/AID COLONIAL PEACE UTIL WEALTH ...GOV/COMP 20. PAGE 25 A0518 — ECO/UNDEV NEUTRAL DIPLOM PLAN

S67
FELDMAN H.,"AID AS IMPERIALISM?" INDIA PAKISTAN UK USA+45 BAL/PWR CAP/ISM DIPLOM ECO/TAC DOMIN BAL/PAY WEALTH...POLICY 20. PAGE 45 A0914 — COLONIAL FOR/AID S/ASIA ECO/UNDEV

S67
FRANK I.,"NEW PERSPECTIVES ON TRADE AND DEVELOPMENT." PROB/SOLV BARGAIN DIPLOM FOR/AID CONFER GP/REL WEALTH 20 UN GATT. PAGE 48 A0980 — ECO/UNDEV INT/ORG INT/TRADE ECO/TAC

S67
GLOBERSON A.,"SOCIAL GROWTH IN THE DEVELOPING COUNTRIES." CULTURE SOCIETY CONSULT PROB/SOLV SOC. PAGE 53 A1082 — ECO/UNDEV FOR/AID EDU/PROP PLAN

S67
GODUNSKY Y.,"'APOSTLES OF PEACE' IN LATIN AMERICA." L/A+17C USA+45 BAL/PWR DIPLOM FOR/AID DOMIN COLONIAL CIVMIL/REL MARXIST. PAGE 53 A1086 — ECO/UNDEV REV VOL/ASSN EDU/PROP

S67
GRUNDY K.W.,"AFRICA IN THE WORLD ARENA." ECO/UNDEV BAL/PWR FOR/AID NEUTRAL REV NAT/LISM GOV/COMP. PAGE 58 A1183 — AFR DIPLOM INT/ORG COLONIAL

S67
HIBBERT R.A.,"THE MONGOLIAN PEOPLE'S REPUBLIC IN THE 1960'S." INT/ORG PLAN FOR/AID 20. PAGE 64 A1326 — ASIA ECO/UNDEV PROB/SOLV DIPLOM

S67
JAVITS J.K.,"LAST CHANCE FOR A COMMON MARKET." L/A+17C INT/ORG 20 EEC LAFTA. PAGE 73 A1501 — FOR/AID ECO/UNDEV INT/TRADE ECO/TAC

S67
KAISER R.G.,"THE TRUMAN DOCTRINE* HOW IT ALL BEGAN." COM EUR+WWI USA+45 R+D INT/ORG BAL/PWR ECO/TAC PEACE TRUMAN/DOC. PAGE 76 A1550 — DIPLOM ECO/UNDEV FOR/AID

S67
KINGSLEY R.E.,"THE US BUSINESS IMAGE IN LATIN AMERICA." L/A+17C USA+45 NAT/G TEC/DEV CAP/ISM FOR/AID DOMIN EDU/PROP...CONCPT LING IDEA/COMP 20. PAGE 79 A1626 — ATTIT LOVE DIPLOM ECO/UNDEV

S67
LOSMAN D.L.,"FOREIGN AID, SOCIALISM AND THE EMERGING COUNTRIES" WOR+45 ADMIN CONTROL PWR 20. PAGE 91 A1864 — ECO/UNDEV FOR/AID SOC

S67
MCCORD W.,"ARMIES AND POLITICS; A PROBLEM IN THE THIRD WORLD." AFR ISLAM USA+45 ECO/UNDEV TOTALISM 20. PAGE 98 A2002 — FOR/AID POLICY NAT/G FORCES

S67
MONTALVA E.F.,"THE ALLIANCE THAT LOST ITS WAY." L/A+17C USA+45 R+D BAL/PWR INT/TRADE RECEIVE REV PEACE...POLICY 20. PAGE 103 A2111 — ECO/UNDEV DIPLOM FOR/AID INT/ORG

S67
PAUKER G.J.,"TOWARD A NEW ORDER IN INDONESIA." COM INDONESIA S/ASIA ECO/UNDEV POL/PAR EX/STRUC TOP/EX BAL/PWR ECO/TAC FOR/AID DOMIN NAT/LISM AUTHORIT ORD/FREE PWR 20. PAGE 114 A2342 — REV NAT/G DIPLOM CIVMIL/REL

S67
ROSE S.,"ASIAN NATIONALISM* THE SECOND STAGE." ASIA COM ECO/UNDEV NAT/G PROB/SOLV DIPLOM FOR/AID DOMIN NEUTRAL REGION TASK...METH/COMP 20. PAGE 123 A2528 — NAT/LISM S/ASIA BAL/PWR COLONIAL

S67
SAPP B.B.,"TRIBAL CULTURES AND COMMUNISM." AFR USA+45 STRATA DIPLOM FOR/AID REGION CENTRAL ATTIT AUTHORIT RIGID/FLEX KNOWL. PAGE 127 A2604 — KIN MARXISM ECO/UNDEV STRUCT

S67
SARBADHIKARI P.,"A NOTE ON THE DOMESTIC CRISIS OF NON-ALIGNMENT." ELITES INTELL ECO/UNDEV FOR/AID DOMIN. PAGE 127 A2605 — NEUTRAL WEALTH TOTALISM BAL/PWR

S67
STEEL R.,"WHAT CAN THE UN DO?" RHODESIA ECO/UNDEV DIPLOM ECO/TAC SANCTION...INT/LAW UN. PAGE 137 A2810 — INT/ORG BAL/PWR PEACE FOR/AID

S67
STEELE R.,"A TASTE FOR INTERVENTION." USA+45 FOR/AID INT/TRADE EDU/PROP COLONIAL WAR PWR...TREND 20 COLD/WAR. PAGE 137 A2812 — POLICY DIPLOM DOMIN ATTIT

S67
THIEN T.T.,"VIETNAM: A CASE OF SOCIAL ALIENATION." VIETNAM AGRI FORCES FOR/AID ADMIN REPRESENT INGP/REL PWR 19/20. PAGE 143 A2918
NAT/G ELITES WORKER STRANGE

S67
YOUNG K.T.,"UNITED STATES POLICY AND VIETNAMESE POLITICAL VIABILITY 1954-1967." VIETNAM/S LOC/G MUNIC FOR/AID ORD/FREE...POLICY 20. PAGE 169 A3437
LEAD ADMIN GP/REL EFFICIENCY

N67
US GOVERNMENT,TREATIES IN FORCE. NAT/G ECO/TAC FOR/AID INT/TRADE NUC/PWR 20. PAGE 153 A3117
DIPLOM INT/ORG BAL/PWR

N67
US SENATE COMM ON FOREIGN REL,ARMS SALES AND FOREIGN POLICY (PAMPHLET). FINAN FOR/AID CONTROL 20. PAGE 156 A3187
ARMS/CONT ADMIN OP/RES DIPLOM

B68
ANTWERP-INST UNIVERSITAIRE,BIBLIOGRAPHIC COMPENDIUM: DEVELOPING COUNTRIES (ANTWERP-INST UNIVERSITAIRE DES TERRITOIRES D'OUTRE-MER). AFR EUR+WWI SOCIETY AGRI FINAN NEIGH VOL/ASSN PROB/SOLV TEC/DEV FOR/AID INT/TRADE 20. PAGE 8 A0166
BIBLIOG ECO/UNDEV DIPLOM PLAN

FORBES H.W. A0959

FORCE AND VIOLENCE....SEE COERCE

FORCES....ARMED FORCES AND POLICE

N
LIBRARY INTERNATIONAL REL,INTERNATIONAL INFORMATION SERVICE. WOR+45 CULTURE INT/ORG FORCES...GEOG HUM SOC. PAGE 88 A1808
BIBLIOG/A DIPLOM INT/TRADE INT/LAW

B
CURRENT THOUGHT ON PEACE AND WAR. WOR+45 INT/ORG FORCES PROB/SOLV DIPLOM NUC/PWR PERCEPT...POLICY SOC 20 UN NATO. PAGE 1 A0008
BIBLIOG/A PEACE ATTIT WAR

B
DEUTSCHE BIBLIOTH FRANKF A M,DEUTSCHE BIBLIOGRAPHIE. EUR+WWI GERMANY ECO/DEV FORCES DIPLOM LEAD...POLICY PHIL/SCI SOC 20. PAGE 36 A0743
BIBLIOG LAW ADMIN NAT/G

N
BACKGROUND; JOURNAL OF INTERNATIONAL STUDIES ASSOCIATION. INT/ORG FORCES ACT/RES EDU/PROP COERCE NAT/LISM PEACE ATTIT...INT/LAW CONCPT 20. PAGE 1 A0005
BIBLIOG DIPLOM POLICY

N
CANADIAN GOVERNMENT PUBLICATIONS (1955-). CANADA AGRI FINAN LABOR FORCES INT/TRADE HEALTH...JURID 20 PARLIAMENT. PAGE 1 A0007
BIBLIOG/A NAT/G DIPLOM INT/ORG

N
JOURNAL OF CONFLICT RESOLUTION. FUT WOR+45 INT/ORG NAT/G FORCES CREATE PROB/SOLV ARMS/CONT NUC/PWR WEAPON SOC. PAGE 1 A0014
BIBLIOG/A DIPLOM WAR

N
INDIA: A REFERENCE ANNUAL. INDIA CULTURE COM/IND R+D FORCES PLAN RECEIVE EDU/PROP HEALTH...STAT CHARTS BIBLIOG 20. PAGE 2 A0036
CONSTN LABOR INT/ORG

N
AIR UNIVERSITY LIBRARY,INDEX TO MILITARY PERIODICALS. FUT SPACE WOR+45 REGION ARMS/CONT NUC/PWR WAR PEACE INT/LAW. PAGE 5 A0105
BIBLIOG/A FORCES NAT/G DIPLOM

N
ATLANTIC INSTITUTE,ATLANTIC STUDIES. COM EUR+WWI USA+45 CULTURE STRUCT ECO/DEV FORCES LEAD ARMS/CONT ...INT/LAW JURID SOC. PAGE 10 A0193
BIBLIOG/A DIPLOM POLICY GOV/REL

N
UNITED NATIONS,UNITED NATIONS PUBLICATIONS. WOR+45 ECO/UNDEV AGRI FINAN FORCES ADMIN LEAD WAR PEACE ...POLICY INT/LAW 20 UN. PAGE 148 A3034
BIBLIOG INT/ORG DIPLOM

N
US SUPERINTENDENT OF DOCUMENTS,MONTHLY CATALOG OF UNITED STATES GOVERNMENT PUBLICATIONS. USA+45 USA-45 AGRI LABOR FORCES INT/TRADE TARIFFS TAX EDU/PROP CT/SYS ARMS/CONT RACE/REL 19/20 CONGRESS PRESIDENT. PAGE 157 A3203
BIBLIOG NAT/G VOL/ASSN POLICY

NLO
WHITE J.A.,THE DIPLOMACY OF THE RUSSO-JAPANESE WAR. ASIA KOREA RUSSIA FORCES CONFER CONTROL PEACE ...BIBLIOG 19 CHINJAP. PAGE 164 A3336
DIPLOM WAR BAL/PWR

B00
OMAN C.,A HISTORY OF THE ART OF WAR: THE MIDDLE AGES FROM THE FOURTH TO THE FOURTEENTH CENTURY. CHRIST-17C MEDIT-7 CULTURE SOCIETY INT/ORG ROUTINE PERSON...CONT/OBS HIST/WRIT CHARTS VAL/FREE. PAGE 112 A2291
FORCES SKILL WAR

B00
VOLPICELLI Z.,RUSSIA ON THE PACIFIC AND THE SIBERIAN RAILWAY. MOD/EUR ECO/UNDEV INT/ORG FORCES PLAN DOMIN COLONIAL ROUTINE ATTIT ALL/VALS...OBS HIST/WRIT TIME/SEQ TREND CON/ANAL AUD/VIS CHARTS 18/19. PAGE 159 A3248
NAT/G ACT/RES RUSSIA

B01
HART A.B.,AMERICAN HISTORY TOLD BY CONTEMPORARIES. UK CULTURE FINAN SECT FORCES DIPLOM TAX RUMOR CT/SYS REV GOV/REL GP/REL...ANTHOL 17/18 PRE/US/AM FEDERALIST. PAGE 62 A1273
USA-45 COLONIAL SOVEREIGN

B02
SEELEY J.R.,THE EXPANSION OF ENGLAND. MOD/EUR S/ASIA UK CULTURE NAT/G FORCES PLAN DOMIN EDU/PROP COLONIAL ROUTINE ATTIT ALL/VALS SOVEREIGN...CONCPT HIST/WRIT PARLIAMENT 18 CMN/WLTH. PAGE 131 A2679
INT/ORG ACT/RES CAP/ISM INDIA

B03
FORTESCUE G.K.,SUBJECT INDEX OF THE MODERN WORKS ADDED TO THE LIBRARY OF THE BRITISH MUSEUM IN THE YEARS 1881-1900 (3 VOLS.). UK LAW CONSTN FINAN NAT/G FORCES INT/TRADE COLONIAL 19. PAGE 47 A0968
BIBLIOG INDEX WRITING

B07
GRIFFIN A.P.C.,LIST OF WORKS RELATING TO THE FRENCH ALLIANCE IN THE AMERICAN REVOLUTION. FRANCE FORCES DIPLOM 18 PRE/US/AM. PAGE 56 A1155
BIBLIOG/A REV WAR

B09
HOLLAND T.E.,LETTERS UPON WAR AND NEUTRALITY. WOR-45 NAT/G FORCES JUDGE ECO/TAC LEGIT CT/SYS NEUTRAL ROUTINE COERCE...JURID TIME/SEQ 20. PAGE 67 A1368
LAW INT/LAW INT/ORG WAR

B14
BERNHARDI F.,ON THE WAR OF TODAY. MOD/EUR INT/ORG NAT/G TOP/EX PWR CHARTS. PAGE 14 A0278
FORCES SKILL WAR

B14
DE BLOCH J.,THE FUTURE OF WAR IN ITS TECHNICAL, ECONOMIC, AND POLITICAL RELATIONS (1899). MOD/EUR TEC/DEV BUDGET INT/TRADE DETER GUERRILLA WEAPON COST PEACE 20. PAGE 34 A0698
WAR BAL/PWR PREDICT FORCES

B16
ROOT E.,THE MILITARY AND COLONIAL POLICY OF THE US. L/A+17C USA-45 LAW SOCIETY STRATA STRUCT INT/ORG NAT/G SCHOOL FORCES EDU/PROP ALL/VALS...OBS VAL/FREE 19/20. PAGE 123 A2522
ACT/RES PLAN DIPLOM WAR

L16
WRIGHT Q.,"THE ENFORCEMENT OF INTERNATIONAL LAW THROUGH MUNICIPAL LAW IN THE US." USA-45 LOC/G NAT/G PUB/INST FORCES LEGIT CT/SYS PERCEPT ALL/VALS ...JURID 20. PAGE 167 A3401
INT/ORG LAW INT/LAW WAR

B17
MEYER H.H.B.,THE UNITED STATES AT WAR, ORGANIZATIONS AND LITERATURE. USA-45 AGRI FINAN INDUS CHIEF FORCES DIPLOM FOR/AID INT/TRADE...SOC 20 PRESIDENT. PAGE 100 A2050
BIBLIOG/A WAR NAT/G VOL/ASSN

B17
UPTON E.,THE MILITARY POLICY OF THE US. USA-45 STRUCT INT/ORG EXEC ATTIT PERCEPT...MGT CONCPT OBS HIST/WRIT CHARTS CONGRESS 18/20. PAGE 149 A3049
FORCES SKILL WAR

B19
VANDERPOL A.,LA DOCTRINE SCOLASTIQUE DU DROIT DE GUERRE. CHRIST-17C FORCES DIPLOM LEGIT SUPEGO MORAL ...BIOG AQUINAS/T SUAREZ/F CHRISTIAN. PAGE 158 A3220
WAR SECT INT/LAW

N19
BARROS J.F.P.,THE INTERNATIONAL POLICE: THE USE OF FORCE IN THE STRUCTURE OF PEACE (PAMPHLET). BRAZIL WOR+45 WOR-45 FORCES DISCRIM NAT/LISM ORD/FREE SOVEREIGN...POLICY NEW/IDEA WORSHIP 20. PAGE 11 A0229
PEACE INT/ORG COERCE BAL/PWR

N19
BENTHAM J.,A PLAN FOR AN UNIVERSAL AND PERPETUAL PEACE (1838) (PAMPHLET). NAT/G FORCES BAL/PWR INT/TRADE ADMIN AGREE CT/SYS ARMS/CONT SOVEREIGN WEALTH GEN/LAWS. PAGE 13 A0269
INT/ORG INT/LAW PEACE COLONIAL

N19
HALPERN M.,THE MORALITY AND POLITICS OF INTERVENTION (PAMPHLET). USA+45 INT/ORG FORCES ECO/TAC MORAL ORD/FREE 20 INTERVENT CHRISTIAN. PAGE 61 A1243
POLICY DIPLOM SOVEREIGN DOMIN

N19
MEZERIK A.G.,U-2 AND OPEN SKIES (PAMPHLET). USA+45 USSR INT/ORG CHIEF FORCES PLAN EDU/PROP CONTROL SANCTION ARMS/CONT 20 UN EISNHWR/DD. PAGE 100 A2060
DIPLOM RISK DEBATE

N19
MEZERIK AG,OUTER SPACE: UN, US, USSR (PAMPHLET). USSR DELIB/GP FORCES DETER NUC/PWR SOVEREIGN ...POLICY 20 UN TREATY. PAGE 101 A2063
SPACE CONTROL DIPLOM INT/ORG

N19
MORGENSTERN O.,THE COMMAND AND CONTROL STRUCTURE (PAMPHLET). USSR COM/IND INT/ORG WEAPON PEACE UTIL ...TREND 20 NATO. PAGE 104 A2132
CONTROL FORCES EFFICIENCY PLAN

B21
STUART G.H.,FRENCH FOREIGN POLICY. CONSTN INT/ORG NAT/G POL/PAR EX/STRUC FORCES PLAN ECO/TAC DOMIN EDU/PROP ADJUD COERCE ATTIT DRIVE RIGID/FLEX ALL/VALS...POLICY OBS RECORD BIOG TIME/SEQ TREND. PAGE 139 A2852
MOD/EUR DIPLOM FRANCE

B22
WALSH E.,THE HISTORY AND NATURE OF INTERNATIONAL RELATIONS. ASIA L/A+17C MOD/EUR USA-45 WOR-45 NAT/G FORCES TOP/EX BAL/PWR REGION ATTIT ORD/FREE RESPECT ...CONCPT HIST/WRIT TREND. PAGE 161 A3270
INT/ORG TIME/SEQ DIPLOM

C25
MOON P.T.,"SYLLABUS ON INTERNATIONAL RELATIONS." EUR+WWI MOD/EUR USA-45 FORCES COLONIAL WAR WEAPON NAT/LISM...POLICY BIBLIOG T 19/20. PAGE 103 A2120
INT/ORG DIPLOM NAT/G

B27
BRANDENBURG E.,FROM BISMARCK TO THE WORLD WAR; A HISTORY OF GERMAN FOREIGN POLICY, 1870-1914 (TRANS. BY ANNIE ELIZABETH ADAMS). GERMANY MOD/EUR FORCES AGREE PWR 19/20 TREATY CHAMBRLN/J WWI BISMARCK/O. PAGE 18 A0368
DIPLOM POLICY WAR

B27
GOOCH G.P.,ENGLISH DEMOCRATIC IDEAS IN THE SEVENTEENTH CENTURY (2ND ED.). UK LAW SECT FORCES DIPLOM LEAD PARL/PROC REV ATTIT AUTHORIT...ANARCH CONCPT 17 PARLIAMENT CMN/WLTH REFORMERS. PAGE 54 A1100
IDEA/COMP MAJORIT EX/STRUC CONSERVE

B28
CORBETT P.E.,CANADA AND WORLD POLITICS. LAW CULTURE SOCIETY STRUCT MARKET INT/ORG FORCES ACT/RES PLAN ECO/TAC LEGIT ORD/FREE PWR RESPECT...SOC CONCPT TIME/SEQ TREND CMN/WLTH 20 LEAGUE/NAT. PAGE 30 A0612
NAT/G CANADA

B28
HOWARD-ELLIS C.,THE ORIGIN, STRUCTURE AND WORKING OF THE LEAGUE OF NATIONS. EUR+WWI MOD/EUR USA-45 CONSTN FORCES LEGIS ECO/TAC LEGIT COERCE ORD/FREE ...JURID SOC CONCPT LEAGUE/NAT 20 ILO ICJ. PAGE 68 A1401
INT/ORG ADJUD

B29
BUELL R.,INTERNATIONAL RELATIONS. WOR+45 WOR-45 CONSTN STRATA FORCES TOP/EX ADMIN ATTIT DRIVE SUPEGO MORAL ORD/FREE PWR SOVEREIGN...JURID SOC CONCPT 20. PAGE 21 A0428
INT/ORG BAL/PWR DIPLOM

B29
CONWELL-EVANS T.P.,THE LEAGUE COUNCIL IN ACTION. EUR+WWI TURKEY UK USSR WOR-45 INT/ORG FORCES JUDGE ECO/TAC EDU/PROP LEGIT ROUTINE ARMS/CONT COERCE ATTIT PWR...MAJORIT GEOG JURID CONCPT LEAGUE/NAT TOT/POP VAL/FREE TUNIS 20. PAGE 30 A0605
DELIB/GP INT/LAW

B29
LANGER W.L.,THE FRANCO-RUSSIAN ALLIANCE: 1890-1894. FRANCE MOD/EUR UK USSR NAT/G CHIEF FORCES BAL/PWR AGREE WAR PEACE PWR...TIME/SEQ TREATY 19 BISMARCK/O. PAGE 84 A1724
DIPLOM

B30
BYNKERSHOEK C.,QUAESTIONUM JURIS PUBLICI LIBRI DUO. CHRIST-17C MOD/EUR CONSTN ELITES SOCIETY NAT/G PROVS EX/STRUC FORCES TOP/EX BAL/PWR DIPLOM ATTIT MORAL...TRADIT CONCPT. PAGE 23 A0460
INT/ORG LAW NAT/LISM INT/LAW

B31
STOWELL E.C.,INTERNATIONAL LAW. FUT UNIV WOR-45 SOCIETY CONSULT EX/STRUC FORCES ACT/RES PLAN DIPLOM EDU/PROP LEGIT DISPL PWR SKILL...POLICY CONCPT OBS TREND TOT/POP 20. PAGE 139 A2839
INT/ORG ROUTINE INT/LAW

B32
BLUM L.,PEACE AND DISARMAMENT (TRANS. BY A. WERTH). NAT/G FORCES WORKER DIPLOM AGREE WAR ATTIT AUTHORIT ORD/FREE. PAGE 16 A0322
SOCIALIST PEACE INT/ORG ARMS/CONT

C32
MARRARO H.R.,"AMERICAN OPINION ON THE UNIFICATION OF ITALY." ITALY MOD/EUR USA-45 FORCES DIPLOM PRESS REV CATHISM...BIOG 19 PRESIDENT. PAGE 95 A1944
BIBLIOG/A NAT/LISM ATTIT ORD/FREE

B33
AMERICAN FOREIGN LAW ASSN,BIOGRAPHICAL NOTES ON THE LAWS AND LEGAL LITERATURE OF URUGUAY AND CURACAO. URUGUAY CONSTN FINAN SECT FORCES JUDGE DIPLOM INT/TRADE ADJUD CT/SYS CRIME 20. PAGE 7 A0147
BIBLIOG/A LAW JURID ADMIN

B33
GENTILI A.,DE JURE BELLI, LIBRI TRES (1612) (VOL. 2). FORCES DIPLOM AGREE PEACE SOVEREIGN. PAGE 52 A1059
WAR INT/LAW MORAL SUPEGO

B33
LAUTERPACHT H.,THE FUNCTION OF LAW IN THE INTERNATIONAL COMMUNITY. WOR-45 NAT/G FORCES CREATE DOMIN LEGIT COERCE WAR PEACE ATTIT ORD/FREE PWR SOVEREIGN...JURID CONCPT METH/CNCPT TIME/SEQ GEN/LAWS GEN/METH LEAGUE/NAT TOT/POP VAL/FREE 20. PAGE 85 A1749
INT/ORG LAW INT/LAW

B34
EINSTEIN A.,THE WORLD AS I SEE IT. WOR-45 INTELL R+D INT/ORG NAT/G SECT VOL/ASSN FORCES CREATE EDU/PROP LEGIT ARMS/CONT WAR WEAPON NAT/LISM ALL/VALS...POLICY CONCPT 20. PAGE 41 A0828
SOCIETY PHIL/SCI DIPLOM PACIFISM

B35
FOREIGN AFFAIRS BIBLIOGRAPHY: A SELECTED AND ANNOTATED LIST OF BOOKS ON INTERNATIONAL RELATIONS 1919-1962 (4 VOLS.). CONSTN FORCES COLONIAL ARMS/CONT WAR NAT/LISM PEACE ATTIT DRIVE...POLICY INT/LAW 20. PAGE 3 A0050
BIBLIOG/A DIPLOM INT/ORG

B35
WEINBERG A.K.,MANIFEST DESTINY: A STUDY OF NATIONALIST EXPANSIONISM IN AMERICAN HISTORY. USA+45 USA-45 FORCES DIPLOM COLONIAL WAR ATTIT 18/20 INTERVENT. PAGE 162 A3305
NAT/LISM GEOG COERCE NAT/G

B36
METZ I.,DIE DEUTSCHE FLOTTE IN DER ENGLISCHEN PRESSE, DER NAVY SCARE VOM WINTER 1904/05. GERMANY UK FORCES DIPLOM WAR 20 NAVY. PAGE 100 A2047
EDU/PROP ATTIT DOMIN PRESS

B36
ROBINSON H.,DEVELOPMENT OF THE BRITISH EMPIRE. WOR-45 CULTURE SOCIETY STRUCT ECO/DEV ECO/UNDEV INT/ORG VOL/ASSN FORCES CREATE PLAN DOMIN EDU/PROP ADMIN COLONIAL PWR WEALTH...POLICY GEOG CHARTS CMN/WLTH 16/20. PAGE 122 A2503
NAT/G HIST/WRIT UK

B37
BOURNE H.E.,THE WORLD WAR: A LIST OF THE MORE IMPORTANT BOOKS PUBLISHED BEFORE 1937 (PAMPHLET). EUR+WWI NAT/G DIPLOM ATTIT SOC. PAGE 17 A0351
BIBLIOG/A WAR FORCES PLAN

B37
UNION OF SOUTH AFRICA,REPORT CONCERNING ADMINISTRATION OF SOUTH WEST AFRICA (6 VOLS.). SOUTH/AFR INDUS PUB/INST FORCES LEGIS BUDGET DIPLOM EDU/PROP ADJUD CT/SYS...GEOG CHARTS 20 AFRICA/SW LEAGUE/NAT. PAGE 148 A3028
NAT/G ADMIN COLONIAL CONSTN

B38
SAINT-PIERRE C.I.,SCHEME FOR LASTING PEACE (TRANS. BY H. BELLOT). INDUS NAT/G CHIEF FORCES INT/TRADE CT/SYS WAR PWR SOVEREIGN WEALTH...POLICY 18. PAGE 126 A2587
INT/ORG PEACE AGREE INT/LAW

B39
DULLES J.,WAR, PEACE AND CHANGE. FRANCE ITALY UK USA-45 WOR-45 LAW INT/ORG NAT/G SECT VOL/ASSN FORCES TOP/EX DOMIN ARMS/CONT COERCE ATTIT PERSON RIGID/FLEX MORAL PWR...JURID STERTYP TOT/POP LEAGUE/NAT 20. PAGE 39 A0796
EDU/PROP TOTALISM WAR

B39
FULLER G.H.,A SELECTED LIST OF REFERENCES ON THE EXPANSION OF THE US NAVY, 1933-1939 (PAMPHLET). MOD/EUR USA-45 NAT/G PLAN DIPLOM DOMIN RISK ARMS/CONT EQUILIB PWR 20 NAVY. PAGE 50 A1019
BIBLIOG FORCES WEAPON WAR

B39
KOHN H.,REVOLUTIONS AND DICTATORSHIPS. COM EUR+WWI ISLAM MOD/EUR NAT/G CHIEF FORCES WAR CIVMIL/REL PWR MARXISM 18/20. PAGE 81 A1661
NAT/LISM TOTALISM REV FASCISM

B39
SPEIER H.,WAR IN OUR TIME. WOR-45 AGRI FINAN FORCES TEC/DEV BAL/PWR EDU/PROP WEAPON PEACE PWR...ANTHOL 20. PAGE 136 A2779
FASCISM WAR DIPLOM NAT/G

B39
TAGGART F.J.,ROME AND CHINA. MEDIT-7 INT/ORG NAT/G FORCES LEGIS TOP/EX PLAN PWR SOVEREIGN...CHARTS TOT/POP ROM/EMP. PAGE 141 A2883
ASIA WAR

C39
REISCHAUER R.,"JAPAN'S GOVERNMENT--POLITICS." CONSTN STRATA POL/PAR FORCES LEGIS DIPLOM ADMIN EXEC CENTRAL...POLICY BIBLIOG 20 CHINJAP. PAGE 120 A2462
NAT/G S/ASIA CONCPT ROUTINE

B40
CONOVER H.F.,A BRIEF LIST OF REFERENCES ON WESTERN HEMISPHERE DEFENSE (PAMPHLET). USA-45 NAT/G CONSULT DELIB/GP FORCES BAL/PWR CONFER DETER...PREDICT CON/ANAL 20. PAGE 29 A0591
BIBLIOG DIPLOM PLAN INT/ORG

B40
CONOVER H.F.,JAPAN-ECONOMIC DEVELOPMENT AND FOREIGN POLICY, A SELECTED LIST OF REFERENCES (PAMPHLET). CULTURE FINAN INDUS NAT/G FORCES INT/TRADE WAR ...SOC TREND 20 CHINJAP. PAGE 29 A0593
BIBLIOG ASIA ECO/DEV DIPLOM

B40
NAFZIGER R.O.,INTERNATIONAL NEWS AND THE PRESS: COMMUNICATIONS, ORGANIZATION OF NEWS-GATHERING INTERNATIONAL AFFAIRS AND FOREIGN... COM/IND FORCES WAR ATTIT...POLICY 20. PAGE 107 A2191
BIBLIOG/A PRESS DIPLOM EDU/PROP

C40
FAHS C.B.,"GOVERNMENT IN JAPAN." FINAN FORCES LEGIS TOP/EX BUDGET INT/TRADE EDU/PROP SOVEREIGN ...CON/ANAL BIBLIOG/A 20 CHINJAP. PAGE 43 A0884
ASIA DIPLOM NAT/G ADMIN

B41
BIRDSALL P.,VERSAILLES TWENTY YEARS AFTER. MOD/EUR
DIPLOM

POL/PAR CHIEF CONSULT FORCES LEGIS REPAR PEACE ORD/FREE...BIBLIOG 20 PRESIDENT TREATY. PAGE 14 A0290
NAT/LISM WAR

B41
SCHWARZENBERGER G.,POWER POLITICS: AN INTRODUCTION TO THE STUDY OF INTERNATIONAL RELATIONS AND POST-WAR PLANNING. INT/ORG FORCES COERCE WAR FEDERAL PEACE MORAL...POLICY CONCPT CON/ANAL BIBLIOG 20. PAGE 130 A2660
DIPLOM UTOPIA PWR

S41
LASSWELL H.D.,"THE GARRISON STATE" (BMR)" FUT WOR+45 ELITES INTELL FORCES ECO/TAC DOMIN EDU/PROP COERCE INGP/REL 20. PAGE 85 A1739
NAT/G DIPLOM PWR CIVMIL/REL

S41
WRIGHT Q.,"FUNDAMENTAL PROBLEMS OF INTERNATIONAL ORGANIZATION." UNIV WOR-45 STRUCT FORCES ACT/RES CREATE DOMIN EDU/PROP LEGIT REGION NAT/LISM ORD/FREE PWR RESPECT SOVEREIGN...JURID SOC CONCPT METH/CNCPT TIME/SEQ 20. PAGE 167 A3405
INT/ORG ATTIT PEACE

B42
CONOVER H.F.,FRENCH COLONIES IN AFRICA: A LIST OF REFERENCES. ALGERIA FRANCE MOROCCO SOMALIA SUDAN CULTURE AGRI LOC/G SECT FORCES DIPLOM INT/TRADE NAT/LISM HEALTH...CON/ANAL 20. PAGE 29 A0594
BIBLIOG AFR ECO/UNDEV COLONIAL

B42
CONOVER H.F.,NEW ZEALAND: A SELECTED LIST OF REFERENCES (PAMPHLET). NEW/ZEALND ECO/UNDEV AGRI INDUS LABOR NAT/G SCHOOL FORCES DIPLOM COLONIAL WAR ...HUM 20. PAGE 29 A0595
BIBLIOG/A S/ASIA CULTURE

B42
CORBETT P.E.,POST WAR WORLDS. ASIA EUR+WWI FUT S/ASIA USA-45 ECO/DEV ECO/UNDEV NAT/G DELIB/GP FORCES PLAN ROUTINE ATTIT PWR 20. PAGE 30 A0613
WOR-45 INT/ORG

B42
CROWE S.E.,THE BERLIN WEST AFRICA CONFERENCE, 1884-85. GERMANY ELITES MARKET INT/ORG DELIB/GP FORCES PROB/SOLV BAL/PWR CAP/ISM DOMIN COLONIAL ...INT/LAW 19. PAGE 33 A0664
AFR CONFER INT/TRADE DIPLOM

B42
FULLER G.H.,DEFENSE FINANCING: A SUPPLEMENTARY LIST OF REFERENCES (PAMPHLET). CANADA UK USA-45 ECO/DEV NAT/G DELIB/GP BUDGET ADJUD ARMS/CONT WEAPON COST PEACE PWR 20 AUSTRAL CHINJAP CONGRESS. PAGE 50 A1021
BIBLIOG/A FINAN FORCES DIPLOM

B42
FULLER G.H.,AUSTRALIA: A SELECT LIST OF REFERENCES. FORCES DIPLOM WAR 20 AUSTRAL. PAGE 50 A1022
BIBLIOG SOC

B42
JACKSON M.V.,EUROPEAN POWERS AND SOUTH-EAST AFRICA: A STUDY OF INTERNATIONAL RELATIONS ON SOUTH-EAST COAST OF AFRICA, 1796-1856. AFR FRANCE PORTUGAL SOUTH/AFR UK USA-45 FORCES INT/TRADE PWR...CHARTS BIBLIOG 18/19 TREATY. PAGE 72 A1477
DOMIN POLICY ORD/FREE DIPLOM

B43
US DEPARTMENT OF STATE,NATIONAL SOCIALISM; BASIC PRINCIPLES, THEIR APPLICATION BY THE NAZI PARTY'S FOREIGN ORGANIZATION... GERMANY WOR-45 ECO/DEV LOC/G POL/PAR FORCES DIPLOM DOMIN COLONIAL ARMS/CONT COERCE NAT/LISM PWR 20 NAZI. PAGE 151 A3081
FASCISM SOCISM NAT/G TOTALISM

B44
BRIERLY J.L.,THE OUTLOOK FOR INTERNATIONAL LAW. FUT WOR-45 CONSTN NAT/G VOL/ASSN FORCES ECO/TAC DOMIN LEGIT ADJUD ROUTINE PEACE ORD/FREE...INT/LAW JURID METH LEAGUE/NAT 20. PAGE 18 A0376
INT/ORG LAW

B44
COMM. STUDY ORGAN. PEACE,UNITED NATIONS GUARDS AND TECHNICAL FIELD SERVICES. WOR+45 DELIB/GP EDU/PROP DRIVE PWR SKILL...CONCPT GEN/LAWS UN TOT/POP 20. PAGE 28 A0576
INT/ORG FORCES PEACE

B44
FULLER G.H.,MILITARY GOVERNMENT: A LIST OF REFERENCES (A PAMPHLET). ITALY UK USA-45 WOR-45 LAW FORCES DOMIN ADMIN ARMS/CONT ORD/FREE PWR ...DECISION 20 CHINJAP. PAGE 50 A1023
BIBLIOG DIPLOM CIVMIL/REL SOVEREIGN

B44
MATTHEWS M.A.,INTERNATIONAL POLICE (PAMPHLET). WOR-45 DIPLOM ARMS/CONT WAR 20. PAGE 96 A1977
BIBLIOG INT/ORG FORCES PEACE

B44
RUDIN H.R.,ARMISTICE 1918. FRANCE GERMANY MOD/EUR UK USA-45 NAT/G CHIEF DELIB/GP FORCES BAL/PWR REPAR ARMS/CONT 20 WILSON/W TREATY. PAGE 125 A2566
AGREE WAR PEACE DIPLOM

S44
WRIGHT Q.,"CONSTITUTIONAL PROCEDURES OF THE US FOR CARRYING OUT OBLIGATIONS FOR MILITARY SANCTIONS." EUR+WWI FUT USA-45 WOR-45 CONSTN INTELL NAT/G CONSULT EX/STRUC LEGIS ROUTINE DRIVE...POLICY JURID CONCPT OBS TREND TOT/POP 20. PAGE 167 A3406
TOP/EX FORCES INT/LAW WAR

B45
BEVERIDGE W.,THE PRICE OF PEACE. GERMANY UK WOR+45 WOR-45 NAT/G FORCES CREATE LEGIT REGION WAR ATTIT KNOWL ORD/FREE PWR...POLICY NEW/IDEA GEN/LAWS LEAGUE/NAT 20 TREATY. PAGE 14 A0284
INT/ORG TREND PEACE

B45
CONOVER H.F.,THE GOVERNMENTS OF THE MAJOR FOREIGN POWERS: A BIBLIOGRAPHY. FRANCE GERMANY ITALY UK USSR CONSTN LOC/G POL/PAR EX/STRUC FORCES ADMIN CT/SYS CIVMIL/REL TOTALISM...POLICY 19/20. PAGE 29 A0598
BIBLIOG NAT/G DIPLOM

B45
CONOVER H.F.,ITALY: ECONOMICS, POLITICS AND MILITARY AFFAIRS, 1940-1945. ITALY ELITES NAT/G POL/PAR EX/STRUC TOP/EX DIPLOM DOMIN CONTROL COERCE WAR CIVMIL/REL EFFICIENCY 20. PAGE 29 A0599
BIBLIOG TOTALISM FORCES

B45
CONOVER H.F.,THE NAZI STATE: WAR CRIMES AND WAR CRIMINALS. GERMANY CULTURE NAT/G SECT FORCES DIPLOM INT/TRADE EDU/PROP...INT/LAW BIOG HIST/WRIT TIME/SEQ 20. PAGE 30 A0600
BIBLIOG WAR CRIME

B45
STRAUSZ-HUPE R.,THE BALANCE OF TOMORROW: POWER AND FOREIGN POLICY IN THE UNITED STATES. FUT USA+45 ECO/DEV EXTR/IND INT/ORG FORCES BAL/PWR REGION NUC/PWR...GEOG CHARTS 20 COLD/WAR EUROPE/W. PAGE 139 A2845
DIPLOM PWR POLICY WAR

B45
VANCE H.L.,GUIDE TO THE LAW AND LEGAL LITERATURE OF MEXICO. LAW CONSTN FINAN LABOR FORCES ADJUD ADMIN ...CRIMLGY PHIL/SCI CON/ANAL 20 MEXIC/AMER. PAGE 158 A3217
BIBLIOG/A INT/LAW JURID CT/SYS

B46
KEETON G.W.,MAKING INTERNATIONAL LAW WORK. FUT WOR-45 NAT/G DELIB/GP FORCES LEGIT COERCE PEACE ATTIT RIGID/FLEX ORD/FREE PWR...JURID CONCPT HIST/WRIT GEN/METH LEAGUE/NAT 20. PAGE 77 A1578
INT/ORG ADJUD INT/LAW

S46
SILBERNER E.,"THE PROBLEM OF WAR IN NINETEENTH CENTURY ECONOMIC THOUGHT." EUR+WWI MOD/EUR UNIV LAW ECO/DEV ECO/UNDEV FINAN INDUS MARKET INT/ORG NAT/G CONSULT FORCES...CONCPT GEN/LAWS GEN/METH 19. PAGE 133 A2715
ATTIT ECO/TAC WAR

B47
BORGESE G.,COMMON CAUSE. LAW CONSTN SOCIETY STRATA ECO/DEV INT/ORG POL/PAR FORCES LEGIS TOP/EX CAP/ISM DIPLOM ADMIN EXEC ATTIT PWR 20. PAGE 17 A0339
WOR+45 NAT/G SOVEREIGN REGION

B47
BROOKINGS INST.,MAJOR PROBLEMS OF UNITED STATES FOREIGN POLICY. USA+45 WOR+45 STRUCT ECO/DEV ECO/UNDEV INT/ORG NAT/G POL/PAR VOL/ASSN DELIB/GP FORCES ECO/TAC LEGIT COERCE ORD/FREE PWR WEALTH ...POLICY STAT TREND CHARTS TOT/POP. PAGE 19 A0392
ACT/RES DIPLOM

B47
GORDON D.L.,THE HIDDEN WEAPON: THE STORY OF ECONOMIC WARFARE. EUR+WWI USA-45 LAW FINAN INDUS NAT/G CONSULT FORCES PLAN DOMIN PWR WEALTH ...INT/LAW CONCPT OBS TOT/POP NAZI 20. PAGE 54 A1112
INT/ORG ECO/TAC INT/TRADE WAR

B47
HEIMANN E.,FREEDOM AND ORDER: LESSONS FROM THE WAR. WOR-45 CONSTN FORCES CHOOSE CIVMIL/REL PERSON ALL/IDEOS SOCISM...SOC IDEA/COMP WORSHIP 20. PAGE 64 A1308
NAT/G SOCIETY ORD/FREE DIPLOM

N47
FOX W.T.R.,UNITED STATES POLICY IN A TWO POWER WORLD. COM USA+45 USSR FORCES DOMIN AGREE NEUTRAL NUC/PWR ORD/FREE SOVEREIGN 20 COLD/WAR TREATY EUROPE/W INTERVENT. PAGE 48 A0972
DIPLOM FOR/AID POLICY

B48
CHURCHILL W.,THE GATHERING STORM. UK WOR-45 INT/ORG NAT/G FORCES TOP/EX DIPLOM ECO/TAC COERCE ATTIT ORD/FREE PWR WEALTH...POLICY SELF/OBS RECORD NAZI PARLIAMENT 20. PAGE 26 A0538
BIOG

B48
GRIFFITH E.S.,RESEARCH IN POLITICAL SCIENCE: THE WORK OF PANELS OF RESEARCH COMMITTEE, APSA. WOR+45 WOR-45 COM/IND R+D FORCES ACT/RES WAR...GOV/COMP ANTHOL 20. PAGE 56 A1160
BIBLIOG PHIL/SCI DIPLOM JURID

B48
NAMIER L.B.,DIPLOMATIC PRELUDE 1938-1939. CZECHOSLVK EUR+WWI GERMANY POLAND UK FORCES DOMIN PWR 20 HITLER/A. PAGE 107 A2193
WAR TOTALISM DIPLOM

C49
YANAGA C.,"JAPAN SINCE PERRY." S/ASIA CULTURE ECO/DEV FORCES WAR 19/20 CHINJAP. PAGE 168 A3430
DIPLOM POL/PAR CIVMIL/REL NAT/LISM

B50
BERLE A.A.,NATURAL SELECTION OF POLITICAL FORCES. FUT WOR+45 WOR-45 CULTURE SOCIETY INT/ORG NAT/G FORCES EDU/PROP LEGIT COERCE...CONCPT HIST/WRIT TREND 20. PAGE 13 A0274
POL/PAR BAL/PWR DIPLOM

B50
CHURCHILL W.,TRIUMPH AND TRAGEDY. UK WOR-45 INT/ORG NAT/G DELIB/GP FORCES TOP/EX DIPLOM COERCE CHOOSE ATTIT ORD/FREE PWR WEALTH...SELF/OBS CHARTS NAZI 20. PAGE 26 A0539
BIOG PEACE WAR

B50
DE RUSETT A.,STRENGTHENING THE FRAMEWORK OF PEACE. WOR+45 VOL/ASSN FORCES CREATE INSPECT ADJUD CONTROL WAR EQUILIB FEDERAL ORD/FREE 20 UN EUROPE. PAGE 35 A0711
INT/ORG DIPLOM PEACE METH/COMP

B50
DULLES J.F.,WAR OR PEACE. CHINA/COM USA+45 USSR INT/ORG SECT FORCES PLAN NUC/PWR WAR CENTRAL MARXISM...POLICY 20 UN ROOSEVLT/F STALIN/J. PAGE 39 A0797
PEACE DIPLOM TREND ORD/FREE

B50
FEIS H.,THE ROAD TO PEARL HARBOR. USA-45 WOR-45 SOCIETY NAT/G FORCES WAR ORD/FREE 20 CHINJAP TREATY. PAGE 44 A0909
DIPLOM POLICY ATTIT

B50
GATZKE H.W.,GERMANY'S DRIVE TO THE WEST. BELGIUM GERMANY MOD/EUR AGRI INDUS POL/PAR FORCES DOMIN AGREE CONTROL REGION COERCE 20 TREATY WWI. PAGE 51 A1053
WAR POLICY NAT/G DIPLOM

B50
LINCOLN G.,ECONOMICS OF NATIONAL SECURITY. USA+45 ELITES COM/IND DIST/IND INDUS NAT/G VOL/ASSN DELIB/GP EX/STRUC FOR/AID EDU/PROP COERCE NUC/PWR WAR ATTIT KNOWL ORD/FREE PWR COLD/WAR TOT/POP VAL/FREE 20. PAGE 89 A1818
FORCES ECO/TAC

B51
LEONARD L.L.,INTERNATIONAL ORGANIZATION. WOR+45 WOR-45 EX/STRUC FORCES LEGIS ECO/TAC INT/TRADE COLONIAL ARMS/CONT...SOC/WK GOV/COMP BIBLIOG. PAGE 87 A1778
NAT/G DIPLOM INT/ORG DELIB/GP

B51
US HOUSE COMM APPROPRIATIONS,MUTUAL SECURITY PROGRAM APPROPRIATIONS FOR 1952: HEARINGS BEFORE A SUBCOMMITTEE OF THE COMMITTEE ON APPROPRIATIONS. KOREA L/A+17C ECO/DEV ECO/UNDEV INT/ORG INSPECT BAL/PWR DIPLOM DEBATE WAR...POLICY STAT ASIA/S 20 CONGRESS NATO COLD/WAR MID/EAST. PAGE 153 A3118
LEGIS FORCES BUDGET FOR/AID

L51
WHITAKER A.P.,"DEVELOPMENT OF AMERICAN REGIONALISM: THE ORGANIZATION OF AMERICAN STATES." L/A+17C USA+45 VOL/ASSN DELIB/GP FORCES TOP/EX ACT/RES ECO/TAC CT/SYS REGION PEACE ALL/VALS OAS 20. PAGE 163 A3330
INT/ORG TIME/SEQ DETER

S51
CONNERY R.H.,"THE MUTUAL DEFENSE ASSISTANCE PROGRAM." COM EUR+WWI KOREA USA+45 NAT/G VOL/ASSN CREATE PLAN BAL/PWR EDU/PROP PERCEPT...POLICY DECISION CONCPT NATO 20. PAGE 29 A0587
INT/ORG FORCES FOR/AID

B52
ALBERTINI L.,THE ORIGINS OF THE WAR OF 1914 (3 VOLS.). AUSTRIA FRANCE GERMANY MOD/EUR RUSSIA UK PROB/SOLV NEUTRAL PWR...BIBLIOG 19/20. PAGE 5 A0107
WAR DIPLOM FORCES BAL/PWR

B52
BARR S.,CITIZENS OF THE WORLD. USA+45 WOR+45 CULTURE FORCES LEGIS ACT/RES BAL/PWR LEGIT PEACE ATTIT ORD/FREE PWR...PLURIST CONCPT OBS TIME/SEQ COLD/WAR 20. PAGE 11 A0227
NAT/G INT/ORG DIPLOM

B52
FERRELL R.H.,PEACE IN THEIR TIME. FRANCE UK USA-45 INT/ORG NAT/G FORCES CREATE AGREE ARMS/CONT COERCE WAR TREATY 20 WILSON/W LEAGUE/NAT BRIAND/A. PAGE 45 A0920
PEACE DIPLOM

B52
MACARTHUR D.,REVITALIZING A NATION. ASIA COM FUT KOREA WOR+45 NAT/G FOR/AID TAX GIVE WAR ATTIT SOCISM 20 CHINJAP EUROPE. PAGE 92 A1885
LEAD FORCES TOP/EX POLICY

B52
MANTOUX E.,THE CARTHAGINIAN PEACE. GERMANY WOR-45 SOCIETY FINAN INT/ORG DELIB/GP FORCES PLAN LEGIT ...CONCPT TIME/SEQ 20 KEYNES/JM HITLER/A. PAGE 94 A1935
ECO/DEV INT/TRADE WAR

B52
RIGGS F.W.,FORMOSA UNDER CHINESE NATIONALIST RULE. CHINA/COM USA+45 CONSTN AGRI FINAN LABOR LOC/G NAT/G POL/PAR FORCES HEALTH KNOWL...STAT WORK VAL/FREE 20. PAGE 121 A2479
ASIA FOR/AID DIPLOM

B52
SMITH C.M.,INTERNATIONAL COMMUNICATION AND POLITICAL WARFARE: AN ANNOTATED BIBLIOGRAPHY (A PAPER). WOR+45 INTELL R+D NAT/G FORCES ACT/RES DIPLOM COERCE ALL/IDEOS. PAGE 134 A2745
BIBLIOG/A EDU/PROP WAR COM/IND

B52
SPENCER F.A.,WAR AND POSTWAR GREECE: AN ANALYSIS BASED ON GREEK WRITINGS. GREECE SOCIETY NAT/G POL/PAR FORCES CREATE DIPLOM LEAD MARXISM...SOC 20. PAGE 136 A2784
BIBLIOG/A WAR REV

B53
BRETTON H.L.,STRESEMANN AND THE REVISION OF VERSAILLES: A FIGHT FOR REASON. EUR+WWI GERMANY FORCES BUDGET ARMS/CONT WAR SUPEGO...BIBLIOG 20 TREATY VERSAILLES STRESEMN/G. PAGE 18 A0373
POLICY DIPLOM BIOG

B53
FEIS H.,THE CHINA TANGLE. ASIA COM USA+45 USA-45 FORCES ECO/TAC REV ATTIT 20 INTERVENT. PAGE 45 A0910
POLICY DIPLOM WAR FOR/AID

B53
LANGER W.L.,THE UNDECLARED WAR, 1940-1941. EUR+WWI GERMANY USA-45 USSR AIR FORCES TEC/DEV CONFER CONTROL COERCE PERCEPT ORD/FREE PWR 20 CHINJAP EUROPE. PAGE 84 A1727
WAR POLICY DIPLOM

B53
MANSERGH N.,DOCUMENTS AND SPEECHES ON BRITISH COMMONWEALTH AFFAIRS 1931-1952. INDIA IRELAND PAKISTAN UK CONSTN POL/PAR CHIEF FORCES COLONIAL ORD/FREE SOVEREIGN...JURID 20 COMMONWLTH. PAGE 94 A1929
BIBLIOG/A DIPLOM ECO/TAC

B53
MATLOFF M.,STRATEGIC PLANNING FOR COALITION WARFARE. UK USA-45 CHIEF DIPLOM EXEC GOV/REL ...METH/COMP 20. PAGE 96 A1967
WAR PLAN DECISION FORCES

B53
MCNEILL W.H.,AMERICA, BRITAIN, AND RUSSIA; THEIR COOPERATION AND CONFLICT. UK USA-45 USSR ECO/DEV ECO/UNDEV FORCES PLAN ADMIN AGREE PERS/REL ...DECISION 20 TREATY. PAGE 98 A2021
WAR DIPLOM DOMIN

B53
SHIRATO I.,JAPANESE SOURCES ON THE HISTORY OF THE CHINESE COMMUNIST MOVEMENT (PAMPHLET). CHINA/COM USSR CONSTRUC NAT/G POL/PAR FORCES DIPLOM DOMIN EDU/PROP CONTROL WAR TOTALISM SOCISM 20. PAGE 132 A2702
BIBLIOG/A MARXISM ECO/UNDEV

S53
LINCOLN G.,"FACTORS DETERMINING ARMS AID." COM FUT USA+45 USSR WOR+45 ECO/DEV NAT/G CONSULT PLAN TEC/DEV DIPLOM DOMIN EDU/PROP PERCEPT PWR ...DECISION CONCPT TREND MARX/KARL 20. PAGE 89 A1819
FORCES POLICY BAL/PWR FOR/AID

B54
ARON R.,CENTURY OF TOTAL WAR. FUT WOR+45 WOR-45 SOCIETY INT/ORG NAT/G FORCES TOP/EX CREATE BAL/PWR DOMIN EDU/PROP COERCE DETER PEACE TOTALISM PWR ...TIME/SEQ TREND COLD/WAR TOT/POP VAL/FREE LEAGUE/NAT 20. PAGE 9 A0179
ATTIT WAR

B54
BUCHANAN W.,AN INTERNATIONAL POLICE FORCE AND PUBLIC OPINION IN THE UNITED STATES, 1939-1953. USA+45 PROB/SOLV CONTROL ATTIT ORD/FREE...STAT TREND 20. PAGE 21 A0425
IDEA/COMP FORCES DIPLOM PLAN

B54
BUTOW R.J.C.,JAPAN'S DECISION TO SURRENDER. USA-45 USSR CHIEF FORCES DOMIN NUC/PWR...BIBLIOG 20 TREATY CHINJAP. PAGE 22 A0453
ELITES DIPLOM WAR PEACE

B54
BUTZ O.,GERMANY: DILEMMA FOR AMERICAN POLICY. GERMANY USA+45 USA-45 USSR WOR+45 INT/ORG FORCES NUC/PWR EFFICIENCY PEACE PWR...GOV/COMP 20 COLD/WAR. PAGE 23 A0459
DIPLOM NAT/G WAR POLICY

B54
GERMANY FOREIGN MINISTRY,DOCUMENTS ON GERMAN FOREIGN POLICY 1918-1945, SERIES C (1933-1937) VOLS. I-V. GERMANY MOD/EUR FORCES PLAN ECO/TAC ...FASCIST CHARTS ANTHOL 20. PAGE 52 A1065
NAT/G DIPLOM POLICY

B54
NATION ASSOCIATES,SECURITY AND THE MIDDLE EAST - THE PROBLEM AND ITS SOLUTION. ISRAEL JORDAN LEBANON SYRIA UAR FORCES FOR/AID GP/REL NAT/LISM PEACE TOTALISM...POLICY 20. PAGE 107 A2198
DIPLOM ECO/UNDEV WAR PLAN

B54
REYNOLDS P.A.,BRITISH FOREIGN POLICY IN THE INTER-WAR YEARS. CZECHOSLVK GERMANY POLAND UK USA-45 POL/PAR FORCES ECO/TAC ARMS/CONT WAR ATTIT 20. PAGE 120 A2470
DIPLOM POLICY NAT/G

B54
TAYLOR A.J.P.,THE STRUGGLE FOR MASTERY IN EUROPE 1848-1918. MOD/EUR VOL/ASSN FORCES BAL/PWR DOMIN CONTROL PEACE MORAL 19/20 TREATY EUROPE WWI. PAGE 142 A2897
DIPLOM WAR PWR

B54
US DEPARTMENT OF STATE,PUBLICATIONS OF THE DEPARTMENT OF STATE, OCTOBER 1,1929 TO JANUARY 1, 1953. AGRI INT/ORG FORCES FOR/AID EDU/PROP ARMS/CONT NUC/PWR ATTIT 20 DEPT/STATE OAS UN NATO. PAGE 151 A3089
BIBLIOG DIPLOM

L54
CHARLESWORTH J.C.,"AMERICA AND A NEW ASIA." ASIA INDIA ISLAM S/ASIA USA+45 USA-45 ECO/UNDEV NAT/G POL/PAR FORCES FOR/AID DOMIN EDU/PROP COERCE DRIVE ALL/VALS MARXISM SOCISM TOT/POP 20. PAGE 26 A0522
ECO/TAC DIPLOM NAT/LISM

S54
FOX W.T.R.,"CIVIL-MILITARY RELATIONS." USA+45 USA-45 R+D ACT/RES DIPLOM INT/TRADE EDU/PROP DETER DISPL DRIVE ORD/FREE...METH/CNCPT TREND COLD/WAR 20. PAGE 48 A0974
POLICY FORCES PLAN SOCIETY

C54
BOWIE R.R.,"STUDIES IN FEDERALISM." AGRI FINAN LABOR EX/STRUC FORCES LEGIS DIPLOM INT/TRADE ADJUD ...BIBLIOG 20 EEC. PAGE 17 A0357
FEDERAL EUR+WWI INT/ORG

CONSTN

B55
COMM. STUDY ORGAN. PEACE,REPORTS. WOR-45 ECO/DEV WOR+45
ECO/UNDEV VOL/ASSN CONSULT FORCES PLAN TEC/DEV INT/ORG
DOMIN EDU/PROP NUC/PWR ATTIT PWR WEALTH...JURID ARMS/CONT
STERTYP FAO ILO 20 UN. PAGE 28 A0579

B55
CRAIG G.A.,THE POLITICS OF THE PRUSSIAN ARMY FORCES
1640-1945. CHRIST-17C EUR+WWI MOD/EUR PRUSSIA NAT/G
STRUCT DIPLOM ADMIN REV WAR...SOC BIBLIOG 17/20. ROLE
PAGE 32 A0652 CHIEF

B55
GULICK E.V.,EUROPE'S CLASSICAL BALANCE OF POWER: IDEA/COMP
CASE HISTORY OF THEORY AND PRACTICE OF GREAT BAL/PWR
CONCEPTS OF EUROPEAN STATECRAFT. MOD/EUR INT/ORG PWR
VOL/ASSN FORCES ORD/FREE 18/19 TREATY. PAGE 58 DIPLOM
A1192

B55
HOGAN W.N.,INTERNATIONAL CONFLICT AND COLLECTIVE INT/ORG
SECURITY: THE PRINCIPLE OF CONCERN IN INTERNATIONAL WAR
ORGANIZATION. CONSTN EX/STRUC BAL/PWR DIPLOM ADJUD ORD/FREE
CONTROL CENTRAL CONSEN PEACE...INT/LAW CONCPT FORCES
METH/COMP 20 UN LEAGUE/NAT. PAGE 66 A1361

B55
JOY C.T.,HOW COMMUNISTS NEGOTIATE. COM USA+45 ASIA
CONSTN CULTURE ECO/UNDEV NAT/G CONSULT DELIB/GP INT/ORG
FORCES PLAN ECO/TAC DOMIN EDU/PROP LEGIT EXEC DIPLOM
ROUTINE COERCE WAR CHOOSE PEACE ATTIT RIGID/FLEX
ORD/FREE PWR...POLICY 20. PAGE 75 A1539

B55
OECD,MARSHALL PLAN IN TURKEY. TURKEY USA+45 COM/IND FOR/AID
CONSTRUC SERV/IND FORCES BUDGET...STAT 20 ECO/UNDEV
MARSHL/PLN. PAGE 111 A2277 AGRI
INDUS

B55
PLISCHKE E.,AMERICAN FOREIGN RELATIONS: A BIBLIOG/A
BIBLIOGRAPHY OF OFFICIAL SOURCES. USA+45 USA-45 DIPLOM
INT/ORG FORCES PRESS WRITING DEBATE EXEC...POLICY NAT/G
INT/LAW 18/20 CONGRESS. PAGE 116 A2390

B55
TAN C.C.,THE BOXER CATASTROPHE. ASIA UK USSR ELITES REV
POL/PAR VOL/ASSN FORCES PROB/SOLV DIPLOM ADMIN NAT/G
COLONIAL NAT/LISM PEACE TREATY 19/20 BOXER/REBL. WAR
PAGE 141 A2885

B55
VIGON J.,TEORIA DEL MILITARISMO. NAT/G DIPLOM FORCES
COLONIAL COERCE GUERRILLA CIVMIL/REL NAT/LISM MORAL PHIL/SCI
ALL/IDEOS PACIFISM 18/20. PAGE 159 A3234 WAR
POLICY

B56
BLACKETT P.M.S.,ATOMIC WEAPONS AND EAST-WEST FORCES
RELATIONS. FUT WOR+45 INT/ORG DELIB/GP COERCE ATTIT PWR
RIGID/FLEX KNOWL...RELATIV HIST/WRIT TREND GEN/METH ARMS/CONT
COLD/WAR 20. PAGE 15 A0299 NUC/PWR

B56
CHANG C.J.,THE MINORITY GROUPS OF YUNN AN AND GP/REL
CHINESE POLITICAL EXPANSION INTO SOUTHEAST ASIA REGION
(DOCTORAL THESIS). ASIA CHINA/COM S/ASIA FORCES DOMIN
TEC/DEV DIPLOM EDU/PROP...GEOG BIBLIOG 20. PAGE 26 MARXISM
A0520

B56
ESTEP R.,AN AIR POWER BIBLIOGRAPHY. USA+45 TEC/DEV BIBLIOG/A
BUDGET DIPLOM EDU/PROP DETER CIVMIL/REL...DECISION FORCES
INT/LAW 20. PAGE 42 A0862 WEAPON
PLAN

B56
FOSTER J.G.,BRITAIN IN WESTERN EUROPE: WEU AND THE INT/ORG
ATLANTIC ALLIANCE. EUR+WWI FRANCE GERMANY GERMANY/W FORCES
ITALY UK STRATA NAT/G DELIB/GP ECO/TAC ORD/FREE PWR WEAPON
...TRADIT TIME/SEQ TREND OEEC PARLIAMENT 20
EUROPE/W. PAGE 47 A0969

B56
GREECE PRESBEIA U.S.,BRITISH OPINION ON CYPRUS. ATTIT
CYPRUS UK FORCES DIPLOM INT/TRADE DOMIN GOV/REL COLONIAL
ORD/FREE SOVEREIGN...POLICY 20. PAGE 55 A1137 LEGIS
PRESS

B56
HAAS E.B.,DYNAMICS OF INTERNATIONAL RELATIONS. WOR+45
WOR-45 ELITES INT/ORG VOL/ASSN EX/STRUC FORCES NAT/G
ECO/TAC DOMIN LEGIT COERCE ATTIT PERSON PWR DIPLOM
...CONCPT TIME/SEQ CHARTS COLD/WAR 20. PAGE 58
A1202

B56
ROBERTS H.L.,RUSSIA AND AMERICA. CHINA/COM S/ASIA DIPLOM
USSR FORCES TEC/DEV FOR/AID NUC/PWR ALL/IDEOS INT/ORG
...MAJORIT TREND NAT/COMP 20 COLD/WAR UN NATO. BAL/PWR
PAGE 122 A2494 TOTALISM

B56
SNELL J.L.,THE MEANING OF YALTA: BIG THREE CONFER
DIPLOMACY AND THE NEW BALANCE OF POWER. EUR+WWI CHIEF
GERMANY USA-45 USSR FORCES PLAN BAL/PWR DIPLOM WAR POLICY
CHOOSE PEACE...CHARTS BIBLIOG 20 UN CHINJAP PROB/SOLV
ROOSEVLT/F. PAGE 134 A2749

B56
WHITAKER A.P.,ARGENTINE UPHEAVAL. STRUCT FORCES REV
DIPLOM COERCE PWR 20 ARGEN. PAGE 164 A3332 POL/PAR

STRATA
NAT/G

B56
WILSON P.,GOVERNMENT AND POLITICS OF INDIA AND BIBLIOG
PAKISTAN: 1885-1955; A BIBLIOGRAPHY OF WORKS IN COLONIAL
WESTERN LANGUAGES. INDIA PAKISTAN CONSTN LOC/G NAT/G
POL/PAR FORCES DIPLOM ADMIN WAR CHOOSE...BIOG S/ASIA
CON/ANAL 19/20. PAGE 165 A3361

C56
DUPUY R.E.,"MILITARY HERITAGE OF AMERICA." USA+45 FORCES
USA-45 TEC/DEV DIPLOM ROUTINE...POLICY TREND CHARTS WAR
IDEA/COMP BIBLIOG COLD/WAR. PAGE 39 A0804 CONCPT

C56
VAGTS A.,"DEFENSE AND DIPLOMACY: THE SOLDIER AND DIPLOM
THE CONDUCT OF FOREIGN RELATIONS." OP/RES CONFER FORCES
DETER WAR PEACE RESPECT...POLICY DECISION CONCPT HIST/WRIT
BIBLIOG 17/20. PAGE 158 A3209

B57
ARON R.,FRANCE DEFEATS EDC. EUR+WWI GERMANY LEGIS INT/ORG
DIPLOM DOMIN EDU/PROP ADMIN...HIST/WRIT 20. PAGE 9 FORCES
A0180 DETER
FRANCE

B57
BLOOMFIELD L.M.,EGYPT, ISRAEL AND THE GULF OF ISLAM
AQABA: IN INTERNATIONAL LAW. LAW NAT/G CONSULT INT/LAW
FORCES PLAN ECO/TAC ROUTINE COERCE ATTIT DRIVE UAR
PERCEPT PERSON RIGID/FLEX LOVE PWR WEALTH...GEOG
CONCPT MYTH TREND. PAGE 15 A0314

B57
BROMBERGER M.,LES SECRETS DE L'EXPEDITION D'EGYPTE. COERCE
FRANCE ISLAM UAR UK USA+45 USSR WOR+45 INT/ORG DIPLOM
NAT/G FORCES BAL/PWR ECO/TAC DOMIN WAR NAT/LISM
ATTIT PWR SOVEREIGN...MAJORIT TIME/SEQ CHARTS SUEZ
COLD/WAR 20. PAGE 19 A0387

B57
COMM. STUDY ORGAN. PEACE,STRENGTHENING THE UNITED INT/ORG
NATIONS. FUT USA+45 WOR+45 CONSTN NAT/G DELIB/GP ORD/FREE
FORCES LEGIS ECO/TAC LEGIT COERCE PEACE...JURID
CONCPT UN COLD/WAR 20. PAGE 28 A0580

B57
DEUTSCH K.W.,POLITICAL COMMUNITY AND THE NORTH EUR+WWI
ATLANTIC AREA: INTERNATIONAL ORGANIZATION IN THE INT/ORG
LIGHT OF HISTORICAL EXPERIENCE. MOD/EUR USA+45 PEACE
USA-45 SOCIETY FORCES TOP/EX CREATE PLAN DIPLOM REGION
DOMIN EDU/PROP LEGIT ATTIT ORD/FREE PWR...SAMP/SIZ
TIME/SEQ CHARTS TOT/POP. PAGE 36 A0736

B57
FREUND G.,UNHOLY ALLIANCE. EUR+WWI GERMANY USSR DIPLOM
FORCES ECO/TAC CONTROL WAR PWR...TREND TREATY. PLAN
PAGE 49 A0999 POLICY

B57
FURNISS E.S.,AMERICAN MILITARY POLICY: STRATEGIC FORCES
ASPECTS OF WORLD POLITICAL GEOGRAPHY. COM EUR+WWI DIPLOM
ISLAM L/A+17C USA+45 WOR+45 INT/ORG ACT/RES
ARMS/CONT COERCE NUC/PWR ATTIT PWR...GEOG NEW/IDEA
VAL/FREE COLD/WAR 20. PAGE 50 A1027

B57
KENNAN G.F.,RUSSIA, THE ATOM AND THE WEST. COM NAT/G
EUR+WWI FUT WOR+45 SOCIETY ECO/DEV FORCES DIPLOM INT/ORG
ECO/TAC DOMIN EDU/PROP COERCE NUC/PWR ATTIT DRIVE USSR
ORD/FREE PWR...POLICY OBS TIME/SEQ TREND COLD/WAR
NATO 20. PAGE 77 A1574

B57
KISSINGER H.A.,NUCLEAR WEAPONS AND FOREIGN POLICY. PLAN
FUT USA+45 WOR+45 INT/ORG FORCES ACT/RES TEC/DEV DETER
DIPLOM ARMS/CONT COERCE ATTIT KNOWL PWR...DECISION NUC/PWR
GEOG CHARTS 20. PAGE 80 A1640

B57
LISKA G.,INTERNATIONAL EQUILIBRIUM. WOR+45 WOR-45 NAT/G
SOCIETY INT/ORG FORCES DETER ATTIT ORD/FREE PWR BAL/PWR
...GEN/LAWS 19/20. PAGE 90 A1836 REGION
DIPLOM

B57
NEHRU J.,MILITARY ALLIANCE (PAMPHLET). INDIA WOR+45 INT/ORG
NAT/G PLAN DETER NUC/PWR WAR...POLICY ANTHOL DIPLOM
NEHRU/J SEATO UN. PAGE 108 A2212 FORCES
PEACE

B57
REISS J.,GEORGE KENNANS POLITIK DER EINDAMMUNG. DIPLOM
USSR NAT/G FORCES TOTALISM ATTIT ORD/FREE...POLICY DETER
20 NATO TRUMAN/HS MARSHL/PLN KENNAN/G. PAGE 120 PEACE
A2463

B57
SPEIER H.,GERMAN REARMAMENT AND ATOMIC WAR: THE TOP/EX
VIEWS OF GERMAN MILITARY AND POLITICAL LEADERS. FUT FORCES
WOR+45 INT/ORG NAT/G WEAPON ATTIT PWR...INT QU NUC/PWR
TOT/POP VAL/FREE COLD/WAR 20. PAGE 136 A2780 GERMANY

B57
US PRES CITIZEN ADVISERS,REPORT TO THE PRESIDENT ON BAL/PWR
THE MUTUAL SECURITY PROGRAM. COM USA+45 WOR+45 FORCES
FINAN INDUS PLAN BUDGET CAP/ISM DIPLOM FOR/AID INT/ORG
INT/TRADE REGION 20 SECUR/PROG. PAGE 155 A3163 ECO/TAC

B57
US SENATE SPEC COMM FOR AID,HEARINGS BEFORE THE FOR/AID
SPECIAL COMMITTEE TO STUDY THE FOREIGN AID PROGRAM. DIPLOM
USA+45 USSR ECO/UNDEV INT/ORG FORCES WEAPON ORD/FREE

TOTALISM ATTIT SUPEGO...NAT/COMP CONGRESS. PAGE 157 A3198 TEC/DEV

L57
FURNISS E.S.,"SOME PERSPECTIVES ON AMERICAN MILITARY ASSISTANCE." USA+45 WOR+45 ECO/UNDEV INT/ORG ECO/TAC ORD/FREE...GEOG TIME/SEQ TREND COLD/WAR 20. PAGE 50 A1028 FORCES FOR/AID WEAPON

S57
HOAG M.W.,"ECONOMIC PROBLEMS OF ALLIANCE." COM EUR+WWI WOR+45 ECO/DEV ECO/UNDEV NAT/G VOL/ASSN FORCES PLAN TEC/DEV DIPLOM COERCE ORD/FREE PWR WEALTH...DECISION GEN/LAWS NATO COLD/WAR. PAGE 65 A1345 INT/ORG ECO/TAC

S57
SCHELLING T.C.,"BARGAINING COMMUNICATION, AND LIMITED WAR." UNIV WOR+45 FACE/GP INT/ORG NAT/G FORCES ACT/RES WAR PERCEPT ALL/VALS...PSY OBS PROJ/TEST CHARTS HYPO/EXP GEN/LAWS TOT/POP 20. PAGE 128 A2622 ROUTINE DECISION

S57
SPEIER H.,"SOVIET ATOMIC BLACKMAIL AND THE NORTH ATLANTIC ALLIANCE." EUR+WWI USA+45 USSR INT/ORG NAT/G FORCES DIPLOM DRIVE ORD/FREE PWR NATO VAL/FREE COLD/WAR 20. PAGE 136 A2781 COM COERCE NUC/PWR

S57
WRIGHT Q.,"THE VALUE OF CONFLICT RESOLUTION OF A GENERAL DISCIPLINE OF INTERNATIONAL RELATIONS." WOR+45 SOCIETY INT/ORG NAT/G FORCES TOP/EX PLAN TEC/DEV ECO/TAC DOMIN LEGIT COERCE ATTIT PWR ...GEN/METH COLD/WAR VAL/FREE. PAGE 168 A3412 ORD/FREE SOC DIPLOM

C57
TANG P.S.H.,"COMMUNIST CHINA TODAY: DOMESTIC AND FOREIGN POLICIES." CHINA/COM COM S/ASIA USSR STRATA FORCES DIPLOM EDU/PROP COERCE GOV/REL...POLICY MAJORIT BIBLIOG 20. PAGE 141 A2886 POL/PAR LEAD ADMIN CONSTN

B58
ANGELL N.,DEFENCE AND THE ENGLISH-SPEAKING ROLE. CHINA/COM UK USSR INT/ORG FORCES EDU/PROP NEUTRAL NUC/PWR NAT/LISM PEACE TOTALISM 20 COLD/WAR COEXIST. PAGE 8 A0161 DIPLOM WAR MARXISM ORD/FREE

B58
ARON R.,ON WAR: ATOMIC WEAPONS AND GLOBAL DIPLOMACY (TRANS. BY TERENCE KILMARTIN). WOR+45 SOCIETY FORCES BAL/PWR WAR WEAPON PERSON...SOC 20. PAGE 9 A0182 ARMS/CONT NUC/PWR COERCE DIPLOM

B58
CAMPBELL J.C.,DEFENSE OF THE MIDDLE EAST: PROBLEMS OF AMERICAN POLICY. ISLAM USA+45 INT/ORG NAT/G EX/STRUC FORCES ECO/TAC DOMIN EDU/PROP LEGIT REGION COERCE...METH/CNCPT COLD/WAR TOT/POP 20. PAGE 23 A0474 TOP/EX ORD/FREE DIPLOM

B58
CRAIG G.A.,FROM BISMARCK TO ADENAUER: ASPECTS OF GERMAN STATECRAFT. GERMANY INTELL FORCES ECO/TAC CONFER COERCE WAR GP/REL ORD/FREE PWR CONSERVE 19/20 BISMARCK/O ADENAUER/K. PAGE 32 A0653 DIPLOM LEAD NAT/G

B58
GARTHOFF R.L.,SOVIET STRATEGY IN THE NUCLEAR AGE. FUT USSR R+D INT/ORG NAT/G ACT/RES TEC/DEV DOMIN DETER WAR ATTIT PWR...RELATIV METH/CNCPT SELF/OBS TREND CON/ANAL STERTYP GEN/LAWS 20. PAGE 51 A1052 COM FORCES BAL/PWR NUC/PWR

B58
GAVIN J.M.,WAR AND PEACE IN THE SPACE AGE. SPACE USA+45 USSR FORCES PLAN TEC/DEV BAL/PWR DIPLOM ARMS/CONT WEAPON CIVMIL/REL...CHARTS GP/COMP 20 NATO COLD/WAR. PAGE 52 A1055 WAR DETER NUC/PWR PEACE

B58
HOLT R.T.,RADIO FREE EUROPE. FUT USA+45 CULTURE ECO/DEV INT/ORG KIN POL/PAR SECT FORCES ACT/RES DIPLOM COERCE REV CHOOSE PEACE ATTIT PWR...MAJORIT CONCPT COLD/WAR WORK 20 RFE. PAGE 67 A1374 COM EDU/PROP COM/IND

B58
INDIAN COUNCIL WORLD AFFAIRS,DEFENCE AND SECURITY IN THE INDIAN OCEAN AREA. INDIA S/ASIA CULTURE CONSULT DELIB/GP FORCES PROB/SOLV DIPLOM INT/TRADE 20 CMN/WLTH. PAGE 70 A1438 GEOG HABITAT ECO/UNDEV ORD/FREE

B58
KENNAN G.F.,THE DECISION TO INTERVENE: SOVIET-AMERICAN RELATIONS, 1917-1920 (VOL. II). CZECHOSLVK EUR+WWI USA-45 USSR ELITES NAT/G FORCES PROB/SOLV REV WAR TOTALISM PWR...CHARTS BIBLIOG 20 TREATY PRESIDENT CHINJAP. PAGE 78 A1588 DIPLOM POLICY ATTIT

B58
MILLIS W.,FOREIGN POLICY AND THE FREE SOCIETY. USA+45 WOR+45 SOCIETY NAT/G FORCES BAL/PWR FOR/AID EDU/PROP DETER ATTIT PWR 20 COLD/WAR. PAGE 102 A2084 DIPLOM POLICY ORD/FREE CONSULT

B58
MOORE B.T.,NATO AND THE FUTURE OF EUROPE. EUR+WWI FUT USA+45 ECO/DEV INDUS MARKET NAT/G VOL/ASSN FORCES DIPLOM NUC/PWR ORD/FREE...CONCPT CHARTS ORG/CHARTS CMN/WLTH 20 NATO. PAGE 103 A2122 INT/ORG REGION

B58
ROCKEFELLER BROTH FUND INC,INTERNATIONAL SECURITY - THE MILITARY ASPECT. USA+45 INT/ORG NAT/G BUDGET ARMS/CONT WAR WEAPON PEACE ORD/FREE 20 NATO. PAGE 123 A2511 NUC/PWR DETER FORCES DIPLOM

B58
SCHUMAN F.,INTERNATIONAL POLITICS. WOR+45 WOR-45 INTELL NAT/G FORCES DOMIN LEGIT COERCE NUC/PWR ATTIT DISPL ORD/FREE PWR SOVEREIGN...POLICY CONCPT GEN/LAWS SUEZ 20. PAGE 129 A2650 FUT INT/ORG NAT/LISM DIPLOM

B58
SLICK T.,PERMANENT PEACE: A CHECK AND BALANCE PLAN. FUT WOR+45 NAT/G FORCES CREATE PLAN EDU/PROP LEGIT ADJUD COERCE NAT/LISM RIGID/FLEX MORAL...HUM CONCPT METH/CNCPT NEW/IDEA TREND CHARTS TOT/POP 20. PAGE 134 A2742 INT/ORG ORD/FREE PEACE ARMS/CONT

B58
US DEPARTMENT OF STATE,PUBLICATIONS OF THE DEPARTMENT OF STATE, JANUARY 1,1953 TO DECEMBER 31, 1957. AGRI INT/ORG FORCES FOR/AID EDU/PROP ARMS/CONT NUC/PWR ATTIT 20 DEPT/STATE OAS UN NATO. PAGE 151 A3092 BIBLIOG DIPLOM

S58
BURNS A.L.,"THE INTERNATIONAL CONSEQUENCES OF EXPECTING SURPRISE." WOR+45 INT/ORG NAT/G FORCES DIPLOM COERCE NUC/PWR WAR CHOOSE ORD/FREE ...METH/CNCPT STYLE OBS STERTYP TOT/POP VAL/FREE. PAGE 22 A0440 PLAN PWR DETER

S58
DAVENPORT J.,"ARMS AND THE WELFARE STATE." INTELL STRUCT FORCES CREATE ECO/TAC FOR/AID DOMIN LEGIT ADMIN WAR ORD/FREE PWR...POLICY SOC CONCPT MYTH OBS TREND COLD/WAR TOT/POP 20. PAGE 34 A0685 USA+45 NAT/G USSR

S58
JORDAN A.,"MILITARY ASSISTANCE AND NATIONAL POLICY." ASIA FUT USA+45 WOR+45 ECO/DEV ECO/UNDEV INT/ORG NAT/G PLAN ECO/TAC ROUTINE WEAPON ATTIT RIGID/FLEX PWR...CONCPT TREND 20. PAGE 75 A1533 FORCES POLICY FOR/AID DIPLOM

S58
THOMPSON K.W.,"NATIONAL SECURITY IN A NUCLEAR AGE." USA+45 WOR+45 SOCIETY INT/ORG NAT/G TOP/EX DIPLOM DOMIN EDU/PROP LEGIT ARMS/CONT COERCE ORD/FREE ...TREND STERTYP TOT/POP VAL/FREE COLD/WAR 20. PAGE 143 A2929 FORCES PWR BAL/PWR

N58
US HOUSE COMM FOREIGN AFFAIRS,HEARINGS ON DRAFT LEGISLATION TO AMEND FURTHER THE MUTUAL SECURITY ACT OF 1954 (PAMPHLET). USA+45 CONSULT FORCES BUDGET DIPLOM DETER COST ORD/FREE...JURID 20 DEPT/DEFEN UN DEPT/STATE. PAGE 153 A3123 LEGIS DELIB/GP CONFER WEAPON

N58
US HOUSE COMM FOREIGN AFFAIRS,HEARINGS ON THE FAR EAST AND THE PACIFIC (PAMPHLET). LAOS USA+45 NAT/G CONSULT FORCES CONFER DEBATE ORD/FREE 20. PAGE 153 A3124 FOR/AID DIPLOM DELIB/GP LEGIS

B59
AIR FORCE ACADEMY ASSEMBLY '59,INTERNATIONAL STABILITY AND PROGRESS (PAMPHLET). USA+45 USSR ECO/UNDEV PROB/SOLV BUDGET DIPLOM ADMIN DETER COST ATTIT...TREND 20. PAGE 5 A0103 FOR/AID FORCES WAR PLAN

B59
AMERICAN FRIENDS OF VIETNAM,AID TO VIETNAM: AN AMERICAN SUCCESS STORY (PAMPHLET). ASIA FUT USA+45 VIETNAM ECO/UNDEV WAR CIVMIL/REL GOV/REL...ANTHOL 20. PAGE 7 A0148 DIPLOM NAT/G FOR/AID FORCES

B59
BALL M.M.,NATO AND THE EUROPEAN MOVEMENT. EUR+WWI USA+45 INT/ORG FORCES BAL/PWR EDU/PROP LEGIT REGION ATTIT ORD/FREE PWR...STAT OBS TIME/SEQ TREND CHARTS ORG/CHARTS STERTYP COLD/WAR EEC OEEC 20 NATO. PAGE 10 A0212 DELIB/GP STRUCT

B59
BRODIE B.,STRATEGY IN THE MISSILE AGE. FUT WOR+45 CONSULT PLAN COERCE DETER RIGID/FLEX PWR...CONCPT TIME/SEQ TREND 20. PAGE 19 A0381 ACT/RES FORCES ARMS/CONT NUC/PWR

B59
EMME E.M.,THE IMPACT OF AIR POWER - NATIONAL SECURITY AND WORLD POLITICS. USA+45 USSR FORCES DIPLOM WEAPON PEACE TOTALISM...POLICY NAT/COMP 20 EUROPE. PAGE 42 A0850 DETER AIR WAR ORD/FREE

B59
GOULD L.P.,THE PRICE OF SURVIVAL. EUR+WWI SPACE USA+45 FORCES ECO/TAC NUC/PWR WAR ORD/FREE MARXISM ...IDEA/COMP 20 COLD/WAR NATO. PAGE 54 A1117 POLICY PROB/SOLV DIPLOM PEACE

B59
GREENSPAN M.,THE MODERN LAW OF LAND WARFARE. WOR+45 INT/ORG NAT/G DELIB/GP FORCES ATTIT...POLICY HYPO/EXP STERTYP 20. PAGE 56 A1142 ADJUD PWR WAR

B59
HERZ J.H.,INTERNATIONAL POLITICS IN THE ATOMIC AGE. FUT USA+45 WOR+45 WOR-45 SOCIETY NAT/G FORCES PLAN COERCE DETER ATTIT DRIVE ORD/FREE PWR...TREND COLD/WAR 20. PAGE 64 A1319 INT/ORG ARMS/CONT NUC/PWR

B59
MODELSKI G.,ATOMIC ENERGY IN THE COMMUNIST BLOC. FUT INT/ORG CONSULT FORCES ACT/RES PLAN KNOWL SKILL ...PHIL/SCI STAT CHARTS 20. PAGE 102 A2096 TEC/DEV NUC/PWR USSR COM

B59
COLUMBIA U BUR APPL SOC RES,ATTITUDES OF PROMINENT AMERICANS TOWARD "WORLD PEACE THROUGH WORLD LAW" (SUPRA-NATL ORGANIZATION FOR WAR PREVENTION). USA+45 USSR ELITES FORCES PLAN PROB/SOLV CONTROL WAR PWR...POLICY SOC QU IDEA/COMP 20 UN. PAGE 117 A2403
ATTIT ACT/RES INT/LAW STAT

B59
ROBERTSON A.H.,EUROPEAN INSTITUTIONS: COOPERATION, INTEGRATION, UNIFICATION. EUR+WWI FINAN INT/ORG FORCES INT/TRADE TARIFFS 20 EEC EURATOM ECSC NATO TREATY. PAGE 122 A2496
ECO/DEV DIPLOM INDUS ECO/TAC

B59
SCHURZ W.L.,AMERICAN FOREIGN AFFAIRS: A GUIDE TO INTERNATIONAL AFFAIRS. USA+45 WOR+45 WOR-45 NAT/G FORCES LEGIS TOP/EX PLAN EDU/PROP LEGIT ADMIN ROUTINE ATTIT ORD/FREE PWR...SOC CONCPT STAT SAMP/SIZ CHARTS STERTYP 20. PAGE 129 A2653
INT/ORG SOCIETY DIPLOM

B59
STERNBERG F.,THE MILITARY AND INDUSTRIAL REVOLUTION OF OUR TIME. USA+45 USSR WOR+45 WORKER COMPUTER PLAN TEC/DEV NUC/PWR GP/REL...POLICY NAT/COMP 20. PAGE 138 A2818
DIPLOM FORCES INDUS CIVMIL/REL

B59
STRAUSZ-HUPE R.,PROTRACTED CONFLICT. CHINA/COM KOREA WOR+45 INT/ORG FORCES ACT/RES ECO/TAC LEGIT COERCE DRIVE PERCEPT KNOWL PWR...PSY CONCPT RECORD GEN/METH COLD/WAR VAL/FREE 20. PAGE 139 A2847
COM PLAN USSR

B59
THOMAS N.,THE PREREQUISITES FOR PEACE. ASIA EUR+WWI FUT ISLAM S/ASIA WOR+45 FORCES PLAN BAL/PWR EDU/PROP LEGIT ATTIT PWR...SOCIALIST CONCPT COLD/WAR 20 UN. PAGE 143 A2924
INT/ORG ORD/FREE ARMS/CONT PEACE

B59
TUNSTALL W.C.B.,THE COMMONWEALTH AND REGIONAL DEFENCE (PAMPHLET). UK LAW VOL/ASSN PLAN AGREE REGION WAR ORD/FREE 20 CMN/WLTH NATO SEATO TREATY. PAGE 146 A2977
INT/ORG FORCES DIPLOM

B59
US HOUSE COMM GOVT OPERATIONS,UNITED STATES AID OPERATIONS IN LAOS. LAOS USA+45 PLAN INSPECT HOUSE/REP. PAGE 154 A3136
FOR/AID ADMIN FORCES ECO/UNDEV

B59
US PRES COMM STUDY MIL ASSIST,COMPOSITE REPORT. USA+45 ECO/UNDEV PLAN BUDGET DIPLOM EFFICIENCY ...POLICY MGT 20. PAGE 155 A3164
FOR/AID FORCES WEAPON ORD/FREE

B59
VAN WAGENEN R.W.,SOME VIEWS OF AMERICAN DEFENSE OFFICIALS ABOUT THE UNITED NATIONS (PAPER). FUT USA+45 NAT/G DIPLOM WAR EFFICIENCY PEACE...POLICY INT 20 UN DEPT/DEFEN. PAGE 158 A3216
INT/ORG LEAD ATTIT FORCES

B59
WARD B.,5 IDEAS THAT CHANGE THE WORLD. WOR+45 WOR-45 SOCIETY STRUCT AGRI INDUS INT/ORG NAT/G FORCES ACT/RES ARMS/CONT TOTALISM ATTIT DRIVE GEN/LAWS. PAGE 161 A3278
ECO/UNDEV ALL/VALS NAT/LISM COLONIAL

B59
WOLFERS A.,ALLIANCE POLICY IN THE COLD WAR. COM INT/ORG FORCES COLONIAL CONTROL NUC/PWR 20 NATO UN COLD/WAR. PAGE 166 A3384
DIPLOM DETER BAL/PWR

B59
YOUNG J.,CHECKLIST OF MICROFILM REPRODUCTIONS OF SELECTED ARCHIVES OF THE JAPANESE ARMY, NAVY, AND OTHER GOVT AGENCIES, 1868-1945. DELIB/GP LEGIS DIPLOM EDU/PROP CIVMIL/REL 19/20 CHINJAP. PAGE 169 A3436
BIBLIOG ASIA FORCES WAR

S59
PUGWASH CONFERENCE,"ON BIOLOGICAL AND CHEMICAL WARFARE." WOR+45 SOCIETY PROC/MFG INT/ORG FORCES EDU/PROP ADJUD RIGID/FLEX ORD/FREE PWR...DECISION PSY NEW/IDEA MATH VAL/FREE 20. PAGE 118 A2417
ACT/RES BIO/SOC WAR WEAPON

S59
SOHN L.B.,"THE DEFINITION OF AGGRESSION." FUT LAW FORCES LEGIT ADJUD ROUTINE COERCE ORD/FREE PWR ...MAJORIT JURID QUANT COLD/WAR 20. PAGE 135 A2762
INT/ORG CT/SYS DETER SOVEREIGN

S59
SUTTON F.X.,"REPRESENTATION AND THE NATURE OF POLITICAL SYSTEMS." UNIV WOR-45 CULTURE SOCIETY STRATA INT/ORG FORCES JUDGE DOMIN LEGIT EXEC REGION REPRESENT ATTIT ORD/FREE RESPECT...SOC HIST/WRIT TIME/SEQ. PAGE 140 A2867
NAT/G CONCPT

N59
BRITISH COMMONWEALTH REL CONF,EXTRACTS FROM THE PROCEEDINGS OF THE SIXTH UNOFFICIAL CONFERENCE (PAMPHLET). GHANA INDIA RHODESIA UK FINAN FORCES DETER FEDERAL...LING 20 PARLIAMENT. PAGE 19 A0379
DIPLOM PARL/PROC INT/TRADE ORD/FREE

N59
US HOUSE COMM FOREIGN AFFAIRS,HEARINGS ON DRAFT LEGISLATION TO AMEND FURTHER THE MUTUAL SECURITY ACT OF 1954 (PAMPHLET). USA+45 USSR CONSULT DELIB/GP FORCES ECO/TAC CONFER...POLICY 20 CONGRESS. PAGE 153 A3126
DIPLOM FOR/AID ORD/FREE LEGIS

B60
ALBRECHT-CARRIE R.,FRANCE, EUROPE AND THE TWO WORLD WARS. EUR+WWI FRANCE GERMANY MOD/EUR UK ECO/DEV NAT/G FORCES BAL/PWR DOMIN ARMS/CONT PEACE PWR 20 TREATY EUROPE. PAGE 5 A0109
DIPLOM WAR

B60
BARNET R.,WHO WANTS DISARMAMENT. COM EUR+WWI USA+45 USSR INT/ORG NAT/G BAL/PWR DIPLOM EDU/PROP COERCE DETER NUC/PWR WAR WEAPON ATTIT PWR...TIME/SEQ COLD/WAR CONGRESS 20. PAGE 11 A0225
PLAN FORCES ARMS/CONT

B60
BILLERBECK K.,SOVIET BLOC FOREIGN AID TO UNDERDEVELOPED COUNTRIES. COM FUT USSR FINAN FORCES TEC/DEV DIPLOM INT/TRADE EDU/PROP NUC/PWR...TREND 20. PAGE 14 A0287
FOR/AID ECO/UNDEV ECO/TAC MARXISM

B60
BROWN H.,COMMUNITY OF FEAR. FORCES TEC/DEV ARMS/CONT COERCE PEACE 20. PAGE 20 A0402
NUC/PWR WAR DIPLOM DETER

B60
BUCHAN A.,NATO IN THE 1960'S. EUR+WWI USA+45 WOR+45 INT/ORG ACT/RES PLAN LEGIT COERCE DETER ATTIT DRIVE RIGID/FLEX ORD/FREE...METH/CNCPT TIME/SEQ TREND GEN/LAWS COLD/WAR 20 NATO. PAGE 21 A0421
VOL/ASSN FORCES ARMS/CONT SOVEREIGN

B60
CONN S.,THE FRAMEWORK OF HEMISPHERE DEFENSE. CANADA L/A+17C USA-45 NAT/G FORCES BAL/PWR DOMIN WAR PEACE DISPL PWR RESPECT...PLURIST CONCPT HIST/WRIT HYPO/EXP MEXIC/AMER 20 ROOSEVLT/F. PAGE 29 A0585
USA+45 INT/ORG DIPLOM

B60
DAVIDS J.,AMERICA AND THE WORLD OF OUR TIME: UNITED STATES DIPLOMACY IN THE TWENTIETH CENTURY. USA-45 SOCIETY ECO/DEV INT/ORG NAT/G POL/PAR FORCES ECO/TAC DOMIN EDU/PROP EXEC COERCE WAR CHOOSE ATTIT PERSON ORD/FREE...CONCPT TIME/SEQ TOT/POP 20. PAGE 34 A0686
USA+45 PWR DIPLOM

B60
DE GAULLE C.,THE EDGE OF THE SWORD. EUR+WWI FRANCE ELITES CHIEF DIPLOM ROLE...REALPOL TRADIT. PAGE 34 A0701
FORCES SUPEGO LEAD WAR

B60
ENGEL J.,THE SECURITY OF THE FREE WORLD. USSR WOR+45 STRATA STRUCT ECO/DEV ECO/UNDEV INT/ORG DELIB/GP FORCES DOMIN LEGIT ADJUD EXEC ARMS/CONT COERCE...POLICY CONCPT NEW/IDEA TIME/SEQ GEN/LAWS COLD/WAR WORK UN 20 NATO. PAGE 42 A0851
COM TREND DIPLOM

B60
ENGELMAN F.L.,THE PEACE OF CHRISTMAS EVE. UK USA-45 NAT/G FORCES CONFER PERS/REL...AUD/VIS BIBLIOG 19 TREATY. PAGE 42 A0853
WAR PEACE DIPLOM PERSON

B60
FISCHER L.,RUSSIA, AMERICA, AND THE WORLD. FUT USA+45 USSR WOR+45 FORCES PLAN BAL/PWR ECO/TAC FOR/AID NEUTRAL TASK NUC/PWR PWR 20 COLD/WAR. PAGE 46 A0937
DIPLOM POLICY MARXISM ECO/UNDEV

B60
FOREIGN POLICY CLEARING HOUSE,STRATEGY FOR THE 60'S. FUT USA+45 WOR+45 ECO/UNDEV FORCES BAL/PWR TASK ARMS/CONT DETER PWR MARXISM 20 SENATE. PAGE 47 A0963
DIPLOM NAT/G POLICY ACT/RES

B60
FURNIA A.H.,THE DIPLOMACY OF APPEASEMENT: ANGLO-FRENCH RELATIONS AND THE PRELUDE TO WORLD WAR II 1931-1938. FRANCE GERMANY UK ELITES NAT/G DELIB/GP FORCES WAR PEACE RIGID/FLEX 20. PAGE 50 A1026
DIPLOM BAL/PWR COERCE

B60
GLUBB J.B.,WAR IN THE DESERT: AN R.A.F. FRONTIER CAMPAIGN. SAUDI/ARAB UK KIN SECT LEAD...GEOG 20 RAF. PAGE 53 A1083
COLONIAL WAR FORCES DIPLOM

B60
KINGSTON-MCCLOUG E.,DEFENSE; POLICY AND STRATEGY. UK SEA AIR TEC/DEV DIPLOM ADMIN LEAD WAR ORD/FREE ...CHARTS 20. PAGE 79 A1627
FORCES PLAN POLICY DECISION

B60
LIEUWEN E.,ARMS AND POLITICS IN LATIN AMERICA. FUT USA+45 USA-45 ECO/UNDEV INT/ORG NAT/G FORCES DIPLOM COERCE ATTIT ALL/VALS VAL/FREE OAS 20. PAGE 88 A1811
L/A+17C FOR/AID

B60
MCCLELLAND C.A.,NUCLEAR WEAPONS, MISSILES, AND FUTURE WAR: PROBLEM FOR THE SIXTIES. WOR+45 FORCES ARMS/CONT DETER MARXISM...POLICY ANTHOL COLD/WAR. PAGE 97 A1998
DIPLOM NUC/PWR WAR WEAPON

B60
MINIFIE J.M.,PEACEMAKER OR POWDER-MONKEY. CANADA INT/ORG NAT/G FORCES LEAD WAR...PREDICT 20. PAGE 102 A2086
DIPLOM POLICY NEUTRAL PEACE

B60
MORAES F.,THE REVOLT IN TIBET. ASIA CHINA/COM INDIA CULTURE CONTROL COERCE WAR TOTALISM...POLICY SOC
COLONIAL FORCES

WORSHIP 20 TIBET INTERVENT. PAGE 104 A2127 DIPLOM ORD/FREE

B60
MORISON E.E.,TURMOIL AND TRADITION: A STUDY OF THE LIFE AND TIMES OF HENRY L. STIMSON. USA+45 USA-45 POL/PAR CHIEF DELIB/GP FORCES BAL/PWR DIPLOM ARMS/CONT WAR PEACE 19/20 STIMSON/HL ROOSEVLT/F TAFT/WH HOOVER/H REPUBLICAN. PAGE 104 A2142 BIOG NAT/G EX/STRUC

B60
MUGRIDGE D.H.,A GUIDE TO THE STUDY OF THE UNITED STATES OF AMERICA: REPRESENTATIVE BOOKS REFLECTING THE DEVELOPMENT OF AMERICAN LIFE. USA+45 USA-45 CONSTN POL/PAR FORCES DIPLOM PRESS CHOOSE...SOC 17/20. PAGE 105 A2165 BIBLIOG/A CULTURE NAT/G POLICY

B60
PAN AMERICAN UNION,FIFTH MEETING OF CONSULTATION OF MINISTERS OF FOREIGN AFFAIRS OF AMERICAN STATES. L/A+17C FORCES PLAN PROB/SOLV ADJUD PEACE...POLICY INT/LAW 20 OAS. PAGE 113 A2327 INT/ORG DIPLOM DELIB/GP ECO/UNDEV

B60
SETON-WATSON H.,NEITHER WAR NOR PEACE. ASIA USSR WOR+45 ELITES INT/ORG NAT/G EX/STRUC FORCES BAL/PWR ECO/TAC EDU/PROP COERCE NAT/LISM ORD/FREE WEALTH TOT/POP 20. PAGE 131 A2688 ATTIT PWR DIPLOM TOTALISM

B60
TAYLOR M.D.,THE UNCERTAIN TRUMPET. USA+45 USSR WOR+45 INT/ORG NAT/G CONSULT DOMIN COERCE NUC/PWR WAR ATTIT ORD/FREE PWR...POLICY CONCPT TREND GEN/METH COLD/WAR UN NATO 20. PAGE 142 A2900 PLAN FORCES DIPLOM

B60
TURNER G.B.,NATIONAL SECURITY IN THE NUCLEAR AGE. KOREA USA+45 PLAN DIPLOM ARMS/CONT DETER WAR WEAPON ...BIBLIOG 20 COLD/WAR NATO. PAGE 146 A2982 NAT/G POLICY FORCES NUC/PWR

B60
US HOUSE COMM FOREIGN AFFAIRS,HEARINGS ON A BILL TO AMEND FURTHER THE MUTUAL SECURITY ACT OF 1954. USA+45 CONSULT FORCES BUDGET FOR/AID CONFER DETER ...CHARTS 20 DEPT/DEFEN DEPT/STATE UNEF. PAGE 153 A3127 DIPLOM ORD/FREE DELIB/GP LEGIS

B60
US HOUSE COMM. SCI. ASTRONAUT.,OCEAN SCIENCES AND NATIONAL SECURITY. FUT SEA ECO/DEV EXTR/IND INT/ORG NAT/G FORCES ACT/RES TEC/DEV ECO/TAC COERCE WAR BIO/SOC KNOWL PWR...CONCPT RECORD LAB/EXP 20. PAGE 154 A3141 R+D ORD/FREE

L60
BRENNAN D.G.,"SETTING AND GOALS OF ARMS CONTROL." FUT USA+45 USSR WOR+45 INTELL INT/ORG NAT/G VOL/ASSN CONSULT PLAN DIPLOM ECO/TAC ADMIN KNOWL PWR...POLICY CONCPT TREND COLD/WAR 20. PAGE 18 A0371 FORCES COERCE ARMS/CONT DETER

L60
HOLTON G.,"ARMS CONTROL." FUT WOR+45 CULTURE INT/ORG NAT/G FORCES TOP/EX PLAN EDU/PROP COERCE ATTIT RIGID/FLEX ORD/FREE...POLICY PHIL/SCI SOC TREND COLD/WAR. PAGE 67 A1377 ACT/RES CONSULT ARMS/CONT NUC/PWR

L60
LAUTERPACHT E.,"THE UNITED NATIONS EMERGENCY FORCE." R+D LEGIT ROUTINE COERCE KNOWL ORD/FREE SKILL...JURID UN 20. PAGE 85 A1746 INT/ORG FORCES

S60
BRODY R.A.,"DETERRENCE STRATEGIES: AN ANNOTATED BIBLIOGRAPHY." WOR+45 PLAN ARMS/CONT NUC/PWR WAR WEAPON DECISION. PAGE 19 A0383 BIBLIOG/A FORCES DETER DIPLOM

S60
DOUGHERTY J.E.,"KEY TO SECURITY: DISARMAMENT OR ARMS STABILITY." COM USA+45 USSR INT/ORG NAT/G CREATE EDU/PROP COERCE DETER ATTIT PWR...DECISION CONCPT MYTH NEW/IDEA TREND 20 COLD/WAR. PAGE 38 A0777 FORCES ORD/FREE ARMS/CONT NUC/PWR

S60
GINSBURGS G.,"PEKING-LHASA-NEW DELHI." CHINA/COM FUT INDIA S/ASIA KIN NAT/G PROVS SECT FORCES BAL/PWR ECO/TAC DOMIN EDU/PROP LEGIT ADMIN REGION GUERRILLA PWR...TREND TIBET 20. PAGE 52 A1074 ASIA COERCE DIPLOM

S60
HAVILAND H.F.,"PROBLEMS OF AMERICAN FOREIGN POLICY." ASIA COM USA+45 WOR+45 INT/ORG NAT/G CONSULT ECO/TAC FOR/AID DOMIN COERCE NUC/PWR ATTIT DRIVE ORD/FREE PWR RESPECT SKILL...POLICY GEOG OBS SAMP TREND GEN/METH METH COLD/WAR UN 20. PAGE 63 A1292 ECO/UNDEV FORCES DIPLOM

S60
MAGATHAN W.,"SOME BASES OF WEST GERMAN MILITARY POLICY." EUR+WWI FUT INT/ORG TOP/EX ECO/TAC DOMIN DRIVE ORD/FREE PWR...TRADIT GEOG OBS TREND. PAGE 93 A1904 NAT/G FORCES GERMANY

S60
MORGENSTERN O.,"GOAL: AN ARMED, INSPECTED, OPEN WORLD." COM EUR+WWI USA+45 R+D INT/ORG NAT/G TEC/DEV BAL/PWR COERCE NUC/PWR ORD/FREE PWR...TREND 20. PAGE 104 A2133 FORCES CONCPT ARMS/CONT DETER

S60
MUNRO L.,"CAN THE UNITED NATIONS ENFORCE PEACE." FORCES WOR+45 LAW INT/ORG VOL/ASSN BAL/PWR LEGIT ARMS/CONT COERCE DETER PEACE PWR...CONCPT REC/INT TREND UN 20 HAMMARSK/D. PAGE 106 A2173 ORD/FREE

S60
O'BRIEN W.,"THE ROLE OF FORCE IN THE INTERNATIONAL JURIDICAL ORDER." WOR+45 NAT/G FORCES DOMIN ADJUD ARMS/CONT DETER NUC/PWR WAR ATTIT PWR...CATH INT/LAW JURID CONCPT TREND STERTYP GEN/LAWS 20. PAGE 110 A2266 INT/ORG COERCE

S60
WRIGHT Q.,"LEGAL ASPECTS OF THE U-2 INCIDENT." COM USA+45 USSR STRUCT NAT/G FORCES PLAN TEC/DEV ADJUD RIGID/FLEX MORAL ORD/FREE...DECISION INT/LAW JURID PSY TREND GEN/LAWS COLD/WAR VAL/FREE 20 U-2. PAGE 168 A3413 PWR POLICY SPACE

C60
WRIGGINS W.H.,"CEYLON: DILEMMAS OF A NEW NATION." ASIA CEYLON CONSTN STRUCT POL/PAR SECT FORCES DIPLOM GOV/REL NAT/LISM...CHARTS BIBLIOG 20. PAGE 167 A3399 PROB/SOLV NAT/G ECO/UNDEV

B61
BRENNAN D.G.,ARMS CONTROL, DISARMAMENT, AND NATIONAL SECURITY. WOR+45 NAT/G FORCES CREATE PROB/SOLV PARTIC WAR PEACE...DECISION INT/LAW ANTHOL BIBLIOG 20. PAGE 18 A0372 ARMS/CONT ORD/FREE DIPLOM POLICY

B61
BULL H.,THE CONTROL OF THE ARMS RACE. COM USA+45 INT/ORG NAT/G PLAN TEC/DEV DIPLOM ATTIT...RELATIV DECISION CONCPT SELF/OBS TREND CON/ANAL GEN/METH 20 COLD/WAR. PAGE 21 A0429 FORCES PWR ARMS/CONT NUC/PWR

B61
CONFERENCE ATLANTIC COMMUNITY,AN INTRODUCTORY BIBLIOGRAPHY. COM WOR+45 FORCES DIPLOM ECO/TAC WAR ...INT/LAW HIST/WRIT COLD/WAR NATO. PAGE 29 A0584 BIBLIOG/A CON/ANAL INT/ORG

B61
DALLIN D.J.,SOVIET FOREIGN POLICY AFTER STALIN. ASIA CHINA/COM EUR+WWI GERMANY IRAN UK YUGOSLAVIA INT/ORG NAT/G VOL/ASSN FORCES TOP/EX BAL/PWR DOMIN EDU/PROP COERCE ATTIT PWR 20. PAGE 33 A0679 COM DIPLOM USSR

B61
FRISCH D.,ARMS REDUCTION: PROGRAM AND ISSUES. USA+45 INT/ORG NAT/G ACT/RES REGION NUC/PWR ATTIT PWR...POLICY 20. PAGE 49 A1010 PLAN FORCES ARMS/CONT DIPLOM

B61
FULLER J.F.C.,THE CONDUCT OF WAR, 1789-1961. FRANCE RUSSIA SOCIETY NAT/G FORCES PROB/SOLV AGREE NUC/PWR WEAPON PEACE...SOC 18/20 TREATY COLD/WAR. PAGE 50 A1025 WAR POLICY REV ROLE

B61
GALLOIS P.,THE BALANCE OF TERROR: STRATEGY FOR THE NUCLEAR AGE. FUT WOR+45 INT/ORG FORCES TOP/EX DETER WAR ATTIT RIGID/FLEX ORD/FREE PWR...HYPO/EXP 20. PAGE 50 A1032 PLAN DECISION DIPLOM NUC/PWR

B61
GOLDWERT M.,CONSTABULARY IN THE DOMINICAN REPUBLIC AND NICARAGUA. DOMIN/REP L/A+17C NICARAGUA USA-45 NAT/G PLAN CONTROL TASK REV...POLICY 20 INTERVENT. PAGE 53 A1093 DIPLOM PEACE FORCES

B61
HARDT J.P.,THE COLD WAR ECONOMIC GAP. USA+45 USSR ECO/DEV FORCES INT/TRADE NUC/PWR PWR 20 COLD/WAR. PAGE 61 A1258 DIPLOM ECO/TAC NAT/COMP POLICY

B61
HARRISON J.P.,GUIDE TO MATERIALS ON LATIN AMERICA IN THE NATIONAL ARCHIVES (2 VOLS.). USA+45 ECO/UNDEV FINAN LOC/G FORCES 20. PAGE 62 A1271 BIBLIOG L/A+17C NAT/G DIPLOM

B61
KERTESZ S.D.,AMERICAN DIPLOMACY IN A NEW ERA. COM S/ASIA UK USA+45 FORCES PROB/SOLV BAL/PWR ECO/TAC ADMIN COLONIAL WAR PEACE ORD/FREE 20 NATO CONGRESS UN COLD/WAR. PAGE 78 A1601 ANTHOL DIPLOM TREND

B61
LERCHE C.O. JR.,FOREIGN POLICY OF THE AMERICAN PEOPLE (REV. ED.). USA+45 USSR FORCES TEC/DEV EDU/PROP WAR PRODUC ORD/FREE MARXISM...POLICY TREND BIBLIOG 20 COLD/WAR. PAGE 87 A1781 DECISION PLAN PEACE DIPLOM

B61
LIPPMANN W.,THE COMING TESTS WITH RUSSIA. COM CUBA GERMANY USSR FORCES CONTROL NEUTRAL COERCE NUC/PWR REV WAR PWR...INT 20 KHRUSH/N BERLIN. PAGE 89 A1830 BAL/PWR DIPLOM MARXISM ARMS/CONT

B61
MECHAM J.L.,THE UNITED STATES AND INTER-AMERICAN SECURITY, 1889-1960. L/A+17C USA+45 USA-45 CONSTN FORCES INT/TRADE PEACE TOTALISM ATTIT...JURID 19/20 UN OAS. PAGE 99 A2030 DIPLOM WAR ORD/FREE INT/ORG

B61
MENDEL D.H. JR.,THE JAPANESE PEOPLE AND FOREIGN POLICY. CHINA/COM KOREA USA+45 USSR SOCIETY FORCES CHOOSE 20 CHINJAP. PAGE 99 A2037 NAT/G DIPLOM POLICY ATTIT

B61
MICHAEL D.N.,PROPOSED STUDIES ON THE IMPLICATIONS FUT

OF PEACEFUL SPACE ACTIVITIES FOR HUMAN AFFAIRS. COM/IND INDUS FORCES DIPLOM PEACE PERSON...PSY SOC 20. PAGE 101 A2066
SPACE ACT/RES PROB/SOLV

B61
NOLLAU G.,INTERNATIONAL COMMUNISM AND WORLD REVOLUTION: HISTORY AND METHODS. RUSSIA USSR INT/ORG NAT/G POL/PAR VOL/ASSN FORCES BAL/PWR DIPLOM EXEC REGION WAR ATTIT PWR MARXISM...CONCPT TIME/SEQ COLD/WAR 19/20. PAGE 102 A2100
COM REV

B61
MORLEY L.,THE PATCHWORK HISTORY OF FOREIGN AID. KOREA/S USA+45 USSR LAW FINAN INT/ORG TEC/DEV BAL/PWR GIVE 20 COLD/WAR NATO. PAGE 104 A2144
FOR/AID ECO/UNDEV FORCES DIPLOM

B61
PANIKKAR K.M.,THE VOICE OF FREEDOM: SELECTED SPEECHES OF PANDIT MOTILAL NEHRU. INDIA UK CONSTN FINAN FORCES LEGIS DIPLOM TAX COLONIAL...POLICY MAJORIT ANTHOL 20 NEHRU/PM. PAGE 114 A2331
NAT/LISM ORD/FREE CHIEF NAT/G

B61
SCHMIDT H.,VERTEIDIGUNG ODER VERGELTUNG. COM CUBA GERMANY/W USSR FORCES DIPLOM ARMS/CONT DETER NUC/PWR...POLICY CHARTS HYPO/EXP SIMUL BIBLIOG 20 NATO COLD/WAR. PAGE 128 A2630
PLAN WAR BAL/PWR ORD/FREE

B61
SCOTT A.M.,POLITICS, USA; CASES ON THE AMERICAN DEMOCRATIC PROCESS. USA+45 CHIEF FORCES DIPLOM LOBBY CHOOSE RACE/REL FEDERAL ATTIT...JURID ANTHOL T 20 PRESIDENT CONGRESS CIVIL/LIB. PAGE 130 A2669
CT/SYS CONSTN NAT/G PLAN

B61
SLESSOR J.,WHAT PRICE COEXISTENCE? COM INT/ORG NAT/G FORCES COLONIAL ARMS/CONT WAR...POLICY TREND 20 NATO COLD/WAR. PAGE 134 A2741
DIPLOM PEACE WOR+45 NUC/PWR

B61
SOKOL A.E.,SEAPOWER IN THE NUCLEAR AGE. USA+45 USSR DIST/IND FORCES INT/TRADE DETER WAR...POLICY NAT/COMP BIBLIOG COLD/WAR. PAGE 135 A2763
SEA PWR WEAPON NUC/PWR

B61
STILLMAN E.,THE NEW POLITICS: AMERICA AND THE END OF THE POSTWAR WORLD. FUT WOR+45 CULTURE SOCIETY ECO/UNDEV INT/ORG NAT/G FORCES TOP/EX ACT/RES DIPLOM EDU/PROP LEGIT ROUTINE DETER ATTIT ORD/FREE PWR...OBS STERTYP COLD/WAR TOT/POP VAL/FREE. PAGE 138 A2827
USA+45 PLAN

B61
STRAUSZ-HUPE R.,A FORWARD STRATEGY FOR AMERICA. FUT WOR+45 ECO/DEV INT/ORG NAT/G POL/PAR DELIB/GP FORCES ACT/RES CREATE ECO/TAC DOMIN EDU/PROP ATTIT DRIVE PWR...MAJORIT CONCPT STAT OBS TIME/SEQ TREND COLD/WAR TOT/POP. PAGE 139 A2848
USA+45 PLAN DIPLOM

B61
US SENATE COMM GOVT OPERATIONS,ORGANIZING FOR NATIONAL SECURITY. COM USA+45 BUDGET DIPLOM DETER NUC/PWR WAR WEAPON ORD/FREE...BIBLIOG 20 COLD/WAR. PAGE 156 A3172
POLICY PLAN FORCES COERCE

B61
US SENATE COMM ON FOREIGN RELS,INTERNATIONAL DEVELOPMENT AND SECURITY: HEARINGS ON BILL (2 VOLS.). ECO/UNDEV FINAN FORCES REV COST WEALTH ...CHARTS 20 AID PRESIDENT. PAGE 157 A3191
FOR/AID CIVMIL/REL ORD/FREE ECO/TAC

B61
WARNER D.,HURRICANE FROM CHINA. ASIA CHINA/COM FUT L/A+17C USA+45 CULTURE NAT/G FORCES TOP/EX FOR/AID DRIVE PWR...CONCPT TIME/SEQ SEATO WORK 20. PAGE 161 A3284
ATTIT TREND REV

B61
WRINCH P.,THE MILITARY STRATEGY OF WINSTON CHURCHILL. UK WOR-45 SEA VOL/ASSN TEC/DEV BAL/PWR LEAD WAR PEACE ATTIT...POLICY 20 CHURCHLL/W. PAGE 168 A3421
CIVMIL/REL FORCES PLAN DIPLOM

L61
CLAUDE I.,"THE UNITED NATIONS AND THE USE OF FORCE." FUT WOR+45 SOCIETY DIPLOM EDU/PROP LEGIT ADMIN ROUTINE COERCE WAR PEACE ORD/FREE...CONCPT TREND UN 20. PAGE 27 A0545
INT/ORG FORCES

L61
HILSMAN R. JR.,"THE NEW COMMUNIST TACTIC: PRECIS-INTERNAL WAR." COM FUT USA+45 ECO/UNDEV POL/PAR FOR/AID RIGID/FLEX ALL/VALS...TREND COLD/WAR 20. PAGE 65 A1334
FORCES COERCE USSR GUERRILLA

L61
HOYT E.C.,"UNITED STATES REACTION TO THE KOREAN ATTACK." COM KOREA USA+45 CONSTN DELIB/GP FORCES PLAN ECO/TAC DOMIN EDU/PROP LEGIT ROUTINE COERCE WAR ATTIT DISPL RIGID/FLEX ORD/FREE PWR...POLICY INT/LAW TREND UN 20. PAGE 68 A1402
ASIA INT/ORG BAL/PWR DIPLOM

L61
WRIGHT Q.,"STUDIES IN DETERRENCE: LIMITED WARS AND THE ROLE OF SEABORNE WEAPONS SYSTEMS." FUT USA+45 WOR+45 SEA INT/ORG NAT/G FORCES ACT/RES WAR WEAPON ORD/FREE TOT/POP 20. PAGE 168 A3415
TEC/DEV SKILL BAL/PWR DETER

S61
KRANNHALS H.V.,"COMMAND INTEGRATION WITHIN THE WARSAW PACT." COM USSR WOR+45 DELIB/GP EDU/PROP ...CONCPT AUD/VIS CHARTS COLD/WAR TOT/POP VAL/FREE 20 TREATY WARSAW/P. PAGE 82 A1675
INT/ORG FORCES TOTALISM

S61
LEWY G.,"SUPERIOR ORDERS, NUCLEAR WARFARE AND THE DICTATES OF CONSCIENCE: THE DILEMMA OF MILITARY OBEDIENCE IN THE ATOMIC." FUT UNIV WOR+45 INTELL SOCIETY FORCES TOP/EX ACT/RES ADMIN ROUTINE NUC/PWR PERCEPT RIGID/FLEX ALL/VALS...POLICY CONCPT 20. PAGE 88 A1805
DETER INT/ORG LAW INT/LAW

S61
MIKSCHE F.O.,"DEFENSE ORGANIZATION FOR WESTERN EUROPE." USA+45 INT/ORG NAT/G VOL/ASSN ACT/RES DOMIN LEGIT COERCE ORD/FREE PWR...RELATIV TREND 20 NATO. PAGE 101 A2071
EUR+WWI FORCES WEAPON NUC/PWR

B62
ABOSCH H.,THE MENACE OF THE MIRACLE: GERMANY FROM HITLER TO ADENAUER. EUR+WWI GERMANY/W CULTURE FORCES PRESS NUC/PWR WAR CHOOSE 20 HITLER/A ADENAUER/K. PAGE 4 A0082
DIPLOM PEACE POLICY

B62
AIR FORCE ACADEMY LIBRARY,INTERNATIONAL ORGANIZATIONS AND MILITARY SECURITY SYSTEMS (PAMPHLET) (SPECIAL BIBLIOGRAPHY SERIES, NUMBER 25). DIPLOM FOR/AID INT/TRADE NUC/PWR PEACE 20 UN NATO OAS SEATO LEAGUE/NAT. PAGE 5 A0104
BIBLIOG INT/ORG FORCES DETER

B62
BELL C.,NEGOTIATION FROM STRENGTH. WOR+45 FACE/GP INT/ORG DELIB/GP FORCES PLAN DOMIN COERCE NUC/PWR PEACE DRIVE PWR...POLICY LOG OBS RECORD INT SAMP TREND COLD/WAR 20. PAGE 13 A0255
NAT/G CONCPT DIPLOM

B62
BLACKETT P.M.S.,STUDIES OF WAR: NUCLEAR AND CONVENTIONAL. EUR+WWI USA+45 DELIB/GP ACT/RES CREATE PLAN TEC/DEV LEGIT COERCE WAR ORD/FREE PWR ...POLICY TECHNIC TIME/SEQ 20. PAGE 15 A0300
INT/ORG FORCES ARMS/CONT NUC/PWR

B62
BOWLES C.,THE CONSCIENCE OF A LIBERAL. COM USA+45 WOR+45 STRUCT LOC/G NAT/G FORCES LEGIS GOV/REL DISCRIM 20 UN CIV/RIGHTS. PAGE 18 A0361
DIPLOM POLICY

B62
BRIMMER B.,A GUIDE TO THE USE OF UNITED NATIONS DOCUMENTS. WOR+45 ECO/UNDEV AGRI EX/STRUC FORCES PROB/SOLV ADMIN WAR PEACE WEALTH...POLICY UN. PAGE 19 A0378
BIBLIOG/A INT/ORG DIPLOM

B62
BURTON J.W.,PEACE THEORY: PRECONDITIONS OF DISARMAMENT. COM EUR+WWI USA+45 NAT/G FORCES BAL/PWR DIPLOM ECO/TAC EDU/PROP REGION COERCE DETER PEACE ATTIT PWR TOT/POP COLD/WAR 20. PAGE 22 A0446
INT/ORG PLAN ARMS/CONT

B62
CLUBB O.E. JR.,THE UNITED STATES AND THE SINO-SOVIET BLOC IN SOUTHEAST ASIA. ASIA CHINA/COM COM USA+45 USSR ECO/UNDEV INT/ORG NAT/G FORCES TOP/EX PLAN ECO/TAC DOMIN COERCE GUERRILLA ATTIT RIGID/FLEX...POLICY OBS TREND 20. PAGE 27 A0553
S/ASIA PWR BAL/PWR DIPLOM

B62
DOUGLAS W.O.,DEMOCRACY'S MANIFESTO. COM USA+45 ECO/UNDEV INT/ORG FORCES PLAN NEUTRAL TASK MARXISM ...JURID 20 NATO SEATO. PAGE 38 A0779
DIPLOM POLICY NAT/G ORD/FREE

B62
DREIER J.C.,THE ORGANIZATION OF AMERICAN STATES AND THE HEMISPHERE CRISIS. CUBA USA+45 CULTURE STRATA NAT/G VOL/ASSN CONSULT FORCES ACT/RES CREATE DIPLOM ECO/TAC FOR/AID ALL/VALS...POLICY OBS OAS 20. PAGE 38 A0786
L/A+17C CONCPT

B62
DUROSELLE J.B.,HISTOIRE DIPLOMATIQUE DE 1919 A NOS JOURS (3RD ED.). FRANCE INT/ORG CHIEF FORCES CONFER ARMS/CONT WAR PEACE ORD/FREE...T TREATY 20 COLD/WAR. PAGE 39 A0807
DIPLOM WOR+45 WOR-45

B62
EVANS M.S.,THE FRINGE ON TOP. USSR EX/STRUC FORCES DIPLOM ECO/TAC PEACE CONSERVE SOCISM...TREND 20 KENNEDY/JF. PAGE 43 A0877
NAT/G PWR CENTRAL POLICY

B62
FORBES H.W.,THE STRATEGY OF DISARMAMENT. FUT WOR+45 INT/ORG VOL/ASSN CONSULT ARMS/CONT COERCE NUC/PWR WAR DRIVE RIGID/FLEX ORD/FREE PWR...POLICY CONCPT OBS TREND STERTYP 20. PAGE 47 A0959
PLAN FORCES DIPLOM

B62
GILPIN R.,AMERICAN SCIENTISTS AND NUCLEAR WEAPONS POLICY. COM FUT USA+45 WOR+45 INT/ORG NAT/G PROF/ORG CONSULT FORCES CREATE TEC/DEV BAL/PWR EDU/PROP ARMS/CONT WAR PERCEPT KNOWL MORAL PWR ...PHIL/SCI SOC CONCPT GEN/LAWS 20. PAGE 52 A1073
INTELL ATTIT DETER NUC/PWR

B62
HUNTINGTON S.P.,CHANGING PATTERNS OF MILITARY POLITICS. EUR+WWI L/A+17C S/ASIA USA+45 WOR+45 CULTURE INT/ORG NAT/G CONSULT PLAN DOMIN EDU/PROP LEGIT DETER WAR ATTIT PERSON PWR...DECISION CONCPT SIMUL GEN/LAWS ANTHOL COLD/WAR 20. PAGE 69 A1419
FORCES RIGID/FLEX

B62
HUTTENBACK R.A.,BRITISH RELATIONS WITH THE SIND, 1799-1843. FRANCE INDIA UK FORCES...POLICY CHARTS
COLONIAL DIPLOM

BIBLIOG 18/19 SIND. PAGE 69 A1425 DOMIN S/ASIA

B62

JORDAN A.A. JR.,FOREIGN AID AND THE DEFENSE OF SOUTHEAST ASIA. PAKISTAN VIETNAM/S FINAN PLAN BUDGET ECO/TAC DETER WAR ORD/FREE...POLICY DECISION CENSUS CHARTS BIBLIOG 20. PAGE 75 A1535 FOR/AID S/ASIA FORCES ECO/UNDEV

B62

KAHN H.,THINKING ABOUT THE UNTHINKABLE. FUT USA+45 LAW NAT/G CONSULT FORCES ACT/RES CREATE PLAN TEC/DEV BAL/PWR DIPLOM EDU/PROP ARMS/CONT DETER ATTIT...CONCPT OBS TREND COLD/WAR 20. PAGE 76 A1547 INT/ORG ORD/FREE NUC/PWR PEACE

B62

KENNEDY J.F.,TO TURN THE TIDE. SPACE AGRI INT/ORG FORCES TEC/DEV ADMIN NUC/PWR PEACE WEALTH...ANTHOL 20 KENNEDY/JF CIV/RIGHTS. PAGE 78 A1592 DIPLOM CHIEF POLICY NAT/G

B62

KING G.,THE UNITED NATIONS IN THE CONGO: A QUEST FOR PEACE. WOR+45 NAT/G CONSULT FORCES LEGIT COERCE WAR ORD/FREE...JURID METH/CNCPT OBS INT HIST/WRIT TIME/SEQ CONGO UN 20 COLD/WAR. PAGE 79 A1624 AFR INT/ORG

B62

MONCRIEFF A.,THE STRATEGY OF SURVIVAL. UK FORCES BAL/PWR CONFER DETER WAR...ANTHOL 20 COLD/WAR. PAGE 102 A2104 PLAN DECISION DIPLOM ARMS/CONT

B62

MORGENSTERN O.,STRATEGIE - HEUTE (2ND ED.). USA+45 USSR ECO/DEV DELIB/GP WAR PEACE ORD/FREE...GOV/COMP NAT/COMP 20 COLD/WAR NATO. PAGE 104 A2134 NUC/PWR DIPLOM FORCES TEC/DEV

B62

MORTON L.,STRATEGY AND COMMAND: THE FIRST TWO YEARS. USA-45 NAT/G CONTROL EXEC LEAD WEAPON CIVMIL/REL PWR...POLICY AUD/VIS CHARTS 20 CHINJAP. PAGE 105 A2150 WAR FORCES PLAN DIPLOM

B62

MULLEY F.W.,THE POLITICS OF WESTERN DEFENSE. EUR+WWI USA-45 WOR+45 VOL/ASSN EX/STRUC FORCES COERCE DETER PEACE ATTIT ORD/FREE PWR...RECORD TIME/SEQ CHARTS COLD/WAR 20 NATO. PAGE 106 A2168 INT/ORG DELIB/GP NUC/PWR

B62

NEAL F.W.,WAR AND PEACE AND GERMANY. EUR+WWI USSR STRUCT INT/ORG NAT/G FORCES DOMIN EDU/PROP LEGIT EXEC COERCE ORD/FREE...HUM SOC NEW/IDEA OBS TIME/SEQ TOT/POP COLD/WAR 20 BERLIN. PAGE 108 A2208 USA+45 POLICY DIPLOM GERMANY

B62

OSGOOD R.E.,NATO: THE ENTANGLING ALLIANCE. USA+45 WOR+45 VOL/ASSN FORCES TOP/EX PLAN DETER WEAPON DRIVE RIGID/FLEX ORD/FREE PWR...TREND 20 NATO. PAGE 112 A2301 INT/ORG ARMS/CONT PEACE

B62

PERRE J.,LES MUTATIONS DE LA GUERRE MODERNE: DE LA REVOLUTION FRANCAISE A LA REVOLUTION NUCLEAIRE. DIPLOM ARMS/CONT DEATH REV WEAPON GP/REL PEACE ATTIT...STAT PREDICT BIBLIOG 18/20 WWI. PAGE 115 A2365 WAR FORCES NUC/PWR

B62

RIVKIN A.,AFRICA AND THE WEST. AFR EUR+WWI FUT ISLAM ISRAEL USA+45 SOCIETY INT/ORG FORCES CREATE PLAN FOR/AID EDU/PROP ATTIT...CONCPT TREND EEC 20 CONGRESS UN. PAGE 121 A2488 ECO/UNDEV ECO/TAC

B62

ROOSEVELT J.,THE LIBERAL PAPERS. USA+45 WOR+45 ECO/DEV INT/ORG DELIB/GP ACT/RES PROB/SOLV DETER ATTIT...TREND IDEA/COMP ANTHOL. PAGE 123 A2520 DIPLOM NEW/LIB POLICY FORCES

B62

SCOTT W.E.,ALLIANCE AGAINST HITLER. EUR+WWI FRANCE GERMANY USSR BAL/PWR LEAD TOTALISM PWR FASCISM MARXISM...POLICY BIBLIOG 20 HITLER/A. PAGE 131 A2675 WAR DIPLOM FORCES

B62

SHAPIRO D.,A SELECT BIBLIOGRAPHY OF WORKS IN ENGLISH ON RUSSIAN HISTORY, 1801-1917. COM USSR STRATA FORCES EDU/PROP ADMIN REV RACE/REL ATTIT 19/20. PAGE 131 A2693 BIBLIOG DIPLOM COLONIAL

B62

SPIRO H.J.,POLITICS IN AFRICA: PROSPECTS SOUTH OF THE SAHARA. INT/ORG KIN FORCES LEGIS PROB/SOLV COERCE RACE/REL FEDERAL...TREND CHARTS BIBLIOG 20. PAGE 136 A2790 AFR NAT/LISM DIPLOM

B62

STEEL R.,THE END OF THE ALLIANCE. FRANCE FUT GERMANY/E GERMANY/W UK USA+45 NAT/G FORCES FOR/AID 20 NATO. PAGE 137 A2809 EUR+WWI POLICY DIPLOM INT/ORG

B62

STRACHEY J.,ON THE PREVENTION OF WAR. FUT WOR+45 INT/ORG NAT/G ACT/RES PLAN BAL/PWR DOMIN EDU/PROP PEACE ATTIT...POLICY TREND TOT/POP COLD/WAR 20 UN. PAGE 139 A2842 FORCES ORD/FREE ARMS/CONT NUC/PWR

B62

STRAUSS L.L.,MEN AND DECISIONS. USA+45 USA-45 USSR CONSULT FORCES TOP/EX WAR PEACE 20. PAGE 139 A2844 DECISION PWR NUC/PWR DIPLOM

B62

THOMSON G.P.,NUCLEAR ENERGY IN BRITAIN DURING THE LAST WAR: THE CHERWELL SIMON LECTURE (MONOGRAPH). UK R+D CONSULT FORCES PLAN DIPLOM TASK CIVMIL/REL ROLE...PHIL/SCI NEW/IDEA LAB/EXP 20 MAUD. PAGE 143 A2934 CREATE TEC/DEV WAR NUC/PWR

B62

US DEPARTMENT OF THE ARMY,GUIDE TO JAPANESE MONOGRAPHS AND JAPANESE STUDIES ON MANCHURIA: 1945-1960. CHINA/COM NAT/G DIPLOM LEAD COERCE WAR ...CHARTS 19/20 CHINJAP. PAGE 152 A3105 BIBLIOG/A FORCES ASIA S/ASIA

B62

US SENATE COMM ON JUDICIARY,CONSTITUTIONAL RIGHTS OF MILITARY PERSONNEL. USA+45 USA-45 FORCES DIPLOM WAR CONGRESS. PAGE 157 A3193 CONSTN ORD/FREE JURID CT/SYS

B62

WRIGHT Q.,PREVENTING WORLD WAR THREE. FUT WOR+45 CULTURE INT/ORG NAT/G CONSULT FORCES ADMIN ARMS/CONT DRIVE RIGID/FLEX ORD/FREE SOVEREIGN ...POLICY CONCPT TREND STERTYP COLD/WAR 20. PAGE 168 A3416 CREATE ATTIT

B62

YALEN R.,REGIONALISM AND WORLD ORDER. EUR+WWI WOR+45 WOR-45 INT/ORG VOL/ASSN DELIB/GP FORCES TOP/EX BAL/PWR DIPLOM DOMIN REGION ARMS/CONT PWR ...JURID HYPO/EXP COLD/WAR 20. PAGE 168 A3427 ORD/FREE POLICY

L62

STEIN E.,"MR HAMMARSKJOLD, THE CHARTER LAW AND THE FUTURE ROLE OF THE UNITED NATIONS SECRETARY-GENERAL." WOR+45 CONSTN INT/ORG DELIB/GP FORCES TOP/EX BAL/PWR LEGIT ROUTINE RIGID/FLEX PWR ...POLICY JURID OBS STERTYP UN COLD/WAR 20 HAMMARSK/D. PAGE 137 A2815 CONCPT BIOG

L62

ULYSSES,"THE INTERNATIONAL AIMS AND POLICIES OF THE SOVIET UNION: THE NEW CONCEPTS AND STRATEGY OF KHRUSHCHEV." FUT USSR WOR+45 SOCIETY INT/ORG NAT/G POL/PAR FORCES TOP/EX PLAN DOMIN EDU/PROP COERCE ATTIT PERSON PWR...TREND COLD/WAR 20 KHRUSH/N. PAGE 146 A2994 COM POLICY BAL/PWR DIPLOM

S62

CRANE R.D.,"LAW AND STRATEGY IN SPACE." FUT USA+45 WOR+45 AIR LAW INT/ORG NAT/G FORCES ACT/RES PLAN BAL/PWR LEGIT ARMS/CONT COERCE ORD/FREE...POLICY INT/LAW JURID SOC/EXP 20 TREATY. PAGE 32 A0656 CONCPT SPACE

S62

GREENSPAN M.,"INTERNATIONAL LAW AND ITS PROTECTION FOR PARTICIPANTS IN UNCONVENTIONAL WARFARE." WOR+45 LAW INT/ORG NAT/G POL/PAR COERCE REV ORD/FREE ...INT/LAW TOT/POP 20. PAGE 56 A1143 FORCES JURID GUERRILLA WAR

S62

NANES A.,"DISARMAMENT: THE LAST SEVEN YEARS." COM EUR+WWI USA+45 USSR INT/ORG FORCES TOP/EX CREATE LEGIT NUC/PWR DISPL ORD/FREE...CONCPT TIME/SEQ CON/ANAL 20. PAGE 107 A2195 DELIB/GP RIGID/FLEX ARMS/CONT

S62

RUSSETT B.M.,"CAUSE, SURPRISE, AND NO ESCAPE." FUT WOR-45 CULTURE SOCIETY INT/ORG FORCES TEC/DEV BAL/PWR EDU/PROP ARMS/CONT NUC/PWR WAR WEAPON PEACE KNOWL ORD/FREE PWR...POLICY CONCPT RECORD TIME/SEQ TREND GEN/LAWS 20 WWI. PAGE 126 A2578 COERCE DIPLOM

S62

SINGER J.D.,"STABLE DETERRENCE AND ITS LIMITS." FUT WOR+45 R+D INT/ORG CONSULT ACT/RES TEC/DEV ARMS/CONT COERCE DRIVE PERCEPT RIGID/FLEX ORD/FREE PWR...MYTH SIMUL TOT/POP 20. PAGE 133 A2728 NAT/G FORCES DETER NUC/PWR

S62

STRACHEY J.,"COMMUNIST INTENTIONS." ASIA USSR YUGOSLAVIA INT/ORG NAT/G FORCES DOMIN EDU/PROP COERCE NUC/PWR NAT/LISM PEACE RIGID/FLEX PWR MARXISM...CONCPT MYTH OBS TIME/SEQ TREND COLD/WAR TOT/POP 20. PAGE 139 A2843 COM ATTIT WAR

S62

THOMAS J.R.T.,"SOVIET BEHAVIOR IN THE QUEMOY CRISES OF 1958." CHINA/COM FUT USSR WOR+45 INT/ORG VOL/ASSN FORCES PLAN BAL/PWR DOMIN COERCE NUC/PWR REV WAR ATTIT DRIVE ORD/FREE...POLICY OBS RECORD COLD/WAR FOR/POL 20. PAGE 143 A2923 COM PWR

S62

TOWSTER J.,"THE USSR AND THE USA: CHALLENGE AND RESPONSE." COM GERMANY USA+45 USSR WOR+45 ECO/UNDEV INT/ORG VOL/ASSN EX/STRUC FORCES TOP/EX CREATE PLAN TEC/DEV DIPLOM ECO/TAC EDU/PROP COLONIAL COERCE PWR ...GEN/METH COLD/WAR 20 KENNEDY/JF. PAGE 145 A2956 ACT/RES GEN/LAWS

C62

BACON F.,"OF THE TRUE GREATNESS OF KINGDOMS AND ESTATES" (1612) IN F. BACON, ESSAYS." ELITES FORCES DOMIN EDU/PROP LEGIT...POLICY GEN/LAWS 16/17 TREATY. PAGE 10 A0200 WAR PWR DIPLOM CONSTN

B63

ABSHIRE D.M.,NATIONAL SECURITY: POLITICAL, MILITARY, AND ECONOMIC STRATEGIES IN THE DECADE AHEAD. ASIA COM USA+45 WOR+45 ECO/DEV ECO/UNDEV FUT ACT/RES BAL/PWR

INT/ORG DELIB/GP FORCES ECO/TAC COERCE ATTIT RIGID/FLEX HEALTH ORD/FREE PWR WEALTH...POLICY STAT CHARTS ANTHOL COLD/WAR VAL/FREE. PAGE 4 A0083

B63
ADLER G.J.,BRITISH INDIA'S NORTHERN FRONTIER: 1865-95. AFGHANISTN RUSSIA UK PROVS COLONIAL COERCE PEACE...GEOG CHARTS BIBLIOG 19 TREATY. PAGE 4 A0091 S/ASIA FORCES DIPLOM POLICY

B63
BLOCH-MORHANGE J.,VINGT ANNEES D'HISTOIRE CONTEMPORAINE. FORCES FOR/AID CONFER LEAD 20 COLD/WAR. PAGE 15 A0311 WAR DIPLOM INT/ORG CHIEF

B63
BOISSIER P.,HISTORIE DU COMITE INTERNATIONAL DE LA CROIX ROUGE. MOD/EUR WOR-45 CONSULT FORCES PLAN DIPLOM EDU/PROP ADMIN MORAL ORD/FREE...SOC CONCPT RECORD TIME/SEQ GEN/LAWS TOT/POP VAL/FREE 19/20. PAGE 16 A0332 INT/ORG HEALTH ARMS/CONT WAR

B63
BROEKMEIJER M.W.,DEVELOPING COUNTRIES AND NATO. USSR FORCES DIPLOM NUC/PWR WAR PEACE TOTALISM 20 NATO. PAGE 19 A0384 ECO/UNDEV FOR/AID ORD/FREE NAT/G

B63
BURNS A.L.,PEACE-KEEPING BY U.N.FORCES - FROM SUEZ TO THE CONGO. AFR FUT ISLAM ISRAEL USSR WOR+45 NAT/G DELIB/GP BAL/PWR DOMIN LEGIT EXEC COERCE PEACE ATTIT PWR RESPECT SOVEREIGN...CONCPT UN 20. PAGE 22 A0441 INT/ORG FORCES ORD/FREE

B63
DEENER D.R.,CANADA - UNITED STATES TREATY RELATIONS. CANADA USA+45 USA-45 NAT/G FORCES PLAN PROB/SOLV AGREE NUC/PWR...TREND 18/20 TREATY. PAGE 35 A0722 DIPLOM INT/LAW POLICY

B63
DUNN F.S.,PEACE-MAKING AND THE SETTLEMENT WITH JAPAN. ASIA USA+45 USA-45 FORCES BAL/PWR ECO/TAC CONFER WAR PWR SOVEREIGN 20 CHINJAP COLD/WAR TREATY. PAGE 39 A0802 POLICY PEACE PLAN DIPLOM

B63
EL-NAGGAR S.,FOREIGN AID TO UNITED ARAB REPUBLIC. UAR USA+45 USSR AGRI FINAN INDUS FORCES EATING DEMAND...CHARTS METH/COMP 20 RESOURCE/N AID. PAGE 41 A0838 FOR/AID ECO/UNDEV RECEIVE PLAN

B63
ELLENDER A.J.,A REPORT ON UNITED STATES FOREIGN OPERATIONS IN AFRICA. SOUTH/AFR USA+45 STRATA EXTR/IND FORCES RACE/REL ISOLAT SOVEREIGN...CHARTS 20 NEGRO. PAGE 41 A0840 FOR/AID DIPLOM WEALTH ECO/UNDEV

B63
ELLERT R.B.,NATO 'FAIR TRIAL' SAFEGUARDS: PRECURSOR TO AN INTERNATIONAL BILL OF PROCEDURAL RIGHTS. WOR+45 FORCES CRIME CIVMIL/REL ATTIT ORD/FREE 20 NATO. PAGE 41 A0841 JURID INT/LAW INT/ORG CT/SYS

B63
FALK R.A.,LAW, MORALITY, AND WAR IN THE CONTEMPORARY WORLD. WOR+45 LAW INT/ORG EX/STRUC FORCES EDU/PROP LEGIT DETER NUC/PWR MORAL ORD/FREE ...JURID TOT/POP 20. PAGE 43 A0888 ADJUD ARMS/CONT PEACE INT/LAW

B63
FRANKEL J.,THE MAKING OF FOREIGN POLICY: AN ANALYSIS OF DECISION-MAKING. CHINA/COM EUR+WWI USA+45 ELITES INTELL FORCES LEGIS PLAN ATTIT ALL/VALS MORAL CONSERVE...GOV/COMP 20 PRESIDENT UN TREATY. PAGE 48 A0981 POLICY DECISION PROB/SOLV DIPLOM

B63
GOLDWIN R.A.,FOREIGN AND MILITARY POLICY. COM USSR WOR+45 ECO/DEV INT/ORG FORCES PLAN ECO/TAC REGION ARMS/CONT MARXISM 20 UN. PAGE 54 A1097 DIPLOM POLICY PWR NAT/G

B63
GREAT BRITAIN CENTRAL OFF INF,CONSULTATION AND CO-OPERATION IN THE COMMONWEALTH. LAW R+D FORCES PLAN EDU/PROP CONFER INGP/REL...GEOG CENSUS 19/20 CMN/WLTH. PAGE 55 A1133 DIPLOM DELIB/GP VOL/ASSN REGION

B63
HALASZ DE BEKY I.L.,A BIBLIOGRAPHY OF THE HUNGARIAN REVOLUTION 1956. COM HUNGARY USSR DIPLOM COERCE MARXISM...POLICY AUD/VIS 20 UN COLD/WAR. PAGE 59 A1221 BIBLIOG REV FORCES ATTIT

B63
HALPERIN M.H.,LIMITED WAR IN A NUCLEAR AGE. CUBA KOREA USA+45 USSR INT/ORG FORCES PLAN DIPLOM DETER PWR...BIBLIOG/A 20. PAGE 60 A1238 WAR NUC/PWR CONTROL WEAPON

B63
HAMM H.,ALBANIA - CHINA'S BEACHHEAD IN EUROPE. ALBANIA CHINA/COM USSR YUGOSLAVIA ELITES SOCIETY POL/PAR DELIB/GP FORCES ECO/TAC COERCE ISOLAT PEACE MARXISM...IDEA/COMP 20 MAO. PAGE 61 A1248 DIPLOM REV NAT/G POLICY

B63
KHADDURI M.,MODERN LIBYA: A STUDY IN POLITICAL DEVELOPMENT. EUR+WWI ISLAM LIBYA ELITES INT/ORG POL/PAR FORCES DIPLOM FOR/AID DOMIN EDU/PROP LEGIT NAT/LISM DRIVE RIGID/FLEX SKILL...CONCPT TIME/SEQ TREND 20. PAGE 78 A1606 NAT/G STRUCT

B63
KLEIMAN R.,ATLANTIC CRISIS; AMERICAN DIPLOMACY CONFRONTS A RESURGENT EUROPE. EUR+WWI USA+45 ECO/DEV AGRI NAT/G CHIEF FORCES PLAN LEAD ATTIT ...CONCPT 20 NATO KENNEDY/JF DEGAULLE/C EEC JOHNSON/LB. PAGE 80 A1648 DIPLOM REGION POLICY

B63
KORBEL J.,POLAND BETWEEN EAST AND WEST: SOVIET AND GERMAN DIPLOMACY TOWARD POLAND 1919-1933. EUR+WWI GERMANY POLAND USSR FORCES AGREE WAR SOVEREIGN ...BIBLIOG 20 TREATY. PAGE 81 A1670 BAL/PWR DIPLOM DOMIN NAT/LISM

B63
LERCHE C.O. JR.,AMERICA IN WORLD AFFAIRS. COM UK USA+45 INT/ORG FORCES ECO/TAC INT/TRADE EDU/PROP WAR NAT/LISM PEACE...BIBLIOG 18/20 UN CONGRESS PRESIDENT COLD/WAR. PAGE 87 A1783 NAT/G DIPLOM PLAN

B63
LILIENTHAL D.E.,CHANGE, HOPE, AND THE BOMB. USA+45 WOR+45 R+D INT/ORG NAT/G DELIB/GP FORCES ACT/RES DETER RIGID/FLEX ORD/FREE...POLICY CONCPT OBS AEC 20. PAGE 89 A1815 ATTIT MYTH ARMS/CONT NUC/PWR

B63
MANSERGH N.,DOCUMENTS AND SPEECHES ON COMMONWEALTH AFFAIRS 1952-1962. CANADA INDIA PAKISTAN UK CONSTN FORCES ECO/TAC EDU/PROP COLONIAL DETER WAR ORD/FREE SOVEREIGN...POLICY 20 AUSTRAL. PAGE 94 A1932 BIBLIOG/A FEDERAL INT/TRADE DIPLOM

B63
ROSNER G.,THE UNITED NATIONS EMERGENCY FORCE. FRANCE ISRAEL UAR UK WOR+45 CREATE WAR PEACE ORD/FREE PWR...INT/LAW JURID HIST/WRIT TIME/SEQ UN. PAGE 124 A2539 INT/ORG FORCES

B63
RUSK D.,THE WINDS OF FREEDOM. S/ASIA SOUTH/AFR INT/ORG FORCES NUC/PWR PEACE ORD/FREE 20 UN COLD/WAR. PAGE 125 A2569 DIPLOM FOR/AID INT/TRADE

B63
SALENT W.S.,THE UNITED STATES BALANCE OF PAYMENTS IN 1968. EUR+WWI UK USA+45 AGRI R+D LABOR FORCES PRODUC...GEOG CONCPT CHARTS 20 CHINJAP EEC. PAGE 126 A2589 BAL/PAY DEMAND FINAN INT/TRADE

B63
SCHRADER R.,SCIENCE AND POLICY. WOR+45 ECO/DEV ECO/UNDEV R+D FORCES PLAN DIPLOM GOV/REL TECHRACY BIBLIOG. PAGE 129 A2644 TEC/DEV NAT/G POLICY ADMIN

B63
SMITH J.E.,THE DEFENSE OF BERLIN. COM GUATEMALA WOR+45 ECO/TAC ADMIN NEUTRAL ATTIT ORD/FREE SOVEREIGN...DECISION 20 DEPT/STATE. PAGE 134 A2747 DIPLOM FORCES BAL/PWR PLAN

B63
STROMBERG R.N.,COLLECTIVE SECURITY AND AMERICAN FOREIGN POLICY FROM THE LEAGUE OF NATIONS TO NATO. USA+45 USA-45 WOR-45 INT/ORG VOL/ASSN EX/STRUC FORCES LEGIT ROUTINE DRIVE...CONCPT TREND UN LEAGUE/NAT 20 NATO. PAGE 139 A2851 ORD/FREE TIME/SEQ DIPLOM

B63
SWEARER H.R.,CONTEMPORARY COMMUNISM: THEORY AND PRACTICE. COM USSR SOCIETY ECO/DEV POL/PAR FORCES PLAN ADMIN LEAD NAT/LISM...POLICY ANTHOL 20 LENIN/VI COM/PARTY. PAGE 140 A2869 MARXISM CONCPT DIPLOM NAT/G

B63
THUCYDIDES,THE PELOPONESIAN WARS. MEDIT-7 CULTURE INT/ORG NAT/G FORCES TOP/EX PLAN ROUTINE PWR ...CONCPT. PAGE 144 A2938 ATTIT COERCE WAR

B63
US HOUSE COMM FOREIGN AFFAIRS,HEARINGS ON H.R. 5490 TO AMEND FURTHER THE FOREIGN ASSISTANCE ACT OF 1961. CUBA EUR+WWI INDIA INT/ORG DELIB/GP LEGIS DIPLOM CONFER ORD/FREE 20 DEPT/STATE DEPT/DEFEN UN. PAGE 153 A3129 FOR/AID INT/TRADE FORCES WEAPON

B63
US SENATE COMM GOVT OPERATIONS,REPORT OF A STUDY OF US FOREIGN AID IN TEN MIDDLE EASTERN AND AFRICAN COUNTRIES. AFR ISLAM USA+45 FORCES PLAN BUDGET DIPLOM TAX DETER WEALTH...STAT CHARTS 20 CONGRESS AID MID/EAST. PAGE 156 A3174 FOR/AID EFFICIENCY ECO/TAC FINAN

B63
US SENATE COMM ON FOREIGN REL,HEARINGS ON S 1276 A BILL TO AMEND FURTHER THE FOREIGN ASSISTANCE ACT OF 1961. USA+45 WOR+45 INDUS INT/ORG FORCES TAX WEAPON SUPEGO...NAT/COMP 20 UN CONGRESS PRESIDENT. PAGE 156 A3182 FOR/AID DIPLOM ECO/UNDEV ORD/FREE

B63
VAN SLYCK P.,PEACE: THE CONTROL OF NATIONAL POWER. CUBA WOR+45 FINAN NAT/G FORCES PROB/SOLV TEC/DEV BAL/PWR ADMIN CONTROL ORD/FREE...POLICY INT/LAW UN COLD/WAR TREATY. PAGE 158 A3214 ARMS/CONT PEACE INT/ORG DIPLOM

B63
VOSS E.H.,NUCLEAR AMBUSH: THE TEST-BAN TRAP. WOR+45 COM/IND INT/ORG NAT/G DELIB/GP FORCES LEGIS TOP/EX ACT/RES DOMIN EDU/PROP LEGIT ROUTINE COERCE ATTIT PERCEPT RIGID/FLEX HEALTH MORAL ORD/FREE PWR. PAGE 160 A3255 TEC/DEV HIST/WRIT ARMS/CONT NUC/PWR

L63
CRANE R.D.,"THE CUBAN CRISIS: A STRATEGIC ANALYSIS OF AMERICAN AND SOVIET POLICY." CUBA USA+45 USSR BAL/PWR RISK DETER NUC/PWR PERCEPT ORD/FREE 20. PAGE 32 A0658 DIPLOM POLICY FORCES

L63
LISSITZYN O.J.,"INTERNATIONAL LAW IN A DIVIDED WORLD." FUT WOR+45 CONSTN CULTURE ECO/DEV ECO/UNDEV DIST/IND NAT/G FORCES ECO/TAC LEGIT ADJUD ADMIN COERCE ATTIT HEALTH MORAL ORD/FREE PWR RESPECT WEALTH VAL/FREE. PAGE 90 A1841 INT/ORG LAW

L63
PADELFORD N.J.,"FINANCIAL CRISIS AND THE UNITED NATIONS." FUT USSR WOR+45 LAW CONSTN FINAN INT/ORG DELIB/GP FORCES PLAN BUDGET DIPLOM COST WEALTH ...STAT CHARTS UN CONGO 20. PAGE 113 A2311 CREATE ECO/TAC

L63
PHELPS J.,"STUDIES IN DETERRENCE VIII: MILITARY STABILITARY AND ARMS CONTROL: A CRITICAL SURVEY." FUT WOR+45 INT/ORG ACT/RES EDU/PROP COERCE NUC/PWR WAR HEALTH PWR...POLICY TECHNIC TREND SIMUL TOT/POP 20. PAGE 116 A2373 FORCES ORD/FREE ARMS/CONT DETER

L63
SCHELLING T.C.,"STRATEGIC PROBLEMS OF AN INTERNATIONAL ARMED FORCE." WOR+45 ECO/DEV INT/ORG NAT/G PLAN BAL/PWR LEGIT ARMS/CONT COERCE DETER ORD/FREE PWR...POLICY CONCPT COLD/WAR 20. PAGE 128 A2624 CREATE FORCES

L63
SINGER J.D.,"WEAPONS MANAGEMENT IN WORLD POLITICS: PROCEEDINGS OF THE INTERNATIONAL ARMS CONTROL SYMPOSIUM, DECEMBER, 1962." FUT WOR+45 SOCIETY ECO/DEV INDUS INT/ORG DELIB/GP FORCES ACT/RES ECO/TAC EDU/PROP ARMS/CONT SUPEGO HEALTH ORD/FREE PWR SKILL...POLICY CHARTS SIMUL ANTHOL VAL/FREE 20. PAGE 133 A2729 CONSULT ATTIT DIPLOM NUC/PWR

S63
ALPHAND H.,"FRANCE AND HER ALLIES." EUR+WWI UK USA+45 ECO/DEV INT/ORG NAT/G VOL/ASSN FORCES TOP/EX DIPLOM ECO/TAC LEGIT ATTIT DRIVE ORD/FREE PWR WEALTH...STAT EEC TOT/POP 20. PAGE 6 A0130 ACT/RES FRANCE

S63
BECHHOEFER B.G.,"UNITED NATIONS PROCEDURES IN CASE OF VIOLATIONS OF DISARMAMENT AGREEMENTS." COM USA+45 USSR LAW CONSTN NAT/G EX/STRUC FORCES LEGIS BAL/PWR EDU/PROP CT/SYS ARMS/CONT ORD/FREE PWR ...POLICY STERTYP UN VAL/FREE 20. PAGE 12 A0245 INT/ORG DELIB/GP

S63
BLOOMFIELD L.P.,"INTERNATIONAL FORCE IN A DISARMING BUT REVOLUTIONARY WORLD." INT/ORG COERCE REV DRIVE PWR...CONCPT STERTYP GEN/LAWS 20. PAGE 16 A0318 FORCES ORD/FREE ARMS/CONT GUERRILLA

S63
BLOOMFIELD L.P.,"HEADQUARTERS-FIELD RELATIONS: SOME NOTES ON THE BEGINNING AND END OF ONUC." AFR INT/ORG ROUTINE COERCE WAR WEAPON UN CONGO 20. PAGE 16 A0319 FORCES ORD/FREE

S63
BRZEZINSKI Z.,"SOVIET QUIESCENCE." EUR+WWI USA+45 USSR FORCES CREATE PLAN COERCE DETER WAR ATTIT 20 TREATY EUROPE. PAGE 20 A0415 DIPLOM ARMS/CONT NUC/PWR AGREE

S63
CLEVELAND H.,"CRISIS DIPLOMACY." USA+45 WOR+45 LAW FORCES TASK NUC/PWR PWR 20. PAGE 27 A0551 DECISION DIPLOM PROB/SOLV POLICY

S63
DARLING F.C.,"THE GEOPOLITICS OF AMERICAN FOREIGN POLITICS IN ASIA." COM S/ASIA USA+45 USSR ECO/UNDEV NAT/G VOL/ASSN CONSULT PLAN GUERRILLA...STAT TOT/POP 20. PAGE 34 A0682 FORCES ECO/TAC FOR/AID DIPLOM

S63
DICKS H.V.,"NATIONAL LOYALTY, IDENTITY, AND THE INTERNATIONAL SOLDIER." FUT NAT/G COERCE ATTIT DRIVE PERCEPT PERSON RIGID/FLEX SUPEGO ALL/VALS ...PSY VAL/FREE. PAGE 37 A0758 INT/ORG FORCES

S63
GIRAUD E.,"L'INTERDICTION DU RECOURS A LA FORCE, LA THEORIE ET LA PRATIQUE DES NATIONS UNIES." ALGERIA COM CUBA HUNGARY WOR+45 ADJUD TOTALISM ATTIT RIGID/FLEX PWR...POLICY JURID CONCPT UN 20 CONGO. PAGE 53 A1077 INT/ORG FORCES DIPLOM

S63
HUMPHREY H.H.,"REGIONAL ARMS CONTROL AGREEMENTS." WOR+45 FORCES PLAN LEGIT COERCE ATTIT HEALTH ORD/FREE...HUM METH/CNCPT MYTH OBS INT TREND TOT/POP 20. PAGE 69 A1416 L/A+17C INT/ORG ARMS/CONT REGION

S63
KINTNER W.R.,"THE PROJECTED EUROPEAN UNION AND AMERICAN RESPONSIBILITIES." EUR+WWI USA+45 STRATA INT/ORG NAT/G DOMIN DETER NUC/PWR ATTIT ORD/FREE PWR 20 NATO. PAGE 79 A1628 FUT FORCES DIPLOM REGION

S63
LIGOT M.,"LA COOPERATION MILITAIRE DANS LES ACCORDS, PASSES ENTRE LA FRANCE ET LES ETATS AFRICAINS ET MALGACHE D'EXPRESSION." ECO/UNDEV INT/ORG NAT/G VOL/ASSN...CONCPT TIME/SEQ 20. PAGE 89 A1814 AFR FORCES FOR/AID FRANCE

S63
MODELSKI G.,"STUDY OF ALLIANCES." WOR+45 WOR-45 INT/ORG NAT/G FORCES LEGIT ADMIN CHOOSE ALL/VALS PWR SKILL...INT/LAW CONCPT GEN/LAWS 20 TREATY. PAGE 102 A2099 VOL/ASSN CON/ANAL DIPLOM

S63
MORGENTHAU H.J.,"THE POLITICAL CONDITIONS FOR AN INTERNATIONAL POLICE FORCE." FUT WOR+45 CREATE LEGIT ADMIN PEACE ORD/FREE 20. PAGE 104 A2141 INT/ORG FORCES ARMS/CONT DETER

S63
MULLEY F.W.,"NUCLEAR WEAPONS: CHALLENGE TO NATIONAL SOVEREIGNTY." EUR+WWI FRANCE UK USA+45 VOL/ASSN EX/STRUC FORCES TOP/EX ACT/RES REGION DRIVE PWR 20 NATO DEGAULLE/C. PAGE 106 A2169 INT/ORG ATTIT DIPLOM NUC/PWR

S63
MURRAY J.N.,"UNITED NATIONS PEACE-KEEPING AND PROBLEMS OF POLITICAL CONTROL." FUT WOR+45 CONSTN DELIB/GP FORCES TOP/EX ACT/RES CREATE LEGIT PEACE PWR...METH/CNCPT CONGO UN 20. PAGE 106 A2182 INT/ORG ORD/FREE

S63
NADLER E.B.,"SOME ECONOMIC DISADVANTAGES OF THE ARMS RACE." USA+45 INDUS R+D FORCES PLAN TEC/DEV ECO/TAC FOR/AID EDU/PROP PWR WEALTH...TREND COLD/WAR 20. PAGE 107 A2190 ECO/DEV MGT BAL/PAY

S63
NICHOLAS H.G.,"UN PEACE FORCES AND THE CHANGING GLOBE: THE LESSONS OF SUEZ AND CONGO." FUT WOR+45 CONSTN INT/ORG CONSULT DELIB/GP TOP/EX CREATE DIPLOM DOMIN LEGIT COERCE WAR PERSON RIGID/FLEX PWR UN SUEZ CONGO UNEF 20. PAGE 109 A2229 ACT/RES FORCES

S63
NOGEE J.L.,"PROPOGANDA AND NEGOTIATION: THE CASE OF THE TEN NATION DISARMAMENT COMMITTEE." COM EUR+WWI USA+45 VOL/ASSN DELIB/GP FORCES DIPLOM DOMIN LEGIT PWR...METH/CNCPT STERTYP COLD/WAR VAL/FREE 20. PAGE 110 A2248 INT/ORG EDU/PROP ARMS/CONT

S63
SONNENFELDT H.,"FOREIGN POLICY FROM MALENKOV TO KHRUSHCHEV." WOR+45 NAT/G FORCES BAL/PWR DIPLOM ECO/TAC COERCE ATTIT PWR...CONCPT HIST/WRIT COLD/WAR 20. PAGE 135 A2768 COM DOMIN FOR/AID USSR

S63
STANLEY T.W.,"DECENTRALIZING NUCLEAR CONTROL IN NATO." EUR+WWI USA+45 ELITES FORCES ACT/RES ATTIT ORD/FREE PWR...NEW/IDEA HYPO/EXP TOT/POP 20 NATO. PAGE 137 A2805 INT/ORG EX/STRUC NUC/PWR

S63
WYZNER E.,"NIEKTORE ASPEKTY PRAWNE FINANSOWANIA OPERACJI ONZ W KONGO I NA BEIZKIM WSCHODZIE." S/ASIA CONSTN FINAN INT/ORG TOP/EX...TIME/SEQ UN 20 CONGRESS. PAGE 168 A3426 FORCES JURID DIPLOM

C63
ATTIA G.E.O.,"LES FORCES ARMEES DES NATIONS UNIES EN COREE ET AU MOYENORIENT." KOREA CONSTN DELIB/GP LEGIS PWR...IDEA/COMP NAT/COMP BIBLIOG UN SUEZ. PAGE 10 A0194 FORCES NAT/G INT/LAW

N63
PATEL H.M.,THE DEFENCE OF INDIA (PAMPHLET). CHINA/COM INDIA PAKISTAN WOR+45 TEC/DEV BAL/PWR DIPLOM CONTROL WAR. PAGE 114 A2340 FORCES POLICY SOVEREIGN DETER

B64
AHLUWALIA K.,THE LEGAL STATUS, PRIVILEGES AND IMMUNITIES OF SPECIALIZED AGENCIES OF UN AND CERTAIN OTHER INTERNATIONAL ORGANIZATIONS. WOR+45 LAW CONSULT DELIB/GP FORCES. PAGE 5 A0102 PRIVIL DIPLOM INT/ORG INT/LAW

B64
BARKER A.J.,SUEZ: THE SEVEN DAY WAR. EUR+WWI ISLAM UAR INT/ORG NAT/G PLAN DIPLOM ECO/TAC DOMIN NAT/LISM DRIVE RIGID/FLEX PWR SOVEREIGN...POLICY JURID TREND CHARTS SUEZ UN 20. PAGE 11 A0221 FORCES COERCE UK

B64
BELL C.,THE DEBATABLE ALLIANCE. COM UK USA+45 NAT/G FORCES PLAN BAL/PWR NUC/PWR WAR ATTIT...GOV/COMP 20. PAGE 13 A0256 DIPLOM PWR PEACE POLICY

B64
BLACKSTOCK P.W.,THE STRATEGY OF SUBVERSION. USA+45 FORCES EDU/PROP ADMIN COERCE GOV/REL...DECISION MGT 20 DEPT/DEFEN CIA DEPT/STATE. PAGE 15 A0301 ORD/FREE DIPLOM CONTROL

B64
BLANCHARD C.H.,KOREAN WAR BIBLIOGRAPHY. KOREA FAM BAL/PWR RATION MURDER WEAPON MARXISM...CHARTS 20. PAGE 15 A0306 BIBLIOG/A WAR DIPLOM FORCES

B64
BLOOMFIELD L.P.,INTERNATIONAL MILITARY FORCES: THE QUESTION OF PEACE-KEEPING IN AN ARMED AND DISARMING WORLD. WOR+45 ACADEM ARMS/CONT REV PEACE 20 UN. PAGE 16 A0320 INT/ORG FORCES FUT DIPLOM

B64
COTTRELL A.J.,THE POLITICS OF THE ATLANTIC VOL/ASSN

ALLIANCE. EUR+WWI USA+45 INT/ORG NAT/G DELIB/GP EX/STRUC BAL/PWR DIPLOM REGION DETER ATTIT ORD/FREE ...CONCPT RECORD GEN/LAWS GEN/METH NATO 20. PAGE 31 A0632
FORCES

B64
DEITCHMAN S.J.,LIMITED WAR AND AMERICAN DEFENSE POLICY. USA+45 WOR+45 INT/ORG NAT/G PLAN TEC/DEV COERCE NUC/PWR RIGID/FLEX PWR SKILL...DECISION METH/CNCPT TIME/SEQ TOT/POP COLD/WAR 20. PAGE 36 A0726
FORCES WAR WEAPON

B64
DEUTSCHE GES AUSWARTIGE POL,STRATEGIE UND ABRUSTUNGSPOLITIK DER SOWJETUNION. USSR TEC/DEV DIPLOM COERCE DETER WEAPON...POLICY PSY 20 ABM/DEFSYS. PAGE 37 A0747
NUC/PWR WAR FORCES ARMS/CONT

B64
EAYRS J.,THE COMMONWEALTH AND SUEZ: A DOCUMENTARY SURVEY. FRANCE ISLAM VOL/ASSN FORCES CONFER COLONIAL WAR INGP/REL 20 CMN/WLTH SUEZ UN. PAGE 40 A0818
DIPLOM NAT/LISM DIST/IND SOVEREIGN

B64
EPSTEIN H.M.,REVOLT IN THE CONGO. AFR CONGO/BRAZ WOR+45 NAT/G FORCES DOMIN WAR CIVMIL/REL INGP/REL MARXISM...RECORD GP/COMP 20 CONGO/LEOP UN. PAGE 42 A0856
REV COLONIAL NAT/LISM DIPLOM

B64
ESTHUS R.A.,FROM ENMITY TO ALLIANCE: US AUSTRALIAN RELATIONS. S/ASIA DIST/IND VOL/ASSN FORCES ATTIT 20 AUSTRAL TREATY CMN/WLTH. PAGE 42 A0863
DIPLOM WAR INT/TRADE FOR/AID

B64
ETZIONI A.,WINNING WITHOUT WAR. FUT MOD/EUR USA+45 WOR+45 ECO/DEV ECO/UNDEV INT/ORG NAT/G FORCES TOP/EX PLAN TEC/DEV ECO/TAC DOMIN EDU/PROP LEGIT COERCE CHOOSE ATTIT MORAL ORD/FREE RESPECT WEALTH MAJORIT. PAGE 43 A0871
PWR TREND DIPLOM USSR

B64
FALL B.,STREET WITHOUT JOY. FRANCE USA+45 DIPLOM ECO/TAC FOR/AID GUERRILLA REV WEAPON...TREND 20. PAGE 44 A0894
WAR S/ASIA FORCES COERCE

B64
FISHER R.,INTERNATIONAL CONFLICT AND BEHAVIORAL SCIENCE: THE CRAIGVILLE PAPERS. COM FUT USA+45 WOR+45 NAT/G DELIB/GP EX/STRUC FORCES ECO/TAC DOMIN EDU/PROP LEGIT COERCE ATTIT PERCEPT ORD/FREE PWR RESPECT...PSY SOC VAL/FREE. PAGE 46 A0940
INT/ORG PLAN DIPLOM

B64
FRYDENSBERG P.,PEACE-KEEPING: EXPERIENCE AND EVALUATION: THE OSLO PAPERS. NORWAY FORCES PLAN CONTROL...INT/LAW 20 UN. PAGE 49 A1012
INT/ORG DIPLOM PEACE COERCE

B64
GESELLSCHAFT RECHTSVERGLEICH,BIBLIOGRAPHIE DES DEUTSCHEN RECHTS (BIBLIOGRAPHY OF GERMAN LAW, TRANS. BY COURTLAND PETERSON). GERMANY FINAN INDUS LABOR SECT FORCES CT/SYS PARL/PROC CRIME...INT/LAW SOC NAT/COMP 20. PAGE 52 A1066
BIBLIOG/A JURID CONSTN ADMIN

B64
GRZYBOWSKI K.,THE SOCIALIST COMMONWEALTH OF NATIONS: ORGANIZATIONS AND INSTITUTIONS. FORCES DIPLOM INT/TRADE ADJUD ADMIN LEAD WAR MARXISM SOCISM...BIBLIOG 20 COMECON WARSAW/P. PAGE 58 A1185
INT/LAW COM REGION INT/ORG

B64
HEKHUIS D.J.,INTERNATIONAL STABILITY: MILITARY, ECONOMIC AND POLITICAL DIMENSIONS. FUT WOR+45 LAW ECO/UNDEV INT/ORG NAT/G VOL/ASSN FORCES ACT/RES BAL/PWR PWR WEALTH...STAT UN 20. PAGE 64 A1310
TEC/DEV DETER REGION

B64
JANOWITZ M.,THE MILITARY IN THE POLITICAL DEVELOPMENT OF NEW NATIONS: AN ESSAY IN COMPARATIVE ANALYSIS. AFR ASIA ISLAM L/A+17C S/ASIA USA+45 ECO/UNDEV INT/ORG NAT/G POL/PAR DELIB/GP PLAN ECO/TAC DOMIN LEGIT COERCE ATTIT DRIVE RESPECT ...SOC CONCPT CENSUS VAL/FREE. PAGE 73 A1495
FORCES PWR

B64
JOHNSON E.A.J.,THE DIMENSIONS OF DIPLOMACY. INT/ORG FORCES TEC/DEV WAR PEACE PWR...SOC ANTHOL 20. PAGE 74 A1522
DIPLOM POLICY METH

B64
KAUFMANN W.W.,THE MC NAMARA STRATEGY. TOP/EX INSPECT BAL/PWR DIPLOM CONTROL DETER GUERRILLA NUC/PWR WEAPON COST PWR...METH/COMP 20 MCNAMARA/R KENNEDY/JF JOHNSON/LB NATO DEPT/DEFEN. PAGE 77 A1572
FORCES WAR PLAN PROB/SOLV

B64
KIMMINICH O.,RUSTUNG UND POLITISCHE SPANNUNG. INDUS ARMS/CONT COERCE NAT/LISM PEACE PERSON ORD/FREE ...POLICY GEOG 20. PAGE 79 A1619
DIPLOM FORCES WEAPON WAR

B64
KITCHEN H.,A HANDBOOK OF AFRICAN AFFAIRS. ECO/UNDEV CREATE DIPLOM COLONIAL RACE/REL...ART/METH GEOG CHARTS 20. PAGE 80 A1646
AFR NAT/G INT/ORG FORCES

B64
LEGGE J.D.,INDONESIA. INDONESIA ELITES ECO/UNDEV POL/PAR CHIEF FORCES INT/TRADE COERCE CHOOSE ORD/FREE...SOC CHARTS BIBLIOG 16/20 CHINJAP. PAGE 86 A1765
S/ASIA DOMIN NAT/LISM POLICY

B64
LENSEN G.A.,REVELATIONS OF A RUSSIAN DIPLOMAT: THE MEMOIRS OF DMITRII I. ABRIKOSSOV. ASIA MOD/EUR RUSSIA USA-45 ELITES ACADEM CHIEF FORCES REV WAR PWR CONSERVE MARXISM 19/20 ABRIKSSV/D CHINJAP BOLSHEVISM. PAGE 87 A1775
DIPLOM POLICY OBS

B64
LIEVWEN E.,GENERALS VS PRESIDENTS: WEOMILITARISM IN LATIN AMERICA. L/A+17C FORCES DIPLOM FOR/AID LEAD ...NAT/COMP 20 PRESIDENT. PAGE 89 A1813
CIVMIL/REL REV CONSERVE ORD/FREE

B64
LISKA G.,EUROPE ASCENDANT. EUR+WWI ECO/DEV FORCES INT/TRADE MARXISM 20 EEC. PAGE 90 A1838
DIPLOM BAL/PWR TARIFFS CENTRAL

B64
LOCKHART W.B.,CASES AND MATERIALS ON CONSTITUTIONAL RIGHTS AND LIBERTIES. USA+45 FORCES LEGIS DIPLOM PRESS CONTROL CRIME WAR PWR...AUD/VIS T WORSHIP 20 NEGRO. PAGE 90 A1849
ORD/FREE CONSTN NAT/G

B64
LUARD E.,THE COLD WAR: A RE-APPRAISAL. FUT USSR WOR+45 FORCES NUC/PWR NAT/LISM ORD/FREE SOVEREIGN ...INT 20 COLD/WAR STALIN/J TREATY UN. PAGE 91 A1870
DIPLOM WAR PEACE TOTALISM

B64
MACKESY P.,THE WAR FOR AMERICA, 1775-1783. UK FORCES DIPLOM...POLICY 18. PAGE 93 A1895
WAR COLONIAL LEAD REV

B64
MEYER F.S.,WHAT IS CONSERVATISM? USA+45 NAT/G FORCES DIPLOM ORD/FREE IDEA/COMP. PAGE 100 A2048
CONSERVE CONCPT EDU/PROP CAP/ISM

B64
PITTMAN J.,PEACEFUL COEXISTENCE. USSR NAT/G NUC/PWR WAR ATTIT 20. PAGE 116 A2385
DIPLOM PEACE POLICY FORCES

B64
REES D.,KOREA: THE LIMITED WAR. ASIA KOREA WOR+45 NAT/G CIVMIL/REL PERS/REL PERSON...POLICY CHARTS 20 UN TRUMAN/HS MACARTHR/D. PAGE 120 A2455
DIPLOM WAR INT/ORG FORCES

B64
REGALA R.,WORLD PEACE THROUGH DIPLOMACY AND LAW. S/ASIA WOR+45 ECO/UNDEV INT/ORG FORCES PLAN PROB/SOLV FOR/AID NUC/PWR WAR...POLICY INT/LAW 20. PAGE 120 A2456
DIPLOM PEACE ADJUD

B64
ROCK V.P.,A STRATEGY OF INTERDEPENDENCE. COM USSR WOR+45 NAT/G FORCES PROB/SOLV TEC/DEV DETER WAR ORD/FREE...CONCPT NEW/IDEA METH/COMP 20. PAGE 122 A2509
DIPLOM NUC/PWR PEACE POLICY

B64
ROSECRANCE R.N.,THE DISPERSION OF NUCLEAR WEAPONS: STRATEGY AND POLITICS. ASIA COM FUT S/ASIA USA+45 INT/ORG NAT/G DELIB/GP FORCES ACT/RES TEC/DEV BAL/PWR COERCE DETER ATTIT RIGID/FLEX ORD/FREE ...POLICY CHARTS VAL/FREE. PAGE 123 A2530
EUR+WWI PWR PEACE

B64
RUSSELL R.B.,UNITED NATIONS EXPERIENCE WITH MILITARY FORCES: POLITICAL AND LEGAL ASPECTS. AFR KOREA WOR+45 LEGIS PROB/SOLV ADMIN CONTROL EFFICIENCY PEACE...POLICY INT/LAW BIBLIOG UN. PAGE 126 A2576
FORCES DIPLOM SANCTION ORD/FREE

B64
SCHWARTZ M.D.,CONFERENCE ON SPACE SCIENCE AND SPACE LAW. FUT COM/IND NAT/G FORCES ACT/RES PLAN BUDGET DIPLOM NUC/PWR WEAPON...POLICY ANTHOL 20. PAGE 130 A2658
SPACE LAW PEACE TEC/DEV

B64
SINGH N.,THE DEFENCE MECHANISM OF THE MODERN STATE. COM UK USA+45 CONSTN INT/ORG NUC/PWR WAR INGP/REL ROLE 20 DEPT/DEFEN COMMONWLTH. PAGE 134 A2735
FORCES TOP/EX NAT/G CIVMIL/REL

B64
TAUBENFELD H.J.,SPACE AND SOCIETY. USA+45 LAW FORCES CREATE TEC/DEV ADJUD CONTROL COST PEACE ...PREDICT ANTHOL 20. PAGE 142 A2895
SPACE SOCIETY ADJUST DIPLOM

B64
TEPASKE J.J.,EXPLOSIVE FORCES IN LATIN AMERICA. CULTURE INTELL ECO/UNDEV INT/ORG NAT/G SECT FORCES ECO/TAC EDU/PROP PWR WEALTH SOC. PAGE 142 A2903
L/A+17C RIGID/FLEX FOR/AID USSR

B64
US AGENCY INTERNATIONAL DEV,REPORT TO CONGRESS ON THE FOREIGN ASSISTANCE PROGRAM. AFR ASIA L/A+17C
FOR/AID ECO/UNDEV

USA+45 INT/ORG VOL/ASSN FORCES CAP/ISM ADMIN WEAPON. PAGE 149 A3052 TEC/DEV BUDGET B64

US SENATE COMM GOVT OPERATIONS,THE SECRETARY OF STATE AND THE AMBASSADOR. USA+45 CHIEF CONSULT EX/STRUC FORCES PLAN ADMIN EXEC INGP/REL ROLE ...ANTHOL 20 PRESIDENT DEPT/STATE. PAGE 156 A3175 DIPLOM DELIB/GP NAT/G B64

US SENATE COMM GOVT OPERATIONS,ADMINISTRATION OF NATIONAL SECURITY. USA+45 CHIEF TOP/EX PLAN DIPLOM CONTROL PEACE...POLICY DECISION 20 PRESIDENT CONGRESS. PAGE 156 A3176 ADMIN FORCES ORD/FREE NAT/G B64

WILLIAMS S.P.,TOWARD A GENUINE WORLD SECURITY SYSTEM (PAMPHLET). WOR+45 INT/ORG FORCES PLAN NUC/PWR ORD/FREE...INT/LAW CONCPT UN PRESIDENT. PAGE 165 A3353 BIBLIOG/A ARMS/CONT DIPLOM PEACE L64

BARROS J.,"THE GREEK-BULGARIAN INCIDENT OF 1925: THE LEAGUE OF NATIONS AND THE GREAT POWERS." BULGARIA EUR+WWI NAT/G FORCES ECO/TAC EDU/PROP LEGIT ROUTINE COERCE WAR PEACE DRIVE PWR...JURID CONCPT METH/CNCPT GEN/LAWS GEN/METH LEAGUE/NAT TOT/POP 20. PAGE 11 A0228 INT/ORG ORD/FREE DIPLOM L64

CARNEGIE ENDOWMENT INT. PEACE,"POLITICAL QUESTIONS (ISSUES BEFORE THE NINETEENTH GENERAL ASSEMBLY)." SPACE WOR+45 CONSTN FINAN NAT/G CONSULT DELIB/GP FORCES LEGIS TEC/DEV EDU/PROP LEGIT ARMS/CONT COERCE NUC/PWR ATTIT ALL/VALS...CONCPT OBS UN COLD/WAR 20. PAGE 24 A0490 INT/ORG PEACE L64

CURTIS G.L.,"THE UNITED NATIONS OBSERVER GROUP IN LEBANON." ISLAM USA+45 NAT/G CONSULT ACT/RES PLAN BAL/PWR LEGIT ATTIT KNOWL...HIST/WRIT UN 20 UN. PAGE 33 A0669 INT/ORG FORCES DIPLOM LEBANON L64

POUNDS N.J.G.,"THE POLITICS OF PARTITION." AFR ASIA COM EUR+WWI FUT ISLAM S/ASIA USA-45 LAW ECO/DEV ECO/UNDEV AGRI INDUS INT/ORG POL/PAR PROVS SECT FORCES TOP/EX EDU/PROP LEGIT ATTIT MORAL ORD/FREE PWR RESPECT WEALTH. PAGE 117 A2402 NAT/G NAT/LISM L64

WARD C.,"THE 'NEW MYTHS' AND 'OLD REALITIES' OF NUCLEAR WAR." COM FUT USA+45 USSR WOR+45 INT/ORG NAT/G DOMIN LEGIT EXEC ATTIT PERCEPT ALL/VALS ...POLICY RELATIV PSY MYTH TREND 20. PAGE 161 A3280 FORCES COERCE ARMS/CONT NUC/PWR S64

ASHRAF S.,"INDIA AND WORLD AFFAIRS: AN ANNUAL BIBLIOGRAPHY, 1962." WOR+45 LAW ECO/UNDEV INT/ORG FORCES PLAN ECO/TAC COERCE ORD/FREE PWR WEALTH ...HIST/WRIT VAL/FREE. PAGE 9 A0188 S/ASIA NAT/G S64

BUCHAN A.,"THE MULTILATERAL FORCE." EUR+WWI FUT USA+45 NAT/G LEGIT PWR SKILL...CONCPT OEEC MLF 20. PAGE 21 A0422 INT/ORG FORCES S64

COFFEY J.,"THE SOVIET VIEW OF A DISARMED WORLD." COM USA+45 INT/ORG NAT/G EX/STRUC EDU/PROP COERCE PERCEPT ORD/FREE PWR...TREND STERTYP VAL/FREE 20 UN. PAGE 27 A0556 FORCES ATTIT ARMS/CONT USSR S64

DELGADO J.,"EL MOMENTO POLITICO HISPANOAMERICA." CHINA/COM FUT PANAMA USA+45 USSR INT/ORG NAT/G POL/PAR FORCES DOMIN REGION COERCE ATTIT ALL/VALS ...TRADIT CONCPT COLD/WAR 20. PAGE 36 A0728 L/A+17C EDU/PROP NAT/LISM S64

GARDNER R.N.,"THE SOVIET UNION AND THE UNITED NATIONS." WOR+45 FINAN POL/PAR VOL/ASSN FORCES ECO/TAC DOMIN EDU/PROP LEGIT ADJUD ADMIN ARMS/CONT COERCE ATTIT ALL/VALS...POLICY MAJORIT CONCPT OBS TIME/SEQ TREND STERTYP UN. PAGE 51 A1046 COM INT/ORG USSR S64

GREENBERG S.,"JUDAISM AND WORLD JUSTICE." MEDIT-7 WOR+45 LAW CULTURE SOCIETY INT/ORG NAT/G FORCES EDU/PROP ATTIT DRIVE PERSON SUPEGO ALL/VALS ...POLICY PSY CONCPT GEN/LAWS JEWS. PAGE 55 A1140 SECT JURID PEACE S64

HOWARD M.,"MILITARY POWER AND INTERNATIONAL ORDER." WOR+45 SOCIETY INT/ORG NAT/G BAL/PWR DOMIN COERCE NUC/PWR WEAPON PWR...NEW/IDEA 20. PAGE 68 A1400 FORCES ATTIT WAR S64

JORDAN A.,"POLITICAL COMMUNICATION: THE THIRD DIMENSION OF STRATEGY." USA+45 WOR+45 INT/ORG NAT/G CONSULT FORCES PLAN LEGIT EXEC PERCEPT ALL/VALS ...POLICY RELATIV PSY NEW/IDEA AUD/VIS EXHIBIT TOT/POP 20. PAGE 75 A1534 EDU/PROP RIGID/FLEX ATTIT S64

KARPOV P.V.,"PEACEFUL COEXISTENCE AND INTERNATIONAL LAW." WOR+45 LAW SOCIETY INT/ORG VOL/ASSN FORCES CREATE CAP/ISM DIPLOM ADJUD NUC/PWR PEACE MORAL ORD/FREE PWR MARXISM...MARXIST JURID CONCPT OBS TREND COLD/WAR MARX/KARL 20. PAGE 77 A1568 COM ATTIT INT/LAW USSR S64

KHAN M.Z.,"ISLAM AND INTERNATIONAL RELATIONS." FUT WOR+45 LAW CULTURE SOCIETY NAT/G SECT DELIB/GP FORCES EDU/PROP ATTIT PERSON SUPEGO ALL/VALS ...POLICY PSY CONCPT MYTH HIST/WRIT GEN/LAWS. PAGE 78 A1608 ISLAM INT/ORG DIPLOM S64

KISSINGER H.A.,"COALITION DIPLOMACY IN A NUCLEAR AGE." COM EUR+WWI USA+45 WOR+45 INT/ORG NAT/G FORCES ACT/RES DOMIN LEGIT COERCE PERCEPT ALL/VALS ...POLICY TOT/POP 20. PAGE 80 A1644 CONSULT ATTIT DIPLOM NUC/PWR S64

KOTANI H.,"PEACE-KEEPING: PROBLEMS FOR SMALLER COUNTRIES." FUT WOR+45 NAT/G ACT/RES PLAN DOMIN EDU/PROP COERCE ALL/VALS...POLICY UN TOT/POP 20. PAGE 82 A1673 INT/ORG FORCES S64

LEVI W.,"CHINA AND THE UNITED NATIONS." ASIA CHINA CHINA/COM WOR+45 WOR-45 CONSTN NAT/G DELIB/GP EX/STRUC FORCES ACT/RES EDU/PROP PWR...POLICY RECORD TIME/SEQ GEN/LAWS UN COLD/WAR 20. PAGE 88 A1794 INT/ORG ATTIT NAT/LISM S64

MAGGS P.B.,"SOVIET VIEWPOINT ON NUCLEAR WEAPONS IN INTERNATIONAL LAW." USSR WOR+45 INT/ORG FORCES DIPLOM ARMS/CONT ATTIT ORD/FREE PWR...POLICY JURID CONCPT OBS TREND CON/ANAL GEN/LAWS VAL/FREE 20. PAGE 93 A1905 COM LAW INT/LAW NUC/PWR S64

RUBINSTEIN A.Z.,"THE SOVIET IMAGE OF WESTERN EUROPE." COM EUR+WWI FRANCE GERMANY GERMANY/W USA+45 USSR INT/ORG NAT/G VOL/ASSN FORCES TOP/EX BAL/PWR EDU/PROP ORD/FREE PWR...MYTH RECORD NATO EEC 20. PAGE 125 A2564 RIGID/FLEX ATTIT S64

SAAB H.,"THE ARAB SEARCH FOR A FEDERAL UNION." SOCIETY INT/ORG NAT/G DELIB/GP FORCES ACT/RES TEC/DEV ECO/TAC DOMIN LEGIT REGION ROUTINE ATTIT DRIVE RIGID/FLEX ALL/VALS...SOC CONCPT NEW/IDEA TIME/SEQ TREND. PAGE 126 A2580 ISLAM PLAN S64

WASKOW A.I.,"NEW ROADS TO A WORLD WITHOUT WAR." FUT WOR+45 CULTURE INTELL SOCIETY NAT/G DOMIN LEGIT EXEC COERCE PEACE ATTIT DISPL PERCEPT RIGID/FLEX ALL/VALS...POLICY RELATIV SOC NEW/IDEA 20. PAGE 161 A3288 INT/ORG FORCES B65

ADENAUER K.,MEMOIRS 1945-53. EUR+WWI GERMANY/W ECO/DEV CHIEF FORCES ECO/TAC WAR GOV/REL PWR SOVEREIGN 20 NATO ADENAUER/K. PAGE 4 A0088 BIOG DIPLOM NAT/G PERS/REL B65

ADENAUER K.,MEINE ERINNERUNGEN, 1945-53 (VOL. I), 1953-55 (VOL. II). EUR+WWI GERMANY CHIEF FORCES PROB/SOLV DIPLOM ARMS/CONT INGP/REL PEACE SOVEREIGN ...OBS/ENVIR RECORD 20. PAGE 4 A0089 NAT/G BIOG SELF/OBS B65

AIR UNIVERSITY LIBRARY,LATIN AMERICA, SELECTED REFERENCES. ECO/UNDEV FORCES EDU/PROP MARXISM 20 OAS. PAGE 5 A0106 BIBLIOG L/A+17C NAT/G DIPLOM B65

FRANKLAND N.,THE BOMBING OFFENSIVE AGAINST GERMANY. GERMANY UK TEC/DEV DIPLOM WAR...METH/COMP 20. PAGE 48 A0985 WEAPON PLAN DECISION FORCES B65

GRAHAM G.S.,THE POLITICS OF NAVAL SUPREMACY; STUDIES IN BRITISH MARITIME ASCENDANCY. UK SEA NAT/G BAL/PWR LEAD WAR WEAPON PEACE...POLICY 18/19 COMMONWLTH. PAGE 55 A1126 FORCES PWR COLONIAL DIPLOM B65

GRETTON P.,MARITIME STRATEGY - A STUDY OF DEFENSE PROBLEMS. ASIA UK USSR DIPLOM COERCE DETER NUC/PWR WEAPON...CONCPT NAT/COMP 20. PAGE 56 A1147 FORCES PLAN WAR SEA B65

HART B.H.L.,THE MEMOIRS OF CAPTAIN LIDDELL HART (VOL. I). UK NAT/G PLAN TEC/DEV DIPLOM ADMIN WEAPON GOV/REL PERS/REL ATTIT PWR FASCISM...POLICY 20. PAGE 62 A1274 FORCES BIOG LEAD WAR B65

HUSS P.J.,RED SPIES IN THE UN. CZECHOSLVK USA+45 USSR COM/IND FORCES EDU/PROP NUC/PWR MARXISM 20 UN COLD/WAR. PAGE 69 A1421 PEACE INT/ORG BAL/PWR DIPLOM B65

KAHN H.,ON ESCALATION; METAPHORS AND SCENARIOS. FORCES DIPLOM ARMS/CONT WAR CIVMIL/REL...INT/LAW 20. PAGE 76 A1548 NUC/PWR ACT/RES INT/ORG ORD/FREE B65

LARUS J.,FROM COLLECTIVE SECURITY TO PREVENTIVE DIPLOMACY. FUT FORCES PROB/SOLV DEBATE AGREE COERCE WAR PWR...ANTHOL 20 LEAGUE/NAT UN. PAGE 85 A1736 INT/ORG PEACE DIPLOM ORD/FREE B65

LEE M.,THE UNITED NATIONS AND WORLD REALITIES. ECO/UNDEV FORCES WAR PEACE ATTIT ROLE WEALTH 20 UN. INT/ORG COLONIAL

PAGE 86 A1761 ARMS/CONT DIPLOM

B65
LEISS A.C.,APARTHEID AND UNITED NATIONS COLLECTIVE MEASURES. SOUTH/AFR ECO/UNDEV EXTR/IND FORCES WORKER ECO/TAC FOR/AID INT/TRADE WEALTH...TREND CHARTS 20 UN NEGRO. PAGE 86 A1770 DISCRIM RACE/REL STRATA DIPLOM

B65
MALLIN J.,FORTRESS CUBA; RUSSIA'S AMERICAN BASE. COM CUBA L/A+17C FORCES PLAN DIPLOM LEAD REV WAR ...POLICY 20 CASTRO/F GUEVARA/C INTERVENT. PAGE 93 A1914 MARXISM CHIEF GUERRILLA DOMIN

B65
MOSKOWITZ H.,US SECURITY, ARMS CONTROL, AND DISARMAMENT 1961-1965. FORCES DIPLOM DETER WAR WEAPON...CHARTS 20 UN COLD/WAR NATO. PAGE 105 A2154 BIBLIOG/A ARMS/CONT NUC/PWR PEACE

B65
MUNGER E.S.,NOTES ON THE FORMATION OF SOUTH AFRICAN FOREIGN POLICY. ACADEM POL/PAR SECT CHIEF DELIB/GP FORCES LEGIS PRESS ATTIT...TREND 20 NEGRO. PAGE 106 A2170 AFR DOMIN POLICY DIPLOM

B65
PANJAB U EXTENSION LIBRARY,INDIAN NEWS INDEX. INDIA ECO/UNDEV INDUS INT/ORG SCHOOL FORCES ADJUD WAR ATTIT WEALTH 20. PAGE 114 A2333 BIBLIOG PRESS WRITING DIPLOM

B65
RANSOM H.H.,AN AMERICAN FOREIGN POLICY READER. USA+45 FORCES EDU/PROP COERCE NUC/PWR WAR PEACE ...DECISION 20. PAGE 119 A2443 NAT/G DIPLOM POLICY

B65
SCOTT A.M.,THE REVOLUTION IN STATECRAFT: INFORMAL PENETRATION. WOR+45 WOR-45 CULTURE INT/ORG FORCES ECO/TAC ROUTINE...BIBLIOG 20. PAGE 130 A2670 DIPLOM EDU/PROP FOR/AID

B65
THAYER F.C. JR.,AIR TRANSPORT POLICY AND NATIONAL SECURITY: A POLITICAL, ECONOMIC, AND MILITARY ANALYSIS. DIST/IND OP/RES PLAN TEC/DEV DIPLOM DETER WAR COST EFFICIENCY...POLICY BIBLIOG 20 DEPT/DEFEN FAA CAB. PAGE 142 A2908 AIR FORCES CIVMIL/REL ORD/FREE

B65
US CONGRESS JT ATOM ENRGY COMM,ATOMIC ENERGY LEGISLATION THROUGH 89TH CONGRESS, 1ST SESSION. USA+45 LAW INT/ORG DELIB/GP BUDGET DIPLOM 20 AEC CONGRESS CASEBOOK EURATOM IAEA. PAGE 150 A3071 NUC/PWR FORCES PEACE LEGIS

B65
US DEPARTMENT OF DEFENSE,US SECURITY ARMS CONTROL, AND DISARMAMENT 1961-1965 (PAMPHLET). CHINA/COM COM GERMANY/W ISRAEL SPACE USA+45 USSR WOR+45 FORCES EDU/PROP DETER EQUILIB PEACE ALL/VALS...GOV/COMP 20 NATO. PAGE 151 A3077 BIBLIOG/A ARMS/CONT NUC/PWR DIPLOM

B65
US DEPARTMENT OF THE ARMY,NUCLEAR WEAPONS AND THE ATLANTIC ALLIANCE: A BIBLIOGRAPHIC SURVEY. ASIA COM EUR+WWI USA+45 FORCES DIPLOM WEAPON...STAT 20 NATO. PAGE 152 A3108 BIBLIOG/A ARMS/CONT NUC/PWR BAL/PWR

B65
US SENATE COMM ON FOREIGN REL,HEARINGS ON THE FOREIGN ASSISTANCE PROGRAM. AFR ASIA L/A+17C USA+45 WOR+45 FORCES TEC/DEV BUDGET CONTROL WEAPON ORD/FREE 20 UN CONGRESS SEC/STATE. PAGE 156 A3183 FOR/AID DIPLOM INT/ORG ECO/UNDEV

B65
WASKOW A.I.,KEEPING THE WORLD DISARMED. AFR GERMANY/E DIPLOM CONTROL WAR 20 UN. PAGE 161 A3289 ARMS/CONT PEACE FORCES PROB/SOLV

B65
WEISNER J.B.,WHERE SCIENCE AND POLITICS MEET. USA+45 ECO/DEV R+D FORCES PROB/SOLV DIPLOM FOR/AID CONTROL...PHIL/SCI PRESIDENT KENNEDY/JF JOHNSON/LB. PAGE 163 A3310 CHIEF NAT/G POLICY TEC/DEV

L65
MATTHEWS D.G.,"A CURRENT BIBLIOGRAPHY ON ETHIOPIAN AFFAIRS: A SELECT BIBLIOGRAPHY FROM 1950-1964." ETHIOPIA LAW CULTURE ECO/UNDEV INDUS LABOR SECT FORCES DIPLOM CIVMIL/REL RACE/REL...LING STAT 20. PAGE 96 A1969 BIBLIOG/A ADMIN POL/PAR NAT/G

S65
"FURTHER READING." INDIA USSR FORCES ATTIT SOCISM 20. PAGE 3 A0068 BIBLIOG DIPLOM MARXISM

S65
AFRICAN BIBLIOGRAPHIC CENTER,"US TREATIES AND AGREEMENTS WITH COUNTRIES IN AFRICA, 1957 TO MID-1963." AFR USA+45 AGRI FINAN FORCES TEC/DEV CAP/ISM FOR/AID 20. PAGE 5 A0097 BIBLIOG DIPLOM INT/ORG INT/TRADE

S65
BROWN S.,"AN ALTERNATIVE TO THE GRAND DESIGN." EUR+WWI FUT USA+45 INT/ORG NAT/G EX/STRUC FORCES CREATE BAL/PWR DOMIN RIGID/FLEX ORD/FREE PWR ...NEW/IDEA RECORD EEC NATO 20. PAGE 20 A0407 VOL/ASSN CONCPT DIPLOM

S65
KHOURI F.J.,"THE JORDON RIVER CONTROVERSY." LAW SOCIETY ECO/UNDEV AGRI FINAN INDUS SECT FORCES ACT/RES PLAN TEC/DEV ECO/TAC EDU/PROP COERCE ATTIT DRIVE PERCEPT RIGID/FLEX ALL/VALS...GEOG SOC MYTH WORK. PAGE 78 A1610 ISLAM INT/ORG ISRAEL JORDAN

S65
MERRITT R.L.,"SELECTED ARTICLES AND DOCUMENTS ON INTERNATIONAL LAW AND RELATIONS." WOR+45 INT/ORG FORCES INT/TRADE. PAGE 100 A2045 BIBLIOG DIPLOM INT/LAW GOV/REL

S65
RODNEY W.,"THE ENTENTE STATES OF WEST AFRICA." AFR FRANCE USA+45 POL/PAR SCHOOL FORCES ECO/TAC COLONIAL PWR 20 AFRICA/W. PAGE 123 A2512 DIPLOM POLICY NAT/G ECO/UNDEV

S65
SPAAK P.H.,"THE SEARCH FOR CONSENSUS: A NEW EFFORT TO BUILD EUROPE." FRANCE GERMANY ECO/DEV NAT/G CONSULT FORCES PLAN EDU/PROP REGION CONSEN ATTIT ...SOC METH/CNCPT OBS TREND EEC NATO WORK 20. PAGE 135 A2770 EUR+WWI INT/ORG

C65
SCHWEBEL M.,"BEHAVIORAL SCIENCE AND HUMAN SURVIVAL." FORCES ARMS/CONT COERCE NUC/PWR WAR GP/REL NAT/LISM PERCEPT...POLICY PSY ANTHOL BIBLIOG/A 20 COLD/WAR. PAGE 130 A2662 PEACE ACT/RES DIPLOM HEAL

C65
US AIR FORCE ACADEMY,"AMERICAN DEFENSE POLICY." COM INT/ORG TEC/DEV FOR/AID ARMS/CONT DETER NUC/PWR ...POLICY DECISION CONCPT ANTHOL BIBLIOG/A 20 COLD/WAR NATO. PAGE 149 A3054 PLAN FORCES WAR COERCE

B66
AMERICAN ASSEMBLY COLUMBIA U,THE UNITED STATES AND THE PHILIPPINES. PHILIPPINE S/ASIA USA+45 USA-45 SOCIETY FORCES INT/TRADE...POLICY 20. PAGE 7 A0138 COLONIAL DIPLOM NAT/LISM

B66
BIRMINGHAM D.,TRADE AND CONFLICT IN ANGOLA. PORTUGAL CULTURE FORCES DIPLOM GP/REL PROFIT HABITAT NAT/COMP. PAGE 14 A0291 WAR INT/TRADE ECO/UNDEV COLONIAL

B66
BRACKMAN A.C.,SOUTHEAST ASIA'S SECOND FRONT: THE POWER STRUGGLE IN THE MALAY ARCHIPELAGO. CHINA/COM INDONESIA MALAYSIA ECO/UNDEV INT/ORG NAT/G FORCES DIPLOM EDU/PROP REGION COERCE GUERRILLA AUTHORIT POPULISM...MAJORIT 20 KENNEDY/JF SEATO. PAGE 18 A0367 S/ASIA MARXISM REV

B66
CLARK G.,WORLD PEACE THROUGH WORLD LAW; TWO ALTERNATIVE PLANS. WOR+45 DELIB/GP FORCES TAX CONFER ADJUD SANCTION ARMS/CONT WAR CHOOSE PRIVIL 20 UN COLD/WAR. PAGE 27 A0541 INT/LAW PEACE PLAN INT/ORG

B66
CLAUSEWITZ C.V.,ON WAR (VOL. III). UNIV EDU/PROP ...POLICY DECISION METH 18/20. PAGE 27 A0548 WAR FORCES PLAN CIVMIL/REL

B66
CRAIG G.A.,WAR, POLITICS, AND DIPLOMACY. PRUSSIA CONSTN FORCES CIVMIL/REL TOTALISM PWR 19/20 BISMARCK/O DULLES/JF NAPOLEON/B. PAGE 32 A0654 WAR DIPLOM BAL/PWR

B66
DAENIKER G.,STRATEGIE DES KLEIN STAATS. SWITZERLND ACT/RES CREATE DIPLOM NEUTRAL DETER WAR WEAPON PWR SOVEREIGN...IDEA/COMP 20 COLD/WAR. PAGE 33 A0673 NUC/PWR PLAN FORCES NAT/G

B66
DAVIS V.,POSTWAR DEFENSE POLICY AND THE US NAVY, 1943-1946. USA+45 DIPLOM CONFER LEAD ATTIT...POLICY IDEA/COMP 20 NAVY. PAGE 34 A0692 FORCES PLAN PROB/SOLV CIVMIL/REL

B66
EMBREE A.T.,ASIA: A GUIDE TO BASIC BOOKS (PAMPHLET). ECO/UNDEV SECT FORCES DIPLOM ALL/IDEOS ...SOC 20. PAGE 41 A0846 BIBLIOG/A ASIA S/ASIA NAT/G

B66
EPSTEIN F.T.,THE AMERICAN BIBLIOGRAPHY OF RUSSIAN AND EAST EUROPEAN STUDIES FOR 1964. USSR LOC/G NAT/G POL/PAR FORCES ADMIN ARMS/CONT...JURID CONCPT 20 UN. PAGE 42 A0855 BIBLIOG COM MARXISM DIPLOM

B66
ESTHUS R.A.,THEODORE ROOSEVELT AND JAPAN. ASIA USA-45 FORCES CONFER WAR SOVEREIGN...BIBLIOG 20 CHINJAP. PAGE 42 A0864 DIPLOM DELIB/GP

B66
EWING L.L.,THE REFERENCE HANDBOOK OF THE ARMED FORCES OF THE WORLD. WOR+45 ECO/TAC FOR/AID COERCE WAR PWR 20. PAGE 43 A0879 FORCES STAT DIPLOM PLAN

B66
FREUND L.,POLITISCHE WAFFEN. EUR+WWI GERMANY CONSULT FORCES CONFER NUC/PWR 20. PAGE 49 A1000 EDU/PROP DIPLOM ATTIT

B66
GERARD-LIBOIS J.,KATANGA SECESSION. INT/ORG FORCES DIPLOM ADMIN CONTROL WAR CHOOSE PWR...CHARTS 20 KATANGA TSHOMBE/M UN. PAGE 52 A1062 NAT/G REGION ORD/FREE REV

B66
GORDON B.K.,THE DIMENSIONS OF CONFLICT IN SOUTHEAST ASIA. S/ASIA FORCES ADJUD REGION...CHARTS 20. PAGE 54 A1111
DIPLOM NAT/COMP INT/ORG VOL/ASSN

B66
GRAHAM I.C.C.,PUBLICATIONS OF THE SOCIAL SCIENCE DEPARTMENT, THE RAND CORPORATION, 1948-1966. USSR WOR+45 NAT/G ARMS/CONT DETER WAR NAT/LISM...SOC GOV/COMP. PAGE 55 A1127
BIBLIOG DIPLOM NUC/PWR FORCES

B66
HALPERIN M.H.,CHINA AND NUCLEAR PROLIFERATION (PAMPHLET). CHINA/COM FUT INDIA USA+45 USSR ARMS/CONT WAR 20 CHINJAP. PAGE 60 A1239
NUC/PWR FORCES POLICY DIPLOM

B66
HORELICK A.L.,STRATEGIC POWER AND SOVIET FOREIGN POLICY. CUBA USSR FORCES PLAN CIVMIL/REL...POLICY DECISION 20 COLD/WAR. PAGE 67 A1383
DIPLOM BAL/PWR DETER NUC/PWR

B66
HORMANN K.,PEACE AND MODERN WAR IN THE JUDGEMENT OF THE CHURCH. INT/ORG FORCES EDU/PROP ATTIT 20. PAGE 67 A1384
PEACE WAR CATH MORAL

B66
JACK H.A.,RELIGION AND PEACE: PAPERS FROM THE NATIONAL INTER-RELIGIOUS CONFERENCE ON PEACE, WASHINGTON, 1966. CHINA/COM USA+45 VIETNAM WOR+45 FORCES FOR/AID LEAD PERS/REL. PAGE 72 A1472
PEACE SECT SUPEGO DIPLOM

B66
KEYES J.G.,A BIBLIOGRAPHY OF WESTERN LANGUAGE PUBLICATIONS CONCERNING NORTH VIETNAM IN THE CORNELL LIBRARY. VIETNAM/N NAT/G FORCES TEC/DEV DIPLOM LEAD RACE/REL...GEOG SOC 20. PAGE 78 A1603
BIBLIOG/A CULTURE ECO/UNDEV S/ASIA

B66
KNORR K.E.,ON THE USES OF MILITARY POWER IN THE NUCLEAR AGE. WOR+45 INT/ORG TEC/DEV ADMIN CONTROL WAR COST 20. PAGE 81 A1656
FORCES DIPLOM DETER NUC/PWR

B66
KUENNE R.E.,THE POLARIS MISSILE STRIKE* A GENERAL ECONOMIC SYSTEMS ANALYSIS. USA+45 USSR NAT/G BAL/PWR ARMS/CONT WAR...MATH PROBABIL COMPUT/IR CHARTS HYPO/EXP SIMUL. PAGE 82 A1689
NUC/PWR FORCES DETER DIPLOM

B66
LONG B.,THE WAR DIARY OF BRECKINRIDGE LONG: SELECTIONS FROM THE YEARS 1939-1944. USA-45 INT/ORG FORCES FOR/AID CHOOSE 20. PAGE 91 A1859
DIPLOM WAR DELIB/GP

B66
NIEDERGANG M.,LA REVOLUTION DE SAINT-DOMINGUE. DOMIN/REP INT/ORG NAT/G CONTROL LEAD GP/REL ORD/FREE MARXISM 20. PAGE 109 A2239
REV FORCES DIPLOM

B66
OBERMANN E.,VERTEIDIGUNG PER FREIHEIT. GERMANY/W WOR+45 INT/ORG COERCE NUC/PWR WEAPON MARXISM 20 UN NATO WARSAW/P TREATY. PAGE 111 A2273
FORCES ORD/FREE WAR PEACE

B66
SAPIN B.M.,THE MAKING OF UNITED STATES FOREIGN POLICY. USA+45 INT/ORG DELIB/GP FORCES PLAN ECO/TAC CIVMIL/REL PRESIDENT. PAGE 127 A2603
DIPLOM EX/STRUC DECISION NAT/G

B66
SCHWARZ U.,AMERICAN STRATEGY: A NEW PERSPECTIVE. USA+45 USA-45 INT/ORG TEC/DEV BAL/PWR DIPLOM LEAD ARMS/CONT DETER NUC/PWR WAR 20 NATO. PAGE 130 A2659
NAT/G POLICY FORCES PWR

B66
SKILLING H.G.,THE GOVERNMENTS OF COMMUNIST EAST EUROPE. COM EUR+WWI ELITES FORCES DIPLOM ECO/TAC CONTROL HABITAT SOCISM...DECISION BIBLIOG 20 EUROPE/E COM/PARTY. PAGE 134 A2738
MARXISM NAT/COMP GP/COMP DOMIN

B66
SMITH D.M.,AMERICAN INTERVENTION, 1917. GERMANY UK USA-45 SEA FORCES DIPLOM INT/TRADE EDU/PROP COERCE WEAPON PEACE 20 WILSON/W WWI. PAGE 134 A2746
WAR ATTIT POLICY NEUTRAL

B66
SOBEL L.A.,SOUTH VIETNAM: US-COMMUNIST CONFRONTATION IN SOUTHEAST ASIA 1961-65. VIETNAM FOR/AID CROWD DETER REV PEACE...GEOG 20 INTERVENT DIEM COLD/WAR. PAGE 134 A2754
WAR TIME/SEQ FORCES NAT/G

B66
SPEARS E.L.,TWO MEN WHO SAVED FRANCE: PETAIN AND DE GAULLE. FRANCE CONSTN FORCES DIPLOM WAR PERSON 20 WWI PETAIN/HP DEGAULLE/C. PAGE 135 A2773
BIOG LEAD CHIEF NAT/G

B66
US DEPARTMENT OF STATE,RESEARCH ON WESTERN EUROPE, GREAT BRITAIN, AND CANADA (EXTERNAL RESEARCH LIST NO 3-25). CANADA GERMANY/W UK LAW CULTURE NAT/G POL/PAR FORCES EDU/PROP REGION MARXISM...GEOG SOC WORSHIP 20 CMN/WLTH. PAGE 152 A3098
BIBLIOG/A EUR+WWI DIPLOM

B66
US DEPARTMENT OF THE ARMY,COMMUNIST CHINA: A STRATEGIC SURVEY: A BIBLIOGRAPHY (PAMPHLET NO. 20-67). CHINA/COM COM INDIA USSR NAT/G POL/PAR EX/STRUC FORCES NUC/PWR REV ATTIT...POLICY GEOG CHARTS. PAGE 152 A3109
BIBLIOG/A MARXISM S/ASIA DIPLOM

B66
US DEPARTMENT OF THE ARMY,SOUTH ASIA: A STRATEGIC SURVEY (PAMPHLET NO. 550-3). AFGHANISTN INDIA NEPAL PAKISTAN ECO/UNDEV INT/ORG POL/PAR FORCES FOR/AID INT/TRADE LEAD WAR...POLICY SOC TREND 20. PAGE 152 A3110
BIBLIOG/A S/ASIA DIPLOM NAT/G

B66
US HOUSE COMM APPROPRIATIONS,HEARINGS ON FOREIGN OPERATIONS AND RELATED AGENCIES APPROPRIATIONS. CUBA USA+45 VOL/ASSN DELIB/GP DIPLOM CONFER ORD/FREE 20 CONGRESS MIGRATION INT/AM/DEV PEACE/CORP. PAGE 153 A3120
FOR/AID BUDGET ECO/UNDEV FORCES

B66
US HOUSE COMM GOVT OPERATIONS,AN INVESTIGATION OF THE US ECONOMIC AND MILITARY ASSISTANCE PROGRAMS IN VIETNAM. USA+45 VIETNAM/S SOCIETY CONSTRUC FINAN FORCES BUDGET INT/TRADE PEACE HEALTH...MGT HOUSE/REP AID. PAGE 154 A3139
FOR/AID ECO/UNDEV WAR INSPECT

B66
US SENATE COMM AERO SPACE SCI,SOVIET SPACE PROGRAMS, 1962-65; GOALS AND PURPOSES, ACHIEVEMENTS, PLANS, AND INTERNATIONAL IMPLICATIONS. USA+45 USSR R+D FORCES PLAN EDU/PROP PRESS ADJUD ARMS/CONT ATTIT MARXISM. PAGE 155 A3168
CONSULT SPACE FUT DIPLOM

B66
US SENATE COMM ON FOREIGN REL,HEARINGS ON S 2859 AND S 2861. USA+45 WOR+45 FORCES BUDGET CAP/ISM ADMIN DETER WEAPON TOTALISM...NAT/COMP 20 UN CONGRESS. PAGE 156 A3185
FOR/AID DIPLOM ORD/FREE ECO/UNDEV

B66
WELCH R.H.W.,THE NEW AMERICANISM, AND OTHER SPEECHES AND ESSAYS. USA+45 ACADEM POL/PAR SCHOOL VOL/ASSN FORCES CAP/ISM TAX REV DISCRIM 20 CIV/RIGHTS COLD/WAR BIRCH/SOC. PAGE 163 A3313
DIPLOM FASCISM MARXISM RACE/REL

B66
WESTWOOD A.F.,FOREIGN AID IN A FOREIGN POLICY FRAMEWORK. AFR ASIA INDIA IRAN L/A+17C USA+45 USSR ECO/UNDEV AGRI FORCES LEGIS PLAN PROB/SOLV ...DECISION 20 COLD/WAR. PAGE 163 A3324
FOR/AID DIPLOM POLICY ECO/TAC

B66
ZABLOCKI C.J.,SINO-SOVIET RIVALRY. AFR ASIA CHINA/COM CUBA EUR+WWI L/A+17C USA+45 USSR WOR+45 POL/PAR FORCES COERCE NUC/PWR...GOV/COMP IDEA/COMP 20 MAO KHRUSH/N. PAGE 169 A3442
DIPLOM MARXISM COM

S66
DINH TRANS V.A.N.,"VIETNAM: A THIRD WAY" S/ASIA USA+45 USSR VIETNAM VIETNAM/S NAT/G SECT FORCES CAP/ISM DIPLOM COLONIAL NEUTRAL MARXISM SOCISM 20 BUDDHISM UNIFICA. PAGE 38 A0766
WAR PLAN ORD/FREE SOCIALIST

S66
FRIEND A.,"THE MIDDLE EAST CRISIS" COM ISLAM ISRAEL SYRIA UAR USA+45 USSR FORCES PLAN FOR/AID CONTROL ORD/FREE PWR...SOCIALIST TIME/SEQ 20 NASSER/G. PAGE 49 A1009
WAR INT/ORG DIPLOM PEACE

S66
ORVIK N.,"NATO: THE ROLE OF THE SMALL MEMBERS." EUR+WWI FUT USA+45 CONSULT FORCES PROB/SOLV ARMS/CONT DETER NUC/PWR PWR 20 NATO. PAGE 112 A2298
NAT/G DIPLOM INT/ORG POLICY

C66
BLAISDELL D.C.,"INTERNATIONAL ORGANIZATION." FUT WOR+45 ECO/DEV DELIB/GP FORCES EFFICIENCY PEACE ORD/FREE...INT/LAW 20 UN LEAGUE/NAT NATO. PAGE 15 A0304
BIBLIOG INT/ORG DIPLOM ARMS/CONT

C66
TARLING N.,"A CONCISE HISTORY OF SOUTHEAST ASIA." BURMA CAMBODIA LAOS S/ASIA THAILAND VIETNAM ECO/UNDEV POL/PAR FORCES ADMIN REV WAR CIVMIL/REL ORD/FREE MARXISM SOCISM 13/20. PAGE 141 A2890
COLONIAL DOMIN INT/TRADE NAT/LISM

B67
ADAMS A.E.,AN ATLAS OF RUSSIAN AND EAST EUROPEAN HISTORY. CHRIST-17C COM MOD/EUR INDUS SECT FORCES DIPLOM COLONIAL REV WAR 4/20. PAGE 4 A0086
CHARTS REGION TREND

B67
BURNS E.L.M.,MEGAMURDER. WOR+45 LAW INT/ORG NAT/G BAL/PWR DIPLOM DETER MURDER WEAPON CIVMIL/REL PEACE ...INT/LAW TREND 20. PAGE 22 A0444
FORCES PLAN WAR NUC/PWR

B67
CHO S.S.,KOREA IN WORLD POLITICS 1940-1950; AN EVALUATION OF AMERICAN RESPONSIBILITY. KOREA USA+45 USSR CONSTN INT/ORG NAT/G FORCES FOR/AID ANOMIE SUPEGO MARXISM...DECISION BIBLIOG 20. PAGE 26 A0533
POLICY DIPLOM PROB/SOLV WAR

B67
EUROPA-ARCHIV,DEUTSCHES AND AUSLANDISCHES SCHRIFTTUM ZU DEN REGIONALEN SICHERHEITSVEREINBARUNGEN 1945-1956. WOR+45 FORCES BAL/PWR REGION. PAGE 43 A0875
BIBLIOG INT/ORG PEACE DETER

B67
GRIFFITH SB I.I.,THE CHINESE PEOPLE'S LIBERATION ARMY. CHINA/COM DIPLOM DOMIN GUERRILLA NUC/PWR REV ...CHARTS BIBLIOG 20. PAGE 57 A1163
FORCES CIVMIL/REL NAT/LISM

PWR

B67
HALPERIN M.H.,CONTEMPORARY MILITARY STRATEGY. ASIA CHINA/COM USA+45 USSR INT/ORG FORCES ACT/RES PLAN TEC/DEV BAL/PWR COERCE WAR...METH/COMP BIBLIOG 20 NATO. PAGE 60 A1240
DIPLOM NUC/PWR DETER ARMS/CONT

B67
KAROL K.S.,CHINA, THE OTHER COMMUNISM (TRANS. BY TOM BAISTOW). CHINA/COM CULTURE INDUS FORCES DIPLOM EDU/PROP CONTROL EXEC NUC/PWR ATTIT...SOC CHARTS 20. PAGE 77 A1567
NAT/G POL/PAR MARXISM INGP/REL

B67
KATZ R.,DEATH IN ROME. EUR+WWI ITALY POL/PAR DIPLOM LEAD ATTIT PERSON ROLE CATHISM. PAGE 77 A1570
WAR MURDER FORCES DEATH

B67
MAW B.,BREAKTHROUGH IN BURMA: MEMOIRS OF A REVOLUTION, 1939-1946. BURMA UK FORCES PROB/SOLV DIPLOM FOR/AID DOMIN LEAD...BIOG 20. PAGE 97 A1980
REV ORD/FREE NAT/LISM COLONIAL

B67
MAZRUI A.A.,TOWARDS A PAX AFRICANA. AFR STRUCT ECO/UNDEV NAT/G DIPLOM COLONIAL REGION WAR ATTIT 20. PAGE 97 A1988
PEACE FORCES PROB/SOLV SOVEREIGN

B67
MCBRIDE J.H.,THE TEST BAN TREATY: MILITARY, TECHNOLOGICAL, AND POLITICAL IMPLICATIONS. USA+45 USSR DELIB/GP FORCES LEGIS TEC/DEV BAL/PWR TREATY. PAGE 97 A1995
ARMS/CONT DIPLOM NUC/PWR

B67
MCCLINTOCK R.,THE MEANING OF LIMITED WAR. FUT WOR+45 NAT/G FORCES GUERRILLA REV...POLICY SAMP/SIZ TREND NAT/COMP 45 COLD/WAR. PAGE 97 A1999
WAR NUC/PWR BAL/PWR DIPLOM

B67
PADELFORD N.J.,THE DYNAMICS OF INTERNATIONAL POLITICS (2ND ED.). WOR+45 LAW INT/ORG FORCES TEC/DEV REGION NAT/LISM PEACE ATTIT PWR ALL/IDEOS UN COLD/WAR NATO TREATY. PAGE 113 A2314
DIPLOM NAT/G POLICY DECISION

B67
POGANY A.H.,POLITICAL SCIENCE AND INTERNATIONAL RELATIONS, BOOKS RECOMMENDED FOR AMERICAN CATHOLIC COLLEGE LIBRARIES. INT/ORG LOC/G NAT/G FORCES BAL/PWR ECO/TAC NUC/PWR...CATH INT/LAW TREATY 20. PAGE 117 A2393
BIBLIOG DIPLOM

B67
RALSTON D.B.,THE ARMY OF THE REPUBLIC; THE PLACE OF THE MILITARY IN THE POLITICAL EVOLUTION OF FRANCE 1871-1914. FRANCE MOD/EUR EX/STRUC LEGIS TOP/EX DIPLOM ADMIN WAR GP/REL ROLE...BIBLIOG 19/20. PAGE 119 A2436
FORCES NAT/G CIVMIL/REL POLICY

B67
RUSSELL B.,WAR CRIMES IN VIETNAM. USA+45 VIETNAM FORCES DIPLOM WEAPON RACE/REL DISCRIM ISOLAT BIO/SOC 20 COLD/WAR RUSSELL/B. PAGE 126 A2574
WAR CRIME ATTIT POLICY

B67
SABLE M.H.,A GUIDE TO LATIN AMERICAN STUDIES (2 VOLS). CONSTN FINAN INT/ORG LABOR MUNIC POL/PAR FORCES CAP/ISM FOR/AID ADMIN MARXISM SOCISM OAS. PAGE 126 A2584
BIBLIOG/A L/A+17C DIPLOM NAT/LISM

B67
THORNE C.,THE APPROACH OF WAR, 1938-1939. EUR+WWI POL/PAR CHIEF FORCES LEAD DRIVE PWR FASCISM ...BIBLIOG/A 20 HITLER/A. PAGE 144 A2936
DIPLOM WAR ELITES

B67
US DEPARTMENT OF THE ARMY,CIVILIAN IN PEACE, SOLDIER IN WAR: A BIBLIOGRAPHIC SURVEY OF THE ARMY AND AIR NATIONAL GUARD (PAMPHLET, NOS. 130-2). USA+45 USA-45 LOC/G NAT/G PROVS LEGIS PLAN ADMIN ATTIT ORD/FREE...POLICY 19/20. PAGE 152 A3111
BIBLIOG/A FORCES ROLE DIPLOM

B67
US SENATE COMM AERO SPACE SCI,TREATY ON PRINCIPLES GOVERNING ACTIVITIES OF STATES IN EXPLORATION AND USE OF OUTER SPACE, INCLUDING...BODIES. DELIB/GP FORCES LEGIS DIPLOM...JURID 20 DEPT/STATE NASA DEPT/DEFEN UN. PAGE 155 A3169
SPACE INT/LAW ORD/FREE PEACE

B67
US SENATE COMM ON FOREIGN REL,UNITED STATES ARMAMENT AND DISARMAMENT PROBLEMS. USA+45 AIR BAL/PWR DIPLOM FOR/AID NUC/PWR ORD/FREE SENATE TREATY. PAGE 156 A3190
ARMS/CONT WEAPON FORCES PROB/SOLV

B67
WATERS M.,THE UNITED NATIONS* INTERNATIONAL ORGANIZATION AND ADMINISTRATION. WOR+45 EX/STRUC FORCES DIPLOM LEAD REGION ARMS/CONT REPRESENT INGP/REL ROLE...METH/COMP ANTHOL 20 UN LEAGUE/NAT. PAGE 162 A3291
CONSTN INT/ORG ADMIN ADJUD

B67
WILLIS F.R.,DE GAULLE: ANACHRONISM, REALIST, OR PROPHET? FRANCE POL/PAR FORCES DIPLOM WAR PEACE ROLE ORD/FREE...POLICY IDEA/COMP ANTHOL 20 DEGAULLE/C. PAGE 165 A3356
BIOG PERSON CHIEF LEAD

L67
BODENHEIMER S.J.,"THE 'POLITICAL UNION' DEBATE IN EUROPE* A CASE STUDY IN INTERGOVERNMENTAL DIPLOMACY." EUR+WWI FUT NAT/G FORCES PLAN DEBATE SOVEREIGN...CONCPT PREDICT EEC NATO. PAGE 16 A0326
DIPLOM REGION INT/ORG

L67
GENEVEY P.,"LE DESARMEMENT APRES LE TRAITE DE VERSAILLES." EUR+WWI GERMANY INT/ORG PROB/SOLV CONFER WAR...POLICY PREDICT 20. PAGE 52 A1057
ARMS/CONT PEACE DIPLOM FORCES

L67
MOORE N.,"THE LAWFULNESS OF MILITARY ASSISTANCE TO THE REPUBLIC OF VIET NAM." USA+45 VIETNAM WOR+45 FOR/AID DOMIN DETER WAR WEAPON...DECISION INT/LAW 20 UN. PAGE 103 A2123
PWR DIPLOM FORCES GOV/REL

S67
AFRICAN BIBLIOGRAPHIC CENTER,"THE SWORD AND GOVERNMENT: A PRELIMINARY AND SELECTED BIBLIOGRAPHICAL GUIDE TO AFRICAN MILITARY AFFAIRS; PART I." AFR USA+45 USSR INT/ORG POL/PAR FOR/AID COLONIAL ARMS/CONT PWR 20 UN. PAGE 5 A0101
BIBLIOG/A FORCES CIVMIL/REL DIPLOM

S67
BELGION M.,"THE CASE FOR REHABILITATING MARSHAL PETAIN." EUR+WWI FRANCE NAT/G DIPLOM ATTIT PERSON MORAL PETAIN/HP. PAGE 12 A0253
WAR FORCES LEAD

S67
CARROLL K.J.,"SECOND STEP TOWARD ARMS CONTROL." WOR+45 INT/ORG VOL/ASSN FORCES PROB/SOLV RISK WEAPON 20 COLD/WAR. PAGE 25 A0503
ARMS/CONT DIPLOM PLAN NUC/PWR

S67
HALL M.,"GERMANY, EAST AND WEST* DANGER AT THE CROSSROADS." GERMANY ELITES CHIEF FORCES DIPLOM ECO/TAC REPAR ARMS/CONT...SOCIALIST 20. PAGE 60 A1227
NAT/LISM ATTIT FASCISM WEAPON

S67
HAZARD J.N.,"POST-DISARMAMENT INTERNATIONAL LAW." FUT USSR WOR+45 INT/ORG DELIB/GP FORCES DETER EQUILIB SOVEREIGN MARXISM 20 UN. PAGE 63 A1301
INT/LAW ARMS/CONT PWR PLAN

S67
KIPP K.,"DIE POLITISCHE BEDEUTUNG DER 'GEGENKUSTE' DARGESTELLT AM BEISPIEL DER USA IM 20. JAHRHUNDERT" USA+45 USA-45 SEA NAT/G CONTROL COERCE WAR...POLICY GEOG 20. PAGE 79 A1629
FORCES ORD/FREE DIPLOM DETER

S67
MCCORD W.,"ARMIES AND POLITICS; A PROBLEM IN THE THIRD WORLD." AFR ISLAM USA+45 ECO/UNDEV TOTALISM 20. PAGE 98 A2002
FOR/AID POLICY NAT/G FORCES

S67
SHOEMAKER R.L.,"JAPANESE ARMY AND THE WEST." ASIA ELITES EX/STRUC DIPLOM DOMIN EDU/PROP COERCE ATTIT AUTHORIT PWR 1/20 CHINJAP. PAGE 132 A2703
FORCES TEC/DEV WAR TOTALISM

S67
TACKABERRY R.B.,"ORGANIZING AND TRAINING PEACE-KEEPING FORCES* THE CANADIAN VIEW." CANADA PLAN DIPLOM CONFER ADJUD ADMIN CIVMIL/REL 20 UN. PAGE 141 A2882
PEACE FORCES INT/ORG CONSULT

S67
TERRILL R.,"THE SIEGE MENTALITY." CHINA/COM NAT/G FORCES DIPLOM REV EFFICIENCY NAT/LISM MARXISM ...TREND 20. PAGE 142 A2904
EDU/PROP WAR DOMIN

S67
THIEN T.T.,"VIETNAM: A CASE OF SOCIAL ALIENATION." VIETNAM AGRI FORCES FOR/AID ADMIN REPRESENT INGP/REL PWR 19/20. PAGE 143 A2918
NAT/G ELITES WORKER STRANGE

C67
SPANIER J.W.,"WORLD POLITICS IN AN AGE OF REVOLUTION." COM WOR+45 FORCES COERCE WAR NAT/LISM SOVEREIGN...POLICY BIBLIOG 20. PAGE 135 A2772
DIPLOM TEC/DEV REV ECO/UNDEV

C83
BURKE E.,"RESOLUTIONS FOR CONCILIATION WITH AMERICA" (1775), IN E. BURKE, COLLECTED WORKS, VOL. 2." UK USA-45 FORCES INT/TRADE TARIFFS TAX SANCTION PEACE...POLICY 18 PRE/US/AM. PAGE 21 A0436
COLONIAL WAR SOVEREIGN ECO/TAC

B86
MAS LATRIE L.,RELATIONS ET COMMERCE DE L'AFRIQUE SEPTENTRIONALE OU MAGREB AVEC LES NATIONS CHRETIENNES AU MOYEN AGE. CULTURE CHIEF FORCES WAR ...SOC CENSUS TREATY 10/16. PAGE 95 A1954
ISLAM SECT DIPLOM INT/TRADE

C93
PLAYFAIR R.L.,"A BIBLIOGRAPHY OF MOROCCO." MOROCCO CULTURE AGRI FORCES DIPLOM WAR HEALTH...GEOG JURID SOC CHARTS. PAGE 116 A2387
BIBLIOG ISLAM MEDIT-7

B96
SMITH A.,LECTURES ON JUSTICE, POLICE, REVENUE AND ARMS (1763). UK LAW FAM FORCES TARIFFS AGREE COERCE INCOME OWN WEALTH LAISSEZ...GEN/LAWS 17/18. PAGE 134 A2743
DIPLOM JURID OLD/LIB TAX

FORD A.G. A0960

PAGE 40 A0816

B32
MASTERS R.D.,INTERNATIONAL LAW IN INTERNATIONAL COURTS. BELGIUM EUR+WWI FRANCE GERMANY MOD/EUR SWITZERLND WOR-45 SOCIETY STRATA STRUCT LEGIT EXEC ALL/VALS...JURID HIST/WRIT TIME/SEQ TREND GEN/LAWS 20. PAGE 96 A1961
INT/ORG LAW INT/LAW

B33
DAHLIN E.,FRENCH AND GERMAN PUBLIC OPINION ON DECLARED WAR AIMS 1914-1918. BELGIUM FRANCE GERMANY NAT/G POL/PAR DIPLOM COERCE REV WAR PEACE 20 WWI WILSON/W. PAGE 33 A0674
ATTIT EDU/PROP DOMIN NAT/COMP

B33
REID H.D.,RECUEIL DES COURS; TOME 45: LES SERVITUDES INTERNATIONALES III. FRANCE CONSTN DELIB/GP PRESS CONTROL REV WAR CHOOSE PEACE MORAL MARITIME TREATY. PAGE 120 A2457
ORD/FREE DIPLOM LAW

B35
LANGER W.L.,THE DIPLOMACY OF IMPERIALISM 1890-1902. FRANCE GERMANY ITALY UK WOR-45 BAL/PWR INT/TRADE LEGIT ADJUD CONTROL WAR PWR SOVEREIGN...CHARTS BIBLIOG/A 19/20. PAGE 84 A1726
DIPLOM COLONIAL DOMIN

B35
SIMONDS F.H.,THE GREAT POWERS IN WORLD POLITICS. FRANCE GERMANY UK WOR-45 INT/ORG NAT/G ARMS/CONT PEACE FASCISM...POLICY GEOG 20 DEPRESSION NAZI. PAGE 133 A2718
DIPLOM WEALTH WAR

B36
BOYCE A.N.,EUROPE AND SOUTH AFRICA. FRANCE GERMANY ITALY SOUTH/AFR UK INDUS NAT/G CONTROL REV WAR NAT/LISM...CONCPT HIST/WRIT 20. PAGE 18 A0362
COLONIAL GOV/COMP NAT/COMP DIPLOM

B36
HUGENDUBEL P.,DIE KRIEGSMACHE DER FRANZOSISCHEN PRESSE. FRANCE GERMANY MOD/EUR COM/IND NAT/G DIPLOM DOMIN PWR 20. PAGE 69 A1412
PRESS EDU/PROP WAR ATTIT

B37
BLAKE J.W.,EUROPEAN BEGINNINGS IN WEST AFRICA 1454-1578. FRANCE GUINEA PORTUGAL UK PWR WEALTH 16/16 AFRICA/W. PAGE 15 A0305
DIPLOM COLONIAL INT/TRADE DOMIN

B38
PETTEE G.S.,THE PROCESS OF REVOLUTION. COM FRANCE ITALY MOD/EUR RUSSIA SPAIN WOR-45 ELITES INTELL SOCIETY STRATA STRUCT INT/ORG NAT/G POL/PAR ACT/RES PLAN EDU/PROP LEGIT EXEC...SOC MYTH TIME/SEQ TOT/POP 18/20. PAGE 115 A2370
COERCE CONCPT REV

B39
DULLES J.,WAR, PEACE AND CHANGE. FRANCE ITALY UK USA-45 WOR-45 LAW INT/ORG NAT/G SECT VOL/ASSN FORCES TOP/EX DOMIN ARMS/CONT COERCE ATTIT PERSON RIGID/FLEX MORAL PWR...JURID STERTYP TOT/POP LEAGUE/NAT 20. PAGE 39 A0796
EDU/PROP TOTALISM WAR

B40
WANDERSCHECK H.,FRANKREICHS PROPAGANDA GEGEN DEUTSCHLAND. FRANCE GERMANY MOD/EUR UK NAT/G DIPLOM WAR 20 JEWS. PAGE 161 A3273
EDU/PROP ATTIT DOMIN PRESS

B40
WOLFERS A.,BRITAIN AND FRANCE BETWEEN TWO WORLD WARS. FRANCE UK INT/ORG NAT/G PLAN BARGAIN ECO/TAC AGREE ISOLAT ALL/IDEOS...DECISION GEOG 20 TREATY VERSAILLES INTERVENT. PAGE 166 A3380
DIPLOM WAR POLICY

B41
BAUMANN G.,GRUNDLAGEN UND PRAXIS DER INTERNATIONALEN PROPAGANDA. FRANCE GERMANY UK CULTURE COM/IND PRESS PWR...PSY METH/COMP 20. PAGE 12 A0236
EDU/PROP DOMIN ATTIT DIPLOM

B42
CONOVER H.F.,FRENCH COLONIES IN AFRICA: A LIST OF REFERENCES. ALGERIA FRANCE MOROCCO SOMALIA SUDAN CULTURE AGRI LOC/G SECT FORCES DIPLOM INT/TRADE NAT/LISM HEALTH...CON/ANAL 20. PAGE 29 A0594
BIBLIOG AFR ECO/UNDEV COLONIAL

B42
JACKSON M.V.,EUROPEAN POWERS AND SOUTH-EAST AFRICA: A STUDY OF INTERNATIONAL RELATIONS ON SOUTH-EAST COAST OF AFRICA, 1796-1856. AFR FRANCE PORTUGAL SOUTH/AFR UK USA-45 FORCES INT/TRADE PWR...CHARTS BIBLIOG 18/19 TREATY. PAGE 72 A1477
DOMIN POLICY ORD/FREE DIPLOM

B44
RUDIN H.R.,ARMISTICE 1918. FRANCE GERMANY MOD/EUR UK USA-45 NAT/G CHIEF DELIB/GP FORCES BAL/PWR REPAR ARMS/CONT 20 WILSON/W TREATY. PAGE 125 A2566
AGREE WAR PEACE DIPLOM

C44
VAN VALKENBURG S.,"ELEMENTS OF POLITICAL GEOGRAPHY." FRANCE COM/IND INDUS NAT/G SECT RACE/REL...LING TREND GEN/LAWS BIBLIOG 20. PAGE 158 A3215
GEOG DIPLOM COLONIAL

B45
CONOVER H.F.,THE GOVERNMENTS OF THE MAJOR FOREIGN POWERS: A BIBLIOGRAPHY. FRANCE GERMANY ITALY UK USSR CONSTN LOC/G POL/PAR EX/STRUC FORCES ADMIN CT/SYS CIVMIL/REL TOTALISM...POLICY 19/20. PAGE 29 A0598
BIBLIOG NAT/G DIPLOM

B45
HARVARD WIDENER LIBRARY,INDOCHINA: A SELECTED LIST OF REFERENCES. CAMBODIA FRANCE S/ASIA VIETNAM COLONIAL...POLICY 19/20. PAGE 62 A1282
BIBLIOG/A ACADEM DIPLOM NAT/G

B45
NELSON M.F.,KOREA AND THE OLD ORDERS IN EASTERN ASIA. ASIA FRANCE KOREA RUSSIA DELIB/GP INT/TRADE DOMIN CONTROL WAR ORD/FREE...POLICY BIBLIOG. PAGE 108 A2218
DIPLOM BAL/PWR ATTIT CONSERVE

B46
BLUM L.,FOR ALL MANKIND (TRANS. BY W. PICKLES). FRANCE GERMANY USSR LAW SOCIETY STRUCT POL/PAR WORKER DIPLOM DOMIN CHOOSE ORD/FREE FASCISM 20. PAGE 16 A0323
POPULISM SOCIALIST NAT/G WAR

B47
CONOVER H.F.,NON-SELF-GOVERNING AREAS. BELGIUM FRANCE ITALY UK WOR+45 CULTURE ECO/UNDEV INT/ORG LOC/G NAT/G ECO/TAC INT/TRADE ADMIN HEALTH...SOC UN. PAGE 30 A0601
BIBLIOG/A COLONIAL DIPLOM

B48
HOWARD J.E.,PARLIAMENT AND FOREIGN POLICY IN FRANCE. FRANCE CONSTN DELIB/GP BUDGET ADMIN PARL/PROC CHOOSE...BIBLIOG/A 20 PARLIAMENT. PAGE 68 A1399
LEGIS CONTROL DIPLOM ATTIT

B48
MINISTERE FINANCES ET ECO,BULLETIN BIBLIOGRAPHIQUE. AFR EUR+WWI FRANCE CULTURE STRUCT FINAN NAT/G ACT/RES INT/TRADE ADMIN REGION PRODUC STAT. PAGE 102 A2088
BIBLIOG/A ECO/UNDEV TEC/DEV COLONIAL

B48
VISSON A.,AS OTHERS SEE US. EUR+WWI FRANCE UK USA+45 CULTURE INTELL SOCIETY STRATA NAT/G POL/PAR FOR/AID ATTIT DRIVE LOVE ORD/FREE RESPECT WEALTH ...PLURIST SOC OBS TOT/POP 20. PAGE 159 A3244
USA-45 PERCEPT

B48
WHEELER-BENNETT J.W.,MUNICH: PROLOGUE TO TRAGEDY. EUR+WWI FRANCE GERMANY UK PLAN PROB/SOLV SOVEREIGN ...POLICY DECISION 20 HITLER/A. PAGE 163 A3327
DIPLOM WAR PEACE

B49
JACKSON R.H.,INTERNATIONAL CONFERENCE ON MILITARY TRIALS. FRANCE GERMANY UK USA+45 USSR VOL/ASSN DELIB/GP REPAR ADJUD CT/SYS CRIME WAR 20 WAR/TRIAL. PAGE 72 A1479
DIPLOM INT/ORG INT/LAW CIVMIL/REL

B51
BROGAN D.W.,THE PRICE OF REVOLUTION. FRANCE USA+45 USA-45 USSR CONSTN NAT/G DIPLOM COLONIAL NAT/LISM ORD/FREE POPULISM...CONCPT 18/20 PRE/US/AM. PAGE 19 A0386
REV METH/COMP COST MARXISM

B51
US DEPARTMENT OF STATE,LIVRES AMERICAINS TRADUITS EN FRANCAIS ET LIVRES FRANCAIS SUR LES ETATS-UNIS D'AMERIQUE (2ND ED.). FRANCE USA+45 SECT DIPLOM EDU/PROP LEISURE...ART/METH GEOG HUM 20. PAGE 151 A3086
BIBLIOG/A SOC

B51
WELLES S.,SEVEN DECISIONS THAT SHAPED HISTORY. ASIA FRANCE FUT USA+45 WOR+45 WOR-45 CONSTN STRUCT INT/ORG NAT/G ACT/RES EDU/PROP DRIVE...POLICY CONCPT TIME/SEQ TREND TOT/POP UN 20 CHINJAP. PAGE 163 A3315
USA-45 DIPLOM WAR

B52
ALBERTINI L.,THE ORIGINS OF THE WAR OF 1914 (3 VOLS.). AUSTRIA FRANCE GERMANY MOD/EUR RUSSIA UK PROB/SOLV NEUTRAL PWR...BIBLIOG 19/20. PAGE 5 A0107
WAR DIPLOM FORCES BAL/PWR

B52
FERRELL R.H.,PEACE IN THEIR TIME. FRANCE UK USA-45 INT/ORG NAT/G FORCES CREATE AGREE ARMS/CONT COERCE WAR TREATY 20 WILSON/W LEAGUE/NAT BRIAND/A. PAGE 45 A0920
PEACE DIPLOM

B52
SKALWEIT S.,FRANKREICH UND FRIEDRICH DER GROSSE. FRANCE GERMANY PRUSSIA NAT/G DOMIN WAR 18 FREDERICK. PAGE 134 A2737
ATTIT EDU/PROP DIPLOM SOC

S52
HAAS E.B.,"THE RECONCILIATION OF CONFLICT, COLONIAL POLICY AIMS: ACCEPTANCE OF THE LEAGUE OF NATIONS MANDATE SYSTEM." FRANCE GERMANY UK WOR+45 WOR-45 LEGIT ATTIT DRIVE ORD/FREE...OLD/LIB INT SYS/QU TIME/SEQ TREND LEAGUE/NAT 20. PAGE 58 A1201
INT/ORG COLONIAL

B53
NEISSER H.,NATIONAL INCOMES AND INTERNATIONAL TRADE. FRANCE GERMANY SWEDEN UK USA-45 EXTR/IND FINAN INDUS TEC/DEV PRICE BAL/PAY EQUILIB INCOME WEALTH...CHARTS METH 19 CHINJAP. PAGE 108 A2215
INT/TRADE PRODUC MARKET CON/ANAL

B54
COOKSON J.,BEFORE THE AFRICAN STORM. BELGIUM CENTRL/AFR FRANCE UK ECO/UNDEV POL/PAR CREATE BAL/PWR RACE/REL NAT/LISM ORD/FREE CONSERVE MARXISM SOC/INTEG 20 CONGO/LEOP. PAGE 30 A0607
COLONIAL REV DISCRIM DIPLOM

B55
ROWE C.,VOLTAIRE AND THE STATE. FRANCE MOD/EUR BAL/PWR CONTROL TASK SUPEGO ORD/FREE PWR...CONCPT 18 VOLTAIRE. PAGE 125 A2553
NAT/G DIPLOM NAT/LISM

ATTIT

B56
FOSTER J.G.,BRITAIN IN WESTERN EUROPE: WEU AND THE ATLANTIC ALLIANCE. EUR+WWI FRANCE GERMANY GERMANY/W ITALY UK STRATA NAT/G DELIB/GP ECO/TAC ORD/FREE PWR ...TRADIT TIME/SEQ TREND OEEC PARLIAMENT 20 EUROPE/W. PAGE 47 A0969
INT/ORG FORCES WEAPON

B57
ARON R.,FRANCE DEFEATS EDC. EUR+WWI GERMANY LEGIS DIPLOM DOMIN EDU/PROP ADMIN...HIST/WRIT 20. PAGE 9 A0180
INT/ORG FORCES DETER FRANCE

B57
BEERS H.P.,THE FRENCH IN NORTH AMERICA. FRANCE USA-45...TIME/SEQ BIBLIOG. PAGE 12 A0247
HIST/WRIT DIPLOM BIOG WRITING

B57
BROMBERGER M.,LES SECRETS DE L'EXPEDITION D'EGYPTE. FRANCE ISLAM UAR UK USA+45 USSR WOR+45 INT/ORG NAT/G FORCES BAL/PWR ECO/TAC DOMIN WAR NAT/LISM ATTIT PWR SOVEREIGN...MAJORIT TIME/SEQ CHARTS SUEZ COLD/WAR 20. PAGE 19 A0387
COERCE DIPLOM

B57
BUCK P.W.,CONTOL OF FOREIGN RELATIONS IN MODERN NATIONS. FRANCE L/A+17C NETHERLAND USSR WOR+45 INT/ORG TOP/EX BAL/PWR DOMIN EDU/PROP COERCE PEACE ATTIT...CONCPT TREND 20 CMN/WLTH. PAGE 21 A0427
NAT/G PWR DIPLOM

C57
BEERS H.P.,"THE FRENCH IN NORTH AFRICA: A BIBLIOGRAPHICAL GUIDE TO FRENCH ARCHIVES, REPRODUCTIONS, AND RESEARCH MISSIONS." AFR CANADA FRANCE USA-45 NAT/LISM ATTIT 20. PAGE 12 A0248
BIBLIOG DIPLOM COLONIAL

B58
DUCLOUX L.,FROM BLACKMAIL TO TREASON. FRANCE PLAN DIPLOM EDU/PROP PRESS RUMOR NAT/LISM...CRIMLGY 20. PAGE 39 A0793
COERCE CRIME NAT/G PWR

B58
MACLES L.M.,LES SOURCES DU TRAVAIL BIBLIOGRAPHIQUE (3 VOLS.). FRANCE WOR+45 DIPLOM...GEOG PHIL/SCI SOC 20. PAGE 93 A1897
BIBLIOG/A NAT/G HUM

B58
TILLION G.,ALGERIA: THE REALITIES. ALGERIA FRANCE ISLAM CULTURE STRATA PROB/SOLV DOMIN REV NAT/LISM WEALTH MARXISM...GEOG 20. PAGE 144 A2940
ECO/UNDEV SOC COLONIAL DIPLOM

N58
INVESTMENT FUND ECO SOC DEV,FRENCH AFRICA: A DECADE OF PROGRESS 1948-1958 (PAMPHLET). AFR FRANCE EXTR/IND INDUS EDU/PROP HEALTH 20. PAGE 71 A1465
FOR/AID DIPLOM ECO/UNDEV AGRI

B59
ALWAN M.,ALGERIA BEFORE THE UNITED NATIONS. AFR ASIA FRANCE ISLAM S/ASIA CONSTN SOCIETY STRUCT INT/ORG NAT/G ECO/TAC ADMIN COLONIAL NAT/LISM ATTIT PWR...DECISION TREND 420 UN. PAGE 7 A0133
PLAN RIGID/FLEX DIPLOM ALGERIA

B59
DEHIO L.,GERMANY AND WORLD POLITICS IN THE TWENTIETH CENTURY. EUR+WWI FRANCE GERMANY MOD/EUR UK USSR NAT/G CHIEF BAL/PWR DOMIN COLONIAL CONTROL LEAD...IDEA/COMP 20 VERSAILLES. PAGE 36 A0724
DIPLOM WAR NAT/LISM SOVEREIGN

B59
DIEBOLD W. JR.,THE SCHUMAN PLAN: A STUDY IN ECONOMIC COOPERATION, 1950-1959. EUR+WWI FRANCE GERMANY USA+45 EXTR/IND CONSULT DELIB/GP PLAN DIPLOM ECO/TAC INT/TRADE ROUTINE ORD/FREE WEALTH ...METH/CNCPT STAT CONT/OBS INT TIME/SEQ ECSC 20. PAGE 37 A0759
INT/ORG REGION

B59
EGYPTIAN SOCIETY OF INT LAW,THE MONROVIA CONFERENCE (PAMPHLET). AFR ALGERIA FRANCE UAR CONFER REGION NUC/PWR WAR DISCRIM 20 SAHARA AFR/STATES. PAGE 40 A0826
COLONIAL SOVEREIGN RACE/REL DIPLOM

B59
FREE L.A.,SIX ALLIES AND A NEUTRAL. ASIA COM EUR+WWI FRANCE GERMANY/W INDIA S/ASIA UK USA+45 INT/ORG NAT/G NUC/PWR PEACE ATTIT PERCEPT RIGID/FLEX ALL/VALS...STAT REC/INT COLD/WAR 20 CHINJAP. PAGE 48 A0992
PSY DIPLOM

B59
LINK R.G.,ENGLISH THEORIES OF ECONOMIC FLUCTUATIONS: 1815-1848. FRANCE UK AGRI WORKER DIPLOM PRICE TASK WAR DEMAND PRODUC...POLICY BIBLIOG 18 MALTHUS MILL/JS WILSON/J. PAGE 89 A1826
IDEA/COMP ECO/DEV WEALTH EQUILIB

B60
ALBRECHT-CARRIE R.,FRANCE, EUROPE AND THE TWO WORLD WARS. EUR+WWI FRANCE GERMANY MOD/EUR UK ECO/DEV NAT/G FORCES BAL/PWR DOMIN ARMS/CONT PEACE PWR 20 TREATY EUROPE. PAGE 5 A0109
DIPLOM WAR

B60
DE GAULLE C.,THE EDGE OF THE SWORD. EUR+WWI FRANCE ELITES CHIEF DIPLOM ROLE...REALPOL TRADIT. PAGE 34 A0701
FORCES SUPEGO LEAD WAR

B60
DUMON F.,LA COMMUNAUTE FRANCO-AFRO-MALGACHE: SES ORIGINES, SES INSTITUTIONS, SON EVOLUTION. FRANCE MADAGASCAR POL/PAR DIPLOM ADMIN ATTIT...TREND T 20. PAGE 39 A0798
JURID INT/ORG AFR CONSTN

B60
FOOTMAN D.,INTERNATIONAL COMMUNISM. ASIA EUR+WWI FRANCE FUT GERMANY MOD/EUR S/ASIA USA-45 WOR+45 WOR-45 INTELL LABOR TOTALISM MARXISM WORK 20. PAGE 47 A0958
COM INT/ORG STRUCT REV

B60
FURNIA A.H.,THE DIPLOMACY OF APPEASEMENT: ANGLO-FRENCH RELATIONS AND THE PRELUDE TO WORLD WAR II 1931-1938. FRANCE GERMANY UK ELITES NAT/G DELIB/GP FORCES WAR PEACE RIGID/FLEX 20. PAGE 50 A1026
DIPLOM BAL/PWR COERCE

B60
LISTER L.,EUROPE'S COAL AND STEEL COMMUNITY. FRANCE GERMANY STRUCT ECO/DEV EXTR/IND INDUS MARKET NAT/G DELIB/GP ECO/TAC INT/TRADE EDU/PROP ATTIT RIGID/FLEX ORD/FREE PWR WEALTH...CONCPT STAT TIME/SEQ CHARTS ECSC 20. PAGE 90 A1843
EUR+WWI INT/ORG REGION

B60
MEYRIAT J.,LA SCIENCE POLITIQUE EN FRANCE, 1945-1958; BIBLIOGRAPHIES FRANCAISES DE SCIENCES SOCIALES (VOL. I). EUR+WWI FRANCE POL/PAR DIPLOM ADMIN CHOOSE ATTIT...IDEA/COMP METH/COMP NAT/COMP 20. PAGE 100 A2057
BIBLIOG/A NAT/G CONCPT PHIL/SCI

L60
LAUTERPACHT E.,"THE SUEZ CANAL SETTLEMENT." FRANCE ISLAM ISRAEL UAR UK BAL/PWR DIPLOM LEGIT...JURID GEN/LAWS ANTHOL SUEZ VAL/FREE 20. PAGE 85 A1747
INT/ORG LAW

S60
KREININ M.E.,"THE 'OUTER-SEVEN' AND EUROPEAN INTEGRATION." EUR+WWI FRANCE GERMANY ITALY UK ECO/DEV DIST/IND INT/TRADE DRIVE WEALTH...MYTH CHARTS EEC OEEC 20. PAGE 82 A1682
ECO/TAC GEN/LAWS

B61
ANSPRENGER F.,POLITIK IM SCHWARZEN AFRIKA. FRANCE NAT/G DIPLOM REGION REV NAT/LISM...CHARTS BIBLIOG 19/20. PAGE 8 A0164
AFR COLONIAL SOVEREIGN

B61
FULLER J.F.C.,THE CONDUCT OF WAR, 1789-1961. FRANCE RUSSIA SOCIETY NAT/G FORCES PROB/SOLV AGREE NUC/PWR WEAPON PEACE...SOC 18/20 TREATY COLD/WAR. PAGE 50 A1025
WAR POLICY REV ROLE

B61
HAYTER W.,THE DIPLOMACY OF THE GREAT POWERS. FRANCE UK USSR WOR+45 EX/STRUC TOP/EX NUC/PWR PEACE...OBS 20. PAGE 63 A1296
DIPLOM POLICY NAT/G

B61
MATTHEWS T.,WAR IN ALGERIA. ALGERIA FRANCE CONTROL ATTIT SOVEREIGN 20. PAGE 96 A1978
REV COLONIAL DIPLOM WAR

B61
SCHNAPPER B.,LA POLITIQUE ET LE COMMERCE FRANCAIS DANS LE GOLFE DE GUINEE DE 1838 A 1871. FRANCE GUINEA UK SEA EXTR/IND NAT/G DELIB/GP LEGIS ADMIN ORD/FREE...POLICY GEOG CENSUS CHARTS BIBLIOG 19. PAGE 129 A2636
COLONIAL INT/TRADE DOMIN AFR

S61
RAY J.,"THE EUROPEAN FREE-TRADE ASSOCIATION AND ITS IMPACT ON INDIA'S TRADE." EUR+WWI FRANCE GERMANY INDIA S/ASIA UK NAT/G VOL/ASSN PLAN INT/TRADE ROUTINE WEALTH...STAT CHARTS CMN/WLTH EEC OEEC 20 EFTA. PAGE 120 A2453
ECO/DEV ECO/TAC

B62
DEHIO L.,THE PRECARIOUS BALANCE: FOUR CENTURIES OF THE EUROPEAN POWER STRUGGLE. FRANCE GERMANY SPAIN NAT/G DOMIN PWR...GOV/COMP 8/20. PAGE 36 A0725
BAL/PWR WAR DIPLOM COERCE

B62
DUROSELLE J.B.,LES NOUVEAUX ETATS DANS LES RELATIONS INTERNATIONALES. AFR CHINA/COM FRANCE MOROCCO S/ASIA USSR ECO/UNDEV INT/ORG PLAN ECO/TAC EDU/PROP ATTIT DRIVE...TREND TOT/POP TUNIS 20. PAGE 39 A0806
NAT/G CONSTN DIPLOM

B62
DUROSELLE J.B.,HISTOIRE DIPLOMATIQUE DE 1919 A NOS JOURS (3RD ED.). FRANCE INT/ORG CHIEF FORCES CONFER ARMS/CONT WAR PEACE ORD/FREE...T TREATY 20 COLD/WAR. PAGE 39 A0807
DIPLOM WOR+45 WOR-45

B62
FRIEDMANN W.,METHODS AND POLICIES OF PRINCIPAL DONOR COUNTRIES IN PUBLIC INTERNATIONAL DEVELOPMENT FINANCING: PRELIMINARY APPRAISAL. FRANCE GERMANY/W UK USA+45 USSR WOR+45 FINAN TEC/DEV CAP/ISM DIPLOM ECO/TAC ATTIT 20 EEC. PAGE 49 A1002
INT/ORG FOR/AID NAT/COMP ADMIN

B62
GUENA Y.,HISTORIQUE DE LA COMMUNAUTE. FUT ECO/UNDEV NAT/G PLAN EDU/PROP COLONIAL REGION NAT/LISM ALL/VALS SOVEREIGN...CONCPT OBS CHARTS 20. PAGE 58 A1186
AFR VOL/ASSN FOR/AID FRANCE

B62
HUTTENBACK R.A.,BRITISH RELATIONS WITH THE SIND, 1799-1843. FRANCE INDIA UK FORCES...POLICY CHARTS
COLONIAL DIPLOM

BIBLIOG 18/19 SIND. PAGE 69 A1425 DOMIN S/ASIA

B62
KENT R.K.,FROM MADAGASCAR TO THE MALAGASY REPUBLIC. FRANCE MADAGASCAR DIPLOM NAT/LISM ORD/FREE...MGT 18/20. PAGE 78 A1596 COLONIAL SOVEREIGN REV POL/PAR

B62
LIPPMANN W.,WESTERN UNITY AND THE COMMON MARKET. EUR+WWI FRANCE GERMANY/W UK USA+45 ECO/DEV AGRI FINAN MARKET INT/ORG NAT/G FOR/AID AGREE WEALTH 20 EEC. PAGE 89 A1831 DIPLOM INT/TRADE VOL/ASSN

B62
NOBECOURT R.G.,LES SECRETS DE LA PROPAGANDE EN FRANCE OCCUPEE. FRANCE ELITES NAT/G DIPLOM GP/REL NAT/LISM TOTALISM ORD/FREE 20 VICHY VICHY. PAGE 109 A2244 METH/COMP EDU/PROP WAR CONTROL

B62
ROBERTSON B.C.,REGIONAL DEVELOPMENT IN THE EUROPEAN ECONOMIC COMMUNITY. EUR+WWI FRANCE FUT ITALY UK ECO/UNDEV WORKER ACT/RES PROB/SOLV TEC/DEV ECO/TAC INT/TRADE EEC. PAGE 122 A2499 PLAN ECO/DEV INT/ORG REGION

B62
SCOTT W.E.,ALLIANCE AGAINST HITLER. EUR+WWI FRANCE GERMANY USSR BAL/PWR LEAD TOTALISM PWR FASCISM MARXISM...POLICY BIBLIOG 20 HITLER/A. PAGE 131 A2675 WAR DIPLOM FORCES

B62
STEEL R.,THE END OF THE ALLIANCE. FRANCE FUT GERMANY/E GERMANY/W UK USA+45 NAT/G FORCES FOR/AID 20 NATO. PAGE 137 A2809 EUR+WWI POLICY DIPLOM INT/ORG

S62
GUETZKOW H.,"THE POTENTIAL OF CASE STUDY IN ANALYZING INTERNATIONAL CONFLICT." EUR+WWI FUT GERMANY INTELL SOCIETY STRUCT INT/ORG LOC/G NAT/G CONSULT CREATE PLAN CHOOSE ATTIT RIGID/FLEX ...POLICY SAAR 20. PAGE 58 A1188 EDU/PROP METH/CNCPT COERCE FRANCE

S62
MANGIN G.,"LES ACCORDS DE COOPERATION EN MATIERE DE JUSTICE ENTRE LA FRANCE ET LES ETATS AFRICAINS ET MALGACHE." AFR ISLAM WOR+45 STRUCT ECO/UNDEV NAT/G DELIB/GP PERCEPT ALL/VALS...JURID MGT TIME/SEQ 20. PAGE 94 A1919 INT/ORG LAW FRANCE

S62
PIQUEMAL M.,"LES PROBLEMES DES UNIONS D'ETATS EN AFRIQUE NOIRE." FRANCE SOCIETY INT/ORG NAT/G DELIB/GP PLAN LEGIT ADMIN COLONIAL ROUTINE ATTIT ORD/FREE PWR...GEOG METH/CNCPT 20. PAGE 116 A2382 AFR ECO/UNDEV REGION

S62
PIQUEMAL M.,"LA COOPERATION FINANCIERE ENTRE LA FRANCE ET LES ETATS AFRICAINS ET MALGACHE." ISLAM INT/ORG TOP/EX ECO/TAC...JURID CHARTS 20. PAGE 116 A2383 AFR FINAN FRANCE MADAGASCAR

S62
VIGNES D.,"L'AUTORITE DES TRAITES INTERNATIONAUX EN DROIT INTERNE." EUR+WWI UNIV LAW CONSTN INTELL NAT/G POL/PAR DIPLOM ATTIT PERCEPT ALL/VALS ...POLICY INT/LAW JURID CONCPT TIME/SEQ 20 TREATY. PAGE 159 A3233 STRUCT LEGIT FRANCE

B63
GARDINIER D.E.,CAMEROON: UNITED NATIONS CHALLENGE TO FRENCH POLICY. AFR CAMEROON FRANCE NAT/G LEGIS CONTROL SOVEREIGN 20 UN. PAGE 51 A1042 DIPLOM POLICY INT/ORG COLONIAL

B63
MONGER G.W.,THE END OF ISOLATION. FRANCE MOD/EUR RUSSIA UK NAT/G LEGIS TOP/EX GOV/REL PWR 20 TREATY CHINJAP. PAGE 103 A2106 DIPLOM POLICY WAR

B63
ROSNER G.,THE UNITED NATIONS EMERGENCY FORCE. FRANCE ISRAEL UAR UK WOR+45 CREATE WAR PEACE ORD/FREE PWR...INT/LAW JURID HIST/WRIT TIME/SEQ UN. PAGE 124 A2539 INT/ORG FORCES

S63
ALPHAND H.,"FRANCE AND HER ALLIES." EUR+WWI UK USA+45 ECO/DEV INT/ORG NAT/G VOL/ASSN FORCES TOP/EX DIPLOM ECO/TAC LEGIT ATTIT DRIVE ORD/FREE PWR WEALTH...STAT EEC TOT/POP 20. PAGE 6 A0130 ACT/RES FRANCE

S63
DIEBOLD W. JR.,"THE NEW SITUATION OF INTERNATIONAL TRADE POLICY." EUR+WWI FRANCE FUT UK USA+45 WOR+45 DIST/IND PLAN INT/TRADE EDU/PROP PWR WEALTH ...RECORD TREND GEN/LAWS EEC VAL/FREE 20. PAGE 37 A0760 MARKET ECO/TAC

S63
GANDILHON J.,"LA SCIENCE ET LA TECHNIQUE A L'AIDE DES REGIONS PEU DEVELOPPEES." FRANCE FUT WOR+45 ECO/DEV R+D PROF/ORG ACT/RES PLAN...MGT TOT/POP VAL/FREE 20 UN. PAGE 51 A1037 ECO/UNDEV TEC/DEV FOR/AID

S63
GANDOLFI A.,"LES ACCORDS DE COOPERATION EN MATIERE DE POLITIQUE ETRANGERE ENTRE LA FRANCE ET LES NOUVEAUX ETATS AFRICAINS ET." AFR ISLAM MADAGASCAR WOR+45 ECO/DEV INT/ORG NAT/G DELIB/GP ECO/TAC ALL/VALS...CON/ANAL 20. PAGE 51 A1038 VOL/ASSN ECO/UNDEV DIPLOM FRANCE

S63
GROSSER A.,"FRANCE AND GERMANY IN THE ATLANTIC COMMUNITY." INT/ORG NAT/G TOP/EX DIPLOM REGION PEACE ATTIT ORD/FREE PWR...CONCPT RECORD TIME/SEQ GEN/LAWS VAL/FREE COLD/WAR 20. PAGE 57 A1178 EUR+WWI VOL/ASSN FRANCE GERMANY

S63
KISSINGER H.A.,"STRAINS ON THE ALLIANCE." EUR+WWI FRANCE GERMANY GERMANY/W USA+45 ECO/DEV INT/ORG NAT/G TOP/EX EDU/PROP NUC/PWR ATTIT PWR...PSY TREND 20. PAGE 80 A1643 VOL/ASSN DRIVE DIPLOM

S63
LERNER D.,"FRENCH ELITE PERSPECTIVES ON THE UNITED NATIONS." EUR+WWI INT/ORG HEALTH ORD/FREE PWR RESPECT...STAT INT SAMP/SIZ VAL/FREE UN 20. PAGE 87 A1786 ATTIT STERTYP ELITES FRANCE

S63
LIGOT M.,"LA COOPERATION MILITAIRE DANS LES ACCORDS, PASSES ENTRE LA FRANCE ET LES ETATS AFRICAINS ET MALGACHE D'EXPRESSION." ECO/UNDEV INT/ORG NAT/G VOL/ASSN...CONCPT TIME/SEQ 20. PAGE 89 A1814 AFR FORCES FOR/AID FRANCE

S63
MULLEY F.W.,"NUCLEAR WEAPONS: CHALLENGE TO NATIONAL SOVEREIGNTY." EUR+WWI FRANCE UK USA+45 VOL/ASSN EX/STRUC FORCES TOP/EX ACT/RES REGION DRIVE PWR 20 NATO DEGAULLE/C. PAGE 106 A2169 INT/ORG ATTIT DIPLOM NUC/PWR

S63
SHONFIELD A.,"AFTER BRUSSELS." EUR+WWI FRANCE GERMANY UK ECO/DEV DIST/IND MARKET VOL/ASSN DELIB/GP CREATE INT/TRADE ATTIT RIGID/FLEX...RECORD TREND GEN/LAWS EEC CMN/WLTH 20. PAGE 132 A2705 PLAN ECO/TAC

S63
SPINELLI A.,"IL TRATTATO DI MOSCA E I PROBLEMI DELLA COESISTENZA PACIFICA." CHINA/COM COM FRANCE FUT WOR+45 INT/ORG VOL/ASSN PEACE...POLICY MYTH 20. PAGE 136 A2788 ATTIT ARMS/CONT TOTALISM

S63
WRIGHT Q.,"PROJECTED EUROPEAN UNION AND AMERICAN INTERNATIONAL PRESTIGE." EUR+WWI FRANCE GERMANY UK USA+45 INT/ORG NAT/G EDU/PROP ATTIT PERCEPT PWR ...CONCPT OBS EEC 20 UN. PAGE 168 A3417 FUT ORD/FREE REGION

B64
DUROSELLE J.B.,POLITIQUES NATIONALES ENVERS LES JEUNES ETATS. FRANCE ISRAEL ITALY UK USA+45 USSR YUGOSLAVIA ECO/DEV FINAN ECO/TAC INT/TRADE ADMIN PWR 20. PAGE 40 A0809 DIPLOM ECO/UNDEV COLONIAL DOMIN

B64
EAYRS J.,THE COMMONWEALTH AND SUEZ: A DOCUMENTARY SURVEY. FRANCE ISLAM VOL/ASSN FORCES CONFER COLONIAL WAR INGP/REL 20 CMN/WLTH SUEZ UN. PAGE 40 A0818 DIPLOM NAT/LISM DIST/IND SOVEREIGN

B64
FALL B.,STREET WITHOUT JOY. FRANCE USA+45 DIPLOM ECO/TAC FOR/AID GUERRILLA REV WEAPON...TREND 20. PAGE 44 A0894 WAR S/ASIA FORCES COERCE

B64
FINER H.,DULLES OVER SUEZ. FRANCE FUT UAR UK WOR+45 NAT/G PROB/SOLV CONTROL NUC/PWR WAR 20 DULLES/JF SUEZ. PAGE 46 A0932 DIPLOM POLICY REC/INT

B64
GOWING M.,BRITAIN AND ATOMIC ENERGY 1939-1945. FRANCE UK USA+45 USA-45 NAT/G CREATE...PHIL/SCI 20 AEA. PAGE 54 A1118 NUC/PWR DIPLOM TEC/DEV

B64
JENSEN D.L.,DIPLOMACY AND DOGMATISM. FRANCE SPAIN REV WAR PERSON CATHISM...POLICY BIOG 16. PAGE 74 A1513 DIPLOM ATTIT SECT

B64
QUIGG P.W.,AFRICA: A FOREIGN AFFAIRS READER. AFR FRANCE PORTUGAL UK DIPLOM LEAD PARL/PROC MARXISM ...MAJORIT METH/CNCPT GOV/COMP IDEA/COMP ANTHOL 19/20. PAGE 118 A2426 COLONIAL SOVEREIGN NAT/LISM RACE/REL

B64
WITHERELL J.W.,OFFICIAL PUBLICATIONS OF FRENCH EQUATORIAL AFRICA, FRENCH CAMEROONS, AND TOGO, 1946-1958 (PAMPHLET). CAMEROON CHAD FRANCE GABON TOGO LAW ECO/UNDEV EXTR/IND INT/TRADE...GEOG HEAL 20. PAGE 165 A3370 BIBLIOG/A AFR NAT/G ADMIN

S64
DE GAULLE C.,"FRENCH WORLD VIEW." AFR ASIA CHINA/COM EUR+WWI ISLAM ECO/UNDEV INT/ORG NAT/G VOL/ASSN ACT/RES DIPLOM ECO/TAC EDU/PROP ATTIT DRIVE WEALTH 20. PAGE 35 A0702 TOP/EX PWR FOR/AID FRANCE

S64
GROSSER A.,"Y A-T-IL UN CONFLIT FRANCO-AMERICAIN." EUR+WWI USA+45 INT/ORG NAT/G PLAN BAL/PWR DIPLOM EDU/PROP NUC/PWR ATTIT DRIVE ORD/FREE PWR...CONCPT OBS TIME/SEQ TREND STERTYP VAL/FREE COLD/WAR. PAGE 57 A1179 VOL/ASSN NAT/LISM FRANCE

S64
HOFFMANN S.,"CE QU'EN PENSENT LES AMERICAINS." EUR+WWI INT/ORG VOL/ASSN PLAN BAL/PWR DIPLOM DOMIN EDU/PROP REGION ARMS/CONT DRIVE ORD/FREE PWR ...POLICY CONCPT OBS TREND STERTYP COLD/WAR VAL/FREE 20. PAGE 66 A1357 USA+45 ATTIT FRANCE

S64
RUBINSTEIN A.Z.,"THE SOVIET IMAGE OF WESTERN EUROPE." COM EUR+WWI FRANCE GERMANY GERMANY/W USA+45 USSR INT/ORG NAT/G VOL/ASSN FORCES TOP/EX BAL/PWR EDU/PROP ORD/FREE PWR...MYTH RECORD NATO EEC 20. PAGE 125 A2564 RIGID/FLEX ATTIT

S64
ZARTMAN I.W.,"LES RELATIONS ENTRE LA FRANCE ET L'ALGERIA DEPUIS LES ACCORDS D'EVIAN." EUR+WWI FUT ISLAM CULTURE AGRI EXTR/IND FINAN INDUS POL/PAR DIPLOM ECO/TAC FOR/AID PEACE ATTIT DRIVE ALL/VALS ...TIME/SEQ VAL/FREE 20. PAGE 169 A3446 ECO/UNDEV ALGERIA FRANCE

B65
COLLINS H.,KARL MARX AND THE BRITISH LABOUR MOVEMENT; YEARS OF THE FIRST INTERNATIONAL. FRANCE SWITZERLND UK CAP/ISM WAR...MARXIST IDEA/COMP BIBLIOG 19. PAGE 28 A0567 MARXISM LABOR INT/ORG REV

B65
FANON F.,STUDIES IN A DYING COLONIALISM. ALGERIA FRANCE STRATA FAM DIPLOM DOMIN WAR RACE/REL DISCRIM HEALTH 20. PAGE 44 A0897 NAT/LISM COLONIAL REV SOVEREIGN

B65
FORGAC A.A.,NEW DIPLOMACY AND THE UNITED NATIONS. FRANCE GERMANY UK USSR INT/ORG DELIB/GP EX/STRUC PEACE...INT/LAW CONCPT UN. PAGE 47 A0965 DIPLOM ETIQUET NAT/G

B65
JOHNSTONE A.,UNITED STATES DIRECT INVESTMENT IN FRANCE: AN INVESTIGATION OF THE FRENCH CHARGES. FRANCE USA+45 ECO/DEV INDUS LG/CO NAT/G ECO/TAC CONTROL WEALTH...BIBLIOG 20 INTERVENT. PAGE 75 A1529 FINAN DIPLOM POLICY SOVEREIGN

B65
O'CONNELL M.R.,IRISH POLITICS AND SOCIAL CONFLICT IN THE AGE OF THE AMERICAN REVOLUTION. FRANCE IRELAND MOD/EUR STRATA SECT LEGIS DIPLOM INT/TRADE DOMIN REV WAR...BIBLIOG 18 PARLIAMENT. PAGE 111 A2268 CATHISM ATTIT NAT/G DELIB/GP

B65
ROSENBERG A.,DEMOCRACY AND SOCIALISM. COM EUR+WWI FRANCE MOD/EUR STRUCT INT/ORG NAT/G POL/PAR TOP/EX EDU/PROP COERCE PERSON PWR FASCISM MARXISM...CONCPT TIME/SEQ MARX/KARL 19/20. PAGE 124 A2535 ATTIT

B65
WARBEY W.,VIETNAM: THE TRUTH. FRANCE S/ASIA USA+45 VIETNAM CULTURE INT/ORG NAT/G DIPLOM FOR/AID EDU/PROP ARMS/CONT PEACE 20 TREATY NLF UN. PAGE 161 A3274 WAR AGREE

B65
WEIL G.L.,A HANDBOOK ON THE EUROPEAN ECONOMIC COMMUNITY. BELGIUM EUR+WWI FRANCE GERMANY/W ITALY CONSTN ECO/DEV CREATE PARTIC GP/REL...DECISION MGT CHARTS 20 EEC. PAGE 162 A3299 INT/TRADE INT/ORG TEC/DEV INT/LAW

B65
WITHERELL J.W.,MADAGASCAR AND ADJACENT ISLANDS; A GUIDE TO OFFICIAL PUBLICATIONS (PAMPHLET). FRANCE MADAGASCAR S/ASIA UK LAW OP/RES PLAN DIPLOM ...POLICY CON/ANAL 19/20. PAGE 165 A3371 BIBLIOG COLONIAL LOC/G ADMIN

S65
RODNEY W.,"THE ENTENTE STATES OF WEST AFRICA." AFR FRANCE USA+45 POL/PAR SCHOOL FORCES ECO/TAC COLONIAL PWR 20 AFRICA/W. PAGE 123 A2512 DIPLOM POLICY NAT/G ECO/UNDEV

S65
SPAAK P.H.,"THE SEARCH FOR CONSENSUS: A NEW EFFORT TO BUILD EUROPE." FRANCE GERMANY ECO/DEV NAT/G CONSULT FORCES PLAN EDU/PROP REGION CONSEN ATTIT ...SOC METH/CNCPT OBS TREND EEC NATO WORK 20. PAGE 135 A2770 EUR+WWI INT/ORG

B66
FRANK E.,LAWMAKERS IN A CHANGING WORLD. FRANCE UK USSR WOR+45 PARTIC EFFICIENCY ROLE ALL/IDEOS ...CHARTS ANTHOL PARLIAMENT 20 UN COLD/WAR. PAGE 48 A0979 GOV/COMP LEGIS NAT/G DIPLOM

B66
HAYER T.,FRENCH AID. AFR FRANCE AGRI FINAN BUDGET ADMIN WAR PRODUC...CHARTS 18/20 THIRD/WRLD OVRSEA/DEV. PAGE 63 A1295 TEC/DEV COLONIAL FOR/AID ECO/UNDEV

B66
KINDLEBERGER C.P.,EUROPE AND THE DOLLAR. EUR+WWI FRANCE GERMANY/W USA+45 CONSTN INT/ORG DIPLOM INT/TRADE...ANTHOL 20 GOLD/STAND. PAGE 79 A1623 BAL/PAY BUDGET FINAN ECO/DEV

B66
PAN S.,VIETNAM CRISIS. ASIA FRANCE USA+45 USA-45 VIETNAM CULTURE SOCIETY INT/ORG ECO/TAC AGREE CONTROL WAR MARXISM 20. PAGE 113 A2325 ECO/UNDEV POLICY DIPLOM NAT/COMP

B66
SPEARS E.L.,TWO MEN WHO SAVED FRANCE: PETAIN AND DE GAULLE. FRANCE CONSTN FORCES DIPLOM WAR PERSON 20 WWI PETAIN/HP DEGAULLE/C. PAGE 135 A2773 BIOG LEAD CHIEF NAT/G

B66
VIEN N.C.,SEEKING THE TRUTH. FRANCE VIETNAM AGRI ADMIN WAR...BIOG 20 BAO/DAI INTERVENT. PAGE 159 A3231 NAT/G CONSULT CONSTN

B66
WOHL R.,FRENCH COMMUNISM IN THE MAKING 1914-1924. FRANCE USSR LEAD REV...IDEA/COMP 20 COM/PARTY. PAGE 166 A3377 MARXISM WORKER DIPLOM

C66
KULSKI W.W.,"DEGAULLE AND THE WORLD: THE FOREIGN POLICY OF THE FIFTH FRENCH REPUBLIC." FRANCE ECO/UNDEV POL/PAR BAL/PWR DETER NUC/PWR ATTIT PWR ...RECORD BIBLIOG DEGAULLE NATO EEC. PAGE 83 A1694 POLICY SOVEREIGN PERSON DIPLOM

B67
ISENBERG I.,FRANCE UNDER DE GAULLE (THE REFERENCE SHELF VOL. 39 NO. 1). EUR+WWI FRANCE ECO/DEV ...BIBLIOG 20 DEGAULLE/C NATO EEC. PAGE 72 A1469 ATTIT DIPLOM POLICY CHIEF

B67
RALSTON D.B.,THE ARMY OF THE REPUBLIC; THE PLACE OF THE MILITARY IN THE POLITICAL EVOLUTION OF FRANCE 1871-1914. FRANCE MOD/EUR EX/STRUC LEGIS TOP/EX DIPLOM ADMIN WAR GP/REL ROLE...BIBLIOG 19/20. PAGE 119 A2436 FORCES NAT/G CIVMIL/REL POLICY

B67
WILLIS F.R.,DE GAULLE: ANACHRONISM, REALIST, OR PROPHET? FRANCE POL/PAR FORCES DIPLOM WAR PEACE ROLE ORD/FREE...POLICY IDEA/COMP ANTHOL 20 DEGAULLE/C. PAGE 165 A3356 BIOG PERSON CHIEF LEAD

S67
BELGION M.,"THE CASE FOR REHABILITATING MARSHAL PETAIN." EUR+WWI FRANCE NAT/G DIPLOM ATTIT PERSON MORAL PETAIN/HP. PAGE 12 A0253 WAR FORCES LEAD

S67
D'AMATO D.,"LEGAL ASPECTS OF THE FRENCH NUCLEAR TESTS." FRANCE WOR+45 ACT/RES COLONIAL RISK GOV/REL EQUILIB ORD/FREE PWR DECISION. PAGE 33 A0672 INT/LAW DIPLOM NUC/PWR ADJUD

S67
HALLE L.J.,"DE GAULLE AND THE FUTURE OF EUROPE." FRANCE DIPLOM 20. PAGE 60 A1232 NAT/LISM LEAD INT/ORG PREDICT

FRANCHISE....FRANCHISE

FRANCK P.G. A0977,A0978

FRANCO/F....FRANCISCO FRANCO

FRANK E. A0979

FRANK I. A0980

FRANK/PARL....FRANKFURT PARLIAMENT

B22
FICHTE J.G.,ADDRESSES TO THE GERMAN NATION. GERMANY PRUSSIA ELITES NAT/G SECT CREATE INT/TRADE HEREDITY ...ART/METH LING 19 FRANK/PARL. PAGE 45 A0923 NAT/LISM CULTURE EDU/PROP REGION

FRANKEL J. A0981

FRANKEL M. A0982

FRANKEL S.H. A0983,A0984

FRANKFUR/F....FELIX FRANKFURTER

FRANKFURT PARLIAMENT....SEE FRANK/PARL

FRANKLAND N. A0985

FRANKLIN W.O. A0986

FRANKLIN/B....BENJAMIN FRANKLIN

B27
PARRINGTON V.L.,MAIN CURRENTS IN AMERICAN THOUGHT (VOL.I). USA-45 AGRI POL/PAR DIPLOM TAX REGION REV 17/18 FRANKLIN/B JEFFERSN/T. PAGE 114 A2336 COLONIAL SECT FEEDBACK ALL/IDEOS

FRANZ G. A0987

FRASER L. A0988

FRASER S. A0989

FRASER-TYTLER W.K. A0990

FRAZIER E.F. A0991

FREDERICK....FREDERICK THE GREAT

B52
SKALWEIT S.,FRANKREICH UND FRIEDRICH DER GROSSE. FRANCE GERMANY PRUSSIA NAT/G DOMIN WAR 18 FREDERICK. PAGE 134 A2737 — ATTIT EDU/PROP DIPLOM SOC

FREDRKSBRG....FREDERICKSBURG, VIRGINIA

FREE L.A. A0992,A0993

FREE/SOIL....FREE-SOIL DEBATE (U.S.)

FREE/SPEE....FREE SPEECH MOVEMENT

FREEDOM....SEE ORD/FREE

FREEDOM/HS....FREEDOM HOUSE

B65
LEVENSTEIN A.,FREEDOM'S ADVOCATE - A TWENTY-FIVE YEAR CHRONICLE. USA+45 POL/PAR LEGIS DIPLOM WAR PEACE TOTALISM DRIVE MARXISM 20 FREEDOM/HS. PAGE 87 A1791 — ORD/FREE VOL/ASSN POLICY ATTIT

FREEMAN H.A. A0994

FREIDEL F. A0995

FRELIMO....MOZAMBIQUE LIBERATION FRONT

FREMANTLE H.E.S. A0996

FRENCH D.S. A0997

FRENCH/CAN....FRENCH CANADA

FREUD A. A0998

FREUD/S....SIGMUND FREUD

B66
MAYER P.,THE PACIFIST CONSCIENCE. SECT CREATE ARMS/CONT WAR RACE/REL ATTIT LOVE...ANTHOL PACIFIST WORSHIP FREUD/S GANDHI/M LAO/TZU KING/MAR/L CONSCN/OBJ. PAGE 97 A1984 — DIPLOM PACIFISM SUPEGO

FREUND G. A0999

FREUND L. A1000

FREYMOND J. A1001

FRIEDMANN W. A1002,A1003

FRIEDMANN W.G. A1004,A1005,A1006

FRIEDRICH C.J. A0357,A1007

FRIEDRICH-EBERT-STIFTUNG A1008

FRIEND A. A1009

FRIENDSHIP....SEE LOVE

FRISCH D. A1010

FRNCO/PRUS....FRANCO-PRUSSIAN WAR

FROMM/E....ERICH FROMM

FRONTIER....FRONTIER

FRUSTRATION....SEE BIO/SOC, ANOMIE, DRIVE

FRUTKIN A.W. A1011

FRYDENSBERG P. A1012

FTC....FEDERAL TRADE COMMISSION

FUCHS G. A1013

FULBRGHT/J....J. WILLIAM FULBRIGHT

B49
BOYD A.,WESTERN UNION: A STUDY OF THE TREND TOWARD EUROPEAN UNITY. FUT REGION NAT/LISM...POLICY IDEA/COMP BIBLIOG 14/20 OEEC ERASMUS/D COUNCL/EUR FULBRGHT/J NATO. PAGE 18 A0363 — DIPLOM AGREE TREND INT/ORG

FULBRIGHT J.W. A1014,A1015,A1016

FULLER C.D. A1017

FULLER G.H. A1018, A1019, A1020, A1021, A1022, A1023, A1024

FULLER J.F.C. A1025

FULLER/MW....MELVILLE WESTON FULLER

FUNCTIONAL ANALYSIS....SEE OP/RES

FURNIA A.H. A1026

FURNISS E.S. A1027,A1028,A2752

FURNIVALL/J....J.S. FURNIVALL

FURNIVALL J.S. A1029

FUT....FUTURE (PAST AND PRESENT ATTEMPTS TO DEPICT IT)

N
JOURNAL OF CONFLICT RESOLUTION. FUT WOR+45 INT/ORG NAT/G FORCES CREATE PROB/SOLV ARMS/CONT NUC/PWR WEAPON SOC. PAGE 1 A0014 — BIBLIOG/A DIPLOM WAR

N
AIR UNIVERSITY LIBRARY,INDEX TO MILITARY PERIODICALS. FUT SPACE WOR+45 REGION ARMS/CONT NUC/PWR WAR PEACE INT/LAW. PAGE 5 A0105 — BIBLIOG/A FORCES NAT/G DIPLOM

N
AMER COUNCIL OF LEARNED SOCIET,THE ACLS CONSTITUENT SOCIETY JOURNAL PROJECT. FUT USA+45 LAW NAT/G PLAN DIPLOM PHIL/SCI. PAGE 7 A0134 — BIBLIOG/A HUM COMPUT/IR COMPUTER

B15
HOBSON J.A.,TOWARDS INTERNATIONAL GOVERNMENT. MOD/EUR STRUCT ECO/TAC EDU/PROP ADJUD ALL/VALS ...SOCIALIST CONCPT GEN/LAWS TOT/POP 20. PAGE 65 A1347 — FUT INT/ORG CENTRAL

B19
KEYNES J.M.,THE ECONOMIC CONSEQUENCES OF THE PEACE. FUT GERMANY MOD/EUR RUSSIA UK USA-45 CULTURE ECO/DEV FINAN INDUS INT/ORG TOP/EX ECO/TAC ROUTINE WAR ATTIT PERCEPT ALL/VALS...OLD/LIB MYTH OBS TIME/SEQ TREND 20 TREATY. PAGE 78 A1605 — EUR+WWI SOCIETY PEACE

N19
TAYLOR T.G.,CANADA'S ROLE IN GEOPOLITICS (PAMPHLET). CANADA FUT USSR COLONIAL REGION WEALTH ...CHARTS 20. PAGE 142 A2901 — GEOG DIPLOM SOCIETY ECO/DEV

N19
ZLOTNICK M.,WEAPONS IN SPACE (PAMPHLET). FUT WOR+45 TEC/DEV DIPLOM ARMS/CONT CIVMIL/REL PEACE HABITAT ...CONCPT NEW/IDEA CHARTS. PAGE 170 A3457 — SPACE WEAPON NUC/PWR WAR

B22
REINSCH P.,SECRET DIPLOMACY: HOW FAR CAN IT BE ELIMINATED. FUT WOR-45 CULTURE INT/ORG NAT/G EDU/PROP WAR...MYTH HIST/WRIT CON/ANAL 20. PAGE 120 A2460 — RIGID/FLEX PWR DIPLOM

S23
DEWEY J.,"ETHICS AND INTERNATIONAL RELATIONS." FUT WOR-45 SOCIETY INT/ORG VOL/ASSN DIPLOM LEGIT ORD/FREE...JURID CONCPT GEN/METH 20. PAGE 37 A0752 — LAW MORAL

B28
HALL W.P.,EMPIRE TO COMMONWEALTH. FUT WOR-45 CONSTN ECO/DEV ECO/UNDEV INT/ORG PROVS PLAN DIPLOM EDU/PROP ADMIN COLONIAL PEACE PERSON ALL/VALS ...POLICY GEOG SOC OBS RECORD TREND CMN/WLTH PARLIAMENT 19/20. PAGE 60 A1229 — VOL/ASSN NAT/G UK

B30
FLEMMING D.,THE TREATY VETO OF THE AMERICAN SENATE. FUT USA+45 USA-45 CONSTN INT/ORG NAT/G TOP/EX LEGIT GOV/REL PWR...POLICY MAJORIT CONCPT OBS TIME/SEQ CONGRESS 20. PAGE 46 A0949 — LEGIS RIGID/FLEX

B31
STOWELL E.C.,INTERNATIONAL LAW. FUT UNIV WOR-45 SOCIETY CONSULT EX/STRUC FORCES ACT/RES PLAN DIPLOM EDU/PROP LEGIT DISPL PWR SKILL...POLICY CONCPT OBS TREND TOT/POP 20. PAGE 139 A2839 — INT/ORG ROUTINE INT/LAW

B32
FLEMMING D.,THE UNITED STATES AND THE LEAGUE OF NATIONS, 1918-1920. FUT USA-45 NAT/G LEGIS TOP/EX DEBATE CHOOSE PEACE ATTIT SOVEREIGN...TIME/SEQ CON/ANAL CONGRESS LEAGUE/NAT 20 TREATY. PAGE 46 A0950 — INT/ORG EDU/PROP

B32
WRIGHT Q.,GOLD AND MONETARY STABILIZATION. FUT USA-45 WOR-45 INTELL ECO/DEV INT/ORG NAT/G CONSULT PLAN ECO/TAC ADMIN ATTIT WEALTH...CONCPT TREND 20. PAGE 167 A3404 — FINAN POLICY

B34
GRAHAM F.D.,PROTECTIVE TARIFFS. FUT USA+45 WOR-45 INDUS MARKET VOL/ASSN PLAN CAP/ISM ECO/TAC PEACE ATTIT DRIVE HEALTH ORD/FREE...OBS TREND GEN/LAWS 20. PAGE 55 A1124 — INT/ORG TARIFFS

B36
RUSSEL F.M.,THEORIES OF INTERNATIONAL RELATIONS. EUR+WWI FUT MOD/EUR USA-45 INT/ORG DIPLOM...JURID CONCPT. PAGE 125 A2571 — PWR POLICY BAL/PWR SOVEREIGN

B38
DE MADARIAGA S.,THE WORLD'S DESIGN. WOR-45 SOCIETY STRUCT EDU/PROP PEACE ATTIT PERSON ALL/VALS ...SOCIALIST CONCPT TIME/SEQ TREND GEN/LAWS LEAGUE/NAT. PAGE 35 A0706 — FUT INT/ORG DIPLOM

B38
FLEMMING D.,THE UNITED STATES AND WORLD ORGANIZATION, 1920-1933. ASIA FUT WOR-45 NAT/G TOP/EX DIPLOM ECO/TAC EDU/PROP LEGIT COERCE WAR ...TIME/SEQ LEAGUE/NAT 20 CHINJAP. PAGE 47 A0951 — USA-45 INT/ORG PEACE

B39
MARRIOTT J.,COMMONWEALTH OR ANARCHY: A SURVEY OF PROJECTS OF PEACE. WOR-45 STRATA DOMIN ATTIT ORD/FREE PWR...TRADIT TIME/SEQ GEN/METH 16/20 CMN/WLTH. PAGE 95 A1945 — FUT INT/ORG PEACE

B39
WILSON G.G.,HANDBOOK OF INTERNATIONAL LAW. FUT UNIV USA-45 WOR-45 SOCIETY LEGIT ATTIT DISPL DRIVE ALL/VALS...INT/LAW TIME/SEQ TREND. PAGE 165 A3359 — INT/ORG LAW CONCPT WAR

L39
NEARING S.,"A WARLESS WORLD." FUT WOR-45 SOCIETY INT/ORG NAT/G EX/STRUC PLAN DOMIN WAR ATTIT DRIVE PWR...POLICY PSY CONCPT OBS TREND HYPO/EXP MARX/KARL 20 MARX/KARL LENIN/VI. PAGE 108 A2210 — COERCE PEACE

B40
CARR E.H.,THE TWENTY YEARS' CRISIS 1919-1939. FUT WOR-45 BAL/PWR ECO/TAC LEGIT TOTALISM ATTIT ALL/VALS...POLICY JURID CONCPT TIME/SEQ TREND GEN/LAWS TOT/POP 20. PAGE 24 A0498 — INT/ORG DIPLOM PEACE

S41
LASSWELL H.D.,"THE GARRISON STATE" (BMR)" FUT WOR+45 ELITES INTELL FORCES ECO/TAC DOMIN EDU/PROP COERCE INGP/REL 20. PAGE 85 A1739 — NAT/G DIPLOM PWR CIVMIL/REL

B42
BONNET H.,THE UNITED NATIONS, WHAT THEY ARE, WHAT THEY MAY BECOME. FUT WOR-45 CREATE BAL/PWR ECO/TAC PWR...TREND GEN/LAWS 20. PAGE 16 A0335 — INT/ORG ORD/FREE

B42
CORBETT P.E.,POST WAR WORLDS. ASIA EUR+WWI FUT S/ASIA USA-45 ECO/DEV ECO/UNDEV NAT/G DELIB/GP FORCES PLAN ROUTINE ATTIT PWR 20. PAGE 30 A0613 — WOR-45 INT/ORG

B42
HAMBRO C.J.,HOW TO WIN THE PEACE. ECO/TAC EDU/PROP ADJUD PERSON ALL/VALS...SOCIALIST TREND GEN/LAWS 20. PAGE 61 A1246 — FUT INT/ORG PEACE

B42
KELSEN H.,LAW AND PEACE IN INTERNATIONAL RELATIONS. FUT WOR-45 NAT/G DELIB/GP DIPLOM LEGIT RIGID/FLEX ORD/FREE SOVEREIGN...JURID CONCPT TREND STERTYP GEN/LAWS LEAGUE/NAT 20. PAGE 77 A1580 — INT/ORG ADJUD PEACE INT/LAW

S42
SHOTWELL J.,"AFTER THE WAR." COM EUR+WWI USA+45 USA-45 NAT/G DIPLOM INT/TRADE ARMS/CONT SOVEREIGN ...CONCPT LEAGUE/NAT TOT/POP FAO 20. PAGE 132 A2707 — FUT INT/ORG PEACE

B43
FULLER G.F.,FOREIGN RELIEF AND REHABILITATION (PAMPHLET). FUT GERMANY UK USA-45 INT/ORG PROB/SOLV DIPLOM FOR/AID ADMIN ADJUST PEACE ALL/VALS...SOC/WK 20 UN JEWS. PAGE 50 A1018 — BIBLIOG/A PLAN GIVE WAR

B43
SULZBACH W.,NATIONAL CONSCIOUSNESS. FUT WOR-45 INT/ORG PEACE MORAL FASCISM MARXISM...MAJORIT TREND WORSHIP 19/20 LEAGUE/NAT INTERVENT WWI. PAGE 140 A2862 — NAT/LISM NAT/G DIPLOM WAR

B44
BARTLETT R.J.,THE LEAGUE TO ENFORCE PEACE. FUT USA-45 NAT/G POL/PAR CREATE EDU/PROP ADMIN RIGID/FLEX PWR...CONCPT TREND GEN/METH LEAGUE/NAT 20. PAGE 11 A0231 — INT/ORG ORD/FREE DIPLOM

B44
BRIERLY J.L.,THE OUTLOOK FOR INTERNATIONAL LAW. FUT WOR-45 CONSTN NAT/G VOL/ASSN FORCES ECO/TAC DOMIN LEGIT ADJUD ROUTINE PEACE ORD/FREE...INT/LAW JURID METH LEAGUE/NAT 20. PAGE 18 A0376 — INT/ORG LAW

B44
HUDSON M.,INTERNATIONAL TRIBUNALS PAST AND FUTURE. FUT WOR-45 LAW EDU/PROP ADJUD ORD/FREE...CONCPT TIME/SEQ TREND GEN/LAWS TOT/POP VAL/FREE 18/20. PAGE 69 A1408 — INT/ORG STRUCT INT/LAW

B44
LIPPMANN W.,US WAR AIMS. USA-45 DIPLOM ATTIT MORAL ORD/FREE PWR...CONCPT TIME/SEQ GEN/LAWS TOT/POP 20. PAGE 89 A1828 — FUT INT/ORG PEACE WAR

B44
WEIGERT H.W.,COMPASS OF THE WORLD, A SYMPOSIUM ON POLITICAL GEOGRAPHY. EUR+WWI FUT MOD/EUR S/ASIA USA-45 WOR-45 SOCIETY AGRI INDUS MARKET ECO/TAC INT/TRADE PERSON 20. PAGE 162 A3298 — TEC/DEV CAP/ISM RUSSIA GEOG

L44
CORWIN E.S.,"THE CONSTITUTION AND WORLD ORGANIZATION." FUT USA+45 USA-45 NAT/G EX/STRUC LEGIS PEACE KNOWL...CON/ANAL UN 20. PAGE 31 A0627 — INT/ORG CONSTN SOVEREIGN

L44
WRIGHT Q.,"THE US AND INTERNATIONAL AGREEMENTS." FUT USA-45 CONSTN INTELL INT/ORG LOC/G NAT/G CHIEF CONSULT EX/STRUC DIPLOM LEGIT DRIVE PERCEPT PWR ...CONCPT CONGRESS 20. PAGE 167 A3407 — DELIB/GP TOP/EX PEACE

S44
WRIGHT Q.,"CONSTITUTIONAL PROCEDURES OF THE US FOR CARRYING OUT OBLIGATIONS FOR MILITARY SANCTIONS." EUR+WWI FUT USA-45 WOR-45 CONSTN INTELL NAT/G CONSULT EX/STRUC LEGIS ROUTINE DRIVE...POLICY JURID CONCPT OBS TREND TOT/POP 20. PAGE 167 A3406 — TOP/EX FORCES INT/LAW WAR

B45
CARR E.H.,NATIONALISM AND AFTER. FUT WOR-45 NAT/G VOL/ASSN EX/STRUC PLAN ROUTINE TOTALISM ATTIT HEALTH ORD/FREE PWR...CONCPT 20. PAGE 25 A0499 — INT/ORG TREND NAT/LISM REGION

B45
RANSHOFFEN-WERTHEIMER EF,THE INTERNATIONAL SECRETARIAT: A GREAT EXPERIMENT IN INTERNATIONAL ADMINISTRATION. EUR+WWI FUT CONSTN FACE/GP CONSULT DELIB/GP ACT/RES ADMIN ROUTINE PEACE ORD/FREE...MGT RECORD ORG/CHARTS LEAGUE/NAT WORK 20. PAGE 119 A2442 — INT/ORG EXEC

B45
STRAUSZ-HUPE R.,THE BALANCE OF TOMORROW: POWER AND FOREIGN POLICY IN THE UNITED STATES. FUT USA+45 ECO/DEV EXTR/IND INT/ORG FORCES BAL/PWR REGION NUC/PWR...GEOG CHARTS 20 COLD/WAR EUROPE/W. PAGE 139 A2845 — DIPLOM PWR POLICY WAR

B45
WEST R.,CONSCIENCE AND SOCIETY: A STUDY OF THE PSYCHOLOGICAL PREREQUISITES OF LAW AND ORDER. FUT UNIV LAW SOCIETY STRUCT DIPLOM WAR PERS/REL SUPEGO ...SOC 20. PAGE 163 A3321 — COERCE INT/LAW ORD/FREE PERSON

B46
KEETON G.W.,MAKING INTERNATIONAL LAW WORK. FUT WOR-45 NAT/G DELIB/GP FORCES LEGIT COERCE PEACE ATTIT RIGID/FLEX ORD/FREE PWR...JURID CONCPT HIST/WRIT GEN/METH LEAGUE/NAT 20. PAGE 77 A1578 — INT/ORG ADJUD INT/LAW

B46
LOWENSTEIN R.,POLITICAL RECONSTRUCTION. WOR+45 EX/STRUC EDU/PROP NAT/LISM ATTIT KNOWL ORD/FREE PWR ...SOCIALIST CONCPT GEN/LAWS TOT/POP 20. PAGE 91 A1869 — FUT INT/ORG DIPLOM

L46
MASTERS D.,"ONE WORLD OR NONE." FUT WOR+45 INTELL INT/ORG ACT/RES EDU/PROP DETER ATTIT RIGID/FLEX SUPEGO KNOWL...STAT TREND ORG/CHARTS 20. PAGE 96 A1960 — POLICY PHIL/SCI ARMS/CONT NUC/PWR

S46
DOUGLAS W.O.,"SYMPOSIUM ON WORLD ORGANIZATION." FUT USA+45 WOR+45 CONSTN SOCIETY NAT/G PLAN EDU/PROP LEGIT RIGID/FLEX KNOWL...INT/LAW JURID STERTYP TOT/POP 20. PAGE 38 A0778 — INT/ORG LAW

B47
KIRK G.,THE STUDY OF INTERNATIONAL RELATIONS. FUT USA-45 R+D ACADEM INT/ORG CONSULT DELIB/GP INT/TRADE EDU/PROP PEACE RIGID/FLEX KNOWL VAL/FREE 20. PAGE 80 A1632 — USA+45 DIPLOM

L47
BRUNER J.S.,"TOWARD A COMMON GROUND-INTERNATIONAL SOCIAL SCIENCE." FUT WOR+45 INTELL R+D NAT/G VOL/ASSN CONSULT DELIB/GP ACT/RES CREATE PLAN TEC/DEV ATTIT ORD/FREE...PSY SOC CONCPT ANTHOL UNESCO 20. PAGE 20 A0410 — INT/ORG KNOWL

L47
COMM. STUDY ORGAN. PEACE,"SECURITY THROUGH THE UNITED NATIONS." COM FUT WOR+45 TOP/EX ACT/RES BAL/PWR ARMS/CONT NUC/PWR...CONCPT GEN/LAWS UN TOT/POP COLD/WAR 20. PAGE 28 A0577 — INT/ORG ORD/FREE PEACE

B48
CHAMBERLAIN L.H.,AMERICAN FOREIGN POLICY. FUT USA+45 USA-45 WOR+45 WOR-45 NAT/G LEGIS TOP/EX ECO/TAC FOR/AID EDU/PROP EXEC ATTIT ORD/FREE ...JURID TREND TOT/POP 20. PAGE 25 A0517 — CONSTN DIPLOM

B48
GRAHAM F.D.,THE THEORY OF INTERNATIONAL VALUES. FUT WOR+45 WOR-45 ECO/DEV FINAN INT/ORG PLAN TEC/DEV CAP/ISM DIPLOM ECO/TAC TARIFFS ROUTINE BAL/PAY DRIVE PWR WEALTH SOCISM...POLICY STAT HYPO/EXP GEN/LAWS 20. PAGE 55 A1125 — NEW/IDEA INT/TRADE

B48
JESSUP P.C.,A MODERN LAW OF NATIONS. FUT WOR+45 WOR-45 SOCIETY NAT/G DELIB/GP LEGIS BAL/PWR EDU/PROP LEGIT PWR...INT/LAW JURID TIME/SEQ LEAGUE/NAT 20. PAGE 74 A1514 — INT/ORG ADJUD

B48
KULISCHER E.M.,EUROPE ON THE MOVE: WAR AND POPULATION CHANGES, 1917-1947. COM EUR+WWI FUT GERMANY USSR DIST/IND PLAN INT/TRADE CONTROL WAR DRIVE...CENSUS TREND COLD/WAR 20. PAGE 82 A1690 ECO/TAC GEOG

B48
MORGENTHAL H.J.,POLITICS AMONG NATIONS: THE STRUGGLE FOR POWER AND PEACE. FUT WOR+45 INT/ORG OP/RES PROB/SOLV BAL/PWR CONTROL ATTIT MORAL ...INT/LAW BIBLIOG 20 COLD/WAR. PAGE 104 A2135 DIPLOM PEACE PWR POLICY

B49
BOYD A.,WESTERN UNION: A STUDY OF THE TREND TOWARD EUROPEAN UNITY. FUT REGION NAT/LISM...POLICY IDEA/COMP BIBLIOG 14/20 OEEC ERASMUS/D COUNCL/EUR FULBRGHT/J NATO. PAGE 18 A0363 DIPLOM AGREE TREND INT/ORG

B49
PARMELEE M.,GEO-ECONOMIC REGIONAL AND WORLD FEDERATION. FUT WOR+45 WOR-45 SOCIETY VOL/ASSN PLAN ...METH/CNCPT SIMUL GEN/METH TOT/POP 20. PAGE 114 A2335 INT/ORG GEOG REGION

L49
COMM. STUDY ORGAN. PEACE,"A TEN YEAR RECORD, 1939-1949." FUT WOR+45 LAW R+D CONSULT DELIB/GP CREATE LEGIT ROUTINE ORD/FREE...TIME/SEQ UN 20. PAGE 28 A0578 INT/ORG CONSTN PEACE

S49
KIRK G.,"MATTERIALS FOR THE STUDY OF INTERNATIONAL RELATIONS." FUT UNIV WOR+45 INTELL EDU/PROP ROUTINE PEACE ATTIT...INT/LAW JURID CONCPT OBS. PAGE 80 A1633 INT/ORG ACT/RES DIPLOM

B50
BERLE A.A.,NATURAL SELECTION OF POLITICAL FORCES. FUT WOR+45 WOR-45 CULTURE SOCIETY INT/ORG NAT/G FORCES EDU/PROP LEGIT COERCE...CONCPT HIST/WRIT TREND 20. PAGE 13 A0274 POL/PAR BAL/PWR DIPLOM

B50
SOHN L.B.,CASES AND OTHER MATERIALS ON WORLD LAW. FUT WOR+45 LAW INT/ORG...INT/LAW JURID METH/CNCPT 20 UN. PAGE 135 A2760 CT/SYS CONSTN

L50
US SENATE COMM. GOVT. OPER.,"REVISION OF THE UN CHARTER." FUT USA+45 WOR+45 CONSTN ECO/DEV ECO/UNDEV NAT/G DELIB/GP ACT/RES CREATE PLAN EXEC ROUTINE CHOOSE ALL/VALS...POLICY CONCPT CONGRESS UN TOT/POP 20 COLD/WAR. PAGE 157 A3196 INT/ORG LEGIS PEACE

S50
UNESCO,"MEETING ON UNIVERSITY TEACHING OF INTERNATIONAL RELATIONS." FUT WOR+45 R+D VOL/ASSN CONSULT PLAN EDU/PROP ATTIT...CONCPT TREND 20. PAGE 147 A3012 INT/ORG KNOWL DIPLOM

B51
CORBETT P.E.,LAW AND SOCIETY IN THE RELATIONS OF STATES. FUT WOR+45 WOR-45 CONTROL WAR PEACE PWR ...POLICY JURID 16/20 TREATY. PAGE 30 A0615 INT/LAW DIPLOM INT/ORG

B51
UNESCO,FREEDOM AND CULTURE. FUT WOR+45 CONSTN CULTURE PERF/ART VOL/ASSN EDU/PROP PEACE ATTIT ALL/VALS SOVEREIGN...POLICY MAJORIT CONCPT TREND STERTYP GEN/LAWS UN TOT/POP 20. PAGE 147 A3013 INT/ORG SOCIETY

B51
WELLES S.,SEVEN DECISIONS THAT SHAPED HISTORY. ASIA FRANCE FUT USA+45 WOR+45 CONSTN STRUCT INT/ORG NAT/G ACT/RES EDU/PROP DRIVE...POLICY CONCPT TIME/SEQ TREND TOT/POP UN 20 CHINJAP. PAGE 163 A3315 USA-45 DIPLOM WAR

L51
MANGONE G.,"THE IDEA AND PRACTICE OF WORLD GOVERNMENT." FUT WOR+45 WOR-45 ECO/DEV LEGIS CREATE LEGIT ROUTINE ATTIT MORAL PWR WEALTH...CONCPT GEN/LAWS 20. PAGE 94 A1920 INT/ORG SOCIETY INT/LAW

B52
HOSELITZ B.F.,THE PROGRESS OF UNDERDEVELOPED AREAS. FUT WOR+45 WOR-45 ECO/DEV ECO/TAC INT/TRADE WEALTH ...SOC TREND GEN/LAWS TOT/POP VAL/FREE COLD/WAR 20. PAGE 68 A1391 ECO/UNDEV PLAN FOR/AID

B52
MACARTHUR D.,REVITALIZING A NATION. ASIA COM FUT KOREA WOR+45 NAT/G FOR/AID TAX GIVE WAR ATTIT SOCISM 20 CHINJAP EUROPE. PAGE 92 A1885 LEAD FORCES TOP/EX POLICY

S52
MASTERS R.D.,"RUSSIA AND THE UNITED NATIONS." FUT USA+45 USSR WOR+45 CONSTN VOL/ASSN DELIB/GP TOP/EX CREATE DIPLOM ADMIN...TREND STERTYP UN 20. PAGE 96 A1962 INT/ORG PWR

S52
SCHWEBEL S.M.,"THE SECRETARY-GENERAL OF THE UN." FUT INTELL CONSULT DELIB/GP ADMIN PEACE ATTIT ...JURID MGT CONCPT TREND UN CONGRESS 20. PAGE 130 A2663 INT/ORG TOP/EX

B53
BORGESE G.,FOUNDATIONS OF THE WORLD REPUBLIC. FUT SOCIETY NAT/G CREATE LEGIT PERSON MORAL...MAJORIT CON/ANAL LEAGUE/NAT TOT/POP 20. PAGE 17 A0340 INT/ORG CONSTN PEACE

B53
MENDE T.,WORLD POWER IN THE BALANCE. FUT USA+45 USSR WOR-45 ECO/DEV ECO/TAC INT/TRADE EDU/PROP UTOPIA ATTIT...HUM CONCPT TREND COLD/WAR TOT/POP 20. PAGE 99 A2036 WOR+45 PWR BAL/PWR

B53
MURPHY G.,IN THE MINDS OF MEN: THE STUDY OF HUMAN BEHAVIOR AND SOCIAL TENSIONS IN INDIA. FUT S/ASIA FAM INT/ORG NAT/G DIPLOM EDU/PROP GP/REL ATTIT RIGID/FLEX ALL/VALS...SOC QU UNESCO 20. PAGE 106 A2176 SECT STRATA INDIA

S53
CORY R.H. JR.,"FORGING A PUBLIC INFORMATION POLICY FOR THE UNITED NATIONS." FUT WOR+45 SOCIETY ADMIN PEACE ATTIT PERSON SKILL...CONCPT 20 UN. PAGE 31 A0628 INT/ORG EDU/PROP BAL/PWR

S53
LINCOLN G.,"FACTORS DETERMINING ARMS AID." COM FUT USA+45 USSR WOR+45 ECO/DEV NAT/G CONSULT PLAN TEC/DEV DIPLOM DOMIN EDU/PROP PERCEPT PWR ...DECISION CONCPT TREND MARX/KARL 20. PAGE 89 A1819 FORCES POLICY BAL/PWR FOR/AID

B54
ARON R.,CENTURY OF TOTAL WAR. FUT WOR+45 WOR-45 SOCIETY INT/ORG NAT/G FORCES TOP/EX CREATE BAL/PWR DOMIN EDU/PROP COERCE DETER PEACE TOTALISM PWR ...TIME/SEQ TREND COLD/WAR TOT/POP VAL/FREE LEAGUE/NAT 20. PAGE 9 A0179 ATTIT WAR

B54
CHEEVER D.S.,ORGANIZING FOR PEACE. FUT WOR+45 WOR-45 STRATA STRUCT NAT/G CREATE DIPLOM LEGIT REGION COERCE DETER PEACE ATTIT DRIVE ALL/VALS ...TIME/SEQ TREND UN LEAGUE/NAT. PAGE 26 A0525 INT/ORG

B54
MILLARD E.L.,FREEDOM IN A FEDERAL WORLD. FUT WOR+45 VOL/ASSN TOP/EX LEGIT ROUTINE FEDERAL PEACE ATTIT DISPL ORD/FREE PWR...MAJORIT INT/LAW JURID TREND COLD/WAR 20. PAGE 101 A2073 INT/ORG CREATE ADJUD BAL/PWR

B54
STALEY E.,THE FUTURE OF UNDERDEVELOPED COUNTRIES: POLITICAL IMPLICATIONS OF ECONOMIC DEVELOPMENT. COM FUT USA+45 SOCIETY ECO/UNDEV CREATE PLAN CAP/ISM ATTIT DRIVE MARXISM SOCISM...POLICY CONCPT CHARTS COLD/WAR 20. PAGE 137 A2801 EDU/PROP ECO/TAC FOR/AID

B54
WRIGHT Q.,PROBLEMS OF STABILITY AND PROGRESS IN INTERNATIONAL RELATIONSHIPS. FUT WOR+45 WOR-45 SOCIETY LEGIS CREATE TEC/DEV ECO/TAC EDU/PROP ADJUD WAR PEACE ORD/FREE PWR...KNO/TEST TREND GEN/LAWS 20. PAGE 167 A3409 INT/ORG CONCPT DIPLOM

S54
DODD S.C.,"THE SCIENTIFIC MEASUREMENT OF FITNESS FOR SELF-GOVERNMENT." FUT CONSTN ECO/UNDEV INT/ORG PLAN PWR...CONCPT QUANT CON/ANAL SOC/EXP UN LEAGUE/NAT 20. PAGE 38 A0767 NAT/G STAT SOVEREIGN

B55
COTTRELL W.F.,ENERGY AND SOCIETY. FUT WOR+45 WOR-45 ECO/DEV ECO/UNDEV INT/ORG NAT/G DETER ORD/FREE PWR SKILL WEALTH...SOC TIME/SEQ TOT/POP VAL/FREE 20. PAGE 31 A0634 TEC/DEV BAL/PWR PEACE

B55
MACMAHON A.W.,FEDERALISM: MATURE AND EMERGENT. EUR+WWI FUT WOR+45 WOR-45 INT/ORG NAT/G REPRESENT FEDERAL...POLICY MGT RECORD TREND GEN/LAWS 20. PAGE 93 A1900 STRUCT CONCPT

B55
MOCH J.,HUMAN FOLLY: DISARM OR PERISH. USA+45 WOR+45 SOCIETY INT/ORG NAT/G ACT/RES EDU/PROP ATTIT PERSON KNOWL ORD/FREE PWR...MAJORIT TOT/POP COLD/WAR 20. PAGE 102 A2093 FUT DELIB/GP ARMS/CONT NUC/PWR

B55
MYRDAL A.R.,AMERICA'S ROLE IN INTERNATIONATIONAL SOCIAL WELFARE. FUT WOR+45 SOCIETY R+D VOL/ASSN ECO/TAC EDU/PROP HEALTH KNOWL WEALTH...SOC CHARTS ORG/CHARTS TOT/POP 20. PAGE 107 A2188 PLAN SKILL FOR/AID

B56
BLACKETT P.M.S.,ATOMIC WEAPONS AND EAST-WEST RELATIONS. FUT WOR+45 INT/ORG DELIB/GP COERCE ATTIT RIGID/FLEX KNOWL...RELATIV HIST/WRIT TREND GEN/METH COLD/WAR 20. PAGE 15 A0299 FORCES PWR ARMS/CONT NUC/PWR

B56
BROOK D.,THE UNITED NATIONS AND CHINA DILEMMA. CHINA/COM FUT WOR+45 ECO/UNDEV NAT/G DELIB/GP ACT/RES DIPLOM ROUTINE NAT/LISM TOTALISM ATTIT DRIVE...CONCPT OBS TIME/SEQ UN TOT/POP TIME UN 20. PAGE 19 A0390 ASIA INT/ORG BAL/PWR

B56
JESSUP P.C.,TRANSNATIONAL LAW. FUT WOR+45 JUDGE CREATE ADJUD ORD/FREE...CONCPT VAL/FREE 20. PAGE 74 A1515 LAW JURID INT/LAW

B56
KIRK G.,THE CHANGING ENVIRONMENT OF INTERNATIONAL RELATIONS. ASIA S/ASIA USA+45 WOR+45 ECO/UNDEV INT/ORG NAT/G FOR/AID EDU/PROP PEACE KNOWL ...PLURIST COLD/WAR TOT/POP 20. PAGE 80 A1634 FUT EXEC DIPLOM

B56
WOLFF R.L.,THE BALKANS IN OUR TIME. ALBANIA FUT MOD/EUR USSR YUGOSLAVIA CULTURE INT/ORG SECT DIPLOM GEOG COM

EDU/PROP COERCE WAR ORD/FREE...CHARTS 4/20 BALKANS COMINFORM. PAGE 166 A3388

B57
COMM. STUDY ORGAN. PEACE,STRENGTHENING THE UNITED NATIONS. FUT USA+45 WOR+45 CONSTN NAT/G DELIB/GP FORCES LEGIS ECO/TAC LEGIT COERCE PEACE...JURID CONCPT UN COLD/WAR 20. PAGE 28 A0580 INT/ORG ORD/FREE

B57
FULLER C.D.,TRAINING OF SPECIALISTS IN INTERNATIONAL RELATIONS. FUT USA+45 USA-45 INTELL INT/ORG...MGT METH/CNCPT INT QU GEN/METH 20. PAGE 50 A1017 KNOWL DIPLOM

B57
JENKS C.W.,THE INTERNATIONAL PROTECTION OF TRADE UNION FREEDOM. FUT WOR+45 WOR-45 VOL/ASSN DELIB/GP CT/SYS REGION ROUTINE...JURID METH/CNCPT RECORD TIME/SEQ CHARTS ILO WORK OAS 20. PAGE 73 A1504 LABOR INT/ORG

B57
KAPLAN M.A.,SYSTEM AND PROCESS OF INTERNATIONAL POLITICS. FUT WOR+45 WOR-45 SOCIETY PLAN BAL/PWR ADMIN ATTIT PERSON RIGID/FLEX PWR SOVEREIGN ...DECISION TREND VAL/FREE. PAGE 76 A1560 INT/ORG DIPLOM

B57
KENNAN G.F.,RUSSIA, THE ATOM AND THE WEST. COM EUR+WWI FUT WOR+45 SOCIETY ECO/DEV FORCES DIPLOM ECO/TAC DOMIN EDU/PROP COERCE NUC/PWR ATTIT DRIVE ORD/FREE PWR...POLICY OBS TIME/SEQ TREND COLD/WAR NATO 20. PAGE 77 A1574 NAT/G INT/ORG USSR

B57
KISSINGER H.A.,NUCLEAR WEAPONS AND FOREIGN POLICY. FUT USA+45 WOR+45 INT/ORG FORCES ACT/RES TEC/DEV DIPLOM ARMS/CONT COERCE ATTIT KNOWL PWR...DECISION GEOG CHARTS 20. PAGE 80 A1640 PLAN DETER NUC/PWR

B57
LAVES W.H.C.,UNESCO. FUT WOR+45 NAT/G CONSULT DELIB/GP TEC/DEV ECO/TAC EDU/PROP PEACE ORD/FREE ...CONCPT TIME/SEQ TREND UNESCO VAL/FREE 20. PAGE 86 A1751 INT/ORG KNOWL

B57
LEVONTIN A.V.,THE MYTH OF INTERNATIONAL SECURITY: A JURIDICAL AND CRITICAL ANALYSIS. FUT WOR+45 WOR-45 LAW NAT/G VOL/ASSN ACT/RES BAL/PWR ATTIT ORD/FREE ...JURID METH/CNCPT TIME/SEQ TREND STERTYP 20. PAGE 88 A1797 INT/ORG INT/LAW SOVEREIGN MYTH

B57
SPEIER H.,GERMAN REARMAMENT AND ATOMIC WAR: THE VIEWS OF GERMAN MILITARY AND POLITICAL LEADERS. FUT WOR+45 INT/ORG NAT/G WEAPON ATTIT PWR...INT QU TOT/POP VAL/FREE COLD/WAR 20. PAGE 136 A2780 TOP/EX FORCES NUC/PWR GERMANY

S57
DEUTSCH K.W.,"MASS COMMUNICATIONS AND THE LOSS OF FREEDOM IN NATIONAL DECISION MAKING." FUT WOR+45 SOCIETY COM/IND INT/ORG NAT/G ACT/RES CREATE TEC/DEV EDU/PROP MAJORITY PERCEPT...METH/CNCPT 20. PAGE 36 A0737 COERCE DECISION WAR

B58
BOWLES C.,IDEAS, PEOPLE AND PEACE. ASIA CHINA/COM FUT INDIA USA+45 USSR ECO/UNDEV INT/ORG LEAD TASK MARXISM 20 NATO UN COLD/WAR. PAGE 18 A0359 PEACE POLICY NAT/G DIPLOM

B58
GARTHOFF R.L.,SOVIET STRATEGY IN THE NUCLEAR AGE. FUT USSR R+D INT/ORG NAT/G ACT/RES TEC/DEV DOMIN DETER WAR ATTIT PWR...RELATIV METH/CNCPT SELF/OBS TREND CON/ANAL STERTYP GEN/LAWS 20. PAGE 51 A1052 COM FORCES BAL/PWR NUC/PWR

B58
HAUSER P.H.,POPULATION AND WORLD POLITICS. FUT WOR+45 WOR-45 AGRI DIST/IND INDUS INT/ORG PLAN ECO/TAC DISPL HEALTH COLD/WAR 20. PAGE 63 A1288 NAT/G ECO/UNDEV FOR/AID

B58
HOLT R.T.,RADIO FREE EUROPE. FUT USA+45 CULTURE ECO/DEV INT/ORG KIN POL/PAR SECT FORCES ACT/RES DIPLOM COERCE REV CHOOSE PEACE ATTIT PWR...MAJORIT CONCPT COLD/WAR WORK 20 RFE. PAGE 67 A1374 COM EDU/PROP COM/IND

B58
MELMAN S.,INSPECTION FOR DISARMAMENT. USA+45 WOR+45 SOCIETY INT/ORG NAT/G CONSULT ACT/RES PLAN EDU/PROP CONTROL DETER PEACE ATTIT PERSON KNOWL...PSY STAT OBS CHARTS TOT/POP VAL/FREE 20. PAGE 99 A2035 FUT ORD/FREE ARMS/CONT NUC/PWR

B58
MOORE B.T.,NATO AND THE FUTURE OF EUROPE. EUR+WWI FUT USA+45 ECO/DEV INDUS MARKET NAT/G VOL/ASSN FORCES DIPLOM NUC/PWR ORD/FREE...CONCPT CHARTS ORG/CHARTS CMN/WLTH 20 NATO. PAGE 103 A2122 INT/ORG REGION

B58
NOEL-BAKER D.,THE ARMS RACE. WOR+45 NAT/G DELIB/GP ACT/RES TEC/DEV EDU/PROP NUC/PWR ATTIT KNOWL PWR ...CONCPT OBS LEAGUE/NAT 20 COLD/WAR. PAGE 109 A2245 FUT INT/ORG ARMS/CONT PEACE

B58
ORGANSKI A.F.K.,WORLD POLITICS. FUT WOR+45 SOCIETY STRUCT NAT/G BAL/PWR ECO/TAC DOMIN NAT/LISM ATTIT KNOWL ORD/FREE PWR...CONCPT METH/CNCPT TREND STERTYP GEN/LAWS TOT/POP 20. PAGE 112 A2297 INT/ORG DIPLOM

B58
SCHUMAN F.,INTERNATIONAL POLITICS. WOR+45 WOR-45 INTELL NAT/G FORCES DOMIN LEGIT COERCE NUC/PWR ATTIT DISPL ORD/FREE PWR SOVEREIGN...POLICY CONCPT GEN/LAWS SUEZ 20. PAGE 129 A2650 FUT INT/ORG NAT/LISM DIPLOM

B58
SLICK T.,PERMANENT PEACE: A CHECK AND BALANCE PLAN. FUT WOR+45 NAT/G FORCES CREATE PLAN EDU/PROP LEGIT ADJUD COERCE NAT/LISM RIGID/FLEX MORAL...HUM CONCPT METH/CNCPT NEW/IDEA TREND CHARTS TOT/POP 20. PAGE 134 A2742 INT/ORG ORD/FREE PEACE ARMS/CONT

S58
JORDAN A.,"MILITARY ASSISTANCE AND NATIONAL POLICY." ASIA FUT USA+45 WOR+45 ECO/DEV ECO/UNDEV INT/ORG NAT/G PLAN ECO/TAC ROUTINE WEAPON ATTIT RIGID/FLEX PWR...CONCPT TREND 20. PAGE 75 A1533 FORCES POLICY FOR/AID DIPLOM

S58
MCDOUGAL M.S.,"PERSPECTIVES FOR A LAW OF OUTER SPACE." FUT WOR+45 AIR CONSULT DELIB/GP TEC/DEV CT/SYS ORD/FREE...POLICY JURID 20 UN. PAGE 98 A2004 INT/ORG SPACE INT/LAW

B59
AMERICAN FRIENDS OF VIETNAM,AID TO VIETNAM: AN AMERICAN SUCCESS STORY (PAMPHLET). ASIA FUT USA+45 VIETNAM ECO/UNDEV WAR CIVMIL/REL GOV/REL...ANTHOL 20. PAGE 7 A0148 DIPLOM NAT/G FOR/AID FORCES

B59
BLOOMFIELD L.P.,WESTERN EUROPE AND THE UN - TRENDS AND PROSPECTS. EUR+WWI BAL/PWR DIPLOM ECO/TAC COLONIAL ATTIT PWR...POLICY 20 UN EUROPE/W. PAGE 16 A0316 INT/ORG TREND FUT NAT/G

B59
BRODIE B.,STRATEGY IN THE MISSILE AGE. FUT WOR+45 CONSULT PLAN COERCE DETER RIGID/FLEX PWR...CONCPT TIME/SEQ TREND 20. PAGE 19 A0381 ACT/RES FORCES ARMS/CONT NUC/PWR

B59
CHINA INSTITUTE OF AMERICA.,CHINA AND THE UNITED NATIONS. CHINA/COM FUT STRUCT EDU/PROP LEGIT ADMIN ATTIT KNOWL ORD/FREE PWR...OBS RECORD STAND/INT TIME/SEQ UN LEAGUE/NAT UNESCO 20. PAGE 26 A0531 ASIA INT/ORG

B59
COMM. STUDY ORGAN. PEACE,ORGANIZING PEACE IN THE NUCLEAR AGE. FUT CONSULT DELIB/GP DOMIN ADJUD ROUTINE COERCE ORD/FREE...TECHNIC INT/LAW JURID NEW/IDEA UN COLD/WAR 20. PAGE 29 A0581 INT/ORG ACT/RES NUC/PWR

B59
COUDENHOVE-KALERGI,FROM WAR TO PEACE. USA+45 USSR WOR+45 WOR-45 LAW INT/ORG NAT/G LEGIT COERCE LOVE ...POLICY PLURIST METH/CNCPT STERTYP TOT/POP UN 20 NATO. PAGE 31 A0636 FUT ORD/FREE

B59
HERZ J.H.,INTERNATIONAL POLITICS IN THE ATOMIC AGE. FUT USA+45 WOR+45 WOR-45 SOCIETY NAT/G FORCES PLAN COERCE DETER ATTIT DRIVE ORD/FREE PWR...TREND COLD/WAR 20. PAGE 64 A1319 INT/ORG ARMS/CONT NUC/PWR

B59
JACKSON B.W.,FIVE IDEAS THAT CHANGE THE WORLD. FUT WOR+45 WOR-45 ECO/UNDEV INDUS DIPLOM DOMIN CONTROL ...IDEA/COMP 20. PAGE 72 A1473 MARXISM NAT/LISM COLONIAL ECO/TAC

B59
MATHISEN T.,METHODOLOGY IN THE STUDY OF INTERNATIONAL RELATIONS. FUT WOR+45 SOCIETY INT/ORG NAT/G POL/PAR WAR PEACE KNOWL PWR...RELATIV CONCPT METH/CNCPT TREND HYPO/EXP METH TOT/POP 20. PAGE 96 A1965 GEN/METH CON/ANAL DIPLOM CREATE

B59
MODELSKI G.,ATOMIC ENERGY IN THE COMMUNIST BLOC. FUT INT/ORG CONSULT FORCES ACT/RES PLAN KNOWL SKILL ...PHIL/SCI STAT CHARTS 20. PAGE 102 A2096 TEC/DEV NUC/PWR USSR COM

B59
SANNWALD R.E.,ECONOMIC INTEGRATION: THEORETICAL ASSUMPTIONS AND CONSEQUENCES OF EUROPEAN UNIFICATION. EUR+WWI FUT FINAN INDUS VOL/ASSN ACT/RES ECO/TAC...PLURIST EEC OEEC 20. PAGE 127 A2601 INT/ORG ECO/DEV INT/TRADE

B59
SCHNEIDER J.,TREATY-MAKING POWER OF INTERNATIONAL ORGANIZATIONS. FUT WOR+45 WOR-45 LAW NAT/G JUDGE DIPLOM LEGIT CT/SYS ORD/FREE PWR...INT/LAW JURID GEN/LAWS TOT/POP UNESCO 20 TREATY. PAGE 129 A2639 INT/ORG ROUTINE

B59
STANFORD RESEARCH INSTITUTE,POSSIBLE NONMILITARY SCIENTIFIC DEVELOPMENTS AND THEIR POTENTIAL IMPACT ON FOREIGN POLICY PROBLEMS OF THE UNITED. FUT USA+45 INT/ORG PROF/ORG CONSULT ACT/RES CREATE PLAN PEACE KNOWL SKILL...TECHNIC PHIL/SCI NEW/IDEA UNESCO 20. PAGE 137 A2802 R+D TEC/DEV

B59
THOMAS N.,THE PREREQUISITES FOR PEACE. ASIA EUR+WWI FUT ISLAM S/ASIA WOR+45 FORCES PLAN BAL/PWR EDU/PROP LEGIT ATTIT PWR...SOCIALIST CONCPT COLD/WAR 20 UN. PAGE 143 A2924 INT/ORG ORD/FREE ARMS/CONT PEACE

B59
VAN WAGENEN R.W.,SOME VIEWS OF AMERICAN DEFENSE OFFICIALS ABOUT THE UNITED NATIONS (PAPER). FUT USA+45 NAT/G DIPLOM WAR EFFICIENCY PEACE...POLICY INT/ORG LEAD ATTIT

INT 20 UN DEPT/DEFEN. PAGE 158 A3216 FORCES

L59
WOLFERS A.,"ACTORS IN INTERNATIONAL POLITICS. IN (FOX,WTR. THEORETICAL ASPECTS OF INTERNATIONAL." FUT WOR+45 CONSTN INT/ORG NAT/G CREATE...CONCPT 20. PAGE 166 A3383 PERSON PWR DIPLOM

S59
BAILEY S.D.,"THE FUTURE COMPOSITION OF THE TRUSTEESHIP COUNCIL." FUT WOR+45 CONSTN VOL/ASSN ADMIN ATTIT PWR...OBS TREND CON/ANAL VAL/FREE UN 20. PAGE 10 A0203 INT/ORG NAT/LISM SOVEREIGN

S59
BOULDING K.E.,"NATIONAL IMAGES AND INTERNATIONAL SYSTEMS." FUT WOR+45 CULTURE INT/ORG TOP/EX ROUTINE ...METH/CNCPT MYTH CONT/OBS TREND HYPO/EXP GEN/METH TOT/POP 20. PAGE 17 A0346 NAT/G DIPLOM

S59
HARTT J.,"ANTARCTICA: ITS IMMEDIATE PRACTICALITIES." FUT USA+45 USSR WOR+45 INT/ORG NAT/G CREATE TEC/DEV REGION KNOWL WEALTH...GEOG 20 ANTARTICA. PAGE 62 A1276 VOL/ASSN ORD/FREE DIPLOM

S59
KINDLEBERGER C.P.,"UNITED STATES ECONOMIC FOREIGN POLICY: RESEARCH REQUIREMENTS FOR 1965." FUT USA+45 WOR+45 DIST/IND MARKET INT/ORG ECO/TAC INT/TRADE WEALTH...OBS TREND CON/ANAL GEN/LAWS VAL/FREE 20. PAGE 79 A1621 FINAN ECO/DEV FOR/AID

S59
KISSINGER H.A.,"THE SEARCH FOR STABILITY." COM GERMANY MOD/EUR USA+45 USA-45 USSR INT/ORG ARMS/CONT NUC/PWR ORD/FREE PWR COLD/WAR 20 NATO. PAGE 80 A1641 FUT ATTIT BAL/PWR

S59
KOHN L.Y.,"ISRAEL AND NEW NATION STATES OF ASIA AND AFRICA." AFR ASIA FUT S/ASIA VOL/ASSN TEC/DEV NAT/LISM RIGID/FLEX SKILL WEALTH...RELATIV OBS TREND CON/ANAL 20. PAGE 81 A1663 ECO/UNDEV ECO/TAC FOR/AID ISRAEL

S59
LASSWELL H.D.,"UNIVERSALITY IN PERSPECTIVE." FUT UNIV SOCIETY CONSULT TOP/EX PLAN EDU/PROP ADJUD ROUTINE ARMS/CONT COERCE PEACE ATTIT PERSON ALL/VALS. PAGE 85 A1741 INT/ORG JURID TOTALISM

S59
PADELFORD N.J.,"REGIONAL COOPERATION IN THE SOUTH PACIFIC: THE SOUTH PACIFIC COMMISSION." FUT NEW/ZEALND UK WOR+45 CULTURE ECO/UNDEV LOC/G VOL/ASSN...OBS CON/ANAL UNESCO VAL/FREE AUSTRAL 20. PAGE 112 A2308 INT/ORG ADMIN

S59
PLAZA G.,"FOR A REGIONAL MARKET IN LATIN AMERICA." FUT L/A+17C CULTURE INDUS NAT/G ECO/TAC INT/TRADE ATTIT WEALTH...NEW/IDEA TREND OAS 20. PAGE 116 A2389 MARKET INT/ORG REGION

S59
SIMONS H.,"WORLD-WIDE CAPABILITIES FOR PRODUCTION AND CONTROL OF NUCLEAR WEAPONS." FUT WOR+45 INDUS INT/ORG NAT/G ECO/TAC ATTIT PWR SKILL...TREND CHARTS VAL/FREE 20. PAGE 133 A2719 TEC/DEV ARMS/CONT NUC/PWR

S59
SOHN L.B.,"THE DEFINITION OF AGGRESSION." FUT LAW FORCES LEGIT ADJUD ROUTINE COERCE ORD/FREE PWR ...MAJORIT JURID QUANT COLD/WAR 20. PAGE 135 A2762 INT/ORG CT/SYS DETER SOVEREIGN

S59
SOLDATI A.,"EOCNOMIC DISINTEGRATION IN EUROPE." EUR+WWI FUT WOR+45 INDUS INT/ORG NAT/G CAP/ISM WEALTH...NEW/IDEA OBS TREND CHARTS EEC 20. PAGE 135 A2764 FINAN ECO/TAC

S59
STOESSINGER J.G.,"THE INTERNATIONAL ATOMIC ENERGY AGENCY: THE FIRST PHASE." FUT WOR+45 NAT/G VOL/ASSN DELIB/GP BAL/PWR LEGIT ADMIN ROUTINE PWR...OBS CON/ANAL GEN/LAWS VAL/FREE 20 IAEA. PAGE 138 A2829 INT/ORG ECO/DEV FOR/AID NUC/PWR

B60
ARMS CONTROL. FUT UNIV WOR+45 INTELL R+D INT/ORG NAT/G VOL/ASSN CONSULT CREATE EDU/PROP PEACE...HUM GEN/LAWS TOT/POP 20. PAGE 3 A0060 DELIB/GP ORD/FREE ARMS/CONT NUC/PWR

B60
ALLEN H.C.,THE ANGLO-AMERICAN PREDICAMENT: THE BRITISH COMMONWEALTH, THE UNITED STATES AND EUROPEAN UNITY. EUR+WWI FUT UK USA+45 WOR+45 ECO/DEV NAT/G PLAN DETER...CONCPT OBS TIME/SEQ TREND COLD/WAR VAL/FREE CMN/WLTH 20. PAGE 6 A0123 INT/ORG PWR BAL/PWR

B60
APTHEKER H.,DISARMAMENT AND THE AMERICAN ECONOMY: A SYMPOSIUM. FUT USA+45 ECO/DEV DIST/IND FINAN INDUS PROC/MFG LABOR NAT/G POL/PAR CONSULT PLAN CAP/ISM INT/TRADE PEACE ATTIT MORAL WEALTH...TREND GEN/LAWS TOT/POP 20. PAGE 9 A0172 MARXIST ARMS/CONT

B60
BAILEY S.D.,THE GENERAL ASSEMBLY OF THE UNITED NATIONS. FUT WOR+45 STRUCT LEGIS ACT/RES PLAN EDU/PROP LEGIT ADMIN EXEC PEACE ATTIT HEALTH PWR ...CONCPT TREND CHARTS GEN/LAWS UN TOT/POP VAL/FREE COLD/WAR 20. PAGE 10 A0204 INT/ORG DELIB/GP DIPLOM

B60
BILLERBECK K.,SOVIET BLOC FOREIGN AID TO UNDERDEVELOPED COUNTRIES. COM FUT USSR FINAN FORCES TEC/DEV DIPLOM INT/TRADE EDU/PROP NUC/PWR...TREND 20. PAGE 14 A0287 FOR/AID ECO/UNDEV ECO/TAC MARXISM

B60
CARNEGIE ENDOWMENT INT. PEACE,PERSPECTIVES ON PEACE - 1910-1960. WOR+45 WOR-45 INTELL INT/ORG CONSULT ACT/RES EDU/PROP ATTIT KNOWL ORD/FREE...TIME/SEQ TREND EEC OAS UNESCO NAZI 20. PAGE 24 A0489 FUT CONCPT ARMS/CONT PEACE

B60
EINSTEIN A.,EINSTEIN ON PEACE. FUT WOR+45 WOR-45 SOCIETY NAT/G PLAN BAL/PWR CAP/ISM DIPLOM ARMS/CONT DETER NAT/LISM...POLICY RELATIV HUM PHIL/SCI CONCPT BIOG COLD/WAR LEAGUE/NAT NAZI. PAGE 41 A0829 INT/ORG ATTIT NUC/PWR PEACE

B60
FISCHER L.,RUSSIA, AMERICA, AND THE WORLD. FUT USA+45 USSR WOR+45 FORCES PLAN BAL/PWR ECO/TAC FOR/AID NEUTRAL TASK NUC/PWR PWR 20 COLD/WAR. PAGE 46 A0937 DIPLOM POLICY MARXISM ECO/UNDEV

B60
FOOTMAN D.,INTERNATIONAL COMMUNISM. ASIA EUR+WWI FRANCE FUT GERMANY MOD/EUR S/ASIA USA-45 WOR+45 WOR-45 INTELL LABOR TOTALISM MARXISM WORK 20. PAGE 47 A0958 COM INT/ORG STRUCT REV

B60
FOREIGN POLICY CLEARING HOUSE,STRATEGY FOR THE 60'S. FUT USA+45 WOR+45 ECO/UNDEV FORCES BAL/PWR TASK ARMS/CONT DETER PWR MARXISM 20 SENATE. PAGE 47 A0963 DIPLOM NAT/G POLICY ACT/RES

B60
JENNINGS R.,PROGRESS OF INTERNATIONAL LAW. FUT WOR+45 WOR-45 SOCIETY NAT/G VOL/ASSN DELIB/GP DIPLOM EDU/PROP LEGIT COERCE ATTIT DRIVE MORAL ORD/FREE...JURID CONCPT OBS TIME/SEQ TREND GEN/LAWS. PAGE 74 A1509 INT/ORG LAW INT/LAW

B60
KHRUSHCHEV N.,FOR VICTORY IN PEACEFUL COMPETITION WITH CAPITALISM. COM FUT USSR WOR+45 CONSTN SOCIETY INDUS INT/ORG DELIB/GP PLAN BAL/PWR DIPLOM PERSON MARXISM...MARXIST WORK 20 COLD/WAR. PAGE 79 A1611 TOP/EX PWR CAP/ISM SOCISM

B60
KRISTENSEN T.,THE ECONOMIC WORLD BALANCE. FUT WOR+45 CULTURE ECO/DEV BAL/PWR INT/TRADE REGION PWR WEALTH...STAT TREND CHARTS 20. PAGE 82 A1685 ECO/UNDEV ECO/TAC FOR/AID

B60
LANDHEER B.,ETHICAL VALUES IN INTERNATIONAL DECISION-MAKING. FUT LAW SOCIETY INT/ORG NAT/G DELIB/GP CREATE NAT/LISM ATTIT PERSON...DECISION CONCPT LEAGUE/NAT TOT/POP 20. PAGE 84 A1718 HYPO/EXP POLICY PEACE

B60
LIEUWEN E.,ARMS AND POLITICS IN LATIN AMERICA. FUT USA+45 USA-45 ECO/UNDEV INT/ORG NAT/G FORCES DIPLOM COERCE ATTIT ALL/VALS VAL/FREE OAS 20. PAGE 88 A1811 L/A+17C FOR/AID

B60
MCKINNEY R.,REVIEW OF THE INTERNATIONAL ATOMIC POLICIES AND PROGRAMS OF THE UNITED STATES (5 VOLS.). COM FUT USA+45 ECO/DEV ECO/UNDEV INT/ORG DELIB/GP PLAN ADMIN 20 THIRD/WRLD. PAGE 98 A2016 NUC/PWR PEACE DIPLOM POLICY

B60
MUNRO L.,UNITED NATIONS, HOPE FOR A DIVIDED WORLD. FUT WOR+45 CONSTN DELIB/GP CREATE TEC/DEV DIPLOM EDU/PROP LEGIT PEACE ATTIT HEALTH ORD/FREE PWR ...CONCPT TREND UN VAL/FREE 20. PAGE 106 A2172 INT/ORG ROUTINE

B60
PENTONY D.E.,THE UNDERDEVELOPED LANDS. FUT WOR+45 CULTURE AGRI FINAN INDUS MARKET INT/ORG LABOR NAT/G VOL/ASSN CONSULT TEC/DEV ECO/TAC EDU/PROP COLONIAL ATTIT WEALTH...OBS RECORD SAMP TREND GEN/METH WORK UN 20. PAGE 115 A2351 ECO/UNDEV POLICY FOR/AID INT/TRADE

B60
PHILLIPS J.F.V.,KWAME NKRUMAH AND THE FUTURE OF AFRICA. FUT GHANA ISLAM ECO/UNDEV CHIEF DIPLOM COLONIAL RACE/REL NAT/LISM...TREND IDEA/COMP BIBLIOG 20 NKRUMAH/K. PAGE 116 A2376 BIOG LEAD SOVEREIGN AFR

B60
PLAMENATZ J.,ON ALIEN RULE AND SELF-GOVERNMENT. AFR FUT S/ASIA WOR+45 CULTURE SOCIETY ECO/UNDEV INT/ORG DOMIN EDU/PROP ATTIT RIGID/FLEX ALL/VALS...POLICY CONCPT OBS TREND CON/ANAL GEN/LAWS TOT/POP VAL/FREE. PAGE 116 A2386 NAT/G CONSTN NAT/LISM SOVEREIGN

B60
RITNER P.,THE DEATH OF AFRICA. USA+45 ECO/UNDEV DIPLOM ECO/TAC REGION RACE/REL NAT/LISM ORD/FREE ...POLICY 20 NEGRO. PAGE 121 A2485 AFR SOCIETY FUT TASK

B60
STEIN E.,AMERICAN ENTERPRISE IN THE EUROPEAN COMMON MARKET: A LEGAL PROFILE. EUR+WWI FUT USA+45 SOCIETY STRUCT ECO/DEV NAT/G VOL/ASSN CONSULT PLAN TEC/DEV ECO/TAC INT/TRADE ADMIN ATTIT RIGID/FLEX PWR...MGT NEW/IDEA STAT TREND COMPUT/IR SIMUL EEC 20. PAGE 137 A2814 MARKET ADJUD INT/LAW

B60
STOLPER W.F.,GERMANY BETWEEN EAST AND WEST: THE ECO/DEV

ECONOMICS OF COMPETITIVE COEXISTENCE. FUT GERMANY/E GERMANY/W WOR+45 FINAN POL/PAR BUDGET ECO/TAC FOR/AID INT/TRADE...STAT CHARTS METH/COMP 20 COLD/WAR. PAGE 138 A2832 DIPLOM GOV/COMP BAL/PWR B60

US HOUSE COMM. SCI. ASTRONAUT.,OCEAN SCIENCES AND NATIONAL SECURITY. FUT SEA ECO/DEV EXTR/IND INT/ORG NAT/G FORCES ACT/RES TEC/DEV ECO/TAC COERCE WAR BIO/SOC KNOWL PWR...CONCPT RECORD LAB/EXP 20. PAGE 154 A3141 R+D ORD/FREE B60

WOETZEL R.K.,THE INTERNATIONAL CONTROL OF AIRSPACE AND OUTERSPACE. FUT WOR+45 AIR CONSTN STRUCT CONSULT PLAN TEC/DEV ADJUD RIGID/FLEX KNOWL ORD/FREE PWR...TECHNIC GEOG MGT NEW/IDEA TREND COMPUT/IR VAL/FREE 20 TREATY. PAGE 166 A3375 INT/ORG JURID SPACE INT/LAW L60

BRENNAN D.G.,"SETTING AND GOALS OF ARMS CONTROL." FUT USA+45 USSR WOR+45 INTELL INT/ORG NAT/G VOL/ASSN CONSULT PLAN DIPLOM ECO/TAC ADMIN KNOWL PWR...POLICY CONCPT TREND COLD/WAR 20. PAGE 18 A0371 FORCES COERCE ARMS/CONT DETER L60

DEAN A.W.,"SECOND GENEVA CONFERENCE OF THE LAW OF THE SEA: THE FIGHT FOR FREEDOM OF THE SEAS." FUT USA+45 USSR WOR+45 WOR-45 SEA CONSTN STRUCT PLAN INT/TRADE ADJUD ADMIN ORD/FREE...DECISION RECORD TREND GEN/LAWS 20 TREATY. PAGE 35 A0717 INT/ORG JURID INT/LAW L60

HOLTON G.,"ARMS CONTROL." FUT WOR+45 CULTURE INT/ORG NAT/G FORCES TOP/EX PLAN EDU/PROP COERCE ATTIT RIGID/FLEX ORD/FREE...POLICY PHIL/SCI SOC TREND COLD/WAR. PAGE 67 A1377 ACT/RES CONSULT ARMS/CONT NUC/PWR S60

"THE EMERGING COMMON MARKETS IN LATIN AMERICA." FUT L/A+17C STRATA DIST/IND INDUS LABOR NAT/G LEGIS ECO/TAC ADMIN RIGID/FLEX HEALTH...NEW/IDEA TIME/SEQ OAS 20. PAGE 3 A0059 FINAN ECO/UNDEV INT/TRADE S60

BOGARDUS E.S.,"THE SOCIOLOGY OF A STRUCTURED PEACE." FUT SOCIETY CREATE DIPLOM EDU/PROP ADJUD ROUTINE ATTIT RIGID/FLEX KNOWL ORD/FREE RESPECT ...POLICY INT/LAW JURID NEW/IDEA SELF/OBS TOT/POP 20 UN. PAGE 16 A0327 INT/ORG SOC NAT/LISM PEACE S60

BOWIE R.,"POLICY FORMATION IN AMERICAN FOREIGN POLICY." FUT USA+45 WOR+45 STRUCT ECO/DEV INT/ORG POL/PAR LEGIS ACT/RES EXEC ALL/VALS...POLICY OBS VAL/FREE 20. PAGE 17 A0355 PLAN DRIVE DIPLOM S60

CLARK W.,"NEW FORCES IN THE UN." FUT UK WOR+45 CONSTN BAL/PWR DIPLOM DRIVE PWR SKILL...CONCPT TREND UN TOT/POP 20. PAGE 27 A0543 INT/ORG ECO/UNDEV SOVEREIGN S60

COHEN A.,"THE NEW AFRICA AND THE UN." FUT ECO/UNDEV NAT/G ECO/TAC INT/TRADE CHOOSE ATTIT ORD/FREE PWR ...POLICY METH/CNCPT OBS TREND CON/ANAL GEN/LAWS TOT/POP VAL/FREE UN 20. PAGE 27 A0558 AFR INT/ORG BAL/PWR FOR/AID S60

DYSON F.J.,"THE FUTURE DEVELOPMENT OF NUCLEAR WEAPONS." FUT WOR+45 DELIB/GP ACT/RES PLAN DETER WEAPON ATTIT PWR...POLICY 20. PAGE 40 A0815 INT/ORG ARMS/CONT NUC/PWR S60

FITZGIBBON R.H.,"DICTATORSHIP AND DEMOCRACY IN LATIN AMERICA." FUT ECO/DEV ECO/UNDEV INT/ORG LOC/G NAT/G TOP/EX PLAN TEC/DEV ECO/TAC CHOOSE ATTIT DRIVE PERSON ALL/VALS OAS TOT/POP 20. PAGE 46 A0943 L/A+17C ACT/RES INT/TRADE S60

FRANKEL S.H.,"ECONOMIC ASPECTS OF POLITICAL INDEPENDENCE IN AFRICA." AFR FUT SOCIETY ECO/UNDEV COM/IND FINAN LEGIS PLAN TEC/DEV CAP/ISM ECO/TAC INT/TRADE ADMIN ATTIT DRIVE RIGID/FLEX PWR WEALTH ...MGT NEW/IDEA MATH TIME/SEQ VAL/FREE 20. PAGE 48 A0984 NAT/G FOR/AID S60

GINSBURGS G.,"PEKING-LHASA-NEW DELHI." CHINA/COM FUT INDIA S/ASIA KIN NAT/G PROVS SECT FORCES BAL/PWR ECO/TAC DOMIN EDU/PROP LEGIT ADMIN REGION GUERRILLA PWR...TREND TIBET 20. PAGE 52 A1074 ASIA COERCE DIPLOM S60

GOODRICH L.,"GEOGRAPHICAL DISTRIBUTION OF THE STAFF OF THE UN SECRETARIAT." FUT WOR+45 CONSTN BAL/PWR DIPLOM EDU/PROP LEGIT ROUTINE RIGID/FLEX...CHARTS UN 20. PAGE 54 A1105 INT/ORG EX/STRUC S60

GULICK E.U.,"OUR BALANCE OF POWER SYSTEM IN PERSPECTIVE." FUT WOR+45 WOR-45 ECO/DEV DOMIN ROUTINE NUC/PWR PEACE PWR WEALTH...PLURIST CONCPT HIST/WRIT GEN/METH TOT/POP 20. PAGE 58 A1191 INT/ORG TREND ARMS/CONT BAL/PWR S60

HAYTON R.D.,"THE ANTARCTIC SETTLEMENT OF 1959." FUT USA+45 WOR+45 WOR-45 STRUCT R+D INT/ORG EX/STRUC CREATE TEC/DEV LEGIT PEACE ATTIT SOVEREIGN ...TIME/SEQ 20 TREATY IGY. PAGE 63 A1297 DELIB/GP JURID DIPLOM REGION S60

IKLE F.C.,"NTH COUNTRIES AND DISARMAMENT." WOR+45 DELIB/GP ECO/TAC DOMIN EDU/PROP LEGIT ROUTINE COERCE RIGID/FLEX ORD/FREE...MARXIST TREND 20. PAGE 70 A1432 FUT INT/ORG ARMS/CONT NUC/PWR S60

KAPLAN M.A.,"THEORETICAL ANALYSIS OF THE BALANCE OF POWER." FUT USA+45 WOR+45 INTELL ECO/DEV INT/ORG NAT/G CONSULT TOP/EX ACT/RES PLAN TEC/DEV ATTIT ALL/VALS...METH/CNCPT TOT/POP 20. PAGE 76 A1562 CREATE NEW/IDEA DIPLOM NUC/PWR S60

KISTIAKOWSKY G.B.,"SCIENCE AND FOREIGN AFFAIRS." FUT WOR+45 NAT/G PROF/ORG PLAN ECO/TAC EDU/PROP NUC/PWR...TREND COLD/WAR 20. PAGE 80 A1645 CONSULT TEC/DEV FOR/AID DIPLOM S60

MAGATHAN W.,"SOME BASES OF WEST GERMAN MILITARY POLICY." EUR+WWI FUT INT/ORG TOP/EX ECO/TAC DOMIN DRIVE ORD/FREE PWR...TRADIT GEOG OBS TREND. PAGE 93 A1904 NAT/G FORCES GERMANY S60

MIKESELL R.F.,"AMERICA'S ECONOMIC RESPONSIBILITY AS A GREAT POWER." COM FUT USA+45 USSR WOR+45 INT/ORG PLAN ECO/TAC FOR/AID EDU/PROP CHOOSE WEALTH ...POLICY 20. PAGE 101 A2069 ECO/UNDEV BAL/PWR CAP/ISM S60

MORALES C.J.,"TRADE AND ECONOMIC INTEGRATION IN LATIN AMERICA." FUT L/A+17C LAW STRATA ECO/UNDEV DIST/IND INDUS LABOR NAT/G LEGIS ECO/TAC ADMIN RIGID/FLEX WEALTH...CONCPT NEW/IDEA CONT/OBS TIME/SEQ WORK 20. PAGE 104 A2128 FINAN INT/TRADE REGION S60

PADELFORD N.J.,"POLITICS AND CHANGE IN THE SECURITY COUNCIL." FUT WOR+45 CONSTN NAT/G EX/STRUC LEGIS ORD/FREE...CONCPT CHARTS UN 20. PAGE 113 A2309 INT/ORG DELIB/GP S60

PETERSON E.N.,"HISTORICAL SCHOLARSHIP AND WORLD UNITY." FUT UNIV WOR-45 CULTURE INTELL INT/ORG NAT/G ACT/RES EDU/PROP ATTIT PERCEPT RIGID/FLEX ...NEW/IDEA OBS HIST/WRIT TREND COLD/WAR TOT/POP 20. PAGE 115 A2367 PLAN KNOWL NAT/LISM S60

RHYNE C.S.,"LAW AS AN INSTRUMENT FOR PEACE." FUT WOR+45 PLAN LEGIT ROUTINE ARMS/CONT NUC/PWR ATTIT ORD/FREE...JURID METH/CNCPT TREND CON/ANAL HYPO/EXP COLD/WAR 20. PAGE 120 A2471 ADJUD EDU/PROP INT/LAW PEACE S60

RIESELBACH Z.N.,"QUANTITATIVE TECHNIQUES FOR STUDYING VOTING BEHAVIOR IN THE UNITED NATIONS GENERAL ASSEMBLY." FUT S/ASIA USA+45 INT/ORG BAL/PWR DIPLOM ECO/TAC FOR/AID ADMIN PWR...POLICY METH/CNCPT METH UN 20. PAGE 121 A2478 QUANT CHOOSE S60

RUSSEL R.W.,"ROLES FOR PSYCHOLOGISTS IN THE MAINTENANCE OF PEACE." FUT USA+45 CULTURE INT/ORG DIPLOM FOR/AID EDU/PROP ATTIT KNOWL MORAL PWR ...POLICY SOC COLD/WAR 20. PAGE 125 A2572 PSY GEN/METH S60

SCHWELB E.,"INTERNATIONAL CONVENTIONS ON HUMAN RIGHTS." FUT WOR+45 LAW CONSTN CULTURE SOCIETY STRUCT VOL/ASSN DELIB/GP PLAN ADJUD SUPEGO LOVE MORAL...SOC CONCPT STAT RECORD HIST/WRIT TREND 20 UN. PAGE 130 A2664 INT/ORG HUM B61

ANAND R.P.,COMPULSORY JURISDICTION OF INTERNATIONAL COURT OF JUSTICE. FUT WOR+45 SOCIETY PLAN LEGIT ADJUD ATTIT DRIVE PERSON ORD/FREE...JURID CONCPT TREND 20 ICJ. PAGE 8 A0156 INT/ORG COERCE INT/LAW B61

EINZIG P.,A DYNAMIC THEORY OF FORWARD EXCHANGE. FUT WOR+45 WOR-45 INT/TRADE BAL/PAY WEALTH...OLD/LIB NEW/IDEA OBS TREND 20. PAGE 41 A0830 FINAN ECO/TAC B61

FLEMING D.F.,THE COLD WAR AND ITS ORIGINS: 1950-1960 (VOL. II). ASIA FUT HUNGARY POLAND WOR+45 TEC/DEV DOMIN NUC/PWR REV PEACE...T 20 COLD/WAR EISNHWR/DD SUEZ. PAGE 46 A0946 MARXISM DIPLOM BAL/PWR B61

GALLOIS P.,THE BALANCE OF TERROR: STRATEGY FOR THE NUCLEAR AGE. FUT WOR+45 INT/ORG FORCES TOP/EX DETER WAR ATTIT RIGID/FLEX ORD/FREE PWR...HYPO/EXP 20. PAGE 50 A1032 PLAN DECISION DIPLOM NUC/PWR B61

HANCOCK W.K.,FOUR STUDIES OF WAR AND PEACE IN THIS CENTURY. FUT WOR+45 WOR-45 ACT/RES LEGIT DETER HEALTH...TREND ANTHOL TOT/POP VAL/FREE UN 20. PAGE 61 A1250 INT/ORG POLICY ARMS/CONT B61

HARRISON S.,INDIA AND THE UNITED STATES. FUT S/ASIA USA+45 WOR+45 INTELL ECO/DEV ECO/UNDEV AGRI INDUS INT/ORG NAT/G CONSULT EX/STRUC TOP/EX PLAN ECO/TAC NEUTRAL ALL/VALS...MGT TOT/POP 20. PAGE 62 A1272 DELIB/GP ACT/RES FOR/AID INDIA B61

HENKIN L.,ARMS CONTROL: ISSUES FOR THE PUBLIC. EUR+WWI FUT USA+45 USSR INT/ORG NAT/G DIPLOM EDU/PROP DETER NUC/PWR ATTIT PWR...CONCPT RECORD HIST/WRIT TIME/SEQ TOT/POP COLD/WAR 20. PAGE 64 A1316 WOR+45 DELIB/GP ARMS/CONT

B61
KISSINGER H.A.,THE NECESSITY FOR CHOICE. FUT USA+45 ECO/UNDEV NAT/G PLAN BAL/PWR ECO/TAC ARMS/CONT DETER NUC/PWR ATTIT...POLICY CONCPT RECORD GEN/LAWS COLD/WAR 20. PAGE 80 A1642
TOP/EX
TREND
DIPLOM

B61
KNORR K.E.,THE INTERNATIONAL SYSTEM. FUT SOCIETY INT/ORG NAT/G PLAN BAL/PWR DIPLOM WAR PWR ...DECISION METH/CNCPT CONT/OBS GAME METH UN 20. PAGE 81 A1655
ACT/RES
SIMUL
ECO/UNDEV

B61
LETHBRIDGE H.J.,CHINA'S URBAN COMMUNES. CHINA/COM FUT ECO/UNDEV DIPLOM EDU/PROP DEMAND INCOME MARXISM ...POLICY 20. PAGE 87 A1790
MUNIC
CONTROL
ECO/TAC
NAT/G

B61
MICHAEL D.N.,PROPOSED STUDIES ON THE IMPLICATIONS OF PEACEFUL SPACE ACTIVITIES FOR HUMAN AFFAIRS. COM/IND INDUS FORCES DIPLOM PEACE PERSON...PSY SOC 20. PAGE 101 A2066
FUT
SPACE
ACT/RES
PROB/SOLV

B61
MILLIKAW M.F.,THE EMERGING NATIONS: THEIR GROWTH AND UNITED STATES POLICY. FUT USA+45 WOR+45 WOR-45 NAT/G PLAN TEC/DEV BAL/PWR GOV/REL PEACE ORD/FREE 20. PAGE 101 A2082
ECO/UNDEV
POLICY
DIPLOM
FOR/AID

B61
SCHELLING T.C.,STRATEGY AND ARMS CONTROL. FUT UNIV WOR+45 INT/ORG PLAN TEC/DEV BAL/PWR LEGIT PERCEPT HEALTH...CONCPT VAL/FREE 20. PAGE 128 A2623
ROUTINE
POLICY
ARMS/CONT

B61
SHARP W.R.,FIELD ADMINISTRATION IN THE UNITED NATION SYSTEM: THE CONDUCT OF INTERNATIONAL ECONOMIC AND SOCIAL PROGRAMS. FUT WOR+45 CONSTN SOCIETY ECO/UNDEV R+D DELIB/GP ACT/RES PLAN TEC/DEV EDU/PROP EXEC ROUTINE HEALTH WEALTH...HUM CONCPT CHARTS METH ILO UNESCO VAL/FREE UN 20. PAGE 132 A2697
INT/ORG
CONSULT

B61
STARK H.,SOCIAL AND ECONOMIC FRONTIERS IN LATIN AMERICA (2ND ED.). CUBA FUT CULTURE AGRI INDUS ECO/TAC PRODUC ATTIT MARXISM...NAT/COMP BIBLIOG T 20. PAGE 137 A2807
L/A+17C
SOCIETY
DIPLOM
ECO/UNDEV

B61
STILLMAN E.,THE NEW POLITICS: AMERICA AND THE END OF THE POSTWAR WORLD. FUT WOR+45 CULTURE SOCIETY ECO/UNDEV INT/ORG NAT/G FORCES TOP/EX ACT/RES DIPLOM EDU/PROP LEGIT ROUTINE DETER ATTIT ORD/FREE PWR...OBS STERTYP COLD/WAR TOT/POP VAL/FREE. PAGE 138 A2827
USA+45
PLAN

B61
STRAUSZ-HUPE R.,A FORWARD STRATEGY FOR AMERICA. FUT WOR+45 ECO/DEV INT/ORG NAT/G POL/PAR DELIB/GP FORCES ACT/RES CREATE ECO/TAC DOMIN EDU/PROP ATTIT DRIVE PWR...MAJORIT CONCPT STAT OBS TIME/SEQ TREND COLD/WAR TOT/POP. PAGE 139 A2848
USA+45
PLAN
DIPLOM

B61
WARNER D.,HURRICANE FROM CHINA. ASIA CHINA/COM FUT L/A+17C USA+45 CULTURE NAT/G FORCES TOP/EX FOR/AID DRIVE PWR...CONCPT TIME/SEQ SEATO WORK 20. PAGE 161 A3284
ATTIT
TREND
REV

B61
WRIGHT Q.,THE ROLE OF INTERNATIONAL LAW IN THE ELIMINATION OF WAR. FUT WOR+45 WOR-45 NAT/G BAL/PWR DIPLOM DOMIN LEGIT PWR...POLICY INT/LAW JURID CONCPT TIME/SEQ TREND GEN/LAWS COLD/WAR 20. PAGE 168 A3414
INT/ORG
ADJUD
ARMS/CONT

B61
YDIT M.,INTERNATIONALISED TERRITORIES. FUT WOR+45 WOR-45 CONSTN VOL/ASSN CREATE PLAN LEGIT PEACE ORD/FREE...GEOG INT/LAW JURID SOC NEW/IDEA OBS RECORD SAMP TIME/SEQ TREND 19/20 BERLIN. PAGE 169 A3431
LOC/G
INT/ORG
DIPLOM
SOVEREIGN

L61
CLAUDE I.,"THE UNITED NATIONS AND THE USE OF FORCE." FUT WOR+45 SOCIETY DIPLOM EDU/PROP LEGIT ADMIN ROUTINE COERCE WAR PEACE ORD/FREE...CONCPT TREND UN 20. PAGE 27 A0545
INT/ORG
FORCES

L61
HALPERIN M.H.,"NUCLEAR WEAPONS AND LIMITED WARS." FUT UNIV WOR+45 INTELL SOCIETY ECO/DEV ACT/RES DRIVE PERCEPT RIGID/FLEX...CONCPT TIME/SEQ TREND TOT/POP 20. PAGE 60 A1237
PLAN
COERCE
NUC/PWR
WAR

L61
HILSMAN R. JR.,"THE NEW COMMUNIST TACTIC: PRECIS-INTERNAL WAR." COM FUT USA+45 ECO/UNDEV POL/PAR FOR/AID RIGID/FLEX ALL/VALS...TREND COLD/WAR 20. PAGE 65 A1334
FORCES
COERCE
USSR
GUERRILLA

L61
LEVINE R.A.,"THE ANTHROPOLOGY OF CONFLICT." FUT CULTURE INTELL FAM INT/ORG LG/CO SML/CO ATTIT KNOWL ...METH/CNCPT VAL/FREE 20. PAGE 88 A1796
SOCIETY
ACT/RES

L61
TAUBENFELD H.J.,"A TREATY FOR ANTARCTICA." FUT USA+45 INTELL INT/ORG LABOR 20 TREATY ANTARCTICA. PAGE 141 A2893
R+D
ACT/RES
DIPLOM

L61
TAUBENFELD H.J.,"A REGIME FOR OUTER SPACE." FUT UNIV R+D ACT/RES PLAN BAL/PWR LEGIT ARMS/CONT ORD/FREE...POLICY JURID TREND UN TOT/POP 20 COLD/WAR. PAGE 142 A2894
INT/ORG
ADJUD
SPACE

L61
WRIGHT Q.,"STUDIES IN DETERRENCE: LIMITED WARS AND THE ROLE OF SEABORNE WEAPONS SYSTEMS." FUT USA+45 WOR+45 SEA INT/ORG NAT/G FORCES ACT/RES WAR WEAPON ORD/FREE TOT/POP 20. PAGE 168 A3415
TEC/DEV
SKILL
BAL/PWR
DETER

S61
BARNET R.,"RUSSIA, CHINA, AND THE WORLD: THE SOVIET ATTITUDE ON DISARMAMENT (PART 3)." ASIA CHINA/COM FUT INT/ORG NAT/G POL/PAR VOL/ASSN ARMS/CONT ATTIT ...POLICY CONCPT TIME/SEQ TREND TOT/POP VAL/FREE 20. PAGE 11 A0226
COM
PLAN
TOTALISM
USSR

S61
CARLETON W.G.,"AMERICAN FOREIGN POLICY: MYTHS AND REALITIES." FUT USA+45 WOR+45 ECO/UNDEV INT/ORG EX/STRUC ARMS/CONT NUC/PWR WAR ATTIT...POLICY CONCPT CONT/OBS GEN/METH COLD/WAR TOT/POP 20. PAGE 24 A0484
PLAN
MYTH
DIPLOM

S61
CASTANEDA J.,"THE UNDERDEVELOPED NATIONS AND THE DEVELOPMENT OF INTERNATIONAL LAW." FUT UNIV LAW ACT/RES FOR/AID LEGIT PERCEPT SKILL...JURID METH/CNCPT TIME/SEQ TOT/POP 20 UN. PAGE 25 A0507
INT/ORG
ECO/UNDEV
PEACE
INT/LAW

S61
DELLA PORT G.,"PROBLEMI E PROSPETTIVE DI COESISTENZA FRA ORIENTE ED OCCIDENTE, (PART 3)." COM FUT WOR+45 NAT/G BAL/PWR FOR/AID BAL/PAY PWR WEALTH...SOC CONCPT GEN/LAWS COLD/WAR 20. PAGE 36 A0729
INT/TRADE

S61
DEUTSCH K.W.,"NATIONAL INDUSTRIALIZATION AND THE DECLINING SHARE OF THE INTERNATIONAL ECONOMIC SECTOR." EUR+WWI FUT WOR+45 WOR-45 MARKET PLAN EDU/PROP WEALTH...WELF/ST OBS TESTS 20. PAGE 36 A0740
DIST/IND
ECO/DEV
INT/TRADE

S61
GALBRAITH J.K.,"A POSITIVE APPROACH TO ECONOMIC AID." FUT USA+45 INTELL NAT/G CONSULT ACT/RES DIPLOM ECO/TAC EDU/PROP ATTIT KNOWL PWR WEALTH ...SOC STERTYP 20. PAGE 50 A1030
ECO/UNDEV
ROUTINE
FOR/AID

S61
HAAS E.B.,"INTERNATIONAL INTEGRATION: THE EUROPEAN AND THE UNIVERSAL PROCESS." EUR+WWI FUT WOR+45 NAT/G EX/STRUC ATTIT DRIVE ORD/FREE PWR...CONCPT GEN/LAWS OEEC 20 NATO COUNCL/EUR. PAGE 59 A1207
INT/ORG
TREND
REGION

S61
HAZARD J.N.,"CODIFYING PEACEFUL COEXISTANCE." FUT INTELL INT/ORG TEC/DEV PEACE HEALTH...INT/LAW CONT/OBS 20. PAGE 63 A1299
VOL/ASSN
JURID

S61
HEILBRONER R.L.,"DYNAMICS OF FOREIGN AID: PROBLEMS OF UNDERDEVELOPED NATIONS PLAGUE ASSISTANCE PROGRAM." FUT USA+45 WOR+45 STRATA NAT/G PLAN TEC/DEV ATTIT DRIVE WEALTH WORK 20. PAGE 64 A1307
ECO/UNDEV
ECO/TAC
FOR/AID

S61
JACKSON E.,"CONSTITUTIONAL DEVELOPMENTS OF THE UNITED NATIONS: THE GROWTH OF ITS EXECUTIVE CAPACITY." FUT WOR+45 CONSTN STRUCT ACT/RES PLAN ALL/VALS...NEW/IDEA OBS COLD/WAR UN 20. PAGE 72 A1475
INT/ORG
EXEC

S61
JACKSON E.,"THE FUTURE DEVELOPMENT OF THE UNITED NATIONS: SOME SUGGESTIONS FOR RESEARCH." FUT LAW CONSTN ECO/DEV FINAN PEACE WEALTH...WELF/ST CONCPT UN 20. PAGE 72 A1476
INT/ORG
PWR

S61
JUVILER P.H.,"INTERPARLIAMENTARY CONTACTS IN SOVIET FOREIGN POLICY." COM FUT WOR+45 WOR-45 SOCIETY CONSULT ACT/RES DIPLOM ADMIN PEACE ATTIT RIGID/FLEX WEALTH...WELF/ST SOC TOT/POP CONGRESS 19/20. PAGE 75 A1543
INT/ORG
DELIB/GP
USSR

S61
LEWY G.,"SUPERIOR ORDERS, NUCLEAR WARFARE AND THE DICTATES OF CONSCIENCE: THE DILEMMA OF MILITARY OBEDIENCE IN THE ATOMIC." FUT UNIV WOR+45 INTELL SOCIETY FORCES TOP/EX ACT/RES ADMIN ROUTINE NUC/PWR PERCEPT RIGID/FLEX ALL/VALS...POLICY CONCPT 20. PAGE 88 A1805
DETER
INT/ORG
LAW
INT/LAW

S61
MACHOWSKI K.,"SELECTED PROBLEMS OF NATIONAL SOVEREIGNTY WITH REFERENCE TO THE LAW OF OUTER SPACE." FUT WOR+45 AIR LAW INTELL SOCIETY ECO/DEV PLAN EDU/PROP DETER DRIVE PERCEPT SOVEREIGN ...POLICY INT/LAW OBS TREND TOT/POP 20. PAGE 92 A1889
UNIV
ACT/RES
NUC/PWR
SPACE

S61
MASTERS R.D.,"A MULTI-BLOC MODEL OF THE INTERNATIONAL SYSTEM." FUT UNIV WOR+45 SOCIETY ACT/RES PLAN...GEOG SOC TREND SIMUL TOT/POP 20. PAGE 96 A1963
INT/ORG
CONCPT

S61
NOVE A.,"THE SOVIET MODEL AND UNDERDEVELOPED
ECO/UNDEV

COUNTRIES." COM FUT USSR WOR+45 CULTURE ECO/DEV POL/PAR FOR/AID EDU/PROP ADMIN MORAL WEALTH ...POLICY RECORD HIST/WRIT 20. PAGE 110 A2258 — PLAN

S61
OCHENG D.,"AN ECONOMIST LOOKS AT UGANDA'S FUTURE." FUT UGANDA AGRI INDUS PLAN PROB/SOLV INT/TRADE SOVEREIGN 20. PAGE 111 A2275 — ECO/UNDEV INCOME ECO/TAC OWN

S61
RALEIGH J.S.,"THE MIDDLE EAST IN 1960: A POLITICAL SURVEY." FUT ISLAM INTELL KIN BAL/PWR EDU/PROP NAT/LISM...TREND VAL/FREE 20. PAGE 119 A2435 — INT/ORG EX/STRUC

S61
ROSTOW W.W.,"THE FUTURE OF FOREIGN AID." COM FUT WOR+45 ECO/DEV INDUS INT/ORG NAT/G CONSULT ACT/RES PLAN DOMIN LEGIT CHOOSE RIGID/FLEX ALL/VALS ...MAJORIT CONCPT TREND TOT/POP 20. PAGE 124 A2544 — ECO/UNDEV ECO/TAC FOR/AID

S61
SINGER J.D.,"THE LEVEL OF ANALYSIS: PROBLEMS IN INTERNATIONAL RELATIONS." FUT INTELL R+D INT/ORG CREATE EDU/PROP...METH/CNCPT HYPO/EXP GEN/METH METH VAL/FREE. PAGE 133 A2725 — SOCIETY SOC DIPLOM

S61
TANNENBAUM F.,"THE UNITED STATES AND LATIN AMERICA." FUT USA+45 NAT/G FOR/AID CHOOSE ATTIT ALL/VALS VAL/FREE 20. PAGE 141 A2888 — L/A+17C ECO/DEV DIPLOM

S61
TAUBENFELD H.J.,"OUTER SPACE--PAST POLITICS AND FUTURE POLICY." FUT USA+45 USA-45 WOR+45 AIR INTELL STRUCT ECO/DEV NAT/G TOP/EX ACT/RES ADMIN ROUTINE NUC/PWR ATTIT DRIVE...CONCPT TIME/SEQ TREND TOT/POP 20. PAGE 141 A2892 — PLAN SPACE INT/ORG

S61
VERNON R.,"A TRADE POLICY FOR THE 1960'S." COM FUT USA+45 WOR+45 ECO/DEV ECO/UNDEV FINAN TOP/EX ACT/RES...WELF/ST METH/CNCPT CONT/OBS TOT/POP 20. PAGE 159 A3229 — PLAN INT/TRADE

S61
VIRALLY M.,"VERS UNE REFORME DU SECRETARIAT DES NATIONS UNIES." FUT WOR+45 CONSTN ECO/DEV TOP/EX BAL/PWR ADMIN ALL/VALS...CONCPT BIOG UN VAL/FREE 20. PAGE 159 A3243 — INT/ORG INTELL DIPLOM

S61
WHELAN J.G.,"KHRUSHCHEV AND THE BALANCE OF WORLD POWER." FUT WOR+45 INT/ORG VOL/ASSN CAP/ISM DIPLOM SKILL...POLICY COLD/WAR 20 KHRUSH/N. PAGE 163 A3328 — COM PWR BAL/PWR USSR

B62
BAILEY S.D.,THE SECRETARIAT OF THE UNITED NATIONS. FUT WOR+45 DELIB/GP PLAN BAL/PWR DOMIN EDU/PROP ADMIN PEACE ATTIT PWR...DECISION CONCPT TREND CON/ANAL CHARTS UN VAL/FREE COLD/WAR 20. PAGE 10 A0205 — INT/ORG EXEC DIPLOM

B62
BAULIN J.,THE ARAB ROLE IN AFRICA. AFR ALGERIA FUT ISLAM MOROCCO UAR COLONIAL NEUTRAL REV...SOC 20 TUNIS BOURGUIBA. PAGE 12 A0235 — NAT/LISM DIPLOM NAT/G SECT

B62
BEATON L.,THE SPREAD OF NUCLEAR WEAPONS. WOR+45 NAT/G PLAN PROB/SOLV DIPLOM ECO/TAC DETER...POLICY 20 COLD/WAR. PAGE 12 A0242 — ARMS/CONT NUC/PWR TEC/DEV FUT

B62
BOULDING K.E.,CONFLICT AND DEFENSE: A GENERAL THEORY. FUT SOCIETY INT/ORG NAT/G CREATE BAL/PWR COERCE NAT/LISM DRIVE ALL/VALS...PLURIST DECISION CONCPT METH/CNCPT TREND HYPO/EXP TOT/POP 20. PAGE 17 A0347 — MATH SIMUL PEACE WAR

B62
BRYANT A.,A CHOICE FOR DESTINY: COMMONWEALTH AND THE COMMON MARKET. EUR+WWI FUT UK INT/TRADE COLONIAL ATTIT SOVEREIGN 20 CMN/WLTH EEC. PAGE 20 A0411 — INT/ORG VOL/ASSN DIPLOM CHOOSE

B62
FORBES H.W.,THE STRATEGY OF DISARMAMENT. FUT WOR+45 INT/ORG VOL/ASSN CONSULT ARMS/CONT COERCE NUC/PWR WAR DRIVE RIGID/FLEX ORD/FREE PWR...POLICY CONCPT OBS TREND STERTYP 20. PAGE 47 A0959 — PLAN FORCES DIPLOM

B62
GILPIN R.,AMERICAN SCIENTISTS AND NUCLEAR WEAPONS POLICY. COM FUT USA+45 WOR+45 INT/ORG NAT/G PROF/ORG CONSULT FORCES CREATE TEC/DEV BAL/PWR EDU/PROP ARMS/CONT WAR PERCEPT KNOWL MORAL PWR ...PHIL/SCI SOC CONCPT GEN/LAWS 20. PAGE 52 A1073 — INTELL ATTIT DETER NUC/PWR

B62
GUENA Y.,HISTORIQUE DE LA COMMUNAUTE. FUT ECO/UNDEV NAT/G PLAN EDU/PROP COLONIAL REGION NAT/LISM ALL/VALS SOVEREIGN...CONCPT OBS CHARTS 20. PAGE 58 A1186 — AFR VOL/ASSN FOR/AID FRANCE

B62
HATCH J.,AFRICA TODAY-AND TOMORROW: AN OUTLINE OF BASIC FACTS AND MAJOR PROBLEMS. AFR FUT ISLAM STRATA ECO/UNDEV INT/ORG NAT/G POL/PAR DELIB/GP TOP/EX EDU/PROP LEGIT CHOOSE ATTIT...TIME/SEQ TOT/POP COLD/WAR 20. PAGE 63 A1287 — PLAN CONSTN NAT/LISM

B62
HIGGANS B.,UNITED NATIONS AND U.S. FOREIGN ECONOMIC POLICY. FUT USA+45 WOR+45 ECO/DEV ECO/UNDEV NAT/G ECO/TAC WEALTH...TIME/SEQ TOT/POP UN 20. PAGE 65 A1328 — INT/ORG ACT/RES FOR/AID DIPLOM

B62
HOFFMAN P.,WORLD WITHOUT WANT. FUT WOR+45 ECO/UNDEV INT/ORG HEALTH KNOWL...TREND TOT/POP FAO 20. PAGE 66 A1353 — CONCPT POLICY FOR/AID

B62
KAHN H.,THINKING ABOUT THE UNTHINKABLE. FUT USA+45 LAW NAT/G CONSULT FORCES ACT/RES CREATE PLAN TEC/DEV BAL/PWR DIPLOM EDU/PROP ARMS/CONT DETER ATTIT...CONCPT OBS TREND COLD/WAR 20. PAGE 76 A1547 — INT/ORG ORD/FREE NUC/PWR PEACE

B62
LAQUEUR W.,THE FUTURE OF COMMUNIST SOCIETY. CHINA/COM USSR LAW ECO/DEV NAT/G POL/PAR PLAN PROB/SOLV DIPLOM LEAD...POLICY CONCPT IDEA/COMP ANTHOL 20. PAGE 85 A1731 — MARXISM COM FUT SOCIETY

B62
MACKENTOSH J.M.,STRATEGY AND TACTICS OF SOVIET FOREIGN POLICY. CHINA/COM FUT USA+45 WOR+45 INT/ORG PLAN DOMIN LEGIT ROUTINE COERCE NUC/PWR WAR ATTIT DRIVE ORD/FREE PWR...CONCPT OBS TIME/SEQ TREND GEN/METH COLD/WAR 20. PAGE 92 A1894 — COM POLICY DIPLOM USSR

B62
MANDER J.,BERLIN: HOSTAGE FOR THE WEST. FUT GERMANY WOR+45 FOR/AID RISK ATTIT ORD/FREE 20 BERLIN COLD/WAR. PAGE 93 A1916 — DIPLOM BAL/PWR DOMIN DETER

B62
MANNING C.A.W.,THE NATURE OF INTERNATIONAL SOCIETY. FUT LAW NAT/G TOP/EX NAT/LISM PEACE PERCEPT PERSON ALL/VALS PLURISM...METH/CNCPT MYTH HYPO/EXP TOT/POP 20. PAGE 94 A1926 — INT/ORG SOCIETY SIMUL DIPLOM

B62
MORGENTHAU H.J.,POLITICS IN THE TWENTIETH CENTURY: IMPASSE OF AMERICAN FOREIGN POLICY. FUT GERMANY USA+45 USSR WOR+45 INT/ORG NAT/G ACT/RES PLAN FOR/AID EDU/PROP LEGIT COERCE WAR PWR...TIME/SEQ TREND COLD/WAR 20. PAGE 104 A2138 — SKILL DIPLOM

B62
OSGOOD C.E.,AN ALTERNATIVE TO WAR OR SURRENDER. FUT UNIV CULTURE INTELL SOCIETY R+D INT/ORG CONSULT DELIB/GP ACT/RES PLAN CHOOSE ATTIT PERCEPT KNOWL ...PHIL/SCI PSY SOC TREND GEN/LAWS 20. PAGE 112 A2300 — ORD/FREE EDU/PROP PEACE WAR

B62
RIVKIN A.,AFRICA AND THE WEST. AFR EUR+WWI FUT ISLAM ISRAEL USA+45 SOCIETY INT/ORG FORCES CREATE PLAN FOR/AID EDU/PROP ATTIT...CONCPT TREND EEC 20 CONGRESS UN. PAGE 121 A2488 — ECO/UNDEV ECO/TAC

B62
ROBERTSON B.C.,REGIONAL DEVELOPMENT IN THE EUROPEAN ECONOMIC COMMUNITY. EUR+WWI FRANCE FUT ITALY UK ECO/UNDEV WORKER ACT/RES PROB/SOLV TEC/DEV ECO/TAC INT/TRADE EEC. PAGE 122 A2499 — PLAN ECO/DEV INT/ORG REGION

B62
SCHUMAN F.L.,THE COLD WAR: RETROSPECT AND PROSPECT. FUT USA+45 USSR WOR+45 BAL/PWR EDU/PROP ARMS/CONT ATTIT...MAJORIT IDEA/COMP ANTHOL BIBLIOG 20 COLD/WAR. PAGE 129 A2651 — MARXISM TEC/DEV DIPLOM NUC/PWR

B62
SINGER J.D.,DETERRENCE, ARMS CONTROL AND DISARMAMENT: TOWARD A SYNTHESIS IN NATIONAL SECURITY POLICY. COM USA+45 INT/ORG BAL/PWR DETER ORD/FREE...POLICY COLD/WAR 20. PAGE 133 A2727 — FUT ACT/RES ARMS/CONT

B62
SNYDER L.L.D.,THE IMPERIALISM READER. AFR ASIA CHINA/COM COM EUR+WWI FUT MOD/EUR USA+45 WOR+45 WOR-45 INT/ORG COLONIAL SOVEREIGN CMN/WLTH OAS 20. PAGE 134 A2751 — DOMIN PWR DIPLOM

B62
STEEL R.,THE END OF THE ALLIANCE. FRANCE FUT GERMANY/E GERMANY/W UK USA+45 NAT/G FORCES FOR/AID 20 NATO. PAGE 137 A2809 — EUR+WWI POLICY DIPLOM INT/ORG

B62
STRACHEY J.,ON THE PREVENTION OF WAR. FUT WOR+45 INT/ORG NAT/G ACT/RES PLAN BAL/PWR DOMIN EDU/PROP PEACE ATTIT...POLICY TREND TOT/POP COLD/WAR 20 UN. PAGE 139 A2842 — FORCES ORD/FREE ARMS/CONT NUC/PWR

B62
WRIGHT Q.,PREVENTING WORLD WAR THREE. FUT WOR+45 CULTURE INT/ORG NAT/G CONSULT FORCES ADMIN ARMS/CONT DRIVE RIGID/FLEX ORD/FREE SOVEREIGN ...POLICY CONCPT TREND STERTYP COLD/WAR 20. PAGE 168 A3416 — CREATE ATTIT

L62
BAILEY S.D.,"THE TROIKA AND THE FUTURE OF THE UN." CONSTN CREATE LEGIT EXEC CHOOSE ORD/FREE PWR ...CONCPT NEW/IDEA UN COLD/WAR 20. PAGE 10 A0206 — FUT INT/ORG USSR

L62
ULYSSES,"THE INTERNATIONAL AIMS AND POLICIES OF THE SOVIET UNION: THE NEW CONCEPTS AND STRATEGY OF KHRUSHCHEV." FUT USSR WOR+45 SOCIETY INT/ORG NAT/G — COM POLICY BAL/PWR

POL/PAR FORCES TOP/EX PLAN DOMIN EDU/PROP COERCE ATTIT PERSON PWR...TREND COLD/WAR 20 KHRUSH/N. PAGE 146 A2994
DIPLOM

S62
ALBONETTI A.,"IL SECONDO PROGRAMMA QUINQUENNALE 1963-67 ED IL BILANCIO RICERCHE ED INVESTIMENTI PER IL 1963 DELL'ERATOM." EUR+WWI FUT ITALY WOR+45 ECO/DEV SERV/IND INT/ORG TEC/DEV ECO/TAC ATTIT SKILL WEALTH...MGT TIME/SEQ OEEC 20. PAGE 5 A0108
R+D PLAN NUC/PWR

S62
BELSHAW C.,"TRAINING AND RECRUITMENT: SOME PRINCIPLES OF INTERNATIONAL AID." FUT WOR+45 SOCIETY INT/ORG NAT/G CREATE PLAN TEC/DEV ECO/TAC FOR/AID EDU/PROP ATTIT PERCEPT...HUM UN FAO ILO UNESCO 20. PAGE 13 A0263
VOL/ASSN ECO/UNDEV

S62
BERKES R.N.B.,"THE NEW FRONTIER IN THE UN." FUT USA+45 WOR+45 INT/ORG DELIB/GP NAT/LISM PERCEPT RESPECT UN OAS 20. PAGE 13 A0272
GEN/LAWS DIPLOM

S62
BIERZANECK R.,"LA NON-RECONAISSANCE ET LE DROIT INTERNATIONAL CONTEMPORAIN." EUR+WWI FUT WOR+45 LAW ECO/DEV ATTIT RIGID/FLEX...CONCPT TIME/SEQ TOT/POP 20. PAGE 14 A0286
EDU/PROP JURID DIPLOM INT/LAW

S62
BLOOMFIELD L.P.,"THE UNITED NATIONS IN CRISIS: THE ROLE OF THE UN IN USA FOREIGN POLICY." FUT USA+45 WOR+45 ECO/UNDEV DIPLOM ATTIT ORD/FREE...CONCPT UN. PAGE 16 A0317
INT/ORG TREND REV

S62
BOULDING K.E.,"THE PREVENTION OF WORLD WAR THREE." FUT WOR+45 INT/ORG PLAN BAL/PWR PEACE ORD/FREE PWR ...NEW/IDEA TREND TOT/POP COLD/WAR 20. PAGE 17 A0348
VOL/ASSN NAT/G ARMS/CONT DIPLOM

S62
CLEVELAND H.,"THE FUTURE ROLE OF THE UNITED STATES IN THE UNITED NATIONS." USA+45 ECO/UNDEV INT/ORG EX/STRUC DIPLOM FOR/AID ROUTINE SKILL SOVEREIGN WEALTH UN 20. PAGE 27 A0550
FUT ATTIT

S62
CORET A.,"LE STATUT DE L'ILE CHRISTMAS DE L'OCEAN INDIEN." FUT S/ASIA ECO/DEV ECO/UNDEV VOL/ASSN DELIB/GP PLAN...RELATIV OBS TIME/SEQ TREND AUSTRAL 20. PAGE 30 A0619
NAT/G INT/ORG NEW/ZEALND

S62
CRANE R.D.,"LAW AND STRATEGY IN SPACE." FUT USA+45 WOR+45 AIR LAW INT/ORG NAT/G FORCES ACT/RES PLAN BAL/PWR LEGIT ARMS/CONT COERCE ORD/FREE...POLICY INT/LAW JURID SOC/EXP 20 TREATY. PAGE 32 A0656
CONCPT SPACE

S62
CRANE R.D.,"SOVIET ATTITUDE TOWARD INTERNATIONAL SPACE LAW." COM FUT USA+45 USSR AIR CONSTN DELIB/GP DOMIN PWR...JURID TREND TOT/POP 20. PAGE 32 A0657
LAW ATTIT INT/LAW SPACE

S62
DE MADARIAGA S.,"TOWARD THE UNITED STATES OF EUROPE." EUR+WWI PLAN DOMIN FEDERAL ATTIT PWR SOVEREIGN...GEOG TOT/POP 20. PAGE 35 A0707
FUT INT/ORG

S62
DRACHKOVITCH M.M.,"THE EMERGING PATTERN OF YUGOSLAV-SOVIET RELATIONS." COM FUT USSR WOR+45 INT/ORG ECO/TAC FOR/AID DOMIN COERCE ATTIT PERSON ORD/FREE PWR...TIME/SEQ 20 TITO/MARSH KHRUSH/N STALIN/J. PAGE 38 A0783
TOP/EX DIPLOM YUGOSLAVIA

S62
FINKELSTEIN L.S.,"THE UNITED NATIONS AND ORGANIZATIONS FOR CONTROL OF ARMAMENT." FUT WOR+45 VOL/ASSN DELIB/GP TOP/EX CREATE EDU/PROP LEGIT ADJUD NUC/PWR ATTIT RIGID/FLEX ORD/FREE...POLICY DECISION CONCPT OBS TREND GEN/LAWS TOT/POP COLD/WAR. PAGE 46 A0933
INT/ORG PWR ARMS/CONT

S62
FOSTER W.C.,"ARMS CONTROL AND DISARMAMENT IN A DIVIDED WORLD." COM FUT USA+45 USSR WOR+45 INTELL INT/ORG NAT/G VOL/ASSN CONSULT CREATE PLAN TEC/DEV EDU/PROP LEGIT NUC/PWR ATTIT RIGID/FLEX...CONCPT TREND TOT/POP 20 UN. PAGE 47 A0971
DELIB/GP POLICY ARMS/CONT DIPLOM

S62
GUETZKOW H.,"THE POTENTIAL OF CASE STUDY IN ANALYZING INTERNATIONAL CONFLICT." EUR+WWI FUT GERMANY INTELL SOCIETY STRUCT INT/ORG LOC/G NAT/G CONSULT CREATE PLAN CHOOSE ATTIT RIGID/FLEX ...POLICY SAAR 20. PAGE 58 A1188
EDU/PROP METH/CNCPT COERCE FRANCE

S62
JACOBSON H.K.,"THE UNITED NATIONS AND COLONIALISM: A TENTATIVE APPRAISAL." AFR FUT S/ASIA USA+45 USSR WOR+45 NAT/G DELIB/GP PLAN DIPLOM ECO/TAC DOMIN ADMIN ROUTINE COERCE ATTIT RIGID/FLEX ORD/FREE PWR ...OBS STERTYP UN 20. PAGE 73 A1486
INT/ORG CONCPT COLONIAL

S62
KOLARZ W.,"THE IMPACT OF COMMUNISM ON WEST AFRICA." AFR FUT SOCIETY INT/ORG NAT/G CREATE PLAN DOMIN EDU/PROP COERCE NAT/LISM ATTIT RIGID/FLEX SOCISM ...POLICY CONCPT TREND MARX/KARL 20. PAGE 81 A1666
COM POL/PAR COLONIAL

S62
LISSITZYN O.J.,"SOME LEGAL IMPLICATIONS OF THE U-2 AND RB-47 INCIDENTS." FUT USA+45 USSR WOR+45 AIR NAT/G DIPLOM LEGIT MORAL ORD/FREE SOVEREIGN...JURID GEN/LAWS GEN/METH COLD/WAR 20 U-2. PAGE 90 A1840
LAW CONCPT SPACE INT/LAW

S62
MILLAR T.B.,"THE COMMONWEALTH AND THE UNITED NATIONS." FUT WOR+45 STRUCT NAT/G VOL/ASSN CONSULT DELIB/GP EDU/PROP LEGIT ATTIT...POLICY CONCPT TREND CMN/WLTH UN 20. PAGE 101 A2072
INT/ORG

S62
ORBAN M.,"L'EUROPE EN FORMATION ET SES PROBLEMES." EUR+WWI FUT WOR+45 WOR-45 INTELL STRUCT DELIB/GP ACT/RES FEDERAL RIGID/FLEX WEALTH...CONCPT TIME/SEQ OEEC 20. PAGE 112 A2295
INT/ORG PLAN REGION

S62
PYE L.W.,"THE POLITICAL IMPULSES AND FANTASIES BEHIND FOREIGN AID." FUT USA+45 ECO/UNDEV DIPLOM ECO/TAC ROUTINE DRIVE KNOWL...SOC METH/CNCPT NEW/IDEA TREND HYPO/EXP STERTYP GEN/METH 20. PAGE 118 A2420
ACT/RES ATTIT FOR/AID

S62
RUSSETT B.M.,"CAUSE, SURPRISE, AND NO ESCAPE." FUT WOR-45 CULTURE SOCIETY INT/ORG FORCES TEC/DEV BAL/PWR EDU/PROP ARMS/CONT NUC/PWR WAR WEAPON PEACE KNOWL ORD/FREE PWR...POLICY CONCPT RECORD TIME/SEQ TREND GEN/LAWS 20 WWI. PAGE 126 A2578
COERCE DIPLOM

S62
SCHACHTER O.,"DAG HAMMARSKJOLD AND THE RELATION OF LAW TO POLITICS." FUT WOR+45 INT/ORG CONSULT PLAN TEC/DEV BAL/PWR DIPLOM LEGIT ATTIT PERCEPT ORD/FREE ...POLICY JURID CONCPT OBS TESTS STERTYP GEN/LAWS 20 HAMMARSK/D. PAGE 128 A2616
ACT/RES ADJUD

S62
SCOTT J.B.,"ANGLO-SOVIET TRADE AND ITS EFFECTS ON THE COMMONWEALTH." COM FUT UK USSR WOR+45 ECO/DEV MARKET INT/ORG CONSULT WEALTH...POLICY TREND CMN/WLTH 20. PAGE 130 A2673
NAT/G ECO/TAC

S62
SINGER J.D.,"STABLE DETERRENCE AND ITS LIMITS." FUT WOR+45 R+D INT/ORG CONSULT ACT/RES TEC/DEV ARMS/CONT COERCE DRIVE PERCEPT RIGID/FLEX ORD/FREE PWR...MYTH SIMUL TOT/POP 20. PAGE 133 A2728
NAT/G FORCES DETER NUC/PWR

S62
SPENSER J.H.,"AFRICA AT THE UNITED NATIONS: SOME OBSERVATIONS." FUT ECO/UNDEV NAT/G CONSULT DELIB/GP PLAN BAL/PWR ECO/TAC EDU/PROP ATTIT RIGID/FLEX HEALTH ORD/FREE PWR WEALTH...POLICY CONCPT OBS TREND STERTYP GEN/METH UN VAL/FREE. PAGE 136 A2786
AFR INT/ORG REGION

S62
THOMAS J.R.T.,"SOVIET BEHAVIOR IN THE QUEMOY CRISES OF 1958." CHINA/COM FUT USSR WOR+45 INT/ORG VOL/ASSN FORCES PLAN BAL/PWR DOMIN COERCE NUC/PWR REV WAR ATTIT DRIVE ORD/FREE...POLICY OBS RECORD COLD/WAR FOR/POL 20. PAGE 143 A2923
COM PWR

B63
ABSHIRE D.M.,NATIONAL SECURITY: POLITICAL, MILITARY, AND ECONOMIC STRATEGIES IN THE DECADE AHEAD. ASIA COM USA+45 WOR+45 ECO/DEV ECO/UNDEV INT/ORG DELIB/GP FORCES ECO/TAC COERCE ATTIT RIGID/FLEX HEALTH ORD/FREE PWR WEALTH...POLICY STAT CHARTS ANTHOL COLD/WAR VAL/FREE. PAGE 4 A0083
FUT ACT/RES BAL/PWR

B63
BAILEY S.D.,THE UNITED NATIONS: A SHORT POLITICAL GUIDE. FUT PROB/SOLV LEAD...INT/LAW 20 UN. PAGE 10 A0207
INT/ORG PEACE DETER DIPLOM

B63
BLACK J.E.,FOREIGN POLICIES IN A WORLD OF CHANGE. FUT INT/ORG ALL/VALS...POLICY MAJORIT MARXIST SOCIALIST TRADIT TIME/SEQ TREND ANTHOL 20. PAGE 15 A0298
WOR+45 NAT/G DIPLOM

B63
BURNS A.L.,PEACE-KEEPING BY U.N.FORCES - FROM SUEZ TO THE CONGO. AFR FUT ISLAM ISRAEL USSR WOR+45 NAT/G DELIB/GP BAL/PWR DOMIN LEGIT EXEC COERCE PEACE ATTIT PWR RESPECT SOVEREIGN...CONCPT UN 20. PAGE 22 A0441
INT/ORG FORCES ORD/FREE

B63
CREMEANS C.,THE ARABS AND THE WORLD: NASSER'S ARAB NATIONALIST POLICY. FUT ISLAM UAR USA+45 SOCIETY STRATA NAT/G POL/PAR PLAN DIPLOM EDU/PROP LEGIT DRIVE ALL/VALS...INT TIME/SEQ CHARTS 20 NASSER/G. PAGE 33 A0662
TOP/EX ATTIT REGION NAT/LISM

B63
HALEY A.G.,SPACE LAW AND GOVERNMENT. FUT USA+45 WOR+45 LEGIS ACT/RES CREATE ATTIT RIGID/FLEX ORD/FREE PWR SOVEREIGN...POLICY JURID CONCPT CHARTS VAL/FREE 20. PAGE 60 A1226
INT/ORG LAW SPACE

B63
LUNDBERG F.,THE COMING WORLD TRANSFORMATION. CULTURE SOCIETY ECO/DEV INT/ORG NAT/G DIPLOM ECO/TAC EDU/PROP 15/21. PAGE 91 A1873
PREDICT FUT WOR+45 TEC/DEV

B63
MANGER W.,THE ALLIANCE FOR PROGRESS: A CRITICAL APPRAISAL. FUT L/A+17C USA+45 CULTURE ECO/UNDEV ACADEM NAT/G SCHOOL PLAN FOR/AID...POLICY OAS.
DIPLOM INT/ORG ECO/TAC

PAGE 94 A1918 — REGION

B63
MARITANO N.,AN ALLIANCE FOR PROGRESS. FUT L/A+17C USA+45 CULTURE ECO/UNDEV NAT/G PLAN CONTROL POLICY. PAGE 95 A1941
DIPLOM INT/ORG ECO/TAC FOR/AID

B63
MCDOUGAL M.S.,LAW AND PUBLIC ORDER IN SPACE. FUT USA+45 ACT/RES TEC/DEV ADJUD...POLICY INT/LAW JURID 20. PAGE 98 A2009
SPACE ORD/FREE DIPLOM DECISION

B63
ROSECRANCE R.N.,ACTION AND REACTION IN WORLD POLITICS. FUT WOR-45 SOCIETY DELIB/GP ACT/RES CREATE DIPLOM ECO/TAC DOMIN EDU/PROP COERCE ATTIT PERSON SUPEGO ORD/FREE PWR...CHARTS SIMUL LEAGUE/NAT VAL/FREE UN 19/20. PAGE 123 A2529
WOR+45 INT/ORG BAL/PWR

B63
ROSSI M.,THE THIRD WORLD. FUT WOR+45 INT/ORG NAT/G CAP/ISM COLONIAL PEACE PWR MARXISM 20 UN THIRD/WRLD. PAGE 124 A2542
ECO/UNDEV DIPLOM BAL/PWR NEUTRAL

B63
WELLESLEY COLLEGE,SYMPOSIUM ON LATIN AMERICA. FUT L/A+17C USA+45 INT/ORG ECO/TAC PARL/PROC REGION ANTHOL. PAGE 163 A3316
ECO/UNDEV CULTURE ORD/FREE DIPLOM

L63
LISSITZYN O.J.,"INTERNATIONAL LAW IN A DIVIDED WORLD." FUT WOR+45 CONSTN CULTURE ECO/DEV ECO/UNDEV DIST/IND NAT/G FORCES ECO/TAC LEGIT ADJUD ADMIN COERCE ATTIT HEALTH MORAL ORD/FREE PWR RESPECT WEALTH VAL/FREE. PAGE 90 A1841
INT/ORG LAW

L63
MOUSKHELY M.,"LE BLOC COMMUNISTE ET LA COMMUNAUTE ECONOMIQUE EUROPEENNE." AFR COM EUR+WWI FUT USSR WOR+45 INTELL ECO/UNDEV LABOR POL/PAR NUC/PWR RIGID/FLEX...TIME/SEQ ORG/CHARTS EEC TOT/POP 20. PAGE 105 A2158
INT/ORG ECO/DEV

L63
PADELFORD N.J.,"FINANCIAL CRISIS AND THE UNITED NATIONS." FUT USSR WOR+45 LAW CONSTN FINAN INT/ORG DELIB/GP FORCES PLAN BUDGET DIPLOM COST WEALTH ...STAT CHARTS UN CONGO 20. PAGE 113 A2311
CREATE ECO/TAC

L63
PHELPS J.,"STUDIES IN DETERRENCE VIII: MILITARY STABILITARY AND ARMS CONTROL: A CRITICAL SURVEY." FUT WOR+45 INT/ORG ACT/RES EDU/PROP COERCE NUC/PWR WAR HEALTH PWR...POLICY TECHNIC TREND SIMUL TOT/POP 20. PAGE 116 A2373
FORCES ORD/FREE ARMS/CONT DETER

L63
PRINCETON UNIV. CONFERENCE,"ARAB DEVELOPMENT IN THE EMERGING INTERNATIONAL ECONOMY." FUT USA+45 DIST/IND FINAN DELIB/GP PLAN ECO/TAC WEALTH VAL/FREE 20. PAGE 118 A2413
ISLAM ECO/UNDEV FOR/AID INT/TRADE

L63
SINGER J.D.,"WEAPONS MANAGEMENT IN WORLD POLITICS: PROCEEDINGS OF THE INTERNATIONAL ARMS CONTROL SYMPOSIUM, DECEMBER, 1962." FUT WOR+45 SOCIETY ECO/DEV INDUS INT/ORG DELIB/GP FORCES ACT/RES ECO/TAC EDU/PROP ARMS/CONT SUPEGO HEALTH ORD/FREE PWR SKILL...POLICY CHARTS SIMUL ANTHOL VAL/FREE 20. PAGE 133 A2729
CONSULT ATTIT DIPLOM NUC/PWR

L63
SZASZY E.,"L'EVOLUTION DES PRINCIPES GENERAUX DU DROIT INTERNATIONAL PRIVE DANS LES PAYS DE DEMOCRATIE POPULAIRE." COM FUT WOR+45 LAW ECO/DEV PERF/ART POL/PAR PROF/ORG ECO/TAC INT/TRADE EDU/PROP ATTIT RIGID/FLEX ALL/VALS SOCISM...JURID TREND GEN/LAWS WORK 20. PAGE 141 A2876
DIPLOM TOTALISM INT/LAW INT/ORG

L63
WILCOX F.O.,"THE ATLANTIC COMMUNITY: PROGRESS AND PROSPECTS." EUR+WWI FUT USA+45 WOR+45 SOCIETY CREATE ECO/TAC EDU/PROP LEGIT REGION ATTIT ALL/VALS ...POLICY ANTHOL VAL/FREE 20. PAGE 164 A3346
INT/ORG ACT/RES

S63
BALOGH T.,"L'INFLUENCE DES INSTITUTIONS MONETAIRES ET COMMERCIALES SUR LA STRUCTURE ECONOMIQUE AFRICAIN." AFR EUR+WWI FUT USA+45 USA-45 WOR+45 SERV/IND INT/ORG NAT/G TOP/EX ROUTINE...INDEX EEC 20. PAGE 11 A0215
FINAN

S63
BARTHELEMY G.,"LE NOUVEAU FRANC (CFA) ET LA BANQUE CENTRALE DES ETATS DE L'AFRIQUE DE L'OUEST." FUT STRUCT INT/ORG PLAN ATTIT ALL/VALS 20. PAGE 11 A0230
AFR FINAN

S63
COSER L.,"AMERICA AND THE WORLD REVOLUTION." COM FUT USA+45 WOR+45 INTELL SOCIETY NAT/G ECO/TAC EDU/PROP ALL/VALS SOCISM...PSY GEN/LAWS TOT/POP 20 COLD/WAR. PAGE 31 A0629
ECO/UNDEV PLAN FOR/AID DIPLOM

S63
COUTY P.,"L'ASSISTANCE POUR LE DEVELOPPEMENT: POINT DE VUE SCANDINAVES." EUR+WWI FINLAND FUT SWEDEN WOR+45 ECO/DEV ECO/UNDEV COM/IND LABOR NAT/G PROF/ORG ACT/RES SKILL WEALTH TOT/POP 20. PAGE 32 A0643
FINAN ROUTINE FOR/AID

S63
DAVEE R.,"POUR UN FONDS DE DEVELOPPEMENT SOCIAL." FUT WOR+45 INTELL SOCIETY ECO/DEV FINAN TEC/DEV ROUTINE WEALTH...TREND TOT/POP VAL/FREE UN 20. PAGE 34 A0684
INT/ORG SOC FOR/AID

S63
DICKS H.V.,"NATIONAL LOYALTY, IDENTITY, AND THE INTERNATIONAL SOLDIER." FUT NAT/G COERCE ATTIT DRIVE PERCEPT PERSON RIGID/FLEX SUPEGO ALL/VALS ...PSY VAL/FREE. PAGE 37 A0758
INT/ORG FORCES

S63
DIEBOLD W. JR.,"THE NEW SITUATION OF INTERNATIONAL TRADE POLICY." EUR+WWI FRANCE FUT UK USA+45 WOR+45 DIST/IND PLAN INT/TRADE EDU/PROP PWR WEALTH ...RECORD TREND GEN/LAWS EEC VAL/FREE 20. PAGE 37 A0760
MARKET ECO/TAC

S63
EMERSON R.,"THE ATLANTIC COMMUNITY AND THE EMERGING COUNTRIES." FUT WOR+45 ECO/DEV ECO/UNDEV R+D NAT/G DELIB/GP BAL/PWR ECO/TAC EDU/PROP ROUTINE ORD/FREE PWR WEALTH...POLICY CONCPT TREND GEN/METH EEC 20 NATO. PAGE 42 A0848
ATTIT INT/TRADE

S63
ETIENNE G.,"'LOIS OBJECTIVES' ET PROBLEMES DE DEVELOPPEMENT DANS LE CONTEXTE CHINE-URSS." ASIA CHINA/COM COM FUT STRUCT INT/ORG VOL/ASSN TOP/EX TEC/DEV ECO/TAC ATTIT RIGID/FLEX...GEOG MGT TIME/SEQ TOT/POP 20. PAGE 42 A0866
TOTALISM USSR

S63
ETZIONI A.,"EUROPEAN UNIFICATION AND PERSPECTIVES ON SOVEREIGNTY." EUR+WWI FUT DELIB/GP TEC/DEV ECO/TAC EDU/PROP DETER NUC/PWR ATTIT DRIVE ORD/FREE PWR WEALTH...CONCPT RECORD TIME/SEQ EEC VAL/FREE 20. PAGE 43 A0870
INT/ORG ECO/DEV SOVEREIGN

S63
GANDILHON J.,"LA SCIENCE ET LA TECHNIQUE A L'AIDE DES REGIONS PEU DEVELOPPEES." FRANCE FUT WOR+45 ECO/DEV R+D PROF/ORG ACT/RES PLAN...MGT TOT/POP VAL/FREE 20 UN. PAGE 51 A1037
ECO/UNDEV TEC/DEV FOR/AID

S63
GARDNER R.N.,"COOPERATION IN OUTER SPACE." FUT USSR WOR+45 AIR LAW COM/IND CONSULT DELIB/GP CREATE KNOWL 20 TREATY. PAGE 51 A1045
INT/ORG ACT/RES PEACE SPACE

S63
GORDON B.,"ECONOMIC IMPEDIMENTS TO REGIONALISM IN SOUTH EAST ASIA." BURMA FUT S/ASIA THAILAND USA+45 AGRI INDUS R+D NAT/G PLAN ECO/TAC WEALTH...STAT CONT/OBS 20. PAGE 54 A1110
VOL/ASSN ECO/UNDEV INT/TRADE REGION

S63
GROSS F.,"THE US NATIONAL INTEREST AND THE UN." FUT CONSTN NAT/G DELIB/GP CREATE DIPLOM RIGID/FLEX ORD/FREE...CONCPT GEN/LAWS 20 UN. PAGE 57 A1172
USA+45 INT/ORG PEACE

S63
HAVILAND H.F.,"BUILDING A POLITICAL COMMUNITY." EUR+WWI FUT UK USA+45 ECO/DEV ECO/UNDEV INT/ORG NAT/G DELIB/GP BAL/PWR ECO/TAC NEUTRAL ROUTINE ATTIT PWR WEALTH...CONCPT COLD/WAR TOT/POP 20. PAGE 63 A1293
VOL/ASSN DIPLOM

S63
HORVATH J.,"MOSCOW'S AID PROGRAM: THE PERFORMANCE SO FAR." COM FUT USSR WOR+45 ECO/DEV FINAN PLAN TEC/DEV FOR/AID EDU/PROP ATTIT ORD/FREE PWR WEALTH ...POLICY STAT CHARTS VAL/FREE 20. PAGE 68 A1389
ECO/UNDEV ECO/TAC

S63
KAWALKOWSKI A.,"POUR UNE EUROPE INDEPENDENTE ET REUNIFIEE." EUR+WWI FUT USA+45 USSR WOR+45 ECO/DEV PROC/MFG INT/ORG NAT/G ACT/RES TEC/DEV FEDERAL RIGID/FLEX...CONCPT METH/CNCPT OEEC TOT/POP 20 DEGAULLE/C. PAGE 77 A1573
R+D PLAN NUC/PWR

S63
KINTNER W.R.,"THE PROJECTED EUROPEAN UNION AND AMERICAN RESPONSIBILITIES." EUR+WWI USA+45 STRATA INT/ORG NAT/G DOMIN DETER NUC/PWR ATTIT ORD/FREE PWR 20 NATO. PAGE 79 A1628
FUT FORCES DIPLOM REGION

S63
KRAVIS I.B.,"THE POLITICAL ARITHMETIC OF INTERNATIONAL BURDENSHARING." FUT USA+45 WOR+45 FINAN DELIB/GP ACT/RES CREATE TEC/DEV ATTIT PWR WEALTH...POLICY MATH STAT VAL/FREE 20. PAGE 82 A1681
INT/ORG ECO/TAC

S63
LEDUC G.,"L'AIDE INTERNATIONALE AU DEVELOPPEMENT." FUT WOR+45 ECO/DEV ECO/UNDEV R+D PROF/ORG TEC/DEV ECO/TAC ROUTINE ATTIT ALL/VALS...MGT TIME/SEQ TOT/POP 20. PAGE 86 A1758
FINAN PLAN FOR/AID

S63
LOPEZIBOR J.,"L'EUROPE, FORME DE VIE." CHRIST-17C EUR+WWI FUT MOD/EUR SOCIETY INT/ORG SECT EDU/PROP ATTIT RIGID/FLEX ALL/VALS...POLICY HUM SOC TIME/SEQ TREND GEN/LAWS. PAGE 91 A1862
NAT/G CULTURE

S63
MACWHINNEY E.,"LES CONCEPT SOVIETIQUE DE 'COEXISTENCE PACIFIQUE' ET LES RAPPORTS JURIDIQUES ENTRE L'URSS ET LES ETATS OCIDENTAUX." COM FUT
NAT/G CONCPT DIPLOM

WOR+45 LAW CULTURE INTELL POL/PAR ACT/RES BAL/PWR ...INT/LAW 20. PAGE 93 A1903 — USSR

S63
MANOLIU F.,"PERSPECTIVES D'UNE INTEGRATION ECONOMIQUE LATINOAMERICAINE." FUT L/A+17C STRUCT MARKET LABOR POL/PAR VOL/ASSN PLAN RIGID/FLEX PWR ...METH/CNCPT OAS TOT/POP 20. PAGE 94 A1927 — FINAN INT/ORG PEACE

S63
MEYROWITZ H.,"LES JURISTES DEVANT L'ARME NUCLAIRE." FUT WOR+45 INTELL SOCIETY BAL/PWR DETER WAR...JURID CONCPT 20. PAGE 100 A2058 — ACT/RES ADJUD INT/LAW NUC/PWR

S63
MORGENTHAU H.J.,"THE POLITICAL CONDITIONS FOR AN INTERNATIONAL POLICE FORCE." FUT WOR+45 CREATE LEGIT ADMIN PEACE ORD/FREE 20. PAGE 104 A2141 — INT/ORG FORCES ARMS/CONT DETER

S63
MURRAY J.N.,"UNITED NATIONS PEACE-KEEPING AND PROBLEMS OF POLITICAL CONTROL." FUT WOR+45 CONSTN DELIB/GP FORCES TOP/EX ACT/RES CREATE LEGIT PEACE PWR...METH/CNCPT CONGO UN 20. PAGE 106 A2182 — INT/ORG ORD/FREE

S63
NICHOLAS H.G.,"UN PEACE FORCES AND THE CHANGING GLOBE: THE LESSONS OF SUEZ AND CONGO." FUT WOR+45 CONSTN INT/ORG CONSULT DELIB/GP TOP/EX CREATE DIPLOM DOMIN LEGIT COERCE WAR PERSON RIGID/FLEX PWR UN SUEZ CONGO UNEF 20. PAGE 109 A2229 — ACT/RES FORCES

S63
ROUGEMONT D.,"LES NOUVELLES CHANCES DE L'EUROPE." EUR+WWI FUT ECO/DEV INT/ORG NAT/G ACT/RES PLAN TEC/DEV EDU/PROP ADMIN COLONIAL FEDERAL ATTIT PWR SKILL...TREND 20. PAGE 124 A2549 — ECO/UNDEV PERCEPT

S63
SCHMIDT W.E.,"THE CASE AGAINST COMMODITY AGREEMENTS." FUT L/A+17C STRATA CONSULT PLAN ECO/TAC EDU/PROP ATTIT DRIVE RIGID/FLEX WEALTH ...MYTH 20. PAGE 128 A2631 — ECO/UNDEV ACT/RES INT/TRADE

S63
SPINELLI A.,"IL TRATTATO DI MOSCA E I PROBLEMI DELLA COESISTENZA PACIFICA." CHINA/COM COM FRANCE FUT WOR+45 INT/ORG VOL/ASSN PEACE...POLICY MYTH 20. PAGE 136 A2788 — ATTIT ARMS/CONT TOTALISM

S63
WALKER H.,"THE INTERNATIONAL LAW OF COMMODITY AGREEMENTS." FUT WOR+45 ECO/DEV ECO/UNDEV FINAN INT/ORG NAT/G CONSULT CREATE PLAN ECO/TAC ATTIT PERCEPT...CONCPT GEN/LAWS TOT/POP GATT 20. PAGE 160 A3265 — MARKET VOL/ASSN INT/LAW INT/TRADE

S63
WEILLER J.,"UNIONS MONETAIRES ET RAPPORTS DE COOPERATION INTERNATIONALE DANS UN MONDE EN TRANSITION: L'EXAMPLE." AFR FUT UNIV WOR+45 SOCIETY ECO/UNDEV MARKET R+D NAT/G FOR/AID PERCEPT RIGID/FLEX...NEW/IDEA 20. PAGE 162 A3303 — FINAN INT/ORG

S63
WRIGHT Q.,"PROJECTED EUROPEAN UNION AND AMERICAN INTERNATIONAL PRESTIGE." EUR+WWI FRANCE GERMANY UK USA+45 INT/ORG NAT/G EDU/PROP ATTIT PERCEPT PWR ...CONCPT OBS EEC 20 UN. PAGE 168 A3417 — FUT ORD/FREE REGION

B64
APTER D.E.,IDEOLOGY AND DISCONTENT. FUT WOR+45 CONSTN CULTURE INTELL SOCIETY STRUCT INT/ORG NAT/G DELIB/GP LEGIS CREATE PLAN TEC/DEV EDU/PROP EXEC PERCEPT PERSON RIGID/FLEX ALL/VALS...POLICY TOT/POP. PAGE 8 A0171 — ACT/RES ATTIT

B64
BLOOMFIELD L.P.,INTERNATIONAL MILITARY FORCES: THE QUESTION OF PEACE-KEEPING IN AN ARMED AND DISARMING WORLD. WOR+45 ACADEM ARMS/CONT REV PEACE 20 UN. PAGE 16 A0320 — INT/ORG FORCES FUT DIPLOM

B64
CEPEDE M.,POPULATION AND FOOD. USA+45 STRUCT ECO/UNDEV FAM PLAN TEC/DEV FOR/AID CONTROL...CATH SOC TREND 19/20. PAGE 25 A0513 — FUT GEOG AGRI CENSUS

B64
CLAUDE I.,SWORDS INTO PLOWSHARES. FUT WOR+45 WOR-45 DELIB/GP EX/STRUC LEGIT ATTIT ORD/FREE...CONCPT TIME/SEQ TREND UN TOT/POP 20. PAGE 27 A0547 — INT/ORG STRUCT

B64
DUBOIS J.,DANGER OVER PANAMA. FUT PANAMA SCHOOL PROB/SOLV EDU/PROP MARXISM...POLICY 19/20 TREATY INTERVENT CANAL/ZONE. PAGE 39 A0790 — DIPLOM COERCE

B64
ETZIONI A.,WINNING WITHOUT WAR. FUT MOD/EUR USA+45 WOR+45 ECO/DEV ECO/UNDEV INT/ORG NAT/G FORCES TOP/EX PLAN TEC/DEV ECO/TAC DOMIN EDU/PROP LEGIT COERCE CHOOSE ATTIT MORAL ORD/FREE RESPECT WEALTH MAJORIT. PAGE 43 A0871 — PWR TREND DIPLOM USSR

B64
FALK R.A.,THE ROLE OF DOMESTIC COURTS IN THE INTERNATIONAL LEGAL ORDER. FUT WOR+45 INT/ORG NAT/G JUDGE EDU/PROP LEGIT CT/SYS...POLICY RELATIV JURID CONCPT GEN/LAWS 20. PAGE 43 A0889 — LAW INT/LAW

B64
FINER H.,DULLES OVER SUEZ. FRANCE FUT UAR UK WOR+45 NAT/G PROB/SOLV CONTROL NUC/PWR WAR 20 DULLES/JF SUEZ. PAGE 46 A0932 — DIPLOM POLICY REC/INT

B64
FISHER R.,INTERNATIONAL CONFLICT AND BEHAVIORAL SCIENCE: THE CRAIGVILLE PAPERS. COM FUT USA+45 WOR+45 NAT/G DELIB/GP EX/STRUC FORCES ECO/TAC DOMIN EDU/PROP LEGIT COERCE ATTIT PERCEPT ORD/FREE PWR RESPECT...PSY SOC VAL/FREE. PAGE 46 A0940 — INT/ORG PLAN DIPLOM

B64
GIBSON J.S.,IDEOLOGY AND WORLD AFFAIRS. FUT WOR+45 ECO/UNDEV NAT/G CAP/ISM TOTALISM ORD/FREE FASCISM MARXISM 20. PAGE 52 A1067 — ALL/IDEOS DIPLOM POLICY IDEA/COMP

B64
GRODZINS M.,THE ATOMIC AGE: FORTY-FIVE SCIENTISTS AND SCHOLARS SPEAK ON NATIONAL AND WORLD AFFAIRS. FUT USA+45 WOR+45 R+D INT/ORG NAT/G CONSULT TEC/DEV EDU/PROP ATTIT PERSON ORD/FREE...HUM CONCPT TIME/SEQ CON/ANAL. PAGE 57 A1169 — INTELL ARMS/CONT NUC/PWR

B64
HEKHUIS D.J.,INTERNATIONAL STABILITY: MILITARY, ECONOMIC AND POLITICAL DIMENSIONS. FUT WOR+45 LAW ECO/UNDEV INT/ORG NAT/G VOL/ASSN FORCES ACT/RES BAL/PWR PWR WEALTH...STAT UN 20. PAGE 64 A1310 — TEC/DEV DETER REGION

B64
JOHNSON L.B.,MY HOPE FOR AMERICA. FUT USA+45 USSR LAW PLAN DIPLOM GIVE INCOME PEACE ATTIT ORD/FREE WEALTH 20 JOHNSON/LB PRESIDENT DEMOCRAT. PAGE 74 A1525 — POLICY POL/PAR NAT/G GOV/REL

B64
KENNEDY J.F.,THE BURDEN AND THE GLORY. FUT USA+45 TEC/DEV ECO/TAC EDU/PROP ARMS/CONT MURDER RACE/REL PEACE...ANTHOL 20 KENNEDY/JF COLD/WAR NATO PRESIDENT. PAGE 78 A1593 — ADMIN POLICY GOV/REL DIPLOM

B64
KOHNSTAMM M.,THE EUROPEAN COMMUNITY AND ITS ROLE IN THE WORLD. FUT MOD/EUR UK USA+45 ECO/DEV 20. PAGE 81 A1664 — INT/ORG NAT/G REGION DIPLOM

B64
LATOURETTE K.S.,CHINA. ASIA CHINA/COM FUT USSR ECO/UNDEV ECO/TAC WAR 19/20. PAGE 85 A1744 — MARXISM NAT/G POLICY DIPLOM

B64
LUARD E.,THE COLD WAR: A RE-APPRAISAL. FUT USSR WOR+45 FORCES NUC/PWR NAT/LISM ORD/FREE SOVEREIGN ...INT 20 COLD/WAR STALIN/J TREATY UN. PAGE 91 A1870 — DIPLOM WAR PEACE TOTALISM

B64
MARKHAM J.W.,THE COMMON MARKET: FRIEND OR COMPETITOR. EUR+WWI FUT USA+45 INT/ORG LG/CO NAT/G VOL/ASSN DELIB/GP EX/STRUC PLAN TARIFFS ORD/FREE PWR WEALTH...POLICY STAT TREND EEC VAL/FREE 20. PAGE 95 A1943 — ECO/DEV ECO/TAC

B64
NASA,PROCEEDINGS OF CONFERENCE ON THE LAW OF SPACE AND OF SATELLITE COMMUNICATIONS: CHICAGO 1963. FUT WOR+45 DELIB/GP PROB/SOLV TEC/DEV CONFER ADJUD NUC/PWR...POLICY IDEA/COMP 20 NASA. PAGE 107 A2197 — SPACE COM/IND LAW DIPLOM

B64
OWEN W.,STRATEGY FOR MOBILITY. FUT WOR+45 WOR-45 DIST/IND INT/ORG NAT/G DELIB/GP PLAN TEC/DEV ECO/TAC ORD/FREE PWR WEALTH...STAT TIME/SEQ VAL/FREE 20. PAGE 112 A2304 — COM/IND ECO/UNDEV

B64
ROSECRANCE R.N.,THE DISPERSION OF NUCLEAR WEAPONS: STRATEGY AND POLITICS. ASIA COM FUT S/ASIA USA+45 INT/ORG NAT/G DELIB/GP FORCES ACT/RES TEC/DEV BAL/PWR COERCE DETER ATTIT RIGID/FLEX ORD/FREE ...POLICY CHARTS VAL/FREE. PAGE 123 A2530 — EUR+WWI PWR PEACE

B64
SCHWARTZ M.D.,CONFERENCE ON SPACE SCIENCE AND SPACE LAW. FUT COM/IND NAT/G FORCES ACT/RES PLAN BUDGET DIPLOM NUC/PWR WEAPON...POLICY ANTHOL 20. PAGE 130 A2658 — SPACE LAW PEACE TEC/DEV

B64
STOESSINGER J.G.,FINANCING THE UNITED NATIONS SYSTEM. FUT WOR+45 CONSTN NAT/G VOL/ASSN DELIB/GP EX/STRUC ECO/TAC LEGIT CT/SYS PWR WEALTH...STAT TIME/SEQ TREND CHARTS VAL/FREE. PAGE 138 A2830 — FINAN INT/ORG

B64
US AIR FORCE ACADEMY ASSEMBLY,OUTER SPACE: FINAL REPORT APRIL 1-4, 1964. FUT USA+45 WOR+45 LAW DELIB/GP CONFER ARMS/CONT WAR PEACE ATTIT MORAL ...ANTHOL 20 NASA. PAGE 150 A3055 — SPACE CIVMIL/REL NUC/PWR DIPLOM

B64
WAINHOUSE D.W.,REMNANTS OF EMPIRE: THE UNITED NATIONS AND THE END OF COLONIALISM. FUT PORTUGAL WOR+45 NAT/G CONSULT DOMIN LEGIT ADMIN ROUTINE ATTIT ORD/FREE...POLICY JURID RECORD INT TIME/SEQ UN CMN/WLTH 20. PAGE 160 A3260 — INT/ORG TREND COLONIAL

L64
ARMENGALD A.,"ECONOMIE ET COEXISTENCE." COM EUR+WWI — MARKET

FUT USA+45 WOR+45 ECO/DEV ECO/UNDEV FINAN INT/ORG NAT/G EXEC CHOOSE ATTIT ALL/VALS...POLICY RELATIV DECISION TREND SOC/EXP COLD/WAR WORK 20. PAGE 9 A0173
ECO/TAC CAP/ISM

L64
HOFFMANN S.,"EUROPE'S IDENTITY CRISIS: BETWEEN THE PAST AND AMERICA." EUR+WWI FUT USA+45 INT/ORG NAT/G LEGIT RIGID/FLEX ALL/VALS...RELATIV TOT/POP 20. PAGE 66 A1358
COERCE POLICY

L64
MILLIS W.,"THE DEMILITARIZED WORLD." COM USA+45 USSR WOR+45 CONSTN NAT/G EX/STRUC PLAN LEGIT ATTIT DRIVE...CONCPT TIME/SEQ STERTYP TOT/POP COLD/WAR 20. PAGE 102 A2085
FUT INT/ORG BAL/PWR PEACE

L64
POUNDS N.J.G.,"THE POLITICS OF PARTITION." AFR ASIA COM EUR+WWI FUT ISLAM S/ASIA USA-45 LAW ECO/DEV ECO/UNDEV AGRI INDUS INT/ORG POL/PAR PROVS SECT FORCES TOP/EX EDU/PROP LEGIT ATTIT MORAL ORD/FREE PWR RESPECT WEALTH. PAGE 117 A2402
NAT/G NAT/LISM

L64
WARD C.,"THE 'NEW MYTHS' AND 'OLD REALITIES' OF NUCLEAR WAR." COM FUT USA+45 USSR WOR+45 INT/ORG NAT/G DOMIN LEGIT EXEC ATTIT PERCEPT ALL/VALS ...POLICY RELATIV PSY MYTH TREND 20. PAGE 161 A3280
FORCES COERCE ARMS/CONT NUC/PWR

S64
BUCHAN A.,"THE MULTILATERAL FORCE." EUR+WWI FUT USA+45 NAT/G LEGIT PWR SKILL...CONCPT OEEC MLF 20. PAGE 21 A0422
INT/ORG FORCES

S64
CRANE R.D.,"BASIC PRINCIPLES IN SOVIET SPACE LAW." FUT WOR+45 AIR INT/ORG DIPLOM DOMIN ARMS/CONT COERCE NUC/PWR PEACE ATTIT DRIVE PWR...INT/LAW METH/CNCPT NEW/IDEA OBS TREND GEN/LAWS VAL/FREE MARX/KARL 20. PAGE 32 A0659
COM LAW USSR SPACE

S64
DELGADO J.,"EL MOMENTO POLITICO HISPANOAMERICA." CHINA/COM FUT PANAMA USA+45 USSR INT/ORG NAT/G POL/PAR FORCES DOMIN REGION COERCE ATTIT ALL/VALS ...TRADIT CONCPT COLD/WAR 20. PAGE 36 A0728
L/A+17C EDU/PROP NAT/LISM

S64
DRAKE S.T.C.,"DEMOCRACY ON TRIAL IN AFRICA." EUR+WWI FUT USA+45 ECO/UNDEV INT/ORG NAT/G POL/PAR TOP/EX EDU/PROP LEGIT ATTIT ALL/VALS...POLICY TREND GEN/LAWS VAL/FREE 20. PAGE 38 A0785
AFR STERTYP

S64
GARMARNIKOW M.,"INFLUENCE-BUYING IN WEST AFRICA." COM FUT USSR INTELL NAT/G PLAN TEC/DEV ECO/TAC DOMIN EDU/PROP REGION NAT/LISM ATTIT DRIVE ALL/VALS SOVEREIGN...POLICY PSY SOC CONCPT TREND STERTYP WORK COLD/WAR 20. PAGE 51 A1049
AFR ECO/UNDEV FOR/AID SOCISM

S64
HABERLER G.,"INTEGRATION AND GROWTH OF THE WORLD ECONOMY IN HISTORICAL PERSPECTIVE." FUT WOR+45 WOR-45 ECO/DEV ECO/UNDEV...TIME/SEQ TREND VAL/FREE 20. PAGE 59 A1209
WEALTH INT/TRADE

S64
HICKEY D.,"THE PHILOSOPHICAL ARGUMENT FOR WORLD GOVERNMENT." WOR+45 SOCIETY ACT/RES PLAN LEGIT ADJUD PEACE PERCEPT PERSON ORD/FREE...HUM JURID PHIL/SCI METH/CNCPT CON/ANAL STERTYP GEN/LAWS TOT/POP 20. PAGE 65 A1327
FUT INT/ORG

S64
HOVET T. JR.,"THE ROLE OF AFRICA IN THE UNITED NATIONS." FUT WOR+45 NAT/G DELIB/GP DOMIN EDU/PROP LEGIT ORD/FREE PWR RESPECT SKILL...OBS TIME/SEQ TREND VAL/FREE UN 20. PAGE 68 A1398
AFR INT/ORG DIPLOM

S64
HUTCHINSON E.C.,"AMERICAN AID TO AFRICA." FUT USA+45 MARKET INT/ORG LOC/G NAT/G PUB/INST PLAN ECO/TAC ATTIT RIGID/FLEX...POLICY CONCPT TREND 20. PAGE 69 A1423
AFR ECO/UNDEV FOR/AID

S64
KHAN M.Z.,"ISLAM AND INTERNATIONAL RELATIONS." FUT WOR+45 LAW CULTURE SOCIETY NAT/G SECT DELIB/GP FORCES EDU/PROP ATTIT PERSON SUPEGO ALL/VALS ...POLICY PSY CONCPT MYTH HIST/WRIT GEN/LAWS. PAGE 78 A1608
ISLAM INT/ORG DIPLOM

S64
KOTANI H.,"PEACE-KEEPING: PROBLEMS FOR SMALLER COUNTRIES." FUT WOR+45 NAT/G ACT/RES PLAN DOMIN EDU/PROP COERCE ALL/VALS...POLICY UN TOT/POP 20. PAGE 82 A1673
INT/ORG FORCES

S64
KUNZ J.,"THE CHANGING SCIENCE OF INTERNATIONAL LAW." FUT WOR+45 WOR-45 INT/ORG LEGIT ORD/FREE ...JURID TIME/SEQ GEN/LAWS 20. PAGE 83 A1696
ADJUD CONCPT INT/LAW

S64
NEISSER H.,"THE EXTERNAL EQUILIBRIUM OF THE UNITED STATES ECONOMY." FUT USA+45 NAT/G ACT/RES PLAN ECO/TAC ATTIT WEALTH...METH/CNCPT GEN/METH VAL/FREE 20. PAGE 108 A2216
FINAN ECO/DEV BAL/PAY INT/TRADE

S64
REIDY J.W.,"LATIN AMERICA AND THE ATLANTIC TRIANGLE." EUR+WWI FUT USA+45 INT/ORG NAT/G REGION COERCE ORD/FREE PWR...TIME/SEQ VAL/FREE 20. PAGE 120 A2458
L/A+17C WEALTH POLICY

S64
SKUBISZEWSKI K.,"FORMS OF PARTICIPATION OF INTERNATIONAL ORGANIZATION IN THE LAW MAKING PROCESS." FUT WOR+45 NAT/G DELIB/GP DOMIN LEGIT KNOWL PWR...JURID TREND 20. PAGE 134 A2740
INT/ORG LAW INT/LAW

S64
WASKOW A.I.,"NEW ROADS TO A WORLD WITHOUT WAR." FUT WOR+45 CULTURE INTELL SOCIETY NAT/G DOMIN LEGIT EXEC COERCE PEACE ATTIT DISPL PERCEPT RIGID/FLEX ALL/VALS...POLICY RELATIV SOC NEW/IDEA 20. PAGE 161 A3288
INT/ORG FORCES

S64
ZARTMAN I.W.,"LES RELATIONS ENTRE LA FRANCE ET L'ALGERIA DEPUIS LES ACCORDS D'EVIAN." EUR+WWI FUT ISLAM CULTURE AGRI EXTR/IND FINAN INDUS POL/PAR DIPLOM ECO/TAC FOR/AID PEACE ATTIT DRIVE ALL/VALS ...TIME/SEQ VAL/FREE 20. PAGE 169 A3446
ECO/UNDEV ALGERIA FRANCE

B65
PEACE RESEARCH ABSTRACTS. FUT WOR+45 R+D INT/ORG NAT/G PLAN TEC/DEV BAL/PWR DIPLOM FOR/AID NUC/PWR HEALTH. PAGE 4 A0072
BIBLIOG/A PEACE ARMS/CONT WAR

B65
CALLEO D.P.,EUROPE'S FUTURE: THE GRAND ALTERNATIVES. UK INT/ORG DIPLOM PWR SOVEREIGN ...CONCPT IDEA/COMP NAT/COMP BIBLIOG 20 EEC EUROPE DEGAULLE/C NATO. PAGE 23 A0468
FUT EUR+WWI FEDERAL NAT/LISM

B65
LARUS J.,FROM COLLECTIVE SECURITY TO PREVENTIVE DIPLOMACY. FUT FORCES PROB/SOLV DEBATE AGREE COERCE WAR PWR...ANTHOL 20 LEAGUE/NAT UN. PAGE 85 A1736
INT/ORG PEACE DIPLOM ORD/FREE

B65
MERKL P.H.,GERMANY: YESTERDAY AND TOMORROW. GERMANY POL/PAR PLAN DIPLOM LEAD FEDERAL 19/20. PAGE 100 A2043
NAT/G FUT

B65
MIDDLETON D.,CRISIS IN THE WEST. EUR+WWI FUT WOR+45 CHIEF PLAN ECO/TAC LEAD REGION NUC/PWR NAT/LISM MARXISM 20 COLD/WAR NATO EEC. PAGE 101 A2068
INT/ORG DIPLOM NAT/G POLICY

B65
US SENATE COMM AERO SPACE SCI,INTERNATIONAL COOPERATION AND ORGANIZATION FOR OUTER SPACE. FUT USA+45 WOR+45 PROF/ORG VOL/ASSN CONSULT DELIB/GP PLAN TEC/DEV ARMS/CONT GP/REL PEACE 20 UN NASA. PAGE 155 A3167
DIPLOM SPACE R+D NAT/G

S65
BROWN S.,"AN ALTERNATIVE TO THE GRAND DESIGN." EUR+WWI FUT USA+45 INT/ORG NAT/G EX/STRUC FORCES CREATE BAL/PWR DOMIN RIGID/FLEX ORD/FREE PWR ...NEW/IDEA RECORD EEC NATO 20. PAGE 20 A0407
VOL/ASSN CONCPT DIPLOM

S65
TURNER F.C.,"THE IMPLICATIONS OF DEMOGRAPHIC CHANGE FOR NATIONALISM AND INTERNATIONALISM." FUT WOR+45 NAT/LISM AGE SEX CONCPT. PAGE 146 A2980
SOCIETY EDU/PROP DIPLOM ORD/FREE

B66
AMERICAN ASSEMBLY COLUMBIA U,A WORLD OF NUCLEAR POWERS? FUT WOR+45 ECO/DEV BAL/PWR ECO/TAC CONTROL RISK EFFICIENCY ATTIT PWR...METH/COMP ANTHOL 20. PAGE 7 A0137
NUC/PWR DIPLOM TEC/DEV ARMS/CONT

B66
HALPERIN M.H.,CHINA AND NUCLEAR PROLIFERATION (PAMPHLET). CHINA/COM FUT INDIA USA+45 USSR ARMS/CONT WAR 20 CHINJAP. PAGE 60 A1239
NUC/PWR FORCES POLICY DIPLOM

B66
INTL ATOMIC ENERGY AGENCY,INTERNATIONAL CONVENTIONS ON CIVIL LIABILITY FOR NUCLEAR DAMAGE. FUT WOR+45 ADJUD WAR COST PEACE SOVEREIGN...JURID 20. PAGE 71 A1462
DIPLOM INT/ORG DELIB/GP NUC/PWR

B66
LENGYEL E.,AFRICA: PAST, PRESENT, AND FUTURE. FUT SOUTH/AFR COLONIAL RACE/REL SOVEREIGN...GEOG AUD/VIS CHARTS T 20 CONGO/LEOP NEGRO. PAGE 87 A1771
AFR CONSTN ECO/UNDEV

B66
THOMPSON J.H.,MODERNIZATION OF THE ARAB WORLD. FUT ISRAEL STRUCT ECO/UNDEV DIPLOM INGP/REL ATTIT ...CENSUS ANTHOL 20 ARABS. PAGE 143 A2926
ADJUST ISLAM PROB/SOLV NAT/COMP

B66
UNITED NATIONS,INTERNATIONAL SPACE BIBLIOGRAPHY. FUT INT/ORG TEC/DEV DIPLOM ARMS/CONT NUC/PWR ...JURID SOC UN. PAGE 149 A3037
BIBLIOG SPACE PEACE R+D

B66
US SENATE COMM AERO SPACE SCI,SOVIET SPACE PROGRAMS, 1962-65; GOALS AND PURPOSES, ACHIEVEMENTS, PLANS, AND INTERNATIONAL IMPLICATIONS. USA+45 USSR R+D FORCES PLAN EDU/PROP PRESS ADJUD ARMS/CONT ATTIT MARXISM. PAGE 155 A3168
CONSULT SPACE FUT DIPLOM

L66
CHENERY H.B.,"FOREIGN ASSISTANCE AND ECONOMIC DEVELOPMENT" FUT WOR+45 NAT/G DIPLOM GIVE PRODUC
FOR/AID EFFICIENCY

...METH/CNCPT CHARTS 20. PAGE 26 A0526 — ECO/UNDEV TEC/DEV

S66
DUROSELLE J.B.,"THE FUTURE OF THE ATLANTIC COMMUNITY." EUR+WWI USA+45 USSR NAT/G CAP/ISM REGION DETER NUC/PWR ATTIT MARXISM...INT/LAW 20 NATO. PAGE 40 A0811 — FUT DIPLOM MYTH POLICY

S66
ORVIK N.,"NATO: THE ROLE OF THE SMALL MEMBERS." EUR+WWI FUT USA+45 CONSULT FORCES PROB/SOLV ARMS/CONT DETER NUC/PWR PWR 20 NATO. PAGE 112 A2298 — NAT/G DIPLOM INT/ORG POLICY

C66
BLAISDELL D.C.,"INTERNATIONAL ORGANIZATION." FUT WOR+45 ECO/DEV DELIB/GP FORCES EFFICIENCY PEACE ORD/FREE...INT/LAW 20 UN LEAGUE/NAT NATO. PAGE 15 A0304 — BIBLIOG INT/ORG DIPLOM ARMS/CONT

B67
BARANSON J.,TECHNOLOGY FOR UNDERDEVELOPED AREAS: AN ANNOTATED BIBLIOGRAPHY. FUT WOR+45 CULTURE INDUS INT/ORG CREATE PROB/SOLV INT/TRADE EDU/PROP AUTOMAT ...CONCPT METH. PAGE 11 A0218 — BIBLIOG/A ECO/UNDEV TEC/DEV R+D

B67
MCCLINTOCK R.,THE MEANING OF LIMITED WAR. FUT WOR+45 NAT/G FORCES GUERRILLA REV...POLICY SAMP/SIZ TREND NAT/COMP 45 COLD/WAR. PAGE 97 A1999 — WAR NUC/PWR BAL/PWR DIPLOM

B67
MURTY B.S.,PROPAGANDA AND WORLD PUBLIC ORDER. FUT WOR+45 COM/IND INT/ORG PROB/SOLV ATTIT KNOWL ORD/FREE...POLICY UN. PAGE 106 A2183 — EDU/PROP DIPLOM CONTROL JURID

L67
BODENHEIMER S.J.,"THE 'POLITICAL UNION' DEBATE IN EUROPE* A CASE STUDY IN INTERGOVERNMENTAL DIPLOMACY." EUR+WWI FUT NAT/G FORCES PLAN DEBATE SOVEREIGN...CONCPT PREDICT EEC NATO. PAGE 16 A0326 — DIPLOM REGION INT/ORG

L67
GRAUBARD S.R.,"TOWARD THE YEAR 2000: WORK IN PROGRESS." FUT ACADEM SECT DELIB/GP DIPLOM EDU/PROP AGE/Y PERSON ROLE...PSY ANTHOL. PAGE 55 A1131 — PREDICT PROB/SOLV SOCIETY CULTURE

S67
GRIFFITHS F.,"THE POLITICAL SIDE OF 'DISARMAMENT'." FUT WOR+45 NUC/PWR NAT/LISM PEACE...NEW/IDEA PREDICT METH/COMP GEN/LAWS 20. PAGE 57 A1164 — ARMS/CONT DIPLOM

S67
HAZARD J.N.,"POST-DISARMAMENT INTERNATIONAL LAW." FUT USSR WOR+45 INT/ORG DELIB/GP FORCES DETER EQUILIB SOVEREIGN MARXISM 20 UN. PAGE 63 A1301 — INT/LAW ARMS/CONT PWR PLAN

S67
HULL E.W.S.,"THE POLITICAL OCEAN." FUT UNIV WOR+45 EXTR/IND R+D VOL/ASSN PLAN BAL/PWR ECO/TAC PEACE WEALTH 20 UN. PAGE 69 A1414 — DIPLOM ECO/UNDEV INT/ORG INT/LAW

S67
JACKSON W.G.F.,"NUCLEAR PROLIFERATION AND THE GREAT POWERS." FUT UK WOR+45 INT/ORG DOMIN ARMS/CONT DETER ORD/FREE PACIFIST. PAGE 72 A1480 — NUC/PWR ATTIT BAL/PWR NAT/LISM

S67
KELLY F.K.,"A PROPOSAL FOR AN ANNUAL REPORT ON THE STATE OF MANKIND." FUT INTELL COM/IND INT/ORG CREATE PROB/SOLV PERS/REL...CONCPT 20 UN. PAGE 77 A1579 — SOCIETY UNIV ATTIT NEW/IDEA

S67
KRISTENSEN T.,"THE SOUTH AS AN INDUSTRIAL POWER." FUT WOR+45 ECO/DEV AGRI INDUS TEC/DEV...CENSUS TREND CHARTS 20. PAGE 82 A1686 — DIPLOM ECO/UNDEV PREDICT PRODUC

S67
SCHACTER O.,"SCIENTIFIC ADVANCES AND INTERNATIONAL LAWMAKING." FUT R+D PLAN PROB/SOLV CONFER CONTROL ...POLICY PREDICT 20 UN. PAGE 128 A2617 — TEC/DEV INT/LAW INT/ORG ACT/RES

S67
SHARP G.,"THE NEED OF A FUNCTIONAL SUBSTITUTE FOR WAR." FUT UNIV WOR+45 CULTURE SOCIETY INT/ORG CONSULT DELIB/GP ACT/RES CREATE BAL/PWR CONFER ARMS/CONT NUC/PWR 20. PAGE 132 A2696 — PEACE WAR DIPLOM PROB/SOLV

S67
VLASCIC I.A.,"THE SPACE TREATY* A PRELIMINARY EVALUATION." FUT USSR WOR+45 R+D ACT/RES TEC/DEV DIPLOM CONFER ARMS/CONT PEACE...PREDICT UN TREATY. PAGE 159 A3245 — SPACE INT/LAW INT/ORG NEUTRAL

FUTURE....SEE FUT

G

GABLE R.W. A0934

GABON....SEE ALSO AFR

S63
ANGUILE G.,"CIVILISATION DU PLAN DANS L'EUROPE ET L'AFRIQUE DE DEMAIN." AFR EUR+WWI GABON ECO/DEV FINAN MARKET DELIB/GP ECO/TAC WEALTH...TREND 20. PAGE 8 A0163 — ECO/UNDEV PLAN INT/TRADE

B64
WITHERELL J.W.,OFFICIAL PUBLICATIONS OF FRENCH EQUATORIAL AFRICA, FRENCH CAMEROONS, AND TOGO, 1946-1958 (PAMPHLET). CAMEROON CHAD FRANCE GABON TOGO LAW ECO/UNDEV EXTR/IND INT/TRADE...GEOG HEAL 20. PAGE 165 A3370 — BIBLIOG/A AFR NAT/G ADMIN

GALBRAITH J.K. A1030

GALBRAITH, JOHN KENNETH....SEE GALBRTH/JK

GALBRTH/JK....JOHN KENNETH GALBRAITH

GALLAGHER M.P. A1031

GALLOIS P. A1032

GALLOWAY E. A1033

GALLOWAY G.B. A1034

GALTUNG J. A1035

GAMBIA....SEE ALSO AFR

B63
WALKER A.A.,OFFICIAL PUBLICATIONS OF SIERRA LEONE AND GAMBIA. GAMBIA SIER/LEONE UK LAW CONSTN LEGIS PLAN BUDGET DIPLOM...SOC SAMP CON/ANAL 20. PAGE 160 A3262 — BIBLIOG NAT/G COLONIAL ADMIN

GAMBLE....SPECULATION ON AN UNCERTAIN EVENT

B67
JOHNSON A.M.,BOSTON CAPITALISTS AND WESTERN RAILROADS: A STUDY IN THE NINETEENTH CENTURY RAILROAD INVESTMENT PROCESS. CREATE BARGAIN INT/TRADE GAMBLE KNOWL 19 BOSTON. PAGE 74 A1519 — FINAN DIST/IND CAP/ISM ECO/UNDEV

GAMBLING....SEE RISK, GAMBLE

GAME....GAME THEORY AND DECISION THEORY IN MODELS

S57
KAPLAN M.,"BALANCE OF POWER, BIPOLARITY AND OTHER MODELS OF INTERNATIONAL SYSTEMS" (BMR)" ACT/RES BAL/PWR...PHIL/SCI METH 20. PAGE 76 A1559 — DIPLOM GAME METH/CNCPT SIMUL

B61
KNORR K.E.,THE INTERNATIONAL SYSTEM. FUT SOCIETY INT/ORG NAT/G PLAN BAL/PWR DIPLOM WAR PWR ...DECISION METH/CNCPT CONT/OBS GAME METH UN 20. PAGE 81 A1655 — ACT/RES SIMUL ECO/UNDEV

B61
ROSENAU J.N.,INTERNATIONAL POLITICS AND FOREIGN POLICY: A READER IN RESEARCH AND THEORY. ELITES ATTIT SOVEREIGN...DECISION CHARTS HYPO/EXP GAME SIMUL ANTHOL BIBLIOG METH 20. PAGE 124 A2531 — ACT/RES DIPLOM CONCPT POLICY

B63
THORELLI H.B.,INTOP: INTERNATIONAL OPERATIONS SIMULATION: PLAYER'S MANUAL. BRAZIL FINAN OP/RES ADMIN GP/REL INGP/REL PRODUC PERCEPT...DECISION MGT EEC. PAGE 144 A2935 — GAME INT/TRADE EDU/PROP LG/CO

S64
BEIM D.,"THE COMMUNIST BLOC AND THE FOREIGN-AID GAME." WOR+45 NAT/G PLAN ROUTINE ATTIT KNOWL ORD/FREE...DECISION QUANT CONT/OBS TIME/SEQ CHARTS GAME SIMUL COLD/WAR 20. PAGE 12 A0252 — COM ECO/UNDEV ECO/TAC FOR/AID

S67
SUINN R.M.,"THE DISARMAMENT FANTASY* PSYCHOLOGICAL FACTORS THAT MAY PRODUCE WARFARE." DIPLOM RISK ARMS/CONT DETER ANOMIE PERSON GAME. PAGE 140 A2860 — DECISION NUC/PWR WAR PSY

GAMER R.E. A1036

GANDHI/I....MME. INDIRA GANDHI

GANDHI/M....MAHATMA GANDHI

B54
SHARMA J.S.,MAHATMA GANDHI: A DESCRIPTIVE BIBLIOGRAPHY. INDIA S/ASIA PROB/SOLV DIPLOM COLONIAL WAR NAT/LISM PEACE ATTIT PERSON SOVEREIGN ...CONCPT 20 GANDHI/M. PAGE 132 A2695 — BIBLIOG/A BIOG CHIEF LEAD

S59
KRIPALANI A.J.B.,"FOR PRINCIPLED NEUTRALITY." CHINA/COM INDIA S/ASIA PLAN ECO/TAC RIGID/FLEX MORAL PWR...MYSTIC SOC RECORD 20 GANDHI/M. PAGE 82 A1684 — ATTIT FOR/AID DIPLOM

B60
MC CLELLAN G.S.,INDIA. CHINA/COM INDIA CONSTN ELITES STRATA AGRI POL/PAR FOR/AID ARMS/CONT REV MARXISM...CENSUS BIBLIOG 20 COLD/WAR GANDHI/M — DIPLOM NAT/G SOCIETY

ECO/UNDEV PRESS LEAD ATTIT...GEOG SOC 20. PAGE 24 A0482 L/A+17C DIPLOM N

CORDIER H.,BIBLIOTECA SINICA. SOCIETY STRUCT SECT DIPLOM COLONIAL...GEOG SOC CON/ANAL. PAGE 30 A0618 BIBLIOG/A NAT/G CULTURE ASIA N

KAPLAN L.,REVIEW INDEX. USA+45 USA-45 FINAN INDUS LABOR RACE/REL...GEOG PSY SOC 20. PAGE 76 A1558 BIBLIOG PROF/ORG ECO/DEV DIPLOM N

KYRIAK T.E.,EAST EUROPE: BIBLIOGRAPHY--INDEX TO US JPRS RESEARCH TRANSLATIONS. ALBANIA BULGARIA COM CZECHOSLVK HUNGARY POLAND ROMANIA AGRI EXTR/IND FINAN SERV/IND INT/TRADE WEAPON...GEOG MGT SOC 20. PAGE 83 A1701 BIBLIOG/A PRESS MARXISM INDUS B00

MORRIS H.C.,THE HISTORY OF COLONIZATION. WOR+45 WOR-45 ECO/DEV ECO/UNDEV INT/ORG ACT/RES PLAN ECO/TAC LEGIT ROUTINE COERCE ATTIT DRIVE ALL/VALS ...GEOG TREND 19. PAGE 105 A2148 DOMIN SOVEREIGN COLONIAL B01

GRIFFIN A.P.C.,LIST OF BOOKS ON SAMOA (PAMPHLET). GERMANY S/ASIA UK USA-45 WOR-45 ECO/UNDEV REGION ALL/VALS ORD/FREE ALL/IDEOS...GEOG INT/LAW 19 SAMOA GUAM. PAGE 56 A1150 BIBLIOG/A COLONIAL DIPLOM B10

MENDELSSOHN S.,SOUTH AFRICAN BIBLIOGRAPHY (2 VOLS.). SOUTH/AFR EXTR/IND LABOR SECT DIPLOM INT/TRADE COLONIAL RACE/REL DISCRIM...GEOG 20. PAGE 99 A2038 BIBLIOG/A AFR NAT/G NAT/LISM B14

HARRIS N.D.,INTERVENTION AND COLONIZATION IN AFRICA. BELGIUM FRANCE GERMANY MOD/EUR PORTUGAL UK ECO/UNDEV BAL/PWR DOMIN CONTROL PWR...GEOG 19/20. PAGE 62 A1267 AFR COLONIAL DIPLOM N19

FRANCK P.G.,AFGHANISTAN BETWEEN EAST AND WEST: THE ECONOMICS OF COMPETITIVE COEXISTENCE (PAMPHLET). AFGHANISTN USA+45 USA-45 USSR INDUS ECO/TAC INT/TRADE CONTROL NEUTRAL ORD/FREE MARXISM...GEOG 20 UN. PAGE 48 A0977 FOR/AID PLAN DIPLOM ECO/UNDEV N19

SALKEVER L.R.,SUB-SAHARA AFRICA (PAMPHLET). AFR USSR EXTR/IND NAT/G SCHOOL DIPLOM COLONIAL WEALTH ...GEOG CHARTS 16/20. PAGE 127 A2594 ECO/UNDEV TEC/DEV TASK INT/TRADE N19

TAYLOR T.G.,CANADA'S ROLE IN GEOPOLITICS (PAMPHLET). CANADA FUT USSR COLONIAL REGION WEALTH ...CHARTS 20. PAGE 142 A2901 GEOG DIPLOM SOCIETY ECO/DEV L21

HALDEMAN E.,"SERIALS OF AN INTERNATIONAL CHARACTER." WOR-45 DIPLOM...ART/METH GEOG HEAL HUM INT/LAW JURID PSY SOC. PAGE 60 A1224 BIBLIOG PHIL/SCI B23

KADEN E.H.,DER POLITISCHE CHARAKTER DER FRANZOSISCHEN KULTURPROPAGANDA AM RHEIN. FRANCE MOD/EUR DOMIN PRESS...GEOG METH/COMP 20. PAGE 75 A1544 EDU/PROP ATTIT DIPLOM NAT/G B27

HARRIS N.D.,EUROPE AND AFRICA. BELGIUM FRANCE GERMANY MOD/EUR PORTUGAL UK ECO/UNDEV BAL/PWR PWR ...GEOG 19/20. PAGE 62 A1268 AFR COLONIAL DIPLOM B28

HALL W.P.,EMPIRE TO COMMONWEALTH. FUT WOR-45 CONSTN ECO/DEV ECO/UNDEV INT/ORG PROVS PLAN DIPLOM EDU/PROP ADMIN COLONIAL PEACE PERSON ALL/VALS ...POLICY GEOG SOC OBS RECORD TREND CMN/WLTH PARLIAMENT 19/20. PAGE 60 A1229 VOL/ASSN NAT/G UK B28

STUART G.H.,LATIN AMERICA AND THE UNITED STATES. USA-45 ECO/UNDEV INT/ORG NAT/G POL/PAR PLAN DOMIN EDU/PROP COLONIAL REGION COERCE ATTIT ALL/VALS ...POLICY GEOG TREND 19/20. PAGE 139 A2853 L/A+17C DIPLOM B29

BOUDET P.,BIBLIOGRAPHIE DE L'INDOCHINE FRANCAISE. S/ASIA VIETNAM SECT...GEOG LING 20. PAGE 17 A0344 BIBLIOG ADMIN COLONIAL DIPLOM B29

CONWELL-EVANS T.P.,THE LEAGUE COUNCIL IN ACTION. EUR+WWI TURKEY UK USSR WOR-45 INT/ORG FORCES JUDGE ECO/TAC EDU/PROP LEGIT ROUTINE ARMS/CONT COERCE ATTIT PWR...MAJORIT GEOG JURID CONCPT LEAGUE/NAT TOT/POP VAL/FREE TUNIS 20. PAGE 30 A0605 DELIB/GP INT/LAW B29

DE REPARAZ G.,GEOGRAFIA Y POLITICA. CHILE SPAIN USSR NAT/G DIPLOM REV MARXISM...POLICY 19/20. PAGE 35 A0709 GEOG MOD/EUR B29

PRATT I.A.,MODERN EGYPT: A LIST OF REFERENCES TO MATERIAL IN THE NEW YORK PUBLIC LIBRARY. UAR BIBLIOG ISLAM

ECO/UNDEV...GEOG JURID SOC LING 20. PAGE 117 A2407 DIPLOM NAT/G B32

BRYCE J.,THE HOLY ROMAN EMPIRE. GERMANY ITALY MOD/EUR CULTURE SOCIETY STRUCT INT/ORG NAT/G SECT DIPLOM DOMIN WAR SUPEGO ALL/VALS SOVEREIGN...GEOG SOC TIME/SEQ CHARTS STERTYP. PAGE 20 A0413 CHRIST-17C NAT/LISM B32

EAGLETON C.,INTERNATIONAL GOVERNMENT. BRAZIL FRANCE GERMANY ITALY UK USSR WOR-45 DELIB/GP TOP/EX PLAN ECO/TAC EDU/PROP LEGIT ADJUD REGION ARMS/CONT COERCE ATTIT PWR...GEOG MGT VAL/FREE LEAGUE/NAT 20. PAGE 40 A0816 INT/ORG JURID DIPLOM INT/LAW B35

BUREAU ECONOMIC RES LAT AM,THE ECONOMIC LITERATURE OF LATIN AMERICA (2 VOLS.). CHRIST-17C AGRI DIST/IND EXTR/IND INDUS WORKER INT/TRADE...GEOG 16/20. PAGE 21 A0433 BIBLIOG L/A+17C ECO/UNDEV FINAN B35

SIMONDS F.H.,THE GREAT POWERS IN WORLD POLITICS. FRANCE GERMANY UK WOR-45 INT/ORG NAT/G ARMS/CONT PEACE FASCISM...POLICY GEOG 20 DEPRESSION NAZI. PAGE 133 A2718 DIPLOM WEALTH WAR B35

WEINBERG A.K.,MANIFEST DESTINY: A STUDY OF NATIONALIST EXPANSIONISM IN AMERICAN HISTORY. USA+45 USA-45 FORCES DIPLOM COLONIAL WAR ATTIT 18/20 INTERVENT. PAGE 162 A3305 NAT/LISM GEOG COERCE NAT/G S35

MCMAHON A.H.,"INTERNATIONAL BOUNDARIES." WOR-45 INT/ORG NAT/G LEGIT SKILL...CHARTS GEN/LAWS 20. PAGE 98 A2017 GEOG VOL/ASSN INT/LAW B36

ROBINSON H.,DEVELOPMENT OF THE BRITISH EMPIRE. WOR-45 CULTURE SOCIETY STRUCT ECO/DEV ECO/UNDEV INT/ORG VOL/ASSN FORCES CREATE PLAN DOMIN EDU/PROP ADMIN COLONIAL PWR WEALTH...POLICY GEOG CHARTS CMN/WLTH 16/20. PAGE 122 A2503 NAT/G HIST/WRIT UK B37

UNION OF SOUTH AFRICA,REPORT CONCERNING ADMINISTRATION OF SOUTH WEST AFRICA (6 VOLS.). SOUTH/AFR INDUS PUB/INST FORCES LEGIS BUDGET DIPLOM EDU/PROP ADJUD CT/SYS...GEOG CHARTS 20 AFRICA/SW LEAGUE/NAT. PAGE 148 A3028 NAT/G ADMIN COLONIAL CONSTN B38

COLBY C.C.,GEOGRAPHICAL ASPECTS OF INTERNATIONAL RELATIONS. WOR-45 ECO/DEV ECO/UNDEV AGRI EXTR/IND INDUS MARKET R+D INT/ORG NAT/G TEC/DEV ECO/TAC INT/TRADE NAT/LISM WEALTH...METH/CNCPT CHARTS GEN/LAWS 20. PAGE 28 A0565 PLAN GEOG DIPLOM B39

KERNER R.J.,NORTHEAST ASIA: A SELECTED BIBLIOGRAPHY (2 VOLS.). KOREA RUSSIA NAT/G DIPLOM...GEOG 19/20 CHINJAP. PAGE 78 A1599 BIBLIOG ASIA SOCIETY CULTURE B40

BOGGS S.W.,INTERNATIONAL BOUNDARIES. WOR-45 SOCIETY ECO/DEV INT/ORG NAT/G NEIGH LEGIT PERSON ORD/FREE PWR...POLICY GEOG MYTH LEAGUE/NAT 20. PAGE 16 A0329 ATTIT CONCPT NAT/LISM B40

BROWN A.D.,PANAMA CANAL AND PANAMA CANAL ZONE: A SELECTED LIST OF REFERENCES. PANAMA NAT/G SCHOOL DIPLOM HEALTH...GEOG SOC 20 CANAL/ZONE. PAGE 19 A0397 BIBLIOG/A ECO/UNDEV B40

WOLFERS A.,BRITAIN AND FRANCE BETWEEN TWO WORLD WARS. FRANCE UK INT/ORG NAT/G PLAN BARGAIN ECO/TAC AGREE ISOLAT ALL/IDEOS...DECISION GEOG 20 TREATY VERSAILLES INTERVENT. PAGE 166 A3380 DIPLOM WAR POLICY B41

GRISMER R.,A NEW BIBLIOGRAPHY OF THE LITERATURES OF SPAIN AND SPANISH AMERICA. CHRIST-17C MOD/EUR PRE/AMER SPAIN CULTURE DIPLOM EDU/PROP...ART/METH GEOG HUM PHIL/SCI 20. PAGE 57 A1165 BIBLIOG LAW NAT/G ECO/UNDEV B43

BROWN A.D.,BRITISH POSSESSIONS IN THE CARIBBEAN AREA: A SELECTED LIST OF REFERENCES. UK NAT/G DIPLOM...GEOG 20 CARIBBEAN. PAGE 20 A0398 BIBLIOG COLONIAL ECO/UNDEV L/A+17C B43

GRIERSON P.,BOOKS ON SOVIET RUSSIA 1917-42: A BIBLIOGRAPHY AND A GUIDE TO READING. USSR CULTURE ELITES NAT/G PLAN DIPLOM REV...GEOG 20. PAGE 56 A1148 BIBLIOG/A COM MARXISM LEAD B44

FULLER G.H.,TURKEY: A SELECTED LIST OF REFERENCES. ISLAM TURKEY CULTURE ECO/UNDEV AGRI DIPLOM NAT/LISM CONSERVE...GEOG HUM INT/LAW SOC 7/20 MAPS. PAGE 50 A1024 BIBLIOG/A ALL/VALS B44

SHELBY C.,LATIN AMERICAN PERIODICALS CURRENTLY RECEIVED IN THE LIBRARY OF CONGRESS AND IN LIBRARY OF DEPARTMENT OF AGRICULTURE. SOCIETY AGRI INDUS LABOR POL/PAR INT/TRADE...GEOG SOC 20. PAGE 132 A2699 BIBLIOG ECO/UNDEV CULTURE L/A+17C

B44
WEIGERT H.W.,COMPASS OF THE WORLD, A SYMPOSIUM ON POLITICAL GEOGRAPHY. EUR+WWI FUT MOD/EUR S/ASIA USA-45 WOR-45 SOCIETY AGRI INDUS MARKET ECO/TAC INT/TRADE PERSON 20. PAGE 162 A3298
TEC/DEV CAP/ISM RUSSIA GEOG

C44
VAN VALKENBURG S.,"ELEMENTS OF POLITICAL GEOGRAPHY." FRANCE COM/IND INDUS NAT/G SECT RACE/REL...LING TREND GEN/LAWS BIBLIOG 20. PAGE 158 A3215
GEOG DIPLOM COLONIAL

B45
HILL N.,CLAIMS TO TERRITORY IN INTERNATIONAL LAW AND RELATIONS. WOR-45 NAT/G DOMIN EDU/PROP LEGIT REGION ROUTINE ORD/FREE PWR WEALTH...GEOG INT/LAW JURID 20. PAGE 65 A1332
INT/ORG ADJUD SOVEREIGN

B45
PERAZA SARAUSA F.,BIBLIOGRAFIAS CUBANAS. CUBA CULTURE ECO/UNDEV AGRI EDU/PROP PRESS CIVMIL/REL ...POLICY GEOG PHIL/SCI BIOG 19/20. PAGE 115 A2353
BIBLIOG/A L/A+17C NAT/G DIPLOM

B45
STRAUSZ-HUPE R.,THE BALANCE OF TOMORROW: POWER AND FOREIGN POLICY IN THE UNITED STATES. FUT USA+45 ECO/DEV EXTR/IND INT/ORG FORCES BAL/PWR REGION NUC/PWR...GEOG CHARTS 20 COLD/WAR EUROPE/W. PAGE 139 A2845
DIPLOM PWR POLICY WAR

B45
WOOLBERT R.G.,FOREIGN AFFAIRS BIBLIOGRAPHY, 1932-1942. INT/ORG SECT INT/TRADE COLONIAL RACE/REL NAT/LISM...GEOG INT/LAW GOV/COMP IDEA/COMP 20. PAGE 167 A3393
BIBLIOG/A DIPLOM WAR

B46
GRIFFIN G.G.,A GUIDE TO MANUSCRIPTS RELATING TO AMERICAN HISTORY IN BRITISH DEPOSITORIES. CANADA IRELAND MOD/EUR UK USA-45 LAW DIPLOM ADMIN COLONIAL WAR NAT/LISM SOVEREIGN...GEOG INT/LAW 15/19 CMN/WLTH. PAGE 56 A1159
BIBLIOG/A ALL/VALS NAT/G

N46
HOBBS C.C.,SOUTHEAST ASIA, 1935-45: A SELECTED LIST OF REFERENCE BOOKS (PAMPHLET). S/ASIA AGRI INDUS NAT/G SECT DIPLOM WAR...ART/METH GEOG SOC LING 20. PAGE 65 A1346
BIBLIOG/A CULTURE HABITAT

B48
FLOREN LOZANO L.,BIBLIOGRAFIA DE LA BIBLIOGRAFIA DOMINICANA. DOMIN/REP NAT/G DIPLOM EDU/PROP CIVMIL/REL...POLICY ART/METH GEOG PHIL/SCI HIST/WRIT 20. PAGE 47 A0952
BIBLIOG/A BIOG L/A+17C CULTURE

B48
KULISCHER E.M.,EUROPE ON THE MOVE: WAR AND POPULATION CHANGES, 1917-1947. COM EUR+WWI FUT GERMANY USSR DIST/IND PLAN INT/TRADE CONTROL WAR DRIVE...CENSUS TREND COLD/WAR 20. PAGE 82 A1690
ECO/TAC GEOG

B49
BEHRENDT R.F.,MODERN LATIN AMERICA IN SOCIAL SCIENCE LITERATURE. STRUCT ECO/UNDEV SCHOOL DIPLOM INT/TRADE EDU/PROP...GEOG 20. PAGE 12 A0250
BIBLIOG/A SOC L/A+17C

B49
PARMELEE M.,GEO-ECONOMIC REGIONAL AND WORLD FEDERATION. FUT WOR+45 WOR-45 SOCIETY VOL/ASSN PLAN ...METH/CNCPT SIMUL GEN/METH TOT/POP 20. PAGE 114 A2335
INT/ORG GEOG REGION

B49
US DEPARTMENT OF STATE,SOVIET BIBLIOGRAPHY (PAMPHLET). CHINA/COM COM USSR LAW AGRI INT/ORG ECO/TAC EDU/PROP...POLICY GEOG 20. PAGE 151 A3084
BIBLIOG/A MARXISM CULTURE DIPLOM

B50
BEHRENDT R.F.,MODERN LATIN AMERICA IN SOCIAL SCIENCE LITERATURE (SUPPLEMENTS I AND II). STRUCT ECO/UNDEV SCHOOL DIPLOM INT/TRADE...GEOG 20. PAGE 12 A0251
BIBLIOG/A SOC L/A+17C

B50
DAVIS E.P.,PERIODICALS OF INTERNATIONAL ORGANIZATIONS; PART I, THE UN AND SPECIALIZED AGENCIES; PART II, INTER-AMERICAN ORGS. CULTURE AGRI FINAN INDUS LABOR INT/TRADE...GEOG HEAL STAT 20 UN OAS UNESCO. PAGE 34 A0689
BIBLIOG/A INT/ORG DIPLOM L/A+17C

B51
BISSAINTHE M.,DICTIONNAIRE DE BIBLIOGRAPHIE HAITIENNE. HAITI ELITES AGRI LEGIS DIPLOM INT/TRADE WRITING ORD/FREE CATHISM...ART/METH GEOG 19/20 NEGRO TREATY. PAGE 15 A0295
BIBLIOG L/A+17C SOCIETY NAT/G

B51
RAPPAPORT A.,THE BRITISH PRESS AND WILSONIAN NEUTRALITY. UK WOR-45 SEA POL/PAR WAR CHOOSE PEACE ATTIT PERCEPT...GEOG 20 WILSON/W. PAGE 119 A2446
PRESS DIPLOM NEUTRAL POLICY

B51
US DEPARTMENT OF STATE,LIVRES AMERICAINS TRADUITS EN FRANCAIS ET LIVRES FRANCAIS SUR LES ETATS-UNIS D'AMERIQUE (2ND ED.). FRANCE USA+45 SECT DIPLOM EDU/PROP LEISURE...ART/METH GEOG HUM 20. PAGE 151 A3086
BIBLIOG/A SOC

C51
BEST H.,"THE SOVIET STATE AND ITS INCEPTION." USSR CULTURE INDUS DIPLOM WEALTH...GEOG SOC BIBLIOG 20. PAGE 14 A0281
COM GEN/METH REV MARXISM

B52
SURANYI-UNGER T.,COMPARATIVE ECONOMIC SYSTEMS. FINAN MARKET DIPLOM PRICE WEALTH...GEOG SOC BIBLIOG METH T 20. PAGE 140 A2865
LAISSEZ PLAN ECO/DEV IDEA/COMP

B52
UN DEPT. SOC. AFF.,PRELIMINARY REPORT ON THE WORLD SOCIAL SITUATION. ISLAM L/A+17C WOR+45 STRATA AGRI EXTR/IND INDUS INT/ORG SCHOOL ADMIN...GEOG SOC TREND UNESCO WORK FAO 20. PAGE 147 A2998
R+D HEALTH FOR/AID

B52
UNESCO,THESES DE SCIENCES SOCIALES: CATALOGUE ANALYTIQUE INTERNATIONAL DE THESES INEDITES DE DOCTORAT, 1940-1950. INT/ORG DIPLOM EDU/PROP...GEOG INT/LAW MGT PSY SOC 20. PAGE 147 A3015
BIBLIOG ACADEM WRITING

B54
GIRAUD A.,CIVILISATION ET PRODUCTIVITE. UNIV INDUS WORKER DIPLOM REV INCOME UTOPIA...GEOG 20. PAGE 53 A1076
SOCIETY PRODUC ROLE

B54
WHITAKER A.P.,THE WESTERN HEMISPHERE IDEA. USA+45 USA-45 CONSTN INT/ORG NAT/G DIPLOM SOVEREIGN...GEOG TIME/SEQ OAS 19/20 MONROE/DOC. PAGE 164 A3331
L/A+17C CONCPT REGION

B55
BUSS C.,THE FAR EAST: A HISTORY OF RECENT AND CONTEMPORARY INTERNATIONAL RELATIONS IN EAST ASIA. WOR+45 WOR-45 CONSTN INT/ORG NAT/G BAL/PWR ATTIT PWR SOVEREIGN...GEOG JURID SOC CONCPT METH/CNCPT 19/20. PAGE 22 A0449
ASIA DIPLOM

B55
SEMJONOW J.M.,DIE FASCHISTISCHE GEOPOLITIK IM DIENSTE DES AMERIKANISCHEN IMPERIALISMUS. USA+45 USA-45 CAP/ISM PEACE ORD/FREE MARXISM SOCISM ...POLICY GEOG 20. PAGE 131 A2684
DIPLOM COERCE FASCISM WAR

B55
THOMPSON V.,MINORITY PROBLEMS IN SOUTHEAST ASIA. CAMBODIA CHINA/COM LAOS S/ASIA KIN NAT/G SECT PROB/SOLV EDU/PROP REGION GP/REL RACE/REL MARXISM ...SOC 20 BUDDHISM UN. PAGE 143 A2933
INGP/REL GEOG DIPLOM STRUCT

B55
TROTIER A.H.,DOCTORAL DISSERTATIONS ACCEPTED BY AMERICAN UNIVERSITIES 1954-55. SECT DIPLOM HEALTH ...ART/METH GEOG INT/LAW SOC LING CHARTS 20. PAGE 145 A2968
BIBLIOG ACADEM USA+45 WRITING

B56
CHANG C.J.,THE MINORITY GROUPS OF YUNN AN AND CHINESE POLITICAL EXPANSION INTO SOUTHEAST ASIA (DOCTORAL THESIS). ASIA CHINA/COM S/ASIA FORCES TEC/DEV DIPLOM EDU/PROP...GEOG BIBLIOG 20. PAGE 26 A0520
GP/REL REGION DOMIN MARXISM

B56
SPROUT H.,MAN-MILIEU RELATIONSHIP HYPOTHESES IN THE CONTEXT OF INTERNATIONAL POLITICS. UNIV PROB/SOLV BIO/SOC PERSON...DECISION GEOG SOC METH/CNCPT PREDICT 20. PAGE 136 A2792
HABITAT DIPLOM CONCPT DRIVE

B56
WOLFF R.L.,THE BALKANS IN OUR TIME. ALBANIA FUT MOD/EUR USSR YUGOSLAVIA CULTURE INT/ORG SECT DIPLOM EDU/PROP COERCE WAR ORD/FREE...CHARTS 4/20 BALKANS COMINFORM. PAGE 166 A3388
GEOG COM

B57
ALEXANDER L.M.,WORLD POLITICAL PATTERNS. NAT/G PROVS CAP/ISM DIPLOM COLONIAL NAT/LISM...POLICY GEOG CHARTS METH/COMP NAT/COMP 20. PAGE 5 A0111
CONTROL METH GOV/COMP

B57
BLOOMFIELD L.M.,EGYPT, ISRAEL AND THE GULF OF AQABA: IN INTERNATIONAL LAW. LAW NAT/G CONSULT FORCES PLAN ECO/TAC ROUTINE COERCE ATTIT DRIVE PERCEPT PERSON RIGID/FLEX LOVE PWR WEALTH...GEOG CONCPT MYTH TREND. PAGE 15 A0314
ISLAM INT/LAW UAR

B57
BYRNES R.F.,BIBLIOGRAPHY OF AMERICAN PUBLICATIONS ON EAST CENTRAL EUROPE, 1945-1957 (VOL. XXII). SECT DIPLOM EDU/PROP RACE/REL...ART/METH GEOG JURID SOC LING 20 JEWS. PAGE 23 A0462
BIBLIOG/A COM MARXISM NAT/G

B57
DRUCKER P.F.,AMERICA'S NEXT TWENTY YEARS. USA+45 DIST/IND ACADEM MUNIC SCHOOL DIPLOM ECO/TAC AUTOMAT HABITAT HEALTH...SOC/WK TREND 20 URBAN/RNWL PUB/TRANS. PAGE 39 A0788
WORKER FOR/AID CENSUS GEOG

B57
FURNISS E.S.,AMERICAN MILITARY POLICY: STRATEGIC ASPECTS OF WORLD POLITICAL GEOGRAPHY. COM EUR+WWI ISLAM L/A+17C USA+45 WOR+45 INT/ORG ACT/RES ARMS/CONT COERCE NUC/PWR ATTIT PWR...GEOG NEW/IDEA VAL/FREE COLD/WAR 20. PAGE 50 A1027
FORCES DIPLOM

B57
KISSINGER H.A.,NUCLEAR WEAPONS AND FOREIGN POLICY. FUT USA+45 WOR+45 INT/ORG FORCES ACT/RES TEC/DEV DIPLOM ARMS/CONT COERCE ATTIT KNOWL PWR...DECISION GEOG CHARTS 20. PAGE 80 A1640
PLAN DETER NUC/PWR

L57
FURNISS E.S.,"SOME PERSPECTIVES ON AMERICAN MILITARY ASSISTANCE." USA+45 WOR+45 ECO/UNDEV
FORCES FOR/AID

INT/ORG ECO/TAC ORD/FREE...GEOG TIME/SEQ TREND COLD/WAR 20. PAGE 50 A1028 — WEAPON

B58
INDIAN COUNCIL WORLD AFFAIRS,DEFENCE AND SECURITY IN THE INDIAN OCEAN AREA. INDIA S/ASIA CULTURE CONSULT DELIB/GP FORCES PROB/SOLV DIPLOM INT/TRADE 20 CMN/WLTH. PAGE 70 A1438 — GEOG HABITAT ECO/UNDEV ORD/FREE

B58
INSTITUTE MEDITERRANEAN AFF,THE PALESTINE REFUGEE PROBLEM. UAR WOR+45 INT/ORG PLAN PROB/SOLV PEACE ...POLICY GEOG STAT CHARTS 20 JEWS UN MIGRATION. PAGE 70 A1444 — STRANGE HABITAT GP/REL INGP/REL

B58
MACLES L.M.,LES SOURCES DU TRAVAIL BIBLIOGRAPHIQUE (3 VOLS.). FRANCE WOR+45 DIPLOM...GEOG PHIL/SCI SOC 20. PAGE 93 A1897 — BIBLIOG/A NAT/G HUM

B58
MANSERGH N.,COMMONWEALTH PERSPECTIVES. GHANA UK LAW VOL/ASSN CONFER HEALTH SOVEREIGN...GEOG CHARTS ANTHOL 20 CMN/WLTH AUSTRAL. PAGE 94 A1930 — DIPLOM COLONIAL INT/ORG INGP/REL

B58
MASON J.B.,THAILAND BIBLIOGRAPHY. S/ASIA THAILAND CULTURE EDU/PROP ADMIN...GEOG SOC LING 20. PAGE 95 A1958 — BIBLIOG/A ECO/UNDEV DIPLOM NAT/G

B58
TILLION G.,ALGERIA: THE REALITIES. ALGERIA FRANCE ISLAM CULTURE STRATA PROB/SOLV DOMIN REV NAT/LISM WEALTH MARXISM...GEOG 20. PAGE 144 A2940 — ECO/UNDEV SOC COLONIAL DIPLOM

B58
YUAN TUNG-LI,CHINA IN WESTERN LITERATURE. SECT DIPLOM...ART/METH GEOG JURID SOC BIOG CON/ANAL. PAGE 169 A3440 — BIBLIOG ASIA CULTURE HUM

C58
BLANCHARD W.,"THAILAND." THAILAND CULTURE AGRI FINAN INDUS FAM LABOR INT/TRADE ATTIT...GEOG HEAL SOC BIBLIOG 20. PAGE 15 A0307 — NAT/G DIPLOM ECO/UNDEV S/ASIA

B59
HAZLEWOOD A.,THE ECONOMICS OF "UNDER-DEVELOPED" AREAS. WOR+45 DIST/IND EXTR/IND FINAN INDUS MARKET PLAN FOR/AID...GEOG 20. PAGE 63 A1302 — BIBLIOG/A ECO/UNDEV AGRI INT/TRADE

B59
KAPLAN D.,THE ARAB REFUGEES: AN ABNORMAL PROBLEM. UAR WOR+45 PROB/SOLV DIPLOM GOV/REL ADJUST EFFICIENCY...POLICY GEOG INT/LAW 20 UN JEWS MIGRATION. PAGE 76 A1557 — STRANGE HABITAT GP/REL INGP/REL

B59
OKINSHEVICH L.A.,LATIN AMERICA IN SOVIET WRITINGS, 1945-1958: A BIBLIOGRAPHY. USSR LAW ECO/UNDEV LABOR DIPLOM EDU/PROP REV...GEOG SOC 20. PAGE 111 A2287 — BIBLIOG WRITING COM L/A+17C

B59
REIFF H.,THE UNITED STATES AND THE TREATY LAW OF THE SEA. USA+45 USA-45 SEA SOCIETY INT/ORG CONSULT DELIB/GP LEGIS DIPLOM LEGIT ATTIT ORD/FREE PWR WEALTH...GEOG JURID TOT/POP 20 TREATY. PAGE 120 A2459 — ADJUD INT/LAW

S59
HARTT J.,"ANTARCTICA: ITS IMMEDIATE PRACTICALITIES." FUT USA+45 USSR WOR+45 INT/ORG NAT/G CREATE TEC/DEV REGION KNOWL WEALTH...GEOG 20 ANTARTICA. PAGE 62 A1276 — VOL/ASSN ORD/FREE DIPLOM

B60
ASPREMONT-LYNDEN H.,RAPPORT SUR L'ADMINISTRATION BELGE DU RUANDA-URUNDI PENDANT L'ANNEE 1959. BELGIUM RWANDA AGRI INDUS DIPLOM ECO/TAC INT/TRADE DOMIN ADMIN RACE/REL...GEOG CENSUS 20 UN. PAGE 9 A0192 — AFR COLONIAL ECO/UNDEV INT/ORG

B60
GLUBB J.B.,WAR IN THE DESERT: AN R.A.F. FRONTIER CAMPAIGN. SAUDI/ARAB UK KIN SECT LEAD...GEOG 20 RAF. PAGE 53 A1083 — COLONIAL WAR FORCES DIPLOM

B60
HEYSE T.,PROBLEMS FONCIERS ET REGIME DES TERRES (ASPECTS ECONOMIQUES, JURIDIQUES ET SOCIAUX). AFR CONGO/BRAZ INT/ORG DIPLOM SOVEREIGN...GEOG TREATY 20. PAGE 64 A1325 — BIBLIOG AGRI ECO/UNDEV LEGIS

B60
HOFFMANN P.G.,ONE HUNDRED COUNTRIES, ONE AND ONE QUARTER BILLION PEOPLE. MARKET INT/ORG TEC/DEV CAP/ISM...GEOG CHARTS METH/COMP 20 UN. PAGE 66 A1354 — FOR/AID ECO/TAC ECO/UNDEV INT/TRADE

B60
ROPKE W.,A HUMANE ECONOMY. CULTURE ECO/DEV FINAN INDUS GP/REL CENTRAL WEALTH...GEOG SOC IDEA/COMP 20 EEC. PAGE 123 A2525 — ECO/TAC INT/ORG DIPLOM ORD/FREE

B60
THEOBALD R.,THE RICH AND THE POOR: A STUDY OF THE ECONOMICS OF RISING EXPECTATIONS. WOR+45 CONSTN ECO/DEV ECO/UNDEV INT/ORG NAT/G PLAN FOR/AID ROUTINE BAL/PAY ORD/FREE PWR WEALTH...GEOG TREND WORK 20. PAGE 142 A2912 — ECO/TAC INT/TRADE

B60
WOETZEL R.K.,THE INTERNATIONAL CONTROL OF AIRSPACE AND OUTERSPACE. FUT WOR+45 AIR CONSTN STRUCT CONSULT PLAN TEC/DEV ADJUD RIGID/FLEX KNOWL ORD/FREE PWR...TECHNIC GEOG MGT NEW/IDEA TREND COMPUT/IR VAL/FREE 20 TREATY. PAGE 166 A3375 — INT/ORG JURID SPACE INT/LAW

S60
HAVILAND H.F.,"PROBLEMS OF AMERICAN FOREIGN POLICY." ASIA COM USA+45 WOR+45 INT/ORG NAT/G CONSULT ECO/TAC FOR/AID DOMIN COERCE NUC/PWR ATTIT DRIVE ORD/FREE PWR RESPECT SKILL...POLICY GEOG OBS SAMP TREND GEN/METH METH COLD/WAR UN 20. PAGE 63 A1292 — ECO/UNDEV FORCES DIPLOM

S60
MAGATHAN W.,"SOME BASES OF WEST GERMAN MILITARY POLICY." EUR+WWI FUT INT/ORG TOP/EX ECO/TAC DOMIN DRIVE ORD/FREE PWR...TRADIT GEOG OBS TREND. PAGE 93 A1904 — NAT/G FORCES GERMANY

B61
SCHIEDER T.,DOCUMENTS ON THE EXPULSION OF THE GERMANS FROM EASTERN-CENTRAL-EUROPE (VOL. II/III). COM EUR+WWI GERMANY HUNGARY ROMANIA USSR DIPLOM RACE/REL 20 MIGRATION. PAGE 128 A2625 — GEOG CULTURE

B61
SCHNAPPER B.,LA POLITIQUE ET LE COMMERCE FRANCAIS DANS LE GOLFE DE GUINEE DE 1838 A 1871. FRANCE GUINEA UK SEA EXTR/IND NAT/G DELIB/GP LEGIS ADMIN ORD/FREE...POLICY GEOG CENSUS CHARTS BIBLIOG 19. PAGE 129 A2636 — COLONIAL INT/TRADE DOMIN AFR

B61
UAR MINISTRY OF CULTURE,A BIBLIOGRAPHICAL LIST OF AL MAGHRIB. ALGERIA ISLAM MOROCCO UAR SECT INT/TRADE COLONIAL 19/20 TUNIS. PAGE 146 A2987 — BIBLIOG DIPLOM GEOG

B61
UAR MINISTRY OF CULTURE,A BIBLIOGRAPHICAL LIST OF LIBYA. ISLAM LIBYA DIPLOM COLONIAL REV WAR 19/20. PAGE 146 A2988 — BIBLIOG GEOG SECT NAT/LISM

B61
UAR MINISTRY OF CULTURE,A BIBLIOGRAPHICAL LIST OF TUNISIA. ISLAM CULTURE NAT/G EDU/PROP COLONIAL ...GEOG 19/20 TUNIS. PAGE 146 A2989 — BIBLIOG DIPLOM SECT

B61
YDIT M.,INTERNATIONALISED TERRITORIES. FUT WOR+45 WOR-45 CONSTN VOL/ASSN CREATE PLAN LEGIT PEACE ORD/FREE...GEOG INT/LAW JURID SOC NEW/IDEA OBS RECORD SAMP TIME/SEQ TREND 19/20 BERLIN. PAGE 169 A3431 — LOC/G INT/ORG DIPLOM SOVEREIGN

B61
ZIMMERMAN I.,A GUIDE TO CURRENT LATIN AMERICAN PERIODICALS: HUMANITIES AND SOCIAL SCIENCES. LABOR SECT EDU/PROP...GEOG HUM SOC LING STAT NAT/COMP 20. PAGE 170 A3452 — BIBLIOG/A DIPLOM L/A+17C PHIL/SCI

S61
LANFALUSSY A.,"EUROPE'S PROGRESS: DUE TO COMMON MARKET." EUR+WWI ECO/DEV DELIB/GP PLAN ECO/TAC ROUTINE WEALTH...GEOG TREND EEC 20. PAGE 84 A1721 — INT/ORG MARKET

S61
MASTERS R.D.,"A MULTI-BLOC MODEL OF THE INTERNATIONAL SYSTEM." FUT UNIV WOR+45 SOCIETY ACT/RES PLAN...GEOG SOC TREND SIMUL TOT/POP 20. PAGE 96 A1963 — INT/ORG CONCPT

B62
CALDER R.,COMMON SENSE ABOUT A STARVING WORLD. WOR+45 STRATA ECO/DEV PLAN GP/REL BIO/SOC HABITAT ...POLICY GEOG STAT RECORD 20 UN BIRTH/CON. PAGE 23 A0466 — FOR/AID CENSUS ECO/UNDEV AGRI

B62
COLLISON R.L.,BIBLIOGRAPHIES, SUBJECT AND NATIONAL: A GUIDE TO THEIR CONTENTS, ARRANGEMENT, AND USE (2ND REV. ED.). SECT DIPLOM...ART/METH GEOG HUM PHIL/SCI SOC MATH BIOG 20. PAGE 28 A0569 — BIBLIOG/A CON/ANAL BIBLIOG

B62
FAO,FOOD AND AGRICULTURE ORGANIZATION AFRICAN SURVEY. AFR CONGO/BRAZ GHANA STRATA AGRI INT/ORG TEC/DEV FOR/AID INT/TRADE RACE/REL DEMAND EFFICIENCY PRODUC...GEOG 20 UN CONGO/LEOP. PAGE 44 A0898 — ECO/TAC WEALTH EXTR/IND ECO/UNDEV

B62
JELAVICH C.,TSARIST RUSSIA AND BALKAN NATIONALISM. BULGARIA MOD/EUR RUSSIA DOMIN GOV/REL...GEOG 19 SERBIA. PAGE 73 A1503 — NAT/LISM DIPLOM WAR

B62
KIDDER F.E.,THESES ON PAN AMERICAN TOPICS. LAW CULTURE NAT/G SECT DIPLOM HEALTH...ART/METH GEOG SOC 13/20. PAGE 79 A1615 — BIBLIOG CHRIST-17C L/A+17C SOCIETY

B62
LOWENSTEIN A.K.,BRUTAL MANDATE: A JOURNEY TO SOUTH WEST AFRICA. CULTURE INT/ORG NAT/G DIPLOM...GEOG 20 UN AFRICA/SW. PAGE 91 A1868 — AFR POLICY RACE/REL PROB/SOLV

B62
MCDOUGAL M.S.,THE PUBLIC ORDER OF THE OCEANS. WOR+45 WOR-45 SEA INT/ORG NAT/G CONSULT DELIB/GP DIPLOM LEGIT PEACE RIGID/FLEX...GEOG INT/LAW JURID RECORD TOT/POP 20 TREATY. PAGE 98 A2007
ADJUD ORD/FREE

B62
ROY P.A.,SOUTH WIND RED. L/A+17C USA+45 ECO/UNDEV NAT/G CAP/ISM MARXISM SOCISM...OLD/LIB GEOG RECORD INT CENSUS 20 COLD/WAR. PAGE 125 A2554
DIPLOM INDUS POLICY ECO/TAC

B62
UNECA LIBRARY,NEW ACQUISITIONS IN THE UNECA LIBRARY. LAW NAT/G PLAN PROB/SOLV TEC/DEV ADMIN REGION...GEOG SOC 20 UN. PAGE 147 A3009
BIBLIOG AFR ECO/UNDEV INT/ORG

B62
US DEPARTMENT OF THE ARMY,AFRICA: ITS PROBLEMS AND PROSPECTS. CHINA/COM USSR INT/ORG FOR/AID COLONIAL LEAD FEDERAL DRIVE SOVEREIGN MARXISM...GEOG 20 COLD/WAR. PAGE 152 A3104
BIBLIOG/A AFR NAT/LISM DIPLOM

B62
US LIBRARY OF CONGRESS,UNITED STATES AND CANADIAN PUBLICATIONS ON AFRICA IN 1960. CANADA USA+45 CULTURE TEC/DEV DIPLOM FOR/AID RACE/REL...GEOG HUM SOC SOC/WK LING 20. PAGE 155 A3156
BIBLIOG/A AFR

B62
US LIBRARY OF CONGRESS,A LIST OF AMERICAN DOCTORAL DISSERTATIONS ON AFRICA. SOCIETY SECT DIPLOM EDU/PROP ADMIN...GEOG 19/20. PAGE 155 A3157
BIBLIOG AFR ACADEM CULTURE

S62
DE MADARIAGA S.,"TOWARD THE UNITED STATES OF EUROPE." EUR+WWI PLAN DOMIN FEDERAL ATTIT PWR SOVEREIGN...GEOG TOT/POP 20. PAGE 35 A0707
FUT INT/ORG

S62
PIQUEMAL M.,"LES PROBLEMES DES UNIONS D'ETATS EN AFRIQUE NOIRE." FRANCE SOCIETY INT/ORG NAT/G DELIB/GP PLAN LEGIT ADMIN COLONIAL ROUTINE ATTIT ORD/FREE PWR...GEOG METH/CNCPT 20. PAGE 116 A2382
AFR ECO/UNDEV REGION

S62
SPRINGER H.W.,"FEDERATION IN THE CARIBBEAN: AN ATTEMPT THAT FAILED." L/A+17C ECO/UNDEV INT/ORG POL/PAR PROVS LEGIS CREATE PLAN LEGIT ADMIN FEDERAL ATTIT DRIVE PERSON ORD/FREE PWR...POLICY GEOG PSY CONCPT OBS CARIBBEAN CMN/WLTH 20. PAGE 136 A2791
VOL/ASSN NAT/G REGION

C62
DUFFY J.,"PORTUGAL IN AFRICA." PORTUGAL SIER/LEONE INDUS WORKER INT/TRADE WAR CONSERVE...CATH GEOG TREND 16/20. PAGE 39 A0795
BIBLIOG RACE/REL ECO/UNDEV COLONIAL

B63
ADLER G.J.,BRITISH INDIA'S NORTHERN FRONTIER: 1865-95. AFGHANISTN RUSSIA UK PROVS COLONIAL COERCE PEACE...GEOG CHARTS BIBLIOG 19 TREATY. PAGE 4 A0091
S/ASIA FORCES DIPLOM POLICY

B63
GREAT BRITAIN CENTRAL OFF INF,CONSULTATION AND CO-OPERATION IN THE COMMONWEALTH. LAW R+D FORCES PLAN EDU/PROP CONFER INGP/REL...GEOG CENSUS 19/20 CMN/WLTH. PAGE 55 A1133
DIPLOM DELIB/GP VOL/ASSN REGION

B63
HONEY P.J.,COMMUNISM IN NORTH VIETNAM: ITS ROLE IN THE SINO-SOVIET DISPUTE. CHINA/COM INDIA USSR VIETNAM/N AGRI POL/PAR LEGIS ECO/TAC WAR PEACE ATTIT...GEOG IDEA/COMP 20. PAGE 67 A1378
POLICY MARXISM CHIEF DIPLOM

B63
SALENT W.S.,THE UNITED STATES BALANCE OF PAYMENTS IN 1968. EUR+WWI UK USA+45 AGRI R+D LABOR FORCES PRODUC...GEOG CONCPT CHARTS 20 CHINJAP EEC. PAGE 126 A2589
BAL/PAY DEMAND FINAN INT/TRADE

B63
UAR MINISTRY OF CULTURE,A BIBLIOGRAPHICAL LIST OF ARABIAN PENINSULA. ISLAM SAUDI/ARAB YEMEN FINAN NAT/G DIPLOM 19/20. PAGE 146 A2990
BIBLIOG GEOG INDUS SECT

S63
ETIENNE G.,"'LOIS OBJECTIVES' ET PROBLEMES DE DEVELOPPEMENT DANS LE CONTEXTE CHINE-URSS." ASIA CHINA/COM COM FUT STRUCT INT/ORG VOL/ASSN TOP/EX TEC/DEV ECO/TAC ATTIT RIGID/FLEX...GEOG MGT TIME/SEQ TOT/POP 20. PAGE 42 A0866
TOTALISM USSR

S63
WEISSBERG G.,"MAPS AS EVIDENCE IN INTERNATIONAL BOUNDARY DISPUTES: A REAPPRAISAL." CHINA/COM EUR+WWI INDIA MOD/EUR S/ASIA INT/ORG NAT/G LEGIT PERCEPT...JURID CHARTS 20. PAGE 163 A3311
LAW GEOG SOVEREIGN

B64
CEPEDE M.,POPULATION AND FOOD. USA+45 STRUCT ECO/UNDEV FAM PLAN TEC/DEV FOR/AID CONTROL...CATH SOC TREND 19/20. PAGE 25 A0513
FUT GEOG AGRI CENSUS

B64
FREE L.A.,THE ATTITUDES, HOPES AND FEARS OF NIGERIANS. AFR NIGERIA ECO/UNDEV AGRI ACADEM PLAN TASK...GEOG CHARTS METH 20. PAGE 49 A0993
NAT/LISM SYS/QU DIPLOM

B64
INTL INF CTR LOCAL CREDIT,GOVERNMENT MEASURES FOR THE PROMOTION OF REGIONAL ECONOMIC DEVELOPMENT. WOR+45 ECO/UNDEV FINAN INT/ORG DIPLOM ORD/FREE ...POLICY GEOG 20. PAGE 71 A1464
FOR/AID PLAN ECO/TAC REGION

B64
JACOB P.E.,THE INTEGRATION OF POLITICAL COMMUNITIES. USA+45 WOR+45 CULTURE LOC/G MUNIC NAT/G CREATE PLAN LEGIT REGION COERCE ALL/VALS ...POLICY GEOG PSY SOC TREND HYPO/EXP GEN/LAWS VAL/FREE 20. PAGE 72 A1483
INT/ORG METH/CNCPT SIMUL STAT

B64
KIMMINICH O.,RUSTUNG UND POLITISCHE SPANNUNG. INDUS ARMS/CONT COERCE NAT/LISM PEACE PERSON ORD/FREE ...POLICY GEOG 20. PAGE 79 A1619
DIPLOM FORCES WEAPON WAR

B64
KITCHEN H.,A HANDBOOK OF AFRICAN AFFAIRS. ECO/UNDEV CREATE DIPLOM COLONIAL RACE/REL...ART/METH GEOG CHARTS 20. PAGE 80 A1646
AFR NAT/G INT/ORG FORCES

B64
MYINT H.,THE ECONOMICS OF THE DEVELOPING COUNTRIES. WOR+45 AGRI PLAN COST...POLICY GEOG 20 MONEY. PAGE 107 A2187
ECO/UNDEV INT/TRADE EXTR/IND FINAN

B64
OECD,DEVELOPMENT ASSISTANCE EFFORTS - POLICIES OF THE MEMBERS. AGRI INDUS BUDGET...GEOG NAT/COMP 20 OECD. PAGE 111 A2280
INT/ORG FOR/AID ECO/UNDEV TEC/DEV

B64
RUSSET B.M.,WORLD HANDBOOK OF POLITICAL AND SOCIAL INDICATORS. WOR+45 COM/IND ADMIN WEALTH...GEOG 20. PAGE 126 A2577
DIPLOM STAT NAT/G NAT/COMP

B64
SINGER H.W.,INTERNATIONAL DEVELOPMENT: GROWTH AND CHANGE. AFR BRAZIL L/A+17C WOR+45 CULTURE AGRI INDUS NAT/G ACT/RES ECO/TAC EDU/PROP WEALTH...GEOG CONCPT METH/CNCPT STAT HYPO/EXP WORK TOT/POP 20. PAGE 133 A2723
FINAN ECO/UNDEV FOR/AID INT/TRADE

B64
US HOUSE COMM ON JUDICIARY,IMMIGRATION HEARINGS. DELIB/GP STRANGE HABITAT...GEOG JURID 20 CONGRESS MIGRATION. PAGE 154 A3140
NAT/G POLICY DIPLOM NAT/LISM

B64
WITHERELL J.W.,OFFICIAL PUBLICATIONS OF FRENCH EQUATORIAL AFRICA, FRENCH CAMEROONS, AND TOGO, 1946-1958 (PAMPHLET). CAMEROON CHAD FRANCE GABON TOGO LAW ECO/UNDEV EXTR/IND INT/TRADE...GEOG HEAL 20. PAGE 165 A3370
BIBLIOG/A AFR NAT/G ADMIN

B65
DEMAS W.G.,THE ECONOMICS OF DEVELOPMENT IN SMALL COUNTRIES WITH SPECIAL REFERENCE TO THE CARIBBEAN. WOR+45 BAL/PAY DEMAND EFFICIENCY PRODUC...GEOG CARIBBEAN. PAGE 36 A0731
ECO/UNDEV PLAN WEALTH INT/TRADE

B65
ROTBERG R.I.,A POLITICAL HISTORY OF TROPICAL AFRICA. EX/STRUC DIPLOM INT/TRADE DOMIN ADMIN RACE/REL NAT/LISM PWR SOVEREIGN...GEOG TIME/SEQ BIBLIOG 1/20. PAGE 124 A2545
AFR CULTURE COLONIAL

B65
UNESCO,INTERNATIONAL ORGANIZATIONS IN THE SOCIAL SCIENCES(REV. ED.). LAW ADMIN ATTIT...CRIMLGY GEOG INT/LAW PSY SOC STAT 20 UNESCO. PAGE 148 A3024
INT/ORG R+D PROF/ORG ACT/RES

B65
UNIVERSAL REFERENCE SYSTEM,INTERNATIONAL AFFAIRS: VOLUME I IN THE POLITICAL SCIENCE, GOVERNMENT, AND PUBLIC POLICY SERIES....DECISION ECOMETRIC GEOG INT/LAW JURID MGT PHIL/SCI PSY SOC. PAGE 149 A3041
BIBLIOG/A GEN/METH COMPUT/IR DIPLOM

B65
US SENATE COMM ON JUDICIARY,REFUGEE PROBLEMS IN SOUTH VIETNAM AND LAOS: HEARINGS BEFORE SUBCOMMITTEE TO INVESTIGATE PROBLEMS OF REFUGEES, ESCAPEES. CHINA/COM LAOS USA+45 VIETNAM/S PROB/SOLV DIPLOM GOV/REL GP/REL EFFICIENCY ORD/FREE...POLICY GEOG 20 CONGRESS MIGRATION. PAGE 157 A3194
STRANGE HABITAT FOR/AID CIVMIL/REL

B65
VON GLAHN G.,LAW AMONG NATIONS: AN INTRODUCTION TO PUBLIC INTERNATIONAL LAW. WOR+45 WOR-45 INT/ORG NAT/G CREATE ADJUD WAR...GEOG CLASSIF TREND BIBLIOG. PAGE 160 A3250
ACADEM INT/LAW GEN/LAWS LAW

B65
WINT G.,ASIA: A HANDBOOK. ASIA COM INDIA USSR CULTURE INTELL NAT/G...GEOG STAT CENSUS NAT/COMP WORSHIP 20 TREATY CHINJAP. PAGE 165 A3365
DIPLOM SOC

S65
KHOURI F.J.,"THE JORDON RIVER CONTROVERSY." LAW SOCIETY ECO/UNDEV AGRI FINAN INDUS SECT FORCES ACT/RES PLAN TEC/DEV ECO/TAC EDU/PROP COERCE ATTIT DRIVE PERCEPT RIGID/FLEX ALL/VALS...GEOG SOC MYTH WORK. PAGE 78 A1610
ISLAM INT/ORG ISRAEL JORDAN

S65
QUADE Q.L.,"THE TRUMAN ADMINISTRATION AND THE SEPARATION OF POWERS: THE CASE OF THE MARSHALL PLAN." SOCIETY INT/ORG NAT/G CONSULT DELIB/GP LEGIS PLAN ECO/TAC ROUTINE DRIVE PERCEPT RIGID/FLEX ORD/FREE PWR WEALTH...DECISION GEOG NEW/IDEA TREND 20 TRUMAN/HS. PAGE 118 A2422 USA+45 ECO/UNDEV DIPLOM

B66
CLENDENON C.,AMERICANS IN AFRICA 1865-1900. AFR USA-45 ECO/UNDEV SECT REV RACE/REL CONSERVE ...TRADIT GEOG BIBLIOG 16/18. PAGE 27 A0549 DIPLOM COLONIAL INT/TRADE

B66
DAVIDSON A.B.,RUSSIA AND AFRICA. USSR AGRI INT/TRADE...GEOG BIBLIOG/A 18/20. PAGE 34 A0687 MARXISM COLONIAL RACE/REL DIPLOM

B66
HALLET R.,PEOPLE AND PROGRESS IN WEST AFRICA: AN INTRODUCTION TO THE PROBLEMS OF DEVELOPMENT. COM/IND INDUS KIN DIPLOM FOR/AID INT/TRADE HEALTH ...GEOG TREND CHARTS BIBLIOG/A 20 AFRICA/W. PAGE 60 A1233 AFR SOCIETY ECO/UNDEV ECO/TAC

B66
HAMILTON W.B.,A DECADE OF THE COMMONWEALTH, 1955-1964. UK LAW ELITES FINAN FOR/AID CONFER COLONIAL PWR...GEOG CHARTS ANTHOL 20 CMN/WLTH UN. PAGE 61 A1247 INT/ORG INGP/REL DIPLOM NAT/G

B66
KEYES J.G.,A BIBLIOGRAPHY OF WESTERN LANGUAGE PUBLICATIONS CONCERNING NORTH VIETNAM IN THE CORNELL LIBRARY. VIETNAM/N NAT/G FORCES TEC/DEV DIPLOM LEAD RACE/REL...GEOG SOC 20. PAGE 78 A1603 BIBLIOG/A CULTURE ECO/UNDEV S/ASIA

B66
LENGYEL E.,AFRICA: PAST, PRESENT, AND FUTURE. FUT SOUTH/AFR COLONIAL RACE/REL SOVEREIGN...GEOG AUD/VIS CHARTS T 20 CONGO/LEOP NEGRO. PAGE 87 A1771 AFR CONSTN ECO/UNDEV

B66
MALLORY W.H.,POLITICAL HANDBOOK AND ATLAS OF THE WORLD: PARLIAMENTS, PARTIES AND PRESS AS OF JANUARY 1, 1966. WOR+45 LEGIS PRESS...GEOG 20. PAGE 93 A1915 CHARTS DIPLOM NAT/G

B66
O'CONNER A.M.,AN ECONOMIC GEOGRAPHY OF EAST AFRICA. AFR TANZANIA UGANDA AGRI WORKER INT/TRADE COLONIAL GOV/REL...CHARTS METH/COMP 20 AFRICA/E. PAGE 111 A2269 ECO/UNDEV EXTR/IND GEOG HABITAT

B66
ROBOCK S.H.,INTERNATIONAL DEVELOPMENT 1965. AGRI INDUS VOL/ASSN PLAN TEC/DEV EDU/PROP HEALTH...JURID 20 UN PEACE/CORP. PAGE 122 A2508 FOR/AID INT/ORG GEOG ECO/UNDEV

B66
SOBEL L.A.,SOUTH VIETNAM: US-COMMUNIST CONFRONTATION IN SOUTHEAST ASIA 1961-65. VIETNAM FOR/AID CROWD DETER REV PEACE...GEOG 20 INTERVENT DIEM COLD/WAR. PAGE 134 A2754 WAR TIME/SEQ FORCES NAT/G

B66
US DEPARTMENT OF STATE,RESEARCH ON AFRICA (EXTERNAL RESEARCH LIST NO 5-25). LAW CULTURE ECO/UNDEV POL/PAR DIPLOM EDU/PROP LEAD REGION MARXISM...GEOG LING WORSHIP 20. PAGE 152 A3094 BIBLIOG/A ASIA S/ASIA NAT/G

B66
US DEPARTMENT OF STATE,RESEARCH ON THE MIDDLE EAST (EXTERNAL RESEARCH LIST NO 4-25). GREECE ISRAEL SYRIA UAR YEMEN CULTURE SOCIETY POL/PAR SECT DIPLOM EDU/PROP WAR NAT/LISM...GEOG GOV/COMP 20. PAGE 152 A3096 BIBLIOG/A ISLAM NAT/G REGION

B66
US DEPARTMENT OF STATE,RESEARCH ON THE USSR AND EASTERN EUROPE (EXTERNAL RESEARCH LIST NO 1-25). USSR LAW CULTURE SOCIETY NAT/G TEC/DEV DIPLOM EDU/PROP REGION...GEOG LING. PAGE 152 A3097 BIBLIOG/A EUR+WWI COM MARXISM

B66
US DEPARTMENT OF STATE,RESEARCH ON WESTERN EUROPE, GREAT BRITAIN, AND CANADA (EXTERNAL RESEARCH LIST NO 3-25). CANADA GERMANY/W UK LAW CULTURE NAT/G POL/PAR FORCES EDU/PROP REGION MARXISM...GEOG SOC WORSHIP 20 CMN/WLTH. PAGE 152 A3098 BIBLIOG/A EUR+WWI DIPLOM

B66
US DEPARTMENT OF THE ARMY,COMMUNIST CHINA: A STRATEGIC SURVEY: A BIBLIOGRAPHY (PAMPHLET NO. 20-67). CHINA/COM COM INDIA USSR NAT/G POL/PAR EX/STRUC FORCES NUC/PWR REV ATTIT...POLICY GEOG CHARTS. PAGE 152 A3109 BIBLIOG/A MARXISM S/ASIA DIPLOM

B66
US SENATE COMM GOVT OPERATIONS,POPULATION CRISIS. USA+45 ECO/DEV ECO/UNDEV AGRI SECT DELIB/GP PROB/SOLV FOR/AID REPRESENT ATTIT...GEOG CHARTS 20 CONGRESS DEPT/STATE DEPT/HEW BIRTH/CON. PAGE 156 A3178 CENSUS CONTROL LEGIS CONSULT

C66
DUROSELLE J.B.,"LE CONFLIT DE TRIESTE 1943-1954: ETUDES DE CAS DE CONFLITS INTERNATIONAUX III." ITALY USA+45 YUGOSLAVIA ELITES DELIB/GP PLAN ADJUST ...POLICY GEOG CHARTS IDEA/COMP TIME 20 TREATY UN COLD/WAR. PAGE 40 A0810 BIBLIOG WAR DIPLOM GEN/LAWS

B67
DE BLIJ H.J.,SYSTEMATIC POLITICAL GEOGRAPHY. WOR+45 STRUCT INT/ORG NAT/G EDU/PROP ADMIN COLONIAL ROUTINE ORD/FREE PWR...IDEA/COMP T 20. PAGE 34 A0697 GEOG CONCPT METH

B67
FRASER-TYTLER W.K.,AFGHANISTAN: A STUDY OF POLITICAL DEVELOPMENTS IN CENTRAL AND SOUTHERN ASIA (3RD ED.). AFGHANISTN INDIA KIN FOR/AID PWR ...BIBLIOG. PAGE 48 A0990 DIPLOM NAT/G CONSTN GEOG

B67
PIKE F.B.,FREEDOM AND REFORM IN LATIN AMERICA. BRAZIL URUGUAY CONSTN CULTURE SECT DIPLOM EDU/PROP PARTIC DRIVE ALL/VALS CATHISM...GEOG ANTHOL BIBLIOG REFORMERS BOLIV. PAGE 116 A2379 L/A+17C ORD/FREE ECO/UNDEV REV

B67
PIPER D.C.,THE INTERNATIONAL LAW OF THE GREAT LAKES. CANADA EXTR/IND MUNIC LICENSE ARMS/CONT CRIME...GEOG 19/20. PAGE 116 A2381 CONCPT DIPLOM INT/LAW

S67
KIPP K.,"DIE POLITISCHE BEDEUTUNG DER 'GEGENKUSTE' DARGESTELLT AM BEISPIEL DER USA IM 20. JAHRHUNDERT" USA+45 USA-45 SEA NAT/G CONTROL COERCE WAR...POLICY GEOG 20. PAGE 79 A1629 FORCES ORD/FREE DIPLOM DETER

S67
LIVNEH E.,"A NEW BEGINNING." ISRAEL USSR WOR+45 NAT/G DIPLOM INGP/REL FEDERAL HABITAT PWR...GEOG PSY JEWS. PAGE 90 A1847 WAR PERSON PEACE PLAN

S67
STEEL R.,"BEYOND THE POWER BLOCS." USA+45 USSR ECO/UNDEV NEUTRAL NUC/PWR NAT/LISM ATTIT...GEOG NATO WARSAW/P COLD/WAR. PAGE 137 A2811 DIPLOM TREND BAL/PWR PLAN

S67
STEGER H.S.,"RESEARCH ON LATIN AMERICA IN THE FEDERAL REPUBLIC OF GERMANY AND WEST BERLIN." FINAN DIPLOM INT/TRADE EDU/PROP...GEOG JURID CHARTS 19/20. PAGE 137 A2813 SOCIETY ECO/UNDEV ACADEM L/A+17C

S67
SYRKIN M.,"I.F. STONE RECONSIDERS ISRAEL." ISRAEL WOR+45 DIPLOM NAT/LISM HABITAT...POLICY GEOG JEWS. PAGE 141 A2875 ISLAM WAR ATTIT MORAL

S67
VELIKONJA J.,"ITALIAN IMMIGRANTS IN THE UNITED STATES IN THE MID-SIXTIES" ITALY USA+45 KIN MUNIC NAT/G WORKER DIPLOM REGION GP/REL ADJUST...GEOG CHARTS SOC/INTEG 20. PAGE 158 A3226 HABITAT ORD/FREE TREND STAT

S67
ZARTMAN I.W.,"AFRICA AS A SUBORDINATE STATE SYSTEM IN INTERNATIONAL RELATIONS." LAW BAL/PWR REGION CENTRAL...GEOG 20. PAGE 169 A3447 DIPLOM INT/ORG CONSTN AFR

C93
PLAYFAIR R.L.,"A BIBLIOGRAPHY OF MOROCCO." MOROCCO CULTURE AGRI FORCES DIPLOM WAR HEALTH...GEOG JURID SOC CHARTS. PAGE 116 A2387 BIBLIOG ISLAM MEDIT-7

B98
GRIFFIN A.P.C.,LIST OF BOOKS RELATING TO CUBA (PAMPHLET). CUBA L/A+17C USA-45 INT/TRADE DOMIN WAR GP/REL ALL/VALS...GEOG SOC CHARTS 19/20. PAGE 56 A1158 BIBLIOG/A NAT/G COLONIAL

GEOGRAPHY....SEE GEOG

GEOPOLITIC....GEOPOLITICS

GEOPOLITICS....SEE GEOG+POL, GEOPOLITIC

GEORGE A.L. A1060

GEORGE J.L. A1060

GEORGE M. A1061

GEORGE/DL....DAVID LLOYD GEORGE

GEORGE/III....GEORGE THE THIRD OF ENGLAND

GEORGIA....GEORGIA(USA)

GER/CONFED....GERMAN CONFEDERATION

GERARD-LIBOIS J. A1062

GERASSI J. A1063

GERBET P. A1064

GERMAN CONFEDERATION....SEE GER/CONFED

GERMAN/AM....GERMAN-AMERICANS

GERMANS/PA....GERMANS IN PENNSYLVANIA

GERMANY....GERMANY IN GENERAL; SEE ALSO APPROPRIATE TIME/SPACE/CULTURE INDEX

B
DEUTSCHE BIBLIOTH FRANKF A M,DEUTSCHE BIBLIOGRAPHIE. EUR+WWI GERMANY ECO/DEV FORCES DIPLOM LEAD...POLICY PHIL/SCI SOC 20. PAGE 36 A0743
BIBLIOG LAW ADMIN NAT/G

N
NEUE POLITISCHE LITERATUR. AFR ASIA EUR+WWI GERMANY RUSSIA SOCIETY ECO/DEV ECO/UNDEV PLAN PROB/SOLV LEAD MARXISM...PHIL/SCI CONCPT 20. PAGE 1 A0021
BIBLIOG DIPLOM COM NAT/G

N
DEUTSCHE BUCHEREI,DEUTSCHE NATIONALBIBLIOGRAPHIE. GERMANY ECO/DEV DIPLOM AGE/Y ATTIT...PHIL/SCI SOC 20. PAGE 37 A0744
BIBLIOG NAT/G LEAD POLICY

N
DEUTSCHE BUCHEREI,JAHRESVERZEICHNIS DES DEUTSCHEN SCHRIFTUMS. AUSTRIA EUR+WWI GERMANY SWITZERLND LAW LOC/G DIPLOM ADMIN...MGT SOC 19/20. PAGE 37 A0745
BIBLIOG WRITING NAT/G

N
DEUTSCHE BUCHEREI,DEUTSCHES BUCHERVERZEICHNIS. GERMANY LAW CULTURE POL/PAR ADMIN LEAD ATTIT PERSON ...SOC 20. PAGE 37 A0746
BIBLIOG NAT/G DIPLOM ECO/DEV

B00
GRIFFIN A.P.C.,LIST OF BOOKS RELATING TO THE THEORY OF COLONIZATION, GOVERNMENT OF DEPENDENCIES, PROTECTORATES, AND RELATED TOPICS. FRANCE GERMANY ITALY SPAIN UK USA-45 WOR-45 ECO/TAC ADMIN CONTROL REGION NAT/LISM ALL/VALS PWR...INT/LAW SOC 16/19. PAGE 56 A1149
BIBLIOG/A COLONIAL GOV/REL DOMIN

B00
MOCKLER-FERRYMAN A.,BRITISH WEST AFRICA. FRANCE GERMANY NIGER SIER/LEONE UK CULTURE DIPLOM WAR RACE/REL PRODUC PROFIT WEALTH...POLICY PREDICT 19. PAGE 102 A2095
AFR COLONIAL INT/TRADE CAP/ISM

B01
GRIFFIN A.P.C.,LIST OF BOOKS ON SAMOA (PAMPHLET). GERMANY S/ASIA UK USA-45 WOR-45 ECO/UNDEV REGION ALL/VALS ORD/FREE ALL/IDEOS...GEOG INT/LAW 19 SAMOA GUAM. PAGE 56 A1150
BIBLIOG/A COLONIAL DIPLOM

B05
GRIFFIN A.P.C.,LIST OF REFERENCES ON THE US CONSULAR SERVICE (PAMPHLET). FRANCE GERMANY SPAIN UK USA-45 WOR-45 OP/RES DOMIN ADMIN FEEDBACK ROUTINE GOV/REL...DECISION 19. PAGE 56 A1153
BIBLIOG/A NAT/G DIPLOM CONSULT

B14
HARRIS N.D.,INTERVENTION AND COLONIZATION IN AFRICA. BELGIUM FRANCE GERMANY MOD/EUR PORTUGAL UK ECO/UNDEV BAL/PWR DOMIN CONTROL PWR...GEOG 19/20. PAGE 62 A1267
AFR COLONIAL DIPLOM

B19
KEYNES J.M.,THE ECONOMIC CONSEQUENCES OF THE PEACE. FUT GERMANY MOD/EUR RUSSIA UK USA-45 CULTURE ECO/DEV FINAN INDUS INT/ORG TOP/EX ECO/TAC ROUTINE WAR ATTIT PERCEPT ALL/VALS...OLD/LIB MYTH OBS TIME/SEQ TREND 20 TREATY. PAGE 78 A1605
EUR+WWI SOCIETY PEACE

B22
FICHTE J.G.,ADDRESSES TO THE GERMAN NATION. GERMANY PRUSSIA ELITES NAT/G SECT CREATE INT/TRADE HEREDITY ...ART/METH LING 19 FRANK/PARL. PAGE 45 A0923
NAT/LISM CULTURE EDU/PROP REGION

B27
BRANDENBURG E.,FROM BISMARCK TO THE WORLD WAR; A HISTORY OF GERMAN FOREIGN POLICY, 1870-1914 (TRANS. BY ANNIE ELIZABETH ADAMS). GERMANY MOD/EUR FORCES AGREE PWR 19/20 TREATY CHAMBRLN/J WWI BISMARCK/O. PAGE 18 A0368
DIPLOM POLICY WAR

B27
HARRIS N.D.,EUROPE AND AFRICA. BELGIUM FRANCE GERMANY MOD/EUR PORTUGAL UK ECO/UNDEV BAL/PWR PWR ...GEOG 19/20. PAGE 62 A1268
AFR COLONIAL DIPLOM

B28
HUBER G.,DIE FRANZOSISCHE PROPAGANDA IM WELTKRIEG GEGEN DEUTSCHLAND 1914 BIS 1918. FRANCE GERMANY MOD/EUR DIPLOM WAR...EXHIBIT 20 WWI. PAGE 68 A1403
EDU/PROP ATTIT DOMIN PRESS

B28
PLAYNE C.E.,THE PRE-WAR MIND IN BRITAIN. GERMANY MOD/EUR UK STRATA SECT DIPLOM EDU/PROP CROWD SUFF ...POLICY ANARCH PSY SOC IDEA/COMP 20 WWI. PAGE 116 A2388
PRESS WAR DOMIN ATTIT

B30
SCHMITT B.E.,THE COMING OF THE WAR, 1914 (2 VOLS.). AUSTRIA FRANCE GERMANY MOD/EUR RUSSIA UK PLAN ROUTINE ORD/FREE. PAGE 128 A2633
WAR DIPLOM

B30
SCHNEIDER G.,HANDBUCH DER BIBLIOGRAPHIE. GERMANY WOR-45 CULTURE SOCIETY LEAD. PAGE 129 A2637
BIBLIOG/A NAT/G DIPLOM

B32
BRYCE J.,THE HOLY ROMAN EMPIRE. GERMANY ITALY MOD/EUR CULTURE SOCIETY STRUCT INT/ORG NAT/G SECT DIPLOM DOMIN WAR SUPEGO ALL/VALS SOVEREIGN...GEOG SOC TIME/SEQ CHARTS STERTYP. PAGE 20 A0413
CHRIST-17C NAT/LISM

B32
EAGLETON C.,INTERNATIONAL GOVERNMENT. BRAZIL FRANCE GERMANY ITALY UK USSR WOR-45 DELIB/GP TOP/EX PLAN ECO/TAC EDU/PROP LEGIT ADJUD REGION ARMS/CONT COERCE ATTIT PWR...GEOG MGT VAL/FREE LEAGUE/NAT 20. PAGE 40 A0816
INT/ORG JURID DIPLOM INT/LAW

B32
MASTERS R.D.,INTERNATIONAL LAW IN INTERNATIONAL COURTS. BELGIUM EUR+WWI FRANCE GERMANY MOD/EUR SWITZERLND WOR-45 SOCIETY STRATA STRUCT LEGIT EXEC ALL/VALS...JURID HIST/WRIT TIME/SEQ TREND GEN/LAWS 20. PAGE 96 A1961
INT/ORG LAW INT/LAW

B33
DAHLIN E.,FRENCH AND GERMAN PUBLIC OPINION ON DECLARED WAR AIMS 1914-1918. BELGIUM FRANCE GERMANY NAT/G POL/PAR DIPLOM COERCE REV WAR PEACE 20 WWI WILSON/W. PAGE 33 A0674
ATTIT EDU/PROP DOMIN NAT/COMP

B34
LOVELL R.I.,THE STRUGGLE FOR SOUTH AFRICA, 1875-1899. GERMANY RHODESIA SOUTH/AFR UK NAT/G ECO/TAC HABITAT WEALTH...POLICY 19. PAGE 91 A1866
COLONIAL DIPLOM WAR GP/REL

B35
LANGER W.L.,THE DIPLOMACY OF IMPERIALISM 1890-1902. FRANCE GERMANY ITALY UK WOR-45 BAL/PWR INT/TRADE LEGIT ADJUD CONTROL WAR PWR SOVEREIGN...CHARTS BIBLIOG/A 19/20. PAGE 84 A1726
DIPLOM COLONIAL DOMIN

B35
MARRIOTT J.A.,DICTATORSHIP AND DEMOCRACY. GERMANY GREECE UK CHIEF DIPLOM DOMIN LEGIT PEACE ORD/FREE CONSERVE...TREND ROME HITLER/A. PAGE 95 A1946
TOTALISM POPULISM PLURIST NAT/G

B35
SIMONDS F.H.,THE GREAT POWERS IN WORLD POLITICS. FRANCE GERMANY UK WOR-45 INT/ORG NAT/G ARMS/CONT PEACE FASCISM...POLICY GEOG 20 DEPRESSION NAZI. PAGE 133 A2718
DIPLOM WEALTH WAR

B36
BOYCE A.N.,EUROPE AND SOUTH AFRICA. FRANCE GERMANY ITALY SOUTH/AFR UK INDUS NAT/G CONTROL REV WAR NAT/LISM...CONCPT HIST/WRIT 20. PAGE 18 A0362
COLONIAL GOV/COMP NAT/COMP DIPLOM

B36
HUGENDUBEL P.,DIE KRIEGSMACHE DER FRANZOSISCHEN PRESSE. FRANCE GERMANY MOD/EUR COM/IND NAT/G DIPLOM DOMIN PWR 20. PAGE 69 A1412
PRESS EDU/PROP WAR ATTIT

B36
METZ I.,DIE DEUTSCHE FLOTTE IN DER ENGLISCHEN PRESSE, DER NAVY SCARE VOM WINTER 1904/05. GERMANY UK FORCES DIPLOM WAR 20 NAVY. PAGE 100 A2047
EDU/PROP ATTIT DOMIN PRESS

B37
BORGESE G.A.,GOLIATH: THE MARCH OF FASCISM. GERMANY ITALY LAW POL/PAR SECT DIPLOM SOCISM...JURID MYTH 20 DANTE MACHIAVELL MUSSOLIN/B. PAGE 17 A0341
POLICY NAT/LISM FASCISM NAT/G

B39
BENES E.,INTERNATIONAL SECURITY. GERMANY UK NAT/G DELIB/GP PLAN BAL/PWR ATTIT ORD/FREE PWR LEAGUE/NAT 20 TREATY. PAGE 13 A0267
EUR+WWI INT/ORG WAR

B39
CARR E.H.,PROPAGANDA IN INTERNATIONAL POLITICS (PAMPHLET). EUR+WWI GERMANY MOD/EUR NAT/G AGREE WAR MORAL...POLICY 20 TREATY. PAGE 24 A0497
DIPLOM EDU/PROP CONTROL ATTIT

B39
WHEELER-BENNET J.W.,THE FORGOTTEN PEACE: BREST-LITOVSK. COM GERMANY USSR TOP/EX AGREE WAR PWR ...BIBLIOG 20 TREATY LENIN/VI UKRAINE. PAGE 163 A3326
PEACE DIPLOM CONFER

B40
WANDERSCHECK H.,FRANKREICHS PROPAGANDA GEGEN DEUTSCHLAND. FRANCE GERMANY MOD/EUR UK NAT/G DIPLOM WAR 20 JEWS. PAGE 161 A3273
EDU/PROP ATTIT DOMIN PRESS

S40
FLORIN J.,"BOLSHEVIST AND NATIONAL SOCIALIST DOCTRINES OF INTERNATIONAL LAW." EUR+WWI GERMANY USSR R+D INT/ORG NAT/G DIPLOM DOMIN EDU/PROP SOCISM ...CONCPT TIME/SEQ 20. PAGE 47 A0955
LAW ATTIT TOTALISM INT/LAW

B41
BAUMANN G.,GRUNDLAGEN UND PRAXIS DER INTERNATIONALEN PROPAGANDA. FRANCE GERMANY UK CULTURE COM/IND PRESS PWR...PSY METH/COMP 20. PAGE 12 A0236
EDU/PROP DOMIN ATTIT DIPLOM

B42
BORNSTEIN J.,ACTION AGAINST THE ENEMY'S MIND. EUR+WWI GERMANY USA-45 DIPLOM DOMIN PRESS LEAD GP/REL DISCRIM PERCEPT FASCISM MARXISM 20 JEWS NAZI ANTI/SEMIT. PAGE 17 A0343
EDU/PROP PSY WAR CONTROL

B42
CROWE S.E.,THE BERLIN WEST AFRICA CONFERENCE, 1884-85. GERMANY ELITES MARKET INT/ORG DELIB/GP
AFR CONFER

FORCES PROB/SOLV BAL/PWR CAP/ISM DOMIN COLONIAL ...INT/LAW 19. PAGE 33 A0664 INT/TRADE DIPLOM

B42
PAGINSKY P.,GERMAN WORKS RELATING TO AMERICA, 1493-1800; A LIST COMPILED FROM THE COLLECTIONS OF THE NEW YORK PUBLIC LIBRARY. GERMANY PRE/AMER CULTURE COLONIAL ATTIT...POLICY SOC 15/19. PAGE 113 A2317 BIBLIOG/A NAT/G L/A+17C DIPLOM

B43
FULLER G.F.,FOREIGN RELIEF AND REHABILITATION (PAMPHLET). FUT GERMANY UK USA-45 INT/ORG PROB/SOLV DIPLOM FOR/AID ADMIN ADJUST PEACE ALL/VALS...SOC/WK 20 UN JEWS. PAGE 50 A1018 BIBLIOG/A PLAN GIVE WAR

B43
MICAUD C.A.,THE FRENCH RIGHT AND NAZI GERMANY 1933-1939: A STUDY OF PUBLIC OPINION. GERMANY UK USSR POL/PAR ARMS/CONT COERCE DETER PEACE RIGID/FLEX PWR MARXISM...FASCIST TREND 20 LEAGUE/NAT TREATY. PAGE 101 A2065 DIPLOM AGREE

B43
US DEPARTMENT OF STATE,NATIONAL SOCIALISM; BASIC PRINCIPLES, THEIR APPLICATION BY THE NAZI PARTY'S FOREIGN ORGANIZATION... GERMANY WOR-45 ECO/DEV LOC/G POL/PAR FORCES DIPLOM DOMIN COLONIAL ARMS/CONT COERCE NAT/LISM PWR 20 NAZI. PAGE 151 A3081 FASCISM SOCISM NAT/G TOTALISM

B44
RUDIN H.R.,ARMISTICE 1918. FRANCE GERMANY MOD/EUR UK USA-45 NAT/G CHIEF DELIB/GP FORCES BAL/PWR REPAR ARMS/CONT 20 WILSON/W TREATY. PAGE 125 A2566 AGREE WAR PEACE DIPLOM

B45
BEVERIDGE W.,THE PRICE OF PEACE. GERMANY UK WOR+45 WOR-45 NAT/G FORCES CREATE LEGIT REGION WAR ATTIT KNOWL ORD/FREE PWR...POLICY NEW/IDEA GEN/LAWS LEAGUE/NAT 20 TREATY. PAGE 14 A0284 INT/ORG TREND PEACE

B45
CONOVER H.F.,THE GOVERNMENTS OF THE MAJOR FOREIGN POWERS: A BIBLIOGRAPHY. FRANCE GERMANY ITALY UK USSR CONSTN LOC/G POL/PAR EX/STRUC FORCES ADMIN CT/SYS CIVMIL/REL TOTALISM...POLICY 19/20. PAGE 29 A0598 BIBLIOG NAT/G DIPLOM

B45
CONOVER H.F.,THE NAZI STATE: WAR CRIMES AND WAR CRIMINALS. GERMANY CULTURE NAT/G SECT FORCES DIPLOM INT/TRADE EDU/PROP...INT/LAW BIOG HIST/WRIT TIME/SEQ 20. PAGE 30 A0600 BIBLIOG WAR CRIME

B46
BLUM L.,FOR ALL MANKIND (TRANS. BY W. PICKLES). FRANCE GERMANY USSR LAW SOCIETY STRUCT POL/PAR WORKER DIPLOM DOMIN CHOOSE ORD/FREE FASCISM 20. PAGE 16 A0323 POPULISM SOCIALIST NAT/G WAR

B48
KULISCHER E.M.,EUROPE ON THE MOVE: WAR AND POPULATION CHANGES, 1917-1947. COM EUR+WWI FUT GERMANY USSR DIST/IND PLAN INT/TRADE CONTROL WAR DRIVE...CENSUS TREND COLD/WAR 20. PAGE 82 A1690 ECO/TAC GEOG

B48
LOGAN R.W.,THE AFRICAN MANDATES IN WORLD POLITICS. EUR+WWI GERMANY ISLAM INT/ORG BARGAIN...POLICY INT/LAW 20. PAGE 90 A1853 WAR COLONIAL AFR DIPLOM

B48
NAMIER L.B.,DIPLOMATIC PRELUDE 1938-1939. CZECHOSLVK EUR+WWI GERMANY POLAND UK FORCES DOMIN PWR 20 HITLER/A. PAGE 107 A2193 WAR TOTALISM DIPLOM

B48
WHEELER-BENNETT J.W.,MUNICH: PROLOGUE TO TRAGEDY. EUR+WWI FRANCE GERMANY UK PLAN PROB/SOLV SOVEREIGN ...POLICY DECISION 20 HITLER/A. PAGE 163 A3327 DIPLOM WAR PEACE

B49
JACKSON R.H.,INTERNATIONAL CONFERENCE ON MILITARY TRIALS. FRANCE GERMANY UK USA+45 USSR VOL/ASSN DELIB/GP REPAR ADJUD CT/SYS CRIME WAR 20 WAR/TRIAL. PAGE 72 A1479 DIPLOM INT/ORG INT/LAW CIVMIL/REL

B49
MANSERGH N.,THE COMING OF THE FIRST WORLD WAR: A STUDY IN EUROPEAN BALANCE, 1878-1914. GERMANY MOD/EUR VOL/ASSN COLONIAL CONTROL PWR 19/20 TREATY. PAGE 94 A1928 DIPLOM WAR BAL/PWR

B50
GATZKE H.W.,GERMANY'S DRIVE TO THE WEST. BELGIUM GERMANY MOD/EUR AGRI INDUS POL/PAR FORCES DOMIN AGREE CONTROL REGION COERCE 20 TREATY WWI. PAGE 51 A1053 WAR POLICY NAT/G DIPLOM

B50
MOCKFORD J.,SOUTH-WEST AFRICA AND THE INTERNATIONAL COURT (PAMPHLET). AFR GERMANY SOUTH/AFR UK ECO/UNDEV DIPLOM CONTROL DISCRIM...DECISION JURID 20 AFRICA/SW. PAGE 102 A2094 COLONIAL SOVEREIGN INT/LAW DOMIN

B50
US LIBRARY OF CONGRESS,THE UNITED STATES AND EUROPE: BIBLIOGRAPHY OF THOUGHT EXPRESSED IN AMERICAN PUBLICATIONS DURING 1950. EUR+WWI GERMANY USA+45 USSR INT/ORG DIPLOM COLONIAL SOVEREIGN ...POLICY 20 COLD/WAR UN BERLIN/BLO. PAGE 154 A3150 BIBLIOG/A SOC ATTIT

B51
BORKENAU F.,EUROPEAN COMMUNISM. COM EUR+WWI GERMANY SPAIN USSR INT/ORG PLAN REV WAR ATTIT 20 STALIN/J HITLER/A. PAGE 17 A0342 MARXISM POLICY DIPLOM NAT/G

B52
ALBERTINI L.,THE ORIGINS OF THE WAR OF 1914 (3 VOLS.). AUSTRIA FRANCE GERMANY MOD/EUR RUSSIA UK PROB/SOLV NEUTRAL PWR...BIBLIOG 19/20. PAGE 5 A0107 WAR DIPLOM FORCES BAL/PWR

B52
MANTOUX E.,THE CARTHAGINIAN PEACE. GERMANY WOR-45 SOCIETY FINAN INT/ORG DELIB/GP FORCES PLAN LEGIT ...CONCPT TIME/SEQ 20 KEYNES/JM HITLER/A. PAGE 94 A1935 ECO/DEV INT/TRADE WAR

B52
SKALWEIT S.,FRANKREICH UND FRIEDRICH DER GROSSE. FRANCE GERMANY PRUSSIA NAT/G DOMIN WAR 18 FREDERICK. PAGE 134 A2737 ATTIT EDU/PROP DIPLOM SOC

S52
HAAS E.B.,"THE RECONCILIATION OF CONFLICT, COLONIAL POLICY AIMS: ACCEPTANCE OF THE LEAGUE OF NATIONS MANDATE SYSTEM." FRANCE GERMANY UK WOR+45 WOR-45 LEGIT ATTIT DRIVE ORD/FREE...OLD/LIB INT SYS/QU TIME/SEQ TREND LEAGUE/NAT 20. PAGE 58 A1201 INT/ORG COLONIAL

B53
BRETTON H.L.,STRESEMANN AND THE REVISION OF VERSAILLES: A FIGHT FOR REASON. EUR+WWI GERMANY FORCES BUDGET ARMS/CONT WAR SUPEGO...BIBLIOG 20 TREATY VERSAILLES STRESEMN/G. PAGE 18 A0373 POLICY DIPLOM BIOG

B53
COUSINS N.,WHO SPEAKS FOR MAN. GERMANY KOREA WOR+45 SOCIETY INT/ORG NAT/G CREATE EDU/PROP HEALTH KNOWL LOVE MORAL...OBS SELF/OBS BIOG HYPO/EXP TOT/POP 20 CHINJAP. PAGE 32 A0642 ATTIT WAR PEACE

B53
LANGER W.L.,THE UNDECLARED WAR, 1940-1941. EUR+WWI GERMANY USA-45 USSR AIR FORCES TEC/DEV CONFER CONTROL COERCE PERCEPT ORD/FREE PWR 20 CHINJAP EUROPE. PAGE 84 A1727 WAR POLICY DIPLOM

B53
NEISSER H.,NATIONAL INCOMES AND INTERNATIONAL TRADE. FRANCE GERMANY SWEDEN UK USA-45 EXTR/IND FINAN INDUS TEC/DEV PRICE BAL/PAY EQUILIB INCOME WEALTH...CHARTS METH 19 CHINJAP. PAGE 108 A2215 INT/TRADE PRODUC MARKET CON/ANAL

B54
BUTZ O.,GERMANY: DILEMMA FOR AMERICAN POLICY. GERMANY USA+45 USA-45 USSR WOR+45 INT/ORG FORCES NUC/PWR EFFICIENCY PEACE PWR...GOV/COMP 20 COLD/WAR. PAGE 23 A0459 DIPLOM NAT/G WAR POLICY

B54
GERMANY FOREIGN MINISTRY,DOCUMENTS ON GERMAN FOREIGN POLICY 1918-1945, SERIES C (1933-1937) VOLS. I-V. GERMANY MOD/EUR FORCES PLAN ECO/TAC ...FASCIST CHARTS ANTHOL 20. PAGE 52 A1065 NAT/G DIPLOM POLICY

B54
REYNOLDS P.A.,BRITISH FOREIGN POLICY IN THE INTER-WAR YEARS. CZECHOSLVK GERMANY POLAND UK USA-45 POL/PAR FORCES ECO/TAC ARMS/CONT WAR ATTIT 20. PAGE 120 A2470 DIPLOM POLICY NAT/G

B54
TOTOK W.,HANDBUCH DER BIBLIOGRAPHISCHEN NACHSCHLAGEWERKE. GERMANY LAW CULTURE ADMIN...SOC 20. PAGE 144 A2952 BIBLIOG/A NAT/G DIPLOM POLICY

B56
FOSTER J.G.,BRITAIN IN WESTERN EUROPE: WEU AND THE ATLANTIC ALLIANCE. EUR+WWI FRANCE GERMANY GERMANY/W ITALY UK STRATA NAT/G DELIB/GP ECO/TAC ORD/FREE PWR ...TRADIT TIME/SEQ TREND OEEC PARLIAMENT 20 EUROPE/W. PAGE 47 A0969 INT/ORG FORCES WEAPON

B56
SNELL J.L.,THE MEANING OF YALTA: BIG THREE DIPLOMACY AND THE NEW BALANCE OF POWER. EUR+WWI GERMANY USA-45 USSR FORCES PLAN BAL/PWR DIPLOM WAR CHOOSE PEACE...CHARTS BIBLIOG 20 UN CHINJAP ROOSEVLT/F. PAGE 134 A2749 CONFER CHIEF POLICY PROB/SOLV

B56
VON BECKERATH E.,HANDWORTERBUCH DER SOCIALWISSENSCHAFTEN (II VOLS.). EUR+WWI GERMANY POL/PAR WORKER DIPLOM LEAD CHOOSE SUFF WEALTH...SOC 20. PAGE 159 A3249 BIBLIOG INT/TRADE NAT/G ECO/DEV

B56
VON HARPE W.,DIE SOWJETUNION FINNLAND UND SKANDANAVIEN, 1945-1955. EUR+WWI FINLAND GERMANY USSR WAR INGP/REL ORD/FREE SOVEREIGN MARXISM ...POLICY GOV/COMP BIBLIOG 20 STALIN/J. PAGE 160 A3252 DIPLOM COM NEUTRAL BAL/PWR

B57
ARON R.,FRANCE DEFEATS EDC. EUR+WWI GERMANY LEGIS DIPLOM DOMIN EDU/PROP ADMIN...HIST/WRIT 20. PAGE 9 A0180 INT/ORG FORCES DETER FRANCE

B57
FRASER L.,PROPAGANDA. GERMANY USSR WOR+45 WOR-45 EDU/PROP

NAT/G POL/PAR CONTROL FEEDBACK LOBBY CROWD WAR CONSEN NAT/LISM 20. PAGE 48 A0988
FASCISM MARXISM DIPLOM

B57
FREUND G.,UNHOLY ALLIANCE. EUR+WWI GERMANY USSR FORCES ECO/TAC CONTROL WAR PWR...TREND TREATY. PAGE 49 A0999
DIPLOM PLAN POLICY

B57
SINEY M.C.,THE ALLIED BLOCKADE OF GERMANY: 1914-1916. EUR+WWI GERMANY MOD/EUR USA-45 DIPLOM CONTROL NEUTRAL PWR 20. PAGE 133 A2721
DETER INT/TRADE INT/LAW WAR

B57
SPEIER H.,GERMAN REARMAMENT AND ATOMIC WAR: THE VIEWS OF GERMAN MILITARY AND POLITICAL LEADERS. FUT WOR+45 INT/ORG NAT/G WEAPON ATTIT PWR...INT QU TOT/POP VAL/FREE COLD/WAR 20. PAGE 136 A2780
TOP/EX FORCES NUC/PWR GERMANY

B58
CRAIG G.A.,FROM BISMARCK TO ADENAUER: ASPECTS OF GERMAN STATECRAFT. GERMANY INTELL FORCES ECO/TAC CONFER COERCE WAR GP/REL ORD/FREE PWR CONSERVE 19/20 BISMARCK/O ADENAUER/K. PAGE 32 A0653
DIPLOM LEAD NAT/G

B58
SCHOEDER P.W.,THE AXIS ALLIANCE AND JAPANESE-AMERICAN RELATIONS 1941. ASIA GERMANY UK USA-45 PEACE ATTIT...POLICY BIBLIOG 20 CHINJAP TREATY. PAGE 129 A2641
AGREE DIPLOM WAR

S58
ROTHFELS H.,"THE GERMAN RESISTANCE IN ITS INTERNATIONAL ASPECTS" (BMR)" EUR+WWI GERMANY UNIV CHIEF DIPLOM WAR NAT/LISM ATTIT...POLICY 20 HITLER/A NAZI. PAGE 124 A2548
VOL/ASSN MORAL FASCISM CIVMIL/REL

B59
DAWSON R.H.,THE DECISION TO AID RUSSIA* FOREIGN POLICY AND DOMESTIC POLITICS. GERMANY USSR CHIEF EX/STRUC LEGIS TOP/EX PROB/SOLV WAR ATTIT...POLICY CONGRESS. PAGE 34 A0695
DECISION DELIB/GP DIPLOM FOR/AID

B59
DEHIO L.,GERMANY AND WORLD POLITICS IN THE TWENTIETH CENTURY. EUR+WWI FRANCE GERMANY MOD/EUR UK USSR NAT/G CHIEF BAL/PWR DOMIN COLONIAL CONTROL LEAD...IDEA/COMP 20 VERSAILLES. PAGE 36 A0724
DIPLOM WAR NAT/LISM SOVEREIGN

B59
DIEBOLD W. JR.,THE SCHUMAN PLAN: A STUDY IN ECONOMIC COOPERATION, 1950-1959. EUR+WWI FRANCE GERMANY USA+45 EXTR/IND CONSULT DELIB/GP PLAN DIPLOM ECO/TAC INT/TRADE ROUTINE ORD/FREE WEALTH ...METH/CNCPT STAT CONT/OBS INT TIME/SEQ ECSC 20. PAGE 37 A0759
INT/ORG REGION

B59
KNIERIEM A.,THE NUREMBERG TRIALS. EUR+WWI GERMANY VOL/ASSN LEAD COERCE WAR INGP/REL TOTALISM SUPEGO ORD/FREE...CONCPT METH/COMP. PAGE 80 A1651
INT/LAW CRIME PARTIC JURID

S59
KISSINGER H.A.,"THE SEARCH FOR STABILITY." COM GERMANY MOD/EUR USA+45 USA-45 USSR INT/ORG ARMS/CONT NUC/PWR ORD/FREE PWR COLD/WAR 20 NATO. PAGE 80 A1641
FUT ATTIT BAL/PWR

S59
WARBURG J.P.,"THE CENTRAL EUROPEAN CRISIS: A PROPOSAL FOR WESTERN INITIATIVE." EUR+WWI INT/ORG NAT/G LEGIT DETER WAR...CONCPT BER/BLOC UN 20. PAGE 161 A3276
PLAN GERMANY

B60
ALBRECHT-CARRIE R.,FRANCE, EUROPE AND THE TWO WORLD WARS. EUR+WWI FRANCE GERMANY MOD/EUR UK ECO/DEV NAT/G FORCES BAL/PWR DOMIN ARMS/CONT PEACE PWR 20 TREATY EUROPE. PAGE 5 A0109
DIPLOM WAR

B60
FOOTMAN D.,INTERNATIONAL COMMUNISM. ASIA EUR+WWI FRANCE FUT GERMANY MOD/EUR S/ASIA USA-45 WOR+45 WOR-45 INTELL LABOR TOTALISM MARXISM WORK 20. PAGE 47 A0958
COM INT/ORG STRUCT REV

B60
FURNIA A.H.,THE DIPLOMACY OF APPEASEMENT: ANGLO-FRENCH RELATIONS AND THE PRELUDE TO WORLD WAR II 1931-1938. FRANCE GERMANY UK ELITES NAT/G DELIB/GP FORCES WAR PEACE RIGID/FLEX 20. PAGE 50 A1026
DIPLOM BAL/PWR COERCE

B60
JAECKH A.,WELTSAAT; ERLEBTES UND ERSTREBTES. GERMANY WOR+45 WOR-45 PLAN WAR...POLICY OBS/ENVIR NAT/COMP PERS/COMP 20. PAGE 73 A1489
BIOG NAT/G SELF/OBS DIPLOM

B60
KENNAN G.F.,RUSSIA AND THE WEST. ASIA COM EUR+WWI GERMANY UK USA+45 USSR INT/ORG NAT/G VOL/ASSN DOMIN REV WAR PWR...TIME/SEQ 20. PAGE 78 A1590
EXEC DIPLOM

B60
LISTER L.,EUROPE'S COAL AND STEEL COMMUNITY. FRANCE GERMANY STRUCT ECO/DEV EXTR/IND INDUS MARKET NAT/G DELIB/GP ECO/TAC INT/TRADE EDU/PROP ATTIT RIGID/FLEX ORD/FREE PWR WEALTH...CONCPT STAT TIME/SEQ CHARTS ECSC 20. PAGE 90 A1843
EUR+WWI INT/ORG REGION

B60
MOSELY P.E.,THE KREMLIN AND WORLD POLITICS. EUR+WWI GERMANY USA+45 USSR CHIEF TOP/EX BAL/PWR DOMIN PEACE PWR...METH 20 COLD/WAR STALIN/J EUROPE/E. PAGE 105 A2151
COM DIPLOM POLICY WAR

B60
PRITTIE T.,GERMANY DIVIDED: THE LEGACY OF THE NAZI ERA. EUR+WWI GERMANY RACE/REL SUPEGO...PSY AUD/VIS BIBLIOG/A 20 NAZI. PAGE 118 A2414
STERTYP PERSON ATTIT DIPLOM

B60
SPEIER H.,DIVIDED BERLIN: THE ANATOMY OF SOVIET POLITICAL BLACKMAIL. COM GERMANY USA+45 USSR WOR+45 NAT/G TOP/EX DOMIN EDU/PROP ALL/VALS...POLICY CONCPT COLD/WAR 20 U-2. PAGE 136 A2782
INT/ORG ACT/RES DIPLOM

B60
THE AFRICA 1960 COMMITTEE,MANDATE IN TRUST; THE PROBLEM OF SOUTH WEST AFRICA. GERMANY STRUCT REGION SANCTION CHOOSE DISCRIM...INT/LAW 20 AFRICA/SW UN LEAGUE/NAT TRUST/TERR. PAGE 142 A2910
NAT/G DIPLOM COLONIAL RACE/REL

S60
KREININ M.E.,"THE 'OUTER-SEVEN' AND EUROPEAN INTEGRATION." EUR+WWI FRANCE GERMANY ITALY UK ECO/DEV DIST/IND INT/TRADE DRIVE WEALTH...MYTH CHARTS EEC OEEC 20. PAGE 82 A1682
ECO/TAC GEN/LAWS

S60
MAGATHAN W.,"SOME BASES OF WEST GERMAN MILITARY POLICY." EUR+WWI FUT INT/ORG TOP/EX ECO/TAC DOMIN DRIVE ORD/FREE PWR...TRADIT GEOG OBS TREND. PAGE 93 A1904
NAT/G FORCES GERMANY

B61
DALLIN D.J.,SOVIET FOREIGN POLICY AFTER STALIN. ASIA CHINA/COM EUR+WWI GERMANY IRAN UK YUGOSLAVIA INT/ORG NAT/G VOL/ASSN FORCES TOP/EX BAL/PWR DOMIN EDU/PROP COERCE ATTIT PWR 20. PAGE 33 A0679
COM DIPLOM USSR

B61
FUCHS G.,GEGEN HITLER UND HENLEIN. CZECHOSLVK GERMANY DIPLOM CHOOSE GP/REL TOTALISM SOVEREIGN 20 HITLER/A. PAGE 50 A1013
FASCISM WORKER POL/PAR NAT/LISM

B61
JAKOBSON M.,THE DIPLOMACY OF THE WINTER WAR. EUR+WWI FINLAND GERMANY USSR INT/ORG NAT/G PEACE TOTALISM PWR...POLICY CONCPT 20 TREATY. PAGE 73 A1492
WAR ORD/FREE DIPLOM

B61
LIPPMANN W.,THE COMING TESTS WITH RUSSIA. COM CUBA GERMANY USSR FORCES CONTROL NEUTRAL COERCE NUC/PWR REV WAR PWR...INT 20 KHRUSH/N BERLIN. PAGE 89 A1830
BAL/PWR DIPLOM MARXISM ARMS/CONT

B61
SCHIEDER T.,DOCUMENTS ON THE EXPULSION OF THE GERMANS FROM EASTERN-CENTRAL-EUROPE (VOL. II/III). COM EUR+WWI GERMANY HUNGARY ROMANIA USSR DIPLOM RACE/REL 20 MIGRATION. PAGE 128 A2625
GEOG CULTURE

S61
RAY J.,"THE EUROPEAN FREE-TRADE ASSOCIATION AND ITS IMPACT ON INDIA'S TRADE." EUR+WWI FRANCE GERMANY INDIA S/ASIA UK NAT/G VOL/ASSN PLAN INT/TRADE ROUTINE WEALTH...STAT CHARTS CMN/WLTH EEC OEEC 20 EFTA. PAGE 120 A2453
ECO/DEV ECO/TAC

B62
ALIX C.,LE SAINT-SIEGE ET LES NATIONALISMES EN EUROPE 1870-1960. COM GERMANY IRELAND ITALY SOCIETY SECT TOTALISM RIGID/FLEX MORAL 19/20. PAGE 6 A0122
CATH NAT/LISM ATTIT DIPLOM

B62
DEHIO L.,THE PRECARIOUS BALANCE: FOUR CENTURIES OF THE EUROPEAN POWER STRUGGLE. FRANCE GERMANY SPAIN NAT/G DOMIN PWR...GOV/COMP 8/20. PAGE 36 A0725
BAL/PWR WAR DIPLOM COERCE

B62
HENDRICKS D.,PAMPHLETS ON THE FIRST WORLD WAR: AN ANNOTATED BIBLIOGRAPHY (OCCASIONAL PAPER NO. 79). GERMANY WOR-45 EDU/PROP NAT/LISM ATTIT PWR ALL/IDEOS 20. PAGE 64 A1314
BIBLIOG/A WAR DIPLOM NAT/G

B62
KENT G.O.,A CATALOG OF FILES AND MICROFILMS OF THE GERMAN FOREIGN MINISTRY ARCHIVES, 1920-1945 (3 VOLS.). GERMANY WOR-45 WRITING WAR 20. PAGE 78 A1595
BIBLIOG NAT/G DIPLOM FASCISM

B62
MANDER J.,BERLIN: HOSTAGE FOR THE WEST. FUT GERMANY WOR+45 FOR/AID RISK ATTIT ORD/FREE 20 BERLIN COLD/WAR. PAGE 93 A1916
DIPLOM BAL/PWR DOMIN DETER

B62
MORGENTHAU H.J.,POLITICS IN THE TWENTIETH CENTURY: IMPASSE OF AMERICAN FOREIGN POLICY. FUT GERMANY USA+45 USSR WOR+45 INT/ORG NAT/G ACT/RES PLAN FOR/AID EDU/PROP LEGIT COERCE WAR PWR...TIME/SEQ TREND COLD/WAR 20. PAGE 104 A2138
SKILL DIPLOM

B62
MORGENTHAU H.J.,POLITICS IN THE 20TH CENTURY: RESTORATION OF AMERICAN POLITICS. ASIA GERMANY USA+45 USSR WOR+45 NAT/G PLAN EDU/PROP LEGIT
INT/ORG DIPLOM

NUC/PWR ATTIT PWR SKILL...CONCPT TREND COLD/WAR 20. PAGE 104 A2139

B62
NEAL F.W.,WAR AND PEACE AND GERMANY. EUR+WWI USSR STRUCT INT/ORG NAT/G FORCES DOMIN EDU/PROP LEGIT EXEC COERCE ORD/FREE...HUM SOC NEW/IDEA OBS TIME/SEQ TOT/POP COLD/WAR 20 BERLIN. PAGE 108 A2208
USA+45 POLICY DIPLOM GERMANY

B62
SCHMIDT-VOLKMAR E.,DER KULTURKAMPF IN DEUTSCHLAND 1871-1890. GERMANY PRUSSIA SOCIETY STRUCT SECT DIPLOM GP/REL NAT/LISM 19 CHURCH/STA BISMARCK/O. PAGE 128 A2632
POL/PAR CATHISM ATTIT NAT/G

B62
SCOTT W.E.,ALLIANCE AGAINST HITLER. EUR+WWI FRANCE GERMANY USSR BAL/PWR LEAD TOTALISM PWR FASCISM MARXISM...POLICY BIBLIOG 20 HITLER/A. PAGE 131 A2675
WAR DIPLOM FORCES

B62
SOMMER T.,DEUTSCHLAND UND JAPAN ZWISCHEN DEN MACHTEN. GERMANY DELIB/GP BAL/PWR AGREE COERCE TOTALISM PWR 20 CHINJAP TREATY. PAGE 135 A2765
DIPLOM WAR ATTIT

B62
WELLEQUET J.,LE CONGO BELGE ET LA WELTPOLITIK (1894-1914. GERMANY DOMIN EDU/PROP WAR ATTIT ...BIBLIOG T CONGO/LEOP. PAGE 163 A3314
ADMIN DIPLOM GP/REL COLONIAL

S62
GUETZKOW H.,"THE POTENTIAL OF CASE STUDY IN ANALYZING INTERNATIONAL CONFLICT." EUR+WWI FUT GERMANY INTELL SOCIETY STRUCT INT/ORG LOC/G NAT/G CONSULT CREATE PLAN CHOOSE ATTIT RIGID/FLEX ...POLICY SAAR 20. PAGE 58 A1188
EDU/PROP METH/CNCPT COERCE FRANCE

S62
TOWSTER J.,"THE USSR AND THE USA: CHALLENGE AND RESPONSE." COM GERMANY USA+45 USSR WOR+45 ECO/UNDEV INT/ORG VOL/ASSN EX/STRUC FORCES TOP/EX CREATE PLAN TEC/DEV DIPLOM ECO/TAC EDU/PROP COLONIAL COERCE PWR ...GEN/METH COLD/WAR 20 KENNEDY/JF. PAGE 145 A2956
ACT/RES GEN/LAWS

B63
FABER K.,DIE NATIONALISTISCHE PUBLIZISTIK DEUTSCHLANDS VON 1866 BIS 1871 (2 VOLS.). EUR+WWI GERMANY DIPLOM EDU/PROP 19. PAGE 43 A0881
BIBLIOG/A NAT/G NAT/LISM POL/PAR

B63
FRANZ G.,TEILUNG UND WIEDERVEREINIGUNG. GERMANY IRELAND ITALY NETHERLAND POLAND CULTURE BAL/PWR CHOOSE NAT/LISM ORD/FREE SOVEREIGN 19/20. PAGE 48 A0987
DIPLOM WAR NAT/COMP ATTIT

B63
GILBERT M.,THE APPEASERS. COM GERMANY UK PLAN ECO/TAC COLONIAL CONTROL EXEC ORD/FREE PWR FASCISM 20 PARLIAMENT. PAGE 52 A1068
DIPLOM WAR POLICY DECISION

B63
KORBEL J.,POLAND BETWEEN EAST AND WEST: SOVIET AND GERMAN DIPLOMACY TOWARD POLAND 1919-1933. EUR+WWI GERMANY POLAND USSR FORCES AGREE WAR SOVEREIGN ...BIBLIOG 20 TREATY. PAGE 81 A1670
BAL/PWR DIPLOM DOMIN NAT/LISM

B63
RAVENS J.P.,STAAT UND KATHOLISCHE KIRCHE IN PREUSSENS POLNISCHEN TEILUNGSGEBIETEN. GERMANY POLAND PRUSSIA PROVS DIPLOM EDU/PROP DEBATE NAT/LISM...JURID 18 CHURCH/STA. PAGE 119 A2451
GP/REL CATHISM SECT NAT/G

S63
GROSSER A.,"FRANCE AND GERMANY IN THE ATLANTIC COMMUNITY." INT/ORG NAT/G TOP/EX DIPLOM REGION PEACE ATTIT ORD/FREE PWR...CONCPT RECORD TIME/SEQ GEN/LAWS VAL/FREE COLD/WAR 20. PAGE 57 A1178
EUR+WWI VOL/ASSN FRANCE GERMANY

S63
KISSINGER H.A.,"STRAINS ON THE ALLIANCE." EUR+WWI FRANCE GERMANY GERMANY/W USA+45 ECO/DEV INT/ORG NAT/G TOP/EX EDU/PROP NUC/PWR ATTIT PWR...PSY TREND 20. PAGE 80 A1643
VOL/ASSN DRIVE DIPLOM

S63
SHONFIELD A.,"AFTER BRUSSELS." EUR+WWI FRANCE GERMANY UK ECO/DEV DIST/IND MARKET VOL/ASSN DELIB/GP CREATE INT/TRADE ATTIT RIGID/FLEX...RECORD TREND GEN/LAWS EEC CMN/WLTH 20. PAGE 132 A2705
PLAN ECO/TAC

S63
WRIGHT Q.,"PROJECTED EUROPEAN UNION AND AMERICAN INTERNATIONAL PRESTIGE." EUR+WWI FRANCE GERMANY UK USA+45 INT/ORG NAT/G EDU/PROP ATTIT PERCEPT PWR ...CONCPT OBS EEC 20 UN. PAGE 168 A3417
FUT ORD/FREE REGION

B64
EHRENBURG I.,THE WAR: 1941-1945 (VOL. V OF "MEN, YEARS - LIFE," TRANS. BY TATIANA SHEBUNINA). GERMANY USSR PRESS WRITING PERS/REL PEACE ANOMIE ATTIT PERSON...CONCPT RECORD BIOG 20 STALIN/J HITLER/A. PAGE 40 A0827
WAR DIPLOM COM MARXIST

B64
GESELLSCHAFT RECHTSVERGLEICH,BIBLIOGRAPHIE DES DEUTSCHEN RECHTS (BIBLIOGRAPHY OF GERMAN LAW, TRANS. BY COURTLAND PETERSON). GERMANY FINAN INDUS LABOR SECT FORCES CT/SYS PARL/PROC CRIME...INT/LAW SOC NAT/COMP 20. PAGE 52 A1066
BIBLIOG/A JURID CONSTN ADMIN

B64
KALDOR N.,ESSAYS ON ECONOMIC POLICY (VOL. II). CHILE GERMANY INDIA FINAN...GOV/COMP METH/COMP 20 KEYNES/JM. PAGE 76 A1551
BAL/PAY INT/TRADE METH/CNCPT ECO/UNDEV

B64
MARTIN J.J.,AMERICAN LIBERALISM AND WORLD POLITICS, 1931-41 (2 VOLS.). GERMANY USA-45 POL/PAR DISCRIM NAT/LISM PEACE RATIONAL ATTIT RIGID/FLEX MARXISM PACIFISM 20. PAGE 95 A1950
NEW/LIB DIPLOM NAT/G POLICY

B64
REMAK J.,THE GENTLE CRITIC: THEODOR FONTANE AND GERMAN POLITICS, 1848-1898. GERMANY PRUSSIA CULTURE ELITES BAL/PWR DIPLOM WRITING GOV/REL...HUM BIOG 19 BISMARCK/O JUNKER FONTANE/T. PAGE 120 A2465
PERSON SOCIETY WORKER CHIEF

S64
RUBINSTEIN A.Z.,"THE SOVIET IMAGE OF WESTERN EUROPE." COM EUR+WWI FRANCE GERMANY GERMANY/W USA+45 USSR INT/ORG NAT/G VOL/ASSN FORCES TOP/EX BAL/PWR EDU/PROP ORD/FREE PWR...MYTH RECORD NATO EEC 20. PAGE 125 A2564
RIGID/FLEX ATTIT

B65
ADENAUER K.,MEINE ERINNERUNGEN, 1945-53 (VOL. I), 1953-55 (VOL. II). EUR+WWI GERMANY CHIEF FORCES PROB/SOLV DIPLOM ARMS/CONT INGP/REL PEACE SOVEREIGN ...OBS/ENVIR RECORD 20. PAGE 4 A0089
NAT/G BIOG SELF/OBS

B65
FORGAC A.A.,NEW DIPLOMACY AND THE UNITED NATIONS. FRANCE GERMANY UK USSR INT/ORG DELIB/GP EX/STRUC PEACE...INT/LAW CONCPT UN. PAGE 47 A0965
DIPLOM ETIQUET NAT/G

B65
FRANKLAND N.,THE BOMBING OFFENSIVE AGAINST GERMANY. GERMANY UK TEC/DEV DIPLOM WAR...METH/COMP 20. PAGE 48 A0985
WEAPON PLAN DECISION FORCES

B65
MERKL P.H.,GERMANY: YESTERDAY AND TOMORROW. GERMANY POL/PAR PLAN DIPLOM LEAD FEDERAL 19/20. PAGE 100 A2043
NAT/G FUT

B65
SCHREIBER H.,TEUTON AND SLAV - THE STRUGGLE FOR CENTRAL EUROPE (TRANS. BY J. CLEUGH). GERMANY POLAND PRUSSIA USSR SOCIETY STRUCT SECT DIPLOM BALTIC. PAGE 129 A2646
GP/REL WAR RACE/REL NAT/LISM

B65
SMITH A.L. JR.,THE DEUTSCHTUM OF NAZI GERMANY AND THE UNITED STATES. GERMANY USA-45 DIPLOM ATTIT FASCISM...BIBLIOG 20 MIGRATION NAZI. PAGE 134 A2744
INGP/REL NAT/LISM STRANGE DELIB/GP

S65
KORBONSKI A.,"USA POLICY IN EAST EUROPE." COM EUR+WWI GERMANY USA+45 CULTURE ECO/UNDEV EDU/PROP RIGID/FLEX WEALTH 20. PAGE 82 A1672
ACT/RES ECO/TAC FOR/AID

S65
ROGGER H.,"EAST GERMANY: STABLE OR IMMOBILE." COM EUR+WWI GERMANY/E NAT/G INT/TRADE DOMIN EDU/PROP COERCE TOTALISM COLD/WAR 20. PAGE 123 A2516
TOP/EX RIGID/FLEX GERMANY

S65
SPAAK P.H.,"THE SEARCH FOR CONSENSUS: A NEW EFFORT TO BUILD EUROPE." FRANCE GERMANY ECO/DEV NAT/G CONSULT FORCES PLAN EDU/PROP REGION CONSEN ATTIT ...SOC METH/CNCPT OBS TREND EEC NATO WORK 20. PAGE 135 A2770
EUR+WWI INT/ORG

B66
DYCK H.V.,WEIMAR GERMANY AND SOVIET RUSSIA 1926-1933. EUR+WWI GERMANY UK USSR ECO/TAC INT/TRADE NEUTRAL WAR ATTIT 20 WEIMAR/REP TREATY. PAGE 40 A0814
DIPLOM GOV/REL POLICY

B66
FREUND L.,POLITISCHE WAFFEN. EUR+WWI GERMANY CONSULT FORCES CONFER NUC/PWR 20. PAGE 49 A1000
EDU/PROP DIPLOM ATTIT

B66
GILBERT M.,THE ROOTS OF APPEASEMENT. EUR+WWI GERMANY UK MUNIC BAL/PWR FASCISM...NEW/IDEA 20. PAGE 52 A1070
DIPLOM REPAR PROB/SOLV POLICY

B66
HENKYS R.,DEUTSCHLAND UND DIE OSTLICHEN NACHBARN. GERMANY POLAND NAT/G POL/PAR INGP/REL ATTIT 20 MIGRATION. PAGE 64 A1317
GP/REL JURID INT/LAW DIPLOM

B66
VON BORCH H.,FRIEDE TROTZ KRIEG. GERMANY USSR WOR+45 PEACE ANOMIE ATTIT 20. PAGE 112 A2305
DIPLOM NUC/PWR WAR COERCE

B66
SMITH D.M.,AMERICAN INTERVENTION, 1917. GERMANY UK USA-45 SEA FORCES DIPLOM INT/TRADE EDU/PROP COERCE WEAPON PEACE 20 WILSON/W WWI. PAGE 134 A2746
WAR ATTIT POLICY NEUTRAL

B66
US SENATE COMM ON FOREIGN REL,UNITED STATES POLICY TOWARD EUROPE (AND RELATED MATTERS). COM EUR+WWI GERMANY PROB/SOLV REGION NUC/PWR WAR NAT/LISM PEACE
DIPLOM INT/ORG POLICY

PWR...NAT/COMP 20 NATO CONGRESS DEGAULLE/C. PAGE 156 A3184 — WOR+45

B67
CECIL L.,ALBERT BALLIN; BUSINESS AND POLITICS IN IMPERIAL GERMANY 1888-1918. GERMANY UK INT/TRADE LEAD WAR PERS/REL ADJUST PWR WEALTH...MGT BIBLIOG 19/20. PAGE 25 A0510 — DIPLOM CONSTN ECO/DEV TOP/EX

L67
GENEVEY P.,"LE DESARMEMENT APRES LE TRAITE DE VERSAILLES." EUR+WWI GERMANY INT/ORG PROB/SOLV CONFER WAR...POLICY PREDICT 20. PAGE 52 A1057 — ARMS/CONT PEACE DIPLOM FORCES

S67
APEL H.,"LES NOUVEAUX ASPECTS DE LA POLITIQUE ETRANGERE ALLEMANDE." EUR+WWI GERMANY POL/PAR BAL/PWR ECO/TAC INT/TRADE NUC/PWR NAT/LISM PEACE ...POLICY 20 EEC COLD/WAR. PAGE 8 A0168 — DIPLOM INT/ORG FEDERAL

S67
COHN K.,"CRIMES AGAINST HUMANITY." GERMANY INT/ORG SANCTION ATTIT ORD/FREE...MARXIST CRIMLGY 20 UN. PAGE 28 A0564 — WAR INT/LAW CRIME ADJUD

S67
HALL M.,"GERMANY, EAST AND WEST* DANGER AT THE CROSSROADS." GERMANY ELITES CHIEF FORCES DIPLOM ECO/TAC REPAR ARMS/CONT...SOCIALIST 20. PAGE 60 A1227 — NAT/LISM ATTIT FASCISM WEAPON

S67
KRUSCHE H.,"THE STRIVING OF THE KIESINGER-STRAUS GOVERNMENT FOR NUCLEAR WEAPONS IS A THREAT TO EUROPEAN SECURITY." EUR+WWI GERMANY BAL/PWR SANCTION WEAPON PEACE ORD/FREE...MARXIST 20 NATO COLD/WAR. PAGE 82 A1688 — ARMS/CONT INT/ORG NUC/PWR DIPLOM

S67
PEUKERT W.,"WEST GERMANY'S 'RED TRADE'." COM GERMANY INDUS CAP/ISM DOMIN SANCTION DEMAND PEACE UTIL...MARXIST 20 COLD/WAR. PAGE 115 A2371 — DIPLOM ECO/TAC INT/TRADE

S67
SPENCER R.,"GERMANY AFTER THE AUTUMN CRISIS." GERMANY CHOOSE GP/REL PERS/REL. PAGE 136 A2785 — DIPLOM POL/PAR PROB/SOLV

S67
WILPERT C.,"A LOOK IN THE MIRROR AND OVER THE WALL." GERMANY POL/PAR...KNO/TEST COLD/WAR. PAGE 165 A3358 — NAT/G PLAN DIPLOM ATTIT

B96
LOWELL A.L.,GOVERNMENTS AND PARTIES IN CONTINENTAL EUROPE, VOL. II. AUSTRIA GERMANY HUNGARY MOD/EUR SWITZERLND SOCIETY EX/STRUC LEGIS DIPLOM AGREE LEAD PARL/PROC PWR...POLICY 19. PAGE 91 A1867 — POL/PAR NAT/G GOV/REL ELITES

GERMANY FOREIGN MINISTRY A1065

GERMANY/E....EAST GERMANY; SEE ALSO COM

B18
KERNER R.J.,SLAVIC EUROPE: A SELECTED BIBLIOGRAPHY IN THE WESTERN EUROPEAN LANGUAGES. BULGARIA CZECHOSLVK GERMANY/E POLAND RUSSIA YUGOSLAVIA NAT/G DIPLOM MARXISM...LING 19/20. PAGE 78 A1598 — BIBLIOG SOCIETY CULTURE COM

B59
BUNDESMIN FUR VERTRIEBENE,ZEITTAFEL DER VORGESCHICHTE UND DES ABLAUFS DER VERTREIBUNG SOWIE DER UNTERBRINGUNG UND EINGLIEDERUNG DER (2 VOLS.). GERMANY/E GERMANY/W NAT/G PROVS PROB/SOLV DIPLOM PARL/PROC ATTIT...BIBLIOG SOC/INTEG 20 MIGRATION PARLIAMENT. PAGE 21 A0431 — JURID GP/REL INT/LAW

B60
STOLPER W.F.,GERMANY BETWEEN EAST AND WEST: THE ECONOMICS OF COMPETITIVE COEXISTENCE. FUT GERMANY/E GERMANY/W WOR+45 FINAN POL/PAR BUDGET ECO/TAC FOR/AID INT/TRADE...STAT CHARTS METH/COMP 20 COLD/WAR. PAGE 138 A2832 — ECO/DEV DIPLOM GOV/COMP BAL/PWR

B62
FRIEDRICH-EBERT-STIFTUNG,THE SOVIET BLOC AND DEVELOPING COUNTRIES. CHINA/COM COM GERMANY/E USSR WOR+45 ECO/UNDEV INT/ORG NAT/G TEC/DEV NEUTRAL PWR ...POLICY 20. PAGE 49 A1008 — MARXISM DIPLOM ECO/TAC FOR/AID

B62
STEEL R.,THE END OF THE ALLIANCE. FRANCE FUT GERMANY/E GERMANY/W UK USA+45 NAT/G FORCES FOR/AID 20 NATO. PAGE 137 A2809 — EUR+WWI POLICY DIPLOM INT/ORG

B63
KHRUSHCHEV N.S.,THE NEW CONTENT OF PEACEFUL COEXISTENCE IN THE NUCLEAR AGE. GERMANY/E WORKER NUC/PWR REV SOCISM 20 COLD/WAR. PAGE 79 A1614 — MARXISM POL/PAR PEACE DIPLOM

B65
WASKOW A.I.,KEEPING THE WORLD DISARMED. AFR GERMANY/E DIPLOM CONTROL WAR 20 UN. PAGE 161 A3289 — ARMS/CONT PEACE FORCES PROB/SOLV

S65
ROGGER H.,"EAST GERMANY: STABLE OR IMMOBILE." COM EUR+WWI GERMANY/E NAT/G INT/TRADE DOMIN EDU/PROP COERCE TOTALISM COLD/WAR 20. PAGE 123 A2516 — TOP/EX RIGID/FLEX GERMANY

S67
SCHUMANN H.,"IMPERIALISMUS-KRITIK UND KOLONIALISMUS-FORSCHUNG." GERMANY/E DIPLOM SOVEREIGN...SOC HIST/WRIT 20. PAGE 129 A2652 — COLONIAL ATTIT DOMIN CAP/ISM

GERMANY/W....WEST GERMANY

N
LITERATUR-VERZEICHNIS DER POLITISCHEN WISSENSCHAFTEN. GERMANY/W WOR+45 CONSTN SOCIETY ECO/DEV INT/ORG POL/PAR LEAD REPRESENT GOV/REL GP/REL...POLICY PHIL/SCI. PAGE 1 A0018 — BIBLIOG EUR+WWI DIPLOM NAT/G

N
JAHRBUCH DER DISSERTATIONEN. GERMANY/W WOR+45 ...TREND 20. PAGE 3 A0048 — BIBLIOG/A NAT/G ACADEM DIPLOM

B52
GURLAND A.R.L.,POLITICAL SCIENCE IN WESTERN GERMANY: THOUGHTS AND WRITINGS, 1950-1952 (PAMPHLET). EUR+WWI GERMANY/W ELITES SOCIETY NAT/G NAT/LISM TOTALISM 20. PAGE 58 A1196 — BIBLIOG/A DIPLOM CIVMIL/REL FASCISM

B56
FOSTER J.G.,BRITAIN IN WESTERN EUROPE: WEU AND THE ATLANTIC ALLIANCE. EUR+WWI FRANCE GERMANY GERMANY/W ITALY UK STRATA NAT/G DELIB/GP ECO/TAC ORD/FREE PWR ...TRADIT TIME/SEQ TREND OEEC PARLIAMENT 20 EUROPE/W. PAGE 47 A0969 — INT/ORG FORCES WEAPON

B58
DEUTSCHE GESCHAFT VOLKERRECHT,DIE VOLKERRECHTLICHEN DISSERTATIONEN AN DEN WESTDEUTSCHEN UNIVERSITATEN, 1945-1957. GERMANY/W NAT/G DIPLOM ADJUD CT/SYS ...POLICY 20. PAGE 37 A0748 — BIBLIOG INT/LAW ACADEM JURID

C58
GOLAY J.F.,"THE FOUNDING OF THE FEDERAL REPUBLIC OF GERMANY." GERMANY/W CONSTN EX/STRUC DIPLOM ADMIN CHOOSE...DECISION BIBLIOG 20. PAGE 53 A1088 — FEDERAL NAT/G PARL/PROC POL/PAR

B59
BUNDESMIN FUR VERTRIEBENE,ZEITTAFEL DER VORGESCHICHTE UND DES ABLAUFS DER VERTREIBUNG SOWIE DER UNTERBRINGUNG UND EINGLIEDERUNG DER (2 VOLS.). GERMANY/E GERMANY/W NAT/G PROVS PROB/SOLV DIPLOM PARL/PROC ATTIT...BIBLIOG SOC/INTEG 20 MIGRATION PARLIAMENT. PAGE 21 A0431 — JURID GP/REL INT/LAW

B59
FREE L.A.,SIX ALLIES AND A NEUTRAL. ASIA COM EUR+WWI FRANCE GERMANY/W INDIA S/ASIA UK USA+45 INT/ORG NAT/G NUC/PWR PEACE ATTIT PERCEPT RIGID/FLEX ALL/VALS...STAT REC/INT COLD/WAR 20 CHINJAP. PAGE 48 A0992 — PSY DIPLOM

B60
STOLPER W.F.,GERMANY BETWEEN EAST AND WEST: THE ECONOMICS OF COMPETITIVE COEXISTENCE. FUT GERMANY/E GERMANY/W WOR+45 FINAN POL/PAR BUDGET ECO/TAC FOR/AID INT/TRADE...STAT CHARTS METH/COMP 20 COLD/WAR. PAGE 138 A2832 — ECO/DEV DIPLOM GOV/COMP BAL/PWR

B61
PECKERT J.,DIE GROSSEN UND DIE KLEINEN MAECHTE. COM GERMANY/W ECO/DEV ECO/UNDEV NAT/G WAR RACE/REL PEACE...POLICY GP/COMP GOV/COMP 20 COLD/WAR. PAGE 114 A2346 — DIPLOM ECO/TAC BAL/PWR

B61
SCHMIDT H.,VERTEIDIGUNG ODER VERGELTUNG. COM CUBA GERMANY/W USSR FORCES DIPLOM ARMS/CONT DETER NUC/PWR...POLICY CHARTS HYPO/EXP SIMUL BIBLIOG 20 NATO COLD/WAR. PAGE 128 A2630 — PLAN WAR BAL/PWR ORD/FREE

B61
TETENS T.H.,THE NEW GERMANY AND THE OLD NAZIS. EUR+WWI GERMANY/W USA+45 NAT/G CRIME CHOOSE RACE/REL TOTALISM AGE/Y ATTIT 20 JEWS NAZI ADENAUER/K. PAGE 142 A2905 — FASCISM DIPLOM FOR/AID POL/PAR

B62
ABOSCH H.,THE MENACE OF THE MIRACLE: GERMANY FROM HITLER TO ADENAUER. EUR+WWI GERMANY/W CULTURE FORCES PRESS NUC/PWR WAR CHOOSE 20 HITLER/A ADENAUER/K. PAGE 4 A0082 — DIPLOM PEACE POLICY

B62
FRIEDMANN W.,METHODS AND POLICIES OF PRINCIPAL DONOR COUNTRIES IN PUBLIC INTERNATIONAL DEVELOPMENT FINANCING: PRELIMINARY APPRAISAL. FRANCE GERMANY/W UK USA+45 USSR WOR+45 FINAN TEC/DEV CAP/ISM DIPLOM ECO/TAC ATTIT 20 EEC. PAGE 49 A1002 — INT/ORG FOR/AID NAT/COMP ADMIN

B62
LIPPMANN W.,WESTERN UNITY AND THE COMMON MARKET. EUR+WWI FRANCE GERMANY/W UK USA+45 ECO/DEV AGRI FINAN MARKET INT/ORG NAT/G FOR/AID AGREE WEALTH 20 EEC. PAGE 89 A1831 — DIPLOM INT/TRADE VOL/ASSN

B62
STEEL R.,THE END OF THE ALLIANCE. FRANCE FUT GERMANY/E GERMANY/W UK USA+45 NAT/G FORCES FOR/AID 20 NATO. PAGE 137 A2809 — EUR+WWI POLICY DIPLOM INT/ORG

B63
ERHARD L.,THE ECONOMICS OF SUCCESS. GERMANY/W WOR+45 LABOR CHIEF TAX REGION COST DEMAND ANTHOL. PAGE 42 A0860
ECO/DEV INT/TRADE PLAN DIPLOM

S63
KISSINGER H.A.,"STRAINS ON THE ALLIANCE." EUR+WWI FRANCE GERMANY GERMANY/W USA+45 ECO/DEV INT/ORG NAT/G TOP/EX EDU/PROP NUC/PWR ATTIT PWR...PSY TREND 20. PAGE 80 A1643
VOL/ASSN DRIVE DIPLOM

B64
COLUMBIA U SCHOOL OF LAW,PUBLIC INTERNATIONAL DEVELOPMENT FINANCING IN INDIA. GERMANY/W INDIA UK USA+45 INDUS PLAN TEC/DEV DIPLOM ECO/TAC GIVE ADMIN UTIL ATTIT 20. PAGE 28 A0572
ECO/UNDEV FINAN FOR/AID INT/ORG

B64
KRETZSCHMAR W.W.,AUSLANDSHILFE ALS MITTEL DER AUSSENWIRTSCHAFTS- UND AUSSENPOLITIK. ASIA GERMANY/W UK USA+45 SOCIETY STRUCT ECO/UNDEV LOBBY EFFICIENCY 20. PAGE 82 A1683
FOR/AID DIPLOM AGRI DIST/IND

S64
RUBINSTEIN A.Z.,"THE SOVIET IMAGE OF WESTERN EUROPE." COM EUR+WWI FRANCE GERMANY GERMANY/W USA+45 USSR INT/ORG NAT/G VOL/ASSN FORCES TOP/EX BAL/PWR EDU/PROP ORD/FREE PWR...MYTH RECORD NATO EEC 20. PAGE 125 A2564
RIGID/FLEX ATTIT

B65
ADENAUER K.,MEMOIRS 1945-53. EUR+WWI GERMANY/W ECO/DEV CHIEF FORCES ECO/TAC WAR GOV/REL PWR SOVEREIGN 20 NATO ADENAUER/K. PAGE 4 A0088
BIOG DIPLOM NAT/G PERS/REL

B65
US DEPARTMENT OF DEFENSE,US SECURITY ARMS CONTROL, AND DISARMAMENT 1961-1965 (PAMPHLET). CHINA/COM COM GERMANY/W ISRAEL SPACE USA+45 USSR WOR+45 FORCES EDU/PROP DETER EQUILIB PEACE ALL/VALS...GOV/COMP 20 NATO. PAGE 151 A3077
BIBLIOG/A ARMS/CONT NUC/PWR DIPLOM

B65
WEIL G.L.,A HANDBOOK ON THE EUROPEAN ECONOMIC COMMUNITY. BELGIUM EUR+WWI FRANCE GERMANY/W ITALY CONSTN ECO/DEV CREATE PARTIC GP/REL...DECISION MGT CHARTS 20 EEC. PAGE 162 A3299
INT/TRADE INT/ORG TEC/DEV INT/LAW

B65
WHITE J.,GERMAN AID. GERMANY/W FINAN PLAN TEC/DEV INT/TRADE ADMIN ATTIT...POLICY 20. PAGE 164 A3335
FOR/AID ECO/UNDEV DIPLOM ECO/TAC

S65
PLISCHKE E.,"INTEGRATING BERLIN AND THE FEDERAL REPUBLIC OF GERMANY." EUR+WWI GERMANY/W LEGIS TEC/DEV DOMIN ORD/FREE PWR...JURID 20 BERLIN. PAGE 117 A2392
DIPLOM NAT/G MUNIC

B66
KINDLEBERGER C.P.,EUROPE AND THE DOLLAR. EUR+WWI FRANCE GERMANY/W USA+45 CONSTN INT/ORG DIPLOM INT/TRADE...ANTHOL 20 GOLD/STAND. PAGE 79 A1623
BAL/PAY BUDGET FINAN ECO/DEV

B66
NEUMANN R.G.,THE GOVERNMENT OF THE GERMAN FEDERAL REPUBLIC. EUR+WWI GERMANY/W LOC/G EX/STRUC LEGIS CT/SYS INGP/REL PWR...BIBLIOG 20 ADENAUER/K. PAGE 108 A2222
NAT/G POL/PAR DIPLOM CONSTN

B66
OBERMANN E.,VERTEIDIGUNG PER FREIHEIT. GERMANY/W WOR+45 INT/ORG COERCE NUC/PWR WEAPON MARXISM 20 UN NATO WARSAW/P TREATY. PAGE 111 A2273
FORCES ORD/FREE WAR PEACE

B66
US DEPARTMENT OF STATE,RESEARCH ON WESTERN EUROPE, GREAT BRITAIN, AND CANADA (EXTERNAL RESEARCH LIST NO 3-25). CANADA GERMANY/W UK LAW CULTURE NAT/G POL/PAR FORCES EDU/PROP REGION MARXISM...GEOG SOC WORSHIP 20 CMN/WLTH. PAGE 152 A3098
BIBLIOG/A EUR+WWI DIPLOM

B66
ZISCHKA A.,WAR ES EIN WUNDER? GERMANY/W ECO/DEV FINAN LG/CO BARGAIN CAP/ISM FOR/AID RATION 20 MARSHL/PLN. PAGE 170 A3456
ECO/TAC INT/TRADE INDUS WAR

S67
SOMMER T.,"BONN CHANGES COURSE." GERMANY/W NAT/G POL/PAR PROB/SOLV NAT/LISM 20 NATO BERLIN/BLO. PAGE 135 A2766
DIPLOM BAL/PWR INT/ORG

S67
YEFROMEV A.,"THE TRUE FACE OF THE WEST GERMAN NATIONAL-DEMOCRATS." GERMANY/W NAT/G DOMIN LEAD SANCTION WAR ATTIT PERSON...MARXIST 20. PAGE 169 A3433
POL/PAR TOTALISM PARL/PROC DIPLOM

GESELLSCHAFT RECHTSVERGLEICH A1066

GETTYSBURG....BATTLE OF GETTYSBURG

GHANA....SEE ALSO AFR

B58
MANSERGH N.,COMMONWEALTH PERSPECTIVES. GHANA UK LAW VOL/ASSN CONFER HEALTH SOVEREIGN...GEOG CHARTS ANTHOL 20 CMN/WLTH AUSTRAL. PAGE 94 A1930
DIPLOM COLONIAL INT/ORG INGP/REL

N59
BRITISH COMMONWEALTH REL CONF,EXTRACTS FROM THE PROCEEDINGS OF THE SIXTH UNOFFICIAL CONFERENCE (PAMPHLET). GHANA INDIA RHODESIA UK FINAN FORCES DETER FEDERAL...LING 20 PARLIAMENT. PAGE 19 A0379
DIPLOM PARL/PROC INT/TRADE ORD/FREE

B60
JEFFRIES C.,TRANSFER OF POWER: PROBLEMS OF THE PASSAGE TO SELFGOVERNMENT. CEYLON GHANA MALAYSIA NIGERIA UK INT/ORG CONSULT DELIB/GP LEGIS DIPLOM CONFER PARL/PROC 20. PAGE 73 A1502
SOVEREIGN COLONIAL ORD/FREE NAT/G

B60
PHILLIPS J.F.V.,KWAME NKRUMAH AND THE FUTURE OF AFRICA. FUT GHANA ISLAM ECO/UNDEV CHIEF DIPLOM COLONIAL RACE/REL NAT/LISM...TREND IDEA/COMP BIBLIOG 20 NKRUMAH/K. PAGE 116 A2376
BIOG LEAD SOVEREIGN AFR

B60
THEOBOLD R.,THE NEW NATIONS OF WEST AFRICA. GHANA NIGERIA CULTURE INT/ORG ECO/TAC FOR/AID COLONIAL RACE/REL POPULISM...ANTHOL BIBLIOG 20 UN. PAGE 143 A2916
AFR SOVEREIGN ECO/UNDEV DIPLOM

B62
FAO,FOOD AND AGRICULTURE ORGANIZATION AFRICAN SURVEY. AFR CONGO/BRAZ GHANA STRATA AGRI INT/ORG TEC/DEV FOR/AID INT/TRADE RACE/REL DEMAND EFFICIENCY PRODUC...GEOG 20 UN CONGO/LEOP. PAGE 44 A0898
ECO/TAC WEALTH EXTR/IND ECO/UNDEV

B62
TOURE S.,THE INTERNATIONAL POLICY OF THE DEMOCRATIC PARTY OF GUINEA (VOL. VII). AFR ALGERIA GHANA GUINEA MALI CONSTN VOL/ASSN CHIEF WAR PEACE ATTIT ...WELF/ST 20 DEMOCRAT. PAGE 144 A2953
DIPLOM POLICY POL/PAR NEW/LIB

S62
GAREAU F.H.,"BLOC POLITICS IN WEST AFRICA." AFR CONGO/BRAZ GHANA GUINEA MALI WOR+45 STRUCT ECO/UNDEV INT/ORG VOL/ASSN CHOOSE ORD/FREE PWR UN 20. PAGE 51 A1048
NAT/G NAT/LISM

B66
SCHATTEN F.,COMMUNISM IN AFRICA. AFR GHANA GUINEA MALI CULTURE ECO/UNDEV LABOR SECT ECO/TAC EDU/PROP REV 20. PAGE 128 A2619
COLONIAL NAT/LISM MARXISM DIPLOM

S67
KRAUS J.,"A MARXIST IN GHANA." GHANA ELITES CHIEF PROB/SOLV TEC/DEV DIPLOM ECO/TAC COLONIAL PARTIC PWR 20 NKRUMAH/K. PAGE 82 A1676
MARXISM PLAN ATTIT CREATE

GIBBON/EDW....EDWARD GIBBON

GIBBS H.P. A1199

GIBRALTAR....SEE UK

GIBSON J.S. A1067

GILBERT F. A0651

GILBERT M. A1068,A1069,A1070

GILBERT R. A1071,A1072

GILPIN R. A1073

GINSBURGS G. A1074,A1075

GIRAUD A. A1076

GIRAUD E. A1077

GIVE....GIVING, PHILANTHROPY

N19
BASCH A.,THE FUTURE OF FOREIGN LENDING FOR DEVELOPMENT (PAMPHLET). WOR+45 ECO/UNDEV FINAN INT/ORG ECO/TAC ATTIT...PREDICT 20. PAGE 11 A0232
FOR/AID ECO/DEV DIPLOM GIVE

N19
HAUSER P.M.,WORLD POPULATION PROBLEMS (PAMPHLET). USA+45 WOR+45 ECO/DEV ECO/UNDEV FAM ACT/RES PLAN PROB/SOLV FOR/AID GIVE EATING...CHARTS 20 BIRTH/CON RESOURCE/N. PAGE 63 A1289
CONTROL CENSUS ATTIT PREDICT

N19
JACKSON R.G.A.,THE CASE FOR AN INTERNATIONAL DEVELOPMENT AUTHORITY (PAMPHLET). WOR+45 ECO/DEV DIPLOM GIVE CONTROL GP/REL EFFICIENCY NAT/LISM SOVEREIGN 20. PAGE 72 A1478
FOR/AID INT/ORG ECO/UNDEV ADMIN

N19
LANGE O.R.,"DISARMAMENT ECONOMIC GROWTH AND INTERNATIONAL CO-OPERATION" (PAMPHLET). WOR+45 DIST/IND PLAN INT/TRADE GIVE TASK DETER WEALTH SOCISM 18/19 BOLIVAR/S. PAGE 84 A1723
ARMS/CONT DIPLOM ECO/DEV ECO/UNDEV

B43
FULLER G.F.,FOREIGN RELIEF AND REHABILITATION
BIBLIOG/A

(PAMPHLET). FUT GERMANY UK USA-45 INT/ORG PROB/SOLV DIPLOM FOR/AID ADMIN ADJUST PEACE ALL/VALS...SOC/WK 20 UN JEWS. PAGE 50 A1018 — PLAN GIVE WAR

B50
LEVI W.,FUNDAMENTALS OF WORLD ORGANIZATION. WOR+45 WOR-45 CULTURE ECO/TAC GIVE RECEIVE PERSON WEALTH ...METH/COMP 19/20 UN LEAGUE/NAT. PAGE 88 A1793 — INT/ORG PEACE ORD/FREE DIPLOM

C51
LEONARD L.L.,"INTERNATIONAL ORGANIZATION (1ST ED.)" WOR+45 FINAN DELIB/GP ECO/TAC GIVE DOMIN SANCTION PEACE BIO/SOC ORD/FREE...INT/LAW 20 UN LEAGUE/NAT. PAGE 87 A1779 — BIBLIOG POLICY DIPLOM INT/ORG

B52
MACARTHUR D.,REVITALIZING A NATION. ASIA COM FUT KOREA WOR+45 NAT/G FOR/AID TAX GIVE WAR ATTIT SOCISM 20 CHINJAP EUROPE. PAGE 92 A1885 — LEAD FORCES TOP/EX POLICY

B57
CASTLE E.W.,THE GREAT GIVEAWAY: THE REALITIES OF FOREIGN AID. USA+45 DIPLOM EDU/PROP NEUTRAL ...DECISION 20. PAGE 25 A0508 — FOR/AID GIVE ECO/UNDEV PROB/SOLV

B57
MILLIKAN M.F.,A PROPOSAL: KEY TO AN EFFECTIVE FOREIGN POLICY. USA+45 AGRI FINAN DELIB/GP DIPLOM REPRESENT MAJORITY...NEW/IDEA CHARTS. PAGE 101 A2081 — FOR/AID GIVE ECO/UNDEV PLAN

B58
PALMER E.E.,AMERICAN FOREIGN POLICY. USA+45 CULTURE ECO/UNDEV NAT/G PLAN GIVE BAL/PAY ORD/FREE WEALTH POPULISM...DECISION ANTHOL 20. PAGE 113 A2319 — DIPLOM ECO/TAC POLICY

B59
CHANDLER E.H.S.,THE HIGH TOWER OF REFUGE: THE INSPIRING STORY OF REFUGEE RELIEF THROUGHOUT THE WORLD. WOR+45 NEIGH SECT WORKER PROB/SOLV DIPLOM ECO/TAC EDU/PROP COST HABITAT. PAGE 25 A0519 — GIVE WEALTH STRANGE INT/ORG

B60
VOGT W.,PEOPLE: CHALLENGE TO SURVIVAL. WOR+45 ECO/DEV ECO/UNDEV FAM INT/ORG NAT/G PLAN PROB/SOLV FOR/AID GIVE EATING 20 BIRTH/CON. PAGE 159 A3247 — CENSUS CONTROL ATTIT TEC/DEV

B61
MEZERIK A.G.,ECONOMIC DEVELOPMENT AIDS FOR UNDERDEVELOPED COUNTRIES. WOR+45 FINAN LEGIS PROB/SOLV TEC/DEV DIPLOM FOR/AID GIVE TASK WAR 20 UN. PAGE 101 A2062 — ECO/UNDEV INT/ORG WEALTH PLAN

B61
MORLEY L.,THE PATCHWORK HISTORY OF FOREIGN AID. KOREA/S USA+45 USSR LAW FINAN INT/ORG TEC/DEV BAL/PWR GIVE 20 COLD/WAR NATO. PAGE 104 A2144 — FOR/AID ECO/UNDEV FORCES DIPLOM

B61
WARD B.J.,INDIA AND THE WEST. INDIA UK USA+45 INT/TRADE GIVE COLONIAL ATTIT MARXISM 19/20. PAGE 161 A3279 — PLAN ECO/UNDEV ECO/TAC FOR/AID

B62
MONTGOMERY J.D.,THE POLITICS OF FOREIGN AID: AMERICAN EXPERIENCE IN SOUTHEAST ASIA. S/ASIA USA+45 NAT/G PROB/SOLV COLONIAL 20. PAGE 103 A2115 — FOR/AID DIPLOM GOV/REL GIVE

B62
MOUSSA P.,THE UNDERPRIVILEGED NATIONS. FINAN INT/ORG PLAN PROB/SOLV CAP/ISM GIVE TASK WEALTH ...POLICY SOC 20. PAGE 105 A2159 — ECO/UNDEV NAT/G DIPLOM FOR/AID

B62
SNOW J.H.,GOVERNMENT BY TREASON. USA+45 USA-45 LEGIS DIPLOM FOR/AID GIVE CONTROL WEALTH MARXISM ...MAJORIT 20 CONGRESS COLD/WAR. PAGE 134 A2750 — FINAN TAX PWR POLICY

B62
WEIDNER E.W.,THE WORLD ROLE OF UNIVERSITIES. USA+45 WOR+45 SECT ACT/RES PROB/SOLV GIVE EFFICIENCY KNOWL ...LING CHARTS BIBLIOG 20. PAGE 162 A3297 — ACADEM EDU/PROP DIPLOM POLICY

B63
COLUMBIA U SCHOOL OF LAW,PUBLIC INTERNATIONAL DEVELOPMENT FINANCING IN SENEGAL. SENEGAL FINAN DELIB/GP GIVE EFFICIENCY...CHARTS GOV/COMP ANTHOL 20. PAGE 28 A0571 — FOR/AID PLAN RECEIVE ECO/UNDEV

B63
INTERAMERICAN ECO AND SOC COUN,THE ALLIANCE FOR PROGRESS: ITS FIRST YEAR: 1961-1962. AGRI SCHOOL PLAN TEC/DEV INT/TRADE TAX GIVE ADMIN WEALTH...SOC 20 SOUTH/AMER. PAGE 71 A1449 — INT/ORG PROB/SOLV ECO/TAC L/A+17C

B63
YOUNG A.N.,CHINA AND THE HELPING HAND. ASIA USA+45 FINAN INDUS ECO/TAC GIVE WEALTH...METH/COMP 20 LEND/LEASE GOLD/STAND. PAGE 169 A3434 — FOR/AID DIPLOM WAR

B64
COLUMBIA U SCHOOL OF LAW,PUBLIC INTERNATIONAL DEVELOPMENT FINANCING IN INDIA. GERMANY/W INDIA UK USA+45 INDUS PLAN TEC/DEV DIPLOM ECO/TAC GIVE ADMIN UTIL ATTIT 20. PAGE 28 A0572 — ECO/UNDEV FINAN FOR/AID INT/ORG

B64
JOHNSON L.B.,MY HOPE FOR AMERICA. FUT USA+45 USSR LAW PLAN DIPLOM GIVE INCOME PEACE ATTIT ORD/FREE WEALTH 20 JOHNSON/LB PRESIDENT DEMOCRAT. PAGE 74 A1525 — POLICY POL/PAR NAT/G GOV/REL

B64
MC GOVERN G.S.,WAR AGAINST WANT. USA+45 AGRI DIPLOM INT/TRADE GIVE RECEIVE DEMAND HEALTH 20 KENNEDY/JF FOOD/PEACE. PAGE 97 A1993 — FOR/AID ECO/DEV POLICY EATING

B65
MEAGHER R.F.,PUBLIC INTERNATIONAL DEVELOPMENT FINANCING IN SUDAN. SUDAN FINAN DELIB/GP GIVE ...CHARTS GOV/COMP 20. PAGE 99 A2029 — FOR/AID PLAN RECEIVE ECO/UNDEV

B65
MONCRIEFF A.,SECOND THOUGHTS ON AID. WOR+45 ECO/UNDEV AGRI FINAN VOL/ASSN PLAN TEC/DEV GIVE EDU/PROP ROLE WEALTH 20. PAGE 102 A2105 — FOR/AID ECO/TAC INT/ORG IDEA/COMP

B66
BALDWIN D.A.,ECONOMIC DEVELOPMENT AND AMERICAN FOREIGN POLICY. USA+45 FINAN LG/CO LEGIS DIPLOM GIVE 20. PAGE 10 A0210 — ECO/TAC FOR/AID ECO/UNDEV POLICY

B66
BRYNES A.,WE GIVE TO CONQUER. USA+45 USSR STRATA ECO/UNDEV INT/ORG NAT/G DIPLOM DRIVE...TREND IDEA/COMP 20. PAGE 20 A0414 — FOR/AID CONTROL GIVE WAR

B66
GLAZER M.,THE FEDERAL GOVERNMENT AND THE UNIVERSITY. CHILE PROB/SOLV DIPLOM GIVE ADMIN WAR ...POLICY SOC 20. PAGE 53 A1079 — BIBLIOG/A NAT/G PLAN ACADEM

B66
HOROWITZ D.,HEMISPHERES NORTH AND SOUTH: ECONOMIC DISPARITY AMONG NATIONS. WOR+45 ECO/DEV ECO/UNDEV INT/ORG PLAN DIPLOM INT/TRADE GIVE PARTIC GP/REL ...WELF/ST 20. PAGE 67 A1387 — ECO/TAC FOR/AID STRATA WEALTH

B66
KIRDAR U.,THE STRUCTURE OF UNITED NATIONS ECONOMIC AID TO UNDERDEVELOPED COUNTRIES. AGRI FINAN INDUS NAT/G EX/STRUC PLAN GIVE TASK...POLICY 20 UN. PAGE 79 A1631 — INT/ORG FOR/AID ECO/UNDEV ADMIN

B66
LEAGUE OF WOMEN VOTERS OF US,FOREIGN AID AT THE CROSSROADS. USA+45 WOR+45 DELIB/GP PROB/SOLV DIPLOM INT/TRADE RECEIVE BAL/PAY...CHARTS 20 UN. PAGE 86 A1756 — FOR/AID GIVE ECO/UNDEV PLAN

B66
OHLIN G.,FOREIGN AID POLICIES RECONSIDERED. ECO/DEV ECO/UNDEV VOL/ASSN CONSULT PLAN CONTROL ATTIT ...CONCPT CHARTS BIBLIOG 20. PAGE 111 A2286 — FOR/AID DIPLOM GIVE

L66
CHENERY H.B.,"FOREIGN ASSISTANCE AND ECONOMIC DEVELOPMENT" FUT WOR+45 NAT/G DIPLOM GIVE PRODUC ...METH/CNCPT CHARTS 20. PAGE 26 A0526 — FOR/AID EFFICIENCY ECO/UNDEV TEC/DEV

GJUPANOVIC H. A1078

GLADSTON/W....WILLIAM GLADSTONE

GLAZER M. A1079

GLEASON J.H. A1080

GLEASON S.E. A1727

GLENN N.D. A1081

GLOBERSON A. A1082

GLUBB J.B. A1083

GMP/REG....GOOD MANUFACTURING PRACTICE REGULATIONS

GOA....SEE ALSO INDIA

L62
CORET A.,"LES PROVINCES PORTUGALLES D'OUTREMER ET L'ONU." AFR PORTUGAL S/ASIA WOR+45 LOC/G NAT/G DOMIN...CONCPT TIME/SEQ UN 20 GOA. PAGE 31 A0620 — INT/ORG SOVEREIGN COLONIAL

GOBLET Y.M. A1084

GOD AND GODS....SEE DEITY

GODET M. A1085

GODUNSKY Y. A1086

GOEBBELS/J....JOSEPH GOEBBELS

GOEBEL J. A1087

GOETHE/J....JOHANN WOLFGANG VON GOETHE

GOLAY J.F. A1088

GOLD J. A1089

GOLD....GOLD

GOLD/COAST....GOLD COAST (PRE-GHANA)

GOLD/STAND....GOLD STANDARD

B58
AVRAMOVIC D.,POSTWAR GROWTH IN INTERNATIONAL INDEBTEDNESS. WOR+45 AGRI INDUS CAP/ISM PRICE INCOME...NAT/COMP 20 GOLD/STAND SILVER. PAGE 10 A0199 — INT/TRADE FINAN COST BAL/PAY

B58
PALYI M.,MANAGED MONEY AT THE CROSSROADS: THE EUROPEAN EXPERIENCE. WOR+45 WOR-45 TEC/DEV DIPLOM INT/TRADE DEMAND WEALTH...CHARTS BIBLIOG 19/20 EUROPE GOLD/STAND SILVER. PAGE 113 A2324 — FINAN ECO/TAC ECO/DEV PRODUC

B59
WENTHOLT W.,SOME COMMENTS ON THE LIQUIDATION OF THE EUROPEAN PAYMENT UNION AND RELATED PROBLEMS (PAMPHLET). WOR+45 PLAN BUDGET PRICE CONTROL 20 EEC GOLD/STAND. PAGE 163 A3319 — FINAN ECO/DEV INT/ORG ECO/TAC

B61
BUSSCHAU W.J.,GOLD AND INTERNATIONAL LIQUIDITY. WOR+45 PRICE EQUILIB WEALTH...CHARTS 20 GOLD/STAND. PAGE 22 A0450 — FINAN DIPLOM PROB/SOLV

B61
HARRIS S.E.,THE DOLLAR IN CRISIS. USA+45 MARKET INT/ORG ECO/TAC PRICE CONTROL WEALTH...METH/COMP ANTHOL 20 GOLD/STAND. PAGE 62 A1269 — BAL/PAY DIPLOM FINAN INT/TRADE

B61
NATIONAL BANK OF LIBYA,INFLATION IN LIBYA (PAMPHLET). LIBYA SOCIETY NAT/G PLAN INT/TRADE ...STAT CHARTS 20 GOLD/STAND. PAGE 107 A2200 — ECO/TAC ECO/UNDEV FINAN BUDGET

B61
TRIFFIN R.,GOLD AND THE DOLLAR CRISIS: THE FUTURE OF CONVERTIBILITY. USA+45 USA-45 INT/ORG PROB/SOLV BUDGET INT/TRADE PRICE...STAT CHARTS 19/20 GOLD/STAND. PAGE 145 A2963 — FINAN ECO/DEV ECO/TAC BAL/PAY

B62
FORD A.G.,THE GOLD STANDARD 1880-1914: BRITAIN AND ARGENTINA. UK ECO/UNDEV INT/TRADE ADMIN GOV/REL DEMAND EFFICIENCY...STAT CHARTS 19/20 ARGEN GOLD/STAND. PAGE 47 A0960 — FINAN ECO/TAC BUDGET BAL/PAY

B62
LUTZ F.A.,GELD UND WAHRUNG. MARKET LABOR BUDGET 20 GOLD/STAND EUROPE. PAGE 92 A1875 — ECO/TAC FINAN DIPLOM POLICY

B63
US CONGRESS JOINT ECO COMM,THE UNITED STATES BALANCE OF PAYMENTS. USA+45 DELIB/GP BUDGET PRICE PRODUC 20 CONGRESS GOLD/STAND MONEY. PAGE 150 A3067 — BAL/PAY INT/TRADE FINAN ECO/TAC

B63
YOUNG A.N.,CHINA AND THE HELPING HAND. ASIA USA+45 FINAN INDUS ECO/TAC GIVE WEALTH...METH/COMP 20 LEND/LEASE GOLD/STAND. PAGE 169 A3434 — FOR/AID DIPLOM WAR

B64
REUSS H.S.,THE CRITICAL DECADE - AN ECONOMIC POLICY FOR AMERICA AND THE FREE WORLD. USA+45 FINAN POL/PAR WORKER PLAN DIPLOM ECO/TAC TARIFFS BAL/PAY ...POLICY 20 CONGRESS GOLD/STAND. PAGE 120 A2468 — FOR/AID INT/TRADE LABOR LEGIS

B65
CASSELL F.,GOLD OR CREDIT? THE ECONOMICS AND POLITICS OF INTERNATIONAL MONEY. WOR+45 PLAN PROB/SOLV BAL/PAY SOVEREIGN WEALTH 20 OEEC GOLD/STAND. PAGE 25 A0506 — FINAN INT/ORG DIPLOM ECO/TAC

B65
ROLFE S.E.,GOLD AND WORLD POWER. UK USA+45 WOR-45 INDUS WORKER INT/TRADE DEMAND...MGT CHARTS 20 GOLD/STAND. PAGE 123 A2517 — BAL/PAY EQUILIB ECO/TAC DIPLOM

B65
US SENATE COMM BANKING CURR,BALANCE OF PAYMENTS - 1965. USA+45 ECO/TAC PRICE WEALTH...CHARTS 20 CONGRESS GOLD/STAND. PAGE 156 A3171 — BAL/PAY FINAN DIPLOM INT/TRADE

B66
KINDLEBERGER C.P.,EUROPE AND THE DOLLAR. EUR+WWI FRANCE GERMANY/W USA+45 CONSTN INT/ORG DIPLOM INT/TRADE...ANTHOL 20 GOLD/STAND. PAGE 79 A1623 — BAL/PAY BUDGET FINAN ECO/DEV

B66
PIQUET H.S.,THE US BALANCE OF PAYMENTS AND INTERNATIONAL MONETARY RESERVES. USA+45 PROB/SOLV INT/TRADE GOV/REL EQUILIB...POLICY STAT CHARTS 20 GOLD/STAND. PAGE 116 A2384 — BAL/PAY DIPLOM FINAN ECO/TAC

B66
TRIFFIN R.,THE WORLD MONEY MAZE. INT/ORG ECO/TAC PRICE OPTIMAL WEALTH...METH/COMP 20 EEC OEEC GOLD/STAND SILVER. PAGE 145 A2964 — BAL/PAY FINAN INT/TRADE DIPLOM

B66
TRIFFIN R.,THE BALANCE OF PAYMENTS AND THE FOREIGN INVESTMENT POSITION OF THE UNITED STATES. USA+45 INT/ORG INT/TRADE PRICE CONTROL...POLICY 20 GOLD/STAND. PAGE 145 A2965 — BAL/PAY DIPLOM FINAN ECO/TAC

B66
WOOLLEY H.B.,MEASURING TRANSACTIONS BETWEEN WORLD AREAS. WOR+45 FINAN...STAT NET/THEORY CHARTS DICTIONARY 20 GOLD/STAND. PAGE 167 A3395 — INT/TRADE BAL/PAY DIPLOM ECOMETRIC

N66
EOMMITTEE ECONOMIC DEVELOPMENT,THE DOLLAR AND THE WORLD MONETARY SYSTEM: A STATEMENT ON NATIONAL POLICY (PAMPHLET). USA+45 NAT/G PLAN PROB/SOLV BUDGET ECO/TAC FOR/AID INCOME...POLICY 20 GOLD/STAND EUROPE. PAGE 42 A0854 — FINAN BAL/PAY DIPLOM ECO/DEV

GOLDMAN M.I. A1090

GOLDMAN/E....ERIC GOLDMAN

S64
RUSK D.,"THE MAKING OF FOREIGN POLICY" USA+45 CHIEF DELIB/GP WORKER PROB/SOLV ADMIN ATTIT PWR ...DECISION 20 DEPT/STATE RUSK/D GOLDMAN/E. PAGE 125 A2570 — DIPLOM INT POLICY

GOLDSCHMIDT W. A1091

GOLDWATER B.M. A1092

GOLDWATR/B....BARRY GOLDWATER

B64
MORGAN T.,GOLDWATER EITHER/OR; A SELF-PORTRAIT BASED UPON HIS OWN WORDS. USA+45 CONSTN AGRI LABOR DIPLOM RACE/REL WEALTH POPULISM...POLICY MAJORIT 20 GOLDWATR/B REPUBLICAN. PAGE 104 A2131 — LEAD POL/PAR CHOOSE ATTIT

GOLDWERT M. A1093

GOLDWIN R.A. A1094,A1095,A1096,A1097

GOMILLN/CG....C.G. GOMILLION

GOMULKA W. A1098

GONZALEZ PEDRERO E. A1099

GOOCH G.P. A1100

GOODMAN E. A1101

GOODMAN R.M. A2010

GOODRICH L.M. A1102,A1103,A1104,A1105,A1106

GOODWIN C.D.W. A1247

GOODWIN G.L. A1107,A1108

GORDENKER L. A1109

GORDON B. A1110

GORDON B.K. A1111

GORDON D.L. A1112

GORDON G.N. A1113

GORDON L. A1114,A1115

GORDON/K....K. GORDON

GORDON/W....WILLIAM GORDON

GORER G. A1116

GOROKHOFF C.J. A2287

GOTT R. A1068

GOULD L.P. A1117

GOV/COMP....COMPARISON OF GOVERNMENTS

N
AMERICAN POLITICAL SCIENCE REVIEW. USA+45 USA-45 WOR+45 WOR-45 INT/ORG ADMIN...INT/LAW PHIL/SCI CONCPT METH 20 UN. PAGE 1 A0003 — BIBLIOG/A DIPLOM NAT/G GOV/COMP

N
CARNEGIE ENDOWMENT,CURRENT RESEARCH IN INTERNATIONAL AFFAIRS: SELECTED BIBLIOGRAPHY OF WORK IN PROGRESS BY PRIVATE RESEARCH AGENCIES. WOR+45 NAT/G ACT/RES GOV/COMP. PAGE 24 A0488 — BIBLIOG/A DIPLOM R+D

N
US DEPARTMENT OF STATE,BIBLIOGRAPHY (PAMPHLETS). AGRI INDUS INT/ORG FOR/AID EDU/PROP WAR MARXISM ...SOC GOV/COMP METH/COMP 20. PAGE 151 A3079 — BIBLIOG DIPLOM ECO/DEV NAT/G

B13
BORCHARD E.M.,BIBLIOGRAPHY OF INTERNATIONAL LAW AND CONTINENTAL LAW. EUR+WWI MOD/EUR UK LAW INT/TRADE WAR PEACE...GOV/COMP NAT/COMP 19/20. PAGE 17 A0338 — BIBLIOG INT/LAW JURID DIPLOM

N17
BURKE E.,THOUGHTS ON THE PROSPECT OF A REGICIDE PEACE (PAMPHLET). FRANCE UK SECT DOMIN MURDER PEACE ORD/FREE SOVEREIGN POPULISM...POLICY GOV/COMP IDEA/COMP 18 JACOBINISM COEXIST. PAGE 21 A0435 — REV CHIEF NAT/G DIPLOM

N19
FREEMAN H.A.,COERCION OF STATES IN FEDERAL UNIONS (PAMPHLET). WOR-45 DIPLOM CONTROL COERCE PEACE ORD/FREE...GOV/COMP METH/COMP NAT/COMP PACIFIST 20. PAGE 49 A0994 — FEDERAL WAR INT/ORG PACIFISM

B36
BOYCE A.N.,EUROPE AND SOUTH AFRICA. FRANCE GERMANY ITALY SOUTH/AFR UK INDUS NAT/G CONTROL REV WAR NAT/LISM...CONCPT HIST/WRIT 20. PAGE 18 A0362 — COLONIAL GOV/COMP NAT/COMP DIPLOM

B41
KEESING F.M.,THE SOUTH SEAS IN THE MODERN WORLD. INDONESIA STRUCT FAM SECT EDU/PROP LEAD INCOME WEALTH...HEAL SOC 20. PAGE 77 A1577 — CULTURE ECO/UNDEV GOV/COMP DIPLOM

B45
WOOLBERT R.G.,FOREIGN AFFAIRS BIBLIOGRAPHY, 1932-1942. INT/ORG SECT INT/TRADE COLONIAL RACE/REL NAT/LISM...GEOG INT/LAW GOV/COMP IDEA/COMP 20. PAGE 167 A3393 — BIBLIOG/A DIPLOM WAR

B48
GRIFFITH E.S.,RESEARCH IN POLITICAL SCIENCE: THE WORK OF PANELS OF RESEARCH COMMITTEE, APSA. WOR+45 WOR-45 COM/IND R+D FORCES ACT/RES WAR...GOV/COMP ANTHOL 20. PAGE 56 A1160 — BIBLIOG PHIL/SCI DIPLOM JURID

B50
DUCLOS P.,L'EVOLUTION DES RAPPORTS POLITIQUES DEPUIS 1750 (LIBERTE, INTEGRATION, UNITE). LAW INT/ORG FEDERAL TOTALISM ATTIT PWR...MAJORIT BIBLIOG 18/20 PARLIAMENT EUROPE. PAGE 39 A0792 — ORD/FREE DIPLOM NAT/G GOV/COMP

B51
LEONARD L.L.,INTERNATIONAL ORGANIZATION. WOR+45 WOR-45 EX/STRUC FORCES LEGIS ECO/TAC INT/TRADE COLONIAL ARMS/CONT...SOC/WK GOV/COMP BIBLIOG. PAGE 87 A1778 — NAT/G DIPLOM INT/ORG DELIB/GP

B54
BUTZ O.,GERMANY: DILEMMA FOR AMERICAN POLICY. GERMANY USA+45 USA-45 USSR WOR+45 INT/ORG FORCES NUC/PWR EFFICIENCY PEACE PWR...GOV/COMP 20 COLD/WAR. PAGE 23 A0459 — DIPLOM NAT/G WAR POLICY

L55
ROSTOW W.W.,"RUSSIA AND CHINA UNDER COMMUNISM." CHINA/COM USSR INTELL STRUCT INT/ORG NAT/G POL/PAR TOP/EX ACT/RES PLAN ADMIN ATTIT ALL/VALS MARXISM ...CONCPT OBS TIME/SEQ TREND GOV/COMP VAL/FREE 20. PAGE 124 A2543 — COM ASIA

B56
VON HARPE W.,DIE SOWJETUNION FINNLAND UND SKANDANAVIEN, 1945-1955. EUR+WWI FINLAND GERMANY USSR WAR INGP/REL ORD/FREE SOVEREIGN MARXISM ...POLICY GOV/COMP BIBLIOG 20 STALIN/J. PAGE 160 A3252 — DIPLOM COM NEUTRAL BAL/PWR

B57
ALEXANDER L.M.,WORLD POLITICAL PATTERNS. NAT/G PROVS CAP/ISM DIPLOM COLONIAL NAT/LISM...POLICY GEOG CHARTS METH/COMP NAT/COMP 20. PAGE 5 A0111 — CONTROL METH GOV/COMP

B59
MEZERK A.G.,FINANCIAL ASSISTANCE FOR ECONOMIC DEVELOPMENT. WOR+45 INDUS DIPLOM INT/TRADE...CHARTS GOV/COMP UN. PAGE 101 A2064 — FOR/AID FINAN ECO/TAC ECO/UNDEV

B60
KENNEDY J.F.,THE STRATEGY OF PEACE. USA+45 WOR+45 BAL/PWR DIPLOM INGP/REL ORD/FREE...GOV/COMP NAT/COMP 20. PAGE 78 A1591 — PEACE PLAN POLICY NAT/G

B60
STOLPER W.F.,GERMANY BETWEEN EAST AND WEST: THE ECONOMICS OF COMPETITIVE COEXISTENCE. FUT GERMANY/E GERMANY/W WOR+45 FINAN POL/PAR BUDGET ECO/TAC FOR/AID INT/TRADE...STAT CHARTS METH/COMP 20 COLD/WAR. PAGE 138 A2832 — ECO/DEV DIPLOM GOV/COMP BAL/PWR

B60
STRACHEY J.,THE END OF EMPIRE. UK WOR+45 WOR-45 DIPLOM INT/TRADE DOMIN ADJUST ORD/FREE WEALTH ...SOCIALIST GOV/COMP TIME COMMONWLTH. PAGE 139 A2841 — COLONIAL ECO/DEV BAL/PWR LAISSEZ

B61
BURDETTE F.L.,POLITICAL SCIENCE: A SELECTED BIBLIOGRAPHY OF BOOKS IN PRINT, WITH ANNOTATIONS (PAMPHLET). LAW LOC/G NAT/G POL/PAR PROVS DIPLOM EDU/PROP ADMIN CHOOSE ATTIT 20. PAGE 21 A0432 — BIBLIOG/A GOV/COMP CONCPT ROUTINE

B61
CARNELL F.,THE POLITICS OF THE NEW STATES: A SELECT ANNOTATED BIBLIOGRAPHY WITH SPECIAL REFERENCE TO THE COMMONWEALTH. CONSTN ELITES LABOR NAT/G POL/PAR EX/STRUC DIPLOM ADJUD ADMIN...GOV/COMP 20 COMMONWLTH. PAGE 24 A0496 — BIBLIOG/A AFR ASIA COLONIAL

B61
PECKERT J.,DIE GROSSEN UND DIE KLEINEN MAECHTE. COM GERMANY/W ECO/DEV ECO/UNDEV NAT/G WAR RACE/REL PEACE...POLICY GP/COMP GOV/COMP 20 COLD/WAR. PAGE 114 A2346 — DIPLOM ECO/TAC BAL/PWR

B62
DEHIO L.,THE PRECARIOUS BALANCE: FOUR CENTURIES OF THE EUROPEAN POWER STRUGGLE. FRANCE GERMANY SPAIN NAT/G DOMIN PWR...GOV/COMP 8/20. PAGE 36 A0725 — BAL/PWR WAR DIPLOM COERCE

B62
EBENSTEIN W.,TWO WAYS OF LIFE. USA+45 CULTURE ECO/DEV PLAN EDU/PROP CONTROL ORD/FREE...GOV/COMP IDEA/COMP T 20 MARX/KARL ENGELS/F LENIN/VI LOCKE/JOHN MILL/JS. PAGE 40 A0819 — MARXISM POPULISM ECO/TAC DIPLOM

B62
KINDLEBERGER C.P.,FOREIGN TRADE AND THE NATIONAL ECONOMY. WOR+45 ECO/DEV ECO/UNDEV ECO/TAC COST DEMAND 20. PAGE 79 A1622 — INT/TRADE GOV/COMP BAL/PAY POLICY

B62
MORGENSTERN O.,STRATEGIE - HEUTE (2ND ED.). USA+45 USSR ECO/DEV DELIB/GP WAR PEACE ORD/FREE...GOV/COMP NAT/COMP 20 COLD/WAR NATO. PAGE 104 A2134 — NUC/PWR DIPLOM FORCES TEC/DEV

B63
COLUMBIA U SCHOOL OF LAW,PUBLIC INTERNATIONAL DEVELOPMENT FINANCING IN SENEGAL. SENEGAL FINAN DELIB/GP GIVE EFFICIENCY...CHARTS GOV/COMP ANTHOL 20. PAGE 28 A0571 — FOR/AID PLAN RECEIVE ECO/UNDEV

B63
DECOTTIGNIES R.,LES NATIONALITES AFRICAINES. AFR NAT/G PROB/SOLV DIPLOM COLONIAL ORD/FREE...CHARTS GOV/COMP 20. PAGE 35 A0721 — NAT/LISM JURID LEGIS LAW

B63
FRANKEL J.,THE MAKING OF FOREIGN POLICY: AN ANALYSIS OF DECISION-MAKING. CHINA/COM EUR+WWI USA+45 ELITES INTELL FORCES LEGIS PLAN ATTIT ALL/VALS MORAL CONSERVE...GOV/COMP 20 PRESIDENT UN TREATY. PAGE 48 A0981 — POLICY DECISION PROB/SOLV DIPLOM

B63
JENNINGS W.I.,DEMOCRACY IN AFRICA. UK CULTURE STRUCT ECO/UNDEV DIPLOM COLONIAL GP/REL ADJUST NAT/LISM ORD/FREE...GOV/COMP 20 THIRD/WRLD. PAGE 74 A1512 — PROB/SOLV AFR CONSTN POPULISM

B63
KAHIN G.M.,MAJOR GOVERNMENTS OF ASIA (2ND ED.). ASIA INDIA INDONESIA PAKISTAN S/ASIA DIPLOM...SOC 20 CHINJAP. PAGE 75 A1546 — GOV/COMP POL/PAR ELITES

B63
RIVKIN A.,THE AFRICAN PRESENCE IN WORLD AFFAIRS. ECO/UNDEV AGRI INT/ORG LOC/G NAT/LISM...OBS PREDICT GOV/COMP 20. PAGE 121 A2489 — AFR NAT/G DIPLOM BAL/PWR

B64
BELL C.,THE DEBATABLE ALLIANCE. COM UK USA+45 NAT/G FORCES PLAN BAL/PWR NUC/PWR WAR ATTIT...GOV/COMP 20. PAGE 13 A0256 — DIPLOM PWR PEACE POLICY

B64
DICKEY J.S.,THE UNITED STATES AND CANADA. CANADA USA+45...SOC 20. PAGE 37 A0756 — DIPLOM TREND GOV/COMP PROB/SOLV

B64
GRIFFITH W.E.,COMMUNISM IN EUROPE (2 VOLS.). CZECHOSLVK USSR WOR+45 WOR-45 YUGOSLAVIA INGP/REL MARXISM SOCISM...ANTHOL 20 EUROPE/E. PAGE 57 A1162 — COM POL/PAR DIPLOM GOV/COMP

B64
HALPERN J.M.,GOVERNMENT, POLITICS, AND SOCIAL STRUCTURE IN LAOS. LAOS CULTURE SOCIETY STRATA STRUCT FAM DIPLOM DOMIN MARXISM...INT GOV/COMP WORSHIP SOC/INTEG 20. PAGE 60 A1242 — NAT/G SOC LOC/G

B64
HORNE D.,THE LUCKY COUNTRY: AUSTRALIA TODAY. UK CULTURE STRATA ATTIT PWR PLURISM...GOV/COMP 20 AUSTRAL. PAGE 67 A1386 — RACE/REL DIPLOM NAT/G

STRUCT

B64
KALDOR N.,ESSAYS ON ECONOMIC POLICY (VOL. II). CHILE GERMANY INDIA FINAN...GOV/COMP METH/COMP 20 KEYNES/JM. PAGE 76 A1551
BAL/PAY INT/TRADE METH/CNCPT ECO/UNDEV

B64
KNIGHT R.,BIBLIOGRAPHY ON INCOME AND WEALTH, 1957-1960 (VOL VIII). WOR+45 ECO/DEV FINAN INT/TRADE...GOV/COMP METH/COMP. PAGE 80 A1652
BIBLIOG/A ECO/UNDEV WEALTH INCOME

B64
KOLARZ W.,BOOKS ON COMMUNISM. USSR WOR+45 CULTURE NAT/G POL/PAR DIPLOM LEAD...CONCPT GOV/COMP IDEA/COMP. PAGE 81 A1667
BIBLIOG/A SOCIETY COM MARXISM

B64
MAUD J.,AID FOR DEVELOPING COUNTRIES. COM EUR+WWI UK INT/TRADE ORD/FREE...GOV/COMP 20. PAGE 96 A1979
FOR/AID DIPLOM ECO/TAC ECO/UNDEV

B64
QUIGG P.W.,AFRICA: A FOREIGN AFFAIRS READER. AFR FRANCE PORTUGAL UK DIPLOM LEAD PARL/PROC MARXISM ...MAJORIT METH/CNCPT GOV/COMP IDEA/COMP ANTHOL 19/20. PAGE 118 A2426
COLONIAL SOVEREIGN NAT/LISM RACE/REL

B64
ROBERTS HL,FOREIGN AFFAIRS BIBLIOGRAPHY, 1952-1962. ECO/DEV SECT PLAN FOR/AID INT/TRADE ARMS/CONT NAT/LISM ATTIT...INT/LAW GOV/COMP IDEA/COMP 20. PAGE 122 A2495
BIBLIOG/A DIPLOM INT/ORG WAR

B65
COX R.H.,THE STATE IN INTERNATIONAL RELATIONS. INT/ORG DIPLOM REV WAR PEACE MARXISM...CONCPT GOV/COMP. PAGE 32 A0647
SOVEREIGN NAT/G FASCISM ORD/FREE

B65
FAGG J.E.,CUBA, HAITI, AND THE DOMINICAN REPUBLIC. CUBA DOMIN/REP HAITI L/A+17C NAT/G DIPLOM ECO/TAC DOMIN CHOOSE AUTHORIT ROLE SOVEREIGN POPULISM 17/20. PAGE 43 A0883
COLONIAL ECO/UNDEV REV GOV/COMP

B65
HARMON R.B.,POLITICAL SCIENCE: A BIBLIOGRAPHICAL GUIDE TO THE LITERATURE. WOR+45 WOR-45 R+D INT/ORG LOC/G NAT/G DIPLOM ADMIN...CONCPT METH. PAGE 61 A1261
BIBLIOG POL/PAR LAW GOV/COMP

B65
LARUS J.,COMPARATIVE WORLD POLITICS. ASIA INDIA WOR+45 WOR-45 BAL/PWR WAR PEACE RATIONAL MORAL PWR ...REALPOL INT/LAW MUSLIM. PAGE 85 A1735
GOV/COMP IDEA/COMP DIPLOM NAT/COMP

B65
MEAGHER R.F.,PUBLIC INTERNATIONAL DEVELOPMENT FINANCING IN SUDAN. SUDAN FINAN DELIB/GP GIVE ...CHARTS GOV/COMP 20. PAGE 99 A2029
FOR/AID PLAN RECEIVE ECO/UNDEV

B65
UN,SPACE ACTIVITIES AND RESOURCES: REVIEW OF UNITED NATION'S NATIONAL AND INTERNATIONAL PROGRAMS. INT/ORG LABOR PLAN TEC/DEV DIPLOM EFFICIENCY HEALTH ...GOV/COMP 20 UN. PAGE 146 A2995
SPACE NUC/PWR FOR/AID PEACE

B65
US DEPARTMENT OF DEFENSE,US SECURITY ARMS CONTROL, AND DISARMAMENT 1961-1965 (PAMPHLET). CHINA/COM COM GERMANY/W ISRAEL SPACE USA+45 USSR WOR+45 FORCES EDU/PROP DETER EQUILIB PEACE ALL/VALS...GOV/COMP 20 NATO. PAGE 151 A3077
BIBLIOG/A ARMS/CONT NUC/PWR DIPLOM

B66
FRANK E.,LAWMAKERS IN A CHANGING WORLD. FRANCE UK USSR WOR+45 PARTIC EFFICIENCY ROLE ALL/IDEOS ...CHARTS ANTHOL PARLIAMENT 20 UN COLD/WAR. PAGE 48 A0979
GOV/COMP LEGIS NAT/G DIPLOM

B66
GRAHAM I.C.C.,PUBLICATIONS OF THE SOCIAL SCIENCE DEPARTMENT, THE RAND CORPORATION, 1948-1966. USSR WOR+45 NAT/G ARMS/CONT DETER WAR NAT/LISM...SOC GOV/COMP. PAGE 55 A1127
BIBLIOG DIPLOM NUC/PWR FORCES

B66
HOLT R.T.,THE POLITICAL BASIS OF ECONOMIC DEVELOPMENT. STRATA STRUCT NAT/G DIPLOM ADMIN...SOC NAT/COMP BIBLIOG 20. PAGE 67 A1376
ECO/TAC GOV/COMP CONSTN EX/STRUC

B66
MCKAY V.,AFRICAN DIPLOMACY STUDIES IN THE DETERMINANTS OF FOREIGN POLICY. AFR SOUTH/AFR CULTURE NEUTRAL REGION SOVEREIGN...INT/LAW GOV/COMP ANTHOL 20. PAGE 98 A2013
ECO/UNDEV RACE/REL CIVMIL/REL DIPLOM

B66
US DEPARTMENT OF STATE,RESEARCH ON THE MIDDLE EAST (EXTERNAL RESEARCH LIST NO 4-25). GREECE ISRAEL SYRIA UAR YEMEN CULTURE SOCIETY POL/PAR SECT DIPLOM EDU/PROP WAR NAT/LISM...GEOG GOV/COMP 20. PAGE 152 A3096
BIBLIOG/A ISLAM NAT/G REGION

B66
ZABLOCKI C.J.,SINO-SOVIET RIVALRY. AFR ASIA CHINA/COM CUBA EUR+WWI L/A+17C USA+45 USSR WOR+45 POL/PAR FORCES COERCE NUC/PWR...GOV/COMP IDEA/COMP 20 MAO KHRUSH/N. PAGE 169 A3442
DIPLOM MARXISM COM

L66
SEYLER W.C.,"DOCTORAL DISSERTATIONS IN POLITICAL SCIENCE IN UNIVERSITIES OF THE UNITED STATES AND CANADA." INT/ORG LOC/G ADMIN...INT/LAW MGT GOV/COMP. PAGE 131 A2690
BIBLIOG LAW NAT/G

S66
GRUNDY K.W.,"RECENT CONTRIBUTIONS TO THE STUDY OF AFRICAN POLITICAL THOUGHT." DIPLOM NAT/LISM ALL/IDEOS...NEW/IDEA GOV/COMP 20. PAGE 58 A1182
BIBLIOG/A AFR ATTIT IDEA/COMP

S66
MERRITT R.L.,"SELECTED ARTICLES AND DOCUMENTS ON COMPARATIVE GOVERNMENT AND CROSS-NATIONAL RESEARCH." AFR ASIA EUR+WWI L/A+17C MOD/EUR ELITES R+D ACT/RES DIPLOM PWR...SOC CONCPT 18/20. PAGE 100 A2046
BIBLIOG GOV/COMP NAT/G GOV/REL

S67
CHAND A.,"INDIA AND TANZANIA." INDIA TANZANIA TEC/DEV ECO/TAC FOR/AID COLONIAL PEACE UTIL WEALTH ...GOV/COMP 20. PAGE 25 A0518
ECO/UNDEV NEUTRAL DIPLOM PLAN

S67
GRUNDY K.W.,"AFRICA IN THE WORLD ARENA." ECO/UNDEV BAL/PWR FOR/AID NEUTRAL REV NAT/LISM GOV/COMP. PAGE 58 A1183
AFR DIPLOM INT/ORG COLONIAL

S67
NIEBUHR R.,"THE SOCIAL MYTHS IN THE COLD WAR." USA+45 USSR VIETNAM PROB/SOLV BAL/PWR ARMS/CONT NAT/LISM PWR ALL/IDEOS CONCPT. PAGE 109 A2238
MYTH DIPLOM GOV/COMP

GOV/REL....RELATIONS BETWEEN GOVERNMENTS

N
UNIVERSITY OF FLORIDA LIBRARY,DOORS TO LATIN AMERICA; RECENT BOOKS AND PAMPHLETS. CONSTN CULTURE SOCIETY ECO/UNDEV COLONIAL LEAD GOV/REL NAT/LISM ATTIT...HUM SOC 20. PAGE 149 A3047
BIBLIOG/A L/A+17C DIPLOM NAT/G

N
LITERATUR-VERZEICHNIS DER POLITISCHEN WISSENSCHAFTEN. GERMANY/W WOR+45 CONSTN SOCIETY ECO/DEV INT/ORG POL/PAR LEAD REPRESENT GOV/REL GP/REL...POLICY PHIL/SCI. PAGE 1 A0018
BIBLIOG EUR+WWI DIPLOM NAT/G

N
MIDDLE EAST JOURNAL. CULTURE SECT DIPLOM LEAD GOV/REL ATTIT...POLICY PHIL/SCI SOC LING BIOG 20. PAGE 1 A0019
BIBLIOG ISLAM NAT/G ECO/UNDEV

N
MIDWEST JOURNAL OF POLITICAL SCIENCE. USA+45 CONSTN ECO/DEV LEGIS PROB/SOLV CT/SYS LEAD GOV/REL ATTIT POLICY. PAGE 1 A0020
BIBLIOG/A NAT/G DIPLOM POL/PAR

N
CHINA QUARTERLY. COM AGRI INDUS ACADEM POL/PAR INT/TRADE CONFER GOV/REL...TIME/SEQ CON/ANAL INDEX 20. PAGE 2 A0032
BIBLIOG/A ASIA DIPLOM POLICY

N
AVTOREFERATY DISSERTATSII. USSR INTELL ACADEM NAT/G DIPLOM GOV/REL KNOWL CONCPT. PAGE 3 A0047
BIBLIOG MARXISM MARXIST COM

N
"PROLOG",DIGEST OF THE SOVIET UKRANIAN PRESS. USSR LAW AGRI INDUS PROVS SCHOOL DIPLOM GOV/REL ATTIT ...HUM LING 20. PAGE 4 A0081
BIBLIOG/A NAT/G PRESS COM

N
ATLANTIC INSTITUTE,ATLANTIC STUDIES. COM EUR+WWI USA+45 CULTURE STRUCT ECO/DEV FORCES LEAD ARMS/CONT ...INT/LAW JURID SOC. PAGE 10 A0193
BIBLIOG/A DIPLOM POLICY GOV/REL

N
FOREIGN TRADE LIBRARY,NEW TITLES RECEIVED IN THE LIBRARY. WOR+45 ECO/UNDEV FINAN NAT/G PLAN TEC/DEV BUDGET ECO/TAC TARIFFS GOV/REL STAT. PAGE 47 A0964
BIBLIOG/A INT/TRADE INDUS ECO/DEV

N
INTERNATIONAL STUDIES,"INDIA AND WORLD AFFAIRS: AN ANNUAL BIBLIOGRAPHY" INDIA INT/TRADE PARTIC GOV/REL 20. PAGE 71 A1461
BIBLIOG POLICY DIPLOM ATTIT

N
UNESCO,INTERNATIONAL BIBLIOGRAPHY OF POLITICAL SCIENCE (VOLUMES 1-8). WOR+45 LAW NAT/G EX/STRUC LEGIS PROB/SOLV DIPLOM ADMIN GOV/REL 20 UNESCO. PAGE 147 A3010
BIBLIOG CONCPT IDEA/COMP

NCO
CARRINGTON C.E.,THE COMMONWEALTH IN AFRICA (PAMPHLET). UK STRUCT NAT/G COLONIAL REPRESENT GOV/REL RACE/REL NAT/LISM...MAJORIT 20 EEC NEGRO COLD/WAR. PAGE 25 A0500
ECO/UNDEV AFR DIPLOM PLAN

B00
GRIFFIN A.P.C.,LIST OF BOOKS RELATING TO THE THEORY OF COLONIZATION, GOVERNMENT OF DEPENDENCIES, PROTECTORATES, AND RELATED TOPICS. FRANCE GERMANY ITALY SPAIN UK USA-45 WOR-45 ECO/TAC ADMIN CONTROL REGION NAT/LISM ALL/VALS PWR...INT/LAW SOC 16/19. PAGE 56 A1149 BIBLIOG/A COLONIAL GOV/REL DOMIN

B01
HART A.B.,AMERICAN HISTORY TOLD BY CONTEMPORARIES. UK CULTURE FINAN SECT FORCES DIPLOM TAX RUMOR CT/SYS REV GOV/REL GP/REL...ANTHOL 17/18 PRE/US/AM FEDERALIST. PAGE 62 A1273 USA-45 COLONIAL SOVEREIGN

B05
AMES J.G.,COMPREHENSIVE INDEX TO THE PUBLICATIONS OF THE UNITED STATES GOVERNMENT , 1881-1893. USA-45 CONSTN POL/PAR DELIB/GP TOP/EX DIPLOM PARL/PROC INGP/REL...INDEX 19 CONGRESS. PAGE 8 A0153 BIBLIOG/A LEGIS NAT/G GOV/REL

B05
GRIFFIN A.P.C.,LIST OF REFERENCES ON THE US CONSULAR SERVICE (PAMPHLET). FRANCE GERMANY SPAIN UK USA-45 WOR-45 OP/RES DOMIN ADMIN FEEDBACK ROUTINE GOV/REL...DECISION 19. PAGE 56 A1153 BIBLIOG/A NAT/G DIPLOM CONSULT

B19
LONDON SCHOOL ECONOMICS-POL,ANNUAL DIGEST OF PUBLIC INTERNATIONAL LAW CASES. INT/ORG MUNIC NAT/G PROVS ADMIN NEUTRAL WAR GOV/REL PRIVIL 20. PAGE 91 A1858 BIBLIOG/A INT/LAW ADJUD DIPLOM

B19
SUTHERLAND G.,CONSTITUTIONAL POWER AND WORLD AFFAIRS. CONSTN STRUCT INT/ORG NAT/G CHIEF LEGIS ACT/RES PLAN GOV/REL ALL/VALS...OBS TIME/SEQ CONGRESS VAL/FREE 20 PRESIDENT. PAGE 140 A2866 USA-45 EXEC DIPLOM

N19
HIGGINS R.,THE ADMINISTRATION OF UNITED KINGDOM FOREIGN POLICY THROUGH THE UNITED NATIONS (PAMPHLET). UK NAT/G ADMIN GOV/REL...CHARTS 20 UN PARLIAMENT. PAGE 65 A1329 DIPLOM POLICY INT/ORG

B26
INTERNATIONAL BIBLIOGRAPHY OF POLITICAL SCIENCE. WOR+45 NAT/G POL/PAR EX/STRUC LEGIS CT/SYS LEAD CHOOSE GOV/REL ATTIT...PHIL/SCI 20. PAGE 3 A0049 BIBLIOG DIPLOM CONCPT ADMIN

B30
FLEMMING D.,THE TREATY VETO OF THE AMERICAN SENATE. FUT USA+45 USA-45 CONSTN INT/ORG NAT/G TOP/EX LEGIT GOV/REL PWR...POLICY MAJORIT CONCPT OBS TIME/SEQ CONGRESS 20. PAGE 46 A0949 LEGIS RIGID/FLEX

B30
SMUTS J.C.,AFRICA AND SOME WORLD PROBLEMS. RHODESIA SOUTH/AFR CULTURE ECO/UNDEV INDUS INT/ORG SECT PROB/SOLV REGION GOV/REL DISCRIM ATTIT 19/20 LEAGUE/NAT LIVNGSTN/D NEGRO. PAGE 134 A2748 LEGIS AFR COLONIAL RACE/REL

B35
LEAGUE OF NATIONS,CATALOGUE OF PUBLICATIONS, 1920-1935. GOV/REL 20 LEAGUE/NAT. PAGE 86 A1755 BIBLIOG INT/ORG DIPLOM

B44
RAGATZ L.J.,LITERATURE OF EUROPEAN IMPERIALISM. ECO/TAC INT/TRADE DOMIN GOV/REL DEMAND NAT/LISM PWR WEALTH 19/20. PAGE 119 A2432 BIBLIOG COLONIAL INT/ORG ECO/UNDEV

B48
BELOFF M.,THOMAS JEFFERSON AND AMERICAN DEMOCRACY. USA-45 NAT/G DIPLOM GOV/REL PEACE 18/19 JEFFERSN/T PRESIDENT VIRGINIA. PAGE 13 A0258 BIOG CHIEF REV

B48
CHILDS J.R.,AMERICAN FOREIGN SERVICE. USA+45 SOCIETY NAT/G ROUTINE GOV/REL 20 DEPT/STATE CIVIL/SERV. PAGE 26 A0530 DIPLOM ADMIN GP/REL

B48
PELCOVITS N.A.,OLD CHINA HANDS AND THE FOREIGN OFFICE. ASIA BURMA UK ECO/UNDEV NAT/G ECO/TAC FOR/AID TARIFFS DOMIN COLONIAL GOV/REL SOVEREIGN 19 HONG/KONG TREATY. PAGE 114 A2348 INT/TRADE ATTIT DIPLOM

B49
HEADLAM-MORLEY,BIBLIOGRAPHY IN POLITICS FOR THE HONOUR SCHOOL OF PHILOSOPHY, POLITICS AND ECONOMICS (PAMPHLET). UK CONSTN LABOR MUNIC DIPLOM ADMIN 19/20. PAGE 64 A1305 BIBLIOG NAT/G PHIL/SCI GOV/REL

B50
PERHAM M.,COLONIAL GOVERNMENT: ANNOTATED READING LIST ON BRITISH COLONIAL GOVERNMENT. UK WOR+45 WOR-45 ECO/UNDEV INT/ORG LEGIS FOR/AID INT/TRADE DOMIN ADMIN REV 20. PAGE 115 A2356 BIBLIOG/A COLONIAL GOV/REL NAT/G

B51
CATALOGO GENERAL DE LA LIBRERIA ESPANOLA E HISPANOAMERICANA 1901-1930; AUTORES (5 VOLS., 1932-1951). SPAIN COLONIAL GOV/REL...SOC 20. PAGE 3 A0058 BIBLIOG L/A+17C DIPLOM NAT/G

B51
SWISHER C.B.,THE THEORY AND PRACTICE OF AMERICAN NATIONAL GOVERNMENT. CULTURE LEGIS DIPLOM ADJUD ADMIN WAR PEACE ORD/FREE...MAJORIT 17/20. PAGE 140 A2872 CONSTN NAT/G GOV/REL GEN/LAWS

B52
THOM J.M.,GUIDE TO RESEARCH MATERIAL IN POLITICAL SCIENCE (PAMPHLET). ELITES LOC/G MUNIC NAT/G LEGIS DIPLOM ADJUD CIVMIL/REL GOV/REL PWR MGT. PAGE 143 A2919 BIBLIOG/A KNOWL

L52
WRIGHT Q.,"CONGRESS AND THE TREATY-MAKING POWER." USA+45 WOR+45 CONSTN INTELL NAT/G CHIEF CONSULT EX/STRUC LEGIS TOP/EX CREATE GOV/REL DISPL DRIVE RIGID/FLEX...TREND TOT/POP CONGRESS CONGRESS 20 TREATY. PAGE 167 A3408 ROUTINE DIPLOM INT/LAW DELIB/GP

B53
MATLOFF M.,STRATEGIC PLANNING FOR COALITION WARFARE. UK USA-45 CHIEF DIPLOM EXEC GOV/REL ...METH/COMP 20. PAGE 96 A1967 WAR PLAN DECISION FORCES

B55
LANDHEER B.,EUROPEAN YEARBOOK, 1955. CONSTN ECO/DEV DIST/IND FINAN DELIB/GP ECO/TAC DETER NUC/PWR ...BIBLIOG 20 EEC. PAGE 84 A1717 EUR+WWI INT/ORG GOV/REL INT/TRADE

B55
STILLMAN C.W.,AFRICA IN THE MODERN WORLD. AFR USA+45 WOR+45 INT/TRADE COLONIAL PARTIC REGION GOV/REL RACE/REL 20. PAGE 138 A2826 ECO/UNDEV DIPLOM POLICY STRUCT

B55
VINSON J.C.,THE PARCHMENT PEACE: THE UNITED STATES SENATE AND THE WASHINGTON CONFERENCE, 1921-1922. USA-45 INT/ORG DELIB/GP PLAN ARMS/CONT GOV/REL ISOLAT PEACE ATTIT SOVEREIGN...INT/LAW BIBLIOG 20 SENATE PRESIDENT CONGRESS LEAGUE/NAT CHINJAP. PAGE 159 A3242 POLICY DIPLOM NAT/G LEGIS

C55
APTER D.E.,"THE GOLD COAST IN TRANSITION." AFR CONSTN LOC/G LEGIS DIPLOM COLONIAL CONTROL GOV/REL ...CHARTS BIBLIOG 20 CMN/WLTH. PAGE 8 A0170 ORD/FREE REPRESENT PARL/PROC NAT/G

B56
GREECE PRESBEIA U.S.,BRITISH OPINION ON CYPRUS. CYPRUS UK FORCES DIPLOM INT/TRADE DOMIN GOV/REL ORD/FREE SOVEREIGN...POLICY 20. PAGE 55 A1137 ATTIT COLONIAL LEGIS PRESS

B56
KOENIG L.W.,THE TRUMAN ADMINISTRATION: ITS PRINCIPLES AND PRACTICE. USA+45 POL/PAR CHIEF LEGIS DIPLOM DEATH NUC/PWR WAR CIVMIL/REL PEACE ...DECISION 20 TRUMAN/HS PRESIDENT TREATY. PAGE 81 A1658 ADMIN POLICY EX/STRUC GOV/REL

B57
NEUMANN F.,THE DEMOCRATIC AND THE AUTHORITARIAN STATE: ESSAYS IN POLITICAL AND LEGAL THEORY. USA+45 USA-45 CONTROL REV GOV/REL PEACE ALL/IDEOS ...INT/LAW CONCPT GEN/LAWS BIBLIOG 20. PAGE 108 A2221 DOMIN NAT/G ORD/FREE POLICY

C57
TANG P.S.H.,"COMMUNIST CHINA TODAY: DOMESTIC AND FOREIGN POLICIES." CHINA/COM COM S/ASIA USSR STRATA FORCES DIPLOM EDU/PROP COERCE GOV/REL...POLICY MAJORIT BIBLIOG 20. PAGE 141 A2886 POL/PAR LEAD ADMIN CONSTN

B58
PAN AMERICAN UNION,REPERTORIO DE PUBLICACIONES PERIODICAS ACTUALES LATINO-AMERICANAS. CULTURE ECO/UNDEV ADMIN LEAD GOV/REL 20 OAS. PAGE 113 A2326 BIBLIOG L/A+17C NAT/G DIPLOM

L58
HAVILAND H.F.,"FOREIGN AID AND THE POLICY PROCESS: 1957." USA+45 FACE/GP POL/PAR VOL/ASSN CHIEF DELIB/GP ACT/RES LEGIT EXEC GOV/REL ATTIT DRIVE PWR ...POLICY TESTS CONGRESS 20. PAGE 63 A1291 LEGIS PLAN FOR/AID

B59
AMERICAN FRIENDS OF VIETNAM,AID TO VIETNAM: AN AMERICAN SUCCESS STORY (PAMPHLET). ASIA FUT USA+45 VIETNAM ECO/UNDEV WAR CIVMIL/REL GOV/REL...ANTHOL 20. PAGE 7 A0148 DIPLOM NAT/G FOR/AID FORCES

B59
KAPLAN D.,THE ARAB REFUGEES: AN ABNORMAL PROBLEM. UAR WOR+45 PROB/SOLV DIPLOM GOV/REL ADJUST EFFICIENCY...POLICY GEOG INT/LAW 20 UN JEWS MIGRATION. PAGE 76 A1557 STRANGE HABITAT GP/REL INGP/REL

B60
AMERICAN ASSEMBLY COLUMBIA U,THE SECRETARY OF STATE. USA+45 ELITES NAT/G PLAN ADMIN GOV/REL CENTRAL ATTIT...POLICY MGT 20 SEC/STATE CONGRESS PRESIDENT. PAGE 7 A0136 DELIB/GP EX/STRUC GP/REL DIPLOM

B60
BROOKINGS INSTITUTION,UNITED STATES FOREIGN POLICY: STUDY NO 9: THE FORMULATION AND ADMINISTRATION OF UNITED STATES FOREIGN POLICY. USA+45 WOR+45 EX/STRUC LEGIS BAL/PWR FOR/AID EDU/PROP CIVMIL/REL GOV/REL...INT COLD/WAR. PAGE 19 A0394 DIPLOM INT/ORG CREATE

B60
BYRD E.M. JR.,TREATIES AND EXECUTIVE AGREEMENTS IN THE UNITED STATES: THEIR SEPARATE ROLES AND LIMITATIONS. USA+45 USA-45 EX/STRUC TARIFFS CT/SYS GOV/REL FEDERAL...IDEA/COMP BIBLIOG SUPREME/CT SENATE CONGRESS. PAGE 23 A0461 CHIEF INT/LAW DIPLOM

B60
FLORES R.H.,CATALOGO DE TESIS DOCTORALES DE LAS FACULTADES DE LA UNIVERSIDAD DE EL SALVADOR. EL/SALVADR LAW DIPLOM ADMIN LEAD GOV/REL...SOC 19/20. PAGE 47 A0954
BIBLIOG ACADEM L/A+17C NAT/G

B60
US HOUSE COMM GOVT OPERATIONS,OPERATIONS OF THE DEVELOPMENT LOAN FUND: HEARINGS (COMMITTEE ON GOVERNMENT OPERATIONS). USA+45 PLAN BUDGET DIPLOM GOV/REL COST...CHARTS 20 CONGRESS DEPT/STATE AID. PAGE 154 A3137
FINAN FOR/AID ECO/TAC EFFICIENCY

B60
VAN HOOGSTRATE D.J.,AMERICAN FOREIGN POLICY: REALISTS AND IDEALISTS: A CATHOLIC INTERPRETATION. BAL/PWR FOR/AID ARMS/CONT GOV/REL PEACE LOVE MORAL SOVEREIGN CATHISM...BIBLIOG 20. PAGE 158 A3213
CATH DIPLOM POLICY IDEA/COMP

C60
WRIGGINS W.H.,"CEYLON: DILEMMAS OF A NEW NATION." ASIA CEYLON CONSTN STRUCT POL/PAR SECT FORCES DIPLOM GOV/REL NAT/LISM...CHARTS BIBLIOG 20. PAGE 167 A3399
PROB/SOLV NAT/G ECO/UNDEV

B61
MILLIKAW M.F.,THE EMERGING NATIONS: THEIR GROWTH AND UNITED STATES POLICY. FUT USA+45 WOR+45 WOR-45 NAT/G PLAN TEC/DEV BAL/PWR GOV/REL PEACE ORD/FREE 20. PAGE 101 A2082
ECO/UNDEV POLICY DIPLOM FOR/AID

B62
AMERICAN LAW INSTITUTE,FOREIGN RELATIONS LAW OF THE UNITED STATES: RESTATEMENT, SECOND. USA+45 NAT/G LEGIS ADJUD EXEC ROUTINE GOV/REL...INT/LAW JURID CONCPT 20 TREATY. PAGE 7 A0152
PROF/ORG LAW DIPLOM ORD/FREE

B62
BOWLES C.,THE CONSCIENCE OF A LIBERAL. COM USA+45 WOR+45 STRUCT LOC/G NAT/G FORCES LEGIS GOV/REL DISCRIM 20 UN CIV/RIGHTS. PAGE 18 A0361
DIPLOM POLICY

B62
FORD A.G.,THE GOLD STANDARD 1880-1914: BRITAIN AND ARGENTINA. UK ECO/UNDEV INT/TRADE ADMIN GOV/REL DEMAND EFFICIENCY...STAT CHARTS 19/20 ARGEN GOLD/STAND. PAGE 47 A0960
FINAN ECO/TAC BUDGET BAL/PAY

B62
JELAVICH C.,TSARIST RUSSIA AND BALKAN NATIONALISM. BULGARIA MOD/EUR RUSSIA DOMIN GOV/REL...GEOG 19 SERBIA. PAGE 73 A1503
NAT/LISM DIPLOM WAR

B62
MONTGOMERY J.D.,THE POLITICS OF FOREIGN AID: AMERICAN EXPERIENCE IN SOUTHEAST ASIA. S/ASIA USA+45 NAT/G PROB/SOLV COLONIAL 20. PAGE 103 A2115
FOR/AID DIPLOM GOV/REL GIVE

B62
SELOSOEMARDJAN O.,SOCIAL CHANGES IN JOGJAKARTA. INDONESIA NETHERLAND ELITES STRATA STRUCT FAM POL/PAR CREATE DIPLOM INT/TRADE EDU/PROP ADMIN GOV/REL...SOC 20 JAVA CHINJAP. PAGE 131 A2683
ECO/UNDEV CULTURE REV COLONIAL

B62
US CONGRESS,COMMUNICATIONS SATELLITE LEGISLATION: HEARINGS BEFORE COMM ON AERON AND SPACE SCIENCES ON BILLS S2550 AND 2814. WOR+45 LAW VOL/ASSN PLAN DIPLOM CONTROL OWN PEACE...NEW/IDEA CONGRESS NASA. PAGE 150 A3062
SPACE COM/IND ADJUD GOV/REL

C62
ROBINSON J.A.,"CONGRESS AND FOREIGN POLICY-MAKING: A STUDY IN LEGISLATIVE INFLUENCE AND INITIATIVE." USA+45 CHIEF DELIB/GP CREATE CONTROL EXEC GOV/REL PERCEPT...TREND BIBLIOG 20 CONGRESS. PAGE 122 A2505
LEGIS DIPLOM POLICY DECISION

B63
FISCHER-GALATI S.,EASTERN EUROPE IN THE SIXTIES. ALBANIA USSR YUGOSLAVIA ECO/UNDEV AGRI MARKET LABOR WORKER DIPLOM INT/TRADE EDU/PROP GOV/REL PRODUC UTOPIA SOCISM 20. PAGE 46 A0939
MARXISM TEC/DEV BAL/PWR ECO/TAC

B63
GOLDSCHMIDT W.,THE UNITED STATES AND AFRICA. USA+45 CULTURE ECO/TAC INT/TRADE GOV/REL...SOC ANTHOL 20 INTERVENT. PAGE 53 A1091
AFR ECO/UNDEV DIPLOM

B63
GONZALEZ PEDRERO E.,ANATOMIA DE UN CONFLICTO. WOR+45 ECO/DEV ECO/UNDEV ECO/TAC FOR/AID CONTROL ARMS/CONT GOV/REL...NAT/COMP 20 COLD/WAR. PAGE 54 A1099
DIPLOM DETER BAL/PWR

B63
GRIFFITH W.E.,ALBANIA AND THE SINO-SOVIET RIFT. ALBANIA CHINA/COM USSR POL/PAR CHIEF LEGIS DIPLOM DOMIN ATTIT PWR...POLICY 20 KHRUSH/N MAO. PAGE 57 A1161
EDU/PROP MARXISM NAT/LISM GOV/REL

B63
MONGER G.W.,THE END OF ISOLATION. FRANCE MOD/EUR RUSSIA UK NAT/G LEGIS TOP/EX GOV/REL PWR 20 TREATY CHINJAP. PAGE 103 A2106
DIPLOM POLICY WAR

B63
SCHRADER R.,SCIENCE AND POLICY. WOR+45 ECO/DEV ECO/UNDEV R+D FORCES PLAN DIPLOM GOV/REL TECHRACY BIBLIOG. PAGE 129 A2644
TEC/DEV NAT/G POLICY ADMIN

B63
US SENATE,DOCUMENTS ON INTERNATIONAL AS"ECTS OF EXPLORATION AND USE OF OUTER SPACE, 1954-62: STAFF REPORT FOR COMM AERON SPACE SCI. USA+45 USSR LEGIS LEAD CIVMIL/REL PEACE...POLICY INT/LAW ANTHOL 20 CONGRESS NASA KHRUSH/N. PAGE 155 A3165
SPACE UTIL GOV/REL DIPLOM

B64
ADAMS V.,THE PEACE CORPS IN ACTION. USA+45 VOL/ASSN EX/STRUC GOV/REL PERCEPT ORD/FREE...OBS 20 KENNEDY/JF PEACE/CORP. PAGE 4 A0087
DIPLOM FOR/AID PERSON DRIVE

B64
ANDREWS D.H.,LATIN AMERICA: A BIBLIOGRAPHY OF PAPERBACK BOOKS. SECT INT/TRADE EDU/PROP WAR GOV/REL ADJUST NAT/LISM ATTIT...ART/METH LING BIOG 20. PAGE 8 A0160
BIBLIOG L/A+17C CULTURE NAT/G

B64
BLACKSTOCK P.W.,THE STRATEGY OF SUBVERSION. USA+45 FORCES EDU/PROP ADMIN COERCE GOV/REL...DECISION MGT 20 DEPT/DEFEN CIA DEPT/STATE. PAGE 15 A0301
ORD/FREE DIPLOM CONTROL

B64
HARMON R.B.,BIBLIOGRAPHY OF BIBLIOGRAPHIES IN POLITICAL SCIENCE (MIMEOGRAPHED PAPER: LIMITED EDITION). WOR+45 WOR-45 INT/ORG POL/PAR GOV/REL ALL/IDEOS...INT/LAW JURID MGT 19/20. PAGE 61 A1260
BIBLIOG NAT/G DIPLOM LOC/G

B64
JOHNSON L.B.,MY HOPE FOR AMERICA. FUT USA+45 USSR LAW PLAN DIPLOM GIVE INCOME PEACE ATTIT ORD/FREE WEALTH 20 JOHNSON/LB PRESIDENT DEMOCRAT. PAGE 74 A1525
POLICY POL/PAR NAT/G GOV/REL

B64
KENNEDY J.F.,THE BURDEN AND THE GLORY. FUT USA+45 TEC/DEV ECO/TAC EDU/PROP ARMS/CONT MURDER RACE/REL PEACE...ANTHOL 20 KENNEDY/JF COLD/WAR NATO PRESIDENT. PAGE 78 A1593
ADMIN POLICY GOV/REL DIPLOM

B64
KNOX V.H.,PUBLIC FINANCE: INFORMATION SOURCES. USA+45 DIPLOM ADMIN GOV/REL COST...POLICY 20. PAGE 81 A1657
BIBLIOG/A FINAN TAX BUDGET

B64
NEWBURY C.W.,THE WEST AFRICAN COMMONWEALTH. CONSTN INTELL ECO/UNDEV VOL/ASSN CHIEF DELIB/GP LEGIS INT/TRADE COLONIAL FEDERAL ATTIT 20 COMMONWLTH AFRICA/W. PAGE 108 A2223
INT/ORG SOVEREIGN GOV/REL AFR

B64
NICOL D.,AFRICA - A SUBJECTIVE VIEW. AFR INT/ORG PLAN ADMIN COLONIAL PARL/PROC PARTIC REGION GOV/REL LITERACY ATTIT...BIBLIOG 20 CIVIL/SERV. PAGE 109 A2230
NAT/G LEAD CULTURE ACADEM

B64
REMAK J.,THE GENTLE CRITIC: THEODOR FONTANE AND GERMAN POLITICS, 1848-1898. GERMANY PRUSSIA CULTURE ELITES BAL/PWR DIPLOM WRITING GOV/REL...HUM BIOG 19 BISMARCK/O JUNKER FONTANE/T. PAGE 120 A2465
PERSON SOCIETY WORKER CHIEF

B64
SARROS P.P.,CONGRESS AND THE NEW DIPLOMACY: THE FORMULATION OF MUTUAL SECURITY POLICY: 1953-60 (THESIS). USA+45 CHIEF EX/STRUC REGION ROUTINE CHOOSE GOV/REL PEACE ROLE...POLICY 20 PRESIDENT CONGRESS. PAGE 127 A2606
DIPLOM POL/PAR NAT/G

S64
HORECKY P.L.,"LIBRARY OF CONGRESS PUBLICATIONS IN AID OF USSR AND EAST EUROPEAN RESEARCH." BULGARIA CZECHOSLVK POLAND USSR YUGOSLAVIA NAT/G POL/PAR DIPLOM ADMIN GOV/REL...CLASSIF 20. PAGE 67 A1382
BIBLIOG/A COM MARXISM

S64
PRASAD B.,"SURVEY OF RECENT RESEARCH: STUDIES ON INDIA'S FOREIGN POLIC AND RELATIONS." ASIA INDIA PAKISTAN USA+45 NAT/G INT/TRADE GOV/REL 20 UN CMN/WLTH. PAGE 117 A2406
BIBLIOG DIPLOM ROLE POLICY

B65
ADENAUER K.,MEMOIRS 1945-53. EUR+WWI GERMANY/W ECO/DEV CHIEF FORCES ECO/TAC WAR GOV/REL PWR SOVEREIGN 20 NATO ADENAUER/K. PAGE 4 A0088
BIOG DIPLOM NAT/G PERS/REL

B65
GEORGE M.,THE WARPED VISION. EUR+WWI UK NAT/G POL/PAR LEGIS PARL/PROC SANCTION COERCE WAR GOV/REL PEACE RESPECT 20 CONSRV/PAR. PAGE 52 A1061
LEAD ATTIT DIPLOM POLICY

B65
HART B.H.L.,THE MEMOIRS OF CAPTAIN LIDDELL HART (VOL. I). UK NAT/G PLAN TEC/DEV DIPLOM ADMIN WEAPON GOV/REL PERS/REL ATTIT PWR FASCISM...POLICY 20. PAGE 62 A1274
FORCES BIOG LEAD WAR

B65
LAFAVE W.R.,LAW AND SOVIET SOCIETY. EX/STRUC DIPLOM DOMIN EDU/PROP PRESS ADMIN CRIME OWN MARXISM 20 KHRUSH/N. PAGE 84 A1710
JURID CT/SYS ADJUD GOV/REL

B65
NKRUMAH K.,NEO-COLONIALISM: THE LAST STAGE OF IMPERIALISM. AFR INT/ORG WORKER FOR/AID INT/TRADE EDU/PROP GOV/REL NAT/LISM SOVEREIGN POPULISM SOCISM ...SOCIALIST 20 THIRD/WRLD INTRVN/ECO. PAGE 109 A2243
COLONIAL DIPLOM ECO/UNDEV ECO/TAC

B65
SPENCE J.E.,REPUBLIC UNDER PRESSURE: A STUDY OF
DIPLOM

SOUTH AFRICAN FOREIGN POLICY. SOUTH/AFR ADMIN POLICY
COLONIAL GOV/REL RACE/REL DISCRIM NAT/LISM ATTIT AFR
ROLE...TREND 20 NEGRO. PAGE 136 A2783

B65
US SENATE,US INTERNATIONAL SPACE PROGRAMS, 1959-65: SPACE
STAFF REPORT FOR COMM ON AERONAUTICAL AND SPACE DIPLOM
SCIENCES. WOR+45 VOL/ASSN CIVMIL/REL 20 CONGRESS PLAN
NASA TREATY. PAGE 155 A3166 GOV/REL

B65
US SENATE COMM ON JUDICIARY,REFUGEE PROBLEMS IN STRANGE
SOUTH VIETNAM AND LAOS: HEARINGS BEFORE HABITAT
SUBCOMMITTEE TO INVESTIGATE PROBLEMS OF REFUGEES, FOR/AID
ESCAPEES. CHINA/COM LAOS USA+45 VIETNAM/S PROB/SOLV CIVMIL/REL
DIPLOM GOV/REL GP/REL EFFICIENCY ORD/FREE...POLICY
GEOG 20 CONGRESS MIGRATION. PAGE 157 A3194

S65
"FURTHER READING." INDIA ADMIN COLONIAL WAR GOV/REL BIBLIOG
ATTIT 20. PAGE 3 A0069 DIPLOM
NAT/G
POLICY

S65
FLEMING D.F.,"CAN PAX AMERICANA SUCCEED?" ASIA DECISION
CHINA/COM EUR+WWI USSR VIETNAM BAL/PWR DIPLOM DOMIN ATTIT
COERCE GOV/REL 20. PAGE 46 A0948 ECO/TAC

S65
GANGAL S.C.,"SURVEY OF RECENT RESEARCH: INDIA AND BIBLIOG
THE COMMONWEALTH" INDIA UK NAT/G INT/TRADE PARTIC POLICY
GOV/REL ROLE 20 CMN/WLTH. PAGE 51 A1039 REGION
DIPLOM

S65
MERRITT R.L.,"SELECTED ARTICLES AND DOCUMENTS ON BIBLIOG
INTERNATIONAL LAW AND RELATIONS." WOR+45 INT/ORG DIPLOM
FORCES INT/TRADE. PAGE 100 A2045 INT/LAW
GOV/REL

B66
CANFIELD L.H.,THE PRESIDENCY OF WOODROW WILSON: PERSON
PRELUDE TO A WORLD IN CRISIS. USA-45 ADJUD NEUTRAL POLICY
WAR CHOOSE INGP/REL PEACE ORD/FREE 20 WILSON/W DIPLOM
PRESIDENT TREATY LEAGUE/NAT. PAGE 24 A0477 GOV/REL

B66
DYCK H.V.,WEIMAR GERMANY AND SOVIET RUSSIA DIPLOM
1926-1933. EUR+WWI GERMANY UK USSR ECO/TAC GOV/REL
INT/TRADE NEUTRAL WAR ATTIT 20 WEIMAR/REP TREATY. POLICY
PAGE 40 A0814

B66
EUDIN X.J.,SOVIET FOREIGN POLICY 1928-34: DOCUMENTS DIPLOM
AND MATERIALS (VOL. I). ASIA USSR WOR-45 INT/ORG POLICY
POL/PAR WORKER WAR PEACE...ANTHOL 20 TREATY GOV/REL
LEAGUE/NAT INTERVENT. PAGE 43 A0873 MARXISM

B66
HARMON R.B.,SOURCES AND PROBLEMS OF BIBLIOGRAPHY IN BIBLIOG
POLITICAL SCIENCE (PAMPHLET). INT/ORG LOC/G MUNIC DIPLOM
POL/PAR ADMIN GOV/REL ALL/IDEOS...JURID MGT CONCPT INT/LAW
19/20. PAGE 61 A1262 NAT/G

B66
O'CONNER A.M.,AN ECONOMIC GEOGRAPHY OF EAST AFRICA. ECO/UNDEV
AFR TANZANIA UGANDA AGRI WORKER INT/TRADE COLONIAL EXTR/IND
GOV/REL...CHARTS METH/COMP 20 AFRICA/E. PAGE 111 GEOG
A2269 HABITAT

B66
PIQUET H.S.,THE US BALANCE OF PAYMENTS AND BAL/PAY
INTERNATIONAL MONETARY RESERVES. USA+45 PROB/SOLV DIPLOM
INT/TRADE GOV/REL EQUILIB...POLICY STAT CHARTS 20 FINAN
GOLD/STAND. PAGE 116 A2384 ECO/TAC

B66
UN ECAFE,ADMINISTRATIVE ASPECTS OF FAMILY PLANNING PLAN
PROGRAMMES (PAMPHLET). ASIA THAILAND WOR+45 CENSUS
VOL/ASSN PROB/SOLV BUDGET FOR/AID EDU/PROP CONFER FAM
CONTROL GOV/REL TIME 20 UN BIRTH/CON. PAGE 147 ADMIN
A2999

S66
MERRITT R.L.,"SELECTED ARTICLES AND DOCUMENTS ON BIBLIOG
COMPARATIVE GOVERNMENT AND CROSS-NATIONAL GOV/COMP
RESEARCH." AFR ASIA EUR+WWI L/A+17C MOD/EUR ELITES NAT/G
R+D ACT/RES DIPLOM PWR...SOC CONCPT 18/20. PAGE 100 GOV/REL
A2046

B67
ATTWOOD W.,THE REDS AND THE BLACKS. AFR POL/PAR DIPLOM
CHOOSE GOV/REL RACE/REL NAT/LISM...BIOG 20. PAGE 10 PWR
A0195 MARXISM

B67
BRZEZINSKI Z.K.,THE SOVIET BLOC: UNITY AND CONFLICT NAT/G
(2ND ED., REV., ENLARGED). COM POLAND USSR INTELL DIPLOM
CHIEF EX/STRUC CONTROL EXEC GOV/REL PWR MARXISM
...TREND IDEA/COMP 20 LENIN/VI MARX/KARL STALIN/J.
PAGE 21 A0420

B67
UNIVERSAL REFERENCE SYSTEM,ECONOMIC REGULATION, BIBLIOG/A
BUSINESS, AND GOVERNMENT (VOLUME VIII). WOR+45 CONTROL
WOR-45 ECO/DEV ECO/UNDEV FINAN LABOR TEC/DEV NAT/G
ECO/TAC INT/TRADE GOV/REL...POLICY COMPUT/IR.
PAGE 149 A3043

B67
US DEPARTMENT OF STATE,THE COUNTRY TEAM - AN DIPLOM
ILLUSTRATED PROFILE OF OUR AMERICAN MISSIONS NAT/G
ABROAD. ECO/TAC FOR/AID EDU/PROP TASK PERS/REL VOL/ASSN
ATTIT 20. PAGE 152 A3099 GOV/REL

L67
"RESTRICTIVE SOVEREIGN IMMUNITY, THE STATE SOVEREIGN
DEPARTMENT, AND THE COURTS." USA+45 USA-45 EX/STRUC ORD/FREE
DIPLOM ADJUD CONTROL GOV/REL 19/20 DEPT/STATE PRIVIL
SUPREME/CT. PAGE 4 A0080 CT/SYS

L67
MOORE N.,"THE LAWFULNESS OF MILITARY ASSISTANCE TO PWR
THE REPUBLIC OF VIET NAM." USA+45 VIETNAM WOR+45 DIPLOM
FOR/AID DOMIN DETER WAR WEAPON...DECISION INT/LAW FORCES
20 UN. PAGE 103 A2123 GOV/REL

S67
D'AMATO D.,"LEGAL ASPECTS OF THE FRENCH NUCLEAR INT/LAW
TESTS." FRANCE WOR+45 ACT/RES COLONIAL RISK GOV/REL DIPLOM
EQUILIB ORD/FREE PWR DECISION. PAGE 33 A0672 NUC/PWR
ADJUD

S67
MOBERG E.,"THE EFFECT OF SECURITY POLICY MEASURES: POLICY
DISCUSSION RELATED TO SWEDEN'S SECURITY POLICY." ORD/FREE
SWEDEN PLAN PROB/SOLV DIPLOM GOV/REL MORAL...CHARTS BUDGET
20. PAGE 102 A2092 FINAN

B91
SIDGWICK H.,THE ELEMENTS OF POLITICS. LOC/G NAT/G POLICY
LEGIS DIPLOM ADJUD CONTROL EXEC PARL/PROC REPRESENT LAW
GOV/REL SOVEREIGN ALL/IDEOS 19 MILL/JS BENTHAM/J. CONCPT
PAGE 132 A2713

B96
LOWELL A.L.,GOVERNMENTS AND PARTIES IN CONTINENTAL POL/PAR
EUROPE, VOL. II. AUSTRIA GERMANY HUNGARY MOD/EUR NAT/G
SWITZERLND SOCIETY EX/STRUC LEGIS DIPLOM AGREE LEAD GOV/REL
PARL/PROC PWR...POLICY 19. PAGE 91 A1867 ELITES

GOVERNMENT....SEE NAT/G, LOC/G, PROVS

GOVERNOR....GOVERNOR; SEE ALSO PROVS, CHIEF, LEAD

GOWING M. A1118

GP/COMP....COMPARISON OF GROUPS

B27
SIEGFRIED A.,AMERICA COMES OF AGE: A FRENCH USA-45
ANALYSIS (TRANS. BY H.H. HEMMING AND DORIS CULTURE
HEMMING). FRANCE UK POL/PAR WORKER TEC/DEV DIPLOM ECO/DEV
REGION RACE/REL ADJUST PRODUC HEREDITY...TIME/SEQ SOC
GP/COMP SOC/INTEG 20 DEMOCRAT REPUBLICAN KKK.
PAGE 132 A2714

B58
GAVIN J.M.,WAR AND PEACE IN THE SPACE AGE. SPACE WAR
USA+45 USSR FORCES PLAN TEC/DEV BAL/PWR DIPLOM DETER
ARMS/CONT WEAPON CIVMIL/REL...CHARTS GP/COMP 20 NUC/PWR
NATO COLD/WAR. PAGE 52 A1055 PEACE

B58
SCOTT W.A.,THE UNITED STATES AND THE UNITED ATTIT
NATIONS: THE PUBLIC VIEW 1945-1955. USA+45 EDU/PROP DIPLOM
...INT QU KNO/TEST SAMP GP/COMP 20 UN. PAGE 130 INT/ORG
A2674

B61
PATAI R.,CULTURES IN CONFLICT; AN INQUIRY INTO THE NAT/COMP
SOCIO-CULTURAL PROBLEMS OF ISRAEL AND HER NEIGHBORS CULTURE
(2ND REV. ED.). ISLAM ISRAEL SOCIETY STRUCT DIPLOM GP/COMP
GP/REL ALL/VALS...SOC 20 JEWS ARABS. PAGE 114 A2339 ATTIT

B61
PEASLEE A.J.,INTERNATIONAL GOVERNMENTAL BIBLIOG
ORGANIZATIONS (2 VOLS.). CONSTN VOL/ASSN DIPLOM INT/ORG
...GP/COMP 20 UN OAS EEC EFTA ECSC. PAGE 114 A2345 INDEX
LAW

B61
PECKERT J.,DIE GROSSEN UND DIE KLEINEN MAECHTE. COM DIPLOM
GERMANY/W ECO/DEV ECO/UNDEV NAT/G WAR RACE/REL ECO/TAC
PEACE...POLICY GP/COMP GOV/COMP 20 COLD/WAR. BAL/PWR
PAGE 114 A2346

S61
TUCKER R.C.,"TOWARDS A COMPARATIVE POLITICS OF MARXISM
MOVEMENT-REGIMES" (BMR)" USSR CONSTN NAT/G CREATE POLICY
PROB/SOLV DIPLOM DOMIN REV...GP/COMP IDEA/COMP METH GEN/LAWS
20 STALIN/J BOLSHEVISM. PAGE 145 A2971 PWR

B64
ECONOMIDES C.P.,LE POUVOIR DE DECISION DES INT/ORG
ORGANISATIONS INTERNATIONALES EUROPEENNES. DIPLOM PWR
DOMIN INGP/REL EFFICIENCY...INT/LAW JURID 20 NATO DECISION
OEEC EEC COUNCL/EUR EURATOM. PAGE 40 A0821 GP/COMP

B64
EPSTEIN H.M.,REVOLT IN THE CONGO. AFR CONGO/BRAZ REV
WOR+45 NAT/G FORCES DOMIN WAR CIVMIL/REL INGP/REL COLONIAL
MARXISM...RECORD GP/COMP 20 CONGO/LEOP UN. PAGE 42 NAT/LISM
A0856 DIPLOM

B64
STEWART C.F.,A BIBLIOGRAPHY OF INTERNATIONAL BIBLIOG
BUSINESS. WOR+45 FINAN LG/CO NAT/G PLAN ECO/TAC INT/ORG
TARIFFS...DECISION MGT GP/COMP NAT/COMP 20 EEC. OP/RES
PAGE 138 A2824 INT/TRADE

B65
EDUCATION AND WORLD AFFAIRS,THE UNIVERSITY LOOKS ACADEM
ABROAD: APPROACHES TO WORLD AFFAIRS AT SIX AMERICAN DIPLOM
UNIVERSITIES. USA+45 CREATE EDU/PROP CONFER LEAD ATTIT

KNOWL 20 CORNELL/U MICH/STA/U STANFORD/U TULANE/U WISCONSN/U. PAGE 40 A0822 — GP/COMP

B66
SINGH L.P.,THE POLITICS OF ECONOMIC COOPERATION IN ASIA; A STUDY OF ASIAN INTERNATIONAL ORGANIZATIONS. ASIA INT/ORG ACT/RES PLAN GP/REL...POLICY GP/COMP BIBLIOG 20 UN SEATO. PAGE 133 A2733 — ECO/UNDEV ECO/TAC REGION DIPLOM

B66
SKILLING H.G.,THE GOVERNMENTS OF COMMUNIST EAST EUROPE. COM EUR+WWI ELITES FORCES DIPLOM ECO/TAC CONTROL HABITAT SOCISM...DECISION BIBLIOG 20 EUROPE/E COM/PARTY. PAGE 134 A2738 — MARXISM NAT/COMP GP/COMP DOMIN

S67
GLENN N.D.,"ARE REGIONAL CULTURAL DIFFERENCES DIMINISHING?" USA+45 DIPLOM RACE/REL AGE/Y AGE/A PERSON MORAL...GP/COMP 20. PAGE 53 A1081 — SAMP ATTIT REGION CULTURE

S67
INGLEHART R.,"AN END TO EUROPEAN INTEGRATION." PROB/SOLV BAL/PWR NAT/LISM...PSY SOC INT CHARTS GP/COMP 20. PAGE 70 A1440 — DIPLOM EUR+WWI REGION ATTIT

S67
ROGERS W.C.,"A COMPARISON OF INFORMED AND GENERAL PUBLIC OPINION ON US FOREIGN POLICY." USA+45 DIPLOM EDU/PROP ORD/FREE...POLICY SAMP IDEA/COMP 20. PAGE 123 A2515 — KNOWL ATTIT GP/COMP ELITES

GP/REL....RELATIONS AMONG GROUPS

N
LITERATUR-VERZEICHNIS DER POLITISCHEN WISSENSCHAFTEN. GERMANY/W WOR+45 CONSTN SOCIETY ECO/DEV INT/ORG POL/PAR LEAD REPRESENT GOV/REL GP/REL...POLICY PHIL/SCI. PAGE 1 A0018 — BIBLIOG EUR+WWI DIPLOM NAT/G

N
SOCIAL RESEARCH. WOR+45 WOR-45 R+D LEAD GP/REL ATTIT...SOC TREND 20. PAGE 2 A0025 — BIBLIOG/A DIPLOM NAT/G SOCIETY

N
RAND SCHOOL OF SOCIAL SCIENCE,INDEX TO LABOR ARTICLES. ECO/DEV INT/ORG LEGIS DIPLOM GP/REL ...NAT/COMP 20. PAGE 119 A2440 — BIBLIOG LABOR MGT ADJUD

N
US CONSOLATE GENERAL HONG KONG,REVIEW OF THE HONG KONG CHINESE PRESS. ECO/UNDEV LOC/G NAT/G PLAN DIPLOM EDU/PROP LEAD GP/REL MARXISM...POLICY INDEX 20. PAGE 150 A3073 — BIBLIOG/A ASIA PRESS ATTIT

N
US LIBRARY OF CONGRESS,ACCESSIONS LIST - INDIA. INDIA CULTURE AGRI LOC/G POL/PAR PLAN PROB/SOLV TEC/DEV DIPLOM EDU/PROP LEAD GP/REL ATTIT 20. PAGE 154 A3142 — BIBLIOG S/ASIA ECO/UNDEV NAT/G

N
US LIBRARY OF CONGRESS,ACCESSIONS LIST -- ISRAEL. ISRAEL CULTURE ECO/UNDEV POL/PAR PLAN PROB/SOLV TEC/DEV DIPLOM EDU/PROP LEAD WAR ATTIT 20 JEWS. PAGE 154 A3143 — BIBLIOG ISLAM NAT/G GP/REL

B01
HART A.B.,AMERICAN HISTORY TOLD BY CONTEMPORARIES. UK CULTURE FINAN SECT FORCES DIPLOM TAX RUMOR CT/SYS REV GOV/REL GP/REL...ANTHOL 17/18 PRE/US/AM FEDERALIST. PAGE 62 A1273 — USA-45 COLONIAL SOVEREIGN

B17
DOS SANTOS M.,BIBLIOGRAPHIA GERAL, A DESCRIPCAO BIBLIOGRAFICA DE LIVROS TANTO DE AUTORES PORTUGUEZES COMO BRASILEIROS... BRAZIL PORTUGAL NAT/G LEAD GP/REL 15/20. PAGE 38 A0774 — BIBLIOG/A L/A+17C DIPLOM COLONIAL

N19
JACKSON R.G.A.,THE CASE FOR AN INTERNATIONAL DEVELOPMENT AUTHORITY (PAMPHLET). WOR+45 ECO/DEV DIPLOM GIVE CONTROL GP/REL EFFICIENCY NAT/LISM SOVEREIGN 20. PAGE 72 A1478 — FOR/AID INT/ORG ECO/UNDEV ADMIN

N19
UNITED ARAB REPUBLIC,THE PROBLEM OF THE PALESTINIAN REFUGEES (PAMPHLET). ISRAEL UAR LAW PROB/SOLV EDU/PROP CONFER ADJUD CONTROL NAT/LISM HEALTH 20 JEWS UN MIGRATION. PAGE 148 A3029 — STRANGE GP/REL INGP/REL DIPLOM

B24
NAVILLE A.,LIBERTE, EGALITE, SOLIDARITE: ESSAIS D'ANALYSE. STRATA FAM VOL/ASSN INT/TRADE GP/REL MORAL MARXISM SOCISM...PSY TREATY. PAGE 107 A2205 — ORD/FREE SOC IDEA/COMP DIPLOM

B28
MAIR L.P.,THE PROTECTION OF MINORITIES. EUR+WWI WOR-45 CONSTN INT/ORG NAT/G LEGIT CT/SYS GP/REL RACE/REL DISCRIM ORD/FREE RESPECT...JURID CONCPT TIME/SEQ 20. PAGE 93 A1909 — LAW SOVEREIGN

B33
PUBLIC OPINION AND WORLD POLITICS. UNIV LAW CULTURE NAT/G PRESS REV GP/REL...MAJORIT METH/COMP ANTHOL 20. PAGE 167 A3400 — DIPLOM EDU/PROP ATTIT MAJORITY

B34
LOVELL R.I.,THE STRUGGLE FOR SOUTH AFRICA, 1875-1899. GERMANY RHODESIA SOUTH/AFR UK NAT/G ECO/TAC HABITAT WEALTH...POLICY 19. PAGE 91 A1866 — COLONIAL DIPLOM WAR GP/REL

B40
NIEBUHR R.,CHRISTIANITY AND POWER POLITICS. WOR-45 SECT DIPLOM GP/REL SUPEGO ALL/IDEOS WORSHIP 20 CHRISTIAN. PAGE 109 A2234 — PARTIC PEACE MORAL

B41
PERHAM M.,AFRICANS AND BRITISH RULE. AFR UK ECO/TAC CONTROL GP/REL ATTIT 20. PAGE 115 A2355 — DIPLOM COLONIAL ADMIN ECO/UNDEV

B42
BORNSTEIN J.,ACTION AGAINST THE ENEMY'S MIND. EUR+WWI GERMANY USA-45 DIPLOM DOMIN PRESS LEAD GP/REL DISCRIM PERCEPT FASCISM MARXISM 20 JEWS NAZI ANTI/SEMIT. PAGE 17 A0343 — EDU/PROP PSY WAR CONTROL

B43
WALKER E.A.,BRITAIN AND SOUTH AFRICA. SOUTH/AFR POL/PAR GP/REL RACE/REL ATTIT ORD/FREE 17/20. PAGE 160 A3264 — COLONIAL WAR DIPLOM SOVEREIGN

B46
GAULD W.A.,MAN, NATURE, AND TIME, AN INTRODUCTION TO WORLD STUDY. WOR-45 CULTURE CREATE DIPLOM GP/REL DRIVE...SOC LING CENSUS CHARTS TIME 18/20. PAGE 52 A1054 — HABITAT PERSON

B47
NIEBUHR R.,THE CHILDREN OF LIGHT AND THE CHILDREN OF DARKNESS: A VINDICATION OF DEMOCRACY AND CRITIQUE OF TRADITIONAL DEFENSE. UNIV STRUCT NAT/G SECT INGP/REL OWN PEACE ORD/FREE MARXISM ...IDEA/COMP GEN/LAWS 20 CHRISTIAN. PAGE 109 A2235 — POPULISM DIPLOM NEIGH GP/REL

B48
CHILDS J.R.,AMERICAN FOREIGN SERVICE. USA+45 SOCIETY NAT/G ROUTINE GOV/REL 20 DEPT/STATE CIVIL/SERV. PAGE 26 A0530 — DIPLOM ADMIN GP/REL

C50
NUMELIN R.,"THE BEGINNINGS OF DIPLOMACY." INT/TRADE WAR GP/REL PEACE STRANGE ATTIT...INT/LAW CONCPT BIBLIOG. PAGE 110 A2260 — DIPLOM KIN CULTURE LAW

B51
CARRINGTON C.E.,THE LIQUIDATION OF THE BRITISH EMPIRE. AFR NAT/G INT/TRADE COLONIAL RACE/REL ATTIT ORD/FREE...POLICY NAT/COMP 20 CMN/WLTH. PAGE 25 A0501 — SOVEREIGN NAT/LISM DIPLOM GP/REL

B51
PRICE D.K.,THE NEW DIMENSIONS OF DIPLOMACY: THE ORGANIZATION OF THE US GOVERNMENT FOR ITS NEW ROLE IN WORLD AFFAIRS (PAMPHLET). USA+45 WOR+45 INT/ORG VOL/ASSN CONSULT DELIB/GP PLAN PROB/SOLV 20 PRESIDENT. PAGE 117 A2411 — DIPLOM GP/REL NAT/G

B52
UNESCO,CURRENT SOCIOLOGY (2 VOLS.). SOCIETY STRATA R+D GP/REL ATTIT PERSON 20 UN. PAGE 147 A3014 — BIBLIOG SOC INT/ORG CULTURE

B53
MARITAIN J.,L'HOMME ET L'ETAT. SECT DIPLOM GP/REL PEACE ORD/FREE...IDEA/COMP 17/20 CHURCH/STA NATURL/LAW. PAGE 95 A1940 — CONCPT NAT/G SOVEREIGN COERCE

B53
MURPHY G.,IN THE MINDS OF MEN: THE STUDY OF HUMAN BEHAVIOR AND SOCIAL TENSIONS IN INDIA. FUT S/ASIA FAM INT/ORG NAT/G DIPLOM EDU/PROP GP/REL ATTIT RIGID/FLEX ALL/VALS...SOC QU UNESCO 20. PAGE 106 A2176 — SECT STRATA INDIA

B54
NATION ASSOCIATES,SECURITY AND THE MIDDLE EAST - THE PROBLEM AND ITS SOLUTION. ISRAEL JORDAN LEBANON SYRIA UAR FORCES FOR/AID GP/REL NAT/LISM PEACE TOTALISM...POLICY 20. PAGE 107 A2198 — DIPLOM ECO/UNDEV WAR PLAN

B55
KOHN H.,NATIONALISM: ITS MEANING AND HISTORY. GP/REL INGP/REL ATTIT...CONCPT NAT/COMP 16/20 MACHIAVELL. PAGE 81 A1662 — NAT/LISM DIPLOM FASCISM REV

B55
THOMPSON V.,MINORITY PROBLEMS IN SOUTHEAST ASIA. CAMBODIA CHINA/COM LAOS S/ASIA KIN NAT/G SECT PROB/SOLV EDU/PROP REGION GP/REL RACE/REL MARXISM ...SOC 20 BUDDHISM UN. PAGE 143 A2933 — INGP/REL GEOG DIPLOM STRUCT

B56
CHANG C.J.,THE MINORITY GROUPS OF YUNN AN AND CHINESE POLITICAL EXPANSION INTO SOUTHEAST ASIA (DOCTORAL THESIS). ASIA CHINA/COM S/ASIA FORCES TEC/DEV DIPLOM EDU/PROP...GEOG BIBLIOG 20. PAGE 26 A0520 — GP/REL REGION DOMIN MARXISM

B56
COMMONWEALTH OF WORLD CITIZENS,THE BIRTH OF A WORLD PEOPLE. WOR+45 CONSTN PROB/SOLV CONTROL TASK WAR GP/REL UTOPIA PWR...POLICY NEW/IDEA 20. PAGE 29 — DIPLOM VOL/ASSN PEACE

A0582 INT/ORG

B57
ALIGHIERI D.,ON WORLD GOVERNMENT. ROMAN/EMP LAW SOCIETY INT/ORG NAT/G POL/PAR ADJUD WAR GP/REL PEACE WORSHIP 15 WORLDUNITY DANTE. PAGE 6 A0121 POLICY CONCPT DIPLOM SECT

B57
STRACHEY A.,THE UNCONSCIOUS MOTIVES OF WAR; A PSYCHO-ANALYTICAL CONTRIBUTION. UNIV SOCIETY DIPLOM DREAM GP/REL ADJUST ATTIT DISPL PERCEPT PERSON KNOWL MORAL. PAGE 139 A2840 WAR DRIVE LOVE PSY

B58
CRAIG G.A.,FROM BISMARCK TO ADENAUER: ASPECTS OF GERMAN STATECRAFT. GERMANY INTELL FORCES ECO/TAC CONFER COERCE WAR GP/REL ORD/FREE PWR CONSERVE 19/20 BISMARCK/O ADENAUER/K. PAGE 32 A0653 DIPLOM LEAD NAT/G

B58
HUNT B.I.,BIPARTISANSHIP: A CASE STUDY OF THE FOREIGN ASSISTANCE PROGRAM, 1947-56 (DOCTORAL THESIS). USA+45 INT/ORG CONSULT LEGIS TEC/DEV ...BIBLIOG PRESIDENT TREATY NATO TRUMAN/HS EISNHWR/DD CONGRESS. PAGE 69 A1418 FOR/AID POL/PAR GP/REL DIPLOM

B58
INSTITUTE MEDITERRANEAN AFF,THE PALESTINE REFUGEE PROBLEM. UAR WOR+45 INT/ORG PLAN PROB/SOLV PEACE ...POLICY GEOG STAT CHARTS 20 JEWS UN MIGRATION. PAGE 70 A1444 STRANGE HABITAT GP/REL INGP/REL

B58
JENNINGS W.I.,PROBLEMS OF THE NEW COMMONWEALTH. CEYLON INDIA MALAYSIA PAKISTAN ECO/UNDEV VOL/ASSN RACE/REL NAT/LISM ROLE 20 CMN/WLTH. PAGE 74 A1511 GP/REL INGP/REL COLONIAL INT/ORG

B58
REUTER P.,INTERNATIONAL INSTITUTIONS. WOR+45 WOR-45 CULTURE SOCIETY VOL/ASSN LEGIT ROUTINE GP/REL INGP/REL KNOWL...JURID METH/CNCPT TIME/SEQ 20. PAGE 120 A2469 INT/ORG PSY

B58
UNESCO,REPERTORIO DE PUBLICACIONES PERIODICAS ACTUALES LATINO AMERICANAS (VOL. VIII). LAW DIPLOM GP/REL...PHIL/SCI SOC 20 UNESCO. PAGE 148 A3021 BIBLIOG/A COM/IND L/A+17C

B59
BUNDESMIN FUR VERTRIEBENE,ZEITTAFEL DER VORGESCHICHTE UND DES ABLAUFS DER VERTREIBUNG SOWIE DER UNTERBRINGUNG UND EINGLIEDERUNG DER (2 VOLS.). GERMANY/E GERMANY/W NAT/G PROVS PROB/SOLV DIPLOM PARL/PROC ATTIT...BIBLIOG SOC/INTEG 20 MIGRATION PARLIAMENT. PAGE 21 A0431 JURID GP/REL INT/LAW

B59
GILBERT R.,GENOCIDE IN TIBET. ASIA SECT CHIEF DIPLOM 20. PAGE 52 A1072 MARXISM MURDER WAR GP/REL

B59
KAPLAN D.,THE ARAB REFUGEES: AN ABNORMAL PROBLEM. UAR WOR+45 PROB/SOLV DIPLOM GOV/REL ADJUST EFFICIENCY...POLICY GEOG INT/LAW 20 UN JEWS MIGRATION. PAGE 76 A1557 STRANGE HABITAT GP/REL INGP/REL

B59
KIRCHHEIMER O.,GEGENWARTSPROBLEME DER ASYLGEWAHRUNG. DOMIN GP/REL ATTIT...NAT/COMP 20. PAGE 79 A1630 DIPLOM INT/LAW JURID ORD/FREE

B59
MAC MILLAN W.M.,THE ROAD TO SELF-RULE. SOUTH/AFR UK CULTURE SOCIETY AGRI LABOR NAT/G INT/TRADE CONTROL GP/REL...SOC 19/20. PAGE 92 A1884 AFR COLONIAL SOVEREIGN POLICY

B59
STERNBERG F.,THE MILITARY AND INDUSTRIAL REVOLUTION OF OUR TIME. USA+45 USSR WOR+45 WORKER COMPUTER PLAN TEC/DEV NUC/PWR GP/REL...POLICY NAT/COMP 20. PAGE 138 A2818 DIPLOM FORCES INDUS CIVMIL/REL

B59
VINACKE H.M.,A HISTORY OF THE FAR EAST IN MODERN TIMES (6TH ED.). KOREA S/ASIA USSR CONSTN CULTURE STRATA ECO/UNDEV NAT/G CHIEF FOR/AID INT/TRADE GP/REL...SOC NAT/COMP 19/20 CHINJAP. PAGE 159 A3235 STRUCT ASIA

B59
VORSPAN A.,JUSTICE AND JUDAISM. FAM DIPLOM ECO/TAC EDU/PROP CRIME RACE/REL MARRIAGE ANOMIE ATTIT ORD/FREE...POLICY 20 UN. PAGE 160 A3254 SECT CULTURE ACT/RES GP/REL

B60
AMERICAN ASSEMBLY COLUMBIA U,THE SECRETARY OF STATE. USA+45 ELITES NAT/G PLAN ADMIN GOV/REL CENTRAL ATTIT...POLICY MGT 20 SEC/STATE CONGRESS PRESIDENT. PAGE 7 A0136 DELIB/GP EX/STRUC GP/REL DIPLOM

B60
ROPKE W.,A HUMANE ECONOMY. CULTURE ECO/DEV FINAN INDUS GP/REL CENTRAL WEALTH...GEOG SOC IDEA/COMP 20 EEC. PAGE 123 A2525 ECO/TAC INT/ORG DIPLOM ORD/FREE

B61
DELZELL C.F.,MUSSOLINI'S ENEMIES - THE ITALIAN ANTI-FASCIST RESISTANCE. ITALY DIPLOM PRESS DETER WAR TOTALISM ORD/FREE MARXISM 20. PAGE 36 A0730 FASCISM GP/REL POL/PAR REV

B61
FUCHS G.,GEGEN HITLER UND HENLEIN. CZECHOSLVK GERMANY DIPLOM CHOOSE GP/REL TOTALISM SOVEREIGN 20 HITLER/A. PAGE 50 A1013 FASCISM WORKER POL/PAR NAT/LISM

B61
KHAN A.W.,INDIA WINS FREEDOM: THE OTHER SIDE. INDIA PAKISTAN CULTURE LEGIS DIPLOM PARL/PROC REV WAR NAT/LISM 20. PAGE 78 A1607 SOVEREIGN GP/REL RACE/REL ORD/FREE

B61
PATAI R.,CULTURES IN CONFLICT; AN INQUIRY INTO THE SOCIO-CULTURAL PROBLEMS OF ISRAEL AND HER NEIGHBORS (2ND REV. ED.). ISLAM ISRAEL SOCIETY STRUCT DIPLOM GP/REL ALL/VALS...SOC 20 JEWS ARABS. PAGE 114 A2339 NAT/COMP CULTURE GP/COMP ATTIT

B61
SHAPP W.R.,FIELD ADMINISTRATION IN THE UNITED NATIONS SYSTEM. FINAN PROB/SOLV INSPECT DIPLOM EXEC REGION ROUTINE EFFICIENCY ROLE...INT CHARTS 20 UN. PAGE 131 A2694 INT/ORG ADMIN GP/REL FOR/AID

B61
WALLERSTEIN I.M.,AFRICA; THE POLITICS OF INDEPENDENCE. AFR SOCIETY STRUCT LEAD PARL/PROC PARTIC GP/REL...POLICY 20. PAGE 160 A3269 ECO/UNDEV DIPLOM COLONIAL ORD/FREE

B61
WARD R.E.,JAPANESE POLITICAL SCIENCE: A GUIDE TO JAPANESE REFERENCE AND RESEARCH MATERIALS (2ND ED.). LAW CONSTN STRATA NAT/G POL/PAR DELIB/GP LEGIS ADMIN CHOOSE GP/REL...INT/LAW 19/20 CHINJAP. PAGE 161 A3282 BIBLIOG/A PHIL/SCI

B62
BLANSHARD P.,FREEDOM AND CATHOLIC POWER IN SPAIN AND PORTUGAL: AN AMERICAN INTERPRETATION. AFR PORTUGAL SPAIN USA+45 LAW LABOR DIPLOM EDU/PROP DISCRIM ISOLAT TOTALISM 20 CHURCH/STA. PAGE 15 A0309 GP/REL FASCISM CATHISM PWR

B62
BUCHMANN J.,L'AFRIQUE NOIRE INDEPENDANTE. POL/PAR DIPLOM COLONIAL PARTIC CHOOSE GP/REL ATTIT ORD/FREE WEALTH NEGRO. PAGE 21 A0426 AFR NAT/LISM DECISION

B62
CALDER R.,COMMON SENSE ABOUT A STARVING WORLD. WOR+45 STRATA ECO/DEV PLAN GP/REL BIO/SOC HABITAT ...POLICY GEOG STAT RECORD 20 UN BIRTH/CON. PAGE 23 A0466 FOR/AID CENSUS ECO/UNDEV AGRI

B62
LEVY H.V.,LIBERDADE E JUSTICA SOCIAL (2ND ED.). BRAZIL COM L/A+17C USSR INT/ORG PARTIC GP/REL WEALTH 20 UN COM/PARTY. PAGE 88 A1798 ORD/FREE MARXISM CAP/ISM LAW

B62
MOON P.,DIVIDE AND QUIT. INDIA PAKISTAN STRATA DELIB/GP PLAN DIPLOM REPRESENT GP/REL INGP/REL CONSEN DISCRIM...OBS 20. PAGE 103 A2119 WAR REGION ISOLAT SECT

B62
NOBECOURT R.G.,LES SECRETS DE LA PROPAGANDE EN FRANCE OCCUPEE. FRANCE ELITES NAT/G DIPLOM GP/REL NAT/LISM TOTALISM ORD/FREE 20 VICHY VICHY. PAGE 109 A2244 METH/COMP EDU/PROP WAR CONTROL

B62
PERRE J.,LES MUTATIONS DE LA GUERRE MODERNE: DE LA REVOLUTION FRANCAISE A LA REVOLUTION NUCLEAIRE. DIPLOM ARMS/CONT DEATH REV WEAPON GP/REL PEACE ATTIT...STAT PREDICT BIBLIOG 18/20 WWI. PAGE 115 A2365 WAR FORCES NUC/PWR

B62
SCHMIDT-VOLKMAR E.,DER KULTURKAMPF IN DEUTSCHLAND 1871-1890. GERMANY PRUSSIA SOCIETY STRUCT SECT DIPLOM GP/REL NAT/LISM 19 CHURCH/STA BISMARCK/O. PAGE 128 A2632 POL/PAR CATHISM ATTIT NAT/G

B62
WELLEQUET J.,LE CONGO BELGE ET LA WELTPOLITIK (1894-1914. GERMANY DOMIN EDU/PROP WAR ATTIT ...BIBLIOG T CONGO/LEOP. PAGE 163 A3314 ADMIN DIPLOM GP/REL COLONIAL

B63
CROZIER B.,THE MORNING AFTER; A STUDY OF INDEPENDENCE. WOR+45 EX/STRUC PLAN BAL/PWR COLONIAL GP/REL 20 COLD/WAR. PAGE 33 A0666 SOVEREIGN NAT/LISM NAT/G DIPLOM

B63
JAIRAZBHOY R.A.,FOREIGN INFLUENCE IN ANCIENT INDIA. INDIA ELITES SECT DIPLOM EDU/PROP COLONIAL REGION GP/REL...ART/METH LING WORSHIP +/14 GRECO/ROMN MESOPOTAM PERSIA PARTH/SASS. PAGE 73 A1491 CULTURE SOCIETY COERCE DOMIN

B63
JENNINGS W.I.,DEMOCRACY IN AFRICA. UK CULTURE STRUCT ECO/UNDEV DIPLOM COLONIAL GP/REL ADJUST NAT/LISM ORD/FREE...GOV/COMP 20 THIRD/WRLD. PAGE 74 A1512 PROB/SOLV AFR CONSTN POPULISM

B63
LIU K.C.,AMERICANS AND CHINESE: A HISTORICAL ESSAY BIBLIOG/A

AND BIBLIOGRAPHY. ASIA USA+45 USA-45 SOCIETY SECT 18/20. PAGE 90 A1845
GP/REL DIPLOM ATTIT

B63
PRESTON W. JR.,ALIENS AND DISSENTERS: FEDERAL SUPPRESSION OF RADICALS 1903-1933. USA-45 DIPLOM ADJUD REPRESENT RACE/REL MAJORITY...BIBLIOG/A 19/20. PAGE 117 A2409
DISCRIM GP/REL INGP/REL ATTIT

B63
RAVENS J.P.,STAAT UND KATHOLISCHE KIRCHE IN PREUSSENS POLNISCHEN TEILUNGSGEBIETEN. GERMANY POLAND PRUSSIA PROVS DIPLOM EDU/PROP DEBATE NAT/LISM...JURID 18 CHURCH/STA. PAGE 119 A2451
GP/REL CATHISM SECT NAT/G

B63
THORELLI H.B.,INTOP: INTERNATIONAL OPERATIONS SIMULATION: PLAYER'S MANUAL. BRAZIL FINAN OP/RES ADMIN GP/REL INGP/REL PRODUC PERCEPT...DECISION MGT EEC. PAGE 144 A2935
GAME INT/TRADE EDU/PROP LG/CO

B63
US DEPARTMENT OF STATE,POLITICAL BEHAVIOR--A LIST OF CURRENT STUDIES. USA+45 COM/IND DIPLOM LEAD PERS/REL DRIVE PERCEPT KNOWL...DECISION SIMUL METH. PAGE 151 A3093
BIBLIOG METH/COMP GP/REL ATTIT

B63
WEINBERG A.,INSTEAD OF VIOLENCE: WRITINGS BY THE GREAT ADVOCATES OF PEACE AND NONVIOLENCE THROUGHOUT HISTORY. WOR+45 WOR-45 SOCIETY SECT PROB/SOLV DIPLOM GP/REL PERS/REL PEACE...ANTHOL PACIFIST. PAGE 162 A3304
PACIFISM WAR IDEA/COMP

B63
WILCOX W.A.,PAKISTAN; THE CONSOLIDATION OF A NATION. INDIA PAKISTAN CONSTN SECT PROB/SOLV COLONIAL PARTIC GP/REL FEDERAL...POLICY 19/20. PAGE 164 A3348
NAT/LISM ECO/UNDEV DIPLOM STRUCT

N63
US AGENCY INTERNATIONAL DEV,PRINCIPLES OF FOREIGN ECONOMIC ASSISTANCE (PAMPHLET). USA+45 FINAN GP/REL BAL/PAY EFFICIENCY 20 AID. PAGE 149 A3051
FOR/AID PLAN ECO/UNDEV ATTIT

B64
ARNOLD G.,TOWARDS PEACE AND A MULTIRACIAL COMMONWEALTH. UK TEC/DEV BAL/PWR COLONIAL GP/REL NAT/LISM PEACE SOVEREIGN...POLICY SOC/INTEG 20 CMN/WLTH. PAGE 9 A0175
DIPLOM INT/TRADE FOR/AID ORD/FREE

B64
COFFIN F.M.,WITNESS FOR AID. COM EUR+WWI USA+45 DIPLOM GP/REL CONSEN ORD/FREE MARXISM...NEW/IDEA 20 CONGRESS AID. PAGE 27 A0557
FOR/AID ECO/UNDEV DELIB/GP PLAN

B64
CURRIE D.P.,FEDERALISM AND THE NEW NATIONS OF AFRICA. CANADA USA+45 INT/TRADE TAX GP/REL ...NAT/COMP SOC/INTEG 20. PAGE 33 A0667
FEDERAL AFR ECO/UNDEV INT/LAW

B64
DESHMUKH C.D.,THE COMMONWEALTH AS INDIA SEES IT. INDIA UK ECO/UNDEV TEC/DEV INT/TRADE GP/REL RACE/REL SOVEREIGN SOC/INTEG 19/20 COMMONWLTH. PAGE 36 A0733
DIPLOM COLONIAL NAT/LISM ATTIT

B64
TONG T.,UNITED STATES DIPLOMACY IN CHINA, 1844-1860. ASIA USA-45 ECO/UNDEV ECO/TAC COERCE GP/REL...INT/LAW 19 TREATY. PAGE 144 A2949
DIPLOM INT/TRADE COLONIAL

B64
WALLBANK T.W.,DOCUMENTS ON MODERN AFRICA. NAT/G COLONIAL GP/REL ATTIT PWR...BIBLIOG 19/20. PAGE 160 A3267
AFR NAT/LISM ECO/UNDEV DIPLOM

S64
"FURTHER READING." INDIA PAKISTAN SECT WAR PEACE ATTIT...POLICY 20. PAGE 3 A0067
BIBLIOG GP/REL DIPLOM NAT/G

S64
CARNEGIE ENDOWMENT INT. PEACE,"HUMAN RIGHTS (ISSUES BEFORE THE NINETEENTH GENERAL ASSEMBLY)." AFR WOR+45 LAW CONSTN NAT/G EDU/PROP GP/REL DISCRIM PEACE ATTIT MORAL ORD/FREE...INT/LAW PSY CONCPT RECORD UN 20. PAGE 24 A0492
INT/ORG PERSON RACE/REL

B65
BRACKETT R.D.,PATHWAYS TO PEACE. SECT VOL/ASSN GP/REL PERS/REL DISCRIM...LING 20 UN PEACE/CORP. PAGE 18 A0366
PEACE INT/ORG EDU/PROP PARTIC

B65
COWEN Z.,THE BRITISH COMMONWEALTH OF NATIONS IN A CHANGING WORLD. UK ECO/UNDEV INT/ORG ECO/TAC INT/TRADE COLONIAL WAR GP/REL RACE/REL SOVEREIGN SOC/INTEG 20 TREATY EEC COMMONWLTH. PAGE 32 A0644
JURID DIPLOM PARL/PROC NAT/LISM

B65
FORM W.H.,INDUSTRIAL RELATIONS AND SOCIAL CHANGE IN LATIN AMERICA. L/A+17C AGRI LABOR NAT/G PLAN PROB/SOLV DIPLOM...MGT SOC ANTHOL BIBLIOG/A METH 20. PAGE 47 A0966
INDUS GP/REL NAT/COMP ECO/UNDEV

B65
LINDBLOM C.E.,THE INTELLIGENCE OF DEMOCRACY; DECISION MAKING THROUGH MUTUAL ADJUSTMENT. WOR+45 SOCIETY NAT/G PROB/SOLV DOMIN PARTIC GP/REL ORD/FREE...POLICY IDEA/COMP BIBLIOG 20. PAGE 89 A1821
PLURISM DECISION ADJUST DIPLOM

B65
MEDIVA J.T.,LA IMPRENTA EN MEXICO, 1539-1821 (8 VOLS.). SOCIETY ECO/UNDEV DIPLOM COLONIAL GP/REL 16/19 MEXIC/AMER. PAGE 99 A2031
BIBLIOG WRITING NAT/G L/A+17C

B65
MEHROTRA S.R.,INDIA AND THE COMMONWEALTH 1885-1929. INDIA UK INT/ORG VOL/ASSN GP/REL ATTIT...POLICY BIBLIOG 19/20 CMN/WLTH. PAGE 99 A2034
DIPLOM NAT/G POL/PAR NAT/LISM

B65
MONCONDUIT F.,LA COMMISSION EUROPEENNE DES DROITS DE L'HOMME. DIPLOM AGREE GP/REL ORD/FREE PWR ...BIBLIOG 20 TREATY. PAGE 102 A2103
INT/LAW INT/ORG ADJUD JURID

B65
QURESHI I.H.,THE STRUGGLE FOR PAKISTAN. INDIA PAKISTAN UK CULTURE LEGIS DIPLOM EDU/PROP COLONIAL ATTIT SOVEREIGN 19/20 MUSLIM. PAGE 118 A2429
GP/REL RACE/REL WAR SECT

B65
RUBINSTEIN A.Z.,THE CHALLENGE OF POLITICS: IDEAS AND ISSUES (2ND ED.). UNIV ELITES SOCIETY EX/STRUC BAL/PWR PARL/PROC AUTHORIT...DECISION ANTHOL 20. PAGE 125 A2565
NAT/G DIPLOM GP/REL ORD/FREE

B65
SCHREIBER H.,TEUTON AND SLAV - THE STRUGGLE FOR CENTRAL EUROPE (TRANS. BY J. CLEUGH). GERMANY POLAND PRUSSIA USSR SOCIETY STRUCT SECT DIPLOM BALTIC. PAGE 129 A2646
GP/REL WAR RACE/REL NAT/LISM

B65
SILVA SOLAR J.,EL DESARROLLO DE LA NUEVA SOCIEDAD EN AMERICA. L/A+17C SOCIETY AGRI PROB/SOLV DIPLOM PARTIC GP/REL OWN...POLICY SOC 20 REFORMERS. PAGE 133 A2716
STRUCT ECO/UNDEV REGION CONTROL

B65
US SENATE COMM AERO SPACE SCI,INTERNATIONAL COOPERATION AND ORGANIZATION FOR OUTER SPACE. FUT USA+45 WOR+45 PROF/ORG VOL/ASSN CONSULT DELIB/GP PLAN TEC/DEV ARMS/CONT GP/REL PEACE 20 UN NASA. PAGE 155 A3167
DIPLOM SPACE R+D NAT/G

B65
US SENATE COMM ON JUDICIARY,REFUGEE PROBLEMS IN SOUTH VIETNAM AND LAOS: HEARINGS BEFORE SUBCOMMITTEE TO INVESTIGATE PROBLEMS OF REFUGEES, ESCAPEES. CHINA/COM LAOS USA+45 VIETNAM/S PROB/SOLV DIPLOM GOV/REL GP/REL EFFICIENCY ORD/FREE...POLICY GEOG 20 CONGRESS MIGRATION. PAGE 157 A3194
STRANGE HABITAT FOR/AID CIVMIL/REL

B65
VAN DEN BERGHE P.L.,AFRICA: SOCIAL PROBLEMS OF CHANGE AND CONFLICT. ELITES STRATA ECO/UNDEV KIN MUNIC DIPLOM GP/REL RACE/REL NAT/LISM...ANTHOL BIBLIOG 20. PAGE 158 A3210
SOC CULTURE AFR STRUCT

B65
WEIL G.L.,A HANDBOOK ON THE EUROPEAN ECONOMIC COMMUNITY. BELGIUM EUR+WWI FRANCE GERMANY/W ITALY CONSTN ECO/DEV CREATE PARTIC GP/REL...DECISION MGT CHARTS 20 EEC. PAGE 162 A3299
INT/TRADE INT/ORG TEC/DEV INT/LAW

C65
SCHWEBEL M.,"BEHAVIORAL SCIENCE AND HUMAN SURVIVAL." FORCES ARMS/CONT COERCE NUC/PWR WAR GP/REL NAT/LISM PERCEPT...POLICY PSY ANTHOL BIBLIOG/A 20 COLD/WAR. PAGE 130 A2662
PEACE ACT/RES DIPLOM HEAL

B66
BIRMINGHAM D.,TRADE AND CONFLICT IN ANGOLA. PORTUGAL CULTURE FORCES DIPLOM GP/REL PROFIT HABITAT NAT/COMP. PAGE 14 A0291
WAR INT/TRADE ECO/UNDEV COLONIAL

B66
FELKER J.L.,SOVIET ECONOMIC CONTROVERSIES. USSR INDUS PLAN INT/TRADE GP/REL MARXISM SOCISM...POLICY 20. PAGE 45 A0915
ECO/DEV MARKET PROFIT PRICE

B66
GROSS F.,WORLD POLITICS AND TENSION AREAS. CHINA/COM SOMALIA VENEZUELA COERCE GP/REL RACE/REL ATTIT HABITAT 19/20 CASEBOOK NEWYORK/C. PAGE 57 A1173
DIPLOM WAR PROB/SOLV

B66
GUPTA S.,KASHMIR - A STUDY IN INDIA-PAKISTAN RELATIONS. INDIA KASHMIR PAKISTAN CONSTN INT/ORG REV RACE/REL NAT/LISM 20 UN MUSLIM/LG. PAGE 58 A1194
DIPLOM GP/REL SOVEREIGN WAR

B66
HENKYS R.,DEUTSCHLAND UND DIE OSTLICHEN NACHBARN. GERMANY POLAND NAT/G POL/PAR INGP/REL ATTIT 20 MIGRATION. PAGE 64 A1317
GP/REL JURID INT/LAW DIPLOM

B66
HOROWITZ D.,HEMISPHERES NORTH AND SOUTH: ECONOMIC DISPARITY AMONG NATIONS. WOR+45 ECO/DEV ECO/UNDEV INT/ORG PLAN DIPLOM INT/TRADE GIVE PARTIC GP/REL
ECO/TAC FOR/AID STRATA

...WELF/ST 20. PAGE 67 A1387 WEALTH

B66
KAREFA-SMART J.,AFRICA: PROGRESS THROUGH COOPERATION. AFR FINAN TEC/DEV DIPLOM FOR/AID EDU/PROP CONFER REGION GP/REL WEALTH...HEAL SOC/INTEG 20. PAGE 76 A1566 ORD/FREE ECO/UNDEV VOL/ASSN PLAN

B66
LEE L.T.,VIENNA CONVENTION ON CONSULAR RELATIONS. WOR+45 LAW INT/ORG CONFER GP/REL PRIVIL...INT/LAW 20 TREATY VIENNA/CNV. PAGE 86 A1760 AGREE DIPLOM ADMIN

B66
LEIGH M.B.,CHECK LIST OF HOLDINGS ON BORNEO IN THE CORNELL UNIVERSITY LIBRARIES (PAMPHLET). BORNEO MALAYSIA LAW CONSTN GP/REL SOC. PAGE 86 A1769 BIBLIOG S/ASIA DIPLOM NAT/G

B66
MORRIS B.S.,INTERNATIONAL COMMUNISM AND AMERICAN POLICY. CHINA/COM USA+45 USSR INT/ORG POL/PAR GP/REL NAT/LISM ATTIT PERCEPT 20. PAGE 105 A2147 DIPLOM POLICY MARXISM

B66
NIEDERGANG M.,LA REVOLUTION DE SAINT-DOMINGUE. DOMIN/REP INT/ORG NAT/G CONTROL LEAD GP/REL ORD/FREE MARXISM 20. PAGE 109 A2239 REV FORCES DIPLOM

B66
SANDERS R.E.,SPAIN AND THE UNITED NATIONS 1945-1950. SPAIN CHIEF DIPLOM CONFER SANCTION ATTIT ...POLICY 20 UN COLD/WAR. PAGE 127 A2599 INT/ORG FASCISM GP/REL STRANGE

B66
SINGH L.P.,THE POLITICS OF ECONOMIC COOPERATION IN ASIA; A STUDY OF ASIAN INTERNATIONAL ORGANIZATIONS. ASIA INT/ORG ACT/RES PLAN GP/REL...POLICY GP/COMP BIBLIOG 20 UN SEATO. PAGE 133 A2733 ECO/UNDEV ECO/TAC REGION DIPLOM

B66
WESTIN A.F.,VIEWS OF AMERICA. COM USA+45 USSR SOCIETY ECO/UNDEV POL/PAR ECO/TAC GP/REL STRANGE MARXISM...MARXIST 20. PAGE 163 A3323 CONCPT ATTIT DIPLOM IDEA/COMP

S66
CHIU H.,"COMMUNIST CHINA'S ATTITUDE TOWARD INTERNATIONAL LAW" CHINA/COM USSR LAW CONSTN DIPLOM GP/REL 20 LENIN/VI. PAGE 26 A0532 INT/LAW MARXISM CONCPT IDEA/COMP

S66
MANSERGH N.,"THE PARTITION OF INDIA IN RETROSPECT." INDIA PAKISTAN S/ASIA UK DIPLOM COLONIAL GP/REL PWR 20. PAGE 94 A1933 NAT/G PARL/PROC POLICY POL/PAR

B67
MEHDI M.T.,PEACE IN THE MIDDLE EAST. ISRAEL SOCIETY NAT/G PLAN EDU/PROP NAT/LISM DRIVE...IDEA/COMP 20 JEWS. PAGE 99 A2033 ISLAM DIPLOM GP/REL COERCE

B67
RALSTON D.B.,THE ARMY OF THE REPUBLIC; THE PLACE OF THE MILITARY IN THE POLITICAL EVOLUTION OF FRANCE 1871-1914. FRANCE MOD/EUR EX/STRUC LEGIS TOP/EX DIPLOM ADMIN WAR GP/REL ROLE...BIBLIOG 19/20. PAGE 119 A2436 FORCES NAT/G CIVMIL/REL POLICY

B67
SCHWARTZ M.A.,PUBLIC OPINION AND CANADIAN IDENTITY. CANADA SOCIETY LOC/G DIPLOM ADMIN LEAD REGION GP/REL SAMP. PAGE 130 A2657 ATTIT NAT/G NAT/LISM POL/PAR

B67
ZUCKERMAN S.,SCIENTISTS AND WAR. ELITES INDUS DIPLOM CENTRAL EFFICIENCY KNOWL 20. PAGE 170 A3459 R+D CONSULT ACT/RES GP/REL

S67
BENTLEY E.,"VIETNAM: THE STATE OF OUR FEELINGS." USA+45 VIETNAM PROB/SOLV DIPLOM GP/REL INGP/REL RACE/REL WEALTH. PAGE 13 A0271 WAR PARTIC ATTIT PEACE

S67
CONNOR W.,"SELF-DETERMINATION: THE NEW PHASE." WOR+45 WOR-45 CULTURE INT/ORG COLONIAL 19/20. PAGE 29 A0588 NAT/LISM SOVEREIGN INGP/REL GP/REL

S67
ECKHARDT A.R.,"SILENCE IN THE CHURCHES." ISRAEL WOR+45 CONSTN GP/REL DISCRIM DRIVE JEWS. PAGE 40 A0820 SECT ATTIT DIPLOM ISLAM

S67
FRANK I.,"NEW PERSPECTIVES ON TRADE AND DEVELOPMENT." PROB/SOLV BARGAIN DIPLOM FOR/AID CONFER GP/REL WEALTH 20 UN GATT. PAGE 48 A0980 ECO/UNDEV INT/ORG INT/TRADE ECO/TAC

S67
HERRERA F.,"EUROPEAN PARTICIPATION IN THE LATIN AMERICAN REGIONAL INTEGRATION" EUR+WWI L/A+17C GP/REL INGP/REL 20. PAGE 64 A1318 DIPLOM REGION INT/ORG FINAN

S67
KIERNAN V.G.,"INDIA AND THE LABOUR PARTY." INDIA UK CAP/ISM GP/REL EFFICIENCY NAT/LISM PWR SOCISM ...SOCIALIST TIME/SEQ 20. PAGE 79 A1616 COLONIAL DIPLOM POL/PAR ECO/UNDEV

S67
NORTH R.C.,"COMMUNICATION AS AN APPROACH TO POLITICS." UNIV INTELL DIPLOM PERCEPT PERSON ...CONCPT TIME. PAGE 110 A2254 PERS/REL GP/REL ACT/RES

S67
ROCKE J.R.M.,"THE BRITISH EXPORT BATTLE FOR THE CARIBBEAN" GP/REL...POLICY 20 CMN/WLTH. PAGE 122 A2510 INT/TRADE DIPLOM MARKET ECO/TAC

S67
SPENCER R.,"GERMANY AFTER THE AUTUMN CRISIS." GERMANY CHOOSE GP/REL PERS/REL. PAGE 136 A2785 DIPLOM POL/PAR PROB/SOLV

S67
VELIKONJA J.,"ITALIAN IMMIGRANTS IN THE UNITED STATES IN THE MID-SIXTIES" ITALY USA+45 KIN MUNIC NAT/G WORKER DIPLOM REGION GP/REL ADJUST...GEOG CHARTS SOC/INTEG 20. PAGE 158 A3226 HABITAT ORD/FREE TREND STAT

S67
YOUNG K.T.,"UNITED STATES POLICY AND VIETNAMESE POLITICAL VIABILITY 1954-1967." VIETNAM/S LOC/G MUNIC FOR/AID ORD/FREE...POLICY 20. PAGE 169 A3437 LEAD ADMIN GP/REL EFFICIENCY

B98
GRIFFIN A.P.C.,LIST OF BOOKS RELATING TO CUBA (PAMPHLET). CUBA L/A+17C USA-45 INT/TRADE DOMIN WAR GP/REL ALL/VALS...GEOG SOC CHARTS 19/20. PAGE 56 A1158 BIBLIOG/A NAT/G COLONIAL

GRABENER J. A2813

GRACIA-MORA M.R. A1119

GRAEBNER N. A1120,A1121,A1122,A1123

GRAHAM F.D. A1124,A1125

GRAHAM G.S. A1126

GRAHAM I.C.C. A1127

GRAND/JURY....GRAND JURIES

GRANDIN T. A1128

GRANGE....GRANGE AND GRANGERS

GRANT N. A1129

GRANT/US....PRESIDENT ULYSSES S. GRANT

GRANTS....SEE GIVE+FOR/AID

GRASES P. A1130

GRAUBARD S.R. A1131

GRAVEN J. A1132

GRAVES R.L. A2935

GREAT BRITAIN....SEE UK

GREAT BRITAIN CENTRAL OFF INF A1133,A1134,A1135

GREAT/SOC....GREAT SOCIETY

GREAVES H.R.G. A1136

GRECO/ROMN....GRECO-ROMAN CIVILIZATION

B63
JAIRAZBHOY R.A.,FOREIGN INFLUENCE IN ANCIENT INDIA. INDIA ELITES SECT DIPLOM EDU/PROP COLONIAL REGION GP/REL...ART/METH LING WORSHIP +/14 GRECO/ROMN MESOPOTAM PERSIA PARTH/SASS. PAGE 73 A1491 CULTURE SOCIETY COERCE DOMIN

GREECE....MODERN GREECE

B20
VINOGRADOFF P.,OUTLINES OF HISTORICAL JURISPRUDENCE (2 VOLS.). GREECE MEDIT-7 LAW CONSTN FACE/GP FAM KIN MUNIC CRIME OWN...INT/LAW IDEA/COMP BIBLIOG. PAGE 159 A3241 JURID METH

B35
MARRIOTT J.A.,DICTATORSHIP AND DEMOCRACY. GERMANY GREECE UK CHIEF DIPLOM DOMIN LEGIT PEACE ORD/FREE TOTALISM POPULISM

CONSERVE...TREND ROME HITLER/A. PAGE 95 A1946 PLURIST NAT/G

B43
BROWN A.D.,GREECE: SELECTED LIST OF REFERENCES. GREECE ECO/UNDEV AGRI FINAN INDUS LABOR SECT TEC/DEV INT/TRADE LEAD...SOC 20. PAGE 20 A0399 BIBLIOG/A WAR DIPLOM NAT/G

B52
SPENCER F.A.,WAR AND POSTWAR GREECE: AN ANALYSIS BASED ON GREEK WRITINGS. GREECE SOCIETY NAT/G POL/PAR FORCES CREATE DIPLOM LEAD MARXISM...SOC 20. PAGE 136 A2784 BIBLIOG/A WAR REV

B57
MCNEILL W.H.,GREECE: AMERICAN AID IN ACTION. GREECE UK USA+45 FINAN CAP/ISM INT/TRADE BAL/PAY PRODUC WEALTH...POLICY METH/COMP 20. PAGE 99 A2022 FOR/AID DIPLOM ECO/UNDEV

B58
MUNKMAN C.A.,AMERICAN AID TO GREECE. GREECE USA+45 AGRI FINAN PROB/SOLV WAR PWR...CHARTS 20 UN. PAGE 106 A2171 FOR/AID PLAN ECO/DEV INT/TRADE

B58
SALETORE B.A.,INDIA'S DIPLOMATIC RELATIONS WITH THE WEST. GREECE INDIA CULTURE ETIQUET...IDEA/COMP 3 ROM/EMP PERSIA. PAGE 126 A2590 DIPLOM CONCPT INT/TRADE

S58
BOGART L.,"MEASURING THE EFFECTIVENESS OF AN OVERSEAS INFORMATION CAMPAIGN." EUR+WWI GREECE USA+45 INT/ORG MUNIC PLAN DIPLOM PEACE PERCEPT RIGID/FLEX KNOWL...TECHNIC PSY SOC NEW/IDEA CONT/OBS REC/INT STAND/INT SAMP/SIZ COLD/WAR 20. PAGE 16 A0328 ATTIT EDU/PROP

B66
US DEPARTMENT OF STATE,RESEARCH ON THE MIDDLE EAST (EXTERNAL RESEARCH LIST NO 4-25). GREECE ISRAEL SYRIA UAR YEMEN CULTURE SOCIETY POL/PAR SECT DIPLOM EDU/PROP WAR NAT/LISM...GEOG GOV/COMP 20. PAGE 152 A3096 BIBLIOG/A ISLAM NAT/G REGION

S67
ANTHEM T.,"CYPRUS* WHAT NOW?" CYPRUS GREECE TURKEY NAT/G BUDGET MAJORITY 20 NATO. PAGE 8 A0165 DIPLOM COERCE INT/TRADE ADJUD

GREECE PRESBEIA U.S. A1137

GREECE/ANC....ANCIENT GREECE

GREEN L.C. A1138,A1139

GREEN/TH....T.H. GREEN

GREENBACK....GREENBACK PARTY

GREENBERG S. A1140

GREENE K.R.C. A1141

GREENSPAN M. A1142,A1143

GREENWICH VILLAGE....SEE GRNWCH/VIL

GREENWICH....GREENWICH, ENGLAND

GREGORY W. A1144,A1145

GRENADA....GRENADA (WEST INDIES)

GRENVILLE J.A.S. A1146

GRENVILLES....GRENVILLES - ENGLISH FAMILY; SEE ALSO UK

GRESHAM-YANG TREATY....SEE GRESHMYANG

GRESHAMOS LAW....SEE GRESHM/LAW

GRESHM/LAW....GRESHAM'S LAW

GRESHMYANG....GRESHAM-YANG TREATY

GRETTON P. A1147

GRIERSON P. A1148

GRIFFIN A.P.C. A1149,A1150,A1151,A1152,A1153,A1154,A1155,A1156 , A1157,A1158

GRIFFIN G.G. A0264,A1159

GRIFFITH E.S. A1160

GRIFFITH W.E. A1161,A1162

GRIFFITH SB I.I. A1163

GRIFFITHS F. A0321,A1164

GRISMER R. A1165

GRISWOLD A.W. A1166

GRNWCH/VIL....GREENWICH VILLAGE

GROB F. A1167

GROBLER J.H. A1168

GRODZINS M. A1169

GROND L. A0513

GROPP A.E. A1170

GROSS F. A1171,A1172,A1173

GROSS J.A. A1174

GROSS L. A1175,A1176,A1177

GROSS NATIONAL PRODUCT....WEALTH+ECO+PRODUC

GROSSER A. A1178,A1179

GROTIUS H. A1180

GROUP RELATIONS....SEE GP/REL

GROWTH....SEE CREATE, CREATE+ECO/UNDEV

GRUNDER G.A. A1181

GRUNDY K.W. A1182,A1183

GRZYBOWSKI K. A1184,A1185

GT BRIT MIN OVERSEAS DEV, LIB A2089

GUAM....GUAM

B01
GRIFFIN A.P.C.,LIST OF BOOKS ON SAMOA (PAMPHLET). GERMANY S/ASIA UK USA-45 WOR-45 ECO/UNDEV REGION ALL/VALS ORD/FREE ALL/IDEOS...GEOG INT/LAW 19 SAMOA GUAM. PAGE 56 A1150 BIBLIOG/A COLONIAL DIPLOM

GUATEMALA....SEE ALSO L/A+17C

B47
PERKINS D.,THE UNITED STATES AND THE CARIBBEAN. CUBA DOMIN/REP GUATEMALA HAITI PANAMA CULTURE ECO/UNDEV FOR/AID ADMIN COERCE HABITAT...POLICY 19/20. PAGE 115 A2359 DIPLOM L/A+17C USA-45

B63
SMITH J.E.,THE DEFENSE OF BERLIN. COM GUATEMALA WOR+45 ECO/TAC ADMIN NEUTRAL ATTIT ORD/FREE SOVEREIGN...DECISION 20 DEPT/STATE. PAGE 134 A2747 DIPLOM FORCES BAL/PWR PLAN

GUEMES/M....MARTIN GUEMES

GUENA Y. A1186

GUERRANT E.O. A1187

GUERRILLA....GUERRILLA WARFARE

N
PEKING REVIEW. CHINA/COM CULTURE AGRI INDUS DIPLOM EDU/PROP GUERRILLA ATTIT MARXISM...BIBLIOG 20. PAGE 1 A0022 MARXIST NAT/G POL/PAR PRESS

B14
DE BLOCH J.,THE FUTURE OF WAR IN ITS TECHNICAL, ECONOMIC, AND POLITICAL RELATIONS (1899). MOD/EUR TEC/DEV BUDGET INT/TRADE DETER GUERRILLA WEAPON COST PEACE 20. PAGE 34 A0698 WAR BAL/PWR PREDICT FORCES

B36
THWAITE D.,THE SEETHING AFRICAN POT: A STUDY OF BLACK NATIONALISM 1882-1935. ETHIOPIA SECT VOL/ASSN COERCE GUERRILLA MURDER DISCRIM MARXISM...PSY TIME/SEQ 18/20 NEGRO. PAGE 144 A2939 NAT/LISM AFR RACE/REL DIPLOM

B45
CLAGETT H.L.,COMMUNIST CHINA: RUTHLESS ENEMY OR PAPER TIGER (PAMPHLET). CHINA/COM ECO/UNDEV AGRI INDUS NAT/G POL/PAR ECO/TAC INT/TRADE GUERRILLA ATTIT...CHARTS NAT/COMP ORG/CHARTS 20. PAGE 26 A0540 BIBLIOG/A MARXISM DIPLOM COERCE

B55
VIGON J.,TEORIA DEL MILITARISMO. NAT/G DIPLOM COLONIAL COERCE GUERRILLA CIVMIL/REL NAT/LISM MORAL ALL/IDEOS PACIFISM 18/20. PAGE 159 A3234 FORCES PHIL/SCI WAR POLICY

S60
GINSBURGS G.,"PEKING-LHASA-NEW DELHI." CHINA/COM FUT INDIA S/ASIA KIN NAT/G PROVS SECT FORCES BAL/PWR ECO/TAC DOMIN EDU/PROP LEGIT ADMIN REGION GUERRILLA PWR...TREND TIBET 20. PAGE 52 A1074
ASIA COERCE DIPLOM

L61
HILSMAN R. JR.,"THE NEW COMMUNIST TACTIC: PRECIS-INTERNAL WAR." COM FUT USA+45 ECO/UNDEV POL/PAR FOR/AID RIGID/FLEX ALL/VALS...TREND COLD/WAR 20. PAGE 65 A1334
FORCES COERCE USSR GUERRILLA

B62
CLUBB O.E. JR.,THE UNITED STATES AND THE SINO-SOVIET BLOC IN SOUTHEAST ASIA. ASIA CHINA/COM COM USA+45 USSR ECO/UNDEV INT/ORG NAT/G FORCES TOP/EX PLAN ECO/TAC DOMIN COERCE GUERRILLA ATTIT RIGID/FLEX...POLICY OBS TREND 20. PAGE 27 A0553
S/ASIA PWR BAL/PWR DIPLOM

B62
LAUERHAUSS L.,COMMUNISM IN LATIN AMERICA: THE POST-WAR YEARS (1945 -1960) (PAPER). INTELL STRATA ECO/UNDEV AGRI WORKER FOR/AID INT/TRADE COLONIAL GUERRILLA 20. PAGE 85 A1745
BIBLIOG L/A+17C MARXISM REV

B62
MORRAY J.P.,THE SECOND REVOLUTION IN CUBA. CUBA AGRI LABOR POL/PAR DIPLOM FOR/AID GUERRILLA TOTALISM MARXISM 20. PAGE 104 A2146
REV MARXIST ECO/TAC NAT/LISM

S62
GREENSPAN M.,"INTERNATIONAL LAW AND ITS PROTECTION FOR PARTICIPANTS IN UNCONVENTIONAL WARFARE." WOR+45 LAW INT/ORG NAT/G POL/PAR COERCE REV ORD/FREE ...INT/LAW TOT/POP 20. PAGE 56 A1143
FORCES JURID GUERRILLA WAR

B63
US DEPARTMENT OF THE ARMY,SOVIET RUSSIA: STRATEGIC SURVEY (PAMPHLET). USSR POL/PAR PLAN DOMIN EDU/PROP ARMS/CONT GUERRILLA WAR WEAPON...TREND CHARTS ORG/CHARTS 20. PAGE 152 A3106
BIBLIOG/A MARXISM DIPLOM COERCE

S63
BLOOMFIELD L.P.,"INTERNATIONAL FORCE IN A DISARMING BUT REVOLUTIONARY WORLD." INT/ORG COERCE REV DRIVE PWR...CONCPT STERTYP GEN/LAWS 20. PAGE 16 A0318
FORCES ORD/FREE ARMS/CONT GUERRILLA

S63
DARLING F.C.,"THE GEOPOLITICS OF AMERICAN FOREIGN POLITICS IN ASIA." COM S/ASIA USA+45 USSR ECO/UNDEV NAT/G VOL/ASSN CONSULT PLAN GUERRILLA...STAT TOT/POP 20. PAGE 34 A0682
FORCES ECO/TAC FOR/AID DIPLOM

B64
FALL B.,STREET WITHOUT JOY. FRANCE USA+45 DIPLOM ECO/TAC FOR/AID GUERRILLA REV WEAPON...TREND 20. PAGE 44 A0894
WAR S/ASIA FORCES COERCE

B64
KAUFMANN W.W.,THE MC NAMARA STRATEGY. TOP/EX INSPECT BAL/PWR DIPLOM CONTROL DETER GUERRILLA NUC/PWR WEAPON COST PWR...METH/COMP 20 MCNAMARA/R KENNEDY/JF JOHNSON/LB NATO DEPT/DEFEN. PAGE 77 A1572
FORCES WAR PLAN PROB/SOLV

S64
GINSBURGS G.,"WARS OF NATIONAL LIBERATION - THE SOVIET THESIS." COM USSR WOR+45 WOR-45 LAW CULTURE INT/ORG DIPLOM LEGIT COLONIAL GUERRILLA WAR NAT/LISM ATTIT PERSON MORAL PWR...JURID OBS TREND MARX/KARL 20. PAGE 53 A1075
COERCE CONCPT INT/LAW REV

S64
TINKER H.,"POLITICS IN SOUTHEAST ASIA." INT/ORG NAT/G CREATE PLAN TEC/DEV GUERRILLA KNOWL ORD/FREE COLD/WAR. PAGE 144 A2944
S/ASIA ACT/RES REGION

B65
MALLIN J.,FORTRESS CUBA; RUSSIA'S AMERICAN BASE. COM CUBA L/A+17C FORCES PLAN DIPLOM LEAD REV WAR ...POLICY 20 CASTRO/F GUEVARA/C INTERVENT. PAGE 93 A1914
MARXISM CHIEF GUERRILLA DOMIN

B66
SUPPLEMENTAL FOREIGN ASSISTANCE FISCAL YEAR 1966: VIETNAM. CHINA/COM COM S/ASIA USA+45 VIETNAM EXTR/IND FINAN DIPLOM TAX GUERRILLA HABITAT ORD/FREE...STAT CHARTS 20 SENATE PRESIDENT. PAGE 4 A0077
CONFER LEGIS WAR FOR/AID

B66
BRACKMAN A.C.,SOUTHEAST ASIA'S SECOND FRONT: THE POWER STRUGGLE IN THE MALAY ARCHIPELAGO. CHINA/COM INDONESIA MALAYSIA ECO/UNDEV INT/ORG NAT/G FORCES DIPLOM EDU/PROP REGION COERCE GUERRILLA AUTHORIT POPULISM...MAJORIT 20 KENNEDY/JF SEATO. PAGE 18 A0367
S/ASIA MARXISM REV

B66
DRACHOVITCH M.M.,THE COMINTERN HISTORICAL HIGHLIGHTS. USSR INT/ORG EX/STRUC LEGIT LEAD GUERRILLA...ANTHOL 20 COMINTERN LENIN/VI. PAGE 38 A0784
DIPLOM REV MARXISM PERSON

B66
FALL B.B.,VIET-NAM WITNESS, 1953-66. S/ASIA VIETNAM SECT PROB/SOLV COLONIAL GUERRILLA...CHARTS BIBLIOG 20. PAGE 44 A0895
MARXIST WAR DIPLOM

B67
GRIFFITH SB I.I.,THE CHINESE PEOPLE'S LIBERATION ARMY. CHINA/COM DIPLOM DOMIN GUERRILLA NUC/PWR REV ...CHARTS BIBLIOG 20. PAGE 57 A1163
FORCES CIVMIL/REL NAT/LISM PWR

B67
MCCLINTOCK R.,THE MEANING OF LIMITED WAR. FUT WOR+45 NAT/G FORCES GUERRILLA REV...POLICY SAMP/SIZ TREND NAT/COMP 45 COLD/WAR. PAGE 97 A1999
WAR NUC/PWR BAL/PWR DIPLOM

B67
SALISBURY H.E.,BEHIND THE LINES - HANOI. VIETNAM/N NAT/G GUERRILLA CIVMIL/REL NAT/LISM KNOWL 20. PAGE 126 A2592
WAR PROB/SOLV DIPLOM OBS

S67
FRANKEL M.,"THE WAR IN VIETNAM." VIETNAM ECO/UNDEV DIPLOM CONFER INGP/REL PEACE PWR...POLICY PREDICT 20. PAGE 48 A0982
WAR COERCE PLAN GUERRILLA

S67
FRANKLIN W.O.,"CLAUSEWITZ ON LIMITED WAR." VIETNAM WOR+45 WOR-45 PROB/SOLV DIPLOM ECO/TAC DOMIN COLONIAL...METH/COMP 19/20. PAGE 48 A0986
COERCE WAR PLAN GUERRILLA

S67
NEUCHTERLEIN D.E.,"THAILAND* ANOTHER VIETNAM?" THAILAND ECO/UNDEV DIPLOM ADMIN REGION CENTRAL NAT/LISM...POLICY 20. PAGE 108 A2220
WAR GUERRILLA S/ASIA NAT/G

GUETZKOW H. A1188

GUEVARA/E....ERNESTO CHE GUEVARA

B65
MALLIN J.,FORTRESS CUBA; RUSSIA'S AMERICAN BASE. COM CUBA L/A+17C FORCES PLAN DIPLOM LEAD REV WAR ...POLICY 20 CASTRO/F GUEVARA/C INTERVENT. PAGE 93 A1914
MARXISM CHIEF GUERRILLA DOMIN

GUIANA/BR....BRITISH GUIANA; SEE ALSO GUYANA

GUIANA/FR....FRENCH GUIANA

GUILDS....SEE PROF/ORG

GUIMARAES A.P. A1189

GUINEA....SEE ALSO AFR

B37
BLAKE J.W.,EUROPEAN BEGINNINGS IN WEST AFRICA 1454-1578. FRANCE GUINEA PORTUGAL UK PWR WEALTH 16/16 AFRICA/W. PAGE 15 A0305
DIPLOM COLONIAL INT/TRADE DOMIN

B61
PANIKKAR K.M.,REVOLUTION IN AFRICA. AFR GUINEA ECO/UNDEV POL/PAR DIPLOM COLONIAL EXEC LEAD SOVEREIGN...CHARTS 20. PAGE 114 A2332
NAT/LISM NAT/G CHIEF

B61
SCHNAPPER B.,LA POLITIQUE ET LE COMMERCE FRANCAIS DANS LE GOLFE DE GUINEE DE 1838 A 1871. FRANCE GUINEA UK SEA EXTR/IND NAT/G DELIB/GP LEGIS ADMIN ORD/FREE...POLICY GEOG CENSUS CHARTS BIBLIOG 19. PAGE 129 A2636
COLONIAL INT/TRADE DOMIN AFR

B62
TOURE S.,THE INTERNATIONAL POLICY OF THE DEMOCRATIC PARTY OF GUINEA (VOL. VII). AFR ALGERIA GHANA GUINEA MALI CONSTN VOL/ASSN CHIEF WAR PEACE ATTIT ...WELF/ST 20 DEMOCRAT. PAGE 144 A2953
DIPLOM POLICY POL/PAR NEW/LIB

S62
GAREAU F.H.,"BLOC POLITICS IN WEST AFRICA." AFR CONGO/BRAZ GHANA GUINEA MALI WOR+45 STRUCT ECO/UNDEV INT/ORG VOL/ASSN CHOOSE ORD/FREE PWR UN 20. PAGE 51 A1048
NAT/G NAT/LISM

B63
AFRICAN BIBLIOGRAPHIC CENTER,THE SCENE IS GUINEA AND THE PERSONAGE IS SEKOU TOURE: A SELECTED CURRENT READING LIST, 1959-1962 (PAMPHLET). GUINEA ECO/UNDEV CHIEF FOR/AID COLONIAL...BIOG 20. PAGE 5 A0095
BIBLIOG AFR POL/PAR COM

B66
SCHATTEN F.,COMMUNISM IN AFRICA. AFR GHANA GUINEA MALI CULTURE ECO/UNDEV LABOR SECT ECO/TAC EDU/PROP REV 20. PAGE 128 A2619
COLONIAL NAT/LISM MARXISM DIPLOM

GUJARAT....GUJARAT (STATE OF INDIA)

GULICK C.A. A1190

GULICK E.V. A1191,A1192

GUNTHER F. A1193

GUPTA S. A1194

GUPTA S.C. A1195

GURLAND A.R.L. A1196

GURTOO D.H.N. A1197

GUTTMAN A. A1198

GUTTMAN/L....LOUIS GUTTMAN (AND GUTTMAN SCALE)

GUYANA....GUYANA; SEE ALSO GUIANA/BR, L/A+17C

B67
JAGAN C.,THE WEST ON TRIAL. GUYANA CONSTN ECO/UNDEV DIPLOM COERCE PWR SOVEREIGN...BIOG 20. PAGE 73 A1490 — SOCISM CREATE PLAN COLONIAL

GYORGY A. A1199

GYR J. A1200

H

HAAS E.B. A1201,A1202,A1203,A1204,A1205,A1206,A1207,A1208

HABERLER G. A1209

HABITAT....ECOLOGY

N19
ZLOTNICK M.,WEAPONS IN SPACE (PAMPHLET). FUT WOR+45 TEC/DEV DIPLOM ARMS/CONT CIVMIL/REL PEACE HABITAT ...CONCPT NEW/IDEA CHARTS. PAGE 170 A3457 — SPACE WEAPON NUC/PWR WAR

B34
LOVELL R.I.,THE STRUGGLE FOR SOUTH AFRICA, 1875-1899. GERMANY RHODESIA SOUTH/AFR UK NAT/G ECO/TAC HABITAT WEALTH...POLICY 19. PAGE 91 A1866 — COLONIAL DIPLOM WAR GP/REL

B46
GAULD W.A.,MAN, NATURE, AND TIME, AN INTRODUCTION TO WORLD STUDY. WOR-45 CULTURE CREATE DIPLOM GP/REL DRIVE...SOC LING CENSUS CHARTS TIME 18/20. PAGE 52 A1054 — HABITAT PERSON

N46
HOBBS C.C.,SOUTHEAST ASIA, 1935-45: A SELECTED LIST OF REFERENCE BOOKS (PAMPHLET). S/ASIA AGRI INDUS NAT/G SECT DIPLOM WAR...ART/METH GEOG SOC LING 20. PAGE 65 A1346 — BIBLIOG/A CULTURE HABITAT

B47
PERKINS D.,THE UNITED STATES AND THE CARIBBEAN. CUBA DOMIN/REP GUATEMALA HAITI PANAMA CULTURE ECO/UNDEV FOR/AID ADMIN COERCE HABITAT...POLICY 19/20. PAGE 115 A2359 — DIPLOM L/A+17C USA-45

B51
YOUNG T.C.,NEAR EASTERN CULTURE AND SOCIETY. ISLAM ECO/UNDEV SECT WRITING ATTIT HABITAT ORD/FREE 20. PAGE 169 A3438 — CULTURE STRUCT REGION DIPLOM

B55
BURR R.N.,DOCUMENTS ON INTER-AMERICAN COOPERATION: VOL. I, 1810-1881; VOL. II, 1881-1948. DELIB/GP BAL/PWR INT/TRADE REPRESENT NAT/LISM PEACE HABITAT ORD/FREE PWR SOVEREIGN...INT/LAW 20 OAS. PAGE 22 A0445 — BIBLIOG DIPLOM INT/ORG L/A+17C

B55
UN ECONOMIC AND SOCIAL COUNCIL,BIBLIOGRAPHY OF PUBLICATIONS OF THE UN AND SPECIALIZED AGENCIES IN THE SOCIAL WELFARE FIELD, 1946-1952. WOR+45 FAM INT/ORG MUNIC ACT/RES PLAN PROB/SOLV EDU/PROP AGE/C AGE/Y HABITAT...HEAL UN. PAGE 147 A3000 — BIBLIOG/A SOC/WK ADMIN WEALTH

B56
SPROUT H.,MAN-MILIEU RELATIONSHIP HYPOTHESES IN THE CONTEXT OF INTERNATIONAL POLITICS. UNIV PROB/SOLV BIO/SOC PERSON...DECISION GEOG SOC METH/CNCPT PREDICT 20. PAGE 136 A2792 — HABITAT DIPLOM CONCPT DRIVE

B57
DRUCKER P.F.,AMERICA'S NEXT TWENTY YEARS. USA+45 DIST/IND ACADEM MUNIC SCHOOL DIPLOM ECO/TAC AUTOMAT HABITAT HEALTH...SOC/WK TREND 20 URBAN/RNWL PUB/TRANS. PAGE 39 A0788 — WORKER FOR/AID CENSUS GEOG

B58
INDIAN COUNCIL WORLD AFFAIRS,DEFENCE AND SECURITY IN THE INDIAN OCEAN AREA. INDIA S/ASIA CULTURE CONSULT DELIB/GP FORCES PROB/SOLV DIPLOM INT/TRADE 20 CMN/WLTH. PAGE 70 A1438 — GEOG HABITAT ECO/UNDEV ORD/FREE

B58
INSTITUTE MEDITERRANEAN AFF,THE PALESTINE REFUGEE PROBLEM. UAR WOR+45 INT/ORG PLAN PROB/SOLV PEACE ...POLICY GEOG STAT CHARTS 20 JEWS UN MIGRATION. PAGE 70 A1444 — STRANGE HABITAT GP/REL INGP/REL

B59
CHANDLER E.H.S.,THE HIGH TOWER OF REFUGE: THE INSPIRING STORY OF REFUGEE RELIEF THROUGHOUT THE WORLD. WOR+45 NEIGH SECT WORKER PROB/SOLV DIPLOM ECO/TAC EDU/PROP COST HABITAT. PAGE 25 A0519 — GIVE WEALTH STRANGE INT/ORG

B59
KAPLAN D.,THE ARAB REFUGEES: AN ABNORMAL PROBLEM. UAR WOR+45 PROB/SOLV DIPLOM GOV/REL ADJUST EFFICIENCY...POLICY GEOG INT/LAW 20 UN JEWS MIGRATION. PAGE 76 A1557 — STRANGE HABITAT GP/REL INGP/REL

B61
HOLDSWORTH M.,SOVIET AFRICAN STUDIES 1918-1959. USSR ACADEM NAT/G DIPLOM REGION KNOWL 20. PAGE 66 A1366 — BIBLIOG/A AFR HABITAT NAT/COMP

B62
CALDER R.,COMMON SENSE ABOUT A STARVING WORLD. WOR+45 STRATA ECO/DEV PLAN GP/REL BIO/SOC HABITAT ...POLICY GEOG STAT RECORD 20 UN BIRTH/CON. PAGE 23 A0466 — FOR/AID CENSUS ECO/UNDEV AGRI

B63
LOOMIE A.J.,THE SPANISH ELIZABETHANS: THE ENGLISH EXILES AT THE COURT OF PHILIP II. SPAIN UK WAR INGP/REL DRIVE HABITAT CATHISM...BIOG 16/17 MIGRATION. PAGE 91 A1860 — NAT/G STRANGE POLICY DIPLOM

B64
HARPER F.,OUT OF CHINA. CHINA/COM ELITES STRATA ATTIT PERSON...BIOG 20 MAO HONG/KONG MIGRATION. PAGE 62 A1264 — HABITAT DEEP/INT DIPLOM MARXISM

B64
US HOUSE COMM ON JUDICIARY,IMMIGRATION HEARINGS. DELIB/GP STRANGE HABITAT...GEOG JURID 20 CONGRESS MIGRATION. PAGE 154 A3140 — NAT/G POLICY DIPLOM NAT/LISM

B65
US SENATE COMM ON JUDICIARY,REFUGEE PROBLEMS IN SOUTH VIETNAM AND LAOS: HEARINGS BEFORE SUBCOMMITTEE TO INVESTIGATE PROBLEMS OF REFUGEES, ESCAPEES. CHINA/COM LAOS USA+45 VIETNAM/S PROB/SOLV DIPLOM GOV/REL GP/REL EFFICIENCY ORD/FREE...POLICY GEOG 20 CONGRESS MIGRATION. PAGE 157 A3194 — STRANGE HABITAT FOR/AID CIVMIL/REL

B66
SUPPLEMENTAL FOREIGN ASSISTANCE FISCAL YEAR 1966: VIETNAM. CHINA/COM COM S/ASIA USA+45 VIETNAM EXTR/IND FINAN DIPLOM TAX GUERRILLA HABITAT ORD/FREE...STAT CHARTS 20 SENATE PRESIDENT. PAGE 4 A0077 — CONFER LEGIS WAR FOR/AID

B66
BIRMINGHAM D.,TRADE AND CONFLICT IN ANGOLA. PORTUGAL CULTURE FORCES DIPLOM GP/REL PROFIT HABITAT NAT/COMP. PAGE 14 A0291 — WAR INT/TRADE ECO/UNDEV COLONIAL

B66
GROSS F.,WORLD POLITICS AND TENSION AREAS. CHINA/COM SOMALIA VENEZUELA COERCE GP/REL RACE/REL ATTIT HABITAT 19/20 CASEBOOK NEWYORK/C. PAGE 57 A1173 — DIPLOM WAR PROB/SOLV

B66
O'CONNER A.M.,AN ECONOMIC GEOGRAPHY OF EAST AFRICA. AFR TANZANIA UGANDA AGRI WORKER INT/TRADE COLONIAL GOV/REL...CHARTS METH/COMP 20 AFRICA/E. PAGE 111 A2269 — ECO/UNDEV EXTR/IND GEOG HABITAT

B66
SKILLING H.G.,THE GOVERNMENTS OF COMMUNIST EAST EUROPE. COM EUR+WWI ELITES FORCES DIPLOM ECO/TAC CONTROL HABITAT SOCISM...DECISION BIBLIOG 20 EUROPE/E COM/PARTY. PAGE 134 A2738 — MARXISM NAT/COMP GP/COMP DOMIN

S67
LIVNEH E.,"A NEW BEGINNING." ISRAEL USSR WOR+45 NAT/G DIPLOM INGP/REL FEDERAL HABITAT PWR...GEOG PSY JEWS. PAGE 90 A1847 — WAR PERSON PEACE PLAN

S67
SYRKIN M.,"I.F. STONE RECONSIDERS ISRAEL." ISRAEL WOR+45 DIPLOM NAT/LISM HABITAT...POLICY GEOG JEWS. PAGE 141 A2875 — ISLAM WAR ATTIT MORAL

S67
VELIKONJA J.,"ITALIAN IMMIGRANTS IN THE UNITED STATES IN THE MID-SIXTIES" ITALY USA+45 KIN MUNIC NAT/G WORKER DIPLOM REGION GP/REL ADJUST...GEOG CHARTS SOC/INTEG 20. PAGE 158 A3226 — HABITAT ORD/FREE TREND STAT

HADDAD J.A. A1210

HADDOW A. A1211

HADWEN J.G. A1212

HAGRAS K.M. A1213

HAGUE PERMANENT CT INTL JUSTIC A1214,A1215

HAGUE/F....FRANK HAGUE

HAHN W.F. A1216

HAIGHT D.E. A1217

HAILEY W.M.H. A1218

HAILEY L. A1219

HAINDS J.R. A1901

HAITI....SEE ALSO L/A+17C

B47
PERKINS D.,THE UNITED STATES AND THE CARIBBEAN. CUBA DOMIN/REP GUATEMALA HAITI PANAMA CULTURE ECO/UNDEV FOR/AID ADMIN COERCE HABITAT...POLICY 19/20. PAGE 115 A2359 — DIPLOM L/A+17C USA-45

B51
BISSAINTHE M.,DICTIONNAIRE DE BIBLIOGRAPHIE HAITIENNE. HAITI ELITES AGRI LEGIS DIPLOM INT/TRADE WRITING ORD/FREE CATHISM...ART/METH GEOG 19/20 NEGRO TREATY. PAGE 15 A0295 — BIBLIOG L/A+17C SOCIETY NAT/G

B65
FAGG J.E.,CUBA, HAITI, AND THE DOMINICAN REPUBLIC. CUBA DOMIN/REP HAITI L/A+17C NAT/G DIPLOM ECO/TAC DOMIN CHOOSE AUTHORIT ROLE SOVEREIGN POPULISM 17/20. PAGE 43 A0883 — COLONIAL ECO/UNDEV REV GOV/COMP

HAJDA J. A1220

HAKLUYT/R....RICHARD HAKLUYT

HALASZ DE BEKY I.L. A1221

HALD M. A1222

HALDANE R.B. A1223

HALDEMAN E. A1224

HALEY A.G. A1225,A1226

HALL M. A1227

HALL W.E. A1228

HALL W.P. A1229

HALLE L.J. A1230,A1231,A1232

HALLECK/C....CHARLES HALLECK

HALLET R. A1233

HALLETT D. A1234

HALLSTEIN W. A1235

HALPERIN E. A1236

HALPERIN M.H. A1237,A1238,A1239,A1240

HALPERIN S.W. A1241

HALPERN J.M. A1242

HALPERN M. A1243

HAMADY S. A1244

HAMBRIDGE G. A1245

HAMBRO C.J. A1246

HAMBRO E. A1106

HAMBURG....HAMBURG, GERMANY

HAMILTON W.B. A1247

HAMILTON/A....ALEXANDER HAMILTON

B64
BOYD J.P.,NUMBER 7: ALEXANDER HAMILTON'S SECRET ATTEMPTS TO CONTROL AMERICAN FOREIGN POLICY. AFR UK DIPLOM WAR RESPECT WEALTH...POLICY HIST/WRIT 18 HAMILTON/A. PAGE 18 A0364 — USA-45 NAT/G TOP/EX PWR

HAMM H. A1248

HAMMARSK/D....DAG HAMMARSKJOLD

S60
MUNRO L.,"CAN THE UNITED NATIONS ENFORCE PEACE." WOR+45 LAW INT/ORG VOL/ASSN BAL/PWR LEGIT ARMS/CONT COERCE DETER PEACE PWR...CONCPT REC/INT TREND UN 20 HAMMARSK/D. PAGE 106 A2173 — FORCES ORD/FREE

B61
MILLER R.I.,DAG HAMMARSKJOLD AND CRISES DIPLOMACY. WOR+45 NAT/G PROB/SOLV LEAD ROLE...DECISION BIOG UN HAMMARSK/D. PAGE 101 A2079 — DIPLOM INT/ORG CHIEF

L62
STEIN E.,"MR HAMMARSKJOLD, THE CHARTER LAW AND THE FUTURE ROLE OF THE UNITED NATIONS SECRETARY-GENERAL." WOR+45 CONSTN INT/ORG DELIB/GP FORCES TOP/EX BAL/PWR LEGIT ROUTINE RIGID/FLEX PWR ...POLICY JURID OBS STERTYP UN COLD/WAR 20 HAMMARSK/D. PAGE 137 A2815 — CONCPT BIOG

S62
SCHACHTER O.,"DAG HAMMARSKJOLD AND THE RELATION OF LAW TO POLITICS." FUT WOR+45 INT/ORG CONSULT PLAN TEC/DEV BAL/PWR DIPLOM LEGIT ATTIT PERCEPT ORD/FREE ...POLICY JURID CONCPT OBS TESTS STERTYP GEN/LAWS 20 HAMMARSK/D. PAGE 128 A2616 — ACT/RES ADJUD

HAMMARSKJOLD, DAG....SEE HAMMARSK/D

HAMRELL S. A1249

HANCOCK W.K. A1250

HANDLIN O. A1251

HANNA A.J. A1252

HANNA/MARK....MARK HANNA

HANSEN A.H. A1253

HANSEN B. A1254

HANSEN G.H. A1255

HANSON J.W. A1256

HAPPINESS.... HAPPINESS AS A CONDITION (UNHAPPINESS)

B42
TOLMAN E.C.,DRIVES TOWARD WAR. UNIV PLAN DIPLOM ECO/TAC COERCE PERS/REL ADJUST HAPPINESS BIO/SOC HEREDITY HEALTH KNOWL. PAGE 144 A2947 — PSY WAR UTOPIA DRIVE

HAPSBURG....HAPSBURG MONARCHY

HAPTHEKER....HAPTHEKER THEORY

HARARI M. A1257

HARDING/WG....PRESIDENT WARREN G. HARDING

HARDT J.P. A1258

HARGIS/BJ....BILLY JAMES HARGIS

HARGREAVES J.D. A1259

HARLAN/JM....JOHN MARSHALL HARLAN

B65
FALK R.A.,THE AFTERMATH OF SABBATINO: BACKGROUND PAPERS AND PROCEEDINGS OF SEVENTH HAMMARSKJOLD FORUM. USA+45 LAW ACT/RES ADJUD ROLE...BIBLIOG 20 EXPROPRIAT SABBATINO HARLAN/JM. PAGE 44 A0891 — SOVEREIGN CT/SYS INT/LAW OWN

HARLEM....HARLEM

HARMAN M. A2968

HARMON R.B. A1260,A1261,A1262

HARNETTY P. A1263

HARPER F. A1264

HARPER S.N. A1265

HARRIMAN A. A1266

HARRIMAN/A....AVERILL HARRIMAN

HARRIS J. A0677

HARRIS N.D. A1267,A1268

HARRIS S.E. A1269

HARRISN/WH....PRESIDENT WILLIAM HENRY HARRISON

HARRISON H.V. A1270

HARRISON J.P. A1271

HARRISON S. A1272

HARRISON/B....PRESIDENT BENJAMIN HARRISON

HART A.B. A1273

HART B.H.L. A1274

HARTLEY A. A1275

HARTT J. A1276

HARVARD BUREAU ECO RES LAT AM A1277

HARVARD LAW SCHOOL LIBRARY A1278,A1279

HARVARD UNIVERSITY LAW LIBRARY A1280

HARVARD UNIVERSITY LAW SCHOOL A1281

HARVARD WIDENER LIBRARY A1282

HARVARD/U....HARVARD UNIVERSITY

HARVEY M.F. A1283

HASAN H.S. A1284

HASSE A.R. A1285

HASSON J.A. A1286

HATCH J. A1287

HATCHER/R....RICHARD HATCHER

HATRED....SEE LOVE

HAUSER P.H. A1288

HAUSER P.M. A1289

HAVILAND H.F. A0525,A1290,A1291,A1292,A1293,A3346

HAWAII....HAWAII

B66
GRENVILLE J.A.S.,POLITICS, STRATEGY, AND AMERICAN DEMOCRACY: STUDIES IN FOREIGN POLICY, 1873-1917. CUBA PHILIPPINE SPAIN USA-45 VENEZUELA ELITES NAT/G CREATE PARTIC WAR RIGID/FLEX ORD/FREE...DECISION TREND 19/20 HAWAII. PAGE 56 A1146
DIPLOM COLONIAL POLICY

HAY P. A1294

HAYDEN T. A1877

HAYEK/V....FRIEDRICH AUGUST VON HAYEK

HAYER T. A1295

HAYES/RB....PRESIDENT RUTHERFORD B. HAYES

HAYTER W. A1296

HAYTON R.D. A1297

HAZARD J.N. A1298,A1299,A1300,A1301

HAZLEWOOD A. A1302,A1303

HEAD/START....THE "HEAD START" PROGRAM

HEADICAR B.M. A1304

HEADLAM-MORLEY A1305

HEAL....HEALTH SCIENCES

B
UN DEPARTMENT SOCIAL AFFAIRS,SOCIAL WELFARE INFORMATION SERIES: CURRENT LITERATURE AND NATIONAL CONFERENCES. WOR+45 INDUS SERV/IND INT/ORG CONSULT ACT/RES WEALTH...HEAL UN. PAGE 147 A2997
BIBLIOG/A SOC/WK DIPLOM ADMIN

N
INTERNATIONAL BOOK NEWS, 1928-1934. ECO/UNDEV FINAN INDUS LABOR INT/TRADE CONFER ADJUD COLONIAL...HEAL SOC/WK CHARTS 20 LEAGUE/NAT. PAGE 1 A0010
BIBLIOG/A DIPLOM INT/LAW INT/ORG

N
AUSTRALIAN PUBLIC AFFAIRS INFORMATION SERVICE. LAW ...HEAL HUM MGT SOC CON/ANAL 20 AUSTRAL. PAGE 2 A0028
BIBLIOG NAT/G CULTURE DIPLOM

L21
HALDEMAN E.,"SERIALS OF AN INTERNATIONAL CHARACTER." WOR-45 DIPLOM...ART/METH GEOG HEAL HUM INT/LAW JURID PSY SOC. PAGE 60 A1224
BIBLIOG PHIL/SCI

B41
KEESING F.M.,THE SOUTH SEAS IN THE MODERN WORLD. INDONESIA STRUCT FAM SECT EDU/PROP LEAD INCOME WEALTH...HEAL SOC 20. PAGE 77 A1577
CULTURE ECO/UNDEV GOV/COMP DIPLOM

B50
DAVIS E.P.,PERIODICALS OF INTERNATIONAL ORGANIZATIONS; PART I, THE UN AND SPECIALIZED AGENCIES; PART II, INTER-AMERICAN ORGS. CULTURE AGRI FINAN INDUS LABOR INT/TRADE...GEOG HEAL STAT 20 UN OAS UNESCO. PAGE 34 A0689
BIBLIOG/A INT/ORG DIPLOM L/A+17C

B55
UN ECONOMIC AND SOCIAL COUNCIL,BIBLIOGRAPHY OF PUBLICATIONS OF THE UN AND SPECIALIZED AGENCIES IN THE SOCIAL WELFARE FIELD, 1946-1952. WOR+45 FAM INT/ORG MUNIC ACT/RES PLAN PROB/SOLV EDU/PROP AGE/C AGE/Y HABITAT...HEAL UN. PAGE 147 A3000
BIBLIOG/A SOC/WK ADMIN WEALTH

C58
BLANCHARD W.,"THAILAND." THAILAND CULTURE AGRI FINAN INDUS FAM LABOR INT/TRADE ATTIT...GEOG HEAL SOC BIBLIOG 20. PAGE 15 A0307
NAT/G DIPLOM ECO/UNDEV S/ASIA

B63
PANAMERICAN UNION,DOCUMENTOS OFICIALES DE LA ORGANIZACION DE LOS ESTADOS AMERICANOS, INDICE Y LISTA (VOL. III, 1962). L/A+17C DELIB/GP INT/TRADE EDU/PROP REGION NUC/PWR...HEAL INT/LAW SOC/WK 20 OAS. PAGE 113 A2329
BIBLIOG INT/ORG DIPLOM

B64
SULLIVAN G.,THE STORY OF THE PEACE CORPS. USA+45 WOR+45 INTELL FACE/GP NAT/G SCHOOL VOL/ASSN CONSULT EX/STRUC PLAN EDU/PROP ADMIN ATTIT DRIVE ALL/VALS ...POLICY HEAL SOC CONCPT INT QU BIOG TREND SOC/EXP WORK. PAGE 140 A2861
INT/ORG ECO/UNDEV FOR/AID PEACE

B64
WITHERELL J.W.,OFFICIAL PUBLICATIONS OF FRENCH EQUATORIAL AFRICA, FRENCH CAMEROONS, AND TOGO, 1946-1958 (PAMPHLET). CAMEROON CHAD FRANCE GABON TOGO LAW ECO/UNDEV EXTR/IND INT/TRADE...GEOG HEAL 20. PAGE 165 A3370
BIBLIOG/A AFR NAT/G ADMIN

C65
SCHWEBEL M.,"BEHAVIORAL SCIENCE AND HUMAN SURVIVAL." FORCES ARMS/CONT COERCE NUC/PWR WAR GP/REL NAT/LISM PERCEPT...POLICY PSY ANTHOL BIBLIOG/A 20 COLD/WAR. PAGE 130 A2662
PEACE ACT/RES DIPLOM HEAL

B66
KAREFA-SMART J.,AFRICA: PROGRESS THROUGH COOPERATION. AFR FINAN TEC/DEV DIPLOM FOR/AID EDU/PROP CONFER REGION GP/REL WEALTH...HEAL SOC/INTEG 20. PAGE 76 A1566
ORD/FREE ECO/UNDEV VOL/ASSN PLAN

HEALEY/D....DOROTHY HEALEY

HEALTH....WELL-BEING, BODILY AND PSYCHIC INTEGRITY

N
CANADIAN GOVERNMENT PUBLICATIONS (1955-). CANADA AGRI FINAN LABOR FORCES INT/TRADE HEALTH...JURID 20 PARLIAMENT. PAGE 1 A0007
BIBLIOG/A NAT/G DIPLOM INT/ORG

N
INDIA: A REFERENCE ANNUAL. INDIA CULTURE COM/IND R+D FORCES PLAN RECEIVE EDU/PROP HEALTH...STAT CHARTS BIBLIOG 20. PAGE 2 A0036
CONSTN LABOR INT/ORG

N
SCHOLARLY BOOKS IN AMERICA; A QUARTERLY BIBLIOGRAPHY OF UNIVERSITY PRESS PUBLICATIONS. WOR+45 AGRI COM/IND NAT/G HEALTH...GEOG PHIL/SCI PSY SOC LING 20. PAGE 3 A0046
BIBLIOG/A LAW MUNIC DIPLOM

N
HOOVER INSTITUTION,UNITED STATES AND CANADIAN PUBLICATIONS ON AFRICA. CULTURE ECO/UNDEV AGRI TEC/DEV EDU/PROP COLONIAL RACE/REL NAT/LISM ATTIT HEALTH...SOC SOC/WK 20. PAGE 67 A1381
BIBLIOG DIPLOM NAT/G AFR

N
US BUREAU OF THE CENSUS,BIBLIOGRAPHY OF SOCIAL SCIENCE PERIODICALS AND MONOGRAPH SERIES. WOR+45 LAW DIPLOM EDU/PROP HEALTH...PSY SOC LING STAT. PAGE 150 A3058
BIBLIOG/A CULTURE NAT/G SOCIETY

N
US SUPERINTENDENT OF DOCUMENTS,FOREIGN RELATIONS OF THE UNITED STATES; PUBLICATIONS RELATING TO FOREIGN COUNTRIES (PRICE LIST 65). UAR USA+45 VIETNAM ECO/UNDEV VOL/ASSN FOR/AID EDU/PROP ARMS/CONT HEALTH MARXISM...POLICY INT/LAW UN NATO. PAGE 157 A3201
BIBLIOG/A DIPLOM INT/ORG NAT/G

N
US SUPERINTENDENT OF DOCUMENTS,GOVERNMENT PERIODICALS AND SUBSCRIPTION SERVICES (PRICE LIST 36). LAW WORKER CT/SYS HEALTH. PAGE 157 A3202
BIBLIOG/A USA+45 NAT/G DIPLOM

B02
MOREL E.D.,AFFAIRS OF WEST AFRICA. UK FINAN INDUS FAM KIN SECT CHIEF WORKER DIPLOM RACE/REL LITERACY
COLONIAL ADMIN

HEALTH...CHARTS 18/20 AFRICA/W NEGRO. PAGE 104 A2129
AFR

N19
MEZERIK A.G.,ATOM TESTS AND RADIATION HAZARDS (PAMPHLET). WOR+45 INT/ORG DIPLOM DETER 20 UN TREATY. PAGE 100 A2059
NUC/PWR ARMS/CONT CONFER HEALTH

N19
NATIONAL ACADEMY OF SCIENCES,THE GROWTH OF WORLD POPULATION: ANALYSIS OF THE PROBLEMS AND RECOMMENDATIONS FOR RESEARCH AND TRAINING (PAMPHLET). WOR+45 CULTURE ECO/UNDEV EDU/PROP MARRIAGE AGE HEALTH...ANTHOL 20 BIRTH/CON. PAGE 107 A2199
CENSUS PLAN FAM INT/ORG

N19
UNITED ARAB REPUBLIC,THE PROBLEM OF THE PALESTINIAN REFUGEES (PAMPHLET). ISRAEL UAR LAW PROB/SOLV EDU/PROP CONFER ADJUD CONTROL NAT/LISM HEALTH 20 JEWS UN MIGRATION. PAGE 148 A3029
STRANGE GP/REL INGP/REL DIPLOM

B32
HANSEN A.H.,ECONOMIC STABILIZATION IN AN UNBALANCED WORLD. COM EUR+WWI USA-45 WOR-45 AGRI FINAN INDUS MARKET INT/ORG LABOR VOL/ASSN EDU/PROP ATTIT HEALTH KNOWL WEALTH...HIST/WRIT TREND VAL/FREE 20. PAGE 61 A1253
NAT/G ECO/DEV CAP/ISM SOCISM

B34
GRAHAM F.D.,PROTECTIVE TARIFFS. FUT USA+45 WOR-45 INDUS MARKET VOL/ASSN PLAN CAP/ISM ECO/TAC PEACE ATTIT DRIVE HEALTH ORD/FREE...OBS TREND GEN/LAWS 20. PAGE 55 A1124
INT/ORG TARIFFS

B40
BROWN A.D.,PANAMA CANAL AND PANAMA CANAL ZONE: A SELECTED LIST OF REFERENCES. PANAMA NAT/G SCHOOL DIPLOM HEALTH...GEOG SOC 20 CANAL/ZONE. PAGE 19 A0397
BIBLIOG/A ECO/UNDEV

B40
MILLER E.,THE NEUROSES OF WAR. UNIV INTELL SOCIETY INT/ORG NAT/G EDU/PROP DISPL DRIVE PERCEPT PERSON RIGID/FLEX...SOC TIME/SEQ 20. PAGE 101 A2075
HEALTH PSY WAR

B42
CONOVER H.F.,FRENCH COLONIES IN AFRICA: A LIST OF REFERENCES. ALGERIA FRANCE MOROCCO SOMALIA SUDAN CULTURE AGRI LOC/G SECT FORCES DIPLOM INT/TRADE NAT/LISM HEALTH...CON/ANAL 20. PAGE 29 A0594
BIBLIOG AFR ECO/UNDEV COLONIAL

B42
TOLMAN E.C.,DRIVES TOWARD WAR. UNIV PLAN DIPLOM ECO/TAC COERCE PERS/REL ADJUST HAPPINESS BIO/SOC HEREDITY HEALTH KNOWL. PAGE 144 A2947
PSY WAR UTOPIA DRIVE

B45
CARR E.H.,NATIONALISM AND AFTER. FUT WOR-45 NAT/G VOL/ASSN EX/STRUC PLAN ROUTINE TOTALISM ATTIT HEALTH ORD/FREE PWR...CONCPT 20. PAGE 25 A0499
INT/ORG TREND NAT/LISM REGION

B47
CONOVER H.F.,NON-SELF-GOVERNING AREAS. BELGIUM FRANCE ITALY UK WOR+45 CULTURE ECO/UNDEV INT/ORG LOC/G NAT/G ECO/TAC INT/TRADE ADMIN HEALTH...SOC UN. PAGE 30 A0601
BIBLIOG/A COLONIAL DIPLOM

L51
KELSEN H.,"RECENT TRENDS IN THE LAW OF THE UNITED NATIONS." KOREA WOR+45 CONSTN LEGIS DIPLOM LEGIT DETER WAR RIGID/FLEX HEALTH ORD/FREE RESPECT ...JURID CON/ANAL UN VAL/FREE 20 NATO. PAGE 77 A1582
INT/ORG LAW INT/LAW

B52
RIGGS F.W.,FORMOSA UNDER CHINESE NATIONALIST RULE. CHINA/COM USA+45 CONSTN AGRI FINAN LABOR LOC/G NAT/G POL/PAR FORCES HEALTH KNOWL...STAT WORK VAL/FREE 20. PAGE 121 A2479
ASIA FOR/AID DIPLOM

B52
UN DEPT. SOC. AFF.,PRELIMINARY REPORT ON THE WORLD SOCIAL SITUATION. ISLAM L/A+17C WOR+45 STRATA AGRI EXTR/IND INDUS INT/ORG SCHOOL ADMIN...GEOG SOC TREND UNESCO WORK FAO 20. PAGE 147 A2998
R+D HEALTH FOR/AID

B52
US MUTUAL SECURITY AGENCY,U. S. TECHNICAL AND ECONOMIC ASSISTANCE IN THE FAR EAST (PAMPHLET). ASIA BURMA INDONESIA PHILIPPINE TAIWAN THAILAND USA+45 AGRI INDUS PLAN EDU/PROP ADMIN HEALTH. PAGE 155 A3161
FOR/AID TEC/DEV ECO/UNDEV BUDGET

B53
COUSINS N.,WHO SPEAKS FOR MAN. GERMANY KOREA WOR+45 SOCIETY INT/ORG NAT/G CREATE EDU/PROP HEALTH KNOWL LOVE MORAL...OBS SELF/OBS BIOG HYPO/EXP TOT/POP 20 CHINJAP. PAGE 32 A0642
ATTIT WAR PEACE

B53
SCHAAF R.W.,DOCUMENTS OF INTERNATIONAL MEETINGS. AGRI INDUS ACADEM DIPLOM NUC/PWR RACE/REL AGE/Y HEALTH...SOC 20. PAGE 127 A2614
BIBLIOG/A DELIB/GP INT/ORG POLICY

B54
NORTHROP F.S.C.,EUROPEAN UNION AND UNITED STATES FOREIGN POLICY: A STUDY IN SOCIOLOGICAL JURISPRUDENCE. EUR+WWI MOD/EUR USA+45 SOCIETY STRUCT NAT/G CREATE ECO/TAC DOMIN EDU/PROP REGION ATTIT RIGID/FLEX HEALTH ORD/FREE WEALTH ...METH/CNCPT TIME/SEQ TREND. PAGE 110 A2256
INT/ORG SOC DIPLOM

B55
MYRDAL A.R.,AMERICA'S ROLE IN INTERNATIONAL SOCIAL WELFARE. FUT WOR+45 SOCIETY R+D VOL/ASSN ECO/TAC EDU/PROP HEALTH KNOWL WEALTH...SOC CHARTS ORG/CHARTS TOT/POP 20. PAGE 107 A2188
PLAN SKILL FOR/AID

B55
TROTIER A.H.,DOCTORAL DISSERTATIONS ACCEPTED BY AMERICAN UNIVERSITIES 1954-55. SECT DIPLOM HEALTH ...ART/METH GEOG INT/LAW SOC LING CHARTS 20. PAGE 145 A2968
BIBLIOG ACADEM USA+45 WRITING

B57
ASHER R.E.,THE UNITED NATIONS AND THE PROMOTION OF THE GENERAL WELFARE. WOR+45 WOR-45 ECO/UNDEV EX/STRUC ACT/RES PLAN EDU/PROP ROUTINE HEALTH...HUM CONCPT CHARTS UNESCO UN ILO 20. PAGE 9 A0185
INT/ORG CONSULT

B57
DRUCKER P.F.,AMERICA'S NEXT TWENTY YEARS. USA+45 DIST/IND ACADEM MUNIC SCHOOL DIPLOM ECO/TAC AUTOMAT HABITAT HEALTH...SOC/WK TREND 20 URBAN/RNWL PUB/TRANS. PAGE 39 A0788
WORKER FOR/AID CENSUS GEOG

B58
HAUSER P.H.,POPULATION AND WORLD POLITICS. FUT WOR+45 WOR-45 AGRI DIST/IND INDUS INT/ORG PLAN ECO/TAC DISPL HEALTH COLD/WAR 20. PAGE 63 A1288
NAT/G ECO/UNDEV FOR/AID

B58
MANSERGH N.,COMMONWEALTH PERSPECTIVES. GHANA UK LAW VOL/ASSN CONFER HEALTH SOVEREIGN...GEOG CHARTS ANTHOL 20 CMN/WLTH AUSTRAL. PAGE 94 A1930
DIPLOM COLONIAL INT/ORG INGP/REL

B58
US OPERATIONS MISSION TO VIET,BUILDING ECONOMIC STRENGTH (PAMPHLET). USA+45 VIETNAM/S INDUS TEC/DEV BUDGET ADMIN EATING HEALTH...STAT 20. PAGE 155 A3162
FOR/AID ECO/UNDEV AGRI EDU/PROP

N58
INVESTMENT FUND ECO SOC DEV,FRENCH AFRICA: A DECADE OF PROGRESS 1948-1958 (PAMPHLET). AFR FRANCE EXTR/IND INDUS EDU/PROP HEALTH 20. PAGE 71 A1465
FOR/AID DIPLOM ECO/UNDEV AGRI

B59
JOSEPH F.M.,AS OTHERS SEE US: THE UNITED STATES THROUGH FOREIGN EYES. AFR EUR+WWI ISLAM L/A+17C S/ASIA USA+45 CULTURE SOCIETY ECO/DEV ECO/UNDEV INT/ORG NAT/G DIPLOM ECO/TAC REV ATTIT RIGID/FLEX HEALTH ORD/FREE WEALTH 20. PAGE 75 A1537
RESPECT DOMIN NAT/LISM SOVEREIGN

S59
HARVEY M.F.,"THE PALESTINE REFUGEE PROBLEM: ELEMENTS OF A SOLUTION." ISLAM LAW INT/ORG DELIB/GP TOP/EX ECO/TAC ROUTINE DRIVE HEALTH LOVE ORD/FREE PWR WEALTH...MAJORIT FAO 20. PAGE 62 A1283
ACT/RES LEGIT PEACE ISRAEL

B60
BAILEY S.D.,THE GENERAL ASSEMBLY OF THE UNITED NATIONS. FUT WOR+45 STRUCT LEGIS ACT/RES PLAN EDU/PROP LEGIT ADMIN EXEC PEACE ATTIT HEALTH PWR ...CONCPT TREND CHARTS GEN/LAWS UN TOT/POP VAL/FREE COLD/WAR 20. PAGE 10 A0204
INT/ORG DELIB/GP DIPLOM

B60
MUNRO L.,UNITED NATIONS, HOPE FOR A DIVIDED WORLD. FUT WOR+45 CONSTN DELIB/GP CREATE TEC/DEV DIPLOM EDU/PROP LEGIT PEACE ATTIT HEALTH ORD/FREE PWR ...CONCPT TREND UN VAL/FREE 20. PAGE 106 A2172
INT/ORG ROUTINE

S60
"THE EMERGING COMMON MARKETS IN LATIN AMERICA." FUT L/A+17C STRATA DIST/IND INDUS LABOR NAT/G LEGIS ECO/TAC ADMIN RIGID/FLEX HEALTH...NEW/IDEA TIME/SEQ OAS 20. PAGE 3 A0059
FINAN ECO/UNDEV INT/TRADE

B61
HANCOCK W.K.,FOUR STUDIES OF WAR AND PEACE IN THIS CENTURY. FUT WOR+45 WOR-45 ACT/RES LEGIT DETER HEALTH...TREND ANTHOL TOT/POP VAL/FREE UN 20. PAGE 61 A1250
INT/ORG POLICY ARMS/CONT

B61
SCHELLING T.C.,STRATEGY AND ARMS CONTROL. FUT UNIV WOR+45 INT/ORG PLAN TEC/DEV BAL/PWR LEGIT PERCEPT HEALTH...CONCPT VAL/FREE 20. PAGE 128 A2623
ROUTINE POLICY ARMS/CONT

B61
SHARP W.R.,FIELD ADMINISTRATION IN THE UNITED NATION SYSTEM: THE CONDUCT OF INTERNATIONAL ECONOMIC AND SOCIAL PROGRAMS. FUT WOR+45 CONSTN SOCIETY ECO/UNDEV R+D DELIB/GP ACT/RES PLAN TEC/DEV EDU/PROP EXEC ROUTINE HEALTH WEALTH...HUM CONCPT CHARTS METH ILO UNESCO VAL/FREE UN 20. PAGE 132 A2697
INT/ORG CONSULT

S61
HAZARD J.N.,"CODIFYING PEACEFUL COEXISTANCE." FUT INTELL INT/ORG TEC/DEV PEACE HEALTH...INT/LAW CONT/OBS 20. PAGE 63 A1299
VOL/ASSN JURID

B62
ALEXANDROWICZ C.H.,WORLD ECONOMIC AGENCIES: LAW AND PRACTICE. WOR+45 DIST/IND FINAN LABOR CONSULT INT/TRADE TARIFFS REPRESENT HEALTH...JURID 20 UN GATT EEC OAS ECSC. PAGE 6 A0115
INT/LAW INT/ORG DIPLOM ADJUD

B62
HOFFMAN P.,WORLD WITHOUT WANT. FUT WOR+45 ECO/UNDEV
CONCPT

INT/ORG HEALTH KNOWL...TREND TOT/POP FAO 20. PAGE 66 A1353 POLICY FOR/AID

B62
KIDDER F.E.,THESES ON PAN AMERICAN TOPICS. LAW CULTURE NAT/G SECT DIPLOM HEALTH...ART/METH GEOG SOC 13/20. PAGE 79 A1615 BIBLIOG CHRIST-17C L/A+17C SOCIETY

B62
LAWSON R.,INTERNATIONAL REGIONAL ORGANIZATIONS. WOR+45 NAT/G VOL/ASSN CONSULT LEGIS EDU/PROP LEGIT ADMIN EXEC ROUTINE HEALTH PWR WEALTH...JURID EEC COLD/WAR 20 UN. PAGE 86 A1752 INT/ORG DELIB/GP REGION

S62
DIHN N.Q.,"L'INTERNATIONALISATION DU MEKONG." CAMBODIA LAOS VIETNAM WOR+45 INT/ORG NAT/G VOL/ASSN PEACE HEALTH...CONCPT TIME/SEQ CHARTS METH VAL/FREE 20. PAGE 37 A0761 S/ASIA DELIB/GP

S62
SPENSER J.H.,"AFRICA AT THE UNITED NATIONS: SOME OBSERVATIONS." FUT ECO/UNDEV NAT/G CONSULT DELIB/GP PLAN BAL/PWR ECO/TAC EDU/PROP ATTIT RIGID/FLEX HEALTH ORD/FREE PWR WEALTH...POLICY CONCPT OBS TREND STERTYP GEN/METH UN VAL/FREE. PAGE 136 A2786 AFR INT/ORG REGION

B63
ABSHIRE D.M.,NATIONAL SECURITY: POLITICAL, MILITARY, AND ECONOMIC STRATEGIES IN THE DECADE AHEAD. ASIA COM USA+45 WOR+45 ECO/DEV ECO/UNDEV INT/ORG DELIB/GP FORCES ECO/TAC COERCE ATTIT RIGID/FLEX HEALTH ORD/FREE PWR WEALTH...POLICY STAT CHARTS ANTHOL COLD/WAR VAL/FREE. PAGE 4 A0083 FUT ACT/RES BAL/PWR

B63
BOISSIER P.,HISTORIE DU COMITE INTERNATIONAL DE LA CROIX ROUGE. MOD/EUR WOR-45 CONSULT FORCES PLAN DIPLOM EDU/PROP ADMIN MORAL ORD/FREE...SOC CONCPT RECORD TIME/SEQ GEN/LAWS TOT/POP VAL/FREE 19/20. PAGE 16 A0332 INT/ORG HEALTH ARMS/CONT WAR

B63
JACOBSON H.K.,THE USSR AND THE UN'S ECONOMIC AND SOCIAL ACTIVITIES. COM WOR+45 DELIB/GP ACT/RES ECO/TAC EDU/PROP RIGID/FLEX SUPEGO HEALTH PWR SKILL ...POLICY CHARTS GEN/METH VAL/FREE UNESCO 20 UN. PAGE 73 A1487 INT/ORG ATTIT USSR

B63
KATZ S.M.,A SELECTED LIST OF US READINGS ON DEVELOPMENT. AGRI COM/IND DIST/IND INDUS LABOR PLAN FOR/AID EDU/PROP HEALTH...POLICY SOC/WK 20. PAGE 77 A1571 BIBLIOG/A ECO/UNDEV TEC/DEV ACT/RES

B63
KRAVIS I.B.,DOMESTIC INTERESTS AND INTERNATIONAL OBLIGATIONS: SAFEGUARDS IN INTERNATIONAL TRADE ORGANIZATIONS. EUR+WWI USA+45 WOR+45 FINAN DELIB/GP ATTIT RIGID/FLEX HEALTH...STAT EEC VAL/FREE OEEC ECSC 20. PAGE 82 A1680 INT/ORG ECO/TAC INT/TRADE

B63
MULLENBACH P.,CIVILIAN NUCLEAR POWER: ECONOMIC ISSUES AND POLICY FORMATION. FINAN INT/ORG DELIB/GP ACT/RES ECO/TAC ATTIT SUPEGO HEALTH ORD/FREE PWR ...POLICY CONCPT MATH STAT CHARTS VAL/FREE 20 COLD/WAR. PAGE 105 A2166 USA+45 ECO/DEV NUC/PWR

B63
US GOVERNMENT,REPORT TO INTER-AMERICAN ECONOMIC AND SOCIAL COUNCIL AT SECOND ANNUAL MEETING. L/A+17C USA+45 VOL/ASSN TEC/DEV DIPLOM TAX EATING EFFICIENCY HEALTH...STAT CHARTS 20 AID. PAGE 153 A3116 ECO/TAC FOR/AID FINAN PLAN

B63
VOSS E.H.,NUCLEAR AMBUSH: THE TEST-BAN TRAP. WOR+45 COM/IND INT/ORG NAT/G DELIB/GP FORCES LEGIS TOP/EX ACT/RES DOMIN EDU/PROP LEGIT ROUTINE COERCE ATTIT PERCEPT RIGID/FLEX HEALTH MORAL ORD/FREE PWR. PAGE 160 A3255 TEC/DEV HIST/WRIT ARMS/CONT NUC/PWR

L63
LISSITZYN O.J.,"INTERNATIONAL LAW IN A DIVIDED WORLD." FUT WOR+45 CONSTN CULTURE ECO/DEV ECO/UNDEV DIST/IND NAT/G FORCES ECO/TAC LEGIT ADJUD ADMIN COERCE ATTIT HEALTH MORAL ORD/FREE PWR RESPECT WEALTH VAL/FREE. PAGE 90 A1841 INT/ORG LAW

L63
PHELPS J.,"STUDIES IN DETERRENCE VIII: MILITARY STABILITARY AND ARMS CONTROL: A CRITICAL SURVEY." FUT WOR+45 INT/ORG ACT/RES EDU/PROP COERCE NUC/PWR WAR HEALTH PWR...POLICY TECHNIC TREND SIMUL TOT/POP 20. PAGE 116 A2373 FORCES ORD/FREE ARMS/CONT DETER

L63
SINGER J.D.,"WEAPONS MANAGEMENT IN WORLD POLITICS: PROCEEDINGS OF THE INTERNATIONAL ARMS CONTROL SYMPOSIUM, DECEMBER, 1962." FUT WOR+45 SOCIETY ECO/DEV INDUS INT/ORG DELIB/GP FORCES ACT/RES ECO/TAC EDU/PROP ARMS/CONT SUPEGO HEALTH ORD/FREE PWR SKILL...POLICY CHARTS SIMUL ANTHOL VAL/FREE 20. PAGE 133 A2729 CONSULT ATTIT DIPLOM NUC/PWR

S63
HUMPHREY H.H.,"REGIONAL ARMS CONTROL AGREEMENTS." WOR+45 FORCES PLAN LEGIT COERCE ATTIT HEALTH ORD/FREE...HUM METH/CNCPT MYTH OBS INT TREND TOT/POP 20. PAGE 69 A1416 L/A+17C INT/ORG ARMS/CONT REGION

S63
LERNER D.,"FRENCH ELITE PERSPECTIVES ON THE UNITED NATIONS." EUR+WWI INT/ORG HEALTH ORD/FREE PWR RESPECT...STAT INT SAMP/SIZ VAL/FREE UN 20. PAGE 87 A1786 ATTIT STERTYP ELITES FRANCE

B64
FEIS H.,FOREIGN AID AND FOREIGN POLICY. USA+45 WOR+45 NAT/G VOL/ASSN ACT/RES TEC/DEV ATTIT HEALTH WEALTH...SOC GEN/LAWS 20. PAGE 45 A0912 ECO/UNDEV ECO/TAC FOR/AID DIPLOM

B64
HAMBRIDGE G.,DYNAMICS OF DEVELOPMENT. AGRI FINAN INDUS LABOR INT/TRADE EDU/PROP ADMIN LEAD OWN HEALTH...ANTHOL BIBLIOG 20. PAGE 61 A1245 ECO/UNDEV ECO/TAC OP/RES ACT/RES

B64
MC GOVERN G.S.,WAR AGAINST WANT. USA+45 AGRI DIPLOM INT/TRADE GIVE RECEIVE DEMAND HEALTH 20 KENNEDY/JF FOOD/PEACE. PAGE 97 A1993 FOR/AID ECO/DEV POLICY EATING

B64
SPECTOR S.D.,A CHECKLIST OF PAPERBOUND BOOKS ON RUSSIA. USSR SECT DIPLOM EDU/PROP HEALTH...PHIL/SCI PSY SOC SOC/WK WORSHIP 20. PAGE 135 A2775 BIBLIOG COM PERF/ART

B65
PEACE RESEARCH ABSTRACTS. FUT WOR+45 R+D INT/ORG NAT/G PLAN TEC/DEV BAL/PWR DIPLOM FOR/AID NUC/PWR HEALTH. PAGE 4 A0072 BIBLIOG/A PEACE ARMS/CONT WAR

B65
FANON F.,STUDIES IN A DYING COLONIALISM. ALGERIA FRANCE STRATA FAM DIPLOM DOMIN WAR RACE/REL DISCRIM HEALTH 20. PAGE 44 A0897 NAT/LISM COLONIAL REV SOVEREIGN

B65
UN,SPACE ACTIVITIES AND RESOURCES: REVIEW OF UNITED NATION'S NATIONAL AND INTERNATIONAL PROGRAMS. INT/ORG LABOR PLAN TEC/DEV DIPLOM EFFICIENCY HEALTH ...GOV/COMP 20 UN. PAGE 146 A2995 SPACE NUC/PWR FOR/AID PEACE

L65
WIONCZEK M.,"LATIN AMERICA FREE TRADE ASSOCIATION." AGRI DIST/IND FINAN INDUS INT/ORG LABOR NAT/G TEC/DEV ECO/TAC HEALTH SKILL WEALTH...POLICY RELATIV MGT LAFTA 20. PAGE 165 A3369 L/A+17C MARKET REGION

S65
GROSS L.,"PROBLEMS OF INTERNATIONAL ADJUDICATION AND COMPLIANCE WITH INTERNATIONAL LAW: SOME SIMPLE SOLUTIONS." WOR+45 SOCIETY NAT/G DOMIN LEGIT ADJUD CT/SYS RIGID/FLEX HEALTH PWR...JURID NEW/IDEA COLD/WAR 20. PAGE 57 A1177 LAW METH/CNCPT INT/LAW

B66
EWING B.G.,PEACE THROUGH NEGOTIATION: THE AUSTRIAN EXPERIENCE. AUSTRIA USSR VIETNAM CONFER CONTROL DETER WAR ATTIT HEALTH PWR...POLICY 20. PAGE 43 A0878 PEACE DIPLOM MARXISM

B66
HALLET R.,PEOPLE AND PROGRESS IN WEST AFRICA: AN INTRODUCTION TO THE PROBLEMS OF DEVELOPMENT. COM/IND INDUS KIN DIPLOM FOR/AID INT/TRADE HEALTH ...GEOG TREND CHARTS BIBLIOG/A 20 AFRICA/W. PAGE 60 A1233 AFR SOCIETY ECO/UNDEV ECO/TAC

B66
LEWIS S.,TOWARDS INTERNATIONAL CO-OPERATION (1ST ED.). WOR+45 AGRI INDUS EDU/PROP RACE/REL ISOLAT NAT/LISM ATTIT HEALTH WEALTH...CHARTS WORSHIP 20 UN. PAGE 88 A1803 DIPLOM ANOMIE PROB/SOLV INT/ORG

B66
ROBOCK S.H.,INTERNATIONAL DEVELOPMENT 1965. AGRI INDUS VOL/ASSN PLAN TEC/DEV EDU/PROP HEALTH...JURID 20 UN PEACE/CORP. PAGE 122 A2508 FOR/AID INT/ORG GEOG ECO/UNDEV

B66
US HOUSE COMM GOVT OPERATIONS,AN INVESTIGATION OF THE US ECONOMIC AND MILITARY ASSISTANCE PROGRAMS IN VIETNAM. USA+45 VIETNAM/S SOCIETY CONSTRUC FINAN FORCES BUDGET INT/TRADE PEACE HEALTH...MGT HOUSE/REP AID. PAGE 154 A3139 FOR/AID ECO/UNDEV WAR INSPECT

B67
JOHNSON D.G.,THE STRUGGLE AGAINST WORLD HUNGER (HEADLINE SERIES, NO. 184) (PAMPHLET). PLAN TEC/DEV FOR/AID...CHARTS 20 FAO MEXIC/AMER. PAGE 74 A1520 AGRI PROB/SOLV ECO/UNDEV HEALTH

B67
US AGENCY INTERNATIONAL DEV,PROPOSED FOREIGN AID PROGRAM FOR 1968: SUMMARY PRESENTATION TO THE CONGRESS. AFR S/ASIA USA+45 AGRI TEC/DEV DIPLOM ECO/TAC BAL/PAY COST HEALTH KNOWL SKILL 20 AID CONGRESS. PAGE 149 A3053 ECO/UNDEV BUDGET FOR/AID STAT

S67
CLINGHAM T.A. JR.,"LEGISLATIVE FLOTSAM AND INTERNATIONAL ACTION IN THE 'YARMOUTH CASTLE'S' WAKE." WOR+45 PROB/SOLV CONFER COST HEALTH...POLICY INT/LAW CONGRESS. PAGE 27 A0552 DIPLOM DIST/IND INT/ORG LAW

N67
US SUPERINTENDENT OF DOCUMENTS,SPACE: MISSILES, THE MOON, NASA, AND SATELLITES (PRICE LIST 79A). USA+45 BIBLIOG/A SPACE

B27
LAUTERPACHT H.,PRIVATE LAW SOURCES AND ANALOGIES OF INTERNATIONAL LAW. WOR-45 NAT/G DELIB/GP LEGIT COERCE ATTIT ORD/FREE PWR SOVEREIGN...JURID CONCPT HIST/WRIT TIME/SEQ GEN/METH LEAGUE/NAT 20. PAGE 85 A1748
INT/ORG ADJUD PEACE INT/LAW

B28
BUTLER G.,THE DEVELOPMENT OF INTERNATIONAL LAW. WOR-45 SOCIETY NAT/G KNOWL ORD/FREE PWR...JURID CONCPT HIST/WRIT GEN/LAWS. PAGE 22 A0451
LAW INT/LAW DIPLOM INT/ORG

B32
HANSEN A.H.,ECONOMIC STABILIZATION IN AN UNBALANCED WORLD. COM EUR+WWI USA-45 WOR-45 AGRI FINAN INDUS MARKET INT/ORG LABOR VOL/ASSN EDU/PROP ATTIT HEALTH KNOWL WEALTH...HIST/WRIT TREND VAL/FREE 20. PAGE 61 A1253
NAT/G ECO/DEV CAP/ISM SOCISM

B32
MASTERS R.D.,INTERNATIONAL LAW IN INTERNATIONAL COURTS. BELGIUM EUR+WWI FRANCE GERMANY MOD/EUR SWITZERLND WOR-45 SOCIETY STRATA STRUCT LEGIT EXEC ALL/VALS...JURID HIST/WRIT TIME/SEQ TREND GEN/LAWS 20. PAGE 96 A1961
INT/ORG LAW INT/LAW

B36
BOYCE A.N.,EUROPE AND SOUTH AFRICA. FRANCE GERMANY ITALY SOUTH/AFR UK INDUS NAT/G CONTROL REV WAR NAT/LISM...CONCPT HIST/WRIT 20. PAGE 18 A0362
COLONIAL GOV/COMP NAT/COMP DIPLOM

B36
ROBINSON H.,DEVELOPMENT OF THE BRITISH EMPIRE. WOR-45 CULTURE SOCIETY STRUCT ECO/DEV ECO/UNDEV INT/ORG VOL/ASSN FORCES CREATE PLAN DOMIN EDU/PROP ADMIN COLONIAL PWR WEALTH...POLICY GEOG CHARTS CMN/WLTH 16/20. PAGE 122 A2503
NAT/G HIST/WRIT UK

B38
RAPPARD W.E.,THE CRISIS OF DEMOCRACY. EUR+WWI UNIV WOR-45 CULTURE SOCIETY ECO/DEV INT/ORG POL/PAR ACT/RES EDU/PROP EXEC CHOOSE ATTIT ALL/VALS...SOC OBS HIST/WRIT TIME/SEQ LEAGUE/NAT NAZI TOT/POP 20. PAGE 119 A2449
NAT/G CONCPT

B39
BROWN J.F.,CONTEMPORARY WORLD POLITICS. WOR-45 NAT/G PLAN BAL/PWR EDU/PROP LEGIT REGION NAT/LISM ORD/FREE PWR SOVEREIGN...POLICY CONCPT HIST/WRIT TIME/SEQ GEN/LAWS LEAGUE/NAT. PAGE 20 A0403
INT/ORG DIPLOM PEACE

B45
CONOVER H.F.,THE NAZI STATE: WAR CRIMES AND WAR CRIMINALS. GERMANY CULTURE NAT/G SECT FORCES DIPLOM INT/TRADE EDU/PROP...INT/LAW BIOG HIST/WRIT TIME/SEQ 20. PAGE 30 A0600
BIBLIOG WAR CRIME

B46
KEETON G.W.,MAKING INTERNATIONAL LAW WORK. FUT WOR-45 NAT/G DELIB/GP FORCES LEGIT COERCE PEACE ATTIT RIGID/FLEX ORD/FREE PWR...JURID CONCPT HIST/WRIT GEN/METH LEAGUE/NAT 20. PAGE 77 A1578
INT/ORG ADJUD INT/LAW

B48
FLOREN LOZANO L.,BIBLIOGRAFIA DE LA BIBLIOGRAFIA DOMINICANA. DOMIN/REP NAT/G DIPLOM EDU/PROP CIVMIL/REL...POLICY ART/METH GEOG PHIL/SCI HIST/WRIT 20. PAGE 47 A0952
BIBLIOG/A BIOG L/A+17C CULTURE

B50
BERLE A.A.,NATURAL SELECTION OF POLITICAL FORCES. FUT WOR+45 WOR-45 CULTURE SOCIETY INT/ORG NAT/G FORCES EDU/PROP LEGIT COERCE...CONCPT HIST/WRIT TREND 20. PAGE 13 A0274
POL/PAR BAL/PWR DIPLOM

B50
MACIVER R.M.,GREAT EXPRESSIONS OF HUMAN RIGHTS. LAW CONSTN CULTURE INTELL SOCIETY R+D INT/ORG ATTIT DRIVE...JURID OBS HIST/WRIT GEN/LAWS. PAGE 92 A1891
UNIV CONCPT

S50
WITTFOGEL K.A.,"RUSSIA AND ASIA: PROBLEMS OF CONTEMPORARY AREA STUDIES AND INTERNATIONAL RELATIONS." ASIA COM USA+45 SOCIETY NAT/G DIPLOM ECO/TAC FOR/AID EDU/PROP KNOWL...HIST/WRIT TOT/POP 20. PAGE 166 A3373
ECO/DEV ADMIN RUSSIA USSR

L51
ULAM A.B.,"THE COMIMFORM AND THE PEOPLE'S DEMOCRACIES." EUR+WWI WOR+45 STRUCT NAT/G POL/PAR TOP/EX ACT/RES PLAN ECO/TAC DOMIN ATTIT ALL/VALS ...HIST/WRIT TIME/SEQ 20 COMINFORM. PAGE 146 A2992
COM INT/ORG USSR TOTALISM

B53
LENZ F.,DIE BEWEGUNGEN DER GROSSEN MACHTE. USA+45 USA-45 USSR SOCIETY STRATA STRUCT NAT/G PERSON MARXISM...CONCPT IDEA/COMP NAT/COMP 18/20. PAGE 87 A1777
BAL/PWR TREND DIPLOM HIST/WRIT

B54
NUSSBAUM D.,A CONCISE HISTORY OF THE LAW OF NATIONS. ASIA CHRIST-17C EUR+WWI ISLAM MEDIT-7 MOD/EUR S/ASIA UNIV WOR+45 WOR-45 SOCIETY STRUCT EXEC ATTIT ALL/VALS...CONCPT HIST/WRIT TIME/SEQ. PAGE 110 A2263
INT/ORG LAW PEACE INT/LAW

B54
SCHIFFER W.,THE LEGAL COMMUNITY OF MANKIND. UNIV WOR+45 WOR-45 SOCIETY NAT/G EDU/PROP LEGIT ATTIT PERSON ORD/FREE PWR...CONCPT HIST/WRIT TREND LEAGUE/NAT UN 20. PAGE 128 A2626
INT/ORG PHIL/SCI

B55
PERKINS B.,THE FIRST RAPPROCHEMENTS: ENGLAND AND THE UNITED STATES, 1795-1805. UK USA-45 ATTIT ...HIST/WRIT BIBLIOG 18/19 MADISON/J WAR/1812. PAGE 115 A2357
DIPLOM COLONIAL WAR

B56
BLACKETT P.M.S.,ATOMIC WEAPONS AND EAST-WEST RELATIONS. FUT WOR+45 INT/ORG DELIB/GP COERCE ATTIT RIGID/FLEX KNOWL...RELATIV HIST/WRIT TREND GEN/METH COLD/WAR 20. PAGE 15 A0299
FORCES PWR ARMS/CONT NUC/PWR

C56
VAGTS A.,"DEFENSE AND DIPLOMACY: THE SOLDIER AND THE CONDUCT OF FOREIGN RELATIONS." OP/RES CONFER DETER WAR PEACE RESPECT...POLICY DECISION CONCPT BIBLIOG 17/20. PAGE 158 A3209
DIPLOM FORCES HIST/WRIT

B57
ARON R.,FRANCE DEFEATS EDC. EUR+WWI GERMANY LEGIS DIPLOM DOMIN EDU/PROP ADMIN...HIST/WRIT 20. PAGE 9 A0180
INT/ORG FORCES DETER FRANCE

B57
BEERS H.P.,THE FRENCH IN NORTH AMERICA. FRANCE USA-45...TIME/SEQ BIBLIOG. PAGE 12 A0247
HIST/WRIT DIPLOM BIOG WRITING

B57
BLOOMFIELD L.P.,EVOLUTION OR REVOLUTION: THE UNITED NATIONS AND THE PROBLEM OF PEACEFUL TERRITORIAL CHANGE. WOR+45 WOR-45 INT/ORG NAT/G DIPLOM ROUTINE REV ATTIT RIGID/FLEX PWR...CONCPT OBS HIST/WRIT UN LEAGUE/NAT 20. PAGE 15 A0315
ORD/FREE LEGIT

B58
RIGGS R.,POLITICS IN THE UNITED NATIONS: A STUDY OF UNITED STATES INFLUENCE IN THE GENERAL ASSEMBLY. USA+45 WOR+45 LEGIS TOP/EX CREATE BAL/PWR DIPLOM DOMIN EDU/PROP COLONIAL ROUTINE ATTIT RIGID/FLEX PWR...CONCPT OBS HIST/WRIT CHARTS STERTYP GEN/LAWS UN COLD/WAR 20. PAGE 121 A2480
INT/ORG

B59
KULSKI W.W.,PEACEFUL CO-EXISTENCE: AN ANALYSIS OF SOVIET FOREIGN POLICY. WOR+45 INTELL SOCIETY ECO/UNDEV POL/PAR EDU/PROP COERCE DRIVE RIGID/FLEX PWR SKILL...PSY CONCPT HIST/WRIT CON/ANAL GEN/METH WORK VAL/FREE 20. PAGE 83 A1691
PLAN DIPLOM USSR

S59
SUTTON F.X.,"REPRESENTATION AND THE NATURE OF POLITICAL SYSTEMS." UNIV WOR-45 CULTURE SOCIETY STRATA INT/ORG FORCES JUDGE DOMIN LEGIT EXEC REGION REPRESENT ATTIT ORD/FREE RESPECT...SOC HIST/WRIT TIME/SEQ. PAGE 140 A2867
NAT/G CONCPT

S59
TIPTON J.B.,"PARTICIPATION OF THE UNITED STATES IN THE INTERNATIONAL LABOR ORGANIZATION." USA+45 LAW STRUCT ECO/DEV ECO/UNDEV INDUS TEC/DEV ECO/TAC ADMIN PERCEPT ORD/FREE SKILL...STAT HIST/WRIT GEN/METH ILO WORK 20. PAGE 144 A2946
LABOR INT/ORG

B60
CONN S.,THE FRAMEWORK OF HEMISPHERE DEFENSE. CANADA L/A+17C USA-45 NAT/G FORCES BAL/PWR DOMIN WAR PEACE DISPL PWR RESPECT...PLURIST CONCPT HIST/WRIT HYPO/EXP MEXIC/AMER 20 ROOSEVLT/F. PAGE 29 A0585
USA+45 INT/ORG DIPLOM

B60
LISKA G.,THE NEW STATECRAFT. WOR+45 WOR-45 LEGIS DIPLOM ADMIN ATTIT PWR WEALTH...HIST/WRIT TREND COLD/WAR 20. PAGE 90 A1837
ECO/TAC CONCPT FOR/AID

S60
GULICK E.U.,"OUR BALANCE OF POWER SYSTEM IN PERSPECTIVE." FUT WOR+45 WOR-45 ECO/DEV DOMIN ROUTINE NUC/PWR PEACE PWR WEALTH...PLURIST CONCPT HIST/WRIT GEN/METH TOT/POP 20. PAGE 58 A1191
INT/ORG TREND ARMS/CONT BAL/PWR

S60
KENNAN G.F.,"PEACEFUL CO-EXISTENCE: A WESTERN VIEW." COM EUR+WWI USA+45 USSR WOR+45 PLAN BAL/PWR DIPLOM INT/TRADE PWR...POLICY CONCPT OBS HIST/WRIT TREND GEN/LAWS COLD/WAR 20 KHRUSH/N. PAGE 78 A1589
ATTIT COERCE

S60
PETERSON E.N.,"HISTORICAL SCHOLARSHIP AND WORLD UNITY." FUT UNIV WOR-45 CULTURE INTELL INT/ORG NAT/G ACT/RES EDU/PROP ATTIT PERCEPT RIGID/FLEX ...NEW/IDEA OBS HIST/WRIT TREND COLD/WAR TOT/POP 20. PAGE 115 A2367
PLAN KNOWL NAT/LISM

S60
SCHWELB E.,"INTERNATIONAL CONVENTIONS ON HUMAN RIGHTS." FUT WOR+45 LAW CONSTN CULTURE SOCIETY STRUCT VOL/ASSN DELIB/GP PLAN ADJUD SUPEGO LOVE MORAL...SOC CONCPT STAT RECORD HIST/WRIT TREND 20 UN. PAGE 130 A2664
INT/ORG HUM

B61
CONFERENCE ATLANTIC COMMUNITY,AN INTRODUCTORY BIBLIOGRAPHY. COM WOR+45 FORCES DIPLOM ECO/TAC WAR ...INT/LAW HIST/WRIT COLD/WAR NATO. PAGE 29 A0584
BIBLIOG/A CON/ANAL INT/ORG

B61
HENKIN L.,ARMS CONTROL: ISSUES FOR THE PUBLIC. EUR+WWI FUT USA+45 USSR INT/ORG NAT/G DIPLOM EDU/PROP DETER NUC/PWR ATTIT PWR...CONCPT RECORD HIST/WRIT TIME/SEQ TOT/POP COLD/WAR 20. PAGE 64
WOR+45 DELIB/GP ARMS/CONT

A1316

S61
NOVE A.,"THE SOVIET MODEL AND UNDERDEVELOPED COUNTRIES." COM FUT USSR WOR+45 CULTURE ECO/DEV POL/PAR FOR/AID EDU/PROP ADMIN MORAL WEALTH ...POLICY RECORD HIST/WRIT 20. PAGE 110 A2258 ECO/UNDEV PLAN

B62
BOUSCAREN A.T.,SOVIET FOREIGN POLICY: A PATTERN OF PERSISTANCE. WOR+45 WOR-45 SOCIETY STRUCT INT/ORG POL/PAR CREATE PLAN EDU/PROP ROUTINE ATTIT RIGID/FLEX...POLICY CONCPT RECORD HIST/WRIT TIME/SEQ MARX/KARL 20. PAGE 17 A0352 COM NAT/G DIPLOM USSR

B62
DALLIN A.,THE SOVIET UNION AT THE UNITED NATIONS: AN INQUIRY INTO SOVIET MOTIVES AND OBJECTIVES. ACT/RES EDU/PROP LEGIT ATTIT KNOWL PWR...POLICY RECORD HIST/WRIT TIME/SEQ TREND ORG/CHARTS GEN/METH COLD/WAR FAO 20 UN. PAGE 33 A0675 COM INT/ORG USSR

B62
GRAEBNER N.,COLD WAR DIPLOMACY 1945-1960. WOR+45 INT/ORG ECO/TAC EDU/PROP COERCE ORD/FREE PWR WEALTH ...HIST/WRIT TOT/POP VAL/FREE COLD/WAR 20. PAGE 55 A1122 USA+45 DIPLOM

B62
KING G.,THE UNITED NATIONS IN THE CONGO: A QUEST FOR PEACE. WOR+45 NAT/G CONSULT FORCES LEGIT COERCE WAR ORD/FREE...JURID METH/CNCPT OBS INT HIST/WRIT TIME/SEQ CONGO UN 20 COLD/WAR. PAGE 79 A1624 AFR INT/ORG

S62
DALLIN A.,"THE SOVIET VIEW OF THE UNITED NATIONS." WOR+45 VOL/ASSN TOP/EX DIPLOM DOMIN EDU/PROP LEGIT ATTIT RIGID/FLEX PWR...CONCPT OBS HIST/WRIT TIME/SEQ STERTYP GEN/LAWS COLD/WAR UN 20. PAGE 33 A0676 COM INT/ORG USSR

B63
GALLAGHER M.P.,THE SOVIET HISTORY OF WORLD WAR II. EUR+WWI USSR DIPLOM DOMIN WRITING CONTROL WAR MARXISM...PSY TIME/SEQ 20 STALIN/J. PAGE 50 A1031 CIVMIL/REL EDU/PROP HIST/WRIT PRESS

B63
ROSNER G.,THE UNITED NATIONS EMERGENCY FORCE. FRANCE ISRAEL UAR UK WOR+45 CREATE WAR PEACE ORD/FREE PWR...INT/LAW JURID HIST/WRIT TIME/SEQ UN. PAGE 124 A2539 INT/ORG FORCES

B63
VOSS E.H.,NUCLEAR AMBUSH: THE TEST-BAN TRAP. WOR+45 COM/IND INT/ORG NAT/G DELIB/GP FORCES LEGIS TOP/EX ACT/RES DOMIN EDU/PROP LEGIT ROUTINE COERCE ATTIT PERCEPT RIGID/FLEX HEALTH MORAL ORD/FREE PWR. PAGE 160 A3255 TEC/DEV HIST/WRIT ARMS/CONT NUC/PWR

L63
ZARTMAN I.W.,"THE SAHARA--BRIDGE OR BARRIER." ISLAM CULTURE SOCIETY NAT/G DELIB/GP DOMIN EDU/PROP LEGIT ATTIT...HIST/WRIT TIME/SEQ CHARTS TOT/POP VAL/FREE 20. PAGE 169 A3445 INT/ORG PWR NAT/LISM

S63
SONNENFELDT H.,"FOREIGN POLICY FROM MALENKOV TO KHRUSHCHEV." WOR+45 NAT/G FORCES BAL/PWR DIPLOM ECO/TAC COERCE ATTIT PWR...CONCPT HIST/WRIT COLD/WAR 20. PAGE 135 A2768 COM DOMIN FOR/AID USSR

S63
WOLFERS A.,"INTEGRATION IN THE WEST: THE CONFLICT OF PERSPECTIVES." EUR+WWI USA+45 ECO/DEV INT/ORG DELIB/GP CREATE TEC/DEV DIPLOM ATTIT PWR...CONCPT HIST/WRIT TREND GEN/LAWS COLD/WAR EEC 20. PAGE 166 A3386 RIGID/FLEX ECO/TAC

S63
WRIGHT Q.,"DECLINE OF CLASSIC DIPLOMACY." CHRIST-17C EUR+WWI MOD/EUR WOR+45 WOR-45 INT/ORG NAT/G DELIB/GP BAL/PWR ATTIT PWR...HIST/WRIT LEAGUE/NAT. PAGE 168 A3418 TEC/DEV CONCPT DIPLOM

B64
BOYD J.P.,NUMBER 7: ALEXANDER HAMILTON'S SECRET ATTEMPTS TO CONTROL AMERICAN FOREIGN POLICY. AFR UK DIPLOM WAR RESPECT WEALTH...POLICY HIST/WRIT 18 HAMILTON/A. PAGE 18 A0364 USA-45 NAT/G TOP/EX PWR

B64
KEEP J.,CONTEMPORARY HISTORY IN THE SOVIET MIRROR. COM USSR POL/PAR CREATE DIPLOM AGREE WAR ATTIT ...MYTH TREND ANTHOL 20 COLD/WAR STALIN/J MARX/KARL LENIN/VI. PAGE 77 A1576 HIST/WRIT METH MARXISM IDEA/COMP

L64
CURTIS G.L.,"THE UNITED NATIONS OBSERVER GROUP IN LEBANON." ISLAM USA+45 NAT/G CONSULT ACT/RES PLAN BAL/PWR LEGIT ATTIT KNOWL...HIST/WRIT UN 20 UN. PAGE 33 A0669 INT/ORG FORCES DIPLOM LEBANON

S64
ASHRAF S.,"INDIA AND WORLD AFFAIRS: AN ANNUAL BIBLIOGRAPHY, 1962." WOR+45 LAW ECO/UNDEV INT/ORG FORCES PLAN ECO/TAC COERCE ORD/FREE PWR WEALTH ...HIST/WRIT VAL/FREE. PAGE 9 A0188 S/ASIA NAT/G

S64
DEVILLERS P.H.,"L'URSS, LA CHINE ET LES ORIGINES DE LA GUERRE DE COREE." ASIA CHINA/COM USSR INT/ORG ECO/TAC EDU/PROP ATTIT RIGID/FLEX PWR...STAND/INT HIST/WRIT COLD/WAR 20. PAGE 37 A0751 WOR+45 KOREA

S64
KHAN M.Z.,"ISLAM AND INTERNATIONAL RELATIONS." FUT WOR+45 LAW CULTURE SOCIETY NAT/G SECT DELIB/GP FORCES EDU/PROP ATTIT PERSON SUPEGO ALL/VALS ...POLICY PSY CONCPT MYTH HIST/WRIT GEN/LAWS. PAGE 78 A1608 ISLAM INT/ORG DIPLOM

S64
SALVADORI M.,"EL CAPITALISMO EN LA EUROPA DE LA POSGUERRA." INT/ORG NAT/G POL/PAR PLAN ECO/TAC ATTIT ORD/FREE WEALTH...HIST/WRIT COLD/WAR EEC 20. PAGE 127 A2596 EUR+WWI ECO/DEV CAP/ISM

B66
BLACKSTOCK P.W.,AGENTS OF DECEIT: FRAUDS, FORGERIES AND POLITICAL INTRIGUES AMONG NATIONS. USSR EDU/PROP WRITING KNOWL 18/20 COLD/WAR KENNAN/G. PAGE 15 A0302 CON/ANAL DIPLOM HIST/WRIT

B67
STEVENS R.P.,LESOTHO, BATSWANA, AND SWAZILAND* THE FORMER HIGH COMMISSION TERRITORIES IN SOUTHERN AFRICA. ECO/DEV KIN POL/PAR HIST/WRIT. PAGE 138 A2821 COLONIAL DIPLOM ORD/FREE

B67
WALLERSTEIN I.,AFRICA* THE POLITICS OF UNITY. AFR INT/ORG REV SOVEREIGN...HIST/WRIT 20. PAGE 160 A3268 TREND DIPLOM ATTIT

S67
FARQUHAR D.M.,"CHINESE COMMUNIST ASSESSMENTS OF A FOREIGN CONQUEST DYNASTY." CHINA/COM DIPLOM CONTROL ...METH 20. PAGE 44 A0900 MARXISM HIST/WRIT POLICY COLONIAL

S67
SCHUMANN H.,"IMPERIALISMUS-KRITIK UND KOLONIALISMUS-FORSCHUNG." GERMANY/E DIPLOM SOVEREIGN...SOC HIST/WRIT 20. PAGE 129 A2652 COLONIAL ATTIT DOMIN CAP/ISM

HISTORICAL RESEARCH INSTITUTE A1343

HISTORICUS A1344

HITLER/A....ADOLF HITLER

B35
MARRIOTT J.A.,DICTATORSHIP AND DEMOCRACY. GERMANY GREECE UK CHIEF DIPLOM DOMIN LEGIT PEACE ORD/FREE CONSERVE...TREND ROME HITLER/A. PAGE 95 A1946 TOTALISM POPULISM PLURIST NAT/G

B48
NAMIER L.B.,DIPLOMATIC PRELUDE 1938-1939. CZECHOSLVK EUR+WWI GERMANY POLAND UK FORCES DOMIN PWR 20 HITLER/A. PAGE 107 A2193 WAR TOTALISM DIPLOM

B48
WHEELER-BENNETT J.W.,MUNICH: PROLOGUE TO TRAGEDY. EUR+WWI FRANCE GERMANY UK PLAN PROB/SOLV SOVEREIGN ...POLICY DECISION 20 HITLER/A. PAGE 163 A3327 DIPLOM WAR PEACE

B51
BORKENAU F.,EUROPEAN COMMUNISM. COM EUR+WWI GERMANY SPAIN USSR INT/ORG PLAN REV WAR ATTIT 20 STALIN/J HITLER/A. PAGE 17 A0342 MARXISM POLICY DIPLOM NAT/G

B52
MANTOUX E.,THE CARTHAGINIAN PEACE. GERMANY WOR-45 SOCIETY FINAN INT/ORG DELIB/GP FORCES PLAN LEGIT ...CONCPT TIME/SEQ 20 KEYNES/JM HITLER/A. PAGE 94 A1935 ECO/DEV INT/TRADE WAR

B54
SALVEMINI G.,PRELUDE TO WORLD WAR II. ITALY MOD/EUR INT/ORG BAL/PWR EDU/PROP CONTROL TOTALISM...TREND NAT/COMP BIBLIOG 19 HITLER/A LEAGUE/NAT MUSSOLIN/B. PAGE 127 A2597 WAR FASCISM LEAD PWR

B55
ALFIERI D.,DICTATORS FACE TO FACE. NAT/G TOP/EX DIPLOM EXEC COERCE ORD/FREE FASCISM...POLICY OBS 20 HITLER/A MUSSOLIN/B. PAGE 6 A0116 WAR CHIEF TOTALISM PERS/REL

S58
ROTHFELS H.,"THE GERMAN RESISTANCE IN ITS INTERNATIONAL ASPECTS" (BMR)" EUR+WWI GERMANY UNIV CHIEF DIPLOM WAR NAT/LISM ATTIT...POLICY 20 HITLER/A NAZI. PAGE 124 A2548 VOL/ASSN MORAL FASCISM CIVMIL/REL

B61
FUCHS G.,GEGEN HITLER UND HENLEIN. CZECHOSLVK GERMANY DIPLOM CHOOSE GP/REL TOTALISM SOVEREIGN 20 HITLER/A. PAGE 50 A1013 FASCISM WORKER POL/PAR NAT/LISM

B62
ABOSCH H.,THE MENACE OF THE MIRACLE: GERMANY FROM HITLER TO ADENAUER. EUR+WWI GERMANY/W CULTURE FORCES PRESS NUC/PWR WAR CHOOSE 20 HITLER/A ADENAUER/K. PAGE 4 A0082 DIPLOM PEACE POLICY

B62
SCOTT W.E.,ALLIANCE AGAINST HITLER. EUR+WWI FRANCE GERMANY USSR BAL/PWR LEAD TOTALISM PWR FASCISM MARXISM...POLICY BIBLIOG 20 HITLER/A. PAGE 131 A2675 WAR DIPLOM FORCES

B64
EHRENBURG I.,THE WAR: 1941-1945 (VOL. V OF "MEN, YEARS - LIFE," TRANS. BY TATIANA SHEBUNINA). GERMANY USSR PRESS WRITING PERS/REL PEACE ANOMIE ATTIT PERSON...CONCPT RECORD BIOG 20 STALIN/J HITLER/A. PAGE 40 A0827 WAR DIPLOM COM MARXIST

B65
LOEWENHEIM F.L.,PEACE OR APPEASEMENT? HITLER, CHAMBERLAIN AND THE MUNICH CRISIS. MUNIC DELIB/GP WAR TOTALISM ATTIT SOVEREIGN...TIME/SEQ ANTHOL BIBLIOG 20 HITLER/A CHAMBRLN/N. PAGE 90 A1851 DIPLOM LEAD PEACE

B66
RISTIC D.N.,YUGOSLAVIA'S REVOLUTION OF 1941. EUR+WWI YUGOSLAVIA NAT/G WAR ORD/FREE...RECORD BIBLIOG 20 HITLER/A TREATY. PAGE 121 A2484 REV ATTIT FASCISM DIPLOM

B67
THORNE C.,THE APPROACH OF WAR, 1938-1939. EUR+WWI POL/PAR CHIEF FORCES LEAD DRIVE PWR FASCISM ...BIBLIOG/A 20 HITLER/A. PAGE 144 A2936 DIPLOM WAR ELITES

HO/CHI/MIN....HO CHI MINH

HOAG M.W. A1345

HOBBES/T....THOMAS HOBBES

HOBBS C.C. A1346

HOBSON J.A. A1347,A1348

HODAPP W. A1113

HODES F. A0330

HODGE G. A1349

HODGES C. A0403,A1350

HODGKIN T. A1351

HODNETT G. A0677

HOEVELER H.J. A1352

HOFFA/J....JAMES HOFFA

HOFFMAN P. A1353

HOFFMANN P.G. A1354

HOFFMANN S. A1355,A1356,A1357,A1358,A1359

HOFMANN L. A1360

HOGAN W.N. A1361,A3218

HOHENBERG J. A1362

HOLBO P.S. A1363

HOLBORN H. A1364

HOLCOMBE A.N. A1365

HOLDSWORTH M. A1366

HOLIFLD/C....CHET HOLIFIELD

HOLLAND T.E. A1367,A1368

HOLLAND....SEE NETHERLAND

HOLLERMAN L. A1369

HOLLINS E.J. A1370

HOLMAN A.G. A1371

HOLMES/OW....OLIVER WENDELL HOLMES

HOLMES/OWJ....OLIVER WENDELL HOLMES, JR.

HOLMQUIST F.W. A0650

HOLSTI K.J. A1372

HOLSTI O.R. A1373

HOLSTI/KJ....K.J. HOLSTI

HOLT R.T. A1374,A1375,A1376

HOLTON G. A1377

HOMEOSTASIS....SEE FEEDBACK

HOMER....HOMER

HOMEST/ACT....HOMESTEAD ACT OF 1862

HOMESTEAD ACT OF 1862....SEE HOMEST/ACT

HOMICIDE....SEE MURDER

HOMOSEXUAL....HOMOSEXUALITY; SEE ALSO BIO/SOC, CRIME, SEX

HOMOSEXUALITY....SEE BIO/SOC, SEX, CRIME, HOMOSEXUAL

HONDURAS....SEE ALSO L/A+17C

HONEY P.J. A1378

HONG/KONG....HONG KONG

B48
PELCOVITS N.A.,OLD CHINA HANDS AND THE FOREIGN OFFICE. ASIA BURMA UK ECO/UNDEV NAT/G ECO/TAC FOR/AID TARIFFS DOMIN COLONIAL GOV/REL SOVEREIGN 19 HONG/KONG TREATY. PAGE 114 A2348 INT/TRADE ATTIT DIPLOM

B64
HARPER F.,OUT OF CHINA. CHINA/COM ELITES STRATA ATTIT PERSON...BIOG 20 MAO HONG/KONG MIGRATION. PAGE 62 A1264 HABITAT DEEP/INT DIPLOM MARXISM

HONORD S. A1379

HOOK S. A1380

HOOVER INSTITUTION A1381

HOOVER/H....HERBERT HOOVER

B60
MORISON E.E.,TURMOIL AND TRADITION: A STUDY OF THE LIFE AND TIMES OF HENRY L. STIMSON. USA+45 USA-45 POL/PAR CHIEF DELIB/GP FORCES BAL/PWR DIPLOM ARMS/CONT WAR PEACE 19/20 STIMSON/HL ROOSEVLT/F TAFT/WH HOOVER/H REPUBLICAN. PAGE 104 A2142 BIOG NAT/G EX/STRUC

HOPI....HOPI INDIANS

HOPKINS/H....HARRY HOPKINS

HORECKY P.L. A1382

HORELICK A.L. A1383

HORMANN K. A1384

HORN O.B. A1385

HORNE D. A1386

HOROWITZ D. A1387

HOROWITZ I.L. A1388

HORVATH J. A1389

HOSCH L.G. A1390

HOSELITZ B.F. A1391,A1392

HOSKYNS C. A1393

HOSMAR J.K. A1394

HOSPITALS....SEE PUB/INST

HOUSE COMMITTEE ON SCIENCE AND ASTRONAUTICS....SEE HS/SCIASTR

HOUSE OF REPRESENTATIVES....SEE HOUSE/REP

HOUSE RULES COMMITTEE....SEE RULES/COMM, HOUSE/REP

HOUSE/CMNS....HOUSE OF COMMONS (ALL NATIONS)

HOUSE/LORD....HOUSE OF LORDS (ALL NATIONS)

HOUSE/REP....HOUSE OF REPRESENTATIVES (ALL NATIONS); SEE ALSO CONGRESS, LEGIS

B56
US HOUSE COMM FOREIGN AFFAIRS,SURVEY OF ACTIVITIES OF THE COMMITTEE ON FOREIGN AFFAIRS HOUSE OF REPRESENTATIVES: 84TH THROUGH 86TH CONGRESS. USA+45 LEGIS DELIB/GP NAT/G

LAW ADJUD...POLICY STAT CHARTS 20 CONGRESS HOUSE/REP. PAGE 153 A3122 — DIPLOM

B58
US HOUSE COMM GOVT OPERATIONS,HEARINGS BEFORE A SUBCOMMITTEE OF THE COMMITTEE ON GOVERNMENT OPERATIONS. CAMBODIA PHILIPPINE USA+45 CONSTRUC TEC/DEV ADMIN CONTROL WEAPON EFFICIENCY HOUSE/REP. PAGE 154 A3135 — FOR/AID DIPLOM ORD/FREE ECO/UNDEV

B59
US HOUSE COMM GOVT OPERATIONS,UNITED STATES AID OPERATIONS IN LAOS. LAOS USA+45 PLAN INSPECT HOUSE/REP. PAGE 154 A3136 — FOR/AID ADMIN FORCES ECO/UNDEV

B66
US HOUSE COMM GOVT OPERATIONS,AN INVESTIGATION OF THE US ECONOMIC AND MILITARY ASSISTANCE PROGRAMS IN VIETNAM. USA+45 VIETNAM/S SOCIETY CONSTRUC FINAN FORCES BUDGET INT/TRADE PEACE HEALTH...MGT HOUSE/REP AID. PAGE 154 A3139 — FOR/AID ECO/UNDEV WAR INSPECT

HOUSTON J.A. A1395

HOUSTON....HOUSTON, TEXAS

HOUTART F. A0513

HOVET T. A1396,A1397,A1398

HOW J.L. A3343

HOWARD J.E. A1399

HOWARD M. A1400

HOWARD-ELLIS C. A1401

HOWELLS L.T. A2935

HOYT E.C. A1402

HS/SCIASTR....HOUSE COMMITTEE ON SCIENCE AND ASTRONAUTICS

HU/FENG....HU FENG

HUAC....HOUSE UNAMERICAN ACTIVITIES COMMITTEE

HUBER G. A1403

HUDSON G.F. A1404,A1405

HUDSON M. A1406,A1407,A1408

HUDSON M.O. A1406, A1407, A1408, A1409

HUDSON R. A1410

HUELIN D. A1411

HUGENDUBEL P. A1412

HUGHES E.M. A1413

HUKS....HUKS (PHILIPPINES)

HULL E.W.S. A1414

HUM....METHODS OF HUMANITIES, LITERARY ANALYSIS

N
LIBRARY INTERNATIONAL REL,INTERNATIONAL INFORMATION SERVICE. WOR+45 CULTURE INT/ORG FORCES...GEOG HUM SOC. PAGE 88 A1808 — BIBLIOG/A DIPLOM INT/TRADE INT/LAW

N
UNIVERSITY OF FLORIDA LIBRARY,DOORS TO LATIN AMERICA; RECENT BOOKS AND PAMPHLETS. CONSTN CULTURE SOCIETY ECO/UNDEV COLONIAL LEAD GOV/REL NAT/LISM ATTIT...HUM SOC 20. PAGE 149 A3047 — BIBLIOG/A L/A+17C DIPLOM NAT/G

N
AUSTRALIAN PUBLIC AFFAIRS INFORMATION SERVICE. LAW ...HEAL HUM MGT SOC CON/ANAL 20 AUSTRAL. PAGE 2 A0028 — BIBLIOG NAT/G CULTURE DIPLOM

N
LATIN AMERICA IN PERIODICAL LITERATURE. LAW TEC/DEV DIPLOM RECEIVE EDU/PROP...GEOG HUM MGT 20. PAGE 2 A0037 — BIBLIOG/A L/A+17C SOCIETY ECO/UNDEV

N
PUBLISHERS' CIRCULAR, THE OFFICIAL ORGAN OF THE PUBLISHERS' ASSOCIATION OF GREAT BRITAIN AND IRELAND. EUR+WWI MOD/EUR UK LAW PROB/SOLV DIPLOM COLONIAL ATTIT...HUM 19/20 CMN/WLTH. PAGE 2 A0039 — BIBLIOG NAT/G WRITING LEAD

N
"PROLOG",DIGEST OF THE SOVIET UKRANIAN PRESS. USSR LAW AGRI INDUS PROVS SCHOOL DIPLOM GOV/REL ATTIT ...HUM LING 20. PAGE 4 A0081 — BIBLIOG/A NAT/G PRESS COM

N
AMER COUNCIL OF LEARNED SOCIET,THE ACLS CONSTITUENT SOCIETY JOURNAL PROJECT. FUT USA+45 LAW NAT/G PLAN DIPLOM PHIL/SCI. PAGE 7 A0134 — BIBLIOG/A HUM COMPUT/IR COMPUTER

N
INSTITUTE OF HISPANIC STUDIES,HISPANIC AMERICAN REPORT. EUR+WWI SPAIN LAW CONSTN ECO/UNDEV POL/PAR EX/STRUC LEGIS LEAD...HUM SOC 20. PAGE 70 A1445 — BIBLIOG/A L/A+17C NAT/G DIPLOM

N
MINISTERE DE L'EDUC NATIONALE,CATALOGUE DES THESES DE DOCTORAT SOUTENNES DEVANT LES UNIVERSITAIRES FRANCAISES. FRANCE LAW DIPLOM ADMIN...HUM SOC 20. PAGE 102 A2087 — BIBLIOG ACADEM KNOWL NAT/G

L21
HALDEMAN E.,"SERIALS OF AN INTERNATIONAL CHARACTER." WOR-45 DIPLOM...ART/METH GEOG HEAL HUM INT/LAW JURID PSY SOC. PAGE 60 A1224 — BIBLIOG PHIL/SCI

B40
THE GUIDE TO CATHOLIC LITERATURE, 1888-1940. ALL/VALS...POLICY MYSTIC HUM PHIL/SCI 19/20. PAGE 3 A0051 — BIBLIOG/A CATHISM DIPLOM CULTURE

B41
EVANS C.,AMERICAN BIBLIOGRAPHY... (12 VOLUMES). USA-45 LAW DIPLOM ADMIN PERSON...HUM SOC 17/18. PAGE 43 A0876 — BIBLIOG NAT/G ALL/VALS ALL/IDEOS

B41
GRISMER R.,A NEW BIBLIOGRAPHY OF THE LITERATURES OF SPAIN AND SPANISH AMERICA. CHRIST-17C MOD/EUR PRE/AMER SPAIN CULTURE DIPLOM EDU/PROP...ART/METH GEOG HUM PHIL/SCI 20. PAGE 57 A1165 — BIBLIOG LAW NAT/G ECO/UNDEV

B42
CONOVER H.F.,NEW ZEALAND: A SELECTED LIST OF REFERENCES (PAMPHLET). NEW/ZEALND ECO/UNDEV AGRI INDUS LABOR NAT/G SCHOOL FORCES DIPLOM COLONIAL WAR ...HUM 20. PAGE 29 A0595 — BIBLIOG/A S/ASIA CULTURE

B44
FULLER G.H.,TURKEY: A SELECTED LIST OF REFERENCES. ISLAM TURKEY CULTURE ECO/UNDEV AGRI DIPLOM NAT/LISM CONSERVE...GEOG HUM INT/LAW SOC 7/20 MAPS. PAGE 50 A1024 — BIBLIOG/A ALL/VALS

B49
MARITAIN J.,HUMAN RIGHTS: COMMENTS AND INTERPRETATIONS. COM UNIV WOR+45 LAW CONSTN CULTURE SOCIETY ECO/DEV ECO/UNDEV SCHOOL DELIB/GP EDU/PROP ATTIT PERCEPT ALL/VALS...HUM SOC TREND UNESCO 20. PAGE 95 A1939 — INT/ORG CONCPT

B50
COUNCIL BRITISH NATIONAL BIB,BRITISH NATIONAL BIBLIOGRAPHY. UK AGRI CONSTRUC PERF/ART POL/PAR SECT CREATE INT/TRADE LEAD...HUM JURID PHIL/SCI 20. PAGE 31 A0637 — BIBLIOG/A NAT/G TEC/DEV DIPLOM

B51
MACLAURIN J.,THE UNITED NATIONS AND POWER POLITICS. WOR+45 CONSULT EDU/PROP LEGIT ADJUD EXEC MORAL ORD/FREE...HUM JURID CONCPT RECORD TIME/SEQ UN COLD/WAR 20. PAGE 93 A1896 — INT/ORG ROUTINE

B51
US DEPARTMENT OF STATE,LIVRES AMERICAINS TRADUITS EN FRANCAIS ET LIVRES FRANCAIS SUR LES ETATS-UNIS D'AMERIQUE (2ND ED.). FRANCE USA+45 SECT DIPLOM EDU/PROP LEISURE...ART/METH GEOG HUM 20. PAGE 151 A3086 — BIBLIOG/A SOC

B51
WABEKE B.H.,A GUIDE TO DUTCH BIBLIOGRAPHIES. BELGIUM INDONESIA NETHERLAND DIPLOM INT/TRADE WAR NAT/LISM KNOWL...ART/METH HUM JURID CON/ANAL 14/20. PAGE 160 A3257 — BIBLIOG/A NAT/G CULTURE COLONIAL

B51
WHITE L.C.,INTERNATIONAL NON-GOVERNMENTAL ORGANIZATIONS. AFR ASIA COM EUR+WWI USA+45 WOR+45 INT/ORG DIPLOM INT/TRADE ALL/VALS...HUM FAO ILO EEC 20. PAGE 164 A3337 — VOL/ASSN CONSULT

B53
MENDE T.,WORLD POWER IN THE BALANCE. FUT USA+45 USSR WOR-45 ECO/DEV ECO/TAC INT/TRADE EDU/PROP UTOPIA ATTIT...HUM CONCPT TREND COLD/WAR TOT/POP 20. PAGE 99 A2036 — WOR+45 PWR BAL/PWR

B56
WU E.,LEADERS OF TWENTIETH-CENTURY CHINA; AN ANNOTATED BIBLIOGRAPHY OF SELECTED CHINESE BIOGRAPHICAL WORKS IN HOOVER LIBRARY. ASIA INDUS POL/PAR DIPLOM ADMIN REV WAR...HUM MGT 20. PAGE 168 A3422 — BIBLIOG/A BIOG INTELL CHIEF

B57
ASHER R.E.,THE UNITED NATIONS AND THE PROMOTION OF THE GENERAL WELFARE. WOR+45 WOR-45 ECO/UNDEV EX/STRUC ACT/RES PLAN EDU/PROP ROUTINE HEALTH...HUM CONCPT CHARTS UNESCO UN ILO 20. PAGE 9 A0185 — INT/ORG CONSULT

B58
MACLES L.M.,LES SOURCES DU TRAVAIL BIBLIOGRAPHIQUE — BIBLIOG/A

(3 VOLS.). FRANCE WOR+45 DIPLOM...GEOG PHIL/SCI SOC 20. PAGE 93 A1897 NAT/G HUM

B58
MASON H.L.,TOYNBEE'S APPROACH TO WORLD POLITICS. AFR USA+45 USSR LAW WAR NAT/LISM ALL/IDEOS...HUM BIBLIOG. PAGE 95 A1957 DIPLOM CONCPT PHIL/SCI SECT

B58
SLICK T.,PERMANENT PEACE: A CHECK AND BALANCE PLAN. FUT WOR+45 NAT/G FORCES CREATE PLAN EDU/PROP LEGIT ADJUD COERCE NAT/LISM RIGID/FLEX MORAL...HUM CONCPT METH/CNCPT NEW/IDEA TREND CHARTS TOT/POP 20. PAGE 134 A2742 INT/ORG ORD/FREE PEACE ARMS/CONT

B58
YUAN TUNG-LI,CHINA IN WESTERN LITERATURE. SECT DIPLOM...ART/METH GEOG JURID SOC BIOG CON/ANAL. PAGE 169 A3440 BIBLIOG ASIA CULTURE HUM

B59
SWIFT R.W.,WORLD AFFAIRS AND THE COLLEGE CURRICULUM. USA+45 PLAN EFFICIENCY PERCEPT...HUM METH/CNCPT. PAGE 140 A2871 ACADEM DIPLOM METH/COMP EDU/PROP

B60
ARMS CONTROL. FUT UNIV WOR+45 INTELL R+D INT/ORG NAT/G VOL/ASSN CONSULT CREATE EDU/PROP PEACE...HUM GEN/LAWS TOT/POP 20. PAGE 3 A0060 DELIB/GP ORD/FREE ARMS/CONT NUC/PWR

B60
CENTRAL ASIAN RESEARCH CENTRE,RUSSIA LOOKS AT AFRICA (PAMPHLET). AFR USSR COLONIAL RACE/REL...HUM 19/20 STALIN/J. PAGE 25 A0511 BIBLIOG MARXISM TREND DIPLOM

B60
EINSTEIN A.,EINSTEIN ON PEACE. FUT WOR+45 WOR-45 SOCIETY NAT/G PLAN BAL/PWR CAP/ISM DIPLOM ARMS/CONT DETER NAT/LISM...POLICY RELATIV HUM PHIL/SCI CONCPT BIOG COLD/WAR LEAGUE/NAT NAZI. PAGE 41 A0829 INT/ORG ATTIT NUC/PWR PEACE

B60
THOMPSON K.W.,POLITICAL REALISM AND THE CRISIS IN WORLD POLITICS. USA+45 USA-45 SOCIETY INT/ORG NAT/G LEGIS TOP/EX LEGIT DETER ATTIT ORD/FREE PWR ...GEN/LAWS TOT/POP 20. PAGE 143 A2931 PLAN HUM BAL/PWR DIPLOM

S60
SCHWELB E.,"INTERNATIONAL CONVENTIONS ON HUMAN RIGHTS." FUT WOR+45 LAW CONSTN CULTURE SOCIETY STRUCT VOL/ASSN DELIB/GP PLAN ADJUD SUPEGO LOVE MORAL...SOC CONCPT STAT RECORD HIST/WRIT TREND 20 UN. PAGE 130 A2664 INT/ORG HUM

B61
SHARP W.R.,FIELD ADMINISTRATION IN THE UNITED NATION SYSTEM: THE CONDUCT OF INTERNATIONAL ECONOMIC AND SOCIAL PROGRAMS. FUT WOR+45 CONSTN SOCIETY ECO/UNDEV R+D DELIB/GP ACT/RES PLAN TEC/DEV EDU/PROP EXEC ROUTINE HEALTH WEALTH...HUM CONCPT CHARTS METH ILO UNESCO VAL/FREE UN 20. PAGE 132 A2697 INT/ORG CONSULT

B61
YUAN TUNG-LI,A GUIDE TO DOCTORAL DISSERTATIONS BY CHINESE STUDENTS IN AMERICA, 1905-1960. ASIA CULTURE SOCIETY ECO/UNDEV NAT/G PROB/SOLV DIPLOM LEAD ATTIT...HUM SOC STAT 20. PAGE 169 A3441 BIBLIOG ACADEM ACT/RES OP/RES

B61
ZIMMERMAN I.,A GUIDE TO CURRENT LATIN AMERICAN PERIODICALS: HUMANITIES AND SOCIAL SCIENCES. LABOR SECT EDU/PROP...GEOG HUM SOC LING STAT NAT/COMP 20. PAGE 170 A3452 BIBLIOG/A DIPLOM L/A+17C PHIL/SCI

B62
COLLISON R.L.,BIBLIOGRAPHIES, SUBJECT AND NATIONAL: A GUIDE TO THEIR CONTENTS, ARRANGEMENT, AND USE (2ND REV. ED.). SECT DIPLOM...ART/METH GEOG HUM PHIL/SCI SOC MATH BIOG 20. PAGE 28 A0569 BIBLIOG/A CON/ANAL BIBLIOG

B62
NEAL F.W.,WAR AND PEACE AND GERMANY. EUR+WWI USSR STRUCT INT/ORG NAT/G FORCES DOMIN EDU/PROP LEGIT EXEC COERCE ORD/FREE...HUM SOC NEW/IDEA OBS TIME/SEQ TOT/POP COLD/WAR 20 BERLIN. PAGE 108 A2208 USA+45 POLICY DIPLOM GERMANY

B62
UNESCO,GENERAL CATALOGUE OF UNESCO PUBLICATIONS AND UNESCO SPONSORED PUBLICATIONS, 1946-1959. WOR+45 ...POLICY ART/METH HUM PHIL/SCI UN. PAGE 148 A3022 BIBLIOG INT/ORG ECO/UNDEV SOC

B62
US LIBRARY OF CONGRESS,UNITED STATES AND CANADIAN PUBLICATIONS ON AFRICA IN 1960. CANADA USA+45 CULTURE TEC/DEV DIPLOM FOR/AID RACE/REL...GEOG HUM SOC SOC/WK LING 20. PAGE 155 A3156 BIBLIOG/A AFR

L62
WILCOX F.O.,"THE UN AND THE NON-ALIGNED NATIONS." AFR S/ASIA USA+45 ECO/UNDEV INT/ORG TEC/DEV EDU/PROP RIGID/FLEX ORD/FREE PWR...POLICY HUM CONCPT STAT OBS TIME/SEQ STERTYP GEN/METH UN 20. PAGE 164 A3345 ATTIT TREND

S62
BELSHAW C.,"TRAINING AND RECRUITMENT: SOME PRINCIPLES OF INTERNATIONAL AID." FUT WOR+45 SOCIETY INT/ORG NAT/G CREATE PLAN TEC/DEV ECO/TAC FOR/AID EDU/PROP ATTIT PERCEPT...HUM UN FAO ILO UNESCO 20. PAGE 13 A0263 VOL/ASSN ECO/UNDEV

B63
STEVENSON A.E.,LOOKING OUTWARD: YEARS OF CRISIS AT THE UNITED NATIONS. COM CUBA USA+45 WOR+45 SOCIETY NAT/G EX/STRUC ACT/RES LEGIT COLONIAL ATTIT PERSON SUPEGO ALL/VALS...POLICY HUM UN COLD/WAR CONGO 20. PAGE 138 A2823 INT/ORG CONCPT ARMS/CONT

S63
CHAKRAVARTI P.C.,"INDIAN NON-ALIGNMENT AND UNITED STATES POLICY." ASIA INDIA S/ASIA USA+45 CULTURE ECO/UNDEV NAT/G VOL/ASSN DELIB/GP TOP/EX FOR/AID NEUTRAL...POLICY HUM CONCPT RECORD GEN/LAWS 20. PAGE 25 A0515 ATTIT ALL/VALS COLONIAL DIPLOM

S63
HUMPHREY H.H.,"REGIONAL ARMS CONTROL AGREEMENTS." WOR+45 FORCES PLAN LEGIT COERCE ATTIT HEALTH ORD/FREE...HUM METH/CNCPT MYTH OBS INT TREND TOT/POP 20. PAGE 69 A1416 L/A+17C INT/ORG ARMS/CONT REGION

S63
LOPEZIBOR J.,"L'EUROPE, FORME DE VIE." CHRIST-17C EUR+WWI FUT MOD/EUR SOCIETY INT/ORG SECT EDU/PROP ATTIT RIGID/FLEX ALL/VALS...POLICY HUM SOC TIME/SEQ TREND GEN/LAWS. PAGE 91 A1862 NAT/G CULTURE

B64
GRODZINS M.,THE ATOMIC AGE: FORTY-FIVE SCIENTISTS AND SCHOLARS SPEAK ON NATIONAL AND WORLD AFFAIRS. FUT USA+45 WOR+45 R+D INT/ORG NAT/G CONSULT TEC/DEV EDU/PROP ATTIT PERSON ORD/FREE...HUM CONCPT TIME/SEQ CON/ANAL. PAGE 57 A1169 INTELL ARMS/CONT NUC/PWR

B64
REMAK J.,THE GENTLE CRITIC: THEODOR FONTANE AND GERMAN POLITICS, 1848-1898. GERMANY PRUSSIA CULTURE ELITES BAL/PWR DIPLOM WRITING GOV/REL...HUM BIOG 19 BISMARCK/O JUNKER FONTANE/T. PAGE 120 A2465 PERSON SOCIETY WORKER CHIEF

B64
TREADGOLD D.W.,THE DEVELOPMENT OF THE USSR. COM USSR ECO/DEV CREATE BAL/PWR DEBATE COLONIAL TOTALISM...HUM ANTHOL BIBLIOG 19/20. PAGE 145 A2960 MARXISM CONSERVE DIPLOM DOMIN

B64
TURNER M.C.,LIBROS EN VENTA EN HISPANOAMERICA Y ESPANA. SPAIN LAW CONSTN CULTURE ADMIN LEAD...HUM SOC 20. PAGE 146 A2983 BIBLIOG L/A+17C NAT/G DIPLOM

B64
UN PUB. INFORM. ORGAN.,EVERY MAN'S UNITED NATIONS. UNIV WOR+45 CONSTN CULTURE SOCIETY ECO/DEV ECO/UNDEV NAT/G ACT/RES PLAN ECO/TAC INT/TRADE EDU/PROP LEGIT PEACE ATTIT ALL/VALS...POLICY HUM INT/LAW CONCPT CHARTS UN TOT/POP 20. PAGE 147 A3004 INT/ORG ROUTINE

S64
HICKEY D.,"THE PHILOSOPHICAL ARGUMENT FOR WORLD GOVERNMENT." WOR+45 SOCIETY ACT/RES PLAN LEGIT ADJUD PEACE PERCEPT PERSON ORD/FREE...HUM JURID PHIL/SCI METH/CNCPT CON/ANAL STERTYP GEN/LAWS TOT/POP 20. PAGE 65 A1327 FUT INT/ORG

S65
DOSSICK J.J.,"DOCTORAL DISSERTATIONS ON RUSSIA, THE SOVIET UNION, AND EASTERN EUROPE." USSR ACADEM DIPLOM EDU/PROP MARXISM 19/20 COLD/WAR. PAGE 38 A0775 BIBLIOG HUM SOC

B66
HOFMANN L.,UNITED STATES AND CANADIAN PUBLICATIONS ON AFRICA IN 1964. LAW AGRI INDUS SCHOOL...HUM SOC 20. PAGE 66 A1360 BIBLIOG AFR DIPLOM

B82
POOLE W.F.,INDEX TO PERIODICAL LITERATURE. LOC/G NAT/G DIPLOM ADMIN...HUM PHIL/SCI SOC 19. PAGE 117 A2396 BIBLIOG USA-45 ALL/VALS SOCIETY

HUM/RIGHTS....HUMAN RIGHTS, DECLARATIONS OF HUMAN RIGHTS, AND HUMAN RIGHTS COMMISSIONS (OFFICIAL ORGANIZATIONS)

HUMAN NATURE....SEE PERSON

HUMAN RELATIONS....SEE RELATIONS INDEX

HUMAN RIGHTS, DECLARATIONS OF HUMAN RIGHTS, AND HUMAN RIGHTS COMMISSIONS (OFFICIAL ORGANIZATIONS)....SEE HUM/RIGHTS

HUMANISM....HUMANISM AND HUMANISTS

HUMANITARIANISM....SEE HUMANISM

HUMANITIES....SEE HUM

HUME/D....DAVID HUME

HUMPHREY D.D. A1415

HUMPHREY H.H. A1416

HUMPHREY/H....HUBERT HORATIO HUMPHREY

HUMPHREYS R.A. A1417

HUNGARY....SEE ALSO COM

N
KYRIAK T.E.,EAST EUROPE: BIBLIOGRAPHY--INDEX TO US JPRS RESEARCH TRANSLATIONS. ALBANIA BULGARIA COM CZECHOSLVK HUNGARY POLAND ROMANIA AGRI EXTR/IND FINAN SERV/IND INT/TRADE WEAPON...GEOG MGT SOC 20. PAGE 83 A1701 — BIBLIOG/A PRESS MARXISM INDUS

B57
BRODY H.,UN DIARY: THE SEARCH FOR PEACE. HUNGARY WOR+45 DELIB/GP ROUTINE REV WAR ORD/FREE...AUD/VIS 20 UN SUEZ. PAGE 19 A0382 — INT/ORG PEACE DIPLOM POLICY

B59
ETSCHMANN R.,DIE WAHRUNGS- UND DEVISENPOLITIK DES OSTBLOCKS UND IHRE AUSWIRKUNGEN AUF DIE WIRTSCHAFTSBEZIEHUNGEN ZWISCHEN OST U WEST. BULGARIA CZECHOSLVK HUNGARY POLAND USSR MARKET NAT/G PLAN DIPLOM...NAT/COMP 20. PAGE 42 A0867 — ECO/TAC FINAN POLICY INT/TRADE

B59
GOLDWIN R.A.,READINGS IN RUSSIAN FOREIGN POLICY. HUNGARY USSR YUGOSLAVIA ELITES INT/ORG NAT/G REV WAR NAT/LISM PERSON SOCISM...CHARTS 20 MAPS BOLSHEVISM. PAGE 53 A1095 — COM MARXISM DIPLOM POLICY

B60
SZTARAY Z.,BIBLIOGRAPHY ON HUNGARY. HUNGARY MOD/EUR CULTURE INDUS SECT DIPLOM REV...ART/METH SOC LING 18/20. PAGE 141 A2879 — BIBLIOG NAT/G COM MARXISM

B61
FLEMING D.F.,THE COLD WAR AND ITS ORIGINS: 1950-1960 (VOL. II). ASIA FUT HUNGARY POLAND WOR+45 TEC/DEV DOMIN NUC/PWR REV PEACE...T 20 COLD/WAR EISNHWR/DD SUEZ. PAGE 46 A0946 — MARXISM DIPLOM BAL/PWR

B61
SCHIEDER T.,DOCUMENTS ON THE EXPULSION OF THE GERMANS FROM EASTERN-CENTRAL-EUROPE (VOL. II/III). COM EUR+WWI GERMANY HUNGARY ROMANIA USSR DIPLOM RACE/REL 20 MIGRATION. PAGE 128 A2625 — GEOG CULTURE

S62
BROWN B.E.,"L'ONU ABANDONNE LA HONGRIE." COM USSR WOR+45 CONSTN NAT/G POL/PAR DELIB/GP ACT/RES TEC/DEV PWR...TIME/SEQ 20 UN. PAGE 20 A0400 — INT/ORG TOTALISM HUNGARY POLICY

B63
HALASZ DE BEKY I.L.,A BIBLIOGRAPHY OF THE HUNGARIAN REVOLUTION 1956. COM HUNGARY USSR DIPLOM COERCE MARXISM...POLICY AUD/VIS 20 UN COLD/WAR. PAGE 59 A1221 — BIBLIOG REV FORCES ATTIT

S63
GIRAUD E.,"L'INTERDICTION DU RECOURS A LA FORCE, LA THEORIE ET LA PRATIQUE DES NATIONS UNIES." ALGERIA COM CUBA HUNGARY WOR+45 ADJUD TOTALISM ATTIT RIGID/FLEX PWR...POLICY JURID CONCPT UN 20 CONGO. PAGE 53 A1077 — INT/ORG FORCES DIPLOM

N63
LIBRARY HUNGARIAN ACADEMY SCI,HUNGARIAN PUBLICATIONS ON ASIA AND AFRICA, 1950-1962: A SELECTED BIBLIOGRAPHY (PAMPHLET). AFR ASIA HUNGARY S/ASIA ECO/UNDEV NAT/G EDU/PROP ATTIT 20 UNESCO. PAGE 88 A1807 — BIBLIOG REGION DIPLOM WRITING

S65
HELMREICH E.C.,"KADAR'S HUNGARY." COM EUR+WWI HUNGARY USSR INTELL ECO/DEV AGRI INT/ORG TOP/EX DOMIN ALL/VALS WORK COLD/WAR 20. PAGE 64 A1311 — NAT/G RIGID/FLEX TOTALISM

B66
BROWN J.F.,THE NEW EASTERN EUROPE. ALBANIA BULGARIA HUNGARY POLAND ROMANIA CULTURE AGRI POL/PAR WAR NAT/LISM MARXISM...CHARTS BIBLIOG 20. PAGE 20 A0404 — DIPLOM COM NAT/G ECO/UNDEV

B66
SPULBER N.,THE STATE AND ECONOMIC DEVELOPMENT IN EASTERN EUROPE. BULGARIA COM CZECHOSLVK HUNGARY POLAND YUGOSLAVIA CULTURE PLAN CAP/ISM INT/TRADE CONTROL...POLICY CHARTS METH/COMP BIBLIOG/A 19/20. PAGE 136 A2793 — ECO/DEV ECO/UNDEV NAT/G TOTALISM

B96
LOWELL A.L.,GOVERNMENTS AND PARTIES IN CONTINENTAL EUROPE, VOL. II. AUSTRIA GERMANY HUNGARY MOD/EUR SWITZERLND SOCIETY EX/STRUC LEGIS DIPLOM AGREE LEAD PARL/PROC PWR...POLICY 19. PAGE 91 A1867 — POL/PAR NAT/G GOV/REL ELITES

HUNT B.I. A1418

HUNTINGTON S.P. A1419

HUNTNGTN/S....SAMUEL P. HUNTINGTON

HUNTON/P....PHILIP HUNTON

HURLEY/PJ....PATRICK J. HURLEY

HURST C. A1420

HUSS P.J. A1421

HUSSEIN....KING HUSSEIN I, KING OF JORDAN

HUSSEY R.D. A0445

HUSSEY W.D. A1422

HUTCHINS/R....ROBERT HUTCHINS

HUTCHINSON E.C. A1423

HUTTENBACK R.A. A1424,A1425

HYDE C.C. A1426

HYDE D. A1427

HYDE L.K.G. A1428

HYPO/EXP....INTELLECTUAL CONSTRUCTS

B00
LORIMER J.,THE INSTITUTES OF THE LAW OF NATIONS. WOR-45 CULTURE SOCIETY NAT/G VOL/ASSN DIPLOM LEGIT WAR PEACE DRIVE ORD/FREE SOVEREIGN...CONCPT RECORD INT TREND HYPO/EXP GEN/METH TOT/POP VAL/FREE 20. PAGE 91 A1863 — INT/ORG LAW INT/LAW

L39
NEARING S.,"A WARLESS WORLD." FUT WOR-45 SOCIETY INT/ORG NAT/G EX/STRUC PLAN DOMIN WAR ATTIT DRIVE PWR...POLICY PSY CONCPT OBS TREND HYPO/EXP MARX/KARL 20 MARX/KARL LENIN/VI. PAGE 108 A2210 — COERCE PEACE

B48
GRAHAM F.D.,THE THEORY OF INTERNATIONAL VALUES. FUT WOR+45 WOR-45 ECO/DEV FINAN INT/ORG PLAN TEC/DEV CAP/ISM DIPLOM ECO/TAC TARIFFS ROUTINE BAL/PAY DRIVE PWR WEALTH SOCISM...POLICY STAT HYPO/EXP GEN/LAWS 20. PAGE 55 A1125 — NEW/IDEA INT/TRADE

L52
HILSMAN R. JR.,"INTELLIGENCE AND POLICY MAKING IN FOREIGN AFFAIRS." USA+45 CONSULT ACT/RES DIPLOM EDU/PROP ROUTINE PEACE PERCEPT PWR SKILL...POLICY MGT HYPO/EXP CONGRESS 20 CIA. PAGE 65 A1333 — PROF/ORG SIMUL WAR

B53
COUSINS N.,WHO SPEAKS FOR MAN. GERMANY KOREA WOR+45 SOCIETY INT/ORG NAT/G CREATE EDU/PROP HEALTH KNOWL LOVE MORAL...OBS SELF/OBS BIOG HYPO/EXP TOT/POP 20 CHINJAP. PAGE 32 A0642 — ATTIT WAR PEACE

B54
MANNING C.A.W.,THE UNIVERSITY TEACHING OF SOCIAL SCIENCES: INTERNATIONAL RELATIONS. WOR+45 INTELL STRATA R+D ACADEM INT/ORG NAT/G CONSULT DELIB/GP ACT/RES EDU/PROP NAT/LISM ATTIT...POLICY CONT/OBS HYPO/EXP VAL/FREE LEAGUE/NAT UNESCO 20. PAGE 94 A1925 — KNOWL PHIL/SCI DIPLOM

S57
SCHELLING T.C.,"BARGAINING COMMUNICATION, AND LIMITED WAR." UNIV WOR+45 FACE/GP INT/ORG NAT/G FORCES ACT/RES WAR PERCEPT ALL/VALS...PSY OBS PROJ/TEST CHARTS HYPO/EXP GEN/LAWS TOT/POP 20. PAGE 128 A2622 — ROUTINE DECISION

B59
GREENSPAN M.,THE MODERN LAW OF LAND WARFARE. WOR+45 INT/ORG NAT/G DELIB/GP FORCES ATTIT...POLICY HYPO/EXP STERTYP 20. PAGE 56 A1142 — ADJUD PWR WAR

B59
MATHISEN T.,METHODOLOGY IN THE STUDY OF INTERNATIONAL RELATIONS. FUT WOR+45 SOCIETY INT/ORG NAT/G POL/PAR WAR PEACE KNOWL PWR...RELATIV CONCPT METH/CNCPT TREND HYPO/EXP METH TOT/POP 20. PAGE 96 A1965 — GEN/METH CON/ANAL DIPLOM CREATE

L59
KAPLAN M.A.,"SOME PROBLEMS IN THE STRATEGIC ANALYSIS OF INTERNATIONAL POLITICS." UNIV R+D INT/ORG CREATE PLAN DIPLOM EDU/PROP COERCE DISPL PWR...METH/CNCPT NEW/IDEA HYPO/EXP TOT/POP 20. PAGE 76 A1561 — DECISION BAL/PWR

S59
BOULDING K.E.,"NATIONAL IMAGES AND INTERNATIONAL SYSTEMS." FUT WOR+45 CULTURE INT/ORG TOP/EX ROUTINE ...METH/CNCPT MYTH CONT/OBS TREND HYPO/EXP GEN/METH TOT/POP 20. PAGE 17 A0346 — NAT/G DIPLOM

B60
CONN S.,THE FRAMEWORK OF HEMISPHERE DEFENSE. CANADA L/A+17C USA-45 NAT/G FORCES BAL/PWR DOMIN WAR PEACE DISPL PWR RESPECT...PLURIST CONCPT HIST/WRIT HYPO/EXP MEXIC/AMER 20 ROOSEVLT/F. PAGE 29 A0585 — USA+45 INT/ORG DIPLOM

B60
LANDHEER B.,ETHICAL VALUES IN INTERNATIONAL — HYPO/EXP

DECISION-MAKING. FUT LAW SOCIETY INT/ORG NAT/G DELIB/GP CREATE NAT/LISM ATTIT PERSON...DECISION CONCPT LEAGUE/NAT TOT/POP 20. PAGE 84 A1718 POLICY PEACE

S60
OSGOOD C.E.,"COGNITIVE DYNAMICS IN THE CONDUCT OF HUMAN AFFAIRS." USA+45 INTELL INT/ORG CONSULT PLAN ATTIT PERSON...PSY CHARTS HYPO/EXP 20. PAGE 112 A2299 R+D SOCIETY

S60
RHYNE C.S.,"LAW AS AN INSTRUMENT FOR PEACE." FUT WOR+45 PLAN LEGIT ROUTINE ARMS/CONT NUC/PWR ATTIT ORD/FREE...JURID METH/CNCPT TREND CON/ANAL HYPO/EXP COLD/WAR 20. PAGE 120 A2471 ADJUD EDU/PROP INT/LAW PEACE

B61
GALLOIS P.,THE BALANCE OF TERROR: STRATEGY FOR THE NUCLEAR AGE. FUT WOR+45 INT/ORG FORCES TOP/EX DETER WAR ATTIT RIGID/FLEX ORD/FREE PWR...HYPO/EXP 20. PAGE 50 A1032 PLAN DECISION DIPLOM NUC/PWR

B61
ROSENAU J.N.,INTERNATIONAL POLITICS AND FOREIGN POLICY: A READER IN RESEARCH AND THEORY. ELITES ATTIT SOVEREIGN...DECISION CHARTS HYPO/EXP GAME SIMUL ANTHOL BIBLIOG METH 20. PAGE 124 A2531 ACT/RES DIPLOM CONCPT POLICY

B61
SCHMIDT H.,VERTEIDIGUNG ODER VERGELTUNG. COM CUBA GERMANY/W USSR FORCES DIPLOM ARMS/CONT DETER NUC/PWR...POLICY CHARTS HYPO/EXP SIMUL BIBLIOG 20 NATO COLD/WAR. PAGE 128 A2630 PLAN WAR BAL/PWR ORD/FREE

S61
SINGER J.D.,"THE LEVEL OF ANALYSIS: PROBLEMS IN INTERNATIONAL RELATIONS." FUT INTELL R+D INT/ORG CREATE EDU/PROP...METH/CNCPT HYPO/EXP GEN/METH METH VAL/FREE. PAGE 133 A2725 SOCIETY SOC DIPLOM

B62
BOULDING K.E.,CONFLICT AND DEFENSE: A GENERAL THEORY. FUT SOCIETY INT/ORG NAT/G CREATE BAL/PWR COERCE NAT/LISM DRIVE ALL/VALS...PLURIST DECISION CONCPT METH/CNCPT TREND HYPO/EXP TOT/POP 20. PAGE 17 A0347 MATH SIMUL PEACE WAR

B62
MANNING C.A.W.,THE NATURE OF INTERNATIONAL SOCIETY. FUT LAW NAT/G TOP/EX NAT/LISM PEACE PERCEPT PERSON ALL/VALS PLURISM...METH/CNCPT MYTH HYPO/EXP TOT/POP 20. PAGE 94 A1926 INT/ORG SOCIETY SIMUL DIPLOM

B62
YALEN R.,REGIONALISM AND WORLD ORDER. EUR+WWI WOR+45 WOR-45 INT/ORG VOL/ASSN DELIB/GP FORCES TOP/EX BAL/PWR DIPLOM DOMIN REGION ARMS/CONT PWR ...JURID HYPO/EXP COLD/WAR 20. PAGE 168 A3427 ORD/FREE POLICY

S62
PYE L.W.,"THE POLITICAL IMPULSES AND FANTASIES BEHIND FOREIGN AID." FUT USA+45 ECO/UNDEV DIPLOM ECO/TAC ROUTINE DRIVE KNOWL...SOC METH/CNCPT NEW/IDEA TREND HYPO/EXP STERTYP GEN/METH 20. PAGE 118 A2420 ACT/RES ATTIT FOR/AID

S63
PINCUS J.,"THE COST OF FOREIGN AID." WOR+45 ECO/DEV FINAN NAT/G VOL/ASSN CREATE ECO/TAC EDU/PROP WEALTH ...METH/CNCPT STAT CHARTS HYPO/EXP TOT/POP VAL/FREE 20. PAGE 116 A2380 USA+45 ECO/UNDEV FOR/AID

S63
STANLEY T.W.,"DECENTRALIZING NUCLEAR CONTROL IN NATO." EUR+WWI USA+45 ELITES FORCES ACT/RES ATTIT ORD/FREE PWR...NEW/IDEA HYPO/EXP TOT/POP 20 NATO. PAGE 137 A2805 INT/ORG EX/STRUC NUC/PWR

B64
HARRISON H.V.,THE ROLE OF THEORY IN INTERNATIONAL RELATIONS. UNIV WOR+45 R+D INT/ORG NAT/G PERCEPT KNOWL...DECISION CONCPT GEN/METH METH 20. PAGE 62 A1270 METH/CNCPT HYPO/EXP DIPLOM

B64
JACOB P.E.,THE INTEGRATION OF POLITICAL COMMUNITIES. USA+45 WOR+45 CULTURE LOC/G MUNIC NAT/G CREATE PLAN LEGIT REGION COERCE ALL/VALS ...POLICY GEOG PSY SOC TREND HYPO/EXP GEN/LAWS VAL/FREE 20. PAGE 72 A1483 INT/ORG METH/CNCPT SIMUL STAT

B64
SINGER H.W.,INTERNATIONAL DEVELOPMENT: GROWTH AND CHANGE. AFR BRAZIL L/A+17C WOR+45 CULTURE AGRI INDUS NAT/G ACT/RES ECO/TAC EDU/PROP WEALTH...GEOG CONCPT METH/CNCPT STAT HYPO/EXP WORK TOT/POP 20. PAGE 133 A2723 FINAN ECO/UNDEV FOR/AID INT/TRADE

B66
KUENNE R.E.,THE POLARIS MISSILE STRIKE* A GENERAL ECONOMIC SYSTEMS ANALYSIS. USA+45 USSR NAT/G BAL/PWR ARMS/CONT WAR...MATH PROBABIL COMPUT/IR CHARTS HYPO/EXP SIMUL. PAGE 82 A1689 NUC/PWR FORCES DETER DIPLOM

B66
RIESELBACH L.N.,THE ROOTS OF ISOLATIONISM* CONGRESSIONAL VOTING AND PRESIDENTIAL LEADERSHIP IN FOREIGN POLICY. POL/PAR LEGIS DIPLOM EDU/PROP LEAD REGION REPRESENT...SOC STAT IDEA/COMP HYPO/EXP BIBLIOG 19/20 CONGRESS. PAGE 121 A2477 ISOLAT CHOOSE CHIEF POLICY

HYPOTHETICAL EXPERIMENTS....SEE HYPO/EXP

HYVARINEN R. A1429

IADB....INTER-ASIAN DEVELOPMENT BANK

IAEA....INTERNATIONAL ATOMIC ENERGY AGENCY

S59
STOESSINGER J.G.,"THE INTERNATIONAL ATOMIC ENERGY AGENCY: THE FIRST PHASE." FUT WOR+45 NAT/G VOL/ASSN DELIB/GP BAL/PWR LEGIT ADMIN ROUTINE PWR...OBS CON/ANAL GEN/LAWS VAL/FREE 20 IAEA. PAGE 138 A2829 INT/ORG ECO/DEV FOR/AID NUC/PWR

B65
US CONGRESS JT ATOM ENRGY COMM,ATOMIC ENERGY LEGISLATION THROUGH 89TH CONGRESS, 1ST SESSION. USA+45 LAW INT/ORG DELIB/GP BUDGET DIPLOM 20 AEC CONGRESS CASEBOOK EURATOM IAEA. PAGE 150 A3071 NUC/PWR FORCES PEACE LEGIS

IBERO-AMERICAN INSTITUTES A1430

IBO....IBO TRIBE

IBRD....INTERNATIONAL BANK FOR RECONSTRUCTION AND DEVELOPMENT

B63
INTERNATIONAL BANK RECONST DEV,THE WORLD BANK GROUP IN ASIA. ASIA S/ASIA INDUS TEC/DEV ECO/TAC...RECORD 20 IBRD WORLD/BANK. PAGE 71 A1451 INT/ORG DIPLOM ECO/UNDEV FINAN

B66
MEERHAEGHE M.,INTERNATIONAL ECONOMIC INSTITUTIONS. EUR+WWI FINAN INDUS MARKET PLAN TARIFFS BAL/PAY EQUILIB...POLICY BIBLIOG/A 20 GATT OEEC EEC IBRD EURCOALSTL. PAGE 99 A2032 ECO/TAC ECO/DEV INT/TRADE INT/ORG

ICA....INTERNATIONAL COOPERATION ADMINISTRATION

B61
ROBINSON M.E.,EDUCATION FOR SOCIAL CHANGE: ESTABLISHING INSTITUTES OF PUBLIC AND BUSINESS ADMINISTRATION ABROAD (PAMPHLET). WOR+45 SOCIETY ACADEM CONFER INGP/REL ROLE...SOC CHARTS BIBLIOG 20 ICA. PAGE 122 A2506 FOR/AID EDU/PROP MGT ADJUST

ICC....U.S. INTERSTATE COMMERCE COMMISSION

ICELAND....ICELAND

B53
ORFIELD L.B.,THE GROWTH OF SCANDINAVIAN LAW. DENMARK ICELAND NORWAY SWEDEN LAW DIPLOM...BIBLIOG 9/20. PAGE 112 A2296 JURID CT/SYS NAT/G

C65
WUORINEN J.H.,"SCANDINAVIA." DENMARK FINLAND ICELAND NORWAY SWEDEN SOCIETY AGRI POL/PAR DELIB/GP DIPLOM INT/TRADE NEUTRAL WAR...CHARTS TREATY 20. PAGE 168 A3423 BIBLIOG NAT/G POLICY

ICHHEISER G. A1431

ICJ....INTERNATIONAL COURT OF JUSTICE; SEE ALSO WORLD/CT

L25
HUDSON M.,"THE PERMANENT COURT OF INTERNATIONAL JUSTICE AND THE QUESTION OF AMERICAN PARTICIPATION." WOR-45 LEGIT CT/SYS ORD/FREE ...JURID CONCPT TIME/SEQ GEN/LAWS VAL/FREE 20 ICJ. PAGE 68 A1406 INT/ORG ADJUD DIPLOM INT/LAW

B28
HOWARD-ELLIS C.,THE ORIGIN, STRUCTURE AND WORKING OF THE LEAGUE OF NATIONS. EUR+WWI MOD/EUR USA-45 CONSTN FORCES LEGIS ECO/TAC LEGIT COERCE ORD/FREE ...JURID SOC CONCPT LEAGUE/NAT 20 ILO ICJ. PAGE 68 A1401 INT/ORG ADJUD

B47
INTERNATIONAL COURT OF JUSTICE,CHARTER OF THE UNITED NATIONS, STATUTE AND RULES OF COURT AND OTHER CONSTITUTIONAL DOCUMENTS. SWITZERLND LAW ADJUD INGP/REL...JURID 20 ICJ UN. PAGE 71 A1453 INT/LAW INT/ORG CT/SYS DIPLOM

L51
LISSITZYN O.J.,"THE INTERNATIONAL COURT OF JUSTICE." WOR+45 INT/ORG LEGIT ORD/FREE...CONCPT TIME/SEQ TREND GEN/LAWS VAL/FREE 20 ICJ. PAGE 90 A1839 ADJUD JURID INT/LAW

B57
ROSENNE S.,THE INTERNATIONAL COURT OF JUSTICE. WOR+45 LAW DOMIN LEGIT PEACE PWR SOVEREIGN...JURID CONCPT RECORD TIME/SEQ CON/ANAL CHARTS UN TOT/POP VAL/FREE LEAGUE/NAT 20 ICJ. PAGE 124 A2537 INT/ORG CT/SYS INT/LAW

B61
ANAND R.P.,COMPULSORY JURISDICTION OF INTERNATIONAL COURT OF JUSTICE. FUT WOR+45 SOCIETY PLAN LEGIT ADJUD ATTIT DRIVE PERSON ORD/FREE...JURID CONCPT TREND 20 ICJ. PAGE 8 A0156 INT/ORG COERCE INT/LAW

ICSU....INTERNATIONAL COUNCIL OF SCIENTIFIC UNIONS

IDEA/COMP....COMPARISON OF IDEAS

N
IMF AND IBRD, JOINT LIBRARY, LIST OF RECENT ADDITIONS. WOR+45 ECO/DEV ECO/UNDEV BUDGET FOR/AID RATION...CONCPT IDEA/COMP. PAGE 70 A1434
BIBLIOG INT/ORG INT/TRADE FINAN

N
IMF AND IBRD, JOINT LIBRARY, LIST OF RECENT PERIODICAL ARTICLES. WOR+45 ECO/DEV ECO/UNDEV BUDGET FOR/AID RATION...CONCPT IDEA/COMP. PAGE 70 A1435
BIBLIOG INT/ORG INT/TRADE FINAN

N
UNESCO, INTERNATIONAL BIBLIOGRAPHY OF POLITICAL SCIENCE (VOLUMES 1-8). WOR+45 LAW NAT/G EX/STRUC LEGIS PROB/SOLV DIPLOM ADMIN GOV/REL 20 UNESCO. PAGE 147 A3010
BIBLIOG CONCPT IDEA/COMP

B15
INTERNATIONAL LAW ASSOCIATION, A FORTY YEARS' CATALOGUE OF THE BOOKS, PAMPHLETS AND PAPERS IN THE LIBRARY OF THE INTERNATIONAL LAW ASSOCIATION. INT/ORG DIPLOM ADJUD NEUTRAL...IDEA/COMP 19/20. PAGE 71 A1458
BIBLIOG LAW INT/LAW

N17
BURKE E., THOUGHTS ON THE PROSPECT OF A REGICIDE PEACE (PAMPHLET). FRANCE UK SECT DOMIN MURDER PEACE ORD/FREE SOVEREIGN POPULISM...POLICY GOV/COMP IDEA/COMP 18 JACOBINISM COEXIST. PAGE 21 A0435
REV CHIEF NAT/G DIPLOM

B20
VINOGRADOFF P., OUTLINES OF HISTORICAL JURISPRUDENCE (2 VOLS.). GREECE MEDIT-7 LAW CONSTN FACE/GP FAM KIN MUNIC CRIME OWN...INT/LAW IDEA/COMP BIBLIOG. PAGE 159 A3241
JURID METH

B24
NAVILLE A., LIBERTE, EGALITE, SOLIDARITE: ESSAIS D'ANALYSE. STRATA FAM VOL/ASSN INT/TRADE GP/REL MORAL MARXISM SOCISM...PSY TREATY. PAGE 107 A2205
ORD/FREE SOC IDEA/COMP DIPLOM

B27
GOOCH G.P., ENGLISH DEMOCRATIC IDEAS IN THE SEVENTEENTH CENTURY (2ND ED.). UK LAW SECT FORCES DIPLOM LEAD PARL/PROC REV ATTIT AUTHORIT...ANARCH CONCPT 17 PARLIAMENT CMN/WLTH REFORMERS. PAGE 54 A1100
IDEA/COMP MAJORIT EX/STRUC CONSERVE

B28
PLAYNE C.E., THE PRE-WAR MIND IN BRITAIN. GERMANY MOD/EUR UK STRATA SECT DIPLOM EDU/PROP CROWD SUFF ...POLICY ANARCH PSY SOC IDEA/COMP 20 WWI. PAGE 116 A2388
PRESS WAR DOMIN ATTIT

C28
WARD P.W., "SOVEREIGNTY: A STUDY OF A CONTEMPORARY POLITICAL NOTION." CONSTN NAT/G DIPLOM REPRESENT PLURISM...IDEA/COMP BIBLIOG. PAGE 161 A3281
SOVEREIGN CONCPT NAT/LISM

B29
STURZO L., THE INTERNATIONAL COMMUNITY AND THE RIGHT OF WAR (TRANS. BY BARBARA BARCLAY CARTER). CULTURE CREATE PROB/SOLV DIPLOM ADJUD CONTROL PEACE PERSON ORD/FREE...INT/LAW IDEA/COMP PACIFIST 20 LEAGUE/NAT. PAGE 140 A2858
INT/ORG PLAN WAR CONCPT

B37
KOHN H., FORCE OR REASON; ISSUES OF THE TWENTIETH CENTURY. WOR+45 NAT/G DIPLOM WAR DRIVE ORD/FREE ALL/IDEOS FASCISM PLURISM...POLICY IDEA/COMP 20. PAGE 81 A1660
COERCE DOMIN RATIONAL COLONIAL

B37
TUPPER E., JAPAN IN AMERICAN PUBLIC OPINION. USA-45 POL/PAR VOL/ASSN INT/TRADE DISCRIM...BIBLIOG 20 CHINJAP TREATY. PAGE 146 A2979
ATTIT IDEA/COMP DIPLOM PRESS

C37
TUPPER E., "JAPAN IN AMERICAN PUBLIC OPINION." USA+45 POL/PAR VOL/ASSN INT/TRADE DISCRIM ...IDEA/COMP 20 CHINJAP. PAGE 146 A2978
BIBLIOG ATTIT DIPLOM PRESS

B41
NIEMEYER G., LAW WITHOUT FORCE: THE FUNCTION OF POLITICS IN INTERNATIONAL LAW. PLAN INSPECT DIPLOM REPAR LEGIT ADJUD WAR ORD/FREE...IDEA/COMP METH/COMP GEN/LAWS 20. PAGE 109 A2240
COERCE LAW PWR INT/LAW

B43
MC DOWELL R.B., IRISH PUBLIC OPINION, 1750-1800. IRELAND CONSTN VOL/ASSN WORKER ORD/FREE CATHISM CONSERVE...POLICY IDEA/COMP BIBLIOG 18/ PARLIAMENT. PAGE 97 A1992
ATTIT NAT/G DIPLOM REV

B45
WOOLBERT R.G., FOREIGN AFFAIRS BIBLIOGRAPHY, 1932-1942. INT/ORG SECT INT/TRADE COLONIAL RACE/REL NAT/LISM...GEOG INT/LAW GOV/COMP IDEA/COMP 20. PAGE 167 A3393
BIBLIOG/A DIPLOM WAR

B47
HEIMANN E., FREEDOM AND ORDER: LESSONS FROM THE WAR. WOR-45 CONSTN FORCES CHOOSE CIVMIL/REL PERSON ALL/IDEOS SOCISM...SOC IDEA/COMP WORSHIP 20. PAGE 64 A1308
NAT/G SOCIETY ORD/FREE DIPLOM

B47
NIEBUHR R., THE CHILDREN OF LIGHT AND THE CHILDREN OF DARKNESS: A VINDICATION OF DEMOCRACY AND CRITIQUE OF TRADITIONAL DEFENSE. UNIV STRUCT NAT/G SECT INGP/REL OWN PEACE ORD/FREE MARXISM ...IDEA/COMP GEN/LAWS 20 CHRISTIAN. PAGE 109 A2235
POPULISM DIPLOM NEIGH GP/REL

S48
MORGENTHAU H.J., "THE TWILIGHT OF INTERNATIONAL MORALITY" (BMR)" WOR+45 WOR-45 BAL/PWR WAR NAT/LISM PEACE...POLICY INT/LAW IDEA/COMP 15/20 TREATY INTERVENT. PAGE 104 A2137
MORAL DIPLOM NAT/G

B49
BOYD A., WESTERN UNION: A STUDY OF THE TREND TOWARD EUROPEAN UNITY. FUT REGION NAT/LISM...POLICY IDEA/COMP BIBLIOG 14/20 OEEC ERASMUS/D COUNCL/EUR FULBRGHT/J NATO. PAGE 18 A0363
DIPLOM AGREE TREND INT/ORG

B49
GROB F., THE RELATIVITY OF WAR AND PEACE: A STUDY IN LAW, HISTORY, AND POLLTICS. WOR+45 WOR-45 LAW DIPLOM DEBATE...CONCPT LING IDEA/COMP BIBLIOG 18/20. PAGE 57 A1167
WAR PEACE INT/LAW STYLE

B49
KAFKA G., FREIHEIT UND ANARCHIE. SECT COERCE DETER WAR ATTIT...IDEA/COMP 20 NATO. PAGE 75 A1545
CONCPT ORD/FREE JURID INT/ORG

B50
GUERRANT E.O., ROOSEVELT'S GOOD NEIGHBOR POLICY. L/A+17C USA+45 USA-45 FOR/AID...IDEA/COMP 20 ROOSEVLT/F TRUMAN/HS. PAGE 58 A1187
DIPLOM NAT/G CHIEF POLICY

B52
FLECHTHEIM O.K., FUNDAMENTALS OF POLITICAL SCIENCE. WOR+45 WOR-45 LAW POL/PAR EX/STRUC LEGIS ADJUD ATTIT PWR...INT/LAW. PAGE 46 A0945
NAT/G DIPLOM IDEA/COMP CONSTN

B52
SURANYI-UNGER T., COMPARATIVE ECONOMIC SYSTEMS. FINAN MARKET DIPLOM PRICE WEALTH...GEOG SOC BIBLIOG METH T 20. PAGE 140 A2865
LAISSEZ PLAN ECO/DEV IDEA/COMP

B53
LANDHEER B., FUNDAMENTALS OF PUBLIC INTERNATIONAL LAW (SELECTIVE BIBLIOGRAPHIES OF THE LIBRARY OF THE PEACE PALACE, VOL. I; PAMPH). INT/ORG OP/RES PEACE ...IDEA/COMP 20. PAGE 84 A1715
BIBLIOG/A INT/LAW DIPLOM PHIL/SCI

B53
LENZ F., DIE BEWEGUNGEN DER GROSSEN MACHTE. USA+45 USA-45 USSR SOCIETY STRATA STRUCT NAT/G PERSON MARXISM...CONCPT IDEA/COMP NAT/COMP 18/20. PAGE 87 A1777
BAL/PWR TREND DIPLOM HIST/WRIT

B53
MARITAIN J., L'HOMME ET L'ETAT. SECT DIPLOM GP/REL PEACE ORD/FREE...IDEA/COMP 17/20 CHURCH/STA NATURL/LAW. PAGE 95 A1940
CONCPT NAT/G SOVEREIGN COERCE

C53
DEUTSCH K.W., "NATIONALISM AND SOCIAL COMMUNICATION: AN INQUIRY INTO THE FOUNDATIONS OF NATIONALITY." CULTURE STRUCT DIPLOM DOMIN ATTIT ORD/FREE SOVEREIGN...SOC STAT CHARTS IDEA/COMP BIBLIOG. PAGE 36 A0735
NAT/LISM CONCPT PERCEPT STRATA

B54
BUCHANAN W., AN INTERNATIONAL POLICE FORCE AND PUBLIC OPINION IN THE UNITED STATES, 1939-1953. USA+45 PROB/SOLV CONTROL ATTIT ORD/FREE...STAT TREND 20. PAGE 21 A0425
IDEA/COMP FORCES DIPLOM PLAN

B55
GULICK E.V., EUROPE'S CLASSICAL BALANCE OF POWER: CASE HISTORY OF THEORY AND PRACTICE OF GREAT CONCEPTS OF EUROPEAN STATECRAFT. MOD/EUR INT/ORG VOL/ASSN FORCES ORD/FREE 18/19 TREATY. PAGE 58 A1192
IDEA/COMP BAL/PWR PWR DIPLOM

B55
HEUSS E., WIRTSCHAFTSSYSTEME UND INTERNATIONALER HANDEL. ECO/DEV FINAN MARKET DIPLOM ECO/TAC COST ...METH/COMP NAT/COMP 20. PAGE 112 A2306
CAP/ISM SOCISM INT/TRADE IDEA/COMP

B56
BEARDSLEY S.W., HUMAN RELATIONS IN INTERNATIONAL AFFAIRS: A GUIDE TO SIGNIFICANT INTERPRETATION AND RESEARCH. UNIV PERS/REL NAT/LISM DRIVE PERSON ...POLICY PSY SOC CON/ANAL IDEA/COMP 20. PAGE 12 A0241
BIBLIOG/A ATTIT CULTURE DIPLOM

B56
FIELD G.C., POLITICAL THEORY. POL/PAR REPRESENT MORAL SOVEREIGN...JURID IDEA/COMP. PAGE 45 A0924
CONCPT NAT/G ORD/FREE DIPLOM

S56
POTTER P.B., "NEUTRALITY, 1955." WOR+45 WOR-45
NEUTRAL

INT/ORG NAT/G WAR ATTIT...POLICY IDEA/COMP 17/20 LEAGUE/NAT UN COLD/WAR. PAGE 117 A2399
INT/LAW DIPLOM CONCPT

C56
DUPUY R.E.,"MILITARY HERITAGE OF AMERICA." USA+45 USA-45 TEC/DEV DIPLOM ROUTINE...POLICY TREND CHARTS IDEA/COMP BIBLIOG COLD/WAR. PAGE 39 A0804
FORCES WAR CONCPT

B57
UNESCO,A REGISTER OF LEGAL DOCUMENTATION IN THE WORLD (2ND ED.). CT/SYS...JURID IDEA/COMP METH/COMP NAT/COMP 20. PAGE 148 A3019
BIBLIOG LAW INT/LAW CONSTN

B57
YAMADA H.,ANNALS OF THE SOCIAL SCIENCES. WOR+45 WOR-45 LAW CULTURE SOCIETY STRUCT DIPLOM...EPIST PSY CONCPT 15/20. PAGE 168 A3428
BIBLIOG/A TREND IDEA/COMP SOC

B58
CHANG H.,WITHIN THE FOUR SEAS. ASIA WAR MORAL MARXISM...IDEA/COMP NAT/COMP 20 CONFUCIUS. PAGE 26 A0521
PEACE DIPLOM KNOWL CULTURE

B58
PALMER E.E.,THE COMMUNIST CHALLENGE. COM USA+45 USA-45 ECO/DEV ECO/UNDEV NEUTRAL ORD/FREE POPULISM ...CONCPT NAT/COMP ANTHOL 19/20 LENIN/VI STALIN/J MAO MARX/KARL COM/PARTY. PAGE 113 A2320
MARXISM DIPLOM IDEA/COMP POLICY

B58
SALETORE B.A.,INDIA'S DIPLOMATIC RELATIONS WITH THE WEST. GREECE INDIA CULTURE ETIQUET...IDEA/COMP 3 ROM/EMP PERSIA. PAGE 126 A2590
DIPLOM CONCPT INT/TRADE

B58
STONE J.,AGGRESSION AND WORLD ORDER: A CRITIQUE OF UNITED NATIONS THEORIES OF AGGRESSION. LAW CONSTN DELIB/GP PROB/SOLV BAL/PWR DIPLOM DEBATE ADJUD CRIME PWR...POLICY IDEA/COMP 20 UN SUEZ LEAGUE/NAT. PAGE 138 A2835
ORD/FREE INT/ORG WAR CONCPT

C58
RAJAN M.S.,"UNITED NATIONS AND DOMESTIC JURISDICTION." WOR+45 WOR-45 PARL/PROC...IDEA/COMP BIBLIOG 20 UN. PAGE 119 A2434
INT/LAW DIPLOM CONSTN INT/ORG

B59
BROOKES E.H.,THE COMMONWEALTH TODAY. UK ROMAN/EMP INT/ORG RACE/REL NAT/LISM SOVEREIGN...TREND SOC/INTEG 20. PAGE 19 A0391
FEDERAL DIPLOM JURID IDEA/COMP

B59
DEHIO L.,GERMANY AND WORLD POLITICS IN THE TWENTIETH CENTURY. EUR+WWI FRANCE GERMANY MOD/EUR UK USSR NAT/G CHIEF BAL/PWR DOMIN COLONIAL CONTROL LEAD...IDEA/COMP 20 VERSAILLES. PAGE 36 A0724
DIPLOM WAR NAT/LISM SOVEREIGN

B59
GOULD L.P.,THE PRICE OF SURVIVAL. EUR+WWI SPACE USA+45 FORCES ECO/TAC NUC/PWR WAR ORD/FREE MARXISM ...IDEA/COMP 20 COLD/WAR NATO. PAGE 54 A1117
POLICY PROB/SOLV DIPLOM PEACE

B59
JACKSON B.W.,FIVE IDEAS THAT CHANGE THE WORLD. FUT WOR+45 WOR-45 ECO/UNDEV INDUS DIPLOM DOMIN CONTROL ...IDEA/COMP 20. PAGE 72 A1473
MARXISM NAT/LISM COLONIAL ECO/TAC

B59
LINK R.G.,ENGLISH THEORIES OF ECONOMIC FLUCTUATIONS: 1815-1848. FRANCE UK AGRI WORKER DIPLOM PRICE TASK WAR DEMAND PRODUC...POLICY BIBLIOG 18 MALTHUS MILL/JS WILSON/J. PAGE 89 A1826
IDEA/COMP ECO/DEV WEALTH EQUILIB

B59
COLUMBIA U BUR APPL SOC RES,ATTITUDES OF PROMINENT AMERICANS TOWARD "WORLD PEACE THROUGH WORLD LAW" (SUPRA-NATL ORGANIZATION FOR WAR PREVENTION). USA+45 USSR ELITES FORCES PLAN PROB/SOLV CONTROL WAR PWR...POLICY SOC QU IDEA/COMP 20 UN. PAGE 117 A2403
ATTIT ACT/RES INT/LAW STAT

B60
AMERICAN ASSOCIATION LAW LIB,INDEX TO FOREIGN LEGAL PERIODICALS. WOR+45 MUNIC...IDEA/COMP 20. PAGE 7 A0139
INDEX LAW JURID DIPLOM

B60
BYRD E.M. JR.,TREATIES AND EXECUTIVE AGREEMENTS IN THE UNITED STATES: THEIR SEPARATE ROLES AND LIMITATIONS. USA+45 USA-45 EX/STRUC TARIFFS CT/SYS GOV/REL FEDERAL...IDEA/COMP BIBLIOG SUPREME/CT SENATE CONGRESS. PAGE 23 A0461
CHIEF INT/LAW DIPLOM

B60
DEUTSCHER I.,THE GREAT CONTEST: RUSSIA AND THE WEST. USA+45 USSR SOCIETY INDUS ARMS/CONT ATTIT ...CONCPT IDEA/COMP 20 COLD/WAR. PAGE 37 A0749
PEACE DIPLOM PWR

B60
KARDELJE,SOCIALISM AND WAR. CHINA/COM WOR+45 YUGOSLAVIA DIPLOM EDU/PROP ATTIT...POLICY CONCPT IDEA/COMP COLD/WAR. PAGE 76 A1565
MARXIST WAR MARXISM BAL/PWR

B60
MEYRIAT J.,LA SCIENCE POLITIQUE EN FRANCE, 1945-1958; BIBLIOGRAPHIES FRANCAISES DE SCIENCES SOCIALES (VOL. I). EUR+WWI FRANCE POL/PAR DIPLOM ADMIN CHOOSE ATTIT...IDEA/COMP METH/COMP NAT/COMP 20. PAGE 100 A2057
BIBLIOG/A NAT/G CONCPT PHIL/SCI

B60
PHILLIPS J.F.V.,KWAME NKRUMAH AND THE FUTURE OF AFRICA. FUT GHANA ISLAM ECO/UNDEV CHIEF DIPLOM COLONIAL RACE/REL NAT/LISM...TREND IDEA/COMP BIBLIOG 20 NKRUMAH/K. PAGE 116 A2376
BIOG LEAD SOVEREIGN AFR

B60
ROPKE W.,A HUMANE ECONOMY. CULTURE ECO/DEV FINAN INDUS GP/REL CENTRAL WEALTH...GEOG SOC IDEA/COMP 20 EEC. PAGE 123 A2525
ECO/TAC INT/ORG DIPLOM ORD/FREE

B60
VAN HOOGSTRATE D.J.,AMERICAN FOREIGN POLICY: REALISTS AND IDEALISTS: A CATHOLIC INTERPRETATION. BAL/PWR FOR/AID ARMS/CONT GOV/REL PEACE LOVE MORAL SOVEREIGN CATHISM...BIBLIOG 20. PAGE 158 A3213
CATH DIPLOM POLICY IDEA/COMP

C60
COX R.H.,"LOCKE ON WAR AND PEACE." UK DIPLOM DOMIN PWR...BIOG IDEA/COMP BIBLIOG 18. PAGE 32 A0646
CONCPT NAT/G PEACE WAR

B61
AMORY J.F.,AROUND THE EDGE OF WAR: A NEW APPROACH TO THE PROBLEMS OF AMERICAN FOREIGN POLICY. COM L/A+17C USA+45 USSR FOR/AID EDU/PROP AGREE CONTROL ARMS/CONT NUC/PWR WAR PWR...IDEA/COMP 20 TREATY ESPIONAGE. PAGE 8 A0154
NAT/G DIPLOM POLICY

B61
DEAN V.M.,BUILDERS OF EMERGING NATIONS. WOR+45 ECO/UNDEV ECO/TAC NEUTRAL TOTALISM ORD/FREE PWR ...BIOG AUD/VIS IDEA/COMP BIBLIOG 20 COLD/WAR. PAGE 35 A0719
NAT/G CHIEF POLICY DIPLOM

B61
HUDSON G.F.,THE SINO-SOVIET DISPUTE. CHINA/COM USSR INTELL INT/TRADE DEBATE REV...IDEA/COMP 20. PAGE 68 A1404
DIPLOM MARXISM PRESS ATTIT

B61
NEWMAN R.P.,RECOGNITION OF COMMUNIST CHINA? A STUDY IN ARGUMENT. CHINA/COM NAT/G PROB/SOLV RATIONAL ...INT/LAW LOG IDEA/COMP BIBLIOG 20. PAGE 108 A2226
MARXISM ATTIT DIPLOM POLICY

B61
OAKES J.B.,THE EDGE OF FREEDOM. EUR+WWI USA+45 USSR ECO/UNDEV BAL/PWR DIPLOM DOMIN COLONIAL PWR MARXISM POPULISM...IDEA/COMP 20 COLD/WAR. PAGE 111 A2271
AFR ORD/FREE SOVEREIGN NEUTRAL

S61
TUCKER R.C.,"TOWARDS A COMPARATIVE POLITICS OF MOVEMENT-REGIMES" (BMR)" USSR CONSTN NAT/G CREATE PROB/SOLV DIPLOM DOMIN REV...GP/COMP IDEA/COMP METH 20 STALIN/J BOLSHEVISM. PAGE 145 A2971
MARXISM POLICY GEN/LAWS PWR

B62
DELANEY R.F.,THE LITERATURE OF COMMUNISM IN AMERICA. COM USA+45 USA-45 INT/ORG LABOR NAT/G POL/PAR INGP/REL...MAJORIT 20. PAGE 36 A0727
BIBLIOG/A MARXISM EDU/PROP IDEA/COMP

B62
EBENSTEIN W.,TWO WAYS OF LIFE. USA+45 CULTURE ECO/DEV PLAN EDU/PROP CONTROL ORD/FREE...GOV/COMP IDEA/COMP T 20 MARX/KARL ENGELS/F LENIN/VI LOCKE/JOHN MILL/JS. PAGE 40 A0819
MARXISM POPULISM ECO/TAC DIPLOM

B62
KLUCKHOHN F.L.,THE NAKED RISE OF COMMUNISM. CHINA/COM COM USSR WOR+45 CONSTN POL/PAR PLAN CONTROL LEAD NEUTRAL CONSERVE 20 STALIN/J EUROPE/E COM/PARTY. PAGE 80 A1650
MARXISM IDEA/COMP DIPLOM DOMIN

B62
LAQUEUR W.,THE FUTURE OF COMMUNIST SOCIETY. CHINA/COM USSR LAW ECO/DEV NAT/G POL/PAR PLAN PROB/SOLV DIPLOM LEAD...POLICY CONCPT IDEA/COMP ANTHOL 20. PAGE 85 A1731
MARXISM COM FUT SOCIETY

B62
ROOSEVELT J.,THE LIBERAL PAPERS. USA+45 WOR+45 ECO/DEV INT/ORG DELIB/GP ACT/RES PROB/SOLV DETER ATTIT...TREND IDEA/COMP ANTHOL. PAGE 123 A2520
DIPLOM NEW/LIB POLICY FORCES

B62
SCHUMAN F.L.,THE COLD WAR: RETROSPECT AND PROSPECT. FUT USA+45 USSR WOR+45 BAL/PWR EDU/PROP ARMS/CONT ATTIT...MAJORIT IDEA/COMP ANTHOL BIBLIOG 20 COLD/WAR. PAGE 129 A2651
MARXISM TEC/DEV DIPLOM NUC/PWR

B63
GRAEBNER N.A.,THE COLD WAR: IDEOLOGICAL CONFLICT OR POWER STRUGGLE? USSR WOR+45 WOR-45 PROB/SOLV EDU/PROP ARMS/CONT REV NAT/LISM PEACE ORD/FREE ...IDEA/COMP ANTHOL BIBLIOG/A 20 COLD/WAR. PAGE 55 A1123
DIPLOM BAL/PWR MARXISM

B63
HAMM H.,ALBANIA - CHINA'S BEACHHEAD IN EUROPE. ALBANIA CHINA/COM USSR YUGOSLAVIA ELITES SOCIETY POL/PAR DELIB/GP FORCES ECO/TAC COERCE ISOLAT PEACE MARXISM...IDEA/COMP 20 MAO. PAGE 61 A1248
DIPLOM REV NAT/G POLICY

B63
HONEY P.J.,COMMUNISM IN NORTH VIETNAM: ITS ROLE IN POLICY
THE SINO-SOVIET DISPUTE. CHINA/COM INDIA USSR MARXISM
VIETNAM/N AGRI POL/PAR LEGIS ECO/TAC WAR PEACE CHIEF
ATTIT...GEOG IDEA/COMP 20. PAGE 67 A1378 DIPLOM

B63
LYON P.,NEUTRALISM. ECO/UNDEV EDU/PROP COLONIAL NAT/COMP
ALL/IDEOS...IDEA/COMP 20 COLD/WAR UN. PAGE 92 A1879 NAT/LISM
DIPLOM
NEUTRAL

B63
MALIK C.,MAN IN THE STRUGGLE FOR PEACE. USSR WOR+45 PEACE
CHIEF PLAN PROB/SOLV PARTIC NUC/PWR REV ORD/FREE MARXISM
...IDEA/COMP METH/COMP 20 UN COLD/WAR. PAGE 93 DIPLOM
A1912 EDU/PROP

B63
ROSS H.,THE COLD WAR: CONTAINMENT AND ITS CRITICSS. MARXISM
WOR+45 POL/PAR BAL/PWR ECO/TAC PEACE ORD/FREE ARMS/CONT
...POLICY IDEA/COMP ANTHOL T 20 COLD/WAR DULLES/JF DIPLOM
TRUMAN/HS EISNHWR/DD. PAGE 124 A2541

B63
RUSSELL B.,UNARMED VICTORY. CHINA/COM CUBA INDIA DIPLOM
USA+45 WAR MARXISM...POLICY IDEA/COMP 20 KHRUSH/N ATTIT
COLD/WAR. PAGE 125 A2573 SOCISM
ORD/FREE

B63
WEINBERG A.,INSTEAD OF VIOLENCE: WRITINGS BY THE PACIFISM
GREAT ADVOCATES OF PEACE AND NONVIOLENCE THROUGHOUT WAR
HISTORY. WOR+45 WOR-45 SOCIETY SECT PROB/SOLV IDEA/COMP
DIPLOM GP/REL PERS/REL PEACE...ANTHOL PACIFIST.
PAGE 162 A3304

S63
LIPSHART A.,"THE ANALYSIS OF BLOC VOTING IN THE CHOOSE
GENERAL ASSEMBLY." L/A+17C WOR+45 ACT/RES INGP/REL INT/ORG
...POLICY DECISION NEW/IDEA STAT IDEA/COMP UN. DELIB/GP
PAGE 90 A1832

C63
ATTIA G.E.O.,"LES FORCES ARMEES DES NATIONS UNIES FORCES
EN COREE ET AU MOYENORIENT." KOREA CONSTN DELIB/GP NAT/G
LEGIS PWR...IDEA/COMP NAT/COMP BIBLIOG UN SUEZ. INT/LAW
PAGE 10 A0194

B64
COHEN M.L.,SELECTED BIBLIOGRAPHY OF FOREIGN AND BIBLIOG/A
INTERNATIONAL LAW....IDEA/COMP METH/COMP 20. JURID
PAGE 28 A0562 LAW
INT/LAW

B64
GIBSON J.S.,IDEOLOGY AND WORLD AFFAIRS. FUT WOR+45 ALL/IDEOS
ECO/UNDEV NAT/G CAP/ISM TOTALISM ORD/FREE FASCISM DIPLOM
MARXISM 20. PAGE 52 A1067 POLICY
IDEA/COMP

B64
KEEP J.,CONTEMPORARY HISTORY IN THE SOVIET MIRROR. HIST/WRIT
COM USSR POL/PAR CREATE DIPLOM AGREE WAR ATTIT METH
...MYTH TREND ANTHOL 20 COLD/WAR STALIN/J MARX/KARL MARXISM
LENIN/VI. PAGE 77 A1576 IDEA/COMP

B64
KOLARZ W.,BOOKS ON COMMUNISM. USSR WOR+45 CULTURE BIBLIOG/A
NAT/G POL/PAR DIPLOM LEAD...CONCPT GOV/COMP SOCIETY
IDEA/COMP. PAGE 81 A1667 COM
MARXISM

B64
MCWHINNEY E.,"PEACEFUL COEXISTENCE" AND SOVIET- PEACE
WESTERN INTERNATIONAL LAW. USSR DIPLOM LEAD...JURID IDEA/COMP
20 COLD/WAR. PAGE 99 A2027 INT/LAW
ATTIT

B64
MEYER F.S.,WHAT IS CONSERVATISM? USA+45 NAT/G CONSERVE
FORCES DIPLOM ORD/FREE IDEA/COMP. PAGE 100 A2048 CONCPT
EDU/PROP
CAP/ISM

B64
NASA,PROCEEDINGS OF CONFERENCE ON THE LAW OF SPACE SPACE
AND OF SATELLITE COMMUNICATIONS: CHICAGO 1963. FUT COM/IND
WOR+45 DELIB/GP PROB/SOLV TEC/DEV CONFER ADJUD LAW
NUC/PWR...POLICY IDEA/COMP 20 NASA. PAGE 107 A2197 DIPLOM

B64
QUIGG P.W.,AFRICA: A FOREIGN AFFAIRS READER. AFR COLONIAL
FRANCE PORTUGAL UK DIPLOM LEAD PARL/PROC MARXISM SOVEREIGN
...MAJORIT METH/CNCPT GOV/COMP IDEA/COMP ANTHOL NAT/LISM
19/20. PAGE 118 A2426 RACE/REL

B64
ROBERTS HL,FOREIGN AFFAIRS BIBLIOGRAPHY, 1952-1962. BIBLIOG/A
ECO/DEV SECT PLAN FOR/AID INT/TRADE ARMS/CONT DIPLOM
NAT/LISM ATTIT...INT/LAW GOV/COMP IDEA/COMP 20. INT/ORG
PAGE 122 A2495 WAR

B64
STANKIEWICZ W.J.,POLITICAL THOUGHT SINCE WORLD WAR IDEA/COMP
II. WOR+45 CAP/ISM DIPLOM COLONIAL COERCE REV DOMIN
REPRESENT ADJUST ANOMIE ALL/IDEOS 20. PAGE 137 ORD/FREE
A2804 AUTHORIT

B64
STILLMAN E.O.,THE POLITICS OF HYSTERIA: THE SOURCES DIPLOM
OF TWENTIETH-CENTURY CONFLICT. WOR+45 WOR-45 IDEA/COMP
CULTURE ECO/UNDEV PLAN CAP/ISM WAR MARXISM COLONIAL
...PREDICT BIBLIOG 20 COLD/WAR. PAGE 138 A2828 CONTROL

S64
BARKUN M.,"CONFLICT RESOLUTION THROUGH IMPLICIT CONSULT
MEDIATION." UNIV BARGAIN CONSEN FEDERAL JURID. CENTRAL
PAGE 11 A0222 INT/LAW
IDEA/COMP

S64
MCGHEE G.C.,"EAST-WEST RELATIONS TODAY." WOR+45 IDEA/COMP
PROB/SOLV BAL/PWR PEACE 20 COLD/WAR. PAGE 98 A2011 DIPLOM
ADJUD

B65
CALLEO D.P.,EUROPE'S FUTURE: THE GRAND FUT
ALTERNATIVES. UK INT/ORG DIPLOM PWR SOVEREIGN EUR+WWI
...CONCPT IDEA/COMP NAT/COMP BIBLIOG 20 EEC EUROPE FEDERAL
DEGAULLE/C NATO. PAGE 23 A0468 NAT/LISM

B65
COLLINS H.,KARL MARX AND THE BRITISH LABOUR MARXISM
MOVEMENT; YEARS OF THE FIRST INTERNATIONAL. FRANCE LABOR
SWITZERLND UK CAP/ISM WAR...MARXIST IDEA/COMP INT/ORG
BIBLIOG 19. PAGE 28 A0567 REV

B65
DU BOIS W.E.B.,THE WORLD AND AFRICA. USA+45 CAP/ISM AFR
DISCRIM STRANGE SOCISM...TIME/SEQ TREND IDEA/COMP DIPLOM
19/20 NEGRO. PAGE 39 A0789 COLONIAL
CULTURE

B65
LARUS J.,COMPARATIVE WORLD POLITICS. ASIA INDIA GOV/COMP
WOR+45 WOR-45 BAL/PWR WAR PEACE RATIONAL MORAL PWR IDEA/COMP
...REALPOL INT/LAW MUSLIM. PAGE 85 A1735 DIPLOM
NAT/COMP

B65
LERCHE C.O.,THE COLD WAR AND AFTER. AFR COM S/ASIA DIPLOM
USA+45 USSR NUC/PWR SOVEREIGN MARXISM...TIME/SEQ BAL/PWR
TREND BIBLIOG 20 COLD/WAR. PAGE 87 A1784 IDEA/COMP

B65
LINDBLOM C.E.,THE INTELLIGENCE OF DEMOCRACY; PLURISM
DECISION MAKING THROUGH MUTUAL ADJUSTMENT. WOR+45 DECISION
SOCIETY NAT/G PROB/SOLV DOMIN PARTIC GP/REL ADJUST
ORD/FREE...POLICY IDEA/COMP BIBLIOG 20. PAGE 89 DIPLOM
A1821

B65
MONCRIEFF A.,SECOND THOUGHTS ON AID. WOR+45 FOR/AID
ECO/UNDEV AGRI FINAN VOL/ASSN PLAN TEC/DEV GIVE ECO/TAC
EDU/PROP ROLE WEALTH 20. PAGE 102 A2105 INT/ORG
IDEA/COMP

B65
THOMAS A.V.,NONINTERVENTION: THE LAW AND ITS IMPORT INT/LAW
IN THE AMERICAS. L/A+17C USA+45 USA-45 WOR+45 PWR
DIPLOM ADJUD...JURID IDEA/COMP 20 UN INTERVENT. COERCE
PAGE 143 A2920

B65
WINT G.,COMMUNIST CHINA'S CRUSADE: MAO'S ROAD TO DIPLOM
POWER AND THE NEW CAMPAIGN FOR WORLD REVOLUTION. MARXISM
ASIA CHINA/COM USA+45 USSR NAT/G POL/PAR DOMIN REV
COERCE WAR PWR...POLICY CHARTS IDEA/COMP BIBLIOG 20 COLONIAL
MAO. PAGE 165 A3364

C65
BURTON J.W.,"INTERNATIONAL RELATIONS: A GENERAL DIPLOM
THEORY." WOR+45 NAT/G CREATE BAL/PWR NEUTRAL COERCE GEN/LAWS
DETER ADJUST...TREND IDEA/COMP GEN/METH BIBLIOG. ACT/RES
PAGE 22 A0447 ORD/FREE

C65
SEARA M.V.,"COSMIC INTERNATIONAL LAW." LAW ACADEM SPACE
ACT/RES DIPLOM COLONIAL CONTROL NUC/PWR SOVEREIGN INT/LAW
...GEN/LAWS BIBLIOG UN. PAGE 131 A2678 IDEA/COMP
INT/ORG

B66
AMERICAN JOURNAL COMP LAW,THE AMERICAN JOURNAL OF IDEA/COMP
COMPARATIVE LAW READER. EUR+WWI USA+45 USA-45 LAW JURID
CONSTN LOC/G MUNIC NAT/G DIPLOM...ANTHOL 20 INT/LAW
SUPREME/CT EURCT/JUST. PAGE 7 A0151 CT/SYS

B66
BESSON W.,DIE GROSSEN MACHTE - STRUKTURFRAGEN DER NAT/COMP
GEGENWARTIGEN WELTPOLITIK. ASIA USSR WOR+45 ATTIT DIPLOM
...IDEA/COMP 20 KENNEDY/JF. PAGE 14 A0280 STRUCT

B66
BRYNES A.,WE GIVE TO CONQUER. USA+45 USSR STRATA FOR/AID
ECO/UNDEV INT/ORG NAT/G DIPLOM DRIVE...TREND CONTROL
IDEA/COMP 20. PAGE 20 A0414 GIVE
WAR

B66
DAENIKER G.,STRATEGIE DES KLEIN STAATS. SWITZERLND NUC/PWR
ACT/RES CREATE DIPLOM NEUTRAL DETER WAR WEAPON PWR PLAN
SOVEREIGN...IDEA/COMP 20 COLD/WAR. PAGE 33 A0673 FORCES
NAT/G

B66
DAVIS V.,POSTWAR DEFENSE POLICY AND THE US NAVY, FORCES
1943-1946. USA+45 DIPLOM CONFER LEAD ATTIT...POLICY PLAN
IDEA/COMP 20 NAVY. PAGE 34 A0692 PROB/SOLV
CIVMIL/REL

B66
FRIEDRICH C.J.,REVOLUTION: NOMOS VIII. NAT/G SOCISM REV
...OBS TREND IDEA/COMP ANTHOL 18/20. PAGE 49 A1007 MARXISM
CONCPT
DIPLOM

B66
MONTGOMERY J.D.,APPROACHES TO DEVELOPMENT: ECO/UNDEV

POLITICS, ADMINISTRATION AND CHANGE. USA+45 AGRI FOR/AID ORD/FREE...CONCPT IDEA/COMP METH/COMP ANTHOL. PAGE 103 A2116 — ADMIN POLICY ECO/TAC

B66
RIESELBACH L.N.,THE ROOTS OF ISOLATIONISM* CONGRESSIONAL VOTING AND PRESIDENTIAL LEADERSHIP IN FOREIGN POLICY. POL/PAR LEGIS DIPLOM EDU/PROP LEAD REGION REPRESENT...SOC STAT IDEA/COMP HYPO/EXP BIBLIOG 19/20 CONGRESS. PAGE 121 A2477 — ISOLAT CHOOSE CHIEF POLICY

B66
WESTIN A.F.,VIEWS OF AMERICA. COM USA+45 USSR SOCIETY ECO/UNDEV POL/PAR ECO/TAC GP/REL STRANGE MARXISM...MARXIST 20. PAGE 163 A3323 — CONCPT ATTIT DIPLOM IDEA/COMP

B66
WOHL R.,FRENCH COMMUNISM IN THE MAKING 1914-1924. FRANCE USSR LEAD REV...IDEA/COMP 20 COM/PARTY. PAGE 166 A3377 — MARXISM WORKER DIPLOM

B66
YEAGER L.B.,INTERNATIONAL MONETARY RELATIONS: THEORY, HISTORY, AND POLICY. WOR+45 WOR-45 INT/TRADE BAL/PAY...NAT/COMP 18/20 MONEY. PAGE 169 A3432 — FINAN DIPLOM ECO/TAC IDEA/COMP

B66
ZABLOCKI C.J.,SINO-SOVIET RIVALRY. AFR ASIA CHINA/COM CUBA EUR+WWI L/A+17C USA+45 USSR WOR+45 POL/PAR FORCES COERCE NUC/PWR...GOV/COMP IDEA/COMP 20 MAO KHRUSH/N. PAGE 169 A3442 — DIPLOM MARXISM COM

L66
MCDOUGAL M.S.,"CHINESE PARTICIPATION IN THE UNITED NATIONS: THE LEGAL IMPERATIVES OF A NEGOTIATED SOLUTION" CHINA/COM WOR+45 VOL/ASSN DIPLOM PARTIC ...DECISION IDEA/COMP 20 UN. PAGE 98 A2010 — INT/ORG REPRESENT POLICY PROB/SOLV

S66
CHIU H.,"COMMUNIST CHINA'S ATTITUDE TOWARD INTERNATIONAL LAW" CHINA/COM USSR LAW CONSTN DIPLOM GP/REL 20 LENIN/VI. PAGE 26 A0532 — INT/LAW MARXISM CONCPT IDEA/COMP

S66
GRUNDY K.W.,"RECENT CONTRIBUTIONS TO THE STUDY OF AFRICAN POLITICAL THOUGHT." DIPLOM NAT/LISM ALL/IDEOS...NEW/IDEA GOV/COMP 20. PAGE 58 A1182 — BIBLIOG/A AFR ATTIT IDEA/COMP

C66
DUROSELLE J.B.,"LE CONFLIT DE TRIESTE 1943-1954: ETUDES DE CAS DE CONFLITS INTERNATIONAUX III." ITALY USA+45 YUGOSLAVIA ELITES DELIB/GP PLAN ADJUST ...POLICY GEOG CHARTS IDEA/COMP TIME 20 TREATY UN COLD/WAR. PAGE 40 A0810 — BIBLIOG WAR DIPLOM GEN/LAWS

B67
BLOOMFIELD L.,THE UNITED NATIONS AND US FOREIGN POLICY. USA+45 DIPLOM LEAD ARMS/CONT DETER PWR 20 UN. PAGE 15 A0313 — INT/ORG PLAN CONFER IDEA/COMP

B67
BRZEZINSKI Z.K.,THE SOVIET BLOC: UNITY AND CONFLICT (2ND ED., REV., ENLARGED). COM POLAND USSR INTELL CHIEF EX/STRUC CONTROL EXEC GOV/REL PWR MARXISM ...TREND IDEA/COMP 20 LENIN/VI MARX/KARL STALIN/J. PAGE 21 A0420 — NAT/G DIPLOM

B67
DE BLIJ H.J.,SYSTEMATIC POLITICAL GEOGRAPHY. WOR+45 STRUCT INT/ORG NAT/G EDU/PROP ADMIN COLONIAL ROUTINE ORD/FREE PWR...IDEA/COMP T 20. PAGE 34 A0697 — GEOG CONCPT METH

B67
FINE S.,RECENT AMERICA* CONFLICTING INTERPRETATIONS OF THE GREAT ISSUES (2ND ED.). USA+45 USA-45 POL/PAR SECT CONFER NUC/PWR WAR ATTIT...POLICY TREND ANTHOL PRESIDENT 20. PAGE 46 A0931 — IDEA/COMP DIPLOM NAT/G

B67
KNOLES G.H.,THE RESPONSIBILITIES OF POWER, 1900-1929. USA-45 SOCIETY SECT JUDGE COLONIAL REPRESENT WEALTH POPULISM...IDEA/COMP ANTHOL PRESIDENT 20 LEAGUE/NAT. PAGE 81 A1653 — PWR DIPLOM NAT/LISM WAR

B67
MACRIDIS R.C.,FOREIGN POLICY IN WORLD POLITICS (3RD ED.). EX/STRUC BAL/PWR COLONIAL NAT/LISM SKILL SOVEREIGN WEALTH...CONCPT TIME/SEQ ANTHOL 20 COLD/WAR. PAGE 93 A1902 — DIPLOM POLICY NAT/G IDEA/COMP

B67
MEHDI M.T.,PEACE IN THE MIDDLE EAST. ISRAEL SOCIETY NAT/G PLAN EDU/PROP NAT/LISM DRIVE...IDEA/COMP 20 JEWS. PAGE 99 A2033 — ISLAM DIPLOM GP/REL COERCE

B67
RUEFF J.,BALANCE OF PAYMENTS. WOR+45 FINAN TEC/DEV DIPLOM TARIFFS PRICE CONTROL...POLICY CONCPT IDEA/COMP. PAGE 125 A2567 — INT/TRADE BAL/PAY ECO/TAC NAT/COMP

B67
SHAFFER H.G.,THE COMMUNIST WORLD: MARXIST AND NON-MARXIST VIEWS. WOR+45 SOCIETY DIPLOM ECO/TAC CONTROL SOCISM...MARXIST ANTHOL BIBLIOG/A 20. PAGE 131 A2691 — MARXISM NAT/COMP IDEA/COMP COM

B67
TROTSKY L.,PROBLEMS OF THE CHINESE REVOLUTION (3RD ED. TRANS. BY MAX SCHACTMAN). ASIA USSR DIPLOM MARXISM SOCISM...IDEA/COMP ANTHOL DICTIONARY 20 STALIN/J. PAGE 145 A2969 — MARXIST REV

B67
WAELDER R.,PROGRESS AND REVOLUTION* A STUDY OF THE ISSUES OF OUR AGE. WOR+45 WOR-45 BAL/PWR DIPLOM COERCE ROLE MORAL ALL/IDEOS...IDEA/COMP NAT/COMP 19/20. PAGE 160 A3259 — PWR NAT/G REV TEC/DEV

B67
WILLIS F.R.,DE GAULLE: ANACHRONISM, REALIST, OR PROPHET? FRANCE POL/PAR FORCES DIPLOM WAR PEACE ROLE ORD/FREE...POLICY IDEA/COMP ANTHOL 20 DEGAULLE/C. PAGE 165 A3356 — BIOG PERSON CHIEF LEAD

S67
KINGSLEY R.E.,"THE US BUSINESS IMAGE IN LATIN AMERICA." L/A+17C USA+45 NAT/G TEC/DEV CAP/ISM FOR/AID DOMIN EDU/PROP...CONCPT LING IDEA/COMP 20. PAGE 79 A1626 — ATTIT LOVE DIPLOM ECO/UNDEV

S67
ROGERS W.C.,"A COMPARISON OF INFORMED AND GENERAL PUBLIC OPINION ON US FOREIGN POLICY." USA+45 DIPLOM EDU/PROP ORD/FREE...POLICY SAMP IDEA/COMP 20. PAGE 123 A2515 — KNOWL ATTIT GP/COMP ELITES

S67
THOMPSON K.W.,"THE EMPIRICAL, NORMATIVE, AND THEORETICAL FOUNDATIONS OF INTERNATIONAL STUDIES." WOR+45 INGP/REL RATIONAL...CONCPT RECORD IDEA/COMP. PAGE 143 A2932 — DIPLOM INTELL METH/COMP KNOWL

C67
GEHLEN M.P.,"THE POLITICS OF COEXISTENCE: SOVIET METHODS AND MOTIVES." COM USSR NAT/G INT/TRADE EDU/PROP ARMS/CONT DETER KNOWL...CHARTS IDEA/COMP 20 COLD/WAR. PAGE 52 A1056 — BIBLIOG PEACE DIPLOM MARXISM

IDEOLOGY....SEE ATTIT, STERTYP, ALSO IDEOLOGICAL TOPIC INDEX, P. XIII

IFC....INTERNATIONAL FINANCE CORPORATION

IGNORANCE....SEE KNOWL

IGY....INTERNATIONAL GEOPHYSICAL YEAR

S60
HAYTON R.D.,"THE ANTARCTIC SETTLEMENT OF 1959." FUT USA+45 WOR+45 WOR-45 STRUCT R+D INT/ORG EX/STRUC CREATE TEC/DEV LEGIT PEACE ATTIT SOVEREIGN ...TIME/SEQ 20 TREATY IGY. PAGE 63 A1297 — DELIB/GP JURID DIPLOM REGION

IKLE F.C. A1432,A1433

ILLEGIT....BASTARDY

ILLEGITIMACY....SEE ILLEGIT

ILLINOIS....ILLINOIS

ILO....INTERNATIONAL LABOR ORGANIZATION

B28
HOWARD-ELLIS C.,THE ORIGIN, STRUCTURE AND WORKING OF THE LEAGUE OF NATIONS. EUR+WWI MOD/EUR USA-45 CONSTN FORCES LEGIS ECO/TAC LEGIT COERCE ORD/FREE ...JURID SOC CONCPT LEAGUE/NAT 20 ILO ICJ. PAGE 68 A1401 — INT/ORG ADJUD

B45
PASTUHOV V.D.,A GUIDE TO THE PRACTICE OF INTERNATIONAL CONFERENCES. WOR+45 PLAN LEGIT ORD/FREE...MGT OBS RECORD VAL/FREE ILO LEAGUE/NAT 20. PAGE 114 A2338 — INT/ORG DELIB/GP

B47
MANDER L.,FOUNDATIONS OF MODERN WORLD SOCIETY. WOR+45 DELIB/GP ECO/TAC INT/TRADE EDU/PROP ALL/VALS ...TIME/SEQ GEN/LAWS TOT/POP VAL/FREE ILO 20. PAGE 94 A1917 — INT/ORG EX/STRUC DIPLOM

B47
TOWLE L.W.,INTERNATIONAL TRADE AND COMMERCIAL POLICY. WOR+45 LAW ECO/DEV FINAN INDUS NAT/G ECO/TAC WEALTH...TIME/SEQ ILO 20. PAGE 144 A2955 — MARKET INT/ORG INT/TRADE

C50
ELLSWORTH P.T.,"INTERNATIONAL ECONOMY." ECO/DEV ECO/UNDEV FINAN LABOR DIPLOM FOR/AID TARIFFS BAL/PAY EQUILIB NAT/LISM OPTIMAL...INT/LAW 20 ILO GATT. PAGE 41 A0843 — BIBLIOG INT/TRADE ECO/TAC INT/ORG

B51
WHITE L.C.,INTERNATIONAL NON-GOVERNMENTAL ORGANIZATIONS. AFR ASIA COM EUR+WWI USA+45 WOR+45 INT/ORG DIPLOM INT/TRADE ALL/VALS...HUM FAO ILO EEC 20. PAGE 164 A3337 — VOL/ASSN CONSULT

B52
ALEXANDROWICZ C.H.,INTERNATIONAL ECONOMIC ORGANIZATION. WOR+45 ECO/DEV ECO/UNDEV DIST/IND FINAN MARKET PLAN ECO/TAC LEGIT DRIVE WEALTH ...POLICY CONCPT QUANT OBS TIME/SEQ GEN/LAWS WORK — INT/ORG INT/TRADE

EEC ILO OEEC UNESCO 20. PAGE 6 A0114

B52
SCHUMAN F.,THE COMMONWEALTH OF MAN. WOR+45 WOR-45 LAW CULTURE ELITES SOCIETY FAM INT/ORG NAT/G VOL/ASSN TOP/EX PLAN BAL/PWR LEGIT ATTIT DISPL DRIVE...POLICY MYTH TREND TOT/POP ILO OEEC 20. PAGE 129 A2649 CONCPT GEN/LAWS

B53
OPPENHEIM L.,INTERNATIONAL LAW: A TREATISE (7TH ED., 2 VOLS.). LAW CONSTN PROB/SOLV INT/TRADE ADJUD AGREE NEUTRAL WAR ORD/FREE SOVEREIGN...BIBLIOG 20 LEAGUE/NAT UN ILO. PAGE 112 A2294 INT/LAW INT/ORG DIPLOM

B55
COMM. STUDY ORGAN. PEACE,REPORTS. WOR-45 ECO/DEV ECO/UNDEV VOL/ASSN CONSULT FORCES PLAN TEC/DEV DOMIN EDU/PROP NUC/PWR ATTIT PWR WEALTH...JURID STERTYP FAO ILO 20 UN. PAGE 28 A0579 WOR+45 INT/ORG ARMS/CONT

B56
SOHN L.B.,BASIC DOCUMENTS OF THE UNITED NATIONS. WOR+45 LAW INT/ORG LEGIT EXEC ROUTINE CHOOSE PWR ...JURID CONCPT GEN/LAWS ANTHOL UN TOT/POP OAS FAO ILO 20. PAGE 135 A2761 DELIB/GP CONSTN

B57
ASHER R.E.,THE UNITED NATIONS AND THE PROMOTION OF THE GENERAL WELFARE. WOR+45 WOR-45 ECO/UNDEV EX/STRUC ACT/RES PLAN EDU/PROP ROUTINE HEALTH...HUM CONCPT CHARTS UNESCO UN ILO 20. PAGE 9 A0185 INT/ORG CONSULT

B57
JENKS C.W.,THE INTERNATIONAL PROTECTION OF TRADE UNION FREEDOM. FUT WOR+45 WOR-45 VOL/ASSN DELIB/GP CT/SYS REGION ROUTINE...JURID METH/CNCPT RECORD TIME/SEQ CHARTS ILO WORK OAS 20. PAGE 73 A1504 LABOR INT/ORG

L59
BEGUIN B.,"ILO AND THE TRIPARTITE SYSTEM." EUR+WWI WOR+45 WOR-45 CONSTN ECO/DEV ECO/UNDEV INDUS INT/ORG NAT/G VOL/ASSN DELIB/GP PLAN TEC/DEV LEGIT ORD/FREE WEALTH...CONCPT TIME/SEQ WORK ILO 20. PAGE 12 A0249 LABOR

S59
TIPTON J.B.,"PARTICIPATION OF THE UNITED STATES IN THE INTERNATIONAL LABOR ORGANIZATION." USA+45 LAW STRUCT ECO/DEV ECO/UNDEV INDUS TEC/DEV ECO/TAC ADMIN PERCEPT ORD/FREE SKILL...STAT HIST/WRIT GEN/METH ILO WORK 20. PAGE 144 A2946 LABOR INT/ORG

L60
FERNBACH A.P.,"SOVIET COEXISTENCE STRATEGY." WOR+45 PROF/ORG VOL/ASSN DIPLOM DOMIN EDU/PROP ATTIT DRIVE PERSON PWR SKILL WEALTH...POLICY OBS SAMP TREND STERTYP ILO WORK COLD/WAR 420. PAGE 45 A0919 LABOR INT/ORG USSR

S60
JACOBSON H.K.,"THE USSR AND ILO." COM STRUCT ECO/DEV ECO/UNDEV CONSULT DELIB/GP ECO/TAC ILO WORK COLD/WAR 20. PAGE 72 A1484 INT/ORG LABOR USSR

B61
SHARP W.R.,FIELD ADMINISTRATION IN THE UNITED NATION SYSTEM: THE CONDUCT OF INTERNATIONAL ECONOMIC AND SOCIAL PROGRAMS. FUT WOR+45 CONSTN SOCIETY ECO/UNDEV R+D DELIB/GP ACT/RES PLAN TEC/DEV EDU/PROP EXEC ROUTINE HEALTH WEALTH...HUM CONCPT CHARTS METH ILO UNESCO VAL/FREE UN 20. PAGE 132 A2697 INT/ORG CONSULT

S62
BELSHAW C.,"TRAINING AND RECRUITMENT: SOME PRINCIPLES OF INTERNATIONAL AID." FUT WOR+45 SOCIETY INT/ORG NAT/G CREATE PLAN TEC/DEV ECO/TAC FOR/AID EDU/PROP ATTIT PERCEPT...HUM UN FAO ILO UNESCO 20. PAGE 13 A0263 VOL/ASSN ECO/UNDEV

S62
TATOMIR N.,"ORGANIZATIA INTERNATIONALA A MUNCII: ASPECTE NOI ALE PROBLEMEI IMBUNATATIRII MECANISMULUI EI." EUR+WWI ECO/DEV VOL/ASSN ADMIN ...METH/CNCPT WORK ILO 20. PAGE 141 A2891 INT/ORG INT/TRADE

B64
SCHECHTER A.H.,INTERPRETATION OF AMBIGUOUS DOCUMENTS BY INTERNATIONAL ADMINISTRATIVE TRIBUNALS. WOR+45 EX/STRUC INT/TRADE CT/SYS SOVEREIGN 20 UN ILO EURCT/JUST. PAGE 128 A2620 INT/LAW DIPLOM INT/ORG ADJUD

S64
GRZYBOWSKI K.,"INTERNATIONAL ORGANIZATIONS FROM THE SOVIET POINT OF VIEW." WOR+45 WOR-45 CULTURE ECO/DEV VOL/ASSN EDU/PROP ATTIT RIGID/FLEX KNOWL ...SOC OBS TIME/SEQ TREND GEN/LAWS VAL/FREE ILO UN 20. PAGE 58 A1184 COM INT/ORG DIPLOM USSR

S64
SCHWELB E.,"OPERATION OF THE EUROPEAN CONVENTION ON HUMAN RIGHTS." EUR+WWI LAW SOCIETY CREATE EDU/PROP ADJUD ADMIN PEACE ATTIT ORD/FREE PWR...POLICY INT/LAW CONCPT OBS GEN/LAWS UN VAL/FREE ILO 20 ECHR. PAGE 130 A2665 INT/ORG MORAL

B66
LUARD E.,THE EVOLUTION OF INTERNATIONAL ORGANIZATIONS. UK WOR+45 BUDGET INT/TRADE WAR BAL/PAY PEACE ORD/FREE...POLICY 19/20 EEC ILO LEAGUE/NAT UN. PAGE 91 A1871 INT/ORG EFFICIENCY CREATE TREND

B67
MEYNAUD J.,TRADE UNIONISM IN AFRICA; A STUDY OF ITS GROWTH AND ORIENTATION (TRANS. BY ANGELA BRENCH). INT/ORG PROB/SOLV COLONIAL PWR...TIME/SEQ TREND ILO. PAGE 100 A2055 LABOR AFR NAT/LISM ORD/FREE

IMF....INTERNATIONAL MONETARY FUND

B58
SEYID MUHAMMAD V.A.,THE LEGAL FRAMEWORK OF WORLD TRADE. WOR+45 INT/ORG DIPLOM CONTROL...BIBLIOG 20 TREATY UN IMF GATT. PAGE 131 A2689 INT/LAW VOL/ASSN INT/TRADE TARIFFS

B62
SHAW C.,LEGAL PROBLEMS IN INTERNATIONAL TRADE AND INVESTMENT. WOR+45 ECO/DEV ECO/UNDEV MARKET DIPLOM TAX INCOME ROLE...ANTHOL BIBLIOG 20 TREATY UN IMF GATT. PAGE 132 A2698 INT/LAW INT/TRADE FINAN ECO/TAC

B63
INTERNATIONAL MONETARY FUND,COMPENSATORY FINANCING OF EXPORT FLUCTUATIONS (PAMPHLET). WOR+45 ECO/DEV ECO/UNDEV INT/ORG WEALTH...TREND 20 IMF MONEY. PAGE 71 A1459 BAL/PAY FINAN BUDGET INT/TRADE

B65
US CONGRESS JOINT ECO COMM,GUIDELINES FOR INTERNATIONAL MONETARY REFORM. USA+45 WOR+45 DELIB/GP BAL/PAY 20 CONGRESS IMF MONEY. PAGE 150 A3069 DIPLOM FINAN PLAN INT/ORG

IMF AND IBRD, JOINT LIBRARY A1434,A1435

IMITATION....SEE NEW/IDEA, CONSEN, CREATE

IMLAH A.H. A1436

IMMUNITY....SEE PRIVIL

IMPERIALISM....SEE COLONIAL, SOVEREIGN, DOMIN

IMPERSONALITY....SEE STRANGE

INAUGURATE....INAUGURATIONS AND CORONATIONS

INCOME....SEE ALSO FINAN, WEALTH

N
US SUPERINTENDENT OF DOCUMENTS,TARIFF AND TAXATION (PRICE LIST 37). USA+45 LAW INT/TRADE ADJUD ADMIN CT/SYS INCOME OWN...DECISION GATT. PAGE 157 A3204 BIBLIOG/A TAX TARIFFS NAT/G

B41
KEESING F.M.,THE SOUTH SEAS IN THE MODERN WORLD. INDONESIA STRUCT FAM SECT EDU/PROP LEAD INCOME WEALTH...HEAL SOC 20. PAGE 77 A1577 CULTURE ECO/UNDEV GOV/COMP DIPLOM

B53
NEISSER H.,NATIONAL INCOMES AND INTERNATIONAL TRADE. FRANCE GERMANY SWEDEN UK USA-45 EXTR/IND FINAN INDUS TEC/DEV PRICE BAL/PAY EQUILIB INCOME WEALTH...CHARTS METH 19 CHINJAP. PAGE 108 A2215 INT/TRADE PRODUC MARKET CON/ANAL

B54
GIRAUD A.,CIVILISATION ET PRODUCTIVITE. UNIV INDUS WORKER DIPLOM REV INCOME UTOPIA...GEOG 20. PAGE 53 A1076 SOCIETY PRODUC ROLE

B58
AVRAMOVIC D.,POSTWAR GROWTH IN INTERNATIONAL INDEBTEDNESS. WOR+45 AGRI INDUS CAP/ISM PRICE INCOME...NAT/COMP 20 GOLD/STAND SILVER. PAGE 10 A0199 INT/TRADE FINAN COST BAL/PAY

B60
LEVIN J.V.,THE EXPORT ECONOMIES: THEIR PATTERN OF DEVELOPMENT IN HISTORICAL PERSPECTIVE. BURMA PERU AGRI WORKER COLONIAL COST DEMAND INCOME 20. PAGE 88 A1795 INT/TRADE ECO/UNDEV BAL/PAY EXTR/IND

B60
THE ECONOMIST (LONDON),THE COMMONWEALTH AND EUROPE. EUR+WWI WOR+45 AGRI FINAN INCOME...STAT CENSUS CHARTS CMN/WLTH EEC. PAGE 142 A2911 INT/TRADE INDUS INT/ORG NAT/COMP

B61
LETHBRIDGE H.J.,CHINA'S URBAN COMMUNES. CHINA/COM FUT ECO/UNDEV DIPLOM EDU/PROP DEMAND INCOME MARXISM ...POLICY 20. PAGE 87 A1790 MUNIC CONTROL ECO/TAC NAT/G

B61
LIEFMANN-KEIL E.,OKONOMISCHE THEORIE DER SOZIALPOLITIK. INT/ORG LABOR WORKER COST INCOME NEW/LIB...CONCPT SOC/INTEG 20. PAGE 88 A1810 ECO/DEV INDUS NAT/G SOC/WK

S61
OCHENG D.,"ECONOMIC FORCES AND UGANDA'S FOREIGN POLICY." AFR UGANDA INT/TRADE TARIFFS INCOME SOVEREIGN WEALTH 20 EACM EEC TANGANYIKA. PAGE 111 A2274 ECO/TAC DIPLOM ECO/UNDEV INT/ORG

S61
OCHENG D.,"AN ECONOMIST LOOKS AT UGANDA'S FUTURE." ECO/UNDEV

FUT UGANDA AGRI INDUS PLAN PROB/SOLV INT/TRADE SOVEREIGN 20. PAGE 111 A2275
INCOME ECO/TAC OWN

B62
HOLMAN A.G.,SOME MEASURES AND INTERPRETATIONS OF EFFECTS OF US FOREIGN ENTERPRISES ON US BALANCE OF PAYMENTS. USA+45 COST INCOME WEALTH...MATH CHARTS 20. PAGE 67 A1371
BAL/PAY INT/TRADE FINAN ECO/TAC

B62
SHAW C.,LEGAL PROBLEMS IN INTERNATIONAL TRADE AND INVESTMENT. WOR+45 ECO/DEV ECO/UNDEV MARKET DIPLOM TAX INCOME ROLE...ANTHOL BIBLIOG 20 TREATY UN IMF GATT. PAGE 132 A2698
INT/LAW INT/TRADE FINAN ECO/TAC

B63
ROBOCK S.H.,OVERVIEW OF TOTAL BRAZILIAN SETTING, NEWER REGIONAL PATTERNS NING AND FOREIGN AID. BRAZIL ECO/UNDEV AGRI FINAN INDUS INT/ORG INCOME UTIL...CHARTS 20. PAGE 122 A2507
ECO/TAC REGION PLAN FOR/AID

B63
THEOBALD R.,FREE MEN AND FREE MARKETS. USA+45 USA-45 ECO/DEV NAT/G TEC/DEV DIPLOM INT/TRADE INCOME ORD/FREE WEALTH...TREND 19/20 KEYNES/JM. PAGE 143 A2915
CONCPT ECO/TAC CAP/ISM MARKET

B64
HAZLEWOOD A.,THE ECONOMICS OF DEVELOPMENT: AN ANNOTATED LIST OF BOOKS AND ARTICLES PUBLISHED 1958-1962. AGRI FINAN INDUS LABOR NAT/G DIPLOM INT/TRADE INCOME...MGT 20. PAGE 63 A1303
BIBLIOG/A ECO/UNDEV TEC/DEV

B64
JOHNSON L.B.,MY HOPE FOR AMERICA. FUT USA+45 USSR LAW PLAN DIPLOM GIVE INCOME PEACE ATTIT ORD/FREE WEALTH 20 JOHNSON/LB PRESIDENT DEMOCRAT. PAGE 74 A1525
POLICY POL/PAR NAT/G GOV/REL

B64
KNIGHT R.,BIBLIOGRAPHY ON INCOME AND WEALTH, 1957-1960 (VOL VIII). WOR+45 ECO/DEV FINAN INT/TRADE...GOV/COMP METH/COMP. PAGE 80 A1652
BIBLIOG/A ECO/UNDEV WEALTH INCOME

B64
LITTLE I.M.D.,AID TO AFRICA. AFR UK TEC/DEV DIPLOM ECO/TAC INCOME WEALTH 20. PAGE 90 A1844
FOR/AID ECO/UNDEV ADMIN POLICY

L65
LOFTUS M.L.,"INTERNATIONAL MONETARY FUND, 1962-1965: A SELECTED BIBLIOGRAPHY." WOR+45 PLAN BUDGET INCOME PROFIT WEALTH. PAGE 90 A1852
BIBLIOG FINAN INT/TRADE INT/ORG

B66
MURPHY G.G.,SOVIET MONGOLIA: A STUDY OF THE OLDEST POLITICAL SATELLITE. USSR STRATA STRUCT COST INCOME ATTIT SOCISM 20. PAGE 106 A2177
DIPLOM ECO/TAC PLAN DOMIN

N66
EOMMITTEE ECONOMIC DEVELOPMENT,THE DOLLAR AND THE WORLD MONETARY SYSTEM: A STATEMENT ON NATIONAL POLICY (PAMPHLET). USA+45 NAT/G PLAN PROB/SOLV BUDGET ECO/TAC FOR/AID INCOME...POLICY 20 GOLD/STAND EUROPE. PAGE 42 A0854
FINAN BAL/PAY DIPLOM ECO/DEV

B96
SMITH A.,LECTURES ON JUSTICE, POLICE, REVENUE AND ARMS (1763). UK LAW FAM FORCES TARIFFS AGREE COERCE INCOME OWN WEALTH LAISSEZ...GEN/LAWS 17/18. PAGE 134 A2743
DIPLOM JURID OLD/LIB TAX

INCOMPETENCE....SEE SKILL

IND/WRK/AF....INDUSTRIAL AND WORKERS' COMMERCIAL UNION OF AFRICA

INDEX....INDEX SYSTEM

N
CHINA QUARTERLY. COM AGRI INDUS ACADEM POL/PAR INT/TRADE CONFER GOV/REL...TIME/SEQ CON/ANAL INDEX 20. PAGE 2 A0032
BIBLIOG/A ASIA DIPLOM POLICY

N
LONDON TIMES OFFICIAL INDEX. UK LAW ECO/DEV NAT/G DIPLOM LEAD ATTIT 20. PAGE 2 A0038
BIBLIOG INDEX PRESS WRITING

N
THE MIDDLE EAST AND NORTH AFRICA. AFR ISLAM CULTURE ECO/UNDEV AGRI NAT/G TEC/DEV FOR/AID INT/TRADE EDU/PROP...CHARTS 20. PAGE 2 A0043
INDEX INDUS FINAN STAT

N
DE MARTENS G.F.,RECUEIL GENERALE DE TRAITES ET AUTRES ACTES RELATIFS AUX RAPPORTS DE DROIT INTERNATIONAL (41 VOLS.). EUR+WWI MOD/EUR USA-45 ...INDEX TREATY 18/20. PAGE 35 A0708
BIBLIOG INT/LAW DIPLOM

N
UNIVERSITY MICROFILMS INC,DISSERTATION ABSTRACTS: ABSTRACTS OF DISSERTATIONS AND MONOGRAPHS IN MICROFILM. CANADA DIPLOM ADMIN...INDEX 20. PAGE 149 A3045
BIBLIOG/A ACADEM PRESS WRITING

N
US CONSOLATE GENERAL HONG KONG,REVIEW OF THE HONG KONG CHINESE PRESS. ECO/UNDEV LOC/G NAT/G PLAN DIPLOM EDU/PROP LEAD GP/REL MARXISM...POLICY INDEX 20. PAGE 150 A3073
BIBLIOG/A ASIA PRESS ATTIT

N
US CONSULATE GENERAL HONG KONG,CURRENT BACKGROUND. CHINA/COM ECO/UNDEV LOC/G NAT/G PLAN DIPLOM EDU/PROP LEAD REV ATTIT...POLICY INDEX 20. PAGE 151 A3074
BIBLIOG/A MARXIST ASIA PRESS

N
US CONSULATE GENERAL HONG KONG,SURVEY OF CHINA MAINLAND PRESS. CHINA/COM ECO/UNDEV LOC/G NAT/G PLAN DIPLOM EDU/PROP LEAD REV ATTIT...POLICY INDEX 20. PAGE 151 A3075
BIBLIOG/A MARXIST ASIA PRESS

N
US CONSULATE GENERAL HONG KONG,US CONSULATE GENERAL, HONG KONG, PRESS SUMMARIES. CHINA/COM ECO/UNDEV LOC/G NAT/G PLAN DIPLOM EDU/PROP LEAD REV ATTIT...POLICY INDEX 20. PAGE 151 A3076
BIBLIOG/A MARXIST ASIA PRESS

B03
FORTESCUE G.K.,SUBJECT INDEX OF THE MODERN WORKS ADDED TO THE LIBRARY OF THE BRITISH MUSEUM IN THE YEARS 1881-1900 (3 VOLS.). UK LAW CONSTN FINAN NAT/G FORCES INT/TRADE COLONIAL 19. PAGE 47 A0968
BIBLIOG INDEX WRITING

B05
AMES J.G.,COMPREHENSIVE INDEX TO THE PUBLICATIONS OF THE UNITED STATES GOVERNMENT , 1881-1893. USA-45 CONSTN POL/PAR DELIB/GP TOP/EX DIPLOM PARL/PROC INGP/REL...INDEX 19 CONGRESS. PAGE 8 A0153
BIBLIOG/A LEGIS NAT/G GOV/REL

B14
HASSE A.R.,INDEX TO UNITED STATES DOCUMENTS RELATING TO FOREIGN AFFAIRS, 1828-1861 (3 VOLS.). USA-45 CHIEF 19 CONGRESS. PAGE 63 A1285
INDEX DIPLOM LEGIS

B28
LODGE H.C.,THE HISTORY OF NATIONS (25 VOLS.). UNIV LEAD...ANTHOL BIBLIOG INDEX. PAGE 90 A1850
DIPLOM SOCIETY NAT/G

B53
GREENE K.R.C.,INSTITUTIONS AND INDIVIDUALS: AN ANNOTATED LIST OF DIRECTORIES USEFUL IN INTERNATIONAL ADMINISTRATION. USA+45 NAT/G VOL/ASSN ...INDEX 20. PAGE 56 A1141
BIBLIOG INT/ORG ADMIN DIPLOM

B54
BINANI G.D.,INDIA AT A GLANCE (REV. ED.). INDIA COM/IND FINAN INDUS LABOR PROVS SCHOOL PLAN DIPLOM INT/TRADE ADMIN...JURID 20. PAGE 14 A0288
INDEX CON/ANAL NAT/G ECO/UNDEV

B59
UNION OF INTERNATIONAL ASSNS,DIRECTORY OF PERIODICALS PUBLISHED BY INTERNATIONAL ORGANIZATIONS (2ND ED.)....INDEX 20. PAGE 148 A3027
BIBLIOG INT/ORG DIPLOM VOL/ASSN

B60
AMERICAN ASSOCIATION LAW LIB,INDEX TO FOREIGN LEGAL PERIODICALS. WOR+45 MUNIC...IDEA/COMP 20. PAGE 7 A0139
INDEX LAW JURID DIPLOM

B60
LERNER A.P.,THE ECONOMICS OF CONTROL. USA+45 ECO/UNDEV INT/ORG ACT/RES PLAN CAP/ISM INT/TRADE ATTIT WEALTH...SOC MATH STAT GEN/LAWS INDEX 20. PAGE 87 A1785
ECO/DEV ROUTINE ECO/TAC SOCISM

L60
HAAS E.B.,"CONSENSUS FORMATION IN THE COUNCIL OF EUROPE." EUR+WWI NAT/G DELIB/GP DIPLOM REGION CHOOSE PWR SOVEREIGN...RELATIV NEW/IDEA QUANT CHARTS INDEX TOT/POP OEEC 20 COUNCL/EUR. PAGE 59 A1206
POL/PAR INT/ORG STAT

B61
ASIA SOCIETY,AMERICAN INSTITUTIONS ANS ORGANIZATIONS INTERESTED IN ASIA; A REFERENCE DIRECTORY (2ND ED.). ASIA USA+45 CULTURE SECT DIPLOM EDU/PROP...INDEX 20. PAGE 9 A0190
VOL/ASSN ACADEM PROF/ORG

B61
PEASLEE A.J.,INTERNATIONAL GOVERNMENTAL ORGANIZATIONS (2 VOLS.). CONSTN VOL/ASSN DIPLOM ...GP/COMP 20 UN OAS EEC EFTA ECSC. PAGE 114 A2345
BIBLIOG INT/ORG INDEX LAW

B62
BLAUSTEIN A.P.,MANUAL ON FOREIGN LEGAL PERIODICALS AND THEIR INDEX. WOR+45 DIPLOM 20. PAGE 15 A0310
BIBLIOG INDEX LAW JURID

S63
BALOGH T.,"L'INFLUENCE DES INSTITUTIONS MONETAIRES ET COMMERCIALES SUR LA STRUCTURE ECONOMIQUE AFRICAIN." AFR EUR+WWI FUT USA+45 USA-45 WOR+45 SERV/IND INT/ORG NAT/G TOP/EX ROUTINE...INDEX EEC 20. PAGE 11 A0215
FINAN

B65
SABLE M.H.,MASTER DIRECTORY FOR LATIN AMERICA. AGRI COM/IND FINAN R+D ACADEM LABOR NAT/G POL/PAR VOL/ASSN INT/TRADE EDU/PROP 20. PAGE 126 A2582
INDEX L/A+17C INT/ORG DIPLOM

B65
UNESCO,HANDBOOK OF INTERNATIONAL EXCHANGES. COM/IND R+D ACADEM PROF/ORG VOL/ASSN CREATE TEC/DEV EDU/PROP AGREE 20 TREATY. PAGE 148 A3025
INDEX INT/ORG DIPLOM PRESS

B67
US DEPARTMENT OF STATE,FOREIGN AFFAIRS RESEARCH (PAMPHLET). USA+45 WOR+45 ACADEM NAT/G...PSY SOC CHARTS 20. PAGE 152 A3100
BIBLIOG INDEX R+D DIPLOM

INDIA....SEE ALSO S/ASIA

N
INDIA: A REFERENCE ANNUAL. INDIA CULTURE COM/IND R+D FORCES PLAN RECEIVE EDU/PROP HEALTH...STAT CHARTS BIBLIOG 20. PAGE 2 A0036
CONSTN LABOR INT/ORG

N
SEMINAR: THE MONTHLY SYMPOSIUM. INDIA ACT/RES TEC/DEV DIPLOM ATTIT...BIBLIOG 20. PAGE 2 A0041
NAT/G ECO/UNDEV SOVEREIGN POLICY

N
AMERICAN BIBLIOGRAPHIC SERVICE,INTERNATIONAL GUIDE TO INDIC STUDIES - A QUARTERLY INDEX TO PERIODICAL LITERATURE. INDIA CULTURE NAT/G DIPLOM...EPIST SOC BIOG 20. PAGE 7 A0140
BIBLIOG S/ASIA CON/ANAL

N
INTERNATIONAL STUDIES,"INDIA AND WORLD AFFAIRS: AN ANNUAL BIBLIOGRAPHY" INDIA INT/TRADE PARTIC GOV/REL 20. PAGE 71 A1461
BIBLIOG POLICY DIPLOM ATTIT

N
US LIBRARY OF CONGRESS,ACCESSIONS LIST - INDIA. INDIA CULTURE AGRI LOC/G POL/PAR PLAN PROB/SOLV TEC/DEV DIPLOM EDU/PROP LEAD GP/REL ATTIT 20. PAGE 154 A3142
BIBLIOG S/ASIA ECO/UNDEV NAT/G

B02
SEELEY J.R.,THE EXPANSION OF ENGLAND. MOD/EUR S/ASIA UK CULTURE NAT/G FORCES PLAN DOMIN EDU/PROP COLONIAL ROUTINE ATTIT ALL/VALS SOVEREIGN...CONCPT HIST/WRIT PARLIAMENT 18 CMN/WLTH. PAGE 131 A2679
INT/ORG ACT/RES CAP/ISM INDIA

N19
MASON E.S.,THE DIPLOMACY OF ECONOMIC ASSISTANCE (PAMPHLET). INDIA PAKISTAN USA+45 ECO/UNDEV NAT/G BUDGET ATTIT...POLICY 20. PAGE 95 A1955
FOR/AID DIPLOM FINAN

B39
FURNIVALL J.S.,NETHERLANDS INDIA. INDIA NETHERLAND CULTURE INDUS NAT/G DIPLOM ADMIN WEALTH...POLICY CHARTS 17/20. PAGE 50 A1029
COLONIAL ECO/UNDEV SOVEREIGN PLURISM

B42
JOSHI P.S.,THE TYRANNY OF COLOUR. INDIA SOUTH/AFR UK ECO/UNDEV NAT/G POL/PAR DIPLOM ECO/TAC WAR ...POLICY 19/20. PAGE 75 A1538
COLONIAL DISCRIM RACE/REL

N45
INDIA QUARTERLY, A JOURNAL OF INTERNATIONAL AFFAIRS. INDIA LAW CONSTN ECO/UNDEV INT/ORG POL/PAR COLONIAL LEAD PARL/PROC WAR ATTIT...SOC 20 CMN/WLTH. PAGE 3 A0053
BIBLIOG/A S/ASIA DIPLOM NAT/G

B45
ELTON G.E.,IMPERIAL COMMONWEALTH. INDIA UK DIPLOM DOMIN WAR NAT/LISM SOVEREIGN...TRADIT CHARTS T 15/20 CMN/WLTH AUSTRAL PRE/US/AM. PAGE 41 A0844
REGION CONCPT COLONIAL

B50
BROOKINGS INSTITUTION,MAJOR PROBLEMS OF UNITED STATES FOREIGN POLICY. AFR ASIA INDIA UK USA+45 USSR BAL/PWR FOR/AID WAR PEACE TOTALISM MARXISM SOCISM 20 CHINJAP COLD/WAR. PAGE 19 A0393
DIPLOM POLICY ORD/FREE

B51
JENNINGS I.,THE COMMONWEALTH IN ASIA. CEYLON INDIA PAKISTAN CULTURE STRATA NAT/G LEGIS DIPLOM COLONIAL ATTIT...DECISION 20 CMN/WLTH. PAGE 74 A1507
CONSTN INT/ORG POLICY PLAN

B51
JENNINGS S.I.,THE COMMONWEALTH IN ASIA. CEYLON INDIA PAKISTAN S/ASIA UK CONSTN CULTURE SOCIETY STRATA STRUCT NAT/G POL/PAR EDU/PROP LEAD WAR 20 CMN/WLTH. PAGE 74 A1510
NAT/LISM REGION COLONIAL DIPLOM

B53
MANSERGH N.,DOCUMENTS AND SPEECHES ON BRITISH COMMONWEALTH AFFAIRS 1931-1952. INDIA IRELAND PAKISTAN UK CONSTN POL/PAR CHIEF FORCES COLONIAL ORD/FREE SOVEREIGN...JURID 20 COMMONWLTH. PAGE 94 A1929
BIBLIOG/A DIPLOM ECO/TAC

B53
MURPHY G.,IN THE MINDS OF MEN: THE STUDY OF HUMAN BEHAVIOR AND SOCIAL TENSIONS IN INDIA. FUT S/ASIA FAM INT/ORG NAT/G DIPLOM EDU/PROP GP/REL ATTIT RIGID/FLEX ALL/VALS...SOC QU UNESCO 20. PAGE 106 A2176
SECT STRATA INDIA

B54
BINANI G.D.,INDIA AT A GLANCE (REV. ED.). INDIA COM/IND FINAN INDUS LABOR PROVS SCHOOL PLAN DIPLOM INT/TRADE ADMIN...JURID 20. PAGE 14 A0288
INDEX CON/ANAL NAT/G ECO/UNDEV

B54
SHARMA J.S.,MAHATMA GANDHI: A DESCRIPTIVE BIBLIOGRAPHY. INDIA S/ASIA PROB/SOLV DIPLOM COLONIAL WAR NAT/LISM PEACE ATTIT PERSON SOVEREIGN ...CONCPT 20 GANDHI/M. PAGE 132 A2695
BIBLIOG/A BIOG CHIEF LEAD

L54
CHARLESWORTH J.C.,"AMERICA AND A NEW ASIA." ASIA INDIA ISLAM S/ASIA USA+45 USA-45 ECO/UNDEV NAT/G POL/PAR FORCES FOR/AID DOMIN EDU/PROP COERCE DRIVE ALL/VALS MARXISM SOCISM TOT/POP 20. PAGE 26 A0522
ECO/TAC DIPLOM NAT/LISM

B55
PANT Y.P.,PLANNING IN UNDERDEVELOPED ECONOMIES. INDIA NEPAL INT/TRADE COLONIAL SOVEREIGN ALL/IDEOS ...TIME/SEQ METH/COMP 20. PAGE 114 A2334
ECO/UNDEV PLAN ECO/TAC DIPLOM

B56
WILSON P.,GOVERNMENT AND POLITICS OF INDIA AND PAKISTAN: 1885-1955; A BIBLIOGRAPHY OF WORKS IN WESTERN LANGUAGES. INDIA PAKISTAN CONSTN LOC/G POL/PAR FORCES DIPLOM ADMIN WAR CHOOSE...BIOG CON/ANAL 19/20. PAGE 165 A3361
BIBLIOG COLONIAL NAT/G S/ASIA

B57
NEHRU J.,MILITARY ALLIANCE (PAMPHLET). INDIA WOR+45 NAT/G PLAN DETER NUC/PWR WAR...POLICY ANTHOL NEHRU/J SEATO UN. PAGE 108 A2212
INT/ORG DIPLOM FORCES PEACE

B57
WILSON P.,SOUTH ASIA; A SELECTED BIBLIOGRAPHY ON INDIA, PAKISTAN, CEYLON (PAMPHLET). CEYLON INDIA PAKISTAN LAW ECO/UNDEV PLAN DIPLOM 20. PAGE 165 A3362
BIBLIOG S/ASIA CULTURE NAT/G

B58
ALEXANDROWICZ,A BIBLIOGRAPHY OF INDIAN LAW. INDIA S/ASIA CONSTN CT/SYS...INT/LAW 19/20. PAGE 6 A0113
BIBLIOG LAW ADJUD JURID

B58
BOWLES C.,IDEAS, PEOPLE AND PEACE. ASIA CHINA/COM FUT INDIA USA+45 USSR ECO/UNDEV INT/ORG LEAD TASK MARXISM 20 NATO UN COLD/WAR. PAGE 18 A0359
PEACE POLICY NAT/G DIPLOM

B58
INDIAN COUNCIL WORLD AFFAIRS,DEFENCE AND SECURITY IN THE INDIAN OCEAN AREA. INDIA S/ASIA CULTURE CONSULT DELIB/GP FORCES PROB/SOLV DIPLOM INT/TRADE 20 CMN/WLTH. PAGE 70 A1438
GEOG HABITAT ECO/UNDEV ORD/FREE

B58
JENNINGS I.,PROBLEMS OF THE NEW COMMONWEALTH. CEYLON INDIA PAKISTAN S/ASIA ECO/UNDEV INT/ORG LOC/G DIPLOM ECO/TAC INT/TRADE COLONIAL RACE/REL DISCRIM 20 COMMONWLTH PARLIAMENT. PAGE 74 A1508
NAT/LISM NEUTRAL FOR/AID POL/PAR

B58
JENNINGS W.I.,PROBLEMS OF THE NEW COMMONWEALTH. CEYLON INDIA MALAYSIA PAKISTAN ECO/UNDEV VOL/ASSN RACE/REL NAT/LISM ROLE 20 CMN/WLTH. PAGE 74 A1511
GP/REL INGP/REL COLONIAL INT/ORG

B58
MANSERGH N.,SURVEY OF BRITISH COMMONWEALTH AFFAIRS: PROBLEMS OF WARTIME CO-OPERATION AND POST-WAR CHANGE 1939-1952. INDIA IRELAND S/ASIA CONSTN INT/ORG BAL/PWR COLONIAL NEUTRAL WAR ADJUST PEACE ROLE ORD/FREE...CHARTS 20 CMN/WLTH NATO UN. PAGE 94 A1931
VOL/ASSN CONSEN PROB/SOLV INGP/REL

B58
NEHRU J.,SPEECHES. INDIA ECO/UNDEV AGRI INDUS INT/ORG POL/PAR DIPLOM FOR/AID NAT/LISM...ANTHOL 20. PAGE 108 A2213
PLAN CHIEF COLONIAL NEUTRAL

B58
SALETORE B.A.,INDIA'S DIPLOMATIC RELATIONS WITH THE WEST. GREECE INDIA CULTURE ETIQUET...IDEA/COMP 3 ROM/EMP PERSIA. PAGE 126 A2590
DIPLOM CONCPT INT/TRADE

B59
FREE L.A.,SIX ALLIES AND A NEUTRAL. ASIA COM EUR+WWI FRANCE GERMANY/W INDIA S/ASIA UK USA+45 INT/ORG NAT/G NUC/PWR PEACE ATTIT PERCEPT RIGID/FLEX ALL/VALS...STAT REC/INT COLD/WAR 20 CHINJAP. PAGE 48 A0992
PSY DIPLOM

B59
KARUNAKARAN K.P.,INDIA IN WORLD AFFAIRS, 1952-1958 (VOL. II). INDIA ECO/UNDEV SECT FOR/AID INT/TRADE ADJUD NEUTRAL REV WAR DISCRIM ORD/FREE MARXISM ...BIBLIOG 20. PAGE 77 A1569
DIPLOM INT/ORG S/ASIA COLONIAL

B59
US GENERAL ACCOUNTING OFFICE,EXAM OF ECONOMIC AND TECHNICAL ASSISTANCE PROGRAM FOR INDIA INT'NAT'L COOP ADMIN REPORT TO CONGRESS 1955-1958. INDIA USA+45 ECO/UNDEV FINAN PLAN DIPLOM COST UTIL WEALTH ...CHARTS 20 CONGRESS AID. PAGE 153 A3114
FOR/AID EFFICIENCY ECO/TAC TEC/DEV

S59
KRIPALANI A.J.B.,"FOR PRINCIPLED NEUTRALITY." CHINA/COM INDIA S/ASIA PLAN ECO/TAC RIGID/FLEX MORAL PWR...MYSTIC SOC RECORD 20 GANDHI/M. PAGE 82 A1684
ATTIT FOR/AID DIPLOM

N59
BRITISH COMMONWEALTH REL CONF,EXTRACTS FROM THE
DIPLOM

PROCEEDINGS OF THE SIXTH UNOFFICIAL CONFERENCE (PAMPHLET). GHANA INDIA RHODESIA UK FINAN FORCES DETER FEDERAL...LING 20 PARLIAMENT. PAGE 19 A0379
PARL/PROC INT/TRADE ORD/FREE

B60
LATIFI D.,INDIA AND UNITED STATES AID. ASIA INDIA UK USA+45 AGRI FINAN INDUS COLONIAL ORD/FREE SOVEREIGN WEALTH...METH/COMP 20. PAGE 85 A1743
FOR/AID DIPLOM ECO/UNDEV

B60
MC CLELLAN G.S.,INDIA. CHINA/COM INDIA CONSTN ELITES STRATA AGRI POL/PAR FOR/AID ARMS/CONT REV MARXISM...CENSUS BIBLIOG 20 COLD/WAR GANDHI/M NEHRU/J. PAGE 97 A1990
DIPLOM NAT/G SOCIETY ECO/UNDEV

B60
MORAES F.,THE REVOLT IN TIBET. ASIA CHINA/COM INDIA CULTURE CONTROL COERCE WAR TOTALISM...POLICY SOC WORSHIP 20 TIBET INTERVENT. PAGE 104 A2127
COLONIAL FORCES DIPLOM ORD/FREE

B60
PENTONY D.E.,UNITED STATES FOREIGN AID. INDIA LAOS USA+45 ECO/UNDEV INT/TRADE ADMIN PEACE ATTIT ...POLICY METH/COMP ANTHOL 20. PAGE 115 A2352
FOR/AID DIPLOM ECO/TAC

B60
SALETORE B.A.,INDIA'S DIPLOMATIC RELATIONS WITH THE EAST. ASIA CEYLON INDIA NEPAL S/ASIA CULTURE 7/14 PERSIA. PAGE 126 A2591
DIPLOM NAT/COMP ETIQUET

S60
GINSBURGS G.,"PEKING-LHASA-NEW DELHI." CHINA/COM FUT INDIA S/ASIA KIN NAT/G PROVS SECT FORCES BAL/PWR ECO/TAC DOMIN EDU/PROP LEGIT ADMIN REGION GUERRILLA PWR...TREND TIBET 20. PAGE 52 A1074
ASIA COERCE DIPLOM

B61
BAINS J.S.,STUDIES IN POLITICAL SCIENCE. INDIA WOR+45 WOR-45 CONSTN BAL/PWR ADJUD ADMIN PARL/PROC SOVEREIGN...SOC METH/COMP ANTHOL 17/20 UN. PAGE 10 A0209
DIPLOM INT/LAW NAT/G

B61
GURTOO D.H.N.,INDIA'S BALANCE OF PAYMENTS (1920-1960). INDIA FINAN DIPLOM FOR/AID INT/TRADE PRICE COLONIAL...CHARTS BIBLIOG 20. PAGE 58 A1197
BAL/PAY STAT ECO/TAC ECO/UNDEV

B61
HARRISON S.,INDIA AND THE UNITED STATES. FUT S/ASIA USA+45 WOR+45 INTELL ECO/DEV ECO/UNDEV AGRI INDUS INT/ORG NAT/G CONSULT EX/STRUC TOP/EX PLAN ECO/TAC NEUTRAL ALL/VALS...MGT TOT/POP 20. PAGE 62 A1272
DELIB/GP ACT/RES FOR/AID INDIA

B61
HISTORICAL RESEARCH INSTITUTE,A SHORT BIBLIOGRAPHY OF INDO-MUSLIM HISTORY. INDIA S/ASIA DIPLOM EDU/PROP COLONIAL LEAD NAT/LISM ATTIT...BIOG 19/20. PAGE 65 A1343
BIBLIOG NAT/G SECT POL/PAR

B61
KHAN A.W.,INDIA WINS FREEDOM: THE OTHER SIDE. INDIA PAKISTAN CULTURE LEGIS DIPLOM PARL/PROC REV WAR NAT/LISM 20. PAGE 78 A1607
SOVEREIGN GP/REL RACE/REL ORD/FREE

B61
PALMER N.D.,THE INDIAN POLITICAL SYSTEM. INDIA ECO/UNDEV SECT CHIEF COLONIAL CHOOSE ALL/IDEOS SOCISM...CHARTS BIBLIOG/A 20. PAGE 113 A2322
NAT/LISM POL/PAR NAT/G DIPLOM

B61
PANIKKAR K.M.,THE VOICE OF FREEDOM: SELECTED SPEECHES OF PANDIT MOTILAL NEHRU. INDIA UK CONSTN FINAN FORCES LEGIS DIPLOM TAX COLONIAL...POLICY MAJORIT ANTHOL 20 NEHRU/PM. PAGE 114 A2331
NAT/LISM ORD/FREE CHIEF NAT/G

B61
SYATAUW J.J.G.,SOME NEWLY ESTABLISHED ASIAN STATES AND THE DEVELOPMENT OF INTERNATIONAL LAW. BURMA CEYLON INDIA INDONESIA ECO/UNDEV COLONIAL NEUTRAL WAR PEACE SOVEREIGN...CHARTS 19/20. PAGE 140 A2873
INT/LAW ADJUST SOCIETY S/ASIA

B61
WARD B.J.,INDIA AND THE WEST. INDIA UK USA+45 INT/TRADE GIVE COLONIAL ATTIT MARXISM 19/20. PAGE 161 A3279
PLAN ECO/UNDEV ECO/TAC FOR/AID

S61
RAY J.,"THE EUROPEAN FREE-TRADE ASSOCIATION AND ITS IMPACT ON INDIA'S TRADE." EUR+WWI FRANCE GERMANY INDIA S/ASIA UK NAT/G VOL/ASSN PLAN INT/TRADE ROUTINE WEALTH...STAT CHARTS CMN/WLTH EEC OEEC 20 EFTA. PAGE 120 A2453
ECO/DEV ECO/TAC

B62
DAVAR F.C.,IRAN AND INDIA THROUGH THE AGES. INDIA IRAN ELITES SECT CREATE ORD/FREE...LING BIBLIOG. PAGE 34 A0683
NAT/COMP DIPLOM CULTURE

B62
HUTTENBACK R.A.,BRITISH RELATIONS WITH THE SIND, 1799-1843. FRANCE INDIA UK FORCES...POLICY CHARTS BIBLIOG 18/19 SIND. PAGE 69 A1425
COLONIAL DIPLOM DOMIN S/ASIA

B62
LEWIS J.P.,QUIET CRISIS IN INDIA. INDIA USA+45 CULTURE ECO/UNDEV AGRI INDUS PROC/MFG NAT/G PLAN TEC/DEV DRIVE PWR SKILL WEALTH...MYTH 20. PAGE 88 A1801
S/ASIA ECO/TAC FOR/AID

B62
MODELSKI G.,SEATO-SIX STUDIES. ASIA CHINA/COM INDIA S/ASIA INT/ORG NAT/G ECO/TAC DETER ATTIT ORD/FREE PWR...TIME/SEQ COLD/WAR TOT/POP 20 SEATO. PAGE 102 A2098
MARKET ECO/UNDEV INT/TRADE

B62
MOON P.,DIVIDE AND QUIT. INDIA PAKISTAN STRATA DELIB/GP PLAN DIPLOM REPRESENT GP/REL INGP/REL CONSEN DISCRIM...OBS 20. PAGE 103 A2119
WAR REGION ISOLAT SECT

S62
RUBINSTEIN A.Z.,"RUSSIA AND THE UNCOMMITTED NATIONS." AFR INDIA ISLAM L/A+17C LAOS S/ASIA ELITES ECO/UNDEV INT/ORG KIN CREATE PLAN TEC/DEV NAT/LISM RIGID/FLEX PWR WEALTH...METH/CNCPT TIME/SEQ GEN/LAWS WORK. PAGE 125 A2562
ECO/TAC TREND COLONIAL USSR

S62
SPECTOR I.,"SOVIET POLICY IN ASIA: A REAPPRAISAL." ASIA CHINA/COM COM INDIA INDONESIA ECO/UNDEV INT/ORG DOMIN EDU/PROP REGION RESPECT...CONCPT TREND TOT/POP COLD/WAR 20 CHINJAP. PAGE 135 A2774
S/ASIA PWR FOR/AID USSR

B63
BROWN W.N.,THE UNITED STATES AND INDIA AND PAKISTAN (REV. ED.). INDIA PAKISTAN S/ASIA WOR+45 POL/PAR SECT INT/TRADE COLONIAL COERCE DISCRIM. PAGE 20 A0408
DIPLOM ECO/UNDEV SOVEREIGN STRUCT

B63
HONEY P.J.,COMMUNISM IN NORTH VIETNAM: ITS ROLE IN THE SINO-SOVIET DISPUTE. CHINA/COM INDIA USSR VIETNAM/N AGRI POL/PAR LEGIS ECO/TAC WAR PEACE ATTIT...GEOG IDEA/COMP 20. PAGE 67 A1378
POLICY MARXISM CHIEF DIPLOM

B63
JAIRAZBHOY R.A.,FOREIGN INFLUENCE IN ANCIENT INDIA. INDIA ELITES SECT DIPLOM EDU/PROP COLONIAL REGION GP/REL...ART/METH LING WORSHIP +/14 GRECO/ROMN MESOPOTAM PERSIA PARTH/SASS. PAGE 73 A1491
CULTURE SOCIETY COERCE DOMIN

B63
KAHIN G.M.,MAJOR GOVERNMENTS OF ASIA (2ND ED.). ASIA INDIA INDONESIA PAKISTAN S/ASIA DIPLOM...SOC 20 CHINJAP. PAGE 75 A1546
GOV/COMP POL/PAR ELITES

B63
MANSERGH N.,DOCUMENTS AND SPEECHES ON COMMONWEALTH AFFAIRS 1952-1962. CANADA INDIA PAKISTAN UK CONSTN FORCES ECO/TAC EDU/PROP COLONIAL DETER WAR ORD/FREE SOVEREIGN...POLICY 20 AUSTRAL. PAGE 94 A1932
BIBLIOG/A FEDERAL INT/TRADE DIPLOM

B63
PATRA A.C.,THE ADMINISTRATION OF JUSTICE UNDER THE EAST INDIA COMPANY IN BENGAL, BIHAR AND ORISSA. INDIA UK LG/CO CAP/ISM INT/TRADE ADJUD COLONIAL CONTROL CT/SYS...POLICY 20. PAGE 114 A2341
ADMIN JURID CONCPT

B63
RAO V.K.R.,FOREIGN AID AND INDIA'S ECONOMIC DEVELOPMENT. INDIA INT/ORG PROB/SOLV TEC/DEV ECO/TAC CONTROL WEALTH...TREND 20. PAGE 119 A2445
FOR/AID ECO/UNDEV RECEIVE DIPLOM

B63
RUSSELL B.,UNARMED VICTORY. CHINA/COM CUBA INDIA USA+45 WAR MARXISM...POLICY IDEA/COMP 20 KHRUSH/N COLD/WAR. PAGE 125 A2573
DIPLOM ATTIT SOCISM ORD/FREE

B63
THIEN T.T.,INDIA AND SOUTHEAST ASIA 1947-1960. COM INDIA S/ASIA SECT DELIB/GP FOR/AID RACE/REL NAT/LISM SOCISM...CHARTS BIBLIOG 20 UN NEHRU/J TREATY. PAGE 143 A2917
DRIVE DIPLOM POLICY

B63
US HOUSE COMM FOREIGN AFFAIRS,HEARINGS ON H.R. 5490 TO AMEND FURTHER THE FOREIGN ASSISTANCE ACT OF 1961. CUBA EUR+WWI INDIA INT/ORG DELIB/GP LEGIS DIPLOM CONFER ORD/FREE 20 DEPT/STATE DEPT/DEFEN UN. PAGE 153 A3129
FOR/AID INT/TRADE FORCES WEAPON

B63
WILCOX W.A.,PAKISTAN; THE CONSOLIDATION OF A NATION. INDIA PAKISTAN CONSTN SECT PROB/SOLV COLONIAL PARTIC GP/REL FEDERAL...POLICY 19/20. PAGE 164 A3348
NAT/LISM ECO/UNDEV DIPLOM STRUCT

S63
CHAKRAVARTI P.C.,"INDIAN NON-ALIGNMENT AND UNITED STATES POLICY." ASIA INDIA S/ASIA USA+45 CULTURE ECO/UNDEV NAT/G VOL/ASSN DELIB/GP TOP/EX FOR/AID NEUTRAL...POLICY HUM CONCPT RECORD GEN/LAWS 20. PAGE 25 A0515
ATTIT ALL/VALS COLONIAL DIPLOM

S63
GUPTA S.C.,"INDIA AND THE SOVIET UNION." CHINA/COM COM INDIA S/ASIA VOL/ASSN TOP/EX FOR/AID EDU/PROP PEACE PWR...RECORD COLD/WAR 20. PAGE 58 A1195
DISPL MYTH USSR

S63
WEISSBERG G.,"MAPS AS EVIDENCE IN INTERNATIONAL BOUNDARY DISPUTES: A REAPPRAISAL." CHINA/COM EUR+WWI INDIA MOD/EUR S/ASIA INT/ORG NAT/G LEGIT PERCEPT...JURID CHARTS 20. PAGE 163 A3311
LAW GEOG SOVEREIGN

N63
PATEL H.M.,THE DEFENCE OF INDIA (PAMPHLET). CHINA/COM INDIA PAKISTAN WOR+45 TEC/DEV BAL/PWR DIPLOM CONTROL WAR. PAGE 114 A2340
FORCES POLICY SOVEREIGN DETER

B64
THE SPECIAL COMMONWEALTH AFRICAN ASSISTANCE PLAN. AFR CANADA INDIA NIGERIA UK FINAN SCHOOL...CHARTS 20 COMMONWLTH. PAGE 3 A0065
ECO/UNDEV TREND FOR/AID ADMIN

B64
CASEY R.G.,THE FUTURE OF THE COMMONWEALTH. INDIA PAKISTAN UK ECO/UNDEV INT/ORG TEC/DEV COLONIAL SUPEGO 20 EEC AUSTRAL. PAGE 25 A0505
DIPLOM SOVEREIGN NAT/LISM FOR/AID

B64
COLUMBIA U SCHOOL OF LAW,PUBLIC INTERNATIONAL DEVELOPMENT FINANCING IN INDIA. GERMANY/W INDIA UK USA+45 INDUS PLAN TEC/DEV DIPLOM ECO/TAC GIVE ADMIN UTIL ATTIT 20. PAGE 28 A0572
ECO/UNDEV FINAN FOR/AID INT/ORG

B64
DESHMUKH C.D.,THE COMMONWEALTH AS INDIA SEES IT. INDIA UK ECO/UNDEV TEC/DEV INT/TRADE GP/REL RACE/REL SOVEREIGN SOC/INTEG 19/20 COMMONWLTH. PAGE 36 A0733
DIPLOM COLONIAL NAT/LISM ATTIT

B64
KALDOR N.,ESSAYS ON ECONOMIC POLICY (VOL. II). CHILE GERMANY INDIA FINAN...GOV/COMP METH/COMP 20 KEYNES/JM. PAGE 76 A1551
BAL/PAY INT/TRADE METH/CNCPT ECO/UNDEV

B64
MAHAR J.M.,INDIA: A CRITICAL BIBLIOGRAPHY. INDIA PAKISTAN CULTURE ECO/UNDEV LOC/G POL/PAR SECT PROB/SOLV DIPLOM ADMIN COLONIAL PARL/PROC ATTIT 20. PAGE 93 A1906
BIBLIOG/A S/ASIA NAT/G LEAD

B64
PRAKASH B.,INDIA AND THE WORLD. INDIA INT/ORG CREATE ORD/FREE...POLICY TREND 20. PAGE 117 A2405
DIPLOM PEACE ATTIT

B64
RAGHAVAN M.D.,INDIA IN CEYLONESE HISTORY, SOCIETY AND CULTURE. CEYLON INDIA S/ASIA LAW SOCIETY INT/TRADE ATTIT...ART/METH JURID SOC LING 20. PAGE 119 A2433
DIPLOM CULTURE SECT STRUCT

B64
TAYLOR E.,RICHER BY ASIA. S/ASIA CULTURE VOL/ASSN ACT/RES ATTIT DISPL PERSON ALL/VALS...INT/LAW MYTH SELF/OBS 20. PAGE 142 A2899
SOCIETY RIGID/FLEX INDIA

B64
US HOUSE COMM GOVT OPERATIONS,US OWNED FOREIGN CURRENCIES: HEARINGS (COMMITTEE ON GOVERNMENT OPERATIONS). INDIA ECO/DEV PLAN BUDGET TAX DEMAND EFFICIENCY 20 AID CONGRESS. PAGE 154 A3138
FINAN ECO/TAC FOR/AID OWN

L64
LLOYD W.B.,"PEACE REQUIRES PEACEMAKERS." AFR INDIA S/ASIA SWITZERLND WOR+45 INT/ORG VOL/ASSN PLAN PERSON PWR 20. PAGE 90 A1848
CONSULT PEACE

L64
RIPLEY R.B.,"INTERAGENCY COMMITTEES AND INCREMENTALISM: THE CASE OF AID TO INDIA." INDIA USA+45 INTELL NAT/G DELIB/GP ACT/RES DIPLOM ROUTINE NAT/LISM ATTIT PWR...SOC CONCPT NEW/IDEA TIME/SEQ CON/ANAL VAL/FREE 20. PAGE 121 A2483
EXEC MGT FOR/AID

L64
WORLD PEACE FOUNDATION,"INTERNATIONAL ORGANIZATIONS: SUMMARY OF ACTIVITIES." INDIA PAKISTAN TURKEY WOR+45 CONSTN CONSULT EX/STRUC ECO/TAC EDU/PROP LEGIT ORD/FREE...JURID SOC UN 20 CYPRESS. PAGE 167 A3397
INT/ORG ROUTINE

S64
"FURTHER READING." INDIA PAKISTAN SECT WAR PEACE ATTIT...POLICY 20. PAGE 3 A0067
BIBLIOG GP/REL DIPLOM NAT/G

S64
PALMER N.D.,"INDIA AS A FACTOR IN UNITED STATES FOREIGN POLICY." INDIA USA+45 USA-45 ECO/UNDEV NAT/G TOP/EX ECO/TAC EDU/PROP...METH/CNCPT TIME/SEQ 20. PAGE 113 A2323
S/ASIA ATTIT FOR/AID DIPLOM

S64
PRASAD B.,"SURVEY OF RECENT RESEARCH: STUDIES ON INDIA'S FOREIGN POLIC AND RELATIONS." ASIA INDIA PAKISTAN USA+45 NAT/G INT/TRADE GOV/REL 20 UN CMN/WLTH. PAGE 117 A2406
BIBLIOG DIPLOM ROLE POLICY

S64
SINGH N.,"THE CONTEMPORARY PRACTICE OF INDIA IN THE FIELD OF INTERNATIONAL LAW." INDIA S/ASIA INT/ORG NAT/G DOMIN EDU/PROP LEGIT KNOWL...CONCPT TOT/POP 20. PAGE 133 A2734
LAW ATTIT DIPLOM INT/LAW

B65
ANALYSIS AND ASSESSMENT OF THE ECONOMIC EFFECTS: PUBLIC LAW 480 TITLE I PROGRAM TURKEY. INDIA TURKEY USA+45 AGRI NAT/G PLAN BUDGET DIPLOM COST EFFICIENCY...CHARTS 20. PAGE 3 A0070
ECO/TAC FOR/AID FINAN ECO/UNDEV

B65
HASSON J.A.,THE ECONOMICS OF NUCLEAR POWER. INDIA UK USA+45 WOR+45 INT/ORG TEC/DEV COST...SOC STAT CHARTS 20 EURATOM. PAGE 63 A1286
NUC/PWR INDUS ECO/DEV METH

B65
INGRAM D.,COMMONWEALTH FOR A COLOUR-BLIND WORLD. AFR INDIA UK STRATA ECO/UNDEV VOL/ASSN CREATE PLAN CONFER COLONIAL ORD/FREE SOC/INTEG 20 COMMONWLTH. PAGE 70 A1441
RACE/REL INT/ORG INGP/REL PROB/SOLV

B65
LARUS J.,COMPARATIVE WORLD POLITICS. ASIA INDIA WOR+45 WOR-45 BAL/PWR WAR PEACE RATIONAL MORAL PWR ...REALPOL INT/LAW MUSLIM. PAGE 85 A1735
GOV/COMP IDEA/COMP DIPLOM NAT/COMP

B65
MEHROTRA S.R.,INDIA AND THE COMMONWEALTH 1885-1929. INDIA UK INT/ORG VOL/ASSN GP/REL ATTIT...POLICY BIBLIOG 19/20 CMN/WLTH. PAGE 99 A2034
DIPLOM NAT/G POL/PAR NAT/LISM

B65
MENON K.P.S.,MANY WORLDS. INDIA BAL/PWR CAP/ISM COLONIAL REV ORD/FREE PWR MARXISM...POLICY 20 COLD/WAR. PAGE 100 A2042
BIOG DIPLOM NAT/G

B65
PANJAB U EXTENSION LIBRARY,INDIAN NEWS INDEX. INDIA ECO/UNDEV INDUS INT/ORG SCHOOL FORCES ADJUD WAR ATTIT WEALTH 20. PAGE 114 A2333
BIBLIOG PRESS WRITING DIPLOM

B65
QURESHI I.H.,THE STRUGGLE FOR PAKISTAN. INDIA PAKISTAN UK CULTURE LEGIS DIPLOM EDU/PROP COLONIAL ATTIT SOVEREIGN 19/20 MUSLIM. PAGE 118 A2429
GP/REL RACE/REL WAR SECT

B65
SOPER T.,EVOLVING COMMONWEALTH. AFR CANADA INDIA IRELAND UK LAW CONSTN POL/PAR DOMIN CONTROL WAR PWR ...AUD/VIS 18/20 COMMONWLTH OEEC. PAGE 135 A2769
INT/ORG COLONIAL VOL/ASSN

B65
WINT G.,ASIA: A HANDBOOK. ASIA COM INDIA USSR CULTURE INTELL NAT/G...GEOG STAT CENSUS NAT/COMP WORSHIP 20 TREATY CHINJAP. PAGE 165 A3365
DIPLOM SOC

S65
"FURTHER READING." INDIA USSR FORCES ATTIT SOCISM 20. PAGE 3 A0068
BIBLIOG DIPLOM MARXISM

S65
"FURTHER READING." INDIA ADMIN COLONIAL WAR GOV/REL ATTIT 20. PAGE 3 A0069
BIBLIOG DIPLOM NAT/G POLICY

S65
GANGAL S.C.,"SURVEY OF RECENT RESEARCH: INDIA AND THE COMMONWEALTH" INDIA UK NAT/G INT/TRADE PARTIC GOV/REL ROLE 20 CMN/WLTH. PAGE 51 A1039
BIBLIOG POLICY REGION DIPLOM

S65
PRABHAKAR P.,"SURVEY OF RESEARCH AND SOURCE MATERIALS; THE SINO-INDIAN BORDER DISPUTE." CHINA/COM INDIA LAW NAT/G PLAN BAL/PWR WAR...POLICY 20 COLD/WAR. PAGE 117 A2404
BIBLIOG ASIA S/ASIA DIPLOM

S65
RAY H.,"THE POLICY OF RUSSIA TOWARDS SINO-INDIAN CONFLICT." ASIA CHINA/COM COM INDIA USSR NAT/G TOP/EX FOR/AID EDU/PROP NEUTRAL COERCE PEACE RIGID/FLEX PWR...METH/CNCPT TIME/SEQ VAL/FREE 20. PAGE 120 A2452
S/ASIA ATTIT DIPLOM WAR

B66
GUPTA S.,KASHMIR - A STUDY IN INDIA-PAKISTAN RELATIONS. INDIA KASHMIR PAKISTAN CONSTN INT/ORG REV RACE/REL NAT/LISM 20 UN MUSLIM/LG. PAGE 58 A1194
DIPLOM GP/REL SOVEREIGN WAR

B66
HALPERIN M.H.,CHINA AND NUCLEAR PROLIFERATION (PAMPHLET). CHINA/COM FUT INDIA USA+45 USSR ARMS/CONT WAR 20 CHINJAP. PAGE 60 A1239
NUC/PWR FORCES POLICY DIPLOM

B66
KEENLEYSIDE H.L.,INTERNATIONAL AID: A SUMMARY. AFR INDIA S/ASIA UK STRATA EXTR/IND TEC/DEV ADMIN RACE/REL DEMAND NAT/LISM WEALTH...TREND CHINJAP. PAGE 77 A1575
ECO/UNDEV FOR/AID DIPLOM TASK

B66
KOH S.J.,STAGES OF INDUSTRIAL DEVELOPMENT IN ASIA. ASIA INDIA KOREA STRATA STRUCT NAT/G INT/TRADE ...CHARTS 19/20 CHINJAP. PAGE 81 A1659
INDUS ECO/UNDEV ECO/DEV LABOR

B66
MOORE R.J.,SIR CHARLES WOOD'S INDIAN POLICY: 1853-66. INDIA POL/PAR CHIEF DELIB/GP DIPLOM CONTROL LEAD WOOD/CHAS. PAGE 103 A2124
COLONIAL ADMIN CONSULT DECISION

B66
NATIONAL COUN APPLIED ECO RES,DEVELOPMENT WITHOUT AID. INDIA FINAN TEC/DEV EFFICIENCY...ANTHOL 20. PAGE 107 A2203
FOR/AID PLAN SOVEREIGN ECO/UNDEV

B66
SAGER P.,MOSKAUS HAND IN INDIEN. INDIA USSR DIPLOM DOMIN...PSY CONCPT 20 COM/PARTY. PAGE 126 A2586
PRESS EDU/PROP METH POL/PAR

B66
SPICER K.,A SAMARITAN STATE? AFR CANADA INDIA PAKISTAN UK USA+45 FINAN INDUS PRODUC...CHARTS 20 NATO. PAGE 136 A2787
DIPLOM FOR/AID ECO/DEV ADMIN

B66
TYSON G.,NEHRU: THE YEARS OF POWER. INDIA UK STRATA ECO/UNDEV FINAN SECT TASK WAR ORD/FREE MARXISM ...POLICY BIBLIOG 20 NEHRU/J. PAGE 146 A2985
CHIEF PWR DIPLOM NAT/G

B66
US DEPARTMENT OF THE ARMY,COMMUNIST CHINA: A STRATEGIC SURVEY: A BIBLIOGRAPHY (PAMPHLET NO. 20-67). CHINA/COM COM INDIA USSR NAT/G POL/PAR EX/STRUC FORCES NUC/PWR REV ATTIT...POLICY GEOG CHARTS. PAGE 152 A3109
BIBLIOG/A MARXISM S/ASIA DIPLOM

B66
US DEPARTMENT OF THE ARMY,SOUTH ASIA: A STRATEGIC SURVEY (PAMPHLET NO. 550-3). AFGHANISTN INDIA NEPAL PAKISTAN ECO/UNDEV INT/ORG POL/PAR FORCES FOR/AID INT/TRADE LEAD WAR...POLICY SOC TREND 20. PAGE 152 A3110
BIBLIOG/A S/ASIA DIPLOM NAT/G

B66
VYAS R.,DAWNING ON THE CAPITOL: US CONGRESS AND INDIA. INDIA S/ASIA USA+45 ELITES ECO/DEV ECO/UNDEV PLAN FOR/AID...BIBLIOG 20 CONGRESS. PAGE 160 A3256
POLICY LEGIS NAT/G DIPLOM

B66
WESTWOOD A.F.,FOREIGN AID IN A FOREIGN POLICY FRAMEWORK. AFR ASIA INDIA IRAN L/A+17C USA+45 USSR ECO/UNDEV AGRI FORCES LEGIS PLAN PROB/SOLV ...DECISION 20 COLD/WAR. PAGE 163 A3324
FOR/AID DIPLOM POLICY ECO/TAC

L66
BARMAN R.K.,"INDO-PAKISTANI RELATIONS 1947-1965: A SELECTED BIBLIOGRAPHY." INDIA PAKISTAN NAT/G 20. PAGE 11 A0223
BIBLIOG DIPLOM S/ASIA

S66
"FURTHER READING." INDIA LEAD ATTIT...CONCPT 20. PAGE 4 A0075
BIBLIOG NAT/G DIPLOM POLICY

S66
MANSERGH N.,"THE PARTITION OF INDIA IN RETROSPECT." INDIA PAKISTAN S/ASIA UK DIPLOM COLONIAL GP/REL PWR 20. PAGE 94 A1933
NAT/G PARL/PROC POLICY POL/PAR

B67
FRASER-TYTLER W.K.,AFGHANISTAN: A STUDY OF POLITICAL DEVELOPMENTS IN CENTRAL AND SOUTHERN ASIA (3RD ED.). AFGHANISTN INDIA KIN FOR/AID PWR ...BIBLIOG. PAGE 48 A0990
DIPLOM NAT/G CONSTN GEOG

L67
"POLITICAL PARTIES ON FOREIGN POLICY IN THE INTER-ELECTION YEARS 1962-66." ASIA COM INDIA USA+45 PLAN ATTIT...DECISION 20. PAGE 4 A0079
POL/PAR DIPLOM POLICY

L67
DEVADHAR Y.C.,"THE ROLE OF FOREIGN PRIVATE CAPITAL IN INDIA'S ECONOMIC DEVELOPMENT* ASSESSMENT OF POLICY AND PERFORMANCE." INDIA INDUS PLAN TEC/DEV BUDGET DIPLOM ECO/TAC BAL/PAY PRODUC WEALTH ...CHARTS 20. PAGE 37 A0750
CAP/ISM FOR/AID POLICY ACT/RES

S67
CHAND A.,"INDIA AND TANZANIA." INDIA TANZANIA TEC/DEV ECO/TAC FOR/AID COLONIAL PEACE UTIL WEALTH ...GOV/COMP 20. PAGE 25 A0518
ECO/UNDEV NEUTRAL DIPLOM PLAN

S67
FELDMAN H.,"AID AS IMPERIALISM?" INDIA PAKISTAN UK USA+45 BAL/PWR CAP/ISM DIPLOM ECO/TAC DOMIN BAL/PAY WEALTH...POLICY 20. PAGE 45 A0914
COLONIAL FOR/AID S/ASIA ECO/UNDEV

S67
KIERNAN V.G.,"INDIA AND THE LABOUR PARTY." INDIA UK CAP/ISM GP/REL EFFICIENCY NAT/LISM PWR SOCISM ...SOCIALIST TIME/SEQ 20. PAGE 79 A1616
COLONIAL DIPLOM POL/PAR ECO/UNDEV

INDIAN COUNCIL WORLD AFFAIRS A1437,A1438

INDIAN/AM....AMERICAN INDIANS

B17
DE VICTORIA F.,DE INDIS ET DE JURE BELLI (1557) IN F. DE VICTORIA, DE INDIS ET DE JURE BELLI REFLECTIONES. UNIV NAT/G SECT CHIEF PARTIC COERCE PEACE MORAL...POLICY 16 INDIAN/AM CHRISTIAN CONSCN/OBJ. PAGE 35 A0715
WAR INT/LAW OWN

INDIANA....INDIANA

INDICATOR....NUMERICAL INDICES AND INDICATORS

INDIVIDUAL....SEE PERSON

INDOCTRINATION....SEE EDU/PROP

INDONESIA....SEE ALSO S/ASIA

N
KYRIAK T.E.,ASIAN DEVELOPMENTS: A BIBLIOGRAPHY. INDONESIA KOREA/N VIETNAM/N CULTURE SOCIETY ECO/UNDEV NAT/G DIPLOM...SOC TREND 20 MONGOLIA. PAGE 83 A1699
BIBLIOG/A ALL/IDEOS S/ASIA ASIA

B41
KEESING F.M.,THE SOUTH SEAS IN THE MODERN WORLD. INDONESIA STRUCT FAM SECT EDU/PROP LEAD INCOME WEALTH...HEAL SOC 20. PAGE 77 A1577
CULTURE ECO/UNDEV GOV/COMP DIPLOM

B50
CORNELL U DEPT ASIAN STUDIES,SOUTHEAST ASIA PROGRAM DATA PAPER. BURMA CAMBODIA INDONESIA MALAYSIA VIETNAM SOCIETY STRUCT NAT/G SECT DIPLOM FOR/AID PWR WEALTH...SOC 20. PAGE 31 A0625
BIBLIOG/A CULTURE S/ASIA ECO/UNDEV

B51
WABEKE B.H.,A GUIDE TO DUTCH BIBLIOGRAPHIES. BELGIUM INDONESIA NETHERLAND DIPLOM INT/TRADE WAR NAT/LISM KNOWL...ART/METH HUM JURID CON/ANAL 14/20. PAGE 160 A3257
BIBLIOG/A NAT/G CULTURE COLONIAL

B52
US MUTUAL SECURITY AGENCY,U. S. TECHNICAL AND ECONOMIC ASSISTANCE IN THE FAR EAST (PAMPHLET). ASIA BURMA INDONESIA PHILIPPINE TAIWAN THAILAND USA+45 AGRI INDUS PLAN EDU/PROP ADMIN HEALTH. PAGE 155 A3161
FOR/AID TEC/DEV ECO/UNDEV BUDGET

B58
WIGGINS J.W.,FOREIGN AID REEXAMINED: A CRITICAL APPRAISAL. CHINA/COM INDONESIA USA+45 FINAN INT/TRADE REGION NAT/LISM ATTIT...CENSUS 20. PAGE 164 A3342
FOR/AID DIPLOM ECO/UNDEV SOVEREIGN

B60
WOLF C.,FOREIGN AID: THEORY AND PRACTICE IN SOUTHERN ASIA. CEYLON INDONESIA PHILIPPINE S/ASIA CULTURE STRATA ECO/UNDEV PLAN EDU/PROP ATTIT ...METH/CNCPT MATH QUANT STAT CONT/OBS TIME/SEQ SIMUL TOT/POP 20. PAGE 166 A3378
ACT/RES ECO/TAC FOR/AID

B61
SYATAUW J.J.G.,SOME NEWLY ESTABLISHED ASIAN STATES AND THE DEVELOPMENT OF INTERNATIONAL LAW. BURMA CEYLON INDIA INDONESIA ECO/UNDEV COLONIAL NEUTRAL WAR PEACE SOVEREIGN...CHARTS 19/20. PAGE 140 A2873
INT/LAW ADJUST SOCIETY S/ASIA

B62
SELOSOEMARDJAN O.,SOCIAL CHANGES IN JOGJAKARTA. INDONESIA NETHERLAND ELITES STRATA STRUCT FAM POL/PAR CREATE DIPLOM INT/TRADE EDU/PROP ADMIN GOV/REL...SOC 20 JAVA CHINJAP. PAGE 131 A2683
ECO/UNDEV CULTURE REV COLONIAL

S62
SPECTOR I.,"SOVIET POLICY IN ASIA: A REAPPRAISAL." ASIA CHINA/COM COM INDIA INDONESIA ECO/UNDEV INT/ORG DOMIN EDU/PROP REGION RESPECT...CONCPT TREND TOT/POP COLD/WAR 20 CHINJAP. PAGE 135 A2774
S/ASIA PWR FOR/AID USSR

B63
KAHIN G.M.,MAJOR GOVERNMENTS OF ASIA (2ND ED.). ASIA INDIA INDONESIA PAKISTAN S/ASIA DIPLOM...SOC 20 CHINJAP. PAGE 75 A1546
GOV/COMP POL/PAR ELITES

B63
US ECON SURVEY TEAM INDONESIA,INDONESIA - PERSPECTIVE AND PROPOSALS FOR UNITED STATES ECONOMIC AID. INDONESIA AGRI MARKET TEC/DEV DIPLOM INT/TRADE EDU/PROP 20. PAGE 153 A3113
FOR/AID ECO/UNDEV PLAN INDUS

S63
HINDLEY D.,"FOREIGN AID TO INDONESIA AND ITS POLITICAL IMPLICATIONS." INDONESIA POL/PAR ATTIT SOVEREIGN...CHARTS 20. PAGE 65 A1336
FOR/AID NAT/G WEALTH ECO/TAC

B64
LEGGE J.D.,INDONESIA. INDONESIA ELITES ECO/UNDEV POL/PAR CHIEF FORCES INT/TRADE COERCE CHOOSE ORD/FREE...SOC CHARTS BIBLIOG 16/20 CHINJAP. PAGE 86 A1765
S/ASIA DOMIN NAT/LISM POLICY

B66
BRACKMAN A.C.,SOUTHEAST ASIA'S SECOND FRONT: THE POWER STRUGGLE IN THE MALAY ARCHIPELAGO. CHINA/COM INDONESIA MALAYSIA ECO/UNDEV INT/ORG NAT/G FORCES DIPLOM EDU/PROP REGION COERCE GUERRILLA AUTHORIT POPULISM...MAJORIT 20 KENNEDY/JF SEATO. PAGE 18 A0367
S/ASIA MARXISM REV

S67
BLUM Y.Z.,"INDONESIA'S RETURN TO THE UNITED NATIONS." INDONESIA ADJUD SANCTION REPRESENT ...JURID 20 UN. PAGE 16 A0324
CONSTN LAW DIPLOM INT/ORG

S67
PAUKER G.J.,"TOWARD A NEW ORDER IN INDONESIA." COM INDONESIA S/ASIA ECO/UNDEV POL/PAR EX/STRUC TOP/EX BAL/PWR ECO/TAC FOR/AID DOMIN NAT/LISM AUTHORIT ORD/FREE PWR 20. PAGE 114 A2342
REV NAT/G DIPLOM CIVMIL/REL

INDUS....ALL OR MOST INDUSTRY; SEE ALSO SPECIFIC INDUSTRIES, INSTITUTIONAL INDEX, PART C, P. XII

B
UN DEPARTMENT SOCIAL AFFAIRS,SOCIAL WELFARE
BIBLIOG/A

INFORMATION SERIES: CURRENT LITERATURE AND NATIONAL CONFERENCES. WOR+45 INDUS SERV/IND INT/ORG CONSULT ACT/RES WEALTH...HEAL UN. PAGE 147 A2997
SOC/WK DIPLOM ADMIN

N
INTERNATIONAL BOOK NEWS, 1928-1934. ECO/UNDEV FINAN INDUS LABOR INT/TRADE CONFER ADJUD COLONIAL...HEAL SOC/WK CHARTS 20 LEAGUE/NAT. PAGE 1 A0010
BIBLIOG/A DIPLOM INT/LAW INT/ORG

N
PEKING REVIEW. CHINA/COM CULTURE AGRI INDUS DIPLOM EDU/PROP GUERRILLA ATTIT MARXISM...BIBLIOG 20. PAGE 1 A0022
MARXIST NAT/G POL/PAR PRESS

N
ARBITRATION JOURNAL. WOR+45 LAW INDUS JUDGE DIPLOM CT/SYS INGP/REL 20. PAGE 2 A0027
BIBLIOG MGT LABOR ADJUD

N
CHINA QUARTERLY. COM AGRI INDUS ACADEM POL/PAR INT/TRADE CONFER GOV/REL...TIME/SEQ CON/ANAL INDEX 20. PAGE 2 A0032
BIBLIOG/A ASIA DIPLOM POLICY

N
THE JAPAN SCIENCE REVIEW: LAW AND POLITICS: LIST OF BOOKS AND ARTICLES ON LAW AND POLITICS. CONSTN AGRI INDUS LABOR DIPLOM TAX ADMIN CRIME...INT/LAW SOC 20 CHINJAP. PAGE 2 A0042
BIBLIOG LAW S/ASIA PHIL/SCI

N
THE MIDDLE EAST AND NORTH AFRICA. AFR ISLAM CULTURE ECO/UNDEV AGRI NAT/G TEC/DEV FOR/AID INT/TRADE EDU/PROP...CHARTS 20. PAGE 2 A0043
INDEX INDUS FINAN STAT

N
"PROLOG",DIGEST OF THE SOVIET UKRANIAN PRESS. USSR LAW AGRI INDUS PROVS SCHOOL DIPLOM GOV/REL ATTIT ...HUM LING 20. PAGE 4 A0081
BIBLIOG/A NAT/G PRESS COM

N
EUROPA PUBLICATIONS LIMITED,THE EUROPA YEAR BOOK. CONSTN FINAN INDUS POL/PAR DIPLOM TV CT/SYS...STAT BIOG CHARTS WORSHIP 20. PAGE 43 A0874
BIBLIOG NAT/G PRESS INT/ORG

N
FOREIGN TRADE LIBRARY,NEW TITLES RECEIVED IN THE LIBRARY. WOR+45 ECO/UNDEV FINAN NAT/G PLAN TEC/DEV BUDGET ECO/TAC TARIFFS GOV/REL STAT. PAGE 47 A0964
BIBLIOG/A INT/TRADE INDUS ECO/DEV

N
KAPLAN L.,REVIEW INDEX. USA+45 USA-45 FINAN INDUS LABOR RACE/REL...GEOG PSY SOC 20. PAGE 76 A1558
BIBLIOG PROF/ORG ECO/DEV DIPLOM

N
KYRIAK T.E.,CHINA: A BIBLIOGRAPHY. ASIA CHINA/COM AGRI FINAN INDUS NAT/G INT/TRADE PRESS...SOC 20. PAGE 83 A1700
BIBLIOG/A MARXISM TOP/EX POL/PAR

N
KYRIAK T.E.,EAST EUROPE: BIBLIOGRAPHY--INDEX TO US JPRS RESEARCH TRANSLATIONS. ALBANIA BULGARIA COM CZECHOSLVK HUNGARY POLAND ROMANIA AGRI EXTR/IND FINAN SERV/IND INT/TRADE WEAPON...GEOG MGT SOC 20. PAGE 83 A1701
BIBLIOG/A PRESS MARXISM INDUS

N
KYRIAK T.E.,SOVIET UNION: BIBLIOGRAPHY INDEX TO US JPRS RESEARCH TRANSLATIONS. USSR ECO/DEV AGRI COM/IND CONSTRUC DIST/IND EXTR/IND PROC/MFG R+D INT/TRADE...SOC 20. PAGE 83 A1703
BIBLIOG/A INDUS MARXISM PRESS

N
MURRA R.O.,POST-WAR PROBLEMS: A CURRENT LIST OF UNITED STATES GOVERNMENT PUBLICATIONS (PAMPHLET). WOR+45 SOCIETY FINAN INT/ORG SCHOOL WORKER TEC/DEV ECO/TAC...SOC 20. PAGE 106 A2180
BIBLIOG/A ADJUST AGRI INDUS

N
US DEPARTMENT OF STATE,BIBLIOGRAPHY (PAMPHLETS). AGRI INDUS INT/ORG FOR/AID EDU/PROP WAR MARXISM ...SOC GOV/COMP METH/COMP 20. PAGE 151 A3079
BIBLIOG DIPLOM ECO/DEV NAT/G

B02
MOREL E.D.,AFFAIRS OF WEST AFRICA. UK FINAN INDUS FAM KIN SECT CHIEF WORKER DIPLOM RACE/REL LITERACY HEALTH...CHARTS 18/20 AFRICA/W NEGRO. PAGE 104 A2129
COLONIAL ADMIN AFR

B17
MEYER H.H.B.,THE UNITED STATES AT WAR, ORGANIZATIONS AND LITERATURE. USA-45 AGRI FINAN INDUS CHIEF FORCES DIPLOM FOR/AID INT/TRADE...SOC 20 PRESIDENT. PAGE 100 A2050
BIBLIOG/A WAR NAT/G VOL/ASSN

B19
KEYNES J.M.,THE ECONOMIC CONSEQUENCES OF THE PEACE. FUT GERMANY MOD/EUR RUSSIA UK USA-45 CULTURE ECO/DEV FINAN INDUS INT/ORG TOP/EX ECO/TAC ROUTINE WAR ATTIT PERCEPT ALL/VALS...OLD/LIB MYTH OBS TIME/SEQ TREND 20 TREATY. PAGE 78 A1605
EUR+WWI SOCIETY PEACE

N19
FRANCK P.G.,AFGHANISTAN BETWEEN EAST AND WEST: THE ECONOMICS OF COMPETITIVE COEXISTENCE (PAMPHLET). AFGHANISTN USA+45 USA-45 USSR INDUS ECO/TAC INT/TRADE CONTROL NEUTRAL ORD/FREE MARXISM...GEOG 20 UN. PAGE 48 A0977
FOR/AID PLAN DIPLOM ECO/UNDEV

B20
WOOLF L.,EMPIRE AND COMMERCE IN AFRICA. EUR+WWI MOD/EUR FINAN INDUS MARKET INT/ORG PLAN COERCE ATTIT DRIVE PWR WEALTH...CONCPT TIME/SEQ TREND CHARTS 20. PAGE 167 A3394
AFR DOMIN COLONIAL SOVEREIGN

B30
SMUTS J.C.,AFRICA AND SOME WORLD PROBLEMS. RHODESIA SOUTH/AFR CULTURE ECO/UNDEV INDUS INT/ORG SECT PROB/SOLV REGION GOV/REL DISCRIM ATTIT 19/20 LEAGUE/NAT LIVNGSTN/D NEGRO. PAGE 134 A2748
LEGIS AFR COLONIAL RACE/REL

B31
BORCHARD E.H.,GUIDE TO THE LAW AND LEGAL LITERATURE OF FRANCE. FRANCE FINAN INDUS LABOR SECT LEGIS ADMIN COLONIAL CRIME OWN...INT/LAW 20. PAGE 17 A0337
BIBLIOG/A LAW CONSTN METH

B32
HANSEN A.H.,ECONOMIC STABILIZATION IN AN UNBALANCED WORLD. COM EUR+WWI USA-45 WOR-45 AGRI FINAN INDUS MARKET INT/ORG LABOR VOL/ASSN EDU/PROP ATTIT HEALTH KNOWL WEALTH...HIST/WRIT TREND VAL/FREE 20. PAGE 61 A1253
NAT/G ECO/DEV CAP/ISM SOCISM

B34
GRAHAM F.D.,PROTECTIVE TARIFFS. FUT USA+45 WOR-45 INDUS MARKET VOL/ASSN PLAN CAP/ISM ECO/TAC PEACE ATTIT DRIVE HEALTH ORD/FREE...OBS TREND GEN/LAWS 20. PAGE 55 A1124
INT/ORG TARIFFS

B35
BUREAU ECONOMIC RES LAT AM,THE ECONOMIC LITERATURE OF LATIN AMERICA (2 VOLS.). CHRIST-17C AGRI DIST/IND EXTR/IND INDUS WORKER INT/TRADE...GEOG 16/20. PAGE 21 A0433
BIBLIOG L/A+17C ECO/UNDEV FINAN

B36
BOYCE A.N.,EUROPE AND SOUTH AFRICA. FRANCE GERMANY ITALY SOUTH/AFR UK INDUS NAT/G CONTROL REV WAR NAT/LISM...CONCPT HIST/WRIT 20. PAGE 18 A0362
COLONIAL GOV/COMP NAT/COMP DIPLOM

B37
ROBBINS L.,ECONOMIC PLANNING AND INTERNATIONAL ORDER. WOR-45 SOCIETY FINAN INDUS NAT/G ECO/TAC ROUTINE WEALTH...SOC TIME/SEQ GEN/METH WORK 20 KEYNES/JM. PAGE 122 A2492
INT/ORG PLAN INT/TRADE

B37
UNION OF SOUTH AFRICA,REPORT CONCERNING ADMINISTRATION OF SOUTH WEST AFRICA (6 VOLS.). SOUTH/AFR INDUS PUB/INST FORCES LEGIS BUDGET DIPLOM EDU/PROP ADJUD CT/SYS...GEOG CHARTS 20 AFRICA/SW LEAGUE/NAT. PAGE 148 A3028
NAT/G ADMIN COLONIAL CONSTN

B37
VINER J.,STUDIES IN THE THEORY OF INTERNATIONAL TRADE. WOR-45 CONSTN ECO/DEV AGRI INDUS MARKET INT/ORG LABOR NAT/G ECO/TAC TARIFFS COLONIAL ATTIT WEALTH...POLICY CONCPT MATH STAT OBS SAMP TREND GEN/LAWS MARX/KARL 20. PAGE 159 A3236
CAP/ISM INT/TRADE

B38
COLBY C.C.,GEOGRAPHICAL ASPECTS OF INTERNATIONAL RELATIONS. WOR-45 ECO/DEV ECO/UNDEV AGRI EXTR/IND INDUS MARKET R+D INT/ORG NAT/G TEC/DEV ECO/TAC INT/TRADE NAT/LISM WEALTH...METH/CNCPT CHARTS GEN/LAWS 20. PAGE 28 A0565
PLAN GEOG DIPLOM

B38
SAINT-PIERRE C.I.,SCHEME FOR LASTING PEACE (TRANS. BY H. BELLOT). INDUS NAT/G CHIEF FORCES INT/TRADE CT/SYS WAR PWR SOVEREIGN WEALTH...POLICY 18. PAGE 126 A2587
INT/ORG PEACE AGREE INT/LAW

B39
FURNIVALL J.S.,NETHERLANDS INDIA. INDIA NETHERLAND CULTURE INDUS NAT/G DIPLOM ADMIN WEALTH...POLICY CHARTS 17/20. PAGE 50 A1029
COLONIAL ECO/UNDEV SOVEREIGN PLURISM

B40
CONOVER H.F.,JAPAN-ECONOMIC DEVELOPMENT AND FOREIGN POLICY, A SELECTED LIST OF REFERENCES (PAMPHLET). CULTURE FINAN INDUS NAT/G FORCES INT/TRADE WAR ...SOC TREND 20 CHINJAP. PAGE 29 A0593
BIBLIOG ASIA ECO/DEV DIPLOM

C40
NORMAN E.H.,"JAPAN'S EMERGENCE AS A MODERN STATE: POLITICAL AND ECONOMIC PROBLEMS OF THE MEIJI PERIOD." CONSTN STRATA AGRI INDUS POL/PAR TEC/DEV CAP/ISM CIVMIL/REL...BIBLIOG 19/20 CHINJAP. PAGE 110 A2250
CENTRAL DIPLOM POLICY NAT/LISM

B42
CONOVER H.F.,NEW ZEALAND: A SELECTED LIST OF REFERENCES (PAMPHLET). NEW/ZEALND ECO/UNDEV AGRI INDUS LABOR NAT/G SCHOOL FORCES DIPLOM COLONIAL WAR ...HUM 20. PAGE 29 A0595
BIBLIOG/A S/ASIA CULTURE

B42
US LIBRARY OF CONGRESS,ECONOMICS OF WAR (APRIL 1941-MARCH 1942). WOR-45 FINAN INDUS LOC/G NAT/G PLAN BUDGET RATION COST DEMAND...POLICY 20. PAGE 154 A3146
BIBLIOG/A INT/TRADE ECO/TAC WAR

L42
SHOTWELL J.,"LESSON OF THE LAST WORLD WAR." EUR+WWI MOD/EUR USA-45 SOCIETY ECO/UNDEV INDUS VOL/ASSN CONSULT ACT/RES CREATE CAP/ISM INT/TRADE DRIVE ALL/VALS...CONCPT NEW/IDEA SELF/OBS GEN/LAWS LEAGUE/NAT NAZI 20. PAGE 132 A2708
INT/ORG ORD/FREE

B43
BROWN A.D.,GREECE: SELECTED LIST OF REFERENCES. GREECE ECO/UNDEV AGRI FINAN INDUS LABOR SECT TEC/DEV INT/TRADE LEAD...SOC 20. PAGE 20 A0399
BIBLIOG/A WAR DIPLOM NAT/G

B43
CONOVER H.F.,SOVIET RUSSIA: SELECTED LIST OF REFERENCES. USSR CULTURE INDUS NAT/G TOP/EX TEC/DEV BUDGET WAR CIVMIL/REL EFFICIENCY MARXISM 20. PAGE 29 A0597
BIBLIOG ECO/DEV COM DIPLOM

B44
SHELBY C.,LATIN AMERICAN PERIODICALS CURRENTLY RECEIVED IN THE LIBRARY OF CONGRESS AND IN LIBRARY OF DEPARTMENT OF AGRICULTURE. SOCIETY AGRI INDUS LABOR POL/PAR INT/TRADE...GEOG SOC 20. PAGE 132 A2699
BIBLIOG ECO/UNDEV CULTURE L/A+17C

B44
WEIGERT H.W.,COMPASS OF THE WORLD, A SYMPOSIUM ON POLITICAL GEOGRAPHY. EUR+WWI FUT MOD/EUR S/ASIA USA-45 WOR-45 SOCIETY AGRI INDUS MARKET ECO/TAC INT/TRADE PERSON 20. PAGE 162 A3298
TEC/DEV CAP/ISM RUSSIA GEOG

C44
VAN VALKENBURG S.,"ELEMENTS OF POLITICAL GEOGRAPHY." FRANCE COM/IND INDUS NAT/G SECT RACE/REL...LING TREND GEN/LAWS BIBLIOG 20. PAGE 158 A3215
GEOG DIPLOM COLONIAL

B45
CLAGETT H.L.,COMMUNIST CHINA: RUTHLESS ENEMY OR PAPER TIGER (PAMPHLET). CHINA/COM ECO/UNDEV AGRI INDUS NAT/G POL/PAR ECO/TAC INT/TRADE GUERRILLA ATTIT...CHARTS NAT/COMP ORG/CHARTS 20. PAGE 26 A0540
BIBLIOG/A MARXISM DIPLOM COERCE

B45
GALLOWAY E.,ABSTRACTS OF POSTWAR LITERATURE (VOL. IV) JAN.-JULY, 1945 NOS. 901-1074. POLAND USA+45 USSR WOR+45 INDUS LABOR PLAN ECO/TAC INT/TRADE TAX EDU/PROP ADMIN COLONIAL INT/LAW. PAGE 51 A1033
BIBLIOG/A NUC/PWR NAT/G DIPLOM

S46
SILBERNER E.,"THE PROBLEM OF WAR IN NINETEENTH CENTURY ECONOMIC THOUGHT." EUR+WWI MOD/EUR UNIV LAW ECO/DEV ECO/UNDEV FINAN INDUS MARKET INT/ORG NAT/G CONSULT FORCES...CONCPT GEN/LAWS GEN/METH 19. PAGE 133 A2715
ATTIT ECO/TAC WAR

N46
HOBBS C.C.,SOUTHEAST ASIA, 1935-45: A SELECTED LIST OF REFERENCE BOOKS (PAMPHLET). S/ASIA AGRI INDUS NAT/G SECT DIPLOM WAR...ART/METH GEOG SOC LING 20. PAGE 65 A1346
BIBLIOG/A CULTURE HABITAT

B47
DE HUSZAR G.B.,PERSISTENT INTERNATIONAL ISSUES. WOR+45 WOR-45 AGRI INDUS INT/ORG PROB/SOLV EFFICIENCY WEALTH...CON/ANAL ANTHOL UN. PAGE 35 A0704
DIPLOM PEACE ECO/TAC FOR/AID

B47
GORDON D.L.,THE HIDDEN WEAPON: THE STORY OF ECONOMIC WARFARE. EUR+WWI USA-45 LAW FINAN INDUS NAT/G CONSULT FORCES PLAN DOMIN PWR WEALTH ...INT/LAW CONCPT OBS TOT/POP NAZI 20. PAGE 54 A1112
INT/ORG ECO/TAC INT/TRADE WAR

B47
TOWLE L.W.,INTERNATIONAL TRADE AND COMMERCIAL POLICY. WOR+45 LAW ECO/DEV FINAN INDUS NAT/G ECO/TAC WEALTH...TIME/SEQ ILO 20. PAGE 144 A2955
MARKET INT/ORG INT/TRADE

B50
CHUKWUEMEKA N.,AFRICAN DEPENDENCIES: A CHALLENGE TO WESTERN DEMOCRACY. NIGERIA ECO/DEV INDUS FOR/AID INT/TRADE DOMIN 20. PAGE 26 A0536
DIPLOM ECO/UNDEV COLONIAL AFR

B50
DAVIS E.P.,PERIODICALS OF INTERNATIONAL ORGANIZATIONS; PART I, THE UN AND SPECIALIZED AGENCIES; PART II, INTER-AMERICAN ORGS. CULTURE AGRI FINAN INDUS LABOR INT/TRADE...GEOG HEAL STAT 20 UN OAS UNESCO. PAGE 34 A0689
BIBLIOG/A INT/ORG DIPLOM L/A+17C

B50
GATZKE H.W.,GERMANY'S DRIVE TO THE WEST. BELGIUM GERMANY MOD/EUR AGRI INDUS POL/PAR FORCES DOMIN AGREE CONTROL REGION COERCE 20 TREATY WWI. PAGE 51 A1053
WAR POLICY NAT/G DIPLOM

B50
LINCOLN G.,ECONOMICS OF NATIONAL SECURITY. USA+45 ELITES COM/IND DIST/IND INDUS NAT/G VOL/ASSN DELIB/GP EX/STRUC FOR/AID EDU/PROP COERCE NUC/PWR WAR ATTIT KNOWL ORD/FREE PWR COLD/WAR TOT/POP VAL/FREE 20. PAGE 89 A1818
FORCES ECO/TAC

B50
US DEPARTMENT OF STATE,POINT FOUR: COOPERATIVE PROGRAM FOR AID IN THE DEVELOPMENT OF ECONOMICALLY UNDERDEVELOPED AREAS. WOR+45 AGRI INDUS INT/ORG PLAN TEC/DEV DIPLOM EDU/PROP ADMIN PEACE PRODUC WEALTH 20 CONGRESS UN. PAGE 151 A3085
ECO/UNDEV FOR/AID FINAN INT/TRADE

B51
CHRISTENSEN A.N.,THE EVOLUTION OF LATIN AMERICAN GOVERNMENT: A BOOK OF READINGS. ECO/UNDEV INDUS LOC/G POL/PAR EX/STRUC LEGIS FOR/AID CT/SYS ...SOC/WK 20 SOUTH/AMER. PAGE 26 A0535
NAT/G CONSTN DIPLOM L/A+17C

B51
US DEPARTMENT OF STATE,POINT FOUR, NEAR EAST AND AFRICA, A SELECTED BIBLIOGRAPHY OF STUDIES ON ECONOMICALLY UNDERDEVELOPED COUNTRIES. AGRI COM/IND FINAN INDUS PLAN INT/TRADE...SOC TREND 20. PAGE 151 A3087
BIBLIOG/A AFR S/ASIA ISLAM

B51
US TARIFF COMMISSION,LIST OF PUBLICATIONS OF THE TARIFF COMMISSION (PAMPHLET). USA+45 USA-45 AGRI EXTR/IND INDUS INT/TRADE...STAT 20. PAGE 157 A3207
BIBLIOG TARIFFS NAT/G ADMIN

B51
VINER J.,INTERNATIONAL ECONOMICS. USA-45 WOR-45 ECO/DEV INDUS NAT/G ECO/TAC ALL/VALS...TIME/SEQ 20. PAGE 159 A3238
FINAN INT/ORG WAR INT/TRADE

C51
BEST H.,"THE SOVIET STATE AND ITS INCEPTION." USSR CULTURE INDUS DIPLOM WEALTH...GEOG SOC BIBLIOG 20. PAGE 14 A0281
COM GEN/METH REV MARXISM

B52
JACKSON E.,MEETING OF THE MINDS: A WAY TO PEACE THROUGH MEDIATION. WOR+45 INDUS INT/ORG NAT/G DELIB/GP DIPLOM EDU/PROP LEGIT ORD/FREE...NEW/IDEA SELF/OBS TIME/SEQ CHARTS GEN/LAWS TOT/POP 20 UN TREATY. PAGE 72 A1474
LABOR JUDGE

B52
UN DEPT. SOC. AFF.,PRELIMINARY REPORT ON THE WORLD SOCIAL SITUATION. ISLAM L/A+17C WOR+45 STRATA AGRI EXTR/IND INDUS INT/ORG SCHOOL ADMIN...GEOG SOC TREND UNESCO WORK FAO 20. PAGE 147 A2998
R+D HEALTH FOR/AID

B52
US MUTUAL SECURITY AGENCY,U. S. TECHNICAL AND ECONOMIC ASSISTANCE IN THE FAR EAST (PAMPHLET). ASIA BURMA INDONESIA PHILIPPINE TAIWAN THAILAND USA+45 AGRI INDUS PLAN EDU/PROP ADMIN HEALTH. PAGE 155 A3161
FOR/AID TEC/DEV ECO/UNDEV BUDGET

B53
NEISSER H.,NATIONAL INCOMES AND INTERNATIONAL TRADE. FRANCE GERMANY SWEDEN UK USA-45 EXTR/IND FINAN INDUS TEC/DEV PRICE BAL/PAY EQUILIB INCOME WEALTH...CHARTS METH 19 CHINJAP. PAGE 108 A2215
INT/TRADE PRODUC MARKET CON/ANAL

B53
SCHAAF R.W.,DOCUMENTS OF INTERNATIONAL MEETINGS. AGRI INDUS ACADEM DIPLOM NUC/PWR RACE/REL AGE/Y HEALTH...SOC 20. PAGE 127 A2614
BIBLIOG/A DELIB/GP INT/ORG POLICY

B54
BINANI G.D.,INDIA AT A GLANCE (REV. ED.). INDIA COM/IND FINAN INDUS LABOR PROVS SCHOOL PLAN DIPLOM INT/TRADE ADMIN...JURID 20. PAGE 14 A0288
INDEX CON/ANAL NAT/G ECO/UNDEV

B54
GIRAUD A.,CIVILISATION ET PRODUCTIVITE. UNIV INDUS WORKER DIPLOM REV INCOME UTOPIA...GEOG 20. PAGE 53 A1076
SOCIETY PRODUC ROLE

B55
JAPAN MOMBUSHO DAIGAKU GAKIYUT,BIBLIOGRAPHY OF THE STUDIES ON LAW AND POLITICS (PAMPHLET). CONSTN INDUS LABOR DIPLOM TAX ADMIN...CRIMLGY INT/LAW 20 CHINJAP. PAGE 73 A1496
BIBLIOG LAW PHIL/SCI

B55
OECD,MARSHALL PLAN IN TURKEY. TURKEY USA+45 COM/IND CONSTRUC SERV/IND FORCES BUDGET...STAT 20 MARSHL/PLN. PAGE 111 A2277
FOR/AID ECO/UNDEV AGRI INDUS

S55
HALLETT D.,"THE HISTORY AND STRUCTURE OF OEEC." EUR+WWI USA+45 CONSTN INDUS INT/ORG NAT/G DELIB/GP ACT/RES PLAN ORD/FREE WEALTH...CONCPT OEEC 20 CMN/WLTH. PAGE 60 A1234
VOL/ASSN ECO/DEV

B56
JUAN T.L.,ECONOMIC AND SOCIAL DEVELOPMENT OF MODERN CHINA: A BIBLIOGRAPHICAL GUIDE. ASIA AGRI COM/IND DIST/IND FINAN INDUS DIPLOM...STAT 20. PAGE 75 A1541
BIBLIOG SOC

B56
UNITED NATIONS,BIBLIOGRAPHY ON INDUSTRIALIZATION IN UNDER-DEVELOPED COUNTRIES. WOR+45 R+D INT/ORG NAT/G FOR/AID ADMIN LEAD 20 UN. PAGE 149 A3036
BIBLIOG ECO/UNDEV INDUS TEC/DEV

B56
US DEPARTMENT OF STATE,ECONOMIC PROBLEMS OF UNDERDEVELOPED AREAS (PAMPHLET). AFR ASIA ISLAM L/A+17C AGRI FINAN INDUS INT/ORG LABOR INT/TRADE ...PSY SOC 20. PAGE 151 A3090
BIBLIOG ECO/UNDEV TEC/DEV R+D

B56
WU E.,LEADERS OF TWENTIETH-CENTURY CHINA; AN ANNOTATED BIBLIOGRAPHY OF SELECTED CHINESE
BIBLIOG/A BIOG

BIOGRAPHICAL WORKS IN HOOVER LIBRARY. ASIA INDUS POL/PAR DIPLOM ADMIN REV WAR...HUM MGT 20. PAGE 168 A3422
INTELL CHIEF

S56
GORDON L.,"THE ORGANIZATION FOR EUROPEAN ECONOMIC COOPERATION." EUR+WWI INDUS INT/ORG NAT/G CONSULT DELIB/GP ACT/RES CREATE PLAN TEC/DEV EDU/PROP LEGIT WEALTH OEEC 20. PAGE 54 A1114
VOL/ASSN ECO/DEV

B57
FRAZIER E.F.,RACE AND CULTURE CONTACTS IN THE MODERN WORLD. WOR+45 WOR-45 SOCIETY ECO/DEV AGRI INDUS INT/ORG LABOR NAT/G PERSON RIGID/FLEX ALL/VALS...SOC TIME/SEQ WORK 19/20. PAGE 48 A0991
CULTURE RACE/REL

B57
US PRES CITIZEN ADVISERS,REPORT TO THE PRESIDENT ON THE MUTUAL SECURITY PROGRAM. COM USA+45 WOR+45 FINAN INDUS PLAN BUDGET CAP/ISM DIPLOM FOR/AID INT/TRADE REGION 20 SECUR/PROG. PAGE 155 A3163
BAL/PWR FORCES INT/ORG ECO/TAC

L57
WARREN S.,"FOREIGN AID AND FOREIGN POLICY." USA+45 WOR+45 WOR-45 DIST/IND INDUS MARKET CONSULT CREATE DIPLOM EDU/PROP LEGIT ATTIT RIGID/FLEX...TIME/SEQ GEN/LAWS WORK 20. PAGE 161 A3285
ECO/UNDEV ALL/VALS ECO/TAC FOR/AID

S57
ALLEN R.L.,"UNITED NATIONS TECHNICAL ASSISTANCE: SOVIET AND EAST-EUROPEAN PARTICIPATION." COM WOR+45 AGRI INDUS INT/ORG NAT/G FOR/AID SKILL UN 20. PAGE 6 A0124
ECO/UNDEV TEC/DEV USSR

B58
AVRAMOVIC D.,POSTWAR GROWTH IN INTERNATIONAL INDEBTEDNESS. WOR+45 AGRI INDUS CAP/ISM PRICE INCOME...NAT/COMP 20 GOLD/STAND SILVER. PAGE 10 A0199
INT/TRADE FINAN COST BAL/PAY

B58
HAUSER P.H.,POPULATION AND WORLD POLITICS. FUT WOR+45 WOR-45 AGRI DIST/IND INDUS INT/ORG PLAN ECO/TAC DISPL HEALTH COLD/WAR 20. PAGE 63 A1288
NAT/G ECO/UNDEV FOR/AID

B58
MOORE B.T.,NATO AND THE FUTURE OF EUROPE. EUR+WWI FUT USA+45 ECO/DEV INDUS MARKET NAT/G VOL/ASSN FORCES DIPLOM NUC/PWR ORD/FREE...CONCPT CHARTS ORG/CHARTS CMN/WLTH 20 NATO. PAGE 103 A2122
INT/ORG REGION

B58
NEHRU J.,SPEECHES. INDIA ECO/UNDEV AGRI INDUS INT/ORG POL/PAR DIPLOM FOR/AID NAT/LISM...ANTHOL 20. PAGE 108 A2213
PLAN CHIEF COLONIAL NEUTRAL

B58
US OPERATIONS MISSION TO VIET,BUILDING ECONOMIC STRENGTH (PAMPHLET). USA+45 VIETNAM/S INDUS TEC/DEV BUDGET ADMIN EATING HEALTH...STAT 20. PAGE 155 A3162
FOR/AID ECO/UNDEV AGRI EDU/PROP

L58
INT. SOC. SCI. BULL.,"TECHNIQUES OF MEDIATION AND CONCILIATION." EUR+WWI USA+45 SOCIETY INDUS INT/ORG LABOR NAT/G LEGIS DIPLOM EDU/PROP CHOOSE ATTIT RIGID/FLEX...JURID CONCPT GEN/LAWS 20. PAGE 70 A1447
VOL/ASSN DELIB/GP INT/LAW

L58
TRAGER F.N.,"A SELECTED AND ANNOTATED BIBLIOGRAPHY ON ECONOMIC DEVELOPMENT, 1953-1957." WOR+45 AGRI FINAN INDUS MARKET LABOR MUNIC WORKER PLAN INT/TRADE PRODUC CENSUS. PAGE 145 A2958
BIBLIOG/A ECO/UNDEV ECO/DEV

S58
ELKIN A.B.,"OEEC-ITS STRUCTURE AND POWERS." EUR+WWI CONSTN INDUS INT/ORG NAT/G VOL/ASSN DELIB/GP ACT/RES PLAN ORD/FREE WEALTH...CHARTS ORG/CHARTS OEEC 20. PAGE 41 A0839
ECO/DEV EX/STRUC

C58
BLANCHARD W.,"THAILAND." THAILAND CULTURE AGRI FINAN INDUS FAM LABOR INT/TRADE ATTIT...GEOG HEAL SOC BIBLIOG 20. PAGE 15 A0307
NAT/G DIPLOM ECO/UNDEV S/ASIA

N58
INVESTMENT FUND ECO SOC DEV,FRENCH AFRICA: A DECADE OF PROGRESS 1948-1958 (PAMPHLET). AFR FRANCE EXTR/IND INDUS EDU/PROP HEALTH 20. PAGE 71 A1465
FOR/AID DIPLOM ECO/UNDEV AGRI

N58
US HOUSE COMM FOREIGN AFFAIRS,HEARINGS ON REVIEW OF THE MUTUAL SECURITY PROGRAMS; EXAMINATION OF SELECTED PROJECTS IN FORMOSA AND PAKISTAN (PAMPHLET). ASIA PAKISTAN TAIWAN INDUS CONSULT DELIB/GP LEGIS BUDGET CONFER DEBATE 20. PAGE 153 A3125
FOR/AID ECO/UNDEV DIPLOM ECO/TAC

B59
HARVARD UNIVERSITY LAW SCHOOL,INTERNATIONAL PROBLEMS OF FINANCIAL PROTECTION AGAINST NUCLEAR RISK. WOR+45 NAT/G DELIB/GP PROB/SOLV DIPLOM CONTROL ATTIT...POLICY INT/LAW MATH 20. PAGE 62 A1281
NUC/PWR ADJUD INDUS FINAN

B59
HAZLEWOOD A.,THE ECONOMICS OF "UNDER-DEVELOPED" AREAS. WOR+45 DIST/IND EXTR/IND FINAN INDUS MARKET PLAN FOR/AID...GEOG 20. PAGE 63 A1302
BIBLIOG/A ECO/UNDEV AGRI INT/TRADE

B59
JACKSON B.W.,FIVE IDEAS THAT CHANGE THE WORLD. FUT WOR+45 WOR-45 ECO/UNDEV INDUS DIPLOM DOMIN CONTROL ...IDEA/COMP 20. PAGE 72 A1473
MARXISM NAT/LISM COLONIAL ECO/TAC

B59
MEZERK A.G.,FINANCIAL ASSISTANCE FOR ECONOMIC DEVELOPMENT. WOR+45 INDUS DIPLOM INT/TRADE...CHARTS GOV/COMP UN. PAGE 101 A2064
FOR/AID FINAN ECO/TAC ECO/UNDEV

B59
NOVE A.,COMMUNIST ECONOMIC STRATEGY: SOVIET GROWTH AND CAPABILITIES. USSR AGRI LABOR PLAN TEC/DEV CAP/ISM INT/TRADE EFFICIENCY MARXISM 20 THIRD/WRLD. PAGE 110 A2257
FOR/AID ECO/TAC DIPLOM INDUS

B59
ROBERTSON A.H.,EUROPEAN INSTITUTIONS: COOPERATION, INTEGRATION, UNIFICATION. EUR+WWI FINAN INT/ORG FORCES INT/TRADE TARIFFS 20 EEC EURATOM ECSC NATO TREATY. PAGE 122 A2496
ECO/DEV DIPLOM INDUS ECO/TAC

B59
ROPKE W.,INTERNATIONAL ORDER AND ECONOMIC INTEGRATION. ECO/DEV ECO/UNDEV AGRI FINAN INDUS INT/ORG WAR PEACE ORD/FREE...SOC METH/COMP 20 EEC. PAGE 123 A2524
INT/TRADE DIPLOM BAL/PAY ALL/IDEOS

B59
SANNWALD R.E.,ECONOMIC INTEGRATION: THEORETICAL ASSUMPTIONS AND CONSEQUENCES OF EUROPEAN UNIFICATION. EUR+WWI FUT FINAN INDUS VOL/ASSN ACT/RES ECO/TAC...PLURIST EEC OEEC 20. PAGE 127 A2601
INT/ORG ECO/DEV INT/TRADE

B59
STERNBERG F.,THE MILITARY AND INDUSTRIAL REVOLUTION OF OUR TIME. USA+45 USSR WOR+45 WORKER COMPUTER PLAN TEC/DEV NUC/PWR GP/REL...POLICY NAT/COMP 20. PAGE 138 A2818
DIPLOM FORCES INDUS CIVMIL/REL

B59
WARD B.,5 IDEAS THAT CHANGE THE WORLD. WOR+45 WOR-45 SOCIETY STRUCT AGRI INDUS INT/ORG NAT/G FORCES ACT/RES ARMS/CONT TOTALISM ATTIT DRIVE GEN/LAWS. PAGE 161 A3278
ECO/UNDEV ALL/VALS NAT/LISM COLONIAL

B59
YRARRAZAVAL E.,AMERICA LATINE EN LA GUERRA FRIA. EUR+WWI L/A+17C USA+45 USSR WOR+45 INDUS INT/ORG NAT/LISM...POLICY COLD/WAR. PAGE 169 A3439
REGION DIPLOM ECO/UNDEV INT/TRADE

L59
BEGUIN B.,"ILO AND THE TRIPARTITE SYSTEM." EUR+WWI WOR+45 WOR-45 CONSTN ECO/DEV ECO/UNDEV INDUS INT/ORG NAT/G VOL/ASSN DELIB/GP PLAN TEC/DEV LEGIT ORD/FREE WEALTH...CONCPT TIME/SEQ WORK ILO 20. PAGE 12 A0249
LABOR

L59
MURPHY J.C.,"SOME IMPLICATIONS OF EUROPE'S COMMON MARKET. IN (COOK P. ECONOMIC DEVELOPMENT AND INTERNATIONAL TRADE.." EUR+WWI ECO/DEV DIST/IND INDUS NAT/G PLAN ECO/TAC INT/TRADE WEALTH...STAT TREND OEEC TOT/POP 20 EEC. PAGE 106 A2178
MARKET INT/ORG REGION

S59
CARLSTON K.S.,"NATIONALIZATION: AN ANALYTIC APPROACH." WOR+45 INT/ORG ECO/TAC DOMIN LEGIT ADJUD COERCE ORD/FREE PWR WEALTH SOCISM...JURID CONCPT TREND STERTYP TOT/POP VAL/FREE 20. PAGE 24 A0486
INDUS NAT/G NAT/LISM SOVEREIGN

S59
PLAZA G.,"FOR A REGIONAL MARKET IN LATIN AMERICA." FUT L/A+17C CULTURE INDUS NAT/G ECO/TAC INT/TRADE ATTIT WEALTH...NEW/IDEA TREND OAS 20. PAGE 116 A2389
MARKET INT/ORG REGION

S59
SIMONS H.,"WORLD-WIDE CAPABILITIES FOR PRODUCTION AND CONTROL OF NUCLEAR WEAPONS." FUT WOR+45 INDUS INT/ORG NAT/G ECO/TAC ATTIT PWR SKILL...TREND CHARTS VAL/FREE 20. PAGE 133 A2719
TEC/DEV ARMS/CONT NUC/PWR

S59
SOLDATI A.,"EOCNOMIC DISINTEGRATION IN EUROPE." EUR+WWI FUT WOR+45 INDUS INT/ORG NAT/G CAP/ISM WEALTH...NEW/IDEA OBS TREND CHARTS EEC 20. PAGE 135 A2764
FINAN ECO/TAC

S59
TIPTON J.B.,"PARTICIPATION OF THE UNITED STATES IN THE INTERNATIONAL LABOR ORGANIZATION." USA+45 LAW STRUCT ECO/DEV ECO/UNDEV INDUS TEC/DEV ECO/TAC ADMIN PERCEPT ORD/FREE SKILL...STAT HIST/WRIT GEN/METH ILO WORK 20. PAGE 144 A2946
LABOR INT/ORG

S59
ZAUBERMAN A.,"SOVIET BLOC ECONOMIC INTEGRATION." COM CULTURE INTELL ECO/DEV INDUS TOP/EX ACT/RES PLAN ECO/TAC INT/TRADE ROUTINE CHOOSE ATTIT ...TIME/SEQ 20. PAGE 169 A3448
MARKET INT/ORG USSR TOTALISM

B60
ALLEN R.L.,SOVIET ECONOMIC WARFARE. USSR FINAN INDUS NAT/G PLAN TEC/DEV FOR/AID DETER WEALTH ...TREND GEN/LAWS 20. PAGE 6 A0126
COM ECO/TAC

B60
APTHEKER H.,DISARMAMENT AND THE AMERICAN ECONOMY: A SYMPOSIUM. FUT USA+45 ECO/DEV DIST/IND FINAN INDUS
MARXIST ARMS/CONT

PROC/MFG LABOR NAT/G POL/PAR CONSULT PLAN CAP/ISM INT/TRADE PEACE ATTIT MORAL WEALTH...TREND GEN/LAWS TOT/POP 20. PAGE 9 A0172

B60

ASPREMONT-LYNDEN H.,RAPPORT SUR L'ADMINISTRATION BELGE DU RUANDA-URUNDI PENDANT L'ANNEE 1959. BELGIUM RWANDA AGRI INDUS DIPLOM ECO/TAC INT/TRADE DOMIN ADMIN RACE/REL...GEOG CENSUS 20 UN. PAGE 9 A0192

AFR COLONIAL ECO/UNDEV INT/ORG

B60

DEUTSCHER I.,THE GREAT CONTEST: RUSSIA AND THE WEST. USA+45 USSR SOCIETY INDUS ARMS/CONT ATTIT ...CONCPT IDEA/COMP 20 COLD/WAR. PAGE 37 A0749

PEACE DIPLOM PWR

B60

KHRUSHCHEV N.,FOR VICTORY IN PEACEFUL COMPETITION WITH CAPITALISM. COM FUT USSR WOR+45 CONSTN SOCIETY INDUS INT/ORG DELIB/GP PLAN BAL/PWR DIPLOM PERSON MARXISM...MARXIST WORK 20 COLD/WAR. PAGE 79 A1611

TOP/EX PWR CAP/ISM SOCISM

B60

LATIFI D.,INDIA AND UNITED STATES AID. ASIA INDIA UK USA+45 AGRI FINAN INDUS COLONIAL ORD/FREE SOVEREIGN WEALTH...METH/COMP 20. PAGE 85 A1743

FOR/AID DIPLOM ECO/UNDEV

B60

LEWIS P.R.,LITERATURE OF THE SOCIAL SCIENCES: AN INTRODUCTORY SURVEY AND GUIDE. UK LAW INDUS DIPLOM INT/TRADE ADMIN...MGT 19/20. PAGE 88 A1802

BIBLIOG/A SOC

B60

LISTER L.,EUROPE'S COAL AND STEEL COMMUNITY. FRANCE GERMANY STRUCT ECO/DEV EXTR/IND INDUS MARKET NAT/G DELIB/GP ECO/TAC INT/TRADE EDU/PROP ATTIT RIGID/FLEX ORD/FREE PWR WEALTH...CONCPT STAT TIME/SEQ CHARTS ECSC 20. PAGE 90 A1843

EUR+WWI INT/ORG REGION

B60

NEALE A.D.,THE FLOW OF RESOURCES FROM RICH TO POOR. WOR+45 ECO/DEV ECO/UNDEV FINAN INDUS NAT/G PLAN EFFICIENCY WEALTH...POLICY NAT/COMP 20 RESOURCE/N. PAGE 108 A2209

FOR/AID DIPLOM METH/CNCPT

B60

PENTONY D.E.,THE UNDERDEVELOPED LANDS. FUT WOR+45 CULTURE AGRI FINAN INDUS MARKET INT/ORG LABOR NAT/G VOL/ASSN CONSULT TEC/DEV ECO/TAC EDU/PROP COLONIAL ATTIT WEALTH...OBS RECORD SAMP TREND GEN/METH WORK UN 20. PAGE 115 A2351

ECO/UNDEV POLICY FOR/AID INT/TRADE

B60

ROPKE W.,A HUMANE ECONOMY. CULTURE ECO/DEV FINAN INDUS GP/REL CENTRAL WEALTH...GEOG SOC IDEA/COMP 20 EEC. PAGE 123 A2525

ECO/TAC INT/ORG DIPLOM ORD/FREE

B60

SZTARAY Z.,BIBLIOGRAPHY ON HUNGARY. HUNGARY MOD/EUR CULTURE INDUS SECT DIPLOM REV...ART/METH SOC LING 18/20. PAGE 141 A2879

BIBLIOG NAT/G COM MARXISM

B60

THE ECONOMIST (LONDON),THE COMMONWEALTH AND EUROPE. EUR+WWI WOR+45 AGRI FINAN INCOME...STAT CENSUS CHARTS CMN/WLTH EEC. PAGE 142 A2911

INT/TRADE INDUS INT/ORG NAT/COMP

S60

"THE EMERGING COMMON MARKETS IN LATIN AMERICA." FUT L/A+17C STRATA DIST/IND INDUS LABOR NAT/G LEGIS ECO/TAC ADMIN RIGID/FLEX HEALTH...NEW/IDEA TIME/SEQ OAS 20. PAGE 3 A0059

FINAN ECO/UNDEV INT/TRADE

S60

GARNICK D.H.,"ON THE ECONOMIC FEASIBILITY OF A MIDDLE EASTERN COMMON MARKET." AFR ISLAM CULTURE INDUS NAT/G PLAN TEC/DEV ECO/TAC ADMIN ATTIT DRIVE RIGID/FLEX...PLURIST STAT TREND GEN/LAWS 20. PAGE 51 A1051

MARKET INT/TRADE

S60

LINDHOLM R.W.,"ACCELERATED DEVELOPMENT WITH A MINIMUM OF FOREIGN AID AND ECONOMIC CONTROLS." SOCIETY INDUS ECO/TAC WEALTH...CONCPT 20. PAGE 89 A1822

ECO/DEV FINAN FOR/AID

S60

MORALES C.J.,"TRADE AND ECONOMIC INTEGRATION IN LATIN AMERICA." FUT L/A+17C LAW STRATA ECO/UNDEV DIST/IND INDUS LABOR NAT/G LEGIS ECO/TAC ADMIN RIGID/FLEX WEALTH...CONCPT NEW/IDEA CONT/OBS TIME/SEQ WORK 20. PAGE 104 A2128

FINAN INT/TRADE REGION

C60

HAZARD J.N.,"THE SOVIET SYSTEM OF GOVERNMENT." USSR SOCIETY INDUS NAT/G POL/PAR DIPLOM CT/SYS...JURID CHARTS BIBLIOG/A 20. PAGE 63 A1298

COM NAT/COMP STRUCT ADMIN

B61

BAGU S.,ARGENTINA EN EL MUNDO. L/A+17C INDUS INT/TRADE WAR ATTIT ROLE...TREND 19/20 ARGEN OAS. PAGE 10 A0202

DIPLOM INT/ORG REGION ECO/UNDEV

B61

DETHINE P.,BIBLIOGRAPHIE DES ASPECTS ECONOMIQUES ET SOCIAUX DE L'INDUSTRIALISATION EN AFRIQUE. AFR FINAN LABOR FOR/AID...SOC 20. PAGE 36 A0734

BIBLIOG/A ECO/UNDEV INDUS TEC/DEV

B61

DIMOCK M.E.,BUSINESS AND GOVERNMENT (4TH ED.). AGRI FINAN OP/RES PLAN BUDGET DIPLOM LOBBY NUC/PWR NEW/LIB SOCISM...POLICY BIBLIOG 20. PAGE 37 A0765

NAT/G INDUS LABOR ECO/TAC

B61

HARRISON S.,INDIA AND THE UNITED STATES. FUT S/ASIA USA+45 WOR+45 INTELL ECO/DEV ECO/UNDEV AGRI INDUS INT/ORG NAT/G CONSULT EX/STRUC TOP/EX PLAN ECO/TAC NEUTRAL ALL/VALS...MGT TOT/POP 20. PAGE 62 A1272

DELIB/GP ACT/RES FOR/AID INDIA

B61

INTERNATIONAL BANK RECONST DEV,THE WORLD BANK IN AFRICA: SUMMARY OF ACTIVITIES. AGRI COM/IND DIST/IND EXTR/IND INDUS TAX COST...CHARTS 20. PAGE 71 A1450

FINAN ECO/UNDEV INT/ORG AFR

B61

LIEFMANN-KEIL E.,OKONOMISCHE THEORIE DER SOZIALPOLITIK. INT/ORG LABOR WORKER COST INCOME NEW/LIB...CONCPT SOC/INTEG 20. PAGE 88 A1810

ECO/DEV INDUS NAT/G SOC/WK

B61

MICHAEL D.N.,PROPOSED STUDIES ON THE IMPLICATIONS OF PEACEFUL SPACE ACTIVITIES FOR HUMAN AFFAIRS. COM/IND INDUS FORCES DIPLOM PEACE PERSON...PSY SOC 20. PAGE 101 A2066

FUT SPACE ACT/RES PROB/SOLV

B61

STARK H.,SOCIAL AND ECONOMIC FRONTIERS IN LATIN AMERICA (2ND ED.). CUBA FUT CULTURE AGRI INDUS ECO/TAC PRODUC ATTIT MARXISM...NAT/COMP BIBLIOG T 20. PAGE 137 A2807

L/A+17C SOCIETY DIPLOM ECO/UNDEV

B61

US GENERAL ACCOUNTING OFFICE,EXAMINATION OF ECONOMIC AND TECHNICAL ASSISTANCE PROGRAM FOR IRAN. IRAN USA+45 AGRI INDUS DIPLOM CONTROL COST 20. PAGE 153 A3115

FOR/AID ADMIN TEC/DEV ECO/UNDEV

S61

OCHENG D.,"AN ECONOMIST LOOKS AT UGANDA'S FUTURE." FUT UGANDA AGRI INDUS PLAN PROB/SOLV INT/TRADE SOVEREIGN 20. PAGE 111 A2275

ECO/UNDEV INCOME ECO/TAC OWN

S61

PADELFORD N.J.,"POLITICS AND THE FUTURE OF ECOSOC." AFR S/ASIA ECO/UNDEV INDUS NAT/G DELIB/GP ACT/RES ORD/FREE WEALTH...CONCPT CHARTS UN 20 ECOSOC. PAGE 113 A2310

INT/ORG TEC/DEV

S61

ROSTOW W.W.,"THE FUTURE OF FOREIGN AID." COM FUT WOR+45 ECO/DEV INDUS INT/ORG NAT/G CONSULT ACT/RES PLAN DOMIN LEGIT CHOOSE RIGID/FLEX ALL/VALS ...MAJORIT CONCPT TREND TOT/POP 20. PAGE 124 A2544

ECO/UNDEV ECO/TAC FOR/AID

S61

VINER J.,"ECONOMIC FOREIGN POLICY ON THE NEW FRONTIER." USA+45 ECO/UNDEV AGRI FINAN INDUS MARKET INT/ORG NAT/G FOR/AID INT/TRADE ADMIN ATTIT PWR 20 KENNEDY/JF. PAGE 159 A3239

TOP/EX ECO/TAC BAL/PAY TARIFFS

B62

CADWELL R.,COMMUNISM IN THE MODERN WORLD. USSR WOR+45 SOCIETY AGRI INDUS INT/ORG SECT EDU/PROP COLONIAL PEACE...SOC 20. PAGE 23 A0463

COM DIPLOM POLICY CONCPT

B62

FATOUROS A.A.,GOVERNMENT GUARANTEES TO FOREIGN INVESTORS. WOR+45 ECO/UNDEV INDUS WORKER ADJUD ...NAT/COMP BIBLIOG TREATY. PAGE 44 A0903

NAT/G FINAN INT/TRADE ECO/DEV

B62

HUMPHREY D.D.,THE UNITED STATES AND THE COMMON MARKET. USA+45 INDUS MARKET INT/ORG PLAN EDU/PROP BAL/PAY DRIVE PWR WEALTH...TREND STERTYP EEC 20. PAGE 69 A1415

ATTIT ECO/TAC

B62

KRAFT J.,THE GRAND DESIGN. EUR+WWI USA+45 AGRI FINAN INDUS MARKET INT/ORG NAT/G PLAN ECO/TAC TARIFFS REGION DRIVE ORD/FREE WEALTH...POLICY OBS TREND EEC 20. PAGE 82 A1674

VOL/ASSN ECO/DEV INT/TRADE

B62

LEWIS J.P.,QUIET CRISIS IN INDIA. INDIA USA+45 CULTURE ECO/UNDEV AGRI INDUS PROC/MFG NAT/G PLAN TEC/DEV DRIVE PWR SKILL WEALTH...MYTH 20. PAGE 88 A1801

S/ASIA ECO/TAC FOR/AID

B62

ROY P.A.,SOUTH WIND RED. L/A+17C USA+45 ECO/UNDEV NAT/G CAP/ISM MARXISM SOCISM...OLD/LIB GEOG RECORD INT CENSUS 20 COLD/WAR. PAGE 125 A2554

DIPLOM INDUS POLICY ECO/TAC

B62

TAYLOR D.,THE BRITISH IN AFRICA. UK CULTURE ECO/UNDEV INDUS DIPLOM INT/TRADE ADMIN WAR RACE/REL ORD/FREE SOVEREIGN...POLICY BIBLIOG 15/20 CMN/WLTH. PAGE 142 A2898

AFR COLONIAL DOMIN

C62

DUFFY J.,"PORTUGAL IN AFRICA." PORTUGAL SIER/LEONE INDUS WORKER INT/TRADE WAR CONSERVE...CATH GEOG TREND 16/20. PAGE 39 A0795

BIBLIOG RACE/REL ECO/UNDEV COLONIAL

B63
BRITISH AID. UK AGRI DIST/IND INDUS SCHOOL TEC/DEV INT/TRADE COLONIAL DEMAND...TREND CHARTS 20. PAGE 3 A0064
FOR/AID ECO/UNDEV NAT/G FINAN

B63
CERAMI C.A.,ALLIANCE BORN OF DANGER. EUR+WWI USA+45 USSR ECO/DEV INDUS VOL/ASSN ECO/TAC REGION ATTIT MARXISM ATLAN/ALL 20 NATO EEC. PAGE 25 A0514
DIPLOM INT/ORG NAT/G POLICY

B63
EL-NAGGAR S.,FOREIGN AID TO UNITED ARAB REPUBLIC. UAR USA+45 USSR AGRI FINAN INDUS FORCES EATING DEMAND...CHARTS METH/COMP 20 RESOURCE/N AID. PAGE 41 A0838
FOR/AID ECO/UNDEV RECEIVE PLAN

B63
FATEMI N.S.,THE DOLLAR CRISIS. USA+45 INDUS NAT/G LEGIS BUDGET TAX COST...CHARTS METH/COMP 20 EEC. PAGE 44 A0902
PROB/SOLV BAL/PAY FOR/AID PLAN

B63
INTERNATIONAL BANK RECONST DEV,THE WORLD BANK GROUP IN ASIA. ASIA S/ASIA INDUS TEC/DEV ECO/TAC...RECORD 20 IBRD WORLD/BANK. PAGE 71 A1451
INT/ORG DIPLOM ECO/UNDEV FINAN

B63
KATZ S.M.,A SELECTED LIST OF US READINGS ON DEVELOPMENT. AGRI COM/IND DIST/IND INDUS LABOR PLAN FOR/AID EDU/PROP HEALTH...POLICY SOC/WK 20. PAGE 77 A1571
BIBLIOG/A ECO/UNDEV TEC/DEV ACT/RES

B63
LAFEBER W.,THE NEW EMPIRE: AN INTERPRETATION OF AMERICAN EXPANSION, 1860-1898. USA-45 CONSTN NAT/LISM SOVEREIGN...TREND BIBLIOG 19/20. PAGE 84 A1711
INDUS NAT/G DIPLOM CAP/ISM

B63
ROBOCK S.H.,OVERVIEW OF TOTAL BRAZILIAN SETTING, NEWER REGIONAL PATTERNS NING AND FOREIGN AID. BRAZIL ECO/UNDEV AGRI FINAN INDUS INT/ORG INCOME UTIL...CHARTS 20. PAGE 122 A2507
ECO/TAC REGION PLAN FOR/AID

B63
SCHMELTZ G.W.,LA POLITIQUE MONDIALE CONTEMPORAINE. SOCIETY ECO/UNDEV INDUS INT/ORG NAT/G POL/PAR CONSULT DELIB/GP PLAN TEC/DEV ECO/TAC DOMIN EDU/PROP ROUTINE COERCE PERCEPT PERSON LOVE SKILL ...SOC RECORD TOT/POP. PAGE 128 A2629
WOR+45 COLONIAL

B63
UAR MINISTRY OF CULTURE,A BIBLIOGRAPHICAL LIST OF ARABIAN PENINSULA. ISLAM SAUDI/ARAB YEMEN FINAN NAT/G DIPLOM 19/20. PAGE 146 A2990
BIBLIOG GEOG INDUS SECT

B63
UNITED STATES GOVERNMENT,REPORT TO THE INTER-AMERICAN ECONOMIC AND SOCIAL COUNCIL. L/A+17C INDUS PLAN INT/TRADE TARIFFS CONFER...CHARTS 20 LAFTA. PAGE 149 A3038
FOR/AID ECO/TAC ECO/UNDEV DIPLOM

B63
US ECON SURVEY TEAM INDONESIA,INDONESIA - PERSPECTIVE AND PROPOSALS FOR UNITED STATES ECONOMIC AID. INDONESIA AGRI MARKET TEC/DEV DIPLOM INT/TRADE EDU/PROP 20. PAGE 153 A3113
FOR/AID ECO/UNDEV PLAN INDUS

B63
US SENATE COMM ON FOREIGN REL,HEARINGS ON S 1276 A BILL TO AMEND FURTHER THE FOREIGN ASSISTANCE ACT OF 1961. USA+45 WOR+45 INDUS INT/ORG FORCES TAX WEAPON SUPEGO...NAT/COMP 20 UN CONGRESS PRESIDENT. PAGE 156 A3182
FOR/AID DIPLOM ECO/UNDEV ORD/FREE

B63
WHITTON J.B.,PROPAGANDA AND THE COLD WAR. USA+45 USSR INDUS NAT/G PLAN WRITING EFFICIENCY...POLICY 20 COLD/WAR. PAGE 164 A3341
ATTIT EDU/PROP COM/IND DIPLOM

B63
YOUNG A.N.,CHINA AND THE HELPING HAND. ASIA USA+45 FINAN INDUS ECO/TAC GIVE WEALTH...METH/COMP 20 LEND/LEASE GOLD/STAND. PAGE 169 A3434
FOR/AID DIPLOM WAR

L63
SINGER J.D.,"WEAPONS MANAGEMENT IN WORLD POLITICS: PROCEEDINGS OF THE INTERNATIONAL ARMS CONTROL SYMPOSIUM, DECEMBER, 1962." FUT WOR+45 SOCIETY ECO/DEV INDUS INT/ORG DELIB/GP FORCES ACT/RES ECO/TAC EDU/PROP ARMS/CONT SUPEGO HEALTH ORD/FREE PWR SKILL...POLICY CHARTS SIMUL ANTHOL VAL/FREE 20. PAGE 133 A2729
CONSULT ATTIT DIPLOM NUC/PWR

S63
GORDON B.,"ECONOMIC IMPEDIMENTS TO REGIONALISM IN SOUTH EAST ASIA." BURMA FUT S/ASIA THAILAND USA+45 AGRI INDUS R+D NAT/G PLAN ECO/TAC WEALTH...STAT CONT/OBS 20. PAGE 54 A1110
VOL/ASSN ECO/UNDEV INT/TRADE REGION

S63
MATHUR P.N.,"GAINS IN ECONOMIC GROWTH FROM INTERNATIONAL TRADE." USA-45 ECO/DEV FINAN INDUS ATTIT WEALTH...MATH QUANT STAT BIOG TREND GEN/LAWS WORK 20. PAGE 96 A1966
MARKET ECO/TAC CAP/ISM INT/TRADE

S63
NADLER E.B.,"SOME ECONOMIC DISADVANTAGES OF THE ARMS RACE." USA+45 INDUS R+D FORCES PLAN TEC/DEV ECO/TAC FOR/AID EDU/PROP PWR WEALTH...TREND COLD/WAR 20. PAGE 107 A2190
ECO/DEV MGT BAL/PAY

S63
SHWADRAN B.,"MIDDLE EAST OIL, 1962." ISLAM USSR ECO/DEV DIST/IND INDUS PLAN BAL/PWR DISPL DRIVE ...POLICY STAT TREND GEN/LAWS EEC OEEC 20 OIL. PAGE 132 A2712
MARKET ECO/TAC INT/TRADE

B64
CHENG C.,ECONOMIC RELATIONS BETWEEN PEKING AND MOSCOW: 1949-63. ASIA CHINA/COM COM USSR FINAN INDUS CONSULT TEC/DEV INT/TRADE...PREDICT CHARTS BIBLIOG 20. PAGE 26 A0527
DIPLOM FOR/AID MARXISM

B64
COLUMBIA U SCHOOL OF LAW,PUBLIC INTERNATIONAL DEVELOPMENT FINANCING IN INDIA. GERMANY/W INDIA UK USA+45 INDUS PLAN TEC/DEV DIPLOM ECO/TAC GIVE ADMIN UTIL ATTIT 20. PAGE 28 A0572
ECO/UNDEV FINAN FOR/AID INT/ORG

B64
FREUD A.,OF HUMAN SOVEREIGNTY. WOR+45 INDUS SECT ECO/TAC CRIME CHOOSE ATTIT MORAL MARXISM...POLICY BIBLIOG 20. PAGE 49 A0998
NAT/LISM DIPLOM WAR PEACE

B64
GESELLSCHAFT RECHTSVERGLEICH,BIBLIOGRAPHIE DES DEUTSCHEN RECHTS (BIBLIOGRAPHY OF GERMAN LAW, TRANS. BY COURTLAND PETERSON). GERMANY FINAN INDUS LABOR SECT FORCES CT/SYS PARL/PROC CRIME...INT/LAW SOC NAT/COMP 20. PAGE 52 A1066
BIBLIOG/A JURID CONSTN ADMIN

B64
HAMBRIDGE G.,DYNAMICS OF DEVELOPMENT. AGRI FINAN INDUS LABOR INT/TRADE EDU/PROP ADMIN LEAD OWN HEALTH...ANTHOL BIBLIOG 20. PAGE 61 A1245
ECO/UNDEV ECO/TAC OP/RES ACT/RES

B64
HAZLEWOOD A.,THE ECONOMICS OF DEVELOPMENT: AN ANNOTATED LIST OF BOOKS AND ARTICLES PUBLISHED 1958-1962. AGRI FINAN INDUS LABOR NAT/G DIPLOM INT/TRADE INCOME...MGT 20. PAGE 63 A1303
BIBLIOG/A ECO/UNDEV TEC/DEV

B64
HINSHAW R.,THE EUROPEAN COMMUNITY AND AMERICAN TRADE: A STUDY IN ATLANTIC ECONOMICS AND POLICY. EUR+WWI UK USA+45 ECO/DEV ECO/UNDEV AGRI INDUS INT/ORG NAT/G ECO/TAC TARIFFS REGION...STAT CHARTS EEC 20. PAGE 65 A1337
MARKET TREND INT/TRADE

B64
KIMMINICH O.,RUSTUNG UND POLITISCHE SPANNUNG. INDUS ARMS/CONT COERCE NAT/LISM PEACE PERSON ORD/FREE ...POLICY GEOG 20. PAGE 79 A1619
DIPLOM FORCES WEAPON WAR

B64
MASON E.S.,FOREIGN AID AND FOREIGN POLICY. USA+45 AGRI INDUS NAT/G EX/STRUC ACT/RES RIGID/FLEX ALL/VALS...POLICY GEN/LAWS MARSHL/PLN CONGRESS 20. PAGE 95 A1956
ECO/UNDEV ECO/TAC FOR/AID DIPLOM

B64
NEHEMKIS P.,LATIN AMERICA: MYTH AND REALITY. INDUS INT/ORG MUNIC PROB/SOLV CAP/ISM DIPLOM REV...SOC 20. PAGE 108 A2211
REGION MYTH L/A+17C ECO/UNDEV

B64
OECD,DEVELOPMENT ASSISTANCE EFFORTS - POLICIES OF THE MEMBERS. AGRI INDUS BUDGET...GEOG NAT/COMP 20 OECD. PAGE 111 A2280
INT/ORG FOR/AID ECO/UNDEV TEC/DEV

B64
RUBIN J.A.,YOUR HUNDRED BILLION DOLLARS. USA+45 USSR INDUS INT/ORG TEC/DEV ECO/TAC...METH/COMP 20 PEACE/CORP. PAGE 125 A2559
FOR/AID DIPLOM ECO/UNDEV

B64
SINGER H.W.,INTERNATIONAL DEVELOPMENT: GROWTH AND CHANGE. AFR BRAZIL L/A+17C WOR+45 CULTURE AGRI INDUS NAT/G ACT/RES ECO/TAC EDU/PROP WEALTH...GEOG CONCPT METH/CNCPT STAT HYPO/EXP WORK TOT/POP 20. PAGE 133 A2723
FINAN ECO/UNDEV FOR/AID INT/TRADE

B64
SZLADITS C.,BIBLIOGRAPHY ON FOREIGN AND COMPARATIVE LAW: BOOKS AND ARTICLES IN ENGLISH (SUPPLEMENT 1962). FINAN INDUS JUDGE LICENSE ADMIN CT/SYS PARL/PROC OWN...INT/LAW CLASSIF METH/COMP NAT/COMP 20. PAGE 141 A2877
BIBLIOG/A JURID ADJUD LAW

L64
CARNEGIE ENDOWMENT INT. PEACE,"ECONOMIC AND SOCIAL QUESTION (ISSUES BEFORE THE NINETEENTH GENERAL ASSEMBLY)." WOR+45 ECO/DEV ECO/UNDEV INDUS R+D DELIB/GP CREATE PLAN TEC/DEV ECO/TAC FOR/AID BAL/PAY...RECORD UN 20. PAGE 24 A0493
INT/ORG INT/TRADE

L64
POUNDS N.J.G.,"THE POLITICS OF PARTITION." AFR ASIA COM EUR+WWI FUT ISLAM S/ASIA USA-45 LAW ECO/DEV ECO/UNDEV AGRI INDUS INT/ORG POL/PAR PROVS SECT FORCES TOP/EX EDU/PROP LEGIT ATTIT MORAL ORD/FREE PWR RESPECT WEALTH. PAGE 117 A2402
NAT/G NAT/LISM

S64
HUELIN D.,"ECONOMIC INTEGRATION IN LATIN AMERICAN: PROGRESS AND PROBLEMS." L/A+17C ECO/DEV AGRI
MARKET ECO/UNDEV

DIST/IND FINAN INDUS NAT/G VOL/ASSN CONSULT DELIB/GP EX/STRUC ACT/RES PLAN TEC/DEV ECO/TAC ROUTINE BAL/PAY WEALTH WORK 20. PAGE 69 A1411 — INT/TRADE

S64
ROTHCHILD D.,"EAST AFRICAN FEDERATION." AFR TANZANIA UGANDA INDUS REGION 20. PAGE 124 A2547 — INT/ORG DIPLOM ECO/UNDEV ECO/TAC

S64
TAUBENFELD R.K.,"INDEPENDENT REVENUE FOR THE UNITED NATIONS." WOR+45 SOCIETY STRUCT INDUS NAT/G CONSULT ACT/RES PLAN ECO/TAC LEGIT WEALTH...DECISION CON/ANAL GEN/METH UN 20. PAGE 142 A2896 — INT/ORG FINAN

S64
TRISKA J.F.,"SOVIET TREATY LAW: A QUANTITATIVE ANALYSIS." WOR+45 LAW ECO/UNDEV AGRI COM/IND INDUS CREATE TEC/DEV DIPLOM ATTIT PWR WEALTH...JURID SAMP TIME/SEQ TREND CHARTS VAL/FREE 20 TREATY. PAGE 145 A2967 — COM ECO/TAC INT/LAW USSR

S64
ZARTMAN I.W.,"LES RELATIONS ENTRE LA FRANCE ET L'ALGERIA DEPUIS LES ACCORDS D'EVIAN." EUR+WWI FUT ISLAM CULTURE AGRI EXTR/IND FINAN INDUS POL/PAR DIPLOM ECO/TAC FOR/AID PEACE ATTIT DRIVE ALL/VALS ...TIME/SEQ VAL/FREE 20. PAGE 169 A3446 — ECO/UNDEV ALGERIA FRANCE

B65
AMERICAN ECONOMIC ASSOCIATION,INDEX OF ECONOMIC JOURNALS 1886-1965 (7 VOLS.). UK USA+45 USA-45 AGRI FINAN PLAN ECO/TAC INT/TRADE ADMIN...STAT CENSUS 19/20. PAGE 7 A0145 — BIBLIOG WRITING INDUS

B65
FORM W.H.,INDUSTRIAL RELATIONS AND SOCIAL CHANGE IN LATIN AMERICA. L/A+17C AGRI LABOR NAT/G PLAN PROB/SOLV DIPLOM...MGT SOC ANTHOL BIBLIOG/A METH 20. PAGE 47 A0966 — INDUS GP/REL NAT/COMP ECO/UNDEV

B65
FRUTKIN A.W.,SPACE AND THE INTERNATIONAL COOPERATION YEAR: A NATIONAL CHALLENGE (PAMPHLET). EUR+WWI USA+45 FINAN TEC/DEV BUDGET...MGT 20 NASA. PAGE 49 A1011 — SPACE INDUS NAT/G DIPLOM

B65
HASSON J.A.,THE ECONOMICS OF NUCLEAR POWER. INDIA UK USA+45 WOR+45 INT/ORG TEC/DEV COST...SOC STAT CHARTS 20 EURATOM. PAGE 63 A1286 — NUC/PWR INDUS ECO/DEV METH

B65
HOSELITZ B.F.,ECONOMICS AND THE IDEA OF MANKIND. UNIV ECO/DEV ECO/UNDEV DIST/IND INDUS INT/ORG NAT/G ACT/RES ECO/TAC WEALTH...CONCPT STAT. PAGE 68 A1392 — CREATE INT/TRADE

B65
INTERNATIONAL SOCIAL SCI COUN,SOCIAL SCIENCES IN THE USSR. USSR ECO/DEV AGRI FINAN INDUS PLAN CAP/ISM...INT/LAW PHIL/SCI PSY SOC 20. PAGE 71 A1460 — BIBLIOG/A ACT/RES MARXISM JURID

B65
JALEE P.,THE PILLAGE OF THE THIRD WORLD (TRANS. BY MARY KLOPPER). WOR+45 AGRI INDUS ECO/TAC FOR/AID COLONIAL CONTROL PRODUC PWR WEALTH...STAT CHARTS 20 RESOURCE/N. PAGE 73 A1493 — ECO/UNDEV DOMIN INT/TRADE DIPLOM

B65
JOHNSON H.G.,THE WORLD ECONOMY AT THE CROSSROADS. COM WOR-45 ECO/DEV AGRI INDUS INT/TRADE REGION NAT/LISM 20. PAGE 74 A1523 — FINAN DIPLOM INT/ORG ECO/UNDEV

B65
JOHNSTONE A.,UNITED STATES DIRECT INVESTMENT IN FRANCE: AN INVESTIGATION OF THE FRENCH CHARGES. FRANCE USA+45 ECO/DEV INDUS LG/CO NAT/G ECO/TAC CONTROL WEALTH...BIBLIOG 20 INTERVENT. PAGE 75 A1529 — FINAN DIPLOM POLICY SOVEREIGN

B65
LYONS G.M.,AMERICA: PURPOSE AND POWER. UK USA+45 FINAN INDUS MARKET WORKER TEC/DEV DIPLOM AUTOMAT NUC/PWR WAR RACE/REL ORD/FREE 20 EEC CONGRESS SUPREME/CT CIV/RIGHTS. PAGE 92 A1881 — PWR PROB/SOLV ECO/DEV TASK

B65
MURUMBI J.,PROBLEMS OF ECONOMIC DEVELOPMENT IN EAST AFRICA. FINAN INDUS WORKER TEC/DEV INT/TRADE TAX DEMAND EFFICIENCY PRODUC SOCISM...TREND CHARTS 20 AFRICA/E. PAGE 106 A2184 — AGRI ECO/TAC ECO/UNDEV PROC/MFG

B65
PANJAB U EXTENSION LIBRARY,INDIAN NEWS INDEX. INDIA ECO/UNDEV INDUS INT/ORG SCHOOL FORCES ADJUD WAR ATTIT WEALTH 20. PAGE 114 A2333 — BIBLIOG PRESS WRITING DIPLOM

B65
REQUA E.G.,THE DEVELOPING NATIONS: A GUIDE TO INFORMATION SOURCES CONCERNING THEIR ECON, POLIT, TECHNICAL, AND SOCIAL PROBLEMS. AFR ASIA ISLAM L/A+17C INDUS INT/ORG CONSULT PLAN PROB/SOLV...SOC 20 UN. PAGE 120 A2466 — BIBLIOG/A ECO/UNDEV FOR/AID TEC/DEV

B65
ROLFE S.E.,GOLD AND WORLD POWER. UK USA+45 WOR-45 INDUS WORKER INT/TRADE DEMAND...MGT CHARTS 20 GOLD/STAND. PAGE 123 A2517 — BAL/PAY EQUILIB ECO/TAC DIPLOM

B65
US BUREAU EDUC CULTURAL AFF,RESOURCES SURVEY FOR LATIN AMERICAN COUNTRIES. L/A+17C USA+45 CULTURE INDUS INT/ORG SECT PLAN EDU/PROP POLICY. PAGE 150 A3056 — NAT/G ECO/UNDEV FOR/AID DIPLOM

L65
MATTHEWS D.G.,"A CURRENT BIBLIOGRAPHY ON ETHIOPIAN AFFAIRS: A SELECT BIBLIOGRAPHY FROM 1950-1964." ETHIOPIA LAW CULTURE ECO/UNDEV INDUS LABOR SECT FORCES DIPLOM CIVMIL/REL RACE/REL...LING STAT 20. PAGE 96 A1969 — BIBLIOG/A ADMIN POL/PAR NAT/G

L65
MATTHEWS D.G.,"A CURRENT BIBLIOGRAPHY ON SUDANESE AFFAIRS; A SELECT BIBLIOGRAPHY FROM 1960-1964." SUDAN LAW CULTURE AGRI FINAN INDUS LABOR POL/PAR TEC/DEV FOR/AID RACE/REL LITERACY...LING 20. PAGE 96 A1970 — BIBLIOG ECO/UNDEV NAT/G DIPLOM

L65
MATTHEWS D.G.,"LE TIERS MONDE: A SELECT AND PRELIMINARY BIBLIOGRAPHIC SURVEY OF MANPOWER IN DEVELOPING COUNTRIES, 1960-1964." AFR ISLAM L/A+17C INDUS PLAN PROB/SOLV TEC/DEV INT/TRADE EFFICIENCY WEALTH...STAT 20. PAGE 96 A1971 — BIBLIOG/A ECO/UNDEV LABOR WORKER

L65
WIONCZEK M.,"LATIN AMERICA FREE TRADE ASSOCIATION." AGRI DIST/IND FINAN INDUS INT/ORG LABOR NAT/G TEC/DEV ECO/TAC HEALTH SKILL WEALTH...POLICY RELATIV MGT LAFTA 20. PAGE 165 A3369 — L/A+17C MARKET REGION

S65
KHOURI F.J.,"THE JORDON RIVER CONTROVERSY." LAW SOCIETY ECO/UNDEV AGRI FINAN INDUS SECT FORCES ACT/RES PLAN TEC/DEV ECO/TAC EDU/PROP COERCE ATTIT DRIVE PERCEPT RIGID/FLEX ALL/VALS...GEOG SOC MYTH WORK. PAGE 78 A1610 — ISLAM INT/ORG ISRAEL JORDAN

B66
BROEKMEIJER M.W.J.,FICTION AND TRUTH ABOUT THE "DECADE OF DEVELOPMENT" WOR+45 AGRI FINAN INDUS NAT/G TEC/DEV DIPLOM EDU/PROP LEAD SKILL 20 THIRD/WRLD. PAGE 19 A0385 — FOR/AID POLICY ECO/UNDEV PLAN

B66
BROWN L.C.,STATE AND SOCIETY IN INDEPENDENT NORTH AFRICA. ALGERIA LIBYA MOROCCO AGRI INDUS INT/ORG POL/PAR SECT PLAN DIPLOM COLONIAL...LING NAT/COMP ANTHOL BIBLIOG 20 TUNIS MUSLIM. PAGE 20 A0406 — NAT/G SOCIETY CULTURE ECO/UNDEV

B66
CURRIE L.,ACCELERATING DEVELOPMENT: THE NECESSITY AND MEANS. COLOMBIA USA+45 INDUS DIPLOM EFFICIENCY WEALTH...METH/CNCPT NEW/IDEA 20. PAGE 33 A0668 — PLAN ECO/UNDEV FOR/AID TEC/DEV

B66
FELKER J.L.,SOVIET ECONOMIC CONTROVERSIES. USSR INDUS PLAN INT/TRADE GP/REL MARXISM SOCISM...POLICY 20. PAGE 45 A0915 — ECO/DEV MARKET PROFIT PRICE

B66
HALLET R.,PEOPLE AND PROGRESS IN WEST AFRICA: AN INTRODUCTION TO THE PROBLEMS OF DEVELOPMENT. COM/IND INDUS KIN DIPLOM FOR/AID INT/TRADE HEALTH ...GEOG TREND CHARTS BIBLIOG/A 20 AFRICA/W. PAGE 60 A1233 — AFR SOCIETY ECO/UNDEV ECO/TAC

B66
HOFMANN L.,UNITED STATES AND CANADIAN PUBLICATIONS ON AFRICA IN 1964. LAW AGRI INDUS SCHOOL...HUM SOC 20. PAGE 66 A1360 — BIBLIOG AFR DIPLOM

B66
KIRDAR U.,THE STRUCTURE OF UNITED NATIONS ECONOMIC AID TO UNDERDEVELOPED COUNTRIES. AGRI FINAN INDUS NAT/G EX/STRUC PLAN GIVE TASK...POLICY 20 UN. PAGE 79 A1631 — INT/ORG FOR/AID ECO/UNDEV ADMIN

B66
KOH S.J.,STAGES OF INDUSTRIAL DEVELOPMENT IN ASIA. ASIA INDIA KOREA STRATA STRUCT NAT/G INT/TRADE ...CHARTS 19/20 CHINJAP. PAGE 81 A1659 — INDUS ECO/UNDEV ECO/DEV LABOR

B66
LEWIS S.,TOWARDS INTERNATIONAL CO-OPERATION (1ST ED.). WOR+45 AGRI INDUS EDU/PROP RACE/REL ISOLAT NAT/LISM ATTIT HEALTH WEALTH...CHARTS WORSHIP 20 UN. PAGE 88 A1803 — DIPLOM ANOMIE PROB/SOLV INT/ORG

B66
MEERHAEGHE M.,INTERNATIONAL ECONOMIC INSTITUTIONS. EUR+WWI FINAN INDUS MARKET PLAN TARIFFS BAL/PAY EQUILIB...POLICY BIBLIOG/A 20 GATT OEEC EEC IBRD EURCOALSTL. PAGE 99 A2032 — ECO/TAC ECO/DEV INT/TRADE INT/ORG

B66
PASSIN H.,THE UNITED STATES AND JAPAN. USA+45 INDUS CAP/ISM...TREND 20 CHINJAP TREATY. PAGE 114 A2337 — DIPLOM INT/TRADE ECO/DEV ECO/TAC

B66
ROBERTSON D.J.,THE BRITISH BALANCE OF PAYMENTS. UK WOR+45 INDUS BUDGET TAX ADJUST...CHARTS ANTHOL 20. PAGE 122 A2500 — FINAN BAL/PAY ECO/DEV INT/TRADE

B66
ROBOCK S.H.,INTERNATIONAL DEVELOPMENT 1965. AGRI — FOR/AID

INDUS VOL/ASSN PLAN TEC/DEV EDU/PROP HEALTH...JURID 20 UN PEACE/CORP. PAGE 122 A2508 INT/ORG GEOG ECO/UNDEV B66

SPICER K.,A SAMARITAN STATE? AFR CANADA INDIA PAKISTAN UK USA+45 FINAN INDUS PRODUC...CHARTS 20 NATO. PAGE 136 A2787 DIPLOM FOR/AID ECO/DEV ADMIN B66

ZISCHKA A.,WAR ES EIN WUNDER? GERMANY/W ECO/DEV FINAN LG/CO BARGAIN CAP/ISM FOR/AID RATION 20 MARSHL/PLN. PAGE 170 A3456 ECO/TAC INT/TRADE INDUS WAR S66

AFRICAN BIBLIOGRAPHIC CENTER,"A CURRENT VIEW OF AFRICANA: A SELECT AND ANNOTATED BIBLIOGRAPHICAL PUBLISHING GUIDE, 1965-1966." AFR CULTURE INDUS LABOR SECT FOR/AID ADMIN COLONIAL REV RACE/REL SOCISM...LING 20. PAGE 5 A0098 BIBLIOG/A NAT/G TEC/DEV POL/PAR C66

WINT G.,"ASIA: A HANDBOOK." ASIA S/ASIA INDUS LABOR SECT PRESS RACE/REL MARXISM...STAT CHARTS BIBLIOG 20. PAGE 165 A3366 ECO/UNDEV DIPLOM NAT/G SOCIETY B67

ADAMS A.E.,AN ATLAS OF RUSSIAN AND EAST EUROPEAN HISTORY. CHRIST-17C COM MOD/EUR INDUS SECT FORCES DIPLOM COLONIAL REV WAR 4/20. PAGE 4 A0086 CHARTS REGION TREND B67

AUBREY H.G.,ATLANTIC ECONOMIC COOPERATION. ECO/DEV INDUS VOL/ASSN PROB/SOLV DIPLOM INT/TRADE TARIFFS CONFER 20. PAGE 10 A0197 INT/ORG ECO/TAC TEC/DEV CAP/ISM B67

BARANSON J.,TECHNOLOGY FOR UNDERDEVELOPED AREAS: AN ANNOTATED BIBLIOGRAPHY. FUT WOR+45 CULTURE INDUS INT/ORG CREATE PROB/SOLV INT/TRADE EDU/PROP AUTOMAT ...CONCPT METH. PAGE 11 A0218 BIBLIOG/A ECO/UNDEV TEC/DEV R+D B67

DILLARD D.,ECONOMIC DEVELOPMENT OF THE NORTH ATLANTIC COMMUNITY. EUR+WWI MOD/EUR USA+45 USA-45 ECO/UNDEV LABOR CAP/ISM WAR BAL/PAY...NAT/COMP 15/20. PAGE 37 A0763 ECO/DEV INT/TRADE INDUS DIPLOM B67

HIRSCHMAN A.O.,DEVELOPMENT PROJECTS OBSERVED. INDUS INT/ORG CONSULT EX/STRUC CREATE OP/RES ECO/TAC DEMAND...POLICY MGT METH/COMP 20 WORLD/BANK. PAGE 65 A1339 ECO/UNDEV R+D FINAN PLAN B67

HOLLERMAN L.,JAPAN'S DEPENDENCE ON THE WORLD ECONOMY. INDUS MARKET LABOR NAT/G DIPLOM 20 CHINJAP. PAGE 67 A1369 PLAN ECO/DEV ECO/TAC INT/TRADE B67

KAROL K.S.,CHINA, THE OTHER COMMUNISM (TRANS. BY TOM BAISTOW). CHINA/COM CULTURE INDUS FORCES DIPLOM EDU/PROP CONTROL EXEC NUC/PWR ATTIT...SOC CHARTS 20. PAGE 77 A1567 NAT/G POL/PAR MARXISM INGP/REL B67

MACDONALD D.F.,THE AGE OF TRANSITION: BRITAIN IN THE NINETEENTH & TWENTIETH CENTURIES. UK ECO/DEV LEGIS DIPLOM NEW/LIB...POLICY 19/20. PAGE 92 A1886 TREND INDUS SOCISM B67

ZUCKERMAN S.,SCIENTISTS AND WAR. ELITES INDUS DIPLOM CENTRAL EFFICIENCY KNOWL 20. PAGE 170 A3459 R+D CONSULT ACT/RES GP/REL L67

DEVADHAR Y.C.,"THE ROLE OF FOREIGN PRIVATE CAPITAL IN INDIA'S ECONOMIC DEVELOPMENT* ASSESSMENT OF POLICY AND PERFORMANCE." INDIA INDUS PLAN TEC/DEV BUDGET DIPLOM ECO/TAC BAL/PAY PRODUC WEALTH ...CHARTS 20. PAGE 37 A0750 CAP/ISM FOR/AID POLICY ACT/RES S67

FALKOWSKI M.,"SOCIALIST ECONOMISTS AND THE DEVELOPING COUNTRIES." COM PLAN TEC/DEV ROUTINE DEMAND EFFICIENCY PRODUC WEALTH...MARXIST TREND GEN/METH. PAGE 44 A0893 DIPLOM SOCISM ECO/UNDEV INDUS S67

GOLDMAN M.I.,"SOVIET ECONOMIC GROWTH SINCE THE REVOLUTION." USSR WORKER INT/TRADE PRODUC MARXISM ...POLICY TIME/SEQ 20. PAGE 53 A1090 ECO/DEV AGRI ECO/TAC INDUS S67

KRISTENSEN T.,"THE SOUTH AS AN INDUSTRIAL POWER." FUT WOR+45 ECO/DEV AGRI INDUS TEC/DEV...CENSUS TREND CHARTS 20. PAGE 82 A1686 DIPLOM ECO/UNDEV PREDICT PRODUC S67

PEUKERT W.,"WEST GERMANY'S 'RED TRADE'." COM GERMANY INDUS CAP/ISM DOMIN SANCTION DEMAND PEACE UTIL...MARXIST 20 COLD/WAR. PAGE 115 A2371 DIPLOM ECO/TAC INT/TRADE

INDUS/REV....INDUSTRIAL REVOLUTION

INDUSTRIAL RELATIONS....SEE LABOR, MGT, INDUS

INDUSTRIALIZATION....SEE ECO/DEV, ECO/UNDEV

INDUSTRY....SEE INDUS

INDUSTRY, COMMUNICATION....SEE COM/IND

INDUSTRY, CONSTRUCTION....SEE CONSTRUC

INDUSTRY, EXTRACTIVE....SEE EXTR/IND

INDUSTRY, MANUFACTURING....SEE PROC/MFG

INDUSTRY, PROCESSING....SEE PROC/MFG

INDUSTRY, SERVICE....SEE SERV/IND

INDUSTRY, TRANSPORTATION....SEE DIST/IND

INDUSTRY, WAREHOUSING....SEE DIST/IND

INFLATION....INFLATION

INFLUENCING....SEE MORE SPECIFIC FORMS, E.G., DOMIN, PWR, WEALTH, EDU/PROP, SKILL, CHANGE, LOBBY

INGHAM K. A1439

INGLEHART R. A1440

INGP/REL....INTRAGROUP RELATIONS

N

ARBITRATION JOURNAL. WOR+45 LAW INDUS JUDGE DIPLOM CT/SYS INGP/REL 20. PAGE 2 A0027 BIBLIOG MGT LABOR ADJUD B05

AMES J.G.,COMPREHENSIVE INDEX TO THE PUBLICATIONS OF THE UNITED STATES GOVERNMENT , 1881-1893. USA-45 CONSTN POL/PAR DELIB/GP TOP/EX DIPLOM PARL/PROC INGP/REL...INDEX 19 CONGRESS. PAGE 8 A0153 BIBLIOG/A LEGIS NAT/G GOV/REL N19

UNITED ARAB REPUBLIC,THE PROBLEM OF THE PALESTINIAN REFUGEES (PAMPHLET). ISRAEL UAR LAW PROB/SOLV EDU/PROP CONFER ADJUD CONTROL NAT/LISM HEALTH 20 JEWS UN MIGRATION. PAGE 148 A3029 STRANGE GP/REL INGP/REL DIPLOM S41

LASSWELL H.D.,"THE GARRISON STATE" (BMR)" FUT WOR+45 ELITES INTELL FORCES ECO/TAC DOMIN EDU/PROP COERCE INGP/REL 20. PAGE 85 A1739 NAT/G DIPLOM PWR CIVMIL/REL B45

MACMINN N.,BIBLIOGRAPHY OF THE PUBLISHED WRITINGS OF JOHN STUART MILL. MOD/EUR UK CAP/ISM DIPLOM KNOWL...EPIST CONCPT 19 MILL/JS. PAGE 93 A1901 BIBLIOG/A SOCIETY INGP/REL LAISSEZ B47

INTERNATIONAL COURT OF JUSTICE,CHARTER OF THE UNITED NATIONS, STATUTE AND RULES OF COURT AND OTHER CONSTITUTIONAL DOCUMENTS. SWITZERLND LAW ADJUD INGP/REL...JURID 20 ICJ UN. PAGE 71 A1453 INT/LAW INT/ORG CT/SYS DIPLOM B47

NIEBUHR R.,THE CHILDREN OF LIGHT AND THE CHILDREN OF DARKNESS: A VINDICATION OF DEMOCRACY AND CRITIQUE OF TRADITIONAL DEFENSE. UNIV STRUCT NAT/G SECT INGP/REL OWN PEACE ORD/FREE MARXISM ...IDEA/COMP GEN/LAWS 20 CHRISTIAN. PAGE 109 A2235 POPULISM DIPLOM NEIGH GP/REL B51

STANTON A.H.,PERSONALITY AND POLITICAL CRISIS. WOR+45 WOR-45 STRUCT DIPLOM INGP/REL TOTALISM MORAL ...ANTHOL 20 LASSWELL/H PARSONS/T RIESMAN/D. PAGE 137 A2806 EDU/PROP WAR PERSON PSY B54

GROSS F.,FOREIGN POLICY ANALYSIS. USA+45 TOP/EX PLAN INGP/REL ATTIT TECHRACY...CONCPT 20. PAGE 57 A1171 POLICY DIPLOM DECISION EDU/PROP B55

KOHN H.,NATIONALISM: ITS MEANING AND HISTORY. GP/REL INGP/REL ATTIT...CONCPT NAT/COMP 16/20 MACHIAVELL. PAGE 81 A1662 NAT/LISM DIPLOM FASCISM REV B55

KROPOTKIN P.,MUTUAL AID, A FACTOR OF EVOLUTION (1902). UNIV ADJUST ATTIT HEREDITY PERSON LOVE DARWIN/C. PAGE 82 A1687 INGP/REL SOCIETY GEN/LAWS BIO/SOC B55

THOMPSON V.,MINORITY PROBLEMS IN SOUTHEAST ASIA. CAMBODIA CHINA/COM LAOS S/ASIA KIN NAT/G SECT PROB/SOLV EDU/PROP REGION GP/REL RACE/REL MARXISM ...SOC 20 BUDDHISM UN. PAGE 143 A2933 INGP/REL GEOG DIPLOM STRUCT

S55
DE SMITH S.A.,"CONSTITUTIONAL MONARCHY IN BURGANDA." AFR UGANDA UK STRUCT CHIEF REGION INGP/REL ADJUST NAT/LISM SOVEREIGN CONSERVE ...POLICY 19/20 BURGANDA. PAGE 35 A0712 NAT/G DIPLOM CONSTN COLONIAL

B56
JAMESON J.F.,THE AMERICAN REVOLUTION CONSIDERED AS A SOCIAL MOVEMENT. USA-45 AGRI FINAN SECT INT/TRADE REPRESENT SUFF INGP/REL RACE/REL DISCRIM...MAJORIT 18/19 CHURCH/STA. PAGE 73 A1494 ORD/FREE REV FEDERAL CONSTN

B56
VON HARPE W.,DIE SOWJETUNION FINNLAND UND SKANDANAVIEN, 1945-1955. EUR+WWI FINLAND GERMANY USSR WAR INGP/REL ORD/FREE SOVEREIGN MARXISM ...POLICY GOV/COMP BIBLIOG 20 STALIN/J. PAGE 160 A3252 DIPLOM COM NEUTRAL BAL/PWR

B58
INSTITUTE MEDITERRANEAN AFF,THE PALESTINE REFUGEE PROBLEM. UAR WOR+45 INT/ORG PLAN PROB/SOLV PEACE ...POLICY GEOG STAT CHARTS 20 JEWS UN MIGRATION. PAGE 70 A1444 STRANGE HABITAT GP/REL INGP/REL

B58
JENNINGS W.I.,PROBLEMS OF THE NEW COMMONWEALTH. CEYLON INDIA MALAYSIA PAKISTAN ECO/UNDEV VOL/ASSN RACE/REL NAT/LISM ROLE 20 CMN/WLTH. PAGE 74 A1511 GP/REL INGP/REL COLONIAL INT/ORG

B58
MANSERGH N.,COMMONWEALTH PERSPECTIVES. GHANA UK LAW VOL/ASSN CONFER HEALTH SOVEREIGN...GEOG CHARTS ANTHOL 20 CMN/WLTH AUSTRAL. PAGE 94 A1930 DIPLOM COLONIAL INT/ORG INGP/REL

B58
MANSERGH N.,SURVEY OF BRITISH COMMONWEALTH AFFAIRS: PROBLEMS OF WARTIME CO-OPERATION AND POST-WAR CHANGE 1939-1952. INDIA IRELAND S/ASIA CONSTN INT/ORG BAL/PWR COLONIAL NEUTRAL WAR ADJUST PEACE ROLE ORD/FREE...CHARTS 20 CMN/WLTH NATO UN. PAGE 94 A1931 VOL/ASSN CONSEN PROB/SOLV INGP/REL

B58
REUTER P.,INTERNATIONAL INSTITUTIONS. WOR+45 WOR-45 CULTURE SOCIETY VOL/ASSN LEGIT ROUTINE GP/REL INGP/REL KNOWL...JURID METH/CNCPT TIME/SEQ 20. PAGE 120 A2469 INT/ORG PSY

C58
WILDING N.,"AN ENCYCLOPEDIA OF PARLIAMENT." UK LAW CONSTN CHIEF PROB/SOLV DIPLOM DEBATE WAR INGP/REL PRIVIL...BIBLIOG DICTIONARY 13/20 CMN/WLTH PARLIAMENT. PAGE 164 A3349 PARL/PROC POL/PAR NAT/G ADMIN

B59
JONES A.C.,NEW FABIAN COLONIAL ESSAYS. UK SOCIETY POL/PAR EDU/PROP ADMIN ORD/FREE SOVEREIGN SOCISM ...ANTHOL 20 CMN/WLTH LABOR/PAR. PAGE 75 A1530 COLONIAL INT/ORG INGP/REL DOMIN

B59
KAPLAN D.,THE ARAB REFUGEES: AN ABNORMAL PROBLEM. UAR WOR+45 PROB/SOLV DIPLOM GOV/REL ADJUST EFFICIENCY...POLICY GEOG INT/LAW 20 UN JEWS MIGRATION. PAGE 76 A1557 STRANGE HABITAT GP/REL INGP/REL

B59
KNIERIEM A.,THE NUREMBERG TRIALS. EUR+WWI GERMANY VOL/ASSN LEAD COERCE WAR INGP/REL TOTALISM SUPEGO ORD/FREE...CONCPT METH/COMP. PAGE 80 A1651 INT/LAW CRIME PARTIC JURID

B59
PANHUYS H.F.,THE ROLE OF NATIONALITY IN INTERNATIONAL LAW. ADJUD CRIME WAR STRANGE...JURID TREND. PAGE 114 A2330 INT/LAW NAT/LISM INGP/REL

B60
KENNEDY J.F.,THE STRATEGY OF PEACE. USA+45 WOR+45 BAL/PWR DIPLOM INGP/REL ORD/FREE...GOV/COMP NAT/COMP 20. PAGE 78 A1591 PEACE PLAN POLICY NAT/G

B60
WHEARE K.C.,THE CONSTITUTIONAL STRUCTURE OF THE COMMONWEALTH. UK EX/STRUC DIPLOM DOMIN ADMIN COLONIAL CONTROL LEAD INGP/REL SUPEGO 20 CMN/WLTH. PAGE 163 A3325 CONSTN INT/ORG VOL/ASSN SOVEREIGN

B61
NOLLAU G.,INTERNATIONAL COMMUNISM AND WORLD REVOLUTION; HISTORY AND METHODS (TRANS. BY VICTOR ANDERSEN). COM WORKER DIPLOM CONFER INGP/REL ...CONCPT BIBLIOG 20 STALIN/J LENIN/VI COMINTERN COMINFORM WORLD/CONG. PAGE 110 A2249 MARXISM POL/PAR INT/ORG REV

B61
ROBINSON M.E.,EDUCATION FOR SOCIAL CHANGE: ESTABLISHING INSTITUTES OF PUBLIC AND BUSINESS ADMINISTRATION ABROAD (PAMPHLET). WOR+45 SOCIETY ACADEM CONFER INGP/REL ROLE...SOC CHARTS BIBLIOG 20 ICA. PAGE 122 A2506 FOR/AID EDU/PROP MGT ADJUST

B62
DELANEY R.F.,THE LITERATURE OF COMMUNISM IN AMERICA. COM USA+45 USA-45 INT/ORG LABOR NAT/G POL/PAR INGP/REL...MAJORIT 20. PAGE 36 A0727 BIBLIOG/A MARXISM EDU/PROP IDEA/COMP

B62
MOON P.,DIVIDE AND QUIT. INDIA PAKISTAN STRATA DELIB/GP PLAN DIPLOM REPRESENT GP/REL INGP/REL CONSEN DISCRIM...OBS 20. PAGE 103 A2119 WAR REGION ISOLAT SECT

B63
GREAT BRITAIN CENTRAL OFF INF,CONSULTATION AND CO-OPERATION IN THE COMMONWEALTH. LAW R+D FORCES PLAN EDU/PROP CONFER INGP/REL...GEOG CENSUS 19/20 CMN/WLTH. PAGE 55 A1133 DIPLOM DELIB/GP VOL/ASSN REGION

B63
HARTLEY A.,A STATE OF ENGLAND. UK ELITES SOCIETY ACADEM NAT/G SCHOOL INGP/REL CONSEN ORD/FREE NEW/LIB...POLICY 20. PAGE 62 A1275 DIPLOM ATTIT INTELL ECO/DEV

B63
LADOR-LEDERER J.J.,INTERNATIONAL NON-GOVERNMENTAL ORGANIZATIONS: A STUDY IN AUTONOMOUS ORGANIZATION AND IUS GENTIUM. LAW DELIB/GP LEGIS DIPLOM 20. PAGE 83 A1709 INT/ORG INT/LAW INGP/REL VOL/ASSN

B63
LOOMIE A.J.,THE SPANISH ELIZABETHANS: THE ENGLISH EXILES AT THE COURT OF PHILIP II. SPAIN UK WAR INGP/REL DRIVE HABITAT CATHISM...BIOG 16/17 MIGRATION. PAGE 91 A1860 NAT/G STRANGE POLICY DIPLOM

B63
PRESTON W. JR.,ALIENS AND DISSENTERS: FEDERAL SUPPRESSION OF RADICALS 1903-1933. USA-45 DIPLOM ADJUD REPRESENT RACE/REL MAJORITY...BIBLIOG/A 19/20. PAGE 117 A2409 DISCRIM GP/REL INGP/REL ATTIT

B63
THORELLI H.B.,INTOP: INTERNATIONAL OPERATIONS SIMULATION: PLAYER'S MANUAL. BRAZIL FINAN OP/RES ADMIN GP/REL INGP/REL PRODUC PERCEPT...DECISION MGT EEC. PAGE 144 A2935 GAME INT/TRADE EDU/PROP LG/CO

S63
LIPSHART A.,"THE ANALYSIS OF BLOC VOTING IN THE GENERAL ASSEMBLY." L/A+17C WOR+45 ACT/RES INGP/REL ...POLICY DECISION NEW/IDEA STAT IDEA/COMP UN. PAGE 90 A1832 CHOOSE INT/ORG DELIB/GP

B64
CALVO SERER R.,LAS NUEVAS DEMOCRACIAS. AFR ASIA ISLAM USA+45 WOR+45 BAL/PWR DOMIN PARTIC INGP/REL AUTHORIT POPULISM...CONCPT 20 COM/PARTY. PAGE 23 A0469 ORD/FREE MARXISM DIPLOM POLICY

B64
EAYRS J.,THE COMMONWEALTH AND SUEZ: A DOCUMENTARY SURVEY. FRANCE ISLAM VOL/ASSN FORCES CONFER COLONIAL WAR INGP/REL 20 CMN/WLTH SUEZ UN. PAGE 40 A0818 DIPLOM NAT/LISM DIST/IND SOVEREIGN

B64
ECONOMIDES C.P.,LE POUVOIR DE DECISION DES ORGANISATIONS INTERNATIONALES EUROPEENNES. DIPLOM DOMIN INGP/REL EFFICIENCY...INT/LAW JURID 20 NATO OEEC EEC COUNCL/EUR EURATOM. PAGE 40 A0821 INT/ORG PWR DECISION GP/COMP

B64
EPSTEIN H.M.,REVOLT IN THE CONGO. AFR CONGO/BRAZ WOR+45 NAT/G FORCES DOMIN WAR CIVMIL/REL INGP/REL MARXISM...RECORD GP/COMP 20 CONGO/LEOP UN. PAGE 42 A0856 REV COLONIAL NAT/LISM DIPLOM

B64
GREAT BRITAIN CENTRAL OFF INF,CONSTITUTIONAL DEVELOPMENT IN THE COMMONWEALTH. VOL/ASSN PLAN DIPLOM COLONIAL INGP/REL NAT/LISM ORD/FREE PWR 17/20 CMN/WLTH. PAGE 55 A1135 REGION CONSTN NAT/G SOVEREIGN

B64
GRIFFITH W.E.,COMMUNISM IN EUROPE (2 VOLS.). CZECHOSLVK USSR WOR+45 WOR-45 YUGOSLAVIA INGP/REL MARXISM SOCISM...ANTHOL 20 EUROPE/E. PAGE 57 A1162 COM POL/PAR DIPLOM GOV/COMP

B64
SINGH N.,THE DEFENCE MECHANISM OF THE MODERN STATE. COM UK USA+45 CONSTN INT/ORG NUC/PWR WAR INGP/REL ROLE 20 DEPT/DEFEN COMMONWLTH. PAGE 134 A2735 FORCES TOP/EX NAT/G CIVMIL/REL

B64
US SENATE COMM GOVT OPERATIONS,THE SECRETARY OF STATE AND THE AMBASSADOR. USA+45 CHIEF CONSULT EX/STRUC FORCES PLAN ADMIN EXEC INGP/REL ROLE ...ANTHOL 20 PRESIDENT DEPT/STATE. PAGE 156 A3175 DIPLOM DELIB/GP NAT/G

B65
ADENAUER K.,MEINE ERINNERUNGEN, 1945-53 (VOL. I), 1953-55 (VOL. II). EUR+WWI GERMANY CHIEF FORCES PROB/SOLV DIPLOM ARMS/CONT INGP/REL PEACE SOVEREIGN ...OBS/ENVIR RECORD 20. PAGE 4 A0089 NAT/G BIOG SELF/OBS

B65
BROMKE A.,THE COMMUNIST STATES AT THE CROSSROADS BETWEEN MOSCOW AND PEKING. CHINA/COM USSR INGP/REL NAT/LISM TOTALISM 20. PAGE 19 A0389 COM DIPLOM MARXISM REGION

B65
EISENHOWER D.D.,WAGING PEACE 1956-61: THE WHITE HOUSE YEARS. USA+45 DIPLOM LEAD INGP/REL RACE/REL PEACE ATTIT...TRADIT TIME/SEQ 20 EISNHWR/DD PRESIDENT COLD/WAR CIV/RIGHTS BERLIN. PAGE 41 A0833 TOP/EX BIOG ORD/FREE POLICY

B65
INGRAM D.,COMMONWEALTH FOR A COLOUR-BLIND WORLD. AFR INDIA UK STRATA ECO/UNDEV VOL/ASSN CREATE PLAN RACE/REL INT/ORG

CONFER COLONIAL ORD/FREE SOC/INTEG 20 COMMONWLTH. PAGE 70 A1441 INGP/REL PROB/SOLV

B65
MILLER J.D.B.,THE COMMONWEALTH IN THE WORLD (3RD ED.). CONSTN COLONIAL PWR SOVEREIGN 20 CMN/WLTH. PAGE 101 A2077 VOL/ASSN INT/ORG INGP/REL DIPLOM

B65
SMITH A.L. JR.,THE DEUTSCHTUM OF NAZI GERMANY AND THE UNITED STATES. GERMANY USA-45 DIPLOM ATTIT FASCISM...BIBLIOG 20 MIGRATION NAZI. PAGE 134 A2744 INGP/REL NAT/LISM STRANGE DELIB/GP

B65
WILLIAMSON J.A.,GREAT BRITAIN AND THE COMMONWEALTH. UK DOMIN COLONIAL INGP/REL...POLICY 18/20 CMN/WLTH. PAGE 165 A3355 NAT/G DIPLOM INT/ORG SOVEREIGN

B66
CANFIELD L.H.,THE PRESIDENCY OF WOODROW WILSON: PRELUDE TO A WORLD IN CRISIS. USA-45 ADJUD NEUTRAL WAR CHOOSE INGP/REL PEACE ORD/FREE 20 WILSON/W PRESIDENT TREATY LEAGUE/NAT. PAGE 24 A0477 PERSON POLICY DIPLOM GOV/REL

B66
FINKLE J.L.,POLITICAL DEVELOPMENT AND SOCIAL CHANGE. WOR+45 CULTURE NAT/G OP/RES PROB/SOLV DIPLOM ECO/TAC INGP/REL...METH/COMP ANTHOL 20. PAGE 46 A0934 ECO/UNDEV SOCIETY CREATE

B66
HAMILTON W.B.,A DECADE OF THE COMMONWEALTH, 1955-1964. UK LAW ELITES FINAN FOR/AID CONFER COLONIAL PWR...GEOG CHARTS ANTHOL 20 CMN/WLTH UN. PAGE 61 A1247 INT/ORG INGP/REL DIPLOM NAT/G

B66
HENKYS R.,DEUTSCHLAND UND DIE OSTLICHEN NACHBARN. GERMANY POLAND NAT/G POL/PAR INGP/REL ATTIT 20 MIGRATION. PAGE 64 A1317 GP/REL JURID INT/LAW DIPLOM

B66
NEUMANN R.G.,THE GOVERNMENT OF THE GERMAN FEDERAL REPUBLIC. EUR+WWI GERMANY/W LOC/G EX/STRUC LEGIS CT/SYS INGP/REL PWR...BIBLIOG 20 ADENAUER/K. PAGE 108 A2222 NAT/G POL/PAR DIPLOM CONSTN

B66
SPINELLI A.,THE EUROCRATS; CONFLICT AND CRISIS IN THE EUROPEAN COMMUNITY (TRANS. BY C. GROVE HAINES). EUR+WWI MARKET POL/PAR ECO/TAC PARL/PROC EEC OEEC ECSC EURATOM. PAGE 136 A2789 INT/ORG INGP/REL CONSTN ADMIN

B66
THOMPSON J.H.,MODERNIZATION OF THE ARAB WORLD. FUT ISRAEL STRUCT ECO/UNDEV DIPLOM INGP/REL ATTIT ...CENSUS ANTHOL 20 ARABS. PAGE 143 A2926 ADJUST ISLAM PROB/SOLV NAT/COMP

B66
WILSON H.A.,THE IMPERIAL POLICY OF SIR ROBERT BORDEN. CANADA UK ELITES INT/ORG VOL/ASSN CONTROL LEAD WAR ROLE 20 CMN/WLTH BORDEN/R. PAGE 165 A3360 INGP/REL COLONIAL CONSTN CHIEF

B67
BODENHEIMER E.,TREATISE ON JUSTICE. INT/ORG NAT/G PUB/INST ACT/RES RISK CRIME INGP/REL DISCRIM DRIVE LAISSEZ 20. PAGE 16 A0325 ALL/VALS STRUCT JURID CONCPT

B67
KAROL K.S.,CHINA, THE OTHER COMMUNISM (TRANS. BY TOM BAISTOW). CHINA/COM CULTURE INDUS FORCES DIPLOM EDU/PROP CONTROL EXEC NUC/PWR ATTIT...SOC CHARTS 20. PAGE 77 A1567 NAT/G POL/PAR MARXISM INGP/REL

B67
SINGER D.,QUANTITATIVE INTERNATIONAL POLITICS* INSIGHTS AND EVIDENCE. WOR+45 WOR-45 PARTIC WAR INGP/REL ATTIT PERSON ROLE...PREDICT BIBLIOG 19/20 UN SENATE. PAGE 133 A2722 DIPLOM NAT/G INT/ORG DECISION

B67
WATERS M.,THE UNITED NATIONS* INTERNATIONAL ORGANIZATION AND ADMINISTRATION. WOR+45 EX/STRUC FORCES DIPLOM LEAD REGION ARMS/CONT REPRESENT INGP/REL ROLE...METH/COMP ANTHOL 20 UN LEAGUE/NAT. PAGE 162 A3291 CONSTN INT/ORG ADMIN ADJUD

S67
ADIE W.A.C.,"CHINA'S 'SECOND LIBERATION'." CHINA/COM SOCIETY WORKER DIPLOM TASK 20 MAO. PAGE 4 A0090 MARXISM REV INGP/REL ANOMIE

S67
BENTLEY E.,"VIETNAM: THE STATE OF OUR FEELINGS." USA+45 VIETNAM PROB/SOLV DIPLOM GP/REL INGP/REL RACE/REL WEALTH. PAGE 13 A0271 WAR PARTIC ATTIT PEACE

S67
BURNS E.B.,"TRADITIONS AND VARIATIONS IN BRAZILIAN FOREIGN POLICY." BRAZIL L/A+17C POL/PAR INT/TRADE COLONIAL INGP/REL ATTIT ORD/FREE PWR 20. PAGE 22 A0443 DIPLOM NAT/LISM CREATE

S67
CONNOR W.,"SELF-DETERMINATION: THE NEW PHASE." WOR+45 WOR-45 CULTURE INT/ORG COLONIAL 19/20. PAGE 29 A0588 NAT/LISM SOVEREIGN INGP/REL GP/REL

S67
EGBERT D.D.,"POLITICS AND ART IN COMMUNIST BULGARIA" BULGARIA COM USSR CULTURE DIPLOM INGP/REL TOTALISM...TREND 20. PAGE 40 A0825 CREATE ART/METH CONTROL MARXISM

S67
FRANKEL M.,"THE WAR IN VIETNAM." VIETNAM ECO/UNDEV DIPLOM CONFER INGP/REL PEACE PWR...POLICY PREDICT 20. PAGE 48 A0982 WAR COERCE PLAN GUERRILLA

S67
HERRERA F.,"EUROPEAN PARTICIPATION IN THE LATIN AMERICAN REGIONAL INTEGRATION" EUR+WWI L/A+17C GP/REL INGP/REL 20. PAGE 64 A1318 DIPLOM REGION INT/ORG FINAN

S67
HODGE G.,"THE RISE AND DEMISE OF THE UN TECHNICAL ASSISTANCE ADMINISTRATION." RISK TASK INGP/REL CONSEN EFFICIENCY 20 UN. PAGE 66 A1349 ADMIN TEC/DEV EX/STRUC INT/ORG

S67
LIVNEH E.,"A NEW BEGINNING." ISRAEL USSR WOR+45 NAT/G DIPLOM INGP/REL FEDERAL HABITAT PWR...GEOG PSY JEWS. PAGE 90 A1847 WAR PERSON PEACE PLAN

S67
ROTBERG R.I.,"COLONIALISM AND AFTER: THE POLITICAL LITERATURE OF CENTRAL AFRICA - A BIBLIOGRAPHIC ESSAY." AFR CHIEF EX/STRUC REV INGP/REL RACE/REL SOVEREIGN 20. PAGE 124 A2546 BIBLIOG/A COLONIAL DIPLOM NAT/G

S67
THIEN T.T.,"VIETNAM: A CASE OF SOCIAL ALIENATION." VIETNAM AGRI FORCES FOR/AID ADMIN REPRESENT INGP/REL PWR 19/20. PAGE 143 A2918 NAT/G ELITES WORKER STRANGE

S67
THOMPSON K.W.,"THE EMPIRICAL, NORMATIVE, AND THEORETICAL FOUNDATIONS OF INTERNATIONAL STUDIES." WOR+45 INGP/REL RATIONAL...CONCPT RECORD IDEA/COMP. PAGE 143 A2932 DIPLOM INTELL METH/COMP KNOWL

S67
WEIL G.L.,"THE EUROPEAN COMMUNITY* WHAT LIES BEYOND THE POINT OF NO RETURN?" VOL/ASSN PROB/SOLV DIPLOM REGION INGP/REL CENTRAL PWR 20 EEC. PAGE 162 A3301 INT/ORG ECO/DEV INT/TRADE PREDICT

INGRAM D. A1441

INNIS/H....HAROLD ADAMS INNIS

INNOVATION....SEE CREATE

INONU/I....ISMET INONU

INSPECT....EXAMINING FOR QUALITY, OUTPUT, LEGALITY

B41
NIEMEYER G.,LAW WITHOUT FORCE: THE FUNCTION OF POLITICS IN INTERNATIONAL LAW. PLAN INSPECT DIPLOM REPAR LEGIT ADJUD WAR ORD/FREE...IDEA/COMP METH/COMP GEN/LAWS 20. PAGE 109 A2240 COERCE LAW PWR INT/LAW

B50
DE RUSETT A.,STRENGTHENING THE FRAMEWORK OF PEACE. WOR+45 VOL/ASSN FORCES CREATE INSPECT ADJUD CONTROL WAR EQUILIB FEDERAL ORD/FREE 20 UN EUROPE. PAGE 35 A0711 INT/ORG DIPLOM PEACE METH/COMP

B51
US HOUSE COMM APPROPRIATIONS,MUTUAL SECURITY PROGRAM APPROPRIATIONS FOR 1952: HEARINGS BEFORE A SUBCOMMITTEE OF THE COMMITTEE ON APPROPRIATIONS. KOREA L/A+17C ECO/DEV ECO/UNDEV INT/ORG INSPECT BAL/PWR DIPLOM DEBATE WAR...POLICY STAT ASIA/S 20 CONGRESS NATO COLD/WAR MID/EAST. PAGE 153 A3118 LEGIS FORCES BUDGET FOR/AID

B59
US HOUSE COMM GOVT OPERATIONS,UNITED STATES AID OPERATIONS IN LAOS. LAOS USA+45 PLAN INSPECT HOUSE/REP. PAGE 154 A3136 FOR/AID ADMIN FORCES ECO/UNDEV

B60
US SENATE COMM ON FOREIGN REL,SITUATION IN VIETNAM (2 VOLS.). USA+45 VIETNAM ECO/TAC COST SENATE DEPT/STATE. PAGE 156 A3181 FOR/AID PLAN EFFICIENCY INSPECT

B61
SHAPP W.R.,FIELD ADMINISTRATION IN THE UNITED NATIONS SYSTEM. FINAN PROB/SOLV INSPECT DIPLOM EXEC REGION ROUTINE EFFICIENCY ROLE...INT CHARTS 20 UN. PAGE 131 A2694 INT/ORG ADMIN GP/REL FOR/AID

B64
KAUFMANN W.W.,THE MC NAMARA STRATEGY. TOP/EX INSPECT BAL/PWR DIPLOM CONTROL DETER GUERRILLA NUC/PWR WEAPON COST PWR...METH/COMP 20 MCNAMARA/R KENNEDY/JF JOHNSON/LB NATO DEPT/DEFEN. PAGE 77 A1572 FORCES WAR PLAN PROB/SOLV

S64
ARMSTRONG J.A.,"THE SOVIET-AMERICAN CONFRONTATION: A NEW STAGE?" CUBA USA+45 USSR PLAN PROB/SOLV INT/TRADE CONTROL ARMS/CONT NUC/PWR MARXISM 20 COLD/WAR INTERVENT. PAGE 9 A0174 DIPLOM POLICY INSPECT

B66
US HOUSE COMM GOVT OPERATIONS,AN INVESTIGATION OF THE US ECONOMIC AND MILITARY ASSISTANCE PROGRAMS IN VIETNAM. USA+45 VIETNAM/S SOCIETY CONSTRUC FINAN FORCES BUDGET INT/TRADE PEACE HEALTH...MGT HOUSE/REP AID. PAGE 154 A3139 FOR/AID ECO/UNDEV WAR INSPECT

B99
BROOKS S.,BRITAIN AND THE BOERS. AFR SOUTH/AFR UK CULTURE INSPECT LEGIT...INT/LAW 19/20 BOER/WAR. PAGE 19 A0396 WAR DIPLOM NAT/G

INSTITUT DE DROIT INTL A1442

INSTITUT INTERMEDIAIRE INTL A1443

INSTITUTE MEDITERRANEAN AFF A1444

INSTITUTE OF HISPANIC STUDIES A1445

INSTITUTE POLITISCHE WISSEN A1446

INSTITUTION, EDUCATIONAL....SEE SCHOOL, ACADEM

INSTITUTION, MENTAL....SEE PUB/INST

INSTITUTION, RELIGIOUS....SEE SECT

INSTITUTIONS....SEE DESCRIPTORS IN INSTITUTIONAL INDEX (TOPICAL INDEX, NO. 2)

INSURANCE....SEE FINAN, SERV/IND

INSURRECTION....SEE REV

INT....INTERVIEW; SEE ALSO INTERVIEWS INDEX, P. XIV

B00
LORIMER J.,THE INSTITUTES OF THE LAW OF NATIONS. WOR-45 CULTURE SOCIETY NAT/G VOL/ASSN DIPLOM LEGIT WAR PEACE DRIVE ORD/FREE SOVEREIGN...CONCPT RECORD INT TREND HYPO/EXP GEN/METH TOT/POP VAL/FREE 20. PAGE 91 A1863 INT/ORG LAW INT/LAW

B35
STALEY E.,WAR AND THE PRIVATE INVESTOR. UNIV WOR-45 INTELL SOCIETY INT/ORG NAT/G TOP/EX CAP/ISM ECO/TAC WAR ATTIT ALL/VALS...INT TIME/SEQ TREND CON/ANAL WORK TOT/POP 20. PAGE 137 A2799 FINAN INT/TRADE DIPLOM

S51
BELKNAP G.,"POLITICAL PARTY IDENTIFICATION AND ATTITUDES TOWARD FOREIGN POLICY" (BMR)" USA+45 VOL/ASSN CONTROL CHOOSE...STAT INT CHARTS 20. PAGE 12 A0254 POL/PAR ATTIT POLICY DIPLOM

S51
BUCHANAN W.,"STEREOTYPES AND TENSIONS AS REVEALED BY THE UNESCO INTERNATIONAL POLL." WOR+45 INT/ORG ATTIT DISPL PERCEPT RIGID/FLEX...INT TESTS SAMP 20. PAGE 21 A0424 R+D STERTYP

S51
GYR J.,"ANALYSIS OF COMMITTEE MEMBER BEHAVIOUR IN FOUR CULTURES." ASIA ISLAM L/A+17C USA+45 INT/ORG VOL/ASSN LEGIT ATTIT...INT DEEP/QU SAMP CHARTS 20. PAGE 58 A1200 DELIB/GP CULTURE

S52
HAAS E.B.,"THE RECONCILIATION OF CONFLICT, COLONIAL POLICY AIMS: ACCEPTANCE OF THE LEAGUE OF NATIONS MANDATE SYSTEM." FRANCE GERMANY UK WOR+45 WOR-45 LEGIT ATTIT DRIVE ORD/FREE...OLD/LIB INT SYS/QU TIME/SEQ TREND LEAGUE/NAT 20. PAGE 58 A1201 INT/ORG COLONIAL

B53
COHEN B.C.,CITIZEN EDUCATION IN WORLD AFFAIRS. USA+45 INT/ORG VOL/ASSN CONSULT ATTIT PWR...INT TIME/SEQ 20. PAGE 27 A0559 KNOWL EDU/PROP DIPLOM

B53
MACK R.T.,RAISING THE WORLDS STANDARD OF LIVING. IRAN INT/ORG VOL/ASSN EX/STRUC ECO/TAC WEALTH...MGT METH/CNCPT STAT CONT/OBS INT TOT/POP VAL/FREE 20 UN. PAGE 92 A1893 WOR+45 FOR/AID INT/TRADE

B56
GEORGE A.L.,WOODROW WILSON AND COLONEL HOUSE. WOR-45 CONSTN FACE/GP INT/ORG NAT/G POL/PAR CONSULT LEGIT EXEC COERCE CHOOSE ATTIT DRIVE PERSON MORAL ORD/FREE PWR RESPECT...POLICY MGT PSY OBS RECORD INT LEAGUE/NAT. PAGE 52 A1060 USA-45 BIOG DIPLOM

B57
FULLER C.D.,TRAINING OF SPECIALISTS IN INTERNATIONAL RELATIONS. FUT USA+45 USA-45 INTELL INT/ORG...MGT METH/CNCPT INT QU GEN/METH 20. PAGE 50 A1017 KNOWL DIPLOM

B57
MURRAY J.N.,THE UNITED NATIONS TRUSTEESHIP SYSTEM. AFR WOR+45 CONSTN CONSULT LEGIS EDU/PROP LEGIT EXEC ROUTINE...INT TIME/SEQ SOMALI UN 20. PAGE 106 A2181 INT/ORG DELIB/GP

B57
SPEIER H.,GERMAN REARMAMENT AND ATOMIC WAR: THE VIEWS OF GERMAN MILITARY AND POLITICAL LEADERS. FUT WOR+45 INT/ORG NAT/G WEAPON ATTIT PWR...INT QU TOT/POP VAL/FREE COLD/WAR 20. PAGE 136 A2780 TOP/EX FORCES NUC/PWR GERMANY

B58
GANGE J.,UNIVERSITY RESEARCH ON INTERNATIONAL AFFAIRS. USA+45 ACADEM INT/ORG CONSULT CREATE EXEC ROUTINE...QUANT STAT INT STERTYP GEN/METH TOT/POP VAL/FREE 20. PAGE 51 A1040 R+D MGT DIPLOM

B58
HAAS E.B.,THE UNITING OF EUROPE. EUR+WWI INT/ORG NAT/G POL/PAR TOP/EX ECO/TAC EDU/PROP LEGIT FEDERAL NAT/LISM DRIVE RIGID/FLEX ORD/FREE PWR PLURISM ...POLICY CONCPT INT GEN/LAWS ECSC EEC 20. PAGE 59 A1204 VOL/ASSN ECO/DEV

B58
SCOTT W.A.,THE UNITED STATES AND THE UNITED NATIONS: THE PUBLIC VIEW 1945-1955. USA+45 EDU/PROP ...INT QU KNO/TEST SAMP GP/COMP 20 UN. PAGE 130 A2674 ATTIT DIPLOM INT/ORG

B59
DIEBOLD W. JR.,THE SCHUMAN PLAN: A STUDY IN ECONOMIC COOPERATION, 1950-1959. EUR+WWI FRANCE GERMANY USA+45 EXTR/IND CONSULT DELIB/GP PLAN DIPLOM ECO/TAC INT/TRADE ROUTINE ORD/FREE WEALTH ...METH/CNCPT STAT CONT/OBS INT TIME/SEQ ECSC 20. PAGE 37 A0759 INT/ORG REGION

B59
GORDENKER L.,THE UNITED NATIONS AND THE PEACEFUL UNIFICATION OF KOREA. ASIA LAW LOC/G CONSULT ACT/RES DIPLOM DOMIN LEGIT ADJUD ADMIN ORD/FREE SOVEREIGN...INT GEN/METH UN COLD/WAR 20. PAGE 54 A1109 DELIB/GP KOREA INT/ORG

B59
VAN WAGENEN R.W.,SOME VIEWS OF AMERICAN DEFENSE OFFICIALS ABOUT THE UNITED NATIONS (PAPER). FUT USA+45 NAT/G DIPLOM WAR EFFICIENCY PEACE...POLICY INT 20 UN DEPT/DEFEN. PAGE 158 A3216 INT/ORG LEAD ATTIT FORCES

B60
BROOKINGS INSTITUTION,UNITED STATES FOREIGN POLICY: STUDY NO 9: THE FORMULATION AND ADMINISTRATION OF UNITED STATES FOREIGN POLICY. USA+45 WOR+45 EX/STRUC LEGIS BAL/PWR FOR/AID EDU/PROP CIVMIL/REL GOV/REL...INT COLD/WAR. PAGE 19 A0394 DIPLOM INT/ORG CREATE

B60
KHRUSHCHEV N.S.,KHRUSHCHEV IN AMERICA. USA+45 USSR INT/TRADE EDU/PROP PRESS PEACE...MARXIST RECORD INT 20 COLD/WAR KHRUSH/N. PAGE 79 A1613 MARXISM CHIEF DIPLOM

B61
LIPPMANN W.,THE COMING TESTS WITH RUSSIA. COM CUBA GERMANY USSR FORCES CONTROL NEUTRAL COERCE NUC/PWR REV WAR PWR...INT 20 KHRUSH/N BERLIN. PAGE 89 A1830 BAL/PWR DIPLOM MARXISM ARMS/CONT

B61
SHAPP W.R.,FIELD ADMINISTRATION IN THE UNITED NATIONS SYSTEM. FINAN PROB/SOLV INSPECT DIPLOM EXEC REGION ROUTINE EFFICIENCY ROLE...INT CHARTS 20 UN. PAGE 131 A2694 INT/ORG ADMIN GP/REL FOR/AID

B62
BELL C.,NEGOTIATION FROM STRENGTH. WOR+45 FACE/GP INT/ORG DELIB/GP FORCES PLAN DOMIN COERCE NUC/PWR PEACE DRIVE PWR...POLICY LOG OBS RECORD INT SAMP TREND COLD/WAR 20. PAGE 13 A0255 NAT/G CONCPT DIPLOM

B62
KING G.,THE UNITED NATIONS IN THE CONGO: A QUEST FOR PEACE. WOR+45 NAT/G CONSULT FORCES LEGIT COERCE WAR ORD/FREE...JURID METH/CNCPT OBS INT HIST/WRIT TIME/SEQ CONGO UN 20 COLD/WAR. PAGE 79 A1624 AFR INT/ORG

B62
ROY P.A.,SOUTH WIND RED. L/A+17C USA+45 ECO/UNDEV NAT/G CAP/ISM MARXISM SOCISM...OLD/LIB GEOG RECORD INT CENSUS 20 COLD/WAR. PAGE 125 A2554 DIPLOM INDUS POLICY ECO/TAC

B63
CREMEANS C.,THE ARABS AND THE WORLD: NASSER'S ARAB NATIONALIST POLICY. FUT ISLAM UAR USA+45 SOCIETY STRATA NAT/G POL/PAR PLAN DIPLOM EDU/PROP LEGIT DRIVE ALL/VALS...INT TIME/SEQ CHARTS 20 NASSER/G. PAGE 33 A0662 TOP/EX ATTIT REGION NAT/LISM

S63
ALGER C.F.,"UNITED NATIONS PARTICIPATION AS A LEARNING EXPERIENCE." WOR+45 KNOWL ORD/FREE PWR ...INT VAL/FREE UN 20. PAGE 6 A0120 INT/ORG ATTIT

S63
HUMPHREY H.H.,"REGIONAL ARMS CONTROL AGREEMENTS." WOR+45 FORCES PLAN LEGIT COERCE ATTIT HEALTH ORD/FREE...HUM METH/CNCPT MYTH OBS INT TREND TOT/POP 20. PAGE 69 A1416 L/A+17C INT/ORG ARMS/CONT REGION

S63
LERNER D.,"FRENCH ELITE PERSPECTIVES ON THE UNITED NATIONS." EUR+WWI INT/ORG HEALTH ORD/FREE PWR RESPECT...STAT INT SAMP/SIZ VAL/FREE UN 20. PAGE 87 A1786 ATTIT STERTYP ELITES FRANCE

B64
AFRO ASIAN SOLIDARITY AGAINST IMPERIALISM. AFR ISLAM S/ASIA ECO/UNDEV NAT/G POL/PAR TOP/EX PRESS ...INT ANTHOL 20 CHOU/ENLAI. PAGE 3 A0066
MARXISM DIPLOM EDU/PROP CHIEF

B64
HALPERN J.M.,GOVERNMENT, POLITICS, AND SOCIAL STRUCTURE IN LAOS. LAOS CULTURE SOCIETY STRATA STRUCT FAM DIPLOM DOMIN MARXISM...INT GOV/COMP WORSHIP SOC/INTEG 20. PAGE 60 A1242
NAT/G SOC LOC/G

B64
LUARD E.,THE COLD WAR: A RE-APPRAISAL. FUT USSR WOR+45 FORCES NUC/PWR NAT/LISM ORD/FREE SOVEREIGN ...INT 20 COLD/WAR STALIN/J TREATY UN. PAGE 91 A1870
DIPLOM WAR PEACE TOTALISM

B64
RUBINSTEIN A.Z.,THE SOVIETS IN INTERNATIONAL ORGANIZATIONS: CHANGING POLICY TOWARD DEVELOPING COUNTRIES, 1953-1963. COM DELIB/GP ACT/RES ECO/TAC EDU/PROP ADMIN ATTIT ORD/FREE PWR...INT VAL/FREE UN 20. PAGE 125 A2563
ECO/UNDEV INT/ORG USSR

B64
SULLIVAN G.,THE STORY OF THE PEACE CORPS. USA+45 WOR+45 INTELL FACE/GP NAT/G SCHOOL VOL/ASSN CONSULT EX/STRUC PLAN EDU/PROP ADMIN ATTIT DRIVE ALL/VALS ...POLICY HEAL SOC CONCPT INT QU BIOG TREND SOC/EXP WORK. PAGE 140 A2861
INT/ORG ECO/UNDEV FOR/AID PEACE

B64
WAINHOUSE D.W.,REMNANTS OF EMPIRE: THE UNITED NATIONS AND THE END OF COLONIALISM. FUT PORTUGAL WOR+45 NAT/G CONSULT DOMIN LEGIT ADMIN ROUTINE ATTIT ORD/FREE...POLICY JURID RECORD INT TIME/SEQ UN CMN/WLTH 20. PAGE 160 A3260
INT/ORG TREND COLONIAL

B64
WARREN S.,THE PRESIDENT AS WORLD LEADER. USA+45 WOR+45 ELITES COM/IND INT/ORG NAT/G VOL/ASSN CHIEF EX/STRUC LEGIT COERCE ATTIT PERSON RIGID/FLEX...INT TIME/SEQ COLD/WAR 20 ROOSEVLT/F TRUMAN/HS EISNHWR/DD KENNEDY/JF. PAGE 161 A3286
TOP/EX PWR DIPLOM

S64
RUSK D.,"THE MAKING OF FOREIGN POLICY" USA+45 CHIEF DELIB/GP WORKER PROB/SOLV ADMIN ATTIT PWR ...DECISION 20 DEPT/STATE RUSK/D GOLDMAN/E. PAGE 125 A2570
DIPLOM INT POLICY

B65
CBS,CONVERSATIONS WITH WALTER LIPPMANN. USA+45 INT/ORG NAT/G POL/PAR PLAN DIPLOM PWR ALL/IDEOS ...POLICY 20 LIPPMANN/W. PAGE 25 A0509
TV ATTIT INT

C65
SCHEINGOLD S.A.,"THE RULE OF LAW IN EUROPEAN INTEGRATION: THE PATH OF THE SCHUMAN PLAN." EUR+WWI JUDGE ADJUD FEDERAL ATTIT PWR...RECORD INT BIBLIOG EEC ECSC. PAGE 128 A2621
INT/LAW CT/SYS REGION CENTRAL

B66
LENT H.B.,THE PEACE CORPS: AMBASSADORS OF GOOD WILL. USA+45 ECO/UNDEV...INT TESTS BIOG AUD/VIS SOC/INTEG 20 PEACE/CORP. PAGE 87 A1776
VOL/ASSN FOR/AID DIPLOM CONSULT

C66
ZAWODNY J.K.,"GUIDE TO THE STUDY OF INTERNATIONAL RELATIONS." OP/RES PRESS...STAT INT 20. PAGE 169 A3449
BIBLIOG/A DIPLOM INT/LAW INT/ORG

B67
BELL W.,THE DEMOCRATIC REVOLUTION IN THE WEST INDIES. WEST/IND WOR+45 DIPLOM RACE/REL NAT/LISM ...INT QU ANTHOL 20. PAGE 13 A0257
REGION ATTIT ORD/FREE ECO/UNDEV

B67
HOHENBERG J.,BETWEEN TWO WORLDS. ASIA S/ASIA USA+45 PRESS TV PERS/REL ISOLAT...INT CHARTS METH/COMP 20. PAGE 66 A1362
COM/IND DIPLOM EFFICIENCY KNOWL

B67
SALISBURY H.E.,ORBIT OF CHINA. ASIA CHINA/COM DIPLOM PEACE PWR 20. PAGE 126 A2593
EDU/PROP OBS INT ARMS/CONT

S67
DEUTSCH K.W.,"ARMS CONTROL AND EUROPEAN UNITY* THE NEXT TEN YEARS." USA+45 ELITES NAT/G BAL/PWR DIPLOM NUC/PWR...INT KNO/TEST NATO EEC. PAGE 36 A0742
ARMS/CONT PEACE REGION PLAN

S67
INGLEHART R.,"AN END TO EUROPEAN INTEGRATION." PROB/SOLV BAL/PWR NAT/LISM...PSY SOC INT CHARTS GP/COMP 20. PAGE 70 A1440
DIPLOM EUR+WWI REGION ATTIT

INT. SOC. SCI. BULL. A1447

INT/AM/DEV....INTER-AMERICAN DEVELOPMENT BANK

B62
ROUND TABLE ON EUROPE'S ROLE IN LATIN AMERICAN DEVELOPMENT. EUR+WWI L/A+17C PLAN BAL/PAY UTIL ROLE WEALTH...CHARTS ANTHOL 20 UN INT/AM/DEV. PAGE 3 A0063
ECO/UNDEV FINAN TEC/DEV FOR/AID

B66
US HOUSE COMM APPROPRIATIONS,HEARINGS ON FOREIGN OPERATIONS AND RELATED AGENCIES APPROPRIATIONS. CUBA USA+45 VOL/ASSN DELIB/GP DIPLOM CONFER ORD/FREE 20 CONGRESS MIGRATION INT/AM/DEV PEACE/CORP. PAGE 153 A3120
FOR/AID BUDGET ECO/UNDEV FORCES

INT/AVIATN....INTERNATIONAL CIVIL AVIATION ORGANIZATION

INT/LAW....INTERNATIONAL LAW

N
INDIAN COUNCIL WORLD AFFAIRS,SELECT ARTICLES ON CURRENT AFFAIRS (BIBLIOGRAPHICAL SERIES: 7). AFR ASIA COM EUR+WWI S/ASIA UK COLONIAL NUC/PWR PEACE ATTIT...INT/LAW SOC 20. PAGE 70 A1437
BIBLIOG DIPLOM INT/ORG ECO/UNDEV

N
LIBRARY INTERNATIONAL REL,INTERNATIONAL INFORMATION SERVICE. WOR+45 CULTURE INT/ORG FORCES...GEOG HUM SOC. PAGE 88 A1808
BIBLIOG/A DIPLOM INT/TRADE INT/LAW

N
LONDON INSTITUTE WORLD AFFAIRS,THE YEAR BOOK OF WORLD AFFAIRS. FINAN BAL/PWR ARMS/CONT WAR ...INT/LAW BIBLIOG 20. PAGE 91 A1856
DIPLOM FOR/AID INT/ORG

N
AMERICAN JOURNAL OF INTERNATIONAL LAW. WOR+45 WOR-45 CONSTN INT/ORG NAT/G CT/SYS ARMS/CONT WAR ...DECISION JURID NAT/COMP 20. PAGE 1 A0002
BIBLIOG/A INT/LAW DIPLOM ADJUD

N
AMERICAN POLITICAL SCIENCE REVIEW. USA+45 USA-45 WOR+45 WOR-45 INT/ORG ADMIN...INT/LAW PHIL/SCI CONCPT METH 20 UN. PAGE 1 A0003
BIBLIOG/A DIPLOM NAT/G GOV/COMP

N
BACKGROUND; JOURNAL OF INTERNATIONAL STUDIES ASSOCIATION. INT/ORG FORCES ACT/RES EDU/PROP COERCE NAT/LISM PEACE ATTIT...INT/LAW CONCPT 20. PAGE 1 A0005
BIBLIOG DIPLOM POLICY

N
INTERNATIONAL AFFAIRS. WOR+45 WOR-45 ECO/UNDEV INT/ORG NAT/G PROB/SOLV FOR/AID WAR...POLICY 20. PAGE 1 A0009
BIBLIOG/A DIPLOM INT/LAW INT/TRADE

N
INTERNATIONAL BOOK NEWS, 1928-1934. ECO/UNDEV FINAN INDUS LABOR INT/TRADE CONFER ADJUD COLONIAL...HEAL SOC/WK CHARTS 20 LEAGUE/NAT. PAGE 1 A0010
BIBLIOG/A DIPLOM INT/LAW INT/ORG

N
INTERNATIONAL STUDIES. ASIA S/ASIA WOR+45 ECO/UNDEV INT/ORG NAT/G LEAD ATTIT WEALTH...SOC 20. PAGE 1 A0012
BIBLIOG/A DIPLOM INT/LAW INT/TRADE

N
JOURNAL OF INTERNATIONAL AFFAIRS. WOR+45 ECO/UNDEV POL/PAR ECO/TAC WAR PEACE PERSON ALL/IDEOS ...INT/LAW TREND. PAGE 1 A0015
BIBLIOG DIPLOM INT/ORG NAT/G

N
FOREIGN AFFAIRS. SPACE WOR+45 WOR-45 CULTURE ECO/UNDEV FINAN NAT/G TEC/DEV INT/TRADE ARMS/CONT NUC/PWR...POLICY 20 UN EURATOM ECSC EEC. PAGE 2 A0034
BIBLIOG DIPLOM INT/ORG INT/LAW

N
THE JAPAN SCIENCE REVIEW: LAW AND POLITICS: LIST OF BOOKS AND ARTICLES ON LAW AND POLITICS. CONSTN AGRI INDUS LABOR DIPLOM TAX ADMIN CRIME...INT/LAW SOC 20 CHINJAP. PAGE 2 A0042
BIBLIOG LAW S/ASIA PHIL/SCI

N
THE WORLD IN FOCUS. WOR+45 LEAD ATTIT...POLICY TREND. PAGE 2 A0044
BIBLIOG INT/ORG INT/LAW DIPLOM

N
AIR UNIVERSITY LIBRARY,INDEX TO MILITARY PERIODICALS. FUT SPACE WOR+45 REGION ARMS/CONT NUC/PWR WAR PEACE INT/LAW. PAGE 5 A0105
BIBLIOG/A FORCES NAT/G DIPLOM

N
ATLANTIC INSTITUTE,ATLANTIC STUDIES. COM EUR+WWI USA+45 CULTURE STRUCT ECO/DEV FORCES LEAD ARMS/CONT ...INT/LAW JURID SOC. PAGE 10 A0193
BIBLIOG/A DIPLOM POLICY GOV/REL

N
DE MARTENS G.F.,RECUEIL GENERALE DE TRAITES ET AUTRES ACTES RELATIFS AUX RAPPORTS DE DROIT INTERNATIONAL (41 VOLS.). EUR+WWI MOD/EUR USA-45 ...INDEX TREATY 18/20. PAGE 35 A0708
BIBLIOG INT/LAW DIPLOM

N
HARVARD LAW SCHOOL LIBRARY,ANNUAL LEGAL BIBLIOGRAPHY. USA+45 CONSTN LEGIS ADJUD CT/SYS ...POLICY 20. PAGE 62 A1278
BIBLIOG JURID LAW

N
HARVARD UNIVERSITY LAW LIBRARY,CATALOG OF INTERNATIONAL LAW AND RELATIONS. WOR+45 WOR-45 INT/ORG NAT/G JUDGE DIPLOM INT/TRADE ADJUD CT/SYS 19/20. PAGE 62 A1280
BIBLIOG INT/LAW JURID

N
JOHNS HOPKINS UNIVERSITY LIB,RECENT ADDITIONS. WOR+45 ECO/UNDEV NAT/G POL/PAR FOR/AID INT/TRADE LEAD REGION ATTIT ALL/IDEOS TREND. PAGE 74 A1518
BIBLIOG DIPLOM INT/LAW INT/ORG

N
SOCIETE DES NATIONS,TRAITES INTERNATIONAUX ET ACTES LEGISLATIFS. WOR-45 INT/ORG NAT/G...INT/LAW JURID 20 LEAGUE/NAT TREATY. PAGE 135 A2759
BIBLIOG DIPLOM LEGIS ADJUD

N
TURNER R.K.,BIBLIOGRAPHY ON WORLD ORGANIZATION. INT/TRADE CT/SYS ARMS/CONT WEALTH...INT/LAW 20. PAGE 146 A2984
BIBLIOG/A INT/ORG PEACE WAR

N
UNITED NATIONS,OFFICIAL RECORDS OF THE UNITED NATIONS' GENERAL ASSEMBLY. WOR+45 BUDGET DIPLOM ADMIN 20 UN. PAGE 148 A3033
INT/ORG DELIB/GP INT/LAW WRITING

N
UNITED NATIONS,UNITED NATIONS PUBLICATIONS. WOR+45 ECO/UNDEV AGRI FINAN FORCES ADMIN LEAD WAR PEACE ...POLICY INT/LAW 20 UN. PAGE 148 A3034
BIBLIOG INT/ORG DIPLOM

N
UNITED NATIONS,YEARBOOK OF THE INTERNATIONAL LAW COMMISSION....CON/ANAL 20 UN. PAGE 149 A3035
BIBLIOG INT/ORG INT/LAW DELIB/GP

N
US SUPERINTENDENT OF DOCUMENTS,FOREIGN RELATIONS OF THE UNITED STATES; PUBLICATIONS RELATING TO FOREIGN COUNTRIES (PRICE LIST 65). UAR USA+45 VIETNAM ECO/UNDEV VOL/ASSN FOR/AID EDU/PROP ARMS/CONT HEALTH MARXISM...POLICY INT/LAW UN NATO. PAGE 157 A3201
BIBLIOG/A DIPLOM INT/ORG NAT/G

B00
DARBY W.E.,INTERNATIONAL TRIBUNALS. WOR-45 NAT/G ECO/TAC DOMIN LEGIT CT/SYS COERCE ORD/FREE PWR SOVEREIGN JURID. PAGE 33 A0681
INT/ORG ADJUD PEACE INT/LAW

B00
GRIFFIN A.P.C.,LIST OF BOOKS RELATING TO THE THEORY OF COLONIZATION, GOVERNMENT OF DEPENDENCIES, PROTECTORATES, AND RELATED TOPICS. FRANCE GERMANY ITALY SPAIN UK USA-45 WOR-45 ECO/TAC ADMIN CONTROL REGION NAT/LISM ALL/VALS PWR...INT/LAW SOC 16/19. PAGE 56 A1149
BIBLIOG/A COLONIAL GOV/REL DOMIN

B00
GROTIUS H.,DE JURE BELLI AC PACIS. CHRIST-17C UNIV LAW SOCIETY PROVS LEGIT PEACE PERCEPT MORAL PWR ...CONCPT CON/ANAL GEN/LAWS. PAGE 57 A1180
JURID INT/LAW WAR

B00
HOLLAND T.E.,STUDIES IN INTERNATIONAL LAW. TURKEY USSR WOR-45 CONSTN NAT/G DIPLOM DOMIN LEGIT COERCE WAR PEACE ORD/FREE PWR SOVEREIGN...JURID CHARTS 20 PARLIAMENT SUEZ TREATY. PAGE 66 A1367
INT/ORG LAW INT/LAW

B00
LORIMER J.,THE INSTITUTES OF THE LAW OF NATIONS. WOR-45 CULTURE SOCIETY NAT/G VOL/ASSN DIPLOM LEGIT WAR PEACE DRIVE ORD/FREE SOVEREIGN...CONCPT RECORD INT TREND HYPO/EXP GEN/METH TOT/POP VAL/FREE 20. PAGE 91 A1863
INT/ORG LAW INT/LAW

B00
MAINE H.S.,INTERNATIONAL LAW. MOD/EUR UNIV SOCIETY STRUCT ACT/RES EXEC WAR ATTIT PERSON ALL/VALS ...POLICY JURID CONCPT OBS TIME/SEQ TOT/POP. PAGE 93 A1908
INT/ORG LAW PEACE INT/LAW

L00
HISTORICUS,"LETTERS AND SOME QUESTIONS OF INTERNATIONAL LAW." FRANCE NETHERLAND UK USA-45 WOR-45 LAW NAT/G COERCE...SOC CONCPT GEN/LAWS TOT/POP 19 CIVIL/WAR. PAGE 65 A1344
WEALTH JURID WAR INT/LAW

B01
GRIFFIN A.P.C.,LIST OF BOOKS ON SAMOA (PAMPHLET). GERMANY S/ASIA UK USA-45 WOR-45 ECO/UNDEV REGION ALL/VALS ORD/FREE ALL/IDEOS...GEOG INT/LAW 19 SAMOA GUAM. PAGE 56 A1150
BIBLIOG/A COLONIAL DIPLOM

B03
MOREL E.D.,THE BRITISH CASE IN FRENCH CONGO. CONGO/BRAZ FRANCE UK COERCE MORAL WEALTH...POLICY INT/LAW 20 CONGO/LEOP. PAGE 104 A2130
DIPLOM INT/TRADE COLONIAL AFR

B06
FOSTER J.W.,THE PRACTICE OF DIPLOMACY AS ILLUSTRATED IN THE FOREIGN RELATIONS OF THE UNITED STATES. MOD/EUR USA-45 NAT/G EX/STRUC ADMIN ...POLICY INT/LAW BIBLIOG 19/20. PAGE 47 A0970
DIPLOM ROUTINE PHIL/SCI

B08
GRIFFIN A.P.C.,LIST OF REFERENCES ON INTERNATIONAL ARBITRATION. FRANCE L/A+17C USA-45 WOR-45 DIPLOM CONFER COLONIAL ARMS/CONT BAL/PAY EQUILIB SOVEREIGN ...DECISION 19/20 MEXIC/AMER. PAGE 56 A1156
BIBLIOG/A INT/ORG INT/LAW DELIB/GP

B09
HOLLAND T.E.,LETTERS UPON WAR AND NEUTRALITY. WOR-45 NAT/G FORCES JUDGE ECO/TAC LEGIT CT/SYS NEUTRAL ROUTINE COERCE...JURID TIME/SEQ 20. PAGE 67 A1368
LAW INT/LAW INT/ORG WAR

B11
PHILLIPSON C.,THE INTERNATIONAL LAW AND CUSTOM OF ANCIENT GREECE AND ROME. MEDIT-7 UNIV INTELL SOCIETY STRUCT NAT/G LEGIS EXEC PERSON...CONCPT OBS CON/ANAL ROM/EMP. PAGE 116 A2377
INT/ORG LAW INT/LAW

B13
BORCHARD E.M.,BIBLIOGRAPHY OF INTERNATIONAL LAW AND CONTINENTAL LAW. EUR+WWI MOD/EUR UK LAW INT/TRADE WAR PEACE...GOV/COMP NAT/COMP 19/20. PAGE 17 A0338
BIBLIOG INT/LAW JURID DIPLOM

B13
BUTLER N.M.,THE INTERNATIONAL MIND. WOR-45 INT/ORG LEGIT PWR...JURID CONCPT 20. PAGE 22 A0452
ADJUD ORD/FREE INT/LAW

B15
INTERNATIONAL LAW ASSOCIATION,A FORTY YEARS' CATALOGUE OF THE BOOKS, PAMPHLETS AND PAPERS IN THE LIBRARY OF THE INTERNATIONAL LAW ASSOCIATION. INT/ORG DIPLOM ADJUD NEUTRAL...IDEA/COMP 19/20. PAGE 71 A1458
BIBLIOG LAW INT/LAW

B16
PUFENDORF S.,LAW OF NATURE AND OF NATIONS (ABRIDGED). UNIV LAW NAT/G DIPLOM AGREE WAR PERSON ALL/VALS PWR...POLICY 18 DEITY NATURL/LAW. PAGE 118 A2416
CONCPT INT/LAW SECT MORAL

B16
ROOT E.,ADDRESSES ON INTERNATIONAL SUBJECTS. MOD/EUR UNIV USA-45 LAW SOCIETY EXEC ATTIT ALL/VALS ...POLICY JURID CONCPT 20 CHINJAP. PAGE 123 A2521
INT/ORG ACT/RES PEACE INT/LAW

L16
WRIGHT Q.,"THE ENFORCEMENT OF INTERNATIONAL LAW THROUGH MUNICIPAL LAW IN THE US." USA-45 LOC/G NAT/G PUB/INST FORCES LEGIT CT/SYS PERCEPT ALL/VALS ...JURID 20. PAGE 167 A3401
INT/ORG LAW INT/LAW WAR

B17
DE VICTORIA F.,DE INDIS ET DE JURE BELLI (1557) IN F. DE VICTORIA, DE INDIS ET DE JURE BELLI REFLECTIONES. UNIV NAT/G SECT CHIEF PARTIC COERCE PEACE MORAL...POLICY 16 INDIAN/AM CHRISTIAN CONSCN/OBJ. PAGE 35 A0715
WAR INT/LAW OWN

B17
MEYER H.H.B.,LIST OF REFERENCES ON EMBARGOES (PAMPHLET). USA-45 AGRI DIPLOM WRITING DEBATE WEAPON...INT/LAW 18/20 CONGRESS. PAGE 100 A2049
BIBLIOG DIST/IND ECO/TAC INT/TRADE

S17
ROOT E.,"THE EFFECT OF DEMOCRACY ON INTERNATIONAL LAW." USA-45 WOR-45 INTELL SOCIETY INT/ORG NAT/G CONSULT ACT/RES CREATE PLAN EDU/PROP PEACE SKILL ...CONCPT METH/CNCPT OBS 20. PAGE 123 A2523
LEGIS JURID INT/LAW

B19
DE CALLIERES F.,THE PRACTICE OF DIPLOMACY. MOD/EUR INT/ORG NAT/G DELIB/GP LEGIS TOP/EX DOMIN ATTIT KNOWL LEAGUE/NAT 20. PAGE 34 A0699
CONSULT ACT/RES DIPLOM INT/LAW

B19
LONDON SCHOOL ECONOMICS-POL,ANNUAL DIGEST OF PUBLIC INTERNATIONAL LAW CASES. INT/ORG MUNIC NAT/G PROVS ADMIN NEUTRAL WAR GOV/REL PRIVIL 20. PAGE 91 A1858
BIBLIOG/A INT/LAW ADJUD DIPLOM

B19
VANDERPOL A.,LA DOCTRINE SCOLASTIQUE DU DROIT DE GUERRE. CHRIST-17C FORCES DIPLOM LEGIT SUPEGO MORAL ...BIOG AQUINAS/T SUAREZ/F CHRISTIAN. PAGE 158 A3220
WAR SECT INT/LAW

N19
BENTHAM J.,A PLAN FOR AN UNIVERSAL AND PERPETUAL PEACE (1838) (PAMPHLET). NAT/G FORCES BAL/PWR INT/TRADE ADMIN AGREE CT/SYS ARMS/CONT SOVEREIGN WEALTH GEN/LAWS. PAGE 13 A0269
INT/ORG INT/LAW PEACE COLONIAL

B20
MEYER H.H.B.,LIST OF REFERENCES ON THE TREATY-MAKING POWER. USA-45 CONTROL PWR...INT/LAW TIME/SEQ 18/20 TREATY. PAGE 100 A2052
BIBLIOG DIPLOM CONSTN

B20
VINOGRADOFF P.,OUTLINES OF HISTORICAL JURISPRUDENCE (2 VOLS.). GREECE MEDIT-7 LAW CONSTN FACE/GP FAM KIN MUNIC CRIME OWN...INT/LAW IDEA/COMP BIBLIOG. PAGE 159 A3241
JURID METH

B21
BALFOUR A.J.,ESSAYS SPECULATIVE AND POLITICAL. SEA CULTURE CREATE WAR NAT/LISM PEACE LOVE...ART/METH INT/LAW CONCPT ANTHOL 20 JEWS. PAGE 10 A0211
PHIL/SCI SOCIETY DIPLOM

B21
OPPENHEIM L.,THE FUTURE OF INTERNATIONAL LAW. EUR+WWI MOD/EUR LAW LEGIS JUDGE LEGIT ORD/FREE ...JURID TIME/SEQ GEN/LAWS 20. PAGE 112 A2293
INT/ORG CT/SYS INT/LAW

L21
HALDEMAN E.,"SERIALS OF AN INTERNATIONAL CHARACTER." WOR-45 DIPLOM...ART/METH GEOG HEAL HUM INT/LAW JURID PSY SOC. PAGE 60 A1224
BIBLIOG PHIL/SCI

B22
MYERS D.P.,MANUAL OF COLLECTIONS OF TREATIES AND OF COLLECTIONS RELATING TO TREATIES. MOD/EUR INT/ORG LEGIS WRITING ADMIN SOVEREIGN...INT/LAW 19/20. PAGE 106 A2186
BIBLIOG/A DIPLOM CONFER

B23
HEADICAR B.M.,CATALOGUE OF THE BOOKS, PAMPHLETS, AND OTHER DOCUMENTS IN THE EDWARD FRY LIBRARY OF INTERNATIONAL LAW... UK INT/ORG 20. PAGE 63 A1304
BIBLIOG INT/LAW DIPLOM

B24
GENTILI A.,DE LEGATIONIBUS. CHRIST-17C NAT/G SECT CONSULT LEGIT...POLICY CATH JURID CONCPT MYTH. PAGE 52 A1058
DIPLOM INT/LAW INT/ORG LAW

B24
HALL W.E.,A TREATISE ON INTERNATIONAL LAW. WOR-45 CONSTN INT/ORG NAT/G DIPLOM ORD/FREE LEAGUE/NAT 20 TREATY. PAGE 60 A1228
PWR JURID WAR INT/LAW

L25
HUDSON M.,"THE PERMANENT COURT OF INTERNATIONAL JUSTICE AND THE QUESTION OF AMERICAN PARTICIPATION." WOR-45 LEGIT CT/SYS ORD/FREE ...JURID CONCPT TIME/SEQ GEN/LAWS VAL/FREE 20 ICJ. PAGE 68 A1406
INT/ORG ADJUD DIPLOM INT/LAW

B27
LAUTERPACHT H.,PRIVATE LAW SOURCES AND ANALOGIES OF INTERNATIONAL LAW. WOR-45 NAT/G DELIB/GP LEGIT COERCE ATTIT ORD/FREE PWR SOVEREIGN...JURID CONCPT HIST/WRIT TIME/SEQ GEN/METH LEAGUE/NAT 20. PAGE 85 A1748
INT/ORG ADJUD PEACE INT/LAW

B28
BUTLER G.,THE DEVELOPMENT OF INTERNATIONAL LAW. WOR-45 SOCIETY NAT/G KNOWL ORD/FREE PWR...JURID CONCPT HIST/WRIT GEN/LAWS. PAGE 22 A0451
LAW INT/LAW DIPLOM INT/ORG

B28
LAPRADELLE,ANNUAIRE DE LA VIE INTERNATIONALE: POLITIQUE, ECONOMIQUE, JURIDIQUE. INT/ORG CONFER ARMS/CONT 20. PAGE 85 A1729
BIBLIOG DIPLOM INT/LAW

B29
CONWELL-EVANS T.P.,THE LEAGUE COUNCIL IN ACTION. EUR+WWI TURKEY UK USSR WOR-45 INT/ORG FORCES JUDGE ECO/TAC EDU/PROP LEGIT ROUTINE ARMS/CONT COERCE ATTIT PWR...MAJORIT GEOG JURID CONCPT LEAGUE/NAT TOT/POP VAL/FREE TUNIS 20. PAGE 30 A0605
DELIB/GP INT/LAW

B29
STURZO L.,THE INTERNATIONAL COMMUNITY AND THE RIGHT OF WAR (TRANS. BY BARBARA BARCLAY CARTER). CULTURE CREATE PROB/SOLV DIPLOM ADJUD CONTROL PEACE PERSON ORD/FREE...INT/LAW IDEA/COMP PACIFIST 20 LEAGUE/NAT. PAGE 140 A2858
INT/ORG PLAN WAR CONCPT

B30
BYNKERSHOEK C.,QUAESTIONUM JURIS PUBLICI LIBRI DUO. CHRIST-17C MOD/EUR CONSTN ELITES SOCIETY NAT/G PROVS EX/STRUC FORCES TOP/EX BAL/PWR DIPLOM ATTIT MORAL...TRADIT CONCPT. PAGE 23 A0460
INT/ORG LAW NAT/LISM INT/LAW

B30
WRIGHT Q.,MANDATES UNDER THE LEAGUE OF NATIONS. WOR-45 CONSTN ECO/DEV ECO/UNDEV NAT/G DELIB/GP TOP/EX LEGIT ALL/VALS...JURID CONCPT LEAGUE/NAT 20. PAGE 167 A3403
INT/ORG LAW INT/LAW

B31
BORCHARD E.H.,GUIDE TO THE LAW AND LEGAL LITERATURE OF FRANCE. FRANCE FINAN INDUS LABOR SECT LEGIS ADMIN COLONIAL CRIME OWN...INT/LAW 20. PAGE 17 A0337
BIBLIOG/A LAW CONSTN METH

B31
STOWELL E.C.,INTERNATIONAL LAW. FUT UNIV WOR-45 SOCIETY CONSULT EX/STRUC FORCES ACT/RES PLAN DIPLOM EDU/PROP LEGIT DISPL PWR SKILL...POLICY CONCPT OBS TREND TOT/POP 20. PAGE 139 A2839
INT/ORG ROUTINE INT/LAW

B31
STUART G.H.,THE INTERNATIONAL CITY OF TANGIER. AFR EUR+WWI MOD/EUR MOROCCO CONSTN PROVS CREATE PLAN LEGIT PEACE ORD/FREE PWR...INT/LAW OBS TIME/SEQ CON/ANAL 20 TANGIER. PAGE 139 A2854
LOC/G INT/ORG DIPLOM SOVEREIGN

B32
EAGLETON C.,INTERNATIONAL GOVERNMENT. BRAZIL FRANCE GERMANY ITALY UK USSR WOR-45 DELIB/GP TOP/EX PLAN ECO/TAC EDU/PROP LEGIT ADJUD REGION ARMS/CONT COERCE ATTIT PWR...GEOG MGT VAL/FREE LEAGUE/NAT 20. PAGE 40 A0816
INT/ORG JURID DIPLOM INT/LAW

B32
MASTERS R.D.,INTERNATIONAL LAW IN INTERNATIONAL COURTS. BELGIUM EUR+WWI FRANCE GERMANY MOD/EUR SWITZERLND WOR-45 SOCIETY STRATA STRUCT LEGIT EXEC ALL/VALS...JURID HIST/WRIT TIME/SEQ TREND GEN/LAWS 20. PAGE 96 A1961
INT/ORG LAW INT/LAW

B33
GENTILI A.,DE JURE BELLI, LIBRI TRES (1612) (VOL. 2). FORCES DIPLOM AGREE PEACE SOVEREIGN. PAGE 52 A1059
WAR INT/LAW MORAL SUPEGO

B33
LAUTERPACHT H.,THE FUNCTION OF LAW IN THE INTERNATIONAL COMMUNITY. WOR-45 NAT/G FORCES CREATE DOMIN LEGIT COERCE WAR PEACE ATTIT ORD/FREE PWR SOVEREIGN...JURID CONCPT METH/CNCPT TIME/SEQ GEN/LAWS GEN/METH LEAGUE/NAT TOT/POP VAL/FREE 20. PAGE 85 A1749
INT/ORG LAW INT/LAW

B33
MATTHEWS M.A.,THE AMERICAN INSTITUTE OF INTERNATIONAL LAW AND THE CODIFICATION OF INTERNATIONAL LAW (PAMPHLET). USA-45 CONSTN ADJUD CT/SYS...JURID 20. PAGE 96 A1973
BIBLIOG/A INT/LAW L/A+17C DIPLOM

B34
WOLFF C.,JUS GENTIUM METHODO SCIENTIFICA PERTRACTATUM. MOD/EUR INT/ORG VOL/ASSN LEGIT PEACE ATTIT...JURID 20. PAGE 166 A3387
NAT/G LAW INT/LAW WAR

B35
FOREIGN AFFAIRS BIBLIOGRAPHY: A SELECTED AND ANNOTATED LIST OF BOOKS ON INTERNATIONAL RELATIONS 1919-1962 (4 VOLS.). CONSTN FORCES COLONIAL ARMS/CONT WAR NAT/LISM PEACE ATTIT DRIVE...POLICY INT/LAW 20. PAGE 3 A0050
BIBLIOG/A DIPLOM INT/ORG

S35
MCMAHON A.H.,"INTERNATIONAL BOUNDARIES." WOR-45 INT/ORG NAT/G LEGIT SKILL...CHARTS GEN/LAWS 20. PAGE 98 A2017
GEOG VOL/ASSN INT/LAW

B36
BRIERLY J.L.,THE LAW OF NATIONS (2ND ED.). WOR+45 WOR-45 INT/ORG AGREE CONTROL COERCE WAR NAT/LISM PEACE PWR 16/20 TREATY LEAGUE/NAT. PAGE 18 A0375
DIPLOM INT/LAW NAT/G

B36
HUDSON M.O.,INTERNATIONAL LEGISLATION: 1929-1931. WOR-45 SEA AIR AGRI FINAN LABOR DIPLOM ECO/TAC REPAR CT/SYS ARMS/CONT WAR WEAPON...JURID 20 TREATY LEAGUE/NAT. PAGE 69 A1409
INT/LAW PARL/PROC ADJUD LAW

B36
MATTHEWS M.A.,DIPLOMACY: SELECT LIST ON DIPLOMACY, DIPLOMATIC AND CONSULAR PRACTICE, AND FOREIGN OFFICE ORGANIZATION (PAMPHLET). EUR+WWI MOD/EUR USA-45 WOR-45...INT/LAW 20. PAGE 96 A1974
BIBLIOG/A DIPLOM NAT/G

B36
MATTHEWS M.A.,INTERNATIONAL LAW: SELECT LIST OF WORKS IN ENGLISH ON PUBLIC INTERNATIONAL LAW: WITH COLLECTIONS OF CASES AND OPINIONS. CHRIST-17C EUR+WWI MOD/EUR WOR-45 CONSTN ADJUD JURID. PAGE 96 A1975
BIBLIOG/A INT/LAW ATTIT DIPLOM

B37
KETCHAM E.H.,PRELIMINARY SELECT BIBLIOGRAPHY OF INTERNATIONAL LAW (PAMPHLET). WOR-45 LAW INT/ORG NAT/G PROB/SOLV CT/SYS NEUTRAL WAR 19/20. PAGE 78 A1602
BIBLIOG DIPLOM ADJUD INT/LAW

B38
MCNAIR A.D.,THE LAW OF TREATIES: BRITISH PRACTICE AND OPINIONS. UK CREATE DIPLOM LEGIT WRITING ADJUD WAR...INT/LAW JURID TREATY. PAGE 98 A2018
AGREE LAW CT/SYS NAT/G

B38
SAINT-PIERRE C.I.,SCHEME FOR LASTING PEACE (TRANS. BY H. BELLOT). INDUS NAT/G CHIEF FORCES INT/TRADE CT/SYS WAR PWR SOVEREIGN WEALTH...POLICY 18. PAGE 126 A2587
INT/ORG PEACE AGREE INT/LAW

B39
WILSON G.G.,HANDBOOK OF INTERNATIONAL LAW. FUT UNIV USA-45 WOR-45 SOCIETY LEGIT ATTIT DISPL DRIVE ALL/VALS...INT/LAW TIME/SEQ TREND. PAGE 165 A3359
INT/ORG LAW CONCPT WAR

C39
HADDOW A.,"POLITICAL SCIENCE IN AMERICAN COLLEGES AND UNIVERSITIES 1636-1900." CONSTN MORAL...POLICY INT/LAW CON/ANAL BIBLIOG T 17/20. PAGE 59 A1211
USA-45 LAW ACADEM KNOWL

C39
SCOTT J.B.,"LAW, THESTATE, AND THE INTERNATIONAL COMMUNITY (2 VOLS.)" INTELL INT/ORG NAT/G SECT INT/TRADE WAR...INT/LAW GEN/LAWS BIBLIOG. PAGE 130 A2672
LAW PHIL/SCI DIPLOM CONCPT

B40
CONOVER H.F.,FOREIGN RELATIONS OF THE UNITED STATES: A LIST OF RECENT BOOKS (PAMPHLET). ASIA CANADA L/A+17C UK INT/ORG INT/TRADE TARIFFS NEUTRAL WAR PEACE...INT/LAW CON/ANAL 20 CHINJAP. PAGE 29 A0592
BIBLIOG/A USA-45 DIPLOM

S40
FLORIN J.,"BOLSHEVIST AND NATIONAL SOCIALIST DOCTRINES OF INTERNATIONAL LAW." EUR+WWI GERMANY USSR R+D INT/ORG NAT/G DIPLOM DOMIN EDU/PROP SOCISM ...CONCPT TIME/SEQ 20. PAGE 47 A0955
LAW ATTIT TOTALISM INT/LAW

B41
NIEMEYER G.,LAW WITHOUT FORCE: THE FUNCTION OF POLITICS IN INTERNATIONAL LAW. PLAN INSPECT DIPLOM REPAR LEGIT ADJUD WAR ORD/FREE...IDEA/COMP METH/COMP GEN/LAWS 20. PAGE 109 A2240
COERCE LAW PWR INT/LAW

B42
CROWE S.E.,THE BERLIN WEST AFRICA CONFERENCE, 1884-85. GERMANY ELITES MARKET INT/ORG DELIB/GP FORCES PROB/SOLV BAL/PWR CAP/ISM DOMIN COLONIAL ...INT/LAW 19. PAGE 33 A0664
AFR CONFER INT/TRADE DIPLOM

B42
FEILCHENFELD E.H.,THE INTERNATIONAL ECONOMIC LAW OF BELLIGERENT OCCUPATION. EUR+WWI MOD/EUR USA-45 INT/ORG DIPLOM ADJUD ARMS/CONT LEAGUE/NAT 20. PAGE 44 A0907
ECO/TAC INT/LAW WAR

B42
KELSEN H.,LAW AND PEACE IN INTERNATIONAL RELATIONS. FUT WOR-45 NAT/G DELIB/GP DIPLOM LEGIT RIGID/FLEX ORD/FREE SOVEREIGN...JURID CONCPT TREND STERTYP GEN/LAWS LEAGUE/NAT 20. PAGE 77 A1580
INT/ORG ADJUD PEACE INT/LAW

B43
BEMIS S.F.,THE LATIN AMERICAN POLICY OF THE UNITED STATES: AN HISTORICAL INTERPRETATION. INT/ORG AGREE COLONIAL WAR PEACE ATTIT ORD/FREE...POLICY INT/LAW CHARTS 18/20 MEXIC/AMER WILSON/W MONROE/DOC. PAGE 13 A0265
DIPLOM SOVEREIGN USA-45 L/A+17C

B43
SERENI A.P.,THE ITALIAN CONCEPTION OF INTERNATIONAL LAW. EUR+WWI MOD/EUR INT/ORG NAT/G DOMIN COERCE ORD/FREE FASCISM...OBS/ENVIR TREND 20. PAGE 131 A2686
LAW TIME/SEQ INT/LAW ITALY

C43
BENTHAM J.,"PRINCIPLES OF INTERNATIONAL LAW" IN J. BOWRING, ED., THE WORKS OF JEREMY BENTHAM." UNIV NAT/G PLAN PROB/SOLV DIPLOM CONTROL SANCTION MORAL ORD/FREE PWR SOVEREIGN 19. PAGE 13 A0270
INT/LAW JURID WAR PEACE

B44
BRIERLY J.L.,THE OUTLOOK FOR INTERNATIONAL LAW. FUT WOR-45 CONSTN NAT/G VOL/ASSN FORCES ECO/TAC DOMIN LEGIT ADJUD ROUTINE PEACE ORD/FREE...INT/LAW JURID METH LEAGUE/NAT 20. PAGE 18 A0376
INT/ORG LAW

B44
FULLER G.H.,TURKEY: A SELECTED LIST OF REFERENCES. ISLAM TURKEY CULTURE ECO/UNDEV AGRI DIPLOM NAT/LISM CONSERVE...GEOG HUM INT/LAW SOC 7/20 MAPS. PAGE 50 A1024
BIBLIOG/A ALL/VALS

B44
HUDSON M.,INTERNATIONAL TRIBUNALS PAST AND FUTURE. FUT WOR-45 LAW EDU/PROP ADJUD ORD/FREE...CONCPT TIME/SEQ TREND GEN/LAWS TOT/POP VAL/FREE 18/20. PAGE 69 A1408
INT/ORG STRUCT INT/LAW

B44
MACIVER R.M.,TOWARDS AN ABIDING PEACE. USA-45 ECO/TAC EDU/PROP DRIVE ORD/FREE PWR WEALTH...CONCPT TIME/SEQ GEN/METH TOT/POP 20. PAGE 92 A1890
INT/ORG PEACE INT/LAW

B44
PUTTKAMMER E.W.,WAR AND THE LAW. UNIV USA-45 CONSTN CULTURE SOCIETY NAT/G POL/PAR ROUTINE ALL/VALS ...JURID CONCPT OBS WORK VAL/FREE 20. PAGE 118 A2418
INT/ORG LAW WAR INT/LAW

S44
WRIGHT Q.,"CONSTITUTIONAL PROCEDURES OF THE US FOR CARRYING OUT OBLIGATIONS FOR MILITARY SANCTIONS." EUR+WWI FUT USA-45 WOR-45 CONSTN INTELL NAT/G CONSULT EX/STRUC LEGIS ROUTINE DRIVE...POLICY JURID CONCPT OBS TREND TOT/POP 20. PAGE 167 A3406
TOP/EX FORCES INT/LAW WAR

C44
SUAREZ F.,"ON WAR" (1621) IN SELECTIONS FROM THREE WORKS, VOL. I." NAT/G SECT CHIEF DIPLOM LEGIT MORAL PWR...POLICY INT/LAW 17. PAGE 140 A2859
WAR REV ORD/FREE CATH

B45
CONOVER H.F.,THE NAZI STATE: WAR CRIMES AND WAR CRIMINALS. GERMANY CULTURE NAT/G SECT FORCES DIPLOM INT/TRADE EDU/PROP...INT/LAW BIOG HIST/WRIT TIME/SEQ 20. PAGE 30 A0600
BIBLIOG WAR CRIME

B45
GALLOWAY E.,ABSTRACTS OF POSTWAR LITERATURE (VOL. IV) JAN.-JULY, 1945 NOS. 901-1074. POLAND USA+45 USSR WOR+45 INDUS LABOR PLAN ECO/TAC INT/TRADE TAX EDU/PROP ADMIN COLONIAL INT/LAW. PAGE 51 A1033
BIBLIOG/A NUC/PWR NAT/G DIPLOM

B45
HILL N.,CLAIMS TO TERRITORY IN INTERNATIONAL LAW AND RELATIONS. WOR-45 NAT/G DOMIN EDU/PROP LEGIT REGION ROUTINE ORD/FREE PWR WEALTH...GEOG INT/LAW JURID 20. PAGE 65 A1332
INT/ORG ADJUD SOVEREIGN

B45
TINGSTERN H.,PEACE AND SECURITY AFTER WW II. WOR-45 DELIB/GP TOP/EX LEGIT CT/SYS COERCE PEACE ATTIT PERCEPT...CONCPT LEAGUE/NAT 20. PAGE 144 A2943
INT/ORG ORD/FREE WAR INT/LAW

B45
UNCIO CONFERENCE LIBRARY,SHORT TITLE CLASSIFIED CATALOG. WOR-45 DOMIN COLONIAL WAR...SOC/WK 20 LEAGUE/NAT UN. PAGE 147 A3006
BIBLIOG DIPLOM INT/ORG INT/LAW

B45
US DEPARTMENT OF STATE,PUBLICATIONS OF THE DEPARTMENT OF STATE: A LIST CUMULATIVE FROM OCTOBER 1, 1929 (PAMPHLET). ASIA EUR+WWI ISLAM L/A+17C USA-45 ADJUD...INT/LAW 20. PAGE 151 A3082
BIBLIOG DIPLOM INT/TRADE

B45
VANCE H.L.,GUIDE TO THE LAW AND LEGAL LITERATURE OF MEXICO. LAW CONSTN FINAN LABOR FORCES ADJUD ADMIN ...CRIMLGY PHIL/SCI CON/ANAL 20 MEXIC/AMER. PAGE 158 A3217
BIBLIOG/A INT/LAW JURID CT/SYS

B45
WEST R.,CONSCIENCE AND SOCIETY: A STUDY OF THE PSYCHOLOGICAL PREREQUISITES OF LAW AND ORDER. FUT UNIV LAW SOCIETY STRUCT DIPLOM WAR PERS/REL SUPEGO ...SOC 20. PAGE 163 A3321
COERCE INT/LAW ORD/FREE PERSON

B45
WOOLBERT R.G.,FOREIGN AFFAIRS BIBLIOGRAPHY, 1932-1942. INT/ORG SECT INT/TRADE COLONIAL RACE/REL NAT/LISM...GEOG INT/LAW GOV/COMP IDEA/COMP 20. PAGE 167 A3393
BIBLIOG/A DIPLOM WAR

B46
GRIFFIN G.G.,A GUIDE TO MANUSCRIPTS RELATING TO AMERICAN HISTORY IN BRITISH DEPOSITORIES. CANADA IRELAND MOD/EUR UK USA-45 LAW DIPLOM ADMIN COLONIAL WAR NAT/LISM SOVEREIGN...GEOG INT/LAW 15/19 CMN/WLTH. PAGE 56 A1159
BIBLIOG/A ALL/VALS NAT/G

B46
KEETON G.W.,MAKING INTERNATIONAL LAW WORK. FUT WOR-45 NAT/G DELIB/GP FORCES LEGIT COERCE PEACE ATTIT RIGID/FLEX ORD/FREE PWR...JURID CONCPT HIST/WRIT GEN/METH LEAGUE/NAT 20. PAGE 77 A1578
INT/ORG ADJUD INT/LAW

B46
SCANLON H.L.,INTERNATIONAL LAW: A SELECTIVE LIST OF WORKS IN ENGLISH ON PUBLIC INTERNATIONAL LAW (A PAMPHLET). CHRIST-17C EUR+WWI MOD/EUR WOR-45 CT/SYS ...JURID 20. PAGE 127 A2613
BIBLIOG/A INT/LAW ADJUD DIPLOM

S46
DOUGLAS W.O.,"SYMPOSIUM ON WORLD ORGANIZATION." FUT USA+45 WOR+45 CONSTN SOCIETY NAT/G PLAN EDU/PROP LEGIT RIGID/FLEX KNOWL...INT/LAW JURID STERTYP TOT/POP 20. PAGE 38 A0778
INT/ORG LAW

C46
GOODRICH L.M.,"CHARTER OF THE UNITED NATIONS: COMMENTARY AND DOCUMENTS." EX/STRUC ADMIN...INT/LAW CON/ANAL BIBLIOG 20 UN. PAGE 54 A1106
CONSTN INT/ORG DIPLOM

B47
GORDON D.L.,THE HIDDEN WEAPON: THE STORY OF ECONOMIC WARFARE. EUR+WWI USA-45 LAW FINAN INDUS NAT/G CONSULT FORCES PLAN DOMIN PWR WEALTH ...INT/LAW CONCPT OBS TOT/POP NAZI 20. PAGE 54 A1112
INT/ORG ECO/TAC INT/TRADE WAR

B47
HYDE C.C.,INTERNATIONAL LAW, CHIEFLY AS INTERPRETED AND APPLIED BY THE UNITED STATES (3 VOLS., 2ND REV. ED.). USA-45 WOR+45 WOR-45 INT/ORG CT/SYS WAR NAT/LISM PEACE ORD/FREE...JURID 19/20 TREATY. PAGE 69 A1426
INT/LAW DIPLOM NAT/G POLICY

B47
INTERNATIONAL COURT OF JUSTICE,CHARTER OF THE UNITED NATIONS, STATUTE AND RULES OF COURT AND OTHER CONSTITUTIONAL DOCUMENTS. SWITZERLND LAW ADJUD INGP/REL...JURID 20 ICJ UN. PAGE 71 A1453
INT/LAW INT/ORG CT/SYS DIPLOM

B48
FENWICK C.G.,INTERNATIONAL LAW. WOR+45 WOR-45 CONSTN NAT/G LEGIT CT/SYS REGION...CONCPT LEAGUE/NAT UN 20. PAGE 45 A0916
INT/ORG JURID INT/LAW

B48
JESSUP P.C.,A MODERN LAW OF NATIONS. FUT WOR+45 WOR-45 SOCIETY NAT/G DELIB/GP LEGIS BAL/PWR EDU/PROP LEGIT PWR...INT/LAW JURID TIME/SEQ LEAGUE/NAT 20. PAGE 74 A1514
INT/ORG ADJUD

B48
LOGAN R.W.,THE AFRICAN MANDATES IN WORLD POLITICS. EUR+WWI GERMANY ISLAM INT/ORG BARGAIN...POLICY INT/LAW 20. PAGE 90 A1853
WAR COLONIAL AFR DIPLOM

B48
MORGENTHAL H.J.,POLITICS AMONG NATIONS: THE STRUGGLE FOR POWER AND PEACE. FUT WOR+45 INT/ORG OP/RES PROB/SOLV BAL/PWR CONTROL ATTIT MORAL ...INT/LAW BIBLIOG 20 COLD/WAR. PAGE 104 A2135
DIPLOM PEACE PWR POLICY

S48
GROSS L.,"THE PEACE OF WESTPHALIA, 1648-1948." WOR+45 WOR-45 CONSTN BAL/PWR FEDERAL 17/20 TREATY WESTPHALIA. PAGE 57 A1175
INT/LAW AGREE CONCPT DIPLOM

S48
MORGENTHAU H.J.,"THE TWILIGHT OF INTERNATIONAL MORALITY" (BMR)" WOR+45 WOR-45 BAL/PWR WAR NAT/LISM PEACE...POLICY INT/LAW IDEA/COMP 15/20 TREATY INTERVENT. PAGE 104 A2137
MORAL DIPLOM NAT/G

B49
GROB F.,THE RELATIVITY OF WAR AND PEACE: A STUDY IN LAW, HISTORY, AND POLLTICS. WOR+45 WOR-45 LAW DIPLOM DEBATE...CONCPT LING IDEA/COMP BIBLIOG 18/20. PAGE 57 A1167
WAR PEACE INT/LAW STYLE

B49
JACKSON R.H.,INTERNATIONAL CONFERENCE ON MILITARY TRIALS. FRANCE GERMANY UK USA+45 USSR VOL/ASSN DELIB/GP REPAR ADJUD CT/SYS CRIME WAR 20 WAR/TRIAL. PAGE 72 A1479
DIPLOM INT/ORG INT/LAW CIVMIL/REL

S49
KIRK G.,"MATTERIALS FOR THE STUDY OF INTERNATIONAL RELATIONS." FUT UNIV WOR+45 INTELL EDU/PROP ROUTINE PEACE ATTIT...INT/LAW JURID CONCPT OBS. PAGE 80 A1633 — INT/ORG ACT/RES DIPLOM

B50
LAUTERPACHT H.,INTERNATIONAL LAW AND HUMAN RIGHTS. USA+45 CONSTN STRUCT INT/ORG ACT/RES EDU/PROP PEACE PERSON ALL/VALS...CONCPT CON/ANAL GEN/LAWS UN 20. PAGE 86 A1750 — DELIB/GP LAW INT/LAW

B50
MOCKFORD J.,SOUTH-WEST AFRICA AND THE INTERNATIONAL COURT (PAMPHLET). AFR GERMANY SOUTH/AFR UK ECO/UNDEV DIPLOM CONTROL DISCRIM...DECISION JURID 20 AFRICA/SW. PAGE 102 A2094 — COLONIAL SOVEREIGN INT/LAW DOMIN

B50
MONPIED E.,BIBLIOGRAPHIE FEDERALISTE: OUVRAGES CHOISIS (VOL. I, MIMEOGRAPHED PAPER). EUR+WWI DIPLOM ADMIN REGION ATTIT PACIFISM SOCISM...INT/LAW 19/20. PAGE 103 A2109 — BIBLIOG/A FEDERAL CENTRAL INT/ORG

B50
ROSS A.,CONSTITUTION OF THE UNITED NATIONS. CONSTN CONSULT DELIB/GP ECO/TAC...INT/LAW JURID 20 UN LEAGUE/NAT. PAGE 124 A2540 — PEACE DIPLOM ORD/FREE INT/ORG

B50
SOHN L.B.,CASES AND OTHER MATERIALS ON WORLD LAW. FUT WOR+45 LAW INT/ORG...INT/LAW JURID METH/CNCPT 20 UN. PAGE 135 A2760 — CT/SYS CONSTN

C50
ELLSWORTH P.T.,"INTERNATIONAL ECONOMY." ECO/DEV ECO/UNDEV FINAN LABOR DIPLOM FOR/AID TARIFFS BAL/PAY EQUILIB NAT/LISM OPTIMAL...INT/LAW 20 ILO GATT. PAGE 41 A0843 — BIBLIOG INT/TRADE ECO/TAC INT/ORG

C50
NUMELIN R.,"THE BEGINNINGS OF DIPLOMACY." INT/TRADE WAR GP/REL PEACE STRANGE ATTIT...INT/LAW CONCPT BIBLIOG. PAGE 110 A2260 — DIPLOM KIN CULTURE LAW

N51
MONPIED E.,FEDERALIST BIBLIOGRAPHY: ARTICLES AND DOCUMENTS PUBLISHED IN BRITISH PERIODICALS 1945-1951 (MIMEOGRAPHED). EUR+WWI UK WOR+45 DIPLOM REGION ATTIT SOCISM...INT/LAW 20. PAGE 103 A2110 — BIBLIOG/A INT/ORG FEDERAL CENTRAL

B51
CORBETT P.E.,LAW AND SOCIETY IN THE RELATIONS OF STATES. FUT WOR+45 WOR-45 CONTROL WAR PEACE PWR ...POLICY JURID 16/20 TREATY. PAGE 30 A0615 — INT/LAW DIPLOM INT/ORG

B51
KELSEN H.,THE LAW OF THE UNITED NATIONS. WOR+45 STRUCT RIGID/FLEX ORD/FREE...INT/LAW JURID CONCPT CON/ANAL GEN/METH UN TOT/POP VAL/FREE 20. PAGE 77 A1581 — INT/ORG ADJUD

L51
KELSEN H.,"RECENT TRENDS IN THE LAW OF THE UNITED NATIONS." KOREA WOR+45 CONSTN LEGIS DIPLOM LEGIT DETER WAR RIGID/FLEX HEALTH ORD/FREE RESPECT ...JURID CON/ANAL UN VAL/FREE 20 NATO. PAGE 77 A1582 — INT/ORG LAW INT/LAW

L51
LISSITZYN O.J.,"THE INTERNATIONAL COURT OF JUSTICE." WOR+45 INT/ORG LEGIT ORD/FREE...CONCPT TIME/SEQ TREND GEN/LAWS VAL/FREE 20 ICJ. PAGE 90 A1839 — ADJUD JURID INT/LAW

L51
MANGONE G.,"THE IDEA AND PRACTICE OF WORLD GOVERNMENT." FUT WOR+45 WOR-45 ECO/DEV LEGIS CREATE LEGIT ROUTINE ATTIT MORAL PWR WEALTH...CONCPT GEN/LAWS 20. PAGE 94 A1920 — INT/ORG SOCIETY INT/LAW

C51
LEONARD L.L.,"INTERNATIONAL ORGANIZATION (1ST ED.)" WOR+45 FINAN DELIB/GP ECO/TAC GIVE DOMIN SANCTION PEACE BIO/SOC ORD/FREE...INT/LAW 20 UN LEAGUE/NAT. PAGE 87 A1779 — BIBLIOG POLICY DIPLOM INT/ORG

B52
DUNN F.S.,CURRENT RESEARCH IN INTERNATIONAL AFFAIRS. UK USA+45...POLICY TREATY. PAGE 39 A0801 — BIBLIOG/A DIPLOM INT/LAW

B52
FLECHTHEIM O.K.,FUNDAMENTALS OF POLITICAL SCIENCE. WOR+45 WOR-45 LAW POL/PAR EX/STRUC LEGIS ADJUD ATTIT PWR...INT/LAW. PAGE 46 A0945 — NAT/G DIPLOM IDEA/COMP CONSTN

B52
KELSEN H.,PRINCIPLES OF INTERNATIONAL LAW. WOR+45 WOR-45 INT/ORG ORD/FREE...JURID GEN/LAWS TOT/POP 20. PAGE 77 A1583 — ADJUD CONSTN INT/LAW

B52
UNESCO,THESES DE SCIENCES SOCIALES: CATALOGUE ANALYTIQUE INTERNATIONAL DE THESES INEDITES DE DOCTORAT, 1940-1950. INT/ORG DIPLOM EDU/PROP...GEOG INT/LAW MGT PSY SOC 20. PAGE 147 A3015 — BIBLIOG ACADEM WRITING

L52
WRIGHT Q.,"CONGRESS AND THE TREATY-MAKING POWER." USA+45 WOR+45 CONSTN INTELL NAT/G CHIEF CONSULT EX/STRUC LEGIS TOP/EX CREATE GOV/REL DISPL DRIVE RIGID/FLEX...TREND TOT/POP CONGRESS CONGRESS 20 TREATY. PAGE 167 A3408 — ROUTINE DIPLOM INT/LAW DELIB/GP

B53
KALIJARVI T.V.,MODERN WORLD POLITICS (3RD ED.). AFR L/A+17C MOD/EUR S/ASIA UK USSR WOR+45 INT/ORG BAL/PWR WAR PWR 20. PAGE 76 A1552 — DIPLOM INT/LAW PEACE

B53
KANTOR H.,A BIBLIOGRAPHY OF UNPUBLISHED DOCTORAL DISSERTATIONS AND MASTERS' THESES DEALING WITH GOVTS, POL, INT REL OF LAT AM. L/A+17C INT/ORG POL/PAR ACT/RES OP/RES CONFER ATTIT...INT/LAW PHIL/SCI 20. PAGE 76 A1556 — BIBLIOG ACADEM DIPLOM NAT/G

B53
LANDHEER B.,FUNDAMENTALS OF PUBLIC INTERNATIONAL LAW (SELECTIVE BIBLIOGRAPHIES OF THE LIBRARY OF THE PEACE PALACE, VOL. I; PAMPH). INT/ORG OP/RES PEACE ...IDEA/COMP 20. PAGE 84 A1715 — BIBLIOG/A INT/LAW DIPLOM PHIL/SCI

B53
OPPENHEIM L.,INTERNATIONAL LAW: A TREATISE (7TH ED., 2 VOLS.). LAW CONSTN PROB/SOLV INT/TRADE ADJUD AGREE NEUTRAL WAR ORD/FREE SOVEREIGN...BIBLIOG 20 LEAGUE/NAT UN ILO. PAGE 112 A2294 — INT/LAW INT/ORG DIPLOM

B54
LANDHEER B.,RECOGNITION IN INTERNATIONAL LAW (SELECTIVE BIBLIOGRAPHIES OF THE LIBRARY OF THE PEACE PALACE, VOL. II; PAMPHLET). NAT/G LEGIT SANCTION 20. PAGE 84 A1716 — BIBLIOG/A INT/LAW INT/ORG DIPLOM

B54
MANGONE G.,A SHORT HISTORY OF INTERNATIONAL ORGANIZATION. MOD/EUR USA+45 USA-45 WOR+45 WOR-45 LAW LEGIS CREATE LEGIT ROUTINE RIGID/FLEX PWR ...JURID CONCPT OBS TIME/SEQ STERTYP GEN/LAWS UN TOT/POP VAL/FREE 18/20. PAGE 94 A1921 — INT/ORG INT/LAW

B54
MILLARD E.L.,FREEDOM IN A FEDERAL WORLD. FUT WOR+45 VOL/ASSN TOP/EX LEGIT ROUTINE FEDERAL PEACE ATTIT DISPL ORD/FREE PWR...MAJORIT INT/LAW JURID TREND COLD/WAR 20. PAGE 101 A2073 — INT/ORG CREATE ADJUD BAL/PWR

B54
NUSSBAUM D.,A CONCISE HISTORY OF THE LAW OF NATIONS. ASIA CHRIST-17C EUR+WWI ISLAM MEDIT-7 MOD/EUR S/ASIA UNIV WOR+45 WOR-45 SOCIETY STRUCT EXEC ATTIT ALL/VALS...CONCPT HIST/WRIT TIME/SEQ. PAGE 110 A2263 — INT/ORG LAW PEACE INT/LAW

B54
STONE J.,LEGAL CONTROLS OF INTERNATIONAL CONFLICT: A TREATISE ON THE DYNAMICS OF DISPUTES AND WAR LAW. WOR+45 WOR-45 NAT/G DIPLOM CT/SYS SOVEREIGN...JURID CONCPT METH/CNCPT GEN/LAWS TOT/POP VAL/FREE COLD/WAR LEAGUE/NAT 20. PAGE 138 A2834 — INT/ORG LAW WAR INT/LAW

B54
US SENATE COMM ON FOREIGN REL,REVIEW OF THE UNITED NATIONS CHARTER: A COLLECTION OF DOCUMENTS. LEGIS DIPLOM ADMIN ARMS/CONT WAR REPRESENT SOVEREIGN ...INT/LAW 20 UN. PAGE 156 A3180 — BIBLIOG CONSTN INT/ORG DEBATE

B55
BURR R.N.,DOCUMENTS ON INTER-AMERICAN COOPERATION: VOL. I, 1810-1881; VOL. II, 1881-1948. DELIB/GP BAL/PWR INT/TRADE REPRESENT NAT/LISM PEACE HABITAT ORD/FREE PWR SOVEREIGN...INT/LAW 20 OAS. PAGE 22 A0445 — BIBLIOG DIPLOM INT/ORG L/A+17C

B55
HOGAN W.N.,INTERNATIONAL CONFLICT AND COLLECTIVE SECURITY: THE PRINCIPLE OF CONCERN IN INTERNATIONAL ORGANIZATION. CONSTN EX/STRUC BAL/PWR DIPLOM ADJUD CONTROL CENTRAL CONSEN PEACE...INT/LAW CONCPT METH/COMP 20 UN LEAGUE/NAT. PAGE 66 A1361 — INT/ORG WAR ORD/FREE FORCES

B55
JAPAN MOMBUSHO DAIGAKU GAKIYUT,BIBLIOGRAPHY OF THE STUDIES ON LAW AND POLITICS (PAMPHLET). CONSTN INDUS LABOR DIPLOM TAX ADMIN...CRIMLGY INT/LAW 20 CHINJAP. PAGE 73 A1496 — BIBLIOG LAW PHIL/SCI

B55
PLISCHKE E.,AMERICAN FOREIGN RELATIONS: A BIBLIOGRAPHY OF OFFICIAL SOURCES. USA+45 USA-45 INT/ORG FORCES PRESS WRITING DEBATE EXEC...POLICY INT/LAW 18/20 CONGRESS. PAGE 116 A2390 — BIBLIOG/A DIPLOM NAT/G

B55
SVARLIEN O.,AN INTRODUCTION TO THE LAW OF NATIONS. SEA AIR INT/ORG NAT/G CHIEF ADMIN AGREE WAR PRIVIL ORD/FREE SOVEREIGN...BIBLIOG 16/20. PAGE 140 A2868 — INT/LAW DIPLOM

B55
TROTIER A.H.,DOCTORAL DISSERTATIONS ACCEPTED BY AMERICAN UNIVERSITIES 1954-55. SECT DIPLOM HEALTH ...ART/METH GEOG INT/LAW SOC LING CHARTS 20. PAGE 145 A2968 — BIBLIOG ACADEM USA+45 WRITING

B55
UN HEADQUARTERS LIBRARY,BIBLIOGRAPHIE DE LA CHARTE DES NATIONS UNIES. CHINA/COM KOREA WOR+45 VOL/ASSN CONFER ADMIN COERCE PEACE ATTIT ORD/FREE SOVEREIGN ...INT/LAW 20 UNESCO UN. PAGE 147 A3001 — BIBLIOG/A INT/ORG DIPLOM

B55
VINSON J.C.,THE PARCHMENT PEACE: THE UNITED STATES SENATE AND THE WASHINGTON CONFERENCE, 1921-1922. USA-45 INT/ORG DELIB/GP PLAN ARMS/CONT GOV/REL ISOLAT PEACE ATTIT SOVEREIGN...INT/LAW BIBLIOG 20 — POLICY DIPLOM NAT/G LEGIS

SENATE PRESIDENT CONGRESS LEAGUE/NAT CHINJAP. PAGE 159 A3242

S55
WRIGHT Q.,"THE PEACEFUL ADJUSTMENT OF INTERNATIONAL RELATIONS: PROBLEMS AND RESEARCH APPROACHES." UNIV INTELL EDU/PROP ADJUD ROUTINE KNOWL SKILL...INT/LAW JURID PHIL/SCI CLASSIF 20. PAGE 167 A3411
R+D METH/CNCPT PEACE

B56
ESTEP R.,AN AIR POWER BIBLIOGRAPHY. USA+45 TEC/DEV BUDGET DIPLOM EDU/PROP DETER CIVMIL/REL...DECISION INT/LAW 20. PAGE 42 A0862
BIBLIOG/A FORCES WEAPON PLAN

B56
HOUSTON J.A.,LATIN AMERICA IN THE UNITED NATIONS. CONSULT DIPLOM LEGIT ROUTINE ATTIT ORD/FREE PWR ...JURID OBS RECORD TIME/SEQ CHARTS 20 UN. PAGE 68 A1395
L/A+17C INT/ORG INT/LAW REGION

B56
JESSUP P.C.,TRANSNATIONAL LAW. FUT WOR+45 JUDGE CREATE ADJUD ORD/FREE...CONCPT VAL/FREE 20. PAGE 74 A1515
LAW JURID INT/LAW

B56
SIPKOV I.,LEGAL SOURCES AND BIBLIOGRAPHY OF BULGARIA. BULGARIA COM LEGIS WRITING ADJUD CT/SYS ...INT/LAW TREATY 20. PAGE 134 A2736
BIBLIOG LAW TOTALISM MARXISM

B56
WATT D.C.,BRITAIN AND THE SUEZ CANAL. COM UAR UK ...INT/LAW 20 SUEZ TREATY. PAGE 162 A3294
DIPLOM INT/TRADE DIST/IND NAT/G

B56
WEIS P.,NATIONALITY AND STATELESSNESS IN INTERNATIONAL LAW. UK WOR+45 WOR-45 LAW CONSTN NAT/G DIPLOM EDU/PROP LEGIT ROUTINE RIGID/FLEX ...JURID RECORD CMN/WLTH 20. PAGE 162 A3309
INT/ORG SOVEREIGN INT/LAW

S56
POTTER P.B.,"NEUTRALITY, 1955." WOR+45 WOR-45 INT/ORG NAT/G WAR ATTIT...POLICY IDEA/COMP 17/20 LEAGUE/NAT UN COLD/WAR. PAGE 117 A2399
NEUTRAL INT/LAW DIPLOM CONCPT

B57
BLOOMFIELD L.M.,EGYPT, ISRAEL AND THE GULF OF AQABA: IN INTERNATIONAL LAW. LAW NAT/G CONSULT FORCES PLAN ECO/TAC ROUTINE COERCE ATTIT DRIVE PERCEPT PERSON RIGID/FLEX LOVE PWR WEALTH...GEOG CONCPT MYTH TREND. PAGE 15 A0314
ISLAM INT/LAW UAR

B57
DE VISSCHER C.,THEORY AND REALITY IN PUBLIC INTERNATIONAL LAW. WOR+45 WOR-45 SOCIETY NAT/G CT/SYS ATTIT MORAL ORD/FREE PWR...JURID CONCPT METH/CNCPT TIME/SEQ GEN/LAWS LEAGUE/NAT TOT/POP VAL/FREE COLD/WAR. PAGE 35 A0716
INT/ORG LAW INT/LAW

B57
INSTITUT DE DROIT INTL,TABLEAU GENERAL DES RESOLUTIONS (1873-1956). LAW NEUTRAL CRIME WAR MARRIAGE PEACE...JURID 19/20. PAGE 70 A1442
INT/LAW DIPLOM ORD/FREE ADJUD

B57
LEVONTIN A.V.,THE MYTH OF INTERNATIONAL SECURITY: A JURIDICAL AND CRITICAL ANALYSIS. FUT WOR+45 WOR-45 LAW NAT/G VOL/ASSN ACT/RES BAL/PWR ATTIT ORD/FREE ...JURID METH/CNCPT TIME/SEQ TREND STERTYP 20. PAGE 88 A1797
INT/ORG INT/LAW SOVEREIGN MYTH

B57
NEUMANN F.,THE DEMOCRATIC AND THE AUTHORITARIAN STATE: ESSAYS IN POLITICAL AND LEGAL THEORY. USA+45 USA-45 CONTROL REV GOV/REL PEACE ALL/IDEOS ...INT/LAW CONCPT GEN/LAWS BIBLIOG 20. PAGE 108 A2221
DOMIN NAT/G ORD/FREE POLICY

B57
ROSENNE S.,THE INTERNATIONAL COURT OF JUSTICE. WOR+45 LAW DOMIN LEGIT PEACE PWR SOVEREIGN...JURID CONCPT RECORD TIME/SEQ CON/ANAL CHARTS UN TOT/POP VAL/FREE LEAGUE/NAT 20 ICJ. PAGE 124 A2537
INT/ORG CT/SYS INT/LAW

B57
SINEY M.C.,THE ALLIED BLOCKADE OF GERMANY: 1914-1916. EUR+WWI GERMANY MOD/EUR USA-45 DIPLOM CONTROL NEUTRAL PWR 20. PAGE 133 A2721
DETER INT/TRADE INT/LAW WAR

B57
UNESCO,A REGISTER OF LEGAL DOCUMENTATION IN THE WORLD (2ND ED.). CT/SYS...JURID IDEA/COMP METH/COMP NAT/COMP 20. PAGE 148 A3019
BIBLIOG LAW INT/LAW CONSTN

B57
WASSENBERGH H.A.,POST-WAR INTERNATIONAL CIVIL AVIATION POLICY AND THE LAW OF THE AIR. WOR+45 AIR INT/ORG DOMIN LEGIT PEACE ORD/FREE...POLICY JURID NEW/IDEA OBS TIME/SEQ TREND CHARTS 20 TREATY. PAGE 162 A3290
COM/IND NAT/G INT/LAW

B58
ALEXANDROWICZ,A BIBLIOGRAPHY OF INDIAN LAW. INDIA S/ASIA CONSTN CT/SYS...INT/LAW 19/20. PAGE 6 A0113
BIBLIOG LAW ADJUD JURID

B58
APPADORAI A.,THE USE OF FORCE IN INTERNATIONAL RELATIONS. WOR+45 CULTURE ECO/UNDEV CAP/ISM ARMS/CONT REV WAR ATTIT PERSON SOVEREIGN MARXISM ...INT/LAW PACIFIST 20 UN INTERVENT THIRD/WRLD COLD/WAR. PAGE 8 A0169
PEACE FEDERAL INT/ORG

B58
BOWETT D.W.,SELF-DEFENSE IN INTERNATIONAL LAW. EUR+WWI MOD/EUR WOR+45 WOR-45 SOCIETY INT/ORG CONSULT DIPLOM LEGIT COERCE ATTIT ORD/FREE...JURID 20 UN. PAGE 17 A0353
ADJUD CONCPT WAR INT/LAW

B58
BRIERLY J.L.,THE BASIS OF OBLIGATION IN INTERNATIONAL LAW, AND OTHER PAPERS. WOR+45 WOR-45 LEGIS...JURID CONCPT NAT/COMP ANTHOL 20. PAGE 19 A0377
INT/LAW DIPLOM ADJUD SOVEREIGN

B58
DEUTSCHE GESCHAFT VOLKERRECHT,DIE VOLKERRECHTLICHEN DISSERTATIONEN AN DEN WESTDEUTSCHEN UNIVERSITATEN, 1945-1957. GERMANY/W NAT/G DIPLOM ADJUD CT/SYS ...POLICY 20. PAGE 37 A0748
BIBLIOG INT/LAW ACADEM JURID

B58
MARTIN L.J.,INTERNATIONAL PROPAGANDA: ITS LEGAL AND DIPLOMATIC CONTROL. UK USA+45 USSR CONSULT DELIB/GP DOMIN CONTROL 20. PAGE 95 A1951
EDU/PROP DIPLOM INT/LAW ATTIT

B58
SEYID MUHAMMAD V.A.,THE LEGAL FRAMEWORK OF WORLD TRADE. WOR+45 INT/ORG DIPLOM CONTROL...BIBLIOG 20 TREATY UN IMF GATT. PAGE 131 A2689
INT/LAW VOL/ASSN INT/TRADE TARIFFS

B58
SOC OF COMP LEGIS AND INT LAW,THE LAW OF THE SEA... (PAMPHLET). WOR+45 NAT/G INT/TRADE ADJUD CONTROL NUC/PWR WAR PEACE ATTIT ORD/FREE...JURID CHARTS 20 UN TREATY RESOURCE/N. PAGE 135 A2756
INT/LAW INT/ORG DIPLOM SEA

L58
HYVARINEN R.,"MONISTIC AND PLURALISTIC INTERPRETATIONS IN THE STUDY OF INTERNATIONAL POLITICS." COLONIAL REGION RACE/REL DISCRIM TOTALISM SOVEREIGN...INT/LAW PHIL/SCI CONCPT BIBLIOG 20. PAGE 70 A1429
DIPLOM PLURISM INT/ORG METH

L58
INT. SOC. SCI. BULL.,"TECHNIQUES OF MEDIATION AND CONCILIATION." EUR+WWI USA+45 SOCIETY INDUS INT/ORG LABOR NAT/G LEGIS DIPLOM EDU/PROP CHOOSE ATTIT RIGID/FLEX...JURID CONCPT GEN/LAWS 20. PAGE 70 A1447
VOL/ASSN DELIB/GP INT/LAW

S58
MCDOUGAL M.S.,"PERSPECTIVES FOR A LAW OF OUTER SPACE." FUT WOR+45 AIR CONSULT DELIB/GP TEC/DEV CT/SYS ORD/FREE...POLICY JURID 20 UN. PAGE 98 A2004
INT/ORG SPACE INT/LAW

C58
RAJAN M.S.,"UNITED NATIONS AND DOMESTIC JURISDICTION." WOR+45 WOR-45 PARL/PROC...IDEA/COMP BIBLIOG 20 UN. PAGE 119 A2434
INT/LAW DIPLOM CONSTN INT/ORG

B59
BUNDESMIN FUR VERTRIEBENE,ZEITTAFEL DER VORGESCHICHTE UND DES ABLAUFS DER VERTREIBUNG SOWIE DER UNTERBRINGUNG UND EINGLIEDERUNG DER (2 VOLS.). GERMANY/E GERMANY/W NAT/G PROVS PROB/SOLV DIPLOM PARL/PROC ATTIT...BIBLIOG SOC/INTEG 20 MIGRATION PARLIAMENT. PAGE 21 A0431
JURID GP/REL INT/LAW

B59
COMM. STUDY ORGAN. PEACE,ORGANIZING PEACE IN THE NUCLEAR AGE. FUT CONSULT DELIB/GP DOMIN ADJUD ROUTINE COERCE ORD/FREE...TECHNIC INT/LAW JURID NEW/IDEA UN COLD/WAR 20. PAGE 29 A0581
INT/ORG ACT/RES NUC/PWR

B59
GOLDWIN R.A.,READINGS IN AMERICAN FOREIGN POLICY. USA+45 USA-45 ARMS/CONT NUC/PWR...INT/LAW 18/20. PAGE 53 A1094
ANTHOL DIPLOM INT/ORG ECO/UNDEV

B59
HARVARD UNIVERSITY LAW SCHOOL,INTERNATIONAL PROBLEMS OF FINANCIAL PROTECTION AGAINST NUCLEAR RISK. WOR+45 NAT/G DELIB/GP PROB/SOLV DIPLOM CONTROL ATTIT...POLICY INT/LAW MATH 20. PAGE 62 A1281
NUC/PWR ADJUD INDUS FINAN

B59
KAPLAN D.,THE ARAB REFUGEES: AN ABNORMAL PROBLEM. UAR WOR+45 PROB/SOLV DIPLOM GOV/REL ADJUST EFFICIENCY...POLICY GEOG INT/LAW 20 UN JEWS MIGRATION. PAGE 76 A1557
STRANGE HABITAT GP/REL INGP/REL

B59
KIRCHHEIMER O.,GEGENWARTSPROBLEME DER ASYLGEWAHRUNG. DOMIN GP/REL ATTIT...NAT/COMP 20. PAGE 79 A1630
DIPLOM INT/LAW JURID ORD/FREE

B59
KNIERIEM A.,THE NUREMBERG TRIALS. EUR+WWI GERMANY VOL/ASSN LEAD COERCE WAR INGP/REL TOTALISM SUPEGO ORD/FREE...CONCPT METH/COMP. PAGE 80 A1651
INT/LAW CRIME PARTIC JURID

B59
MAYER A.J.,POLITICAL ORIGINS OF THE NEW DIPLOMACY, 1917-1918. EUR+WWI MOD/EUR USA-45 WAR PWR...POLICY INT/LAW BIBLIOG. PAGE 97 A1983
TREND DIPLOM

B59
PANAMERICAN UNION,PUBLICATIONS: PAU AND OFFICIAL RECORDS OF THE OAS, IN ENGLISH, SPANISH, PORTUGUESE, AND FRENCH, 1958-59. NAT/G ATTIT...SOC 20 OAS. PAGE 113 A2328
BIBLIOG L/A+17C INT/LAW DIPLOM

B59
PANHUYS H.F.,THE ROLE OF NATIONALITY IN INTERNATIONAL LAW. ADJUD CRIME WAR STRANGE...JURID TREND. PAGE 114 A2330
INT/LAW NAT/LISM INGP/REL

B59
COLUMBIA U BUR APPL SOC RES,ATTITUDES OF PROMINENT AMERICANS TOWARD "WORLD PEACE THROUGH WORLD LAW" (SUPRA-NATL ORGANIZATION FOR WAR PREVENTION). USA+45 USSR ELITES FORCES PLAN PROB/SOLV CONTROL WAR PWR...POLICY SOC QU IDEA/COMP 20 UN. PAGE 117 A2403
ATTIT ACT/RES INT/LAW STAT

B59
REIFF H.,THE UNITED STATES AND THE TREATY LAW OF THE SEA. USA+45 USA-45 SEA SOCIETY INT/ORG CONSULT DELIB/GP LEGIS DIPLOM LEGIT ATTIT ORD/FREE PWR WEALTH...GEOG JURID TOT/POP 20 TREATY. PAGE 120 A2459
ADJUD INT/LAW

B59
SCHNEIDER J.,TREATY-MAKING POWER OF INTERNATIONAL ORGANIZATIONS. FUT WOR+45 WOR-45 LAW NAT/G JUDGE DIPLOM LEGIT CT/SYS ORD/FREE PWR...INT/LAW JURID GEN/LAWS TOT/POP UNESCO 20 TREATY. PAGE 129 A2639
INT/ORG ROUTINE

B59
SIMPSON J.L.,INTERNATIONAL ARBITRATION: LAW AND PRACTICE. WOR+45 WOR-45 INT/ORG DELIB/GP ADJUD PEACE MORAL ORD/FREE...METH 18/20. PAGE 133 A2720
INT/LAW DIPLOM CT/SYS CONSULT

B59
TARDIFF G.,LA LIBERTAD; LA LIBERTAD DE EXPRESION, IDEALES Y REALIDADES AMERICANAS. ISLAM INT/ORG PROB/SOLV PRESS CONFER PARTIC CATHISM...INT/LAW SOC/INTEG UN MID/EAST. PAGE 141 A2889
ORD/FREE ATTIT DIPLOM CONCPT

L59
MCDOUGAL M.S.,"THE IDENTIFICATION AND APPRAISAL OF DIVERSE SYSTEMS OF PUBLIC ORDER (BMR)" WOR+45 NAT/G CONSULT EDU/PROP POLICY. PAGE 98 A2005
INT/LAW DIPLOM ALL/IDEOS

S59
POTTER P.B.,"OBSTACLES AND ALTERNATIVES TO INTERNATIONAL LAW." WOR+45 NAT/G VOL/ASSN DELIB/GP BAL/PWR DOMIN ROUTINE...JURID VAL/FREE 20. PAGE 117 A2400
INT/ORG LAW DIPLOM INT/LAW

B60
BYRD E.M. JR.,TREATIES AND EXECUTIVE AGREEMENTS IN THE UNITED STATES: THEIR SEPARATE ROLES AND LIMITATIONS. USA+45 USA-45 EX/STRUC TARIFFS CT/SYS GOV/REL FEDERAL...IDEA/COMP BIBLIOG SUPREME/CT SENATE CONGRESS. PAGE 23 A0461
CHIEF INT/LAW DIPLOM

B60
HARVARD LAW SCHOOL LIBRARY,CURRENT LEGAL BIBLIOGRAPHY. USA+45 CONSTN LEGIS ADJUD CT/SYS POLICY. PAGE 62 A1279
BIBLIOG JURID LAW INT/LAW

B60
JENNINGS R.,PROGRESS OF INTERNATIONAL LAW. FUT WOR+45 WOR-45 SOCIETY NAT/G VOL/ASSN DELIB/GP DIPLOM EDU/PROP LEGIT COERCE ATTIT DRIVE MORAL ORD/FREE...JURID CONCPT OBS TIME/SEQ TREND GEN/LAWS. PAGE 74 A1509
INT/ORG LAW INT/LAW

B60
PAN AMERICAN UNION,FIFTH MEETING OF CONSULTATION OF MINISTERS OF FOREIGN AFFAIRS OF AMERICAN STATES. L/A+17C FORCES PLAN PROB/SOLV ADJUD PEACE...POLICY INT/LAW 20 OAS. PAGE 113 A2327
INT/ORG DIPLOM DELIB/GP ECO/UNDEV

B60
PRICE D.,THE SECRETARY OF STATE. USA+45 CONSTN ELITES INTELL CHIEF EX/STRUC TOP/EX LEGIT ATTIT PWR SKILL...DECISION 20 CONGRESS. PAGE 117 A2410
CONSULT DIPLOM INT/LAW

B60
STEIN E.,AMERICAN ENTERPRISE IN THE EUROPEAN COMMON MARKET: A LEGAL PROFILE. EUR+WWI FUT USA+45 SOCIETY STRUCT ECO/DEV NAT/G VOL/ASSN CONSULT PLAN TEC/DEV ECO/TAC INT/TRADE ADMIN ATTIT RIGID/FLEX PWR...MGT NEW/IDEA STAT TREND COMPUT/IR SIMUL EEC 20. PAGE 137 A2814
MARKET ADJUD INT/LAW

B60
THE AFRICA 1960 COMMITTEE,MANDATE IN TRUST; THE PROBLEM OF SOUTH WEST AFRICA. GERMANY STRUCT REGION SANCTION CHOOSE DISCRIM...INT/LAW 20 AFRICA/SW UN LEAGUE/NAT TRUST/TERR. PAGE 142 A2910
NAT/G DIPLOM COLONIAL RACE/REL

B60
UNITED WORLD FEDERALISTS,UNITED WORLD FEDERALISTS; PANORAMA OF RECENT BOOKS, FILMS, AND JOURNALS ON WORLD FEDERATION, THE UN, AND WORLD PEACE. CULTURE ECO/UNDEV PROB/SOLV FOR/AID ARMS/CONT NUC/PWR ...INT/LAW PHIL/SCI 20 UN. PAGE 149 A3039
BIBLIOG/A DIPLOM INT/ORG PEACE

B60
WOETZEL R.K.,THE INTERNATIONAL CONTROL OF AIRSPACE AND OUTERSPACE. FUT WOR+45 AIR CONSTN STRUCT CONSULT PLAN TEC/DEV ADJUD RIGID/FLEX KNOWL ORD/FREE PWR...TECHNIC GEOG MGT NEW/IDEA TREND COMPUT/IR VAL/FREE 20 TREATY. PAGE 166 A3375
INT/ORG JURID SPACE INT/LAW

L60
DEAN A.W.,"SECOND GENEVA CONFERENCE OF THE LAW OF THE SEA: THE FIGHT FOR FREEDOM OF THE SEAS." FUT USA+45 USSR WOR+45 WOR-45 SEA CONSTN STRUCT PLAN INT/TRADE ADJUD ADMIN ORD/FREE...DECISION RECORD TREND GEN/LAWS 20 TREATY. PAGE 35 A0717
INT/ORG JURID INT/LAW

L60
KUNZ J.,"SANCTIONS IN INTERNATIONAL LAW." WOR+45 WOR-45 LEGIT ARMS/CONT COERCE PEACE ATTIT ...METH/CNCPT TIME/SEQ TREND 20. PAGE 83 A1695
INT/ORG ADJUD INT/LAW

S60
BOGARDUS E.S.,"THE SOCIOLOGY OF A STRUCTURED PEACE." FUT SOCIETY CREATE DIPLOM EDU/PROP ADJUD ROUTINE ATTIT RIGID/FLEX KNOWL ORD/FREE RESPECT ...POLICY INT/LAW JURID NEW/IDEA SELF/OBS TOT/POP 20 UN. PAGE 16 A0327
INT/ORG SOC NAT/LISM PEACE

S60
GRACIA-MORA M.R.,"INTERNATIONAL RESPONSIBILITY FOR SUBVERSIVE ACTIVITIES AND HOSTILE PROPAGANDA BY PRIVATE PERSONS AGAINST." COM EUR+WWI L/A+17C UK USA+45 USSR WOR-45 CONSTN NAT/G LEGIT ADJUD REV PEACE TOTALISM ORD/FREE...INT/LAW 20. PAGE 55 A1119
INT/ORG JURID SOVEREIGN

S60
O'BRIEN W.,"THE ROLE OF FORCE IN THE INTERNATIONAL JURIDICAL ORDER." WOR+45 NAT/G FORCES DOMIN ADJUD ARMS/CONT DETER NUC/PWR WAR ATTIT PWR...CATH INT/LAW JURID CONCPT TREND STERTYP GEN/LAWS 20. PAGE 110 A2266
INT/ORG COERCE

S60
POTTER P.B.,"RELATIVE VALUES OF INTERNATIONAL RELATIONS, LAW, AND ORGANIZATIONS." WOR+45 NAT/G LEGIT ADJUD ORD/FREE...CONCPT TOT/POP COLD/WAR 20. PAGE 117 A2401
INT/ORG LEGIS DIPLOM INT/LAW

S60
RHYNE C.S.,"LAW AS AN INSTRUMENT FOR PEACE." FUT WOR+45 PLAN LEGIT ROUTINE ARMS/CONT NUC/PWR ATTIT ORD/FREE...JURID METH/CNCPT TREND CON/ANAL HYPO/EXP COLD/WAR 20. PAGE 120 A2471
ADJUD EDU/PROP INT/LAW PEACE

S60
SCHACHTER O.,"THE ENFORCEMENT OF INTERNATIONAL JUDICIAL AND ARBITRAL DECISIONS." WOR+45 NAT/G ECO/TAC DOMIN LEGIT ROUTINE COERCE ATTIT DRIVE ALL/VALS PWR...METH/CNCPT TREND TOT/POP 20 UN. PAGE 128 A2615
INT/ORG ADJUD INT/LAW

S60
WRIGHT Q.,"LEGAL ASPECTS OF THE U-2 INCIDENT." COM USA+45 USSR STRUCT NAT/G FORCES PLAN TEC/DEV ADJUD RIGID/FLEX MORAL ORD/FREE...DECISION INT/LAW JURID PSY TREND GEN/LAWS COLD/WAR VAL/FREE 20 U-2. PAGE 168 A3413
PWR POLICY SPACE

B61
ANAND R.P.,COMPULSORY JURISDICTION OF INTERNATIONAL COURT OF JUSTICE. FUT WOR+45 SOCIETY PLAN LEGIT ADJUD ATTIT DRIVE PERSON ORD/FREE...JURID CONCPT TREND 20 ICJ. PAGE 8 A0156
INT/ORG COERCE INT/LAW

B61
BAINS J.S.,STUDIES IN POLITICAL SCIENCE. INDIA WOR+45 WOR-45 CONSTN BAL/PWR ADJUD ADMIN PARL/PROC SOVEREIGN...SOC METH/COMP ANTHOL 17/20 UN. PAGE 10 A0209
DIPLOM INT/LAW NAT/G

B61
BRENNAN D.G.,ARMS CONTROL, DISARMAMENT, AND NATIONAL SECURITY. WOR+45 NAT/G FORCES CREATE PROB/SOLV PARTIC WAR PEACE...DECISION INT/LAW ANTHOL BIBLIOG 20. PAGE 18 A0372
ARMS/CONT ORD/FREE DIPLOM POLICY

B61
CONFERENCE ATLANTIC COMMUNITY,AN INTRODUCTORY BIBLIOGRAPHY. COM WOR+45 FORCES DIPLOM ECO/TAC WAR ...INT/LAW HIST/WRIT COLD/WAR NATO. PAGE 29 A0584
BIBLIOG/A CON/ANAL INT/ORG

B61
LARSON A.,WHEN NATIONS DISAGREE. USA+45 WOR+45 INT/ORG ADJUD COERCE CRIME OWN SOVEREIGN...POLICY JURID 20. PAGE 85 A1734
INT/LAW DIPLOM WAR

B61
MCDOUGAL M.S.,LAW AND MINIMUM WORLD PUBLIC ORDER. WOR+45 SOCIETY NAT/G DELIB/GP EDU/PROP LEGIT ADJUD COERCE ATTIT PERSON...JURID CONCPT RECORD TREND TOT/POP 20. PAGE 98 A2006
INT/ORG ORD/FREE INT/LAW

B61
NEWMAN R.P.,RECOGNITION OF COMMUNIST CHINA? A STUDY IN ARGUMENT. CHINA/COM NAT/G PROB/SOLV RATIONAL ...INT/LAW LOG IDEA/COMP BIBLIOG 20. PAGE 108 A2226
MARXISM ATTIT DIPLOM POLICY

B61
RIENOW R.,CONTEMPORARY INTERNATIONAL POLITICS. WOR+45 INT/ORG BAL/PWR EDU/PROP COLONIAL NEUTRAL REGION WAR PEACE...INT/LAW 20 COLD/WAR UN. PAGE 121 A2476
DIPLOM PWR POLICY NAT/G

B61
STONE J.,QUEST FOR SURVIVAL. WOR+45 NAT/G VOL/ASSN LEGIT ADMIN ARMS/CONT COERCE DISPL ORD/FREE PWR ...POLICY INT/LAW JURID COLD/WAR 20. PAGE 139 A2836
INT/ORG ADJUD SOVEREIGN

B61
SYATAUW J.J.G.,SOME NEWLY ESTABLISHED ASIAN STATES AND THE DEVELOPMENT OF INTERNATIONAL LAW. BURMA CEYLON INDIA INDONESIA ECO/UNDEV COLONIAL NEUTRAL WAR PEACE SOVEREIGN...CHARTS 19/20. PAGE 140 A2873
INT/LAW ADJUST SOCIETY S/ASIA

B61
WARD R.E.,JAPANESE POLITICAL SCIENCE: A GUIDE TO JAPANESE REFERENCE AND RESEARCH MATERIALS (2ND ED.). LAW CONSTN STRATA NAT/G POL/PAR DELIB/GP LEGIS ADMIN CHOOSE GP/REL...INT/LAW 19/20 CHINJAP. PAGE 161 A3282
BIBLIOG/A PHIL/SCI

B61
WECHSLER H.,PRINCIPLES, POLITICS AND FUNDAMENTAL LAW: SELECTED ESSAYS. USA+45 USA-45 LAW SOCIETY NAT/G PROVS DELIB/GP EX/STRUC ACT/RES LEGIT PERSON KNOWL PWR...JURID 20 NUREMBERG. PAGE 162 A3296
CT/SYS CONSTN INT/LAW

B61
WRIGHT Q.,THE ROLE OF INTERNATIONAL LAW IN THE ELIMINATION OF WAR. FUT WOR+45 WOR-45 NAT/G BAL/PWR DIPLOM DOMIN LEGIT PWR...POLICY INT/LAW JURID CONCPT TIME/SEQ TREND GEN/LAWS COLD/WAR 20. PAGE 168 A3414
INT/ORG ADJUD ARMS/CONT

B61
YDIT M.,INTERNATIONALISED TERRITORIES. FUT WOR+45 WOR-45 CONSTN VOL/ASSN CREATE PLAN LEGIT PEACE ORD/FREE...GEOG INT/LAW JURID SOC NEW/IDEA OBS RECORD SAMP TIME/SEQ TREND 19/20 BERLIN. PAGE 169 A3431
LOC/G INT/ORG DIPLOM SOVEREIGN

L61
HOYT E.C.,"UNITED STATES REACTION TO THE KOREAN ATTACK." COM KOREA USA+45 CONSTN DELIB/GP FORCES PLAN ECO/TAC DOMIN EDU/PROP LEGIT ROUTINE COERCE WAR ATTIT DISPL RIGID/FLEX ORD/FREE PWR...POLICY INT/LAW TREND UN 20. PAGE 68 A1402
ASIA INT/ORG BAL/PWR DIPLOM

L61
SAND P.T.,"AN HISTORICAL SURVEY OF INTERNATIONAL AIR LAW SINCE 1944." USA+45 USA-45 WOR+45 WOR-45 SOCIETY ECO/DEV NAT/G CONSULT EX/STRUC ACT/RES PLAN LEGIT ROUTINE...JURID CONCPT METH/CNCPT TREND 20. PAGE 127 A2598
INT/ORG LAW INT/LAW SPACE

S61
ALGER C.F.,"NON-RESOLUTION CONSEQUENCES OF THE UNITED NATIONS AND THEIR EFFECT ON INTERNATIONAL CONFLICT." WOR+45 CONSTN ECO/DEV NAT/G CONSULT DELIB/GP TOP/EX ACT/RES PLAN DIPLOM EDU/PROP ROUTINE ATTIT ALL/VALS...INT/LAW TOT/POP UN 20. PAGE 6 A0117
INT/ORG DRIVE BAL/PWR

S61
CASTANEDA J.,"THE UNDERDEVELOPED NATIONS AND THE DEVELOPMENT OF INTERNATIONAL LAW." FUT UNIV LAW ACT/RES FOR/AID LEGIT PERCEPT SKILL...JURID METH/CNCPT TIME/SEQ TOT/POP 20 UN. PAGE 25 A0507
INT/ORG ECO/UNDEV PEACE INT/LAW

S61
HAZARD J.N.,"CODIFYING PEACEFUL COEXISTANCE." FUT INTELL INT/ORG TEC/DEV PEACE HEALTH...INT/LAW CONT/OBS 20. PAGE 63 A1299
VOL/ASSN JURID

S61
LEWY G.,"SUPERIOR ORDERS, NUCLEAR WARFARE AND THE DICTATES OF CONSCIENCE: THE DILEMMA OF MILITARY OBEDIENCE IN THE ATOMIC." FUT UNIV WOR+45 INTELL SOCIETY FORCES TOP/EX ACT/RES ADMIN ROUTINE NUC/PWR PERCEPT RIGID/FLEX ALL/VALS...POLICY CONCPT 20. PAGE 88 A1805
DETER INT/ORG LAW INT/LAW

S61
LIPSON L.,"AN ARGUMENT ON THE LEGALITY OF RECONNAISSANCE STATELLITES." COM USA+45 USSR WOR+45 AIR INTELL NAT/G CONSULT PLAN DIPLOM LEGIT ROUTINE ATTIT...INT/LAW JURID CONCPT METH/CNCPT TREND COLD/WAR 20. PAGE 90 A1833
INT/ORG LAW SPACE

S61
MACHOWSKI K.,"SELECTED PROBLEMS OF NATIONAL SOVEREIGNTY WITH REFERENCE TO THE LAW OF OUTER SPACE." FUT WOR+45 AIR LAW INTELL SOCIETY ECO/DEV PLAN EDU/PROP DETER DRIVE PERCEPT SOVEREIGN ...POLICY INT/LAW OBS TREND TOT/POP 20. PAGE 92 A1889
UNIV ACT/RES NUC/PWR SPACE

B62
ALEXANDROWICZ C.H.,WORLD ECONOMIC AGENCIES: LAW AND PRACTICE. WOR+45 DIST/IND FINAN LABOR CONSULT INT/TRADE TARIFFS REPRESENT HEALTH...JURID 20 UN GATT EEC OAS ECSC. PAGE 6 A0115
INT/LAW INT/ORG DIPLOM ADJUD

B62
AMERICAN LAW INSTITUTE,FOREIGN RELATIONS LAW OF THE UNITED STATES: RESTATEMENT, SECOND. USA+45 NAT/G LEGIS ADJUD EXEC ROUTINE GOV/REL...INT/LAW JURID CONCPT 20 TREATY. PAGE 7 A0152
PROF/ORG LAW DIPLOM ORD/FREE

B62
BIBLIOTHEQUE PALAIS DE LA PAIX,CATALOGUE OF THE PEACE PALACE LIBRARY, SUPPLEMENT 1937-1952 (7 VOLS.). WOR+45 WOR-45 INT/ORG NAT/G ADJUD WAR PEACE ...JURID 20. PAGE 14 A0285
BIBLIOG INT/LAW DIPLOM

B62
COLOMBOS C.J.,THE INTERNATIONAL LAW OF THE SEA. WOR+45 EXTR/IND DIPLOM INT/TRADE TARIFFS AGREE WAR ...TIME/SEQ 20 TREATY. PAGE 28 A0570
INT/LAW SEA JURID ADJUD

B62
GOLDWATER B.M.,WHY NOT VICTORY? A FRESH LOOK AT AMERICAN FOREIGN POLICY. USA+45 WOR+45 FOR/AID LEAD ARMS/CONT WAR PEACE ATTIT ORD/FREE PWR MARXISM ...INT/LAW 20 TREATY ECHR COUNCL/EUR. PAGE 53 A1092
DIPLOM POLICY CONSERVE NAT/LISM

B62
LILLICH R.B.,INTERNATIONAL CLAIMS: THEIR ADJUDICATION BY NATIONAL COMMISSIONS. WOR+45 WOR-45 INT/ORG LEGIT CT/SYS TOT/POP 20. PAGE 89 A1816
ADJUD JURID INT/LAW

B62
MCDOUGAL M.S.,THE PUBLIC ORDER OF THE OCEANS. WOR+45 WOR-45 SEA INT/ORG NAT/G CONSULT DELIB/GP DIPLOM LEGIT PEACE RIGID/FLEX...GEOG INT/LAW JURID RECORD TOT/POP 20 TREATY. PAGE 98 A2007
ADJUD ORD/FREE

B62
PERKINS D.,AMERICA'S QUEST FOR PEACE. USA+45 WOR+45 DIPLOM CONFER NAT/LISM ATTIT 20 UN TREATY. PAGE 115 A2361
INT/LAW INT/ORG ARMS/CONT PEACE

B62
ROSENNE S.,THE WORLD COURT: WHAT IT IS AND HOW IT WORKS. WOR+45 WOR-45 LAW CONSTN JUDGE EDU/PROP LEGIT ROUTINE CHOOSE PEACE ORD/FREE...JURID OBS TIME/SEQ CHARTS UN TOT/POP VAL/FREE 20. PAGE 124 A2538
INT/ORG ADJUD INT/LAW

B62
SCHMITT H.A.,THE PATH TO EUROPEAN UNITY. EUR+WWI USA+45 PLAN TEC/DEV DIPLOM FOR/AID CONFER...INT/LAW 20 EEC EURCOALSTL MARSHL/PLN UNIFICA. PAGE 128 A2634
INT/ORG INT/TRADE REGION ECO/DEV

B62
SCHWARTZ L.E.,INTERNATIONAL ORGANIZATIONS AND SPACE COOPERATION. VOL/ASSN CONSULT CREATE TEC/DEV SANCTION...POLICY INT/LAW PHIL/SCI 20 UN. PAGE 130 A2656
INT/ORG DIPLOM R+D SPACE

B62
SCHWARZENBERGER G.,THE FRONTIERS OF INTERNATIONAL LAW. WOR+45 WOR-45 NAT/G LEGIT CT/SYS ROUTINE MORAL ORD/FREE PWR...JURID SOC GEN/METH 20 COLD/WAR. PAGE 130 A2661
INT/ORG LAW INT/LAW

B62
SHAW C.,LEGAL PROBLEMS IN INTERNATIONAL TRADE AND INVESTMENT. WOR+45 ECO/DEV ECO/UNDEV MARKET DIPLOM TAX INCOME ROLE...ANTHOL BIBLIOG 20 TREATY UN IMF GATT. PAGE 132 A2698
INT/LAW INT/TRADE FINAN ECO/TAC

B62
TRISKA J.F.,THE THEORY, LAW, AND POLICY OF SOVIET TREATIES. WOR+45 WOR-45 CONSTN INT/ORG NAT/G VOL/ASSN DOMIN LEGIT COERCE ATTIT PWR RESPECT ...POLICY JURID CONCPT OBS SAMP TIME/SEQ TREND GEN/LAWS 20. PAGE 145 A2966
COM LAW INT/LAW USSR

L62
GROSS L.,"IMMUNITIES AND PRIVILEGES OF DELIGATIONS TO THE UNITED NATIONS." USA+45 WOR+45 STRATA NAT/G VOL/ASSN CONSULT DIPLOM EDU/PROP ROUTINE RESPECT ...POLICY INT/LAW CONCPT UN 20. PAGE 57 A1176
INT/ORG LAW ELITES

L62
PETKOFF D.K.,"RECOGNITION AND NON-RECOGNITION OF STATES AND GOVERNMENTS IN INTERNATIONAL LAW." ASIA COM USA+45 WOR+45 NAT/G ACT/RES DIPLOM DOMIN LEGIT COERCE ORD/FREE PWR...CONCPT GEN/LAWS 20. PAGE 115 A2369
INT/ORG LAW INT/LAW

L62
SCHWERIN K.,"LAW LIBRARIES AND FOREIGN LAW COLLECTION IN THE USA." USA+45 USA-45...INT/LAW STAT 20. PAGE 130 A2667
BIBLIOG LAW ACADEM ADMIN

S62
BIERZANECK R.,"LA NON-RECONAISSANCE ET LE DROIT INTERNATIONAL CONTEMPORAIN." EUR+WWI FUT WOR+45 LAW ECO/DEV ATTIT RIGID/FLEX...CONCPT TIME/SEQ TOT/POP 20. PAGE 14 A0286
EDU/PROP JURID DIPLOM INT/LAW

S62
CRANE R.D.,"LAW AND STRATEGY IN SPACE." FUT USA+45 WOR+45 AIR LAW INT/ORG NAT/G FORCES ACT/RES PLAN BAL/PWR LEGIT ARMS/CONT COERCE ORD/FREE...POLICY INT/LAW JURID SOC/EXP 20 TREATY. PAGE 32 A0656
CONCPT SPACE

S62
CRANE R.D.,"SOVIET ATTITUDE TOWARD INTERNATIONAL SPACE LAW." COM FUT USA+45 USSR AIR CONSTN DELIB/GP DOMIN PWR...JURID TREND TOT/POP 20. PAGE 32 A0657
LAW ATTIT INT/LAW SPACE

S62
FALK R.A.,"THE REALITY OF INTERNATIONAL LAW." WOR+45 NAT/G LEGIT COERCE DETER WAR MORAL ORD/FREE PWR SOVEREIGN...JURID CONCPT VAL/FREE COLD/WAR 20. PAGE 43 A0887
INT/ORG ADJUD NUC/PWR INT/LAW

S62
GRAVEN J.,"LE MOUVEAU DROIT PENAL INTERNATIONAL." UNIV STRUCT LEGIS ACT/RES CRIME ATTIT PERCEPT PERSON...JURID CONCPT 20. PAGE 55 A1132
CT/SYS PUB/INST INT/ORG INT/LAW

S62
GREEN L.C.,"POLITICAL OFFENSES, WAR CRIMES AND EXTRADITION." WOR+45 YUGOSLAVIA INT/ORG LEGIT ROUTINE WAR ORD/FREE SOVEREIGN...JURID NAZI 20
LAW CONCPT INT/LAW

INTERPOL. PAGE 55 A1138

S62
GREENSPAN M.,"INTERNATIONAL LAW AND ITS PROTECTION FOR PARTICIPANTS IN UNCONVENTIONAL WARFARE." WOR+45 LAW INT/ORG NAT/G POL/PAR COERCE REV ORD/FREE ...INT/LAW TOT/POP 20. PAGE 56 A1143
FORCES JURID GUERRILLA WAR

S62
JOHNSON O.H.,"THE ENGLISH TRADITION IN INTERNATIONAL LAW." CHRIST-17C MOD/EUR EDU/PROP LEGIT CT/SYS ORD/FREE...JURID CONCPT TIME/SEQ. PAGE 75 A1526
LAW INT/LAW UK

S62
LISSITZYN O.J.,"SOME LEGAL IMPLICATIONS OF THE U-2 AND RB-47 INCIDENTS." FUT USA+45 USSR WOR+45 AIR NAT/G DIPLOM LEGIT MORAL ORD/FREE SOVEREIGN...JURID GEN/LAWS GEN/METH COLD/WAR 20 U-2. PAGE 90 A1840
LAW CONCPT SPACE INT/LAW

S62
MCWHINNEY E.,"CO-EXISTENCE, THE CUBA CRISIS, AND COLD WAR-INTERNATIONAL WAR." CUBA USA+45 USSR WOR+45 NAT/G TOP/EX BAL/PWR DIPLOM DOMIN LEGIT PEACE RIGID/FLEX ORD/FREE...STERTYP COLD/WAR 20. PAGE 99 A2026
CONCPT INT/LAW

S62
MONNIER J.P.,"LA SUCCESSION D'ETATS EN MATIERE DE RESPONSABILITE INTERNATIONALE." UNIV CONSTN INTELL SOCIETY ADJUD ROUTINE PERCEPT SUPEGO...GEN/LAWS TOT/POP 20. PAGE 103 A2107
NAT/G JURID INT/LAW

S62
MOUSKHELY M.,"LA NAISSANCE DES ETATS EN DROIT INTERNATIONAL PUBLIC." UNIV SOCIETY INT/ORG VOL/ASSN LEGIT ATTIT RIGID/FLEX...JURID TIME/SEQ 20. PAGE 105 A2157
NAT/G STRUCT INT/LAW

S62
VIGNES D.,"L'AUTORITE DES TRAITES INTERNATIONAUX EN DROIT INTERNE." EUR+WWI UNIV LAW CONSTN INTELL NAT/G POL/PAR DIPLOM ATTIT PERCEPT ALL/VALS ...POLICY INT/LAW JURID CONCPT TIME/SEQ 20 TREATY. PAGE 159 A3233
STRUCT LEGIT FRANCE

C62
LILLICH R.B.,"INTERNATIONAL CLAIMS: THEIR ADJUDICATION BY NATIONAL COMMISSIONS." WOR+45 WOR-45 NAT/G ADJUD...JURID BIBLIOG 18/20. PAGE 89 A1817
INT/LAW DIPLOM PROB/SOLV

B63
BAILEY S.D.,THE UNITED NATIONS: A SHORT POLITICAL GUIDE. FUT PROB/SOLV LEAD...INT/LAW 20 UN. PAGE 10 A0207
INT/ORG PEACE DETER DIPLOM

B63
DEENER D.R.,CANADA - UNITED STATES TREATY RELATIONS. CANADA USA+45 USA-45 NAT/G FORCES PLAN PROB/SOLV AGREE NUC/PWR...TREND 18/20 TREATY. PAGE 35 A0722
DIPLOM INT/LAW POLICY

B63
ELLERT R.B.,NATO 'FAIR TRIAL' SAFEGUARDS: PRECURSOR TO AN INTERNATIONAL BILL OF PROCEDURAL RIGHTS. WOR+45 FORCES CRIME CIVMIL/REL ATTIT ORD/FREE 20 NATO. PAGE 41 A0841
JURID INT/LAW INT/ORG CT/SYS

B63
FALK R.A.,LAW, MORALITY, AND WAR IN THE CONTEMPORARY WORLD. WOR+45 LAW INT/ORG EX/STRUC FORCES EDU/PROP LEGIT DETER NUC/PWR MORAL ORD/FREE ...JURID TOT/POP 20. PAGE 43 A0888
ADJUD ARMS/CONT PEACE INT/LAW

B63
HINSLEY F.H.,POWER AND THE PURSUIT OF PEACE. WOR+45 WOR-45 PLAN RIGID/FLEX ALL/VALS ALL/IDEOS...POLICY DECISION INT/LAW 12/20 ROUSSEAU/J KANT/I BENTHAM/J LEAGUE/NAT. PAGE 65 A1338
DIPLOM CONSTN PEACE COERCE

B63
LADOR-LEDERER J.J.,INTERNATIONAL NON-GOVERNMENTAL ORGANIZATIONS: A STUDY IN AUTONOMOUS ORGANIZATION AND IUS GENTIUM. LAW DELIB/GP LEGIS DIPLOM 20. PAGE 83 A1709
INT/ORG INT/LAW INGP/REL VOL/ASSN

B63
LIVNEH E.,ISRAEL LEGAL BIBLIOGRAPHY IN EUROPEAN LANGUAGES. ISRAEL LOC/G JUDGE TAX...INT/LAW 20. PAGE 90 A1846
BIBLIOG LAW NAT/G CONSTN

B63
MCDOUGAL M.S.,LAW AND PUBLIC ORDER IN SPACE. FUT USA+45 ACT/RES TEC/DEV ADJUD...POLICY INT/LAW JURID 20. PAGE 98 A2009
SPACE ORD/FREE DIPLOM DECISION

B63
PACHTER H.M.,COLLISION COURSE; THE CUBAN MISSILE CRISIS AND COEXISTENCE. CUBA USA+45 DIPLOM ARMS/CONT PEACE MARXISM...DECISION INT/LAW 20 COLD/WAR KHRUSH/N KENNEDY/JF CASTRO/F. PAGE 112 A2307
WAR BAL/PWR NUC/PWR DETER

B63
PANAMERICAN UNION,DOCUMENTOS OFICIALES DE LA ORGANIZACION DE LOS ESTADOS AMERICANOS, INDICE Y LISTA (VOL. III, 1962). L/A+17C DELIB/GP INT/TRADE EDU/PROP REGION NUC/PWR...HEAL INT/LAW SOC/WK 20 OAS. PAGE 113 A2329
BIBLIOG INT/ORG DIPLOM

B63
PEREZ ORTIZ R.,ANUARIO BIBLIOGRAFICO COLOMBIANO, 1961. AGRI...INT/LAW JURID SOC LING 20 COLOMB. PAGE 115 A2354
BIBLIOG L/A+17C NAT/G

B63
ROSNER G.,THE UNITED NATIONS EMERGENCY FORCE. FRANCE ISRAEL UAR UK WOR+45 CREATE WAR PEACE ORD/FREE PWR...INT/LAW JURID HIST/WRIT TIME/SEQ UN. PAGE 124 A2539
INT/ORG FORCES

B63
US SENATE,DOCUMENTS ON INTERNATIONAL AS"ECTS OF EXPLORATION AND USE OF OUTER SPACE, 1954-62: STAFF REPORT FOR COMM AERON SPACE SCI. USA+45 USSR LEGIS LEAD CIVMIL/REL PEACE...POLICY INT/LAW ANTHOL 20 CONGRESS NASA KHRUSH/N. PAGE 155 A3165
SPACE UTIL GOV/REL DIPLOM

B63
VAN SLYCK P.,PEACE: THE CONTROL OF NATIONAL POWER. CUBA WOR+45 FINAN NAT/G FORCES PROB/SOLV TEC/DEV BAL/PWR ADMIN CONTROL ORD/FREE...POLICY INT/LAW UN COLD/WAR TREATY. PAGE 158 A3214
ARMS/CONT PEACE INT/ORG DIPLOM

L63
SZASZY E.,"L'EVOLUTION DES PRINCIPES GENERAUX DU DROIT INTERNATIONAL PRIVE DANS LES PAYS DE DEMOCRATIE POPULAIRE." COM FUT WOR+45 LAW ECO/DEV PERF/ART POL/PAR PROF/ORG ECO/TAC INT/TRADE EDU/PROP ATTIT RIGID/FLEX ALL/VALS SOCISM...JURID TREND GEN/LAWS WORK 20. PAGE 141 A2876
DIPLOM TOTALISM INT/LAW INT/ORG

S63
CAHIER P.,"LE DROIT INTERNE DES ORGANISATIONS INTERNATIONALES." UNIV CONSTN SOCIETY ECO/DEV R+D NAT/G TOP/EX LEGIT ATTIT PERCEPT...TIME/SEQ 19/20. PAGE 23 A0464
INT/ORG JURID DIPLOM INT/LAW

S63
FRIEDMANN W.G.,"THE USES OF 'GENERAL PRINCIPLES' IN THE DEVELOPMENT OF INTERNATIONAL LAW." WOR+45 NAT/G DIPLOM INT/TRADE LEGIT ROUTINE RIGID/FLEX ORD/FREE ...JURID CONCPT STERTYP GEN/METH 20. PAGE 49 A1005
LAW INT/LAW INT/ORG

S63
MACWHINNEY E.,"LES CONCEPT SOVIETIQUE DE 'COEXISTENCE PACIFIQUE' ET LES RAPPORTS JURIDIQUES ENTRE L'URSS ET LES ETATS OCIDENTAUX." COM FUT WOR+45 LAW CULTURE INTELL POL/PAR ACT/RES BAL/PWR ...INT/LAW 20. PAGE 93 A1903
NAT/G CONCPT DIPLOM USSR

S63
MEYROWITZ H.,"LES JURISTES DEVANT L'ARME NUCLAIRE." FUT WOR+45 INTELL SOCIETY BAL/PWR DETER WAR...JURID CONCPT 20. PAGE 100 A2058
ACT/RES ADJUD INT/LAW NUC/PWR

S63
MODELSKI G.,"STUDY OF ALLIANCES." WOR+45 WOR-45 INT/ORG NAT/G FORCES LEGIT ADMIN CHOOSE ALL/VALS PWR SKILL...INT/LAW CONCPT GEN/LAWS 20 TREATY. PAGE 102 A2099
VOL/ASSN CON/ANAL DIPLOM

S63
TALLON D.,"L'ETUDE DU DROIT COMPARE COMME MOYEN DE RECHERCHER LES MATIERES SUSCEPTIBLES D'UNIFICATION INTERNATIONALE." WOR+45 LAW SOCIETY VOL/ASSN CONSULT LEGIT CT/SYS RIGID/FLEX KNOWL 20. PAGE 141 A2884
INT/ORG JURID INT/LAW

S63
WALKER H.,"THE INTERNATIONAL LAW OF COMMODITY AGREEMENTS." FUT WOR+45 ECO/DEV ECO/UNDEV FINAN INT/ORG NAT/G CONSULT CREATE PLAN ECO/TAC ATTIT PERCEPT...CONCPT GEN/LAWS TOT/POP GATT 20. PAGE 160 A3265
MARKET VOL/ASSN INT/LAW INT/TRADE

S63
WENGLER W.,"LES CONFLITS DE LOIS ET LE PRINCIPE D'EGALITE." UNIV LAW SOCIETY ACT/RES LEGIT ATTIT PERCEPT 20. PAGE 163 A3318
JURID CONCPT INT/LAW

C63
ATTIA G.E.O.,"LES FORCES ARMEES DES NATIONS UNIES EN COREE ET AU MOYENORIENT." KOREA CONSTN DELIB/GP LEGIS PWR...IDEA/COMP NAT/COMP BIBLIOG UN SUEZ. PAGE 10 A0194
FORCES NAT/G INT/LAW

B64
AHLUWALIA K.,THE LEGAL STATUS, PRIVILEGES AND IMMUNITIES OF SPECIALIZED AGENCIES OF UN AND CERTAIN OTHER INTERNATIONAL ORGANIZATIONS. WOR+45 LAW CONSULT DELIB/GP FORCES. PAGE 5 A0102
PRIVIL DIPLOM INT/ORG INT/LAW

B64
COHEN M.,LAW AND POLITICS IN SPACE: SPECIFIC AND URGENT PROBLEMS IN THE LAW OF OUTER SPACE. CHINA/COM COM USA+45 USSR WOR+45 COM/IND INT/ORG NAT/G LEGIT NUC/PWR ATTIT BIO/SOC...JURID CONCPT CONGRESS 20 STALIN/J. PAGE 28 A0561
DELIB/GP LAW INT/LAW SPACE

B64
COHEN M.L.,SELECTED BIBLIOGRAPHY OF FOREIGN AND INTERNATIONAL LAW....IDEA/COMP METH/COMP 20. PAGE 28 A0562
BIBLIOG/A JURID LAW INT/LAW

B64
CURRIE D.P.,FEDERALISM AND THE NEW NATIONS OF AFRICA. CANADA USA+45 INT/TRADE TAX GP/REL ...NAT/COMP SOC/INTEG 20. PAGE 33 A0667
FEDERAL AFR ECO/UNDEV INT/LAW

B64
DIAS R.W.M.,A BIBLIOGRAPHY OF JURISPRUDENCE (2ND ED.). VOL/ASSN LEGIS ADJUD CT/SYS OWN...INT/LAW 18/20. PAGE 37 A0754
BIBLIOG/A JURID LAW CONCPT

B64
ECONOMIDES C.P.,LE POUVOIR DE DECISION DES ORGANISATIONS INTERNATIONALES EUROPEENNES. DIPLOM DOMIN INGP/REL EFFICIENCY...INT/LAW JURID 20 NATO OEEC EEC COUNCL/EUR EURATOM. PAGE 40 A0821
INT/ORG PWR DECISION GP/COMP

B64
FALK R.A.,THE ROLE OF DOMESTIC COURTS IN THE INTERNATIONAL LEGAL ORDER. FUT WOR+45 INT/ORG NAT/G JUDGE EDU/PROP LEGIT CT/SYS...POLICY RELATIV JURID CONCPT GEN/LAWS 20. PAGE 43 A0889
LAW INT/LAW

B64
FRIEDMANN W.G.,THE CHANGING STRUCTURE OF INTERNATIONAL LAW. WOR+45 INT/ORG NAT/G PROVS LEGIT ORD/FREE PWR...JURID CONCPT GEN/LAWS TOT/POP UN 20. PAGE 49 A1006
ADJUD TREND INT/LAW

B64
FRYDENSBERG P.,PEACE-KEEPING: EXPERIENCE AND EVALUATION: THE OSLO PAPERS. NORWAY FORCES PLAN CONTROL...INT/LAW 20 UN. PAGE 49 A1012
INT/ORG DIPLOM PEACE COERCE

B64
GESELLSCHAFT RECHTSVERGLEICH,BIBLIOGRAPHIE DES DEUTSCHEN RECHTS (BIBLIOGRAPHY OF GERMAN LAW, TRANS. BY COURTLAND PETERSON). GERMANY FINAN INDUS LABOR SECT FORCES CT/SYS PARL/PROC CRIME...INT/LAW SOC NAT/COMP 20. PAGE 52 A1066
BIBLIOG/A JURID CONSTN ADMIN

B64
GRZYBOWSKI K.,THE SOCIALIST COMMONWEALTH OF NATIONS: ORGANIZATIONS AND INSTITUTIONS. FORCES DIPLOM INT/TRADE ADJUD ADMIN LEAD WAR MARXISM SOCISM...BIBLIOG 20 COMECON WARSAW/P. PAGE 58 A1185
INT/LAW COM REGION INT/ORG

B64
HARMON R.B.,BIBLIOGRAPHY OF BIBLIOGRAPHIES IN POLITICAL SCIENCE (MIMEOGRAPHED PAPER: LIMITED EDITION). WOR+45 WOR-45 INT/ORG POL/PAR GOV/REL ALL/IDEOS...INT/LAW JURID MGT 19/20. PAGE 61 A1260
BIBLIOG NAT/G DIPLOM LOC/G

B64
KULSKI W.W.,INTERNATIONAL POLITICS IN A REVOLUTIONARY AGE. NEUTRAL NAT/LISM...POLICY DECISION INT/LAW CONCPT 20 UN. PAGE 83 A1693
DIPLOM WAR NUC/PWR INT/ORG

B64
MCWHINNEY E.,"PEACEFUL COEXISTENCE" AND SOVIET-WESTERN INTERNATIONAL LAW. USSR DIPLOM LEAD...JURID 20 COLD/WAR. PAGE 99 A2027
PEACE IDEA/COMP INT/LAW ATTIT

B64
NICE R.W.,TREASURY OF LAW. WOR+45 WOR-45 SECT ADJUD MORAL ORD/FREE...INT/LAW JURID PHIL/SCI ANTHOL. PAGE 108 A2227
LAW WRITING PERS/REL DIPLOM

B64
REGALA R.,WORLD PEACE THROUGH DIPLOMACY AND LAW. S/ASIA WOR+45 ECO/UNDEV INT/ORG FORCES PLAN PROB/SOLV FOR/AID NUC/PWR WAR...POLICY INT/LAW 20. PAGE 120 A2456
DIPLOM PEACE ADJUD

B64
ROBERTS HL,FOREIGN AFFAIRS BIBLIOGRAPHY, 1952-1962. ECO/DEV SECT PLAN FOR/AID INT/TRADE ARMS/CONT NAT/LISM ATTIT...INT/LAW GOV/COMP IDEA/COMP 20. PAGE 122 A2495
BIBLIOG/A DIPLOM INT/ORG WAR

B64
RUSSELL R.B.,UNITED NATIONS EXPERIENCE WITH MILITARY FORCES: POLITICAL AND LEGAL ASPECTS. AFR KOREA WOR+45 LEGIS PROB/SOLV ADMIN CONTROL EFFICIENCY PEACE...POLICY INT/LAW BIBLIOG UN. PAGE 126 A2576
FORCES DIPLOM SANCTION ORD/FREE

B64
SCHECHTER A.H.,INTERPRETATION OF AMBIGUOUS DOCUMENTS BY INTERNATIONAL ADMINISTRATIVE TRIBUNALS. WOR+45 EX/STRUC INT/TRADE CT/SYS SOVEREIGN 20 UN ILO EURCT/JUST. PAGE 128 A2620
INT/LAW DIPLOM INT/ORG ADJUD

B64
SCHWELB E.,HUMAN RIGHTS AND THE INTERNATIONAL COMMUNITY. WOR+45 WOR-45 NAT/G SECT DELIB/GP DIPLOM PEACE RESPECT TREATY 20 UN. PAGE 130 A2666
INT/ORG ORD/FREE INT/LAW

B64
SEGAL R.,SANCTIONS AGAINST SOUTH AFRICA. AFR SOUTH/AFR NAT/G INT/TRADE RACE/REL PEACE PWR ...INT/LAW ANTHOL 20 UN. PAGE 131 A2681
SANCTION DISCRIM ECO/TAC POLICY

B64
STANGER R.J.,ESSAYS ON INTERVENTION. PLAN PROB/SOLV BAL/PWR ADJUD COERCE WAR ROLE PWR...INT/LAW CONCPT 20 UN INTERVENT. PAGE 137 A2803
SOVEREIGN DIPLOM POLICY LEGIT

B64
SZLADITS C.,BIBLIOGRAPHY ON FOREIGN AND COMPARATIVE LAW: BOOKS AND ARTICLES IN ENGLISH (SUPPLEMENT 1962). FINAN INDUS JUDGE LICENSE ADMIN CT/SYS PARL/PROC OWN...INT/LAW CLASSIF METH/COMP NAT/COMP 20. PAGE 141 A2877
BIBLIOG/A JURID ADJUD LAW

B64
TAYLOR E.,RICHER BY ASIA. S/ASIA CULTURE VOL/ASSN ACT/RES ATTIT DISPL PERSON ALL/VALS...INT/LAW MYTH SELF/OBS 20. PAGE 142 A2899
SOCIETY RIGID/FLEX INDIA

B64
THANT U.,TOWARD WORLD PEACE. DELIB/GP TEC/DEV EDU/PROP WAR SOVEREIGN...INT/LAW 20 UN MID/EAST. PAGE 142 A2907
DIPLOM BIOG PEACE COERCE

B64
TONG T.,UNITED STATES DIPLOMACY IN CHINA, 1844-1860. ASIA USA-45 ECO/UNDEV ECO/TAC COERCE GP/REL...INT/LAW 19 TREATY. PAGE 144 A2949
DIPLOM INT/TRADE COLONIAL

B64
UN PUB. INFORM. ORGAN.,EVERY MAN'S UNITED NATIONS. UNIV WOR+45 CONSTN CULTURE SOCIETY ECO/DEV ECO/UNDEV NAT/G ACT/RES PLAN ECO/TAC INT/TRADE EDU/PROP LEGIT PEACE ATTIT ALL/VALS...POLICY HUM INT/LAW CONCPT CHARTS UN TOT/POP 20. PAGE 147 A3004
INT/ORG ROUTINE

B64
VECCHIO G.D.,L'ETAT ET LE DROIT. ITALY CONSTN EX/STRUC LEGIS DIPLOM CT/SYS...JURID 20 UN. PAGE 158 A3225
NAT/G SOVEREIGN CONCPT INT/LAW

B64
WILLIAMS S.P.,TOWARD A GENUINE WORLD SECURITY SYSTEM (PAMPHLET). WOR+45 INT/ORG FORCES PLAN NUC/PWR ORD/FREE...INT/LAW CONCPT UN PRESIDENT. PAGE 165 A3353
BIBLIOG/A ARMS/CONT DIPLOM PEACE

S64
BARKUN M.,"CONFLICT RESOLUTION THROUGH IMPLICIT MEDIATION." UNIV BARGAIN CONSEN FEDERAL JURID. PAGE 11 A0222
CONSULT CENTRAL INT/LAW IDEA/COMP

S64
CARNEGIE ENDOWMENT INT. PEACE,"HUMAN RIGHTS (ISSUES BEFORE THE NINETEENTH GENERAL ASSEMBLY)." AFR WOR+45 LAW CONSTN NAT/G EDU/PROP GP/REL DISCRIM PEACE ATTIT MORAL ORD/FREE...INT/LAW PSY CONCPT RECORD UN 20. PAGE 24 A0492
INT/ORG PERSON RACE/REL

S64
CARNEGIE ENDOWMENT INT. PEACE,"LEGAL QUESTIONS (ISSUES BEFORE THE NINETEENTH GENERAL ASSEMBLY)." WOR+45 CONSTN NAT/G DELIB/GP ADJUD PEACE MORAL ORD/FREE...RECORD UN 20 TREATY. PAGE 24 A0494
INT/ORG LAW INT/LAW

S64
COHEN M.,"BASIC PRINCIPLES OF INTERNATIONAL LAW." UNIV WOR+45 WOR-45 BAL/PWR LEGIT ADJUD WAR ATTIT MORAL ORD/FREE PWR...JURID CONCPT MYTH TOT/POP 20. PAGE 27 A0560
INT/ORG INT/LAW

S64
CRANE R.D.,"BASIC PRINCIPLES IN SOVIET SPACE LAW." FUT WOR+45 AIR INT/ORG DIPLOM DOMIN ARMS/CONT COERCE NUC/PWR PEACE ATTIT DRIVE PWR...INT/LAW METH/CNCPT NEW/IDEA OBS TREND GEN/LAWS VAL/FREE MARX/KARL 20. PAGE 32 A0659
COM LAW USSR SPACE

S64
GINSBURGS G.,"WARS OF NATIONAL LIBERATION - THE SOVIET THESIS." COM USSR WOR+45 WOR-45 LAW CULTURE INT/ORG DIPLOM LEGIT COLONIAL GUERRILLA WAR NAT/LISM ATTIT PERSON MORAL PWR...JURID OBS TREND MARX/KARL 20. PAGE 53 A1075
COERCE CONCPT INT/LAW REV

S64
KARPOV P.V.,"PEACEFUL COEXISTENCE AND INTERNATIONAL LAW." WOR+45 LAW SOCIETY INT/ORG VOL/ASSN FORCES CREATE CAP/ISM DIPLOM ADJUD NUC/PWR PEACE MORAL ORD/FREE PWR MARXISM...MARXIST JURID CONCPT OBS TREND COLD/WAR MARX/KARL 20. PAGE 77 A1568
COM ATTIT INT/LAW USSR

S64
KUNZ J.,"THE CHANGING SCIENCE OF INTERNATIONAL LAW." FUT WOR+45 WOR-45 INT/ORG LEGIT ORD/FREE ...JURID TIME/SEQ GEN/LAWS 20. PAGE 83 A1696
ADJUD CONCPT INT/LAW

S64
LIPSON L.,"PEACEFUL COEXISTENCE." COM USSR WOR+45 LAW INT/ORG DIPLOM LEGIT ADJUD ORD/FREE...CONCPT OBS TREND GEN/LAWS VAL/FREE COLD/WAR 20. PAGE 90 A1834
ATTIT JURID INT/LAW PEACE

S64
MAGGS P.B.,"SOVIET VIEWPOINT ON NUCLEAR WEAPONS IN INTERNATIONAL LAW." USSR WOR+45 INT/ORG FORCES DIPLOM ARMS/CONT ATTIT ORD/FREE PWR...POLICY JURID CONCPT OBS TREND CON/ANAL GEN/LAWS VAL/FREE 20. PAGE 93 A1905
COM LAW INT/LAW NUC/PWR

S64
SCHWELB E.,"OPERATION OF THE EUROPEAN CONVENTION ON HUMAN RIGHTS." EUR+WWI LAW SOCIETY CREATE EDU/PROP ADJUD ADMIN PEACE ATTIT ORD/FREE PWR...POLICY INT/LAW CONCPT OBS GEN/LAWS UN VAL/FREE ILO 20 ECHR. PAGE 130 A2665
INT/ORG MORAL

S64
SINGH N.,"THE CONTEMPORARY PRACTICE OF INDIA IN THE FIELD OF INTERNATIONAL LAW." INDIA S/ASIA INT/ORG NAT/G DOMIN EDU/PROP LEGIT KNOWL...CONCPT TOT/POP 20. PAGE 133 A2734
LAW ATTIT DIPLOM INT/LAW

S64
SKUBISZEWSKI K.,"FORMS OF PARTICIPATION OF INTERNATIONAL ORGANIZATION IN THE LAW MAKING PROCESS." FUT WOR+45 NAT/G DELIB/GP DOMIN LEGIT KNOWL PWR...JURID TREND 20. PAGE 134 A2740
INT/ORG LAW INT/LAW

S64
TRISKA J.F.,"SOVIET TREATY LAW: A QUANTITATIVE ANALYSIS." WOR+45 LAW ECO/UNDEV AGRI COM/IND INDUS CREATE TEC/DEV DIPLOM ATTIT PWR WEALTH...JURID SAMP TIME/SEQ TREND CHARTS VAL/FREE 20 TREATY. PAGE 145 A2967
COM ECO/TAC INT/LAW USSR

B65
FALK R.A.,THE AFTERMATH OF SABBATINO: BACKGROUND PAPERS AND PROCEEDINGS OF SEVENTH HAMMARSKJOLD FORUM. USA+45 LAW ACT/RES ADJUD ROLE...BIBLIOG 20 EXPROPRIAT SABBATINO HARLAN/JM. PAGE 44 A0891
SOVEREIGN CT/SYS INT/LAW OWN

B65
FORGAC A.A.,NEW DIPLOMACY AND THE UNITED NATIONS. FRANCE GERMANY UK USSR INT/ORG DELIB/GP EX/STRUC PEACE...INT/LAW CONCPT UN. PAGE 47 A0965
DIPLOM ETIQUET NAT/G

B65
INTERNATIONAL SOCIAL SCI COUN,SOCIAL SCIENCES IN THE USSR. USSR ECO/DEV AGRI FINAN INDUS PLAN CAP/ISM...INT/LAW PHIL/SCI PSY SOC 20. PAGE 71 A1460
BIBLIOG/A ACT/RES MARXISM JURID

B65
KAHN H.,ON ESCALATION; METAPHORS AND SCENARIOS. FORCES DIPLOM ARMS/CONT WAR CIVMIL/REL...INT/LAW 20. PAGE 76 A1548
NUC/PWR ACT/RES INT/ORG ORD/FREE

B65
LARUS J.,COMPARATIVE WORLD POLITICS. ASIA INDIA WOR+45 WOR-45 BAL/PWR WAR PEACE RATIONAL MORAL PWR ...REALPOL INT/LAW MUSLIM. PAGE 85 A1735
GOV/COMP IDEA/COMP DIPLOM NAT/COMP

B65
MONCONDUIT F.,LA COMMISSION EUROPEENNE DES DROITS DE L'HOMME. DIPLOM AGREE GP/REL ORD/FREE PWR ...BIBLIOG 20 TREATY. PAGE 102 A2103
INT/LAW INT/ORG ADJUD JURID

B65
MOODY M.,CATALOG OF INTERNATIONAL LAW AND RELATIONS (20 VOLS.). WOR+45 INT/ORG NAT/G ADJUD ADMIN CT/SYS POLICY. PAGE 103 A2117
BIBLIOG INT/LAW DIPLOM

B65
MOSTECKY V.,SOVIET LEGAL BIBLIOGRAPHY. USSR LEGIS PRESS WRITING CONFER ADJUD CT/SYS REV MARXISM ...INT/LAW JURID DICTIONARY 20. PAGE 105 A2155
BIBLIOG/A LAW COM CONSTN

B65
RUBINSTEIN A.,THE CHALLENGE OF POLITICS: IDEAS AND ISSUES. BAL/PWR COLONIAL WAR TOTALISM ORD/FREE PWR MARXISM SOCISM...INT/LAW 20. PAGE 125 A2561
NAT/G SOVEREIGN DIPLOM NAT/LISM

B65
SEABURY P.,BALANCE OF POWER. INT/ORG DETER PEACE ATTIT...INT/LAW. PAGE 131 A2677
BAL/PWR DIPLOM WAR

B65
SHUKRI A.,THE CONCEPT OF SELF-DETERMINATION IN THE UNITED NATIONS. WOR+45 DIPLOM INT/TRADE SANCTION NAT/LISM...BIBLIOG 20 UN. PAGE 132 A2709
COLONIAL INT/ORG INT/LAW SOVEREIGN

B65
STOETZER O.C.,THE ORGANIZATION OF AMERICAN STATES. L/A+17C EX/STRUC FOR/AID CONFER PARL/PROC ORD/FREE SOVEREIGN...POLICY INT/LAW 20 OAS. PAGE 138 A2831
INT/ORG REGION DIPLOM BAL/PWR

B65
THOMAS A.V.,NONINTERVENTION: THE LAW AND ITS IMPORT IN THE AMERICAS. L/A+17C USA+45 USA-45 WOR+45 DIPLOM ADJUD...JURID IDEA/COMP 20 UN INTERVENT. PAGE 143 A2920
INT/LAW PWR COERCE

B65
UNESCO,INTERNATIONAL ORGANIZATIONS IN THE SOCIAL SCIENCES(REV. ED.). LAW ADMIN ATTIT...CRIMLGY GEOG INT/LAW PSY SOC STAT 20 UNESCO. PAGE 148 A3024
INT/ORG R+D PROF/ORG ACT/RES

B65
UNIVERSAL REFERENCE SYSTEM,INTERNATIONAL AFFAIRS: VOLUME I IN THE POLITICAL SCIENCE, GOVERNMENT, AND PUBLIC POLICY SERIES....DECISION ECOMETRIC GEOG INT/LAW JURID MGT PHIL/SCI PSY SOC. PAGE 149 A3041
BIBLIOG/A GEN/METH COMPUT/IR DIPLOM

B65
VON GLAHN G.,LAW AMONG NATIONS: AN INTRODUCTION TO PUBLIC INTERNATIONAL LAW. WOR+45 WOR-45 INT/ORG NAT/G CREATE ADJUD WAR...GEOG CLASSIF TREND BIBLIOG. PAGE 160 A3250
ACADEM INT/LAW GEN/LAWS LAW

B65
VONGLAHN G.,LAW AMONG NATIONS: AN INTRODUCTION TO PUBLIC INTERNATIONAL LAW. UNIV WOR+45 LAW INT/ORG NAT/G LEGIT EXEC RIGID/FLEX...CONCPT TIME/SEQ GEN/LAWS UN TOT/POP 20. PAGE 160 A3253
CONSTN JURID INT/LAW

B65
WEIL G.L.,A HANDBOOK ON THE EUROPEAN ECONOMIC COMMUNITY. BELGIUM EUR+WWI FRANCE GERMANY/W ITALY CONSTN ECO/DEV CREATE PARTIC GP/REL...DECISION MGT CHARTS 20 EEC. PAGE 162 A3299
INT/TRADE INT/ORG TEC/DEV INT/LAW

B65
WHITE G.M.,THE USE OF EXPERTS BY INTERNATIONAL TRIBUNALS. WOR+45 WOR-45 INT/ORG NAT/G PAY ADJUD COST...OBS BIBLIOG 20. PAGE 164 A3334
INT/LAW ROUTINE CONSULT CT/SYS

L65
RUBIN A.P.,"UNITED STATES CONTEMPORARY PRACTICE RELATING TO INTERNATIONAL LAW." USA+45 WOR+45 CONSTN INT/ORG NAT/G DELIB/GP EX/STRUC DIPLOM DOMIN CT/SYS ROUTINE ORD/FREE...CONCPT COLD/WAR 20. PAGE 125 A2558
LAW LEGIT INT/LAW

S65
AMRAM P.W.,"REPORT ON THE TENTH SESSION OF THE HAGUE CONFERENCE ON PRIVATE INTERNATIONAL LAW." USA+45 WOR+45 INT/ORG CREATE LEGIT ADJUD ALL/VALS ...JURID CONCPT METH/CNCPT OBS GEN/METH 20. PAGE 8 A0155
VOL/ASSN DELIB/GP INT/LAW

S65
FALK R.A.,"INTERNATIONAL LEGAL ORDER." USA+45 INTELL FACE/GP INT/ORG LEGIT KNOWL...CONCPT METH/CNCPT STYLE RECORD GEN/METH 20. PAGE 44 A0890
ATTIT GEN/LAWS INT/LAW

S65
GROSS L.,"PROBLEMS OF INTERNATIONAL ADJUDICATION AND COMPLIANCE WITH INTERNATIONAL LAW: SOME SIMPLE SOLUTIONS." WOR+45 SOCIETY NAT/G DOMIN LEGIT ADJUD CT/SYS RIGID/FLEX HEALTH PWR...JURID NEW/IDEA COLD/WAR 20. PAGE 57 A1177
LAW METH/CNCPT INT/LAW

S65
MERRITT R.L.,"SELECTED ARTICLES AND DOCUMENTS ON INTERNATIONAL LAW AND RELATIONS." WOR+45 INT/ORG FORCES INT/TRADE. PAGE 100 A2045
BIBLIOG DIPLOM INT/LAW GOV/REL

S65
STEIN E.,"TOWARD SUPREMACY OF TREATY-CONSTITUTION BY JUDICIAL FIAT: ON THE MARGIN OF THE COSTA CASE." EUR+WWI ITALY WOR+45 INT/ORG NAT/G LEGIT REGION NAT/LISM PWR...JURID CONCPT TREND TOT/POP VAL/FREE 20. PAGE 138 A2816
ADJUD CONSTN SOVEREIGN INT/LAW

C65
SCHEINGOLD S.A.,"THE RULE OF LAW IN EUROPEAN INTEGRATION: THE PATH OF THE SCHUMAN PLAN." EUR+WWI JUDGE ADJUD FEDERAL ATTIT PWR...RECORD INT BIBLIOG EEC ECSC. PAGE 128 A2621
INT/LAW CT/SYS REGION CENTRAL

C65
SEARA M.V.,"COSMIC INTERNATIONAL LAW." LAW ACADEM ACT/RES DIPLOM COLONIAL CONTROL NUC/PWR SOVEREIGN ...GEN/LAWS BIBLIOG UN. PAGE 131 A2678
SPACE INT/LAW IDEA/COMP INT/ORG

B66
AMERICAN JOURNAL COMP LAW,THE AMERICAN JOURNAL OF COMPARATIVE LAW READER. EUR+WWI USA+45 USA-45 LAW CONSTN LOC/G MUNIC NAT/G DIPLOM...ANTHOL 20 SUPREME/CT EURCT/JUST. PAGE 7 A0151
IDEA/COMP JURID INT/LAW CT/SYS

B66
ASAMOAH O.Y.,THE LEGAL SIGNIFICANCE OF THE DECLARATIONS OF THE GENERAL ASSEMBLY OF THE UNITED NATIONS. WOR+45 CREATE CONTROL...BIBLIOG 20 UN. PAGE 9 A0184
INT/LAW INT/ORG DIPLOM

B66
BROWNLIE I.,PRINCIPLES OF PUBLIC INTERNATIONAL LAW. WOR+45 WOR-45 LAW JUDGE REPAR ADJUD SOVEREIGN ...JURID T. PAGE 20 A0409
INT/LAW DIPLOM INT/ORG

B66
CLARK G.,WORLD PEACE THROUGH WORLD LAW; TWO ALTERNATIVE PLANS. WOR+45 DELIB/GP FORCES TAX CONFER ADJUD SANCTION ARMS/CONT WAR CHOOSE PRIVIL 20 UN COLD/WAR. PAGE 27 A0541
INT/LAW PEACE PLAN INT/ORG

B66
COPLIN W.D.,THE FUNCTIONS OF INTERNATIONAL LAW. WOR+45 ECO/DEV ECO/UNDEV ADJUD COLONIAL WAR OWN SOVEREIGN...POLICY GEN/LAWS 20. PAGE 30 A0611
INT/LAW DIPLOM INT/ORG

B66
COUNCIL OF EUROPE,EUROPEAN CONVENTION ON HUMAN RIGHTS - COLLECTED TEXTS (5TH ED.). EUR+WWI DIPLOM ADJUD CT/SYS...INT/LAW 20 ECHR. PAGE 31 A0638
ORD/FREE DELIB/GP INT/ORG JURID

B66
EDWARDS C.D.,TRADE REGULATIONS OVERSEAS. IRELAND NEW/ZEALND SOUTH/AFR NAT/G CAP/ISM TARIFFS CONTROL ...POLICY JURID 20 EEC CHINJAP. PAGE 40 A0823
INT/TRADE DIPLOM INT/LAW ECO/TAC

B66
HARMON R.B.,SOURCES AND PROBLEMS OF BIBLIOGRAPHY IN POLITICAL SCIENCE (PAMPHLET). INT/ORG LOC/G MUNIC POL/PAR ADMIN GOV/REL ALL/IDEOS...JURID MGT CONCPT 19/20. PAGE 61 A1262
BIBLIOG DIPLOM INT/LAW NAT/G

B66
HAY P.,FEDERALISM AND SUPRANATIONAL ORGANIZATIONS: PATTERNS FOR NEW LEGAL STRUCTURES. EUR+WWI LAW NAT/G VOL/ASSN DIPLOM PWR...NAT/COMP TREATY EEC. PAGE 63 A1294
SOVEREIGN FEDERAL INT/ORG INT/LAW

B66
HENKYS R.,DEUTSCHLAND UND DIE OSTLICHEN NACHBARN. GERMANY POLAND NAT/G POL/PAR INGP/REL ATTIT 20
GP/REL JURID

MIGRATION. PAGE 64 A1317 INT/LAW DIPLOM

B66
HOEVELER H.J.,INTERNATIONALE BEKAMPFUNG DES VERBRECHENS. AUSTRIA SWITZERLND WOR+45 INT/ORG CONTROL BIO/SOC...METH/COMP NAT/COMP 20 MAFIA SCOT/YARD FBI. PAGE 66 A1352 CRIMLGY CRIME DIPLOM INT/LAW

B66
LALL A.,MODERN INTERNATIONAL NEGOTIATION: PRINCIPLES AND PRACTICE. WOR+45 INT/ORG DELIB/GP PROB/SOLV DETER...INT/LAW TREATY. PAGE 84 A1712 DIPLOM ECO/TAC ATTIT

B66
LEE L.T.,VIENNA CONVENTION ON CONSULAR RELATIONS. WOR+45 LAW INT/ORG CONFER GP/REL PRIVIL...INT/LAW 20 TREATY VIENNA/CNV. PAGE 86 A1760 AGREE DIPLOM ADMIN

B66
MCKAY V.,AFRICAN DIPLOMACY STUDIES IN THE DETERMINANTS OF FOREIGN POLICY. AFR SOUTH/AFR CULTURE NEUTRAL REGION SOVEREIGN...INT/LAW GOV/COMP ANTHOL 20. PAGE 98 A2013 ECO/UNDEV RACE/REL CIVMIL/REL DIPLOM

B66
NANTWI E.K.,THE ENFORCEMENT OF INTERNATIONAL JUDICIAL DECISIONS AND ARBITAL AWARDS IN PUBLIC INTERNATIONAL LAW. WOR+45 WOR-45 JUDGE PROB/SOLV DIPLOM CT/SYS SUPEGO MORAL PWR RESPECT...METH/CNCPT 18/20 CASEBOOK. PAGE 107 A2196 INT/LAW ADJUD SOVEREIGN INT/ORG

B66
OLSON W.C.,THE THEORY AND PRACTICE OF INTERNATIONAL RELATIONS (2ND ED.). WOR+45 LEAD SUPEGO...INT/LAW PHIL/SCI. PAGE 112 A2290 DIPLOM NAT/G INT/ORG POLICY

B66
POLLACK R.S.,THE INDIVIDUAL'S RIGHTS AND INTERNATIONAL ORGANIZATION. LAW INT/ORG DELIB/GP SUPEGO...JURID SOC/INTEG 20 TREATY UN. PAGE 117 A2394 INT/LAW ORD/FREE DIPLOM PERSON

B66
SALTER L.M.,RESOLUTION OF INTERNATIONAL CONFLICT. USA+45 INT/ORG SECT DIPLOM ECO/TAC FOR/AID DETER NUC/PWR WAR 20. PAGE 127 A2595 PROB/SOLV PEACE INT/LAW POLICY

B66
SZLADITS C.,A BIBLIOGRAPHY ON FOREIGN AND COMPARATIVE LAW (SUPPLEMENT 1964). FINAN FAM LABOR LG/CO LEGIS JUDGE ADMIN CRIME...CRIMLGY 20. PAGE 141 A2878 BIBLIOG/A CT/SYS INT/LAW

B66
VAN DYKE V.,INTERNATIONAL POLITICS. WOR+45 ECO/DEV ECO/UNDEV INT/ORG BAL/PWR AGREE ARMS/CONT NAT/LISM PEACE PWR...INT/LAW 20 TREATY UN. PAGE 158 A3212 DIPLOM NAT/G WAR SOVEREIGN

B66
WELCH C.E.,DREAM OF UNITY; PAN-AFRICANISM AND POLITICAL UNIFICATION IN WEST AFRICA. AFR ECO/UNDEV CONFER COLONIAL LEAD...INT/LAW 20. PAGE 163 A3312 INT/ORG REGION NAT/LISM DIPLOM

L66
SEYLER W.C.,"DOCTORAL DISSERTATIONS IN POLITICAL SCIENCE IN UNIVERSITIES OF THE UNITED STATES AND CANADA." INT/ORG LOC/G ADMIN...INT/LAW MGT GOV/COMP. PAGE 131 A2690 BIBLIOG LAW NAT/G

S66
CHIU H.,"COMMUNIST CHINA'S ATTITUDE TOWARD INTERNATIONAL LAW" CHINA/COM USSR LAW CONSTN DIPLOM GP/REL 20 LENIN/VI. PAGE 26 A0532 INT/LAW MARXISM CONCPT IDEA/COMP

S66
DUROSELLE J.B.,"THE FUTURE OF THE ATLANTIC COMMUNITY." EUR+WWI USA+45 USSR NAT/G CAP/ISM REGION DETER NUC/PWR ATTIT MARXISM...INT/LAW 20 NATO. PAGE 40 A0811 FUT DIPLOM MYTH POLICY

S66
GREEN L.C.,"RHODESIAN OIL: BOOTLEGGERS OR PIRATES?" AFR RHODESIA UK WOR+45 INT/ORG NAT/G DIPLOM LEGIT COLONIAL SOVEREIGN 20 UN OAU. PAGE 55 A1139 INT/TRADE SANCTION INT/LAW POLICY

C66
BLAISDELL D.C.,"INTERNATIONAL ORGANIZATION." FUT WOR+45 ECO/DEV DELIB/GP FORCES EFFICIENCY PEACE ORD/FREE...INT/LAW 20 UN LEAGUE/NAT NATO. PAGE 15 A0304 BIBLIOG INT/ORG DIPLOM ARMS/CONT

C66
ZAWODNY J.K.,"GUIDE TO THE STUDY OF INTERNATIONAL RELATIONS." OP/RES PRESS...STAT INT 20. PAGE 169 A3449 BIBLIOG/A DIPLOM INT/LAW INT/ORG

B67
BLOM-COOPER L.,THE LITERATURE OF THE LAW AND THE LANGUAGE OF THE LAW (2 VOLS.). CANADA ISRAEL UK WOR+45 WOR-45 JUDGE CT/SYS ATTIT...CRIMLGY JURID ANTHOL CMN/WLTH. PAGE 15 A0312 BIBLIOG LAW INT/LAW ADJUD

B67
BURNS E.L.M.,MEGAMURDER. WOR+45 LAW INT/ORG NAT/G BAL/PWR DIPLOM DETER MURDER WEAPON CIVMIL/REL PEACE ...INT/LAW TREND 20. PAGE 22 A0444 FORCES PLAN WAR NUC/PWR

B67
HOLSTI K.J.,INTERNATIONAL POLITICS* A FRAMEWORK FOR ANALYSIS. WOR+45 WOR-45 NAT/G EDU/PROP DETER WAR WEAPON PWR BIBLIOG. PAGE 67 A1372 DIPLOM BARGAIN POLICY INT/LAW

B67
LAWYERS COMM AMER POLICY VIET,VIETNAM AND INTERNATIONAL LAW: AN ANALYSIS OF THE LEGALITY OF THE US MILITARY INVOLVEMENT. VIETNAM LAW INT/ORG COERCE WEAPON PEACE ORD/FREE 20 UN SEATO TREATY. PAGE 86 A1753 INT/LAW DIPLOM ADJUD WAR

B67
ROBINSON R.D.,INTERNATIONAL MANAGEMENT. USA+45 FINAN R+D PLAN PRODUC...DECISION T. PAGE 92 A1882 INT/TRADE MGT INT/LAW MARKET

B67
PIPER D.C.,THE INTERNATIONAL LAW OF THE GREAT LAKES. CANADA EXTR/IND MUNIC LICENSE ARMS/CONT CRIME...GEOG 19/20. PAGE 116 A2381 CONCPT DIPLOM INT/LAW

B67
POGANY A.H.,POLITICAL SCIENCE AND INTERNATIONAL RELATIONS, BOOKS RECOMMENDED FOR AMERICAN CATHOLIC COLLEGE LIBRARIES. INT/ORG LOC/G NAT/G FORCES BAL/PWR ECO/TAC NUC/PWR...CATH INT/LAW TREATY 20. PAGE 117 A2393 BIBLIOG DIPLOM

B67
UNIVERSAL REFERENCE SYSTEM,LAW, JURISPRUDENCE, AND JUDICIAL PROCESS (VOLUME VII). WOR+45 WOR-45 CONSTN NAT/G LEGIS JUDGE CT/SYS...INT/LAW COMPUT/IR GEN/METH METH. PAGE 149 A3044 BIBLIOG/A LAW JURID ADJUD

B67
US SENATE COMM AERO SPACE SCI,TREATY ON PRINCIPLES GOVERNING ACTIVITIES OF STATES IN EXPLORATION AND USE OF OUTER SPACE, INCLUDING...BODIES. DELIB/GP FORCES LEGIS DIPLOM...JURID 20 DEPT/STATE NASA DEPT/DEFEN UN. PAGE 155 A3169 SPACE INT/LAW ORD/FREE PEACE

B67
US SENATE COMM ON FOREIGN REL,HUMAN RIGHTS CONVENTIONS. USA+45 LABOR VOL/ASSN DELIB/GP DOMIN ADJUD REPRESENT...INT/LAW MGT CONGRESS. PAGE 156 A3189 LEGIS ORD/FREE WORKER LOBBY

L67
ANAND R.P.,"SOVEREIGN EQUALITY OF STATES IN INTERNATIONAL LAW." UNIV DIPLOM DOMIN CONFER DEBATE SANCTION ATTIT UN. PAGE 8 A0157 INT/LAW INT/ORG CONCPT POLICY

L67
LANDIS E.S.,"THE SOUTH WEST AFRICA CASES* REMAND TO THE UNITED NATIONS." ETHIOPIA LIBERIA SOUTH/AFR BAL/PWR 20 UN. PAGE 84 A1719 INT/LAW INT/ORG DIPLOM ADJUD

L67
LISSITZYN O.J.,"TREATIES AND CHANGED CIRCUMSTANCES (REBUS SIC STANTIBUS)" WOR+45 CONSEN...JURID 20. PAGE 90 A1842 AGREE DIPLOM INT/LAW

L67
MOORE N.,"THE LAWFULNESS OF MILITARY ASSISTANCE TO THE REPUBLIC OF VIET NAM." USA+45 VIETNAM WOR+45 FOR/AID DOMIN DETER WAR WEAPON...DECISION INT/LAW 20 UN. PAGE 103 A2123 PWR DIPLOM FORCES GOV/REL

S67
CLINGHAM T.A. JR.,"LEGISLATIVE FLOTSAM AND INTERNATIONAL ACTION IN THE 'YARMOUTH CASTLE'S' WAKE." WOR+45 PROB/SOLV CONFER COST HEALTH...POLICY INT/LAW CONGRESS. PAGE 27 A0552 DIPLOM DIST/IND INT/ORG LAW

S67
COHN K.,"CRIMES AGAINST HUMANITY." GERMANY INT/ORG SANCTION ATTIT ORD/FREE...MARXIST CRIMLGY 20 UN. PAGE 28 A0564 WAR INT/LAW CRIME ADJUD

S67
D'AMATO D.,"LEGAL ASPECTS OF THE FRENCH NUCLEAR TESTS." FRANCE WOR+45 ACT/RES COLONIAL RISK GOV/REL EQUILIB ORD/FREE PWR DECISION. PAGE 33 A0672 INT/LAW DIPLOM NUC/PWR ADJUD

S67
DOYLE S.E.,"COMMUNICATION SATELLITES* INTERNAL ORGANIZATION FOR DEVELOPMENT AND CONTROL." USA+45 R+D ACT/RES DIPLOM NAT/LISM...POLICY INT/LAW PREDICT UN. PAGE 38 A0781 TEC/DEV SPACE COM/IND INT/ORG

S67
EISENDRATH C.,"THE OUTER SPACE TREATY." CHINA/COM COM USA+45 DIPLOM CONTROL NUC/PWR...INT/LAW 20 UN COLD/WAR TREATY. PAGE 41 A0831 SPACE INT/ORG PEACE ARMS/CONT

S67
FAWCETT J.E.S.,"GIBRALTAR* THE LEGAL ISSUES." SPAIN UK INT/ORG BAL/PWR LICENSE CONFER SANCTION PRIVIL ...JURID CHARTS 20. PAGE 44 A0905 INT/LAW DIPLOM COLONIAL ADJUD

S67
FOREIGN POLICY ASSOCIATION,"US CONCERN FOR WORLD LAW." USA+45 WOR+45 DELIB/GP JUDGE BAL/PWR CONFER PEACE ORD/FREE 20 UN. PAGE 47 A0962 INT/LAW INT/ORG DIPLOM ARMS/CONT

S67
HAZARD J.N.,"POST-DISARMAMENT INTERNATIONAL LAW." FUT USSR WOR+45 INT/ORG DELIB/GP FORCES DETER EQUILIB SOVEREIGN MARXISM 20 UN. PAGE 63 A1301
INT/LAW ARMS/CONT PWR PLAN

S67
HULL E.W.S.,"THE POLITICAL OCEAN." FUT UNIV WOR+45 EXTR/IND R+D VOL/ASSN PLAN BAL/PWR ECO/TAC PEACE WEALTH 20 UN. PAGE 69 A1414
DIPLOM ECO/UNDEV INT/ORG INT/LAW

S67
JOHNSON D.H.N.,"THE SOUTH-WEST AFRICA CASES." AFR ETHIOPIA LIBERIA SOUTH/AFR CONSULT JUDGE BAL/PWR 20. PAGE 74 A1521
INT/LAW DIPLOM INT/ORG ADJUD

S67
JOHNSTON D.M.,"LAW, TECHNOLOGY AND THE SEA." WOR+45 PLAN PROB/SOLV TEC/DEV CONFER ADJUD ORD/FREE ...POLICY JURID. PAGE 75 A1528
INT/LAW INT/ORG DIPLOM NEUTRAL

S67
MANN F.A.,"THE BRETTON WOODS AGREEMENT IN THE ENGLISH COURTS." UK JUDGE ADJUD CT/SYS...JURID PREDICT CON/ANAL 20. PAGE 94 A1923
LAW INT/LAW CONSTN

S67
MUDGE G.A.,"DOMESTIC POLICIES AND UN ACTIVITIES* THE CASE OF RHODESIA AND THE REPUBLIC OF SOUTH AFRICA." RHODESIA SOUTH/AFR POL/PAR LEAD SANCTION CHOOSE RACE/REL CONSEN DISCRIM ATTIT...INT/LAW UN PARLIAMENT 20. PAGE 105 A2163
AFR NAT/G POLICY

S67
ODA S.,"THE NORMALIZATION OF RELATIONS BETWEEN JAPAN AND THE REPUBLIC OF KOREA." NAT/G BAL/PWR REPAR INT/LAW. PAGE 111 A2276
DIPLOM LEGIS DECISION

S67
RAMSEY J.A.,"THE STATUS OF INTERNATIONAL COPYRIGHTS." WOR+45 CREATE TEC/DEV DIPLOM CONFER CONTROL SANCTION OWN...POLICY JURID. PAGE 119 A2439
INT/LAW INT/ORG COM/IND PRESS

S67
REINTANZ G.,"THE SPACE TREATY." WOR+45 DIPLOM CONTROL ARMS/CONT NUC/PWR WAR...MARXIST 20 COLD/WAR UN TREATY. PAGE 120 A2461
SPACE INT/LAW INT/ORG PEACE

S67
SCHACTER O.,"SCIENTIFIC ADVANCES AND INTERNATIONAL LAWMAKING." FUT R+D PLAN PROB/SOLV CONFER CONTROL ...POLICY PREDICT 20 UN. PAGE 128 A2617
TEC/DEV INT/LAW INT/ORG ACT/RES

S67
STEEL R.,"WHAT CAN THE UN DO?" RHODESIA ECO/UNDEV DIPLOM ECO/TAC SANCTION...INT/LAW UN. PAGE 137 A2810
INT/ORG BAL/PWR PEACE FOR/AID

S67
VAN DUSEN H.P.,"HAMMARSKOLD IN THE WORLD'S SERVICE." DIPLOM CONFER LEAD PEACE STRANGE UTOPIA MORAL SKILL OBJECTIVE...INT/LAW SELF/OBS 20. PAGE 158 A3211
INT/ORG CONSULT TOP/EX NEUTRAL

S67
VLASCIC I.A.,"THE SPACE TREATY* A PRELIMINARY EVALUATION." FUT USSR WOR+45 R+D ACT/RES TEC/DEV DIPLOM CONFER ARMS/CONT PEACE...PREDICT UN TREATY. PAGE 159 A3245
SPACE INT/LAW INT/ORG NEUTRAL

S67
WEIL G.L.,"THE MERGER OF THE INSTITUTIONS OF THE EUROPEAN COMMUNITIES" EUR+WWI ECO/DEV INT/TRADE CONSEN PLURISM...DECISION MGT 20 EEC EURATOM ECSC TREATY. PAGE 162 A3300
ECO/TAC INT/ORG CENTRAL INT/LAW

B91
DOLE C.F.,THE AMERICAN CITIZEN. USA-45 LAW PARTIC ATTIT...INT/LAW 19. PAGE 38 A0769
NAT/G MORAL NAT/LISM MAJORITY

B96
DE VATTEL E.,THE LAW OF NATIONS. AGRI FINAN CHIEF DIPLOM INT/TRADE AGREE OWN ALL/VALS MORAL ORD/FREE SOVEREIGN...GEN/LAWS 18 NATURL/LAW WOLFF/C. PAGE 35 A0714
LAW CONCPT NAT/G INT/LAW

B97
US DEPARTMENT OF STATE,CATALOGUE OF WORKS RELATING TO THE LAW OF NATIONS AND DIPLOMACY IN THE LIBRARY OF THE DEPARTMENT OF STATE (PAMPHLET). WOR-45 NAT/G ADJUD CT/SYS...INT/LAW JURID 19. PAGE 152 A3102
BIBLIOG/A DIPLOM LAW

B99
BROOKS S.,BRITAIN AND THE BOERS. AFR SOUTH/AFR UK CULTURE INSPECT LEGIT...INT/LAW 19/20 BOER/WAR. PAGE 19 A0396
WAR DIPLOM NAT/G

INT/ORG....INTERNATIONAL ORGANIZATIONS; SEE ALSO VOL/ASSN AND APPROPRIATE ORGANIZATION

INT/REL....INTERNATIONAL RELATIONS

INT/TRADE....INTERNATIONAL TRADE

N
LIBRARY INTERNATIONAL REL,INTERNATIONAL INFORMATION SERVICE. WOR+45 CULTURE INT/ORG FORCES...GEOG HUM SOC. PAGE 88 A1808
BIBLIOG/A DIPLOM INT/TRADE INT/LAW

N
CANADIAN GOVERNMENT PUBLICATIONS (1955-). CANADA AGRI FINAN LABOR FORCES INT/TRADE HEALTH...JURID 20 PARLIAMENT. PAGE 1 A0007
BIBLIOG/A NAT/G DIPLOM INT/ORG

N
INTERNATIONAL AFFAIRS. WOR+45 WOR-45 ECO/UNDEV INT/ORG NAT/G PROB/SOLV FOR/AID WAR...POLICY 20. PAGE 1 A0009
BIBLIOG/A DIPLOM INT/LAW INT/TRADE

N
INTERNATIONAL BOOK NEWS, 1928-1934. ECO/UNDEV FINAN INDUS LABOR INT/TRADE CONFER ADJUD COLONIAL...HEAL SOC/WK CHARTS 20 LEAGUE/NAT. PAGE 1 A0010
BIBLIOG/A DIPLOM INT/LAW INT/ORG

N
INTERNATIONAL STUDIES. ASIA S/ASIA WOR+45 ECO/UNDEV INT/ORG NAT/G LEAD ATTIT WEALTH...SOC 20. PAGE 1 A0012
BIBLIOG/A DIPLOM INT/LAW INT/TRADE

N
CHINA QUARTERLY. COM AGRI INDUS ACADEM POL/PAR INT/TRADE CONFER GOV/REL...TIME/SEQ CON/ANAL INDEX 20. PAGE 2 A0032
BIBLIOG/A ASIA DIPLOM POLICY

N
FOREIGN AFFAIRS. SPACE WOR+45 WOR-45 CULTURE ECO/UNDEV FINAN NAT/G TEC/DEV INT/TRADE ARMS/CONT NUC/PWR...POLICY 20 UN EURATOM ECSC EEC. PAGE 2 A0034
BIBLIOG DIPLOM INT/ORG INT/LAW

N
THE MIDDLE EAST AND NORTH AFRICA. AFR ISLAM CULTURE ECO/UNDEV AGRI NAT/G TEC/DEV FOR/AID INT/TRADE EDU/PROP...CHARTS 20. PAGE 2 A0043
INDEX INDUS FINAN STAT

N
FOREIGN TRADE LIBRARY,NEW TITLES RECEIVED IN THE LIBRARY. WOR+45 ECO/UNDEV FINAN NAT/G PLAN TEC/DEV BUDGET ECO/TAC TARIFFS GOV/REL STAT. PAGE 47 A0964
BIBLIOG/A INT/TRADE INDUS ECO/DEV

N
HARVARD UNIVERSITY LAW LIBRARY,CATALOG OF INTERNATIONAL LAW AND RELATIONS. WOR+45 WOR-45 INT/ORG NAT/G JUDGE DIPLOM INT/TRADE ADJUD CT/SYS 19/20. PAGE 62 A1280
BIBLIOG INT/LAW JURID

N
IMF AND IBRD, JOINT LIBRARY,LIST OF RECENT ADDITIONS. WOR+45 ECO/DEV ECO/UNDEV BUDGET FOR/AID RATION...CONCPT IDEA/COMP. PAGE 70 A1434
BIBLIOG INT/ORG INT/TRADE FINAN

N
IMF AND IBRD, JOINT LIBRARY,LIST OF RECENT PERIODICAL ARTICLES. WOR+45 ECO/DEV ECO/UNDEV BUDGET FOR/AID RATION...CONCPT IDEA/COMP. PAGE 70 A1435
BIBLIOG INT/ORG INT/TRADE FINAN

N
INTERNATIONAL STUDIES,"INDIA AND WORLD AFFAIRS: AN ANNUAL BIBLIOGRAPHY" INDIA INT/TRADE PARTIC GOV/REL 20. PAGE 71 A1461
BIBLIOG POLICY DIPLOM ATTIT

N
JOHNS HOPKINS UNIVERSITY LIB,RECENT ADDITIONS. WOR+45 ECO/UNDEV NAT/G POL/PAR FOR/AID INT/TRADE LEAD REGION ATTIT ALL/IDEOS TREND. PAGE 74 A1518
BIBLIOG DIPLOM INT/LAW INT/ORG

N
KYRIAK T.E.,CHINA: A BIBLIOGRAPHY. ASIA CHINA/COM AGRI FINAN INDUS NAT/G INT/TRADE PRESS...SOC 20. PAGE 83 A1700
BIBLIOG/A MARXISM TOP/EX POL/PAR

N
KYRIAK T.E.,EAST EUROPE: BIBLIOGRAPHY--INDEX TO US JPRS RESEARCH TRANSLATIONS. ALBANIA BULGARIA COM CZECHOSLVK HUNGARY POLAND ROMANIA AGRI EXTR/IND FINAN SERV/IND INT/TRADE WEAPON...GEOG MGT SOC 20. PAGE 83 A1701
BIBLIOG/A PRESS MARXISM INDUS

N
KYRIAK T.E.,SOVIET UNION: BIBLIOGRAPHY INDEX TO US JPRS RESEARCH TRANSLATIONS. USSR ECO/DEV AGRI COM/IND CONSTRUC DIST/IND EXTR/IND PROC/MFG R+D INT/TRADE...SOC 20. PAGE 83 A1703
BIBLIOG/A INDUS MARXISM PRESS

N
TURNER R.K.,BIBLIOGRAPHY ON WORLD ORGANIZATION. INT/TRADE CT/SYS ARMS/CONT WEALTH...INT/LAW 20. PAGE 146 A2984
BIBLIOG/A INT/ORG PEACE WAR

N
UNITED NATIONS,OFFICIAL RECORDS OF THE ECONOMIC AND SOCIAL COUNCIL OF THE UNITED NATIONS. WOR+45 DIPLOM INT/TRADE CONFER...SOC SOC/WK 20 UN UNESCO. PAGE 148 A3031
INT/ORG DELIB/GP WRITING

N
US SUPERINTENDENT OF DOCUMENTS,MONTHLY CATALOG OF UNITED STATES GOVERNMENT PUBLICATIONS. USA+45 USA-45 AGRI LABOR FORCES INT/TRADE TARIFFS TAX EDU/PROP CT/SYS ARMS/CONT RACE/REL 19/20 CONGRESS PRESIDENT. PAGE 157 A3203
BIBLIOG NAT/G VOL/ASSN POLICY

N
US SUPERINTENDENT OF DOCUMENTS,TARIFF AND TAXATION (PRICE LIST 37). USA+45 LAW INT/TRADE ADJUD ADMIN CT/SYS INCOME OWN...DECISION GATT. PAGE 157 A3204
BIBLIOG/A TAX TARIFFS NAT/G

N
WORLD PEACE FOUNDATION,DOCUMENTS OF INTERNATIONAL ORGANIZATIONS: A SELECTED BIBLIOGRAPHY. WOR+45 WOR-45 AGRI FINAN ACT/RES OP/RES INT/TRADE ADMIN ...CON/ANAL 20 UN UNESCO LEAGUE/NAT. PAGE 167 A3396
BIBLIOG DIPLOM INT/ORG REGION

B00
MOCKLER-FERRYMAN A.,BRITISH WEST AFRICA. FRANCE GERMANY NIGER SIER/LEONE UK CULTURE DIPLOM WAR RACE/REL PRODUC PROFIT WEALTH...POLICY PREDICT 19. PAGE 102 A2095
AFR COLONIAL INT/TRADE CAP/ISM

B03
FORTESCUE G.K.,SUBJECT INDEX OF THE MODERN WORKS ADDED TO THE LIBRARY OF THE BRITISH MUSEUM IN THE YEARS 1881-1900 (3 VOLS.). UK LAW CONSTN FINAN NAT/G FORCES INT/TRADE COLONIAL 19. PAGE 47 A0968
BIBLIOG INDEX WRITING

B03
MOREL E.D.,THE BRITISH CASE IN FRENCH CONGO. CONGO/BRAZ FRANCE UK COERCE MORAL WEALTH...POLICY INT/LAW 20 CONGO/LEOP. PAGE 104 A2130
DIPLOM INT/TRADE COLONIAL AFR

B06
GRIFFIN A.P.C.,SELECT LIST OF REFERENCES ON THE BRITISH TARIFF MOVEMENT. MOD/EUR UK BAL/PWR BARGAIN ECO/TAC LAISSEZ 20. PAGE 56 A1154
BIBLIOG/A INT/TRADE TARIFFS COLONIAL

B08
ARON R.,WAR AND INDUSTRIAL SOCIETY. EUR+WWI MOD/EUR WOR+45 WOR-45 CONSTN SOCIETY INT/ORG POL/PAR VOL/ASSN DIPLOM INT/TRADE PEACE ATTIT...BIOG GEN/LAWS 19/20. PAGE 9 A0178
ECO/DEV WAR

B08
LABRIOLA A.,ESSAYS ON THE MATERIALISTIC CONCEPTION OF HISTORY. STRATA POL/PAR CAP/ISM DIPLOM INT/TRADE WAR 20. PAGE 83 A1706
MARXIST WORKER REV COLONIAL

B10
MENDELSSOHN S.,SOUTH AFRICAN BIBLIOGRAPHY (2 VOLS.). SOUTH/AFR EXTR/IND LABOR SECT DIPLOM INT/TRADE COLONIAL RACE/REL DISCRIM...GEOG 20. PAGE 99 A2038
BIBLIOG/A AFR NAT/G NAT/LISM

B13
BORCHARD E.M.,BIBLIOGRAPHY OF INTERNATIONAL LAW AND CONTINENTAL LAW. EUR+WWI MOD/EUR UK LAW INT/TRADE WAR PEACE...GOV/COMP NAT/COMP 19/20. PAGE 17 A0338
BIBLIOG INT/LAW JURID DIPLOM

B14
DE BLOCH J.,THE FUTURE OF WAR IN ITS TECHNICAL, ECONOMIC, AND POLITICAL RELATIONS (1899). MOD/EUR TEC/DEV BUDGET INT/TRADE DETER GUERRILLA WEAPON COST PEACE 20. PAGE 34 A0698
WAR BAL/PWR PREDICT FORCES

B17
MEYER H.H.B.,LIST OF REFERENCES ON EMBARGOES (PAMPHLET). USA-45 AGRI DIPLOM WRITING DEBATE WEAPON...INT/LAW 18/20 CONGRESS. PAGE 100 A2049
BIBLIOG DIST/IND ECO/TAC INT/TRADE

B17
MEYER H.H.B.,THE UNITED STATES AT WAR, ORGANIZATIONS AND LITERATURE. USA-45 AGRI FINAN INDUS CHIEF FORCES DIPLOM FOR/AID INT/TRADE...SOC 20 PRESIDENT. PAGE 100 A2050
BIBLIOG/A WAR NAT/G VOL/ASSN

B19
MEYER H.H.B.,SELECT LIST OF REFERENCES ON ECONOMIC RECONSTRUCTION: INCLUDING REPORTS OF THE BRITISH MINISTRY OF RECONSTRUCTION. UK LABOR PLAN PROB/SOLV ECO/TAC INT/TRADE WAR DEMAND PRODUC 20. PAGE 100 A2051
BIBLIOG/A EUR+WWI ECO/DEV WORKER

B19
SUMNER W.G.,WAR AND OTHER ESSAYS. USA-45 DELIB/GP DIPLOM TARIFFS COLONIAL PEACE SOVEREIGN 20. PAGE 140 A2864
INT/TRADE ORD/FREE CAP/ISM ECO/TAC

B19
US DEPARTMENT OF STATE,A TENTATIVE LIST OF TREATY COLLECTIONS. WOR-45 BAL/PWR INT/TRADE TARIFFS WAR PEACE ORD/FREE 20. PAGE 151 A3080
ANTHOL DIPLOM DELIB/GP

N19
BENTHAM J.,A PLAN FOR AN UNIVERSAL AND PERPETUAL PEACE (1838) (PAMPHLET). NAT/G FORCES BAL/PWR INT/TRADE ADMIN AGREE CT/SYS ARMS/CONT SOVEREIGN WEALTH GEN/LAWS. PAGE 13 A0269
INT/ORG INT/LAW PEACE COLONIAL

N19
FRANCK P.G.,AFGHANISTAN BETWEEN EAST AND WEST: THE ECONOMICS OF COMPETITIVE COEXISTENCE (PAMPHLET). AFGHANISTN USA+45 USA-45 USSR INDUS ECO/TAC INT/TRADE CONTROL NEUTRAL ORD/FREE MARXISM...GEOG 20 UN. PAGE 48 A0977
FOR/AID PLAN DIPLOM ECO/UNDEV

N19
LANGE O.R.,"DISARMAMENT ECONOMIC GROWTH AND INTERNATIONAL CO-OPERATION" (PAMPHLET). WOR+45 DIST/IND PLAN INT/TRADE GIVE TASK DETER WEALTH SOCISM 18/19 BOLIVAR/S. PAGE 84 A1723
ARMS/CONT DIPLOM ECO/DEV ECO/UNDEV

N19
SALKEVER L.R.,SUB-SAHARA AFRICA (PAMPHLET). AFR USSR EXTR/IND NAT/G SCHOOL DIPLOM COLONIAL WEALTH ...GEOG CHARTS 16/20. PAGE 127 A2594
ECO/UNDEV TEC/DEV TASK INT/TRADE

N19
STEUBER F.A.,THE CONTRIBUTION OF SWITZERLAND TO THE ECONOMIC AND SOCIAL DEVELOPMENT OF LOW-INCOME COUNTRIES (PAMPHLET). SWITZERLND FINAN NAT/G VOL/ASSN INT/TRADE DRIVE...CHARTS 20. PAGE 138 A2820
FOR/AID ECO/UNDEV PLAN DIPLOM

N19
VELYAMINOV G.,AFRICA AND THE COMMON MARKET (PAMPHLET). AFR MARKET VOL/ASSN ECO/TAC COLONIAL ORD/FREE...SOCIALIST 20 THIRD/WRLD. PAGE 158 A3227
INT/ORG INT/TRADE SOVEREIGN ECO/UNDEV

B22
FICHTE J.G.,ADDRESSES TO THE GERMAN NATION. GERMANY PRUSSIA ELITES NAT/G SECT CREATE INT/TRADE HEREDITY ...ART/METH LING 19 FRANK/PARL. PAGE 45 A0923
NAT/LISM CULTURE EDU/PROP REGION

B24
NAVILLE A.,LIBERTE, EGALITE, SOLIDARITE: ESSAIS D'ANALYSE. STRATA FAM VOL/ASSN INT/TRADE GP/REL MORAL MARXISM SOCISM...PSY TREATY. PAGE 107 A2205
ORD/FREE SOC IDEA/COMP DIPLOM

B26
INSTITUT INTERMEDIAIRE INTL,REPERTOIRE GENERAL DES TRAITES ET AUTRES ACTES DIPLOMATIQUES CONCLUS DEPUIS 1895 JUSQU'EN 1920. MOD/EUR WOR-45 INT/ORG VOL/ASSN DELIB/GP INT/TRADE WAR TREATY 19/20. PAGE 70 A1443
BIBLIOG DIPLOM

B33
AMERICAN FOREIGN LAW ASSN,BIOGRAPHICAL NOTES ON THE LAWS AND LEGAL LITERATURE OF URUGUAY AND CURACAO. URUGUAY CONSTN FINAN SECT FORCES JUDGE DIPLOM INT/TRADE ADJUD CT/SYS CRIME 20. PAGE 7 A0147
BIBLIOG/A LAW JURID ADMIN

B33
OHLIN B.,INTERREGIONAL AND INTERNATIONAL TRADE. USA-45 WOR-45 CULTURE FINAN MARKET CONSULT PLAN ECO/TAC ATTIT WEALTH...CONCPT MATH TOT/POP 20. PAGE 111 A2285
INT/ORG ECO/DEV INT/TRADE REGION

B35
BEMIS S.F.,GUIDE TO THE DIPLOMATIC HISTORY OF THE UNITED STATES, 17751921. NAT/G LEGIS TOP/EX PROB/SOLV CAP/ISM INT/TRADE TARIFFS ADJUD ...CON/ANAL 18/20. PAGE 13 A0264
BIBLIOG/A DIPLOM USA-45

B35
BUREAU ECONOMIC RES LAT AM,THE ECONOMIC LITERATURE OF LATIN AMERICA (2 VOLS.). CHRIST-17C AGRI DIST/IND EXTR/IND INDUS WORKER INT/TRADE...GEOG 16/20. PAGE 21 A0433
BIBLIOG L/A+17C ECO/UNDEV FINAN

B35
CONOVER H.F.,A SELECTED LIST OF REFERENCES ON THE DIPLOMATIC & TRADE RELATIONS OF THE US WITH THE USSR, 1919-1935 (PAMPHLET). USA-45 USSR DELIB/GP LEGIS OP/RES PROB/SOLV BAL/PWR BARGAIN 20. PAGE 29 A0590
BIBLIOG DIPLOM INT/TRADE

B35
LANGER W.L.,THE DIPLOMACY OF IMPERIALISM 1890-1902. FRANCE GERMANY ITALY UK WOR-45 BAL/PWR INT/TRADE LEGIT ADJUD CONTROL WAR PWR SOVEREIGN...CHARTS BIBLIOG/A 19/20. PAGE 84 A1726
DIPLOM COLONIAL DOMIN

B35
STALEY E.,WAR AND THE PRIVATE INVESTOR. UNIV WOR-45 INTELL SOCIETY INT/ORG NAT/G TOP/EX CAP/ISM ECO/TAC WAR ATTIT ALL/VALS...INT TIME/SEQ TREND CON/ANAL WORK TOT/POP 20. PAGE 137 A2799
FINAN INT/TRADE DIPLOM

B36
HARVARD BUREAU ECO RES LAT AM,THE ECONOMIC LITERATURE OF LATIN AMERICA: A TENTATIVE BIBLIOGRAPHY. NAT/G TARIFFS CENTRAL COST DEMAND 20. PAGE 62 A1277
BIBLIOG ECO/UNDEV L/A+17C INT/TRADE

B36
VARLEY D.H.,A BIBLIOGRAPHY OF ITALIAN COLONISATION IN AFRICA WITH A SECTION ON ABYSSINIA. AFR ETHIOPIA ITALY LIBYA SOMALIA AGRI FINAN LABOR TEC/DEV DIPLOM INT/TRADE RACE/REL DISCRIM 19/20. PAGE 158 A3222
BIBLIOG COLONIAL ADMIN LAW

B37
BLAKE J.W.,EUROPEAN BEGINNINGS IN WEST AFRICA 1454-1578. FRANCE GUINEA PORTUGAL UK PWR WEALTH 16/16 AFRICA/W. PAGE 15 A0305
DIPLOM COLONIAL INT/TRADE DOMIN

B37
ROBBINS L.,ECONOMIC PLANNING AND INTERNATIONAL ORDER. WOR-45 SOCIETY FINAN INDUS NAT/G ECO/TAC ROUTINE WEALTH...SOC TIME/SEQ GEN/METH WORK 20 KEYNES/JM. PAGE 122 A2492
INT/ORG PLAN INT/TRADE

B37
TUPPER E.,JAPAN IN AMERICAN PUBLIC OPINION. USA-45
ATTIT

POL/PAR VOL/ASSN INT/TRADE DISCRIM...BIBLIOG 20 CHINJAP TREATY. PAGE 146 A2979 — IDEA/COMP DIPLOM PRESS

B37
VINER J.,STUDIES IN THE THEORY OF INTERNATIONAL TRADE. WOR-45 CONSTN ECO/DEV AGRI INDUS MARKET INT/ORG LABOR NAT/G ECO/TAC TARIFFS COLONIAL ATTIT WEALTH...POLICY CONCPT MATH STAT OBS SAMP TREND GEN/LAWS MARX/KARL 20. PAGE 159 A3236 — CAP/ISM INT/TRADE

C37
TUPPER E.,"JAPAN IN AMERICAN PUBLIC OPINION." USA+45 POL/PAR VOL/ASSN INT/TRADE DISCRIM ...IDEA/COMP 20 CHINJAP. PAGE 146 A2978 — BIBLIOG ATTIT DIPLOM PRESS

B38
COLBY C.C.,GEOGRAPHICAL ASPECTS OF INTERNATIONAL RELATIONS. WOR-45 ECO/DEV ECO/UNDEV AGRI EXTR/IND INDUS MARKET R+D INT/ORG NAT/G TEC/DEV ECO/TAC INT/TRADE NAT/LISM WEALTH...METH/CNCPT CHARTS GEN/LAWS 20. PAGE 28 A0565 — PLAN GEOG DIPLOM

B38
GRISWOLD A.W.,THE FAR EASTERN POLICY OF THE UNITED STATES. ASIA S/ASIA USA-45 INT/ORG INT/TRADE WAR NAT/LISM...BIBLIOG 19/20 LEAGUE/NAT ROOSEVLT/T ROOSEVLT/F WILSON/W TREATY. PAGE 57 A1166 — DIPLOM POLICY CHIEF

B38
HARPER S.N.,THE GOVERNMENT OF THE SOVIET UNION. COM USSR LAW CONSTN ECO/DEV PLAN TEC/DEV DIPLOM INT/TRADE ADMIN REV NAT/LISM...POLICY 20. PAGE 62 A1265 — MARXISM NAT/G LEAD POL/PAR

B38
SAINT-PIERRE C.I.,SCHEME FOR LASTING PEACE (TRANS. BY H. BELLOT). INDUS NAT/G CHIEF FORCES INT/TRADE CT/SYS WAR PWR SOVEREIGN WEALTH...POLICY 18. PAGE 126 A2587 — INT/ORG PEACE AGREE INT/LAW

B38
WARE E.E.,THE STUDY OF INTERNATIONAL RELATIONS IN THE UNITED STATES. USA+45 USA-45 WOR-45 INTELL SERV/IND INT/ORG NAT/G PROF/ORG SECT CONSULT INT/TRADE EDU/PROP ARMS/CONT...CONCPT 20. PAGE 161 A3283 — KNOWL DIPLOM

B39
LENIN V.I.,IMPERIALISM: THE HIGHEST STAGE OF CAPITALISM. USSR WOR-45 DIST/IND INT/TRADE ATTIT MARXISM SOCISM...CHARTS 20. PAGE 87 A1773 — MARXIST CAP/ISM COLONIAL DOMIN

B39
STALEY E.,WORLD ECONOMY IN TRANSITION. WOR-45 SOCIETY INT/ORG PROF/ORG ECO/TAC ATTIT WEALTH ...METH/CNCPT TREND GEN/LAWS 20. PAGE 137 A2800 — TEC/DEV INT/TRADE

B39
ZIMMERN A.,MODERN POLITICAL DOCTRINE. WOR-45 CULTURE SOCIETY ECO/UNDEV DELIB/GP EX/STRUC CREATE DOMIN COERCE NAT/LISM ATTIT RIGID/FLEX ORD/FREE PWR WEALTH...POLICY CONCPT OBS TIME/SEQ TREND TOT/POP LEAGUE/NAT 20. PAGE 170 A3454 — NAT/G ECO/TAC BAL/PWR INT/TRADE

C39
SCOTT J.B.,"LAW, THESTATE, AND THE INTERNATIONAL COMMUNITY (2 VOLS.)" INTELL INT/ORG NAT/G SECT INT/TRADE WAR...INT/LAW GEN/LAWS BIBLIOG. PAGE 130 A2672 — LAW PHIL/SCI DIPLOM CONCPT

B40
CONOVER H.F.,FOREIGN RELATIONS OF THE UNITED STATES: A LIST OF RECENT BOOKS (PAMPHLET). ASIA CANADA L/A+17C UK INT/ORG INT/TRADE TARIFFS NEUTRAL WAR PEACE...INT/LAW CON/ANAL 20 CHINJAP. PAGE 29 A0592 — BIBLIOG/A USA-45 DIPLOM

B40
CONOVER H.F.,JAPAN-ECONOMIC DEVELOPMENT AND FOREIGN POLICY, A SELECTED LIST OF REFERENCES (PAMPHLET). CULTURE FINAN INDUS NAT/G FORCES INT/TRADE WAR ...SOC TREND 20 CHINJAP. PAGE 29 A0593 — BIBLIOG ASIA ECO/DEV DIPLOM

C40
FAHS C.B.,"GOVERNMENT IN JAPAN." FINAN FORCES LEGIS TOP/EX BUDGET INT/TRADE EDU/PROP SOVEREIGN ...CON/ANAL BIBLIOG/A 20 CHINJAP. PAGE 43 A0884 — ASIA DIPLOM NAT/G ADMIN

B42
CONOVER H.F.,FRENCH COLONIES IN AFRICA: A LIST OF REFERENCES. ALGERIA FRANCE MOROCCO SOMALIA SUDAN CULTURE AGRI LOC/G SECT FORCES DIPLOM INT/TRADE NAT/LISM HEALTH...CON/ANAL 20. PAGE 29 A0594 — BIBLIOG AFR ECO/UNDEV COLONIAL

B42
CROWE S.E.,THE BERLIN WEST AFRICA CONFERENCE, 1884-85. GERMANY ELITES MARKET INT/ORG DELIB/GP FORCES PROB/SOLV BAL/PWR CAP/ISM DOMIN COLONIAL ...INT/LAW 19. PAGE 33 A0664 — AFR CONFER INT/TRADE DIPLOM

B42
JACKSON M.V.,EUROPEAN POWERS AND SOUTH-EAST AFRICA: A STUDY OF INTERNATIONAL RELATIONS ON SOUTH-EAST COAST OF AFRICA, 1796-1856. AFR FRANCE PORTUGAL SOUTH/AFR UK USA-45 FORCES INT/TRADE PWR...CHARTS BIBLIOG 18/19 TREATY. PAGE 72 A1477 — DOMIN POLICY ORD/FREE DIPLOM

B42
US LIBRARY OF CONGRESS,ECONOMICS OF WAR (APRIL 1941-MARCH 1942). WOR-45 FINAN INDUS LOC/G NAT/G PLAN BUDGET RATION COST DEMAND...POLICY 20. PAGE 154 A3146 — BIBLIOG/A INT/TRADE ECO/TAC WAR

L42
SHOTWELL J.,"LESSON OF THE LAST WORLD WAR." EUR+WWI MOD/EUR USA-45 SOCIETY ECO/UNDEV INDUS VOL/ASSN CONSULT ACT/RES CREATE CAP/ISM INT/TRADE DRIVE ALL/VALS...CONCPT NEW/IDEA SELF/OBS GEN/LAWS LEAGUE/NAT NAZI 20. PAGE 132 A2708 — INT/ORG ORD/FREE

S42
SHOTWELL J.,"AFTER THE WAR." COM EUR+WWI USA+45 USA-45 NAT/G DIPLOM INT/TRADE ARMS/CONT SOVEREIGN ...CONCPT LEAGUE/NAT TOT/POP FAO 20. PAGE 132 A2707 — FUT INT/ORG PEACE

B43
BROWN A.D.,GREECE: SELECTED LIST OF REFERENCES. GREECE ECO/UNDEV AGRI FINAN INDUS LABOR SECT TEC/DEV INT/TRADE LEAD...SOC 20. PAGE 20 A0399 — BIBLIOG/A WAR DIPLOM NAT/G

B43
VINER J.,TRADE RELATIONS BETWEEN FREE-MARKET AND CONTROLLED ECONOMIES. WOR-45 MARKET PLAN TARIFFS DEMAND...POLICY STAT 20. PAGE 159 A3237 — INT/TRADE DIPLOM CONTROL NAT/G

B44
RAGATZ L.J.,LITERATURE OF EUROPEAN IMPERIALISM. ECO/TAC INT/TRADE DOMIN GOV/REL DEMAND NAT/LISM PWR WEALTH 19/20. PAGE 119 A2432 — BIBLIOG COLONIAL INT/ORG ECO/UNDEV

B44
SHELBY C.,LATIN AMERICAN PERIODICALS CURRENTLY RECEIVED IN THE LIBRARY OF CONGRESS AND IN LIBRARY OF DEPARTMENT OF AGRICULTURE. SOCIETY AGRI INDUS LABOR POL/PAR INT/TRADE...GEOG SOC 20. PAGE 132 A2699 — BIBLIOG ECO/UNDEV CULTURE L/A+17C

B44
WEIGERT H.W.,COMPASS OF THE WORLD, A SYMPOSIUM ON POLITICAL GEOGRAPHY. EUR+WWI FUT MOD/EUR S/ASIA USA+45 WOR-45 SOCIETY AGRI INDUS MARKET ECO/TAC INT/TRADE PERSON 20. PAGE 162 A3298 — TEC/DEV CAP/ISM RUSSIA GEOG

B45
CLAGETT H.L.,COMMUNIST CHINA: RUTHLESS ENEMY OR PAPER TIGER (PAMPHLET). CHINA/COM ECO/UNDEV AGRI INDUS NAT/G POL/PAR ECO/TAC INT/TRADE GUERRILLA ATTIT...CHARTS NAT/COMP ORG/CHARTS 20. PAGE 26 A0540 — BIBLIOG/A MARXISM DIPLOM COERCE

B45
CONOVER H.F.,THE NAZI STATE: WAR CRIMES AND WAR CRIMINALS. GERMANY CULTURE NAT/G SECT FORCES DIPLOM INT/TRADE EDU/PROP...INT/LAW BIOG HIST/WRIT TIME/SEQ 20. PAGE 30 A0600 — BIBLIOG WAR CRIME

B45
GALLOWAY E.,ABSTRACTS OF POSTWAR LITERATURE (VOL. IV) JAN.-JULY, 1945 NOS. 901-1074. POLAND USA+45 USSR WOR+45 INDUS LABOR PLAN ECO/TAC INT/TRADE TAX EDU/PROP ADMIN COLONIAL INT/LAW. PAGE 51 A1033 — BIBLIOG/A NUC/PWR NAT/G DIPLOM

B45
NELSON M.F.,KOREA AND THE OLD ORDERS IN EASTERN ASIA. ASIA FRANCE KOREA RUSSIA DELIB/GP INT/TRADE DOMIN CONTROL WAR ORD/FREE...POLICY BIBLIOG. PAGE 108 A2218 — DIPLOM BAL/PWR ATTIT CONSERVE

B45
US DEPARTMENT OF STATE,PUBLICATIONS OF THE DEPARTMENT OF STATE: A LIST CUMULATIVE FROM OCTOBER 1, 1929 (PAMPHLET). ASIA EUR+WWI ISLAM L/A+17C USA-45 ADJUD...INT/LAW 20. PAGE 151 A3082 — BIBLIOG DIPLOM INT/TRADE

B45
WOOLBERT R.G.,FOREIGN AFFAIRS BIBLIOGRAPHY, 1932-1942. INT/ORG SECT INT/TRADE COLONIAL RACE/REL NAT/LISM...GEOG INT/LAW GOV/COMP IDEA/COMP 20. PAGE 167 A3393 — BIBLIOG/A DIPLOM WAR

C45
NELSON M.F.,"KOREA AND THE OLD ORDERS IN EASTERN ASIA." KOREA WOR-45 DELIB/GP INT/TRADE DOMIN CONTROL WAR ATTIT ORD/FREE CONSERVE...POLICY TREATY. PAGE 108 A2217 — BIBLIOG DIPLOM BAL/PWR ASIA

B47
CONOVER H.F.,NON-SELF-GOVERNING AREAS. BELGIUM FRANCE ITALY UK WOR+45 CULTURE ECO/UNDEV INT/ORG LOC/G NAT/G ECO/TAC INT/TRADE ADMIN HEALTH...SOC UN. PAGE 30 A0601 — BIBLIOG/A COLONIAL DIPLOM

B47
FEIS H.,SEEN FROM E A, THREE INTERNATIONAL EPISODES. EUR+WWI ITALY USA-45 WOR-45 AGRI INT/ORG NAT/G INT/TRADE LEGIT EXEC ATTIT ORD/FREE...POLICY LEAGUE/NAT TOT/POP 20 OIL. PAGE 44 A0908 — EXTR/IND ECO/TAC DIPLOM

B47
GORDON D.L.,THE HIDDEN WEAPON: THE STORY OF ECONOMIC WARFARE. EUR+WWI USA-45 LAW FINAN INDUS NAT/G CONSULT FORCES PLAN DOMIN PWR WEALTH ...INT/LAW CONCPT OBS TOT/POP NAZI 20. PAGE 54 A1112 — INT/ORG ECO/TAC INT/TRADE WAR

B47
KIRK G.,THE STUDY OF INTERNATIONAL RELATIONS. FUT USA-45 R+D ACADEM INT/ORG CONSULT DELIB/GP INT/TRADE EDU/PROP PEACE RIGID/FLEX KNOWL VAL/FREE 20. PAGE 80 A1632 — USA+45 DIPLOM

B47
MANDER L.,FOUNDATIONS OF MODERN WORLD SOCIETY. WOR+45 DELIB/GP ECO/TAC INT/TRADE EDU/PROP ALL/VALS ...TIME/SEQ GEN/LAWS TOT/POP VAL/FREE ILO 20. PAGE 94 A1917
INT/ORG EX/STRUC DIPLOM

B47
TOWLE L.W.,INTERNATIONAL TRADE AND COMMERCIAL POLICY. WOR+45 LAW ECO/DEV FINAN INDUS NAT/G ECO/TAC WEALTH...TIME/SEQ ILO 20. PAGE 144 A2955
MARKET INT/ORG INT/TRADE

B48
CLYDE P.H.,THE FAR EAST: A HISTORY OF THE IMPACT OF THE WEST ON EASTERN ASIA. CHINA/COM CULTURE INT/TRADE DOMIN COLONIAL WAR PWR...CHARTS BIBLIOG 19/20 CHINJAP. PAGE 27 A0554
DIPLOM ASIA

B48
GRAHAM F.D.,THE THEORY OF INTERNATIONAL VALUES. FUT WOR+45 WOR-45 ECO/DEV FINAN INT/ORG PLAN TEC/DEV CAP/ISM DIPLOM ECO/TAC TARIFFS ROUTINE BAL/PAY DRIVE PWR WEALTH SOCISM...POLICY STAT HYPO/EXP GEN/LAWS 20. PAGE 55 A1125
NEW/IDEA INT/TRADE

B48
KULISCHER E.M.,EUROPE ON THE MOVE: WAR AND POPULATION CHANGES, 1917-1947. COM EUR+WWI FUT GERMANY USSR DIST/IND PLAN INT/TRADE CONTROL WAR DRIVE...CENSUS TREND COLD/WAR 20. PAGE 82 A1690
ECO/TAC GEOG

B48
MINISTERE FINANCES ET ECO,BULLETIN BIBLIOGRAPHIQUE. AFR EUR+WWI FRANCE CULTURE STRUCT FINAN NAT/G ACT/RES INT/TRADE ADMIN REGION PRODUC STAT. PAGE 102 A2088
BIBLIOG/A ECO/UNDEV TEC/DEV COLONIAL

B48
PELCOVITS N.A.,OLD CHINA HANDS AND THE FOREIGN OFFICE. ASIA BURMA UK ECO/UNDEV NAT/G ECO/TAC FOR/AID TARIFFS DOMIN COLONIAL GOV/REL SOVEREIGN 19 HONG/KONG TREATY. PAGE 114 A2348
INT/TRADE ATTIT DIPLOM

B49
BEHRENDT R.F.,MODERN LATIN AMERICA IN SOCIAL SCIENCE LITERATURE. STRUCT ECO/UNDEV SCHOOL DIPLOM INT/TRADE EDU/PROP...GEOG 20. PAGE 12 A0250
BIBLIOG/A SOC L/A+17C

B49
HINDEN R.,EMPIRE AND AFTER. UK POL/PAR BAL/PWR DIPLOM INT/TRADE WAR NAT/LISM PWR 17/20. PAGE 65 A1335
NAT/G COLONIAL ATTIT POLICY

B50
BEHRENDT R.F.,MODERN LATIN AMERICA IN SOCIAL SCIENCE LITERATURE (SUPPLEMENTS I AND II). STRUCT ECO/UNDEV SCHOOL DIPLOM INT/TRADE...GEOG 20. PAGE 12 A0251
BIBLIOG/A SOC L/A+17C

B50
CHUKWUEMEKA N.,AFRICAN DEPENDENCIES: A CHALLENGE TO WESTERN DEMOCRACY. NIGERIA ECO/DEV INDUS FOR/AID INT/TRADE DOMIN 20. PAGE 26 A0536
DIPLOM ECO/UNDEV COLONIAL AFR

B50
COUNCIL BRITISH NATIONAL BIB,BRITISH NATIONAL BIBLIOGRAPHY. UK AGRI CONSTRUC PERF/ART POL/PAR SECT CREATE INT/TRADE LEAD...HUM JURID PHIL/SCI 20. PAGE 31 A0637
BIBLIOG/A NAT/G TEC/DEV DIPLOM

B50
DAVIS E.P.,PERIODICALS OF INTERNATIONAL ORGANIZATIONS; PART I, THE UN AND SPECIALIZED AGENCIES; PART II, INTER-AMERICAN ORGS. CULTURE AGRI FINAN INDUS LABOR INT/TRADE...GEOG HEAL STAT 20 UN OAS UNESCO. PAGE 34 A0689
BIBLIOG/A INT/ORG DIPLOM L/A+17C

B50
MCCAMY J.,THE ADMINISTRATION OF AMERICAN FOREIGN AFFAIRS. USA+45 SOCIETY INT/ORG NAT/G ACT/RES PLAN INT/TRADE EDU/PROP ADJUD ALL/VALS...METH/CNCPT TIME/SEQ CONGRESS 20. PAGE 97 A1996
EXEC STRUCT DIPLOM

B50
PERHAM M.,COLONIAL GOVERNMENT: ANNOTATED READING LIST ON BRITISH COLONIAL GOVERNMENT. UK WOR+45 WOR-45 ECO/UNDEV INT/ORG LEGIS FOR/AID INT/TRADE DOMIN ADMIN REV 20. PAGE 115 A2356
BIBLIOG/A COLONIAL GOV/REL NAT/G

B50
US DEPARTMENT OF STATE,POINT FOUR: COOPERATIVE PROGRAM FOR AID IN THE DEVELOPMENT OF ECONOMICALLY UNDERDEVELOPED AREAS. WOR+45 AGRI INDUS INT/ORG PLAN TEC/DEV DIPLOM EDU/PROP ADMIN PEACE PRODUC WEALTH 20 CONGRESS UN. PAGE 151 A3085
ECO/UNDEV FOR/AID FINAN INT/TRADE

C50
ELLSWORTH P.T.,"INTERNATIONAL ECONOMY." ECO/DEV ECO/UNDEV FINAN LABOR DIPLOM FOR/AID TARIFFS BAL/PAY EQUILIB NAT/LISM OPTIMAL...INT/LAW 20 ILO GATT. PAGE 41 A0843
BIBLIOG INT/TRADE ECO/TAC INT/ORG

C50
NUMELIN R.,"THE BEGINNINGS OF DIPLOMACY." INT/TRADE WAR GP/REL PEACE STRANGE ATTIT...INT/LAW CONCPT BIBLIOG. PAGE 110 A2260
DIPLOM KIN CULTURE LAW

B51
BISSAINTHE M.,DICTIONNAIRE DE BIBLIOGRAPHIE HAITIENNE. HAITI ELITES AGRI LEGIS DIPLOM INT/TRADE WRITING ORD/FREE CATHISM...ART/METH GEOG 19/20 NEGRO TREATY. PAGE 15 A0295
BIBLIOG L/A+17C SOCIETY NAT/G

B51
CARRINGTON C.E.,THE LIQUIDATION OF THE BRITISH EMPIRE. AFR NAT/G INT/TRADE COLONIAL RACE/REL ATTIT ORD/FREE...POLICY NAT/COMP 20 CMN/WLTH. PAGE 25 A0501
SOVEREIGN NAT/LISM DIPLOM GP/REL

B51
LEONARD L.L.,INTERNATIONAL ORGANIZATION. WOR+45 WOR-45 EX/STRUC FORCES LEGIS ECO/TAC INT/TRADE COLONIAL ARMS/CONT...SOC/WK GOV/COMP BIBLIOG. PAGE 87 A1778
NAT/G DIPLOM INT/ORG DELIB/GP

B51
US DEPARTMENT OF STATE,POINT FOUR, NEAR EAST AND AFRICA, A SELECTED BIBLIOGRAPHY OF STUDIES ON ECONOMICALLY UNDERDEVELOPED COUNTRIES. AGRI COM/IND FINAN INDUS PLAN INT/TRADE...SOC TREND 20. PAGE 151 A3087
BIBLIOG/A AFR S/ASIA ISLAM

B51
US LIBRARY OF CONGRESS,PUBLIC AFFAIRS ABSTRACTS. USA+45 INT/ORG INT/TRADE ARMS/CONT...NAT/COMP 20 CONGRESS. PAGE 155 A3151
BIBLIOG/A DIPLOM POLICY

B51
US TARIFF COMMISSION,LIST OF PUBLICATIONS OF THE TARIFF COMMISSION (PAMPHLET). USA+45 USA-45 AGRI EXTR/IND INDUS INT/TRADE...STAT 20. PAGE 157 A3207
BIBLIOG TARIFFS NAT/G ADMIN

B51
VINER J.,INTERNATIONAL ECONOMICS. USA-45 WOR-45 ECO/DEV INDUS NAT/G ECO/TAC ALL/VALS...TIME/SEQ 20. PAGE 159 A3238
FINAN INT/ORG WAR INT/TRADE

B51
WABEKE B.H.,A GUIDE TO DUTCH BIBLIOGRAPHIES. BELGIUM INDONESIA NETHERLAND DIPLOM INT/TRADE WAR NAT/LISM KNOWL...ART/METH HUM JURID CON/ANAL 14/20. PAGE 160 A3257
BIBLIOG/A NAT/G CULTURE COLONIAL

B51
WHITE L.C.,INTERNATIONAL NON-GOVERNMENTAL ORGANIZATIONS. AFR ASIA COM EUR+WWI USA+45 WOR+45 INT/ORG DIPLOM INT/TRADE ALL/VALS...HUM FAO ILO EEC 20. PAGE 164 A3337
VOL/ASSN CONSULT

B52
ALEXANDROWICZ C.H.,INTERNATIONAL ECONOMIC ORGANIZATION. WOR+45 ECO/DEV ECO/UNDEV DIST/IND FINAN MARKET PLAN ECO/TAC LEGIT DRIVE WEALTH ...POLICY CONCPT QUANT OBS TIME/SEQ GEN/LAWS WORK EEC ILO OEEC UNESCO 20. PAGE 6 A0114
INT/ORG INT/TRADE

B52
HOSELITZ B.F.,THE PROGRESS OF UNDERDEVELOPED AREAS. FUT WOR+45 WOR-45 ECO/DEV ECO/TAC INT/TRADE WEALTH ...SOC TREND GEN/LAWS TOT/POP VAL/FREE COLD/WAR 20. PAGE 68 A1391
ECO/UNDEV PLAN FOR/AID

B52
MANTOUX E.,THE CARTHAGINIAN PEACE. GERMANY WOR-45 SOCIETY FINAN INT/ORG DELIB/GP FORCES PLAN LEGIT ...CONCPT TIME/SEQ 20 KEYNES/JM HITLER/A. PAGE 94 A1935
ECO/DEV INT/TRADE WAR

C52
STUART G.H.,"AMERICAN DIPLOMATIC AND CONSULAR PRACTICE (2ND ED.)" EUR+WWI MOD/EUR USA-45 DELIB/GP INT/TRADE ADJUD...BIBLIOG 20. PAGE 140 A2855
DIPLOM ADMIN INT/ORG

B53
MACK R.T.,RAISING THE WORLDS STANDARD OF LIVING. IRAN INT/ORG VOL/ASSN EX/STRUC ECO/TAC WEALTH...MGT METH/CNCPT STAT CONT/OBS INT TOT/POP VAL/FREE 20 UN. PAGE 92 A1893
WOR+45 FOR/AID INT/TRADE

B53
MENDE T.,WORLD POWER IN THE BALANCE. FUT USA+45 USSR WOR-45 ECO/DEV ECO/TAC INT/TRADE EDU/PROP UTOPIA ATTIT...HUM CONCPT TREND COLD/WAR TOT/POP 20. PAGE 99 A2036
WOR+45 PWR BAL/PWR

B53
NEISSER H.,NATIONAL INCOMES AND INTERNATIONAL TRADE. FRANCE GERMANY SWEDEN UK USA-45 EXTR/IND FINAN INDUS TEC/DEV PRICE BAL/PAY EQUILIB INCOME WEALTH...CHARTS METH 19 CHINJAP. PAGE 108 A2215
INT/TRADE PRODUC MARKET CON/ANAL

B53
OPPENHEIM L.,INTERNATIONAL LAW: A TREATISE (7TH ED., 2 VOLS.). LAW CONSTN PROB/SOLV INT/TRADE ADJUD AGREE NEUTRAL WAR ORD/FREE SOVEREIGN...BIBLIOG 20 LEAGUE/NAT UN ILO. PAGE 112 A2294
INT/LAW INT/ORG DIPLOM

B54
BINANI G.D.,INDIA AT A GLANCE (REV. ED.). INDIA COM/IND FINAN INDUS LABOR PROVS SCHOOL PLAN DIPLOM INT/TRADE ADMIN...JURID 20. PAGE 14 A0288
INDEX CON/ANAL NAT/G ECO/UNDEV

B54
EPSTEIN L.D.,BRITAIN - UNEASY ALLY. KOREA UK USA+45 NAT/G POL/PAR ECO/TAC FOR/AID INT/TRADE WAR LABOR/PAR CONSRV/PAR. PAGE 42 A0857
DIPLOM ATTIT POLICY NAT/COMP

B54
KENWORTHY L.S.,FREE AND INEXPENSIVE MATERIALS ON WORLD AFFAIRS (PAMPHLET). WOR+45 CULTURE ECO/UNDEV INT/TRADE ARMS/CONT NUC/PWR UN. PAGE 78 A1597
BIBLIOG/A NAT/G INT/ORG DIPLOM

B54
TINBERGEN J.,INTERNATIONAL ECONOMIC INTEGRATION. WOR+45 WOR-45 ECO/UNDEV NAT/G ECO/TAC BAL/PAY ...METH/CNCPT STAT TIME/SEQ GEN/METH OEEC 20. PAGE 144 A2941
INT/ORG ECO/DEV INT/TRADE

S54
FOX W.T.R.,"CIVIL-MILITARY RELATIONS." USA+45 USA-45 R+D ACT/RES DIPLOM INT/TRADE EDU/PROP DETER DISPL DRIVE ORD/FREE...METH/CNCPT TREND COLD/WAR 20. PAGE 48 A0974
POLICY FORCES PLAN SOCIETY

C54
BOWIE R.R.,"STUDIES IN FEDERALISM." AGRI FINAN LABOR EX/STRUC FORCES LEGIS DIPLOM INT/TRADE ADJUD ...BIBLIOG 20 EEC. PAGE 17 A0357
FEDERAL EUR+WWI INT/ORG CONSTN

B55
ARNOLD G.L.,THE PATTERN OF WORLD CONFLICT. USA+45 INT/ORG ECO/TAC INT/TRADE PEACE 20 EUROPE. PAGE 9 A0176
DIPLOM BAL/PWR NAT/LISM PLAN

B55
BURR R.N.,DOCUMENTS ON INTER-AMERICAN COOPERATION: VOL. I, 1810-1881; VOL. II, 1881-1948. DELIB/GP BAL/PWR INT/TRADE REPRESENT NAT/LISM PEACE HABITAT ORD/FREE PWR SOVEREIGN...INT/LAW 20 OAS. PAGE 22 A0445
BIBLIOG DIPLOM INT/ORG L/A+17C

B55
LANDHEER B.,EUROPEAN YEARBOOK, 1955. CONSTN ECO/DEV DIST/IND FINAN DELIB/GP ECO/TAC DETER NUC/PWR ...BIBLIOG 20 EEC. PAGE 84 A1717
EUR+WWI INT/ORG GOV/REL INT/TRADE

B55
O3HEVSS E.,WIRTSCHAFTSSYSTEME UND INTERNATIONALER HANDEL. ECO/DEV FINAN MARKET DIPLOM ECO/TAC COST ...METH/COMP NAT/COMP 20. PAGE 112 A2306
CAP/ISM SOCISM INT/TRADE IDEA/COMP

B55
PANT Y.P.,PLANNING IN UNDERDEVELOPED ECONOMIES. INDIA NEPAL INT/TRADE COLONIAL SOVEREIGN ALL/IDEOS ...TIME/SEQ METH/COMP 20. PAGE 114 A2334
ECO/UNDEV PLAN ECO/TAC DIPLOM

B55
STILLMAN C.W.,AFRICA IN THE MODERN WORLD. AFR USA+45 WOR+45 INT/TRADE COLONIAL PARTIC REGION GOV/REL RACE/REL 20. PAGE 138 A2826
ECO/UNDEV DIPLOM POLICY STRUCT

B55
STUART G.H.,LATIN AMERICA AND THE UNITED STATES (5TH ED.). L/A+17C USA+45 USA-45 INT/TRADE COLONIAL ...POLICY CHARTS T 19/20. PAGE 140 A2856
NAT/G DIPLOM

B55
WRIGHT Q.,THE STUDY OF INTERNATIONAL RELATIONS. WOR+45 WOR-45 SOCIETY ECO/TAC INT/TRADE EDU/PROP ALL/VALS...CONCPT GEN/METH 20. PAGE 167 A3410
INT/ORG DIPLOM

L55
KISER M.,"ORGANIZATION OF AMERICAN STATES." L/A+17C USA+45 ECO/UNDEV INT/ORG NAT/G PLAN TEC/DEV DIPLOM ECO/TAC INT/TRADE EDU/PROP ADMIN ALL/VALS...POLICY MGT RECORD ORG/CHARTS OAS 20. PAGE 80 A1639
VOL/ASSN ECO/DEV REGION

B56
BUREAU OF PUBLIC AFFAIRS,AMERICAN FOREIGN POLICY: CURRENT DOCUMENTS. COM USA+45 USSR WOR+45 DELIB/GP FOR/AID INT/TRADE ARMS/CONT NUC/PWR ALL/VALS ALL/IDEOS...DECISION 20 NATO. PAGE 21 A0434
BIBLIOG/A DIPLOM POLICY

B56
FORSTMANN A.,DIE GRUNDLAGEN DER AUSSENWIRTSCHAFTSTHEORIE. ECO/TAC TARIFFS PRICE WAR ...NAT/COMP 20. PAGE 47 A0967
INT/TRADE CONCPT DIPLOM ECO/DEV

B56
GREECE PRESBEIA U.S.,BRITISH OPINION ON CYPRUS. CYPRUS UK FORCES DIPLOM INT/TRADE DOMIN GOV/REL ORD/FREE SOVEREIGN...POLICY 20. PAGE 55 A1137
ATTIT COLONIAL LEGIS PRESS

B56
JAMESON J.F.,THE AMERICAN REVOLUTION CONSIDERED AS A SOCIAL MOVEMENT. USA-45 AGRI FINAN SECT INT/TRADE REPRESENT SUFF INGP/REL RACE/REL DISCRIM...MAJORIT 18/19 CHURCH/STA. PAGE 73 A1494
ORD/FREE REV FEDERAL CONSTN

B56
KNORR K.E.,RUBLE DIPLOMACY: CHALLENGE TO AMERICAN FOREIGN AID(PAMPHLET). CHINA/COM USA+45 USSR PLAN TEC/DEV CAP/ISM INT/TRADE DOMIN EDU/PROP CONTROL LEAD 20 COLD/WAR. PAGE 81 A1654
ECO/UNDEV COM DIPLOM FOR/AID

B56
KRAUS O.,THEORIE DER ZWISCHENSTAATLICHEN WIRTSCHAFTSBEZIEHUNGEN. TARIFFS WAR COST 20. PAGE 82 A1677
INT/TRADE DIPLOM BAL/PAY ECO/TAC

B56
TOYNBEE A.,THE WAR AND THE NEUTRALS. L/A+17C PORTUGAL SPAIN SWEDEN SWITZERLND TURKEY WOR+45 WOR-45 ECO/TAC CONFER CONTROL REGION 20. PAGE 145 A2957
NEUTRAL WAR INT/TRADE DIPLOM

B56
US DEPARTMENT OF STATE,ECONOMIC PROBLEMS OF UNDERDEVELOPED AREAS (PAMPHLET). AFR ASIA ISLAM L/A+17C AGRI FINAN INDUS INT/ORG LABOR INT/TRADE ...PSY SOC 20. PAGE 151 A3090
BIBLIOG ECO/UNDEV TEC/DEV R+D

B56
US DEPARTMENT OF STATE,THE SUEZ CANAL PROBLEM; JULY 26-SEPTEMBER 22, 1956. UAR WOR+45 BAL/PWR COERCE NAT/LISM ATTIT ORD/FREE SOVEREIGN 20 SUEZ. PAGE 151 A3091
DIPLOM CONFER INT/TRADE

B56
VON BECKERATH E.,HANDWORTERBUCH DER SOCIALWISSENSCHAFTEN (II VOLS.). EUR+WWI GERMANY POL/PAR WORKER DIPLOM LEAD CHOOSE SUFF WEALTH...SOC 20. PAGE 159 A3249
BIBLIOG INT/TRADE NAT/G ECO/DEV

B56
WATT D.C.,BRITAIN AND THE SUEZ CANAL. COM UAR UK ...INT/LAW 20 SUEZ TREATY. PAGE 162 A3294
DIPLOM INT/TRADE DIST/IND NAT/G

B57
ASHER R.E.,THE UNITED NATIONS AND ECONOMIC AND SOCIAL COOPERATION. ECO/UNDEV COM/IND DIST/IND FINAN PLAN PROB/SOLV INT/TRADE TASK WEALTH...SOC 20 UN. PAGE 9 A0186
INT/ORG DIPLOM FOR/AID

B57
MCNEILL W.H.,GREECE: AMERICAN AID IN ACTION. GREECE UK USA+45 FINAN CAP/ISM INT/TRADE BAL/PAY PRODUC WEALTH...POLICY METH/COMP 20. PAGE 99 A2022
FOR/AID DIPLOM ECO/UNDEV

B57
SINEY M.C.,THE ALLIED BLOCKADE OF GERMANY: 1914-1916. EUR+WWI GERMANY MOD/EUR USA-45 DIPLOM CONTROL NEUTRAL PWR 20. PAGE 133 A2721
DETER INT/TRADE INT/LAW WAR

B57
US PRES CITIZEN ADVISERS,REPORT TO THE PRESIDENT ON THE MUTUAL SECURITY PROGRAM. COM USA+45 WOR+45 FINAN INDUS PLAN BUDGET CAP/ISM DIPLOM FOR/AID INT/TRADE REGION 20 SECUR/PROG. PAGE 155 A3163
BAL/PWR FORCES INT/ORG ECO/TAC

B57
WARBURG J.P.,AGENDA FOR ACTION. ISLAM ISRAEL USA+45 FOR/AID INT/TRADE WAR NAT/LISM 20 MID/EAST EUROPE ARABS. PAGE 161 A3275
DIPLOM POLICY INT/ORG BAL/PWR

B58
ALMEYDA M.C.,REFLEXIONES POLITICAS. CHILE L/A+17C USA+45 INT/ORG POL/PAR ECO/TAC PARTIC ATTIT 20. PAGE 6 A0128
ECO/UNDEV REGION DIPLOM INT/TRADE

B58
AVRAMOVIC D.,POSTWAR GROWTH IN INTERNATIONAL INDEBTEDNESS. WOR+45 AGRI INDUS CAP/ISM PRICE INCOME...NAT/COMP 20 GOLD/STAND SILVER. PAGE 10 A0199
INT/TRADE FINAN COST BAL/PAY

B58
INDIAN COUNCIL WORLD AFFAIRS,DEFENCE AND SECURITY IN THE INDIAN OCEAN AREA. INDIA S/ASIA CULTURE CONSULT DELIB/GP FORCES PROB/SOLV DIPLOM INT/TRADE 20 CMN/WLTH. PAGE 70 A1438
GEOG HABITAT ECO/UNDEV ORD/FREE

B58
JENNINGS I.,PROBLEMS OF THE NEW COMMONWEALTH. CEYLON INDIA PAKISTAN S/ASIA ECO/UNDEV INT/ORG LOC/G DIPLOM ECO/TAC INT/TRADE COLONIAL RACE/REL DISCRIM 20 COMMONWLTH PARLIAMENT. PAGE 74 A1508
NAT/LISM NEUTRAL FOR/AID POL/PAR

B58
MUNKMAN C.A.,AMERICAN AID TO GREECE. GREECE USA+45 AGRI FINAN PROB/SOLV WAR PWR...CHARTS 20 UN. PAGE 106 A2171
FOR/AID PLAN ECO/DEV INT/TRADE

B58
PALYI M.,MANAGED MONEY AT THE CROSSROADS: THE EUROPEAN EXPERIENCE. WOR+45 WOR-45 TEC/DEV DIPLOM INT/TRADE DEMAND WEALTH...CHARTS BIBLIOG 19/20 EUROPE GOLD/STAND SILVER. PAGE 113 A2324
FINAN ECO/TAC ECO/DEV PRODUC

B58
SALETORE B.A.,INDIA'S DIPLOMATIC RELATIONS WITH THE WEST. GREECE INDIA CULTURE ETIQUET...IDEA/COMP 3 ROM/EMP PERSIA. PAGE 126 A2590
DIPLOM CONCPT INT/TRADE

B58
SCITOUSKY T.,ECONOMIC THEORY AND WESTERN EUROPEAN INTEGRATION. EUR+WWI INT/ORG ACT/RES INT/TRADE REGION BAL/PAY WEALTH...METH/CNCPT STAT CHARTS GEN/METH ECSC TOT/POP EEC OEEC 20. PAGE 130 A2668
ECO/TAC

B58
SEYID MUHAMMAD V.A.,THE LEGAL FRAMEWORK OF WORLD TRADE. WOR+45 INT/ORG DIPLOM CONTROL...BIBLIOG 20 TREATY UN IMF GATT. PAGE 131 A2689
INT/LAW VOL/ASSN INT/TRADE TARIFFS

B58
SOC OF COMP LEGIS AND INT LAW,THE LAW OF THE SEA... (PAMPHLET). WOR+45 NAT/G INT/TRADE ADJUD CONTROL NUC/PWR WAR PEACE ATTIT ORD/FREE...JURID CHARTS 20 UN TREATY RESOURCE/N. PAGE 135 A2756
INT/LAW INT/ORG DIPLOM SEA

B58
WIGGINS J.W.,FOREIGN AID REEXAMINED: A CRITICAL APPRAISAL. CHINA/COM INDONESIA USA+45 FINAN INT/TRADE REGION NAT/LISM ATTIT...CENSUS 20. PAGE 164 A3342
FOR/AID DIPLOM ECO/UNDEV SOVEREIGN

L58
TRAGER F.N.,"A SELECTED AND ANNOTATED BIBLIOGRAPHY ON ECONOMIC DEVELOPMENT, 1953-1957." WOR+45 AGRI FINAN INDUS MARKET LABOR MUNIC WORKER PLAN INT/TRADE PRODUC CENSUS. PAGE 145 A2958
BIBLIOG/A ECO/UNDEV ECO/DEV

C58
BLANCHARD W.,"THAILAND." THAILAND CULTURE AGRI FINAN INDUS FAM LABOR INT/TRADE ATTIT...GEOG HEAL SOC BIBLIOG 20. PAGE 15 A0307
NAT/G DIPLOM ECO/UNDEV S/ASIA

B59
ALLEN R.L.,SOVIET INFLUENCE IN LATIN AMERICA. ECO/UNDEV FINAN PROC/MFG NAT/G TEC/DEV EDU/PROP EXEC ROUTINE ATTIT DRIVE PERSON ALL/VALS PWR...STAT CHARTS WORK 20. PAGE 6 A0125
L/A+17C ECO/TAC INT/TRADE USSR

B59
ALLEN W.R.,FOREIGN TRADE AND FINANCE. ECO/DEV DIPLOM BAL/PAY...POLICY CONCPT ANTHOL 20. PAGE 6 A0127
INT/TRADE EQUILIB FINAN

B59
DIEBOLD W. JR.,THE SCHUMAN PLAN: A STUDY IN ECONOMIC COOPERATION, 1950-1959. EUR+WWI FRANCE GERMANY USA+45 EXTR/IND CONSULT DELIB/GP PLAN DIPLOM ECO/TAC INT/TRADE ROUTINE ORD/FREE WEALTH ...METH/CNCPT STAT CONT/OBS INT TIME/SEQ ECSC 20. PAGE 37 A0759
INT/ORG REGION

B59
ETSCHMANN R.,DIE WAHRUNGS- UND DEVISENPOLITIK DES OSTBLOCKS UND IHRE AUSWIRKUNGEN AUF DIE WIRTSCHAFTSBEZIEHUNGEN ZWISCHEN OST U WEST. BULGARIA CZECHOSLVK HUNGARY POLAND USSR MARKET NAT/G PLAN DIPLOM...NAT/COMP 20. PAGE 42 A0867
ECO/TAC FINAN POLICY INT/TRADE

B59
HAZLEWOOD A.,THE ECONOMICS OF "UNDER-DEVELOPED" AREAS. WOR+45 DIST/IND EXTR/IND FINAN INDUS MARKET PLAN FOR/AID...GEOG 20. PAGE 63 A1302
BIBLIOG/A ECO/UNDEV AGRI INT/TRADE

B59
KARUNAKARAN K.P.,INDIA IN WORLD AFFAIRS, 1952-1958 (VOL. II). INDIA ECO/UNDEV SECT FOR/AID INT/TRADE ADJUD NEUTRAL REV WAR DISCRIM ORD/FREE MARXISM ...BIBLIOG 20. PAGE 77 A1569
DIPLOM INT/ORG S/ASIA COLONIAL

B59
MAC MILLAN W.M.,THE ROAD TO SELF-RULE. SOUTH/AFR UK CULTURE SOCIETY AGRI LABOR NAT/G INT/TRADE CONTROL GP/REL...SOC 19/20. PAGE 92 A1884
AFR COLONIAL SOVEREIGN POLICY

B59
MEZERK A.G.,FINANCIAL ASSISTANCE FOR ECONOMIC DEVELOPMENT. WOR+45 INDUS DIPLOM INT/TRADE...CHARTS GOV/COMP UN. PAGE 101 A2064
FOR/AID FINAN ECO/TAC ECO/UNDEV

B59
NOVE A.,COMMUNIST ECONOMIC STRATEGY: SOVIET GROWTH AND CAPABILITIES. USSR AGRI LABOR PLAN TEC/DEV CAP/ISM INT/TRADE EFFICIENCY MARXISM 20 THIRD/WRLD. PAGE 110 A2257
FOR/AID ECO/TAC DIPLOM INDUS

B59
ROBERTSON A.H.,EUROPEAN INSTITUTIONS: COOPERATION, INTEGRATION, UNIFICATION. EUR+WWI FINAN INT/ORG FORCES INT/TRADE TARIFFS 20 EEC EURATOM ECSC NATO TREATY. PAGE 122 A2496
ECO/DEV DIPLOM INDUS ECO/TAC

B59
ROBINSON J.A.,THE MONRONEY RESOULUTION: CONGRESSIONAL INITIATIVE IN FOREIGN POLICY MAKING. USA+45 POL/PAR TOP/EX DIPLOM INT/TRADE 20 CONGRESS WORLD/BANK INTL/DEV. PAGE 122 A2504
LEGIS FINAN ECO/UNDEV CHIEF

B59
ROPKE W.,INTERNATIONAL ORDER AND ECONOMIC INTEGRATION. ECO/DEV ECO/UNDEV AGRI FINAN INDUS INT/ORG WAR PEACE ORD/FREE...SOC METH/COMP 20 EEC. PAGE 123 A2524
INT/TRADE DIPLOM BAL/PAY ALL/IDEOS

B59
SANNWALD R.E.,ECONOMIC INTEGRATION: THEORETICAL ASSUMPTIONS AND CONSEQUENCES OF EUROPEAN UNIFICATION. EUR+WWI FUT FINAN INDUS VOL/ASSN ACT/RES ECO/TAC...PLURIST EEC OEEC 20. PAGE 127 A2601
INT/ORG ECO/DEV INT/TRADE

B59
STOVEL J.A.,CANADA IN THE WORLD ECONOMY. CANADA PRICE DEMAND...STAT CHARTS BIBLIOG 20 VINER/J. PAGE 139 A2838
INT/TRADE BAL/PAY FINAN ECO/TAC

B59
THOMAS D.H.,GUIDE TO THE DIPLOMATIC ARCHIVES OF WESTERN EUROPE. EUR+WWI ELITES INT/ORG NAT/G BAL/PWR INT/TRADE PEACE. PAGE 143 A2921
BIBLIOG DIPLOM CONFER

B59
VINACKE H.M.,A HISTORY OF THE FAR EAST IN MODERN TIMES (6TH ED.). KOREA S/ASIA USSR CONSTN CULTURE STRATA ECO/UNDEV NAT/G CHIEF FOR/AID INT/TRADE GP/REL...SOC NAT/COMP 19/20 CHINJAP. PAGE 159 A3235
STRUCT ASIA

B59
YRARRAZAVAL E.,AMERICA LATINE EN LA GUERRA FRIA. EUR+WWI L/A+17C USA+45 USSR WOR+45 INDUS INT/ORG NAT/LISM...POLICY COLD/WAR. PAGE 169 A3439
REGION DIPLOM ECO/UNDEV

INT/TRADE
L59
MURPHY J.C.,"SOME IMPLICATIONS OF EUROPE'S COMMON MARKET. IN (COOK P, ECONOMIC DEVELOPMENT AND INTERNATIONAL TRADE.." EUR+WWI ECO/DEV DIST/IND INDUS NAT/G PLAN ECO/TAC INT/TRADE WEALTH...STAT TREND OEEC TOT/POP 20 EEC. PAGE 106 A2178
MARKET INT/ORG REGION

S59
KINDLEBERGER C.P.,"UNITED STATES ECONOMIC FOREIGN POLICY: RESEARCH REQUIREMENTS FOR 1965." FUT USA+45 WOR+45 DIST/IND MARKET INT/ORG ECO/TAC INT/TRADE WEALTH...OBS TREND CON/ANAL GEN/LAWS VAL/FREE 20. PAGE 79 A1621
FINAN ECO/DEV FOR/AID

S59
PLAZA G.,"FOR A REGIONAL MARKET IN LATIN AMERICA." FUT L/A+17C CULTURE INDUS NAT/G ECO/TAC INT/TRADE ATTIT WEALTH...NEW/IDEA TREND OAS 20. PAGE 116 A2389
MARKET INT/ORG REGION

S59
ZAUBERMAN A.,"SOVIET BLOC ECONOMIC INTEGRATION." COM CULTURE INTELL ECO/DEV INDUS TOP/EX ACT/RES PLAN ECO/TAC INT/TRADE ROUTINE CHOOSE ATTIT ...TIME/SEQ 20. PAGE 169 A3448
MARKET INT/ORG USSR TOTALISM

N59
BRITISH COMMONWEALTH REL CONF,EXTRACTS FROM THE PROCEEDINGS OF THE SIXTH UNOFFICIAL CONFERENCE (PAMPHLET). GHANA INDIA RHODESIA UK FINAN FORCES DETER FEDERAL...LING 20 PARLIAMENT. PAGE 19 A0379
DIPLOM PARL/PROC INT/TRADE ORD/FREE

B60
APTHEKER H.,DISARMAMENT AND THE AMERICAN ECONOMY: A SYMPOSIUM. FUT USA+45 ECO/DEV DIST/IND FINAN INDUS PROC/MFG LABOR NAT/G POL/PAR CONSULT PLAN CAP/ISM INT/TRADE PEACE ATTIT MORAL WEALTH...TREND GEN/LAWS TOT/POP 20. PAGE 9 A0172
MARXIST ARMS/CONT

B60
ASPREMONT-LYNDEN H.,RAPPORT SUR L'ADMINISTRATION BELGE DU RUANDA-URUNDI PENDANT L'ANNEE 1959. BELGIUM RWANDA AGRI INDUS DIPLOM ECO/TAC INT/TRADE DOMIN ADMIN RACE/REL...GEOG CENSUS 20 UN. PAGE 9 A0192
AFR COLONIAL ECO/UNDEV INT/ORG

B60
BILLERBECK K.,SOVIET BLOC FOREIGN AID TO UNDERDEVELOPED COUNTRIES. COM FUT USSR FINAN FORCES TEC/DEV DIPLOM INT/TRADE EDU/PROP NUC/PWR...TREND 20. PAGE 14 A0287
FOR/AID ECO/UNDEV ECO/TAC MARXISM

B60
HOFFMANN P.G.,ONE HUNDRED COUNTRIES, ONE AND ONE QUARTER BILLION PEOPLE. MARKET INT/ORG TEC/DEV CAP/ISM...GEOG CHARTS METH/COMP 20 UN. PAGE 66 A1354
FOR/AID ECO/TAC ECO/UNDEV INT/TRADE

B60
JACOBSON H.K.,AMERICAN FOREIGN POLICY. COM EUR+WWI USA+45 USA-45 ECO/DEV ECO/UNDEV INT/ORG NAT/G INT/TRADE EDU/PROP COLONIAL CHOOSE MARXISM 20 NATO. PAGE 72 A1485
POL/PAR PWR DIPLOM

B60
KENEN P.B.,GIANT AMONG NATIONS: PROBLEMS IN UNITED STATES FOREIGN ECONOMIC POLICY. USA+45 FINAN DIPLOM TARIFFS BAL/PAY WEALTH 20 COLD/WAR. PAGE 77 A1584
FOR/AID ECO/UNDEV INT/TRADE PLAN

B60
KENEN P.B.,BRITISH MONETARY POLICY AND THE BALANCE OF PAYMENTS 1951-57. UK PLAN BUDGET ECO/TAC INT/TRADE PAY PRICE COST ATTIT 20. PAGE 77 A1585
BAL/PAY PROB/SOLV FINAN NAT/G

B60
KHRUSHCHEV N.S.,KHRUSHCHEV IN AMERICA. USA+45 USSR INT/TRADE EDU/PROP PRESS PEACE...MARXIST RECORD INT 20 COLD/WAR KHRUSH/N. PAGE 79 A1613
MARXISM CHIEF DIPLOM

B60
KRISTENSEN T.,THE ECONOMIC WORLD BALANCE. FUT WOR+45 CULTURE ECO/DEV BAL/PWR INT/TRADE REGION PWR WEALTH...STAT TREND CHARTS 20. PAGE 82 A1685
ECO/UNDEV ECO/TAC FOR/AID

B60
LERNER A.P.,THE ECONOMICS OF CONTROL. USA+45 ECO/UNDEV INT/ORG ACT/RES PLAN CAP/ISM INT/TRADE ATTIT WEALTH...SOC MATH STAT GEN/LAWS INDEX 20. PAGE 87 A1785
ECO/DEV ROUTINE ECO/TAC SOCISM

B60
LEVIN J.V.,THE EXPORT ECONOMIES: THEIR PATTERN OF DEVELOPMENT IN HISTORICAL PERSPECTIVE. BURMA PERU AGRI WORKER COLONIAL COST DEMAND INCOME 20. PAGE 88 A1795
INT/TRADE ECO/UNDEV BAL/PAY EXTR/IND

B60
LEWIS P.R.,LITERATURE OF THE SOCIAL SCIENCES: AN INTRODUCTORY SURVEY AND GUIDE. UK LAW INDUS DIPLOM INT/TRADE ADMIN...MGT 19/20. PAGE 88 A1802
BIBLIOG/A SOC

B60
LISTER L.,EUROPE'S COAL AND STEEL COMMUNITY. FRANCE GERMANY STRUCT ECO/DEV EXTR/IND INDUS MARKET NAT/G DELIB/GP ECO/TAC INT/TRADE EDU/PROP ATTIT RIGID/FLEX ORD/FREE PWR WEALTH...CONCPT STAT TIME/SEQ CHARTS ECSC 20. PAGE 90 A1843
EUR+WWI INT/ORG REGION

B60
MENEZES A.J.,O BRASIL E O MUNDO ASIO-AFRICANO (REV. ED.). AFR ASIA BRAZIL WOR+45 INT/TRADE ORD/FREE PWR
DIPLOM BAL/PWR

SOVEREIGN...POLICY 20. PAGE 99 A2040 LEAD ECO/UNDEV

B60
PENTONY D.E.,THE UNDERDEVELOPED LANDS. FUT WOR+45 CULTURE AGRI FINAN INDUS MARKET INT/ORG LABOR NAT/G VOL/ASSN CONSULT TEC/DEV ECO/TAC EDU/PROP COLONIAL ATTIT WEALTH...OBS RECORD SAMP TREND GEN/METH WORK UN 20. PAGE 115 A2351 ECO/UNDEV POLICY FOR/AID INT/TRADE

B60
PENTONY D.E.,UNITED STATES FOREIGN AID. INDIA LAOS USA+45 ECO/UNDEV INT/TRADE ADMIN PEACE ATTIT ...POLICY METH/COMP ANTHOL 20. PAGE 115 A2352 FOR/AID DIPLOM ECO/TAC

B60
SCHLESINGER J.R.,THE POLITICAL ECONOMY OF NATIONAL SECURITY. USA+45 USSR WOR+45 ECO/DEV ECO/UNDEV NAT/G DELIB/GP TOP/EX BAL/PWR DIPLOM INT/TRADE ATTIT PWR...STERTYP TOT/POP 20. PAGE 128 A2628 PLAN ECO/TAC

B60
SHONFIELD A.,THE ATTACK ON WORLD POVERTY. WOR+45 ECO/DEV ECO/UNDEV FINAN VOL/ASSN PLAN EDU/PROP DRIVE KNOWL WEALTH...CONT/OBS STAND/INT ORG/CHARTS TOT/POP UNESCO 20. PAGE 132 A2704 INT/ORG ECO/TAC FOR/AID INT/TRADE

B60
STEIN E.,AMERICAN ENTERPRISE IN THE EUROPEAN COMMON MARKET: A LEGAL PROFILE. EUR+WWI FUT USA+45 SOCIETY STRUCT ECO/DEV NAT/G VOL/ASSN CONSULT PLAN TEC/DEV ECO/TAC INT/TRADE ADMIN ATTIT RIGID/FLEX PWR...MGT NEW/IDEA STAT TREND COMPUT/IR SIMUL EEC 20. PAGE 137 A2814 MARKET ADJUD INT/LAW

B60
STOLPER W.F.,GERMANY BETWEEN EAST AND WEST: THE ECONOMICS OF COMPETITIVE COEXISTENCE. FUT GERMANY/E GERMANY/W WOR+45 FINAN POL/PAR BUDGET ECO/TAC FOR/AID INT/TRADE...STAT CHARTS METH/COMP 20 COLD/WAR. PAGE 138 A2832 ECO/DEV DIPLOM GOV/COMP BAL/PWR

B60
STRACHEY J.,THE END OF EMPIRE. UK WOR+45 WOR-45 DIPLOM INT/TRADE DOMIN ADJUST ORD/FREE WEALTH ...SOCIALIST GOV/COMP TIME COMMONWLTH. PAGE 139 A2841 COLONIAL ECO/DEV BAL/PWR LAISSEZ

B60
THE ECONOMIST (LONDON),THE COMMONWEALTH AND EUROPE. EUR+WWI WOR+45 AGRI FINAN INCOME...STAT CENSUS CHARTS CMN/WLTH EEC. PAGE 142 A2911 INT/TRADE INDUS INT/ORG NAT/COMP

B60
THEOBALD R.,THE RICH AND THE POOR: A STUDY OF THE ECONOMICS OF RISING EXPECTATIONS. WOR+45 CONSTN ECO/DEV ECO/UNDEV INT/ORG NAT/G PLAN FOR/AID ROUTINE BAL/PAY ORD/FREE PWR WEALTH...GEOG TREND WORK 20. PAGE 142 A2912 ECO/TAC INT/TRADE

B60
WODDIS J.,AFRICA: THE ROOTS OF REVOLT. SOUTH/AFR WORKER INT/TRADE RACE/REL DISCRIM ORD/FREE 20. PAGE 166 A3374 COLONIAL SOVEREIGN WAR ECO/UNDEV

L60
DEAN A.W.,"SECOND GENEVA CONFERENCE OF THE LAW OF THE SEA: THE FIGHT FOR FREEDOM OF THE SEAS." FUT USA+45 USSR WOR+45 WOR-45 SEA CONSTN STRUCT PLAN INT/TRADE ADJUD ADMIN ORD/FREE...DECISION RECORD TREND GEN/LAWS 20 TREATY. PAGE 35 A0717 INT/ORG JURID INT/LAW

S60
"THE EMERGING COMMON MARKETS IN LATIN AMERICA." FUT L/A+17C STRATA DIST/IND INDUS LABOR NAT/G LEGIS ECO/TAC ADMIN RIGID/FLEX HEALTH...NEW/IDEA TIME/SEQ OAS 20. PAGE 3 A0059 FINAN ECO/UNDEV INT/TRADE

S60
COHEN A.,"THE NEW AFRICA AND THE UN." FUT ECO/UNDEV NAT/G ECO/TAC INT/TRADE CHOOSE ATTIT ORD/FREE PWR ...POLICY METH/CNCPT OBS TREND CON/ANAL GEN/LAWS TOT/POP VAL/FREE UN 20. PAGE 27 A0558 AFR INT/ORG BAL/PWR FOR/AID

S60
FITZGIBBON R.H.,"DICTATORSHIP AND DEMOCRACY IN LATIN AMERICA." FUT ECO/DEV ECO/UNDEV INT/ORG LOC/G NAT/G TOP/EX PLAN TEC/DEV ECO/TAC CHOOSE ATTIT DRIVE PERSON ALL/VALS OAS TOT/POP 20. PAGE 46 A0943 L/A+17C ACT/RES INT/TRADE

S60
FRANKEL S.H.,"ECONOMIC ASPECTS OF POLITICAL INDEPENDENCE IN AFRICA." AFR FUT SOCIETY ECO/UNDEV COM/IND FINAN LEGIS PLAN TEC/DEV CAP/ISM ECO/TAC INT/TRADE ADMIN ATTIT DRIVE RIGID/FLEX PWR WEALTH ...MGT NEW/IDEA MATH TIME/SEQ VAL/FREE 20. PAGE 48 A0984 NAT/G FOR/AID

S60
GARNICK D.H.,"ON THE ECONOMIC FEASIBILITY OF A MIDDLE EASTERN COMMON MARKET." AFR ISLAM CULTURE INDUS NAT/G PLAN TEC/DEV ECO/TAC ADMIN ATTIT DRIVE RIGID/FLEX...PLURIST STAT TREND GEN/LAWS 20. PAGE 51 A1051 MARKET INT/TRADE

S60
KENNAN G.F.,"PEACEFUL CO-EXISTENCE: A WESTERN VIEW." COM EUR+WWI USA+45 USSR WOR+45 PLAN BAL/PWR DIPLOM INT/TRADE PWR...POLICY CONCPT OBS HIST/WRIT TREND GEN/LAWS COLD/WAR 20 KHRUSH/N. PAGE 78 A1589 ATTIT COERCE

S60
KREININ M.E.,"THE 'OUTER-SEVEN' AND EUROPEAN INTEGRATION." EUR+WWI FRANCE GERMANY ITALY UK ECO/DEV DIST/IND INT/TRADE DRIVE WEALTH...MYTH CHARTS EEC OEEC 20. PAGE 82 A1682 ECO/TAC GEN/LAWS

S60
MARTIN E.M.,"NEW TRENDS IN UNITED STATES ECONOMIC FOREIGN POLICY." USA+45 INTELL DELIB/GP FOR/AID INT/TRADE ROUTINE BAL/PAY...RELATIV 20. PAGE 95 A1949 NAT/G PLAN DIPLOM

S60
MORALES C.J.,"TRADE AND ECONOMIC INTEGRATION IN LATIN AMERICA." FUT L/A+17C LAW STRATA ECO/UNDEV DIST/IND INDUS LABOR NAT/G LEGIS ECO/TAC ADMIN RIGID/FLEX WEALTH...CONCPT NEW/IDEA CONT/OBS TIME/SEQ WORK 20. PAGE 104 A2128 FINAN INT/TRADE REGION

S60
OWEN C.F.,"US AND SOVIET RELATIONS WITH UNDERDEVELOPED COUNTRIES: LATIN AMERICA-A CASE STUDY." AFR COM L/A+17C USA+45 USSR EXTR/IND MARKET TEC/DEV DIPLOM ECO/TAC NAT/LISM ORD/FREE PWR ...TREND WORK 20. PAGE 112 A2303 ECO/UNDEV DRIVE INT/TRADE

N60
ERDMAN P.E.,COMMON MARKETS AND FREE TRADE AREAS (PAMPHLET). USA+45 MARKET INT/ORG TEC/DEV DIPLOM UTIL...CON/ANAL CHARTS BIBLIOG 20 EEC OEEC. PAGE 42 A0859 TREND PROB/SOLV INT/TRADE ECO/DEV

B61
AUBREY H.G.,COEXISTENCE: ECONOMIC CHALLENGE AND RESPONSE. USSR WOR+45 ACT/RES BAL/PWR CAP/ISM DIPLOM ECO/TAC FOR/AID INT/TRADE PEACE SOCISM ...METH/COMP NAT/COMP COLD/WAR. PAGE 10 A0196 POLICY ECO/UNDEV PLAN COM

B61
BAGU S.,ARGENTINA EN EL MUNDO. L/A+17C INDUS INT/TRADE WAR ATTIT ROLE...TREND 19/20 ARGEN OAS. PAGE 10 A0202 DIPLOM INT/ORG REGION ECO/UNDEV

B61
BONNEFOUS M.,EUROPE ET TIERS MONDE. EUR+WWI SOCIETY INT/ORG NAT/G VOL/ASSN ACT/RES TEC/DEV CAP/ISM ECO/TAC ATTIT ORD/FREE SOVEREIGN...POLICY CONCPT TREND 20. PAGE 16 A0334 AFR ECO/UNDEV FOR/AID INT/TRADE

B61
DIA M.,THE AFRICAN NATIONS AND WORLD SOLIDARITY. ISLAM CULTURE ELITES ECO/DEV ECO/UNDEV INT/ORG NAT/G PLAN ECO/TAC INT/TRADE EDU/PROP NAT/LISM ATTIT DRIVE ORD/FREE WEALTH...SOCIALIST CONCPT CON/ANAL GEN/LAWS TOT/POP 20. PAGE 37 A0753 AFR REGION SOCISM

B61
EINZIG P.,A DYNAMIC THEORY OF FORWARD EXCHANGE. FUT WOR+45 WOR-45 INT/TRADE BAL/PAY WEALTH...OLD/LIB NEW/IDEA OBS TREND 20. PAGE 41 A0830 FINAN ECO/TAC

B61
FRIEDMANN W.G.,JOINT INTERNATIONAL BUSINESS VENTURES. ASIA ISLAM L/A+17C ECO/DEV DIST/IND FINAN PROC/MFG FACE/GP LG/CO NAT/G VOL/ASSN CONSULT EX/STRUC PLAN ADMIN ROUTINE WEALTH...OLD/LIB WORK 20. PAGE 49 A1004 ECO/UNDEV INT/TRADE

B61
GURTOO D.H.N.,INDIA'S BALANCE OF PAYMENTS (1920-1960). INDIA FINAN DIPLOM FOR/AID INT/TRADE PRICE COLONIAL...CHARTS BIBLIOG 20. PAGE 58 A1197 BAL/PAY STAT ECO/TAC ECO/UNDEV

B61
HARDT J.P.,THE COLD WAR ECONOMIC GAP. USA+45 USSR ECO/DEV FORCES INT/TRADE NUC/PWR PWR 20 COLD/WAR. PAGE 61 A1258 DIPLOM ECO/TAC NAT/COMP POLICY

B61
HARRIS S.E.,THE DOLLAR IN CRISIS. USA+45 MARKET INT/ORG ECO/TAC PRICE CONTROL WEALTH...METH/COMP ANTHOL 20 GOLD/STAND. PAGE 62 A1269 BAL/PAY DIPLOM FINAN INT/TRADE

B61
HUDSON G.F.,THE SINO-SOVIET DISPUTE. CHINA/COM USSR INTELL INT/TRADE DEBATE REV...IDEA/COMP 20. PAGE 68 A1404 DIPLOM MARXISM PRESS ATTIT

B61
KITZINGER V.W.,THE CHALLENGE OF THE COMMON MARKET. EUR+WWI ECO/DEV DIST/IND PLAN ECO/TAC INT/TRADE LEGIT ATTIT PWR WEALTH...TIME/SEQ TREND CHARTS EEC 20. PAGE 80 A1647 MARKET INT/ORG UK

B61
MECHAM J.L.,THE UNITED STATES AND INTER-AMERICAN SECURITY, 1889-1960. L/A+17C USA+45 USA-45 CONSTN FORCES INT/TRADE PEACE TOTALISM ATTIT...JURID 19/20 UN OAS. PAGE 99 A2030 DIPLOM WAR ORD/FREE INT/ORG

B61
NATIONAL BANK OF LIBYA,INFLATION IN LIBYA (PAMPHLET). LIBYA SOCIETY NAT/G PLAN INT/TRADE ...STAT CHARTS 20 GOLD/STAND. PAGE 107 A2200 ECO/TAC ECO/UNDEV FINAN BUDGET

B61
OECD,STATISTICS OF BALANCE OF PAYMENTS 1950-61. WOR+45 FINAN ECO/TAC INT/TRADE DEMAND WEALTH...STAT BAL/PAY ECO/DEV

NAT/COMP 20 OEEC OECD. PAGE 111 A2278 INT/ORG CHARTS

B61
OEEC,LIBERALISATION OF CURRENT INVISIBLES AND CAPITAL MOVEMENTS BY THE OEEC (PAMPHLET). WOR+45 ECO/DEV BUDGET ECO/TAC ORD/FREE 20. PAGE 111 A2282 FINAN INT/ORG INT/TRADE BAL/PAY

B61
PERKINS D.,THE UNITED STATES AND LATIN AMERICAN. L/A+17C USA+45 USA-45 STRUCT COLONIAL REV ORD/FREE 19/20. PAGE 115 A2360 DIPLOM INT/TRADE NAT/G

B61
PERLO V.,EL IMPERIALISMO NORTHEAMERICANO. USA+45 USA-45 FINAN CAP/ISM DIPLOM DOMIN CONTROL DISCRIM 19/20. PAGE 115 A2363 SOCIALIST ECO/DEV INT/TRADE ECO/TAC

B61
SCHNAPPER B.,LA POLITIQUE ET LE COMMERCE FRANCAIS DANS LE GOLFE DE GUINEE DE 1838 A 1871. FRANCE GUINEA UK SEA EXTR/IND NAT/G DELIB/GP LEGIS ADMIN ORD/FREE...POLICY GEOG CENSUS CHARTS BIBLIOG 19. PAGE 129 A2636 COLONIAL INT/TRADE DOMIN AFR

B61
SOKOL A.E.,SEAPOWER IN THE NUCLEAR AGE. USA+45 USSR DIST/IND FORCES INT/TRADE DETER WAR...POLICY NAT/COMP BIBLIOG COLD/WAR. PAGE 135 A2763 SEA PWR WEAPON NUC/PWR

B61
TRIFFIN R.,GOLD AND THE DOLLAR CRISIS: THE FUTURE OF CONVERTIBILITY. USA+45 USA-45 INT/ORG PROB/SOLV BUDGET INT/TRADE PRICE...STAT CHARTS 19/20 GOLD/STAND. PAGE 145 A2963 FINAN ECO/DEV ECO/TAC BAL/PAY

B61
UAR MINISTRY OF CULTURE,A BIBLIOGRAPHICAL LIST OF AL MAGHRIB. ALGERIA ISLAM MOROCCO UAR SECT INT/TRADE COLONIAL 19/20 TUNIS. PAGE 146 A2987 BIBLIOG DIPLOM GEOG

B61
US CONGRESS JOINT ECO COMM,INTERNATIONAL PAYMENTS IMBALANCES AND NEED FOR STRENGTHENING INTERNATIONAL FINANCIAL ARRANGEMENTS. USA+45 WOR+45 DELIB/GP DIPLOM INT/TRADE...CHARTS 20 CONGRESS OEEC. PAGE 150 A3063 BAL/PAY INT/ORG FINAN PROB/SOLV

B61
US HOUSE COMM FOREIGN AFFAIRS,THE INTERNATIONAL DEVELOPMENT AND SECURITY ACT: HEARINGS BEFORE COMMITTEE ON FOREIGN AFFAIRS, HOUSE OF REP: HR7372. USA+45 AGRI INT/ORG NAT/G CONSULT DELIB/GP DIPLOM ECO/TAC INT/TRADE LOBBY REPRESENT 20 MCNAMARA/R DILLON/D RUSK/D CONGRESS. PAGE 153 A3128 FOR/AID CONFER LEGIS ECO/UNDEV

B61
WARD B.J.,INDIA AND THE WEST. INDIA UK USA+45 INT/TRADE GIVE COLONIAL ATTIT MARXISM 19/20. PAGE 161 A3279 PLAN ECO/UNDEV ECO/TAC FOR/AID

B61
WILLOUGHBY W.R.,THE ST LAWRENCE WATERWAY: A STUDY IN POLITICS AND DIPLOMACY. USA+45 ECO/DEV COM/IND INT/ORG CONSULT DELIB/GP ACT/RES TEC/DEV DIPLOM ECO/TAC ROUTINE...TIME/SEQ 20. PAGE 165 A3357 LEGIS INT/TRADE CANADA DIST/IND

S61
BRZEZINSKI Z.K.,"THE ORGANIZATION OF THE COMMUNIST CAMP." COM CZECHOSLVK COM/IND NAT/G DELIB/GP INT/TRADE DOMIN EDU/PROP EXEC ROUTINE COERCE ATTIT PWR...MGT CONCPT TIME/SEQ CHARTS VAL/FREE 20 TREATY. PAGE 20 A0416 VOL/ASSN DIPLOM USSR

S61
DELLA PORT G.,"PROBLEMI E PROSPETTIVE DI COESISTENZA FRA ORIENTE ED OCCIDENTE, (PART 3)." COM FUT WOR+45 NAT/G BAL/PWR FOR/AID BAL/PAY PWR WEALTH...SOC CONCPT GEN/LAWS COLD/WAR 20. PAGE 36 A0729 INT/TRADE

S61
DEUTSCH K.W.,"NATIONAL INDUSTRIALIZATION AND THE DECLINING SHARE OF THE INTERNATIONAL ECONOMIC SECTOR." EUR+WWI FUT WOR+45 WOR-45 MARKET PLAN EDU/PROP WEALTH...WELF/ST OBS TESTS 20. PAGE 36 A0740 DIST/IND ECO/DEV INT/TRADE

S61
OCHENG D.,"ECONOMIC FORCES AND UGANDA'S FOREIGN POLICY." AFR UGANDA INT/TRADE TARIFFS INCOME SOVEREIGN WEALTH 20 EACM EEC TANGANYIKA. PAGE 111 A2274 ECO/TAC DIPLOM ECO/UNDEV INT/ORG

S61
OCHENG D.,"AN ECONOMIST LOOKS AT UGANDA'S FUTURE." FUT UGANDA AGRI INDUS PLAN PROB/SOLV INT/TRADE SOVEREIGN 20. PAGE 111 A2275 ECO/UNDEV INCOME ECO/TAC OWN

S61
RAY J.,"THE EUROPEAN FREE-TRADE ASSOCIATION AND ITS IMPACT ON INDIA'S TRADE." EUR+WWI FRANCE GERMANY INDIA S/ASIA UK NAT/G VOL/ASSN PLAN INT/TRADE ROUTINE WEALTH...STAT CHARTS CMN/WLTH EEC OEEC 20 EFTA. PAGE 120 A2453 ECO/DEV ECO/TAC

S61
VERNON R.,"A TRADE POLICY FOR THE 1960'S." COM FUT USA+45 WOR+45 ECO/DEV ECO/UNDEV FINAN TOP/EX ACT/RES...WELF/ST METH/CNCPT CONT/OBS TOT/POP 20. PAGE 159 A3229 PLAN INT/TRADE

S61
VINER J.,"ECONOMIC FOREIGN POLICY ON THE NEW FRONTIER." USA+45 ECO/UNDEV AGRI FINAN INDUS MARKET INT/ORG NAT/G FOR/AID INT/TRADE ADMIN ATTIT PWR 20 KENNEDY/JF. PAGE 159 A3239 TOP/EX ECO/TAC BAL/PAY TARIFFS

S61
ZAGORIA D.S.,"SINO-SOVIET FRICTION IN UNDERDEVELOPED AREAS." ASIA CHINA/COM COM ACT/RES PLAN ATTIT ORD/FREE PWR COLD/WAR 20. PAGE 169 A3443 ECO/UNDEV ECO/TAC INT/TRADE USSR

B62
AIR FORCE ACADEMY LIBRARY,INTERNATIONAL ORGANIZATIONS AND MILITARY SECURITY SYSTEMS (PAMPHLET) (SPECIAL BIBLIOGRAPHY SERIES, NUMBER 25). DIPLOM FOR/AID INT/TRADE NUC/PWR PEACE 20 UN NATO OAS SEATO LEAGUE/NAT. PAGE 5 A0104 BIBLIOG INT/ORG FORCES DETER

B62
ALEXANDROWICZ C.H.,WORLD ECONOMIC AGENCIES: LAW AND PRACTICE. WOR+45 DIST/IND FINAN LABOR CONSULT INT/TRADE TARIFFS REPRESENT HEALTH...JURID 20 UN GATT EEC OAS ECSC. PAGE 6 A0115 INT/LAW INT/ORG DIPLOM ADJUD

B62
ALTHING F.A.M.,EUROPEAN ORGANIZATIONS AND FOREIGN RELATIONS OF STATES: A COMPARATIVE ANALYSIS OF DECISION-MAKING. EUR+WWI INT/ORG CONSTN ELITES BAL/PWR INT/TRADE SOVEREIGN TREATY. PAGE 6 A0131 DELIB/GP INT/ORG DECISION DIPLOM

B62
BRYANT A.,A CHOICE FOR DESTINY: COMMONWEALTH AND THE COMMON MARKET. EUR+WWI FUT UK INT/TRADE COLONIAL ATTIT SOVEREIGN 20 CMN/WLTH EEC. PAGE 20 A0411 INT/ORG VOL/ASSN DIPLOM CHOOSE

B62
COLOMBOS C.J.,THE INTERNATIONAL LAW OF THE SEA. WOR+45 EXTR/IND DIPLOM INT/TRADE TARIFFS AGREE WAR ...TIME/SEQ 20 TREATY. PAGE 28 A0570 INT/LAW SEA JURID ADJUD

B62
FAO,FOOD AND AGRICULTURE ORGANIZATION AFRICAN SURVEY. AFR CONGO/BRAZ GHANA STRATA AGRI INT/ORG TEC/DEV FOR/AID INT/TRADE RACE/REL DEMAND EFFICIENCY PRODUC...GEOG 20 UN CONGO/LEOP. PAGE 44 A0898 ECO/TAC WEALTH EXTR/IND ECO/UNDEV

B62
FATOUROS A.A.,GOVERNMENT GUARANTEES TO FOREIGN INVESTORS. WOR+45 ECO/UNDEV INDUS WORKER ADJUD ...NAT/COMP BIBLIOG TREATY. PAGE 44 A0903 NAT/G FINAN INT/TRADE ECO/DEV

B62
FORD A.G.,THE GOLD STANDARD 1880-1914: BRITAIN AND ARGENTINA. UK ECO/UNDEV INT/TRADE ADMIN GOV/REL DEMAND EFFICIENCY...STAT CHARTS 19/20 ARGEN GOLD/STAND. PAGE 47 A0960 FINAN ECO/TAC BUDGET BAL/PAY

B62
HOLMAN A.G.,SOME MEASURES AND INTERPRETATIONS OF EFFECTS OF US FOREIGN ENTERPRISES ON US BALANCE OF PAYMENTS. USA+45 COST INCOME WEALTH...MATH CHARTS 20. PAGE 67 A1371 BAL/PAY INT/TRADE FINAN ECO/TAC

B62
KINDLEBERGER C.P.,FOREIGN TRADE AND THE NATIONAL ECONOMY. WOR+45 ECO/DEV ECO/UNDEV ECO/TAC COST DEMAND 20. PAGE 79 A1622 INT/TRADE GOV/COMP BAL/PAY POLICY

B62
KRAFT J.,THE GRAND DESIGN. EUR+WWI USA+45 AGRI FINAN INDUS MARKET INT/ORG NAT/G PLAN ECO/TAC TARIFFS REGION DRIVE ORD/FREE WEALTH...POLICY OBS TREND EEC 20. PAGE 82 A1674 VOL/ASSN ECO/DEV INT/TRADE

B62
LAUERHAUSS L.,COMMUNISM IN LATIN AMERICA: THE POST-WAR YEARS (1945 -1960) (PAPER). INTELL STRATA ECO/UNDEV AGRI WORKER FOR/AID INT/TRADE COLONIAL GUERRILLA 20. PAGE 85 A1745 BIBLIOG L/A+17C MARXISM REV

B62
LEOPOLD R.W.,THE GROWTH OF AMERICAN FOREIGN POLICY: A HISTORY. USA+45 USA-45 EX/STRUC LEGIS INT/TRADE WAR...CHARTS BIBLIOG/A T 18/20. PAGE 87 A1780 NAT/G DIPLOM POLICY

B62
LIPPMANN W.,WESTERN UNITY AND THE COMMON MARKET. EUR+WWI FRANCE GERMANY/W UK USA+45 ECO/DEV AGRI FINAN MARKET INT/ORG NAT/G FOR/AID AGREE WEALTH 20 EEC. PAGE 89 A1831 DIPLOM INT/TRADE VOL/ASSN

B62
MEADE J.E.,CASE STUDIES IN EUROPEAN ECONOMIC UNION. BELGIUM EUR+WWI LUXEMBOURG NAT/G INT/TRADE REGION ROUTINE WEALTH...METH/CNCPT STAT CHARTS ECSC TOT/POP OEEC EEC 20. PAGE 99 A2028 INT/ORG ECO/TAC

B62
MODELSKI G.,SEATO-SIX STUDIES. ASIA CHINA/COM INDIA S/ASIA INT/ORG NAT/G ECO/TAC DETER ATTIT ORD/FREE PWR...TIME/SEQ COLD/WAR TOT/POP 20 SEATO. PAGE 102 A2098 MARKET ECO/UNDEV INT/TRADE

B62
RIMALOV V.V.,ECONOMIC COOPERATION BETWEEN USSR AND UNDERDEVELOPED COUNTRIES. USSR FINAN TEC/DEV FOR/AID PLAN

INT/TRADE DOMIN EDU/PROP COLONIAL NAT/LISM DRIVE SOVEREIGN...AUD/VIS 20. PAGE 121 A2482 — ECO/UNDEV DIPLOM

B62
ROBERTSON B.C.,REGIONAL DEVELOPMENT IN THE EUROPEAN ECONOMIC COMMUNITY. EUR+WWI FRANCE FUT ITALY UK ECO/UNDEV WORKER ACT/RES PROB/SOLV TEC/DEV ECO/TAC INT/TRADE EEC. PAGE 122 A2499 — PLAN ECO/DEV INT/ORG REGION

B62
ROBINSON A.D.,DUTCH ORGANIZED AGRICULTURE IN INTERNATIONAL POLITICS, 1945-1960. EUR+WWI NETHERLAND STRUCT ECO/DEV NAT/G VOL/ASSN CONSULT DELIB/GP PLAN TEC/DEV INT/TRADE EDU/PROP ATTIT RIGID/FLEX ALL/VALS...NEW/IDEA TREND EEC 20. PAGE 122 A2502 — AGRI INT/ORG

B62
SCHMITT H.A.,THE PATH TO EUROPEAN UNITY. EUR+WWI USA+45 PLAN TEC/DEV DIPLOM FOR/AID CONFER...INT/LAW 20 EEC EURCOALSTL MARSHL/PLN UNIFICA. PAGE 128 A2634 — INT/ORG INT/TRADE REGION ECO/DEV

B62
SELOSOEMARDJAN O.,SOCIAL CHANGES IN JOGJAKARTA. INDONESIA NETHERLAND ELITES STRATA STRUCT FAM POL/PAR CREATE DIPLOM INT/TRADE EDU/PROP ADMIN GOV/REL...SOC 20 JAVA CHINJAP. PAGE 131 A2683 — ECO/UNDEV CULTURE REV COLONIAL

B62
SHAW C.,LEGAL PROBLEMS IN INTERNATIONAL TRADE AND INVESTMENT. WOR+45 ECO/DEV ECO/UNDEV MARKET DIPLOM TAX INCOME ROLE...ANTHOL BIBLIOG 20 TREATY UN IMF GATT. PAGE 132 A2698 — INT/LAW INT/TRADE FINAN ECO/TAC

B62
TAYLOR D.,THE BRITISH IN AFRICA. UK CULTURE ECO/UNDEV INDUS DIPLOM INT/TRADE ADMIN WAR RACE/REL ORD/FREE SOVEREIGN...POLICY BIBLIOG 15/20 CMN/WLTH. PAGE 142 A2898 — AFR COLONIAL DOMIN

B62
THEOBALD R.,NATIONAL DEVELOPMENT EFFORTS (PAMPHLET). WOR+45 AGRI BUDGET FOR/AID INT/TRADE TAX 20. PAGE 142 A2914 — ECO/UNDEV PLAN BAL/PAY WEALTH

B62
US CONGRESS JOINT ECO COMM,FACTORS AFFECTING THE UNITED STATES BALANCE OF PAYMENTS. USA+45 DELIB/GP PLAN DIPLOM FOR/AID PRODUC WEALTH...CHARTS 20 CONGRESS OEEC. PAGE 150 A3064 — BAL/PAY INT/TRADE ECO/TAC FINAN

B62
US CONGRESS JOINT ECO COMM,ECONOMIC DEVELOPMENTS IN SOUTH AMERICA. USA+45 SOCIETY FINAN NAT/G PROB/SOLV TEC/DEV INT/TRADE TAX EFFICIENCY PRODUC ATTIT ...POLICY 20 CONGRESS SOUTH/AMER. PAGE 150 A3065 — L/A+17C ECO/UNDEV FOR/AID DIPLOM

B62
ZOOK P.D.,FOREIGN TRADE AND HUMAN CAPITAL. L/A+17C USA+45 FINAN DIPLOM ECO/TAC PRODUC...POLICY 20. PAGE 170 A3458 — INT/TRADE ECO/UNDEV FOR/AID BAL/PAY

L62
MURACCIOLE L.,"LA BANQUE CENTRALE DES ETATS DE L'AFRIQUE DE L'OUEST." AFR LAW ECO/UNDEV INT/ORG NAT/G CONSULT ECO/TAC ROUTINE...CHARTS 20. PAGE 106 A2175 — ISLAM FINAN INT/TRADE

S62
DEUTSCH K.W.,"TOWARDS WESTERN EUROPEAN INTEGRATION: AN INTERIM ASSESSMENT." EUR+WWI STRUCT ECO/DEV INT/ORG ECO/TAC INT/TRADE EDU/PROP PEACE ATTIT DRIVE PWR SOVEREIGN...PSY SOC TIME/SEQ CHARTS STERTYP 20. PAGE 36 A0741 — VOL/ASSN RIGID/FLEX REGION

S62
TATOMIR N.,"ORGANIZATIA INTERNATIONALA A MUNCII: ASPECTE NOI ALE PROBLEMEI IMBUNATATIRII MECANISMULUI EI." EUR+WWI ECO/DEV VOL/ASSN ADMIN ...METH/CNCPT WORK ILO 20. PAGE 141 A2891 — INT/ORG INT/TRADE

S62
THOMPSON D.,"THE UNITED KINGDOM AND THE TREATY OF ROME." EUR+WWI INT/ORG NAT/G DELIB/GP LEGIS INT/TRADE RIGID/FLEX...CONCPT EEC PARLIAMENT CMN/WLTH 20. PAGE 143 A2925 — ADJUD JURID

C62
DUFFY J.,"PORTUGAL IN AFRICA." PORTUGAL SIER/LEONE INDUS WORKER INT/TRADE WAR CONSERVE...CATH GEOG TREND 16/20. PAGE 39 A0795 — BIBLIOG RACE/REL ECO/UNDEV COLONIAL

B63
BRITISH AID. UK AGRI DIST/IND INDUS SCHOOL TEC/DEV INT/TRADE COLONIAL DEMAND...TREND CHARTS 20. PAGE 3 A0064 — FOR/AID ECO/UNDEV NAT/G FINAN

B63
BROWN W.N.,THE UNITED STATES AND INDIA AND PAKISTAN (REV. ED.). INDIA PAKISTAN S/ASIA WOR+45 POL/PAR SECT INT/TRADE COLONIAL COERCE DISCRIM. PAGE 20 A0408 — DIPLOM ECO/UNDEV SOVEREIGN STRUCT

B63
CENTRO PARA EL DESARROLLO,LA ALIANZA PARA EL PROGRESO Y EL DESARROLLO SOCIAL DE AMERICA LATINA. L/A+17C INT/ORG DIPLOM ECO/TAC INT/TRADE ATTIT 20. PAGE 25 A0512 — ECO/UNDEV FOR/AID PLAN REGION

B63
ERHARD L.,THE ECONOMICS OF SUCCESS. GERMANY/W WOR+45 LABOR CHIEF TAX REGION COST DEMAND ANTHOL. PAGE 42 A0860 — ECO/DEV INT/TRADE PLAN DIPLOM

B63
FISCHER-GALATI S.,EASTERN EUROPE IN THE SIXTIES. ALBANIA USSR YUGOSLAVIA ECO/UNDEV AGRI MARKET LABOR WORKER DIPLOM INT/TRADE EDU/PROP GOV/REL PRODUC UTOPIA SOCISM 20. PAGE 46 A0939 — MARXISM TEC/DEV BAL/PWR ECO/TAC

B63
GOLDSCHMIDT W.,THE UNITED STATES AND AFRICA. USA+45 CULTURE ECO/TAC INT/TRADE GOV/REL...SOC ANTHOL 20 INTERVENT. PAGE 53 A1091 — AFR ECO/UNDEV DIPLOM

B63
GUIMARAES A.P.,INFLACAO E MONOPOLIO NO BRASIL. BRAZIL FINAN NAT/G PLAN PAY...METH/COMP 20. PAGE 58 A1189 — ECO/UNDEV PRICE INT/TRADE BAL/PAY

B63
HUSSEY W.D.,THE BRITISH EMPIRE AND COMMONWEALTH 1500 TO 1961. UK USA-45 SOCIETY ECO/UNDEV NAT/G VOL/ASSN INT/TRADE DOMIN CONTROL WAR PWR ...DICTIONARY 16/20 COMMONWLTH TRUST/TERR. PAGE 69 A1422 — COLONIAL SOVEREIGN INT/ORG

B63
INTERAMERICAN ECO AND SOC COUN,THE ALLIANCE FOR PROGRESS: ITS FIRST YEAR: 1961-1962. AGRI SCHOOL PLAN TEC/DEV INT/TRADE TAX GIVE ADMIN WEALTH...SOC 20 SOUTH/AMER. PAGE 71 A1449 — INT/ORG PROB/SOLV ECO/TAC L/A+17C

B63
INTERNATIONAL MONETARY FUND,COMPENSATORY FINANCING OF EXPORT FLUCTUATIONS (PAMPHLET). WOR+45 ECO/DEV ECO/UNDEV INT/ORG WEALTH...TREND 20 IMF MONEY. PAGE 71 A1459 — BAL/PAY FINAN BUDGET INT/TRADE

B63
KRAVIS I.B.,DOMESTIC INTERESTS AND INTERNATIONAL OBLIGATIONS: SAFEGUARDS IN INTERNATIONAL TRADE ORGANIZATIONS. EUR+WWI USA+45 WOR+45 FINAN DELIB/GP ATTIT RIGID/FLEX HEALTH...STAT EEC VAL/FREE OEEC ECSC 20. PAGE 82 A1680 — INT/ORG ECO/TAC INT/TRADE

B63
LANGE O.,ECONOMIC DEVELOPMENT, PLANNING, AND INTERNATIONAL COOPERATION. UAR WOR+45 FINAN CAP/ISM PERS/REL 20. PAGE 84 A1722 — ECO/UNDEV DIPLOM INT/TRADE PLAN

B63
LARY M.B.,PROBLEMS OF THE UNITED STATES AS WORLD TRADER AND BANKER. USA+45 NAT/G PLAN DIPLOM FOR/AID ...TREND CHARTS. PAGE 85 A1737 — ECO/DEV FINAN BAL/PAY INT/TRADE

B63
LERCHE C.O. JR.,CONCEPTS OF INTERNATIONAL POLITICS. WOR+45 WOR-45 LAW DELIB/GP EX/STRUC TEC/DEV ECO/TAC INT/TRADE LEGIT ROUTINE COERCE ATTIT ORD/FREE PWR RESPECT...STERTYP GEN/LAWS VAL/FREE. PAGE 87 A1782 — INT/ORG WAR

B63
LERCHE C.O. JR.,AMERICA IN WORLD AFFAIRS. COM UK USA+45 INT/ORG FORCES ECO/TAC INT/TRADE EDU/PROP WAR NAT/LISM PEACE...BIBLIOG 18/20 UN CONGRESS PRESIDENT COLD/WAR. PAGE 87 A1783 — NAT/G DIPLOM PLAN

B63
LICHTHEIM G.,THE NEW EUROPE: TODAY AND TOMORROW. EUR+WWI FINAN 20 EEC EUROPE/W. PAGE 88 A1809 — DIPLOM ECO/DEV INT/ORG INT/TRADE

B63
LYONS F.S.L.,INTERNATIONALISM IN EUROPE 1815-1914. LAW AGRI COM/IND DIST/IND LABOR SECT INT/TRADE TARIFFS...BIBLIOG 19/20. PAGE 92 A1880 — DIPLOM MOD/EUR INT/ORG

B63
MANSERGH N.,DOCUMENTS AND SPEECHES ON COMMONWEALTH AFFAIRS 1952-1962. CANADA INDIA PAKISTAN UK CONSTN FORCES ECO/TAC EDU/PROP COLONIAL DETER WAR ORD/FREE SOVEREIGN...POLICY 20 AUSTRAL. PAGE 94 A1932 — BIBLIOG/A FEDERAL INT/TRADE DIPLOM

B63
MENDES C.,NACIONALISMO E DESENVOLVIMENTO. AFR ASIA L/A+17C STRATA INT/TRADE COLONIAL. PAGE 99 A2039 — NAT/LISM ECO/UNDEV DIPLOM REV

B63
MOSELY P.E.,THE SOVIET UNION, 1922-1962: A FOREIGN AFFAIRS READER. ASIA POLAND USSR CULTURE INTELL AGRI POL/PAR WORKER INT/TRADE DOMIN WAR NAT/LISM MARXISM SOCISM 20 KHRUSH/N. PAGE 105 A2152 — PWR POLICY DIPLOM

B63
MYRDAL G.,CHALLENGE TO AFFLUENCE. USA+45 WOR+45 FINAN INT/ORG NAT/G PLAN ECO/TAC INT/TRADE BAL/PAY ORD/FREE 20 EUROPE/W. PAGE 107 A2189 — ECO/DEV WEALTH DIPLOM PRODUC

B63
PAENSON I.,SYSTEMATIC GLOSSARY ENGLISH, FRENCH, SPANISH, RUSSIAN OF SELECTED ECONOMIC AND SOCIAL TERMS. WOR+45 FINAN LABOR INT/TRADE DEMAND PRODUC 20. PAGE 113 A2315 — DICTIONARY SOC LING

B63
PANAMERICAN UNION,DOCUMENTOS OFICIALES DE LA ORGANIZACION DE LOS ESTADOS AMERICANOS, INDICE Y LISTA (VOL. III, 1962). L/A+17C DELIB/GP INT/TRADE EDU/PROP REGION NUC/PWR...HEAL INT/LAW SOC/WK 20 OAS. PAGE 113 A2329 — BIBLIOG INT/ORG DIPLOM

B63
PATRA A.C.,THE ADMINISTRATION OF JUSTICE UNDER THE EAST INDIA COMPANY IN BENGAL, BIHAR AND ORISSA. INDIA UK LG/CO CAP/ISM INT/TRADE ADJUD COLONIAL CONTROL CT/SYS...POLICY 20. PAGE 114 A2341 — ADMIN JURID CONCPT

B63
RUSK D.,THE WINDS OF FREEDOM. S/ASIA SOUTH/AFR INT/ORG FORCES NUC/PWR PEACE ORD/FREE 20 UN COLD/WAR. PAGE 125 A2569 — DIPLOM FOR/AID INT/TRADE

B63
SALENT W.S.,THE UNITED STATES BALANCE OF PAYMENTS IN 1968. EUR+WWI UK USA+45 AGRI R+D LABOR FORCES PRODUC...GEOG CONCPT CHARTS 20 CHINJAP EEC. PAGE 126 A2589 — BAL/PAY DEMAND FINAN INT/TRADE

B63
THEOBALD R.,FREE MEN AND FREE MARKETS. USA+45 USA-45 ECO/DEV NAT/G TEC/DEV DIPLOM INT/TRADE INCOME ORD/FREE WEALTH...TREND 19/20 KEYNES/JM. PAGE 143 A2915 — CONCPT ECO/TAC CAP/ISM MARKET

B63
THORELLI H.B.,INTOP: INTERNATIONAL OPERATIONS SIMULATION: PLAYER'S MANUAL. BRAZIL FINAN OP/RES ADMIN GP/REL INGP/REL PRODUC PERCEPT...DECISION MGT EEC. PAGE 144 A2935 — GAME INT/TRADE EDU/PROP LG/CO

B63
UN SECRETARY GENERAL,PLANNING FOR ECONOMIC DEVELOPMENT. ECO/UNDEV FINAN BUDGET INT/TRADE TARIFFS TAX ADMIN 20 UN. PAGE 147 A3005 — PLAN ECO/TAC MGT NAT/COMP

B63
UNITED STATES GOVERNMENT,REPORT TO THE INTER-AMERICAN ECONOMIC AND SOCIAL COUNCIL. L/A+17C INDUS PLAN INT/TRADE TARIFFS CONFER...CHARTS 20 LAFTA. PAGE 149 A3038 — FOR/AID ECO/TAC ECO/UNDEV DIPLOM

B63
US CONGRESS JOINT ECO COMM,DISCRIMINATORY OCEAN FREIGHT RATES AND BALANCE OF PAYMENTS. USA+45 SEA DELIB/GP DISCRIM...CHARTS 20 CONGRESS. PAGE 150 A3066 — BAL/PAY DIST/IND PRICE INT/TRADE

B63
US CONGRESS JOINT ECO COMM,THE UNITED STATES BALANCE OF PAYMENTS. USA+45 DELIB/GP BUDGET PRICE PRODUC 20 CONGRESS GOLD/STAND MONEY. PAGE 150 A3067 — BAL/PAY INT/TRADE FINAN ECO/TAC

B63
US CONGRESS JOINT ECO COMM,THE UNITED STATES BALANCE OF PAYMENTS. USA+45 DELIB/GP CONFER...MATH PREDICT CHARTS 20 CONGRESS. PAGE 150 A3068 — BAL/PAY ECO/TAC INT/TRADE CONSULT

B63
US ECON SURVEY TEAM INDONESIA,INDONESIA - PERSPECTIVE AND PROPOSALS FOR UNITED STATES ECONOMIC AID. INDONESIA AGRI MARKET TEC/DEV DIPLOM INT/TRADE EDU/PROP 20. PAGE 153 A3113 — FOR/AID ECO/UNDEV PLAN INDUS

B63
US HOUSE COMM FOREIGN AFFAIRS,HEARINGS ON H.R. 5490 TO AMEND FURTHER THE FOREIGN ASSISTANCE ACT OF 1961. CUBA EUR+WWI INDIA INT/ORG DELIB/GP LEGIS DIPLOM CONFER ORD/FREE 20 DEPT/STATE DEPT/DEFEN UN. PAGE 153 A3129 — FOR/AID INT/TRADE FORCES WEAPON

B63
VON HALLER A.,DIE LETZTEN WOLLEN DIE ERSTEN SEIN. AFR S/ASIA INT/TRADE REV ORD/FREE SOVEREIGN 20. PAGE 160 A3251 — FOR/AID ECO/UNDEV MARXISM CAP/ISM

B63
WESTERFIELD H.,THE INSTRUMENTS OF AMERICA'S FOREIGN POLICY. WOR+45 ECO/DEV NAT/G CONSULT EX/STRUC LEGIS BAL/PWR FOR/AID INT/TRADE DOMIN EDU/PROP LEGIT ATTIT KNOWL ORD/FREE PWR WEALTH...OBS COLD/WAR TOT/POP VAL/FREE. PAGE 163 A3322 — USA+45 INT/ORG DIPLOM

L63
PRINCETON UNIV. CONFERENCE,"ARAB DEVELOPMENT IN THE EMERGING INTERNATIONAL ECONOMY." FUT USA+45 DIST/IND FINAN DELIB/GP PLAN ECO/TAC WEALTH VAL/FREE 20. PAGE 118 A2413 — ISLAM ECO/UNDEV FOR/AID INT/TRADE

L63
SZASZY E.,"L'EVOLUTION DES PRINCIPES GENERAUX DU DROIT INTERNATIONAL PRIVE DANS LES PAYS DE DEMOCRATIE POPULAIRE." COM FUT WOR+45 LAW ECO/DEV PERF/ART POL/PAR PROF/ORG ECO/TAC INT/TRADE EDU/PROP ATTIT RIGID/FLEX ALL/VALS SOCISM...JURID TREND GEN/LAWS WORK 20. PAGE 141 A2876 — DIPLOM TOTALISM INT/LAW INT/ORG

S63
ANGUILE G.,"CIVILISATION DU PLAN DANS L'EUROPE ET L'AFRIQUE DE DEMAIN." AFR EUR+WWI GABON ECO/DEV FINAN MARKET DELIB/GP ECO/TAC WEALTH...TREND 20. PAGE 8 A0163 — ECO/UNDEV PLAN INT/TRADE

S63
DIEBOLD W. JR.,"THE NEW SITUATION OF INTERNATIONAL TRADE POLICY." EUR+WWI FRANCE FUT UK USA+45 WOR+45 DIST/IND PLAN INT/TRADE EDU/PROP PWR WEALTH ...RECORD TREND GEN/LAWS EEC VAL/FREE 20. PAGE 37 A0760 — MARKET ECO/TAC

S63
EMERSON R.,"THE ATLANTIC COMMUNITY AND THE EMERGING COUNTRIES." FUT WOR+45 ECO/DEV ECO/UNDEV R+D NAT/G DELIB/GP BAL/PWR ECO/TAC EDU/PROP ROUTINE ORD/FREE PWR WEALTH...POLICY CONCPT TREND GEN/METH EEC 20 NATO. PAGE 42 A0848 — ATTIT INT/TRADE

S63
FRIEDMANN W.G.,"THE USES OF 'GENERAL PRINCIPLES' IN THE DEVELOPMENT OF INTERNATIONAL LAW." WOR+45 NAT/G DIPLOM INT/TRADE LEGIT ROUTINE RIGID/FLEX ORD/FREE ...JURID CONCPT STERTYP GEN/METH 20. PAGE 49 A1005 — LAW INT/LAW INT/ORG

S63
GORDON B.,"ECONOMIC IMPEDIMENTS TO REGIONALISM IN SOUTH EAST ASIA." BURMA FUT S/ASIA THAILAND USA+45 AGRI INDUS R+D NAT/G PLAN ECO/TAC WEALTH...STAT CONT/OBS 20. PAGE 54 A1110 — VOL/ASSN ECO/UNDEV INT/TRADE REGION

S63
MATHUR P.N.,"GAINS IN ECONOMIC GROWTH FROM INTERNATIONAL TRADE." USA-45 ECO/DEV FINAN INDUS ATTIT WEALTH...MATH QUANT STAT BIOG TREND GEN/LAWS WORK 20. PAGE 96 A1966 — MARKET ECO/TAC CAP/ISM INT/TRADE

S63
NYE J.S. JR.,"EAST AFRICAN ECONOMIC INTEGRATION." AFR UGANDA PROVS DELIB/GP PLAN ECO/TAC INT/TRADE ADMIN ROUTINE ORD/FREE PWR WEALTH...OBS TIME/SEQ VAL/FREE 20. PAGE 110 A2264 — ECO/UNDEV INT/ORG

S63
RAMERIE L.,"TENSION AU SEIN DU COMECON: LE CAS ROUMAIN." COM EUR+WWI USSR WOR+45 ECO/DEV DIST/IND NAT/G POL/PAR VOL/ASSN EDU/PROP TOTALISM ATTIT WEALTH...TIME/SEQ 20 COMECON. PAGE 119 A2438 — INT/ORG ECO/TAC INT/TRADE ROMANIA

S63
SCHMIDT W.E.,"THE CASE AGAINST COMMODITY AGREEMENTS." FUT L/A+17C STRATA CONSULT PLAN ECO/TAC EDU/PROP ATTIT DRIVE RIGID/FLEX WEALTH ...MYTH 20. PAGE 128 A2631 — ECO/UNDEV ACT/RES INT/TRADE

S63
SHONFIELD A.,"AFTER BRUSSELS." EUR+WWI FRANCE GERMANY UK ECO/DEV DIST/IND MARKET VOL/ASSN DELIB/GP CREATE INT/TRADE ATTIT RIGID/FLEX...RECORD TREND GEN/LAWS EEC CMN/WLTH 20. PAGE 132 A2705 — PLAN ECO/TAC

S63
SHWADRAN B.,"MIDDLE EAST OIL, 1962." ISLAM USSR ECO/DEV DIST/IND INDUS PLAN BAL/PWR DISPL DRIVE ...POLICY STAT TREND GEN/LAWS EEC OEEC 20 OIL. PAGE 132 A2712 — MARKET ECO/TAC INT/TRADE

S63
WALKER H.,"THE INTERNATIONAL LAW OF COMMODITY AGREEMENTS." FUT WOR+45 ECO/DEV ECO/UNDEV FINAN INT/ORG NAT/G CONSULT CREATE PLAN ECO/TAC ATTIT PERCEPT...CONCPT GEN/LAWS TOT/POP GATT 20. PAGE 160 A3265 — MARKET VOL/ASSN INT/LAW INT/TRADE

B64
ALVIM J.C.,A REVOLUCAO SEM RUMO. BRAZIL NAT/G BAL/PWR DIPLOM INT/TRADE PARTIC WEALTH...POLICY SOC SOC/INTEG 20. PAGE 6 A0132 — REV CIVMIL/REL ECO/UNDEV ORD/FREE

B64
ANDREWS D.H.,LATIN AMERICA: A BIBLIOGRAPHY OF PAPERBACK BOOKS. SECT INT/TRADE EDU/PROP WAR GOV/REL ADJUST NAT/LISM ATTIT...ART/METH LING BIOG 20. PAGE 8 A0160 — BIBLIOG L/A+17C CULTURE NAT/G

B64
ARNOLD G.,TOWARDS PEACE AND A MULTIRACIAL COMMONWEALTH. UK TEC/DEV BAL/PWR COLONIAL GP/REL NAT/LISM PEACE SOVEREIGN...POLICY SOC/INTEG 20 CMN/WLTH. PAGE 9 A0175 — DIPLOM INT/TRADE FOR/AID ORD/FREE

B64
CHENG C.,ECONOMIC RELATIONS BETWEEN PEKING AND MOSCOW: 1949-63. ASIA CHINA/COM COM USSR FINAN INDUS CONSULT TEC/DEV INT/TRADE...PREDICT CHARTS BIBLIOG 20. PAGE 26 A0527 — DIPLOM FOR/AID MARXISM

B64
CURRIE D.P.,FEDERALISM AND THE NEW NATIONS OF AFRICA. CANADA USA+45 INT/TRADE TAX GP/REL ...NAT/COMP SOC/INTEG 20. PAGE 33 A0667 — FEDERAL AFR ECO/UNDEV INT/LAW

B64
DESHMUKH C.D.,THE COMMONWEALTH AS INDIA SEES IT. INDIA UK ECO/UNDEV TEC/DEV INT/TRADE GP/REL RACE/REL SOVEREIGN SOC/INTEG 19/20 COMMONWLTH. PAGE 36 A0733 — DIPLOM COLONIAL NAT/LISM ATTIT

B64
DUROSELLE J.B.,POLITIQUES NATIONALES ENVERS LES JEUNES ETATS. FRANCE ISRAEL ITALY UK USA+45 USSR YUGOSLAVIA ECO/DEV FINAN ECO/TAC INT/TRADE ADMIN PWR 20. PAGE 40 A0809 — DIPLOM ECO/UNDEV COLONIAL DOMIN

B64
ESTHUS R.A.,FROM ENMITY TO ALLIANCE: US AUSTRALIAN RELATIONS. S/ASIA DIST/IND VOL/ASSN FORCES ATTIT 20 AUSTRAL TREATY CMN/WLTH. PAGE 42 A0863 — DIPLOM WAR INT/TRADE FOR/AID

B64
FULBRIGHT J.W.,OLD MYTHS AND NEW REALITIES. USA+45 USSR LEGIS INT/TRADE DETER ATTIT...POLICY 20 COLD/WAR TREATY. PAGE 50 A1016 DIPLOM INT/ORG ORD/FREE

B64
GRZYBOWSKI K.,THE SOCIALIST COMMONWEALTH OF NATIONS: ORGANIZATIONS AND INSTITUTIONS. FORCES DIPLOM INT/TRADE ADJUD ADMIN LEAD WAR MARXISM SOCISM...BIBLIOG 20 COMECON WARSAW/P. PAGE 58 A1185 INT/LAW COM REGION INT/ORG

B64
HAMBRIDGE G.,DYNAMICS OF DEVELOPMENT. AGRI FINAN INDUS LABOR INT/TRADE EDU/PROP ADMIN LEAD OWN HEALTH...ANTHOL BIBLIOG 20. PAGE 61 A1245 ECO/UNDEV ECO/TAC OP/RES ACT/RES

B64
HANSEN B.,INTERNATIONAL LIQUIDITY. USA+45 INT/ORG ECO/TAC PRICE CONTROL WEALTH...POLICY 20. PAGE 61 A1254 BAL/PAY INT/TRADE DIPLOM FINAN

B64
HAZLEWOOD A.,THE ECONOMICS OF DEVELOPMENT: AN ANNOTATED LIST OF BOOKS AND ARTICLES PUBLISHED 1958-1962. AGRI FINAN INDUS LABOR NAT/G DIPLOM INT/TRADE INCOME...MGT 20. PAGE 63 A1303 BIBLIOG/A ECO/UNDEV TEC/DEV

B64
HINSHAW R.,THE EUROPEAN COMMUNITY AND AMERICAN TRADE: A STUDY IN ATLANTIC ECONOMICS AND POLICY. EUR+WWI UK USA+45 ECO/DEV ECO/UNDEV AGRI INDUS INT/ORG NAT/G ECO/TAC TARIFFS REGION...STAT CHARTS EEC 20. PAGE 65 A1337 MARKET TREND INT/TRADE

B64
KALDOR N.,ESSAYS ON ECONOMIC POLICY (VOL. II). CHILE GERMANY INDIA FINAN...GOV/COMP METH/COMP 20 KEYNES/JM. PAGE 76 A1551 BAL/PAY INT/TRADE METH/CNCPT ECO/UNDEV

B64
KNIGHT R.,BIBLIOGRAPHY ON INCOME AND WEALTH, 1957-1960 (VOL VIII). WOR+45 ECO/DEV FINAN INT/TRADE...GOV/COMP METH/COMP. PAGE 80 A1652 BIBLIOG/A ECO/UNDEV WEALTH INCOME

B64
KRAUSE L.B.,THE COMMON MARKET: PROGRESS AND CONTROVERSY. EUR+WWI UK ECO/DEV REGION...ANTHOL NATO EEC. PAGE 82 A1678 DIPLOM MARKET INT/TRADE INT/ORG

B64
LEGGE J.D.,INDONESIA. INDONESIA ELITES ECO/UNDEV POL/PAR CHIEF FORCES INT/TRADE COERCE CHOOSE ORD/FREE...SOC CHARTS BIBLIOG 16/20 CHINJAP. PAGE 86 A1765 S/ASIA DOMIN NAT/LISM POLICY

B64
LISKA G.,EUROPE ASCENDANT. EUR+WWI ECO/DEV FORCES INT/TRADE MARXISM 20 EEC. PAGE 90 A1838 DIPLOM BAL/PWR TARIFFS CENTRAL

B64
MAUD J.,AID FOR DEVELOPING COUNTRIES. COM EUR+WWI UK INT/TRADE ORD/FREE...GOV/COMP 20. PAGE 96 A1979 FOR/AID DIPLOM ECO/TAC ECO/UNDEV

B64
MC GOVERN G.S.,WAR AGAINST WANT. USA+45 AGRI DIPLOM INT/TRADE GIVE RECEIVE DEMAND HEALTH 20 KENNEDY/JF FOOD/PEACE. PAGE 97 A1993 FOR/AID ECO/DEV POLICY EATING

B64
MYINT H.,THE ECONOMICS OF THE DEVELOPING COUNTRIES. WOR+45 AGRI PLAN COST...POLICY GEOG 20 MONEY. PAGE 107 A2187 ECO/UNDEV INT/TRADE EXTR/IND FINAN

B64
NEWBURY C.W.,THE WEST AFRICAN COMMONWEALTH. CONSTN INTELL ECO/UNDEV VOL/ASSN CHIEF DELIB/GP LEGIS INT/TRADE COLONIAL FEDERAL ATTIT 20 COMMONWLTH AFRICA/W. PAGE 108 A2223 INT/ORG SOVEREIGN GOV/REL AFR

B64
NEWCOMER H.A.,INTERNATIONAL AIDS TO OVERSEAS INVESTMENTS AND TRADE. ECO/UNDEV TARIFFS PROFIT ...BIBLIOG 20 GATT UN. PAGE 108 A2225 INT/TRADE FINAN DIPLOM FOR/AID

B64
RAGHAVAN M.D.,INDIA IN CEYLONESE HISTORY, SOCIETY AND CULTURE. CEYLON INDIA S/ASIA LAW SOCIETY INT/TRADE ATTIT...ART/METH JURID SOC LING 20. PAGE 119 A2433 DIPLOM CULTURE SECT STRUCT

B64
RAMAZANI R.K.,THE MIDDLE EAST AND THE EUROPEAN COMMON MARKET. EUR+WWI ISLAM ECO/DEV EXTR/IND MARKET PROC/MFG INT/ORG NAT/G TEC/DEV ECO/TAC REGION DRIVE WEALTH...STAT CHARTS EEC TOT/POP 20. PAGE 119 A2437 ECO/UNDEV ATTIT INT/TRADE

B64
RANIS G.,THE UNITED STATES AND THE DEVELOPING ECONOMIES. COM USA+45 AGRI FINAN TEC/DEV CAP/ISM ECO/TAC INT/TRADE...POLICY METH/COMP ANTHOL 20 AID. PAGE 119 A2441 ECO/UNDEV DIPLOM FOR/AID

B64
REUSS H.S.,THE CRITICAL DECADE - AN ECONOMIC POLICY FOR AMERICA AND THE FREE WORLD. USA+45 FINAN POL/PAR WORKER PLAN DIPLOM ECO/TAC TARIFFS BAL/PAY ...POLICY 20 CONGRESS GOLD/STAND. PAGE 120 A2468 FOR/AID INT/TRADE LABOR LEGIS

B64
RIVKIN A.,AFRICA AND THE EUROPEAN COMMON MARKET (PAMPHLET). AFR MOD/EUR WOR+45 TEC/DEV FOR/AID TARIFFS BAL/PAY...POLICY 20 EEC. PAGE 121 A2490 INT/ORG INT/TRADE ECO/TAC ECO/UNDEV

B64
ROBERTS HL,FOREIGN AFFAIRS BIBLIOGRAPHY, 1952-1962. ECO/DEV SECT PLAN FOR/AID INT/TRADE ARMS/CONT NAT/LISM ATTIT...INT/LAW GOV/COMP IDEA/COMP 20. PAGE 122 A2495 BIBLIOG/A DIPLOM INT/ORG WAR

B64
SCHECHTER A.H.,INTERPRETATION OF AMBIGUOUS DOCUMENTS BY INTERNATIONAL ADMINISTRATIVE TRIBUNALS. WOR+45 EX/STRUC INT/TRADE CT/SYS SOVEREIGN 20 UN ILO EURCT/JUST. PAGE 128 A2620 INT/LAW DIPLOM INT/ORG ADJUD

B64
SEGAL R.,SANCTIONS AGAINST SOUTH AFRICA. AFR SOUTH/AFR NAT/G INT/TRADE RACE/REL PEACE PWR ...INT/LAW ANTHOL 20 UN. PAGE 131 A2681 SANCTION DISCRIM ECO/TAC POLICY

B64
SINGER H.W.,INTERNATIONAL DEVELOPMENT: GROWTH AND CHANGE. AFR BRAZIL L/A+17C WOR+45 CULTURE AGRI INDUS NAT/G ACT/RES ECO/TAC EDU/PROP WEALTH...GEOG CONCPT METH/CNCPT STAT HYPO/EXP WORK TOT/POP 20. PAGE 133 A2723 FINAN ECO/UNDEV FOR/AID INT/TRADE

B64
STEWART C.F.,A BIBLIOGRAPHY OF INTERNATIONAL BUSINESS. WOR+45 FINAN LG/CO NAT/G PLAN ECO/TAC TARIFFS...DECISION MGT GP/COMP NAT/COMP 20 EEC. PAGE 138 A2824 BIBLIOG INT/ORG OP/RES INT/TRADE

B64
TONG T.,UNITED STATES DIPLOMACY IN CHINA, 1844-1860. ASIA USA-45 ECO/UNDEV ECO/TAC COERCE GP/REL...INT/LAW 19 TREATY. PAGE 144 A2949 DIPLOM INT/TRADE COLONIAL

B64
UN PUB. INFORM. ORGAN.,EVERY MAN'S UNITED NATIONS. UNIV WOR+45 CONSTN CULTURE SOCIETY ECO/DEV ECO/UNDEV NAT/G ACT/RES PLAN ECO/TAC INT/TRADE EDU/PROP LEGIT PEACE ATTIT ALL/VALS...POLICY HUM INT/LAW CONCPT CHARTS UN TOT/POP 20. PAGE 147 A3004 INT/ORG ROUTINE

B64
WITHERELL J.W.,OFFICIAL PUBLICATIONS OF FRENCH EQUATORIAL AFRICA, FRENCH CAMEROONS, AND TOGO, 1946-1958 (PAMPHLET). CAMEROON CHAD FRANCE GABON TOGO LAW ECO/UNDEV EXTR/IND INT/TRADE...GEOG HEAL 20. PAGE 165 A3370 BIBLIOG/A AFR NAT/G ADMIN

B64
WYTHE G.,THE UNITED STATES AND INTER-AMERICAN RELATIONS: A CONTEMPORARY APPRAISAL. L/A+17C USA+45 ECO/UNDEV INT/ORG NAT/G VOL/ASSN INT/TRADE EDU/PROP DRIVE...SOC TREND OAS UN 20. PAGE 168 A3425 ATTIT ECO/TAC FOR/AID

L64
CARNEGIE ENDOWMENT INT. PEACE,"ECONOMIC AND SOCIAL QUESTION (ISSUES BEFORE THE NINETEENTH GENERAL ASSEMBLY)." WOR+45 ECO/DEV ECO/UNDEV INDUS R+D DELIB/GP CREATE PLAN TEC/DEV ECO/TAC FOR/AID BAL/PAY...RECORD UN 20. PAGE 24 A0493 INT/ORG INT/TRADE

L64
KORBONSKI A.,"COMECON." ASIA ECO/DEV ECO/UNDEV ECO/TAC BAL/PAY NAT/LISM 20 COMECON. PAGE 81 A1671 COM INT/ORG INT/TRADE

S64
ARMSTRONG J.A.,"THE SOVIET-AMERICAN CONFRONTATION: A NEW STAGE?" CUBA USA+45 USSR PLAN PROB/SOLV INT/TRADE CONTROL ARMS/CONT NUC/PWR MARXISM 20 COLD/WAR INTERVENT. PAGE 9 A0174 DIPLOM POLICY INSPECT

S64
COCHRANE J.D.,"US ATTITUDES TOWARD CENTRAL-AMERICAN INTEGRATION." L/A+17C USA+45 ECO/UNDEV FACE/GP VOL/ASSN DELIB/GP ECO/TAC INT/TRADE EDU/PROP RIGID/FLEX ORD/FREE WEALTH...TIME/SEQ TOT/POP 20. PAGE 27 A0555 NAT/G ATTIT REGION

S64
DERWINSKI E.J.,"THE COST OF THE INTERNATIONAL COFFEE AGREEMENT." L/A+17C USA+45 WOR+45 ECO/UNDEV NAT/G VOL/ASSN LEGIS DIPLOM ECO/TAC FOR/AID LEGIT ATTIT...TIME/SEQ CONGRESS 20 TREATY. PAGE 36 A0732 MARKET DELIB/GP INT/TRADE

S64
GARDNER R.N.,"GATT AND THE UNITED NATIONS CONFERENCE ON TRADE AND DEVELOPMENT." USA+45 WOR+45 SOCIETY ECO/UNDEV MARKET NAT/G DELIB/GP ACT/RES PLAN ECO/TAC TARIFFS EDU/PROP ROUTINE DRIVE RIGID/FLEX WEALTH...DECISION MGT TREND UN TOT/POP 20 GATT. PAGE 51 A1047 INT/ORG INT/TRADE

S64
HABERLER G.,"INTEGRATION AND GROWTH OF THE WORLD ECONOMY IN HISTORICAL PERSPECTIVE." FUT WOR+45 WOR-45 ECO/DEV ECO/UNDEV...TIME/SEQ TREND VAL/FREE 20. PAGE 59 A1209 WEALTH INT/TRADE

S64
HUELIN D.,"ECONOMIC INTEGRATION IN LATIN AMERICAN: PROGRESS AND PROBLEMS." L/A+17C ECO/DEV AGRI DIST/IND FINAN INDUS NAT/G VOL/ASSN CONSULT DELIB/GP EX/STRUC ACT/RES PLAN TEC/DEV ECO/TAC ROUTINE BAL/PAY WEALTH WORK 20. PAGE 69 A1411
MARKET ECO/UNDEV INT/TRADE

S64
KOJIMA K.,"THE PATTERN OF INTERNATIONAL TRADE AMONG ADVANCED COUNTRIES." EUR+WWI UK USA+45 WOR+45 MARKET NAT/G ECO/TAC WEALTH...MATH STAT CON/ANAL CHARTS EEC CHINJAP 20 CHINJAP. PAGE 81 A1665
ECO/DEV TREND INT/TRADE

S64
MCCREARY E.A.,"THOSE AMERICAN MANAGERS DON'T IMPRESS EUROPE." EUR+WWI USA+45 CULTURE STRATA ECO/DEV TOP/EX INT/TRADE ATTIT DRIVE PERSON RIGID/FLEX...CONCPT 20. PAGE 98 A2003
MARKET ACT/RES BAL/PAY CAP/ISM

S64
NEISSER H.,"THE EXTERNAL EQUILIBRIUM OF THE UNITED STATES ECONOMY." FUT USA+45 NAT/G ACT/RES PLAN ECO/TAC ATTIT WEALTH...METH/CNCPT GEN/METH VAL/FREE 20. PAGE 108 A2216
FINAN ECO/DEV BAL/PAY INT/TRADE

S64
PRASAD B.,"SURVEY OF RECENT RESEARCH: STUDIES ON INDIA'S FOREIGN POLIC AND RELATIONS." ASIA INDIA PAKISTAN USA+45 NAT/G INT/TRADE GOV/REL 20 UN CMN/WLTH. PAGE 117 A2406
BIBLIOG DIPLOM ROLE POLICY

B65
AMERICAN ECONOMIC ASSOCIATION,INDEX OF ECONOMIC JOURNALS 1886-1965 (7 VOLS.). UK USA+45 USA-45 AGRI FINAN PLAN ECO/TAC INT/TRADE ADMIN...STAT CENSUS 19/20. PAGE 7 A0145
BIBLIOG WRITING INDUS

B65
COWEN Z.,THE BRITISH COMMONWEALTH OF NATIONS IN A CHANGING WORLD. UK ECO/UNDEV INT/ORG ECO/TAC INT/TRADE COLONIAL WAR GP/REL RACE/REL SOVEREIGN SOC/INTEG 20 TREATY EEC COMMONWLTH. PAGE 32 A0644
JURID DIPLOM PARL/PROC NAT/LISM

B65
DEMAS W.G.,THE ECONOMICS OF DEVELOPMENT IN SMALL COUNTRIES WITH SPECIAL REFERENCE TO THE CARIBBEAN. WOR+45 BAL/PAY DEMAND EFFICIENCY PRODUC...GEOG CARIBBEAN. PAGE 36 A0731
ECO/UNDEV PLAN WEALTH INT/TRADE

B65
FRIEDMANN W.,AN INTRODUCTION TO WORLD POLITICS (5TH ED.). WOR+45 ECO/UNDEV BAL/PWR FOR/AID INT/TRADE PEACE...STAT CENSUS CHARTS BIBLIOG T 20 COLD/WAR UN THIRD/WRLD. PAGE 49 A1003
DIPLOM INT/ORG PROB/SOLV

B65
HAGRAS K.M.,UNITED NATIONS CONFERENCE ON TRADE AND DEVELOPMENT: A CASE STUDY OF UN DIPLOMACY. CONSULT ACT/RES TEC/DEV FOR/AID INT/TRADE...BIBLIOG 20 UN LEAGUE/NAT UNCTAD. PAGE 59 A1213
INT/ORG ADMIN DELIB/GP DIPLOM

B65
HOSELITZ B.F.,ECONOMICS AND THE IDEA OF MANKIND. UNIV ECO/DEV ECO/UNDEV DIST/IND INDUS INT/ORG NAT/G ACT/RES ECO/TAC WEALTH...CONCPT STAT. PAGE 68 A1392
CREATE INT/TRADE

B65
JADOS S.S.,DOCUMENTS ON RUSSIAN-AMERICAN RELATIONS: WASHINGTON TO EISENHOWER. USA+45 USA-45 USSR INT/ORG LEGIS INT/TRADE WAR PEACE...ANTHOL BIBLIOG 18/20 PRESIDENT. PAGE 73 A1488
DIPLOM CHIEF CONTROL

B65
JALEE P.,THE PILLAGE OF THE THIRD WORLD (TRANS. BY MARY KLOPPER). WOR+45 AGRI INDUS ECO/TAC FOR/AID COLONIAL CONTROL PRODUC PWR WEALTH...STAT CHARTS 20 RESOURCE/N. PAGE 73 A1493
ECO/UNDEV DOMIN INT/TRADE DIPLOM

B65
JOHNSON H.G.,THE WORLD ECONOMY AT THE CROSSROADS. COM WOR-45 ECO/DEV AGRI INDUS INT/TRADE REGION NAT/LISM 20. PAGE 74 A1523
FINAN DIPLOM INT/ORG ECO/UNDEV

B65
LEISS A.C.,APARTHEID AND UNITED NATIONS COLLECTIVE MEASURES. SOUTH/AFR ECO/UNDEV EXTR/IND FORCES WORKER ECO/TAC FOR/AID INT/TRADE WEALTH...TREND CHARTS 20 UN NEGRO. PAGE 86 A1770
DISCRIM RACE/REL STRATA DIPLOM

B65
MCCOLL G.D.,THE AUSTRALIAN BALANCE OF PAYMENTS. UK USA+45 AGRI WORKER DIPLOM EQUILIB PRODUC...STAT TREND CHARTS BIBLIOG/A 20 AUSTRAL. PAGE 97 A2001
ECO/DEV BAL/PAY INT/TRADE COST

B65
MORGENTHAU H.,MORGENTHAU DIARY (CHINA) (2 VOLS.). ASIA USA+45 USA-45 LAW DELIB/GP EX/STRUC PLAN FOR/AID INT/TRADE CONFER WAR MARXISM 20 CHINJAP. PAGE 104 A2136
DIPLOM ADMIN

B65
MOWRY G.E.,THE URBAN NATION 1920-1960. USA+45 USA-45 SOCIETY ECO/DEV MUNIC FOR/AID INT/TRADE AUTOMAT...BIBLIOG/A 20. PAGE 105 A2161
TEC/DEV NAT/G TOTALISM DIPLOM

B65
MURUMBI J.,PROBLEMS OF ECONOMIC DEVELOPMENT IN EAST AFRICA. FINAN INDUS WORKER TEC/DEV INT/TRADE TAX DEMAND EFFICIENCY PRODUC SOCISM...TREND CHARTS 20 AFRICA/E. PAGE 106 A2184
AGRI ECO/TAC ECO/UNDEV PROC/MFG

B65
NATIONAL CENTRAL LIBRARY,LATIN AMERICAN ECONOMIC AND SOCIAL SERIALS. UK SOCIETY NAT/G PLAN PROB/SOLV ...SOC 20. PAGE 107 A2202
BIBLIOG INT/TRADE ECO/UNDEV L/A+17C

B65
NEWBURY C.W.,BRITISH POLICY TOWARDS WEST AFRICA: SELECT DOCUMENTS 1786-1874. AFR UK INT/TRADE DOMIN ADMIN COLONIAL CT/SYS COERCE ORD/FREE...BIBLIOG/A 18/19. PAGE 108 A2224
DIPLOM POLICY NAT/G WRITING

B65
NKRUMAH K.,NEO-COLONIALISM: THE LAST STAGE OF IMPERIALISM. AFR INT/ORG WORKER FOR/AID INT/TRADE EDU/PROP GOV/REL NAT/LISM SOVEREIGN POPULISM SOCISM ...SOCIALIST 20 THIRD/WRLD INTRVN/ECO. PAGE 109 A2243
COLONIAL DIPLOM ECO/UNDEV ECO/TAC

B65
O'CONNELL M.R.,IRISH POLITICS AND SOCIAL CONFLICT IN THE AGE OF THE AMERICAN REVOLUTION. FRANCE IRELAND MOD/EUR STRATA SECT LEGIS DIPLOM INT/TRADE DOMIN REV WAR...BIBLIOG 18 PARLIAMENT. PAGE 111 A2268
CATHISM ATTIT NAT/G DELIB/GP

B65
RODRIGUES J.H.,BRAZIL AND AFRICA. AFR BRAZIL PORTUGAL UK USA+45 USA-45 CULTURE ECO/UNDEV INT/ORG INT/TRADE RACE/REL ORD/FREE 15/20 UN MISCEGEN. PAGE 123 A2513
DIPLOM COLONIAL POLICY ATTIT

B65
ROLFE S.E.,GOLD AND WORLD POWER. UK USA+45 WOR-45 INDUS WORKER INT/TRADE DEMAND...MGT CHARTS 20 GOLD/STAND. PAGE 123 A2517
BAL/PAY EQUILIB ECO/TAC DIPLOM

B65
ROTBERG R.I.,A POLITICAL HISTORY OF TROPICAL AFRICA. EX/STRUC DIPLOM INT/TRADE DOMIN ADMIN RACE/REL NAT/LISM PWR SOVEREIGN...GEOG TIME/SEQ BIBLIOG 1/20. PAGE 124 A2545
AFR CULTURE COLONIAL

B65
SABLE M.H.,MASTER DIRECTORY FOR LATIN AMERICA. AGRI COM/IND FINAN R+D ACADEM LABOR NAT/G POL/PAR VOL/ASSN INT/TRADE EDU/PROP 20. PAGE 126 A2582
INDEX L/A+17C INT/ORG DIPLOM

B65
SABLE M.H.,PERIODICALS FOR LATIN AMERICAN ECONOMIC DEVELOPMENT, TRADE, AND FINANCE: AN ANNOTATED BIBLIOGRAPHY (A PAMPHLET). ECO/TAC PRODUC PROFIT ...STAT NAT/COMP 20 OAS. PAGE 126 A2583
BIBLIOG/A L/A+17C ECO/UNDEV INT/TRADE

B65
SHUKRI A.,THE CONCEPT OF SELF-DETERMINATION IN THE UNITED NATIONS. WOR+45 DIPLOM INT/TRADE SANCTION NAT/LISM...BIBLIOG 20 UN. PAGE 132 A2709
COLONIAL INT/ORG INT/LAW SOVEREIGN

B65
STEWART I.G.,AFRICAN PRIMARY PRODUCTS AND INTERNATIONAL TRADE. ECO/UNDEV AGRI FINAN DIPLOM CONTROL 20. PAGE 138 A2825
AFR INT/TRADE INT/ORG

B65
US SENATE COMM BANKING CURR,BALANCE OF PAYMENTS - 1965. USA+45 ECO/TAC PRICE WEALTH...CHARTS 20 CONGRESS GOLD/STAND. PAGE 156 A3171
BAL/PAY FINAN DIPLOM INT/TRADE

B65
US SENATE COMM ON JUDICIARY,ANTITRUST EXEMPTIONS FOR AGREEMENTS RELATING TO BALANCE OF PAYMENTS. FINAN ECO/TAC CONTROL WEALTH...POLICY 20 CONGRESS. PAGE 157 A3195
BAL/PAY ADJUD MARKET INT/TRADE

B65
WEIL G.L.,A HANDBOOK ON THE EUROPEAN ECONOMIC COMMUNITY. BELGIUM EUR+WWI FRANCE GERMANY/W ITALY CONSTN ECO/DEV CREATE PARTIC GP/REL...DECISION MGT CHARTS 20 EEC. PAGE 162 A3299
INT/TRADE INT/ORG TEC/DEV INT/LAW

B65
WEILER J.,L'ECONOMIE INTERNATIONALE DEPUIS 1950. WOR+45 DIPLOM TARIFFS CONFER...POLICY TREATY. PAGE 162 A3302
FINAN INT/TRADE REGION FOR/AID

B65
WHITE J.,GERMAN AID. GERMANY/W FINAN PLAN TEC/DEV INT/TRADE ADMIN ATTIT...POLICY 20. PAGE 164 A3335
FOR/AID ECO/UNDEV DIPLOM ECO/TAC

L65
LOFTUS M.L.,"INTERNATIONAL MONETARY FUND, 1962-1965: A SELECTED BIBLIOGRAPHY." WOR+45 PLAN BUDGET INCOME PROFIT WEALTH. PAGE 90 A1852
BIBLIOG FINAN INT/TRADE INT/ORG

L65
MATTHEWS D.G.,"LE TIERS MONDE: A SELECT AND PRELIMINARY BIBLIOGRAPHIC SURVEY OF MANPOWER IN DEVELOPING COUNTRIES, 1960-1964." AFR ISLAM L/A+17C INDUS PLAN PROB/SOLV TEC/DEV INT/TRADE EFFICIENCY WEALTH...STAT 20. PAGE 96 A1971
BIBLIOG/A ECO/UNDEV LABOR WORKER

S65
AFRICAN BIBLIOGRAPHIC CENTER,"US TREATIES AND AGREEMENTS WITH COUNTRIES IN AFRICA, 1957 TO MID-1963." AFR USA+45 AGRI FINAN FORCES TEC/DEV
BIBLIOG DIPLOM INT/ORG

CAP/ISM FOR/AID 20. PAGE 5 A0097 INT/TRADE

S65
GANGAL S.C.,"SURVEY OF RECENT RESEARCH: INDIA AND THE COMMONWEALTH" INDIA UK NAT/G INT/TRADE PARTIC GOV/REL ROLE 20 CMN/WLTH. PAGE 51 A1039 BIBLIOG POLICY REGION DIPLOM

S65
MERRITT R.L.,"SELECTED ARTICLES AND DOCUMENTS ON INTERNATIONAL LAW AND RELATIONS." WOR+45 INT/ORG FORCES INT/TRADE. PAGE 100 A2045 BIBLIOG DIPLOM INT/LAW GOV/REL

S65
ROGGER H.,"EAST GERMANY: STABLE OR IMMOBILE." COM EUR+WWI GERMANY/E NAT/G INT/TRADE DOMIN EDU/PROP COERCE TOTALISM COLD/WAR 20. PAGE 123 A2516 TOP/EX RIGID/FLEX GERMANY

C65
MARK M.,"BEYOND SOVEREIGNTY." WOR+45 WOR-45 ECO/UNDEV BAL/PWR INT/TRADE NUC/PWR REV WAR MARXISM NEW/LIB BIBLIOG. PAGE 95 A1942 NAT/LISM NAT/G DIPLOM INTELL

C65
WUORINEN J.H.,"SCANDINAVIA." DENMARK FINLAND ICELAND NORWAY SWEDEN SOCIETY AGRI POL/PAR DELIB/GP DIPLOM INT/TRADE NEUTRAL WAR...CHARTS TREATY 20. PAGE 168 A3423 BIBLIOG NAT/G POLICY

B66
AMERICAN ASSEMBLY COLUMBIA U,THE UNITED STATES AND THE PHILIPPINES. PHILIPPINE S/ASIA USA+45 USA-45 SOCIETY FORCES INT/TRADE...POLICY 20. PAGE 7 A0138 COLONIAL DIPLOM NAT/LISM

B66
ENTWICKLUNGSPOLITIK - HANDBUCH UND LEXIKON. MARKET SECT DIPLOM INT/TRADE EDU/PROP CATHISM 20. PAGE 14 A0283 ECO/UNDEV FOR/AID ECO/TAC PLAN

B66
BIRMINGHAM D.,TRADE AND CONFLICT IN ANGOLA. PORTUGAL CULTURE FORCES DIPLOM GP/REL PROFIT HABITAT NAT/COMP. PAGE 14 A0291 WAR INT/TRADE ECO/UNDEV COLONIAL

B66
CLENDENON C.,AMERICANS IN AFRICA 1865-1900. AFR USA-45 ECO/UNDEV SECT REV RACE/REL CONSERVE ...TRADIT GEOG BIBLIOG 16/18. PAGE 27 A0549 DIPLOM COLONIAL INT/TRADE

B66
CONNEL-SMITH G.,THE INTERAMERICAN SYSTEM. CUBA L/A+17C DELIB/GP FOR/AID COLONIAL PEACE PWR MARXISM ...BIBLIOG 19/20 OAS. PAGE 29 A0586 DIPLOM INT/TRADE REGION INT/ORG

B66
COYLE D.C.,THE UNITED NATIONS AND HOW IT WORKS. ECO/UNDEV DELIB/GP BAL/PWR EDU/PROP ARMS/CONT NUC/PWR WAR 20 UN. PAGE 32 A0648 INT/ORG PEACE DIPLOM INT/TRADE

B66
DAVIDSON A.B.,RUSSIA AND AFRICA. USSR AGRI INT/TRADE...GEOG BIBLIOG/A 18/20. PAGE 34 A0687 MARXISM COLONIAL RACE/REL DIPLOM

B66
DYCK H.V.,WEIMAR GERMANY AND SOVIET RUSSIA 1926-1933. EUR+WWI GERMANY UK USSR ECO/TAC INT/TRADE NEUTRAL WAR ATTIT 20 WEIMAR/REP TREATY. PAGE 40 A0814 DIPLOM GOV/REL POLICY

B66
EDWARDS C.D.,TRADE REGULATIONS OVERSEAS. IRELAND NEW/ZEALND SOUTH/AFR NAT/G CAP/ISM TARIFFS CONTROL ...POLICY JURID 20 EEC CHINJAP. PAGE 40 A0823 INT/TRADE DIPLOM INT/LAW ECO/TAC

B66
FELKER J.L.,SOVIET ECONOMIC CONTROVERSIES. USSR INDUS PLAN INT/TRADE GP/REL MARXISM SOCISM...POLICY 20. PAGE 45 A0915 ECO/DEV MARKET PROFIT PRICE

B66
FITZGERALD C.P.,THE BIRTH OF COMMUNIST CHINA (2ND ED.). ASIA CHINA/COM STRUCT BAL/PWR DIPLOM ECO/TAC INT/TRADE WEALTH 20. PAGE 46 A0942 REV MARXISM ECO/UNDEV

B66
HALLET R.,PEOPLE AND PROGRESS IN WEST AFRICA: AN INTRODUCTION TO THE PROBLEMS OF DEVELOPMENT. COM/IND INDUS KIN DIPLOM FOR/AID INT/TRADE HEALTH ...GEOG TREND CHARTS BIBLIOG/A 20 AFRICA/W. PAGE 60 A1233 AFR SOCIETY ECO/UNDEV ECO/TAC

B66
HOROWITZ D.,HEMISPHERES NORTH AND SOUTH: ECONOMIC DISPARITY AMONG NATIONS. WOR+45 ECO/DEV ECO/UNDEV INT/ORG PLAN DIPLOM INT/TRADE GIVE PARTIC GP/REL ...WELF/ST 20. PAGE 67 A1387 ECO/TAC FOR/AID STRATA WEALTH

B66
HUTTENBACK R.A.,BRITISH IMPERIAL EXPERIENCE. S/ASIA UK WOR-45 INT/ORG TEC/DEV...CHARTS 16/20 COMMONWLTH MERCANTLST. PAGE 69 A1424 COLONIAL TIME/SEQ INT/TRADE

B66
INTERNATIONAL ECO POLICY ASSN,THE UNITED STATES BALANCE OF PAYMENTS. INT/ORG NAT/G PROB/SOLV BUDGET DIPLOM INT/TRADE WEALTH 20. PAGE 71 A1454 BAL/PAY ECO/TAC POLICY FINAN

B66
INTERNATIONAL ECONOMIC ASSN,STABILITY AND PROGRESS IN THE WORLD ECONOMY: THE FIRST CONGRESS OF THE INTERNATIONAL ECONOMIC ASSOCIATION. WOR+45 ECO/DEV ECO/UNDEV DELIB/GP FOR/AID BAL/PAY...TREND CMN/WLTH 20. PAGE 71 A1455 INT/TRADE

B66
KIM Y.K.,PATTERNS OF COMPETITIVE COEXISTENCE: USA VS. USSR. USA+45 USSR ECO/DEV ECO/UNDEV INT/ORG FOR/AID INT/TRADE ARMS/CONT...BIBLIOG 20 COLD/WAR. PAGE 79 A1618 DIPLOM PEACE BAL/PWR DETER

B66
KINDLEBERGER C.P.,EUROPE AND THE DOLLAR. EUR+WWI FRANCE GERMANY/W USA+45 CONSTN INT/ORG DIPLOM INT/TRADE...ANTHOL 20 GOLD/STAND. PAGE 79 A1623 BAL/PAY BUDGET FINAN ECO/DEV

B66
KOH S.J.,STAGES OF INDUSTRIAL DEVELOPMENT IN ASIA. ASIA INDIA KOREA STRATA STRUCT NAT/G INT/TRADE ...CHARTS 19/20 CHINJAP. PAGE 81 A1659 INDUS ECO/UNDEV ECO/DEV LABOR

B66
LAMBERG R.F.,PRAG UND DIE DRITTE WELT. AFR ASIA CZECHOSLVK L/A+17C MARKET TEC/DEV ECO/TAC REV ATTIT 20 TREATY. PAGE 84 A1713 DIPLOM ECO/UNDEV INT/TRADE FOR/AID

B66
LEAGUE OF WOMEN VOTERS OF US,FOREIGN AID AT THE CROSSROADS. USA+45 WOR+45 DELIB/GP PROB/SOLV DIPLOM INT/TRADE RECEIVE BAL/PAY...CHARTS 20 UN. PAGE 86 A1756 FOR/AID GIVE ECO/UNDEV PLAN

B66
LUARD E.,THE EVOLUTION OF INTERNATIONAL ORGANIZATIONS. UK WOR+45 BUDGET INT/TRADE WAR BAL/PAY PEACE ORD/FREE...POLICY 19/20 EEC ILO LEAGUE/NAT UN. PAGE 91 A1871 INT/ORG EFFICIENCY CREATE TREND

B66
MCNAIR A.D.,THE LEGAL EFFECTS OF WAR. UK FINAN DIPLOM ORD/FREE 20 ENGLSH/LAW. PAGE 98 A2019 JURID WAR INT/TRADE LABOR

B66
MEERHAEGHE M.,INTERNATIONAL ECONOMIC INSTITUTIONS. EUR+WWI FINAN INDUS MARKET PLAN TARIFFS BAL/PAY EQUILIB...POLICY BIBLIOG/A 20 GATT OEEC EEC IBRD EURCOALSTL. PAGE 99 A2032 ECO/TAC ECO/DEV INT/TRADE INT/ORG

B66
NIJHOFF M.,ANNUAIRE EUROPEEN (VOL. XII). INT/TRADE REGION PEACE 20 EFTA EEC ECSC EURATOM. PAGE 109 A2241 BIBLIOG INT/ORG EUR+WWI DIPLOM

B66
O'CONNER A.M.,AN ECONOMIC GEOGRAPHY OF EAST AFRICA. AFR TANZANIA UGANDA AGRI WORKER INT/TRADE COLONIAL GOV/REL...CHARTS METH/COMP 20 AFRICA/E. PAGE 111 A2269 ECO/UNDEV EXTR/IND GEOG HABITAT

B66
PASSIN H.,THE UNITED STATES AND JAPAN. USA+45 INDUS CAP/ISM...TREND 20 CHINJAP TREATY. PAGE 114 A2337 DIPLOM INT/TRADE ECO/DEV ECO/TAC

B66
PIQUET H.S.,THE US BALANCE OF PAYMENTS AND INTERNATIONAL MONETARY RESERVES. USA+45 PROB/SOLV INT/TRADE GOV/REL EQUILIB...POLICY STAT CHARTS 20 GOLD/STAND. PAGE 116 A2384 BAL/PAY DIPLOM FINAN ECO/TAC

B66
ROBERTSON D.J.,THE BRITISH BALANCE OF PAYMENTS. UK WOR+45 INDUS BUDGET TAX ADJUST...CHARTS ANTHOL 20. PAGE 122 A2500 FINAN BAL/PAY ECO/DEV INT/TRADE

B66
SMITH D.M.,AMERICAN INTERVENTION, 1917. GERMANY UK USA-45 SEA FORCES DIPLOM INT/TRADE EDU/PROP COERCE WEAPON PEACE 20 WILSON/W WWI. PAGE 134 A2746 WAR ATTIT POLICY NEUTRAL

B66
SPULBER N.,THE STATE AND ECONOMIC DEVELOPMENT IN EASTERN EUROPE. BULGARIA COM CZECHOSLVK HUNGARY POLAND YUGOSLAVIA CULTURE PLAN CAP/ISM INT/TRADE CONTROL...POLICY CHARTS METH/COMP BIBLIOG/A 19/20. PAGE 136 A2793 ECO/DEV ECO/UNDEV NAT/G TOTALISM

B66
TRIFFIN R.,THE WORLD MONEY MAZE. INT/ORG ECO/TAC PRICE OPTIMAL WEALTH...METH/COMP 20 EEC OEEC GOLD/STAND SILVER. PAGE 145 A2964 BAL/PAY FINAN INT/TRADE DIPLOM

B66
TRIFFIN R.,THE BALANCE OF PAYMENTS AND THE FOREIGN INVESTMENT POSITION OF THE UNITED STATES. USA+45 INT/ORG INT/TRADE PRICE CONTROL...POLICY 20 GOLD/STAND. PAGE 145 A2965 BAL/PAY DIPLOM FINAN ECO/TAC

B66
US DEPARTMENT OF THE ARMY,SOUTH ASIA: A STRATEGIC SURVEY (PAMPHLET NO. 550-3). AFGHANISTN INDIA NEPAL BIBLIOG/A S/ASIA

PAKISTAN ECO/UNDEV INT/ORG POL/PAR FORCES FOR/AID INT/TRADE LEAD WAR...POLICY SOC TREND 20. PAGE 152 A3110 — DIPLOM NAT/G

B66
US HOUSE COMM FOREIGN AFFAIRS,HEARINGS ON HR 12449 A BILL TO AMEND FURTHER THE FOREIGN ASSISTANCE ACT OF 1961. AFR ASIA L/A+17C USA+45 VIETNAM INT/ORG TEC/DEV INT/TRADE ATTIT ORD/FREE 20 UN NATO CONGRESS AID. PAGE 154 A3132 — FOR/AID ECO/TAC ECO/UNDEV DIPLOM

B66
US HOUSE COMM GOVT OPERATIONS,AN INVESTIGATION OF THE US ECONOMIC AND MILITARY ASSISTANCE PROGRAMS IN VIETNAM. USA+45 VIETNAM/S SOCIETY CONSTRUC FINAN FORCES BUDGET INT/TRADE PEACE HEALTH...MGT HOUSE/REP AID. PAGE 154 A3139 — FOR/AID ECO/UNDEV WAR INSPECT

B66
WOOLLEY H.B.,MEASURING TRANSACTIONS BETWEEN WORLD AREAS. WOR+45 FINAN...STAT NET/THEORY CHARTS DICTIONARY 20 GOLD/STAND. PAGE 167 A3395 — INT/TRADE BAL/PAY DIPLOM ECOMETRIC

B66
YEAGER L.B.,INTERNATIONAL MONETARY RELATIONS: THEORY, HISTORY, AND POLICY. WOR+45 WOR-45 INT/TRADE BAL/PAY...NAT/COMP 18/20 MONEY. PAGE 169 A3432 — FINAN DIPLOM ECO/TAC IDEA/COMP

B66
ZISCHKA A.,WAR ES EIN WUNDER? GERMANY/W ECO/DEV FINAN LG/CO BARGAIN CAP/ISM FOR/AID RATION 20 MARSHL/PLN. PAGE 170 A3456 — ECO/TAC INT/TRADE INDUS WAR

L66
AMERICAN ECONOMIC REVIEW,"SIXTY-THIRD LIST OF DOCTORAL DISSERTATIONS IN POLITICAL ECONOMY IN AMERICAN UNIVERSITIES AND COLLEGES." ECO/DEV AGRI FINAN LABOR WORKER PLAN BUDGET INT/TRADE ADMIN DEMAND...MGT STAT 20. PAGE 7 A0146 — BIBLIOG/A CONCPT ACADEM

S66
"WORLD BANK CONVENTION ON INVESTMENT DISPUTES; A BIBLIOGRAPH ICAL NOTE." VOL/ASSN CONSULT CAP/ISM DIPLOM INT/TRADE 20 SENATE PRESIDENT. PAGE 4 A0074 — BIBLIOG ADJUD FINAN INT/ORG

S66
AFRICAN BIBLIOGRAPHIC CENTER,"THE NEW AFRO-ASIAN STATES IN PERSPECTIVE, 1960-1963: A SELECT BIBLIOGRAPHY." AFR ASIA CULTURE SOCIETY INT/ORG LABOR TEC/DEV LITERACY 20 UN. PAGE 5 A0100 — BIBLIOG DIPLOM FOR/AID INT/TRADE

S66
ERB GF,"THE UNITED NATIONS CONFERENCE ON TRADE AND DEVELOPMENT (UNCTAD): A SELECTED CURRENT READING LIST." FINAN FOR/AID CONFER 20 UN. PAGE 42 A0858 — BIBLIOG/A INT/TRADE ECO/UNDEV INT/ORG

S66
GREEN L.C.,"RHODESIAN OIL: BOOTLEGGERS OR PIRATES?" AFR RHODESIA UK WOR+45 INT/ORG NAT/G DIPLOM LEGIT COLONIAL SOVEREIGN 20 UN OAU. PAGE 55 A1139 — INT/TRADE SANCTION INT/LAW POLICY

S66
JAVITS J.K.,"POLITICAL ACTION VITAL FOR LATIN AMERICAN INTEGRATION." ECO/UNDEV INT/ORG POL/PAR VOL/ASSN PLAN PROB/SOLV INT/TRADE EFFICIENCY 20 OAS LAFTA. PAGE 73 A1500 — L/A+17C ECO/TAC REGION

S66
KLEIN S.,"A SURVEY OF SINO-JAPANESE TRADE, 1950-1966" TAIWAN EDU/PROP 20 CHINJAP. PAGE 80 A1649 — INT/TRADE DIPLOM MARXISM

C66
TARLING N.,"A CONCISE HISTORY OF SOUTHEAST ASIA." BURMA CAMBODIA LAOS S/ASIA THAILAND VIETNAM ECO/UNDEV POL/PAR FORCES ADMIN REV WAR CIVMIL/REL ORD/FREE MARXISM SOCISM 13/20. PAGE 141 A2890 — COLONIAL DOMIN INT/TRADE NAT/LISM

N66
BRITISH DEVELOPMENT POLICIES: 1966 (PAMPHLET). UK AGRI TARIFFS BAL/PAY...TREND CHARTS 20 OVRSEA/DEV. PAGE 4 A0076 — WEALTH DIPLOM INT/TRADE FOR/AID

B67
AUBREY H.G.,ATLANTIC ECONOMIC COOPERATION. ECO/DEV INDUS VOL/ASSN PROB/SOLV DIPLOM INT/TRADE TARIFFS CONFER 20. PAGE 10 A0197 — INT/ORG ECO/TAC TEC/DEV CAP/ISM

B67
BARANSON J.,TECHNOLOGY FOR UNDERDEVELOPED AREAS: AN ANNOTATED BIBLIOGRAPHY. FUT WOR+45 CULTURE INDUS INT/ORG CREATE PROB/SOLV INT/TRADE EDU/PROP AUTOMAT ...CONCPT METH. PAGE 11 A0218 — BIBLIOG/A ECO/UNDEV TEC/DEV R+D

B67
CECIL L.,ALBERT BALLIN; BUSINESS AND POLITICS IN IMPERIAL GERMANY 1888-1918. GERMANY UK INT/TRADE LEAD WAR PERS/REL ADJUST PWR WEALTH...MGT BIBLIOG 19/20. PAGE 25 A0510 — DIPLOM CONSTN ECO/DEV TOP/EX

B67
DILLARD D.,ECONOMIC DEVELOPMENT OF THE NORTH ATLANTIC COMMUNITY. EUR+WWI MOD/EUR USA+45 USA-45 ECO/UNDEV LABOR CAP/ISM WAR BAL/PAY...NAT/COMP 15/20. PAGE 37 A0763 — ECO/DEV INT/TRADE INDUS DIPLOM

B67
HOLLERMAN L.,JAPAN'S DEPENDENCE ON THE WORLD ECONOMY. INDUS MARKET LABOR NAT/G DIPLOM 20 CHINJAP. PAGE 67 A1369 — PLAN ECO/DEV ECO/TAC INT/TRADE

B67
JOHNSON A.M.,BOSTON CAPITALISTS AND WESTERN RAILROADS: A STUDY IN THE NINETEENTH CENTURY RAILROAD INVESTMENT PROCESS. CREATE BARGAIN INT/TRADE GAMBLE KNOWL 19 BOSTON. PAGE 74 A1519 — FINAN DIST/IND CAP/ISM ECO/UNDEV

B67
LANDEN R.G.,OMAN SINCE 1856: DISRUPTIVE MODERNIZATION IN A TRADITIONAL ARAB SOCIETY. UK DIST/IND EXTR/IND SECT DIPLOM INT/TRADE...SOC LING CHARTS BIBLIOG 19/20. PAGE 84 A1714 — ISLAM CULTURE ECO/UNDEV NAT/G

B67
ROBINSON R.D.,INTERNATIONAL MANAGEMENT. USA+45 FINAN R+D PLAN PRODUC...DECISION T. PAGE 92 A1882 — INT/TRADE MGT INT/LAW MARKET

B67
ROYAL INSTITUTE INTL AFFAIRS,SURVEY OF INTERNATIONAL AFFAIRS. WOR+45 WOR-45 FINAN INT/TRADE PWR...CHARTS 20. PAGE 125 A2557 — DIPLOM BAL/PWR INT/ORG

B67
RUEFF J.,BALANCE OF PAYMENTS. WOR+45 FINAN TEC/DEV DIPLOM TARIFFS PRICE CONTROL...POLICY CONCPT IDEA/COMP. PAGE 125 A2567 — INT/TRADE BAL/PAY ECO/TAC NAT/COMP

B67
SACHS M.Y.,THE WORLDMARK ENCYCLOPEDIA OF THE NATIONS (5 VOLS.). ELITES SOCIETY STRATA ECO/DEV ECO/UNDEV AGRI EXTR/IND FINAN LABOR LOC/G NAT/G POL/PAR SECT INT/TRADE SOVEREIGN...SOC 20. PAGE 126 A2585 — WOR+45 INT/ORG BAL/PWR

B67
UNIVERSAL REFERENCE SYSTEM,ECONOMIC REGULATION, BUSINESS, AND GOVERNMENT (VOLUME VIII). WOR+45 WOR-45 ECO/DEV ECO/UNDEV FINAN LABOR TEC/DEV ECO/TAC INT/TRADE GOV/REL...POLICY COMPUT/IR. PAGE 149 A3043 — BIBLIOG/A CONTROL NAT/G

B67
US CONGRESS SENATE,SURVEY OF THE ALLIANCE FOR PROGRESS; INFLATION IN LATIN AMERICA (PAMPHLET). USA+45 MARKET INT/ORG DIPLOM INT/TRADE BAL/PAY SENATE. PAGE 150 A3072 — L/A+17C FINAN POLICY FOR/AID

L67
GALTUNG J.,"ON THE EFFECTS OF INTERNATIONAL ECONOMIC SANCTIONS, WITH EXAMPLES FROM THE CASE OF RHODESIA." NAT/G DIPLOM EDU/PROP ADJUST EFFICIENCY ATTIT MORAL...OBS CHARTS 20. PAGE 51 A1035 — SANCTION ECO/TAC INT/TRADE ECO/UNDEV

L67
GOLD J.,"INTERPRETATION BY THE INTERNATIONAL MONETARY FUND OF ITS ARTICLES OF AGREEMENT." INT/TRADE ADJUD ATTIT...POLICY JURID. PAGE 53 A1089 — CONSTN INT/ORG LAW DIPLOM

L67
MACDONALD R.S.J.,"THE RESORT TO ECONOMIC COERCION BY INTERNATIONAL POLITICAL ORGANIZATIONS." CUBA ETHIOPIA RHODESIA SOUTH/AFR NAT/G FOR/AID INT/TRADE DOMIN CONTROL SANCTION...DECISION LEAGUE/NAT UN OAS 20. PAGE 92 A1887 — INT/ORG COERCE ECO/TAC DIPLOM

L67
SEGAL A.,"THE INTEGRATION OF DEVELOPING COUNTRIES: SOME THOUGHTS ON EAST AFRICA AND CENTRAL AMERICA." AFR L/A+17C INT/ORG NAT/G VOL/ASSN FOR/AID INT/TRADE EQUILIB NAT/LISM PWR 20. PAGE 131 A2680 — ECO/UNDEV DIPLOM REGION

S67
ANTHEM T.,"CYPRUS* WHAT NOW?" CYPRUS GREECE TURKEY NAT/G BUDGET MAJORITY 20 NATO. PAGE 8 A0165 — DIPLOM COERCE INT/TRADE ADJUD

S67
APEL H.,"LES NOUVEAUX ASPECTS DE LA POLITIQUE ETRANGERE ALLEMANDE." EUR+WWI GERMANY POL/PAR BAL/PWR ECO/TAC INT/TRADE NUC/PWR NAT/LISM PEACE ...POLICY 20 EEC COLD/WAR. PAGE 8 A0168 — DIPLOM INT/ORG FEDERAL

S67
BURNS E.B.,"TRADITIONS AND VARIATIONS IN BRAZILIAN FOREIGN POLICY." BRAZIL L/A+17C POL/PAR INT/TRADE COLONIAL INGP/REL ATTIT ORD/FREE PWR 20. PAGE 22 A0443 — DIPLOM NAT/LISM CREATE

S67
BUTT R.,"THE COMMON MARKET AND CONSERVATIVE POLITICS, 1961-2." UK CHIEF DIPLOM ECO/TAC INT/TRADE CONFER DEBATE REGION ATTIT...POLICY 20 EEC. PAGE 22 A0454 — EUR+WWI INT/ORG POL/PAR

S67
COSGROVE C.A.,"AGRICULTURE, FINANCE AND POLITICS IN THE EUROPEAN COMMUNITY." EUR+WWI DIST/IND MARKET INT/ORG VOL/ASSN DELIB/GP TEC/DEV BAL/PWR BARGAIN ECO/TAC RATION CONFER 20 EEC. PAGE 31 A0630 — ECO/DEV DIPLOM AGRI INT/TRADE

S67
FRANK I.,"NEW PERSPECTIVES ON TRADE AND DEVELOPMENT." PROB/SOLV BARGAIN DIPLOM FOR/AID CONFER GP/REL WEALTH 20 UN GATT. PAGE 48 A0980 — ECO/UNDEV INT/ORG INT/TRADE

ECO/TAC
S67
FRENCH D.S.,"DOES THE U.S. EXPLOIT THE DEVELOPING NATIONS?" INT/ORG NAT/G CAP/ISM BAL/PAY WEALTH POLICY. PAGE 49 A0997 ECO/UNDEV INT/TRADE ECO/TAC COLONIAL
S67
GOLDMAN M.I.,"SOVIET ECONOMIC GROWTH SINCE THE REVOLUTION." USSR WORKER INT/TRADE PRODUC MARXISM ...POLICY TIME/SEQ 20. PAGE 53 A1090 ECO/DEV AGRI ECO/TAC INDUS
S67
JAVITS J.K.,"LAST CHANCE FOR A COMMON MARKET." L/A+17C INT/ORG 20 EEC LAFTA. PAGE 73 A1501 FOR/AID ECO/UNDEV INT/TRADE ECO/TAC
S67
JOHNSON J.,"THE UNITED STATES AND THE LATIN AMERICAN LEFT WINGS." L/A+17C STRATA POL/PAR INT/TRADE 20. PAGE 74 A1524 ECO/UNDEV WORKER ECO/TAC REGION
S67
LEFF N.H.,"EXPORT STAGNATION AND AUTARKIC DEVELOPMENT IN BRAZIL, 19471962." BRAZIL ECO/TAC TARIFFS 20. PAGE 86 A1764 BAL/PAY INT/TRADE WEALTH DIPLOM
S67
LEVI M.,"LES DIFFICULTES ECONOMIQUES DE LA GRANDE-BRETAGNE." UK INT/ORG TEC/DEV BARGAIN DIPLOM DOMIN REPRESENT DEMAND WEALTH...POLICY 20 EEC. PAGE 88 A1792 BAL/PAY INT/TRADE PRODUC
S67
MONTALVA E.F.,"THE ALLIANCE THAT LOST ITS WAY." L/A+17C USA+45 R+D BAL/PWR INT/TRADE RECEIVE REV PEACE...POLICY 20. PAGE 103 A2111 ECO/UNDEV DIPLOM FOR/AID INT/ORG
S67
OLIVIER G.,"ASPECTS JURIDIQUES DE L'ADOPTION DU TRAITE CECA A LA CRISE CHARBONNIERE (SUITE ET FIN)" LAW DIST/IND PLAN DIPLOM RATION PRICE ADMIN COST DEMAND...POLICY CON/ANAL ECSC TREATY. PAGE 112 A2288 INT/TRADE INT/ORG EXTR/IND CONSTN
S67
PERLO V.,"NEW DIMENSIONS IN EAST-WEST TRADE." UK USA+45 USSR WOR+45 ECO/DEV NAT/G CAP/ISM PEACE WEALTH LAISSEZ...SOCIALIST MGT 20. PAGE 115 A2364 BAL/PWR ECO/TAC INT/TRADE
S67
PEUKERT W.,"WEST GERMANY'S 'RED TRADE'." COM GERMANY INDUS CAP/ISM DOMIN SANCTION DEMAND PEACE UTIL...MARXIST 20 COLD/WAR. PAGE 115 A2371 DIPLOM ECO/TAC INT/TRADE
S67
ROCKE J.R.M.,"THE BRITISH EXPORT BATTLE FOR THE CARIBBEAN" GP/REL...POLICY 20 CMN/WLTH. PAGE 122 A2510 INT/TRADE DIPLOM MARKET ECO/TAC
S67
SHERSHNEV Y.,"THE KENNEDY ROUND* PLANS AND REALITY." EUR+WWI USA+45 INT/ORG DIPLOM TARIFFS DOMIN CONFER PWR...MARXIST PREDICT. PAGE 132 A2701 ECO/TAC ECO/DEV INT/TRADE BAL/PWR
S67
STEELE R.,"A TASTE FOR INTERVENTION." USA+45 FOR/AID INT/TRADE EDU/PROP COLONIAL WAR PWR...TREND 20 COLD/WAR. PAGE 137 A2812 POLICY DIPLOM DOMIN ATTIT
S67
STEGER H.S.,"RESEARCH ON LATIN AMERICA IN THE FEDERAL REPUBLIC OF GERMANY AND WEST BERLIN." FINAN DIPLOM INT/TRADE EDU/PROP...GEOG JURID CHARTS 19/20. PAGE 137 A2813 SOCIETY ECO/UNDEV ACADEM L/A+17C
S67
WALKER R.L.,"THE WEST AND THE 'NEW ASIA'." CHINA/COM ECO/UNDEV DIPLOM...PREDICT 20. PAGE 160 A3266 ASIA INT/TRADE COLONIAL REGION
S67
WEIL G.L.,"THE MERGER OF THE INSTITUTIONS OF THE EUROPEAN COMMUNITIES" EUR+WWI ECO/DEV INT/TRADE CONSEN PLURISM...DECISION MGT 20 EEC EURATOM ECSC TREATY. PAGE 162 A3300 ECO/TAC INT/ORG CENTRAL INT/LAW
S67
WEIL G.L.,"THE EUROPEAN COMMUNITY* WHAT LIES BEYOND THE POINT OF NO RETURN?" VOL/ASSN PROB/SOLV DIPLOM REGION INGP/REL CENTRAL PWR 20 EEC. PAGE 162 A3301 INT/ORG ECO/DEV INT/TRADE PREDICT
C67
GEHLEN M.P.,"THE POLITICS OF COEXISTENCE: SOVIET METHODS AND MOTIVES." COM USSR NAT/G INT/TRADE EDU/PROP ARMS/CONT DETER KNOWL...CHARTS IDEA/COMP 20 COLD/WAR. PAGE 52 A1056 BIBLIOG PEACE DIPLOM MARXISM
N67
US GOVERNMENT,TREATIES IN FORCE. NAT/G ECO/TAC FOR/AID INT/TRADE NUC/PWR 20. PAGE 153 A3117 DIPLOM INT/ORG BAL/PWR
B68
ANTWERP-INST UNIVERSITAIRE,BIBLIOGRAPHIC COMPENDIUM: DEVELOPING COUNTRIES (ANTWERP-INST UNIVERSITAIRE DES TERRITOIRES D'OUTRE-MER). AFR EUR+WWI SOCIETY AGRI FINAN NEIGH VOL/ASSN PROB/SOLV TEC/DEV FOR/AID INT/TRADE 20. PAGE 8 A0166 BIBLIOG ECO/UNDEV DIPLOM PLAN
C83
BURKE E.,"RESOLUTIONS FOR CONCILIATION WITH AMERICA" (1775), IN E. BURKE, COLLECTED WORKS, VOL. 2." UK USA-45 FORCES INT/TRADE TARIFFS TAX SANCTION PEACE...POLICY 18 PRE/US/AM. PAGE 21 A0436 COLONIAL WAR SOVEREIGN ECO/TAC
B86
MAS LATRIE L.,RELATIONS ET COMMERCE DE L'AFRIQUE SEPTENTRIONALE OU MAGREB AVEC LES NATIONS CHRETIENNES AU MOYEN AGE. CULTURE CHIEF FORCES WAR ...SOC CENSUS TREATY 10/16. PAGE 95 A1954 ISLAM SECT DIPLOM INT/TRADE
B96
DE VATTEL E.,THE LAW OF NATIONS. AGRI FINAN CHIEF DIPLOM INT/TRADE AGREE OWN ALL/VALS MORAL ORD/FREE SOVEREIGN...GEN/LAWS 18 NATURL/LAW WOLFF/C. PAGE 35 A0714 LAW CONCPT NAT/G INT/LAW
B98
GRIFFIN A.P.C.,LIST OF BOOKS RELATING TO CUBA (PAMPHLET). CUBA L/A+17C USA-45 INT/TRADE DOMIN WAR GP/REL ALL/VALS...GEOG SOC CHARTS 19/20. PAGE 56 A1158 BIBLIOG/A NAT/G COLONIAL

INTEGRATION....SEE NEGRO, SOUTH/US, RACE/REL, SOC/INTEG, CIV/RIGHTS, DISCRIM, ISOLAT, SCHOOL, STRANGE

INTEGRATION, POLITICAL+ECONOMIC....SEE REGION+INT/ORG+ VOL/ASSN+CENTRAL

INTELL....INTELLIGENTSIA

N
THE WORLD OF LEARNING. INTELL ACT/RES EDU/PROP 20 UNESCO. PAGE 2 A0045 BIBLIOG/A ACADEM R+D INT/ORG
N
AVTOREFERATY DISSERTATSII. USSR INTELL ACADEM NAT/G DIPLOM GOV/REL KNOWL CONCPT. PAGE 3 A0047 BIBLIOG MARXISM MARXIST COM
N
AMERICAN HISTORICAL SOCIETY,LIST OF DOCTORAL DISSERTATIONS IN HISTORY IN PROGRESS OR COMPLETED IN COLLEGES AND UNIVERSITIES IN THE UNITED STATES. WOR+45 WOR-45 CULTURE SOCIETY NAT/G DIPLOM LEAD TREND. PAGE 7 A0150 BIBLIOG ACADEM INTELL
B11
PHILLIPSON C.,THE INTERNATIONAL LAW AND CUSTOM OF ANCIENT GREECE AND ROME. MEDIT-7 UNIV INTELL SOCIETY STRUCT NAT/G LEGIS EXEC PERSON...CONCPT OBS CON/ANAL ROM/EMP. PAGE 116 A2377 INT/ORG LAW INT/LAW
S17
ROOT E.,"THE EFFECT OF DEMOCRACY ON INTERNATIONAL LAW." USA-45 WOR-45 INTELL SOCIETY INT/ORG NAT/G CONSULT ACT/RES CREATE PLAN EDU/PROP PEACE SKILL ...CONCPT METH/CNCPT OBS 20. PAGE 123 A2523 LEGIS JURID INT/LAW
B22
BRYCE J.,INTERNATIONAL RELATIONS. CHRIST-17C EUR+WWI MOD/EUR CULTURE INTELL NAT/G DELIB/GP CREATE BAL/PWR DIPLOM ATTIT DRIVE RIGID/FLEX ALL/VALS...PLURIST JURID CONCPT TIME/SEQ GEN/LAWS TOT/POP. PAGE 20 A0412 INT/ORG POLICY
B28
MILLER D.H.,THE DRAFTING OF THE COVENANT. UNIV WOR-45 INTELL NAT/G DELIB/GP PLAN ECO/TAC LEGIT WAR ATTIT PERCEPT...CONCPT TIME/SEQ LEAGUE/NAT TOT/POP 20. PAGE 101 A2074 INT/ORG STRUCT PEACE
B32
WRIGHT Q.,GOLD AND MONETARY STABILIZATION. FUT USA-45 WOR-45 INTELL ECO/DEV INT/ORG NAT/G CONSULT PLAN ECO/TAC ADMIN ATTIT WEALTH...CONCPT TREND 20. PAGE 167 A3404 FINAN POLICY
B34
EINSTEIN A.,THE WORLD AS I SEE IT. WOR-45 INTELL R+D INT/ORG NAT/G SECT VOL/ASSN FORCES CREATE EDU/PROP LEGIT ARMS/CONT WAR WEAPON NAT/LISM ALL/VALS...POLICY CONCPT 20. PAGE 41 A0828 SOCIETY PHIL/SCI DIPLOM PACIFISM
B35
STALEY E.,WAR AND THE PRIVATE INVESTOR. UNIV WOR-45 INTELL SOCIETY INT/ORG NAT/G TOP/EX CAP/ISM ECO/TAC WAR ATTIT ALL/VALS...INT TIME/SEQ TREND CON/ANAL WORK TOT/POP 20. PAGE 137 A2799 FINAN INT/TRADE DIPLOM
B38
PETTEE G.S.,THE PROCESS OF REVOLUTION. COM FRANCE ITALY MOD/EUR RUSSIA SPAIN WOR-45 ELITES INTELL SOCIETY STRATA STRUCT INT/ORG NAT/G POL/PAR ACT/RES PLAN EDU/PROP LEGIT EXEC...SOC MYTH TIME/SEQ TOT/POP 18/20. PAGE 115 A2370 COERCE CONCPT REV
B38
WARE E.E.,THE STUDY OF INTERNATIONAL RELATIONS IN THE UNITED STATES. USA+45 USA-45 WOR-45 INTELL SERV/IND INT/ORG NAT/G PROF/ORG SECT CONSULT INT/TRADE EDU/PROP ARMS/CONT...CONCPT 20. PAGE 161 KNOWL DIPLOM

A3283

C39
SCOTT J.B.,"LAW, THESTATE, AND THE INTERNATIONAL COMMUNITY (2 VOLS.)" INTELL INT/ORG NAT/G SECT INT/TRADE WAR...INT/LAW GEN/LAWS BIBLIOG. PAGE 130 A2672 LAW PHIL/SCI DIPLOM CONCPT

B40
MILLER E.,THE NEUROSES OF WAR. UNIV INTELL SOCIETY INT/ORG NAT/G EDU/PROP DISPL DRIVE PERCEPT PERSON RIGID/FLEX...SOC TIME/SEQ 20. PAGE 101 A2075 HEALTH PSY WAR

S41
LASSWELL H.D.,"THE GARRISON STATE" (BMR)" FUT WOR+45 ELITES INTELL FORCES ECO/TAC DOMIN EDU/PROP COERCE INGP/REL 20. PAGE 85 A1739 NAT/G DIPLOM PWR CIVMIL/REL

S42
TURNER F.J.,"AMERICAN SECTIONALISM AND WORLD ORGANIZATION." EUR+WWI UNIV USA-45 WOR-45 INTELL ECO/DEV TOP/EX ACT/RES PLAN EDU/PROP LEGIT ALL/VALS ...CONCPT NEW/IDEA OBS TREND LEAGUE/NAT TOT/POP 20. PAGE 146 A2981 INT/ORG DRIVE BAL/PWR

L44
WRIGHT Q.,"THE US AND INTERNATIONAL AGREEMENTS." FUT USA-45 CONSTN INTELL INT/ORG LOC/G NAT/G CHIEF CONSULT EX/STRUC DIPLOM LEGIT DRIVE PERCEPT PWR ...CONCPT CONGRESS 20. PAGE 167 A3407 DELIB/GP TOP/EX PEACE

S44
WRIGHT Q.,"CONSTITUTIONAL PROCEDURES OF THE US FOR CARRYING OUT OBLIGATIONS FOR MILITARY SANCTIONS." EUR+WWI FUT USA-45 WOR-45 CONSTN INTELL NAT/G CONSULT EX/STRUC LEGIS ROUTINE DRIVE...POLICY JURID CONCPT OBS TREND TOT/POP 20. PAGE 167 A3406 TOP/EX FORCES INT/LAW WAR

L46
MASTERS D.,"ONE WORLD OR NONE." FUT WOR+45 INTELL INT/ORG ACT/RES EDU/PROP DETER ATTIT RIGID/FLEX SUPEGO KNOWL...STAT TREND ORG/CHARTS 20. PAGE 96 A1960 POLICY PHIL/SCI ARMS/CONT NUC/PWR

L47
BRUNER J.S.,"TOWARD A COMMON GROUND-INTERNATIONAL SOCIAL SCIENCE." FUT WOR+45 INTELL R+D NAT/G VOL/ASSN CONSULT DELIB/GP ACT/RES CREATE PLAN TEC/DEV ATTIT ORD/FREE...PSY SOC CONCPT ANTHOL UNESCO 20. PAGE 20 A0410 INT/ORG KNOWL

B48
VISSON A.,AS OTHERS SEE US. EUR+WWI FRANCE UK USA+45 CULTURE INTELL SOCIETY STRATA NAT/G POL/PAR FOR/AID ATTIT DRIVE LOVE ORD/FREE RESPECT WEALTH ...PLURIST SOC OBS TOT/POP 20. PAGE 159 A3244 USA-45 PERCEPT

B49
ROSENHAUPT H.W.,HOW TO WAGE PEACE. USA+45 SOCIETY STRATA STRUCT R+D INT/ORG POL/PAR LEGIS ACT/RES CREATE PLAN EDU/PROP ADMIN EXEC ATTIT ALL/VALS ...TIME/SEQ TREND COLD/WAR 20. PAGE 124 A2536 INTELL CONCPT DIPLOM

B49
SINGER K.,THE IDEA OF CONFLICT. UNIV INTELL INT/ORG NAT/G PLAN ROUTINE ATTIT DRIVE ALL/VALS...POLICY CONCPT TIME/SEQ. PAGE 133 A2730 ACT/RES SOC

B49
STREIT C.,UNION NOW. UNIV USA-45 WOR-45 INTELL STRUCT INT/ORG NAT/G PLAN DIPLOM EXEC ATTIT ...CONCPT TIME/SEQ. PAGE 139 A2849 SOCIETY ACT/RES WAR

S49
FOX W.T.R.,"INTERWAR INTERNATIONAL RELATIONS RESEARCH: THE AMERICAN EXPERIENCE." USA+45 USA-45 INTELL INT/ORG VOL/ASSN OP/RES ATTIT SKILL ...TIME/SEQ LEAGUE/NAT 20. PAGE 48 A0973 ACT/RES CON/ANAL

S49
KIRK G.,"MATTERIALS FOR THE STUDY OF INTERNATIONAL RELATIONS." FUT UNIV WOR+45 INTELL EDU/PROP ROUTINE PEACE ATTIT...INT/LAW JURID CONCPT OBS. PAGE 80 A1633 INT/ORG ACT/RES DIPLOM

B50
MACIVER R.M.,GREAT EXPRESSIONS OF HUMAN RIGHTS. LAW CONSTN CULTURE INTELL SOCIETY R+D INT/ORG ATTIT DRIVE...JURID OBS HIST/WRIT GEN/LAWS. PAGE 92 A1891 UNIV CONCPT

B50
STONE J.,THE PROVINCE AND FUNCTION OF LAW. UNIV WOR+45 WOR-45 CULTURE INTELL SOCIETY ECO/DEV ECO/UNDEV NAT/G LEGIT ROUTINE ATTIT PERCEPT PERSON ...JURID CONCPT GEN/LAWS GEN/METH 20. PAGE 138 A2833 INT/ORG LAW

B51
BLANSHARD P.,COMMUNISM, DEMOCRACY AND CATHOLIC POWER. USSR VATICAN WOR+45 WOR-45 CULTURE ELITES INTELL SOCIETY STRUCT INT/ORG POL/PAR EDU/PROP COERCE ATTIT KNOWL PWR MARXISM...CONCPT COLD/WAR 20. PAGE 15 A0308 COM SECT TOTALISM

B51
MCKEON R.,DEMOCRACY IN A WORLD OF TENSION. UNIV LAW INTELL STRUCT R+D INT/ORG SCHOOL EDU/PROP LEGIT ATTIT DRIVE PERCEPT PERSON...POLICY JURID PSY SOC CONCPT METH/CNCPT OBS UNESCO TOT/POP VAL/FREE. PAGE 98 A2015 SOCIETY ALL/VALS ORD/FREE

B52
SMITH C.M.,INTERNATIONAL COMMUNICATION AND POLITICAL WARFARE: AN ANNOTATED BIBLIOGRAPHY (A PAPER). WOR+45 INTELL R+D NAT/G FORCES ACT/RES DIPLOM COERCE ALL/IDEOS. PAGE 134 A2745 BIBLIOG/A EDU/PROP WAR COM/IND

L52
WRIGHT Q.,"CONGRESS AND THE TREATY-MAKING POWER." USA+45 WOR+45 CONSTN INTELL NAT/G CHIEF CONSULT EX/STRUC LEGIS TOP/EX CREATE GOV/REL DISPL DRIVE RIGID/FLEX...TREND TOT/POP CONGRESS CONGRESS 20 TREATY. PAGE 167 A3408 ROUTINE DIPLOM INT/LAW DELIB/GP

S52
SCHWEBEL S.M.,"THE SECRETARY-GENERAL OF THE UN." FUT INTELL CONSULT DELIB/GP ADMIN PEACE ATTIT ...JURID MGT CONCPT TREND UN CONGRESS 20. PAGE 130 A2663 INT/ORG TOP/EX

B54
MANNING C.A.W.,THE UNIVERSITY TEACHING OF SOCIAL SCIENCES: INTERNATIONAL RELATIONS. WOR+45 INTELL STRATA R+D ACADEM INT/ORG NAT/G CONSULT DELIB/GP ACT/RES EDU/PROP NAT/LISM ATTIT...POLICY CONT/OBS HYPO/EXP VAL/FREE LEAGUE/NAT UNESCO 20. PAGE 94 A1925 KNOWL PHIL/SCI DIPLOM

S54
DAWSON K.H.,"THE UNITED NATIONS IN A DISUNITED WORLD." WOR+45 WOR-45 LAW INTELL NAT/G PEACE ATTIT PERCEPT MORAL LEAGUE/NAT TOT/POP VAL/FREE 20 UN. PAGE 34 A0694 INT/ORG LEGIT

L55
ROSTOW W.W.,"RUSSIA AND CHINA UNDER COMMUNISM." CHINA/COM USSR INTELL STRUCT INT/ORG NAT/G POL/PAR TOP/EX ACT/RES PLAN ADMIN ATTIT ALL/VALS MARXISM ...CONCPT OBS TIME/SEQ TREND GOV/COMP VAL/FREE 20. PAGE 124 A2543 COM ASIA

S55
WRIGHT Q.,"THE PEACEFUL ADJUSTMENT OF INTERNATIONAL RELATIONS: PROBLEMS AND RESEARCH APPROACHES." UNIV INTELL EDU/PROP ADJUD ROUTINE KNOWL SKILL...INT/LAW JURID PHIL/SCI CLASSIF 20. PAGE 167 A3411 R+D METH/CNCPT PEACE

B56
WU E.,LEADERS OF TWENTIETH-CENTURY CHINA; AN ANNOTATED BIBLIOGRAPHY OF SELECTED CHINESE BIOGRAPHICAL WORKS IN HOOVER LIBRARY. ASIA INDUS POL/PAR DIPLOM ADMIN REV WAR...HUM MGT 20. PAGE 168 A3422 BIBLIOG/A BIOG INTELL CHIEF

S56
CUTLER R.,"THE DEVELOPMENT OF THE NATIONAL SECURITY COUNCIL." USA+45 INTELL CONSULT EX/STRUC DIPLOM LEAD 20 TRUMAN/HS EISNHWR/DD NSC. PAGE 33 A0670 ORD/FREE DELIB/GP PROB/SOLV NAT/G

B57
FULLER C.D.,TRAINING OF SPECIALISTS IN INTERNATIONAL RELATIONS. FUT USA+45 USA-45 INTELL INT/ORG...MGT METH/CNCPT INT QU GEN/METH 20. PAGE 50 A1017 KNOWL DIPLOM

B58
CRAIG G.A.,FROM BISMARCK TO ADENAUER: ASPECTS OF GERMAN STATECRAFT. GERMANY INTELL FORCES ECO/TAC CONFER COERCE WAR GP/REL ORD/FREE PWR CONSERVE 19/20 BISMARCK/O ADENAUER/K. PAGE 32 A0653 DIPLOM LEAD NAT/G

B58
SCHUMAN F.,INTERNATIONAL POLITICS. WOR+45 WOR-45 INTELL NAT/G FORCES DOMIN LEGIT COERCE NUC/PWR ATTIT DISPL ORD/FREE PWR SOVEREIGN...POLICY CONCPT GEN/LAWS SUEZ 20. PAGE 129 A2650 FUT INT/ORG NAT/LISM DIPLOM

S58
DAVENPORT J.,"ARMS AND THE WELFARE STATE." INTELL STRUCT FORCES CREATE ECO/TAC FOR/AID DOMIN LEGIT ADMIN WAR ORD/FREE PWR...POLICY SOC CONCPT MYTH OBS TREND COLD/WAR TOT/POP 20. PAGE 34 A0685 USA+45 NAT/G USSR

B59
KULSKI W.W.,PEACEFUL CO-EXISTENCE: AN ANALYSIS OF SOVIET FOREIGN POLICY. WOR+45 INTELL SOCIETY ECO/UNDEV POL/PAR EDU/PROP COERCE DRIVE RIGID/FLEX PWR SKILL...PSY CONCPT HIST/WRIT CON/ANAL GEN/METH WORK VAL/FREE 20. PAGE 83 A1691 PLAN DIPLOM USSR

S59
FOX W.T.R.,"THE USES OF INTERNATIONAL RELATIONS THEORY. IN (FOX, THE THEORETICAL ASPECTS OF INTERNATIONAL RELATIONS,. WOR+45 INTELL SOCIETY STRATA INT/ORG CONSULT ACT/RES PWR...POLICY 20. PAGE 48 A0976 PLAN DIPLOM METH/CNCPT

S59
ZAUBERMAN A.,"SOVIET BLOC ECONOMIC INTEGRATION." COM CULTURE INTELL ECO/DEV INDUS TOP/EX ACT/RES PLAN ECO/TAC INT/TRADE ROUTINE CHOOSE ATTIT ...TIME/SEQ 20. PAGE 169 A3448 MARKET INT/ORG USSR TOTALISM

B60
ARMS CONTROL. FUT UNIV WOR+45 INTELL R+D INT/ORG NAT/G VOL/ASSN CONSULT CREATE EDU/PROP PEACE...HUM GEN/LAWS TOT/POP 20. PAGE 3 A0060 DELIB/GP ORD/FREE ARMS/CONT NUC/PWR

B60
CARNEGIE ENDOWMENT INT. PEACE,PERSPECTIVES ON PEACE - 1910-1960. WOR+45 WOR-45 INTELL INT/ORG CONSULT ACT/RES EDU/PROP ATTIT KNOWL ORD/FREE...TIME/SEQ TREND EEC OAS UNESCO NAZI 20. PAGE 24 A0489 FUT CONCPT ARMS/CONT PEACE

B60
FOOTMAN D.,INTERNATIONAL COMMUNISM. ASIA EUR+WWI COM

FRANCE FUT GERMANY MOD/EUR S/ASIA USA-45 WOR+45 WOR-45 INTELL LABOR TOTALISM MARXISM WORK 20. PAGE 47 A0958 — INT/ORG STRUCT REV

B60
PRICE D.,THE SECRETARY OF STATE. USA+45 CONSTN ELITES INTELL CHIEF EX/STRUC TOP/EX LEGIT ATTIT PWR SKILL...DECISION 20 CONGRESS. PAGE 117 A2410 — CONSULT DIPLOM INT/LAW

L60
BRENNAN D.G.,"SETTING AND GOALS OF ARMS CONTROL." FUT USA+45 USSR WOR+45 INTELL INT/ORG NAT/G VOL/ASSN CONSULT PLAN DIPLOM ECO/TAC ADMIN KNOWL PWR...POLICY CONCPT TREND COLD/WAR 20. PAGE 18 A0371 — FORCES COERCE ARMS/CONT DETER

S60
KAPLAN M.A.,"THEORETICAL ANALYSIS OF THE BALANCE OF POWER." FUT USA+45 WOR+45 INTELL ECO/DEV INT/ORG NAT/G CONSULT TOP/EX ACT/RES PLAN TEC/DEV ATTIT ALL/VALS...METH/CNCPT TOT/POP 20. PAGE 76 A1562 — CREATE NEW/IDEA DIPLOM NUC/PWR

S60
MARTIN E.M.,"NEW TRENDS IN UNITED STATES ECONOMIC FOREIGN POLICY." USA+45 INTELL DELIB/GP FOR/AID INT/TRADE ROUTINE BAL/PAY...RELATIV 20. PAGE 95 A1949 — NAT/G PLAN DIPLOM

S60
MODELSKI G.,"AUSTRALIA AND SEATO." S/ASIA USA+45 CULTURE INTELL ECO/DEV NAT/G PLAN DIPLOM ADMIN ROUTINE ATTIT SKILL...MGT TIME/SEQ AUSTRAL 20 SEATO. PAGE 102 A2097 — INT/ORG ACT/RES

S60
OSGOOD C.E.,"COGNITIVE DYNAMICS IN THE CONDUCT OF HUMAN AFFAIRS." USA+45 INTELL INT/ORG CONSULT PLAN ATTIT PERSON...PSY CHARTS HYPO/EXP 20. PAGE 112 A2299 — R+D SOCIETY

S60
PETERSON E.N.,"HISTORICAL SCHOLARSHIP AND WORLD UNITY." FUT UNIV WOR-45 CULTURE INTELL INT/ORG NAT/G ACT/RES EDU/PROP ATTIT PERCEPT RIGID/FLEX ...NEW/IDEA OBS HIST/WRIT TREND COLD/WAR TOT/POP 20. PAGE 115 A2367 — PLAN KNOWL NAT/LISM

B61
HARRISON S.,INDIA AND THE UNITED STATES. FUT S/ASIA USA+45 WOR+45 INTELL ECO/DEV ECO/UNDEV AGRI INDUS INT/ORG NAT/G CONSULT EX/STRUC TOP/EX PLAN ECO/TAC NEUTRAL ALL/VALS...MGT TOT/POP 20. PAGE 62 A1272 — DELIB/GP ACT/RES FOR/AID INDIA

B61
HUDSON G.F.,THE SINO-SOVIET DISPUTE. CHINA/COM USSR INTELL INT/TRADE DEBATE REV...IDEA/COMP 20. PAGE 68 A1404 — DIPLOM MARXISM PRESS ATTIT

B61
NOGEE J.L.,SOVIET POLICY TOWARD INTERNATIONAL CONTROL OF ATOMIC ENERGY. COM USA+45 WOR+45 INTELL NAT/G ACT/RES DIPLOM EDU/PROP NUC/PWR TOTALISM PERCEPT KNOWL PWR...TIME/SEQ COLD/WAR 20. PAGE 109 A2247 — INT/ORG ATTIT ARMS/CONT USSR

L61
HALPERIN M.H.,"NUCLEAR WEAPONS AND LIMITED WARS." FUT UNIV WOR+45 INTELL SOCIETY ECO/DEV ACT/RES DRIVE PERCEPT RIGID/FLEX...CONCPT TIME/SEQ TREND TOT/POP 20. PAGE 60 A1237 — PLAN COERCE NUC/PWR WAR

L61
LEVINE R.A.,"THE ANTHROPOLOGY OF CONFLICT." FUT CULTURE INTELL FAM INT/ORG LG/CO SML/CO ATTIT KNOWL ...METH/CNCPT VAL/FREE 20. PAGE 88 A1796 — SOCIETY ACT/RES

L61
TAUBENFELD H.J.,"A TREATY FOR ANTARCTICA." FUT USA+45 INTELL INT/ORG LABOR 20 TREATY ANTARCTICA. PAGE 141 A2893 — R+D ACT/RES DIPLOM

S61
BALL M.M.,"ISSUES FOR THE AMERICAS: NON-INTERVENTION VS HUMAN RIGHTS AND THE PRESERVATION OF DEMOCRATIC INSTITUTIONS." USA+45 INTELL INT/ORG NAT/G DIPLOM ECO/TAC LEGIT...TREND OAS TOT/POP 20. PAGE 11 A0213 — L/A+17C MORAL

S61
DANIELS R.V.,"THE CHINESE REVOLUTION IN RUSSIAN PERSPECTIVE." ASIA CHINA/COM COM USSR INTELL INT/ORG TOP/EX REV TOTALISM PWR...POLICY WORK VAL/FREE 20. PAGE 33 A0680 — POL/PAR PLAN

S61
GALBRAITH J.K.,"A POSITIVE APPROACH TO ECONOMIC AID." FUT USA+45 INTELL NAT/G CONSULT ACT/RES DIPLOM ECO/TAC EDU/PROP ATTIT KNOWL PWR WEALTH ...SOC STERTYP 20. PAGE 50 A1030 — ECO/UNDEV ROUTINE FOR/AID

S61
HAZARD J.N.,"CODIFYING PEACEFUL COEXISTANCE." FUT INTELL INT/ORG TEC/DEV PEACE HEALTH...INT/LAW CONT/OBS 20. PAGE 63 A1299 — VOL/ASSN JURID

S61
LEWY G.,"SUPERIOR ORDERS, NUCLEAR WARFARE AND THE DICTATES OF CONSCIENCE: THE DILEMMA OF MILITARY OBEDIENCE IN THE ATOMIC." FUT UNIV WOR+45 INTELL SOCIETY FORCES TOP/EX ACT/RES ADMIN ROUTINE NUC/PWR PERCEPT RIGID/FLEX ALL/VALS...POLICY CONCPT 20. PAGE 88 A1805 — DETER INT/ORG LAW INT/LAW

S61
LIPSON L.,"AN ARGUMENT ON THE LEGALITY OF RECONNAISSANCE STATELLITES." COM USA+45 USSR WOR+45 AIR INTELL NAT/G CONSULT PLAN DIPLOM LEGIT ROUTINE ATTIT...INT/LAW JURID CONCPT METH/CNCPT TREND COLD/WAR 20. PAGE 90 A1833 — INT/ORG LAW SPACE

S61
MACHOWSKI K.,"SELECTED PROBLEMS OF NATIONAL SOVEREIGNTY WITH REFERENCE TO THE LAW OF OUTER SPACE." FUT WOR+45 AIR LAW INTELL SOCIETY ECO/DEV PLAN EDU/PROP DETER DRIVE PERCEPT SOVEREIGN ...POLICY INT/LAW OBS TREND TOT/POP 20. PAGE 92 A1889 — UNIV ACT/RES NUC/PWR SPACE

S61
RALEIGH J.S.,"THE MIDDLE EAST IN 1960: A POLITICAL SURVEY." FUT ISLAM INTELL KIN BAL/PWR EDU/PROP NAT/LISM...TREND VAL/FREE 20. PAGE 119 A2435 — INT/ORG EX/STRUC

S61
SINGER J.D.,"THE LEVEL OF ANALYSIS: PROBLEMS IN INTERNATIONAL RELATIONS." FUT INTELL R+D INT/ORG CREATE EDU/PROP...METH/CNCPT HYPO/EXP GEN/METH METH VAL/FREE. PAGE 133 A2725 — SOCIETY SOC DIPLOM

S61
TAUBENFELD H.J.,"OUTER SPACE--PAST POLITICS AND FUTURE POLICY." FUT USA+45 USA-45 WOR+45 AIR INTELL STRUCT ECO/DEV NAT/G TOP/EX ACT/RES ADMIN ROUTINE NUC/PWR ATTIT DRIVE...CONCPT TIME/SEQ TREND TOT/POP 20. PAGE 141 A2892 — PLAN SPACE INT/ORG

S61
VIRALLY M.,"VERS UNE REFORME DU SECRETARIAT DES NATIONS UNIES." FUT WOR+45 CONSTN ECO/DEV TOP/EX BAL/PWR ADMIN ALL/VALS...CONCPT BIOG UN VAL/FREE 20. PAGE 159 A3243 — INT/ORG INTELL DIPLOM

B62
GILPIN R.,AMERICAN SCIENTISTS AND NUCLEAR WEAPONS POLICY. COM FUT USA+45 WOR+45 INT/ORG NAT/G PROF/ORG CONSULT FORCES CREATE TEC/DEV BAL/PWR EDU/PROP ARMS/CONT WAR PERCEPT KNOWL MORAL PWR ...PHIL/SCI SOC CONCPT GEN/LAWS 20. PAGE 52 A1073 — INTELL ATTIT DETER NUC/PWR

B62
LAUERHAUSS L.,COMMUNISM IN LATIN AMERICA: THE POST-WAR YEARS (1945 -1960) (PAPER). INTELL STRATA ECO/UNDEV AGRI WORKER FOR/AID INT/TRADE COLONIAL GUERRILLA 20. PAGE 85 A1745 — BIBLIOG L/A+17C MARXISM REV

B62
OSGOOD C.E.,AN ALTERNATIVE TO WAR OR SURRENDER. FUT UNIV CULTURE INTELL SOCIETY R+D INT/ORG CONSULT DELIB/GP ACT/RES PLAN CHOOSE ATTIT PERCEPT KNOWL ...PHIL/SCI PSY SOC TREND GEN/LAWS 20. PAGE 112 A2300 — ORD/FREE EDU/PROP PEACE WAR

L62
"HIGHER EDUCATION AND ECONOMIC AND SOCIAL DEVELOPMENT IN LATIN AMERICA: A BIBLIOGRAPHY." L/A+17C SOCIETY ECO/UNDEV PROF/ORG DIPLOM CONFER ...SOC 20. PAGE 3 A0062 — BIBLIOG/A ACADEM INTELL EDU/PROP

S62
FOSTER W.C.,"ARMS CONTROL AND DISARMAMENT IN A DIVIDED WORLD." COM FUT USA+45 USSR WOR+45 INTELL INT/ORG NAT/G VOL/ASSN CONSULT CREATE PLAN TEC/DEV EDU/PROP LEGIT NUC/PWR ATTIT RIGID/FLEX...CONCPT TREND TOT/POP 20 UN. PAGE 47 A0971 — DELIB/GP POLICY ARMS/CONT DIPLOM

S62
GUETZKOW H.,"THE POTENTIAL OF CASE STUDY IN ANALYZING INTERNATIONAL CONFLICT." EUR+WWI FUT GERMANY INTELL SOCIETY STRUCT INT/ORG LOC/G NAT/G CONSULT CREATE PLAN CHOOSE ATTIT RIGID/FLEX ...POLICY SAAR 20. PAGE 58 A1188 — EDU/PROP METH/CNCPT COERCE FRANCE

S62
MONNIER J.P.,"LA SUCCESSION D'ETATS EN MATIERE DE RESPONSABILITE INTERNATIONALE." UNIV CONSTN INTELL SOCIETY ADJUD ROUTINE PERCEPT SUPEGO...GEN/LAWS TOT/POP 20. PAGE 103 A2107 — NAT/G JURID INT/LAW

S62
ORBAN M.,"L'EUROPE EN FORMATION ET SES PROBLEMES." EUR+WWI FUT WOR+45 WOR-45 INTELL STRUCT DELIB/GP ACT/RES FEDERAL RIGID/FLEX WEALTH...CONCPT TIME/SEQ OEEC 20. PAGE 112 A2295 — INT/ORG PLAN REGION

S62
SCHILLING W.R.,"SCIENTISTS, FOREIGN POLICY AND POLITICS." WOR+45 WOR-45 INTELL INT/ORG CONSULT TOP/EX ACT/RES PLAN ADMIN KNOWL...CONCPT OBS TREND LEAGUE/NAT 20. PAGE 128 A2627 — NAT/G TEC/DEV DIPLOM NUC/PWR

S62
VIGNES D.,"L'AUTORITE DES TRAITES INTERNATIONAUX EN DROIT INTERNE." EUR+WWI UNIV LAW CONSTN INTELL NAT/G POL/PAR DIPLOM ATTIT PERCEPT ALL/VALS ...POLICY INT/LAW JURID CONCPT TIME/SEQ 20 TREATY. PAGE 159 A3233 — STRUCT LEGIT FRANCE

B63
BUTTS R.F.,AMERICAN EDUCATION IN INTERNATIONAL DEVELOPMENT. USA+45 WOR+45 INTELL SCHOOL DIPLOM EDU/PROP...BIBLIOG 20. PAGE 23 A0457 — ACADEM FOR/AID CONSULT ECO/UNDEV

B63
FRANKEL J.,THE MAKING OF FOREIGN POLICY: AN ANALYSIS OF DECISION-MAKING. CHINA/COM EUR+WWI — POLICY DECISION

USA+45 ELITES INTELL FORCES LEGIS PLAN ATTIT ALL/VALS MORAL CONSERVE...GOV/COMP 20 PRESIDENT UN TREATY. PAGE 48 A0981 PROB/SOLV DIPLOM

B63
HARTLEY A.,A STATE OF ENGLAND. UK ELITES SOCIETY ACADEM NAT/G SCHOOL INGP/REL CONSEN ORD/FREE NEW/LIB...POLICY 20. PAGE 62 A1275 DIPLOM ATTIT INTELL ECO/DEV

B63
MOSELY P.E.,THE SOVIET UNION, 1922-1962: A FOREIGN AFFAIRS READER. ASIA POLAND USSR CULTURE INTELL AGRI POL/PAR WORKER INT/TRADE DOMIN WAR NAT/LISM MARXISM SOCISM 20 KHRUSH/N. PAGE 105 A2152 PWR POLICY DIPLOM

B63
QUAISON-SACKEY A.,AFRICA UNBOUND: REFLECTIONS OF AN AFRICAN STATESMAN. ISLAM CULTURE INTELL INT/ORG POL/PAR TOP/EX DOMIN EDU/PROP LEGIT ATTIT PERSON ...CONCPT OBS TIME/SEQ CHARTS STERTYP 20 UN. PAGE 118 A2423 AFR BIOG

L63
MOUSKHELY M.,"LE BLOC COMMUNISTE ET LA COMMUNAUTE ECONOMIQUE EUROPEENNE." AFR COM EUR+WWI FUT USSR WOR+45 INTELL ECO/UNDEV LABOR POL/PAR NUC/PWR RIGID/FLEX...TIME/SEQ ORG/CHARTS EEC TOT/POP 20. PAGE 105 A2158 INT/ORG ECO/DEV

S63
COSER L.,"AMERICA AND THE WORLD REVOLUTION." COM FUT USA+45 WOR+45 INTELL SOCIETY NAT/G ECO/TAC EDU/PROP ALL/VALS SOCISM...PSY GEN/LAWS TOT/POP 20 COLD/WAR. PAGE 31 A0629 ECO/UNDEV PLAN FOR/AID DIPLOM

S63
DAVEE R.,"POUR UN FONDS DE DEVELOPPEMENT SOCIAL." FUT WOR+45 INTELL SOCIETY ECO/DEV FINAN TEC/DEV ROUTINE WEALTH...TREND TOT/POP VAL/FREE UN 20. PAGE 34 A0684 INT/ORG SOC FOR/AID

S63
MACWHINNEY E.,"LES CONCEPT SOVIETIQUE DE 'COEXISTENCE PACIFIQUE' ET LES RAPPORTS JURIDIQUES ENTRE L'URSS ET LES ETATS OCIDENTAUX." COM FUT WOR+45 LAW CULTURE INTELL POL/PAR ACT/RES BAL/PWR ...INT/LAW 20. PAGE 93 A1903 NAT/G CONCPT DIPLOM USSR

S63
MARTHELOT P.,"PROGRES DE LA REFORME AGRAIRE." INTELL ECO/DEV R+D FOR/AID ADMIN KNOWL...OBS VAL/FREE UN 20. PAGE 95 A1948 AGRI INT/ORG

S63
MEYROWITZ H.,"LES JURISTES DEVANT L'ARME NUCLAIRE." FUT WOR+45 INTELL SOCIETY BAL/PWR DETER WAR...JURID CONCPT 20. PAGE 100 A2058 ACT/RES ADJUD INT/LAW NUC/PWR

B64
APTER D.E.,IDEOLOGY AND DISCONTENT. FUT WOR+45 CONSTN CULTURE INTELL SOCIETY STRUCT INT/ORG NAT/G DELIB/GP LEGIS CREATE PLAN TEC/DEV EDU/PROP EXEC PERCEPT PERSON RIGID/FLEX ALL/VALS...POLICY TOT/POP. PAGE 8 A0171 ACT/RES ATTIT

B64
GRODZINS M.,THE ATOMIC AGE: FORTY-FIVE SCIENTISTS AND SCHOLARS SPEAK ON NATIONAL AND WORLD AFFAIRS. FUT USA+45 WOR+45 R+D INT/ORG NAT/G CONSULT TEC/DEV EDU/PROP ATTIT PERSON ORD/FREE...HUM CONCPT TIME/SEQ CON/ANAL. PAGE 57 A1169 INTELL ARMS/CONT NUC/PWR

B64
IKLE F.C.,HOW NATIONS NEGOTIATE. COM EUR+WWI USA+45 INTELL INT/ORG VOL/ASSN DELIB/GP ACT/RES CREATE DOMIN EDU/PROP ADJUD ROUTINE ATTIT PERSON ORD/FREE RESPECT SKILL...PSY SOC OBS VAL/FREE. PAGE 70 A1433 NAT/G PWR POLICY

B64
NEWBURY C.W.,THE WEST AFRICAN COMMONWEALTH. CONSTN INTELL ECO/UNDEV VOL/ASSN CHIEF DELIB/GP LEGIS INT/TRADE COLONIAL FEDERAL ATTIT 20 COMMONWLTH AFRICA/W. PAGE 108 A2223 INT/ORG SOVEREIGN GOV/REL AFR

B64
SULLIVAN G.,THE STORY OF THE PEACE CORPS. USA+45 WOR+45 INTELL FACE/GP NAT/G SCHOOL VOL/ASSN CONSULT EX/STRUC PLAN EDU/PROP ADMIN ATTIT DRIVE ALL/VALS ...POLICY HEAL SOC CONCPT INT QU BIOG TREND SOC/EXP WORK. PAGE 140 A2861 INT/ORG ECO/UNDEV FOR/AID PEACE

B64
TEPASKE J.J.,EXPLOSIVE FORCES IN LATIN AMERICA. CULTURE INTELL ECO/UNDEV INT/ORG NAT/G SECT FORCES ECO/TAC EDU/PROP PWR WEALTH SOC. PAGE 142 A2903 L/A+17C RIGID/FLEX FOR/AID USSR

L64
RIPLEY R.B.,"INTERAGENCY COMMITTEES AND INCREMENTALISM: THE CASE OF AID TO INDIA." INDIA USA+45 INTELL NAT/G DELIB/GP ACT/RES DIPLOM ROUTINE NAT/LISM ATTIT PWR...SOC CONCPT NEW/IDEA TIME/SEQ CON/ANAL VAL/FREE 20. PAGE 121 A2483 EXEC MGT FOR/AID

S64
GARMARNIKOW M.,"INFLUENCE-BUYING IN WEST AFRICA." COM FUT USSR INTELL NAT/G PLAN TEC/DEV ECO/TAC DOMIN EDU/PROP REGION NAT/LISM ATTIT DRIVE ALL/VALS SOVEREIGN...POLICY PSY SOC CONCPT TREND STERTYP WORK COLD/WAR 20. PAGE 51 A1049 AFR ECO/UNDEV FOR/AID SOCISM

S64
WASKOW A.I.,"NEW ROADS TO A WORLD WITHOUT WAR." FUT WOR+45 CULTURE INTELL SOCIETY NAT/G DOMIN LEGIT EXEC COERCE PEACE ATTIT DISPL PERCEPT RIGID/FLEX ALL/VALS...POLICY RELATIV SOC NEW/IDEA 20. PAGE 161 A3288 INT/ORG FORCES

B65
PENNICK JL J.R.,THE POLITICS OF AMERICAN SCIENCE, 1939 TO THE PRESENT. USA+45 USA-45 INTELL TEC/DEV DIPLOM NEW/LIB...ANTHOL 20 COLD/WAR. PAGE 114 A2349 POLICY ADMIN PHIL/SCI NAT/G

B65
WINT G.,ASIA: A HANDBOOK. ASIA COM INDIA USSR CULTURE INTELL NAT/G...GEOG STAT CENSUS NAT/COMP WORSHIP 20 TREATY CHINJAP. PAGE 165 A3365 DIPLOM SOC

B65
WRESZIN M.,OSWALD GARRISON VILLARD: PACIFIST AT WAR. EDU/PROP MORAL ORD/FREE. PAGE 167 A3398 USA-45 NAT/G INT/ORG INTELL

S65
FALK R.A.,"INTERNATIONAL LEGAL ORDER." USA+45 INTELL FACE/GP INT/ORG LEGIT KNOWL...CONCPT METH/CNCPT STYLE RECORD GEN/METH 20. PAGE 44 A0890 ATTIT GEN/LAWS INT/LAW

S65
HELMREICH E.C.,"KADAR'S HUNGARY." COM EUR+WWI HUNGARY USSR INTELL ECO/DEV AGRI INT/ORG TOP/EX DOMIN ALL/VALS WORK COLD/WAR 20. PAGE 64 A1311 NAT/G RIGID/FLEX TOTALISM

C65
MARK M.,"BEYOND SOVEREIGNTY." WOR+45 WOR-45 ECO/UNDEV BAL/PWR INT/TRADE NUC/PWR REV WAR MARXISM NEW/LIB BIBLIOG. PAGE 95 A1942 NAT/LISM NAT/G DIPLOM INTELL

B67
BRZEZINSKI Z.K.,THE SOVIET BLOC: UNITY AND CONFLICT (2ND ED., REV., ENLARGED). COM POLAND USSR INTELL CHIEF EX/STRUC CONTROL EXEC GOV/REL PWR MARXISM ...TREND IDEA/COMP 20 LENIN/VI MARX/KARL STALIN/J. PAGE 21 A0420 NAT/G DIPLOM

B67
FILENE P.G.,AMERICANS AND THE SOVIET EXPERIMENT, 1917-1933. USA-45 USSR INTELL NAT/G CAP/ISM DIPLOM EDU/PROP PRESS REV SOCISM...PSY 20. PAGE 45 A0930 ATTIT RIGID/FLEX MARXISM SOCIETY

S67
BREGMAN A.,"WHITHER RUSSIA?" COM RUSSIA INTELL POL/PAR DIPLOM PARTIC NAT/LISM TOTALISM ATTIT ORD/FREE 20. PAGE 18 A0370 MARXISM ELITES ADMIN CREATE

S67
CRAWFORD E.T.,"FOREIGN AREA RESEARCH: A BACKGROUND STATEMENT." USA+45 CONSULT DELIB/GP DIPLOM. PAGE 32 A0661 INTELL NAT/G POLICY ACT/RES

S67
DE ROUGEMENT D.,"THE CAMPAIGN OF THE EUROPEAN CONGRESSES." ELITES INTELL DIPLOM ECO/TAC CONFER PEACE...POLICY PREDICT. PAGE 35 A0710 EUR+WWI REGION FEDERAL INT/ORG

S67
KELLY F.K.,"A PROPOSAL FOR AN ANNUAL REPORT ON THE STATE OF MANKIND." FUT INTELL COM/IND INT/ORG CREATE PROB/SOLV PERS/REL...CONCPT 20 UN. PAGE 77 A1579 SOCIETY UNIV ATTIT NEW/IDEA

S67
NORTH R.C.,"COMMUNICATION AS AN APPROACH TO POLITICS." UNIV INTELL DIPLOM PERCEPT PERSON ...CONCPT TIME. PAGE 110 A2254 PERS/REL GP/REL ACT/RES

S67
ROMANOVSKY S.,"MISUSE OF CULTURAL COOPERATION." USA+45 INTELL DIPLOM DOMIN ATTIT COLD/WAR. PAGE 123 A2518 EDU/PROP POLICY MARXISM CAP/ISM

S67
SARBADHIKARI P.,"A NOTE ON THE DOMESTIC CRISIS OF NON-ALIGNMENT." ELITES INTELL ECO/UNDEV FOR/AID DOMIN. PAGE 127 A2605 NEUTRAL WEALTH TOTALISM BAL/PWR

S67
THOMPSON K.W.,"THE EMPIRICAL, NORMATIVE, AND THEORETICAL FOUNDATIONS OF INTERNATIONAL STUDIES." WOR+45 INGP/REL RATIONAL...CONCPT RECORD IDEA/COMP. PAGE 143 A2932 DIPLOM INTELL METH/COMP KNOWL

INTELLIGENCE, MILITARY....SEE ACT/RES+FORCES+KNOWL

INTELLIGENTSIA....SEE INTELL

INTERAMERICAN CULTURAL COUN A1448

INTERAMERICAN ECO AND SOC COUN A1449

INTEREST....INTEREST

INTER-AMERICAN DEVELOPMENT BANK....SEE INT/AM/DEV

INTER-ASIAN DEVELOPMENT BANK....SEE IADB

INTERNAL REVENUE SERVICE....SEE IRS

INTERNAL WARFARE....SEE REV

INTERNATIONAL BANK RECONST DEV A1450,A1451

INTERNATIONAL COMN JURISTS A1452

INTERNATIONAL COURT OF JUSTICE A1453

INTERNATIONAL ECO POLICY ASSN A1454

INTERNATIONAL ECONOMIC ASSN A1455

INTERNATIONAL FEDN DOCUMENTTN A1456

INTERNATIONAL LABOUR OFFICE A1457

INTERNATIONAL LAW ASSOCIATION A1458

INTERNATIONAL MONETARY FUND A1459

INTERNATIONAL SOCIAL SCI COUN A1460

INTERNATIONAL STUDIES A1461

INTERNATIONAL ATOMIC ENERGY AGENCY....SEE IAEA

INTERNATIONAL BANK FOR RECONSTRUCT. AND DEV....SEE IBRD

INTERNATIONAL CIVIL AVIATION ORGANIZATION....SEE INT/AVIATN

INTERNATIONAL COOPERATION ADMINISTRATION....SEE ICA

INTERNATIONAL COUNCIL OF SCIENTIFIC UNIONS....SEE ICSU

INTERNATIONAL COURT OF JUSTICE....SEE ICJ

INTERNATIONAL DEVELOPMENT ASSOCIATION....SEE INTL/DEV

INTERNATIONAL ECONOMIC ASSOCIATION....SEE INTL/ECON

INTERNATIONAL FINANCE CORPORATION....SEE INTL/FINAN

INTERNATIONAL GEOPHYSICAL YEAR....SEE IGY

INTERNATIONAL INTEGRATION....SEE INT/ORG, INT/REL

INTERNATIONAL LABOR ORGANIZATION....SEE ILO

INTERNATIONAL LAW....SEE INT/LAW

INTERNATIONAL MONETARY FUND....SEE IMF

INTERNATIONAL ORGANIZATIONS....SEE INT/ORG

INTERNATIONAL RELATIONS....SEE INT/REL

INTERNATIONAL SYSTEMS....SEE NET/THEORY+INT/REL+WOR+45

INTERNATIONAL TELECOMMUNICATIONS UNION....SEE ITU

INTERNATIONAL TRADE....SEE INT/TRADE

INTERNATIONAL WORKERS OF THE WORLD....SEE IWW

INTERPOL

S62
GREEN L.C.,"POLITICAL OFFENSES, WAR CRIMES AND EXTRADITION." WOR+45 YUGOSLAVIA INT/ORG LEGIT ROUTINE WAR ORD/FREE SOVEREIGN...JURID NAZI 20 INTERPOL. PAGE 55 A1138 — LAW CONCPT INT/LAW

INTERSTATE COMMERCE COMMISSION....SEE ICC

INTERSTATE COMMISSION ON CRIME....SEE INTST/CRIM

INTERVENT....INTERVENTIONISM (MILITARY, POLITICAL, AND/OR ECONOMIC INTERFERENCE BY A SOVEREIGN STATE OR AN INTERNATIONAL AGENCY IN THE AFFAIRS OF ANOTHER SOVEREIGN STATE)

N19
DEANE H.,THE WAR IN VIETNAM (PAMPHLET). CHINA/COM VIETNAM BAL/PWR DIPLOM ECO/TAC SOCISM INTERVENT COLD/WAR INTERVENT COLD/WAR. PAGE 35 A0720 — WAR SOCIALIST MORAL CAP/ISM

N19
DEANE H.,THE WAR IN VIETNAM (PAMPHLET). CHINA/COM VIETNAM BAL/PWR DIPLOM ECO/TAC SOCISM INTERVENT COLD/WAR INTERVENT COLD/WAR. PAGE 35 A0720 — WAR SOCIALIST MORAL CAP/ISM

N19
HALPERN M.,THE MORALITY AND POLITICS OF INTERVENTION (PAMPHLET). USA+45 INT/ORG FORCES ECO/TAC MORAL ORD/FREE 20 INTERVENT CHRISTIAN. PAGE 61 A1243 — POLICY DIPLOM SOVEREIGN DOMIN

B35
WEINBERG A.K.,MANIFEST DESTINY: A STUDY OF NATIONALIST EXPANSIONISM IN AMERICAN HISTORY. USA+45 USA-45 FORCES DIPLOM COLONIAL WAR ATTIT 18/20 INTERVENT. PAGE 162 A3305 — NAT/LISM GEOG COERCE NAT/G

B40
WOLFERS A.,BRITAIN AND FRANCE BETWEEN TWO WORLD WARS. FRANCE UK INT/ORG NAT/G PLAN BARGAIN ECO/TAC AGREE ISOLAT ALL/IDEOS...DECISION GEOG 20 TREATY VERSAILLES INTERVENT. PAGE 166 A3380 — DIPLOM WAR POLICY

B43
SULZBACH W.,NATIONAL CONSCIOUSNESS. FUT WOR-45 INT/ORG PEACE MORAL FASCISM MARXISM...MAJORIT TREND WORSHIP 19/20 LEAGUE/NAT INTERVENT WWI. PAGE 140 A2862 — NAT/LISM NAT/G DIPLOM WAR

N47
FOX W.T.R.,UNITED STATES POLICY IN A TWO POWER WORLD. COM USA+45 USSR FORCES DOMIN AGREE NEUTRAL NUC/PWR ORD/FREE SOVEREIGN 20 COLD/WAR TREATY EUROPE/W INTERVENT. PAGE 48 A0972 — DIPLOM FOR/AID POLICY

S48
MORGENTHAU H.J.,"THE TWILIGHT OF INTERNATIONAL MORALITY" (BMR)" WOR+45 WOR-45 BAL/PWR WAR NAT/LISM PEACE...POLICY INT/LAW IDEA/COMP 15/20 TREATY INTERVENT. PAGE 104 A2137 — MORAL DIPLOM NAT/G

B52
LIPPMANN W.,ISOLATION AND ALLIANCES: AN AMERICAN SPEAKS TO THE BRITISH. USA+45 USA-45 INT/ORG AGREE COERCE DETER WAR PEACE MORAL 20 TREATY INTERVENT. PAGE 89 A1829 — DIPLOM SOVEREIGN COLONIAL ATTIT

B53
FEIS H.,THE CHINA TANGLE. ASIA COM USA+45 USA-45 FORCES ECO/TAC REV ATTIT 20 INTERVENT. PAGE 45 A0910 — POLICY DIPLOM WAR FOR/AID

B53
SQUIRES J.D.,BRITISH PROPAGANDA AT HOME AND IN THE UNITED STATES FROM 1914 TO 1917. UK NAT/G PROB/SOLV DOMIN PRESS EFFICIENCY...PSY PREDICT 20 WWI INTERVENT PSY/WAR. PAGE 136 A2794 — EDU/PROP CONTROL WAR DIPLOM

B57
BURNS A.,IN DEFENCE OF COLONIES; BRITISH COLONIAL TERRITORIES IN INTERNATIONAL AFFAIRS. UK ECO/UNDEV PLAN DOMIN SOVEREIGN...MAJORIT 18/20 CMN/WLTH INTERVENT. PAGE 22 A0439 — COLONIAL POLICY ATTIT DIPLOM

B58
APPADORAI A.,THE USE OF FORCE IN INTERNATIONAL RELATIONS. WOR+45 CULTURE ECO/UNDEV CAP/ISM ARMS/CONT REV WAR ATTIT PERSON SOVEREIGN MARXISM ...INT/LAW PACIFIST 20 UN INTERVENT THIRD/WRLD COLD/WAR. PAGE 8 A0169 — PEACE FEDERAL INT/ORG

B60
MORAES F.,THE REVOLT IN TIBET. ASIA CHINA/COM INDIA CULTURE CONTROL COERCE WAR TOTALISM...POLICY SOC WORSHIP 20 TIBET INTERVENT. PAGE 104 A2127 — COLONIAL FORCES DIPLOM ORD/FREE

B60
SOBEL R.,THE ORIGINS OF INTERVENTIONISM: THE UNITED STATES AND THE RUSSO-FINNISH WAR. FINLAND USA-45 USSR LEGIS ATTIT RIGID/FLEX...BIBLIOG 20 INTERVENT. PAGE 135 A2755 — DIPLOM WAR PROB/SOLV NEUTRAL

B61
GOLDWERT M.,CONSTABULARY IN THE DOMINICAN REPUBLIC AND NICARAGUA. DOMIN/REP L/A+17C NICARAGUA USA-45 NAT/G PLAN CONTROL TASK REV...POLICY 20 INTERVENT. PAGE 53 A1093 — DIPLOM PEACE FORCES

B62
APATHEKER H.,AMERICAN FOREIGN POLICY AND THE COLD WAR. USA+45 NAT/G POL/PAR COLONIAL NAT/LISM SOVEREIGN MARXISM SOCISM 20 COLD/WAR MARX/KARL LENIN/VI INTERVENT. PAGE 8 A0167 — DIPLOM WAR PEACE

B62
LESSING P.,AFRICA'S RED HARVEST. AFR CHINA/COM COM USSR ECO/UNDEV BAL/PWR DIPLOM CONTROL PWR 20 COLD/WAR INTERVENT. PAGE 87 A1789 — NAT/LISM MARXISM FOR/AID EDU/PROP

B63
GOLDSCHMIDT W.,THE UNITED STATES AND AFRICA. USA+45 CULTURE ECO/TAC INT/TRADE GOV/REL...SOC ANTHOL 20 INTERVENT. PAGE 53 A1091 — AFR ECO/UNDEV DIPLOM

B64
DUBOIS J.,DANGER OVER PANAMA. FUT PANAMA SCHOOL PROB/SOLV EDU/PROP MARXISM...POLICY 19/20 TREATY INTERVENT CANAL/ZONE. PAGE 39 A0790 — DIPLOM COERCE

B64
IRISH M.D.,WORLD PRESSURES ON AMERICAN FOREIGN POLICY. ASIA COM L/A+17C SOUTH/AFR UK WOR+45 ECO/DEV ECO/UNDEV COLONIAL SANCTION COERCE REV TOTALISM...ANTHOL 20 COLD/WAR EUROPE/W INTERVENT. PAGE 72 A1467 — DIPLOM POLICY

B64
LEGUM C.,SOUTH AFRICA: CRISIS FOR THE WEST. SOUTH/AFR COERCE DISCRIM ATTIT...TREND 20 INTERVENT. PAGE 86 A1767 RACE/REL STRATA DIPLOM PROB/SOLV

B64
STANGER R.J.,ESSAYS ON INTERVENTION. PLAN PROB/SOLV BAL/PWR ADJUD COERCE WAR ROLE PWR...INT/LAW CONCPT 20 UN INTERVENT. PAGE 137 A2803 SOVEREIGN DIPLOM POLICY LEGIT

B64
WRIGHT T.P. JR.,AMERICAN SUPPORT OF FREE ELECTIONS ABROAD. USA+45 USA-45 DOMIN LEAD NEUTRAL MARXISM ...POLICY TIME/SEQ BIBLIOG 19/20 COLD/WAR INTERVENT. PAGE 168 A3420 DIPLOM CHOOSE L/A+17C POPULISM

S64
ARMSTRONG J.A.,"THE SOVIET-AMERICAN CONFRONTATION: A NEW STAGE?" CUBA USA+45 USSR PLAN PROB/SOLV INT/TRADE CONTROL ARMS/CONT NUC/PWR MARXISM 20 COLD/WAR INTERVENT. PAGE 9 A0174 DIPLOM POLICY INSPECT

B65
JOHNSTONE A.,UNITED STATES DIRECT INVESTMENT IN FRANCE: AN INVESTIGATION OF THE FRENCH CHARGES. FRANCE USA+45 ECO/DEV INDUS LG/CO NAT/G ECO/TAC CONTROL WEALTH...BIBLIOG 20 INTERVENT. PAGE 75 A1529 FINAN DIPLOM POLICY SOVEREIGN

B65
MALLIN J.,FORTRESS CUBA; RUSSIA'S AMERICAN BASE. COM CUBA L/A+17C FORCES PLAN DIPLOM LEAD REV WAR ...POLICY 20 CASTRO/F GUEVARA/C INTERVENT. PAGE 93 A1914 MARXISM CHIEF GUERRILLA DOMIN

B65
MOLNAR T.,AFRICA: A POLITICAL TRAVELOGUE. STRUCT ECO/UNDEV DIPLOM EDU/PROP LEAD RACE/REL MARXISM 20 INTERVENT EUROPE. PAGE 102 A2101 COLONIAL AFR ORD/FREE

B65
THOMAS A.V.,NONINTERVENTION: THE LAW AND ITS IMPORT IN THE AMERICAS. L/A+17C USA+45 USA-45 WOR+45 DIPLOM ADJUD...JURID IDEA/COMP 20 UN INTERVENT. PAGE 143 A2920 INT/LAW PWR COERCE

B66
EUDIN X.J.,SOVIET FOREIGN POLICY 1928-34: DOCUMENTS AND MATERIALS (VOL. I). ASIA USSR WOR-45 INT/ORG POL/PAR WORKER WAR PEACE...ANTHOL 20 TREATY LEAGUE/NAT INTERVENT. PAGE 43 A0873 DIPLOM POLICY GOV/REL MARXISM

B66
KANET R.E.,THE SOVIET UNION AND SUB-SAHARAN AFRICA: COMMUNIST POLICY TOWARD AFRICA, 1917-1965. AFR USSR ECO/UNDEV TEC/DEV EDU/PROP TASK DISCRIM PEACE WEALTH ALL/IDEOS...CHARTS BIBLIOG SOC/INTEG 19/20 NEGRO UN INTERVENT. PAGE 76 A1555 DIPLOM ECO/TAC MARXISM

B66
SOBEL L.A.,SOUTH VIETNAM: US-COMMUNIST CONFRONTATION IN SOUTHEAST ASIA 1961-65. VIETNAM FOR/AID CROWD DETER REV PEACE...GEOG 20 INTERVENT DIEM COLD/WAR. PAGE 134 A2754 WAR TIME/SEQ FORCES NAT/G

B66
VIEN N.C.,SEEKING THE TRUTH. FRANCE VIETNAM AGRI ADMIN WAR...BIOG 20 BAO/DAI INTERVENT. PAGE 159 A3231 NAT/G CONSULT CONSTN

INTERVIEWING....SEE INT, REC/INT

INTERVIEWS....SEE INTERVIEWS INDEX, P. XIV

INTGOV/REL....ADVISORY COMMISSION ON INTERGOVERNMENTAL RELATIONS

INTL ATOMIC ENERGY AGENCY A1462

INTL CONF ON WORLD POLITICS-5 A1463

INTL INF CTR LOCAL CREDIT A1464

INTL/DEV....INTERNATIONAL DEVELOPMENT ASSOCIATION

B59
ROBINSON J.A.,THE MONRONEY RESOULUTION: CONGRESSIONAL INITIATIVE IN FOREIGN POLICY MAKING. USA+45 POL/PAR TOP/EX DIPLOM INT/TRADE 20 CONGRESS WORLD/BANK INTL/DEV. PAGE 122 A2504 LEGIS FINAN ECO/UNDEV CHIEF

INTL/ECON....INTERNATIONAL ECONOMIC ASSOCIATION

INTL/FINAN....INTERNATIONAL FINANCE CORPORATION

B57
MATECKI B.,ESTABLISHMENT OF THE INTERNATIONAL FINANCE CORPORATION AND UNITED STATES POLICY. USA+45 WOR+45 CONSTN NAT/G CREATE RIGID/FLEX KNOWL ...METH/CNCPT TIME/SEQ SIMUL TOT/POP 20 INTL/FINAN. PAGE 96 A1964 FINAN INT/ORG DIPLOM

INTRAGROUP RELATIONS....SEE INGP/REL

INTRVN/ECO....INTERVENTION (ECONOMIC) - PHILOSOPHY OF GOVERNMENTAL INTERFERENCE IN DOMESTIC ECONOMIC AFFAIRS

B65
NKRUMAH K.,NEO-COLONIALISM: THE LAST STAGE OF IMPERIALISM. AFR INT/ORG WORKER FOR/AID INT/TRADE EDU/PROP GOV/REL NAT/LISM SOVEREIGN POPULISM SOCISM ...SOCIALIST 20 THIRD/WRLD INTRVN/ECO. PAGE 109 A2243 COLONIAL DIPLOM ECO/UNDEV ECO/TAC

INTST/CRIM....U.S. INTERSTATE COMMISSION ON CRIME

INVENTION....SEE CREATE

INVESTMENT FUND ECO SOC DEV A1465

INVESTMENT....SEE FINAN

IOWA....IOWA

IRAN....SEE ALSO ISLAM

B53
MACK R.T.,RAISING THE WORLDS STANDARD OF LIVING. IRAN INT/ORG VOL/ASSN EX/STRUC ECO/TAC WEALTH...MGT METH/CNCPT STAT CONT/OBS INT TOT/POP VAL/FREE 20 UN. PAGE 92 A1893 WOR+45 FOR/AID INT/TRADE

B61
DALLIN D.J.,SOVIET FOREIGN POLICY AFTER STALIN. ASIA CHINA/COM EUR+WWI GERMANY IRAN UK YUGOSLAVIA INT/ORG NAT/G VOL/ASSN FORCES TOP/EX BAL/PWR DOMIN EDU/PROP COERCE ATTIT PWR 20. PAGE 33 A0679 COM DIPLOM USSR

B61
US GENERAL ACCOUNTING OFFICE,EXAMINATION OF ECONOMIC AND TECHNICAL ASSISTANCE PROGRAM FOR IRAN. IRAN USA+45 AGRI INDUS DIPLOM CONTROL COST 20. PAGE 153 A3115 FOR/AID ADMIN TEC/DEV ECO/UNDEV

B62
DAVAR F.C.,IRAN AND INDIA THROUGH THE AGES. INDIA IRAN ELITES SECT CREATE ORD/FREE...LING BIBLIOG. PAGE 34 A0683 NAT/COMP DIPLOM CULTURE

B66
WESTWOOD A.F.,FOREIGN AID IN A FOREIGN POLICY FRAMEWORK. AFR ASIA INDIA IRAN L/A+17C USA+45 USSR ECO/UNDEV AGRI FORCES LEGIS PLAN PROB/SOLV ...DECISION 20 COLD/WAR. PAGE 163 A3324 FOR/AID DIPLOM POLICY ECO/TAC

IRAQ....SEE ALSO ISLAM

IRELAND....SEE ALSO UK

B43
MC DOWELL R.B.,IRISH PUBLIC OPINION, 1750-1800. IRELAND CONSTN VOL/ASSN WORKER ORD/FREE CATHISM CONSERVE...POLICY IDEA/COMP BIBLIOG 18/ PARLIAMENT. PAGE 97 A1992 ATTIT NAT/G DIPLOM REV

B46
GRIFFIN G.G.,A GUIDE TO MANUSCRIPTS RELATING TO AMERICAN HISTORY IN BRITISH DEPOSITORIES. CANADA IRELAND MOD/EUR UK USA-45 LAW DIPLOM ADMIN COLONIAL WAR NAT/LISM SOVEREIGN...GEOG INT/LAW 15/19 CMN/WLTH. PAGE 56 A1159 BIBLIOG/A ALL/VALS NAT/G

B53
MANSERGH N.,DOCUMENTS AND SPEECHES ON BRITISH COMMONWEALTH AFFAIRS 1931-1952. INDIA IRELAND PAKISTAN UK CONSTN POL/PAR CHIEF FORCES COLONIAL ORD/FREE SOVEREIGN...JURID 20 COMMONWLTH. PAGE 94 A1929 BIBLIOG/A DIPLOM ECO/TAC

B58
MANSERGH N.,SURVEY OF BRITISH COMMONWEALTH AFFAIRS: PROBLEMS OF WARTIME CO-OPERATION AND POST-WAR CHANGE 1939-1952. INDIA IRELAND S/ASIA CONSTN INT/ORG BAL/PWR COLONIAL NEUTRAL WAR ADJUST PEACE ROLE ORD/FREE...CHARTS 20 CMN/WLTH NATO UN. PAGE 94 A1931 VOL/ASSN CONSEN PROB/SOLV INGP/REL

B62
ALIX C.,LE SAINT-SIEGE ET LES NATIONALISMES EN EUROPE 1870-1960. COM GERMANY IRELAND ITALY SOCIETY SECT TOTALISM RIGID/FLEX MORAL 19/20. PAGE 6 A0122 CATH NAT/LISM ATTIT DIPLOM

B63
FRANZ G.,TEILUNG UND WIEDERVEREINIGUNG. GERMANY IRELAND ITALY NETHERLAND POLAND CULTURE BAL/PWR CHOOSE NAT/LISM ORD/FREE SOVEREIGN 19/20. PAGE 48 A0987 DIPLOM WAR NAT/COMP ATTIT

B65
O'CONNELL M.R.,IRISH POLITICS AND SOCIAL CONFLICT IN THE AGE OF THE AMERICAN REVOLUTION. FRANCE IRELAND MOD/EUR STRATA SECT LEGIS DIPLOM INT/TRADE DOMIN REV WAR...BIBLIOG 18 PARLIAMENT. PAGE 111 A2268 CATHISM ATTIT NAT/G DELIB/GP

B65
SOPER T.,EVOLVING COMMONWEALTH. AFR CANADA INDIA IRELAND UK LAW CONSTN POL/PAR DOMIN CONTROL WAR PWR ...AUD/VIS 18/20 COMMONWLTH OEEC. PAGE 135 A2769 INT/ORG COLONIAL VOL/ASSN

B66
EDWARDS C.D.,TRADE REGULATIONS OVERSEAS. IRELAND INT/TRADE

NEW/ZEALND SOUTH/AFR NAT/G CAP/ISM TARIFFS CONTROL ...POLICY JURID 20 EEC CHINJAP. PAGE 40 A0823 — DIPLOM INT/LAW ECO/TAC

IRGUN....IRGUN - PALESTINE REVOLUTIONARY ORGANIZATION

IRIKURA J.K. A1466

IRISH M.D. A1467

IRISH/AMER....IRISH AMERICANS

IRIYE A. A1468

IRS....U.S. INTERNAL REVENUE SERVICE

ISENBERG I. A1469

ISLAM R. A1470

ISLAM....ISLAMIC WORLD; SEE ALSO APPROPRIATE NATIONS

N
MIDDLE EAST JOURNAL. CULTURE SECT DIPLOM LEAD GOV/REL ATTIT...POLICY PHIL/SCI SOC LING BIOG 20. PAGE 1 A0019 — BIBLIOG ISLAM NAT/G ECO/UNDEV

N
THE MIDDLE EAST AND NORTH AFRICA. AFR ISLAM CULTURE ECO/UNDEV AGRI NAT/G TEC/DEV FOR/AID INT/TRADE EDU/PROP...CHARTS 20. PAGE 2 A0043 — INDEX INDUS FINAN STAT

N
US LIBRARY OF CONGRESS,ACCESSIONS LIST -- ISRAEL. ISRAEL CULTURE ECO/UNDEV POL/PAR PLAN PROB/SOLV TEC/DEV DIPLOM EDU/PROP LEAD WAR ATTIT 20 JEWS. PAGE 154 A3143 — BIBLIOG ISLAM NAT/G GP/REL

N19
KUWAIT ARABIA,KUWAIT FUND FOR ARAB ECONOMIC DEVELOPMENT (PAMPHLET). ISLAM KUWAIT UAR ECO/UNDEV LEGIS ECO/TAC WEALTH 20. PAGE 83 A1697 — FOR/AID DIPLOM FINAN ADMIN

N19
LISKA G.,THE GREATER MAGHREB: FROM INDEPENDENCE TO UNITY? (PAMPHLET). ALGERIA ISLAM MOROCCO PROB/SOLV BAL/PWR CONFER COLONIAL REPRESENT NAT/LISM 20 TUNIS. PAGE 90 A1835 — ECO/UNDEV REGION DIPLOM DOMIN

B29
PRATT I.A.,MODERN EGYPT: A LIST OF REFERENCES TO MATERIAL IN THE NEW YORK PUBLIC LIBRARY. UAR ECO/UNDEV...GEOG JURID SOC LING 20. PAGE 117 A2407 — BIBLIOG ISLAM DIPLOM NAT/G

B39
KOHN H.,REVOLUTIONS AND DICTATORSHIPS. COM EUR+WWI ISLAM MOD/EUR NAT/G CHIEF FORCES WAR CIVMIL/REL PWR MARXISM 18/20. PAGE 81 A1661 — NAT/LISM TOTALISM REV FASCISM

B44
FULLER G.H.,TURKEY: A SELECTED LIST OF REFERENCES. ISLAM TURKEY CULTURE ECO/UNDEV AGRI DIPLOM NAT/LISM CONSERVE...GEOG HUM INT/LAW SOC 7/20 MAPS. PAGE 50 A1024 — BIBLIOG/A ALL/VALS

B45
US DEPARTMENT OF STATE,PUBLICATIONS OF THE DEPARTMENT OF STATE: A LIST CUMULATIVE FROM OCTOBER 1, 1929 (PAMPHLET). ASIA EUR+WWI ISLAM L/A+17C USA-45 ADJUD...INT/LAW 20. PAGE 151 A3082 — BIBLIOG DIPLOM INT/TRADE

B48
LOGAN R.W.,THE AFRICAN MANDATES IN WORLD POLITICS. EUR+WWI GERMANY ISLAM INT/ORG BARGAIN...POLICY INT/LAW 20. PAGE 90 A1853 — WAR COLONIAL AFR DIPLOM

B51
US DEPARTMENT OF STATE,POINT FOUR, NEAR EAST AND AFRICA, A SELECTED BIBLIOGRAPHY OF STUDIES ON ECONOMICALLY UNDERDEVELOPED COUNTRIES. AGRI COM/IND FINAN INDUS PLAN INT/TRADE...SOC TREND 20. PAGE 151 A3087 — BIBLIOG/A AFR S/ASIA ISLAM

B51
YOUNG T.C.,NEAR EASTERN CULTURE AND SOCIETY. ISLAM ECO/UNDEV SECT WRITING ATTIT HABITAT ORD/FREE 20. PAGE 169 A3438 — CULTURE STRUCT REGION DIPLOM

S51
GYR J.,"ANALYSIS OF COMMITTEE MEMBER BEHAVIOUR IN FOUR CULTURES." ASIA ISLAM L/A+17C USA+45 INT/ORG VOL/ASSN LEGIT ATTIT...INT DEEP/QU SAMP CHARTS 20. PAGE 58 A1200 — DELIB/GP CULTURE

B52
UN DEPT. SOC. AFF.,PRELIMINARY REPORT ON THE WORLD SOCIAL SITUATION. ISLAM L/A+17C WOR+45 STRATA AGRI EXTR/IND INDUS INT/ORG SCHOOL ADMIN...GEOG SOC TREND UNESCO WORK FAO 20. PAGE 147 A2998 — R+D HEALTH FOR/AID

B52
US LIBRARY OF CONGRESS,EGYPT AND THE ANGLO-EGYPTIAN SUDAN: A SELECTIVE GUIDE TO BACKGROUND READING (PAMPHLET). SUDAN UAR UK DIPLOM...POLICY 20. PAGE 155 A3153 — BIBLIOG/A COLONIAL ISLAM NAT/G

B54
NUSSBAUM D.,A CONCISE HISTORY OF THE LAW OF NATIONS. ASIA CHRIST-17C EUR+WWI ISLAM MEDIT-7 MOD/EUR S/ASIA UNIV WOR+45 WOR-45 SOCIETY STRUCT EXEC ATTIT ALL/VALS...CONCPT HIST/WRIT TIME/SEQ. PAGE 110 A2263 — INT/ORG LAW PEACE INT/LAW

L54
CHARLESWORTH J.C.,"AMERICA AND A NEW ASIA." ASIA INDIA ISLAM S/ASIA USA+45 USA-45 ECO/UNDEV NAT/G POL/PAR FORCES FOR/AID DOMIN EDU/PROP COERCE DRIVE ALL/VALS MARXISM SOCISM TOT/POP 20. PAGE 26 A0522 — ECO/TAC DIPLOM NAT/LISM

B56
US DEPARTMENT OF STATE,ECONOMIC PROBLEMS OF UNDERDEVELOPED AREAS (PAMPHLET). AFR ASIA ISLAM L/A+17C AGRI FINAN INDUS INT/ORG LABOR INT/TRADE ...PSY SOC 20. PAGE 151 A3090 — BIBLIOG ECO/UNDEV TEC/DEV R+D

B57
BLOOMFIELD L.M.,EGYPT, ISRAEL AND THE GULF OF AQABA: IN INTERNATIONAL LAW. LAW NAT/G CONSULT FORCES PLAN ECO/TAC ROUTINE COERCE ATTIT DRIVE PERCEPT PERSON RIGID/FLEX LOVE PWR WEALTH...GEOG CONCPT MYTH TREND. PAGE 15 A0314 — ISLAM INT/LAW UAR

B57
BROMBERGER M.,LES SECRETS DE L'EXPEDITION D'EGYPTE. FRANCE ISLAM UAR UK USA+45 USSR WOR+45 INT/ORG NAT/G FORCES BAL/PWR ECO/TAC DOMIN WAR NAT/LISM ATTIT PWR SOVEREIGN...MAJORIT TIME/SEQ CHARTS SUEZ COLD/WAR 20. PAGE 19 A0387 — COERCE DIPLOM

B57
CRABB C.,BIPARTISAN FOREIGN POLICY: MYTH OR REALITY. ASIA COM EUR+WWI ISLAM USA+45 USA-45 INT/ORG NAT/G LEGIS TOP/EX PWR CONGRESS 20. PAGE 32 A0649 — POL/PAR ATTIT DIPLOM

B57
FURNISS E.S.,AMERICAN MILITARY POLICY: STRATEGIC ASPECTS OF WORLD POLITICAL GEOGRAPHY. COM EUR+WWI ISLAM L/A+17C USA+45 WOR+45 INT/ORG ACT/RES ARMS/CONT COERCE NUC/PWR ATTIT PWR...GEOG NEW/IDEA VAL/FREE COLD/WAR 20. PAGE 50 A1027 — FORCES DIPLOM

B57
MOYER K.E.,FROM IRAN TO MORROCCO; FROM TURKEY TO THE SUDAN: A SELECTED AND ANNOTATED BIBLIOGRAPHY OF NORTH AFRICA AND NEAR EAST... ISLAM DIPLOM EDU/PROP 20. PAGE 105 A2162 — BIBLIOG/A ECO/UNDEV SECT NAT/G

B57
WARBURG J.P.,AGENDA FOR ACTION. ISLAM ISRAEL USA+45 FOR/AID INT/TRADE WAR NAT/LISM 20 MID/EAST EUROPE ARABS. PAGE 161 A3275 — DIPLOM POLICY INT/ORG BAL/PWR

B58
BERLINER J.S.,SOVIET ECONOMIC AID: THE AID AND TRADE POLICY IN UNDERDEVELOPED COUNTRIES. AFR COM ISLAM L/A+17C S/ASIA USSR ECO/DEV DIST/IND FINAN MARKET INT/ORG ACT/RES PLAN BAL/PWR WEAPON PWR WEALTH...CHARTS 20. PAGE 14 A0277 — ECO/UNDEV ECO/TAC FOR/AID

B58
CAMPBELL J.C.,DEFENSE OF THE MIDDLE EAST: PROBLEMS OF AMERICAN POLICY. ISLAM USA+45 INT/ORG NAT/G EX/STRUC FORCES ECO/TAC DOMIN EDU/PROP LEGIT REGION COERCE...METH/CNCPT COLD/WAR TOT/POP 20. PAGE 23 A0474 — TOP/EX ORD/FREE DIPLOM

B58
TILLION G.,ALGERIA: THE REALITIES. ALGERIA FRANCE ISLAM CULTURE STRATA PROB/SOLV DOMIN REV NAT/LISM WEALTH MARXISM...GEOG 20. PAGE 144 A2940 — ECO/UNDEV SOC COLONIAL DIPLOM

B59
ALWAN M.,ALGERIA BEFORE THE UNITED NATIONS. AFR ASIA FRANCE ISLAM S/ASIA CONSTN SOCIETY STRUCT INT/ORG NAT/G ECO/TAC ADMIN COLONIAL NAT/LISM ATTIT PWR...DECISION TREND 420 UN. PAGE 7 A0133 — PLAN RIGID/FLEX DIPLOM ALGERIA

B59
JOSEPH F.M.,AS OTHERS SEE US: THE UNITED STATES THROUGH FOREIGN EYES. AFR EUR+WWI ISLAM L/A+17C S/ASIA USA+45 CULTURE SOCIETY ECO/DEV ECO/UNDEV INT/ORG NAT/G DIPLOM ECO/TAC REV ATTIT RIGID/FLEX HEALTH ORD/FREE WEALTH 20. PAGE 75 A1537 — RESPECT DOMIN NAT/LISM SOVEREIGN

B59
LAQUER W.Z.,THE SOVIET UNION AND THE MIDDLE EAST. COM UAR USSR ECO/UNDEV NAT/G VOL/ASSN ECO/TAC EDU/PROP COLONIAL EXEC PWR...TIME/SEQ TREND COLD/WAR 20. PAGE 85 A1730 — ISLAM DRIVE FOR/AID NAT/LISM

B59
TARDIFF G.,LA LIBERTAD; LA LIBERTAD DE EXPRESION, IDEALES Y REALIDADES AMERICANAS. ISLAM INT/ORG PROB/SOLV PRESS CONFER PARTIC CATHISM...INT/LAW SOC/INTEG UN MID/EAST. PAGE 141 A2889 — ORD/FREE ATTIT DIPLOM CONCPT

B59
THOMAS N.,THE PREREQUISITES FOR PEACE. ASIA EUR+WWI FUT ISLAM S/ASIA WOR+45 FORCES PLAN BAL/PWR EDU/PROP LEGIT ATTIT PWR...SOCIALIST CONCPT COLD/WAR 20 UN. PAGE 143 A2924 — INT/ORG ORD/FREE ARMS/CONT PEACE

S59
HARVEY M.F.,"THE PALESTINE REFUGEE PROBLEM: — ACT/RES

ELEMENTS OF A SOLUTION." ISLAM LAW INT/ORG DELIB/GP TOP/EX ECO/TAC ROUTINE DRIVE HEALTH LOVE ORD/FREE PWR WEALTH...MAJORIT FAO 20. PAGE 62 A1283
LEGIT PEACE ISRAEL

S59
SAYEGH F.,"ARAB NATIONALISM AND SOVIET-AMERICAN RELATIONS." ISLAM USA+45 ECO/UNDEV PLAN ECO/TAC LEGIT NAT/LISM DRIVE PERCEPT KNOWL PWR...DECISION CONCPT STAT RECORD TREND CON/ANAL VAL/FREE 20 COLD/WAR. PAGE 127 A2610
DIPLOM USSR

B60
HAMADY S.,TEMPERAMENT AND CHARACTER OF THE ARABS. FAM NAT/G SECT DIPLOM NAT/LISM...POLICY 20 ARABS. PAGE 61 A1244
NAT/COMP PERSON CULTURE ISLAM

B60
PHILLIPS J.F.V.,KWAME NKRUMAH AND THE FUTURE OF AFRICA. FUT GHANA ISLAM ECO/UNDEV CHIEF DIPLOM COLONIAL RACE/REL NAT/LISM...TREND IDEA/COMP BIBLIOG 20 NKRUMAH/K. PAGE 116 A2376
BIOG LEAD SOVEREIGN AFR

B60
QUBAIN F.I.,INSIDE THE ARAB MIND: A BIBLIOGRAPHIC SURVEY OF LITERATURE IN ARABIC ON ARAB NATIONALISM AND UNITY. ISLAM POL/PAR SECT LEAD SOVEREIGN MARXISM SOCISM. PAGE 118 A2425
BIBLIOG/A FEDERAL DIPLOM NAT/LISM

L60
LAUTERPACHT E.,"THE SUEZ CANAL SETTLEMENT." FRANCE ISLAM ISRAEL UAR UK BAL/PWR DIPLOM LEGIT...JURID GEN/LAWS ANTHOL SUEZ VAL/FREE 20. PAGE 85 A1747
INT/ORG LAW

S60
GARNICK D.H.,"ON THE ECONOMIC FEASIBILITY OF A MIDDLE EASTERN COMMON MARKET." AFR ISLAM CULTURE INDUS NAT/G PLAN TEC/DEV ECO/TAC ADMIN ATTIT DRIVE RIGID/FLEX...PLURIST STAT TREND GEN/LAWS 20. PAGE 51 A1051
MARKET INT/TRADE

B61
DIA M.,THE AFRICAN NATIONS AND WORLD SOLIDARITY. ISLAM CULTURE ELITES ECO/DEV ECO/UNDEV INT/ORG NAT/G PLAN ECO/TAC INT/TRADE EDU/PROP NAT/LISM ATTIT DRIVE ORD/FREE WEALTH...SOCIALIST CONCPT CON/ANAL GEN/LAWS TOT/POP 20. PAGE 37 A0753
AFR REGION SOCISM

B61
FRIEDMANN W.G.,JOINT INTERNATIONAL BUSINESS VENTURES. ASIA ISLAM L/A+17C ECO/DEV DIST/IND FINAN PROC/MFG FACE/GP LG/CO NAT/G VOL/ASSN CONSULT EX/STRUC PLAN ADMIN ROUTINE WEALTH...OLD/LIB WORK 20. PAGE 49 A1004
ECO/UNDEV INT/TRADE

B61
HASAN H.S.,PAKISTAN AND THE UN. ISLAM WOR+45 ECO/DEV ECO/UNDEV NAT/G TOP/EX ECO/TAC FOR/AID EDU/PROP ADMIN DRIVE PERCEPT...OBS TIME/SEQ UN 20. PAGE 62 A1284
INT/ORG ATTIT PAKISTAN

B61
PATAI R.,CULTURES IN CONFLICT; AN INQUIRY INTO THE SOCIO-CULTURAL PROBLEMS OF ISRAEL AND HER NEIGHBORS (2ND REV. ED.). ISLAM ISRAEL SOCIETY STRUCT DIPLOM GP/REL ALL/VALS...SOC 20 JEWS ARABS. PAGE 114 A2339
NAT/COMP CULTURE GP/COMP ATTIT

B61
ROBINS D.B.,EVOLVING UNITED STATES POLICIES TOWARD THE EMERGING NATIONS OF ASIA AND AFRICA (PAMPHLET). ISLAM ECO/UNDEV INT/ORG CONSULT CREATE PLAN TEC/DEV FOR/AID CONFER ALL/VALS 20 KENNEDY/JF EISNHWR/DD UN AID. PAGE 122 A2501
AFR S/ASIA DIPLOM BIBLIOG

B61
UAR MINISTRY OF CULTURE,A BIBLIOGRAPHICAL LIST OF AL MAGHRIB. ALGERIA ISLAM MOROCCO UAR SECT INT/TRADE COLONIAL 19/20 TUNIS. PAGE 146 A2987
BIBLIOG DIPLOM GEOG

B61
UAR MINISTRY OF CULTURE,A BIBLIOGRAPHICAL LIST OF LIBYA. ISLAM LIBYA DIPLOM COLONIAL REV WAR 19/20. PAGE 146 A2988
BIBLIOG GEOG SECT NAT/LISM

B61
UAR MINISTRY OF CULTURE,A BIBLIOGRAPHICAL LIST OF TUNISIA. ISLAM CULTURE NAT/G EDU/PROP COLONIAL ...GEOG 19/20 TUNIS. PAGE 146 A2989
BIBLIOG DIPLOM SECT

S61
RALEIGH J.S.,"THE MIDDLE EAST IN 1960: A POLITICAL SURVEY." FUT ISLAM INTELL KIN BAL/PWR EDU/PROP NAT/LISM...TREND VAL/FREE 20. PAGE 119 A2435
INT/ORG EX/STRUC

B62
BAULIN J.,THE ARAB ROLE IN AFRICA. AFR ALGERIA FUT ISLAM MOROCCO UAR COLONIAL NEUTRAL REV...SOC 20 TUNIS BOURGUIBA. PAGE 12 A0235
NAT/LISM DIPLOM NAT/G SECT

B62
HARARI M.,GOVERNMENT AND POLITICS OF THE MIDDLE EAST. ISLAM USA+45 NAT/G SECT CHIEF ADMIN ORD/FREE 20. PAGE 61 A1257
DIPLOM ECO/UNDEV TEC/DEV POLICY

B62
HATCH J.,AFRICA TODAY-AND TOMORROW: AN OUTLINE OF BASIC FACTS AND MAJOR PROBLEMS. AFR FUT ISLAM STRATA ECO/UNDEV INT/ORG NAT/G POL/PAR DELIB/GP TOP/EX EDU/PROP LEGIT CHOOSE ATTIT...TIME/SEQ TOT/POP COLD/WAR 20. PAGE 63 A1287
PLAN CONSTN NAT/LISM

B62
RIVKIN A.,AFRICA AND THE WEST. AFR EUR+WWI FUT ISLAM ISRAEL USA+45 SOCIETY INT/ORG FORCES CREATE PLAN FOR/AID EDU/PROP ATTIT...CONCPT TREND EEC 20 CONGRESS UN. PAGE 121 A2488
ECO/UNDEV ECO/TAC

L62
MURACCIOLE L.,"LA BANQUE CENTRALE DES ETATS DE L'AFRIQUE DE L'OUEST." AFR LAW ECO/UNDEV INT/ORG NAT/G CONSULT ECO/TAC ROUTINE...CHARTS 20. PAGE 106 A2175
ISLAM FINAN INT/TRADE

S62
CORET A.,"LA DECLARATION DE L'ASSEMBLEE GENERAL DE L'ONU SUR L'OCTROI DE L'INDEPENDENCE AUX PAYS ET AUX PEUPLES." AFR ASIA ISLAM NIGERIA S/ASIA USSR WOR+45 ECO/UNDEV NAT/G DELIB/GP COLONIAL ALL/VALS ...CONCPT TIME/SEQ TREND UN TOT/POP 20 MEXIC/AMER. PAGE 31 A0621
INT/ORG STRUCT SOVEREIGN

S62
MANGIN G.,"LES ACCORDS DE COOPERATION EN MATIERE DE JUSTICE ENTRE LA FRANCE ET LES ETATS AFRICAINS ET MALGACHE." AFR ISLAM WOR+45 STRUCT ECO/UNDEV NAT/G DELIB/GP PERCEPT ALL/VALS...JURID MGT TIME/SEQ 20. PAGE 94 A1919
INT/ORG LAW FRANCE

S62
PIQUEMAL M.,"LA COOPERATION FINANCIERE ENTRE LA FRANCE ET LES ETATS AFRICAINS ET MALGACHE." ISLAM INT/ORG TOP/EX ECO/TAC...JURID CHARTS 20. PAGE 116 A2383
AFR FINAN FRANCE MADAGASCAR

S62
RAZAFIMBAHINY J.,"L'ORGANISATION AFRICAINE ET MALGACHE DE COOPERATION ECONOMIQUE." AFR ISLAM MADAGASCAR NAT/G ACT/RES ECO/TAC ALL/VALS ...TIME/SEQ 20. PAGE 120 A2454
INT/ORG ECO/UNDEV

S62
RUBINSTEIN A.Z.,"RUSSIA AND THE UNCOMMITTED NATIONS." AFR INDIA ISLAM L/A+17C LAOS S/ASIA ELITES ECO/UNDEV INT/ORG KIN CREATE PLAN TEC/DEV NAT/LISM RIGID/FLEX PWR WEALTH...METH/CNCPT TIME/SEQ GEN/LAWS WORK. PAGE 125 A2562
ECO/TAC TREND COLONIAL USSR

S62
VASAK K.,"DE LA CONVENTION EUROPEENNE A LA CONVENTION AFRICAINE DES DROITS DE L'HOMME." AFR ISLAM WOR+45 LAW CONSTN ECO/UNDEV INT/ORG PERCEPT ALL/VALS 20. PAGE 158 A3223
DELIB/GP CONCPT COLONIAL

B63
BURNS A.L.,PEACE-KEEPING BY U.N.FORCES - FROM SUEZ TO THE CONGO. AFR FUT ISLAM ISRAEL USSR WOR+45 NAT/G DELIB/GP BAL/PWR DOMIN LEGIT EXEC COERCE PEACE ATTIT PWR RESPECT SOVEREIGN...CONCPT UN 20. PAGE 22 A0441
INT/ORG FORCES ORD/FREE

B63
CREMEANS C.,THE ARABS AND THE WORLD: NASSER'S ARAB NATIONALIST POLICY. FUT ISLAM UAR USA+45 SOCIETY STRATA NAT/G POL/PAR PLAN DIPLOM EDU/PROP LEGIT DRIVE ALL/VALS...INT TIME/SEQ CHARTS 20 NASSER/G. PAGE 33 A0662
TOP/EX ATTIT REGION NAT/LISM

B63
KHADDURI M.,MODERN LIBYA: A STUDY IN POLITICAL DEVELOPMENT. EUR+WWI ISLAM LIBYA ELITES INT/ORG POL/PAR FORCES DIPLOM FOR/AID DOMIN EDU/PROP LEGIT NAT/LISM DRIVE RIGID/FLEX SKILL...CONCPT TIME/SEQ TREND 20. PAGE 78 A1606
NAT/G STRUCT

B63
QUAISON-SACKEY A.,AFRICA UNBOUND: REFLECTIONS OF AN AFRICAN STATESMAN. ISLAM CULTURE INTELL INT/ORG POL/PAR TOP/EX DOMIN EDU/PROP LEGIT ATTIT PERSON ...CONCPT OBS TIME/SEQ CHARTS STERTYP 20 UN. PAGE 118 A2423
AFR BIOG

B63
UAR MINISTRY OF CULTURE,A BIBLIOGRAPHICAL LIST OF ARABIAN PENINSULA. ISLAM SAUDI/ARAB YEMEN FINAN NAT/G DIPLOM 19/20. PAGE 146 A2990
BIBLIOG GEOG INDUS SECT

B63
US SENATE COMM GOVT OPERATIONS,REPORT OF A STUDY OF US FOREIGN AID IN TEN MIDDLE EASTERN AND AFRICAN COUNTRIES. AFR ISLAM USA+45 FORCES PLAN BUDGET DIPLOM TAX DETER WEALTH...STAT CHARTS 20 CONGRESS AID MID/EAST. PAGE 156 A3174
FOR/AID EFFICIENCY ECO/TAC FINAN

L63
PRINCETON UNIV. CONFERENCE,"ARAB DEVELOPMENT IN THE EMERGING INTERNATIONAL ECONOMY." FUT USA+45 DIST/IND FINAN DELIB/GP PLAN ECO/TAC WEALTH VAL/FREE 20. PAGE 118 A2413
ISLAM ECO/UNDEV FOR/AID INT/TRADE

L63
ZARTMAN I.W.,"THE SAHARA--BRIDGE OR BARRIER." ISLAM CULTURE SOCIETY NAT/G DELIB/GP DOMIN EDU/PROP LEGIT ATTIT...HIST/WRIT TIME/SEQ CHARTS TOT/POP VAL/FREE 20. PAGE 169 A3445
INT/ORG PWR NAT/LISM

S63
GANDOLFI A.,"LES ACCORDS DE COOPERATION EN MATIERE DE POLITIQUE ETRANGERE ENTRE LA FRANCE ET LES NOUVEAUX ETATS AFRICAINS ET." AFR ISLAM MADAGASCAR WOR+45 ECO/DEV INT/ORG NAT/G DELIB/GP ECO/TAC ALL/VALS...CON/ANAL 20. PAGE 51 A1038
VOL/ASSN ECO/UNDEV DIPLOM FRANCE

S63
SHWADRAN B.,"MIDDLE EAST OIL, 1962." ISLAM USSR ECO/DEV DIST/IND INDUS PLAN BAL/PWR DISPL DRIVE ...POLICY STAT TREND GEN/LAWS EEC OEEC 20 OIL. PAGE 132 A2712
MARKET ECO/TAC INT/TRADE

B64
AFRO ASIAN SOLIDARITY AGAINST IMPERIALISM. AFR ISLAM S/ASIA ECO/UNDEV NAT/G POL/PAR TOP/EX PRESS ...INT ANTHOL 20 CHOU/ENLAI. PAGE 3 A0066
MARXISM DIPLOM EDU/PROP CHIEF

B64
AMERICAN ASSEMBLY,THE UNITED STATES AND THE MIDDLE EAST. ISRAEL USA+45 STRUCT ECO/DEV ECO/UNDEV INT/ORG NAT/G SCHOOL SECT VOL/ASSN EX/STRUC TEC/DEV NAT/LISM...SOC 20. PAGE 7 A0135
ISLAM DRIVE REGION

B64
BARKER A.J.,SUEZ: THE SEVEN DAY WAR. EUR+WWI ISLAM UAR INT/ORG NAT/G PLAN DIPLOM ECO/TAC DOMIN NAT/LISM DRIVE RIGID/FLEX PWR SOVEREIGN...POLICY JURID TREND CHARTS SUEZ UN 20. PAGE 11 A0221
FORCES COERCE UK

B64
BINDER L.,THE IDEOLOGICAL REVOLUTION IN THE MIDDLE EAST. ISLAM STRUCT INT/ORG KIN SECT EX/STRUC TOP/EX PLAN ATTIT DRIVE RIGID/FLEX PWR...MYTH TOT/POP 20. PAGE 14 A0289
POL/PAR NAT/G NAT/LISM

B64
CALVO SERER R.,LAS NUEVAS DEMOCRACIAS. AFR ASIA ISLAM USA+45 WOR+45 BAL/PWR DOMIN PARTIC INGP/REL AUTHORIT POPULISM...CONCPT 20 COM/PARTY. PAGE 23 A0469
ORD/FREE MARXISM DIPLOM POLICY

B64
EAYRS J.,THE COMMONWEALTH AND SUEZ: A DOCUMENTARY SURVEY. FRANCE ISLAM VOL/ASSN FORCES CONFER COLONIAL WAR INGP/REL 20 CMN/WLTH SUEZ UN. PAGE 40 A0818
DIPLOM NAT/LISM DIST/IND SOVEREIGN

B64
JANOWITZ M.,THE MILITARY IN THE POLITICAL DEVELOPMENT OF NEW NATIONS: AN ESSAY IN COMPARATIVE ANALYSIS. AFR ASIA ISLAM L/A+17C S/ASIA USA+45 ECO/UNDEV INT/ORG NAT/G POL/PAR DELIB/GP PLAN ECO/TAC DOMIN LEGIT COERCE ATTIT DRIVE RESPECT ...SOC CONCPT CENSUS VAL/FREE. PAGE 73 A1495
FORCES PWR

B64
RAMAZANI R.K.,THE MIDDLE EAST AND THE EUROPEAN COMMON MARKET. EUR+WWI ISLAM ECO/DEV EXTR/IND MARKET PROC/MFG INT/ORG NAT/G TEC/DEV ECO/TAC REGION DRIVE WEALTH...STAT CHARTS EEC TOT/POP 20. PAGE 119 A2437
ECO/UNDEV ATTIT INT/TRADE

B64
UAR NATIONAL LIBRARY,A BIBLIOGRAPHICAL LIST OF WORKS ABOUT PALESTINE AND JORDAN (2ND ED.). ISRAEL JORDAN SECT DIPLOM...SOC 20 JEWS. PAGE 146 A2991
BIBLIOG ISLAM

L64
CAMPBELL J.C.,"THE MIDDLE EAST IN THE MUTED COLD WAR." COM EUR+WWI UAR USA+45 USSR STRUCT ECO/UNDEV NAT/G VOL/ASSN EX/STRUC TOP/EX DIPLOM ECO/TAC EDU/PROP...TIME/SEQ COLD/WAR 20. PAGE 23 A0475
ISLAM FOR/AID NAT/LISM

L64
CURTIS G.L.,"THE UNITED NATIONS OBSERVER GROUP IN LEBANON." ISLAM USA+45 NAT/G CONSULT ACT/RES PLAN BAL/PWR LEGIT ATTIT KNOWL...HIST/WRIT UN 20 UN. PAGE 33 A0669
INT/ORG FORCES DIPLOM LEBANON

L64
POUNDS N.J.G.,"THE POLITICS OF PARTITION." AFR ASIA COM EUR+WWI FUT ISLAM S/ASIA USA-45 LAW ECO/DEV ECO/UNDEV AGRI INDUS INT/ORG POL/PAR PROVS SECT FORCES TOP/EX EDU/PROP LEGIT ATTIT MORAL ORD/FREE PWR RESPECT WEALTH. PAGE 117 A2402
NAT/G NAT/LISM

S64
CARNEGIE ENDOWMENT INT. PEACE,"COLONIAL COUNTRIES AND PEOPLES (ISSUES BEFORE THE NINETEENTH GENERAL ASSEMBLY)." AFR ISLAM L/A+17C WOR+45 DELIB/GP LEGIS ECO/TAC EDU/PROP NAT/LISM PEACE ALL/VALS...RECORD UN CMN/WLTH 20. PAGE 24 A0491
INT/ORG ECO/UNDEV COLONIAL

S64
DE GAULLE C.,"FRENCH WORLD VIEW." AFR ASIA CHINA/COM EUR+WWI ISLAM ECO/UNDEV INT/ORG NAT/G VOL/ASSN ACT/RES DIPLOM ECO/TAC EDU/PROP ATTIT DRIVE WEALTH 20. PAGE 35 A0702
TOP/EX PWR FOR/AID FRANCE

S64
KHAN M.Z.,"ISLAM AND INTERNATIONAL RELATIONS." FUT WOR+45 LAW CULTURE SOCIETY NAT/G SECT DELIB/GP FORCES EDU/PROP ATTIT PERSON SUPEGO ALL/VALS ...POLICY PSY CONCPT MYTH HIST/WRIT GEN/LAWS. PAGE 78 A1608
ISLAM INT/ORG DIPLOM

S64
SAAB H.,"THE ARAB SEARCH FOR A FEDERAL UNION." SOCIETY INT/ORG NAT/G DELIB/GP FORCES ACT/RES TEC/DEV ECO/TAC DOMIN LEGIT REGION ROUTINE ATTIT DRIVE RIGID/FLEX ALL/VALS...SOC CONCPT NEW/IDEA TIME/SEQ TREND. PAGE 126 A2580
ISLAM PLAN

S64
TOUVAL S.,"THE SOMALI REPUBLIC." AFR ISLAM SOMALIA FAM KIN NAT/G CREATE FOR/AID LEGIT ATTIT ALL/VALS ...RECORD TREND 20. PAGE 144 A2954
ECO/UNDEV RIGID/FLEX

S64
ZARTMAN I.W.,"LES RELATIONS ENTRE LA FRANCE ET L'ALGERIA DEPUIS LES ACCORDS D'EVIAN." EUR+WWI FUT ISLAM CULTURE AGRI EXTR/IND FINAN INDUS POL/PAR DIPLOM ECO/TAC FOR/AID PEACE ATTIT DRIVE ALL/VALS ...TIME/SEQ VAL/FREE 20. PAGE 169 A3446
ECO/UNDEV ALGERIA FRANCE

C64
EASTON S.C.,"THE RISE AND FALL OF WESTERN COLONIALISM." AFR ISLAM L/A+17C ECO/UNDEV REV NAT/LISM...CHARTS BIBLIOG 15/20. PAGE 40 A0817
COLONIAL DIPLOM ORD/FREE WAR

B65
MACDONALD R.W.,THE LEAGUE OF ARAB STATES: A STUDY IN THE DYNAMICS OF REGIONAL ORGANIZATION. ISRAEL UAR USSR FINAN INT/ORG DELIB/GP ECO/TAC AGREE NEUTRAL ORD/FREE PWR...DECISION BIBLIOG 20 TREATY UN. PAGE 92 A1888
ISLAM REGION DIPLOM ADMIN

B65
MANSFIELD P.,NASSER'S EGYPT. AFR ISLAM UAR ECO/UNDEV AGRI COLONIAL SOVEREIGN...CHARTS 20 NASSER/G MID/EAST. PAGE 94 A1934
CHIEF ECO/TAC DIPLOM POLICY

B65
REQUA E.G.,THE DEVELOPING NATIONS: A GUIDE TO INFORMATION SOURCES CONCERNING THEIR ECON, POLIT, TECHNICAL, AND SOCIAL PROBLEMS. AFR ASIA ISLAM L/A+17C INDUS INT/ORG CONSULT PLAN PROB/SOLV...SOC 20 UN. PAGE 120 A2466
BIBLIOG/A ECO/UNDEV FOR/AID TEC/DEV

B65
SANDERSON G.N.,ENGLAND, EUROPE, AND THE UPPER NILE 1882-1899. ISLAM MOD/EUR UAR UK CHIEF...POLICY CHARTS BIBLIOG/A 19 ARABS NEGRO. PAGE 127 A2600
AFR DIPLOM COLONIAL

L65
MATTHEWS D.G.,"LE TIERS MONDE: A SELECT AND PRELIMINARY BIBLIOGRAPHIC SURVEY OF MANPOWER IN DEVELOPING COUNTRIES, 1960-1964." AFR ISLAM L/A+17C INDUS PLAN PROB/SOLV TEC/DEV INT/TRADE EFFICIENCY WEALTH...STAT 20. PAGE 96 A1971
BIBLIOG/A ECO/UNDEV LABOR WORKER

S65
KHOURI F.J.,"THE JORDON RIVER CONTROVERSY." LAW SOCIETY ECO/UNDEV AGRI FINAN INDUS SECT FORCES ACT/RES PLAN TEC/DEV ECO/TAC EDU/PROP COERCE ATTIT DRIVE PERCEPT RIGID/FLEX ALL/VALS...GEOG SOC MYTH WORK. PAGE 78 A1610
ISLAM INT/ORG ISRAEL JORDAN

B66
THOMPSON J.H.,MODERNIZATION OF THE ARAB WORLD. FUT ISRAEL STRUCT ECO/UNDEV DIPLOM INGP/REL ATTIT ...CENSUS ANTHOL 20 ARABS. PAGE 143 A2926
ADJUST ISLAM PROB/SOLV NAT/COMP

B66
US DEPARTMENT OF STATE,RESEARCH ON THE MIDDLE EAST (EXTERNAL RESEARCH LIST NO 4-25). GREECE ISRAEL SYRIA UAR YEMEN CULTURE SOCIETY POL/PAR SECT DIPLOM EDU/PROP WAR NAT/LISM...GEOG GOV/COMP 20. PAGE 152 A3096
BIBLIOG/A ISLAM NAT/G REGION

B66
ZEINE Z.N.,THE EMERGENCE OF ARAB NATIONALISM (REV. ED.). TURKEY UK NAT/G SECT TEC/DEV LEAD REV WAR AGE/Y ROLE ORD/FREE...TRADIT CHARTS BIBLIOG 20 ARABS OTTOMAN. PAGE 170 A3451
ISLAM NAT/LISM DIPLOM

S66
FRIEND A.,"THE MIDDLE EAST CRISIS" COM ISLAM ISRAEL SYRIA UAR USA+45 USSR FORCES PLAN FOR/AID CONTROL ORD/FREE PWR...SOCIALIST TIME/SEQ 20 NASSER/G. PAGE 49 A1009
WAR INT/ORG DIPLOM PEACE

B67
LANDEN R.G.,OMAN SINCE 1856: DISRUPTIVE MODERNIZATION IN A TRADITIONAL ARAB SOCIETY. UK DIST/IND EXTR/IND SECT DIPLOM INT/TRADE...SOC LING CHARTS BIBLIOG 19/20. PAGE 84 A1714
ISLAM CULTURE ECO/UNDEV NAT/G

B67
MEHDI M.T.,PEACE IN THE MIDDLE EAST. ISRAEL SOCIETY NAT/G PLAN EDU/PROP NAT/LISM DRIVE...IDEA/COMP 20 JEWS. PAGE 99 A2033
ISLAM DIPLOM GP/REL COERCE

S67
ECKHARDT A.R.,"SILENCE IN THE CHURCHES." ISRAEL WOR+45 CONSTN GP/REL DISCRIM DRIVE JEWS. PAGE 40 A0820
SECT ATTIT DIPLOM ISLAM

S67
KYLE K.,"BACKGROUND TO THE CRISIS" ISLAM ISRAEL UAR UK USSR NAT/G PROB/SOLV LEGIT CONTROL REGION STRANGE MORAL 20 JEWS. PAGE 83 A1698
DIPLOM POLICY SOVEREIGN COERCE

S67
MCCORD W.,"ARMIES AND POLITICS; A PROBLEM IN THE THIRD WORLD." AFR ISLAM USA+45 ECO/UNDEV TOTALISM 20. PAGE 98 A2002
FOR/AID POLICY NAT/G FORCES

S67
SYRKIN M.,"I.F. STONE RECONSIDERS ISRAEL." ISRAEL WOR+45 DIPLOM NAT/LISM HABITAT...POLICY GEOG JEWS. PAGE 141 A2875
ISLAM WAR ATTIT MORAL

B86
MAS LATRIE L.,RELATIONS ET COMMERCE DE L'AFRIQUE SEPTENTRIONALE OU MAGREB AVEC LES NATIONS CHRETIENNES AU MOYEN AGE. CULTURE CHIEF FORCES WAR ...SOC CENSUS TREATY 10/16. PAGE 95 A1954
ISLAM SECT DIPLOM INT/TRADE

B93
ROYAL GEOGRAPHIC SOCIETY,BIBLIOGRAPHY OF BARBARY STATES (4 SUPPLEMENTARY PAPERS). ALGERIA LIBYA MOROCCO SOCIETY STRUCT DIPLOM LEAD 14/19 TUNIS. PAGE 125 A2555
BIBLIOG ISLAM NAT/G COLONIAL

C93
PLAYFAIR R.L.,"A BIBLIOGRAPHY OF MOROCCO." MOROCCO CULTURE AGRI FORCES DIPLOM WAR HEALTH...GEOG JURID SOC CHARTS. PAGE 116 A2387
BIBLIOG ISLAM MEDIT-7

ISOLAT....ISOLATION AND COMMUNITY, CONDITIONS OF HIGH GROUP SEGREGATION

N
US LIBRARY OF CONGRESS,EAST EUROPEAN ACCESSIONS INDEX. NAT/G ISOLAT ATTIT KNOWL...POLICY 20. PAGE 154 A3144
BIBLIOG COM MARXIST DIPLOM

B03
GRIFFIN A.P.C.,LISTS PUBLISHED 1902-03: ANGLO-SAXON INTERESTS (PAMPHLET). UK USA-45 ELITES SOCIETY DIPLOM ISOLAT 19/20. PAGE 56 A1152
BIBLIOG COLONIAL RACE/REL DOMIN

S26
COHEN P.A.,"WANG T'AO AND INCIPIENT CHINESE NATIONALISM." ASIA ADMIN ATTIT 19/20 BUREAUCRCY. PAGE 28 A0563
NAT/LISM ISOLAT CONSERVE DIPLOM

B36
BEARD C.A.,THE DEVIL THEORY OF WAR; AN INQUIRY INTO NATURE OF HISTORY AND THE POSSIBILITY OF KEEPING OUT OF WAR. USA-45 INT/ORG PROB/SOLV NEUTRAL ISOLAT ...CONCPT 20 LEAGUE/NAT WWI. PAGE 12 A0240
GEN/LAWS WAR POLICY DIPLOM

B40
WOLFERS A.,BRITAIN AND FRANCE BETWEEN TWO WORLD WARS. FRANCE UK INT/ORG NAT/G PLAN BARGAIN ECO/TAC AGREE ISOLAT ALL/IDEOS...DECISION GEOG 20 TREATY VERSAILLES INTERVENT. PAGE 166 A3380
DIPLOM WAR POLICY

B49
GORER G.,THE PEOPLE OF GREAT RUSSIA: A PSYCHOLOGICAL STUDY. RUSSIA USSR NAT/G DIPLOM LEAD AGE/C ANOMIE ATTIT DRIVE...POLICY 20. PAGE 54 A1116
ISOLAT PERSON PSY SOCIETY

B55
VINSON J.C.,THE PARCHMENT PEACE: THE UNITED STATES SENATE AND THE WASHINGTON CONFERENCE, 1921-1922. USA-45 INT/ORG DELIB/GP PLAN ARMS/CONT GOV/REL ISOLAT PEACE ATTIT SOVEREIGN...INT/LAW BIBLIOG 20 SENATE PRESIDENT CONGRESS LEAGUE/NAT CHINJAP. PAGE 159 A3242
POLICY DIPLOM NAT/G LEGIS

B57
ADLER S.,THE ISOLATIONIST IMPULSE: ITS TWENTIETH-CENTURY REACTION. USA+45 USA-45 POL/PAR WAR ISOLAT NAT/LISM 20. PAGE 5 A0093
DIPLOM POLICY ATTIT

B57
DUDDEN A.P.,WOODROW WILSON AND THE WORLD OF TODAY. USA-45 NAT/G PROVS CONTROL PARTIC WAR ISOLAT PWR SKILL...PERS/COMP ANTHOL 19/20 WILSON/W UN LEAGUE/NAT WWI. PAGE 39 A0794
CHIEF DIPLOM POL/PAR LEAD

B57
SEABURY P.,THE WANING OF SOUTHERN "INTERNATIONALISM" (PAMPHLET). USA+45 USA-45 INT/ORG LEGIS MAJORITY...TREND 20 SOUTH/US MIDWEST/US. PAGE 131 A2676
DIPLOM REGION ATTIT ISOLAT

C58
BUTTINGER J.,"THE SMALLER DRAGON; A POLITICAL HISTORY OF VIETNAM." VIETNAM SECT DIPLOM CIVMIL/REL ISOLAT NAT/LISM...BIBLIOG/A 3/20. PAGE 22 A0455
COLONIAL DOMIN SOVEREIGN REV

B59
BEMIS S.F.,A SHORT HISTORY OF AMERICAN FOREIGN POLICY AND DIPLOMACY. USA+45 USA-45 INT/ORG NEUTRAL REV WAR ISOLAT ORD/FREE...CHARTS T 18/20. PAGE 13 A0266
DIPLOM ATTIT

B62
BLANSHARD P.,FREEDOM AND CATHOLIC POWER IN SPAIN AND PORTUGAL: AN AMERICAN INTERPRETATION. AFR PORTUGAL SPAIN USA+45 LAW LABOR DIPLOM EDU/PROP DISCRIM ISOLAT TOTALISM 20 CHURCH/STA. PAGE 15 A0309
GP/REL FASCISM CATHISM PWR

B62
MOON P.,DIVIDE AND QUIT. INDIA PAKISTAN STRATA DELIB/GP PLAN DIPLOM REPRESENT GP/REL INGP/REL CONSEN DISCRIM...OBS 20. PAGE 103 A2119
WAR REGION ISOLAT SECT

B63
ELLENDER A.J.,A REPORT ON UNITED STATES FOREIGN OPERATIONS IN AFRICA. SOUTH/AFR USA+45 STRATA EXTR/IND FORCES RACE/REL ISOLAT SOVEREIGN...CHARTS 20 NEGRO. PAGE 41 A0840
FOR/AID DIPLOM WEALTH ECO/UNDEV

B63
HAMM H.,ALBANIA - CHINA'S BEACHHEAD IN EUROPE. ALBANIA CHINA/COM USSR YUGOSLAVIA ELITES SOCIETY POL/PAR DELIB/GP FORCES ECO/TAC COERCE ISOLAT PEACE MARXISM...IDEA/COMP 20 MAO. PAGE 61 A1248
DIPLOM REV NAT/G POLICY

C63
CHARLETON W.G.,"THE REVOLUTION IN AMERICAN FOREIGN POLICY." COM PROB/SOLV FOR/AID DOMIN COLONIAL NEUTRAL DETER WAR ISOLAT NAT/LISM...BIBLIOG 19/20 UN COLD/WAR NATO. PAGE 26 A0523
DIPLOM INT/ORG BAL/PWR

B66
EKIRCH A.A. JR.,IDEAS, IDEALS, AND AMERICAN DIPLOMACY. USA+45 USA-45 INT/ORG DOMIN COLONIAL ARMS/CONT DETER ISOLAT NAT/LISM...MAJORIT BIBLIOG 19/20 COLD/WAR. PAGE 41 A0834
DIPLOM LEAD PEACE

B66
LEWIS S.,TOWARDS INTERNATIONAL CO-OPERATION (1ST ED.). WOR+45 AGRI INDUS EDU/PROP RACE/REL ISOLAT NAT/LISM ATTIT HEALTH WEALTH...CHARTS WORSHIP 20 UN. PAGE 88 A1803
DIPLOM ANOMIE PROB/SOLV INT/ORG

B66
RIESELBACH L.N.,THE ROOTS OF ISOLATIONISM* CONGRESSIONAL VOTING AND PRESIDENTIAL LEADERSHIP IN FOREIGN POLICY. POL/PAR LEGIS DIPLOM EDU/PROP LEAD REGION REPRESENT...SOC STAT IDEA/COMP HYPO/EXP BIBLIOG 19/20 CONGRESS. PAGE 121 A2477
ISOLAT CHOOSE CHIEF POLICY

B67
HOHENBERG J.,BETWEEN TWO WORLDS. ASIA S/ASIA USA+45 PRESS TV PERS/REL ISOLAT...INT CHARTS METH/COMP 20. PAGE 66 A1362
COM/IND DIPLOM EFFICIENCY KNOWL

B67
RUSSELL B.,WAR CRIMES IN VIETNAM. USA+45 VIETNAM FORCES DIPLOM WEAPON RACE/REL DISCRIM ISOLAT BIO/SOC 20 COLD/WAR RUSSELL/B. PAGE 126 A2574
WAR CRIME ATTIT POLICY

S67
KAHN H.,"CRITERIA FOR LONG-RANGE NUCLEAR CONTROL POLICIES." WOR+45 INT/ORG TEC/DEV DOMIN DETER WAR WEAPON ISOLAT ORD/FREE POLICY. PAGE 76 A1549
NUC/PWR ARMS/CONT BAL/PWR DIPLOM

ISOLATION....SEE ISOLAT

ISRAEL....SEE ALSO JEWS, ISLAM

N
US LIBRARY OF CONGRESS,ACCESSIONS LIST -- ISRAEL. ISRAEL CULTURE ECO/UNDEV POL/PAR PLAN PROB/SOLV TEC/DEV DIPLOM EDU/PROP LEAD WAR ATTIT 20 JEWS. PAGE 154 A3143
BIBLIOG ISLAM NAT/G GP/REL

N19
UNITED ARAB REPUBLIC,THE PROBLEM OF THE PALESTINIAN REFUGEES (PAMPHLET). ISRAEL UAR LAW PROB/SOLV EDU/PROP CONFER ADJUD CONTROL NAT/LISM HEALTH 20 JEWS UN MIGRATION. PAGE 148 A3029
STRANGE GP/REL INGP/REL DIPLOM

B54
NATION ASSOCIATES,SECURITY AND THE MIDDLE EAST - THE PROBLEM AND ITS SOLUTION. ISRAEL JORDAN LEBANON SYRIA UAR FORCES FOR/AID GP/REL NAT/LISM PEACE TOTALISM...POLICY 20. PAGE 107 A2198
DIPLOM ECO/UNDEV WAR PLAN

B57
WARBURG J.P.,AGENDA FOR ACTION. ISLAM ISRAEL USA+45 FOR/AID INT/TRADE WAR NAT/LISM 20 MID/EAST EUROPE ARABS. PAGE 161 A3275
DIPLOM POLICY INT/ORG BAL/PWR

S59
HARVEY M.F.,"THE PALESTINE REFUGEE PROBLEM: ELEMENTS OF A SOLUTION." ISLAM LAW INT/ORG DELIB/GP TOP/EX ECO/TAC ROUTINE DRIVE HEALTH LOVE ORD/FREE PWR WEALTH...MAJORIT FAO 20. PAGE 62 A1283
ACT/RES LEGIT PEACE ISRAEL

S59
KOHN L.Y.,"ISRAEL AND NEW NATION STATES OF ASIA AND AFRICA." AFR ASIA FUT S/ASIA VOL/ASSN TEC/DEV NAT/LISM RIGID/FLEX SKILL WEALTH...RELATIV OBS TREND CON/ANAL 20. PAGE 81 A1663
ECO/UNDEV ECO/TAC FOR/AID ISRAEL

L60
LAUTERPACHT E.,"THE SUEZ CANAL SETTLEMENT." FRANCE ISLAM ISRAEL UAR UK BAL/PWR DIPLOM LEGIT...JURID GEN/LAWS ANTHOL SUEZ VAL/FREE 20. PAGE 85 A1747
INT/ORG LAW

B61
PATAI R.,CULTURES IN CONFLICT; AN INQUIRY INTO THE SOCIO-CULTURAL PROBLEMS OF ISRAEL AND HER NEIGHBORS (2ND REV. ED.). ISLAM ISRAEL SOCIETY STRUCT DIPLOM GP/REL ALL/VALS...SOC 20 JEWS ARABS. PAGE 114 A2339
NAT/COMP CULTURE GP/COMP ATTIT

B62
RIVKIN A.,AFRICA AND THE WEST. AFR EUR+WWI FUT ISLAM ISRAEL USA+45 SOCIETY INT/ORG FORCES CREATE PLAN FOR/AID EDU/PROP ATTIT...CONCPT TREND EEC 20 CONGRESS UN. PAGE 121 A2488
ECO/UNDEV ECO/TAC

B63
BURNS A.L.,PEACE-KEEPING BY U.N.FORCES - FROM SUEZ TO THE CONGO. AFR FUT ISLAM ISRAEL USSR WOR+45 NAT/G DELIB/GP BAL/PWR DOMIN LEGIT EXEC COERCE PEACE ATTIT PWR RESPECT SOVEREIGN...CONCPT UN 20. PAGE 22 A0441
INT/ORG FORCES ORD/FREE

B63
LIVNEH E.,ISRAEL LEGAL BIBLIOGRAPHY IN EUROPEAN LANGUAGES. ISRAEL LOC/G JUDGE TAX...INT/LAW 20. PAGE 90 A1846
BIBLIOG LAW NAT/G CONSTN

B63
ROSNER G.,THE UNITED NATIONS EMERGENCY FORCE. FRANCE ISRAEL UAR UK WOR+45 CREATE WAR PEACE ORD/FREE PWR...INT/LAW JURID HIST/WRIT TIME/SEQ UN. PAGE 124 A2539
INT/ORG FORCES

B64
AMERICAN ASSEMBLY,THE UNITED STATES AND THE MIDDLE EAST. ISRAEL USA+45 STRUCT ECO/DEV ECO/UNDEV INT/ORG NAT/G SCHOOL SECT VOL/ASSN EX/STRUC TEC/DEV NAT/LISM...SOC 20. PAGE 7 A0135
ISLAM DRIVE REGION

B64
DUROSELLE J.B.,POLITIQUES NATIONALES ENVERS LES JEUNES ETATS. FRANCE ISRAEL ITALY UK USA+45 USSR YUGOSLAVIA ECO/DEV FINAN ECO/TAC INT/TRADE ADMIN PWR 20. PAGE 40 A0809
DIPLOM ECO/UNDEV COLONIAL DOMIN

B64
SAKAI R.K.,STUDIES ON ASIA, 1964. ASIA CHINA/COM ISRAEL MALAYSIA S/ASIA USA+45 USSR ECO/UNDEV FAM POL/PAR SECT CONSULT NAT/LISM...POLICY SOC 20 CHINJAP. PAGE 126 A2588
PWR DIPLOM

B64
UAR NATIONAL LIBRARY,A BIBLIOGRAPHICAL LIST OF WORKS ABOUT PALESTINE AND JORDAN (2ND ED.). ISRAEL JORDAN SECT DIPLOM...SOC 20 JEWS. PAGE 146 A2991
BIBLIOG ISLAM

B65
MACDONALD R.W.,THE LEAGUE OF ARAB STATES: A STUDY IN THE DYNAMICS OF REGIONAL ORGANIZATION. ISRAEL UAR USSR FINAN INT/ORG DELIB/GP ECO/TAC AGREE NEUTRAL ORD/FREE PWR...DECISION BIBLIOG 20 TREATY UN. PAGE 92 A1888
ISLAM REGION DIPLOM ADMIN

B65
US DEPARTMENT OF DEFENSE,US SECURITY ARMS CONTROL, AND DISARMAMENT 1961-1965 (PAMPHLET). CHINA/COM COM GERMANY/W ISRAEL SPACE USA+45 USSR WOR+45 FORCES EDU/PROP DETER EQUILIB PEACE ALL/VALS...GOV/COMP 20 NATO. PAGE 151 A3077
BIBLIOG/A ARMS/CONT NUC/PWR DIPLOM

S65
KHOURI F.J.,"THE JORDON RIVER CONTROVERSY." LAW SOCIETY ECO/UNDEV AGRI FINAN INDUS SECT FORCES ACT/RES PLAN TEC/DEV ECO/TAC EDU/PROP COERCE ATTIT DRIVE PERCEPT RIGID/FLEX ALL/VALS...GEOG SOC MYTH WORK. PAGE 78 A1610
ISLAM INT/ORG ISRAEL JORDAN

B66
THOMPSON J.H.,MODERNIZATION OF THE ARAB WORLD. FUT ISRAEL STRUCT ECO/UNDEV DIPLOM INGP/REL ATTIT ...CENSUS ANTHOL 20 ARABS. PAGE 143 A2926
ADJUST ISLAM PROB/SOLV NAT/COMP

B66
US DEPARTMENT OF STATE,RESEARCH ON THE MIDDLE EAST (EXTERNAL RESEARCH LIST NO 4-25). GREECE ISRAEL SYRIA UAR YEMEN CULTURE SOCIETY POL/PAR SECT DIPLOM EDU/PROP WAR NAT/LISM...GEOG GOV/COMP 20. PAGE 152 A3096
BIBLIOG/A ISLAM NAT/G REGION

S66
FRIEND A.,"THE MIDDLE EAST CRISIS" COM ISLAM ISRAEL SYRIA UAR USA+45 USSR FORCES PLAN FOR/AID CONTROL ORD/FREE PWR...SOCIALIST TIME/SEQ 20 NASSER/G. PAGE 49 A1009
WAR INT/ORG DIPLOM PEACE

B67
BLOM-COOPER L.,THE LITERATURE OF THE LAW AND THE LANGUAGE OF THE LAW (2 VOLS.). CANADA ISRAEL UK WOR+45 WOR-45 JUDGE CT/SYS ATTIT...CRIMLGY JURID ANTHOL CMN/WLTH. PAGE 15 A0312
BIBLIOG LAW INT/LAW ADJUD

B67
MEHDI M.T.,PEACE IN THE MIDDLE EAST. ISRAEL SOCIETY NAT/G PLAN EDU/PROP NAT/LISM DRIVE...IDEA/COMP 20 JEWS. PAGE 99 A2033
ISLAM DIPLOM GP/REL COERCE

S67
ECKHARDT A.R.,"SILENCE IN THE CHURCHES." ISRAEL WOR+45 CONSTN GP/REL DISCRIM DRIVE JEWS. PAGE 40 A0820
SECT ATTIT DIPLOM ISLAM

S67
KYLE K.,"BACKGROUND TO THE CRISIS" ISLAM ISRAEL UAR UK USSR NAT/G PROB/SOLV LEGIT CONTROL REGION STRANGE MORAL 20 JEWS. PAGE 83 A1698
DIPLOM POLICY SOVEREIGN COERCE

S67
LIVNEH E.,"A NEW BEGINNING." ISRAEL USSR WOR+45 NAT/G DIPLOM INGP/REL FEDERAL HABITAT PWR...GEOG PSY JEWS. PAGE 90 A1847
WAR PERSON PEACE PLAN

S67
SYRKIN M.,"I.F. STONE RECONSIDERS ISRAEL." ISRAEL WOR+45 DIPLOM NAT/LISM HABITAT...POLICY GEOG JEWS. PAGE 141 A2875
ISLAM WAR ATTIT MORAL

ISSUES (CURRENT SUBJECTS OF DISCOURSE)....SEE CONCPT, POLICY

ITAL/AMER....ITALIAN-AMERICANS

ITALY....SEE ALSO APPROPRIATE TIME/SPACE/CULTURE INDEX

B00
GRIFFIN A.P.C.,LIST OF BOOKS RELATING TO THE THEORY OF COLONIZATION, GOVERNMENT OF DEPENDENCIES, PROTECTORATES, AND RELATED TOPICS. FRANCE GERMANY ITALY SPAIN UK USA-45 WOR-45 ECO/TAC ADMIN CONTROL REGION NAT/LISM ALL/VALS PWR...INT/LAW SOC 16/19. PAGE 56 A1149
BIBLIOG/A COLONIAL GOV/REL DOMIN

C28
SCHNEIDER H.W.,"MAKING THE FASCIST STATE." ITALY CULTURE LABOR DIPLOM REV WAR NAT/LISM TOTALISM ATTIT DRIVE SOCISM...BIBLIOG PARLIAMENT 20. PAGE 129 A2638
FASCISM POLICY POL/PAR

B32
BRYCE J.,THE HOLY ROMAN EMPIRE. GERMANY ITALY MOD/EUR CULTURE SOCIETY STRUCT INT/ORG NAT/G SECT DIPLOM DOMIN WAR SUPEGO ALL/VALS SOVEREIGN...GEOG SOC TIME/SEQ CHARTS STERTYP. PAGE 20 A0413
CHRIST-17C NAT/LISM

B32
EAGLETON C.,INTERNATIONAL GOVERNMENT. BRAZIL FRANCE GERMANY ITALY UK USSR WOR-45 DELIB/GP TOP/EX PLAN ECO/TAC EDU/PROP LEGIT ADJUD REGION ARMS/CONT COERCE ATTIT PWR...GEOG MGT VAL/FREE LEAGUE/NAT 20. PAGE 40 A0816
INT/ORG JURID DIPLOM INT/LAW

C32
MARRARO H.R.,"AMERICAN OPINION ON THE UNIFICATION OF ITALY." ITALY MOD/EUR USA-45 FORCES DIPLOM PRESS REV CATHISM...BIOG 19 PRESIDENT. PAGE 95 A1944
BIBLIOG/A NAT/LISM ATTIT ORD/FREE

B35
LANGER W.L.,THE DIPLOMACY OF IMPERIALISM 1890-1902. FRANCE GERMANY ITALY UK WOR-45 BAL/PWR INT/TRADE LEGIT ADJUD CONTROL WAR PWR SOVEREIGN...CHARTS BIBLIOG/A 19/20. PAGE 84 A1726
DIPLOM COLONIAL DOMIN

B36
BOYCE A.N.,EUROPE AND SOUTH AFRICA. FRANCE GERMANY ITALY SOUTH/AFR UK INDUS NAT/G CONTROL REV WAR NAT/LISM...CONCPT HIST/WRIT 20. PAGE 18 A0362
COLONIAL GOV/COMP NAT/COMP DIPLOM

B36
VARLEY D.H.,A BIBLIOGRAPHY OF ITALIAN COLONISATION IN AFRICA WITH A SECTION ON ABYSSINIA. AFR ETHIOPIA ITALY LIBYA SOMALIA AGRI FINAN LABOR TEC/DEV DIPLOM INT/TRADE RACE/REL DISCRIM 19/20. PAGE 158 A3222
BIBLIOG COLONIAL ADMIN LAW

B37
BORGESE G.A.,GOLIATH: THE MARCH OF FASCISM. GERMANY ITALY LAW POL/PAR SECT DIPLOM SOCISM...JURID MYTH 20 DANTE MACHIAVELL MUSSOLIN/B. PAGE 17 A0341
POLICY NAT/LISM FASCISM NAT/G

B38
PETTEE G.S.,THE PROCESS OF REVOLUTION. COM FRANCE ITALY MOD/EUR RUSSIA SPAIN WOR-45 ELITES INTELL SOCIETY STRATA STRUCT INT/ORG NAT/G POL/PAR ACT/RES PLAN EDU/PROP LEGIT EXEC...SOC MYTH TIME/SEQ TOT/POP 18/20. PAGE 115 A2370
COERCE CONCPT REV

B39
DULLES J.,WAR, PEACE AND CHANGE. FRANCE ITALY UK USA-45 WOR-45 LAW INT/ORG NAT/G SECT VOL/ASSN FORCES TOP/EX DOMIN ARMS/CONT COERCE ATTIT PERSON RIGID/FLEX MORAL PWR...JURID STERTYP TOT/POP LEAGUE/NAT 20. PAGE 39 A0796
EDU/PROP TOTALISM WAR

B40
ITALIAN LIBRARY OF INFORMATION: OUTLINE STUDIES (VOL. V). ITALY LIBYA CONTROL...FASCIST 20. PAGE 3 A0052
COLONIAL DIPLOM ECO/TAC POLICY

B43
SERENI A.P.,THE ITALIAN CONCEPTION OF INTERNATIONAL LAW. EUR+WWI MOD/EUR INT/ORG NAT/G DOMIN COERCE ORD/FREE FASCISM...OBS/ENVIR TREND 20. PAGE 131 A2686
LAW TIME/SEQ INT/LAW ITALY

B44
FULLER G.H.,MILITARY GOVERNMENT: A LIST OF REFERENCES (A PAMPHLET). ITALY UK USA-45 WOR-45 LAW FORCES DOMIN ADMIN ARMS/CONT ORD/FREE PWR ...DECISION 20 CHINJAP. PAGE 50 A1023
BIBLIOG DIPLOM CIVMIL/REL SOVEREIGN

B45
CONOVER H.F.,THE GOVERNMENTS OF THE MAJOR FOREIGN POWERS: A BIBLIOGRAPHY. FRANCE GERMANY ITALY UK USSR CONSTN LOC/G POL/PAR EX/STRUC FORCES ADMIN CT/SYS CIVMIL/REL TOTALISM...POLICY 19/20. PAGE 29 A0598
BIBLIOG NAT/G DIPLOM

B45
CONOVER H.F.,ITALY: ECONOMICS, POLITICS AND MILITARY AFFAIRS, 1940-1945. ITALY ELITES NAT/G POL/PAR EX/STRUC TOP/EX DIPLOM DOMIN CONTROL COERCE WAR CIVMIL/REL EFFICIENCY 20. PAGE 29 A0599
BIBLIOG TOTALISM FORCES

B47
CONOVER H.F.,NON-SELF-GOVERNING AREAS. BELGIUM FRANCE ITALY UK WOR+45 CULTURE ECO/UNDEV INT/ORG LOC/G NAT/G ECO/TAC INT/TRADE ADMIN HEALTH...SOC UN. PAGE 30 A0601
BIBLIOG/A COLONIAL DIPLOM

B47
FEIS H.,SEEN FROM E A, THREE INTERNATIONAL EPISODES. EUR+WWI ITALY USA-45 WOR-45 AGRI INT/ORG NAT/G INT/TRADE LEGIT EXEC ATTIT ORD/FREE...POLICY LEAGUE/NAT TOT/POP 20 OIL. PAGE 44 A0908 — EXTR/IND ECO/TAC DIPLOM

B49
BOZZA T.,SCRITTORI POLITICI ITALIANI DAL 1550 AL 1650. CHRIST-17C ITALY DIPLOM DOMIN 16/17. PAGE 18 A0365 — BIBLIOG/A NAT/G CONCPT WRITING

B54
SALVEMINI G.,PRELUDE TO WORLD WAR II. ITALY MOD/EUR INT/ORG BAL/PWR EDU/PROP CONTROL TOTALISM...TREND NAT/COMP BIBLIOG 19 HITLER/A LEAGUE/NAT MUSSOLIN/B. PAGE 127 A2597 — WAR FASCISM LEAD PWR

B56
FOSTER J.G.,BRITAIN IN WESTERN EUROPE: WEU AND THE ATLANTIC ALLIANCE. EUR+WWI FRANCE GERMANY GERMANY/W ITALY UK STRATA NAT/G DELIB/GP ECO/TAC ORD/FREE PWR ...TRADIT TIME/SEQ TREND OEEC PARLIAMENT 20 EUROPE/W. PAGE 47 A0969 — INT/ORG FORCES WEAPON

B60
HOLT R.T.,STRATEGIC PSYCHOLOGICAL OPERATIONS AND AMERICAN FOREIGN POLICY. ITALY USA+45 FOR/AID DOMIN RUMOR ADMIN TASK WAR CHOOSE ATTIT ALL/IDEOS...PSY COLD/WAR. PAGE 67 A1375 — EDU/PROP ACT/RES DIPLOM POLICY

S60
KREININ M.E.,"THE 'OUTER-SEVEN' AND EUROPEAN INTEGRATION." EUR+WWI FRANCE GERMANY ITALY UK ECO/DEV DIST/IND INT/TRADE DRIVE WEALTH...MYTH CHARTS EEC OEEC 20. PAGE 82 A1682 — ECO/TAC GEN/LAWS

B61
DELZELL C.F.,MUSSOLINI'S ENEMIES - THE ITALIAN ANTI-FASCIST RESISTANCE. ITALY DIPLOM PRESS DETER WAR TOTALISM ORD/FREE MARXISM 20. PAGE 36 A0730 — FASCISM GP/REL POL/PAR REV

B62
ALIX C.,LE SAINT-SIEGE ET LES NATIONALISMES EN EUROPE 1870-1960. COM GERMANY IRELAND ITALY SOCIETY SECT TOTALISM RIGID/FLEX MORAL 19/20. PAGE 6 A0122 — CATH NAT/LISM ATTIT DIPLOM

B62
ROBERTSON B.C.,REGIONAL DEVELOPMENT IN THE EUROPEAN ECONOMIC COMMUNITY. EUR+WWI FRANCE FUT ITALY UK ECO/UNDEV WORKER ACT/RES PROB/SOLV TEC/DEV ECO/TAC INT/TRADE EEC. PAGE 122 A2499 — PLAN ECO/DEV INT/ORG REGION

S62
ALBONETTI A.,"IL SECONDO PROGRAMMA QUINQUENNALE 1963-67 ED IL BILANCIO RICERCHE ED INVESTIMENTI PER IL 1963 DELL'ERATOM." EUR+WWI FUT ITALY WOR+45 ECO/DEV SERV/IND INT/ORG TEC/DEV ECO/TAC ATTIT SKILL WEALTH...MGT TIME/SEQ OEEC 20. PAGE 5 A0108 — R+D PLAN NUC/PWR

B63
FRANZ G.,TEILUNG UND WIEDERVEREINIGUNG. GERMANY IRELAND ITALY NETHERLAND POLAND CULTURE BAL/PWR CHOOSE NAT/LISM ORD/FREE SOVEREIGN 19/20. PAGE 48 A0987 — DIPLOM WAR NAT/COMP ATTIT

B64
DUROSELLE J.B.,POLITIQUES NATIONALES ENVERS LES JEUNES ETATS. FRANCE ISRAEL ITALY UK USA+45 USSR YUGOSLAVIA ECO/DEV FINAN ECO/TAC INT/TRADE ADMIN PWR 20. PAGE 40 A0809 — DIPLOM ECO/UNDEV COLONIAL DOMIN

B64
HALPERIN S.W.,MUSSOLINI AND ITALIAN FASCISM. ITALY NAT/G POL/PAR SECT ECO/TAC LEAD PWR SOCISM...POLICY 20 MUSSOLIN/B. PAGE 60 A1241 — FASCISM NAT/LISM EDU/PROP CHIEF

B64
VECCHIO G.D.,L'ETAT ET LE DROIT. ITALY CONSTN EX/STRUC LEGIS DIPLOM CT/SYS...JURID 20 UN. PAGE 158 A3225 — NAT/G SOVEREIGN CONCPT INT/LAW

B65
GILBERT M.,THE EUROPEAN POWERS 1900-45. EUR+WWI ITALY MOD/EUR USSR REV WAR PWR ALL/IDEOS FASCISM ...AUD/VIS CHARTS BIBLIOG 20. PAGE 52 A1069 — DIPLOM NAT/G POLICY BAL/PWR

B65
WEIL G.L.,A HANDBOOK ON THE EUROPEAN ECONOMIC COMMUNITY. BELGIUM EUR+WWI FRANCE GERMANY/W ITALY CONSTN ECO/DEV CREATE PARTIC GP/REL...DECISION MGT CHARTS 20 EEC. PAGE 162 A3299 — INT/TRADE INT/ORG TEC/DEV INT/LAW

S65
STEIN E.,"TOWARD SUPREMACY OF TREATY-CONSTITUTION BY JUDICIAL FIAT: ON THE MARGIN OF THE COSTA CASE." EUR+WWI ITALY WOR+45 INT/ORG NAT/G LEGIT REGION NAT/LISM PWR...JURID CONCPT TREND TOT/POP VAL/FREE 20. PAGE 138 A2816 — ADJUD CONSTN SOVEREIGN INT/LAW

C66
DUROSELLE J.B.,"LE CONFLIT DE TRIESTE 1943-1954: ETUDES DE CAS DE CONFLITS INTERNATIONAUX III." ITALY USA+45 YUGOSLAVIA ELITES DELIB/GP PLAN ADJUST ...POLICY GEOG CHARTS IDEA/COMP TIME 20 TREATY UN COLD/WAR. PAGE 40 A0810 — BIBLIOG WAR DIPLOM GEN/LAWS

B67
KATZ R.,DEATH IN ROME. EUR+WWI ITALY POL/PAR DIPLOM LEAD ATTIT PERSON ROLE CATHISM. PAGE 77 A1570 — WAR MURDER FORCES DEATH

S67
VELIKONJA J.,"ITALIAN IMMIGRANTS IN THE UNITED STATES IN THE MID-SIXTIES" ITALY USA+45 KIN MUNIC NAT/G WORKER DIPLOM REGION GP/REL ADJUST...GEOG CHARTS SOC/INTEG 20. PAGE 158 A3226 — HABITAT ORD/FREE TREND STAT

ITO....INTERNATIONAL TRADE ORGANIZATION

ITU....INTERNATIONAL TELECOMMUNICATIONS UNION

IVORY COAST....SEE IVORY/CST

IVORY/CST....IVORY COAST; SEE ALSO AFR

IWW....INTERNATIONAL WORKERS OF THE WORLD

B57
PETERSON H.C.,OPPONENTS OF WAR 1917-1918. USA-45 POL/PAR DOMIN ORD/FREE PWR PACIFISM SOCISM 20 IWW CONSCN/OBJ. PAGE 115 A2368 — WAR PEACE ATTIT EDU/PROP

J

JACK H. A1471

JACK H.A. A1472

JACKSON B.W. A1473

JACKSON E. A1474,A1475,A1476

JACKSON M.V. A1477

JACKSON R.G.A. A1478

JACKSON R.H. A1479

JACKSON W.G.F. A1480

JACKSON W.V. A1481

JACKSON/A....PRESIDENT ANDREW JACKSON

JACKSON/RH....R.H. JACKSON

JACOB P.E. A1482,A1483

JACOBINISM....JACOBINISM: FRENCH DEMOCRATIC REVOLUTIONARY DOCTRINE, 1789

N17
BURKE E.,THOUGHTS ON THE PROSPECT OF A REGICIDE PEACE (PAMPHLET). FRANCE UK SECT DOMIN MURDER PEACE ORD/FREE SOVEREIGN POPULISM...POLICY GOV/COMP IDEA/COMP 18 JACOBINISM COEXIST. PAGE 21 A0435 — REV CHIEF NAT/G DIPLOM

JACOBSON H.K. A1484,A1485,A1486,A1487

JADOS S.S. A1488

JAECKH A. A1489

JAFFA/HU....H.U. JAFFA

JAGAN C. A1490

JAIRAZBHOY R.A. A1491

JAKARTA....JAKARTA, INDONESIA

JAKOBSON M. A1492

JALEE P. A1493

JAMAICA....SEE ALSO L/A+17C

JAMESON J.F. A1494

JANET/P....PIERRE JANET

JANOWITZ M. A1495

JAPAN....SEE ALSO ASIA

JAPAN MOMBUSHO DAIGAKU GAKIYUT A1496

JAPANESE AMERICANS....SEE NISEI

JAPANESE ASSOCIATION INT. LAW A1497

JARMO....JARMO, A PRE- OR EARLY HISTORIC SOCIETY

JASPERS/K....KARL JASPERS

JASZI O. A1498

JAT....A POLITICAL SYSTEM OF INDIA

JAURES/JL....JEAN LEON JAURES (FRENCH SOCIALIST 1859-1914)

JAVA....JAVA, INDONESIA; SEE ALSO INDONESIA

B62
SELOSOEMARDJAN O.,SOCIAL CHANGES IN JOGJAKARTA. INDONESIA NETHERLAND ELITES STRATA STRUCT FAM POL/PAR CREATE DIPLOM INT/TRADE EDU/PROP ADMIN GOV/REL...SOC 20 JAVA CHINJAP. PAGE 131 A2683
ECO/UNDEV CULTURE REV COLONIAL

JAVITS B.A. A1499

JAVITS J.K. A1500,A1501

JEFFERSN/T....PRESIDENT THOMAS JEFFERSON

B27
PARRINGTON V.L.,MAIN CURRENTS IN AMERICAN THOUGHT (VOL.I). USA-45 AGRI POL/PAR DIPLOM TAX REGION REV 17/18 FRANKLIN/B JEFFERSN/T. PAGE 114 A2336
COLONIAL SECT FEEDBACK ALL/IDEOS

B48
BELOFF M.,THOMAS JEFFERSON AND AMERICAN DEMOCRACY. USA-45 NAT/G DIPLOM GOV/REL PEACE 18/19 JEFFERSN/T PRESIDENT VIRGINIA. PAGE 13 A0258
BIOG CHIEF REV

JEFFRIES C. A1502

JEHOVA/WIT....JEHOVAHOS WITNESSES

JELAVICH C. A1503

JENCKS/C....C. JENCKS

JENKS C.W. A1504,A1505,A1506

JENNINGS R. A1509

JENNINGS W.I. A1507,A1508,A1510,A1511,A1512

JENSEN D.L. A1513

JESSUP P.C. A1514,A1515

JEWELL M.E. A1516

JEWS....JEWS, JUDAISM

N
US LIBRARY OF CONGRESS,ACCESSIONS LIST -- ISRAEL. ISRAEL CULTURE ECO/UNDEV POL/PAR PLAN PROB/SOLV TEC/DEV DIPLOM EDU/PROP LEAD WAR ATTIT 20 JEWS. PAGE 154 A3143
BIBLIOG ISLAM NAT/G GP/REL

N19
UNITED ARAB REPUBLIC,THE PROBLEM OF THE PALESTINIAN REFUGEES (PAMPHLET). ISRAEL UAR LAW PROB/SOLV EDU/PROP CONFER ADJUD CONTROL NAT/LISM HEALTH 20 JEWS UN MIGRATION. PAGE 148 A3029
STRANGE GP/REL INGP/REL DIPLOM

B21
BALFOUR A.J.,ESSAYS SPECULATIVE AND POLITICAL. SEA CULTURE CREATE WAR NAT/LISM PEACE LOVE...ART/METH INT/LAW CONCPT ANTHOL 20 JEWS. PAGE 10 A0211
PHIL/SCI SOCIETY DIPLOM

B40
WANDERSCHECK H.,FRANKREICHS PROPAGANDA GEGEN DEUTSCHLAND. FRANCE GERMANY MOD/EUR UK NAT/G DIPLOM WAR 20 JEWS. PAGE 161 A3273
EDU/PROP ATTIT DOMIN PRESS

B42
BORNSTEIN J.,ACTION AGAINST THE ENEMY'S MIND. EUR+WWI GERMANY USA-45 DIPLOM DOMIN PRESS LEAD GP/REL DISCRIM PERCEPT FASCISM MARXISM 20 JEWS NAZI ANTI/SEMIT. PAGE 17 A0343
EDU/PROP PSY WAR CONTROL

B43
FULLER G.F.,FOREIGN RELIEF AND REHABILITATION (PAMPHLET). FUT GERMANY UK USA-45 INT/ORG PROB/SOLV DIPLOM FOR/AID ADMIN ADJUST PEACE ALL/VALS...SOC/WK 20 UN JEWS. PAGE 50 A1018
BIBLIOG/A PLAN GIVE WAR

B57
BYRNES R.F.,BIBLIOGRAPHY OF AMERICAN PUBLICATIONS ON EAST CENTRAL EUROPE, 1945-1957 (VOL. XXII). SECT DIPLOM EDU/PROP RACE/REL...ART/METH GEOG JURID SOC LING 20 JEWS. PAGE 23 A0462
BIBLIOG/A COM MARXISM NAT/G

B58
INSTITUTE MEDITERRANEAN AFF,THE PALESTINE REFUGEE PROBLEM. UAR WOR+45 INT/ORG PLAN PROB/SOLV PEACE ...POLICY GEOG STAT CHARTS 20 JEWS UN MIGRATION. PAGE 70 A1444
STRANGE HABITAT GP/REL INGP/REL

B59
KAPLAN D.,THE ARAB REFUGEES: AN ABNORMAL PROBLEM. UAR WOR+45 PROB/SOLV DIPLOM GOV/REL ADJUST EFFICIENCY...POLICY GEOG INT/LAW 20 UN JEWS MIGRATION. PAGE 76 A1557
STRANGE HABITAT GP/REL INGP/REL

B61
PATAI R.,CULTURES IN CONFLICT; AN INQUIRY INTO THE SOCIO-CULTURAL PROBLEMS OF ISRAEL AND HER NEIGHBORS (2ND REV. ED.). ISLAM ISRAEL SOCIETY STRUCT DIPLOM GP/REL ALL/VALS...SOC 20 JEWS ARABS. PAGE 114 A2339
NAT/COMP CULTURE GP/COMP ATTIT

B61
TETENS T.H.,THE NEW GERMANY AND THE OLD NAZIS. EUR+WWI GERMANY/W USA+45 NAT/G CRIME CHOOSE RACE/REL TOTALISM AGE/Y ATTIT 20 JEWS NAZI ADENAUER/K. PAGE 142 A2905
FASCISM DIPLOM FOR/AID POL/PAR

B64
UAR NATIONAL LIBRARY,A BIBLIOGRAPHICAL LIST OF WORKS ABOUT PALESTINE AND JORDAN (2ND ED.). ISRAEL JORDAN SECT DIPLOM...SOC 20 JEWS. PAGE 146 A2991
BIBLIOG ISLAM

S64
GREENBERG S.,"JUDAISM AND WORLD JUSTICE." MEDIT-7 WOR+45 LAW CULTURE SOCIETY INT/ORG NAT/G FORCES EDU/PROP ATTIT DRIVE PERSON SUPEGO ALL/VALS ...POLICY PSY CONCPT GEN/LAWS JEWS. PAGE 55 A1140
SECT JURID PEACE

B67
MEHDI M.T.,PEACE IN THE MIDDLE EAST. ISRAEL SOCIETY NAT/G PLAN EDU/PROP NAT/LISM DRIVE...IDEA/COMP 20 JEWS. PAGE 99 A2033
ISLAM DIPLOM GP/REL COERCE

S67
ECKHARDT A.R.,"SILENCE IN THE CHURCHES." ISRAEL WOR+45 CONSTN GP/REL DISCRIM DRIVE JEWS. PAGE 40 A0820
SECT ATTIT DIPLOM ISLAM

S67
KYLE K.,"BACKGROUND TO THE CRISIS" ISLAM ISRAEL UAR UK USSR NAT/G PROB/SOLV LEGIT CONTROL REGION STRANGE MORAL 20 JEWS. PAGE 83 A1698
DIPLOM POLICY SOVEREIGN COERCE

S67
LIVNEH E.,"A NEW BEGINNING." ISRAEL USSR WOR+45 NAT/G DIPLOM INGP/REL FEDERAL HABITAT PWR...GEOG PSY JEWS. PAGE 90 A1847
WAR PERSON PEACE PLAN

S67
SYRKIN M.,"I.F. STONE RECONSIDERS ISRAEL." ISRAEL WOR+45 DIPLOM NAT/LISM HABITAT...POLICY GEOG JEWS. PAGE 141 A2875
ISLAM WAR ATTIT MORAL

JIMENEZ E. A1517

JOHN BIRCH SOCIETY....SEE BIRCH/SOC

JOHN/XXII....POPE JOHN XXII

JOHN/XXIII....POPE JOHN XXIII

B66
HOLLINS E.J.,PEACE IS POSSIBLE: A READER FOR LAYMEN. WOR+45 CULTURE PLAN RISK AGE/Y ALL/VALS SOVEREIGN...PSY CONCPT TREND 20 UN JOHN/XXIII KENNAN/G MYRDAL/G. PAGE 67 A1370
PEACE DIPLOM INT/ORG NUC/PWR

JOHNS HOPKINS UNIVERSITY LIB A1518

JOHNSN/ALB....ALBERT JOHNSON

JOHNSN/AND....PRESIDENT ANDREW JOHNSON

JOHNSON A.M. A1519

JOHNSON D.G. A1520

JOHNSON D.H.N. A1521

JOHNSON E.A.J. A1522

JOHNSON H.G. A1523

JOHNSON J. A1524

JOHNSON L.B. A1525

JOHNSON O.H. A1526

JOHNSON/D....D. JOHNSON

JOHNSON/LB ....PRESIDENT LYNDON BAINES JOHNSON

B63
KLEIMAN R.,ATLANTIC CRISIS; AMERICAN DIPLOMACY CONFRONTS A RESURGENT EUROPE. EUR+WWI USA+45 ECO/DEV AGRI NAT/G CHIEF FORCES PLAN LEAD ATTIT
DIPLOM REGION POLICY

...CONCPT 20 NATO KENNEDY/JF DEGAULLE/C EEC JOHNSON/LB. PAGE 80 A1648

B64
JOHNSON L.B.,MY HOPE FOR AMERICA. FUT USA+45 USSR LAW PLAN DIPLOM GIVE INCOME PEACE ATTIT ORD/FREE WEALTH 20 JOHNSON/LB PRESIDENT DEMOCRAT. PAGE 74 A1525
POLICY POL/PAR NAT/G GOV/REL

B64
KAUFMANN W.W.,THE MC NAMARA STRATEGY. TOP/EX INSPECT BAL/PWR DIPLOM CONTROL DETER GUERRILLA NUC/PWR WEAPON COST PWR...METH/COMP 20 MCNAMARA/R KENNEDY/JF JOHNSON/LB NATO DEPT/DEFEN. PAGE 77 A1572
FORCES WAR PLAN PROB/SOLV

B65
WEISNER J.B.,WHERE SCIENCE AND POLITICS MEET. USA+45 ECO/DEV R+D FORCES PROB/SOLV DIPLOM FOR/AID CONTROL...PHIL/SCI PRESIDENT KENNEDY/JF JOHNSON/LB. PAGE 163 A3310
CHIEF NAT/G POLICY TEC/DEV

JOHNSTN/GD....GEORGE D. JOHNSTON

JOHNSTON D.M. A1527,A1528

JOHNSTON L.P. A1217

JOHNSTONE A. A1529

JONES A.C. A1530

JONES H.D. A0399,A1531

JONES J.M. A1532

JONESVILLE....JONESVILLE: LOCATION OF W.L. WARNEROS "DEMOCRACY IN JONESVILLE"

JORDAN A. A1533,A1534

JORDAN A.A. A1535

JORDAN D.C. A3333

JORDAN N. A1536

JORDAN....SEE ALSO ISLAM

B54
NATION ASSOCIATES,SECURITY AND THE MIDDLE EAST - THE PROBLEM AND ITS SOLUTION. ISRAEL JORDAN LEBANON SYRIA UAR FORCES FOR/AID GP/REL NAT/LISM PEACE TOTALISM...POLICY 20. PAGE 107 A2198
DIPLOM ECO/UNDEV WAR PLAN

B64
UAR NATIONAL LIBRARY,A BIBLIOGRAPHICAL LIST OF WORKS ABOUT PALESTINE AND JORDAN (2ND ED.). ISRAEL JORDAN SECT DIPLOM...SOC 20 JEWS. PAGE 146 A2991
BIBLIOG ISLAM

S65
KHOURI F.J.,"THE JORDON RIVER CONTROVERSY." LAW SOCIETY ECO/UNDEV AGRI FINAN INDUS SECT FORCES ACT/RES PLAN TEC/DEV ECO/TAC EDU/PROP COERCE ATTIT DRIVE PERCEPT RIGID/FLEX ALL/VALS...GEOG SOC MYTH WORK. PAGE 78 A1610
ISLAM INT/ORG ISRAEL JORDAN

JOSEPH F.M. A1537

JOSHI P.S. A1538

JOURNALISM....SEE PRESS

JOY C.T. A1539

JOYCE W. A1540

JUAN T.L. A1541

JUDD P. A1542

JUDGE....JUDGES; SEE ALSO ADJUD

N
ARBITRATION JOURNAL. WOR+45 LAW INDUS JUDGE DIPLOM CT/SYS INGP/REL 20. PAGE 2 A0027
BIBLIOG MGT LABOR ADJUD

N
HARVARD UNIVERSITY LAW LIBRARY,CATALOG OF INTERNATIONAL LAW AND RELATIONS. WOR+45 WOR-45 INT/ORG NAT/G JUDGE DIPLOM INT/TRADE ADJUD CT/SYS 19/20. PAGE 62 A1280
BIBLIOG INT/LAW JURID

B09
HOLLAND T.E.,LETTERS UPON WAR AND NEUTRALITY. WOR-45 NAT/G FORCES JUDGE ECO/TAC LEGIT CT/SYS NEUTRAL ROUTINE COERCE...JURID TIME/SEQ 20. PAGE 67 A1368
LAW INT/LAW INT/ORG WAR

B21
OPPENHEIM L.,THE FUTURE OF INTERNATIONAL LAW. EUR+WWI MOD/EUR LAW LEGIS JUDGE LEGIT ORD/FREE ...JURID TIME/SEQ GEN/LAWS 20. PAGE 112 A2293
INT/ORG CT/SYS INT/LAW

B29
CONWELL-EVANS T.P.,THE LEAGUE COUNCIL IN ACTION. EUR+WWI TURKEY UK USSR WOR-45 INT/ORG FORCES JUDGE ECO/TAC EDU/PROP LEGIT ROUTINE ARMS/CONT COERCE ATTIT PWR...MAJORIT GEOG JURID CONCPT LEAGUE/NAT TOT/POP VAL/FREE TUNIS 20. PAGE 30 A0605
DELIB/GP INT/LAW

B33
AMERICAN FOREIGN LAW ASSN,BIOGRAPHICAL NOTES ON THE LAWS AND LEGAL LITERATURE OF URUGUAY AND CURACAO. URUGUAY CONSTN FINAN SECT FORCES JUDGE DIPLOM INT/TRADE ADJUD CT/SYS CRIME 20. PAGE 7 A0147
BIBLIOG/A LAW JURID ADMIN

B52
JACKSON E.,MEETING OF THE MINDS: A WAY TO PEACE THROUGH MEDIATION. WOR+45 INDUS INT/ORG NAT/G DELIB/GP DIPLOM EDU/PROP LEGIT ORD/FREE...NEW/IDEA SELF/OBS TIME/SEQ CHARTS GEN/LAWS TOT/POP 20 UN TREATY. PAGE 72 A1474
LABOR JUDGE

B56
JESSUP P.C.,TRANSNATIONAL LAW. FUT WOR+45 JUDGE CREATE ADJUD ORD/FREE...CONCPT VAL/FREE 20. PAGE 74 A1515
LAW JURID INT/LAW

B59
CORBETT P.E.,LAW IN DIPLOMACY. UK USA+45 USSR CONSTN SOCIETY INT/ORG JUDGE LEGIT ATTIT ORD/FREE TOT/POP LEAGUE/NAT 20. PAGE 30 A0616
NAT/G ADJUD JURID DIPLOM

B59
SCHNEIDER J.,TREATY-MAKING POWER OF INTERNATIONAL ORGANIZATIONS. FUT WOR+45 WOR-45 LAW NAT/G JUDGE DIPLOM LEGIT CT/SYS ORD/FREE PWR...INT/LAW JURID GEN/LAWS TOT/POP UNESCO 20 TREATY. PAGE 129 A2639
INT/ORG ROUTINE

S59
HOFFMANN S.,"IMPLEMENTATION OF INTERNATIONAL INSTRUMENTS ON HUMAN RIGHTS." WOR+45 VOL/ASSN DELIB/GP JUDGE EDU/PROP LEGIT ROUTINE PEACE COLD/WAR 20. PAGE 66 A1355
INT/ORG MORAL

S59
SUTTON F.X.,"REPRESENTATION AND THE NATURE OF POLITICAL SYSTEMS." UNIV WOR-45 CULTURE SOCIETY STRATA INT/ORG FORCES JUDGE DOMIN LEGIT EXEC REGION REPRESENT ATTIT ORD/FREE RESPECT...SOC HIST/WRIT TIME/SEQ. PAGE 140 A2867
NAT/G CONCPT

B62
ROSENNE S.,THE WORLD COURT: WHAT IT IS AND HOW IT WORKS. WOR+45 WOR-45 LAW CONSTN JUDGE EDU/PROP LEGIT ROUTINE CHOOSE PEACE ORD/FREE...JURID OBS TIME/SEQ CHARTS UN TOT/POP VAL/FREE 20. PAGE 124 A2538
INT/ORG ADJUD INT/LAW

B63
BOWETT D.W.,THE LAW OF INTERNATIONAL INSTITUTIONS. WOR+45 WOR-45 CONSTN DELIB/GP EX/STRUC JUDGE EDU/PROP LEGIT CT/SYS EXEC ROUTINE RIGID/FLEX ORD/FREE PWR...JURID CONCPT ORG/CHARTS GEN/METH LEAGUE/NAT OAS OEEC 20 UN. PAGE 17 A0354
INT/ORG ADJUD DIPLOM

B63
LIVNEH E.,ISRAEL LEGAL BIBLIOGRAPHY IN EUROPEAN LANGUAGES. ISRAEL LOC/G JUDGE TAX...INT/LAW 20. PAGE 90 A1846
BIBLIOG LAW NAT/G CONSTN

B64
FALK R.A.,THE ROLE OF DOMESTIC COURTS IN THE INTERNATIONAL LEGAL ORDER. FUT WOR+45 INT/ORG NAT/G JUDGE EDU/PROP LEGIT CT/SYS...POLICY RELATIV JURID CONCPT GEN/LAWS 20. PAGE 43 A0889
LAW INT/LAW

B64
SZLADITS C.,BIBLIOGRAPHY ON FOREIGN AND COMPARATIVE LAW: BOOKS AND ARTICLES IN ENGLISH (SUPPLEMENT 1962). FINAN INDUS JUDGE LICENSE ADMIN CT/SYS PARL/PROC OWN...INT/LAW CLASSIF METH/COMP NAT/COMP 20. PAGE 141 A2877
BIBLIOG/A JURID ADJUD LAW

C65
SCHEINGOLD S.A.,"THE RULE OF LAW IN EUROPEAN INTEGRATION: THE PATH OF THE SCHUMAN PLAN." EUR+WWI JUDGE ADJUD FEDERAL ATTIT PWR...RECORD INT BIBLIOG EEC ECSC. PAGE 128 A2621
INT/LAW CT/SYS REGION CENTRAL

B66
BROWNLIE I.,PRINCIPLES OF PUBLIC INTERNATIONAL LAW. WOR+45 WOR-45 LAW JUDGE REPAR ADJUD SOVEREIGN ...JURID T. PAGE 20 A0409
INT/LAW DIPLOM INT/ORG

B66
NANTWI E.K.,THE ENFORCEMENT OF INTERNATIONAL JUDICIAL DECISIONS AND ARBITAL AWARDS IN PUBLIC INTERNATIONAL LAW. WOR+45 WOR-45 JUDGE PROB/SOLV DIPLOM CT/SYS SUPEGO MORAL PWR RESPECT...METH/CNCPT 18/20 CASEBOOK. PAGE 107 A2196
INT/LAW ADJUD SOVEREIGN INT/ORG

B66
SZLADITS C.,A BIBLIOGRAPHY ON FOREIGN AND COMPARATIVE LAW (SUPPLEMENT 1964). FINAN FAM LABOR LG/CO LEGIS JUDGE ADMIN CRIME...CRIMLGY 20. PAGE 141 A2878
BIBLIOG/A CT/SYS INT/LAW

B67
BLOM-COOPER L.,THE LITERATURE OF THE LAW AND THE LANGUAGE OF THE LAW (2 VOLS.). CANADA ISRAEL UK WOR+45 WOR-45 JUDGE CT/SYS ATTIT...CRIMLGY JURID ANTHOL CMN/WLTH. PAGE 15 A0312
BIBLIOG LAW INT/LAW ADJUD

B67
KNOLES G.H.,THE RESPONSIBILITIES OF POWER, 1900-1929. USA-45 SOCIETY SECT JUDGE COLONIAL REPRESENT WEALTH POPULISM...IDEA/COMP ANTHOL PRESIDENT 20 LEAGUE/NAT. PAGE 81 A1653
PWR DIPLOM NAT/LISM WAR

B67
UNIVERSAL REFERENCE SYSTEM,LAW, JURISPRUDENCE, AND JUDICIAL PROCESS (VOLUME VII). WOR+45 WOR-45 CONSTN NAT/G LEGIS JUDGE CT/SYS...INT/LAW COMPUT/IR GEN/METH METH. PAGE 149 A3044
BIBLIOG/A LAW JURID ADJUD

S67
FOREIGN POLICY ASSOCIATION,"US CONCERN FOR WORLD LAW." USA+45 WOR+45 DELIB/GP JUDGE BAL/PWR CONFER PEACE ORD/FREE 20 UN. PAGE 47 A0962
INT/LAW INT/ORG DIPLOM ARMS/CONT

S67
JOHNSON D.H.N.,"THE SOUTH-WEST AFRICA CASES." AFR ETHIOPIA LIBERIA SOUTH/AFR CONSULT JUDGE BAL/PWR 20. PAGE 74 A1521
INT/LAW DIPLOM INT/ORG ADJUD

S67
MANN F.A.,"THE BRETTON WOODS AGREEMENT IN THE ENGLISH COURTS." UK JUDGE ADJUD CT/SYS...JURID PREDICT CON/ANAL 20. PAGE 94 A1923
LAW INT/LAW CONSTN

JUDICIAL PROCESS....SEE ADJUD

JUGOSLAVIA....SEE YUGOSLAVIA

JUNKER ....JUNKER: REACTIONARY PRUSSIAN ARISTOCRACY

B64
REMAK J.,THE GENTLE CRITIC: THEODOR FONTANE AND GERMAN POLITICS, 1848-1898. GERMANY PRUSSIA CULTURE ELITES BAL/PWR DIPLOM WRITING GOV/REL...HUM BIOG 19 BISMARCK/O JUNKER FONTANE/T. PAGE 120 A2465
PERSON SOCIETY WORKER CHIEF

JURID....LAW

N
INTERNATIONAL COMN JURISTS,AFRICAN CONFERENCE ON THE RULE OF LAW. AFR INT/ORG LEGIS DIPLOM CONFER COLONIAL ORD/FREE...CONCPT METH/COMP 20. PAGE 71 A1452
CT/SYS JURID DELIB/GP

N
AMERICAN JOURNAL OF INTERNATIONAL LAW. WOR+45 WOR-45 CONSTN INT/ORG NAT/G CT/SYS ARMS/CONT WAR ...DECISION JURID NAT/COMP 20. PAGE 1 A0002
BIBLIOG/A INT/LAW DIPLOM ADJUD

N
CANADIAN GOVERNMENT PUBLICATIONS (1955-). CANADA AGRI FINAN LABOR FORCES INT/TRADE HEALTH...JURID 20 PARLIAMENT. PAGE 1 A0007
BIBLIOG/A NAT/G DIPLOM INT/ORG

N
ATLANTIC INSTITUTE,ATLANTIC STUDIES. COM EUR+WWI USA+45 CULTURE STRUCT ECO/DEV FORCES LEAD ARMS/CONT ...INT/LAW JURID SOC. PAGE 10 A0193
BIBLIOG/A DIPLOM POLICY GOV/REL

N
HARVARD LAW SCHOOL LIBRARY,ANNUAL LEGAL BIBLIOGRAPHY. USA+45 CONSTN LEGIS ADJUD CT/SYS ...POLICY 20. PAGE 62 A1278
BIBLIOG JURID LAW INT/LAW

N
HARVARD UNIVERSITY LAW LIBRARY,CATALOG OF INTERNATIONAL LAW AND RELATIONS. WOR+45 WOR-45 INT/ORG NAT/G JUDGE DIPLOM INT/TRADE ADJUD CT/SYS 19/20. PAGE 62 A1280
BIBLIOG INT/LAW JURID

N
SOCIETE DES NATIONS,TRAITES INTERNATIONAUX ET ACTES LEGISLATIFS. WOR-45 INT/ORG NAT/G...INT/LAW JURID 20 LEAGUE/NAT TREATY. PAGE 135 A2759
BIBLIOG DIPLOM LEGIS ADJUD

B00
DARBY W.E.,INTERNATIONAL TRIBUNALS. WOR-45 NAT/G ECO/TAC DOMIN LEGIT CT/SYS COERCE ORD/FREE PWR SOVEREIGN JURID. PAGE 33 A0681
INT/ORG ADJUD PEACE INT/LAW

B00
GROTIUS H.,DE JURE BELLI AC PACIS. CHRIST-17C UNIV LAW SOCIETY PROVS LEGIT PEACE PERCEPT MORAL PWR ...CONCPT CON/ANAL GEN/LAWS. PAGE 57 A1180
JURID INT/LAW WAR

B00
HOLLAND T.E.,STUDIES IN INTERNATIONAL LAW. TURKEY USSR WOR-45 CONSTN NAT/G DIPLOM DOMIN LEGIT COERCE WAR PEACE ORD/FREE PWR SOVEREIGN...JURID CHARTS 20 PARLIAMENT SUEZ TREATY. PAGE 66 A1367
INT/ORG LAW INT/LAW

B00
MAINE H.S.,INTERNATIONAL LAW. MOD/EUR UNIV SOCIETY STRUCT ACT/RES EXEC WAR ATTIT PERSON ALL/VALS ...POLICY JURID CONCPT OBS TIME/SEQ TOT/POP. PAGE 93 A1908
INT/ORG LAW PEACE INT/LAW

L00
HISTORICUS,"LETTERS AND SOME QUESTIONS OF INTERNATIONAL LAW." FRANCE NETHERLAND UK USA-45 WOR-45 LAW NAT/G COERCE...SOC CONCPT GEN/LAWS TOT/POP 19 CIVIL/WAR. PAGE 65 A1344
WEALTH JURID WAR INT/LAW

B04
CRANDALL S.B.,TREATIES: THEIR MAKING AND ENFORCEMENT. MOD/EUR USA-45 CONSTN INT/ORG NAT/G LEGIS EDU/PROP LEGIT EXEC PEACE KNOWL MORAL...JURID CONGRESS 19/20 TREATY. PAGE 32 A0655
LAW

B09
HOLLAND T.E.,LETTERS UPON WAR AND NEUTRALITY. WOR-45 NAT/G FORCES JUDGE ECO/TAC LEGIT CT/SYS NEUTRAL ROUTINE COERCE...JURID TIME/SEQ 20. PAGE 67 A1368
LAW INT/LAW INT/ORG WAR

B13
BORCHARD E.M.,BIBLIOGRAPHY OF INTERNATIONAL LAW AND CONTINENTAL LAW. EUR+WWI MOD/EUR UK LAW INT/TRADE WAR PEACE...GOV/COMP NAT/COMP 19/20. PAGE 17 A0338
BIBLIOG INT/LAW JURID DIPLOM

B13
BUTLER N.M.,THE INTERNATIONAL MIND. WOR-45 INT/ORG LEGIT PWR...JURID CONCPT 20. PAGE 22 A0452
ADJUD ORD/FREE INT/LAW

B16
ROOT E.,ADDRESSES ON INTERNATIONAL SUBJECTS. MOD/EUR UNIV USA-45 LAW SOCIETY EXEC ATTIT ALL/VALS ...POLICY JURID CONCPT 20 CHINJAP. PAGE 123 A2521
INT/ORG ACT/RES PEACE INT/LAW

L16
WRIGHT Q.,"THE ENFORCEMENT OF INTERNATIONAL LAW THROUGH MUNICIPAL LAW IN THE US." USA-45 LOC/G NAT/G PUB/INST FORCES LEGIT CT/SYS PERCEPT ALL/VALS ...JURID 20. PAGE 167 A3401
INT/ORG LAW INT/LAW WAR

S17
ROOT E.,"THE EFFECT OF DEMOCRACY ON INTERNATIONAL LAW." USA-45 WOR-45 INTELL SOCIETY INT/ORG NAT/G CONSULT ACT/RES CREATE PLAN EDU/PROP PEACE SKILL ...CONCPT METH/CNCPT OBS 20. PAGE 123 A2523
LEGIS JURID INT/LAW

B20
DICKINSON E.,THE EQUALITY OF STATES IN INTERNATIONAL LAW. WOR-45 INT/ORG NAT/G DIPLOM EDU/PROP LEGIT PEACE ATTIT ALL/VALS...JURID TIME/SEQ LEAGUE/NAT. PAGE 37 A0757
LAW CONCPT SOVEREIGN

B20
VINOGRADOFF P.,OUTLINES OF HISTORICAL JURISPRUDENCE (2 VOLS.). GREECE MEDIT-7 LAW CONSTN FACE/GP FAM KIN MUNIC CRIME OWN...INT/LAW IDEA/COMP BIBLIOG. PAGE 159 A3241
JURID METH

B21
OPPENHEIM L.,THE FUTURE OF INTERNATIONAL LAW. EUR+WWI MOD/EUR LAW LEGIS JUDGE LEGIT ORD/FREE ...JURID TIME/SEQ GEN/LAWS 20. PAGE 112 A2293
INT/ORG CT/SYS INT/LAW

L21
HALDEMAN E.,"SERIALS OF AN INTERNATIONAL CHARACTER." WOR-45 DIPLOM...ART/METH GEOG HEAL HUM INT/LAW JURID PSY SOC. PAGE 60 A1224
BIBLIOG PHIL/SCI

B22
BRYCE J.,INTERNATIONAL RELATIONS. CHRIST-17C EUR+WWI MOD/EUR CULTURE INTELL NAT/G DELIB/GP CREATE BAL/PWR DIPLOM ATTIT DRIVE RIGID/FLEX ALL/VALS...PLURIST JURID CONCPT TIME/SEQ GEN/LAWS TOT/POP. PAGE 20 A0412
INT/ORG POLICY

B22
WRIGHT Q.,THE CONTROL OF AMERICAN FOREIGN RELATIONS. USA-45 WOR-45 CONSTN INT/ORG CONSULT LEGIS LEGIT ROUTINE ORD/FREE PWR...POLICY JURID CONCPT METH/CNCPT RECORD LEAGUE/NAT 20. PAGE 167 A3402
NAT/G EXEC DIPLOM

S23
DEWEY J.,"ETHICS AND INTERNATIONAL RELATIONS." FUT WOR-45 SOCIETY INT/ORG VOL/ASSN DIPLOM LEGIT ORD/FREE...JURID CONCPT GEN/METH 20. PAGE 37 A0752
LAW MORAL

B24
GENTILI A.,DE LEGATIONIBUS. CHRIST-17C NAT/G SECT CONSULT LEGIT...POLICY CATH JURID CONCPT MYTH. PAGE 52 A1058
DIPLOM INT/LAW INT/ORG LAW

B24
HALL W.E.,A TREATISE ON INTERNATIONAL LAW. WOR-45 CONSTN INT/ORG NAT/G DIPLOM ORD/FREE LEAGUE/NAT 20 TREATY. PAGE 60 A1228
PWR JURID WAR INT/LAW

B25
GODET M.,INDEX BIBLIOGRAPHICUS: INTERNATIONAL CATALOGUE OF SOURCES OF CURRENT BIBLIOGRAPHIC INFORMATION. EUR+WWI MOD/EUR SOCIETY SECT TAX ...JURID PHIL/SCI SOC MATH. PAGE 53 A1085
BIBLIOG/A DIPLOM EDU/PROP LAW

L25
HUDSON M.,"THE PERMANENT COURT OF INTERNATIONAL JUSTICE AND THE QUESTION OF AMERICAN PARTICIPATION." WOR-45 LEGIT CT/SYS ORD/FREE ...JURID CONCPT TIME/SEQ GEN/LAWS VAL/FREE 20 ICJ. PAGE 68 A1406
INT/ORG ADJUD DIPLOM INT/LAW

B27
LAUTERPACHT H.,PRIVATE LAW SOURCES AND ANALOGIES OF INTERNATIONAL LAW. WOR-45 NAT/G DELIB/GP LEGIT COERCE ATTIT ORD/FREE PWR SOVEREIGN...JURID CONCPT HIST/WRIT TIME/SEQ GEN/METH LEAGUE/NAT 20. PAGE 85
INT/ORG ADJUD PEACE INT/LAW

A1748

B28
BUTLER G.,THE DEVELOPMENT OF INTERNATIONAL LAW. WOR-45 SOCIETY NAT/G KNOWL ORD/FREE PWR...JURID CONCPT HIST/WRIT GEN/LAWS. PAGE 22 A0451
LAW INT/LAW DIPLOM INT/ORG

B28
HOWARD-ELLIS C.,THE ORIGIN, STRUCTURE AND WORKING OF THE LEAGUE OF NATIONS. EUR+WWI MOD/EUR USA-45 CONSTN FORCES LEGIS ECO/TAC LEGIT COERCE ORD/FREE ...JURID SOC CONCPT LEAGUE/NAT 20 ILO ICJ. PAGE 68 A1401
INT/ORG ADJUD

B28
MAIR L.P.,THE PROTECTION OF MINORITIES. EUR+WWI WOR-45 CONSTN INT/ORG NAT/G LEGIT CT/SYS GP/REL RACE/REL DISCRIM ORD/FREE RESPECT...JURID CONCPT TIME/SEQ 20. PAGE 93 A1909
LAW SOVEREIGN

B29
BUELL R.,INTERNATIONAL RELATIONS. WOR+45 WOR-45 CONSTN STRATA FORCES TOP/EX ADMIN ATTIT DRIVE SUPEGO MORAL ORD/FREE PWR SOVEREIGN...JURID SOC CONCPT 20. PAGE 21 A0428
INT/ORG BAL/PWR DIPLOM

B29
CONWELL-EVANS T.P.,THE LEAGUE COUNCIL IN ACTION. EUR+WWI TURKEY UK USSR WOR-45 INT/ORG FORCES JUDGE ECO/TAC EDU/PROP LEGIT ROUTINE ARMS/CONT COERCE ATTIT PWR...MAJORIT GEOG JURID CONCPT LEAGUE/NAT TOT/POP VAL/FREE TUNIS 20. PAGE 30 A0605
DELIB/GP INT/LAW

B29
DUNN F.,THE PRACTICE AND PROCEDURE OF INTERNATIONAL CONFERENCES. WOR-45 NAT/G DELIB/GP BAL/PWR LEGIT EXEC ROUTINE PEACE ORD/FREE RESPECT...JURID CONCPT METH/CNCPT OBS RECORD TIME/SEQ 20. PAGE 39 A0799
INT/ORG DIPLOM

B29
PRATT I.A.,MODERN EGYPT: A LIST OF REFERENCES TO MATERIAL IN THE NEW YORK PUBLIC LIBRARY. UAR ECO/UNDEV...GEOG JURID SOC LING 20. PAGE 117 A2407
BIBLIOG ISLAM DIPLOM NAT/G

B30
WRIGHT Q.,MANDATES UNDER THE LEAGUE OF NATIONS. WOR-45 CONSTN ECO/DEV ECO/UNDEV NAT/G DELIB/GP TOP/EX LEGIT ALL/VALS...JURID CONCPT LEAGUE/NAT 20. PAGE 167 A3403
INT/ORG LAW INT/LAW

B32
EAGLETON C.,INTERNATIONAL GOVERNMENT. BRAZIL FRANCE GERMANY ITALY UK USSR WOR-45 DELIB/GP TOP/EX PLAN ECO/TAC EDU/PROP LEGIT ADJUD REGION ARMS/CONT COERCE ATTIT PWR...GEOG MGT VAL/FREE LEAGUE/NAT 20. PAGE 40 A0816
INT/ORG JURID DIPLOM INT/LAW

B32
GREGORY W.,LIST OF THE SERIAL PUBLICATIONS OF FOREIGN GOVERNMENTS, 1815-1931. WOR-45 DIPLOM ADJUD ...POLICY 20. PAGE 56 A1144
BIBLIOG NAT/G LAW JURID

B32
MASTERS R.D.,INTERNATIONAL LAW IN INTERNATIONAL COURTS. BELGIUM EUR+WWI FRANCE GERMANY MOD/EUR SWITZERLND WOR-45 SOCIETY STRATA STRUCT LEGIT EXEC ALL/VALS...JURID HIST/WRIT TIME/SEQ TREND GEN/LAWS 20. PAGE 96 A1961
INT/ORG LAW INT/LAW

B33
AMERICAN FOREIGN LAW ASSN,BIOGRAPHICAL NOTES ON THE LAWS AND LEGAL LITERATURE OF URUGUAY AND CURACAO. URUGUAY CONSTN FINAN SECT FORCES JUDGE DIPLOM INT/TRADE ADJUD CT/SYS CRIME 20. PAGE 7 A0147
BIBLIOG/A LAW JURID ADMIN

B33
LAUTERPACHT H.,THE FUNCTION OF LAW IN THE INTERNATIONAL COMMUNITY. WOR-45 NAT/G FORCES CREATE DOMIN LEGIT COERCE WAR PEACE ATTIT ORD/FREE PWR SOVEREIGN...JURID CONCPT METH/CNCPT TIME/SEQ GEN/LAWS GEN/METH LEAGUE/NAT TOT/POP VAL/FREE 20. PAGE 85 A1749
INT/ORG LAW INT/LAW

B33
MATTHEWS M.A.,THE AMERICAN INSTITUTE OF INTERNATIONAL LAW AND THE CODIFICATION OF INTERNATIONAL LAW (PAMPHLET). USA-45 CONSTN ADJUD CT/SYS...JURID 20. PAGE 96 A1973
BIBLIOG/A INT/LAW L/A+17C DIPLOM

B34
WOLFF C.,JUS GENTIUM METHODO SCIENTIFICA PERTRACTATUM. MOD/EUR INT/ORG VOL/ASSN LEGIT PEACE ATTIT...JURID 20. PAGE 166 A3387
NAT/G LAW INT/LAW WAR

B35
KENNEDY W.P.,THE LAW AND CUSTOM OF THE SOUTH AFRICAN CONSTITUTION. AFR SOUTH/AFR KIN LOC/G PROVS DIPLOM ADJUD ADMIN EXEC 20. PAGE 78 A1594
CT/SYS CONSTN JURID PARL/PROC

B36
HUDSON M.O.,INTERNATIONAL LEGISLATION: 1929-1931. WOR-45 SEA AIR AGRI FINAN LABOR DIPLOM ECO/TAC REPAR CT/SYS ARMS/CONT WAR WEAPON...JURID 20 TREATY LEAGUE/NAT. PAGE 69 A1409
INT/LAW PARL/PROC ADJUD LAW

B36
MATTHEWS M.A.,INTERNATIONAL LAW: SELECT LIST OF WORKS IN ENGLISH ON PUBLIC INTERNATIONAL LAW: WITH COLLECTIONS OF CASES AND OPINIONS. CHRIST-17C EUR+WWI MOD/EUR WOR-45 CONSTN ADJUD JURID. PAGE 96 A1975
BIBLIOG/A INT/LAW ATTIT DIPLOM

B36
RUSSEL F.M.,THEORIES OF INTERNATIONAL RELATIONS. EUR+WWI FUT MOD/EUR USA-45 INT/ORG DIPLOM...JURID CONCPT. PAGE 125 A2571
PWR POLICY BAL/PWR SOVEREIGN

B37
BORGESE G.A.,GOLIATH: THE MARCH OF FASCISM. GERMANY ITALY LAW POL/PAR SECT DIPLOM SOCISM...JURID MYTH 20 DANTE MACHIAVELL MUSSOLIN/B. PAGE 17 A0341
POLICY NAT/LISM FASCISM NAT/G

B37
SCHUSTER E.,GUIDE TO LAW AND LEGAL LITERATURE OF CENTRAL AMERICAN REPUBLICS. L/A+17C INT/ORG ADJUD SANCTION CRIME...JURID 19/20. PAGE 129 A2654
BIBLIOG/A REGION CT/SYS LAW

B38
MCNAIR A.D.,THE LAW OF TREATIES: BRITISH PRACTICE AND OPINIONS. UK CREATE DIPLOM LEGIT WRITING ADJUD WAR...INT/LAW JURID TREATY. PAGE 98 A2018
AGREE LAW CT/SYS NAT/G

B39
DULLES J.,WAR, PEACE AND CHANGE. FRANCE ITALY UK USA-45 WOR-45 LAW INT/ORG NAT/G SECT VOL/ASSN FORCES TOP/EX DOMIN ARMS/CONT COERCE ATTIT PERSON RIGID/FLEX MORAL PWR...JURID STERTYP TOT/POP LEAGUE/NAT 20. PAGE 39 A0796
EDU/PROP TOTALISM WAR

B39
MAXWELL B.W.,INTERNATIONAL RELATIONS. EUR+WWI WOR-45 NAT/G CONSULT DIPLOM LEGIT ADJUD NAT/LISM ATTIT ORD/FREE SOVEREIGN...JURID LEAGUE/NAT TOT/POP VAL/FREE 20. PAGE 97 A1981
INT/ORG

B40
CARR E.H.,THE TWENTY YEARS' CRISIS 1919-1939. FUT WOR-45 BAL/PWR ECO/TAC LEGIT TOTALISM ATTIT ALL/VALS...POLICY JURID CONCPT TIME/SEQ TREND GEN/LAWS TOT/POP 20. PAGE 24 A0498
INT/ORG DIPLOM PEACE

B40
MIDDLEBUSH F.,ELEMENTS OF INTERNATIONAL RELATIONS. WOR-45 PROVS CONSULT EDU/PROP LEGIT WAR NAT/LISM ATTIT KNOWL MORAL ORD/FREE PWR...JURID LEAGUE/NAT TOT/POP VAL/FREE. PAGE 101 A2067
NAT/G INT/ORG PEACE DIPLOM

S41
WRIGHT Q.,"FUNDAMENTAL PROBLEMS OF INTERNATIONAL ORGANIZATION." UNIV WOR-45 STRUCT FORCES ACT/RES CREATE DOMIN EDU/PROP LEGIT REGION NAT/LISM ORD/FREE PWR RESPECT SOVEREIGN...JURID SOC CONCPT METH/CNCPT TIME/SEQ 20. PAGE 167 A3405
INT/ORG ATTIT PEACE

B42
KELSEN H.,LAW AND PEACE IN INTERNATIONAL RELATIONS. FUT WOR-45 NAT/G DELIB/GP DIPLOM LEGIT RIGID/FLEX ORD/FREE SOVEREIGN...JURID CONCPT TREND STERTYP GEN/LAWS LEAGUE/NAT 20. PAGE 77 A1580
INT/ORG ADJUD PEACE INT/LAW

B43
HAGUE PERMANENT CT INTL JUSTIC,WORLD COURT REPORTS: COLLECTION OF THE JUDGEMENTS ORDERS AND OPINIONS VOLUME 4 1936-42. WOR-45 CONFER PEACE ATTIT ...DECISION JURID ANTHOL 20 WORLD/CT CASEBOOK. PAGE 59 A1215
INT/ORG CT/SYS DIPLOM ADJUD

C43
BENTHAM J.,"PRINCIPLES OF INTERNATIONAL LAW" IN J. BOWRING, ED., THE WORKS OF JEREMY BENTHAM." UNIV NAT/G PLAN PROB/SOLV DIPLOM CONTROL SANCTION MORAL ORD/FREE PWR SOVEREIGN 19. PAGE 13 A0270
INT/LAW JURID WAR PEACE

B44
BRIERLY J.L.,THE OUTLOOK FOR INTERNATIONAL LAW. FUT WOR-45 CONSTN NAT/G VOL/ASSN FORCES ECO/TAC DOMIN LEGIT ADJUD ROUTINE PEACE ORD/FREE...INT/LAW JURID METH LEAGUE/NAT 20. PAGE 18 A0376
INT/ORG LAW

B44
DAVIS H.E.,PIONEERS IN WORLD ORDER. WOR-45 CONSTN ECO/TAC DOMIN EDU/PROP LEGIT ADJUD ADMIN ARMS/CONT CHOOSE KNOWL ORD/FREE...POLICY JURID SOC STAT OBS CENSUS TIME/SEQ ANTHOL LEAGUE/NAT 20. PAGE 34 A0691
INT/ORG ROUTINE

B44
PUTTKAMMER E.W.,WAR AND THE LAW. UNIV USA-45 CONSTN CULTURE SOCIETY NAT/G POL/PAR ROUTINE ALL/VALS ...JURID CONCPT OBS WORK VAL/FREE 20. PAGE 118 A2418
INT/ORG LAW WAR INT/LAW

S44
WRIGHT Q.,"CONSTITUTIONAL PROCEDURES OF THE US FOR CARRYING OUT OBLIGATIONS FOR MILITARY SANCTIONS." EUR+WWI FUT USA-45 WOR-45 CONSTN INTELL NAT/G CONSULT EX/STRUC LEGIS ROUTINE DRIVE...POLICY JURID CONCPT OBS TREND TOT/POP 20. PAGE 167 A3406
TOP/EX FORCES INT/LAW WAR

B45
HILL N.,CLAIMS TO TERRITORY IN INTERNATIONAL LAW AND RELATIONS. WOR-45 NAT/G DOMIN EDU/PROP LEGIT REGION ROUTINE ORD/FREE PWR WEALTH...GEOG INT/LAW JURID 20. PAGE 65 A1332
INT/ORG ADJUD SOVEREIGN

B45
VANCE H.L.,GUIDE TO THE LAW AND LEGAL LITERATURE OF MEXICO. LAW CONSTN FINAN LABOR FORCES ADJUD ADMIN ...CRIMLGY PHIL/SCI CON/ANAL 20 MEXIC/AMER. PAGE 158 A3217
BIBLIOG/A INT/LAW JURID CT/SYS

B46
KEETON G.W.,MAKING INTERNATIONAL LAW WORK. FUT WOR-45 NAT/G DELIB/GP FORCES LEGIT COERCE PEACE ATTIT RIGID/FLEX ORD/FREE PWR...JURID CONCPT HIST/WRIT GEN/METH LEAGUE/NAT 20. PAGE 77 A1578 — INT/ORG ADJUD INT/LAW

B46
SCANLON H.L.,INTERNATIONAL LAW: A SELECTIVE LIST OF WORKS IN ENGLISH ON PUBLIC INTERNATIONAL LAW (A PAMPHLET). CHRIST-17C EUR+WWI MOD/EUR WOR-45 CT/SYS ...JURID 20. PAGE 127 A2613 — BIBLIOG/A INT/LAW ADJUD DIPLOM

S46
DOUGLAS W.O.,"SYMPOSIUM ON WORLD ORGANIZATION." FUT USA+45 WOR+45 CONSTN SOCIETY NAT/G PLAN EDU/PROP LEGIT RIGID/FLEX KNOWL...INT/LAW JURID STERTYP TOT/POP 20. PAGE 38 A0778 — INT/ORG LAW

B47
HYDE C.C.,INTERNATIONAL LAW, CHIEFLY AS INTERPRETED AND APPLIED BY THE UNITED STATES (3 VOLS., 2ND REV. ED.). USA-45 WOR+45 WOR-45 INT/ORG CT/SYS WAR NAT/LISM PEACE ORD/FREE...JURID 19/20 TREATY. PAGE 69 A1426 — INT/LAW DIPLOM NAT/G POLICY

B47
INTERNATIONAL COURT OF JUSTICE,CHARTER OF THE UNITED NATIONS, STATUTE AND RULES OF COURT AND OTHER CONSTITUTIONAL DOCUMENTS. SWITZERLND LAW ADJUD INGP/REL...JURID 20 ICJ UN. PAGE 71 A1453 — INT/LAW INT/ORG CT/SYS DIPLOM

B48
CHAMBERLAIN L.H.,AMERICAN FOREIGN POLICY. FUT USA+45 USA-45 WOR+45 WOR-45 NAT/G LEGIS TOP/EX ECO/TAC FOR/AID EDU/PROP EXEC ATTIT ORD/FREE ...JURID TREND TOT/POP 20. PAGE 25 A0517 — CONSTN DIPLOM

B48
FENWICK C.G.,INTERNATIONAL LAW. WOR+45 WOR-45 CONSTN NAT/G LEGIT CT/SYS REGION...CONCPT LEAGUE/NAT UN 20. PAGE 45 A0916 — INT/ORG JURID INT/LAW

B48
GRIFFITH E.S.,RESEARCH IN POLITICAL SCIENCE: THE WORK OF PANELS OF RESEARCH COMMITTEE, APSA. WOR+45 WOR-45 COM/IND R+D FORCES ACT/RES WAR...GOV/COMP ANTHOL 20. PAGE 56 A1160 — BIBLIOG PHIL/SCI DIPLOM JURID

B48
JESSUP P.C.,A MODERN LAW OF NATIONS. FUT WOR+45 WOR-45 SOCIETY NAT/G DELIB/GP LEGIS BAL/PWR EDU/PROP LEGIT PWR...INT/LAW JURID TIME/SEQ LEAGUE/NAT 20. PAGE 74 A1514 — INT/ORG ADJUD

B49
KAFKA G.,FREIHEIT UND ANARCHIE. SECT COERCE DETER WAR ATTIT...IDEA/COMP 20 NATO. PAGE 75 A1545 — CONCPT ORD/FREE JURID INT/ORG

S49
KIRK G.,"MATTERIALS FOR THE STUDY OF INTERNATIONAL RELATIONS." FUT UNIV WOR+45 INTELL EDU/PROP ROUTINE PEACE ATTIT...INT/LAW JURID CONCPT OBS. PAGE 80 A1633 — INT/ORG ACT/RES DIPLOM

B50
COUNCIL BRITISH NATIONAL BIB,BRITISH NATIONAL BIBLIOGRAPHY. UK AGRI CONSTRUC PERF/ART POL/PAR SECT CREATE INT/TRADE LEAD...HUM JURID PHIL/SCI 20. PAGE 31 A0637 — BIBLIOG/A NAT/G TEC/DEV DIPLOM

B50
JIMENEZ E.,VOTING AND HANDLING OF DISPUTES IN THE SECURITY COUNCIL. WOR+45 CONSTN INT/ORG DIPLOM LEGIT DETER CHOOSE MORAL ORD/FREE PWR...JURID TIME/SEQ COLD/WAR UN 20. PAGE 74 A1517 — DELIB/GP ROUTINE

B50
MACIVER R.M.,GREAT EXPRESSIONS OF HUMAN RIGHTS. LAW CONSTN CULTURE INTELL SOCIETY R+D INT/ORG ATTIT DRIVE...JURID OBS HIST/WRIT GEN/LAWS. PAGE 92 A1891 — UNIV CONCPT

B50
MOCKFORD J.,SOUTH-WEST AFRICA AND THE INTERNATIONAL COURT (PAMPHLET). AFR GERMANY SOUTH/AFR UK ECO/UNDEV DIPLOM CONTROL DISCRIM...DECISION JURID 20 AFRICA/SW. PAGE 102 A2094 — COLONIAL SOVEREIGN INT/LAW DOMIN

B50
ROSS A.,CONSTITUTION OF THE UNITED NATIONS. CONSTN CONSULT DELIB/GP ECO/TAC...INT/LAW JURID 20 UN LEAGUE/NAT. PAGE 124 A2540 — PEACE DIPLOM ORD/FREE INT/ORG

B50
SOHN L.B.,CASES AND OTHER MATERIALS ON WORLD LAW. FUT WOR+45 LAW INT/ORG...INT/LAW JURID METH/CNCPT 20 UN. PAGE 135 A2760 — CT/SYS CONSTN

B50
STONE J.,THE PROVINCE AND FUNCTION OF LAW. UNIV WOR+45 WOR-45 CULTURE INTELL SOCIETY ECO/DEV ECO/UNDEV NAT/G LEGIT ROUTINE ATTIT PERCEPT PERSON ...JURID CONCPT GEN/LAWS GEN/METH 20. PAGE 138 A2833 — INT/ORG LAW

B51
CORBETT P.E.,LAW AND SOCIETY IN THE RELATIONS OF STATES. FUT WOR+45 WOR-45 CONTROL WAR PEACE PWR ...POLICY JURID 16/20 TREATY. PAGE 30 A0615 — INT/LAW DIPLOM INT/ORG

B51
KELSEN H.,THE LAW OF THE UNITED NATIONS. WOR+45 STRUCT RIGID/FLEX ORD/FREE...INT/LAW JURID CONCPT CON/ANAL GEN/METH UN TOT/POP VAL/FREE 20. PAGE 77 A1581 — INT/ORG ADJUD

B51
MACLAURIN J.,THE UNITED NATIONS AND POWER POLITICS. WOR+45 CONSULT EDU/PROP LEGIT ADJUD EXEC MORAL ORD/FREE...HUM JURID CONCPT RECORD TIME/SEQ UN COLD/WAR 20. PAGE 93 A1896 — INT/ORG ROUTINE

B51
MCKEON R.,DEMOCRACY IN A WORLD OF TENSION. UNIV LAW INTELL STRUCT R+D INT/ORG SCHOOL EDU/PROP LEGIT ATTIT DRIVE PERCEPT PERSON...POLICY JURID PSY SOC CONCPT METH/CNCPT OBS UNESCO TOT/POP VAL/FREE. PAGE 98 A2015 — SOCIETY ALL/VALS ORD/FREE

B51
WABEKE B.H.,A GUIDE TO DUTCH BIBLIOGRAPHIES. BELGIUM INDONESIA NETHERLAND DIPLOM INT/TRADE WAR NAT/LISM KNOWL...ART/METH HUM JURID CON/ANAL 14/20. PAGE 160 A3257 — BIBLIOG/A NAT/G CULTURE COLONIAL

L51
KELSEN H.,"RECENT TRENDS IN THE LAW OF THE UNITED NATIONS." KOREA WOR+45 CONSTN LEGIS DIPLOM LEGIT DETER WAR RIGID/FLEX HEALTH ORD/FREE RESPECT ...JURID CON/ANAL UN VAL/FREE 20 NATO. PAGE 77 A1582 — INT/ORG LAW INT/LAW

L51
LISSITZYN O.J.,"THE INTERNATIONAL COURT OF JUSTICE." WOR+45 INT/ORG LEGIT ORD/FREE...CONCPT TIME/SEQ TREND GEN/LAWS VAL/FREE 20 ICJ. PAGE 90 A1839 — ADJUD JURID INT/LAW

B52
KELSEN H.,PRINCIPLES OF INTERNATIONAL LAW. WOR+45 WOR-45 INT/ORG ORD/FREE...JURID GEN/LAWS TOT/POP 20. PAGE 77 A1583 — ADJUD CONSTN INT/LAW

S52
SCHWEBEL S.M.,"THE SECRETARY-GENERAL OF THE UN." FUT INTELL CONSULT DELIB/GP ADMIN PEACE ATTIT ...JURID MGT CONCPT TREND UN CONGRESS 20. PAGE 130 A2663 — INT/ORG TOP/EX

B53
MANSERGH N.,DOCUMENTS AND SPEECHES ON BRITISH COMMONWEALTH AFFAIRS 1931-1952. INDIA IRELAND PAKISTAN UK CONSTN POL/PAR CHIEF FORCES COLONIAL ORD/FREE SOVEREIGN...JURID 20 COMMONWLTH. PAGE 94 A1929 — BIBLIOG/A DIPLOM ECO/TAC

B53
ORFIELD L.B.,THE GROWTH OF SCANDINAVIAN LAW. DENMARK ICELAND NORWAY SWEDEN LAW DIPLOM...BIBLIOG 9/20. PAGE 112 A2296 — JURID CT/SYS NAT/G

B53
STOUT H.M.,BRITISH GOVERNMENT. UK FINAN LOC/G POL/PAR DELIB/GP DIPLOM ADMIN COLONIAL CHOOSE ORD/FREE...JURID BIBLIOG 20 COMMONWLTH. PAGE 139 A2837 — NAT/G PARL/PROC CONSTN NEW/LIB

B53
THAYER P.W.,SOUTHEAST ASIA IN THE COMING WORLD. ASIA S/ASIA USA+45 USA-45 SOCIETY INT/ORG ACT/RES ECO/TAC EDU/PROP COERCE TOTALISM ALL/VALS...JURID 20. PAGE 142 A2909 — ECO/UNDEV ATTIT FOR/AID DIPLOM

B54
BINANI G.D.,INDIA AT A GLANCE (REV. ED.). INDIA COM/IND FINAN INDUS LABOR PROVS SCHOOL PLAN DIPLOM INT/TRADE ADMIN...JURID 20. PAGE 14 A0288 — INDEX CON/ANAL NAT/G ECO/UNDEV

B54
MANGONE G.,A SHORT HISTORY OF INTERNATIONAL ORGANIZATION. MOD/EUR USA+45 USA-45 WOR+45 WOR-45 LAW LEGIS CREATE LEGIT ROUTINE RIGID/FLEX PWR ...JURID CONCPT OBS TIME/SEQ STERTYP GEN/LAWS UN TOT/POP VAL/FREE 18/20. PAGE 94 A1921 — INT/ORG INT/LAW

B54
MILLARD E.L.,FREEDOM IN A FEDERAL WORLD. FUT WOR+45 VOL/ASSN TOP/EX LEGIT ROUTINE FEDERAL PEACE ATTIT DISPL ORD/FREE PWR...MAJORIT INT/LAW JURID TREND COLD/WAR 20. PAGE 101 A2073 — INT/ORG CREATE ADJUD BAL/PWR

B54
STONE J.,LEGAL CONTROLS OF INTERNATIONAL CONFLICT: A TREATISE ON THE DYNAMICS OF DISPUTES AND WAR LAW. WOR+45 WOR-45 NAT/G DIPLOM CT/SYS SOVEREIGN...JURID CONCPT METH/CNCPT GEN/LAWS TOT/POP VAL/FREE COLD/WAR LEAGUE/NAT 20. PAGE 138 A2834 — INT/ORG LAW WAR INT/LAW

B55
BUSS C.,THE FAR EAST: A HISTORY OF RECENT AND CONTEMPORARY INTERNATIONAL RELATIONS IN EAST ASIA. WOR+45 WOR-45 CONSTN INT/ORG NAT/G BAL/PWR ATTIT PWR SOVEREIGN...GEOG JURID SOC CONCPT METH/CNCPT 19/20. PAGE 22 A0449 — ASIA DIPLOM

B55
COMM. STUDY ORGAN. PEACE,REPORTS. WOR-45 ECO/DEV ECO/UNDEV VOL/ASSN CONSULT FORCES PLAN TEC/DEV DOMIN EDU/PROP NUC/PWR ATTIT PWR WEALTH...JURID STERTYP FAO ILO 20 UN. PAGE 28 A0579 — WOR+45 INT/ORG ARMS/CONT

S55
WRIGHT Q.,"THE PEACEFUL ADJUSTMENT OF INTERNATIONAL RELATIONS: PROBLEMS AND RESEARCH APPROACHES." UNIV INTELL EDU/PROP ADJUD ROUTINE KNOWL SKILL...INT/LAW JURID PHIL/SCI CLASSIF 20. PAGE 167 A3411 — R+D METH/CNCPT PEACE

B56
FIELD G.C.,POLITICAL THEORY. POL/PAR REPRESENT MORAL SOVEREIGN...JURID IDEA/COMP. PAGE 45 A0924 — CONCPT NAT/G ORD/FREE DIPLOM

B56
GOODRICH L.,KOREA: A STUDY OF US POLICY IN THE UNITED NATIONS. ASIA USA+45 STRUCT CONSULT DELIB/GP ATTIT DRIVE PWR...JURID GEN/LAWS COLD/WAR 20 UN. PAGE 54 A1103 — INT/ORG DIPLOM KOREA

B56
HOUSTON J.A.,LATIN AMERICA IN THE UNITED NATIONS. CONSULT DIPLOM LEGIT ROUTINE ATTIT ORD/FREE PWR ...JURID OBS RECORD TIME/SEQ CHARTS 20 UN. PAGE 68 A1395 — L/A+17C INT/ORG INT/LAW REGION

B56
JESSUP P.C.,TRANSNATIONAL LAW. FUT WOR+45 JUDGE CREATE ADJUD ORD/FREE...CONCPT VAL/FREE 20. PAGE 74 A1515 — LAW JURID INT/LAW

B56
SOHN L.B.,BASIC DOCUMENTS OF THE UNITED NATIONS. WOR+45 LAW INT/ORG LEGIT EXEC ROUTINE CHOOSE PWR ...JURID CONCPT GEN/LAWS ANTHOL UN TOT/POP OAS FAO ILO 20. PAGE 135 A2761 — DELIB/GP CONSTN

B56
WEIS P.,NATIONALITY AND STATELESSNESS IN INTERNATIONAL LAW. UK WOR+45 WOR-45 LAW CONSTN NAT/G DIPLOM EDU/PROP LEGIT ROUTINE RIGID/FLEX ...JURID RECORD CMN/WLTH 20. PAGE 162 A3309 — INT/ORG SOVEREIGN INT/LAW

B57
BYRNES R.F.,BIBLIOGRAPHY OF AMERICAN PUBLICATIONS ON EAST CENTRAL EUROPE, 1945-1957 (VOL. XXII). SECT DIPLOM EDU/PROP RACE/REL...ART/METH GEOG JURID SOC LING 20 JEWS. PAGE 23 A0462 — BIBLIOG/A COM MARXISM NAT/G

B57
COMM. STUDY ORGAN. PEACE,STRENGTHENING THE UNITED NATIONS. FUT USA+45 WOR+45 CONSTN NAT/G DELIB/GP FORCES LEGIS ECO/TAC LEGIT COERCE PEACE...JURID CONCPT UN COLD/WAR 20. PAGE 28 A0580 — INT/ORG ORD/FREE

B57
DE VISSCHER C.,THEORY AND REALITY IN PUBLIC INTERNATIONAL LAW. WOR+45 WOR-45 SOCIETY NAT/G CT/SYS ATTIT MORAL ORD/FREE PWR...JURID CONCPT METH/CNCPT TIME/SEQ GEN/LAWS LEAGUE/NAT TOT/POP VAL/FREE COLD/WAR. PAGE 35 A0716 — INT/ORG LAW INT/LAW

B57
INSTITUT DE DROIT INTL,TABLEAU GENERAL DES RESOLUTIONS (1873-1956). LAW NEUTRAL CRIME WAR MARRIAGE PEACE...JURID 19/20. PAGE 70 A1442 — INT/LAW DIPLOM ORD/FREE ADJUD

B57
JENKS C.W.,THE INTERNATIONAL PROTECTION OF TRADE UNION FREEDOM. FUT WOR+45 WOR-45 VOL/ASSN DELIB/GP CT/SYS REGION ROUTINE...JURID METH/CNCPT RECORD TIME/SEQ CHARTS ILO WORK OAS 20. PAGE 73 A1504 — LABOR INT/ORG

B57
LEVONTIN A.V.,THE MYTH OF INTERNATIONAL SECURITY: A JURIDICAL AND CRITICAL ANALYSIS. FUT WOR+45 WOR-45 LAW NAT/G VOL/ASSN ACT/RES BAL/PWR ATTIT ORD/FREE ...JURID METH/CNCPT TIME/SEQ TREND STERTYP 20. PAGE 88 A1797 — INT/ORG INT/LAW SOVEREIGN MYTH

B57
ROSENNE S.,THE INTERNATIONAL COURT OF JUSTICE. WOR+45 LAW DOMIN LEGIT PEACE PWR SOVEREIGN...JURID CONCPT RECORD TIME/SEQ CON/ANAL CHARTS UN TOT/POP VAL/FREE LEAGUE/NAT 20 ICJ. PAGE 124 A2537 — INT/ORG CT/SYS INT/LAW

B57
UNESCO,A REGISTER OF LEGAL DOCUMENTATION IN THE WORLD (2ND ED.). CT/SYS...JURID IDEA/COMP METH/COMP NAT/COMP 20. PAGE 148 A3019 — BIBLIOG LAW INT/LAW CONSTN

B57
WASSENBERGH H.A.,POST-WAR INTERNATIONAL CIVIL AVIATION POLICY AND THE LAW OF THE AIR. WOR+45 AIR INT/ORG DOMIN LEGIT PEACE ORD/FREE...POLICY JURID NEW/IDEA OBS TIME/SEQ TREND CHARTS 20 TREATY. PAGE 162 A3290 — COM/IND NAT/G INT/LAW

B58
ALEXANDROWICZ,A BIBLIOGRAPHY OF INDIAN LAW. INDIA S/ASIA CONSTN CT/SYS...INT/LAW 19/20. PAGE 6 A0113 — BIBLIOG LAW ADJUD JURID

B58
BOWETT D.W.,SELF-DEFENSE IN INTERNATIONAL LAW. EUR+WWI MOD/EUR WOR+45 WOR-45 SOCIETY INT/ORG CONSULT DIPLOM LEGIT COERCE ATTIT ORD/FREE...JURID 20 UN. PAGE 17 A0353 — ADJUD CONCPT WAR INT/LAW

B58
BRIERLY J.L.,THE BASIS OF OBLIGATION IN INTERNATIONAL LAW, AND OTHER PAPERS. WOR+45 WOR-45 LEGIS...JURID CONCPT NAT/COMP ANTHOL 20. PAGE 19 A0377 — INT/LAW DIPLOM ADJUD SOVEREIGN

B58
DEUTSCHE GESCHAFT VOLKERRECHT,DIE VOLKERRECHTLICHEN DISSERTATIONEN AN DEN WESTDEUTSCHEN UNIVERSITATEN, 1945-1957. GERMANY/W NAT/G DIPLOM ADJUD CT/SYS ...POLICY 20. PAGE 37 A0748 — BIBLIOG INT/LAW ACADEM JURID

B58
HENKIN L.,ARMS CONTROL AND INSPECTION IN AMERICAN LAW. LAW CONSTN INT/ORG LOC/G MUNIC NAT/G PROVS EDU/PROP LEGIT EXEC NUC/PWR KNOWL ORD/FREE...OBS TOT/POP CONGRESS 20. PAGE 64 A1315 — USA+45 JURID ARMS/CONT

B58
JENKS C.W.,THE COMMON LAW OF MANKIND. EUR+WWI MOD/EUR SPACE WOR+45 INT/ORG BAL/PWR ARMS/CONT COERCE SUPEGO MORAL...TREND 20. PAGE 73 A1505 — JURID SOVEREIGN

B58
REUTER P.,INTERNATIONAL INSTITUTIONS. WOR+45 WOR-45 CULTURE SOCIETY VOL/ASSN LEGIT ROUTINE GP/REL INGP/REL KNOWL...JURID METH/CNCPT TIME/SEQ 20. PAGE 120 A2469 — INT/ORG PSY

B58
RUSSELL R.B.,A HISTORY OF THE UNITED NATIONS CHARTER: THE ROLE OF THE UNITED STATES. SOCIETY NAT/G CONSULT DOMIN LEGIT ATTIT ORD/FREE PWR ...POLICY JURID CONCPT UN LEAGUE/NAT. PAGE 126 A2575 — USA-45 INT/ORG CONSTN

B58
SOC OF COMP LEGIS AND INT LAW,THE LAW OF THE SEA... (PAMPHLET). WOR+45 NAT/G INT/TRADE ADJUD CONTROL NUC/PWR WAR PEACE ATTIT ORD/FREE...JURID CHARTS 20 UN TREATY RESOURCE/N. PAGE 135 A2756 — INT/LAW INT/ORG DIPLOM SEA

B58
YUAN TUNG-LI,CHINA IN WESTERN LITERATURE. SECT DIPLOM...ART/METH GEOG JURID SOC BIOG CON/ANAL. PAGE 169 A3440 — BIBLIOG ASIA CULTURE HUM

L58
INT. SOC. SCI. BULL.,"TECHNIQUES OF MEDIATION AND CONCILIATION." EUR+WWI USA+45 SOCIETY INDUS INT/ORG LABOR NAT/G LEGIS DIPLOM EDU/PROP CHOOSE ATTIT RIGID/FLEX...JURID CONCPT GEN/LAWS 20. PAGE 70 A1447 — VOL/ASSN DELIB/GP INT/LAW

S58
MCDOUGAL M.S.,"PERSPECTIVES FOR A LAW OF OUTER SPACE." FUT WOR+45 AIR CONSULT DELIB/GP TEC/DEV CT/SYS ORD/FREE...POLICY JURID 20 UN. PAGE 98 A2004 — INT/ORG SPACE INT/LAW

N58
US HOUSE COMM FOREIGN AFFAIRS,HEARINGS ON DRAFT LEGISLATION TO AMEND FURTHER THE MUTUAL SECURITY ACT OF 1954 (PAMPHLET). USA+45 CONSULT FORCES BUDGET DIPLOM DETER COST ORD/FREE...JURID 20 DEPT/DEFEN UN DEPT/STATE. PAGE 153 A3123 — LEGIS DELIB/GP CONFER WEAPON

B59
BROOKES E.H.,THE COMMONWEALTH TODAY. UK ROMAN/EMP INT/ORG RACE/REL NAT/LISM SOVEREIGN...TREND SOC/INTEG 20. PAGE 19 A0391 — FEDERAL DIPLOM JURID IDEA/COMP

B59
BUNDESMIN FUR VERTRIEBENE,ZEITTAFEL DER VORGESCHICHTE UND DES ABLAUFS DER VERTREIBUNG SOWIE DER UNTERBRINGUNG UND EINGLIEDERUNG DER (2 VOLS.). GERMANY/E GERMANY/W NAT/G PROVS PROB/SOLV DIPLOM PARL/PROC ATTIT...BIBLIOG SOC/INTEG 20 MIGRATION PARLIAMENT. PAGE 21 A0431 — JURID GP/REL INT/LAW

B59
COMM. STUDY ORGAN. PEACE,ORGANIZING PEACE IN THE NUCLEAR AGE. FUT CONSULT DELIB/GP DOMIN ADJUD ROUTINE COERCE ORD/FREE...TECHNIC INT/LAW JURID NEW/IDEA UN COLD/WAR 20. PAGE 29 A0581 — INT/ORG ACT/RES NUC/PWR

B59
CORBETT P.E.,LAW IN DIPLOMACY. UK USA+45 USSR CONSTN SOCIETY INT/ORG JUDGE LEGIT ATTIT ORD/FREE TOT/POP LEAGUE/NAT 20. PAGE 30 A0616 — NAT/G ADJUD JURID DIPLOM

B59
HALEY A.G.,FIRST COLLOQUIUM ON THE LAW OF OUTER SPACE. WOR+45 INT/ORG ACT/RES PLAN BAL/PWR CONFER ATTIT PWR...POLICY JURID CHARTS ANTHOL 20. PAGE 60 A1225 — SPACE LAW SOVEREIGN CONTROL

B59
KIRCHHEIMER O.,GEGENWARTSPROBLEME DER ASYLGEWAHRUNG. DOMIN GP/REL ATTIT...NAT/COMP 20. PAGE 79 A1630 — DIPLOM INT/LAW JURID ORD/FREE

B59
KNIERIEM A.,THE NUREMBERG TRIALS. EUR+WWI GERMANY VOL/ASSN LEAD COERCE WAR INGP/REL TOTALISM SUPEGO ORD/FREE...CONCPT METH/COMP. PAGE 80 A1651 — INT/LAW CRIME PARTIC JURID

B59
PANHUYS H.F.,THE ROLE OF NATIONALITY IN INTERNATIONAL LAW. ADJUD CRIME WAR STRANGE...JURID TREND. PAGE 114 A2330 — INT/LAW NAT/LISM INGP/REL

B59
REIFF H.,THE UNITED STATES AND THE TREATY LAW OF THE SEA. USA+45 USA-45 SEA SOCIETY INT/ORG CONSULT DELIB/GP LEGIS DIPLOM LEGIT ATTIT ORD/FREE PWR WEALTH...GEOG JURID TOT/POP 20 TREATY. PAGE 120 A2459 — ADJUD INT/LAW

B59
SCHNEIDER J.,TREATY-MAKING POWER OF INTERNATIONAL — INT/ORG

ORGANIZATIONS. FUT WOR+45 WOR-45 LAW NAT/G JUDGE DIPLOM LEGIT CT/SYS ORD/FREE PWR...INT/LAW JURID GEN/LAWS TOT/POP UNESCO 20 TREATY. PAGE 129 A2639 ROUTINE

S59
CARLSTON K.S.,"NATIONALIZATION: AN ANALYTIC APPROACH." WOR+45 INT/ORG ECO/TAC DOMIN LEGIT ADJUD COERCE ORD/FREE PWR WEALTH SOCISM...JURID CONCPT TREND STERTYP TOT/POP VAL/FREE 20. PAGE 24 A0486 INDUS NAT/G NAT/LISM SOVEREIGN

S59
LASSWELL H.D.,"UNIVERSALITY IN PERSPECTIVE." FUT UNIV SOCIETY CONSULT TOP/EX PLAN EDU/PROP ADJUD ROUTINE ARMS/CONT COERCE PEACE ATTIT PERSON ALL/VALS. PAGE 85 A1741 INT/ORG JURID TOTALISM

S59
POTTER P.B.,"OBSTACLES AND ALTERNATIVES TO INTERNATIONAL LAW." WOR+45 NAT/G VOL/ASSN DELIB/GP BAL/PWR DOMIN ROUTINE...JURID VAL/FREE 20. PAGE 117 A2400 INT/ORG LAW DIPLOM INT/LAW

S59
SOHN L.B.,"THE DEFINITION OF AGGRESSION." FUT LAW FORCES LEGIT ADJUD ROUTINE COERCE ORD/FREE PWR ...MAJORIT JURID QUANT COLD/WAR 20. PAGE 135 A2762 INT/ORG CT/SYS DETER SOVEREIGN

B60
AMERICAN ASSOCIATION LAW LIB,INDEX TO FOREIGN LEGAL PERIODICALS. WOR+45 MUNIC...IDEA/COMP 20. PAGE 7 A0139 INDEX LAW JURID DIPLOM

B60
DUMON F.,LA COMMUNAUTE FRANCO-AFRO-MALGACHE: SES ORIGINES, SES INSTITUTIONS, SON EVOLUTION. FRANCE MADAGASCAR POL/PAR DIPLOM ADMIN ATTIT...TREND T 20. PAGE 39 A0798 JURID INT/ORG AFR CONSTN

B60
HARVARD LAW SCHOOL LIBRARY,CURRENT LEGAL BIBLIOGRAPHY. USA+45 CONSTN LEGIS ADJUD CT/SYS POLICY. PAGE 62 A1279 BIBLIOG JURID LAW INT/LAW

B60
JENNINGS R.,PROGRESS OF INTERNATIONAL LAW. FUT WOR+45 WOR-45 SOCIETY NAT/G VOL/ASSN DELIB/GP DIPLOM EDU/PROP LEGIT COERCE ATTIT DRIVE MORAL ORD/FREE...JURID CONCPT OBS TIME/SEQ TREND GEN/LAWS. PAGE 74 A1509 INT/ORG LAW INT/LAW

B60
WOETZEL R.K.,THE INTERNATIONAL CONTROL OF AIRSPACE AND OUTERSPACE. FUT WOR+45 AIR CONSTN STRUCT CONSULT PLAN TEC/DEV ADJUD RIGID/FLEX KNOWL ORD/FREE PWR...TECHNIC GEOG MGT NEW/IDEA TREND COMPUT/IR VAL/FREE 20 TREATY. PAGE 166 A3375 INT/ORG JURID SPACE INT/LAW

L60
DEAN A.W.,"SECOND GENEVA CONFERENCE OF THE LAW OF THE SEA: THE FIGHT FOR FREEDOM OF THE SEAS." FUT USA+45 USSR WOR+45 WOR-45 SEA CONSTN STRUCT PLAN INT/TRADE ADJUD ADMIN ORD/FREE...DECISION RECORD TREND GEN/LAWS 20 TREATY. PAGE 35 A0717 INT/ORG JURID INT/LAW

L60
LAUTERPACHT E.,"THE UNITED NATIONS EMERGENCY FORCE." R+D LEGIT ROUTINE COERCE KNOWL ORD/FREE SKILL...JURID UN 20. PAGE 85 A1746 INT/ORG FORCES

L60
LAUTERPACHT E.,"THE SUEZ CANAL SETTLEMENT." FRANCE ISLAM ISRAEL UAR UK BAL/PWR DIPLOM LEGIT...JURID GEN/LAWS ANTHOL SUEZ VAL/FREE 20. PAGE 85 A1747 INT/ORG LAW

S60
BOGARDUS E.S.,"THE SOCIOLOGY OF A STRUCTURED PEACE." FUT SOCIETY CREATE DIPLOM EDU/PROP ADJUD ROUTINE ATTIT RIGID/FLEX KNOWL ORD/FREE RESPECT ...POLICY INT/LAW JURID NEW/IDEA SELF/OBS TOT/POP 20 UN. PAGE 16 A0327 INT/ORG SOC NAT/LISM PEACE

S60
GRACIA-MORA M.R.,"INTERNATIONAL RESPONSIBILITY FOR SUBVERSIVE ACTIVITIES AND HOSTILE PROPAGANDA BY PRIVATE PERSONS AGAINST." COM EUR+WWI L/A+17C UK USA+45 USSR WOR-45 CONSTN NAT/G LEGIT ADJUD REV PEACE TOTALISM ORD/FREE...INT/LAW 20. PAGE 55 A1119 INT/ORG JURID SOVEREIGN

S60
HAYTON R.D.,"THE ANTARCTIC SETTLEMENT OF 1959." FUT USA+45 WOR+45 WOR-45 STRUCT R+D INT/ORG EX/STRUC CREATE TEC/DEV LEGIT PEACE ATTIT SOVEREIGN ...TIME/SEQ 20 TREATY IGY. PAGE 63 A1297 DELIB/GP JURID DIPLOM REGION

S60
O'BRIEN W.,"THE ROLE OF FORCE IN THE INTERNATIONAL JURIDICAL ORDER." WOR+45 NAT/G FORCES DOMIN ADJUD ARMS/CONT DETER NUC/PWR WAR ATTIT PWR...CATH INT/LAW JURID CONCPT TREND STERTYP GEN/LAWS 20. PAGE 110 A2266 INT/ORG COERCE

S60
RHYNE C.S.,"LAW AS AN INSTRUMENT FOR PEACE." FUT WOR+45 PLAN LEGIT ROUTINE ARMS/CONT NUC/PWR ATTIT ORD/FREE...JURID METH/CNCPT TREND CON/ANAL HYPO/EXP COLD/WAR 20. PAGE 120 A2471 ADJUD EDU/PROP INT/LAW PEACE

S60
THOMPSON K.W.,"MORAL PURPOSE IN FOREIGN POLICY: REALITIES AND ILLUSIONS." WOR+45 WOR-45 LAW CULTURE SOCIETY INT/ORG PLAN ADJUD ADMIN COERCE RIGID/FLEX SUPEGO KNOWL ORD/FREE PWR...SOC TREND SOC/EXP TOT/POP 20. PAGE 143 A2930 MORAL JURID DIPLOM

S60
WRIGHT Q.,"LEGAL ASPECTS OF THE U-2 INCIDENT." COM USA+45 USSR STRUCT NAT/G FORCES PLAN TEC/DEV ADJUD RIGID/FLEX MORAL ORD/FREE...DECISION INT/LAW JURID PSY TREND GEN/LAWS COLD/WAR VAL/FREE 20 U-2. PAGE 168 A3413 PWR POLICY SPACE

C60
HAZARD J.N.,"THE SOVIET SYSTEM OF GOVERNMENT." USSR SOCIETY INDUS NAT/G POL/PAR DIPLOM CT/SYS...JURID CHARTS BIBLIOG/A 20. PAGE 63 A1298 COM NAT/COMP STRUCT ADMIN

B61
ANAND R.P.,COMPULSORY JURISDICTION OF INTERNATIONAL COURT OF JUSTICE. FUT WOR+45 SOCIETY PLAN LEGIT ADJUD ATTIT DRIVE PERSON ORD/FREE...JURID CONCPT TREND 20 ICJ. PAGE 8 A0156 INT/ORG COERCE INT/LAW

B61
JENKS C.W.,INTERNATIONAL IMMUNITIES. PLAN EDU/PROP ADMIN PERCEPT...OLD/LIB JURID CONCPT TREND TOT/POP. PAGE 74 A1506 INT/ORG DIPLOM

B61
LARSON A.,WHEN NATIONS DISAGREE. USA+45 WOR+45 INT/ORG ADJUD COERCE CRIME OWN SOVEREIGN...POLICY JURID 20. PAGE 85 A1734 INT/LAW DIPLOM WAR

B61
MCDOUGAL M.S.,LAW AND MINIMUM WORLD PUBLIC ORDER. WOR+45 SOCIETY NAT/G DELIB/GP EDU/PROP LEGIT ADJUD COERCE ATTIT PERSON...JURID CONCPT RECORD TREND TOT/POP 20. PAGE 98 A2006 INT/ORG ORD/FREE INT/LAW

B61
MECHAM J.L.,THE UNITED STATES AND INTER-AMERICAN SECURITY, 1889-1960. L/A+17C USA+45 USA-45 CONSTN FORCES INT/TRADE PEACE TOTALISM ATTIT...JURID 19/20 UN OAS. PAGE 99 A2030 DIPLOM WAR ORD/FREE INT/ORG

B61
ROBERTSON A.H.,THE LAW OF INTERNATIONAL INSTITUTIONS IN EUROPE. EUR+WWI MOD/EUR INT/ORG NAT/G VOL/ASSN DELIB/GP...JURID TIME/SEQ TOT/POP 20 TREATY. PAGE 122 A2497 RIGID/FLEX ORD/FREE

B61
SCOTT A.M.,POLITICS, USA; CASES ON THE AMERICAN DEMOCRATIC PROCESS. USA+45 CHIEF FORCES DIPLOM LOBBY CHOOSE RACE/REL FEDERAL ATTIT...JURID ANTHOL T 20 PRESIDENT CONGRESS CIVIL/LIB. PAGE 130 A2669 CT/SYS CONSTN NAT/G PLAN

B61
STONE J.,QUEST FOR SURVIVAL. WOR+45 NAT/G VOL/ASSN LEGIT ADMIN ARMS/CONT COERCE DISPL ORD/FREE PWR ...POLICY INT/LAW JURID COLD/WAR 20. PAGE 139 A2836 INT/ORG ADJUD SOVEREIGN

B61
WECHSLER H.,PRINCIPLES, POLITICS AND FUNDAMENTAL LAW: SELECTED ESSAYS. USA+45 USA-45 LAW SOCIETY NAT/G PROVS DELIB/GP EX/STRUC ACT/RES LEGIT PERSON KNOWL PWR...JURID 20 NUREMBERG. PAGE 162 A3296 CT/SYS CONSTN INT/LAW

B61
WRIGHT Q.,THE ROLE OF INTERNATIONAL LAW IN THE ELIMINATION OF WAR. FUT WOR+45 WOR-45 NAT/G BAL/PWR DIPLOM DOMIN LEGIT PWR...POLICY INT/LAW JURID CONCPT TIME/SEQ TREND GEN/LAWS COLD/WAR 20. PAGE 168 A3414 INT/ORG ADJUD ARMS/CONT

B61
YDIT M.,INTERNATIONALISED TERRITORIES. FUT WOR+45 WOR-45 CONSTN VOL/ASSN CREATE PLAN LEGIT PEACE ORD/FREE...GEOG INT/LAW JURID SOC NEW/IDEA OBS RECORD SAMP TIME/SEQ TREND 19/20 BERLIN. PAGE 169 A3431 LOC/G INT/ORG DIPLOM SOVEREIGN

L61
SAND P.T.,"AN HISTORICAL SURVEY OF INTERNATIONAL AIR LAW SINCE 1944." USA+45 USA-45 WOR+45 WOR-45 SOCIETY ECO/DEV NAT/G CONSULT EX/STRUC ACT/RES PLAN LEGIT ROUTINE...JURID CONCPT METH/CNCPT TREND 20. PAGE 127 A2598 INT/ORG LAW INT/LAW SPACE

L61
TAUBENFELD H.J.,"A REGIME FOR OUTER SPACE." FUT UNIV R+D ACT/RES PLAN BAL/PWR LEGIT ARMS/CONT ORD/FREE...POLICY JURID TREND UN TOT/POP 20 COLD/WAR. PAGE 142 A2894 INT/ORG ADJUD SPACE

S61
CASTANEDA J.,"THE UNDERDEVELOPED NATIONS AND THE DEVELOPMENT OF INTERNATIONAL LAW." FUT UNIV LAW ACT/RES FOR/AID LEGIT PERCEPT SKILL...JURID METH/CNCPT TIME/SEQ TOT/POP 20 UN. PAGE 25 A0507 INT/ORG ECO/UNDEV PEACE INT/LAW

S61
HAZARD J.N.,"CODIFYING PEACEFUL COEXISTANCE." FUT INTELL INT/ORG TEC/DEV PEACE HEALTH...INT/LAW CONT/OBS 20. PAGE 63 A1299 VOL/ASSN JURID

S61
LIPSON L.,"AN ARGUMENT ON THE LEGALITY OF RECONNAISSANCE STATELLITES." COM USA+45 USSR WOR+45 AIR INTELL NAT/G CONSULT PLAN DIPLOM LEGIT ROUTINE ATTIT...INT/LAW JURID CONCPT METH/CNCPT TREND COLD/WAR 20. PAGE 90 A1833 INT/ORG LAW SPACE

S61
MILLER E.,"LEGAL ASPECTS OF UN ACTION IN THE CONGO." AFR CULTURE ADMIN PEACE DRIVE RIGID/FLEX INT/ORG LEGIT

ORD/FREE...WELF/ST JURID OBS UN CONGO 20. PAGE 101 A2076

B62
ALEXANDROWICZ C.H.,WORLD ECONOMIC AGENCIES: LAW AND PRACTICE. WOR+45 DIST/IND FINAN LABOR CONSULT INT/TRADE TARIFFS REPRESENT HEALTH...JURID 20 UN GATT EEC OAS ECSC. PAGE 6 A0115
INT/LAW INT/ORG DIPLOM ADJUD

B62
AMERICAN LAW INSTITUTE,FOREIGN RELATIONS LAW OF THE UNITED STATES: RESTATEMENT, SECOND. USA+45 NAT/G LEGIS ADJUD EXEC ROUTINE GOV/REL...INT/LAW JURID CONCPT 20 TREATY. PAGE 7 A0152
PROF/ORG LAW DIPLOM ORD/FREE

B62
BIBLIOTHEQUE PALAIS DE LA PAIX,CATALOGUE OF THE PEACE PALACE LIBRARY, SUPPLEMENT 1937-1952 (7 VOLS.). WOR+45 WOR-45 INT/ORG NAT/G ADJUD WAR PEACE ...JURID 20. PAGE 14 A0285
BIBLIOG INT/LAW DIPLOM

B62
BLAUSTEIN A.P.,MANUAL ON FOREIGN LEGAL PERIODICALS AND THEIR INDEX. WOR+45 DIPLOM 20. PAGE 15 A0310
BIBLIOG INDEX LAW JURID

B62
CARLSTON K.S.,LAW AND ORGANIZATION IN WORLD SOCIETY. WOR+45 FINAN ECO/TAC DOMIN LEGIT CT/SYS ROUTINE COERCE ORD/FREE PWR WEALTH...PLURIST DECISION JURID MGT METH/CNCPT GEN/LAWS 20. PAGE 24 A0487
INT/ORG LAW

B62
COLOMBOS C.J.,THE INTERNATIONAL LAW OF THE SEA. WOR+45 EXTR/IND DIPLOM INT/TRADE TARIFFS AGREE WAR ...TIME/SEQ 20 TREATY. PAGE 28 A0570
INT/LAW SEA JURID ADJUD

B62
DOUGLAS W.O.,DEMOCRACY'S MANIFESTO. COM USA+45 ECO/UNDEV INT/ORG FORCES PLAN NEUTRAL TASK MARXISM ...JURID 20 NATO SEATO. PAGE 38 A0779
DIPLOM POLICY NAT/G ORD/FREE

B62
KING G.,THE UNITED NATIONS IN THE CONGO: A QUEST FOR PEACE. WOR+45 NAT/G CONSULT FORCES LEGIT COERCE WAR ORD/FREE...JURID METH/CNCPT OBS INT HIST/WRIT TIME/SEQ CONGO UN 20 COLD/WAR. PAGE 79 A1624
AFR INT/ORG

B62
LAWSON R.,INTERNATIONAL REGIONAL ORGANIZATIONS. WOR+45 NAT/G VOL/ASSN CONSULT LEGIS EDU/PROP LEGIT ADMIN EXEC ROUTINE HEALTH PWR WEALTH...JURID EEC COLD/WAR 20 UN. PAGE 86 A1752
INT/ORG DELIB/GP REGION

B62
LILLICH R.B.,INTERNATIONAL CLAIMS: THEIR ADJUDICATION BY NATIONAL COMMISSIONS. WOR+45 WOR-45 INT/ORG LEGIT CT/SYS TOT/POP 20. PAGE 89 A1816
ADJUD JURID INT/LAW

B62
MCDOUGAL M.S.,THE PUBLIC ORDER OF THE OCEANS. WOR+45 WOR-45 SEA INT/ORG NAT/G CONSULT DELIB/GP DIPLOM LEGIT PEACE RIGID/FLEX...GEOG INT/LAW JURID RECORD TOT/POP 20 TREATY. PAGE 98 A2007
ADJUD ORD/FREE

B62
ROSENNE S.,THE WORLD COURT: WHAT IT IS AND HOW IT WORKS. WOR+45 WOR-45 LAW CONSTN JUDGE EDU/PROP LEGIT ROUTINE CHOOSE PEACE ORD/FREE...JURID OBS TIME/SEQ CHARTS UN TOT/POP VAL/FREE 20. PAGE 124 A2538
INT/ORG ADJUD INT/LAW

B62
SCHWARZENBERGER G.,THE FRONTIERS OF INTERNATIONAL LAW. WOR+45 WOR-45 NAT/G LEGIT CT/SYS ROUTINE MORAL ORD/FREE PWR...JURID SOC GEN/METH 20 COLD/WAR. PAGE 130 A2661
INT/ORG LAW INT/LAW

B62
TRISKA J.F.,THE THEORY, LAW, AND POLICY OF SOVIET TREATIES. WOR+45 WOR-45 CONSTN INT/ORG NAT/G VOL/ASSN DOMIN LEGIT COERCE ATTIT PWR RESPECT ...POLICY JURID CONCPT OBS SAMP TIME/SEQ TREND GEN/LAWS 20. PAGE 145 A2966
COM LAW INT/LAW USSR

B62
US SENATE COMM ON JUDICIARY,CONSTITUTIONAL RIGHTS OF MILITARY PERSONNEL. USA+45 USA-45 FORCES DIPLOM WAR CONGRESS. PAGE 157 A3193
CONSTN ORD/FREE JURID CT/SYS

B62
WOETZEL R.K.,THE NURENBERG TRIALS IN INTERNATIONAL LAW. CHRIST-17C MOD/EUR WOR+45 SOCIETY NAT/G DELIB/GP DOMIN LEGIT ROUTINE ATTIT DRIVE PERSON SUPEGO MORAL ORD/FREE...POLICY MAJORIT JURID PSY SOC SELF/OBS RECORD NAZI TOT/POP. PAGE 166 A3376
INT/ORG ADJUD WAR

B62
YALEN R.,REGIONALISM AND WORLD ORDER. EUR+WWI WOR+45 WOR-45 INT/ORG VOL/ASSN DELIB/GP FORCES TOP/EX BAL/PWR DIPLOM DOMIN REGION ARMS/CONT PWR ...JURID HYPO/EXP COLD/WAR 20. PAGE 168 A3427
ORD/FREE POLICY

L62
NIZARD L.,"CUBAN QUESTION AND SECURITY COUNCIL." L/A+17C USA+45 ECO/UNDEV NAT/G POL/PAR DELIB/GP ECO/TAC PWR...RELATIV OBS TIME/SEQ TREND GEN/LAWS UN 20 UN. PAGE 109 A2242
INT/ORG JURID DIPLOM CUBA

L62
STEIN E.,"MR HAMMARSKJOLD, THE CHARTER LAW AND THE FUTURE ROLE OF THE UNITED NATIONS SECRETARY-GENERAL." WOR+45 CONSTN INT/ORG DELIB/GP FORCES TOP/EX BAL/PWR LEGIT ROUTINE RIGID/FLEX PWR ...POLICY JURID OBS STERTYP UN COLD/WAR 20 HAMMARSK/D. PAGE 137 A2815
CONCPT BIOG

S62
BIERZANECK R.,"LA NON-RECONAISSANCE ET LE DROIT INTERNATIONAL CONTEMPORAIN." EUR+WWI FUT WOR+45 LAW ECO/DEV ATTIT RIGID/FLEX...CONCPT TIME/SEQ TOT/POP 20. PAGE 14 A0286
EDU/PROP JURID DIPLOM INT/LAW

S62
CRANE R.D.,"LAW AND STRATEGY IN SPACE." FUT USA+45 WOR+45 AIR LAW INT/ORG NAT/G FORCES ACT/RES PLAN BAL/PWR LEGIT ARMS/CONT COERCE ORD/FREE...POLICY INT/LAW JURID SOC/EXP 20 TREATY. PAGE 32 A0656
CONCPT SPACE

S62
CRANE R.D.,"SOVIET ATTITUDE TOWARD INTERNATIONAL SPACE LAW." COM FUT USA+45 USSR AIR CONSTN DELIB/GP DOMIN PWR...JURID TREND TOT/POP 20. PAGE 32 A0657
LAW ATTIT INT/LAW SPACE

S62
FALK R.A.,"THE REALITY OF INTERNATIONAL LAW." WOR+45 NAT/G LEGIT COERCE DETER WAR MORAL ORD/FREE PWR SOVEREIGN...JURID CONCPT VAL/FREE COLD/WAR 20. PAGE 43 A0887
INT/ORG ADJUD NUC/PWR INT/LAW

S62
GRAVEN J.,"LE MOUVEAU DROIT PENAL INTERNATIONAL." UNIV STRUCT LEGIS ACT/RES CRIME ATTIT PERCEPT PERSON...JURID CONCPT 20. PAGE 55 A1132
CT/SYS PUB/INST INT/ORG INT/LAW

S62
GREEN L.C.,"POLITICAL OFFENSES, WAR CRIMES AND EXTRADITION." WOR+45 YUGOSLAVIA INT/ORG LEGIT ROUTINE WAR ORD/FREE SOVEREIGN...JURID NAZI 20 INTERPOL. PAGE 55 A1138
LAW CONCPT INT/LAW

S62
GREENSPAN M.,"INTERNATIONAL LAW AND ITS PROTECTION FOR PARTICIPANTS IN UNCONVENTIONAL WARFARE." WOR+45 LAW INT/ORG NAT/G POL/PAR COERCE REV ORD/FREE ...INT/LAW TOT/POP 20. PAGE 56 A1143
FORCES JURID GUERRILLA WAR

S62
JOHNSON O.H.,"THE ENGLISH TRADITION IN INTERNATIONAL LAW." CHRIST-17C MOD/EUR EDU/PROP LEGIT CT/SYS ORD/FREE...JURID CONCPT TIME/SEQ. PAGE 75 A1526
LAW INT/LAW UK

S62
LISSITZYN O.J.,"SOME LEGAL IMPLICATIONS OF THE U-2 AND RB-47 INCIDENTS." FUT USA+45 USSR WOR+45 AIR NAT/G DIPLOM LEGIT MORAL ORD/FREE SOVEREIGN...JURID GEN/LAWS GEN/METH COLD/WAR 20 U-2. PAGE 90 A1840
LAW CONCPT SPACE INT/LAW

S62
MANGIN G.,"LES ACCORDS DE COOPERATION EN MATIERE DE JUSTICE ENTRE LA FRANCE ET LES ETATS AFRICAINS ET MALGACHE." AFR ISLAM WOR+45 STRUCT ECO/UNDEV NAT/G DELIB/GP PERCEPT ALL/VALS...JURID MGT TIME/SEQ 20. PAGE 94 A1919
INT/ORG LAW FRANCE

S62
MONNIER J.P.,"LA SUCCESSION D'ETATS EN MATIERE DE RESPONSABILITE INTERNATIONALE." UNIV CONSTN INTELL SOCIETY ADJUD ROUTINE PERCEPT SUPEGO...GEN/LAWS TOT/POP 20. PAGE 103 A2107
NAT/G JURID INT/LAW

S62
MOUSKHELY M.,"LA NAISSANCE DES ETATS EN DROIT INTERNATIONAL PUBLIC." UNIV SOCIETY INT/ORG VOL/ASSN LEGIT ATTIT RIGID/FLEX...JURID TIME/SEQ 20. PAGE 105 A2157
NAT/G STRUCT INT/LAW

S62
PIQUEMAL M.,"LA COOPERATION FINANCIERE ENTRE LA FRANCE ET LES ETATS AFRICAINS ET MALGACHE." ISLAM INT/ORG TOP/EX ECO/TAC...JURID CHARTS 20. PAGE 116 A2383
AFR FINAN FRANCE MADAGASCAR

S62
SCHACHTER O.,"DAG HAMMARSKJOLD AND THE RELATION OF LAW TO POLITICS." FUT WOR+45 INT/ORG CONSULT PLAN TEC/DEV BAL/PWR DIPLOM LEGIT ATTIT PERCEPT ORD/FREE ...POLICY JURID CONCPT OBS TESTS STERTYP GEN/LAWS 20 HAMMARSK/D. PAGE 128 A2616
ACT/RES ADJUD

S62
THOMPSON D.,"THE UNITED KINGDOM AND THE TREATY OF ROME." EUR+WWI INT/ORG NAT/G DELIB/GP LEGIS INT/TRADE RIGID/FLEX...CONCPT EEC PARLIAMENT CMN/WLTH 20. PAGE 143 A2925
ADJUD JURID

S62
VIGNES D.,"L'AUTORITE DES TRAITES INTERNATIONAUX EN DROIT INTERNE." EUR+WWI UNIV LAW CONSTN INTELL NAT/G POL/PAR DIPLOM ATTIT PERCEPT ALL/VALS ...POLICY INT/LAW JURID CONCPT TIME/SEQ 20 TREATY. PAGE 159 A3233
STRUCT LEGIT FRANCE

C62
LILLICH R.B.,"INTERNATIONAL CLAIMS: THEIR ADJUDICATION BY NATIONAL COMMISSIONS." WOR+45 WOR-45 NAT/G ADJUD...JURID BIBLIOG 18/20. PAGE 89 A1817
INT/LAW DIPLOM PROB/SOLV

B63
BOWETT D.W.,THE LAW OF INTERNATIONAL INSTITUTIONS. WOR+45 WOR-45 CONSTN DELIB/GP EX/STRUC JUDGE EDU/PROP LEGIT CT/SYS EXEC ROUTINE RIGID/FLEX ORD/FREE PWR...JURID CONCPT ORG/CHARTS GEN/METH LEAGUE/NAT OAS OEEC 20 UN. PAGE 17 A0354
INT/ORG ADJUD DIPLOM

B63
DECOTTIGNIES R.,LES NATIONALITES AFRICAINES. AFR NAT/G PROB/SOLV DIPLOM COLONIAL ORD/FREE...CHARTS GOV/COMP 20. PAGE 35 A0721
NAT/LISM JURID LEGIS LAW

B63
ELLERT R.B.,NATO 'FAIR TRIAL' SAFEGUARDS: PRECURSOR TO AN INTERNATIONAL BILL OF PROCEDURAL RIGHTS. WOR+45 FORCES CRIME CIVMIL/REL ATTIT ORD/FREE 20 NATO. PAGE 41 A0841
JURID INT/LAW INT/ORG CT/SYS

B63
FALK R.A.,LAW, MORALITY, AND WAR IN THE CONTEMPORARY WORLD. WOR+45 LAW INT/ORG EX/STRUC FORCES EDU/PROP LEGIT DETER NUC/PWR MORAL ORD/FREE ...JURID TOT/POP 20. PAGE 43 A0888
ADJUD ARMS/CONT PEACE INT/LAW

B63
HALEY A.G.,SPACE LAW AND GOVERNMENT. FUT USA+45 WOR+45 LEGIS ACT/RES CREATE ATTIT RIGID/FLEX ORD/FREE PWR SOVEREIGN...POLICY JURID CONCPT CHARTS VAL/FREE 20. PAGE 60 A1226
INT/ORG LAW SPACE

B63
LANOUE G.R.,A BIBLIOGRAPHY OF DOCTORAL DISSERTATIONS ON POLITICS AND RELIGION. USA+45 USA-45 CONSTN PROVS DIPLOM CT/SYS MORAL...POLICY JURID CONCPT 20. PAGE 84 A1728
BIBLIOG NAT/G LOC/G SECT

B63
MCDOUGAL M.S.,LAW AND PUBLIC ORDER IN SPACE. FUT USA+45 ACT/RES TEC/DEV ADJUD...POLICY INT/LAW JURID 20. PAGE 98 A2009
SPACE ORD/FREE DIPLOM DECISION

B63
PATRA A.C.,THE ADMINISTRATION OF JUSTICE UNDER THE EAST INDIA COMPANY IN BENGAL, BIHAR AND ORISSA. INDIA UK LG/CO CAP/ISM INT/TRADE ADJUD COLONIAL CONTROL CT/SYS...POLICY 20. PAGE 114 A2341
ADMIN JURID CONCPT

B63
PEREZ ORTIZ R.,ANUARIO BIBLIOGRAFICO COLOMBIANO, 1961. AGRI...INT/LAW JURID SOC LING 20 COLOMB. PAGE 115 A2354
BIBLIOG L/A+17C NAT/G

B63
RAVENS J.P.,STAAT UND KATHOLISCHE KIRCHE IN PREUSSENS POLNISCHEN TEILUNGSGEBIETEN. GERMANY POLAND PRUSSIA PROVS DIPLOM EDU/PROP DEBATE NAT/LISM...JURID 18 CHURCH/STA. PAGE 119 A2451
GP/REL CATHISM SECT NAT/G

B63
ROBERTSON A.H.,HUMAN RIGHTS IN EUROPE. CONSTN SOCIETY INT/ORG NAT/G VOL/ASSN DELIB/GP ACT/RES PLAN ADJUD REGION ROUTINE ATTIT LOVE ORD/FREE RESPECT...JURID SOC CONCPT SOC/EXP UN 20. PAGE 122 A2498
EUR+WWI PERSON

B63
ROSNER G.,THE UNITED NATIONS EMERGENCY FORCE. FRANCE ISRAEL UAR UK WOR+45 CREATE WAR PEACE ORD/FREE PWR...INT/LAW JURID HIST/WRIT TIME/SEQ UN. PAGE 124 A2539
INT/ORG FORCES

L63
SZASZY E.,"L'EVOLUTION DES PRINCIPES GENERAUX DU DROIT INTERNATIONAL PRIVE DANS LES PAYS DE DEMOCRATIE POPULAIRE." COM FUT WOR+45 LAW ECO/DEV PERF/ART POL/PAR PROF/ORG ECO/TAC INT/TRADE EDU/PROP ATTIT RIGID/FLEX ALL/VALS SOCISM...JURID TREND GEN/LAWS WORK 20. PAGE 141 A2876
DIPLOM TOTALISM INT/LAW INT/ORG

S63
ALGER C.F.,"HYPOTHESES ON RELATIONSHIPS BETWEEN THE ORGANIZATION OF INTERNATIONAL SOCIETY AND INTERNATIONAL ORDER." WOR+45 WOR-45 ORD/FREE PWR ...JURID GEN/LAWS VAL/FREE 20. PAGE 6 A0119
INT/ORG LAW

S63
CAHIER P.,"LE DROIT INTERNE DES ORGANISATIONS INTERNATIONALES." UNIV CONSTN SOCIETY ECO/DEV R+D NAT/G TOP/EX LEGIT ATTIT PERCEPT...TIME/SEQ 19/20. PAGE 23 A0464
INT/ORG JURID DIPLOM INT/LAW

S63
FRIEDMANN W.G.,"THE USES OF 'GENERAL PRINCIPLES' IN THE DEVELOPMENT OF INTERNATIONAL LAW." WOR+45 NAT/G DIPLOM INT/TRADE LEGIT ROUTINE RIGID/FLEX ORD/FREE ...JURID CONCPT STERTYP GEN/METH 20. PAGE 49 A1005
LAW INT/LAW INT/ORG

S63
GIRAUD E.,"L'INTERDICTION DU RECOURS A LA FORCE, LA THEORIE ET LA PRATIQUE DES NATIONS UNIES." ALGERIA COM CUBA HUNGARY WOR+45 ADJUD TOTALISM ATTIT RIGID/FLEX PWR...POLICY JURID CONCPT UN 20 CONGO. PAGE 53 A1077
INT/ORG FORCES DIPLOM

S63
MCDOUGAL M.S.,"THE SOVIET-CUBAN QUARANTINE AND SELF-DEFENSE." CUBA USA+45 USSR WOR+45 INT/ORG NAT/G BAL/PWR NUC/PWR ATTIT...JURID CONCPT. PAGE 98 A2008
ORD/FREE LEGIT SOVEREIGN

S63
MEYROWITZ H.,"LES JURISTES DEVANT L'ARME NUCLAIRE." FUT WOR+45 INTELL SOCIETY BAL/PWR DETER WAR...JURID CONCPT 20. PAGE 100 A2058
ACT/RES ADJUD INT/LAW NUC/PWR

S63
TALLON D.,"L'ETUDE DU DROIT COMPARE COMME MOYEN DE RECHERCHER LES MATIERES SUSCEPTIBLES D'UNIFICATION INTERNATIONALE." WOR+45 LAW SOCIETY VOL/ASSN CONSULT LEGIT CT/SYS RIGID/FLEX KNOWL 20. PAGE 141 A2884
INT/ORG JURID INT/LAW

S63
WEISSBERG G.,"MAPS AS EVIDENCE IN INTERNATIONAL BOUNDARY DISPUTES: A REAPPRAISAL." CHINA/COM EUR+WWI INDIA MOD/EUR S/ASIA INT/ORG NAT/G LEGIT PERCEPT...JURID CHARTS 20. PAGE 163 A3311
LAW GEOG SOVEREIGN

S63
WENGLER W.,"LES CONFLITS DE LOIS ET LE PRINCIPE D'EGALITE." UNIV LAW SOCIETY ACT/RES LEGIT ATTIT PERCEPT 20. PAGE 163 A3318
JURID CONCPT INT/LAW

S63
WYZNER E.,"NIEKTORE ASPEKTY PRAWNE FINANSOWANIA OPERACJI ONZ W KONGO I NA BEIZKIM WSCHODZIE." S/ASIA CONSTN FINAN INT/ORG TOP/EX...TIME/SEQ UN 20 CONGRESS. PAGE 168 A3426
FORCES JURID DIPLOM

B64
BARKER A.J.,SUEZ: THE SEVEN DAY WAR. EUR+WWI ISLAM UAR INT/ORG NAT/G PLAN DIPLOM ECO/TAC DOMIN NAT/LISM DRIVE RIGID/FLEX PWR SOVEREIGN...POLICY JURID TREND CHARTS SUEZ UN 20. PAGE 11 A0221
FORCES COERCE UK

B64
COHEN M.,LAW AND POLITICS IN SPACE: SPECIFIC AND URGENT PROBLEMS IN THE LAW OF OUTER SPACE. CHINA/COM COM USA+45 USSR WOR+45 COM/IND INT/ORG NAT/G LEGIT NUC/PWR ATTIT BIO/SOC...JURID CONCPT CONGRESS 20 STALIN/J. PAGE 28 A0561
DELIB/GP LAW INT/LAW SPACE

B64
COHEN M.L.,SELECTED BIBLIOGRAPHY OF FOREIGN AND INTERNATIONAL LAW....IDEA/COMP METH/COMP 20. PAGE 28 A0562
BIBLIOG/A JURID LAW INT/LAW

B64
DIAS R.W.M.,A BIBLIOGRAPHY OF JURISPRUDENCE (2ND ED.). VOL/ASSN LEGIS ADJUD CT/SYS OWN...INT/LAW 18/20. PAGE 37 A0754
BIBLIOG/A JURID LAW CONCPT

B64
ECONOMIDES C.P.,LE POUVOIR DE DECISION DES ORGANISATIONS INTERNATIONALES EUROPEENNES. DIPLOM DOMIN INGP/REL EFFICIENCY...INT/LAW JURID 20 NATO OEEC EEC COUNCL/EUR EURATOM. PAGE 40 A0821
INT/ORG PWR DECISION GP/COMP

B64
FALK R.A.,THE ROLE OF DOMESTIC COURTS IN THE INTERNATIONAL LEGAL ORDER. FUT WOR+45 INT/ORG NAT/G JUDGE EDU/PROP LEGIT CT/SYS...POLICY RELATIV JURID CONCPT GEN/LAWS 20. PAGE 43 A0889
LAW INT/LAW

B64
FRIEDMANN W.G.,THE CHANGING STRUCTURE OF INTERNATIONAL LAW. WOR+45 INT/ORG NAT/G PROVS LEGIT ORD/FREE PWR...JURID CONCPT GEN/LAWS TOT/POP UN 20. PAGE 49 A1006
ADJUD TREND INT/LAW

B64
GESELLSCHAFT RECHTSVERGLEICH,BIBLIOGRAPHIE DES DEUTSCHEN RECHTS (BIBLIOGRAPHY OF GERMAN LAW, TRANS. BY COURTLAND PETERSON). GERMANY FINAN INDUS LABOR SECT FORCES CT/SYS PARL/PROC CRIME...INT/LAW SOC NAT/COMP 20. PAGE 52 A1066
BIBLIOG/A JURID CONSTN ADMIN

B64
GJUPANOVIC H.,LEGAL SOURCES AND BIBLIOGRAPHY OF YUGOSLAVIA. COM YUGOSLAVIA LAW LEGIS DIPLOM ADMIN PARL/PROC REGION CRIME CENTRAL 20. PAGE 53 A1078
BIBLIOG/A JURID CONSTN ADJUD

B64
HARMON R.B.,BIBLIOGRAPHY OF BIBLIOGRAPHIES IN POLITICAL SCIENCE (MIMEOGRAPHED PAPER: LIMITED EDITION). WOR+45 WOR-45 INT/ORG POL/PAR GOV/REL ALL/IDEOS...INT/LAW JURID MGT 19/20. PAGE 61 A1260
BIBLIOG NAT/G DIPLOM LOC/G

B64
KIS T.I.,LES PAYS DE L'EUROPE DE L'EST: LEURS RAPPORTS MUTUELS ET LE PROBLEME DE LEUR INTEGRATION DANS L'ORBITE DE L'USSR. EUR+WWI RUSSIA USSR INT/ORG NAT/G REV ATTIT...JURID SOC BIBLIOG WARSAW/P COMECON EUROPE/E. PAGE 80 A1638
DIPLOM COM MARXISM REGION

B64
MCWHINNEY E.,"PEACEFUL COEXISTENCE" AND SOVIET-WESTERN INTERNATIONAL LAW. USSR DIPLOM LEAD...JURID 20 COLD/WAR. PAGE 99 A2027
PEACE IDEA/COMP INT/LAW ATTIT

B64
NICE R.W.,TREASURY OF LAW. WOR+45 WOR-45 SECT ADJUD MORAL ORD/FREE...INT/LAW JURID PHIL/SCI ANTHOL. PAGE 108 A2227
LAW WRITING PERS/REL DIPLOM

B64
RAGHAVAN M.D.,INDIA IN CEYLONESE HISTORY, SOCIETY AND CULTURE. CEYLON INDIA S/ASIA LAW SOCIETY INT/TRADE ATTIT...ART/METH JURID SOC LING 20. PAGE 119 A2433
DIPLOM CULTURE SECT STRUCT

B64
SZLADITS C.,BIBLIOGRAPHY ON FOREIGN AND COMPARATIVE LAW: BOOKS AND ARTICLES IN ENGLISH (SUPPLEMENT 1962). FINAN INDUS JUDGE LICENSE ADMIN CT/SYS PARL/PROC OWN...INT/LAW CLASSIF METH/COMP NAT/COMP 20. PAGE 141 A2877
BIBLIOG/A JURID ADJUD LAW

B64
US HOUSE COMM ON JUDICIARY,IMMIGRATION HEARINGS. DELIB/GP STRANGE HABITAT...GEOG JURID 20 CONGRESS MIGRATION. PAGE 154 A3140
NAT/G POLICY DIPLOM NAT/LISM

B64
VECCHIO G.D.,L'ETAT ET LE DROIT. ITALY CONSTN EX/STRUC LEGIS DIPLOM CT/SYS...JURID 20 UN. PAGE 158 A3225
NAT/G SOVEREIGN CONCPT INT/LAW

B64
WAINHOUSE D.W.,REMNANTS OF EMPIRE: THE UNITED NATIONS AND THE END OF COLONIALISM. FUT PORTUGAL WOR+45 NAT/G CONSULT DOMIN LEGIT ADMIN ROUTINE ATTIT ORD/FREE...POLICY JURID RECORD INT TIME/SEQ UN CMN/WLTH 20. PAGE 160 A3260
INT/ORG TREND COLONIAL

L64
BARROS J.,"THE GREEK-BULGARIAN INCIDENT OF 1925: THE LEAGUE OF NATIONS AND THE GREAT POWERS." BULGARIA EUR+WWI NAT/G FORCES ECO/TAC EDU/PROP LEGIT ROUTINE COERCE WAR PEACE DRIVE PWR...JURID CONCPT METH/CNCPT GEN/LAWS GEN/METH LEAGUE/NAT TOT/POP 20. PAGE 11 A0228
INT/ORG ORD/FREE DIPLOM

L64
WORLD PEACE FOUNDATION,"INTERNATIONAL ORGANIZATIONS: SUMMARY OF ACTIVITIES." INDIA PAKISTAN TURKEY WOR+45 CONSTN CONSULT EX/STRUC ECO/TAC EDU/PROP LEGIT ORD/FREE...JURID SOC UN 20 CYPRESS. PAGE 167 A3397
INT/ORG ROUTINE

S64
BARKUN M.,"CONFLICT RESOLUTION THROUGH IMPLICIT MEDIATION." UNIV BARGAIN CONSEN FEDERAL JURID. PAGE 11 A0222
CONSULT CENTRAL INT/LAW IDEA/COMP

S64
COHEN M.,"BASIC PRINCIPLES OF INTERNATIONAL LAW." UNIV WOR+45 WOR-45 BAL/PWR LEGIT ADJUD WAR ATTIT MORAL ORD/FREE PWR...JURID CONCPT MYTH TOT/POP 20. PAGE 27 A0560
INT/ORG INT/LAW

S64
GINSBURGS G.,"WARS OF NATIONAL LIBERATION - THE SOVIET THESIS." COM USSR WOR+45 WOR-45 LAW CULTURE INT/ORG DIPLOM LEGIT COLONIAL GUERRILLA WAR NAT/LISM ATTIT PERSON MORAL PWR...JURID OBS TREND MARX/KARL 20. PAGE 53 A1075
COERCE CONCPT INT/LAW REV

S64
GREENBERG S.,"JUDAISM AND WORLD JUSTICE." MEDIT-7 WOR+45 LAW CULTURE SOCIETY INT/ORG NAT/G FORCES EDU/PROP ATTIT DRIVE PERSON SUPEGO ALL/VALS ...POLICY PSY CONCPT GEN/LAWS JEWS. PAGE 55 A1140
SECT JURID PEACE

S64
HICKEY D.,"THE PHILOSOPHICAL ARGUMENT FOR WORLD GOVERNMENT." WOR+45 SOCIETY ACT/RES PLAN LEGIT ADJUD PEACE PERCEPT PERSON ORD/FREE...HUM JURID PHIL/SCI METH/CNCPT CON/ANAL STERTYP GEN/LAWS TOT/POP 20. PAGE 65 A1327
FUT INT/ORG

S64
KARPOV P.V.,"PEACEFUL COEXISTENCE AND INTERNATIONAL LAW." WOR+45 LAW SOCIETY INT/ORG VOL/ASSN FORCES CREATE CAP/ISM DIPLOM ADJUD NUC/PWR PEACE MORAL ORD/FREE PWR MARXISM...MARXIST JURID CONCPT OBS TREND COLD/WAR MARX/KARL 20. PAGE 77 A1568
COM ATTIT INT/LAW USSR

S64
KUNZ J.,"THE CHANGING SCIENCE OF INTERNATIONAL LAW." FUT WOR+45 WOR-45 INT/ORG LEGIT ORD/FREE ...JURID TIME/SEQ GEN/LAWS 20. PAGE 83 A1696
ADJUD CONCPT INT/LAW

S64
LIPSON L.,"PEACEFUL COEXISTENCE." COM USSR WOR+45 LAW INT/ORG DIPLOM LEGIT ADJUD ORD/FREE...CONCPT OBS TREND GEN/LAWS VAL/FREE COLD/WAR 20. PAGE 90 A1834
ATTIT JURID INT/LAW PEACE

S64
MAGGS P.B.,"SOVIET VIEWPOINT ON NUCLEAR WEAPONS IN INTERNATIONAL LAW." USSR WOR+45 INT/ORG FORCES DIPLOM ARMS/CONT ATTIT ORD/FREE PWR...POLICY JURID CONCPT OBS TREND CON/ANAL GEN/LAWS VAL/FREE 20. PAGE 93 A1905
COM LAW INT/LAW NUC/PWR

S64
SKUBISZEWSKI K.,"FORMS OF PARTICIPATION OF INTERNATIONAL ORGANIZATION IN THE LAW MAKING PROCESS." FUT WOR+45 NAT/G DELIB/GP DOMIN LEGIT KNOWL PWR...JURID TREND 20. PAGE 134 A2740
INT/ORG LAW INT/LAW

S64
TRISKA J.F.,"SOVIET TREATY LAW: A QUANTITATIVE ANALYSIS." WOR+45 LAW ECO/UNDEV AGRI COM/IND INDUS CREATE TEC/DEV DIPLOM ATTIT PWR WEALTH...JURID SAMP TIME/SEQ TREND CHARTS VAL/FREE 20 TREATY. PAGE 145 A2967
COM ECO/TAC INT/LAW USSR

B65
COWEN Z.,THE BRITISH COMMONWEALTH OF NATIONS IN A CHANGING WORLD. UK ECO/UNDEV INT/ORG ECO/TAC INT/TRADE COLONIAL WAR GP/REL RACE/REL SOVEREIGN SOC/INTEG 20 TREATY EEC COMMONWLTH. PAGE 32 A0644
JURID DIPLOM PARL/PROC NAT/LISM

B65
INTERNATIONAL SOCIAL SCI COUN,SOCIAL SCIENCES IN THE USSR. USSR ECO/DEV AGRI FINAN INDUS PLAN CAP/ISM...INT/LAW PHIL/SCI PSY SOC 20. PAGE 71 A1460
BIBLIOG/A ACT/RES MARXISM JURID

B65
JOHNSTON D.M.,THE INTERNATIONAL LAW OF FISHERIES: A FRAMEWORK FOR POLICYORIENTED INQUIRIES. WOR+45 ACT/RES PLAN PROB/SOLV CONTROL SOVEREIGN. PAGE 75 A1527
CONCPT EXTR/IND JURID DIPLOM

B65
LAFAVE W.R.,LAW AND SOVIET SOCIETY. EX/STRUC DIPLOM DOMIN EDU/PROP PRESS ADMIN CRIME OWN MARXISM 20 KHRUSH/N. PAGE 84 A1710
JURID CT/SYS ADJUD GOV/REL

B65
MONCONDUIT F.,LA COMMISSION EUROPEENNE DES DROITS DE L'HOMME. DIPLOM AGREE GP/REL ORD/FREE PWR ...BIBLIOG 20 TREATY. PAGE 102 A2103
INT/LAW INT/ORG ADJUD JURID

B65
MOSTECKY V.,SOVIET LEGAL BIBLIOGRAPHY. USSR LEGIS PRESS WRITING CONFER ADJUD CT/SYS REV MARXISM ...INT/LAW JURID DICTIONARY 20. PAGE 105 A2155
BIBLIOG/A LAW COM CONSTN

B65
THOMAS A.V.,NONINTERVENTION: THE LAW AND ITS IMPORT IN THE AMERICAS. L/A+17C USA+45 USA-45 WOR+45 DIPLOM ADJUD...JURID IDEA/COMP 20 UN INTERVENT. PAGE 143 A2920
INT/LAW PWR COERCE

B65
UNIVERSAL REFERENCE SYSTEM,INTERNATIONAL AFFAIRS: VOLUME I IN THE POLITICAL SCIENCE, GOVERNMENT, AND PUBLIC POLICY SERIES....DECISION ECOMETRIC GEOG INT/LAW JURID MGT PHIL/SCI PSY SOC. PAGE 149 A3041
BIBLIOG/A GEN/METH COMPUT/IR DIPLOM

B65
VONGLAHN G.,LAW AMONG NATIONS: AN INTRODUCTION TO PUBLIC INTERNATIONAL LAW. UNIV WOR+45 LAW INT/ORG NAT/G LEGIT EXEC RIGID/FLEX...CONCPT TIME/SEQ GEN/LAWS UN TOT/POP 20. PAGE 160 A3253
CONSTN JURID INT/LAW

S65
AMRAM P.W.,"REPORT ON THE TENTH SESSION OF THE HAGUE CONFERENCE ON PRIVATE INTERNATIONAL LAW." USA+45 WOR+45 INT/ORG CREATE LEGIT ADJUD ALL/VALS ...JURID CONCPT METH/CNCPT OBS GEN/METH 20. PAGE 8 A0155
VOL/ASSN DELIB/GP INT/LAW

S65
GROSS L.,"PROBLEMS OF INTERNATIONAL ADJUDICATION AND COMPLIANCE WITH INTERNATIONAL LAW: SOME SIMPLE SOLUTIONS." WOR+45 SOCIETY NAT/G DOMIN LEGIT ADJUD CT/SYS RIGID/FLEX HEALTH PWR...JURID NEW/IDEA COLD/WAR 20. PAGE 57 A1177
LAW METH/CNCPT INT/LAW

S65
HAZARD J.N.,"CO-EXISTENCE LAW BOWS OUT." WOR+45 R+D INT/ORG VOL/ASSN CONSULT DELIB/GP ACT/RES CREATE PEACE KNOWL...JURID CONCPT COLD/WAR VAL/FREE 20. PAGE 63 A1300
PROF/ORG ADJUD

S65
MAC CHESNEY B.,"SOME COMMENTS ON THE 'QUARANTINE' OF CUBA." USA+45 WOR+45 NAT/G BAL/PWR DIPLOM LEGIT ROUTINE ATTIT ORD/FREE...JURID METH/CNCPT 20. PAGE 92 A1883
INT/ORG LAW CUBA USSR

S65
PLISCHKE E.,"INTEGRATING BERLIN AND THE FEDERAL REPUBLIC OF GERMANY." EUR+WWI GERMANY/W LEGIS TEC/DEV DOMIN ORD/FREE PWR...JURID 20 BERLIN. PAGE 117 A2392
DIPLOM NAT/G MUNIC

S65
STEIN E.,"TOWARD SUPREMACY OF TREATY-CONSTITUTION BY JUDICIAL FIAT: ON THE MARGIN OF THE COSTA CASE." EUR+WWI ITALY WOR+45 INT/ORG NAT/G LEGIT REGION NAT/LISM PWR...JURID CONCPT TREND TOT/POP VAL/FREE 20. PAGE 138 A2816
ADJUD CONSTN SOVEREIGN INT/LAW

B66
AMERICAN JOURNAL COMP LAW,THE AMERICAN JOURNAL OF COMPARATIVE LAW READER. EUR+WWI USA+45 USA-45 LAW CONSTN LOC/G MUNIC NAT/G DIPLOM...ANTHOL 20 SUPREME/CT EURCT/JUST. PAGE 7 A0151
IDEA/COMP JURID INT/LAW CT/SYS

B66
BROWNLIE I.,PRINCIPLES OF PUBLIC INTERNATIONAL LAW. WOR+45 WOR-45 LAW JUDGE REPAR ADJUD SOVEREIGN ...JURID T. PAGE 20 A0409
INT/LAW DIPLOM INT/ORG

B66
COUNCIL OF EUROPE,EUROPEAN CONVENTION ON HUMAN RIGHTS - COLLECTED TEXTS (5TH ED.). EUR+WWI DIPLOM ADJUD CT/SYS...INT/LAW 20 ECHR. PAGE 31 A0638
ORD/FREE DELIB/GP INT/ORG JURID

B66
DOUMA J.,BIBLIOGRAPHY ON THE INTERNATIONAL COURT INCLUDING THE PERMANENT COURT, 1918-1964. WOR+45 WOR-45 DELIB/GP WAR PRIVIL...JURID NAT/COMP 20 UN LEAGUE/NAT. PAGE 38 A0780
BIBLIOG/A INT/ORG CT/SYS DIPLOM

B66
EDWARDS C.D.,TRADE REGULATIONS OVERSEAS. IRELAND NEW/ZEALND SOUTH/AFR NAT/G CAP/ISM TARIFFS CONTROL ...POLICY JURID 20 EEC CHINJAP. PAGE 40 A0823
INT/TRADE DIPLOM INT/LAW ECO/TAC

B66
EPSTEIN F.T.,THE AMERICAN BIBLIOGRAPHY OF RUSSIAN AND EAST EUROPEAN STUDIES FOR 1964. USSR LOC/G NAT/G POL/PAR FORCES ADMIN ARMS/CONT...JURID CONCPT 20 UN. PAGE 42 A0855
BIBLIOG COM MARXISM DIPLOM

B66
HARMON R.B.,SOURCES AND PROBLEMS OF BIBLIOGRAPHY IN POLITICAL SCIENCE (PAMPHLET). INT/ORG LOC/G MUNIC POL/PAR ADMIN GOV/REL ALL/IDEOS...JURID MGT CONCPT 19/20. PAGE 61 A1262
BIBLIOG DIPLOM INT/LAW NAT/G

B66
HENKYS R.,DEUTSCHLAND UND DIE OSTLICHEN NACHBARN. GERMANY POLAND NAT/G POL/PAR INGP/REL ATTIT 20 MIGRATION. PAGE 64 A1317
GP/REL JURID INT/LAW DIPLOM

B66
INTL ATOMIC ENERGY AGENCY,INTERNATIONAL CONVENTIONS ON CIVIL LIABILITY FOR NUCLEAR DAMAGE. FUT WOR+45 ADJUD WAR COST PEACE SOVEREIGN...JURID 20. PAGE 71 A1462
DIPLOM INT/ORG DELIB/GP NUC/PWR

B66
MCNAIR A.D.,THE LEGAL EFFECTS OF WAR. UK FINAN DIPLOM ORD/FREE 20 ENGLSH/LAW. PAGE 98 A2019
JURID WAR INT/TRADE LABOR

B66
POLLACK R.S.,THE INDIVIDUAL'S RIGHTS AND INTERNATIONAL ORGANIZATION. LAW INT/ORG DELIB/GP SUPEGO...JURID SOC/INTEG 20 TREATY UN. PAGE 117 A2394
INT/LAW ORD/FREE DIPLOM PERSON

B66
ROBOCK S.H.,INTERNATIONAL DEVELOPMENT 1965. AGRI INDUS VOL/ASSN PLAN TEC/DEV EDU/PROP HEALTH...JURID 20 UN PEACE/CORP. PAGE 122 A2508
FOR/AID INT/ORG GEOG ECO/UNDEV

B66
UNITED NATIONS,INTERNATIONAL SPACE BIBLIOGRAPHY. FUT INT/ORG TEC/DEV DIPLOM ARMS/CONT NUC/PWR ...JURID SOC UN. PAGE 149 A3037
BIBLIOG SPACE PEACE R+D

B67
BLOM-COOPER L.,THE LITERATURE OF THE LAW AND THE LANGUAGE OF THE LAW (2 VOLS.). CANADA ISRAEL UK WOR+45 WOR-45 JUDGE CT/SYS ATTIT...CRIMLGY JURID ANTHOL CMN/WLTH. PAGE 15 A0312
BIBLIOG LAW INT/LAW ADJUD

B67
BODENHEIMER E.,TREATISE ON JUSTICE. INT/ORG NAT/G PUB/INST ACT/RES RISK CRIME INGP/REL DISCRIM DRIVE LAISSEZ 20. PAGE 16 A0325
ALL/VALS STRUCT JURID CONCPT

B67
MURTY B.S.,PROPAGANDA AND WORLD PUBLIC ORDER. FUT WOR+45 COM/IND INT/ORG PROB/SOLV ATTIT KNOWL ORD/FREE...POLICY UN. PAGE 106 A2183
EDU/PROP DIPLOM CONTROL JURID

B67
UNIVERSAL REFERENCE SYSTEM,LAW, JURISPRUDENCE, AND JUDICIAL PROCESS (VOLUME VII). WOR+45 WOR-45 CONSTN NAT/G LEGIS JUDGE CT/SYS...INT/LAW COMPUT/IR GEN/METH METH. PAGE 149 A3044
BIBLIOG/A LAW JURID ADJUD

B67
US SENATE COMM AERO SPACE SCI,TREATY ON PRINCIPLES GOVERNING ACTIVITIES OF STATES IN EXPLORATION AND USE OF OUTER SPACE, INCLUDING...BODIES. DELIB/GP FORCES LEGIS DIPLOM...JURID 20 DEPT/STATE NASA DEPT/DEFEN UN. PAGE 155 A3169
SPACE INT/LAW ORD/FREE PEACE

L67
CAHIERS P.,"LE RECOURS EN CONSTATATION DE MANQUEMENTS DES ETATS MEMBRES DEVANT LA COUR DES COMMUNAUTES EUROPEENNES." LAW PROB/SOLV DIPLOM ADMIN CT/SYS SANCTION ATTIT...POLICY DECISION JURID ECSC EEC. PAGE 23 A0465
INT/ORG CONSTN ROUTINE ADJUD

L67
GOLD J.,"INTERPRETATION BY THE INTERNATIONAL MONETARY FUND OF ITS ARTICLES OF AGREEMENT." INT/TRADE ADJUD ATTIT...POLICY JURID. PAGE 53 A1089
CONSTN INT/ORG LAW DIPLOM

L67
LISSITZYN O.J.,"TREATIES AND CHANGED CIRCUMSTANCES (REBUS SIC STANTIBUS)" WOR+45 CONSEN...JURID 20. PAGE 90 A1842
AGREE DIPLOM INT/LAW

S67
BLUM Y.Z.,"INDONESIA'S RETURN TO THE UNITED NATIONS." INDONESIA ADJUD SANCTION REPRESENT ...JURID 20 UN. PAGE 16 A0324
CONSTN LAW DIPLOM INT/ORG

S67
FABREGA J.,"ANTECEDENTES EXTRANJEROS EN LA CONSTITUCION PANAMENA." CUBA L/A+17C PANAMA URUGUAY EX/STRUC LEGIS DIPLOM ORD/FREE 19/20 COLOMB MEXIC/AMER. PAGE 43 A0882
CONSTN JURID NAT/G PARL/PROC

S67
FAWCETT J.E.S.,"GIBRALTAR* THE LEGAL ISSUES." SPAIN UK INT/ORG BAL/PWR LICENSE CONFER SANCTION PRIVIL ...JURID CHARTS 20. PAGE 44 A0905
INT/LAW DIPLOM COLONIAL ADJUD

S67
JOHNSTON D.M.,"LAW, TECHNOLOGY AND THE SEA." WOR+45 PLAN PROB/SOLV TEC/DEV CONFER ADJUD ORD/FREE ...POLICY JURID. PAGE 75 A1528
INT/LAW INT/ORG DIPLOM NEUTRAL

S67
MANN F.A.,"THE BRETTON WOODS AGREEMENT IN THE ENGLISH COURTS." UK JUDGE ADJUD CT/SYS...JURID PREDICT CON/ANAL 20. PAGE 94 A1923
LAW INT/LAW CONSTN

S67
RAMSEY J.A.,"THE STATUS OF INTERNATIONAL COPYRIGHTS." WOR+45 CREATE TEC/DEV DIPLOM CONFER CONTROL SANCTION OWN...POLICY JURID. PAGE 119 A2439
INT/LAW INT/ORG COM/IND PRESS

S67
STEGER H.S.,"RESEARCH ON LATIN AMERICA IN THE FEDERAL REPUBLIC OF GERMANY AND WEST BERLIN." FINAN DIPLOM INT/TRADE EDU/PROP...GEOG JURID CHARTS 19/20. PAGE 137 A2813
SOCIETY ECO/UNDEV ACADEM L/A+17C

C93
PLAYFAIR R.L.,"A BIBLIOGRAPHY OF MOROCCO." MOROCCO CULTURE AGRI FORCES DIPLOM WAR HEALTH...GEOG JURID SOC CHARTS. PAGE 116 A2387
BIBLIOG ISLAM MEDIT-7

B96
SMITH A.,LECTURES ON JUSTICE, POLICE, REVENUE AND ARMS (1763). UK LAW FAM FORCES TARIFFS AGREE COERCE INCOME OWN WEALTH LAISSEZ...GEN/LAWS 17/18. PAGE 134 A2743
DIPLOM JURID OLD/LIB TAX

B97
US DEPARTMENT OF STATE,CATALOGUE OF WORKS RELATING TO THE LAW OF NATIONS AND DIPLOMACY IN THE LIBRARY OF THE DEPARTMENT OF STATE (PAMPHLET). WOR-45 NAT/G ADJUD CT/SYS...INT/LAW JURID 19. PAGE 152 A3102
BIBLIOG/A DIPLOM LAW

JURISPRUDENCE....SEE LAW

JURY....JURIES AND JURY BEHAVIOR; SEE ALSO DELIB/GP, ADJUD

JUSTICE DEPARTMENT....SEE DEPT/JUST

JUVILER P.H. A1543

JWAIDEH A.R. A2745

K

KADALIE/C....CLEMENTS KADALIE

KADEN E.H. A1544

KAFKA G. A1545

KAHIN G.M. A1546

KAHLER A. A2779

KAHN H. A1547,A1548,A1549

KAISER R.G. A1550

KAISR/ALUM....KAISER ALUMINUM

KALDOR N. A1551

KALIJARVI T.V. A1309, A1552

KALMANOFF G. A1004

KALUODA J. A1553

KAMCHATKA....KAMCHATKA, U.S.S.R.

KAMISAR Y. A1849

KANDELL I.L. A1554

KANET R.E. A1555

KANSAS....KANSAS

KANT/I....IMMANUEL KANT

B63
HINSLEY F.H.,POWER AND THE PURSUIT OF PEACE. WOR+45 WOR-45 PLAN RIGID/FLEX ALL/VALS ALL/IDEOS...POLICY DECISION INT/LAW 12/20 ROUSSEAU/J KANT/I BENTHAM/J LEAGUE/NAT. PAGE 65 A1338
DIPLOM CONSTN PEACE COERCE

KANTOR H. A1556

KAPINGAMAR....KAPINGAMARANGI

KAPLAN D. A1557

KAPLAN L. A1558

KAPLAN M. A1559

KAPLAN M.A. A1560,A1561,A1562,A1563,A1564,A2464

KARDELJE A1565

KAREFA-SMART J. A1566

KAROL K.S. A1567

KARPOV P.V. A1568

KARUNAKARAN K.P. A1569

KASHMIR....SEE ALSO S/ASIA

B66
GUPTA S.,KASHMIR - A STUDY IN INDIA-PAKISTAN RELATIONS. INDIA KASHMIR PAKISTAN CONSTN INT/ORG REV RACE/REL NAT/LISM 20 UN MUSLIM/LG. PAGE 58 A1194 — DIPLOM GP/REL SOVEREIGN WAR

KATANGA....SEE ALSO AFR

B66
GERARD-LIBOIS J.,KATANGA SECESSION. INT/ORG FORCES DIPLOM ADMIN CONTROL WAR CHOOSE PWR...CHARTS 20 KATANGA TSHOMBE/M UN. PAGE 52 A1062 — NAT/G REGION ORD/FREE REV

KATZ R. A1570

KATZ S.M. A1571

KATZENBACH N. A1563

KAUFMANN J. A1212

KAUFMANN W.W. A1572

KAUNDA K. A1874

KAUNDA/K....KENNETH KAUNDA, PRESIDENT OF ZAMBIA

KAWALKOWSKI A. A1573

KEEFE G.M. A0902

KENNAN G.F. A1574

KEENLEYSIDE H.L. A1575

KEEP J. A1576

KEESING F.M. A1577

KEETON G.W. A1578

KEFAUVER/E....ESTES KEFAUVER

KEITA/M....MOBIDO KEITA

KEL/BRIAND....KELLOGG BRIAND PEACE PACT

KELLY F.K. A1579

KELSEN H. A1580,A1581,A1582,A1583

KELSEN/H....HANS KELSEN

KELSON R N. A0904

KENEN P.B. A1584,A1585

KENJI M. A2795

KENNAN G.F. A1586,A1587,A1588,A1589,A1590

KENNAN/G....GEORGE KENNAN

B57
REISS J.,GEORGE KENNANS POLITIK DER EINDAMMUNG. USSR NAT/G FORCES TOTALISM ATTIT ORD/FREE...POLICY 20 NATO TRUMAN/HS MARSHL/PLN KENNAN/G. PAGE 120 A2463 — DIPLOM DETER PEACE

B66
BLACKSTOCK P.W.,AGENTS OF DECEIT: FRAUDS, FORGERIES AND POLITICAL INTRIGUES AMONG NATIONS. USSR EDU/PROP WRITING KNOWL 18/20 COLD/WAR KENNAN/G. PAGE 15 A0302 — CON/ANAL DIPLOM HIST/WRIT

B66
HOLLINS E.J.,PEACE IS POSSIBLE: A READER FOR LAYMEN. WOR+45 CULTURE PLAN RISK AGE/Y ALL/VALS SOVEREIGN...PSY CONCPT TREND 20 UN JOHN/XXIII KENNAN/G MYRDAL/G. PAGE 67 A1370 — PEACE DIPLOM INT/ORG NUC/PWR

KENNEDY J.F. A1591,A1592,A1593

KENNEDY W.P. A1594

KENNEDY/JF....PRESIDENT JOHN F. KENNEDY

B61
ROBINS D.B.,EVOLVING UNITED STATES POLICIES TOWARD THE EMERGING NATIONS OF ASIA AND AFRICA (PAMPHLET). ISLAM ECO/UNDEV INT/ORG CONSULT CREATE PLAN TEC/DEV FOR/AID CONFER ALL/VALS 20 KENNEDY/JF EISNHWR/DD UN AID. PAGE 122 A2501 — AFR S/ASIA DIPLOM BIBLIOG

S61
VINER J.,"ECONOMIC FOREIGN POLICY ON THE NEW FRONTIER." USA+45 ECO/UNDEV AGRI FINAN INDUS MARKET INT/ORG NAT/G FOR/AID INT/TRADE ADMIN ATTIT PWR 20 KENNEDY/JF. PAGE 159 A3239 — TOP/EX ECO/TAC BAL/PAY TARIFFS

B62
EVANS M.S.,THE FRINGE ON TOP. USSR EX/STRUC FORCES DIPLOM ECO/TAC PEACE CONSERVE SOCISM...TREND 20 KENNEDY/JF. PAGE 43 A0877 — NAT/G PWR CENTRAL POLICY

B62
GOLDWIN R.A.,WHY FOREIGN AID? - TWO MESSAGES BY PRESIDENT KENNEDY AND ESSAYS. S/ASIA USA+45 ECO/UNDEV 20 KENNEDY/JF THIRD/WRLD. PAGE 54 A1096 — DIPLOM FOR/AID POLICY

B62
KENNEDY J.F.,TO TURN THE TIDE. SPACE AGRI INT/ORG FORCES TEC/DEV ADMIN NUC/PWR PEACE WEALTH...ANTHOL 20 KENNEDY/JF CIV/RIGHTS. PAGE 78 A1592 — DIPLOM CHIEF POLICY NAT/G

B62
US SENATE COMM GOVT OPERATIONS,ADMINISTRATION OF NATIONAL SECURITY. USA+45 CHIEF PLAN PROB/SOLV TEC/DEV DIPLOM ATTIT...POLICY DECISION 20 KENNEDY/JF RUSK/D MCNAMARA/R BUNDY/M HERTER/C. PAGE 156 A3173 — ORD/FREE ADMIN NAT/G CONTROL

B62
WILLIAMS W.A.,THE UNITED STATES, CUBA, AND CASTRO: AN ESSAY ON THE DYNAMICS OF REVOLUTION AND THE DISSOLUTION OF EMPIRE. CUBA USA+45 AGRI VOL/ASSN DIPLOM ECO/TAC DOMIN COERCE...POLICY 20 EISNHWR/DD CIA KENNEDY/JF CASTRO/F. PAGE 165 A3354 — REV CONSTN COM LEAD

S62
TOWSTER J.,"THE USSR AND THE USA: CHALLENGE AND RESPONSE." COM GERMANY USA+45 USSR WOR+45 ECO/UNDEV INT/ORG VOL/ASSN EX/STRUC FORCES TOP/EX CREATE PLAN TEC/DEV DIPLOM ECO/TAC EDU/PROP COLONIAL COERCE PWR ...GEN/METH COLD/WAR 20 KENNEDY/JF. PAGE 145 A2956 — ACT/RES GEN/LAWS

B63
KLEIMAN R.,ATLANTIC CRISIS; AMERICAN DIPLOMACY CONFRONTS A RESURGENT EUROPE. EUR+WWI USA+45 ECO/DEV AGRI NAT/G CHIEF FORCES PLAN LEAD ATTIT ...CONCPT 20 NATO KENNEDY/JF DEGAULLE/C EEC JOHNSON/LB. PAGE 80 A1648 — DIPLOM REGION POLICY

B63
PACHTER H.M.,COLLISION COURSE; THE CUBAN MISSILE CRISIS AND COEXISTENCE. CUBA USA+45 DIPLOM ARMS/CONT PEACE MARXISM...DECISION INT/LAW 20 COLD/WAR KHRUSH/N KENNEDY/JF CASTRO/F. PAGE 112 A2307 — WAR BAL/PWR NUC/PWR DETER

B64
ADAMS V.,THE PEACE CORPS IN ACTION. USA+45 VOL/ASSN EX/STRUC GOV/REL PERCEPT ORD/FREE...OBS 20 KENNEDY/JF PEACE/CORP. PAGE 4 A0087 — DIPLOM FOR/AID PERSON DRIVE

B64
DAVIES U.P. JR.,FOREIGN AND OTHER AFFAIRS. EUR+WWI L/A+17C S/ASIA USA+45 ECO/UNDEV CHIEF PLAN ECO/TAC PWR MARXISM 20 KENNEDY/JF UN. PAGE 34 A0688 — DIPLOM NAT/G POLICY FOR/AID

B64
KAUFMANN W.W.,THE MC NAMARA STRATEGY. TOP/EX INSPECT BAL/PWR DIPLOM CONTROL DETER GUERRILLA NUC/PWR WEAPON COST PWR...METH/COMP 20 MCNAMARA/R KENNEDY/JF JOHNSON/LB NATO DEPT/DEFEN. PAGE 77 A1572 — FORCES WAR PLAN PROB/SOLV

B64
KENNEDY J.F.,THE BURDEN AND THE GLORY. FUT USA+45 TEC/DEV ECO/TAC EDU/PROP ARMS/CONT MURDER RACE/REL PEACE...ANTHOL 20 KENNEDY/JF COLD/WAR NATO PRESIDENT. PAGE 78 A1593 — ADMIN POLICY GOV/REL DIPLOM

B64
MC GOVERN G.S.,WAR AGAINST WANT. USA+45 AGRI DIPLOM INT/TRADE GIVE RECEIVE DEMAND HEALTH 20 KENNEDY/JF FOOD/PEACE. PAGE 97 A1993 — FOR/AID ECO/DEV POLICY EATING

B64
WARREN S.,THE PRESIDENT AS WORLD LEADER. USA+45 WOR+45 ELITES COM/IND INT/ORG NAT/G VOL/ASSN CHIEF — TOP/EX PWR

EX/STRUC LEGIT COERCE ATTIT PERSON RIGID/FLEX...INT TIME/SEQ COLD/WAR 20 ROOSEVLT/F TRUMAN/HS EISNHWR/DD KENNEDY/JF. PAGE 161 A3286 — DIPLOM

B65
TREFOUSSE H.L.,THE COLD WAR: A BOOK OF DOCUMENTS. ASIA L/A+17C USSR WOR+45 WOR-45 ECO/TAC FOR/AID ARMS/CONT NUC/PWR PEACE ORD/FREE...ANTHOL 20 COLD/WAR KENNEDY/JF EISNHWR/DD. PAGE 145 A2961 — BAL/PWR DIPLOM MARXISM

B65
WEISNER J.B.,WHERE SCIENCE AND POLITICS MEET. USA+45 ECO/DEV R+D FORCES PROB/SOLV DIPLOM FOR/AID CONTROL...PHIL/SCI PRESIDENT KENNEDY/JF JOHNSON/LB. PAGE 163 A3310 — CHIEF NAT/G POLICY TEC/DEV

B66
BESSON W.,DIE GROSSEN MACHTE - STRUKTURFRAGEN DER GEGENWARTIGEN WELTPOLITIK. ASIA USSR WOR+45 ATTIT ...IDEA/COMP 20 KENNEDY/JF. PAGE 14 A0280 — NAT/COMP DIPLOM STRUCT

B66
BRACKMAN A.C.,SOUTHEAST ASIA'S SECOND FRONT: THE POWER STRUGGLE IN THE MALAY ARCHIPELAGO. CHINA/COM INDONESIA MALAYSIA ECO/UNDEV INT/ORG NAT/G FORCES DIPLOM EDU/PROP REGION COERCE GUERRILLA AUTHORIT POPULISM...MAJORIT 20 KENNEDY/JF SEATO. PAGE 18 A0367 — S/ASIA MARXISM REV

B66
FREIDEL F.,AMERICAN ISSUES IN THE TWENTIETH CENTURY. SOCIETY FINAN ECO/TAC FOR/AID CONTROL NUC/PWR WAR RACE/REL PEACE ATTIT...ANTHOL T 20 WILSON/W ROOSEVLT/F KENNEDY/JF TRUMAN/HS. PAGE 49 A0995 — DIPLOM POLICY NAT/G ORD/FREE

B66
MAY E.R.,ANXIETY AND AFFLUENCE: 1945-1965. USA+45 DIPLOM FOR/AID ARMS/CONT RACE/REL CONSEN...ANTHOL 20 COLD/WAR KENNEDY/JF EISNHWR/DD TRUMAN/HS BERLIN/BLO. PAGE 97 A1982 — ANOMIE ECO/DEV NUC/PWR WEALTH

KENNEDY/RF....ROBERT F. KENNEDY

KENT G.O. A1595

KENT R.K. A1596

KENTUCKY....KENTUCKY

KENWORTHY L.S. A1597

KENYA....KENYA

KENYATTA....JOMO KENYATTA

KERNER R.J. A1598,A1599

KERTESZ S.D. A1600,A1601

KETCHAM E.H. A1602

KEYES J.G. A1603

KEYFITZ N. A1604

KEYNES J.M. A1605

KEYNES/G....GEOFFREY KEYNES

KEYNES/JM....JOHN MAYNARD KEYNES

B37
ROBBINS L.,ECONOMIC PLANNING AND INTERNATIONAL ORDER. WOR-45 SOCIETY FINAN INDUS NAT/G ECO/TAC ROUTINE WEALTH...SOC TIME/SEQ GEN/METH WORK 20 KEYNES/JM. PAGE 122 A2492 — INT/ORG PLAN INT/TRADE

B52
MANTOUX E.,THE CARTHAGINIAN PEACE. GERMANY WOR-45 SOCIETY FINAN INT/ORG DELIB/GP FORCES PLAN LEGIT ...CONCPT TIME/SEQ 20 KEYNES/JM HITLER/A. PAGE 94 A1935 — ECO/DEV INT/TRADE WAR

B63
THEOBALD R.,FREE MEN AND FREE MARKETS. USA+45 USA-45 ECO/DEV NAT/G TEC/DEV DIPLOM INT/TRADE INCOME ORD/FREE WEALTH...TREND 19/20 KEYNES/JM. PAGE 143 A2915 — CONCPT ECO/TAC CAP/ISM MARKET

B64
KALDOR N.,ESSAYS ON ECONOMIC POLICY (VOL. II). CHILE GERMANY INDIA FINAN...GOV/COMP METH/COMP 20 KEYNES/JM. PAGE 76 A1551 — BAL/PAY INT/TRADE METH/CNCPT ECO/UNDEV

KEYSERLING L.H. A1499

KHADDURI M. A1606

KHAN A.W. A1607

KHAN M.Z. A1608,A1609

KHASAS....KHASAS (ANCIENT COMMUNITY)

KHOURI F.J. A1610

KHRUSH/N....NIKITA KHRUSHCHEV

N19
GRANT N.,COMMUNIST PSYCHOLOGICAL OFFENSIVE: DISTORTION IN THE TRANSLATION OF OFFICIAL DOCUMENTS (PAMPHLET). USSR POL/PAR CHIEF FOR/AID PRESS WRITING COLONIAL LEAD WAR PEACE 20 KHRUSH/N. PAGE 55 A1129 — MARXISM DIPLOM EDU/PROP

B59
HARRIMAN A.,PEACE WITH RUSSIA? USA+45 USSR SOCIETY ECO/TAC CONTROL TOTALISM ATTIT MARXISM...POLICY 20 STALIN/J KHRUSH/N. PAGE 62 A1266 — DIPLOM PEACE NAT/G TASK

B59
SHANNON D.A.,THE DECLINE OF AMERICAN COMMUNISM; A HISTORY OF THE COMMUNIST PARTY OF THE UNITED STATES SINCE 1945. USA+45 LAW SOCIETY LABOR NAT/G WORKER DIPLOM EDU/PROP LEAD...POLICY BIBLIOG 20 KHRUSH/N NEGRO AFL/CIO COLD/WAR COM/PARTY. PAGE 131 A2692 — MARXISM POL/PAR ATTIT POPULISM

B60
KHRUSHCHEV N.S.,KHRUSHCHEV IN NEW YORK. USA+45 USSR ATTIT...ANTHOL 20 UN KHRUSH/N. PAGE 79 A1612 — DIPLOM PEACE ARMS/CONT

B60
KHRUSHCHEV N.S.,KHRUSHCHEV IN AMERICA. USA+45 USSR INT/TRADE EDU/PROP PRESS PEACE...MARXIST RECORD INT 20 COLD/WAR KHRUSH/N. PAGE 79 A1613 — MARXISM CHIEF DIPLOM

B60
MONTGOMERY B.L.,AN APPROACH TO SANITY; A STUDY OF EAST-WEST RELATIONS. CONFER WAR EFFICIENCY ATTIT ...POLICY 20 NATO COLD/WAR KHRUSH/N. PAGE 103 A2113 — DIPLOM INT/ORG BAL/PWR DETER

S60
KENNAN G.F.,"PEACEFUL CO-EXISTENCE: A WESTERN VIEW." COM EUR+WWI USA+45 USSR WOR+45 PLAN BAL/PWR DIPLOM INT/TRADE PWR...POLICY CONCPT OBS HIST/WRIT TREND GEN/LAWS COLD/WAR 20 KHRUSH/N. PAGE 78 A1589 — ATTIT COERCE

B61
LIPPMANN W.,THE COMING TESTS WITH RUSSIA. COM CUBA GERMANY USSR FORCES CONTROL NEUTRAL COERCE NUC/PWR REV WAR PWR...INT 20 KHRUSH/N BERLIN. PAGE 89 A1830 — BAL/PWR DIPLOM MARXISM ARMS/CONT

B61
OVERSTREET H.,THE WAR CALLED PEACE. USSR WOR+45 COM/IND INT/ORG POL/PAR BAL/PWR EDU/PROP PEACE ATTIT...CONCPT 20 KHRUSH/N. PAGE 112 A2302 — DIPLOM COM POLICY LEAD

S61
WHELAN J.G.,"KHRUSHCHEV AND THE BALANCE OF WORLD POWER." FUT WOR+45 INT/ORG VOL/ASSN CAP/ISM DIPLOM SKILL...POLICY COLD/WAR 20 KHRUSH/N. PAGE 163 A3328 — COM PWR BAL/PWR USSR

S61
ZAGORIA D.S.,"THE FUTURE OF SINO-SOVIET RELATIONS." CHINA/COM INT/ORG NAT/G POL/PAR VOL/ASSN ACT/RES PLAN PERSON...METH/CNCPT TIME/SEQ TOT/POP VAL/FREE 20 MAO KHRUSH/N. PAGE 169 A3444 — ASIA COM TOTALISM USSR

L62
ULYSSES,"THE INTERNATIONAL AIMS AND POLICIES OF THE SOVIET UNION: THE NEW CONCEPTS AND STRATEGY OF KHRUSHCHEV." FUT USSR WOR+45 SOCIETY INT/ORG NAT/G POL/PAR FORCES TOP/EX PLAN DOMIN EDU/PROP COERCE ATTIT PERSON PWR...TREND COLD/WAR 20 KHRUSH/N. PAGE 146 A2994 — COM POLICY BAL/PWR DIPLOM

S62
DRACHKOVITCH M.M.,"THE EMERGING PATTERN OF YUGOSLAV-SOVIET RELATIONS." COM FUT USSR WOR+45 INT/ORG ECO/TAC FOR/AID DOMIN COERCE ATTIT PERSON ORD/FREE PWR...TIME/SEQ 20 TITO/MARSH KHRUSH/N STALIN/J. PAGE 38 A0783 — TOP/EX DIPLOM YUGOSLAVIA

B63
GRIFFITH W.E.,ALBANIA AND THE SINO-SOVIET RIFT. ALBANIA CHINA/COM USSR POL/PAR CHIEF LEGIS DIPLOM DOMIN ATTIT PWR...POLICY 20 KHRUSH/N MAO. PAGE 57 A1161 — EDU/PROP MARXISM NAT/LISM GOV/REL

B63
MOSELY P.E.,THE SOVIET UNION, 1922-1962: A FOREIGN AFFAIRS READER. ASIA POLAND USSR CULTURE INTELL AGRI POL/PAR WORKER INT/TRADE DOMIN WAR NAT/LISM MARXISM SOCISM 20 KHRUSH/N. PAGE 105 A2152 — PWR POLICY DIPLOM

B63
PACHTER H.M.,COLLISION COURSE; THE CUBAN MISSILE CRISIS AND COEXISTENCE. CUBA USA+45 DIPLOM ARMS/CONT PEACE MARXISM...DECISION INT/LAW 20 COLD/WAR KHRUSH/N KENNEDY/JF CASTRO/F. PAGE 112 A2307 — WAR BAL/PWR NUC/PWR DETER

B63
RUSSELL B.,UNARMED VICTORY. CHINA/COM CUBA INDIA USA+45 WAR MARXISM...POLICY IDEA/COMP 20 KHRUSH/N COLD/WAR. PAGE 125 A2573 — DIPLOM ATTIT SOCISM ORD/FREE

B63
US SENATE,DOCUMENTS ON INTERNATIONAL AS"ECTS OF EXPLORATION AND USE OF OUTER SPACE, 1954-62: STAFF — SPACE UTIL

REPORT FOR COMM AERON SPACE SCI. USA+45 USSR LEGIS LEAD CIVMIL/REL PEACE...POLICY INT/LAW ANTHOL 20 CONGRESS NASA KHRUSH/N. PAGE 155 A3165 — GOV/REL DIPLOM

B63
WHITNEY T.P.,KHRUSHCHEV SPEAKS. USSR AGRI LEAD ...BIOG ANTHOL 20 KHRUSH/N STALIN/J ESPIONAGE. PAGE 164 A3339 — DIPLOM MARXISM CHIEF

B65
LAFAVE W.R.,LAW AND SOVIET SOCIETY. EX/STRUC DIPLOM DOMIN EDU/PROP PRESS ADMIN CRIME OWN MARXISM 20 KHRUSH/N. PAGE 84 A1710 — JURID CT/SYS ADJUD GOV/REL

B66
BLOOMFIELD L.P.,KHRUSHCHEV AND THE ARMS RACE. USA+45 USSR ECO/DEV BAL/PWR EDU/PROP CONFER NUC/PWR ATTIT...CHARTS 20 KHRUSH/N. PAGE 16 A0321 — ARMS/CONT COM POLICY DIPLOM

B66
ZABLOCKI C.J.,SINO-SOVIET RIVALRY. AFR ASIA CHINA/COM CUBA EUR+WWI L/A+17C USA+45 USSR WOR+45 POL/PAR FORCES COERCE NUC/PWR...GOV/COMP IDEA/COMP 20 MAO KHRUSH/N. PAGE 169 A3442 — DIPLOM MARXISM COM

KHRUSHCHEV N. A1611

KHRUSHCHEV N.S. A1612,A1613,A1614

KIDDER F.E. A1615

KIERKE/S....SOREN KIERKEGAARD

KIERNAN V.G. A1616

KILSON M. A0849

KIM Y.H. A1617

KIM Y.K. A1618

KIM/IL-SON....IL-SON KIM

KIMMINICH O. A1619

KIN....KINSHIP (EXCEPT NUCLEAR FAMILY)

B02
MOREL E.D.,AFFAIRS OF WEST AFRICA. UK FINAN INDUS FAM KIN SECT CHIEF WORKER DIPLOM RACE/REL LITERACY HEALTH...CHARTS 18/20 AFRICA/W NEGRO. PAGE 104 A2129 — COLONIAL ADMIN AFR

B20
VINOGRADOFF P.,OUTLINES OF HISTORICAL JURISPRUDENCE (2 VOLS.). GREECE MEDIT-7 LAW CONSTN FACE/GP FAM KIN MUNIC CRIME OWN...INT/LAW IDEA/COMP BIBLIOG. PAGE 159 A3241 — JURID METH

B35
KENNEDY W.P.,THE LAW AND CUSTOM OF THE SOUTH AFRICAN CONSTITUTION. AFR SOUTH/AFR KIN LOC/G PROVS DIPLOM ADJUD ADMIN EXEC 20. PAGE 78 A1594 — CT/SYS CONSTN JURID PARL/PROC

C50
NUMELIN R.,"THE BEGINNINGS OF DIPLOMACY." INT/TRADE WAR GP/REL PEACE STRANGE ATTIT...INT/LAW CONCPT BIBLIOG. PAGE 110 A2260 — DIPLOM KIN CULTURE LAW

B55
THOMPSON V.,MINORITY PROBLEMS IN SOUTHEAST ASIA. CAMBODIA CHINA/COM LAOS S/ASIA KIN NAT/G SECT PROB/SOLV EDU/PROP REGION GP/REL RACE/REL MARXISM ...SOC 20 BUDDHISM UN. PAGE 143 A2933 — INGP/REL GEOG DIPLOM STRUCT

B58
GROBLER J.H.,AFRICA'S DESTINY. AFR EUR+WWI SOUTH/AFR UK USA+45 ELITES KIN LOC/G DIPLOM DISCRIM ATTIT CONSERVE MARXISM 20 ROOSEVLT/T NEGRO. PAGE 57 A1168 — POLICY ORD/FREE COLONIAL CONSTN

B58
HOLT R.T.,RADIO FREE EUROPE. FUT USA+45 CULTURE ECO/DEV INT/ORG KIN POL/PAR SECT FORCES ACT/RES DIPLOM COERCE REV CHOOSE PEACE ATTIT PWR...MAJORIT CONCPT COLD/WAR WORK 20 RFE. PAGE 67 A1374 — COM EDU/PROP COM/IND

B60
GLUBB J.B.,WAR IN THE DESERT: AN R.A.F. FRONTIER CAMPAIGN. SAUDI/ARAB UK KIN SECT LEAD...GEOG 20 RAF. PAGE 53 A1083 — COLONIAL WAR FORCES DIPLOM

S60
GINSBURGS G.,"PEKING-LHASA-NEW DELHI." CHINA/COM FUT INDIA S/ASIA KIN NAT/G PROVS SECT FORCES BAL/PWR ECO/TAC DOMIN EDU/PROP LEGIT ADMIN REGION GUERRILLA PWR...TREND TIBET 20. PAGE 52 A1074 — ASIA COERCE DIPLOM

S61
RALEIGH J.S.,"THE MIDDLE EAST IN 1960: A POLITICAL SURVEY." FUT ISLAM INTELL KIN BAL/PWR EDU/PROP NAT/LISM...TREND VAL/FREE 20. PAGE 119 A2435 — INT/ORG EX/STRUC

B62
SPIRO H.J.,POLITICS IN AFRICA: PROSPECTS SOUTH OF THE SAHARA. INT/ORG KIN FORCES LEGIS PROB/SOLV COERCE RACE/REL FEDERAL...TREND CHARTS BIBLIOG 20. PAGE 136 A2790 — AFR NAT/LISM DIPLOM

S62
RUBINSTEIN A.Z.,"RUSSIA AND THE UNCOMMITTED NATIONS." AFR INDIA ISLAM L/A+17C LAOS S/ASIA ELITES ECO/UNDEV INT/ORG KIN CREATE PLAN TEC/DEV NAT/LISM RIGID/FLEX PWR WEALTH...METH/CNCPT TIME/SEQ GEN/LAWS WORK. PAGE 125 A2562 — ECO/TAC TREND COLONIAL USSR

B63
JUDD P.,AFRICAN INDEPENDENCE: THE EXPLODING EMERGENCE OF THE NEW AFRICAN NATIONS. AFR UK LAW CONSTN CULTURE KIN DIPLOM ATTIT...CHARTS BIBLIOG 20 UN DEGAULLE/C NEGRO THIRD/WRLD. PAGE 75 A1542 — ORD/FREE POLICY DOMIN LOC/G

S63
MAZRUI A.A.,"ON THE CONCEPT 'WE ARE ALL AFRICANS'." AFR CULTURE KIN LOC/G NAT/G DOMIN EDU/PROP LEGIT ATTIT PERCEPT PERSON KNOWL ORD/FREE...TIME/SEQ TOT/POP 20. PAGE 97 A1986 — PROVS INT/ORG NAT/LISM

B64
BINDER L.,THE IDEOLOGICAL REVOLUTION IN THE MIDDLE EAST. ISLAM STRUCT INT/ORG KIN SECT EX/STRUC TOP/EX PLAN ATTIT DRIVE RIGID/FLEX PWR...MYTH TOT/POP 20. PAGE 14 A0289 — POL/PAR NAT/G NAT/LISM

B64
BURKE F.G.,AFRICA'S QUEST FOR ORDER. AFR CULTURE KIN MUNIC NAT/G DIPLOM COLONIAL REV DISCRIM NAT/LISM AGE/Y 20. PAGE 21 A0437 — ORD/FREE CONSEN RACE/REL LEAD

B64
LUTHULI A.,AFRICA'S FREEDOM. KIN LABOR POL/PAR SCHOOL DIPLOM NEUTRAL REGION REV NAT/LISM PWR WEALTH SOCISM SOC/INTEG 20. PAGE 92 A1874 — AFR ECO/UNDEV COLONIAL

S64
TOUVAL S.,"THE SOMALI REPUBLIC." AFR ISLAM SOMALIA FAM KIN NAT/G CREATE FOR/AID LEGIT ATTIT ALL/VALS ...RECORD TREND 20. PAGE 144 A2954 — ECO/UNDEV RIGID/FLEX

B65
VAN DEN BERGHE P.L.,AFRICA: SOCIAL PROBLEMS OF CHANGE AND CONFLICT. ELITES STRATA ECO/UNDEV KIN MUNIC DIPLOM GP/REL RACE/REL NAT/LISM...ANTHOL BIBLIOG 20. PAGE 158 A3210 — SOC CULTURE AFR STRUCT

B66
HALLET R.,PEOPLE AND PROGRESS IN WEST AFRICA: AN INTRODUCTION TO THE PROBLEMS OF DEVELOPMENT. COM/IND INDUS KIN DIPLOM FOR/AID INT/TRADE HEALTH ...GEOG TREND CHARTS BIBLIOG/A 20 AFRICA/W. PAGE 60 A1233 — AFR SOCIETY ECO/UNDEV ECO/TAC

B67
FRASER-TYTLER W.K.,AFGHANISTAN: A STUDY OF POLITICAL DEVELOPMENTS IN CENTRAL AND SOUTHERN ASIA (3RD ED.). AFGHANISTN INDIA KIN FOR/AID PWR ...BIBLIOG. PAGE 48 A0990 — DIPLOM NAT/G CONSTN GEOG

B67
STEVENS R.P.,LESOTHO, BATSWANA, AND SWAZILAND* THE FORMER HIGH COMMISSION TERRITORIES IN SOUTHERN AFRICA. ECO/DEV KIN POL/PAR HIST/WRIT. PAGE 138 A2821 — COLONIAL DIPLOM ORD/FREE

S67
SAPP B.B.,"TRIBAL CULTURES AND COMMUNISM." AFR USA+45 STRATA DIPLOM FOR/AID REGION CENTRAL ATTIT AUTHORIT RIGID/FLEX KNOWL. PAGE 127 A2604 — KIN MARXISM ECO/UNDEV STRUCT

S67
VELIKONJA J.,"ITALIAN IMMIGRANTS IN THE UNITED STATES IN THE MID-SIXTIES" ITALY USA+45 KIN MUNIC NAT/G WORKER DIPLOM REGION GP/REL ADJUST...GEOG CHARTS SOC/INTEG 20. PAGE 158 A3226 — HABITAT ORD/FREE TREND STAT

KINDLEBERGER C.P. A1620,A1621,A1622,A1623

KING G. A1624

KING....KING AND KINGSHIP; SEE ALSO CHIEF, CONSERVE, TRADIT

C62
BACON F.,"OF EMPIRE" (1612) IN F. BACON, ESSAYS." ELITES NAT/G PROB/SOLV DIPLOM ADMIN CONTROL WEALTH 16/17 KING. PAGE 10 A0201 — PWR CHIEF DOMIN GEN/LAWS

KING/MAR/L....REVEREND MARTIN LUTHER KING

B66
MAYER P.,THE PACIFIST CONSCIENCE. SECT CREATE ARMS/CONT WAR RACE/REL ATTIT LOVE...ANTHOL PACIFIST WORSHIP FREUD/S GANDHI/M LAO/TZU KING/MAR/L CONSCN/OBJ. PAGE 97 A1984 — DIPLOM PACIFISM SUPEGO

KING-HALL S. A1625

KINGSLEY R.E. A1626

KINGSTON-MCCLOUG E. A1627

KINSEY/A....ALFRED KINSEY

KINTNER W.R. A1628,A2847,A2848

KIPLING/R....RUDYARD KIPLING

B66
FABAR R.,THE VISION AND THE NEED: LATE VICTORIAN IMPERIALIST AIMS. MOD/EUR UK WOR-45 CULTURE NAT/G DIPLOM...TIME/SEQ METH/COMP 19 KIPLING/R COMMONWLTH. PAGE 43 A0880 — COLONIAL CONCPT ADMIN ATTIT

KIPP K. A1629

KIRCHHEIMER O. A1630

KIRDAR U. A1631

KIRK G. A1632,A1633,A1634

KIRK R. A1635

KIRK/GRAY....GRAYSON KIRK

KIRKWOOD K. A1636

KIRPICEVA I.K. A1637

KIS T.I. A1638

KISER M. A1639

KISSINGER H.A. A1640,A1641,A1642,A1643,A1644

KISTIAKOWSKY G.B. A1645

KITCHEN H. A1646

KITZINGER V.W. A1647

KKK....KU KLUX KLAN

B27
SIEGFRIED A.,AMERICA COMES OF AGE: A FRENCH ANALYSIS (TRANS. BY H.H. HEMMING AND DORIS HEMMING). FRANCE UK POL/PAR WORKER TEC/DEV DIPLOM REGION RACE/REL ADJUST PRODUC HEREDITY...TIME/SEQ GP/COMP SOC/INTEG 20 DEMOCRAT REPUBLICAN KKK. PAGE 132 A2714 — USA-45 CULTURE ECO/DEV SOC

KLEIMAN R. A1648

KLEIN S. A1649

KLUCKHN/C....CLYDE KLUCKHOHN

KLUCKHOHN F.L. A1650

KNIERIEM A. A1651

KNIGHT R. A1652

KNO/TEST....TESTS FOR FACTUAL KNOWLEDGE

S47
RADVANYI L.,"PROBLEMS OF INTERNATIONAL OPINION SURVEYS." WOR+45 INT/ORG NAT/G CREATE ATTIT...PSY SOC METH/CNCPT REC/INT KNO/TEST SAMP/SIZ METH VAL/FREE 20. PAGE 118 A2431 — QU/SEMANT SAMP DIPLOM

B54
WRIGHT Q.,PROBLEMS OF STABILITY AND PROGRESS IN INTERNATIONAL RELATIONSHIPS. FUT WOR+45 WOR-45 SOCIETY LEGIS CREATE TEC/DEV ECO/TAC EDU/PROP ADJUD WAR PEACE ORD/FREE PWR...KNO/TEST TREND GEN/LAWS 20. PAGE 167 A3409 — INT/ORG CONCPT DIPLOM

B58
SCOTT W.A.,THE UNITED STATES AND THE UNITED NATIONS: THE PUBLIC VIEW 1945-1955. USA+45 EDU/PROP ...INT QU KNO/TEST SAMP GP/COMP 20 UN. PAGE 130 A2674 — ATTIT DIPLOM INT/ORG

S67
DEUTSCH K.W.,"ARMS CONTROL AND EUROPEAN UNITY* THE NEXT TEN YEARS." USA+45 ELITES NAT/G BAL/PWR DIPLOM NUC/PWR...INT KNO/TEST NATO EEC. PAGE 36 A0742 — ARMS/CONT PEACE REGION PLAN

S67
VERBA S.,"PUBLIC OPINION AND THE WAR IN VIETNAM." USA+45 VIETNAM DIPLOM WAR...CORREL STAT QU CHARTS 20. PAGE 158 A3228 — ATTIT KNO/TEST NAT/G PLAN

S67
WILPERT C.,"A LOOK IN THE MIRROR AND OVER THE WALL." GERMANY POL/PAR...KNO/TEST COLD/WAR. PAGE 165 A3358 — NAT/G PLAN DIPLOM ATTIT

KNOLES G.H. A1653

KNORR K.E. A1654,A1655,A1656

KNOWL....ENLIGHTENMENT, KNOWLEDGE

N
AMERICAN DOCUMENTATION INST,DOCUMENTATION ABSTRACTS. WOR+45 NAT/G COMPUTER CREATE TEC/DEV DIPLOM EDU/PROP REGION KNOWL...PHIL/SCI CLASSIF LING. PAGE 7 A0143 — BIBLIOG/A AUTOMAT COMPUT/IR R+D

N
AVTOREFERATY DISSERTATSII. USSR INTELL ACADEM NAT/G DIPLOM GOV/REL KNOWL CONCPT. PAGE 3 A0047 — BIBLIOG MARXISM MARXIST COM

N
MINISTERE DE L'EDUC NATIONALE,CATALOGUE DES THESES DE DOCTORAT SOUTENNES DEVANT LES UNIVERSITAIRES FRANCAISES. FRANCE LAW DIPLOM ADMIN...HUM SOC 20. PAGE 102 A2087 — BIBLIOG ACADEM KNOWL NAT/G

N
US LIBRARY OF CONGRESS,EAST EUROPEAN ACCESSIONS INDEX. NAT/G ISOLAT ATTIT KNOWL...POLICY 20. PAGE 154 A3144 — BIBLIOG COM MARXIST DIPLOM

B04
CRANDALL S.B.,TREATIES: THEIR MAKING AND ENFORCEMENT. MOD/EUR USA-45 CONSTN INT/ORG NAT/G LEGIS EDU/PROP LEGIT EXEC PEACE KNOWL MORAL...JURID CONGRESS 19/20 TREATY. PAGE 32 A0655 — LAW

B19
DE CALLIERES F.,THE PRACTICE OF DIPLOMACY. MOD/EUR INT/ORG NAT/G DELIB/GP LEGIS TOP/EX DOMIN ATTIT KNOWL LEAGUE/NAT 20. PAGE 34 A0699 — CONSULT ACT/RES DIPLOM INT/LAW

B22
POTTER P.B.,AN INTRODUCTION TO THE STUDY OF INTERNATIONAL ORGANIZATION. WOR-45 ACT/RES CREATE EDU/PROP ROUTINE PERCEPT KNOWL...CONT/OBS RECORD GEN/LAWS TOT/POP VAL/FREE 20. PAGE 117 A2398 — INT/ORG CONCPT

B24
POOLE D.C.,THE CONDUCT OF FOREIGN RELATIONS UNDER MODERN DEMOCRATIC CONDITIONS. EUR+WWI USA-45 INT/ORG PLAN LEGIT ADMIN KNOWL PWR...MAJORIT OBS/ENVIR HIST/WRIT GEN/LAWS 20. PAGE 117 A2395 — NAT/G EDU/PROP DIPLOM

B28
BUTLER G.,THE DEVELOPMENT OF INTERNATIONAL LAW. WOR-45 SOCIETY NAT/G KNOWL ORD/FREE PWR...JURID CONCPT HIST/WRIT GEN/LAWS. PAGE 22 A0451 — LAW INT/LAW DIPLOM INT/ORG

B32
HANSEN A.H.,ECONOMIC STABILIZATION IN AN UNBALANCED WORLD. COM EUR+WWI USA-45 WOR-45 AGRI FINAN INDUS MARKET INT/ORG LABOR VOL/ASSN EDU/PROP ATTIT HEALTH KNOWL WEALTH...HIST/WRIT TREND VAL/FREE 20. PAGE 61 A1253 — NAT/G ECO/DEV CAP/ISM SOCISM

B33
LANGER W.L.,FOREIGN AFFAIRS BIBLIOGRAPHY. WOR-45 INT/ORG CONSULT EDU/PROP ROUTINE NAT/LISM ATTIT SOVEREIGN...STAT RECORD GEN/METH LEAGUE/NAT TOT/POP. PAGE 84 A1725 — KNOWL

B38
WARE E.E.,THE STUDY OF INTERNATIONAL RELATIONS IN THE UNITED STATES. USA+45 USA-45 WOR-45 INTELL SERV/IND INT/ORG NAT/G PROF/ORG SECT CONSULT INT/TRADE EDU/PROP ARMS/CONT...CONCPT 20. PAGE 161 A3283 — KNOWL DIPLOM

C39
HADDOW A.,"POLITICAL SCIENCE IN AMERICAN COLLEGES AND UNIVERSITIES 1636-1900." CONSTN MORAL...POLICY INT/LAW CON/ANAL BIBLIOG T 17/20. PAGE 59 A1211 — USA-45 LAW ACADEM KNOWL

B40
MIDDLEBUSH F.,ELEMENTS OF INTERNATIONAL RELATIONS. WOR-45 PROVS CONSULT EDU/PROP LEGIT WAR NAT/LISM ATTIT KNOWL MORAL ORD/FREE PWR...JURID LEAGUE/NAT TOT/POP VAL/FREE. PAGE 101 A2067 — NAT/G INT/ORG PEACE DIPLOM

B42
TOLMAN E.C.,DRIVES TOWARD WAR. UNIV PLAN DIPLOM ECO/TAC COERCE PERS/REL ADJUST HAPPINESS BIO/SOC HEREDITY HEALTH KNOWL. PAGE 144 A2947 — PSY WAR UTOPIA DRIVE

B44
ADLER M.J.,HOW TO THINK ABOUT WAR AND PEACE. WOR-45 LAW SOCIETY EX/STRUC DIPLOM KNOWL ORD/FREE...POLICY TREND GEN/LAWS 20. PAGE 4 A0092 — INT/ORG CREATE ARMS/CONT PEACE

B44
DAVIS H.E.,PIONEERS IN WORLD ORDER. WOR-45 CONSTN ECO/TAC DOMIN EDU/PROP LEGIT ADJUD ADMIN ARMS/CONT CHOOSE KNOWL ORD/FREE...POLICY JURID SOC STAT OBS CENSUS TIME/SEQ ANTHOL LEAGUE/NAT 20. PAGE 34 A0691 — INT/ORG ROUTINE

L44
CORWIN E.S.,"THE CONSTITUTION AND WORLD ORGANIZATION." FUT USA+45 USA-45 NAT/G EX/STRUC LEGIS PEACE KNOWL...CON/ANAL UN 20. PAGE 31 A0627 — INT/ORG CONSTN SOVEREIGN

B45
BEVERIDGE W.,THE PRICE OF PEACE. GERMANY UK WOR+45 WOR-45 NAT/G FORCES CREATE LEGIT REGION WAR ATTIT KNOWL ORD/FREE PWR...POLICY NEW/IDEA GEN/LAWS LEAGUE/NAT 20 TREATY. PAGE 14 A0284
INT/ORG TREND PEACE

B45
KANDELL I.L.,UNITED STATES ACTIVITIES IN INTERNATIONAL CULTURAL RELATIONS. INT/ORG NAT/G VOL/ASSN CREATE DIPLOM EDU/PROP ATTIT RIGID/FLEX KNOWL...PLURIST CONCPT OBS TREND GEN/LAWS TOT/POP UNESCO 20. PAGE 76 A1554
USA-45 CULTURE

B45
MACMINN N.,BIBLIOGRAPHY OF THE PUBLISHED WRITINGS OF JOHN STUART MILL. MOD/EUR UK CAP/ISM DIPLOM KNOWL...EPIST CONCPT 19 MILL/JS. PAGE 93 A1901
BIBLIOG/A SOCIETY INGP/REL LAISSEZ

B46
BIBLIOGRAFIIA DISSERTATSII: DOKTORSKIE DISSERTATSII ZA 19411944 (2 VOLS.). COM USSR LAW POL/PAR DIPLOM ADMIN LEAD...PHIL/SCI SOC 20. PAGE 3 A0054
BIBLIOG ACADEM KNOWL MARXIST

B46
LOWENSTEIN R.,POLITICAL RECONSTRUCTION. WOR+45 EX/STRUC EDU/PROP NAT/LISM ATTIT KNOWL ORD/FREE PWR ...SOCIALIST CONCPT GEN/LAWS TOT/POP 20. PAGE 91 A1869
FUT INT/ORG DIPLOM

L46
MASTERS D.,"ONE WORLD OR NONE." FUT WOR+45 INTELL INT/ORG ACT/RES EDU/PROP DETER ATTIT RIGID/FLEX SUPEGO KNOWL...STAT TREND ORG/CHARTS 20. PAGE 96 A1960
POLICY PHIL/SCI ARMS/CONT NUC/PWR

S46
DOUGLAS W.O.,"SYMPOSIUM ON WORLD ORGANIZATION." FUT USA+45 WOR+45 CONSTN SOCIETY NAT/G PLAN EDU/PROP LEGIT RIGID/FLEX KNOWL...INT/LAW JURID STERTYP TOT/POP 20. PAGE 38 A0778
INT/ORG LAW

B47
KIRK G.,THE STUDY OF INTERNATIONAL RELATIONS. FUT USA-45 R+D ACADEM INT/ORG CONSULT DELIB/GP INT/TRADE EDU/PROP PEACE RIGID/FLEX KNOWL VAL/FREE 20. PAGE 80 A1632
USA+45 DIPLOM

L47
BRUNER J.S.,"TOWARD A COMMON GROUND-INTERNATIONAL SOCIAL SCIENCE." FUT WOR+45 INTELL R+D NAT/G VOL/ASSN CONSULT DELIB/GP ACT/RES CREATE PLAN TEC/DEV ATTIT ORD/FREE...PSY SOC CONCPT ANTHOL UNESCO 20. PAGE 20 A0410
INT/ORG KNOWL

B49
FORD FOUNDATION,REPORT OF THE STUDY FOR THE FORD FOUNDATION ON POLICY AND PROGRAM. SOCIETY R+D ACT/RES CAP/ISM FOR/AID EDU/PROP ADMIN KNOWL ...POLICY PSY SOC 20. PAGE 47 A0961
WEALTH GEN/LAWS

L49
UNESCO,"SOME SUGGESTIONS ON TEACHING ABOUT THE UN AND ITS SPECIALIZED AGENCIES." UNIV WOR+45 SOCIETY STRATA SCHOOL WAR ALL/VALS KNOWL...SOC CONCPT UNESCO 20 UN. PAGE 147 A3011
INT/ORG EDU/PROP

B50
LINCOLN G.,ECONOMICS OF NATIONAL SECURITY. USA+45 ELITES COM/IND DIST/IND INDUS NAT/G VOL/ASSN DELIB/GP EX/STRUC FOR/AID EDU/PROP COERCE NUC/PWR WAR ATTIT KNOWL ORD/FREE PWR COLD/WAR TOT/POP VAL/FREE 20. PAGE 89 A1818
FORCES ECO/TAC

S50
CORBETT P.E.,"OBJECTIVITY IN THE STUDY OF INTERNATIONAL AFFAIRS." WOR+45 SOCIETY ACT/RES EDU/PROP PERSON RIGID/FLEX KNOWL TOT/POP 20. PAGE 30 A0614
INT/ORG DIPLOM

S50
UNESCO,"MEETING ON UNIVERSITY TEACHING OF INTERNATIONAL RELATIONS." FUT WOR+45 R+D VOL/ASSN CONSULT PLAN EDU/PROP ATTIT...CONCPT TREND 20. PAGE 147 A3012
INT/ORG KNOWL DIPLOM

S50
WITTFOGEL K.A.,"RUSSIA AND ASIA: PROBLEMS OF CONTEMPORARY AREA STUDIES AND INTERNATIONAL RELATIONS." ASIA COM USA+45 SOCIETY NAT/G DIPLOM ECO/TAC FOR/AID EDU/PROP KNOWL...HIST/WRIT TOT/POP 20. PAGE 166 A3373
ECO/DEV ADMIN RUSSIA USSR

B51
BLANSHARD P.,COMMUNISM, DEMOCRACY AND CATHOLIC POWER. USSR VATICAN WOR+45 WOR-45 CULTURE ELITES INTELL SOCIETY STRUCT INT/ORG POL/PAR EDU/PROP COERCE ATTIT KNOWL PWR MARXISM...CONCPT COLD/WAR 20. PAGE 15 A0308
COM SECT TOTALISM

B51
WABEKE B.H.,A GUIDE TO DUTCH BIBLIOGRAPHIES. BELGIUM INDONESIA NETHERLAND DIPLOM INT/TRADE WAR NAT/LISM KNOWL...ART/METH HUM JURID CON/ANAL 14/20. PAGE 160 A3257
BIBLIOG/A NAT/G CULTURE COLONIAL

B52
RIGGS F.W.,FORMOSA UNDER CHINESE NATIONALIST RULE. CHINA/COM USA+45 CONSTN AGRI FINAN LABOR LOC/G NAT/G POL/PAR FORCES HEALTH KNOWL...STAT WORK VAL/FREE 20. PAGE 121 A2479
ASIA FOR/AID DIPLOM

B52
THOM J.M.,GUIDE TO RESEARCH MATERIAL IN POLITICAL SCIENCE (PAMPHLET). ELITES LOC/G MUNIC NAT/G LEGIS DIPLOM ADJUD CIVMIL/REL GOV/REL PWR MGT. PAGE 143 A2919
BIBLIOG/A KNOWL

N52
COORDINATING COMM DOC SOC SCI,INTERNATIONAL REPERTORY OF SOCIAL SCIENCE DOCUMENTATION CENTERS (PAMPHLET). ACT/RES OP/RES WRITING KNOWL...CON/ANAL METH. PAGE 30 A0610
BIBLIOG/A R+D NAT/G INT/ORG

B53
BARBER H.W.,FOREIGN POLICIES OF THE UNITED STATES. USA+45 USA-45 WOR+45 INT/ORG NAT/G EX/STRUC ECO/TAC DOMIN EDU/PROP LEGIT COERCE KNOWL PWR COLD/WAR COLD/WAR 20. PAGE 11 A0219
CONCPT DIPLOM

B53
COHEN B.C.,CITIZEN EDUCATION IN WORLD AFFAIRS. USA+45 INT/ORG VOL/ASSN CONSULT ATTIT PWR...INT TIME/SEQ 20. PAGE 27 A0559
KNOWL EDU/PROP DIPLOM

B53
COUSINS N.,WHO SPEAKS FOR MAN. GERMANY KOREA WOR+45 SOCIETY INT/ORG NAT/G CREATE EDU/PROP HEALTH KNOWL LOVE MORAL...OBS SELF/OBS BIOG HYPO/EXP TOT/POP 20 CHINJAP. PAGE 32 A0642
ATTIT WAR PEACE

L53
UNESCO,"THE TECHNIQUE OF INTERNATIONAL CONFERENCES." WOR+45 INT/ORG VOL/ASSN EDU/PROP ROUTINE ATTIT DRIVE KNOWL ORD/FREE...SOC UNESCO 20. PAGE 148 A3016
DELIB/GP ACT/RES

S53
MANNING C.A.W.,"THE PRETENTIONS OF INTERNATIONAL RELATIONS." WOR+45 SOCIETY CREATE EDU/PROP ATTIT PERSON KNOWL...GEN/LAWS TOT/POP VAL/FREE 20. PAGE 94 A1924
INT/ORG DIPLOM UK

B54
COUDENHOVE-KALERGI,AN IDEA CONQUERS THE WORLD. EUR+WWI MOD/EUR USA-45 CONSTN FAM CREATE EDU/PROP ATTIT PERSON KNOWL...CONCPT SELF/OBS TIME/SEQ. PAGE 31 A0635
INT/ORG BIOG DIPLOM

B54
MANNING C.A.W.,THE UNIVERSITY TEACHING OF SOCIAL SCIENCES: INTERNATIONAL RELATIONS. WOR+45 INTELL STRATA R+D ACADEM INT/ORG NAT/G CONSULT DELIB/GP ACT/RES EDU/PROP NAT/LISM ATTIT...POLICY CONT/OBS HYPO/EXP VAL/FREE LEAGUE/NAT UNESCO 20. PAGE 94 A1925
KNOWL PHIL/SCI DIPLOM

B55
MOCH J.,HUMAN FOLLY: DISARM OR PERISH. USA+45 WOR+45 SOCIETY INT/ORG NAT/G ACT/RES EDU/PROP ATTIT PERSON KNOWL ORD/FREE PWR...MAJORIT TOT/POP COLD/WAR 20. PAGE 102 A2093
FUT DELIB/GP ARMS/CONT NUC/PWR

B55
MYRDAL A.R.,AMERICA'S ROLE IN INTERNATIONATIONAL SOCIAL WELFARE. FUT WOR+45 SOCIETY R+D VOL/ASSN ECO/TAC EDU/PROP HEALTH KNOWL WEALTH...SOC CHARTS ORG/CHARTS TOT/POP 20. PAGE 107 A2188
PLAN SKILL FOR/AID

S55
TORRE M.,"PSYCHIATRIC OBSERVATIONS OF INTERNATIONAL CONFERENCES." WOR+45 INT/ORG PROF/ORG VOL/ASSN CONSULT EDU/PROP ROUTINE ATTIT DRIVE KNOWL...PSY METH/CNCPT OBS/ENVIR STERTYP 20. PAGE 144 A2950
DELIB/GP OBS DIPLOM

S55
WRIGHT Q.,"THE PEACEFUL ADJUSTMENT OF INTERNATIONAL RELATIONS: PROBLEMS AND RESEARCH APPROACHES." UNIV INTELL EDU/PROP ADJUD ROUTINE KNOWL SKILL...INT/LAW JURID PHIL/SCI CLASSIF 20. PAGE 167 A3411
R+D METH/CNCPT PEACE

B56
BLACKETT P.M.S.,ATOMIC WEAPONS AND EAST-WEST RELATIONS. FUT WOR+45 INT/ORG DELIB/GP COERCE ATTIT RIGID/FLEX KNOWL...RELATIV HIST/WRIT TREND GEN/METH COLD/WAR 20. PAGE 15 A0299
FORCES PWR ARMS/CONT NUC/PWR

B56
KIRK G.,THE CHANGING ENVIRONMENT OF INTERNATIONAL RELATIONS. ASIA S/ASIA USA+45 WOR+45 ECO/UNDEV INT/ORG NAT/G FOR/AID EDU/PROP PEACE KNOWL ...PLURIST COLD/WAR TOT/POP 20. PAGE 80 A1634
FUT EXEC DIPLOM

B56
SPEECKAERT G.P.,INTERNATIONAL INSTITUTIONS AND INTERNATIONAL ORGANIZATIONS. PROF/ORG DELIB/GP KNOWL 19/20. PAGE 136 A2776
BIBLIOG INT/ORG DIPLOM VOL/ASSN

B57
FULLER C.D.,TRAINING OF SPECIALISTS IN INTERNATIONAL RELATIONS. FUT USA+45 USA-45 INTELL INT/ORG...MGT METH/CNCPT INT QU GEN/METH 20. PAGE 50 A1017
KNOWL DIPLOM

B57
KISSINGER H.A.,NUCLEAR WEAPONS AND FOREIGN POLICY. FUT USA+45 WOR+45 INT/ORG FORCES ACT/RES TEC/DEV DIPLOM ARMS/CONT COERCE ATTIT KNOWL PWR...DECISION GEOG CHARTS 20. PAGE 80 A1640
PLAN DETER NUC/PWR

B57
LAVES W.H.C.,UNESCO. FUT WOR+45 NAT/G CONSULT DELIB/GP TEC/DEV ECO/TAC EDU/PROP PEACE ORD/FREE ...CONCPT TIME/SEQ TREND UNESCO VAL/FREE 20. PAGE 86 A1751
INT/ORG KNOWL

B57
MATECKI B.,ESTABLISHMENT OF THE INTERNATIONAL FINANCE CORPORATION AND UNITED STATES POLICY. USA+45 WOR+45 CONSTN NAT/G CREATE RIGID/FLEX KNOWL ...METH/CNCPT TIME/SEQ SIMUL TOT/POP 20 INTL/FINAN. PAGE 96 A1964 FINAN INT/ORG DIPLOM

B57
STRACHEY A.,THE UNCONSCIOUS MOTIVES OF WAR; A PSYCHO-ANALYTICAL CONTRIBUTION. UNIV SOCIETY DIPLOM DREAM GP/REL ADJUST ATTIT DISPL PERCEPT PERSON KNOWL MORAL. PAGE 139 A2840 WAR DRIVE LOVE PSY

L57
HAAS E.B.,"REGIONAL INTEGRATION AND NATIONAL POLICY." WOR+45 VOL/ASSN DELIB/GP EX/STRUC ECO/TAC DOMIN EDU/PROP LEGIT COERCE ATTIT PERCEPT KNOWL ...TIME/SEQ COLD/WAR 20 UN. PAGE 59 A1203 INT/ORG ORD/FREE REGION

B58
CHANG H.,WITHIN THE FOUR SEAS. ASIA WAR MORAL MARXISM...IDEA/COMP NAT/COMP 20 CONFUCIUS. PAGE 26 A0521 PEACE DIPLOM KNOWL CULTURE

B58
HENKIN L.,ARMS CONTROL AND INSPECTION IN AMERICAN LAW. LAW CONSTN INT/ORG LOC/G MUNIC NAT/G PROVS EDU/PROP LEGIT EXEC NUC/PWR KNOWL ORD/FREE...OBS TOT/POP CONGRESS 20. PAGE 64 A1315 USA+45 JURID ARMS/CONT

B58
MELMAN S.,INSPECTION FOR DISARMAMENT. USA+45 WOR+45 SOCIETY INT/ORG NAT/G CONSULT ACT/RES PLAN EDU/PROP CONTROL DETER PEACE ATTIT PERSON KNOWL...PSY STAT OBS CHARTS TOT/POP VAL/FREE 20. PAGE 99 A2035 FUT ORD/FREE ARMS/CONT NUC/PWR

B58
NOEL-BAKER D.,THE ARMS RACE. WOR+45 NAT/G DELIB/GP ACT/RES TEC/DEV EDU/PROP NUC/PWR ATTIT KNOWL PWR ...CONCPT OBS LEAGUE/NAT 20 COLD/WAR. PAGE 109 A2245 FUT INT/ORG ARMS/CONT PEACE

B58
ORGANSKI A.F.K.,WORLD POLITICS. FUT WOR+45 SOCIETY STRUCT NAT/G BAL/PWR ECO/TAC DOMIN NAT/LISM ATTIT KNOWL ORD/FREE PWR...CONCPT METH/CNCPT TREND STERTYP GEN/LAWS TOT/POP 20. PAGE 112 A2297 INT/ORG DIPLOM

B58
REUTER P.,INTERNATIONAL INSTITUTIONS. WOR+45 WOR-45 CULTURE SOCIETY VOL/ASSN LEGIT ROUTINE GP/REL INGP/REL KNOWL...JURID METH/CNCPT TIME/SEQ 20. PAGE 120 A2469 INT/ORG PSY

S58
ANDERSON N.,"INTERNATIONAL SEMINARS: AN ANALYSIS AND AN EVALUATION." WOR+45 R+D ACT/RES CREATE PLAN REGION ATTIT KNOWL SKILL...SOC REC/INT PERS/TEST CHARTS 20. PAGE 8 A0158 INT/ORG DELIB/GP

S58
BOGART L.,"MEASURING THE EFFECTIVENESS OF AN OVERSEAS INFORMATION CAMPAIGN." EUR+WWI GREECE USA+45 INT/ORG MUNIC PLAN DIPLOM PEACE PERCEPT RIGID/FLEX KNOWL...TECHNIC PSY SOC NEW/IDEA CONT/OBS REC/INT STAND/INT SAMP/SIZ COLD/WAR 20. PAGE 16 A0328 ATTIT EDU/PROP

B59
CHINA INSTITUTE OF AMERICA.,CHINA AND THE UNITED NATIONS. CHINA/COM FUT STRUCT EDU/PROP LEGIT ADMIN ATTIT KNOWL ORD/FREE PWR...OBS RECORD STAND/INT TIME/SEQ UN LEAGUE/NAT UNESCO 20. PAGE 26 A0531 ASIA INT/ORG

B59
GOODRICH L.,THE UNITED NATIONS. WOR+45 CONSTN STRUCT ACT/RES LEGIT COERCE KNOWL ORD/FREE PWR ...GEN/LAWS UN 20. PAGE 54 A1104 INT/ORG ROUTINE

B59
MATHISEN T.,METHODOLOGY IN THE STUDY OF INTERNATIONAL RELATIONS. FUT WOR+45 SOCIETY INT/ORG NAT/G POL/PAR WAR PEACE KNOWL PWR...RELATIV CONCPT METH/CNCPT TREND HYPO/EXP METH TOT/POP 20. PAGE 96 A1965 GEN/METH CON/ANAL DIPLOM CREATE

B59
MODELSKI G.,ATOMIC ENERGY IN THE COMMUNIST BLOC. FUT INT/ORG CONSULT FORCES ACT/RES PLAN KNOWL SKILL ...PHIL/SCI STAT CHARTS 20. PAGE 102 A2096 TEC/DEV NUC/PWR USSR COM

B59
STANFORD RESEARCH INSTITUTE,POSSIBLE NONMILITARY SCIENTIFIC DEVELOPMENTS AND THEIR POTENTIAL IMPACT ON FOREIGN POLICY PROBLEMS OF THE UNITED. FUT USA+45 INT/ORG PROF/ORG CONSULT ACT/RES CREATE PLAN PEACE KNOWL SKILL...TECHNIC PHIL/SCI NEW/IDEA UNESCO 20. PAGE 137 A2802 R+D TEC/DEV

B59
STRAUSZ-HUPE R.,PROTRACTED CONFLICT. CHINA/COM KOREA WOR+45 INT/ORG FORCES ACT/RES ECO/TAC LEGIT COERCE DRIVE PERCEPT KNOWL PWR...PSY CONCPT RECORD GEN/METH COLD/WAR VAL/FREE 20. PAGE 139 A2847 COM PLAN USSR

S59
HARTT J.,"ANTARCTICA: ITS IMMEDIATE PRACTICALITIES." FUT USA+45 USSR WOR+45 INT/ORG NAT/G CREATE TEC/DEV REGION KNOWL WEALTH...GEOG 20 ANTARTICA. PAGE 62 A1276 VOL/ASSN ORD/FREE DIPLOM

S59
QUIGLEY H.S.,"TOWARD REAPPRAISAL OF OUR CHINA POLICY." CHINA/COM USA+45 INT/ORG PLAN ECO/TAC PERCEPT ORD/FREE...DECISION PSY CON/ANAL GEN/METH VAL/FREE 20. PAGE 118 A2427 ASIA KNOWL DIPLOM

S59
SAYEGH F.,"ARAB NATIONALISM AND SOVIET-AMERICAN RELATIONS." ISLAM USA+45 ECO/UNDEV PLAN ECO/TAC LEGIT NAT/LISM DRIVE PERCEPT KNOWL PWR...DECISION CONCPT STAT RECORD TREND CON/ANAL VAL/FREE 20 COLD/WAR. PAGE 127 A2610 DIPLOM USSR

B60
CARNEGIE ENDOWMENT INT. PEACE,PERSPECTIVES ON PEACE - 1910-1960. WOR+45 WOR-45 INTELL INT/ORG CONSULT ACT/RES EDU/PROP ATTIT KNOWL ORD/FREE...TIME/SEQ TREND EEC OAS UNESCO NAZI 20. PAGE 24 A0489 FUT CONCPT ARMS/CONT PEACE

B60
SHONFIELD A.,THE ATTACK ON WORLD POVERTY. WOR+45 ECO/DEV ECO/UNDEV FINAN VOL/ASSN PLAN EDU/PROP DRIVE KNOWL WEALTH...CONT/OBS STAND/INT ORG/CHARTS TOT/POP UNESCO 20. PAGE 132 A2704 INT/ORG ECO/TAC FOR/AID INT/TRADE

B60
US HOUSE COMM. SCI. ASTRONAUT.,OCEAN SCIENCES AND NATIONAL SECURITY. FUT SEA ECO/DEV EXTR/IND INT/ORG NAT/G FORCES ACT/RES TEC/DEV ECO/TAC COERCE WAR BIO/SOC KNOWL PWR...CONCPT RECORD LAB/EXP 20. PAGE 154 A3141 R+D ORD/FREE

B60
WOETZEL R.K.,THE INTERNATIONAL CONTROL OF AIRSPACE AND OUTERSPACE. FUT WOR+45 AIR CONSTN STRUCT CONSULT PLAN TEC/DEV ADJUD RIGID/FLEX KNOWL ORD/FREE PWR...TECHNIC GEOG MGT NEW/IDEA TREND COMPUT/IR VAL/FREE 20 TREATY. PAGE 166 A3375 INT/ORG JURID SPACE INT/LAW

L60
BRENNAN D.G.,"SETTING AND GOALS OF ARMS CONTROL." FUT USA+45 USSR WOR+45 INTELL INT/ORG NAT/G VOL/ASSN CONSULT PLAN DIPLOM ECO/TAC ADMIN KNOWL PWR...POLICY CONCPT TREND COLD/WAR 20. PAGE 18 A0371 FORCES COERCE ARMS/CONT DETER

L60
DEUTSCH K.W.,"TOWARD AN INVENTORY OF BASIC TRENDS AND PATTERNS IN COMPARATIVE AND INTERNATIONAL POLITICS." UNIV WOR+45 SOCIETY STRUCT INT/ORG NAT/G CREATE PLAN EDU/PROP KNOWL...PHIL/SCI METH/CNCPT STAT SELF/OBS OBS/ENVIR SAMP TREND CON/ANAL CHARTS SOC/EXP GEN/METH 20. PAGE 36 A0739 R+D PERCEPT

L60
LAUTERPACHT E.,"THE UNITED NATIONS EMERGENCY FORCE." R+D LEGIT ROUTINE COERCE KNOWL ORD/FREE SKILL...JURID UN 20. PAGE 85 A1746 INT/ORG FORCES

S60
BOGARDUS E.S.,"THE SOCIOLOGY OF A STRUCTURED PEACE." FUT SOCIETY CREATE DIPLOM EDU/PROP ADJUD ROUTINE ATTIT RIGID/FLEX KNOWL ORD/FREE RESPECT ...POLICY INT/LAW JURID NEW/IDEA SELF/OBS TOT/POP 20 UN. PAGE 16 A0327 INT/ORG SOC NAT/LISM PEACE

S60
LEAR J.,"PEACE: SCIENCE'S NEXT GREAT EXPLORATION." USA+45 INT/ORG TOP/EX TEC/DEV EDU/PROP ROUTINE PEACE KNOWL SKILL 20. PAGE 86 A1757 EX/STRUC ARMS/CONT NUC/PWR

S60
PETERSON E.N.,"HISTORICAL SCHOLARSHIP AND WORLD UNITY." FUT UNIV WOR-45 CULTURE INTELL INT/ORG NAT/G ACT/RES EDU/PROP ATTIT PERCEPT RIGID/FLEX ...NEW/IDEA OBS HIST/WRIT TREND COLD/WAR TOT/POP 20. PAGE 115 A2367 PLAN KNOWL NAT/LISM

S60
RUSSEL R.W.,"ROLES FOR PSYCHOLOGISTS IN THE MAINTENANCE OF PEACE." FUT USA+45 CULTURE INT/ORG DIPLOM FOR/AID EDU/PROP ATTIT KNOWL MORAL PWR ...POLICY SOC COLD/WAR 20. PAGE 125 A2572 PSY GEN/METH

S60
THOMPSON K.W.,"MORAL PURPOSE IN FOREIGN POLICY: REALITIES AND ILLUSIONS." WOR+45 WOR-45 LAW CULTURE SOCIETY INT/ORG PLAN ADJUD ADMIN COERCE RIGID/FLEX SUPEGO KNOWL ORD/FREE PWR...SOC TREND SOC/EXP TOT/POP 20. PAGE 143 A2930 MORAL JURID DIPLOM

B61
HOLDSWORTH M.,SOVIET AFRICAN STUDIES 1918-1959. USSR ACADEM NAT/G DIPLOM REGION KNOWL 20. PAGE 66 A1366 BIBLIOG/A AFR HABITAT NAT/COMP

B61
NOGEE J.L.,SOVIET POLICY TOWARD INTERNATIONAL CONTROL OF ATOMIC ENERGY. COM USA+45 WOR+45 INTELL NAT/G ACT/RES DIPLOM EDU/PROP NUC/PWR TOTALISM PERCEPT KNOWL PWR...TIME/SEQ COLD/WAR 20. PAGE 109 A2247 INT/ORG ATTIT ARMS/CONT USSR

B61
PEASLEE A.J.,INTERNATIONAL GOVERNMENT ORGANIZATIONS, CONSTITUTIONAL DOCUMENTS. WOR+45 WOR-45 CONSTN VOL/ASSN DELIB/GP EX/STRUC ROUTINE KNOWL TOT/POP 20. PAGE 114 A2344 INT/ORG STRUCT

B61
SINGER J.D.,FINANCING INTERNATIONAL ORGANIZATION: THE UNITED NATIONS BUDGET PROCESS. WOR+45 FINAN INT/ORG MGT

ACT/RES CREATE PLAN BUDGET ECO/TAC ADMIN ROUTINE ATTIT KNOWL...DECISION METH/CNCPT TIME/SEQ UN 20. PAGE 133 A2726

B61
WECHSLER H.,PRINCIPLES, POLITICS AND FUNDAMENTAL LAW: SELECTED ESSAYS. USA+45 USA-45 LAW SOCIETY NAT/G PROVS DELIB/GP EX/STRUC ACT/RES LEGIT PERSON KNOWL PWR...JURID 20 NUREMBERG. PAGE 162 A3296
CT/SYS CONSTN INT/LAW

L61
LEVINE R.A.,"THE ANTHROPOLOGY OF CONFLICT." FUT CULTURE INTELL FAM INT/ORG LG/CO SML/CO ATTIT KNOWL ...METH/CNCPT VAL/FREE 20. PAGE 88 A1796
SOCIETY ACT/RES

S61
BARALL M.,"THE UNITED STATES GOVERNMENT RESPONDS." L/A+17C USA+45 SOCIETY NAT/G CREATE PLAN DIPLOM ECO/TAC ATTIT DRIVE RIGID/FLEX KNOWL SKILL WEALTH ...METH/CNCPT TIME/SEQ GEN/METH 20. PAGE 11 A0217
ECO/UNDEV ACT/RES FOR/AID

S61
GALBRAITH J.K.,"A POSITIVE APPROACH TO ECONOMIC AID." FUT USA+45 INTELL NAT/G CONSULT ACT/RES DIPLOM ECO/TAC EDU/PROP ATTIT KNOWL PWR WEALTH ...SOC STERTYP 20. PAGE 50 A1030
ECO/UNDEV ROUTINE FOR/AID

B62
CARDOZA M.H.,DIPLOMATS IN INTERNATIONAL COOPERATION: STEPCHILDREN OF THE FOREIGN SERVICE. EUR+WWI USA+45 NAT/G CONSULT ACT/RES EDU/PROP ROUTINE RIGID/FLEX KNOWL SKILL...SOC OBS TIME/SEQ EEC OEEC NATO 20. PAGE 24 A0480
INT/ORG METH/CNCPT DIPLOM

B62
COUNCIL ON WORLD TENSIONS,A STUDY OF WORLD TENSIONS AND DEVELOPMENT. WOR+45 ECO/DEV ECO/UNDEV INT/ORG PLAN DIPLOM ECO/TAC EDU/PROP ATTIT KNOWL ORD/FREE PWR WEALTH...CONCPT TREND CHARTS STERTYP COLD/WAR TOT/POP 20. PAGE 31 A0640
TEC/DEV SOC

B62
DALLIN A.,THE SOVIET UNION AT THE UNITED NATIONS: AN INQUIRY INTO SOVIET MOTIVES AND OBJECTIVES. ACT/RES EDU/PROP LEGIT ATTIT KNOWL PWR...POLICY RECORD HIST/WRIT TIME/SEQ TREND ORG/CHARTS GEN/METH COLD/WAR FAO 20 UN. PAGE 33 A0675
COM INT/ORG USSR

B62
GILPIN R.,AMERICAN SCIENTISTS AND NUCLEAR WEAPONS POLICY. COM FUT USA+45 WOR+45 INT/ORG NAT/G PROF/ORG CONSULT FORCES CREATE TEC/DEV BAL/PWR EDU/PROP ARMS/CONT WAR PERCEPT KNOWL MORAL PWR ...PHIL/SCI SOC CONCPT GEN/LAWS 20. PAGE 52 A1073
INTELL ATTIT DETER NUC/PWR

B62
HOFFMAN P.,WORLD WITHOUT WANT. FUT WOR+45 ECO/UNDEV INT/ORG HEALTH KNOWL...TREND TOT/POP FAO 20. PAGE 66 A1353
CONCPT POLICY FOR/AID

B62
NICHOLAS H.G.,THE UNITED NATIONS AS A POLITICAL INSTITUTION. WOR+45 CONSTN EX/STRUC ACT/RES LEGIT PERCEPT KNOWL PWR...CONCPT TIME/SEQ CON/ANAL ORG/CHARTS UN 20. PAGE 109 A2228
INT/ORG ROUTINE

B62
OSGOOD C.E.,AN ALTERNATIVE TO WAR OR SURRENDER. FUT UNIV CULTURE INTELL SOCIETY R+D INT/ORG CONSULT DELIB/GP ACT/RES PLAN CHOOSE ATTIT PERCEPT KNOWL ...PHIL/SCI PSY SOC TREND GEN/LAWS 20. PAGE 112 A2300
ORD/FREE EDU/PROP PEACE WAR

B62
SAVORD R.,AMERICAN AGENCIES INTERESTED IN INTERNATIONAL AFFAIRS. USA-45 R+D NAT/G VOL/ASSN ACT/RES EDU/PROP KNOWL...CONCPT 20. PAGE 127 A2608
INT/ORG CONSULT DIPLOM

B62
WEIDNER E.W.,THE WORLD ROLE OF UNIVERSITIES. USA+45 WOR+45 SECT ACT/RES PROB/SOLV GIVE EFFICIENCY KNOWL ...LING CHARTS BIBLIOG 20. PAGE 162 A3297
ACADEM EDU/PROP DIPLOM POLICY

S62
MILLIKEN M.,"NEW AND OLD CRITERIA FOR AID." WOR+45 ECO/DEV ECO/UNDEV ACT/RES PLAN ATTIT KNOWL...TREND CON/ANAL SIMUL GEN/METH 20. PAGE 102 A2083
USA+45 ECO/TAC FOR/AID

S62
NORTH R.C.,"DECISION MAKING IN CRISIS: AN INTRODUCTION." WOR+45 WOR-45 NAT/G CONSULT DELIB/GP TEC/DEV PERCEPT KNOWL...POLICY DECISION PSY METH/CNCPT CONT/OBS TREND VAL/FREE 20. PAGE 110 A2251
INT/ORG ROUTINE DIPLOM

S62
PYE L.W.,"THE POLITICAL IMPULSES AND FANTASIES BEHIND FOREIGN AID." FUT USA+45 ECO/UNDEV DIPLOM ECO/TAC ROUTINE DRIVE KNOWL...SOC METH/CNCPT NEW/IDEA TREND HYPO/EXP STERTYP GEN/METH 20. PAGE 118 A2420
ACT/RES ATTIT FOR/AID

S62
RUSSETT B.M.,"CAUSE, SURPRISE, AND NO ESCAPE." FUT WOR-45 CULTURE SOCIETY INT/ORG FORCES TEC/DEV BAL/PWR EDU/PROP ARMS/CONT NUC/PWR WAR WEAPON PEACE KNOWL ORD/FREE PWR...POLICY CONCPT RECORD TIME/SEQ TREND GEN/LAWS 20 WWI. PAGE 126 A2578
COERCE DIPLOM

S62
SCHILLING W.R.,"SCIENTISTS, FOREIGN POLICY AND POLITICS." WOR+45 WOR-45 INTELL INT/ORG CONSULT TOP/EX ACT/RES PLAN ADMIN KNOWL...CONCPT OBS TREND LEAGUE/NAT 20. PAGE 128 A2627
NAT/G TEC/DEV DIPLOM NUC/PWR

B63
US DEPARTMENT OF STATE,POLITICAL BEHAVIOR--A LIST OF CURRENT STUDIES. USA+45 COM/IND DIPLOM LEAD PERS/REL DRIVE PERCEPT KNOWL...DECISION SIMUL METH. PAGE 151 A3093
BIBLIOG METH/COMP GP/REL ATTIT

B63
WESTERFIELD H.,THE INSTRUMENTS OF AMERICA'S FOREIGN POLICY. WOR+45 ECO/DEV NAT/G CONSULT EX/STRUC LEGIS BAL/PWR FOR/AID INT/TRADE DOMIN EDU/PROP LEGIT ATTIT KNOWL ORD/FREE PWR WEALTH...OBS COLD/WAR TOT/POP VAL/FREE. PAGE 163 A3322
USA+45 INT/ORG DIPLOM

S63
ALGER C.F.,"UNITED NATIONS PARTICIPATION AS A LEARNING EXPERIENCE." WOR+45 KNOWL ORD/FREE PWR ...INT VAL/FREE UN 20. PAGE 6 A0120
INT/ORG ATTIT

S63
GARDNER R.N.,"COOPERATION IN OUTER SPACE." FUT USSR WOR+45 AIR LAW COM/IND CONSULT DELIB/GP CREATE KNOWL 20 TREATY. PAGE 51 A1045
INT/ORG ACT/RES PEACE SPACE

S63
JORDAN N.,"INTERNATIONAL RELATIONS AND THE PSYCHOLOGIST." USA+45 WOR+45 DIPLOM...POLICY VAL/FREE 20. PAGE 75 A1536
KNOWL PSY

S63
MARTHELOT P.,"PROGRES DE LA REFORME AGRAIRE." INTELL ECO/DEV R+D FOR/AID ADMIN KNOWL...OBS VAL/FREE UN 20. PAGE 95 A1948
AGRI INT/ORG

S63
MAZRUI A.A.,"ON THE CONCEPT 'WE ARE ALL AFRICANS'." AFR CULTURE KIN LOC/G NAT/G DOMIN EDU/PROP LEGIT ATTIT PERCEPT PERSON KNOWL ORD/FREE...TIME/SEQ TOT/POP 20. PAGE 97 A1986
PROVS INT/ORG NAT/LISM

S63
PHELPS J.,"INFORMATION AND ARMS CONTROL." COM SPACE USA+45 USSR WOR+45 R+D INT/ORG NAT/G DELIB/GP DIPLOM ORD/FREE...CONCPT 20. PAGE 116 A2374
KNOWL ARMS/CONT NUC/PWR

S63
TALLON D.,"L'ETUDE DU DROIT COMPARE COMME MOYEN DE RECHERCHER LES MATIERES SUSCEPTIBLES D'UNIFICATION INTERNATIONALE." WOR+45 LAW SOCIETY VOL/ASSN CONSULT LEGIT CT/SYS RIGID/FLEX KNOWL 20. PAGE 141 A2884
INT/ORG JURID INT/LAW

S63
VEROFF J.,"AFRICAN STUDENTS IN THE UNITED STATES." AFR USA+45 CULTURE ACT/RES FOR/AID PEACE ATTIT KNOWL...SOC RECORD DEEP/QU SYS/QU CHARTS STERTYP TOT/POP 20. PAGE 159 A3230
PERCEPT RIGID/FLEX RACE/REL

B64
HARRISON H.V.,THE ROLE OF THEORY IN INTERNATIONAL RELATIONS. UNIV WOR+45 R+D INT/ORG NAT/G PERCEPT KNOWL...DECISION CONCPT GEN/METH METH 20. PAGE 62 A1270
METH/CNCPT HYPO/EXP DIPLOM

L64
CURTIS G.L.,"THE UNITED NATIONS OBSERVER GROUP IN LEBANON." ISLAM USA+45 NAT/G CONSULT ACT/RES PLAN BAL/PWR LEGIT ATTIT KNOWL...HIST/WRIT UN 20 UN. PAGE 33 A0669
INT/ORG FORCES DIPLOM LEBANON

L64
SYMONDS R.,"REFLECTIONS IN LOCALISATION." AFR S/ASIA UK STRATA INT/ORG NAT/G SCHOOL EDU/PROP LEGIT KNOWL ORD/FREE PWR RESPECT CMN/WLTH 20. PAGE 140 A2874
ADMIN MGT COLONIAL

S64
BEIM D.,"THE COMMUNIST BLOC AND THE FOREIGN-AID GAME." WOR+45 NAT/G PLAN ROUTINE ATTIT KNOWL ORD/FREE...DECISION QUANT CONT/OBS TIME/SEQ CHARTS GAME SIMUL COLD/WAR 20. PAGE 12 A0252
COM ECO/UNDEV ECO/TAC FOR/AID

S64
GRZYBOWSKI K.,"INTERNATIONAL ORGANIZATIONS FROM THE SOVIET POINT OF VIEW." WOR+45 WOR-45 CULTURE ECO/DEV VOL/ASSN EDU/PROP ATTIT RIGID/FLEX KNOWL ...SOC OBS TIME/SEQ TREND GEN/LAWS VAL/FREE ILO UN 20. PAGE 58 A1184
COM INT/ORG DIPLOM USSR

S64
HOSCH L.G.,"PUBLIC ADMINISTRATION ON THE INTERNATIONAL FRONTIER." WOR+45 R+D NAT/G EDU/PROP EXEC KNOWL ORD/FREE VAL/FREE 20 UN. PAGE 68 A1390
INT/ORG MGT

S64
JACK H.,"NONALIGNMENT AND A TEST BAN AGREEMENT: THE ROLE OF THE NON-ALIGNED STATES." WOR+45 INT/ORG CONSULT DOMIN EDU/PROP LEGIT CHOOSE PEACE ATTIT DRIVE KNOWL ORD/FREE...TREND CHARTS GEN/LAWS UN VAL/FREE 20. PAGE 72 A1471
PWR CONCPT NUC/PWR

S64
RUBIN R.,"THE UN CORRESPONDENT." WOR+45 FACE/GP PROF/ORG EDU/PROP ROUTINE PERCEPT KNOWL...RECORD STAND/INT QU UN WORK TOT/POP VAL/FREE 20. PAGE 125 A2560
INT/ORG ATTIT DIPLOM

S64
SINGH N.,"THE CONTEMPORARY PRACTICE OF INDIA IN THE FIELD OF INTERNATIONAL LAW." INDIA S/ASIA INT/ORG NAT/G DOMIN EDU/PROP LEGIT KNOWL...CONCPT TOT/POP 20. PAGE 133 A2734
LAW ATTIT DIPLOM INT/LAW

S64
SKUBISZEWSKI K.,"FORMS OF PARTICIPATION OF INTERNATIONAL ORGANIZATION IN THE LAW MAKING PROCESS." FUT WOR+45 NAT/G DELIB/GP DOMIN LEGIT KNOWL PWR...JURID TREND 20. PAGE 134 A2740
INT/ORG LAW INT/LAW

S64
TINKER H.,"POLITICS IN SOUTHEAST ASIA." INT/ORG NAT/G CREATE PLAN TEC/DEV GUERRILLA KNOWL ORD/FREE COLD/WAR. PAGE 144 A2944
S/ASIA ACT/RES REGION

B65
COOMBS P.H.,EDUCATION AND FOREIGN AID. AFR USA+45 DIPLOM EFFICIENCY KNOWL ORD/FREE...ANTHOL 20 AID. PAGE 30 A0608
EDU/PROP FOR/AID SCHOOL ECO/UNDEV

B65
EDUCATION AND WORLD AFFAIRS,THE UNIVERSITY LOOKS ABROAD: APPROACHES TO WORLD AFFAIRS AT SIX AMERICAN UNIVERSITIES. USA+45 CREATE EDU/PROP CONFER LEAD KNOWL 20 CORNELL/U MICH/STA/U STANFORD/U TULANE/U WISCONSN/U. PAGE 40 A0822
ACADEM DIPLOM ATTIT GP/COMP

S65
FALK R.A.,"INTERNATIONAL LEGAL ORDER." USA+45 INTELL FACE/GP INT/ORG LEGIT KNOWL...CONCPT METH/CNCPT STYLE RECORD GEN/METH 20. PAGE 44 A0890
ATTIT GEN/LAWS INT/LAW

S65
HAZARD J.N.,"CO-EXISTENCE LAW BOWS OUT." WOR+45 R+D INT/ORG VOL/ASSN CONSULT DELIB/GP ACT/RES CREATE PEACE KNOWL...JURID CONCPT COLD/WAR VAL/FREE 20. PAGE 63 A1300
PROF/ORG ADJUD

B66
BLACKSTOCK P.W.,AGENTS OF DECEIT: FRAUDS, FORGERIES AND POLITICAL INTRIGUES AMONG NATIONS. USSR EDU/PROP WRITING KNOWL 18/20 COLD/WAR KENNAN/G. PAGE 15 A0302
CON/ANAL DIPLOM HIST/WRIT

B67
HOHENBERG J.,BETWEEN TWO WORLDS. ASIA S/ASIA USA+45 PRESS TV PERS/REL ISOLAT...INT CHARTS METH/COMP 20. PAGE 66 A1362
COM/IND DIPLOM EFFICIENCY KNOWL

B67
JOHNSON A.M.,BOSTON CAPITALISTS AND WESTERN RAILROADS: A STUDY IN THE NINETEENTH CENTURY RAILROAD INVESTMENT PROCESS. CREATE BARGAIN INT/TRADE GAMBLE KNOWL 19 BOSTON. PAGE 74 A1519
FINAN DIST/IND CAP/ISM ECO/UNDEV

B67
MURTY B.S.,PROPAGANDA AND WORLD PUBLIC ORDER. FUT WOR+45 COM/IND INT/ORG PROB/SOLV ATTIT KNOWL ORD/FREE...POLICY UN. PAGE 106 A2183
EDU/PROP DIPLOM CONTROL JURID

B67
SALISBURY H.E.,BEHIND THE LINES - HANOI. VIETNAM/N NAT/G GUERRILLA CIVMIL/REL NAT/LISM KNOWL 20. PAGE 126 A2592
WAR PROB/SOLV DIPLOM OBS

B67
US AGENCY INTERNATIONAL DEV,PROPOSED FOREIGN AID PROGRAM FOR 1968: SUMMARY PRESENTATION TO THE CONGRESS. AFR S/ASIA USA+45 AGRI TEC/DEV DIPLOM ECO/TAC BAL/PAY COST HEALTH KNOWL SKILL 20 AID CONGRESS. PAGE 149 A3053
ECO/UNDEV BUDGET FOR/AID STAT

B67
ZUCKERMAN S.,SCIENTISTS AND WAR. ELITES INDUS DIPLOM CENTRAL EFFICIENCY KNOWL 20. PAGE 170 A3459
R+D CONSULT ACT/RES GP/REL

S67
ROGERS W.C.,"A COMPARISON OF INFORMED AND GENERAL PUBLIC OPINION ON US FOREIGN POLICY." USA+45 DIPLOM EDU/PROP ORD/FREE...POLICY SAMP IDEA/COMP 20. PAGE 123 A2515
KNOWL ATTIT GP/COMP ELITES

S67
SAPP B.B.,"TRIBAL CULTURES AND COMMUNISM." AFR USA+45 STRATA DIPLOM FOR/AID REGION CENTRAL ATTIT AUTHORIT RIGID/FLEX KNOWL. PAGE 127 A2604
KIN MARXISM ECO/UNDEV STRUCT

S67
THOMPSON K.W.,"THE EMPIRICAL, NORMATIVE, AND THEORETICAL FOUNDATIONS OF INTERNATIONAL STUDIES." WOR+45 INGP/REL RATIONAL...CONCPT RECORD IDEA/COMP. PAGE 143 A2932
DIPLOM INTELL METH/COMP KNOWL

C67
GEHLEN M.P.,"THE POLITICS OF COEXISTENCE: SOVIET METHODS AND MOTIVES." COM USSR NAT/G INT/TRADE EDU/PROP ARMS/CONT DETER KNOWL...CHARTS IDEA/COMP 20 COLD/WAR. PAGE 52 A1056
BIBLIOG PEACE DIPLOM MARXISM

KNOWLEDGE TEST....SEE KNO/TEST

KNOX V.H. A1657

KNOX/HENRY....HENRY KNOX (SECRETARY OF WAR 1789)

KOENIG L.W. A1658

KOH S.J. A1659

KOHLER/J....JOSEF KOHLER

KOHN H. A1660,A1661,A1662

KOHN L.Y. A1663

KOHNSTAMM M. A1664

KOJIMA K. A1665

KOLAJA J. A1220

KOLARZ W. A1666,A1667,A1668

KOMESAR N.K. A1669

KORBEL J. A1670

KORBONSKI A. A1671,A1672

KOREA....SEE ALSO KOREA/N, KOREA/S, ASIA

NLO
WHITE J.A.,THE DIPLOMACY OF THE RUSSO-JAPANESE WAR. ASIA KOREA RUSSIA FORCES CONFER CONTROL PEACE ...BIBLIOG 19 CHINJAP. PAGE 164 A3336
DIPLOM WAR BAL/PWR

B39
KERNER R.J.,NORTHEAST ASIA: A SELECTED BIBLIOGRAPHY (2 VOLS.). KOREA RUSSIA NAT/G DIPLOM...GEOG 19/20 CHINJAP. PAGE 78 A1599
BIBLIOG ASIA SOCIETY CULTURE

B45
NELSON M.F.,KOREA AND THE OLD ORDERS IN EASTERN ASIA. ASIA FRANCE KOREA RUSSIA DELIB/GP INT/TRADE DOMIN CONTROL WAR ORD/FREE...POLICY BIBLIOG. PAGE 108 A2218
DIPLOM BAL/PWR ATTIT CONSERVE

C45
NELSON M.F.,"KOREA AND THE OLD ORDERS IN EASTERN ASIA." KOREA WOR-45 DELIB/GP INT/TRADE DOMIN CONTROL WAR ATTIT ORD/FREE CONSERVE...POLICY TREATY. PAGE 108 A2217
BIBLIOG DIPLOM BAL/PWR ASIA

B50
NORTHROP F.S.C.,THE TAMING OF THE NATIONS. KOREA USA+45 USSR WOR+45 STRUCT ECO/UNDEV INT/ORG NAT/G TOP/EX NUC/PWR ATTIT ALL/VALS...TIME/SEQ 20 HIROSHIMA. PAGE 110 A2255
CONCPT BAL/PWR

B51
US HOUSE COMM APPROPRIATIONS,MUTUAL SECURITY PROGRAM APPROPRIATIONS FOR 1952: HEARINGS BEFORE A SUBCOMMITTEE OF THE COMMITTEE ON APPROPRIATIONS. KOREA L/A+17C ECO/DEV ECO/UNDEV INT/ORG INSPECT BAL/PWR DIPLOM DEBATE WAR...POLICY STAT ASIA/S 20 CONGRESS NATO COLD/WAR MID/EAST. PAGE 153 A3118
LEGIS FORCES BUDGET FOR/AID

L51
KELSEN H.,"RECENT TRENDS IN THE LAW OF THE UNITED NATIONS." KOREA WOR+45 CONSTN LEGIS DIPLOM LEGIT DETER WAR RIGID/FLEX HEALTH ORD/FREE RESPECT ...JURID CON/ANAL UN VAL/FREE 20 NATO. PAGE 77 A1582
INT/ORG LAW INT/LAW

S51
CONNERY R.H.,"THE MUTUAL DEFENSE ASSISTANCE PROGRAM." COM EUR+WWI KOREA USA+45 NAT/G VOL/ASSN CREATE PLAN BAL/PWR EDU/PROP PERCEPT...POLICY DECISION CONCPT NATO 20. PAGE 29 A0587
INT/ORG FORCES FOR/AID

B52
MACARTHUR D.,REVITALIZING A NATION. ASIA COM FUT KOREA WOR+45 NAT/G FOR/AID TAX GIVE WAR ATTIT SOCISM 20 CHINJAP EUROPE. PAGE 92 A1885
LEAD FORCES TOP/EX POLICY

B53
COUSINS N.,WHO SPEAKS FOR MAN. GERMANY KOREA WOR+45 SOCIETY INT/ORG NAT/G CREATE EDU/PROP HEALTH KNOWL LOVE MORAL...OBS SELF/OBS BIOG HYPO/EXP TOT/POP 20 CHINJAP. PAGE 32 A0642
ATTIT WAR PEACE

B54
EPSTEIN L.D.,BRITAIN - UNEASY ALLY. KOREA UK USA+45 NAT/G POL/PAR ECO/TAC FOR/AID INT/TRADE WAR LABOR/PAR CONSRV/PAR. PAGE 42 A0857
DIPLOM ATTIT POLICY NAT/COMP

S54
WOLFERS A.,"COLLECTIVE SECURITY AND THE WAR IN KOREA." ASIA KOREA USA+45 INT/ORG DIPLOM ROUTINE ...GEN/LAWS UN COLD/WAR 20. PAGE 166 A3381
ACT/RES LEGIT

B55
UN HEADQUARTERS LIBRARY,BIBLIOQRAPHIE DE LA CHARTE DES NATIONS UNIES. CHINA/COM KOREA WOR+45 VOL/ASSN CONFER ADMIN COERCE PEACE ATTIT ORD/FREE SOVEREIGN ...INT/LAW 20 UNESCO UN. PAGE 147 A3001
BIBLIOG/A INT/ORG DIPLOM

B56
BALL W.M.,NATIONALISM AND COMMUNISM IN EAST ASIA. ASIA BURMA EUR+WWI KOREA USA+45 ECO/UNDEV NAT/G POL/PAR DIPLOM ECO/TAC FOR/AID EDU/PROP COERCE RACE/REL NAT/LISM DRIVE SOVEREIGN...TREND 20 CHINJAP. PAGE 11 A0214
S/ASIA ATTIT

B56
GOODRICH L.,KOREA: A STUDY OF US POLICY IN THE
INT/ORG

UNITED NATIONS. ASIA USA+45 STRUCT CONSULT DELIB/GP ATTIT DRIVE PWR...JURID GEN/LAWS COLD/WAR 20 UN. PAGE 54 A1103 — DIPLOM KOREA

L58
SNYDER R.N.,"THE UNITED STATES DECISION TO RESIST AGGRESSION IN KOREA." ASIA KOREA S/ASIA USA+45 USA-45 WOR+45 INT/ORG DELIB/GP BAL/PWR COERCE PWR ...CONCPT REC/INT RESIST/INT COLD/WAR 20. PAGE 134 A2753 — QUANT METH/CNCPT DIPLOM

B59
GORDENKER L.,THE UNITED NATIONS AND THE PEACEFUL UNIFICATION OF KOREA. ASIA LAW LOC/G CONSULT ACT/RES DIPLOM DOMIN LEGIT ADJUD ADMIN ORD/FREE SOVEREIGN...INT GEN/METH UN COLD/WAR 20. PAGE 54 A1109 — DELIB/GP KOREA INT/ORG

B59
NAHM A.C.,JAPANESE PENETRATION OF KOREA, 1894-1910. ASIA KOREA NAT/G...POLICY 20 CHINJAP. PAGE 107 A2192 — BIBLIOG/A DIPLOM WAR COLONIAL

B59
STRAUSZ-HUPE R.,PROTRACTED CONFLICT. CHINA/COM KOREA WOR+45 INT/ORG FORCES ACT/RES ECO/TAC LEGIT COERCE DRIVE PERCEPT KNOWL PWR...PSY CONCPT RECORD GEN/METH COLD/WAR VAL/FREE 20. PAGE 139 A2847 — COM PLAN USSR

B59
VINACKE H.M.,A HISTORY OF THE FAR EAST IN MODERN TIMES (6TH ED.). KOREA S/ASIA USSR CONSTN CULTURE STRATA ECO/UNDEV NAT/G CHIEF FOR/AID INT/TRADE GP/REL...SOC NAT/COMP 19/20 CHINJAP. PAGE 159 A3235 — STRUCT ASIA

B60
TURNER G.B.,NATIONAL SECURITY IN THE NUCLEAR AGE. KOREA USA+45 PLAN DIPLOM ARMS/CONT DETER WAR WEAPON ...BIBLIOG 20 COLD/WAR NATO. PAGE 146 A2982 — NAT/G POLICY FORCES NUC/PWR

B60
WHITING A.S.,CHINA CROSSES THE YALU: THE DECISION TO ENTER THE KOREAN WAR. ASIA CHINA/COM KOREA ECO/UNDEV R+D INT/ORG TOP/EX ACT/RES BAL/PWR ATTIT PWR...GEN/METH 20. PAGE 164 A3338 — PLAN COERCE WAR

B61
MENDEL D.H. JR.,THE JAPANESE PEOPLE AND FOREIGN POLICY. CHINA/COM KOREA USA+45 USSR SOCIETY FORCES CHOOSE 20 CHINJAP. PAGE 99 A2037 — NAT/G DIPLOM POLICY ATTIT

L61
HOYT E.C.,"UNITED STATES REACTION TO THE KOREAN ATTACK." COM KOREA USA+45 CONSTN DELIB/GP FORCES PLAN ECO/TAC DOMIN EDU/PROP LEGIT ROUTINE COERCE WAR ATTIT DISPL RIGID/FLEX ORD/FREE PWR...POLICY INT/LAW TREND UN 20. PAGE 68 A1402 — ASIA INT/ORG BAL/PWR DIPLOM

B63
HALPERIN M.H.,LIMITED WAR IN A NUCLEAR AGE. CUBA KOREA USA+45 USSR INT/ORG FORCES PLAN DIPLOM DETER PWR...BIBLIOG/A 20. PAGE 60 A1238 — WAR NUC/PWR CONTROL WEAPON

B63
LEE C.,THE POLITICS OF KOREAN NATIONALISM. KOREA S/ASIA DIPLOM REV WAR 14/20 CHINJAP. PAGE 86 A1759 — NAT/LISM SOVEREIGN COLONIAL

C63
ATTIA G.E.O.,"LES FORCES ARMEES DES NATIONS UNIES EN COREE ET AU MOYENORIENT." KOREA CONSTN DELIB/GP LEGIS PWR...IDEA/COMP NAT/COMP BIBLIOG UN SUEZ. PAGE 10 A0194 — FORCES NAT/G INT/LAW

B64
BLANCHARD C.H.,KOREAN WAR BIBLIOGRAPHY. KOREA FAM BAL/PWR RATION MURDER WEAPON MARXISM...CHARTS 20. PAGE 15 A0306 — BIBLIOG/A WAR DIPLOM FORCES

B64
REES D.,KOREA: THE LIMITED WAR. ASIA KOREA WOR+45 NAT/G CIVMIL/REL PERS/REL PERSON...POLICY CHARTS 20 UN TRUMAN/HS MACARTHR/D. PAGE 120 A2455 — DIPLOM WAR INT/ORG FORCES

B64
RUSSELL R.B.,UNITED NATIONS EXPERIENCE WITH MILITARY FORCES: POLITICAL AND LEGAL ASPECTS. AFR KOREA WOR+45 LEGIS PROB/SOLV ADMIN CONTROL EFFICIENCY PEACE...POLICY INT/LAW BIBLIOG UN. PAGE 126 A2576 — FORCES DIPLOM SANCTION ORD/FREE

S64
DEVILLERS P.H.,"L'URSS, LA CHINE ET LES ORIGINES DE LA GUERRE DE COREE." ASIA CHINA/COM USSR INT/ORG ECO/TAC EDU/PROP ATTIT RIGID/FLEX PWR...STAND/INT HIST/WRIT COLD/WAR 20. PAGE 37 A0751 — WOR+45 KOREA

B65
CHUNG Y.S.,KOREA: A SELECTED BIBLIOGRAPHY 1959-1963. ASIA KOREA NAT/G DIPLOM 20. PAGE 26 A0537 — BIBLIOG/A SOC

B66
KOH S.J.,STAGES OF INDUSTRIAL DEVELOPMENT IN ASIA. ASIA INDIA KOREA STRATA STRUCT NAT/G INT/TRADE ...CHARTS 19/20 CHINJAP. PAGE 81 A1659 — INDUS ECO/UNDEV ECO/DEV LABOR

B67
CHO S.S.,KOREA IN WORLD POLITICS 1940-1950; AN EVALUATION OF AMERICAN RESPONSIBILITY. KOREA USA+45 USSR CONSTN INT/ORG NAT/G FORCES FOR/AID ANOMIE SUPEGO MARXISM...DECISION BIBLIOG 20. PAGE 26 A0533 — POLICY DIPLOM PROB/SOLV WAR

B67
MCNELLY T.,SOURCES IN MODERN EAST ASIAN HISTORY AND POLITICS. KOREA VIETNAM CULTURE DIPLOM COLONIAL REV WAR PWR ALL/IDEOS MARXISM...ANTHOL 20 CHINJAP. PAGE 99 A2023 — NAT/COMP ASIA S/ASIA SOCIETY

KOREA/N....NORTH KOREA ; SEE ALSO KOREA

N
KYRIAK T.E.,ASIAN DEVELOPMENTS: A BIBLIOGRAPHY. INDONESIA KOREA/N VIETNAM/N CULTURE SOCIETY ECO/UNDEV NAT/G DIPLOM...SOC TREND 20 MONGOLIA. PAGE 83 A1699 — BIBLIOG/A ALL/IDEOS S/ASIA ASIA

B64
WEINTRAUB S.,THE WAR IN THE WARDS. KOREA/N WOR+45 DIPLOM COERCE ORD/FREE SKILL 20 TREATY. PAGE 162 A3308 — EDU/PROP PEACE CROWD PUB/INST

KOREA/S....SOUTH KOREA; SEE ALSO KOREA

B61
MORLEY L.,THE PATCHWORK HISTORY OF FOREIGN AID. KOREA/S USA+45 USSR LAW FINAN INT/ORG TEC/DEV BAL/PWR GIVE 20 COLD/WAR NATO. PAGE 104 A2144 — FOR/AID ECO/UNDEV FORCES DIPLOM

KORNILOV/L....LAVR GEORGIEVICH KORNILOV

KOTANI H. A1673

KOTSCHING W.M. A0186

KRAFT J. A1674

KRAMER M.N. A1786

KRANNHALS H.V. A1675

KRAUS J. A1676

KRAUS O. A1677

KRAUSE L.B. A1678

KRAUSE W. A1679

KRAVIS I.B. A1680,A1681

KREININ M.E. A1682

KRETZSCHMAR W.W. A1683

KRIPALANI J.B. A1684

KRISTENSEN T. A1685,A1686

KROPOTKIN P. A1687

KRUGMAN H.E. A0425

KRUSCHE H. A1688

KU KLUX KLAN....SEE KKK

KUENNE R.E. A1689

KULISCHER E.M. A1690

KULSKI W.W. A1691,A1692,A1693,A1694

KUNZ J. A1695,A1696

KUOMINTANG....KUOMINTANG

KUWAIT....SEE ALSO ISLAM

N19
KUWAIT ARABIA,KUWAIT FUND FOR ARAB ECONOMIC DEVELOPMENT (PAMPHLET). ISLAM KUWAIT UAR ECO/UNDEV LEGIS ECO/TAC WEALTH 20. PAGE 83 A1697 — FOR/AID DIPLOM FINAN ADMIN

KUWAIT ARABIA A1697

KUZNETS....KUZNETS SCALE

KY/NGUYEN....NGUYEN KY

KYLE K. A1698

KYRIAK T.E. A1699,A1700,A1701,A1702,A1703,A1704

L/A+17C....LATIN AMERICA SINCE 1700; SEE ALSO APPROPRIATE NATIONS

L

N
SABIN J.,BIBLIOTHECA AMERICANA: A DICTIONARY OF BOOKS RELATING TO AMERICA, FROM ITS DISCOVERY TO THE PRESENT TIME(29 VOLS.). CONSTN CULTURE SOCIETY ECO/DEV LOC/G EDU/PROP NAT/LISM...POLICY GEOG SOC 19. PAGE 126 A2581
BIBLIOG L/A+17C DIPLOM NAT/G

N
UNIVERSITY OF FLORIDA LIBRARY,DOORS TO LATIN AMERICA; RECENT BOOKS AND PAMPHLETS. CONSTN CULTURE SOCIETY ECO/UNDEV COLONIAL LEAD GOV/REL NAT/LISM ATTIT...HUM SOC 20. PAGE 149 A3047
BIBLIOG/A L/A+17C DIPLOM NAT/G

N
HANDBOOK OF LATIN AMERICAN STUDIES. LAW CULTURE ECO/UNDEV POL/PAR ADMIN LEAD...SOC 20. PAGE 2 A0035
BIBLIOG/A L/A+17C NAT/G DIPLOM

N
LATIN AMERICA IN PERIODICAL LITERATURE. LAW TEC/DEV DIPLOM RECEIVE EDU/PROP...GEOG HUM MGT 20. PAGE 2 A0037
BIBLIOG/A L/A+17C SOCIETY ECO/UNDEV

N
CARIBBEAN COMMISSION,CURRENT CARIBBEAN BIBLIOGRAPHY. FRANCE NETHERLAND UK CULTURE ECO/UNDEV PRESS LEAD ATTIT...GEOG SOC 20. PAGE 24 A0482
BIBLIOG NAT/G L/A+17C DIPLOM

N
DOHERTY D.K.,PRELIMINARY BIBLIOGRAPHY OF COLONIZATION AND SETTLEMENT IN LATIN AMERICA AND ANGLO-AMERICA. L/A+17C PRE/AMER USA-45 ECO/UNDEV NAT/G 15/20. PAGE 38 A0768
BIBLIOG COLONIAL ADMIN DIPLOM

N
INSTITUTE OF HISPANIC STUDIES,HISPANIC AMERICAN REPORT. EUR+WWI SPAIN LAW CONSTN ECO/UNDEV POL/PAR EX/STRUC LEGIS LEAD...HUM SOC 20. PAGE 70 A1445
BIBLIOG/A L/A+17C NAT/G DIPLOM

N
OAS,DOCUMENTOS OFICIALES DE LA ORGANIZACION DE LOS ESTADOS AMERICANOS. L/A+17C ATTIT 20 OAS. PAGE 111 A2272
BIBLIOG INT/ORG DIPLOM POLICY

N
UNIVERSITY OF CALIFORNIA,STATISTICAL ABSTRACT OF LATIN AMERICA. L/A+17C DIPLOM 20. PAGE 149 A3046
BIBLIOG NAT/G ECO/UNDEV STAT

B03
GRIFFIN A.P.C.,SELECT LIST OF REFERENCES ON THE MONROE DOCTRINE (PAMPHLET). L/A+17C NAT/G TOP/EX 19/20. PAGE 56 A1151
BIBLIOG DIPLOM COLONIAL

B08
GRIFFIN A.P.C.,LIST OF REFERENCES ON INTERNATIONAL ARBITRATION. FRANCE L/A+17C USA-45 WOR-45 DIPLOM CONFER COLONIAL ARMS/CONT BAL/PAY EQUILIB SOVEREIGN ...DECISION 19/20 MEXIC/AMER. PAGE 56 A1156
BIBLIOG/A INT/ORG INT/LAW DELIB/GP

B16
ROOT E.,THE MILITARY AND COLONIAL POLICY OF THE US. L/A+17C USA-45 LAW SOCIETY STRATA STRUCT INT/ORG NAT/G SCHOOL FORCES EDU/PROP ALL/VALS...OBS VAL/FREE 19/20. PAGE 123 A2522
ACT/RES PLAN DIPLOM WAR

B17
DOS SANTOS M.,BIBLIOGRAPHIA GERAL, A DESCRIPCAO BIBLIOGRAFICA DE LIVROS TANTO DE AUTORES PORTUGUEZES COMO BRASILEIROS... BRAZIL PORTUGAL NAT/G LEAD GP/REL 15/20. PAGE 38 A0774
BIBLIOG/A L/A+17C DIPLOM COLONIAL

B22
WALSH E.,THE HISTORY AND NATURE OF INTERNATIONAL RELATIONS. ASIA L/A+17C MOD/EUR USA-45 WOR-45 NAT/G FORCES TOP/EX BAL/PWR REGION ATTIT ORD/FREE RESPECT ...CONCPT HIST/WRIT TREND. PAGE 161 A3270
INT/ORG TIME/SEQ DIPLOM

B28
STUART G.H.,LATIN AMERICA AND THE UNITED STATES. USA-45 ECO/UNDEV INT/ORG NAT/G POL/PAR PLAN DOMIN EDU/PROP COLONIAL REGION COERCE ATTIT ALL/VALS ...POLICY GEOG TREND 19/20. PAGE 139 A2853
L/A+17C DIPLOM

B33
MATTHEWS M.A.,THE AMERICAN INSTITUTE OF INTERNATIONAL LAW AND THE CODIFICATION OF INTERNATIONAL LAW (PAMPHLET). USA-45 CONSTN ADJUD CT/SYS...JURID 20. PAGE 96 A1973
BIBLIOG/A INT/LAW L/A+17C DIPLOM

B35
BUREAU ECONOMIC RES LAT AM,THE ECONOMIC LITERATURE OF LATIN AMERICA (2 VOLS.). CHRIST-17C AGRI DIST/IND EXTR/IND INDUS WORKER INT/TRADE...GEOG 16/20. PAGE 21 A0433
BIBLIOG L/A+17C ECO/UNDEV FINAN

B36
HARVARD BUREAU ECO RES LAT AM,THE ECONOMIC LITERATURE OF LATIN AMERICA: A TENTATIVE BIBLIOGRAPHY. NAT/G TARIFFS CENTRAL COST DEMAND 20. PAGE 62 A1277
BIBLIOG ECO/UNDEV L/A+17C INT/TRADE

B37
SCHUSTER E.,GUIDE TO LAW AND LEGAL LITERATURE OF CENTRAL AMERICAN REPUBLICS. L/A+17C INT/ORG ADJUD SANCTION CRIME...JURID 19/20. PAGE 129 A2654
BIBLIOG/A REGION CT/SYS LAW

B40
CONOVER H.F.,FOREIGN RELATIONS OF THE UNITED STATES: A LIST OF RECENT BOOKS (PAMPHLET). ASIA CANADA L/A+17C UK INT/ORG INT/TRADE TARIFFS NEUTRAL WAR PEACE...INT/LAW CON/ANAL 20 CHINJAP. PAGE 29 A0592
BIBLIOG/A USA-45 DIPLOM

B41
WHITAKER A.P.,THE UNITED STATES AND THE INDEPENDENCE OF LATIN AMERICA, 1800-1830. PORTUGAL SPAIN USA-45 COLONIAL REGION SOVEREIGN...POLICY TIME/SEQ BIBLIOG/A 18/20. PAGE 163 A3329
DIPLOM L/A+17C CONCPT ORD/FREE

B42
PAGINSKY P.,GERMAN WORKS RELATING TO AMERICA, 1493-1800; A LIST COMPILED FROM THE COLLECTIONS OF THE NEW YORK PUBLIC LIBRARY. GERMANY PRE/AMER CULTURE COLONIAL ATTIT...POLICY SOC 15/19. PAGE 113 A2317
BIBLIOG/A NAT/G L/A+17C DIPLOM

B42
SIMOES DOS REIS A.,BIBLIOGRAFIA DAS BIBLIOGRAFIAS BRASILEIRAS. BRAZIL ADMIN COLONIAL 20. PAGE 133 A2717
BIBLIOG NAT/G DIPLOM L/A+17C

B43
BEMIS S.F.,THE LATIN AMERICAN POLICY OF THE UNITED STATES: AN HISTORICAL INTERPRETATION. INT/ORG AGREE COLONIAL WAR PEACE ATTIT ORD/FREE...POLICY INT/LAW CHARTS 18/20 MEXIC/AMER WILSON/W MONROE/DOC. PAGE 13 A0265
DIPLOM SOVEREIGN USA-45 L/A+17C

B43
BROWN A.D.,BRITISH POSSESSIONS IN THE CARIBBEAN AREA: A SELECTED LIST OF REFERENCES. UK NAT/G DIPLOM...GEOG 20 CARIBBEAN. PAGE 20 A0398
BIBLIOG COLONIAL ECO/UNDEV L/A+17C

B43
CARLO A.M.,ENSAYO DE UNA BIBLIOGRAFIA DE BIBLIOGRAFIAS MEXICANAS. ECO/UNDEV LOC/G ADMIN LEAD 20 MEXIC/AMER. PAGE 24 A0485
BIBLIOG L/A+17C NAT/G DIPLOM

B44
SHELBY C.,LATIN AMERICAN PERIODICALS CURRENTLY RECEIVED IN THE LIBRARY OF CONGRESS AND IN LIBRARY OF DEPARTMENT OF AGRICULTURE. SOCIETY AGRI INDUS LABOR POL/PAR INT/TRADE...GEOG SOC 20. PAGE 132 A2699
BIBLIOG ECO/UNDEV CULTURE L/A+17C

B45
PERAZA SARAUSA F.,BIBLIOGRAFIAS CUBANAS. CUBA CULTURE ECO/UNDEV AGRI EDU/PROP PRESS CIVMIL/REL ...POLICY GEOG PHIL/SCI BIOG 19/20. PAGE 115 A2353
BIBLIOG/A L/A+17C NAT/G DIPLOM

B45
US DEPARTMENT OF STATE,PUBLICATIONS OF THE DEPARTMENT OF STATE: A LIST CUMULATIVE FROM OCTOBER 1, 1929 (PAMPHLET). ASIA EUR+WWI ISLAM L/A+17C USA-45 ADJUD...INT/LAW 20. PAGE 151 A3082
BIBLIOG DIPLOM INT/TRADE

B47
PERKINS D.,THE UNITED STATES AND THE CARIBBEAN. CUBA DOMIN/REP GUATEMALA HAITI PANAMA CULTURE ECO/UNDEV FOR/AID ADMIN COERCE HABITAT...POLICY 19/20. PAGE 115 A2359
DIPLOM L/A+17C USA-45

B48
GUIDE TO THE RECORDS IN THE NATIONAL ARCHIVES. ECO/UNDEV ADMIN COLONIAL 16/20. PAGE 3 A0055
BIBLIOG NAT/G L/A+17C DIPLOM

B48
FLOREN LOZANO L.,BIBLIOGRAFIA DE LA BIBLIOGRAFIA DOMINICANA. DOMIN/REP NAT/G DIPLOM EDU/PROP CIVMIL/REL...POLICY ART/METH GEOG PHIL/SCI HIST/WRIT 20. PAGE 47 A0952
BIBLIOG/A BIOG L/A+17C CULTURE

B49
BEHRENDT R.F.,MODERN LATIN AMERICA IN SOCIAL SCIENCE LITERATURE. STRUCT ECO/UNDEV SCHOOL DIPLOM INT/TRADE EDU/PROP...GEOG 20. PAGE 12 A0250
BIBLIOG/A SOC L/A+17C

B49
BORBA DE MORAES R.,MANUAL BIBLIOGRAFICO DE ESTUDOS BRASILEIROS. BRAZIL DIPLOM ADMIN LEAD...SOC 20. PAGE 17 A0336
BIBLIOG L/A+17C NAT/G ECO/UNDEV

B50
BEHRENDT R.F.,MODERN LATIN AMERICA IN SOCIAL SCIENCE LITERATURE (SUPPLEMENTS I AND II). STRUCT ECO/UNDEV SCHOOL DIPLOM INT/TRADE...GEOG 20. PAGE 12 A0251
BIBLIOG/A SOC L/A+17C

B50
DAVIS E.P.,PERIODICALS OF INTERNATIONAL ORGANIZATIONS; PART I, THE UN AND SPECIALIZED AGENCIES; PART II, INTER-AMERICAN ORGS. CULTURE AGRI FINAN INDUS LABOR INT/TRADE...GEOG HEAL STAT 20 UN OAS UNESCO. PAGE 34 A0689
BIBLIOG/A INT/ORG DIPLOM L/A+17C

B50
GUERRANT E.O.,ROOSEVELT'S GOOD NEIGHBOR POLICY.
DIPLOM

L/A+17C USA+45 USA-45 FOR/AID...IDEA/COMP 20 ROOSEVLT/F TRUMAN/HS. PAGE 58 A1187
NAT/G CHIEF POLICY

B51
CATALOGO GENERAL DE LA LIBRERIA ESPANOLA E HISPANOAMERICANA 1901-1930; AUTORES (5 VOLS., 1932-1951). SPAIN COLONIAL GOV/REL...SOC 20. PAGE 3 A0058
BIBLIOG L/A+17C DIPLOM NAT/G

B51
BISSAINTHE M.,DICTIONNAIRE DE BIBLIOGRAPHIE HAITIENNE. HAITI ELITES AGRI LEGIS DIPLOM INT/TRADE WRITING ORD/FREE CATHISM...ART/METH GEOG 19/20 NEGRO TREATY. PAGE 15 A0295
BIBLIOG L/A+17C SOCIETY NAT/G

B51
CHRISTENSEN A.N.,THE EVOLUTION OF LATIN AMERICAN GOVERNMENT: A BOOK OF READINGS. ECO/UNDEV INDUS LOC/G POL/PAR EX/STRUC LEGIS FOR/AID CT/SYS ...SOC/WK 20 SOUTH/AMER. PAGE 26 A0535
NAT/G CONSTN DIPLOM L/A+17C

B51
US HOUSE COMM APPROPRIATIONS,MUTUAL SECURITY PROGRAM APPROPRIATIONS FOR 1952: HEARINGS BEFORE A SUBCOMMITTEE OF THE COMMITTEE ON APPROPRIATIONS. KOREA L/A+17C ECO/DEV ECO/UNDEV INT/ORG INSPECT BAL/PWR DIPLOM DEBATE WAR...POLICY STAT ASIA/S 20 CONGRESS NATO COLD/WAR MID/EAST. PAGE 153 A3118
LEGIS FORCES BUDGET FOR/AID

L51
WHITAKER A.P.,"DEVELOPMENT OF AMERICAN REGIONALISM: THE ORGANIZATION OF AMERICAN STATES." L/A+17C USA+45 VOL/ASSN DELIB/GP FORCES TOP/EX ACT/RES ECO/TAC CT/SYS REGION PEACE ALL/VALS OAS 20. PAGE 163 A3330
INT/ORG TIME/SEQ DETER

S51
GYR J.,"ANALYSIS OF COMMITTEE MEMBER BEHAVIOUR IN FOUR CULTURES." ASIA ISLAM L/A+17C USA+45 INT/ORG VOL/ASSN LEGIT ATTIT...INT DEEP/QU SAMP CHARTS 20. PAGE 58 A1200
DELIB/GP CULTURE

B52
DILLON D.R.,LATIN AMERICA, 1935-1949; A SELECTED BIBLIOGRAPHY. LAW EDU/PROP...SOC 20. PAGE 37 A0764
BIBLIOG L/A+17C NAT/G DIPLOM

B52
UN DEPT. SOC. AFF.,PRELIMINARY REPORT ON THE WORLD SOCIAL SITUATION. ISLAM L/A+17C WOR+45 STRATA AGRI EXTR/IND INDUS INT/ORG SCHOOL ADMIN...GEOG SOC TREND UNESCO WORK FAO 20. PAGE 147 A2998
R+D HEALTH FOR/AID

B53
GROPP A.E.,UNION LIST OF LATIN AMERICAN NEWSPAPERS IN LIBRARIES IN THE UNITED STATES. USA+45 DIPLOM ATTIT 20. PAGE 57 A1170
BIBLIOG PRESS L/A+17C NAT/G

B53
KALIJARVI T.V.,MODERN WORLD POLITICS (3RD ED.). AFR L/A+17C MOD/EUR S/ASIA UK USSR WOR+45 INT/ORG BAL/PWR WAR PWR 20. PAGE 76 A1552
DIPLOM INT/LAW PEACE

B53
KANTOR H.,A BIBLIOGRAPHY OF UNPUBLISHED DOCTORAL DISSERTATIONS AND MASTERS' THESES DEALING WITH GOVTS, POL, INT REL OF LAT AM. L/A+17C INT/ORG POL/PAR ACT/RES OP/RES CONFER ATTIT...INT/LAW PHIL/SCI 20. PAGE 76 A1556
BIBLIOG ACADEM DIPLOM NAT/G

B53
ROSCIO J.G.,OBRAS. L/A+17C SPAIN DIPLOM REV WAR NAT/LISM TOTALISM PWR SOVEREIGN 19. PAGE 123 A2527
ORD/FREE COLONIAL NAT/G PHIL/SCI

B54
WHITAKER A.P.,THE WESTERN HEMISPHERE IDEA. USA+45 USA-45 CONSTN INT/ORG NAT/G DIPLOM SOVEREIGN...GEOG TIME/SEQ OAS 19/20 MONROE/DOC. PAGE 164 A3331
L/A+17C CONCPT REGION

B55
BURR R.N.,DOCUMENTS ON INTER-AMERICAN COOPERATION: VOL. I, 1810-1881; VOL. II, 1881-1948. DELIB/GP BAL/PWR INT/TRADE REPRESENT NAT/LISM PEACE HABITAT ORD/FREE PWR SOVEREIGN...INT/LAW 20 OAS. PAGE 22 A0445
BIBLIOG DIPLOM INT/ORG L/A+17C

B55
STUART G.H.,LATIN AMERICA AND THE UNITED STATES (5TH ED.). L/A+17C USA+45 USA-45 INT/TRADE COLONIAL ...POLICY CHARTS T 19/20. PAGE 140 A2856
NAT/G DIPLOM

L55
KISER M.,"ORGANIZATION OF AMERICAN STATES." L/A+17C USA+45 ECO/UNDEV INT/ORG NAT/G PLAN TEC/DEV DIPLOM ECO/TAC INT/TRADE EDU/PROP ADMIN ALL/VALS...POLICY MGT RECORD ORG/CHARTS OAS 20. PAGE 80 A1639
VOL/ASSN ECO/DEV REGION

B56
HOUSTON J.A.,LATIN AMERICA IN THE UNITED NATIONS. CONSULT DIPLOM LEGIT ROUTINE ATTIT ORD/FREE PWR ...JURID OBS RECORD TIME/SEQ CHARTS 20 UN. PAGE 68 A1395
L/A+17C INT/ORG INT/LAW REGION

B56
TOYNBEE A.,THE WAR AND THE NEUTRALS. L/A+17C PORTUGAL SPAIN SWEDEN SWITZERLND TURKEY WOR+45 WOR-45 ECO/TAC CONFER CONTROL REGION 20. PAGE 145 A2957
NEUTRAL WAR INT/TRADE DIPLOM

B56
US DEPARTMENT OF STATE,ECONOMIC PROBLEMS OF UNDERDEVELOPED AREAS (PAMPHLET). AFR ASIA ISLAM L/A+17C AGRI FINAN INDUS INT/ORG LABOR INT/TRADE ...PSY SOC 20. PAGE 151 A3090
BIBLIOG ECO/UNDEV TEC/DEV R+D

B57
BUCK P.W.,CONTOL OF FOREIGN RELATIONS IN MODERN NATIONS. FRANCE L/A+17C NETHERLAND USSR WOR+45 INT/ORG TOP/EX BAL/PWR DOMIN EDU/PROP COERCE PEACE ATTIT...CONCPT TREND 20 CMN/WLTH. PAGE 21 A0427
NAT/G PWR DIPLOM

B57
CARIBBEAN COMMISSION,A CATALOGUE OF CARIBBEAN COMMISSION PUBLICATIONS (PAMPHLET). WEST/IND CULTURE ECO/UNDEV LOC/G DIPLOM SOC. PAGE 24 A0483
BIBLIOG L/A+17C INT/ORG NAT/G

B57
DEAN V.M.,THE NATURE OF THE NON-WESTERN WORLD. AFR ASIA L/A+17C S/ASIA CULTURE SOCIETY STRATA ECO/DEV DIPLOM ECO/TAC FOR/AID ATTIT DRIVE ALL/VALS ...RELATIV SOC CONCPT TIME/SEQ TREND TOT/POP 20. PAGE 35 A0718
ECO/UNDEV STERTYP NAT/LISM

B57
FURNISS E.S.,AMERICAN MILITARY POLICY: STRATEGIC ASPECTS OF WORLD POLITICAL GEOGRAPHY. COM EUR+WWI ISLAM L/A+17C USA+45 WOR+45 INT/ORG ACT/RES ARMS/CONT COERCE NUC/PWR ATTIT PWR...GEOG NEW/IDEA VAL/FREE COLD/WAR 20. PAGE 50 A1027
FORCES DIPLOM

B57
US SENATE SPEC COMM FOR AID,COMPILATION OF STUDIES AND SURVEYS. AFR ASIA L/A+17C USA+45 ECO/UNDEV AGRI INT/ORG CONSULT TEC/DEV CONFER TOTALISM...NAT/COMP 20 CONGRESS. PAGE 157 A3197
FOR/AID DIPLOM ORD/FREE DELIB/GP

B58
ALMEYDA M.C.,REFLEXIONES POLITICAS. CHILE L/A+17C USA+45 INT/ORG POL/PAR ECO/TAC PARTIC ATTIT 20. PAGE 6 A0128
ECO/UNDEV REGION DIPLOM INT/TRADE

B58
BERLINER J.S.,SOVIET ECONOMIC AID: THE AID AND TRADE POLICY IN UNDERDEVELOPED COUNTRIES. AFR COM ISLAM L/A+17C S/ASIA USSR ECO/DEV DIST/IND FINAN MARKET INT/ORG ACT/RES PLAN BAL/PWR WEAPON PWR WEALTH...CHARTS 20. PAGE 14 A0277
ECO/UNDEV ECO/TAC FOR/AID

B58
HUMPHREYS R.A.,LATIN AMERICAN HISTORY: A GUIDE TO THE LITERATURE IN ENGLISH. CULTURE NAT/G DIPLOM BIOG. PAGE 69 A1417
BIBLIOG/A L/A+17C

B58
PAN AMERICAN UNION,REPERTORIO DE PUBLICACIONES PERIODICAS ACTUALES LATINO-AMERICANAS. CULTURE ECO/UNDEV ADMIN LEAD GOV/REL 20 OAS. PAGE 113 A2326
BIBLIOG L/A+17C NAT/G DIPLOM

B58
UNESCO,REPERTORIO DE PUBLICACIONES PERIODICAS ACTUALES LATINO AMERICANAS (VOL. VIII). LAW DIPLOM GP/REL...PHIL/SCI SOC 20 UNESCO. PAGE 148 A3021
BIBLIOG/A COM/IND L/A+17C

B59
ALLEN R.L.,SOVIET INFLUENCE IN LATIN AMERICA. ECO/UNDEV FINAN PROC/MFG NAT/G TEC/DEV EDU/PROP EXEC ROUTINE ATTIT DRIVE PERSON ALL/VALS PWR...STAT CHARTS WORK 20. PAGE 6 A0125
L/A+17C ECO/TAC INT/TRADE USSR

B59
INTERAMERICAN CULTURAL COUN,LISTA DE LIBROS REPRESENTAVOS DE AMERICA. CULTURE DIPLOM ADMIN 20. PAGE 71 A1448
BIBLIOG/A NAT/G L/A+17C SOC

B59
JOSEPH F.M.,AS OTHERS SEE US: THE UNITED STATES THROUGH FOREIGN EYES. AFR EUR+WWI ISLAM L/A+17C S/ASIA USA+45 CULTURE SOCIETY ECO/DEV ECO/UNDEV INT/ORG NAT/G DIPLOM ECO/TAC REV ATTIT RIGID/FLEX HEALTH ORD/FREE WEALTH 20. PAGE 75 A1537
RESPECT DOMIN NAT/LISM SOVEREIGN

B59
LOPEZ M.M.,CATALOGOS DE PUBLICACIONES PERIODICAS MEXICANAS. L/A+17C CULTURE NAT/G DIPLOM 20 MEXIC/AMER. PAGE 91 A1861
BIBLIOG PRESS CON/ANAL

B59
NUNEZ JIMENEZ A.,LA LIBERACION DE LAS ISLAS. CUBA L/A+17C USA+45 LAW CHIEF PLAN DIPLOM FOR/AID OWN WEALTH 20 CASTRO/F. PAGE 110 A2261
AGRI REV ECO/UNDEV NAT/G

B59
OKINSHEVICH L.A.,LATIN AMERICA IN SOVIET WRITINGS, 1945-1958: A BIBLIOGRAPHY. USSR LAW ECO/UNDEV LABOR DIPLOM EDU/PROP REV...GEOG SOC 20. PAGE 111 A2287
BIBLIOG WRITING COM L/A+17C

B59
PANAMERICAN UNION,PUBLICATIONS: PAU AND OFFICIAL RECORDS OF THE OAS, IN ENGLISH, SPANISH, PORTUGUESE, AND FRENCH, 1958-59. NAT/G ATTIT...SOC 20 OAS. PAGE 113 A2328
BIBLIOG L/A+17C INT/LAW DIPLOM

B59
YRARRAZAVAL E.,AMERICA LATINE EN LA GUERRA FRIA. EUR+WWI L/A+17C USA+45 USSR WOR+45 INDUS INT/ORG NAT/LISM...POLICY COLD/WAR. PAGE 169 A3439
REGION DIPLOM ECO/UNDEV INT/TRADE

S59
PLAZA G.,"FOR A REGIONAL MARKET IN LATIN AMERICA." FUT L/A+17C CULTURE INDUS NAT/G ECO/TAC INT/TRADE ATTIT WEALTH...NEW/IDEA TREND OAS 20. PAGE 116 A2389
MARKET INT/ORG REGION

B60
CONN S.,THE FRAMEWORK OF HEMISPHERE DEFENSE. CANADA L/A+17C USA-45 NAT/G FORCES BAL/PWR DOMIN WAR PEACE DISPL PWR RESPECT...PLURIST CONCPT HIST/WRIT HYPO/EXP MEXIC/AMER 20 ROOSEVLT/F. PAGE 29 A0585
USA+45 INT/ORG DIPLOM

B60
DE HERRERA C.D.,LISTA BIBLIOGRAFICA DE LOS TRABAJOS DE GRADUACION Y TESIS PRESENTADOS EN LA UNIVERSIDAD, 1939-1960. PANAMA DIPLOM LEAD...SOC 20. PAGE 35 A0703
BIBLIOG L/A+17C NAT/G ACADEM

B60
FLORES R.H.,CATALOGO DE TESIS DOCTORALES DE LAS FACULTADES DE LA UNIVERSIDAD DE EL SALVADOR. EL/SALVADR LAW DIPLOM ADMIN LEAD GOV/REL...SOC 19/20. PAGE 47 A0954
BIBLIOG ACADEM L/A+17C NAT/G

B60
LIEUWEN E.,ARMS AND POLITICS IN LATIN AMERICA. FUT USA+45 USA-45 ECO/UNDEV INT/ORG NAT/G FORCES DIPLOM COERCE ATTIT ALL/VALS VAL/FREE OAS 20. PAGE 88 A1811
L/A+17C FOR/AID

B60
PAN AMERICAN UNION,FIFTH MEETING OF CONSULTATION OF MINISTERS OF FOREIGN AFFAIRS OF AMERICAN STATES. L/A+17C FORCES PLAN PROB/SOLV ADJUD PEACE...POLICY INT/LAW 20 OAS. PAGE 113 A2327
INT/ORG DIPLOM DELIB/GP ECO/UNDEV

S60
"THE EMERGING COMMON MARKETS IN LATIN AMERICA." FUT L/A+17C STRATA DIST/IND INDUS LABOR NAT/G LEGIS ECO/TAC ADMIN RIGID/FLEX HEALTH...NEW/IDEA TIME/SEQ OAS 20. PAGE 3 A0059
FINAN ECO/UNDEV INT/TRADE

S60
FITZGIBBON R.H.,"DICTATORSHIP AND DEMOCRACY IN LATIN AMERICA." FUT ECO/DEV ECO/UNDEV INT/ORG LOC/G NAT/G TOP/EX PLAN TEC/DEV ECO/TAC CHOOSE ATTIT DRIVE PERSON ALL/VALS OAS TOT/POP 20. PAGE 46 A0943
L/A+17C ACT/RES INT/TRADE

S60
GRACIA-MORA M.R.,"INTERNATIONAL RESPONSIBILITY FOR SUBVERSIVE ACTIVITIES AND HOSTILE PROPAGANDA BY PRIVATE PERSONS AGAINST." COM EUR+WWI L/A+17C UK USA+45 USSR WOR-45 CONSTN NAT/G LEGIT ADJUD REV PEACE TOTALISM ORD/FREE...INT/LAW 20. PAGE 55 A1119
INT/ORG JURID SOVEREIGN

S60
KALUODA J.,"COMMUNIST STRATEGY IN LATIN AMERICA." L/A+17C USA+45 INT/ORG NAT/G POL/PAR DIPLOM ECO/TAC EDU/PROP COERCE WEALTH...CONCPT OAS COLD/WAR 20. PAGE 76 A1553
COM PWR CUBA

S60
MORA J.A.,"THE ORGANIZATION OF AMERICAN STATES." USA+45 LAW ECO/UNDEV VOL/ASSN DELIB/GP PLAN BAL/PWR EDU/PROP ADMIN DRIVE RIGID/FLEX ORD/FREE WEALTH ...TIME/SEQ GEN/LAWS OAS 20. PAGE 103 A2126
L/A+17C INT/ORG REGION

S60
MORALES C.J.,"TRADE AND ECONOMIC INTEGRATION IN LATIN AMERICA." FUT L/A+17C LAW STRATA ECO/UNDEV DIST/IND INDUS LABOR NAT/G LEGIS ECO/TAC ADMIN RIGID/FLEX WEALTH...CONCPT NEW/IDEA CONT/OBS TIME/SEQ WORK 20. PAGE 104 A2128
FINAN INT/TRADE REGION

S60
OWEN C.F.,"US AND SOVIET RELATIONS WITH UNDERDEVELOPED COUNTRIES: LATIN AMERICA-A CASE STUDY." AFR COM L/A+17C USA+45 USSR EXTR/IND MARKET TEC/DEV DIPLOM ECO/TAC NAT/LISM ORD/FREE PWR ...TREND WORK 20. PAGE 112 A2303
ECO/UNDEV DRIVE INT/TRADE

B61
AMORY J.F.,AROUND THE EDGE OF WAR: A NEW APPROACH TO THE PROBLEMS OF AMERICAN FOREIGN POLICY. COM L/A+17C USA+45 USSR FOR/AID EDU/PROP AGREE CONTROL ARMS/CONT NUC/PWR WAR PWR...IDEA/COMP 20 TREATY ESPIONAGE. PAGE 8 A0154
NAT/G DIPLOM POLICY

B61
BAGU S.,ARGENTINA EN EL MUNDO. L/A+17C INDUS INT/TRADE WAR ATTIT ROLE...TREND 19/20 ARGEN OAS. PAGE 10 A0202
DIPLOM INT/ORG REGION ECO/UNDEV

B61
FRIEDMANN W.G.,JOINT INTERNATIONAL BUSINESS VENTURES. ASIA ISLAM L/A+17C ECO/DEV DIST/IND FINAN PROC/MFG FACE/GP LG/CO NAT/G VOL/ASSN CONSULT EX/STRUC PLAN ADMIN ROUTINE WEALTH...OLD/LIB WORK 20. PAGE 49 A1004
ECO/UNDEV INT/TRADE

B61
GOLDWERT M.,CONSTABULARY IN THE DOMINICAN REPUBLIC AND NICARAGUA. DOMIN/REP L/A+17C NICARAGUA USA-45 NAT/G PLAN CONTROL TASK REV...POLICY 20 INTERVENT. PAGE 53 A1093
DIPLOM PEACE FORCES

B61
GRASES P.,ESTUDIOS BIBLIOGRAFICOS. VENEZUELA...SOC 20. PAGE 55 A1130
BIBLIOG NAT/G DIPLOM L/A+17C

B61
HADDAD J.A.,REVOLUCAO CUBANA E REVOLUCAO BRASILEIRA. BRAZIL CUBA L/A+17C STRATA AGRI WORKER EDU/PROP REGION...POLICY NAT/COMP 20. PAGE 59 A1210
REV ORD/FREE DIPLOM ECO/UNDEV

B61
HARRISON J.P.,GUIDE TO MATERIALS ON LATIN AMERICA IN THE NATIONAL ARCHIVES (2 VOLS.). USA+45 ECO/UNDEV FINAN LOC/G FORCES 20. PAGE 62 A1271
BIBLIOG L/A+17C NAT/G DIPLOM

B61
MECHAM J.L.,THE UNITED STATES AND INTER-AMERICAN SECURITY, 1889-1960. L/A+17C USA+45 USA-45 CONSTN FORCES INT/TRADE PEACE TOTALISM ATTIT...JURID 19/20 UN OAS. PAGE 99 A2030
DIPLOM WAR ORD/FREE INT/ORG

B61
PERKINS D.,THE UNITED STATES AND LATIN AMERICAN. L/A+17C USA+45 USA-45 STRUCT COLONIAL REV ORD/FREE 19/20. PAGE 115 A2360
DIPLOM INT/TRADE NAT/G

B61
STARK H.,SOCIAL AND ECONOMIC FRONTIERS IN LATIN AMERICA (2ND ED.). CUBA FUT CULTURE AGRI INDUS ECO/TAC PRODUC ATTIT MARXISM...NAT/COMP BIBLIOG T 20. PAGE 137 A2807
L/A+17C SOCIETY DIPLOM ECO/UNDEV

B61
US HOUSE COMM APPROPRIATIONS,INTER-AMERICAN PROGRAMS FOR 1961: DENIAL OF 1962 BUDGET INFORMATION. CHILE L/A+17C USA+45 FINAN CONSULT BUDGET ADJUD COST EFFICIENCY WEALTH...POLICY CHARTS 20 CONGRESS. PAGE 153 A3119
LEGIS FOR/AID DELIB/GP ECO/UNDEV

B61
WARNER D.,HURRICANE FROM CHINA. ASIA CHINA/COM FUT L/A+17C USA+45 CULTURE NAT/G FORCES TOP/EX FOR/AID DRIVE PWR...CONCPT TIME/SEQ SEATO WORK 20. PAGE 161 A3284
ATTIT TREND REV

B61
WOOD B.,THE MAKING OF THE GOOD NEIGHBOR POLICY. L/A+17C USA-45 COERCE CIVMIL/REL DISCRIM. PAGE 166 A3389
DIPLOM DELIB/GP POLICY

B61
ZIMMERMAN I.,A GUIDE TO CURRENT LATIN AMERICAN PERIODICALS: HUMANITIES AND SOCIAL SCIENCES. LABOR SECT EDU/PROP...GEOG HUM SOC LING STAT NAT/COMP 20. PAGE 170 A3452
BIBLIOG/A DIPLOM L/A+17C PHIL/SCI

S61
ANGLIN D.,"UNITED STATES OPPOSITION TO CANADIAN MEMBERSHIP IN THE PAN AMERICAN UNION: A CANADIAN VIEW." L/A+17C UK USA+45 VOL/ASSN DELIB/GP EX/STRUC PLAN DIPLOM DOMIN REGION ATTIT RIGID/FLEX PWR ...RELATIV CONCPT STERTYP CMN/WLTH OAS 20. PAGE 8 A0162
INT/ORG CANADA

S61
BALL M.M.,"ISSUES FOR THE AMERICAS: NON-INTERVENTION VS HUMAN RIGHTS AND THE PRESERVATION OF DEMOCRATIC INSTITUTIONS." USA+45 INTELL INT/ORG NAT/G DIPLOM ECO/TAC LEGIT...TREND OAS TOT/POP 20. PAGE 11 A0213
L/A+17C MORAL

S61
BARALL M.,"THE UNITED STATES GOVERNMENT RESPONDS." L/A+17C USA+45 SOCIETY NAT/G CREATE PLAN DIPLOM ECO/TAC ATTIT DRIVE RIGID/FLEX KNOWL SKILL WEALTH ...METH/CNCPT TIME/SEQ GEN/METH 20. PAGE 11 A0217
ECO/UNDEV ACT/RES FOR/AID

S61
TANNENBAUM F.,"THE UNITED STATES AND LATIN AMERICA." FUT USA+45 NAT/G FOR/AID CHOOSE ATTIT ALL/VALS VAL/FREE 20. PAGE 141 A2888
L/A+17C ECO/DEV DIPLOM

B62
ROUND TABLE ON EUROPE'S ROLE IN LATIN AMERICAN DEVELOPMENT. EUR+WWI L/A+17C PLAN BAL/PAY UTIL ROLE WEALTH...CHARTS ANTHOL 20 UN INT/AM/DEV. PAGE 3 A0063
ECO/UNDEV FINAN TEC/DEV FOR/AID

B62
BROWN L.C.,LATIN AMERICA, A BIBLIOGRAPHY. EX/STRUC ADMIN LEAD ATTIT...POLICY 20. PAGE 20 A0405
BIBLIOG L/A+17C DIPLOM NAT/G

B62
DIAZ J.S.,MANUAL DE BIBLIOGRAFIA DE LA LITERATURA ESPANOLA. PRE/AMER SPAIN ECO/UNDEV DIPLOM LEAD ATTIT...SOC 15/20. PAGE 37 A0755
BIBLIOG L/A+17C NAT/G COLONIAL

B62
DREIER J.C.,THE ORGANIZATION OF AMERICAN STATES AND THE HEMISPHERE CRISIS. CUBA USA+45 CULTURE STRATA NAT/G VOL/ASSN CONSULT FORCES ACT/RES CREATE DIPLOM ECO/TAC FOR/AID ALL/VALS...POLICY OBS OAS 20. PAGE 38 A0786
L/A+17C CONCPT

B62
DREIER J.C.,THE ALLIANCE FOR PROGRESS. L/A+17C USA+45 CULTURE ECO/DEV ECO/UNDEV NAT/G PLAN DIPLOM PWR 20 OAS. PAGE 39 A0787
FOR/AID INT/ORG ECO/TAC POLICY

B62
HOOK S.,WORLD COMMUNISM: KEY DOCUMENTARY MATERIAL. CHINA/COM L/A+17C USA+45 USSR POL/PAR DIPLOM COLONIAL REV WAR...ANTHOL 20 MARX/KARL LENIN/VI
MARXISM COM GEN/LAWS

COM/PARTY. PAGE 67 A1380 — NAT/G

B62
HUNTINGTON S.P.,CHANGING PATTERNS OF MILITARY POLITICS. EUR+WWI L/A+17C S/ASIA USA+45 WOR+45 CULTURE INT/ORG NAT/G CONSULT PLAN DOMIN EDU/PROP LEGIT DETER WAR ATTIT PERSON PWR...DECISION CONCPT SIMUL GEN/LAWS ANTHOL COLD/WAR 20. PAGE 69 A1419 — FORCES RIGID/FLEX

B62
KIDDER F.E.,THESES ON PAN AMERICAN TOPICS. LAW CULTURE NAT/G SECT DIPLOM HEALTH...ART/METH GEOG SOC 13/20. PAGE 79 A1615 — BIBLIOG CHRIST-17C L/A+17C SOCIETY

B62
LAUERHAUSS L.,COMMUNISM IN LATIN AMERICA: THE POST-WAR YEARS (1945 -1960) (PAPER). INTELL STRATA ECO/UNDEV AGRI WORKER FOR/AID INT/TRADE COLONIAL GUERRILLA 20. PAGE 85 A1745 — BIBLIOG L/A+17C MARXISM REV

B62
LEVY H.V.,LIBERDADE E JUSTICA SOCIAL (2ND ED.). BRAZIL COM L/A+17C USSR INT/ORG PARTIC GP/REL WEALTH 20 UN COM/PARTY. PAGE 88 A1798 — ORD/FREE MARXISM CAP/ISM LAW

B62
POSTON R.W.,DEMOCRACY SPEAKS MANY TONGUES. L/A+17C USA+45 ECO/UNDEV ACT/RES ECO/TAC ADMIN ORD/FREE ...METH/COMP 20. PAGE 117 A2397 — FOR/AID DIPLOM CAP/ISM MARXISM

B62
QUIRK R.E.,AN AFFAIR OF HONOR: WOODROW WILSON AND THE OCCUPATION OF VERACRUZ. L/A+17C USA-45 COLONIAL SUPEGO PWR 20 WILSON/W MEXIC/AMER. PAGE 118 A2428 — DOMIN DIPLOM COERCE PROB/SOLV

B62
ROY P.A.,SOUTH WIND RED. L/A+17C USA+45 ECO/UNDEV NAT/G CAP/ISM MARXISM SOCISM...OLD/LIB GEOG RECORD INT CENSUS 20 COLD/WAR. PAGE 125 A2554 — DIPLOM INDUS POLICY ECO/TAC

B62
US CONGRESS JOINT ECO COMM,ECONOMIC DEVELOPMENTS IN SOUTH AMERICA. USA+45 SOCIETY FINAN NAT/G PROB/SOLV TEC/DEV INT/TRADE TAX EFFICIENCY PRODUC ATTIT ...POLICY 20 CONGRESS SOUTH/AMER. PAGE 150 A3065 — L/A+17C ECO/UNDEV FOR/AID DIPLOM

B62
ZOOK P.D.,FOREIGN TRADE AND HUMAN CAPITAL. L/A+17C USA+45 FINAN DIPLOM ECO/TAC PRODUC...POLICY 20. PAGE 170 A3458 — INT/TRADE ECO/UNDEV FOR/AID BAL/PAY

L62
"HIGHER EDUCATION AND ECONOMIC AND SOCIAL DEVELOPMENT IN LATIN AMERICA: A BIBLIOGRAPHY." L/A+17C SOCIETY ECO/UNDEV PROF/ORG DIPLOM CONFER ...SOC 20. PAGE 3 A0062 — BIBLIOG/A ACADEM INTELL EDU/PROP

L62
NIZARD L.,"CUBAN QUESTION AND SECURITY COUNCIL." L/A+17C USA+45 ECO/UNDEV NAT/G POL/PAR DELIB/GP ECO/TAC PWR...RELATIV OBS TIME/SEQ TREND GEN/LAWS UN 20 UN. PAGE 109 A2242 — INT/ORG JURID DIPLOM CUBA

S62
FENWICK C.G.,"ISSUES AT PUNTA DEL ESTE: NON-INTERVENTION VS COLLECTIVE SECURITY." L/A+17C USA+45 VOL/ASSN DELIB/GP ECO/TAC LEGIT ADJUD REGION ORD/FREE OAS COLD/WAR 20. PAGE 45 A0917 — INT/ORG CUBA

S62
RUBINSTEIN A.Z.,"RUSSIA AND THE UNCOMMITTED NATIONS." AFR INDIA ISLAM L/A+17C LAOS S/ASIA ELITES ECO/UNDEV INT/ORG KIN CREATE PLAN TEC/DEV NAT/LISM RIGID/FLEX PWR WEALTH...METH/CNCPT TIME/SEQ GEN/LAWS WORK. PAGE 125 A2562 — ECO/TAC TREND COLONIAL USSR

S62
SPRINGER H.W.,"FEDERATION IN THE CARIBBEAN: AN ATTEMPT THAT FAILED." L/A+17C ECO/UNDEV INT/ORG POL/PAR PROVS LEGIS CREATE PLAN LEGIT ADMIN FEDERAL ATTIT DRIVE PERSON ORD/FREE PWR...POLICY GEOG PSY CONCPT OBS CARIBBEAN CMN/WLTH 20. PAGE 136 A2791 — VOL/ASSN NAT/G REGION

B63
CANELAS O.A.,RADIOGRAFIA DE LA ALIANZA PARA EL ATRASO. L/A+17C USA+45 ECO/TAC DOMIN COLONIAL NAT/LISM...SOCIALIST NAT/COMP 20. PAGE 23 A0476 — REV DIPLOM ECO/UNDEV REGION

B63
CENTRO PARA EL DESARROLLO,LA ALIANZA PARA EL PROGRESO Y EL DESARROLLO SOCIAL DE AMERICA LATINA. L/A+17C INT/ORG DIPLOM ECO/TAC INT/TRADE ATTIT 20. PAGE 25 A0512 — ECO/UNDEV FOR/AID PLAN REGION

B63
COMISION DE HISTORIO,GUIA DE LOS DOCUMENTOS MICROFOTOGRAFIADOS POR LA UNIDAD MOVIL DE LA UNESCO. SOCIETY ECO/UNDEV INT/ORG ADMIN...SOC 20 UNESCO. PAGE 28 A0573 — BIBLIOG NAT/G L/A+17C DIPLOM

B63
FLORES E.,LAND REFORM AND THE ALLIANCE FOR PROGRESS (PAMPHLET). L/A+17C USA+45 STRUCT ECO/UNDEV NAT/G WORKER CREATE PLAN ECO/TAC COERCE REV 20. PAGE 47 A0953 — AGRI INT/ORG DIPLOM POLICY

B63
GORDON L.,A NEW DEAL FOR LATIN AMERICA. L/A+17C USA+45 CULTURE NAT/G TEC/DEV DIPLOM FOR/AID REGION TASK...POLICY 20 DEPT/STATE. PAGE 54 A1115 — ECO/UNDEV ECO/TAC INT/ORG PLAN

B63
INTERAMERICAN ECO AND SOC COUN,THE ALLIANCE FOR PROGRESS: ITS FIRST YEAR: 1961-1962. AGRI SCHOOL PLAN TEC/DEV INT/TRADE TAX GIVE ADMIN WEALTH...SOC 20 SOUTH/AMER. PAGE 71 A1449 — INT/ORG PROB/SOLV ECO/TAC L/A+17C

B63
MANGER W.,THE ALLIANCE FOR PROGRESS: A CRITICAL APPRAISAL. FUT L/A+17C USA+45 CULTURE ECO/UNDEV ACADEM NAT/G SCHOOL PLAN FOR/AID...POLICY OAS. PAGE 94 A1918 — DIPLOM INT/ORG ECO/TAC REGION

B63
MARITANO N.,AN ALLIANCE FOR PROGRESS. FUT L/A+17C USA+45 CULTURE ECO/UNDEV NAT/G PLAN CONTROL POLICY. PAGE 95 A1941 — DIPLOM INT/ORG ECO/TAC FOR/AID

B63
MENDES C.,NACIONALISMO E DESENVOLVIMENTO. AFR ASIA L/A+17C STRATA INT/TRADE COLONIAL. PAGE 99 A2039 — NAT/LISM ECO/UNDEV DIPLOM REV

B63
PANAMERICAN UNION,DOCUMENTOS OFICIALES DE LA ORGANIZACION DE LOS ESTADOS AMERICANOS, INDICE Y LISTA (VOL. III, 1962). L/A+17C DELIB/GP INT/TRADE EDU/PROP REGION NUC/PWR...HEAL INT/LAW SOC/WK 20 OAS. PAGE 113 A2329 — BIBLIOG INT/ORG DIPLOM

B63
PEREZ ORTIZ R.,ANUARIO BIBLIOGRAFICO COLOMBIANO, 1961. AGRI...INT/LAW JURID SOC LING 20 COLOMB. PAGE 115 A2354 — BIBLIOG L/A+17C NAT/G

B63
SZULC T.,THE WINDS OF REVOLUTION; LATIN AMERICA TODAY - AND TOMORROW. L/A+17C ORD/FREE SOCISM ...PREDICT TREND 20. PAGE 141 A2880 — REV INT/ORG MARXISM ECO/UNDEV

B63
UNITED STATES GOVERNMENT,REPORT TO THE INTER-AMERICAN ECONOMIC AND SOCIAL COUNCIL. L/A+17C INDUS PLAN INT/TRADE TARIFFS CONFER...CHARTS 20 LAFTA. PAGE 149 A3038 — FOR/AID ECO/TAC ECO/UNDEV DIPLOM

B63
US GOVERNMENT,REPORT TO INTER-AMERICAN ECONOMIC AND SOCIAL COUNCIL AT SECOND ANNUAL MEETING. L/A+17C USA+45 VOL/ASSN TEC/DEV DIPLOM TAX EATING EFFICIENCY HEALTH...STAT CHARTS 20 AID. PAGE 153 A3116 — ECO/TAC FOR/AID FINAN PLAN

B63
WELLESLEY COLLEGE,SYMPOSIUM ON LATIN AMERICA. FUT L/A+17C USA+45 INT/ORG ECO/TAC PARL/PROC REGION ANTHOL. PAGE 163 A3316 — ECO/UNDEV CULTURE ORD/FREE DIPLOM

S63
ALEXANDER R.,"LATIN AMERICA AND THE COMMUNIST BLOC." ASIA COM CUBA L/A+17C USA+45 USSR NAT/G VOL/ASSN TEC/DEV FOR/AID LEGIT PWR WEALTH COLD/WAR 20. PAGE 6 A0112 — ECO/UNDEV RECORD

S63
HOLBO P.S.,"COLD WAR DRIFT IN LATIN AMERICA." CUBA L/A+17C USA+45 USA-45 INT/ORG NAT/G NEIGH VOL/ASSN ACT/RES PLAN ECO/TAC ATTIT RIGID/FLEX ALL/VALS ...RECORD TIME/SEQ OAS LAFTA 20 COLD/WAR. PAGE 66 A1363 — DELIB/GP CREATE FOR/AID

S63
HUMPHREY H.H.,"REGIONAL ARMS CONTROL AGREEMENTS." WOR+45 FORCES PLAN LEGIT COERCE ATTIT HEALTH ORD/FREE...HUM METH/CNCPT MYTH OBS INT TREND TOT/POP 20. PAGE 69 A1416 — L/A+17C INT/ORG ARMS/CONT REGION

S63
LIPSHART A.,"THE ANALYSIS OF BLOC VOTING IN THE GENERAL ASSEMBLY." L/A+17C WOR+45 ACT/RES INGP/REL ...POLICY DECISION NEW/IDEA STAT IDEA/COMP UN. PAGE 90 A1832 — CHOOSE INT/ORG DELIB/GP

S63
MANOLIU F.,"PERSPECTIVES D'UNE INTEGRATION ECONOMIQUE LATINOAMERICAINE." FUT L/A+17C STRUCT MARKET LABOR POL/PAR VOL/ASSN PLAN RIGID/FLEX PWR ...METH/CNCPT OAS TOT/POP 20. PAGE 94 A1927 — FINAN INT/ORG PEACE

S63
SCHMIDT W.E.,"THE CASE AGAINST COMMODITY AGREEMENTS." FUT L/A+17C STRATA CONSULT PLAN ECO/TAC EDU/PROP ATTIT DRIVE RIGID/FLEX WEALTH ...MYTH 20. PAGE 128 A2631 — ECO/UNDEV ACT/RES INT/TRADE

S63
WELLS H.,"THE OAS AND THE DOMINICAN ELECTIONS." L/A+17C INT/ORG NAT/G POL/PAR TEC/DEV ECO/TAC EDU/PROP PERCEPT...TIME/SEQ OAS TOT/POP 20. PAGE 163 A3317 — CONSULT CHOOSE DOMIN/REP

C63
SCHMITT K.M.,"EVOLUTION OR CHAOS: DYNAMICS OF LATIN AMERICAN GOVERNMENT AND POLITICS." L/A+17C AGRI FINAN CAP/ISM EXEC LEAD BAL/PAY TOTALISM ATTIT ...TREND BIBLIOG 20. PAGE 129 A2635 — DIPLOM POLICY POL/PAR LOBBY

B64
ANDREWS D.H.,LATIN AMERICA: A BIBLIOGRAPHY OF PAPERBACK BOOKS. SECT INT/TRADE EDU/PROP WAR GOV/REL ADJUST NAT/LISM ATTIT...ART/METH LING BIOG 20. PAGE 8 A0160
BIBLIOG L/A+17C CULTURE NAT/G

B64
CORFO,CHILE, A SELECTED BIBLIOGRAPHY IN ENGLISH (PAMPHLET). CHILE DIPLOM...SOC 20. PAGE 31 A0623
BIBLIOG NAT/G POLICY L/A+17C

B64
DAVIES U.P. JR.,FOREIGN AND OTHER AFFAIRS. EUR+WWI L/A+17C S/ASIA USA+45 ECO/UNDEV CHIEF PLAN ECO/TAC PWR MARXISM 20 KENNEDY/JF UN. PAGE 34 A0688
DIPLOM NAT/G POLICY FOR/AID

B64
HOROWITZ I.L.,REVOLUTION IN BRAZIL. BRAZIL L/A+17C ELITES STRATA NAT/G BAL/PWR PARTIC ATTIT 20. PAGE 68 A1388
ECO/UNDEV DIPLOM POLICY ORD/FREE

B64
IBERO-AMERICAN INSTITUTES,IBEROAMERICANA. STRUCT ADMIN SOC. PAGE 70 A1430
BIBLIOG L/A+17C NAT/G DIPLOM

B64
IRISH M.D.,WORLD PRESSURES ON AMERICAN FOREIGN POLICY. ASIA COM L/A+17C SOUTH/AFR UK WOR+45 ECO/DEV ECO/UNDEV COLONIAL SANCTION COERCE REV TOTALISM...ANTHOL 20 COLD/WAR EUROPE/W INTERVENT. PAGE 72 A1467
DIPLOM POLICY

B64
JACKSON W.V.,LIBRARY GUIDE FOR BRAZILIAN STUDIES. BRAZIL USA+45 STRUCT DIPLOM ADMIN...SOC 20. PAGE 72 A1481
BIBLIOG L/A+17C NAT/G LOC/G

B64
JANOWITZ M.,THE MILITARY IN THE POLITICAL DEVELOPMENT OF NEW NATIONS: AN ESSAY IN COMPARATIVE ANALYSIS. AFR ASIA ISLAM L/A+17C S/ASIA USA+45 ECO/UNDEV INT/ORG NAT/G POL/PAR DELIB/GP PLAN ECO/TAC DOMIN LEGIT COERCE ATTIT DRIVE RESPECT ...SOC CONCPT CENSUS VAL/FREE. PAGE 73 A1495
FORCES PWR

B64
LENS S.,THE FUTILE CRUSADE. ASIA CHINA/COM L/A+17C USA+45 USSR WOR+45 ECO/DEV BAL/PWR DIPLOM NUC/PWR WAR NAT/LISM PEACE 20 COLD/WAR PRESIDENT CIA. PAGE 87 A1774
ORD/FREE ANOMIE COM MARXISM

B64
LIEVWEN E.,GENERALS VS PRESIDENTS: WEOMILITARISM IN LATIN AMERICA. L/A+17C FORCES DIPLOM FOR/AID LEAD ...NAT/COMP 20 PRESIDENT. PAGE 89 A1813
CIVMIL/REL REV CONSERVE ORD/FREE

B64
MAIER J.,POLITICS OF CHANGE IN LATIN AMERICA. BRAZIL L/A+17C STRATA INT/ORG NAT/G POL/PAR FOR/AID REV 20. PAGE 93 A1907
SOCIETY NAT/LISM DIPLOM REGION

B64
MUSSO AMBROSI L.A.,BIBLIOGRAFIA DE BIBLIOGRAFIAS URUGUAYAS. URUGUAY DIPLOM ADMIN ATTIT...SOC 20. PAGE 106 A2185
BIBLIOG NAT/G L/A+17C PRESS

B64
NEHEMKIS P.,LATIN AMERICA: MYTH AND REALITY. INDUS INT/ORG MUNIC PROB/SOLV CAP/ISM DIPLOM REV...SOC 20. PAGE 108 A2211
REGION MYTH L/A+17C ECO/UNDEV

B64
SEGUNDO-SANCHEZ M.,OBRAS (2 VOLS.). VENEZUELA EX/STRUC DIPLOM ADMIN 19/20. PAGE 131 A2682
BIBLIOG LEAD NAT/G L/A+17C

B64
SINGER H.W.,INTERNATIONAL DEVELOPMENT: GROWTH AND CHANGE. AFR BRAZIL L/A+17C WOR+45 CULTURE AGRI INDUS NAT/G ACT/RES ECO/TAC EDU/PROP WEALTH...GEOG CONCPT METH/CNCPT STAT HYPO/EXP WORK TOT/POP 20. PAGE 133 A2723
FINAN ECO/UNDEV FOR/AID INT/TRADE

B64
TEPASKE J.J.,EXPLOSIVE FORCES IN LATIN AMERICA. CULTURE INTELL ECO/UNDEV INT/ORG NAT/G SECT FORCES ECO/TAC EDU/PROP PWR WEALTH SOC. PAGE 142 A2903
L/A+17C RIGID/FLEX FOR/AID USSR

B64
TURNER M.C.,LIBROS EN VENTA EN HISPANOAMERICA Y ESPANA. SPAIN LAW CONSTN CULTURE ADMIN LEAD...HUM SOC 20. PAGE 146 A2983
BIBLIOG L/A+17C NAT/G DIPLOM

B64
US AGENCY INTERNATIONAL DEV,REPORT TO CONGRESS ON THE FOREIGN ASSISTANCE PROGRAM. AFR ASIA L/A+17C USA+45 INT/ORG VOL/ASSN FORCES CAP/ISM ADMIN WEAPON. PAGE 149 A3052
FOR/AID ECO/UNDEV TEC/DEV BUDGET

B64
US HOUSE COMM FOREIGN AFFAIRS,HEARINGS ON H.R. 10502 TO AMEND FURTHER THE FOREIGN ASSISTANCE ACT OF 1961. AFR ASIA L/A+17C INT/ORG CONSULT DELIB/GP TEC/DEV ECO/TAC EDU/PROP CONFER 20 UN NATO CONGRESS AID. PAGE 153 A3130
FOR/AID DIPLOM ORD/FREE ECO/UNDEV

B64
WITHERS W.,THE ECONOMIC CRISIS IN LATIN AMERICA. BRAZIL CHILE STRATA AGRI DIPLOM FOR/AID PWR SOCISM ...POLICY 20 MEXIC/AMER ARGEN. PAGE 166 A3372
L/A+17C ECO/UNDEV CAP/ISM ALL/IDEOS

B64
WRIGHT T.P. JR.,AMERICAN SUPPORT OF FREE ELECTIONS ABROAD. USA+45 USA-45 DOMIN LEAD NEUTRAL MARXISM ...POLICY TIME/SEQ BIBLIOG 19/20 COLD/WAR INTERVENT. PAGE 168 A3420
DIPLOM CHOOSE L/A+17C POPULISM

B64
WYTHE G.,THE UNITED STATES AND INTER-AMERICAN RELATIONS: A CONTEMPORARY APPRAISAL. L/A+17C USA+45 ECO/UNDEV INT/ORG NAT/G VOL/ASSN INT/TRADE EDU/PROP DRIVE...SOC TREND OAS UN 20. PAGE 168 A3425
ATTIT ECO/TAC FOR/AID

L64
CLAUDE I.,"THE OAS, THE UN, AND THE UNITED STATES." L/A+17C USA+45 CONSTN NAT/G DELIB/GP DOMIN EDU/PROP LEGIT REGION COERCE ORD/FREE PWR...TIME/SEQ TREND STERTYP OAS UN 20. PAGE 27 A0546
INT/ORG POLICY

L64
HAAS E.B.,"ECONOMICS AND DIFFERENTIAL PATTERNS OF POLITICAL INTEGRATION: PROJECTIONS ABOUT UNITY IN LATIN AMERICA." SOCIETY NAT/G DELIB/GP ACT/RES CREATE PLAN ECO/TAC REGION ROUTINE ATTIT DRIVE PWR WEALTH...CONCPT TREND CHARTS LAFTA 20. PAGE 59 A1208
L/A+17C INT/ORG MARKET

S64
CARNEGIE ENDOWMENT INT. PEACE,"COLONIAL COUNTRIES AND PEOPLES (ISSUES BEFORE THE NINETEENTH GENERAL ASSEMBLY)." AFR ISLAM L/A+17C WOR+45 DELIB/GP LEGIS ECO/TAC EDU/PROP NAT/LISM PEACE ALL/VALS...RECORD UN CMN/WLTH 20. PAGE 24 A0491
INT/ORG ECO/UNDEV COLONIAL

S64
COCHRANE J.D.,"US ATTITUDES TOWARD CENTRAL-AMERICAN INTEGRATION." L/A+17C USA+45 ECO/UNDEV FACE/GP VOL/ASSN DELIB/GP ECO/TAC INT/TRADE EDU/PROP RIGID/FLEX ORD/FREE WEALTH...TIME/SEQ TOT/POP 20. PAGE 27 A0555
NAT/G ATTIT REGION

S64
DELGADO J.,"EL MOMENTO POLITICO HISPANOAMERICA." CHINA/COM FUT PANAMA USA+45 USSR INT/ORG NAT/G POL/PAR FORCES DOMIN REGION COERCE ATTIT ALL/VALS ...TRADIT CONCPT COLD/WAR 20. PAGE 36 A0728
L/A+17C EDU/PROP NAT/LISM

S64
DERWINSKI E.J.,"THE COST OF THE INTERNATIONAL COFFEE AGREEMENT." L/A+17C USA+45 WOR+45 ECO/UNDEV NAT/G VOL/ASSN LEGIS DIPLOM ECO/TAC FOR/AID LEGIT ATTIT...TIME/SEQ CONGRESS 20 TREATY. PAGE 36 A0732
MARKET DELIB/GP INT/TRADE

S64
HUELIN D.,"ECONOMIC INTEGRATION IN LATIN AMERICAN: PROGRESS AND PROBLEMS." L/A+17C ECO/DEV AGRI DIST/IND FINAN INDUS NAT/G VOL/ASSN CONSULT DELIB/GP EX/STRUC ACT/RES PLAN TEC/DEV ECO/TAC ROUTINE BAL/PAY WEALTH WORK 20. PAGE 69 A1411
MARKET ECO/UNDEV INT/TRADE

S64
REIDY J.W.,"LATIN AMERICA AND THE ATLANTIC TRIANGLE." EUR+WWI FUT USA+45 INT/ORG NAT/G REGION COERCE ORD/FREE PWR...TIME/SEQ VAL/FREE 20. PAGE 120 A2458
L/A+17C WEALTH POLICY

C64
EASTON S.C.,"THE RISE AND FALL OF WESTERN COLONIALISM." AFR ISLAM L/A+17C ECO/UNDEV REV NAT/LISM...CHARTS BIBLIOG 15/20. PAGE 40 A0817
COLONIAL DIPLOM ORD/FREE WAR

B65
AIR UNIVERSITY LIBRARY,LATIN AMERICA, SELECTED REFERENCES. ECO/UNDEV FORCES EDU/PROP MARXISM 20 OAS. PAGE 5 A0106
BIBLIOG L/A+17C NAT/G DIPLOM

B65
FAGG J.E.,CUBA, HAITI, AND THE DOMINICAN REPUBLIC. CUBA DOMIN/REP HAITI L/A+17C NAT/G DIPLOM ECO/TAC DOMIN CHOOSE AUTHORIT ROLE SOVEREIGN POPULISM 17/20. PAGE 43 A0883
COLONIAL ECO/UNDEV REV GOV/COMP

B65
FORM W.H.,INDUSTRIAL RELATIONS AND SOCIAL CHANGE IN LATIN AMERICA. L/A+17C AGRI LABOR NAT/G PLAN PROB/SOLV DIPLOM...MGT SOC ANTHOL BIBLIOG/A METH 20. PAGE 47 A0966
INDUS GP/REL NAT/COMP ECO/UNDEV

B65
GERASSI J.,THE GREAT FEAR IN LATIN AMERICA. L/A+17C USA+45 ELITES STRUCT INT/ORG REV ORD/FREE WEALTH 20 LAFTA. PAGE 52 A1063
SOCIETY FOR/AID DIPLOM

B65
HALPERIN E.,NATIONALISM AND COMMUNISM. CHILE L/A+17C CAP/ISM EDU/PROP CHOOSE DISCRIM SOCISM ...BIBLIOG 20 COM/PARTY. PAGE 60 A1236
NAT/LISM MARXISM POL/PAR REV

B65
HISPANIC SOCIETY OF AMERICA,CATALOGUE (10 VOLS.). PORTUGAL PRE/AMER SPAIN NAT/G ADMIN...POLICY SOC
BIBLIOG L/A+17C

15/20. PAGE 65 A1341 COLONIAL DIPLOM

B65
LIEUWEN E.,U.S. POLICY IN LATIN AMERICA: A SHORT HISTORY. L/A+17C USA+45 USA-45 DELIB/GP ECO/TAC 19/20 COLD/WAR MONROE/DOC. PAGE 89 A1812 DIPLOM COLONIAL NAT/G FOR/AID

B65
MALLIN J.,FORTRESS CUBA; RUSSIA'S AMERICAN BASE. COM CUBA L/A+17C FORCES PLAN DIPLOM LEAD REV WAR ...POLICY 20 CASTRO/F GUEVARA/C INTERVENT. PAGE 93 A1914 MARXISM CHIEF GUERRILLA DOMIN

B65
MEDIVA J.T.,LA IMPRENTA EN MEXICO, 1539-1821 (8 VOLS.). SOCIETY ECO/UNDEV DIPLOM COLONIAL GP/REL 16/19 MEXIC/AMER. PAGE 99 A2031 BIBLIOG WRITING NAT/G L/A+17C

B65
NATIONAL CENTRAL LIBRARY,LATIN AMERICAN ECONOMIC AND SOCIAL SERIALS. UK SOCIETY NAT/G PLAN PROB/SOLV ...SOC 20. PAGE 107 A2202 BIBLIOG INT/TRADE ECO/UNDEV L/A+17C

B65
RAPPAPORT A.,ISSUES IN AMERICAN DIPLOMACY: WORLD POWER AND LEADERSHIP SINCE 1895 (VOL. II). CHINA/COM EUR+WWI L/A+17C USA+45 USA-45 NAT/G ECO/TAC DOMIN CONFER LEAD NUC/PWR WEAPON...DECISION 19/20 WILSON/W ROOSEVLT/F CHINJAP. PAGE 119 A2447 WAR POLICY DIPLOM

B65
REQUA E.G.,THE DEVELOPING NATIONS: A GUIDE TO INFORMATION SOURCES CONCERNING THEIR ECON, POLIT, TECHNICAL, AND SOCIAL PROBLEMS. AFR ASIA ISLAM L/A+17C INDUS INT/ORG CONSULT PLAN PROB/SOLV...SOC 20 UN. PAGE 120 A2466 BIBLIOG/A ECO/UNDEV FOR/AID TEC/DEV

B65
SABLE M.H.,MASTER DIRECTORY FOR LATIN AMERICA. AGRI COM/IND FINAN R+D ACADEM LABOR NAT/G POL/PAR VOL/ASSN INT/TRADE EDU/PROP 20. PAGE 126 A2582 INDEX L/A+17C INT/ORG DIPLOM

B65
SABLE M.H.,PERIODICALS FOR LATIN AMERICAN ECONOMIC DEVELOPMENT, TRADE, AND FINANCE: AN ANNOTATED BIBLIOGRAPHY (A PAMPHLET). ECO/TAC PRODUC PROFIT ...STAT NAT/COMP 20 OAS. PAGE 126 A2583 BIBLIOG/A L/A+17C ECO/UNDEV INT/TRADE

B65
SILVA SOLAR J.,EL DESARROLLO DE LA NUEVA SOCIEDAD EN AMERICA. L/A+17C SOCIETY AGRI PROB/SOLV DIPLOM PARTIC GP/REL OWN...POLICY SOC 20 REFORMERS. PAGE 133 A2716 STRUCT ECO/UNDEV REGION CONTROL

B65
STOETZER O.C.,THE ORGANIZATION OF AMERICAN STATES. L/A+17C EX/STRUC FOR/AID CONFER PARL/PROC ORD/FREE SOVEREIGN...POLICY INT/LAW 20 OAS. PAGE 138 A2831 INT/ORG REGION DIPLOM BAL/PWR

B65
THOMAS A.V.,NONINTERVENTION: THE LAW AND ITS IMPORT IN THE AMERICAS. L/A+17C USA+45 USA-45 WOR+45 DIPLOM ADJUD...JURID IDEA/COMP 20 UN INTERVENT. PAGE 143 A2920 INT/LAW PWR COERCE

B65
TREFOUSSE H.L.,THE COLD WAR: A BOOK OF DOCUMENTS. ASIA L/A+17C USSR WOR+45 WOR-45 ECO/TAC FOR/AID ARMS/CONT NUC/PWR PEACE ORD/FREE...ANTHOL 20 COLD/WAR KENNEDY/JF EISNHWR/DD. PAGE 145 A2961 BAL/PWR DIPLOM MARXISM

B65
US BUREAU EDUC CULTURAL AFF,RESOURCES SURVEY FOR LATIN AMERICAN COUNTRIES. L/A+17C USA+45 CULTURE INDUS INT/ORG SECT PLAN EDU/PROP POLICY. PAGE 150 A3056 NAT/G ECO/UNDEV FOR/AID DIPLOM

B65
US HOUSE COMM FOREIGN AFFAIRS,HEARINGS ON DRAFT BILL TO AMEND FURTHER THE FOREIGN ASSISTANCE ACT OF 1961. AFR ASIA L/A+17C USA+45 INT/ORG DELIB/GP TEC/DEV ECO/TAC CONFER TOTALISM 20 CONGRESS AID. PAGE 153 A3131 FOR/AID ECO/UNDEV DIPLOM ORD/FREE

B65
US SENATE COMM ON FOREIGN REL,HEARINGS ON THE FOREIGN ASSISTANCE PROGRAM. AFR ASIA L/A+17C USA+45 WOR+45 FORCES TEC/DEV BUDGET CONTROL WEAPON ORD/FREE 20 UN CONGRESS SEC/STATE. PAGE 156 A3183 FOR/AID DIPLOM INT/ORG ECO/UNDEV

B65
WILGUS A.C.,HISTORIES AND HISTORIANS OF HISPANIC AMERICA (REPRINT ED.). CHRIST-17C SECT DIPLOM REV 16/20. PAGE 164 A3350 BIBLIOG/A L/A+17C REGION COLONIAL

L65
MATTHEWS D.G.,"LE TIERS MONDE: A SELECT AND PRELIMINARY BIBLIOGRAPHIC SURVEY OF MANPOWER IN DEVELOPING COUNTRIES, 1960-1964." AFR ISLAM L/A+17C INDUS PLAN PROB/SOLV TEC/DEV INT/TRADE EFFICIENCY WEALTH...STAT 20. PAGE 96 A1971 BIBLIOG/A ECO/UNDEV LABOR WORKER

L65
WIONCZEK M.,"LATIN AMERICA FREE TRADE ASSOCIATION." AGRI DIST/IND FINAN INDUS INT/ORG LABOR NAT/G TEC/DEV ECO/TAC HEALTH SKILL WEALTH...POLICY RELATIV MGT LAFTA 20. PAGE 165 A3369 L/A+17C MARKET REGION

S65
SCHNEIDER R.M.,"THE US IN LATIN AMERICA." L/A+17C USA+45 NAT/G POL/PAR PLAN RIGID/FLEX ALL/VALS OAS 20. PAGE 129 A2640 VOL/ASSN ECO/UNDEV FOR/AID

B66
CANNING HOUSE LIBRARY,AUTHOR AND SUBJECT CATALOGUES OF THE CANNING HOUSE LIBRARY (5 VOLS.). UK CULTURE LEAD...SOC 19/20. PAGE 24 A0478 BIBLIOG L/A+17C NAT/G DIPLOM

B66
CONNEL-SMITH G.,THE INTERAMERICAN SYSTEM. CUBA L/A+17C DELIB/GP FOR/AID COLONIAL PEACE PWR MARXISM ...BIBLIOG 19/20 OAS. PAGE 29 A0586 DIPLOM INT/TRADE REGION INT/ORG

B66
GARNER W.R.,THE CHACO DISPUTE; A STUDY OF PRESTIGE DIPLOMACY. L/A+17C PARAGUAY USA-45 INT/ORG AGREE PEACE...TIME/SEQ 20 BOLIV LEAGUE/NAT ARGEN CHACO/WAR. PAGE 51 A1050 WAR DIPLOM CONCPT PWR

B66
LAMBERG R.F.,PRAG UND DIE DRITTE WELT. AFR ASIA CZECHOSLVK L/A+17C MARKET TEC/DEV ECO/TAC REV ATTIT 20 TREATY. PAGE 84 A1713 DIPLOM ECO/UNDEV INT/TRADE FOR/AID

B66
US DEPARTMENT OF STATE,RESEARCH ON THE AMERICAN REPUBLICS (EXTERNAL RESEARCH LIST NO 6-25). CULTURE SOCIETY POL/PAR DIPLOM EDU/PROP MARXISM WORSHIP 20 OAS. PAGE 152 A3095 BIBLIOG/A L/A+17C REGION NAT/G

B66
US HOUSE COMM FOREIGN AFFAIRS,HEARINGS ON HR 12449 A BILL TO AMEND FURTHER THE FOREIGN ASSISTANCE ACT OF 1961. AFR ASIA L/A+17C USA+45 VIETNAM INT/ORG TEC/DEV INT/TRADE ATTIT ORD/FREE 20 UN NATO CONGRESS AID. PAGE 154 A3132 FOR/AID ECO/TAC ECO/UNDEV DIPLOM

B66
WESTWOOD A.F.,FOREIGN AID IN A FOREIGN POLICY FRAMEWORK. AFR ASIA INDIA IRAN L/A+17C USA+45 USSR ECO/UNDEV AGRI FORCES LEGIS PLAN PROB/SOLV ...DECISION 20 COLD/WAR. PAGE 163 A3324 FOR/AID DIPLOM POLICY ECO/TAC

B66
WHITAKER A.P.,NATIONALISM IN CONTEMPORARY LATIN AMERICA. AGRI NAT/G WEALTH...POLICY SOC CONCPT OBS TREND 20. PAGE 164 A3333 NAT/LISM L/A+17C DIPLOM ECO/UNDEV

B66
ZABLOCKI C.J.,SINO-SOVIET RIVALRY. AFR ASIA CHINA/COM CUBA EUR+WWI L/A+17C USA+45 USSR WOR+45 POL/PAR FORCES COERCE NUC/PWR...GOV/COMP IDEA/COMP 20 MAO KHRUSH/N. PAGE 169 A3442 DIPLOM MARXISM COM

S66
JAVITS J.K.,"POLITICAL ACTION VITAL FOR LATIN AMERICAN INTEGRATION." ECO/UNDEV INT/ORG POL/PAR VOL/ASSN PLAN PROB/SOLV INT/TRADE EFFICIENCY 20 OAS LAFTA. PAGE 73 A1500 L/A+17C ECO/TAC REGION

S66
MERRITT R.L.,"SELECTED ARTICLES AND DOCUMENTS ON COMPARATIVE GOVERNMENT AND CROSS-NATIONAL RESEARCH." AFR ASIA EUR+WWI L/A+17C MOD/EUR ELITES R+D ACT/RES DIPLOM PWR...SOC CONCPT 18/20. PAGE 100 A2046 BIBLIOG GOV/COMP NAT/G GOV/REL

B67
PIKE F.B.,FREEDOM AND REFORM IN LATIN AMERICA. BRAZIL URUGUAY CONSTN CULTURE SECT DIPLOM EDU/PROP PARTIC DRIVE ALL/VALS CATHISM...GEOG ANTHOL BIBLIOG REFORMERS BOLIV. PAGE 116 A2379 L/A+17C ORD/FREE ECO/UNDEV REV

B67
SABLE M.H.,A GUIDE TO LATIN AMERICAN STUDIES (2 VOLS). CONSTN FINAN INT/ORG LABOR MUNIC POL/PAR FORCES CAP/ISM FOR/AID ADMIN MARXISM SOCISM OAS. PAGE 126 A2584 BIBLIOG/A L/A+17C DIPLOM NAT/LISM

B67
US CONGRESS SENATE,SURVEY OF THE ALLIANCE FOR PROGRESS; INFLATION IN LATIN AMERICA (PAMPHLET). USA+45 MARKET INT/ORG DIPLOM INT/TRADE BAL/PAY SENATE. PAGE 150 A3072 L/A+17C FINAN POLICY FOR/AID

L67
SEGAL A.,"THE INTEGRATION OF DEVELOPING COUNTRIES: SOME THOUGHTS ON EAST AFRICA AND CENTRAL AMERICA." AFR L/A+17C INT/ORG NAT/G VOL/ASSN FOR/AID INT/TRADE EQUILIB NAT/LISM PWR 20. PAGE 131 A2680 ECO/UNDEV DIPLOM REGION

S67
BURNS E.B.,"TRADITIONS AND VARIATIONS IN BRAZILIAN FOREIGN POLICY." BRAZIL L/A+17C POL/PAR INT/TRADE COLONIAL INGP/REL ATTIT ORD/FREE PWR 20. PAGE 22 A0443 DIPLOM NAT/LISM CREATE

S67
FABREGA J.,"ANTECEDENTES EXTRANJEROS EN LA CONSTITUCION PANAMENA." CUBA L/A+17C PANAMA URUGUAY EX/STRUC LEGIS DIPLOM ORD/FREE 19/20 COLOMB MEXIC/AMER. PAGE 43 A0882 CONSTN JURID NAT/G PARL/PROC

S67
GODUNSKY Y.,"'APOSTLES OF PEACE' IN LATIN AMERICA." L/A+17C USA+45 BAL/PWR DIPLOM FOR/AID DOMIN COLONIAL CIVMIL/REL MARXIST. PAGE 53 A1086 ECO/UNDEV REV VOL/ASSN EDU/PROP

S67
HEATH D.B.,"BOLIVIA UNDER BARRIENTOS." L/A+17C NAT/G CHIEF DIPLOM ECO/TAC...POLICY 20 BOLIV. PAGE 64 A1306 — ECO/UNDEV POL/PAR REV CONSTN

S67
HERRERA F.,"EUROPEAN PARTICIPATION IN THE LATIN AMERICAN REGIONAL INTEGRATION" EUR+WWI L/A+17C GP/REL INGP/REL 20. PAGE 64 A1318 — DIPLOM REGION INT/ORG FINAN

S67
JAVITS J.K.,"LAST CHANCE FOR A COMMON MARKET." L/A+17C INT/ORG 20 EEC LAFTA. PAGE 73 A1501 — FOR/AID ECO/UNDEV INT/TRADE ECO/TAC

S67
JOHNSON J.,"THE UNITED STATES AND THE LATIN AMERICAN LEFT WINGS." L/A+17C STRATA POL/PAR INT/TRADE 20. PAGE 74 A1524 — ECO/UNDEV WORKER ECO/TAC REGION

S67
KINGSLEY R.E.,"THE US BUSINESS IMAGE IN LATIN AMERICA." L/A+17C USA+45 NAT/G TEC/DEV CAP/ISM FOR/AID DOMIN EDU/PROP...CONCPT LING IDEA/COMP 20. PAGE 79 A1626 — ATTIT LOVE DIPLOM ECO/UNDEV

S67
MONTALVA E.F.,"THE ALLIANCE THAT LOST ITS WAY." L/A+17C USA+45 R+D BAL/PWR INT/TRADE RECEIVE REV PEACE...POLICY 20. PAGE 103 A2111 — ECO/UNDEV DIPLOM FOR/AID INT/ORG

S67
STEGER H.S.,"RESEARCH ON LATIN AMERICA IN THE FEDERAL REPUBLIC OF GERMANY AND WEST BERLIN." FINAN DIPLOM INT/TRADE EDU/PROP...GEOG JURID CHARTS 19/20. PAGE 137 A2813 — SOCIETY ECO/UNDEV ACADEM L/A+17C

B98
GRIFFIN A.P.C.,LIST OF BOOKS RELATING TO CUBA (PAMPHLET). CUBA L/A+17C USA-45 INT/TRADE DOMIN WAR GP/REL ALL/VALS...GEOG SOC CHARTS 19/20. PAGE 56 A1158 — BIBLIOG/A NAT/G COLONIAL

LA DOCUMENTATION FRANCAISE A1705

LAB/EXP....LABORATORY EXPERIMENTS

B60
US HOUSE COMM. SCI. ASTRONAUT.,OCEAN SCIENCES AND NATIONAL SECURITY. FUT SEA ECO/DEV EXTR/IND INT/ORG NAT/G FORCES ACT/RES TEC/DEV ECO/TAC COERCE WAR BIO/SOC KNOWL PWR...CONCPT RECORD LAB/EXP 20. PAGE 154 A3141 — R+D ORD/FREE

B62
THOMSON G.P.,NUCLEAR ENERGY IN BRITAIN DURING THE LAST WAR: THE CHERWELL SIMON LECTURE (MONOGRAPH). UK R+D CONSULT FORCES PLAN DIPLOM TASK CIVMIL/REL ROLE...PHIL/SCI NEW/IDEA LAB/EXP 20 MAUD. PAGE 143 A2934 — CREATE TEC/DEV WAR NUC/PWR

LABEDZ L. A1731,A1732

LABOR FORCE....SEE WORKER

LABOR RELATIONS....SEE LABOR, ALSO RELATIONS INDEX

LABOR UNIONS....SEE LABOR

LABOR....LABOR UNIONS (BUT NOT GUILDS)

N
CANADIAN GOVERNMENT PUBLICATIONS (1955-). CANADA AGRI FINAN LABOR FORCES INT/TRADE HEALTH...JURID 20 PARLIAMENT. PAGE 1 A0007 — BIBLIOG/A NAT/G DIPLOM INT/ORG

N
INTERNATIONAL BOOK NEWS, 1928-1934. ECO/UNDEV FINAN INDUS LABOR INT/TRADE CONFER ADJUD COLONIAL...HEAL SOC/WK CHARTS 20 LEAGUE/NAT. PAGE 1 A0010 — BIBLIOG/A DIPLOM INT/LAW INT/ORG

N
ARBITRATION JOURNAL. WOR+45 LAW INDUS JUDGE DIPLOM CT/SYS INGP/REL 20. PAGE 2 A0027 — BIBLIOG MGT LABOR ADJUD

N
INDIA: A REFERENCE ANNUAL. INDIA CULTURE COM/IND R+D FORCES PLAN RECEIVE EDU/PROP HEALTH...STAT CHARTS BIBLIOG 20. PAGE 2 A0036 — CONSTN LABOR INT/ORG

N
THE JAPAN SCIENCE REVIEW: LAW AND POLITICS: LIST OF BOOKS AND ARTICLES ON LAW AND POLITICS. CONSTN AGRI INDUS LABOR DIPLOM TAX ADMIN CRIME...INT/LAW SOC 20 CHINJAP. PAGE 2 A0042 — BIBLIOG LAW S/ASIA PHIL/SCI

N
AFRICAN BIBLIOGRAPHIC CENTER,A CURRENT BIBLIOGRAPHY ON AFRICAN AFFAIRS. LAW CULTURE ECO/UNDEV LABOR SECT DIPLOM FOR/AID COLONIAL NAT/LISM...LING 20. PAGE 5 A0094 — BIBLIOG/A AFR NAT/G REGION

N
AMERICAN ECONOMIC ASSOCIATION,THE JOURNAL OF ECONOMIC ABSTRACTS. ECO/UNDEV MARKET LABOR DIPLOM ...MGT CONCPT METH 20. PAGE 7 A0144 — BIBLIOG/A R+D FINAN

N
KAPLAN L.,REVIEW INDEX. USA+45 USA-45 FINAN INDUS LABOR RACE/REL...GEOG PSY SOC 20. PAGE 76 A1558 — BIBLIOG PROF/ORG ECO/DEV DIPLOM

N
RAND SCHOOL OF SOCIAL SCIENCE,INDEX TO LABOR ARTICLES. ECO/DEV INT/ORG LEGIS DIPLOM GP/REL ...NAT/COMP 20. PAGE 119 A2440 — BIBLIOG LABOR MGT ADJUD

N
US SUPERINTENDENT OF DOCUMENTS,MONTHLY CATALOG OF UNITED STATES GOVERNMENT PUBLICATIONS. USA+45 USA-45 AGRI LABOR FORCES INT/TRADE TARIFFS TAX EDU/PROP CT/SYS ARMS/CONT RACE/REL 19/20 CONGRESS PRESIDENT. PAGE 157 A3203 — BIBLIOG NAT/G VOL/ASSN POLICY

C06
MONTGOMERY H.,"A DICTIONARY OF POLITICAL PHRASES AND ILLUSIONS WITH A SHORT BIBLIOGRAPHY." EUR+WWI MOD/EUR UK AGRI LABOR LOC/G NAT/G COLONIAL CHOOSE RACE/REL. PAGE 103 A2114 — BIBLIOG DICTIONARY POLICY DIPLOM

B10
MENDELSSOHN S.,SOUTH AFRICAN BIBLIOGRAPHY (2 VOLS.). SOUTH/AFR EXTR/IND LABOR SECT DIPLOM INT/TRADE COLONIAL RACE/REL DISCRIM...GEOG 20. PAGE 99 A2038 — BIBLIOG/A AFR NAT/G NAT/LISM

B19
MEYER H.H.B.,SELECT LIST OF REFERENCES ON ECONOMIC RECONSTRUCTION: INCLUDING REPORTS OF THE BRITISH MINISTRY OF RECONSTRUCTION. UK LABOR PLAN PROB/SOLV ECO/TAC INT/TRADE WAR DEMAND PRODUC 20. PAGE 100 A2051 — BIBLIOG/A EUR+WWI ECO/DEV WORKER

C28
SCHNEIDER H.W.,"MAKING THE FASCIST STATE." ITALY CULTURE LABOR DIPLOM REV WAR NAT/LISM TOTALISM ATTIT DRIVE SOCISM...BIBLIOG PARLIAMENT 20. PAGE 129 A2638 — FASCISM POLICY POL/PAR

B31
BORCHARD E.H.,GUIDE TO THE LAW AND LEGAL LITERATURE OF FRANCE. FRANCE FINAN INDUS LABOR SECT LEGIS ADMIN COLONIAL CRIME OWN...INT/LAW 20. PAGE 17 A0337 — BIBLIOG/A LAW CONSTN METH

B32
HANSEN A.H.,ECONOMIC STABILIZATION IN AN UNBALANCED WORLD. COM EUR+WWI USA-45 WOR-45 AGRI FINAN INDUS MARKET INT/ORG LABOR VOL/ASSN EDU/PROP ATTIT HEALTH KNOWL WEALTH...HIST/WRIT TREND VAL/FREE 20. PAGE 61 A1253 — NAT/G ECO/DEV CAP/ISM SOCISM

B36
HUDSON M.O.,INTERNATIONAL LEGISLATION: 1929-1931. WOR-45 SEA AIR AGRI FINAN LABOR DIPLOM ECO/TAC REPAR CT/SYS ARMS/CONT WAR WEAPON...JURID 20 TREATY LEAGUE/NAT. PAGE 69 A1409 — INT/LAW PARL/PROC ADJUD LAW

B36
VARLEY D.H.,A BIBLIOGRAPHY OF ITALIAN COLONISATION IN AFRICA WITH A SECTION ON ABYSSINIA. AFR ETHIOPIA ITALY LIBYA SOMALIA AGRI FINAN LABOR TEC/DEV DIPLOM INT/TRADE RACE/REL DISCRIM 19/20. PAGE 158 A3222 — BIBLIOG COLONIAL ADMIN LAW

B37
GALLOWAY G.B.,AMERICAN PAMPHLET LITERATURE OF PUBLIC AFFAIRS (PAMPHLET). USA-45 ECO/DEV LABOR ADMIN...MGT 20. PAGE 51 A1034 — BIBLIOG/A PLAN DIPLOM NAT/G

B37
VINER J.,STUDIES IN THE THEORY OF INTERNATIONAL TRADE. WOR-45 CONSTN ECO/DEV AGRI INDUS MARKET INT/ORG LABOR NAT/G ECO/TAC TARIFFS COLONIAL ATTIT WEALTH...POLICY CONCPT MATH STAT OBS SAMP TREND GEN/LAWS MARX/KARL 20. PAGE 159 A3236 — CAP/ISM INT/TRADE

B42
CONOVER H.F.,NEW ZEALAND: A SELECTED LIST OF REFERENCES (PAMPHLET). NEW/ZEALND ECO/UNDEV AGRI INDUS LABOR NAT/G SCHOOL FORCES DIPLOM COLONIAL WAR ...HUM 20. PAGE 29 A0595 — BIBLIOG/A S/ASIA CULTURE

B43
BROWN A.D.,GREECE: SELECTED LIST OF REFERENCES. GREECE ECO/UNDEV AGRI FINAN INDUS LABOR SECT TEC/DEV INT/TRADE LEAD...SOC 20. PAGE 20 A0399 — BIBLIOG/A WAR DIPLOM NAT/G

B44
SHELBY C.,LATIN AMERICAN PERIODICALS CURRENTLY RECEIVED IN THE LIBRARY OF CONGRESS AND IN LIBRARY OF DEPARTMENT OF AGRICULTURE. SOCIETY AGRI INDUS LABOR POL/PAR INT/TRADE...GEOG SOC 20. PAGE 132 A2699 — BIBLIOG ECO/UNDEV CULTURE L/A+17C

B45
GALLOWAY E.,ABSTRACTS OF POSTWAR LITERATURE (VOL. IV) JAN.-JULY, 1945 NOS. 901-1074. POLAND USA+45 USSR WOR+45 INDUS LABOR PLAN ECO/TAC INT/TRADE TAX EDU/PROP ADMIN COLONIAL INT/LAW. PAGE 51 A1033 — BIBLIOG/A NUC/PWR NAT/G DIPLOM

B45
VANCE H.L.,GUIDE TO THE LAW AND LEGAL LITERATURE OF MEXICO. LAW CONSTN FINAN LABOR FORCES ADJUD ADMIN ...CRIMLGY PHIL/SCI CON/ANAL 20 MEXIC/AMER. PAGE 158 A3217 BIBLIOG/A INT/LAW JURID CT/SYS

B46
STURZO D.L.,NATIONALISM AND INTERNATIONALISM. WOR-45 INT/ORG LABOR NAT/G POL/PAR TOTALISM MORAL ORD/FREE FASCISM...MAJORIT 19/20 UN LEAGUE/NAT MUSSOLIN/B. PAGE 140 A2857 NAT/LISM DIPLOM WAR PEACE

B49
HEADLAM-MORLEY,BIBLIOGRAPHY IN POLITICS FOR THE HONOUR SCHOOL OF PHILOSOPHY, POLITICS AND ECONOMICS (PAMPHLET). UK CONSTN LABOR MUNIC DIPLOM ADMIN 19/20. PAGE 64 A1305 BIBLIOG NAT/G PHIL/SCI GOV/REL

B50
DAVIS E.P.,PERIODICALS OF INTERNATIONAL ORGANIZATIONS; PART I, THE UN AND SPECIALIZED AGENCIES; PART II, INTER-AMERICAN ORGS. CULTURE AGRI FINAN INDUS LABOR INT/TRADE...GEOG HEAL STAT 20 UN OAS UNESCO. PAGE 34 A0689 BIBLIOG/A INT/ORG DIPLOM L/A+17C

C50
ELLSWORTH P.T.,"INTERNATIONAL ECONOMY." ECO/DEV ECO/UNDEV FINAN LABOR DIPLOM FOR/AID TARIFFS BAL/PAY EQUILIB NAT/LISM OPTIMAL...INT/LAW 20 ILO GATT. PAGE 41 A0843 BIBLIOG INT/TRADE ECO/TAC INT/ORG

N50
SCHAPIRO J.S.,THE WORLD IN CRISES: POLITICAL AND SOCIAL MOVEMENTS IN THE TWENTIETH CENTURY. USA+45 INT/ORG LABOR PLAN CAP/ISM DIPLOM COLONIAL PEACE TOTALISM ATTIT LAISSEZ...BIBLIOG 20 COLD/WAR. PAGE 128 A2618 NAT/LISM TEC/DEV REV WAR

B52
JACKSON E.,MEETING OF THE MINDS: A WAY TO PEACE THROUGH MEDIATION. WOR+45 INDUS INT/ORG NAT/G DELIB/GP DIPLOM EDU/PROP LEGIT ORD/FREE...NEW/IDEA SELF/OBS TIME/SEQ CHARTS GEN/LAWS TOT/POP 20 UN TREATY. PAGE 72 A1474 LABOR JUDGE

B52
RIGGS F.W.,FORMOSA UNDER CHINESE NATIONALIST RULE. CHINA/COM USA+45 CONSTN AGRI FINAN LABOR LOC/G NAT/G POL/PAR FORCES HEALTH KNOWL...STAT WORK VAL/FREE 20. PAGE 121 A2479 ASIA FOR/AID DIPLOM

B54
BINANI G.D.,INDIA AT A GLANCE (REV. ED.). INDIA COM/IND FINAN INDUS LABOR PROVS SCHOOL PLAN DIPLOM INT/TRADE ADMIN...JURID 20. PAGE 14 A0288 INDEX CON/ANAL NAT/G ECO/UNDEV

C54
BOWIE R.R.,"STUDIES IN FEDERALISM." AGRI FINAN LABOR EX/STRUC FORCES LEGIS DIPLOM INT/TRADE ADJUD ...BIBLIOG 20 EEC. PAGE 17 A0357 FEDERAL EUR+WWI INT/ORG CONSTN

B55
GULICK C.A.,HISTORY AND THEORIES OF WORKING-CLASS MOVEMENTS: A SELECT BIBLIOGRAPHY. EUR+WWI MOD/EUR UK USA-45 INT/ORG. PAGE 58 A1190 BIBLIOG WORKER LABOR ADMIN

B55
JAPAN MOMBUSHO DAIGAKU GAKIYUT,BIBLIOGRAPHY OF THE STUDIES ON LAW AND POLITICS (PAMPHLET). CONSTN INDUS LABOR DIPLOM TAX ADMIN...CRIMLGY INT/LAW 20 CHINJAP. PAGE 73 A1496 BIBLIOG LAW PHIL/SCI

B56
US DEPARTMENT OF STATE,ECONOMIC PROBLEMS OF UNDERDEVELOPED AREAS (PAMPHLET). AFR ASIA ISLAM L/A+17C AGRI FINAN INDUS INT/ORG LABOR INT/TRADE ...PSY SOC 20. PAGE 151 A3090 BIBLIOG ECO/UNDEV TEC/DEV R+D

B57
FRAZIER E.F.,RACE AND CULTURE CONTACTS IN THE MODERN WORLD. WOR+45 WOR-45 SOCIETY ECO/DEV AGRI INDUS INT/ORG LABOR NAT/G PERSON RIGID/FLEX ALL/VALS...SOC TIME/SEQ WORK 19/20. PAGE 48 A0991 CULTURE RACE/REL

B57
JENKS C.W.,THE INTERNATIONAL PROTECTION OF TRADE UNION FREEDOM. FUT WOR+45 WOR-45 VOL/ASSN DELIB/GP CT/SYS REGION ROUTINE...JURID METH/CNCPT RECORD TIME/SEQ CHARTS ILO WORK OAS 20. PAGE 73 A1504 LABOR INT/ORG

L58
INT. SOC. SCI. BULL.,"TECHNIQUES OF MEDIATION AND CONCILIATION." EUR+WWI USA+45 SOCIETY INDUS INT/ORG LABOR NAT/G LEGIS DIPLOM EDU/PROP CHOOSE ATTIT RIGID/FLEX...JURID CONCPT GEN/LAWS 20. PAGE 70 A1447 VOL/ASSN DELIB/GP INT/LAW

L58
TRAGER F.N.,"A SELECTED AND ANNOTATED BIBLIOGRAPHY ON ECONOMIC DEVELOPMENT, 1953-1957." WOR+45 AGRI FINAN INDUS MARKET LABOR MUNIC WORKER PLAN INT/TRADE PRODUC CENSUS. PAGE 145 A2958 BIBLIOG/A ECO/UNDEV ECO/DEV

C58
BLANCHARD W.,"THAILAND." THAILAND CULTURE AGRI FINAN INDUS FAM LABOR INT/TRADE ATTIT...GEOG HEAL SOC BIBLIOG 20. PAGE 15 A0307 NAT/G DIPLOM ECO/UNDEV S/ASIA

B59
MAC MILLAN W.M.,THE ROAD TO SELF-RULE. SOUTH/AFR UK AFR CULTURE SOCIETY AGRI LABOR NAT/G INT/TRADE CONTROL GP/REL...SOC 19/20. PAGE 92 A1884 COLONIAL SOVEREIGN POLICY

B59
NOVE A.,COMMUNIST ECONOMIC STRATEGY: SOVIET GROWTH AND CAPABILITIES. USSR AGRI LABOR PLAN TEC/DEV CAP/ISM INT/TRADE EFFICIENCY MARXISM 20 THIRD/WRLD. PAGE 110 A2257 FOR/AID ECO/TAC DIPLOM INDUS

B59
OKINSHEVICH L.A.,LATIN AMERICA IN SOVIET WRITINGS, 1945-1958: A BIBLIOGRAPHY. USSR LAW ECO/UNDEV LABOR DIPLOM EDU/PROP REV...GEOG SOC 20. PAGE 111 A2287 BIBLIOG WRITING COM L/A+17C

B59
SHANNON D.A.,THE DECLINE OF AMERICAN COMMUNISM; A HISTORY OF THE COMMUNIST PARTY OF THE UNITED STATES SINCE 1945. USA+45 LAW SOCIETY LABOR NAT/G WORKER DIPLOM EDU/PROP LEAD...POLICY BIBLIOG 20 KHRUSH/N NEGRO AFL/CIO COLD/WAR COM/PARTY. PAGE 131 A2692 MARXISM POL/PAR ATTIT POPULISM

L59
BEGUIN B.,"ILO AND THE TRIPARTITE SYSTEM." EUR+WWI WOR+45 WOR-45 CONSTN ECO/DEV ECO/UNDEV INDUS INT/ORG NAT/G VOL/ASSN DELIB/GP PLAN TEC/DEV LEGIT ORD/FREE WEALTH...CONCPT TIME/SEQ WORK ILO 20. PAGE 12 A0249 LABOR

S59
TIPTON J.B.,"PARTICIPATION OF THE UNITED STATES IN THE INTERNATIONAL LABOR ORGANIZATION." USA+45 LAW STRUCT ECO/DEV ECO/UNDEV INDUS TEC/DEV ECO/TAC ADMIN PERCEPT ORD/FREE SKILL...STAT HIST/WRIT GEN/METH ILO WORK 20. PAGE 144 A2946 LABOR INT/ORG

B60
APTHEKER H.,DISARMAMENT AND THE AMERICAN ECONOMY: A SYMPOSIUM. FUT USA+45 ECO/DEV DIST/IND FINAN INDUS PROC/MFG LABOR NAT/G POL/PAR CONSULT PLAN CAP/ISM INT/TRADE PEACE ATTIT MORAL WEALTH...TREND GEN/LAWS TOT/POP 20. PAGE 9 A0172 MARXIST ARMS/CONT

B60
FOOTMAN D.,INTERNATIONAL COMMUNISM. ASIA EUR+WWI FRANCE FUT GERMANY MOD/EUR S/ASIA USA-45 WOR+45 WOR-45 INTELL LABOR TOTALISM MARXISM WORK 20. PAGE 47 A0958 COM INT/ORG STRUCT REV

B60
PENTONY D.E.,THE UNDERDEVELOPED LANDS. FUT WOR+45 CULTURE AGRI FINAN INDUS MARKET INT/ORG LABOR NAT/G VOL/ASSN CONSULT TEC/DEV ECO/TAC EDU/PROP COLONIAL ATTIT WEALTH...OBS RECORD SAMP TREND GEN/METH WORK UN 20. PAGE 115 A2351 ECO/UNDEV POLICY FOR/AID INT/TRADE

L60
FERNBACH A.P.,"SOVIET COEXISTENCE STRATEGY." WOR+45 PROF/ORG VOL/ASSN DIPLOM DOMIN EDU/PROP ATTIT DRIVE PERSON PWR SKILL WEALTH...POLICY OBS SAMP TREND STERTYP ILO WORK COLD/WAR 420. PAGE 45 A0919 LABOR INT/ORG USSR

S60
"THE EMERGING COMMON MARKETS IN LATIN AMERICA." FUT L/A+17C STRATA DIST/IND INDUS LABOR NAT/G LEGIS ECO/TAC ADMIN RIGID/FLEX HEALTH...NEW/IDEA TIME/SEQ OAS 20. PAGE 3 A0059 FINAN ECO/UNDEV INT/TRADE

S60
JACOBSON H.K.,"THE USSR AND ILO." COM STRUCT ECO/DEV ECO/UNDEV CONSULT DELIB/GP ECO/TAC ILO WORK COLD/WAR 20. PAGE 72 A1484 INT/ORG LABOR USSR

S60
MORALES C.J.,"TRADE AND ECONOMIC INTEGRATION IN LATIN AMERICA." FUT L/A+17C LAW STRATA ECO/UNDEV DIST/IND INDUS LABOR NAT/G LEGIS ECO/TAC ADMIN RIGID/FLEX WEALTH...CONCPT NEW/IDEA CONT/OBS TIME/SEQ WORK 20. PAGE 104 A2128 FINAN INT/TRADE REGION

B61
CARNELL F.,THE POLITICS OF THE NEW STATES: A SELECT ANNOTATED BIBLIOGRAPHY WITH SPECIAL REFERENCE TO THE COMMONWEALTH. CONSTN ELITES LABOR NAT/G POL/PAR EX/STRUC DIPLOM ADJUD ADMIN...GOV/COMP 20 COMMONWLTH. PAGE 24 A0496 BIBLIOG/A AFR ASIA COLONIAL

B61
DETHINE P.,BIBLIOGRAPHIE DES ASPECTS ECONOMIQUES ET SOCIAUX DE L'INDUSTRIALISATION EN AFRIQUE. AFR FINAN LABOR FOR/AID...SOC 20. PAGE 36 A0734 BIBLIOG/A ECO/UNDEV INDUS TEC/DEV

B61
DIMOCK M.E.,BUSINESS AND GOVERNMENT (4TH ED.). AGRI FINAN OP/RES PLAN BUDGET DIPLOM LOBBY NUC/PWR NEW/LIB SOCISM...POLICY BIBLIOG 20. PAGE 37 A0765 NAT/G INDUS LABOR ECO/TAC

B61
GANGULI B.N.,ECONOMIC INTEGRATION. FINAN LABOR CAP/ISM DIPLOM WEALTH...NAT/COMP 20. PAGE 51 A1041 ECO/TAC METH/CNCPT EQUILIB ECO/UNDEV

B61
LIEFMANN-KEIL E.,OKONOMISCHE THEORIE DER SOZIALPOLITIK. INT/ORG LABOR WORKER COST INCOME NEW/LIB...CONCPT SOC/INTEG 20. PAGE 88 A1810 ECO/DEV INDUS NAT/G SOC/WK

B61
ZIMMERMAN I.,A GUIDE TO CURRENT LATIN AMERICAN BIBLIOG/A

PERIODICALS: HUMANITIES AND SOCIAL SCIENCES. LABOR SECT EDU/PROP...GEOG HUM SOC LING STAT NAT/COMP 20. PAGE 170 A3452 — DIPLOM L/A+17C PHIL/SCI

L61
TAUBENFELD H.J.,"A TREATY FOR ANTARCTICA." FUT USA+45 INTELL INT/ORG LABOR 20 TREATY ANTARCTICA. PAGE 141 A2893 — R+D ACT/RES DIPLOM

B62
ALEXANDROWICZ C.H.,WORLD ECONOMIC AGENCIES: LAW AND PRACTICE. WOR+45 DIST/IND FINAN LABOR CONSULT INT/TRADE TARIFFS REPRESENT HEALTH...JURID 20 UN GATT EEC OAS ECSC. PAGE 6 A0115 — INT/LAW INT/ORG DIPLOM ADJUD

B62
BLANSHARD P.,FREEDOM AND CATHOLIC POWER IN SPAIN AND PORTUGAL: AN AMERICAN INTERPRETATION. AFR PORTUGAL SPAIN USA+45 LAW LABOR DIPLOM EDU/PROP DISCRIM ISOLAT TOTALISM 20 CHURCH/STA. PAGE 15 A0309 — GP/REL FASCISM CATHISM PWR

B62
DELANEY R.F.,THE LITERATURE OF COMMUNISM IN AMERICA. COM USA+45 USA-45 INT/ORG LABOR NAT/G POL/PAR INGP/REL...MAJORIT 20. PAGE 36 A0727 — BIBLIOG/A MARXISM EDU/PROP IDEA/COMP

B62
KYRIAK T.E.,INTERNATIONAL COMMUNIST DEVELOPMENTS 1957-1961: INDEX TO TRANSLATIONS FROM AFRICA, ASIA, LATIN AMERICA, WEST EUROPE. COM WOR+45 NAT/G WORKER DIPLOM NAT/LISM. PAGE 83 A1704 — BIBLIOG/A MARXISM LABOR POL/PAR

B62
LUTZ F.A.,GELD UND WAHRUNG. MARKET LABOR BUDGET 20 GOLD/STAND EUROPE. PAGE 92 A1875 — ECO/TAC FINAN DIPLOM POLICY

B62
MORRAY J.P.,THE SECOND REVOLUTION IN CUBA. CUBA AGRI LABOR POL/PAR DIPLOM FOR/AID GUERRILLA TOTALISM MARXISM 20. PAGE 104 A2146 — REV MARXIST ECO/TAC NAT/LISM

B63
AFRICAN BIBLIOGRAPHIC CENTER,THE SCENE IS KENYA AND THE PERSONAGE IS TOM MBOYA: A SELECTED CURRENT READING LIST FROM 1956-1962 (PAMPHLET). ECO/UNDEV LABOR POL/PAR CHIEF COLONIAL CHOOSE NAT/LISM ORD/FREE 20. PAGE 5 A0096 — BIBLIOG DIPLOM AFR NAT/G

B63
ERHARD L.,THE ECONOMICS OF SUCCESS. GERMANY/W WOR+45 LABOR CHIEF TAX REGION COST DEMAND ANTHOL. PAGE 42 A0860 — ECO/DEV INT/TRADE PLAN DIPLOM

B63
FISCHER-GALATI S.,EASTERN EUROPE IN THE SIXTIES. ALBANIA USSR YUGOSLAVIA ECO/UNDEV AGRI MARKET LABOR WORKER DIPLOM INT/TRADE EDU/PROP GOV/REL PRODUC UTOPIA SOCISM 20. PAGE 46 A0939 — MARXISM TEC/DEV BAL/PWR ECO/TAC

B63
KATZ S.M.,A SELECTED LIST OF US READINGS ON DEVELOPMENT. AGRI COM/IND DIST/IND INDUS LABOR PLAN FOR/AID EDU/PROP HEALTH...POLICY SOC/WK 20. PAGE 77 A1571 — BIBLIOG/A ECO/UNDEV TEC/DEV ACT/RES

B63
LYONS F.S.L.,INTERNATIONALISM IN EUROPE 1815-1914. LAW AGRI COM/IND DIST/IND LABOR SECT INT/TRADE TARIFFS...BIBLIOG 19/20. PAGE 92 A1880 — DIPLOM MOD/EUR INT/ORG

B63
MBOYA T.,FREEDOM AND AFTER. AFR LABOR POL/PAR DIPLOM EDU/PROP COERCE SOCISM 20. PAGE 97 A1989 — COLONIAL ECO/UNDEV NAT/LISM INT/ORG

B63
PAENSON I.,SYSTEMATIC GLOSSARY ENGLISH, FRENCH, SPANISH, RUSSIAN OF SELECTED ECONOMIC AND SOCIAL TERMS. WOR+45 FINAN LABOR INT/TRADE DEMAND PRODUC 20. PAGE 113 A2315 — DICTIONARY SOC LING

B63
SALENT W.S.,THE UNITED STATES BALANCE OF PAYMENTS IN 1968. EUR+WWI UK USA+45 AGRI R+D LABOR FORCES PRODUC...GEOG CONCPT CHARTS 20 CHINJAP EEC. PAGE 126 A2589 — BAL/PAY DEMAND FINAN INT/TRADE

L63
MOUSKHELY M.,"LE BLOC COMMUNISTE ET LA COMMUNAUTE ECONOMIQUE EUROPEENNE." AFR COM EUR+WWI FUT USSR WOR+45 INTELL ECO/UNDEV LABOR POL/PAR NUC/PWR RIGID/FLEX...TIME/SEQ ORG/CHARTS EEC TOT/POP 20. PAGE 105 A2158 — INT/ORG ECO/DEV

S63
COUTY P.,"L'ASSISTANCE POUR LE DEVELOPPEMENT: POINT DE VUE SCANDINAVES." EUR+WWI FINLAND FUT SWEDEN WOR+45 ECO/DEV ECO/UNDEV COM/IND LABOR NAT/G PROF/ORG ACT/RES SKILL WEALTH TOT/POP 20. PAGE 32 A0643 — FINAN ROUTINE FOR/AID

S63
MANOLIU F.,"PERSPECTIVES D'UNE INTEGRATION ECONOMIQUE LATINOAMERICAINE." FUT L/A+17C STRUCT MARKET LABOR POL/PAR VOL/ASSN PLAN RIGID/FLEX PWR ...METH/CNCPT OAS TOT/POP 20. PAGE 94 A1927 — FINAN INT/ORG PEACE

B64
GESELLSCHAFT RECHTSVERGLEICH,BIBLIOGRAPHIE DES DEUTSCHEN RECHTS (BIBLIOGRAPHY OF GERMAN LAW, TRANS. BY COURTLAND PETERSON). GERMANY FINAN INDUS LABOR SECT FORCES CT/SYS PARL/PROC CRIME...INT/LAW SOC NAT/COMP 20. PAGE 52 A1066 — BIBLIOG/A JURID CONSTN ADMIN

B64
HAMBRIDGE G.,DYNAMICS OF DEVELOPMENT. AGRI FINAN INDUS LABOR INT/TRADE EDU/PROP ADMIN LEAD OWN HEALTH...ANTHOL BIBLIOG 20. PAGE 61 A1245 — ECO/UNDEV ECO/TAC OP/RES ACT/RES

B64
HAZLEWOOD A.,THE ECONOMICS OF DEVELOPMENT: AN ANNOTATED LIST OF BOOKS AND ARTICLES PUBLISHED 1958-1962. AGRI FINAN INDUS LABOR NAT/G DIPLOM INT/TRADE INCOME...MGT 20. PAGE 63 A1303 — BIBLIOG/A ECO/UNDEV TEC/DEV

B64
LUTHULI A.,AFRICA'S FREEDOM. KIN LABOR POL/PAR SCHOOL DIPLOM NEUTRAL REGION REV NAT/LISM PWR WEALTH SOCISM SOC/INTEG 20. PAGE 92 A1874 — AFR ECO/UNDEV COLONIAL

B64
MORGAN T.,GOLDWATER EITHER/OR; A SELF-PORTRAIT BASED UPON HIS OWN WORDS. USA+45 CONSTN AGRI LABOR DIPLOM RACE/REL WEALTH POPULISM...POLICY MAJORIT 20 GOLDWATR/B REPUBLICAN. PAGE 104 A2131 — LEAD POL/PAR CHOOSE ATTIT

B64
REUSS H.S.,THE CRITICAL DECADE - AN ECONOMIC POLICY FOR AMERICA AND THE FREE WORLD. USA+45 FINAN POL/PAR WORKER PLAN DIPLOM ECO/TAC TARIFFS BAL/PAY ...POLICY 20 CONGRESS GOLD/STAND. PAGE 120 A2468 — FOR/AID INT/TRADE LABOR LEGIS

B65
WHITE HOUSE CONFERENCE ON INTERNATIONAL COOPERATION(VOL.II). SPACE WOR+45 EXTR/IND INT/ORG LABOR WORKER NUC/PWR PEACE AGE/Y...CENSUS ANTHOL 20 RESOURCE/N URBAN/RNWL PUB/TRANS. PAGE 3 A0071 — R+D CONFER TEC/DEV DIPLOM

B65
COLLINS H.,KARL MARX AND THE BRITISH LABOUR MOVEMENT; YEARS OF THE FIRST INTERNATIONAL. FRANCE SWITZERLND UK CAP/ISM WAR...MARXIST IDEA/COMP BIBLIOG 19. PAGE 28 A0567 — MARXISM LABOR INT/ORG REV

B65
FORM W.H.,INDUSTRIAL RELATIONS AND SOCIAL CHANGE IN LATIN AMERICA. L/A+17C AGRI LABOR NAT/G PLAN PROB/SOLV DIPLOM...MGT SOC ANTHOL BIBLIOG/A METH 20. PAGE 47 A0966 — INDUS GP/REL NAT/COMP ECO/UNDEV

B65
SABLE M.H.,MASTER DIRECTORY FOR LATIN AMERICA. AGRI COM/IND FINAN R+D ACADEM LABOR NAT/G POL/PAR VOL/ASSN INT/TRADE EDU/PROP 20. PAGE 126 A2582 — INDEX L/A+17C INT/ORG DIPLOM

B65
UN,SPACE ACTIVITIES AND RESOURCES: REVIEW OF UNITED NATION'S NATIONAL AND INTERNATIONAL PROGRAMS. INT/ORG LABOR PLAN TEC/DEV DIPLOM EFFICIENCY HEALTH ...GOV/COMP 20 UN. PAGE 146 A2995 — SPACE NUC/PWR FOR/AID PEACE

B65
US LIBRARY OF CONGRESS,A DIRECTORY OF INFORMATION RESOURCES IN THE UNITED STATES: SOCIAL SCIENCES. USA+45 ACADEM INT/ORG LABOR PROF/ORG PUB/INST SCHOOL SECT 20. PAGE 155 A3159 — BIBLIOG R+D COMPUT/IR

L65
MATTHEWS D.G.,"A CURRENT BIBLIOGRAPHY ON ETHIOPIAN AFFAIRS: A SELECT BIBLIOGRAPHY FROM 1950-1964." ETHIOPIA LAW CULTURE ECO/UNDEV INDUS LABOR SECT FORCES DIPLOM CIVMIL/REL RACE/REL...LING STAT 20. PAGE 96 A1969 — BIBLIOG/A ADMIN POL/PAR NAT/G

L65
MATTHEWS D.G.,"A CURRENT BIBLIOGRAPHY ON SUDANESE AFFAIRS; A SELECT BIBLIOGRAPHY FROM 1960-1964." SUDAN LAW CULTURE AGRI FINAN INDUS LABOR POL/PAR TEC/DEV FOR/AID RACE/REL LITERACY...LING 20. PAGE 96 A1970 — BIBLIOG ECO/UNDEV NAT/G DIPLOM

L65
MATTHEWS D.G.,"LE TIERS MONDE: A SELECT AND PRELIMINARY BIBLIOGRAPHIC SURVEY OF MANPOWER IN DEVELOPING COUNTRIES, 1960-1964." AFR ISLAM L/A+17C INDUS PLAN PROB/SOLV TEC/DEV INT/TRADE EFFICIENCY WEALTH...STAT 20. PAGE 96 A1971 — BIBLIOG/A ECO/UNDEV LABOR WORKER

L65
WIONCZEK M.,"LATIN AMERICA FREE TRADE ASSOCIATION." AGRI DIST/IND FINAN INDUS INT/ORG LABOR NAT/G TEC/DEV ECO/TAC HEALTH SKILL WEALTH...POLICY RELATIV MGT LAFTA 20. PAGE 165 A3369 — L/A+17C MARKET REGION

B66
BERNSTEIN B.J.,THE TRUMAN ADMINISTRATION. WOR+45 LABOR POL/PAR LEGIS DIPLOM NUC/PWR WAR ATTIT ...POLICY 20 TRUMAN/HS. PAGE 14 A0279 — LEAD TOP/EX NAT/G

B66
COLE A.B.,SOCIALIST PARTIES IN POSTWAR JAPAN. STRATA AGRI LABOR PLAN DIPLOM ECO/TAC AGREE LEAD CHOOSE ATTIT...CHARTS 20 CHINJAP SOC/DEMPAR. PAGE 28 A0566 — POL/PAR POLICY SOCISM NAT/G

B66
KOH S.J.,STAGES OF INDUSTRIAL DEVELOPMENT IN ASIA. ASIA INDIA KOREA STRATA STRUCT NAT/G INT/TRADE ...CHARTS 19/20 CHINJAP. PAGE 81 A1659 — INDUS ECO/UNDEV ECO/DEV

LABOR

MCNAIR A.D.,THE LEGAL EFFECTS OF WAR. UK FINAN DIPLOM ORD/FREE 20 ENGLSH/LAW. PAGE 98 A2019 — B66 — JURID WAR INT/TRADE LABOR

SCHATTEN F.,COMMUNISM IN AFRICA. AFR GHANA GUINEA MALI CULTURE ECO/UNDEV LABOR SECT ECO/TAC EDU/PROP REV 20. PAGE 128 A2619 — B66 — COLONIAL NAT/LISM MARXISM DIPLOM

SZLADITS C.,A BIBLIOGRAPHY ON FOREIGN AND COMPARATIVE LAW (SUPPLEMENT 1964). FINAN FAM LABOR LG/CO LEGIS JUDGE ADMIN CRIME...CRIMLGY 20. PAGE 141 A2878 — B66 — BIBLIOG/A CT/SYS INT/LAW

AMERICAN ECONOMIC REVIEW,"SIXTY-THIRD LIST OF DOCTORAL DISSERTATIONS IN POLITICAL ECONOMY IN AMERICAN UNIVERSITIES AND COLLEGES." ECO/DEV AGRI FINAN LABOR WORKER PLAN BUDGET INT/TRADE ADMIN DEMAND...MGT STAT 20. PAGE 7 A0146 — L66 — BIBLIOG/A CONCPT ACADEM

AFRICAN BIBLIOGRAPHIC CENTER,"A CURRENT VIEW OF AFRICANA: A SELECT AND ANNOTATED BIBLIOGRAPHICAL PUBLISHING GUIDE, 1965-1966." AFR CULTURE INDUS LABOR SECT FOR/AID ADMIN COLONIAL REV RACE/REL SOCISM...LING 20. PAGE 5 A0098 — S66 — BIBLIOG/A NAT/G TEC/DEV POL/PAR

AFRICAN BIBLIOGRAPHIC CENTER,"THE NEW AFRO-ASIAN STATES IN PERSPECTIVE, 1960-1963: A SELECT BIBLIOGRAPHY." AFR ASIA CULTURE SOCIETY INT/ORG LABOR TEC/DEV LITERACY 20 UN. PAGE 5 A0100 — S66 — BIBLIOG DIPLOM FOR/AID INT/TRADE

MATTHEWS D.G.,"ETHIOPIAN OUTLINE: A BIBLIOGRAPHIC RESEARCH GUIDE." ETHIOPIA LAW STRUCT ECO/UNDEV AGRI LABOR SECT CHIEF DELIB/GP EX/STRUC ADMIN...LING ORG/CHARTS 20. PAGE 96 A1972 — S66 — BIBLIOG NAT/G DIPLOM POL/PAR

WINT G.,"ASIA: A HANDBOOK." ASIA S/ASIA INDUS LABOR SECT PRESS RACE/REL MARXISM...STAT CHARTS BIBLIOG 20. PAGE 165 A3366 — C66 — ECO/UNDEV DIPLOM NAT/G SOCIETY

DILLARD D.,ECONOMIC DEVELOPMENT OF THE NORTH ATLANTIC COMMUNITY. EUR+WWI MOD/EUR USA+45 USA-45 ECO/UNDEV LABOR CAP/ISM WAR BAL/PAY...NAT/COMP 15/20. PAGE 37 A0763 — B67 — ECO/DEV INT/TRADE INDUS DIPLOM

HOLLERMAN L.,JAPAN'S DEPENDENCE ON THE WORLD ECONOMY. INDUS MARKET LABOR NAT/G DIPLOM 20 CHINJAP. PAGE 67 A1369 — B67 — PLAN ECO/DEV ECO/TAC INT/TRADE

INTERNATIONAL LABOUR OFFICE,SUBJECT GUIDE TO PUBLICATIONS OF THE INTERNATIONAL LABOUR OFFICE, 1919-1964. DIPLOM 20. PAGE 71 A1457 — B67 — BIBLIOG LABOR INT/ORG WORKER

KIRK R.,THE POLITICAL PRINCIPLES OF ROBERT A. TAFT. USA+45 LABOR DIPLOM ADJUD ADJUST ORD/FREE TAFT/RA. PAGE 80 A1635 — B67 — POL/PAR LEAD LEGIS ATTIT

MEYNAUD J.,TRADE UNIONISM IN AFRICA; A STUDY OF ITS GROWTH AND ORIENTATION (TRANS. BY ANGELA BRENCH). INT/ORG PROB/SOLV COLONIAL PWR...TIME/SEQ TREND ILO. PAGE 100 A2055 — B67 — LABOR AFR NAT/LISM ORD/FREE

SABLE M.H.,A GUIDE TO LATIN AMERICAN STUDIES (2 VOLS). CONSTN FINAN INT/ORG LABOR MUNIC POL/PAR FORCES CAP/ISM FOR/AID ADMIN MARXISM SOCISM OAS. PAGE 126 A2584 — B67 — BIBLIOG/A L/A+17C DIPLOM NAT/LISM

SACHS M.Y.,THE WORLDMARK ENCYCLOPEDIA OF THE NATIONS (5 VOLS.). ELITES SOCIETY STRATA ECO/DEV ECO/UNDEV AGRI EXTR/IND FINAN LABOR LOC/G NAT/G POL/PAR SECT INT/TRADE SOVEREIGN...SOC 20. PAGE 126 A2585 — B67 — WOR+45 INT/ORG BAL/PWR

UNIVERSAL REFERENCE SYSTEM,ECONOMIC REGULATION, BUSINESS, AND GOVERNMENT (VOLUME VIII). WOR+45 WOR-45 ECO/DEV ECO/UNDEV FINAN LABOR TEC/DEV ECO/TAC INT/TRADE GOV/REL...POLICY COMPUT/IR. PAGE 149 A3043 — B67 — BIBLIOG/A CONTROL NAT/G

US SENATE COMM ON FOREIGN REL,HUMAN RIGHTS CONVENTIONS. USA+45 LABOR VOL/ASSN DELIB/GP DOMIN ADJUD REPRESENT...INT/LAW MGT CONGRESS. PAGE 156 A3189 — B67 — LEGIS ORD/FREE WORKER LOBBY

LABOR/PAR....LABOR PARTY (ALL NATIONS)

EPSTEIN L.D.,BRITAIN - UNEASY ALLY. KOREA UK USA+45 NAT/G POL/PAR ECO/TAC FOR/AID INT/TRADE WAR LABOR/PAR CONSRV/PAR. PAGE 42 A0857 — B54 — DIPLOM ATTIT POLICY NAT/COMP

JONES A.C.,NEW FABIAN COLONIAL ESSAYS. UK SOCIETY POL/PAR EDU/PROP ADMIN ORD/FREE SOVEREIGN SOCISM ...ANTHOL 20 CMN/WLTH LABOR/PAR. PAGE 75 A1530 — B59 — COLONIAL INT/ORG INGP/REL DOMIN

LABORATORY EXPERIMENTS....SEE LAB/EXP

LABRIOLA A. A1706

LACOUTRE J. A1707,A1708

LADOR-LEDERER J.J. A1709

LAFAVE W.R. A1710

LAFEBER W. A1711

LAFTA....LATIN AMERICAN FREE TRADE ASSOCIATION; SEE ALSO INT/ORG, VOL/ASSN, INT/TRADE

UNITED STATES GOVERNMENT,REPORT TO THE INTER-AMERICAN ECONOMIC AND SOCIAL COUNCIL. L/A+17C INDUS PLAN INT/TRADE TARIFFS CONFER...CHARTS 20 LAFTA. PAGE 149 A3038 — B63 — FOR/AID ECO/TAC ECO/UNDEV DIPLOM

HOLBO P.S.,"COLD WAR DRIFT IN LATIN AMERICA." CUBA L/A+17C USA+45 USA-45 INT/ORG NAT/G NEIGH VOL/ASSN ACT/RES PLAN ECO/TAC ATTIT RIGID/FLEX ALL/VALS ...RECORD TIME/SEQ OAS LAFTA 20 COLD/WAR. PAGE 66 A1363 — S63 — DELIB/GP CREATE FOR/AID

HAAS E.B.,"ECONOMICS AND DIFFERENTIAL PATTERNS OF POLITICAL INTEGRATION: PROJECTIONS ABOUT UNITY IN LATIN AMERICA." SOCIETY NAT/G DELIB/GP ACT/RES CREATE PLAN ECO/TAC REGION ROUTINE ATTIT DRIVE PWR WEALTH...CONCPT TREND CHARTS LAFTA 20. PAGE 59 A1208 — L64 — L/A+17C INT/ORG MARKET

GERASSI J.,THE GREAT FEAR IN LATIN AMERICA. L/A+17C USA+45 ELITES STRUCT INT/ORG REV ORD/FREE WEALTH 20 LAFTA. PAGE 52 A1063 — B65 — SOCIETY FOR/AID DIPLOM

WIONCZEK M.,"LATIN AMERICA FREE TRADE ASSOCIATION." AGRI DIST/IND FINAN INDUS INT/ORG LABOR NAT/G TEC/DEV ECO/TAC HEALTH SKILL WEALTH...POLICY RELATIV MGT LAFTA 20. PAGE 165 A3369 — L65 — L/A+17C MARKET REGION

JAVITS J.K.,"POLITICAL ACTION VITAL FOR LATIN AMERICAN INTEGRATION." ECO/UNDEV INT/ORG POL/PAR VOL/ASSN PLAN PROB/SOLV INT/TRADE EFFICIENCY 20 OAS LAFTA. PAGE 73 A1500 — S66 — L/A+17C ECO/TAC REGION

JAVITS J.K.,"LAST CHANCE FOR A COMMON MARKET." L/A+17C INT/ORG 20 EEC LAFTA. PAGE 73 A1501 — S67 — FOR/AID ECO/UNDEV INT/TRADE ECO/TAC

LAGUARD/F....FIORELLO LAGUARDIA

LAISSEZ....LAISSEZ-FAIRE-ISM; SEE ALSO OLD/LIB

GRIFFIN A.P.C.,SELECT LIST OF REFERENCES ON THE BRITISH TARIFF MOVEMENT. MOD/EUR UK BAL/PWR BARGAIN ECO/TAC LAISSEZ 20. PAGE 56 A1154 — B06 — BIBLIOG/A INT/TRADE TARIFFS COLONIAL

MACMINN N.,BIBLIOGRAPHY OF THE PUBLISHED WRITINGS OF JOHN STUART MILL. MOD/EUR UK CAP/ISM DIPLOM KNOWL...EPIST CONCPT 19 MILL/JS. PAGE 93 A1901 — B45 — BIBLIOG/A SOCIETY INGP/REL LAISSEZ

SCHAPIRO J.S.,THE WORLD IN CRISES: POLITICAL AND SOCIAL MOVEMENTS IN THE TWENTIETH CENTURY. USA+45 INT/ORG LABOR PLAN CAP/ISM DIPLOM COLONIAL PEACE TOTALISM ATTIT LAISSEZ...BIBLIOG 20 COLD/WAR. PAGE 128 A2618 — N50 — NAT/LISM TEC/DEV REV WAR

SURANYI-UNGER T.,COMPARATIVE ECONOMIC SYSTEMS. FINAN MARKET DIPLOM PRICE WEALTH...GEOG SOC BIBLIOG METH T 20. PAGE 140 A2865 — B52 — LAISSEZ PLAN ECO/DEV IDEA/COMP

STRACHEY J.,THE END OF EMPIRE. UK WOR+45 WOR-45 DIPLOM INT/TRADE DOMIN ADJUST ORD/FREE WEALTH ...SOCIALIST GOV/COMP TIME COMMONWLTH. PAGE 139 A2841 — B60 — COLONIAL ECO/DEV BAL/PWR LAISSEZ

ALBRECHT-CARRIE R.,THE MEANING OF THE FIRST WORLD WAR. MOD/EUR USA-45 INT/ORG BAL/PWR PEACE ATTIT LAISSEZ MARXISM...CONCPT BIBLIOG 19/20 LEAGUE/NAT WWI. PAGE 5 A0110 — B65 — DIPLOM WAR

B67
BODENHEIMER E.,TREATISE ON JUSTICE. INT/ORG NAT/G PUB/INST ACT/RES RISK CRIME INGP/REL DISCRIM DRIVE LAISSEZ 20. PAGE 16 A0325 — ALL/VALS STRUCT JURID CONCPT

S67
PERLO V.,"NEW DIMENSIONS IN EAST-WEST TRADE." UK USA+45 USSR WOR+45 ECO/DEV NAT/G CAP/ISM PEACE WEALTH LAISSEZ...SOCIALIST MGT 20. PAGE 115 A2364 — BAL/PWR ECO/TAC INT/TRADE

B96
SMITH A.,LECTURES ON JUSTICE, POLICE, REVENUE AND ARMS (1763). UK LAW FAM FORCES TARIFFS AGREE COERCE INCOME OWN WEALTH LAISSEZ...GEN/LAWS 17/18. PAGE 134 A2743 — DIPLOM JURID OLD/LIB TAX

LAKEWOOD....LAKEWOOD, CALIFORNIA

LAKOFF/SA....SANFORD A. LAKOFF

LALL A. A1712

LAMBERG R.F. A1713

LAND REFORM....SEE AGRI + CREATE

LAND/LEAG....LAND LEAGUE (IRELAND)

LAND/VALUE....LAND VALUE TAX

LANDEN R.G. A1714

LANDHEER B. A1715,A1716,A1717,A1718

LANDIS E.S. A1719

LANDRAT....COUNTY CHIEF EXECUTIVE (GERMANY)

LANDRM/GRF....LANDRUM-GRIFFIN ACT

LANDSKROY W.A. A1720

LANFALUSSY A. A1721

LANGE O. A1722

LANGE O.R. A1723

LANGER W.L. A1724,A1725,A1726,A1727

LANGLEY....LANGLEY-PORTER NEUROPSYCHIATRIC INSTITUTE

LANGUAGE....SEE LING, ALSO LOGIC, MATHEMATICS, AND LANGUAGE INDEX, P. XIV

LANGUEDOC....LANGUEDOC, SOUTHERN FRANCE

LANOUE G.R. A1728

LAO/TZU....LAO TZU

B66
MAYER P.,THE PACIFIST CONSCIENCE. SECT CREATE ARMS/CONT WAR RACE/REL ATTIT LOVE...ANTHOL PACIFIST WORSHIP FREUD/S GANDHI/M LAO/TZU KING/MAR/L CONSCN/OBJ. PAGE 97 A1984 — DIPLOM PACIFISM SUPEGO

LAOS....SEE ALSO S/ASIA

B55
THOMPSON V.,MINORITY PROBLEMS IN SOUTHEAST ASIA. CAMBODIA CHINA/COM LAOS S/ASIA KIN NAT/G SECT PROB/SOLV EDU/PROP REGION GP/REL RACE/REL MARXISM ...SOC 20 BUDDHISM UN. PAGE 143 A2933 — INGP/REL GEOG DIPLOM STRUCT

N58
US HOUSE COMM FOREIGN AFFAIRS,HEARINGS ON THE FAR EAST AND THE PACIFIC (PAMPHLET). LAOS USA+45 NAT/G CONSULT FORCES CONFER DEBATE ORD/FREE 20. PAGE 153 A3124 — FOR/AID DIPLOM DELIB/GP LEGIS

B59
US HOUSE COMM GOVT OPERATIONS,UNITED STATES AID OPERATIONS IN LAOS. LAOS USA+45 PLAN INSPECT HOUSE/REP. PAGE 154 A3136 — FOR/AID ADMIN FORCES ECO/UNDEV

B60
PENTONY D.E.,UNITED STATES FOREIGN AID. INDIA LAOS USA+45 ECO/UNDEV INT/TRADE ADMIN PEACE ATTIT ...POLICY METH/COMP ANTHOL 20. PAGE 115 A2352 — FOR/AID DIPLOM ECO/TAC

S62
DIHN N.Q.,"L'INTERNATIONALISATION DU MEKONG." CAMBODIA LAOS VIETNAM WOR+45 INT/ORG NAT/G VOL/ASSN PEACE HEALTH...CONCPT TIME/SEQ CHARTS METH VAL/FREE 20. PAGE 37 A0761 — S/ASIA DELIB/GP

S62
RUBINSTEIN A.Z.,"RUSSIA AND THE UNCOMMITTED NATIONS." AFR INDIA ISLAM L/A+17C LAOS S/ASIA ELITES ECO/UNDEV INT/ORG KIN CREATE PLAN TEC/DEV NAT/LISM RIGID/FLEX PWR WEALTH...METH/CNCPT TIME/SEQ GEN/LAWS WORK. PAGE 125 A2562 — ECO/TAC TREND COLONIAL USSR

B64
HALPERN J.M.,GOVERNMENT, POLITICS, AND SOCIAL STRUCTURE IN LAOS. LAOS CULTURE SOCIETY STRATA STRUCT FAM DIPLOM DOMIN MARXISM...INT GOV/COMP WORSHIP SOC/INTEG 20. PAGE 60 A1242 — NAT/G SOC LOC/G

B65
US SENATE COMM ON JUDICIARY,REFUGEE PROBLEMS IN SOUTH VIETNAM AND LAOS: HEARINGS BEFORE SUBCOMMITTEE TO INVESTIGATE PROBLEMS OF REFUGEES, ESCAPEES. CHINA/COM LAOS USA+45 VIETNAM/S PROB/SOLV DIPLOM GOV/REL GP/REL EFFICIENCY ORD/FREE...POLICY GEOG 20 CONGRESS MIGRATION. PAGE 157 A3194 — STRANGE HABITAT FOR/AID CIVMIL/REL

C66
TARLING N.,"A CONCISE HISTORY OF SOUTHEAST ASIA." BURMA CAMBODIA LAOS S/ASIA THAILAND VIETNAM ECO/UNDEV POL/PAR FORCES ADMIN REV WAR CIVMIL/REL ORD/FREE MARXISM SOCISM 13/20. PAGE 141 A2890 — COLONIAL DOMIN INT/TRADE NAT/LISM

LAPRADELLE A1729

LAQUEUR W.Z. A1730,A1731,A1732

LARCENY....LARCENY

LARSEN K. A1733

LARSON A. A1734

LARTEH....LARTEH, GHANA

LARUS J. A1735,A1736

LARY M.B. A1737

LASKI/H....HAROLD LASKI

LASKY V. A1738

LASSALLE/F....FERDINAND LASSALLE

LASSWELL H.D. A1739,A1740,A1741,A2005,A2009

LASSWELL/H....HAROLD D. LASSWELL

B51
STANTON A.H.,PERSONALITY AND POLITICAL CRISIS. WOR+45 WOR-45 STRUCT DIPLOM INGP/REL TOTALISM MORAL ...ANTHOL 20 LASSWELL/H PARSONS/T RIESMAN/D. PAGE 137 A2806 — EDU/PROP WAR PERSON PSY

LATHAM E. A1742

LATIFI D. A1743

LATIN AMERICA....SEE L/A+17C

LATIN AMERICAN FREE TRADE ASSOCIATION....SEE LAFTA

LATOURETTE K.S. A1744

LATVIA....SEE ALSO USSR

LAUERHAUSS L. A1745

LAUNDY P. A3349

LAURIER/W....SIR WILFRED LAURIER

LAUTERPACHT E. A1746,A1747

LAUTERPACHT H. A1748,A1749,A1750,A2294

LAVES W.H.C. A1751

LAW....LAW, ETHICAL DIRECTIVES IN A COMMUNITY; SEE ALSO JURID

B
DEUTSCHE BIBLIOTH FRANKF A M,DEUTSCHE BIBLIOGRAPHIE. EUR+WWI GERMANY ECO/DEV FORCES DIPLOM LEAD...POLICY PHIL/SCI SOC 20. PAGE 36 A0743 — BIBLIOG LAW ADMIN NAT/G

N
JOURNAL OF POLITICS. USA+45 USA-45 CONSTN POL/PAR EX/STRUC LEGIS PROB/SOLV DIPLOM CT/SYS CHOOSE RACE/REL 20. PAGE 1 A0017 — BIBLIOG/A NAT/G LAW LOC/G

N
POLITICAL SCIENCE QUARTERLY. USA+45 USA-45 LAW CONSTN ECO/DEV INT/ORG LOC/G POL/PAR LEGIS LEAD — BIBLIOG/A NAT/G

NUC/PWR...CONCPT 20. PAGE 1 A0023 — DIPLOM POLICY

N
ARBITRATION JOURNAL. WOR+45 LAW INDUS JUDGE DIPLOM CT/SYS INGP/REL 20. PAGE 2 A0027 — BIBLIOG MGT LABOR ADJUD

N
AUSTRALIAN PUBLIC AFFAIRS INFORMATION SERVICE. LAW ...HEAL HUM MGT SOC CON/ANAL 20 AUSTRAL. PAGE 2 A0028 — BIBLIOG NAT/G CULTURE DIPLOM

N
BIBLIOGRAPHIE DER SOZIALWISSENSCHAFTEN. WOR-45 CONSTN SOCIETY ECO/DEV ECO/UNDEV DIPLOM LEAD WAR PEACE...PHIL/SCI SOC 19/20. PAGE 2 A0030 — BIBLIOG LAW CONCPT NAT/G

N
HANDBOOK OF LATIN AMERICAN STUDIES. LAW CULTURE ECO/UNDEV POL/PAR ADMIN LEAD...SOC 20. PAGE 2 A0035 — BIBLIOG/A L/A+17C NAT/G DIPLOM

N
LATIN AMERICA IN PERIODICAL LITERATURE. LAW TEC/DEV DIPLOM RECEIVE EDU/PROP...GEOG HUM MGT 20. PAGE 2 A0037 — BIBLIOG/A L/A+17C SOCIETY ECO/UNDEV

N
LONDON TIMES OFFICIAL INDEX. UK LAW ECO/DEV NAT/G DIPLOM LEAD ATTIT 20. PAGE 2 A0038 — BIBLIOG INDEX PRESS WRITING

N
PUBLISHERS' CIRCULAR, THE OFFICIAL ORGAN OF THE PUBLISHERS' ASSOCIATION OF GREAT BRITAIN AND IRELAND. EUR+WWI MOD/EUR UK LAW PROB/SOLV DIPLOM COLONIAL ATTIT...HUM 19/20 CMN/WLTH. PAGE 2 A0039 — BIBLIOG NAT/G WRITING LEAD

N
THE JAPAN SCIENCE REVIEW: LAW AND POLITICS: LIST OF BOOKS AND ARTICLES ON LAW AND POLITICS. CONSTN AGRI INDUS LABOR DIPLOM TAX ADMIN CRIME...INT/LAW SOC 20 CHINJAP. PAGE 2 A0042 — BIBLIOG LAW S/ASIA PHIL/SCI

N
SCHOLARLY BOOKS IN AMERICA; A QUARTERLY BIBLIOGRAPHY OF UNIVERSITY PRESS PUBLICATIONS. WOR+45 AGRI COM/IND NAT/G HEALTH...GEOG PHIL/SCI PSY SOC LING 20. PAGE 3 A0046 — BIBLIOG/A LAW MUNIC DIPLOM

N
"PROLOG",DIGEST OF THE SOVIET UKRANIAN PRESS. USSR LAW AGRI INDUS PROVS SCHOOL DIPLOM GOV/REL ATTIT ...HUM LING 20. PAGE 4 A0081 — BIBLIOG/A NAT/G PRESS COM

N
AFRICAN BIBLIOGRAPHIC CENTER,A CURRENT BIBLIOGRAPHY ON AFRICAN AFFAIRS. LAW CULTURE ECO/UNDEV LABOR SECT DIPLOM FOR/AID COLONIAL NAT/LISM...LING 20. PAGE 5 A0094 — BIBLIOG/A AFR NAT/G REGION

N
AMER COUNCIL OF LEARNED SOCIET,THE ACLS CONSTITUENT SOCIETY JOURNAL PROJECT. FUT USA+45 LAW NAT/G PLAN DIPLOM PHIL/SCI. PAGE 7 A0134 — BIBLIOG/A HUM COMPUT/IR COMPUTER

N
ASIA FOUNDATION,LIBRARY NOTES. LAW CONSTN CULTURE SOCIETY ECO/UNDEV INT/ORG NAT/G COLONIAL LEAD REGION NAT/LISM ATTIT 20 UN. PAGE 9 A0189 — BIBLIOG/A ASIA S/ASIA DIPLOM

N
CORNELL UNIVERSITY LIBRARY,SOUTHEAST ASIA ACCESSIONS LIST. LAW SOCIETY STRUCT ECO/UNDEV POL/PAR TEC/DEV DIPLOM LEAD REGION. PAGE 31 A0626 — BIBLIOG S/ASIA NAT/G CULTURE

N
DEUTSCHE BUCHEREI,JAHRESVERZEICHNIS DES DEUTSCHEN SCHRIFTUMS. AUSTRIA EUR+WWI GERMANY SWITZERLND LAW LOC/G DIPLOM ADMIN...MGT SOC 19/20. PAGE 37 A0745 — BIBLIOG WRITING NAT/G

N
DEUTSCHE BUCHEREI,DEUTSCHES BUCHERVERZEICHNIS. GERMANY LAW CULTURE POL/PAR ADMIN LEAD ATTIT PERSON ...SOC 20. PAGE 37 A0746 — BIBLIOG NAT/G DIPLOM ECO/DEV

N
HARVARD LAW SCHOOL LIBRARY,ANNUAL LEGAL BIBLIOGRAPHY. USA+45 CONSTN LEGIS ADJUD CT/SYS ...POLICY 20. PAGE 62 A1278 — BIBLIOG JURID LAW INT/LAW

N
INSTITUTE OF HISPANIC STUDIES,HISPANIC AMERICAN REPORT. EUR+WWI SPAIN LAW CONSTN ECO/UNDEV POL/PAR EX/STRUC LEGIS LEAD...HUM SOC 20. PAGE 70 A1445 — BIBLIOG/A L/A+17C NAT/G DIPLOM

N
MCSPADDEN J.W.,THE AMERICAN STATESMAN'S YEARBOOK. WOR-45 LAW CONSTN AGRI FINAN DEBATE ADMIN PARL/PROC ...CHARTS BIBLIOG/A 20. PAGE 99 A2025 — DIPLOM NAT/G PROVS LEGIS

N
MINISTERE DE L'EDUC NATIONALE,CATALOGUE DES THESES DE DOCTORAT SOUTENNES DEVANT LES UÑIVERSITAIRES FRANCAISES. FRANCE LAW DIPLOM ADMIN...HUM SOC 20. PAGE 102 A2087 — BIBLIOG ACADEM KNOWL NAT/G

N
MINISTRY OF OVERSEAS DEVELOPME,TECHNICAL CO-OPERATION -- A BIBLIOGRAPHY. UK LAW SOCIETY DIPLOM ECO/TAC FOR/AID...STAT 20 CMN/WLTH. PAGE 102 A2089 — BIBLIOG TEC/DEV ECO/DEV NAT/G

N
UNESCO,INTERNATIONAL BIBLIOGRAPHY OF POLITICAL SCIENCE (VOLUMES 1-8). WOR+45 LAW NAT/G EX/STRUC LEGIS PROB/SOLV DIPLOM ADMIN GOV/REL 20 UNESCO. PAGE 147 A3010 — BIBLIOG CONCPT IDEA/COMP

N
US BUREAU OF THE CENSUS,BIBLIOGRAPHY OF SOCIAL SCIENCE PERIODICALS AND MONOGRAPH SERIES. WOR+45 LAW DIPLOM EDU/PROP HEALTH...PSY SOC LING STAT. PAGE 150 A3058 — BIBLIOG/A CULTURE NAT/G SOCIETY

N
US SUPERINTENDENT OF DOCUMENTS,GOVERNMENT PERIODICALS AND SUBSCRIPTION SERVICES (PRICE LIST 36). LAW WORKER CT/SYS HEALTH. PAGE 157 A3202 — BIBLIOG/A USA+45 NAT/G DIPLOM

N
US SUPERINTENDENT OF DOCUMENTS,TARIFF AND TAXATION (PRICE LIST 37). USA+45 LAW INT/TRADE ADJUD ADMIN CT/SYS INCOME OWN...DECISION GATT. PAGE 157 A3204 — BIBLIOG/A TAX TARIFFS NAT/G

B00
GROTIUS H.,DE JURE BELLI AC PACIS. CHRIST-17C UNIV LAW SOCIETY PROVS LEGIT PEACE PERCEPT MORAL PWR ...CONCPT CON/ANAL GEN/LAWS. PAGE 57 A1180 — JURID INT/LAW WAR

B00
HOLLAND T.E.,STUDIES IN INTERNATIONAL LAW. TURKEY USSR WOR-45 CONSTN NAT/G DIPLOM DOMIN LEGIT COERCE WAR PEACE ORD/FREE PWR SOVEREIGN...JURID CHARTS 20 PARLIAMENT SUEZ TREATY. PAGE 66 A1367 — INT/ORG LAW INT/LAW

B00
LORIMER J.,THE INSTITUTES OF THE LAW OF NATIONS. WOR-45 CULTURE SOCIETY NAT/G VOL/ASSN DIPLOM LEGIT WAR PEACE DRIVE ORD/FREE SOVEREIGN...CONCPT RECORD INT TREND HYPO/EXP GEN/METH TOT/POP VAL/FREE 20. PAGE 91 A1863 — INT/ORG LAW INT/LAW

B00
MAINE H.S.,INTERNATIONAL LAW. MOD/EUR UNIV SOCIETY STRUCT ACT/RES EXEC WAR ATTIT PERSON ALL/VALS ...POLICY JURID CONCPT OBS TIME/SEQ TOT/POP. PAGE 93 A1908 — INT/ORG LAW PEACE INT/LAW

L00
HISTORICUS,"LETTERS AND SOME QUESTIONS OF INTERNATIONAL LAW." FRANCE NETHERLAND UK USA-45 WOR-45 LAW NAT/G COERCE...SOC CONCPT GEN/LAWS TOT/POP 19 CIVIL/WAR. PAGE 65 A1344 — WEALTH JURID WAR INT/LAW

B03
FORTESCUE G.K.,SUBJECT INDEX OF THE MODERN WORKS ADDED TO THE LIBRARY OF THE BRITISH MUSEUM IN THE YEARS 1881-1900 (3 VOLS.). UK LAW CONSTN FINAN NAT/G FORCES INT/TRADE COLONIAL 19. PAGE 47 A0968 — BIBLIOG INDEX WRITING

B04
CRANDALL S.B.,TREATIES: THEIR MAKING AND ENFORCEMENT. MOD/EUR USA-45 CONSTN INT/ORG NAT/G LEGIS EDU/PROP LEGIT EXEC PEACE KNOWL MORAL...JURID CONGRESS 19/20 TREATY. PAGE 32 A0655 — LAW

C05
DUNNING W.A.,"HISTORY OF POLITICAL THEORIES FROM LUTHER TO MONTESQUIEU." LAW NAT/G SECT DIPLOM REV WAR ORD/FREE SOVEREIGN CONSERVE...TRADIT BIBLIOG 16/18. PAGE 39 A0803 — PHIL/SCI CONCPT GEN/LAWS

B09
HOLLAND T.E.,LETTERS UPON WAR AND NEUTRALITY. WOR-45 NAT/G FORCES JUDGE ECO/TAC LEGIT CT/SYS NEUTRAL ROUTINE COERCE...JURID TIME/SEQ 20. PAGE 67 A1368 — LAW INT/LAW INT/ORG WAR

B11
PHILLIPSON C.,THE INTERNATIONAL LAW AND CUSTOM OF ANCIENT GREECE AND ROME. MEDIT-7 UNIV INTELL SOCIETY STRUCT NAT/G LEGIS EXEC PERSON...CONCPT OBS CON/ANAL ROM/EMP. PAGE 116 A2377 — INT/ORG LAW INT/LAW

B13
BORCHARD E.M.,BIBLIOGRAPHY OF INTERNATIONAL LAW AND CONTINENTAL LAW. EUR+WWI MOD/EUR UK LAW INT/TRADE WAR PEACE...GOV/COMP NAT/COMP 19/20. PAGE 17 A0338 — BIBLIOG INT/LAW JURID DIPLOM

B15
INTERNATIONAL LAW ASSOCIATION,A FORTY YEARS' CATALOGUE OF THE BOOKS, PAMPHLETS AND PAPERS IN THE LIBRARY OF THE INTERNATIONAL LAW ASSOCIATION. INT/ORG DIPLOM ADJUD NEUTRAL...IDEA/COMP 19/20. PAGE 71 A1458 — BIBLIOG LAW INT/LAW

B16
PUFENDORF S.,LAW OF NATURE AND OF NATIONS (ABRIDGED). UNIV LAW NAT/G DIPLOM AGREE WAR PERSON ALL/VALS PWR...POLICY 18 DEITY NATURL/LAW. PAGE 118 A2416 — CONCPT INT/LAW SECT MORAL

B16
ROOT E.,ADDRESSES ON INTERNATIONAL SUBJECTS. MOD/EUR UNIV USA-45 LAW SOCIETY EXEC ATTIT ALL/VALS ...POLICY JURID CONCPT 20 CHINJAP. PAGE 123 A2521 INT/ORG ACT/RES PEACE INT/LAW

B16
ROOT E.,THE MILITARY AND COLONIAL POLICY OF THE US. L/A+17C USA-45 LAW SOCIETY STRATA STRUCT INT/ORG NAT/G SCHOOL FORCES EDU/PROP ALL/VALS...OBS VAL/FREE 19/20. PAGE 123 A2522 ACT/RES PLAN DIPLOM WAR

L16
WRIGHT Q.,"THE ENFORCEMENT OF INTERNATIONAL LAW THROUGH MUNICIPAL LAW IN THE US." USA-45 LOC/G NAT/G PUB/INST FORCES LEGIT CT/SYS PERCEPT ALL/VALS ...JURID 20. PAGE 167 A3401 INT/ORG LAW INT/LAW WAR

N19
UNITED ARAB REPUBLIC,THE PROBLEM OF THE PALESTINIAN REFUGEES (PAMPHLET). ISRAEL UAR LAW PROB/SOLV EDU/PROP CONFER ADJUD CONTROL NAT/LISM HEALTH 20 JEWS UN MIGRATION. PAGE 148 A3029 STRANGE GP/REL INGP/REL DIPLOM

B20
DICKINSON E.,THE EQUALITY OF STATES IN INTERNATIONAL LAW. WOR-45 INT/ORG NAT/G DIPLOM EDU/PROP LEGIT PEACE ATTIT ALL/VALS...JURID TIME/SEQ LEAGUE/NAT. PAGE 37 A0757 LAW CONCPT SOVEREIGN

B20
VINOGRADOFF P.,OUTLINES OF HISTORICAL JURISPRUDENCE (2 VOLS.). GREECE MEDIT-7 LAW CONSTN FACE/GP FAM KIN MUNIC CRIME OWN...INT/LAW IDEA/COMP BIBLIOG. PAGE 159 A3241 JURID METH

B21
OPPENHEIM L.,THE FUTURE OF INTERNATIONAL LAW. EUR+WWI MOD/EUR LAW LEGIS JUDGE LEGIT ORD/FREE ...JURID TIME/SEQ GEN/LAWS 20. PAGE 112 A2293 INT/ORG CT/SYS INT/LAW

S23
DEWEY J.,"ETHICS AND INTERNATIONAL RELATIONS." FUT WOR-45 SOCIETY INT/ORG VOL/ASSN DIPLOM LEGIT ORD/FREE...JURID CONCPT GEN/METH 20. PAGE 37 A0752 LAW MORAL

B24
GENTILI A.,DE LEGATIONIBUS. CHRIST-17C NAT/G SECT CONSULT LEGIT...POLICY CATH JURID CONCPT MYTH. PAGE 52 A1058 DIPLOM INT/LAW INT/ORG LAW

B25
GODET M.,INDEX BIBLIOGRAPHICUS: INTERNATIONAL CATALOGUE OF SOURCES OF CURRENT BIBLIOGRAPHIC INFORMATION. EUR+WWI MOD/EUR SOCIETY SECT TAX ...JURID PHIL/SCI SOC MATH. PAGE 53 A1085 BIBLIOG/A DIPLOM EDU/PROP LAW

B27
GOOCH G.P.,ENGLISH DEMOCRATIC IDEAS IN THE SEVENTEENTH CENTURY (2ND ED.). UK LAW SECT FORCES DIPLOM LEAD PARL/PROC REV ATTIT AUTHORIT...ANARCH CONCPT 17 PARLIAMENT CMN/WLTH REFORMERS. PAGE 54 A1100 IDEA/COMP MAJORIT EX/STRUC CONSERVE

B28
BUTLER G.,THE DEVELOPMENT OF INTERNATIONAL LAW. WOR-45 SOCIETY NAT/G KNOWL ORD/FREE PWR...JURID CONCPT HIST/WRIT GEN/LAWS. PAGE 22 A0451 LAW INT/LAW DIPLOM INT/ORG

B28
CORBETT P.E.,CANADA AND WORLD POLITICS. LAW CULTURE SOCIETY STRUCT MARKET INT/ORG FORCES ACT/RES PLAN ECO/TAC LEGIT ORD/FREE PWR RESPECT...SOC CONCPT TIME/SEQ TREND CMN/WLTH 20 LEAGUE/NAT. PAGE 30 A0612 NAT/G CANADA

B28
MAIR L.P.,THE PROTECTION OF MINORITIES. EUR+WWI WOR-45 CONSTN INT/ORG NAT/G LEGIT CT/SYS GP/REL RACE/REL DISCRIM ORD/FREE RESPECT...JURID CONCPT TIME/SEQ 20. PAGE 93 A1909 LAW SOVEREIGN

B30
BYNKERSHOEK C.,QUAESTIONUM JURIS PUBLICI LIBRI DUO. CHRIST-17C MOD/EUR CONSTN ELITES SOCIETY NAT/G PROVS EX/STRUC FORCES TOP/EX BAL/PWR DIPLOM ATTIT MORAL...TRADIT CONCPT. PAGE 23 A0460 INT/ORG LAW NAT/LISM INT/LAW

B30
WRIGHT Q.,MANDATES UNDER THE LEAGUE OF NATIONS. WOR-45 CONSTN ECO/DEV ECO/UNDEV NAT/G DELIB/GP TOP/EX LEGIT ALL/VALS...JURID CONCPT LEAGUE/NAT 20. PAGE 167 A3403 INT/ORG LAW INT/LAW

B31
BORCHARD E.H.,GUIDE TO THE LAW AND LEGAL LITERATURE OF FRANCE. FRANCE FINAN INDUS LABOR SECT LEGIS ADMIN COLONIAL CRIME OWN...INT/LAW 20. PAGE 17 A0337 BIBLIOG/A LAW CONSTN METH

B32
GREGORY W.,LIST OF THE SERIAL PUBLICATIONS OF FOREIGN GOVERNMENTS, 1815-1931. WOR-45 DIPLOM ADJUD ...POLICY 20. PAGE 56 A1144 BIBLIOG NAT/G LAW JURID

B32
MASTERS R.D.,INTERNATIONAL LAW IN INTERNATIONAL COURTS. BELGIUM EUR+WWI FRANCE GERMANY MOD/EUR SWITZERLND WOR-45 SOCIETY STRATA STRUCT LEGIT EXEC ALL/VALS...JURID HIST/WRIT TIME/SEQ TREND GEN/LAWS 20. PAGE 96 A1961 INT/ORG LAW INT/LAW

B32
MORLEY F.,THE SOCIETY OF NATIONS. EUR+WWI UNIV WOR-45 LAW CONSTN ACT/RES PLAN EDU/PROP LEGIT ROUTINE...POLICY TIME/SEQ LEAGUE/NAT TOT/POP 20. PAGE 104 A2143 INT/ORG CONCPT

B33
AMERICAN FOREIGN LAW ASSN,BIOGRAPHICAL NOTES ON THE LAWS AND LEGAL LITERATURE OF URUGUAY AND CURACAO. URUGUAY CONSTN FINAN SECT FORCES JUDGE DIPLOM INT/TRADE ADJUD CT/SYS CRIME 20. PAGE 7 A0147 BIBLIOG/A LAW JURID ADMIN

B33
LAUTERPACHT H.,THE FUNCTION OF LAW IN THE INTERNATIONAL COMMUNITY. WOR-45 NAT/G FORCES CREATE DOMIN LEGIT COERCE WAR PEACE ATTIT ORD/FREE PWR SOVEREIGN...JURID CONCPT METH/CNCPT TIME/SEQ GEN/LAWS GEN/METH LEAGUE/NAT TOT/POP VAL/FREE 20. PAGE 85 A1749 INT/ORG LAW INT/LAW

B33
REID H.D.,RECUEIL DES COURS; TOME 45: LES SERVITUDES INTERNATIONALES III. FRANCE CONSTN DELIB/GP PRESS CONTROL REV WAR CHOOSE PEACE MORAL MARITIME TREATY. PAGE 120 A2457 ORD/FREE DIPLOM LAW

B33
PUBLIC OPINION AND WORLD POLITICS. UNIV LAW CULTURE NAT/G PRESS REV GP/REL...MAJORIT METH/COMP ANTHOL 20. PAGE 167 A3400 DIPLOM EDU/PROP ATTIT MAJORITY

B34
US TARIFF COMMISSION,THE TARIFF; A BIBLIOGRAPHY: A SELECT LIST OF REFERENCES. USA-45 LAW DIPLOM TAX ADMIN...POLICY TREATY 20. PAGE 157 A3208 BIBLIOG/A TARIFFS ECO/TAC

B34
WOLFF C.,JUS GENTIUM METHODO SCIENTIFICA PERTRACTATUM. MOD/EUR INT/ORG VOL/ASSN LEGIT PEACE ATTIT...JURID 20. PAGE 166 A3387 NAT/G LAW INT/LAW WAR

B36
HUDSON M.O.,INTERNATIONAL LEGISLATION: 1929-1931. WOR-45 SEA AIR AGRI FINAN LABOR DIPLOM ECO/TAC REPAR CT/SYS ARMS/CONT WAR WEAPON...JURID 20 TREATY LEAGUE/NAT. PAGE 69 A1409 INT/LAW PARL/PROC ADJUD LAW

B36
VARLEY D.H.,A BIBLIOGRAPHY OF ITALIAN COLONISATION IN AFRICA WITH A SECTION ON ABYSSINIA. AFR ETHIOPIA ITALY LIBYA SOMALIA AGRI FINAN LABOR TEC/DEV DIPLOM INT/TRADE RACE/REL DISCRIM 19/20. PAGE 158 A3222 BIBLIOG COLONIAL ADMIN LAW

B37
BORGESE G.A.,GOLIATH: THE MARCH OF FASCISM. GERMANY ITALY LAW POL/PAR SECT DIPLOM SOCISM...JURID MYTH 20 DANTE MACHIAVELL MUSSOLIN/B. PAGE 17 A0341 POLICY NAT/LISM FASCISM NAT/G

B37
KETCHAM E.H.,PRELIMINARY SELECT BIBLIOGRAPHY OF INTERNATIONAL LAW (PAMPHLET). WOR-45 LAW INT/ORG NAT/G PROB/SOLV CT/SYS NEUTRAL WAR 19/20. PAGE 78 A1602 BIBLIOG DIPLOM ADJUD INT/LAW

B37
ROYAL INST. INT. AFF.,THE COLONIAL PROBLEM. WOR-45 LAW ECO/DEV ECO/UNDEV NAT/G PLAN ECO/TAC EDU/PROP ADMIN ATTIT ALL/VALS...CONCPT 20. PAGE 125 A2556 INT/ORG ACT/RES SOVEREIGN COLONIAL

B37
SCHUSTER E.,GUIDE TO LAW AND LEGAL LITERATURE OF CENTRAL AMERICAN REPUBLICS. L/A+17C INT/ORG ADJUD SANCTION CRIME...JURID 19/20. PAGE 129 A2654 BIBLIOG/A REGION CT/SYS LAW

B38
HAGUE PERMANENT CT INTL JUSTIC,WORLD COURT REPORTS: COLLECTION OF THE JUDGEMENTS ORDERS AND OPINIONS VOLUME 3 1932-35. WOR-45 LAW DELIB/GP CONFER WAR PEACE ATTIT...DECISION ANTHOL 20 WORLD/CT CASEBOOK. PAGE 59 A1214 INT/ORG CT/SYS DIPLOM ADJUD

B38
HARPER S.N.,THE GOVERNMENT OF THE SOVIET UNION. COM USSR LAW CONSTN ECO/DEV PLAN TEC/DEV DIPLOM INT/TRADE ADMIN REV NAT/LISM...POLICY 20. PAGE 62 A1265 MARXISM NAT/G LEAD POL/PAR

B38
MCNAIR A.D.,THE LAW OF TREATIES: BRITISH PRACTICE AND OPINIONS. UK CREATE DIPLOM LEGIT WRITING ADJUD WAR...INT/LAW JURID TREATY. PAGE 98 A2018 AGREE LAW CT/SYS NAT/G

B39
DULLES J.,WAR, PEACE AND CHANGE. FRANCE ITALY UK USA-45 WOR-45 LAW INT/ORG NAT/G SECT VOL/ASSN FORCES TOP/EX DOMIN ARMS/CONT COERCE ATTIT PERSON RIGID/FLEX MORAL PWR...JURID STERTYP TOT/POP LEAGUE/NAT 20. PAGE 39 A0796 EDU/PROP TOTALISM WAR

B39
THOMAS J.A.,THE HOUSE OF COMMONS, 1832-1901; A STUDY OF ITS ECONOMIC AND FUNCTIONAL CHARACTER. UK LAW STRATA FINAN DIPLOM CONTROL LEAD LOBBY REPRESENT WEALTH...POLICY STAT BIBLIOG 19/20 PARLIAMENT. PAGE 143 A2922 PARL/PROC LEGIS POL/PAR ECO/DEV

B39
WILSON G.G.,HANDBOOK OF INTERNATIONAL LAW. FUT UNIV INT/ORG

USA-45 WOR-45 SOCIETY LEGIT ATTIT DISPL DRIVE ALL/VALS...INT/LAW TIME/SEQ TREND. PAGE 165 A3359 — LAW CONCPT WAR

B39
ZIMMERN A.,THE LEAGUE OF NATIONS AND THE RULE OF LAW. WOR-45 STRUCT NAT/G DELIB/GP EX/STRUC BAL/PWR DOMIN LEGIT COERCE ORD/FREE PWR...POLICY RECORD LEAGUE/NAT TOT/POP VAL/FREE 20 LEAGUE/NAT. PAGE 170 A3453 — INT/ORG LAW DIPLOM

C39
HADDOW A.,"POLITICAL SCIENCE IN AMERICAN COLLEGES AND UNIVERSITIES 1636-1900." CONSTN MORAL...POLICY INT/LAW CON/ANAL BIBLIOG T 17/20. PAGE 59 A1211 — USA-45 LAW ACADEM KNOWL

C39
SCOTT J.B.,"LAW, THESTATE, AND THE INTERNATIONAL COMMUNITY (2 VOLS.)" INTELL INT/ORG NAT/G SECT INT/TRADE WAR...INT/LAW GEN/LAWS BIBLIOG. PAGE 130 A2672 — LAW PHIL/SCI DIPLOM CONCPT

S40
FLORIN J.,"BOLSHEVIST AND NATIONAL SOCIALIST DOCTRINES OF INTERNATIONAL LAW." EUR+WWI GERMANY USSR R+D INT/ORG NAT/G DIPLOM DOMIN EDU/PROP SOCISM ...CONCPT TIME/SEQ 20. PAGE 47 A0955 — LAW ATTIT TOTALISM INT/LAW

B41
EVANS C.,AMERICAN BIBLIOGRAPHY... (12 VOLUMES). USA-45 LAW DIPLOM ADMIN PERSON...HUM SOC 17/18. PAGE 43 A0876 — BIBLIOG NAT/G ALL/VALS ALL/IDEOS

B41
GRISMER R.,A NEW BIBLIOGRAPHY OF THE LITERATURES OF SPAIN AND SPANISH AMERICA. CHRIST-17C MOD/EUR PRE/AMER SPAIN CULTURE DIPLOM EDU/PROP...ART/METH GEOG HUM PHIL/SCI 20. PAGE 57 A1165 — BIBLIOG LAW NAT/G ECO/UNDEV

B41
NIEMEYER G.,LAW WITHOUT FORCE: THE FUNCTION OF POLITICS IN INTERNATIONAL LAW. PLAN INSPECT DIPLOM REPAR LEGIT ADJUD WAR ORD/FREE...IDEA/COMP METH/COMP GEN/LAWS 20. PAGE 109 A2240 — COERCE LAW PWR INT/LAW

B43
SERENI A.P.,THE ITALIAN CONCEPTION OF INTERNATIONAL LAW. EUR+WWI MOD/EUR INT/ORG NAT/G DOMIN COERCE ORD/FREE FASCISM...OBS/ENVIR TREND 20. PAGE 131 A2686 — LAW TIME/SEQ INT/LAW ITALY

B44
ADLER M.J.,HOW TO THINK ABOUT WAR AND PEACE. WOR-45 LAW SOCIETY EX/STRUC DIPLOM KNOWL ORD/FREE...POLICY TREND GEN/LAWS 20. PAGE 4 A0092 — INT/ORG CREATE ARMS/CONT PEACE

B44
BRIERLY J.L.,THE OUTLOOK FOR INTERNATIONAL LAW. FUT WOR-45 CONSTN NAT/G VOL/ASSN FORCES ECO/TAC DOMIN LEGIT ADJUD ROUTINE PEACE ORD/FREE...INT/LAW JURID METH LEAGUE/NAT 20. PAGE 18 A0376 — INT/ORG LAW

B44
FULLER G.H.,MILITARY GOVERNMENT: A LIST OF REFERENCES (A PAMPHLET). ITALY UK USA-45 WOR-45 LAW FORCES DOMIN ADMIN ARMS/CONT ORD/FREE PWR ...DECISION 20 CHINJAP. PAGE 50 A1023 — BIBLIOG DIPLOM CIVMIL/REL SOVEREIGN

B44
HUDSON M.,INTERNATIONAL TRIBUNALS PAST AND FUTURE. FUT WOR-45 LAW EDU/PROP ADJUD ORD/FREE...CONCPT TIME/SEQ TREND GEN/LAWS TOT/POP VAL/FREE 18/20. PAGE 69 A1408 — INT/ORG STRUCT INT/LAW

B44
PUTTKAMMER E.W.,WAR AND THE LAW. UNIV USA-45 CONSTN CULTURE SOCIETY NAT/G POL/PAR ROUTINE ALL/VALS ...JURID CONCPT OBS WORK VAL/FREE 20. PAGE 118 A2418 — INT/ORG LAW WAR INT/LAW

N45
INDIA QUARTERLY, A JOURNAL OF INTERNATIONAL AFFAIRS. INDIA LAW CONSTN ECO/UNDEV INT/ORG POL/PAR COLONIAL LEAD PARL/PROC WAR ATTIT...SOC 20 CMN/WLTH. PAGE 3 A0053 — BIBLIOG/A S/ASIA DIPLOM NAT/G

B45
VANCE H.L.,GUIDE TO THE LAW AND LEGAL LITERATURE OF MEXICO. LAW CONSTN FINAN LABOR FORCES ADJUD ADMIN ...CRIMLGY PHIL/SCI CON/ANAL 20 MEXIC/AMER. PAGE 158 A3217 — BIBLIOG/A INT/LAW JURID CT/SYS

B45
WEST R.,CONSCIENCE AND SOCIETY: A STUDY OF THE PSYCHOLOGICAL PREREQUISITES OF LAW AND ORDER. FUT UNIV LAW SOCIETY STRUCT DIPLOM WAR PERS/REL SUPEGO ...SOC 20. PAGE 163 A3321 — COERCE INT/LAW ORD/FREE PERSON

B45
WING D.,SHORT-TITLE CATALOGUE OF BOOKS PRINTED IN THE BRITISH ISLES, AND OF ENGLISH BOOKS PRINTED OVERSEAS; 1641-1700 (3 VOLS.). UK USA-45 LAW DIPLOM ADMIN COLONIAL LEAD ATTIT 17. PAGE 165 A3363 — BIBLIOG MOD/EUR NAT/G

B46
BIBLIOGRAFIIA DISSERTATSII: DOKTORSKIE DISSERTATSII ZA 19411944 (2 VOLS.). COM USSR LAW POL/PAR DIPLOM ADMIN LEAD...PHIL/SCI SOC 20. PAGE 3 A0054 — BIBLIOG ACADEM KNOWL MARXIST

B46
BLUM L.,FOR ALL MANKIND (TRANS. BY W. PICKLES). FRANCE GERMANY USSR LAW SOCIETY STRUCT POL/PAR WORKER DIPLOM DOMIN CHOOSE ORD/FREE FASCISM 20. PAGE 16 A0323 — POPULISM SOCIALIST NAT/G WAR

B46
GRIFFIN G.G.,A GUIDE TO MANUSCRIPTS RELATING TO AMERICAN HISTORY IN BRITISH DEPOSITORIES. CANADA IRELAND MOD/EUR UK USA-45 LAW DIPLOM ADMIN COLONIAL WAR NAT/LISM SOVEREIGN...GEOG INT/LAW 15/19 CMN/WLTH. PAGE 56 A1159 — BIBLIOG/A ALL/VALS NAT/G

S46
DOUGLAS W.O.,"SYMPOSIUM ON WORLD ORGANIZATION." FUT USA+45 WOR+45 CONSTN SOCIETY NAT/G PLAN EDU/PROP LEGIT RIGID/FLEX KNOWL...INT/LAW JURID STERTYP TOT/POP 20. PAGE 38 A0778 — INT/ORG LAW

S46
SILBERNER E.,"THE PROBLEM OF WAR IN NINETEENTH CENTURY ECONOMIC THOUGHT." EUR+WWI MOD/EUR UNIV LAW ECO/DEV ECO/UNDEV FINAN INDUS MARKET INT/ORG NAT/G CONSULT FORCES...CONCPT GEN/LAWS GEN/METH 19. PAGE 133 A2715 — ATTIT ECO/TAC WAR

B47
BORGESE G.,COMMON CAUSE. LAW CONSTN SOCIETY STRATA ECO/DEV INT/ORG POL/PAR FORCES LEGIS TOP/EX CAP/ISM DIPLOM ADMIN EXEC ATTIT PWR 20. PAGE 17 A0339 — WOR+45 NAT/G SOVEREIGN REGION

B47
GORDON D.L.,THE HIDDEN WEAPON: THE STORY OF ECONOMIC WARFARE. EUR+WWI USA-45 LAW FINAN INDUS NAT/G CONSULT FORCES PLAN DOMIN PWR WEALTH ...INT/LAW CONCPT OBS TOT/POP NAZI 20. PAGE 54 A1112 — INT/ORG ECO/TAC INT/TRADE WAR

B47
HILL M.,IMMUNITIES AND PRIVILEGES OF INTERNATIONAL OFFICIALS. CANADA EUR+WWI NETHERLAND SWITZERLND LAW LEGIS DIPLOM LEGIT RESPECT...TIME/SEQ LEAGUE/NAT UN VAL/FREE 20. PAGE 65 A1330 — INT/ORG ADMIN

B47
HIRSHBERG H.S.,SUBJECT GUIDE TO UNITED STATES GOVERNMENT PUBLICATIONS. USA+45 USA-45 LAW ADMIN ...SOC 20. PAGE 65 A1340 — BIBLIOG NAT/G DIPLOM LOC/G

B47
INTERNATIONAL COURT OF JUSTICE,CHARTER OF THE UNITED NATIONS, STATUTE AND RULES OF COURT AND OTHER CONSTITUTIONAL DOCUMENTS. SWITZERLND LAW ADJUD INGP/REL...JURID 20 ICJ UN. PAGE 71 A1453 — INT/LAW INT/ORG CT/SYS DIPLOM

B47
TOWLE L.W.,INTERNATIONAL TRADE AND COMMERCIAL POLICY. WOR+45 LAW ECO/DEV FINAN INDUS NAT/G ECO/TAC WEALTH...TIME/SEQ ILO 20. PAGE 144 A2955 — MARKET INT/ORG INT/TRADE

B48
NEUBURGER O.,GUIDE TO OFFICIAL PUBLICATIONS OF THE OTHER AMERICAN REPUBLICS: VENEZUELA (VOL. XIX). VENEZUELA FINAN LEGIS PLAN BUDGET DIPLOM CT/SYS PARL/PROC 19/20. PAGE 108 A2219 — BIBLIOG/A NAT/G CONSTN LAW

B49
GROB F.,THE RELATIVITY OF WAR AND PEACE: A STUDY IN LAW, HISTORY, AND POLLTICS. WOR+45 WOR-45 LAW DIPLOM DEBATE...CONCPT LING IDEA/COMP BIBLIOG 18/20. PAGE 57 A1167 — WAR PEACE INT/LAW STYLE

B49
MARITAIN J.,HUMAN RIGHTS: COMMENTS AND INTERPRETATIONS. COM UNIV WOR+45 LAW CONSTN CULTURE SOCIETY ECO/DEV ECO/UNDEV SCHOOL DELIB/GP EDU/PROP ATTIT PERCEPT ALL/VALS...HUM SOC TREND UNESCO 20. PAGE 95 A1939 — INT/ORG CONCPT

B49
US DEPARTMENT OF STATE,SOVIET BIBLIOGRAPHY (PAMPHLET). CHINA/COM COM USSR LAW AGRI INT/ORG ECO/TAC EDU/PROP...POLICY GEOG 20. PAGE 151 A3084 — BIBLIOG/A MARXISM CULTURE DIPLOM

L49
COMM. STUDY ORGAN. PEACE,"A TEN YEAR RECORD, 1939-1949." FUT WOR+45 LAW R+D CONSULT DELIB/GP CREATE LEGIT ROUTINE ORD/FREE...TIME/SEQ UN 20. PAGE 28 A0578 — INT/ORG CONSTN PEACE

B50
BOHATTA H.,INTERNATIONALE BIBLIOGRAPHIE. WOR+45 LAW CULTURE PRESS. PAGE 16 A0330 — BIBLIOG DIPLOM NAT/G WRITING

B50
BROWN E.S.,MANUAL OF GOVERNMENT PUBLICATIONS. WOR+45 WOR-45 CONSTN INT/ORG MUNIC PROVS DIPLOM ADMIN 20. PAGE 20 A0401 — BIBLIOG/A NAT/G LAW

B50
DUCLOS P.,L'EVOLUTION DES RAPPORTS POLITIQUES DEPUIS 1750 (LIBERTE, INTEGRATION, UNITE). LAW INT/ORG FEDERAL TOTALISM ATTIT PWR...MAJORIT BIBLIOG 18/20 PARLIAMENT EUROPE. PAGE 39 A0792 — ORD/FREE DIPLOM NAT/G GOV/COMP

B50
LAUTERPACHT H.,INTERNATIONAL LAW AND HUMAN RIGHTS. USA+45 CONSTN STRUCT INT/ORG ACT/RES EDU/PROP PEACE PERSON ALL/VALS...CONCPT CON/ANAL GEN/LAWS UN 20. PAGE 86 A1750 — DELIB/GP LAW INT/LAW

B50
MACIVER R.M.,GREAT EXPRESSIONS OF HUMAN RIGHTS. LAW CONSTN CULTURE INTELL SOCIETY R+D INT/ORG ATTIT DRIVE...JURID OBS HIST/WRIT GEN/LAWS. PAGE 92 A1891
UNIV CONCPT

B50
SOHN L.B.,CASES AND OTHER MATERIALS ON WORLD LAW. FUT WOR+45 LAW INT/ORG...INT/LAW JURID METH/CNCPT 20 UN. PAGE 135 A2760
CT/SYS CONSTN

B50
STONE J.,THE PROVINCE AND FUNCTION OF LAW. UNIV WOR+45 WOR-45 CULTURE INTELL SOCIETY ECO/DEV ECO/UNDEV NAT/G LEGIT ROUTINE ATTIT PERCEPT PERSON ...JURID CONCPT GEN/LAWS GEN/METH 20. PAGE 138 A2833
INT/ORG LAW

C50
NUMELIN R.,"THE BEGINNINGS OF DIPLOMACY." INT/TRADE WAR GP/REL PEACE STRANGE ATTIT...INT/LAW CONCPT BIBLIOG. PAGE 110 A2260
DIPLOM KIN CULTURE LAW

B51
MCKEON R.,DEMOCRACY IN A WORLD OF TENSION. UNIV LAW INTELL STRUCT R+D INT/ORG SCHOOL EDU/PROP LEGIT ATTIT DRIVE PERCEPT PERSON...POLICY JURID PSY SOC CONCPT METH/CNCPT OBS UNESCO TOT/POP VAL/FREE. PAGE 98 A2015
SOCIETY ALL/VALS ORD/FREE

L51
KELSEN H.,"RECENT TRENDS IN THE LAW OF THE UNITED NATIONS." KOREA WOR+45 CONSTN LEGIS DIPLOM LEGIT DETER WAR RIGID/FLEX HEALTH ORD/FREE RESPECT ...JURID CON/ANAL UN VAL/FREE 20 NATO. PAGE 77 A1582
INT/ORG LAW INT/LAW

B52
DILLON D.R.,LATIN AMERICA, 1935-1949; A SELECTED BIBLIOGRAPHY. LAW EDU/PROP...SOC 20. PAGE 37 A0764
BIBLIOG L/A+17C NAT/G DIPLOM

B52
FLECHTHEIM O.K.,FUNDAMENTALS OF POLITICAL SCIENCE. WOR+45 WOR-45 LAW POL/PAR EX/STRUC LEGIS ADJUD ATTIT PWR...INT/LAW. PAGE 46 A0945
NAT/G DIPLOM IDEA/COMP CONSTN

B52
SCHUMAN F.,THE COMMONWEALTH OF MAN. WOR+45 WOR-45 LAW CULTURE ELITES SOCIETY FAM INT/ORG NAT/G VOL/ASSN TOP/EX PLAN BAL/PWR LEGIT ATTIT DISPL DRIVE...POLICY MYTH TREND TOT/POP ILO OEEC 20. PAGE 129 A2649
CONCPT GEN/LAWS

B52
US DEPARTMENT OF STATE,RESEARCH ON EASTERN EUROPE (EXCLUDING USSR). EUR+WWI LAW ECO/DEV NAT/G PROB/SOLV DIPLOM ADMIN LEAD MARXISM...TREND 19/20. PAGE 151 A3088
BIBLIOG R+D ACT/RES COM

B52
VANDENBOSCH A.,THE UN: BACKGROUND, ORGANIZATION, FUNCTIONS, ACTIVITIES. WOR+45 LAW CONSTN STRUCT INT/ORG CONSULT BAL/PWR EDU/PROP EXEC ALL/VALS ...POLICY CONCPT UN 20. PAGE 158 A3218
DELIB/GP TIME/SEQ PEACE

B53
OPPENHEIM L.,INTERNATIONAL LAW: A TREATISE (7TH ED., 2 VOLS.). LAW CONSTN PROB/SOLV INT/TRADE ADJUD AGREE NEUTRAL WAR ORD/FREE SOVEREIGN...BIBLIOG 20 LEAGUE/NAT UN ILO. PAGE 112 A2294
INT/LAW INT/ORG DIPLOM

B53
ORFIELD L.B.,THE GROWTH OF SCANDINAVIAN LAW. DENMARK ICELAND NORWAY SWEDEN LAW DIPLOM...BIBLIOG 9/20. PAGE 112 A2296
JURID CT/SYS NAT/G

B53
ZIMMERN A.,THE AMERICAN ROAD TO PEACE. USA+45 LAW INT/ORG NAT/G EX/STRUC TOP/EX EDU/PROP LEGIT COERCE PEACE ATTIT ORD/FREE PWR...CONCPT TIME/SEQ LEAGUE/NAT TOT/POP VAL/FREE 20 UN. PAGE 170 A3455
USA-45 DIPLOM

B54
MANGONE G.,A SHORT HISTORY OF INTERNATIONAL ORGANIZATION. MOD/EUR USA+45 USA-45 WOR+45 WOR-45 LAW LEGIS CREATE LEGIT ROUTINE RIGID/FLEX PWR ...JURID CONCPT OBS TIME/SEQ STERTYP GEN/LAWS UN TOT/POP VAL/FREE 18/20. PAGE 94 A1921
INT/ORG INT/LAW

B54
NUSSBAUM D.,A CONCISE HISTORY OF THE LAW OF NATIONS. ASIA CHRIST-17C EUR+WWI ISLAM MEDIT-7 MOD/EUR S/ASIA UNIV WOR+45 WOR-45 SOCIETY STRUCT EXEC ATTIT ALL/VALS...CONCPT HIST/WRIT TIME/SEQ. PAGE 110 A2263
INT/ORG LAW PEACE INT/LAW

B54
STONE J.,LEGAL CONTROLS OF INTERNATIONAL CONFLICT: A TREATISE ON THE DYNAMICS OF DISPUTES AND WAR LAW. WOR+45 WOR-45 NAT/G DIPLOM CT/SYS SOVEREIGN...JURID CONCPT METH/CNCPT GEN/LAWS TOT/POP VAL/FREE COLD/WAR LEAGUE/NAT 20. PAGE 138 A2834
INT/ORG LAW WAR INT/LAW

B54
STREIT C.K.,FREEDOM AGAINST ITSELF. LAW SOCIETY DIPLOM UTOPIA PWR SOVEREIGN ALL/IDEOS 17/20 NATO UN. PAGE 139 A2850
ORD/FREE CREATE INT/ORG CONCPT

B54
TOTOK W.,HANDBUCH DER BIBLIOGRAPHISCHEN NACHSCHLAGEWERKE. GERMANY LAW CULTURE ADMIN...SOC 20. PAGE 144 A2952
BIBLIOG/A NAT/G DIPLOM POLICY

S54
DAWSON K.H.,"THE UNITED NATIONS IN A DISUNITED WORLD." WOR+45 WOR-45 LAW INTELL NAT/G PEACE ATTIT PERCEPT MORAL LEAGUE/NAT TOT/POP VAL/FREE 20 UN. PAGE 34 A0694
INT/ORG LEGIT

B55
JAPAN MOMBUSHO DAIGAKU GAKIYUT,BIBLIOGRAPHY OF THE STUDIES ON LAW AND POLITICS (PAMPHLET). CONSTN INDUS LABOR DIPLOM TAX ADMIN...CRIMLGY INT/LAW 20 CHINJAP. PAGE 73 A1496
BIBLIOG LAW PHIL/SCI

B56
JESSUP P.C.,TRANSNATIONAL LAW. FUT WOR+45 JUDGE CREATE ADJUD ORD/FREE...CONCPT VAL/FREE 20. PAGE 74 A1515
LAW JURID INT/LAW

B56
SIPKOV I.,LEGAL SOURCES AND BIBLIOGRAPHY OF BULGARIA. BULGARIA COM LEGIS WRITING ADJUD CT/SYS ...INT/LAW TREATY 20. PAGE 134 A2736
BIBLIOG LAW TOTALISM MARXISM

B56
SOHN L.B.,BASIC DOCUMENTS OF THE UNITED NATIONS. WOR+45 LAW INT/ORG LEGIT EXEC ROUTINE CHOOSE PWR ...JURID CONCPT GEN/LAWS ANTHOL UN TOT/POP OAS FAO ILO 20. PAGE 135 A2761
DELIB/GP CONSTN

B56
US HOUSE COMM FOREIGN AFFAIRS,SURVEY OF ACTIVITIES OF THE COMMITTEE ON FOREIGN AFFAIRS HOUSE OF REPRESENTATIVES: 84TH THROUGH 86TH CONGRESS. USA+45 LAW ADJUD...POLICY STAT CHARTS 20 CONGRESS HOUSE/REP. PAGE 153 A3122
LEGIS DELIB/GP NAT/G DIPLOM

B56
WEIS P.,NATIONALITY AND STATELESSNESS IN INTERNATIONAL LAW. UK WOR+45 WOR-45 LAW CONSTN NAT/G DIPLOM EDU/PROP LEGIT ROUTINE RIGID/FLEX ...JURID RECORD CMN/WLTH 20. PAGE 162 A3309
INT/ORG SOVEREIGN INT/LAW

B57
ALIGHIERI D.,ON WORLD GOVERNMENT. ROMAN/EMP LAW SOCIETY INT/ORG NAT/G POL/PAR ADJUD WAR GP/REL PEACE WORSHIP 15 WORLDUNITY DANTE. PAGE 6 A0121
POLICY CONCPT DIPLOM SECT

B57
BLOOMFIELD L.M.,EGYPT, ISRAEL AND THE GULF OF AQABA: IN INTERNATIONAL LAW. LAW NAT/G CONSULT FORCES PLAN ECO/TAC ROUTINE COERCE ATTIT DRIVE PERCEPT PERSON RIGID/FLEX LOVE PWR WEALTH...GEOG CONCPT MYTH TREND. PAGE 15 A0314
ISLAM INT/LAW UAR

B57
DE VISSCHER C.,THEORY AND REALITY IN PUBLIC INTERNATIONAL LAW. WOR+45 WOR-45 SOCIETY NAT/G CT/SYS ATTIT MORAL ORD/FREE PWR...JURID CONCPT METH/CNCPT TIME/SEQ GEN/LAWS LEAGUE/NAT TOT/POP VAL/FREE COLD/WAR. PAGE 35 A0716
INT/ORG LAW INT/LAW

B57
INSTITUT DE DROIT INTL,TABLEAU GENERAL DES RESOLUTIONS (1873-1956). LAW NEUTRAL CRIME WAR MARRIAGE PEACE...JURID 19/20. PAGE 70 A1442
INT/LAW DIPLOM ORD/FREE ADJUD

B57
LEVONTIN A.V.,THE MYTH OF INTERNATIONAL SECURITY: A JURIDICAL AND CRITICAL ANALYSIS. FUT WOR+45 WOR-45 LAW NAT/G VOL/ASSN ACT/RES BAL/PWR ATTIT ORD/FREE ...JURID METH/CNCPT TIME/SEQ TREND STERTYP 20. PAGE 88 A1797
INT/ORG INT/LAW SOVEREIGN MYTH

B57
ROSENNE S.,THE INTERNATIONAL COURT OF JUSTICE. WOR+45 LAW DOMIN LEGIT PEACE PWR SOVEREIGN...JURID CONCPT RECORD TIME/SEQ CON/ANAL CHARTS UN TOT/POP VAL/FREE LEAGUE/NAT 20 ICJ. PAGE 124 A2537
INT/ORG CT/SYS INT/LAW

B57
UNESCO,A REGISTER OF LEGAL DOCUMENTATION IN THE WORLD (2ND ED.). CT/SYS...JURID IDEA/COMP METH/COMP NAT/COMP 20. PAGE 148 A3019
BIBLIOG LAW INT/LAW CONSTN

B57
US COMMISSION GOVT SECURITY,RECOMMENDATIONS; AREA: IMMIGRANT PROGRAM. USA+45 LAW WORKER DIPLOM EDU/PROP WRITING ADMIN PEACE ATTIT...CONCPT ANTHOL 20 MIGRATION SUBVERT. PAGE 150 A3060
POLICY CONTROL PLAN NAT/G

B57
WILSON P.,SOUTH ASIA; A SELECTED BIBLIOGRAPHY ON INDIA, PAKISTAN, CEYLON (PAMPHLET). CEYLON INDIA PAKISTAN LAW ECO/UNDEV PLAN DIPLOM 20. PAGE 165 A3362
BIBLIOG S/ASIA CULTURE NAT/G

B57
YAMADA H.,ANNALS OF THE SOCIAL SCIENCES. WOR+45 WOR-45 LAW CULTURE SOCIETY STRUCT DIPLOM...EPIST PSY CONCPT 15/20. PAGE 168 A3428
BIBLIOG/A TREND IDEA/COMP SOC

B58
ALEXANDROWICZ,A BIBLIOGRAPHY OF INDIAN LAW. INDIA S/ASIA CONSTN CT/SYS...INT/LAW 19/20. PAGE 6 A0113
BIBLIOG LAW ADJUD JURID

B58
HENKIN L.,ARMS CONTROL AND INSPECTION IN AMERICAN LAW. LAW CONSTN INT/ORG LOC/G MUNIC NAT/G PROVS EDU/PROP LEGIT EXEC NUC/PWR KNOWL ORD/FREE...OBS TOT/POP CONGRESS 20. PAGE 64 A1315
USA+45 JURID ARMS/CONT

B58
MANSERGH N.,COMMONWEALTH PERSPECTIVES. GHANA UK LAW VOL/ASSN CONFER HEALTH SOVEREIGN...GEOG CHARTS ANTHOL 20 CMN/WLTH AUSTRAL. PAGE 94 A1930
DIPLOM COLONIAL INT/ORG INGP/REL

B58
MASON H.L.,TOYNBEE'S APPROACH TO WORLD POLITICS. AFR USA+45 USSR LAW WAR NAT/LISM ALL/IDEOS...HUM BIBLIOG. PAGE 95 A1957
DIPLOM CONCPT PHIL/SCI SECT

B58
STONE J.,AGGRESSION AND WORLD ORDER: A CRITIQUE OF UNITED NATIONS THEORIES OF AGGRESSION. LAW CONSTN DELIB/GP PROB/SOLV BAL/PWR DIPLOM DEBATE ADJUD CRIME PWR...POLICY IDEA/COMP 20 UN SUEZ LEAGUE/NAT. PAGE 138 A2835
ORD/FREE INT/ORG WAR CONCPT

B58
UNESCO,REPERTORIO DE PUBLICACIONES PERIODICAS ACTUALES LATINO AMERICANAS (VOL. VIII). LAW DIPLOM GP/REL...PHIL/SCI SOC 20 UNESCO. PAGE 148 A3021
BIBLIOG/A COM/IND L/A+17C

C58
WILDING N.,"AN ENCYCLOPEDIA OF PARLIAMENT." UK LAW CONSTN CHIEF PROB/SOLV DIPLOM DEBATE WAR INGP/REL PRIVIL...BIBLIOG DICTIONARY 13/20 CMN/WLTH PARLIAMENT. PAGE 164 A3349
PARL/PROC POL/PAR NAT/G ADMIN

B59
COUDENHOVE-KALERGI,FROM WAR TO PEACE. USA+45 USSR WOR+45 WOR-45 LAW INT/ORG NAT/G LEGIT COERCE LOVE ...POLICY PLURIST METH/CNCPT STERTYP TOT/POP UN 20 NATO. PAGE 31 A0636
FUT ORD/FREE

B59
GORDENKER L.,THE UNITED NATIONS AND THE PEACEFUL UNIFICATION OF KOREA. ASIA LAW LOC/G CONSULT ACT/RES DIPLOM DOMIN LEGIT ADJUD ADMIN ORD/FREE SOVEREIGN...INT GEN/METH UN COLD/WAR 20. PAGE 54 A1109
DELIB/GP KOREA INT/ORG

B59
HALEY A.G.,FIRST COLLOQUIUM ON THE LAW OF OUTER SPACE. WOR+45 INT/ORG ACT/RES PLAN BAL/PWR CONFER ATTIT PWR...POLICY JURID CHARTS ANTHOL 20. PAGE 60 A1225
SPACE LAW SOVEREIGN CONTROL

B59
NUNEZ JIMENEZ A.,LA LIBERACION DE LAS ISLAS. CUBA L/A+17C USA+45 LAW CHIEF PLAN DIPLOM FOR/AID OWN WEALTH 20 CASTRO/F. PAGE 110 A2261
AGRI REV ECO/UNDEV NAT/G

B59
OKINSHEVICH L.A.,LATIN AMERICA IN SOVIET WRITINGS, 1945-1958: A BIBLIOGRAPHY. USSR LAW ECO/UNDEV LABOR DIPLOM EDU/PROP REV...GEOG SOC 20. PAGE 111 A2287
BIBLIOG WRITING COM L/A+17C

B59
SCHNEIDER J.,TREATY-MAKING POWER OF INTERNATIONAL ORGANIZATIONS. FUT WOR+45 WOR-45 LAW NAT/G JUDGE DIPLOM LEGIT CT/SYS ORD/FREE PWR...INT/LAW JURID GEN/LAWS TOT/POP UNESCO 20 TREATY. PAGE 129 A2639
INT/ORG ROUTINE

B59
SHANNON D.A.,THE DECLINE OF AMERICAN COMMUNISM; A HISTORY OF THE COMMUNIST PARTY OF THE UNITED STATES SINCE 1945. USA+45 LAW SOCIETY LABOR NAT/G WORKER DIPLOM EDU/PROP LEAD...POLICY BIBLIOG 20 KHRUSH/N NEGRO AFL/CIO COLD/WAR COM/PARTY. PAGE 131 A2692
MARXISM POL/PAR ATTIT POPULISM

B59
TUNSTALL W.C.B.,THE COMMONWEALTH AND REGIONAL DEFENCE (PAMPHLET). UK LAW VOL/ASSN PLAN AGREE REGION WAR ORD/FREE 20 CMN/WLTH NATO SEATO TREATY. PAGE 146 A2977
INT/ORG FORCES DIPLOM

S59
HARVEY M.F.,"THE PALESTINE REFUGEE PROBLEM: ELEMENTS OF A SOLUTION." ISLAM LAW INT/ORG DELIB/GP TOP/EX ECO/TAC ROUTINE DRIVE HEALTH LOVE ORD/FREE PWR WEALTH...MAJORIT FAO 20. PAGE 62 A1283
ACT/RES LEGIT PEACE ISRAEL

S59
POTTER P.B.,"OBSTACLES AND ALTERNATIVES TO INTERNATIONAL LAW." WOR+45 NAT/G VOL/ASSN DELIB/GP BAL/PWR DOMIN ROUTINE...JURID VAL/FREE 20. PAGE 117 A2400
INT/ORG LAW DIPLOM INT/LAW

S59
SOHN L.B.,"THE DEFINITION OF AGGRESSION." FUT LAW FORCES LEGIT ADJUD ROUTINE COERCE ORD/FREE PWR ...MAJORIT JURID QUANT COLD/WAR 20. PAGE 135 A2762
INT/ORG CT/SYS DETER SOVEREIGN

S59
TIPTON J.B.,"PARTICIPATION OF THE UNITED STATES IN THE INTERNATIONAL LABOR ORGANIZATION." USA+45 LAW STRUCT ECO/DEV ECO/UNDEV INDUS TEC/DEV ECO/TAC ADMIN PERCEPT ORD/FREE SKILL...STAT HIST/WRIT GEN/METH ILO WORK 20. PAGE 144 A2946
LABOR INT/ORG

B60
AMERICAN ASSOCIATION LAW LIB,INDEX TO FOREIGN LEGAL PERIODICALS. WOR+45 MUNIC...IDEA/COMP 20. PAGE 7 A0139
INDEX LAW JURID DIPLOM

B60
FLORES R.H.,CATALOGO DE TESIS DOCTORALES DE LAS FACULTADES DE LA UNIVERSIDAD DE EL SALVADOR. EL/SALVADR LAW DIPLOM ADMIN LEAD GOV/REL...SOC 19/20. PAGE 47 A0954
BIBLIOG ACADEM L/A+17C NAT/G

B60
HARVARD LAW SCHOOL LIBRARY,CURRENT LEGAL BIBLIOGRAPHY. USA+45 CONSTN LEGIS ADJUD CT/SYS POLICY. PAGE 62 A1279
BIBLIOG JURID LAW INT/LAW

B60
JENNINGS R.,PROGRESS OF INTERNATIONAL LAW. FUT WOR+45 WOR-45 SOCIETY NAT/G VOL/ASSN DELIB/GP DIPLOM EDU/PROP LEGIT COERCE ATTIT DRIVE MORAL ORD/FREE...JURID CONCPT OBS TIME/SEQ TREND GEN/LAWS. PAGE 74 A1509
INT/ORG LAW INT/LAW

B60
LANDHEER B.,ETHICAL VALUES IN INTERNATIONAL DECISION-MAKING. FUT LAW SOCIETY INT/ORG NAT/G DELIB/GP CREATE NAT/LISM ATTIT PERSON...DECISION CONCPT LEAGUE/NAT TOT/POP 20. PAGE 84 A1718
HYPO/EXP POLICY PEACE

B60
LEWIS P.R.,LITERATURE OF THE SOCIAL SCIENCES: AN INTRODUCTORY SURVEY AND GUIDE. UK LAW INDUS DIPLOM INT/TRADE ADMIN...MGT 19/20. PAGE 88 A1802
BIBLIOG/A SOC

L60
LAUTERPACHT E.,"THE SUEZ CANAL SETTLEMENT." FRANCE ISLAM ISRAEL UAR UK BAL/PWR DIPLOM LEGIT...JURID GEN/LAWS ANTHOL SUEZ VAL/FREE 20. PAGE 85 A1747
INT/ORG LAW

S60
MORA J.A.,"THE ORGANIZATION OF AMERICAN STATES." USA+45 LAW ECO/UNDEV VOL/ASSN DELIB/GP PLAN BAL/PWR EDU/PROP ADMIN DRIVE RIGID/FLEX ORD/FREE WEALTH ...TIME/SEQ GEN/LAWS OAS 20. PAGE 103 A2126
L/A+17C INT/ORG REGION

S60
MORALES C.J.,"TRADE AND ECONOMIC INTEGRATION IN LATIN AMERICA." FUT L/A+17C LAW STRATA ECO/UNDEV DIST/IND INDUS LABOR NAT/G LEGIS ECO/TAC ADMIN RIGID/FLEX WEALTH...CONCPT NEW/IDEA CONT/OBS TIME/SEQ WORK 20. PAGE 104 A2128
FINAN INT/TRADE REGION

S60
MUNRO L.,"CAN THE UNITED NATIONS ENFORCE PEACE." WOR+45 LAW INT/ORG VOL/ASSN BAL/PWR LEGIT ARMS/CONT COERCE DETER PEACE PWR...CONCPT REC/INT TREND UN 20 HAMMARSK/D. PAGE 106 A2173
FORCES ORD/FREE

S60
SCHWELB E.,"INTERNATIONAL CONVENTIONS ON HUMAN RIGHTS." FUT WOR+45 LAW CONSTN CULTURE SOCIETY STRUCT VOL/ASSN DELIB/GP PLAN ADJUD SUPEGO LOVE MORAL...SOC CONCPT STAT RECORD HIST/WRIT TREND 20 UN. PAGE 130 A2664
INT/ORG HUM

S60
THOMPSON K.W.,"MORAL PURPOSE IN FOREIGN POLICY: REALITIES AND ILLUSIONS." WOR+45 WOR-45 LAW CULTURE SOCIETY INT/ORG PLAN ADJUD ADMIN COERCE RIGID/FLEX SUPEGO KNOWL ORD/FREE PWR...SOC TREND SOC/EXP TOT/POP 20. PAGE 143 A2930
MORAL JURID DIPLOM

B61
BURDETTE F.L.,POLITICAL SCIENCE: A SELECTED BIBLIOGRAPHY OF BOOKS IN PRINT, WITH ANNOTATIONS (PAMPHLET). LAW LOC/G NAT/G POL/PAR PROVS DIPLOM EDU/PROP ADMIN CHOOSE ATTIT 20. PAGE 21 A0432
BIBLIOG/A GOV/COMP CONCPT ROUTINE

B61
KAPLAN M.A.,THE POLITICAL FOUNDATIONS OF INTERNATIONAL LAW. WOR+45 WOR-45 CULTURE SOCIETY ECO/DEV DIPLOM PERCEPT...TECHNIC METH/CNCPT. PAGE 76 A1563
INT/ORG LAW

B61
MORLEY L.,THE PATCHWORK HISTORY OF FOREIGN AID. KOREA/S USA+45 USSR LAW FINAN INT/ORG TEC/DEV BAL/PWR GIVE 20 COLD/WAR NATO. PAGE 104 A2144
FOR/AID ECO/UNDEV FORCES DIPLOM

B61
PEASLEE A.J.,INTERNATIONAL GOVERNMENTAL ORGANIZATIONS (2 VOLS.). CONSTN VOL/ASSN DIPLOM ...GP/COMP 20 UN OAS EEC EFTA ECSC. PAGE 114 A2345
BIBLIOG INT/ORG INDEX LAW

B61
WARD R.E.,JAPANESE POLITICAL SCIENCE: A GUIDE TO JAPANESE REFERENCE AND RESEARCH MATERIALS (2ND ED.). LAW CONSTN STRATA NAT/G POL/PAR DELIB/GP LEGIS ADMIN CHOOSE GP/REL...INT/LAW 19/20 CHINJAP. PAGE 161 A3282
BIBLIOG/A PHIL/SCI

B61
WECHSLER H.,PRINCIPLES, POLITICS AND FUNDAMENTAL LAW: SELECTED ESSAYS. USA+45 USA-45 LAW SOCIETY NAT/G PROVS DELIB/GP EX/STRUC ACT/RES LEGIT PERSON KNOWL PWR...JURID 20 NUREMBERG. PAGE 162 A3296
CT/SYS CONSTN INT/LAW

L61
SAND P.T.,"AN HISTORICAL SURVEY OF INTERNATIONAL AIR LAW SINCE 1944." USA+45 USA-45 WOR+45 WOR-45 SOCIETY ECO/DEV NAT/G CONSULT EX/STRUC ACT/RES PLAN LEGIT ROUTINE...JURID CONCPT METH/CNCPT TREND 20. PAGE 127 A2598
INT/ORG LAW INT/LAW SPACE

S61
CASTANEDA J.,"THE UNDERDEVELOPED NATIONS AND THE DEVELOPMENT OF INTERNATIONAL LAW." FUT UNIV LAW ACT/RES FOR/AID LEGIT PERCEPT SKILL...JURID METH/CNCPT TIME/SEQ TOT/POP 20 UN. PAGE 25 A0507
INT/ORG ECO/UNDEV PEACE INT/LAW

S61
JACKSON E.,"THE FUTURE DEVELOPMENT OF THE UNITED NATIONS: SOME SUGGESTIONS FOR RESEARCH." FUT LAW CONSTN ECO/DEV FINAN PEACE WEALTH...WELF/ST CONCPT UN 20. PAGE 72 A1476
INT/ORG PWR

S61
LEWY G.,"SUPERIOR ORDERS, NUCLEAR WARFARE AND THE DICTATES OF CONSCIENCE: THE DILEMMA OF MILITARY OBEDIENCE IN THE ATOMIC." FUT UNIV WOR+45 INTELL SOCIETY FORCES TOP/EX ACT/RES ADMIN ROUTINE NUC/PWR PERCEPT RIGID/FLEX ALL/VALS...POLICY CONCPT 20. PAGE 88 A1805
DETER INT/ORG LAW INT/LAW

S61
LIPSON L.,"AN ARGUMENT ON THE LEGALITY OF RECONNAISSANCE STATELLITES." COM USA+45 USSR WOR+45 AIR INTELL NAT/G CONSULT PLAN DIPLOM LEGIT ROUTINE ATTIT...INT/LAW JURID CONCPT METH/CNCPT TREND COLD/WAR 20. PAGE 90 A1833
INT/ORG LAW SPACE

S61
MACHOWSKI K.,"SELECTED PROBLEMS OF NATIONAL SOVEREIGNTY WITH REFERENCE TO THE LAW OF OUTER SPACE." FUT WOR+45 AIR LAW INTELL SOCIETY ECO/DEV PLAN EDU/PROP DETER DRIVE PERCEPT SOVEREIGN ...POLICY INT/LAW OBS TREND TOT/POP 20. PAGE 92 A1889
UNIV ACT/RES NUC/PWR SPACE

B62
AMERICAN LAW INSTITUTE,FOREIGN RELATIONS LAW OF THE UNITED STATES: RESTATEMENT, SECOND. USA+45 NAT/G LEGIS ADJUD EXEC ROUTINE GOV/REL...INT/LAW JURID CONCPT 20 TREATY. PAGE 7 A0152
PROF/ORG LAW DIPLOM ORD/FREE

B62
BLANSHARD P.,FREEDOM AND CATHOLIC POWER IN SPAIN AND PORTUGAL: AN AMERICAN INTERPRETATION. AFR PORTUGAL SPAIN USA+45 LAW LABOR DIPLOM EDU/PROP DISCRIM ISOLAT TOTALISM 20 CHURCH/STA. PAGE 15 A0309
GP/REL FASCISM CATHISM PWR

B62
BLAUSTEIN A.P.,MANUAL ON FOREIGN LEGAL PERIODICALS AND THEIR INDEX. WOR+45 DIPLOM 20. PAGE 15 A0310
BIBLIOG INDEX LAW JURID

B62
CARLSTON K.S.,LAW AND ORGANIZATION IN WORLD SOCIETY. WOR+45 FINAN ECO/TAC DOMIN LEGIT CT/SYS ROUTINE COERCE ORD/FREE PWR WEALTH...PLURIST DECISION JURID MGT METH/CNCPT GEN/LAWS 20. PAGE 24 A0487
INT/ORG LAW

B62
COSTA RICA UNIVERSIDAD BIBL,LISTA DE TESIS DE GRADO DE LA UNIVERSIDAD DE COSTA RICA. COSTA/RICA LAW LOC/G ADMIN LEAD...SOC 20. PAGE 31 A0631
BIBLIOG/A NAT/G DIPLOM ECO/UNDEV

B62
HADWEN J.G.,HOW UNITED NATIONS DECISIONS ARE MADE. WOR+45 LAW EDU/PROP LEGIT ADMIN PWR...DECISION SELF/OBS GEN/LAWS UN 20. PAGE 59 A1212
INT/ORG ROUTINE

B62
KAHN H.,THINKING ABOUT THE UNTHINKABLE. FUT USA+45 LAW NAT/G CONSULT FORCES ACT/RES CREATE PLAN TEC/DEV BAL/PWR DIPLOM EDU/PROP ARMS/CONT DETER ATTIT...CONCPT OBS TREND COLD/WAR 20. PAGE 76 A1547
INT/ORG ORD/FREE NUC/PWR PEACE

B62
KIDDER F.E.,THESES ON PAN AMERICAN TOPICS. LAW CULTURE NAT/G SECT DIPLOM HEALTH...ART/METH GEOG SOC 13/20. PAGE 79 A1615
BIBLIOG CHRIST-17C L/A+17C SOCIETY

B62
LAQUEUR W.,THE FUTURE OF COMMUNIST SOCIETY. CHINA/COM USSR LAW ECO/DEV NAT/G POL/PAR PLAN PROB/SOLV DIPLOM LEAD...POLICY CONCPT IDEA/COMP ANTHOL 20. PAGE 85 A1731
MARXISM COM FUT SOCIETY

B62
LEVY H.V.,LIBERDADE E JUSTICA SOCIAL (2ND ED.). BRAZIL COM L/A+17C USSR INT/ORG PARTIC GP/REL WEALTH 20 UN COM/PARTY. PAGE 88 A1798
ORD/FREE MARXISM CAP/ISM LAW

B62
MANNING C.A.W.,THE NATURE OF INTERNATIONAL SOCIETY. FUT LAW NAT/G TOP/EX NAT/LISM PEACE PERCEPT PERSON ALL/VALS PLURISM...METH/CNCPT MYTH HYPO/EXP TOT/POP 20. PAGE 94 A1926
INT/ORG SOCIETY SIMUL DIPLOM

B62
ROSENNE S.,THE WORLD COURT: WHAT IT IS AND HOW IT WORKS. WOR+45 WOR-45 LAW CONSTN JUDGE EDU/PROP LEGIT ROUTINE CHOOSE PEACE ORD/FREE...JURID OBS TIME/SEQ CHARTS UN TOT/POP VAL/FREE 20. PAGE 124 A2538
INT/ORG ADJUD INT/LAW

B62
SCHWARZENBERGER G.,THE FRONTIERS OF INTERNATIONAL LAW. WOR+45 WOR-45 NAT/G LEGIT CT/SYS ROUTINE MORAL ORD/FREE PWR...JURID SOC GEN/METH 20 COLD/WAR. PAGE 130 A2661
INT/ORG LAW INT/LAW

B62
TRISKA J.F.,THE THEORY, LAW, AND POLICY OF SOVIET TREATIES. WOR+45 WOR-45 CONSTN INT/ORG NAT/G VOL/ASSN DOMIN LEGIT COERCE ATTIT PWR RESPECT ...POLICY JURID CONCPT OBS SAMP TIME/SEQ TREND GEN/LAWS 20. PAGE 145 A2966
COM LAW INT/LAW USSR

B62
UNECA LIBRARY,NEW ACQUISITIONS IN THE UNECA LIBRARY. LAW NAT/G PLAN PROB/SOLV TEC/DEV ADMIN REGION...GEOG SOC 20 UN. PAGE 147 A3009
BIBLIOG AFR ECO/UNDEV INT/ORG

B62
US CONGRESS,LEGISLATIVE HISTORY OF UNITED STATES TAX CONVENTIONS(VOL. 1). USA+45 USA-45 DELIB/GP WEALTH...CHARTS 20 CONGRESS. PAGE 150 A3061
TAX LEGIS LAW DIPLOM

B62
US CONGRESS,COMMUNICATIONS SATELLITE LEGISLATION: HEARINGS BEFORE COMM ON AERON AND SPACE SCIENCES ON BILLS S2550 AND 2814. WOR+45 LAW VOL/ASSN PLAN DIPLOM CONTROL OWN PEACE...NEW/IDEA CONGRESS NASA. PAGE 150 A3062
SPACE COM/IND ADJUD GOV/REL

L62
CORET A.,"L'INDEPENDANCE DU SAMOA OCCIDENTAL." S/ASIA LAW INT/ORG EXEC ALL/VALS SAMOA UN 20. PAGE 31 A0622
NAT/G STRUCT SOVEREIGN

L62
GROSS L.,"IMMUNITIES AND PRIVILEGES OF DELIGATIONS TO THE UNITED NATIONS." USA+45 WOR+45 STRATA NAT/G VOL/ASSN CONSULT DIPLOM EDU/PROP ROUTINE RESPECT ...POLICY INT/LAW CONCPT UN 20. PAGE 57 A1176
INT/ORG LAW ELITES

L62
MURACCIOLE L.,"LA BANQUE CENTRALE DES ETATS DE L'AFRIQUE DE L'OUEST." AFR LAW ECO/UNDEV INT/ORG NAT/G CONSULT ECO/TAC ROUTINE...CHARTS 20. PAGE 106 A2175
ISLAM FINAN INT/TRADE

L62
PETKOFF D.K.,"RECOGNITION AND NON-RECOGNITION OF STATES AND GOVERNMENTS IN INTERNATIONAL LAW." ASIA COM USA+45 WOR+45 NAT/G ACT/RES DIPLOM DOMIN LEGIT COERCE ORD/FREE PWR...CONCPT GEN/LAWS 20. PAGE 115 A2369
INT/ORG LAW INT/LAW

L62
SCHWERIN K.,"LAW LIBRARIES AND FOREIGN LAW COLLECTION IN THE USA." USA+45 USA-45...INT/LAW STAT 20. PAGE 130 A2667
BIBLIOG LAW ACADEM ADMIN

S62
BIERZANECK R.,"LA NON-RECONAISSANCE ET LE DROIT INTERNATIONAL CONTEMPORAIN." EUR+WWI FUT WOR+45 LAW ECO/DEV ATTIT RIGID/FLEX...CONCPT TIME/SEQ TOT/POP 20. PAGE 14 A0286
EDU/PROP JURID DIPLOM INT/LAW

S62
CRANE R.D.,"LAW AND STRATEGY IN SPACE." FUT USA+45 WOR+45 AIR LAW INT/ORG NAT/G FORCES ACT/RES PLAN BAL/PWR LEGIT ARMS/CONT COERCE ORD/FREE...POLICY INT/LAW JURID SOC/EXP 20 TREATY. PAGE 32 A0656
CONCPT SPACE

S62
CRANE R.D.,"SOVIET ATTITUDE TOWARD INTERNATIONAL SPACE LAW." COM FUT USA+45 USSR AIR CONSTN DELIB/GP DOMIN PWR...JURID TREND TOT/POP 20. PAGE 32 A0657
LAW ATTIT INT/LAW SPACE

S62
GREEN L.C.,"POLITICAL OFFENSES, WAR CRIMES AND EXTRADITION." WOR+45 YUGOSLAVIA INT/ORG LEGIT ROUTINE WAR ORD/FREE SOVEREIGN...JURID NAZI 20 INTERPOL. PAGE 55 A1138
LAW CONCPT INT/LAW

S62
GREENSPAN M.,"INTERNATIONAL LAW AND ITS PROTECTION FOR PARTICIPANTS IN UNCONVENTIONAL WARFARE." WOR+45 LAW INT/ORG NAT/G POL/PAR COERCE REV ORD/FREE ...INT/LAW TOT/POP 20. PAGE 56 A1143
FORCES JURID GUERRILLA WAR

S62
JOHNSON O.H.,"THE ENGLISH TRADITION IN INTERNATIONAL LAW." CHRIST-17C MOD/EUR EDU/PROP LEGIT CT/SYS ORD/FREE...JURID CONCPT TIME/SEQ. PAGE 75 A1526
LAW INT/LAW UK

S62
LISSITZYN O.J.,"SOME LEGAL IMPLICATIONS OF THE U-2 AND RB-47 INCIDENTS." FUT USA+45 USSR WOR+45 AIR NAT/G DIPLOM LEGIT MORAL ORD/FREE SOVEREIGN...JURID GEN/LAWS GEN/METH COLD/WAR 20 U-2. PAGE 90 A1840
LAW CONCPT SPACE INT/LAW

S62
MANGIN G.,"LES ACCORDS DE COOPERATION EN MATIERE DE JUSTICE ENTRE LA FRANCE ET LES ETATS AFRICAINS ET MALGACHE." AFR ISLAM WOR+45 STRUCT ECO/UNDEV NAT/G DELIB/GP PERCEPT ALL/VALS...JURID MGT TIME/SEQ 20. PAGE 94 A1919
INT/ORG LAW FRANCE

S62
VASAK K.,"DE LA CONVENTION EUROPEENNE A LA CONVENTION AFRICAINE DES DROITS DE L'HOMME." AFR ISLAM WOR+45 LAW CONSTN ECO/UNDEV INT/ORG PERCEPT ALL/VALS 20. PAGE 158 A3223
DELIB/GP CONCPT COLONIAL

S62
VIGNES D.,"L'AUTORITE DES TRAITES INTERNATIONAUX EN
STRUCT

DROIT INTERNE." EUR+WWI UNIV LAW CONSTN INTELL NAT/G POL/PAR DIPLOM ATTIT PERCEPT ALL/VALS ...POLICY INT/LAW JURID CONCPT TIME/SEQ 20 TREATY. PAGE 159 A3233
LEGIT FRANCE

B63
DECOTTIGNIES R.,LES NATIONALITES AFRICAINES. AFR NAT/G PROB/SOLV DIPLOM COLONIAL ORD/FREE...CHARTS GOV/COMP 20. PAGE 35 A0721
NAT/LISM JURID LEGIS LAW

B63
ELIAS T.O.,GOVERNMENT AND POLITICS IN AFRICA. CONSTN CULTURE SOCIETY NAT/G POL/PAR DIPLOM REPRESENT PERSON...SOC TREND BIBLIOG 4/20. PAGE 41 A0837
AFR NAT/LISM COLONIAL LAW

B63
FALK R.A.,LAW, MORALITY, AND WAR IN THE CONTEMPORARY WORLD. WOR+45 LAW INT/ORG EX/STRUC FORCES EDU/PROP LEGIT DETER NUC/PWR MORAL ORD/FREE ...JURID TOT/POP 20. PAGE 43 A0888
ADJUD ARMS/CONT PEACE INT/LAW

B63
GREAT BRITAIN CENTRAL OFF INF,CONSULTATION AND CO-OPERATION IN THE COMMONWEALTH. LAW R+D FORCES PLAN EDU/PROP CONFER INGP/REL...GEOG CENSUS 19/20 CMN/WLTH. PAGE 55 A1133
DIPLOM DELIB/GP VOL/ASSN REGION

B63
HALEY A.G.,SPACE LAW AND GOVERNMENT. FUT USA+45 WOR+45 LEGIS ACT/RES CREATE ATTIT RIGID/FLEX ORD/FREE PWR SOVEREIGN...POLICY JURID CONCPT CHARTS VAL/FREE 20. PAGE 60 A1226
INT/ORG LAW SPACE

B63
JUDD P.,AFRICAN INDEPENDENCE: THE EXPLODING EMERGENCE OF THE NEW AFRICAN NATIONS. AFR UK LAW CONSTN CULTURE KIN DIPLOM ATTIT...CHARTS BIBLIOG 20 UN DEGAULLE/C NEGRO THIRD/WRLD. PAGE 75 A1542
ORD/FREE POLICY DOMIN LOC/G

B63
LADOR-LEDERER J.J.,INTERNATIONAL NON-GOVERNMENTAL ORGANIZATIONS: A STUDY IN AUTONOMOUS ORGANIZATION AND IUS GENTIUM. LAW DELIB/GP LEGIS DIPLOM 20. PAGE 83 A1709
INT/ORG INT/LAW INGP/REL VOL/ASSN

B63
LERCHE C.O. JR.,CONCEPTS OF INTERNATIONAL POLITICS. WOR+45 WOR-45 LAW DELIB/GP EX/STRUC TEC/DEV ECO/TAC INT/TRADE LEGIT ROUTINE COERCE ATTIT ORD/FREE PWR RESPECT...STERTYP GEN/LAWS VAL/FREE. PAGE 87 A1782
INT/ORG WAR

B63
LIVNEH E.,ISRAEL LEGAL BIBLIOGRAPHY IN EUROPEAN LANGUAGES. ISRAEL LOC/G JUDGE TAX...INT/LAW 20. PAGE 90 A1846
BIBLIOG LAW NAT/G CONSTN

B63
LYONS F.S.L.,INTERNATIONALISM IN EUROPE 1815-1914. LAW AGRI COM/IND DIST/IND LABOR SECT INT/TRADE TARIFFS...BIBLIOG 19/20. PAGE 92 A1880
DIPLOM MOD/EUR INT/ORG

B63
WALKER A.A.,OFFICIAL PUBLICATIONS OF SIERRA LEONE AND GAMBIA. GAMBIA SIER/LEONE UK LAW CONSTN LEGIS PLAN BUDGET DIPLOM...SOC SAMP CON/ANAL 20. PAGE 160 A3262
BIBLIOG NAT/G COLONIAL ADMIN

L63
LISSITZYN O.J.,"INTERNATIONAL LAW IN A DIVIDED WORLD." FUT WOR+45 CONSTN CULTURE ECO/DEV ECO/UNDEV DIST/IND NAT/G FORCES ECO/TAC LEGIT ADJUD ADMIN COERCE ATTIT HEALTH MORAL ORD/FREE PWR RESPECT WEALTH VAL/FREE. PAGE 90 A1841
INT/ORG LAW

L63
PADELFORD N.J.,"FINANCIAL CRISIS AND THE UNITED NATIONS." FUT USSR WOR+45 LAW CONSTN FINAN INT/ORG DELIB/GP FORCES PLAN BUDGET DIPLOM COST WEALTH ...STAT CHARTS UN CONGO 20. PAGE 113 A2311
CREATE ECO/TAC

L63
SZASZY E.,"L'EVOLUTION DES PRINCIPES GENERAUX DU DROIT INTERNATIONAL PRIVE DANS LES PAYS DE DEMOCRATIE POPULAIRE." COM FUT WOR+45 LAW ECO/DEV PERF/ART POL/PAR PROF/ORG ECO/TAC INT/TRADE EDU/PROP ATTIT RIGID/FLEX ALL/VALS SOCISM...JURID TREND GEN/LAWS WORK 20. PAGE 141 A2876
DIPLOM TOTALISM INT/LAW INT/ORG

S63
ALGER C.F.,"HYPOTHESES ON RELATIONSHIPS BETWEEN THE ORGANIZATION OF INTERNATIONAL SOCIETY AND INTERNATIONAL ORDER." WOR+45 WOR-45 ORD/FREE PWR ...JURID GEN/LAWS VAL/FREE 20. PAGE 6 A0119
INT/ORG LAW

S63
BECHHOEFER B.G.,"UNITED NATIONS PROCEDURES IN CASE OF VIOLATIONS OF DISARMAMENT AGREEMENTS." COM USA+45 USSR LAW CONSTN NAT/G EX/STRUC FORCES LEGIS BAL/PWR EDU/PROP CT/SYS ARMS/CONT ORD/FREE PWR ...POLICY STERTYP UN VAL/FREE 20. PAGE 12 A0245
INT/ORG DELIB/GP

S63
CLEVELAND H.,"CRISIS DIPLOMACY." USA+45 WOR+45 LAW FORCES TASK NUC/PWR PWR 20. PAGE 27 A0551
DECISION DIPLOM PROB/SOLV POLICY

S63
FRIEDMANN W.G.,"THE USES OF 'GENERAL PRINCIPLES' IN THE DEVELOPMENT OF INTERNATIONAL LAW." WOR+45 NAT/G DIPLOM INT/TRADE LEGIT ROUTINE RIGID/FLEX ORD/FREE ...JURID CONCPT STERTYP GEN/METH 20. PAGE 49 A1005
LAW INT/LAW INT/ORG

S63
GARDNER R.N.,"COOPERATION IN OUTER SPACE." FUT USSR WOR+45 AIR LAW COM/IND CONSULT DELIB/GP CREATE KNOWL 20 TREATY. PAGE 51 A1045
INT/ORG ACT/RES PEACE SPACE

S63
HARNETTY P.,"CANADA, SOUTH AFRICA AND THE COMMONWEALTH." CANADA SOUTH/AFR LAW INT/ORG VOL/ASSN DELIB/GP LEGIS TOP/EX ECO/TAC LEGIT DRIVE MORAL...CONCPT CMN/WLTH 20. PAGE 62 A1263
AFR ATTIT

S63
MACWHINNEY E.,"LES CONCEPT SOVIETIQUE DE 'COEXISTENCE PACIFIQUE' ET LES RAPPORTS JURIDIQUES ENTRE L'URSS ET LES ETATS OCIDENTAUX." COM FUT WOR+45 LAW CULTURE INTELL POL/PAR ACT/RES BAL/PWR ...INT/LAW 20. PAGE 93 A1903
NAT/G CONCPT DIPLOM USSR

S63
TALLON D.,"L'ETUDE DU DROIT COMPARE COMME MOYEN DE RECHERCHER LES MATIERES SUSCEPTIBLES D'UNIFICATION INTERNATIONALE." WOR+45 LAW SOCIETY VOL/ASSN CONSULT LEGIT CT/SYS RIGID/FLEX KNOWL 20. PAGE 141 A2884
INT/ORG JURID INT/LAW

S63
WEISSBERG G.,"MAPS AS EVIDENCE IN INTERNATIONAL BOUNDARY DISPUTES: A REAPPRAISAL." CHINA/COM EUR+WWI INDIA MOD/EUR S/ASIA INT/ORG NAT/G LEGIT PERCEPT...JURID CHARTS 20. PAGE 163 A3311
LAW GEOG SOVEREIGN

S63
WENGLER W.,"LES CONFLITS DE LOIS ET LE PRINCIPE D'EGALITE." UNIV LAW SOCIETY ACT/RES LEGIT ATTIT PERCEPT 20. PAGE 163 A3318
JURID CONCPT INT/LAW

B64
AHLUWALIA K.,THE LEGAL STATUS, PRIVILEGES AND IMMUNITIES OF SPECIALIZED AGENCIES OF UN AND CERTAIN OTHER INTERNATIONAL ORGANIZATIONS. WOR+45 LAW CONSULT DELIB/GP FORCES. PAGE 5 A0102
PRIVIL DIPLOM INT/ORG INT/LAW

B64
COHEN M.,LAW AND POLITICS IN SPACE: SPECIFIC AND URGENT PROBLEMS IN THE LAW OF OUTER SPACE. CHINA/COM COM USA+45 USSR WOR+45 COM/IND INT/ORG NAT/G LEGIT NUC/PWR ATTIT BIO/SOC...JURID CONCPT CONGRESS 20 STALIN/J. PAGE 28 A0561
DELIB/GP LAW INT/LAW SPACE

B64
COHEN M.L.,SELECTED BIBLIOGRAPHY OF FOREIGN AND INTERNATIONAL LAW....IDEA/COMP METH/COMP 20. PAGE 28 A0562
BIBLIOG/A JURID LAW INT/LAW

B64
DIAS R.W.M.,A BIBLIOGRAPHY OF JURISPRUDENCE (2ND ED.). VOL/ASSN LEGIS ADJUD CT/SYS OWN...INT/LAW 18/20. PAGE 37 A0754
BIBLIOG/A JURID LAW CONCPT

B64
FALK R.A.,THE ROLE OF DOMESTIC COURTS IN THE INTERNATIONAL LEGAL ORDER. FUT WOR+45 INT/ORG NAT/G JUDGE EDU/PROP LEGIT CT/SYS...POLICY RELATIV JURID CONCPT GEN/LAWS 20. PAGE 43 A0889
LAW INT/LAW

B64
GARDNER L.C.,ECONOMIC ASPECTS OF NEW DEAL DIPLOMACY. USA-45 WOR-45 LAW ECO/DEV INT/ORG NAT/G VOL/ASSN LEGIS TOP/EX EDU/PROP ORD/FREE PWR WEALTH ...POLICY TIME/SEQ VAL/FREE 20 ROOSEVLT/F. PAGE 51 A1043
ECO/TAC DIPLOM

B64
GJUPANOVIC H.,LEGAL SOURCES AND BIBLIOGRAPHY OF YUGOSLAVIA. COM YUGOSLAVIA LAW LEGIS DIPLOM ADMIN PARL/PROC REGION CRIME CENTRAL 20. PAGE 53 A1078
BIBLIOG/A JURID CONSTN ADJUD

B64
HEKHUIS D.J.,INTERNATIONAL STABILITY: MILITARY, ECONOMIC AND POLITICAL DIMENSIONS. FUT WOR+45 LAW ECO/UNDEV INT/ORG NAT/G VOL/ASSN FORCES ACT/RES BAL/PWR PWR WEALTH...STAT UN 20. PAGE 64 A1310
TEC/DEV DETER REGION

B64
JOHNSON L.B.,MY HOPE FOR AMERICA. FUT USA+45 USSR LAW PLAN DIPLOM GIVE INCOME PEACE ATTIT ORD/FREE WEALTH 20 JOHNSON/LB PRESIDENT DEMOCRAT. PAGE 74 A1525
POLICY POL/PAR NAT/G GOV/REL

B64
NASA,PROCEEDINGS OF CONFERENCE ON THE LAW OF SPACE AND OF SATELLITE COMMUNICATIONS: CHICAGO 1963. FUT WOR+45 DELIB/GP PROB/SOLV TEC/DEV CONFER ADJUD NUC/PWR...POLICY IDEA/COMP 20 NASA. PAGE 107 A2197
SPACE COM/IND LAW DIPLOM

B64
NICE R.W.,TREASURY OF LAW. WOR+45 WOR-45 SECT ADJUD MORAL ORD/FREE...INT/LAW JURID PHIL/SCI ANTHOL. PAGE 108 A2227
LAW WRITING PERS/REL DIPLOM

B64
PERKINS D.,THE AMERICAN DEMOCRACY: ITS RISE TO POWER. ASIA USSR LAW CULTURE FINAN EDU/PROP COLONIAL CHOOSE...POLICY CHARTS BIBLIOG WORSHIP PRESIDENT 15/20 NEGRO. PAGE 115 A2362
LOC/G ECO/TAC WAR DIPLOM

B64
RAGHAVAN M.D.,INDIA IN CEYLONESE HISTORY, SOCIETY
DIPLOM

AND CULTURE. CEYLON INDIA S/ASIA LAW SOCIETY INT/TRADE ATTIT...ART/METH JURID SOC LING 20. PAGE 119 A2433
CULTURE SECT STRUCT

B64
RICHARDSON I.L.,BIBLIOGRAFIA BRASILEIRA DE ADMINISTRACAO PUBLICA E ASSUNTOS CORRELATOS. BRAZIL CONSTN FINAN LOC/G NAT/G POL/PAR PLAN DIPLOM RECEIVE ATTIT...METH 20. PAGE 121 A2474
BIBLIOG MGT ADMIN LAW

B64
SCHWARTZ M.D.,CONFERENCE ON SPACE SCIENCE AND SPACE LAW. FUT COM/IND NAT/G FORCES ACT/RES PLAN BUDGET DIPLOM NUC/PWR WEAPON...POLICY ANTHOL 20. PAGE 130 A2658
SPACE LAW PEACE TEC/DEV

B64
SZLADITS C.,BIBLIOGRAPHY ON FOREIGN AND COMPARATIVE LAW: BOOKS AND ARTICLES IN ENGLISH (SUPPLEMENT 1962). FINAN INDUS JUDGE LICENSE ADMIN CT/SYS PARL/PROC OWN...INT/LAW CLASSIF METH/COMP NAT/COMP 20. PAGE 141 A2877
BIBLIOG/A JURID ADJUD LAW

B64
TAUBENFELD H.J.,SPACE AND SOCIETY. USA+45 LAW FORCES CREATE TEC/DEV ADJUD CONTROL COST PEACE ...PREDICT ANTHOL 20. PAGE 142 A2895
SPACE SOCIETY ADJUST DIPLOM

B64
TURNER M.C.,LIBROS EN VENTA EN HISPANOAMERICA Y ESPANA. SPAIN LAW CONSTN CULTURE ADMIN LEAD...HUM SOC 20. PAGE 146 A2983
BIBLIOG L/A+17C NAT/G DIPLOM

B64
US AIR FORCE ACADEMY ASSEMBLY,OUTER SPACE: FINAL REPORT APRIL 1-4, 1964. FUT USA+45 WOR+45 LAW DELIB/GP CONFER ARMS/CONT WAR PEACE ATTIT MORAL ...ANTHOL 20 NASA. PAGE 150 A3055
SPACE CIVMIL/REL NUC/PWR DIPLOM

B64
WITHERELL J.W.,OFFICIAL PUBLICATIONS OF FRENCH EQUATORIAL AFRICA, FRENCH CAMEROONS, AND TOGO, 1946-1958 (PAMPHLET). CAMEROON CHAD FRANCE GABON TOGO LAW ECO/UNDEV EXTR/IND INT/TRADE...GEOG HEAL 20. PAGE 165 A3370
BIBLIOG/A AFR NAT/G ADMIN

B64
WRIGHT Q.,A STUDY OF WAR. LAW NAT/G PROB/SOLV BAL/PWR NAT/LISM PEACE ATTIT SOVEREIGN...CENSUS SOC/INTEG. PAGE 168 A3419
WAR CONCPT DIPLOM CONTROL

L64
BERKS R.N.,"THE US AND WEAPONS CONTROL." WOR+45 LAW INT/ORG NAT/G LEGIS EXEC COERCE PEACE ATTIT RIGID/FLEX ALL/VALS PWR...POLICY TOT/POP 20. PAGE 13 A0273
USA+45 PLAN ARMS/CONT

L64
POUNDS N.J.G.,"THE POLITICS OF PARTITION." AFR ASIA COM EUR+WWI FUT ISLAM S/ASIA USA-45 LAW ECO/DEV ECO/UNDEV AGRI INDUS INT/ORG POL/PAR PROVS SECT FORCES TOP/EX EDU/PROP LEGIT ATTIT MORAL ORD/FREE PWR RESPECT WEALTH. PAGE 117 A2402
NAT/G NAT/LISM

S64
ASHRAF S.,"INDIA AND WORLD AFFAIRS: AN ANNUAL BIBLIOGRAPHY, 1962." WOR+45 LAW ECO/UNDEV INT/ORG FORCES PLAN ECO/TAC COERCE ORD/FREE PWR WEALTH ...HIST/WRIT VAL/FREE. PAGE 9 A0188
S/ASIA NAT/G

S64
CARNEGIE ENDOWMENT INT. PEACE,"HUMAN RIGHTS (ISSUES BEFORE THE NINETEENTH GENERAL ASSEMBLY)." AFR WOR+45 LAW CONSTN NAT/G EDU/PROP GP/REL DISCRIM PEACE ATTIT MORAL ORD/FREE...INT/LAW PSY CONCPT RECORD UN 20. PAGE 24 A0492
INT/ORG PERSON RACE/REL

S64
CARNEGIE ENDOWMENT INT. PEACE,"LEGAL QUESTIONS (ISSUES BEFORE THE NINETEENTH GENERAL ASSEMBLY)." WOR+45 CONSTN NAT/G DELIB/GP ADJUD PEACE MORAL ORD/FREE...RECORD UN 20 TREATY. PAGE 24 A0494
INT/ORG LAW INT/LAW

S64
CRANE R.D.,"BASIC PRINCIPLES IN SOVIET SPACE LAW." FUT WOR+45 AIR INT/ORG DIPLOM DOMIN ARMS/CONT COERCE NUC/PWR PEACE ATTIT DRIVE PWR...INT/LAW METH/CNCPT NEW/IDEA OBS TREND GEN/LAWS VAL/FREE MARX/KARL 20. PAGE 32 A0659
COM LAW USSR SPACE

S64
GINSBURGS G.,"WARS OF NATIONAL LIBERATION - THE SOVIET THESIS." COM USSR WOR+45 WOR-45 LAW CULTURE INT/ORG DIPLOM LEGIT COLONIAL GUERRILLA WAR NAT/LISM ATTIT PERSON MORAL PWR...JURID OBS TREND MARX/KARL 20. PAGE 53 A1075
COERCE CONCPT INT/LAW REV

S64
GREENBERG S.,"JUDAISM AND WORLD JUSTICE." MEDIT-7 WOR+45 LAW CULTURE SOCIETY INT/ORG NAT/G FORCES EDU/PROP ATTIT DRIVE PERSON SUPEGO ALL/VALS ...POLICY PSY CONCPT GEN/LAWS JEWS. PAGE 55 A1140
SECT JURID PEACE

S64
KARPOV P.V.,"PEACEFUL COEXISTENCE AND INTERNATIONAL LAW." WOR+45 LAW SOCIETY INT/ORG VOL/ASSN FORCES CREATE CAP/ISM DIPLOM ADJUD NUC/PWR PEACE MORAL ORD/FREE PWR MARXISM...MARXIST JURID CONCPT OBS TREND COLD/WAR MARX/KARL 20. PAGE 77 A1568
COM ATTIT INT/LAW USSR

S64
KHAN M.Z.,"ISLAM AND INTERNATIONAL RELATIONS." FUT WOR+45 LAW CULTURE SOCIETY NAT/G SECT DELIB/GP FORCES EDU/PROP ATTIT PERSON SUPEGO ALL/VALS ...POLICY PSY CONCPT MYTH HIST/WRIT GEN/LAWS. PAGE 78 A1608
ISLAM INT/ORG DIPLOM

S64
LIPSON L.,"PEACEFUL COEXISTENCE." COM USSR WOR+45 LAW INT/ORG DIPLOM LEGIT ADJUD ORD/FREE...CONCPT OBS TREND GEN/LAWS VAL/FREE COLD/WAR 20. PAGE 90 A1834
ATTIT JURID INT/LAW PEACE

S64
MAGGS P.B.,"SOVIET VIEWPOINT ON NUCLEAR WEAPONS IN INTERNATIONAL LAW." USSR WOR+45 INT/ORG FORCES DIPLOM ARMS/CONT ATTIT ORD/FREE PWR...POLICY JURID CONCPT OBS TREND CON/ANAL GEN/LAWS VAL/FREE 20. PAGE 93 A1905
COM LAW INT/LAW NUC/PWR

S64
SCHWELB E.,"OPERATION OF THE EUROPEAN CONVENTION ON HUMAN RIGHTS." EUR+WWI LAW SOCIETY CREATE EDU/PROP ADJUD ADMIN PEACE ATTIT ORD/FREE PWR...POLICY INT/LAW CONCPT OBS GEN/LAWS UN VAL/FREE ILO 20 ECHR. PAGE 130 A2665
INT/ORG MORAL

S64
SINGH N.,"THE CONTEMPORARY PRACTICE OF INDIA IN THE FIELD OF INTERNATIONAL LAW." INDIA S/ASIA INT/ORG NAT/G DOMIN EDU/PROP LEGIT KNOWL...CONCPT TOT/POP 20. PAGE 133 A2734
LAW ATTIT DIPLOM INT/LAW

S64
SKUBISZEWSKI K.,"FORMS OF PARTICIPATION OF INTERNATIONAL ORGANIZATION IN THE LAW MAKING PROCESS." FUT WOR+45 NAT/G DELIB/GP DOMIN LEGIT KNOWL PWR...JURID TREND 20. PAGE 134 A2740
INT/ORG LAW INT/LAW

S64
TRISKA J.F.,"SOVIET TREATY LAW: A QUANTITATIVE ANALYSIS." WOR+45 LAW ECO/UNDEV AGRI COM/IND INDUS CREATE TEC/DEV DIPLOM ATTIT PWR WEALTH...JURID SAMP TIME/SEQ TREND CHARTS VAL/FREE 20 TREATY. PAGE 145 A2967
COM ECO/TAC INT/LAW USSR

B65
FALK R.A.,THE AFTERMATH OF SABBATINO: BACKGROUND PAPERS AND PROCEEDINGS OF SEVENTH HAMMARSKJOLD FORUM. USA+45 LAW ACT/RES ADJUD ROLE...BIBLIOG 20 EXPROPRIAT SABBATINO HARLAN/JM. PAGE 44 A0891
SOVEREIGN CT/SYS INT/LAW OWN

B65
HARMON R.B.,POLITICAL SCIENCE: A BIBLIOGRAPHICAL GUIDE TO THE LITERATURE. WOR+45 WOR-45 R+D INT/ORG LOC/G NAT/G DIPLOM ADMIN...CONCPT METH. PAGE 61 A1261
BIBLIOG POL/PAR LAW GOV/COMP

B65
MORGENTHAU H.,MORGENTHAU DIARY (CHINA) (2 VOLS.). ASIA USA+45 USA-45 LAW DELIB/GP EX/STRUC PLAN FOR/AID INT/TRADE CONFER WAR MARXISM 20 CHINJAP. PAGE 104 A2136
DIPLOM ADMIN

B65
MOSTECKY V.,SOVIET LEGAL BIBLIOGRAPHY. USSR LEGIS PRESS WRITING CONFER ADJUD CT/SYS REV MARXISM ...INT/LAW JURID DICTIONARY 20. PAGE 105 A2155
BIBLIOG/A LAW COM CONSTN

B65
SOPER T.,EVOLVING COMMONWEALTH. AFR CANADA INDIA IRELAND UK LAW CONSTN POL/PAR DOMIN CONTROL WAR PWR ...AUD/VIS 18/20 COMMONWLTH OEEC. PAGE 135 A2769
INT/ORG COLONIAL VOL/ASSN

B65
UNESCO,INTERNATIONAL ORGANIZATIONS IN THE SOCIAL SCIENCES(REV. ED.). LAW ADMIN ATTIT...CRIMLGY GEOG INT/LAW PSY SOC STAT 20 UNESCO. PAGE 148 A3024
INT/ORG R+D PROF/ORG ACT/RES

B65
US CONGRESS JT ATOM ENRGY COMM,ATOMIC ENERGY LEGISLATION THROUGH 89TH CONGRESS, 1ST SESSION. USA+45 LAW INT/ORG DELIB/GP BUDGET DIPLOM 20 AEC CONGRESS CASEBOOK EURATOM IAEA. PAGE 150 A3071
NUC/PWR FORCES PEACE LEGIS

B65
VON GLAHN G.,LAW AMONG NATIONS: AN INTRODUCTION TO PUBLIC INTERNATIONAL LAW. WOR+45 WOR-45 INT/ORG NAT/G CREATE ADJUD WAR...GEOG CLASSIF TREND BIBLIOG. PAGE 160 A3250
ACADEM INT/LAW GEN/LAWS LAW

B65
VONGLAHN G.,LAW AMONG NATIONS: AN INTRODUCTION TO PUBLIC INTERNATIONAL LAW. UNIV WOR+45 LAW INT/ORG NAT/G LEGIT EXEC RIGID/FLEX...CONCPT TIME/SEQ GEN/LAWS UN TOT/POP 20. PAGE 160 A3253
CONSTN JURID INT/LAW

B65
WITHERELL J.W.,MADAGASCAR AND ADJACENT ISLANDS; A GUIDE TO OFFICIAL PUBLICATIONS (PAMPHLET). FRANCE MADAGASCAR S/ASIA UK LAW OP/RES PLAN DIPLOM ...POLICY CON/ANAL 19/20. PAGE 165 A3371
BIBLIOG COLONIAL LOC/G ADMIN

L65
MATTHEWS D.G.,"A CURRENT BIBLIOGRAPHY ON ETHIOPIAN AFFAIRS: A SELECT BIBLIOGRAPHY FROM 1950-1964." ETHIOPIA LAW CULTURE ECO/UNDEV INDUS LABOR SECT FORCES DIPLOM CIVMIL/REL RACE/REL...LING STAT 20. PAGE 96 A1969
BIBLIOG/A ADMIN POL/PAR NAT/G

L65
MATTHEWS D.G.,"A CURRENT BIBLIOGRAPHY ON SUDANESE
BIBLIOG

AFFAIRS; A SELECT BIBLIOGRAPHY FROM 1960-1964." SUDAN LAW CULTURE AGRI FINAN INDUS LABOR POL/PAR TEC/DEV FOR/AID RACE/REL LITERACY...LING 20. PAGE 96 A1970 — ECO/UNDEV NAT/G DIPLOM

L65
RUBIN A.P.,"UNITED STATES CONTEMPORARY PRACTICE RELATING TO INTERNATIONAL LAW." USA+45 WOR+45 CONSTN INT/ORG NAT/G DELIB/GP EX/STRUC DIPLOM DOMIN CT/SYS ROUTINE ORD/FREE...CONCPT COLD/WAR 20. PAGE 125 A2558 — LAW LEGIT INT/LAW

S65
GROSS L.,"PROBLEMS OF INTERNATIONAL ADJUDICATION AND COMPLIANCE WITH INTERNATIONAL LAW: SOME SIMPLE SOLUTIONS." WOR+45 SOCIETY NAT/G DOMIN LEGIT ADJUD CT/SYS RIGID/FLEX HEALTH PWR...JURID NEW/IDEA COLD/WAR 20. PAGE 57 A1177 — LAW METH/CNCPT INT/LAW

S65
KHOURI F.J.,"THE JORDON RIVER CONTROVERSY." LAW SOCIETY ECO/UNDEV AGRI FINAN INDUS SECT FORCES ACT/RES PLAN TEC/DEV ECO/TAC EDU/PROP COERCE ATTIT DRIVE PERCEPT RIGID/FLEX ALL/VALS...GEOG SOC MYTH WORK. PAGE 78 A1610 — ISLAM INT/ORG ISRAEL JORDAN

S65
MAC CHESNEY B.,"SOME COMMENTS ON THE 'QUARANTINE' OF CUBA." USA+45 WOR+45 NAT/G BAL/PWR DIPLOM LEGIT ROUTINE ATTIT ORD/FREE...JURID METH/CNCPT 20. PAGE 92 A1883 — INT/ORG LAW CUBA USSR

S65
PRABHAKAR P.,"SURVEY OF RESEARCH AND SOURCE MATERIALS; THE SINO-INDIAN BORDER DISPUTE." CHINA/COM INDIA LAW NAT/G PLAN BAL/PWR WAR...POLICY 20 COLD/WAR. PAGE 117 A2404 — BIBLIOG ASIA S/ASIA DIPLOM

C65
SEARA M.V.,"COSMIC INTERNATIONAL LAW." LAW ACADEM ACT/RES DIPLOM COLONIAL CONTROL NUC/PWR SOVEREIGN ...GEN/LAWS BIBLIOG UN. PAGE 131 A2678 — SPACE INT/LAW IDEA/COMP INT/ORG

B66
AMERICAN JOURNAL COMP LAW,THE AMERICAN JOURNAL OF COMPARATIVE LAW READER. EUR+WWI USA+45 USA-45 LAW CONSTN LOC/G MUNIC NAT/G DIPLOM...ANTHOL 20 SUPREME/CT EURCT/JUST. PAGE 7 A0151 — IDEA/COMP JURID INT/LAW CT/SYS

B66
BESTERMAN T.,A WORLD BIBLIOGRAPHY OF BIBLIOGRAPHIES (4TH ED.). WOR+45 WOR-45 LAW INT/ORG ADMIN CON/ANAL. PAGE 14 A0282 — BIBLIOG/A DIPLOM

B66
BOULDING K.E.,THE IMPACT OF THE SOCIAL SCIENCES. UNIV LAW SOCIETY CREATE PROB/SOLV...TREND WORSHIP. PAGE 17 A0349 — SOC DIPLOM

B66
BROWNLIE I.,PRINCIPLES OF PUBLIC INTERNATIONAL LAW. WOR+45 WOR-45 LAW JUDGE REPAR ADJUD SOVEREIGN ...JURID T. PAGE 20 A0409 — INT/LAW DIPLOM INT/ORG

B66
HAMILTON W.B.,A DECADE OF THE COMMONWEALTH, 1955-1964. UK LAW ELITES FINAN FOR/AID CONFER COLONIAL PWR...GEOG CHARTS ANTHOL 20 CMN/WLTH UN. PAGE 61 A1247 — INT/ORG INGP/REL DIPLOM NAT/G

B66
HAY P.,FEDERALISM AND SUPRANATIONAL ORGANIZATIONS: PATTERNS FOR NEW LEGAL STRUCTURES. EUR+WWI LAW NAT/G VOL/ASSN DIPLOM PWR...NAT/COMP TREATY EEC. PAGE 63 A1294 — SOVEREIGN FEDERAL INT/ORG INT/LAW

B66
HOFMANN L.,UNITED STATES AND CANADIAN PUBLICATIONS ON AFRICA IN 1964. LAW AGRI INDUS SCHOOL...HUM SOC 20. PAGE 66 A1360 — BIBLIOG AFR DIPLOM

B66
LEE L.T.,VIENNA CONVENTION ON CONSULAR RELATIONS. WOR+45 LAW INT/ORG CONFER GP/REL PRIVIL...INT/LAW 20 TREATY VIENNA/CNV. PAGE 86 A1760 — AGREE DIPLOM ADMIN

B66
LEIGH M.B.,CHECK LIST OF HOLDINGS ON BORNEO IN THE CORNELL UNIVERSITY LIBRARIES (PAMPHLET). BORNEO MALAYSIA LAW CONSTN GP/REL SOC. PAGE 86 A1769 — BIBLIOG S/ASIA DIPLOM NAT/G

B66
MULLER C.F.J.,A SELECT BIBLIOGRAPHY OF SOUTH AFRICAN HISTORY; A GUIDE FOR HISTORICAL RESEARCH. SOUTH/AFR UK LAW CONSTN SOCIETY STRUCT AGRI SECT DIPLOM COLONIAL LEAD RACE/REL...POLICY 17/20 NEGRO. PAGE 106 A2167 — BIBLIOG AFR NAT/G

B66
POLLACK R.S.,THE INDIVIDUAL'S RIGHTS AND INTERNATIONAL ORGANIZATION. LAW INT/ORG DELIB/GP SUPEGO...JURID SOC/INTEG 20 TREATY UN. PAGE 117 A2394 — INT/LAW ORD/FREE DIPLOM PERSON

B66
SOCIAL SCIENCE RESEARCH COUN,BIBLIOGRAPHY OF RESEARCH IN THE SOCIAL SCIENCES IN AUSTRALIA 1957-1960. LAW R+D DIPLOM 20 AUSTRAL. PAGE 135 A2758 — BIBLIOG SOC PSY

B66
TINKER H.,SOUTH ASIA. UK LAW ECO/UNDEV AGRI ACADEM SECT DIPLOM EDU/PROP REV WEALTH ALL/IDEOS...CHARTS BIBLIOG GANDHI/M NEHRU/J. PAGE 144 A2945 — S/ASIA COLONIAL TREND

B66
US DEPARTMENT OF STATE,RESEARCH ON AFRICA (EXTERNAL RESEARCH LIST NO 5-25). LAW CULTURE ECO/UNDEV POL/PAR DIPLOM EDU/PROP LEAD REGION MARXISM...GEOG LING WORSHIP 20. PAGE 152 A3094 — BIBLIOG/A ASIA S/ASIA NAT/G

B66
US DEPARTMENT OF STATE,RESEARCH ON THE USSR AND EASTERN EUROPE (EXTERNAL RESEARCH LIST NO 1-25). USSR LAW CULTURE SOCIETY NAT/G TEC/DEV DIPLOM EDU/PROP REGION...GEOG LING. PAGE 152 A3097 — BIBLIOG/A EUR+WWI COM MARXISM

B66
US DEPARTMENT OF STATE,RESEARCH ON WESTERN EUROPE, GREAT BRITAIN, AND CANADA (EXTERNAL RESEARCH LIST NO 3-25). CANADA GERMANY/W UK LAW CULTURE NAT/G POL/PAR FORCES EDU/PROP REGION MARXISM...GEOG SOC WORSHIP 20 CMN/WLTH. PAGE 152 A3098 — BIBLIOG/A EUR+WWI DIPLOM

B66
US SENATE COMM ON FOREIGN REL,ASIAN DEVELOPMENT BANK ACT. USA+45 LAW DIPLOM...CHARTS 20 BLACK/EUG S/EASTASIA. PAGE 156 A3186 — FOR/AID FINAN ECO/UNDEV S/ASIA

L66
SEYLER W.C.,"DOCTORAL DISSERTATIONS IN POLITICAL SCIENCE IN UNIVERSITIES OF THE UNITED STATES AND CANADA." INT/ORG LOC/G ADMIN...INT/LAW MGT GOV/COMP. PAGE 131 A2690 — BIBLIOG LAW NAT/G

S66
CHIU H.,"COMMUNIST CHINA'S ATTITUDE TOWARD INTERNATIONAL LAW" CHINA/COM USSR LAW CONSTN DIPLOM GP/REL 20 LENIN/VI. PAGE 26 A0532 — INT/LAW MARXISM CONCPT IDEA/COMP

S66
MATTHEWS D.G.,"ETHIOPIAN OUTLINE: A BIBLIOGRAPHIC RESEARCH GUIDE." ETHIOPIA LAW STRUCT ECO/UNDEV AGRI LABOR SECT CHIEF DELIB/GP EX/STRUC ADMIN...LING ORG/CHARTS 20. PAGE 96 A1972 — BIBLIOG NAT/G DIPLOM POL/PAR

S66
PRATT R.C.,"AFRICAN REACTIONS TO THE RHODESIAN CRISIS." RHODESIA UK LAW DIPLOM...POLICY 20. PAGE 117 A2408 — ATTIT AFR COLONIAL RACE/REL

B67
BLOM-COOPER L.,THE LITERATURE OF THE LAW AND THE LANGUAGE OF THE LAW (2 VOLS.). CANADA ISRAEL UK WOR+45 WOR-45 JUDGE CT/SYS ATTIT...CRIMLGY JURID ANTHOL CMN/WLTH. PAGE 15 A0312 — BIBLIOG LAW INT/LAW ADJUD

B67
BURNS E.L.M.,MEGAMURDER. WOR+45 LAW INT/ORG NAT/G BAL/PWR DIPLOM DETER MURDER WEAPON CIVMIL/REL PEACE ...INT/LAW TREND 20. PAGE 22 A0444 — FORCES PLAN WAR NUC/PWR

B67
LAWYERS COMM AMER POLICY VIET,VIETNAM AND INTERNATIONAL LAW: AN ANALYSIS OF THE LEGALITY OF THE US MILITARY INVOLVEMENT. VIETNAM LAW INT/ORG COERCE WEAPON PEACE ORD/FREE 20 UN SEATO TREATY. PAGE 86 A1753 — INT/LAW DIPLOM ADJUD WAR

B67
PADELFORD N.J.,THE DYNAMICS OF INTERNATIONAL POLITICS (2ND ED.). WOR+45 LAW INT/ORG FORCES TEC/DEV REGION NAT/LISM PEACE ATTIT PWR ALL/IDEOS UN COLD/WAR NATO TREATY. PAGE 113 A2314 — DIPLOM NAT/G POLICY DECISION

B67
UNIVERSAL REFERENCE SYSTEM,BIBLIOGRAPHY OF BIBLIOGRAPHIES IN POLITICAL SCIENCE, GOVERNMENT, AND PUBLIC POLICY (VOLUME III). WOR+45 WOR-45 LAW ADMIN...SOC CON/ANAL COMPUT/IR GEN/METH. PAGE 149 A3042 — BIBLIOG/A NAT/G DIPLOM POLICY

B67
UNIVERSAL REFERENCE SYSTEM,LAW, JURISPRUDENCE, AND JUDICIAL PROCESS (VOLUME VII). WOR+45 WOR-45 CONSTN NAT/G LEGIS JUDGE CT/SYS...INT/LAW COMPUT/IR GEN/METH METH. PAGE 149 A3044 — BIBLIOG/A LAW JURID ADJUD

B67
US SUPERINTENDENT OF DOCUMENTS,LIBRARY OF CONGRESS (PRICE LIST 83). AFR ASIA EUR+WWI USA-45 USSR NAT/G DIPLOM CONFER CT/SYS WAR...DECISION PHIL/SCI CLASSIF 19/20 CONGRESS PRESIDENT. PAGE 157 A3205 — BIBLIOG/A USA+45 AUTOMAT LAW

L67
CAHIERS P.,"LE RECOURS EN CONSTATATION DE MANQUEMENTS DES ETATS MEMBRES DEVANT LA COUR DES COMMUNAUTES EUROPEENNES." LAW PROB/SOLV DIPLOM ADMIN CT/SYS SANCTION ATTIT...POLICY DECISION JURID ECSC EEC. PAGE 23 A0465 — INT/ORG CONSTN ROUTINE ADJUD

L67
GOLD J.,"INTERPRETATION BY THE INTERNATIONAL MONETARY FUND OF ITS ARTICLES OF AGREEMENT." INT/TRADE ADJUD ATTIT...POLICY JURID. PAGE 53 A1089 — CONSTN INT/ORG LAW DIPLOM

S67
BLUM Y.Z.,"INDONESIA'S RETURN TO THE UNITED NATIONS." INDONESIA ADJUD SANCTION REPRESENT ...JURID 20 UN. PAGE 16 A0324 — CONSTN LAW DIPLOM INT/ORG

S67
CLINGHAM T.A. JR.,"LEGISLATIVE FLOTSAM AND INTERNATIONAL ACTION IN THE 'YARMOUTH CASTLE'S' WAKE." WOR+45 PROB/SOLV CONFER COST HEALTH...POLICY INT/LAW CONGRESS. PAGE 27 A0552
DIPLOM DIST/IND INT/ORG LAW

S67
MANN F.A.,"THE BRETTON WOODS AGREEMENT IN THE ENGLISH COURTS." UK JUDGE ADJUD CT/SYS...JURID PREDICT CON/ANAL 20. PAGE 94 A1923
LAW INT/LAW CONSTN

S67
OLIVIER G.,"ASPECTS JURIDIQUES DE L'ADOPTION DU TRAITE CECA A LA CRISE CHARBONNIERE (SUITE ET FIN)" LAW DIST/IND PLAN DIPLOM RATION PRICE ADMIN COST DEMAND...POLICY CON/ANAL ECSC TREATY. PAGE 112 A2288
INT/TRADE INT/ORG EXTR/IND CONSTN

S67
ZARTMAN I.W.,"AFRICA AS A SUBORDINATE STATE SYSTEM IN INTERNATIONAL RELATIONS." LAW BAL/PWR REGION CENTRAL...GEOG 20. PAGE 169 A3447
DIPLOM INT/ORG CONSTN AFR

B91
DOLE C.F.,THE AMERICAN CITIZEN. USA-45 LAW PARTIC ATTIT...INT/LAW 19. PAGE 38 A0769
NAT/G MORAL NAT/LISM MAJORITY

B91
SIDGWICK H.,THE ELEMENTS OF POLITICS. LOC/G NAT/G LEGIS DIPLOM ADJUD CONTROL EXEC PARL/PROC REPRESENT GOV/REL SOVEREIGN ALL/IDEOS 19 MILL/JS BENTHAM/J. PAGE 132 A2713
POLICY LAW CONCPT

B96
DE VATTEL E.,THE LAW OF NATIONS. AGRI FINAN CHIEF DIPLOM INT/TRADE AGREE OWN ALL/VALS MORAL ORD/FREE SOVEREIGN...GEN/LAWS 18 NATURL/LAW WOLFF/C. PAGE 35 A0714
LAW CONCPT NAT/G INT/LAW

B96
SMITH A.,LECTURES ON JUSTICE, POLICE, REVENUE AND ARMS (1763). UK LAW FAM FORCES TARIFFS AGREE COERCE INCOME OWN WEALTH LAISSEZ...GEN/LAWS 17/18. PAGE 134 A2743
DIPLOM JURID OLD/LIB TAX

B97
US DEPARTMENT OF STATE,CATALOGUE OF WORKS RELATING TO THE LAW OF NATIONS AND DIPLOMACY IN THE LIBRARY OF THE DEPARTMENT OF STATE (PAMPHLET). WOR-45 NAT/G ADJUD CT/SYS...INT/LAW JURID 19. PAGE 152 A3102
BIBLIOG/A DIPLOM LAW

LAW/ETHIC....ETHICS OF LAW AND COURT PROCESSES

LAWRENC/TE....THOMAS EDWARD LAWRENCE

LAWSON R. A1752

LAWYERS COMM AMER POLICY VIET A1753

LAZITCH B. A0784

LAZRSFLD/P....PAUL LAZARSFELD (AND LAZARSFELD SCALE)

LE GHAIT E. A1754

LEAD....LEADING, CONTRIBUTING MORE THAN AVERAGE

N
UNIVERSITY OF FLORIDA LIBRARY,DOORS TO LATIN AMERICA; RECENT BOOKS AND PAMPHLETS. CONSTN CULTURE SOCIETY ECO/UNDEV COLONIAL LEAD GOV/REL NAT/LISM ATTIT...HUM SOC 20. PAGE 149 A3047
BIBLIOG/A L/A+17C DIPLOM NAT/G

B
DEUTSCHE BIBLIOTH FRANKF A M,DEUTSCHE BIBLIOGRAPHIE. EUR+WWI GERMANY ECO/DEV FORCES DIPLOM LEAD...POLICY PHIL/SCI SOC 20. PAGE 36 A0743
BIBLIOG LAW ADMIN NAT/G

N
BULLETIN ANALYTIQUE DE DOCUMENTATION POLITIQUE, ECONOMIQUE, ET SOCIAL CONTEMPORAIRE. FRANCE WOR+45 SOCIETY ECO/DEV ECO/UNDEV INT/ORG LOC/G PROB/SOLV FOR/AID LEAD REGION SOC. PAGE 1 A0006
BIBLIOG/A DIPLOM NAT/COMP NAT/G

N
INTERNATIONAL STUDIES. ASIA S/ASIA WOR+45 ECO/UNDEV INT/ORG NAT/G LEAD ATTIT WEALTH...SOC 20. PAGE 1 A0012
BIBLIOG/A DIPLOM INT/LAW INT/TRADE

N
JOURNAL OF MODERN HISTORY. WOR+45 WOR-45 LEAD WAR ...TIME/SEQ TREND NAT/COMP 20. PAGE 1 A0016
BIBLIOG/A DIPLOM NAT/G

N
LITERATUR-VERZEICHNIS DER POLITISCHEN WISSENSCHAFTEN. GERMANY/W WOR+45 CONSTN SOCIETY ECO/DEV INT/ORG POL/PAR LEAD REPRESENT GOV/REL GP/REL...POLICY PHIL/SCI. PAGE 1 A0018
BIBLIOG EUR+WWI DIPLOM NAT/G

N
MIDDLE EAST JOURNAL. CULTURE SECT DIPLOM LEAD GOV/REL ATTIT...POLICY PHIL/SCI SOC LING BIOG 20. PAGE 1 A0019
BIBLIOG ISLAM NAT/G ECO/UNDEV

N
MIDWEST JOURNAL OF POLITICAL SCIENCE. USA+45 CONSTN ECO/DEV LEGIS PROB/SOLV CT/SYS LEAD GOV/REL ATTIT POLICY. PAGE 1 A0020
BIBLIOG/A NAT/G DIPLOM POL/PAR

N
NEUE POLITISCHE LITERATUR. AFR ASIA EUR+WWI GERMANY RUSSIA SOCIETY ECO/DEV ECO/UNDEV PLAN PROB/SOLV LEAD MARXISM...PHIL/SCI CONCPT 20. PAGE 1 A0021
BIBLIOG DIPLOM COM NAT/G

N
POLITICAL SCIENCE QUARTERLY. USA+45 USA-45 LAW CONSTN ECO/DEV INT/ORG LOC/G POL/PAR LEGIS LEAD NUC/PWR...CONCPT 20. PAGE 1 A0023
BIBLIOG/A NAT/G DIPLOM POLICY

N
REVIEW OF POLITICS. WOR+45 WOR-45 CONSTN LEGIS PROB/SOLV ADMIN LEAD ALL/IDEOS...PHIL/SCI 20. PAGE 2 A0024
BIBLIOG/A DIPLOM INT/ORG NAT/G

N
SOCIAL RESEARCH. WOR+45 WOR-45 R+D LEAD GP/REL ATTIT...SOC TREND 20. PAGE 2 A0025
BIBLIOG/A DIPLOM NAT/G SOCIETY

N
BIBLIO, CATALOGUE DES OUVRAGES PARUS EN LANGUE FRANCAISE DANS LE MONDE ENTIER. FRANCE WOR+45 ADMIN LEAD PERSON...SOC 20. PAGE 2 A0029
BIBLIOG NAT/G DIPLOM ECO/DEV

N
BIBLIOGRAPHIE DER SOZIALWISSENSCHAFTEN. WOR-45 CONSTN SOCIETY ECO/DEV ECO/UNDEV DIPLOM LEAD WAR PEACE...PHIL/SCI SOC 19/20. PAGE 2 A0030
BIBLIOG LAW CONCPT NAT/G

N
DAILY SUMMARY OF THE JAPANESE PRESS. NAT/G DIPLOM LEAD 20 CHINJAP. PAGE 2 A0031
BIBLIOG PRESS ASIA ATTIT

N
HANDBOOK OF LATIN AMERICAN STUDIES. LAW CULTURE ECO/UNDEV POL/PAR ADMIN LEAD...SOC 20. PAGE 2 A0035
BIBLIOG/A L/A+17C NAT/G DIPLOM

N
LONDON TIMES OFFICIAL INDEX. UK LAW ECO/DEV NAT/G DIPLOM LEAD ATTIT 20. PAGE 2 A0038
BIBLIOG INDEX PRESS WRITING

N
PUBLISHERS' CIRCULAR, THE OFFICIAL ORGAN OF THE PUBLISHERS' ASSOCIATION OF GREAT BRITAIN AND IRELAND. EUR+WWI MOD/EUR UK LAW PROB/SOLV DIPLOM COLONIAL ATTIT...HUM 19/20 CMN/WLTH. PAGE 2 A0039
BIBLIOG NAT/G WRITING LEAD

N
THE WORLD IN FOCUS. WOR+45 LEAD ATTIT...POLICY TREND. PAGE 2 A0044
BIBLIOG INT/ORG INT/LAW DIPLOM

N
AMERICAN HISTORICAL SOCIETY,LIST OF DOCTORAL DISSERTATIONS IN HISTORY IN PROGRESS OR COMPLETED IN COLLEGES AND UNIVERSITIES IN THE UNITED STATES. WOR+45 WOR-45 CULTURE SOCIETY NAT/G DIPLOM LEAD TREND. PAGE 7 A0150
BIBLIOG ACADEM INTELL

N
ASIA FOUNDATION,LIBRARY NOTES. LAW CONSTN CULTURE SOCIETY ECO/UNDEV INT/ORG NAT/G COLONIAL LEAD REGION NAT/LISM ATTIT 20 UN. PAGE 9 A0189
BIBLIOG/A ASIA S/ASIA DIPLOM

N
ATLANTIC INSTITUTE,ATLANTIC STUDIES. COM EUR+WWI USA+45 CULTURE STRUCT ECO/DEV FORCES LEAD ARMS/CONT ...INT/LAW JURID SOC. PAGE 10 A0193
BIBLIOG/A DIPLOM POLICY GOV/REL

N
CARIBBEAN COMMISSION,CURRENT CARIBBEAN BIBLIOGRAPHY. FRANCE NETHERLAND UK CULTURE ECO/UNDEV PRESS LEAD ATTIT...GEOG SOC 20. PAGE 24 A0482
BIBLIOG NAT/G L/A+17C DIPLOM

N
CORNELL UNIVERSITY LIBRARY,SOUTHEAST ASIA ACCESSIONS LIST. LAW SOCIETY STRUCT ECO/UNDEV POL/PAR TEC/DEV DIPLOM LEAD REGION. PAGE 31 A0626
BIBLIOG S/ASIA NAT/G CULTURE

N
DEUTSCHE BUCHEREI,DEUTSCHE NATIONALBIBLIOGRAPHIE. GERMANY ECO/DEV DIPLOM AGE/Y ATTIT...PHIL/SCI SOC 20. PAGE 37 A0744
BIBLIOG NAT/G LEAD POLICY

N
DEUTSCHE BUCHEREI,DEUTSCHES BUCHERVERZEICHNIS. GERMANY LAW CULTURE POL/PAR ADMIN LEAD ATTIT PERSON ...SOC 20. PAGE 37 A0746
BIBLIOG NAT/G DIPLOM ECO/DEV

N
INSTITUTE OF HISPANIC STUDIES,HISPANIC AMERICAN REPORT. EUR+WWI SPAIN LAW CONSTN ECO/UNDEV POL/PAR EX/STRUC LEGIS LEAD...HUM SOC 20. PAGE 70 A1445
BIBLIOG/A L/A+17C NAT/G DIPLOM

N
JOHNS HOPKINS UNIVERSITY LIB,RECENT ADDITIONS. WOR+45 ECO/UNDEV NAT/G POL/PAR FOR/AID INT/TRADE LEAD REGION ATTIT ALL/IDEOS TREND. PAGE 74 A1518
BIBLIOG DIPLOM INT/LAW INT/ORG

N
LA DOCUMENTATION FRANCAISE,CHRONOLOGIE INTERNATIONAL. FRANCE WOR+45 CHIEF PROB/SOLV BAL/PWR CONFER LEAD...POLICY CON/ANAL 20. PAGE 83 A1705
BIBLIOG/A DIPLOM TIME/SEQ

N
UNITED NATIONS,UNITED NATIONS PUBLICATIONS. WOR+45 ECO/UNDEV AGRI FINAN FORCES ADMIN LEAD WAR PEACE ...POLICY INT/LAW 20 UN. PAGE 148 A3034
BIBLIOG INT/ORG DIPLOM

N
US CONSOLATE GENERAL HONG KONG,REVIEW OF THE HONG KONG CHINESE PRESS. ECO/UNDEV LOC/G NAT/G PLAN DIPLOM EDU/PROP LEAD GP/REL MARXISM...POLICY INDEX 20. PAGE 150 A3073
BIBLIOG/A ASIA PRESS ATTIT

N
US CONSULATE GENERAL HONG KONG,CURRENT BACKGROUND. CHINA/COM ECO/UNDEV LOC/G NAT/G PLAN DIPLOM EDU/PROP LEAD REV ATTIT...POLICY INDEX 20. PAGE 151 A3074
BIBLIOG/A MARXIST ASIA PRESS

N
US CONSULATE GENERAL HONG KONG,SURVEY OF CHINA MAINLAND PRESS. CHINA/COM ECO/UNDEV LOC/G NAT/G PLAN DIPLOM EDU/PROP LEAD REV ATTIT...POLICY INDEX 20. PAGE 151 A3075
BIBLIOG/A MARXIST ASIA PRESS

N
US CONSULATE GENERAL HONG KONG,US CONSULATE GENERAL, HONG KONG, PRESS SUMMARIES. CHINA/COM ECO/UNDEV LOC/G NAT/G PLAN DIPLOM EDU/PROP LEAD REV ATTIT...POLICY INDEX 20. PAGE 151 A3076
BIBLIOG/A MARXIST ASIA PRESS

N
US LIBRARY OF CONGRESS,ACCESSIONS LIST - INDIA. INDIA CULTURE AGRI LOC/G POL/PAR PLAN PROB/SOLV TEC/DEV DIPLOM EDU/PROP LEAD GP/REL ATTIT 20. PAGE 154 A3142
BIBLIOG S/ASIA ECO/UNDEV NAT/G

N
US LIBRARY OF CONGRESS,ACCESSIONS LIST -- ISRAEL. ISRAEL CULTURE ECO/UNDEV POL/PAR PLAN PROB/SOLV TEC/DEV DIPLOM EDU/PROP LEAD WAR ATTIT 20 JEWS. PAGE 154 A3143
BIBLIOG ISLAM NAT/G GP/REL

B17
DOS SANTOS M.,BIBLIOGRAPHIA GERAL, A DESCRIPCAO BIBLIOGRAFICA DE LIVROS TANTO DE AUTORES PORTUGUEZES COMO BRASILEIROS... BRAZIL PORTUGAL NAT/G LEAD GP/REL 15/20. PAGE 38 A0774
BIBLIOG/A L/A+17C DIPLOM COLONIAL

N19
GRANT N.,COMMUNIST PSYCHOLOGICAL OFFENSIVE: DISTORTION IN THE TRANSLATION OF OFFICIAL DOCUMENTS (PAMPHLET). USSR POL/PAR CHIEF FOR/AID PRESS WRITING COLONIAL LEAD WAR PEACE 20 KHRUSH/N. PAGE 55 A1129
MARXISM DIPLOM EDU/PROP

N19
HAJDA J.,THE COLD WAR VIEWED AS A SOCIOLOGICAL PROBLEM (PAMPHLET). COM CZECHOSLVK EUR+WWI SOCIETY PLAN EDU/PROP CONTROL TASK ATTIT MARXISM...POLICY 20 COLD/WAR MIGRATION. PAGE 59 A1220
DIPLOM LEAD PWR NAT/G

N19
MEZERIK A.G.,COLONIALISM AND THE UNITED NATIONS (PAMPHLET). WOR+45 NAT/G ADMIN LEAD WAR CHOOSE EFFICIENCY PEACE ATTIT ORD/FREE...POLICY CHARTS UN COLD/WAR. PAGE 100 A2061
COLONIAL DIPLOM BAL/PWR INT/ORG

B26
INTERNATIONAL BIBLIOGRAPHY OF POLITICAL SCIENCE. WOR+45 NAT/G POL/PAR EX/STRUC LEGIS CT/SYS LEAD CHOOSE GOV/REL ATTIT...PHIL/SCI 20. PAGE 3 A0049
BIBLIOG DIPLOM CONCPT ADMIN

B27
GOOCH G.P.,ENGLISH DEMOCRATIC IDEAS IN THE SEVENTEENTH CENTURY (2ND ED.). UK LAW SECT FORCES DIPLOM LEAD PARL/PROC REV ATTIT AUTHORIT...ANARCH CONCPT 17 PARLIAMENT CMN/WLTH REFORMERS. PAGE 54 A1100
IDEA/COMP MAJORIT EX/STRUC CONSERVE

B28
LODGE H.C.,THE HISTORY OF NATIONS (25 VOLS.). UNIV LEAD...ANTHOL BIBLIOG INDEX. PAGE 90 A1850
DIPLOM SOCIETY NAT/G

B30
SCHNEIDER G.,HANDBUCH DER BIBLIOGRAPHIE. GERMANY WOR-45 CULTURE SOCIETY LEAD. PAGE 129 A2637
BIBLIOG/A NAT/G DIPLOM

B38
HARPER S.N.,THE GOVERNMENT OF THE SOVIET UNION. COM USSR LAW CONSTN ECO/DEV PLAN TEC/DEV DIPLOM INT/TRADE ADMIN REV NAT/LISM...POLICY 20. PAGE 62 A1265
MARXISM NAT/G LEAD POL/PAR

B39
THOMAS J.A.,THE HOUSE OF COMMONS, 1832-1901; A STUDY OF ITS ECONOMIC AND FUNCTIONAL CHARACTER. UK LAW STRATA FINAN DIPLOM CONTROL LEAD LOBBY REPRESENT WEALTH...POLICY STAT BIBLIOG 19/20 PARLIAMENT. PAGE 143 A2922
PARL/PROC LEGIS POL/PAR ECO/DEV

B41
KEESING F.M.,THE SOUTH SEAS IN THE MODERN WORLD. INDONESIA STRUCT FAM SECT EDU/PROP LEAD INCOME WEALTH...HEAL SOC 20. PAGE 77 A1577
CULTURE ECO/UNDEV GOV/COMP DIPLOM

B42
BORNSTEIN J.,ACTION AGAINST THE ENEMY'S MIND. EUR+WWI GERMANY USA-45 DIPLOM DOMIN PRESS LEAD GP/REL DISCRIM PERCEPT FASCISM MARXISM 20 JEWS NAZI ANTI/SEMIT. PAGE 17 A0343
EDU/PROP PSY WAR CONTROL

B43
BROWN A.D.,GREECE: SELECTED LIST OF REFERENCES. GREECE ECO/UNDEV AGRI FINAN INDUS LABOR SECT TEC/DEV INT/TRADE LEAD...SOC 20. PAGE 20 A0399
BIBLIOG/A WAR DIPLOM NAT/G

B43
CARLO A.M.,ENSAYO DE UNA BIBLIOGRAFIA DE BIBLIOGRAFIAS MEXICANAS. ECO/UNDEV LOC/G ADMIN LEAD 20 MEXIC/AMER. PAGE 24 A0485
BIBLIOG L/A+17C NAT/G DIPLOM

B43
GRIERSON P.,BOOKS ON SOVIET RUSSIA 1917-42: A BIBLIOGRAPHY AND A GUIDE TO READING. USSR CULTURE ELITES NAT/G PLAN DIPLOM REV...GEOG 20. PAGE 56 A1148
BIBLIOG/A COM MARXISM LEAD

B43
LEWIN E.,ROYAL EMPIRE SOCIETY BIBLIOGRAPHIES NO. 9: SUB-SAHARA AFRICA. ECO/UNDEV TEC/DEV DIPLOM ADMIN COLONIAL LEAD 20. PAGE 88 A1800
BIBLIOG AFR NAT/G SOCIETY

N45
INDIA QUARTERLY, A JOURNAL OF INTERNATIONAL AFFAIRS. INDIA LAW CONSTN ECO/UNDEV INT/ORG POL/PAR COLONIAL LEAD PARL/PROC WAR ATTIT...SOC 20 CMN/WLTH. PAGE 3 A0053
BIBLIOG/A S/ASIA DIPLOM NAT/G

B45
WING D.,SHORT-TITLE CATALOGUE OF BOOKS PRINTED IN THE BRITISH ISLES, AND OF ENGLISH BOOKS PRINTED OVERSEAS; 1641-1700 (3 VOLS.). UK USA-45 LAW DIPLOM ADMIN COLONIAL LEAD ATTIT 17. PAGE 165 A3363
BIBLIOG MOD/EUR NAT/G

B46
BIBLIOGRAFIIA DISSERTATSII: DOKTORSKIE DISSERTATSII ZA 19411944 (2 VOLS.). COM USSR LAW POL/PAR DIPLOM ADMIN LEAD...PHIL/SCI SOC 20. PAGE 3 A0054
BIBLIOG ACADEM KNOWL MARXIST

B49
BORBA DE MORAES R.,MANUAL BIBLIOGRAFICO DE ESTUDOS BRASILEIROS. BRAZIL DIPLOM ADMIN LEAD...SOC 20. PAGE 17 A0336
BIBLIOG L/A+17C NAT/G ECO/UNDEV

B49
GORER G.,THE PEOPLE OF GREAT RUSSIA: A PSYCHOLOGICAL STUDY. RUSSIA USSR NAT/G DIPLOM LEAD AGE/C ANOMIE ATTIT DRIVE...POLICY 20. PAGE 54 A1116
ISOLAT PERSON PSY SOCIETY

L49
HEINDEL R.H.,"THE NORTH ATLANTIC TREATY IN THE UNITED STATES SENATE." CONSTN POL/PAR CHIEF DEBATE LEAD ROUTINE WAR PEACE...CHARTS UN SENATE NATO. PAGE 64 A1309
DECISION PARL/PROC LEGIS INT/ORG

B50
COUNCIL BRITISH NATIONAL BIB,BRITISH NATIONAL BIBLIOGRAPHY. UK AGRI CONSTRUC PERF/ART POL/PAR SECT CREATE INT/TRADE LEAD...HUM JURID PHIL/SCI 20. PAGE 31 A0637
BIBLIOG/A NAT/G TEC/DEV DIPLOM

B51
JENNINGS S.I.,THE COMMONWEALTH IN ASIA. CEYLON INDIA PAKISTAN S/ASIA UK CONSTN CULTURE SOCIETY STRATA STRUCT NAT/G POL/PAR EDU/PROP LEAD WAR 20 CMN/WLTH. PAGE 74 A1510
NAT/LISM REGION COLONIAL DIPLOM

B51
US LIBRARY OF CONGRESS,EAST EUROPEAN ACCESSIONS LIST (VOL. I). POL/PAR DIPLOM ADMIN LEAD 20. PAGE 155 A3152
BIBLIOG/A COM SOCIETY NAT/G

B52
MACARTHUR D.,REVITALIZING A NATION. ASIA COM FUT KOREA WOR+45 NAT/G FOR/AID TAX GIVE WAR ATTIT SOCISM 20 CHINJAP EUROPE. PAGE 92 A1885
LEAD FORCES TOP/EX POLICY

B52
SPENCER F.A.,WAR AND POSTWAR GREECE: AN ANALYSIS BASED ON GREEK WRITINGS. GREECE SOCIETY NAT/G POL/PAR FORCES CREATE DIPLOM LEAD MARXISM...SOC 20. PAGE 136 A2784
BIBLIOG/A WAR REV

B52
US DEPARTMENT OF STATE,RESEARCH ON EASTERN EUROPE (EXCLUDING USSR). EUR+WWI LAW ECO/DEV NAT/G PROB/SOLV DIPLOM ADMIN LEAD MARXISM...TREND 19/20. PAGE 151 A3088
BIBLIOG R+D ACT/RES COM

B53
ELAHI K.N.,A GUIDE TO WORKS OF REFERENCE PUBLISHED
BIBLIOG

IN PAKISTAN (PAMPHLET). PAKISTAN DIPLOM COLONIAL LEAD. PAGE 41 A0835
S/ASIA NAT/G

B54
SALVEMINI G.,PRELUDE TO WORLD WAR II. ITALY MOD/EUR INT/ORG BAL/PWR EDU/PROP CONTROL TOTALISM...TREND NAT/COMP BIBLIOG 19 HITLER/A LEAGUE/NAT MUSSOLIN/B. PAGE 127 A2597
WAR FASCISM LEAD PWR

B54
SHARMA J.S.,MAHATMA GANDHI: A DESCRIPTIVE BIBLIOGRAPHY. INDIA S/ASIA PROB/SOLV DIPLOM COLONIAL WAR NAT/LISM PEACE ATTIT PERSON SOVEREIGN ...CONCPT 20 GANDHI/M. PAGE 132 A2695
BIBLIOG/A BIOG CHIEF LEAD

B55
JAPANESE STUDIES OF MODERN CHINA. ASIA DIPLOM LEAD REV MARXISM 19/20 CHINJAP. PAGE 43 A0885
BIBLIOG/A SOC

B55
INSTITUTE POLITISCHE WISSEN,POLITISCHE LITERATUR (3 VOLS.). INT/ORG LEAD WAR PEACE...CONCPT TREND NAT/COMP 20. PAGE 70 A1446
BIBLIOG/A NAT/G DIPLOM POLICY

B56
GUNTHER F.,BUCHERKUNDE ZUR WELTGESCHICHTE VON UNTERGANG DES ROMISCHEN WELTREICHES BIS ZUR GEGENWART. WOR+45 WOR-45 LEAD PERSON. PAGE 58 A1193
BIBLIOG DIPLOM NAT/G TREND

B56
KNORR K.E.,RUBLE DIPLOMACY: CHALLENGE TO AMERICAN FOREIGN AID(PAMPHLET). CHINA/COM USA+45 USSR PLAN TEC/DEV CAP/ISM INT/TRADE DOMIN EDU/PROP CONTROL LEAD 20 COLD/WAR. PAGE 81 A1654
ECO/UNDEV COM DIPLOM FOR/AID

B56
PHILIPPINE STUDIES PROGRAM,SELECTED BIBLIOGRAPHY ON THE PHILIPPINES, TOPICALLY ARRANGED AND ANNOTATED. PHILIPPINE SECT DIPLOM COLONIAL LEAD...SOC 18/20. PAGE 116 A2375
BIBLIOG/A S/ASIA NAT/G ECO/UNDEV

B56
UNITED NATIONS,BIBLIOGRAPHY ON INDUSTRIALIZATION IN UNDER-DEVELOPED COUNTRIES. WOR+45 R+D INT/ORG NAT/G FOR/AID ADMIN LEAD 20 UN. PAGE 149 A3036
BIBLIOG ECO/UNDEV INDUS TEC/DEV

B56
VON BECKERATH E.,HANDWORTERBUCH DER SOCIALWISSENSCHAFTEN (II VOLS.). EUR+WWI GERMANY POL/PAR WORKER DIPLOM LEAD CHOOSE SUFF WEALTH...SOC 20. PAGE 159 A3249
BIBLIOG INT/TRADE NAT/G ECO/DEV

B56
WILBUR C.M.,DOCUMENTS ON COMMUNISM, NATIONALISM, AND SOVIET ADVISERS IN CHINA, 1918-1927. CHINA/COM USSR STRUCT DIPLOM LEAD NAT/LISM...BIBLIOG/A 20. PAGE 164 A3343
REV POL/PAR MARXISM COM

S56
CUTLER R.,"THE DEVELOPMENT OF THE NATIONAL SECURITY COUNCIL." USA+45 INTELL CONSULT EX/STRUC DIPLOM LEAD 20 TRUMAN/HS EISNHWR/DD NSC. PAGE 33 A0670
ORD/FREE DELIB/GP PROB/SOLV NAT/G

B57
BISHOP O.B.,PUBLICATIONS OF THE GOVERNMENTS OF NOVA SCOTIA, PRINCE EDWARD ISLAND, NEW BRUNSWICK 1758-1952. CANADA UK ADMIN COLONIAL LEAD...POLICY 18/20. PAGE 14 A0293
BIBLIOG NAT/G DIPLOM

B57
DUDDEN A.P.,WOODROW WILSON AND THE WORLD OF TODAY. USA-45 NAT/G PROVS CONTROL PARTIC WAR ISOLAT PWR SKILL...PERS/COMP ANTHOL 19/20 WILSON/W UN LEAGUE/NAT WWI. PAGE 39 A0794
CHIEF DIPLOM POL/PAR LEAD

C57
TANG P.S.H.,"COMMUNIST CHINA TODAY: DOMESTIC AND FOREIGN POLICIES." CHINA/COM COM S/ASIA USSR STRATA FORCES DIPLOM EDU/PROP COERCE GOV/REL...POLICY MAJORIT BIBLIOG 20. PAGE 141 A2886
POL/PAR LEAD ADMIN CONSTN

B58
BOWLES C.,IDEAS, PEOPLE AND PEACE. ASIA CHINA/COM FUT INDIA USA+45 USSR ECO/UNDEV INT/ORG LEAD TASK MARXISM 20 NATO UN COLD/WAR. PAGE 18 A0359
PEACE POLICY NAT/G DIPLOM

B58
CRAIG G.A.,FROM BISMARCK TO ADENAUER: ASPECTS OF GERMAN STATECRAFT. GERMANY INTELL FORCES ECO/TAC CONFER COERCE WAR GP/REL ORD/FREE PWR CONSERVE 19/20 BISMARCK/O ADENAUER/K. PAGE 32 A0653
DIPLOM LEAD NAT/G

B58
PAN AMERICAN UNION,REPERTORIO DE PUBLICACIONES PERIODICAS ACTUALES LATINO-AMERICANAS. CULTURE ECO/UNDEV ADMIN LEAD GOV/REL 20 OAS. PAGE 113 A2326
BIBLIOG L/A+17C NAT/G DIPLOM

B59
DEHIO L.,GERMANY AND WORLD POLITICS IN THE TWENTIETH CENTURY. EUR+WWI FRANCE GERMANY MOD/EUR UK USSR NAT/G CHIEF BAL/PWR DOMIN COLONIAL CONTROL LEAD...IDEA/COMP 20 VERSAILLES. PAGE 36 A0724
DIPLOM WAR NAT/LISM SOVEREIGN

B59
KNIERIEM A.,THE NUREMBERG TRIALS. EUR+WWI GERMANY VOL/ASSN LEAD COERCE WAR INGP/REL TOTALISM SUPEGO ORD/FREE...CONCPT METH/COMP. PAGE 80 A1651
INT/LAW CRIME PARTIC JURID

B59
SHANNON D.A.,THE DECLINE OF AMERICAN COMMUNISM; A HISTORY OF THE COMMUNIST PARTY OF THE UNITED STATES SINCE 1945. USA+45 LAW SOCIETY LABOR NAT/G WORKER DIPLOM EDU/PROP LEAD...POLICY BIBLIOG 20 KHRUSH/N NEGRO AFL/CIO COLD/WAR COM/PARTY. PAGE 131 A2692
MARXISM POL/PAR ATTIT POPULISM

B59
VAN WAGENEN R.W.,SOME VIEWS OF AMERICAN DEFENSE OFFICIALS ABOUT THE UNITED NATIONS (PAPER). FUT USA+45 NAT/G DIPLOM WAR EFFICIENCY PEACE...POLICY INT 20 UN DEPT/DEFEN. PAGE 158 A3216
INT/ORG LEAD ATTIT FORCES

B60
DE GAULLE C.,THE EDGE OF THE SWORD. EUR+WWI FRANCE ELITES CHIEF DIPLOM ROLE...REALPOL TRADIT. PAGE 34 A0701
FORCES SUPEGO LEAD WAR

B60
DE HERRERA C.D.,LISTA BIBLIOGRAFICA DE LOS TRABAJOS DE GRADUACION Y TESIS PRESENTADOS EN LA UNIVERSIDAD, 1939-1960. PANAMA DIPLOM LEAD...SOC 20. PAGE 35 A0703
BIBLIOG L/A+17C NAT/G ACADEM

B60
FISCHER L.,THE SOVIETS IN WORLD AFFAIRS. CHINA/COM COM EUR+WWI USSR INT/ORG CONFER LEAD ARMS/CONT REV PWR...CHARTS 20 TREATY VERSAILLES. PAGE 46 A0938
DIPLOM NAT/G POLICY MARXISM

B60
FLORES R.H.,CATALOGO DE TESIS DOCTORALES DE LAS FACULTADES DE LA UNIVERSIDAD DE EL SALVADOR. EL/SALVADR LAW DIPLOM ADMIN LEAD GOV/REL...SOC 19/20. PAGE 47 A0954
BIBLIOG ACADEM L/A+17C NAT/G

B60
GLUBB J.B.,WAR IN THE DESERT: AN R.A.F. FRONTIER CAMPAIGN. SAUDI/ARAB UK KIN SECT LEAD...GEOG 20 RAF. PAGE 53 A1083
COLONIAL WAR FORCES DIPLOM

B60
KINGSTON-MCCLOUG E.,DEFENSE; POLICY AND STRATEGY. UK SEA AIR TEC/DEV DIPLOM ADMIN LEAD WAR ORD/FREE ...CHARTS 20. PAGE 79 A1627
FORCES PLAN POLICY DECISION

B60
MENEZES A.J.,O BRASIL E O MUNDO ASIO-AFRICANO (REV. ED.). AFR ASIA BRAZIL WOR+45 INT/TRADE ORD/FREE PWR SOVEREIGN...POLICY 20. PAGE 99 A2040
DIPLOM BAL/PWR LEAD ECO/UNDEV

B60
MINIFIE J.M.,PEACEMAKER OR POWDER-MONKEY. CANADA INT/ORG NAT/G FORCES LEAD WAR...PREDICT 20. PAGE 102 A2086
DIPLOM POLICY NEUTRAL PEACE

B60
PHILLIPS J.F.V.,KWAME NKRUMAH AND THE FUTURE OF AFRICA. FUT GHANA ISLAM ECO/UNDEV CHIEF DIPLOM COLONIAL RACE/REL NAT/LISM...TREND IDEA/COMP BIBLIOG 20 NKRUMAH/K. PAGE 116 A2376
BIOG LEAD SOVEREIGN AFR

B60
QUBAIN F.I.,INSIDE THE ARAB MIND: A BIBLIOGRAPHIC SURVEY OF LITERATURE IN ARABIC ON ARAB NATIONALISM AND UNITY. ISLAM POL/PAR SECT LEAD SOVEREIGN MARXISM SOCISM. PAGE 118 A2425
BIBLIOG/A FEDERAL DIPLOM NAT/LISM

B60
WHEARE K.C.,THE CONSTITUTIONAL STRUCTURE OF THE COMMONWEALTH. UK EX/STRUC DIPLOM DOMIN ADMIN COLONIAL CONTROL LEAD INGP/REL SUPEGO 20 CMN/WLTH. PAGE 163 A3325
CONSTN INT/ORG VOL/ASSN SOVEREIGN

B61
ACHESON D.,SKETCHES FROM LIFE. WOR+45 20 CHURCHLL/W EDEN/A ADENAUER/K SALAZAR/A. PAGE 4 A0085
BIOG LEAD CHIEF DIPLOM

B61
CONOVER H.F.,SERIALS FOR AFRICAN STUDIES. ECO/UNDEV DIPLOM LEAD NAT/LISM ATTIT...SOC 20. PAGE 30 A0604
BIBLIOG AFR NAT/G

B61
HISTORICAL RESEARCH INSTITUTE,A SHORT BIBLIOGRAPHY OF INDO-MUSLIM HISTORY. INDIA S/ASIA DIPLOM EDU/PROP COLONIAL LEAD NAT/LISM ATTIT...BIOG 19/20. PAGE 65 A1343
BIBLIOG NAT/G SECT POL/PAR

B61
LEGISLATIVE REFERENCE SERVICE,WORLD COMMUNIST MOVEMENT: SELECTIVE CHRONOLOGY, 1818-1957 (4 VOLS.). COM WOR+45 WOR-45 POL/PAR LEAD 19/20. PAGE 86 A1766
BIBLIOG DIPLOM TIME/SEQ MARXISM

B61
MILLER R.I.,DAG HAMMARSKJOLD AND CRISES DIPLOMACY. WOR+45 NAT/G PROB/SOLV LEAD ROLE...DECISION BIOG UN HAMMARSK/D. PAGE 101 A2079
DIPLOM INT/ORG CHIEF

B61
OVERSTREET H.,THE WAR CALLED PEACE. USSR WOR+45 COM/IND INT/ORG POL/PAR BAL/PWR EDU/PROP PEACE ATTIT...CONCPT 20 KHRUSH/N. PAGE 112 A2302
DIPLOM COM POLICY LEAD

B61
PANIKKAR K.M.,REVOLUTION IN AFRICA. AFR GUINEA
NAT/LISM

ECO/UNDEV POL/PAR DIPLOM COLONIAL EXEC LEAD SOVEREIGN...CHARTS 20. PAGE 114 A2332 — NAT/G CHIEF

B61
WALLERSTEIN I.M.,AFRICA; THE POLITICS OF INDEPENDENCE. AFR SOCIETY STRUCT LEAD PARL/PROC PARTIC GP/REL...POLICY 20. PAGE 160 A3269 — ECO/UNDEV DIPLOM COLONIAL ORD/FREE

B61
WRINCH P.,THE MILITARY STRATEGY OF WINSTON CHURCHILL. UK WOR-45 SEA VOL/ASSN TEC/DEV BAL/PWR LEAD WAR PEACE ATTIT...POLICY 20 CHURCHLL/W. PAGE 168 A3421 — CIVMIL/REL FORCES PLAN DIPLOM

B61
YUAN TUNG-LI,A GUIDE TO DOCTORAL DISSERTATIONS BY CHINESE STUDENTS IN AMERICA, 1905-1960. ASIA CULTURE SOCIETY ECO/UNDEV NAT/G PROB/SOLV DIPLOM LEAD ATTIT...HUM SOC STAT 20. PAGE 169 A3441 — BIBLIOG ACADEM ACT/RES OP/RES

B62
BROWN L.C.,LATIN AMERICA, A BIBLIOGRAPHY. EX/STRUC ADMIN LEAD ATTIT...POLICY 20. PAGE 20 A0405 — BIBLIOG L/A+17C DIPLOM NAT/G

B62
COSTA RICA UNIVERSIDAD BIBL,LISTA DE TESIS DE GRADO DE LA UNIVERSIDAD DE COSTA RICA. COSTA/RICA LAW LOC/G ADMIN LEAD...SOC 20. PAGE 31 A0631 — BIBLIOG/A NAT/G DIPLOM ECO/UNDEV

B62
DIAZ J.S.,MANUAL DE BIBLIOGRAFIA DE LA LITERATURA ESPANOLA. PRE/AMER SPAIN ECO/UNDEV DIPLOM LEAD ATTIT...SOC 15/20. PAGE 37 A0755 — BIBLIOG L/A+17C NAT/G COLONIAL

B62
GOLDWATER B.M.,WHY NOT VICTORY? A FRESH LOOK AT AMERICAN FOREIGN POLICY. USA+45 WOR+45 FOR/AID LEAD ARMS/CONT WAR PEACE ATTIT ORD/FREE PWR MARXISM ...INT/LAW 20 TREATY ECHR COUNCL/EUR. PAGE 53 A1092 — DIPLOM POLICY CONSERVE NAT/LISM

B62
KIRPICEVA I.K.,HANDBUCH DER RUSSISCHEN UND SOWJETISCHEN BIBLIOGRAPHIEN (5 VOLS.). USSR STRUCT ECO/DEV DIPLOM LEAD ATTIT 18/20. PAGE 80 A1637 — BIBLIOG/A NAT/G MARXISM COM

B62
KLUCKHOHN F.L.,THE NAKED RISE OF COMMUNISM. CHINA/COM COM USSR WOR+45 CONSTN POL/PAR PLAN CONTROL LEAD NEUTRAL CONSERVE 20 STALIN/J EUROPE/E COM/PARTY. PAGE 80 A1650 — MARXISM IDEA/COMP DIPLOM DOMIN

B62
LAQUEUR W.,THE FUTURE OF COMMUNIST SOCIETY. CHINA/COM USSR LAW ECO/DEV NAT/G POL/PAR PLAN PROB/SOLV DIPLOM LEAD...POLICY CONCPT IDEA/COMP ANTHOL 20. PAGE 85 A1731 — MARXISM COM FUT SOCIETY

B62
LAQUEUR W.,POLYCENTRISM. CHINA/COM COM USSR WOR+45 INT/ORG NAT/G ECO/TAC DOMIN LEAD ATTIT PWR SOVEREIGN...ANTHOL 20. PAGE 85 A1732 — MARXISM DIPLOM BAL/PWR POLICY

B62
MORTON L.,STRATEGY AND COMMAND: THE FIRST TWO YEARS. USA-45 NAT/G CONTROL EXEC LEAD WEAPON CIVMIL/REL PWR...POLICY AUD/VIS CHARTS 20 CHINJAP. PAGE 105 A2150 — WAR FORCES PLAN DIPLOM

B62
SCOTT W.E.,ALLIANCE AGAINST HITLER. EUR+WWI FRANCE GERMANY USSR BAL/PWR LEAD TOTALISM PWR FASCISM MARXISM...POLICY BIBLIOG 20 HITLER/A. PAGE 131 A2675 — WAR DIPLOM FORCES

B62
US DEPARTMENT OF THE ARMY,AFRICA: ITS PROBLEMS AND PROSPECTS. CHINA/COM USSR INT/ORG FOR/AID COLONIAL LEAD FEDERAL DRIVE SOVEREIGN MARXISM...GEOG 20 COLD/WAR. PAGE 152 A3104 — BIBLIOG/A AFR NAT/LISM DIPLOM

B62
US DEPARTMENT OF THE ARMY,GUIDE TO JAPANESE MONOGRAPHS AND JAPANESE STUDIES ON MANCHURIA: 1945-1960. CHINA/COM NAT/G DIPLOM LEAD COERCE WAR ...CHARTS 19/20 CHINJAP. PAGE 152 A3105 — BIBLIOG/A FORCES ASIA S/ASIA

B62
WILLIAMS W.A.,THE UNITED STATES, CUBA, AND CASTRO: AN ESSAY ON THE DYNAMICS OF REVOLUTION AND THE DISSOLUTION OF EMPIRE. CUBA USA+45 AGRI VOL/ASSN DIPLOM ECO/TAC DOMIN COERCE...POLICY 20 EISNHWR/DD CIA KENNEDY/JF CASTRO/F. PAGE 165 A3354 — REV CONSTN COM LEAD

B63
BAILEY S.D.,THE UNITED NATIONS: A SHORT POLITICAL GUIDE. FUT PROB/SOLV LEAD...INT/LAW 20 UN. PAGE 10 A0207 — INT/ORG PEACE DETER DIPLOM

B63
BISHOP O.B.,PUBLICATIONS OF THE GOVERNMENT OF THE PROVINCE OF CANADA 1841-1867. CANADA DIPLOM COLONIAL LEAD...POLICY 18. PAGE 14 A0294 — BIBLIOG NAT/G ATTIT

B63
BLOCH-MORHANGE J.,VINGT ANNEES D'HISTOIRE CONTEMPORAINE. FORCES FOR/AID CONFER LEAD 20 COLD/WAR. PAGE 15 A0311 — WAR DIPLOM INT/ORG CHIEF

B63
DALLIN A.,DIVERSITY IN INTERNATIONAL COMMUNISM: A DOCUMENTARY RECORD, 1961-1963. CHINA/COM CHIEF PRESS WRITING DEBATE LEAD...POLICY ANTHOL 20. PAGE 33 A0677 — COM DIPLOM POL/PAR CONFER

B63
KLEIMAN R.,ATLANTIC CRISIS; AMERICAN DIPLOMACY CONFRONTS A RESURGENT EUROPE. EUR+WWI USA+45 ECO/DEV AGRI NAT/G CHIEF FORCES PLAN LEAD ATTIT ...CONCPT 20 NATO KENNEDY/JF DEGAULLE/C EEC JOHNSON/LB. PAGE 80 A1648 — DIPLOM REGION POLICY

B63
MENEZES A.J.,SUBDESENVOLVIMENTO E POLITICA INTERNACIONAL. BRAZIL WOR+45 PLAN CONTROL LEAD NAT/LISM ORD/FREE 20 THIRD/WRLD. PAGE 99 A2041 — ECO/UNDEV DIPLOM POLICY BAL/PWR

B63
MONTER W.,THE GOVERNMENT OF GENEVA, 1536-1605 (DOCTORAL THESIS). SWITZERLND DIPLOM LEAD ORD/FREE SOVEREIGN 16/17 CALVIN/J ROME. PAGE 103 A2112 — SECT FINAN LOC/G ADMIN

B63
NORTH R.C.,M. N. ROY'S MISSION TO CHINA: THE COMMUNIST-KUOMINTANG SPLIT OF 1927. ASIA USSR STRATA LEGIS WORKER LEAD REV ATTIT ROLE SOCISM 20 ROY/MN COM/PARTY. PAGE 110 A2253 — POL/PAR MARXISM DIPLOM

B63
PECQUET P.,THE DIPLOMACY OF THE CONFEDERATE CABINET OF RICHMOND AND ITS AGENTS ABROAD (LIMITED ED.). MOD/EUR USA-45 LEAD...OBS 19 CIVIL/WAR SOUTH/US. PAGE 114 A2347 — DIPLOM WAR ORD/FREE

B63
SWEARER H.R.,CONTEMPORARY COMMUNISM: THEORY AND PRACTICE. COM USSR SOCIETY ECO/DEV POL/PAR FORCES PLAN ADMIN LEAD NAT/LISM...POLICY ANTHOL 20 LENIN/VI COM/PARTY. PAGE 140 A2869 — MARXISM CONCPT DIPLOM NAT/G

B63
US DEPARTMENT OF STATE,POLITICAL BEHAVIOR--A LIST OF CURRENT STUDIES. USA+45 COM/IND DIPLOM LEAD PERS/REL DRIVE PERCEPT KNOWL...DECISION SIMUL METH. PAGE 151 A3093 — BIBLIOG METH/COMP GP/REL ATTIT

B63
US SENATE,DOCUMENTS ON INTERNATIONAL AS"ECTS OF EXPLORATION AND USE OF OUTER SPACE, 1954-62: STAFF REPORT FOR COMM AERON SPACE SCI. USA+45 USSR LEGIS LEAD CIVMIL/REL PEACE...POLICY INT/LAW ANTHOL 20 CONGRESS NASA KHRUSH/N. PAGE 155 A3165 — SPACE UTIL GOV/REL DIPLOM

B63
US SENATE COMM APPROPRIATIONS,PERSONNEL ADMINISTRATION AND OPERATIONS OF AGENCY FOR INTERNATIONAL DEVELOPMENT: SPECIAL HEARING. FINAN LEAD COST UTIL SKILL...CHARTS 20 CONGRESS AID CIVIL/SERV. PAGE 155 A3170 — ADMIN FOR/AID EFFICIENCY DIPLOM

B63
WHITNEY T.P.,KHRUSHCHEV SPEAKS. USSR AGRI LEAD ...BIOG ANTHOL 20 KHRUSH/N STALIN/J ESPIONAGE. PAGE 164 A3339 — DIPLOM MARXISM CHIEF

C63
SCHMITT K.M.,"EVOLUTION OR CHAOS: DYNAMICS OF LATIN AMERICAN GOVERNMENT AND POLITICS." L/A+17C AGRI FINAN CAP/ISM EXEC LEAD BAL/PAY TOTALISM ATTIT ...TREND BIBLIOG 20. PAGE 129 A2635 — DIPLOM POLICY POL/PAR LOBBY

B64
BURKE F.G.,AFRICA'S QUEST FOR ORDER. AFR CULTURE KIN MUNIC NAT/G DIPLOM COLONIAL REV DISCRIM NAT/LISM AGE/Y 20. PAGE 21 A0437 — ORD/FREE CONSEN RACE/REL LEAD

B64
BUTWELL R.,SOUTHEAST ASIA TODAY - AND TOMORROW. NAT/G COLONIAL LEAD REGION WAR CHOOSE WEALTH MARXISM 20. PAGE 23 A0458 — S/ASIA DIPLOM ECO/UNDEV NAT/LISM

B64
GRZYBOWSKI K.,THE SOCIALIST COMMONWEALTH OF NATIONS: ORGANIZATIONS AND INSTITUTIONS. FORCES DIPLOM INT/TRADE ADJUD ADMIN LEAD WAR MARXISM SOCISM...BIBLIOG 20 COMECON WARSAW/P. PAGE 58 A1185 — INT/LAW COM REGION INT/ORG

B64
HALPERIN S.W.,MUSSOLINI AND ITALIAN FASCISM. ITALY NAT/G POL/PAR SECT ECO/TAC LEAD PWR SOCISM...POLICY 20 MUSSOLIN/B. PAGE 60 A1241 — FASCISM NAT/LISM EDU/PROP CHIEF

B64
HAMBRIDGE G.,DYNAMICS OF DEVELOPMENT. AGRI FINAN INDUS LABOR INT/TRADE EDU/PROP ADMIN LEAD OWN HEALTH...ANTHOL BIBLIOG 20. PAGE 61 A1245 — ECO/UNDEV ECO/TAC OP/RES ACT/RES

B64
KOLARZ W.,BOOKS ON COMMUNISM. USSR WOR+45 CULTURE NAT/G POL/PAR DIPLOM LEAD...CONCPT GOV/COMP IDEA/COMP. PAGE 81 A1667 — BIBLIOG/A SOCIETY COM MARXISM

B64
LIEVWEN E.,GENERALS VS PRESIDENTS: WEOMILITARISM IN LATIN AMERICA. L/A+17C FORCES DIPLOM FOR/AID LEAD — CIVMIL/REL REV

...NAT/COMP 20 PRESIDENT. PAGE 89 A1813
CONSERVE ORD/FREE

B64
MACKESY P.,THE WAR FOR AMERICA, 1775-1783. UK FORCES DIPLOM...POLICY 18. PAGE 93 A1895
WAR COLONIAL LEAD REV

B64
MAHAR J.M.,INDIA: A CRITICAL BIBLIOGRAPHY. INDIA PAKISTAN CULTURE ECO/UNDEV LOC/G POL/PAR SECT PROB/SOLV DIPLOM ADMIN COLONIAL PARL/PROC ATTIT 20. PAGE 93 A1906
BIBLIOG/A S/ASIA NAT/G LEAD

B64
MCWHINNEY E.,"PEACEFUL COEXISTENCE" AND SOVIET-WESTERN INTERNATIONAL LAW. USSR DIPLOM LEAD...JURID 20 COLD/WAR. PAGE 99 A2027
PEACE IDEA/COMP INT/LAW ATTIT

B64
MORGAN T.,GOLDWATER EITHER/OR; A SELF-PORTRAIT BASED UPON HIS OWN WORDS. USA+45 CONSTN AGRI LABOR DIPLOM RACE/REL WEALTH POPULISM...POLICY MAJORIT 20 GOLDWATR/B REPUBLICAN. PAGE 104 A2131
LEAD POL/PAR CHOOSE ATTIT

B64
NICOL D.,AFRICA - A SUBJECTIVE VIEW. AFR INT/ORG PLAN ADMIN COLONIAL PARL/PROC PARTIC REGION GOV/REL LITERACY ATTIT...BIBLIOG 20 CIVIL/SERV. PAGE 109 A2230
NAT/G LEAD CULTURE ACADEM

B64
QUIGG P.W.,AFRICA: A FOREIGN AFFAIRS READER. AFR FRANCE PORTUGAL UK DIPLOM LEAD PARL/PROC MARXISM ...MAJORIT METH/CNCPT GOV/COMP IDEA/COMP ANTHOL 19/20. PAGE 118 A2426
COLONIAL SOVEREIGN NAT/LISM RACE/REL

B64
SEGUNDO-SANCHEZ M.,OBRAS (2 VOLS.). VENEZUELA EX/STRUC DIPLOM ADMIN 19/20. PAGE 131 A2682
BIBLIOG LEAD NAT/G L/A+17C

B64
TURNER M.C.,LIBROS EN VENTA EN HISPANOAMERICA Y ESPANA. SPAIN LAW CONSTN CULTURE ADMIN LEAD...HUM SOC 20. PAGE 146 A2983
BIBLIOG L/A+17C NAT/G DIPLOM

B64
WRIGHT T.P. JR.,AMERICAN SUPPORT OF FREE ELECTIONS ABROAD. USA+45 USA-45 DOMIN LEAD NEUTRAL MARXISM ...POLICY TIME/SEQ BIBLIOG 19/20 COLD/WAR INTERVENT. PAGE 168 A3420
DIPLOM CHOOSE L/A+17C POPULISM

B65
EDUCATION AND WORLD AFFAIRS,THE UNIVERSITY LOOKS ABROAD: APPROACHES TO WORLD AFFAIRS AT SIX AMERICAN UNIVERSITIES. USA+45 CREATE EDU/PROP CONFER LEAD KNOWL 20 CORNELL/U MICH/STA/U STANFORD/U TULANE/U WISCONSN/U. PAGE 40 A0822
ACADEM DIPLOM ATTIT GP/COMP

B65
EISENHOWER D.D.,WAGING PEACE 1956-61: THE WHITE HOUSE YEARS. USA+45 DIPLOM LEAD INGP/REL RACE/REL PEACE ATTIT...TRADIT TIME/SEQ 20 EISNHWR/DD PRESIDENT COLD/WAR CIV/RIGHTS BERLIN. PAGE 41 A0833
TOP/EX BIOG ORD/FREE POLICY

B65
GEORGE M.,THE WARPED VISION. EUR+WWI UK NAT/G POL/PAR LEGIS PARL/PROC SANCTION COERCE WAR GOV/REL PEACE RESPECT 20 CONSRV/PAR. PAGE 52 A1061
LEAD ATTIT DIPLOM POLICY

B65
GRAHAM G.S.,THE POLITICS OF NAVAL SUPREMACY; STUDIES IN BRITISH MARITIME ASCENDANCY. UK SEA NAT/G BAL/PWR LEAD WAR WEAPON PEACE...POLICY 18/19 COMMONWLTH. PAGE 55 A1126
FORCES PWR COLONIAL DIPLOM

B65
HART B.H.L.,THE MEMOIRS OF CAPTAIN LIDDELL HART (VOL. I). UK NAT/G PLAN TEC/DEV DIPLOM ADMIN WEAPON GOV/REL PERS/REL ATTIT PWR FASCISM...POLICY 20. PAGE 62 A1274
FORCES BIOG LEAD WAR

B65
LOEWENHEIM F.L.,PEACE OR APPEASEMENT? HITLER, CHAMBERLAIN AND THE MUNICH CRISIS. MUNIC DELIB/GP WAR TOTALISM ATTIT SOVEREIGN...TIME/SEQ ANTHOL BIBLIOG 20 HITLER/A CHAMBRLN/N. PAGE 90 A1851
DIPLOM LEAD PEACE

B65
MALLIN J.,FORTRESS CUBA; RUSSIA'S AMERICAN BASE. COM CUBA L/A+17C FORCES PLAN DIPLOM LEAD REV WAR ...POLICY 20 CASTRO/F GUEVARA/C INTERVENT. PAGE 93 A1914
MARXISM CHIEF GUERRILLA DOMIN

B65
MERKL P.H.,GERMANY: YESTERDAY AND TOMORROW. GERMANY POL/PAR PLAN DIPLOM LEAD FEDERAL 19/20. PAGE 100 A2043
NAT/G FUT

B65
MIDDLETON D.,CRISIS IN THE WEST. EUR+WWI FUT WOR+45 CHIEF PLAN ECO/TAC LEAD REGION NUC/PWR NAT/LISM MARXISM 20 COLD/WAR NATO EEC. PAGE 101 A2068
INT/ORG DIPLOM NAT/G POLICY

B65
MOLNAR T.,AFRICA: A POLITICAL TRAVELOGUE. STRUCT ECO/UNDEV DIPLOM EDU/PROP LEAD RACE/REL MARXISM 20 INTERVENT EUROPE. PAGE 102 A2101
COLONIAL AFR ORD/FREE

B65
RAPPAPORT A.,ISSUES IN AMERICAN DIPLOMACY: WORLD POWER AND LEADERSHIP SINCE 1895 (VOL. II). CHINA/COM EUR+WWI L/A+17C USA+45 USA-45 NAT/G ECO/TAC DOMIN CONFER LEAD NUC/PWR WEAPON...DECISION 19/20 WILSON/W ROOSEVLT/F CHINJAP. PAGE 119 A2447
WAR POLICY DIPLOM

B66
BERNSTEIN B.J.,THE TRUMAN ADMINISTRATION. WOR+45 LABOR POL/PAR LEGIS DIPLOM NUC/PWR WAR ATTIT ...POLICY 20 TRUMAN/HS. PAGE 14 A0279
LEAD TOP/EX NAT/G

B66
BLACK C.E.,THE DYNAMICS OF MODERNIZATION: A STUDY IN COMPARATIVE HISTORY. STRUCT ECO/DEV ECO/UNDEV NAT/G DIPLOM LEAD REV...PREDICT TIME/SEQ TREND SOC/INTEG 17/20. PAGE 15 A0296
SOCIETY SOC NAT/COMP

B66
BROEKMEIJER M.W.J.,FICTION AND TRUTH ABOUT THE "DECADE OF DEVELOPMENT" WOR+45 AGRI FINAN INDUS NAT/G TEC/DEV DIPLOM EDU/PROP LEAD SKILL 20 THIRD/WRLD. PAGE 19 A0385
FOR/AID POLICY ECO/UNDEV PLAN

B66
CANNING HOUSE LIBRARY,AUTHOR AND SUBJECT CATALOGUES OF THE CANNING HOUSE LIBRARY (5 VOLS.). UK CULTURE LEAD...SOC 19/20. PAGE 24 A0478
BIBLIOG L/A+17C NAT/G DIPLOM

B66
COLE A.B.,SOCIALIST PARTIES IN POSTWAR JAPAN. STRATA AGRI LABOR PLAN DIPLOM ECO/TAC AGREE LEAD CHOOSE ATTIT...CHARTS 20 CHINJAP SOC/DEMPAR. PAGE 28 A0566
POL/PAR POLICY SOCISM NAT/G

B66
DAVIS V.,POSTWAR DEFENSE POLICY AND THE US NAVY, 1943-1946. USA+45 DIPLOM CONFER LEAD ATTIT...POLICY IDEA/COMP 20 NAVY. PAGE 34 A0692
FORCES PLAN PROB/SOLV CIVMIL/REL

B66
DONALD A.D.,JOHN F. KENNEDY AND THE NEW FRONTIER. LEGIS DIPLOM DISCRIM PEACE PWR 20. PAGE 38 A0771
LEAD CHIEF BIOG EFFICIENCY

B66
DRACHOVITCH M.M.,THE COMINTERN HISTORICAL HIGHLIGHTS. USSR INT/ORG EX/STRUC LEGIT LEAD GUERRILLA...ANTHOL 20 COMINTERN LENIN/VI. PAGE 38 A0784
DIPLOM REV MARXISM PERSON

B66
EKIRCH A.A. JR.,IDEAS, IDEALS, AND AMERICAN DIPLOMACY. USA+45 USA-45 INT/ORG DOMIN COLONIAL ARMS/CONT DETER ISOLAT NAT/LISM...MAJORIT BIBLIOG 19/20 COLD/WAR. PAGE 41 A0834
DIPLOM LEAD PEACE

B66
FEHRENBACH T.R.,THIS KIND OF PEACE. WOR+45 LEAD PARTIC WAR EFFICIENCY ATTIT UN. PAGE 44 A0906
PEACE DIPLOM INT/ORG BAL/PWR

B66
JACK H.A.,RELIGION AND PEACE: PAPERS FROM THE NATIONAL INTER-RELIGIOUS CONFERENCE ON PEACE, WASHINGTON, 1966. CHINA/COM USA+45 VIETNAM WOR+45 FORCES FOR/AID LEAD PERS/REL. PAGE 72 A1472
PEACE SECT SUPEGO DIPLOM

B66
KEYES J.G.,A BIBLIOGRAPHY OF WESTERN LANGUAGE PUBLICATIONS CONCERNING NORTH VIETNAM IN THE CORNELL LIBRARY. VIETNAM/N NAT/G FORCES TEC/DEV DIPLOM LEAD RACE/REL...GEOG SOC 20. PAGE 78 A1603
BIBLIOG/A CULTURE ECO/UNDEV S/ASIA

B66
MC LELLAN D.S.,THE COLD WAR IN TRANSITION. USSR WOR+45 CONTROL LEAD NUC/PWR NAT/LISM SOVEREIGN 20 COLD/WAR THIRD/WRLD. PAGE 97 A1994
BAL/PWR DETER DIPLOM POLICY

B66
MOORE R.J.,SIR CHARLES WOOD'S INDIAN POLICY: 1853-66. INDIA POL/PAR CHIEF DELIB/GP DIPLOM CONTROL LEAD WOOD/CHAS. PAGE 103 A2124
COLONIAL ADMIN CONSULT DECISION

B66
MULLER C.F.J.,A SELECT BIBLIOGRAPHY OF SOUTH AFRICAN HISTORY; A GUIDE FOR HISTORICAL RESEARCH. SOUTH/AFR UK LAW CONSTN SOCIETY STRUCT AGRI SECT DIPLOM COLONIAL LEAD RACE/REL...POLICY 17/20 NEGRO. PAGE 106 A2167
BIBLIOG AFR NAT/G

B66
NIEDERGANG M.,LA REVOLUTION DE SAINT-DOMINGUE. DOMIN/REP INT/ORG NAT/G CONTROL LEAD GP/REL ORD/FREE MARXISM 20. PAGE 109 A2239
REV FORCES DIPLOM

B66
OLSON W.C.,THE THEORY AND PRACTICE OF INTERNATIONAL RELATIONS (2ND ED.). WOR+45 LEAD SUPEGO...INT/LAW PHIL/SCI. PAGE 112 A2290
DIPLOM NAT/G INT/ORG POLICY

B66
RIESELBACH L.N.,THE ROOTS OF ISOLATIONISM* CONGRESSIONAL VOTING AND PRESIDENTIAL LEADERSHIP IN FOREIGN POLICY. POL/PAR LEGIS DIPLOM EDU/PROP LEAD REGION REPRESENT...SOC STAT IDEA/COMP HYPO/EXP BIBLIOG 19/20 CONGRESS. PAGE 121 A2477
ISOLAT CHOOSE CHIEF POLICY

B66
SCHWARZ U.,AMERICAN STRATEGY: A NEW PERSPECTIVE. USA+45 USA-45 INT/ORG TEC/DEV BAL/PWR DIPLOM LEAD ARMS/CONT DETER NUC/PWR WAR 20 NATO. PAGE 130 A2659 NAT/G POLICY FORCES PWR

B66
SPEARS E.L.,TWO MEN WHO SAVED FRANCE: PETAIN AND DE GAULLE. FRANCE CONSTN FORCES DIPLOM WAR PERSON 20 WWI PETAIN/HP DEGAULLE/C. PAGE 135 A2773 BIOG LEAD CHIEF NAT/G

B66
US DEPARTMENT OF STATE,RESEARCH ON AFRICA (EXTERNAL RESEARCH LIST NO 5-25). LAW CULTURE ECO/UNDEV POL/PAR DIPLOM EDU/PROP LEAD REGION MARXISM...GEOG LING WORSHIP 20. PAGE 152 A3094 BIBLIOG/A ASIA S/ASIA NAT/G

B66
US DEPARTMENT OF THE ARMY,SOUTH ASIA: A STRATEGIC SURVEY (PAMPHLET NO. 550-3). AFGHANISTN INDIA NEPAL PAKISTAN ECO/UNDEV INT/ORG POL/PAR FORCES FOR/AID INT/TRADE LEAD WAR...POLICY SOC TREND 20. PAGE 152 A3110 BIBLIOG/A S/ASIA DIPLOM NAT/G

B66
WELCH C.E.,DREAM OF UNITY; PAN-AFRICANISM AND POLITICAL UNIFICATION IN WEST AFRICA. AFR ECO/UNDEV CONFER COLONIAL LEAD...INT/LAW 20. PAGE 163 A3312 INT/ORG REGION NAT/LISM DIPLOM

B66
WILSON H.A.,THE IMPERIAL POLICY OF SIR ROBERT BORDEN. CANADA UK ELITES INT/ORG VOL/ASSN CONTROL LEAD WAR ROLE 20 CMN/WLTH BORDEN/R. PAGE 165 A3360 INGP/REL COLONIAL CONSTN CHIEF

B66
WOHL R.,FRENCH COMMUNISM IN THE MAKING 1914-1924. FRANCE USSR LEAD REV...IDEA/COMP 20 COM/PARTY. PAGE 166 A3377 MARXISM WORKER DIPLOM

B66
ZEINE Z.N.,THE EMERGENCE OF ARAB NATIONALISM (REV. ED.). TURKEY UK NAT/G SECT TEC/DEV LEAD REV WAR AGE/Y ROLE ORD/FREE...TRADIT CHARTS BIBLIOG 20 ARABS OTTOMAN. PAGE 170 A3451 ISLAM NAT/LISM DIPLOM

S66
"FURTHER READING." INDIA LEAD ATTIT...CONCPT 20. PAGE 4 A0075 BIBLIOG NAT/G DIPLOM POLICY

S66
GAMER R.E.,"URGENT SINGAPORE, PATIENT MALAYSIA." MALAYSIA S/ASIA ECO/UNDEV POL/PAR CHIEF TARIFFS TAX CONTROL LEAD REGION PWR 20 SINGAPORE. PAGE 51 A1036 DIPLOM NAT/G POLICY ECO/TAC

S66
MCNEAL R.H.,"THE LEGACY OF THE COMINTERN." USSR WOR+45 WOR-45 PROB/SOLV DIPLOM CONFER CONTROL LEAD WAR 20 STALIN/J COMINTERN. PAGE 98 A2020 MARXISM INT/ORG POL/PAR PWR

B67
BLOOMFIELD L.,THE UNITED NATIONS AND US FOREIGN POLICY. USA+45 DIPLOM LEAD ARMS/CONT DETER PWR 20 UN. PAGE 15 A0313 INT/ORG PLAN CONFER IDEA/COMP

B67
CECIL L.,ALBERT BALLIN; BUSINESS AND POLITICS IN IMPERIAL GERMANY 1888-1918. GERMANY UK INT/TRADE LEAD WAR PERS/REL ADJUST PWR WEALTH...MGT BIBLIOG 19/20. PAGE 25 A0510 DIPLOM CONSTN ECO/DEV TOP/EX

B67
KATZ R.,DEATH IN ROME. EUR+WWI ITALY POL/PAR DIPLOM LEAD ATTIT PERSON ROLE CATHISM. PAGE 77 A1570 WAR MURDER FORCES DEATH

B67
KIRK R.,THE POLITICAL PRINCIPLES OF ROBERT A. TAFT. USA+45 LABOR DIPLOM ADJUD ADJUST ORD/FREE TAFT/RA. PAGE 80 A1635 POL/PAR LEAD LEGIS ATTIT

B67
MAW B.,BREAKTHROUGH IN BURMA: MEMOIRS OF A REVOLUTION, 1939-1946. BURMA UK FORCES PROB/SOLV DIPLOM FOR/AID DOMIN LEAD...BIOG 20. PAGE 97 A1980 REV ORD/FREE NAT/LISM COLONIAL

B67
SCHWARTZ M.A.,PUBLIC OPINION AND CANADIAN IDENTITY. CANADA SOCIETY LOC/G DIPLOM ADMIN LEAD REGION GP/REL SAMP. PAGE 130 A2657 ATTIT NAT/G NAT/LISM POL/PAR

B67
THORNE C.,THE APPROACH OF WAR, 1938-1939. EUR+WWI POL/PAR CHIEF FORCES LEAD DRIVE PWR FASCISM ...BIBLIOG/A 20 HITLER/A. PAGE 144 A2936 DIPLOM WAR ELITES

B67
WATERS M.,THE UNITED NATIONS* INTERNATIONAL ORGANIZATION AND ADMINISTRATION. WOR+45 EX/STRUC FORCES DIPLOM LEAD REGION ARMS/CONT REPRESENT INGP/REL ROLE...METH/COMP ANTHOL 20 UN LEAGUE/NAT. PAGE 162 A3291 CONSTN INT/ORG ADMIN ADJUD

B67
WILLIS F.R.,DE GAULLE: ANACHRONISM, REALIST, OR PROPHET? FRANCE POL/PAR FORCES DIPLOM WAR PEACE ROLE ORD/FREE...POLICY IDEA/COMP ANTHOL 20 DEGAULLE/C. PAGE 165 A3356 BIOG PERSON CHIEF LEAD

B67
YAMAMURA K.,ECONOMIC POLICY IN POSTWAR JAPAN. ASIA FINAN POL/PAR DIPLOM LEAD NAT/LISM ATTIT NEW/LIB POPULISM 20 CHINJAP. PAGE 168 A3429 ECO/DEV POLICY NAT/G TEC/DEV

S67
BELGION M.,"THE CASE FOR REHABILITATING MARSHAL PETAIN." EUR+WWI FRANCE NAT/G DIPLOM ATTIT PERSON MORAL PETAIN/HP. PAGE 12 A0253 WAR FORCES LEAD

S67
HALLE L.J.,"DE GAULLE AND THE FUTURE OF EUROPE." FRANCE DIPLOM 20. PAGE 60 A1232 NAT/LISM LEAD INT/ORG PREDICT

S67
LACOUTRE J.,"HO CHI MINH." CHINA/COM USSR VIETNAM/N NAT/G CHIEF TOP/EX LEAD NEUTRAL...REALPOL PREDICT 20. PAGE 83 A1708 NAT/LISM MARXISM REV DIPLOM

S67
MEYER J.,"CUBA S'ENFERME DANS SA REVOLUTION." CHINA/COM CUBA USSR NAT/G TOP/EX DIPLOM LEAD ATTIT ...PREDICT 20. PAGE 100 A2053 MARXISM REV CHIEF NAT/LISM

S67
MUDGE G.A.,"DOMESTIC POLICIES AND UN ACTIVITIES* THE CASE OF RHODESIA AND THE REPUBLIC OF SOUTH AFRICA." RHODESIA SOUTH/AFR POL/PAR LEAD SANCTION CHOOSE RACE/REL CONSEN DISCRIM ATTIT...INT/LAW UN PARLIAMENT 20. PAGE 105 A2163 AFR NAT/G POLICY

S67
SENCOURT R.,"FOREIGN POLICY* AN HISTORIC RECTIFICATION." EUR+WWI UK DIPLOM EDU/PROP LEAD WAR CHOOSE PERS/REL...METH/COMP PARLIAMENT. PAGE 131 A2685 POLICY POL/PAR NAT/G

S67
VAN DUSEN H.P.,"HAMMARSKOLD IN THE WORLD'S SERVICE." DIPLOM CONFER LEAD PEACE STRANGE UTOPIA MORAL SKILL OBJECTIVE...INT/LAW SELF/OBS 20. PAGE 158 A3211 INT/ORG CONSULT TOP/EX NEUTRAL

S67
YEFROMEV A.,"THE TRUE FACE OF THE WEST GERMAN NATIONAL-DEMOCRATS." GERMANY/W NAT/G DOMIN LEAD SANCTION WAR ATTIT PERSON...MARXIST 20. PAGE 169 A3433 POL/PAR TOTALISM PARL/PROC DIPLOM

S67
YOUNG K.T.,"UNITED STATES POLICY AND VIETNAMESE POLITICAL VIABILITY 1954-1967." VIETNAM/S LOC/G MUNIC FOR/AID ORD/FREE...POLICY 20. PAGE 169 A3437 LEAD ADMIN GP/REL EFFICIENCY

B93
ROYAL GEOGRAPHIC SOCIETY,BIBLIOGRAPHY OF BARBARY STATES (4 SUPPLEMENTARY PAPERS). ALGERIA LIBYA MOROCCO SOCIETY STRUCT DIPLOM LEAD 14/19 TUNIS. PAGE 125 A2555 BIBLIOG ISLAM NAT/G COLONIAL

B96
LOWELL A.L.,GOVERNMENTS AND PARTIES IN CONTINENTAL EUROPE, VOL. II. AUSTRIA GERMANY HUNGARY MOD/EUR SWITZERLND SOCIETY EX/STRUC LEGIS DIPLOM AGREE LEAD PARL/PROC PWR...POLICY 19. PAGE 91 A1867 POL/PAR NAT/G GOV/REL ELITES

LEADING....SEE LEAD

LEAGUE OF NATIONS A1755

LEAGUE OF WOMEN VOTERS OF US A1756

LEAGUE/NAT....LEAGUE OF NATIONS; SEE ALSO INT/ORG

N
INTERNATIONAL BOOK NEWS, 1928-1934. ECO/UNDEV FINAN INDUS LABOR INT/TRADE CONFER ADJUD COLONIAL...HEAL SOC/WK CHARTS 20 LEAGUE/NAT. PAGE 1 A0010 BIBLIOG/A DIPLOM INT/LAW INT/ORG

N
SOCIETE DES NATIONS,TRAITES INTERNATIONAUX ET ACTES LEGISLATIFS. WOR-45 INT/ORG NAT/G...INT/LAW JURID 20 LEAGUE/NAT TREATY. PAGE 135 A2759 BIBLIOG DIPLOM LEGIS ADJUD

N
WORLD PEACE FOUNDATION,DOCUMENTS OF INTERNATIONAL ORGANIZATIONS: A SELECTED BIBLIOGRAPHY. WOR+45 WOR-45 AGRI FINAN ACT/RES OP/RES INT/TRADE ADMIN ...CON/ANAL 20 UN UNESCO LEAGUE/NAT. PAGE 167 A3396 BIBLIOG DIPLOM INT/ORG REGION

B18
US LIBRARY OF CONGRESS,LIST OF REFERENCES ON A LEAGUE OF NATIONS. DIPLOM WAR PEACE 20 LEAGUE/NAT. BIBLIOG INT/ORG

PAGE 154 A3145 ADMIN EX/STRUC

B19
DE CALLIERES F.,THE PRACTICE OF DIPLOMACY. MOD/EUR INT/ORG NAT/G DELIB/GP LEGIS TOP/EX DOMIN ATTIT KNOWL LEAGUE/NAT 20. PAGE 34 A0699 CONSULT ACT/RES DIPLOM INT/LAW

B20
DICKINSON E.,THE EQUALITY OF STATES IN INTERNATIONAL LAW. WOR-45 INT/ORG NAT/G DIPLOM EDU/PROP LEGIT PEACE ATTIT ALL/VALS...JURID TIME/SEQ LEAGUE/NAT. PAGE 37 A0757 LAW CONCPT SOVEREIGN

B22
WRIGHT Q.,THE CONTROL OF AMERICAN FOREIGN RELATIONS. USA-45 WOR-45 CONSTN INT/ORG CONSULT LEGIS LEGIT ROUTINE ORD/FREE PWR...POLICY JURID CONCPT METH/CNCPT RECORD LEAGUE/NAT 20. PAGE 167 A3402 NAT/G EXEC DIPLOM

B24
HALL W.E.,A TREATISE ON INTERNATIONAL LAW. WOR-45 CONSTN INT/ORG NAT/G DIPLOM ORD/FREE LEAGUE/NAT 20 TREATY. PAGE 60 A1228 PWR JURID WAR INT/LAW

B27
LAUTERPACHT H.,PRIVATE LAW SOURCES AND ANALOGIES OF INTERNATIONAL LAW. WOR-45 NAT/G DELIB/GP LEGIT COERCE ATTIT ORD/FREE PWR SOVEREIGN...JURID CONCPT HIST/WRIT TIME/SEQ GEN/METH LEAGUE/NAT 20. PAGE 85 A1748 INT/ORG ADJUD PEACE INT/LAW

B28
CORBETT P.E.,CANADA AND WORLD POLITICS. LAW CULTURE SOCIETY STRUCT MARKET INT/ORG FORCES ACT/RES PLAN ECO/TAC LEGIT ORD/FREE PWR RESPECT...SOC CONCPT TIME/SEQ TREND CMN/WLTH 20 LEAGUE/NAT. PAGE 30 A0612 NAT/G CANADA

B28
HOWARD-ELLIS C.,THE ORIGIN, STRUCTURE AND WORKING OF THE LEAGUE OF NATIONS. EUR+WWI MOD/EUR USA-45 CONSTN FORCES LEGIS ECO/TAC LEGIT COERCE ORD/FREE ...JURID SOC CONCPT LEAGUE/NAT 20 ILO ICJ. PAGE 68 A1401 INT/ORG ADJUD

B28
MILLER D.H.,THE DRAFTING OF THE COVENANT. UNIV WOR-45 INTELL NAT/G DELIB/GP PLAN ECO/TAC LEGIT WAR ATTIT PERCEPT...CONCPT TIME/SEQ LEAGUE/NAT TOT/POP 20. PAGE 101 A2074 INT/ORG STRUCT PEACE

B29
CONWELL-EVANS T.P.,THE LEAGUE COUNCIL IN ACTION. EUR+WWI TURKEY UK USSR WOR-45 INT/ORG FORCES JUDGE ECO/TAC EDU/PROP LEGIT ROUTINE ARMS/CONT COERCE ATTIT PWR...MAJORIT GEOG JURID CONCPT LEAGUE/NAT TOT/POP VAL/FREE TUNIS 20. PAGE 30 A0605 DELIB/GP INT/LAW

B29
STURZO L.,THE INTERNATIONAL COMMUNITY AND THE RIGHT OF WAR (TRANS. BY BARBARA BARCLAY CARTER). CULTURE CREATE PROB/SOLV DIPLOM ADJUD CONTROL PEACE PERSON ORD/FREE...INT/LAW IDEA/COMP PACIFIST 20 LEAGUE/NAT. PAGE 140 A2858 INT/ORG PLAN WAR CONCPT

B30
SMUTS J.C.,AFRICA AND SOME WORLD PROBLEMS. RHODESIA SOUTH/AFR CULTURE ECO/UNDEV INDUS INT/ORG SECT PROB/SOLV REGION GOV/REL DISCRIM ATTIT 19/20 LEAGUE/NAT LIVNGSTN/D NEGRO. PAGE 134 A2748 LEGIS AFR COLONIAL RACE/REL

B30
WRIGHT Q.,MANDATES UNDER THE LEAGUE OF NATIONS. WOR-45 CONSTN ECO/DEV ECO/UNDEV NAT/G DELIB/GP TOP/EX LEGIT ALL/VALS...JURID CONCPT LEAGUE/NAT 20. PAGE 167 A3403 INT/ORG LAW INT/LAW

B31
GREAVES H.R.G.,THE LEAGUE COMMITTEES AND WORLD ORDER. WOR-45 DELIB/GP EX/STRUC EDU/PROP ALL/VALS LEAGUE/NAT VAL/FREE 20. PAGE 55 A1136 INT/ORG DIPLOM ROUTINE

B31
HILL N.,INTERNATIONAL ADMINISTRATION. WOR-45 DELIB/GP DIPLOM EDU/PROP ALL/VALS...MGT TIME/SEQ LEAGUE/NAT TOT/POP VAL/FREE 20. PAGE 65 A1331 INT/ORG ADMIN

B31
HODGES C.,THE BACKGROUND OF INTERNATIONAL RELATIONS. WOR-45 SOCIETY ECO/DEV ECO/UNDEV INT/ORG DIPLOM DOMIN EDU/PROP LEGIT WAR ATTIT DRIVE PERSON ALL/VALS...CONCPT METH/CNCPT TIME/SEQ CHARTS WORK LEAGUE/NAT 19/20. PAGE 66 A1350 NAT/G BAL/PWR

B32
EAGLETON C.,INTERNATIONAL GOVERNMENT. BRAZIL FRANCE GERMANY ITALY UK USSR WOR-45 DELIB/GP TOP/EX PLAN ECO/TAC EDU/PROP LEGIT ADJUD REGION ARMS/CONT COERCE ATTIT PWR...GEOG MGT VAL/FREE LEAGUE/NAT 20. PAGE 40 A0816 INT/ORG JURID DIPLOM INT/LAW

B32
FLEMMING D.,THE UNITED STATES AND THE LEAGUE OF NATIONS, 1918-1920. FUT USA-45 NAT/G LEGIS TOP/EX DEBATE CHOOSE PEACE ATTIT SOVEREIGN...TIME/SEQ CON/ANAL CONGRESS LEAGUE/NAT 20 TREATY. PAGE 46 A0950 INT/ORG EDU/PROP

B32
MORLEY F.,THE SOCIETY OF NATIONS. EUR+WWI UNIV WOR-45 LAW CONSTN ACT/RES PLAN EDU/PROP LEGIT ROUTINE...POLICY TIME/SEQ LEAGUE/NAT TOT/POP 20. PAGE 104 A2143 INT/ORG CONCPT

B33
LANGER W.L.,FOREIGN AFFAIRS BIBLIOGRAPHY. WOR-45 INT/ORG CONSULT EDU/PROP ROUTINE NAT/LISM ATTIT SOVEREIGN...STAT RECORD GEN/METH LEAGUE/NAT TOT/POP. PAGE 84 A1725 KNOWL

B33
LAUTERPACHT H.,THE FUNCTION OF LAW IN THE INTERNATIONAL COMMUNITY. WOR-45 NAT/G FORCES CREATE DOMIN LEGIT COERCE WAR PEACE ATTIT ORD/FREE PWR SOVEREIGN...JURID CONCPT METH/CNCPT TIME/SEQ GEN/LAWS GEN/METH LEAGUE/NAT TOT/POP VAL/FREE 20. PAGE 85 A1749 INT/ORG LAW INT/LAW

B35
HUDSON M.,BY PACIFIC MEANS. WOR-45 EDU/PROP ORD/FREE...CONCPT TIME/SEQ GEN/LAWS LEAGUE/NAT TOT/POP 20 TREATY. PAGE 68 A1407 INT/ORG CT/SYS PEACE

B35
LEAGUE OF NATIONS,CATALOGUE OF PUBLICATIONS, 1920-1935. GOV/REL 20 LEAGUE/NAT. PAGE 86 A1755 BIBLIOG INT/ORG DIPLOM

B36
BEARD C.A.,THE DEVIL THEORY OF WAR; AN INQUIRY INTO NATURE OF HISTORY AND THE POSSIBILITY OF KEEPING OUT OF WAR. USA-45 INT/ORG PROB/SOLV NEUTRAL ISOLAT ...CONCPT 20 LEAGUE/NAT WWI. PAGE 12 A0240 GEN/LAWS WAR POLICY DIPLOM

B36
BRIERLY J.L.,THE LAW OF NATIONS (2ND ED.). WOR+45 WOR-45 INT/ORG AGREE CONTROL COERCE WAR NAT/LISM PEACE PWR 16/20 TREATY LEAGUE/NAT. PAGE 18 A0375 DIPLOM INT/LAW NAT/G

B36
HUDSON M.O.,INTERNATIONAL LEGISLATION: 1929-1931. WOR-45 SEA AIR AGRI FINAN LABOR DIPLOM ECO/TAC REPAR CT/SYS ARMS/CONT WAR WEAPON...JURID 20 TREATY LEAGUE/NAT. PAGE 69 A1409 INT/LAW PARL/PROC ADJUD LAW

B36
SHOTWELL J.,ON THE RIM OF THE ABYSS. EUR+WWI USA-45 STRUCT INT/ORG ACT/RES PLAN EDU/PROP EXEC ATTIT ALL/VALS...TIME/SEQ LEAGUE/NAT TOT/POP 20. PAGE 132 A2706 NAT/G BAL/PWR

B37
UNION OF SOUTH AFRICA,REPORT CONCERNING ADMINISTRATION OF SOUTH WEST AFRICA (6 VOLS.). SOUTH/AFR INDUS PUB/INST FORCES LEGIS BUDGET DIPLOM EDU/PROP ADJUD CT/SYS...GEOG CHARTS 20 AFRICA/SW LEAGUE/NAT. PAGE 148 A3028 NAT/G ADMIN COLONIAL CONSTN

B38
DE MADARIAGA S.,THE WORLD'S DESIGN. WOR-45 SOCIETY STRUCT EDU/PROP PEACE ATTIT PERSON ALL/VALS ...SOCIALIST CONCPT TIME/SEQ TREND GEN/LAWS LEAGUE/NAT. PAGE 35 A0706 FUT INT/ORG DIPLOM

B38
FLEMMING D.,THE UNITED STATES AND WORLD ORGANIZATION, 1920-1933. ASIA FUT WOR-45 NAT/G TOP/EX DIPLOM ECO/TAC EDU/PROP LEGIT COERCE WAR ...TIME/SEQ LEAGUE/NAT 20 CHINJAP. PAGE 47 A0951 USA-45 INT/ORG PEACE

B38
GRISWOLD A.W.,THE FAR EASTERN POLICY OF THE UNITED STATES. ASIA S/ASIA USA-45 INT/ORG INT/TRADE WAR NAT/LISM...BIBLIOG 19/20 LEAGUE/NAT ROOSEVLT/T ROOSEVLT/F WILSON/W TREATY. PAGE 57 A1166 DIPLOM POLICY CHIEF

B38
MATTHEWS M.A.,FEDERALISM: SELECT LIST OF REFERENCES ON FEDERAL GOVERNMENT REGIONALISM...EXAMPLES OF FEDERATIONS (PAMPHLET). WOR-45 CONSTN INT/ORG NAT/G 19/20 OAS LEAGUE/NAT. PAGE 96 A1976 BIBLIOG/A FEDERAL REGION DIPLOM

B38
RAPPARD W.E.,THE CRISIS OF DEMOCRACY. EUR+WWI UNIV WOR-45 CULTURE SOCIETY ECO/DEV INT/ORG POL/PAR ACT/RES EDU/PROP EXEC CHOOSE ATTIT ALL/VALS...SOC OBS HIST/WRIT TIME/SEQ LEAGUE/NAT NAZI TOT/POP 20. PAGE 119 A2449 NAT/G CONCPT

B39
BENES E.,INTERNATIONAL SECURITY. GERMANY UK NAT/G DELIB/GP PLAN BAL/PWR ATTIT ORD/FREE PWR LEAGUE/NAT 20 TREATY. PAGE 13 A0267 EUR+WWI INT/ORG WAR

B39
BROWN J.F.,CONTEMPORARY WORLD POLITICS. WOR-45 NAT/G PLAN BAL/PWR EDU/PROP LEGIT REGION NAT/LISM ORD/FREE PWR SOVEREIGN...POLICY CONCPT HIST/WRIT TIME/SEQ GEN/LAWS LEAGUE/NAT. PAGE 20 A0403 INT/ORG DIPLOM PEACE

B39
DULLES J.,WAR, PEACE AND CHANGE. FRANCE ITALY UK USA-45 WOR-45 LAW INT/ORG NAT/G SECT VOL/ASSN FORCES TOP/EX DOMIN ARMS/CONT COERCE ATTIT PERSON RIGID/FLEX MORAL PWR...JURID STERTYP TOT/POP LEAGUE/NAT 20. PAGE 39 A0796 EDU/PROP TOTALISM WAR

B39
MAXWELL B.W.,INTERNATIONAL RELATIONS. EUR+WWI WOR-45 NAT/G CONSULT DIPLOM LEGIT ADJUD NAT/LISM ATTIT ORD/FREE SOVEREIGN...JURID LEAGUE/NAT TOT/POP VAL/FREE 20. PAGE 97 A1981 INT/ORG

B39
ZIMMERN A.,THE LEAGUE OF NATIONS AND THE RULE OF INT/ORG

LAW. WOR-45 STRUCT NAT/G DELIB/GP EX/STRUC BAL/PWR DOMIN LEGIT COERCE ORD/FREE PWR...POLICY RECORD LEAGUE/NAT TOT/POP VAL/FREE 20 LEAGUE/NAT. PAGE 170 A3453
LAW DIPLOM

B39
ZIMMERN A.,THE LEAGUE OF NATIONS AND THE RULE OF LAW. WOR-45 STRUCT NAT/G DELIB/GP EX/STRUC BAL/PWR DOMIN LEGIT COERCE ORD/FREE PWR...POLICY RECORD LEAGUE/NAT TOT/POP VAL/FREE 20 LEAGUE/NAT. PAGE 170 A3453
INT/ORG LAW DIPLOM

B39
ZIMMERN A.,MODERN POLITICAL DOCTRINE. WOR-45 CULTURE SOCIETY ECO/UNDEV DELIB/GP EX/STRUC CREATE DOMIN COERCE NAT/LISM ATTIT RIGID/FLEX ORD/FREE PWR WEALTH...POLICY CONCPT OBS TIME/SEQ TREND TOT/POP LEAGUE/NAT 20. PAGE 170 A3454
NAT/G ECO/TAC BAL/PWR INT/TRADE

B40
BOGGS S.W.,INTERNATIONAL BOUNDARIES. WOR-45 SOCIETY ECO/DEV INT/ORG NAT/G NEIGH LEGIT PERSON ORD/FREE PWR...POLICY GEOG MYTH LEAGUE/NAT 20. PAGE 16 A0329
ATTIT CONCPT NAT/LISM

B40
MIDDLEBUSH F.,ELEMENTS OF INTERNATIONAL RELATIONS. WOR-45 PROVS CONSULT EDU/PROP LEGIT WAR NAT/LISM ATTIT KNOWL MORAL ORD/FREE PWR...JURID LEAGUE/NAT TOT/POP VAL/FREE. PAGE 101 A2067
NAT/G INT/ORG PEACE DIPLOM

B40
RAPPARD W.E.,THE QUEST FOR PEACE. UNIV USA-45 WOR-45 SOCIETY INT/ORG NAT/G PLAN EXEC ROUTINE WAR ATTIT DRIVE ALL/VALS...POLICY CONCPT OBS TIME/SEQ LEAGUE/NAT TOT/POP 20. PAGE 119 A2450
EUR+WWI ACT/RES PEACE

B41
BURTON M.E.,THE ASSEMBLY OF THE LEAGUE OF NATIONS. WOR-45 CONSTN SOCIETY STRUCT INT/ORG NAT/G CREATE ATTIT RIGID/FLEX PWR...POLICY TIME/SEQ LEAGUE/NAT 20. PAGE 22 A0448
DELIB/GP EX/STRUC DIPLOM

B41
YOUNG G.,FEDERALISM AND FREEDOM. EUR+WWI MOD/EUR RUSSIA USA-45 WOR-45 SOCIETY STRUCT ECO/DEV INT/ORG EXEC FEDERAL ATTIT PERSON ALL/VALS...OLD/LIB CONCPT OBS TREND LEAGUE/NAT TOT/POP. PAGE 169 A3435
NAT/G WAR

L41
COMM. STUDY ORGAN. PEACE,"ORGANIZATION OF PEACE." USA-45 WOR-45 STRATA NAT/G ACT/RES DIPLOM ECO/TAC EDU/PROP ADJUD ATTIT ORD/FREE PWR...SOC CONCPT ANTHOL LEAGUE/NAT 20. PAGE 28 A0575
INT/ORG PLAN PEACE

B42
FEILCHENFELD E.H.,THE INTERNATIONAL ECONOMIC LAW OF BELLIGERENT OCCUPATION. EUR+WWI MOD/EUR USA-45 INT/ORG DIPLOM ADJUD ARMS/CONT LEAGUE/NAT 20. PAGE 44 A0907
ECO/TAC INT/LAW WAR

B42
KELSEN H.,LAW AND PEACE IN INTERNATIONAL RELATIONS. FUT WOR-45 NAT/G DELIB/GP DIPLOM LEGIT RIGID/FLEX ORD/FREE SOVEREIGN...JURID CONCPT TREND STERTYP GEN/LAWS LEAGUE/NAT 20. PAGE 77 A1580
INT/ORG ADJUD PEACE INT/LAW

L42
SHOTWELL J.,"LESSON OF THE LAST WORLD WAR." EUR+WWI MOD/EUR USA-45 SOCIETY ECO/UNDEV INDUS VOL/ASSN CONSULT ACT/RES CREATE CAP/ISM INT/TRADE DRIVE ALL/VALS...CONCPT NEW/IDEA SELF/OBS GEN/LAWS LEAGUE/NAT NAZI 20. PAGE 132 A2708
INT/ORG ORD/FREE

S42
SHOTWELL J.,"AFTER THE WAR." COM EUR+WWI USA+45 USA-45 NAT/G DIPLOM INT/TRADE ARMS/CONT SOVEREIGN ...CONCPT LEAGUE/NAT TOT/POP FAO 20. PAGE 132 A2707
FUT INT/ORG PEACE

S42
TURNER F.J.,"AMERICAN SECTIONALISM AND WORLD ORGANIZATION." EUR+WWI UNIV USA-45 WOR-45 INTELL ECO/DEV TOP/EX ACT/RES PLAN EDU/PROP LEGIT ALL/VALS ...CONCPT NEW/IDEA OBS TREND LEAGUE/NAT TOT/POP 20. PAGE 146 A2981
INT/ORG DRIVE BAL/PWR

B43
CONOVER H.F.,THE BALKANS: A SELECTED LIST OF REFERENCES. ALBANIA BULGARIA ROMANIA YUGOSLAVIA INT/ORG PROB/SOLV DIPLOM LEGIT CONFER ADJUD WAR NAT/LISM PEACE PWR 20 LEAGUE/NAT. PAGE 29 A0596
BIBLIOG EUR+WWI

B43
HEMLEBEN S.J.,PLANS FOR WORLD PEACE THROUGH SIX CENTURIES. WOR-45 EDU/PROP DRIVE PWR...CONCPT TIME/SEQ GEN/LAWS TOT/POP LEAGUE/NAT 14/20. PAGE 64 A1312
INT/ORG PEACE

B43
MICAUD C.A.,THE FRENCH RIGHT AND NAZI GERMANY 1933-1939: A STUDY OF PUBLIC OPINION. GERMANY UK USSR POL/PAR ARMS/CONT COERCE DETER PEACE RIGID/FLEX PWR MARXISM...FASCIST TREND 20 LEAGUE/NAT TREATY. PAGE 101 A2065
DIPLOM AGREE

B43
SULZBACH W.,NATIONAL CONSCIOUSNESS. FUT WOR-45 INT/ORG PEACE MORAL FASCISM MARXISM...MAJORIT TREND WORSHIP 19/20 LEAGUE/NAT INTERVENT WWI. PAGE 140 A2862
NAT/LISM NAT/G DIPLOM WAR

B44
BARTLETT R.J.,THE LEAGUE TO ENFORCE PEACE. FUT USA-45 NAT/G POL/PAR CREATE EDU/PROP ADMIN RIGID/FLEX PWR...CONCPT TREND GEN/METH LEAGUE/NAT 20. PAGE 11 A0231
INT/ORG ORD/FREE DIPLOM

B44
BRIERLY J.L.,THE OUTLOOK FOR INTERNATIONAL LAW. FUT WOR-45 CONSTN NAT/G VOL/ASSN FORCES ECO/TAC DOMIN LEGIT ADJUD ROUTINE PEACE ORD/FREE...INT/LAW JURID METH LEAGUE/NAT 20. PAGE 18 A0376
INT/ORG LAW

B44
DAVIS H.E.,PIONEERS IN WORLD ORDER. WOR-45 CONSTN ECO/TAC DOMIN EDU/PROP LEGIT ADJUD ADMIN ARMS/CONT CHOOSE KNOWL ORD/FREE...POLICY JURID SOC STAT OBS CENSUS TIME/SEQ ANTHOL LEAGUE/NAT 20. PAGE 34 A0691
INT/ORG ROUTINE

L44
HAILEY,"THE FUTURE OF COLONIAL PEOPLES." WOR-45 CONSTN CULTURE ECO/UNDEV AGRI MARKET INT/ORG NAT/G SECT CONSULT ECO/TAC LEGIT ADMIN NAT/LISM ALL/VALS ...SOC OBS TREND STERTYP CMN/WLTH LEAGUE/NAT PARLIAMENT 20. PAGE 59 A1218
PLAN CONCPT DIPLOM UK

B45
BEVERIDGE W.,THE PRICE OF PEACE. GERMANY UK WOR+45 WOR-45 NAT/G FORCES CREATE LEGIT REGION WAR ATTIT KNOWL ORD/FREE PWR...POLICY NEW/IDEA GEN/LAWS LEAGUE/NAT 20 TREATY. PAGE 14 A0284
INT/ORG TREND PEACE

B45
PASTUHOV V.D.,A GUIDE TO THE PRACTICE OF INTERNATIONAL CONFERENCES. WOR+45 PLAN LEGIT ORD/FREE...MGT OBS RECORD VAL/FREE ILO LEAGUE/NAT 20. PAGE 114 A2338
INT/ORG DELIB/GP

B45
RANSHOFFEN-WERTHEIMER EF,THE INTERNATIONAL SECRETARIAT: A GREAT EXPERIMENT IN INTERNATIONAL ADMINISTRATION. EUR+WWI FUT CONSTN FACE/GP CONSULT DELIB/GP ACT/RES ADMIN ROUTINE PEACE ORD/FREE...MGT RECORD ORG/CHARTS LEAGUE/NAT WORK 20. PAGE 119 A2442
INT/ORG EXEC

B45
TINGSTERN H.,PEACE AND SECURITY AFTER WW II. WOR-45 DELIB/GP TOP/EX LEGIT CT/SYS COERCE PEACE ATTIT PERCEPT...CONCPT LEAGUE/NAT 20. PAGE 144 A2943
INT/ORG ORD/FREE WAR INT/LAW

B45
UNCIO CONFERENCE LIBRARY,SHORT TITLE CLASSIFIED CATALOG. WOR-45 DOMIN COLONIAL WAR...SOC/WK 20 LEAGUE/NAT UN. PAGE 147 A3006
BIBLIOG DIPLOM INT/ORG INT/LAW

B46
KEETON G.W.,MAKING INTERNATIONAL LAW WORK. FUT WOR-45 NAT/G DELIB/GP FORCES LEGIT COERCE PEACE ATTIT RIGID/FLEX ORD/FREE PWR...JURID CONCPT HIST/WRIT GEN/METH LEAGUE/NAT 20. PAGE 77 A1578
INT/ORG ADJUD INT/LAW

B46
MITRANY D.,A WORKING PEACE SYSTEM. WOR+45 WOR-45 ECO/DEV INT/ORG NAT/G DELIB/GP ECO/TAC REGION ATTIT RIGID/FLEX...TREND GEN/LAWS LEAGUE/NAT 20. PAGE 102 A2091
VOL/ASSN PLAN PEACE SOVEREIGN

B46
STURZO D.L.,NATIONALISM AND INTERNATIONALISM. WOR-45 INT/ORG LABOR NAT/G POL/PAR TOTALISM MORAL ORD/FREE FASCISM...MAJORIT 19/20 UN LEAGUE/NAT MUSSOLIN/B. PAGE 140 A2857
NAT/LISM DIPLOM WAR PEACE

B47
FEIS H.,SEEN FROM E A, THREE INTERNATIONAL EPISODES. EUR+WWI ITALY USA-45 WOR-45 AGRI INT/ORG NAT/G INT/TRADE LEGIT EXEC ATTIT ORD/FREE...POLICY LEAGUE/NAT TOT/POP 20 OIL. PAGE 44 A0908
EXTR/IND ECO/TAC DIPLOM

B47
HILL M.,IMMUNITIES AND PRIVILEGES OF INTERNATIONAL OFFICIALS. CANADA EUR+WWI NETHERLAND SWITZERLND LAW LEGIS DIPLOM LEGIT RESPECT...TIME/SEQ LEAGUE/NAT UN VAL/FREE 20. PAGE 65 A1330
INT/ORG ADMIN

B48
FENWICK C.G.,INTERNATIONAL LAW. WOR+45 WOR-45 CONSTN NAT/G LEGIT CT/SYS REGION...CONCPT LEAGUE/NAT UN 20. PAGE 45 A0916
INT/ORG JURID INT/LAW

B48
JESSUP P.C.,A MODERN LAW OF NATIONS. FUT WOR+45 WOR-45 SOCIETY NAT/G DELIB/GP LEGIS BAL/PWR EDU/PROP LEGIT PWR...INT/LAW JURID TIME/SEQ LEAGUE/NAT 20. PAGE 74 A1514
INT/ORG ADJUD

S49
FOX W.T.R.,"INTERWAR INTERNATIONAL RELATIONS RESEARCH: THE AMERICAN EXPERIENCE." USA+45 USA-45 INTELL INT/ORG VOL/ASSN OP/RES ATTIT SKILL ...TIME/SEQ LEAGUE/NAT 20. PAGE 48 A0973
ACT/RES CON/ANAL

B50
LEVI W.,FUNDAMENTALS OF WORLD ORGANIZATION. WOR+45 WOR-45 CULTURE ECO/TAC GIVE RECEIVE PERSON WEALTH ...METH/COMP 19/20 UN LEAGUE/NAT. PAGE 88 A1793
INT/ORG PEACE ORD/FREE DIPLOM

B50
ROSS A.,CONSTITUTION OF THE UNITED NATIONS. CONSTN CONSULT DELIB/GP ECO/TAC...INT/LAW JURID 20 UN LEAGUE/NAT. PAGE 124 A2540
PEACE DIPLOM ORD/FREE INT/ORG

C51
LEONARD L.L.,"INTERNATIONAL ORGANIZATION (1ST ED.)" WOR+45 FINAN DELIB/GP ECO/TAC GIVE DOMIN SANCTION
BIBLIOG POLICY

PEACE BIO/SOC ORD/FREE...INT/LAW 20 UN LEAGUE/NAT. PAGE 87 A1779 DIPLOM INT/ORG

B52
FERRELL R.H.,PEACE IN THEIR TIME. FRANCE UK USA-45 INT/ORG NAT/G FORCES CREATE AGREE ARMS/CONT COERCE WAR TREATY 20 WILSON/W LEAGUE/NAT BRIAND/A. PAGE 45 A0920 PEACE DIPLOM

B52
FIFIELD R.H.,WOODROW WILSON AND THE FAR EAST. ASIA CHIEF BAL/PWR CONFER COLONIAL ARMS/CONT WAR ...TIME/SEQ NAT/COMP BIBLIOG 19/20 WILSON/W LEAGUE/NAT PRESIDENT. PAGE 45 A0926 DIPLOM DELIB/GP INT/ORG

B52
WALTERS F.P.,A HISTORY OF THE LEAGUE OF NATIONS. EUR+WWI CONSTN NAT/G LEGIS TOP/EX ACT/RES PLAN EDU/PROP LEGIT ROUTINE ATTIT...TREND LEAGUE/NAT 20 CHINJAP. PAGE 161 A3271 INT/ORG TIME/SEQ NAT/LISM

S52
HAAS E.B.,"THE RECONCILIATION OF CONFLICT, COLONIAL POLICY AIMS: ACCEPTANCE OF THE LEAGUE OF NATIONS MANDATE SYSTEM." FRANCE GERMANY UK WOR+45 WOR-45 LEGIT ATTIT DRIVE ORD/FREE...OLD/LIB INT SYS/QU TIME/SEQ TREND LEAGUE/NAT 20. PAGE 58 A1201 INT/ORG COLONIAL

S52
SCHUMAN F.,"INTERNATIONAL IDEALS AND THE NATIONAL INTEREST." WOR+45 WOR-45 INT/ORG VOL/ASSN DELIB/GP CREATE BAL/PWR DOMIN PEACE PERSON MORAL PWR SOVEREIGN...POLICY GEN/LAWS TOT/POP LEAGUE/NAT 20. PAGE 129 A2648 ATTIT CONCPT

C52
FIFIELD R.H.,"WOODROW WILSON AND THE FAR EAST." ASIA CHIEF DELIB/GP BAL/PWR CONFER COLONIAL ARMS/CONT WAR...TIME/SEQ NAT/COMP 19/20 WILSON/W LEAGUE/NAT. PAGE 45 A0925 BIBLIOG DIPLOM INT/ORG

B53
BORGESE G.,FOUNDATIONS OF THE WORLD REPUBLIC. FUT SOCIETY NAT/G CREATE LEGIT PERSON MORAL...MAJORIT CON/ANAL LEAGUE/NAT TOT/POP 20. PAGE 17 A0340 INT/ORG CONSTN PEACE

B53
OPPENHEIM L.,INTERNATIONAL LAW: A TREATISE (7TH ED., 2 VOLS.). LAW CONSTN PROB/SOLV INT/TRADE ADJUD AGREE NEUTRAL WAR ORD/FREE SOVEREIGN...BIBLIOG 20 LEAGUE/NAT UN ILO. PAGE 112 A2294 INT/LAW INT/ORG DIPLOM

B53
ZIMMERN A.,THE AMERICAN ROAD TO PEACE. USA+45 LAW INT/ORG NAT/G EX/STRUC TOP/EX EDU/PROP LEGIT COERCE PEACE ATTIT ORD/FREE PWR...CONCPT TIME/SEQ LEAGUE/NAT TOT/POP VAL/FREE 20 UN. PAGE 170 A3455 USA-45 DIPLOM

B54
ARON R.,CENTURY OF TOTAL WAR. FUT WOR+45 WOR-45 SOCIETY INT/ORG NAT/G FORCES TOP/EX CREATE BAL/PWR DOMIN EDU/PROP COERCE DETER PEACE TOTALISM PWR ...TIME/SEQ TREND COLD/WAR TOT/POP VAL/FREE LEAGUE/NAT 20. PAGE 9 A0179 ATTIT WAR

B54
CHEEVER D.S.,ORGANIZING FOR PEACE. FUT WOR+45 WOR-45 STRATA STRUCT NAT/G CREATE DIPLOM LEGIT REGION COERCE DETER PEACE ATTIT DRIVE ALL/VALS ...TIME/SEQ TREND UN LEAGUE/NAT. PAGE 26 A0525 INT/ORG

B54
COOK T.,POWER THROUGH PURPOSE. USA+45 WOR+45 WOR-45 INT/ORG VOL/ASSN BAL/PWR DIPLOM EDU/PROP LEGIT PERSON...GEN/LAWS LEAGUE/NAT 20. PAGE 30 A0606 ATTIT CONCPT

B54
MANNING C.A.W.,THE UNIVERSITY TEACHING OF SOCIAL SCIENCES: INTERNATIONAL RELATIONS. WOR+45 INTELL STRATA R+D ACADEM INT/ORG NAT/G CONSULT DELIB/GP ACT/RES EDU/PROP NAT/LISM ATTIT...POLICY CONT/OBS HYPO/EXP VAL/FREE LEAGUE/NAT UNESCO 20. PAGE 94 A1925 KNOWL PHIL/SCI DIPLOM

B54
SALVEMINI G.,PRELUDE TO WORLD WAR II. ITALY MOD/EUR INT/ORG BAL/PWR EDU/PROP CONTROL TOTALISM...TREND NAT/COMP BIBLIOG 19 HITLER/A LEAGUE/NAT MUSSOLIN/B. PAGE 127 A2597 WAR FASCISM LEAD PWR

B54
SCHIFFER W.,THE LEGAL COMMUNITY OF MANKIND. UNIV WOR+45 WOR-45 SOCIETY NAT/G EDU/PROP LEGIT ATTIT PERSON ORD/FREE PWR...CONCPT HIST/WRIT TREND LEAGUE/NAT UN 20. PAGE 128 A2626 INT/ORG PHIL/SCI

B54
STONE J.,LEGAL CONTROLS OF INTERNATIONAL CONFLICT: A TREATISE ON THE DYNAMICS OF DISPUTES AND WAR LAW. WOR+45 WOR-45 NAT/G DIPLOM CT/SYS SOVEREIGN...JURID CONCPT METH/CNCPT GEN/LAWS TOT/POP VAL/FREE COLD/WAR LEAGUE/NAT 20. PAGE 138 A2834 INT/ORG LAW WAR INT/LAW

B54
STRAUSZ-HUPE R.,INTERNATIONAL RELATIONS IN THE AGE OF THE CONFLICT BETWEEN DEMOCRACY AND DICTATORSHIP (2ND ED.). INT/ORG BAL/PWR EDU/PROP ADMIN WAR PEACE PWR...CONCPT CHARTS BIBLIOG 20 COLD/WAR UN LEAGUE/NAT. PAGE 139 A2846 DIPLOM POPULISM MARXISM

S54
DAWSON K.H.,"THE UNITED NATIONS IN A DISUNITED WORLD." WOR+45 WOR-45 LAW INTELL NAT/G PEACE ATTIT PERCEPT MORAL LEAGUE/NAT TOT/POP VAL/FREE 20 UN. PAGE 34 A0694 INT/ORG LEGIT

S54
DODD S.C.,"THE SCIENTIFIC MEASUREMENT OF FITNESS FOR SELF-GOVERNMENT." FUT CONSTN ECO/UNDEV INT/ORG PLAN PWR...CONCPT QUANT CON/ANAL SOC/EXP UN LEAGUE/NAT 20. PAGE 38 A0767 NAT/G STAT SOVEREIGN

B55
HOGAN W.N.,INTERNATIONAL CONFLICT AND COLLECTIVE SECURITY: THE PRINCIPLE OF CONCERN IN INTERNATIONAL ORGANIZATION. CONSTN EX/STRUC BAL/PWR DIPLOM ADJUD CONTROL CENTRAL CONSEN PEACE...INT/LAW CONCPT METH/COMP 20 UN LEAGUE/NAT. PAGE 66 A1361 INT/ORG WAR ORD/FREE FORCES

B55
TANNENBAUM F.,THE AMERICAN TRADITION IN FOREIGN POLICY. USA+45 USA-45 CONSTN INT/ORG NAT/G POL/PAR VOL/ASSN TOP/EX LEGIT DRIVE ORD/FREE PWR...CONCPT GEN/LAWS CONGRESS LEAGUE/NAT COLD/WAR OAS 18/20. PAGE 141 A2887 TIME/SEQ

B55
VINSON J.C.,THE PARCHMENT PEACE: THE UNITED STATES SENATE AND THE WASHINGTON CONFERENCE, 1921-1922. USA-45 INT/ORG DELIB/GP PLAN ARMS/CONT GOV/REL ISOLAT PEACE ATTIT SOVEREIGN...INT/LAW BIBLIOG 20 SENATE PRESIDENT CONGRESS LEAGUE/NAT CHINJAP. PAGE 159 A3242 POLICY DIPLOM NAT/G LEGIS

B56
GEORGE A.L.,WOODROW WILSON AND COLONEL HOUSE. WOR-45 CONSTN FACE/GP INT/ORG NAT/G POL/PAR CONSULT LEGIT EXEC COERCE CHOOSE ATTIT DRIVE PERSON MORAL ORD/FREE PWR RESPECT...POLICY MGT PSY OBS RECORD INT LEAGUE/NAT. PAGE 52 A1060 USA-45 BIOG DIPLOM

B56
WATKINS J.T.,GENERAL INTERNATIONAL ORGANIZATION: A SOURCE BOOK. 19/20 LEAGUE/NAT UN. PAGE 162 A3292 BIBLIOG DIPLOM INT/ORG WRITING

S56
POTTER P.B.,"NEUTRALITY, 1955." WOR+45 WOR-45 INT/ORG NAT/G WAR ATTIT...POLICY IDEA/COMP 17/20 LEAGUE/NAT UN COLD/WAR. PAGE 117 A2399 NEUTRAL INT/LAW DIPLOM CONCPT

B57
BLOOMFIELD L.P.,EVOLUTION OR REVOLUTION: THE UNITED NATIONS AND THE PROBLEM OF PEACEFUL TERRITORIAL CHANGE. WOR+45 WOR-45 INT/ORG NAT/G DIPLOM ROUTINE REV ATTIT RIGID/FLEX PWR...CONCPT OBS HIST/WRIT UN LEAGUE/NAT 20. PAGE 15 A0315 ORD/FREE LEGIT

B57
DE VISSCHER C.,THEORY AND REALITY IN PUBLIC INTERNATIONAL LAW. WOR+45 WOR-45 SOCIETY NAT/G CT/SYS ATTIT MORAL ORD/FREE PWR...JURID CONCPT METH/CNCPT TIME/SEQ GEN/LAWS LEAGUE/NAT TOT/POP VAL/FREE COLD/WAR. PAGE 35 A0716 INT/ORG LAW INT/LAW

B57
DUDDEN A.P.,WOODROW WILSON AND THE WORLD OF TODAY. USA-45 NAT/G PROVS CONTROL PARTIC WAR ISOLAT PWR SKILL...PERS/COMP ANTHOL 19/20 WILSON/W UN LEAGUE/NAT WWI. PAGE 39 A0794 CHIEF DIPLOM POL/PAR LEAD

B57
ROSENNE S.,THE INTERNATIONAL COURT OF JUSTICE. WOR+45 LAW DOMIN LEGIT PEACE PWR SOVEREIGN...JURID CONCPT RECORD TIME/SEQ CON/ANAL CHARTS UN TOT/POP VAL/FREE LEAGUE/NAT 20 ICJ. PAGE 124 A2537 INT/ORG CT/SYS INT/LAW

B58
ISLAM R.,INTERNATIONAL ECONOMIC COOPERATION AND THE UNITED NATIONS. FINAN PLAN EXEC TASK WAR PEACE ...SOC METH/CNCPT 20 UN LEAGUE/NAT. PAGE 72 A1470 INT/ORG DIPLOM ADMIN

B58
NOEL-BAKER D.,THE ARMS RACE. WOR+45 NAT/G DELIB/GP ACT/RES TEC/DEV EDU/PROP NUC/PWR ATTIT KNOWL PWR ...CONCPT OBS LEAGUE/NAT 20 COLD/WAR. PAGE 109 A2245 FUT INT/ORG ARMS/CONT PEACE

B58
RUSSELL R.B.,A HISTORY OF THE UNITED NATIONS CHARTER: THE ROLE OF THE UNITED STATES. SOCIETY NAT/G CONSULT DOMIN LEGIT ATTIT ORD/FREE PWR ...POLICY JURID CONCPT UN LEAGUE/NAT. PAGE 126 A2575 USA-45 INT/ORG CONSTN

B58
STONE J.,AGGRESSION AND WORLD ORDER: A CRITIQUE OF UNITED NATIONS THEORIES OF AGGRESSION. LAW CONSTN DELIB/GP PROB/SOLV BAL/PWR DIPLOM DEBATE ADJUD CRIME PWR...POLICY IDEA/COMP 20 UN SUEZ LEAGUE/NAT. PAGE 138 A2835 ORD/FREE INT/ORG WAR CONCPT

B59
CHINA INSTITUTE OF AMERICA.,CHINA AND THE UNITED NATIONS. CHINA/COM FUT STRUCT EDU/PROP LEGIT ADMIN ATTIT KNOWL ORD/FREE PWR...OBS RECORD STAND/INT TIME/SEQ UN LEAGUE/NAT UNESCO 20. PAGE 26 A0531 ASIA INT/ORG

B59
CORBETT P.E.,LAW IN DIPLOMACY. UK USA+45 USSR CONSTN SOCIETY INT/ORG JUDGE LEGIT ATTIT ORD/FREE TOT/POP LEAGUE/NAT 20. PAGE 30 A0616 NAT/G ADJUD JURID DIPLOM

B60
EINSTEIN A.,EINSTEIN ON PEACE. FUT WOR+45 WOR-45 INT/ORG

SOCIETY NAT/G PLAN BAL/PWR CAP/ISM DIPLOM ARMS/CONT DETER NAT/LISM...POLICY RELATIV HUM PHIL/SCI CONCPT BIOG COLD/WAR LEAGUE/NAT NAZI. PAGE 41 A0829
ATTIT NUC/PWR PEACE

B60
LANDHEER B.,ETHICAL VALUES IN INTERNATIONAL DECISION-MAKING. FUT LAW SOCIETY INT/ORG NAT/G DELIB/GP CREATE NAT/LISM ATTIT PERSON...DECISION CONCPT LEAGUE/NAT TOT/POP 20. PAGE 84 A1718
HYPO/EXP POLICY PEACE

B60
THE AFRICA 1960 COMMITTEE,MANDATE IN TRUST; THE PROBLEM OF SOUTH WEST AFRICA. GERMANY STRUCT REGION SANCTION CHOOSE DISCRIM...INT/LAW 20 AFRICA/SW UN LEAGUE/NAT TRUST/TERR. PAGE 142 A2910
NAT/G DIPLOM COLONIAL RACE/REL

B60
US DEPARTMENT OF THE ARMY,DISARMAMENT: A BIBLIOGRAPHIC RECORD: 1916-1960. DETER WAR WEAPON PEACE 20 UN LEAGUE/NAT COLD/WAR NATO. PAGE 152 A3103
BIBLIOG/A ARMS/CONT NUC/PWR DIPLOM

B62
AIR FORCE ACADEMY LIBRARY,INTERNATIONAL ORGANIZATIONS AND MILITARY SECURITY SYSTEMS (PAMPHLET) (SPECIAL BIBLIOGRAPHY SERIES, NUMBER 25). DIPLOM FOR/AID INT/TRADE NUC/PWR PEACE 20 UN NATO OAS SEATO LEAGUE/NAT. PAGE 5 A0104
BIBLIOG INT/ORG FORCES DETER

B62
DUTOIT B.,LA NEUTRALITE SUISSE A L'HEURE EUROPEENNE. EUR+WWI MOD/EUR INT/ORG NAT/G VOL/ASSN PLAN BAL/PWR LEGIT NEUTRAL REGION PEACE ORD/FREE SOVEREIGN...CONCPT OBS TIME/SEQ TREND STERTYP VAL/FREE LEAGUE/NAT UN 20. PAGE 40 A0812
ATTIT DIPLOM SWITZERLND

S62
SCHILLING W.R.,"SCIENTISTS, FOREIGN POLICY AND POLITICS." WOR+45 WOR-45 INTELL INT/ORG CONSULT TOP/EX ACT/RES PLAN ADMIN KNOWL...CONCPT OBS TREND LEAGUE/NAT 20. PAGE 128 A2627
NAT/G TEC/DEV DIPLOM NUC/PWR

B63
BOWETT D.W.,THE LAW OF INTERNATIONAL INSTITUTIONS. WOR+45 WOR-45 CONSTN DELIB/GP EX/STRUC JUDGE EDU/PROP LEGIT CT/SYS EXEC ROUTINE RIGID/FLEX ORD/FREE PWR...JURID CONCPT ORG/CHARTS GEN/METH LEAGUE/NAT OAS OEEC 20 UN. PAGE 17 A0354
INT/ORG ADJUD DIPLOM

B63
HINSLEY F.H.,POWER AND THE PURSUIT OF PEACE. WOR+45 WOR-45 PLAN RIGID/FLEX ALL/VALS ALL/IDEOS...POLICY DECISION INT/LAW 12/20 ROUSSEAU/J KANT/I BENTHAM/J LEAGUE/NAT. PAGE 65 A1338
DIPLOM CONSTN PEACE COERCE

B63
NICOLSON H.,DIPLOMACY (3RD ED.). INT/ORG NAT/G CONSULT DELIB/GP CONFER 19/20 LEAGUE/NAT UN. PAGE 109 A2232
DIPLOM CONCPT NAT/COMP

B63
ROSECRANCE R.N.,ACTION AND REACTION IN WORLD POLITICS. FUT WOR-45 SOCIETY DELIB/GP ACT/RES CREATE DIPLOM ECO/TAC DOMIN EDU/PROP COERCE ATTIT PERSON SUPEGO ORD/FREE PWR...CHARTS SIMUL LEAGUE/NAT VAL/FREE UN 19/20. PAGE 123 A2529
WOR+45 INT/ORG BAL/PWR

B63
STROMBERG R.N.,COLLECTIVE SECURITY AND AMERICAN FOREIGN POLICY FROM THE LEAGUE OF NATIONS TO NATO. USA+45 USA-45 WOR-45 INT/ORG VOL/ASSN EX/STRUC FORCES LEGIT ROUTINE DRIVE...CONCPT TREND UN LEAGUE/NAT 20 NATO. PAGE 139 A2851
ORD/FREE TIME/SEQ DIPLOM

S63
WRIGHT Q.,"DECLINE OF CLASSIC DIPLOMACY." CHRIST-17C EUR+WWI MOD/EUR WOR+45 WOR-45 INT/ORG NAT/G DELIB/GP BAL/PWR ATTIT PWR...HIST/WRIT LEAGUE/NAT. PAGE 168 A3418
TEC/DEV CONCPT DIPLOM

B64
CZERNIN F.,VERSAILLES - 1919. EUR+WWI USA-45 FACE/GP POL/PAR VOL/ASSN DELIB/GP TOP/EX CREATE BAL/PWR DIPLOM LEGIT NAT/LISM PEACE ATTIT RIGID/FLEX ORD/FREE PWR...CON/ANAL LEAGUE/NAT 20 VERSAILLES. PAGE 33 A0671
INT/ORG STRUCT

L64
BARROS J.,"THE GREEK-BULGARIAN INCIDENT OF 1925: THE LEAGUE OF NATIONS AND THE GREAT POWERS." BULGARIA EUR+WWI NAT/G FORCES ECO/TAC EDU/PROP LEGIT ROUTINE COERCE WAR PEACE DRIVE PWR...JURID CONCPT METH/CNCPT GEN/LAWS GEN/METH LEAGUE/NAT TOT/POP 20. PAGE 11 A0228
INT/ORG ORD/FREE DIPLOM

S64
FALK S.L.,"DISARMAMENT IN HISTORICAL PERSPECTIVE." WOR-45 NAT/G PLAN NUC/PWR PEACE ORD/FREE PWR ...TIME/SEQ AUD/VIS VAL/FREE LEAGUE/NAT 20. PAGE 44 A0892
INT/ORG COERCE ARMS/CONT

S64
VANDENBOSCH A.,"THE SMALL STATES IN INTERNATIONAL POLITICS AND ORGANIZATION." EUR+WWI MOD/EUR WOR+45 WOR-45 CONSTN DELIB/GP COERCE ORD/FREE PWR ...TIME/SEQ GEN/LAWS VAL/FREE LEAGUE/NAT UN 19/20. PAGE 158 A3219
NAT/G INT/ORG DIPLOM

B65
ALBRECHT-CARRIE R.,THE MEANING OF THE FIRST WORLD WAR. MOD/EUR USA-45 INT/ORG BAL/PWR PEACE ATTIT LAISSEZ MARXISM...CONCPT BIBLIOG 19/20 LEAGUE/NAT WWI. PAGE 5 A0110
DIPLOM WAR

B65
HAGRAS K.M.,UNITED NATIONS CONFERENCE ON TRADE AND DEVELOPMENT: A CASE STUDY OF UN DIPLOMACY. CONSULT ACT/RES TEC/DEV FOR/AID INT/TRADE...BIBLIOG 20 UN LEAGUE/NAT UNCTAD. PAGE 59 A1213
INT/ORG ADMIN DELIB/GP DIPLOM

B65
LARUS J.,FROM COLLECTIVE SECURITY TO PREVENTIVE DIPLOMACY. FUT FORCES PROB/SOLV DEBATE AGREE COERCE WAR PWR...ANTHOL 20 LEAGUE/NAT UN. PAGE 85 A1736
INT/ORG PEACE DIPLOM ORD/FREE

S65
MERRITT R.L.,"WOODROW WILSON AND THE 'GREAT AND SOLEMN REFERENDUM,' 1920." USA-45 SOCIETY NAT/G CONSULT LEGIS ACT/RES PLAN DOMIN EDU/PROP ROUTINE ATTIT DISPL DRIVE PERSON RIGID/FLEX MORAL ORD/FREE ...PSY SOC CONCPT MYTH LEAGUE/NAT. PAGE 100 A2044
INT/ORG TOP/EX DIPLOM

B66
CANFIELD L.H.,THE PRESIDENCY OF WOODROW WILSON: PRELUDE TO A WORLD IN CRISIS. USA-45 ADJUD NEUTRAL WAR CHOOSE INGP/REL PEACE ORD/FREE 20 WILSON/W PRESIDENT TREATY LEAGUE/NAT. PAGE 24 A0477
PERSON POLICY DIPLOM GOV/REL

B66
DOUMA J.,BIBLIOGRAPHY ON THE INTERNATIONAL COURT INCLUDING THE PERMANENT COURT, 1918-1964. WOR+45 WOR-45 DELIB/GP WAR PRIVIL...JURID NAT/COMP 20 UN LEAGUE/NAT. PAGE 38 A0780
BIBLIOG/A INT/ORG CT/SYS DIPLOM

B66
EUDIN X.J.,SOVIET FOREIGN POLICY 1928-34: DOCUMENTS AND MATERIALS (VOL. I). ASIA USSR WOR-45 INT/ORG POL/PAR WORKER WAR PEACE...ANTHOL 20 TREATY LEAGUE/NAT INTERVENT. PAGE 43 A0873
DIPLOM POLICY GOV/REL MARXISM

B66
GARNER W.R.,THE CHACO DISPUTE; A STUDY OF PRESTIGE DIPLOMACY. L/A+17C PARAGUAY USA-45 INT/ORG AGREE PEACE...TIME/SEQ 20 BOLIV LEAGUE/NAT ARGEN CHACO/WAR. PAGE 51 A1050
WAR DIPLOM CONCPT PWR

B66
LUARD E.,THE EVOLUTION OF INTERNATIONAL ORGANIZATIONS. UK WOR+45 BUDGET INT/TRADE WAR BAL/PAY PEACE ORD/FREE...POLICY 19/20 EEC ILO LEAGUE/NAT UN. PAGE 91 A1871
INT/ORG EFFICIENCY CREATE TREND

B66
US LIBRARY OF CONGRESS,NIGERIA: A GUIDE TO OFFICIAL PUBLICATIONS. CAMEROON NIGERIA UK DIPLOM...POLICY 19/20 UN LEAGUE/NAT. PAGE 155 A3160
BIBLIOG ADMIN NAT/G COLONIAL

B66
WAINHOUSE D.W.,INTERNATIONAL PEACE OBSERVATION: A HISTORY AND FORECAST. INT/ORG PROB/SOLV BAL/PWR AGREE ARMS/CONT COERCE NUC/PWR...PREDICT METH/COMP 20 UN LEAGUE/NAT OAS TREATY. PAGE 160 A3261
PEACE DIPLOM

C66
BLAISDELL D.C.,"INTERNATIONAL ORGANIZATION." FUT WOR+45 ECO/DEV DELIB/GP FORCES EFFICIENCY PEACE ORD/FREE...INT/LAW 20 UN LEAGUE/NAT NATO. PAGE 15 A0304
BIBLIOG INT/ORG DIPLOM ARMS/CONT

B67
KNOLES G.H.,THE RESPONSIBILITIES OF POWER, 1900-1929. USA-45 SOCIETY SECT JUDGE COLONIAL REPRESENT WEALTH POPULISM...IDEA/COMP ANTHOL PRESIDENT 20 LEAGUE/NAT. PAGE 81 A1653
PWR DIPLOM NAT/LISM WAR

B67
WATERS M.,THE UNITED NATIONS* INTERNATIONAL ORGANIZATION AND ADMINISTRATION. WOR+45 EX/STRUC FORCES DIPLOM LEAD REGION ARMS/CONT REPRESENT INGP/REL ROLE...METH/COMP ANTHOL 20 UN LEAGUE/NAT. PAGE 162 A3291
CONSTN INT/ORG ADMIN ADJUD

L67
MACDONALD R.S.J.,"THE RESORT TO ECONOMIC COERCION BY INTERNATIONAL POLITICAL ORGANIZATIONS." CUBA ETHIOPIA RHODESIA SOUTH/AFR NAT/G FOR/AID INT/TRADE DOMIN CONTROL SANCTION...DECISION LEAGUE/NAT UN OAS 20. PAGE 92 A1887
INT/ORG COERCE ECO/TAC DIPLOM

LEAGUE/WV....LEAGUE OF WOMEN VOTERS

LEAR J. A1757

LEARNING....SEE PERCEPT

LEASE....SEE RENT

LEBANON....SEE ALSO ISLAM

B54
NATION ASSOCIATES,SECURITY AND THE MIDDLE EAST - THE PROBLEM AND ITS SOLUTION. ISRAEL JORDAN LEBANON SYRIA UAR FORCES FOR/AID GP/REL NAT/LISM PEACE TOTALISM...POLICY 20. PAGE 107 A2198
DIPLOM ECO/UNDEV WAR PLAN

L64
CURTIS G.L.,"THE UNITED NATIONS OBSERVER GROUP IN LEBANON." ISLAM USA+45 NAT/G CONSULT ACT/RES PLAN BAL/PWR LEGIT ATTIT KNOWL...HIST/WRIT UN 20 UN. PAGE 33 A0669
INT/ORG FORCES DIPLOM LEBANON

LEDUC G. A1758

LEDYARD/J....JOHN LEDYARD

LEE C. A1759

LEE L.T. A1760

LEE M.J. A1761

LEE/IVY....IVY LEE

LEEVILLE....LEEVILLE, TEXAS

LEFEVER E.W. A1762,A1763

LEFF N.H. A1764

LEGAL SYSTEM....SEE LAW

LEGAL PERMIT....SEE LICENSE

LEGGE J.D. A1765

LEGION/DCY....LEGION OF DECENCY

LEGIS....LEGISLATURES; SEE ALSO PARLIAMENT, CONGRESS

N
INTERNATIONAL COMN JURISTS,AFRICAN CONFERENCE ON THE RULE OF LAW. AFR INT/ORG LEGIS DIPLOM CONFER COLONIAL ORD/FREE...CONCPT METH/COMP 20. PAGE 71 A1452
CT/SYS
JURID
DELIB/GP

N
JOURNAL OF POLITICS. USA+45 USA-45 CONSTN POL/PAR EX/STRUC LEGIS PROB/SOLV DIPLOM CT/SYS CHOOSE RACE/REL 20. PAGE 1 A0017
BIBLIOG/A
NAT/G
LAW
LOC/G

N
MIDWEST JOURNAL OF POLITICAL SCIENCE. USA+45 CONSTN ECO/DEV LEGIS PROB/SOLV CT/SYS LEAD GOV/REL ATTIT POLICY. PAGE 1 A0020
BIBLIOG/A
NAT/G
DIPLOM
POL/PAR

N
POLITICAL SCIENCE QUARTERLY. USA+45 USA-45 LAW CONSTN ECO/DEV INT/ORG LOC/G POL/PAR LEGIS LEAD NUC/PWR...CONCPT 20. PAGE 1 A0023
BIBLIOG/A
NAT/G
DIPLOM
POLICY

N
REVIEW OF POLITICS. WOR+45 WOR-45 CONSTN LEGIS PROB/SOLV ADMIN LEAD ALL/IDEOS...PHIL/SCI 20. PAGE 2 A0024
BIBLIOG/A
DIPLOM
INT/ORG
NAT/G

N
HARVARD LAW SCHOOL LIBRARY,ANNUAL LEGAL BIBLIOGRAPHY. USA+45 CONSTN LEGIS ADJUD CT/SYS ...POLICY 20. PAGE 62 A1278
BIBLIOG
JURID
LAW
INT/LAW

N
INSTITUTE OF HISPANIC STUDIES,HISPANIC AMERICAN REPORT. EUR+WWI SPAIN LAW CONSTN ECO/UNDEV POL/PAR EX/STRUC LEGIS LEAD...HUM SOC 20. PAGE 70 A1445
BIBLIOG/A
L/A+17C
NAT/G
DIPLOM

N
MCSPADDEN J.W.,THE AMERICAN STATESMAN'S YEARBOOK. WOR-45 LAW CONSTN AGRI FINAN DEBATE ADMIN PARL/PROC ...CHARTS BIBLIOG/A 20. PAGE 99 A2025
DIPLOM
NAT/G
PROVS
LEGIS

N
RAND SCHOOL OF SOCIAL SCIENCE,INDEX TO LABOR ARTICLES. ECO/DEV INT/ORG LEGIS DIPLOM GP/REL ...NAT/COMP 20. PAGE 119 A2440
BIBLIOG
LABOR
MGT
ADJUD

N
SOCIETE DES NATIONS,TRAITES INTERNATIONAUX ET ACTES LEGISLATIFS. WOR-45 INT/ORG NAT/G...INT/LAW JURID 20 LEAGUE/NAT TREATY. PAGE 135 A2759
BIBLIOG
DIPLOM
LEGIS
ADJUD

N
UNESCO,INTERNATIONAL BIBLIOGRAPHY OF POLITICAL SCIENCE (VOLUMES 1-8). WOR+45 LAW NAT/G EX/STRUC LEGIS PROB/SOLV DIPLOM ADMIN GOV/REL 20 UNESCO. PAGE 147 A3010
BIBLIOG
CONCPT
IDEA/COMP

N/R
FULBRIGHT J.W.,THE ARROGANCE OF POWER. USA+45 WOR+45 ECO/UNDEV ACADEM LEGIS ECO/TAC FOR/AID PEACE ROLE ORD/FREE PWR 20 COLD/WAR CONGRESS. PAGE 50 A1014
DIPLOM
POLICY
REV

B04
CRANDALL S.B.,TREATIES: THEIR MAKING AND ENFORCEMENT. MOD/EUR USA-45 CONSTN INT/ORG NAT/G LEGIS EDU/PROP LEGIT EXEC PEACE KNOWL MORAL...JURID CONGRESS 19/20 TREATY. PAGE 32 A0655
LAW

B05
AMES J.G.,COMPREHENSIVE INDEX TO THE PUBLICATIONS OF THE UNITED STATES GOVERNMENT , 1881-1893. USA-45 CONSTN POL/PAR DELIB/GP TOP/EX DIPLOM PARL/PROC INGP/REL...INDEX 19 CONGRESS. PAGE 8 A0153
BIBLIOG/A
LEGIS
NAT/G
GOV/REL

B11
PHILLIPSON C.,THE INTERNATIONAL LAW AND CUSTOM OF ANCIENT GREECE AND ROME. MEDIT-7 UNIV INTELL SOCIETY STRUCT NAT/G LEGIS EXEC PERSON...CONCPT OBS CON/ANAL ROM/EMP. PAGE 116 A2377
INT/ORG
LAW
INT/LAW

B14
HASSE A.R.,INDEX TO UNITED STATES DOCUMENTS RELATING TO FOREIGN AFFAIRS, 1828-1861 (3 VOLS.). USA-45 CHIEF 19 CONGRESS. PAGE 63 A1285
INDEX
DIPLOM
LEGIS

S17
ROOT E.,"THE EFFECT OF DEMOCRACY ON INTERNATIONAL LAW." USA-45 WOR-45 INTELL SOCIETY INT/ORG NAT/G CONSULT ACT/RES CREATE PLAN EDU/PROP PEACE SKILL ...CONCPT METH/CNCPT OBS 20. PAGE 123 A2523
LEGIS
JURID
INT/LAW

B19
DE CALLIERES F.,THE PRACTICE OF DIPLOMACY. MOD/EUR INT/ORG NAT/G DELIB/GP LEGIS TOP/EX DOMIN ATTIT KNOWL LEAGUE/NAT 20. PAGE 34 A0699
CONSULT
ACT/RES
DIPLOM
INT/LAW

B19
SUTHERLAND G.,CONSTITUTIONAL POWER AND WORLD AFFAIRS. CONSTN STRUCT INT/ORG NAT/G CHIEF LEGIS ACT/RES PLAN GOV/REL ALL/VALS...OBS TIME/SEQ CONGRESS VAL/FREE 20 PRESIDENT. PAGE 140 A2866
USA-45
EXEC
DIPLOM

N19
KUWAIT ARABIA,KUWAIT FUND FOR ARAB ECONOMIC DEVELOPMENT (PAMPHLET). ISLAM KUWAIT UAR ECO/UNDEV LEGIS ECO/TAC WEALTH 20. PAGE 83 A1697
FOR/AID
DIPLOM
FINAN
ADMIN

B21
OPPENHEIM L.,THE FUTURE OF INTERNATIONAL LAW. EUR+WWI MOD/EUR LAW LEGIS JUDGE LEGIT ORD/FREE ...JURID TIME/SEQ GEN/LAWS 20. PAGE 112 A2293
INT/ORG
CT/SYS
INT/LAW

B22
MYERS D.P.,MANUAL OF COLLECTIONS OF TREATIES AND OF COLLECTIONS RELATING TO TREATIES. MOD/EUR INT/ORG LEGIS WRITING ADMIN SOVEREIGN...INT/LAW 19/20. PAGE 106 A2186
BIBLIOG/A
DIPLOM
CONFER

B22
WRIGHT Q.,THE CONTROL OF AMERICAN FOREIGN RELATIONS. USA-45 WOR-45 CONSTN INT/ORG CONSULT LEGIS LEGIT ROUTINE ORD/FREE PWR...POLICY JURID CONCPT METH/CNCPT RECORD LEAGUE/NAT 20. PAGE 167 A3402
NAT/G
EXEC
DIPLOM

B26
INTERNATIONAL BIBLIOGRAPHY OF POLITICAL SCIENCE. WOR+45 NAT/G POL/PAR EX/STRUC LEGIS CT/SYS LEAD CHOOSE GOV/REL ATTIT...PHIL/SCI 20. PAGE 3 A0049
BIBLIOG
DIPLOM
CONCPT
ADMIN

B28
CHILDS J.B.,FOREIGN GOVERNMENT PUBLICATIONS (PAMPHLET). LEGIS DIPLOM 19/20. PAGE 26 A0529
BIBLIOG
PRESS
NAT/G

B28
HOWARD-ELLIS C.,THE ORIGIN, STRUCTURE AND WORKING OF THE LEAGUE OF NATIONS. EUR+WWI MOD/EUR USA-45 CONSTN FORCES LEGIS ECO/TAC LEGIT COERCE ORD/FREE ...JURID SOC CONCPT LEAGUE/NAT 20 ILO ICJ. PAGE 68 A1401
INT/ORG
ADJUD

B30
FLEMMING D.,THE TREATY VETO OF THE AMERICAN SENATE. FUT USA+45 USA-45 CONSTN INT/ORG NAT/G TOP/EX LEGIT GOV/REL PWR...POLICY MAJORIT CONCPT OBS TIME/SEQ CONGRESS 20. PAGE 46 A0949
LEGIS
RIGID/FLEX

B30
SMUTS J.C.,AFRICA AND SOME WORLD PROBLEMS. RHODESIA SOUTH/AFR CULTURE ECO/UNDEV INDUS INT/ORG SECT PROB/SOLV REGION GOV/REL DISCRIM ATTIT 19/20 LEAGUE/NAT LIVNGSTN/D NEGRO. PAGE 134 A2748
LEGIS
AFR
COLONIAL
RACE/REL

B31
BORCHARD E.H.,GUIDE TO THE LAW AND LEGAL LITERATURE OF FRANCE. FRANCE FINAN INDUS LABOR SECT LEGIS ADMIN COLONIAL CRIME OWN...INT/LAW 20. PAGE 17 A0337
BIBLIOG/A
LAW
CONSTN
METH

B32
FLEMMING D.,THE UNITED STATES AND THE LEAGUE OF NATIONS, 1918-1920. FUT USA-45 NAT/G LEGIS TOP/EX DEBATE CHOOSE PEACE ATTIT SOVEREIGN...TIME/SEQ CON/ANAL CONGRESS LEAGUE/NAT 20 TREATY. PAGE 46 A0950
INT/ORG
EDU/PROP

B35
BEMIS S.F.,GUIDE TO THE DIPLOMATIC HISTORY OF THE UNITED STATES, 17751921. NAT/G LEGIS TOP/EX PROB/SOLV CAP/ISM INT/TRADE TARIFFS ADJUD ...CON/ANAL 18/20. PAGE 13 A0264
BIBLIOG/A
DIPLOM
USA-45

B35
CONOVER H.F.,A SELECTED LIST OF REFERENCES ON THE DIPLOMATIC & TRADE RELATIONS OF THE US WITH THE USSR, 1919-1935 (PAMPHLET). USA-45 USSR DELIB/GP LEGIS OP/RES PROB/SOLV BAL/PWR BARGAIN 20. PAGE 29 A0590
BIBLIOG
DIPLOM
INT/TRADE

B37
UNION OF SOUTH AFRICA,REPORT CONCERNING ADMINISTRATION OF SOUTH WEST AFRICA (6 VOLS.).
NAT/G
ADMIN

SOUTH/AFR INDUS PUB/INST FORCES LEGIS BUDGET DIPLOM EDU/PROP ADJUD CT/SYS...GEOG CHARTS 20 AFRICA/SW LEAGUE/NAT. PAGE 148 A3028
COLONIAL CONSTN

B38
GREGORY W.,INTERNATIONAL CONGRESSES AND CONFERENCES 1840-1937: A UNION LIST OF THEIR PUBLICATIONS AVAILABLE IN US AND CANADA. WOR-45 LEGIS ATTIT ...POLICY 19/20. PAGE 56 A1145
BIBLIOG INT/ORG CONFER

B39
TAGGART F.J.,ROME AND CHINA. MEDIT-7 INT/ORG NAT/G FORCES LEGIS TOP/EX PLAN PWR SOVEREIGN...CHARTS TOT/POP ROM/EMP. PAGE 141 A2883
ASIA WAR

B39
THOMAS J.A.,THE HOUSE OF COMMONS, 1832-1901; A STUDY OF ITS ECONOMIC AND FUNCTIONAL CHARACTER. UK LAW STRATA FINAN DIPLOM CONTROL LEAD LOBBY REPRESENT WEALTH...POLICY STAT BIBLIOG 19/20 PARLIAMENT. PAGE 143 A2922
PARL/PROC LEGIS POL/PAR ECO/DEV

C39
REISCHAUER R.,"JAPAN'S GOVERNMENT--POLITICS." CONSTN STRATA POL/PAR FORCES LEGIS DIPLOM ADMIN EXEC CENTRAL...POLICY BIBLIOG 20 CHINJAP. PAGE 120 A2462
NAT/G S/ASIA CONCPT ROUTINE

C40
FAHS C.B.,"GOVERNMENT IN JAPAN." FINAN FORCES LEGIS TOP/EX BUDGET INT/TRADE EDU/PROP SOVEREIGN ...CON/ANAL BIBLIOG/A 20 CHINJAP. PAGE 43 A0884
ASIA DIPLOM NAT/G ADMIN

B41
BIRDSALL P.,VERSAILLES TWENTY YEARS AFTER. MOD/EUR POL/PAR CHIEF CONSULT FORCES LEGIS REPAR PEACE ORD/FREE...BIBLIOG 20 PRESIDENT TREATY. PAGE 14 A0290
DIPLOM NAT/LISM WAR

B44
WHITTON J.B.,THE SECOND CHANCE: AMERICA AND THE PEACE. EUR+WWI USA-45 SOCIETY STRUCT INT/ORG NAT/G LEGIT EXEC WAR ALL/VALS...SOC CONCPT TIME/SEQ TREND CONGRESS 20. PAGE 164 A3340
LEGIS PEACE

L44
CORWIN E.S.,"THE CONSTITUTION AND WORLD ORGANIZATION." FUT USA+45 USA-45 NAT/G EX/STRUC LEGIS PEACE KNOWL...CON/ANAL UN 20. PAGE 31 A0627
INT/ORG CONSTN SOVEREIGN

S44
WRIGHT Q.,"CONSTITUTIONAL PROCEDURES OF THE US FOR CARRYING OUT OBLIGATIONS FOR MILITARY SANCTIONS." EUR+WWI FUT USA-45 WOR-45 CONSTN INTELL NAT/G CONSULT EX/STRUC LEGIS ROUTINE DRIVE...POLICY JURID CONCPT OBS TREND TOT/POP 20. PAGE 167 A3406
TOP/EX FORCES INT/LAW WAR

B45
HORN O.B.,BRITISH PUBLIC OPINION AND THE FIRST PARTITION OF POLAND. POLAND UK LEGIS PRESS RUMOR CONTROL PARTIC NAT/LISM SOVEREIGN 18/19. PAGE 67 A1385
DIPLOM POLICY ATTIT NAT/G

B47
BORGESE G.,COMMON CAUSE. LAW CONSTN SOCIETY STRATA ECO/DEV INT/ORG POL/PAR FORCES LEGIS TOP/EX CAP/ISM DIPLOM ADMIN EXEC ATTIT PWR 20. PAGE 17 A0339
WOR+45 NAT/G SOVEREIGN REGION

B47
HILL M.,IMMUNITIES AND PRIVILEGES OF INTERNATIONAL OFFICIALS. CANADA EUR+WWI NETHERLAND SWITZERLND LAW LEGIS DIPLOM LEGIT RESPECT...TIME/SEQ LEAGUE/NAT UN VAL/FREE 20. PAGE 65 A1330
INT/ORG ADMIN

B48
CHAMBERLAIN L.H.,AMERICAN FOREIGN POLICY. FUT USA+45 USA-45 WOR+45 WOR-45 NAT/G LEGIS TOP/EX ECO/TAC FOR/AID EDU/PROP EXEC ATTIT ORD/FREE ...JURID TREND TOT/POP 20. PAGE 25 A0517
CONSTN DIPLOM

B48
HOWARD J.E.,PARLIAMENT AND FOREIGN POLICY IN FRANCE. FRANCE CONSTN DELIB/GP BUDGET ADMIN PARL/PROC CHOOSE...BIBLIOG/A 20 PARLIAMENT. PAGE 68 A1399
LEGIS CONTROL DIPLOM ATTIT

B48
JESSUP P.C.,A MODERN LAW OF NATIONS. FUT WOR+45 WOR-45 SOCIETY NAT/G DELIB/GP LEGIS BAL/PWR EDU/PROP LEGIT PWR...INT/LAW JURID TIME/SEQ LEAGUE/NAT 20. PAGE 74 A1514
INT/ORG ADJUD

B48
NEUBURGER O.,GUIDE TO OFFICIAL PUBLICATIONS OF THE OTHER AMERICAN REPUBLICS: VENEZUELA (VOL. XIX). VENEZUELA FINAN LEGIS PLAN BUDGET DIPLOM CT/SYS PARL/PROC 19/20. PAGE 108 A2219
BIBLIOG/A NAT/G CONSTN LAW

B49
ROSENHAUPT H.W.,HOW TO WAGE PEACE. USA+45 SOCIETY STRATA STRUCT R+D INT/ORG POL/PAR LEGIS ACT/RES CREATE PLAN EDU/PROP ADMIN EXEC ATTIT ALL/VALS ...TIME/SEQ TREND COLD/WAR 20. PAGE 124 A2536
INTELL CONCPT DIPLOM

L49
HEINDEL R.H.,"THE NORTH ATLANTIC TREATY IN THE UNITED STATES SENATE." CONSTN POL/PAR CHIEF DEBATE LEAD ROUTINE WAR PEACE...CHARTS UN SENATE NATO. PAGE 64 A1309
DECISION PARL/PROC LEGIS INT/ORG

B50
PERHAM M.,COLONIAL GOVERNMENT: ANNOTATED READING LIST ON BRITISH COLONIAL GOVERNMENT. UK WOR+45 WOR-45 ECO/UNDEV INT/ORG LEGIS FOR/AID INT/TRADE DOMIN ADMIN REV 20. PAGE 115 A2356
BIBLIOG/A COLONIAL GOV/REL NAT/G

L50
US SENATE COMM. GOVT. OPER.,"REVISION OF THE UN CHARTER." FUT USA+45 WOR+45 CONSTN ECO/DEV ECO/UNDEV NAT/G DELIB/GP ACT/RES CREATE PLAN EXEC ROUTINE CHOOSE ALL/VALS...POLICY CONCPT CONGRESS UN TOT/POP 20 COLD/WAR. PAGE 157 A3196
INT/ORG LEGIS PEACE

B51
BISSAINTHE M.,DICTIONNAIRE DE BIBLIOGRAPHIE HAITIENNE. HAITI ELITES AGRI LEGIS DIPLOM INT/TRADE WRITING ORD/FREE CATHISM...ART/METH GEOG 19/20 NEGRO TREATY. PAGE 15 A0295
BIBLIOG L/A+17C SOCIETY NAT/G

B51
CHRISTENSEN A.N.,THE EVOLUTION OF LATIN AMERICAN GOVERNMENT: A BOOK OF READINGS. ECO/UNDEV INDUS LOC/G POL/PAR EX/STRUC LEGIS FOR/AID CT/SYS ...SOC/WK 20 SOUTH/AMER. PAGE 26 A0535
NAT/G CONSTN DIPLOM L/A+17C

B51
JENNINGS I.,THE COMMONWEALTH IN ASIA. CEYLON INDIA PAKISTAN CULTURE STRATA NAT/G LEGIS DIPLOM COLONIAL ATTIT...DECISION 20 CMN/WLTH. PAGE 74 A1507
CONSTN INT/ORG POLICY PLAN

B51
LEONARD L.L.,INTERNATIONAL ORGANIZATION. WOR+45 WOR-45 EX/STRUC FORCES LEGIS ECO/TAC INT/TRADE COLONIAL ARMS/CONT...SOC/WK GOV/COMP BIBLIOG. PAGE 87 A1778
NAT/G DIPLOM INT/ORG DELIB/GP

B51
SWISHER C.B.,THE THEORY AND PRACTICE OF AMERICAN NATIONAL GOVERNMENT. CULTURE LEGIS DIPLOM ADJUD ADMIN WAR PEACE ORD/FREE...MAJORIT 17/20. PAGE 140 A2872
CONSTN NAT/G GOV/REL GEN/LAWS

B51
US HOUSE COMM APPROPRIATIONS,MUTUAL SECURITY PROGRAM APPROPRIATIONS FOR 1952: HEARINGS BEFORE A SUBCOMMITTEE OF THE COMMITTEE ON APPROPRIATIONS. KOREA L/A+17C ECO/DEV ECO/UNDEV INT/ORG INSPECT BAL/PWR DIPLOM DEBATE WAR...POLICY STAT ASIA/S 20 CONGRESS NATO COLD/WAR MID/EAST. PAGE 153 A3118
LEGIS FORCES BUDGET FOR/AID

L51
KELSEN H.,"RECENT TRENDS IN THE LAW OF THE UNITED NATIONS." KOREA WOR+45 CONSTN LEGIS DIPLOM LEGIT DETER WAR RIGID/FLEX HEALTH ORD/FREE RESPECT ...JURID CON/ANAL UN VAL/FREE 20 NATO. PAGE 77 A1582
INT/ORG LAW INT/LAW

L51
MANGONE G.,"THE IDEA AND PRACTICE OF WORLD GOVERNMENT." FUT WOR+45 WOR-45 ECO/DEV LEGIS CREATE LEGIT ROUTINE ATTIT MORAL PWR WEALTH...CONCPT GEN/LAWS 20. PAGE 94 A1920
INT/ORG SOCIETY INT/LAW

B52
BARR S.,CITIZENS OF THE WORLD. USA+45 WOR+45 CULTURE FORCES LEGIS ACT/RES BAL/PWR LEGIT PEACE ATTIT ORD/FREE PWR...PLURIST CONCPT OBS TIME/SEQ COLD/WAR 20. PAGE 11 A0227
NAT/G INT/ORG DIPLOM

B52
FLECHTHEIM O.K.,FUNDAMENTALS OF POLITICAL SCIENCE. WOR+45 WOR-45 LAW POL/PAR EX/STRUC LEGIS ADJUD ATTIT PWR...INT/LAW. PAGE 46 A0945
NAT/G DIPLOM IDEA/COMP CONSTN

B52
THOM J.M.,GUIDE TO RESEARCH MATERIAL IN POLITICAL SCIENCE (PAMPHLET). ELITES LOC/G MUNIC NAT/G LEGIS DIPLOM ADJUD CIVMIL/REL GOV/REL PWR MGT. PAGE 143 A2919
BIBLIOG/A KNOWL

B52
WALTERS F.P.,A HISTORY OF THE LEAGUE OF NATIONS. EUR+WWI CONSTN NAT/G LEGIS TOP/EX ACT/RES PLAN EDU/PROP LEGIT ROUTINE ATTIT...TREND LEAGUE/NAT 20 CHINJAP. PAGE 161 A3271
INT/ORG TIME/SEQ NAT/LISM

L52
WRIGHT Q.,"CONGRESS AND THE TREATY-MAKING POWER." USA+45 WOR+45 CONSTN INTELL NAT/G CHIEF CONSULT EX/STRUC LEGIS TOP/EX CREATE GOV/REL DISPL DRIVE RIGID/FLEX...TREND TOT/POP CONGRESS CONGRESS 20 TREATY. PAGE 167 A3408
ROUTINE DIPLOM INT/LAW DELIB/GP

B53
MACMAHON A.W.,ADMINISTRATION IN FOREIGN AFFAIRS. NAT/G CONSULT DELIB/GP LEGIS ACT/RES CREATE ADMIN EXEC RIGID/FLEX PWR...METH/CNCPT TIME/SEQ TOT/POP VAL/FREE 20. PAGE 93 A1899
USA+45 ROUTINE FOR/AID DIPLOM

B54
MANGONE G.,A SHORT HISTORY OF INTERNATIONAL ORGANIZATION. MOD/EUR USA+45 USA-45 WOR+45 WOR-45 LAW LEGIS CREATE LEGIT ROUTINE RIGID/FLEX PWR ...JURID CONCPT OBS TIME/SEQ STERTYP GEN/LAWS UN TOT/POP VAL/FREE 18/20. PAGE 94 A1921
INT/ORG INT/LAW

B54
US SENATE COMM ON FOREIGN REL,REVIEW OF THE UNITED NATIONS CHARTER: A COLLECTION OF DOCUMENTS. LEGIS DIPLOM ADMIN ARMS/CONT WAR REPRESENT SOVEREIGN ...INT/LAW 20 UN. PAGE 156 A3180
BIBLIOG CONSTN INT/ORG DEBATE

B54
WRIGHT Q.,PROBLEMS OF STABILITY AND PROGRESS IN INTERNATIONAL RELATIONSHIPS. FUT WOR+45 WOR-45
INT/ORG CONCPT

SOCIETY LEGIS CREATE TEC/DEV ECO/TAC EDU/PROP ADJUD DIPLOM WAR PEACE ORD/FREE PWR...KNO/TEST TREND GEN/LAWS 20. PAGE 167 A3409

BOWIE R.R.,"STUDIES IN FEDERALISM." AGRI FINAN LABOR EX/STRUC FORCES LEGIS DIPLOM INT/TRADE ADJUD ...BIBLIOG 20 EEC. PAGE 17 A0357 — C54 — FEDERAL EUR+WWI INT/ORG CONSTN

CHOWDHURI R.N.,INTERNATIONAL MANDATES AND TRUSTEESHIP SYSTEMS. WOR+45 STRUCT ECO/UNDEV INT/ORG LEGIS DOMIN EDU/PROP LEGIT ADJUD EXEC PWR ...CONCPT TIME/SEQ UN 20. PAGE 26 A0534 — B55 — DELIB/GP PLAN SOVEREIGN

SNYDER R.C.,AMERICAN FOREIGN POLICY. USA+45 USA-45 WOR+45 WOR-45 CONSTN INT/ORG POL/PAR VOL/ASSN DELIB/GP LEGIS CREATE DOMIN EDU/PROP EXEC COERCE ATTIT DRIVE ORD/FREE PWR...MGT OBS RECORD TIME/SEQ TREND. PAGE 134 A2752 — B55 — NAT/G DIPLOM

VINSON J.C.,THE PARCHMENT PEACE: THE UNITED STATES SENATE AND THE WASHINGTON CONFERENCE, 1921-1922. USA-45 INT/ORG DELIB/GP PLAN ARMS/CONT GOV/REL ISOLAT PEACE ATTIT SOVEREIGN...INT/LAW BIBLIOG 20 SENATE PRESIDENT CONGRESS LEAGUE/NAT CHINJAP. PAGE 159 A3242 — B55 — POLICY DIPLOM NAT/G LEGIS

APTER D.E.,"THE GOLD COAST IN TRANSITION." AFR CONSTN LOC/G LEGIS DIPLOM COLONIAL CONTROL GOV/REL ...CHARTS BIBLIOG 20 CMN/WLTH. PAGE 8 A0170 — C55 — ORD/FREE REPRESENT PARL/PROC NAT/G

BOWLES C.,AFRICA'S CHALLENGE TO AMERICA. USA+45 ECO/UNDEV NAT/G LEGIS COLONIAL CONTROL REV ORD/FREE SOVEREIGN 20 COLD/WAR. PAGE 18 A0358 — B56 — AFR DIPLOM POLICY FOR/AID

GREECE PRESBEIA U.S.,BRITISH OPINION ON CYPRUS. CYPRUS UK FORCES DIPLOM INT/TRADE DOMIN GOV/REL ORD/FREE SOVEREIGN...POLICY 20. PAGE 55 A1137 — B56 — ATTIT COLONIAL LEGIS PRESS

KOENIG L.W.,THE TRUMAN ADMINISTRATION: ITS PRINCIPLES AND PRACTICE. USA+45 POL/PAR CHIEF LEGIS DIPLOM DEATH NUC/PWR WAR CIVMIL/REL PEACE ...DECISION 20 TRUMAN/HS PRESIDENT TREATY. PAGE 81 A1658 — B56 — ADMIN POLICY EX/STRUC GOV/REL

SIPKOV I.,LEGAL SOURCES AND BIBLIOGRAPHY OF BULGARIA. BULGARIA COM LEGIS WRITING ADJUD CT/SYS ...INT/LAW TREATY 20. PAGE 134 A2736 — B56 — BIBLIOG LAW TOTALISM MARXISM

US HOUSE COMM FOREIGN AFFAIRS,SURVEY OF ACTIVITIES OF THE COMMITTEE ON FOREIGN AFFAIRS HOUSE OF REPRESENTATIVES: 84TH THROUGH 86TH CONGRESS. USA+45 LAW ADJUD...POLICY STAT CHARTS 20 CONGRESS HOUSE/REP. PAGE 153 A3122 — B56 — LEGIS DELIB/GP NAT/G DIPLOM

ARON R.,FRANCE DEFEATS EDC. EUR+WWI GERMANY LEGIS DIPLOM DOMIN EDU/PROP ADMIN...HIST/WRIT 20. PAGE 9 A0180 — B57 — INT/ORG FORCES DETER FRANCE

COMM. STUDY ORGAN. PEACE,STRENGTHENING THE UNITED NATIONS. FUT USA+45 WOR+45 CONSTN NAT/G DELIB/GP FORCES LEGIS ECO/TAC LEGIT COERCE PEACE...JURID CONCPT UN COLD/WAR 20. PAGE 28 A0580 — B57 — INT/ORG ORD/FREE

CRABB C.,BIPARTISAN FOREIGN POLICY: MYTH OR REALITY. ASIA COM EUR+WWI ISLAM USA+45 USA-45 INT/ORG NAT/G LEGIS TOP/EX PWR CONGRESS 20. PAGE 32 A0649 — B57 — POL/PAR ATTIT DIPLOM

HODGKIN T.,NATIONALISM IN COLONIAL AFRICA. STRATA STRUCT MUNIC NAT/G POL/PAR LEGIS ATTIT SOVEREIGN ...POLICY TREND BIBLIOG 20. PAGE 66 A1351 — B57 — AFR COLONIAL NAT/LISM DIPLOM

MURRAY J.N.,THE UNITED NATIONS TRUSTEESHIP SYSTEM. AFR WOR+45 CONSTN CONSULT LEGIS EDU/PROP LEGIT EXEC ROUTINE...INT TIME/SEQ SOMALI UN 20. PAGE 106 A2181 — B57 — INT/ORG DELIB/GP

SEABURY P.,THE WANING OF SOUTHERN "INTERNATIONALISM" (PAMPHLET). USA+45 USA-45 INT/ORG LEGIS MAJORITY...TREND 20 SOUTH/US MIDWEST/US. PAGE 131 A2676 — B57 — DIPLOM REGION ATTIT ISOLAT

US SENATE COMM ON JUDICIARY,HEARING BEFORE SUBCOMMITTEE ON COMMITTEE OF JUDICIARY, UNITED STATES SENATE: S. J. RES. 3. USA+45 NAT/G CONSULT DELIB/GP DIPLOM ADJUD LOBBY REPRESENT 20 CONGRESS TREATY. PAGE 157 A3192 — B57 — LEGIS CONSTN CONFER AGREE

US SENATE SPECIAL COMM FOR AFF,REPORT OF THE SPECIAL COMMITTEE TO STUDY THE FOREIGN AID PROGRAM (PAMPHLET). USA+45 CONSULT DELIB/GP LEGIS PLAN TEC/DEV CONFER SUPEGO CONGRESS. PAGE 157 A3199 — N57 — FOR/AID ORD/FREE ECO/UNDEV DIPLOM

BRIERLY J.L.,THE BASIS OF OBLIGATION IN INTERNATIONAL LAW, AND OTHER PAPERS. WOR+45 WOR-45 LEGIS...JURID CONCPT NAT/COMP ANTHOL 20. PAGE 19 A0377 — B58 — INT/LAW DIPLOM ADJUD SOVEREIGN

CARROLL H.N.,THE HOUSE OF REPRESENTATIVES AND FOREIGN AFFAIRS. USA+45 USA-45 NAT/G POL/PAR DIPLOM FOR/AID LEGIT ROUTINE PWR...TIME/SEQ CONGRESS. PAGE 25 A0502 — B58 — DELIB/GP LEGIS

HUNT B.I.,BIPARTISANSHIP: A CASE STUDY OF THE FOREIGN ASSISTANCE PROGRAM, 1947-56 (DOCTORAL THESIS). USA+45 INT/ORG CONSULT LEGIS TEC/DEV ...BIBLIOG PRESIDENT TREATY NATO TRUMAN/HS EISNHWR/DD CONGRESS. PAGE 69 A1418 — B58 — FOR/AID POL/PAR GP/REL DIPLOM

RIGGS R.,POLITICS IN THE UNITED NATIONS: A STUDY OF UNITED STATES INFLUENCE IN THE GENERAL ASSEMBLY. USA+45 WOR+45 LEGIS TOP/EX CREATE BAL/PWR DIPLOM DOMIN EDU/PROP COLONIAL ROUTINE ATTIT RIGID/FLEX PWR...CONCPT OBS HIST/WRIT CHARTS STERTYP GEN/LAWS UN COLD/WAR 20. PAGE 121 A2480 — B58 — INT/ORG

HAVILAND H.F.,"FOREIGN AID AND THE POLICY PROCESS: 1957." USA+45 FACE/GP POL/PAR VOL/ASSN CHIEF DELIB/GP ACT/RES LEGIT EXEC GOV/REL ATTIT DRIVE PWR ...POLICY TESTS CONGRESS 20. PAGE 63 A1291 — L58 — LEGIS PLAN FOR/AID

INT. SOC. SCI. BULL.,"TECHNIQUES OF MEDIATION AND CONCILIATION." EUR+WWI USA+45 SOCIETY INDUS INT/ORG LABOR NAT/G LEGIS DIPLOM EDU/PROP CHOOSE ATTIT RIGID/FLEX...JURID CONCPT GEN/LAWS 20. PAGE 70 A1447 — L58 — VOL/ASSN DELIB/GP INT/LAW

STAAR R.F.,"ELECTIONS IN COMMUNIST POLAND." EUR+WWI SOCIETY INT/ORG NAT/G POL/PAR LEGIS ACT/RES ECO/TAC EDU/PROP ADJUD ADMIN ROUTINE COERCE TOTALISM ATTIT ORD/FREE PWR 20. PAGE 137 A2797 — S58 — COM CHOOSE POLAND

US HOUSE COMM FOREIGN AFFAIRS,HEARINGS ON DRAFT LEGISLATION TO AMEND FURTHER THE MUTUAL SECURITY ACT OF 1954 (PAMPHLET). USA+45 CONSULT FORCES BUDGET DIPLOM DETER COST ORD/FREE...JURID 20 DEPT/DEFEN UN DEPT/STATE. PAGE 153 A3123 — N58 — LEGIS DELIB/GP CONFER WEAPON

US HOUSE COMM FOREIGN AFFAIRS,HEARINGS ON THE FAR EAST AND THE PACIFIC (PAMPHLET). LAOS USA+45 NAT/G CONSULT FORCES CONFER DEBATE ORD/FREE 20. PAGE 153 A3124 — N58 — FOR/AID DIPLOM DELIB/GP LEGIS

US HOUSE COMM FOREIGN AFFAIRS,HEARINGS ON REVIEW OF THE MUTUAL SECURITY PROGRAMS; EXAMINATION OF SELECTED PROJECTS IN FORMOSA AND PAKISTAN (PAMPHLET). ASIA PAKISTAN TAIWAN INDUS CONSULT DELIB/GP LEGIS BUDGET CONFER DEBATE 20. PAGE 153 A3125 — N58 — FOR/AID ECO/UNDEV DIPLOM ECO/TAC

DAWSON R.H.,THE DECISION TO AID RUSSIA* FOREIGN POLICY AND DOMESTIC POLITICS. GERMANY USSR CHIEF EX/STRUC LEGIS TOP/EX PROB/SOLV WAR ATTIT...POLICY CONGRESS. PAGE 34 A0695 — B59 — DECISION DELIB/GP DIPLOM FOR/AID

REIFF H.,THE UNITED STATES AND THE TREATY LAW OF THE SEA. USA+45 USA-45 SEA SOCIETY INT/ORG CONSULT DELIB/GP LEGIS DIPLOM LEGIT ATTIT ORD/FREE PWR WEALTH...GEOG JURID TOT/POP 20 TREATY. PAGE 120 A2459 — B59 — ADJUD INT/LAW

ROBINSON J.A.,THE MONRONEY RESOULUTION: CONGRESSIONAL INITIATIVE IN FOREIGN POLICY MAKING. USA+45 POL/PAR TOP/EX DIPLOM INT/TRADE 20 CONGRESS WORLD/BANK INTL/DEV. PAGE 122 A2504 — B59 — LEGIS FINAN ECO/UNDEV CHIEF

SCHURZ W.L.,AMERICAN FOREIGN AFFAIRS: A GUIDE TO INTERNATIONAL AFFAIRS. USA+45 WOR+45 WOR-45 NAT/G FORCES LEGIS TOP/EX PLAN EDU/PROP LEGIT ADMIN ROUTINE ATTIT ORD/FREE PWR...SOC CONCPT STAT SAMP/SIZ CHARTS STERTYP 20. PAGE 129 A2653 — B59 — INT/ORG SOCIETY DIPLOM

YOUNG J.,CHECKLIST OF MICROFILM REPRODUCTIONS OF SELECTED ARCHIVES OF THE JAPANESE ARMY, NAVY, AND OTHER GOVT AGENCIES, 1868-1945. DELIB/GP LEGIS DIPLOM EDU/PROP CIVMIL/REL 19/20 CHINJAP. PAGE 169 A3436 — B59 — BIBLIOG ASIA FORCES WAR

US HOUSE COMM FOREIGN AFFAIRS,HEARINGS ON DRAFT LEGISLATION TO AMEND FURTHER THE MUTUAL SECURITY ACT OF 1954 (PAMPHLET). USA+45 USSR CONSULT DELIB/GP FORCES ECO/TAC CONFER...POLICY 20 CONGRESS. PAGE 153 A3126 — N59 — DIPLOM FOR/AID ORD/FREE LEGIS

BAILEY S.D.,THE GENERAL ASSEMBLY OF THE UNITED NATIONS. FUT WOR+45 STRUCT LEGIS ACT/RES PLAN — B60 — INT/ORG DELIB/GP

EDU/PROP LEGIT ADMIN EXEC PEACE ATTIT HEALTH PWR ...CONCPT TREND CHARTS GEN/LAWS UN TOT/POP VAL/FREE COLD/WAR 20. PAGE 10 A0204 — DIPLOM
B60

BROOKINGS INSTITUTION,UNITED STATES FOREIGN POLICY: STUDY NO 9: THE FORMULATION AND ADMINISTRATION OF UNITED STATES FOREIGN POLICY. USA+45 WOR+45 EX/STRUC LEGIS BAL/PWR FOR/AID EDU/PROP CIVMIL/REL GOV/REL...INT COLD/WAR. PAGE 19 A0394 — DIPLOM INT/ORG CREATE
B60

HARVARD LAW SCHOOL LIBRARY,CURRENT LEGAL BIBLIOGRAPHY. USA+45 CONSTN LEGIS ADJUD CT/SYS POLICY. PAGE 62 A1279 — BIBLIOG JURID LAW INT/LAW
B60

HEYSE T.,PROBLEMS FONCIERS ET REGIME DES TERRES (ASPECTS ECONOMIQUES, JURIDIQUES ET SOCIAUX). AFR CONGO/BRAZ INT/ORG DIPLOM SOVEREIGN...GEOG TREATY 20. PAGE 64 A1325 — BIBLIOG AGRI ECO/UNDEV LEGIS
B60

JEFFRIES C.,TRANSFER OF POWER: PROBLEMS OF THE PASSAGE TO SELFGOVERNMENT. CEYLON GHANA MALAYSIA NIGERIA UK INT/ORG CONSULT DELIB/GP LEGIS DIPLOM CONFER PARL/PROC 20. PAGE 73 A1502 — SOVEREIGN COLONIAL ORD/FREE NAT/G
B60

LINDSAY K.,EUROPEAN ASSEMBLIES: THE EXPERIMENTAL PERIOD 1949-1959. EUR+WWI ECO/DEV NAT/G POL/PAR LEGIS TOP/EX ACT/RES PLAN ECO/TAC DOMIN LEGIT ROUTINE ATTIT DRIVE ORD/FREE PWR SKILL...SOC CONCPT TREND CHARTS GEN/LAWS VAL/FREE. PAGE 89 A1823 — VOL/ASSN INT/ORG REGION
B60

LISKA G.,THE NEW STATECRAFT. WOR+45 WOR-45 LEGIS DIPLOM ADMIN ATTIT PWR WEALTH...HIST/WRIT TREND COLD/WAR 20. PAGE 90 A1837 — ECO/TAC CONCPT FOR/AID
B60

SOBEL R.,THE ORIGINS OF INTERVENTIONISM: THE UNITED STATES AND THE RUSSO-FINNISH WAR. FINLAND USA-45 USSR LEGIS ATTIT RIGID/FLEX...BIBLIOG 20 INTERVENT. PAGE 135 A2755 — DIPLOM WAR PROB/SOLV NEUTRAL
B60

THOMPSON K.W.,POLITICAL REALISM AND THE CRISIS IN WORLD POLITICS. USA+45 USA-45 SOCIETY INT/ORG NAT/G LEGIS TOP/EX LEGIT DETER ATTIT ORD/FREE PWR ...GEN/LAWS TOT/POP 20. PAGE 143 A2931 — PLAN HUM BAL/PWR DIPLOM
B60

US HOUSE COMM FOREIGN AFFAIRS,HEARINGS ON A BILL TO AMEND FURTHER THE MUTUAL SECURITY ACT OF 1954. USA+45 CONSULT FORCES BUDGET FOR/AID CONFER DETER ...CHARTS 20 DEPT/DEFEN DEPT/STATE UNEF. PAGE 153 A3127 — DIPLOM ORD/FREE DELIB/GP LEGIS
S60

"THE EMERGING COMMON MARKETS IN LATIN AMERICA." FUT L/A+17C STRATA DIST/IND INDUS LABOR NAT/G LEGIS ECO/TAC ADMIN RIGID/FLEX HEALTH...NEW/IDEA TIME/SEQ OAS 20. PAGE 3 A0059 — FINAN ECO/UNDEV INT/TRADE
S60

BOWIE R.,"POLICY FORMATION IN AMERICAN FOREIGN POLICY." FUT USA+45 WOR+45 STRUCT ECO/DEV INT/ORG POL/PAR LEGIS ACT/RES EXEC ALL/VALS...POLICY OBS VAL/FREE 20. PAGE 17 A0355 — PLAN DRIVE DIPLOM
S60

FRANKEL S.H.,"ECONOMIC ASPECTS OF POLITICAL INDEPENDENCE IN AFRICA." AFR FUT SOCIETY ECO/UNDEV COM/IND FINAN LEGIS PLAN TEC/DEV CAP/ISM ECO/TAC INT/TRADE ADMIN ATTIT DRIVE RIGID/FLEX PWR WEALTH ...MGT NEW/IDEA MATH TIME/SEQ VAL/FREE 20. PAGE 48 A0984 — NAT/G FOR/AID
S60

GOODMAN E.,"THE CRY OF NATIONAL LIBERATION: RECENT SOVIET ATTITUDES TOWARDS NATIONAL SELF-DETERMINATION." COM INT/ORG LEGIS ROUTINE PWR ...TIME/SEQ CON/ANAL STERTYP GEN/LAWS 20 UN. PAGE 54 A1101 — ATTIT EDU/PROP SOVEREIGN USSR
S60

MORALES C.J.,"TRADE AND ECONOMIC INTEGRATION IN LATIN AMERICA." FUT L/A+17C LAW STRATA ECO/UNDEV DIST/IND INDUS LABOR NAT/G LEGIS ECO/TAC ADMIN RIGID/FLEX WEALTH...CONCPT NEW/IDEA CONT/OBS TIME/SEQ WORK 20. PAGE 104 A2128 — FINAN INT/TRADE REGION
S60

PADELFORD N.J.,"POLITICS AND CHANGE IN THE SECURITY COUNCIL." FUT WOR+45 CONSTN NAT/G EX/STRUC LEGIS ORD/FREE...CONCPT CHARTS UN 20. PAGE 113 A2309 — INT/ORG DELIB/GP
S60

POTTER P.B.,"RELATIVE VALUES OF INTERNATIONAL RELATIONS, LAW, AND ORGANIZATIONS." WOR+45 NAT/G LEGIT ADJUD ORD/FREE...CONCPT TOT/POP COLD/WAR 20. PAGE 117 A2401 — INT/ORG LEGIS DIPLOM INT/LAW
B61

BARNES W.,THE FOREIGN SERVICE OF THE UNITED STATES. USA+45 USA-45 CONSTN INT/ORG POL/PAR CONSULT DELIB/GP LEGIS DOMIN EDU/PROP EXEC ATTIT RIGID/FLEX ORD/FREE PWR...POLICY CONCPT STAT OBS RECORD BIOG TIME/SEQ TREND. PAGE 11 A0224 — NAT/G MGT DIPLOM
B61

BISHOP D.G.,THE ADMINISTRATION OF BRITISH FOREIGN RELATIONS. EUR+WWI MOD/EUR INT/ORG NAT/G POL/PAR DELIB/GP LEGIS TOP/EX ECO/TAC DOMIN EDU/PROP ADMIN COERCE 20. PAGE 14 A0292 — ROUTINE PWR DIPLOM UK
B61

GRAEBNER N.,THE NEW ISOLATIONISM: A STUDY IN POLITICS AND FOREIGN POLICY SINCE 1960. USA+45 INT/ORG LOC/G NAT/G POL/PAR LEGIS BAL/PWR EDU/PROP CHOOSE ATTIT PERSON ORD/FREE 20 TRUMAN/HS EISNHWR/DD. PAGE 55 A1120 — EXEC PWR DIPLOM
B61

JAVITS B.A.,THE PEACE BY INVESTMENT CORPORATION. WOR+45 NAT/G LEGIS PROB/SOLV PERS/REL WEALTH ...POLICY 20. PAGE 73 A1499 — ECO/UNDEV DIPLOM FOR/AID PEACE
B61

KHAN A.W.,INDIA WINS FREEDOM: THE OTHER SIDE. INDIA PAKISTAN CULTURE LEGIS DIPLOM PARL/PROC REV WAR NAT/LISM 20. PAGE 78 A1607 — SOVEREIGN GP/REL RACE/REL ORD/FREE
B61

MACLURE M.,AFRICA: THE POLITICAL PATTERN. SOUTH/AFR CULTURE LEGIS DIPLOM COLONIAL RACE/REL 20. PAGE 93 A1898 — AFR POLICY NAT/G
B61

MEZERIK A.G.,ECONOMIC DEVELOPMENT AIDS FOR UNDERDEVELOPED COUNTRIES. WOR+45 FINAN LEGIS PROB/SOLV TEC/DEV DIPLOM FOR/AID GIVE TASK WAR 20 UN. PAGE 101 A2062 — ECO/UNDEV INT/ORG WEALTH PLAN
B61

PANIKKAR K.M.,THE VOICE OF FREEDOM: SELECTED SPEECHES OF PANDIT MOTILAL NEHRU. INDIA UK CONSTN FINAN FORCES LEGIS DIPLOM TAX COLONIAL...POLICY MAJORIT ANTHOL 20 NEHRU/PM. PAGE 114 A2331 — NAT/LISM ORD/FREE CHIEF NAT/G
B61

SCHNAPPER B.,LA POLITIQUE ET LE COMMERCE FRANCAIS DANS LE GOLFE DE GUINEE DE 1838 A 1871. FRANCE GUINEA UK SEA EXTR/IND NAT/G DELIB/GP LEGIS ADMIN ORD/FREE...POLICY GEOG CENSUS CHARTS BIBLIOG 19. PAGE 129 A2636 — COLONIAL INT/TRADE DOMIN AFR
B61

US HOUSE COMM APPROPRIATIONS,INTER-AMERICAN PROGRAMS FOR 1961: DENIAL OF 1962 BUDGET INFORMATION. CHILE L/A+17C USA+45 FINAN CONSULT BUDGET ADJUD COST EFFICIENCY WEALTH...POLICY CHARTS 20 CONGRESS. PAGE 153 A3119 — LEGIS FOR/AID DELIB/GP ECO/UNDEV
B61

US HOUSE COMM FOREIGN AFFAIRS,THE INTERNATIONAL DEVELOPMENT AND SECURITY ACT: HEARINGS BEFORE COMMITTEE ON FOREIGN AFFAIRS, HOUSE OF REP: HR7372. USA+45 AGRI INT/ORG NAT/G CONSULT DELIB/GP DIPLOM ECO/TAC INT/TRADE LOBBY REPRESENT 20 MCNAMARA/R DILLON/D RUSK/D CONGRESS. PAGE 153 A3128 — FOR/AID CONFER LEGIS ECO/UNDEV
B61

WARD R.E.,JAPANESE POLITICAL SCIENCE: A GUIDE TO JAPANESE REFERENCE AND RESEARCH MATERIALS (2ND ED.). LAW CONSTN STRATA NAT/G POL/PAR DELIB/GP LEGIS ADMIN CHOOSE GP/REL...INT/LAW 19/20 CHINJAP. PAGE 161 A3282 — BIBLIOG/A PHIL/SCI
B61

WILLOUGHBY W.R.,THE ST LAWRENCE WATERWAY: A STUDY IN POLITICS AND DIPLOMACY. USA+45 ECO/DEV COM/IND INT/ORG CONSULT DELIB/GP ACT/RES TEC/DEV DIPLOM ECO/TAC ROUTINE...TIME/SEQ 20. PAGE 165 A3357 — LEGIS INT/TRADE CANADA DIST/IND
B62

AMERICAN LAW INSTITUTE,FOREIGN RELATIONS LAW OF THE UNITED STATES: RESTATEMENT, SECOND. USA+45 NAT/G LEGIS ADJUD EXEC ROUTINE GOV/REL...INT/LAW JURID CONCPT 20 TREATY. PAGE 7 A0152 — PROF/ORG LAW DIPLOM ORD/FREE
B62

BOWLES C.,THE CONSCIENCE OF A LIBERAL. COM USA+45 WOR+45 STRUCT LOC/G NAT/G FORCES LEGIS GOV/REL DISCRIM 20 UN CIV/RIGHTS. PAGE 18 A0361 — DIPLOM POLICY
B62

GUTTMAN A.,THE WOUND IN THE HEART: AMERICA AND THE SPANISH CIVIL WAR. SPAIN USA-45 POL/PAR LEGIS ECO/TAC CHOOSE ANOMIE ATTIT MARXISM...POLICY ANARCH BIBLIOG 20 ROOSEVLT/F. PAGE 58 A1198 — ALL/IDEOS WAR DIPLOM CATHISM
B62

JEWELL M.E.,SENATORIAL POLITICS AND FOREIGN POLICY. NAT/G POL/PAR CHIEF DELIB/GP TOP/EX FOR/AID EDU/PROP ROUTINE ATTIT PWR SKILL...MAJORIT METH/CNCPT TIME/SEQ CONGRESS 20 PRESIDENT. PAGE 74 A1516 — USA+45 LEGIS DIPLOM
B62

LAWSON R.,INTERNATIONAL REGIONAL ORGANIZATIONS. WOR+45 NAT/G VOL/ASSN CONSULT LEGIS EDU/PROP LEGIT ADMIN EXEC ROUTINE HEALTH PWR WEALTH...JURID EEC COLD/WAR 20 UN. PAGE 86 A1752 — INT/ORG DELIB/GP REGION
B62

LEOPOLD R.W.,THE GROWTH OF AMERICAN FOREIGN POLICY: A HISTORY. USA+45 USA-45 EX/STRUC LEGIS INT/TRADE WAR...CHARTS BIBLIOG/A T 18/20. PAGE 87 A1780 — NAT/G DIPLOM POLICY
B62

SNOW J.H.,GOVERNMENT BY TREASON. USA+45 USA-45 LEGIS DIPLOM FOR/AID GIVE CONTROL WEALTH MARXISM ...MAJORIT 20 CONGRESS COLD/WAR. PAGE 134 A2750 — FINAN TAX PWR

POLICY

B62
SPIRO H.J.,POLITICS IN AFRICA: PROSPECTS SOUTH OF AFR
THE SAHARA. INT/ORG KIN FORCES LEGIS PROB/SOLV NAT/LISM
COERCE RACE/REL FEDERAL...TREND CHARTS BIBLIOG 20. DIPLOM
PAGE 136 A2790

B62
STARR R.E.,POLAND 1944-1962: THE SOVIETIZATION OF A MARXISM
CAPTIVE PEOPLE. COM POLAND USSR POL/PAR SECT LEGIS NAT/G
DIPLOM DOMIN EDU/PROP CHOOSE ORD/FREE...POLICY TOTALISM
CHARTS BIBLIOG 20. PAGE 137 A2808 NAT/COMP

B62
US CONGRESS,LEGISLATIVE HISTORY OF UNITED STATES TAX
TAX CONVENTIONS(VOL. 1). USA+45 USA-45 DELIB/GP LEGIS
WEALTH...CHARTS 20 CONGRESS. PAGE 150 A3061 LAW
DIPLOM

L62
MURACCIOLE L.,"LA LOI FONDAMENTALE DE LA REPUBLIQUE AFR
DU CONGO." WOR+45 SOCIETY ECO/UNDEV INT/ORG NAT/G CONSTN
LEGIS PLAN LEGIT ADJUD COLONIAL ROUTINE ATTIT
SOVEREIGN 20 CONGO. PAGE 106 A2174

S62
GRAVEN J.,"LE MOUVEAU DROIT PENAL INTERNATIONAL." CT/SYS
UNIV STRUCT LEGIS ACT/RES CRIME ATTIT PERCEPT PUB/INST
PERSON...JURID CONCPT 20. PAGE 55 A1132 INT/ORG
INT/LAW

S62
SPRINGER H.W.,"FEDERATION IN THE CARIBBEAN: AN VOL/ASSN
ATTEMPT THAT FAILED." L/A+17C ECO/UNDEV INT/ORG NAT/G
POL/PAR PROVS LEGIS CREATE PLAN LEGIT ADMIN FEDERAL REGION
ATTIT DRIVE PERSON ORD/FREE PWR...POLICY GEOG PSY
CONCPT OBS CARIBBEAN CMN/WLTH 20. PAGE 136 A2791

S62
THOMPSON D.,"THE UNITED KINGDOM AND THE TREATY OF ADJUD
ROME." EUR+WWI INT/ORG NAT/G DELIB/GP LEGIS JURID
INT/TRADE RIGID/FLEX...CONCPT EEC PARLIAMENT
CMN/WLTH 20. PAGE 143 A2925

S62
TRUMAN D.,"THE DOMESTIC POLITICS OF FOREIGN AID." ROUTINE
USA+45 WOR+45 NAT/G POL/PAR LEGIS DIPLOM ECO/TAC FOR/AID
EDU/PROP ADMIN CHOOSE ATTIT PWR CONGRESS 20
CONGRESS. PAGE 145 A2970

C62
ROBINSON J.A.,"CONGRESS AND FOREIGN POLICY-MAKING: LEGIS
A STUDY IN LEGISLATIVE INFLUENCE AND INITIATIVE." DIPLOM
USA+45 CHIEF DELIB/GP CREATE CONTROL EXEC GOV/REL POLICY
PERCEPT...TREND BIBLIOG 20 CONGRESS. PAGE 122 A2505 DECISION

B63
DECOTTIGNIES R.,LES NATIONALITES AFRICAINES. AFR NAT/LISM
NAT/G PROB/SOLV DIPLOM COLONIAL ORD/FREE...CHARTS JURID
GOV/COMP 20. PAGE 35 A0721 LEGIS
LAW

B63
DRACHKOVITCH,UNITED STATES AID TO YUGOSLAVIA AND FOR/AID
POLAND. POLAND USA+45 YUGOSLAVIA LEGIS EXEC POLICY
TOTALISM MARXISM 20 CONGRESS. PAGE 38 A0782 DIPLOM
ATTIT

B63
FATEMI N.S.,THE DOLLAR CRISIS. USA+45 INDUS NAT/G PROB/SOLV
LEGIS BUDGET TAX COST...CHARTS METH/COMP 20 EEC. BAL/PAY
PAGE 44 A0902 FOR/AID
PLAN

B63
FRANKEL J.,THE MAKING OF FOREIGN POLICY: AN POLICY
ANALYSIS OF DECISION-MAKING. CHINA/COM EUR+WWI DECISION
USA+45 ELITES INTELL FORCES LEGIS PLAN ATTIT PROB/SOLV
ALL/VALS MORAL CONSERVE...GOV/COMP 20 PRESIDENT UN DIPLOM
TREATY. PAGE 48 A0981

B63
GARDINIER D.E.,CAMEROON: UNITED NATIONS CHALLENGE DIPLOM
TO FRENCH POLICY. AFR CAMEROON FRANCE NAT/G LEGIS POLICY
CONTROL SOVEREIGN 20 UN. PAGE 51 A1042 INT/ORG
COLONIAL

B63
GRIFFITH W.E.,ALBANIA AND THE SINO-SOVIET RIFT. EDU/PROP
ALBANIA CHINA/COM USSR POL/PAR CHIEF LEGIS DIPLOM MARXISM
DOMIN ATTIT PWR...POLICY 20 KHRUSH/N MAO. PAGE 57 NAT/LISM
A1161 GOV/REL

B63
HALEY A.G.,SPACE LAW AND GOVERNMENT. FUT USA+45 INT/ORG
WOR+45 LEGIS ACT/RES CREATE ATTIT RIGID/FLEX LAW
ORD/FREE PWR SOVEREIGN...POLICY JURID CONCPT CHARTS SPACE
VAL/FREE 20. PAGE 60 A1226

B63
HONEY P.J.,COMMUNISM IN NORTH VIETNAM: ITS ROLE IN POLICY
THE SINO-SOVIET DISPUTE. CHINA/COM INDIA USSR MARXISM
VIETNAM/N AGRI POL/PAR LEGIS ECO/TAC WAR PEACE CHIEF
ATTIT...GEOG IDEA/COMP 20. PAGE 67 A1378 DIPLOM

B63
LADOR-LEDERER J.J.,INTERNATIONAL NON-GOVERNMENTAL INT/ORG
ORGANIZATIONS: A STUDY IN AUTONOMOUS ORGANIZATION INT/LAW
AND IUS GENTIUM. LAW DELIB/GP LEGIS DIPLOM 20. INGP/REL
PAGE 83 A1709 VOL/ASSN

B63
MONGER G.W.,THE END OF ISOLATION. FRANCE MOD/EUR DIPLOM
RUSSIA UK NAT/G LEGIS TOP/EX GOV/REL PWR 20 TREATY POLICY
CHINJAP. PAGE 103 A2106 WAR

B63
NORTH R.C.,M. N. ROY'S MISSION TO CHINA: THE POL/PAR
COMMUNIST-KUOMINTANG SPLIT OF 1927. ASIA USSR MARXISM
STRATA LEGIS WORKER LEAD REV ATTIT ROLE SOCISM 20 DIPLOM
ROY/MN COM/PARTY. PAGE 110 A2253

B63
US HOUSE COMM FOREIGN AFFAIRS,HEARINGS ON H.R. 5490 FOR/AID
TO AMEND FURTHER THE FOREIGN ASSISTANCE ACT OF INT/TRADE
1961. CUBA EUR+WWI INDIA INT/ORG DELIB/GP LEGIS FORCES
DIPLOM CONFER ORD/FREE 20 DEPT/STATE DEPT/DEFEN UN. WEAPON
PAGE 153 A3129

B63
US SENATE,DOCUMENTS ON INTERNATIONAL AS"ECTS OF SPACE
EXPLORATION AND USE OF OUTER SPACE, 1954-62: STAFF UTIL
REPORT FOR COMM AERON SPACE SCI. USA+45 USSR LEGIS GOV/REL
LEAD CIVMIL/REL PEACE...POLICY INT/LAW ANTHOL 20 DIPLOM
CONGRESS NASA KHRUSH/N. PAGE 155 A3165

B63
VOSS E.H.,NUCLEAR AMBUSH: THE TEST-BAN TRAP. WOR+45 TEC/DEV
COM/IND INT/ORG NAT/G DELIB/GP FORCES LEGIS TOP/EX HIST/WRIT
ACT/RES DOMIN EDU/PROP LEGIT ROUTINE COERCE ATTIT ARMS/CONT
PERCEPT RIGID/FLEX HEALTH MORAL ORD/FREE PWR. NUC/PWR
PAGE 160 A3255

B63
WALKER A.A.,OFFICIAL PUBLICATIONS OF SIERRA LEONE BIBLIOG
AND GAMBIA. GAMBIA SIER/LEONE UK LAW CONSTN LEGIS NAT/G
PLAN BUDGET DIPLOM...SOC SAMP CON/ANAL 20. PAGE 160 COLONIAL
A3262 ADMIN

B63
WESTERFIELD H.,THE INSTRUMENTS OF AMERICA'S FOREIGN USA+45
POLICY. WOR+45 ECO/DEV NAT/G CONSULT EX/STRUC LEGIS INT/ORG
BAL/PWR FOR/AID INT/TRADE DOMIN EDU/PROP LEGIT DIPLOM
ATTIT KNOWL ORD/FREE PWR WEALTH...OBS COLD/WAR
TOT/POP VAL/FREE. PAGE 163 A3322

L63
RUSSETT B.M.,"TOWARD A MODEL OF COMPETITIVE ATTIT
INTERNATIONAL POLITICS." USA+45 WOR+45 INT/ORG EDU/PROP
NAT/G POL/PAR VOL/ASSN LEGIS BAL/PWR DIPLOM LEGIT
PWR...CONCPT CONT/OBS STERTYP GEN/LAWS TOT/POP
COLD/WAR 20 UN. PAGE 126 A2579

S63
BANFIELD J.,"FEDERATION IN EAST-AFRICA." AFR UGANDA EX/STRUC
ELITES INT/ORG NAT/G VOL/ASSN LEGIS ECO/TAC FEDERAL PWR
ATTIT SOVEREIGN TOT/POP 20 TANGANYIKA. PAGE 11 REGION
A0216

S63
BECHHOEFER B.G.,"UNITED NATIONS PROCEDURES IN CASE INT/ORG
OF VIOLATIONS OF DISARMAMENT AGREEMENTS." COM DELIB/GP
USA+45 USSR LAW CONSTN NAT/G EX/STRUC FORCES LEGIS
BAL/PWR EDU/PROP CT/SYS ARMS/CONT ORD/FREE PWR
...POLICY STERTYP UN VAL/FREE 20. PAGE 12 A0245

S63
HARNETTY P.,"CANADA, SOUTH AFRICA AND THE AFR
COMMONWEALTH." CANADA SOUTH/AFR LAW INT/ORG ATTIT
VOL/ASSN DELIB/GP LEGIS TOP/EX ECO/TAC LEGIT DRIVE
MORAL...CONCPT CMN/WLTH 20. PAGE 62 A1263

C63
ATTIA G.E.O.,"LES FORCES ARMEES DES NATIONS UNIES FORCES
EN COREE ET AU MOYENORIENT." KOREA CONSTN DELIB/GP NAT/G
LEGIS PWR...IDEA/COMP NAT/COMP BIBLIOG UN SUEZ. INT/LAW
PAGE 10 A0194

B64
APTER D.E.,IDEOLOGY AND DISCONTENT. FUT WOR+45 ACT/RES
CONSTN CULTURE INTELL SOCIETY STRUCT INT/ORG NAT/G ATTIT
DELIB/GP LEGIS CREATE PLAN TEC/DEV EDU/PROP EXEC
PERCEPT PERSON RIGID/FLEX ALL/VALS...POLICY
TOT/POP. PAGE 8 A0171

B64
DE SMITH S.A.,THE NEW COMMONWEALTH AND ITS EX/STRUC
CONSTITUTIONS. AFR CYPRUS PAKISTAN S/ASIA INT/ORG CONSTN
NAT/G LEGIS LEGIT RIGID/FLEX PWR...CONCPT TIME/SEQ SOVEREIGN
CMN/WLTH 20. PAGE 35 A0713

B64
DIAS R.W.M.,A BIBLIOGRAPHY OF JURISPRUDENCE (2ND BIBLIOG/A
ED.). VOL/ASSN LEGIS ADJUD CT/SYS OWN...INT/LAW JURID
18/20. PAGE 37 A0754 LAW
CONCPT

B64
DONOUGHUE B.,BRITISH POLITICS AND THE AMERICAN DIPLOM
REVOLUTION: THE PATH TO WAR 1773-75. UK USA-45 POLICY
NAT/G LEGIS WAR 18 PRE/US/AM. PAGE 38 A0772 COLONIAL
REV

B64
FULBRIGHT J.W.,OLD MYTHS AND NEW REALITIES. USA+45 DIPLOM
USSR LEGIS INT/TRADE DETER ATTIT...POLICY 20 INT/ORG
COLD/WAR TREATY. PAGE 50 A1016 ORD/FREE

B64
GARDNER L.C.,ECONOMIC ASPECTS OF NEW DEAL ECO/TAC
DIPLOMACY. USA-45 WOR-45 LAW ECO/DEV INT/ORG NAT/G DIPLOM
VOL/ASSN LEGIS TOP/EX EDU/PROP ORD/FREE PWR WEALTH
...POLICY TIME/SEQ VAL/FREE 20 ROOSEVLT/F. PAGE 51
A1043

B64
GJUPANOVIC H.,LEGAL SOURCES AND BIBLIOGRAPHY OF BIBLIOG/A
YUGOSLAVIA. COM YUGOSLAVIA LAW LEGIS DIPLOM ADMIN JURID

PARL/PROC REGION CRIME CENTRAL 20. PAGE 53 A1078 — CONSTN ADJUD

B64
LOCKHART W.B.,CASES AND MATERIALS ON CONSTITUTIONAL RIGHTS AND LIBERTIES. USA+45 FORCES LEGIS DIPLOM PRESS CONTROL CRIME WAR PWR...AUD/VIS T WORSHIP 20 NEGRO. PAGE 90 A1849 — ORD/FREE CONSTN NAT/G

B64
NEWBURY C.W.,THE WEST AFRICAN COMMONWEALTH. CONSTN INTELL ECO/UNDEV VOL/ASSN CHIEF DELIB/GP LEGIS INT/TRADE COLONIAL FEDERAL ATTIT 20 COMMONWLTH AFRICA/W. PAGE 108 A2223 — INT/ORG SOVEREIGN GOV/REL AFR

B64
REUSS H.S.,THE CRITICAL DECADE - AN ECONOMIC POLICY FOR AMERICA AND THE FREE WORLD. USA+45 FINAN POL/PAR WORKER PLAN DIPLOM ECO/TAC TARIFFS BAL/PAY ...POLICY 20 CONGRESS GOLD/STAND. PAGE 120 A2468 — FOR/AID INT/TRADE LABOR LEGIS

B64
RUSSELL R.B.,UNITED NATIONS EXPERIENCE WITH MILITARY FORCES: POLITICAL AND LEGAL ASPECTS. AFR KOREA WOR+45 LEGIS PROB/SOLV ADMIN CONTROL EFFICIENCY PEACE...POLICY INT/LAW BIBLIOG UN. PAGE 126 A2576 — FORCES DIPLOM SANCTION ORD/FREE

B64
VECCHIO G.D.,L'ETAT ET LE DROIT. ITALY CONSTN EX/STRUC LEGIS DIPLOM CT/SYS...JURID 20 UN. PAGE 158 A3225 — NAT/G SOVEREIGN CONCPT INT/LAW

L64
BERKS R.N.,"THE US AND WEAPONS CONTROL." WOR+45 LAW INT/ORG NAT/G LEGIS EXEC COERCE PEACE ATTIT RIGID/FLEX ALL/VALS PWR...POLICY TOT/POP 20. PAGE 13 A0273 — USA+45 PLAN ARMS/CONT

L64
CARNEGIE ENDOWMENT INT. PEACE,"POLITICAL QUESTIONS (ISSUES BEFORE THE NINETEENTH GENERAL ASSEMBLY)." SPACE WOR+45 CONSTN FINAN NAT/G CONSULT DELIB/GP FORCES LEGIS TEC/DEV EDU/PROP LEGIT ARMS/CONT COERCE NUC/PWR ATTIT ALL/VALS...CONCPT OBS UN COLD/WAR 20. PAGE 24 A0490 — INT/ORG PEACE

S64
CARNEGIE ENDOWMENT INT. PEACE,"COLONIAL COUNTRIES AND PEOPLES (ISSUES BEFORE THE NINETEENTH GENERAL ASSEMBLY)." AFR ISLAM L/A+17C WOR+45 DELIB/GP LEGIS ECO/TAC EDU/PROP NAT/LISM PEACE ALL/VALS...RECORD UN CMN/WLTH 20. PAGE 24 A0491 — INT/ORG ECO/UNDEV COLONIAL

S64
DERWINSKI E.J.,"THE COST OF THE INTERNATIONAL COFFEE AGREEMENT." L/A+17C USA+45 WOR+45 ECO/UNDEV NAT/G VOL/ASSN LEGIS DIPLOM ECO/TAC FOR/AID LEGIT ATTIT...TIME/SEQ CONGRESS 20 TREATY. PAGE 36 A0732 — MARKET DELIB/GP INT/TRADE

S64
GROSS J.A.,"WHITEHALL AND THE COMMONWEALTH." EUR+WWI MOD/EUR INT/ORG NAT/G CONSULT DELIB/GP LEGIS DOMIN ADMIN COLONIAL ROUTINE PWR CMN/WLTH 19/20. PAGE 57 A1174 — EX/STRUC ATTIT TREND

B65
BROOKINGS INSTITUTION,BROOKINGS PAPERS ON PUBLIC POLICY. USA+45 ECO/UNDEV LEGIS CAP/ISM ECO/TAC TAX EDU/PROP CONTROL APPORT 20. PAGE 19 A0395 — DIPLOM FOR/AID POLICY FINAN

B65
GEORGE M.,THE WARPED VISION. EUR+WWI UK NAT/G POL/PAR LEGIS PARL/PROC SANCTION COERCE WAR GOV/REL PEACE RESPECT 20 CONSRV/PAR. PAGE 52 A1061 — LEAD ATTIT DIPLOM POLICY

B65
HAIGHT D.E.,THE PRESIDENT; ROLES AND POWERS. USA+45 USA-45 POL/PAR PLAN DIPLOM CHOOSE PERS/REL PWR 18/20 PRESIDENT CONGRESS. PAGE 59 A1217 — CHIEF LEGIS TOP/EX EX/STRUC

B65
JADOS S.S.,DOCUMENTS ON RUSSIAN-AMERICAN RELATIONS: WASHINGTON TO EISENHOWER. USA+45 USA-45 USSR INT/ORG LEGIS INT/TRADE WAR PEACE...ANTHOL BIBLIOG 18/20 PRESIDENT. PAGE 73 A1488 — DIPLOM CHIEF CONTROL

B65
LEVENSTEIN A.,FREEDOM'S ADVOCATE - A TWENTY-FIVE YEAR CHRONICLE. USA+45 POL/PAR LEGIS DIPLOM WAR PEACE TOTALISM DRIVE MARXISM 20 FREEDOM/HS. PAGE 87 A1791 — ORD/FREE VOL/ASSN POLICY ATTIT

B65
MOSTECKY V.,SOVIET LEGAL BIBLIOGRAPHY. USSR LEGIS PRESS WRITING CONFER ADJUD CT/SYS REV MARXISM ...INT/LAW JURID DICTIONARY 20. PAGE 105 A2155 — BIBLIOG/A LAW COM CONSTN

B65
MUNGER E.S.,NOTES ON THE FORMATION OF SOUTH AFRICAN FOREIGN POLICY. ACADEM POL/PAR SECT CHIEF DELIB/GP FORCES LEGIS PRESS ATTIT...TREND 20 NEGRO. PAGE 106 A2170 — AFR DOMIN POLICY DIPLOM

B65
O'CONNELL M.R.,IRISH POLITICS AND SOCIAL CONFLICT IN THE AGE OF THE AMERICAN REVOLUTION. FRANCE IRELAND MOD/EUR STRATA SECT LEGIS DIPLOM INT/TRADE DOMIN REV WAR...BIBLIOG 18 PARLIAMENT. PAGE 111 A2268 — CATHISM ATTIT NAT/G DELIB/GP

B65
OGILVY-WEBB M.,THE GOVERNMENT EXPLAINS: A STUDY OF THE INFORMATION SERVICES. UK DELIB/GP LEGIS WORKER BUDGET DIPLOM 20. PAGE 111 A2284 — EDU/PROP ATTIT NAT/G ADMIN

B65
QURESHI I.H.,THE STRUGGLE FOR PAKISTAN. INDIA PAKISTAN UK CULTURE LEGIS DIPLOM EDU/PROP COLONIAL ATTIT SOVEREIGN 19/20 MUSLIM. PAGE 118 A2429 — GP/REL RACE/REL WAR SECT

B65
US CONGRESS JT ATOM ENRGY COMM,ATOMIC ENERGY LEGISLATION THROUGH 89TH CONGRESS, 1ST SESSION. USA+45 LAW INT/ORG DELIB/GP BUDGET DIPLOM 20 AEC CONGRESS CASEBOOK EURATOM IAEA. PAGE 150 A3071 — NUC/PWR FORCES PEACE LEGIS

S65
MERRITT R.L.,"WOODROW WILSON AND THE 'GREAT AND SOLEMN REFERENDUM,' 1920." USA-45 SOCIETY NAT/G CONSULT LEGIS ACT/RES PLAN DOMIN EDU/PROP ROUTINE ATTIT DISPL DRIVE PERSON RIGID/FLEX MORAL ORD/FREE ...PSY SOC CONCPT MYTH LEAGUE/NAT. PAGE 100 A2044 — INT/ORG TOP/EX DIPLOM

S65
PLISCHKE E.,"INTEGRATING BERLIN AND THE FEDERAL REPUBLIC OF GERMANY." EUR+WWI GERMANY/W LEGIS TEC/DEV DOMIN ORD/FREE PWR...JURID 20 BERLIN. PAGE 117 A2392 — DIPLOM NAT/G MUNIC

S65
QUADE Q.L.,"THE TRUMAN ADMINISTRATION AND THE SEPARATION OF POWERS: THE CASE OF THE MARSHALL PLAN." SOCIETY INT/ORG NAT/G CONSULT DELIB/GP LEGIS PLAN ECO/TAC ROUTINE DRIVE PERCEPT RIGID/FLEX ORD/FREE PWR WEALTH...DECISION GEOG NEW/IDEA TREND 20 TRUMAN/HS. PAGE 118 A2422 — USA+45 ECO/UNDEV DIPLOM

B66
SUPPLEMENTAL FOREIGN ASSISTANCE FISCAL YEAR 1966: VIETNAM. CHINA/COM COM S/ASIA USA+45 VIETNAM EXTR/IND FINAN DIPLOM TAX GUERRILLA HABITAT ORD/FREE...STAT CHARTS 20 SENATE PRESIDENT. PAGE 4 A0077 — CONFER LEGIS WAR FOR/AID

B66
BALDWIN D.A.,ECONOMIC DEVELOPMENT AND AMERICAN FOREIGN POLICY. USA+45 FINAN LG/CO LEGIS DIPLOM GIVE 20. PAGE 10 A0210 — ECO/TAC FOR/AID ECO/UNDEV POLICY

B66
BERNSTEIN B.J.,THE TRUMAN ADMINISTRATION. WOR+45 LABOR POL/PAR LEGIS DIPLOM NUC/PWR WAR ATTIT ...POLICY 20 TRUMAN/HS. PAGE 14 A0279 — LEAD TOP/EX NAT/G

B66
DONALD A.D.,JOHN F. KENNEDY AND THE NEW FRONTIER. LEGIS DIPLOM DISCRIM PEACE PWR 20. PAGE 38 A0771 — LEAD CHIEF BIOG EFFICIENCY

B66
FRANK E.,LAWMAKERS IN A CHANGING WORLD. FRANCE UK USSR WOR+45 PARTIC EFFICIENCY ROLE ALL/IDEOS ...CHARTS ANTHOL PARLIAMENT 20 UN COLD/WAR. PAGE 48 A0979 — GOV/COMP LEGIS NAT/G DIPLOM

B66
LATHAM E.,THE COMMUNIST CONTROVERSY IN WASHINGTON. USA+45 USA-45 DELIB/GP EX/STRUC LEGIS DIPLOM NAT/LISM MARXISM 20. PAGE 85 A1742 — POL/PAR TOTALISM ORD/FREE NAT/G

B66
MALLORY W.H.,POLITICAL HANDBOOK AND ATLAS OF THE WORLD: PARLIAMENTS, PARTIES AND PRESS AS OF JANUARY 1, 1966. WOR+45 LEGIS PRESS...GEOG 20. PAGE 93 A1915 — CHARTS DIPLOM NAT/G

B66
NEUMANN R.G.,THE GOVERNMENT OF THE GERMAN FEDERAL REPUBLIC. EUR+WWI GERMANY/W LOC/G EX/STRUC LEGIS CT/SYS INGP/REL PWR...BIBLIOG 20 ADENAUER/K. PAGE 108 A2222 — NAT/G POL/PAR DIPLOM CONSTN

B66
RIESELBACH L.N.,THE ROOTS OF ISOLATIONISM* CONGRESSIONAL VOTING AND PRESIDENTIAL LEADERSHIP IN FOREIGN POLICY. POL/PAR LEGIS DIPLOM EDU/PROP LEAD REGION REPRESENT...SOC STAT IDEA/COMP HYPO/EXP BIBLIOG 19/20 CONGRESS. PAGE 121 A2477 — ISOLAT CHOOSE CHIEF POLICY

B66
SZLADITS C.,A BIBLIOGRAPHY ON FOREIGN AND COMPARATIVE LAW (SUPPLEMENT 1964). FINAN FAM LABOR LG/CO LEGIS JUDGE ADMIN CRIME...CRIMLGY 20. PAGE 141 A2878 — BIBLIOG/A CT/SYS INT/LAW

B66
US HOUSE COMM FOREIGN AFFAIRS,UNITED STATES - SOUTH AFRICAN RELATIONS. SOUTH/AFR USA+45 NAT/G CONSULT DELIB/GP LEGIS CONFER SANCTION RACE/REL ATTIT 20 CONGRESS. PAGE 154 A3134 — DISCRIM DIPLOM POLICY PARL/PROC

B66
US SENATE COMM GOVT OPERATIONS,POPULATION CRISIS. USA+45 ECO/DEV ECO/UNDEV AGRI SECT DELIB/GP PROB/SOLV FOR/AID REPRESENT ATTIT...GEOG CHARTS 20 CONGRESS DEPT/STATE DEPT/HEW BIRTH/CON. PAGE 156 A3178 — CENSUS CONTROL LEGIS CONSULT

B66
VYAS R.,DAWNING ON THE CAPITOL: US CONGRESS AND INDIA. INDIA S/ASIA USA+45 ELITES ECO/DEV ECO/UNDEV PLAN FOR/AID...BIBLIOG 20 CONGRESS. PAGE 160 A3256
POLICY LEGIS NAT/G DIPLOM

B66
WESTWOOD A.F.,FOREIGN AID IN A FOREIGN POLICY FRAMEWORK. AFR ASIA INDIA IRAN L/A+17C USA+45 USSR ECO/UNDEV AGRI FORCES LEGIS PLAN PROB/SOLV ...DECISION 20 COLD/WAR. PAGE 163 A3324
FOR/AID DIPLOM POLICY ECO/TAC

B67
KIRK R.,THE POLITICAL PRINCIPLES OF ROBERT A. TAFT. USA+45 LABOR DIPLOM ADJUD ADJUST ORD/FREE TAFT/RA. PAGE 80 A1635
POL/PAR LEAD LEGIS ATTIT

B67
MACDONALD D.F.,THE AGE OF TRANSITION: BRITAIN IN THE NINETEENTH & TWENTIETH CENTURIES. UK ECO/DEV LEGIS DIPLOM NEW/LIB...POLICY 19/20. PAGE 92 A1886
TREND INDUS SOCISM

B67
MCBRIDE J.H.,THE TEST BAN TREATY: MILITARY, TECHNOLOGICAL, AND POLITICAL IMPLICATIONS. USA+45 USSR DELIB/GP FORCES LEGIS TEC/DEV BAL/PWR TREATY. PAGE 97 A1995
ARMS/CONT DIPLOM NUC/PWR

B67
RALSTON D.B.,THE ARMY OF THE REPUBLIC; THE PLACE OF THE MILITARY IN THE POLITICAL EVOLUTION OF FRANCE 1871-1914. FRANCE MOD/EUR EX/STRUC LEGIS TOP/EX DIPLOM ADMIN WAR GP/REL ROLE...BIBLIOG 19/20. PAGE 119 A2436
FORCES NAT/G CIVMIL/REL POLICY

B67
UNIVERSAL REFERENCE SYSTEM,LAW, JURISPRUDENCE, AND JUDICIAL PROCESS (VOLUME VII). WOR+45 WOR-45 CONSTN NAT/G LEGIS JUDGE CT/SYS...INT/LAW COMPUT/IR GEN/METH METH. PAGE 149 A3044
BIBLIOG/A LAW JURID ADJUD

B67
US DEPARTMENT OF THE ARMY,CIVILIAN IN PEACE, SOLDIER IN WAR: A BIBLIOGRAPHIC SURVEY OF THE ARMY AND AIR NATIONAL GUARD (PAMPHLET, NOS. 130-2). USA+45 LOC/G NAT/G PROVS LEGIS PLAN ADMIN ATTIT ORD/FREE...POLICY 19/20. PAGE 152 A3111
BIBLIOG/A FORCES ROLE DIPLOM

B67
US SENATE COMM AERO SPACE SCI,TREATY ON PRINCIPLES GOVERNING ACTIVITIES OF STATES IN EXPLORATION AND USE OF OUTER SPACE, INCLUDING...BODIES. DELIB/GP FORCES LEGIS DIPLOM...JURID 20 DEPT/STATE NASA DEPT/DEFEN UN. PAGE 155 A3169
SPACE INT/LAW ORD/FREE PEACE

B67
US SENATE COMM ON FOREIGN REL,HUMAN RIGHTS CONVENTIONS. USA+45 LABOR VOL/ASSN DELIB/GP DOMIN ADJUD REPRESENT...INT/LAW MGT CONGRESS. PAGE 156 A3189
LEGIS ORD/FREE WORKER LOBBY

L67
KOMESAR N.K.,"PRESIDENTIAL AMENDMENT & TERMINATION OF TREATIES* THE CASE OF THE WARSAW CONVENTION." POLAND USA+45 NAT/G CHIEF PROB/SOLV DIPLOM PWR 20 CONGRESS. PAGE 81 A1669
TOP/EX LEGIS CONSTN LICENSE

S67
FABREGA J.,"ANTECEDENTES EXTRANJEROS EN LA CONSTITUCION PANAMENA." CUBA L/A+17C PANAMA URUGUAY EX/STRUC LEGIS DIPLOM ORD/FREE 19/20 COLOMB MEXIC/AMER. PAGE 43 A0882
CONSTN JURID NAT/G PARL/PROC

S67
ODA S.,"THE NORMALIZATION OF RELATIONS BETWEEN JAPAN AND THE REPUBLIC OF KOREA." NAT/G BAL/PWR REPAR INT/LAW. PAGE 111 A2276
DIPLOM LEGIS DECISION

B90
HOSMAR J.K.,A SHORT HISTORY OF ANGLO-SAXON FREEDOM. UK USA-45 ROMAN/EMP NAT/G EX/STRUC LEGIS COLONIAL REV NAT/LISM POPULISM PARLIAMENT ANGLO/SAX MAGNA/CART. PAGE 68 A1394
CONSTN ORD/FREE DIPLOM PARL/PROC

B91
SIDGWICK H.,THE ELEMENTS OF POLITICS. LOC/G NAT/G LEGIS DIPLOM ADJUD CONTROL EXEC PARL/PROC REPRESENT GOV/REL SOVEREIGN ALL/IDEOS 19 MILL/JS BENTHAM/J. PAGE 132 A2713
POLICY LAW CONCPT

B96
LOWELL A.L.,GOVERNMENTS AND PARTIES IN CONTINENTAL EUROPE, VOL. II. AUSTRIA GERMANY HUNGARY MOD/EUR SWITZERLND SOCIETY EX/STRUC LEGIS DIPLOM AGREE LEAD PARL/PROC PWR...POLICY 19. PAGE 91 A1867
POL/PAR NAT/G GOV/REL ELITES

LEGISLATION....SEE CONGRESS, LEGIS, SENATE, HOUSE/REP

LEGISLATIVE REFERENCE SERVICE A1766

LEGISLATIVE APPORTIONMENT....SEE APPORT

LEGISLATURES....SEE LEGIS

LEGIT....LEGITIMACY

B00
DARBY W.E.,INTERNATIONAL TRIBUNALS. WOR-45 NAT/G ECO/TAC DOMIN LEGIT CT/SYS COERCE ORD/FREE PWR SOVEREIGN JURID. PAGE 33 A0681
INT/ORG ADJUD PEACE
INT/LAW

B00
GROTIUS H.,DE JURE BELLI AC PACIS. CHRIST-17C UNIV LAW SOCIETY PROVS LEGIT PEACE PERCEPT MORAL PWR ...CONCPT CON/ANAL GEN/LAWS. PAGE 57 A1180
JURID INT/LAW WAR

B00
HOLLAND T.E.,STUDIES IN INTERNATIONAL LAW. TURKEY USSR WOR-45 CONSTN NAT/G DIPLOM DOMIN LEGIT COERCE WAR PEACE ORD/FREE PWR SOVEREIGN...JURID CHARTS 20 PARLIAMENT SUEZ TREATY. PAGE 66 A1367
INT/ORG LAW INT/LAW

B00
LORIMER J.,THE INSTITUTES OF THE LAW OF NATIONS. WOR-45 CULTURE SOCIETY NAT/G VOL/ASSN DIPLOM LEGIT WAR PEACE DRIVE ORD/FREE SOVEREIGN...CONCPT RECORD INT TREND HYPO/EXP GEN/METH TOT/POP VAL/FREE 20. PAGE 91 A1863
INT/ORG LAW INT/LAW

B00
MORRIS H.C.,THE HISTORY OF COLONIZATION. WOR+45 WOR-45 ECO/DEV ECO/UNDEV INT/ORG ACT/RES PLAN ECO/TAC LEGIT ROUTINE COERCE ATTIT DRIVE ALL/VALS ...GEOG TREND 19. PAGE 105 A2148
DOMIN SOVEREIGN COLONIAL

B04
CRANDALL S.B.,TREATIES: THEIR MAKING AND ENFORCEMENT. MOD/EUR USA-45 CONSTN INT/ORG NAT/G LEGIS EDU/PROP LEGIT EXEC PEACE KNOWL MORAL...JURID CONGRESS 19/20 TREATY. PAGE 32 A0655
LAW

B09
HOLLAND T.E.,LETTERS UPON WAR AND NEUTRALITY. WOR-45 NAT/G FORCES JUDGE ECO/TAC LEGIT CT/SYS NEUTRAL ROUTINE COERCE...JURID TIME/SEQ 20. PAGE 67 A1368
LAW INT/LAW INT/ORG WAR

B13
BUTLER N.M.,THE INTERNATIONAL MIND. WOR-45 INT/ORG LEGIT PWR...JURID CONCPT 20. PAGE 22 A0452
ADJUD ORD/FREE INT/LAW

L16
WRIGHT Q.,"THE ENFORCEMENT OF INTERNATIONAL LAW THROUGH MUNICIPAL LAW IN THE US." USA-45 LOC/G NAT/G PUB/INST FORCES LEGIT CT/SYS PERCEPT ALL/VALS ...JURID 20. PAGE 167 A3401
INT/ORG LAW INT/LAW WAR

B17
SATOW E.,A GUIDE TO DIPLOMATIC PRACTICE. MOD/EUR INT/ORG BAL/PWR LEGIT ORD/FREE PWR SOVEREIGN ...POLICY GEN/METH 20. PAGE 127 A2607
GEN/LAWS DIPLOM

B19
VANDERPOL A.,LA DOCTRINE SCOLASTIQUE DU DROIT DE GUERRE. CHRIST-17C FORCES DIPLOM LEGIT SUPEGO MORAL ...BIOG AQUINAS/T SUAREZ/F CHRISTIAN. PAGE 158 A3220
WAR SECT INT/LAW

B20
BURNS C.D.,INTERNATIONAL POLITICS. WOR-45 CULTURE SOCIETY ECO/UNDEV NAT/G VOL/ASSN DELIB/GP ACT/RES CREATE DOMIN EDU/PROP LEGIT ATTIT DRIVE RIGID/FLEX ALL/VALS...PLURIST PSY CONCPT TREND. PAGE 22 A0442
INT/ORG PEACE SOVEREIGN

B20
DICKINSON E.,THE EQUALITY OF STATES IN INTERNATIONAL LAW. WOR-45 INT/ORG NAT/G DIPLOM EDU/PROP LEGIT PEACE ATTIT ALL/VALS...JURID TIME/SEQ LEAGUE/NAT. PAGE 37 A0757
LAW CONCPT SOVEREIGN

B20
HALDANE R.B.,BEFORE THE WAR. MOD/EUR SOCIETY INT/ORG NAT/G DELIB/GP PLAN DOMIN EDU/PROP LEGIT ADMIN COERCE ATTIT DRIVE MORAL ORD/FREE PWR...SOC CONCPT SELF/OBS RECORD BIOG TIME/SEQ. PAGE 60 A1223
POLICY DIPLOM UK

B21
OPPENHEIM L.,THE FUTURE OF INTERNATIONAL LAW. EUR+WWI MOD/EUR LAW LEGIS JUDGE LEGIT ORD/FREE ...JURID TIME/SEQ GEN/LAWS 20. PAGE 112 A2293
INT/ORG CT/SYS INT/LAW

B22
WRIGHT Q.,THE CONTROL OF AMERICAN FOREIGN RELATIONS. USA-45 WOR-45 CONSTN INT/ORG CONSULT LEGIS LEGIT ROUTINE ORD/FREE PWR...POLICY JURID CONCPT METH/CNCPT RECORD LEAGUE/NAT 20. PAGE 167 A3402
NAT/G EXEC DIPLOM

S23
DEWEY J.,"ETHICS AND INTERNATIONAL RELATIONS." FUT WOR-45 SOCIETY INT/ORG VOL/ASSN DIPLOM LEGIT ORD/FREE...JURID CONCPT GEN/METH 20. PAGE 37 A0752
LAW MORAL

B24
GENTILI A.,DE LEGATIONIBUS. CHRIST-17C NAT/G SECT CONSULT LEGIT...POLICY CATH JURID CONCPT MYTH. PAGE 52 A1058
DIPLOM INT/LAW INT/ORG LAW

B24
POOLE D.C.,THE CONDUCT OF FOREIGN RELATIONS UNDER MODERN DEMOCRATIC CONDITIONS. EUR+WWI USA-45 INT/ORG PLAN LEGIT ADMIN KNOWL PWR...MAJORIT OBS/ENVIR HIST/WRIT GEN/LAWS 20. PAGE 117 A2395
NAT/G EDU/PROP DIPLOM

L25
HUDSON M.,"THE PERMANENT COURT OF INTERNATIONAL JUSTICE AND THE QUESTION OF AMERICAN PARTICIPATION." WOR-45 LEGIT CT/SYS ORD/FREE ...JURID CONCPT TIME/SEQ GEN/LAWS VAL/FREE 20 ICJ. PAGE 68 A1406
INT/ORG ADJUD DIPLOM INT/LAW

B27
LAUTERPACHT H.,PRIVATE LAW SOURCES AND ANALOGIES OF
INT/ORG

INTERNATIONAL LAW. WOR-45 NAT/G DELIB/GP LEGIT COERCE ATTIT ORD/FREE PWR SOVEREIGN...JURID CONCPT HIST/WRIT TIME/SEQ GEN/METH LEAGUE/NAT 20. PAGE 85 A1748 — ADJUD PEACE INT/LAW

B28
CORBETT P.E.,CANADA AND WORLD POLITICS. LAW CULTURE SOCIETY STRUCT MARKET INT/ORG FORCES ACT/RES PLAN ECO/TAC LEGIT ORD/FREE PWR RESPECT...SOC CONCPT TIME/SEQ TREND CMN/WLTH 20 LEAGUE/NAT. PAGE 30 A0612 — NAT/G CANADA

B28
HOWARD-ELLIS C.,THE ORIGIN, STRUCTURE AND WORKING OF THE LEAGUE OF NATIONS. EUR+WWI MOD/EUR USA-45 CONSTN FORCES LEGIS ECO/TAC LEGIT COERCE ORD/FREE ...JURID SOC CONCPT LEAGUE/NAT 20 ILO ICJ. PAGE 68 A1401 — INT/ORG ADJUD

B28
MAIR L.P.,THE PROTECTION OF MINORITIES. EUR+WWI WOR-45 CONSTN INT/ORG NAT/G LEGIT CT/SYS GP/REL RACE/REL DISCRIM ORD/FREE RESPECT...JURID CONCPT TIME/SEQ 20. PAGE 93 A1909 — LAW SOVEREIGN

B28
MILLER D.H.,THE DRAFTING OF THE COVENANT. UNIV WOR-45 INTELL NAT/G DELIB/GP PLAN ECO/TAC LEGIT WAR ATTIT PERCEPT...CONCPT TIME/SEQ LEAGUE/NAT TOT/POP 20. PAGE 101 A2074 — INT/ORG STRUCT PEACE

B29
CONWELL-EVANS T.P.,THE LEAGUE COUNCIL IN ACTION. EUR+WWI TURKEY UK USSR WOR-45 INT/ORG FORCES JUDGE ECO/TAC EDU/PROP LEGIT ROUTINE ARMS/CONT COERCE ATTIT PWR...MAJORIT GEOG JURID CONCPT LEAGUE/NAT TOT/POP VAL/FREE TUNIS 20. PAGE 30 A0605 — DELIB/GP INT/LAW

B29
DUNN F.,THE PRACTICE AND PROCEDURE OF INTERNATIONAL CONFERENCES. WOR-45 NAT/G DELIB/GP BAL/PWR LEGIT EXEC ROUTINE PEACE ORD/FREE RESPECT...JURID CONCPT METH/CNCPT OBS RECORD TIME/SEQ 20. PAGE 39 A0799 — INT/ORG DIPLOM

B30
FLEMMING D.,THE TREATY VETO OF THE AMERICAN SENATE. FUT USA+45 USA-45 CONSTN INT/ORG NAT/G TOP/EX LEGIT GOV/REL PWR...POLICY MAJORIT CONCPT OBS TIME/SEQ CONGRESS 20. PAGE 46 A0949 — LEGIS RIGID/FLEX

B30
WRIGHT Q.,MANDATES UNDER THE LEAGUE OF NATIONS. WOR-45 CONSTN ECO/DEV ECO/UNDEV NAT/G DELIB/GP TOP/EX LEGIT ALL/VALS...JURID CONCPT LEAGUE/NAT 20. PAGE 167 A3403 — INT/ORG LAW INT/LAW

B31
HODGES C.,THE BACKGROUND OF INTERNATIONAL RELATIONS. WOR-45 SOCIETY ECO/DEV ECO/UNDEV INT/ORG DIPLOM DOMIN EDU/PROP LEGIT WAR ATTIT DRIVE PERSON ALL/VALS...CONCPT METH/CNCPT TIME/SEQ CHARTS WORK LEAGUE/NAT 19/20. PAGE 66 A1350 — NAT/G BAL/PWR

B31
STOWELL E.C.,INTERNATIONAL LAW. FUT UNIV WOR-45 SOCIETY CONSULT EX/STRUC FORCES ACT/RES PLAN DIPLOM EDU/PROP LEGIT DISPL PWR SKILL...POLICY CONCPT OBS TREND TOT/POP 20. PAGE 139 A2839 — INT/ORG ROUTINE INT/LAW

B31
STUART G.H.,THE INTERNATIONAL CITY OF TANGIER. AFR EUR+WWI MOD/EUR MOROCCO CONSTN PROVS CREATE PLAN LEGIT PEACE ORD/FREE PWR...INT/LAW OBS TIME/SEQ CON/ANAL 20 TANGIER. PAGE 139 A2854 — LOC/G INT/ORG DIPLOM SOVEREIGN

B32
EAGLETON C.,INTERNATIONAL GOVERNMENT. BRAZIL FRANCE GERMANY ITALY UK USSR WOR-45 DELIB/GP TOP/EX PLAN ECO/TAC EDU/PROP LEGIT ADJUD REGION ARMS/CONT COERCE ATTIT PWR...GEOG MGT VAL/FREE LEAGUE/NAT 20. PAGE 40 A0816 — INT/ORG JURID DIPLOM INT/LAW

B32
MASTERS R.D.,INTERNATIONAL LAW IN INTERNATIONAL COURTS. BELGIUM EUR+WWI FRANCE GERMANY MOD/EUR SWITZERLND WOR-45 SOCIETY STRATA STRUCT LEGIT EXEC ALL/VALS...JURID HIST/WRIT TIME/SEQ TREND GEN/LAWS 20. PAGE 96 A1961 — INT/ORG LAW INT/LAW

B32
MORLEY F.,THE SOCIETY OF NATIONS. EUR+WWI UNIV WOR-45 LAW CONSTN ACT/RES PLAN EDU/PROP LEGIT ROUTINE...POLICY TIME/SEQ LEAGUE/NAT TOT/POP 20. PAGE 104 A2143 — INT/ORG CONCPT

B33
LAUTERPACHT H.,THE FUNCTION OF LAW IN THE INTERNATIONAL COMMUNITY. WOR-45 NAT/G FORCES CREATE DOMIN LEGIT COERCE WAR PEACE ATTIT ORD/FREE PWR SOVEREIGN...JURID CONCPT METH/CNCPT TIME/SEQ GEN/LAWS GEN/METH LEAGUE/NAT TOT/POP VAL/FREE 20. PAGE 85 A1749 — INT/ORG LAW INT/LAW

B34
EINSTEIN A.,THE WORLD AS I SEE IT. WOR-45 INTELL R+D INT/ORG NAT/G SECT VOL/ASSN FORCES CREATE EDU/PROP LEGIT ARMS/CONT WAR WEAPON NAT/LISM ALL/VALS...POLICY CONCPT 20. PAGE 41 A0828 — SOCIETY PHIL/SCI DIPLOM PACIFISM

B34
WOLFF C.,JUS GENTIUM METHODO SCIENTIFICA PERTRACTATUM. MOD/EUR INT/ORG VOL/ASSN LEGIT PEACE ATTIT...JURID 20. PAGE 166 A3387 — NAT/G LAW INT/LAW

WAR

B35
LANGER W.L.,THE DIPLOMACY OF IMPERIALISM 1890-1902. FRANCE GERMANY ITALY UK WOR-45 BAL/PWR INT/TRADE LEGIT ADJUD CONTROL WAR PWR SOVEREIGN...CHARTS BIBLIOG/A 19/20. PAGE 84 A1726 — DIPLOM COLONIAL DOMIN

B35
MARRIOTT J.A.,DICTATORSHIP AND DEMOCRACY. GERMANY GREECE UK CHIEF DIPLOM DOMIN LEGIT PEACE ORD/FREE CONSERVE...TREND ROME HITLER/A. PAGE 95 A1946 — TOTALISM POPULISM PLURIST NAT/G

S35
MCMAHON A.H.,"INTERNATIONAL BOUNDARIES." WOR-45 INT/ORG NAT/G LEGIT SKILL...CHARTS GEN/LAWS 20. PAGE 98 A2017 — GEOG VOL/ASSN INT/LAW

B38
FLEMMING D.,THE UNITED STATES AND WORLD ORGANIZATION, 1920-1933. ASIA FUT WOR-45 NAT/G TOP/EX DIPLOM ECO/TAC EDU/PROP LEGIT COERCE WAR ...TIME/SEQ LEAGUE/NAT 20 CHINJAP. PAGE 47 A0951 — USA-45 INT/ORG PEACE

B38
HOBSON J.A.,IMPERIALISM. MOD/EUR UK WOR-45 CULTURE ECO/UNDEV NAT/G VOL/ASSN PLAN EDU/PROP LEGIT REGION COERCE ATTIT PWR...POLICY PLURIST TIME/SEQ GEN/LAWS 19/20. PAGE 66 A1348 — DOMIN ECO/TAC BAL/PWR COLONIAL

B38
MCNAIR A.D.,THE LAW OF TREATIES: BRITISH PRACTICE AND OPINIONS. UK CREATE DIPLOM LEGIT WRITING ADJUD WAR...INT/LAW JURID TREATY. PAGE 98 A2018 — AGREE LAW CT/SYS NAT/G

B38
PETTEE G.S.,THE PROCESS OF REVOLUTION. COM FRANCE ITALY MOD/EUR RUSSIA SPAIN WOR-45 ELITES INTELL SOCIETY STRATA STRUCT INT/ORG NAT/G POL/PAR ACT/RES PLAN EDU/PROP LEGIT EXEC...SOC MYTH TIME/SEQ TOT/POP 18/20. PAGE 115 A2370 — COERCE CONCPT REV

B39
BROWN J.F.,CONTEMPORARY WORLD POLITICS. WOR-45 NAT/G PLAN BAL/PWR EDU/PROP LEGIT REGION NAT/LISM ORD/FREE PWR SOVEREIGN...POLICY CONCPT HIST/WRIT TIME/SEQ GEN/LAWS LEAGUE/NAT. PAGE 20 A0403 — INT/ORG DIPLOM PEACE

B39
MAXWELL B.W.,INTERNATIONAL RELATIONS. EUR+WWI WOR-45 NAT/G CONSULT DIPLOM LEGIT ADJUD NAT/LISM ATTIT ORD/FREE SOVEREIGN...JURID LEAGUE/NAT TOT/POP VAL/FREE 20. PAGE 97 A1981 — INT/ORG

B39
WILSON G.G.,HANDBOOK OF INTERNATIONAL LAW. FUT UNIV USA-45 WOR-45 SOCIETY LEGIT ATTIT DISPL DRIVE ALL/VALS...INT/LAW TIME/SEQ TREND. PAGE 165 A3359 — INT/ORG LAW CONCPT WAR

B39
ZIMMERN A.,THE LEAGUE OF NATIONS AND THE RULE OF LAW. WOR-45 STRUCT NAT/G DELIB/GP EX/STRUC BAL/PWR DOMIN LEGIT COERCE ORD/FREE PWR...POLICY RECORD LEAGUE/NAT TOT/POP VAL/FREE 20 LEAGUE/NAT. PAGE 170 A3453 — INT/ORG LAW DIPLOM

B40
BOGGS S.W.,INTERNATIONAL BOUNDARIES. WOR-45 SOCIETY ECO/DEV INT/ORG NAT/G NEIGH LEGIT PERSON ORD/FREE PWR...POLICY GEOG MYTH LEAGUE/NAT 20. PAGE 16 A0329 — ATTIT CONCPT NAT/LISM

B40
CARR E.H.,THE TWENTY YEARS' CRISIS 1919-1939. FUT WOR-45 BAL/PWR ECO/TAC LEGIT TOTALISM ATTIT ALL/VALS...POLICY JURID CONCPT TIME/SEQ TREND GEN/LAWS TOT/POP 20. PAGE 24 A0498 — INT/ORG DIPLOM PEACE

B40
MIDDLEBUSH F.,ELEMENTS OF INTERNATIONAL RELATIONS. WOR-45 PROVS CONSULT EDU/PROP LEGIT WAR NAT/LISM ATTIT KNOWL MORAL ORD/FREE PWR...JURID LEAGUE/NAT TOT/POP VAL/FREE. PAGE 101 A2067 — NAT/G INT/ORG PEACE DIPLOM

B41
NIEMEYER G.,LAW WITHOUT FORCE: THE FUNCTION OF POLITICS IN INTERNATIONAL LAW. PLAN INSPECT DIPLOM REPAR LEGIT ADJUD WAR ORD/FREE...IDEA/COMP METH/COMP GEN/LAWS 20. PAGE 109 A2240 — COERCE LAW PWR INT/LAW

L41
COMM. STUDY ORGAN. PEACE,"PRELIMINARY REPORT." WOR-45 SOCIETY DELIB/GP PLAN LEGIT WAR ORD/FREE ...CONCPT TOT/POP 20. PAGE 28 A0574 — INT/ORG ACT/RES PEACE

S41
WRIGHT Q.,"FUNDAMENTAL PROBLEMS OF INTERNATIONAL ORGANIZATION." UNIV WOR-45 STRUCT FORCES ACT/RES CREATE DOMIN EDU/PROP LEGIT REGION NAT/LISM ORD/FREE PWR RESPECT SOVEREIGN...JURID SOC CONCPT METH/CNCPT TIME/SEQ 20. PAGE 167 A3405 — INT/ORG ATTIT PEACE

B42
KELSEN H.,LAW AND PEACE IN INTERNATIONAL RELATIONS. FUT WOR-45 NAT/G DELIB/GP DIPLOM LEGIT RIGID/FLEX ORD/FREE SOVEREIGN...JURID CONCPT TREND STERTYP GEN/LAWS LEAGUE/NAT 20. PAGE 77 A1580 — INT/ORG ADJUD PEACE INT/LAW

S42
TURNER F.J.,"AMERICAN SECTIONALISM AND WORLD ORGANIZATION." EUR+WWI UNIV USA-45 WOR-45 INTELL ECO/DEV TOP/EX ACT/RES PLAN EDU/PROP LEGIT ALL/VALS ...CONCPT NEW/IDEA OBS TREND LEAGUE/NAT TOT/POP 20. — INT/ORG DRIVE BAL/PWR

PAGE 146 A2981

B43
CONOVER H.F.,THE BALKANS: A SELECTED LIST OF REFERENCES. ALBANIA BULGARIA ROMANIA YUGOSLAVIA INT/ORG PROB/SOLV DIPLOM LEGIT CONFER ADJUD WAR NAT/LISM PEACE PWR 20 LEAGUE/NAT. PAGE 29 A0596 BIBLIOG EUR+WWI

B44
BRIERLY J.L.,THE OUTLOOK FOR INTERNATIONAL LAW. FUT WOR-45 CONSTN NAT/G VOL/ASSN FORCES ECO/TAC DOMIN LEGIT ADJUD ROUTINE PEACE ORD/FREE...INT/LAW JURID METH LEAGUE/NAT 20. PAGE 18 A0376 INT/ORG LAW

B44
DAVIS H.E.,PIONEERS IN WORLD ORDER. WOR-45 CONSTN ECO/TAC DOMIN EDU/PROP LEGIT ADJUD ADMIN ARMS/CONT CHOOSE KNOWL ORD/FREE...POLICY JURID SOC STAT OBS CENSUS TIME/SEQ ANTHOL LEAGUE/NAT 20. PAGE 34 A0691 INT/ORG ROUTINE

B44
WHITTON J.B.,THE SECOND CHANCE: AMERICA AND THE PEACE. EUR+WWI USA-45 SOCIETY STRUCT INT/ORG NAT/G LEGIT EXEC WAR ALL/VALS...SOC CONCPT TIME/SEQ TREND CONGRESS 20. PAGE 164 A3340 LEGIS PEACE

L44
HAILEY,"THE FUTURE OF COLONIAL PEOPLES." WOR-45 CONSTN CULTURE ECO/UNDEV AGRI MARKET INT/ORG NAT/G SECT CONSULT ECO/TAC LEGIT ADMIN NAT/LISM ALL/VALS ...SOC OBS TREND STERTYP CMN/WLTH LEAGUE/NAT PARLIAMENT 20. PAGE 59 A1218 PLAN CONCPT DIPLOM UK

L44
WRIGHT Q.,"THE US AND INTERNATIONAL AGREEMENTS." FUT USA-45 CONSTN INTELL INT/ORG LOC/G NAT/G CHIEF CONSULT EX/STRUC DIPLOM LEGIT DRIVE PERCEPT PWR ...CONCPT CONGRESS 20. PAGE 167 A3407 DELIB/GP TOP/EX PEACE

C44
SUAREZ F.,"ON WAR" (1621) IN SELECTIONS FROM THREE WORKS, VOL. I." NAT/G SECT CHIEF DIPLOM LEGIT MORAL PWR...POLICY INT/LAW 17. PAGE 140 A2859 WAR REV ORD/FREE CATH

B45
BEVERIDGE W.,THE PRICE OF PEACE. GERMANY UK WOR+45 WOR-45 NAT/G FORCES CREATE LEGIT REGION WAR ATTIT KNOWL ORD/FREE PWR...POLICY NEW/IDEA GEN/LAWS LEAGUE/NAT 20 TREATY. PAGE 14 A0284 INT/ORG TREND PEACE

B45
HILL N.,CLAIMS TO TERRITORY IN INTERNATIONAL LAW AND RELATIONS. WOR-45 NAT/G DOMIN EDU/PROP LEGIT REGION ROUTINE ORD/FREE PWR WEALTH...GEOG INT/LAW JURID 20. PAGE 65 A1332 INT/ORG ADJUD SOVEREIGN

B45
PASTUHOV V.D.,A GUIDE TO THE PRACTICE OF INTERNATIONAL CONFERENCES. WOR+45 PLAN LEGIT ORD/FREE...MGT OBS RECORD VAL/FREE ILO LEAGUE/NAT 20. PAGE 114 A2338 INT/ORG DELIB/GP

B45
TINGSTERN H.,PEACE AND SECURITY AFTER WW II. WOR-45 DELIB/GP TOP/EX LEGIT CT/SYS COERCE PEACE ATTIT PERCEPT...CONCPT LEAGUE/NAT 20. PAGE 144 A2943 INT/ORG ORD/FREE WAR INT/LAW

B46
KEETON G.W.,MAKING INTERNATIONAL LAW WORK. FUT WOR-45 NAT/G DELIB/GP FORCES LEGIT COERCE PEACE ATTIT RIGID/FLEX ORD/FREE PWR...JURID CONCPT HIST/WRIT GEN/METH LEAGUE/NAT 20. PAGE 77 A1578 INT/ORG ADJUD INT/LAW

S46
DOUGLAS W.O.,"SYMPOSIUM ON WORLD ORGANIZATION." FUT USA+45 WOR+45 CONSTN SOCIETY NAT/G PLAN EDU/PROP LEGIT RIGID/FLEX KNOWL...INT/LAW JURID STERTYP TOT/POP 20. PAGE 38 A0778 INT/ORG LAW

B47
BROOKINGS INST.,MAJOR PROBLEMS OF UNITED STATES FOREIGN POLICY. USA+45 WOR+45 STRUCT ECO/DEV ECO/UNDEV INT/ORG NAT/G POL/PAR VOL/ASSN DELIB/GP FORCES ECO/TAC LEGIT COERCE ORD/FREE PWR WEALTH ...POLICY STAT TREND CHARTS TOT/POP. PAGE 19 A0392 ACT/RES DIPLOM

B47
FEIS H.,SEEN FROM E A, THREE INTERNATIONAL EPISODES. EUR+WWI ITALY USA-45 WOR-45 AGRI INT/ORG NAT/G INT/TRADE LEGIT EXEC ATTIT ORD/FREE...POLICY LEAGUE/NAT TOT/POP 20 OIL. PAGE 44 A0908 EXTR/IND ECO/TAC DIPLOM

B47
HILL M.,IMMUNITIES AND PRIVILEGES OF INTERNATIONAL OFFICIALS. CANADA EUR+WWI NETHERLAND SWITZERLND LAW LEGIS DIPLOM LEGIT RESPECT...TIME/SEQ LEAGUE/NAT UN VAL/FREE 20. PAGE 65 A1330 INT/ORG ADMIN

B48
FENWICK C.G.,INTERNATIONAL LAW. WOR+45 WOR-45 CONSTN NAT/G LEGIT CT/SYS REGION...CONCPT LEAGUE/NAT UN 20. PAGE 45 A0916 INT/ORG JURID INT/LAW

B48
JESSUP P.C.,A MODERN LAW OF NATIONS. FUT WOR+45 WOR-45 SOCIETY NAT/G DELIB/GP LEGIS BAL/PWR EDU/PROP LEGIT PWR...INT/LAW JURID TIME/SEQ LEAGUE/NAT 20. PAGE 74 A1514 INT/ORG ADJUD

L49
COMM. STUDY ORGAN. PEACE,"A TEN YEAR RECORD, 1939-1949." FUT WOR+45 LAW R+D CONSULT DELIB/GP CREATE LEGIT ROUTINE ORD/FREE...TIME/SEQ UN 20. INT/ORG CONSTN PEACE

PAGE 28 A0578

B50
BERLE A.A.,NATURAL SELECTION OF POLITICAL FORCES. FUT WOR+45 WOR-45 CULTURE SOCIETY INT/ORG NAT/G FORCES EDU/PROP LEGIT COERCE...CONCPT HIST/WRIT TREND 20. PAGE 13 A0274 POL/PAR BAL/PWR DIPLOM

B50
CHASE E.P.,THE UNITED NATIONS IN ACTION. WOR+45 CONSTN DELIB/GP LEGIT ROUTINE COERCE PEACE ORD/FREE PWR...CON/ANAL GEN/LAWS UN 20. PAGE 26 A0524 INT/ORG STRUCT ARMS/CONT

B50
JIMENEZ E.,VOTING AND HANDLING OF DISPUTES IN THE SECURITY COUNCIL. WOR+45 CONSTN INT/ORG DIPLOM LEGIT DETER CHOOSE MORAL ORD/FREE PWR...JURID TIME/SEQ COLD/WAR UN 20. PAGE 74 A1517 DELIB/GP ROUTINE

B50
STONE J.,THE PROVINCE AND FUNCTION OF LAW. UNIV WOR+45 WOR-45 CULTURE INTELL SOCIETY ECO/DEV ECO/UNDEV NAT/G LEGIT ROUTINE ATTIT PERCEPT PERSON ...JURID CONCPT GEN/LAWS GEN/METH 20. PAGE 138 A2833 INT/ORG LAW

B51
MACLAURIN J.,THE UNITED NATIONS AND POWER POLITICS. WOR+45 CONSULT EDU/PROP LEGIT ADJUD EXEC MORAL ORD/FREE...HUM JURID CONCPT RECORD TIME/SEQ UN COLD/WAR 20. PAGE 93 A1896 INT/ORG ROUTINE

B51
MCKEON R.,DEMOCRACY IN A WORLD OF TENSION. UNIV LAW INTELL STRUCT R+D INT/ORG SCHOOL EDU/PROP LEGIT ATTIT DRIVE PERCEPT PERSON...POLICY JURID PSY SOC CONCPT METH/CNCPT OBS UNESCO TOT/POP VAL/FREE. PAGE 98 A2015 SOCIETY ALL/VALS ORD/FREE

L51
KELSEN H.,"RECENT TRENDS IN THE LAW OF THE UNITED NATIONS." KOREA WOR+45 CONSTN LEGIS DIPLOM LEGIT DETER WAR RIGID/FLEX HEALTH ORD/FREE RESPECT ...JURID CON/ANAL UN VAL/FREE 20 NATO. PAGE 77 A1582 INT/ORG LAW INT/LAW

L51
LISSITZYN O.J.,"THE INTERNATIONAL COURT OF JUSTICE." WOR+45 INT/ORG LEGIT ORD/FREE...CONCPT TIME/SEQ TREND GEN/LAWS VAL/FREE 20 ICJ. PAGE 90 A1839 ADJUD JURID INT/LAW

L51
MANGONE G.,"THE IDEA AND PRACTICE OF WORLD GOVERNMENT." FUT WOR+45 WOR-45 ECO/DEV LEGIS CREATE LEGIT ROUTINE ATTIT MORAL PWR WEALTH...CONCPT GEN/LAWS 20. PAGE 94 A1920 INT/ORG SOCIETY INT/LAW

S51
GYR J.,"ANALYSIS OF COMMITTEE MEMBER BEHAVIOUR IN FOUR CULTURES." ASIA ISLAM L/A+17C USA+45 INT/ORG VOL/ASSN LEGIT ATTIT...INT DEEP/QU SAMP CHARTS 20. PAGE 58 A1200 DELIB/GP CULTURE

B52
ALEXANDROWICZ C.H.,INTERNATIONAL ECONOMIC ORGANIZATION. WOR+45 ECO/DEV ECO/UNDEV DIST/IND FINAN MARKET PLAN ECO/TAC LEGIT DRIVE WEALTH ...POLICY CONCPT QUANT OBS TIME/SEQ GEN/LAWS WORK EEC ILO OEEC UNESCO 20. PAGE 6 A0114 INT/ORG INT/TRADE

B52
BARR S.,CITIZENS OF THE WORLD. USA+45 WOR+45 CULTURE FORCES LEGIS ACT/RES BAL/PWR LEGIT PEACE ATTIT ORD/FREE PWR...PLURIST CONCPT OBS TIME/SEQ COLD/WAR 20. PAGE 11 A0227 NAT/G INT/ORG DIPLOM

B52
JACKSON E.,MEETING OF THE MINDS: A WAY TO PEACE THROUGH MEDIATION. WOR+45 INDUS INT/ORG NAT/G DELIB/GP DIPLOM EDU/PROP LEGIT ORD/FREE...NEW/IDEA SELF/OBS TIME/SEQ CHARTS GEN/LAWS TOT/POP 20 UN TREATY. PAGE 72 A1474 LABOR JUDGE

B52
MANTOUX E.,THE CARTHAGINIAN PEACE. GERMANY WOR-45 SOCIETY FINAN INT/ORG DELIB/GP FORCES PLAN LEGIT ...CONCPT TIME/SEQ 20 KEYNES/JM HITLER/A. PAGE 94 A1935 ECO/DEV INT/TRADE WAR

B52
SCHUMAN F.,THE COMMONWEALTH OF MAN. WOR+45 WOR-45 LAW CULTURE ELITES SOCIETY FAM INT/ORG NAT/G VOL/ASSN TOP/EX PLAN BAL/PWR LEGIT ATTIT DISPL DRIVE...POLICY MYTH TREND TOT/POP ILO OEEC 20. PAGE 129 A2649 CONCPT GEN/LAWS

B52
WALTERS F.P.,A HISTORY OF THE LEAGUE OF NATIONS. EUR+WWI CONSTN NAT/G LEGIS TOP/EX ACT/RES PLAN EDU/PROP LEGIT ROUTINE ATTIT...TREND LEAGUE/NAT 20 CHINJAP. PAGE 161 A3271 INT/ORG TIME/SEQ NAT/LISM

S52
HAAS E.B.,"THE RECONCILIATION OF CONFLICT, COLONIAL POLICY AIMS: ACCEPTANCE OF THE LEAGUE OF NATIONS MANDATE SYSTEM." FRANCE GERMANY UK WOR+45 WOR-45 LEGIT ATTIT DRIVE ORD/FREE...OLD/LIB INT SYS/QU TIME/SEQ TREND LEAGUE/NAT 20. PAGE 58 A1201 INT/ORG COLONIAL

B53
BARBER H.W.,FOREIGN POLICIES OF THE UNITED STATES. USA+45 USA-45 WOR+45 INT/ORG NAT/G EX/STRUC ECO/TAC DOMIN EDU/PROP LEGIT COERCE KNOWL PWR COLD/WAR CONCPT DIPLOM

COLD/WAR 20. PAGE 11 A0219

B53
BORGESE G.,FOUNDATIONS OF THE WORLD REPUBLIC. FUT SOCIETY NAT/G CREATE LEGIT PERSON MORAL...MAJORIT CON/ANAL LEAGUE/NAT TOT/POP 20. PAGE 17 A0340 — INT/ORG CONSTN PEACE

B53
ZIMMERN A.,THE AMERICAN ROAD TO PEACE. USA+45 LAW INT/ORG NAT/G EX/STRUC TOP/EX EDU/PROP LEGIT COERCE PEACE ATTIT ORD/FREE PWR...CONCPT TIME/SEQ LEAGUE/NAT TOT/POP VAL/FREE 20 UN. PAGE 170 A3455 — USA-45 DIPLOM

B54
CHEEVER D.S.,ORGANIZING FOR PEACE. FUT WOR+45 WOR-45 STRATA STRUCT NAT/G CREATE DIPLOM LEGIT REGION COERCE DETER PEACE ATTIT DRIVE ALL/VALS ...TIME/SEQ TREND UN LEAGUE/NAT. PAGE 26 A0525 — INT/ORG

B54
COOK T.,POWER THROUGH PURPOSE. USA+45 WOR+45 WOR-45 INT/ORG VOL/ASSN BAL/PWR DIPLOM EDU/PROP LEGIT PERSON...GEN/LAWS LEAGUE/NAT 20. PAGE 30 A0606 — ATTIT CONCPT

B54
LANDHEER B.,RECOGNITION IN INTERNATIONAL LAW (SELECTIVE BIBLIOGRAPHIES OF THE LIBRARY OF THE PEACE PALACE, VOL. II; PAMPHLET). NAT/G LEGIT SANCTION 20. PAGE 84 A1716 — BIBLIOG/A INT/LAW INT/ORG DIPLOM

B54
MANGONE G.,A SHORT HISTORY OF INTERNATIONAL ORGANIZATION. MOD/EUR USA+45 USA-45 WOR+45 WOR-45 LAW LEGIS CREATE LEGIT ROUTINE RIGID/FLEX PWR ...JURID CONCPT OBS TIME/SEQ STERTYP GEN/LAWS UN TOT/POP VAL/FREE 18/20. PAGE 94 A1921 — INT/ORG INT/LAW

B54
MILLARD E.L.,FREEDOM IN A FEDERAL WORLD. FUT WOR+45 VOL/ASSN TOP/EX LEGIT ROUTINE FEDERAL PEACE ATTIT DISPL ORD/FREE PWR...MAJORIT INT/LAW JURID TREND COLD/WAR 20. PAGE 101 A2073 — INT/ORG CREATE ADJUD BAL/PWR

B54
SCHIFFER W.,THE LEGAL COMMUNITY OF MANKIND. UNIV WOR+45 WOR-45 SOCIETY NAT/G EDU/PROP LEGIT ATTIT PERSON ORD/FREE PWR...CONCPT HIST/WRIT TREND LEAGUE/NAT UN 20. PAGE 128 A2626 — INT/ORG PHIL/SCI

S54
DAWSON K.H.,"THE UNITED NATIONS IN A DISUNITED WORLD." WOR+45 WOR-45 LAW INTELL NAT/G PEACE ATTIT PERCEPT MORAL LEAGUE/NAT TOT/POP VAL/FREE 20 UN. PAGE 34 A0694 — INT/ORG LEGIT

S54
WOLFERS A.,"COLLECTIVE SECURITY AND THE WAR IN KOREA." ASIA KOREA USA+45 INT/ORG DIPLOM ROUTINE ...GEN/LAWS UN COLD/WAR 20. PAGE 166 A3381 — ACT/RES LEGIT

B55
CHOWDHURI R.N.,INTERNATIONAL MANDATES AND TRUSTEESHIP SYSTEMS. WOR+45 STRUCT ECO/UNDEV INT/ORG LEGIS DOMIN EDU/PROP LEGIT ADJUD EXEC PWR ...CONCPT TIME/SEQ UN 20. PAGE 26 A0534 — DELIB/GP PLAN SOVEREIGN

B55
JOY C.T.,HOW COMMUNISTS NEGOTIATE. COM USA+45 CONSTN CULTURE ECO/UNDEV NAT/G CONSULT DELIB/GP FORCES PLAN ECO/TAC DOMIN EDU/PROP LEGIT EXEC ROUTINE COERCE WAR CHOOSE PEACE ATTIT RIGID/FLEX ORD/FREE PWR...POLICY 20. PAGE 75 A1539 — ASIA INT/ORG DIPLOM

B55
TANNENBAUM F.,THE AMERICAN TRADITION IN FOREIGN POLICY. USA+45 USA-45 CONSTN INT/ORG NAT/G POL/PAR VOL/ASSN TOP/EX LEGIT DRIVE ORD/FREE PWR...CONCPT GEN/LAWS CONGRESS LEAGUE/NAT COLD/WAR OAS 18/20. PAGE 141 A2887 — TIME/SEQ

B55
WILCOX F.O.,PROPOSALS FOR CHANGES IN THE UNITED NATIONS. WOR+45 CONSTN ACT/RES CREATE LEGIT ATTIT ORD/FREE...CONCPT ORG/CHARTS UN TOT/POP 20. PAGE 164 A3344 — INT/ORG STRUCT

B56
GEORGE A.L.,WOODROW WILSON AND COLONEL HOUSE. WOR-45 CONSTN FACE/GP INT/ORG NAT/G POL/PAR CONSULT LEGIT EXEC COERCE CHOOSE ATTIT DRIVE PERSON MORAL ORD/FREE PWR RESPECT...POLICY MGT PSY OBS RECORD INT LEAGUE/NAT. PAGE 52 A1060 — USA-45 BIOG DIPLOM

B56
HAAS E.B.,DYNAMICS OF INTERNATIONAL RELATIONS. WOR-45 ELITES INT/ORG VOL/ASSN EX/STRUC FORCES ECO/TAC DOMIN LEGIT COERCE ATTIT PERSON PWR ...CONCPT TIME/SEQ CHARTS COLD/WAR 20. PAGE 58 A1202 — WOR+45 NAT/G DIPLOM

B56
HOUSTON J.A.,LATIN AMERICA IN THE UNITED NATIONS. CONSULT DIPLOM LEGIT ROUTINE ATTIT ORD/FREE PWR ...JURID OBS RECORD TIME/SEQ CHARTS 20 UN. PAGE 68 A1395 — L/A+17C INT/ORG INT/LAW REGION

B56
REITZEL W.,UNITED STATES FOREIGN POLICY, 1945-1955. USA+45 WOR+45 CONSTN INT/ORG EDU/PROP LEGIT EXEC COERCE NUC/PWR PEACE ATTIT ORD/FREE PWR...DECISION CONCPT OBS RECORD TIME/SEQ TREND COLD/WAR UN CONGRESS. PAGE 120 A2464 — NAT/G POLICY DIPLOM

B56
SOHN L.B.,BASIC DOCUMENTS OF THE UNITED NATIONS. WOR+45 LAW INT/ORG LEGIT EXEC ROUTINE CHOOSE PWR ...JURID CONCPT GEN/LAWS ANTHOL UN TOT/POP OAS FAO ILO 20. PAGE 135 A2761 — DELIB/GP CONSTN

B56
WEIS P.,NATIONALITY AND STATELESSNESS IN INTERNATIONAL LAW. UK WOR+45 WOR-45 LAW CONSTN NAT/G DIPLOM EDU/PROP LEGIT ROUTINE RIGID/FLEX ...JURID RECORD CMN/WLTH 20. PAGE 162 A3309 — INT/ORG SOVEREIGN INT/LAW

S56
GORDON L.,"THE ORGANIZATION FOR EUROPEAN ECONOMIC COOPERATION." EUR+WWI INDUS INT/ORG NAT/G CONSULT DELIB/GP ACT/RES CREATE PLAN TEC/DEV EDU/PROP LEGIT WEALTH OEEC 20. PAGE 54 A1114 — VOL/ASSN ECO/DEV

B57
BEAL J.R.,JOHN FOSTER DULLES, A BIOGRAPHY. USA+45 USSR WOR+45 CONSTN INT/ORG NAT/G EX/STRUC LEGIT ADMIN NUC/PWR DISPL PERSON ORD/FREE PWR SKILL ...POLICY PSY OBS RECORD COLD/WAR UN 20 DULLES/JF. PAGE 12 A0237 — BIOG DIPLOM

B57
BLOOMFIELD L.P.,EVOLUTION OR REVOLUTION: THE UNITED NATIONS AND THE PROBLEM OF PEACEFUL TERRITORIAL CHANGE. WOR+45 WOR-45 INT/ORG NAT/G DIPLOM ROUTINE REV ATTIT RIGID/FLEX PWR...CONCPT OBS HIST/WRIT UN LEAGUE/NAT 20. PAGE 15 A0315 — ORD/FREE LEGIT

B57
COMM. STUDY ORGAN. PEACE,STRENGTHENING THE UNITED NATIONS. FUT USA+45 WOR+45 CONSTN NAT/G DELIB/GP FORCES LEGIS ECO/TAC LEGIT COERCE PEACE...JURID CONCPT UN COLD/WAR 20. PAGE 28 A0580 — INT/ORG ORD/FREE

B57
DEUTSCH K.W.,POLITICAL COMMUNITY AND THE NORTH ATLANTIC AREA: INTERNATIONAL ORGANIZATION IN THE LIGHT OF HISTORICAL EXPERIENCE. MOD/EUR USA+45 USA-45 SOCIETY FORCES TOP/EX CREATE PLAN DIPLOM DOMIN EDU/PROP LEGIT ATTIT ORD/FREE PWR...SAMP/SIZ TIME/SEQ CHARTS TOT/POP. PAGE 36 A0736 — EUR+WWI INT/ORG PEACE REGION

B57
MURRAY J.N.,THE UNITED NATIONS TRUSTEESHIP SYSTEM. AFR WOR+45 CONSTN CONSULT LEGIS EDU/PROP LEGIT EXEC ROUTINE...INT TIME/SEQ SOMALI UN 20. PAGE 106 A2181 — INT/ORG DELIB/GP

B57
ROSENNE S.,THE INTERNATIONAL COURT OF JUSTICE. WOR+45 LAW DOMIN LEGIT PEACE PWR SOVEREIGN...JURID CONCPT RECORD TIME/SEQ CON/ANAL CHARTS UN TOT/POP VAL/FREE LEAGUE/NAT 20 ICJ. PAGE 124 A2537 — INT/ORG CT/SYS INT/LAW

B57
WASSENBERGH H.A.,POST-WAR INTERNATIONAL CIVIL AVIATION POLICY AND THE LAW OF THE AIR. WOR+45 AIR INT/ORG DOMIN LEGIT PEACE ORD/FREE...POLICY JURID NEW/IDEA OBS TIME/SEQ TREND CHARTS 20 TREATY. PAGE 162 A3290 — COM/IND NAT/G INT/LAW

L57
HAAS E.B.,"REGIONAL INTEGRATION AND NATIONAL POLICY." WOR+45 VOL/ASSN DELIB/GP EX/STRUC ECO/TAC DOMIN EDU/PROP LEGIT COERCE ATTIT PERCEPT KNOWL ...TIME/SEQ COLD/WAR 20 UN. PAGE 59 A1203 — INT/ORG ORD/FREE REGION

L57
WARREN S.,"FOREIGN AID AND FOREIGN POLICY." USA+45 WOR+45 WOR-45 DIST/IND INDUS MARKET CONSULT CREATE DIPLOM EDU/PROP LEGIT ATTIT RIGID/FLEX...TIME/SEQ GEN/LAWS WORK 20. PAGE 161 A3285 — ECO/UNDEV ALL/VALS ECO/TAC FOR/AID

S57
WRIGHT Q.,"THE VALUE OF CONFLICT RESOLUTION OF A GENERAL DISCIPLINE OF INTERNATIONAL RELATIONS." WOR+45 SOCIETY INT/ORG NAT/G FORCES TOP/EX PLAN TEC/DEV ECO/TAC DOMIN LEGIT COERCE ATTIT PWR ...GEN/METH COLD/WAR VAL/FREE. PAGE 168 A3412 — ORD/FREE SOC DIPLOM

B58
BOWETT D.W.,SELF-DEFENSE IN INTERNATIONAL LAW. EUR+WWI MOD/EUR WOR+45 WOR-45 SOCIETY INT/ORG CONSULT DIPLOM LEGIT COERCE ATTIT ORD/FREE...JURID 20 UN. PAGE 17 A0353 — ADJUD CONCPT WAR INT/LAW

B58
CAMPBELL J.C.,DEFENSE OF THE MIDDLE EAST: PROBLEMS OF AMERICAN POLICY. ISLAM USA+45 INT/ORG NAT/G EX/STRUC FORCES ECO/TAC DOMIN EDU/PROP LEGIT REGION COERCE...METH/CNCPT COLD/WAR TOT/POP 20. PAGE 23 A0474 — TOP/EX ORD/FREE DIPLOM

B58
CARROLL H.N.,THE HOUSE OF REPRESENTATIVES AND FOREIGN AFFAIRS. USA+45 USA-45 NAT/G POL/PAR DIPLOM FOR/AID LEGIT ROUTINE PWR...TIME/SEQ CONGRESS. PAGE 25 A0502 — DELIB/GP LEGIS

B58
HAAS E.B.,THE UNITING OF EUROPE. EUR+WWI INT/ORG NAT/G POL/PAR TOP/EX ECO/TAC EDU/PROP LEGIT FEDERAL NAT/LISM DRIVE RIGID/FLEX ORD/FREE PWR PLURISM ...POLICY CONCPT INT GEN/LAWS ECSC EEC 20. PAGE 59 A1204 — VOL/ASSN ECO/DEV

B58
HENKIN L.,ARMS CONTROL AND INSPECTION IN AMERICAN LAW. LAW CONSTN INT/ORG LOC/G MUNIC NAT/G PROVS EDU/PROP LEGIT EXEC NUC/PWR KNOWL ORD/FREE...OBS TOT/POP CONGRESS 20. PAGE 64 A1315 — USA+45 JURID ARMS/CONT

B58
KINDLEBERGER C.P.,INTERNATIONAL ECONOMICS. WOR+45 WOR-45 ECO/DEV ECO/UNDEV FINAN VOL/ASSN ACT/RES DIPLOM ECO/TAC LEGIT REGION ATTIT DRIVE ORD/FREE WEALTH...POLICY STAT TREND GEN/LAWS EEC ECSC OEEC 20. PAGE 79 A1620 INT/ORG BAL/PWR TARIFFS

B58
REUTER P.,INTERNATIONAL INSTITUTIONS. WOR+45 WOR-45 CULTURE SOCIETY VOL/ASSN LEGIT ROUTINE GP/REL INGP/REL KNOWL...JURID METH/CNCPT TIME/SEQ 20. PAGE 120 A2469 INT/ORG PSY

B58
RUSSELL R.B.,A HISTORY OF THE UNITED NATIONS CHARTER: THE ROLE OF THE UNITED STATES. SOCIETY NAT/G CONSULT DOMIN LEGIT ATTIT ORD/FREE PWR ...POLICY JURID CONCPT UN LEAGUE/NAT. PAGE 126 A2575 USA-45 INT/ORG CONSTN

B58
SCHUMAN F.,INTERNATIONAL POLITICS. WOR+45 WOR-45 INTELL NAT/G FORCES DOMIN LEGIT COERCE NUC/PWR ATTIT DISPL ORD/FREE PWR SOVEREIGN...POLICY CONCPT GEN/LAWS SUEZ 20. PAGE 129 A2650 FUT INT/ORG NAT/LISM DIPLOM

B58
SLICK T.,PERMANENT PEACE: A CHECK AND BALANCE PLAN. FUT WOR+45 NAT/G FORCES CREATE PLAN EDU/PROP LEGIT ADJUD COERCE NAT/LISM RIGID/FLEX MORAL...HUM CONCPT METH/CNCPT NEW/IDEA TREND CHARTS TOT/POP 20. PAGE 134 A2742 INT/ORG ORD/FREE PEACE ARMS/CONT

L58
HAVILAND H.F.,"FOREIGN AID AND THE POLICY PROCESS: 1957." USA+45 FACE/GP POL/PAR VOL/ASSN CHIEF DELIB/GP ACT/RES LEGIT EXEC GOV/REL ATTIT DRIVE PWR ...POLICY TESTS CONGRESS 20. PAGE 63 A1291 LEGIS PLAN FOR/AID

S58
BLAISDELL D.C.,"PRESSURE GROUPS, FOREIGN POLICIES, AND INTERNATIONAL POLITICS." USA+45 WOR+45 INT/ORG PLAN DOMIN EDU/PROP LEGIT ADMIN ROUTINE CHOOSE ...DECISION MGT METH/CNCPT CON/ANAL 20. PAGE 15 A0303 PROF/ORG PWR

S58
DAVENPORT J.,"ARMS AND THE WELFARE STATE." INTELL STRUCT FORCES CREATE ECO/TAC FOR/AID DOMIN LEGIT ADMIN WAR ORD/FREE PWR...POLICY SOC CONCPT MYTH OBS TREND COLD/WAR TOT/POP 20. PAGE 34 A0685 USA+45 NAT/G USSR

S58
SINGER J.D.,"THREAT PERCEPTION AND THE ARMAMENT TENSION DILEMMA." WOR+45 WOR-45 ELITES INT/ORG NAT/G DELIB/GP PLAN LEGIT COERCE DETER ATTIT RIGID/FLEX PWR...DECISION PSY 20. PAGE 133 A2724 PERCEPT ARMS/CONT BAL/PWR

S58
THOMPSON K.W.,"NATIONAL SECURITY IN A NUCLEAR AGE." USA+45 WOR+45 SOCIETY INT/ORG NAT/G TOP/EX DIPLOM DOMIN EDU/PROP LEGIT ARMS/CONT COERCE ORD/FREE ...TREND STERTYP TOT/POP VAL/FREE COLD/WAR 20. PAGE 143 A2929 FORCES PWR BAL/PWR

B59
BALL M.M.,NATO AND THE EUROPEAN MOVEMENT. EUR+WWI USA+45 INT/ORG FORCES BAL/PWR EDU/PROP LEGIT REGION ATTIT ORD/FREE PWR...STAT OBS TIME/SEQ TREND CHARTS ORG/CHARTS STERTYP COLD/WAR EEC OEEC 20 NATO. PAGE 10 A0212 DELIB/GP STRUCT

B59
CHINA INSTITUTE OF AMERICA.,CHINA AND THE UNITED NATIONS. CHINA/COM FUT STRUCT EDU/PROP LEGIT ADMIN ATTIT KNOWL ORD/FREE PWR...OBS RECORD STAND/INT TIME/SEQ UN LEAGUE/NAT UNESCO 20. PAGE 26 A0531 ASIA INT/ORG

B59
CORBETT P.E.,LAW IN DIPLOMACY. UK USA+45 USSR CONSTN SOCIETY INT/ORG JUDGE LEGIT ATTIT ORD/FREE TOT/POP LEAGUE/NAT 20. PAGE 30 A0616 NAT/G ADJUD JURID DIPLOM

B59
COUDENHOVE-KALERGI,FROM WAR TO PEACE. USA+45 USSR WOR+45 WOR-45 LAW INT/ORG NAT/G LEGIT COERCE LOVE ...POLICY PLURIST METH/CNCPT STERTYP TOT/POP UN 20 NATO. PAGE 31 A0636 FUT ORD/FREE

B59
FOX W.T.R.,THEORETICAL ASPECTS OF INTERNATIONAL RELATIONS. WOR+45 INT/ORG NAT/G POL/PAR CONSULT PLAN ECO/TAC DOMIN EDU/PROP LEGIT EXEC COERCE PWR WEALTH...RELATIV CONCPT 20. PAGE 48 A0975 DELIB/GP ANTHOL

B59
GOODRICH L.,THE UNITED NATIONS. WOR+45 CONSTN STRUCT ACT/RES LEGIT COERCE KNOWL ORD/FREE PWR ...GEN/LAWS UN 20. PAGE 54 A1104 INT/ORG ROUTINE

B59
GORDENKER L.,THE UNITED NATIONS AND THE PEACEFUL UNIFICATION OF KOREA. ASIA LAW LOC/G CONSULT ACT/RES DIPLOM DOMIN LEGIT ADJUD ADMIN ORD/FREE SOVEREIGN...INT GEN/METH UN COLD/WAR 20. PAGE 54 A1109 DELIB/GP KOREA INT/ORG

B59
REIFF H.,THE UNITED STATES AND THE TREATY LAW OF THE SEA. USA+45 USA-45 SEA SOCIETY INT/ORG CONSULT DELIB/GP LEGIS DIPLOM LEGIT ATTIT ORD/FREE PWR WEALTH...GEOG JURID TOT/POP 20 TREATY. PAGE 120 A2459 ADJUD INT/LAW

B59
SCHNEIDER J.,TREATY-MAKING POWER OF INTERNATIONAL ORGANIZATIONS. FUT WOR+45 WOR-45 LAW NAT/G JUDGE DIPLOM LEGIT CT/SYS ORD/FREE PWR...INT/LAW JURID GEN/LAWS TOT/POP UNESCO 20 TREATY. PAGE 129 A2639 INT/ORG ROUTINE

B59
SCHURZ W.L.,AMERICAN FOREIGN AFFAIRS: A GUIDE TO INTERNATIONAL AFFAIRS. USA+45 WOR+45 WOR-45 NAT/G FORCES LEGIS TOP/EX PLAN EDU/PROP LEGIT ADMIN ROUTINE ATTIT ORD/FREE PWR...SOC CONCPT STAT SAMP/SIZ CHARTS STERTYP 20. PAGE 129 A2653 INT/ORG SOCIETY DIPLOM

B59
STRAUSZ-HUPE R.,PROTRACTED CONFLICT. CHINA/COM KOREA WOR+45 INT/ORG FORCES ACT/RES ECO/TAC LEGIT COERCE DRIVE PERCEPT KNOWL PWR...PSY CONCPT RECORD GEN/METH COLD/WAR VAL/FREE 20. PAGE 139 A2847 COM PLAN USSR

B59
THOMAS N.,THE PREREQUISITES FOR PEACE. ASIA EUR+WWI FUT ISLAM S/ASIA WOR+45 FORCES PLAN BAL/PWR EDU/PROP LEGIT ATTIT PWR...SOCIALIST CONCPT COLD/WAR 20 UN. PAGE 143 A2924 INT/ORG ORD/FREE ARMS/CONT PEACE

L59
BEGUIN B.,"ILO AND THE TRIPARTITE SYSTEM." EUR+WWI WOR+45 WOR-45 CONSTN ECO/DEV ECO/UNDEV INDUS INT/ORG NAT/G VOL/ASSN DELIB/GP PLAN TEC/DEV LEGIT ORD/FREE WEALTH...CONCPT TIME/SEQ WORK ILO 20. PAGE 12 A0249 LABOR

S59
CARLSTON K.S.,"NATIONALIZATION: AN ANALYTIC APPROACH." WOR+45 INT/ORG ECO/TAC DOMIN LEGIT ADJUD COERCE ORD/FREE PWR WEALTH SOCISM...JURID CONCPT TREND STERTYP TOT/POP VAL/FREE 20. PAGE 24 A0486 INDUS NAT/G NAT/LISM SOVEREIGN

S59
HARVEY M.F.,"THE PALESTINE REFUGEE PROBLEM: ELEMENTS OF A SOLUTION." ISLAM LAW INT/ORG DELIB/GP TOP/EX ECO/TAC ROUTINE DRIVE HEALTH LOVE ORD/FREE PWR WEALTH...MAJORIT FAO 20. PAGE 62 A1283 ACT/RES LEGIT PEACE ISRAEL

S59
HOFFMANN S.,"IMPLEMENTATION OF INTERNATIONAL INSTRUMENTS ON HUMAN RIGHTS." WOR+45 VOL/ASSN DELIB/GP JUDGE EDU/PROP LEGIT ROUTINE PEACE COLD/WAR 20. PAGE 66 A1355 INT/ORG MORAL

S59
SAYEGH F.,"ARAB NATIONALISM AND SOVIET-AMERICAN RELATIONS." ISLAM USA+45 ECO/UNDEV PLAN ECO/TAC LEGIT NAT/LISM DRIVE PERCEPT KNOWL PWR...DECISION CONCPT STAT RECORD TREND CON/ANAL VAL/FREE 20 COLD/WAR. PAGE 127 A2610 DIPLOM USSR

S59
SOHN L.B.,"THE DEFINITION OF AGGRESSION." FUT LAW FORCES LEGIT ADJUD ROUTINE COERCE ORD/FREE PWR ...MAJORIT JURID QUANT COLD/WAR 20. PAGE 135 A2762 INT/ORG CT/SYS DETER SOVEREIGN

S59
STOESSINGER J.G.,"THE INTERNATIONAL ATOMIC ENERGY AGENCY: THE FIRST PHASE." FUT WOR+45 NAT/G VOL/ASSN DELIB/GP BAL/PWR LEGIT ADMIN ROUTINE PWR...OBS CON/ANAL GEN/LAWS VAL/FREE 20 IAEA. PAGE 138 A2829 INT/ORG ECO/DEV FOR/AID NUC/PWR

S59
SUTTON F.X.,"REPRESENTATION AND THE NATURE OF POLITICAL SYSTEMS." UNIV WOR-45 CULTURE SOCIETY STRATA INT/ORG FORCES JUDGE DOMIN LEGIT EXEC REGION REPRESENT ATTIT ORD/FREE RESPECT...SOC HIST/WRIT TIME/SEQ. PAGE 140 A2867 NAT/G CONCPT

S59
WARBURG J.P.,"THE CENTRAL EUROPEAN CRISIS: A PROPOSAL FOR WESTERN INITIATIVE." EUR+WWI INT/ORG NAT/G LEGIT DETER WAR...CONCPT BER/BLOC UN 20. PAGE 161 A3276 PLAN GERMANY

B60
BAILEY S.D.,THE GENERAL ASSEMBLY OF THE UNITED NATIONS. FUT WOR+45 STRUCT LEGIS ACT/RES PLAN EDU/PROP LEGIT ADMIN EXEC PEACE ATTIT HEALTH PWR ...CONCPT TREND CHARTS GEN/LAWS UN TOT/POP VAL/FREE COLD/WAR 20. PAGE 10 A0204 INT/ORG DELIB/GP DIPLOM

B60
BUCHAN A.,NATO IN THE 1960'S. EUR+WWI USA+45 WOR+45 INT/ORG ACT/RES PLAN LEGIT COERCE DETER ATTIT DRIVE RIGID/FLEX ORD/FREE...METH/CNCPT TIME/SEQ TREND GEN/LAWS COLD/WAR 20 NATO. PAGE 21 A0421 VOL/ASSN FORCES ARMS/CONT SOVEREIGN

B60
ENGEL J.,THE SECURITY OF THE FREE WORLD. USSR WOR+45 STRATA STRUCT ECO/DEV ECO/UNDEV INT/ORG DELIB/GP FORCES DOMIN LEGIT ADJUD EXEC ARMS/CONT COERCE...POLICY CONCPT NEW/IDEA TIME/SEQ GEN/LAWS COLD/WAR WORK UN 20 NATO. PAGE 42 A0851 COM TREND DIPLOM

B60
HAAS E.B.,THE COMPARATIVE STUDY OF THE UNITED NATIONS. WOR+45 NAT/G DOMIN LEGIT ROUTINE PEACE ORD/FREE PWR UN VAL/FREE 20. PAGE 59 A1205 INT/ORG DIPLOM

B60
JENNINGS R.,PROGRESS OF INTERNATIONAL LAW. FUT WOR+45 WOR-45 SOCIETY NAT/G VOL/ASSN DELIB/GP DIPLOM EDU/PROP LEGIT COERCE ATTIT DRIVE MORAL ORD/FREE...JURID CONCPT OBS TIME/SEQ TREND INT/ORG LAW INT/LAW

GEN/LAWS. PAGE 74 A1509

B60
LINDSAY K.,EUROPEAN ASSEMBLIES: THE EXPERIMENTAL PERIOD 1949-1959. EUR+WWI ECO/DEV NAT/G POL/PAR LEGIS TOP/EX ACT/RES PLAN ECO/TAC DOMIN LEGIT ROUTINE ATTIT DRIVE ORD/FREE PWR SKILL...SOC CONCPT TREND CHARTS GEN/LAWS VAL/FREE. PAGE 89 A1823 [VOL/ASSN INT/ORG REGION]

B60
MUNRO L.,UNITED NATIONS, HOPE FOR A DIVIDED WORLD. FUT WOR+45 CONSTN DELIB/GP CREATE TEC/DEV DIPLOM EDU/PROP LEGIT PEACE ATTIT HEALTH ORD/FREE PWR ...CONCPT TREND UN VAL/FREE 20. PAGE 106 A2172 [INT/ORG ROUTINE]

B60
PRICE D.,THE SECRETARY OF STATE. USA+45 CONSTN ELITES INTELL CHIEF EX/STRUC TOP/EX LEGIT ATTIT PWR SKILL...DECISION 20 CONGRESS. PAGE 117 A2410 [CONSULT DIPLOM INT/LAW]

B60
THOMPSON K.W.,POLITICAL REALISM AND THE CRISIS IN WORLD POLITICS. USA+45 USA-45 SOCIETY INT/ORG NAT/G LEGIS TOP/EX LEGIT DETER ATTIT ORD/FREE PWR ...GEN/LAWS TOT/POP 20. PAGE 143 A2931 [PLAN HUM BAL/PWR DIPLOM]

L60
KUNZ J.,"SANCTIONS IN INTERNATIONAL LAW." WOR+45 WOR-45 LEGIT ARMS/CONT COERCE PEACE ATTIT ...METH/CNCPT TIME/SEQ TREND 20. PAGE 83 A1695 [INT/ORG ADJUD INT/LAW]

L60
LAUTERPACHT E.,"THE UNITED NATIONS EMERGENCY FORCE." R+D LEGIT ROUTINE COERCE KNOWL ORD/FREE SKILL...JURID UN 20. PAGE 85 A1746 [INT/ORG FORCES]

L60
LAUTERPACHT E.,"THE SUEZ CANAL SETTLEMENT." FRANCE ISLAM ISRAEL UAR UK BAL/PWR DIPLOM LEGIT...JURID GEN/LAWS ANTHOL SUEZ VAL/FREE 20. PAGE 85 A1747 [INT/ORG LAW]

S60
GINSBURGS G.,"PEKING-LHASA-NEW DELHI." CHINA/COM FUT INDIA S/ASIA KIN NAT/G PROVS SECT FORCES BAL/PWR ECO/TAC DOMIN EDU/PROP LEGIT ADMIN REGION GUERRILLA PWR...TREND TIBET 20. PAGE 52 A1074 [ASIA COERCE DIPLOM]

S60
GOODRICH L.,"GEOGRAPHICAL DISTRIBUTION OF THE STAFF OF THE UN SECRETARIAT." FUT WOR+45 CONSTN BAL/PWR DIPLOM EDU/PROP LEGIT ROUTINE RIGID/FLEX...CHARTS UN 20. PAGE 54 A1105 [INT/ORG EX/STRUC]

S60
GRACIA-MORA M.R.,"INTERNATIONAL RESPONSIBILITY FOR SUBVERSIVE ACTIVITIES AND HOSTILE PROPAGANDA BY PRIVATE PERSONS AGAINST." COM EUR+WWI L/A+17C UK USA+45 USSR WOR-45 CONSTN NAT/G LEGIT ADJUD REV PEACE TOTALISM ORD/FREE...INT/LAW 20. PAGE 55 A1119 [INT/ORG JURID SOVEREIGN]

S60
HAYTON R.D.,"THE ANTARCTIC SETTLEMENT OF 1959." FUT USA+45 WOR+45 WOR-45 STRUCT R+D INT/ORG EX/STRUC CREATE TEC/DEV LEGIT PEACE ATTIT SOVEREIGN ...TIME/SEQ 20 TREATY IGY. PAGE 63 A1297 [DELIB/GP JURID DIPLOM REGION]

S60
IKLE F.C.,"NTH COUNTRIES AND DISARMAMENT." WOR+45 DELIB/GP ECO/TAC DOMIN EDU/PROP LEGIT ROUTINE COERCE RIGID/FLEX ORD/FREE...MARXIST TREND 20. PAGE 70 A1432 [FUT INT/ORG ARMS/CONT NUC/PWR]

S60
MUNRO L.,"CAN THE UNITED NATIONS ENFORCE PEACE." WOR+45 LAW INT/ORG VOL/ASSN BAL/PWR LEGIT ARMS/CONT COERCE DETER PEACE PWR...CONCPT REC/INT TREND UN 20 HAMMARSK/D. PAGE 106 A2173 [FORCES ORD/FREE]

S60
NANES A.,"THE EUROPEAN COMMUNITY AND THE UNITED STATES: EVOLVING RELATIONS." EUR+WWI USA+45 WOR+45 ECO/UNDEV MARKET NAT/G DELIB/GP PLAN LEGIT ATTIT PWR WEALTH...CONCPT STAT TIME/SEQ CON/ANAL EEC OEEC 20 EURATOM. PAGE 107 A2194 [INT/ORG REGION]

S60
POTTER P.B.,"RELATIVE VALUES OF INTERNATIONAL RELATIONS, LAW, AND ORGANIZATIONS." WOR+45 NAT/G LEGIT ADJUD ORD/FREE...CONCPT TOT/POP COLD/WAR 20. PAGE 117 A2401 [INT/ORG LEGIS DIPLOM INT/LAW]

S60
RHYNE C.S.,"LAW AS AN INSTRUMENT FOR PEACE." FUT WOR+45 PLAN LEGIT ROUTINE ARMS/CONT NUC/PWR ATTIT ORD/FREE...JURID METH/CNCPT TREND CON/ANAL HYPO/EXP COLD/WAR 20. PAGE 120 A2471 [ADJUD EDU/PROP INT/LAW PEACE]

S60
SCHACHTER O.,"THE ENFORCEMENT OF INTERNATIONAL JUDICIAL AND ARBITRAL DECISIONS." WOR+45 NAT/G ECO/TAC DOMIN LEGIT ROUTINE COERCE ATTIT DRIVE ALL/VALS PWR...METH/CNCPT TREND TOT/POP 20 UN. PAGE 128 A2615 [INT/ORG ADJUD INT/LAW]

B61
ANAND R.P.,COMPULSORY JURISDICTION OF INTERNATIONAL COURT OF JUSTICE. FUT WOR+45 SOCIETY PLAN LEGIT ADJUD ATTIT DRIVE PERSON ORD/FREE...JURID CONCPT TREND 20 ICJ. PAGE 8 A0156 [INT/ORG COERCE INT/LAW]

B61
GRAEBNER N.,AN UNCERTAIN TRADITION: AMERICAN SECRETARIES OF STATE IN THE 20TH CENTURY. USA+45 CONSTN INT/ORG NAT/G DELIB/GP TOP/EX BAL/PWR DOMIN LEGIT ADMIN ARMS/CONT ATTIT DRIVE PERSON SUPEGO ORD/FREE PWR...GEN/LAWS VAL/FREE CONGRESS. PAGE 55 A1121 [USA-45 BIOG DIPLOM]

B61
HANCOCK W.K.,FOUR STUDIES OF WAR AND PEACE IN THIS CENTURY. FUT WOR+45 WOR-45 ACT/RES LEGIT DETER HEALTH...TREND ANTHOL TOT/POP VAL/FREE UN 20. PAGE 61 A1250 [INT/ORG POLICY ARMS/CONT]

B61
KITZINGER V.W.,THE CHALLENGE OF THE COMMON MARKET. EUR+WWI ECO/DEV DIST/IND PLAN ECO/TAC INT/TRADE LEGIT ATTIT PWR WEALTH...TIME/SEQ TREND CHARTS EEC 20. PAGE 80 A1647 [MARKET INT/ORG UK]

B61
LUKACS J.,A HISTORY OF THE COLD WAR. ASIA COM EUR+WWI USA+45 USA-45 INT/ORG NAT/G DELIB/GP ACT/RES BAL/PWR DIPLOM DOMIN EDU/PROP LEGIT DRIVE ORD/FREE...TREND COLD/WAR 20. PAGE 91 A1872 [PWR TIME/SEQ USSR]

B61
MCDOUGAL M.S.,LAW AND MINIMUM WORLD PUBLIC ORDER. WOR+45 SOCIETY NAT/G DELIB/GP EDU/PROP LEGIT ADJUD COERCE ATTIT PERSON...JURID CONCPT RECORD TREND TOT/POP 20. PAGE 98 A2006 [INT/ORG ORD/FREE INT/LAW]

B61
SCAMMEL W.M.,INTERNATIONAL MONETARY POLICY. WOR+45 WOR-45 ACT/RES ECO/TAC LEGIT WEALTH...GEN/METH UN 20. PAGE 127 A2611 [INT/ORG FINAN BAL/PAY]

B61
SCHELLING T.C.,STRATEGY AND ARMS CONTROL. FUT UNIV WOR+45 INT/ORG PLAN TEC/DEV BAL/PWR LEGIT PERCEPT HEALTH...CONCPT VAL/FREE 20. PAGE 128 A2623 [ROUTINE POLICY ARMS/CONT]

B61
STILLMAN E.,THE NEW POLITICS: AMERICA AND THE END OF THE POSTWAR WORLD. FUT WOR+45 CULTURE SOCIETY ECO/UNDEV INT/ORG NAT/G FORCES TOP/EX ACT/RES DIPLOM EDU/PROP LEGIT ROUTINE DETER ATTIT ORD/FREE PWR...OBS STERTYP COLD/WAR TOT/POP VAL/FREE. PAGE 138 A2827 [USA+45 PLAN]

B61
STONE J.,QUEST FOR SURVIVAL. WOR+45 NAT/G VOL/ASSN LEGIT ADMIN ARMS/CONT COERCE DISPL ORD/FREE PWR ...POLICY INT/LAW JURID COLD/WAR 20. PAGE 139 A2836 [INT/ORG ADJUD SOVEREIGN]

B61
WECHSLER H.,PRINCIPLES, POLITICS AND FUNDAMENTAL LAW: SELECTED ESSAYS. USA+45 USA-45 LAW SOCIETY NAT/G PROVS DELIB/GP EX/STRUC ACT/RES LEGIT PERSON KNOWL PWR...JURID 20 NUREMBERG. PAGE 162 A3296 [CT/SYS CONSTN INT/LAW]

B61
WRIGHT Q.,THE ROLE OF INTERNATIONAL LAW IN THE ELIMINATION OF WAR. FUT WOR+45 WOR-45 NAT/G BAL/PWR DIPLOM DOMIN LEGIT PWR...POLICY INT/LAW JURID CONCPT TIME/SEQ TREND GEN/LAWS COLD/WAR 20. PAGE 168 A3414 [INT/ORG ADJUD ARMS/CONT]

B61
YDIT M.,INTERNATIONALISED TERRITORIES. FUT WOR+45 WOR-45 CONSTN VOL/ASSN CREATE PLAN LEGIT PEACE ORD/FREE...GEOG INT/LAW JURID SOC NEW/IDEA OBS RECORD SAMP TIME/SEQ TREND 19/20 BERLIN. PAGE 169 A3431 [LOC/G INT/ORG DIPLOM SOVEREIGN]

L61
CLAUDE I.,"THE UNITED NATIONS AND THE USE OF FORCE." FUT WOR+45 SOCIETY DIPLOM EDU/PROP LEGIT ADMIN ROUTINE COERCE WAR PEACE ORD/FREE...CONCPT TREND UN 20. PAGE 27 A0545 [INT/ORG FORCES]

L61
HOYT E.C.,"UNITED STATES REACTION TO THE KOREAN ATTACK." COM KOREA USA+45 CONSTN DELIB/GP FORCES PLAN ECO/TAC DOMIN EDU/PROP LEGIT ROUTINE COERCE WAR ATTIT DISPL RIGID/FLEX ORD/FREE PWR...POLICY INT/LAW TREND UN 20. PAGE 68 A1402 [ASIA INT/ORG BAL/PWR DIPLOM]

L61
SAND P.T.,"AN HISTORICAL SURVEY OF INTERNATIONAL AIR LAW SINCE 1944." USA+45 USA-45 WOR+45 WOR-45 SOCIETY ECO/DEV NAT/G CONSULT EX/STRUC ACT/RES PLAN LEGIT ROUTINE...JURID CONCPT METH/CNCPT TREND 20. PAGE 127 A2598 [INT/ORG LAW INT/LAW SPACE]

L61
TAUBENFELD H.J.,"A REGIME FOR OUTER SPACE." FUT UNIV R+D ACT/RES PLAN BAL/PWR LEGIT ARMS/CONT ORD/FREE...POLICY JURID TREND UN TOT/POP 20 COLD/WAR. PAGE 142 A2894 [INT/ORG ADJUD SPACE]

S61
BALL M.M.,"ISSUES FOR THE AMERICAS: NON-INTERVENTION VS HUMAN RIGHTS AND THE PRESERVATION OF DEMOCRATIC INSTITUTIONS." USA+45 INTELL INT/ORG NAT/G DIPLOM ECO/TAC LEGIT...TREND OAS TOT/POP 20. PAGE 11 A0213 [L/A+17C MORAL]

S61
CASTANEDA J.,"THE UNDERDEVELOPED NATIONS AND THE DEVELOPMENT OF INTERNATIONAL LAW." FUT UNIV LAW ACT/RES FOR/AID LEGIT PERCEPT SKILL...JURID METH/CNCPT TIME/SEQ TOT/POP 20 UN. PAGE 25 A0507 [INT/ORG ECO/UNDEV PEACE INT/LAW]

S61
LIPSON L.,"AN ARGUMENT ON THE LEGALITY OF RECONNAISSANCE STATELLITES." COM USA+45 USSR WOR+45 AIR INTELL NAT/G CONSULT PLAN DIPLOM LEGIT ROUTINE ATTIT...INT/LAW JURID CONCPT METH/CNCPT TREND [INT/ORG LAW SPACE]

COLD/WAR 20. PAGE 90 A1833

S61
MIKSCHE F.O.,"DEFENSE ORGANIZATION FOR WESTERN EUROPE." USA+45 INT/ORG NAT/G VOL/ASSN ACT/RES DOMIN LEGIT COERCE ORD/FREE PWR...RELATIV TREND 20 NATO. PAGE 101 A2071
EUR+WWI FORCES WEAPON NUC/PWR

S61
MILLER E.,"LEGAL ASPECTS OF UN ACTION IN THE CONGO." AFR CULTURE ADMIN PEACE DRIVE RIGID/FLEX ORD/FREE...WELF/ST JURID OBS UN CONGO 20. PAGE 101 A2076
INT/ORG LEGIT

S61
ROSTOW W.W.,"THE FUTURE OF FOREIGN AID." COM FUT WOR+45 ECO/DEV INDUS INT/ORG NAT/G CONSULT ACT/RES PLAN DOMIN LEGIT CHOOSE RIGID/FLEX ALL/VALS ...MAJORIT CONCPT TREND TOT/POP 20. PAGE 124 A2544
ECO/UNDEV ECO/TAC FOR/AID

S61
WEST F.J.,"THE NEW GUINEA QUESTION: AN AUSTRALIAN VIEW." WOR+45 INT/ORG VOL/ASSN LEGIT PERCEPT ...POLICY TIME/SEQ AUSTRAL VAL/FREE 20 CMN/WLTH. PAGE 163 A3320
S/ASIA ECO/UNDEV

B62
BLACKETT P.M.S.,STUDIES OF WAR: NUCLEAR AND CONVENTIONAL. EUR+WWI USA+45 DELIB/GP ACT/RES CREATE PLAN TEC/DEV LEGIT COERCE WAR ORD/FREE PWR ...POLICY TECHNIC TIME/SEQ 20. PAGE 15 A0300
INT/ORG FORCES ARMS/CONT NUC/PWR

B62
CARLSTON K.S.,LAW AND ORGANIZATION IN WORLD SOCIETY. WOR+45 FINAN ECO/TAC DOMIN LEGIT CT/SYS ROUTINE COERCE ORD/FREE PWR WEALTH...PLURIST DECISION JURID MGT METH/CNCPT GEN/LAWS 20. PAGE 24 A0487
INT/ORG LAW

B62
DALLIN A.,THE SOVIET UNION AT THE UNITED NATIONS: AN INQUIRY INTO SOVIET MOTIVES AND OBJECTIVES. ACT/RES EDU/PROP LEGIT ATTIT KNOWL PWR...POLICY RECORD HIST/WRIT TIME/SEQ TREND ORG/CHARTS GEN/METH COLD/WAR FAO 20 UN. PAGE 33 A0675
COM INT/ORG USSR

B62
DUTOIT B.,LA NEUTRALITE SUISSE A L'HEURE EUROPEENNE. EUR+WWI MOD/EUR INT/ORG NAT/G VOL/ASSN PLAN BAL/PWR LEGIT NEUTRAL REGION PEACE ORD/FREE SOVEREIGN...CONCPT OBS TIME/SEQ TREND STERTYP VAL/FREE LEAGUE/NAT UN 20. PAGE 40 A0812
ATTIT DIPLOM SWITZERLND

B62
HADWEN J.G.,HOW UNITED NATIONS DECISIONS ARE MADE. WOR+45 LAW EDU/PROP LEGIT ADMIN PWR...DECISION SELF/OBS GEN/LAWS UN 20. PAGE 59 A1212
INT/ORG ROUTINE

B62
HATCH J.,AFRICA TODAY-AND TOMORROW: AN OUTLINE OF BASIC FACTS AND MAJOR PROBLEMS. AFR FUT ISLAM STRATA ECO/UNDEV INT/ORG NAT/G POL/PAR DELIB/GP TOP/EX EDU/PROP LEGIT CHOOSE ATTIT...TIME/SEQ TOT/POP COLD/WAR 20. PAGE 63 A1287
PLAN CONSTN NAT/LISM

B62
HUNTINGTON S.P.,CHANGING PATTERNS OF MILITARY POLITICS. EUR+WWI L/A+17C S/ASIA USA+45 WOR+45 CULTURE INT/ORG NAT/G CONSULT PLAN DOMIN EDU/PROP LEGIT DETER WAR ATTIT PERSON PWR...DECISION CONCPT SIMUL GEN/LAWS ANTHOL COLD/WAR 20. PAGE 69 A1419
FORCES RIGID/FLEX

B62
KING G.,THE UNITED NATIONS IN THE CONGO: A QUEST FOR PEACE. WOR+45 NAT/G CONSULT FORCES LEGIT COERCE WAR ORD/FREE...JURID METH/CNCPT OBS INT HIST/WRIT TIME/SEQ CONGO UN 20 COLD/WAR. PAGE 79 A1624
AFR INT/ORG

B62
LAWSON R.,INTERNATIONAL REGIONAL ORGANIZATIONS. WOR+45 NAT/G VOL/ASSN CONSULT LEGIS EDU/PROP LEGIT ADMIN EXEC ROUTINE HEALTH PWR WEALTH...JURID EEC COLD/WAR 20 UN. PAGE 86 A1752
INT/ORG DELIB/GP REGION

B62
LILLICH R.B.,INTERNATIONAL CLAIMS: THEIR ADJUDICATION BY NATIONAL COMMISSIONS. WOR+45 WOR-45 INT/ORG LEGIT CT/SYS TOT/POP 20. PAGE 89 A1816
ADJUD JURID INT/LAW

B62
MACKENTOSH J.M.,STRATEGY AND TACTICS OF SOVIET FOREIGN POLICY. CHINA/COM FUT USA+45 WOR+45 INT/ORG PLAN DOMIN LEGIT ROUTINE COERCE NUC/PWR WAR ATTIT DRIVE ORD/FREE PWR...CONCPT OBS TIME/SEQ TREND GEN/METH COLD/WAR 20. PAGE 92 A1894
COM POLICY DIPLOM USSR

B62
MCDOUGAL M.S.,THE PUBLIC ORDER OF THE OCEANS. WOR+45 WOR-45 SEA INT/ORG NAT/G CONSULT DELIB/GP DIPLOM LEGIT PEACE RIGID/FLEX...GEOG INT/LAW JURID RECORD TOT/POP 20 TREATY. PAGE 98 A2007
ADJUD ORD/FREE

B62
MCKENNA J.,DIPLOMATIC PROTEST IN FOREIGN POLICY: ANALYSIS AND CASE STUDIES. COM USA+45 WOR+45 INT/ORG PUB/INST DELIB/GP TOP/EX ACT/RES PLAN LEGIT ATTIT 20. PAGE 98 A2014
NAT/G POLICY DIPLOM

B62
MORGENTHAU H.J.,POLITICS IN THE TWENTIETH CENTURY: IMPASSE OF AMERICAN FOREIGN POLICY. FUT GERMANY USA+45 USSR WOR+45 INT/ORG NAT/G ACT/RES PLAN FOR/AID EDU/PROP LEGIT COERCE WAR PWR...TIME/SEQ TREND COLD/WAR 20. PAGE 104 A2138
SKILL DIPLOM

B62
MORGENTHAU H.J.,POLITICS IN THE 20TH CENTURY: RESTORATION OF AMERICAN POLITICS. ASIA GERMANY USA+45 USSR WOR+45 NAT/G PLAN EDU/PROP LEGIT NUC/PWR ATTIT PWR SKILL...CONCPT TREND COLD/WAR 20. PAGE 104 A2139
INT/ORG DIPLOM

B62
NEAL F.W.,WAR AND PEACE AND GERMANY. EUR+WWI USSR STRUCT INT/ORG NAT/G FORCES DOMIN EDU/PROP LEGIT EXEC COERCE ORD/FREE...HUM SOC NEW/IDEA OBS TIME/SEQ TOT/POP COLD/WAR 20 BERLIN. PAGE 108 A2208
USA+45 POLICY DIPLOM GERMANY

B62
NICHOLAS H.G.,THE UNITED NATIONS AS A POLITICAL INSTITUTION. WOR+45 CONSTN EX/STRUC ACT/RES LEGIT PERCEPT KNOWL PWR...CONCPT TIME/SEQ CON/ANAL ORG/CHARTS UN 20. PAGE 109 A2228
INT/ORG ROUTINE

B62
ROSENNE S.,THE WORLD COURT: WHAT IT IS AND HOW IT WORKS. WOR+45 WOR-45 LAW CONSTN JUDGE EDU/PROP LEGIT ROUTINE CHOOSE PEACE ORD/FREE...JURID OBS TIME/SEQ CHARTS UN TOT/POP VAL/FREE 20. PAGE 124 A2538
INT/ORG ADJUD INT/LAW

B62
SCHWARZENBERGER G.,THE FRONTIERS OF INTERNATIONAL LAW. WOR+45 WOR-45 NAT/G LEGIT CT/SYS ROUTINE MORAL ORD/FREE PWR...JURID SOC GEN/METH 20 COLD/WAR. PAGE 130 A2661
INT/ORG LAW INT/LAW

B62
TRISKA J.F.,THE THEORY, LAW, AND POLICY OF SOVIET TREATIES. WOR+45 WOR-45 CONSTN INT/ORG NAT/G VOL/ASSN DOMIN LEGIT COERCE ATTIT PWR RESPECT ...POLICY JURID CONCPT OBS SAMP TIME/SEQ TREND GEN/LAWS 20. PAGE 145 A2966
COM LAW INT/LAW USSR

B62
WOETZEL R.K.,THE NURENBERG TRIALS IN INTERNATIONAL LAW. CHRIST-17C MOD/EUR WOR+45 SOCIETY NAT/G DELIB/GP DOMIN LEGIT ROUTINE ATTIT DRIVE PERSON SUPEGO MORAL ORD/FREE...POLICY MAJORIT JURID PSY SOC SELF/OBS RECORD NAZI TOT/POP. PAGE 166 A3376
INT/ORG ADJUD WAR

L62
BAILEY S.D.,"THE TROIKA AND THE FUTURE OF THE UN." CONSTN CREATE LEGIT EXEC CHOOSE ORD/FREE PWR ...CONCPT NEW/IDEA UN COLD/WAR 20. PAGE 10 A0206
FUT INT/ORG USSR

L62
MURACCIOLE L.,"LA LOI FONDAMENTALE DE LA REPUBLIQUE DU CONGO." WOR+45 SOCIETY ECO/UNDEV INT/ORG NAT/G LEGIS PLAN LEGIT ADJUD COLONIAL ROUTINE ATTIT SOVEREIGN 20 CONGO. PAGE 106 A2174
AFR CONSTN

L62
PETKOFF D.K.,"RECOGNITION AND NON-RECOGNITION OF STATES AND GOVERNMENTS IN INTERNATIONAL LAW." ASIA COM USA+45 WOR+45 NAT/G ACT/RES DIPLOM DOMIN LEGIT COERCE ORD/FREE PWR...CONCPT GEN/LAWS 20. PAGE 115 A2369
INT/ORG LAW INT/LAW

L62
STEIN E.,"MR HAMMARSKJOLD, THE CHARTER LAW AND THE FUTURE ROLE OF THE UNITED NATIONS SECRETARY-GENERAL." WOR+45 CONSTN INT/ORG DELIB/GP FORCES TOP/EX BAL/PWR LEGIT ROUTINE RIGID/FLEX PWR ...POLICY JURID OBS STERTYP UN COLD/WAR 20 HAMMARSK/D. PAGE 137 A2815
CONCPT BIOG

S62
CRANE R.D.,"LAW AND STRATEGY IN SPACE." FUT USA+45 WOR+45 AIR LAW INT/ORG NAT/G FORCES ACT/RES PLAN BAL/PWR LEGIT ARMS/CONT COERCE ORD/FREE...POLICY INT/LAW JURID SOC/EXP 20 TREATY. PAGE 32 A0656
CONCPT SPACE

S62
DALLIN A.,"THE SOVIET VIEW OF THE UNITED NATIONS." WOR+45 VOL/ASSN TOP/EX DIPLOM DOMIN EDU/PROP LEGIT ATTIT RIGID/FLEX PWR...CONCPT OBS HIST/WRIT TIME/SEQ STERTYP GEN/LAWS COLD/WAR UN 20. PAGE 33 A0676
COM INT/ORG USSR

S62
FALK R.A.,"THE REALITY OF INTERNATIONAL LAW." WOR+45 NAT/G LEGIT COERCE DETER WAR MORAL ORD/FREE PWR SOVEREIGN...JURID CONCPT VAL/FREE COLD/WAR 20. PAGE 43 A0887
INT/ORG ADJUD NUC/PWR INT/LAW

S62
FENWICK C.G.,"ISSUES AT PUNTA DEL ESTE: NON-INTERVENTION VS COLLECTIVE SECURITY." L/A+17C USA+45 VOL/ASSN DELIB/GP ECO/TAC LEGIT ADJUD REGION ORD/FREE OAS COLD/WAR 20. PAGE 45 A0917
INT/ORG CUBA

S62
FINKELSTEIN L.S.,"THE UNITED NATIONS AND ORGANIZATIONS FOR CONTROL OF ARMAMENT." FUT WOR+45 VOL/ASSN DELIB/GP TOP/EX CREATE EDU/PROP LEGIT ADJUD NUC/PWR ATTIT RIGID/FLEX ORD/FREE...POLICY DECISION CONCPT OBS TREND GEN/LAWS TOT/POP COLD/WAR. PAGE 46 A0933
INT/ORG PWR ARMS/CONT

S62
FOSTER W.C.,"ARMS CONTROL AND DISARMAMENT IN A DIVIDED WORLD." COM FUT USA+45 USSR WOR+45 INTELL INT/ORG NAT/G VOL/ASSN CONSULT CREATE PLAN TEC/DEV EDU/PROP LEGIT NUC/PWR ATTIT RIGID/FLEX...CONCPT TREND TOT/POP 20 UN. PAGE 47 A0971
DELIB/GP POLICY ARMS/CONT DIPLOM

S62
GREEN L.C.,"POLITICAL OFFENSES, WAR CRIMES AND EXTRADITION." WOR+45 YUGOSLAVIA INT/ORG LEGIT ROUTINE WAR ORD/FREE SOVEREIGN...JURID NAZI 20 INTERPOL. PAGE 55 A1138
LAW CONCPT INT/LAW

S62
JOHNSON O.H.,"THE ENGLISH TRADITION IN INTERNATIONAL LAW." CHRIST-17C MOD/EUR EDU/PROP LEGIT CT/SYS ORD/FREE...JURID CONCPT TIME/SEQ. PAGE 75 A1526
LAW INT/LAW UK

S62
LISSITZYN O.J.,"SOME LEGAL IMPLICATIONS OF THE U-2 AND RB-47 INCIDENTS." FUT USA+45 USSR WOR+45 AIR NAT/G DIPLOM LEGIT MORAL ORD/FREE SOVEREIGN...JURID GEN/LAWS GEN/METH COLD/WAR 20 U-2. PAGE 90 A1840
LAW CONCPT SPACE INT/LAW

S62
MCWHINNEY E.,"CO-EXISTENCE, THE CUBA CRISIS, AND COLD WAR-INTERNATIONAL WAR." CUBA USA+45 USSR WOR+45 NAT/G TOP/EX BAL/PWR DIPLOM DOMIN LEGIT PEACE RIGID/FLEX ORD/FREE...STERTYP COLD/WAR 20. PAGE 99 A2026
CONCPT INT/LAW

S62
MILLAR T.B.,"THE COMMONWEALTH AND THE UNITED NATIONS." FUT WOR+45 STRUCT NAT/G VOL/ASSN CONSULT DELIB/GP EDU/PROP LEGIT ATTIT...POLICY CONCPT TREND CMN/WLTH UN 20. PAGE 101 A2072
INT/ORG

S62
MOUSKHELY M.,"LA NAISSANCE DES ETATS EN DROIT INTERNATIONAL PUBLIC." UNIV SOCIETY INT/ORG VOL/ASSN LEGIT ATTIT RIGID/FLEX...JURID TIME/SEQ 20. PAGE 105 A2157
NAT/G STRUCT INT/LAW

S62
NANES A.,"DISARMAMENT: THE LAST SEVEN YEARS." COM EUR+WWI USA+45 USSR INT/ORG FORCES TOP/EX CREATE LEGIT NUC/PWR DISPL ORD/FREE...CONCPT TIME/SEQ CON/ANAL 20. PAGE 107 A2195
DELIB/GP RIGID/FLEX ARMS/CONT

S62
PIQUEMAL M.,"LES PROBLEMES DES UNIONS D'ETATS EN AFRIQUE NOIRE." FRANCE SOCIETY INT/ORG NAT/G DELIB/GP PLAN LEGIT ADMIN COLONIAL ROUTINE ATTIT ORD/FREE PWR...GEOG METH/CNCPT 20. PAGE 116 A2382
AFR ECO/UNDEV REGION

S62
SCHACHTER O.,"DAG HAMMARSKJOLD AND THE RELATION OF LAW TO POLITICS." FUT WOR+45 INT/ORG CONSULT PLAN TEC/DEV BAL/PWR DIPLOM LEGIT ATTIT PERCEPT ORD/FREE ...POLICY JURID CONCPT OBS TESTS STERTYP GEN/LAWS 20 HAMMARSK/D. PAGE 128 A2616
ACT/RES ADJUD

S62
SPRINGER H.W.,"FEDERATION IN THE CARIBBEAN: AN ATTEMPT THAT FAILED." L/A+17C ECO/UNDEV INT/ORG POL/PAR PROVS LEGIS CREATE PLAN LEGIT ADMIN FEDERAL ATTIT DRIVE PERSON ORD/FREE PWR...POLICY GEOG PSY CONCPT OBS CARIBBEAN CMN/WLTH 20. PAGE 136 A2791
VOL/ASSN NAT/G REGION

S62
VIGNES D.,"L'AUTORITE DES TRAITES INTERNATIONAUX EN DROIT INTERNE." EUR+WWI UNIV LAW CONSTN INTELL NAT/G POL/PAR DIPLOM ATTIT PERCEPT ALL/VALS ...POLICY INT/LAW JURID CONCPT TIME/SEQ 20 TREATY. PAGE 159 A3233
STRUCT LEGIT FRANCE

C62
BACON F.,"OF THE TRUE GREATNESS OF KINGDOMS AND ESTATES" (1612) IN F. BACON, ESSAYS." ELITES FORCES DOMIN EDU/PROP LEGIT...POLICY GEN/LAWS 16/17 TREATY. PAGE 10 A0200
WAR PWR DIPLOM CONSTN

B63
BOWETT D.W.,THE LAW OF INTERNATIONAL INSTITUTIONS. WOR+45 WOR-45 CONSTN DELIB/GP EX/STRUC JUDGE EDU/PROP LEGIT CT/SYS EXEC ROUTINE RIGID/FLEX ORD/FREE PWR...JURID CONCPT ORG/CHARTS GEN/METH LEAGUE/NAT OAS OEEC 20 UN. PAGE 17 A0354
INT/ORG ADJUD DIPLOM

B63
BURNS A.L.,PEACE-KEEPING BY U.N.FORCES - FROM SUEZ TO THE CONGO. AFR FUT ISLAM ISRAEL USSR WOR+45 NAT/G DELIB/GP BAL/PWR DOMIN LEGIT EXEC COERCE PEACE ATTIT PWR RESPECT SOVEREIGN...CONCPT UN 20. PAGE 22 A0441
INT/ORG FORCES ORD/FREE

B63
CREMEANS C.,THE ARABS AND THE WORLD: NASSER'S ARAB NATIONALIST POLICY. FUT ISLAM UAR USA+45 SOCIETY STRATA NAT/G POL/PAR PLAN DIPLOM EDU/PROP LEGIT DRIVE ALL/VALS...INT TIME/SEQ CHARTS 20 NASSER/G. PAGE 33 A0662
TOP/EX ATTIT REGION NAT/LISM

B63
FALK R.A.,LAW, MORALITY, AND WAR IN THE CONTEMPORARY WORLD. WOR+45 LAW INT/ORG EX/STRUC FORCES EDU/PROP LEGIT DETER NUC/PWR MORAL ORD/FREE ...JURID TOT/POP 20. PAGE 43 A0888
ADJUD ARMS/CONT PEACE INT/LAW

B63
HENDERSON W.,SOUTHEAST ASIA: PROBLEMS OF UNITED STATES POLICY. COM S/ASIA CULTURE STRATA ECO/UNDEV INT/ORG DELIB/GP ACT/RES ECO/TAC DOMIN EDU/PROP LEGIT COERCE ATTIT ALL/VALS...STAT TIME/SEQ ANTHOL VAL/FREE 20. PAGE 64 A1313
ASIA USA+45 DIPLOM

B63
KHADDURI M.,MODERN LIBYA: A STUDY IN POLITICAL DEVELOPMENT. EUR+WWI ISLAM LIBYA ELITES INT/ORG POL/PAR FORCES DIPLOM FOR/AID DOMIN EDU/PROP LEGIT NAT/LISM DRIVE RIGID/FLEX SKILL...CONCPT TIME/SEQ TREND 20. PAGE 78 A1606
NAT/G STRUCT

B63
LERCHE C.O. JR.,CONCEPTS OF INTERNATIONAL POLITICS. WOR+45 WOR-45 LAW DELIB/GP EX/STRUC TEC/DEV ECO/TAC INT/TRADE LEGIT ROUTINE COERCE ATTIT ORD/FREE PWR RESPECT...STERTYP GEN/LAWS VAL/FREE. PAGE 87 A1782
INT/ORG WAR

B63
MAYNE R.,THE COMMUNITY OF EUROPE. UK CONSTN NAT/G CONSULT DELIB/GP CREATE PLAN ECO/TAC LEGIT ADMIN ROUTINE ORD/FREE PWR WEALTH...CONCPT TIME/SEQ EEC EURATOM 20. PAGE 97 A1985
EUR+WWI INT/ORG REGION

B63
QUAISON-SACKEY A.,AFRICA UNBOUND: REFLECTIONS OF AN AFRICAN STATESMAN. ISLAM CULTURE INTELL INT/ORG POL/PAR TOP/EX DOMIN EDU/PROP LEGIT ATTIT PERSON ...CONCPT OBS TIME/SEQ CHARTS STERTYP 20 UN. PAGE 118 A2423
AFR BIOG

B63
STEVENSON A.E.,LOOKING OUTWARD: YEARS OF CRISIS AT THE UNITED NATIONS. COM CUBA USA+45 WOR+45 SOCIETY NAT/G EX/STRUC ACT/RES LEGIT COLONIAL ATTIT PERSON SUPEGO ALL/VALS...POLICY HUM UN COLD/WAR CONGO 20. PAGE 138 A2823
INT/ORG CONCPT ARMS/CONT

B63
STROMBERG R.N.,COLLECTIVE SECURITY AND AMERICAN FOREIGN POLICY FROM THE LEAGUE OF NATIONS TO NATO. USA+45 USA-45 WOR-45 INT/ORG VOL/ASSN EX/STRUC FORCES LEGIT ROUTINE DRIVE...CONCPT TREND UN LEAGUE/NAT 20 NATO. PAGE 139 A2851
ORD/FREE TIME/SEQ DIPLOM

B63
VOSS E.H.,NUCLEAR AMBUSH: THE TEST-BAN TRAP. WOR+45 COM/IND INT/ORG NAT/G DELIB/GP FORCES LEGIS TOP/EX ACT/RES DOMIN EDU/PROP LEGIT ROUTINE COERCE ATTIT PERCEPT RIGID/FLEX HEALTH MORAL ORD/FREE PWR. PAGE 160 A3255
TEC/DEV HIST/WRIT ARMS/CONT NUC/PWR

B63
WESTERFIELD H.,THE INSTRUMENTS OF AMERICA'S FOREIGN POLICY. WOR+45 ECO/DEV NAT/G CONSULT EX/STRUC LEGIS BAL/PWR FOR/AID INT/TRADE DOMIN EDU/PROP LEGIT ATTIT KNOWL ORD/FREE PWR WEALTH...OBS COLD/WAR TOT/POP VAL/FREE. PAGE 163 A3322
USA+45 INT/ORG DIPLOM

L63
LISSITZYN O.J.,"INTERNATIONAL LAW IN A DIVIDED WORLD." FUT WOR+45 CONSTN CULTURE ECO/DEV ECO/UNDEV DIST/IND NAT/G FORCES ECO/TAC LEGIT ADJUD ADMIN COERCE ATTIT HEALTH MORAL ORD/FREE PWR RESPECT WEALTH VAL/FREE. PAGE 90 A1841
INT/ORG LAW

L63
RUSSETT B.M.,"TOWARD A MODEL OF COMPETITIVE INTERNATIONAL POLITICS." USA+45 WOR+45 INT/ORG NAT/G POL/PAR VOL/ASSN LEGIS BAL/PWR DIPLOM LEGIT PWR...CONCPT CONT/OBS STERTYP GEN/LAWS TOT/POP COLD/WAR 20 UN. PAGE 126 A2579
ATTIT EDU/PROP

L63
SCHELLING T.C.,"STRATEGIC PROBLEMS OF AN INTERNATIONAL ARMED FORCE." WOR+45 ECO/DEV INT/ORG NAT/G PLAN BAL/PWR LEGIT ARMS/CONT COERCE DETER ORD/FREE PWR...POLICY CONCPT COLD/WAR 20. PAGE 128 A2624
CREATE FORCES

L63
WILCOX F.O.,"THE ATLANTIC COMMUNITY: PROGRESS AND PROSPECTS." EUR+WWI FUT USA+45 WOR+45 SOCIETY CREATE ECO/TAC EDU/PROP LEGIT REGION ATTIT ALL/VALS ...POLICY ANTHOL VAL/FREE 20. PAGE 164 A3346
INT/ORG ACT/RES

L63
ZARTMAN I.W.,"THE SAHARA--BRIDGE OR BARRIER." ISLAM CULTURE SOCIETY NAT/G DELIB/GP DOMIN EDU/PROP LEGIT ATTIT...HIST/WRIT TIME/SEQ CHARTS TOT/POP VAL/FREE 20. PAGE 169 A3445
INT/ORG PWR NAT/LISM

S63
ALEXANDER R.,"LATIN AMERICA AND THE COMMUNIST BLOC." ASIA COM CUBA L/A+17C USA+45 USSR NAT/G VOL/ASSN TEC/DEV FOR/AID LEGIT PWR WEALTH COLD/WAR 20. PAGE 6 A0112
ECO/UNDEV RECORD

S63
ALPHAND H.,"FRANCE AND HER ALLIES." EUR+WWI UK USA+45 ECO/DEV INT/ORG NAT/G VOL/ASSN FORCES TOP/EX DIPLOM ECO/TAC LEGIT ATTIT DRIVE ORD/FREE PWR WEALTH...STAT EEC TOT/POP 20. PAGE 6 A0130
ACT/RES FRANCE

S63
CAHIER P.,"LE DROIT INTERNE DES ORGANISATIONS INTERNATIONALES." UNIV CONSTN SOCIETY ECO/DEV R+D NAT/G TOP/EX LEGIT ATTIT PERCEPT...TIME/SEQ 19/20. PAGE 23 A0464
INT/ORG JURID DIPLOM INT/LAW

S63
FRIEDMANN W.G.,"THE USES OF 'GENERAL PRINCIPLES' IN THE DEVELOPMENT OF INTERNATIONAL LAW." WOR+45 NAT/G DIPLOM INT/TRADE LEGIT ROUTINE RIGID/FLEX ORD/FREE ...JURID CONCPT STERTYP GEN/METH 20. PAGE 49 A1005
LAW INT/LAW INT/ORG

S63
HARNETTY P.,"CANADA, SOUTH AFRICA AND THE COMMONWEALTH." CANADA SOUTH/AFR LAW INT/ORG VOL/ASSN DELIB/GP LEGIS TOP/EX ECO/TAC LEGIT DRIVE MORAL...CONCPT CMN/WLTH 20. PAGE 62 A1263
AFR ATTIT

S63
HUMPHREY H.H.,"REGIONAL ARMS CONTROL AGREEMENTS." WOR+45 FORCES PLAN LEGIT COERCE ATTIT HEALTH ORD/FREE...HUM METH/CNCPT MYTH OBS INT TREND TOT/POP 20. PAGE 69 A1416
L/A+17C INT/ORG ARMS/CONT REGION

S63
MANGONE G.,"THE UNITED NATIONS AND UNITED STATES FOREIGN POLICY." USA+45 WOR+45 ECO/UNDEV NAT/G DIPLOM LEGIT ROUTINE ATTIT DRIVE...TIME/SEQ UN COLD/WAR 20. PAGE 94 A1922
INT/ORG ECO/TAC FOR/AID

S63
MAZRUI A.A.,"ON THE CONCEPT 'WE ARE ALL AFRICANS'." AFR CULTURE KIN LOC/G NAT/G DOMIN EDU/PROP LEGIT ATTIT PERCEPT PERSON KNOWL ORD/FREE...TIME/SEQ TOT/POP 20. PAGE 97 A1986
PROVS INT/ORG NAT/LISM

S63
MCDOUGAL M.S.,"THE SOVIET-CUBAN QUARANTINE AND SELF-DEFENSE." CUBA USA+45 USSR WOR+45 INT/ORG NAT/G BAL/PWR NUC/PWR ATTIT...JURID CONCPT. PAGE 98 A2008
ORD/FREE LEGIT SOVEREIGN

S63
MODELSKI G.,"STUDY OF ALLIANCES." WOR+45 WOR-45 INT/ORG NAT/G FORCES LEGIT ADMIN CHOOSE ALL/VALS PWR SKILL...INT/LAW CONCPT GEN/LAWS 20 TREATY. PAGE 102 A2099
VOL/ASSN CON/ANAL DIPLOM

S63
MORGENTHAU H.J.,"THE POLITICAL CONDITIONS FOR AN INTERNATIONAL POLICE FORCE." FUT WOR+45 CREATE LEGIT ADMIN PEACE ORD/FREE 20. PAGE 104 A2141
INT/ORG FORCES ARMS/CONT DETER

S63
MURRAY J.N.,"UNITED NATIONS PEACE-KEEPING AND PROBLEMS OF POLITICAL CONTROL." FUT WOR+45 CONSTN DELIB/GP FORCES TOP/EX ACT/RES CREATE LEGIT PEACE PWR...METH/CNCPT CONGO UN 20. PAGE 106 A2182
INT/ORG ORD/FREE

S63
NEIDLE A.F.,"PEACE KEEPING AND DISARMAMENT." COM USA+45 USSR WOR+45 INT/ORG NAT/G BAL/PWR EDU/PROP LEGIT ATTIT PWR 20. PAGE 108 A2214
DELIB/GP ACT/RES ARMS/CONT PEACE

S63
NICHOLAS H.G.,"UN PEACE FORCES AND THE CHANGING GLOBE: THE LESSONS OF SUEZ AND CONGO." FUT WOR+45 CONSTN INT/ORG CONSULT DELIB/GP TOP/EX CREATE DIPLOM DOMIN LEGIT COERCE WAR PERSON RIGID/FLEX PWR UN SUEZ CONGO UNEF 20. PAGE 109 A2229
ACT/RES FORCES

S63
NOGEE J.L.,"PROPOGANDA AND NEGOTIATION: THE CASE OF THE TEN NATION DISARMAMENT COMMITTEE." COM EUR+WWI USA+45 VOL/ASSN DELIB/GP FORCES DIPLOM DOMIN LEGIT PWR...METH/CNCPT STERTYP COLD/WAR VAL/FREE 20. PAGE 110 A2248
INT/ORG EDU/PROP ARMS/CONT

S63
TALLON D.,"L'ETUDE DU DROIT COMPARE COMME MOYEN DE RECHERCHER LES MATIERES SUSCEPTIBLES D'UNIFICATION INTERNATIONALE." WOR+45 LAW SOCIETY VOL/ASSN CONSULT LEGIT CT/SYS RIGID/FLEX KNOWL 20. PAGE 141 A2884
INT/ORG JURID INT/LAW

S63
WEISSBERG G.,"MAPS AS EVIDENCE IN INTERNATIONAL BOUNDARY DISPUTES: A REAPPRAISAL." CHINA/COM EUR+WWI INDIA MOD/EUR S/ASIA INT/ORG NAT/G LEGIT PERCEPT...JURID CHARTS 20. PAGE 163 A3311
LAW GEOG SOVEREIGN

S63
WENGLER W.,"LES CONFLITS DE LOIS ET LE PRINCIPE D'EGALITE." UNIV LAW SOCIETY ACT/RES LEGIT ATTIT PERCEPT 20. PAGE 163 A3318
JURID CONCPT INT/LAW

B64
CLAUDE I.,SWORDS INTO PLOWSHARES. FUT WOR+45 WOR-45 DELIB/GP EX/STRUC LEGIT ATTIT ORD/FREE...CONCPT TIME/SEQ TREND UN TOT/POP 20. PAGE 27 A0547
INT/ORG STRUCT

B64
COHEN M.,LAW AND POLITICS IN SPACE: SPECIFIC AND URGENT PROBLEMS IN THE LAW OF OUTER SPACE. CHINA/COM COM USA+45 USSR WOR+45 COM/IND INT/ORG NAT/G LEGIT NUC/PWR ATTIT BIO/SOC...JURID CONCPT CONGRESS 20 STALIN/J. PAGE 28 A0561
DELIB/GP LAW INT/LAW SPACE

B64
CZERNIN F.,VERSAILLES - 1919. EUR+WWI USA-45 FACE/GP POL/PAR VOL/ASSN DELIB/GP TOP/EX CREATE BAL/PWR DIPLOM LEGIT NAT/LISM PEACE ATTIT RIGID/FLEX ORD/FREE PWR...CON/ANAL LEAGUE/NAT 20 VERSAILLES. PAGE 33 A0671
INT/ORG STRUCT

B64
DE SMITH S.A.,THE NEW COMMONWEALTH AND ITS CONSTITUTIONS. AFR CYPRUS PAKISTAN S/ASIA INT/ORG NAT/G LEGIS LEGIT RIGID/FLEX PWR...CONCPT TIME/SEQ CMN/WLTH 20. PAGE 35 A0713
EX/STRUC CONSTN SOVEREIGN

B64
ETZIONI A.,WINNING WITHOUT WAR. FUT MOD/EUR USA+45 WOR+45 ECO/DEV ECO/UNDEV INT/ORG NAT/G FORCES TOP/EX PLAN TEC/DEV ECO/TAC DOMIN EDU/PROP LEGIT COERCE CHOOSE ATTIT MORAL ORD/FREE RESPECT WEALTH MAJORIT. PAGE 43 A0871
PWR TREND DIPLOM USSR

B64
FALK R.A.,THE ROLE OF DOMESTIC COURTS IN THE INTERNATIONAL LEGAL ORDER. FUT WOR+45 INT/ORG NAT/G JUDGE EDU/PROP LEGIT CT/SYS...POLICY RELATIV JURID CONCPT GEN/LAWS 20. PAGE 43 A0889
LAW INT/LAW

B64
FISHER R.,INTERNATIONAL CONFLICT AND BEHAVIORAL SCIENCE: THE CRAIGVILLE PAPERS. COM FUT USA+45 WOR+45 NAT/G DELIB/GP EX/STRUC FORCES ECO/TAC DOMIN EDU/PROP LEGIT COERCE ATTIT PERCEPT ORD/FREE PWR RESPECT...PSY SOC VAL/FREE. PAGE 46 A0940
INT/ORG PLAN DIPLOM

B64
FRIEDMANN W.G.,THE CHANGING STRUCTURE OF INTERNATIONAL LAW. WOR+45 INT/ORG NAT/G PROVS LEGIT ORD/FREE PWR...JURID CONCPT GEN/LAWS TOT/POP UN 20. PAGE 49 A1006
ADJUD TREND INT/LAW

B64
JACOB P.E.,THE INTEGRATION OF POLITICAL COMMUNITIES. USA+45 WOR+45 CULTURE LOC/G MUNIC NAT/G CREATE PLAN LEGIT REGION COERCE ALL/VALS ...POLICY GEOG PSY SOC TREND HYPO/EXP GEN/LAWS VAL/FREE 20. PAGE 72 A1483
INT/ORG METH/CNCPT SIMUL STAT

B64
JANOWITZ M.,THE MILITARY IN THE POLITICAL DEVELOPMENT OF NEW NATIONS: AN ESSAY IN COMPARATIVE ANALYSIS. AFR ASIA ISLAM L/A+17C S/ASIA USA+45 ECO/UNDEV INT/ORG NAT/G POL/PAR DELIB/GP PLAN ECO/TAC DOMIN LEGIT COERCE ATTIT DRIVE RESPECT ...SOC CONCPT CENSUS VAL/FREE. PAGE 73 A1495
FORCES PWR

B64
PLISCHKE E.,SYSTEMS OF INTEGRATING THE INTERNATIONAL COMMUNITY. WOR+45 NAT/G VOL/ASSN ECO/TAC LEGIT PWR WEALTH...TIME/SEQ ANTHOL UN TOT/POP 20. PAGE 116 A2391
INT/ORG EX/STRUC REGION

B64
STANGER R.J.,ESSAYS ON INTERVENTION. PLAN PROB/SOLV BAL/PWR ADJUD COERCE WAR ROLE PWR...INT/LAW CONCPT 20 UN INTERVENT. PAGE 137 A2803
SOVEREIGN DIPLOM POLICY LEGIT

B64
STOESSINGER J.G.,FINANCING THE UNITED NATIONS SYSTEM. FUT WOR+45 CONSTN NAT/G VOL/ASSN DELIB/GP EX/STRUC ECO/TAC LEGIT CT/SYS PWR WEALTH...STAT TIME/SEQ TREND CHARTS VAL/FREE. PAGE 138 A2830
FINAN INT/ORG

B64
UN PUB. INFORM. ORGAN.,EVERY MAN'S UNITED NATIONS. UNIV WOR+45 CONSTN CULTURE SOCIETY ECO/DEV ECO/UNDEV NAT/G ACT/RES PLAN ECO/TAC INT/TRADE EDU/PROP LEGIT PEACE ATTIT ALL/VALS...POLICY HUM INT/LAW CONCPT CHARTS UN TOT/POP 20. PAGE 147 A3004
INT/ORG ROUTINE

B64
WAINHOUSE D.W.,REMNANTS OF EMPIRE: THE UNITED NATIONS AND THE END OF COLONIALISM. FUT PORTUGAL WOR+45 NAT/G CONSULT DOMIN LEGIT ADMIN ROUTINE ATTIT ORD/FREE...POLICY JURID RECORD INT TIME/SEQ UN CMN/WLTH 20. PAGE 160 A3260
INT/ORG TREND COLONIAL

B64
WARREN S.,THE PRESIDENT AS WORLD LEADER. USA+45 WOR+45 ELITES COM/IND INT/ORG NAT/G VOL/ASSN CHIEF EX/STRUC LEGIT COERCE ATTIT PERSON RIGID/FLEX...INT TIME/SEQ COLD/WAR 20 ROOSEVLT/F TRUMAN/HS EISNHWR/DD KENNEDY/JF. PAGE 161 A3286
TOP/EX PWR DIPLOM

L64
BARROS J.,"THE GREEK-BULGARIAN INCIDENT OF 1925: THE LEAGUE OF NATIONS AND THE GREAT POWERS." BULGARIA EUR+WWI NAT/G FORCES ECO/TAC EDU/PROP LEGIT ROUTINE COERCE WAR PEACE DRIVE PWR...JURID CONCPT METH/CNCPT GEN/LAWS GEN/METH LEAGUE/NAT TOT/POP 20. PAGE 11 A0228
INT/ORG ORD/FREE DIPLOM

L64
CARNEGIE ENDOWMENT INT. PEACE,"POLITICAL QUESTIONS (ISSUES BEFORE THE NINETEENTH GENERAL ASSEMBLY)." SPACE WOR+45 CONSTN FINAN NAT/G CONSULT DELIB/GP FORCES LEGIS TEC/DEV EDU/PROP LEGIT ARMS/CONT COERCE NUC/PWR ATTIT ALL/VALS...CONCPT OBS UN COLD/WAR 20. PAGE 24 A0490
INT/ORG PEACE

L64
CLAUDE I.,"THE OAS, THE UN, AND THE UNITED STATES." L/A+17C USA+45 CONSTN NAT/G DELIB/GP DOMIN EDU/PROP LEGIT REGION COERCE ORD/FREE PWR...TIME/SEQ TREND STERTYP OAS UN 20. PAGE 27 A0546
INT/ORG POLICY

L64
CURTIS G.L.,"THE UNITED NATIONS OBSERVER GROUP IN LEBANON." ISLAM USA+45 NAT/G CONSULT ACT/RES PLAN BAL/PWR LEGIT ATTIT KNOWL...HIST/WRIT UN 20 UN. PAGE 33 A0669
INT/ORG FORCES DIPLOM LEBANON

L64
HERZ J.H.,"THE RELEVANCY AND IRRELEVANCY OF APPEASEMENT." WOR+45 INT/ORG CONSULT TOP/EX LEGIT ATTIT SUPEGO ORD/FREE...POLICY SOC GEN/LAWS 20. PAGE 64 A1320
ACT/RES RIGID/FLEX

L64
HOFFMANN S.,"EUROPE'S IDENTITY CRISIS: BETWEEN THE PAST AND AMERICA." EUR+WWI FUT USA+45 INT/ORG NAT/G LEGIT RIGID/FLEX ALL/VALS...RELATIV TOT/POP 20. PAGE 66 A1358
COERCE POLICY

L64
MANZER R.A.,"THE UNITED NATIONS SPECIAL FUND."
FINAN

WOR+45 CONSTN ECO/UNDEV NAT/G TOP/EX LEGIT WEALTH ...CHARTS UN 20. PAGE 94 A1936
INT/ORG

L64
MILLIS W.,"THE DEMILITARIZED WORLD." COM USA+45 USSR WOR+45 CONSTN NAT/G EX/STRUC PLAN LEGIT ATTIT DRIVE...CONCPT TIME/SEQ STERTYP TOT/POP COLD/WAR 20. PAGE 102 A2085
FUT INT/ORG BAL/PWR PEACE

L64
POUNDS N.J.G.,"THE POLITICS OF PARTITION." AFR ASIA COM EUR+WWI FUT ISLAM S/ASIA USA-45 LAW ECO/DEV ECO/UNDEV AGRI INDUS INT/ORG POL/PAR PROVS SECT FORCES TOP/EX EDU/PROP LEGIT ATTIT MORAL ORD/FREE PWR RESPECT WEALTH. PAGE 117 A2402
NAT/G NAT/LISM

L64
SYMONDS R.,"REFLECTIONS IN LOCALISATION." AFR S/ASIA UK STRATA INT/ORG NAT/G SCHOOL EDU/PROP LEGIT KNOWL ORD/FREE PWR RESPECT CMN/WLTH 20. PAGE 140 A2874
ADMIN MGT COLONIAL

L64
WARD C.,"THE 'NEW MYTHS' AND 'OLD REALITIES' OF NUCLEAR WAR." COM FUT USA+45 USSR WOR+45 INT/ORG NAT/G DOMIN LEGIT EXEC ATTIT PERCEPT ALL/VALS ...POLICY RELATIV PSY MYTH TREND 20. PAGE 161 A3280
FORCES COERCE ARMS/CONT NUC/PWR

L64
WORLD PEACE FOUNDATION,"INTERNATIONAL ORGANIZATIONS: SUMMARY OF ACTIVITIES." INDIA PAKISTAN TURKEY WOR+45 CONSTN CONSULT EX/STRUC ECO/TAC EDU/PROP LEGIT ORD/FREE...JURID SOC UN 20 CYPRESS. PAGE 167 A3397
INT/ORG ROUTINE

S64
BUCHAN A.,"THE MULTILATERAL FORCE." EUR+WWI FUT USA+45 NAT/G LEGIT PWR SKILL...CONCPT OEEC MLF 20. PAGE 21 A0422
INT/ORG FORCES

S64
COHEN M.,"BASIC PRINCIPLES OF INTERNATIONAL LAW." UNIV WOR+45 WOR-45 BAL/PWR LEGIT ADJUD WAR ATTIT MORAL ORD/FREE PWR...JURID CONCPT MYTH TOT/POP 20. PAGE 27 A0560
INT/ORG INT/LAW

S64
DERWINSKI E.J.,"THE COST OF THE INTERNATIONAL COFFEE AGREEMENT." L/A+17C USA+45 WOR+45 ECO/UNDEV NAT/G VOL/ASSN LEGIS DIPLOM ECO/TAC FOR/AID LEGIT ATTIT...TIME/SEQ CONGRESS 20 TREATY. PAGE 36 A0732
MARKET DELIB/GP INT/TRADE

S64
DRAKE S.T.C.,"DEMOCRACY ON TRIAL IN AFRICA." EUR+WWI FUT USA+45 ECO/UNDEV INT/ORG NAT/G POL/PAR TOP/EX EDU/PROP LEGIT ATTIT ALL/VALS...POLICY TREND GEN/LAWS VAL/FREE 20. PAGE 38 A0785
AFR STERTYP

S64
GARDNER R.N.,"THE SOVIET UNION AND THE UNITED NATIONS." WOR+45 FINAN POL/PAR VOL/ASSN FORCES ECO/TAC DOMIN EDU/PROP LEGIT ADJUD ADMIN ARMS/CONT COERCE ATTIT ALL/VALS...POLICY MAJORIT CONCPT OBS TIME/SEQ TREND STERTYP UN. PAGE 51 A1046
COM INT/ORG USSR

S64
GINSBURGS G.,"WARS OF NATIONAL LIBERATION - THE SOVIET THESIS." COM USSR WOR+45 WOR-45 LAW CULTURE INT/ORG DIPLOM LEGIT COLONIAL GUERRILLA WAR NAT/LISM ATTIT PERSON MORAL PWR...JURID OBS TREND MARX/KARL 20. PAGE 53 A1075
COERCE CONCPT INT/LAW REV

S64
HICKEY D.,"THE PHILOSOPHICAL ARGUMENT FOR WORLD GOVERNMENT." WOR+45 SOCIETY ACT/RES PLAN LEGIT ADJUD PEACE PERCEPT PERSON ORD/FREE...HUM JURID PHIL/SCI METH/CNCPT CON/ANAL STERTYP GEN/LAWS TOT/POP 20. PAGE 65 A1327
FUT INT/ORG

S64
HOVET T. JR.,"THE ROLE OF AFRICA IN THE UNITED NATIONS." FUT WOR+45 NAT/G DELIB/GP DOMIN EDU/PROP LEGIT ORD/FREE PWR RESPECT SKILL...OBS TIME/SEQ TREND VAL/FREE UN 20. PAGE 68 A1398
AFR INT/ORG DIPLOM

S64
JACK H.,"NONALIGNMENT AND A TEST BAN AGREEMENT: THE ROLE OF THE NON-ALIGNED STATES." WOR+45 INT/ORG CONSULT DOMIN EDU/PROP LEGIT CHOOSE PEACE ATTIT DRIVE KNOWL ORD/FREE...TREND CHARTS GEN/LAWS UN VAL/FREE 20. PAGE 72 A1471
PWR CONCPT NUC/PWR

S64
JORDAN A.,"POLITICAL COMMUNICATION: THE THIRD DIMENSION OF STRATEGY." USA+45 WOR+45 INT/ORG NAT/G CONSULT FORCES PLAN LEGIT EXEC PERCEPT ALL/VALS ...POLICY RELATIV PSY NEW/IDEA AUD/VIS EXHIBIT TOT/POP 20. PAGE 75 A1534
EDU/PROP RIGID/FLEX ATTIT

S64
KHAN M.Z.,"THE PRESIDENT OF THE GENERAL ASSEMBLY." WOR+45 CONSTN DELIB/GP EDU/PROP LEGIT ROUTINE PWR RESPECT SKILL...DECISION SOC BIOG TREND UN 20. PAGE 78 A1609
INT/ORG TOP/EX

S64
KISSINGER H.A.,"COALITION DIPLOMACY IN A NUCLEAR AGE." COM EUR+WWI USA+45 WOR+45 INT/ORG NAT/G FORCES ACT/RES DOMIN LEGIT COERCE PERCEPT ALL/VALS ...POLICY TOT/POP 20. PAGE 80 A1644
CONSULT ATTIT DIPLOM NUC/PWR

S64
KUNZ J.,"THE CHANGING SCIENCE OF INTERNATIONAL LAW." FUT WOR+45 WOR-45 INT/ORG LEGIT ORD/FREE ...JURID TIME/SEQ GEN/LAWS 20. PAGE 83 A1696
ADJUD CONCPT INT/LAW

S64
LIPSON L.,"PEACEFUL COEXISTENCE." COM USSR WOR+45 LAW INT/ORG DIPLOM LEGIT ADJUD ORD/FREE...CONCPT OBS TREND GEN/LAWS VAL/FREE COLD/WAR 20. PAGE 90 A1834
ATTIT JURID INT/LAW PEACE

S64
SAAB H.,"THE ARAB SEARCH FOR A FEDERAL UNION." SOCIETY INT/ORG NAT/G DELIB/GP FORCES ACT/RES TEC/DEV ECO/TAC DOMIN LEGIT REGION ROUTINE ATTIT DRIVE RIGID/FLEX ALL/VALS...SOC CONCPT NEW/IDEA TIME/SEQ TREND. PAGE 126 A2580
ISLAM PLAN

S64
SINGH N.,"THE CONTEMPORARY PRACTICE OF INDIA IN THE FIELD OF INTERNATIONAL LAW." INDIA S/ASIA INT/ORG NAT/G DOMIN EDU/PROP LEGIT KNOWL...CONCPT TOT/POP 20. PAGE 133 A2734
LAW ATTIT DIPLOM INT/LAW

S64
SKUBISZEWSKI K.,"FORMS OF PARTICIPATION OF INTERNATIONAL ORGANIZATION IN THE LAW MAKING PROCESS." FUT WOR+45 NAT/G DELIB/GP DOMIN LEGIT KNOWL PWR...JURID TREND 20. PAGE 134 A2740
INT/ORG LAW INT/LAW

S64
TAUBENFELD R.K.,"INDEPENDENT REVENUE FOR THE UNITED NATIONS." WOR+45 SOCIETY STRUCT INDUS NAT/G CONSULT ACT/RES PLAN ECO/TAC LEGIT WEALTH...DECISION CON/ANAL GEN/METH UN 20. PAGE 142 A2896
INT/ORG FINAN

S64
TOUVAL S.,"THE SOMALI REPUBLIC." AFR ISLAM SOMALIA FAM KIN NAT/G CREATE FOR/AID LEGIT ATTIT ALL/VALS ...RECORD TREND 20. PAGE 144 A2954
ECO/UNDEV RIGID/FLEX

S64
WASKOW A.I.,"NEW ROADS TO A WORLD WITHOUT WAR." FUT WOR+45 CULTURE INTELL SOCIETY NAT/G DOMIN LEGIT EXEC COERCE PEACE ATTIT DISPL PERCEPT RIGID/FLEX ALL/VALS...POLICY RELATIV SOC NEW/IDEA 20. PAGE 161 A3288
INT/ORG FORCES

B65
VONGLAHN G.,LAW AMONG NATIONS: AN INTRODUCTION TO PUBLIC INTERNATIONAL LAW. UNIV WOR+45 LAW INT/ORG NAT/G LEGIT EXEC RIGID/FLEX...CONCPT TIME/SEQ GEN/LAWS UN TOT/POP 20. PAGE 160 A3253
CONSTN JURID INT/LAW

L65
KAPLAN M.A.,"OLD REALITIES AND NEW MYTHS." USA+45 WOR+45 INT/ORG NAT/G TOP/EX ACT/RES BAL/PWR ECO/TAC EDU/PROP LEGIT RIGID/FLEX ALL/VALS...RECORD COLD/WAR 20. PAGE 76 A1564
ATTIT MYTH DIPLOM

L65
RUBIN A.P.,"UNITED STATES CONTEMPORARY PRACTICE RELATING TO INTERNATIONAL LAW." USA+45 WOR+45 CONSTN INT/ORG NAT/G DELIB/GP EX/STRUC DIPLOM DOMIN CT/SYS ROUTINE ORD/FREE...CONCPT COLD/WAR 20. PAGE 125 A2558
LAW LEGIT INT/LAW

S65
AMRAM P.W.,"REPORT ON THE TENTH SESSION OF THE HAGUE CONFERENCE ON PRIVATE INTERNATIONAL LAW." USA+45 WOR+45 INT/ORG CREATE LEGIT ADJUD ALL/VALS ...JURID CONCPT METH/CNCPT OBS GEN/METH 20. PAGE 8 A0155
VOL/ASSN DELIB/GP INT/LAW

S65
FALK R.A.,"INTERNATIONAL LEGAL ORDER." USA+45 INTELL FACE/GP INT/ORG LEGIT KNOWL...CONCPT METH/CNCPT STYLE RECORD GEN/METH 20. PAGE 44 A0890
ATTIT GEN/LAWS INT/LAW

S65
GROSS L.,"PROBLEMS OF INTERNATIONAL ADJUDICATION AND COMPLIANCE WITH INTERNATIONAL LAW: SOME SIMPLE SOLUTIONS." WOR+45 SOCIETY NAT/G DOMIN LEGIT ADJUD CT/SYS RIGID/FLEX HEALTH PWR...JURID NEW/IDEA COLD/WAR 20. PAGE 57 A1177
LAW METH/CNCPT INT/LAW

S65
MAC CHESNEY B.,"SOME COMMENTS ON THE 'QUARANTINE' OF CUBA." USA+45 WOR+45 NAT/G BAL/PWR DIPLOM LEGIT ROUTINE ATTIT ORD/FREE...JURID METH/CNCPT 20. PAGE 92 A1883
INT/ORG LAW CUBA USSR

S65
STEIN E.,"TOWARD SUPREMACY OF TREATY-CONSTITUTION BY JUDICIAL FIAT: ON THE MARGIN OF THE COSTA CASE." EUR+WWI ITALY WOR+45 INT/ORG NAT/G LEGIT REGION NAT/LISM PWR...JURID CONCPT TREND TOT/POP VAL/FREE 20. PAGE 138 A2816
ADJUD CONSTN SOVEREIGN INT/LAW

B66
DRACHOVITCH M.M.,THE COMINTERN HISTORICAL HIGHLIGHTS. USSR INT/ORG EX/STRUC LEGIT LEAD GUERRILLA...ANTHOL 20 COMINTERN LENIN/VI. PAGE 38 A0784
DIPLOM REV MARXISM PERSON

B66
WEINSTEIN F.B.,VIETNAM'S UNHELD ELECTIONS: THE FAILURE TO CARRY OUT THE 1956 REUNIFICATION ELECTIONS... (MONOGRAPH). VIETNAM/S VIETNAM/N LEGIT CONFER ADJUD WAR PEACE 20 TREATY GENEVA/CON UNIFICA. PAGE 162 A3306
AGREE NAT/G CHOOSE DIPLOM

S66
GREEN L.C.,"RHODESIAN OIL: BOOTLEGGERS OR PIRATES?" AFR RHODESIA UK WOR+45 INT/ORG NAT/G DIPLOM LEGIT COLONIAL SOVEREIGN 20 UN OAU. PAGE 55 A1139
INT/TRADE SANCTION INT/LAW POLICY

S67
KYLE K.,"BACKGROUND TO THE CRISIS" ISLAM ISRAEL UAR UK USSR NAT/G PROB/SOLV LEGIT CONTROL REGION STRANGE MORAL 20 JEWS. PAGE 83 A1698 DIPLOM POLICY SOVEREIGN COERCE

B99
BROOKS S.,BRITAIN AND THE BOERS. AFR SOUTH/AFR UK CULTURE INSPECT LEGIT...INT/LAW 19/20 BOER/WAR. PAGE 19 A0396 WAR DIPLOM NAT/G

LEGUM C. A1767

LEGUM M. A1767

LEHMAN R.L. A1768

LEIB B.S. A1127

LEIBNITZ/G....GOTTFRIED WILHELM VON LEIBNITZ

LEIGH M.B. A1769

LEISS A.C. A1770

LEISURE....UNOBLIGATED TIME EXPENDITURES

B51
US DEPARTMENT OF STATE,LIVRES AMERICAINS TRADUITS EN FRANCAIS ET LIVRES FRANCAIS SUR LES ETATS-UNIS D'AMERIQUE (2ND ED.). FRANCE USA+45 SECT DIPLOM EDU/PROP LEISURE...ART/METH GEOG HUM 20. PAGE 151 A3086 BIBLIOG/A SOC

B65
COOPER S.,BEHIND THE GOLDEN CURTAIN: A VIEW OF THE USA. UK USA+45 SECT EDU/PROP COERCE LEISURE ORD/FREE WEALTH 20. PAGE 30 A0609 SOCIETY DIPLOM ATTIT ACT/RES

LEND/LEASE....LEND-LEASE PROGRAM(S)

B63
YOUNG A.N.,CHINA AND THE HELPING HAND. ASIA USA+45 FINAN INDUS ECO/TAC GIVE WEALTH...METH/COMP 20 LEND/LEASE GOLD/STAND. PAGE 169 A3434 FOR/AID DIPLOM WAR

LENGYEL E. A1771

LENIN V.I. A1772,A1773

LENIN/VI....VLADIMIR ILYICH LENIN

B39
WHEELER-BENNET J.W.,THE FORGOTTEN PEACE: BREST-LITOVSK. COM GERMANY USSR TOP/EX AGREE WAR PWR ...BIBLIOG 20 TREATY LENIN/VI UKRAINE. PAGE 163 A3326 PEACE DIPLOM CONFER

L39
NEARING S.,"A WARLESS WORLD." FUT WOR-45 SOCIETY INT/ORG NAT/G EX/STRUC PLAN DOMIN WAR ATTIT DRIVE PWR...POLICY PSY CONCPT OBS TREND HYPO/EXP MARX/KARL 20 MARX/KARL LENIN/VI. PAGE 108 A2210 COERCE PEACE

B58
PALMER E.E.,THE COMMUNIST CHALLENGE. COM USA+45 USA-45 ECO/DEV ECO/UNDEV NEUTRAL ORD/FREE POPULISM ...CONCPT NAT/COMP ANTHOL 19/20 LENIN/VI STALIN/J MAO MARX/KARL COM/PARTY. PAGE 113 A2320 MARXISM DIPLOM IDEA/COMP POLICY

B61
NOLLAU G.,INTERNATIONAL COMMUNISM AND WORLD REVOLUTION; HISTORY AND METHODS (TRANS. BY VICTOR ANDERSEN). COM WORKER DIPLOM CONFER INGP/REL ...CONCPT BIBLIOG 20 STALIN/J LENIN/VI COMINTERN COMINFORM WORLD/CONG. PAGE 110 A2249 MARXISM POL/PAR INT/ORG REV

B62
APATHEKER H.,AMERICAN FOREIGN POLICY AND THE COLD WAR. USA+45 NAT/G POL/PAR COLONIAL NAT/LISM SOVEREIGN MARXISM SOCISM 20 COLD/WAR MARX/KARL LENIN/VI INTERVENT. PAGE 8 A0167 DIPLOM WAR PEACE

B62
EBENSTEIN W.,TWO WAYS OF LIFE. USA+45 CULTURE ECO/DEV PLAN EDU/PROP CONTROL ORD/FREE...GOV/COMP IDEA/COMP T 20 MARX/KARL ENGELS/F LENIN/VI LOCKE/JOHN MILL/JS. PAGE 40 A0819 MARXISM POPULISM ECO/TAC DIPLOM

B62
HOOK S.,WORLD COMMUNISM: KEY DOCUMENTARY MATERIAL. CHINA/COM L/A+17C USA+45 USSR POL/PAR DIPLOM COLONIAL REV WAR...ANTHOL 20 MARX/KARL LENIN/VI COM/PARTY. PAGE 67 A1380 MARXISM COM GEN/LAWS NAT/G

B63
MILLER W.J.,THE MEANING OF COMMUNISM. USSR SOCIETY ECO/DEV EX/STRUC WORKER TEC/DEV ADMIN TOTALISM ...POLICY CONCPT CHARTS BIBLIOG T 20 COLD/WAR LENIN/VI STALIN/J. PAGE 101 A2080 MARXISM TRADIT DIPLOM NAT/G

B63
SWEARER H.R.,CONTEMPORARY COMMUNISM: THEORY AND PRACTICE. COM USSR SOCIETY ECO/DEV POL/PAR FORCES PLAN ADMIN LEAD NAT/LISM...POLICY ANTHOL 20 LENIN/VI COM/PARTY. PAGE 140 A2869 MARXISM CONCPT DIPLOM NAT/G

B64
KEEP J.,CONTEMPORARY HISTORY IN THE SOVIET MIRROR. COM USSR POL/PAR CREATE DIPLOM AGREE WAR ATTIT ...MYTH TREND ANTHOL 20 COLD/WAR STALIN/J MARX/KARL LENIN/VI. PAGE 77 A1576 HIST/WRIT METH MARXISM IDEA/COMP

B66
DRACHOVITCH M.M.,THE COMINTERN HISTORICAL HIGHLIGHTS. USSR INT/ORG EX/STRUC LEGIT LEAD GUERRILLA...ANTHOL 20 COMINTERN LENIN/VI. PAGE 38 A0784 DIPLOM REV MARXISM PERSON

S66
CHIU H.,"COMMUNIST CHINA'S ATTITUDE TOWARD INTERNATIONAL LAW" CHINA/COM USSR LAW CONSTN DIPLOM GP/REL 20 LENIN/VI. PAGE 26 A0532 INT/LAW MARXISM CONCPT IDEA/COMP

B67
BRZEZINSKI Z.K.,THE SOVIET BLOC: UNITY AND CONFLICT (2ND ED., REV., ENLARGED). COM POLAND USSR INTELL CHIEF EX/STRUC CONTROL EXEC GOV/REL PWR MARXISM ...TREND IDEA/COMP 20 LENIN/VI MARX/KARL STALIN/J. PAGE 21 A0420 NAT/G DIPLOM

LENS S. A1774

LENSEN G.A. A1775

LENT H.B. A1776

LENZ F. A1777

LEONARD L.L. A1778,A1779

LEOPOLD R.W. A1780

LERCHE C.O. JR. A1781,A1782,A1783,A1784

LERNER A.P. A1785

LERNER D. A1786

LERNER M.P. A1787

LERNER R. A1094

LERNER W. A1788

LESAGE/J....J. LESAGE

LESSING P. A1789

LETHBRIDGE H.J. A1790

LEVELLERS....LEVELLERS PARTY

LEVENSTEIN A. A1791

LEVI M. A1792

LEVI W. A1793,A1794

LEVIN J.V. A1795

LEVINE R.A. A1796

LEVONTIN A.V. A1797

LEVY H.V. A1798

LEWIN E. A1799,A1800

LEWIS J.D. A1498

LEWIS J.P. A1801

LEWIS P.R. A1802

LEWIS S. A1803

LEWIS W.A. A1804

LEWIS/A....ARTHUR LEWIS

LEWIS/JL....JOHN L. LEWIS

LEWY G. A1805

LEYPOLOT F. A1806

LFNA....LEAGUE OF FREE NATIONS ASSOCIATION

LG/CO....LARGE COMPANY

N19
MARCUS W.,US PRIVATE INVESTMENT AND ECONOMIC AID IN UNDERDEVELOPED COUNTRIES (PAMPHLET). USA+45 LG/CO FOR/AID ECO/UNDEV

NAT/G CAP/ISM EDU/PROP 20. PAGE 94 A1937 — FINAN PLAN

C54
BERLE A.A. JR.,"THE 20TH CENTURY CAPITALIST REVOLUTION." ECO/DEV NAT/G DIPLOM PRICE CONTROL ATTIT...BIBLIOG/A 20. PAGE 14 A0275 — LG/CO CAP/ISM MGT PWR

B61
FRIEDMANN W.G.,JOINT INTERNATIONAL BUSINESS VENTURES. ASIA ISLAM L/A+17C ECO/DEV DIST/IND FINAN PROC/MFG FACE/GP LG/CO NAT/G VOL/ASSN CONSULT EX/STRUC PLAN ADMIN ROUTINE WEALTH...OLD/LIB WORK 20. PAGE 49 A1004 — ECO/UNDEV INT/TRADE

L61
LEVINE R.A.,"THE ANTHROPOLOGY OF CONFLICT." FUT CULTURE INTELL FAM INT/ORG LG/CO SML/CO ATTIT KNOWL ...METH/CNCPT VAL/FREE 20. PAGE 88 A1796 — SOCIETY ACT/RES

B63
PATRA A.C.,THE ADMINISTRATION OF JUSTICE UNDER THE EAST INDIA COMPANY IN BENGAL, BIHAR AND ORISSA. INDIA UK LG/CO CAP/ISM INT/TRADE ADJUD COLONIAL CONTROL CT/SYS...POLICY 20. PAGE 114 A2341 — ADMIN JURID CONCPT

B63
THORELLI H.B.,INTOP: INTERNATIONAL OPERATIONS SIMULATION: PLAYER'S MANUAL. BRAZIL FINAN OP/RES ADMIN GP/REL INGP/REL PRODUC PERCEPT...DECISION MGT EEC. PAGE 144 A2935 — GAME INT/TRADE EDU/PROP LG/CO

B64
MARKHAM J.W.,THE COMMON MARKET: FRIEND OR COMPETITOR. EUR+WWI FUT USA+45 INT/ORG LG/CO NAT/G VOL/ASSN DELIB/GP EX/STRUC PLAN TARIFFS ORD/FREE PWR WEALTH...POLICY STAT TREND EEC VAL/FREE 20. PAGE 95 A1943 — ECO/DEV ECO/TAC

B64
STEWART C.F.,A BIBLIOGRAPHY OF INTERNATIONAL BUSINESS. WOR+45 FINAN LG/CO NAT/G PLAN ECO/TAC TARIFFS...DECISION MGT GP/COMP NAT/COMP 20 EEC. PAGE 138 A2824 — BIBLIOG INT/ORG OP/RES INT/TRADE

B65
JOHNSTONE A.,UNITED STATES DIRECT INVESTMENT IN FRANCE: AN INVESTIGATION OF THE FRENCH CHARGES. FRANCE USA+45 ECO/DEV INDUS LG/CO NAT/G ECO/TAC CONTROL WEALTH...BIBLIOG 20 INTERVENT. PAGE 75 A1529 — FINAN DIPLOM POLICY SOVEREIGN

B66
BALDWIN D.A.,ECONOMIC DEVELOPMENT AND AMERICAN FOREIGN POLICY. USA+45 FINAN LG/CO LEGIS DIPLOM GIVE 20. PAGE 10 A0210 — ECO/TAC FOR/AID ECO/UNDEV POLICY

B66
SZLADITS C.,A BIBLIOGRAPHY ON FOREIGN AND COMPARATIVE LAW (SUPPLEMENT 1964). FINAN FAM LABOR LG/CO LEGIS JUDGE ADMIN CRIME...CRIMLGY 20. PAGE 141 A2878 — BIBLIOG/A CT/SYS INT/LAW

B66
ZISCHKA A.,WAR ES EIN WUNDER? GERMANY/W ECO/DEV FINAN LG/CO BARGAIN CAP/ISM FOR/AID RATION 20 MARSHL/PLN. PAGE 170 A3456 — ECO/TAC INT/TRADE INDUS WAR

LIB/INTRNT....LIBERAL INTERNATIONAL

LIB/PARTY....LIBERAL PARTY (ALL NATIONS)

LIBERALISM....SEE NEW/LIB, WELF/ST, OLD/LIB, LAISSEZ

LIBERIA....SEE ALSO AFR

L67
LANDIS E.S.,"THE SOUTH WEST AFRICA CASES* REMAND TO THE UNITED NATIONS." ETHIOPIA LIBERIA SOUTH/AFR BAL/PWR 20 UN. PAGE 84 A1719 — INT/LAW INT/ORG DIPLOM ADJUD

S67
JOHNSON D.H.N.,"THE SOUTH-WEST AFRICA CASES." AFR ETHIOPIA LIBERIA SOUTH/AFR CONSULT JUDGE BAL/PWR 20. PAGE 74 A1521 — INT/LAW DIPLOM INT/ORG ADJUD

LIBERTY....SEE ORD/FREE

LIBRARY HUNGARIAN ACADEMY SCI A1807

LIBRARY INTERNATIONAL REL A1808

LIBYA....SEE ALSO ISLAM

B36
VARLEY D.H.,A BIBLIOGRAPHY OF ITALIAN COLONISATION IN AFRICA WITH A SECTION ON ABYSSINIA. AFR ETHIOPIA ITALY LIBYA SOMALIA AGRI FINAN LABOR TEC/DEV DIPLOM INT/TRADE RACE/REL DISCRIM 19/20. PAGE 158 A3222 — BIBLIOG COLONIAL ADMIN LAW

B40
ITALIAN LIBRARY OF INFORMATION: OUTLINE STUDIES (VOL. V). ITALY LIBYA CONTROL...FASCIST 20. PAGE 3 A0052 — COLONIAL DIPLOM ECO/TAC POLICY

B60
PRINCETON U CONFERENCE,CURRENT PROBLEMS IN NORTH AFRICA. ALGERIA LIBYA MOROCCO USA+45 EXTR/IND POL/PAR PROB/SOLV DIPLOM ECO/TAC WAR...ANTHOL 20 TUNIS. PAGE 118 A2412 — POLICY ECO/UNDEV NAT/G

B61
NATIONAL BANK OF LIBYA,INFLATION IN LIBYA (PAMPHLET). LIBYA SOCIETY NAT/G PLAN INT/TRADE ...STAT CHARTS 20 GOLD/STAND. PAGE 107 A2200 — ECO/TAC ECO/UNDEV FINAN BUDGET

B61
UAR MINISTRY OF CULTURE,A BIBLIOGRAPHICAL LIST OF LIBYA. ISLAM LIBYA DIPLOM COLONIAL REV WAR 19/20. PAGE 146 A2988 — BIBLIOG GEOG SECT NAT/LISM

B63
KHADDURI M.,MODERN LIBYA: A STUDY IN POLITICAL DEVELOPMENT. EUR+WWI ISLAM LIBYA ELITES INT/ORG POL/PAR FORCES DIPLOM FOR/AID DOMIN EDU/PROP LEGIT NAT/LISM DRIVE RIGID/FLEX SKILL...CONCPT TIME/SEQ TREND 20. PAGE 78 A1606 — NAT/G STRUCT

B66
BROWN L.C.,STATE AND SOCIETY IN INDEPENDENT NORTH AFRICA. ALGERIA LIBYA MOROCCO AGRI INDUS INT/ORG POL/PAR SECT PLAN DIPLOM COLONIAL...LING NAT/COMP ANTHOL BIBLIOG 20 TUNIS MUSLIM. PAGE 20 A0406 — NAT/G SOCIETY CULTURE ECO/UNDEV

B93
ROYAL GEOGRAPHIC SOCIETY,BIBLIOGRAPHY OF BARBARY STATES (4 SUPPLEMENTARY PAPERS). ALGERIA LIBYA MOROCCO SOCIETY STRUCT DIPLOM LEAD 14/19 TUNIS. PAGE 125 A2555 — BIBLIOG ISLAM NAT/G COLONIAL

LICENSE....LEGAL PERMIT

B64
SZLADITS C.,BIBLIOGRAPHY ON FOREIGN AND COMPARATIVE LAW: BOOKS AND ARTICLES IN ENGLISH (SUPPLEMENT 1962). FINAN INDUS JUDGE LICENSE ADMIN CT/SYS PARL/PROC OWN...INT/LAW CLASSIF METH/COMP NAT/COMP 20. PAGE 141 A2877 — BIBLIOG/A JURID ADJUD LAW

B67
PIPER D.C.,THE INTERNATIONAL LAW OF THE GREAT LAKES. CANADA EXTR/IND MUNIC LICENSE ARMS/CONT CRIME...GEOG 19/20. PAGE 116 A2381 — CONCPT DIPLOM INT/LAW

L67
KOMESAR N.K.,"PRESIDENTIAL AMENDMENT & TERMINATION OF TREATIES* THE CASE OF THE WARSAW CONVENTION." POLAND USA+45 NAT/G CHIEF PROB/SOLV DIPLOM PWR 20 CONGRESS. PAGE 81 A1669 — TOP/EX LEGIS CONSTN LICENSE

S67
FAWCETT J.E.S.,"GIBRALTAR* THE LEGAL ISSUES." SPAIN UK INT/ORG BAL/PWR LICENSE CONFER SANCTION PRIVIL ...JURID CHARTS 20. PAGE 44 A0905 — INT/LAW DIPLOM COLONIAL ADJUD

LICHTHEIM G. A1809

LIECHTENST....LIECHTENSTEIN; SEE ALSO APPROPRIATE TIME/SPACE/CULTURE INDEX

LIEFMANN-KEIL E. A1810

LIESNER H.H. A2028

LIEUWEN E. A1811,A1812

LIGHTFT/PM....PHIL M. LIGHTFOOT

LIGOT M. A1814

LIKERT/R....RENSIS LIKERT

LILIENTHAL D.E. A1815

LILLICH R.B. A1816,A1817

LIN/PIAO....LIN PIAO

LINCOLN G. A1818,A1819

LINCOLN G.A. A2314

LINCOLN/A....PRESIDENT ABRAHAM LINCOLN

LINDAHL/E....ERIK LINDAHL

LINDBERG L. A1820

LINDBLOM C.E. A1821

LINDHOLM R.W. A1822

LINDSAY K. A1823

LINEBARGER P. A1824

LING D.L. A1825

LING....LINGUISTICS, LANGUAGE

N
AMERICAN DOCUMENTATION INST,DOCUMENTATION ABSTRACTS. WOR+45 NAT/G COMPUTER CREATE TEC/DEV DIPLOM EDU/PROP REGION KNOWL...PHIL/SCI CLASSIF LING. PAGE 7 A0143
BIBLIOG/A AUTOMAT COMPUT/IR R+D

N
MIDDLE EAST JOURNAL. CULTURE SECT DIPLOM LEAD GOV/REL ATTIT...POLICY PHIL/SCI SOC LING BIOG 20. PAGE 1 A0019
BIBLIOG ISLAM NAT/G ECO/UNDEV

N
SCHOLARLY BOOKS IN AMERICA; A QUARTERLY BIBLIOGRAPHY OF UNIVERSITY PRESS PUBLICATIONS. WOR+45 AGRI COM/IND NAT/G HEALTH...GEOG PHIL/SCI PSY SOC LING 20. PAGE 3 A0046
BIBLIOG/A LAW MUNIC DIPLOM

N
"PROLOG",DIGEST OF THE SOVIET UKRANIAN PRESS. USSR LAW AGRI INDUS PROVS SCHOOL DIPLOM GOV/REL ATTIT ...HUM LING 20. PAGE 4 A0081
BIBLIOG/A NAT/G PRESS COM

N
AFRICAN BIBLIOGRAPHIC CENTER,A CURRENT BIBLIOGRAPHY ON AFRICAN AFFAIRS. LAW CULTURE ECO/UNDEV LABOR SECT DIPLOM FOR/AID COLONIAL NAT/LISM...LING 20. PAGE 5 A0094
BIBLIOG/A AFR NAT/G REGION

N
US BUREAU OF THE CENSUS,BIBLIOGRAPHY OF SOCIAL SCIENCE PERIODICALS AND MONOGRAPH SERIES. WOR+45 LAW DIPLOM EDU/PROP HEALTH...PSY SOC LING STAT. PAGE 150 A3058
BIBLIOG/A CULTURE NAT/G SOCIETY

B18
KERNER R.J.,SLAVIC EUROPE: A SELECTED BIBLIOGRAPHY IN THE WESTERN EUROPEAN LANGUAGES. BULGARIA CZECHOSLVK GERMANY/E POLAND RUSSIA YUGOSLAVIA NAT/G DIPLOM MARXISM...LING 19/20. PAGE 78 A1598
BIBLIOG SOCIETY CULTURE COM

B22
FICHTE J.G.,ADDRESSES TO THE GERMAN NATION. GERMANY PRUSSIA ELITES NAT/G SECT CREATE INT/TRADE HEREDITY ...ART/METH LING 19 FRANK/PARL. PAGE 45 A0923
NAT/LISM CULTURE EDU/PROP REGION

B29
BOUDET P.,BIBLIOGRAPHIE DE L'INDOCHINE FRANCAISE. S/ASIA VIETNAM SECT...GEOG LING 20. PAGE 17 A0344
BIBLIOG ADMIN COLONIAL DIPLOM

B29
PRATT I.A.,MODERN EGYPT: A LIST OF REFERENCES TO MATERIAL IN THE NEW YORK PUBLIC LIBRARY. UAR ECO/UNDEV...GEOG JURID SOC LING 20. PAGE 117 A2407
BIBLIOG ISLAM DIPLOM NAT/G

C44
VAN VALKENBURG S.,"ELEMENTS OF POLITICAL GEOGRAPHY." FRANCE COM/IND INDUS NAT/G SECT RACE/REL...LING TREND GEN/LAWS BIBLIOG 20. PAGE 158 A3215
GEOG DIPLOM COLONIAL

B46
GAULD W.A.,MAN, NATURE, AND TIME, AN INTRODUCTION TO WORLD STUDY. WOR-45 CULTURE CREATE DIPLOM GP/REL DRIVE...SOC LING CENSUS CHARTS TIME 18/20. PAGE 52 A1054
HABITAT PERSON

N46
HOBBS C.C.,SOUTHEAST ASIA, 1935-45: A SELECTED LIST OF REFERENCE BOOKS (PAMPHLET). S/ASIA AGRI INDUS NAT/G SECT DIPLOM WAR...ART/METH GEOG SOC LING 20. PAGE 65 A1346
BIBLIOG/A CULTURE HABITAT

B49
GROB F.,THE RELATIVITY OF WAR AND PEACE: A STUDY IN LAW, HISTORY, AND POLLTICS. WOR+45 WOR-45 LAW DIPLOM DEBATE...CONCPT LING IDEA/COMP BIBLIOG 18/20. PAGE 57 A1167
WAR PEACE INT/LAW STYLE

B55
TROTIER A.H.,DOCTORAL DISSERTATIONS ACCEPTED BY AMERICAN UNIVERSITIES 1954-55. SECT DIPLOM HEALTH ...ART/METH GEOG INT/LAW SOC LING CHARTS 20. PAGE 145 A2968
BIBLIOG ACADEM USA+45 WRITING

B57
BYRNES R.F.,BIBLIOGRAPHY OF AMERICAN PUBLICATIONS ON EAST CENTRAL EUROPE, 1945-1957 (VOL. XXII). SECT DIPLOM EDU/PROP RACE/REL...ART/METH GEOG JURID SOC LING 20 JEWS. PAGE 23 A0462
BIBLIOG/A COM MARXISM NAT/G

B58
MASON J.B.,THAILAND BIBLIOGRAPHY. S/ASIA THAILAND CULTURE EDU/PROP ADMIN...GEOG SOC LING 20. PAGE 95 A1958
BIBLIOG/A ECO/UNDEV DIPLOM NAT/G

N59
BRITISH COMMONWEALTH REL CONF,EXTRACTS FROM THE PROCEEDINGS OF THE SIXTH UNOFFICIAL CONFERENCE (PAMPHLET). GHANA INDIA RHODESIA UK FINAN FORCES DETER FEDERAL...LING 20 PARLIAMENT. PAGE 19 A0379
DIPLOM PARL/PROC INT/TRADE ORD/FREE

B60
SZTARAY Z.,BIBLIOGRAPHY ON HUNGARY. HUNGARY MOD/EUR CULTURE INDUS SECT DIPLOM REV...ART/METH SOC LING 18/20. PAGE 141 A2879
BIBLIOG NAT/G COM MARXISM

B61
ZIMMERMAN I.,A GUIDE TO CURRENT LATIN AMERICAN PERIODICALS: HUMANITIES AND SOCIAL SCIENCES. LABOR SECT EDU/PROP...GEOG HUM SOC LING STAT NAT/COMP 20. PAGE 170 A3452
BIBLIOG/A DIPLOM L/A+17C PHIL/SCI

B62
DAVAR F.C.,IRAN AND INDIA THROUGH THE AGES. INDIA IRAN ELITES SECT CREATE ORD/FREE...LING BIBLIOG. PAGE 34 A0683
NAT/COMP DIPLOM CULTURE

B62
US LIBRARY OF CONGRESS,UNITED STATES AND CANADIAN PUBLICATIONS ON AFRICA IN 1960. CANADA USA+45 CULTURE TEC/DEV DIPLOM FOR/AID RACE/REL...GEOG HUM SOC SOC/WK LING 20. PAGE 155 A3156
BIBLIOG/A AFR

B62
WEIDNER E.W.,THE WORLD ROLE OF UNIVERSITIES. USA+45 WOR+45 SECT ACT/RES PROB/SOLV GIVE EFFICIENCY KNOWL ...LING CHARTS BIBLIOG 20. PAGE 162 A3297
ACADEM EDU/PROP DIPLOM POLICY

B63
JAIRAZBHOY R.A.,FOREIGN INFLUENCE IN ANCIENT INDIA. INDIA ELITES SECT DIPLOM EDU/PROP COLONIAL REGION GP/REL...ART/METH LING WORSHIP +/14 GRECO/ROMN MESOPOTAM PERSIA PARTH/SASS. PAGE 73 A1491
CULTURE SOCIETY COERCE DOMIN

B63
PAENSON I.,SYSTEMATIC GLOSSARY ENGLISH, FRENCH, SPANISH, RUSSIAN OF SELECTED ECONOMIC AND SOCIAL TERMS. WOR+45 FINAN LABOR INT/TRADE DEMAND PRODUC 20. PAGE 113 A2315
DICTIONARY SOC LING

B63
PEREZ ORTIZ R.,ANUARIO BIBLIOGRAFICO COLOMBIANO, 1961. AGRI...INT/LAW JURID SOC LING 20 COLOMB. PAGE 115 A2354
BIBLIOG L/A+17C NAT/G

B64
ANDREWS D.H.,LATIN AMERICA: A BIBLIOGRAPHY OF PAPERBACK BOOKS. SECT INT/TRADE EDU/PROP WAR GOV/REL ADJUST NAT/LISM ATTIT...ART/METH LING BIOG 20. PAGE 8 A0160
BIBLIOG L/A+17C CULTURE NAT/G

B64
RAGHAVAN M.D.,INDIA IN CEYLONESE HISTORY, SOCIETY AND CULTURE. CEYLON INDIA S/ASIA LAW SOCIETY INT/TRADE ATTIT...ART/METH JURID SOC LING 20. PAGE 119 A2433
DIPLOM CULTURE SECT STRUCT

B65
BRACKETT R.D.,PATHWAYS TO PEACE. SECT VOL/ASSN GP/REL PERS/REL DISCRIM...LING 20 UN PEACE/CORP. PAGE 18 A0366
PEACE INT/ORG EDU/PROP PARTIC

L65
MATTHEWS D.G.,"A CURRENT BIBLIOGRAPHY ON ETHIOPIAN AFFAIRS: A SELECT BIBLIOGRAPHY FROM 1950-1964." ETHIOPIA LAW CULTURE ECO/UNDEV INDUS LABOR SECT FORCES DIPLOM CIVMIL/REL RACE/REL...LING STAT 20. PAGE 96 A1969
BIBLIOG/A ADMIN POL/PAR NAT/G

L65
MATTHEWS D.G.,"A CURRENT BIBLIOGRAPHY ON SUDANESE AFFAIRS; A SELECT BIBLIOGRAPHY FROM 1960-1964." SUDAN LAW CULTURE AGRI FINAN INDUS LABOR POL/PAR TEC/DEV FOR/AID RACE/REL LITERACY...LING 20. PAGE 96 A1970
BIBLIOG ECO/UNDEV NAT/G DIPLOM

B66
BROWN L.C.,STATE AND SOCIETY IN INDEPENDENT NORTH AFRICA. ALGERIA LIBYA MOROCCO AGRI INDUS INT/ORG POL/PAR SECT PLAN DIPLOM COLONIAL...LING NAT/COMP ANTHOL BIBLIOG 20 TUNIS MUSLIM. PAGE 20 A0406
NAT/G SOCIETY CULTURE ECO/UNDEV

B66
US DEPARTMENT OF STATE,RESEARCH ON AFRICA (EXTERNAL RESEARCH LIST NO 5-25). LAW CULTURE ECO/UNDEV POL/PAR DIPLOM EDU/PROP LEAD REGION MARXISM...GEOG LING WORSHIP 20. PAGE 152 A3094
BIBLIOG/A ASIA S/ASIA NAT/G

B66
US DEPARTMENT OF STATE,RESEARCH ON THE USSR AND EASTERN EUROPE (EXTERNAL RESEARCH LIST NO 1-25). USSR LAW CULTURE SOCIETY NAT/G TEC/DEV DIPLOM EDU/PROP REGION...GEOG LING. PAGE 152 A3097
BIBLIOG/A EUR+WWI COM MARXISM

S66
AFRICAN BIBLIOGRAPHIC CENTER,"A CURRENT VIEW OF AFRICANA: A SELECT AND ANNOTATED BIBLIOGRAPHICAL PUBLISHING GUIDE, 1965-1966." AFR CULTURE INDUS LABOR SECT FOR/AID ADMIN COLONIAL REV RACE/REL SOCISM...LING 20. PAGE 5 A0098
BIBLIOG/A NAT/G TEC/DEV POL/PAR

S66
MATTHEWS D.G.,"ETHIOPIAN OUTLINE: A BIBLIOGRAPHIC RESEARCH GUIDE." ETHIOPIA LAW STRUCT ECO/UNDEV AGRI LABOR SECT CHIEF DELIB/GP EX/STRUC ADMIN...LING ORG/CHARTS 20. PAGE 96 A1972
BIBLIOG NAT/G DIPLOM POL/PAR

B67
LANDEN R.G.,OMAN SINCE 1856: DISRUPTIVE MODERNIZATION IN A TRADITIONAL ARAB SOCIETY. UK
ISLAM CULTURE

DIST/IND EXTR/IND SECT DIPLOM INT/TRADE...SOC LING CHARTS BIBLIOG 19/20. PAGE 84 A1714 ECO/UNDEV NAT/G

S67
KINGSLEY R.E.,"THE US BUSINESS IMAGE IN LATIN AMERICA." L/A+17C USA+45 NAT/G TEC/DEV CAP/ISM FOR/AID DOMIN EDU/PROP...CONCPT LING IDEA/COMP 20. PAGE 79 A1626 ATTIT LOVE DIPLOM ECO/UNDEV

LINGUISTICS....SEE LING

LINK R.G. A1826

LINK/AS....ARTHUR S. LINK

LIPMAN E.J. A3254

LIPPMANN W. A1827,A1828,A1829,A1830,A1831

LIPPMANN/W....WALTER LIPPMANN

B65
CBS,CONVERSATIONS WITH WALTER LIPPMANN. USA+45 INT/ORG NAT/G POL/PAR PLAN DIPLOM PWR ALL/IDEOS ...POLICY 20 LIPPMANN/W. PAGE 25 A0509 TV ATTIT INT

LIPSHART A. A1832

LIPSON L. A1833,A1834,A2004

LISKA G. A1835,A1836,A1837,A1838

LISSITZYN O.J. A1839,A1840,A1841,A1842

LISTER L. A1843

LITERACY....ABILITY TO READ AND WRITE

B02
MOREL E.D.,AFFAIRS OF WEST AFRICA. UK FINAN INDUS FAM KIN SECT CHIEF WORKER DIPLOM RACE/REL LITERACY HEALTH...CHARTS 18/20 AFRICA/W NEGRO. PAGE 104 A2129 COLONIAL ADMIN AFR

B64
NICOL D.,AFRICA - A SUBJECTIVE VIEW. AFR INT/ORG PLAN ADMIN COLONIAL PARL/PROC PARTIC REGION GOV/REL LITERACY ATTIT...BIBLIOG 20 CIVIL/SERV. PAGE 109 A2230 NAT/G LEAD CULTURE ACADEM

L65
MATTHEWS D.G.,"A CURRENT BIBLIOGRAPHY ON SUDANESE AFFAIRS; A SELECT BIBLIOGRAPHY FROM 1960-1964." SUDAN LAW CULTURE AGRI FINAN INDUS LABOR POL/PAR TEC/DEV FOR/AID RACE/REL LITERACY...LING 20. PAGE 96 A1970 BIBLIOG ECO/UNDEV NAT/G DIPLOM

S66
AFRICAN BIBLIOGRAPHIC CENTER,"THE NEW AFRO-ASIAN STATES IN PERSPECTIVE, 1960-1963: A SELECT BIBLIOGRAPHY." AFR ASIA CULTURE SOCIETY INT/ORG LABOR TEC/DEV LITERACY 20 UN. PAGE 5 A0100 BIBLIOG DIPLOM FOR/AID INT/TRADE

LITERARY ANALYSIS....SEE HUM

LITHUANIA....SEE ALSO USSR

LITTLE I.M.D. A1844

LIU K.C. A1845

LIU/SHAO....LIU SHAO-CHI

LIVNEH E. A1846,A1847

LIVNGSTN/D....DAVID LIVINGSTON

B30
SMUTS J.C.,AFRICA AND SOME WORLD PROBLEMS. RHODESIA SOUTH/AFR CULTURE ECO/UNDEV INDUS INT/ORG SECT PROB/SOLV REGION GOV/REL DISCRIM ATTIT 19/20 LEAGUE/NAT LIVNGSTN/D NEGRO. PAGE 134 A2748 LEGIS AFR COLONIAL RACE/REL

LIVY....LIVY

LLOYD W.B. A1848

LLOYD/HD....HENRY D. LLOYD

LLOYD-GEO/D....DAVID LLOYD GEORGE

LOANS....SEE RENT+GIVE+FOR/AID+FINAN

LOBBY....PRESSURE GROUP

B39
THOMAS J.A.,THE HOUSE OF COMMONS, 1832-1901; A STUDY OF ITS ECONOMIC AND FUNCTIONAL CHARACTER. UK LAW STRATA FINAN DIPLOM CONTROL LEAD LOBBY REPRESENT WEALTH...POLICY STAT BIBLIOG 19/20 PARLIAMENT. PAGE 143 A2922 PARL/PROC LEGIS POL/PAR ECO/DEV

B57
FRASER L.,PROPAGANDA. GERMANY USSR WOR+45 WOR-45 NAT/G POL/PAR CONTROL FEEDBACK LOBBY CROWD WAR CONSEN NAT/LISM 20. PAGE 48 A0988 EDU/PROP FASCISM MARXISM DIPLOM

B57
US SENATE COMM ON JUDICIARY,HEARING BEFORE SUBCOMMITTEE ON COMMITTEE OF JUDICIARY, UNITED STATES SENATE: S. J. RES. 3. USA+45 NAT/G CONSULT DELIB/GP DIPLOM ADJUD LOBBY REPRESENT 20 CONGRESS TREATY. PAGE 157 A3192 LEGIS CONSTN CONFER AGREE

B60
HOVET T. JR.,BLOC POLITICS IN THE UNITED NATIONS. WOR+45...POLICY STAT CHARTS METH UN. PAGE 68 A1396 LOBBY INT/ORG DIPLOM CHOOSE

B61
DIMOCK M.E.,BUSINESS AND GOVERNMENT (4TH ED.). AGRI FINAN OP/RES PLAN BUDGET DIPLOM LOBBY NUC/PWR NEW/LIB SOCISM...POLICY BIBLIOG 20. PAGE 37 A0765 NAT/G INDUS LABOR ECO/TAC

B61
ROSENAU J.N.,PUBLIC OPINION AND FOREIGN POLICY; AN OPERATIONAL FORMULA. USA+45 COM/IND OP/RES EDU/PROP LOBBY CROWD...CON/ANAL BIBLIOG 20. PAGE 124 A2532 ATTIT PRESS DIPLOM

B61
SCOTT A.M.,POLITICS, USA; CASES ON THE AMERICAN DEMOCRATIC PROCESS. USA+45 CHIEF FORCES DIPLOM LOBBY CHOOSE RACE/REL FEDERAL ATTIT...JURID ANTHOL T 20 PRESIDENT CONGRESS CIVIL/LIB. PAGE 130 A2669 CT/SYS CONSTN NAT/G PLAN

B61
US HOUSE COMM FOREIGN AFFAIRS,THE INTERNATIONAL DEVELOPMENT AND SECURITY ACT: HEARINGS BEFORE COMMITTEE ON FOREIGN AFFAIRS, HOUSE OF REP: HR7372. USA+45 AGRI INT/ORG NAT/G CONSULT DELIB/GP DIPLOM ECO/TAC INT/TRADE LOBBY REPRESENT 20 MCNAMARA/R DILLON/D RUSK/D CONGRESS. PAGE 153 A3128 FOR/AID CONFER LEGIS ECO/UNDEV

B63
HOVET T. JR.,AFRICA IN THE UNITED NATIONS. AFR DELIB/GP EDU/PROP LOBBY CHOOSE ORD/FREE PWR RESPECT SKILL...STAT TIME/SEQ CON/ANAL CHARTS STERTYP VAL/FREE 20 UN. PAGE 68 A1397 INT/ORG USSR

B63
WATKINS K.W.,BRITAIN DIVIDED; THE EFFECT OF THE SPANISH CIVIL WAR ON BRITISH POLITICAL OPINION. SPAIN UK POL/PAR BAL/PWR LOBBY NEUTRAL 20. PAGE 162 A3293 EDU/PROP WAR POLICY DIPLOM

C63
SCHMITT K.M.,"EVOLUTION OR CHAOS: DYNAMICS OF LATIN AMERICAN GOVERNMENT AND POLITICS." L/A+17C AGRI FINAN CAP/ISM EXEC LEAD BAL/PAY TOTALISM ATTIT ...TREND BIBLIOG 20. PAGE 129 A2635 DIPLOM POLICY POL/PAR LOBBY

B64
KRETZSCHMAR W.W.,AUSLANDSHILFE ALS MITTEL DER AUSSENWIRTSCHAFTS- UND AUSSENPOLITIK. ASIA GERMANY/W UK USA+45 SOCIETY STRUCT ECO/UNDEV LOBBY EFFICIENCY 20. PAGE 82 A1683 FOR/AID DIPLOM AGRI DIST/IND

B67
O'LEARY M.K.,THE POLITICS OF AMERICAN FOREIGN AID. USA+45 POL/PAR CHIEF BUDGET EDU/PROP LOBBY CONGRESS. PAGE 111 A2270 FOR/AID DIPLOM PARL/PROC ATTIT

B67
ROSENAU J.N.,DOMESTIC SOURCES OF FOREIGN POLICY. WOR+45 STRATA COM/IND MUNIC POL/PAR LOBBY PARTIC REGION ATTIT...PSY SOC COLD/WAR. PAGE 124 A2534 DIPLOM POLICY NAT/G CHOOSE

B67
US SENATE COMM ON FOREIGN REL,HUMAN RIGHTS CONVENTIONS. USA+45 LABOR VOL/ASSN DELIB/GP DOMIN ADJUD REPRESENT...INT/LAW MGT CONGRESS. PAGE 156 A3189 LEGIS ORD/FREE WORKER LOBBY

LOBBYING....SEE LOBBY

LOC/G....LOCAL GOVERNMENT

N
SABIN J.,BIBLIOTHECA AMERICANA: A DICTIONARY OF BOOKS RELATING TO AMERICA, FROM ITS DISCOVERY TO THE PRESENT TIME(29 VOLS.). CONSTN CULTURE SOCIETY ECO/DEV LOC/G EDU/PROP NAT/LISM...POLICY GEOG SOC 19. PAGE 126 A2581 BIBLIOG L/A+17C DIPLOM NAT/G

N
BULLETIN ANALYTIQUE DE DOCUMENTATION POLITIQUE, ECONOMIQUE, ET SOCIAL CONTEMPORAIRE. FRANCE WOR+45 SOCIETY ECO/DEV ECO/UNDEV INT/ORG LOC/G PROB/SOLV FOR/AID LEAD REGION SOC. PAGE 1 A0006 BIBLIOG/A DIPLOM NAT/COMP NAT/G

N
JOURNAL OF POLITICS. USA+45 USA-45 CONSTN POL/PAR EX/STRUC LEGIS PROB/SOLV DIPLOM CT/SYS CHOOSE RACE/REL 20. PAGE 1 A0017 BIBLIOG/A NAT/G LAW LOC/G

N
POLITICAL SCIENCE QUARTERLY. USA+45 USA-45 LAW BIBLIOG/A

CONSTN ECO/DEV INT/ORG LOC/G POL/PAR LEGIS LEAD NUC/PWR...CONCPT 20. PAGE 1 A0023
NAT/G DIPLOM POLICY

N

AMERICAN BIBLIOGRAPHIC SERVICE,QUARTERLY CHECKLIST OF ORIENTAL STUDIES. CULTURE LOC/G NAT/G DIPLOM ...HIST/WRIT CON/ANAL 20. PAGE 7 A0141
BIBLIOG S/ASIA ASIA

N

DEUTSCHE BUCHEREI,JAHRESVERZEICHNIS DES DEUTSCHEN SCHRIFTUMS. AUSTRIA EUR+WWI GERMANY SWITZERLND LAW LOC/G DIPLOM ADMIN...MGT SOC 19/20. PAGE 37 A0745
BIBLIOG WRITING NAT/G

N

US CONSOLATE GENERAL HONG KONG,REVIEW OF THE HONG KONG CHINESE PRESS. ECO/UNDEV LOC/G NAT/G PLAN DIPLOM EDU/PROP LEAD GP/REL MARXISM...POLICY INDEX 20. PAGE 150 A3073
BIBLIOG/A ASIA PRESS ATTIT

N

US CONSULATE GENERAL HONG KONG,CURRENT BACKGROUND. CHINA/COM ECO/UNDEV LOC/G NAT/G PLAN DIPLOM EDU/PROP LEAD REV ATTIT...POLICY INDEX 20. PAGE 151 A3074
BIBLIOG/A MARXIST ASIA PRESS

N

US CONSULATE GENERAL HONG KONG,SURVEY OF CHINA MAINLAND PRESS. CHINA/COM ECO/UNDEV LOC/G NAT/G PLAN DIPLOM EDU/PROP LEAD REV ATTIT...POLICY INDEX 20. PAGE 151 A3075
BIBLIOG/A MARXIST ASIA PRESS

N

US CONSULATE GENERAL HONG KONG,US CONSULATE GENERAL, HONG KONG, PRESS SUMMARIES. CHINA/COM ECO/UNDEV LOC/G NAT/G PLAN DIPLOM EDU/PROP LEAD REV ATTIT...POLICY INDEX 20. PAGE 151 A3076
BIBLIOG/A MARXIST ASIA PRESS

N

US LIBRARY OF CONGRESS,ACCESSIONS LIST - INDIA. INDIA CULTURE AGRI LOC/G POL/PAR PLAN PROB/SOLV TEC/DEV DIPLOM EDU/PROP LEAD GP/REL ATTIT 20. PAGE 154 A3142
BIBLIOG S/ASIA ECO/UNDEV NAT/G

C06

MONTGOMERY H.,"A DICTIONARY OF POLITICAL PHRASES AND ILLUSIONS WITH A SHORT BIBLIOGRAPHY." EUR+WWI MOD/EUR UK AGRI LABOR LOC/G NAT/G COLONIAL CHOOSE RACE/REL. PAGE 103 A2114
BIBLIOG DICTIONARY POLICY DIPLOM

L16

WRIGHT Q.,"THE ENFORCEMENT OF INTERNATIONAL LAW THROUGH MUNICIPAL LAW IN THE US." USA-45 LOC/G NAT/G PUB/INST FORCES LEGIT CT/SYS PERCEPT ALL/VALS ...JURID 20. PAGE 167 A3401
INT/ORG LAW INT/LAW WAR

B31

STUART G.H.,THE INTERNATIONAL CITY OF TANGIER. AFR EUR+WWI MOD/EUR MOROCCO CONSTN PROVS CREATE PLAN LEGIT PEACE ORD/FREE PWR...INT/LAW OBS TIME/SEQ CON/ANAL 20 TANGIER. PAGE 139 A2854
LOC/G INT/ORG DIPLOM SOVEREIGN

B35

KENNEDY W.P.,THE LAW AND CUSTOM OF THE SOUTH AFRICAN CONSTITUTION. AFR SOUTH/AFR KIN LOC/G PROVS DIPLOM ADJUD ADMIN EXEC 20. PAGE 78 A1594
CT/SYS CONSTN JURID PARL/PROC

B42

CONOVER H.F.,FRENCH COLONIES IN AFRICA: A LIST OF REFERENCES. ALGERIA FRANCE MOROCCO SOMALIA SUDAN CULTURE AGRI LOC/G SECT FORCES DIPLOM INT/TRADE NAT/LISM HEALTH...CON/ANAL 20. PAGE 29 A0594
BIBLIOG AFR ECO/UNDEV COLONIAL

B42

US LIBRARY OF CONGRESS,ECONOMICS OF WAR (APRIL 1941-MARCH 1942). WOR-45 FINAN INDUS LOC/G NAT/G PLAN BUDGET RATION COST DEMAND...POLICY 20. PAGE 154 A3146
BIBLIOG/A INT/TRADE ECO/TAC WAR

B43

CARLO A.M.,ENSAYO DE UNA BIBLIOGRAFIA DE BIBLIOGRAFIAS MEXICANAS. ECO/UNDEV LOC/G ADMIN LEAD 20 MEXIC/AMER. PAGE 24 A0485
BIBLIOG L/A+17C NAT/G DIPLOM

B43

US DEPARTMENT OF STATE,NATIONAL SOCIALISM; BASIC PRINCIPLES, THEIR APPLICATION BY THE NAZI PARTY'S FOREIGN ORGANIZATION... GERMANY WOR-45 ECO/DEV LOC/G POL/PAR FORCES DIPLOM DOMIN COLONIAL ARMS/CONT COERCE NAT/LISM PWR 20 NAZI. PAGE 151 A3081
FASCISM SOCISM NAT/G TOTALISM

L44

WRIGHT Q.,"THE US AND INTERNATIONAL AGREEMENTS." FUT USA-45 CONSTN INTELL INT/ORG LOC/G NAT/G CHIEF CONSULT EX/STRUC DIPLOM LEGIT DRIVE PERCEPT PWR ...CONCPT CONGRESS 20. PAGE 167 A3407
DELIB/GP TOP/EX PEACE

B45

CONOVER H.F.,THE GOVERNMENTS OF THE MAJOR FOREIGN POWERS: A BIBLIOGRAPHY. FRANCE GERMANY ITALY UK USSR CONSTN LOC/G POL/PAR EX/STRUC FORCES ADMIN CT/SYS CIVMIL/REL TOTALISM...POLICY 19/20. PAGE 29 A0598
BIBLIOG NAT/G DIPLOM

B45

ROGERS W.C.,INTERNATIONAL ADMINISTRATION: A BIBLIOGRAPHY (PUBLICATION NO 92; A PAMPHLET). WOR-45 INT/ORG LOC/G NAT/G CENTRAL 20. PAGE 123 A2514
BIBLIOG/A ADMIN MGT DIPLOM

B47

CONOVER H.F.,NON-SELF-GOVERNING AREAS. BELGIUM FRANCE ITALY UK WOR+45 CULTURE ECO/UNDEV INT/ORG LOC/G NAT/G ECO/TAC INT/TRADE ADMIN HEALTH...SOC UN. PAGE 30 A0601
BIBLIOG/A COLONIAL DIPLOM

B47

HIRSHBERG H.S.,SUBJECT GUIDE TO UNITED STATES GOVERNMENT PUBLICATIONS. USA+45 USA-45 LAW ADMIN ...SOC 20. PAGE 65 A1340
BIBLIOG NAT/G DIPLOM LOC/G

B49

THE CURRENT DIGEST OF THE SOVIET PRESS. USSR WOR+45 LOC/G NAT/G DIPLOM EDU/PROP...MARXIST 20. PAGE 3 A0056
BIBLIOG/A COM ATTIT PRESS

B51

CHRISTENSEN A.N.,THE EVOLUTION OF LATIN AMERICAN GOVERNMENT: A BOOK OF READINGS. ECO/UNDEV INDUS LOC/G POL/PAR EX/STRUC LEGIS FOR/AID CT/SYS ...SOC/WK 20 SOUTH/AMER. PAGE 26 A0535
NAT/G CONSTN DIPLOM L/A+17C

B52

RIGGS F.W.,FORMOSA UNDER CHINESE NATIONALIST RULE. CHINA/COM USA+45 CONSTN AGRI FINAN LABOR LOC/G NAT/G POL/PAR FORCES HEALTH KNOWL...STAT WORK VAL/FREE 20. PAGE 121 A2479
ASIA FOR/AID DIPLOM

B52

THOM J.M.,GUIDE TO RESEARCH MATERIAL IN POLITICAL SCIENCE (PAMPHLET). ELITES LOC/G MUNIC NAT/G LEGIS DIPLOM ADJUD CIVMIL/REL GOV/REL PWR MGT. PAGE 143 A2919
BIBLIOG/A KNOWL

B53

STOUT H.M.,BRITISH GOVERNMENT. UK FINAN LOC/G POL/PAR DELIB/GP DIPLOM ADMIN COLONIAL CHOOSE ORD/FREE...JURID BIBLIOG 20 COMMONWLTH. PAGE 139 A2837
NAT/G PARL/PROC CONSTN NEW/LIB

C55

APTER D.E.,"THE GOLD COAST IN TRANSITION." AFR CONSTN LOC/G LEGIS DIPLOM COLONIAL CONTROL GOV/REL ...CHARTS BIBLIOG 20 CMN/WLTH. PAGE 8 A0170
ORD/FREE REPRESENT PARL/PROC NAT/G

B56

WILSON P.,GOVERNMENT AND POLITICS OF INDIA AND PAKISTAN: 1885-1955; A BIBLIOGRAPHY OF WORKS IN WESTERN LANGUAGES. INDIA PAKISTAN CONSTN LOC/G POL/PAR FORCES DIPLOM ADMIN WAR CHOOSE...BIOG CON/ANAL 19/20. PAGE 165 A3361
BIBLIOG COLONIAL NAT/G S/ASIA

B57

CARIBBEAN COMMISSION,A CATALOGUE OF CARIBBEAN COMMISSION PUBLICATIONS (PAMPHLET). WEST/IND CULTURE ECO/UNDEV LOC/G DIPLOM SOC. PAGE 24 A0483
BIBLIOG L/A+17C INT/ORG NAT/G

N57

BIBLIOGRAPHY OF NEW GUIDES AND AIDS TO PUBLIC DOCUMENTS USE, 1953-1956 (PAMPHLET). WOR+45 MUNIC DIPLOM...CON/ANAL CHARTS METH. PAGE 164 A3347
BIBLIOG/A NAT/G LOC/G INT/ORG

B58

GROBLER J.H.,AFRICA'S DESTINY. AFR EUR+WWI SOUTH/AFR UK USA+45 ELITES KIN LOC/G DIPLOM DISCRIM ATTIT CONSERVE MARXISM 20 ROOSEVLT/T NEGRO. PAGE 57 A1168
POLICY ORD/FREE COLONIAL CONSTN

B58

HENKIN L.,ARMS CONTROL AND INSPECTION IN AMERICAN LAW. LAW CONSTN INT/ORG LOC/G MUNIC NAT/G PROVS EDU/PROP LEGIT EXEC NUC/PWR KNOWL ORD/FREE...OBS TOT/POP CONGRESS 20. PAGE 64 A1315
USA+45 JURID ARMS/CONT

B58

JENNINGS I.,PROBLEMS OF THE NEW COMMONWEALTH. CEYLON INDIA PAKISTAN S/ASIA ECO/UNDEV INT/ORG LOC/G DIPLOM ECO/TAC INT/TRADE COLONIAL RACE/REL DISCRIM 20 COMMONWLTH PARLIAMENT. PAGE 74 A1508
NAT/LISM NEUTRAL FOR/AID POL/PAR

B58

NEAL F.W.,TITOISM IN ACTION. COM YUGOSLAVIA AGRI LOC/G DIPLOM TOTALISM...BIBLIOG 20 TITO/MARSH. PAGE 107 A2206
MARXISM POL/PAR CHIEF ADMIN

B59

GORDENKER L.,THE UNITED NATIONS AND THE PEACEFUL UNIFICATION OF KOREA. ASIA LAW LOC/G CONSULT ACT/RES DIPLOM DOMIN LEGIT ADJUD ADMIN ORD/FREE SOVEREIGN...INT GEN/METH UN COLD/WAR 20. PAGE 54 A1109
DELIB/GP KOREA INT/ORG

S59

PADELFORD N.J.,"REGIONAL COOPERATION IN THE SOUTH PACIFIC: THE SOUTH PACIFIC COMMISSION." FUT NEW/ZEALND UK WOR+45 CULTURE ECO/UNDEV LOC/G VOL/ASSN...OBS CON/ANAL UNESCO VAL/FREE AUSTRAL 20. PAGE 112 A2308
INT/ORG ADMIN

S60

FITZGIBBON R.H.,"DICTATORSHIP AND DEMOCRACY IN LATIN AMERICA." FUT ECO/DEV ECO/UNDEV INT/ORG LOC/G NAT/G TOP/EX PLAN TEC/DEV ECO/TAC CHOOSE ATTIT DRIVE PERSON ALL/VALS OAS TOT/POP 20. PAGE 46 A0943
L/A+17C ACT/RES INT/TRADE

B61

BURDETTE F.L.,POLITICAL SCIENCE: A SELECTED BIBLIOGRAPHY OF BOOKS IN PRINT, WITH ANNOTATIONS (PAMPHLET). LAW LOC/G NAT/G POL/PAR PROVS DIPLOM EDU/PROP ADMIN CHOOSE ATTIT 20. PAGE 21 A0432
BIBLIOG/A GOV/COMP CONCPT ROUTINE

B61
GRAEBNER N.,THE NEW ISOLATIONISM: A STUDY IN POLITICS AND FOREIGN POLICY SINCE 1960. USA+45 INT/ORG LOC/G NAT/G POL/PAR LEGIS BAL/PWR EDU/PROP CHOOSE ATTIT PERSON ORD/FREE 20 TRUMAN/HS EISNHWR/DD. PAGE 55 A1120 — EXEC PWR DIPLOM

B61
HARRISON J.P.,GUIDE TO MATERIALS ON LATIN AMERICA IN THE NATIONAL ARCHIVES (2 VOLS.). USA+45 ECO/UNDEV FINAN LOC/G FORCES 20. PAGE 62 A1271 — BIBLIOG L/A+17C NAT/G DIPLOM

B61
YDIT M.,INTERNATIONALISED TERRITORIES. FUT WOR+45 WOR-45 CONSTN VOL/ASSN CREATE PLAN LEGIT PEACE ORD/FREE...GEOG INT/LAW JURID SOC NEW/IDEA OBS RECORD SAMP TIME/SEQ TREND 19/20 BERLIN. PAGE 169 A3431 — LOC/G INT/ORG DIPLOM SOVEREIGN

B62
BOWLES C.,THE CONSCIENCE OF A LIBERAL. COM USA+45 WOR+45 STRUCT LOC/G NAT/G FORCES LEGIS GOV/REL DISCRIM 20 UN CIV/RIGHTS. PAGE 18 A0361 — DIPLOM POLICY

B62
COSTA RICA UNIVERSIDAD BIBL,LISTA DE TESIS DE GRADO DE LA UNIVERSIDAD DE COSTA RICA. COSTA/RICA LAW LOC/G ADMIN LEAD...SOC 20. PAGE 31 A0631 — BIBLIOG/A NAT/G DIPLOM ECO/UNDEV

L62
CORET A.,"LES PROVINCES PORTUGALLES D'OUTREMER ET L'ONU." AFR PORTUGAL S/ASIA WOR+45 LOC/G NAT/G DOMIN...CONCPT TIME/SEQ UN 20 GOA. PAGE 31 A0620 — INT/ORG SOVEREIGN COLONIAL

S62
GUETZKOW H.,"THE POTENTIAL OF CASE STUDY IN ANALYZING INTERNATIONAL CONFLICT." EUR+WWI FUT GERMANY INTELL SOCIETY STRUCT INT/ORG LOC/G NAT/G CONSULT CREATE PLAN CHOOSE ATTIT RIGID/FLEX ...POLICY SAAR 20. PAGE 58 A1188 — EDU/PROP METH/CNCPT COERCE FRANCE

B63
JUDD P.,AFRICAN INDEPENDENCE: THE EXPLODING EMERGENCE OF THE NEW AFRICAN NATIONS. AFR UK LAW CONSTN CULTURE KIN DIPLOM ATTIT...CHARTS BIBLIOG 20 UN DEGAULLE/C NEGRO THIRD/WRLD. PAGE 75 A1542 — ORD/FREE POLICY DOMIN LOC/G

B63
LANOUE G.R.,A BIBLIOGRAPHY OF DOCTORAL DISSERTATIONS ON POLITICS AND RELIGION. USA+45 USA-45 CONSTN PROVS DIPLOM CT/SYS MORAL...POLICY JURID CONCPT 20. PAGE 84 A1728 — BIBLIOG NAT/G LOC/G SECT

B63
LIVNEH E.,ISRAEL LEGAL BIBLIOGRAPHY IN EUROPEAN LANGUAGES. ISRAEL LOC/G JUDGE TAX...INT/LAW 20. PAGE 90 A1846 — BIBLIOG LAW NAT/G CONSTN

B63
MONTER W.,THE GOVERNMENT OF GENEVA, 1536-1605 (DOCTORAL THESIS). SWITZERLND DIPLOM LEAD ORD/FREE SOVEREIGN 16/17 CALVIN/J ROME. PAGE 103 A2112 — SECT FINAN LOC/G ADMIN

B63
RIVKIN A.,THE AFRICAN PRESENCE IN WORLD AFFAIRS. ECO/UNDEV AGRI INT/ORG LOC/G NAT/LISM...OBS PREDICT GOV/COMP 20. PAGE 121 A2489 — AFR NAT/G DIPLOM BAL/PWR

S63
MAZRUI A.A.,"ON THE CONCEPT 'WE ARE ALL AFRICANS'." AFR CULTURE KIN LOC/G NAT/G DOMIN EDU/PROP LEGIT ATTIT PERCEPT PERSON KNOWL ORD/FREE...TIME/SEQ TOT/POP 20. PAGE 97 A1986 — PROVS INT/ORG NAT/LISM

B64
HALPERN J.M.,GOVERNMENT, POLITICS, AND SOCIAL STRUCTURE IN LAOS. LAOS CULTURE SOCIETY STRATA STRUCT FAM DIPLOM DOMIN MARXISM...INT GOV/COMP WORSHIP SOC/INTEG 20. PAGE 60 A1242 — NAT/G SOC LOC/G

B64
HARMON R.B.,BIBLIOGRAPHY OF BIBLIOGRAPHIES IN POLITICAL SCIENCE (MIMEOGRAPHED PAPER: LIMITED EDITION). WOR+45 WOR-45 INT/ORG POL/PAR GOV/REL ALL/IDEOS...INT/LAW JURID MGT 19/20. PAGE 61 A1260 — BIBLIOG NAT/G DIPLOM LOC/G

B64
JACKSON W.V.,LIBRARY GUIDE FOR BRAZILIAN STUDIES. BRAZIL USA+45 STRUCT DIPLOM ADMIN...SOC 20. PAGE 72 A1481 — BIBLIOG L/A+17C NAT/G LOC/G

B64
JACOB P.E.,THE INTEGRATION OF POLITICAL COMMUNITIES. USA+45 WOR+45 CULTURE LOC/G MUNIC NAT/G CREATE PLAN LEGIT REGION COERCE ALL/VALS ...POLICY GEOG PSY SOC TREND HYPO/EXP GEN/LAWS VAL/FREE 20. PAGE 72 A1483 — INT/ORG METH/CNCPT SIMUL STAT

B64
MAHAR J.M.,INDIA: A CRITICAL BIBLIOGRAPHY. INDIA PAKISTAN CULTURE ECO/UNDEV LOC/G POL/PAR SECT PROB/SOLV DIPLOM ADMIN COLONIAL PARL/PROC ATTIT 20. PAGE 93 A1906 — BIBLIOG/A S/ASIA NAT/G LEAD

B64
PERKINS D.,THE AMERICAN DEMOCRACY: ITS RISE TO POWER. ASIA USSR LAW CULTURE FINAN EDU/PROP COLONIAL CHOOSE...POLICY CHARTS BIBLIOG WORSHIP PRESIDENT 15/20 NEGRO. PAGE 115 A2362 — LOC/G ECO/TAC WAR DIPLOM

B64
RICHARDSON I.L.,BIBLIOGRAFIA BRASILEIRA DE ADMINISTRACAO PUBLICA E ASSUNTOS CORRELATOS. BRAZIL CONSTN FINAN LOC/G NAT/G POL/PAR PLAN DIPLOM RECEIVE ATTIT...METH 20. PAGE 121 A2474 — BIBLIOG MGT ADMIN LAW

S64
HUTCHINSON E.C.,"AMERICAN AID TO AFRICA." FUT USA+45 MARKET INT/ORG LOC/G NAT/G PUB/INST PLAN ECO/TAC ATTIT RIGID/FLEX...POLICY CONCPT TREND 20. PAGE 69 A1423 — AFR ECO/UNDEV FOR/AID

B65
HARMON R.B.,POLITICAL SCIENCE: A BIBLIOGRAPHICAL GUIDE TO THE LITERATURE. WOR+45 WOR-45 R+D INT/ORG LOC/G NAT/G DIPLOM ADMIN...CONCPT METH. PAGE 61 A1261 — BIBLIOG POL/PAR LAW GOV/COMP

B65
US LIBRARY OF CONGRESS,RARE BOOKS DIVISION: GUIDE TO ITS COLLECTION AND SERVICES. LOC/G SECT WAR. PAGE 155 A3158 — BIBLIOG/A NAT/G DIPLOM

B65
WITHERELL J.W.,MADAGASCAR AND ADJACENT ISLANDS; A GUIDE TO OFFICIAL PUBLICATIONS (PAMPHLET). FRANCE MADAGASCAR S/ASIA UK LAW OP/RES PLAN DIPLOM ...POLICY CON/ANAL 19/20. PAGE 165 A3371 — BIBLIOG COLONIAL LOC/G ADMIN

B66
AMERICAN JOURNAL COMP LAW,THE AMERICAN JOURNAL OF COMPARATIVE LAW READER. EUR+WWI USA+45 USA-45 LAW CONSTN LOC/G MUNIC NAT/G DIPLOM...ANTHOL 20 SUPREME/CT EURCT/JUST. PAGE 7 A0151 — IDEA/COMP JURID INT/LAW CT/SYS

B66
EPSTEIN F.T.,THE AMERICAN BIBLIOGRAPHY OF RUSSIAN AND EAST EUROPEAN STUDIES FOR 1964. USSR LOC/G NAT/G POL/PAR FORCES ADMIN ARMS/CONT...JURID CONCPT 20 UN. PAGE 42 A0855 — BIBLIOG COM MARXISM DIPLOM

B66
HARMON R.B.,SOURCES AND PROBLEMS OF BIBLIOGRAPHY IN POLITICAL SCIENCE (PAMPHLET). INT/ORG LOC/G MUNIC POL/PAR ADMIN GOV/REL ALL/IDEOS...JURID MGT CONCPT 19/20. PAGE 61 A1262 — BIBLIOG DIPLOM INT/LAW NAT/G

B66
NEUMANN R.G.,THE GOVERNMENT OF THE GERMAN FEDERAL REPUBLIC. EUR+WWI GERMANY/W LOC/G EX/STRUC LEGIS CT/SYS INGP/REL PWR...BIBLIOG 20 ADENAUER/K. PAGE 108 A2222 — NAT/G POL/PAR DIPLOM CONSTN

L66
SEYLER W.C.,"DOCTORAL DISSERTATIONS IN POLITICAL SCIENCE IN UNIVERSITIES OF THE UNITED STATES AND CANADA." INT/ORG LOC/G ADMIN...INT/LAW MGT GOV/COMP. PAGE 131 A2690 — BIBLIOG LAW NAT/G

S66
"RESEARCH WORK 1965-1966." NEW/ZEALND ELITES ACADEM LOC/G MUNIC POL/PAR PROVS DIPLOM COLONIAL...SOC 20 AUSTRAL. PAGE 4 A0073 — BIBLIOG NAT/G CULTURE S/ASIA

B67
POGANY A.H.,POLITICAL SCIENCE AND INTERNATIONAL RELATIONS, BOOKS RECOMMENDED FOR AMERICAN CATHOLIC COLLEGE LIBRARIES. INT/ORG LOC/G NAT/G FORCES BAL/PWR ECO/TAC NUC/PWR...CATH INT/LAW TREATY 20. PAGE 117 A2393 — BIBLIOG DIPLOM

B67
SACHS M.Y.,THE WORLDMARK ENCYCLOPEDIA OF THE NATIONS (5 VOLS.). ELITES SOCIETY STRATA ECO/DEV ECO/UNDEV AGRI EXTR/IND FINAN LABOR LOC/G NAT/G POL/PAR SECT INT/TRADE SOVEREIGN...SOC 20. PAGE 126 A2585 — WOR+45 INT/ORG BAL/PWR

B67
SCHWARTZ M.A.,PUBLIC OPINION AND CANADIAN IDENTITY. CANADA SOCIETY LOC/G DIPLOM ADMIN LEAD REGION GP/REL SAMP. PAGE 130 A2657 — ATTIT NAT/G NAT/LISM POL/PAR

B67
US DEPARTMENT OF THE ARMY,CIVILIAN IN PEACE, SOLDIER IN WAR: A BIBLIOGRAPHIC SURVEY OF THE ARMY AND AIR NATIONAL GUARD (PAMPHLET, NOS. 130-2). USA+45 USA-45 LOC/G NAT/G PROVS LEGIS PLAN ADMIN ATTIT ORD/FREE...POLICY 19/20. PAGE 152 A3111 — BIBLIOG/A FORCES ROLE DIPLOM

S67
YOUNG K.T.,"UNITED STATES POLICY AND VIETNAMESE POLITICAL VIABILITY 1954-1967." VIETNAM/S LOC/G MUNIC FOR/AID ORD/FREE...POLICY 20. PAGE 169 A3437 — LEAD ADMIN GP/REL EFFICIENCY

B82
POOLE W.F.,INDEX TO PERIODICAL LITERATURE. LOC/G NAT/G DIPLOM ADMIN...HUM PHIL/SCI SOC 19. PAGE 117 A2396 — BIBLIOG USA-45 ALL/VALS SOCIETY

B91
SIDGWICK H.,THE ELEMENTS OF POLITICS. LOC/G NAT/G LEGIS DIPLOM ADJUD CONTROL EXEC PARL/PROC REPRESENT GOV/REL SOVEREIGN ALL/IDEOS 19 MILL/JS BENTHAM/J. PAGE 132 A2713 — POLICY LAW CONCPT

LOCAL GOVERNMENT....SEE LOC/G

LOCKE/JOHN....JOHN LOCKE

B62
EBENSTEIN W.,TWO WAYS OF LIFE. USA+45 CULTURE ECO/DEV PLAN EDU/PROP CONTROL ORD/FREE...GOV/COMP IDEA/COMP T 20 MARX/KARL ENGELS/F LENIN/VI LOCKE/JOHN MILL/JS. PAGE 40 A0819 — MARXISM POPULISM ECO/TAC DIPLOM

LOCKHART W.B. A1849

LODGE H.C. A1850

LODGE/HC....HENRY CABOT LODGE

LOEWENHEIM F.L. A1851

LOFTUS M.L. A1852

LOG....LOGIC

B61
NEWMAN R.P.,RECOGNITION OF COMMUNIST CHINA? A STUDY IN ARGUMENT. CHINA/COM NAT/G PROB/SOLV RATIONAL ...INT/LAW LOG IDEA/COMP BIBLIOG 20. PAGE 108 A2226 — MARXISM ATTIT DIPLOM POLICY

B62
BELL C.,NEGOTIATION FROM STRENGTH. WOR+45 FACE/GP INT/ORG DELIB/GP FORCES PLAN DOMIN COERCE NUC/PWR PEACE DRIVE PWR...POLICY LOG OBS RECORD INT SAMP TREND COLD/WAR 20. PAGE 13 A0255 — NAT/G CONCPT DIPLOM

LOGAN R.W. A1853

LOGIC....SEE LOG

LOGIST/MGT....LOGISTICS MANAGEMENT INSTITUTE

LOGISTICS MANAGEMENT INSTITUTE....SEE LOGIST/MGT

LONDON K. A1854,A1855

LONDON....LONDON, ENGLAND

LONDON INSTITUTE WORLD AFFAIRS A1856

LONDON LIBRARY ASSOCIATION A1857

LONDON SCHOOL ECONOMICS-POL A1858

LONG B. A1859

LONG/FAMLY....THE LONG FAMILY OF LOUISIANA

LONGAKER R.P. A2869

LONGE/FD....F.D. LONGE

LOOMIE A.J. A1860

LOPEZ M.M. A1861

LOPEZIBOR J. A1862

LORIMER J. A1863

LOS/ANG....LOS ANGELES

LOSMAN D.L. A1864

LOUISIANA....LOUISIANA

LOUISVILLE....LOUISVILLE, KENTUCKY

LOUVERT/T....L'OUVERTURE TOUSSANT

LOVE....AFFECTION, FRIENDSHIP, SEX RELATIONS

B21
BALFOUR A.J.,ESSAYS SPECULATIVE AND POLITICAL. SEA CULTURE CREATE WAR NAT/LISM PEACE LOVE...ART/METH INT/LAW CONCPT ANTHOL 20 JEWS. PAGE 10 A0211 — PHIL/SCI SOCIETY DIPLOM

B48
VISSON A.,AS OTHERS SEE US. EUR+WWI FRANCE UK USA+45 CULTURE INTELL SOCIETY STRATA NAT/G POL/PAR FOR/AID ATTIT DRIVE LOVE ORD/FREE RESPECT WEALTH ...PLURIST SOC OBS TOT/POP 20. PAGE 159 A3244 — USA-45 PERCEPT

B50
GLEASON J.H.,THE GENESIS OF RUSSOPHOBIA IN GREAT BRITAIN: A STUDY OF THE INTERACTION OF POLICY AND OPINION. ASIA RUSSIA UK NAT/G AGREE CONTROL REV WAR LOVE PWR TREATY 19. PAGE 53 A1080 — DIPLOM POLICY DOMIN COLONIAL

S51
ICHHEISER G.,"MISUNDERSTANDING IN INTERNATIONAL RELATIONS." UNIV SOCIETY FACE/GP INT/ORG SECT ATTIT PERSON RIGID/FLEX LOVE RESPECT...RELATIV PSY SOC CONCPT MYTH SOC/EXP GEN/LAWS. PAGE 70 A1431 — PERCEPT STERTYP NAT/LISM DIPLOM

L52
NIEBUHR R.,"THE MORAL IMPLICATIONS OF LOYALTY TO THE UNITED NATIONS." WOR+45 WOR-45 SOCIETY ECO/DEV INT/ORG VOL/ASSN PEACE ATTIT PERSON LOVE ORD/FREE PWR RESPECT...CONCPT UN TOT/POP COLD/WAR UNESCO 20. PAGE 109 A2236 — SUPEGO GEN/LAWS

B53
COUSINS N.,WHO SPEAKS FOR MAN. GERMANY KOREA WOR+45 SOCIETY INT/ORG NAT/G CREATE EDU/PROP HEALTH KNOWL LOVE MORAL...OBS SELF/OBS BIOG HYPO/EXP TOT/POP 20 CHINJAP. PAGE 32 A0642 — ATTIT WAR PEACE

B55
KROPOTKIN P.,MUTUAL AID, A FACTOR OF EVOLUTION (1902). UNIV ADJUST ATTIT HEREDITY PERSON LOVE DARWIN/C. PAGE 82 A1687 — INGP/REL SOCIETY GEN/LAWS BIO/SOC

B57
BLOOMFIELD L.M.,EGYPT, ISRAEL AND THE GULF OF AQABA: IN INTERNATIONAL LAW. LAW NAT/G CONSULT FORCES PLAN ECO/TAC ROUTINE COERCE ATTIT DRIVE PERCEPT PERSON RIGID/FLEX LOVE PWR WEALTH...GEOG CONCPT MYTH TREND. PAGE 15 A0314 — ISLAM INT/LAW UAR

B57
STRACHEY A.,THE UNCONSCIOUS MOTIVES OF WAR; A PSYCHO-ANALYTICAL CONTRIBUTION. UNIV SOCIETY DIPLOM DREAM GP/REL ADJUST ATTIT DISPL PERCEPT PERSON KNOWL MORAL. PAGE 139 A2840 — WAR DRIVE LOVE PSY

B59
COUDENHOVE-KALERGI,FROM WAR TO PEACE. USA+45 USSR WOR+45 WOR-45 LAW INT/ORG NAT/G LEGIT COERCE LOVE ...POLICY PLURIST METH/CNCPT STERTYP TOT/POP UN 20 NATO. PAGE 31 A0636 — FUT ORD/FREE

S59
HARVEY M.F.,"THE PALESTINE REFUGEE PROBLEM: ELEMENTS OF A SOLUTION." ISLAM LAW INT/ORG DELIB/GP TOP/EX ECO/TAC ROUTINE DRIVE HEALTH LOVE ORD/FREE PWR WEALTH...MAJORIT FAO 20. PAGE 62 A1283 — ACT/RES LEGIT PEACE ISRAEL

B60
VAN HOOGSTRATE D.J.,AMERICAN FOREIGN POLICY: REALISTS AND IDEALISTS: A CATHOLIC INTERPRETATION. BAL/PWR FOR/AID ARMS/CONT GOV/REL PEACE LOVE MORAL SOVEREIGN CATHISM...BIBLIOG 20. PAGE 158 A3213 — CATH DIPLOM POLICY IDEA/COMP

S60
SCHWELB E.,"INTERNATIONAL CONVENTIONS ON HUMAN RIGHTS." FUT WOR+45 LAW CONSTN CULTURE SOCIETY STRUCT VOL/ASSN DELIB/GP PLAN ADJUD SUPEGO LOVE MORAL...SOC CONCPT STAT RECORD HIST/WRIT TREND 20 UN. PAGE 130 A2664 — INT/ORG HUM

B63
ROBERTSON A.H.,HUMAN RIGHTS IN EUROPE. CONSTN SOCIETY INT/ORG NAT/G VOL/ASSN DELIB/GP ACT/RES PLAN ADJUD REGION ROUTINE ATTIT LOVE ORD/FREE RESPECT...JURID SOC CONCPT SOC/EXP UN 20. PAGE 122 A2498 — EUR+WWI PERSON

B63
SCHMELTZ G.W.,LA POLITIQUE MONDIALE CONTEMPORAINE. SOCIETY ECO/UNDEV INDUS INT/ORG NAT/G POL/PAR CONSULT DELIB/GP PLAN TEC/DEV ECO/TAC DOMIN EDU/PROP ROUTINE COERCE PERCEPT PERSON LOVE SKILL ...SOC RECORD TOT/POP. PAGE 128 A2629 — WOR+45 COLONIAL

B66
MAYER P.,THE PACIFIST CONSCIENCE. SECT CREATE ARMS/CONT WAR RACE/REL ATTIT LOVE...ANTHOL PACIFIST WORSHIP FREUD/S GANDHI/M LAO/TZU KING/MAR/L CONSCN/OBJ. PAGE 97 A1984 — DIPLOM PACIFISM SUPEGO

S67
KINGSLEY R.E.,"THE US BUSINESS IMAGE IN LATIN AMERICA." L/A+17C USA+45 NAT/G TEC/DEV CAP/ISM FOR/AID DOMIN EDU/PROP...CONCPT LING IDEA/COMP 20. PAGE 79 A1626 — ATTIT LOVE DIPLOM ECO/UNDEV

LOVEDAY A. A1865

LOVELL R.I. A1866

LOVESTN/J....JAY LOVESTONE

LOWELL A.L. A1867

LOWENSTEIN A.K. A1868

LOWENSTEIN R. A1869

LOWENTHAL R. A1404

LOWITH

LOYALTY....SEE SUPEGO

LUA....LUA, OR LAWA: VILLAGE PEOPLES OF NORTHERN THAILAND

LUANDA....LUANDA, ANGOLA

LUARD E. A1870,A1871

LUBBOCK/TX....LUBBOCK, TEXAS

LUDWIG/BAV....LUDWIG THE BAVARIAN

LUKACS J. A1872

LUMBERING....SEE EXTR/IND

LUNDBERG F. A1873

LUTHER/M....MARTIN LUTHER

LUTHULI A. A1874

LUTZ F.A. A1875,A1876

LUVALE....LUVALE TRIBE, CENTRAL AFRICA

LUXEMBOURG....SEE ALSO APPROPRIATE TIME/SPACE/CULTURE INDEX

B62
MEADE J.E.,CASE STUDIES IN EUROPEAN ECONOMIC UNION. BELGIUM EUR+WWI LUXEMBOURG NAT/G INT/TRADE REGION ROUTINE WEALTH...METH/CNCPT STAT CHARTS ECSC TOT/POP OEEC EEC 20. PAGE 99 A2028
INT/ORG ECO/TAC

LUZON....LUZON, PHILIPPINES

LYND S. A1877

LYON J.T. A2598

LYON P. A1878,A1879

LYONS D. A2325

LYONS F.S.L. A1880

LYONS G.M. A0661,A1881

M

MAC CHESNEY B. A1883

MAC MILLAN W.M. A1884

MACAO....MACAO

MACAPAGL/D....DIOSDADO MACAPAGAL

MACARTHR/D....DOUGLAS MACARTHUR

B64
REES D.,KOREA: THE LIMITED WAR. ASIA KOREA WOR+45 NAT/G CIVMIL/REL PERS/REL PERSON...POLICY CHARTS 20 UN TRUMAN/HS MACARTHR/D. PAGE 120 A2455
DIPLOM WAR INT/ORG FORCES

MACARTHUR D. A1885

MACDONALD D.F. A1886

MACDONALD R.S.J. A1887

MACDONALD R.W. A1888

MACHIAVELL....NICCOLO MACHIAVELLI

MACHIAVELLISM....SEE REALPOL,

B37
BORGESE G.A.,GOLIATH: THE MARCH OF FASCISM. GERMANY ITALY LAW POL/PAR SECT DIPLOM SOCISM...JURID MYTH 20 DANTE MACHIAVELL MUSSOLIN/B. PAGE 17 A0341
POLICY NAT/LISM FASCISM NAT/G

B55
KOHN H.,NATIONALISM: ITS MEANING AND HISTORY. GP/REL INGP/REL ATTIT...CONCPT NAT/COMP 16/20 MACHIAVELL. PAGE 81 A1662
NAT/LISM DIPLOM FASCISM REV

MACHOWSKI K. A1889

MACIVER R.M. A1890,A1891,A1892

MACK R.T. A1893

MACKENTOSH J.M. A1894

MACKESY P. A1895

MACLAURIN J. A1896

MACLEISH/A....ARCHIBALD MACLEISH

MACLES L.M. A1897

MACLURE M. A1898

MACMAHON A.W. A1899,A1900

MACMILLN/H....HAROLD MACMILLAN, PRIMÈ MINISTER

MACMINN N. A1901

MACOBY S. A0451

MACRIDIS R.C. A1902

MACWHINNEY E. A1903

MADAGASCAR....SEE ALSO AFR

B60
DUMON F.,LA COMMUNAUTE FRANCO-AFRO-MALGACHE: SES ORIGINES, SES INSTITUTIONS, SON EVOLUTION. FRANCE MADAGASCAR POL/PAR DIPLOM ADMIN ATTIT...TREND T 20. PAGE 39 A0798
JURID INT/ORG AFR CONSTN

B62
KENT R.K.,FROM MADAGASCAR TO THE MALAGASY REPUBLIC. FRANCE MADAGASCAR DIPLOM NAT/LISM ORD/FREE...MGT 18/20. PAGE 78 A1596
COLONIAL SOVEREIGN REV POL/PAR

S62
PIQUEMAL M.,"LA COOPERATION FINANCIERE ENTRE LA FRANCE ET LES ETATS AFRICAINS ET MALGACHE." ISLAM INT/ORG TOP/EX ECO/TAC...JURID CHARTS 20. PAGE 116 A2383
AFR FINAN FRANCE MADAGASCAR

S62
RAZAFIMBAHINY J.,"L'ORGANISATION AFRICAINE ET MALGACHE DE COOPERATION ECONOMIQUE." AFR ISLAM MADAGASCAR NAT/G ACT/RES ECO/TAC ALL/VALS ...TIME/SEQ 20. PAGE 120 A2454
INT/ORG ECO/UNDEV

S63
GANDOLFI A.,"LES ACCORDS DE COOPERATION EN MATIERE DE POLITIQUE ETRANGERE ENTRE LA FRANCE ET LES NOUVEAUX ETATS AFRICAINS ET." AFR ISLAM MADAGASCAR WOR+45 ECO/DEV INT/ORG NAT/G DELIB/GP ECO/TAC ALL/VALS...CON/ANAL 20. PAGE 51 A1038
VOL/ASSN ECO/UNDEV DIPLOM FRANCE

B65
WITHERELL J.W.,MADAGASCAR AND ADJACENT ISLANDS; A GUIDE TO OFFICIAL PUBLICATIONS (PAMPHLET). FRANCE MADAGASCAR S/ASIA UK LAW OP/RES PLAN DIPLOM ...POLICY CON/ANAL 19/20. PAGE 165 A3371
BIBLIOG COLONIAL LOC/G ADMIN

MADDOX U. A0242

MADERO/F....FRANCISCO MADERO

MADISON/J....PRESIDENT JAMES MADISON

B55
PERKINS B.,THE FIRST RAPPROCHEMENTS: ENGLAND AND THE UNITED STATES, 1795-1805. UK USA-45 ATTIT ...HIST/WRIT BIBLIOG 18/19 MADISON/J WAR/1812. PAGE 115 A2357
DIPLOM COLONIAL WAR

MAFIA....MAFIA

B66
HOEVELER H.J.,INTERNATIONALE BEKAMPFUNG DES VERBRECHENS. AUSTRIA SWITZERLND WOR+45 INT/ORG CONTROL BIO/SOC...METH/COMP NAT/COMP 20 MAFIA SCOT/YARD FBI. PAGE 66 A1352
CRIMLGY CRIME DIPLOM INT/LAW

MAGATHAN W. A1904

MAGGS P.B. A1905

MAGHREB....SEE ALSO ISLAM

MAGNA/CART....MAGNA CARTA

B90
HOSMAR J.K.,A SHORT HISTORY OF ANGLO-SAXON FREEDOM. UK USA-45 ROMAN/EMP NAT/G EX/STRUC LEGIS COLONIAL REV NAT/LISM POPULISM PARLIAMENT ANGLO/SAX MAGNA/CART. PAGE 68 A1394
CONSTN ORD/FREE DIPLOM PARL/PROC

MAGON/F....FLORES MAGON

MAHAR J.M. A1906

MAIER J. A1907

MAIMONIDES....MAIMONIDES

MAINE H.S. A1908

MAINE....MAINE

MAIR L.P. A1909

MAISEL A.Q. A1910

MAITLAND/F....FREDERIC WILLIAM MAITLAND

MAJORIT....MAJORITARIAN

NCO
CARRINGTON C.E.,THE COMMONWEALTH IN AFRICA (PAMPHLET). UK STRUCT NAT/G COLONIAL REPRESENT GOV/REL RACE/REL NAT/LISM...MAJORIT 20 EEC NEGRO COLD/WAR. PAGE 25 A0500
ECO/UNDEV AFR DIPLOM PLAN

B24
POOLE D.C.,THE CONDUCT OF FOREIGN RELATIONS UNDER MODERN DEMOCRATIC CONDITIONS. EUR+WWI USA-45 INT/ORG PLAN LEGIT ADMIN KNOWL PWR...MAJORIT OBS/ENVIR HIST/WRIT GEN/LAWS 20. PAGE 117 A2395
NAT/G EDU/PROP DIPLOM

B27
GOOCH G.P.,ENGLISH DEMOCRATIC IDEAS IN THE SEVENTEENTH CENTURY (2ND ED.). UK LAW SECT FORCES DIPLOM LEAD PARL/PROC REV ATTIT AUTHORIT...ANARCH CONCPT 17 PARLIAMENT CMN/WLTH REFORMERS. PAGE 54 A1100
IDEA/COMP MAJORIT EX/STRUC CONSERVE

B29
CONWELL-EVANS T.P.,THE LEAGUE COUNCIL IN ACTION. EUR+WWI TURKEY UK USSR WOR-45 INT/ORG FORCES JUDGE ECO/TAC EDU/PROP LEGIT ROUTINE ARMS/CONT COERCE ATTIT PWR...MAJORIT GEOG JURID CONCPT LEAGUE/NAT TOT/POP VAL/FREE TUNIS 20. PAGE 30 A0605
DELIB/GP INT/LAW

B30
FLEMMING D.,THE TREATY VETO OF THE AMERICAN SENATE. FUT USA+45 USA-45 CONSTN INT/ORG NAT/G TOP/EX LEGIT GOV/REL PWR...POLICY MAJORIT CONCPT OBS TIME/SEQ CONGRESS 20. PAGE 46 A0949
LEGIS RIGID/FLEX

B33
WAMBAUCH S.,PLEBISCITES SINCE THE WORLD WAR: WITH A COLLECTION OF OFFICIAL DOCUMENTS. WOR-45 COLONIAL SANCTION...MAJORIT DECISION CHARTS BIBLIOG 19/20 WWI. PAGE 161 A3272
DIPLOM CONSTN NAT/G CHOOSE

B33
PUBLIC OPINION AND WORLD POLITICS. UNIV LAW CULTURE NAT/G PRESS REV GP/REL...MAJORIT METH/COMP ANTHOL 20. PAGE 167 A3400
DIPLOM EDU/PROP ATTIT MAJORITY

B43
SULZBACH W.,NATIONAL CONSCIOUSNESS. FUT WOR-45 INT/ORG PEACE MORAL FASCISM MARXISM...MAJORIT TREND WORSHIP 19/20 LEAGUE/NAT INTERVENT WWI. PAGE 140 A2862
NAT/LISM NAT/G DIPLOM WAR

B46
STURZO D.L.,NATIONALISM AND INTERNATIONALISM. WOR-45 INT/ORG LABOR NAT/G POL/PAR TOTALISM MORAL ORD/FREE FASCISM...MAJORIT 19/20 UN LEAGUE/NAT MUSSOLIN/B. PAGE 140 A2857
NAT/LISM DIPLOM WAR PEACE

B50
DUCLOS P.,L'EVOLUTION DES RAPPORTS POLITIQUES DEPUIS 1750 (LIBERTE, INTEGRATION, UNITE). LAW INT/ORG FEDERAL TOTALISM ATTIT PWR...MAJORIT BIBLIOG 18/20 PARLIAMENT EUROPE. PAGE 39 A0792
ORD/FREE DIPLOM NAT/G GOV/COMP

B51
SWISHER C.B.,THE THEORY AND PRACTICE OF AMERICAN NATIONAL GOVERNMENT. CULTURE LEGIS DIPLOM ADJUD ADMIN WAR PEACE ORD/FREE...MAJORIT 17/20. PAGE 140 A2872
CONSTN NAT/G GOV/REL GEN/LAWS

B51
UNESCO,FREEDOM AND CULTURE. FUT WOR+45 CONSTN CULTURE PERF/ART VOL/ASSN EDU/PROP PEACE ATTIT ALL/VALS SOVEREIGN...POLICY MAJORIT CONCPT TREND STERTYP GEN/LAWS UN TOT/POP 20. PAGE 147 A3013
INT/ORG SOCIETY

B53
BORGESE G.,FOUNDATIONS OF THE WORLD REPUBLIC. FUT SOCIETY NAT/G CREATE LEGIT PERSON MORAL...MAJORIT CON/ANAL LEAGUE/NAT TOT/POP 20. PAGE 17 A0340
INT/ORG CONSTN PEACE

S53
BOULDING K.E.,"ECONOMIC ISSUES IN INTERNATIONAL CONFLICT." WOR+45 ECO/DEV NAT/G TOP/EX DIPLOM ECO/TAC DOMIN ATTIT WEALTH...MAJORIT OBS/ENVIR TREND GEN/LAWS COLD/WAR TOT/POP 20. PAGE 17 A0345
PWR FOR/AID

B54
MILLARD E.L.,FREEDOM IN A FEDERAL WORLD. FUT WOR+45 VOL/ASSN TOP/EX LEGIT ROUTINE FEDERAL PEACE ATTIT DISPL ORD/FREE PWR...MAJORIT INT/LAW JURID TREND COLD/WAR 20. PAGE 101 A2073
INT/ORG CREATE ADJUD BAL/PWR

B55
MOCH J.,HUMAN FOLLY: DISARM OR PERISH. USA+45 WOR+45 SOCIETY INT/ORG NAT/G ACT/RES EDU/PROP ATTIT PERSON KNOWL ORD/FREE PWR...MAJORIT TOT/POP COLD/WAR 20. PAGE 102 A2093
FUT DELIB/GP ARMS/CONT NUC/PWR

B56
JAMESON J.F.,THE AMERICAN REVOLUTION CONSIDERED AS A SOCIAL MOVEMENT. USA-45 AGRI FINAN SECT INT/TRADE REPRESENT SUFF INGP/REL RACE/REL DISCRIM...MAJORIT 18/19 CHURCH/STA. PAGE 73 A1494
ORD/FREE REV FEDERAL CONSTN

B56
ROBERTS H.L.,RUSSIA AND AMERICA. CHINA/COM S/ASIA USSR FORCES TEC/DEV FOR/AID NUC/PWR ALL/IDEOS ...MAJORIT TREND NAT/COMP 20 COLD/WAR UN NATO. PAGE 122 A2494
DIPLOM INT/ORG BAL/PWR TOTALISM

B57
BROMBERGER M.,LES SECRETS DE L'EXPEDITION D'EGYPTE. FRANCE ISLAM UAR UK USA+45 USSR WOR+45 INT/ORG NAT/G FORCES BAL/PWR ECO/TAC DOMIN WAR NAT/LISM ATTIT PWR SOVEREIGN...MAJORIT TIME/SEQ CHARTS SUEZ COLD/WAR 20. PAGE 19 A0387
COERCE DIPLOM

B57
BURNS A.,IN DEFENCE OF COLONIES; BRITISH COLONIAL TERRITORIES IN INTERNATIONAL AFFAIRS. UK ECO/UNDEV PLAN DOMIN SOVEREIGN...MAJORIT 18/20 CMN/WLTH INTERVENT. PAGE 22 A0439
COLONIAL POLICY ATTIT DIPLOM

C57
TANG P.S.H.,"COMMUNIST CHINA TODAY: DOMESTIC AND FOREIGN POLICIES." CHINA/COM COM S/ASIA USSR STRATA FORCES DIPLOM EDU/PROP COERCE GOV/REL...POLICY MAJORIT BIBLIOG 20. PAGE 141 A2886
POL/PAR LEAD ADMIN CONSTN

B58
HOLT R.T.,RADIO FREE EUROPE. FUT USA+45 CULTURE ECO/DEV INT/ORG KIN POL/PAR SECT FORCES ACT/RES DIPLOM COERCE REV CHOOSE PEACE ATTIT PWR...MAJORIT CONCPT COLD/WAR WORK 20 RFE. PAGE 67 A1374
COM EDU/PROP COM/IND

S59
HARVEY M.F.,"THE PALESTINE REFUGEE PROBLEM: ELEMENTS OF A SOLUTION." ISLAM LAW INT/ORG DELIB/GP TOP/EX ECO/TAC ROUTINE DRIVE HEALTH LOVE ORD/FREE PWR WEALTH...MAJORIT FAO 20. PAGE 62 A1283
ACT/RES LEGIT PEACE ISRAEL

S59
SOHN L.B.,"THE DEFINITION OF AGGRESSION." FUT LAW FORCES LEGIT ADJUD ROUTINE COERCE ORD/FREE PWR ...MAJORIT JURID QUANT COLD/WAR 20. PAGE 135 A2762
INT/ORG CT/SYS DETER SOVEREIGN

B61
PANIKKAR K.M.,THE VOICE OF FREEDOM: SELECTED SPEECHES OF PANDIT MOTILAL NEHRU. INDIA UK CONSTN FINAN FORCES LEGIS DIPLOM TAX COLONIAL...POLICY MAJORIT ANTHOL 20 NEHRU/PM. PAGE 114 A2331
NAT/LISM ORD/FREE CHIEF NAT/G

B61
STRAUSZ-HUPE R.,A FORWARD STRATEGY FOR AMERICA. FUT WOR+45 ECO/DEV INT/ORG NAT/G POL/PAR DELIB/GP FORCES ACT/RES CREATE ECO/TAC DOMIN EDU/PROP ATTIT DRIVE PWR...MAJORIT CONCPT STAT OBS TIME/SEQ TREND COLD/WAR TOT/POP. PAGE 139 A2848
USA+45 PLAN DIPLOM

S61
ROSTOW W.W.,"THE FUTURE OF FOREIGN AID." COM FUT WOR+45 ECO/DEV INDUS INT/ORG NAT/G CONSULT ACT/RES PLAN DOMIN LEGIT CHOOSE RIGID/FLEX ALL/VALS ...MAJORIT CONCPT TREND TOT/POP 20. PAGE 124 A2544
ECO/UNDEV ECO/TAC FOR/AID

B62
DELANEY R.F.,THE LITERATURE OF COMMUNISM IN AMERICA. COM USA+45 USA-45 INT/ORG LABOR NAT/G POL/PAR INGP/REL...MAJORIT 20. PAGE 36 A0727
BIBLIOG/A MARXISM EDU/PROP IDEA/COMP

B62
JEWELL M.E.,SENATORIAL POLITICS AND FOREIGN POLICY. NAT/G POL/PAR CHIEF DELIB/GP TOP/EX FOR/AID EDU/PROP ROUTINE ATTIT PWR SKILL...MAJORIT METH/CNCPT TIME/SEQ CONGRESS 20 PRESIDENT. PAGE 74 A1516
USA+45 LEGIS DIPLOM

B62
SCHUMAN F.L.,THE COLD WAR: RETROSPECT AND PROSPECT. FUT USA+45 USSR WOR+45 BAL/PWR EDU/PROP ARMS/CONT ATTIT...MAJORIT IDEA/COMP ANTHOL BIBLIOG 20 COLD/WAR. PAGE 129 A2651
MARXISM TEC/DEV DIPLOM NUC/PWR

B62
SNOW J.H.,GOVERNMENT BY TREASON. USA+45 USA-45 LEGIS DIPLOM FOR/AID GIVE CONTROL WEALTH MARXISM ...MAJORIT 20 CONGRESS COLD/WAR. PAGE 134 A2750
FINAN TAX PWR POLICY

B62
WOETZEL R.K.,THE NURENBERG TRIALS IN INTERNATIONAL LAW. CHRIST-17C MOD/EUR WOR+45 SOCIETY NAT/G DELIB/GP DOMIN LEGIT ROUTINE ATTIT DRIVE PERSON SUPEGO MORAL ORD/FREE...POLICY MAJORIT JURID PSY SOC SELF/OBS RECORD NAZI TOT/POP. PAGE 166 A3376
INT/ORG ADJUD WAR

B63
BLACK J.E.,FOREIGN POLICIES IN A WORLD OF CHANGE. FUT INT/ORG ALL/VALS...POLICY MAJORIT MARXIST SOCIALIST TRADIT TIME/SEQ TREND ANTHOL 20. PAGE 15 A0298
WOR+45 NAT/G DIPLOM

B63
FIFIELD R.H.,SOUTHEAST ASIA IN UNITED STATES POLICY. S/ASIA USA+45 ECO/UNDEV NAT/G DIPLOM ECO/TAC ADMIN COERCE ORD/FREE...POLICY MAJORIT 20. PAGE 45 A0928
INT/ORG PWR

B64
ETZIONI A.,WINNING WITHOUT WAR. FUT MOD/EUR USA+45 WOR+45 ECO/DEV ECO/UNDEV INT/ORG NAT/G FORCES TOP/EX PLAN TEC/DEV ECO/TAC DOMIN EDU/PROP LEGIT COERCE CHOOSE ATTIT MORAL ORD/FREE RESPECT WEALTH MAJORIT. PAGE 43 A0871
PWR TREND DIPLOM USSR

B64
MORGAN T.,GOLDWATER EITHER/OR; A SELF-PORTRAIT BASED UPON HIS OWN WORDS. USA+45 CONSTN AGRI LABOR DIPLOM RACE/REL WEALTH POPULISM...POLICY MAJORIT 20 GOLDWATR/B REPUBLICAN. PAGE 104 A2131
LEAD POL/PAR CHOOSE ATTIT

B64
QUIGG P.W.,AFRICA: A FOREIGN AFFAIRS READER. AFR FRANCE PORTUGAL UK DIPLOM LEAD PARL/PROC MARXISM ...MAJORIT METH/CNCPT GOV/COMP IDEA/COMP ANTHOL 19/20. PAGE 118 A2426 — COLONIAL SOVEREIGN NAT/LISM RACE/REL

S64
GARDNER R.N.,"THE SOVIET UNION AND THE UNITED NATIONS." WOR+45 FINAN POL/PAR VOL/ASSN FORCES ECO/TAC DOMIN EDU/PROP LEGIT ADJUD ADMIN ARMS/CONT COERCE ATTIT ALL/VALS...POLICY MAJORIT CONCPT OBS TIME/SEQ TREND STERTYP UN. PAGE 51 A1046 — COM INT/ORG USSR

C64
SCHRAMM W.,"MASS MEDIA AND NATIONAL DEVELOPMENT: THE ROLE OF INFORMATION IN DEVELOPING COUNTRIES." FINAN R+D ACT/RES PLAN TEC/DEV DIPLOM CHOOSE SUPEGO ORD/FREE...BIBLIOG 20. PAGE 129 A2645 — ECO/UNDEV COM/IND EDU/PROP MAJORIT

B65
NATIONAL BOOK CENTRE PAKISTAN,BOOKS ON PAKISTAN: A BIBLIOGRAPHY. PAKISTAN CULTURE DIPLOM ADMIN ATTIT ...MAJORIT SOC CONCPT 20. PAGE 107 A2201 — BIBLIOG CONSTN S/ASIA NAT/G

B66
BRACKMAN A.C.,SOUTHEAST ASIA'S SECOND FRONT: THE POWER STRUGGLE IN THE MALAY ARCHIPELAGO. CHINA/COM INDONESIA MALAYSIA ECO/UNDEV INT/ORG NAT/G FORCES DIPLOM EDU/PROP REGION COERCE GUERRILLA AUTHORIT POPULISM...MAJORIT 20 KENNEDY/JF SEATO. PAGE 18 A0367 — S/ASIA MARXISM REV

B66
EKIRCH A.A. JR.,IDEAS, IDEALS, AND AMERICAN DIPLOMACY. USA+45 USA-45 INT/ORG DOMIN COLONIAL ARMS/CONT DETER ISOLAT NAT/LISM...MAJORIT BIBLIOG 19/20 COLD/WAR. PAGE 41 A0834 — DIPLOM LEAD PEACE

MAJORITY....BEHAVIOR OF MAJOR PARTS OF A GROUP; SEE ALSO CONSEN, MAJORIT

B33
PUBLIC OPINION AND WORLD POLITICS. UNIV LAW CULTURE NAT/G PRESS REV GP/REL...MAJORIT METH/COMP ANTHOL 20. PAGE 167 A3400 — DIPLOM EDU/PROP ATTIT MAJORITY

B57
MILLIKAN M.F.,A PROPOSAL: KEY TO AN EFFECTIVE FOREIGN POLICY. USA+45 AGRI FINAN DELIB/GP DIPLOM REPRESENT MAJORITY...NEW/IDEA CHARTS. PAGE 101 A2081 — FOR/AID GIVE ECO/UNDEV PLAN

B57
SEABURY P.,THE WANING OF SOUTHERN "INTERNATIONALISM" (PAMPHLET). USA+45 USA-45 INT/ORG LEGIS MAJORITY...TREND 20 SOUTH/US MIDWEST/US. PAGE 131 A2676 — DIPLOM REGION ATTIT ISOLAT

S57
DEUTSCH K.W.,"MASS COMMUNICATIONS AND THE LOSS OF FREEDOM IN NATIONAL DECISION MAKING." FUT WOR+45 SOCIETY COM/IND INT/ORG NAT/G ACT/RES CREATE TEC/DEV EDU/PROP MAJORITY PERCEPT...METH/CNCPT 20. PAGE 36 A0737 — COERCE DECISION WAR

B61
NEAL F.W.,US FOREIGN POLICY AND THE SOVIET UNION. USA+45 USSR INT/ORG ECO/TAC ARMS/CONT MAJORITY NAT/LISM ATTIT RESPECT MARXISM 20. PAGE 108 A2207 — DIPLOM POLICY PEACE

B63
PRESTON W. JR.,ALIENS AND DISSENTERS: FEDERAL SUPPRESSION OF RADICALS 1903-1933. USA-45 DIPLOM ADJUD REPRESENT RACE/REL MAJORITY...BIBLIOG/A 19/20. PAGE 117 A2409 — DISCRIM GP/REL INGP/REL ATTIT

S67
ANTHEM T.,"CYPRUS* WHAT NOW?" CYPRUS GREECE TURKEY NAT/G BUDGET MAJORITY 20 NATO. PAGE 8 A0165 — DIPLOM COERCE INT/TRADE ADJUD

B91
DOLE C.F.,THE AMERICAN CITIZEN. USA-45 LAW PARTIC ATTIT...INT/LAW 19. PAGE 38 A0769 — NAT/G MORAL NAT/LISM MAJORITY

MALAWI....SEE ALSO AFR

MALAYA....MALAYA

MALAYSIA....SEE ALSO S/ASIA

B50
CORNELL U DEPT ASIAN STUDIES,SOUTHEAST ASIA PROGRAM DATA PAPER. BURMA CAMBODIA INDONESIA MALAYSIA VIETNAM SOCIETY STRUCT NAT/G SECT DIPLOM FOR/AID PWR WEALTH...SOC 20. PAGE 31 A0625 — BIBLIOG/A CULTURE S/ASIA ECO/UNDEV

B58
JENNINGS W.I.,PROBLEMS OF THE NEW COMMONWEALTH. CEYLON INDIA MALAYSIA PAKISTAN ECO/UNDEV VOL/ASSN RACE/REL NAT/LISM ROLE 20 CMN/WLTH. PAGE 74 A1511 — GP/REL INGP/REL COLONIAL INT/ORG

B60
JEFFRIES C.,TRANSFER OF POWER: PROBLEMS OF THE PASSAGE TO SELFGOVERNMENT. CEYLON GHANA MALAYSIA NIGERIA UK INT/ORG CONSULT DELIB/GP LEGIS DIPLOM CONFER PARL/PROC 20. PAGE 73 A1502 — SOVEREIGN COLONIAL ORD/FREE NAT/G

B64
SAKAI R.K.,STUDIES ON ASIA, 1964. ASIA CHINA/COM ISRAEL MALAYSIA S/ASIA USA+45 USSR ECO/UNDEV FAM POL/PAR SECT CONSULT NAT/LISM...POLICY SOC 20 CHINJAP. PAGE 126 A2588 — PWR DIPLOM

B66
BRACKMAN A.C.,SOUTHEAST ASIA'S SECOND FRONT: THE POWER STRUGGLE IN THE MALAY ARCHIPELAGO. CHINA/COM INDONESIA MALAYSIA ECO/UNDEV INT/ORG NAT/G FORCES DIPLOM EDU/PROP REGION COERCE GUERRILLA AUTHORIT POPULISM...MAJORIT 20 KENNEDY/JF SEATO. PAGE 18 A0367 — S/ASIA MARXISM REV

B66
LEIGH M.B.,CHECK LIST OF HOLDINGS ON BORNEO IN THE CORNELL UNIVERSITY LIBRARIES (PAMPHLET). BORNEO MALAYSIA LAW CONSTN GP/REL SOC. PAGE 86 A1769 — BIBLIOG S/ASIA DIPLOM NAT/G

S66
GAMER R.E.,"URGENT SINGAPORE, PATIENT MALAYSIA." MALAYSIA S/ASIA ECO/UNDEV POL/PAR CHIEF TARIFFS TAX CONTROL LEAD REGION PWR 20 SINGAPORE. PAGE 51 A1036 — DIPLOM NAT/G POLICY ECO/TAC

MALCLES L.N. A1911

MALCOLM/X....MALCOLM X

MALDIVE....MALDIVE ISLAND; SEE ALSO S/ASIA, COMMONWLTH

MALE/SEX....MALE SEX

MALI....SEE ALSO AFR

B62
TOURE S.,THE INTERNATIONAL POLICY OF THE DEMOCRATIC PARTY OF GUINEA (VOL. VII). AFR ALGERIA GHANA GUINEA MALI CONSTN VOL/ASSN CHIEF WAR PEACE ATTIT ...WELF/ST 20 DEMOCRAT. PAGE 144 A2953 — DIPLOM POLICY POL/PAR NEW/LIB

S62
GAREAU F.H.,"BLOC POLITICS IN WEST AFRICA." AFR CONGO/BRAZ GHANA GUINEA MALI WOR+45 STRUCT ECO/UNDEV INT/ORG VOL/ASSN CHOOSE ORD/FREE PWR UN 20. PAGE 51 A1048 — NAT/G NAT/LISM

B66
SCHATTEN F.,COMMUNISM IN AFRICA. AFR GHANA GUINEA MALI CULTURE ECO/UNDEV LABOR SECT ECO/TAC EDU/PROP REV 20. PAGE 128 A2619 — COLONIAL NAT/LISM MARXISM DIPLOM

MALIK C. A1912

MALINOWSKI W.R. A1913

MALLIN J. A1914

MALLORY W.H. A1915

MALOF P. A0944

MALTA....SEE ALSO APPROPRIATE TIME/SPACE/CULTURE INDEX

MALTHUS....THOMAS ROBERT MALTHUS

B59
LINK R.G.,ENGLISH THEORIES OF ECONOMIC FLUCTUATIONS: 1815-1848. FRANCE UK AGRI WORKER DIPLOM PRICE TASK WAR DEMAND PRODUC...POLICY BIBLIOG 18 MALTHUS MILL/JS WILSON/J. PAGE 89 A1826 — IDEA/COMP ECO/DEV WEALTH EQUILIB

MANAGEMENT....SEE MGT, EX/STRUC, ADMIN

MANAGEMENT BY OBJECTIVES....SEE MGT/OBJECT

MANCHESTER....MANCHESTER, ENGLAND

MANCHU/DYN....MANCHU DYNASTY

MANDER J. A1916

MANDER L. A1917

MANGER W. A1918

MANGIN G. A1919

MANGONE G. A1920,A1921,A1922

MANITOBA....MANITOBA, CANADA

MANN F.A. A1923

MANNERS....SEE ETIQUET

MANNHEIM/K....KARL MANNHEIM

MANNING C.A.W. A1924,A1925,A1926

MANOLIU F. A1927

MANPOWER....SEE LABOR

MANSERGH N. A1928,A1929,A1930,A1931,A1932,A1933

MANSFIELD P. A1934

MANTECON J. A0485

MANTON/M....MART MANTON

MANTOUX E. A1935

MANUFACTURING INDUSTRY....SEE PROC/MFG

MANZER R.A. A1936

MAO....MAO TSE-TUNG

B58
PALMER E.E.,THE COMMUNIST CHALLENGE. COM USA+45 USA-45 ECO/DEV ECO/UNDEV NEUTRAL ORD/FREE POPULISM ...CONCPT NAT/COMP ANTHOL 19/20 LENIN/VI STALIN/J MAO MARX/KARL COM/PARTY. PAGE 113 A2320 — MARXISM DIPLOM IDEA/COMP POLICY

S61
ZAGORIA D.S.,"THE FUTURE OF SINO-SOVIET RELATIONS." CHINA/COM INT/ORG NAT/G POL/PAR VOL/ASSN ACT/RES PLAN PERSON...METH/CNCPT TIME/SEQ TOT/POP VAL/FREE 20 MAO KHRUSH/N. PAGE 169 A3444 — ASIA COM TOTALISM USSR

B63
GRIFFITH W.E.,ALBANIA AND THE SINO-SOVIET RIFT. ALBANIA CHINA/COM USSR POL/PAR CHIEF LEGIS DIPLOM DOMIN ATTIT PWR...POLICY 20 KHRUSH/N MAO. PAGE 57 A1161 — EDU/PROP MARXISM NAT/LISM GOV/REL

B63
HAMM H.,ALBANIA - CHINA'S BEACHHEAD IN EUROPE. ALBANIA CHINA/COM USSR YUGOSLAVIA ELITES SOCIETY POL/PAR DELIB/GP FORCES ECO/TAC COERCE ISOLAT PEACE MARXISM...IDEA/COMP 20 MAO. PAGE 61 A1248 — DIPLOM REV NAT/G POLICY

B64
HARPER F.,OUT OF CHINA. CHINA/COM ELITES STRATA ATTIT PERSON...BIOG 20 MAO HONG/KONG MIGRATION. PAGE 62 A1264 — HABITAT DEEP/INT DIPLOM MARXISM

B65
WINT G.,COMMUNIST CHINA'S CRUSADE: MAO'S ROAD TO POWER AND THE NEW CAMPAIGN FOR WORLD REVOLUTION. ASIA CHINA/COM USA+45 USSR NAT/G POL/PAR DOMIN COERCE WAR PWR...POLICY CHARTS IDEA/COMP BIBLIOG 20 MAO. PAGE 165 A3364 — DIPLOM MARXISM REV COLONIAL

B66
ZABLOCKI C.J.,SINO-SOVIET RIVALRY. AFR ASIA CHINA/COM CUBA EUR+WWI L/A+17C USA+45 USSR WOR+45 POL/PAR FORCES COERCE NUC/PWR...GOV/COMP IDEA/COMP 20 MAO KHRUSH/N. PAGE 169 A3442 — DIPLOM MARXISM COM

S67
ADIE W.A.C.,"CHINA'S 'SECOND LIBERATION'." CHINA/COM SOCIETY WORKER DIPLOM TASK 20 MAO. PAGE 4 A0090 — MARXISM REV INGP/REL ANOMIE

MAPS....MAPS AND ATLASES;

B44
FULLER G.H.,TURKEY: A SELECTED LIST OF REFERENCES. ISLAM TURKEY CULTURE ECO/UNDEV AGRI DIPLOM NAT/LISM CONSERVE...GEOG HUM INT/LAW SOC 7/20 MAPS. PAGE 50 A1024 — BIBLIOG/A ALL/VALS

B59
GOLDWIN R.A.,READINGS IN RUSSIAN FOREIGN POLICY. HUNGARY USSR YUGOSLAVIA ELITES INT/ORG NAT/G REV WAR NAT/LISM PERSON SOCISM...CHARTS 20 MAPS BOLSHEVISM. PAGE 53 A1095 — COM MARXISM DIPLOM POLICY

MARAJO....MARAJO, A BRAZILIAN ISLAND

MARANHAO....MARANHAO, BRAZIL

MARCANT/V....VITO MARCANTONIO

MARCUS W. A1937

MARCUSE/H....HERBERT MARCUSE

MARCY C.M. A3344

MARIAS J. A1938

MARITAIN J. A1939,A1940

MARITAIN/J....JACQUES MARITAIN

MARITANO N. A1941

MARITIME....MARITIME PROVINCES

B33
REID H.D.,RECUEIL DES COURS; TOME 45: LES SERVITUDES INTERNATIONALES III. FRANCE CONSTN DELIB/GP PRESS CONTROL REV WAR CHOOSE PEACE MORAL MARITIME TREATY. PAGE 120 A2457 — ORD/FREE DIPLOM LAW

MARK M. A1942

MARKET RESEARCH....SEE MARKET

MARKET....MARKETING SYSTEM

N
AMERICAN ECONOMIC ASSOCIATION,THE JOURNAL OF ECONOMIC ABSTRACTS. ECO/UNDEV MARKET LABOR DIPLOM ...MGT CONCPT METH 20. PAGE 7 A0144 — BIBLIOG/A R+D FINAN

N19
VELYAMINOV G.,AFRICA AND THE COMMON MARKET (PAMPHLET). AFR MARKET VOL/ASSN ECO/TAC COLONIAL ORD/FREE...SOCIALIST 20 THIRD/WRLD. PAGE 158 A3227 — INT/ORG INT/TRADE SOVEREIGN ECO/UNDEV

B20
WOOLF L.,EMPIRE AND COMMERCE IN AFRICA. EUR+WWI MOD/EUR FINAN INDUS MARKET INT/ORG PLAN COERCE ATTIT DRIVE PWR WEALTH...CONCPT TIME/SEQ TREND CHARTS 20. PAGE 167 A3394 — AFR DOMIN COLONIAL SOVEREIGN

B28
CORBETT P.E.,CANADA AND WORLD POLITICS. LAW CULTURE SOCIETY STRUCT MARKET INT/ORG FORCES ACT/RES PLAN ECO/TAC LEGIT ORD/FREE PWR RESPECT...SOC CONCPT TIME/SEQ TREND CMN/WLTH 20 LEAGUE/NAT. PAGE 30 A0612 — NAT/G CANADA

B32
HANSEN A.H.,ECONOMIC STABILIZATION IN AN UNBALANCED WORLD. COM EUR+WWI USA-45 WOR-45 AGRI FINAN INDUS MARKET INT/ORG LABOR VOL/ASSN EDU/PROP ATTIT HEALTH KNOWL WEALTH...HIST/WRIT TREND VAL/FREE 20. PAGE 61 A1253 — NAT/G ECO/DEV CAP/ISM SOCISM

B33
OHLIN B.,INTERREGIONAL AND INTERNATIONAL TRADE. USA-45 WOR-45 CULTURE FINAN MARKET CONSULT PLAN ECO/TAC ATTIT WEALTH...CONCPT MATH TOT/POP 20. PAGE 111 A2285 — INT/ORG ECO/DEV INT/TRADE REGION

B34
GRAHAM F.D.,PROTECTIVE TARIFFS. FUT USA+45 WOR-45 INDUS MARKET VOL/ASSN PLAN CAP/ISM ECO/TAC PEACE ATTIT DRIVE HEALTH ORD/FREE...OBS TREND GEN/LAWS 20. PAGE 55 A1124 — INT/ORG TARIFFS

B37
VINER J.,STUDIES IN THE THEORY OF INTERNATIONAL TRADE. WOR-45 CONSTN ECO/DEV AGRI INDUS MARKET INT/ORG LABOR NAT/G ECO/TAC TARIFFS COLONIAL ATTIT WEALTH...POLICY CONCPT MATH STAT OBS SAMP TREND GEN/LAWS MARX/KARL 20. PAGE 159 A3236 — CAP/ISM INT/TRADE

B38
COLBY C.C.,GEOGRAPHICAL ASPECTS OF INTERNATIONAL RELATIONS. WOR-45 ECO/DEV ECO/UNDEV AGRI EXTR/IND INDUS MARKET INT/ORG NAT/G TEC/DEV ECO/TAC INT/TRADE NAT/LISM WEALTH...METH/CNCPT CHARTS GEN/LAWS 20. PAGE 28 A0565 — PLAN GEOG DIPLOM

B42
CROWE S.E.,THE BERLIN WEST AFRICA CONFERENCE, 1884-85. GERMANY ELITES MARKET INT/ORG DELIB/GP FORCES PROB/SOLV BAL/PWR CAP/ISM DOMIN COLONIAL ...INT/LAW 19. PAGE 33 A0664 — AFR CONFER INT/TRADE DIPLOM

B43
VINER J.,TRADE RELATIONS BETWEEN FREE-MARKET AND CONTROLLED ECONOMIES. WOR-45 MARKET PLAN TARIFFS DEMAND...POLICY STAT 20. PAGE 159 A3237 — INT/TRADE DIPLOM CONTROL NAT/G

B44
WEIGERT H.W.,COMPASS OF THE WORLD, A SYMPOSIUM ON POLITICAL GEOGRAPHY. EUR+WWI FUT MOD/EUR S/ASIA USA-45 WOR-45 SOCIETY AGRI INDUS MARKET ECO/TAC INT/TRADE PERSON 20. PAGE 162 A3298 — TEC/DEV CAP/ISM RUSSIA GEOG

L44
HAILEY,"THE FUTURE OF COLONIAL PEOPLES." WOR-45 CONSTN CULTURE ECO/UNDEV AGRI MARKET INT/ORG NAT/G SECT CONSULT ECO/TAC LEGIT ADMIN NAT/LISM ALL/VALS ...SOC OBS TREND STERTYP CMN/WLTH LEAGUE/NAT PARLIAMENT 20. PAGE 59 A1218 — PLAN CONCPT DIPLOM UK

S46
SILBERNER E.,"THE PROBLEM OF WAR IN NINETEENTH CENTURY ECONOMIC THOUGHT." EUR+WWI MOD/EUR UNIV LAW ECO/DEV ECO/UNDEV FINAN INDUS MARKET INT/ORG NAT/G CONSULT FORCES...CONCPT GEN/LAWS GEN/METH 19. PAGE 133 A2715 — ATTIT ECO/TAC WAR

B47
TOWLE L.W.,INTERNATIONAL TRADE AND COMMERCIAL POLICY. WOR+45 LAW ECO/DEV FINAN INDUS NAT/G ECO/TAC WEALTH...TIME/SEQ ILO 20. PAGE 144 A2955 — MARKET INT/ORG INT/TRADE

B52
ALEXANDROWICZ C.H.,INTERNATIONAL ECONOMIC ORGANIZATION. WOR+45 ECO/DEV ECO/UNDEV DIST/IND FINAN MARKET PLAN ECO/TAC LEGIT DRIVE WEALTH ...POLICY CONCPT QUANT OBS TIME/SEQ GEN/LAWS WORK EEC ILO OEEC UNESCO 20. PAGE 6 A0114
INT/ORG INT/TRADE

B52
SURANYI-UNGER T.,COMPARATIVE ECONOMIC SYSTEMS. FINAN MARKET DIPLOM PRICE WEALTH...GEOG SOC BIBLIOG METH T 20. PAGE 140 A2865
LAISSEZ PLAN ECO/DEV IDEA/COMP

B53
NEISSER H.,NATIONAL INCOMES AND INTERNATIONAL TRADE. FRANCE GERMANY SWEDEN UK USA-45 EXTR/IND FINAN INDUS TEC/DEV PRICE BAL/PAY EQUILIB INCOME WEALTH...CHARTS METH 19 CHINJAP. PAGE 108 A2215
INT/TRADE PRODUC MARKET CON/ANAL

B55
O3HEVSS E.,WIRTSCHAFTSSYSTEME UND INTERNATIONALER HANDEL. ECO/DEV FINAN MARKET DIPLOM ECO/TAC COST ...METH/COMP NAT/COMP 20. PAGE 112 A2306
CAP/ISM SOCISM INT/TRADE IDEA/COMP

L57
WARREN S.,"FOREIGN AID AND FOREIGN POLICY." USA+45 WOR+45 WOR-45 DIST/IND INDUS MARKET CONSULT CREATE DIPLOM EDU/PROP LEGIT ATTIT RIGID/FLEX...TIME/SEQ GEN/LAWS WORK 20. PAGE 161 A3285
ECO/UNDEV ALL/VALS ECO/TAC FOR/AID

B58
BERLINER J.S.,SOVIET ECONOMIC AID: THE AID AND TRADE POLICY IN UNDERDEVELOPED COUNTRIES. AFR COM ISLAM L/A+17C S/ASIA USSR ECO/DEV DIST/IND FINAN MARKET INT/ORG ACT/RES PLAN BAL/PWR WEAPON PWR WEALTH...CHARTS 20. PAGE 14 A0277
ECO/UNDEV ECO/TAC FOR/AID

B58
IMLAH A.H.,ECONOMIC ELEMENTS IN THE PAX BRITANNICA. MOD/EUR USA+45 USA-45 ECO/DEV INT/ORG NAT/G BAL/PWR ECO/TAC PEACE ATTIT PWR WEALTH...STAT CHARTS VAL/FREE 19. PAGE 70 A1436
MARKET UK

B58
MOORE B.T.,NATO AND THE FUTURE OF EUROPE. EUR+WWI FUT USA+45 ECO/DEV INDUS MARKET NAT/G VOL/ASSN FORCES DIPLOM NUC/PWR ORD/FREE...CONCPT CHARTS ORG/CHARTS CMN/WLTH 20 NATO. PAGE 103 A2122
INT/ORG REGION

L58
TRAGER F.N.,"A SELECTED AND ANNOTATED BIBLIOGRAPHY ON ECONOMIC DEVELOPMENT, 1953-1957." WOR+45 AGRI FINAN INDUS MARKET LABOR MUNIC WORKER PLAN INT/TRADE PRODUC CENSUS. PAGE 145 A2958
BIBLIOG/A ECO/UNDEV ECO/DEV

B59
ETSCHMANN R.,DIE WAHRUNGS- UND DEVISENPOLITIK DES OSTBLOCKS UND IHRE AUSWIRKUNGEN AUF DIE WIRTSCHAFTSBEZIEHUNGEN ZWISCHEN OST U WEST. BULGARIA CZECHOSLVK HUNGARY POLAND USSR MARKET NAT/G PLAN DIPLOM...NAT/COMP 20. PAGE 42 A0867
ECO/TAC FINAN POLICY INT/TRADE

B59
HAZLEWOOD A.,THE ECONOMICS OF "UNDER-DEVELOPED" AREAS. WOR+45 DIST/IND EXTR/IND FINAN INDUS MARKET PLAN FOR/AID...GEOG 20. PAGE 63 A1302
BIBLIOG/A ECO/UNDEV AGRI INT/TRADE

L59
MURPHY J.C.,"SOME IMPLICATIONS OF EUROPE'S COMMON MARKET. IN (COOK P, ECONOMIC DEVELOPMENT AND INTERNATIONAL TRADE.." EUR+WWI ECO/DEV DIST/IND INDUS NAT/G PLAN ECO/TAC INT/TRADE WEALTH...STAT TREND OEEC TOT/POP 20 EEC. PAGE 106 A2178
MARKET INT/ORG REGION

S59
KINDLEBERGER C.P.,"UNITED STATES ECONOMIC FOREIGN POLICY: RESEARCH REQUIREMENTS FOR 1965." FUT USA+45 WOR+45 DIST/IND MARKET INT/ORG ECO/TAC INT/TRADE WEALTH...OBS TREND CON/ANAL GEN/LAWS VAL/FREE 20. PAGE 79 A1621
FINAN ECO/DEV FOR/AID

S59
PLAZA G.,"FOR A REGIONAL MARKET IN LATIN AMERICA." FUT L/A+17C CULTURE INDUS NAT/G ECO/TAC INT/TRADE ATTIT WEALTH...NEW/IDEA TREND OAS 20. PAGE 116 A2389
MARKET INT/ORG REGION

S59
ZAUBERMAN A.,"SOVIET BLOC ECONOMIC INTEGRATION." COM CULTURE INTELL ECO/DEV INDUS TOP/EX ACT/RES PLAN ECO/TAC INT/TRADE ROUTINE CHOOSE ATTIT ...TIME/SEQ 20. PAGE 169 A3448
MARKET INT/ORG USSR TOTALISM

B60
HOFFMANN P.G.,ONE HUNDRED COUNTRIES, ONE AND ONE QUARTER BILLION PEOPLE. MARKET INT/ORG TEC/DEV CAP/ISM...GEOG CHARTS METH/COMP 20 UN. PAGE 66 A1354
FOR/AID ECO/TAC ECO/UNDEV INT/TRADE

B60
LISTER L.,EUROPE'S COAL AND STEEL COMMUNITY. FRANCE GERMANY STRUCT ECO/DEV EXTR/IND INDUS MARKET NAT/G DELIB/GP ECO/TAC INT/TRADE EDU/PROP ATTIT RIGID/FLEX ORD/FREE PWR WEALTH...CONCPT STAT TIME/SEQ CHARTS ECSC 20. PAGE 90 A1843
EUR+WWI INT/ORG REGION

B60
PENTONY D.E.,THE UNDERDEVELOPED LANDS. FUT WOR+45 CULTURE AGRI FINAN INDUS MARKET INT/ORG LABOR NAT/G VOL/ASSN CONSULT TEC/DEV ECO/TAC EDU/PROP COLONIAL ATTIT WEALTH...OBS RECORD SAMP TREND GEN/METH WORK UN 20. PAGE 115 A2351
ECO/UNDEV POLICY FOR/AID INT/TRADE

B60
STEIN E.,AMERICAN ENTERPRISE IN THE EUROPEAN COMMON MARKET: A LEGAL PROFILE. EUR+WWI FUT USA+45 SOCIETY STRUCT ECO/DEV NAT/G VOL/ASSN CONSULT PLAN TEC/DEV ECO/TAC INT/TRADE ADMIN ATTIT RIGID/FLEX PWR...MGT NEW/IDEA STAT TREND COMPUT/IR SIMUL EEC 20. PAGE 137 A2814
MARKET ADJUD INT/LAW

S60
GARNICK D.H.,"ON THE ECONOMIC FEASIBILITY OF A MIDDLE EASTERN COMMON MARKET." AFR ISLAM CULTURE INDUS NAT/G PLAN TEC/DEV ECO/TAC ADMIN ATTIT DRIVE RIGID/FLEX...PLURIST STAT TREND GEN/LAWS 20. PAGE 51 A1051
MARKET INT/TRADE

S60
NANES A.,"THE EUROPEAN COMMUNITY AND THE UNITED STATES: EVOLVING RELATIONS." EUR+WWI USA+45 WOR+45 ECO/UNDEV MARKET NAT/G DELIB/GP PLAN LEGIT ATTIT PWR WEALTH...CONCPT STAT TIME/SEQ CON/ANAL EEC OEEC 20 EURATOM. PAGE 107 A2194
INT/ORG REGION

S60
OWEN C.F.,"US AND SOVIET RELATIONS WITH UNDERDEVELOPED COUNTRIES: LATIN AMERICA-A CASE STUDY." AFR COM L/A+17C USA+45 USSR EXTR/IND MARKET TEC/DEV DIPLOM ECO/TAC NAT/LISM ORD/FREE PWR ...TREND WORK 20. PAGE 112 A2303
ECO/UNDEV DRIVE INT/TRADE

N60
ERDMAN P.E.,COMMON MARKETS AND FREE TRADE AREAS (PAMPHLET). USA+45 MARKET INT/ORG TEC/DEV DIPLOM UTIL...CON/ANAL CHARTS BIBLIOG 20 EEC OEEC. PAGE 42 A0859
TREND PROB/SOLV INT/TRADE ECO/DEV

B61
HARRIS S.E.,THE DOLLAR IN CRISIS. USA+45 MARKET INT/ORG ECO/TAC PRICE CONTROL WEALTH...METH/COMP ANTHOL 20 GOLD/STAND. PAGE 62 A1269
BAL/PAY DIPLOM FINAN INT/TRADE

B61
KITZINGER V.W.,THE CHALLENGE OF THE COMMON MARKET. EUR+WWI ECO/DEV DIST/IND PLAN ECO/TAC INT/TRADE LEGIT ATTIT PWR WEALTH...TIME/SEQ TREND CHARTS EEC 20. PAGE 80 A1647
MARKET INT/ORG UK

B61
THEOBALD R.,THE CHALLENGE OF ABUNDANCE. USA+45 WOR+45 MARKET DIPLOM FOR/AID REV PRODUC UTOPIA SUPEGO...POLICY TREND BIBLIOG/A 20. PAGE 142 A2913
WELF/ST ECO/UNDEV PROB/SOLV ECO/TAC

S61
DEUTSCH K.W.,"NATIONAL INDUSTRIALIZATION AND THE DECLINING SHARE OF THE INTERNATIONAL ECONOMIC SECTOR." EUR+WWI FUT WOR+45 WOR-45 MARKET PLAN EDU/PROP WEALTH...WELF/ST OBS TESTS 20. PAGE 36 A0740
DIST/IND ECO/DEV INT/TRADE

S61
LANFALUSSY A.,"EUROPE'S PROGRESS: DUE TO COMMON MARKET." EUR+WWI ECO/DEV DELIB/GP PLAN ECO/TAC ROUTINE WEALTH...GEOG TREND EEC 20. PAGE 84 A1721
INT/ORG MARKET

S61
VINER J.,"ECONOMIC FOREIGN POLICY ON THE NEW FRONTIER." USA+45 ECO/UNDEV AGRI FINAN INDUS MARKET INT/ORG NAT/G FOR/AID INT/TRADE ADMIN ATTIT PWR 20 KENNEDY/JF. PAGE 159 A3239
TOP/EX ECO/TAC BAL/PAY TARIFFS

B62
HUMPHREY D.D.,THE UNITED STATES AND THE COMMON MARKET. USA+45 INDUS MARKET INT/ORG PLAN EDU/PROP BAL/PAY DRIVE PWR WEALTH...TREND STERTYP EEC 20. PAGE 69 A1415
ATTIT ECO/TAC

B62
KRAFT J.,THE GRAND DESIGN. EUR+WWI USA+45 AGRI FINAN INDUS MARKET INT/ORG NAT/G PLAN ECO/TAC TARIFFS REGION DRIVE ORD/FREE WEALTH...POLICY OBS TREND EEC 20. PAGE 82 A1674
VOL/ASSN ECO/DEV INT/TRADE

B62
LIPPMANN W.,WESTERN UNITY AND THE COMMON MARKET. EUR+WWI FRANCE GERMANY/W UK USA+45 ECO/DEV AGRI FINAN MARKET INT/ORG NAT/G FOR/AID AGREE WEALTH 20 EEC. PAGE 89 A1831
DIPLOM INT/TRADE VOL/ASSN

B62
LUTZ F.A.,GELD UND WAHRUNG. MARKET LABOR BUDGET 20 GOLD/STAND EUROPE. PAGE 92 A1875
ECO/TAC FINAN DIPLOM POLICY

B62
MODELSKI G.,SEATO-SIX STUDIES. ASIA CHINA/COM INDIA S/ASIA INT/ORG NAT/G ECO/TAC DETER ATTIT ORD/FREE PWR...TIME/SEQ COLD/WAR TOT/POP 20 SEATO. PAGE 102 A2098
MARKET ECO/UNDEV INT/TRADE

B62
SHAW C.,LEGAL PROBLEMS IN INTERNATIONAL TRADE AND INVESTMENT. WOR+45 ECO/DEV ECO/UNDEV MARKET DIPLOM TAX INCOME ROLE...ANTHOL BIBLIOG 20 TREATY UN IMF GATT. PAGE 132 A2698
INT/LAW INT/TRADE FINAN ECO/TAC

S62
SCOTT J.B.,"ANGLO-SOVIET TRADE AND ITS EFFECTS ON THE COMMONWEALTH." COM FUT UK USSR WOR+45 ECO/DEV MARKET INT/ORG CONSULT WEALTH...POLICY TREND CMN/WLTH 20. PAGE 130 A2673
NAT/G ECO/TAC

B63
FISCHER-GALATI S.,EASTERN EUROPE IN THE SIXTIES. ALBANIA USSR YUGOSLAVIA ECO/UNDEV AGRI MARKET LABOR WORKER DIPLOM INT/TRADE EDU/PROP GOV/REL PRODUC UTOPIA SOCISM 20. PAGE 46 A0939 MARXISM TEC/DEV BAL/PWR ECO/TAC

B63
LINDBERG L.,POLITICAL DYNAMICS OF EUROPEAN ECONOMIC INTEGRATION. EUR+WWI ECO/DEV INT/ORG VOL/ASSN DELIB/GP ADMIN WEALTH...DECISION EEC 20. PAGE 89 A1820 MARKET ECO/TAC

B63
THEOBALD R.,FREE MEN AND FREE MARKETS. USA+45 USA-45 ECO/DEV NAT/G TEC/DEV DIPLOM INT/TRADE INCOME ORD/FREE WEALTH...TREND 19/20 KEYNES/JM. PAGE 143 A2915 CONCPT ECO/TAC CAP/ISM MARKET

B63
US ECON SURVEY TEAM INDONESIA,INDONESIA - PERSPECTIVE AND PROPOSALS FOR UNITED STATES ECONOMIC AID. INDONESIA AGRI MARKET TEC/DEV DIPLOM INT/TRADE EDU/PROP 20. PAGE 153 A3113 FOR/AID ECO/UNDEV PLAN INDUS

S63
ANGUILE G.,"CIVILISATION DU PLAN DANS L'EUROPE ET L'AFRIQUE DE DEMAIN." AFR EUR+WWI GABON ECO/DEV FINAN MARKET DELIB/GP ECO/TAC WEALTH...TREND 20. PAGE 8 A0163 ECO/UNDEV PLAN INT/TRADE

S63
DIEBOLD W. JR.,"THE NEW SITUATION OF INTERNATIONAL TRADE POLICY." EUR+WWI FRANCE FUT UK USA+45 WOR+45 DIST/IND PLAN INT/TRADE EDU/PROP PWR WEALTH ...RECORD TREND GEN/LAWS EEC VAL/FREE 20. PAGE 37 A0760 MARKET ECO/TAC

S63
HALLSTEIN W.,"THE EUROPEAN COMMUNITY AND ATLANTIC PARTNERSHIP." EUR+WWI USA+45 MARKET NAT/G VOL/ASSN DELIB/GP ARMS/CONT NUC/PWR ATTIT PWR...CONCPT STAT TIME/SEQ TREND OEEC 20 EEC. PAGE 60 A1235 INT/ORG ECO/TAC UK

S63
MANOLIU F.,"PERSPECTIVES D'UNE INTEGRATION ECONOMIQUE LATINOAMERICAINE." FUT L/A+17C STRUCT MARKET LABOR POL/PAR VOL/ASSN PLAN RIGID/FLEX PWR ...METH/CNCPT OAS TOT/POP 20. PAGE 94 A1927 FINAN INT/ORG PEACE

S63
MATHUR P.N.,"GAINS IN ECONOMIC GROWTH FROM INTERNATIONAL TRADE." USA-45 ECO/DEV FINAN INDUS ATTIT WEALTH...MATH QUANT STAT BIOG TREND GEN/LAWS WORK 20. PAGE 96 A1966 MARKET ECO/TAC CAP/ISM INT/TRADE

S63
SCHOFLING J.A.,"EFTA: THE OTHER EUROPE." ECO/DEV MARKET CONSULT ECO/TAC WEALTH...TIME/SEQ EEC OEEC 20 EFTA. PAGE 129 A2642 EUR+WWI INT/ORG REGION

S63
SHONFIELD A.,"AFTER BRUSSELS." EUR+WWI FRANCE GERMANY UK ECO/DEV DIST/IND MARKET VOL/ASSN DELIB/GP CREATE INT/TRADE ATTIT RIGID/FLEX...RECORD TREND GEN/LAWS EEC CMN/WLTH 20. PAGE 132 A2705 PLAN ECO/TAC

S63
SHWADRAN B.,"MIDDLE EAST OIL, 1962." ISLAM USSR ECO/DEV DIST/IND INDUS PLAN BAL/PWR DISPL DRIVE ...POLICY STAT TREND GEN/LAWS EEC OEEC 20 OIL. PAGE 132 A2712 MARKET ECO/TAC INT/TRADE

S63
WALKER H.,"THE INTERNATIONAL LAW OF COMMODITY AGREEMENTS." FUT WOR+45 ECO/DEV ECO/UNDEV FINAN INT/ORG NAT/G CONSULT CREATE PLAN ECO/TAC ATTIT PERCEPT...CONCPT GEN/LAWS TOT/POP GATT 20. PAGE 160 A3265 MARKET VOL/ASSN INT/LAW INT/TRADE

S63
WEILLER J.,"UNIONS MONETAIRES ET RAPPORTS DE COOPERATION INTERNATIONALE DANS UN MONDE EN TRANSITION: L'EXAMPLE." AFR FUT UNIV WOR+45 SOCIETY ECO/UNDEV MARKET R+D NAT/G FOR/AID PERCEPT RIGID/FLEX...NEW/IDEA 20. PAGE 162 A3303 FINAN INT/ORG

B64
HINSHAW R.,THE EUROPEAN COMMUNITY AND AMERICAN TRADE: A STUDY IN ATLANTIC ECONOMICS AND POLICY. EUR+WWI UK USA+45 ECO/DEV ECO/UNDEV AGRI INDUS INT/ORG NAT/G ECO/TAC TARIFFS REGION...STAT CHARTS EEC 20. PAGE 65 A1337 MARKET TREND INT/TRADE

B64
KRAUSE L.B.,THE COMMON MARKET: PROGRESS AND CONTROVERSY. EUR+WWI UK ECO/DEV REGION...ANTHOL NATO EEC. PAGE 82 A1678 DIPLOM MARKET INT/TRADE INT/ORG

B64
RAMAZANI R.K.,THE MIDDLE EAST AND THE EUROPEAN COMMON MARKET. EUR+WWI ISLAM ECO/DEV EXTR/IND MARKET PROC/MFG INT/ORG NAT/G TEC/DEV ECO/TAC REGION DRIVE WEALTH...STAT CHARTS EEC TOT/POP 20. PAGE 119 A2437 ECO/UNDEV ATTIT INT/TRADE

B64
ZEBOT C.A.,THE ECONOMICS OF COMPETITIVE COEXISTENCE. CHINA/COM USSR WOR+45 FINAN MARKET FOR/AID PRICE DEMAND EQUILIB WEALTH ALL/IDEOS 20. PAGE 169 A3450 TEC/DEV DIPLOM METH/COMP

L64
ARMENGALD A.,"ECONOMIE ET COEXISTENCE." COM EUR+WWI FUT USA+45 WOR+45 ECO/DEV ECO/UNDEV FINAN INT/ORG NAT/G EXEC CHOOSE ATTIT ALL/VALS...POLICY RELATIV DECISION TREND SOC/EXP COLD/WAR WORK 20. PAGE 9 A0173 MARKET ECO/TAC CAP/ISM

L64
HAAS E.B.,"ECONOMICS AND DIFFERENTIAL PATTERNS OF POLITICAL INTEGRATION: PROJECTIONS ABOUT UNITY IN LATIN AMERICA." SOCIETY NAT/G DELIB/GP ACT/RES CREATE PLAN ECO/TAC REGION ROUTINE ATTIT DRIVE PWR WEALTH...CONCPT TREND CHARTS LAFTA 20. PAGE 59 A1208 L/A+17C INT/ORG MARKET

S64
DERWINSKI E.J.,"THE COST OF THE INTERNATIONAL COFFEE AGREEMENT." L/A+17C USA+45 WOR+45 ECO/UNDEV NAT/G VOL/ASSN LEGIS DIPLOM ECO/TAC FOR/AID LEGIT ATTIT...TIME/SEQ CONGRESS 20 TREATY. PAGE 36 A0732 MARKET DELIB/GP INT/TRADE

S64
GARDNER R.N.,"GATT AND THE UNITED NATIONS CONFERENCE ON TRADE AND DEVELOPMENT." USA+45 WOR+45 SOCIETY ECO/UNDEV MARKET NAT/G DELIB/GP ACT/RES PLAN ECO/TAC TARIFFS EDU/PROP ROUTINE DRIVE RIGID/FLEX WEALTH...DECISION MGT TREND UN TOT/POP 20 GATT. PAGE 51 A1047 INT/ORG INT/TRADE

S64
GERBET P.,"LA MISE EN OEUVRE DU MARCHE COMMUN AGRICOLE." ECO/DEV MARKET INT/ORG NAT/G PLAN EDU/PROP NAT/LISM WEALTH...OBS EEC VAL/FREE 20. PAGE 52 A1064 EUR+WWI AGRI REGION

S64
HUELIN D.,"ECONOMIC INTEGRATION IN LATIN AMERICAN: PROGRESS AND PROBLEMS." L/A+17C ECO/DEV AGRI DIST/IND FINAN INDUS NAT/G VOL/ASSN CONSULT DELIB/GP EX/STRUC ACT/RES PLAN TEC/DEV ECO/TAC ROUTINE BAL/PAY WEALTH WORK 20. PAGE 69 A1411 MARKET ECO/UNDEV INT/TRADE

S64
HUTCHINSON E.C.,"AMERICAN AID TO AFRICA." FUT USA+45 MARKET INT/ORG LOC/G NAT/G PUB/INST PLAN ECO/TAC ATTIT RIGID/FLEX...POLICY CONCPT TREND 20. PAGE 69 A1423 AFR ECO/UNDEV FOR/AID

S64
KOJIMA K.,"THE PATTERN OF INTERNATIONAL TRADE AMONG ADVANCED COUNTRIES." EUR+WWI UK USA+45 WOR+45 MARKET NAT/G ECO/TAC WEALTH...MATH STAT CON/ANAL CHARTS EEC CHINJAP 20 CHINJAP. PAGE 81 A1665 ECO/DEV TREND INT/TRADE

S64
MCCREARY E.A.,"THOSE AMERICAN MANAGERS DON'T IMPRESS EUROPE." EUR+WWI USA+45 CULTURE STRATA ECO/DEV TOP/EX INT/TRADE ATTIT DRIVE PERSON RIGID/FLEX...CONCPT 20. PAGE 98 A2003 MARKET ACT/RES BAL/PAY CAP/ISM

B65
LYONS G.M.,AMERICA: PURPOSE AND POWER. UK USA+45 FINAN INDUS MARKET WORKER TEC/DEV DIPLOM AUTOMAT NUC/PWR WAR RACE/REL ORD/FREE 20 EEC CONGRESS SUPREME/CT CIV/RIGHTS. PAGE 92 A1881 PWR PROB/SOLV ECO/DEV TASK

B65
US SENATE COMM ON JUDICIARY,ANTITRUST EXEMPTIONS FOR AGREEMENTS RELATING TO BALANCE OF PAYMENTS. FINAN ECO/TAC CONTROL WEALTH...POLICY 20 CONGRESS. PAGE 157 A3195 BAL/PAY ADJUD MARKET INT/TRADE

L65
WIONCZEK M.,"LATIN AMERICA FREE TRADE ASSOCIATION." AGRI DIST/IND FINAN INDUS INT/ORG LABOR NAT/G TEC/DEV ECO/TAC HEALTH SKILL WEALTH...POLICY RELATIV MGT LAFTA 20. PAGE 165 A3369 L/A+17C MARKET REGION

B66
ENTWICKLUNGSPOLITIK - HANDBUCH UND LEXIKON. MARKET SECT DIPLOM INT/TRADE EDU/PROP CATHISM 20. PAGE 14 A0283 ECO/UNDEV FOR/AID ECO/TAC PLAN

B66
FELKER J.L.,SOVIET ECONOMIC CONTROVERSIES. USSR INDUS PLAN INT/TRADE GP/REL MARXISM SOCISM...POLICY 20. PAGE 45 A0915 ECO/DEV MARKET PROFIT PRICE

B66
LAMBERG R.F.,PRAG UND DIE DRITTE WELT. AFR ASIA CZECHOSLVK L/A+17C MARKET TEC/DEV ECO/TAC REV ATTIT 20 TREATY. PAGE 84 A1713 DIPLOM ECO/UNDEV INT/TRADE FOR/AID

B66
MEERHAEGHE M.,INTERNATIONAL ECONOMIC INSTITUTIONS. EUR+WWI FINAN INDUS MARKET PLAN TARIFFS BAL/PAY EQUILIB...POLICY BIBLIOG/A 20 GATT OEEC EEC IBRD EURCOALSTL. PAGE 99 A2032 ECO/TAC ECO/DEV INT/TRADE INT/ORG

B66
SPINELLI A.,THE EUROCRATS; CONFLICT AND CRISIS IN THE EUROPEAN COMMUNITY (TRANS. BY C. GROVE HAINES). EUR+WWI MARKET POL/PAR ECO/TAC PARL/PROC EEC OEEC ECSC EURATOM. PAGE 136 A2789 INT/ORG INGP/REL CONSTN ADMIN

B67
HOLLERMAN L.,JAPAN'S DEPENDENCE ON THE WORLD ECONOMY. INDUS MARKET LABOR NAT/G DIPLOM 20 CHINJAP. PAGE 67 A1369 PLAN ECO/DEV ECO/TAC INT/TRADE

B67
ROBINSON R.D.,INTERNATIONAL MANAGEMENT. USA+45 INT/TRADE

FINAN R+D PLAN PRODUC...DECISION T. PAGE 92 A1882 MGT INT/LAW MARKET

B67
US CONGRESS SENATE,SURVEY OF THE ALLIANCE FOR PROGRESS; INFLATION IN LATIN AMERICA (PAMPHLET). USA+45 MARKET INT/ORG DIPLOM INT/TRADE BAL/PAY SENATE. PAGE 150 A3072 L/A+17C FINAN POLICY FOR/AID

S67
COSGROVE C.A.,"AGRICULTURE, FINANCE AND POLITICS IN THE EUROPEAN COMMUNITY." EUR+WWI DIST/IND MARKET INT/ORG VOL/ASSN DELIB/GP TEC/DEV BAL/PWR BARGAIN ECO/TAC RATION CONFER 20 EEC. PAGE 31 A0630 ECO/DEV DIPLOM AGRI INT/TRADE

S67
ROCKE J.R.M.,"THE BRITISH EXPORT BATTLE FOR THE CARIBBEAN" GP/REL...POLICY 20 CMN/WLTH. PAGE 122 A2510 INT/TRADE DIPLOM MARKET ECO/TAC

MARKETING SYSTEM....SEE MARKET

MARKHAM J.W. A1943

MARRARO H.R. A1944

MARRIAGE....WEDLOCK; SEE ALSO LOVE

N19
NATIONAL ACADEMY OF SCIENCES,THE GROWTH OF WORLD POPULATION: ANALYSIS OF THE PROBLEMS AND RECOMMENDATIONS FOR RESEARCH AND TRAINING (PAMPHLET). WOR+45 CULTURE ECO/UNDEV EDU/PROP MARRIAGE AGE HEALTH...ANTHOL 20 BIRTH/CON. PAGE 107 A2199 CENSUS PLAN FAM INT/ORG

B57
INSTITUT DE DROIT INTL,TABLEAU GENERAL DES RESOLUTIONS (1873-1956). LAW NEUTRAL CRIME WAR MARRIAGE PEACE...JURID 19/20. PAGE 70 A1442 INT/LAW DIPLOM ORD/FREE ADJUD

B59
VORSPAN A.,JUSTICE AND JUDAISM. FAM DIPLOM ECO/TAC EDU/PROP CRIME RACE/REL MARRIAGE ANOMIE ATTIT ORD/FREE...POLICY 20 UN. PAGE 160 A3254 SECT CULTURE ACT/RES GP/REL

MARRIOTT J.A. A1945, A1946

MARSH N.S. A2925

MARSHALL/A....ALFRED MARSHALL

MARSHALL/J....JOHN MARSHALL

MARSHL/PLN....MARSHALL PLAN

B55
JONES J.M.,THE FIFTEEN WEEKS (FEBRUARY 21-JUNE 5, 1947). EUR+WWI USA+45 PROB/SOLV BAL/PWR...POLICY TIME/SEQ 20 COLD/WAR MARSHL/PLN TRUMAN/HS WASHING/DC. PAGE 75 A1532 DIPLOM ECO/TAC FOR/AID

B55
OECD,MARSHALL PLAN IN TURKEY. TURKEY USA+45 COM/IND CONSTRUC SERV/IND FORCES BUDGET...STAT 20 MARSHL/PLN. PAGE 111 A2277 FOR/AID ECO/UNDEV AGRI INDUS

B57
REISS J.,GEORGE KENNANS POLITIK DER EINDAMMUNG. USSR NAT/G FORCES TOTALISM ATTIT ORD/FREE...POLICY 20 NATO TRUMAN/HS MARSHL/PLN KENNAN/G. PAGE 120 A2463 DIPLOM DETER PEACE

B62
SCHMITT H.A.,THE PATH TO EUROPEAN UNITY. EUR+WWI USA+45 PLAN TEC/DEV DIPLOM FOR/AID CONFER...INT/LAW 20 EEC EURCOALSTL MARSHL/PLN UNIFICA. PAGE 128 A2634 INT/ORG INT/TRADE REGION ECO/DEV

B64
MASON E.S.,FOREIGN AID AND FOREIGN POLICY. USA+45 AGRI INDUS NAT/G EX/STRUC ACT/RES RIGID/FLEX ALL/VALS...POLICY GEN/LAWS MARSHL/PLN CONGRESS 20. PAGE 95 A1956 ECO/UNDEV ECO/TAC FOR/AID DIPLOM

B66
ZISCHKA A.,WAR ES EIN WUNDER? GERMANY/W ECO/DEV FINAN LG/CO BARGAIN CAP/ISM FOR/AID RATION 20 MARSHL/PLN. PAGE 170 A3456 ECO/TAC INT/TRADE INDUS WAR

MARSON C.C. A1669

MARTELLI G. A1947

MARTHELOT P. A1948

MARTI/JOSE....JOSE MARTI

MARTIN C.C. A0762

MARTIN E.M. A1949

MARTIN J.J. A1950

MARTIN L.J. A1951

MARTIN L.W. A1952,A1953

MARX/KARL....KARL MARX

B37
VINER J.,STUDIES IN THE THEORY OF INTERNATIONAL TRADE. WOR-45 CONSTN ECO/DEV AGRI INDUS MARKET INT/ORG LABOR NAT/G ECO/TAC TARIFFS COLONIAL ATTIT WEALTH...POLICY CONCPT MATH STAT OBS SAMP TREND GEN/LAWS MARX/KARL 20. PAGE 159 A3236 CAP/ISM INT/TRADE

B39
ROBBINS L.,ECONOMIC CAUSES OF WAR. WOR-45 ECO/DEV ECO/UNDEV INT/ORG NAT/G TEC/DEV DIPLOM DOMIN COLONIAL ATTIT DRIVE PWR WEALTH...POLICY CONCPT OBS SAMP TREND CON/ANAL GEN/LAWS MARX/KARL 20. PAGE 122 A2493 COERCE ECO/TAC WAR

L39
NEARING S.,"A WARLESS WORLD." FUT WOR-45 SOCIETY INT/ORG NAT/G EX/STRUC PLAN DOMIN WAR ATTIT DRIVE PWR...POLICY PSY CONCPT OBS TREND HYPO/EXP MARX/KARL 20 MARX/KARL LENIN/VI. PAGE 108 A2210 COERCE PEACE

L39
NEARING S.,"A WARLESS WORLD." FUT WOR-45 SOCIETY INT/ORG NAT/G EX/STRUC PLAN DOMIN WAR ATTIT DRIVE PWR...POLICY PSY CONCPT OBS TREND HYPO/EXP MARX/KARL 20 MARX/KARL LENIN/VI. PAGE 108 A2210 COERCE PEACE

S53
LINCOLN G.,"FACTORS DETERMINING ARMS AID." COM FUT USA+45 USSR WOR+45 ECO/DEV NAT/G CONSULT PLAN TEC/DEV DIPLOM DOMIN EDU/PROP PERCEPT PWR ...DECISION CONCPT TREND MARX/KARL 20. PAGE 89 A1819 FORCES POLICY BAL/PWR FOR/AID

B58
PALMER E.E.,THE COMMUNIST CHALLENGE. COM USA+45 USA-45 ECO/DEV ECO/UNDEV NEUTRAL ORD/FREE POPULISM ...CONCPT NAT/COMP ANTHOL 19/20 LENIN/VI STALIN/J MAO MARX/KARL COM/PARTY. PAGE 113 A2320 MARXISM DIPLOM IDEA/COMP POLICY

B62
APATHEKER H.,AMERICAN FOREIGN POLICY AND THE COLD WAR. USA+45 NAT/G POL/PAR COLONIAL NAT/LISM SOVEREIGN MARXISM SOCISM 20 COLD/WAR MARX/KARL LENIN/VI INTERVENT. PAGE 8 A0167 DIPLOM WAR PEACE

B62
BOUSCAREN A.T.,SOVIET FOREIGN POLICY: A PATTERN OF PERSISTANCE. WOR+45 WOR-45 SOCIETY STRUCT INT/ORG POL/PAR CREATE PLAN EDU/PROP ROUTINE ATTIT RIGID/FLEX...POLICY CONCPT RECORD HIST/WRIT TIME/SEQ MARX/KARL 20. PAGE 17 A0352 COM NAT/G DIPLOM USSR

B62
EBENSTEIN W.,TWO WAYS OF LIFE. USA+45 CULTURE ECO/DEV PLAN EDU/PROP CONTROL ORD/FREE...GOV/COMP IDEA/COMP T 20 MARX/KARL ENGELS/F LENIN/VI LOCKE/JOHN MILL/JS. PAGE 40 A0819 MARXISM POPULISM ECO/TAC DIPLOM

B62
HOOK S.,WORLD COMMUNISM: KEY DOCUMENTARY MATERIAL. CHINA/COM L/A+17C USA+45 USSR POL/PAR DIPLOM COLONIAL REV WAR...ANTHOL 20 MARX/KARL LENIN/VI COM/PARTY. PAGE 67 A1380 MARXISM COM GEN/LAWS NAT/G

S62
CROAN M.,"POLYCENTRISM: COMMUNIST INTERNATIONAL RELATIONS." ASIA STRUCT INT/ORG NAT/G POL/PAR CONSULT PLAN DOMIN EDU/PROP COERCE ATTIT RIGID/FLEX SOCISM...POLICY CONCPT TREND CON/ANAL GEN/LAWS MARX/KARL. PAGE 33 A0663 COM CREATE DIPLOM NAT/LISM

S62
KOLARZ W.,"THE IMPACT OF COMMUNISM ON WEST AFRICA." AFR FUT SOCIETY INT/ORG NAT/G CREATE PLAN DOMIN EDU/PROP COERCE NAT/LISM ATTIT RIGID/FLEX SOCISM ...POLICY CONCPT TREND MARX/KARL 20. PAGE 81 A1666 COM POL/PAR COLONIAL

B63
TUCKER R.C.,THE SOVIET POLITICAL MIND. WOR+45 ELITES INT/ORG NAT/G POL/PAR PLAN DIPLOM ECO/TAC DOMIN ADMIN NUC/PWR REV DRIVE PERSON SUPEGO PWR WEALTH...POLICY MGT PSY CONCPT OBS BIOG TREND COLD/WAR MARX/KARL 20. PAGE 145 A2972 COM TOP/EX USSR

B64
KEEP J.,CONTEMPORARY HISTORY IN THE SOVIET MIRROR. COM USSR POL/PAR CREATE DIPLOM AGREE WAR ATTIT ...MYTH TREND ANTHOL 20 COLD/WAR STALIN/J MARX/KARL LENIN/VI. PAGE 77 A1576 HIST/WRIT METH MARXISM IDEA/COMP

S64
CRANE R.D.,"BASIC PRINCIPLES IN SOVIET SPACE LAW." FUT WOR+45 AIR INT/ORG DIPLOM DOMIN ARMS/CONT COERCE NUC/PWR PEACE ATTIT DRIVE PWR...INT/LAW METH/CNCPT NEW/IDEA OBS TREND GEN/LAWS VAL/FREE MARX/KARL 20. PAGE 32 A0659 COM LAW USSR SPACE

S64
GINSBURGS G.,"WARS OF NATIONAL LIBERATION - THE COERCE

SOVIET THESIS." COM USSR WOR+45 WOR-45 LAW CULTURE CONCPT
INT/ORG DIPLOM LEGIT COLONIAL GUERRILLA WAR INT/LAW
NAT/LISM ATTIT PERSON MORAL PWR...JURID OBS TREND REV
MARX/KARL 20. PAGE 53 A1075

S64
KARPOV P.V.,"PEACEFUL COEXISTENCE AND INTERNATIONAL COM
LAW." WOR+45 LAW SOCIETY INT/ORG VOL/ASSN FORCES ATTIT
CREATE CAP/ISM DIPLOM ADJUD NUC/PWR PEACE MORAL INT/LAW
ORD/FREE PWR MARXISM...MARXIST JURID CONCPT OBS USSR
TREND COLD/WAR MARX/KARL 20. PAGE 77 A1568

B65
ROSENBERG A.,DEMOCRACY AND SOCIALISM. COM EUR+WWI ATTIT
FRANCE MOD/EUR STRUCT INT/ORG NAT/G POL/PAR TOP/EX
EDU/PROP COERCE PERSON PWR FASCISM MARXISM...CONCPT
TIME/SEQ MARX/KARL 19/20. PAGE 124 A2535

B67
BRZEZINSKI Z.K.,THE SOVIET BLOC: UNITY AND CONFLICT NAT/G
(2ND ED., REV., ENLARGED). COM POLAND USSR INTELL DIPLOM
CHIEF EX/STRUC CONTROL EXEC GOV/REL PWR MARXISM
...TREND IDEA/COMP 20 LENIN/VI MARX/KARL STALIN/J.
PAGE 21 A0420

MARXISM....MARXISM, COMMUNISM; SEE ALSO MARXIST

N
MONPIED E.,BIBLIOGRAPHIE FEDERALISTE: ARTICLES ET BIBLIOG/A
DOCUMENTS PUBLIES DANS LES PERIODIQUES PARUS EN FEDERAL
FRANCE NOV. 1945-OCT. 1950. EUR+WWI WOR+45 ADMIN CENTRAL
REGION ATTIT MARXISM PACIFISM 20 EEC. PAGE 103 INT/ORG
A2108

N
NEUE POLITISCHE LITERATUR. AFR ASIA EUR+WWI GERMANY BIBLIOG
RUSSIA SOCIETY ECO/DEV ECO/UNDEV PLAN PROB/SOLV DIPLOM
LEAD MARXISM...PHIL/SCI CONCPT 20. PAGE 1 A0021 COM
NAT/G

N
PEKING REVIEW. CHINA/COM CULTURE AGRI INDUS DIPLOM MARXIST
EDU/PROP GUERRILLA ATTIT MARXISM...BIBLIOG 20. NAT/G
PAGE 1 A0022 POL/PAR
PRESS

N
AVTOREFERATY DISSERTATSII. USSR INTELL ACADEM NAT/G BIBLIOG
DIPLOM GOV/REL KNOWL CONCPT. PAGE 3 A0047 MARXISM
MARXIST
COM

N
KYRIAK T.E.,CHINA: A BIBLIOGRAPHY. ASIA CHINA/COM BIBLIOG/A
AGRI FINAN INDUS NAT/G INT/TRADE PRESS...SOC 20. MARXISM
PAGE 83 A1700 TOP/EX
POL/PAR

N
KYRIAK T.E.,EAST EUROPE: BIBLIOGRAPHY--INDEX TO US BIBLIOG/A
JPRS RESEARCH TRANSLATIONS. ALBANIA BULGARIA COM PRESS
CZECHOSLVK HUNGARY POLAND ROMANIA AGRI EXTR/IND MARXISM
FINAN SERV/IND INT/TRADE WEAPON...GEOG MGT SOC 20. INDUS
PAGE 83 A1701

N
KYRIAK T.E.,SOVIET UNION: BIBLIOGRAPHY INDEX TO US BIBLIOG/A
JPRS RESEARCH TRANSLATIONS. USSR ECO/DEV AGRI INDUS
COM/IND CONSTRUC DIST/IND EXTR/IND PROC/MFG R+D MARXISM
INT/TRADE...SOC 20. PAGE 83 A1703 PRESS

N
US CONSOLATE GENERAL HONG KONG,REVIEW OF THE HONG BIBLIOG/A
KONG CHINESE PRESS. ECO/UNDEV LOC/G NAT/G PLAN ASIA
DIPLOM EDU/PROP LEAD GP/REL MARXISM...POLICY INDEX PRESS
20. PAGE 150 A3073 ATTIT

N
US DEPARTMENT OF STATE,BIBLIOGRAPHY (PAMPHLETS). BIBLIOG
AGRI INDUS INT/ORG FOR/AID EDU/PROP WAR MARXISM DIPLOM
...SOC GOV/COMP METH/COMP 20. PAGE 151 A3079 ECO/DEV
NAT/G

N
US SUPERINTENDENT OF DOCUMENTS,FOREIGN RELATIONS OF BIBLIOG/A
THE UNITED STATES; PUBLICATIONS RELATING TO FOREIGN DIPLOM
COUNTRIES (PRICE LIST 65). UAR USA+45 VIETNAM INT/ORG
ECO/UNDEV VOL/ASSN FOR/AID EDU/PROP ARMS/CONT NAT/G
HEALTH MARXISM...POLICY INT/LAW UN NATO. PAGE 157
A3201

B18
KERNER R.J.,SLAVIC EUROPE: A SELECTED BIBLIOGRAPHY BIBLIOG
IN THE WESTERN EUROPEAN LANGUAGES. BULGARIA SOCIETY
CZECHOSLVK GERMANY/E POLAND RUSSIA YUGOSLAVIA NAT/G CULTURE
DIPLOM MARXISM...LING 19/20. PAGE 78 A1598 COM

N19
FRANCK P.G.,AFGHANISTAN BETWEEN EAST AND WEST: THE FOR/AID
ECONOMICS OF COMPETITIVE COEXISTENCE (PAMPHLET). PLAN
AFGHANISTN USA+45 USA-45 USSR INDUS ECO/TAC DIPLOM
INT/TRADE CONTROL NEUTRAL ORD/FREE MARXISM...GEOG ECO/UNDEV
20 UN. PAGE 48 A0977

N19
GRANT N.,COMMUNIST PSYCHOLOGICAL OFFENSIVE: MARXISM
DISTORTION IN THE TRANSLATION OF OFFICIAL DOCUMENTS DIPLOM
(PAMPHLET). USSR POL/PAR CHIEF FOR/AID PRESS EDU/PROP
WRITING COLONIAL LEAD WAR PEACE 20 KHRUSH/N.
PAGE 55 A1129

N19
HAJDA J.,THE COLD WAR VIEWED AS A SOCIOLOGICAL DIPLOM
PROBLEM (PAMPHLET). COM CZECHOSLVK EUR+WWI SOCIETY LEAD
PLAN EDU/PROP CONTROL TASK ATTIT MARXISM...POLICY PWR
20 COLD/WAR MIGRATION. PAGE 59 A1220 NAT/G

B24
NAVILLE A.,LIBERTE, EGALITE, SOLIDARITE: ESSAIS ORD/FREE
D'ANALYSE. STRATA FAM VOL/ASSN INT/TRADE GP/REL SOC
MORAL MARXISM SOCISM...PSY TREATY. PAGE 107 A2205 IDEA/COMP
DIPLOM

B29
DE REPARAZ G.,GEOGRAFIA Y POLITICA. CHILE SPAIN GEOG
USSR NAT/G DIPLOM REV MARXISM...POLICY 19/20. MOD/EUR
PAGE 35 A0709

B32
LENIN V.I.,THE WAR AND THE SECOND INTERNATIONAL. POL/PAR
COM MOD/EUR USSR CAP/ISM DIPLOM NAT/LISM ATTIT WAR
MARXISM...CONCPT 20. PAGE 87 A1772 SOCISM
INT/ORG

B36
THWAITE D.,THE SEETHING AFRICAN POT: A STUDY OF NAT/LISM
BLACK NATIONALISM 1882-1935. ETHIOPIA SECT VOL/ASSN AFR
COERCE GUERRILLA MURDER DISCRIM MARXISM...PSY RACE/REL
TIME/SEQ 18/20 NEGRO. PAGE 144 A2939 DIPLOM

B38
HARPER S.N.,THE GOVERNMENT OF THE SOVIET UNION. COM MARXISM
USSR LAW CONSTN ECO/DEV PLAN TEC/DEV DIPLOM NAT/G
INT/TRADE ADMIN REV NAT/LISM...POLICY 20. PAGE 62 LEAD
A1265 POL/PAR

B39
KOHN H.,REVOLUTIONS AND DICTATORSHIPS. COM EUR+WWI NAT/LISM
ISLAM MOD/EUR NAT/G CHIEF FORCES WAR CIVMIL/REL PWR TOTALISM
MARXISM 18/20. PAGE 81 A1661 REV
FASCISM

B39
LENIN V.I.,IMPERIALISM: THE HIGHEST STAGE OF MARXIST
CAPITALISM. USSR WOR-45 DIST/IND INT/TRADE ATTIT CAP/ISM
MARXISM SOCISM...CHARTS 20. PAGE 87 A1773 COLONIAL
DOMIN

B42
BORNSTEIN J.,ACTION AGAINST THE ENEMY'S MIND. EDU/PROP
EUR+WWI GERMANY USA-45 DIPLOM DOMIN PRESS LEAD PSY
GP/REL DISCRIM PERCEPT FASCISM MARXISM 20 JEWS NAZI WAR
ANTI/SEMIT. PAGE 17 A0343 CONTROL

B43
CONOVER H.F.,SOVIET RUSSIA: SELECTED LIST OF BIBLIOG
REFERENCES. USSR CULTURE INDUS NAT/G TOP/EX TEC/DEV ECO/DEV
BUDGET WAR CIVMIL/REL EFFICIENCY MARXISM 20. COM
PAGE 29 A0597 DIPLOM

B43
GRIERSON P.,BOOKS ON SOVIET RUSSIA 1917-42: A BIBLIOG/A
BIBLIOGRAPHY AND A GUIDE TO READING. USSR CULTURE COM
ELITES NAT/G PLAN DIPLOM REV...GEOG 20. PAGE 56 MARXISM
A1148 LEAD

B43
MICAUD C.A.,THE FRENCH RIGHT AND NAZI GERMANY DIPLOM
1933-1939: A STUDY OF PUBLIC OPINION. GERMANY UK AGREE
USSR POL/PAR ARMS/CONT COERCE DETER PEACE
RIGID/FLEX PWR MARXISM...FASCIST TREND 20
LEAGUE/NAT TREATY. PAGE 101 A2065

B43
SULZBACH W.,NATIONAL CONSCIOUSNESS. FUT WOR-45 NAT/LISM
INT/ORG PEACE MORAL FASCISM MARXISM...MAJORIT TREND NAT/G
WORSHIP 19/20 LEAGUE/NAT INTERVENT WWI. PAGE 140 DIPLOM
A2862 WAR

B45
CLAGETT H.L.,COMMUNIST CHINA: RUTHLESS ENEMY OR BIBLIOG/A
PAPER TIGER (PAMPHLET). CHINA/COM ECO/UNDEV AGRI MARXISM
INDUS NAT/G POL/PAR ECO/TAC INT/TRADE GUERRILLA DIPLOM
ATTIT...CHARTS NAT/COMP ORG/CHARTS 20. PAGE 26 COERCE
A0540

B47
NIEBUHR R.,THE CHILDREN OF LIGHT AND THE CHILDREN POPULISM
OF DARKNESS: A VINDICATION OF DEMOCRACY AND DIPLOM
CRITIQUE OF TRADITIONAL DEFENSE. UNIV STRUCT NAT/G NEIGH
SECT INGP/REL OWN PEACE ORD/FREE MARXISM GP/REL
...IDEA/COMP GEN/LAWS 20 CHRISTIAN. PAGE 109 A2235

B48
DURBIN E.F.M.,THE POLITICS OF DEMOCRATIC SOCIALISM; SOCIALIST
AN ESSAY ON SOCIAL POLICY. STRATA POL/PAR PLAN POPULISM
COERCE DRIVE PERSON PWR MARXISM...CHARTS METH/COMP. POLICY
PAGE 39 A0805 SOCIETY

B49
US DEPARTMENT OF STATE,SOVIET BIBLIOGRAPHY BIBLIOG/A
(PAMPHLET). CHINA/COM COM USSR LAW AGRI INT/ORG MARXISM
ECO/TAC EDU/PROP...POLICY GEOG 20. PAGE 151 A3084 CULTURE
DIPLOM

B50
BROOKINGS INSTITUTION,MAJOR PROBLEMS OF UNITED DIPLOM
STATES FOREIGN POLICY. AFR ASIA INDIA UK USA+45 POLICY
USSR BAL/PWR FOR/AID WAR PEACE TOTALISM MARXISM ORD/FREE
SOCISM 20 CHINJAP COLD/WAR. PAGE 19 A0393

B50
DULLES J.F.,WAR OR PEACE. CHINA/COM USA+45 USSR PEACE
INT/ORG SECT FORCES PLAN NUC/PWR WAR CENTRAL DIPLOM
MARXISM...POLICY 20 UN ROOSEVLT/F STALIN/J. PAGE 39 TREND

A0797 ORD/FREE

B51
BLANSHARD P.,COMMUNISM, DEMOCRACY AND CATHOLIC POWER. USSR VATICAN WOR+45 WOR-45 CULTURE ELITES INTELL SOCIETY STRUCT INT/ORG POL/PAR EDU/PROP COERCE ATTIT KNOWL PWR MARXISM...CONCPT COLD/WAR 20. PAGE 15 A0308 — COM SECT TOTALISM

B51
BORKENAU F.,EUROPEAN COMMUNISM. COM EUR+WWI GERMANY SPAIN USSR INT/ORG PLAN REV WAR ATTIT 20 STALIN/J HITLER/A. PAGE 17 A0342 — MARXISM POLICY DIPLOM NAT/G

B51
BROGAN D.W.,THE PRICE OF REVOLUTION. FRANCE USA+45 USA-45 USSR CONSTN NAT/G DIPLOM COLONIAL NAT/LISM ORD/FREE POPULISM...CONCPT 18/20 PRE/US/AM. PAGE 19 A0386 — REV METH/COMP COST MARXISM

C51
BEST H.,"THE SOVIET STATE AND ITS INCEPTION." USSR CULTURE INDUS DIPLOM WEALTH...GEOG SOC BIBLIOG 20. PAGE 14 A0281 — COM GEN/METH REV MARXISM

B52
SPENCER F.A.,WAR AND POSTWAR GREECE: AN ANALYSIS BASED ON GREEK WRITINGS. GREECE SOCIETY NAT/G POL/PAR FORCES CREATE DIPLOM LEAD MARXISM...SOC 20. PAGE 136 A2784 — BIBLIOG/A WAR REV

B52
US DEPARTMENT OF STATE,RESEARCH ON EASTERN EUROPE (EXCLUDING USSR). EUR+WWI LAW ECO/DEV NAT/G PROB/SOLV DIPLOM ADMIN LEAD MARXISM...TREND 19/20. PAGE 151 A3088 — BIBLIOG R+D ACT/RES COM

B53
LENZ F.,DIE BEWEGUNGEN DER GROSSEN MACHTE. USA+45 USA-45 USSR SOCIETY STRATA STRUCT NAT/G PERSON MARXISM...CONCPT IDEA/COMP NAT/COMP 18/20. PAGE 87 A1777 — BAL/PWR TREND DIPLOM HIST/WRIT

B53
SHIRATO I.,JAPANESE SOURCES ON THE HISTORY OF THE CHINESE COMMUNIST MOVEMENT (PAMPHLET). CHINA/COM USSR CONSTRUC NAT/G POL/PAR FORCES DIPLOM DOMIN EDU/PROP CONTROL WAR TOTALISM SOCISM 20. PAGE 132 A2702 — BIBLIOG/A MARXISM ECO/UNDEV

B54
COOKSON J.,BEFORE THE AFRICAN STORM. BELGIUM CENTRL/AFR FRANCE UK ECO/UNDEV POL/PAR CREATE BAL/PWR RACE/REL NAT/LISM ORD/FREE CONSERVE MARXISM SOC/INTEG 20 CONGO/LEOP. PAGE 30 A0607 — COLONIAL REV DISCRIM DIPLOM

B54
STALEY E.,THE FUTURE OF UNDERDEVELOPED COUNTRIES: POLITICAL IMPLICATIONS OF ECONOMIC DEVELOPMENT. COM FUT USA+45 SOCIETY ECO/UNDEV CREATE PLAN CAP/ISM ATTIT DRIVE MARXISM SOCISM...POLICY CONCPT CHARTS COLD/WAR 20. PAGE 137 A2801 — EDU/PROP ECO/TAC FOR/AID

B54
STRAUSZ-HUPE R.,INTERNATIONAL RELATIONS IN THE AGE OF THE CONFLICT BETWEEN DEMOCRACY AND DICTATORSHIP (2ND ED.). INT/ORG BAL/PWR EDU/PROP ADMIN WAR PEACE PWR...CONCPT CHARTS BIBLIOG 20 COLD/WAR UN LEAGUE/NAT. PAGE 139 A2846 — DIPLOM POPULISM MARXISM

L54
CHARLESWORTH J.C.,"AMERICA AND A NEW ASIA." ASIA INDIA ISLAM S/ASIA USA+45 USA-45 ECO/UNDEV NAT/G POL/PAR FORCES FOR/AID DOMIN EDU/PROP COERCE DRIVE ALL/VALS MARXISM SOCISM TOT/POP 20. PAGE 26 A0522 — ECO/TAC DIPLOM NAT/LISM

B55
JAPANESE STUDIES OF MODERN CHINA. ASIA DIPLOM LEAD REV MARXISM 19/20 CHINJAP. PAGE 43 A0885 — BIBLIOG/A SOC

B55
SEMJONOW J.M.,DIE FASCHISTISCHE GEOPOLITIK IM DIENSTE DES AMERIKANISCHEN IMPERIALISMUS. USA+45 USA-45 CAP/ISM PEACE ORD/FREE MARXISM SOCISM ...POLICY GEOG 20. PAGE 131 A2684 — DIPLOM COERCE FASCISM WAR

B55
THOMPSON V.,MINORITY PROBLEMS IN SOUTHEAST ASIA. CAMBODIA CHINA/COM LAOS S/ASIA KIN NAT/G SECT PROB/SOLV EDU/PROP REGION GP/REL RACE/REL MARXISM ...SOC 20 BUDDHISM UN. PAGE 143 A2933 — INGP/REL GEOG DIPLOM STRUCT

L55
ROSTOW W.W.,"RUSSIA AND CHINA UNDER COMMUNISM." CHINA/COM USSR INTELL STRUCT INT/ORG NAT/G POL/PAR TOP/EX ACT/RES PLAN ADMIN ATTIT ALL/VALS MARXISM ...CONCPT OBS TIME/SEQ TREND GOV/COMP VAL/FREE 20. PAGE 124 A2543 — COM ASIA

B56
CHANG C.J.,THE MINORITY GROUPS OF YUNN AN AND CHINESE POLITICAL EXPANSION INTO SOUTHEAST ASIA (DOCTORAL THESIS). ASIA CHINA/COM S/ASIA FORCES TEC/DEV DIPLOM EDU/PROP...GEOG BIBLIOG 20. PAGE 26 A0520 — GP/REL REGION DOMIN MARXISM

B56
GILBERT R.,COMPETITIVE COEXISTENCE: THE NEW SOVIET CHALLENGE. WORKER DIPLOM WAR ORD/FREE 20 COLD/WAR. PAGE 52 A1071 — NUC/PWR DOMIN MARXISM PEACE

B56
SIPKOV I.,LEGAL SOURCES AND BIBLIOGRAPHY OF BULGARIA. BULGARIA COM LEGIS WRITING ADJUD CT/SYS ...INT/LAW TREATY 20. PAGE 134 A2736 — BIBLIOG LAW TOTALISM MARXISM

B56
VON HARPE W.,DIE SOWJETUNION FINNLAND UND SKANDANAVIEN, 1945-1955. EUR+WWI FINLAND GERMANY USSR WAR INGP/REL ORD/FREE SOVEREIGN MARXISM ...POLICY GOV/COMP BIBLIOG 20 STALIN/J. PAGE 160 A3252 — DIPLOM COM NEUTRAL BAL/PWR

B56
WILBUR C.M.,DOCUMENTS ON COMMUNISM, NATIONALISM, AND SOVIET ADVISERS IN CHINA, 1918-1927. CHINA/COM USSR STRUCT DIPLOM LEAD NAT/LISM...BIBLIOG/A 20. PAGE 164 A3343 — REV POL/PAR MARXISM COM

B57
BYRNES R.F.,BIBLIOGRAPHY OF AMERICAN PUBLICATIONS ON EAST CENTRAL EUROPE, 1945-1957 (VOL. XXII). SECT DIPLOM EDU/PROP RACE/REL...ART/METH GEOG JURID SOC LING 20 JEWS. PAGE 23 A0462 — BIBLIOG/A COM MARXISM NAT/G

B57
FRASER L.,PROPAGANDA. GERMANY USSR WOR+45 WOR-45 NAT/G POL/PAR CONTROL FEEDBACK LOBBY CROWD WAR CONSEN NAT/LISM 20. PAGE 48 A0988 — EDU/PROP FASCISM MARXISM DIPLOM

B57
TOMASIC D.A.,NATIONAL COMMUNISM AND SOVIET STRATEGY. UK USSR YUGOSLAVIA NAT/G POL/PAR CHIEF CREATE DOMIN REV WAR PWR...BIOG TREND 20 TITO/MARSH STALIN/J. PAGE 144 A2948 — COM NAT/LISM MARXISM DIPLOM

B58
ANGELL N.,DEFENCE AND THE ENGLISH-SPEAKING ROLE. CHINA/COM UK USSR INT/ORG FORCES EDU/PROP NEUTRAL NUC/PWR NAT/LISM PEACE TOTALISM 20 COLD/WAR COEXIST. PAGE 8 A0161 — DIPLOM WAR MARXISM ORD/FREE

B58
APPADORAI A.,THE USE OF FORCE IN INTERNATIONAL RELATIONS. WOR+45 CULTURE ECO/UNDEV CAP/ISM ARMS/CONT REV WAR ATTIT PERSON SOVEREIGN MARXISM ...INT/LAW PACIFIST 20 UN INTERVENT THIRD/WRLD COLD/WAR. PAGE 8 A0169 — PEACE FEDERAL INT/ORG

B58
BOWLES C.,IDEAS, PEOPLE AND PEACE. ASIA CHINA/COM FUT INDIA USA+45 USSR ECO/UNDEV INT/ORG LEAD TASK MARXISM 20 NATO UN COLD/WAR. PAGE 18 A0359 — PEACE POLICY NAT/G DIPLOM

B58
CHANG H.,WITHIN THE FOUR SEAS. ASIA WAR MORAL MARXISM...IDEA/COMP NAT/COMP 20 CONFUCIUS. PAGE 26 A0521 — PEACE DIPLOM KNOWL CULTURE

B58
GROBLER J.H.,AFRICA'S DESTINY. AFR EUR+WWI SOUTH/AFR UK USA+45 ELITES KIN LOC/G DIPLOM DISCRIM ATTIT CONSERVE MARXISM 20 ROOSEVLT/T NEGRO. PAGE 57 A1168 — POLICY ORD/FREE COLONIAL CONSTN

B58
KENNAN G.F.,RUSSIA, THE ATOM AND THE WEST. USA+45 USSR INT/ORG ARMS/CONT MARXISM 20 NATO. PAGE 77 A1587 — BAL/PWR NUC/PWR CONTROL DIPLOM

B58
NEAL F.W.,TITOISM IN ACTION. COM YUGOSLAVIA AGRI LOC/G DIPLOM TOTALISM...BIBLIOG 20 TITO/MARSH. PAGE 107 A2206 — MARXISM POL/PAR CHIEF ADMIN

B58
PALMER E.E.,THE COMMUNIST CHALLENGE. COM USA+45 USA-45 ECO/DEV ECO/UNDEV NEUTRAL ORD/FREE POPULISM ...CONCPT NAT/COMP ANTHOL 19/20 LENIN/VI STALIN/J MAO MARX/KARL COM/PARTY. PAGE 113 A2320 — MARXISM DIPLOM IDEA/COMP POLICY

B58
TILLION G.,ALGERIA: THE REALITIES. ALGERIA FRANCE ISLAM CULTURE STRATA PROB/SOLV DOMIN REV NAT/LISM WEALTH MARXISM...GEOG 20. PAGE 144 A2940 — ECO/UNDEV SOC COLONIAL DIPLOM

B58
VARG P.A.,MISSIONARIES, CHINESE, AND DIPLOMATS: THE AMERICAN PROTESTANT MISSIONARY MOVEMENT IN CHINA, 1890-1952. ASIA ECO/UNDEV NAT/G PROB/SOLV CAP/ISM EDU/PROP COLONIAL NAT/LISM ATTIT MARXISM...NAT/COMP STERTYP 20 CHINJAP PROTESTANT MISSION. PAGE 158 A3221 — CULTURE DIPLOM SECT

B59
CAREW-HUNT R.C.,BOOKS ON COMMUNISM. NAT/G POL/PAR DIPLOM REV...BIOG 19/20. PAGE 24 A0481 — BIBLIOG/A MARXISM COM ASIA

B59
CHALUPA V.,RISE AND DEVELOPMENT OF A TOTALITARIAN STATE. CZECHOSLVK USSR STRUCT INT/ORG WORKER DIPLOM ECO/TAC COERCE NAT/LISM ATTIT...POLICY 20 COM/PARTY. PAGE 25 A0516 — TOTALISM MARXISM REV POL/PAR

B59
GILBERT R.,GENOCIDE IN TIBET. ASIA SECT CHIEF — MARXISM

DIPLOM 20. PAGE 52 A1072
MURDER WAR GP/REL

B59
GOLDWIN R.A.,READINGS IN RUSSIAN FOREIGN POLICY. HUNGARY USSR YUGOSLAVIA ELITES INT/ORG NAT/G REV WAR NAT/LISM PERSON SOCISM...CHARTS 20 MAPS BOLSHEVISM. PAGE 53 A1095
COM MARXISM DIPLOM POLICY

B59
GOULD L.P.,THE PRICE OF SURVIVAL. EUR+WWI SPACE USA+45 FORCES ECO/TAC NUC/PWR WAR ORD/FREE MARXISM ...IDEA/COMP 20 COLD/WAR NATO. PAGE 54 A1117
POLICY PROB/SOLV DIPLOM PEACE

B59
HARRIMAN A.,PEACE WITH RUSSIA? USA+45 USSR SOCIETY ECO/TAC CONTROL TOTALISM ATTIT MARXISM...POLICY 20 STALIN/J KHRUSH/N. PAGE 62 A1266
DIPLOM PEACE NAT/G TASK

B59
JACKSON B.W.,FIVE IDEAS THAT CHANGE THE WORLD. FUT WOR+45 WOR-45 ECO/UNDEV INDUS DIPLOM DOMIN CONTROL ...IDEA/COMP 20. PAGE 72 A1473
MARXISM NAT/LISM COLONIAL ECO/TAC

B59
KARUNAKARAN K.P.,INDIA IN WORLD AFFAIRS, 1952-1958 (VOL. II). INDIA ECO/UNDEV SECT FOR/AID INT/TRADE ADJUD NEUTRAL REV WAR DISCRIM ORD/FREE MARXISM ...BIBLIOG 20. PAGE 77 A1569
DIPLOM INT/ORG S/ASIA COLONIAL

B59
NIEBUHR R.,NATIONS AND EMPIRES. WOR+45 INT/ORG COLONIAL NUC/PWR TOTALISM UTOPIA ORD/FREE MARXISM WORSHIP 20 COLD/WAR PROTESTANT CHRISTIAN. PAGE 109 A2237
DIPLOM NAT/G POLICY PWR

B59
NOVE A.,COMMUNIST ECONOMIC STRATEGY: SOVIET GROWTH AND CAPABILITIES. USSR AGRI LABOR PLAN TEC/DEV CAP/ISM INT/TRADE EFFICIENCY MARXISM 20 THIRD/WRLD. PAGE 110 A2257
FOR/AID ECO/TAC DIPLOM INDUS

B59
SHANNON D.A.,THE DECLINE OF AMERICAN COMMUNISM; A HISTORY OF THE COMMUNIST PARTY OF THE UNITED STATES SINCE 1945. USA+45 LAW SOCIETY LABOR NAT/G WORKER DIPLOM EDU/PROP LEAD...POLICY BIBLIOG 20 KHRUSH/N NEGRO AFL/CIO COLD/WAR COM/PARTY. PAGE 131 A2692
MARXISM POL/PAR ATTIT POPULISM

C59
KULSKI W.W.,"PEACEFUL COEXISTENCE." USSR ECO/UNDEV INT/ORG POL/PAR EDU/PROP COLONIAL CONTROL REV NAT/LISM PEACE PWR MARXISM...BIBLIOG 20. PAGE 83 A1692
COM DIPLOM DOMIN

B60
BILLERBECK K.,SOVIET BLOC FOREIGN AID TO UNDERDEVELOPED COUNTRIES. COM FUT USSR FINAN FORCES TEC/DEV DIPLOM INT/TRADE EDU/PROP NUC/PWR...TREND 20. PAGE 14 A0287
FOR/AID ECO/UNDEV ECO/TAC MARXISM

B60
CENTRAL ASIAN RESEARCH CENTRE,RUSSIA LOOKS AT AFRICA (PAMPHLET). AFR USSR COLONIAL RACE/REL...HUM 19/20 STALIN/J. PAGE 25 A0511
BIBLIOG MARXISM TREND DIPLOM

B60
EMERSON R.,FROM EMPIRE TO NATION: THE RISE TO SELF-ASSERTION OF ASIAN AND AFRICAN PEOPLES. S/ASIA CULTURE NAT/G SECT DIPLOM ATTIT SOVEREIGN MARXISM ...POLICY BIBLIOG 19/20. PAGE 41 A0847
NAT/LISM COLONIAL AFR ASIA

B60
FISCHER L.,RUSSIA, AMERICA, AND THE WORLD. FUT USA+45 USSR WOR+45 FORCES PLAN BAL/PWR ECO/TAC FOR/AID NEUTRAL TASK NUC/PWR PWR 20 COLD/WAR. PAGE 46 A0937
DIPLOM POLICY MARXISM ECO/UNDEV

B60
FISCHER L.,THE SOVIETS IN WORLD AFFAIRS. CHINA/COM COM EUR+WWI USSR INT/ORG CONFER LEAD ARMS/CONT REV PWR...CHARTS 20 TREATY VERSAILLES. PAGE 46 A0938
DIPLOM NAT/G POLICY MARXISM

B60
FOOTMAN D.,INTERNATIONAL COMMUNISM. ASIA EUR+WWI FRANCE FUT GERMANY MOD/EUR S/ASIA USA-45 WOR+45 WOR-45 INTELL LABOR TOTALISM MARXISM WORK 20. PAGE 47 A0958
COM INT/ORG STRUCT REV

B60
FOREIGN POLICY CLEARING HOUSE,STRATEGY FOR THE 60'S. FUT USA+45 WOR+45 ECO/UNDEV FORCES BAL/PWR TASK ARMS/CONT DETER PWR MARXISM 20 SENATE. PAGE 47 A0963
DIPLOM NAT/G POLICY ACT/RES

B60
HAHN W.F.,AMERICAN STRATEGY FOR THE NUCLEAR AGE. USA+45 NAT/G TEC/DEV ECO/TAC FOR/AID ARMS/CONT NUC/PWR ORD/FREE MARXISM...ANTHOL 20. PAGE 59 A1216
DIPLOM PLAN PEACE

B60
JACOBSON H.K.,AMERICAN FOREIGN POLICY. COM EUR+WWI USA+45 USA-45 ECO/DEV ECO/UNDEV INT/ORG NAT/G INT/TRADE EDU/PROP COLONIAL CHOOSE MARXISM 20 NATO. PAGE 72 A1485
POL/PAR PWR DIPLOM

B60
KARDELJE,SOCIALISM AND WAR. CHINA/COM WOR+45 YUGOSLAVIA DIPLOM EDU/PROP ATTIT...POLICY CONCPT IDEA/COMP COLD/WAR. PAGE 76 A1565
MARXIST WAR MARXISM BAL/PWR

B60
KHRUSHCHEV N.,FOR VICTORY IN PEACEFUL COMPETITION WITH CAPITALISM. COM FUT USSR WOR+45 CONSTN SOCIETY INDUS INT/ORG DELIB/GP PLAN BAL/PWR DIPLOM PERSON MARXISM...MARXIST WORK 20 COLD/WAR. PAGE 79 A1611
TOP/EX PWR CAP/ISM SOCISM

B60
KHRUSHCHEV N.S.,KHRUSHCHEV IN AMERICA. USA+45 USSR INT/TRADE EDU/PROP PRESS PEACE...MARXIST RECORD INT 20 COLD/WAR KHRUSH/N. PAGE 79 A1613
MARXISM CHIEF DIPLOM

B60
MC CLELLAN G.S.,INDIA. CHINA/COM INDIA CONSTN ELITES STRATA AGRI POL/PAR FOR/AID ARMS/CONT REV MARXISM...CENSUS BIBLIOG 20 COLD/WAR GANDHI/M NEHRU/J. PAGE 97 A1990
DIPLOM NAT/G SOCIETY ECO/UNDEV

B60
MCCLELLAND C.A.,NUCLEAR WEAPONS, MISSILES, AND FUTURE WAR: PROBLEM FOR THE SIXTIES. WOR+45 FORCES ARMS/CONT DETER MARXISM...POLICY ANTHOL COLD/WAR. PAGE 97 A1998
DIPLOM NUC/PWR WAR WEAPON

B60
QUBAIN F.I.,INSIDE THE ARAB MIND: A BIBLIOGRAPHIC SURVEY OF LITERATURE IN ARABIC ON ARAB NATIONALISM AND UNITY. ISLAM POL/PAR SECT LEAD SOVEREIGN MARXISM SOCISM. PAGE 118 A2425
BIBLIOG/A FEDERAL DIPLOM NAT/LISM

B60
SZTARAY Z.,BIBLIOGRAPHY ON HUNGARY. HUNGARY MOD/EUR CULTURE INDUS SECT DIPLOM REV...ART/METH SOC LING 18/20. PAGE 141 A2879
BIBLIOG NAT/G COM MARXISM

B61
DELZELL C.F.,MUSSOLINI'S ENEMIES - THE ITALIAN ANTI-FASCIST RESISTANCE. ITALY DIPLOM PRESS DETER WAR TOTALISM ORD/FREE MARXISM 20. PAGE 36 A0730
FASCISM GP/REL POL/PAR REV

B61
FLEMING D.F.,THE COLD WAR AND ITS ORIGINS: 1950-1960 (VOL. II). ASIA FUT HUNGARY POLAND WOR+45 TEC/DEV DOMIN NUC/PWR REV PEACE...T 20 COLD/WAR EISNHWR/DD SUEZ. PAGE 46 A0946
MARXISM DIPLOM BAL/PWR

B61
FLEMING D.F.,THE COLD WAR AND ITS ORIGINS: 1917-1950 (VOL. I). ASIA USSR WOR+45 WOR-45 TEC/DEV FOR/AID NUC/PWR REV WAR PEACE FASCISM...T 20 COLD/WAR NATO BERLIN/BLO. PAGE 46 A0947
DIPLOM MARXISM BAL/PWR

B61
HUDSON G.F.,THE SINO-SOVIET DISPUTE. CHINA/COM USSR INTELL INT/TRADE DEBATE REV...IDEA/COMP 20. PAGE 68 A1404
DIPLOM MARXISM PRESS ATTIT

B61
LEGISLATIVE REFERENCE SERVICE,WORLD COMMUNIST MOVEMENT: SELECTIVE CHRONOLOGY, 1818-1957 (4 VOLS.). COM WOR+45 WOR-45 POL/PAR LEAD 19/20. PAGE 86 A1766
BIBLIOG DIPLOM TIME/SEQ MARXISM

B61
LERCHE C.O. JR.,FOREIGN POLICY OF THE AMERICAN PEOPLE (REV. ED.). USA+45 USSR FORCES TEC/DEV EDU/PROP WAR PRODUC ORD/FREE MARXISM...POLICY TREND BIBLIOG 20 COLD/WAR. PAGE 87 A1781
DECISION PLAN PEACE DIPLOM

B61
LETHBRIDGE H.J.,CHINA'S URBAN COMMUNES. CHINA/COM FUT ECO/UNDEV DIPLOM EDU/PROP DEMAND INCOME MARXISM ...POLICY 20. PAGE 87 A1790
MUNIC CONTROL ECO/TAC NAT/G

B61
LIPPMANN W.,THE COMING TESTS WITH RUSSIA. COM CUBA GERMANY USSR FORCES CONTROL NEUTRAL COERCE NUC/PWR REV WAR PWR...INT 20 KHRUSH/N BERLIN. PAGE 89 A1830
BAL/PWR DIPLOM MARXISM ARMS/CONT

B61
NOLLAU G.,INTERNATIONAL COMMUNISM AND WORLD REVOLUTION: HISTORY AND METHODS. RUSSIA USSR INT/ORG NAT/G POL/PAR VOL/ASSN FORCES BAL/PWR DIPLOM EXEC REGION WAR ATTIT PWR MARXISM...CONCPT TIME/SEQ COLD/WAR 19/20. PAGE 102 A2100
COM REV

B61
NEAL F.W.,US FOREIGN POLICY AND THE SOVIET UNION. USA+45 USSR INT/ORG ECO/TAC ARMS/CONT MAJORITY NAT/LISM ATTIT RESPECT MARXISM 20. PAGE 108 A2207
DIPLOM POLICY PEACE

B61
NEWMAN R.P.,RECOGNITION OF COMMUNIST CHINA? A STUDY IN ARGUMENT. CHINA/COM NAT/G PROB/SOLV RATIONAL ...INT/LAW LOG IDEA/COMP BIBLIOG 20. PAGE 108 A2226
MARXISM ATTIT DIPLOM POLICY

B61
NOLLAU G.,INTERNATIONAL COMMUNISM AND WORLD REVOLUTION; HISTORY AND METHODS (TRANS. BY VICTOR ANDERSEN). COM WORKER DIPLOM CONFER INGP/REL ...CONCPT BIBLIOG 20 STALIN/J LENIN/VI COMINTERN COMINFORM WORLD/CONG. PAGE 110 A2249
MARXISM POL/PAR INT/ORG REV

B61
OAKES J.B.,THE EDGE OF FREEDOM. EUR+WWI USA+45 USSR ECO/UNDEV BAL/PWR DIPLOM DOMIN COLONIAL PWR MARXISM POPULISM...IDEA/COMP 20 COLD/WAR. PAGE 111 A2271
AFR ORD/FREE SOVEREIGN

NEUTRAL

SCHWARTZ H.,THE RED PHOENIX: RUSSIA SINCE WORLD WAR II. USA+45 WOR+45 ELITES POL/PAR TEC/DEV ECO/TAC MARXISM. PAGE 130 A2655 — B61 DIPLOM NAT/G ECO/DEV

STARK H.,SOCIAL AND ECONOMIC FRONTIERS IN LATIN AMERICA (2ND ED.). CUBA FUT CULTURE AGRI INDUS ECO/TAC PRODUC ATTIT MARXISM...NAT/COMP BIBLIOG T 20. PAGE 137 A2807 — B61 L/A+17C SOCIETY DIPLOM ECO/UNDEV

US LIBRARY OF CONGRESS,WORLD COMMUNIST MOVEMENT. USA+45 USSR WOR+45 INT/ORG DIPLOM REV ATTIT 19/20. PAGE 155 A3155 — B61 BIBLIOG/A EDU/PROP MARXISM POL/PAR

WARD B.J.,INDIA AND THE WEST. INDIA UK USA+45 INT/TRADE GIVE COLONIAL ATTIT MARXISM 19/20. PAGE 161 A3279 — B61 PLAN ECO/UNDEV ECO/TAC FOR/AID

TUCKER R.C.,"TOWARDS A COMPARATIVE POLITICS OF MOVEMENT-REGIMES" (BMR)" USSR CONSTN NAT/G CREATE PROB/SOLV DIPLOM DOMIN REV...GP/COMP IDEA/COMP METH 20 STALIN/J BOLSHEVISM. PAGE 145 A2971 — S61 MARXISM POLICY GEN/LAWS PWR

APATHEKER H.,AMERICAN FOREIGN POLICY AND THE COLD WAR. USA+45 NAT/G POL/PAR COLONIAL NAT/LISM SOVEREIGN MARXISM SOCISM 20 COLD/WAR MARX/KARL LENIN/VI INTERVENT. PAGE 8 A0167 — B62 DIPLOM WAR PEACE

DELANEY R.F.,THE LITERATURE OF COMMUNISM IN AMERICA. COM USA+45 USA-45 INT/ORG LABOR NAT/G POL/PAR INGP/REL...MAJORIT 20. PAGE 36 A0727 — B62 BIBLIOG/A MARXISM EDU/PROP IDEA/COMP

DOUGLAS W.O.,DEMOCRACY'S MANIFESTO. COM USA+45 ECO/UNDEV INT/ORG FORCES PLAN NEUTRAL TASK MARXISM ...JURID 20 NATO SEATO. PAGE 38 A0779 — B62 DIPLOM POLICY NAT/G ORD/FREE

EBENSTEIN W.,TWO WAYS OF LIFE. USA+45 CULTURE ECO/DEV PLAN EDU/PROP CONTROL ORD/FREE...GOV/COMP IDEA/COMP T 20 MARX/KARL ENGELS/F LENIN/VI LOCKE/JOHN MILL/JS. PAGE 40 A0819 — B62 MARXISM POPULISM ECO/TAC DIPLOM

ELLIOTT J.R.,THE APPEAL OF COMMUNISM IN THE UNDERDEVELOPED NATIONS. USSR WOR+45 INT/ORG NAT/G DIPLOM DOMIN EDU/PROP ROUTINE ATTIT RIGID/FLEX ORD/FREE PWR WEALTH MARXISM...POLICY SOC METH/CNCPT MYTH TOT/POP COLD/WAR 20. PAGE 41 A0842 — B62 COM ECO/UNDEV

FRIEDRICH-EBERT-STIFTUNG,THE SOVIET BLOC AND DEVELOPING COUNTRIES. CHINA/COM COM GERMANY/E USSR WOR+45 ECO/UNDEV INT/ORG NAT/G TEC/DEV NEUTRAL PWR ...POLICY 20. PAGE 49 A1008 — B62 MARXISM DIPLOM ECO/TAC FOR/AID

GOLDWATER B.M.,WHY NOT VICTORY? A FRESH LOOK AT AMERICAN FOREIGN POLICY. USA+45 WOR+45 FOR/AID LEAD ARMS/CONT WAR PEACE ATTIT ORD/FREE PWR MARXISM ...INT/LAW 20 TREATY ECHR COUNCL/EUR. PAGE 53 A1092 — B62 DIPLOM POLICY CONSERVE NAT/LISM

GUTTMAN A.,THE WOUND IN THE HEART: AMERICA AND THE SPANISH CIVIL WAR. SPAIN USA-45 POL/PAR LEGIS ECO/TAC CHOOSE ANOMIE ATTIT MARXISM...POLICY ANARCH BIBLIOG 20 ROOSEVLT/F. PAGE 58 A1198 — B62 ALL/IDEOS WAR DIPLOM CATHISM

HOOK S.,WORLD COMMUNISM: KEY DOCUMENTARY MATERIAL. CHINA/COM L/A+17C USA+45 USSR POL/PAR DIPLOM COLONIAL REV WAR...ANTHOL 20 MARX/KARL LENIN/VI COM/PARTY. PAGE 67 A1380 — B62 MARXISM COM GEN/LAWS NAT/G

KIRPICEVA I.K.,HANDBUCH DER RUSSISCHEN UND SOWJETISCHEN BIBLIOGRAPHIEN (5 VOLS.). USSR STRUCT ECO/DEV DIPLOM LEAD ATTIT 18/20. PAGE 80 A1637 — B62 BIBLIOG/A NAT/G MARXISM COM

KLUCKHOHN F.L.,THE NAKED RISE OF COMMUNISM. CHINA/COM COM USSR WOR+45 CONSTN POL/PAR PLAN CONTROL LEAD NEUTRAL CONSERVE 20 STALIN/J EUROPE/E COM/PARTY. PAGE 80 A1650 — B62 MARXISM IDEA/COMP DIPLOM DOMIN

KYRIAK T.E.,INTERNATIONAL COMMUNIST DEVELOPMENTS 1957-1961: INDEX TO TRANSLATIONS FROM AFRICA, ASIA, LATIN AMERICA, WEST EUROPE. COM WOR+45 NAT/G WORKER DIPLOM NAT/LISM. PAGE 83 A1704 — B62 BIBLIOG/A MARXISM LABOR POL/PAR

LAQUEUR W.,THE FUTURE OF COMMUNIST SOCIETY. CHINA/COM USSR LAW ECO/DEV NAT/G POL/PAR PLAN PROB/SOLV DIPLOM LEAD...POLICY CONCPT IDEA/COMP ANTHOL 20. PAGE 85 A1731 — B62 MARXISM COM FUT SOCIETY

LAQUEUR W.,POLYCENTRISM. CHINA/COM COM USSR WOR+45 INT/ORG NAT/G ECO/TAC DOMIN LEAD ATTIT PWR SOVEREIGN...ANTHOL 20. PAGE 85 A1732 — B62 MARXISM DIPLOM BAL/PWR POLICY

LAUERHAUSS L.,COMMUNISM IN LATIN AMERICA: THE POST-WAR YEARS (1945 -1960) (PAPER). INTELL STRATA ECO/UNDEV AGRI WORKER FOR/AID INT/TRADE COLONIAL GUERRILLA 20. PAGE 85 A1745 — B62 BIBLIOG L/A+17C MARXISM REV

LERNER M.,THE AGE OF OVERKILL: A PREFACE TO WORLD POLITICS. USA+45 USSR WOR+45 SOCIETY ECO/UNDEV BAL/PWR NEUTRAL PARTIC REV ALL/IDEOS MARXISM ...BIBLIOG/A 20. PAGE 87 A1787 — B62 DIPLOM NUC/PWR PWR DEATH

LESSING P.,AFRICA'S RED HARVEST. AFR CHINA/COM COM USSR ECO/UNDEV BAL/PWR DIPLOM CONTROL PWR 20 COLD/WAR INTERVENT. PAGE 87 A1789 — B62 NAT/LISM MARXISM FOR/AID EDU/PROP

LEVY H.V.,LIBERDADE E JUSTICA SOCIAL (2ND ED.). BRAZIL COM L/A+17C USSR INT/ORG PARTIC GP/REL WEALTH 20 UN COM/PARTY. PAGE 88 A1798 — B62 ORD/FREE MARXISM CAP/ISM LAW

MORRAY J.P.,THE SECOND REVOLUTION IN CUBA. CUBA AGRI LABOR POL/PAR DIPLOM FOR/AID GUERRILLA TOTALISM MARXISM 20. PAGE 104 A2146 — B62 REV MARXIST ECO/TAC NAT/LISM

POSTON R.W.,DEMOCRACY SPEAKS MANY TONGUES. L/A+17C USA+45 ECO/UNDEV ACT/RES ECO/TAC ADMIN ORD/FREE ...METH/COMP 20. PAGE 117 A2397 — B62 FOR/AID DIPLOM CAP/ISM MARXISM

ROSAMOND R.,CRUSADE FOR PEACE: EISENHOWER'S PRESIDENTIAL LEGACY WITH THE PROGRAM FOR ACTION. USA+45 PARTIC ARMS/CONT MORAL MARXISM...TRADIT CONCPT CHARTS GEN/LAWS ANTHOL 20 PRESIDENT EISNHWR/DD. PAGE 123 A2526 — B62 PEACE DIPLOM EDU/PROP POLICY

ROY P.A.,SOUTH WIND RED. L/A+17C USA+45 ECO/UNDEV NAT/G CAP/ISM MARXISM SOCISM...OLD/LIB GEOG RECORD INT CENSUS 20 COLD/WAR. PAGE 125 A2554 — B62 DIPLOM INDUS POLICY ECO/TAC

SCHUMAN F.L.,THE COLD WAR: RETROSPECT AND PROSPECT. FUT USA+45 USSR WOR+45 BAL/PWR EDU/PROP ARMS/CONT ATTIT...MAJORIT IDEA/COMP ANTHOL BIBLIOG 20 COLD/WAR. PAGE 129 A2651 — B62 MARXISM TEC/DEV DIPLOM NUC/PWR

SCOTT W.E.,ALLIANCE AGAINST HITLER. EUR+WWI FRANCE GERMANY USSR BAL/PWR LEAD TOTALISM PWR FASCISM MARXISM...POLICY BIBLIOG 20 HITLER/A. PAGE 131 A2675 — B62 WAR DIPLOM FORCES

SNOW J.H.,GOVERNMENT BY TREASON. USA+45 USA-45 LEGIS DIPLOM FOR/AID GIVE CONTROL WEALTH MARXISM ...MAJORIT 20 CONGRESS COLD/WAR. PAGE 134 A2750 — B62 FINAN TAX PWR POLICY

STARR R.E.,POLAND 1944-1962: THE SOVIETIZATION OF A CAPTIVE PEOPLE. COM POLAND USSR POL/PAR SECT LEGIS DIPLOM DOMIN EDU/PROP CHOOSE ORD/FREE...POLICY CHARTS BIBLIOG 20. PAGE 137 A2808 — B62 MARXISM NAT/G TOTALISM NAT/COMP

US DEPARTMENT OF THE ARMY,AFRICA: ITS PROBLEMS AND PROSPECTS. CHINA/COM USSR INT/ORG FOR/AID COLONIAL LEAD FEDERAL DRIVE SOVEREIGN MARXISM...GEOG 20 COLD/WAR. PAGE 152 A3104 — B62 BIBLIOG/A AFR NAT/LISM DIPLOM

LONDON K.,"SINO-SOVIET RELATIONS IN THE CONTEXT OF THE 'WORLD SOCIALIST SYSTEM'." ASIA CHINA/COM COM USSR INT/ORG NAT/G TOP/EX BAL/PWR DIPLOM DOMIN ATTIT PERCEPT RIGID/FLEX PWR MARXISM...METH/CNCPT TREND 20. PAGE 91 A1854 — S62 DELIB/GP CONCPT SOCISM

STRACHEY J.,"COMMUNIST INTENTIONS." ASIA USSR YUGOSLAVIA INT/ORG NAT/G FORCES DOMIN EDU/PROP COERCE NUC/PWR NAT/LISM PEACE RIGID/FLEX PWR MARXISM...CONCPT MYTH OBS TIME/SEQ TREND COLD/WAR TOT/POP 20. PAGE 139 A2843 — S62 COM ATTIT WAR

CERAMI C.A.,ALLIANCE BORN OF DANGER. EUR+WWI USA+45 USSR ECO/DEV INDUS VOL/ASSN ECO/TAC REGION ATTIT MARXISM ATLAN/ALL 20 NATO EEC. PAGE 25 A0514 — B63 DIPLOM INT/ORG NAT/G POLICY

DRACHKOVITCH,UNITED STATES AID TO YUGOSLAVIA AND POLAND. POLAND USA+45 YUGOSLAVIA LEGIS EXEC TOTALISM MARXISM 20 CONGRESS. PAGE 38 A0782 — B63 FOR/AID POLICY DIPLOM ATTIT

FISCHER-GALATI S.,EASTERN EUROPE IN THE SIXTIES. ALBANIA USSR YUGOSLAVIA ECO/UNDEV AGRI MARKET LABOR WORKER DIPLOM INT/TRADE EDU/PROP GOV/REL PRODUC UTOPIA SOCISM 20. PAGE 46 A0939 — B63 MARXISM TEC/DEV BAL/PWR ECO/TAC

GALLAGHER M.P.,THE SOVIET HISTORY OF WORLD WAR II. EUR+WWI USSR DIPLOM DOMIN WRITING CONTROL WAR — B63 CIVMIL/REL EDU/PROP

MARXISM...PSY TIME/SEQ 20 STALIN/J. PAGE 50 A1031
HIST/WRIT PRESS

B63

GOLDWIN R.A.,FOREIGN AND MILITARY POLICY. COM USSR WOR+45 ECO/DEV INT/ORG FORCES PLAN ECO/TAC REGION ARMS/CONT MARXISM 20 UN. PAGE 54 A1097
DIPLOM POLICY PWR NAT/G

B63

GORDON G.N.,THE IDEA INVADERS. USA+45 USSR CULTURE COM/IND DIPLOM PRESS TV TOTALISM MARXISM 20. PAGE 54 A1113
EDU/PROP ATTIT ORD/FREE CONTROL

B63

GRAEBNER N.A.,THE COLD WAR: IDEOLOGICAL CONFLICT OR POWER STRUGGLE? USSR WOR+45 WOR-45 PROB/SOLV EDU/PROP ARMS/CONT REV NAT/LISM PEACE ORD/FREE ...IDEA/COMP ANTHOL BIBLIOG/A 20 COLD/WAR. PAGE 55 A1123
DIPLOM BAL/PWR MARXISM

B63

GRIFFITH W.E.,ALBANIA AND THE SINO-SOVIET RIFT. ALBANIA CHINA/COM USSR POL/PAR CHIEF LEGIS DIPLOM DOMIN ATTIT PWR...POLICY 20 KHRUSH/N MAO. PAGE 57 A1161
EDU/PROP MARXISM NAT/LISM GOV/REL

B63

HALASZ DE BEKY I.L.,A BIBLIOGRAPHY OF THE HUNGARIAN REVOLUTION 1956. COM HUNGARY USSR DIPLOM COERCE MARXISM...POLICY AUD/VIS 20 UN COLD/WAR. PAGE 59 A1221
BIBLIOG REV FORCES ATTIT

B63

HAMM H.,ALBANIA - CHINA'S BEACHHEAD IN EUROPE. ALBANIA CHINA/COM USSR YUGOSLAVIA ELITES SOCIETY POL/PAR DELIB/GP FORCES ECO/TAC COERCE ISOLAT PEACE MARXISM...IDEA/COMP 20 MAO. PAGE 61 A1248
DIPLOM REV NAT/G POLICY

B63

HONEY P.J.,COMMUNISM IN NORTH VIETNAM: ITS ROLE IN THE SINO-SOVIET DISPUTE. CHINA/COM INDIA USSR VIETNAM/N AGRI POL/PAR LEGIS ECO/TAC WAR PEACE ATTIT...GEOG IDEA/COMP 20. PAGE 67 A1378
POLICY MARXISM CHIEF DIPLOM

B63

HYDE D.,THE PEACEFUL ASSAULT. COM UAR USSR ECO/DEV ECO/UNDEV NAT/G POL/PAR CAP/ISM PWR 20. PAGE 69 A1427
MARXISM CONTROL ECO/TAC DIPLOM

B63

KHRUSHCHEV N.S.,THE NEW CONTENT OF PEACEFUL COEXISTENCE IN THE NUCLEAR AGE. GERMANY/E WORKER NUC/PWR REV SOCISM 20 COLD/WAR. PAGE 79 A1614
MARXISM POL/PAR PEACE DIPLOM

B63

MALIK C.,MAN IN THE STRUGGLE FOR PEACE. USSR WOR+45 CHIEF PLAN PROB/SOLV PARTIC NUC/PWR REV ORD/FREE ...IDEA/COMP METH/COMP 20 UN COLD/WAR. PAGE 93 A1912
PEACE MARXISM DIPLOM EDU/PROP

B63

MILLER W.J.,THE MEANING OF COMMUNISM. USSR SOCIETY ECO/DEV EX/STRUC WORKER TEC/DEV ADMIN TOTALISM ...POLICY CONCPT CHARTS BIBLIOG T 20 COLD/WAR LENIN/VI STALIN/J. PAGE 101 A2080
MARXISM TRADIT DIPLOM NAT/G

B63

MOSELY P.E.,THE SOVIET UNION, 1922-1962: A FOREIGN AFFAIRS READER. ASIA POLAND USSR CULTURE INTELL AGRI POL/PAR WORKER INT/TRADE DOMIN WAR NAT/LISM MARXISM SOCISM 20 KHRUSH/N. PAGE 105 A2152
PWR POLICY DIPLOM

B63

NORTH R.C.,M. N. ROY'S MISSION TO CHINA: THE COMMUNIST-KUOMINTANG SPLIT OF 1927. ASIA USSR STRATA LEGIS WORKER LEAD REV ATTIT ROLE SOCISM 20 ROY/MN COM/PARTY. PAGE 110 A2253
POL/PAR MARXISM DIPLOM

B63

PACHTER H.M.,COLLISION COURSE; THE CUBAN MISSILE CRISIS AND COEXISTENCE. CUBA USA+45 DIPLOM ARMS/CONT PEACE MARXISM...DECISION INT/LAW 20 COLD/WAR KHRUSH/N KENNEDY/JF CASTRO/F. PAGE 112 A2307
WAR BAL/PWR NUC/PWR DETER

B63

ROSS H.,THE COLD WAR: CONTAINMENT AND ITS CRITICSS. WOR+45 POL/PAR BAL/PWR ECO/TAC PEACE ORD/FREE ...POLICY IDEA/COMP ANTHOL T 20 COLD/WAR DULLES/JF TRUMAN/HS EISNHWR/DD. PAGE 124 A2541
MARXISM ARMS/CONT DIPLOM

B63

ROSSI M.,THE THIRD WORLD. FUT WOR+45 INT/ORG NAT/G CAP/ISM COLONIAL PEACE PWR MARXISM 20 UN THIRD/WRLD. PAGE 124 A2542
ECO/UNDEV DIPLOM BAL/PWR NEUTRAL

B63

RUSSELL B.,UNARMED VICTORY. CHINA/COM CUBA INDIA USA+45 WAR MARXISM...POLICY IDEA/COMP 20 KHRUSH/N COLD/WAR. PAGE 125 A2573
DIPLOM ATTIT SOCISM ORD/FREE

B63

SWEARER H.R.,CONTEMPORARY COMMUNISM: THEORY AND PRACTICE. COM USSR SOCIETY ECO/DEV POL/PAR FORCES PLAN ADMIN LEAD NAT/LISM...POLICY ANTHOL 20 LENIN/VI COM/PARTY. PAGE 140 A2869
MARXISM CONCPT DIPLOM NAT/G

B63

SZULC T.,THE WINDS OF REVOLUTION; LATIN AMERICA TODAY - AND TOMORROW. L/A+17C ORD/FREE SOCISM ...PREDICT TREND 20. PAGE 141 A2880
REV INT/ORG MARXISM ECO/UNDEV

B63

US DEPARTMENT OF THE ARMY,SOVIET RUSSIA: STRATEGIC SURVEY (PAMPHLET). USSR POL/PAR PLAN DOMIN EDU/PROP ARMS/CONT GUERRILLA WAR WEAPON...TREND CHARTS ORG/CHARTS 20. PAGE 152 A3106
BIBLIOG/A MARXISM DIPLOM COERCE

B63

VON HALLER A.,DIE LETZTEN WOLLEN DIE ERSTEN SEIN. AFR S/ASIA INT/TRADE REV ORD/FREE SOVEREIGN 20. PAGE 160 A3251
FOR/AID ECO/UNDEV MARXISM CAP/ISM

B63

WHITNEY T.P.,KHRUSHCHEV SPEAKS. USSR AGRI LEAD ...BIOG ANTHOL 20 KHRUSH/N STALIN/J ESPIONAGE. PAGE 164 A3339
DIPLOM MARXISM CHIEF

B64

AFRO ASIAN SOLIDARITY AGAINST IMPERIALISM. AFR ISLAM S/ASIA ECO/UNDEV NAT/G POL/PAR TOP/EX PRESS ...INT ANTHOL 20 CHOU/ENLAI. PAGE 3 A0066
MARXISM DIPLOM EDU/PROP CHIEF

B64

BLANCHARD C.H.,KOREAN WAR BIBLIOGRAPHY. KOREA FAM BAL/PWR RATION MURDER WEAPON MARXISM...CHARTS 20. PAGE 15 A0306
BIBLIOG/A WAR DIPLOM FORCES

B64

BUTWELL R.,SOUTHEAST ASIA TODAY - AND TOMORROW. NAT/G COLONIAL LEAD REGION WAR CHOOSE WEALTH MARXISM 20. PAGE 23 A0458
S/ASIA DIPLOM ECO/UNDEV NAT/LISM

B64

CALVO SERER R.,LAS NUEVAS DEMOCRACIAS. AFR ASIA ISLAM USA+45 WOR+45 BAL/PWR DOMIN PARTIC INGP/REL AUTHORIT POPULISM...CONCPT 20 COM/PARTY. PAGE 23 A0469
ORD/FREE MARXISM DIPLOM POLICY

B64

CHENG C.,ECONOMIC RELATIONS BETWEEN PEKING AND MOSCOW: 1949-63. ASIA CHINA/COM COM USSR FINAN INDUS CONSULT TEC/DEV INT/TRADE...PREDICT CHARTS BIBLIOG 20. PAGE 26 A0527
DIPLOM FOR/AID MARXISM

B64

COFFIN F.M.,WITNESS FOR AID. COM EUR+WWI USA+45 DIPLOM GP/REL CONSEN ORD/FREE MARXISM...NEW/IDEA 20 CONGRESS AID. PAGE 27 A0557
FOR/AID ECO/UNDEV DELIB/GP PLAN

B64

DAVIES U.P. JR.,FOREIGN AND OTHER AFFAIRS. EUR+WWI L/A+17C S/ASIA USA+45 ECO/UNDEV CHIEF PLAN ECO/TAC PWR MARXISM 20 KENNEDY/JF UN. PAGE 34 A0688
DIPLOM NAT/G POLICY FOR/AID

B64

DUBOIS J.,DANGER OVER PANAMA. FUT PANAMA SCHOOL PROB/SOLV EDU/PROP MARXISM...POLICY 19/20 TREATY INTERVENT CANAL/ZONE. PAGE 39 A0790
DIPLOM COERCE

B64

EMBREE A.T.,A GUIDE TO PAPERBACKS ON ASIA; SELECTED AND ANNOTATED (PAMPHLET). CULTURE SOCIETY ECO/UNDEV SECT DIPLOM COLONIAL MARXISM...SOC 20. PAGE 41 A0845
BIBLIOG/A ASIA S/ASIA NAT/G

B64

EPSTEIN H.M.,REVOLT IN THE CONGO. AFR CONGO/BRAZ WOR+45 NAT/G FORCES DOMIN WAR CIVMIL/REL INGP/REL MARXISM...RECORD GP/COMP 20 CONGO/LEOP UN. PAGE 42 A0856
REV COLONIAL NAT/LISM DIPLOM

B64

FREUD A.,OF HUMAN SOVEREIGNTY. WOR+45 INDUS SECT ECO/TAC CRIME CHOOSE ATTIT MORAL MARXISM...POLICY BIBLIOG 20. PAGE 49 A0998
NAT/LISM DIPLOM WAR PEACE

B64

GIBSON J.S.,IDEOLOGY AND WORLD AFFAIRS. FUT WOR+45 ECO/UNDEV NAT/G CAP/ISM TOTALISM ORD/FREE FASCISM MARXISM 20. PAGE 52 A1067
ALL/IDEOS DIPLOM POLICY IDEA/COMP

B64

GRIFFITH W.E.,COMMUNISM IN EUROPE (2 VOLS.). CZECHOSLVK USSR WOR+45 WOR-45 YUGOSLAVIA INGP/REL MARXISM SOCISM...ANTHOL 20 EUROPE/E. PAGE 57 A1162
COM POL/PAR DIPLOM GOV/COMP

B64

GRZYBOWSKI K.,THE SOCIALIST COMMONWEALTH OF NATIONS: ORGANIZATIONS AND INSTITUTIONS. FORCES DIPLOM INT/TRADE ADJUD ADMIN LEAD WAR MARXISM SOCISM...BIBLIOG 20 COMECON WARSAW/P. PAGE 58 A1185
INT/LAW COM REGION INT/ORG

B64

HALPERN J.M.,GOVERNMENT, POLITICS, AND SOCIAL STRUCTURE IN LAOS. LAOS CULTURE SOCIETY STRATA STRUCT FAM DIPLOM DOMIN MARXISM...INT GOV/COMP WORSHIP SOC/INTEG 20. PAGE 60 A1242
NAT/G SOC LOC/G

B64

HAMRELL S.,THE SOVIET BLOC, CHINA, AND AFRICA. AFR CHINA/COM COM USSR ECO/UNDEV EDU/PROP 20. PAGE 61 A1249
MARXISM DIPLOM CONTROL FOR/AID

HARPER F.,OUT OF CHINA. CHINA/COM ELITES STRATA ATTIT PERSON...BIOG 20 MAO HONG/KONG MIGRATION. PAGE 62 A1264
B64 HABITAT DEEP/INT DIPLOM MARXISM

KEEP J.,CONTEMPORARY HISTORY IN THE SOVIET MIRROR. COM USSR POL/PAR CREATE DIPLOM AGREE WAR ATTIT ...MYTH TREND ANTHOL 20 COLD/WAR STALIN/J MARX/KARL LENIN/VI. PAGE 77 A1576
B64 HIST/WRIT METH MARXISM IDEA/COMP

KIS T.I.,LES PAYS DE L'EUROPE DE L'EST: LEURS RAPPORTS MUTUELS ET LE PROBLEME DE LEUR INTEGRATION DANS L'ORBITE DE L'USSR. EUR+WWI RUSSIA USSR INT/ORG NAT/G REV ATTIT...JURID SOC BIBLIOG WARSAW/P COMECON EUROPE/E. PAGE 80 A1638
B64 DIPLOM COM MARXISM REGION

KOLARZ W.,BOOKS ON COMMUNISM. USSR WOR+45 CULTURE NAT/G POL/PAR DIPLOM LEAD...CONCPT GOV/COMP IDEA/COMP. PAGE 81 A1667
B64 BIBLIOG/A SOCIETY COM MARXISM

LATOURETTE K.S.,CHINA. ASIA CHINA/COM FUT USSR ECO/UNDEV ECO/TAC WAR 19/20. PAGE 85 A1744
B64 MARXISM NAT/G POLICY DIPLOM

LENS S.,THE FUTILE CRUSADE. ASIA CHINA/COM L/A+17C USA+45 USSR WOR+45 ECO/DEV BAL/PWR DIPLOM NUC/PWR WAR NAT/LISM PEACE 20 COLD/WAR PRESIDENT CIA. PAGE 87 A1774
B64 ORD/FREE ANOMIE COM MARXISM

LENSEN G.A.,REVELATIONS OF A RUSSIAN DIPLOMAT: THE MEMOIRS OF DMITRII I. ABRIKOSSOV. ASIA MOD/EUR RUSSIA USA-45 ELITES ACADEM CHIEF FORCES REV WAR PWR CONSERVE MARXISM 19/20 ABRIKSSV/D CHINJAP BOLSHEVISM. PAGE 87 A1775
B64 DIPLOM POLICY OBS

LISKA G.,EUROPE ASCENDANT. EUR+WWI ECO/DEV FORCES INT/TRADE MARXISM 20 EEC. PAGE 90 A1838
B64 DIPLOM BAL/PWR TARIFFS CENTRAL

MARTIN J.J.,AMERICAN LIBERALISM AND WORLD POLITICS, 1931-41 (2 VOLS.). GERMANY USA-45 POL/PAR DISCRIM NAT/LISM PEACE RATIONAL ATTIT RIGID/FLEX MARXISM PACIFISM 20. PAGE 95 A1950
B64 NEW/LIB DIPLOM NAT/G POLICY

NOVE A.,COMMUNISM AT THE CROSSROADS. USSR INT/ORG POL/PAR TOTALISM...POLICY CONCPT 20. PAGE 110 A2259
B64 DIPLOM BAL/PWR MARXISM ORD/FREE

QUIGG P.W.,AFRICA: A FOREIGN AFFAIRS READER. AFR FRANCE PORTUGAL UK DIPLOM LEAD PARL/PROC MARXISM ...MAJORIT METH/CNCPT GOV/COMP IDEA/COMP ANTHOL 19/20. PAGE 118 A2426
B64 COLONIAL SOVEREIGN NAT/LISM RACE/REL

STILLMAN E.O.,THE POLITICS OF HYSTERIA: THE SOURCES OF TWENTIETH-CENTURY CONFLICT. WOR+45 WOR-45 CULTURE ECO/UNDEV PLAN CAP/ISM WAR MARXISM ...PREDICT BIBLIOG 20 COLD/WAR. PAGE 138 A2828
B64 DIPLOM IDEA/COMP COLONIAL CONTROL

TREADGOLD D.W.,THE DEVELOPMENT OF THE USSR. COM USSR ECO/DEV CREATE BAL/PWR DEBATE COLONIAL TOTALISM...HUM ANTHOL BIBLIOG 19/20. PAGE 145 A2960
B64 MARXISM CONSERVE DIPLOM DOMIN

WRIGHT T.P. JR.,AMERICAN SUPPORT OF FREE ELECTIONS ABROAD. USA+45 USA-45 DOMIN LEAD NEUTRAL MARXISM ...POLICY TIME/SEQ BIBLIOG 19/20 COLD/WAR INTERVENT. PAGE 168 A3420
B64 DIPLOM CHOOSE L/A+17C POPULISM

ARMSTRONG J.A.,"THE SOVIET-AMERICAN CONFRONTATION: A NEW STAGE?" CUBA USA+45 USSR PLAN PROB/SOLV INT/TRADE CONTROL ARMS/CONT NUC/PWR MARXISM 20 COLD/WAR INTERVENT. PAGE 9 A0174
S64 DIPLOM POLICY INSPECT

HORECKY P.L.,"LIBRARY OF CONGRESS PUBLICATIONS IN AID OF USSR AND EAST EUROPEAN RESEARCH." BULGARIA CZECHOSLVK POLAND USSR YUGOSLAVIA NAT/G POL/PAR DIPLOM ADMIN GOV/REL...CLASSIF 20. PAGE 67 A1382
S64 BIBLIOG/A COM MARXISM

KARPOV P.V.,"PEACEFUL COEXISTENCE AND INTERNATIONAL LAW." WOR+45 LAW SOCIETY INT/ORG VOL/ASSN FORCES CREATE CAP/ISM DIPLOM ADJUD NUC/PWR PEACE MORAL ORD/FREE PWR MARXISM...MARXIST JURID CONCPT OBS TREND COLD/WAR MARX/KARL 20. PAGE 77 A1568
S64 COM ATTIT INT/LAW USSR

LERNER W.,"THE HISTORICAL ORIGINS OF THE SOVIET DOCTRINE OF PEACEFUL COEXISTENCE." COM USSR INT/ORG NAT/G VOL/ASSN PLAN PEACE ATTIT RIGID/FLEX PWR MARXISM...TIME/SEQ COLD/WAR 20. PAGE 87 A1788
S64 EDU/PROP DIPLOM

AIR UNIVERSITY LIBRARY,LATIN AMERICA, SELECTED REFERENCES. ECO/UNDEV FORCES EDU/PROP MARXISM 20 OAS. PAGE 5 A0106
B65 BIBLIOG L/A+17C NAT/G DIPLOM

ALBRECHT-CARRIE R.,THE MEANING OF THE FIRST WORLD WAR. MOD/EUR USA-45 INT/ORG BAL/PWR PEACE ATTIT LAISSEZ MARXISM...CONCPT BIBLIOG 19/20 LEAGUE/NAT WWI. PAGE 5 A0110
B65 DIPLOM WAR

BROMKE A.,THE COMMUNIST STATES AT THE CROSSROADS BETWEEN MOSCOW AND PEKING. CHINA/COM USSR INGP/REL NAT/LISM TOTALISM 20. PAGE 19 A0389
B65 COM DIPLOM MARXISM REGION

COLLINS H.,KARL MARX AND THE BRITISH LABOUR MOVEMENT; YEARS OF THE FIRST INTERNATIONAL. FRANCE SWITZERLND UK CAP/ISM WAR...MARXIST IDEA/COMP BIBLIOG 19. PAGE 28 A0567
B65 MARXISM LABOR INT/ORG REV

COX R.H.,THE STATE IN INTERNATIONAL RELATIONS. INT/ORG DIPLOM REV WAR PEACE MARXISM...CONCPT GOV/COMP. PAGE 32 A0647
B65 SOVEREIGN NAT/G FASCISM ORD/FREE

DOMENACH J.M.,LA PROPAGANDE POLITIQUE. COM/IND INT/ORG POL/PAR DOMIN RIGID/FLEX FASCISM MARXISM ...PSY 20. PAGE 38 A0770
B65 ATTIT EDU/PROP TEC/DEV MYTH

EMERSON R.,THE POLITICAL AWAKENING OF AFRICA. ECO/UNDEV INT/ORG COLONIAL RACE/REL ORD/FREE MARXISM...TREND ANTHOL 20. PAGE 42 A0849
B65 AFR NAT/LISM DIPLOM POL/PAR

FRASER S.,GOVERNMENTAL POLICY AND INTERNATIONAL EDUCATION. CHINA/COM COM USA+45 WOR+45 CONTROL MARXISM...ANTHOL BIBLIOG/A 20 UN. PAGE 48 A0989
B65 EDU/PROP DIPLOM POLICY NAT/G

HALLE L.J.,THE SOCIETY OF MAN. WOR+45 WOR-45 EDU/PROP NAT/LISM MARXISM CONCPT. PAGE 60 A1231
B65 DIPLOM PHIL/SCI CREATE SOCIETY

HALPERIN E.,NATIONALISM AND COMMUNISM. CHILE L/A+17C CAP/ISM EDU/PROP CHOOSE DISCRIM SOCISM ...BIBLIOG 20 COM/PARTY. PAGE 60 A1236
B65 NAT/LISM MARXISM POL/PAR REV

HUSS P.J.,RED SPIES IN THE UN. CZECHOSLVK USA+45 USSR COM/IND FORCES EDU/PROP NUC/PWR MARXISM 20 UN COLD/WAR. PAGE 69 A1421
B65 PEACE INT/ORG BAL/PWR DIPLOM

INTERNATIONAL SOCIAL SCI COUN,SOCIAL SCIENCES IN THE USSR. USSR ECO/DEV AGRI FINAN INDUS PLAN CAP/ISM...INT/LAW PHIL/SCI PSY SOC 20. PAGE 71 A1460
B65 BIBLIOG/A ACT/RES MARXISM JURID

KRAUSE W.,ECONOMIC DEVELOPMENT: THE UNDERDEVELOPED WORLD AND THE AMERICAN INTEREST. USA+45 AGRI PLAN MARXISM...CHARTS 20. PAGE 82 A1679
B65 FOR/AID ECO/UNDEV FINAN PROB/SOLV

LAFAVE W.R.,LAW AND SOVIET SOCIETY. EX/STRUC DIPLOM DOMIN EDU/PROP PRESS ADMIN CRIME OWN MARXISM 20 KHRUSH/N. PAGE 84 A1710
B65 JURID CT/SYS ADJUD GOV/REL

LERCHE C.O.,THE COLD WAR AND AFTER. AFR COM S/ASIA USA+45 USSR NUC/PWR SOVEREIGN MARXISM...TIME/SEQ TREND BIBLIOG 20 COLD/WAR. PAGE 87 A1784
B65 DIPLOM BAL/PWR IDEA/COMP

LEVENSTEIN A.,FREEDOM'S ADVOCATE - A TWENTY-FIVE YEAR CHRONICLE. USA+45 POL/PAR LEGIS DIPLOM WAR PEACE TOTALISM DRIVE MARXISM 20 FREEDOM/HS. PAGE 87 A1791
B65 ORD/FREE VOL/ASSN POLICY ATTIT

MALLIN J.,FORTRESS CUBA; RUSSIA'S AMERICAN BASE. COM CUBA L/A+17C FORCES PLAN DIPLOM LEAD REV WAR ...POLICY 20 CASTRO/F GUEVARA/C INTERVENT. PAGE 93 A1914
B65 MARXISM CHIEF GUERRILLA DOMIN

MENON K.P.S.,MANY WORLDS. INDIA BAL/PWR CAP/ISM COLONIAL REV ORD/FREE PWR MARXISM...POLICY 20 COLD/WAR. PAGE 100 A2042
B65 BIOG DIPLOM NAT/G

MIDDLETON D.,CRISIS IN THE WEST. EUR+WWI FUT WOR+45 CHIEF PLAN ECO/TAC LEAD REGION NUC/PWR NAT/LISM MARXISM 20 COLD/WAR NATO EEC. PAGE 101 A2068
B65 INT/ORG DIPLOM NAT/G POLICY

MOLNAR T.,AFRICA: A POLITICAL TRAVELOGUE. STRUCT ECO/UNDEV DIPLOM EDU/PROP LEAD RACE/REL MARXISM 20 INTERVENT EUROPE. PAGE 102 A2101
B65 COLONIAL AFR ORD/FREE

MORGENTHAU H.,MORGENTHAU DIARY (CHINA) (2 VOLS.).
B65 DIPLOM

ASIA USA+45 USA-45 LAW DELIB/GP EX/STRUC PLAN FOR/AID INT/TRADE CONFER WAR MARXISM 20 CHINJAP. PAGE 104 A2136 — ADMIN

B65
MOSTECKY V.,SOVIET LEGAL BIBLIOGRAPHY. USSR LEGIS PRESS WRITING CONFER ADJUD CT/SYS REV MARXISM ...INT/LAW JURID DICTIONARY 20. PAGE 105 A2155 — BIBLIOG/A LAW COM CONSTN

B65
ROMEIN J.,THE ASIAN CENTURY. ASIA COM S/ASIA DIPLOM COLONIAL TIME 20. PAGE 123 A2519 — REV NAT/LISM CULTURE MARXISM

B65
ROSENBERG A.,DEMOCRACY AND SOCIALISM. COM EUR+WWI FRANCE MOD/EUR STRUCT INT/ORG NAT/G POL/PAR TOP/EX EDU/PROP COERCE PERSON PWR FASCISM MARXISM...CONCPT TIME/SEQ MARX/KARL 19/20. PAGE 124 A2535 — ATTIT

B65
RUBINSTEIN A.,THE CHALLENGE OF POLITICS: IDEAS AND ISSUES. BAL/PWR COLONIAL WAR TOTALISM ORD/FREE PWR MARXISM SOCISM...INT/LAW 20. PAGE 125 A2561 — NAT/G SOVEREIGN DIPLOM NAT/LISM

B65
SULZBERGER C.L.,UNFINISHED REVOLUTION. USA+45 WOR+45 INT/ORG TEC/DEV BAL/PWR FOR/AID COLONIAL NEUTRAL PWR SOVEREIGN MARXISM 20. PAGE 140 A2863 — DIPLOM ECO/UNDEV POLICY NAT/G

B65
TREFOUSSE H.L.,THE COLD WAR: A BOOK OF DOCUMENTS. ASIA L/A+17C USSR WOR+45 WOR-45 ECO/TAC FOR/AID ARMS/CONT NUC/PWR PEACE ORD/FREE...ANTHOL 20 COLD/WAR KENNEDY/JF EISNHWR/DD. PAGE 145 A2961 — BAL/PWR DIPLOM MARXISM

B65
WINT G.,COMMUNIST CHINA'S CRUSADE: MAO'S ROAD TO POWER AND THE NEW CAMPAIGN FOR WORLD REVOLUTION. ASIA CHINA/COM USA+45 USSR NAT/G POL/PAR DOMIN COERCE WAR PWR...POLICY CHARTS IDEA/COMP BIBLIOG 20 MAO. PAGE 165 A3364 — DIPLOM MARXISM REV COLONIAL

S65
"FURTHER READING." INDIA USSR FORCES ATTIT SOCISM 20. PAGE 3 A0068 — BIBLIOG DIPLOM MARXISM

S65
DOSSICK J.J.,"DOCTORAL DISSERTATIONS ON RUSSIA, THE SOVIET UNION, AND EASTERN EUROPE." USSR ACADEM DIPLOM EDU/PROP MARXISM 19/20 COLD/WAR. PAGE 38 A0775 — BIBLIOG HUM SOC

C65
MARK M.,"BEYOND SOVEREIGNTY." WOR+45 WOR-45 ECO/UNDEV BAL/PWR INT/TRADE NUC/PWR REV WAR MARXISM NEW/LIB BIBLIOG. PAGE 95 A1942 — NAT/LISM NAT/G DIPLOM INTELL

B66
BRACKMAN A.C.,SOUTHEAST ASIA'S SECOND FRONT: THE POWER STRUGGLE IN THE MALAY ARCHIPELAGO. CHINA/COM INDONESIA MALAYSIA ECO/UNDEV INT/ORG NAT/G FORCES DIPLOM EDU/PROP REGION COERCE GUERRILLA AUTHORIT POPULISM...MAJORIT 20 KENNEDY/JF SEATO. PAGE 18 A0367 — S/ASIA MARXISM REV

B66
BROWN J.F.,THE NEW EASTERN EUROPE. ALBANIA BULGARIA HUNGARY POLAND ROMANIA CULTURE AGRI POL/PAR WAR NAT/LISM MARXISM...CHARTS BIBLIOG 20. PAGE 20 A0404 — DIPLOM COM NAT/G ECO/UNDEV

B66
CONNEL-SMITH G.,THE INTERAMERICAN SYSTEM. CUBA L/A+17C DELIB/GP FOR/AID COLONIAL PEACE PWR MARXISM ...BIBLIOG 19/20 OAS. PAGE 29 A0586 — DIPLOM INT/TRADE REGION INT/ORG

B66
DAVIDSON A.B.,RUSSIA AND AFRICA. USSR AGRI INT/TRADE...GEOG BIBLIOG/A 18/20. PAGE 34 A0687 — MARXISM COLONIAL RACE/REL DIPLOM

B66
DRACHOVITCH M.M.,THE COMINTERN HISTORICAL HIGHLIGHTS. USSR INT/ORG EX/STRUC LEGIT LEAD GUERRILLA...ANTHOL 20 COMINTERN LENIN/VI. PAGE 38 A0784 — DIPLOM REV MARXISM PERSON

B66
EPSTEIN F.T.,THE AMERICAN BIBLIOGRAPHY OF RUSSIAN AND EAST EUROPEAN STUDIES FOR 1964. USSR LOC/G NAT/G POL/PAR FORCES ADMIN ARMS/CONT...JURID CONCPT 20 UN. PAGE 42 A0855 — BIBLIOG COM MARXISM DIPLOM

B66
EUDIN X.J.,SOVIET FOREIGN POLICY 1928-34: DOCUMENTS AND MATERIALS (VOL. I). ASIA USSR WOR-45 INT/ORG POL/PAR WORKER WAR PEACE...ANTHOL 20 TREATY LEAGUE/NAT INTERVENT. PAGE 43 A0873 — DIPLOM POLICY GOV/REL MARXISM

B66
EWING B.G.,PEACE THROUGH NEGOTIATION: THE AUSTRIAN EXPERIENCE. AUSTRIA USSR VIETNAM CONFER CONTROL DETER WAR ATTIT HEALTH PWR...POLICY 20. PAGE 43 A0878 — PEACE DIPLOM MARXISM

B66
FELKER J.L.,SOVIET ECONOMIC CONTROVERSIES. USSR INDUS PLAN INT/TRADE GP/REL MARXISM SOCISM...POLICY 20. PAGE 45 A0915 — ECO/DEV MARKET PROFIT PRICE

B66
FERKISS V.C.,AFRICA'S SEARCH FOR IDENTITY. AFR USA+45 CULTURE ECO/UNDEV INT/ORG NAT/G COLONIAL MARXISM 20. PAGE 45 A0918 — NAT/LISM SOVEREIGN DIPLOM ROLE

B66
FITZGERALD C.P.,THE BIRTH OF COMMUNIST CHINA (2ND ED.). ASIA CHINA/COM STRUCT BAL/PWR DIPLOM ECO/TAC INT/TRADE WEALTH 20. PAGE 46 A0942 — REV MARXISM ECO/UNDEV

B66
FRIEDRICH C.J.,REVOLUTION: NOMOS VIII. NAT/G SOCISM ...OBS TREND IDEA/COMP ANTHOL 18/20. PAGE 49 A1007 — REV MARXISM CONCPT DIPLOM

B66
INTL CONF ON WORLD POLITICS-5,EASTERN EUROPE IN TRANSITION. EUR+WWI USSR ECO/TAC NAT/LISM ATTIT SOVEREIGN...CHARTS ANTHOL 20 TREATY WARSAW/P. PAGE 71 A1463 — COM NAT/COMP MARXISM DIPLOM

B66
KANET R.E.,THE SOVIET UNION AND SUB-SAHARAN AFRICA: COMMUNIST POLICY TOWARD AFRICA, 1917-1965. AFR USSR ECO/UNDEV TEC/DEV EDU/PROP TASK DISCRIM PEACE WEALTH ALL/IDEOS...CHARTS BIBLIOG SOC/INTEG 19/20 NEGRO UN INTERVENT. PAGE 76 A1555 — DIPLOM ECO/TAC MARXISM

B66
LATHAM E.,THE COMMUNIST CONTROVERSY IN WASHINGTON. USA+45 USA-45 DELIB/GP EX/STRUC LEGIS DIPLOM NAT/LISM MARXISM 20. PAGE 85 A1742 — POL/PAR TOTALISM ORD/FREE NAT/G

B66
MORRIS B.S.,INTERNATIONAL COMMUNISM AND AMERICAN POLICY. CHINA/COM USA+45 USSR INT/ORG POL/PAR GP/REL NAT/LISM ATTIT PERCEPT 20. PAGE 105 A2147 — DIPLOM POLICY MARXISM

B66
NIEDERGANG M.,LA REVOLUTION DE SAINT-DOMINGUE. DOMIN/REP INT/ORG NAT/G CONTROL LEAD GP/REL ORD/FREE MARXISM 20. PAGE 109 A2239 — REV FORCES DIPLOM

B66
OBERMANN E.,VERTEIDIGUNG PER FREIHEIT. GERMANY/W WOR+45 INT/ORG COERCE NUC/PWR WEAPON MARXISM 20 UN NATO WARSAW/P TREATY. PAGE 111 A2273 — FORCES ORD/FREE WAR PEACE

B66
PAN S.,VIETNAM CRISIS. ASIA FRANCE USA+45 USA-45 VIETNAM CULTURE SOCIETY INT/ORG ECO/TAC AGREE CONTROL WAR MARXISM 20. PAGE 113 A2325 — ECO/UNDEV POLICY DIPLOM NAT/COMP

B66
SCHATTEN F.,COMMUNISM IN AFRICA. AFR GHANA GUINEA MALI CULTURE ECO/UNDEV LABOR SECT ECO/TAC EDU/PROP REV 20. PAGE 128 A2619 — COLONIAL NAT/LISM MARXISM DIPLOM

B66
SKILLING H.G.,THE GOVERNMENTS OF COMMUNIST EAST EUROPE. COM EUR+WWI ELITES FORCES DIPLOM ECO/TAC CONTROL HABITAT SOCISM...DECISION BIBLIOG 20 EUROPE/E COM/PARTY. PAGE 134 A2738 — MARXISM NAT/COMP GP/COMP DOMIN

B66
TYSON G.,NEHRU: THE YEARS OF POWER. INDIA UK STRATA ECO/UNDEV FINAN SECT TASK WAR ORD/FREE MARXISM ...POLICY BIBLIOG 20 NEHRU/J. PAGE 146 A2985 — CHIEF PWR DIPLOM NAT/G

B66
US DEPARTMENT OF STATE,RESEARCH ON AFRICA (EXTERNAL RESEARCH LIST NO 5-25). LAW CULTURE ECO/UNDEV POL/PAR DIPLOM EDU/PROP LEAD REGION MARXISM...GEOG LING WORSHIP 20. PAGE 152 A3094 — BIBLIOG/A ASIA S/ASIA NAT/G

B66
US DEPARTMENT OF STATE,RESEARCH ON THE AMERICAN REPUBLICS (EXTERNAL RESEARCH LIST NO 6-25). CULTURE SOCIETY POL/PAR DIPLOM EDU/PROP MARXISM WORSHIP 20 OAS. PAGE 152 A3095 — BIBLIOG/A L/A+17C REGION NAT/G

B66
US DEPARTMENT OF STATE,RESEARCH ON THE USSR AND EASTERN EUROPE (EXTERNAL RESEARCH LIST NO 1-25). USSR LAW CULTURE SOCIETY NAT/G TEC/DEV DIPLOM EDU/PROP REGION...GEOG LING. PAGE 152 A3097 — BIBLIOG/A EUR+WWI COM MARXISM

B66
US DEPARTMENT OF STATE,RESEARCH ON WESTERN EUROPE, GREAT BRITAIN, AND CANADA (EXTERNAL RESEARCH LIST NO 3-25). CANADA GERMANY/W UK LAW CULTURE NAT/G POL/PAR FORCES EDU/PROP REGION MARXISM...GEOG SOC WORSHIP 20 CMN/WLTH. PAGE 152 A3098 — BIBLIOG/A EUR+WWI DIPLOM

B66
US DEPARTMENT OF THE ARMY,COMMUNIST CHINA: A STRATEGIC SURVEY: A BIBLIOGRAPHY (PAMPHLET NO. 20-67). CHINA/COM COM INDIA USSR NAT/G POL/PAR EX/STRUC FORCES NUC/PWR REV ATTIT...POLICY GEOG CHARTS. PAGE 152 A3109 — BIBLIOG/A MARXISM S/ASIA DIPLOM

B66
US SENATE COMM AERO SPACE SCI,SOVIET SPACE PROGRAMS, 1962-65; GOALS AND PURPOSES, ACHIEVEMENTS, PLANS, AND INTERNATIONAL IMPLICATIONS. USA+45 USSR R+D FORCES PLAN EDU/PROP PRESS ADJUD ARMS/CONT ATTIT MARXISM. PAGE 155 A3168 — CONSULT SPACE FUT DIPLOM

B66
WELCH R.H.W.,THE NEW AMERICANISM, AND OTHER SPEECHES AND ESSAYS. USA+45 ACADEM POL/PAR SCHOOL VOL/ASSN FORCES CAP/ISM TAX REV DISCRIM 20 CIV/RIGHTS COLD/WAR BIRCH/SOC. PAGE 163 A3313 — DIPLOM FASCISM MARXISM RACE/REL

B66
WESTIN A.F.,VIEWS OF AMERICA. COM USA+45 USSR SOCIETY ECO/UNDEV POL/PAR ECO/TAC GP/REL STRANGE MARXISM...MARXIST 20. PAGE 163 A3323 — CONCPT ATTIT DIPLOM IDEA/COMP

B66
WOHL R.,FRENCH COMMUNISM IN THE MAKING 1914-1924. FRANCE USSR LEAD REV...IDEA/COMP 20 COM/PARTY. PAGE 166 A3377 — MARXISM WORKER DIPLOM

B66
ZABLOCKI C.J.,SINO-SOVIET RIVALRY. AFR ASIA CHINA/COM CUBA EUR+WWI L/A+17C USA+45 USSR WOR+45 POL/PAR FORCES COERCE NUC/PWR...GOV/COMP IDEA/COMP 20 MAO KHRUSH/N. PAGE 169 A3442 — DIPLOM MARXISM COM

S66
CHIU H.,"COMMUNIST CHINA'S ATTITUDE TOWARD INTERNATIONAL LAW" CHINA/COM USSR LAW CONSTN DIPLOM GP/REL 20 LENIN/VI. PAGE 26 A0532 — INT/LAW MARXISM CONCPT IDEA/COMP

S66
CRANMER-BYNG J.L.,"THE CHINESE ATTITUDE TOWARDS EXTERNAL RELATIONS." ASIA CHINA/COM EXEC NAT/LISM MARXISM...POLICY 20. PAGE 32 A0660 — ATTIT DIPLOM NAT/G

S66
DINH TRANS V.A.N.,"VIETNAM: A THIRD WAY" S/ASIA USA+45 USSR VIETNAM VIETNAM/S NAT/G SECT FORCES CAP/ISM DIPLOM COLONIAL NEUTRAL MARXISM SOCISM 20 BUDDHISM UNIFICA. PAGE 38 A0766 — WAR PLAN ORD/FREE SOCIALIST

S66
DUROSELLE J.B.,"THE FUTURE OF THE ATLANTIC COMMUNITY." EUR+WWI USA+45 USSR NAT/G CAP/ISM REGION DETER NUC/PWR ATTIT MARXISM...INT/LAW 20 NATO. PAGE 40 A0811 — FUT DIPLOM MYTH POLICY

S66
KLEIN S.,"A SURVEY OF SINO-JAPANESE TRADE, 1950-1966" TAIWAN EDU/PROP 20 CHINJAP. PAGE 80 A1649 — INT/TRADE DIPLOM MARXISM

S66
MCNEAL R.H.,"THE LEGACY OF THE COMINTERN." USSR WOR+45 WOR-45 PROB/SOLV DIPLOM CONFER CONTROL LEAD WAR 20 STALIN/J COMINTERN. PAGE 98 A2020 — MARXISM INT/ORG POL/PAR PWR

S66
SKILLING H.G.,"THE RUMANIAN NATIONAL COURSE." COM EUR+WWI ROMANIA NAT/G ECO/TAC PWR 20. PAGE 134 A2739 — NAT/LISM POLICY DIPLOM MARXISM

C66
TARLING N.,"A CONCISE HISTORY OF SOUTHEAST ASIA." BURMA CAMBODIA LAOS S/ASIA THAILAND VIETNAM ECO/UNDEV POL/PAR FORCES ADMIN REV WAR CIVMIL/REL ORD/FREE MARXISM SOCISM 13/20. PAGE 141 A2890 — COLONIAL DOMIN INT/TRADE NAT/LISM

C66
WINT G.,"ASIA: A HANDBOOK." ASIA S/ASIA INDUS LABOR SECT PRESS RACE/REL MARXISM...STAT CHARTS BIBLIOG 20. PAGE 165 A3366 — ECO/UNDEV DIPLOM NAT/G SOCIETY

N66
US HOUSE COMM FOREIGN AFFAIRS,UNITED STATES POLICY TOWARD ASIA (PAMPHLET). CHINA/COM USA+45 USSR VIETNAM INT/ORG NAT/G PWR MARXISM 20 UN. PAGE 154 A3133 — POLICY ASIA DIPLOM PLAN

B67
ATTWOOD W.,THE REDS AND THE BLACKS. AFR POL/PAR CHOOSE GOV/REL RACE/REL NAT/LISM...BIOG 20. PAGE 10 A0195 — DIPLOM PWR MARXISM

B67
BRZEZINSKI Z.K.,IDEOLOGY AND POWER IN SOVIET POLITICS. USSR NAT/G POL/PAR PWR...GEN/LAWS 19/20. PAGE 21 A0419 — DIPLOM EX/STRUC MARXISM

B67
BRZEZINSKI Z.K.,THE SOVIET BLOC: UNITY AND CONFLICT (2ND ED., REV., ENLARGED). COM POLAND USSR INTELL CHIEF EX/STRUC CONTROL EXEC GOV/REL PWR MARXISM ...TREND IDEA/COMP 20 LENIN/VI MARX/KARL STALIN/J. PAGE 21 A0420 — NAT/G DIPLOM

B67
CHO S.S.,KOREA IN WORLD POLITICS 1940-1950; AN EVALUATION OF AMERICAN RESPONSIBILITY. KOREA USA+45 USSR CONSTN INT/ORG NAT/G FORCES FOR/AID ANOMIE SUPEGO MARXISM...DECISION BIBLIOG 20. PAGE 26 A0533 — POLICY DIPLOM PROB/SOLV WAR

B67
FILENE P.G.,AMERICANS AND THE SOVIET EXPERIMENT, 1917-1933. USA-45 USSR INTELL NAT/G CAP/ISM DIPLOM EDU/PROP PRESS REV SOCISM...PSY 20. PAGE 45 A0930 — ATTIT RIGID/FLEX MARXISM SOCIETY

B67
KAROL K.S.,CHINA, THE OTHER COMMUNISM (TRANS. BY TOM BAISTOW). CHINA/COM CULTURE INDUS FORCES DIPLOM EDU/PROP CONTROL EXEC NUC/PWR ATTIT...SOC CHARTS 20. PAGE 77 A1567 — NAT/G POL/PAR MARXISM INGP/REL

B67
MCNELLY T.,SOURCES IN MODERN EAST ASIAN HISTORY AND POLITICS. KOREA VIETNAM CULTURE DIPLOM COLONIAL REV WAR PWR ALL/IDEOS MARXISM...ANTHOL 20 CHINJAP. PAGE 99 A2023 — NAT/COMP ASIA S/ASIA SOCIETY

B67
SABLE M.H.,A GUIDE TO LATIN AMERICAN STUDIES (2 VOLS). CONSTN FINAN INT/ORG LABOR MUNIC POL/PAR FORCES CAP/ISM FOR/AID ADMIN MARXISM SOCISM OAS. PAGE 126 A2584 — BIBLIOG/A L/A+17C DIPLOM NAT/LISM

B67
SHAFFER H.G.,THE COMMUNIST WORLD: MARXIST AND NON-MARXIST VIEWS. WOR+45 SOCIETY DIPLOM ECO/TAC CONTROL SOCISM...MARXIST ANTHOL BIBLIOG/A 20. PAGE 131 A2691 — MARXISM NAT/COMP IDEA/COMP COM

B67
TROTSKY L.,PROBLEMS OF THE CHINESE REVOLUTION (3RD ED. TRANS. BY MAX SCHACTMAN). ASIA USSR DIPLOM MARXISM SOCISM...IDEA/COMP ANTHOL DICTIONARY 20 STALIN/J. PAGE 145 A2969 — MARXIST REV

S67
ABT J.J.,"WORLD OF SENATOR FULBRIGHT." VIETNAM WOR+45 COERCE DETER REV ORD/FREE MARXISM...MARXIST 20. PAGE 4 A0084 — DIPLOM PLAN PWR

S67
ADIE W.A.C.,"CHINA'S 'SECOND LIBERATION'." CHINA/COM SOCIETY WORKER DIPLOM TASK 20 MAO. PAGE 4 A0090 — MARXISM REV INGP/REL ANOMIE

S67
BREGMAN A.,"WHITHER RUSSIA?" COM RUSSIA INTELL POL/PAR DIPLOM PARTIC NAT/LISM TOTALISM ATTIT ORD/FREE 20. PAGE 18 A0370 — MARXISM ELITES ADMIN CREATE

S67
DAVIS H.B.,"LENIN AND NATIONALISM: THE REDIRECTION OF THE MARXIST THEORY OF NATIONALISM." COM MOD/EUR USSR STRATA INT/ORG PLAN DOMIN COLONIAL FEDERAL ...TREND 20. PAGE 34 A0690 — NAT/LISM MARXISM ATTIT CENTRAL

S67
EGBERT D.D.,"POLITICS AND ART IN COMMUNIST BULGARIA" BULGARIA COM USSR CULTURE DIPLOM INGP/REL TOTALISM...TREND 20. PAGE 40 A0825 — CREATE ART/METH CONTROL MARXISM

S67
FARQUHAR D.M.,"CHINESE COMMUNIST ASSESSMENTS OF A FOREIGN CONQUEST DYNASTY." CHINA/COM DIPLOM CONTROL ...METH 20. PAGE 44 A0900 — MARXISM HIST/WRIT POLICY COLONIAL

S67
GOLDMAN M.I.,"SOVIET ECONOMIC GROWTH SINCE THE REVOLUTION." USSR WORKER INT/TRADE PRODUC MARXISM ...POLICY TIME/SEQ 20. PAGE 53 A1090 — ECO/DEV AGRI ECO/TAC INDUS

S67
HAZARD J.N.,"POST-DISARMAMENT INTERNATIONAL LAW." FUT USSR WOR+45 INT/ORG DELIB/GP FORCES DETER EQUILIB SOVEREIGN MARXISM 20 UN. PAGE 63 A1301 — INT/LAW ARMS/CONT PWR PLAN

S67
KRAUS J.,"A MARXIST IN GHANA." GHANA ELITES CHIEF PROB/SOLV TEC/DEV DIPLOM ECO/TAC COLONIAL PARTIC PWR 20 NKRUMAH/K. PAGE 82 A1676 — MARXISM PLAN ATTIT CREATE

S67
LACOUTRE J.,"HO CHI MINH." CHINA/COM USSR VIETNAM/N NAT/G CHIEF TOP/EX LEAD NEUTRAL...REALPOL PREDICT 20. PAGE 83 A1708 — NAT/LISM MARXISM REV DIPLOM

S67
MEYER J.,"CUBA S'ENFERME DANS SA REVOLUTION." CHINA/COM CUBA USSR NAT/G TOP/EX DIPLOM LEAD ATTIT ...PREDICT 20. PAGE 100 A2053 — MARXISM REV CHIEF NAT/LISM

S67
MOSELY P.E.,"EASTERN EUROPE IN WORLD POWER POLITICS: WHERE DE-STALINIZATION HAS LED." ECO/UNDEV NAT/LISM 20. PAGE 105 A2153 — COM NAT/G DIPLOM MARXISM

S67
ROMANOVSKY S.,"MISUSE OF CULTURAL COOPERATION." USA+45 INTELL DIPLOM DOMIN ATTIT COLD/WAR. PAGE 123 A2518 — EDU/PROP POLICY MARXISM CAP/ISM

S67
SAPP B.B.,"TRIBAL CULTURES AND COMMUNISM." AFR USA+45 STRATA DIPLOM FOR/AID REGION CENTRAL ATTIT AUTHORIT RIGID/FLEX KNOWL. PAGE 127 A2604 — KIN MARXISM ECO/UNDEV STRUCT

S67
TERRILL R.,"THE SIEGE MENTALITY." CHINA/COM NAT/G FORCES DIPLOM REV EFFICIENCY NAT/LISM MARXISM ...TREND 20. PAGE 142 A2904 EDU/PROP WAR DOMIN

S67
TUCKER R.C.,"THE DERADICALIZATION OF MARXIST MOVEMENTS." USSR SOCIETY DIPLOM 20. PAGE 145 A2973 MARXISM ADJUST ATTIT REV

C67
GEHLEN M.P.,"THE POLITICS OF COEXISTENCE: SOVIET METHODS AND MOTIVES." COM USSR NAT/G INT/TRADE EDU/PROP ARMS/CONT DETER KNOWL...CHARTS IDEA/COMP 20 COLD/WAR. PAGE 52 A1056 BIBLIOG PEACE DIPLOM MARXISM

MARXIST....MARXIST

N
PEKING REVIEW. CHINA/COM CULTURE AGRI INDUS DIPLOM EDU/PROP GUERRILLA ATTIT MARXISM...BIBLIOG 20. PAGE 1 A0022 MARXIST NAT/G POL/PAR PRESS

N
AVTOREFERATY DISSERTATSII. USSR INTELL ACADEM NAT/G DIPLOM GOV/REL KNOWL CONCPT. PAGE 3 A0047 BIBLIOG MARXISM MARXIST COM

N
US CONSULATE GENERAL HONG KONG,CURRENT BACKGROUND. CHINA/COM ECO/UNDEV LOC/G NAT/G PLAN DIPLOM EDU/PROP LEAD REV ATTIT...POLICY INDEX 20. PAGE 151 A3074 BIBLIOG/A MARXIST ASIA PRESS

N
US CONSULATE GENERAL HONG KONG,SURVEY OF CHINA MAINLAND PRESS. CHINA/COM ECO/UNDEV LOC/G NAT/G PLAN DIPLOM EDU/PROP LEAD REV ATTIT...POLICY INDEX 20. PAGE 151 A3075 BIBLIOG/A MARXIST ASIA PRESS

N
US CONSULATE GENERAL HONG KONG,US CONSULATE GENERAL, HONG KONG, PRESS SUMMARIES. CHINA/COM ECO/UNDEV LOC/G NAT/G PLAN DIPLOM EDU/PROP LEAD REV ATTIT...POLICY INDEX 20. PAGE 151 A3076 BIBLIOG/A MARXIST ASIA PRESS

N
US LIBRARY OF CONGRESS,EAST EUROPEAN ACCESSIONS INDEX. NAT/G ISOLAT ATTIT KNOWL...POLICY 20. PAGE 154 A3144 BIBLIOG COM MARXIST DIPLOM

B08
LABRIOLA A.,ESSAYS ON THE MATERIALISTIC CONCEPTION OF HISTORY. STRATA POL/PAR CAP/ISM DIPLOM INT/TRADE WAR 20. PAGE 83 A1706 MARXIST WORKER REV COLONIAL

B39
LENIN V.I.,IMPERIALISM: THE HIGHEST STAGE OF CAPITALISM. USSR WOR-45 DIST/IND INT/TRADE ATTIT MARXISM SOCISM...CHARTS 20. PAGE 87 A1773 MARXIST CAP/ISM COLONIAL DOMIN

B46
BIBLIOGRAFIIA DISSERTATSII: DOKTORSKIE DISSERTATSII ZA 19411944 (2 VOLS.). COM USSR LAW POL/PAR DIPLOM ADMIN LEAD...PHIL/SCI SOC 20. PAGE 3 A0054 BIBLIOG ACADEM KNOWL MARXIST

B49
THE CURRENT DIGEST OF THE SOVIET PRESS. USSR WOR+45 LOC/G NAT/G DIPLOM EDU/PROP...MARXIST 20. PAGE 3 A0056 BIBLIOG/A COM ATTIT PRESS

S59
FISCHER L.,"THE SOVIET-AMERICAN ANTAGONISM: HOW WILL IT END." CONSTN CULTURE PLAN TEC/DEV RIGID/FLEX SUPEGO ORD/FREE...MARXIST DECISION PSY CONCPT CON/ANAL GEN/LAWS VAL/FREE 20 COLD/WAR. PAGE 46 A0936 USA+45 PWR DIPLOM USSR

B60
APTHEKER H.,DISARMAMENT AND THE AMERICAN ECONOMY: A SYMPOSIUM. FUT USA+45 ECO/DEV DIST/IND FINAN INDUS PROC/MFG LABOR NAT/G POL/PAR CONSULT PLAN CAP/ISM INT/TRADE PEACE ATTIT MORAL WEALTH...TREND GEN/LAWS TOT/POP 20. PAGE 9 A0172 MARXIST ARMS/CONT

B60
KARDELJE,SOCIALISM AND WAR. CHINA/COM WOR+45 YUGOSLAVIA DIPLOM EDU/PROP ATTIT...POLICY CONCPT IDEA/COMP COLD/WAR. PAGE 76 A1565 MARXIST WAR MARXISM BAL/PWR

B60
KHRUSHCHEV N.,FOR VICTORY IN PEACEFUL COMPETITION WITH CAPITALISM. COM FUT USSR WOR+45 CONSTN SOCIETY INDUS INT/ORG DELIB/GP PLAN BAL/PWR DIPLOM PERSON MARXISM...MARXIST WORK 20 COLD/WAR. PAGE 79 A1611 TOP/EX PWR CAP/ISM SOCISM

B60
KHRUSHCHEV N.S.,KHRUSHCHEV IN AMERICA. USA+45 USSR INT/TRADE EDU/PROP PRESS PEACE...MARXIST RECORD INT 20 COLD/WAR KHRUSH/N. PAGE 79 A1613 MARXISM CHIEF DIPLOM

S60
IKLE F.C.,"NTH COUNTRIES AND DISARMAMENT." WOR+45 DELIB/GP ECO/TAC DOMIN EDU/PROP LEGIT ROUTINE COERCE RIGID/FLEX ORD/FREE...MARXIST TREND 20. PAGE 70 A1432 FUT INT/ORG ARMS/CONT NUC/PWR

B61
MORRAY J.P.,FROM YALTA TO DISARMAMENT: COLD WAR DEBATE. USA+45 CAP/ISM FOR/AID CONTROL NUC/PWR 20 UN COLD/WAR CHURCHLL/W. PAGE 104 A2145 MARXIST ARMS/CONT DIPLOM BAL/PWR

B62
MORRAY J.P.,THE SECOND REVOLUTION IN CUBA. CUBA AGRI LABOR POL/PAR DIPLOM FOR/AID GUERRILLA TOTALISM MARXISM 20. PAGE 104 A2146 REV MARXIST ECO/TAC NAT/LISM

B63
BLACK J.E.,FOREIGN POLICIES IN A WORLD OF CHANGE. FUT INT/ORG ALL/VALS...POLICY MAJORIT MARXIST SOCIALIST TRADIT TIME/SEQ TREND ANTHOL 20. PAGE 15 A0298 WOR+45 NAT/G DIPLOM

B64
DUTT R.P.,THE INTERNATIONALE. COM WOR+45 WOR-45 WORKER CAP/ISM WAR ATTIT...TREND GEN/LAWS 18/20 COM/PARTY. PAGE 40 A0813 ALL/IDEOS INT/ORG MARXIST ORD/FREE

B64
EHRENBURG I.,THE WAR: 1941-1945 (VOL. V OF "MEN, YEARS - LIFE," TRANS. BY TATIANA SHEBUNINA). GERMANY USSR PRESS WRITING PERS/REL PEACE ANOMIE ATTIT PERSON...CONCPT RECORD BIOG 20 STALIN/J HITLER/A. PAGE 40 A0827 WAR DIPLOM COM MARXIST

S64
KARPOV P.V.,"PEACEFUL COEXISTENCE AND INTERNATIONAL LAW." WOR+45 LAW SOCIETY INT/ORG VOL/ASSN FORCES CREATE CAP/ISM DIPLOM ADJUD NUC/PWR PEACE MORAL ORD/FREE PWR MARXISM...MARXIST JURID CONCPT OBS TREND COLD/WAR MARX/KARL 20. PAGE 77 A1568 COM ATTIT INT/LAW USSR

B65
COLLINS H.,KARL MARX AND THE BRITISH LABOUR MOVEMENT; YEARS OF THE FIRST INTERNATIONAL. FRANCE SWITZERLND UK CAP/ISM WAR...MARXIST IDEA/COMP BIBLIOG 19. PAGE 28 A0567 MARXISM LABOR INT/ORG REV

B66
FALL B.B.,VIET-NAM WITNESS, 1953-66. S/ASIA VIETNAM SECT PROB/SOLV COLONIAL GUERRILLA...CHARTS BIBLIOG 20. PAGE 44 A0895 MARXIST WAR DIPLOM

B66
WESTIN A.F.,VIEWS OF AMERICA. COM USA+45 USSR SOCIETY ECO/UNDEV POL/PAR ECO/TAC GP/REL STRANGE MARXISM...MARXIST 20. PAGE 163 A3323 CONCPT ATTIT DIPLOM IDEA/COMP

B67
SHAFFER H.G.,THE COMMUNIST WORLD: MARXIST AND NON-MARXIST VIEWS. WOR+45 SOCIETY DIPLOM ECO/TAC CONTROL SOCISM...MARXIST ANTHOL BIBLIOG/A 20. PAGE 131 A2691 MARXISM NAT/COMP IDEA/COMP COM

B67
TROTSKY L.,PROBLEMS OF THE CHINESE REVOLUTION (3RD ED. TRANS. BY MAX SCHACTMAN). ASIA USSR DIPLOM MARXISM SOCISM...IDEA/COMP ANTHOL DICTIONARY 20 STALIN/J. PAGE 145 A2969 MARXIST REV

S67
ABT J.J.,"WORLD OF SENATOR FULBRIGHT." VIETNAM WOR+45 COERCE DETER REV ORD/FREE MARXISM...MARXIST 20. PAGE 4 A0084 DIPLOM PLAN PWR

S67
COHN K.,"CRIMES AGAINST HUMANITY." GERMANY INT/ORG SANCTION ATTIT ORD/FREE...MARXIST CRIMLGY 20 UN. PAGE 28 A0564 WAR INT/LAW CRIME ADJUD

S67
FALKOWSKI M.,"SOCIALIST ECONOMISTS AND THE DEVELOPING COUNTRIES." COM PLAN TEC/DEV ROUTINE DEMAND EFFICIENCY PRODUC WEALTH...MARXIST TREND GEN/METH. PAGE 44 A0893 DIPLOM SOCISM ECO/UNDEV INDUS

S67
GODUNSKY Y.,"'APOSTLES OF PEACE' IN LATIN AMERICA." L/A+17C USA+45 BAL/PWR DIPLOM FOR/AID DOMIN COLONIAL CIVMIL/REL MARXIST. PAGE 53 A1086 ECO/UNDEV REV VOL/ASSN EDU/PROP

S67
KRUSCHE H.,"THE STRIVING OF THE KIESINGER-STRAUS GOVERNMENT FOR NUCLEAR WEAPONS IS A THREAT TO EUROPEAN SECURITY." EUR+WWI GERMANY BAL/PWR SANCTION WEAPON PEACE ORD/FREE...MARXIST 20 NATO COLD/WAR. PAGE 82 A1688 ARMS/CONT INT/ORG NUC/PWR DIPLOM

S67
PEUKERT W.,"WEST GERMANY'S 'RED TRADE'." COM GERMANY INDUS CAP/ISM DOMIN SANCTION DEMAND PEACE UTIL...MARXIST 20 COLD/WAR. PAGE 115 A2371 DIPLOM ECO/TAC INT/TRADE

S67
REINTANZ G.,"THE SPACE TREATY." WOR+45 DIPLOM CONTROL ARMS/CONT NUC/PWR WAR...MARXIST 20 COLD/WAR UN TREATY. PAGE 120 A2461 SPACE INT/LAW INT/ORG PEACE

S67
SHERSHNEV Y.,"THE KENNEDY ROUND* PLANS AND REALITY." EUR+WWI USA+45 INT/ORG DIPLOM TARIFFS DOMIN CONFER PWR...MARXIST PREDICT. PAGE 132 A2701 ECO/TAC ECO/DEV INT/TRADE

YEFROMEV A.,"THE TRUE FACE OF THE WEST GERMAN NATIONAL-DEMOCRATS." GERMANY/W NAT/G DOMIN LEAD SANCTION WAR ATTIT PERSON...MARXIST 20. PAGE 169 A3433 — BAL/PWR S67 POL/PAR TOTALISM PARL/PROC DIPLOM

MARYLAND....MARYLAND

MAS LATRIE L. A1954

MASON E.S. A1955,A1956

MASON H.L. A1957

MASON J.B. A1958

MASS MEDIA....SEE EDU/PROP, COM/IND

MASSACHU....MASSACHUSETTS

MASSEY V. A1959

MASTERS D. A1960

MASTERS R.D. A1961,A1962,A1963

MATECKI B. A1964

MATH....MATHEMATICS

GODET M.,INDEX BIBLIOGRAPHICUS: INTERNATIONAL CATALOGUE OF SOURCES OF CURRENT BIBLIOGRAPHIC INFORMATION. EUR+WWI MOD/EUR SOCIETY SECT TAX ...JURID PHIL/SCI SOC MATH. PAGE 53 A1085 — B25 BIBLIOG/A DIPLOM EDU/PROP LAW

OHLIN B.,INTERREGIONAL AND INTERNATIONAL TRADE. USA-45 WOR-45 CULTURE FINAN MARKET CONSULT PLAN ECO/TAC ATTIT WEALTH...CONCPT MATH TOT/POP 20. PAGE 111 A2285 — B33 INT/ORG ECO/DEV INT/TRADE REGION

VINER J.,STUDIES IN THE THEORY OF INTERNATIONAL TRADE. WOR-45 CONSTN ECO/DEV AGRI INDUS MARKET INT/ORG LABOR NAT/G ECO/TAC TARIFFS COLONIAL ATTIT WEALTH...POLICY CONCPT MATH STAT OBS SAMP TREND GEN/LAWS MARX/KARL 20. PAGE 159 A3236 — B37 CAP/ISM INT/TRADE

HARVARD UNIVERSITY LAW SCHOOL,INTERNATIONAL PROBLEMS OF FINANCIAL PROTECTION AGAINST NUCLEAR RISK. WOR+45 NAT/G DELIB/GP PROB/SOLV DIPLOM CONTROL ATTIT...POLICY INT/LAW MATH 20. PAGE 62 A1281 — B59 NUC/PWR ADJUD INDUS FINAN

PUGWASH CONFERENCE,"ON BIOLOGICAL AND CHEMICAL WARFARE." WOR+45 SOCIETY PROC/MFG INT/ORG FORCES EDU/PROP ADJUD RIGID/FLEX ORD/FREE PWR...DECISION PSY NEW/IDEA MATH VAL/FREE 20. PAGE 118 A2417 — S59 ACT/RES BIO/SOC WAR WEAPON

REUBENS E.D.,"THE BASIS FOR REORIENATION OF AMERICAN FOREIGN AID POLICY." USA+45 USSR STRUCT INT/ORG CONSULT ECO/TAC ADMIN DRIVE MORAL ORD/FREE PWR WEALTH...RELATIV MATH STAT TREND GEN/LAWS VAL/FREE 20. PAGE 120 A2467 — S59 ECO/UNDEV PLAN FOR/AID DIPLOM

LERNER A.P.,THE ECONOMICS OF CONTROL. USA+45 ECO/UNDEV INT/ORG ACT/RES PLAN CAP/ISM INT/TRADE ATTIT WEALTH...SOC MATH STAT GEN/LAWS INDEX 20. PAGE 87 A1785 — B60 ECO/DEV ROUTINE ECO/TAC SOCISM

WOLF C.,FOREIGN AID: THEORY AND PRACTICE IN SOUTHERN ASIA. CEYLON INDONESIA PHILIPPINE S/ASIA CULTURE STRATA ECO/UNDEV PLAN EDU/PROP ATTIT ...METH/CNCPT MATH QUANT STAT CONT/OBS TIME/SEQ SIMUL TOT/POP 20. PAGE 166 A3378 — B60 ACT/RES ECO/TAC FOR/AID

FRANKEL S.H.,"ECONOMIC ASPECTS OF POLITICAL INDEPENDENCE IN AFRICA." AFR FUT SOCIETY ECO/UNDEV COM/IND FINAN LEGIS PLAN TEC/DEV CAP/ISM ECO/TAC INT/TRADE ADMIN ATTIT DRIVE RIGID/FLEX PWR WEALTH ...MGT NEW/IDEA MATH TIME/SEQ VAL/FREE 20. PAGE 48 A0984 — S60 NAT/G FOR/AID

BOULDING K.E.,CONFLICT AND DEFENSE: A GENERAL THEORY. FUT SOCIETY INT/ORG NAT/G CREATE BAL/PWR COERCE NAT/LISM DRIVE ALL/VALS...PLURIST DECISION CONCPT METH/CNCPT TREND HYPO/EXP TOT/POP 20. PAGE 17 A0347 — B62 MATH SIMUL PEACE WAR

COLLISON R.L.,BIBLIOGRAPHIES, SUBJECT AND NATIONAL: A GUIDE TO THEIR CONTENTS, ARRANGEMENT, AND USE (2ND REV. ED.). SECT DIPLOM...ART/METH GEOG HUM PHIL/SCI SOC MATH BIOG 20. PAGE 28 A0569 — B62 BIBLIOG/A CON/ANAL BIBLIOG

HOLMAN A.G.,SOME MEASURES AND INTERPRETATIONS OF EFFECTS OF US FOREIGN ENTERPRISES ON US BALANCE OF PAYMENTS. USA+45 COST INCOME WEALTH...MATH CHARTS 20. PAGE 67 A1371 — B62 BAL/PAY INT/TRADE FINAN ECO/TAC

MULLENBACH P.,CIVILIAN NUCLEAR POWER: ECONOMIC ISSUES AND POLICY FORMATION. FINAN INT/ORG DELIB/GP ACT/RES ECO/TAC ATTIT SUPEGO HEALTH ORD/FREE PWR ...POLICY CONCPT MATH STAT CHARTS VAL/FREE 20 COLD/WAR. PAGE 105 A2166 — B63 USA+45 ECO/DEV NUC/PWR

US CONGRESS JOINT ECO COMM,THE UNITED STATES BALANCE OF PAYMENTS. USA+45 DELIB/GP CONFER...MATH PREDICT CHARTS 20 CONGRESS. PAGE 150 A3068 — B63 BAL/PAY ECO/TAC INT/TRADE CONSULT

KRAVIS I.B.,"THE POLITICAL ARITHMETIC OF INTERNATIONAL BURDENSHARING." FUT USA+45 WOR+45 FINAN DELIB/GP ACT/RES CREATE TEC/DEV ATTIT PWR WEALTH...POLICY MATH STAT VAL/FREE 20. PAGE 82 A1681 — S63 INT/ORG ECO/TAC

MATHUR P.N.,"GAINS IN ECONOMIC GROWTH FROM INTERNATIONAL TRADE." USA-45 ECO/DEV FINAN INDUS ATTIT WEALTH...MATH QUANT STAT BIOG TREND GEN/LAWS WORK 20. PAGE 96 A1966 — S63 MARKET ECO/TAC CAP/ISM INT/TRADE

KOJIMA K.,"THE PATTERN OF INTERNATIONAL TRADE AMONG ADVANCED COUNTRIES." EUR+WWI UK USA+45 WOR+45 MARKET NAT/G ECO/TAC WEALTH...MATH STAT CON/ANAL CHARTS EEC CHINJAP 20 CHINJAP. PAGE 81 A1665 — S64 ECO/DEV TREND INT/TRADE

KUENNE R.E.,THE POLARIS MISSILE STRIKE* A GENERAL ECONOMIC SYSTEMS ANALYSIS. USA+45 USSR NAT/G BAL/PWR ARMS/CONT WAR...MATH PROBABIL COMPUT/IR CHARTS HYPO/EXP SIMUL. PAGE 82 A1689 — B66 NUC/PWR FORCES DETER DIPLOM

MATHEMATICS....SEE MATH, ALSO LOGIC, MATHEMATICS, AND LANGUAGE INDEX, P. XIV

MATHISEN T. A1965

MATHUR P.N. A1966

MATLEY I.M. A0086

MATLOFF M. A1967

MATTEI/E....ENRICO MATTEI

MATTHEWS D.G. A1968,A1969,A1970,A1971,A1972

MATTHEWS M.A. A1973,A1974,A1975,A1976,A1977

MATTHEWS T. A1978

MATUSOW A.J. A0279

MAU/MAU....MAU MAU

MITCHELL P.,AFRICAN AFTERTHOUGHTS. UGANDA CONSTN NAT/G ADJUD COERCE WAR 20 WWI MAU/MAU. PAGE 102 A2090 — B54 BIOG CHIEF COLONIAL DOMIN

MAUD J. A1979

MAUD....MILITARY APPLICATIONS OF URANIUM DETONATION (MAUD) (U.K. - WWII)

THOMSON G.P.,NUCLEAR ENERGY IN BRITAIN DURING THE LAST WAR: THE CHERWELL SIMON LECTURE (MONOGRAPH). UK R+D CONSULT FORCES PLAN DIPLOM TASK CIVMIL/REL ROLE...PHIL/SCI NEW/IDEA LAB/EXP 20 MAUD. PAGE 143 A2934 — B62 CREATE TEC/DEV WAR NUC/PWR

MAURITANIA....SEE ALSO AFR

MAURRAS/C....CHARLES MAURRAS

MAW B. A1980

MAXWELL B.W. A1981

MAY E.R. A1982

MAYER A.J. A1983

MAYER P. A1984

MAYNE R. A1985

MAYO/ELTON....ELTON MAYO

MAYOR....MAYOR; SEE ALSO MUNIC, CHIEF

MELINAT C.H. A1340

MELMAN S. A2035

MENDE T. A2036

MENDEL D.H. A2037

MENDELSSOHN S. A2038

MENDES C. A2039

MENEZES A.J. A2040,A2041

MENON K.P.S. A2042

MENON/KRSH....KRISHNA MENON

MENSHEVIK....MENSHEVIKS

MENTAL DISORDERS....SEE HEALTH

MENTAL HEALTH....SEE HEALTH, PSY

MENTAL INSTITUTION....SEE PUB/INST

MENZIES/RG....ROBERT G. MENZIES

MERCANTILISM....SEE ECO

MERCANTLST....MERCANTILIST ECONOMIC THEORY

B66
HUTTENBACK R.A.,BRITISH IMPERIAL EXPERIENCE. S/ASIA UK WOR-45 INT/ORG TEC/DEV...CHARTS 16/20 COMMONWLTH MERCANTLST. PAGE 69 A1424
COLONIAL
TIME/SEQ
INT/TRADE

MERCIER/E....ERNEST MERCIER

MEREDITH/J....JAMES MEREDITH

MERGERS....SEE INDUS, EX/STRUC, FINAN

MERKL P.H. A2043

MERRITT R.L. A2044,A2045,A2046

MERTHYR....MERTHYR, WALES

MERTON/R....ROBERT MERTON

MESKILL J. A0846

MESOPOTAM....MESOPOTAMIA

B63
JAIRAZBHOY R.A.,FOREIGN INFLUENCE IN ANCIENT INDIA. INDIA ELITES SECT DIPLOM EDU/PROP COLONIAL REGION GP/REL...ART/METH LING WORSHIP +/14 GRECO/ROMN MESOPOTAM PERSIA PARTH/SASS. PAGE 73 A1491
CULTURE
SOCIETY
COERCE
DOMIN

METH....HEAVILY EMPHASIZED METHODOLOGY OR TECHNIQUE OF STUDY

N
AMERICAN POLITICAL SCIENCE REVIEW. USA+45 USA-45 WOR+45 WOR-45 INT/ORG ADMIN...INT/LAW PHIL/SCI CONCPT METH 20 UN. PAGE 1 A0003
BIBLIOG/A
DIPLOM
NAT/G
GOV/COMP

N
AMERICAN ECONOMIC ASSOCIATION,THE JOURNAL OF ECONOMIC ABSTRACTS. ECO/UNDEV MARKET LABOR DIPLOM ...MGT CONCPT METH 20. PAGE 7 A0144
BIBLIOG/A
R+D
FINAN

BLI
MOOR C.C.,HOW TO USE UNITED NATIONS DOCUMENTS (PAPER). WOR+45 ACADEM CONTROL 20 UN. PAGE 103 A2121
BIBLIOG
METH
INT/ORG

B20
VINOGRADOFF P.,OUTLINES OF HISTORICAL JURISPRUDENCE (2 VOLS.). GREECE MEDIT-7 LAW CONSTN FACE/GP FAM KIN MUNIC CRIME OWN...INT/LAW IDEA/COMP BIBLIOG. PAGE 159 A3241
JURID
METH

B31
BORCHARD E.H.,GUIDE TO THE LAW AND LEGAL LITERATURE OF FRANCE. FRANCE FINAN INDUS LABOR SECT LEGIS ADMIN COLONIAL CRIME OWN...INT/LAW 20. PAGE 17 A0337
BIBLIOG/A
LAW
CONSTN
METH

B44
BRIERLY J.L.,THE OUTLOOK FOR INTERNATIONAL LAW. FUT WOR-45 CONSTN NAT/G VOL/ASSN FORCES ECO/TAC DOMIN LEGIT ADJUD ROUTINE PEACE ORD/FREE...INT/LAW JURID METH LEAGUE/NAT 20. PAGE 18 A0376
INT/ORG
LAW

S47
RADVANYI L.,"PROBLEMS OF INTERNATIONAL OPINION SURVEYS." WOR+45 INT/ORG NAT/G CREATE ATTIT...PSY SOC METH/CNCPT REC/INT KNO/TEST SAMP/SIZ METH VAL/FREE 20. PAGE 118 A2431
QU/SEMANT
SAMP
DIPLOM

B52
SURANYI-UNGER T.,COMPARATIVE ECONOMIC SYSTEMS. FINAN MARKET DIPLOM PRICE WEALTH...GEOG SOC BIBLIOG METH T 20. PAGE 140 A2865
LAISSEZ
PLAN
ECO/DEV
IDEA/COMP

N52
COORDINATING COMM DOC SOC SCI,INTERNATIONAL REPERTORY OF SOCIAL SCIENCE DOCUMENTATION CENTERS (PAMPHLET). ACT/RES OP/RES WRITING KNOWL...CON/ANAL METH. PAGE 30 A0610
BIBLIOG/A
R+D
NAT/G
INT/ORG

B53
NEISSER H.,NATIONAL INCOMES AND INTERNATIONAL TRADE. FRANCE GERMANY SWEDEN UK USA-45 EXTR/IND FINAN INDUS TEC/DEV PRICE BAL/PAY EQUILIB INCOME WEALTH...CHARTS METH 19 CHINJAP. PAGE 108 A2215
INT/TRADE
PRODUC
MARKET
CON/ANAL

B57
ALEXANDER L.M.,WORLD POLITICAL PATTERNS. NAT/G PROVS CAP/ISM DIPLOM COLONIAL NAT/LISM...POLICY GEOG CHARTS METH/COMP NAT/COMP 20. PAGE 5 A0111
CONTROL
METH
GOV/COMP

S57
KAPLAN M.,"BALANCE OF POWER, BIPOLARITY AND OTHER MODELS OF INTERNATIONAL SYSTEMS" (BMR)" ACT/RES BAL/PWR...PHIL/SCI METH 20. PAGE 76 A1559
DIPLOM
GAME
METH/CNCPT
SIMUL

N57
BIBLIOGRAPHY OF NEW GUIDES AND AIDS TO PUBLIC DOCUMENTS USE, 1953-1956 (PAMPHLET). WOR+45 MUNIC DIPLOM...CON/ANAL CHARTS METH. PAGE 164 A3347
BIBLIOG/A
NAT/G
LOC/G
INT/ORG

L58
HYVARINEN R.,"MONISTIC AND PLURALISTIC INTERPRETATIONS IN THE STUDY OF INTERNATIONAL POLITICS." COLONIAL REGION RACE/REL DISCRIM TOTALISM SOVEREIGN...INT/LAW PHIL/SCI CONCPT BIBLIOG 20. PAGE 70 A1429
DIPLOM
PLURISM
INT/ORG
METH

B59
MATHISEN T.,METHODOLOGY IN THE STUDY OF INTERNATIONAL RELATIONS. FUT WOR+45 SOCIETY INT/ORG NAT/G POL/PAR WAR PEACE KNOWL PWR...RELATIV CONCPT METH/CNCPT TREND HYPO/EXP METH TOT/POP 20. PAGE 96 A1965
GEN/METH
CON/ANAL
DIPLOM
CREATE

B59
SIMPSON J.L.,INTERNATIONAL ARBITRATION: LAW AND PRACTICE. WOR+45 WOR-45 INT/ORG DELIB/GP ADJUD PEACE MORAL ORD/FREE...METH 18/20. PAGE 133 A2720
INT/LAW
DIPLOM
CT/SYS
CONSULT

B60
HOFFMANN S.H.,CONTEMPORARY THEORY IN INTERNATIONAL RELATIONS. RATIONAL...SOC METH/CNCPT METH/COMP SIMUL ANTHOL 20. PAGE 66 A1359
DIPLOM
METH
PHIL/SCI
DECISION

B60
HOVET T. JR.,BLOC POLITICS IN THE UNITED NATIONS. WOR+45...POLICY STAT CHARTS METH UN. PAGE 68 A1396
LOBBY
INT/ORG
DIPLOM
CHOOSE

B60
MOSELY P.E.,THE KREMLIN AND WORLD POLITICS. EUR+WWI GERMANY USA+45 USSR CHIEF TOP/EX BAL/PWR DOMIN PEACE PWR...METH 20 COLD/WAR STALIN/J EUROPE/E. PAGE 105 A2151
COM
DIPLOM
POLICY
WAR

B60
SCANLON D.G.,INTERNATIONAL EDUCATION: A DOCUMENTARY HISTORY. ADMIN CONTROL ATTIT PERCEPT...BIOG ANTHOL METH 20. PAGE 127 A2612
EDU/PROP
INT/ORG
NAT/COMP
DIPLOM

S60
HAVILAND H.F.,"PROBLEMS OF AMERICAN FOREIGN POLICY." ASIA COM USA+45 WOR+45 INT/ORG NAT/G CONSULT ECO/TAC FOR/AID DOMIN COERCE NUC/PWR ATTIT DRIVE ORD/FREE PWR RESPECT SKILL...POLICY GEOG OBS SAMP TREND GEN/METH METH COLD/WAR UN 20. PAGE 63 A1292
ECO/UNDEV
FORCES
DIPLOM

S60
RIESELBACH Z.N.,"QUANTITATIVE TECHNIQUES FOR STUDYING VOTING BEHAVIOR IN THE UNITED NATIONS GENERAL ASSEMBLY." FUT S/ASIA USA+45 INT/ORG BAL/PWR DIPLOM ECO/TAC FOR/AID ADMIN PWR...POLICY METH/CNCPT METH UN 20. PAGE 121 A2478
QUANT
CHOOSE

B61
KNORR K.E.,THE INTERNATIONAL SYSTEM. FUT SOCIETY INT/ORG NAT/G PLAN BAL/PWR DIPLOM WAR PWR ...DECISION METH/CNCPT CONT/OBS GAME METH UN 20. PAGE 81 A1655
ACT/RES
SIMUL
ECO/UNDEV

B61
NICOLSON H.G.,THE OLD DIPLOMACY AND THE NEW. NAT/G PLAN PROB/SOLV...METH 20. PAGE 109 A2233
DIPLOM
POLICY
INT/ORG

B61
ROSENAU J.N.,INTERNATIONAL POLITICS AND FOREIGN POLICY: A READER IN RESEARCH AND THEORY. ELITES ATTIT SOVEREIGN...DECISION CHARTS HYPO/EXP GAME SIMUL ANTHOL BIBLIOG METH 20. PAGE 124 A2531
ACT/RES
DIPLOM
CONCPT
POLICY

B61
SHARP W.R.,FIELD ADMINISTRATION IN THE UNITED NATION SYSTEM: THE CONDUCT OF INTERNATIONAL
INT/ORG
CONSULT

ECONOMIC AND SOCIAL PROGRAMS. FUT WOR+45 CONSTN SOCIETY ECO/UNDEV R+D DELIB/GP ACT/RES PLAN TEC/DEV EDU/PROP EXEC ROUTINE HEALTH WEALTH...HUM CONCPT CHARTS METH ILO UNESCO VAL/FREE UN 20. PAGE 132 A2697

S61
SINGER J.D.,"THE LEVEL OF ANALYSIS: PROBLEMS IN INTERNATIONAL RELATIONS." FUT INTELL R+D INT/ORG CREATE EDU/PROP...METH/CNCPT HYPO/EXP GEN/METH METH VAL/FREE. PAGE 133 A2725
SOCIETY SOC DIPLOM

S61
TUCKER R.C.,"TOWARDS A COMPARATIVE POLITICS OF MOVEMENT-REGIMES" (BMR)" USSR CONSTN NAT/G CREATE PROB/SOLV DIPLOM DOMIN REV...GP/COMP IDEA/COMP METH 20 STALIN/J BOLSHEVISM. PAGE 145 A2971
MARXISM POLICY GEN/LAWS PWR

S62
DIHN N.Q.,"L'INTERNATIONALISATION DU MEKONG." CAMBODIA LAOS VIETNAM WOR+45 INT/ORG NAT/G VOL/ASSN PEACE HEALTH...CONCPT TIME/SEQ CHARTS METH VAL/FREE 20. PAGE 37 A0761
S/ASIA DELIB/GP

B63
US DEPARTMENT OF STATE,POLITICAL BEHAVIOR--A LIST OF CURRENT STUDIES. USA+45 COM/IND DIPLOM LEAD PERS/REL DRIVE PERCEPT KNOWL...DECISION SIMUL METH. PAGE 151 A3093
BIBLIOG METH/COMP GP/REL ATTIT

B64
FREE L.A.,THE ATTITUDES, HOPES AND FEARS OF NIGERIANS. AFR NIGERIA ECO/UNDEV AGRI ACADEM PLAN TASK...GEOG CHARTS METH 20. PAGE 49 A0993
NAT/LISM SYS/QU DIPLOM

B64
HARRISON H.V.,THE ROLE OF THEORY IN INTERNATIONAL RELATIONS. UNIV WOR+45 R+D INT/ORG NAT/G PERCEPT KNOWL...DECISION CONCPT GEN/METH METH 20. PAGE 62 A1270
METH/CNCPT HYPO/EXP DIPLOM

B64
JOHNSON E.A.J.,THE DIMENSIONS OF DIPLOMACY. INT/ORG FORCES TEC/DEV WAR PEACE PWR...SOC ANTHOL 20. PAGE 74 A1522
DIPLOM POLICY METH

B64
KEEP J.,CONTEMPORARY HISTORY IN THE SOVIET MIRROR. COM USSR POL/PAR CREATE DIPLOM AGREE WAR ATTIT ...MYTH TREND ANTHOL 20 COLD/WAR STALIN/J MARX/KARL LENIN/VI. PAGE 77 A1576
HIST/WRIT METH MARXISM IDEA/COMP

B64
RICHARDSON I.L.,BIBLIOGRAFIA BRASILEIRA DE ADMINISTRACAO PUBLICA E ASSUNTOS CORRELATOS. BRAZIL CONSTN FINAN LOC/G NAT/G POL/PAR PLAN DIPLOM RECEIVE ATTIT...METH 20. PAGE 121 A2474
BIBLIOG MGT ADMIN LAW

B65
FORM W.H.,INDUSTRIAL RELATIONS AND SOCIAL CHANGE IN LATIN AMERICA. L/A+17C AGRI LABOR NAT/G PLAN PROB/SOLV DIPLOM...MGT SOC ANTHOL BIBLIOG/A METH 20. PAGE 47 A0966
INDUS GP/REL NAT/COMP ECO/UNDEV

B65
HARMON R.B.,POLITICAL SCIENCE: A BIBLIOGRAPHICAL GUIDE TO THE LITERATURE. WOR+45 WOR-45 R+D INT/ORG LOC/G NAT/G DIPLOM ADMIN...CONCPT METH. PAGE 61 A1261
BIBLIOG POL/PAR LAW GOV/COMP

B65
HASSON J.A.,THE ECONOMICS OF NUCLEAR POWER. INDIA UK USA+45 WOR+45 INT/ORG TEC/DEV COST...SOC STAT CHARTS 20 EURATOM. PAGE 63 A1286
NUC/PWR INDUS ECO/DEV METH

B66
CLAUSEWITZ C.V.,ON WAR (VOL. III). UNIV EDU/PROP ...POLICY DECISION METH 18/20. PAGE 27 A0548
WAR FORCES PLAN CIVMIL/REL

B66
MC CLELLAND C.A.,THEORY AND THE INTERNATIONAL SYSTEM. EDU/PROP PWR...DECISION SOC METH. PAGE 97 A1991
DIPLOM METH/CNCPT ACT/RES R+D

B66
SAGER P.,MOSKAUS HAND IN INDIEN. INDIA USSR DIPLOM DOMIN...PSY CONCPT 20 COM/PARTY. PAGE 126 A2586
PRESS EDU/PROP METH POL/PAR

B67
BARANSON J.,TECHNOLOGY FOR UNDERDEVELOPED AREAS: AN ANNOTATED BIBLIOGRAPHY. FUT WOR+45 CULTURE INDUS INT/ORG CREATE PROB/SOLV INT/TRADE EDU/PROP AUTOMAT ...CONCPT METH. PAGE 11 A0218
BIBLIOG/A ECO/UNDEV TEC/DEV R+D

B67
DE BLIJ H.J.,SYSTEMATIC POLITICAL GEOGRAPHY. WOR+45 STRUCT INT/ORG NAT/G EDU/PROP ADMIN COLONIAL ROUTINE ORD/FREE PWR...IDEA/COMP T 20. PAGE 34 A0697
GEOG CONCPT METH

B67
UNIVERSAL REFERENCE SYSTEM,LAW, JURISPRUDENCE, AND JUDICIAL PROCESS (VOLUME VII). WOR+45 WOR-45 CONSTN NAT/G LEGIS JUDGE CT/SYS...INT/LAW COMPUT/IR GEN/METH METH. PAGE 149 A3044
BIBLIOG/A LAW JURID ADJUD

S67
FARQUHAR D.M.,"CHINESE COMMUNIST ASSESSMENTS OF A FOREIGN CONQUEST DYNASTY." CHINA/COM DIPLOM CONTROL ...METH 20. PAGE 44 A0900
MARXISM HIST/WRIT POLICY COLONIAL

METH/CNCPT....METHODOLOGICAL CONCEPTS

METH/COMP....COMPARISON OF METHODS

N
INTERNATIONAL COMN JURISTS,AFRICAN CONFERENCE ON THE RULE OF LAW. AFR INT/ORG LEGIS DIPLOM CONFER COLONIAL ORD/FREE...CONCPT METH/COMP 20. PAGE 71 A1452
CT/SYS JURID DELIB/GP

N
US DEPARTMENT OF STATE,BIBLIOGRAPHY (PAMPHLETS). AGRI INDUS INT/ORG FOR/AID EDU/PROP WAR MARXISM ...SOC GOV/COMP METH/COMP 20. PAGE 151 A3079
BIBLIOG DIPLOM ECO/DEV NAT/G

N19
FREEMAN H.A.,COERCION OF STATES IN FEDERAL UNIONS (PAMPHLET). WOR-45 DIPLOM CONTROL COERCE PEACE ORD/FREE...GOV/COMP METH/COMP NAT/COMP PACIFIST 20. PAGE 49 A0994
FEDERAL WAR INT/ORG PACIFISM

B23
KADEN E.H.,DER POLITISCHE CHARAKTER DER FRANZOSISCHEN KULTURPROPAGANDA AM RHEIN. FRANCE MOD/EUR DOMIN PRESS...GEOG METH/COMP 20. PAGE 75 A1544
EDU/PROP ATTIT DIPLOM NAT/G

B33
PUBLIC OPINION AND WORLD POLITICS. UNIV LAW CULTURE NAT/G PRESS REV GP/REL...MAJORIT METH/COMP ANTHOL 20. PAGE 167 A3400
DIPLOM EDU/PROP ATTIT MAJORITY

B40
FULLER G.H.,A LIST OF BIBLIOGRAPHIES ON PROPAGANDA (PAMPHLET). MOD/EUR USA-45 CONSULT ACT/RES PRESS FEEDBACK TASK WAR ATTIT PWR...CON/ANAL METH/COMP 20. PAGE 50 A1020
BIBLIOG/A EDU/PROP DOMIN DIPLOM

B41
BAUMANN G.,GRUNDLAGEN UND PRAXIS DER INTERNATIONALEN PROPAGANDA. FRANCE GERMANY UK CULTURE COM/IND PRESS PWR...PSY METH/COMP 20. PAGE 12 A0236
EDU/PROP DOMIN ATTIT DIPLOM

B41
NIEMEYER G.,LAW WITHOUT FORCE: THE FUNCTION OF POLITICS IN INTERNATIONAL LAW. PLAN INSPECT DIPLOM REPAR LEGIT ADJUD WAR ORD/FREE...IDEA/COMP METH/COMP GEN/LAWS 20. PAGE 109 A2240
COERCE LAW PWR INT/LAW

B48
DURBIN E.F.M.,THE POLITICS OF DEMOCRATIC SOCIALISM; AN ESSAY ON SOCIAL POLICY. STRATA POL/PAR PLAN COERCE DRIVE PERSON PWR MARXISM...CHARTS METH/COMP. PAGE 39 A0805
SOCIALIST POPULISM POLICY SOCIETY

B50
DE RUSETT A.,STRENGTHENING THE FRAMEWORK OF PEACE. WOR+45 VOL/ASSN FORCES CREATE INSPECT ADJUD CONTROL WAR EQUILIB FEDERAL ORD/FREE 20 UN EUROPE. PAGE 35 A0711
INT/ORG DIPLOM PEACE METH/COMP

B50
LEVI W.,FUNDAMENTALS OF WORLD ORGANIZATION. WOR+45 WOR-45 CULTURE ECO/TAC GIVE RECEIVE PERSON WEALTH ...METH/COMP 19/20 UN LEAGUE/NAT. PAGE 88 A1793
INT/ORG PEACE ORD/FREE DIPLOM

B51
BROGAN D.W.,THE PRICE OF REVOLUTION. FRANCE USA+45 USA-45 USSR CONSTN NAT/G DIPLOM COLONIAL NAT/LISM ORD/FREE POPULISM...CONCPT 18/20 PRE/US/AM. PAGE 19 A0386
REV METH/COMP COST MARXISM

B53
MATLOFF M.,STRATEGIC PLANNING FOR COALITION WARFARE. UK USA-45 CHIEF DIPLOM EXEC GOV/REL ...METH/COMP 20. PAGE 96 A1967
WAR PLAN DECISION FORCES

B55
HOGAN W.N.,INTERNATIONAL CONFLICT AND COLLECTIVE SECURITY: THE PRINCIPLE OF CONCERN IN INTERNATIONAL ORGANIZATION. CONSTN EX/STRUC BAL/PWR DIPLOM ADJUD CONTROL CENTRAL CONSEN PEACE...INT/LAW CONCPT METH/COMP 20 UN LEAGUE/NAT. PAGE 66 A1361
INT/ORG WAR ORD/FREE FORCES

B55
O3HEVSS E.,WIRTSCHAFTSSYSTEME UND INTERNATIONALER HANDEL. ECO/DEV FINAN MARKET DIPLOM ECO/TAC COST ...METH/COMP NAT/COMP 20. PAGE 112 A2306
CAP/ISM SOCISM INT/TRADE IDEA/COMP

B55
PANT Y.P.,PLANNING IN UNDERDEVELOPED ECONOMIES. INDIA NEPAL INT/TRADE COLONIAL SOVEREIGN ALL/IDEOS ...TIME/SEQ METH/COMP 20. PAGE 114 A2334
ECO/UNDEV PLAN ECO/TAC DIPLOM

B57
ALEXANDER L.M.,WORLD POLITICAL PATTERNS. NAT/G PROVS CAP/ISM DIPLOM COLONIAL NAT/LISM...POLICY GEOG CHARTS METH/COMP NAT/COMP 20. PAGE 5 A0111
CONTROL METH GOV/COMP

B57
MCNEILL W.H.,GREECE: AMERICAN AID IN ACTION. GREECE UK USA+45 FINAN CAP/ISM INT/TRADE BAL/PAY PRODUC WEALTH...POLICY METH/COMP 20. PAGE 99 A2022
FOR/AID DIPLOM ECO/UNDEV

B57
UNESCO,A REGISTER OF LEGAL DOCUMENTATION IN THE WORLD (2ND ED.). CT/SYS...JURID IDEA/COMP METH/COMP NAT/COMP 20. PAGE 148 A3019
BIBLIOG
LAW
INT/LAW
CONSTN

B59
KNIERIEM A.,THE NUREMBERG TRIALS. EUR+WWI GERMANY VOL/ASSN LEAD COERCE WAR INGP/REL TOTALISM SUPEGO ORD/FREE...CONCPT METH/COMP. PAGE 80 A1651
INT/LAW
CRIME
PARTIC
JURID

B59
ROPKE W.,INTERNATIONAL ORDER AND ECONOMIC INTEGRATION. ECO/DEV ECO/UNDEV AGRI FINAN INDUS INT/ORG WAR PEACE ORD/FREE...SOC METH/COMP 20 EEC. PAGE 123 A2524
INT/TRADE
DIPLOM
BAL/PAY
ALL/IDEOS

B59
SWIFT R.W.,WORLD AFFAIRS AND THE COLLEGE CURRICULUM. USA+45 PLAN EFFICIENCY PERCEPT...HUM METH/CNCPT. PAGE 140 A2871
ACADEM
DIPLOM
METH/COMP
EDU/PROP

B60
HOFFMANN P.G.,ONE HUNDRED COUNTRIES, ONE AND ONE QUARTER BILLION PEOPLE. MARKET INT/ORG TEC/DEV CAP/ISM...GEOG CHARTS METH/COMP 20 UN. PAGE 66 A1354
FOR/AID
ECO/TAC
ECO/UNDEV
INT/TRADE

B60
HOFFMANN S.H.,CONTEMPORARY THEORY IN INTERNATIONAL RELATIONS. RATIONAL...SOC METH/CNCPT METH/COMP SIMUL ANTHOL 20. PAGE 66 A1359
DIPLOM
METH
PHIL/SCI
DECISION

B60
LATIFI D.,INDIA AND UNITED STATES AID. ASIA INDIA UK USA+45 AGRI FINAN INDUS COLONIAL ORD/FREE SOVEREIGN WEALTH...METH/COMP 20. PAGE 85 A1743
FOR/AID
DIPLOM
ECO/UNDEV

B60
MEYRIAT J.,LA SCIENCE POLITIQUE EN FRANCE, 1945-1958; BIBLIOGRAPHIES FRANCAISES DE SCIENCES SOCIALES (VOL. I). EUR+WWI FRANCE POL/PAR DIPLOM ADMIN CHOOSE ATTIT...IDEA/COMP METH/COMP NAT/COMP 20. PAGE 100 A2057
BIBLIOG/A
NAT/G
CONCPT
PHIL/SCI

B60
PENTONY D.E.,UNITED STATES FOREIGN AID. INDIA LAOS USA+45 ECO/UNDEV INT/TRADE ADMIN PEACE ATTIT ...POLICY METH/COMP ANTHOL 20. PAGE 115 A2352
FOR/AID
DIPLOM
ECO/TAC

B60
STOLPER W.F.,GERMANY BETWEEN EAST AND WEST: THE ECONOMICS OF COMPETITIVE COEXISTENCE. FUT GERMANY/E GERMANY/W WOR+45 FINAN POL/PAR BUDGET ECO/TAC FOR/AID INT/TRADE...STAT CHARTS METH/COMP 20 COLD/WAR. PAGE 138 A2832
ECO/DEV
DIPLOM
GOV/COMP
BAL/PWR

B61
AUBREY H.G.,COEXISTENCE: ECONOMIC CHALLENGE AND RESPONSE. USSR WOR+45 ACT/RES BAL/PWR CAP/ISM DIPLOM ECO/TAC FOR/AID INT/TRADE PEACE SOCISM ...METH/COMP NAT/COMP COLD/WAR. PAGE 10 A0196
POLICY
ECO/UNDEV
PLAN
COM

B61
BAINS J.S.,STUDIES IN POLITICAL SCIENCE. INDIA WOR+45 WOR-45 CONSTN BAL/PWR ADJUD ADMIN PARL/PROC SOVEREIGN...SOC METH/COMP ANTHOL 17/20 UN. PAGE 10 A0209
DIPLOM
INT/LAW
NAT/G

B61
HARRIS S.E.,THE DOLLAR IN CRISIS. USA+45 MARKET INT/ORG ECO/TAC PRICE CONTROL WEALTH...METH/COMP ANTHOL 20 GOLD/STAND. PAGE 62 A1269
BAL/PAY
DIPLOM
FINAN
INT/TRADE

B62
NOBECOURT R.G.,LES SECRETS DE LA PROPAGANDE EN FRANCE OCCUPEE. FRANCE ELITES NAT/G DIPLOM GP/REL NAT/LISM TOTALISM ORD/FREE 20 VICHY VICHY. PAGE 109 A2244
METH/COMP
EDU/PROP
WAR
CONTROL

B62
POSTON R.W.,DEMOCRACY SPEAKS MANY TONGUES. L/A+17C USA+45 ECO/UNDEV ACT/RES ECO/TAC ADMIN ORD/FREE ...METH/COMP 20. PAGE 117 A2397
FOR/AID
DIPLOM
CAP/ISM
MARXISM

B63
EL-NAGGAR S.,FOREIGN AID TO UNITED ARAB REPUBLIC. UAR USA+45 USSR AGRI FINAN INDUS FORCES EATING DEMAND...CHARTS METH/COMP 20 RESOURCE/N AID. PAGE 41 A0838
FOR/AID
ECO/UNDEV
RECEIVE
PLAN

B63
FATEMI N.S.,THE DOLLAR CRISIS. USA+45 INDUS NAT/G LEGIS BUDGET TAX COST...CHARTS METH/COMP 20 EEC. PAGE 44 A0902
PROB/SOLV
BAL/PAY
FOR/AID
PLAN

B63
FULBRIGHT J.W.,PROSPECTS FOR THE WEST. COM USA+45 USSR INT/ORG NAT/G SCHOOL PROB/SOLV NUC/PWR WAR PEACE ORD/FREE...PREDICT METH/COMP 20 DEGAULLE/C. PAGE 50 A1015
DIPLOM
BAL/PWR
CONCPT
POLICY

B63
GUIMARAES A.P.,INFLACAO E MONOPOLIO NO BRASIL. BRAZIL FINAN NAT/G PLAN PAY...METH/COMP 20. PAGE 58 A1189
ECO/UNDEV
PRICE
INT/TRADE
BAL/PAY

B63
HONORD S.,PUBLIC RELATIONS IN ADMINISTRATION. WOR+45 NAT/G...SOC/WK BIBLIOG 20. PAGE 67 A1379
PRESS
DIPLOM
MGT
METH/COMP

B63
MALIK C.,MAN IN THE STRUGGLE FOR PEACE. USSR WOR+45 CHIEF PLAN PROB/SOLV PARTIC NUC/PWR REV ORD/FREE ...IDEA/COMP METH/COMP 20 UN COLD/WAR. PAGE 93 A1912
PEACE
MARXISM
DIPLOM
EDU/PROP

B63
US DEPARTMENT OF STATE,POLITICAL BEHAVIOR--A LIST OF CURRENT STUDIES. USA+45 COM/IND DIPLOM LEAD PERS/REL DRIVE PERCEPT KNOWL...DECISION SIMUL METH. PAGE 151 A3093
BIBLIOG
METH/COMP
GP/REL
ATTIT

B63
YOUNG A.N.,CHINA AND THE HELPING HAND. ASIA USA+45 FINAN INDUS ECO/TAC GIVE WEALTH...METH/COMP 20 LEND/LEASE GOLD/STAND. PAGE 169 A3434
FOR/AID
DIPLOM
WAR

B64
COHEN M.L.,SELECTED BIBLIOGRAPHY OF FOREIGN AND INTERNATIONAL LAW....IDEA/COMP METH/COMP 20. PAGE 28 A0562
BIBLIOG/A
JURID
LAW
INT/LAW

B64
KALDOR N.,ESSAYS ON ECONOMIC POLICY (VOL. II). CHILE GERMANY INDIA FINAN...GOV/COMP METH/COMP 20 KEYNES/JM. PAGE 76 A1551
BAL/PAY
INT/TRADE
METH/CNCPT
ECO/UNDEV

B64
KAUFMANN W.W.,THE MC NAMARA STRATEGY. TOP/EX INSPECT BAL/PWR DIPLOM CONTROL DETER GUERRILLA NUC/PWR WEAPON COST PWR...METH/COMP 20 MCNAMARA/R KENNEDY/JF JOHNSON/LB NATO DEPT/DEFEN. PAGE 77 A1572
FORCES
WAR
PLAN
PROB/SOLV

B64
KNIGHT R.,BIBLIOGRAPHY ON INCOME AND WEALTH, 1957-1960 (VOL VIII). WOR+45 ECO/DEV FINAN INT/TRADE...GOV/COMP METH/COMP. PAGE 80 A1652
BIBLIOG/A
ECO/UNDEV
WEALTH
INCOME

B64
RANIS G.,THE UNITED STATES AND THE DEVELOPING ECONOMIES. COM USA+45 AGRI FINAN TEC/DEV CAP/ISM ECO/TAC INT/TRADE...POLICY METH/COMP ANTHOL 20 AID. PAGE 119 A2441
ECO/UNDEV
DIPLOM
FOR/AID

B64
ROCK V.P.,A STRATEGY OF INTERDEPENDENCE. COM USSR WOR+45 NAT/G FORCES PROB/SOLV TEC/DEV DETER WAR ORD/FREE...CONCPT NEW/IDEA METH/COMP 20. PAGE 122 A2509
DIPLOM
NUC/PWR
PEACE
POLICY

B64
RUBIN J.A.,YOUR HUNDRED BILLION DOLLARS. USA+45 USSR INDUS INT/ORG TEC/DEV ECO/TAC...METH/COMP 20 PEACE/CORP. PAGE 125 A2559
FOR/AID
DIPLOM
ECO/UNDEV

B64
SZLADITS C.,BIBLIOGRAPHY ON FOREIGN AND COMPARATIVE LAW: BOOKS AND ARTICLES IN ENGLISH (SUPPLEMENT 1962). FINAN INDUS JUDGE LICENSE ADMIN CT/SYS PARL/PROC OWN...INT/LAW CLASSIF METH/COMP NAT/COMP 20. PAGE 141 A2877
BIBLIOG/A
JURID
ADJUD
LAW

B64
TULLY A.,WHERE DID YOUR MONEY GO. USA+45 USSR ECO/UNDEV ADMIN EFFICIENCY WEALTH...METH/COMP 20. PAGE 146 A2976
FOR/AID
DIPLOM
CONTROL

B64
ZEBOT C.A.,THE ECONOMICS OF COMPETITIVE COEXISTENCE. CHINA/COM USSR WOR+45 FINAN MARKET FOR/AID PRICE DEMAND EQUILIB WEALTH ALL/IDEOS 20. PAGE 169 A3450
TEC/DEV
DIPLOM
METH/COMP

B65
FRANKLAND N.,THE BOMBING OFFENSIVE AGAINST GERMANY. GERMANY UK TEC/DEV DIPLOM WAR...METH/COMP 20. PAGE 48 A0985
WEAPON
PLAN
DECISION
FORCES

B65
MEYERHOFF A.E.,THE STRATEGY OF PERSUASION: THE USE OF ADVERTISING SKILLS IN FIGHTING THE COLD WAR. USA+45 USSR PLAN ATTIT DRIVE...BIBLIOG 20 COLD/WAR. PAGE 100 A2054
EDU/PROP
SERV/IND
METH/COMP
DIPLOM

B65
US BUREAU OF THE BUDGET,THE BALANCE OF PAYMENTS STATISTICS OF THE UNITED STATES: A REVIEW AND APPRAISAL. USA+45 FINAN NAT/G PROB/SOLV DIPLOM. PAGE 150 A3057
BAL/PAY
STAT
METH/COMP
BUDGET

B66
AMERICAN ASSEMBLY COLUMBIA U,A WORLD OF NUCLEAR POWERS? FUT WOR+45 ECO/DEV BAL/PWR ECO/TAC CONTROL RISK EFFICIENCY ATTIT PWR...METH/COMP ANTHOL 20. PAGE 7 A0137
NUC/PWR
DIPLOM
TEC/DEV
ARMS/CONT

B66
FABAR R.,THE VISION AND THE NEED: LATE VICTORIAN IMPERIALIST AIMS. MOD/EUR UK WOR-45 CULTURE NAT/G DIPLOM...TIME/SEQ METH/COMP 19 KIPLING/R COMMONWLTH. PAGE 43 A0880
COLONIAL
CONCPT
ADMIN
ATTIT

B66
FINKLE J.L.,POLITICAL DEVELOPMENT AND SOCIAL
ECO/UNDEV

CHANGE. WOR+45 CULTURE NAT/G OP/RES PROB/SOLV DIPLOM ECO/TAC INGP/REL...METH/COMP ANTHOL 20. PAGE 46 A0934 — SOCIETY CREATE

B66
HOEVELER H.J.,INTERNATIONALE BEKAMPFUNG DES VERBRECHENS. AUSTRIA SWITZERLND WOR+45 INT/ORG CONTROL BIO/SOC...METH/COMP NAT/COMP 20 MAFIA SCOT/YARD FBI. PAGE 66 A1352 — CRIMLGY CRIME DIPLOM INT/LAW

B66
MONTGOMERY J.D.,APPROACHES TO DEVELOPMENT: POLITICS, ADMINISTRATION AND CHANGE. USA+45 AGRI FOR/AID ORD/FREE...CONCPT IDEA/COMP METH/COMP ANTHOL. PAGE 103 A2116 — ECO/UNDEV ADMIN POLICY ECO/TAC

B66
O'CONNER A.M.,AN ECONOMIC GEOGRAPHY OF EAST AFRICA. AFR TANZANIA UGANDA AGRI WORKER INT/TRADE COLONIAL GOV/REL...CHARTS METH/COMP 20 AFRICA/E. PAGE 111 A2269 — ECO/UNDEV EXTR/IND GEOG HABITAT

B66
SPULBER N.,THE STATE AND ECONOMIC DEVELOPMENT IN EASTERN EUROPE. BULGARIA COM CZECHOSLVK HUNGARY POLAND YUGOSLAVIA CULTURE PLAN CAP/ISM INT/TRADE CONTROL...POLICY CHARTS METH/COMP BIBLIOG/A 19/20. PAGE 136 A2793 — ECO/DEV ECO/UNDEV NAT/G TOTALISM

B66
TRIFFIN R.,THE WORLD MONEY MAZE. INT/ORG ECO/TAC PRICE OPTIMAL WEALTH...METH/COMP 20 EEC OEEC GOLD/STAND SILVER. PAGE 145 A2964 — BAL/PAY FINAN INT/TRADE DIPLOM

B66
WAINHOUSE D.W.,INTERNATIONAL PEACE OBSERVATION: A HISTORY AND FORECAST. INT/ORG PROB/SOLV BAL/PWR AGREE ARMS/CONT COERCE NUC/PWR...PREDICT METH/COMP 20 UN LEAGUE/NAT OAS TREATY. PAGE 160 A3261 — PEACE DIPLOM

B67
CLARK S.V.O.,CENTRAL BANK COOPERATION: 1924-31. WOR-45 PROB/SOLV ECO/TAC ADJUST BAL/PAY...TREND CHARTS METH/COMP 20. PAGE 27 A0542 — FINAN EQUILIB DIPLOM POLICY

B67
HALPERIN M.H.,CONTEMPORARY MILITARY STRATEGY. ASIA CHINA/COM USA+45 USSR INT/ORG FORCES ACT/RES PLAN TEC/DEV BAL/PWR COERCE WAR...METH/COMP BIBLIOG 20 NATO. PAGE 60 A1240 — DIPLOM NUC/PWR DETER ARMS/CONT

B67
HIRSCHMAN A.O.,DEVELOPMENT PROJECTS OBSERVED. INDUS INT/ORG CONSULT EX/STRUC CREATE OP/RES ECO/TAC DEMAND...POLICY MGT METH/COMP 20 WORLD/BANK. PAGE 65 A1339 — ECO/UNDEV R+D FINAN PLAN

B67
HOHENBERG J.,BETWEEN TWO WORLDS. ASIA S/ASIA USA+45 PRESS TV PERS/REL ISOLAT...INT CHARTS METH/COMP 20. PAGE 66 A1362 — COM/IND DIPLOM EFFICIENCY KNOWL

B67
WATERS M.,THE UNITED NATIONS* INTERNATIONAL ORGANIZATION AND ADMINISTRATION. WOR+45 EX/STRUC FORCES DIPLOM LEAD REGION ARMS/CONT REPRESENT INGP/REL ROLE...METH/COMP ANTHOL 20 UN LEAGUE/NAT. PAGE 162 A3291 — CONSTN INT/ORG ADMIN ADJUD

S67
FRANKLIN W.O.,"CLAUSEWITZ ON LIMITED WAR." VIETNAM WOR+45 WOR-45 PROB/SOLV DIPLOM ECO/TAC DOMIN COLONIAL...METH/COMP 19/20. PAGE 48 A0986 — COERCE WAR PLAN GUERRILLA

S67
GRIFFITHS F.,"THE POLITICAL SIDE OF 'DISARMAMENT'." FUT WOR+45 NUC/PWR NAT/LISM PEACE...NEW/IDEA PREDICT METH/COMP GEN/LAWS 20. PAGE 57 A1164 — ARMS/CONT DIPLOM

S67
ROSE S.,"ASIAN NATIONALISM* THE SECOND STAGE." ASIA COM ECO/UNDEV NAT/G PROB/SOLV DIPLOM FOR/AID DOMIN NEUTRAL REGION TASK...METH/COMP 20. PAGE 123 A2528 — NAT/LISM S/ASIA BAL/PWR COLONIAL

S67
SENCOURT R.,"FOREIGN POLICY* AN HISTORIC RECTIFICATION." EUR+WWI UK DIPLOM EDU/PROP LEAD WAR CHOOSE PERS/REL...METH/COMP PARLIAMENT. PAGE 131 A2685 — POLICY POL/PAR NAT/G

S67
THOMPSON K.W.,"THE EMPIRICAL, NORMATIVE, AND THEORETICAL FOUNDATIONS OF INTERNATIONAL STUDIES." WOR+45 INGP/REL RATIONAL...CONCPT RECORD IDEA/COMP. PAGE 143 A2932 — DIPLOM INTELL METH/COMP KNOWL

METHOD, COMPARATIVE....SEE IDEA/COMP, METH/COMP

METHODOLOGY....SEE METH, PHIL/SCI, METHODOLOGICAL INDEXES, PP. XIII-XIV

METRO/COUN....METROPOLITAN COUNCIL

METROPOLITAN....SEE MUNIC

METROPOLITAN COUNCIL....SEE METRO/COUN

METTRNCH/K....PRINCE K. VON METTERNICH

B62
SCHRODER P.M.,METTERNICH'S DIPLOMACY AT ITS ZENITH, 1820-1823. MOD/EUR ELITES INT/ORG VOL/ASSN DELIB/GP ECO/TAC EDU/PROP DISPL PWR SOVEREIGN...POLICY CONCPT GEN/LAWS 19 METTRNCH/K. PAGE 129 A2647 — ORD/FREE BIOG BAL/PWR DIPLOM

METZ I. A2047

MEXIC/AMER....MEXICAN-AMERICANS; SEE ALSO SPAN/AMER

B08
GRIFFIN A.P.C.,LIST OF REFERENCES ON INTERNATIONAL ARBITRATION. FRANCE L/A+17C USA-45 WOR-45 DIPLOM CONFER COLONIAL ARMS/CONT BAL/PAY EQUILIB SOVEREIGN ...DECISION 19/20 MEXIC/AMER. PAGE 56 A1156 — BIBLIOG/A INT/ORG INT/LAW DELIB/GP

B43
BEMIS S.F.,THE LATIN AMERICAN POLICY OF THE UNITED STATES: AN HISTORICAL INTERPRETATION. INT/ORG AGREE COLONIAL WAR PEACE ATTIT ORD/FREE...POLICY INT/LAW CHARTS 18/20 MEXIC/AMER WILSON/W MONROE/DOC. PAGE 13 A0265 — DIPLOM SOVEREIGN USA-45 L/A+17C

B43
CARLO A.M.,ENSAYO DE UNA BIBLIOGRAFIA DE BIBLIOGRAFIAS MEXICANAS. ECO/UNDEV LOC/G ADMIN LEAD 20 MEXIC/AMER. PAGE 24 A0485 — BIBLIOG L/A+17C NAT/G DIPLOM

B45
VANCE H.L.,GUIDE TO THE LAW AND LEGAL LITERATURE OF MEXICO. LAW CONSTN FINAN LABOR FORCES ADJUD ADMIN ...CRIMLGY PHIL/SCI CON/ANAL 20 MEXIC/AMER. PAGE 158 A3217 — BIBLIOG/A INT/LAW JURID CT/SYS

B59
LOPEZ M.M.,CATALOGOS DE PUBLICACIONES PERIODICAS MEXICANAS. L/A+17C CULTURE NAT/G DIPLOM 20 MEXIC/AMER. PAGE 91 A1861 — BIBLIOG PRESS CON/ANAL

B59
RICE E.A.,THE DIPLOMATIC RELATIONS BETWEEN THE UNITED STATES AND MEXICO 1925-1929. USA-45 NAT/G DOMIN PEACE ORD/FREE CATHISM 20 MEXIC/AMER. PAGE 121 A2472 — DIPLOM SECT POLICY

B60
CONN S.,THE FRAMEWORK OF HEMISPHERE DEFENSE. CANADA L/A+17C USA-45 NAT/G FORCES BAL/PWR DOMIN WAR PEACE DISPL PWR RESPECT...PLURIST CONCPT HIST/WRIT HYPO/EXP MEXIC/AMER 20 ROOSEVLT/F. PAGE 29 A0585 — USA+45 INT/ORG DIPLOM

B62
QUIRK R.E.,AN AFFAIR OF HONOR: WOODROW WILSON AND THE OCCUPATION OF VERACRUZ. L/A+17C USA-45 COLONIAL SUPEGO PWR 20 WILSON/W MEXIC/AMER. PAGE 118 A2428 — DOMIN DIPLOM COERCE PROB/SOLV

S62
CORET A.,"LA DECLARATION DE L'ASSEMBLEE GENERAL DE L'ONU SUR L'OCTROI DE L'INDEPENDENCE AUX PAYS ET AUX PEUPLES." AFR ASIA ISLAM NIGERIA S/ASIA USSR WOR+45 ECO/UNDEV NAT/G DELIB/GP COLONIAL ALL/VALS ...CONCPT TIME/SEQ TREND UN TOT/POP 20 MEXIC/AMER. PAGE 31 A0621 — INT/ORG STRUCT SOVEREIGN

B64
WITHERS W.,THE ECONOMIC CRISIS IN LATIN AMERICA. BRAZIL CHILE STRATA AGRI DIPLOM FOR/AID PWR SOCISM ...POLICY 20 MEXIC/AMER ARGEN. PAGE 166 A3372 — L/A+17C ECO/UNDEV CAP/ISM ALL/IDEOS

B65
MEDIVA J.T.,LA IMPRENTA EN MEXICO, 1539-1821 (8 VOLS.). SOCIETY ECO/UNDEV DIPLOM COLONIAL GP/REL 16/19 MEXIC/AMER. PAGE 99 A2031 — BIBLIOG WRITING NAT/G L/A+17C

B67
JOHNSON D.G.,THE STRUGGLE AGAINST WORLD HUNGER (HEADLINE SERIES, NO. 184) (PAMPHLET). PLAN TEC/DEV FOR/AID...CHARTS 20 FAO MEXIC/AMER. PAGE 74 A1520 — AGRI PROB/SOLV ECO/UNDEV HEALTH

B67
TEITELBAUM L.M.,WOODROW WILSON AND THE MEXICAN REVOLUTION 1913-1916: A HISTORY OF UNITED STATES-MEXICAN RELATIONS. USA-45 CHIEF TOP/EX WAR 20 MEXIC/AMER WILSON/W VILLA/P CARRANZA/V. PAGE 142 A2902 — REV DIPLOM

S67
FABREGA J.,"ANTECEDENTES EXTRANJEROS EN LA CONSTITUCION PANAMENA." CUBA L/A+17C PANAMA URUGUAY EX/STRUC LEGIS DIPLOM ORD/FREE 19/20 COLOMB MEXIC/AMER. PAGE 43 A0882 — CONSTN JURID NAT/G PARL/PROC

MEXICO....SEE ALSO L/A+17C

MEYER F.S. A2048

MEYER H.H.B. A1157,A2049,A2050,A2051,A2052

MEYER J. A2053

MEYERHOFF A.E. A2054

MEYNAUD J. A2055

MEYRIAT J. A0808,A0809,A2056,A2057

MEYROWITZ H. A2058

MEZERIK A.G. A2059,A2060,A2061,A2062

MEZERIK AG A2063 ,A2064

MGT....MANAGEMENT

N
INTERNATIONAL REVIEW OF ADMINISTRATIVE SCIENCES. WOR+45 WOR-45 STRATA ECO/DEV ECO/UNDEV CREATE PLAN PROB/SOLV DIPLOM CONTROL REPRESENT...MGT 20. PAGE 1 A0011
BIBLIOG/A ADMIN INT/ORG NAT/G

N
ARBITRATION JOURNAL. WOR+45 LAW INDUS JUDGE DIPLOM CT/SYS INGP/REL 20. PAGE 2 A0027
BIBLIOG MGT LABOR ADJUD

N
AUSTRALIAN PUBLIC AFFAIRS INFORMATION SERVICE. LAW ...HEAL HUM MGT SOC CON/ANAL 20 AUSTRAL. PAGE 2 A0028
BIBLIOG NAT/G CULTURE DIPLOM

N
LATIN AMERICA IN PERIODICAL LITERATURE. LAW TEC/DEV DIPLOM RECEIVE EDU/PROP...GEOG HUM MGT 20. PAGE 2 A0037
BIBLIOG/A L/A+17C SOCIETY ECO/UNDEV

N
AMERICAN ECONOMIC ASSOCIATION,THE JOURNAL OF ECONOMIC ABSTRACTS. ECO/UNDEV MARKET LABOR DIPLOM ...MGT CONCPT METH 20. PAGE 7 A0144
BIBLIOG/A R+D FINAN

N
DEUTSCHE BUCHEREI,JAHRESVERZEICHNIS DES DEUTSCHEN SCHRIFTUMS. AUSTRIA EUR+WWI GERMANY SWITZERLND LAW LOC/G DIPLOM ADMIN...MGT SOC 19/20. PAGE 37 A0745
BIBLIOG WRITING NAT/G

N
KYRIAK T.E.,EAST EUROPE: BIBLIOGRAPHY--INDEX TO US JPRS RESEARCH TRANSLATIONS. ALBANIA BULGARIA COM CZECHOSLVK HUNGARY POLAND ROMANIA AGRI EXTR/IND FINAN SERV/IND INT/TRADE WEAPON...GEOG MGT SOC 20. PAGE 83 A1701
BIBLIOG/A PRESS MARXISM INDUS

N
RAND SCHOOL OF SOCIAL SCIENCE,INDEX TO LABOR ARTICLES. ECO/DEV INT/ORG LEGIS DIPLOM GP/REL ...NAT/COMP 20. PAGE 119 A2440
BIBLIOG LABOR MGT ADJUD

B17
UPTON E.,THE MILITARY POLICY OF THE US. USA-45 STRUCT INT/ORG EXEC ATTIT PERCEPT...MGT CONCPT OBS HIST/WRIT CHARTS CONGRESS 18/20. PAGE 149 A3049
FORCES SKILL WAR

B31
HILL N.,INTERNATIONAL ADMINISTRATION. WOR-45 DELIB/GP DIPLOM EDU/PROP ALL/VALS...MGT TIME/SEQ LEAGUE/NAT TOT/POP VAL/FREE 20. PAGE 65 A1331
INT/ORG ADMIN

B32
EAGLETON C.,INTERNATIONAL GOVERNMENT. BRAZIL FRANCE GERMANY ITALY UK USSR WOR-45 DELIB/GP TOP/EX PLAN ECO/TAC EDU/PROP LEGIT ADJUD REGION ARMS/CONT COERCE ATTIT PWR...GEOG MGT VAL/FREE LEAGUE/NAT 20. PAGE 40 A0816
INT/ORG JURID DIPLOM INT/LAW

B37
GALLOWAY G.B.,AMERICAN PAMPHLET LITERATURE OF PUBLIC AFFAIRS (PAMPHLET). USA-45 ECO/DEV LABOR ADMIN...MGT 20. PAGE 51 A1034
BIBLIOG/A PLAN DIPLOM NAT/G

B45
PASTUHOV V.D.,A GUIDE TO THE PRACTICE OF INTERNATIONAL CONFERENCES. WOR+45 PLAN LEGIT ORD/FREE...MGT OBS RECORD VAL/FREE ILO LEAGUE/NAT 20. PAGE 114 A2338
INT/ORG DELIB/GP

B45
RANSHOFFEN-WERTHEIMER EF,THE INTERNATIONAL SECRETARIAT: A GREAT EXPERIMENT IN INTERNATIONAL ADMINISTRATION. EUR+WWI FUT CONSTN FACE/GP CONSULT DELIB/GP ACT/RES ADMIN ROUTINE PEACE ORD/FREE...MGT RECORD ORG/CHARTS LEAGUE/NAT WORK 20. PAGE 119 A2442
INT/ORG EXEC

B45
ROGERS W.C.,INTERNATIONAL ADMINISTRATION: A BIBLIOGRAPHY (PUBLICATION NO 92; A PAMPHLET). WOR-45 INT/ORG LOC/G NAT/G CENTRAL 20. PAGE 123 A2514
BIBLIOG/A ADMIN MGT DIPLOM

B52
THOM J.M.,GUIDE TO RESEARCH MATERIAL IN POLITICAL SCIENCE (PAMPHLET). ELITES LOC/G MUNIC NAT/G LEGIS DIPLOM ADJUD CIVMIL/REL GOV/REL PWR MGT. PAGE 143 A2919
BIBLIOG/A KNOWL

B52
UNESCO,THESES DE SCIENCES SOCIALES: CATALOGUE ANALYTIQUE INTERNATIONAL DE THESES INEDITES DE DOCTORAT, 1940-1950. INT/ORG DIPLOM EDU/PROP...GEOG INT/LAW MGT PSY SOC 20. PAGE 147 A3015
BIBLIOG ACADEM WRITING

L52
HILSMAN R. JR.,"INTELLIGENCE AND POLICY MAKING IN FOREIGN AFFAIRS." USA+45 CONSULT ACT/RES DIPLOM EDU/PROP ROUTINE PEACE PERCEPT PWR SKILL...POLICY MGT HYPO/EXP CONGRESS 20 CIA. PAGE 65 A1333
PROF/ORG SIMUL WAR

S52
SCHWEBEL S.M.,"THE SECRETARY-GENERAL OF THE UN." FUT INTELL CONSULT DELIB/GP ADMIN PEACE ATTIT ...JURID MGT CONCPT TREND UN CONGRESS 20. PAGE 130 A2663
INT/ORG TOP/EX

B53
LARSEN K.,NATIONAL BIBLIOGRAPHIC SERVICES: THEIR CREATION AND OPERATION. WOR+45 COM/IND CREATE PLAN DIPLOM PRESS ADMIN ROUTINE...MGT UNESCO. PAGE 85 A1733
BIBLIOG/A INT/ORG WRITING

B53
MACK R.T.,RAISING THE WORLDS STANDARD OF LIVING. IRAN INT/ORG VOL/ASSN EX/STRUC ECO/TAC WEALTH...MGT METH/CNCPT STAT CONT/OBS INT TOT/POP VAL/FREE 20 UN. PAGE 92 A1893
WOR+45 FOR/AID INT/TRADE

C54
BERLE A.A. JR.,"THE 20TH CENTURY CAPITALIST REVOLUTION." ECO/DEV NAT/G DIPLOM PRICE CONTROL ATTIT...BIBLIOG/A 20. PAGE 14 A0275
LG/CO CAP/ISM MGT PWR

B55
MACMAHON A.W.,FEDERALISM: MATURE AND EMERGENT. EUR+WWI FUT WOR+45 WOR-45 INT/ORG NAT/G REPRESENT FEDERAL...POLICY MGT RECORD TREND GEN/LAWS 20. PAGE 93 A1900
STRUCT CONCPT

B55
SNYDER R.C.,AMERICAN FOREIGN POLICY. USA+45 USA-45 WOR+45 WOR-45 CONSTN INT/ORG POL/PAR VOL/ASSN DELIB/GP LEGIS CREATE DOMIN EDU/PROP EXEC COERCE ATTIT DRIVE ORD/FREE PWR...MGT OBS RECORD TIME/SEQ TREND. PAGE 134 A2752
NAT/G DIPLOM

L55
KISER M.,"ORGANIZATION OF AMERICAN STATES." L/A+17C USA+45 ECO/UNDEV INT/ORG NAT/G PLAN TEC/DEV DIPLOM ECO/TAC INT/TRADE EDU/PROP ADMIN ALL/VALS...POLICY MGT RECORD ORG/CHARTS OAS 20. PAGE 80 A1639
VOL/ASSN ECO/DEV REGION

B56
GEORGE A.L.,WOODROW WILSON AND COLONEL HOUSE. WOR-45 CONSTN FACE/GP INT/ORG NAT/G POL/PAR CONSULT LEGIT EXEC COERCE CHOOSE ATTIT DRIVE PERSON MORAL ORD/FREE PWR RESPECT...POLICY MGT PSY OBS RECORD INT LEAGUE/NAT. PAGE 52 A1060
USA-45 BIOG DIPLOM

B56
LOVEDAY A.,REFLECTIONS ON INTERNATIONAL ADMINISTRATION. WOR+45 WOR-45 DELIB/GP ACT/RES ADMIN EXEC ROUTINE DRIVE...METH/CNCPT TIME/SEQ CON/ANAL SIMUL TOT/POP 20. PAGE 91 A1865
INT/ORG MGT

B56
WU E.,LEADERS OF TWENTIETH-CENTURY CHINA; AN ANNOTATED BIBLIOGRAPHY OF SELECTED CHINESE BIOGRAPHICAL WORKS IN HOOVER LIBRARY. ASIA INDUS POL/PAR DIPLOM ADMIN REV WAR...HUM MGT 20. PAGE 168 A3422
BIBLIOG/A BIOG INTELL CHIEF

B57
FULLER C.D.,TRAINING OF SPECIALISTS IN INTERNATIONAL RELATIONS. FUT USA+45 USA-45 INTELL INT/ORG...MGT METH/CNCPT INT QU GEN/METH 20. PAGE 50 A1017
KNOWL DIPLOM

B58
GANGE J.,UNIVERSITY RESEARCH ON INTERNATIONAL AFFAIRS. USA+45 ACADEM INT/ORG CONSULT CREATE EXEC ROUTINE...QUANT STAT INT STERTYP GEN/METH TOT/POP VAL/FREE 20. PAGE 51 A1040
R+D MGT DIPLOM

S58
BLAISDELL D.C.,"PRESSURE GROUPS, FOREIGN POLICIES, AND INTERNATIONAL POLITICS." USA+45 WOR+45 INT/ORG PLAN DOMIN EDU/PROP LEGIT ADMIN ROUTINE CHOOSE ...DECISION MGT METH/CNCPT CON/ANAL 20. PAGE 15 A0303
PROF/ORG PWR

B59
US PRES COMM STUDY MIL ASSIST,COMPOSITE REPORT. USA+45 ECO/UNDEV PLAN BUDGET DIPLOM EFFICIENCY ...POLICY MGT 20. PAGE 155 A3164
FOR/AID FORCES WEAPON ORD/FREE

B60
AMERICAN ASSEMBLY COLUMBIA U,THE SECRETARY OF STATE. USA+45 ELITES NAT/G PLAN ADMIN GOV/REL CENTRAL ATTIT...POLICY MGT 20 SEC/STATE CONGRESS PRESIDENT. PAGE 7 A0136
DELIB/GP EX/STRUC GP/REL DIPLOM

B60
LEWIS P.R.,LITERATURE OF THE SOCIAL SCIENCES: AN INTRODUCTORY SURVEY AND GUIDE. UK LAW INDUS DIPLOM INT/TRADE ADMIN...MGT 19/20. PAGE 88 A1802
BIBLIOG/A SOC

B60
STEIN E.,AMERICAN ENTERPRISE IN THE EUROPEAN COMMON MARKET: A LEGAL PROFILE. EUR+WWI FUT USA+45 SOCIETY STRUCT ECO/DEV NAT/G VOL/ASSN CONSULT PLAN TEC/DEV ECO/TAC INT/TRADE ADMIN ATTIT RIGID/FLEX PWR...MGT
MARKET ADJUD INT/LAW

NEW/IDEA STAT TREND COMPUT/IR SIMUL EEC 20. PAGE 137 A2814

B60
WOETZEL R.K.,THE INTERNATIONAL CONTROL OF AIRSPACE AND OUTERSPACE. FUT WOR+45 AIR CONSTN STRUCT CONSULT PLAN TEC/DEV ADJUD RIGID/FLEX KNOWL ORD/FREE PWR...TECHNIC GEOG MGT NEW/IDEA TREND COMPUT/IR VAL/FREE 20 TREATY. PAGE 166 A3375
INT/ORG JURID SPACE INT/LAW

S60
FRANKEL S.H.,"ECONOMIC ASPECTS OF POLITICAL INDEPENDENCE IN AFRICA." AFR FUT SOCIETY ECO/UNDEV COM/IND FINAN LEGIS PLAN TEC/DEV CAP/ISM ECO/TAC INT/TRADE ADMIN ATTIT DRIVE RIGID/FLEX PWR WEALTH ...MGT NEW/IDEA MATH TIME/SEQ VAL/FREE 20. PAGE 48 A0984
NAT/G FOR/AID

S60
MODELSKI G.,"AUSTRALIA AND SEATO." S/ASIA USA+45 CULTURE INTELL ECO/DEV NAT/G PLAN DIPLOM ADMIN ROUTINE ATTIT SKILL...MGT TIME/SEQ AUSTRAL 20 SEATO. PAGE 102 A2097
INT/ORG ACT/RES

S60
RIVKIN A.,"AFRICAN ECONOMIC DEVELOPMENT: ADVANCED TECHNOLOGY AND THE STAGES OF GROWTH." CULTURE ECO/UNDEV AGRI COM/IND EXTR/IND PLAN ECO/TAC ATTIT DRIVE RIGID/FLEX SKILL WEALTH...MGT SOC GEN/LAWS WORK TOT/POP 20. PAGE 121 A2487
AFR TEC/DEV FOR/AID

B61
BARNES W.,THE FOREIGN SERVICE OF THE UNITED STATES. USA+45 USA-45 CONSTN INT/ORG POL/PAR CONSULT DELIB/GP LEGIS DOMIN EDU/PROP EXEC ATTIT RIGID/FLEX ORD/FREE PWR...POLICY CONCPT STAT OBS RECORD BIOG TIME/SEQ TREND. PAGE 11 A0224
NAT/G MGT DIPLOM

B61
HARRISON S.,INDIA AND THE UNITED STATES. FUT S/ASIA USA+45 WOR+45 INTELL ECO/DEV ECO/UNDEV AGRI INDUS INT/ORG NAT/G CONSULT EX/STRUC TOP/EX PLAN ECO/TAC NEUTRAL ALL/VALS...MGT TOT/POP 20. PAGE 62 A1272
DELIB/GP ACT/RES FOR/AID INDIA

B61
ROBINSON M.E.,EDUCATION FOR SOCIAL CHANGE: ESTABLISHING INSTITUTES OF PUBLIC AND BUSINESS ADMINISTRATION ABROAD (PAMPHLET). WOR+45 SOCIETY ACADEM CONFER INGP/REL ROLE...SOC CHARTS BIBLIOG 20 ICA. PAGE 122 A2506
FOR/AID EDU/PROP MGT ADJUST

B61
SINGER J.D.,FINANCING INTERNATIONAL ORGANIZATION: THE UNITED NATIONS BUDGET PROCESS. WOR+45 FINAN ACT/RES CREATE PLAN BUDGET ECO/TAC ADMIN ROUTINE ATTIT KNOWL...DECISION METH/CNCPT TIME/SEQ UN 20. PAGE 133 A2726
INT/ORG MGT

S61
BRZEZINSKI Z.K.,"THE ORGANIZATION OF THE COMMUNIST CAMP." COM CZECHOSLVK COM/IND NAT/G DELIB/GP INT/TRADE DOMIN EDU/PROP EXEC ROUTINE COERCE ATTIT PWR...MGT CONCPT TIME/SEQ CHARTS VAL/FREE 20 TREATY. PAGE 20 A0416
VOL/ASSN DIPLOM USSR

B62
CARLSTON K.S.,LAW AND ORGANIZATION IN WORLD SOCIETY. WOR+45 FINAN ECO/TAC DOMIN LEGIT CT/SYS ROUTINE COERCE ORD/FREE PWR WEALTH...PLURIST DECISION JURID MGT METH/CNCPT GEN/LAWS 20. PAGE 24 A0487
INT/ORG LAW

B62
KENT R.K.,FROM MADAGASCAR TO THE MALAGASY REPUBLIC. FRANCE MADAGASCAR DIPLOM NAT/LISM ORD/FREE...MGT 18/20. PAGE 78 A1596
COLONIAL SOVEREIGN REV POL/PAR

B62
THANT U.,THE UNITED NATIONS' DEVELOPMENT DECADE: PROPOSALS FOR ACTION. WOR+45 SOCIETY ECO/UNDEV AGRI COM/IND FINAN R+D MUNIC SCHOOL VOL/ASSN CONSULT PLAN TEC/DEV ECO/TAC EDU/PROP ADMIN ROUTINE RIGID/FLEX...MGT SOC CONCPT UNESCO UN TOT/POP VAL/FREE. PAGE 142 A2906
INT/ORG ALL/VALS

S62
ALBONETTI A.,"IL SECONDO PROGRAMMA QUINQUENNALE 1963-67 ED IL BILANCIO RICERCHE ED INVESTIMENTI PER IL 1963 DELL'ERATOM." EUR+WWI FUT ITALY WOR+45 ECO/DEV SERV/IND INT/ORG TEC/DEV ECO/TAC ATTIT SKILL WEALTH...MGT TIME/SEQ OEEC 20. PAGE 5 A0108
R+D PLAN NUC/PWR

S62
ALGER C.F.,"THE EXTERNAL BUREAUCRACY IN UNITED STATES FOREIGN AFFAIRS." USA+45 WOR+45 SOCIETY COM/IND INT/ORG NAT/G CONSULT EX/STRUC ACT/RES ...MGT SOC CONCPT TREND 20. PAGE 6 A0118
ADMIN ATTIT DIPLOM

S62
MANGIN G.,"LES ACCORDS DE COOPERATION EN MATIERE DE JUSTICE ENTRE LA FRANCE ET LES ETATS AFRICAINS ET MALGACHE." AFR ISLAM WOR+45 STRUCT ECO/UNDEV NAT/G DELIB/GP PERCEPT ALL/VALS...JURID MGT TIME/SEQ 20. PAGE 94 A1919
INT/ORG LAW FRANCE

B63
HONORD S.,PUBLIC RELATIONS IN ADMINISTRATION. WOR+45 NAT/G...SOC/WK BIBLIOG 20. PAGE 67 A1379
PRESS DIPLOM MGT METH/COMP

B63
THORELLI H.B.,INTOP: INTERNATIONAL OPERATIONS SIMULATION: PLAYER'S MANUAL. BRAZIL FINAN OP/RES ADMIN GP/REL INGP/REL PRODUC PERCEPT...DECISION MGT EEC. PAGE 144 A2935
GAME INT/TRADE EDU/PROP LG/CO

B63
TUCKER R.C.,THE SOVIET POLITICAL MIND. WOR+45 ELITES INT/ORG NAT/G POL/PAR PLAN DIPLOM ECO/TAC DOMIN ADMIN NUC/PWR REV DRIVE PERSON SUPEGO PWR WEALTH...POLICY MGT PSY CONCPT OBS BIOG TREND COLD/WAR MARX/KARL 20. PAGE 145 A2972
COM TOP/EX USSR

B63
UN SECRETARY GENERAL,PLANNING FOR ECONOMIC DEVELOPMENT. ECO/UNDEV FINAN BUDGET INT/TRADE TARIFFS TAX ADMIN 20 UN. PAGE 147 A3005
PLAN ECO/TAC MGT NAT/COMP

S63
ETIENNE G.,"'LOIS OBJECTIVES' ET PROBLEMES DE DEVELOPPEMENT DANS LE CONTEXTE CHINE-URSS." ASIA CHINA/COM COM FUT STRUCT INT/ORG VOL/ASSN TOP/EX TEC/DEV ECO/TAC ATTIT RIGID/FLEX...GEOG MGT TIME/SEQ TOT/POP 20. PAGE 42 A0866
TOTALISM USSR

S63
GANDILHON J.,"LA SCIENCE ET LA TECHNIQUE A L'AIDE DES REGIONS PEU DEVELOPPEES." FRANCE FUT WOR+45 ECO/DEV R+D PROF/ORG ACT/RES PLAN...MGT TOT/POP VAL/FREE 20 UN. PAGE 51 A1037
ECO/UNDEV TEC/DEV FOR/AID

S63
LEDUC G.,"L'AIDE INTERNATIONALE AU DEVELOPPEMENT." FUT WOR+45 ECO/DEV ECO/UNDEV R+D PROF/ORG TEC/DEV ECO/TAC ROUTINE ATTIT ALL/VALS...MGT TIME/SEQ TOT/POP 20. PAGE 86 A1758
FINAN PLAN FOR/AID

S63
NADLER E.B.,"SOME ECONOMIC DISADVANTAGES OF THE ARMS RACE." USA+45 INDUS R+D FORCES PLAN TEC/DEV ECO/TAC FOR/AID EDU/PROP PWR WEALTH...TREND COLD/WAR 20. PAGE 107 A2190
ECO/DEV MGT BAL/PAY

S63
VINER J.,"REPORT OF THE CLAY COMMITTEE ON FOREIGN AID: A SYMPOSIUM." USA+45 WOR+45 NAT/G CONSULT PLAN BAL/PWR ATTIT WEALTH...MGT CONCPT TOT/POP 20. PAGE 159 A3240
ACT/RES ECO/TAC FOR/AID

B64
BLACKSTOCK P.W.,THE STRATEGY OF SUBVERSION. USA+45 FORCES EDU/PROP ADMIN COERCE GOV/REL...DECISION MGT 20 DEPT/DEFEN CIA DEPT/STATE. PAGE 15 A0301
ORD/FREE DIPLOM CONTROL

B64
HARMON R.B.,BIBLIOGRAPHY OF BIBLIOGRAPHIES IN POLITICAL SCIENCE (MIMEOGRAPHED PAPER: LIMITED EDITION). WOR+45 WOR-45 INT/ORG POL/PAR GOV/REL ALL/IDEOS...INT/LAW JURID MGT 19/20. PAGE 61 A1260
BIBLIOG NAT/G DIPLOM LOC/G

B64
HAZLEWOOD A.,THE ECONOMICS OF DEVELOPMENT: AN ANNOTATED LIST OF BOOKS AND ARTICLES PUBLISHED 1958-1962. AGRI FINAN INDUS LABOR NAT/G DIPLOM INT/TRADE INCOME...MGT 20. PAGE 63 A1303
BIBLIOG/A ECO/UNDEV TEC/DEV

B64
RICHARDSON I.L.,BIBLIOGRAFIA BRASILEIRA DE ADMINISTRACAO PUBLICA E ASSUNTOS CORRELATOS. BRAZIL CONSTN FINAN LOC/G NAT/G POL/PAR PLAN DIPLOM RECEIVE ATTIT...METH 20. PAGE 121 A2474
BIBLIOG MGT ADMIN LAW

B64
STEWART C.F.,A BIBLIOGRAPHY OF INTERNATIONAL BUSINESS. WOR+45 FINAN LG/CO NAT/G PLAN ECO/TAC TARIFFS...DECISION MGT GP/COMP NAT/COMP 20 EEC. PAGE 138 A2824
BIBLIOG INT/ORG OP/RES INT/TRADE

L64
RIPLEY R.B.,"INTERAGENCY COMMITTEES AND INCREMENTALISM: THE CASE OF AID TO INDIA." INDIA USA+45 INTELL NAT/G DELIB/GP ACT/RES DIPLOM ROUTINE NAT/LISM ATTIT PWR...SOC CONCPT NEW/IDEA TIME/SEQ CON/ANAL VAL/FREE 20. PAGE 121 A2483
EXEC MGT FOR/AID

L64
SYMONDS R.,"REFLECTIONS IN LOCALISATION." AFR S/ASIA UK STRATA INT/ORG NAT/G SCHOOL EDU/PROP LEGIT KNOWL ORD/FREE PWR RESPECT CMN/WLTH 20. PAGE 140 A2874
ADMIN MGT COLONIAL

S64
GARDNER R.N.,"GATT AND THE UNITED NATIONS CONFERENCE ON TRADE AND DEVELOPMENT." USA+45 WOR+45 SOCIETY ECO/UNDEV MARKET NAT/G DELIB/GP ACT/RES PLAN ECO/TAC TARIFFS EDU/PROP ROUTINE DRIVE RIGID/FLEX WEALTH...DECISION MGT TREND UN TOT/POP 20 GATT. PAGE 51 A1047
INT/ORG INT/TRADE

S64
HOSCH L.G.,"PUBLIC ADMINISTRATION ON THE INTERNATIONAL FRONTIER." WOR+45 R+D NAT/G EDU/PROP EXEC KNOWL ORD/FREE VAL/FREE 20 UN. PAGE 68 A1390
INT/ORG MGT

S64
WOOD H.B.,"STRETCHING YOUR FOREIGN-AID DOLLAR." USA+45 WOR+45 CONSULT EDU/PROP ATTIT WEALTH...OBS TOT/POP CONGRESS 20. PAGE 166 A3390
ECO/UNDEV MGT FOR/AID

B65
FORM W.H.,INDUSTRIAL RELATIONS AND SOCIAL CHANGE IN LATIN AMERICA. L/A+17C AGRI LABOR NAT/G PLAN PROB/SOLV DIPLOM...MGT SOC ANTHOL BIBLIOG/A METH
INDUS GP/REL NAT/COMP

20. PAGE 47 A0966 ECO/UNDEV

B65
FRUTKIN A.W.,SPACE AND THE INTERNATIONAL COOPERATION YEAR: A NATIONAL CHALLENGE (PAMPHLET). EUR+WWI USA+45 FINAN TEC/DEV BUDGET...MGT 20 NASA. PAGE 49 A1011 SPACE INDUS NAT/G DIPLOM

B65
ROLFE S.E.,GOLD AND WORLD POWER. UK USA+45 WOR-45 INDUS WORKER INT/TRADE DEMAND...MGT CHARTS 20 GOLD/STAND. PAGE 123 A2517 BAL/PAY EQUILIB ECO/TAC DIPLOM

B65
UNIVERSAL REFERENCE SYSTEM,INTERNATIONAL AFFAIRS: VOLUME I IN THE POLITICAL SCIENCE, GOVERNMENT, AND PUBLIC POLICY SERIES....DECISION ECOMETRIC GEOG INT/LAW JURID MGT PHIL/SCI PSY SOC. PAGE 149 A3041 BIBLIOG/A GEN/METH COMPUT/IR DIPLOM

B65
WEIL G.L.,A HANDBOOK ON THE EUROPEAN ECONOMIC COMMUNITY. BELGIUM EUR+WWI FRANCE GERMANY/W ITALY CONSTN ECO/DEV CREATE PARTIC GP/REL...DECISION MGT CHARTS 20 EEC. PAGE 162 A3299 INT/TRADE INT/ORG TEC/DEV INT/LAW

L65
WIONCZEK M.,"LATIN AMERICA FREE TRADE ASSOCIATION." AGRI DIST/IND FINAN INDUS INT/ORG LABOR NAT/G TEC/DEV ECO/TAC HEALTH SKILL WEALTH...POLICY RELATIV MGT LAFTA 20. PAGE 165 A3369 L/A+17C MARKET REGION

B66
HARMON R.B.,SOURCES AND PROBLEMS OF BIBLIOGRAPHY IN POLITICAL SCIENCE (PAMPHLET). INT/ORG LOC/G MUNIC POL/PAR ADMIN GOV/REL ALL/IDEOS...JURID MGT CONCPT 19/20. PAGE 61 A1262 BIBLIOG DIPLOM INT/LAW NAT/G

B66
US HOUSE COMM GOVT OPERATIONS,AN INVESTIGATION OF THE US ECONOMIC AND MILITARY ASSISTANCE PROGRAMS IN VIETNAM. USA+45 VIETNAM/S SOCIETY CONSTRUC FINAN FORCES BUDGET INT/TRADE PEACE HEALTH...MGT HOUSE/REP AID. PAGE 154 A3139 FOR/AID ECO/UNDEV WAR INSPECT

L66
AMERICAN ECONOMIC REVIEW,"SIXTY-THIRD LIST OF DOCTORAL DISSERTATIONS IN POLITICAL ECONOMY IN AMERICAN UNIVERSITIES AND COLLEGES." ECO/DEV AGRI FINAN LABOR WORKER PLAN BUDGET INT/TRADE ADMIN DEMAND...MGT STAT 20. PAGE 7 A0146 BIBLIOG/A CONCPT ACADEM

L66
SEYLER W.C.,"DOCTORAL DISSERTATIONS IN POLITICAL SCIENCE IN UNIVERSITIES OF THE UNITED STATES AND CANADA." INT/ORG LOC/G ADMIN...INT/LAW MGT GOV/COMP. PAGE 131 A2690 BIBLIOG LAW NAT/G

B67
CECIL L.,ALBERT BALLIN; BUSINESS AND POLITICS IN IMPERIAL GERMANY 1888-1918. GERMANY UK INT/TRADE LEAD WAR PERS/REL ADJUST PWR WEALTH...MGT BIBLIOG 19/20. PAGE 25 A0510 DIPLOM CONSTN ECO/DEV TOP/EX

B67
HIRSCHMAN A.O.,DEVELOPMENT PROJECTS OBSERVED. INDUS INT/ORG CONSULT EX/STRUC CREATE OP/RES ECO/TAC DEMAND...POLICY MGT METH/COMP 20 WORLD/BANK. PAGE 65 A1339 ECO/UNDEV R+D FINAN PLAN

B67
ROBINSON R.D.,INTERNATIONAL MANAGEMENT. USA+45 FINAN R+D PLAN PRODUC...DECISION T. PAGE 92 A1882 INT/TRADE MGT INT/LAW MARKET

B67
US SENATE COMM ON FOREIGN REL,HUMAN RIGHTS CONVENTIONS. USA+45 LABOR VOL/ASSN DELIB/GP DOMIN ADJUD REPRESENT...INT/LAW MGT CONGRESS. PAGE 156 A3189 LEGIS ORD/FREE WORKER LOBBY

S67
PERLO V.,"NEW DIMENSIONS IN EAST-WEST TRADE." UK USA+45 USSR WOR+45 ECO/DEV NAT/G CAP/ISM PEACE WEALTH LAISSEZ...SOCIALIST MGT 20. PAGE 115 A2364 BAL/PWR ECO/TAC INT/TRADE

S67
WEIL G.L.,"THE MERGER OF THE INSTITUTIONS OF THE EUROPEAN COMMUNITIES" EUR+WWI ECO/DEV INT/TRADE CONSEN PLURISM...DECISION MGT 20 EEC EURATOM ECSC TREATY. PAGE 162 A3300 ECO/TAC INT/ORG CENTRAL INT/LAW

MGT/OBJECT....MANAGEMENT BY OBJECTIVES

MICAUD C.A. A2065

MICH/STA/U....MICHIGAN STATE UNIVERSITY

B65
EDUCATION AND WORLD AFFAIRS,THE UNIVERSITY LOOKS ABROAD: APPROACHES TO WORLD AFFAIRS AT SIX AMERICAN UNIVERSITIES. USA+45 CREATE EDU/PROP CONFER LEAD KNOWL 20 CORNELL/U MICH/STA/U STANFORD/U TULANE/U WISCONSN/U. PAGE 40 A0822 ACADEM DIPLOM ATTIT GP/COMP

MICH/U....UNIVERSITY OF MICHIGAN

MICHAEL D.N. A2066

MICHIGAN STATE UNIVERSITY....SEE MICH/STA/U

MICHIGAN....MICHIGAN

MICRONESIA....MICRONESIA

MID/EAST....MIDDLE EAST

B51
US HOUSE COMM APPROPRIATIONS,MUTUAL SECURITY PROGRAM APPROPRIATIONS FOR 1952: HEARINGS BEFORE A SUBCOMMITTEE OF THE COMMITTEE ON APPROPRIATIONS. KOREA L/A+17C ECO/DEV ECO/UNDEV INT/ORG INSPECT BAL/PWR DIPLOM DEBATE WAR...POLICY STAT ASIA/S 20 CONGRESS NATO COLD/WAR MID/EAST. PAGE 153 A3118 LEGIS FORCES BUDGET FOR/AID

B57
WARBURG J.P.,AGENDA FOR ACTION. ISLAM ISRAEL USA+45 FOR/AID INT/TRADE WAR NAT/LISM 20 MID/EAST EUROPE ARABS. PAGE 161 A3275 DIPLOM POLICY INT/ORG BAL/PWR

B59
TARDIFF G.,LA LIBERTAD; LA LIBERTAD DE EXPRESION, IDEALES Y REALIDADES AMERICANAS. ISLAM INT/ORG PROB/SOLV PRESS CONFER PARTIC CATHISM...INT/LAW SOC/INTEG UN MID/EAST. PAGE 141 A2889 ORD/FREE ATTIT DIPLOM CONCPT

B63
US SENATE COMM GOVT OPERATIONS,REPORT OF A STUDY OF US FOREIGN AID IN TEN MIDDLE EASTERN AND AFRICAN COUNTRIES. AFR ISLAM USA+45 FORCES PLAN BUDGET DIPLOM TAX DETER WEALTH...STAT CHARTS 20 CONGRESS AID MID/EAST. PAGE 156 A3174 FOR/AID EFFICIENCY ECO/TAC FINAN

B64
THANT U.,TOWARD WORLD PEACE. DELIB/GP TEC/DEV EDU/PROP WAR SOVEREIGN...INT/LAW 20 UN MID/EAST. PAGE 142 A2907 DIPLOM BIOG PEACE COERCE

B65
MANSFIELD P.,NASSER'S EGYPT. AFR ISLAM UAR ECO/UNDEV AGRI COLONIAL SOVEREIGN...CHARTS 20 NASSER/G MID/EAST. PAGE 94 A1934 CHIEF ECO/TAC DIPLOM POLICY

S67
HUDSON R.,"WAS THIS WAR NECESSARY? THE UN AND THE MIDDLE EAST" WOR+45 STRUCT DIPLOM DOMIN CONTROL REPRESENT PWR...NEW/IDEA 20 UN MID/EAST. PAGE 69 A1410 DELIB/GP INT/ORG PROB/SOLV PEACE

MIDDLEBUSH F. A2067

MIDDLETON D. A2068

MIDDLETOWN....MIDDLETOWN: LOCATION OF LYND STUDY

MIDWEST/US....MIDWESTERN UNITED STATES

B57
SEABURY P.,THE WANING OF SOUTHERN "INTERNATIONALISM" (PAMPHLET). USA+45 USA-45 INT/ORG LEGIS MAJORITY...TREND 20 SOUTH/US MIDWEST/US. PAGE 131 A2676 DIPLOM REGION ATTIT ISOLAT

MIGRATION....MIGRATION; IMMIGRATION AND EMIGRATION; SEE ALSO HABITAT, GEOG

N19
HAJDA J.,THE COLD WAR VIEWED AS A SOCIOLOGICAL PROBLEM (PAMPHLET). COM CZECHOSLVK EUR+WWI SOCIETY PLAN EDU/PROP CONTROL TASK ATTIT MARXISM...POLICY 20 COLD/WAR MIGRATION. PAGE 59 A1220 DIPLOM LEAD PWR NAT/G

N19
UNITED ARAB REPUBLIC,THE PROBLEM OF THE PALESTINIAN REFUGEES (PAMPHLET). ISRAEL UAR LAW PROB/SOLV EDU/PROP CONFER ADJUD CONTROL NAT/LISM HEALTH 20 JEWS UN MIGRATION. PAGE 148 A3029 STRANGE GP/REL INGP/REL DIPLOM

B57
US COMMISSION GOVT SECURITY,RECOMMENDATIONS; AREA: IMMIGRANT PROGRAM. USA+45 LAW WORKER DIPLOM EDU/PROP WRITING ADMIN PEACE ATTIT...CONCPT ANTHOL 20 MIGRATION SUBVERT. PAGE 150 A3060 POLICY CONTROL PLAN NAT/G

B58
INSTITUTE MEDITERRANEAN AFF,THE PALESTINE REFUGEE PROBLEM. UAR WOR+45 INT/ORG PLAN PROB/SOLV PEACE ...POLICY GEOG STAT CHARTS 20 JEWS UN MIGRATION. PAGE 70 A1444 STRANGE HABITAT GP/REL INGP/REL

B59
BUNDESMIN FUR VERTRIEBENE,ZEITTAFEL DER VORGESCHICHTE UND DES ABLAUFS DER VERTREIBUNG SOWIE DER UNTERBRINGUNG UND EINGLIEDERUNG DER (2 VOLS.). GERMANY/E GERMANY/W NAT/G PROVS PROB/SOLV DIPLOM PARL/PROC ATTIT...BIBLIOG SOC/INTEG 20 MIGRATION PARLIAMENT. PAGE 21 A0431 JURID GP/REL INT/LAW

B59
KAPLAN D.,THE ARAB REFUGEES: AN ABNORMAL PROBLEM. UAR WOR+45 PROB/SOLV DIPLOM GOV/REL ADJUST EFFICIENCY...POLICY GEOG INT/LAW 20 UN JEWS MIGRATION. PAGE 76 A1557 STRANGE HABITAT GP/REL INGP/REL

B61
SCHIEDER T.,DOCUMENTS ON THE EXPULSION OF THE GEOG

GERMANS FROM EASTERN-CENTRAL-EUROPE (VOL. II/III). COM EUR+WWI GERMANY HUNGARY ROMANIA USSR DIPLOM RACE/REL 20 MIGRATION. PAGE 128 A2625 — CULTURE

B63
LOOMIE A.J.,THE SPANISH ELIZABETHANS: THE ENGLISH EXILES AT THE COURT OF PHILIP II. SPAIN UK WAR INGP/REL DRIVE HABITAT CATHISM...BIOG 16/17 MIGRATION. PAGE 91 A1860 — NAT/G STRANGE POLICY DIPLOM

B64
HARPER F.,OUT OF CHINA. CHINA/COM ELITES STRATA ATTIT PERSON...BIOG 20 MAO HONG/KONG MIGRATION. PAGE 62 A1264 — HABITAT DEEP/INT DIPLOM MARXISM

B64
US HOUSE COMM ON JUDICIARY,IMMIGRATION HEARINGS. DELIB/GP STRANGE HABITAT...GEOG JURID 20 CONGRESS MIGRATION. PAGE 154 A3140 — NAT/G POLICY DIPLOM NAT/LISM

B65
SMITH A.L. JR.,THE DEUTSCHTUM OF NAZI GERMANY AND THE UNITED STATES. GERMANY USA-45 DIPLOM ATTIT FASCISM...BIBLIOG 20 MIGRATION NAZI. PAGE 134 A2744 — INGP/REL NAT/LISM STRANGE DELIB/GP

B65
US SENATE COMM ON JUDICIARY,REFUGEE PROBLEMS IN SOUTH VIETNAM AND LAOS: HEARINGS BEFORE SUBCOMMITTEE TO INVESTIGATE PROBLEMS OF REFUGEES, ESCAPEES. CHINA/COM LAOS USA+45 VIETNAM/S PROB/SOLV DIPLOM GOV/REL GP/REL EFFICIENCY ORD/FREE...POLICY GEOG 20 CONGRESS MIGRATION. PAGE 157 A3194 — STRANGE HABITAT FOR/AID CIVMIL/REL

B66
HENKYS R.,DEUTSCHLAND UND DIE OSTLICHEN NACHBARN. GERMANY POLAND NAT/G POL/PAR INGP/REL ATTIT 20 MIGRATION. PAGE 64 A1317 — GP/REL JURID INT/LAW DIPLOM

B66
US HOUSE COMM APPROPRIATIONS,HEARINGS ON FOREIGN OPERATIONS AND RELATED AGENCIES APPROPRIATIONS. CUBA USA+45 VOL/ASSN DELIB/GP DIPLOM CONFER ORD/FREE 20 CONGRESS MIGRATION INT/AM/DEV PEACE/CORP. PAGE 153 A3120 — FOR/AID BUDGET ECO/UNDEV FORCES

MIKESELL R.F. A2069,A2070

MIKSCHE F.O. A2071

MIL/ACAD....MILITARY ACADEMY

MILITARY....SEE FORCES

MILITARY APPLICATIONS OF URANIUM DETONATION....SEE MAUD

MILL/JAMES....JAMES MILL

MILL/JS....JOHN STUART MILL

B45
MACMINN N.,BIBLIOGRAPHY OF THE PUBLISHED WRITINGS OF JOHN STUART MILL. MOD/EUR UK CAP/ISM DIPLOM KNOWL...EPIST CONCPT 19 MILL/JS. PAGE 93 A1901 — BIBLIOG/A SOCIETY INGP/REL LAISSEZ

B59
LINK R.G.,ENGLISH THEORIES OF ECONOMIC FLUCTUATIONS: 1815-1848. FRANCE UK AGRI WORKER DIPLOM PRICE TASK WAR DEMAND PRODUC...POLICY BIBLIOG 18 MALTHUS MILL/JS WILSON/J. PAGE 89 A1826 — IDEA/COMP ECO/DEV WEALTH EQUILIB

B62
EBENSTEIN W.,TWO WAYS OF LIFE. USA+45 CULTURE ECO/DEV PLAN EDU/PROP CONTROL ORD/FREE...GOV/COMP IDEA/COMP T 20 MARX/KARL ENGELS/F LENIN/VI LOCKE/JOHN MILL/JS. PAGE 40 A0819 — MARXISM POPULISM ECO/TAC DIPLOM

B91
SIDGWICK H.,THE ELEMENTS OF POLITICS. LOC/G NAT/G LEGIS DIPLOM ADJUD CONTROL EXEC PARL/PROC REPRESENT GOV/REL SOVEREIGN ALL/IDEOS 19 MILL/JS BENTHAM/J. PAGE 132 A2713 — POLICY LAW CONCPT

MILLAR T.B. A2072

MILLARD E.L. A2073

MILLER D.H. A2074

MILLER E. A2075,A2076

MILLER J.D.B. A2077,A2078

MILLER R.I. A2079

MILLER W.J. A2080

MILLIKAN M.F. A2081

MILLIKAW M.F. A2082

MILLIKEN M. A2083

MILLIS W. A2084,A2085

MILLS/CW....C. WRIGHT MILLS

MILNER/A....ALFRED MILNER

MILTON P.R. A0343

MILTON/J....MILTON, JOHN

MINIFIE J.M. A2086

MINING....SEE EXTR/IND

MINISTERE DE L'EDUC NATIONALE A2087

MINISTERE FINANCES ET ECO A2088

MINNESOTA....MINNESOTA

MINORITY....SEE RACE/REL

MISCEGEN....MISCEGENATION

B65
RODRIGUES J.H.,BRAZIL AND AFRICA. AFR BRAZIL PORTUGAL UK USA+45 USA-45 CULTURE ECO/UNDEV INT/ORG INT/TRADE RACE/REL ORD/FREE 15/20 UN MISCEGEN. PAGE 123 A2513 — DIPLOM COLONIAL POLICY ATTIT

MISSION....MISSIONARIES

B58
VARG P.A.,MISSIONARIES, CHINESE, AND DIPLOMATS: THE AMERICAN PROTESTANT MISSIONARY MOVEMENT IN CHINA, 1890-1952. ASIA ECO/UNDEV NAT/G PROB/SOLV CAP/ISM EDU/PROP COLONIAL NAT/LISM ATTIT MARXISM...NAT/COMP STERTYP 20 CHINJAP PROTESTANT MISSION. PAGE 158 A3221 — CULTURE DIPLOM SECT

MISSISSIPP....MISSISSIPPI

MISSOURI....MISSOURI

MITCHELL P. A2090

MITRANY D. A2091

MLF....MULTILATERAL FORCE

S64
BUCHAN A.,"THE MULTILATERAL FORCE." EUR+WWI FUT USA+45 NAT/G LEGIT PWR SKILL...CONCPT OEEC MLF 20. PAGE 21 A0422 — INT/ORG FORCES

MNR....MOVIMIENTO NACIONALISTA REVOLUCIONARIO (BOLIVIA)

MO/BASIN....MISSOURI RIVER BASIN PLAN

MOB....SEE CROWD

MOBERG E. A2092

MOBUTU/J....JOSEPH MOBUTU

MOCH J. A2093

MOCHE....MOCHE, PERU

MOCKFORD J. A2094

MOCKLER-FERRYMAN A. A2095

MOD/EUR....MODERN EUROPE (1700-1918); SEE ALSO APPROPRIATE NATIONS

N
PUBLISHERS' CIRCULAR, THE OFFICIAL ORGAN OF THE PUBLISHERS' ASSOCIATION OF GREAT BRITAIN AND IRELAND. EUR+WWI MOD/EUR UK LAW PROB/SOLV DIPLOM COLONIAL ATTIT...HUM 19/20 CMN/WLTH. PAGE 2 A0039 — BIBLIOG NAT/G WRITING LEAD

N
DE MARTENS G.F.,RECUEIL GENERALE DE TRAITES ET AUTRES ACTES RELATIFS AUX RAPPORTS DE DROIT INTERNATIONAL (41 VOLS.). EUR+WWI MOD/EUR USA-45 ...INDEX TREATY 18/20. PAGE 35 A0708 — BIBLIOG INT/LAW DIPLOM

B00
MAINE H.S.,INTERNATIONAL LAW. MOD/EUR UNIV SOCIETY STRUCT ACT/RES EXEC WAR ATTIT PERSON ALL/VALS ...POLICY JURID CONCPT OBS TIME/SEQ TOT/POP. PAGE 93 A1908 — INT/ORG LAW PEACE INT/LAW

B00
VOLPICELLI Z.,RUSSIA ON THE PACIFIC AND THE SIBERIAN RAILWAY. MOD/EUR ECO/UNDEV INT/ORG FORCES PLAN DOMIN COLONIAL ROUTINE ATTIT ALL/VALS...OBS HIST/WRIT TIME/SEQ TREND CON/ANAL AUD/VIS CHARTS 18/19. PAGE 159 A3248 NAT/G ACT/RES RUSSIA

B02
SEELEY J.R.,THE EXPANSION OF ENGLAND. MOD/EUR S/ASIA UK CULTURE NAT/G FORCES PLAN DOMIN EDU/PROP COLONIAL ROUTINE ATTIT ALL/VALS SOVEREIGN...CONCPT HIST/WRIT PARLIAMENT 18 CMN/WLTH. PAGE 131 A2679 INT/ORG ACT/RES CAP/ISM INDIA

B04
CRANDALL S.B.,TREATIES: THEIR MAKING AND ENFORCEMENT. MOD/EUR USA-45 CONSTN INT/ORG NAT/G LEGIS EDU/PROP LEGIT EXEC PEACE KNOWL MORAL...JURID CONGRESS 19/20 TREATY. PAGE 32 A0655 LAW

B06
FOSTER J.W.,THE PRACTICE OF DIPLOMACY AS ILLUSTRATED IN THE FOREIGN RELATIONS OF THE UNITED STATES. MOD/EUR USA-45 NAT/G EX/STRUC ADMIN ...POLICY INT/LAW BIBLIOG 19/20. PAGE 47 A0970 DIPLOM ROUTINE PHIL/SCI

B06
GRIFFIN A.P.C.,SELECT LIST OF REFERENCES ON THE BRITISH TARIFF MOVEMENT. MOD/EUR UK BAL/PWR BARGAIN ECO/TAC LAISSEZ 20. PAGE 56 A1154 BIBLIOG/A INT/TRADE TARIFFS COLONIAL

C06
MONTGOMERY H.,"A DICTIONARY OF POLITICAL PHRASES AND ILLUSIONS WITH A SHORT BIBLIOGRAPHY." EUR+WWI MOD/EUR UK AGRI LABOR LOC/G NAT/G COLONIAL CHOOSE RACE/REL. PAGE 103 A2114 BIBLIOG DICTIONARY POLICY DIPLOM

B08
ARON R.,WAR AND INDUSTRIAL SOCIETY. EUR+WWI MOD/EUR WOR+45 WOR-45 CONSTN SOCIETY INT/ORG POL/PAR VOL/ASSN DIPLOM INT/TRADE PEACE ATTIT...BIOG GEN/LAWS 19/20. PAGE 9 A0178 ECO/DEV WAR

B13
BORCHARD E.M.,BIBLIOGRAPHY OF INTERNATIONAL LAW AND CONTINENTAL LAW. EUR+WWI MOD/EUR UK LAW INT/TRADE WAR PEACE...GOV/COMP NAT/COMP 19/20. PAGE 17 A0338 BIBLIOG INT/LAW JURID DIPLOM

B14
BERNHARDI F.,ON THE WAR OF TODAY. MOD/EUR INT/ORG NAT/G TOP/EX PWR CHARTS. PAGE 14 A0278 FORCES SKILL WAR

B14
DE BLOCH J.,THE FUTURE OF WAR IN ITS TECHNICAL, ECONOMIC, AND POLITICAL RELATIONS (1899). MOD/EUR TEC/DEV BUDGET INT/TRADE DETER GUERRILLA WEAPON COST PEACE 20. PAGE 34 A0698 WAR BAL/PWR PREDICT FORCES

B14
HARRIS N.D.,INTERVENTION AND COLONIZATION IN AFRICA. BELGIUM FRANCE GERMANY MOD/EUR PORTUGAL UK ECO/UNDEV BAL/PWR DOMIN CONTROL PWR...GEOG 19/20. PAGE 62 A1267 AFR COLONIAL DIPLOM

B15
FARIES J.C.,THE RISE OF INTERNATIONALISM. ASIA MOD/EUR NAT/G VOL/ASSN DELIB/GP BAL/PWR EDU/PROP ARMS/CONT RIGID/FLEX TREND. PAGE 44 A0899 INT/ORG DIPLOM PEACE

B15
HOBSON J.A.,TOWARDS INTERNATIONAL GOVERNMENT. MOD/EUR STRUCT ECO/TAC EDU/PROP ADJUD ALL/VALS ...SOCIALIST CONCPT GEN/LAWS TOT/POP 20. PAGE 65 A1347 FUT INT/ORG CENTRAL

B16
ROOT E.,ADDRESSES ON INTERNATIONAL SUBJECTS. MOD/EUR UNIV USA-45 LAW SOCIETY EXEC ATTIT ALL/VALS ...POLICY JURID CONCPT 20 CHINJAP. PAGE 123 A2521 INT/ORG ACT/RES PEACE INT/LAW

B17
DILLA H.M.,CLASSIFIED LIST OF MAGAZINE ARTICLES ON THE EUROPEAN WAR. MOD/EUR USA-45 WOR-45 PEACE ATTIT 20. PAGE 37 A0762 BIBLIOG WAR DIPLOM POLICY

B17
SATOW E.,A GUIDE TO DIPLOMATIC PRACTICE. MOD/EUR INT/ORG BAL/PWR LEGIT ORD/FREE PWR SOVEREIGN ...POLICY GEN/METH 20. PAGE 127 A2607 GEN/LAWS DIPLOM

B19
DE CALLIERES F.,THE PRACTICE OF DIPLOMACY. MOD/EUR INT/ORG NAT/G DELIB/GP LEGIS TOP/EX DOMIN ATTIT KNOWL LEAGUE/NAT 20. PAGE 34 A0699 CONSULT ACT/RES DIPLOM INT/LAW

B19
KEYNES J.M.,THE ECONOMIC CONSEQUENCES OF THE PEACE. FUT GERMANY MOD/EUR RUSSIA UK USA-45 CULTURE ECO/DEV FINAN INDUS INT/ORG TOP/EX ECO/TAC ROUTINE WAR ATTIT PERCEPT ALL/VALS...OLD/LIB MYTH OBS TIME/SEQ TREND 20 TREATY. PAGE 78 A1605 EUR+WWI SOCIETY PEACE

N19
HANNA A.J.,EUROPEAN RULE IN AFRICA (PAMPHLET). BELGIUM FRANCE MOD/EUR UK WOR+45 WOR-45 ECO/UNDEV NAT/G PARTIC SOVEREIGN...NAT/COMP 19/20. PAGE 61 A1252 DIPLOM COLONIAL AFR NAT/LISM

B20
HALDANE R.B.,BEFORE THE WAR. MOD/EUR SOCIETY INT/ORG NAT/G DELIB/GP PLAN DOMIN EDU/PROP LEGIT ADMIN COERCE ATTIT DRIVE MORAL ORD/FREE PWR...SOC CONCPT SELF/OBS RECORD BIOG TIME/SEQ. PAGE 60 A1223 POLICY DIPLOM UK

B20
WOOLF L.,EMPIRE AND COMMERCE IN AFRICA. EUR+WWI MOD/EUR FINAN INDUS MARKET INT/ORG PLAN COERCE ATTIT DRIVE PWR WEALTH...CONCPT TIME/SEQ TREND CHARTS 20. PAGE 167 A3394 AFR DOMIN COLONIAL SOVEREIGN

B21
OPPENHEIM L.,THE FUTURE OF INTERNATIONAL LAW. EUR+WWI MOD/EUR LAW LEGIS JUDGE LEGIT ORD/FREE ...JURID TIME/SEQ GEN/LAWS 20. PAGE 112 A2293 INT/ORG CT/SYS INT/LAW

B21
STUART G.H.,FRENCH FOREIGN POLICY. CONSTN INT/ORG NAT/G POL/PAR EX/STRUC FORCES PLAN ECO/TAC DOMIN EDU/PROP ADJUD COERCE ATTIT DRIVE RIGID/FLEX ALL/VALS...POLICY OBS RECORD BIOG TIME/SEQ TREND. PAGE 139 A2852 MOD/EUR DIPLOM FRANCE

B22
BRYCE J.,INTERNATIONAL RELATIONS. CHRIST-17C EUR+WWI MOD/EUR CULTURE INTELL NAT/G DELIB/GP CREATE BAL/PWR DIPLOM ATTIT DRIVE RIGID/FLEX ALL/VALS...PLURIST JURID CONCPT TIME/SEQ GEN/LAWS TOT/POP. PAGE 20 A0412 INT/ORG POLICY

B22
MYERS D.P.,MANUAL OF COLLECTIONS OF TREATIES AND OF COLLECTIONS RELATING TO TREATIES. MOD/EUR INT/ORG LEGIS WRITING ADMIN SOVEREIGN...INT/LAW 19/20. PAGE 106 A2186 BIBLIOG/A DIPLOM CONFER

B22
WALSH E.,THE HISTORY AND NATURE OF INTERNATIONAL RELATIONS. ASIA L/A+17C MOD/EUR USA-45 WOR-45 NAT/G FORCES TOP/EX BAL/PWR REGION ATTIT ORD/FREE RESPECT ...CONCPT HIST/WRIT TREND. PAGE 161 A3270 INT/ORG TIME/SEQ DIPLOM

B23
KADEN E.H.,DER POLITISCHE CHARAKTER DER FRANZOSISCHEN KULTURPROPAGANDA AM RHEIN. FRANCE MOD/EUR DOMIN PRESS...GEOG METH/COMP 20. PAGE 75 A1544 EDU/PROP ATTIT DIPLOM NAT/G

B25
GODET M.,INDEX BIBLIOGRAPHICUS: INTERNATIONAL CATALOGUE OF SOURCES OF CURRENT BIBLIOGRAPHIC INFORMATION. EUR+WWI MOD/EUR SOCIETY SECT TAX ...JURID PHIL/SCI SOC MATH. PAGE 53 A1085 BIBLIOG/A DIPLOM EDU/PROP LAW

C25
MOON P.T.,"SYLLABUS ON INTERNATIONAL RELATIONS." EUR+WWI MOD/EUR USA-45 FORCES COLONIAL WAR WEAPON NAT/LISM...POLICY BIBLIOG T 19/20. PAGE 103 A2120 INT/ORG DIPLOM NAT/G

B26
INSTITUT INTERMEDIAIRE INTL,REPERTOIRE GENERAL DES TRAITES ET AUTRES ACTES DIPLOMATIQUES CONCLUS DEPUIS 1895 JUSQU'EN 1920. MOD/EUR WOR-45 INT/ORG VOL/ASSN DELIB/GP INT/TRADE WAR TREATY 19/20. PAGE 70 A1443 BIBLIOG DIPLOM

B27
BRANDENBURG E.,FROM BISMARCK TO THE WORLD WAR; A HISTORY OF GERMAN FOREIGN POLICY, 1870-1914 (TRANS. BY ANNIE ELIZABETH ADAMS). GERMANY MOD/EUR FORCES AGREE PWR 19/20 TREATY CHAMBRLN/J WWI BISMARCK/O. PAGE 18 A0368 DIPLOM POLICY WAR

B27
HARRIS N.D.,EUROPE AND AFRICA. BELGIUM FRANCE GERMANY MOD/EUR PORTUGAL UK ECO/UNDEV BAL/PWR PWR ...GEOG 19/20. PAGE 62 A1268 AFR COLONIAL DIPLOM

B28
HOWARD-ELLIS C.,THE ORIGIN, STRUCTURE AND WORKING OF THE LEAGUE OF NATIONS. EUR+WWI MOD/EUR USA-45 CONSTN FORCES LEGIS ECO/TAC LEGIT COERCE ORD/FREE ...JURID SOC CONCPT LEAGUE/NAT 20 ILO ICJ. PAGE 68 A1401 INT/ORG ADJUD

B28
HUBER G.,DIE FRANZOSISCHE PROPAGANDA IM WELTKRIEG GEGEN DEUTSCHLAND 1914 BIS 1918. FRANCE GERMANY MOD/EUR DIPLOM WAR...EXHIBIT 20 WWI. PAGE 68 A1403 EDU/PROP ATTIT DOMIN PRESS

B28
PLAYNE C.E.,THE PRE-WAR MIND IN BRITAIN. GERMANY MOD/EUR UK STRATA SECT DIPLOM EDU/PROP CROWD SUFF ...POLICY ANARCH PSY SOC IDEA/COMP 20 WWI. PAGE 116 A2388 PRESS WAR DOMIN ATTIT

B29
DE REPARAZ G.,GEOGRAFIA Y POLITICA. CHILE SPAIN USSR NAT/G DIPLOM REV MARXISM...POLICY 19/20. PAGE 35 A0709 GEOG MOD/EUR

B29
LANGER W.L.,THE FRANCO-RUSSIAN ALLIANCE: 1890-1894. FRANCE MOD/EUR UK USSR NAT/G CHIEF FORCES BAL/PWR AGREE WAR PEACE PWR...TIME/SEQ TREATY 19 BISMARCK/O. PAGE 84 A1724 DIPLOM

B30
BYNKERSHOEK C.,QUAESTIONUM JURIS PUBLICI LIBRI DUO. CHRIST-17C MOD/EUR CONSTN ELITES SOCIETY NAT/G PROVS EX/STRUC FORCES TOP/EX BAL/PWR DIPLOM ATTIT MORAL...TRADIT CONCPT. PAGE 23 A0460 INT/ORG LAW NAT/LISM INT/LAW

B30
SCHMITT B.E.,THE COMING OF THE WAR, 1914 (2 VOLS.). WAR

AUSTRIA FRANCE GERMANY MOD/EUR RUSSIA UK PLAN ROUTINE ORD/FREE. PAGE 128 A2633 DIPLOM

B31
STUART G.H.,THE INTERNATIONAL CITY OF TANGIER. AFR EUR+WWI MOD/EUR MOROCCO CONSTN PROVS CREATE PLAN LEGIT PEACE ORD/FREE PWR...INT/LAW OBS TIME/SEQ CON/ANAL 20 TANGIER. PAGE 139 A2854 LOC/G INT/ORG DIPLOM SOVEREIGN

B32
BRYCE J.,THE HOLY ROMAN EMPIRE. GERMANY ITALY MOD/EUR CULTURE SOCIETY STRUCT INT/ORG NAT/G SECT DIPLOM DOMIN WAR SUPEGO ALL/VALS SOVEREIGN...GEOG SOC TIME/SEQ CHARTS STERTYP. PAGE 20 A0413 CHRIST-17C NAT/LISM

B32
LENIN V.I.,THE WAR AND THE SECOND INTERNATIONAL. COM MOD/EUR USSR CAP/ISM DIPLOM NAT/LISM ATTIT MARXISM...CONCPT 20. PAGE 87 A1772 POL/PAR WAR SOCISM INT/ORG

B32
MASTERS R.D.,INTERNATIONAL LAW IN INTERNATIONAL COURTS. BELGIUM EUR+WWI FRANCE GERMANY MOD/EUR SWITZERLND WOR-45 SOCIETY STRATA STRUCT LEGIT EXEC ALL/VALS...JURID HIST/WRIT TIME/SEQ TREND GEN/LAWS 20. PAGE 96 A1961 INT/ORG LAW INT/LAW

C32
MARRARO H.R.,"AMERICAN OPINION ON THE UNIFICATION OF ITALY." ITALY MOD/EUR USA-45 FORCES DIPLOM PRESS REV CATHISM...BIOG 19 PRESIDENT. PAGE 95 A1944 BIBLIOG/A NAT/LISM ATTIT ORD/FREE

B34
WOLFF C.,JUS GENTIUM METHODO SCIENTIFICA PERTRACTATUM. MOD/EUR INT/ORG VOL/ASSN LEGIT PEACE ATTIT...JURID 20. PAGE 166 A3387 NAT/G LAW INT/LAW WAR

B36
HUGENDUBEL P.,DIE KRIEGSMACHE DER FRANZOSISCHEN PRESSE. FRANCE GERMANY MOD/EUR COM/IND NAT/G DIPLOM DOMIN PWR 20. PAGE 69 A1412 PRESS EDU/PROP WAR ATTIT

B36
MATTHEWS M.A.,DIPLOMACY: SELECT LIST ON DIPLOMACY, DIPLOMATIC AND CONSULAR PRACTICE, AND FOREIGN OFFICE ORGANIZATION (PAMPHLET). EUR+WWI MOD/EUR USA-45 WOR-45...INT/LAW 20. PAGE 96 A1974 BIBLIOG/A DIPLOM NAT/G

B36
MATTHEWS M.A.,INTERNATIONAL LAW: SELECT LIST OF WORKS IN ENGLISH ON PUBLIC INTERNATIONAL LAW: WITH COLLECTIONS OF CASES AND OPINIONS. CHRIST-17C EUR+WWI MOD/EUR WOR-45 CONSTN ADJUD JURID. PAGE 96 A1975 BIBLIOG/A INT/LAW ATTIT DIPLOM

B36
RUSSEL F.M.,THEORIES OF INTERNATIONAL RELATIONS. EUR+WWI FUT MOD/EUR USA-45 INT/ORG DIPLOM...JURID CONCPT. PAGE 125 A2571 PWR POLICY BAL/PWR SOVEREIGN

B37
THOMPSON J.W.,SECRET DIPLOMACY: A RECORD OF ESPIONAGE AND DOUBLE-DEALING: 1500-1815. CHRIST-17C MOD/EUR NAT/G WRITING RISK MORAL...ANTHOL BIBLIOG 16/19 ESPIONAGE. PAGE 143 A2927 DIPLOM CRIME

B38
HOBSON J.A.,IMPERIALISM. MOD/EUR UK WOR-45 CULTURE ECO/UNDEV NAT/G VOL/ASSN PLAN EDU/PROP LEGIT REGION COERCE ATTIT PWR...POLICY PLURIST TIME/SEQ GEN/LAWS 19/20. PAGE 66 A1348 DOMIN ECO/TAC BAL/PWR COLONIAL

B38
PETTEE G.S.,THE PROCESS OF REVOLUTION. COM FRANCE ITALY MOD/EUR RUSSIA SPAIN WOR-45 ELITES INTELL SOCIETY STRATA STRUCT INT/ORG NAT/G POL/PAR ACT/RES PLAN EDU/PROP LEGIT EXEC...SOC MYTH TIME/SEQ TOT/POP 18/20. PAGE 115 A2370 COERCE CONCPT REV

B39
CARR E.H.,PROPAGANDA IN INTERNATIONAL POLITICS (PAMPHLET). EUR+WWI GERMANY MOD/EUR NAT/G AGREE WAR MORAL...POLICY 20 TREATY. PAGE 24 A0497 DIPLOM EDU/PROP CONTROL ATTIT

B39
FULLER G.H.,A SELECTED LIST OF REFERENCES ON THE EXPANSION OF THE US NAVY, 1933-1939 (PAMPHLET). MOD/EUR USA-45 NAT/G PLAN DIPLOM DOMIN RISK ARMS/CONT EQUILIB PWR 20 NAVY. PAGE 50 A1019 BIBLIOG FORCES WEAPON WAR

B39
KOHN H.,REVOLUTIONS AND DICTATORSHIPS. COM EUR+WWI ISLAM MOD/EUR NAT/G CHIEF FORCES WAR CIVMIL/REL PWR MARXISM 18/20. PAGE 81 A1661 NAT/LISM TOTALISM REV FASCISM

B40
FULLER G.H.,A LIST OF BIBLIOGRAPHIES ON PROPAGANDA (PAMPHLET). MOD/EUR USA-45 CONSULT ACT/RES PRESS FEEDBACK TASK WAR ATTIT PWR...CON/ANAL METH/COMP 20. PAGE 50 A1020 BIBLIOG/A EDU/PROP DOMIN DIPLOM

B40
WANDERSCHECK H.,FRANKREICHS PROPAGANDA GEGEN DEUTSCHLAND. FRANCE GERMANY MOD/EUR UK NAT/G DIPLOM WAR 20 JEWS. PAGE 161 A3273 EDU/PROP ATTIT DOMIN PRESS

B41
BIRDSALL P.,VERSAILLES TWENTY YEARS AFTER. MOD/EUR POL/PAR CHIEF CONSULT FORCES LEGIS REPAR PEACE ORD/FREE...BIBLIOG 20 PRESIDENT TREATY. PAGE 14 A0290 DIPLOM NAT/LISM WAR

B41
GRISMER R.,A NEW BIBLIOGRAPHY OF THE LITERATURES OF SPAIN AND SPANISH AMERICA. CHRIST-17C MOD/EUR PRE/AMER SPAIN CULTURE DIPLOM EDU/PROP...ART/METH GEOG HUM PHIL/SCI 20. PAGE 57 A1165 BIBLIOG LAW NAT/G ECO/UNDEV

B41
YOUNG G.,FEDERALISM AND FREEDOM. EUR+WWI MOD/EUR RUSSIA USA-45 WOR-45 SOCIETY STRUCT ECO/DEV INT/ORG EXEC FEDERAL ATTIT PERSON ALL/VALS...OLD/LIB CONCPT OBS TREND LEAGUE/NAT TOT/POP. PAGE 169 A3435 NAT/G WAR

B42
FEILCHENFELD E.H.,THE INTERNATIONAL ECONOMIC LAW OF BELLIGERENT OCCUPATION. EUR+WWI MOD/EUR USA-45 INT/ORG DIPLOM ADJUD ARMS/CONT LEAGUE/NAT 20. PAGE 44 A0907 ECO/TAC INT/LAW WAR

L42
SHOTWELL J.,"LESSON OF THE LAST WORLD WAR." EUR+WWI MOD/EUR USA-45 SOCIETY ECO/UNDEV INDUS VOL/ASSN CONSULT ACT/RES CREATE CAP/ISM INT/TRADE DRIVE ALL/VALS...CONCPT NEW/IDEA SELF/OBS GEN/LAWS LEAGUE/NAT NAZI 20. PAGE 132 A2708 INT/ORG ORD/FREE

B43
SERENI A.P.,THE ITALIAN CONCEPTION OF INTERNATIONAL LAW. EUR+WWI MOD/EUR INT/ORG NAT/G DOMIN COERCE ORD/FREE FASCISM...OBS/ENVIR TREND 20. PAGE 131 A2686 LAW TIME/SEQ INT/LAW ITALY

B44
RUDIN H.R.,ARMISTICE 1918. FRANCE GERMANY MOD/EUR UK USA-45 NAT/G CHIEF DELIB/GP FORCES BAL/PWR REPAR ARMS/CONT 20 WILSON/W TREATY. PAGE 125 A2566 AGREE WAR PEACE DIPLOM

B44
WEIGERT H.W.,COMPASS OF THE WORLD, A SYMPOSIUM ON POLITICAL GEOGRAPHY. EUR+WWI FUT MOD/EUR S/ASIA USA-45 WOR-45 SOCIETY AGRI INDUS MARKET ECO/TAC INT/TRADE PERSON 20. PAGE 162 A3298 TEC/DEV CAP/ISM RUSSIA GEOG

B45
MACMINN N.,BIBLIOGRAPHY OF THE PUBLISHED WRITINGS OF JOHN STUART MILL. MOD/EUR UK CAP/ISM DIPLOM KNOWL...EPIST CONCPT 19 MILL/JS. PAGE 93 A1901 BIBLIOG/A SOCIETY INGP/REL LAISSEZ

B45
WING D.,SHORT-TITLE CATALOGUE OF BOOKS PRINTED IN THE BRITISH ISLES, AND OF ENGLISH BOOKS PRINTED OVERSEAS; 1641-1700 (3 VOLS.). UK USA-45 LAW DIPLOM ADMIN COLONIAL LEAD ATTIT 17. PAGE 165 A3363 BIBLIOG MOD/EUR NAT/G

B46
GRIFFIN G.G.,A GUIDE TO MANUSCRIPTS RELATING TO AMERICAN HISTORY IN BRITISH DEPOSITORIES. CANADA IRELAND MOD/EUR UK USA-45 LAW DIPLOM ADMIN COLONIAL WAR NAT/LISM SOVEREIGN...GEOG INT/LAW 15/19 CMN/WLTH. PAGE 56 A1159 BIBLIOG/A ALL/VALS NAT/G

B46
SCANLON H.L.,INTERNATIONAL LAW: A SELECTIVE LIST OF WORKS IN ENGLISH ON PUBLIC INTERNATIONAL LAW (A PAMPHLET). CHRIST-17C EUR+WWI MOD/EUR WOR-45 CT/SYS ...JURID 20. PAGE 127 A2613 BIBLIOG/A INT/LAW ADJUD DIPLOM

S46
SILBERNER E.,"THE PROBLEM OF WAR IN NINETEENTH CENTURY ECONOMIC THOUGHT." EUR+WWI MOD/EUR UNIV LAW ECO/DEV ECO/UNDEV FINAN INDUS MARKET INT/ORG NAT/G CONSULT FORCES...CONCPT GEN/LAWS GEN/METH 19. PAGE 133 A2715 ATTIT ECO/TAC WAR

B49
MANSERGH N.,THE COMING OF THE FIRST WORLD WAR: A STUDY IN EUROPEAN BALANCE, 1878-1914. GERMANY MOD/EUR VOL/ASSN COLONIAL CONTROL PWR 19/20 TREATY. PAGE 94 A1928 DIPLOM WAR BAL/PWR

B50
GATZKE H.W.,GERMANY'S DRIVE TO THE WEST. BELGIUM GERMANY MOD/EUR AGRI INDUS POL/PAR FORCES DOMIN AGREE CONTROL REGION COERCE 20 TREATY WWI. PAGE 51 A1053 WAR POLICY NAT/G DIPLOM

B51
HOLBORN H.,THE POLITICAL COLLAPSE OF EUROPE. EUR+WWI MOD/EUR USA-45 BAL/PWR PEACE POLICY. PAGE 66 A1364 DIPLOM ORD/FREE WAR

B52
ALBERTINI L.,THE ORIGINS OF THE WAR OF 1914 (3 VOLS.). AUSTRIA FRANCE GERMANY MOD/EUR RUSSIA UK PROB/SOLV NEUTRAL PWR...BIBLIOG 19/20. PAGE 5 A0107 WAR DIPLOM FORCES BAL/PWR

C52
STUART G.H.,"AMERICAN DIPLOMATIC AND CONSULAR PRACTICE (2ND ED.)" EUR+WWI MOD/EUR USA-45 DELIB/GP INT/TRADE ADJUD...BIBLIOG 20. PAGE 140 A2855 DIPLOM ADMIN INT/ORG

B53
KALIJARVI T.V.,MODERN WORLD POLITICS (3RD ED.). AFR L/A+17C MOD/EUR S/ASIA UK USSR WOR+45 INT/ORG BAL/PWR WAR PWR 20. PAGE 76 A1552 DIPLOM INT/LAW PEACE

B54
COUDENHOVE-KALERGI,AN IDEA CONQUERS THE WORLD. EUR+WWI MOD/EUR USA-45 CONSTN FAM CREATE EDU/PROP ATTIT PERSON KNOWL...CONCPT SELF/OBS TIME/SEQ. PAGE 31 A0635 — INT/ORG BIOG DIPLOM

B54
GERMANY FOREIGN MINISTRY,DOCUMENTS ON GERMAN FOREIGN POLICY 1918-1945, SERIES C (1933-1937) VOLS. I-V. GERMANY MOD/EUR FORCES PLAN ECO/TAC ...FASCIST CHARTS ANTHOL 20. PAGE 52 A1065 — NAT/G DIPLOM POLICY

B54
MANGONE G.,A SHORT HISTORY OF INTERNATIONAL ORGANIZATION. MOD/EUR USA+45 USA-45 WOR+45 WOR-45 LAW LEGIS CREATE LEGIT ROUTINE RIGID/FLEX PWR ...JURID CONCPT OBS TIME/SEQ STERTYP GEN/LAWS UN TOT/POP VAL/FREE 18/20. PAGE 94 A1921 — INT/ORG INT/LAW

B54
NORTHROP F.S.C.,EUROPEAN UNION AND UNITED STATES FOREIGN POLICY: A STUDY IN SOCIOLOGICAL JURISPRUDENCE. EUR+WWI MOD/EUR USA+45 SOCIETY STRUCT NAT/G CREATE ECO/TAC DOMIN EDU/PROP REGION ATTIT RIGID/FLEX HEALTH ORD/FREE WEALTH ...METH/CNCPT TIME/SEQ TREND. PAGE 110 A2256 — INT/ORG SOC DIPLOM

B54
NUSSBAUM D.,A CONCISE HISTORY OF THE LAW OF NATIONS. ASIA CHRIST-17C EUR+WWI ISLAM MEDIT-7 MOD/EUR S/ASIA UNIV WOR+45 WOR-45 SOCIETY STRUCT EXEC ATTIT ALL/VALS...CONCPT HIST/WRIT TIME/SEQ. PAGE 110 A2263 — INT/ORG LAW PEACE INT/LAW

B54
SALVEMINI G.,PRELUDE TO WORLD WAR II. ITALY MOD/EUR INT/ORG BAL/PWR EDU/PROP CONTROL TOTALISM...TREND NAT/COMP BIBLIOG 19 HITLER/A LEAGUE/NAT MUSSOLIN/B. PAGE 127 A2597 — WAR FASCISM LEAD PWR

B54
TAYLOR A.J.P.,THE STRUGGLE FOR MASTERY IN EUROPE 1848-1918. MOD/EUR VOL/ASSN FORCES BAL/PWR DOMIN CONTROL PEACE MORAL 19/20 TREATY EUROPE WWI. PAGE 142 A2897 — DIPLOM WAR PWR

B55
CRAIG G.A.,THE POLITICS OF THE PRUSSIAN ARMY 1640-1945. CHRIST-17C EUR+WWI MOD/EUR PRUSSIA STRUCT DIPLOM ADMIN REV WAR...SOC BIBLIOG 17/20. PAGE 32 A0652 — FORCES NAT/G ROLE CHIEF

B55
GULICK C.A.,HISTORY AND THEORIES OF WORKING-CLASS MOVEMENTS: A SELECT BIBLIOGRAPHY. EUR+WWI MOD/EUR UK USA-45 INT/ORG. PAGE 58 A1190 — BIBLIOG WORKER LABOR ADMIN

B55
GULICK E.V.,EUROPE'S CLASSICAL BALANCE OF POWER: CASE HISTORY OF THEORY AND PRACTICE OF GREAT CONCEPTS OF EUROPEAN STATECRAFT. MOD/EUR INT/ORG VOL/ASSN FORCES ORD/FREE 18/19 TREATY. PAGE 58 A1192 — IDEA/COMP BAL/PWR PWR DIPLOM

B55
ROWE C.,VOLTAIRE AND THE STATE. FRANCE MOD/EUR BAL/PWR CONTROL TASK SUPEGO ORD/FREE PWR...CONCPT 18 VOLTAIRE. PAGE 125 A2553 — NAT/G DIPLOM NAT/LISM ATTIT

B56
WOLFF R.L.,THE BALKANS IN OUR TIME. ALBANIA FUT MOD/EUR USSR YUGOSLAVIA CULTURE INT/ORG SECT DIPLOM EDU/PROP COERCE WAR ORD/FREE...CHARTS 4/20 BALKANS COMINFORM. PAGE 166 A3388 — GEOG COM

B57
DEUTSCH K.W.,POLITICAL COMMUNITY AND THE NORTH ATLANTIC AREA: INTERNATIONAL ORGANIZATION IN THE LIGHT OF HISTORICAL EXPERIENCE. MOD/EUR USA+45 USA-45 SOCIETY FORCES TOP/EX CREATE PLAN DIPLOM DOMIN EDU/PROP LEGIT ATTIT ORD/FREE PWR...SAMP/SIZ TIME/SEQ CHARTS TOT/POP. PAGE 36 A0736 — EUR+WWI INT/ORG PEACE REGION

B57
SINEY M.C.,THE ALLIED BLOCKADE OF GERMANY: 1914-1916. EUR+WWI GERMANY MOD/EUR USA-45 DIPLOM CONTROL NEUTRAL PWR 20. PAGE 133 A2721 — DETER INT/TRADE INT/LAW WAR

B58
BOWETT D.W.,SELF-DEFENSE IN INTERNATIONAL LAW. EUR+WWI MOD/EUR WOR+45 WOR-45 SOCIETY INT/ORG CONSULT DIPLOM LEGIT COERCE ATTIT ORD/FREE...JURID 20 UN. PAGE 17 A0353 — ADJUD CONCPT WAR INT/LAW

B58
IMLAH A.H.,ECONOMIC ELEMENTS IN THE PAX BRITANNICA. MOD/EUR USA+45 USA-45 ECO/DEV INT/ORG NAT/G BAL/PWR ECO/TAC PEACE ATTIT PWR WEALTH...STAT CHARTS VAL/FREE 19. PAGE 70 A1436 — MARKET UK

B58
JENKS C.W.,THE COMMON LAW OF MANKIND. EUR+WWI MOD/EUR SPACE WOR+45 INT/ORG BAL/PWR ARMS/CONT COERCE SUPEGO MORAL...TREND 20. PAGE 73 A1505 — JURID SOVEREIGN

B59
DEHIO L.,GERMANY AND WORLD POLITICS IN THE TWENTIETH CENTURY. EUR+WWI FRANCE GERMANY MOD/EUR UK USSR NAT/G CHIEF BAL/PWR DOMIN COLONIAL CONTROL LEAD...IDEA/COMP 20 VERSAILLES. PAGE 36 A0724 — DIPLOM WAR NAT/LISM SOVEREIGN

B59
MAYER A.J.,POLITICAL ORIGINS OF THE NEW DIPLOMACY, 1917-1918. EUR+WWI MOD/EUR USA-45 WAR PWR...POLICY INT/LAW BIBLIOG. PAGE 97 A1983 — TREND DIPLOM

S59
KISSINGER H.A.,"THE SEARCH FOR STABILITY." COM GERMANY MOD/EUR USA+45 USA-45 USSR INT/ORG ARMS/CONT NUC/PWR ORD/FREE PWR COLD/WAR 20 NATO. PAGE 80 A1641 — FUT ATTIT BAL/PWR

B60
ALBRECHT-CARRIE R.,FRANCE, EUROPE AND THE TWO WORLD WARS. EUR+WWI FRANCE GERMANY MOD/EUR UK ECO/DEV NAT/G FORCES BAL/PWR DOMIN ARMS/CONT PEACE PWR 20 TREATY EUROPE. PAGE 5 A0109 — DIPLOM WAR

B60
FOOTMAN D.,INTERNATIONAL COMMUNISM. ASIA EUR+WWI FRANCE FUT GERMANY MOD/EUR S/ASIA USA-45 WOR+45 WOR-45 INTELL LABOR TOTALISM MARXISM WORK 20. PAGE 47 A0958 — COM INT/ORG STRUCT REV

B60
NURTY K.S.,STUDIES IN PROBLEMS OF PEACE. CHRIST-17C MOD/EUR S/ASIA WOR+45 WOR-45 INT/ORG NAT/G SECT COERCE REV NAT/LISM ALL/VALS...CONCPT MYTH TIME/SEQ. PAGE 110 A2262 — POLICY PEACE PACIFISM ORD/FREE

B60
SZTARAY Z.,BIBLIOGRAPHY ON HUNGARY. HUNGARY MOD/EUR CULTURE INDUS SECT DIPLOM REV...ART/METH SOC LING 18/20. PAGE 141 A2879 — BIBLIOG NAT/G COM MARXISM

B61
BISHOP D.G.,THE ADMINISTRATION OF BRITISH FOREIGN RELATIONS. EUR+WWI MOD/EUR INT/ORG NAT/G POL/PAR DELIB/GP LEGIS TOP/EX ECO/TAC DOMIN EDU/PROP ADMIN COERCE 20. PAGE 14 A0292 — ROUTINE PWR DIPLOM UK

B61
ROBERTSON A.H.,THE LAW OF INTERNATIONAL INSTITUTIONS IN EUROPE. EUR+WWI MOD/EUR INT/ORG NAT/G VOL/ASSN DELIB/GP...JURID TIME/SEQ TOT/POP 20 TREATY. PAGE 122 A2497 — RIGID/FLEX ORD/FREE

B62
DUTOIT B.,LA NEUTRALITE SUISSE A L'HEURE EUROPEENNE. EUR+WWI MOD/EUR INT/ORG NAT/G VOL/ASSN PLAN BAL/PWR LEGIT NEUTRAL REGION PEACE ORD/FREE SOVEREIGN...CONCPT OBS TIME/SEQ TREND STERTYP VAL/FREE LEAGUE/NAT UN 20. PAGE 40 A0812 — ATTIT DIPLOM SWITZERLND

B62
JELAVICH C.,TSARIST RUSSIA AND BALKAN NATIONALISM. BULGARIA MOD/EUR RUSSIA DOMIN GOV/REL...GEOG 19 SERBIA. PAGE 73 A1503 — NAT/LISM DIPLOM WAR

B62
SCHRODER P.M.,METTERNICH'S DIPLOMACY AT ITS ZENITH, 1820-1823. MOD/EUR ELITES INT/ORG VOL/ASSN DELIB/GP ECO/TAC EDU/PROP DISPL PWR SOVEREIGN...POLICY CONCPT GEN/LAWS 19 METTRNCH/K. PAGE 129 A2647 — ORD/FREE BIOG BAL/PWR DIPLOM

B62
SNYDER L.L.D.,THE IMPERIALISM READER. AFR ASIA CHINA/COM COM EUR+WWI FUT MOD/EUR USA+45 WOR+45 WOR-45 INT/ORG COLONIAL SOVEREIGN CMN/WLTH OAS 20. PAGE 134 A2751 — DOMIN PWR DIPLOM

B62
WOETZEL R.K.,THE NURENBERG TRIALS IN INTERNATIONAL LAW. CHRIST-17C MOD/EUR WOR+45 SOCIETY NAT/G DELIB/GP DOMIN LEGIT ROUTINE ATTIT DRIVE PERSON SUPEGO MORAL ORD/FREE...POLICY MAJORIT JURID PSY SOC SELF/OBS RECORD NAZI TOT/POP. PAGE 166 A3376 — INT/ORG ADJUD WAR

S62
JOHNSON O.H.,"THE ENGLISH TRADITION IN INTERNATIONAL LAW." CHRIST-17C MOD/EUR EDU/PROP LEGIT CT/SYS ORD/FREE...JURID CONCPT TIME/SEQ. PAGE 75 A1526 — LAW INT/LAW UK

B63
BOISSIER P.,HISTORIE DU COMITE INTERNATIONAL DE LA CROIX ROUGE. MOD/EUR WOR-45 CONSULT FORCES PLAN DIPLOM EDU/PROP ADMIN MORAL ORD/FREE...SOC CONCPT RECORD TIME/SEQ GEN/LAWS TOT/POP VAL/FREE 19/20. PAGE 16 A0332 — INT/ORG HEALTH ARMS/CONT WAR

B63
LYONS F.S.L.,INTERNATIONALISM IN EUROPE 1815-1914. LAW AGRI COM/IND DIST/IND LABOR SECT INT/TRADE TARIFFS...BIBLIOG 19/20. PAGE 92 A1880 — DIPLOM MOD/EUR INT/ORG

B63
MONGER G.W.,THE END OF ISOLATION. FRANCE MOD/EUR RUSSIA UK NAT/G LEGIS TOP/EX GOV/REL PWR 20 TREATY CHINJAP. PAGE 103 A2106 — DIPLOM POLICY WAR

B63
NORTH R.C.,CONTENT ANALYSIS: A HANDBOOK WITH APPLICATIONS FOR THE STUDY OF INTERNATIONAL CRISIS. ASIA COM EUR+WWI MOD/EUR INT/ORG TEC/DEV DOMIN EDU/PROP ROUTINE COERCE PERCEPT RIGID/FLEX ALL/VALS ...QUANT TESTS CON/ANAL SIMUL GEN/LAWS VAL/FREE. PAGE 110 A2252 — METH/CNCPT COMPUT/IR USSR

B63
PECQUET P.,THE DIPLOMACY OF THE CONFEDERATE CABINET OF RICHMOND AND ITS AGENTS ABROAD (LIMITED ED.). MOD/EUR USA-45 LEAD...OBS 19 CIVIL/WAR SOUTH/US. PAGE 114 A2347 — DIPLOM WAR ORD/FREE

B63
PERKINS B.,PROLOGUE TO THE WAR: ENGLAND AND THE UNITED STATES, 1805-1812. MOD/EUR UK USA-45 NAT/G ORD/FREE RESPECT SOVEREIGN...POLICY TREATY 19 WAR/1812. PAGE 115 A2358 — WAR DIPLOM NEUTRAL

S63
LOPEZIBOR J.,"L'EUROPE, FORME DE VIE." CHRIST-17C EUR+WWI FUT MOD/EUR SOCIETY INT/ORG SECT EDU/PROP ATTIT RIGID/FLEX ALL/VALS...POLICY HUM SOC TIME/SEQ TREND GEN/LAWS. PAGE 91 A1862 — NAT/G CULTURE

S63
WEISSBERG G.,"MAPS AS EVIDENCE IN INTERNATIONAL BOUNDARY DISPUTES: A REAPPRAISAL." CHINA/COM EUR+WWI INDIA MOD/EUR S/ASIA INT/ORG NAT/G LEGIT PERCEPT...JURID CHARTS 20. PAGE 163 A3311 — LAW GEOG SOVEREIGN

S63
WRIGHT Q.,"DECLINE OF CLASSIC DIPLOMACY." CHRIST-17C EUR+WWI MOD/EUR WOR+45 WOR-45 INT/ORG NAT/G DELIB/GP BAL/PWR ATTIT PWR...HIST/WRIT LEAGUE/NAT. PAGE 168 A3418 — TEC/DEV CONCPT DIPLOM

B64
ETZIONI A.,WINNING WITHOUT WAR. FUT MOD/EUR USA+45 WOR+45 ECO/DEV ECO/UNDEV INT/ORG NAT/G FORCES TOP/EX PLAN TEC/DEV ECO/TAC DOMIN EDU/PROP LEGIT COERCE CHOOSE ATTIT MORAL ORD/FREE RESPECT WEALTH MAJORIT. PAGE 43 A0871 — PWR TREND DIPLOM USSR

B64
KOHNSTAMM M.,THE EUROPEAN COMMUNITY AND ITS ROLE IN THE WORLD. FUT MOD/EUR UK USA+45 ECO/DEV 20. PAGE 81 A1664 — INT/ORG NAT/G REGION DIPLOM

B64
LENSEN G.A.,REVELATIONS OF A RUSSIAN DIPLOMAT: THE MEMOIRS OF DMITRII I. ABRIKOSSOV. ASIA MOD/EUR RUSSIA USA-45 ELITES ACADEM CHIEF FORCES REV WAR PWR CONSERVE MARXISM 19/20 ABRIKSSV/D CHINJAP BOLSHEVISM. PAGE 87 A1775 — DIPLOM POLICY OBS

B64
RIVKIN A.,AFRICA AND THE EUROPEAN COMMON MARKET (PAMPHLET). AFR MOD/EUR WOR+45 TEC/DEV FOR/AID TARIFFS BAL/PAY...POLICY 20 EEC. PAGE 121 A2490 — INT/ORG INT/TRADE ECO/TAC ECO/UNDEV

S64
GROSS J.A.,"WHITEHALL AND THE COMMONWEALTH." EUR+WWI MOD/EUR INT/ORG NAT/G CONSULT DELIB/GP LEGIS DOMIN ADMIN COLONIAL ROUTINE PWR CMN/WLTH 19/20. PAGE 57 A1174 — EX/STRUC ATTIT TREND

S64
VANDENBOSCH A.,"THE SMALL STATES IN INTERNATIONAL POLITICS AND ORGANIZATION." EUR+WWI MOD/EUR WOR+45 WOR-45 CONSTN DELIB/GP COERCE ORD/FREE PWR ...TIME/SEQ GEN/LAWS VAL/FREE LEAGUE/NAT UN 19/20. PAGE 158 A3219 — NAT/G INT/ORG DIPLOM

B65
ALBRECHT-CARRIE R.,THE MEANING OF THE FIRST WORLD WAR. MOD/EUR USA-45 INT/ORG BAL/PWR PEACE ATTIT LAISSEZ MARXISM...CONCPT BIBLIOG 19/20 LEAGUE/NAT WWI. PAGE 5 A0110 — DIPLOM WAR

B65
GILBERT M.,THE EUROPEAN POWERS 1900-45. EUR+WWI ITALY MOD/EUR USSR REV WAR PWR ALL/IDEOS FASCISM ...AUD/VIS CHARTS BIBLIOG 20. PAGE 52 A1069 — DIPLOM NAT/G POLICY BAL/PWR

B65
O'CONNELL M.R.,IRISH POLITICS AND SOCIAL CONFLICT IN THE AGE OF THE AMERICAN REVOLUTION. FRANCE IRELAND MOD/EUR STRATA SECT LEGIS DIPLOM INT/TRADE DOMIN REV WAR...BIBLIOG 18 PARLIAMENT. PAGE 111 A2268 — CATHISM ATTIT NAT/G DELIB/GP

B65
ROSENBERG A.,DEMOCRACY AND SOCIALISM. COM EUR+WWI FRANCE MOD/EUR STRUCT INT/ORG NAT/G POL/PAR TOP/EX EDU/PROP COERCE PERSON PWR FASCISM MARXISM...CONCPT TIME/SEQ MARX/KARL 19/20. PAGE 124 A2535 — ATTIT

B65
SANDERSON G.N.,ENGLAND, EUROPE, AND THE UPPER NILE 1882-1899. ISLAM MOD/EUR UAR UK CHIEF...POLICY CHARTS BIBLIOG/A 19 ARABS NEGRO. PAGE 127 A2600 — AFR DIPLOM COLONIAL

B66
FABAR R.,THE VISION AND THE NEED: LATE VICTORIAN IMPERIALIST AIMS. MOD/EUR UK WOR-45 CULTURE NAT/G DIPLOM...TIME/SEQ METH/COMP 19 KIPLING/R COMMONWLTH. PAGE 43 A0880 — COLONIAL CONCPT ADMIN ATTIT

B66
MARTIN L.W.,DIPLOMACY IN MODERN EUROPEAN HISTORY. EUR+WWI MOD/EUR INT/ORG NAT/G EX/STRUC ROUTINE WAR PEACE TOTALISM PWR 15/20 COLD/WAR EUROPE/W. PAGE 95 A1953 — DIPLOM POLICY

S66
MERRITT R.L.,"SELECTED ARTICLES AND DOCUMENTS ON COMPARATIVE GOVERNMENT AND CROSS-NATIONAL RESEARCH." AFR ASIA EUR+WWI L/A+17C MOD/EUR ELITES R+D ACT/RES DIPLOM PWR...SOC CONCPT 18/20. PAGE 100 A2046 — BIBLIOG GOV/COMP NAT/G GOV/REL

B67
ADAMS A.E.,AN ATLAS OF RUSSIAN AND EAST EUROPEAN HISTORY. CHRIST-17C COM MOD/EUR INDUS SECT FORCES DIPLOM COLONIAL REV WAR 4/20. PAGE 4 A0086 — CHARTS REGION TREND

B67
DILLARD D.,ECONOMIC DEVELOPMENT OF THE NORTH ATLANTIC COMMUNITY. EUR+WWI MOD/EUR USA+45 USA-45 ECO/UNDEV LABOR CAP/ISM WAR BAL/PAY...NAT/COMP 15/20. PAGE 37 A0763 — ECO/DEV INT/TRADE INDUS DIPLOM

B67
RALSTON D.B.,THE ARMY OF THE REPUBLIC; THE PLACE OF THE MILITARY IN THE POLITICAL EVOLUTION OF FRANCE 1871-1914. FRANCE MOD/EUR EX/STRUC LEGIS TOP/EX DIPLOM ADMIN WAR GP/REL ROLE...BIBLIOG 19/20. PAGE 119 A2436 — FORCES NAT/G CIVMIL/REL POLICY

S67
DAVIS H.B.,"LENIN AND NATIONALISM: THE REDIRECTION OF THE MARXIST THEORY OF NATIONALISM." COM MOD/EUR USSR STRATA INT/ORG PLAN DOMIN COLONIAL FEDERAL ...TREND 20. PAGE 34 A0690 — NAT/LISM MARXISM ATTIT CENTRAL

B96
LOWELL A.L.,GOVERNMENTS AND PARTIES IN CONTINENTAL EUROPE, VOL. II. AUSTRIA GERMANY HUNGARY MOD/EUR SWITZERLND SOCIETY EX/STRUC LEGIS DIPLOM AGREE LEAD PARL/PROC PWR...POLICY 19. PAGE 91 A1867 — POL/PAR NAT/G GOV/REL ELITES

MODAL....MODAL TYPES, FASHIONS

MODELS....SEE SIMUL, MATH, ALSO MODELS INDEX, P. XIV

MODELSKI G. A2096,A2097,A2098,A2099

MODERNIZATION....SEE MODERNIZE

MODERNIZE....MODERNIZATION

MODIGLIANI A2215

MOID A. A0835

MOLLAU G. A2100

MOLNAR T. A2101

MONACO R. A2102

MONACO....SEE ALSO APPROPRIATE TIME/SPACE/CULTURE INDEX

MONARCH....SEE CHIEF, KING

MONARCHY....SEE CONSERVE, CHIEF, KING

MONCONDUIT F. A2103

MONCRIEFF A. A2104,A2105

MONETARY POLICY....SEE FINAN, PLAN

MONEY....SEE FINAN, ECO

B62
LUTZ F.A.,THE PROBLEM OF INTERNATIONAL ECONOMIC EQUILIBRIUM. FINAN PRODUC WEALTH 20 MONEY. PAGE 92 A1876 — DIPLOM EQUILIB BAL/PAY PROB/SOLV

B63
INTERNATIONAL MONETARY FUND,COMPENSATORY FINANCING OF EXPORT FLUCTUATIONS (PAMPHLET). WOR+45 ECO/DEV ECO/UNDEV INT/ORG WEALTH...TREND 20 IMF MONEY. PAGE 71 A1459 — BAL/PAY FINAN BUDGET INT/TRADE

B63
US CONGRESS JOINT ECO COMM,THE UNITED STATES BALANCE OF PAYMENTS. USA+45 DELIB/GP BUDGET PRICE PRODUC 20 CONGRESS GOLD/STAND MONEY. PAGE 150 A3067 — BAL/PAY INT/TRADE FINAN ECO/TAC

B64
MYINT H.,THE ECONOMICS OF THE DEVELOPING COUNTRIES. WOR+45 AGRI PLAN COST...POLICY GEOG 20 MONEY. PAGE 107 A2187 — ECO/UNDEV INT/TRADE EXTR/IND FINAN

B65
US CONGRESS JOINT ECO COMM,GUIDELINES FOR INTERNATIONAL MONETARY REFORM. USA+45 WOR+45 DELIB/GP BAL/PAY 20 CONGRESS IMF MONEY. PAGE 150 A3069 — DIPLOM FINAN PLAN INT/ORG

B66
US CONGRESS JOINT ECO COMM,NEW APPROACH TO UNITED STATES INTERNATIONAL ECONOMIC POLICY. USA+45 WOR+45 CHIEF DELIB/GP CONFER...CHARTS 20 CONGRESS MONEY. PAGE 150 A3070 — DIPLOM ECO/TAC BAL/PAY FINAN

B66
YEAGER L.B.,INTERNATIONAL MONETARY RELATIONS: THEORY, HISTORY, AND POLICY. WOR+45 WOR-45 INT/TRADE BAL/PAY...NAT/COMP 18/20 MONEY. PAGE 169 A3432 — FINAN DIPLOM ECO/TAC IDEA/COMP

MONGER G.W. A2106

MONGOLIA....SEE ALSO USSR

N
KYRIAK T.E.,ASIAN DEVELOPMENTS: A BIBLIOGRAPHY. INDONESIA KOREA/N VIETNAM/N CULTURE SOCIETY ECO/UNDEV NAT/G DIPLOM...SOC TREND 20 MONGOLIA. PAGE 83 A1699 — BIBLIOG/A ALL/IDEOS S/ASIA ASIA

MONNIER J.P. A2107

MONOPOLY....MONOPOLIES, OLIGOPOLIES, AND ANTI-TRUST ACTIONS

MONPIED E. A2108,A2109,A2110

MONROE/DOC....MONROE DOCTRINE

B43
BEMIS S.F.,THE LATIN AMERICAN POLICY OF THE UNITED STATES: AN HISTORICAL INTERPRETATION. INT/ORG AGREE COLONIAL WAR PEACE ATTIT ORD/FREE...POLICY INT/LAW CHARTS 18/20 MEXIC/AMER WILSON/W MONROE/DOC. PAGE 13 A0265 — DIPLOM SOVEREIGN USA-45 L/A+17C

B54
WHITAKER A.P.,THE WESTERN HEMISPHERE IDEA. USA+45 USA-45 CONSTN INT/ORG NAT/G DIPLOM SOVEREIGN...GEOG TIME/SEQ OAS 19/20 MONROE/DOC. PAGE 164 A3331 — L/A+17C CONCPT REGION

B65
LIEUWEN E.,U.S. POLICY IN LATIN AMERICA: A SHORT HISTORY. L/A+17C USA+45 USA-45 DELIB/GP ECO/TAC 19/20 COLD/WAR MONROE/DOC. PAGE 89 A1812 — DIPLOM COLONIAL NAT/G FOR/AID

MONROE/J....PRESIDENT JAMES MONROE

MONTALVA E.F. A2111

MONTANA....MONTANA

MONTECARLO....MONTE CARLO - OPERATIONAL RESEARCH DECISION-MAKING MODEL

MONTER W. A2112

MONTESQ....MONTESQUIEU, CHARLES LOUIS DE SECONDAT

MONTGOMERY B.L. A2113

MONTGOMERY H. A2114

MONTGOMERY J.D. A2115,A2116

MONTGOMERY....MONTGOMERY, ALABAMA

MOODY M. A2117

MOOMAW I.W. A2118

MOON P. A2119

MOON P.T. A2120

MOOR C.C. A2121

MOORE B.T. A2122

MOORE N. A2123

MOORE R.J. A2124

MOORE W.E. A2125

MOORTHY S.D. A2372

MOOS M. A0606

MORA J.A. A2126

MORAES F. A2127

MORAL....RECTITUDE, MORALITY, GOODNESS (ALSO IMMORALITY)

B00
GROTIUS H.,DE JURE BELLI AC PACIS. CHRIST-17C UNIV LAW SOCIETY PROVS LEGIT PEACE PERCEPT MORAL PWR ...CONCPT CON/ANAL GEN/LAWS. PAGE 57 A1180 — JURID INT/LAW WAR

B03
MOREL E.D.,THE BRITISH CASE IN FRENCH CONGO. CONGO/BRAZ FRANCE UK COERCE MORAL WEALTH...POLICY INT/LAW 20 CONGO/LEOP. PAGE 104 A2130 — DIPLOM INT/TRADE COLONIAL AFR

B04
CRANDALL S.B.,TREATIES: THEIR MAKING AND ENFORCEMENT. MOD/EUR USA-45 CONSTN INT/ORG NAT/G LEGIS EDU/PROP LEGIT EXEC PEACE KNOWL MORAL...JURID CONGRESS 19/20 TREATY. PAGE 32 A0655 — LAW

B16
PUFENDORF S.,LAW OF NATURE AND OF NATIONS (ABRIDGED). UNIV LAW NAT/G DIPLOM AGREE WAR PERSON ALL/VALS PWR...POLICY 18 DEITY NATURL/LAW. PAGE 118 A2416 — CONCPT INT/LAW SECT MORAL

B17
DE VICTORIA F.,DE INDIS ET DE JURE BELLI (1557) IN F. DE VICTORIA, DE INDIS ET DE JURE BELLI REFLECTIONES. UNIV NAT/G SECT CHIEF PARTIC COERCE PEACE MORAL...POLICY 16 INDIAN/AM CHRISTIAN CONSCN/OBJ. PAGE 35 A0715 — WAR INT/LAW OWN

B17
VEBLEN T.B.,AN INQUIRY INTO THE NATURE OF PEACE AND THE TERMS OF ITS PERPETUATION. UNIV STRATA FINAN EDU/PROP PRICE COST DISCRIM NAT/LISM MORAL ORD/FREE PACIFIST 20 WORLDUNITY. PAGE 158 A3224 — PEACE DIPLOM WAR NAT/G

B19
VANDERPOL A.,LA DOCTRINE SCOLASTIQUE DU DROIT DE GUERRE. CHRIST-17C FORCES DIPLOM LEGIT SUPEGO MORAL ...BIOG AQUINAS/T SUAREZ/F CHRISTIAN. PAGE 158 A3220 — WAR SECT INT/LAW

N19
DEANE H.,THE WAR IN VIETNAM (PAMPHLET). CHINA/COM VIETNAM BAL/PWR DIPLOM ECO/TAC SOCISM INTERVENT COLD/WAR INTERVENT COLD/WAR. PAGE 35 A0720 — WAR SOCIALIST MORAL CAP/ISM

N19
HALPERN M.,THE MORALITY AND POLITICS OF INTERVENTION (PAMPHLET). USA+45 INT/ORG FORCES ECO/TAC MORAL ORD/FREE 20 INTERVENT CHRISTIAN. PAGE 61 A1243 — POLICY DIPLOM SOVEREIGN DOMIN

B20
HALDANE R.B.,BEFORE THE WAR. MOD/EUR SOCIETY INT/ORG NAT/G DELIB/GP PLAN DOMIN EDU/PROP LEGIT ADMIN COERCE ATTIT DRIVE MORAL ORD/FREE PWR...SOC CONCPT SELF/OBS RECORD BIOG TIME/SEQ. PAGE 60 A1223 — POLICY DIPLOM UK

S23
DEWEY J.,"ETHICS AND INTERNATIONAL RELATIONS." FUT WOR-45 SOCIETY INT/ORG VOL/ASSN DIPLOM LEGIT ORD/FREE...JURID CONCPT GEN/METH 20. PAGE 37 A0752 — LAW MORAL

B24
NAVILLE A.,LIBERTE, EGALITE, SOLIDARITE: ESSAIS D'ANALYSE. STRATA FAM VOL/ASSN INT/TRADE GP/REL MORAL MARXISM SOCISM...PSY TREATY. PAGE 107 A2205 — ORD/FREE SOC IDEA/COMP DIPLOM

B29
BUELL R.,INTERNATIONAL RELATIONS. WOR+45 WOR-45 CONSTN STRATA FORCES TOP/EX ADMIN ATTIT DRIVE SUPEGO MORAL ORD/FREE PWR SOVEREIGN...JURID SOC CONCPT 20. PAGE 21 A0428 — INT/ORG BAL/PWR DIPLOM

B30
BYNKERSHOEK C.,QUAESTIONUM JURIS PUBLICI LIBRI DUO. CHRIST-17C MOD/EUR CONSTN ELITES SOCIETY NAT/G PROVS EX/STRUC FORCES TOP/EX BAL/PWR DIPLOM ATTIT MORAL...TRADIT CONCPT. PAGE 23 A0460 — INT/ORG LAW NAT/LISM INT/LAW

B31
BEALES A.C.,THE HISTORY OF PEACE. WOR-45 VOL/ASSN DELIB/GP CREATE PLAN EDU/PROP ATTIT MORAL ...TIME/SEQ VAL/FREE 19/20. PAGE 12 A0239 — INT/ORG ARMS/CONT PEACE

B33
FERRERO G.,PEACE AND WAR (TRANS. BY BERTHA PRITCHARD). CULTURE FINAN SECT ATTIT SUPEGO MORAL ORD/FREE CONSERVE POPULISM SOCISM POLICY. PAGE 45 A0922 — WAR PEACE DIPLOM PROB/SOLV

B33
GENTILI A.,DE JURE BELLI, LIBRI TRES (1612) (VOL. 2). FORCES DIPLOM AGREE PEACE SOVEREIGN. PAGE 52 A1059 — WAR INT/LAW MORAL SUPEGO

B33
REID H.D.,RECUEIL DES COURS; TOME 45: LES SERVITUDES INTERNATIONALES III. FRANCE CONSTN DELIB/GP PRESS CONTROL REV WAR CHOOSE PEACE MORAL MARITIME TREATY. PAGE 120 A2457 — ORD/FREE DIPLOM LAW

B37
THOMPSON J.W.,SECRET DIPLOMACY: A RECORD OF ESPIONAGE AND DOUBLE-DEALING: 1500-1815. CHRIST-17C MOD/EUR NAT/G WRITING RISK MORAL...ANTHOL BIBLIOG 16/19 ESPIONAGE. PAGE 143 A2927 — DIPLOM CRIME

B39
CARR E.H.,PROPAGANDA IN INTERNATIONAL POLITICS (PAMPHLET). EUR+WWI GERMANY MOD/EUR NAT/G AGREE WAR MORAL...POLICY 20 TREATY. PAGE 24 A0497 — DIPLOM EDU/PROP CONTROL ATTIT

B39
DULLES J.,WAR, PEACE AND CHANGE. FRANCE ITALY UK USA-45 WOR-45 LAW INT/ORG NAT/G SECT VOL/ASSN FORCES TOP/EX DOMIN ARMS/CONT COERCE ATTIT PERSON RIGID/FLEX MORAL PWR...JURID STERTYP TOT/POP LEAGUE/NAT 20. PAGE 39 A0796 — EDU/PROP TOTALISM WAR

C39
HADDOW A.,"POLITICAL SCIENCE IN AMERICAN COLLEGES AND UNIVERSITIES 1636-1900." CONSTN MORAL...POLICY INT/LAW CON/ANAL BIBLIOG T 17/20. PAGE 59 A1211 — USA-45 LAW ACADEM KNOWL

B40
MIDDLEBUSH F.,ELEMENTS OF INTERNATIONAL RELATIONS. WOR-45 PROVS CONSULT EDU/PROP LEGIT WAR NAT/LISM ATTIT KNOWL MORAL ORD/FREE PWR...JURID LEAGUE/NAT TOT/POP VAL/FREE. PAGE 101 A2067
NAT/G INT/ORG PEACE DIPLOM

B40
NIEBUHR R.,CHRISTIANITY AND POWER POLITICS. WOR-45 SECT DIPLOM GP/REL SUPEGO ALL/IDEOS WORSHIP 20 CHRISTIAN. PAGE 109 A2234
PARTIC PEACE MORAL

B41
SCHWARZENBERGER G.,POWER POLITICS: AN INTRODUCTION TO THE STUDY OF INTERNATIONAL RELATIONS AND POST-WAR PLANNING. INT/ORG FORCES COERCE WAR FEDERAL PEACE MORAL...POLICY CONCPT CON/ANAL BIBLIOG 20. PAGE 130 A2660
DIPLOM UTOPIA PWR

B43
SULZBACH W.,NATIONAL CONSCIOUSNESS. FUT WOR-45 INT/ORG PEACE MORAL FASCISM MARXISM...MAJORIT TREND WORSHIP 19/20 LEAGUE/NAT INTERVENT WWI. PAGE 140 A2862
NAT/LISM NAT/G DIPLOM WAR

C43
BENTHAM J.,"PRINCIPLES OF INTERNATIONAL LAW" IN J. BOWRING, ED., THE WORKS OF JEREMY BENTHAM." UNIV NAT/G PLAN PROB/SOLV DIPLOM CONTROL SANCTION MORAL ORD/FREE PWR SOVEREIGN 19. PAGE 13 A0270
INT/LAW JURID WAR PEACE

B44
LIPPMANN W.,US WAR AIMS. USA-45 DIPLOM ATTIT MORAL ORD/FREE PWR...CONCPT TIME/SEQ GEN/LAWS TOT/POP 20. PAGE 89 A1828
FUT INT/ORG PEACE WAR

C44
SUAREZ F.,"ON WAR" (1621) IN SELECTIONS FROM THREE WORKS, VOL. I." NAT/G SECT CHIEF DIPLOM LEGIT MORAL PWR...POLICY INT/LAW 17. PAGE 140 A2859
WAR REV ORD/FREE CATH

B46
STURZO D.L.,NATIONALISM AND INTERNATIONALISM. WOR-45 INT/ORG LABOR NAT/G POL/PAR TOTALISM MORAL ORD/FREE FASCISM...MAJORIT 19/20 UN LEAGUE/NAT MUSSOLIN/B. PAGE 140 A2857
NAT/LISM DIPLOM WAR PEACE

B48
MORGENTHAL H.J.,POLITICS AMONG NATIONS: THE STRUGGLE FOR POWER AND PEACE. FUT WOR+45 INT/ORG OP/RES PROB/SOLV BAL/PWR CONTROL ATTIT MORAL ...INT/LAW BIBLIOG 20 COLD/WAR. PAGE 104 A2135
DIPLOM PEACE PWR POLICY

S48
MORGENTHAU H.J.,"THE TWILIGHT OF INTERNATIONAL MORALITY" (BMR)" WOR+45 WOR-45 BAL/PWR WAR NAT/LISM PEACE...POLICY INT/LAW IDEA/COMP 15/20 TREATY INTERVENT. PAGE 104 A2137
MORAL DIPLOM NAT/G

B50
JIMENEZ E.,VOTING AND HANDLING OF DISPUTES IN THE SECURITY COUNCIL. WOR+45 CONSTN INT/ORG DIPLOM LEGIT DETER CHOOSE MORAL ORD/FREE PWR...JURID TIME/SEQ COLD/WAR UN 20. PAGE 74 A1517
DELIB/GP ROUTINE

B51
MACLAURIN J.,THE UNITED NATIONS AND POWER POLITICS. WOR+45 CONSULT EDU/PROP LEGIT ADJUD EXEC MORAL ORD/FREE...HUM JURID CONCPT RECORD TIME/SEQ UN COLD/WAR 20. PAGE 93 A1896
INT/ORG ROUTINE

B51
STANTON A.H.,PERSONALITY AND POLITICAL CRISIS. WOR+45 WOR-45 STRUCT DIPLOM INGP/REL TOTALISM MORAL ...ANTHOL 20 LASSWELL/H PARSONS/T RIESMAN/D. PAGE 137 A2806
EDU/PROP WAR PERSON PSY

L51
MANGONE G.,"THE IDEA AND PRACTICE OF WORLD GOVERNMENT." FUT WOR+45 WOR-45 ECO/DEV LEGIS CREATE LEGIT ROUTINE ATTIT MORAL PWR WEALTH...CONCPT GEN/LAWS 20. PAGE 94 A1920
INT/ORG SOCIETY INT/LAW

B52
LIPPMANN W.,ISOLATION AND ALLIANCES: AN AMERICAN SPEAKS TO THE BRITISH. USA+45 USA-45 INT/ORG AGREE COERCE DETER WAR PEACE MORAL 20 TREATY INTERVENT. PAGE 89 A1829
DIPLOM SOVEREIGN COLONIAL ATTIT

S52
SCHUMAN F.,"INTERNATIONAL IDEALS AND THE NATIONAL INTEREST." WOR+45 WOR-45 INT/ORG VOL/ASSN DELIB/GP CREATE BAL/PWR DOMIN PEACE PERSON MORAL PWR SOVEREIGN...POLICY GEN/LAWS TOT/POP LEAGUE/NAT 20. PAGE 129 A2648
ATTIT CONCPT

B53
BORGESE G.,FOUNDATIONS OF THE WORLD REPUBLIC. FUT SOCIETY NAT/G CREATE LEGIT PERSON MORAL...MAJORIT CON/ANAL LEAGUE/NAT TOT/POP 20. PAGE 17 A0340
INT/ORG CONSTN PEACE

B53
COUSINS N.,WHO SPEAKS FOR MAN. GERMANY KOREA WOR+45 SOCIETY INT/ORG NAT/G CREATE EDU/PROP HEALTH KNOWL LOVE MORAL...OBS SELF/OBS BIOG HYPO/EXP TOT/POP 20 CHINJAP. PAGE 32 A0642
ATTIT WAR PEACE

B54
TAYLOR A.J.P.,THE STRUGGLE FOR MASTERY IN EUROPE 1848-1918. MOD/EUR VOL/ASSN FORCES BAL/PWR DOMIN CONTROL PEACE MORAL 19/20 TREATY EUROPE WWI. PAGE 142 A2897
DIPLOM WAR PWR

S54
DAWSON K.H.,"THE UNITED NATIONS IN A DISUNITED WORLD." WOR+45 WOR-45 LAW INTELL NAT/G PEACE ATTIT PERCEPT MORAL LEAGUE/NAT TOT/POP VAL/FREE 20 UN. PAGE 34 A0694
INT/ORG LEGIT

B55
VIGON J.,TEORIA DEL MILITARISMO. NAT/G DIPLOM COLONIAL COERCE GUERRILLA CIVMIL/REL NAT/LISM MORAL ALL/IDEOS PACIFISM 18/20. PAGE 159 A3234
FORCES PHIL/SCI WAR POLICY

B56
FIELD G.C.,POLITICAL THEORY. POL/PAR REPRESENT MORAL SOVEREIGN...JURID IDEA/COMP. PAGE 45 A0924
CONCPT NAT/G ORD/FREE DIPLOM

B56
GEORGE A.L.,WOODROW WILSON AND COLONEL HOUSE. WOR-45 CONSTN FACE/GP INT/ORG NAT/G POL/PAR CONSULT LEGIT EXEC COERCE CHOOSE ATTIT DRIVE PERSON MORAL ORD/FREE PWR RESPECT...POLICY MGT PSY OBS RECORD INT LEAGUE/NAT. PAGE 52 A1060
USA-45 BIOG DIPLOM

B57
DE VISSCHER C.,THEORY AND REALITY IN PUBLIC INTERNATIONAL LAW. WOR+45 WOR-45 SOCIETY NAT/G CT/SYS ATTIT MORAL ORD/FREE PWR...JURID CONCPT METH/CNCPT TIME/SEQ GEN/LAWS LEAGUE/NAT TOT/POP VAL/FREE COLD/WAR. PAGE 35 A0716
INT/ORG LAW INT/LAW

B57
LEFEVER E.W.,ETHICS AND UNITED STATUS FOREIGN POLICY. SOCIETY INT/ORG NAT/G ACT/RES DIPLOM EDU/PROP COERCE ATTIT MORAL...TREND GEN/LAWS COLD/WAR 20. PAGE 86 A1762
USA+45 CULTURE CONCPT POLICY

B57
STRACHEY A.,THE UNCONSCIOUS MOTIVES OF WAR; A PSYCHO-ANALYTICAL CONTRIBUTION. UNIV SOCIETY DIPLOM DREAM GP/REL ADJUST ATTIT DISPL PERCEPT PERSON KNOWL MORAL. PAGE 139 A2840
WAR DRIVE LOVE PSY

B58
CHANG H.,WITHIN THE FOUR SEAS. ASIA WAR MORAL MARXISM...IDEA/COMP NAT/COMP 20 CONFUCIUS. PAGE 26 A0521
PEACE DIPLOM KNOWL CULTURE

B58
JENKS C.W.,THE COMMON LAW OF MANKIND. EUR+WWI MOD/EUR SPACE WOR+45 INT/ORG BAL/PWR ARMS/CONT COERCE SUPEGO MORAL...TREND 20. PAGE 73 A1505
JURID SOVEREIGN

B58
SLICK T.,PERMANENT PEACE: A CHECK AND BALANCE PLAN. FUT WOR+45 NAT/G FORCES CREATE PLAN EDU/PROP LEGIT ADJUD COERCE NAT/LISM RIGID/FLEX MORAL...HUM CONCPT METH/CNCPT NEW/IDEA TREND CHARTS TOT/POP 20. PAGE 134 A2742
INT/ORG ORD/FREE PEACE ARMS/CONT

S58
BOURBON-BUSSET J.,"HOW DECISIONS ARE MADE IN FOREIGN POLITICS: PSYCHOLOGY IN INTERNATIONAL POLITICS." WOR+45 NAT/G SECT REGION WAR MORAL ...CONCPT OBS STERTYP GEN/LAWS TOT/POP COLD/WAR 20. PAGE 17 A0350
INT/ORG DELIB/GP DIPLOM

S58
ROTHFELS H.,"THE GERMAN RESISTANCE IN ITS INTERNATIONAL ASPECTS" (BMR)" EUR+WWI GERMANY UNIV CHIEF DIPLOM WAR NAT/LISM ATTIT...POLICY 20 HITLER/A NAZI. PAGE 124 A2548
VOL/ASSN MORAL FASCISM CIVMIL/REL

B59
SIMPSON J.L.,INTERNATIONAL ARBITRATION: LAW AND PRACTICE. WOR+45 WOR-45 INT/ORG DELIB/GP ADJUD PEACE MORAL ORD/FREE...METH 18/20. PAGE 133 A2720
INT/LAW DIPLOM CT/SYS CONSULT

S59
HOFFMANN S.,"IMPLEMENTATION OF INTERNATIONAL INSTRUMENTS ON HUMAN RIGHTS." WOR+45 VOL/ASSN DELIB/GP JUDGE EDU/PROP LEGIT ROUTINE PEACE COLD/WAR 20. PAGE 66 A1355
INT/ORG MORAL

S59
KRIPALANI A.J.B.,"FOR PRINCIPLED NEUTRALITY." CHINA/COM INDIA S/ASIA PLAN ECO/TAC RIGID/FLEX MORAL PWR...MYSTIC SOC RECORD 20 GANDHI/M. PAGE 82 A1684
ATTIT FOR/AID DIPLOM

S59
REUBENS E.D.,"THE BASIS FOR REORIENATION OF AMERICAN FOREIGN AID POLICY." USA+45 USSR STRUCT INT/ORG CONSULT ECO/TAC ADMIN DRIVE MORAL ORD/FREE PWR WEALTH...RELATIV MATH STAT TREND GEN/LAWS VAL/FREE 20. PAGE 120 A2467
ECO/UNDEV PLAN FOR/AID DIPLOM

B60
APTHEKER H.,DISARMAMENT AND THE AMERICAN ECONOMY: A SYMPOSIUM. FUT USA+45 ECO/DEV DIST/IND FINAN INDUS PROC/MFG LABOR NAT/G POL/PAR CONSULT PLAN CAP/ISM INT/TRADE PEACE ATTIT MORAL WEALTH...TREND GEN/LAWS TOT/POP 20. PAGE 9 A0172
MARXIST ARMS/CONT

B60
JENNINGS R.,PROGRESS OF INTERNATIONAL LAW. FUT WOR+45 WOR-45 SOCIETY NAT/G VOL/ASSN DELIB/GP DIPLOM EDU/PROP LEGIT COERCE ATTIT DRIVE MORAL ORD/FREE...JURID CONCPT OBS TIME/SEQ TREND GEN/LAWS. PAGE 74 A1509
INT/ORG LAW INT/LAW

B60
VAN HOOGSTRATE D.J.,AMERICAN FOREIGN POLICY: REALISTS AND IDEALISTS: A CATHOLIC INTERPRETATION. BAL/PWR FOR/AID ARMS/CONT GOV/REL PEACE LOVE MORAL SOVEREIGN CATHISM...BIBLIOG 20. PAGE 158 A3213
CATH DIPLOM POLICY IDEA/COMP

L60
RIGGS R.,"OVER-SELLING THE U.N. CHARTER, FACT AND MYTH." USA+45 SOCIETY NAT/G TOP/EX PLAN DIPLOM EDU/PROP PEACE ATTIT PERCEPT MORAL...POLICY SAMP UN 20. PAGE 121 A2481
INT/ORG MYTH

S60
RUSSEL R.W.,"ROLES FOR PSYCHOLOGISTS IN THE MAINTENANCE OF PEACE." FUT USA+45 CULTURE INT/ORG DIPLOM FOR/AID EDU/PROP ATTIT KNOWL MORAL PWR ...POLICY SOC COLD/WAR 20. PAGE 125 A2572
PSY GEN/METH

S60
SCHWELB E.,"INTERNATIONAL CONVENTIONS ON HUMAN RIGHTS." FUT WOR+45 LAW CONSTN CULTURE SOCIETY STRUCT VOL/ASSN DELIB/GP PLAN ADJUD SUPEGO LOVE MORAL...SOC CONCPT STAT RECORD HIST/WRIT TREND 20 UN. PAGE 130 A2664
INT/ORG HUM

S60
THOMPSON K.W.,"MORAL PURPOSE IN FOREIGN POLICY: REALITIES AND ILLUSIONS." WOR+45 WOR-45 LAW CULTURE SOCIETY INT/ORG PLAN ADJUD ADMIN COERCE RIGID/FLEX SUPEGO KNOWL ORD/FREE PWR...SOC TREND SOC/EXP TOT/POP 20. PAGE 143 A2930
MORAL JURID DIPLOM

S60
WRIGHT Q.,"LEGAL ASPECTS OF THE U-2 INCIDENT." COM USA+45 USSR STRUCT NAT/G FORCES PLAN TEC/DEV ADJUD RIGID/FLEX MORAL ORD/FREE...DECISION INT/LAW JURID PSY TREND GEN/LAWS COLD/WAR VAL/FREE 20 U-2. PAGE 168 A3413
PWR POLICY SPACE

B61
EISENHOWER D.D.,PEACE WITH JUSTICE: SELECTED ADDRESSES. USSR PARTIC ARMS/CONT MORAL...TRADIT CONCPT GEN/LAWS ANTHOL 20 PRESIDENT COLD/WAR. PAGE 41 A0832
PEACE DIPLOM EDU/PROP POLICY

S61
BALL M.M.,"ISSUES FOR THE AMERICAS: NON-INTERVENTION VS HUMAN RIGHTS AND THE PRESERVATION OF DEMOCRATIC INSTITUTIONS." USA+45 INTELL INT/ORG NAT/G DIPLOM ECO/TAC LEGIT...TREND OAS TOT/POP 20. PAGE 11 A0213
L/A+17C MORAL

S61
NOVE A.,"THE SOVIET MODEL AND UNDERDEVELOPED COUNTRIES." COM FUT USSR WOR+45 CULTURE ECO/DEV POL/PAR FOR/AID EDU/PROP ADMIN MORAL WEALTH ...POLICY RECORD HIST/WRIT 20. PAGE 110 A2258
ECO/UNDEV PLAN

B62
ALIX C.,LE SAINT-SIEGE ET LES NATIONALISMES EN EUROPE 1870-1960. COM GERMANY IRELAND ITALY SOCIETY SECT TOTALISM RIGID/FLEX MORAL 19/20. PAGE 6 A0122
CATH NAT/LISM ATTIT DIPLOM

B62
BENNETT J.C.,NUCLEAR WEAPONS AND THE CONFLICT OF CONSCIENCE. WOR+45 PROB/SOLV DIPLOM WEAPON SUPEGO MORAL...ANTHOL WORSHIP 20. PAGE 13 A0268
POLICY NUC/PWR WAR

B62
GILPIN R.,AMERICAN SCIENTISTS AND NUCLEAR WEAPONS POLICY. COM FUT USA+45 WOR+45 INT/ORG NAT/G PROF/ORG CONSULT FORCES CREATE TEC/DEV BAL/PWR EDU/PROP ARMS/CONT WAR PERCEPT KNOWL MORAL PWR ...PHIL/SCI SOC CONCPT GEN/LAWS 20. PAGE 52 A1073
INTELL ATTIT DETER NUC/PWR

B62
KING-HALL S.,POWER POLITICS IN THE NUCLEAR AGE: A POLICY FOR BRITAIN. UK WOR+45 PLAN ECO/TAC CONTROL RISK ARMS/CONT MORAL PWR RESPECT...OLD/LIB 20. PAGE 79 A1625
BAL/PWR NUC/PWR POLICY DIPLOM

B62
ROSAMOND R.,CRUSADE FOR PEACE: EISENHOWER'S PRESIDENTIAL LEGACY WITH THE PROGRAM FOR ACTION. USA+45 PARTIC ARMS/CONT MORAL MARXISM...TRADIT CONCPT CHARTS GEN/LAWS ANTHOL 20 PRESIDENT EISNHWR/DD. PAGE 123 A2526
PEACE DIPLOM EDU/PROP POLICY

B62
SCHWARZENBERGER G.,THE FRONTIERS OF INTERNATIONAL LAW. WOR+45 WOR-45 NAT/G LEGIT CT/SYS ROUTINE MORAL ORD/FREE PWR...JURID SOC GEN/METH 20 COLD/WAR. PAGE 130 A2661
INT/ORG LAW INT/LAW

B62
WOETZEL R.K.,THE NURENBERG TRIALS IN INTERNATIONAL LAW. CHRIST-17C MOD/EUR WOR+45 SOCIETY NAT/G DELIB/GP DOMIN LEGIT ROUTINE ATTIT DRIVE PERSON SUPEGO MORAL ORD/FREE...POLICY MAJORIT JURID PSY SOC SELF/OBS RECORD NAZI TOT/POP. PAGE 166 A3376
INT/ORG ADJUD WAR

S62
FALK R.A.,"THE REALITY OF INTERNATIONAL LAW." WOR+45 NAT/G LEGIT COERCE DETER WAR MORAL ORD/FREE PWR SOVEREIGN...JURID CONCPT VAL/FREE COLD/WAR 20. PAGE 43 A0887
INT/ORG ADJUD NUC/PWR INT/LAW

S62
LISSITZYN O.J.,"SOME LEGAL IMPLICATIONS OF THE U-2 AND RB-47 INCIDENTS." FUT USA+45 USSR WOR+45 AIR NAT/G DIPLOM LEGIT MORAL ORD/FREE SOVEREIGN...JURID GEN/LAWS GEN/METH COLD/WAR 20 U-2. PAGE 90 A1840
LAW CONCPT SPACE INT/LAW

B63
BOISSIER P.,HISTORIE DU COMITE INTERNATIONAL DE LA CROIX ROUGE. MOD/EUR WOR-45 CONSULT FORCES PLAN DIPLOM EDU/PROP ADMIN MORAL ORD/FREE...SOC CONCPT RECORD TIME/SEQ GEN/LAWS TOT/POP VAL/FREE 19/20. PAGE 16 A0332
INT/ORG HEALTH ARMS/CONT WAR

B63
FALK R.A.,LAW, MORALITY, AND WAR IN THE CONTEMPORARY WORLD. WOR+45 LAW INT/ORG EX/STRUC FORCES EDU/PROP LEGIT DETER NUC/PWR MORAL ORD/FREE ...JURID TOT/POP 20. PAGE 43 A0888
ADJUD ARMS/CONT PEACE INT/LAW

B63
FRANKEL J.,THE MAKING OF FOREIGN POLICY: AN ANALYSIS OF DECISION-MAKING. CHINA/COM EUR+WWI USA+45 ELITES INTELL FORCES LEGIS PLAN ATTIT ALL/VALS MORAL CONSERVE...GOV/COMP 20 PRESIDENT UN TREATY. PAGE 48 A0981
POLICY DECISION PROB/SOLV DIPLOM

B63
LANOUE G.R.,A BIBLIOGRAPHY OF DOCTORAL DISSERTATIONS ON POLITICS AND RELIGION. USA+45 USA-45 CONSTN PROVS DIPLOM CT/SYS MORAL...POLICY JURID CONCPT 20. PAGE 84 A1728
BIBLIOG NAT/G LOC/G SECT

B63
VOSS E.H.,NUCLEAR AMBUSH: THE TEST-BAN TRAP. WOR+45 COM/IND INT/ORG NAT/G DELIB/GP FORCES LEGIS TOP/EX ACT/RES DOMIN EDU/PROP LEGIT ROUTINE COERCE ATTIT PERCEPT RIGID/FLEX HEALTH MORAL ORD/FREE PWR. PAGE 160 A3255
TEC/DEV HIST/WRIT ARMS/CONT NUC/PWR

L63
LISSITZYN O.J.,"INTERNATIONAL LAW IN A DIVIDED WORLD." FUT WOR+45 CONSTN CULTURE ECO/DEV ECO/UNDEV DIST/IND NAT/G FORCES ECO/TAC LEGIT ADJUD ADMIN COERCE ATTIT HEALTH MORAL ORD/FREE PWR RESPECT WEALTH VAL/FREE. PAGE 90 A1841
INT/ORG LAW

S63
HARNETTY P.,"CANADA, SOUTH AFRICA AND THE COMMONWEALTH." CANADA SOUTH/AFR LAW INT/ORG VOL/ASSN DELIB/GP LEGIS TOP/EX ECO/TAC LEGIT DRIVE MORAL...CONCPT CMN/WLTH 20. PAGE 62 A1263
AFR ATTIT

B64
ETZIONI A.,WINNING WITHOUT WAR. FUT MOD/EUR USA+45 WOR+45 ECO/DEV ECO/UNDEV INT/ORG NAT/G FORCES TOP/EX PLAN TEC/DEV ECO/TAC DOMIN EDU/PROP LEGIT COERCE CHOOSE ATTIT MORAL ORD/FREE RESPECT WEALTH MAJORIT. PAGE 43 A0871
PWR TREND DIPLOM USSR

B64
FREUD A.,OF HUMAN SOVEREIGNTY. WOR+45 INDUS SECT ECO/TAC CRIME CHOOSE ATTIT MORAL MARXISM...POLICY BIBLIOG 20. PAGE 49 A0998
NAT/LISM DIPLOM WAR PEACE

B64
NICE R.W.,TREASURY OF LAW. WOR+45 WOR-45 SECT ADJUD MORAL ORD/FREE...INT/LAW JURID PHIL/SCI ANTHOL. PAGE 108 A2227
LAW WRITING PERS/REL DIPLOM

B64
ROSENAU J.N.,INTERNATIONAL ASPECTS OF CIVIL STRIFE. CHINA/COM CUBA EUR+WWI USA+45 USSR BAL/PWR EDU/PROP NEUTRAL COERCE MORAL...NAT/COMP 20 COLD/WAR UN. PAGE 124 A2533
POLICY DIPLOM REV WAR

B64
US AIR FORCE ACADEMY ASSEMBLY,OUTER SPACE: FINAL REPORT APRIL 1-4, 1964. FUT USA+45 WOR+45 LAW DELIB/GP CONFER ARMS/CONT WAR PEACE ATTIT MORAL ...ANTHOL 20 NASA. PAGE 150 A3055
SPACE CIVMIL/REL NUC/PWR DIPLOM

B64
WOODHOUSE C.M.,THE NEW CONCERT OF NATIONS. WOR+45 ECO/DEV ECO/UNDEV NAT/G BAL/PWR ECO/TAC NAT/LISM PWR SOVEREIGN ALL/IDEOS 20 UN COLD/WAR. PAGE 166 A3391
DIPLOM MORAL FOR/AID COLONIAL

L64
POUNDS N.J.G.,"THE POLITICS OF PARTITION." AFR ASIA COM EUR+WWI FUT ISLAM S/ASIA USA-45 LAW ECO/DEV ECO/UNDEV AGRI INDUS INT/ORG POL/PAR PROVS SECT FORCES TOP/EX EDU/PROP LEGIT ATTIT MORAL ORD/FREE PWR RESPECT WEALTH. PAGE 117 A2402
NAT/G NAT/LISM

S64
CARNEGIE ENDOWMENT INT. PEACE,"HUMAN RIGHTS (ISSUES BEFORE THE NINETEENTH GENERAL ASSEMBLY)." AFR WOR+45 LAW CONSTN NAT/G EDU/PROP GP/REL DISCRIM PEACE ATTIT MORAL ORD/FREE...INT/LAW PSY CONCPT RECORD UN 20. PAGE 24 A0492
INT/ORG PERSON RACE/REL

S64
CARNEGIE ENDOWMENT INT. PEACE,"LEGAL QUESTIONS (ISSUES BEFORE THE NINETEENTH GENERAL ASSEMBLY)." WOR+45 CONSTN NAT/G DELIB/GP ADJUD PEACE MORAL ORD/FREE...RECORD UN 20 TREATY. PAGE 24 A0494
INT/ORG LAW INT/LAW

S64
COHEN M.,"BASIC PRINCIPLES OF INTERNATIONAL LAW." UNIV WOR+45 WOR-45 BAL/PWR LEGIT ADJUD WAR ATTIT MORAL ORD/FREE PWR...JURID CONCPT MYTH TOT/POP 20. PAGE 27 A0560
INT/ORG INT/LAW

S64
GINSBURGS G.,"WARS OF NATIONAL LIBERATION - THE SOVIET THESIS." COM USSR WOR+45 WOR-45 LAW CULTURE INT/ORG DIPLOM LEGIT COLONIAL GUERRILLA WAR
COERCE CONCPT INT/LAW

NAT/LISM ATTIT PERSON MORAL PWR...JURID OBS TREND MARX/KARL 20. PAGE 53 A1075 — REV

S64
HOSKYNS C.,"THE AFRICAN STATES AND THE UNITED NATIONS: 1958-1964." SOUTH/AFR NAT/G VOL/ASSN CONSULT BAL/PWR EDU/PROP MORAL ORD/FREE PWR ...CONCPT TREND UN 20. PAGE 68 A1393 — AFR INT/ORG DIPLOM

S64
KARPOV P.V.,"PEACEFUL COEXISTENCE AND INTERNATIONAL LAW." WOR+45 LAW SOCIETY INT/ORG VOL/ASSN FORCES CREATE CAP/ISM DIPLOM ADJUD NUC/PWR PEACE MORAL ORD/FREE PWR MARXISM...MARXIST JURID CONCPT OBS TREND COLD/WAR MARX/KARL 20. PAGE 77 A1568 — COM ATTIT INT/LAW USSR

S64
MARTELLI G.,"PORTUGAL AND THE UNITED NATIONS." AFR EUR+WWI ELITES INT/ORG NAT/G PROVS PLAN DIPLOM ECO/TAC DOMIN COLONIAL RIGID/FLEX MORAL ORD/FREE PWR WEALTH...MYTH UN 20. PAGE 95 A1947 — ATTIT PORTUGAL

S64
MAZRUI A.A.,"THE UNITED NATIONS AND SOME AFRICAN POLITICAL ATTITUDES." ECO/TAC FOR/AID DOMIN ROUTINE CHOOSE ATTIT DRIVE MORAL PWR RESPECT WEALTH...PSY CONCPT OBS TREND UN VAL/FREE 20. PAGE 97 A1987 — AFR INT/ORG SOVEREIGN

S64
SCHWELB E.,"OPERATION OF THE EUROPEAN CONVENTION ON HUMAN RIGHTS." EUR+WWI LAW SOCIETY CREATE EDU/PROP ADJUD ADMIN PEACE ATTIT ORD/FREE PWR...POLICY INT/LAW CONCPT OBS GEN/LAWS UN VAL/FREE ILO 20 ECHR. PAGE 130 A2665 — INT/ORG MORAL

B65
LARUS J.,COMPARATIVE WORLD POLITICS. ASIA INDIA WOR+45 WOR-45 BAL/PWR WAR PEACE RATIONAL MORAL PWR ...REALPOL INT/LAW MUSLIM. PAGE 85 A1735 — GOV/COMP IDEA/COMP DIPLOM NAT/COMP

B65
WRESZIN M.,OSWALD GARRISON VILLARD: PACIFIST AT WAR. EDU/PROP MORAL ORD/FREE. PAGE 167 A3398 — USA-45 NAT/G INT/ORG INTELL

S65
MERRITT R.L.,"WOODROW WILSON AND THE 'GREAT AND SOLEMN REFERENDUM,' 1920." USA-45 SOCIETY NAT/G CONSULT LEGIS ACT/RES PLAN DOMIN EDU/PROP ROUTINE ATTIT DISPL DRIVE PERSON RIGID/FLEX MORAL ORD/FREE ...PSY SOC CONCPT MYTH LEAGUE/NAT. PAGE 100 A2044 — INT/ORG TOP/EX DIPLOM

B66
HANSEN G.H.,AFRO-ASIA AND NON-ALIGNMENT. AFR ASIA S/ASIA NEUTRAL MORAL 20. PAGE 61 A1255 — DIPLOM CONFER POLICY NAT/LISM

B66
HORMANN K.,PEACE AND MODERN WAR IN THE JUDGEMENT OF THE CHURCH. INT/ORG FORCES EDU/PROP ATTIT 20. PAGE 67 A1384 — PEACE WAR CATH MORAL

B66
LYND S.,THE OTHER SIDE. USA+45 VIETNAM/N NAT/G PEACE SOVEREIGN 20. PAGE 92 A1877 — WAR POLICY MORAL DIPLOM

B66
NANTWI E.K.,THE ENFORCEMENT OF INTERNATIONAL JUDICIAL DECISIONS AND ARBITAL AWARDS IN PUBLIC INTERNATIONAL LAW. WOR+45 WOR-45 JUDGE PROB/SOLV DIPLOM CT/SYS SUPEGO MORAL PWR RESPECT...METH/CNCPT 18/20 CASEBOOK. PAGE 107 A2196 — INT/LAW ADJUD SOVEREIGN INT/ORG

B67
WAELDER R.,PROGRESS AND REVOLUTION* A STUDY OF THE ISSUES OF OUR AGE. WOR+45 WOR-45 BAL/PWR DIPLOM COERCE ROLE MORAL ALL/IDEOS...IDEA/COMP NAT/COMP 19/20. PAGE 160 A3259 — PWR NAT/G REV TEC/DEV

L67
GALTUNG J.,"ON THE EFFECTS OF INTERNATIONAL ECONOMIC SANCTIONS, WITH EXAMPLES FROM THE CASE OF RHODESIA." NAT/G DIPLOM EDU/PROP ADJUST EFFICIENCY ATTIT MORAL...OBS CHARTS 20. PAGE 51 A1035 — SANCTION ECO/TAC INT/TRADE ECO/UNDEV

S67
BELGION M.,"THE CASE FOR REHABILITATING MARSHAL PETAIN." EUR+WWI FRANCE NAT/G DIPLOM ATTIT PERSON MORAL PETAIN/HP. PAGE 12 A0253 — WAR FORCES LEAD

S67
GLENN N.D.,"ARE REGIONAL CULTURAL DIFFERENCES DIMINISHING?" USA+45 DIPLOM RACE/REL AGE/Y AGE/A PERSON MORAL...GP/COMP 20. PAGE 53 A1081 — SAMP ATTIT REGION CULTURE

S67
KYLE K.,"BACKGROUND TO THE CRISIS" ISLAM ISRAEL UAR UK USSR NAT/G PROB/SOLV LEGIT CONTROL REGION STRANGE MORAL 20 JEWS. PAGE 83 A1698 — DIPLOM POLICY SOVEREIGN COERCE

S67
MOBERG E.,"THE EFFECT OF SECURITY POLICY MEASURES: DISCUSSION RELATED TO SWEDEN'S SECURITY POLICY." SWEDEN PLAN PROB/SOLV DIPLOM GOV/REL MORAL...CHARTS 20. PAGE 102 A2092 — POLICY ORD/FREE BUDGET FINAN

S67
SYRKIN M.,"I.F. STONE RECONSIDERS ISRAEL." ISRAEL WOR+45 DIPLOM NAT/LISM HABITAT...POLICY GEOG JEWS. PAGE 141 A2875 — ISLAM WAR ATTIT MORAL

S67
VAN DUSEN H.P.,"HAMMARSKOLD IN THE WORLD'S SERVICE." DIPLOM CONFER LEAD PEACE STRANGE UTOPIA MORAL SKILL OBJECTIVE...INT/LAW SELF/OBS 20. PAGE 158 A3211 — INT/ORG CONSULT TOP/EX NEUTRAL

B91
DOLE C.F.,THE AMERICAN CITIZEN. USA-45 LAW PARTIC ATTIT...INT/LAW 19. PAGE 38 A0769 — NAT/G MORAL NAT/LISM MAJORITY

B96
DE VATTEL E.,THE LAW OF NATIONS. AGRI FINAN CHIEF DIPLOM INT/TRADE AGREE OWN ALL/VALS MORAL ORD/FREE SOVEREIGN...GEN/LAWS 18 NATURL/LAW WOLFF/C. PAGE 35 A0714 — LAW CONCPT NAT/G INT/LAW

MORALES C.J. A2128

MORALITY....SEE MORAL, CULTURE, ALL/VALS

MORDAN H. A0829

MORE/THOM....SIR THOMAS MORE

MOREL E.D. A2129,A2130

MORGAN J. A0224

MORGAN T. A2131

MORGENSTERN O. A2132,A2133,A2134

MORGENTH/H.... HANS MORGENTHAU

S52
TUCKER R.W.,"PROFESSOR MORGENTHAU'S THEORY OF POLITICAL 'REALISM'." USA+45 USA-45 WOR+45 WOR-45 NAT/G...POLICY 20 MORGENTH/H. PAGE 145 A2974 — CONCPT ATTIT DIPLOM

MORGENTHAU H.J. A2135,A2136,A2137,A2138,A2140,A2141

MORISON E.E. A2142

MORL/MINTO....MORLEY-MINTO - ERA OF BRITISH RULE IN INDIA (1905-1910)

MORLEY F. A2143,A2144

MORLEY L. A2144

MORLEY/J....JOHN MORLEY

MORMON....MORMON PEOPLE AND MORMON FAITH

MOROCCO....SEE ALSO ISLAM

N19
LISKA G.,THE GREATER MAGHREB: FROM INDEPENDENCE TO UNITY? (PAMPHLET). ALGERIA ISLAM MOROCCO PROB/SOLV BAL/PWR CONFER COLONIAL REPRESENT NAT/LISM 20 TUNIS. PAGE 90 A1835 — ECO/UNDEV REGION DIPLOM DOMIN

B31
STUART G.H.,THE INTERNATIONAL CITY OF TANGIER. AFR EUR+WWI MOD/EUR MOROCCO CONSTN PROVS CREATE PLAN LEGIT PEACE ORD/FREE PWR...INT/LAW OBS TIME/SEQ CON/ANAL 20 TANGIER. PAGE 139 A2854 — LOC/G INT/ORG DIPLOM SOVEREIGN

B42
CONOVER H.F.,FRENCH COLONIES IN AFRICA: A LIST OF REFERENCES. ALGERIA FRANCE MOROCCO SOMALIA SUDAN CULTURE AGRI LOC/G SECT FORCES DIPLOM INT/TRADE NAT/LISM HEALTH...CON/ANAL 20. PAGE 29 A0594 — BIBLIOG AFR ECO/UNDEV COLONIAL

B57
CONOVER H.F.,NORTH AND NORTHEAST AFRICA; A SELECTED ANNOTATED LIST OF WRITINGS. ALGERIA MOROCCO SUDAN UAR CULTURE INT/ORG PROB/SOLV ADJUD NAT/LISM PWR WEALTH...SOC 20 UN. PAGE 30 A0603 — BIBLIOG/A DIPLOM AFR ECO/UNDEV

B60
PRINCETON U CONFERENCE,CURRENT PROBLEMS IN NORTH AFRICA. ALGERIA LIBYA MOROCCO USA+45 EXTR/IND POL/PAR PROB/SOLV DIPLOM ECO/TAC WAR...ANTHOL 20 TUNIS. PAGE 118 A2412 — POLICY ECO/UNDEV NAT/G

B61
UAR MINISTRY OF CULTURE,A BIBLIOGRAPHICAL LIST OF AL MAGHRIB. ALGERIA ISLAM MOROCCO UAR SECT INT/TRADE COLONIAL 19/20 TUNIS. PAGE 146 A2987 — BIBLIOG DIPLOM GEOG

B62
BAULIN J.,THE ARAB ROLE IN AFRICA. AFR ALGERIA FUT — NAT/LISM

ISLAM MOROCCO UAR COLONIAL NEUTRAL REV...SOC 20 TUNIS BOURGUIBA. PAGE 12 A0235 — DIPLOM NAT/G SECT

B62

DUROSELLE J.B.,LES NOUVEAUX ETATS DANS LES RELATIONS INTERNATIONALES. AFR CHINA/COM FRANCE MOROCCO S/ASIA USSR ECO/UNDEV INT/ORG PLAN ECO/TAC EDU/PROP ATTIT DRIVE...TREND TOT/POP TUNIS 20. PAGE 39 A0806 — NAT/G CONSTN DIPLOM

B66

BROWN L.C.,STATE AND SOCIETY IN INDEPENDENT NORTH AFRICA. ALGERIA LIBYA MOROCCO AGRI INDUS INT/ORG POL/PAR SECT PLAN DIPLOM COLONIAL...LING NAT/COMP ANTHOL BIBLIOG 20 TUNIS MUSLIM. PAGE 20 A0406 — NAT/G SOCIETY CULTURE ECO/UNDEV

B93

ROYAL GEOGRAPHIC SOCIETY,BIBLIOGRAPHY OF BARBARY STATES (4 SUPPLEMENTARY PAPERS). ALGERIA LIBYA MOROCCO SOCIETY STRUCT DIPLOM LEAD 14/19 TUNIS. PAGE 125 A2555 — BIBLIOG ISLAM NAT/G COLONIAL

C93

PLAYFAIR R.L.,"A BIBLIOGRAPHY OF MOROCCO." MOROCCO CULTURE AGRI FORCES DIPLOM WAR HEALTH...GEOG JURID SOC CHARTS. PAGE 116 A2387 — BIBLIOG ISLAM MEDIT-7

MORRAY J.P. A2145,A2146

MORRIS B.S. A2147

MORRIS H.C. A2148

MORRIS R.B. A2149

MORRIS/CW....C.W. MORRIS

MORRIS/G....G. MORRIS

MORROW/DW....DWIGHT W. MORROW

MORTON H.H. A2623

MORTON L. A2150

MOSCA/G....GAETANO MOSCA

MOSCOW....MOSCOW, U.S.S.R.

MOSELY P.E. A2151,A2152,A2153

MOSKOWITZ H. A2154

MOSSI....MOSSI TRIBE

MOSTECKY V. A2155

MOTIVATION....SEE DRIVE

MOUSKHELY M. A2156,A2157,A2158

MOUSSA P. A2159

MOVIES....SEE FILM

MOVIMIENTO NACIONALISTA REVOLUCIONARIO (BOLIVIA)....SEE MNR

MOWER A.G. A2160

MOWRY G.E. A2161

MOYER K.E. A2162

MOYNI/RPRT....MOYNIHAN REPORT

MOZAMBIQUE LIBERATION FRONT....SEE FRELIMO

MOZAMBIQUE....MOZAMBIQUE

MUCKRAKER....MUCKRAKERS

MUDGE G.A. A2163

MUGRIDGE D.H. A2164,A2165

MUGWUMP....MUGWUMP

MULATTO....MULATTO

MULLENBACH P. A2166

MULLER C.F.J. A2167

MULLEY F.W. A2168,A2169

MULTILATERAL FORCE....SEE MLF

MULTIVAR....MULTIVARIATE ANALYSIS

MUNGER E.S. A2170

MUNIC....CITIES, TOWNS, VILLAGES

N

SCHOLARLY BOOKS IN AMERICA; A QUARTERLY BIBLIOGRAPHY OF UNIVERSITY PRESS PUBLICATIONS. WOR+45 AGRI COM/IND NAT/G HEALTH...GEOG PHIL/SCI PSY SOC LING 20. PAGE 3 A0046 — BIBLIOG/A LAW MUNIC DIPLOM

B19

LONDON SCHOOL ECONOMICS-POL,ANNUAL DIGEST OF PUBLIC INTERNATIONAL LAW CASES. INT/ORG MUNIC NAT/G PROVS ADMIN NEUTRAL WAR GOV/REL PRIVIL 20. PAGE 91 A1858 — BIBLIOG/A INT/LAW ADJUD DIPLOM

B20

VINOGRADOFF P.,OUTLINES OF HISTORICAL JURISPRUDENCE (2 VOLS.). GREECE MEDIT-7 LAW CONSTN FACE/GP FAM KIN MUNIC CRIME OWN...INT/LAW IDEA/COMP BIBLIOG. PAGE 159 A3241 — JURID METH

B49

HEADLAM-MORLEY,BIBLIOGRAPHY IN POLITICS FOR THE HONOUR SCHOOL OF PHILOSOPHY, POLITICS AND ECONOMICS (PAMPHLET). UK CONSTN LABOR MUNIC DIPLOM ADMIN 19/20. PAGE 64 A1305 — BIBLIOG NAT/G PHIL/SCI GOV/REL

B50

BROWN E.S.,MANUAL OF GOVERNMENT PUBLICATIONS. WOR+45 WOR-45 CONSTN INT/ORG MUNIC PROVS DIPLOM ADMIN 20. PAGE 20 A0401 — BIBLIOG/A NAT/G LAW

B52

THOM J.M.,GUIDE TO RESEARCH MATERIAL IN POLITICAL SCIENCE (PAMPHLET). ELITES LOC/G MUNIC NAT/G LEGIS DIPLOM ADJUD CIVMIL/REL GOV/REL PWR MGT. PAGE 143 A2919 — BIBLIOG/A KNOWL

B55

UN ECONOMIC AND SOCIAL COUNCIL,BIBLIOGRAPHY OF PUBLICATIONS OF THE UN AND SPECIALIZED AGENCIES IN THE SOCIAL WELFARE FIELD, 1946-1952. WOR+45 FAM INT/ORG MUNIC ACT/RES PLAN PROB/SOLV EDU/PROP AGE/C AGE/Y HABITAT...HEAL UN. PAGE 147 A3000 — BIBLIOG/A SOC/WK ADMIN WEALTH

B57

DRUCKER P.F.,AMERICA'S NEXT TWENTY YEARS. USA+45 DIST/IND ACADEM MUNIC SCHOOL DIPLOM ECO/TAC AUTOMAT HABITAT HEALTH...SOC/WK TREND 20 URBAN/RNWL PUB/TRANS. PAGE 39 A0788 — WORKER FOR/AID CENSUS GEOG

B57

HODGKIN T.,NATIONALISM IN COLONIAL AFRICA. STRATA STRUCT MUNIC NAT/G POL/PAR LEGIS ATTIT SOVEREIGN ...POLICY TREND BIBLIOG 20. PAGE 66 A1351 — AFR COLONIAL NAT/LISM DIPLOM

N57

BIBLIOGRAPHY OF NEW GUIDES AND AIDS TO PUBLIC DOCUMENTS USE, 1953-1956 (PAMPHLET). WOR+45 MUNIC DIPLOM...CON/ANAL CHARTS METH. PAGE 164 A3347 — BIBLIOG/A NAT/G LOC/G INT/ORG

B58

HENKIN L.,ARMS CONTROL AND INSPECTION IN AMERICAN LAW. LAW CONSTN INT/ORG LOC/G MUNIC NAT/G PROVS EDU/PROP LEGIT EXEC NUC/PWR KNOWL ORD/FREE...OBS TOT/POP CONGRESS 20. PAGE 64 A1315 — USA+45 JURID ARMS/CONT

L58

TRAGER F.N.,"A SELECTED AND ANNOTATED BIBLIOGRAPHY ON ECONOMIC DEVELOPMENT, 1953-1957." WOR+45 AGRI FINAN INDUS MARKET LABOR MUNIC WORKER PLAN INT/TRADE PRODUC CENSUS. PAGE 145 A2958 — BIBLIOG/A ECO/UNDEV ECO/DEV

S58

BOGART L.,"MEASURING THE EFFECTIVENESS OF AN OVERSEAS INFORMATION CAMPAIGN." EUR+WWI GREECE USA+45 INT/ORG MUNIC PLAN DIPLOM PEACE PERCEPT RIGID/FLEX KNOWL...TECHNIC PSY SOC NEW/IDEA CONT/OBS REC/INT STAND/INT SAMP/SIZ COLD/WAR 20. PAGE 16 A0328 — ATTIT EDU/PROP

B60

AMERICAN ASSOCIATION LAW LIB,INDEX TO FOREIGN LEGAL PERIODICALS. WOR+45 MUNIC...IDEA/COMP 20. PAGE 7 A0139 — INDEX LAW JURID DIPLOM

B61

LETHBRIDGE H.J.,CHINA'S URBAN COMMUNES. CHINA/COM FUT ECO/UNDEV DIPLOM EDU/PROP DEMAND INCOME MARXISM ...POLICY 20. PAGE 87 A1790 — MUNIC CONTROL ECO/TAC NAT/G

B62

THANT U.,THE UNITED NATIONS' DEVELOPMENT DECADE: PROPOSALS FOR ACTION. WOR+45 SOCIETY ECO/UNDEV AGRI COM/IND FINAN R+D MUNIC SCHOOL VOL/ASSN CONSULT PLAN TEC/DEV ECO/TAC EDU/PROP ADMIN ROUTINE RIGID/FLEX...MGT SOC CONCPT UNESCO UN TOT/POP VAL/FREE. PAGE 142 A2906 — INT/ORG ALL/VALS

B64

BURKE F.G.,AFRICA'S QUEST FOR ORDER. AFR CULTURE KIN MUNIC NAT/G DIPLOM COLONIAL REV DISCRIM NAT/LISM AGE/Y 20. PAGE 21 A0437 — ORD/FREE CONSEN RACE/REL LEAD

B64
JACOB P.E.,THE INTEGRATION OF POLITICAL COMMUNITIES. USA+45 WOR+45 CULTURE LOC/G MUNIC NAT/G CREATE PLAN LEGIT REGION COERCE ALL/VALS ...POLICY GEOG PSY SOC TREND HYPO/EXP GEN/LAWS VAL/FREE 20. PAGE 72 A1483
INT/ORG METH/CNCPT SIMUL STAT

B64
NEHEMKIS P.,LATIN AMERICA: MYTH AND REALITY. INDUS INT/ORG MUNIC PROB/SOLV CAP/ISM DIPLOM REV...SOC 20. PAGE 108 A2211
REGION MYTH L/A+17C ECO/UNDEV

B65
LOEWENHEIM F.L.,PEACE OR APPEASEMENT? HITLER, CHAMBERLAIN AND THE MUNICH CRISIS. MUNIC DELIB/GP WAR TOTALISM ATTIT SOVEREIGN...TIME/SEQ ANTHOL BIBLIOG 20 HITLER/A CHAMBRLN/N. PAGE 90 A1851
DIPLOM LEAD PEACE

B65
MOWRY G.E.,THE URBAN NATION 1920-1960. USA+45 USA-45 SOCIETY ECO/DEV MUNIC FOR/AID INT/TRADE AUTOMAT...BIBLIOG/A 20. PAGE 105 A2161
TEC/DEV NAT/G TOTALISM DIPLOM

B65
VAN DEN BERGHE P.L.,AFRICA: SOCIAL PROBLEMS OF CHANGE AND CONFLICT. ELITES STRATA ECO/UNDEV KIN MUNIC DIPLOM GP/REL RACE/REL NAT/LISM...ANTHOL BIBLIOG 20. PAGE 158 A3210
SOC CULTURE AFR STRUCT

S65
PLISCHKE E.,"INTEGRATING BERLIN AND THE FEDERAL REPUBLIC OF GERMANY." EUR+WWI GERMANY/W LEGIS TEC/DEV DOMIN ORD/FREE PWR...JURID 20 BERLIN. PAGE 117 A2392
DIPLOM NAT/G MUNIC

B66
AMERICAN JOURNAL COMP LAW,THE AMERICAN JOURNAL OF COMPARATIVE LAW READER. EUR+WWI USA+45 USA-45 LAW CONSTN LOC/G MUNIC NAT/G DIPLOM...ANTHOL 20 SUPREME/CT EURCT/JUST. PAGE 7 A0151
IDEA/COMP JURID INT/LAW CT/SYS

B66
EUBANK K.,THE SUMMIT CONFERENCES. EUR+WWI USA+45 USA-45 MUNIC BAL/PWR WAR PEACE PWR...POLICY AUD/VIS 20 GENEVA/CON TEHERAN YALTA POTSDAM. PAGE 43 A0872
CONFER NAT/G CHIEF DIPLOM

B66
GILBERT M.,THE ROOTS OF APPEASEMENT. EUR+WWI GERMANY UK MUNIC BAL/PWR FASCISM...NEW/IDEA 20. PAGE 52 A1070
DIPLOM REPAR PROB/SOLV POLICY

B66
HARMON R.B.,SOURCES AND PROBLEMS OF BIBLIOGRAPHY IN POLITICAL SCIENCE (PAMPHLET). INT/ORG LOC/G MUNIC POL/PAR ADMIN GOV/REL ALL/IDEOS...JURID MGT CONCPT 19/20. PAGE 61 A1262
BIBLIOG DIPLOM INT/LAW NAT/G

S66
"RESEARCH WORK 1965-1966." NEW/ZEALND ELITES ACADEM LOC/G MUNIC POL/PAR PROVS DIPLOM COLONIAL...SOC 20 AUSTRAL. PAGE 4 A0073
BIBLIOG NAT/G CULTURE S/ASIA

B67
PIPER D.C.,THE INTERNATIONAL LAW OF THE GREAT LAKES. CANADA EXTR/IND MUNIC LICENSE ARMS/CONT CRIME...GEOG 19/20. PAGE 116 A2381
CONCPT DIPLOM INT/LAW

B67
ROSENAU J.N.,DOMESTIC SOURCES OF FOREIGN POLICY. WOR+45 STRATA COM/IND MUNIC POL/PAR LOBBY PARTIC REGION ATTIT...PSY SOC COLD/WAR. PAGE 124 A2534
DIPLOM POLICY NAT/G CHOOSE

B67
SABLE M.H.,A GUIDE TO LATIN AMERICAN STUDIES (2 VOLS). CONSTN FINAN INT/ORG LABOR MUNIC POL/PAR FORCES CAP/ISM FOR/AID ADMIN MARXISM SOCISM OAS. PAGE 126 A2584
BIBLIOG/A L/A+17C DIPLOM NAT/LISM

S67
VELIKONJA J.,"ITALIAN IMMIGRANTS IN THE UNITED STATES IN THE MID-SIXTIES" ITALY USA+45 KIN MUNIC NAT/G WORKER DIPLOM REGION GP/REL ADJUST...GEOG CHARTS SOC/INTEG 20. PAGE 158 A3226
HABITAT ORD/FREE TREND STAT

S67
YOUNG K.T.,"UNITED STATES POLICY AND VIETNAMESE POLITICAL VIABILITY 1954-1967." VIETNAM/S LOC/G MUNIC FOR/AID ORD/FREE...POLICY 20. PAGE 169 A3437
LEAD ADMIN GP/REL EFFICIENCY

MUNICH....MUNICH, GERMANY

MUNICIPALITIES....SEE MUNIC

MUNKMAN C.A. A2171

MUNRO L. A2172,A2173

MURACCIOLE L. A2174,A2175

MURDER....MURDER, ASSASSINATION; SEE ALSO CRIME

N17
BURKE E.,THOUGHTS ON THE PROSPECT OF A REGICIDE PEACE (PAMPHLET). FRANCE UK SECT DOMIN MURDER PEACE ORD/FREE SOVEREIGN POPULISM...POLICY GOV/COMP IDEA/COMP 18 JACOBINISM COEXIST. PAGE 21 A0435
REV CHIEF NAT/G DIPLOM

B36
THWAITE D.,THE SEETHING AFRICAN POT: A STUDY OF BLACK NATIONALISM 1882-1935. ETHIOPIA SECT VOL/ASSN COERCE GUERRILLA MURDER DISCRIM MARXISM...PSY TIME/SEQ 18/20 NEGRO. PAGE 144 A2939
NAT/LISM AFR RACE/REL DIPLOM

B57
JASZI O.,AGAINST THE TYRANT. WOR+45 WOR-45 CONSTN DIPLOM CONTROL PARTIC REV WAR...CONCPT. PAGE 73 A1498
TOTALISM ORD/FREE CHIEF MURDER

B59
GILBERT R.,GENOCIDE IN TIBET. ASIA SECT CHIEF DIPLOM 20. PAGE 52 A1072
MARXISM MURDER WAR GP/REL

B64
BLANCHARD C.H.,KOREAN WAR BIBLIOGRAPHY. KOREA FAM BAL/PWR RATION MURDER WEAPON MARXISM...CHARTS 20. PAGE 15 A0306
BIBLIOG/A WAR DIPLOM FORCES

B64
KENNEDY J.F.,THE BURDEN AND THE GLORY. FUT USA+45 TEC/DEV ECO/TAC EDU/PROP ARMS/CONT MURDER RACE/REL PEACE...ANTHOL 20 KENNEDY/JF COLD/WAR NATO PRESIDENT. PAGE 78 A1593
ADMIN POLICY GOV/REL DIPLOM

B67
BURNS E.L.M.,MEGAMURDER. WOR+45 LAW INT/ORG NAT/G BAL/PWR DIPLOM DETER MURDER WEAPON CIVMIL/REL PEACE ...INT/LAW TREND 20. PAGE 22 A0444
FORCES PLAN WAR NUC/PWR

B67
KATZ R.,DEATH IN ROME. EUR+WWI ITALY POL/PAR DIPLOM LEAD ATTIT PERSON ROLE CATHISM. PAGE 77 A1570
WAR MURDER FORCES DEATH

MURNGIN....MURNGIN, AN AUSTRALIAN TRIBE

MURPHY G. A2176

MURPHY G.G. A2177

MURPHY J.C. A2178,A2179

MURRA R.O. A2180

MURRAY J.N. A2181,A2182

MURRAY J.C. A2084

MURRAY/JC....JOHN COURTNEY MURRAY

MURTY B.S. A2183

MURUMBI J. A2184

MUSCAT....MUSCAT AND OMAN; SEE ALSO ISLAM

MUSIC....MUSIC AND SONGS

MUSLIM....MUSLIM PEOPLE AND RELIGION

B65
LARUS J.,COMPARATIVE WORLD POLITICS. ASIA INDIA WOR+45 WOR-45 BAL/PWR WAR PEACE RATIONAL MORAL PWR ...REALPOL INT/LAW MUSLIM. PAGE 85 A1735
GOV/COMP IDEA/COMP DIPLOM NAT/COMP

B65
QURESHI I.H.,THE STRUGGLE FOR PAKISTAN. INDIA PAKISTAN UK CULTURE LEGIS DIPLOM EDU/PROP COLONIAL ATTIT SOVEREIGN 19/20 MUSLIM. PAGE 118 A2429
GP/REL RACE/REL WAR SECT

B66
BROWN L.C.,STATE AND SOCIETY IN INDEPENDENT NORTH AFRICA. ALGERIA LIBYA MOROCCO AGRI INDUS INT/ORG POL/PAR SECT PLAN DIPLOM COLONIAL...LING NAT/COMP ANTHOL BIBLIOG 20 TUNIS MUSLIM. PAGE 20 A0406
NAT/G SOCIETY CULTURE ECO/UNDEV

MUSLIM/LG....MUSLIM LEAGUE

B66
GUPTA S.,KASHMIR - A STUDY IN INDIA-PAKISTAN RELATIONS. INDIA KASHMIR PAKISTAN CONSTN INT/ORG REV RACE/REL NAT/LISM 20 UN MUSLIM/LG. PAGE 58 A1194
DIPLOM GP/REL SOVEREIGN WAR

MUSSO AMBROSI L.A. A2185

MUSSOLIN/B....BENITO MUSSOLINI

B37
BORGESE G.A.,GOLIATH: THE MARCH OF FASCISM. GERMANY ITALY LAW POL/PAR SECT DIPLOM SOCISM...JURID MYTH 20 DANTE MACHIAVELL MUSSOLIN/B. PAGE 17 A0341
POLICY NAT/LISM FASCISM

NAT/G

B46
STURZO D.L.,NATIONALISM AND INTERNATIONALISM. WOR-45 INT/ORG LABOR NAT/G POL/PAR TOTALISM MORAL ORD/FREE FASCISM...MAJORIT 19/20 UN LEAGUE/NAT MUSSOLIN/B. PAGE 140 A2857
NAT/LISM DIPLOM WAR PEACE

B54
SALVEMINI G.,PRELUDE TO WORLD WAR II. ITALY MOD/EUR INT/ORG BAL/PWR EDU/PROP CONTROL TOTALISM...TREND NAT/COMP BIBLIOG 19 HITLER/A LEAGUE/NAT MUSSOLIN/B. PAGE 127 A2597
WAR FASCISM LEAD PWR

B55
ALFIERI D.,DICTATORS FACE TO FACE. NAT/G TOP/EX DIPLOM EXEC COERCE ORD/FREE FASCISM...POLICY OBS 20 HITLER/A MUSSOLIN/B. PAGE 6 A0116
WAR CHIEF TOTALISM PERS/REL

B64
HALPERIN S.W.,MUSSOLINI AND ITALIAN FASCISM. ITALY NAT/G POL/PAR SECT ECO/TAC LEAD PWR SOCISM...POLICY 20 MUSSOLIN/B. PAGE 60 A1241
FASCISM NAT/LISM EDU/PROP CHIEF

MUTHER J.E. A2575

MYERS D.P. A2186

MYINT H. A2187

MYRDAL A.R. A2188

MYRDAL G. A2189

MYRDAL/G....GUNNAR MYRDAL

B66
HOLLINS E.J.,PEACE IS POSSIBLE: A READER FOR LAYMEN. WOR+45 CULTURE PLAN RISK AGE/Y ALL/VALS SOVEREIGN...PSY CONCPT TREND 20 UN JOHN/XXIII KENNAN/G MYRDAL/G. PAGE 67 A1370
PEACE DIPLOM INT/ORG NUC/PWR

MYSTIC....MYSTICAL

B40
THE GUIDE TO CATHOLIC LITERATURE, 1888-1940. ALL/VALS...POLICY MYSTIC HUM PHIL/SCI 19/20. PAGE 3 A0051
BIBLIOG/A CATHISM DIPLOM CULTURE

S59
KRIPALANI A.J.B.,"FOR PRINCIPLED NEUTRALITY." CHINA/COM INDIA S/ASIA PLAN ECO/TAC RIGID/FLEX MORAL PWR...MYSTIC SOC RECORD 20 GANDHI/M. PAGE 82 A1684
ATTIT FOR/AID DIPLOM

MYSTISM....MYSTICISM

MYTH....FICTION

B19
KEYNES J.M.,THE ECONOMIC CONSEQUENCES OF THE PEACE. FUT GERMANY MOD/EUR RUSSIA UK USA-45 CULTURE ECO/DEV FINAN INDUS INT/ORG TOP/EX ECO/TAC ROUTINE WAR ATTIT PERCEPT ALL/VALS...OLD/LIB MYTH OBS TIME/SEQ TREND 20 TREATY. PAGE 78 A1605
EUR+WWI SOCIETY PEACE

B22
REINSCH P.,SECRET DIPLOMACY: HOW FAR CAN IT BE ELIMINATED. FUT WOR-45 CULTURE INT/ORG NAT/G EDU/PROP WAR...MYTH HIST/WRIT CON/ANAL 20. PAGE 120 A2460
RIGID/FLEX PWR DIPLOM

B24
GENTILI A.,DE LEGATIONIBUS. CHRIST-17C NAT/G SECT CONSULT LEGIT...POLICY CATH JURID CONCPT MYTH. PAGE 52 A1058
DIPLOM INT/LAW INT/ORG LAW

B37
BORGESE G.A.,GOLIATH: THE MARCH OF FASCISM. GERMANY ITALY LAW POL/PAR SECT DIPLOM SOCISM...JURID MYTH 20 DANTE MACHIAVELL MUSSOLIN/B. PAGE 17 A0341
POLICY NAT/LISM FASCISM NAT/G

B38
PETTEE G.S.,THE PROCESS OF REVOLUTION. COM FRANCE ITALY MOD/EUR RUSSIA SPAIN WOR-45 ELITES INTELL SOCIETY STRATA STRUCT INT/ORG NAT/G POL/PAR ACT/RES PLAN EDU/PROP LEGIT EXEC...SOC MYTH TIME/SEQ TOT/POP 18/20. PAGE 115 A2370
COERCE CONCPT REV

B40
BOGGS S.W.,INTERNATIONAL BOUNDARIES. WOR-45 SOCIETY ECO/DEV INT/ORG NAT/G NEIGH LEGIT PERSON ORD/FREE PWR...POLICY GEOG MYTH LEAGUE/NAT 20. PAGE 16 A0329
ATTIT CONCPT NAT/LISM

B49
STETTINIUS E.R.,ROOSEVELT AND THE RUSSIANS: THE YALTA CONFERENCE. UK USSR WOR+45 WOR-45 INT/ORG VOL/ASSN TOP/EX ACT/RES EDU/PROP PEACE ATTIT DRIVE PERSON SUPEGO PWR...POLICY CONCPT MYTH OBS TIME/SEQ AUD/VIS COLD/WAR 20 CHURCHLL/W YALTA ROOSEVLT/F. PAGE 138 A2819
DIPLOM DELIB/GP BIOG

S51
ICHHEISER G.,"MISUNDERSTANDING IN INTERNATIONAL RELATIONS." UNIV SOCIETY FACE/GP INT/ORG SECT ATTIT PERSON RIGID/FLEX LOVE RESPECT...RELATIV PSY SOC CONCPT MYTH SOC/EXP GEN/LAWS. PAGE 70 A1431
PERCEPT STERTYP NAT/LISM DIPLOM

B52
SCHUMAN F.,THE COMMONWEALTH OF MAN. WOR+45 WOR-45 LAW CULTURE ELITES SOCIETY FAM INT/ORG NAT/G VOL/ASSN TOP/EX PLAN BAL/PWR LEGIT ATTIT DISPL DRIVE...POLICY MYTH TREND TOT/POP ILO OEEC 20. PAGE 129 A2649
CONCPT GEN/LAWS

B57
BLOOMFIELD L.M.,EGYPT, ISRAEL AND THE GULF OF AQABA: IN INTERNATIONAL LAW. LAW NAT/G CONSULT FORCES PLAN ECO/TAC ROUTINE COERCE ATTIT DRIVE PERCEPT PERSON RIGID/FLEX LOVE PWR WEALTH...GEOG CONCPT MYTH TREND. PAGE 15 A0314
ISLAM INT/LAW UAR

B57
LEVONTIN A.V.,THE MYTH OF INTERNATIONAL SECURITY: A JURIDICAL AND CRITICAL ANALYSIS. FUT WOR+45 WOR-45 LAW NAT/G VOL/ASSN ACT/RES BAL/PWR ATTIT ORD/FREE ...JURID METH/CNCPT TIME/SEQ TREND STERTYP 20. PAGE 88 A1797
INT/ORG INT/LAW SOVEREIGN MYTH

S58
DAVENPORT J.,"ARMS AND THE WELFARE STATE." INTELL STRUCT FORCES CREATE ECO/TAC FOR/AID DOMIN LEGIT ADMIN WAR ORD/FREE PWR...POLICY SOC CONCPT MYTH OBS TREND COLD/WAR TOT/POP 20. PAGE 34 A0685
USA+45 NAT/G USSR

B59
HALLE L.J.,DREAM AND REALITY: ASPECTS OF AMERICAN FOREIGN POLICY. USA+45 CONSTN CONSULT PROB/SOLV NAT/LISM PERSON. PAGE 60 A1230
POLICY MYTH DIPLOM NAT/G

S59
BOULDING K.E.,"NATIONAL IMAGES AND INTERNATIONAL SYSTEMS." FUT WOR+45 CULTURE INT/ORG TOP/EX ROUTINE ...METH/CNCPT MYTH CONT/OBS TREND HYPO/EXP GEN/METH TOT/POP 20. PAGE 17 A0346
NAT/G DIPLOM

B60
CAMPAIGNE J.G.,AMERICAN MIGHT AND SOVIET MYTH. COM EUR+WWI ECO/DEV ECO/UNDEV INT/ORG NAT/G CAP/ISM ECO/TAC FOR/AID EDU/PROP ATTIT PWR WEALTH...POLICY CONCPT MYTH TREND STERTYP GEN/LAWS COLD/WAR. PAGE 23 A0473
USA+45 DOMIN DIPLOM USSR

B60
NURTY K.S.,STUDIES IN PROBLEMS OF PEACE. CHRIST-17C MOD/EUR S/ASIA WOR+45 WOR-45 INT/ORG NAT/G SECT COERCE REV NAT/LISM ALL/VALS...CONCPT MYTH TIME/SEQ. PAGE 110 A2262
POLICY PEACE PACIFISM ORD/FREE

L60
RIGGS R.,"OVER-SELLING THE U.N. CHARTER, FACT AND MYTH." USA+45 SOCIETY NAT/G TOP/EX PLAN DIPLOM EDU/PROP PEACE ATTIT PERCEPT MORAL...POLICY SAMP UN 20. PAGE 121 A2481
INT/ORG MYTH

S60
DOUGHERTY J.E.,"KEY TO SECURITY: DISARMAMENT OR ARMS STABILITY." COM USA+45 USSR INT/ORG NAT/G CREATE EDU/PROP COERCE DETER ATTIT PWR...DECISION CONCPT MYTH NEW/IDEA TREND 20 COLD/WAR. PAGE 38 A0777
FORCES ORD/FREE ARMS/CONT NUC/PWR

S60
KREININ M.E.,"THE 'OUTER-SEVEN' AND EUROPEAN INTEGRATION." EUR+WWI FRANCE GERMANY ITALY UK ECO/DEV DIST/IND INT/TRADE DRIVE WEALTH...MYTH CHARTS EEC OEEC 20. PAGE 82 A1682
ECO/TAC GEN/LAWS

S61
CARLETON W.G.,"AMERICAN FOREIGN POLICY: MYTHS AND REALITIES." FUT USA+45 WOR+45 ECO/UNDEV INT/ORG EX/STRUC ARMS/CONT NUC/PWR WAR ATTIT...POLICY CONCPT CONT/OBS GEN/METH COLD/WAR TOT/POP 20. PAGE 24 A0484
PLAN MYTH DIPLOM

B62
ELLIOTT J.R.,THE APPEAL OF COMMUNISM IN THE UNDERDEVELOPED NATIONS. USSR WOR+45 INT/ORG NAT/G DIPLOM DOMIN EDU/PROP ROUTINE ATTIT RIGID/FLEX ORD/FREE PWR WEALTH MARXISM...POLICY SOC METH/CNCPT MYTH TOT/POP COLD/WAR 20. PAGE 41 A0842
COM ECO/UNDEV

B62
LEWIS J.P.,QUIET CRISIS IN INDIA. INDIA USA+45 CULTURE ECO/UNDEV AGRI INDUS PROC/MFG NAT/G PLAN TEC/DEV DRIVE PWR SKILL WEALTH...MYTH 20. PAGE 88 A1801
S/ASIA ECO/TAC FOR/AID

B62
MANNING C.A.W.,THE NATURE OF INTERNATIONAL SOCIETY. FUT LAW NAT/G TOP/EX NAT/LISM PEACE PERCEPT PERSON ALL/VALS PLURISM...METH/CNCPT MYTH HYPO/EXP TOT/POP 20. PAGE 94 A1926
INT/ORG SOCIETY SIMUL DIPLOM

B62
SPANIER J.W.,THE POLITICS OF DISARMAMENT. COM USA+45 USSR EDU/PROP ATTIT ORD/FREE PWR RESPECT ...MYTH RECORD 20 COLD/WAR. PAGE 135 A2771
INT/ORG DELIB/GP ARMS/CONT

S62
SINGER J.D.,"STABLE DETERRENCE AND ITS LIMITS." FUT WOR+45 R+D INT/ORG CONSULT ACT/RES TEC/DEV ARMS/CONT COERCE DRIVE PERCEPT RIGID/FLEX ORD/FREE
NAT/G FORCES DETER

PWR...MYTH SIMUL TOT/POP 20. PAGE 133 A2728 — NUC/PWR

S62
STRACHEY J.,"COMMUNIST INTENTIONS." ASIA USSR YUGOSLAVIA INT/ORG NAT/G FORCES DOMIN EDU/PROP COERCE NUC/PWR NAT/LISM PEACE RIGID/FLEX PWR MARXISM...CONCPT MYTH OBS TIME/SEQ TREND COLD/WAR TOT/POP 20. PAGE 139 A2843 — COM ATTIT WAR

B63
LILIENTHAL D.E.,CHANGE, HOPE, AND THE BOMB. USA+45 WOR+45 R+D INT/ORG NAT/G DELIB/GP FORCES ACT/RES DETER RIGID/FLEX ORD/FREE...POLICY CONCPT OBS AEC 20. PAGE 89 A1815 — ATTIT MYTH ARMS/CONT NUC/PWR

B63
PIKE F.B.,CHILE AND THE UNITED STATES 1880-1962: THE EMERGENCE OF CHILE'S CRISIS AND THE CHALLENGE TO US DIPLOMACY. CHILE COM USA+45 USA-45 SOCIETY STRATA ECO/UNDEV...MYTH 19/20. PAGE 116 A2378 — FOR/AID DIPLOM ATTIT STRUCT

S63
GUPTA S.C.,"INDIA AND THE SOVIET UNION." CHINA/COM COM INDIA S/ASIA VOL/ASSN TOP/EX FOR/AID EDU/PROP PEACE PWR...RECORD COLD/WAR 20. PAGE 58 A1195 — DISPL MYTH USSR

S63
HUMPHREY H.H.,"REGIONAL ARMS CONTROL AGREEMENTS." WOR+45 FORCES PLAN LEGIT COERCE ATTIT HEALTH ORD/FREE...HUM METH/CNCPT MYTH OBS INT TREND TOT/POP 20. PAGE 69 A1416 — L/A+17C INT/ORG ARMS/CONT REGION

S63
SCHMIDT W.E.,"THE CASE AGAINST COMMODITY AGREEMENTS." FUT L/A+17C STRATA CONSULT PLAN ECO/TAC EDU/PROP ATTIT DRIVE RIGID/FLEX WEALTH ...MYTH 20. PAGE 128 A2631 — ECO/UNDEV ACT/RES INT/TRADE

S63
SPINELLI A.,"IL TRATTATO DI MOSCA E I PROBLEMI DELLA COESISTENZA PACIFICA." CHINA/COM COM FRANCE FUT WOR+45 INT/ORG VOL/ASSN PEACE...POLICY MYTH 20. PAGE 136 A2788 — ATTIT ARMS/CONT TOTALISM

B64
BINDER L.,THE IDEOLOGICAL REVOLUTION IN THE MIDDLE EAST. ISLAM STRUCT INT/ORG KIN SECT EX/STRUC TOP/EX PLAN ATTIT DRIVE RIGID/FLEX PWR...MYTH TOT/POP 20. PAGE 14 A0289 — POL/PAR NAT/G NAT/LISM

B64
KEEP J.,CONTEMPORARY HISTORY IN THE SOVIET MIRROR. COM USSR POL/PAR CREATE DIPLOM AGREE WAR ATTIT ...MYTH TREND ANTHOL 20 COLD/WAR STALIN/J MARX/KARL LENIN/VI. PAGE 77 A1576 — HIST/WRIT METH MARXISM IDEA/COMP

B64
NEHEMKIS P.,LATIN AMERICA: MYTH AND REALITY. INDUS INT/ORG MUNIC PROB/SOLV CAP/ISM DIPLOM REV...SOC 20. PAGE 108 A2211 — REGION MYTH L/A+17C ECO/UNDEV

B64
TAYLOR E.,RICHER BY ASIA. S/ASIA CULTURE VOL/ASSN ACT/RES ATTIT DISPL PERSON ALL/VALS...INT/LAW MYTH SELF/OBS 20. PAGE 142 A2899 — SOCIETY RIGID/FLEX INDIA

L64
WARD C.,"THE 'NEW MYTHS' AND 'OLD REALITIES' OF NUCLEAR WAR." COM FUT USA+45 USSR WOR+45 INT/ORG NAT/G DOMIN LEGIT EXEC ATTIT PERCEPT ALL/VALS ...POLICY RELATIV PSY MYTH TREND 20. PAGE 161 A3280 — FORCES COERCE ARMS/CONT NUC/PWR

S64
COHEN M.,"BASIC PRINCIPLES OF INTERNATIONAL LAW." UNIV WOR+45 WOR-45 BAL/PWR LEGIT ADJUD WAR ATTIT MORAL ORD/FREE PWR...JURID CONCPT MYTH TOT/POP 20. PAGE 27 A0560 — INT/ORG INT/LAW

S64
KHAN M.Z.,"ISLAM AND INTERNATIONAL RELATIONS." FUT WOR+45 LAW CULTURE SOCIETY NAT/G SECT DELIB/GP FORCES EDU/PROP ATTIT PERSON SUPEGO ALL/VALS ...POLICY PSY CONCPT MYTH HIST/WRIT GEN/LAWS. PAGE 78 A1608 — ISLAM INT/ORG DIPLOM

S64
MARTELLI G.,"PORTUGAL AND THE UNITED NATIONS." AFR EUR+WWI ELITES INT/ORG NAT/G PROVS PLAN DIPLOM ECO/TAC DOMIN COLONIAL RIGID/FLEX MORAL ORD/FREE PWR WEALTH...MYTH UN 20. PAGE 95 A1947 — ATTIT PORTUGAL

S64
RUBINSTEIN A.Z.,"THE SOVIET IMAGE OF WESTERN EUROPE." COM EUR+WWI FRANCE GERMANY GERMANY/W USA+45 USSR INT/ORG NAT/G VOL/ASSN FORCES TOP/EX BAL/PWR EDU/PROP ORD/FREE PWR...MYTH RECORD NATO EEC 20. PAGE 125 A2564 — RIGID/FLEX ATTIT

B65
DOMENACH J.M.,LA PROPAGANDE POLITIQUE. COM/IND INT/ORG POL/PAR DOMIN RIGID/FLEX FASCISM MARXISM ...PSY 20. PAGE 38 A0770 — ATTIT EDU/PROP TEC/DEV MYTH

L65
KAPLAN M.A.,"OLD REALITIES AND NEW MYTHS." USA+45 WOR+45 INT/ORG NAT/G TOP/EX ACT/RES BAL/PWR ECO/TAC EDU/PROP LEGIT RIGID/FLEX ALL/VALS...RECORD COLD/WAR 20. PAGE 76 A1564 — ATTIT MYTH DIPLOM

L65
TUCKER R.W.,"PEACE AND WAR." UNIV CULTURE SOCIETY INT/ORG NAT/G ACT/RES DOMIN DETER WAR ATTIT DISPL ...POLICY CONCPT MYTH GEN/LAWS 20. PAGE 145 A2975 — PWR COERCE ARMS/CONT PEACE

S65
KHOURI F.J.,"THE JORDON RIVER CONTROVERSY." LAW SOCIETY ECO/UNDEV AGRI FINAN INDUS SECT FORCES ACT/RES PLAN TEC/DEV ECO/TAC EDU/PROP COERCE ATTIT DRIVE PERCEPT RIGID/FLEX ALL/VALS...GEOG SOC MYTH WORK. PAGE 78 A1610 — ISLAM INT/ORG ISRAEL JORDAN

S65
MERRITT R.L.,"WOODROW WILSON AND THE 'GREAT AND SOLEMN REFERENDUM,' 1920." USA-45 SOCIETY NAT/G CONSULT LEGIS ACT/RES PLAN DOMIN EDU/PROP ROUTINE ATTIT DISPL DRIVE PERSON RIGID/FLEX MORAL ORD/FREE ...PSY SOC CONCPT MYTH LEAGUE/NAT. PAGE 100 A2044 — INT/ORG TOP/EX DIPLOM

S66
DUROSELLE J.B.,"THE FUTURE OF THE ATLANTIC COMMUNITY." EUR+WWI USA+45 USSR NAT/G CAP/ISM REGION DETER NUC/PWR ATTIT MARXISM...INT/LAW 20 NATO. PAGE 40 A0811 — FUT DIPLOM MYTH POLICY

S67
NIEBUHR R.,"THE SOCIAL MYTHS IN THE COLD WAR." USA+45 USSR VIETNAM PROB/SOLV BAL/PWR ARMS/CONT NAT/LISM PWR ALL/IDEOS CONCPT. PAGE 109 A2238 — MYTH DIPLOM GOV/COMP

N

NAACP....NATIONAL ASSOCIATION FOR THE ADVANCEMENT OF COLORED PEOPLE

NABALOI....NABALOI TRIBE, PHILIPPINES

NADLER E.B. A2190

NAFTA....NORTH ATLANTIC FREE TRADE AREA

NAFZIGER R.O. A2191

NAHM A.C. A2192

NAM....NATIONAL ASSOCIATION OF MANUFACTURERS

NAM/TIEN....NAM TIEN

NAMIER L.B. A2193

NANES A. A2194,A2195

NANTWI E.K. A2196

NAPOLEON/B....NAPOLEON BONAPARTE

B66
CRAIG G.A.,WAR, POLITICS, AND DIPLOMACY. PRUSSIA CONSTN FORCES CIVMIL/REL TOTALISM PWR 19/20 BISMARCK/O DULLES/JF NAPOLEON/B. PAGE 32 A0654 — WAR DIPLOM BAL/PWR

NARAIN D. A2445

NARAYAN/J....JAYPRAKASH NARAYAN

NARCO/ACT....UNIFORM NARCOTIC DRUG ACT

NASA A2197

NASA....NATIONAL AERONAUTIC AND SPACE ADMINISTRATION

B62
US CONGRESS,COMMUNICATIONS SATELLITE LEGISLATION: HEARINGS BEFORE COMM ON AERON AND SPACE SCIENCES ON BILLS S2550 AND 2814. WOR+45 LAW VOL/ASSN PLAN DIPLOM CONTROL OWN PEACE...NEW/IDEA CONGRESS NASA. PAGE 150 A3062 — SPACE COM/IND ADJUD GOV/REL

B63
US SENATE,DOCUMENTS ON INTERNATIONAL AS"ECTS OF EXPLORATION AND USE OF OUTER SPACE, 1954-62: STAFF REPORT FOR COMM AERON SPACE SCI. USA+45 USSR LEGIS LEAD CIVMIL/REL PEACE...POLICY INT/LAW ANTHOL 20 CONGRESS NASA KHRUSH/N. PAGE 155 A3165 — SPACE UTIL GOV/REL DIPLOM

B64
NASA,PROCEEDINGS OF CONFERENCE ON THE LAW OF SPACE AND OF SATELLITE COMMUNICATIONS: CHICAGO 1963. FUT WOR+45 DELIB/GP PROB/SOLV TEC/DEV CONFER ADJUD NUC/PWR...POLICY IDEA/COMP 20 NASA. PAGE 107 A2197 — SPACE COM/IND LAW DIPLOM

B64
US AIR FORCE ACADEMY ASSEMBLY,OUTER SPACE: FINAL REPORT APRIL 1-4, 1964. FUT USA+45 WOR+45 LAW DELIB/GP CONFER ARMS/CONT WAR PEACE ATTIT MORAL ...ANTHOL 20 NASA. PAGE 150 A3055 — SPACE CIVMIL/REL NUC/PWR DIPLOM

B65
FRUTKIN A.W.,SPACE AND THE INTERNATIONAL COOPERATION YEAR: A NATIONAL CHALLENGE (PAMPHLET). EUR+WWI USA+45 FINAN TEC/DEV BUDGET...MGT 20 NASA. PAGE 49 A1011 — SPACE INDUS NAT/G DIPLOM

B65
US SENATE,US INTERNATIONAL SPACE PROGRAMS, 1959-65: STAFF REPORT FOR COMM ON AERONAUTICAL AND SPACE SCIENCES. WOR+45 VOL/ASSN CIVMIL/REL 20 CONGRESS NASA TREATY. PAGE 155 A3166 — SPACE DIPLOM PLAN GOV/REL

B65
US SENATE COMM AERO SPACE SCI,INTERNATIONAL COOPERATION AND ORGANIZATION FOR OUTER SPACE. FUT USA+45 WOR+45 PROF/ORG VOL/ASSN CONSULT DELIB/GP PLAN TEC/DEV ARMS/CONT GP/REL PEACE 20 UN NASA. PAGE 155 A3167
DIPLOM SPACE R+D NAT/G

B67
US SENATE COMM AERO SPACE SCI,TREATY ON PRINCIPLES GOVERNING ACTIVITIES OF STATES IN EXPLORATION AND USE OF OUTER SPACE, INCLUDING...BODIES. DELIB/GP FORCES LEGIS DIPLOM...JURID 20 DEPT/STATE NASA DEPT/DEFEN UN. PAGE 155 A3169
SPACE INT/LAW ORD/FREE PEACE

N67
US SUPERINTENDENT OF DOCUMENTS,SPACE: MISSILES, THE MOON, NASA, AND SATELLITES (PRICE LIST 79A). USA+45 COM/IND R+D NAT/G DIPLOM EDU/PROP ADMIN CONTROL HEALTH...POLICY SIMUL NASA CONGRESS. PAGE 157 A3206
BIBLIOG/A SPACE TEC/DEV PEACE

NASHVILLE....NASHVILLE, TENNESSEE

NASSER/G....GAMAL ABDUL NASSER

B63
CREMEANS C.,THE ARABS AND THE WORLD: NASSER'S ARAB NATIONALIST POLICY. FUT ISLAM UAR USA+45 SOCIETY STRATA NAT/G POL/PAR PLAN DIPLOM EDU/PROP LEGIT DRIVE ALL/VALS...INT TIME/SEQ CHARTS 20 NASSER/G. PAGE 33 A0662
TOP/EX ATTIT REGION NAT/LISM

B64
UNITED ARAB REPUBLIC,TOWARDS THE SECOND AFRICAN SUMMIT ASSEMBLY. AFR UAR CONSTN VOL/ASSN CHIEF PLAN DIPLOM AGREE 20 NASSER/G AFR/STATES. PAGE 148 A3030
CONFER DELIB/GP INT/ORG POLICY

B65
MANSFIELD P.,NASSER'S EGYPT. AFR ISLAM UAR ECO/UNDEV AGRI COLONIAL SOVEREIGN...CHARTS 20 NASSER/G MID/EAST. PAGE 94 A1934
CHIEF ECO/TAC DIPLOM POLICY

S66
FRIEND A.,"THE MIDDLE EAST CRISIS" COM ISLAM ISRAEL SYRIA UAR USA+45 USSR FORCES PLAN FOR/AID CONTROL ORD/FREE PWR...SOCIALIST TIME/SEQ 20 NASSER/G. PAGE 49 A1009
WAR INT/ORG DIPLOM PEACE

NAT/COMP....COMPARISON OF NATIONS

N
AMERICAN JOURNAL OF INTERNATIONAL LAW. WOR+45 WOR-45 CONSTN INT/ORG NAT/G CT/SYS ARMS/CONT WAR ...DECISION JURID NAT/COMP 20. PAGE 1 A0002
BIBLIOG/A INT/LAW DIPLOM ADJUD

N
BULLETIN ANALYTIQUE DE DOCUMENTATION POLITIQUE, ECONOMIQUE, ET SOCIAL CONTEMPORAIRE. FRANCE WOR+45 SOCIETY ECO/DEV ECO/UNDEV INT/ORG LOC/G PROB/SOLV FOR/AID LEAD REGION SOC. PAGE 1 A0006
BIBLIOG/A DIPLOM NAT/COMP NAT/G

N
JOURNAL OF MODERN HISTORY. WOR+45 WOR-45 LEAD WAR ...TIME/SEQ TREND NAT/COMP 20. PAGE 1 A0016
BIBLIOG/A DIPLOM NAT/G

N
RAND SCHOOL OF SOCIAL SCIENCE,INDEX TO LABOR ARTICLES. ECO/DEV INT/ORG LEGIS DIPLOM GP/REL ...NAT/COMP 20. PAGE 119 A2440
BIBLIOG LABOR MGT ADJUD

B13
BORCHARD E.M.,BIBLIOGRAPHY OF INTERNATIONAL LAW AND CONTINENTAL LAW. EUR+WWI MOD/EUR UK LAW INT/TRADE WAR PEACE...GOV/COMP NAT/COMP 19/20. PAGE 17 A0338
BIBLIOG INT/LAW JURID DIPLOM

N19
FREEMAN H.A.,COERCION OF STATES IN FEDERAL UNIONS (PAMPHLET). WOR-45 DIPLOM CONTROL COERCE PEACE ORD/FREE...GOV/COMP METH/COMP NAT/COMP PACIFIST 20. PAGE 49 A0994
FEDERAL WAR INT/ORG PACIFISM

N19
HANNA A.J.,EUROPEAN RULE IN AFRICA (PAMPHLET). BELGIUM FRANCE MOD/EUR UK WOR+45 WOR-45 ECO/UNDEV NAT/G PARTIC SOVEREIGN...NAT/COMP 19/20. PAGE 61 A1252
DIPLOM COLONIAL AFR NAT/LISM

B33
DAHLIN E.,FRENCH AND GERMAN PUBLIC OPINION ON DECLARED WAR AIMS 1914-1918. BELGIUM FRANCE GERMANY NAT/G POL/PAR DIPLOM COERCE REV WAR PEACE 20 WWI WILSON/W. PAGE 33 A0674
ATTIT EDU/PROP DOMIN NAT/COMP

B36
BOYCE A.N.,EUROPE AND SOUTH AFRICA. FRANCE GERMANY ITALY SOUTH/AFR UK INDUS NAT/G CONTROL REV WAR NAT/LISM...CONCPT HIST/WRIT 20. PAGE 18 A0362
COLONIAL GOV/COMP NAT/COMP

DIPLOM

B45
CLAGETT H.L.,COMMUNIST CHINA: RUTHLESS ENEMY OR PAPER TIGER (PAMPHLET). CHINA/COM ECO/UNDEV AGRI INDUS NAT/G POL/PAR ECO/TAC INT/TRADE GUERRILLA ATTIT...CHARTS NAT/COMP ORG/CHARTS 20. PAGE 26 A0540
BIBLIOG/A MARXISM DIPLOM COERCE

B51
CARRINGTON C.E.,THE LIQUIDATION OF THE BRITISH EMPIRE. AFR NAT/G INT/TRADE COLONIAL RACE/REL ATTIT ORD/FREE...POLICY NAT/COMP 20 CMN/WLTH. PAGE 25 A0501
SOVEREIGN NAT/LISM DIPLOM GP/REL

B51
US LIBRARY OF CONGRESS,PUBLIC AFFAIRS ABSTRACTS. USA+45 INT/ORG INT/TRADE ARMS/CONT...NAT/COMP 20 CONGRESS. PAGE 155 A3151
BIBLIOG/A DIPLOM POLICY

B52
FIFIELD R.H.,WOODROW WILSON AND THE FAR EAST. ASIA CHIEF BAL/PWR CONFER COLONIAL ARMS/CONT WAR ...TIME/SEQ NAT/COMP BIBLIOG 19/20 WILSON/W LEAGUE/NAT PRESIDENT. PAGE 45 A0926
DIPLOM DELIB/GP INT/ORG

C52
FIFIELD R.H.,"WOODROW WILSON AND THE FAR EAST." ASIA CHIEF DELIB/GP BAL/PWR CONFER COLONIAL ARMS/CONT WAR...TIME/SEQ NAT/COMP 19/20 WILSON/W LEAGUE/NAT. PAGE 45 A0925
BIBLIOG DIPLOM INT/ORG

B53
LENZ F.,DIE BEWEGUNGEN DER GROSSEN MACHTE. USA+45 USA-45 USSR SOCIETY STRATA STRUCT NAT/G PERSON MARXISM...CONCPT IDEA/COMP NAT/COMP 18/20. PAGE 87 A1777
BAL/PWR TREND DIPLOM HIST/WRIT

B54
EPSTEIN L.D.,BRITAIN - UNEASY ALLY. KOREA UK USA+45 NAT/G POL/PAR ECO/TAC FOR/AID INT/TRADE WAR LABOR/PAR CONSRV/PAR. PAGE 42 A0857
DIPLOM ATTIT POLICY NAT/COMP

B54
SALVEMINI G.,PRELUDE TO WORLD WAR II. ITALY MOD/EUR INT/ORG BAL/PWR EDU/PROP CONTROL TOTALISM...TREND NAT/COMP BIBLIOG 19 HITLER/A LEAGUE/NAT MUSSOLIN/B. PAGE 127 A2597
WAR FASCISM LEAD PWR

B55
INSTITUTE POLITISCHE WISSEN,POLITISCHE LITERATUR (3 VOLS.). INT/ORG LEAD WAR PEACE...CONCPT TREND NAT/COMP 20. PAGE 70 A1446
BIBLIOG/A NAT/G DIPLOM POLICY

B55
KOHN H.,NATIONALISM: ITS MEANING AND HISTORY. GP/REL INGP/REL ATTIT...CONCPT NAT/COMP 16/20 MACHIAVELL. PAGE 81 A1662
NAT/LISM DIPLOM FASCISM REV

B55
O3HEVSS E.,WIRTSCHAFTSSYSTEME UND INTERNATIONALER HANDEL. ECO/DEV FINAN MARKET DIPLOM ECO/TAC COST ...METH/COMP NAT/COMP 20. PAGE 112 A2306
CAP/ISM SOCISM INT/TRADE IDEA/COMP

B56
FORSTMANN A.,DIE GRUNDLAGEN DER AUSSENWIRTSCHAFTSTHEORIE. ECO/TAC TARIFFS PRICE WAR ...NAT/COMP 20. PAGE 47 A0967
INT/TRADE CONCPT DIPLOM ECO/DEV

B56
ROBERTS H.L.,RUSSIA AND AMERICA. CHINA/COM S/ASIA USSR FORCES TEC/DEV FOR/AID NUC/PWR ALL/IDEOS ...MAJORIT TREND NAT/COMP 20 COLD/WAR UN NATO. PAGE 122 A2494
DIPLOM INT/ORG BAL/PWR TOTALISM

B57
ALEXANDER L.M.,WORLD POLITICAL PATTERNS. NAT/G PROVS CAP/ISM DIPLOM COLONIAL NAT/LISM...POLICY GEOG CHARTS METH/COMP NAT/COMP 20. PAGE 5 A0111
CONTROL METH GOV/COMP

B57
PALMER N.D.,INTERNATIONAL RELATIONS. WOR+45 INT/ORG NAT/G ECO/TAC EDU/PROP COLONIAL WAR PWR SOVEREIGN ...POLICY T 20 TREATY. PAGE 113 A2321
DIPLOM BAL/PWR NAT/COMP

B57
UNESCO,A REGISTER OF LEGAL DOCUMENTATION IN THE WORLD (2ND ED.). CT/SYS...JURID IDEA/COMP METH/COMP NAT/COMP 20. PAGE 148 A3019
BIBLIOG LAW INT/LAW CONSTN

B57
US SENATE SPEC COMM FOR AID,COMPILATION OF STUDIES AND SURVEYS. AFR ASIA L/A+17C USA+45 ECO/UNDEV AGRI INT/ORG CONSULT TEC/DEV CONFER TOTALISM...NAT/COMP 20 CONGRESS. PAGE 157 A3197
FOR/AID DIPLOM ORD/FREE DELIB/GP

B57
US SENATE SPEC COMM FOR AID,HEARINGS BEFORE THE SPECIAL COMMITTEE TO STUDY THE FOREIGN AID PROGRAM. USA+45 USSR ECO/UNDEV INT/ORG FORCES WEAPON TOTALISM ATTIT SUPEGO...NAT/COMP CONGRESS. PAGE 157 A3198
FOR/AID DIPLOM ORD/FREE TEC/DEV

B58
AVRAMOVIC D.,POSTWAR GROWTH IN INTERNATIONAL INDEBTEDNESS. WOR+45 AGRI INDUS CAP/ISM PRICE INCOME...NAT/COMP 20 GOLD/STAND SILVER. PAGE 10 A0199
INT/TRADE FINAN COST BAL/PAY

B58
BRIERLY J.L.,THE BASIS OF OBLIGATION IN INTERNATIONAL LAW, AND OTHER PAPERS. WOR+45 WOR-45 LEGIS...JURID CONCPT NAT/COMP ANTHOL 20. PAGE 19 A0377
INT/LAW DIPLOM ADJUD SOVEREIGN

B58
CHANG H.,WITHIN THE FOUR SEAS. ASIA WAR MORAL MARXISM...IDEA/COMP NAT/COMP 20 CONFUCIUS. PAGE 26 A0521
PEACE DIPLOM KNOWL CULTURE

B58
PALMER E.E.,THE COMMUNIST CHALLENGE. COM USA+45 USA-45 ECO/DEV ECO/UNDEV NEUTRAL ORD/FREE POPULISM ...CONCPT NAT/COMP ANTHOL 19/20 LENIN/VI STALIN/J MAO MARX/KARL COM/PARTY. PAGE 113 A2320
MARXISM DIPLOM IDEA/COMP POLICY

B58
VARG P.A.,MISSIONARIES, CHINESE, AND DIPLOMATS: THE AMERICAN PROTESTANT MISSIONARY MOVEMENT IN CHINA, 1890-1952. ASIA ECO/UNDEV NAT/G PROB/SOLV CAP/ISM EDU/PROP COLONIAL NAT/LISM ATTIT MARXISM...NAT/COMP STERTYP 20 CHINJAP PROTESTANT MISSION. PAGE 158 A3221
CULTURE DIPLOM SECT

B59
EMME E.M.,THE IMPACT OF AIR POWER - NATIONAL SECURITY AND WORLD POLITICS. USA+45 USSR FORCES DIPLOM WEAPON PEACE TOTALISM...POLICY NAT/COMP 20 EUROPE. PAGE 42 A0850
DETER AIR WAR ORD/FREE

B59
ETSCHMANN R.,DIE WAHRUNGS- UND DEVISENPOLITIK DES OSTBLOCKS UND IHRE AUSWIRKUNGEN AUF DIE WIRTSCHAFTSBEZIEHUNGEN ZWISCHEN OST U WEST. BULGARIA CZECHOSLVK HUNGARY POLAND USSR MARKET NAT/G PLAN DIPLOM...NAT/COMP 20. PAGE 42 A0867
ECO/TAC FINAN POLICY INT/TRADE

B59
KIRCHHEIMER O.,GEGENWARTSPROBLEME DER ASYLGEWAHRUNG. DOMIN GP/REL ATTIT...NAT/COMP 20. PAGE 79 A1630
DIPLOM INT/LAW JURID ORD/FREE

B59
STERNBERG F.,THE MILITARY AND INDUSTRIAL REVOLUTION OF OUR TIME. USA+45 USSR WOR+45 WORKER COMPUTER PLAN TEC/DEV NUC/PWR GP/REL...POLICY NAT/COMP 20. PAGE 138 A2818
DIPLOM FORCES INDUS CIVMIL/REL

B59
VINACKE H.M.,A HISTORY OF THE FAR EAST IN MODERN TIMES (6TH ED.). KOREA S/ASIA USSR CONSTN CULTURE STRATA ECO/UNDEV NAT/G CHIEF FOR/AID INT/TRADE GP/REL...SOC NAT/COMP 19/20 CHINJAP. PAGE 159 A3235
STRUCT ASIA

B60
HAMADY S.,TEMPERAMENT AND CHARACTER OF THE ARABS. FAM NAT/G SECT DIPLOM NAT/LISM...POLICY 20 ARABS. PAGE 61 A1244
NAT/COMP PERSON CULTURE ISLAM

B60
JAECKH A.,WELTSAAT; ERLEBTES UND ERSTREBTES. GERMANY WOR+45 WOR-45 PLAN WAR...POLICY OBS/ENVIR NAT/COMP PERS/COMP 20. PAGE 73 A1489
BIOG NAT/G SELF/OBS DIPLOM

B60
KENNEDY J.F.,THE STRATEGY OF PEACE. USA+45 WOR+45 BAL/PWR DIPLOM INGP/REL ORD/FREE...GOV/COMP NAT/COMP 20. PAGE 78 A1591
PEACE PLAN POLICY NAT/G

B60
MEYRIAT J.,LA SCIENCE POLITIQUE EN FRANCE, 1945-1958; BIBLIOGRAPHIES FRANCAISES DE SCIENCES SOCIALES (VOL. I). EUR+WWI FRANCE POL/PAR DIPLOM ADMIN CHOOSE ATTIT...IDEA/COMP METH/COMP NAT/COMP 20. PAGE 100 A2057
BIBLIOG/A NAT/G CONCPT PHIL/SCI

B60
NEALE A.D.,THE FLOW OF RESOURCES FROM RICH TO POOR. WOR+45 ECO/DEV ECO/UNDEV FINAN INDUS NAT/G PLAN EFFICIENCY WEALTH...POLICY NAT/COMP 20 RESOURCE/N. PAGE 108 A2209
FOR/AID DIPLOM METH/CNCPT

B60
SALETORE B.A.,INDIA'S DIPLOMATIC RELATIONS WITH THE EAST. ASIA CEYLON INDIA NEPAL S/ASIA CULTURE 7/14 PERSIA. PAGE 126 A2591
DIPLOM NAT/COMP ETIQUET

B60
SCANLON D.G.,INTERNATIONAL EDUCATION: A DOCUMENTARY HISTORY. ADMIN CONTROL ATTIT PERCEPT...BIOG ANTHOL METH 20. PAGE 127 A2612
EDU/PROP INT/ORG NAT/COMP DIPLOM

B60
SETHE P.,SCHICKSALSSTUNDEN DER WELTGESCHICHTE (6TH ED.). NAT/G BAL/PWR DOMIN REV PWR...NAT/COMP 16/20. PAGE 131 A2687
DIPLOM WAR PEACE

B60
THE ECONOMIST (LONDON),THE COMMONWEALTH AND EUROPE. EUR+WWI WOR+45 AGRI FINAN INCOME...STAT CENSUS CHARTS CMN/WLTH EEC. PAGE 142 A2911
INT/TRADE INDUS INT/ORG NAT/COMP

C60
HAZARD J.N.,"THE SOVIET SYSTEM OF GOVERNMENT." USSR SOCIETY INDUS NAT/G POL/PAR DIPLOM CT/SYS...JURID CHARTS BIBLIOG/A 20. PAGE 63 A1298
COM NAT/COMP STRUCT

ADMIN

B61
AUBREY H.G.,COEXISTENCE: ECONOMIC CHALLENGE AND RESPONSE. USSR WOR+45 ACT/RES BAL/PWR CAP/ISM DIPLOM ECO/TAC FOR/AID INT/TRADE PEACE SOCISM ...METH/COMP NAT/COMP COLD/WAR. PAGE 10 A0196
POLICY ECO/UNDEV PLAN COM

B61
GANGULI B.N.,ECONOMIC INTEGRATION. FINAN LABOR CAP/ISM DIPLOM WEALTH...NAT/COMP 20. PAGE 51 A1041
ECO/TAC METH/CNCPT EQUILIB ECO/UNDEV

B61
HADDAD J.A.,REVOLUCAO CUBANA E REVOLUCAO BRASILEIRA. BRAZIL CUBA L/A+17C STRATA AGRI WORKER EDU/PROP REGION...POLICY NAT/COMP 20. PAGE 59 A1210
REV ORD/FREE DIPLOM ECO/UNDEV

B61
HARDT J.P.,THE COLD WAR ECONOMIC GAP. USA+45 USSR ECO/DEV FORCES INT/TRADE NUC/PWR PWR 20 COLD/WAR. PAGE 61 A1258
DIPLOM ECO/TAC NAT/COMP POLICY

B61
HOLDSWORTH M.,SOVIET AFRICAN STUDIES 1918-1959. USSR ACADEM NAT/G DIPLOM REGION KNOWL 20. PAGE 66 A1366
BIBLIOG/A AFR HABITAT NAT/COMP

B61
OECD,STATISTICS OF BALANCE OF PAYMENTS 1950-61. WOR+45 FINAN ECO/TAC INT/TRADE DEMAND WEALTH...STAT NAT/COMP 20 OEEC OECD. PAGE 111 A2278
BAL/PAY ECO/DEV INT/ORG CHARTS

B61
PATAI R.,CULTURES IN CONFLICT; AN INQUIRY INTO THE SOCIO-CULTURAL PROBLEMS OF ISRAEL AND HER NEIGHBORS (2ND REV. ED.). ISLAM ISRAEL SOCIETY STRUCT DIPLOM GP/REL ALL/VALS...SOC 20 JEWS ARABS. PAGE 114 A2339
NAT/COMP CULTURE GP/COMP ATTIT

B61
SOKOL A.E.,SEAPOWER IN THE NUCLEAR AGE. USA+45 USSR DIST/IND FORCES INT/TRADE DETER WAR...POLICY NAT/COMP BIBLIOG COLD/WAR. PAGE 135 A2763
SEA PWR WEAPON NUC/PWR

B61
STARK H.,SOCIAL AND ECONOMIC FRONTIERS IN LATIN AMERICA (2ND ED.). CUBA FUT CULTURE AGRI INDUS ECO/TAC PRODUC ATTIT MARXISM...NAT/COMP BIBLIOG T 20. PAGE 137 A2807
L/A+17C SOCIETY DIPLOM ECO/UNDEV

B61
ZIMMERMAN I.,A GUIDE TO CURRENT LATIN AMERICAN PERIODICALS: HUMANITIES AND SOCIAL SCIENCES. LABOR SECT EDU/PROP...GEOG HUM SOC LING STAT NAT/COMP 20. PAGE 170 A3452
BIBLIOG/A DIPLOM L/A+17C PHIL/SCI

B62
COUNCIL ON WORLD TENSIONS,RESTLESS NATIONS. WOR+45 STRUCT INT/ORG NAT/G PLAN ECO/TAC...NAT/COMP ANTHOL 20. PAGE 32 A0641
ECO/UNDEV POLICY DIPLOM TASK

B62
DAVAR F.C.,IRAN AND INDIA THROUGH THE AGES. INDIA IRAN ELITES SECT CREATE ORD/FREE...LING BIBLIOG. PAGE 34 A0683
NAT/COMP DIPLOM CULTURE

B62
FATOUROS A.A.,GOVERNMENT GUARANTEES TO FOREIGN INVESTORS. WOR+45 ECO/UNDEV INDUS WORKER ADJUD ...NAT/COMP BIBLIOG TREATY. PAGE 44 A0903
NAT/G FINAN INT/TRADE ECO/DEV

B62
FRIEDMANN W.,METHODS AND POLICIES OF PRINCIPAL DONOR COUNTRIES IN PUBLIC INTERNATIONAL DEVELOPMENT FINANCING: PRELIMINARY APPRAISAL. FRANCE GERMANY/W UK USA+45 USSR WOR+45 FINAN TEC/DEV CAP/ISM DIPLOM ECO/TAC ATTIT 20 EEC. PAGE 49 A1002
INT/ORG FOR/AID NAT/COMP ADMIN

B62
MORGENSTERN O.,STRATEGIE - HEUTE (2ND ED.). USA+45 USSR ECO/DEV DELIB/GP WAR PEACE ORD/FREE...GOV/COMP NAT/COMP 20 COLD/WAR NATO. PAGE 104 A2134
NUC/PWR DIPLOM FORCES TEC/DEV

B62
STARR R.E.,POLAND 1944-1962: THE SOVIETIZATION OF A CAPTIVE PEOPLE. COM POLAND USSR POL/PAR SECT LEGIS DIPLOM DOMIN EDU/PROP CHOOSE ORD/FREE...POLICY CHARTS BIBLIOG 20. PAGE 137 A2808
MARXISM NAT/G TOTALISM NAT/COMP

B63
CANELAS O.A.,RADIOGRAFIA DE LA ALIANZA PARA EL ATRASO. L/A+17C USA+45 ECO/TAC DOMIN COLONIAL NAT/LISM...SOCIALIST NAT/COMP 20. PAGE 23 A0476
REV DIPLOM ECO/UNDEV REGION

B63
FRANZ G.,TEILUNG UND WIEDERVEREINIGUNG. GERMANY IRELAND ITALY NETHERLAND POLAND CULTURE BAL/PWR CHOOSE NAT/LISM ORD/FREE SOVEREIGN 19/20. PAGE 48 A0987
DIPLOM WAR NAT/COMP ATTIT

B63
GONZALEZ PEDRERO E.,ANATOMIA DE UN CONFLICTO. WOR+45 ECO/DEV ECO/UNDEV ECO/TAC FOR/AID CONTROL ARMS/CONT GOV/REL...NAT/COMP 20 COLD/WAR. PAGE 54 A1099
DIPLOM DETER BAL/PWR

B63
LYON P.,NEUTRALISM. ECO/UNDEV EDU/PROP COLONIAL ALL/IDEOS...IDEA/COMP 20 COLD/WAR UN. PAGE 92 A1879 — NAT/COMP NAT/LISM DIPLOM NEUTRAL

B63
NICOLSON H.,DIPLOMACY (3RD ED.). INT/ORG NAT/G CONSULT DELIB/GP CONFER 19/20 LEAGUE/NAT UN. PAGE 109 A2232 — DIPLOM CONCPT NAT/COMP

B63
UN SECRETARY GENERAL,PLANNING FOR ECONOMIC DEVELOPMENT. ECO/UNDEV FINAN BUDGET INT/TRADE TARIFFS TAX ADMIN 20 UN. PAGE 147 A3005 — PLAN ECO/TAC MGT NAT/COMP

B63
US SENATE COMM ON FOREIGN REL,HEARINGS ON S 1276 A BILL TO AMEND FURTHER THE FOREIGN ASSISTANCE ACT OF 1961. USA+45 WOR+45 INDUS INT/ORG FORCES TAX WEAPON SUPEGO...NAT/COMP 20 UN CONGRESS PRESIDENT. PAGE 156 A3182 — FOR/AID DIPLOM ECO/UNDEV ORD/FREE

C63
ATTIA G.E.O.,"LES FORCES ARMEES DES NATIONS UNIES EN COREE ET AU MOYENORIENT." KOREA CONSTN DELIB/GP LEGIS PWR...IDEA/COMP NAT/COMP BIBLIOG UN SUEZ. PAGE 10 A0194 — FORCES NAT/G INT/LAW

B64
CURRIE D.P.,FEDERALISM AND THE NEW NATIONS OF AFRICA. CANADA USA+45 INT/TRADE TAX GP/REL ...NAT/COMP SOC/INTEG 20. PAGE 33 A0667 — FEDERAL AFR ECO/UNDEV INT/LAW

B64
GESELLSCHAFT RECHTSVERGLEICH,BIBLIOGRAPHIE DES DEUTSCHEN RECHTS (BIBLIOGRAPHY OF GERMAN LAW, TRANS. BY COURTLAND PETERSON). GERMANY FINAN INDUS LABOR SECT FORCES CT/SYS PARL/PROC CRIME...INT/LAW SOC NAT/COMP 20. PAGE 52 A1066 — BIBLIOG/A JURID CONSTN ADMIN

B64
LIEVWEN E.,GENERALS VS PRESIDENTS: WEOMILITARISM IN LATIN AMERICA. L/A+17C FORCES DIPLOM FOR/AID LEAD ...NAT/COMP 20 PRESIDENT. PAGE 89 A1813 — CIVMIL/REL REV CONSERVE ORD/FREE

B64
OECD,DEVELOPMENT ASSISTANCE EFFORTS - POLICIES OF THE MEMBERS. AGRI INDUS BUDGET...GEOG NAT/COMP 20 OECD. PAGE 111 A2280 — INT/ORG FOR/AID ECO/UNDEV TEC/DEV

B64
ROSENAU J.N.,INTERNATIONAL ASPECTS OF CIVIL STRIFE. CHINA/COM CUBA EUR+WWI USA+45 USSR BAL/PWR EDU/PROP NEUTRAL COERCE MORAL...NAT/COMP 20 COLD/WAR UN. PAGE 124 A2533 — POLICY DIPLOM REV WAR

B64
RUSSET B.M.,WORLD HANDBOOK OF POLITICAL AND SOCIAL INDICATORS. WOR+45 COM/IND ADMIN WEALTH...GEOG 20. PAGE 126 A2577 — DIPLOM STAT NAT/G NAT/COMP

B64
STEWART C.F.,A BIBLIOGRAPHY OF INTERNATIONAL BUSINESS. WOR+45 FINAN LG/CO NAT/G PLAN ECO/TAC TARIFFS...DECISION MGT GP/COMP NAT/COMP 20 EEC. PAGE 138 A2824 — BIBLIOG INT/ORG OP/RES INT/TRADE

B64
SZLADITS C.,BIBLIOGRAPHY ON FOREIGN AND COMPARATIVE LAW: BOOKS AND ARTICLES IN ENGLISH (SUPPLEMENT 1962). FINAN INDUS JUDGE LICENSE ADMIN CT/SYS PARL/PROC OWN...INT/LAW CLASSIF METH/COMP NAT/COMP 20. PAGE 141 A2877 — BIBLIOG/A JURID ADJUD LAW

B64
UNESCO,WORLD COMMUNICATIONS: PRESS, RADIO, TELEVISION, FILM (4TH ED.). WOR+45 DIPLOM TV PEACE ...NAT/COMP SOC/INTEG 20 FILM. PAGE 148 A3023 — COM/IND EDU/PROP PRESS TEC/DEV

B64
VOELKMANN K.,HERRSCHER VON MORGEN? BAL/PWR COLONIAL NEUTRAL REGION RACE/REL ALL/VALS SOVEREIGN...RECORD 20 COLD/WAR THIRD/WRLD. PAGE 159 A3246 — DIPLOM ECO/UNDEV CONTROL NAT/COMP

B65
CALLEO D.P.,EUROPE'S FUTURE: THE GRAND ALTERNATIVES. UK INT/ORG DIPLOM PWR SOVEREIGN ...CONCPT IDEA/COMP NAT/COMP BIBLIOG 20 EEC EUROPE DEGAULLE/C NATO. PAGE 23 A0468 — FUT EUR+WWI FEDERAL NAT/LISM

B65
FORM W.H.,INDUSTRIAL RELATIONS AND SOCIAL CHANGE IN LATIN AMERICA. L/A+17C AGRI LABOR NAT/G PLAN PROB/SOLV DIPLOM...MGT SOC ANTHOL BIBLIOG/A METH 20. PAGE 47 A0966 — INDUS GP/REL NAT/COMP ECO/UNDEV

B65
GRETTON P.,MARITIME STRATEGY - A STUDY OF DEFENSE PROBLEMS. ASIA UK USSR DIPLOM COERCE DETER NUC/PWR WEAPON...CONCPT NAT/COMP 20. PAGE 56 A1147 — FORCES PLAN WAR SEA

B65
LARUS J.,COMPARATIVE WORLD POLITICS. ASIA INDIA WOR+45 WOR-45 BAL/PWR WAR PEACE RATIONAL MORAL PWR ...REALPOL INT/LAW MUSLIM. PAGE 85 A1735 — GOV/COMP IDEA/COMP DIPLOM

NAT/COMP
B65
SABLE M.H.,PERIODICALS FOR LATIN AMERICAN ECONOMIC DEVELOPMENT, TRADE, AND FINANCE: AN ANNOTATED BIBLIOGRAPHY (A PAMPHLET). ECO/TAC PRODUC PROFIT ...STAT NAT/COMP 20 OAS. PAGE 126 A2583 — BIBLIOG/A L/A+17C ECO/UNDEV INT/TRADE

B65
WINT G.,ASIA: A HANDBOOK. ASIA COM INDIA USSR CULTURE INTELL NAT/G...GEOG STAT CENSUS NAT/COMP WORSHIP 20 TREATY CHINJAP. PAGE 165 A3365 — DIPLOM SOC

B66
BESSON W.,DIE GROSSEN MACHTE - STRUKTURFRAGEN DER GEGENWARTIGEN WELTPOLITIK. ASIA USSR WOR+45 ATTIT ...IDEA/COMP 20 KENNEDY/JF. PAGE 14 A0280 — NAT/COMP DIPLOM STRUCT

B66
BIRMINGHAM D.,TRADE AND CONFLICT IN ANGOLA. PORTUGAL CULTURE FORCES DIPLOM GP/REL PROFIT HABITAT NAT/COMP. PAGE 14 A0291 — WAR INT/TRADE ECO/UNDEV COLONIAL

B66
BLACK C.E.,THE DYNAMICS OF MODERNIZATION: A STUDY IN COMPARATIVE HISTORY. STRUCT ECO/DEV ECO/UNDEV NAT/G DIPLOM LEAD REV...PREDICT TIME/SEQ TREND SOC/INTEG 17/20. PAGE 15 A0296 — SOCIETY SOC NAT/COMP

B66
BROWN L.C.,STATE AND SOCIETY IN INDEPENDENT NORTH AFRICA. ALGERIA LIBYA MOROCCO AGRI INDUS INT/ORG POL/PAR SECT PLAN DIPLOM COLONIAL...LING NAT/COMP ANTHOL BIBLIOG 20 TUNIS MUSLIM. PAGE 20 A0406 — NAT/G SOCIETY CULTURE ECO/UNDEV

B66
DOUMA J.,BIBLIOGRAPHY ON THE INTERNATIONAL COURT INCLUDING THE PERMANENT COURT, 1918-1964. WOR+45 WOR-45 DELIB/GP WAR PRIVIL...JURID NAT/COMP 20 UN LEAGUE/NAT. PAGE 38 A0780 — BIBLIOG/A INT/ORG CT/SYS DIPLOM

B66
GORDON B.K.,THE DIMENSIONS OF CONFLICT IN SOUTHEAST ASIA. S/ASIA FORCES ADJUD REGION...CHARTS 20. PAGE 54 A1111 — DIPLOM NAT/COMP INT/ORG VOL/ASSN

B66
HAY P.,FEDERALISM AND SUPRANATIONAL ORGANIZATIONS: PATTERNS FOR NEW LEGAL STRUCTURES. EUR+WWI LAW NAT/G VOL/ASSN DIPLOM PWR...NAT/COMP TREATY EEC. PAGE 63 A1294 — SOVEREIGN FEDERAL INT/ORG INT/LAW

B66
HOEVELER H.J.,INTERNATIONALE BEKAMPFUNG DES VERBRECHENS. AUSTRIA SWITZERLND WOR+45 INT/ORG CONTROL BIO/SOC...METH/COMP NAT/COMP 20 MAFIA SCOT/YARD FBI. PAGE 66 A1352 — CRIMLGY CRIME DIPLOM INT/LAW

B66
HOLT R.T.,THE POLITICAL BASIS OF ECONOMIC DEVELOPMENT. STRATA STRUCT NAT/G DIPLOM ADMIN...SOC NAT/COMP BIBLIOG 20. PAGE 67 A1376 — ECO/TAC GOV/COMP CONSTN EX/STRUC

B66
INTL CONF ON WORLD POLITICS-5,EASTERN EUROPE IN TRANSITION. EUR+WWI USSR ECO/TAC NAT/LISM ATTIT SOVEREIGN...CHARTS ANTHOL 20 TREATY WARSAW/P. PAGE 71 A1463 — COM NAT/COMP MARXISM DIPLOM

B66
PAN S.,VIETNAM CRISIS. ASIA FRANCE USA+45 USA-45 VIETNAM CULTURE SOCIETY INT/ORG ECO/TAC AGREE CONTROL WAR MARXISM 20. PAGE 113 A2325 — ECO/UNDEV POLICY DIPLOM NAT/COMP

B66
SKILLING H.G.,THE GOVERNMENTS OF COMMUNIST EAST EUROPE. COM EUR+WWI ELITES FORCES DIPLOM ECO/TAC CONTROL HABITAT SOCISM...DECISION BIBLIOG 20 EUROPE/E COM/PARTY. PAGE 134 A2738 — MARXISM NAT/COMP GP/COMP DOMIN

B66
THOMPSON J.H.,MODERNIZATION OF THE ARAB WORLD. FUT ISRAEL STRUCT ECO/UNDEV DIPLOM INGP/REL ATTIT ...CENSUS ANTHOL 20 ARABS. PAGE 143 A2926 — ADJUST ISLAM PROB/SOLV NAT/COMP

B66
US SENATE COMM ON FOREIGN REL,UNITED STATES POLICY TOWARD EUROPE (AND RELATED MATTERS). COM EUR+WWI GERMANY PROB/SOLV REGION NUC/PWR WAR NAT/LISM PEACE PWR...NAT/COMP 20 NATO CONGRESS DEGAULLE/C. PAGE 156 A3184 — DIPLOM INT/ORG POLICY WOR+45

B66
US SENATE COMM ON FOREIGN REL,HEARINGS ON S 2859 AND S 2861. USA+45 WOR+45 FORCES BUDGET CAP/ISM ADMIN DETER WEAPON TOTALISM...NAT/COMP 20 UN CONGRESS. PAGE 156 A3185 — FOR/AID DIPLOM ORD/FREE ECO/UNDEV

B66
YEAGER L.B.,INTERNATIONAL MONETARY RELATIONS: THEORY, HISTORY, AND POLICY. WOR+45 WOR-45 INT/TRADE BAL/PAY...NAT/COMP 18/20 MONEY. PAGE 169 A3432 — FINAN DIPLOM ECO/TAC IDEA/COMP

B67
DILLARD D.,ECONOMIC DEVELOPMENT OF THE NORTH ATLANTIC COMMUNITY. EUR+WWI MOD/EUR USA+45 USA-45 ECO/UNDEV LABOR CAP/ISM WAR BAL/PAY...NAT/COMP 15/20. PAGE 37 A0763 — ECO/DEV INT/TRADE INDUS DIPLOM

B67
MCCLINTOCK R.,THE MEANING OF LIMITED WAR. FUT WAR
WOR+45 NAT/G FORCES GUERRILLA REV...POLICY SAMP/SIZ NUC/PWR
TREND NAT/COMP 45 COLD/WAR. PAGE 97 A1999 BAL/PWR
DIPLOM

B67
MCNELLY T.,SOURCES IN MODERN EAST ASIAN HISTORY AND NAT/COMP
POLITICS. KOREA VIETNAM CULTURE DIPLOM COLONIAL REV ASIA
WAR PWR ALL/IDEOS MARXISM...ANTHOL 20 CHINJAP. S/ASIA
PAGE 99 A2023 SOCIETY

B67
RUEFF J.,BALANCE OF PAYMENTS. WOR+45 FINAN TEC/DEV INT/TRADE
DIPLOM TARIFFS PRICE CONTROL...POLICY CONCPT BAL/PAY
IDEA/COMP. PAGE 125 A2567 ECO/TAC
NAT/COMP

B67
SHAFFER H.G.,THE COMMUNIST WORLD: MARXIST AND NON- MARXISM
MARXIST VIEWS. WOR+45 SOCIETY DIPLOM ECO/TAC NAT/COMP
CONTROL SOCISM...MARXIST ANTHOL BIBLIOG/A 20. IDEA/COMP
PAGE 131 A2691 COM

B67
UNESCO,PRINCIPLES AND PROBLEMS OF NATIONAL SCIENCE NAT/COMP
POLICIES. WOR+45 ECO/DEV ECO/UNDEV R+D INT/ORG POLICY
PROB/SOLV CONFER...PHIL/SCI CHARTS 20 UNESCO UN. TEC/DEV
PAGE 148 A3026 CREATE

B67
WAELDER R.,PROGRESS AND REVOLUTION* A STUDY OF THE PWR
ISSUES OF OUR AGE. WOR+45 WOR-45 BAL/PWR DIPLOM NAT/G
COERCE ROLE MORAL ALL/IDEOS...IDEA/COMP NAT/COMP REV
19/20. PAGE 160 A3259 TEC/DEV

NAT/FARMER....NATIONAL FARMERS' ASSOCIATION

NAT/G....NATIONAL GOVERNMENT

NAT/LISM....NATIONALISM

N
SABIN J.,BIBLIOTHECA AMERICANA: A DICTIONARY OF BIBLIOG
BOOKS RELATING TO AMERICA, FROM ITS DISCOVERY TO L/A+17C
THE PRESENT TIME(29 VOLS.). CONSTN CULTURE SOCIETY DIPLOM
ECO/DEV LOC/G EDU/PROP NAT/LISM...POLICY GEOG SOC NAT/G
19. PAGE 126 A2581

N
UNIVERSITY OF FLORIDA LIBRARY,DOORS TO LATIN BIBLIOG/A
AMERICA; RECENT BOOKS AND PAMPHLETS. CONSTN CULTURE L/A+17C
SOCIETY ECO/UNDEV COLONIAL LEAD GOV/REL NAT/LISM DIPLOM
ATTIT...HUM SOC 20. PAGE 149 A3047 NAT/G

N
AFRICANA NEWSLETTER. ECO/UNDEV ACADEM SECT DIPLOM BIBLIOG/A
PRESS COLONIAL NAT/LISM 20. PAGE 1 A0001 AFR
NAT/G

N
BACKGROUND; JOURNAL OF INTERNATIONAL STUDIES BIBLIOG
ASSOCIATION. INT/ORG FORCES ACT/RES EDU/PROP COERCE DIPLOM
NAT/LISM PEACE ATTIT...INT/LAW CONCPT 20. PAGE 1 POLICY
A0005

N
JOURNAL OF ASIAN STUDIES. CULTURE ECO/DEV SECT BIBLIOG
DIPLOM EDU/PROP WAR NAT/LISM...PHIL/SCI SOC 20. ASIA
PAGE 1 A0013 S/ASIA
NAT/G

N
AFRICAN BIBLIOGRAPHIC CENTER,A CURRENT BIBLIOGRAPHY BIBLIOG/A
ON AFRICAN AFFAIRS. LAW CULTURE ECO/UNDEV LABOR AFR
SECT DIPLOM FOR/AID COLONIAL NAT/LISM...LING 20. NAT/G
PAGE 5 A0094 REGION

N
ASIA FOUNDATION,LIBRARY NOTES. LAW CONSTN CULTURE BIBLIOG/A
SOCIETY ECO/UNDEV INT/ORG NAT/G COLONIAL LEAD ASIA
REGION NAT/LISM ATTIT 20 UN. PAGE 9 A0189 S/ASIA
DIPLOM

N
HOOVER INSTITUTION,UNITED STATES AND CANADIAN BIBLIOG
PUBLICATIONS ON AFRICA. CULTURE ECO/UNDEV AGRI DIPLOM
TEC/DEV EDU/PROP COLONIAL RACE/REL NAT/LISM ATTIT NAT/G
HEALTH...SOC SOC/WK 20. PAGE 67 A1381 AFR

N
LONDON LIBRARY ASSOCIATION,ATHENAEUM SUBJECT INDEX. BIBLIOG
1915-1918. NAT/G DIPLOM NAT/LISM 20. PAGE 91 A1857 CON/ANAL
SOC

NCO
CARRINGTON C.E.,THE COMMONWEALTH IN AFRICA ECO/UNDEV
(PAMPHLET). UK STRUCT NAT/G COLONIAL REPRESENT AFR
GOV/REL RACE/REL NAT/LISM...MAJORIT 20 EEC NEGRO DIPLOM
COLD/WAR. PAGE 25 A0500 PLAN

B00
GRIFFIN A.P.C.,LIST OF BOOKS RELATING TO THE THEORY BIBLIOG/A
OF COLONIZATION, GOVERNMENT OF DEPENDENCIES, COLONIAL
PROTECTORATES, AND RELATED TOPICS. FRANCE GERMANY GOV/REL
ITALY SPAIN UK USA-45 WOR-45 ECO/TAC ADMIN CONTROL DOMIN
REGION NAT/LISM ALL/VALS PWR...INT/LAW SOC 16/19.
PAGE 56 A1149

B09
FREMANTLE H.E.S.,THE NEW NATION, A SURVEY OF THE NAT/LISM
CONDITION AND PROSPECTS OF SOUTH AFRICA. SOUTH/AFR SOVEREIGN
CONSTN POL/PAR DIPLOM DOMIN COLONIAL WEALTH...SOC RACE/REL
TREND 19. PAGE 49 A0996 REGION

B10
MENDELSSOHN S.,SOUTH AFRICAN BIBLIOGRAPHY (2 BIBLIOG/A
VOLS.). SOUTH/AFR EXTR/IND LABOR SECT DIPLOM AFR
INT/TRADE COLONIAL RACE/REL DISCRIM...GEOG 20. NAT/G
PAGE 99 A2038 NAT/LISM

B17
VEBLEN T.B.,AN INQUIRY INTO THE NATURE OF PEACE AND PEACE
THE TERMS OF ITS PERPETUATION. UNIV STRATA FINAN DIPLOM
EDU/PROP PRICE COST DISCRIM NAT/LISM MORAL ORD/FREE WAR
PACIFIST 20 WORLDUNITY. PAGE 158 A3224 NAT/G

N19
ASIAN-AFRICAN CONFERENCE,SELECTED DOCUMENTS OF THE NEUTRAL
BANDUNG CONFERENCE (PAMPHLET). S/ASIA PLAN ECO/TAC ECO/UNDEV
CONFER REGION REV NAT/LISM 20. PAGE 9 A0191 COLONIAL
DIPLOM

N19
BARROS J.F.P.,THE INTERNATIONAL POLICE: THE USE OF PEACE
FORCE IN THE STRUCTURE OF PEACE (PAMPHLET). BRAZIL INT/ORG
WOR+45 WOR-45 FORCES DISCRIM NAT/LISM ORD/FREE COERCE
SOVEREIGN...POLICY NEW/IDEA WORSHIP 20. PAGE 11 BAL/PWR
A0229

N19
HANNA A.J.,EUROPEAN RULE IN AFRICA (PAMPHLET). DIPLOM
BELGIUM FRANCE MOD/EUR UK WOR+45 WOR-45 ECO/UNDEV COLONIAL
NAT/G PARTIC SOVEREIGN...NAT/COMP 19/20. PAGE 61 AFR
A1252 NAT/LISM

N19
JACKSON R.G.A.,THE CASE FOR AN INTERNATIONAL FOR/AID
DEVELOPMENT AUTHORITY (PAMPHLET). WOR+45 ECO/DEV INT/ORG
DIPLOM GIVE CONTROL GP/REL EFFICIENCY NAT/LISM ECO/UNDEV
SOVEREIGN 20. PAGE 72 A1478 ADMIN

N19
LISKA G.,THE GREATER MAGHREB: FROM INDEPENDENCE TO ECO/UNDEV
UNITY? (PAMPHLET). ALGERIA ISLAM MOROCCO PROB/SOLV REGION
BAL/PWR CONFER COLONIAL REPRESENT NAT/LISM 20 DIPLOM
TUNIS. PAGE 90 A1835 DOMIN

N19
MASSEY V.,CANADIANS AND THEIR COMMONWEALTH: THE ATTIT
ROMANES LECTURE DELIVERED IN THE SHELDONIAN THEATRE DIPLOM
JUNE 1, 1961 (PAMPHLET). CANADA UK CULTURE ECO/DEV NAT/G
REPRESENT NAT/LISM PEACE PWR CONSERVE 20 CMN/WLTH. SOVEREIGN
PAGE 96 A1959

N19
PROVISIONS SECTION OAU,ORGANIZATION OF AFRICAN CONSTN
UNITY: BASIC DOCUMENTS AND RESOLUTIONS (PAMPHLET). EX/STRUC
AFR CULTURE ECO/UNDEV DIPLOM ECO/TAC EDU/PROP SOVEREIGN
COLONIAL ARMS/CONT NUC/PWR RACE/REL DISCRIM INT/ORG
NAT/LISM 20 UN OAU. PAGE 118 A2415

N19
UNITED ARAB REPUBLIC,THE PROBLEM OF THE PALESTINIAN STRANGE
REFUGEES (PAMPHLET). ISRAEL UAR LAW PROB/SOLV GP/REL
EDU/PROP CONFER ADJUD CONTROL NAT/LISM HEALTH 20 INGP/REL
JEWS UN MIGRATION. PAGE 148 A3029 DIPLOM

B21
BALFOUR A.J.,ESSAYS SPECULATIVE AND POLITICAL. SEA PHIL/SCI
CULTURE CREATE WAR NAT/LISM PEACE LOVE...ART/METH SOCIETY
INT/LAW CONCPT ANTHOL 20 JEWS. PAGE 10 A0211 DIPLOM

B22
FICHTE J.G.,ADDRESSES TO THE GERMAN NATION. GERMANY NAT/LISM
PRUSSIA ELITES NAT/G SECT CREATE INT/TRADE HEREDITY CULTURE
...ART/METH LING 19 FRANK/PARL. PAGE 45 A0923 EDU/PROP
REGION

C25
MOON P.T.,"SYLLABUS ON INTERNATIONAL RELATIONS." INT/ORG
EUR+WWI MOD/EUR USA-45 FORCES COLONIAL WAR WEAPON DIPLOM
NAT/LISM...POLICY BIBLIOG T 19/20. PAGE 103 A2120 NAT/G

B26
LEWIN E.,RECENT PUBLICATIONS IN THE LIBRARY OF THE BIBLIOG
ROYAL COLONIAL INSTITUTE (PAMPHLET). CANADA UK COLONIAL
EX/STRUC PARL/PROC NAT/LISM SOVEREIGN 20 CMN/WLTH CONSTN
PARLIAMENT. PAGE 88 A1799 DIPLOM

S26
COHEN P.A.,"WANG T'AO AND INCIPIENT CHINESE NAT/LISM
NATIONALISM." ASIA ADMIN ATTIT 19/20 BUREAUCRCY. ISOLAT
PAGE 28 A0563 CONSERVE
DIPLOM

C28
SCHNEIDER H.W.,"MAKING THE FASCIST STATE." ITALY FASCISM
CULTURE LABOR DIPLOM REV WAR NAT/LISM TOTALISM POLICY
ATTIT DRIVE SOCISM...BIBLIOG PARLIAMENT 20. POL/PAR
PAGE 129 A2638

C28
WARD P.W.,"SOVEREIGNTY: A STUDY OF A CONTEMPORARY SOVEREIGN
POLITICAL NOTION." CONSTN NAT/G DIPLOM REPRESENT CONCPT
PLURISM...IDEA/COMP BIBLIOG. PAGE 161 A3281 NAT/LISM

B30
BYNKERSHOEK C.,QUAESTIONUM JURIS PUBLICI LIBRI DUO. INT/ORG
CHRIST-17C MOD/EUR CONSTN ELITES SOCIETY NAT/G LAW
PROVS EX/STRUC FORCES TOP/EX BAL/PWR DIPLOM ATTIT NAT/LISM
MORAL...TRADIT CONCPT. PAGE 23 A0460 INT/LAW

B32
BRYCE J.,THE HOLY ROMAN EMPIRE. GERMANY ITALY CHRIST-17C
MOD/EUR CULTURE SOCIETY STRUCT INT/ORG NAT/G SECT NAT/LISM
DIPLOM DOMIN WAR SUPEGO ALL/VALS SOVEREIGN...GEOG

SOC TIME/SEQ CHARTS STERTYP. PAGE 20 A0413

B32
LENIN V.I.,THE WAR AND THE SECOND INTERNATIONAL. COM MOD/EUR USSR CAP/ISM DIPLOM NAT/LISM ATTIT MARXISM...CONCPT 20. PAGE 87 A1772
POL/PAR WAR SOCISM INT/ORG

C32
MARRARO H.R.,"AMERICAN OPINION ON THE UNIFICATION OF ITALY." ITALY MOD/EUR USA-45 FORCES DIPLOM PRESS REV CATHISM...BIOG 19 PRESIDENT. PAGE 95 A1944
BIBLIOG/A NAT/LISM ATTIT ORD/FREE

B33
LANGER W.L.,FOREIGN AFFAIRS BIBLIOGRAPHY. WOR-45 INT/ORG CONSULT EDU/PROP ROUTINE NAT/LISM ATTIT SOVEREIGN...STAT RECORD GEN/METH LEAGUE/NAT TOT/POP. PAGE 84 A1725
KNOWL

B34
EINSTEIN A.,THE WORLD AS I SEE IT. WOR-45 INTELL R+D INT/ORG NAT/G SECT VOL/ASSN FORCES CREATE EDU/PROP LEGIT ARMS/CONT WAR WEAPON NAT/LISM ALL/VALS...POLICY CONCPT 20. PAGE 41 A0828
SOCIETY PHIL/SCI DIPLOM PACIFISM

B35
FOREIGN AFFAIRS BIBLIOGRAPHY: A SELECTED AND ANNOTATED LIST OF BOOKS ON INTERNATIONAL RELATIONS 1919-1962 (4 VOLS.). CONSTN FORCES COLONIAL ARMS/CONT WAR NAT/LISM PEACE ATTIT DRIVE...POLICY INT/LAW 20. PAGE 3 A0050
BIBLIOG/A DIPLOM INT/ORG

B35
WEINBERG A.K.,MANIFEST DESTINY: A STUDY OF NATIONALIST EXPANSIONISM IN AMERICAN HISTORY. USA+45 USA-45 FORCES DIPLOM COLONIAL WAR ATTIT 18/20 INTERVENT. PAGE 162 A3305
NAT/LISM GEOG COERCE NAT/G

B36
BOYCE A.N.,EUROPE AND SOUTH AFRICA. FRANCE GERMANY ITALY SOUTH/AFR UK INDUS NAT/G CONTROL REV WAR NAT/LISM...CONCPT HIST/WRIT 20. PAGE 18 A0362
COLONIAL GOV/COMP NAT/COMP DIPLOM

B36
BRIERLY J.L.,THE LAW OF NATIONS (2ND ED.). WOR+45 WOR-45 INT/ORG AGREE CONTROL COERCE WAR NAT/LISM PEACE PWR 16/20 TREATY LEAGUE/NAT. PAGE 18 A0375
DIPLOM INT/LAW NAT/G

B36
THWAITE D.,THE SEETHING AFRICAN POT: A STUDY OF BLACK NATIONALISM 1882-1935. ETHIOPIA SECT VOL/ASSN COERCE GUERRILLA MURDER DISCRIM MARXISM...PSY TIME/SEQ 18/20 NEGRO. PAGE 144 A2939
NAT/LISM AFR RACE/REL DIPLOM

B37
BORGESE G.A.,GOLIATH: THE MARCH OF FASCISM. GERMANY ITALY LAW POL/PAR SECT DIPLOM SOCISM...JURID MYTH 20 DANTE MACHIAVELL MUSSOLIN/B. PAGE 17 A0341
POLICY NAT/LISM FASCISM NAT/G

B38
COLBY C.C.,GEOGRAPHICAL ASPECTS OF INTERNATIONAL RELATIONS. WOR-45 ECO/DEV ECO/UNDEV AGRI EXTR/IND INDUS MARKET R+D INT/ORG NAT/G TEC/DEV ECO/TAC INT/TRADE NAT/LISM WEALTH...METH/CNCPT CHARTS GEN/LAWS 20. PAGE 28 A0565
PLAN GEOG DIPLOM

B38
GRISWOLD A.W.,THE FAR EASTERN POLICY OF THE UNITED STATES. ASIA S/ASIA USA-45 INT/ORG INT/TRADE WAR NAT/LISM...BIBLIOG 19/20 LEAGUE/NAT ROOSEVLT/T ROOSEVLT/F WILSON/W TREATY. PAGE 57 A1166
DIPLOM POLICY CHIEF

B38
HARPER S.N.,THE GOVERNMENT OF THE SOVIET UNION. COM USSR LAW CONSTN ECO/DEV PLAN TEC/DEV DIPLOM INT/TRADE ADMIN REV NAT/LISM...POLICY 20. PAGE 62 A1265
MARXISM NAT/G LEAD POL/PAR

B39
BROWN J.F.,CONTEMPORARY WORLD POLITICS. WOR-45 NAT/G PLAN BAL/PWR EDU/PROP LEGIT REGION NAT/LISM ORD/FREE PWR SOVEREIGN...POLICY CONCPT HIST/WRIT TIME/SEQ GEN/LAWS LEAGUE/NAT. PAGE 20 A0403
INT/ORG DIPLOM PEACE

B39
KOHN H.,REVOLUTIONS AND DICTATORSHIPS. COM EUR+WWI ISLAM MOD/EUR NAT/G CHIEF FORCES WAR CIVMIL/REL PWR MARXISM 18/20. PAGE 81 A1661
NAT/LISM TOTALISM REV FASCISM

B39
MAXWELL B.W.,INTERNATIONAL RELATIONS. EUR+WWI WOR-45 NAT/G CONSULT DIPLOM LEGIT ADJUD NAT/LISM ATTIT ORD/FREE SOVEREIGN...JURID LEAGUE/NAT TOT/POP VAL/FREE 20. PAGE 97 A1981
INT/ORG

B39
ZIMMERN A.,MODERN POLITICAL DOCTRINE. WOR-45 CULTURE SOCIETY ECO/UNDEV DELIB/GP EX/STRUC CREATE DOMIN COERCE NAT/LISM ATTIT RIGID/FLEX ORD/FREE PWR WEALTH...POLICY CONCPT OBS TIME/SEQ TREND TOT/POP LEAGUE/NAT 20. PAGE 170 A3454
NAT/G ECO/TAC BAL/PWR INT/TRADE

B40
BOGGS S.W.,INTERNATIONAL BOUNDARIES. WOR-45 SOCIETY ECO/DEV INT/ORG NAT/G NEIGH LEGIT PERSON ORD/FREE PWR...POLICY GEOG MYTH LEAGUE/NAT 20. PAGE 16 A0329
ATTIT CONCPT NAT/LISM

B40
MIDDLEBUSH F.,ELEMENTS OF INTERNATIONAL RELATIONS. WOR-45 PROVS CONSULT EDU/PROP LEGIT WAR NAT/LISM ATTIT KNOWL MORAL ORD/FREE PWR...JURID LEAGUE/NAT TOT/POP VAL/FREE. PAGE 101 A2067
NAT/G INT/ORG PEACE DIPLOM

C40
NORMAN E.H.,"JAPAN'S EMERGENCE AS A MODERN STATE: POLITICAL AND ECONOMIC PROBLEMS OF THE MEIJI PERIOD." CONSTN STRATA AGRI INDUS POL/PAR TEC/DEV CAP/ISM CIVMIL/REL...BIBLIOG 19/20 CHINJAP. PAGE 110 A2250
CENTRAL DIPLOM POLICY NAT/LISM

B41
BIRDSALL P.,VERSAILLES TWENTY YEARS AFTER. MOD/EUR POL/PAR CHIEF CONSULT FORCES LEGIS REPAR PEACE ORD/FREE...BIBLIOG 20 PRESIDENT TREATY. PAGE 14 A0290
DIPLOM NAT/LISM WAR

S41
WRIGHT Q.,"FUNDAMENTAL PROBLEMS OF INTERNATIONAL ORGANIZATION." UNIV WOR-45 STRUCT FORCES ACT/RES CREATE DOMIN EDU/PROP LEGIT REGION NAT/LISM ORD/FREE PWR RESPECT SOVEREIGN...JURID SOC CONCPT METH/CNCPT TIME/SEQ 20. PAGE 167 A3405
INT/ORG ATTIT PEACE

B42
CONOVER H.F.,FRENCH COLONIES IN AFRICA: A LIST OF REFERENCES. ALGERIA FRANCE MOROCCO SOMALIA SUDAN CULTURE AGRI LOC/G SECT FORCES DIPLOM INT/TRADE NAT/LISM HEALTH...CON/ANAL 20. PAGE 29 A0594
BIBLIOG AFR ECO/UNDEV COLONIAL

B43
CONOVER H.F.,THE BALKANS: A SELECTED LIST OF REFERENCES. ALBANIA BULGARIA ROMANIA YUGOSLAVIA INT/ORG PROB/SOLV DIPLOM LEGIT CONFER ADJUD WAR NAT/LISM PEACE PWR 20 LEAGUE/NAT. PAGE 29 A0596
BIBLIOG EUR+WWI

B43
SULZBACH W.,NATIONAL CONSCIOUSNESS. FUT WOR-45 INT/ORG PEACE MORAL FASCISM MARXISM...MAJORIT TREND WORSHIP 19/20 LEAGUE/NAT INTERVENT WWI. PAGE 140 A2862
NAT/LISM NAT/G DIPLOM WAR

B43
US DEPARTMENT OF STATE,NATIONAL SOCIALISM; BASIC PRINCIPLES, THEIR APPLICATION BY THE NAZI PARTY'S FOREIGN ORGANIZATION... GERMANY WOR-45 ECO/DEV LOC/G POL/PAR FORCES DIPLOM DOMIN COLONIAL ARMS/CONT COERCE NAT/LISM PWR 20 NAZI. PAGE 151 A3081
FASCISM SOCISM NAT/G TOTALISM

B44
FULLER G.H.,TURKEY: A SELECTED LIST OF REFERENCES. ISLAM TURKEY CULTURE ECO/UNDEV AGRI DIPLOM NAT/LISM CONSERVE...GEOG HUM INT/LAW SOC 7/20 MAPS. PAGE 50 A1024
BIBLIOG/A ALL/VALS

B44
RAGATZ L.J.,LITERATURE OF EUROPEAN IMPERIALISM. ECO/TAC INT/TRADE DOMIN GOV/REL DEMAND NAT/LISM PWR WEALTH 19/20. PAGE 119 A2432
BIBLIOG COLONIAL INT/ORG ECO/UNDEV

L44
HAILEY,"THE FUTURE OF COLONIAL PEOPLES." WOR-45 CONSTN CULTURE ECO/UNDEV AGRI MARKET INT/ORG NAT/G SECT CONSULT ECO/TAC LEGIT ADMIN NAT/LISM ALL/VALS ...SOC OBS TREND STERTYP CMN/WLTH LEAGUE/NAT PARLIAMENT 20. PAGE 59 A1218
PLAN CONCPT DIPLOM UK

B45
CARR E.H.,NATIONALISM AND AFTER. FUT WOR-45 NAT/G VOL/ASSN EX/STRUC PLAN ROUTINE TOTALISM ATTIT HEALTH ORD/FREE PWR...CONCPT 20. PAGE 25 A0499
INT/ORG TREND NAT/LISM REGION

B45
ELTON G.E.,IMPERIAL COMMONWEALTH. INDIA UK DIPLOM DOMIN WAR NAT/LISM SOVEREIGN...TRADIT CHARTS T 15/20 CMN/WLTH AUSTRAL PRE/US/AM. PAGE 41 A0844
REGION CONCPT COLONIAL

B45
HORN O.B.,BRITISH PUBLIC OPINION AND THE FIRST PARTITION OF POLAND. POLAND UK LEGIS PRESS RUMOR CONTROL PARTIC NAT/LISM SOVEREIGN 18/19. PAGE 67 A1385
DIPLOM POLICY ATTIT NAT/G

B45
WOOLBERT R.G.,FOREIGN AFFAIRS BIBLIOGRAPHY, 1932-1942. INT/ORG SECT INT/TRADE COLONIAL RACE/REL NAT/LISM...GEOG INT/LAW GOV/COMP IDEA/COMP 20. PAGE 167 A3393
BIBLIOG/A DIPLOM WAR

B46
GRIFFIN G.G.,A GUIDE TO MANUSCRIPTS RELATING TO AMERICAN HISTORY IN BRITISH DEPOSITORIES. CANADA IRELAND MOD/EUR UK USA-45 LAW DIPLOM ADMIN COLONIAL WAR NAT/LISM SOVEREIGN...GEOG INT/LAW 15/19 CMN/WLTH. PAGE 56 A1159
BIBLIOG/A ALL/VALS NAT/G

B46
LOWENSTEIN R.,POLITICAL RECONSTRUCTION. WOR+45 EX/STRUC EDU/PROP NAT/LISM ATTIT KNOWL ORD/FREE PWR ...SOCIALIST CONCPT GEN/LAWS TOT/POP 20. PAGE 91 A1869
FUT INT/ORG DIPLOM

B46
STURZO D.L.,NATIONALISM AND INTERNATIONALISM. WOR-45 INT/ORG LABOR NAT/G POL/PAR TOTALISM MORAL ORD/FREE FASCISM...MAJORIT 19/20 UN LEAGUE/NAT MUSSOLIN/B. PAGE 140 A2857
NAT/LISM DIPLOM WAR PEACE

B47
HYDE C.C.,INTERNATIONAL LAW, CHIEFLY AS INTERPRETED AND APPLIED BY THE UNITED STATES (3 VOLS., 2ND REV. ED.). USA-45 WOR+45 WOR-45 INT/ORG CT/SYS WAR NAT/LISM PEACE ORD/FREE...JURID 19/20 TREATY.
INT/LAW DIPLOM NAT/G POLICY

PAGE 69 A1426

S48
MORGENTHAU H.J.,"THE TWILIGHT OF INTERNATIONAL MORALITY" (BMR)" WOR+45 WOR-45 BAL/PWR WAR NAT/LISM PEACE...POLICY INT/LAW IDEA/COMP 15/20 TREATY INTERVENT. PAGE 104 A2137
MORAL DIPLOM NAT/G

B49
BOYD A.,WESTERN UNION: A STUDY OF THE TREND TOWARD EUROPEAN UNITY. FUT REGION NAT/LISM...POLICY IDEA/COMP BIBLIOG 14/20 OEEC ERASMUS/D COUNCL/EUR FULBRGHT/J NATO. PAGE 18 A0363
DIPLOM AGREE TREND INT/ORG

B49
HINDEN R.,EMPIRE AND AFTER. UK POL/PAR BAL/PWR DIPLOM INT/TRADE WAR NAT/LISM PWR 17/20. PAGE 65 A1335
NAT/G COLONIAL ATTIT POLICY

C49
YANAGA C.,"JAPAN SINCE PERRY." S/ASIA CULTURE ECO/DEV FORCES WAR 19/20 CHINJAP. PAGE 168 A3430
DIPLOM POL/PAR CIVMIL/REL NAT/LISM

B50
BARGHOORN F.C.,THE SOVIET IMAGE OF THE UNITED STATES: A STUDY IN DISTORTION. COM USSR DOMIN WAR NAT/LISM TOTALISM SOCISM...PSY 20. PAGE 11 A0220
PROB/SOLV EDU/PROP DIPLOM ATTIT

C50
ELLSWORTH P.T.,"INTERNATIONAL ECONOMY." ECO/DEV ECO/UNDEV FINAN LABOR DIPLOM FOR/AID TARIFFS BAL/PAY EQUILIB NAT/LISM OPTIMAL...INT/LAW 20 ILO GATT. PAGE 41 A0843
BIBLIOG INT/TRADE ECO/TAC INT/ORG

N50
SCHAPIRO J.S.,THE WORLD IN CRISES: POLITICAL AND SOCIAL MOVEMENTS IN THE TWENTIETH CENTURY. USA+45 INT/ORG LABOR PLAN CAP/ISM DIPLOM COLONIAL PEACE TOTALISM ATTIT LAISSEZ...BIBLIOG 20 COLD/WAR. PAGE 128 A2618
NAT/LISM TEC/DEV REV WAR

B51
BROGAN D.W.,THE PRICE OF REVOLUTION. FRANCE USA+45 USA-45 USSR CONSTN NAT/G DIPLOM COLONIAL NAT/LISM ORD/FREE POPULISM...CONCPT 18/20 PRE/US/AM. PAGE 19 A0386
REV METH/COMP COST MARXISM

B51
CARRINGTON C.E.,THE LIQUIDATION OF THE BRITISH EMPIRE. AFR NAT/G INT/TRADE COLONIAL RACE/REL ATTIT ORD/FREE...POLICY NAT/COMP 20 CMN/WLTH. PAGE 25 A0501
SOVEREIGN NAT/LISM DIPLOM GP/REL

B51
JENNINGS S.I.,THE COMMONWEALTH IN ASIA. CEYLON INDIA PAKISTAN S/ASIA UK CONSTN CULTURE SOCIETY STRATA STRUCT NAT/G POL/PAR EDU/PROP LEAD WAR 20 CMN/WLTH. PAGE 74 A1510
NAT/LISM REGION COLONIAL DIPLOM

B51
WABEKE B.H.,A GUIDE TO DUTCH BIBLIOGRAPHIES. BELGIUM INDONESIA NETHERLAND DIPLOM INT/TRADE WAR NAT/LISM KNOWL...ART/METH HUM JURID CON/ANAL 14/20. PAGE 160 A3257
BIBLIOG/A NAT/G CULTURE COLONIAL

S51
ICHHEISER G.,"MISUNDERSTANDING IN INTERNATIONAL RELATIONS." UNIV SOCIETY FACE/GP INT/ORG SECT ATTIT PERSON RIGID/FLEX LOVE RESPECT...RELATIV PSY SOC CONCPT MYTH SOC/EXP GEN/LAWS. PAGE 70 A1431
PERCEPT STERTYP NAT/LISM DIPLOM

B52
GURLAND A.R.L.,POLITICAL SCIENCE IN WESTERN GERMANY: THOUGHTS AND WRITINGS, 1950-1952 (PAMPHLET). EUR+WWI GERMANY/W ELITES SOCIETY NAT/G NAT/LISM TOTALISM 20. PAGE 58 A1196
BIBLIOG/A DIPLOM CIVMIL/REL FASCISM

B52
WALTERS F.P.,A HISTORY OF THE LEAGUE OF NATIONS. EUR+WWI CONSTN NAT/G LEGIS TOP/EX ACT/RES PLAN EDU/PROP LEGIT ROUTINE ATTIT...TREND LEAGUE/NAT 20 CHINJAP. PAGE 161 A3271
INT/ORG TIME/SEQ NAT/LISM

B53
ROSCIO J.G.,OBRAS. L/A+17C SPAIN DIPLOM REV WAR NAT/LISM TOTALISM PWR SOVEREIGN 19. PAGE 123 A2527
ORD/FREE COLONIAL NAT/G PHIL/SCI

C53
DEUTSCH K.W.,"NATIONALISM AND SOCIAL COMMUNICATION: AN INQUIRY INTO THE FOUNDATIONS OF NATIONALITY." CULTURE STRUCT DIPLOM DOMIN ATTIT ORD/FREE SOVEREIGN...SOC STAT CHARTS IDEA/COMP BIBLIOG. PAGE 36 A0735
NAT/LISM CONCPT PERCEPT STRATA

B54
COOKSON J.,BEFORE THE AFRICAN STORM. BELGIUM CENTRL/AFR FRANCE UK ECO/UNDEV POL/PAR CREATE BAL/PWR RACE/REL NAT/LISM ORD/FREE CONSERVE MARXISM SOC/INTEG 20 CONGO/LEOP. PAGE 30 A0607
COLONIAL REV DISCRIM DIPLOM

B54
MANNING C.A.W.,THE UNIVERSITY TEACHING OF SOCIAL SCIENCES: INTERNATIONAL RELATIONS. WOR+45 INTELL STRATA R+D ACADEM INT/ORG NAT/G CONSULT DELIB/GP ACT/RES EDU/PROP NAT/LISM ATTIT...POLICY CONT/OBS HYPO/EXP VAL/FREE LEAGUE/NAT UNESCO 20. PAGE 94 A1925
KNOWL PHIL/SCI DIPLOM

B54
NATION ASSOCIATES,SECURITY AND THE MIDDLE EAST - THE PROBLEM AND ITS SOLUTION. ISRAEL JORDAN LEBANON SYRIA UAR FORCES FOR/AID GP/REL NAT/LISM PEACE TOTALISM...POLICY 20. PAGE 107 A2198
DIPLOM ECO/UNDEV WAR PLAN

B54
SHARMA J.S.,MAHATMA GANDHI: A DESCRIPTIVE BIBLIOGRAPHY. INDIA S/ASIA PROB/SOLV DIPLOM COLONIAL WAR NAT/LISM PEACE ATTIT PERSON SOVEREIGN ...CONCPT 20 GANDHI/M. PAGE 132 A2695
BIBLIOG/A BIOG CHIEF LEAD

L54
CHARLESWORTH J.C.,"AMERICA AND A NEW ASIA." ASIA INDIA ISLAM S/ASIA USA+45 USA-45 ECO/UNDEV NAT/G POL/PAR FORCES FOR/AID DOMIN EDU/PROP COERCE DRIVE ALL/VALS MARXISM SOCISM TOT/POP 20. PAGE 26 A0522
ECO/TAC DIPLOM NAT/LISM

B55
ARNOLD G.L.,THE PATTERN OF WORLD CONFLICT. USA+45 INT/ORG ECO/TAC INT/TRADE PEACE 20 EUROPE. PAGE 9 A0176
DIPLOM BAL/PWR NAT/LISM PLAN

B55
BURR R.N.,DOCUMENTS ON INTER-AMERICAN COOPERATION: VOL. I, 1810-1881; VOL. II, 1881-1948. DELIB/GP BAL/PWR INT/TRADE REPRESENT NAT/LISM PEACE HABITAT ORD/FREE PWR SOVEREIGN...INT/LAW 20 OAS. PAGE 22 A0445
BIBLIOG DIPLOM INT/ORG L/A+17C

B55
KOHN H.,NATIONALISM: ITS MEANING AND HISTORY. GP/REL INGP/REL ATTIT...CONCPT NAT/COMP 16/20 MACHIAVELL. PAGE 81 A1662
NAT/LISM DIPLOM FASCISM REV

B55
ROWE C.,VOLTAIRE AND THE STATE. FRANCE MOD/EUR BAL/PWR CONTROL TASK SUPEGO ORD/FREE PWR...CONCPT 18 VOLTAIRE. PAGE 125 A2553
NAT/G DIPLOM NAT/LISM ATTIT

B55
TAN C.C.,THE BOXER CATASTROPHE. ASIA UK USSR ELITES POL/PAR VOL/ASSN FORCES PROB/SOLV DIPLOM ADMIN COLONIAL NAT/LISM PEACE TREATY 19/20 BOXER/REBL. PAGE 141 A2885
REV NAT/G WAR

B55
VIGON J.,TEORIA DEL MILITARISMO. NAT/G DIPLOM COLONIAL COERCE GUERRILLA CIVMIL/REL NAT/LISM MORAL ALL/IDEOS PACIFISM 18/20. PAGE 159 A3234
FORCES PHIL/SCI WAR POLICY

S55
DE SMITH S.A.,"CONSTITUTIONAL MONARCHY IN BURGANDA." AFR UGANDA UK STRUCT CHIEF REGION INGP/REL ADJUST NAT/LISM SOVEREIGN CONSERVE ...POLICY 19/20 BURGANDA. PAGE 35 A0712
NAT/G DIPLOM CONSTN COLONIAL

B56
BALL W.M.,NATIONALISM AND COMMUNISM IN EAST ASIA. ASIA BURMA EUR+WWI KOREA USA+45 ECO/UNDEV NAT/G POL/PAR DIPLOM ECO/TAC FOR/AID EDU/PROP COERCE RACE/REL NAT/LISM DRIVE SOVEREIGN...TREND 20 CHINJAP. PAGE 11 A0214
S/ASIA ATTIT

B56
BEARDSLEY S.W.,HUMAN RELATIONS IN INTERNATIONAL AFFAIRS: A GUIDE TO SIGNIFICANT INTERPRETATION AND RESEARCH. UNIV PERS/REL NAT/LISM DRIVE PERSON ...POLICY PSY SOC CON/ANAL IDEA/COMP 20. PAGE 12 A0241
BIBLIOG/A ATTIT CULTURE DIPLOM

B56
BROOK D.,THE UNITED NATIONS AND CHINA DILEMMA. CHINA/COM FUT WOR+45 ECO/UNDEV NAT/G DELIB/GP ACT/RES DIPLOM ROUTINE NAT/LISM TOTALISM ATTIT DRIVE...CONCPT OBS TIME/SEQ UN TOT/POP TIME UN 20. PAGE 19 A0390
ASIA INT/ORG BAL/PWR

B56
UNDERHILL F.H.,THE BRITISH COMMONWEALTH: AN EXPERIMENT IN CO-OPERATION AMONG NATIONS. CANADA UK WOR+45 WOR-45 INT/ORG COLONIAL UTIL SOVEREIGN CONSERVE...OLD/LIB SOC/EXP BIBLIOG/A 19/20 CMN/WLTH. PAGE 147 A3007
VOL/ASSN NAT/LISM DIPLOM

B56
US DEPARTMENT OF STATE,THE SUEZ CANAL PROBLEM; JULY 26-SEPTEMBER 22, 1956. UAR WOR+45 BAL/PWR COERCE NAT/LISM ATTIT ORD/FREE SOVEREIGN 20 SUEZ. PAGE 151 A3091
DIPLOM CONFER INT/TRADE

B56
WILBUR C.M.,DOCUMENTS ON COMMUNISM, NATIONALISM, AND SOVIET ADVISERS IN CHINA, 1918-1927. CHINA/COM USSR STRUCT DIPLOM LEAD NAT/LISM...BIBLIOG/A 20. PAGE 164 A3343
REV POL/PAR MARXISM COM

B57
ADLER S.,THE ISOLATIONIST IMPULSE: ITS TWENTIETH-CENTURY REACTION. USA+45 USA-45 POL/PAR WAR ISOLAT NAT/LISM 20. PAGE 5 A0093
DIPLOM POLICY ATTIT

B57
ALEXANDER L.M.,WORLD POLITICAL PATTERNS. NAT/G PROVS CAP/ISM DIPLOM COLONIAL NAT/LISM...POLICY GEOG CHARTS METH/COMP NAT/COMP 20. PAGE 5 A0111
CONTROL METH GOV/COMP

B57
ARON R.,L'UNIFICATION ECONOMIQUE DE L'EUROPE. EUR+WWI SWITZERLND UK INT/ORG NAT/G REGION NAT/LISM
VOL/ASSN ECO/TAC

ORD/FREE PWR...CONCPT METH/CNCPT OBS TREND STERTYP GEN/LAWS EEC 20. PAGE 9 A0181

B57
BERLE A.A.,TIDES OF CRISIS: A PRIMER OF FOREIGN RELATIONS. USA+45 WOR+45 DOMIN NUC/PWR NAT/LISM PWR ...CONCPT STERTYP GEN/LAWS 20 UN. PAGE 14 A0276
INT/ORG TREND PEACE

B57
BROMBERGER M.,LES SECRETS DE L'EXPEDITION D'EGYPTE. FRANCE ISLAM UAR UK USA+45 USSR WOR+45 INT/ORG NAT/G FORCES BAL/PWR ECO/TAC DOMIN WAR NAT/LISM ATTIT PWR SOVEREIGN...MAJORIT TIME/SEQ CHARTS SUEZ COLD/WAR 20. PAGE 19 A0387
COERCE DIPLOM

B57
CONOVER H.F.,NORTH AND NORTHEAST AFRICA; A SELECTED ANNOTATED LIST OF WRITINGS. ALGERIA MOROCCO SUDAN UAR CULTURE INT/ORG PROB/SOLV ADJUD NAT/LISM PWR WEALTH...SOC 20 UN. PAGE 30 A0603
BIBLIOG/A DIPLOM AFR ECO/UNDEV

B57
DEAN V.M.,THE NATURE OF THE NON-WESTERN WORLD. AFR ASIA L/A+17C S/ASIA CULTURE SOCIETY STRATA ECO/DEV DIPLOM ECO/TAC FOR/AID ATTIT DRIVE ALL/VALS ...RELATIV SOC CONCPT TIME/SEQ TREND TOT/POP 20. PAGE 35 A0718
ECO/UNDEV STERTYP NAT/LISM

B57
FRASER L.,PROPAGANDA. GERMANY USSR WOR+45 WOR-45 NAT/G POL/PAR CONTROL FEEDBACK LOBBY CROWD WAR CONSEN NAT/LISM 20. PAGE 48 A0988
EDU/PROP FASCISM MARXISM DIPLOM

B57
HODGKIN T.,NATIONALISM IN COLONIAL AFRICA. STRATA STRUCT MUNIC NAT/G POL/PAR LEGIS ATTIT SOVEREIGN ...POLICY TREND BIBLIOG 20. PAGE 66 A1351
AFR COLONIAL NAT/LISM DIPLOM

B57
TOMASIC D.A.,NATIONAL COMMUNISM AND SOVIET STRATEGY. UK USSR YUGOSLAVIA NAT/G POL/PAR CHIEF CREATE DOMIN REV WAR PWR...BIOG TREND 20 TITO/MARSH STALIN/J. PAGE 144 A2948
COM NAT/LISM MARXISM DIPLOM

B57
WARBURG J.P.,AGENDA FOR ACTION. ISLAM ISRAEL USA+45 FOR/AID INT/TRADE WAR NAT/LISM 20 MID/EAST EUROPE ARABS. PAGE 161 A3275
DIPLOM POLICY INT/ORG BAL/PWR

C57
BEERS H.P.,"THE FRENCH IN NORTH AFRICA: A BIBLIOGRAPHICAL GUIDE TO FRENCH ARCHIVES, REPRODUCTIONS, AND RESEARCH MISSIONS." AFR CANADA FRANCE USA-45 NAT/LISM ATTIT 20. PAGE 12 A0248
BIBLIOG DIPLOM COLONIAL

B58
ANGELL N.,DEFENCE AND THE ENGLISH-SPEAKING ROLE. CHINA/COM UK USSR INT/ORG FORCES EDU/PROP NEUTRAL NUC/PWR NAT/LISM PEACE TOTALISM 20 COLD/WAR COEXIST. PAGE 8 A0161
DIPLOM WAR MARXISM ORD/FREE

B58
DUCLOUX L.,FROM BLACKMAIL TO TREASON. FRANCE PLAN DIPLOM EDU/PROP PRESS RUMOR NAT/LISM...CRIMLGY 20. PAGE 39 A0793
COERCE CRIME NAT/G PWR

B58
HAAS E.B.,THE UNITING OF EUROPE. EUR+WWI INT/ORG NAT/G POL/PAR TOP/EX ECO/TAC EDU/PROP LEGIT FEDERAL NAT/LISM DRIVE RIGID/FLEX ORD/FREE PWR PLURISM ...POLICY CONCPT INT GEN/LAWS ECSC EEC 20. PAGE 59 A1204
VOL/ASSN ECO/DEV

B58
JENNINGS I.,PROBLEMS OF THE NEW COMMONWEALTH. CEYLON INDIA PAKISTAN S/ASIA ECO/UNDEV INT/ORG LOC/G DIPLOM ECO/TAC INT/TRADE COLONIAL RACE/REL DISCRIM 20 COMMONWLTH PARLIAMENT. PAGE 74 A1508
NAT/LISM NEUTRAL FOR/AID POL/PAR

B58
JENNINGS W.I.,PROBLEMS OF THE NEW COMMONWEALTH. CEYLON INDIA MALAYSIA PAKISTAN ECO/UNDEV VOL/ASSN RACE/REL NAT/LISM ROLE 20 CMN/WLTH. PAGE 74 A1511
GP/REL INGP/REL COLONIAL INT/ORG

B58
MASON H.L.,TOYNBEE'S APPROACH TO WORLD POLITICS. AFR USA+45 USSR LAW WAR NAT/LISM ALL/IDEOS...HUM BIBLIOG. PAGE 95 A1957
DIPLOM CONCPT PHIL/SCI SECT

B58
NEHRU J.,SPEECHES. INDIA ECO/UNDEV AGRI INDUS INT/ORG POL/PAR DIPLOM FOR/AID NAT/LISM...ANTHOL 20. PAGE 108 A2213
PLAN CHIEF COLONIAL NEUTRAL

B58
ORGANSKI A.F.K.,WORLD POLITICS. FUT WOR+45 SOCIETY STRUCT NAT/G BAL/PWR ECO/TAC DOMIN NAT/LISM ATTIT KNOWL ORD/FREE PWR...CONCPT METH/CNCPT TREND STERTYP GEN/LAWS TOT/POP 20. PAGE 112 A2297
INT/ORG DIPLOM

B58
SCHUMAN F.,INTERNATIONAL POLITICS. WOR+45 WOR-45 INTELL NAT/G FORCES DOMIN LEGIT COERCE NUC/PWR ATTIT DISPL ORD/FREE PWR SOVEREIGN...POLICY CONCPT GEN/LAWS SUEZ 20. PAGE 129 A2650
FUT INT/ORG NAT/LISM DIPLOM

B58
SLICK T.,PERMANENT PEACE: A CHECK AND BALANCE PLAN. FUT WOR+45 NAT/G FORCES CREATE PLAN EDU/PROP LEGIT ADJUD COERCE NAT/LISM RIGID/FLEX MORAL...HUM CONCPT METH/CNCPT NEW/IDEA TREND CHARTS TOT/POP 20. PAGE 134 A2742
INT/ORG ORD/FREE PEACE ARMS/CONT

B58
TILLION G.,ALGERIA: THE REALITIES. ALGERIA FRANCE ISLAM CULTURE STRATA PROB/SOLV DOMIN REV NAT/LISM WEALTH MARXISM...GEOG 20. PAGE 144 A2940
ECO/UNDEV SOC COLONIAL DIPLOM

B58
VARG P.A.,MISSIONARIES, CHINESE, AND DIPLOMATS: THE AMERICAN PROTESTANT MISSIONARY MOVEMENT IN CHINA, 1890-1952. ASIA ECO/UNDEV NAT/G PROB/SOLV CAP/ISM EDU/PROP COLONIAL NAT/LISM ATTIT MARXISM...NAT/COMP STERTYP 20 CHINJAP PROTESTANT MISSION. PAGE 158 A3221
CULTURE DIPLOM SECT

B58
WIGGINS J.W.,FOREIGN AID REEXAMINED: A CRITICAL APPRAISAL. CHINA/COM INDONESIA USA+45 FINAN INT/TRADE REGION NAT/LISM ATTIT...CENSUS 20. PAGE 164 A3342
FOR/AID DIPLOM ECO/UNDEV SOVEREIGN

S58
ROTHFELS H.,"THE GERMAN RESISTANCE IN ITS INTERNATIONAL ASPECTS" (BMR)" EUR+WWI GERMANY UNIV CHIEF DIPLOM WAR NAT/LISM ATTIT...POLICY 20 HITLER/A NAZI. PAGE 124 A2548
VOL/ASSN MORAL FASCISM CIVMIL/REL

C58
BUTTINGER J.,"THE SMALLER DRAGON; A POLITICAL HISTORY OF VIETNAM." VIETNAM SECT DIPLOM CIVMIL/REL ISOLAT NAT/LISM...BIBLIOG/A 3/20. PAGE 22 A0455
COLONIAL DOMIN SOVEREIGN REV

C58
FIFIELD R.H.,"THE DIPLOMACY OF SOUTHEAST ASIA: 1945-1958." INT/ORG NAT/G COLONIAL REGION...CHARTS BIBLIOG 20 UN. PAGE 45 A0927
S/ASIA DIPLOM NAT/LISM

B59
ALWAN M.,ALGERIA BEFORE THE UNITED NATIONS. AFR ASIA FRANCE ISLAM S/ASIA CONSTN SOCIETY STRUCT INT/ORG NAT/G ECO/TAC ADMIN COLONIAL NAT/LISM ATTIT PWR...DECISION TREND 420 UN. PAGE 7 A0133
PLAN RIGID/FLEX DIPLOM ALGERIA

B59
BROOKES E.H.,THE COMMONWEALTH TODAY. UK ROMAN/EMP INT/ORG RACE/REL NAT/LISM SOVEREIGN...TREND SOC/INTEG 20. PAGE 19 A0391
FEDERAL DIPLOM JURID IDEA/COMP

B59
CHALUPA V.,RISE AND DEVELOPMENT OF A TOTALITARIAN STATE. CZECHOSLVK USSR STRUCT INT/ORG WORKER DIPLOM ECO/TAC COERCE NAT/LISM ATTIT...POLICY 20 COM/PARTY. PAGE 25 A0516
TOTALISM MARXISM REV POL/PAR

B59
DEHIO L.,GERMANY AND WORLD POLITICS IN THE TWENTIETH CENTURY. EUR+WWI FRANCE GERMANY MOD/EUR UK USSR NAT/G CHIEF BAL/PWR DOMIN COLONIAL CONTROL LEAD...IDEA/COMP 20 VERSAILLES. PAGE 36 A0724
DIPLOM WAR NAT/LISM SOVEREIGN

B59
GOLDWIN R.A.,READINGS IN RUSSIAN FOREIGN POLICY. HUNGARY USSR YUGOSLAVIA ELITES INT/ORG NAT/G REV WAR NAT/LISM PERSON SOCISM...CHARTS 20 MAPS BOLSHEVISM. PAGE 53 A1095
COM MARXISM DIPLOM POLICY

B59
HALLE L.J.,DREAM AND REALITY: ASPECTS OF AMERICAN FOREIGN POLICY. USA+45 CONSTN CONSULT PROB/SOLV NAT/LISM PERSON. PAGE 60 A1230
POLICY MYTH DIPLOM NAT/G

B59
JACKSON B.W.,FIVE IDEAS THAT CHANGE THE WORLD. FUT WOR+45 WOR-45 ECO/UNDEV INDUS DIPLOM DOMIN CONTROL ...IDEA/COMP 20. PAGE 72 A1473
MARXISM NAT/LISM COLONIAL ECO/TAC

B59
JOSEPH F.M.,AS OTHERS SEE US: THE UNITED STATES THROUGH FOREIGN EYES. AFR EUR+WWI ISLAM L/A+17C S/ASIA USA+45 CULTURE SOCIETY ECO/DEV ECO/UNDEV INT/ORG NAT/G DIPLOM ECO/TAC REV ATTIT RIGID/FLEX HEALTH ORD/FREE WEALTH 20. PAGE 75 A1537
RESPECT DOMIN NAT/LISM SOVEREIGN

B59
LAQUER W.Z.,THE SOVIET UNION AND THE MIDDLE EAST. COM UAR USSR ECO/UNDEV NAT/G VOL/ASSN ECO/TAC EDU/PROP COLONIAL EXEC PWR...TIME/SEQ TREND COLD/WAR 20. PAGE 85 A1730
ISLAM DRIVE FOR/AID NAT/LISM

B59
PANHUYS H.F.,THE ROLE OF NATIONALITY IN INTERNATIONAL LAW. ADJUD CRIME WAR STRANGE...JURID TREND. PAGE 114 A2330
INT/LAW NAT/LISM INGP/REL

B59
WARD B.,5 IDEAS THAT CHANGE THE WORLD. WOR+45 WOR-45 SOCIETY STRUCT AGRI INDUS INT/ORG NAT/G FORCES ACT/RES ARMS/CONT TOTALISM ATTIT DRIVE GEN/LAWS. PAGE 161 A3278
ECO/UNDEV ALL/VALS NAT/LISM COLONIAL

B59
YRARRAZAVAL E.,AMERICA LATINE EN LA GUERRA FRIA. EUR+WWI L/A+17C USA+45 USSR WOR+45 INDUS INT/ORG NAT/LISM...POLICY COLD/WAR. PAGE 169 A3439
REGION DIPLOM ECO/UNDEV INT/TRADE

L59
GRANDIN T.,"THE POLITICAL USE OF THE RADIO." EUR+WWI SOCIETY INT/ORG DIPLOM CONTROL ATTIT ORD/FREE...CONCPT STAT RECORD SAMP GEN/LAWS TOT/POP 20. PAGE 55 A1128
COM/IND EDU/PROP NAT/LISM

S59
BAILEY S.D.,"THE FUTURE COMPOSITION OF THE TRUSTEESHIP COUNCIL." FUT WOR+45 CONSTN VOL/ASSN ADMIN ATTIT PWR...OBS TREND CON/ANAL VAL/FREE UN 20. PAGE 10 A0203
INT/ORG NAT/LISM SOVEREIGN

S59
CARLSTON K.S.,"NATIONALIZATION: AN ANALYTIC APPROACH." WOR+45 INT/ORG ECO/TAC DOMIN LEGIT ADJUD COERCE ORD/FREE PWR WEALTH SOCISM...JURID CONCPT TREND STERTYP TOT/POP VAL/FREE 20. PAGE 24 A0486
INDUS NAT/G NAT/LISM SOVEREIGN

S59
KOHN L.Y.,"ISRAEL AND NEW NATION STATES OF ASIA AND AFRICA." AFR ASIA FUT S/ASIA VOL/ASSN TEC/DEV NAT/LISM RIGID/FLEX SKILL WEALTH...RELATIV OBS TREND CON/ANAL 20. PAGE 81 A1663
ECO/UNDEV ECO/TAC FOR/AID ISRAEL

S59
SAYEGH F.,"ARAB NATIONALISM AND SOVIET-AMERICAN RELATIONS." ISLAM USA+45 ECO/UNDEV PLAN ECO/TAC LEGIT NAT/LISM DRIVE PERCEPT KNOWL PWR...DECISION CONCPT STAT RECORD TREND CON/ANAL VAL/FREE 20 COLD/WAR. PAGE 127 A2610
DIPLOM USSR

C59
KULSKI W.W.,"PEACEFUL COEXISTENCE." USSR ECO/UNDEV INT/ORG POL/PAR EDU/PROP COLONIAL CONTROL REV NAT/LISM PEACE PWR MARXISM...BIBLIOG 20. PAGE 83 A1692
COM DIPLOM DOMIN

B60
EINSTEIN A.,EINSTEIN ON PEACE. FUT WOR+45 WOR-45 SOCIETY NAT/G PLAN BAL/PWR CAP/ISM DIPLOM ARMS/CONT DETER NAT/LISM...POLICY RELATIV HUM PHIL/SCI CONCPT BIOG COLD/WAR LEAGUE/NAT NAZI. PAGE 41 A0829
INT/ORG ATTIT NUC/PWR PEACE

B60
EMERSON R.,FROM EMPIRE TO NATION: THE RISE TO SELF-ASSERTION OF ASIAN AND AFRICAN PEOPLES. S/ASIA CULTURE NAT/G SECT DIPLOM ATTIT SOVEREIGN MARXISM ...POLICY BIBLIOG 19/20. PAGE 41 A0847
NAT/LISM COLONIAL AFR ASIA

B60
ENGEL-JANOSI F.,OSTERREICH UND DER VATIKAN (2 VOLS). AUSTRIA VATICAN NAT/LISM PEACE PERSON CATHISM 20. PAGE 42 A0852
DIPLOM ATTIT WAR

B60
HAMADY S.,TEMPERAMENT AND CHARACTER OF THE ARABS. FAM NAT/G SECT DIPLOM NAT/LISM...POLICY 20 ARABS. PAGE 61 A1244
NAT/COMP PERSON CULTURE ISLAM

B60
HANDLIN O.,AMERICAN PRINCIPLES AND ISSUES. USA+45 USA-45 DIPLOM WAR PERSON. PAGE 61 A1251
ORD/FREE NAT/LISM ATTIT

B60
LANDHEER B.,ETHICAL VALUES IN INTERNATIONAL DECISION-MAKING. FUT LAW SOCIETY INT/ORG NAT/G DELIB/GP CREATE NAT/LISM ATTIT PERSON...DECISION CONCPT LEAGUE/NAT TOT/POP 20. PAGE 84 A1718
HYPO/EXP POLICY PEACE

B60
NURTY K.S.,STUDIES IN PROBLEMS OF PEACE. CHRIST-17C MOD/EUR S/ASIA WOR+45 WOR-45 INT/ORG NAT/G SECT COERCE REV NAT/LISM ALL/VALS...CONCPT MYTH TIME/SEQ. PAGE 110 A2262
POLICY PEACE PACIFISM ORD/FREE

B60
PHILLIPS J.F.V.,KWAME NKRUMAH AND THE FUTURE OF AFRICA. FUT GHANA ISLAM ECO/UNDEV CHIEF DIPLOM COLONIAL RACE/REL NAT/LISM...TREND IDEA/COMP BIBLIOG 20 NKRUMAH/K. PAGE 116 A2376
BIOG LEAD SOVEREIGN AFR

B60
PLAMENATZ J.,ON ALIEN RULE AND SELF-GOVERNMENT. AFR FUT S/ASIA WOR+45 CULTURE SOCIETY ECO/UNDEV INT/ORG DOMIN EDU/PROP ATTIT RIGID/FLEX ALL/VALS...POLICY CONCPT OBS TREND CON/ANAL GEN/LAWS TOT/POP VAL/FREE. PAGE 116 A2386
NAT/G CONSTN NAT/LISM SOVEREIGN

B60
QUBAIN F.I.,INSIDE THE ARAB MIND: A BIBLIOGRAPHIC SURVEY OF LITERATURE IN ARABIC ON ARAB NATIONALISM AND UNITY. ISLAM POL/PAR SECT LEAD SOVEREIGN MARXISM SOCISM. PAGE 118 A2425
BIBLIOG/A FEDERAL DIPLOM NAT/LISM

B60
RITNER P.,THE DEATH OF AFRICA. USA+45 ECO/UNDEV DIPLOM ECO/TAC REGION RACE/REL NAT/LISM ORD/FREE ...POLICY 20 NEGRO. PAGE 121 A2485
AFR SOCIETY FUT TASK

B60
SETON-WATSON H.,NEITHER WAR NOR PEACE. ASIA USSR WOR+45 ELITES INT/ORG NAT/G EX/STRUC FORCES BAL/PWR ECO/TAC EDU/PROP COERCE NAT/LISM ORD/FREE WEALTH TOT/POP 20. PAGE 131 A2688
ATTIT PWR DIPLOM TOTALISM

B60
SPEER J.P.,FOR WHAT PURPOSE? CHINA/COM USSR CONSTN PROB/SOLV DIPLOM CONTROL TASK WAR NAT/LISM WORSHIP 20 UN. PAGE 136 A2778
PEACE SECT SUPEGO ALL/IDEOS

S60
BOGARDUS E.S.,"THE SOCIOLOGY OF A STRUCTURED PEACE." FUT SOCIETY CREATE DIPLOM EDU/PROP ADJUD ROUTINE ATTIT RIGID/FLEX KNOWL ORD/FREE RESPECT ...POLICY INT/LAW JURID NEW/IDEA SELF/OBS TOT/POP 20 UN. PAGE 16 A0327
INT/ORG SOC NAT/LISM PEACE

S60
OWEN C.F.,"US AND SOVIET RELATIONS WITH UNDERDEVELOPED COUNTRIES: LATIN AMERICA-A CASE STUDY." AFR COM L/A+17C USA+45 USSR EXTR/IND MARKET TEC/DEV DIPLOM ECO/TAC NAT/LISM ORD/FREE PWR ...TREND WORK 20. PAGE 112 A2303
ECO/UNDEV DRIVE INT/TRADE

S60
PETERSON E.N.,"HISTORICAL SCHOLARSHIP AND WORLD UNITY." FUT UNIV WOR-45 CULTURE INTELL INT/ORG NAT/G ACT/RES EDU/PROP ATTIT PERCEPT RIGID/FLEX ...NEW/IDEA OBS HIST/WRIT TREND COLD/WAR TOT/POP 20. PAGE 115 A2367
PLAN KNOWL NAT/LISM

C60
WRIGGINS W.H.,"CEYLON: DILEMMAS OF A NEW NATION." ASIA CEYLON CONSTN STRUCT POL/PAR SECT FORCES DIPLOM GOV/REL NAT/LISM...CHARTS BIBLIOG 20. PAGE 167 A3399
PROB/SOLV NAT/G ECO/UNDEV

B61
ANSPRENGER F.,POLITIK IM SCHWARZEN AFRIKA. FRANCE NAT/G DIPLOM REGION REV NAT/LISM...CHARTS BIBLIOG 19/20. PAGE 8 A0164
AFR COLONIAL SOVEREIGN

B61
CONOVER H.F.,SERIALS FOR AFRICAN STUDIES. ECO/UNDEV DIPLOM LEAD NAT/LISM ATTIT...SOC 20. PAGE 30 A0604
BIBLIOG AFR NAT/G

B61
DIA M.,THE AFRICAN NATIONS AND WORLD SOLIDARITY. ISLAM CULTURE ELITES ECO/DEV ECO/UNDEV INT/ORG NAT/G PLAN ECO/TAC INT/TRADE EDU/PROP NAT/LISM ATTIT DRIVE ORD/FREE WEALTH...SOCIALIST CONCPT CON/ANAL GEN/LAWS TOT/POP 20. PAGE 37 A0753
AFR REGION SOCISM

B61
FUCHS G.,GEGEN HITLER UND HENLEIN. CZECHOSLVK GERMANY DIPLOM CHOOSE GP/REL TOTALISM SOVEREIGN 20 HITLER/A. PAGE 50 A1013
FASCISM WORKER POL/PAR NAT/LISM

B61
HISTORICAL RESEARCH INSTITUTE,A SHORT BIBLIOGRAPHY OF INDO-MUSLIM HISTORY. INDIA S/ASIA DIPLOM EDU/PROP COLONIAL LEAD NAT/LISM ATTIT...BIOG 19/20. PAGE 65 A1343
BIBLIOG NAT/G SECT POL/PAR

B61
KHAN A.W.,INDIA WINS FREEDOM: THE OTHER SIDE. INDIA PAKISTAN CULTURE LEGIS DIPLOM PARL/PROC REV WAR NAT/LISM 20. PAGE 78 A1607
SOVEREIGN GP/REL RACE/REL ORD/FREE

B61
LEHMAN R.L.,AFRICA SOUTH OF THE SAHARA (PAMPHLET). DIPLOM COLONIAL NAT/LISM. PAGE 86 A1768
BIBLIOG/A AFR CULTURE NAT/G

B61
NEAL F.W.,US FOREIGN POLICY AND THE SOVIET UNION. USA+45 USSR INT/ORG ECO/TAC ARMS/CONT MAJORITY NAT/LISM ATTIT RESPECT MARXISM 20. PAGE 108 A2207
DIPLOM POLICY PEACE

B61
PALMER N.D.,THE INDIAN POLITICAL SYSTEM. INDIA ECO/UNDEV SECT CHIEF COLONIAL CHOOSE ALL/IDEOS SOCISM...CHARTS BIBLIOG/A 20. PAGE 113 A2322
NAT/LISM POL/PAR NAT/G DIPLOM

B61
PANIKKAR K.M.,THE VOICE OF FREEDOM: SELECTED SPEECHES OF PANDIT MOTILAL NEHRU. INDIA UK CONSTN FINAN FORCES LEGIS DIPLOM TAX COLONIAL...POLICY MAJORIT ANTHOL 20 NEHRU/PM. PAGE 114 A2331
NAT/LISM ORD/FREE CHIEF NAT/G

B61
PANIKKAR K.M.,REVOLUTION IN AFRICA. AFR GUINEA ECO/UNDEV POL/PAR DIPLOM COLONIAL EXEC LEAD SOVEREIGN...CHARTS 20. PAGE 114 A2332
NAT/LISM NAT/G CHIEF

B61
UAR MINISTRY OF CULTURE,A BIBLIOGRAPHICAL LIST OF LIBYA. ISLAM LIBYA DIPLOM COLONIAL REV WAR 19/20. PAGE 146 A2988
BIBLIOG GEOG SECT NAT/LISM

S61
RALEIGH J.S.,"THE MIDDLE EAST IN 1960: A POLITICAL SURVEY." FUT ISLAM INTELL KIN BAL/PWR EDU/PROP NAT/LISM...TREND VAL/FREE 20. PAGE 119 A2435
INT/ORG EX/STRUC

B62
ALIX C.,LE SAINT-SIEGE ET LES NATIONALISMES EN EUROPE 1870-1960. COM GERMANY IRELAND ITALY SOCIETY SECT TOTALISM RIGID/FLEX MORAL 19/20. PAGE 6 A0122
CATH NAT/LISM ATTIT DIPLOM

B62
APATHEKER H.,AMERICAN FOREIGN POLICY AND THE COLD WAR. USA+45 NAT/G POL/PAR COLONIAL NAT/LISM SOVEREIGN MARXISM SOCISM 20 COLD/WAR MARX/KARL LENIN/VI INTERVENT. PAGE 8 A0167
DIPLOM WAR PEACE

B62
BAULIN J.,THE ARAB ROLE IN AFRICA. AFR ALGERIA FUT
NAT/LISM

ISLAM MOROCCO UAR COLONIAL NEUTRAL REV...SOC 20 TUNIS BOURGUIBA. PAGE 12 A0235
DIPLOM NAT/G SECT

B62
BOULDING K.E.,CONFLICT AND DEFENSE: A GENERAL THEORY. FUT SOCIETY INT/ORG NAT/G CREATE BAL/PWR COERCE NAT/LISM DRIVE ALL/VALS...PLURIST DECISION CONCPT METH/CNCPT TREND HYPO/EXP TOT/POP 20. PAGE 17 A0347
MATH SIMUL PEACE WAR

B62
BUCHMANN J.,L'AFRIQUE NOIRE INDEPENDANTE. POL/PAR DIPLOM COLONIAL PARTIC CHOOSE GP/REL ATTIT ORD/FREE WEALTH NEGRO. PAGE 21 A0426
AFR NAT/LISM DECISION

B62
GOLDWATER B.M.,WHY NOT VICTORY? A FRESH LOOK AT AMERICAN FOREIGN POLICY. USA+45 WOR+45 FOR/AID LEAD ARMS/CONT WAR PEACE ATTIT ORD/FREE PWR MARXISM ...INT/LAW 20 TREATY ECHR COUNCL/EUR. PAGE 53 A1092
DIPLOM POLICY CONSERVE NAT/LISM

B62
GUENA Y.,HISTORIQUE DE LA COMMUNAUTE. FUT ECO/UNDEV NAT/G PLAN EDU/PROP COLONIAL REGION NAT/LISM ALL/VALS SOVEREIGN...CONCPT OBS CHARTS 20. PAGE 58 A1186
AFR VOL/ASSN FOR/AID FRANCE

B62
HATCH J.,AFRICA TODAY-AND TOMORROW: AN OUTLINE OF BASIC FACTS AND MAJOR PROBLEMS. AFR FUT ISLAM STRATA ECO/UNDEV INT/ORG NAT/G POL/PAR DELIB/GP TOP/EX EDU/PROP LEGIT CHOOSE ATTIT...TIME/SEQ TOT/POP COLD/WAR 20. PAGE 63 A1287
PLAN CONSTN NAT/LISM

B62
HENDRICKS D.,PAMPHLETS ON THE FIRST WORLD WAR: AN ANNOTATED BIBLIOGRAPHY (OCCASIONAL PAPER NO. 79). GERMANY WOR-45 EDU/PROP NAT/LISM ATTIT PWR ALL/IDEOS 20. PAGE 64 A1314
BIBLIOG/A WAR DIPLOM NAT/G

B62
INGHAM K.,A HISTORY OF EAST AFRICA. NAT/G DIPLOM ADMIN WAR NAT/LISM...SOC BIOG BIBLIOG. PAGE 70 A1439
AFR CONSTN COLONIAL

B62
JELAVICH C.,TSARIST RUSSIA AND BALKAN NATIONALISM. BULGARIA MOD/EUR RUSSIA DOMIN GOV/REL...GEOG 19 SERBIA. PAGE 73 A1503
NAT/LISM DIPLOM WAR

B62
KENT R.K.,FROM MADAGASCAR TO THE MALAGASY REPUBLIC. FRANCE MADAGASCAR DIPLOM NAT/LISM ORD/FREE...MGT 18/20. PAGE 78 A1596
COLONIAL SOVEREIGN REV POL/PAR

B62
KYRIAK T.E.,INTERNATIONAL COMMUNIST DEVELOPMENTS 1957-1961: INDEX TO TRANSLATIONS FROM AFRICA, ASIA, LATIN AMERICA, WEST EUROPE. COM WOR+45 NAT/G WORKER DIPLOM NAT/LISM. PAGE 83 A1704
BIBLIOG/A MARXISM LABOR POL/PAR

B62
LESSING P.,AFRICA'S RED HARVEST. AFR CHINA/COM COM USSR ECO/UNDEV BAL/PWR DIPLOM CONTROL PWR 20 COLD/WAR INTERVENT. PAGE 87 A1789
NAT/LISM MARXISM FOR/AID EDU/PROP

B62
MANNING C.A.W.,THE NATURE OF INTERNATIONAL SOCIETY. FUT LAW NAT/G TOP/EX NAT/LISM PEACE PERCEPT PERSON ALL/VALS PLURISM...METH/CNCPT MYTH HYPO/EXP TOT/POP 20. PAGE 94 A1926
INT/ORG SOCIETY SIMUL DIPLOM

B62
MORRAY J.P.,THE SECOND REVOLUTION IN CUBA. CUBA AGRI LABOR POL/PAR DIPLOM FOR/AID GUERRILLA TOTALISM MARXISM 20. PAGE 104 A2146
REV MARXIST ECO/TAC NAT/LISM

B62
NOBECOURT R.G.,LES SECRETS DE LA PROPAGANDE EN FRANCE OCCUPEE. FRANCE ELITES NAT/G DIPLOM GP/REL NAT/LISM TOTALISM ORD/FREE 20 VICHY VICHY. PAGE 109 A2244
METH/COMP EDU/PROP WAR CONTROL

B62
PERKINS D.,AMERICA'S QUEST FOR PEACE. USA+45 WOR+45 DIPLOM CONFER NAT/LISM ATTIT 20 UN TREATY. PAGE 115 A2361
INT/LAW INT/ORG ARMS/CONT PEACE

B62
RIMALOV V.V.,ECONOMIC COOPERATION BETWEEN USSR AND UNDERDEVELOPED COUNTRIES. USSR FINAN TEC/DEV INT/TRADE DOMIN EDU/PROP COLONIAL NAT/LISM DRIVE SOVEREIGN...AUD/VIS 20. PAGE 121 A2482
FOR/AID PLAN ECO/UNDEV DIPLOM

B62
SCHMIDT-VOLKMAR E.,DER KULTURKAMPF IN DEUTSCHLAND 1871-1890. GERMANY PRUSSIA SOCIETY STRUCT SECT DIPLOM GP/REL NAT/LISM 19 CHURCH/STA BISMARCK/O. PAGE 128 A2632
POL/PAR CATHISM ATTIT NAT/G

B62
SPIRO H.J.,POLITICS IN AFRICA: PROSPECTS SOUTH OF THE SAHARA. INT/ORG KIN FORCES LEGIS PROB/SOLV COERCE RACE/REL FEDERAL...TREND CHARTS BIBLIOG 20. PAGE 136 A2790
AFR NAT/LISM DIPLOM

B62
US DEPARTMENT OF THE ARMY,AFRICA: ITS PROBLEMS AND PROSPECTS. CHINA/COM USSR INT/ORG FOR/AID COLONIAL LEAD FEDERAL DRIVE SOVEREIGN MARXISM...GEOG 20 COLD/WAR. PAGE 152 A3104
BIBLIOG/A AFR NAT/LISM DIPLOM

B62
WOLFERS A.,DISCORD AND COLLABORATION: ESSAYS ON INTERNATIONAL POLITICS. WOR+45 CULTURE SOCIETY INT/ORG NAT/G BAL/PWR DIPLOM DOMIN NAT/LISM PEACE PWR...POLICY CONCPT STYLE RECORD TREND GEN/LAWS 20. PAGE 166 A3385
ATTIT ORD/FREE

S62
BERKES R.N.B.,"THE NEW FRONTIER IN THE UN." FUT USA+45 WOR+45 INT/ORG DELIB/GP NAT/LISM PERCEPT RESPECT UN OAS 20. PAGE 13 A0272
GEN/LAWS DIPLOM

S62
CROAN M.,"POLYCENTRISM: COMMUNIST INTERNATIONAL RELATIONS." ASIA STRUCT INT/ORG NAT/G POL/PAR CONSULT PLAN DOMIN EDU/PROP COERCE ATTIT RIGID/FLEX SOCISM...POLICY CONCPT TREND CON/ANAL GEN/LAWS MARX/KARL. PAGE 33 A0663
COM CREATE DIPLOM NAT/LISM

S62
GAREAU F.H.,"BLOC POLITICS IN WEST AFRICA." AFR CONGO/BRAZ GHANA GUINEA MALI WOR+45 STRUCT ECO/UNDEV INT/ORG VOL/ASSN CHOOSE ORD/FREE PWR UN 20. PAGE 51 A1048
NAT/G NAT/LISM

S62
KOLARZ W.,"THE IMPACT OF COMMUNISM ON WEST AFRICA." AFR FUT SOCIETY INT/ORG NAT/G CREATE PLAN DOMIN EDU/PROP COERCE NAT/LISM ATTIT RIGID/FLEX SOCISM ...POLICY CONCPT TREND MARX/KARL 20. PAGE 81 A1666
COM POL/PAR COLONIAL

S62
RUBINSTEIN A.Z.,"RUSSIA AND THE UNCOMMITTED NATIONS." AFR INDIA ISLAM L/A+17C LAOS S/ASIA ELITES ECO/UNDEV INT/ORG KIN CREATE PLAN TEC/DEV NAT/LISM RIGID/FLEX PWR WEALTH...METH/CNCPT TIME/SEQ GEN/LAWS WORK. PAGE 125 A2562
ECO/TAC TREND COLONIAL USSR

S62
STRACHEY J.,"COMMUNIST INTENTIONS." ASIA USSR YUGOSLAVIA INT/ORG NAT/G FORCES DOMIN EDU/PROP COERCE NUC/PWR NAT/LISM PEACE RIGID/FLEX PWR MARXISM...CONCPT MYTH OBS TIME/SEQ TREND COLD/WAR TOT/POP 20. PAGE 139 A2843
COM ATTIT WAR

B63
AFRICAN BIBLIOGRAPHIC CENTER,THE SCENE IS KENYA AND THE PERSONAGE IS TOM MBOYA: A SELECTED CURRENT READING LIST FROM 1956-1962 (PAMPHLET). ECO/UNDEV LABOR POL/PAR CHIEF COLONIAL CHOOSE NAT/LISM ORD/FREE 20. PAGE 5 A0096
BIBLIOG DIPLOM AFR NAT/G

B63
CANELAS O.A.,RADIOGRAFIA DE LA ALIANZA PARA EL ATRASO. L/A+17C USA+45 ECO/TAC DOMIN COLONIAL NAT/LISM...SOCIALIST NAT/COMP 20. PAGE 23 A0476
REV DIPLOM ECO/UNDEV REGION

B63
CREMEANS C.,THE ARABS AND THE WORLD: NASSER'S ARAB NATIONALIST POLICY. FUT ISLAM UAR USA+45 SOCIETY STRATA NAT/G POL/PAR PLAN DIPLOM EDU/PROP LEGIT DRIVE ALL/VALS...INT TIME/SEQ CHARTS 20 NASSER/G. PAGE 33 A0662
TOP/EX ATTIT REGION NAT/LISM

B63
CROZIER B.,THE MORNING AFTER; A STUDY OF INDEPENDENCE. WOR+45 EX/STRUC PLAN BAL/PWR COLONIAL GP/REL 20 COLD/WAR. PAGE 33 A0666
SOVEREIGN NAT/LISM NAT/G DIPLOM

B63
DECOTTIGNIES R.,LES NATIONALITES AFRICAINES. AFR NAT/G PROB/SOLV DIPLOM COLONIAL ORD/FREE...CHARTS GOV/COMP 20. PAGE 35 A0721
NAT/LISM JURID LEGIS LAW

B63
ELIAS T.O.,GOVERNMENT AND POLITICS IN AFRICA. CONSTN CULTURE SOCIETY NAT/G POL/PAR DIPLOM REPRESENT PERSON...SOC TREND BIBLIOG 4/20. PAGE 41 A0837
AFR NAT/LISM COLONIAL LAW

B63
ETHIOPIAN MINISTRY INFORMATION,AFRICAN SUMMIT CONFERENCE ADDIS ABABA, ETHIOPIA, 1963. ETHIOPIA DELIB/GP COLONIAL NAT/LISM...POLICY DECISION 20. PAGE 42 A0865
AFR CONFER REGION DIPLOM

B63
FABER K.,DIE NATIONALISTISCHE PUBLIZISTIK DEUTSCHLANDS VON 1866 BIS 1871 (2 VOLS.). EUR+WWI GERMANY DIPLOM EDU/PROP 19. PAGE 43 A0881
BIBLIOG/A NAT/G NAT/LISM POL/PAR

B63
FRANZ G.,TEILUNG UND WIEDERVEREINIGUNG. GERMANY IRELAND ITALY NETHERLAND POLAND CULTURE BAL/PWR CHOOSE NAT/LISM ORD/FREE SOVEREIGN 19/20. PAGE 48 A0987
DIPLOM WAR NAT/COMP ATTIT

B63
GRAEBNER N.A.,THE COLD WAR: IDEOLOGICAL CONFLICT OR POWER STRUGGLE? USSR WOR+45 WOR-45 PROB/SOLV EDU/PROP ARMS/CONT REV NAT/LISM PEACE ORD/FREE ...IDEA/COMP ANTHOL BIBLIOG/A 20 COLD/WAR. PAGE 55 A1123
DIPLOM BAL/PWR MARXISM

B63
GRIFFITH W.E.,ALBANIA AND THE SINO-SOVIET RIFT. ALBANIA CHINA/COM USSR POL/PAR CHIEF LEGIS DIPLOM DOMIN ATTIT PWR...POLICY 20 KHRUSH/N MAO. PAGE 57
EDU/PROP MARXISM NAT/LISM

A1161 GOV/REL

B63
JENNINGS W.I.,DEMOCRACY IN AFRICA. UK CULTURE STRUCT ECO/UNDEV DIPLOM COLONIAL GP/REL ADJUST NAT/LISM ORD/FREE...GOV/COMP 20 THIRD/WRLD. PAGE 74 A1512 PROB/SOLV AFR CONSTN POPULISM

B63
KHADDURI M.,MODERN LIBYA: A STUDY IN POLITICAL DEVELOPMENT. EUR+WWI ISLAM LIBYA ELITES INT/ORG POL/PAR FORCES DIPLOM FOR/AID DOMIN EDU/PROP LEGIT NAT/LISM DRIVE RIGID/FLEX SKILL...CONCPT TIME/SEQ TREND 20. PAGE 78 A1606 NAT/G STRUCT

B63
KORBEL J.,POLAND BETWEEN EAST AND WEST: SOVIET AND GERMAN DIPLOMACY TOWARD POLAND 1919-1933. EUR+WWI GERMANY POLAND USSR FORCES AGREE WAR SOVEREIGN ...BIBLIOG 20 TREATY. PAGE 81 A1670 BAL/PWR DIPLOM DOMIN NAT/LISM

B63
LAFEBER W.,THE NEW EMPIRE: AN INTERPRETATION OF AMERICAN EXPANSION, 1860-1898. USA-45 CONSTN NAT/LISM SOVEREIGN...TREND BIBLIOG 19/20. PAGE 84 A1711 INDUS NAT/G DIPLOM CAP/ISM

B63
LEE C.,THE POLITICS OF KOREAN NATIONALISM. KOREA S/ASIA DIPLOM REV WAR 14/20 CHINJAP. PAGE 86 A1759 NAT/LISM SOVEREIGN COLONIAL

B63
LERCHE C.O. JR.,AMERICA IN WORLD AFFAIRS. COM UK USA+45 INT/ORG FORCES ECO/TAC INT/TRADE EDU/PROP WAR NAT/LISM PEACE...BIBLIOG 18/20 UN CONGRESS PRESIDENT COLD/WAR. PAGE 87 A1783 NAT/G DIPLOM PLAN

B63
LYON P.,NEUTRALISM. ECO/UNDEV EDU/PROP COLONIAL ALL/IDEOS...IDEA/COMP 20 COLD/WAR UN. PAGE 92 A1879 NAT/COMP NAT/LISM DIPLOM NEUTRAL

B63
MBOYA T.,FREEDOM AND AFTER. AFR LABOR POL/PAR DIPLOM EDU/PROP COERCE SOCISM 20. PAGE 97 A1989 COLONIAL ECO/UNDEV NAT/LISM INT/ORG

B63
MENDES C.,NACIONALISMO E DESENVOLVIMENTO. AFR ASIA L/A+17C STRATA INT/TRADE COLONIAL. PAGE 99 A2039 NAT/LISM ECO/UNDEV DIPLOM REV

B63
MENEZES A.J.,SUBDESENVOLVIMENTO E POLITICA INTERNACIONAL. BRAZIL WOR+45 PLAN CONTROL LEAD NAT/LISM ORD/FREE 20 THIRD/WRLD. PAGE 99 A2041 ECO/UNDEV DIPLOM POLICY BAL/PWR

B63
MOSELY P.E.,THE SOVIET UNION, 1922-1962: A FOREIGN AFFAIRS READER. ASIA POLAND USSR CULTURE INTELL AGRI POL/PAR WORKER INT/TRADE DOMIN WAR NAT/LISM MARXISM SOCISM 20 KHRUSH/N. PAGE 105 A2152 PWR POLICY DIPLOM

B63
RAVENS J.P.,STAAT UND KATHOLISCHE KIRCHE IN PREUSSENS POLNISCHEN TEILUNGSGEBIETEN. GERMANY POLAND PRUSSIA PROVS DIPLOM EDU/PROP DEBATE NAT/LISM...JURID 18 CHURCH/STA. PAGE 119 A2451 GP/REL CATHISM SECT NAT/G

B63
RIUKIN A.,THE AFRICAN PRESENCE IN WORLD AFFAIRS. AFR WOR+45 ECO/UNDEV AGRI INT/ORG BAL/PWR ECO/TAC COLONIAL NEUTRAL NAT/LISM PEACE SOVEREIGN 20 UN. PAGE 121 A2486 DIPLOM NAT/G POLICY PWR

B63
RIVKIN A.,THE AFRICAN PRESENCE IN WORLD AFFAIRS. ECO/UNDEV AGRI INT/ORG LOC/G NAT/LISM...OBS PREDICT GOV/COMP 20. PAGE 121 A2489 AFR NAT/G DIPLOM BAL/PWR

B63
SWEARER H.R.,CONTEMPORARY COMMUNISM: THEORY AND PRACTICE. COM USSR SOCIETY ECO/DEV POL/PAR FORCES PLAN ADMIN LEAD NAT/LISM...POLICY ANTHOL 20 LENIN/VI COM/PARTY. PAGE 140 A2869 MARXISM CONCPT DIPLOM NAT/G

B63
THIEN T.T.,INDIA AND SOUTHEAST ASIA 1947-1960. COM INDIA S/ASIA SECT DELIB/GP FOR/AID RACE/REL NAT/LISM SOCISM...CHARTS BIBLIOG 20 UN NEHRU/J TREATY. PAGE 143 A2917 DRIVE DIPLOM POLICY

B63
WILCOX W.A.,PAKISTAN; THE CONSOLIDATION OF A NATION. INDIA PAKISTAN CONSTN SECT PROB/SOLV COLONIAL PARTIC GP/REL FEDERAL...POLICY 19/20. PAGE 164 A3348 NAT/LISM ECO/UNDEV DIPLOM STRUCT

L63
ZARTMAN I.W.,"THE SAHARA--BRIDGE OR BARRIER." ISLAM CULTURE SOCIETY NAT/G DELIB/GP DOMIN EDU/PROP LEGIT ATTIT...HIST/WRIT TIME/SEQ CHARTS TOT/POP VAL/FREE 20. PAGE 169 A3445 INT/ORG PWR NAT/LISM

S63
MAZRUI A.A.,"ON THE CONCEPT 'WE ARE ALL AFRICANS'." AFR CULTURE KIN LOC/G NAT/G DOMIN EDU/PROP LEGIT ATTIT PERCEPT PERSON KNOWL ORD/FREE...TIME/SEQ TOT/POP 20. PAGE 97 A1986 PROVS INT/ORG NAT/LISM

C63
CHARLETON W.G.,"THE REVOLUTION IN AMERICAN FOREIGN POLICY." COM PROB/SOLV FOR/AID DOMIN COLONIAL NEUTRAL DETER WAR ISOLAT NAT/LISM...BIBLIOG 19/20 UN COLD/WAR NATO. PAGE 26 A0523 DIPLOM INT/ORG BAL/PWR

B64
AMERICAN ASSEMBLY,THE UNITED STATES AND THE MIDDLE EAST. ISRAEL USA+45 STRUCT ECO/DEV ECO/UNDEV INT/ORG NAT/G SCHOOL SECT VOL/ASSN EX/STRUC TEC/DEV NAT/LISM...SOC 20. PAGE 7 A0135 ISLAM DRIVE REGION

B64
ANDREWS D.H.,LATIN AMERICA: A BIBLIOGRAPHY OF PAPERBACK BOOKS. SECT INT/TRADE EDU/PROP WAR GOV/REL ADJUST NAT/LISM ATTIT...ART/METH LING BIOG 20. PAGE 8 A0160 BIBLIOG L/A+17C CULTURE NAT/G

B64
ARNOLD G.,TOWARDS PEACE AND A MULTIRACIAL COMMONWEALTH. UK TEC/DEV BAL/PWR COLONIAL GP/REL NAT/LISM PEACE SOVEREIGN...POLICY SOC/INTEG 20 CMN/WLTH. PAGE 9 A0175 DIPLOM INT/TRADE FOR/AID ORD/FREE

B64
BARKER A.J.,SUEZ: THE SEVEN DAY WAR. EUR+WWI ISLAM UAR INT/ORG NAT/G PLAN DIPLOM ECO/TAC DOMIN NAT/LISM DRIVE RIGID/FLEX PWR SOVEREIGN...POLICY JURID TREND CHARTS SUEZ UN 20. PAGE 11 A0221 FORCES COERCE UK

B64
BINDER L.,THE IDEOLOGICAL REVOLUTION IN THE MIDDLE EAST. ISLAM STRUCT INT/ORG KIN SECT EX/STRUC TOP/EX PLAN ATTIT DRIVE RIGID/FLEX PWR...MYTH TOT/POP 20. PAGE 14 A0289 POL/PAR NAT/G NAT/LISM

B64
BURKE F.G.,AFRICA'S QUEST FOR ORDER. AFR CULTURE KIN MUNIC NAT/G DIPLOM COLONIAL REV DISCRIM NAT/LISM AGE/Y 20. PAGE 21 A0437 ORD/FREE CONSEN RACE/REL LEAD

B64
BUTWELL R.,SOUTHEAST ASIA TODAY - AND TOMORROW. NAT/G COLONIAL LEAD REGION WAR CHOOSE WEALTH MARXISM 20. PAGE 23 A0458 S/ASIA DIPLOM ECO/UNDEV NAT/LISM

B64
CASEY R.G.,THE FUTURE OF THE COMMONWEALTH. INDIA PAKISTAN UK ECO/UNDEV INT/ORG TEC/DEV COLONIAL SUPEGO 20 EEC AUSTRAL. PAGE 25 A0505 DIPLOM SOVEREIGN NAT/LISM FOR/AID

B64
COX R.,PAN-AFRICANISM IN PRACTICE. AFR DIPLOM CONFER RACE/REL ROLE SOVEREIGN...POLICY 20 PANAF/FREE. PAGE 32 A0645 ORD/FREE COLONIAL REGION NAT/LISM

B64
CZERNIN F.,VERSAILLES - 1919. EUR+WWI USA-45 FACE/GP POL/PAR VOL/ASSN DELIB/GP TOP/EX CREATE BAL/PWR DIPLOM LEGIT NAT/LISM PEACE ATTIT RIGID/FLEX ORD/FREE PWR...CON/ANAL LEAGUE/NAT 20 VERSAILLES. PAGE 33 A0671 INT/ORG STRUCT

B64
DESHMUKH C.D.,THE COMMONWEALTH AS INDIA SEES IT. INDIA UK ECO/UNDEV TEC/DEV INT/TRADE GP/REL RACE/REL SOVEREIGN SOC/INTEG 19/20 COMMONWLTH. PAGE 36 A0733 DIPLOM COLONIAL NAT/LISM ATTIT

B64
EAYRS J.,THE COMMONWEALTH AND SUEZ: A DOCUMENTARY SURVEY. FRANCE ISLAM VOL/ASSN FORCES CONFER COLONIAL WAR INGP/REL 20 CMN/WLTH SUEZ UN. PAGE 40 A0818 DIPLOM NAT/LISM DIST/IND SOVEREIGN

B64
EPSTEIN H.M.,REVOLT IN THE CONGO. AFR CONGO/BRAZ WOR+45 NAT/G FORCES DOMIN WAR CIVMIL/REL INGP/REL MARXISM...RECORD GP/COMP 20 CONGO/LEOP UN. PAGE 42 A0856 REV COLONIAL NAT/LISM DIPLOM

B64
FREE L.A.,THE ATTITUDES, HOPES AND FEARS OF NIGERIANS. AFR NIGERIA ECO/UNDEV AGRI ACADEM PLAN TASK...GEOG CHARTS METH 20. PAGE 49 A0993 NAT/LISM SYS/QU DIPLOM

B64
FREUD A.,OF HUMAN SOVEREIGNTY. WOR+45 INDUS SECT ECO/TAC CRIME CHOOSE ATTIT MORAL MARXISM...POLICY BIBLIOG 20. PAGE 49 A0998 NAT/LISM DIPLOM WAR PEACE

B64
GREAT BRITAIN CENTRAL OFF INF,CONSTITUTIONAL DEVELOPMENT IN THE COMMONWEALTH. VOL/ASSN PLAN DIPLOM COLONIAL INGP/REL NAT/LISM ORD/FREE PWR 17/20 CMN/WLTH. PAGE 55 A1135 REGION CONSTN NAT/G SOVEREIGN

B64
HALPERIN S.W.,MUSSOLINI AND ITALIAN FASCISM. ITALY NAT/G POL/PAR SECT ECO/TAC LEAD PWR SOCISM...POLICY 20 MUSSOLIN/B. PAGE 60 A1241 FASCISM NAT/LISM EDU/PROP CHIEF

B64
KIMMINICH O.,RUSTUNG UND POLITISCHE SPANNUNG. INDUS ARMS/CONT COERCE NAT/LISM PEACE PERSON ORD/FREE ...POLICY GEOG 20. PAGE 79 A1619 DIPLOM FORCES WEAPON WAR

B64
KULSKI W.W.,INTERNATIONAL POLITICS IN A REVOLUTIONARY AGE. NEUTRAL NAT/LISM...POLICY DECISION INT/LAW CONCPT 20 UN. PAGE 83 A1693
DIPLOM WAR NUC/PWR INT/ORG

B64
LEGGE J.D.,INDONESIA. INDONESIA ELITES ECO/UNDEV POL/PAR CHIEF FORCES INT/TRADE COERCE CHOOSE ORD/FREE...SOC CHARTS BIBLIOG 16/20 CHINJAP. PAGE 86 A1765
S/ASIA DOMIN NAT/LISM POLICY

B64
LENS S.,THE FUTILE CRUSADE. ASIA CHINA/COM L/A+17C USA+45 USSR WOR+45 ECO/DEV BAL/PWR DIPLOM NUC/PWR WAR NAT/LISM PEACE 20 COLD/WAR PRESIDENT CIA. PAGE 87 A1774
ORD/FREE ANOMIE COM MARXISM

B64
LUARD E.,THE COLD WAR: A RE-APPRAISAL. FUT USSR WOR+45 FORCES NUC/PWR NAT/LISM ORD/FREE SOVEREIGN ...INT 20 COLD/WAR STALIN/J TREATY UN. PAGE 91 A1870
DIPLOM WAR PEACE TOTALISM

B64
LUTHULI A.,AFRICA'S FREEDOM. KIN LABOR POL/PAR SCHOOL DIPLOM NEUTRAL REGION REV NAT/LISM PWR WEALTH SOCISM SOC/INTEG 20. PAGE 92 A1874
AFR ECO/UNDEV COLONIAL

B64
MAIER J.,POLITICS OF CHANGE IN LATIN AMERICA. BRAZIL L/A+17C STRATA INT/ORG NAT/G POL/PAR FOR/AID REV 20. PAGE 93 A1907
SOCIETY NAT/LISM DIPLOM REGION

B64
MARTIN J.J.,AMERICAN LIBERALISM AND WORLD POLITICS, 1931-41 (2 VOLS.). GERMANY USA-45 POL/PAR DISCRIM NAT/LISM PEACE RATIONAL ATTIT RIGID/FLEX MARXISM PACIFISM 20. PAGE 95 A1950
NEW/LIB DIPLOM NAT/G POLICY

B64
MATTHEWS D.G.,A CURRENT VIEW OF AFRICANA (PAMPHLET). CULTURE ECO/UNDEV DIPLOM RACE/REL ATTIT 20. PAGE 96 A1968
BIBLIOG/A AFR NAT/G NAT/LISM

B64
QUIGG P.W.,AFRICA: A FOREIGN AFFAIRS READER. AFR FRANCE PORTUGAL UK DIPLOM LEAD PARL/PROC MARXISM ...MAJORIT METH/CNCPT GOV/COMP IDEA/COMP ANTHOL 19/20. PAGE 118 A2426
COLONIAL SOVEREIGN NAT/LISM RACE/REL

B64
ROBERTS HL,FOREIGN AFFAIRS BIBLIOGRAPHY, 1952-1962. ECO/DEV SECT PLAN FOR/AID INT/TRADE ARMS/CONT NAT/LISM ATTIT...INT/LAW GOV/COMP IDEA/COMP 20. PAGE 122 A2495
BIBLIOG/A DIPLOM INT/ORG WAR

B64
SAKAI R.K.,STUDIES ON ASIA, 1964. ASIA CHINA/COM ISRAEL MALAYSIA S/ASIA USA+45 USSR ECO/UNDEV FAM POL/PAR SECT CONSULT NAT/LISM...POLICY SOC 20 CHINJAP. PAGE 126 A2588
PWR DIPLOM

B64
US HOUSE COMM ON JUDICIARY,IMMIGRATION HEARINGS. DELIB/GP STRANGE HABITAT...GEOG JURID 20 CONGRESS MIGRATION. PAGE 154 A3140
NAT/G POLICY DIPLOM NAT/LISM

B64
WALLBANK T.W.,DOCUMENTS ON MODERN AFRICA. NAT/G COLONIAL GP/REL ATTIT PWR...BIBLIOG 19/20. PAGE 160 A3267
AFR NAT/LISM ECO/UNDEV DIPLOM

B64
WOODHOUSE C.M.,THE NEW CONCERT OF NATIONS. WOR+45 ECO/DEV ECO/UNDEV NAT/G BAL/PWR ECO/TAC NAT/LISM PWR SOVEREIGN ALL/IDEOS 20 UN COLD/WAR. PAGE 166 A3391
DIPLOM MORAL FOR/AID COLONIAL

B64
WRIGHT Q.,A STUDY OF WAR. LAW NAT/G PROB/SOLV BAL/PWR NAT/LISM PEACE ATTIT SOVEREIGN...CENSUS SOC/INTEG. PAGE 168 A3419
WAR CONCPT DIPLOM CONTROL

L64
CAMPBELL J.C.,"THE MIDDLE EAST IN THE MUTED COLD WAR." COM EUR+WWI UAR USA+45 USSR STRUCT ECO/UNDEV NAT/G VOL/ASSN EX/STRUC TOP/EX DIPLOM ECO/TAC EDU/PROP...TIME/SEQ COLD/WAR 20. PAGE 23 A0475
ISLAM FOR/AID NAT/LISM

L64
KORBONSKI A.,"COMECON." ASIA ECO/DEV ECO/UNDEV ECO/TAC BAL/PAY NAT/LISM 20 COMECON. PAGE 81 A1671
COM INT/ORG INT/TRADE

L64
POUNDS N.J.G.,"THE POLITICS OF PARTITION." AFR ASIA COM EUR+WWI FUT ISLAM S/ASIA USA-45 LAW ECO/DEV ECO/UNDEV AGRI INDUS INT/ORG POL/PAR PROVS SECT FORCES TOP/EX EDU/PROP LEGIT ATTIT MORAL ORD/FREE PWR RESPECT WEALTH. PAGE 117 A2402
NAT/G NAT/LISM

L64
RIPLEY R.B.,"INTERAGENCY COMMITTEES AND INCREMENTALISM: THE CASE OF AID TO INDIA." INDIA USA+45 INTELL NAT/G DELIB/GP ACT/RES DIPLOM ROUTINE NAT/LISM ATTIT PWR...SOC CONCPT NEW/IDEA TIME/SEQ CON/ANAL VAL/FREE 20. PAGE 121 A2483
EXEC MGT FOR/AID

S64
CARNEGIE ENDOWMENT INT. PEACE,"COLONIAL COUNTRIES AND PEOPLES (ISSUES BEFORE THE NINETEENTH GENERAL ASSEMBLY)." AFR ISLAM L/A+17C WOR+45 DELIB/GP LEGIS ECO/TAC EDU/PROP NAT/LISM PEACE ALL/VALS...RECORD UN CMN/WLTH 20. PAGE 24 A0491
INT/ORG ECO/UNDEV COLONIAL

S64
DELGADO J.,"EL MOMENTO POLITICO HISPANOAMERICA." CHINA/COM FUT PANAMA USA+45 USSR INT/ORG NAT/G POL/PAR FORCES DOMIN REGION COERCE ATTIT ALL/VALS ...TRADIT CONCPT COLD/WAR 20. PAGE 36 A0728
L/A+17C EDU/PROP NAT/LISM

S64
GARMARNIKOW M.,"INFLUENCE-BUYING IN WEST AFRICA." COM FUT USSR INTELL NAT/G PLAN TEC/DEV ECO/TAC DOMIN EDU/PROP REGION NAT/LISM ATTIT DRIVE ALL/VALS SOVEREIGN...POLICY PSY SOC CONCPT TREND STERTYP WORK COLD/WAR 20. PAGE 51 A1049
AFR ECO/UNDEV FOR/AID SOCISM

S64
GERBET P.,"LA MISE EN OEUVRE DU MARCHE COMMUN AGRICOLE." ECO/DEV MARKET INT/ORG NAT/G PLAN EDU/PROP NAT/LISM WEALTH...OBS EEC VAL/FREE 20. PAGE 52 A1064
EUR+WWI AGRI REGION

S64
GINSBURGS G.,"WARS OF NATIONAL LIBERATION - THE SOVIET THESIS." COM USSR WOR+45 WOR-45 LAW CULTURE INT/ORG DIPLOM LEGIT COLONIAL GUERRILLA WAR NAT/LISM ATTIT PERSON MORAL PWR...JURID OBS TREND MARX/KARL 20. PAGE 53 A1075
COERCE CONCPT INT/LAW REV

S64
GROSSER A.,"Y A-T-IL UN CONFLIT FRANCO-AMERICAIN." EUR+WWI USA+45 INT/ORG NAT/G PLAN BAL/PWR DIPLOM EDU/PROP NUC/PWR ATTIT DRIVE ORD/FREE PWR...CONCPT OBS TIME/SEQ TREND STERTYP VAL/FREE COLD/WAR. PAGE 57 A1179
VOL/ASSN NAT/LISM FRANCE

S64
LEVI W.,"CHINA AND THE UNITED NATIONS." ASIA CHINA CHINA/COM WOR+45 WOR-45 CONSTN NAT/G DELIB/GP EX/STRUC FORCES ACT/RES EDU/PROP PWR...POLICY RECORD TIME/SEQ GEN/LAWS UN COLD/WAR 20. PAGE 88 A1794
INT/ORG ATTIT NAT/LISM

S64
PADELFORD N.J.,"THE ORGANIZATION OF AFRICAN UNITY." ECO/UNDEV INT/ORG PLAN BAL/PWR DIPLOM ECO/TAC NAT/LISM ORD/FREE PWR WEALTH...CONCPT TREND STERTYP VAL/FREE COLD/WAR 20. PAGE 113 A2313
AFR VOL/ASSN REGION

C64
EASTON S.C.,"THE RISE AND FALL OF WESTERN COLONIALISM." AFR ISLAM L/A+17C ECO/UNDEV REV NAT/LISM...CHARTS BIBLIOG 15/20. PAGE 40 A0817
COLONIAL DIPLOM ORD/FREE WAR

B65
BROMKE A.,THE COMMUNIST STATES AT THE CROSSROADS BETWEEN MOSCOW AND PEKING. CHINA/COM USSR INGP/REL NAT/LISM TOTALISM 20. PAGE 19 A0389
COM DIPLOM MARXISM REGION

B65
CALLEO D.P.,EUROPE'S FUTURE: THE GRAND ALTERNATIVES. UK INT/ORG DIPLOM PWR SOVEREIGN ...CONCPT IDEA/COMP NAT/COMP BIBLIOG 20 EEC EUROPE DEGAULLE/C NATO. PAGE 23 A0468
FUT EUR+WWI FEDERAL NAT/LISM

B65
COWEN Z.,THE BRITISH COMMONWEALTH OF NATIONS IN A CHANGING WORLD. UK ECO/UNDEV INT/ORG ECO/TAC INT/TRADE COLONIAL WAR GP/REL RACE/REL SOVEREIGN SOC/INTEG 20 TREATY EEC COMMONWLTH. PAGE 32 A0644
JURID DIPLOM PARL/PROC NAT/LISM

B65
EMERSON R.,THE POLITICAL AWAKENING OF AFRICA. ECO/UNDEV INT/ORG COLONIAL RACE/REL ORD/FREE MARXISM...TREND ANTHOL 20. PAGE 42 A0849
AFR NAT/LISM DIPLOM POL/PAR

B65
FANON F.,STUDIES IN A DYING COLONIALISM. ALGERIA FRANCE STRATA FAM DIPLOM DOMIN WAR RACE/REL DISCRIM HEALTH 20. PAGE 44 A0897
NAT/LISM COLONIAL REV SOVEREIGN

B65
HALLE L.J.,THE SOCIETY OF MAN. WOR+45 WOR-45 EDU/PROP NAT/LISM MARXISM CONCPT. PAGE 60 A1231
DIPLOM PHIL/SCI CREATE SOCIETY

B65
HALPERIN E.,NATIONALISM AND COMMUNISM. CHILE L/A+17C CAP/ISM EDU/PROP CHOOSE DISCRIM SOCISM ...BIBLIOG 20 COM/PARTY. PAGE 60 A1236
NAT/LISM MARXISM POL/PAR REV

B65
JOHNSON H.G.,THE WORLD ECONOMY AT THE CROSSROADS. COM WOR-45 ECO/DEV AGRI INDUS INT/TRADE REGION NAT/LISM 20. PAGE 74 A1523
FINAN DIPLOM INT/ORG ECO/UNDEV

B65
KIRKWOOD K.,BRITAIN AND AFRICA. AFR UK ECO/UNDEV ECO/TAC WAR NAT/LISM SOVEREIGN 19/20. PAGE 80 A1636
NAT/G DIPLOM POLICY COLONIAL

B65
LASKY V.,THE UGLY RUSSIAN. AFR ASIA USSR ECO/UNDEV NAT/LISM TOTALISM PERSON 20. PAGE 85 A1738
FOR/AID ATTIT DIPLOM

B65
MEHROTRA S.R.,INDIA AND THE COMMONWEALTH 1885-1929. INDIA UK INT/ORG VOL/ASSN GP/REL ATTIT...POLICY BIBLIOG 19/20 CMN/WLTH. PAGE 99 A2034
DIPLOM NAT/G POL/PAR NAT/LISM

B65
MIDDLETON D.,CRISIS IN THE WEST. EUR+WWI FUT WOR+45 CHIEF PLAN ECO/TAC LEAD REGION NUC/PWR NAT/LISM MARXISM 20 COLD/WAR NATO EEC. PAGE 101 A2068
INT/ORG DIPLOM NAT/G POLICY

B65
NKRUMAH K.,NEO-COLONIALISM: THE LAST STAGE OF IMPERIALISM. AFR INT/ORG WORKER FOR/AID INT/TRADE EDU/PROP GOV/REL NAT/LISM SOVEREIGN POPULISM SOCISM ...SOCIALIST 20 THIRD/WRLD INTRVN/ECO. PAGE 109 A2243
COLONIAL DIPLOM ECO/UNDEV ECO/TAC

B65
ROMEIN J.,THE ASIAN CENTURY. ASIA COM S/ASIA DIPLOM COLONIAL TIME 20. PAGE 123 A2519
REV NAT/LISM CULTURE MARXISM

B65
ROTBERG R.I.,A POLITICAL HISTORY OF TROPICAL AFRICA. EX/STRUC DIPLOM INT/TRADE DOMIN ADMIN RACE/REL NAT/LISM PWR SOVEREIGN...GEOG TIME/SEQ BIBLIOG 1/20. PAGE 124 A2545
AFR CULTURE COLONIAL

B65
RUBINSTEIN A.,THE CHALLENGE OF POLITICS: IDEAS AND ISSUES. BAL/PWR COLONIAL WAR TOTALISM ORD/FREE PWR MARXISM SOCISM...INT/LAW 20. PAGE 125 A2561
NAT/G SOVEREIGN DIPLOM NAT/LISM

B65
SCHREIBER H.,TEUTON AND SLAV - THE STRUGGLE FOR CENTRAL EUROPE (TRANS. BY J. CLEUGH). GERMANY POLAND PRUSSIA USSR SOCIETY STRUCT SECT DIPLOM BALTIC. PAGE 129 A2646
GP/REL WAR RACE/REL NAT/LISM

B65
SHUKRI A.,THE CONCEPT OF SELF-DETERMINATION IN THE UNITED NATIONS. WOR+45 DIPLOM INT/TRADE SANCTION NAT/LISM...BIBLIOG 20 UN. PAGE 132 A2709
COLONIAL INT/ORG INT/LAW SOVEREIGN

B65
SMITH A.L. JR.,THE DEUTSCHTUM OF NAZI GERMANY AND THE UNITED STATES. GERMANY USA-45 DIPLOM ATTIT FASCISM...BIBLIOG 20 MIGRATION NAZI. PAGE 134 A2744
INGP/REL NAT/LISM STRANGE DELIB/GP

B65
SPENCE J.E.,REPUBLIC UNDER PRESSURE: A STUDY OF SOUTH AFRICAN FOREIGN POLICY. SOUTH/AFR ADMIN COLONIAL GOV/REL RACE/REL DISCRIM NAT/LISM ATTIT ROLE...TREND 20 NEGRO. PAGE 136 A2783
DIPLOM POLICY AFR

B65
VAN DEN BERGHE P.L.,AFRICA: SOCIAL PROBLEMS OF CHANGE AND CONFLICT. ELITES STRATA ECO/UNDEV KIN MUNIC DIPLOM GP/REL RACE/REL NAT/LISM...ANTHOL BIBLIOG 20. PAGE 158 A3210
SOC CULTURE AFR STRUCT

S65
STEIN E.,"TOWARD SUPREMACY OF TREATY-CONSTITUTION BY JUDICIAL FIAT: ON THE MARGIN OF THE COSTA CASE." EUR+WWI ITALY WOR+45 INT/ORG NAT/G LEGIT REGION NAT/LISM PWR...JURID CONCPT TREND TOT/POP VAL/FREE 20. PAGE 138 A2816
ADJUD CONSTN SOVEREIGN INT/LAW

S65
TURNER F.C.,"THE IMPLICATIONS OF DEMOGRAPHIC CHANGE FOR NATIONALISM AND INTERNATIONALISM." FUT WOR+45 NAT/LISM AGE SEX CONCPT. PAGE 146 A2980
SOCIETY EDU/PROP DIPLOM ORD/FREE

C65
MARK M.,"BEYOND SOVEREIGNTY." WOR+45 WOR-45 ECO/UNDEV BAL/PWR INT/TRADE NUC/PWR REV WAR MARXISM NEW/LIB BIBLIOG. PAGE 95 A1942
NAT/LISM NAT/G DIPLOM INTELL

C65
SCHWEBEL M.,"BEHAVIORAL SCIENCE AND HUMAN SURVIVAL." FORCES ARMS/CONT COERCE NUC/PWR WAR GP/REL NAT/LISM PERCEPT...POLICY PSY ANTHOL BIBLIOG/A 20 COLD/WAR. PAGE 130 A2662
PEACE ACT/RES DIPLOM HEAL

B66
AMERICAN ASSEMBLY COLUMBIA U,THE UNITED STATES AND THE PHILIPPINES. PHILIPPINE S/ASIA USA+45 USA-45 SOCIETY FORCES INT/TRADE...POLICY 20. PAGE 7 A0138
COLONIAL DIPLOM NAT/LISM

B66
AMERICAN FRIENDS SERVICE COMM,PEACE IN VIETNAM: A NEW APPROACH IN SOUTHEAST ASIA: A REPORT. ASIA S/ASIA USA+45 VIETNAM ORD/FREE 20 TREATY. PAGE 7 A0149
PEACE WAR NAT/LISM DIPLOM

B66
BROWN J.F.,THE NEW EASTERN EUROPE. ALBANIA BULGARIA HUNGARY POLAND ROMANIA CULTURE AGRI POL/PAR WAR NAT/LISM MARXISM...CHARTS BIBLIOG 20. PAGE 20 A0404
DIPLOM COM NAT/G ECO/UNDEV

B66
EKIRCH A.A. JR.,IDEAS, IDEALS, AND AMERICAN DIPLOMACY. USA+45 USA-45 INT/ORG DOMIN COLONIAL ARMS/CONT DETER ISOLAT NAT/LISM...MAJORIT BIBLIOG 19/20 COLD/WAR. PAGE 41 A0834
DIPLOM LEAD PEACE

B66
FERKISS V.C.,AFRICA'S SEARCH FOR IDENTITY. AFR USA+45 CULTURE ECO/UNDEV INT/ORG NAT/G COLONIAL MARXISM 20. PAGE 45 A0918
NAT/LISM SOVEREIGN DIPLOM ROLE

B66
GRAHAM I.C.C.,PUBLICATIONS OF THE SOCIAL SCIENCE DEPARTMENT, THE RAND CORPORATION, 1948-1966. USSR WOR+45 NAT/G ARMS/CONT DETER WAR NAT/LISM...SOC GOV/COMP. PAGE 55 A1127
BIBLIOG DIPLOM NUC/PWR FORCES

B66
GUPTA S.,KASHMIR - A STUDY IN INDIA-PAKISTAN RELATIONS. INDIA KASHMIR PAKISTAN CONSTN INT/ORG REV RACE/REL NAT/LISM 20 UN MUSLIM/LG. PAGE 58 A1194
DIPLOM GP/REL SOVEREIGN WAR

B66
HANSEN G.H.,AFRO-ASIA AND NON-ALIGNMENT. AFR ASIA S/ASIA NEUTRAL MORAL 20. PAGE 61 A1255
DIPLOM CONFER POLICY NAT/LISM

B66
INTL CONF ON WORLD POLITICS-5,EASTERN EUROPE IN TRANSITION. EUR+WWI USSR ECO/TAC NAT/LISM ATTIT SOVEREIGN...CHARTS ANTHOL 20 TREATY WARSAW/P. PAGE 71 A1463
COM NAT/COMP MARXISM DIPLOM

B66
KEENLEYSIDE H.L.,INTERNATIONAL AID: A SUMMARY. AFR INDIA S/ASIA UK STRATA EXTR/IND TEC/DEV ADMIN RACE/REL DEMAND NAT/LISM WEALTH...TREND CHINJAP. PAGE 77 A1575
ECO/UNDEV FOR/AID DIPLOM TASK

B66
LATHAM E.,THE COMMUNIST CONTROVERSY IN WASHINGTON. USA+45 USA-45 DELIB/GP EX/STRUC LEGIS DIPLOM NAT/LISM MARXISM 20. PAGE 85 A1742
POL/PAR TOTALISM ORD/FREE NAT/G

B66
LEWIS S.,TOWARDS INTERNATIONAL CO-OPERATION (1ST ED.). WOR+45 AGRI INDUS EDU/PROP RACE/REL ISOLAT NAT/LISM ATTIT HEALTH WEALTH...CHARTS WORSHIP 20 UN. PAGE 88 A1803
DIPLOM ANOMIE PROB/SOLV INT/ORG

B66
LONDON K.,EASTERN EUROPE IN TRANSITION. CHINA/COM USSR DOMIN COLONIAL CENTRAL RIGID/FLEX PWR...SOC ANTHOL 20. PAGE 91 A1855
SOVEREIGN COM NAT/LISM DIPLOM

B66
MC LELLAN D.S.,THE COLD WAR IN TRANSITION. USSR WOR+45 CONTROL LEAD NUC/PWR NAT/LISM SOVEREIGN 20 COLD/WAR THIRD/WRLD. PAGE 97 A1994
BAL/PWR DETER DIPLOM POLICY

B66
MORRIS B.S.,INTERNATIONAL COMMUNISM AND AMERICAN POLICY. CHINA/COM USA+45 USSR INT/ORG POL/PAR GP/REL NAT/LISM ATTIT PERCEPT 20. PAGE 105 A2147
DIPLOM POLICY MARXISM

B66
SCHATTEN F.,COMMUNISM IN AFRICA. AFR GHANA GUINEA MALI CULTURE ECO/UNDEV LABOR SECT ECO/TAC EDU/PROP REV 20. PAGE 128 A2619
COLONIAL NAT/LISM MARXISM DIPLOM

B66
US DEPARTMENT OF STATE,RESEARCH ON THE MIDDLE EAST (EXTERNAL RESEARCH LIST NO 4-25). GREECE ISRAEL SYRIA UAR YEMEN CULTURE SOCIETY POL/PAR SECT DIPLOM EDU/PROP WAR NAT/LISM...GEOG GOV/COMP 20. PAGE 152 A3096
BIBLIOG/A ISLAM NAT/G REGION

B66
US SENATE COMM ON FOREIGN REL,UNITED STATES POLICY TOWARD EUROPE (AND RELATED MATTERS). COM EUR+WWI GERMANY PROB/SOLV REGION NUC/PWR WAR NAT/LISM PEACE PWR...NAT/COMP 20 NATO CONGRESS DEGAULLE/C. PAGE 156 A3184
DIPLOM INT/ORG POLICY WOR+45

B66
VAN DYKE V.,INTERNATIONAL POLITICS. WOR+45 ECO/DEV ECO/UNDEV INT/ORG BAL/PWR AGREE ARMS/CONT NAT/LISM PEACE PWR...INT/LAW 20 TREATY UN. PAGE 158 A3212
DIPLOM NAT/G WAR SOVEREIGN

B66
WELCH C.E.,DREAM OF UNITY; PAN-AFRICANISM AND POLITICAL UNIFICATION IN WEST AFRICA. AFR ECO/UNDEV CONFER COLONIAL LEAD...INT/LAW 20. PAGE 163 A3312
INT/ORG REGION NAT/LISM DIPLOM

B66
WHITAKER A.P.,NATIONALISM IN CONTEMPORARY LATIN AMERICA. AGRI NAT/G WEALTH...POLICY SOC CONCPT OBS TREND 20. PAGE 164 A3333
NAT/LISM L/A+17C DIPLOM ECO/UNDEV

B66
ZEINE Z.N.,THE EMERGENCE OF ARAB NATIONALISM (REV. ED.). TURKEY UK NAT/G SECT TEC/DEV LEAD REV WAR AGE/Y ROLE ORD/FREE...TRADIT CHARTS BIBLIOG 20 ARABS OTTOMAN. PAGE 170 A3451
ISLAM NAT/LISM DIPLOM

S66
CRANMER-BYNG J.L.,"THE CHINESE ATTITUDE TOWARDS EXTERNAL RELATIONS." ASIA CHINA/COM EXEC NAT/LISM MARXISM...POLICY 20. PAGE 32 A0660
ATTIT DIPLOM NAT/G

S66
GRUNDY K.W.,"RECENT CONTRIBUTIONS TO THE STUDY OF AFRICAN POLITICAL THOUGHT." DIPLOM NAT/LISM ALL/IDEOS...NEW/IDEA GOV/COMP 20. PAGE 58 A1182
BIBLIOG/A AFR ATTIT IDEA/COMP

S66
O'BRIEN W.V.,"EVENTS AND TRENDS: PATTERNS OF AFRICAN INTERNATIONAL POLITICAL BEHAVIOR." CULTURE SOCIETY NAT/G NAT/LISM SOCISM. PAGE 111 A2267
BIBLIOG/A AFR TREND DIPLOM

S66
SKILLING H.G.,"THE RUMANIAN NATIONAL COURSE." COM EUR+WWI ROMANIA NAT/G ECO/TAC PWR 20. PAGE 134 A2739
NAT/LISM POLICY DIPLOM MARXISM

C66
TARLING N.,"A CONCISE HISTORY OF SOUTHEAST ASIA." BURMA CAMBODIA LAOS S/ASIA THAILAND VIETNAM ECO/UNDEV POL/PAR FORCES ADMIN REV WAR CIVMIL/REL ORD/FREE MARXISM SOCISM 13/20. PAGE 141 A2890
COLONIAL DOMIN INT/TRADE NAT/LISM

B67
ATTWOOD W.,THE REDS AND THE BLACKS. AFR POL/PAR CHOOSE GOV/REL RACE/REL NAT/LISM...BIOG 20. PAGE 10 A0195
DIPLOM PWR MARXISM

B67
BELL W.,THE DEMOCRATIC REVOLUTION IN THE WEST INDIES. WEST/IND WOR+45 DIPLOM RACE/REL NAT/LISM ...INT QU ANTHOL 20. PAGE 13 A0257
REGION ATTIT ORD/FREE ECO/UNDEV

B67
GRIFFITH SB I.I.,THE CHINESE PEOPLE'S LIBERATION ARMY. CHINA/COM DIPLOM DOMIN GUERRILLA NUC/PWR REV ...CHARTS BIBLIOG 20. PAGE 57 A1163
FORCES CIVMIL/REL NAT/LISM PWR

B67
KNOLES G.H.,THE RESPONSIBILITIES OF POWER, 1900-1929. USA-45 SOCIETY SECT JUDGE COLONIAL REPRESENT WEALTH POPULISM...IDEA/COMP ANTHOL PRESIDENT 20 LEAGUE/NAT. PAGE 81 A1653
PWR DIPLOM NAT/LISM WAR

B67
MACRIDIS R.C.,FOREIGN POLICY IN WORLD POLITICS (3RD ED.). EX/STRUC BAL/PWR COLONIAL NAT/LISM SKILL SOVEREIGN WEALTH...CONCPT TIME/SEQ ANTHOL 20 COLD/WAR. PAGE 93 A1902
DIPLOM POLICY NAT/G IDEA/COMP

B67
MAW B.,BREAKTHROUGH IN BURMA: MEMOIRS OF A REVOLUTION, 1939-1946. BURMA UK FORCES PROB/SOLV DIPLOM FOR/AID DOMIN LEAD...BIOG 20. PAGE 97 A1980
REV ORD/FREE NAT/LISM COLONIAL

B67
MEHDI M.T.,PEACE IN THE MIDDLE EAST. ISRAEL SOCIETY NAT/G PLAN EDU/PROP NAT/LISM DRIVE...IDEA/COMP 20 JEWS. PAGE 99 A2033
ISLAM DIPLOM GP/REL COERCE

B67
MEYNAUD J.,TRADE UNIONISM IN AFRICA; A STUDY OF ITS GROWTH AND ORIENTATION (TRANS. BY ANGELA BRENCH). INT/ORG PROB/SOLV COLONIAL PWR...TIME/SEQ TREND ILO. PAGE 100 A2055
LABOR AFR NAT/LISM ORD/FREE

B67
OLSON L.,JAPAN TODAY AND TOMORROW (PAMPHLET) (HEADLINE SERIES, NO. 181). PLAN DIPLOM NAT/LISM ATTIT...PREDICT 20 CHINJAP. PAGE 112 A2289
NAT/G CULTURE ECO/DEV

B67
PADELFORD N.J.,THE DYNAMICS OF INTERNATIONAL POLITICS (2ND ED.). WOR+45 LAW INT/ORG FORCES TEC/DEV REGION NAT/LISM PEACE ATTIT PWR ALL/IDEOS UN COLD/WAR NATO TREATY. PAGE 113 A2314
DIPLOM NAT/G POLICY DECISION

B67
SABLE M.H.,A GUIDE TO LATIN AMERICAN STUDIES (2 VOLS). CONSTN FINAN INT/ORG LABOR MUNIC POL/PAR FORCES CAP/ISM FOR/AID ADMIN MARXISM SOCISM OAS. PAGE 126 A2584
BIBLIOG/A L/A+17C DIPLOM NAT/LISM

B67
SALISBURY H.E.,BEHIND THE LINES - HANOI. VIETNAM/N NAT/G GUERRILLA CIVMIL/REL NAT/LISM KNOWL 20. PAGE 126 A2592
WAR PROB/SOLV DIPLOM OBS

B67
SCHWARTZ M.A.,PUBLIC OPINION AND CANADIAN IDENTITY. CANADA SOCIETY LOC/G DIPLOM ADMIN LEAD REGION GP/REL SAMP. PAGE 130 A2657
ATTIT NAT/G NAT/LISM POL/PAR

B67
YAMAMURA K.,ECONOMIC POLICY IN POSTWAR JAPAN. ASIA FINAN POL/PAR DIPLOM LEAD NAT/LISM ATTIT NEW/LIB POPULISM 20 CHINJAP. PAGE 168 A3429
ECO/DEV POLICY NAT/G TEC/DEV

L67
SEGAL A.,"THE INTEGRATION OF DEVELOPING COUNTRIES: SOME THOUGHTS ON EAST AFRICA AND CENTRAL AMERICA." AFR L/A+17C INT/ORG NAT/G VOL/ASSN FOR/AID INT/TRADE EQUILIB NAT/LISM PWR 20. PAGE 131 A2680
ECO/UNDEV DIPLOM REGION

S67
APEL H.,"LES NOUVEAUX ASPECTS DE LA POLITIQUE ETRANGERE ALLEMANDE." EUR+WWI GERMANY POL/PAR BAL/PWR ECO/TAC INT/TRADE NUC/PWR NAT/LISM PEACE ...POLICY 20 EEC COLD/WAR. PAGE 8 A0168
DIPLOM INT/ORG FEDERAL

S67
BREGMAN A.,"WHITHER RUSSIA?" COM RUSSIA INTELL POL/PAR DIPLOM PARTIC NAT/LISM TOTALISM ATTIT ORD/FREE 20. PAGE 18 A0370
MARXISM ELITES ADMIN CREATE

S67
BURNS E.B.,"TRADITIONS AND VARIATIONS IN BRAZILIAN FOREIGN POLICY." BRAZIL L/A+17C POL/PAR INT/TRADE COLONIAL INGP/REL ATTIT ORD/FREE PWR 20. PAGE 22 A0443
DIPLOM NAT/LISM CREATE

S67
CONNOR W.,"SELF-DETERMINATION: THE NEW PHASE." WOR+45 WOR-45 CULTURE INT/ORG COLONIAL 19/20. PAGE 29 A0588
NAT/LISM SOVEREIGN INGP/REL GP/REL

S67
DAVIS H.B.,"LENIN AND NATIONALISM: THE REDIRECTION OF THE MARXIST THEORY OF NATIONALISM." COM MOD/EUR USSR STRATA INT/ORG PLAN DOMIN COLONIAL FEDERAL ...TREND 20. PAGE 34 A0690
NAT/LISM MARXISM ATTIT CENTRAL

S67
DOYLE S.E.,"COMMUNICATION SATELLITES* INTERNAL ORGANIZATION FOR DEVELOPMENT AND CONTROL." USA+45 R+D ACT/RES DIPLOM NAT/LISM...POLICY INT/LAW PREDICT UN. PAGE 38 A0781
TEC/DEV SPACE COM/IND INT/ORG

S67
GRIFFITHS F.,"THE POLITICAL SIDE OF 'DISARMAMENT'." FUT WOR+45 NUC/PWR NAT/LISM PEACE...NEW/IDEA PREDICT METH/COMP GEN/LAWS 20. PAGE 57 A1164
ARMS/CONT DIPLOM

S67
GRUNDY K.W.,"AFRICA IN THE WORLD ARENA." ECO/UNDEV BAL/PWR FOR/AID NEUTRAL REV NAT/LISM GOV/COMP. PAGE 58 A1183
AFR DIPLOM INT/ORG COLONIAL

S67
HALL M.,"GERMANY, EAST AND WEST* DANGER AT THE CROSSROADS." GERMANY ELITES CHIEF FORCES DIPLOM ECO/TAC REPAR ARMS/CONT...SOCIALIST 20. PAGE 60 A1227
NAT/LISM ATTIT FASCISM WEAPON

S67
HALLE L.J.,"DE GAULLE AND THE FUTURE OF EUROPE." FRANCE DIPLOM 20. PAGE 60 A1232
NAT/LISM LEAD INT/ORG PREDICT

S67
INGLEHART R.,"AN END TO EUROPEAN INTEGRATION." PROB/SOLV BAL/PWR NAT/LISM...PSY SOC INT CHARTS GP/COMP 20. PAGE 70 A1440
DIPLOM EUR+WWI REGION ATTIT

S67
JACKSON W.G.F.,"NUCLEAR PROLIFERATION AND THE GREAT POWERS." FUT UK WOR+45 INT/ORG DOMIN ARMS/CONT DETER ORD/FREE PACIFIST. PAGE 72 A1480
NUC/PWR ATTIT BAL/PWR NAT/LISM

S67
KIERNAN V.G.,"INDIA AND THE LABOUR PARTY." INDIA UK CAP/ISM GP/REL EFFICIENCY NAT/LISM PWR SOCISM ...SOCIALIST TIME/SEQ 20. PAGE 79 A1616
COLONIAL DIPLOM POL/PAR ECO/UNDEV

S67
LACOUTRE J.,"HO CHI MINH." CHINA/COM USSR VIETNAM/N NAT/G CHIEF TOP/EX LEAD NEUTRAL...REALPOL PREDICT 20. PAGE 83 A1708
NAT/LISM MARXISM REV DIPLOM

S67
MEYER J.,"CUBA S'ENFERME DANS SA REVOLUTION." CHINA/COM CUBA USSR NAT/G TOP/EX DIPLOM LEAD ATTIT ...PREDICT 20. PAGE 100 A2053
MARXISM REV CHIEF NAT/LISM

S67
MOSELY P.E.,"EASTERN EUROPE IN WORLD POWER POLITICS: WHERE DE-STALINIZATION HAS LED." ECO/UNDEV NAT/LISM 20. PAGE 105 A2153
COM NAT/G DIPLOM MARXISM

S67
NEUCHTERLEIN D.E.,"THAILAND* ANOTHER VIETNAM?" THAILAND ECO/UNDEV DIPLOM ADMIN REGION CENTRAL NAT/LISM...POLICY 20. PAGE 108 A2220
WAR GUERRILLA S/ASIA NAT/G

S67
NIEBUHR R.,"THE SOCIAL MYTHS IN THE COLD WAR." USA+45 USSR VIETNAM PROB/SOLV BAL/PWR ARMS/CONT NAT/LISM PWR ALL/IDEOS CONCPT. PAGE 109 A2238
MYTH DIPLOM GOV/COMP

S67
PAUKER G.J.,"TOWARD A NEW ORDER IN INDONESIA." COM INDONESIA S/ASIA ECO/UNDEV POL/PAR EX/STRUC TOP/EX BAL/PWR ECO/TAC FOR/AID DOMIN NAT/LISM AUTHORIT ORD/FREE PWR 20. PAGE 114 A2342
REV NAT/G DIPLOM CIVMIL/REL

S67
ROSE S.,"ASIAN NATIONALISM* THE SECOND STAGE." ASIA
NAT/LISM

COM ECO/UNDEV NAT/G PROB/SOLV DIPLOM FOR/AID DOMIN NEUTRAL REGION TASK...METH/COMP 20. PAGE 123 A2528 — S/ASIA BAL/PWR COLONIAL

S67
SOMMER T.,"BONN CHANGES COURSE." GERMANY/W NAT/G POL/PAR PROB/SOLV NAT/LISM 20 NATO BERLIN/BLO. PAGE 135 A2766 — DIPLOM BAL/PWR INT/ORG

S67
STEEL R.,"BEYOND THE POWER BLOCS." USA+45 USSR ECO/UNDEV NEUTRAL NUC/PWR NAT/LISM ATTIT...GEOG NATO WARSAW/P COLD/WAR. PAGE 137 A2811 — DIPLOM TREND BAL/PWR PLAN

S67
SYRKIN M.,"I.F. STONE RECONSIDERS ISRAEL." ISRAEL WOR+45 DIPLOM NAT/LISM HABITAT...POLICY GEOG JEWS. PAGE 141 A2875 — ISLAM WAR ATTIT MORAL

S67
TERRILL R.,"THE SIEGE MENTALITY." CHINA/COM NAT/G FORCES DIPLOM REV EFFICIENCY NAT/LISM MARXISM ...TREND 20. PAGE 142 A2904 — EDU/PROP WAR DOMIN

C67
LING D.L.,"TUNISIA: FROM PROTECTORATE TO REPUBLIC." CULTURE NAT/G POL/PAR CHIEF DIPLOM COERCE WAR PWR ...BIBLIOG 19/20 TUNIS. PAGE 89 A1825 — AFR NAT/LISM COLONIAL PROB/SOLV

C67
SPANIER J.W.,"WORLD POLITICS IN AN AGE OF REVOLUTION." COM WOR+45 FORCES COERCE WAR NAT/LISM SOVEREIGN...POLICY BIBLIOG 20. PAGE 135 A2772 — DIPLOM TEC/DEV REV ECO/UNDEV

B90
HOSMAR J.K.,A SHORT HISTORY OF ANGLO-SAXON FREEDOM. UK USA-45 ROMAN/EMP NAT/G EX/STRUC LEGIS COLONIAL REV NAT/LISM POPULISM PARLIAMENT ANGLO/SAX MAGNA/CART. PAGE 68 A1394 — CONSTN ORD/FREE DIPLOM PARL/PROC

B91
DOLE C.F.,THE AMERICAN CITIZEN. USA-45 LAW PARTIC ATTIT...INT/LAW 19. PAGE 38 A0769 — NAT/G MORAL NAT/LISM MAJORITY

NAT/SAFETY....NATIONAL SAFETY COUNCIL

NAT/SERV....COMPULSORY NATIONAL SERVICE

NAT/UNITY....NATIONAL UNITY COMMITTEE (TURKEY)

NATAL

NATHAN O. A0829

NATION ASSOCIATES A2198

NATIONAL AERONAUTIC AND SPACE ADMINISTRATION....SEE NASA

NATIONAL ASSOCIATION FOR THE ADVANCEMENT OF COLORED PEOPLE....SEE NAACP

NATIONAL ASSOCIATION OF MANUFACTURERS....SEE NAM

NATIONAL BELLAS HESS....SEE BELLAS/HES

NATIONAL COUNCIL OF CHURCHES....SEE NCC

NATIONAL DEBT....SEE DEBT

NATIONAL DIRECTORY (IRELAND)....SEE DIRECT/NAT

NATIONAL EDUCATION ASSOCIATION....SEE NEA

NATIONAL FARMERS' ASSOCIATION....SEE NAT/FARMER

NATIONAL GUARD....SEE NATL/GUARD

NATIONAL INSTITUTE OF HEALTH....SEE NIH

NATIONAL INSTITUTE OF PUBLIC ADMINISTRATION....SEE NIPA

NATIONAL LABOR RELATIONS BOARD....SEE NLRB

NATIONAL LIBERATION COUNCIL IN GHANA....SEE NLC

NATIONAL LIBERATION FRONT (OF SOUTH VIETNAM)....SEE NLF

NATIONAL RECOVERY ADMINISTRATION....SEE NRA

NATIONAL SAFETY COUNCIL....SEE NAT/SAFETY

NATIONAL SCIENCE FOUNDATION....SEE NSF

NATIONAL SECURITY COUNCIL....SEE NSC

NATIONAL SECURITY....SEE ORD/FREE

NATIONAL SOCIAL SCIENCE FOUNDATION....SEE NSSF

NATIONAL UNITY COMMITTEE....SEE NUC

NATIONAL WEALTH....SEE NAT/G+WEALTH

NATIONAL ACADEMY OF SCIENCES A2199

NATIONAL BANK OF LIBYA A2200

NATIONAL BOOK CENTRE PAKISTAN A2201

NATIONAL CENTRAL LIBRARY A2202

NATIONAL COUN APPLIED ECO RES A2203

NATIONAL PLANNING ASSOCIATION A2204

NATIONALISM....SEE NAT/LISM

NATIONALIST CHINA....SEE TAIWAN

NATIONALIZATION....SEE SOCISM

NATL/GUARD....NATIONAL GUARD

NATO....NORTH ATLANTIC TREATY ORGANIZATION; SEE ALSO VOL/ASSN, INT/ORG, FORCES, DETER

N
WEINTAL E.,FACING THE BRINK* AN INTIMATE STUDY OF CRISIS DIPLOMACY. CYPRUS FRANCE USA+45 USSR VIETNAM YEMEN INT/ORG NAT/G...POLICY DECISION PREDICT COLD/WAR PRESIDENT NATO 20. PAGE 162 A3307 — DIPLOM

B
CURRENT THOUGHT ON PEACE AND WAR. WOR+45 INT/ORG FORCES PROB/SOLV DIPLOM NUC/PWR PERCEPT...POLICY SOC 20 UN NATO. PAGE 1 A0008 — BIBLIOG/A PEACE ATTIT WAR

N
US SUPERINTENDENT OF DOCUMENTS,FOREIGN RELATIONS OF THE UNITED STATES; PUBLICATIONS RELATING TO FOREIGN COUNTRIES (PRICE LIST 65). UAR USA+45 VIETNAM ECO/UNDEV VOL/ASSN FOR/AID EDU/PROP ARMS/CONT HEALTH MARXISM...POLICY INT/LAW UN NATO. PAGE 157 A3201 — BIBLIOG/A DIPLOM INT/ORG NAT/G

N19
MORGENSTERN O.,THE COMMAND AND CONTROL STRUCTURE (PAMPHLET). USSR COM/IND INT/ORG WEAPON PEACE UTIL ...TREND 20 NATO. PAGE 104 A2132 — CONTROL FORCES EFFICIENCY PLAN

B48
US DEPARTMENT OF STATE,FOREIGN AFFAIRS HIGHLIGHTS (NEWSLETTER). COM USA+45 INT/ORG PLAN BAL/PWR WAR PWR...BIBLIOG 20 COLD/WAR NATO UN DEPT/STATE. PAGE 151 A3083 — DIPLOM NAT/G POLICY

B49
BOYD A.,WESTERN UNION: A STUDY OF THE TREND TOWARD EUROPEAN UNITY. FUT REGION NAT/LISM...POLICY IDEA/COMP BIBLIOG 14/20 OEEC ERASMUS/D COUNCL/EUR FULBRGHT/J NATO. PAGE 18 A0363 — DIPLOM AGREE TREND INT/ORG

B49
KAFKA G.,FREIHEIT UND ANARCHIE. SECT COERCE DETER WAR ATTIT...IDEA/COMP 20 NATO. PAGE 75 A1545 — CONCPT ORD/FREE JURID INT/ORG

L49
HEINDEL R.H.,"THE NORTH ATLANTIC TREATY IN THE UNITED STATES SENATE." CONSTN POL/PAR CHIEF DEBATE LEAD ROUTINE WAR PEACE...CHARTS UN SENATE NATO. PAGE 64 A1309 — DECISION PARL/PROC LEGIS INT/ORG

B51
CORMACK M.,SELECTED PAMPHLETS ON THE UNITED NATIONS AND INTERNATIONAL RELATIONS (PAMPHLET). USA+45 R+D EX/STRUC PROB/SOLV ROUTINE...POLICY CON/ANAL 20 UN NATO. PAGE 31 A0624 — BIBLIOG/A NAT/G INT/ORG DIPLOM

B51
US HOUSE COMM APPROPRIATIONS,MUTUAL SECURITY PROGRAM APPROPRIATIONS FOR 1952: HEARINGS BEFORE A SUBCOMMITTEE OF THE COMMITTEE ON APPROPRIATIONS. KOREA L/A+17C ECO/DEV ECO/UNDEV INT/ORG INSPECT BAL/PWR DIPLOM DEBATE WAR...POLICY STAT ASIA/S 20 CONGRESS NATO COLD/WAR MID/EAST. PAGE 153 A3118 — LEGIS FORCES BUDGET FOR/AID

L51
KELSEN H.,"RECENT TRENDS IN THE LAW OF THE UNITED NATIONS." KOREA WOR+45 CONSTN LEGIS DIPLOM LEGIT DETER WAR RIGID/FLEX HEALTH ORD/FREE RESPECT ...JURID CON/ANAL UN VAL/FREE 20 NATO. PAGE 77 A1582 — INT/ORG LAW INT/LAW

S51
CONNERY R.H.,"THE MUTUAL DEFENSE ASSISTANCE PROGRAM." COM EUR+WWI KOREA USA+45 NAT/G VOL/ASSN CREATE PLAN BAL/PWR EDU/PROP PERCEPT...POLICY DECISION CONCPT NATO 20. PAGE 29 A0587 — INT/ORG FORCES FOR/AID

B54
SAPIN B.M.,THE ROLE OF THE MILITARY IN AMERICAN FOREIGN POLICY. USA+45 INT/ORG PROB/SOLV DETER NUC/PWR ATTIT PWR...BIBLIOG 20 NATO. PAGE 127 A2602 — DIPLOM POLICY CIVMIL/REL

NAT/G

B54
STREIT C.K.,FREEDOM AGAINST ITSELF. LAW SOCIETY DIPLOM UTOPIA PWR SOVEREIGN ALL/IDEOS 17/20 NATO UN. PAGE 139 A2850
ORD/FREE CREATE INT/ORG CONCPT

B54
US DEPARTMENT OF STATE,PUBLICATIONS OF THE DEPARTMENT OF STATE, OCTOBER 1,1929 TO JANUARY 1, 1953. AGRI INT/ORG FORCES FOR/AID EDU/PROP ARMS/CONT NUC/PWR ATTIT 20 DEPT/STATE OAS UN NATO. PAGE 151 A3089
BIBLIOG DIPLOM

B56
BUREAU OF PUBLIC AFFAIRS,AMERICAN FOREIGN POLICY: CURRENT DOCUMENTS. COM USA+45 USSR WOR+45 DELIB/GP FOR/AID INT/TRADE ARMS/CONT NUC/PWR ALL/VALS ALL/IDEOS...DECISION 20 NATO. PAGE 21 A0434
BIBLIOG/A DIPLOM POLICY

B56
ROBERTS H.L.,RUSSIA AND AMERICA. CHINA/COM S/ASIA USSR FORCES TEC/DEV FOR/AID NUC/PWR ALL/IDEOS ...MAJORIT TREND NAT/COMP 20 COLD/WAR UN NATO. PAGE 122 A2494
DIPLOM INT/ORG BAL/PWR TOTALISM

B57
KENNAN G.F.,RUSSIA, THE ATOM AND THE WEST. COM EUR+WWI FUT WOR+45 SOCIETY ECO/DEV FORCES DIPLOM ECO/TAC DOMIN EDU/PROP COERCE NUC/PWR ATTIT DRIVE ORD/FREE PWR...POLICY OBS TIME/SEQ TREND COLD/WAR NATO 20. PAGE 77 A1574
NAT/G INT/ORG USSR

B57
REISS J.,GEORGE KENNANS POLITIK DER EINDAMMUNG. USSR NAT/G FORCES TOTALISM ATTIT ORD/FREE...POLICY 20 NATO TRUMAN/HS MARSHL/PLN KENNAN/G. PAGE 120 A2463
DIPLOM DETER PEACE

S57
HOAG M.W.,"ECONOMIC PROBLEMS OF ALLIANCE." COM EUR+WWI WOR+45 ECO/DEV ECO/UNDEV NAT/G VOL/ASSN FORCES PLAN TEC/DEV DIPLOM COERCE ORD/FREE PWR WEALTH...DECISION GEN/LAWS NATO COLD/WAR. PAGE 65 A1345
INT/ORG ECO/TAC

S57
SPEIER H.,"SOVIET ATOMIC BLACKMAIL AND THE NORTH ATLANTIC ALLIANCE." EUR+WWI USA+45 USSR INT/ORG NAT/G FORCES DIPLOM DRIVE ORD/FREE PWR NATO VAL/FREE COLD/WAR 20. PAGE 136 A2781
COM COERCE NUC/PWR

B58
BOWLES C.,IDEAS, PEOPLE AND PEACE. ASIA CHINA/COM FUT INDIA USA+45 USSR ECO/UNDEV INT/ORG LEAD TASK MARXISM 20 NATO UN COLD/WAR. PAGE 18 A0359
PEACE POLICY NAT/G DIPLOM

B58
GAVIN J.M.,WAR AND PEACE IN THE SPACE AGE. SPACE USA+45 USSR FORCES PLAN TEC/DEV BAL/PWR DIPLOM ARMS/CONT WEAPON CIVMIL/REL...CHARTS GP/COMP 20 NATO COLD/WAR. PAGE 52 A1055
WAR DETER NUC/PWR PEACE

B58
HUNT B.I.,BIPARTISANSHIP: A CASE STUDY OF THE FOREIGN ASSISTANCE PROGRAM, 1947-56 (DOCTORAL THESIS). USA+45 INT/ORG CONSULT LEGIS TEC/DEV ...BIBLIOG PRESIDENT TREATY NATO TRUMAN/HS EISNHWR/DD CONGRESS. PAGE 69 A1418
FOR/AID POL/PAR GP/REL DIPLOM

B58
KENNAN G.F.,RUSSIA, THE ATOM AND THE WEST. USA+45 USSR INT/ORG ARMS/CONT MARXISM 20 NATO. PAGE 77 A1587
BAL/PWR NUC/PWR CONTROL DIPLOM

B58
MANSERGH N.,SURVEY OF BRITISH COMMONWEALTH AFFAIRS: PROBLEMS OF WARTIME CO-OPERATION AND POST-WAR CHANGE 1939-1952. INDIA IRELAND S/ASIA CONSTN INT/ORG BAL/PWR COLONIAL NEUTRAL WAR ADJUST PEACE ROLE ORD/FREE...CHARTS 20 CMN/WLTH NATO UN. PAGE 94 A1931
VOL/ASSN CONSEN PROB/SOLV INGP/REL

B58
MOORE B.T.,NATO AND THE FUTURE OF EUROPE. EUR+WWI FUT USA+45 ECO/DEV INDUS MARKET NAT/G VOL/ASSN FORCES DIPLOM NUC/PWR ORD/FREE...CONCPT CHARTS ORG/CHARTS CMN/WLTH 20 NATO. PAGE 103 A2122
INT/ORG REGION

B58
ROCKEFELLER BROTH FUND INC,INTERNATIONAL SECURITY - THE MILITARY ASPECT. USA+45 INT/ORG NAT/G BUDGET ARMS/CONT WAR WEAPON PEACE ORD/FREE 20 NATO. PAGE 123 A2511
NUC/PWR DETER FORCES DIPLOM

B58
US DEPARTMENT OF STATE,PUBLICATIONS OF THE DEPARTMENT OF STATE, JANUARY 1,1953 TO DECEMBER 31, 1957. AGRI INT/ORG FORCES FOR/AID EDU/PROP ARMS/CONT NUC/PWR ATTIT 20 DEPT/STATE OAS UN NATO. PAGE 151 A3092
BIBLIOG DIPLOM

B59
BALL M.M.,NATO AND THE EUROPEAN MOVEMENT. EUR+WWI USA+45 INT/ORG FORCES BAL/PWR EDU/PROP LEGIT REGION ATTIT ORD/FREE PWR...STAT OBS TIME/SEQ TREND CHARTS ORG/CHARTS STERTYP COLD/WAR EEC OEEC 20 NATO. PAGE 10 A0212
DELIB/GP STRUCT

B59
COUDENHOVE-KALERGI,FROM WAR TO PEACE. USA+45 USSR WOR+45 WOR-45 LAW INT/ORG NAT/G LEGIT COERCE LOVE ...POLICY PLURIST METH/CNCPT STERTYP TOT/POP UN 20 NATO. PAGE 31 A0636
FUT ORD/FREE

B59
GOULD L.P.,THE PRICE OF SURVIVAL. EUR+WWI SPACE USA+45 FORCES ECO/TAC NUC/PWR WAR ORD/FREE MARXISM ...IDEA/COMP 20 COLD/WAR NATO. PAGE 54 A1117
POLICY PROB/SOLV DIPLOM PEACE

B59
PEARSON L.B.,DIPLOMACY IN THE NUCLEAR AGE. USA+45 USSR INT/ORG PWR...TREND 20 NATO UN. PAGE 114 A2343
NUC/PWR PEACE POLICY DIPLOM

B59
ROBERTSON A.H.,EUROPEAN INSTITUTIONS: COOPERATION, INTEGRATION, UNIFICATION. EUR+WWI FINAN INT/ORG FORCES INT/TRADE TARIFFS 20 EEC EURATOM ECSC NATO TREATY. PAGE 122 A2496
ECO/DEV DIPLOM INDUS ECO/TAC

B59
TUNSTALL W.C.B.,THE COMMONWEALTH AND REGIONAL DEFENCE (PAMPHLET). UK LAW VOL/ASSN PLAN AGREE REGION WAR ORD/FREE 20 CMN/WLTH NATO SEATO TREATY. PAGE 146 A2977
INT/ORG FORCES DIPLOM

B59
WOLFERS A.,ALLIANCE POLICY IN THE COLD WAR. COM INT/ORG FORCES COLONIAL CONTROL NUC/PWR 20 NATO UN COLD/WAR. PAGE 166 A3384
DIPLOM DETER BAL/PWR

S59
KISSINGER H.A.,"THE SEARCH FOR STABILITY." COM GERMANY MOD/EUR USA+45 USA-45 USSR INT/ORG ARMS/CONT NUC/PWR ORD/FREE PWR COLD/WAR 20 NATO. PAGE 80 A1641
FUT ATTIT BAL/PWR

B60
BUCHAN A.,NATO IN THE 1960'S. EUR+WWI USA+45 WOR+45 INT/ORG ACT/RES PLAN LEGIT COERCE DETER ATTIT DRIVE RIGID/FLEX ORD/FREE...METH/CNCPT TIME/SEQ TREND GEN/LAWS COLD/WAR 20 NATO. PAGE 21 A0421
VOL/ASSN FORCES ARMS/CONT SOVEREIGN

B60
ENGEL J.,THE SECURITY OF THE FREE WORLD. USSR WOR+45 STRATA STRUCT ECO/DEV ECO/UNDEV INT/ORG DELIB/GP FORCES DOMIN LEGIT ADJUD EXEC ARMS/CONT COERCE...POLICY CONCPT NEW/IDEA TIME/SEQ GEN/LAWS COLD/WAR WORK UN 20 NATO. PAGE 42 A0851
COM TREND DIPLOM

B60
JACOBSON H.K.,AMERICAN FOREIGN POLICY. COM EUR+WWI USA+45 USA-45 ECO/DEV ECO/UNDEV INT/ORG NAT/G INT/TRADE EDU/PROP COLONIAL CHOOSE MARXISM 20 NATO. PAGE 72 A1485
POL/PAR PWR DIPLOM

B60
LE GHAIT E.,NO CARTE BLANCHE TO CAPRICORN; THE FOLLY OF NUCLEAR WAR. WOR+45 INT/ORG BAL/PWR DIPLOM RISK COERCE...CENSUS 20 NATO. PAGE 86 A1754
DETER NUC/PWR PLAN DECISION

B60
MONTGOMERY B.L.,AN APPROACH TO SANITY; A STUDY OF EAST-WEST RELATIONS. CONFER WAR EFFICIENCY ATTIT ...POLICY 20 NATO COLD/WAR KHRUSH/N. PAGE 103 A2113
DIPLOM INT/ORG BAL/PWR DETER

B60
TAYLOR M.D.,THE UNCERTAIN TRUMPET. USA+45 USSR WOR+45 INT/ORG NAT/G CONSULT DOMIN COERCE NUC/PWR WAR ATTIT ORD/FREE PWR...POLICY CONCPT TREND GEN/METH COLD/WAR UN NATO 20. PAGE 142 A2900
PLAN FORCES DIPLOM

B60
TURNER G.B.,NATIONAL SECURITY IN THE NUCLEAR AGE. KOREA USA+45 PLAN DIPLOM ARMS/CONT DETER WAR WEAPON ...BIBLIOG 20 COLD/WAR NATO. PAGE 146 A2982
NAT/G POLICY FORCES NUC/PWR

B60
US DEPARTMENT OF THE ARMY,DISARMAMENT: A BIBLIOGRAPHIC RECORD: 1916-1960. DETER WAR WEAPON PEACE 20 UN LEAGUE/NAT COLD/WAR NATO. PAGE 152 A3103
BIBLIOG/A ARMS/CONT NUC/PWR DIPLOM

B61
CONFERENCE ATLANTIC COMMUNITY,AN INTRODUCTORY BIBLIOGRAPHY. COM WOR+45 FORCES DIPLOM ECO/TAC WAR ...INT/LAW HIST/WRIT COLD/WAR NATO. PAGE 29 A0584
BIBLIOG/A CON/ANAL INT/ORG

B61
FLEMING D.F.,THE COLD WAR AND ITS ORIGINS: 1917-1950 (VOL. I). ASIA USSR WOR+45 WOR-45 TEC/DEV FOR/AID NUC/PWR REV WAR PEACE FASCISM...T 20 COLD/WAR NATO BERLIN/BLO. PAGE 46 A0947
DIPLOM MARXISM BAL/PWR

B61
KERTESZ S.D.,AMERICAN DIPLOMACY IN A NEW ERA. COM S/ASIA UK USA+45 FORCES PROB/SOLV BAL/PWR ECO/TAC ADMIN COLONIAL WAR PEACE ORD/FREE 20 NATO CONGRESS UN COLD/WAR. PAGE 78 A1601
ANTHOL DIPLOM TREND

B61
MORLEY L.,THE PATCHWORK HISTORY OF FOREIGN AID. KOREA/S USA+45 USSR LAW FINAN INT/ORG TEC/DEV BAL/PWR GIVE 20 COLD/WAR NATO. PAGE 104 A2144
FOR/AID ECO/UNDEV FORCES DIPLOM

B61
SCHMIDT H.,VERTEIDIGUNG ODER VERGELTUNG. COM CUBA GERMANY/W USSR FORCES DIPLOM ARMS/CONT DETER NUC/PWR...POLICY CHARTS HYPO/EXP SIMUL BIBLIOG 20
PLAN WAR BAL/PWR

NATO COLD/WAR. PAGE 128 A2630 — ORD/FREE

B61
SLESSOR J.,WHAT PRICE COEXISTENCE? COM INT/ORG NAT/G FORCES COLONIAL ARMS/CONT WAR...POLICY TREND 20 NATO COLD/WAR. PAGE 134 A2741 — DIPLOM PEACE WOR+45 NUC/PWR

S61
BURNET A.,"TOO MANY ALLIES." COM EUR+WWI UK WOR+45 WOR-45 ACT/RES PLAN DISPL PWR SKILL...TIME/SEQ 20 CMN/WLTH SEATO NATO CENTO. PAGE 22 A0438 — VOL/ASSN INT/ORG DIPLOM

S61
HAAS E.B.,"INTERNATIONAL INTEGRATION: THE EUROPEAN AND THE UNIVERSAL PROCESS." EUR+WWI FUT WOR+45 NAT/G EX/STRUC ATTIT DRIVE ORD/FREE PWR...CONCPT GEN/LAWS OEEC 20 NATO COUNCL/EUR. PAGE 59 A1207 — INT/ORG TREND REGION

S61
MIKSCHE F.O.,"DEFENSE ORGANIZATION FOR WESTERN EUROPE." USA+45 INT/ORG NAT/G VOL/ASSN ACT/RES DOMIN LEGIT COERCE ORD/FREE PWR...RELATIV TREND 20 NATO. PAGE 101 A2071 — EUR+WWI FORCES WEAPON NUC/PWR

B62
AIR FORCE ACADEMY LIBRARY,INTERNATIONAL ORGANIZATIONS AND MILITARY SECURITY SYSTEMS (PAMPHLET) (SPECIAL BIBLIOGRAPHY SERIES, NUMBER 25). DIPLOM FOR/AID INT/TRADE NUC/PWR PEACE 20 UN NATO OAS SEATO LEAGUE/NAT. PAGE 5 A0104 — BIBLIOG INT/ORG FORCES DETER

B62
CARDOZA M.H.,DIPLOMATS IN INTERNATIONAL COOPERATION: STEPCHILDREN OF THE FOREIGN SERVICE. EUR+WWI USA+45 NAT/G CONSULT ACT/RES EDU/PROP ROUTINE RIGID/FLEX KNOWL SKILL...SOC OBS TIME/SEQ EEC OEEC NATO 20. PAGE 24 A0480 — INT/ORG METH/CNCPT DIPLOM

B62
DOUGLAS W.O.,DEMOCRACY'S MANIFESTO. COM USA+45 ECO/UNDEV INT/ORG FORCES PLAN NEUTRAL TASK MARXISM ...JURID 20 NATO SEATO. PAGE 38 A0779 — DIPLOM POLICY NAT/G ORD/FREE

B62
MORGENSTERN O.,STRATEGIE - HEUTE (2ND ED.). USA+45 USSR ECO/DEV DELIB/GP WAR PEACE ORD/FREE...GOV/COMP NAT/COMP 20 COLD/WAR NATO. PAGE 104 A2134 — NUC/PWR DIPLOM FORCES TEC/DEV

B62
MULLEY F.W.,THE POLITICS OF WESTERN DEFENSE. EUR+WWI USA-45 WOR+45 VOL/ASSN EX/STRUC FORCES COERCE DETER PEACE ATTIT ORD/FREE PWR...RECORD TIME/SEQ CHARTS COLD/WAR 20 NATO. PAGE 106 A2168 — INT/ORG DELIB/GP NUC/PWR

B62
OSGOOD R.E.,NATO: THE ENTANGLING ALLIANCE. USA+45 WOR+45 VOL/ASSN FORCES TOP/EX PLAN DETER WEAPON DRIVE RIGID/FLEX ORD/FREE PWR...TREND 20 NATO. PAGE 112 A2301 — INT/ORG ARMS/CONT PEACE

B62
STEEL R.,THE END OF THE ALLIANCE. FRANCE FUT GERMANY/E GERMANY/W UK USA+45 NAT/G FORCES FOR/AID 20 NATO. PAGE 137 A2809 — EUR+WWI POLICY DIPLOM INT/ORG

B63
BELOFF M.,THE UNITED STATES AND THE UNITY OF EUROPE. EUR+WWI UK USA+45 WOR+45 VOL/ASSN DIPLOM REGION ATTIT PWR...CONCPT EEC OEEC 20 NATO. PAGE 13 A0261 — ECO/DEV INT/ORG

B63
BROEKMEIJER M.W.,DEVELOPING COUNTRIES AND NATO. USSR FORCES DIPLOM NUC/PWR WAR PEACE TOTALISM 20 NATO. PAGE 19 A0384 — ECO/UNDEV FOR/AID ORD/FREE NAT/G

B63
CERAMI C.A.,ALLIANCE BORN OF DANGER. EUR+WWI USA+45 USSR ECO/DEV INDUS VOL/ASSN ECO/TAC REGION ATTIT MARXISM ATLAN/ALL 20 NATO EEC. PAGE 25 A0514 — DIPLOM INT/ORG NAT/G POLICY

B63
ELLERT R.B.,NATO 'FAIR TRIAL' SAFEGUARDS: PRECURSOR TO AN INTERNATIONAL BILL OF PROCEDURAL RIGHTS. WOR+45 FORCES CRIME CIVMIL/REL ATTIT ORD/FREE 20 NATO. PAGE 41 A0841 — JURID INT/LAW INT/ORG CT/SYS

B63
KLEIMAN R.,ATLANTIC CRISIS; AMERICAN DIPLOMACY CONFRONTS A RESURGENT EUROPE. EUR+WWI USA+45 ECO/DEV AGRI NAT/G CHIEF FORCES PLAN LEAD ATTIT ...CONCPT 20 NATO KENNEDY/JF DEGAULLE/C EEC JOHNSON/LB. PAGE 80 A1648 — DIPLOM REGION POLICY

B63
STROMBERG R.N.,COLLECTIVE SECURITY AND AMERICAN FOREIGN POLICY FROM THE LEAGUE OF NATIONS TO NATO. USA+45 USA-45 WOR-45 INT/ORG VOL/ASSN EX/STRUC FORCES LEGIT ROUTINE DRIVE...CONCPT TREND UN LEAGUE/NAT 20 NATO. PAGE 139 A2851 — ORD/FREE TIME/SEQ DIPLOM

S63
EMERSON R.,"THE ATLANTIC COMMUNITY AND THE EMERGING COUNTRIES." FUT WOR+45 ECO/DEV ECO/UNDEV R+D NAT/G DELIB/GP BAL/PWR ECO/TAC EDU/PROP ROUTINE ORD/FREE PWR WEALTH...POLICY CONCPT TREND GEN/METH EEC 20 NATO. PAGE 42 A0848 — ATTIT INT/TRADE

S63
KINTNER W.R.,"THE PROJECTED EUROPEAN UNION AND AMERICAN RESPONSIBILITIES." EUR+WWI USA+45 STRATA INT/ORG NAT/G DOMIN DETER NUC/PWR ATTIT ORD/FREE PWR 20 NATO. PAGE 79 A1628 — FUT FORCES DIPLOM REGION

S63
MULLEY F.W.,"NUCLEAR WEAPONS: CHALLENGE TO NATIONAL SOVEREIGNTY." EUR+WWI FRANCE UK USA+45 VOL/ASSN EX/STRUC FORCES TOP/EX ACT/RES REGION DRIVE PWR 20 NATO DEGAULLE/C. PAGE 106 A2169 — INT/ORG ATTIT DIPLOM NUC/PWR

S63
STANLEY T.W.,"DECENTRALIZING NUCLEAR CONTROL IN NATO." EUR+WWI USA+45 ELITES FORCES ACT/RES ATTIT ORD/FREE PWR...NEW/IDEA HYPO/EXP TOT/POP 20 NATO. PAGE 137 A2805 — INT/ORG EX/STRUC NUC/PWR

C63
CHARLETON W.G.,"THE REVOLUTION IN AMERICAN FOREIGN POLICY." COM PROB/SOLV FOR/AID DOMIN COLONIAL NEUTRAL DETER WAR ISOLAT NAT/LISM...BIBLIOG 19/20 UN COLD/WAR NATO. PAGE 26 A0523 — DIPLOM INT/ORG BAL/PWR

B64
COTTRELL A.J.,THE POLITICS OF THE ATLANTIC ALLIANCE. EUR+WWI USA+45 INT/ORG NAT/G DELIB/GP EX/STRUC BAL/PWR DIPLOM REGION DETER ATTIT ORD/FREE ...CONCPT RECORD GEN/LAWS GEN/METH NATO 20. PAGE 31 A0632 — VOL/ASSN FORCES

B64
ECONOMIDES C.P.,LE POUVOIR DE DECISION DES ORGANISATIONS INTERNATIONALES EUROPEENNES. DIPLOM DOMIN INGP/REL EFFICIENCY...INT/LAW JURID 20 NATO OEEC EEC COUNCL/EUR EURATOM. PAGE 40 A0821 — INT/ORG PWR DECISION GP/COMP

B64
FREYMOND J.,WESTERN EUROPE SINCE THE WAR. COM EUR+WWI USA+45 DIPLOM...BIBLIOG 20 NATO UN EEC. PAGE 49 A1001 — INT/ORG POLICY ECO/DEV ECO/TAC

B64
KAUFMANN W.W.,THE MC NAMARA STRATEGY. TOP/EX INSPECT BAL/PWR DIPLOM CONTROL DETER GUERRILLA NUC/PWR WEAPON COST PWR...METH/COMP 20 MCNAMARA/R KENNEDY/JF JOHNSON/LB NATO DEPT/DEFEN. PAGE 77 A1572 — FORCES WAR PLAN PROB/SOLV

B64
KENNEDY J.F.,THE BURDEN AND THE GLORY. FUT USA+45 TEC/DEV ECO/TAC EDU/PROP ARMS/CONT MURDER RACE/REL PEACE...ANTHOL 20 KENNEDY/JF COLD/WAR NATO PRESIDENT. PAGE 78 A1593 — ADMIN POLICY GOV/REL DIPLOM

B64
KRAUSE L.B.,THE COMMON MARKET: PROGRESS AND CONTROVERSY. EUR+WWI UK ECO/DEV REGION...ANTHOL NATO EEC. PAGE 82 A1678 — DIPLOM MARKET INT/TRADE INT/ORG

B64
US HOUSE COMM FOREIGN AFFAIRS,HEARINGS ON H.R. 10502 TO AMEND FURTHER THE FOREIGN ASSISTANCE ACT OF 1961. AFR ASIA L/A+17C INT/ORG CONSULT DELIB/GP TEC/DEV ECO/TAC EDU/PROP CONFER 20 UN NATO CONGRESS AID. PAGE 153 A3130 — FOR/AID DIPLOM ORD/FREE ECO/UNDEV

S64
RUBINSTEIN A.Z.,"THE SOVIET IMAGE OF WESTERN EUROPE." COM EUR+WWI FRANCE GERMANY GERMANY/W USA+45 USSR INT/ORG NAT/G VOL/ASSN FORCES TOP/EX BAL/PWR EDU/PROP ORD/FREE PWR...MYTH RECORD NATO EEC 20. PAGE 125 A2564 — RIGID/FLEX ATTIT

B65
ADENAUER K.,MEMOIRS 1945-53. EUR+WWI GERMANY/W ECO/DEV CHIEF FORCES ECO/TAC WAR GOV/REL PWR SOVEREIGN 20 NATO ADENAUER/K. PAGE 4 A0088 — BIOG DIPLOM NAT/G PERS/REL

B65
CALLEO D.P.,EUROPE'S FUTURE: THE GRAND ALTERNATIVES. UK INT/ORG DIPLOM PWR SOVEREIGN ...CONCPT IDEA/COMP NAT/COMP BIBLIOG 20 EEC EUROPE DEGAULLE/C NATO. PAGE 23 A0468 — FUT EUR+WWI FEDERAL NAT/LISM

B65
MIDDLETON D.,CRISIS IN THE WEST. EUR+WWI FUT WOR+45 CHIEF PLAN ECO/TAC LEAD REGION NUC/PWR NAT/LISM MARXISM 20 COLD/WAR NATO EEC. PAGE 101 A2068 — INT/ORG DIPLOM NAT/G POLICY

B65
MOSKOWITZ H.,US SECURITY, ARMS CONTROL, AND DISARMAMENT 1961-1965. FORCES DIPLOM DETER WAR WEAPON...CHARTS 20 UN COLD/WAR NATO. PAGE 105 A2154 — BIBLIOG/A ARMS/CONT NUC/PWR PEACE

B65
US DEPARTMENT OF DEFENSE,US SECURITY ARMS CONTROL, AND DISARMAMENT 1961-1965 (PAMPHLET). CHINA/COM COM GERMANY/W ISRAEL SPACE USA+45 USSR WOR+45 FORCES EDU/PROP DETER EQUILIB PEACE ALL/VALS...GOV/COMP 20 NATO. PAGE 151 A3077 — BIBLIOG/A ARMS/CONT NUC/PWR DIPLOM

B65
US DEPARTMENT OF THE ARMY,NUCLEAR WEAPONS AND THE ATLANTIC ALLIANCE: A BIBLIOGRAPHIC SURVEY. ASIA COM EUR+WWI USA+45 FORCES DIPLOM WEAPON...STAT 20 NATO. PAGE 152 A3108 — BIBLIOG/A ARMS/CONT NUC/PWR BAL/PWR

S65
BROWN S.,"AN ALTERNATIVE TO THE GRAND DESIGN." EUR+WWI FUT USA+45 INT/ORG NAT/G EX/STRUC FORCES CREATE BAL/PWR DOMIN RIGID/FLEX ORD/FREE PWR ...NEW/IDEA RECORD EEC NATO 20. PAGE 20 A0407
VOL/ASSN CONCPT DIPLOM

S65
SPAAK P.H.,"THE SEARCH FOR CONSENSUS: A NEW EFFORT TO BUILD EUROPE." FRANCE GERMANY ECO/DEV NAT/G CONSULT FORCES PLAN EDU/PROP REGION CONSEN ATTIT ...SOC METH/CNCPT OBS TREND EEC NATO WORK 20. PAGE 135 A2770
EUR+WWI INT/ORG

C65
US AIR FORCE ACADEMY,"AMERICAN DEFENSE POLICY." COM INT/ORG TEC/DEV FOR/AID ARMS/CONT DETER NUC/PWR ...POLICY DECISION CONCPT ANTHOL BIBLIOG/A 20 COLD/WAR NATO. PAGE 149 A3054
PLAN FORCES WAR COERCE

B66
BEAUFRE A.,NATO AND EUROPE. WOR+45 PLAN CONFER EXEC NUC/PWR ATTIT...POLICY 20 NATO EUROPE. PAGE 12 A0243
INT/ORG DETER DIPLOM ADMIN

B66
OBERMANN E.,VERTEIDIGUNG PER FREIHEIT. GERMANY/W WOR+45 INT/ORG COERCE NUC/PWR WEAPON MARXISM 20 UN NATO WARSAW/P TREATY. PAGE 111 A2273
FORCES ORD/FREE WAR PEACE

B66
SCHWARZ U.,AMERICAN STRATEGY: A NEW PERSPECTIVE. USA+45 USA-45 INT/ORG TEC/DEV BAL/PWR DIPLOM LEAD ARMS/CONT DETER NUC/PWR WAR 20 NATO. PAGE 130 A2659
NAT/G POLICY FORCES PWR

B66
SPICER K.,A SAMARITAN STATE? AFR CANADA INDIA PAKISTAN UK USA+45 FINAN INDUS PRODUC...CHARTS 20 NATO. PAGE 136 A2787
DIPLOM FOR/AID ECO/DEV ADMIN

B66
US HOUSE COMM FOREIGN AFFAIRS,HEARINGS ON HR 12449 A BILL TO AMEND FURTHER THE FOREIGN ASSISTANCE ACT OF 1961. AFR ASIA L/A+17C USA+45 VIETNAM INT/ORG TEC/DEV INT/TRADE ATTIT ORD/FREE 20 UN NATO CONGRESS AID. PAGE 154 A3132
FOR/AID ECO/TAC ECO/UNDEV DIPLOM

B66
US SENATE COMM ON FOREIGN REL,UNITED STATES POLICY TOWARD EUROPE (AND RELATED MATTERS). COM EUR+WWI GERMANY PROB/SOLV REGION NUC/PWR WAR NAT/LISM PEACE PWR...NAT/COMP 20 NATO CONGRESS DEGAULLE/C. PAGE 156 A3184
DIPLOM INT/ORG POLICY WOR+45

S66
DUROSELLE J.B.,"THE FUTURE OF THE ATLANTIC COMMUNITY." EUR+WWI USA+45 USSR NAT/G CAP/ISM REGION DETER NUC/PWR ATTIT MARXISM...INT/LAW 20 NATO. PAGE 40 A0811
FUT DIPLOM MYTH POLICY

S66
ORVIK N.,"NATO: THE ROLE OF THE SMALL MEMBERS." EUR+WWI FUT USA+45 CONSULT FORCES PROB/SOLV ARMS/CONT DETER NUC/PWR PWR 20 NATO. PAGE 112 A2298
NAT/G DIPLOM INT/ORG POLICY

S66
SHERMAN M.,"GUARANTEES AND NUCLEAR SPREAD." USA+45 WOR+45 INT/ORG PLAN DETER WAR ORD/FREE 20 NATO. PAGE 132 A2700
DIPLOM POLICY NAT/G NUC/PWR

C66
BLAISDELL D.C.,"INTERNATIONAL ORGANIZATION." FUT WOR+45 ECO/DEV DELIB/GP FORCES EFFICIENCY PEACE ORD/FREE...INT/LAW 20 UN LEAGUE/NAT NATO. PAGE 15 A0304
BIBLIOG INT/ORG DIPLOM ARMS/CONT

C66
KULSKI W.W.,"DEGAULLE AND THE WORLD: THE FOREIGN POLICY OF THE FIFTH FRENCH REPUBLIC." FRANCE ECO/UNDEV POL/PAR BAL/PWR DETER NUC/PWR ATTIT PWR ...RECORD BIBLIOG DEGAULLE NATO EEC. PAGE 83 A1694
POLICY SOVEREIGN PERSON DIPLOM

B67
HALPERIN M.H.,CONTEMPORARY MILITARY STRATEGY. ASIA CHINA/COM USA+45 USSR INT/ORG FORCES ACT/RES PLAN TEC/DEV BAL/PWR COERCE WAR...METH/COMP BIBLIOG 20 NATO. PAGE 60 A1240
DIPLOM NUC/PWR DETER ARMS/CONT

B67
ISENBERG I.,FRANCE UNDER DE GAULLE (THE REFERENCE SHELF VOL. 39 NO. 1). EUR+WWI FRANCE ECO/DEV ...BIBLIOG 20 DEGAULLE/C NATO EEC. PAGE 72 A1469
ATTIT DIPLOM POLICY CHIEF

B67
PADELFORD N.J.,THE DYNAMICS OF INTERNATIONAL POLITICS (2ND ED.). WOR+45 LAW INT/ORG FORCES TEC/DEV REGION NAT/LISM PEACE ATTIT PWR ALL/IDEOS UN COLD/WAR NATO TREATY. PAGE 113 A2314
DIPLOM NAT/G POLICY DECISION

B67
ROACH J.R.,THE UNITED STATES AND THE ATLANTIC COMMUNITY; ISSUES AND PROSPECTS. WOR+45 TEC/DEV ECO/TAC COLONIAL REGION PEACE ROLE...ANTHOL NATO COLD/WAR EEC. PAGE 121 A2491
INT/ORG POLICY ADJUST DIPLOM

L67
BODENHEIMER S.J.,"THE 'POLITICAL UNION' DEBATE IN EUROPE* A CASE STUDY IN INTERGOVERNMENTAL DIPLOMACY." EUR+WWI FUT NAT/G FORCES PLAN DEBATE SOVEREIGN...CONCPT PREDICT EEC NATO. PAGE 16 A0326
DIPLOM REGION INT/ORG

S67
ANTHEM T.,"CYPRUS* WHAT NOW?" CYPRUS GREECE TURKEY NAT/G BUDGET MAJORITY 20 NATO. PAGE 8 A0165
DIPLOM COERCE INT/TRADE ADJUD

S67
DEUTSCH K.W.,"ARMS CONTROL AND EUROPEAN UNITY* THE NEXT TEN YEARS." USA+45 ELITES NAT/G BAL/PWR DIPLOM NUC/PWR...INT KNO/TEST NATO EEC. PAGE 36 A0742
ARMS/CONT PEACE REGION PLAN

S67
KRUSCHE H.,"THE STRIVING OF THE KIESINGER-STRAUS GOVERNMENT FOR NUCLEAR WEAPONS IS A THREAT TO EUROPEAN SECURITY." EUR+WWI GERMANY BAL/PWR SANCTION WEAPON PEACE ORD/FREE...MARXIST 20 NATO COLD/WAR. PAGE 82 A1688
ARMS/CONT INT/ORG NUC/PWR DIPLOM

S67
SOMMER T.,"BONN CHANGES COURSE." GERMANY/W NAT/G POL/PAR PROB/SOLV NAT/LISM 20 NATO BERLIN/BLO. PAGE 135 A2766
DIPLOM BAL/PWR INT/ORG

S67
STEEL R.,"BEYOND THE POWER BLOCS." USA+45 USSR ECO/UNDEV NEUTRAL NUC/PWR NAT/LISM ATTIT...GEOG NATO WARSAW/P COLD/WAR. PAGE 137 A2811
DIPLOM TREND BAL/PWR PLAN

NATURL/LAW....NATURAL LAW

B16
PUFENDORF S.,LAW OF NATURE AND OF NATIONS (ABRIDGED). UNIV LAW NAT/G DIPLOM AGREE WAR PERSON ALL/VALS PWR...POLICY 18 DEITY NATURL/LAW. PAGE 118 A2416
CONCPT INT/LAW SECT MORAL

B53
MARITAIN J.,L'HOMME ET L'ETAT. SECT DIPLOM GP/REL PEACE ORD/FREE...IDEA/COMP 17/20 CHURCH/STA NATURL/LAW. PAGE 95 A1940
CONCPT NAT/G SOVEREIGN COERCE

B96
DE VATTEL E.,THE LAW OF NATIONS. AGRI FINAN CHIEF DIPLOM INT/TRADE AGREE OWN ALL/VALS MORAL ORD/FREE SOVEREIGN...GEN/LAWS 18 NATURL/LAW WOLFF/C. PAGE 35 A0714
LAW CONCPT NAT/G INT/LAW

NAVAHO....NAVAHO INDIANS

NAVAL/RES....OFFICE OF NAVAL RESEARCH

NAVILLE A. A2205

NAVY....NAVY (ALL NATIONS)

B36
METZ I.,DIE DEUTSCHE FLOTTE IN DER ENGLISCHEN PRESSE, DER NAVY SCARE VOM WINTER 1904/05. GERMANY UK FORCES DIPLOM WAR 20 NAVY. PAGE 100 A2047
EDU/PROP ATTIT DOMIN PRESS

B39
FULLER G.H.,A SELECTED LIST OF REFERENCES ON THE EXPANSION OF THE US NAVY, 1933-1939 (PAMPHLET). MOD/EUR USA-45 NAT/G PLAN DIPLOM DOMIN RISK ARMS/CONT EQUILIB PWR 20 NAVY. PAGE 50 A1019
BIBLIOG FORCES WEAPON WAR

B66
DAVIS V.,POSTWAR DEFENSE POLICY AND THE US NAVY, 1943-1946. USA+45 DIPLOM CONFER LEAD ATTIT...POLICY IDEA/COMP 20 NAVY. PAGE 34 A0692
FORCES PLAN PROB/SOLV CIVMIL/REL

NAWAS M.K. A2734

NAZI....NAZI MOVEMENT (ALL NATIONS); SEE ALSO GERMANY, NAT/LISM, FASCIST

B35
SIMONDS F.H.,THE GREAT POWERS IN WORLD POLITICS. FRANCE GERMANY UK WOR-45 INT/ORG NAT/G ARMS/CONT PEACE FASCISM...POLICY GEOG 20 DEPRESSION NAZI. PAGE 133 A2718
DIPLOM WEALTH WAR

B38
RAPPARD W.E.,THE CRISIS OF DEMOCRACY. EUR+WWI UNIV WOR-45 CULTURE SOCIETY ECO/DEV INT/ORG POL/PAR ACT/RES EDU/PROP EXEC CHOOSE ATTIT ALL/VALS...SOC OBS HIST/WRIT TIME/SEQ LEAGUE/NAT NAZI TOT/POP 20. PAGE 119 A2449
NAT/G CONCPT

B42
BORNSTEIN J.,ACTION AGAINST THE ENEMY'S MIND. EUR+WWI GERMANY USA-45 DIPLOM DOMIN PRESS LEAD GP/REL DISCRIM PERCEPT FASCISM MARXISM 20 JEWS NAZI ANTI/SEMIT. PAGE 17 A0343
EDU/PROP PSY WAR CONTROL

L42
SHOTWELL J.,"LESSON OF THE LAST WORLD WAR." EUR+WWI MOD/EUR USA-45 SOCIETY ECO/UNDEV INDUS VOL/ASSN CONSULT ACT/RES CREATE CAP/ISM INT/TRADE DRIVE ALL/VALS...CONCPT NEW/IDEA SELF/OBS GEN/LAWS
INT/ORG ORD/FREE

LEAGUE/NAT NAZI 20. PAGE 132 A2708

B43
US DEPARTMENT OF STATE,NATIONAL SOCIALISM; BASIC PRINCIPLES, THEIR APPLICATION BY THE NAZI PARTY'S FOREIGN ORGANIZATION... GERMANY WOR-45 ECO/DEV LOC/G POL/PAR FORCES DIPLOM DOMIN COLONIAL ARMS/CONT COERCE NAT/LISM PWR 20 NAZI. PAGE 151 A3081
FASCISM SOCISM NAT/G TOTALISM

B47
GORDON D.L.,THE HIDDEN WEAPON: THE STORY OF ECONOMIC WARFARE. EUR+WWI USA-45 LAW FINAN INDUS NAT/G CONSULT FORCES PLAN DOMIN PWR WEALTH ...INT/LAW CONCPT OBS TOT/POP NAZI 20. PAGE 54 A1112
INT/ORG ECO/TAC INT/TRADE WAR

B48
CHURCHILL W.,THE GATHERING STORM. UK WOR-45 INT/ORG NAT/G FORCES TOP/EX DIPLOM ECO/TAC COERCE ATTIT ORD/FREE PWR WEALTH...POLICY SELF/OBS RECORD NAZI PARLIAMENT 20. PAGE 26 A0538
BIOG

B50
CHURCHILL W.,TRIUMPH AND TRAGEDY. UK WOR-45 INT/ORG NAT/G DELIB/GP FORCES TOP/EX DIPLOM COERCE CHOOSE ATTIT ORD/FREE PWR WEALTH...SELF/OBS CHARTS NAZI 20. PAGE 26 A0539
BIOG PEACE WAR

S58
ROTHFELS H.,"THE GERMAN RESISTANCE IN ITS INTERNATIONAL ASPECTS" (BMR)" EUR+WWI GERMANY UNIV CHIEF DIPLOM WAR NAT/LISM ATTIT...POLICY 20 HITLER/A NAZI. PAGE 124 A2548
VOL/ASSN MORAL FASCISM CIVMIL/REL

B60
CARNEGIE ENDOWMENT INT. PEACE,PERSPECTIVES ON PEACE - 1910-1960. WOR+45 WOR-45 INTELL INT/ORG CONSULT ACT/RES EDU/PROP ATTIT KNOWL ORD/FREE...TIME/SEQ TREND EEC OAS UNESCO NAZI 20. PAGE 24 A0489
FUT CONCPT ARMS/CONT PEACE

B60
EINSTEIN A.,EINSTEIN ON PEACE. FUT WOR+45 WOR-45 SOCIETY NAT/G PLAN BAL/PWR CAP/ISM DIPLOM ARMS/CONT DETER NAT/LISM...POLICY RELATIV HUM PHIL/SCI CONCPT BIOG COLD/WAR LEAGUE/NAT NAZI. PAGE 41 A0829
INT/ORG ATTIT NUC/PWR PEACE

B60
PRITTIE T.,GERMANY DIVIDED: THE LEGACY OF THE NAZI ERA. EUR+WWI GERMANY RACE/REL SUPEGO...PSY AUD/VIS BIBLIOG/A 20 NAZI. PAGE 118 A2414
STERTYP PERSON ATTIT DIPLOM

B61
SCHONBRUNN G.,WELTKRIEGE UND REVOLUTIONEN 1914-1945. USSR DIPLOM TOTALISM ORD/FREE 20 TREATY WWI NAZI. PAGE 129 A2643
WAR REV FASCISM SOCISM

B61
TETENS T.H.,THE NEW GERMANY AND THE OLD NAZIS. EUR+WWI GERMANY/W USA+45 NAT/G CRIME CHOOSE RACE/REL TOTALISM AGE/Y ATTIT 20 JEWS NAZI ADENAUER/K. PAGE 142 A2905
FASCISM DIPLOM FOR/AID POL/PAR

B62
WOETZEL R.K.,THE NURENBERG TRIALS IN INTERNATIONAL LAW. CHRIST-17C MOD/EUR WOR+45 SOCIETY NAT/G DELIB/GP DOMIN LEGIT ROUTINE ATTIT DRIVE PERSON SUPEGO MORAL ORD/FREE...POLICY MAJORIT JURID PSY SOC SELF/OBS RECORD NAZI TOT/POP. PAGE 166 A3376
INT/ORG ADJUD WAR

S62
GREEN L.C.,"POLITICAL OFFENSES, WAR CRIMES AND EXTRADITION." WOR+45 YUGOSLAVIA INT/ORG LEGIT ROUTINE WAR ORD/FREE SOVEREIGN...JURID NAZI 20 INTERPOL. PAGE 55 A1138
LAW CONCPT INT/LAW

B65
SMITH A.L. JR.,THE DEUTSCHTUM OF NAZI GERMANY AND THE UNITED STATES. GERMANY USA-45 DIPLOM ATTIT FASCISM...BIBLIOG 20 MIGRATION NAZI. PAGE 134 A2744
INGP/REL NAT/LISM STRANGE DELIB/GP

NCC....NATIONAL COUNCIL OF CHURCHES

NE/WIN....NE WIN

NEA....NATIONAL EDUCATION ASSOCIATION

NEAL F.W. A2206,A2207,A2208

NEALE A.D. A2209

NEAR EAST....SEE MEDIT-7, ISLAM

NEARING S. A2210

NEBRASKA....NEBRASKA

NEFF J.C. A1216

NEG/INCOME....NEGATIVE INCOME TAX

NEGRITO....NEGRITO TRIBE, PHILIPPINES

NEGRO....NEGRO; SEE ALSO BLACK/PWR

NCO
CARRINGTON C.E.,THE COMMONWEALTH IN AFRICA (PAMPHLET). UK STRUCT NAT/G COLONIAL REPRESENT GOV/REL RACE/REL NAT/LISM...MAJORIT 20 EEC NEGRO COLD/WAR. PAGE 25 A0500
ECO/UNDEV AFR DIPLOM PLAN

B02
MOREL E.D.,AFFAIRS OF WEST AFRICA. UK FINAN INDUS FAM KIN SECT CHIEF WORKER DIPLOM RACE/REL LITERACY HEALTH...CHARTS 18/20 AFRICA/W NEGRO. PAGE 104 A2129
COLONIAL ADMIN AFR

B30
SMUTS J.C.,AFRICA AND SOME WORLD PROBLEMS. RHODESIA SOUTH/AFR CULTURE ECO/UNDEV INDUS INT/ORG SECT PROB/SOLV REGION GOV/REL DISCRIM ATTIT 19/20 LEAGUE/NAT LIVNGSTN/D NEGRO. PAGE 134 A2748
LEGIS AFR COLONIAL RACE/REL

B36
THWAITE D.,THE SEETHING AFRICAN POT: A STUDY OF BLACK NATIONALISM 1882-1935. ETHIOPIA SECT VOL/ASSN COERCE GUERRILLA MURDER DISCRIM MARXISM...PSY TIME/SEQ 18/20 NEGRO. PAGE 144 A2939
NAT/LISM AFR RACE/REL DIPLOM

B51
BISSAINTHE M.,DICTIONNAIRE DE BIBLIOGRAPHIE HAITIENNE. HAITI ELITES AGRI LEGIS DIPLOM INT/TRADE WRITING ORD/FREE CATHISM...ART/METH GEOG 19/20 NEGRO TREATY. PAGE 15 A0295
BIBLIOG L/A+17C SOCIETY NAT/G

B58
GROBLER J.H.,AFRICA'S DESTINY. AFR EUR+WWI SOUTH/AFR UK USA+45 ELITES KIN LOC/G DIPLOM DISCRIM ATTIT CONSERVE MARXISM 20 ROOSEVLT/T NEGRO. PAGE 57 A1168
POLICY ORD/FREE COLONIAL CONSTN

B59
SHANNON D.A.,THE DECLINE OF AMERICAN COMMUNISM; A HISTORY OF THE COMMUNIST PARTY OF THE UNITED STATES SINCE 1945. USA+45 LAW SOCIETY LABOR NAT/G WORKER DIPLOM EDU/PROP LEAD...POLICY BIBLIOG 20 KHRUSH/N NEGRO AFL/CIO COLD/WAR COM/PARTY. PAGE 131 A2692
MARXISM POL/PAR ATTIT POPULISM

B60
RITNER P.,THE DEATH OF AFRICA. USA+45 ECO/UNDEV DIPLOM ECO/TAC REGION RACE/REL NAT/LISM ORD/FREE ...POLICY 20 NEGRO. PAGE 121 A2485
AFR SOCIETY FUT TASK

B61
CAMERON J.,THE AFRICAN REVOLUTION. AFR UK ECO/UNDEV POL/PAR REGION RACE/REL DISCRIM PWR CONSERVE ...CONCPT SOC/INTEG 20 NEGRO. PAGE 23 A0472
REV COLONIAL ORD/FREE DIPLOM

B62
BUCHMANN J.,L'AFRIQUE NOIRE INDEPENDANTE. POL/PAR DIPLOM COLONIAL PARTIC CHOOSE GP/REL ATTIT ORD/FREE WEALTH NEGRO. PAGE 21 A0426
AFR NAT/LISM DECISION

B63
ELLENDER A.J.,A REPORT ON UNITED STATES FOREIGN OPERATIONS IN AFRICA. SOUTH/AFR USA+45 STRATA EXTR/IND FORCES RACE/REL ISOLAT SOVEREIGN...CHARTS 20 NEGRO. PAGE 41 A0840
FOR/AID DIPLOM WEALTH ECO/UNDEV

B63
JUDD P.,AFRICAN INDEPENDENCE: THE EXPLODING EMERGENCE OF THE NEW AFRICAN NATIONS. AFR UK LAW CONSTN CULTURE KIN DIPLOM ATTIT...CHARTS BIBLIOG 20 UN DEGAULLE/C NEGRO THIRD/WRLD. PAGE 75 A1542
ORD/FREE POLICY DOMIN LOC/G

B64
LOCKHART W.B.,CASES AND MATERIALS ON CONSTITUTIONAL RIGHTS AND LIBERTIES. USA+45 FORCES LEGIS DIPLOM PRESS CONTROL CRIME WAR PWR...AUD/VIS T WORSHIP 20 NEGRO. PAGE 90 A1849
ORD/FREE CONSTN NAT/G

B64
PERKINS D.,THE AMERICAN DEMOCRACY: ITS RISE TO POWER. ASIA USSR LAW CULTURE FINAN EDU/PROP COLONIAL CHOOSE...POLICY CHARTS BIBLIOG WORSHIP PRESIDENT 15/20 NEGRO. PAGE 115 A2362
LOC/G ECO/TAC WAR DIPLOM

B65
DU BOIS W.E.B.,THE WORLD AND AFRICA. USA+45 CAP/ISM DISCRIM STRANGE SOCISM...TIME/SEQ TREND IDEA/COMP 19/20 NEGRO. PAGE 39 A0789
AFR DIPLOM COLONIAL CULTURE

B65
LEISS A.C.,APARTHEID AND UNITED NATIONS COLLECTIVE MEASURES. SOUTH/AFR ECO/UNDEV EXTR/IND FORCES WORKER ECO/TAC FOR/AID INT/TRADE WEALTH...TREND CHARTS 20 UN NEGRO. PAGE 86 A1770
DISCRIM RACE/REL STRATA DIPLOM

B65
MUNGER E.S.,NOTES ON THE FORMATION OF SOUTH AFRICAN FOREIGN POLICY. ACADEM POL/PAR SECT CHIEF DELIB/GP FORCES LEGIS PRESS ATTIT...TREND 20 NEGRO. PAGE 106 A2170
AFR DOMIN POLICY DIPLOM

B65
SANDERSON G.N.,ENGLAND, EUROPE, AND THE UPPER NILE 1882-1899. ISLAM MOD/EUR UAR UK CHIEF...POLICY CHARTS BIBLIOG/A 19 ARABS NEGRO. PAGE 127 A2600
AFR DIPLOM COLONIAL

B65
SPENCE J.E.,REPUBLIC UNDER PRESSURE: A STUDY OF SOUTH AFRICAN FOREIGN POLICY. SOUTH/AFR ADMIN COLONIAL GOV/REL RACE/REL DISCRIM NAT/LISM ATTIT ROLE...TREND 20 NEGRO. PAGE 136 A2783
DIPLOM POLICY AFR

B66
KANET R.E.,THE SOVIET UNION AND SUB-SAHARAN AFRICA:
DIPLOM

COMMUNIST POLICY TOWARD AFRICA, 1917-1965. AFR USSR ECO/UNDEV TEC/DEV EDU/PROP TASK DISCRIM PEACE WEALTH ALL/IDEOS...CHARTS BIBLIOG SOC/INTEG 19/20 NEGRO UN INTERVENT. PAGE 76 A1555
ECO/TAC MARXISM

B66
LENGYEL E.,AFRICA: PAST, PRESENT, AND FUTURE. FUT SOUTH/AFR COLONIAL RACE/REL SOVEREIGN...GEOG AUD/VIS CHARTS T 20 CONGO/LEOP NEGRO. PAGE 87 A1771
AFR CONSTN ECO/UNDEV

B66
MULLER C.F.J.,A SELECT BIBLIOGRAPHY OF SOUTH AFRICAN HISTORY; A GUIDE FOR HISTORICAL RESEARCH. SOUTH/AFR UK LAW CONSTN SOCIETY STRUCT AGRI SECT DIPLOM COLONIAL LEAD RACE/REL...POLICY 17/20 NEGRO. PAGE 106 A2167
BIBLIOG AFR NAT/G

NEHEMKIS P. A2211

NEHRU J. A2212,A2213

NEHRU/J....JAWAHARLAL NEHRU

B57
NEHRU J.,MILITARY ALLIANCE (PAMPHLET). INDIA WOR+45 NAT/G PLAN DETER NUC/PWR WAR...POLICY ANTHOL NEHRU/J SEATO UN. PAGE 108 A2212
INT/ORG DIPLOM FORCES PEACE

B60
MC CLELLAN G.S.,INDIA. CHINA/COM INDIA CONSTN ELITES STRATA AGRI POL/PAR FOR/AID ARMS/CONT REV MARXISM...CENSUS BIBLIOG 20 COLD/WAR GANDHI/M NEHRU/J. PAGE 97 A1990
DIPLOM NAT/G SOCIETY ECO/UNDEV

B63
THIEN T.T.,INDIA AND SOUTHEAST ASIA 1947-1960. COM INDIA S/ASIA SECT DELIB/GP FOR/AID RACE/REL NAT/LISM SOCISM...CHARTS BIBLIOG 20 UN NEHRU/J TREATY. PAGE 143 A2917
DRIVE DIPLOM POLICY

B66
TINKER H.,SOUTH ASIA. UK LAW ECO/UNDEV AGRI ACADEM SECT DIPLOM EDU/PROP REV WEALTH ALL/IDEOS...CHARTS BIBLIOG GANDHI/M NEHRU/J. PAGE 144 A2945
S/ASIA COLONIAL TREND

B66
TYSON G.,NEHRU: THE YEARS OF POWER. INDIA UK STRATA ECO/UNDEV FINAN SECT TASK WAR ORD/FREE MARXISM ...POLICY BIBLIOG 20 NEHRU/J. PAGE 146 A2985
CHIEF PWR DIPLOM NAT/G

NEHRU/PM....PANDIT MOTILAL NEHRU

B61
PANIKKAR K.M.,THE VOICE OF FREEDOM: SELECTED SPEECHES OF PANDIT MOTILAL NEHRU. INDIA UK CONSTN FINAN FORCES LEGIS DIPLOM TAX COLONIAL...POLICY MAJORIT ANTHOL 20 NEHRU/PM. PAGE 114 A2331
NAT/LISM ORD/FREE CHIEF NAT/G

NEIDLE A.F. A2214

NEIGH....NEIGHBORHOOD

B40
BOGGS S.W.,INTERNATIONAL BOUNDARIES. WOR-45 SOCIETY ECO/DEV INT/ORG NAT/G NEIGH LEGIT PERSON ORD/FREE PWR...POLICY GEOG MYTH LEAGUE/NAT 20. PAGE 16 A0329
ATTIT CONCPT NAT/LISM

B47
NIEBUHR R.,THE CHILDREN OF LIGHT AND THE CHILDREN OF DARKNESS: A VINDICATION OF DEMOCRACY AND CRITIQUE OF TRADITIONAL DEFENSE. UNIV STRUCT NAT/G SECT INGP/REL OWN PEACE ORD/FREE MARXISM ...IDEA/COMP GEN/LAWS 20 CHRISTIAN. PAGE 109 A2235
POPULISM DIPLOM NEIGH GP/REL

B59
CHANDLER E.H.S.,THE HIGH TOWER OF REFUGE: THE INSPIRING STORY OF REFUGEE RELIEF THROUGHOUT THE WORLD. WOR+45 NEIGH SECT WORKER PROB/SOLV DIPLOM ECO/TAC EDU/PROP COST HABITAT. PAGE 25 A0519
GIVE WEALTH STRANGE INT/ORG

B60
STEVENSON A.E.,PUTTING FIRST THINGS FIRST. USA+45 INT/ORG NEIGH FOR/AID DISCRIM...ANTHOL 20. PAGE 138 A2822
DIPLOM ECO/UNDEV ORD/FREE EDU/PROP

S63
HOLBO P.S.,"COLD WAR DRIFT IN LATIN AMERICA." CUBA L/A+17C USA+45 USA-45 INT/ORG NAT/G NEIGH VOL/ASSN ACT/RES PLAN ECO/TAC ATTIT RIGID/FLEX ALL/VALS ...RECORD TIME/SEQ OAS LAFTA 20 COLD/WAR. PAGE 66 A1363
DELIB/GP CREATE FOR/AID

B68
ANTWERP-INST UNIVERSITAIRE,BIBLIOGRAPHIC COMPENDIUM: DEVELOPING COUNTRIES (ANTWERP-INST UNIVERSITAIRE DES TERRITOIRES D'OUTRE-MER). AFR EUR+WWI SOCIETY AGRI FINAN NEIGH VOL/ASSN PROB/SOLV TEC/DEV FOR/AID INT/TRADE 20. PAGE 8 A0166
BIBLIOG ECO/UNDEV DIPLOM PLAN

NEISSER H. A2215,A2216

NELSON M.F. A2217,A2218

NEOLITHIC....NEOLITHIC PERIOD

NEPAL....SEE ALSO S/ASIA

B55
PANT Y.P.,PLANNING IN UNDERDEVELOPED ECONOMIES. INDIA NEPAL INT/TRADE COLONIAL SOVEREIGN ALL/IDEOS ...TIME/SEQ METH/COMP 20. PAGE 114 A2334
ECO/UNDEV PLAN ECO/TAC DIPLOM

B60
SALETORE B.A.,INDIA'S DIPLOMATIC RELATIONS WITH THE EAST. ASIA CEYLON INDIA NEPAL S/ASIA CULTURE 7/14 PERSIA. PAGE 126 A2591
DIPLOM NAT/COMP ETIQUET

B66
US DEPARTMENT OF THE ARMY,SOUTH ASIA: A STRATEGIC SURVEY (PAMPHLET NO. 550-3). AFGHANISTN INDIA NEPAL PAKISTAN ECO/UNDEV INT/ORG POL/PAR FORCES FOR/AID INT/TRADE LEAD WAR...POLICY SOC TREND 20. PAGE 152 A3110
BIBLIOG/A S/ASIA DIPLOM NAT/G

NET/THEORY....NETWORK THEORY

B66
WOOLLEY H.B.,MEASURING TRANSACTIONS BETWEEN WORLD AREAS. WOR+45 FINAN...STAT NET/THEORY CHARTS DICTIONARY 20 GOLD/STAND. PAGE 167 A3395
INT/TRADE BAL/PAY DIPLOM ECOMETRIC

NETH/IND....NETHERLAND EAST INDIES (PRE-INDONESIA)

NETHERLAND....NETHERLANDS; SEE ALSO APPROPRIATE TIME/SPACE/ CULTURE INDEX

N
CARIBBEAN COMMISSION,CURRENT CARIBBEAN BIBLIOGRAPHY. FRANCE NETHERLAND UK CULTURE ECO/UNDEV PRESS LEAD ATTIT...GEOG SOC 20. PAGE 24 A0482
BIBLIOG NAT/G L/A+17C DIPLOM

L00
HISTORICUS,"LETTERS AND SOME QUESTIONS OF INTERNATIONAL LAW." FRANCE NETHERLAND UK USA-45 WOR-45 LAW NAT/G COERCE...SOC CONCPT GEN/LAWS TOT/POP 19 CIVIL/WAR. PAGE 65 A1344
WEALTH JURID WAR INT/LAW

B39
FURNIVALL J.S.,NETHERLANDS INDIA. INDIA NETHERLAND CULTURE INDUS NAT/G DIPLOM ADMIN WEALTH...POLICY CHARTS 17/20. PAGE 50 A1029
COLONIAL ECO/UNDEV SOVEREIGN PLURISM

B47
HILL M.,IMMUNITIES AND PRIVILEGES OF INTERNATIONAL OFFICIALS. CANADA EUR+WWI NETHERLAND SWITZERLND LAW LEGIS DIPLOM LEGIT RESPECT...TIME/SEQ LEAGUE/NAT UN VAL/FREE 20. PAGE 65 A1330
INT/ORG ADMIN

B51
WABEKE B.H.,A GUIDE TO DUTCH BIBLIOGRAPHIES. BELGIUM INDONESIA NETHERLAND DIPLOM INT/TRADE WAR NAT/LISM KNOWL...ART/METH HUM JURID CON/ANAL 14/20. PAGE 160 A3257
BIBLIOG/A NAT/G CULTURE COLONIAL

B57
BUCK P.W.,CONTOL OF FOREIGN RELATIONS IN MODERN NATIONS. FRANCE L/A+17C NETHERLAND USSR WOR+45 INT/ORG TOP/EX BAL/PWR DOMIN EDU/PROP COERCE PEACE ATTIT...CONCPT TREND 20 CMN/WLTH. PAGE 21 A0427
NAT/G PWR DIPLOM

B62
ROBINSON A.D.,DUTCH ORGANIZED AGRICULTURE IN INTERNATIONAL POLITICS, 1945-1960. EUR+WWI NETHERLAND STRUCT ECO/DEV NAT/G VOL/ASSN CONSULT DELIB/GP PLAN TEC/DEV INT/TRADE EDU/PROP ATTIT RIGID/FLEX ALL/VALS...NEW/IDEA TREND EEC 20. PAGE 122 A2502
AGRI INT/ORG

B62
SELOSOEMARDJAN O.,SOCIAL CHANGES IN JOGJAKARTA. INDONESIA NETHERLAND ELITES STRATA STRUCT FAM POL/PAR CREATE DIPLOM INT/TRADE EDU/PROP ADMIN GOV/REL...SOC 20 JAVA CHINJAP. PAGE 131 A2683
ECO/UNDEV CULTURE REV COLONIAL

B63
FRANZ G.,TEILUNG UND WIEDERVEREINIGUNG. GERMANY IRELAND ITALY NETHERLAND POLAND CULTURE BAL/PWR CHOOSE NAT/LISM ORD/FREE SOVEREIGN 19/20. PAGE 48 A0987
DIPLOM WAR NAT/COMP ATTIT

NETWORK THEORY....SEE NET/THEORY

NEUBURGER O. A2219

NEUCHTERLEIN D.E. A2220

NEUMANN F. A2221

NEUMANN R.G. A2222

NEUTRAL....POLITICAL NONALIGNMENT, LEGAL NEUTRALITY

B09
HOLLAND T.E.,LETTERS UPON WAR AND NEUTRALITY. WOR-45 NAT/G FORCES JUDGE ECO/TAC LEGIT CT/SYS NEUTRAL ROUTINE COERCE...JURID TIME/SEQ 20. PAGE 67 A1368
LAW INT/LAW INT/ORG WAR

B15
INTERNATIONAL LAW ASSOCIATION,A FORTY YEARS' CATALOGUE OF THE BOOKS, PAMPHLETS AND PAPERS IN THE LIBRARY OF THE INTERNATIONAL LAW ASSOCIATION. INT/ORG DIPLOM ADJUD NEUTRAL...IDEA/COMP 19/20. PAGE 71 A1458
BIBLIOG LAW INT/LAW

B19
LONDON SCHOOL ECONOMICS-POL,ANNUAL DIGEST OF PUBLIC INTERNATIONAL LAW CASES. INT/ORG MUNIC NAT/G PROVS ADMIN NEUTRAL WAR GOV/REL PRIVIL 20. PAGE 91 A1858
BIBLIOG/A INT/LAW ADJUD DIPLOM

N19
ASIAN-AFRICAN CONFERENCE,SELECTED DOCUMENTS OF THE BANDUNG CONFERENCE (PAMPHLET). S/ASIA PLAN ECO/TAC CONFER REGION REV NAT/LISM 20. PAGE 9 A0191
NEUTRAL ECO/UNDEV COLONIAL DIPLOM

N19
FRANCK P.G.,AFGHANISTAN BETWEEN EAST AND WEST: THE ECONOMICS OF COMPETITIVE COEXISTENCE (PAMPHLET). AFGHANISTN USA+45 USA-45 USSR INDUS ECO/TAC INT/TRADE CONTROL NEUTRAL ORD/FREE MARXISM...GEOG 20 UN. PAGE 48 A0977
FOR/AID PLAN DIPLOM ECO/UNDEV

B36
BEARD C.A.,THE DEVIL THEORY OF WAR; AN INQUIRY INTO NATURE OF HISTORY AND THE POSSIBILITY OF KEEPING OUT OF WAR. USA-45 INT/ORG PROB/SOLV NEUTRAL ISOLAT ...CONCPT 20 LEAGUE/NAT WWI. PAGE 12 A0240
GEN/LAWS WAR POLICY DIPLOM

B37
KETCHAM E.H.,PRELIMINARY SELECT BIBLIOGRAPHY OF INTERNATIONAL LAW (PAMPHLET). WOR-45 LAW INT/ORG NAT/G PROB/SOLV CT/SYS NEUTRAL WAR 19/20. PAGE 78 A1602
BIBLIOG DIPLOM ADJUD INT/LAW

B40
CONOVER H.F.,FOREIGN RELATIONS OF THE UNITED STATES: A LIST OF RECENT BOOKS (PAMPHLET). ASIA CANADA L/A+17C UK INT/ORG INT/TRADE TARIFFS NEUTRAL WAR PEACE...INT/LAW CON/ANAL 20 CHINJAP. PAGE 29 A0592
BIBLIOG/A USA-45 DIPLOM

N47
FOX W.T.R.,UNITED STATES POLICY IN A TWO POWER WORLD. COM USA+45 USSR FORCES DOMIN AGREE NEUTRAL NUC/PWR ORD/FREE SOVEREIGN 20 COLD/WAR TREATY EUROPE/W INTERVENT. PAGE 48 A0972
DIPLOM FOR/AID POLICY

B51
RAPPAPORT A.,THE BRITISH PRESS AND WILSONIAN NEUTRALITY. UK WOR-45 SEA POL/PAR WAR CHOOSE PEACE ATTIT PERCEPT...GEOG 20 WILSON/W. PAGE 119 A2446
PRESS DIPLOM NEUTRAL POLICY

B52
ALBERTINI L.,THE ORIGINS OF THE WAR OF 1914 (3 VOLS.). AUSTRIA FRANCE GERMANY MOD/EUR RUSSIA UK PROB/SOLV NEUTRAL PWR...BIBLIOG 19/20. PAGE 5 A0107
WAR DIPLOM FORCES BAL/PWR

B53
OPPENHEIM L.,INTERNATIONAL LAW: A TREATISE (7TH ED., 2 VOLS.). LAW CONSTN PROB/SOLV INT/TRADE ADJUD AGREE NEUTRAL WAR ORD/FREE SOVEREIGN...BIBLIOG 20 LEAGUE/NAT UN ILO. PAGE 112 A2294
INT/LAW INT/ORG DIPLOM

B56
TOYNBEE A.,THE WAR AND THE NEUTRALS. L/A+17C PORTUGAL SPAIN SWEDEN SWITZERLND TURKEY WOR+45 WOR-45 ECO/TAC CONFER CONTROL REGION 20. PAGE 145 A2957
NEUTRAL WAR INT/TRADE DIPLOM

B56
VON HARPE W.,DIE SOWJETUNION FINNLAND UND SKANDANAVIEN, 1945-1955. EUR+WWI FINLAND GERMANY USSR WAR INGP/REL ORD/FREE SOVEREIGN MARXISM ...POLICY GOV/COMP BIBLIOG 20 STALIN/J. PAGE 160 A3252
DIPLOM COM NEUTRAL BAL/PWR

S56
POTTER P.B.,"NEUTRALITY, 1955." WOR+45 WOR-45 INT/ORG NAT/G WAR ATTIT...POLICY IDEA/COMP 17/20 LEAGUE/NAT UN COLD/WAR. PAGE 117 A2399
NEUTRAL INT/LAW DIPLOM CONCPT

B57
CASTLE E.W.,THE GREAT GIVEAWAY: THE REALITIES OF FOREIGN AID. USA+45 DIPLOM EDU/PROP NEUTRAL ...DECISION 20. PAGE 25 A0508
FOR/AID GIVE ECO/UNDEV PROB/SOLV

B57
INSTITUT DE DROIT INTL,TABLEAU GENERAL DES RESOLUTIONS (1873-1956). LAW NEUTRAL CRIME WAR MARRIAGE PEACE...JURID 19/20. PAGE 70 A1442
INT/LAW DIPLOM ORD/FREE ADJUD

B57
SINEY M.C.,THE ALLIED BLOCKADE OF GERMANY: 1914-1916. EUR+WWI GERMANY MOD/EUR USA-45 DIPLOM CONTROL NEUTRAL PWR 20. PAGE 133 A2721
DETER INT/TRADE INT/LAW WAR

B58
ANGELL N.,DEFENCE AND THE ENGLISH-SPEAKING ROLE. CHINA/COM UK USSR INT/ORG FORCES EDU/PROP NEUTRAL NUC/PWR NAT/LISM PEACE TOTALISM 20 COLD/WAR COEXIST. PAGE 8 A0161
DIPLOM WAR MARXISM ORD/FREE

B58
JENNINGS I.,PROBLEMS OF THE NEW COMMONWEALTH. CEYLON INDIA PAKISTAN S/ASIA ECO/UNDEV INT/ORG LOC/G DIPLOM ECO/TAC INT/TRADE COLONIAL RACE/REL DISCRIM 20 COMMONWLTH PARLIAMENT. PAGE 74 A1508
NAT/LISM NEUTRAL FOR/AID POL/PAR

B58
MANSERGH N.,SURVEY OF BRITISH COMMONWEALTH AFFAIRS: PROBLEMS OF WARTIME CO-OPERATION AND POST-WAR CHANGE 1939-1952. INDIA IRELAND S/ASIA CONSTN INT/ORG BAL/PWR COLONIAL NEUTRAL WAR ADJUST PEACE ROLE ORD/FREE...CHARTS 20 CMN/WLTH NATO UN. PAGE 94 A1931
VOL/ASSN CONSEN PROB/SOLV INGP/REL

B58
NEHRU J.,SPEECHES. INDIA ECO/UNDEV AGRI INDUS INT/ORG POL/PAR DIPLOM FOR/AID NAT/LISM...ANTHOL 20. PAGE 108 A2213
PLAN CHIEF COLONIAL NEUTRAL

B58
PALMER E.E.,THE COMMUNIST CHALLENGE. COM USA+45 USA-45 ECO/DEV ECO/UNDEV NEUTRAL ORD/FREE POPULISM ...CONCPT NAT/COMP ANTHOL 19/20 LENIN/VI STALIN/J MAO MARX/KARL COM/PARTY. PAGE 113 A2320
MARXISM DIPLOM IDEA/COMP POLICY

B59
BEMIS S.F.,A SHORT HISTORY OF AMERICAN FOREIGN POLICY AND DIPLOMACY. USA+45 USA-45 INT/ORG NEUTRAL REV WAR ISOLAT ORD/FREE...CHARTS T 18/20. PAGE 13 A0266
DIPLOM ATTIT

B59
KARUNAKARAN K.P.,INDIA IN WORLD AFFAIRS, 1952-1958 (VOL. II). INDIA ECO/UNDEV SECT FOR/AID INT/TRADE ADJUD NEUTRAL REV WAR DISCRIM ORD/FREE MARXISM ...BIBLIOG 20. PAGE 77 A1569
DIPLOM INT/ORG S/ASIA COLONIAL

S59
BROMKE A.,"DISENGAGEMENT IN EAST EUROPE." COM USSR INT/ORG DIPLOM EDU/PROP NEUTRAL NUC/PWR DRIVE RIGID/FLEX PWR...PSY CONCPT CON/ANAL GEN/METH VAL/FREE 20. PAGE 19 A0388
BAL/PWR

B60
FISCHER L.,RUSSIA, AMERICA, AND THE WORLD. FUT USA+45 USSR WOR+45 FORCES PLAN BAL/PWR ECO/TAC FOR/AID NEUTRAL TASK NUC/PWR PWR 20 COLD/WAR. PAGE 46 A0937
DIPLOM POLICY MARXISM ECO/UNDEV

B60
MINIFIE J.M.,PEACEMAKER OR POWDER-MONKEY. CANADA INT/ORG NAT/G FORCES LEAD WAR...PREDICT 20. PAGE 102 A2086
DIPLOM POLICY NEUTRAL PEACE

B60
SOBEL R.,THE ORIGINS OF INTERVENTIONISM: THE UNITED STATES AND THE RUSSO-FINNISH WAR. FINLAND USA+45 USSR LEGIS ATTIT RIGID/FLEX...BIBLIOG 20 INTERVENT. PAGE 135 A2755
DIPLOM WAR PROB/SOLV NEUTRAL

S60
LYON P.,"NEUTRALITY AND THE EMERGENCE OF THE CONCEPT OF NEUTRALISM." WOR+45 WOR-45 INT/ORG NAT/G BAL/PWR NEUTRAL ATTIT PWR...POLICY TIME/SEQ TREND COLD/WAR TOT/POP VAL/FREE 20 UN. PAGE 92 A1878
CONCPT

B61
DEAN V.M.,BUILDERS OF EMERGING NATIONS. WOR+45 ECO/UNDEV ECO/TAC NEUTRAL TOTALISM ORD/FREE PWR ...BIOG AUD/VIS IDEA/COMP BIBLIOG 20 COLD/WAR. PAGE 35 A0719
NAT/G CHIEF POLICY DIPLOM

B61
HARRISON S.,INDIA AND THE UNITED STATES. FUT S/ASIA USA+45 WOR+45 INTELL ECO/DEV ECO/UNDEV AGRI INDUS INT/ORG NAT/G CONSULT EX/STRUC TOP/EX PLAN ECO/TAC NEUTRAL ALL/VALS...MGT TOT/POP 20. PAGE 62 A1272
DELIB/GP ACT/RES FOR/AID INDIA

B61
LIPPMANN W.,THE COMING TESTS WITH RUSSIA. COM CUBA GERMANY USSR FORCES CONTROL NEUTRAL COERCE NUC/PWR REV WAR PWR...INT 20 KHRUSH/N BERLIN. PAGE 89 A1830
BAL/PWR DIPLOM MARXISM ARMS/CONT

B61
OAKES J.B.,THE EDGE OF FREEDOM. EUR+WWI USA+45 USSR ECO/UNDEV BAL/PWR DIPLOM DOMIN COLONIAL PWR MARXISM POPULISM...IDEA/COMP 20 COLD/WAR. PAGE 111 A2271
AFR ORD/FREE SOVEREIGN NEUTRAL

B61
RIENOW R.,CONTEMPORARY INTERNATIONAL POLITICS. WOR+45 INT/ORG BAL/PWR EDU/PROP COLONIAL NEUTRAL REGION WAR PEACE...INT/LAW 20 COLD/WAR UN. PAGE 121 A2476
DIPLOM PWR POLICY NAT/G

B61
SYATAUW J.J.G.,SOME NEWLY ESTABLISHED ASIAN STATES AND THE DEVELOPMENT OF INTERNATIONAL LAW. BURMA CEYLON INDIA INDONESIA ECO/UNDEV COLONIAL NEUTRAL WAR PEACE SOVEREIGN...CHARTS 19/20. PAGE 140 A2873
INT/LAW ADJUST SOCIETY S/ASIA

B62
BAULIN J.,THE ARAB ROLE IN AFRICA. AFR ALGERIA FUT ISLAM MOROCCO UAR COLONIAL NEUTRAL REV...SOC 20 TUNIS BOURGUIBA. PAGE 12 A0235
NAT/LISM DIPLOM NAT/G SECT

B62
DOUGLAS W.O.,DEMOCRACY'S MANIFESTO. COM USA+45 ECO/UNDEV INT/ORG FORCES PLAN NEUTRAL TASK MARXISM ...JURID 20 NATO SEATO. PAGE 38 A0779
DIPLOM POLICY NAT/G ORD/FREE

B62
DUTOIT B.,LA NEUTRALITE SUISSE A L'HEURE EUROPEENNE. EUR+WWI MOD/EUR INT/ORG NAT/G VOL/ASSN PLAN BAL/PWR LEGIT NEUTRAL REGION PEACE ORD/FREE SOVEREIGN...CONCPT OBS TIME/SEQ TREND STERTYP VAL/FREE LEAGUE/NAT UN 20. PAGE 40 A0812
ATTIT DIPLOM SWITZERLND

B62
FRIEDRICH-EBERT-STIFTUNG,THE SOVIET BLOC AND DEVELOPING COUNTRIES. CHINA/COM COM GERMANY/E USSR WOR+45 ECO/UNDEV INT/ORG NAT/G TEC/DEV NEUTRAL PWR ...POLICY 20. PAGE 49 A1008
MARXISM DIPLOM ECO/TAC FOR/AID

B62
GYORGY A.,PROBLEMS IN INTERNATIONAL RELATIONS. COM CT/SYS NUC/PWR ALL/IDEOS 20 UN EEC ECSC. PAGE 58 A1199
DIPLOM NEUTRAL BAL/PWR REV

B62
KLUCKHOHN F.L.,THE NAKED RISE OF COMMUNISM. CHINA/COM COM USSR WOR+45 CONSTN POL/PAR PLAN CONTROL LEAD NEUTRAL CONSERVE 20 STALIN/J EUROPE/E COM/PARTY. PAGE 80 A1650
MARXISM IDEA/COMP DIPLOM DOMIN

B62
LERNER M.,THE AGE OF OVERKILL: A PREFACE TO WORLD POLITICS. USA+45 USSR WOR+45 SOCIETY ECO/UNDEV BAL/PWR NEUTRAL PARTIC REV ALL/IDEOS MARXISM ...BIBLIOG/A 20. PAGE 87 A1787
DIPLOM NUC/PWR PWR DEATH

B62
MARTIN L.W.,NEUTRALISM AND NONALIGNMENT. WOR+45 ATTIT PWR...POLICY ANTHOL 20 UN. PAGE 95 A1952
DIPLOM NEUTRAL BAL/PWR INT/ORG

B63
BRECHER M.,THE NEW STATES OF ASIA. ASIA S/ASIA INT/ORG BAL/PWR COLONIAL NEUTRAL ORD/FREE PWR 20 UN. PAGE 18 A0369
NAT/G ECO/UNDEV DIPLOM POLICY

B63
LYON P.,NEUTRALISM. ECO/UNDEV EDU/PROP COLONIAL ALL/IDEOS...IDEA/COMP 20 COLD/WAR UN. PAGE 92 A1879
NAT/COMP NAT/LISM DIPLOM NEUTRAL

B63
PERKINS B.,PROLOGUE TO THE WAR: ENGLAND AND THE UNITED STATES, 1805-1812. MOD/EUR UK USA-45 NAT/G ORD/FREE RESPECT SOVEREIGN...POLICY TREATY 19 WAR/1812. PAGE 115 A2358
WAR DIPLOM NEUTRAL

B63
RIUKIN A.,THE AFRICAN PRESENCE IN WORLD AFFAIRS. AFR WOR+45 ECO/UNDEV AGRI INT/ORG BAL/PWR ECO/TAC COLONIAL NEUTRAL NAT/LISM PEACE SOVEREIGN 20 UN. PAGE 121 A2486
DIPLOM NAT/G POLICY PWR

B63
ROSSI M.,THE THIRD WORLD. FUT WOR+45 INT/ORG NAT/G CAP/ISM COLONIAL PEACE PWR MARXISM 20 UN THIRD/WRLD. PAGE 124 A2542
ECO/UNDEV DIPLOM BAL/PWR NEUTRAL

B63
SMITH J.E.,THE DEFENSE OF BERLIN. COM GUATEMALA WOR+45 ECO/TAC ADMIN NEUTRAL ATTIT ORD/FREE SOVEREIGN...DECISION 20 DEPT/STATE. PAGE 134 A2747
DIPLOM FORCES BAL/PWR PLAN

B63
WATKINS K.W.,BRITAIN DIVIDED; THE EFFECT OF THE SPANISH CIVIL WAR ON BRITISH POLITICAL OPINION. SPAIN UK POL/PAR BAL/PWR LOBBY NEUTRAL 20. PAGE 162 A3293
EDU/PROP WAR POLICY DIPLOM

S63
CHAKRAVARTI P.C.,"INDIAN NON-ALIGNMENT AND UNITED STATES POLICY." ASIA INDIA S/ASIA USA+45 CULTURE ECO/UNDEV NAT/G VOL/ASSN DELIB/GP TOP/EX FOR/AID NEUTRAL...POLICY HUM CONCPT RECORD GEN/LAWS 20. PAGE 25 A0515
ATTIT ALL/VALS COLONIAL DIPLOM

S63
HAVILAND H.F.,"BUILDING A POLITICAL COMMUNITY." EUR+WWI FUT UK USA+45 ECO/DEV ECO/UNDEV INT/ORG NAT/G DELIB/GP BAL/PWR ECO/TAC NEUTRAL ROUTINE ATTIT PWR WEALTH...CONCPT COLD/WAR TOT/POP 20. PAGE 63 A1293
VOL/ASSN DIPLOM

C63
CHARLETON W.G.,"THE REVOLUTION IN AMERICAN FOREIGN POLICY." COM PROB/SOLV FOR/AID DOMIN COLONIAL NEUTRAL DETER WAR ISOLAT NAT/LISM...BIBLIOG 19/20 UN COLD/WAR NATO. PAGE 26 A0523
DIPLOM INT/ORG BAL/PWR

B64
KULSKI W.W.,INTERNATIONAL POLITICS IN A REVOLUTIONARY AGE. NEUTRAL NAT/LISM...POLICY DECISION INT/LAW CONCPT 20 UN. PAGE 83 A1693
DIPLOM WAR NUC/PWR INT/ORG

B64
LUTHULI A.,AFRICA'S FREEDOM. KIN LABOR POL/PAR SCHOOL DIPLOM NEUTRAL REGION REV NAT/LISM PWR WEALTH SOCISM SOC/INTEG 20. PAGE 92 A1874
AFR ECO/UNDEV COLONIAL

B64
ROSENAU J.N.,INTERNATIONAL ASPECTS OF CIVIL STRIFE. CHINA/COM CUBA EUR+WWI USA+45 USSR BAL/PWR EDU/PROP NEUTRAL COERCE MORAL...NAT/COMP 20 COLD/WAR UN. PAGE 124 A2533
POLICY DIPLOM REV WAR

B64
VOELKMANN K.,HERRSCHER VON MORGEN? BAL/PWR COLONIAL NEUTRAL REGION RACE/REL ALL/VALS SOVEREIGN...RECORD 20 COLD/WAR THIRD/WRLD. PAGE 159 A3246
DIPLOM ECO/UNDEV CONTROL NAT/COMP

B64
WRIGHT T.P. JR.,AMERICAN SUPPORT OF FREE ELECTIONS ABROAD. USA+45 USA-45 DOMIN LEAD NEUTRAL MARXISM ...POLICY TIME/SEQ BIBLIOG 19/20 COLD/WAR INTERVENT. PAGE 168 A3420
DIPLOM CHOOSE L/A+17C POPULISM

B65
MACDONALD R.W.,THE LEAGUE OF ARAB STATES: A STUDY IN THE DYNAMICS OF REGIONAL ORGANIZATION. ISRAEL UAR USSR FINAN INT/ORG DELIB/GP ECO/TAC AGREE NEUTRAL ORD/FREE PWR...DECISION BIBLIOG 20 TREATY UN. PAGE 92 A1888
ISLAM REGION DIPLOM ADMIN

B65
MORRIS R.B.,THE PEACEMAKERS; THE GREAT POWERS AND AMERICAN INDEPENDENCE. BAL/PWR CONFER COLONIAL NEUTRAL PEACE ORD/FREE TREATY 18 PRE/US/AM. PAGE 105 A2149
SOVEREIGN REV DIPLOM

B65
SULZBERGER C.L.,UNFINISHED REVOLUTION. USA+45 WOR+45 INT/ORG TEC/DEV BAL/PWR FOR/AID COLONIAL NEUTRAL PWR SOVEREIGN MARXISM 20. PAGE 140 A2863
DIPLOM ECO/UNDEV POLICY NAT/G

S65
RAY H.,"THE POLICY OF RUSSIA TOWARDS SINO-INDIAN CONFLICT." ASIA CHINA/COM COM INDIA USSR NAT/G TOP/EX FOR/AID EDU/PROP NEUTRAL COERCE PEACE RIGID/FLEX PWR...METH/CNCPT TIME/SEQ VAL/FREE 20. PAGE 120 A2452
S/ASIA ATTIT DIPLOM WAR

C65
BURTON J.W.,"INTERNATIONAL RELATIONS: A GENERAL THEORY." WOR+45 NAT/G CREATE BAL/PWR NEUTRAL COERCE DETER ADJUST...TREND IDEA/COMP GEN/METH BIBLIOG. PAGE 22 A0447
DIPLOM GEN/LAWS ACT/RES ORD/FREE

C65
WUORINEN J.H.,"SCANDINAVIA." DENMARK FINLAND ICELAND NORWAY SWEDEN SOCIETY AGRI POL/PAR DELIB/GP DIPLOM INT/TRADE NEUTRAL WAR...CHARTS TREATY 20. PAGE 168 A3423
BIBLIOG NAT/G POLICY

B66
CANFIELD L.H.,THE PRESIDENCY OF WOODROW WILSON: PRELUDE TO A WORLD IN CRISIS. USA-45 ADJUD NEUTRAL WAR CHOOSE INGP/REL PEACE ORD/FREE 20 WILSON/W PRESIDENT TREATY LEAGUE/NAT. PAGE 24 A0477
PERSON POLICY DIPLOM GOV/REL

B66
DAENIKER G.,STRATEGIE DES KLEIN STAATS. SWITZERLND ACT/RES CREATE DIPLOM NEUTRAL DETER WAR WEAPON PWR SOVEREIGN...IDEA/COMP 20 COLD/WAR. PAGE 33 A0673
NUC/PWR PLAN FORCES NAT/G

B66
DYCK H.V.,WEIMAR GERMANY AND SOVIET RUSSIA 1926-1933. EUR+WWI GERMANY UK USSR ECO/TAC INT/TRADE NEUTRAL WAR ATTIT 20 WEIMAR/REP TREATY. PAGE 40 A0814
DIPLOM GOV/REL POLICY

B66
HANSEN G.H.,AFRO-ASIA AND NON-ALIGNMENT. AFR ASIA S/ASIA NEUTRAL MORAL 20. PAGE 61 A1255
DIPLOM CONFER POLICY NAT/LISM

B66
MCKAY V.,AFRICAN DIPLOMACY STUDIES IN THE DETERMINANTS OF FOREIGN POLICY. AFR SOUTH/AFR CULTURE NEUTRAL REGION SOVEREIGN...INT/LAW GOV/COMP ANTHOL 20. PAGE 98 A2013
ECO/UNDEV RACE/REL CIVMIL/REL DIPLOM

B66
SMITH D.M.,AMERICAN INTERVENTION, 1917. GERMANY UK USA-45 SEA FORCES DIPLOM INT/TRADE EDU/PROP COERCE WEAPON PEACE 20 WILSON/W WWI. PAGE 134 A2746
WAR ATTIT POLICY NEUTRAL

S66
DINH TRANS V.A.N.,"VIETNAM: A THIRD WAY" S/ASIA USA+45 USSR VIETNAM VIETNAM/S NAT/G SECT FORCES CAP/ISM DIPLOM COLONIAL NEUTRAL MARXISM SOCISM 20 BUDDHISM UNIFICA. PAGE 38 A0766
WAR PLAN ORD/FREE SOCIALIST

S67
CHAND A.,"INDIA AND TANZANIA." INDIA TANZANIA TEC/DEV ECO/TAC FOR/AID COLONIAL PEACE UTIL WEALTH ...GOV/COMP 20. PAGE 25 A0518
ECO/UNDEV NEUTRAL DIPLOM PLAN

S67
GRUNDY K.W.,"AFRICA IN THE WORLD ARENA." ECO/UNDEV BAL/PWR FOR/AID NEUTRAL REV NAT/LISM GOV/COMP. PAGE 58 A1183
AFR DIPLOM INT/ORG COLONIAL

S67
JOHNSTON D.M.,"LAW, TECHNOLOGY AND THE SEA." WOR+45 PLAN PROB/SOLV TEC/DEV CONFER ADJUD ORD/FREE ...POLICY JURID. PAGE 75 A1528
INT/LAW INT/ORG DIPLOM NEUTRAL

S67
LACOUTRE J.,"HO CHI MINH." CHINA/COM USSR VIETNAM/N NAT/G CHIEF TOP/EX LEAD NEUTRAL...REALPOL PREDICT
NAT/LISM MARXISM

20. PAGE 83 A1708 REV DIPLOM

S67
ROSE S.,"ASIAN NATIONALISM* THE SECOND STAGE." ASIA COM ECO/UNDEV NAT/G PROB/SOLV DIPLOM FOR/AID DOMIN NEUTRAL REGION TASK...METH/COMP 20. PAGE 123 A2528 NAT/LISM S/ASIA BAL/PWR COLONIAL

S67
SARBADHIKARI P.,"A NOTE ON THE DOMESTIC CRISIS OF NON-ALIGNMENT." ELITES INTELL ECO/UNDEV FOR/AID DOMIN. PAGE 127 A2605 NEUTRAL WEALTH TOTALISM BAL/PWR

S67
STEEL R.,"BEYOND THE POWER BLOCS." USA+45 USSR ECO/UNDEV NEUTRAL NUC/PWR NAT/LISM ATTIT...GEOG NATO WARSAW/P COLD/WAR. PAGE 137 A2811 DIPLOM TREND BAL/PWR PLAN

S67
VAN DUSEN H.P.,"HAMMARSKOLD IN THE WORLD'S SERVICE." DIPLOM CONFER LEAD PEACE STRANGE UTOPIA MORAL SKILL OBJECTIVE...INT/LAW SELF/OBS 20. PAGE 158 A3211 INT/ORG CONSULT TOP/EX NEUTRAL

S67
VLASCIC I.A.,"THE SPACE TREATY* A PRELIMINARY EVALUATION." FUT USSR WOR+45 R+D ACT/RES TEC/DEV DIPLOM CONFER ARMS/CONT PEACE...PREDICT UN TREATY. PAGE 159 A3245 SPACE INT/LAW INT/ORG NEUTRAL

NEVADA....NEVADA

NEVINS A. A1591

NEW ECONOMICS....SEE NEW/ECONOM

NEW LIBERALISM....SEE NEW/LIB

NEW STATES....SEE ECO/UNDEV+GEOGRAPHIC AREA+COLONIAL+ NAT/LISM

NEW YORK CITY....SEE NEWYORK/C

NEW/BRUNS....NEW BRUNSWICK, CANADA

NEW/DEAL....NEW DEAL OF F.D.R.'S ADMINISTRATION

NEW/DELHI....NEW DELHI (UNCTAD MEETING OF DEVELOPED AND UNDERDEVELOPED NATIONS IN 1968)

NEW/ECO/MN....NEW ECONOMIC MECHANISM OF HUNGARY

NEW/ECONOM....NEW ECONOMICS

NEW/ENGLND....NEW ENGLAND

NEW/FRONTR....NEW FRONTIER OF J.F.KENNEDY

NEW/GUINEA....NEW GUINEA

NEW/HAMPSH....NEW HAMPSHIRE

NEW/HEBRID....NEW HEBRIDES

NEW/IDEA....NEW CONCEPT

NEW/JERSEY....NEW JERSEY

NEW/LEFT....THE NEW LEFT

NEW/LIB....NEW LIBERALISM

B53
STOUT H.M.,BRITISH GOVERNMENT. UK FINAN LOC/G POL/PAR DELIB/GP DIPLOM ADMIN COLONIAL CHOOSE ORD/FREE...JURID BIBLIOG 20 COMMONWLTH. PAGE 139 A2837 NAT/G PARL/PROC CONSTN NEW/LIB

B61
DIMOCK M.E.,BUSINESS AND GOVERNMENT (4TH ED.). AGRI FINAN OP/RES PLAN BUDGET DIPLOM LOBBY NUC/PWR NEW/LIB SOCISM...POLICY BIBLIOG 20. PAGE 37 A0765 NAT/G INDUS LABOR ECO/TAC

B61
LIEFMANN-KEIL E.,OKONOMISCHE THEORIE DER SOZIALPOLITIK. INT/ORG LABOR WORKER COST INCOME NEW/LIB...CONCPT SOC/INTEG 20. PAGE 88 A1810 ECO/DEV INDUS NAT/G SOC/WK

B62
ROOSEVELT J.,THE LIBERAL PAPERS. USA+45 WOR+45 ECO/DEV INT/ORG DELIB/GP ACT/RES PROB/SOLV DETER ATTIT...TREND IDEA/COMP ANTHOL. PAGE 123 A2520 DIPLOM NEW/LIB POLICY FORCES

B62
TOURE S.,THE INTERNATIONAL POLICY OF THE DEMOCRATIC PARTY OF GUINEA (VOL. VII). AFR ALGERIA GHANA GUINEA MALI CONSTN VOL/ASSN CHIEF WAR PEACE ATTIT ...WELF/ST 20 DEMOCRAT. PAGE 144 A2953 DIPLOM POLICY POL/PAR NEW/LIB

B63
HARTLEY A.,A STATE OF ENGLAND. UK ELITES SOCIETY ACADEM NAT/G SCHOOL INGP/REL CONSEN ORD/FREE NEW/LIB...POLICY 20. PAGE 62 A1275 DIPLOM ATTIT INTELL ECO/DEV

B64
MARTIN J.J.,AMERICAN LIBERALISM AND WORLD POLITICS, 1931-41 (2 VOLS.). GERMANY USA-45 POL/PAR DISCRIM NAT/LISM PEACE RATIONAL ATTIT RIGID/FLEX MARXISM PACIFISM 20. PAGE 95 A1950 NEW/LIB DIPLOM NAT/G POLICY

B65
PENNICK JL J.R.,THE POLITICS OF AMERICAN SCIENCE, 1939 TO THE PRESENT. USA+45 USA-45 INTELL TEC/DEV DIPLOM NEW/LIB...ANTHOL 20 COLD/WAR. PAGE 114 A2349 POLICY ADMIN PHIL/SCI NAT/G

C65
MARK M.,"BEYOND SOVEREIGNTY." WOR+45 WOR-45 ECO/UNDEV BAL/PWR INT/TRADE NUC/PWR REV WAR MARXISM NEW/LIB BIBLIOG. PAGE 95 A1942 NAT/LISM NAT/G DIPLOM INTELL

B67
MACDONALD D.F.,THE AGE OF TRANSITION: BRITAIN IN THE NINETEENTH & TWENTIETH CENTURIES. UK ECO/DEV LEGIS DIPLOM NEW/LIB...POLICY 19/20. PAGE 92 A1886 TREND INDUS SOCISM

B67
YAMAMURA K.,ECONOMIC POLICY IN POSTWAR JAPAN. ASIA FINAN POL/PAR DIPLOM LEAD NAT/LISM ATTIT NEW/LIB POPULISM 20 CHINJAP. PAGE 168 A3429 ECO/DEV POLICY NAT/G TEC/DEV

NEW/MEXICO....NEW MEXICO

NEW/YORK....NEW YORK STATE

NEW/ZEALND....NEW ZEALAND; SEE ALSO S/ASIA, COMMONWLTH

B42
CONOVER H.F.,NEW ZEALAND: A SELECTED LIST OF REFERENCES (PAMPHLET). NEW/ZEALND ECO/UNDEV AGRI INDUS LABOR NAT/G SCHOOL FORCES DIPLOM COLONIAL WAR ...HUM 20. PAGE 29 A0595 BIBLIOG/A S/ASIA CULTURE

S59
PADELFORD N.J.,"REGIONAL COOPERATION IN THE SOUTH PACIFIC: THE SOUTH PACIFIC COMMISSION." FUT NEW/ZEALND UK WOR+45 CULTURE ECO/UNDEV LOC/G VOL/ASSN...OBS CON/ANAL UNESCO VAL/FREE AUSTRAL 20. PAGE 112 A2308 INT/ORG ADMIN

S62
CORET A.,"LE STATUT DE L'ILE CHRISTMAS DE L'OCEAN INDIEN." FUT S/ASIA ECO/DEV ECO/UNDEV VOL/ASSN DELIB/GP PLAN...RELATIV OBS TIME/SEQ TREND AUSTRAL 20. PAGE 30 A0619 NAT/G INT/ORG NEW/ZEALND

B66
EDWARDS C.D.,TRADE REGULATIONS OVERSEAS. IRELAND NEW/ZEALND SOUTH/AFR NAT/G CAP/ISM TARIFFS CONTROL ...POLICY JURID 20 EEC CHINJAP. PAGE 40 A0823 INT/TRADE DIPLOM INT/LAW ECO/TAC

S66
"RESEARCH WORK 1965-1966." NEW/ZEALND ELITES ACADEM LOC/G MUNIC POL/PAR PROVS DIPLOM COLONIAL...SOC 20 AUSTRAL. PAGE 4 A0073 BIBLIOG NAT/G CULTURE S/ASIA

NEWARK/NJ....NEWARK, N.J.

NEWBURY C.W. A2223,A2224

NEWCOMER H.A. A2225

NEWFNDLND....NEWFOUNDLAND, CANADA

NEWMAN P.K. A2184

NEWMAN R.P. A2226

NEWY/TIMES....NEW YORK TIMES

NEWYORK/C....NEW YORK CITY

B66
GROSS F.,WORLD POLITICS AND TENSION AREAS. CHINA/COM SOMALIA VENEZUELA COERCE GP/REL RACE/REL ATTIT HABITAT 19/20 CASEBOOK NEWYORK/C. PAGE 57 A1173 DIPLOM WAR PROB/SOLV

NICARAGUA....NICARAGUA; SEE ALSO L/A+17C

B61
GOLDWERT M.,CONSTABULARY IN THE DOMINICAN REPUBLIC AND NICARAGUA. DOMIN/REP L/A+17C NICARAGUA USA-45 NAT/G PLAN CONTROL TASK REV...POLICY 20 INTERVENT. PAGE 53 A1093 DIPLOM PEACE FORCES

NICE R.W. A2227

NICHOLAS H.G. A2228,A2229

NICHOLAS/I....CZAR NICHOLAS I

NICHOLSON T.L. A2814

NICOL D. A2230

NICOLSON H. A2231,A2232

NICOLSON H.G. A2233

NICOLSON/A....SIR ARTHUR NICOLSON

NIEBUHR R. A2234,A2235,A2236,A2237,A2238

NIEBUHR/R....REINHOLD NIEBUHR

NIEBURG/HL....H.L. NIEBURG

NIEDERGANG M. A2239

NIEMEYER G. A2240

NIETZSCH/F....FRIEDRICH NIETZSCHE

NIGERIA....SEE ALSO AFR

B00
MOCKLER-FERRYMAN A.,BRITISH WEST AFRICA. FRANCE GERMANY NIGER SIER/LEONE UK CULTURE DIPLOM WAR RACE/REL PRODUC PROFIT WEALTH...POLICY PREDICT 19. PAGE 102 A2095 — AFR COLONIAL INT/TRADE CAP/ISM

B50
CHUKWUEMEKA N.,AFRICAN DEPENDENCIES: A CHALLENGE TO WESTERN DEMOCRACY. NIGERIA ECO/DEV INDUS FOR/AID INT/TRADE DOMIN 20. PAGE 26 A0536 — DIPLOM ECO/UNDEV COLONIAL AFR

B60
JEFFRIES C.,TRANSFER OF POWER: PROBLEMS OF THE PASSAGE TO SELFGOVERNMENT. CEYLON GHANA MALAYSIA NIGERIA UK INT/ORG CONSULT DELIB/GP LEGIS DIPLOM CONFER PARL/PROC 20. PAGE 73 A1502 — SOVEREIGN COLONIAL ORD/FREE NAT/G

B60
THEOBOLD R.,THE NEW NATIONS OF WEST AFRICA. GHANA NIGERIA CULTURE INT/ORG ECO/TAC FOR/AID COLONIAL RACE/REL POPULISM...ANTHOL BIBLIOG 20 UN. PAGE 143 A2916 — AFR SOVEREIGN ECO/UNDEV DIPLOM

S62
CORET A.,"LA DECLARATION DE L'ASSEMBLEE GENERAL DE L'ONU SUR L'OCTROI DE L'INDEPENDENCE AUX PAYS ET AUX PEUPLES." AFR ASIA ISLAM NIGERIA S/ASIA USSR WOR+45 ECO/UNDEV NAT/G DELIB/GP COLONIAL ALL/VALS ...CONCPT TIME/SEQ TREND UN TOT/POP 20 MEXIC/AMER. PAGE 31 A0621 — INT/ORG STRUCT SOVEREIGN

B64
THE SPECIAL COMMONWEALTH AFRICAN ASSISTANCE PLAN. AFR CANADA INDIA NIGERIA UK FINAN SCHOOL...CHARTS 20 COMMONWLTH. PAGE 3 A0065 — ECO/UNDEV TREND FOR/AID ADMIN

B64
FREE L.A.,THE ATTITUDES, HOPES AND FEARS OF NIGERIANS. AFR NIGERIA ECO/UNDEV AGRI ACADEM PLAN TASK...GEOG CHARTS METH 20. PAGE 49 A0993 — NAT/LISM SYS/QU DIPLOM

B66
US LIBRARY OF CONGRESS,NIGERIA: A GUIDE TO OFFICIAL PUBLICATIONS. CAMEROON NIGERIA UK DIPLOM...POLICY 19/20 UN LEAGUE/NAT. PAGE 155 A3160 — BIBLIOG ADMIN NAT/G COLONIAL

NIH....NATIONAL INSTITUTE OF HEALTH

NIJHOFF M. A2241

NIJKERK K.F. A0158

NIPA....NATIONAL INSTITUTE OF PUBLIC ADMINISTRATION

NISEI....NISEI: JAPANESE AMERICANS

NIXON/RM....PRESIDENT RICHARD M. NIXON

NIZARD L. A2242

NKRUMAH K. A2243

NKRUMAH/K....KWAME NKRUMAH

B60
PHILLIPS J.F.V.,KWAME NKRUMAH AND THE FUTURE OF AFRICA. FUT GHANA ISLAM ECO/UNDEV CHIEF DIPLOM COLONIAL RACE/REL NAT/LISM...TREND IDEA/COMP BIBLIOG 20 NKRUMAH/K. PAGE 116 A2376 — BIOG LEAD SOVEREIGN AFR

S67
KRAUS J.,"A MARXIST IN GHANA." GHANA ELITES CHIEF PROB/SOLV TEC/DEV DIPLOM ECO/TAC COLONIAL PARTIC PWR 20 NKRUMAH/K. PAGE 82 A1676 — MARXISM PLAN ATTIT CREATE

NLC....NATIONAL LIBERATION COUNCIL IN GHANA

NLF....NATIONAL LIBERATION FRONT OF SOUTH VIETNAM

B65
WARBEY W.,VIETNAM: THE TRUTH. FRANCE S/ASIA USA+45 VIETNAM CULTURE INT/ORG NAT/G DIPLOM FOR/AID EDU/PROP ARMS/CONT PEACE 20 TREATY NLF UN. PAGE 161 A3274 — WAR AGREE

NLRB....NATIONAL LABOR RELATIONS BOARD

NOBECOURT R.G. A2244

NOBILITY....SEE ELITES

NOEL-BAKER D. A2245

NOGEE J.L. A2246,A2247,A2248,A2771

NOLLAU G. A2249

NOMAD/MAX....MAX NOMAD

NOMADISM....SEE GEOG

NONALIGNED NATIONS....SEE THIRD/WRLD

NON-WHITE....SEE RACE/REL

NONVIOLENT....NONVIOLENCE (CONCEPT)

NORMAN E.H. A2250

NORMS....SEE AVERAGE, ALSO APPROPRIATE VALUES AND DIMENSIONS OF GROUPS, STAT, LOG, ETC.

NORTH R.C. A2251,A2252,A2253,A2254

NORTH AFRICA....SEE AFRICA/N, ISLAM

NORTH ATLANTIC FREE TRADE AREA....SEE NAFTA

NORTH ATLANTIC TREATY ORGANIZATION....SEE NATO

NORTH KOREA....SEE KOREA/N

NORTH VIETNAM....SEE VIETNAM/N

NORTH/AMER....NORTH AMERICA, EXCLUSIVE OF CENTRAL AMERICA

NORTH/CAR....NORTH CAROLINA

NORTH/DAK....NORTH DAKOTA

NORTH/US....NORTHERN UNITED STATES

NORTHERN RHODESIA....SEE ZAMBIA

NORTHROP F.S.C. A2255,A2256

NORTHW/TER....NORTHWEST TERRITORIES, CANADA

NORTHWST/U....NORTHWESTERN UNIVERSITY

NORWAY....SEE ALSO APPROPRIATE TIME/SPACE/CULTURE INDEX

B53
ORFIELD L.B.,THE GROWTH OF SCANDINAVIAN LAW. DENMARK ICELAND NORWAY SWEDEN LAW DIPLOM...BIBLIOG 9/20. PAGE 112 A2296 — JURID CT/SYS NAT/G

B64
FRYDENSBERG P.,PEACE-KEEPING: EXPERIENCE AND EVALUATION: THE OSLO PAPERS. NORWAY FORCES PLAN CONTROL...INT/LAW 20 UN. PAGE 49 A1012 — INT/ORG DIPLOM PEACE COERCE

C65
WUORINEN J.H.,"SCANDINAVIA." DENMARK FINLAND ICELAND NORWAY SWEDEN SOCIETY AGRI POL/PAR DELIB/GP DIPLOM INT/TRADE NEUTRAL WAR...CHARTS TREATY 20. PAGE 168 A3423 — BIBLIOG NAT/G POLICY

NOVA/SCOT....NOVA SCOTIA, CANADA

NOVE A. A2257,A2258,A2259

NOVOTNY/A....ANTONIN NOVOTNY

NRA....NATIONAL RECOVERY ADMINISTRATION

NSC....NATIONAL SECURITY COUNCIL

S56
CUTLER R.,"THE DEVELOPMENT OF THE NATIONAL SECURITY COUNCIL." USA+45 INTELL CONSULT EX/STRUC DIPLOM LEAD 20 TRUMAN/HS EISNHWR/DD NSC. PAGE 33 A0670
ORD/FREE DELIB/GP PROB/SOLV NAT/G

NSF....NATIONAL SCIENCE FOUNDATION

NSSF....NATIONAL SOCIAL SCIENCE FOUNDATION

NUC....NATIONAL UNITY COMMITTEE (TURKEY)

NUC/PWR....NUCLEAR POWER, INCLUDING NUCLEAR WEAPONS

N
CONOVER H.F.,WORLD GOVERNMENT: A LIST OF SELECTED REFERENCES (PAMPHLET). WOR+45 PROB/SOLV ARMS/CONT WAR PEACE 20 UN. PAGE 29 A0589
BIBLIOG/A NUC/PWR INT/ORG DIPLOM

N
INDIAN COUNCIL WORLD AFFAIRS,SELECT ARTICLES ON CURRENT AFFAIRS (BIBLIOGRAPHICAL SERIES: 7). AFR ASIA COM EUR+WWI S/ASIA UK COLONIAL NUC/PWR PEACE ATTIT...INT/LAW SOC 20. PAGE 70 A1437
BIBLIOG DIPLOM INT/ORG ECO/UNDEV

B
CURRENT THOUGHT ON PEACE AND WAR. WOR+45 INT/ORG FORCES PROB/SOLV DIPLOM NUC/PWR PERCEPT...POLICY SOC 20 UN NATO. PAGE 1 A0008
BIBLIOG/A PEACE ATTIT WAR

N
JOURNAL OF CONFLICT RESOLUTION. FUT WOR+45 INT/ORG NAT/G FORCES CREATE PROB/SOLV ARMS/CONT NUC/PWR WEAPON SOC. PAGE 1 A0014
BIBLIOG/A DIPLOM WAR

N
POLITICAL SCIENCE QUARTERLY. USA+45 USA-45 LAW CONSTN ECO/DEV INT/ORG LOC/G POL/PAR LEGIS LEAD NUC/PWR...CONCPT 20. PAGE 1 A0023
BIBLIOG/A NAT/G DIPLOM POLICY

N
FOREIGN AFFAIRS. SPACE WOR+45 WOR-45 CULTURE ECO/UNDEV FINAN NAT/G TEC/DEV INT/TRADE ARMS/CONT NUC/PWR...POLICY 20 UN EURATOM ECSC EEC. PAGE 2 A0034
BIBLIOG DIPLOM INT/ORG INT/LAW

N
AIR UNIVERSITY LIBRARY,INDEX TO MILITARY PERIODICALS. FUT SPACE WOR+45 REGION ARMS/CONT NUC/PWR WAR PEACE INT/LAW. PAGE 5 A0105
BIBLIOG/A FORCES NAT/G DIPLOM

N
COUNCIL ON FOREIGN RELATIONS,DOCUMENTS ON AMERICAN FOREIGN RELATIONS. INT/ORG ECO/TAC NUC/PWR WAR WEAPON...POLICY CON/ANAL CHARTS 20 OAS UN. PAGE 31 A0639
BIBLIOG USA+45 USA-45 DIPLOM

N
UNITED NATIONS,OFFICIAL RECORDS OF THE UNITED NATIONS' ATOMIC ENERGY COMMISSION - DISARMAMENT COMMISSION. WOR+45 TEC/DEV DIPLOM WRITING NUC/PWR 20 UN. PAGE 148 A3032
ARMS/CONT INT/ORG DELIB/GP CONFER

N19
MEZERIK A.G.,ATOM TESTS AND RADIATION HAZARDS (PAMPHLET). WOR+45 INT/ORG DIPLOM DETER 20 UN TREATY. PAGE 100 A2059
NUC/PWR ARMS/CONT CONFER HEALTH

N19
MEZERIK AG,OUTER SPACE: UN, US, USSR (PAMPHLET). USSR DELIB/GP FORCES DETER NUC/PWR SOVEREIGN ...POLICY 20 UN TREATY. PAGE 101 A2063
SPACE CONTROL DIPLOM INT/ORG

N19
PROVISIONS SECTION OAU,ORGANIZATION OF AFRICAN UNITY: BASIC DOCUMENTS AND RESOLUTIONS (PAMPHLET). AFR CULTURE ECO/UNDEV DIPLOM ECO/TAC EDU/PROP COLONIAL ARMS/CONT NUC/PWR RACE/REL DISCRIM NAT/LISM 20 UN OAU. PAGE 118 A2415
CONSTN EX/STRUC SOVEREIGN INT/ORG

N19
ZLOTNICK M.,WEAPONS IN SPACE (PAMPHLET). FUT WOR+45 TEC/DEV DIPLOM ARMS/CONT CIVMIL/REL PEACE HABITAT ...CONCPT NEW/IDEA CHARTS. PAGE 170 A3457
SPACE WEAPON NUC/PWR WAR

B45
GALLOWAY E.,ABSTRACTS OF POSTWAR LITERATURE (VOL. IV) JAN.-JULY, 1945 NOS. 901-1074. POLAND USA+45 USSR WOR+45 INDUS LABOR PLAN ECO/TAC INT/TRADE TAX EDU/PROP ADMIN COLONIAL INT/LAW. PAGE 51 A1033
BIBLIOG/A NUC/PWR NAT/G DIPLOM

B45
STRAUSZ-HUPE R.,THE BALANCE OF TOMORROW: POWER AND FOREIGN POLICY IN THE UNITED STATES. FUT USA+45 ECO/DEV EXTR/IND INT/ORG FORCES BAL/PWR REGION NUC/PWR...GEOG CHARTS 20 COLD/WAR EUROPE/W. PAGE 139 A2845
DIPLOM PWR POLICY WAR

B46
BRODIE B.,THE OBSOLETE WEAPON: ATOMIC POWER AND WORLD ORDER. COM USA+45 USSR WOR+45 DELIB/GP PLAN ORD/FREE PWR...CONCPT TIME/SEQ TREND UN 20. PAGE 19 A0380
INT/ORG TEC/DEV ARMS/CONT NUC/PWR

L46
MASTERS D.,"ONE WORLD OR NONE." FUT WOR+45 INTELL INT/ORG ACT/RES EDU/PROP DETER ATTIT RIGID/FLEX SUPEGO KNOWL...STAT TREND ORG/CHARTS 20. PAGE 96 A1960
POLICY PHIL/SCI ARMS/CONT NUC/PWR

B47
SOCIAL SCIENCE RESEARCH COUN,PUBLIC REACTION TO THE ATOMIC BOMB AND WORLD AFFAIRS. SOCIETY CONFER ARMS/CONT...STAT QU SAMP CHARTS 20. PAGE 135 A2757
ATTIT NUC/PWR DIPLOM WAR

L47
COMM. STUDY ORGAN. PEACE,"SECURITY THROUGH THE UNITED NATIONS." COM FUT WOR+45 TOP/EX ACT/RES BAL/PWR ARMS/CONT NUC/PWR...CONCPT GEN/LAWS UN TOT/POP COLD/WAR 20. PAGE 28 A0577
INT/ORG ORD/FREE PEACE

N47
FOX W.T.R.,UNITED STATES POLICY IN A TWO POWER WORLD. COM USA+45 USSR FORCES DOMIN AGREE NEUTRAL NUC/PWR ORD/FREE SOVEREIGN 20 COLD/WAR TREATY EUROPE/W INTERVENT. PAGE 48 A0972
DIPLOM FOR/AID POLICY

B48
COTTRELL L.S. JR.,AMERICAN PUBLIC OPINION ON WORLD AFFAIRS IN THE ATOMIC AGE. USA+45 CULTURE INT/ORG NAT/G DIPLOM EDU/PROP PEACE RIGID/FLEX ORD/FREE ...POLICY SOC CONCPT STAND/INT TOT/POP 20. PAGE 31 A0633
SOCIETY ATTIT ARMS/CONT NUC/PWR

B50
DULLES J.F.,WAR OR PEACE. CHINA/COM USA+45 USSR INT/ORG SECT FORCES PLAN NUC/PWR WAR CENTRAL MARXISM...POLICY 20 UN ROOSEVLT/F STALIN/J. PAGE 39 A0797
PEACE DIPLOM TREND ORD/FREE

B50
LINCOLN G.,ECONOMICS OF NATIONAL SECURITY. USA+45 ELITES COM/IND DIST/IND INDUS NAT/G VOL/ASSN DELIB/GP EX/STRUC FOR/AID EDU/PROP COERCE NUC/PWR WAR ATTIT KNOWL ORD/FREE PWR COLD/WAR TOT/POP VAL/FREE 20. PAGE 89 A1818
FORCES ECO/TAC

B50
NORTHROP F.S.C.,THE TAMING OF THE NATIONS. KOREA USA+45 USSR WOR+45 STRUCT ECO/UNDEV INT/ORG NAT/G TOP/EX NUC/PWR ATTIT ALL/VALS...TIME/SEQ 20 HIROSHIMA. PAGE 110 A2255
CONCPT BAL/PWR

B53
SCHAAF R.W.,DOCUMENTS OF INTERNATIONAL MEETINGS. AGRI INDUS ACADEM DIPLOM NUC/PWR RACE/REL AGE/Y HEALTH...SOC 20. PAGE 127 A2614
BIBLIOG/A DELIB/GP INT/ORG POLICY

B54
BUTOW R.J.C.,JAPAN'S DECISION TO SURRENDER. USA-45 USSR CHIEF FORCES DOMIN NUC/PWR...BIBLIOG 20 TREATY CHINJAP. PAGE 22 A0453
ELITES DIPLOM WAR PEACE

B54
BUTZ O.,GERMANY: DILEMMA FOR AMERICAN POLICY. GERMANY USA+45 USA-45 USSR WOR+45 INT/ORG FORCES NUC/PWR EFFICIENCY PEACE PWR...GOV/COMP 20 COLD/WAR. PAGE 23 A0459
DIPLOM NAT/G WAR POLICY

B54
KENNAN G.F.,REALITIES OF AMERICAN FOREIGN POLICY. USA+45 INT/ORG NUC/PWR TOTALISM 20 COLD/WAR. PAGE 77 A1586
DIPLOM BAL/PWR DECISION DETER

B54
KENWORTHY L.S.,FREE AND INEXPENSIVE MATERIALS ON WORLD AFFAIRS (PAMPHLET). WOR+45 CULTURE ECO/UNDEV INT/TRADE ARMS/CONT NUC/PWR UN. PAGE 78 A1597
BIBLIOG/A NAT/G INT/ORG DIPLOM

B54
SAPIN B.M.,THE ROLE OF THE MILITARY IN AMERICAN FOREIGN POLICY. USA+45 INT/ORG PROB/SOLV DETER NUC/PWR ATTIT PWR...BIBLIOG 20 NATO. PAGE 127 A2602
DIPLOM POLICY CIVMIL/REL NAT/G

B54
US DEPARTMENT OF STATE,PUBLICATIONS OF THE DEPARTMENT OF STATE, OCTOBER 1,1929 TO JANUARY 1, 1953. AGRI INT/ORG FORCES FOR/AID EDU/PROP ARMS/CONT NUC/PWR ATTIT 20 DEPT/STATE OAS UN NATO. PAGE 151 A3089
BIBLIOG DIPLOM

B55
COMM. STUDY ORGAN. PEACE,REPORTS. WOR-45 ECO/DEV ECO/UNDEV VOL/ASSN CONSULT FORCES PLAN TEC/DEV DOMIN EDU/PROP NUC/PWR ATTIT PWR WEALTH...JURID STERTYP FAO ILO 20 UN. PAGE 28 A0579
WOR+45 INT/ORG ARMS/CONT

B55
LANDHEER B.,EUROPEAN YEARBOOK, 1955. CONSTN ECO/DEV DIST/IND FINAN DELIB/GP ECO/TAC DETER NUC/PWR ...BIBLIOG 20 EEC. PAGE 84 A1717
EUR+WWI INT/ORG GOV/REL INT/TRADE

B55
MOCH J.,HUMAN FOLLY: DISARM OR PERISH. USA+45 WOR+45 SOCIETY INT/ORG NAT/G ACT/RES EDU/PROP ATTIT PERSON KNOWL ORD/FREE PWR...MAJORIT TOT/POP COLD/WAR 20. PAGE 102 A2093
FUT DELIB/GP ARMS/CONT NUC/PWR

B56
BLACKETT P.M.S.,ATOMIC WEAPONS AND EAST-WEST RELATIONS. FUT WOR+45 INT/ORG DELIB/GP COERCE ATTIT RIGID/FLEX KNOWL...RELATIV HIST/WRIT TREND GEN/METH COLD/WAR 20. PAGE 15 A0299
FORCES PWR ARMS/CONT NUC/PWR

B56
BUREAU OF PUBLIC AFFAIRS,AMERICAN FOREIGN POLICY: CURRENT DOCUMENTS. COM USA+45 USSR WOR+45 DELIB/GP FOR/AID INT/TRADE ARMS/CONT NUC/PWR ALL/VALS ALL/IDEOS...DECISION 20 NATO. PAGE 21 A0434
BIBLIOG/A DIPLOM POLICY

B56
GILBERT R.,COMPETITIVE COEXISTENCE: THE NEW SOVIET CHALLENGE. WORKER DIPLOM WAR ORD/FREE 20 COLD/WAR. PAGE 52 A1071
NUC/PWR DOMIN MARXISM PEACE

B56
KOENIG L.W.,THE TRUMAN ADMINISTRATION: ITS PRINCIPLES AND PRACTICE. USA+45 POL/PAR CHIEF LEGIS DIPLOM DEATH NUC/PWR WAR CIVMIL/REL PEACE ...DECISION 20 TRUMAN/HS PRESIDENT TREATY. PAGE 81 A1658
ADMIN POLICY EX/STRUC GOV/REL

B56
REITZEL W.,UNITED STATES FOREIGN POLICY, 1945-1955. USA+45 WOR+45 CONSTN INT/ORG EDU/PROP LEGIT EXEC COERCE NUC/PWR PEACE ATTIT ORD/FREE PWR...DECISION CONCPT OBS RECORD TIME/SEQ TREND COLD/WAR UN CONGRESS. PAGE 120 A2464
NAT/G POLICY DIPLOM

B56
ROBERTS H.L.,RUSSIA AND AMERICA. CHINA/COM S/ASIA USSR FORCES TEC/DEV FOR/AID NUC/PWR ALL/IDEOS ...MAJORIT TREND NAT/COMP 20 COLD/WAR UN NATO. PAGE 122 A2494
DIPLOM INT/ORG BAL/PWR TOTALISM

B57
BEAL J.R.,JOHN FOSTER DULLES, A BIOGRAPHY. USA+45 USSR WOR+45 CONSTN INT/ORG NAT/G EX/STRUC LEGIT ADMIN NUC/PWR DISPL PERSON ORD/FREE PWR SKILL ...POLICY PSY OBS RECORD COLD/WAR UN 20 DULLES/JF. PAGE 12 A0237
BIOG DIPLOM

B57
BERLE A.A.,TIDES OF CRISIS: A PRIMER OF FOREIGN RELATIONS. USA+45 WOR+45 DOMIN NUC/PWR NAT/LISM PWR ...CONCPT STERTYP GEN/LAWS 20 UN. PAGE 14 A0276
INT/ORG TREND PEACE

B57
FURNISS E.S.,AMERICAN MILITARY POLICY: STRATEGIC ASPECTS OF WORLD POLITICAL GEOGRAPHY. COM EUR+WWI ISLAM L/A+17C USA+45 WOR+45 INT/ORG ACT/RES ARMS/CONT COERCE NUC/PWR ATTIT PWR...GEOG NEW/IDEA VAL/FREE COLD/WAR 20. PAGE 50 A1027
FORCES DIPLOM

B57
KENNAN G.F.,RUSSIA, THE ATOM AND THE WEST. COM EUR+WWI FUT WOR+45 SOCIETY ECO/DEV FORCES DIPLOM ECO/TAC DOMIN EDU/PROP COERCE NUC/PWR ATTIT DRIVE ORD/FREE PWR...POLICY OBS TIME/SEQ TREND COLD/WAR NATO 20. PAGE 77 A1574
NAT/G INT/ORG USSR

B57
KISSINGER H.A.,NUCLEAR WEAPONS AND FOREIGN POLICY. FUT USA+45 WOR+45 INT/ORG FORCES ACT/RES TEC/DEV DIPLOM ARMS/CONT COERCE ATTIT KNOWL PWR...DECISION GEOG CHARTS 20. PAGE 80 A1640
PLAN DETER NUC/PWR

B57
NEHRU J.,MILITARY ALLIANCE (PAMPHLET). INDIA WOR+45 NAT/G PLAN DETER NUC/PWR WAR...POLICY ANTHOL NEHRU/J SEATO UN. PAGE 108 A2212
INT/ORG DIPLOM FORCES PEACE

B57
SPEIER H.,GERMAN REARMAMENT AND ATOMIC WAR: THE VIEWS OF GERMAN MILITARY AND POLITICAL LEADERS. FUT WOR+45 INT/ORG NAT/G WEAPON ATTIT PWR...INT QU TOT/POP VAL/FREE COLD/WAR 20. PAGE 136 A2780
TOP/EX FORCES NUC/PWR GERMANY

S57
SPEIER H.,"SOVIET ATOMIC BLACKMAIL AND THE NORTH ATLANTIC ALLIANCE." EUR+WWI USA+45 USSR INT/ORG NAT/G FORCES DIPLOM DRIVE ORD/FREE PWR NATO VAL/FREE COLD/WAR 20. PAGE 136 A2781
COM COERCE NUC/PWR

B58
ANGELL N.,DEFENCE AND THE ENGLISH-SPEAKING ROLE. CHINA/COM UK USSR INT/ORG FORCES EDU/PROP NEUTRAL NUC/PWR NAT/LISM PEACE TOTALISM 20 COLD/WAR COEXIST. PAGE 8 A0161
DIPLOM WAR MARXISM ORD/FREE

B58
ARON R.,ON WAR: ATOMIC WEAPONS AND GLOBAL DIPLOMACY (TRANS. BY TERENCE KILMARTIN). WOR+45 SOCIETY FORCES BAL/PWR WAR WEAPON PERSON...SOC 20. PAGE 9 A0182
ARMS/CONT NUC/PWR COERCE DIPLOM

B58
GARTHOFF R.L.,SOVIET STRATEGY IN THE NUCLEAR AGE. FUT USSR R+D INT/ORG NAT/G ACT/RES TEC/DEV DOMIN DETER WAR ATTIT PWR...RELATIV METH/CNCPT SELF/OBS TREND CON/ANAL STERTYP GEN/LAWS 20. PAGE 51 A1052
COM FORCES BAL/PWR NUC/PWR

B58
GAVIN J.M.,WAR AND PEACE IN THE SPACE AGE. SPACE USA+45 USSR FORCES PLAN TEC/DEV BAL/PWR DIPLOM ARMS/CONT WEAPON CIVMIL/REL...CHARTS GP/COMP 20 NATO COLD/WAR. PAGE 52 A1055
WAR DETER NUC/PWR PEACE

B58
HENKIN L.,ARMS CONTROL AND INSPECTION IN AMERICAN LAW. LAW CONSTN INT/ORG LOC/G MUNIC NAT/G PROVS EDU/PROP LEGIT EXEC NUC/PWR KNOWL ORD/FREE...OBS TOT/POP CONGRESS 20. PAGE 64 A1315
USA+45 JURID ARMS/CONT

B58
KENNAN G.F.,RUSSIA, THE ATOM AND THE WEST. USA+45 USSR INT/ORG ARMS/CONT MARXISM 20 NATO. PAGE 77 A1587
BAL/PWR NUC/PWR CONTROL DIPLOM

B58
MELMAN S.,INSPECTION FOR DISARMAMENT. USA+45 WOR+45 SOCIETY INT/ORG NAT/G CONSULT ACT/RES PLAN EDU/PROP CONTROL DETER PEACE ATTIT PERSON KNOWL...PSY STAT OBS CHARTS TOT/POP VAL/FREE 20. PAGE 99 A2035
FUT ORD/FREE ARMS/CONT NUC/PWR

B58
MOORE B.T.,NATO AND THE FUTURE OF EUROPE. EUR+WWI FUT USA+45 ECO/DEV INDUS MARKET NAT/G VOL/ASSN FORCES DIPLOM NUC/PWR ORD/FREE...CONCPT CHARTS ORG/CHARTS CMN/WLTH 20 NATO. PAGE 103 A2122
INT/ORG REGION

B58
NATIONAL PLANNING ASSOCIATION,1970 WITHOUT ARMS CONTROL (PAMPHLET). WOR+45 PROB/SOLV TEC/DEV DIPLOM CONFER DETER NUC/PWR WAR...CHARTS 20 COLD/WAR. PAGE 107 A2204
ARMS/CONT ORD/FREE WEAPON PREDICT

B58
NOEL-BAKER D.,THE ARMS RACE. WOR+45 NAT/G DELIB/GP ACT/RES TEC/DEV EDU/PROP NUC/PWR ATTIT KNOWL PWR ...CONCPT OBS LEAGUE/NAT 20 COLD/WAR. PAGE 109 A2245
FUT INT/ORG ARMS/CONT PEACE

B58
ROCKEFELLER BROTH FUND INC,INTERNATIONAL SECURITY THE MILITARY ASPECT. USA+45 INT/ORG NAT/G BUDGET ARMS/CONT WAR WEAPON PEACE ORD/FREE 20 NATO. PAGE 123 A2511
NUC/PWR DETER FORCES DIPLOM

B58
SCHUMAN F.,INTERNATIONAL POLITICS. WOR+45 WOR-45 INTELL NAT/G FORCES DOMIN LEGIT COERCE NUC/PWR ATTIT DISPL ORD/FREE PWR SOVEREIGN...POLICY CONCPT GEN/LAWS SUEZ 20. PAGE 129 A2650
FUT INT/ORG NAT/LISM DIPLOM

B58
SOC OF COMP LEGIS AND INT LAW,THE LAW OF THE SEA... (PAMPHLET). WOR+45 NAT/G INT/TRADE ADJUD CONTROL NUC/PWR WAR PEACE ATTIT ORD/FREE...JURID CHARTS 20 UN TREATY RESOURCE/N. PAGE 135 A2756
INT/LAW INT/ORG DIPLOM SEA

B58
UN INTL CONF ON PEACEFUL USE,PROGRESS IN ATOMIC ENERGY (VOL. I). WOR+45 R+D PLAN TEC/DEV CONFER CONTROL PEACE SKILL...CHARTS ANTHOL 20 UN BAGHDAD. PAGE 147 A3003
NUC/PWR DIPLOM WORKER EDU/PROP

B58
US DEPARTMENT OF STATE,PUBLICATIONS OF THE DEPARTMENT OF STATE, JANUARY 1,1953 TO DECEMBER 31, 1957. AGRI INT/ORG FORCES FOR/AID EDU/PROP ARMS/CONT NUC/PWR ATTIT 20 DEPT/STATE OAS UN NATO. PAGE 151 A3092
BIBLIOG DIPLOM

S58
BURNS A.L.,"THE INTERNATIONAL CONSEQUENCES OF EXPECTING SURPRISE." WOR+45 INT/ORG NAT/G FORCES DIPLOM COERCE NUC/PWR WAR CHOOSE ORD/FREE ...METH/CNCPT STYLE OBS STERTYP TOT/POP VAL/FREE. PAGE 22 A0440
PLAN PWR DETER

B59
BRODIE B.,STRATEGY IN THE MISSILE AGE. FUT WOR+45 CONSULT PLAN COERCE DETER RIGID/FLEX PWR...CONCPT TIME/SEQ TREND 20. PAGE 19 A0381
ACT/RES FORCES ARMS/CONT NUC/PWR

B59
COMM. STUDY ORGAN. PEACE,ORGANIZING PEACE IN THE NUCLEAR AGE. FUT CONSULT DELIB/GP DOMIN ADJUD ROUTINE COERCE ORD/FREE...TECHNIC INT/LAW JURID NEW/IDEA UN COLD/WAR 20. PAGE 29 A0581
INT/ORG ACT/RES NUC/PWR

B59
EGYPTIAN SOCIETY OF INT LAW,THE MONROVIA CONFERENCE (PAMPHLET). AFR ALGERIA FRANCE UAR CONFER REGION NUC/PWR WAR DISCRIM 20 SAHARA AFR/STATES. PAGE 40 A0826
COLONIAL SOVEREIGN RACE/REL DIPLOM

B59
FREE L.A.,SIX ALLIES AND A NEUTRAL. ASIA COM EUR+WWI FRANCE GERMANY/W INDIA S/ASIA UK USA+45 INT/ORG NAT/G NUC/PWR PEACE ATTIT PERCEPT RIGID/FLEX ALL/VALS...STAT REC/INT COLD/WAR 20 CHINJAP. PAGE 48 A0992
PSY DIPLOM

B59
GOLDWIN R.A.,READINGS IN AMERICAN FOREIGN POLICY. USA+45 USA-45 ARMS/CONT NUC/PWR...INT/LAW 18/20. PAGE 53 A1094
ANTHOL DIPLOM INT/ORG ECO/UNDEV

B59
GOULD L.P.,THE PRICE OF SURVIVAL. EUR+WWI SPACE USA+45 FORCES ECO/TAC NUC/PWR WAR ORD/FREE MARXISM ...IDEA/COMP 20 COLD/WAR NATO. PAGE 54 A1117
POLICY PROB/SOLV DIPLOM PEACE

B59
HARVARD UNIVERSITY LAW SCHOOL,INTERNATIONAL PROBLEMS OF FINANCIAL PROTECTION AGAINST NUCLEAR RISK. WOR+45 NAT/G DELIB/GP PROB/SOLV DIPLOM CONTROL ATTIT...POLICY INT/LAW MATH 20. PAGE 62
NUC/PWR ADJUD INDUS FINAN

A1281

B59
HERZ J.H.,INTERNATIONAL POLITICS IN THE ATOMIC AGE. FUT USA+45 WOR-45 SOCIETY NAT/G FORCES PLAN COERCE DETER ATTIT DRIVE ORD/FREE PWR...TREND COLD/WAR 20. PAGE 64 A1319
INT/ORG ARMS/CONT NUC/PWR

B59
HUGHES E.M.,AMERICA THE VINCIBLE. USA+45 FOR/AID ARMS/CONT NUC/PWR PERS/REL RATIONAL ATTIT ALL/VALS 20 COLD/WAR. PAGE 69 A1413
ORD/FREE DIPLOM WAR

B59
MODELSKI G.,ATOMIC ENERGY IN THE COMMUNIST BLOC. FUT INT/ORG CONSULT FORCES ACT/RES PLAN KNOWL SKILL ...PHIL/SCI STAT CHARTS 20. PAGE 102 A2096
TEC/DEV NUC/PWR USSR COM

B59
NIEBUHR R.,NATIONS AND EMPIRES. WOR+45 INT/ORG COLONIAL NUC/PWR TOTALISM UTOPIA ORD/FREE MARXISM WORSHIP 20 COLD/WAR PROTESTANT CHRISTIAN. PAGE 109 A2237
DIPLOM NAT/G POLICY PWR

B59
PEARSON L.B.,DIPLOMACY IN THE NUCLEAR AGE. USA+45 USSR INT/ORG PWR...TREND 20 NATO UN. PAGE 114 A2343
NUC/PWR PEACE POLICY DIPLOM

B59
STERNBERG F.,THE MILITARY AND INDUSTRIAL REVOLUTION OF OUR TIME. USA+45 USSR WOR+45 WORKER COMPUTER PLAN TEC/DEV NUC/PWR GP/REL...POLICY NAT/COMP 20. PAGE 138 A2818
DIPLOM FORCES INDUS CIVMIL/REL

B59
WOLFERS A.,ALLIANCE POLICY IN THE COLD WAR. COM INT/ORG FORCES COLONIAL CONTROL NUC/PWR 20 NATO UN COLD/WAR. PAGE 166 A3384
DIPLOM DETER BAL/PWR

S59
BROMKE A.,"DISENGAGEMENT IN EAST EUROPE." COM USSR INT/ORG DIPLOM EDU/PROP NEUTRAL NUC/PWR DRIVE RIGID/FLEX PWR...PSY CONCPT CON/ANAL GEN/METH VAL/FREE 20. PAGE 19 A0388
BAL/PWR

S59
KISSINGER H.A.,"THE SEARCH FOR STABILITY." COM GERMANY MOD/EUR USA+45 USA-45 USSR INT/ORG ARMS/CONT NUC/PWR ORD/FREE PWR COLD/WAR 20 NATO. PAGE 80 A1641
FUT ATTIT BAL/PWR

S59
SIMONS H.,"WORLD-WIDE CAPABILITIES FOR PRODUCTION AND CONTROL OF NUCLEAR WEAPONS." FUT WOR+45 INDUS INT/ORG NAT/G ECO/TAC ATTIT PWR SKILL...TREND CHARTS VAL/FREE 20. PAGE 133 A2719
TEC/DEV ARMS/CONT NUC/PWR

S59
STOESSINGER J.G.,"THE INTERNATIONAL ATOMIC ENERGY AGENCY: THE FIRST PHASE." FUT WOR+45 NAT/G VOL/ASSN DELIB/GP BAL/PWR LEGIT ADMIN ROUTINE PWR...OBS CON/ANAL GEN/LAWS VAL/FREE 20 IAEA. PAGE 138 A2829
INT/ORG ECO/DEV FOR/AID NUC/PWR

B60
ARMS CONTROL. FUT UNIV WOR+45 INTELL R+D INT/ORG NAT/G VOL/ASSN CONSULT CREATE EDU/PROP PEACE...HUM GEN/LAWS TOT/POP 20. PAGE 3 A0060
DELIB/GP ORD/FREE ARMS/CONT NUC/PWR

B60
BARNET R.,WHO WANTS DISARMAMENT. COM EUR+WWI USA+45 USSR INT/ORG NAT/G BAL/PWR DIPLOM EDU/PROP COERCE DETER NUC/PWR WAR WEAPON ATTIT PWR...TIME/SEQ COLD/WAR CONGRESS 20. PAGE 11 A0225
PLAN FORCES ARMS/CONT

B60
BILLERBECK K.,SOVIET BLOC FOREIGN AID TO UNDERDEVELOPED COUNTRIES. COM FUT USSR FINAN FORCES TEC/DEV DIPLOM INT/TRADE EDU/PROP NUC/PWR...TREND 20. PAGE 14 A0287
FOR/AID ECO/UNDEV ECO/TAC MARXISM

B60
BROWN H.,COMMUNITY OF FEAR. FORCES TEC/DEV ARMS/CONT COERCE PEACE 20. PAGE 20 A0402
NUC/PWR WAR DIPLOM DETER

B60
EINSTEIN A.,EINSTEIN ON PEACE. FUT WOR+45 WOR-45 SOCIETY NAT/G PLAN BAL/PWR CAP/ISM DIPLOM ARMS/CONT DETER NAT/LISM...POLICY RELATIV HUM PHIL/SCI CONCPT BIOG COLD/WAR LEAGUE/NAT NAZI. PAGE 41 A0829
INT/ORG ATTIT NUC/PWR PEACE

B60
FISCHER L.,RUSSIA, AMERICA, AND THE WORLD. FUT USA+45 USSR WOR+45 FORCES PLAN BAL/PWR ECO/TAC FOR/AID NEUTRAL TASK NUC/PWR PWR 20 COLD/WAR. PAGE 46 A0937
DIPLOM POLICY MARXISM ECO/UNDEV

B60
HAHN W.F.,AMERICAN STRATEGY FOR THE NUCLEAR AGE. USA+45 NAT/G TEC/DEV ECO/TAC FOR/AID ARMS/CONT NUC/PWR ORD/FREE MARXISM...ANTHOL 20. PAGE 59 A1216
DIPLOM PLAN PEACE

B60
LE GHAIT E.,NO CARTE BLANCHE TO CAPRICORN; THE FOLLY OF NUCLEAR WAR. WOR+45 INT/ORG BAL/PWR DIPLOM RISK COERCE...CENSUS 20 NATO. PAGE 86 A1754
DETER NUC/PWR PLAN DECISION

B60
MCCLELLAND C.A.,NUCLEAR WEAPONS, MISSILES, AND FUTURE WAR: PROBLEM FOR THE SIXTIES. WOR+45 FORCES ARMS/CONT DETER MARXISM...POLICY ANTHOL COLD/WAR. PAGE 97 A1998
DIPLOM NUC/PWR WAR WEAPON

B60
MCKINNEY R.,REVIEW OF THE INTERNATIONAL ATOMIC POLICIES AND PROGRAMS OF THE UNITED STATES (5 VOLS.). COM FUT USA+45 ECO/DEV ECO/UNDEV INT/ORG DELIB/GP PLAN ADMIN 20 THIRD/WRLD. PAGE 98 A2016
NUC/PWR PEACE DIPLOM POLICY

B60
TAYLOR M.D.,THE UNCERTAIN TRUMPET. USA+45 USSR WOR+45 INT/ORG NAT/G CONSULT DOMIN COERCE NUC/PWR WAR ATTIT ORD/FREE PWR...POLICY CONCPT TREND GEN/METH COLD/WAR UN NATO 20. PAGE 142 A2900
PLAN FORCES DIPLOM

B60
TURNER G.B.,NATIONAL SECURITY IN THE NUCLEAR AGE. KOREA USA+45 PLAN DIPLOM ARMS/CONT DETER WAR WEAPON ...BIBLIOG 20 COLD/WAR NATO. PAGE 146 A2982
NAT/G POLICY FORCES NUC/PWR

B60
UNITED WORLD FEDERALISTS,UNITED WORLD FEDERALISTS; PANORAMA OF RECENT BOOKS, FILMS, AND JOURNALS ON WORLD FEDERATION, THE UN, AND WORLD PEACE. CULTURE ECO/UNDEV PROB/SOLV FOR/AID ARMS/CONT NUC/PWR ...INT/LAW PHIL/SCI 20 UN. PAGE 149 A3039
BIBLIOG/A DIPLOM INT/ORG PEACE

B60
US DEPARTMENT OF THE ARMY,DISARMAMENT: A BIBLIOGRAPHIC RECORD: 1916-1960. DETER WAR WEAPON PEACE 20 UN LEAGUE/NAT COLD/WAR NATO. PAGE 152 A3103
BIBLIOG/A ARMS/CONT NUC/PWR DIPLOM

L60
HOLTON G.,"ARMS CONTROL." FUT WOR+45 CULTURE INT/ORG NAT/G FORCES TOP/EX PLAN EDU/PROP COERCE ATTIT RIGID/FLEX ORD/FREE...POLICY PHIL/SCI SOC TREND COLD/WAR. PAGE 67 A1377
ACT/RES CONSULT ARMS/CONT NUC/PWR

L60
JACOB P.E.,"THE DISARMAMENT CONSENSUS." USA+45 USSR WOR+45 INT/ORG NAT/G ACT/RES TEC/DEV BAL/PWR EDU/PROP ADMIN COERCE DETER NUC/PWR CONSEN RIGID/FLEX PWR...CONCPT RECORD CHARTS COLD/WAR 20. PAGE 72 A1482
DELIB/GP ATTIT ARMS/CONT

L60
NOGEE J.L.,"THE DIPLOMACY OF DISARMAMENT." WOR+45 INT/ORG NAT/G CONSULT DELIB/GP TOP/EX BAL/PWR DIPLOM EDU/PROP COERCE DETER WEAPON PEACE ATTIT ...RECORD TIME/SEQ TOT/POP VAL/FREE COLD/WAR 20. PAGE 109 A2246
PWR ORD/FREE ARMS/CONT NUC/PWR

S60
BRODY R.A.,"DETERRENCE STRATEGIES: AN ANNOTATED BIBLIOGRAPHY." WOR+45 PLAN ARMS/CONT NUC/PWR WAR WEAPON DECISION. PAGE 19 A0383
BIBLIOG/A FORCES DETER DIPLOM

S60
DOUGHERTY J.E.,"KEY TO SECURITY: DISARMAMENT OR ARMS STABILITY." COM USA+45 USSR INT/ORG NAT/G CREATE EDU/PROP COERCE DETER ATTIT PWR...DECISION CONCPT MYTH NEW/IDEA TREND 20 COLD/WAR. PAGE 38 A0777
FORCES ORD/FREE ARMS/CONT NUC/PWR

S60
DYSON F.J.,"THE FUTURE DEVELOPMENT OF NUCLEAR WEAPONS." FUT WOR+45 DELIB/GP ACT/RES PLAN DETER WEAPON ATTIT PWR...POLICY 20. PAGE 40 A0815
INT/ORG ARMS/CONT NUC/PWR

S60
GULICK E.U.,"OUR BALANCE OF POWER SYSTEM IN PERSPECTIVE." FUT WOR+45 WOR-45 ECO/DEV DOMIN ROUTINE NUC/PWR PEACE PWR WEALTH...PLURIST CONCPT HIST/WRIT GEN/METH TOT/POP 20. PAGE 58 A1191
INT/ORG TREND ARMS/CONT BAL/PWR

S60
HAVILAND H.F.,"PROBLEMS OF AMERICAN FOREIGN POLICY." ASIA COM USA+45 WOR+45 INT/ORG NAT/G CONSULT ECO/TAC FOR/AID DOMIN COERCE NUC/PWR ATTIT DRIVE ORD/FREE PWR RESPECT SKILL...POLICY GEOG OBS SAMP TREND GEN/METH METH COLD/WAR UN 20. PAGE 63 A1292
ECO/UNDEV FORCES DIPLOM

S60
IKLE F.C.,"NTH COUNTRIES AND DISARMAMENT." WOR+45 DELIB/GP ECO/TAC DOMIN EDU/PROP LEGIT ROUTINE COERCE RIGID/FLEX ORD/FREE...MARXIST TREND 20. PAGE 70 A1432
FUT INT/ORG ARMS/CONT NUC/PWR

S60
KAPLAN M.A.,"THEORETICAL ANALYSIS OF THE BALANCE OF POWER." FUT USA+45 WOR+45 INTELL ECO/DEV INT/ORG NAT/G CONSULT TOP/EX ACT/RES PLAN TEC/DEV ATTIT ALL/VALS...METH/CNCPT TOT/POP 20. PAGE 76 A1562
CREATE NEW/IDEA DIPLOM NUC/PWR

S60
KISTIAKOWSKY G.B.,"SCIENCE AND FOREIGN AFFAIRS." FUT WOR+45 NAT/G PROF/ORG PLAN ECO/TAC EDU/PROP NUC/PWR...TREND COLD/WAR 20. PAGE 80 A1645
CONSULT TEC/DEV FOR/AID DIPLOM

S60
LEAR J.,"PEACE: SCIENCE'S NEXT GREAT EXPLORATION." USA+45 INT/ORG TOP/EX TEC/DEV EDU/PROP ROUTINE PEACE KNOWL SKILL 20. PAGE 86 A1757
EX/STRUC ARMS/CONT NUC/PWR

S60
MORGENSTERN O.,"GOAL: AN ARMED, INSPECTED, OPEN WORLD." COM EUR+WWI USA+45 R+D INT/ORG NAT/G TEC/DEV BAL/PWR COERCE NUC/PWR ORD/FREE PWR...TREND 20. PAGE 104 A2133
FORCES CONCPT ARMS/CONT DETER

S60
O'BRIEN W.,"THE ROLE OF FORCE IN THE INTERNATIONAL JURIDICAL ORDER." WOR+45 NAT/G FORCES DOMIN ADJUD ARMS/CONT DETER NUC/PWR WAR ATTIT PWR...CATH INT/LAW JURID CONCPT TREND STERTYP GEN/LAWS 20. PAGE 110 A2266
INT/ORG COERCE

S60
RHYNE C.S.,"LAW AS AN INSTRUMENT FOR PEACE." FUT WOR+45 PLAN LEGIT ROUTINE ARMS/CONT NUC/PWR ATTIT ORD/FREE...JURID METH/CNCPT TREND CON/ANAL HYPO/EXP COLD/WAR 20. PAGE 120 A2471
ADJUD EDU/PROP INT/LAW PEACE

B61
AMORY J.F.,AROUND THE EDGE OF WAR: A NEW APPROACH TO THE PROBLEMS OF AMERICAN FOREIGN POLICY. COM L/A+17C USA+45 USSR FOR/AID EDU/PROP AGREE CONTROL ARMS/CONT NUC/PWR WAR PWR...IDEA/COMP 20 TREATY ESPIONAGE. PAGE 8 A0154
NAT/G DIPLOM POLICY

B61
BECHHOEFER B.G.,POSTWAR NEGOTIATIONS FOR ARMS CONTROL. COM EUR+WWI USSR INT/ORG NAT/G ACT/RES BAL/PWR DIPLOM ECO/TAC EDU/PROP ADMIN REGION DETER NUC/PWR WAR WEAPON PEACE ATTIT PWR...POLICY TIME/SEQ COLD/WAR CONGRESS 20. PAGE 12 A0244
USA+45 ARMS/CONT

B61
BULL H.,THE CONTROL OF THE ARMS RACE. COM USA+45 INT/ORG NAT/G PLAN TEC/DEV DIPLOM ATTIT...RELATIV DECISION CONCPT SELF/OBS TREND CON/ANAL GEN/METH 20 COLD/WAR. PAGE 21 A0429
FORCES PWR ARMS/CONT NUC/PWR

B61
DIMOCK M.E.,BUSINESS AND GOVERNMENT (4TH ED.). AGRI FINAN OP/RES PLAN BUDGET DIPLOM LOBBY NUC/PWR NEW/LIB SOCISM...POLICY BIBLIOG 20. PAGE 37 A0765
NAT/G INDUS LABOR ECO/TAC

B61
FLEMING D.F.,THE COLD WAR AND ITS ORIGINS: 1950-1960 (VOL. II). ASIA FUT HUNGARY POLAND WOR+45 TEC/DEV DOMIN NUC/PWR REV PEACE...T 20 COLD/WAR EISNHWR/DD SUEZ. PAGE 46 A0946
MARXISM DIPLOM BAL/PWR

B61
FLEMING D.F.,THE COLD WAR AND ITS ORIGINS: 1917-1950 (VOL. I). ASIA USSR WOR+45 WOR-45 TEC/DEV FOR/AID NUC/PWR REV WAR PEACE FASCISM...T 20 COLD/WAR NATO BERLIN/BLO. PAGE 46 A0947
DIPLOM MARXISM BAL/PWR

B61
FRISCH D.,ARMS REDUCTION: PROGRAM AND ISSUES. USA+45 INT/ORG NAT/G ACT/RES REGION NUC/PWR ATTIT PWR...POLICY 20. PAGE 49 A1010
PLAN FORCES ARMS/CONT DIPLOM

B61
FULLER J.F.C.,THE CONDUCT OF WAR, 1789-1961. FRANCE RUSSIA SOCIETY NAT/G FORCES PROB/SOLV AGREE NUC/PWR WEAPON PEACE...SOC 18/20 TREATY COLD/WAR. PAGE 50 A1025
WAR POLICY REV ROLE

B61
GALLOIS P.,THE BALANCE OF TERROR: STRATEGY FOR THE NUCLEAR AGE. FUT WOR+45 INT/ORG FORCES TOP/EX DETER WAR ATTIT RIGID/FLEX ORD/FREE PWR...HYPO/EXP 20. PAGE 50 A1032
PLAN DECISION DIPLOM NUC/PWR

B61
HARDT J.P.,THE COLD WAR ECONOMIC GAP. USA+45 USSR ECO/DEV FORCES INT/TRADE NUC/PWR PWR 20 COLD/WAR. PAGE 61 A1258
DIPLOM ECO/TAC NAT/COMP POLICY

B61
HAYTER W.,THE DIPLOMACY OF THE GREAT POWERS. FRANCE UK USSR WOR+45 EX/STRUC TOP/EX NUC/PWR PEACE...OBS 20. PAGE 63 A1296
DIPLOM POLICY NAT/G

B61
HENKIN L.,ARMS CONTROL: ISSUES FOR THE PUBLIC. EUR+WWI FUT USA+45 USSR INT/ORG NAT/G DIPLOM EDU/PROP DETER NUC/PWR ATTIT PWR...CONCPT RECORD HIST/WRIT TIME/SEQ TOT/POP COLD/WAR 20. PAGE 64 A1316
WOR+45 DELIB/GP ARMS/CONT

B61
KISSINGER H.A.,THE NECESSITY FOR CHOICE. FUT USA+45 ECO/UNDEV NAT/G PLAN BAL/PWR ECO/TAC ARMS/CONT DETER NUC/PWR ATTIT...POLICY CONCPT RECORD GEN/LAWS COLD/WAR 20. PAGE 80 A1642
TOP/EX TREND DIPLOM

B61
LIPPMANN W.,THE COMING TESTS WITH RUSSIA. COM CUBA GERMANY USSR FORCES CONTROL NEUTRAL COERCE NUC/PWR REV WAR PWR...INT 20 KHRUSH/N BERLIN. PAGE 89 A1830
BAL/PWR DIPLOM MARXISM ARMS/CONT

B61
MORRAY J.P.,FROM YALTA TO DISARMAMENT: COLD WAR DEBATE. USA+45 CAP/ISM FOR/AID CONTROL NUC/PWR 20 UN COLD/WAR CHURCHLL/W. PAGE 104 A2145
MARXIST ARMS/CONT DIPLOM BAL/PWR

B61
NOGEE J.L.,SOVIET POLICY TOWARD INTERNATIONAL CONTROL OF ATOMIC ENERGY. COM USA+45 WOR+45 INTELL NAT/G ACT/RES DIPLOM EDU/PROP NUC/PWR TOTALISM PERCEPT KNOWL PWR...TIME/SEQ COLD/WAR 20. PAGE 109 A2247
INT/ORG ATTIT ARMS/CONT USSR

B61
SCHMIDT H.,VERTEIDIGUNG ODER VERGELTUNG. COM CUBA GERMANY/W USSR FORCES DIPLOM ARMS/CONT DETER NUC/PWR...POLICY CHARTS HYPO/EXP SIMUL BIBLIOG 20 NATO COLD/WAR. PAGE 128 A2630
PLAN WAR BAL/PWR ORD/FREE

B61
SLESSOR J.,WHAT PRICE COEXISTENCE? COM INT/ORG NAT/G FORCES COLONIAL ARMS/CONT WAR...POLICY TREND 20 NATO COLD/WAR. PAGE 134 A2741
DIPLOM PEACE WOR+45 NUC/PWR

B61
SOKOL A.E.,SEAPOWER IN THE NUCLEAR AGE. USA+45 USSR DIST/IND FORCES INT/TRADE DETER WAR...POLICY NAT/COMP BIBLIOG COLD/WAR. PAGE 135 A2763
SEA PWR WEAPON NUC/PWR

B61
US SENATE COMM GOVT OPERATIONS,ORGANIZING FOR NATIONAL SECURITY. COM USA+45 BUDGET DIPLOM DETER NUC/PWR WAR WEAPON ORD/FREE...BIBLIOG 20 COLD/WAR. PAGE 156 A3172
POLICY PLAN FORCES COERCE

L61
HALPERIN M.H.,"NUCLEAR WEAPONS AND LIMITED WARS." FUT UNIV WOR+45 INTELL SOCIETY ECO/DEV ACT/RES DRIVE PERCEPT RIGID/FLEX...CONCPT TIME/SEQ TREND TOT/POP 20. PAGE 60 A1237
PLAN COERCE NUC/PWR WAR

S61
CARLETON W.G.,"AMERICAN FOREIGN POLICY: MYTHS AND REALITIES." FUT USA+45 WOR+45 ECO/UNDEV INT/ORG EX/STRUC ARMS/CONT NUC/PWR WAR ATTIT...POLICY CONCPT CONT/OBS GEN/METH COLD/WAR TOT/POP 20. PAGE 24 A0484
PLAN MYTH DIPLOM

S61
LEWY G.,"SUPERIOR ORDERS, NUCLEAR WARFARE AND THE DICTATES OF CONSCIENCE: THE DILEMMA OF MILITARY OBEDIENCE IN THE ATOMIC." FUT UNIV WOR+45 INTELL SOCIETY FORCES TOP/EX ACT/RES ADMIN ROUTINE NUC/PWR PERCEPT RIGID/FLEX ALL/VALS...POLICY CONCPT 20. PAGE 88 A1805
DETER INT/ORG LAW INT/LAW

S61
MACHOWSKI K.,"SELECTED PROBLEMS OF NATIONAL SOVEREIGNTY WITH REFERENCE TO THE LAW OF OUTER SPACE." FUT WOR+45 AIR LAW INTELL SOCIETY ECO/DEV PLAN EDU/PROP DETER DRIVE PERCEPT SOVEREIGN ...POLICY INT/LAW OBS TREND TOT/POP 20. PAGE 92 A1889
UNIV ACT/RES NUC/PWR SPACE

S61
MIKSCHE F.O.,"DEFENSE ORGANIZATION FOR WESTERN EUROPE." USA+45 INT/ORG NAT/G VOL/ASSN ACT/RES DOMIN LEGIT COERCE ORD/FREE PWR...RELATIV TREND 20 NATO. PAGE 101 A2071
EUR+WWI FORCES WEAPON NUC/PWR

S61
TAUBENFELD H.J.,"OUTER SPACE--PAST POLITICS AND FUTURE POLICY." FUT USA+45 USA-45 WOR+45 AIR INTELL STRUCT ECO/DEV NAT/G TOP/EX ACT/RES ADMIN ROUTINE NUC/PWR ATTIT DRIVE...CONCPT TIME/SEQ TREND TOT/POP 20. PAGE 141 A2892
PLAN SPACE INT/ORG

B62
ABOSCH H.,THE MENACE OF THE MIRACLE: GERMANY FROM HITLER TO ADENAUER. EUR+WWI GERMANY/W CULTURE FORCES PRESS NUC/PWR WAR CHOOSE 20 HITLER/A ADENAUER/K. PAGE 4 A0082
DIPLOM PEACE POLICY

B62
AIR FORCE ACADEMY LIBRARY,INTERNATIONAL ORGANIZATIONS AND MILITARY SECURITY SYSTEMS (PAMPHLET) (SPECIAL BIBLIOGRAPHY SERIES, NUMBER 25). DIPLOM FOR/AID INT/TRADE NUC/PWR PEACE 20 UN NATO OAS SEATO LEAGUE/NAT. PAGE 5 A0104
BIBLIOG INT/ORG FORCES DETER

B62
BEATON L.,THE SPREAD OF NUCLEAR WEAPONS. WOR+45 NAT/G PLAN PROB/SOLV DIPLOM ECO/TAC DETER...POLICY 20 COLD/WAR. PAGE 12 A0242
ARMS/CONT NUC/PWR TEC/DEV FUT

B62
BELL C.,NEGOTIATION FROM STRENGTH. WOR+45 FACE/GP INT/ORG DELIB/GP FORCES PLAN DOMIN COERCE NUC/PWR PEACE DRIVE PWR...POLICY LOG OBS RECORD INT SAMP TREND COLD/WAR 20. PAGE 13 A0255
NAT/G CONCPT DIPLOM

B62
BENNETT J.C.,NUCLEAR WEAPONS AND THE CONFLICT OF CONSCIENCE. WOR+45 PROB/SOLV DIPLOM WEAPON SUPEGO MORAL...ANTHOL WORSHIP 20. PAGE 13 A0268
POLICY NUC/PWR WAR

B62
BLACKETT P.M.S.,STUDIES OF WAR: NUCLEAR AND CONVENTIONAL. EUR+WWI USA+45 DELIB/GP ACT/RES CREATE PLAN TEC/DEV LEGIT COERCE WAR ORD/FREE PWR ...POLICY TECHNIC TIME/SEQ 20. PAGE 15 A0300
INT/ORG FORCES ARMS/CONT NUC/PWR

B62
FORBES H.W.,THE STRATEGY OF DISARMAMENT. FUT WOR+45 INT/ORG VOL/ASSN CONSULT ARMS/CONT COERCE NUC/PWR WAR DRIVE RIGID/FLEX ORD/FREE PWR...POLICY CONCPT OBS TREND STERTYP 20. PAGE 47 A0959
PLAN FORCES DIPLOM

B62
GILPIN R.,AMERICAN SCIENTISTS AND NUCLEAR WEAPONS POLICY. COM FUT USA+45 WOR+45 INT/ORG NAT/G PROF/ORG CONSULT FORCES CREATE TEC/DEV BAL/PWR EDU/PROP ARMS/CONT WAR PERCEPT KNOWL MORAL PWR ...PHIL/SCI SOC CONCPT GEN/LAWS 20. PAGE 52 A1073
INTELL ATTIT DETER NUC/PWR

B62
GYORGY A.,PROBLEMS IN INTERNATIONAL RELATIONS. COM CT/SYS NUC/PWR ALL/IDEOS 20 UN EEC ECSC. PAGE 58 A1199
DIPLOM NEUTRAL BAL/PWR REV

B62
KAHN H.,THINKING ABOUT THE UNTHINKABLE. FUT USA+45 LAW NAT/G CONSULT FORCES ACT/RES CREATE PLAN TEC/DEV BAL/PWR DIPLOM EDU/PROP ARMS/CONT DETER ATTIT...CONCPT OBS TREND COLD/WAR 20. PAGE 76 A1547
INT/ORG ORD/FREE NUC/PWR PEACE

B62
KENNEDY J.F.,TO TURN THE TIDE. SPACE AGRI INT/ORG FORCES TEC/DEV ADMIN NUC/PWR PEACE WEALTH...ANTHOL 20 KENNEDY/JF CIV/RIGHTS. PAGE 78 A1592
DIPLOM CHIEF POLICY NAT/G

B62
KING-HALL S.,POWER POLITICS IN THE NUCLEAR AGE: A POLICY FOR BRITAIN. UK WOR+45 PLAN ECO/TAC CONTROL RISK ARMS/CONT MORAL PWR RESPECT...OLD/LIB 20. PAGE 79 A1625
BAL/PWR NUC/PWR POLICY DIPLOM

B62
LERNER M.,THE AGE OF OVERKILL: A PREFACE TO WORLD POLITICS. USA+45 USSR WOR+45 SOCIETY ECO/UNDEV BAL/PWR NEUTRAL PARTIC REV ALL/IDEOS MARXISM ...BIBLIOG/A 20. PAGE 87 A1787
DIPLOM NUC/PWR PWR DEATH

B62
MACKENTOSH J.M.,STRATEGY AND TACTICS OF SOVIET FOREIGN POLICY. CHINA/COM FUT USA+45 WOR+45 INT/ORG PLAN DOMIN LEGIT ROUTINE COERCE NUC/PWR WAR ATTIT DRIVE ORD/FREE PWR...CONCPT OBS TIME/SEQ TREND GEN/METH COLD/WAR 20. PAGE 92 A1894
COM POLICY DIPLOM USSR

B62
MORGENSTERN O.,STRATEGIE - HEUTE (2ND ED.). USA+45 USSR ECO/DEV DELIB/GP WAR PEACE ORD/FREE...GOV/COMP NAT/COMP 20 COLD/WAR NATO. PAGE 104 A2134
NUC/PWR DIPLOM FORCES TEC/DEV

B62
MORGENTHAU H.J.,POLITICS IN THE 20TH CENTURY: RESTORATION OF AMERICAN POLITICS. ASIA GERMANY USA+45 USSR WOR+45 NAT/G PLAN EDU/PROP LEGIT NUC/PWR ATTIT PWR SKILL...CONCPT TREND COLD/WAR 20. PAGE 104 A2139
INT/ORG DIPLOM

B62
MULLEY F.W.,THE POLITICS OF WESTERN DEFENSE. EUR+WWI USA-45 WOR+45 VOL/ASSN EX/STRUC FORCES COERCE DETER PEACE ATTIT ORD/FREE PWR...RECORD TIME/SEQ CHARTS COLD/WAR 20 NATO. PAGE 106 A2168
INT/ORG DELIB/GP NUC/PWR

B62
PERRE J.,LES MUTATIONS DE LA GUERRE MODERNE: DE LA REVOLUTION FRANCAISE A LA REVOLUTION NUCLEAIRE. DIPLOM ARMS/CONT DEATH REV WEAPON GP/REL PEACE ATTIT...STAT PREDICT BIBLIOG 18/20 WWI. PAGE 115 A2365
WAR FORCES NUC/PWR

B62
SCHUMAN F.L.,THE COLD WAR: RETROSPECT AND PROSPECT. FUT USA+45 USSR WOR+45 BAL/PWR EDU/PROP ARMS/CONT ATTIT...MAJORIT IDEA/COMP ANTHOL BIBLIOG 20 COLD/WAR. PAGE 129 A2651
MARXISM TEC/DEV DIPLOM NUC/PWR

B62
STRACHEY J.,ON THE PREVENTION OF WAR. FUT WOR+45 INT/ORG NAT/G ACT/RES PLAN BAL/PWR DOMIN EDU/PROP PEACE ATTIT...POLICY TREND TOT/POP COLD/WAR 20 UN. PAGE 139 A2842
FORCES ORD/FREE ARMS/CONT NUC/PWR

B62
STRAUSS L.L.,MEN AND DECISIONS. USA+45 USA-45 USSR CONSULT FORCES TOP/EX WAR PEACE 20. PAGE 139 A2844
DECISION PWR NUC/PWR DIPLOM

B62
THOMSON G.P.,NUCLEAR ENERGY IN BRITAIN DURING THE LAST WAR: THE CHERWELL SIMON LECTURE (MONOGRAPH). UK R+D CONSULT FORCES PLAN DIPLOM TASK CIVMIL/REL ROLE...PHIL/SCI NEW/IDEA LAB/EXP 20 MAUD. PAGE 143 A2934
CREATE TEC/DEV WAR NUC/PWR

B62
WADSWORTH J.J.,THE PRICE OF PEACE. WOR+45 TEC/DEV CONTROL NUC/PWR PEACE ATTIT TREATY 20. PAGE 160 A3258
DIPLOM INT/ORG ARMS/CONT POLICY

S62
ALBONETTI A.,"IL SECONDO PROGRAMMA QUINQUENNALE 1963-67 ED IL BILANCIO RICERCHE ED INVESTIMENTI PER IL 1963 DELL'ERATOM." EUR+WWI FUT ITALY WOR+45 ECO/DEV SERV/IND INT/ORG TEC/DEV ECO/TAC ATTIT SKILL WEALTH...MGT TIME/SEQ OEEC 20. PAGE 5 A0108
R+D PLAN NUC/PWR

S62
FALK R.A.,"THE REALITY OF INTERNATIONAL LAW." WOR+45 NAT/G LEGIT COERCE DETER WAR MORAL ORD/FREE PWR SOVEREIGN...JURID CONCPT VAL/FREE COLD/WAR 20. PAGE 43 A0887
INT/ORG ADJUD NUC/PWR INT/LAW

S62
FINKELSTEIN L.S.,"THE UNITED NATIONS AND ORGANIZATIONS FOR CONTROL OF ARMAMENT." FUT WOR+45 VOL/ASSN DELIB/GP TOP/EX CREATE EDU/PROP LEGIT ADJUD NUC/PWR ATTIT RIGID/FLEX ORD/FREE...POLICY DECISION CONCPT OBS TREND GEN/LAWS TOT/POP COLD/WAR. PAGE 46 A0933
INT/ORG PWR ARMS/CONT

S62
FOSTER W.C.,"ARMS CONTROL AND DISARMAMENT IN A DIVIDED WORLD." COM FUT USA+45 USSR WOR+45 INTELL INT/ORG NAT/G VOL/ASSN CONSULT CREATE PLAN TEC/DEV EDU/PROP LEGIT NUC/PWR ATTIT RIGID/FLEX...CONCPT TREND TOT/POP 20 UN. PAGE 47 A0971
DELIB/GP POLICY ARMS/CONT DIPLOM

S62
NANES A.,"DISARMAMENT: THE LAST SEVEN YEARS." COM EUR+WWI USA+45 USSR INT/ORG FORCES TOP/EX CREATE LEGIT NUC/PWR DISPL ORD/FREE...CONCPT TIME/SEQ CON/ANAL 20. PAGE 107 A2195
DELIB/GP RIGID/FLEX ARMS/CONT

S62
RUSSETT B.M.,"CAUSE, SURPRISE, AND NO ESCAPE." FUT WOR-45 CULTURE SOCIETY INT/ORG FORCES TEC/DEV BAL/PWR EDU/PROP ARMS/CONT NUC/PWR WAR WEAPON PEACE KNOWL ORD/FREE PWR...POLICY CONCPT RECORD TIME/SEQ TREND GEN/LAWS 20 WWI. PAGE 126 A2578
COERCE DIPLOM

S62
SCHILLING W.R.,"SCIENTISTS, FOREIGN POLICY AND POLITICS." WOR+45 WOR-45 INTELL INT/ORG CONSULT TOP/EX ACT/RES PLAN ADMIN KNOWL...CONCPT OBS TREND LEAGUE/NAT 20. PAGE 128 A2627
NAT/G TEC/DEV DIPLOM NUC/PWR

S62
SINGER J.D.,"STABLE DETERRENCE AND ITS LIMITS." FUT WOR+45 R+D INT/ORG CONSULT ACT/RES TEC/DEV ARMS/CONT COERCE DRIVE PERCEPT RIGID/FLEX ORD/FREE PWR...MYTH SIMUL TOT/POP 20. PAGE 133 A2728
NAT/G FORCES DETER NUC/PWR

S62
STRACHEY J.,"COMMUNIST INTENTIONS." ASIA USSR YUGOSLAVIA INT/ORG NAT/G FORCES DOMIN EDU/PROP COERCE NUC/PWR NAT/LISM PEACE RIGID/FLEX PWR MARXISM...CONCPT MYTH OBS TIME/SEQ TREND COLD/WAR TOT/POP 20. PAGE 139 A2843
COM ATTIT WAR

S62
THOMAS J.R.T.,"SOVIET BEHAVIOR IN THE QUEMOY CRISES OF 1958." CHINA/COM FUT USSR WOR+45 INT/ORG VOL/ASSN FORCES PLAN BAL/PWR DOMIN COERCE NUC/PWR REV WAR ATTIT DRIVE ORD/FREE...POLICY OBS RECORD COLD/WAR FOR/POL 20. PAGE 143 A2923
COM PWR

B63
BROEKMEIJER M.W.,DEVELOPING COUNTRIES AND NATO. USSR FORCES DIPLOM NUC/PWR WAR PEACE TOTALISM 20 NATO. PAGE 19 A0384
ECO/UNDEV FOR/AID ORD/FREE NAT/G

B63
DEENER D.R.,CANADA - UNITED STATES TREATY RELATIONS. CANADA USA+45 USA-45 NAT/G FORCES PLAN PROB/SOLV AGREE NUC/PWR...TREND 18/20 TREATY. PAGE 35 A0722
DIPLOM INT/LAW POLICY

B63
FALK R.A.,LAW, MORALITY, AND WAR IN THE CONTEMPORARY WORLD. WOR+45 LAW INT/ORG EX/STRUC FORCES EDU/PROP LEGIT DETER NUC/PWR MORAL ORD/FREE ...JURID TOT/POP 20. PAGE 43 A0888
ADJUD ARMS/CONT PEACE INT/LAW

B63
FULBRIGHT J.W.,PROSPECTS FOR THE WEST. COM USA+45 USSR INT/ORG NAT/G SCHOOL PROB/SOLV NUC/PWR WAR PEACE ORD/FREE...PREDICT METH/COMP 20 DEGAULLE/C. PAGE 50 A1015
DIPLOM BAL/PWR CONCPT POLICY

B63
HALPERIN M.H.,LIMITED WAR IN A NUCLEAR AGE. CUBA KOREA USA+45 USSR INT/ORG FORCES PLAN DIPLOM DETER PWR...BIBLIOG/A 20. PAGE 60 A1238
WAR NUC/PWR CONTROL WEAPON

B63
KHRUSHCHEV N.S.,THE NEW CONTENT OF PEACEFUL COEXISTENCE IN THE NUCLEAR AGE. GERMANY/E WORKER NUC/PWR REV SOCISM 20 COLD/WAR. PAGE 79 A1614
MARXISM POL/PAR PEACE DIPLOM

B63
LILIENTHAL D.E.,CHANGE, HOPE, AND THE BOMB. USA+45 WOR+45 R+D INT/ORG NAT/G DELIB/GP FORCES ACT/RES DETER RIGID/FLEX ORD/FREE...POLICY CONCPT OBS AEC 20. PAGE 89 A1815
ATTIT MYTH ARMS/CONT NUC/PWR

B63
MALIK C.,MAN IN THE STRUGGLE FOR PEACE. USSR WOR+45 CHIEF PLAN PROB/SOLV PARTIC NUC/PWR REV ORD/FREE ...IDEA/COMP METH/COMP 20 UN COLD/WAR. PAGE 93 A1912
PEACE MARXISM DIPLOM EDU/PROP

B63
MULLENBACH P.,CIVILIAN NUCLEAR POWER: ECONOMIC ISSUES AND POLICY FORMATION. FINAN INT/ORG DELIB/GP ACT/RES ECO/TAC ATTIT SUPEGO HEALTH ORD/FREE PWR ...POLICY CONCPT MATH STAT CHARTS VAL/FREE 20 COLD/WAR. PAGE 105 A2166
USA+45 ECO/DEV NUC/PWR

B63
PACHTER H.M.,COLLISION COURSE; THE CUBAN MISSILE CRISIS AND COEXISTENCE. CUBA USA+45 DIPLOM ARMS/CONT PEACE MARXISM...DECISION INT/LAW 20 COLD/WAR KHRUSH/N KENNEDY/JF CASTRO/F. PAGE 112 A2307
WAR BAL/PWR NUC/PWR DETER

B63
PANAMERICAN UNION,DOCUMENTOS OFICIALES DE LA ORGANIZACION DE LOS ESTADOS AMERICANOS, INDICE Y LISTA (VOL. III, 1962). L/A+17C DELIB/GP INT/TRADE
BIBLIOG INT/ORG DIPLOM

EDU/PROP REGION NUC/PWR...HEAL INT/LAW SOC/WK 20 OAS. PAGE 113 A2329

B63
RUSK D.,THE WINDS OF FREEDOM. S/ASIA SOUTH/AFR INT/ORG FORCES NUC/PWR PEACE ORD/FREE 20 UN COLD/WAR. PAGE 125 A2569
DIPLOM FOR/AID INT/TRADE

B63
TUCKER R.C.,THE SOVIET POLITICAL MIND. WOR+45 ELITES INT/ORG NAT/G POL/PAR PLAN DIPLOM ECO/TAC DOMIN ADMIN NUC/PWR REV DRIVE PERSON SUPEGO PWR WEALTH...POLICY MGT PSY CONCPT OBS BIOG TREND COLD/WAR MARX/KARL 20. PAGE 145 A2972
COM TOP/EX USSR

B63
US DEPARTMENT OF THE ARMY,US OVERSEAS BASES: PRESENT STATUS AND FUTURE PROSPECTS (PAMPHLET). USA+45 DIPLOM NUC/PWR ATTIT ORD/FREE...POLICY CHARTS 20. PAGE 152 A3107
BIBLIOG/A WAR BAL/PWR DETER

B63
VOSS E.H.,NUCLEAR AMBUSH: THE TEST-BAN TRAP. WOR+45 COM/IND INT/ORG NAT/G DELIB/GP FORCES LEGIS TOP/EX ACT/RES DOMIN EDU/PROP LEGIT ROUTINE COERCE ATTIT PERCEPT RIGID/FLEX HEALTH MORAL ORD/FREE PWR. PAGE 160 A3255
TEC/DEV HIST/WRIT ARMS/CONT NUC/PWR

L63
CRANE R.D.,"THE CUBAN CRISIS: A STRATEGIC ANALYSIS OF AMERICAN AND SOVIET POLICY." CUBA USA+45 USSR BAL/PWR RISK DETER NUC/PWR PERCEPT ORD/FREE 20. PAGE 32 A0658
DIPLOM POLICY FORCES

L63
MOUSKHELY M.,"LE BLOC COMMUNISTE ET LA COMMUNAUTE ECONOMIQUE EUROPEENNE." AFR COM EUR+WWI FUT USSR WOR+45 INTELL ECO/UNDEV LABOR POL/PAR NUC/PWR RIGID/FLEX...TIME/SEQ ORG/CHARTS EEC TOT/POP 20. PAGE 105 A2158
INT/ORG ECO/DEV

L63
PHELPS J.,"STUDIES IN DETERRENCE VIII: MILITARY STABILITARY AND ARMS CONTROL: A CRITICAL SURVEY." FUT WOR+45 INT/ORG ACT/RES EDU/PROP COERCE NUC/PWR WAR HEALTH PWR...POLICY TECHNIC TREND SIMUL TOT/POP 20. PAGE 116 A2373
FORCES ORD/FREE ARMS/CONT DETER

L63
SINGER J.D.,"WEAPONS MANAGEMENT IN WORLD POLITICS: PROCEEDINGS OF THE INTERNATIONAL ARMS CONTROL SYMPOSIUM, DECEMBER, 1962." FUT WOR+45 SOCIETY ECO/DEV INDUS INT/ORG DELIB/GP FORCES ACT/RES ECO/TAC EDU/PROP ARMS/CONT SUPEGO HEALTH ORD/FREE PWR SKILL...POLICY CHARTS SIMUL ANTHOL VAL/FREE 20. PAGE 133 A2729
CONSULT ATTIT DIPLOM NUC/PWR

S63
BOHN L.,"WHOSE NUCLEAR TEST: NON-PHYSICAL INSPECTION AND TEST BAN." WOR+45 R+D INT/ORG VOL/ASSN ORD/FREE...GEN/LAWS GEN/METH COLD/WAR 20. PAGE 16 A0331
ADJUD ARMS/CONT TEC/DEV NUC/PWR

S63
BRZEZINSKI Z.,"SOVIET QUIESCENCE." EUR+WWI USA+45 USSR FORCES CREATE PLAN COERCE DETER WAR ATTIT 20 TREATY EUROPE. PAGE 20 A0415
DIPLOM ARMS/CONT NUC/PWR AGREE

S63
CLEVELAND H.,"CRISIS DIPLOMACY." USA+45 WOR+45 LAW FORCES TASK NUC/PWR PWR 20. PAGE 27 A0551
DECISION DIPLOM PROB/SOLV POLICY

S63
ETZIONI A.,"EUROPEAN UNIFICATION AND PERSPECTIVES ON SOVEREIGNTY." EUR+WWI FUT DELIB/GP TEC/DEV ECO/TAC EDU/PROP DETER NUC/PWR ATTIT DRIVE ORD/FREE PWR WEALTH...CONCPT RECORD TIME/SEQ EEC VAL/FREE 20. PAGE 43 A0870
INT/ORG ECO/DEV SOVEREIGN

S63
HALLSTEIN W.,"THE EUROPEAN COMMUNITY AND ATLANTIC PARTNERSHIP." EUR+WWI USA+45 MARKET NAT/G VOL/ASSN DELIB/GP ARMS/CONT NUC/PWR ATTIT PWR...CONCPT STAT TIME/SEQ TREND OEEC 20 EEC. PAGE 60 A1235
INT/ORG ECO/TAC UK

S63
KAWALKOWSKI A.,"POUR UNE EUROPE INDEPENDENTE ET REUNIFIEE." EUR+WWI FUT USA+45 USSR WOR+45 ECO/DEV PROC/MFG INT/ORG NAT/G ACT/RES TEC/DEV FEDERAL RIGID/FLEX...CONCPT METH/CNCPT OEEC TOT/POP 20 DEGAULLE/C. PAGE 77 A1573
R+D PLAN NUC/PWR

S63
KINTNER W.R.,"THE PROJECTED EUROPEAN UNION AND AMERICAN RESPONSIBILITIES." EUR+WWI USA+45 STRATA INT/ORG NAT/G DOMIN DETER NUC/PWR ATTIT ORD/FREE PWR 20 NATO. PAGE 79 A1628
FUT FORCES DIPLOM REGION

S63
KISSINGER H.A.,"STRAINS ON THE ALLIANCE." EUR+WWI FRANCE GERMANY GERMANY/W USA+45 ECO/DEV INT/ORG NAT/G TOP/EX EDU/PROP NUC/PWR ATTIT PWR...PSY TREND 20. PAGE 80 A1643
VOL/ASSN DRIVE DIPLOM

S63
MCDOUGAL M.S.,"THE SOVIET-CUBAN QUARANTINE AND SELF-DEFENSE." CUBA USA+45 USSR WOR+45 INT/ORG NAT/G BAL/PWR NUC/PWR ATTIT...JURID CONCPT. PAGE 98 A2008
ORD/FREE LEGIT SOVEREIGN

S63
MEYROWITZ H.,"LES JURISTES DEVANT L'ARME NUCLAIRE." FUT WOR+45 INTELL SOCIETY BAL/PWR DETER WAR...JURID CONCPT 20. PAGE 100 A2058
ACT/RES ADJUD INT/LAW NUC/PWR

S63
MULLEY F.W.,"NUCLEAR WEAPONS: CHALLENGE TO NATIONAL SOVEREIGNTY." EUR+WWI FRANCE UK USA+45 VOL/ASSN EX/STRUC FORCES TOP/EX ACT/RES REGION DRIVE PWR 20 NATO DEGAULLE/C. PAGE 106 A2169
INT/ORG ATTIT DIPLOM NUC/PWR

S63
PHELPS J.,"INFORMATION AND ARMS CONTROL." COM SPACE USA+45 USSR WOR+45 R+D INT/ORG NAT/G DELIB/GP DIPLOM ORD/FREE...CONCPT 20. PAGE 116 A2374
KNOWL ARMS/CONT NUC/PWR

S63
STANLEY T.W.,"DECENTRALIZING NUCLEAR CONTROL IN NATO." EUR+WWI USA+45 ELITES FORCES ACT/RES ATTIT ORD/FREE PWR...NEW/IDEA HYPO/EXP TOT/POP 20 NATO. PAGE 137 A2805
INT/ORG EX/STRUC NUC/PWR

B64
BELL C.,THE DEBATABLE ALLIANCE. COM UK USA+45 NAT/G FORCES PLAN BAL/PWR NUC/PWR WAR ATTIT...GOV/COMP 20. PAGE 13 A0256
DIPLOM PWR PEACE POLICY

B64
COHEN M.,LAW AND POLITICS IN SPACE: SPECIFIC AND URGENT PROBLEMS IN THE LAW OF OUTER SPACE. CHINA/COM COM USA+45 USSR WOR+45 COM/IND INT/ORG NAT/G LEGIT NUC/PWR ATTIT BIO/SOC...JURID CONCPT CONGRESS 20 STALIN/J. PAGE 28 A0561
DELIB/GP LAW INT/LAW SPACE

B64
DALLIN A.,THE SOVIET UNION, ARMS CONTROL AND DISARMAMENT. COM INT/ORG VOL/ASSN EX/STRUC DIPLOM NUC/PWR ATTIT PWR TOT/POP COLD/WAR 20. PAGE 33 A0678
ORD/FREE ARMS/CONT USSR

B64
DEITCHMAN S.J.,LIMITED WAR AND AMERICAN DEFENSE POLICY. USA+45 WOR+45 INT/ORG NAT/G PLAN TEC/DEV COERCE NUC/PWR RIGID/FLEX PWR SKILL...DECISION METH/CNCPT TIME/SEQ TOT/POP COLD/WAR 20. PAGE 36 A0726
FORCES WAR WEAPON

B64
DEUTSCHE GES AUSWARTIGE POL,STRATEGIE UND ABRUSTUNGSPOLITIK DER SOWJETUNION. USSR TEC/DEV DIPLOM COERCE DETER WEAPON...POLICY PSY 20 ABM/DEFSYS. PAGE 37 A0747
NUC/PWR WAR FORCES ARMS/CONT

B64
FINER H.,DULLES OVER SUEZ. FRANCE FUT UAR UK WOR+45 NAT/G PROB/SOLV CONTROL NUC/PWR WAR 20 DULLES/JF SUEZ. PAGE 46 A0932
DIPLOM POLICY REC/INT

B64
GOWING M.,BRITAIN AND ATOMIC ENERGY 1939-1945. FRANCE UK USA+45 USA-45 NAT/G CREATE...PHIL/SCI 20 AEA. PAGE 54 A1118
NUC/PWR DIPLOM TEC/DEV

B64
GRODZINS M.,THE ATOMIC AGE: FORTY-FIVE SCIENTISTS AND SCHOLARS SPEAK ON NATIONAL AND WORLD AFFAIRS. FUT USA+45 WOR+45 R+D INT/ORG NAT/G CONSULT TEC/DEV EDU/PROP ATTIT PERSON ORD/FREE...HUM CONCPT TIME/SEQ CON/ANAL. PAGE 57 A1169
INTELL ARMS/CONT NUC/PWR

B64
KAUFMANN W.W.,THE MC NAMARA STRATEGY. TOP/EX INSPECT BAL/PWR DIPLOM CONTROL DETER GUERRILLA NUC/PWR WEAPON COST PWR...METH/COMP 20 MCNAMARA/R KENNEDY/JF JOHNSON/LB NATO DEPT/DEFEN. PAGE 77 A1572
FORCES WAR PLAN PROB/SOLV

B64
KULSKI W.W.,INTERNATIONAL POLITICS IN A REVOLUTIONARY AGE. NEUTRAL NAT/LISM...POLICY DECISION INT/LAW CONCPT 20 UN. PAGE 83 A1693
DIPLOM WAR NUC/PWR INT/ORG

B64
LENS S.,THE FUTILE CRUSADE. ASIA CHINA/COM L/A+17C USA+45 USSR WOR+45 ECO/DEV BAL/PWR DIPLOM NUC/PWR WAR NAT/LISM PEACE 20 COLD/WAR PRESIDENT CIA. PAGE 87 A1774
ORD/FREE ANOMIE COM MARXISM

B64
LUARD E.,THE COLD WAR: A RE-APPRAISAL. FUT USSR WOR+45 FORCES NUC/PWR NAT/LISM ORD/FREE SOVEREIGN ...INT 20 COLD/WAR STALIN/J TREATY UN. PAGE 91 A1870
DIPLOM WAR PEACE TOTALISM

B64
NASA,PROCEEDINGS OF CONFERENCE ON THE LAW OF SPACE AND OF SATELLITE COMMUNICATIONS: CHICAGO 1963. FUT WOR+45 DELIB/GP PROB/SOLV TEC/DEV CONFER ADJUD NUC/PWR...POLICY IDEA/COMP 20 NASA. PAGE 107 A2197
SPACE COM/IND LAW DIPLOM

B64
PITTMAN J.,PEACEFUL COEXISTENCE. USSR NAT/G NUC/PWR WAR ATTIT 20. PAGE 116 A2385
DIPLOM PEACE POLICY FORCES

B64
REGALA R.,WORLD PEACE THROUGH DIPLOMACY AND LAW. S/ASIA WOR+45 ECO/UNDEV INT/ORG FORCES PLAN PROB/SOLV FOR/AID NUC/PWR WAR...POLICY INT/LAW 20. PAGE 120 A2456
DIPLOM PEACE ADJUD

B64
ROCK V.P.,A STRATEGY OF INTERDEPENDENCE. COM USSR DIPLOM
WOR+45 NAT/G FORCES PROB/SOLV TEC/DEV DETER WAR NUC/PWR
ORD/FREE...CONCPT NEW/IDEA METH/COMP 20. PAGE 122 PEACE
A2509 POLICY

B64
SCHWARTZ M.D.,CONFERENCE ON SPACE SCIENCE AND SPACE SPACE
LAW. FUT COM/IND NAT/G FORCES ACT/RES PLAN BUDGET LAW
DIPLOM NUC/PWR WEAPON...POLICY ANTHOL 20. PAGE 130 PEACE
A2658 TEC/DEV

B64
SINGH N.,THE DEFENCE MECHANISM OF THE MODERN STATE. FORCES
COM UK USA+45 CONSTN INT/ORG NUC/PWR WAR INGP/REL TOP/EX
ROLE 20 DEPT/DEFEN COMMONWLTH. PAGE 134 A2735 NAT/G
CIVMIL/REL

B64
US AIR FORCE ACADEMY ASSEMBLY,OUTER SPACE: FINAL SPACE
REPORT APRIL 1-4, 1964. FUT USA+45 WOR+45 LAW CIVMIL/REL
DELIB/GP CONFER ARMS/CONT WAR PEACE ATTIT MORAL NUC/PWR
...ANTHOL 20 NASA. PAGE 150 A3055 DIPLOM

B64
WILLIAMS S.P.,TOWARD A GENUINE WORLD SECURITY BIBLIOG/A
SYSTEM (PAMPHLET). WOR+45 INT/ORG FORCES PLAN ARMS/CONT
NUC/PWR ORD/FREE...INT/LAW CONCPT UN PRESIDENT. DIPLOM
PAGE 165 A3353 PEACE

L64
CARNEGIE ENDOWMENT INT. PEACE,"POLITICAL QUESTIONS INT/ORG
(ISSUES BEFORE THE NINETEENTH GENERAL ASSEMBLY)." PEACE
SPACE WOR+45 CONSTN FINAN NAT/G CONSULT DELIB/GP
FORCES LEGIS TEC/DEV EDU/PROP LEGIT ARMS/CONT
COERCE NUC/PWR ATTIT ALL/VALS...CONCPT OBS UN
COLD/WAR 20. PAGE 24 A0490

L64
WARD C.,"THE 'NEW MYTHS' AND 'OLD REALITIES' OF FORCES
NUCLEAR WAR." COM FUT USA+45 USSR WOR+45 INT/ORG COERCE
NAT/G DOMIN LEGIT EXEC ATTIT PERCEPT ALL/VALS ARMS/CONT
...POLICY RELATIV PSY MYTH TREND 20. PAGE 161 A3280 NUC/PWR

S64
ARMSTRONG J.A.,"THE SOVIET-AMERICAN CONFRONTATION: DIPLOM
A NEW STAGE?" CUBA USA+45 USSR PLAN PROB/SOLV POLICY
INT/TRADE CONTROL ARMS/CONT NUC/PWR MARXISM 20 INSPECT
COLD/WAR INTERVENT. PAGE 9 A0174

S64
CRANE R.D.,"BASIC PRINCIPLES IN SOVIET SPACE LAW." COM
FUT WOR+45 AIR INT/ORG DIPLOM DOMIN ARMS/CONT LAW
COERCE NUC/PWR PEACE ATTIT DRIVE PWR...INT/LAW USSR
METH/CNCPT NEW/IDEA OBS TREND GEN/LAWS VAL/FREE SPACE
MARX/KARL 20. PAGE 32 A0659

S64
FALK S.L.,"DISARMAMENT IN HISTORICAL PERSPECTIVE." INT/ORG
WOR-45 NAT/G PLAN NUC/PWR PEACE ORD/FREE PWR COERCE
...TIME/SEQ AUD/VIS VAL/FREE LEAGUE/NAT 20. PAGE 44 ARMS/CONT
A0892

S64
GROSSER A.,"Y A-T-IL UN CONFLIT FRANCO-AMERICAIN." VOL/ASSN
EUR+WWI USA+45 INT/ORG NAT/G PLAN BAL/PWR DIPLOM NAT/LISM
EDU/PROP NUC/PWR ATTIT DRIVE ORD/FREE PWR...CONCPT FRANCE
OBS TIME/SEQ TREND STERTYP VAL/FREE COLD/WAR.
PAGE 57 A1179

S64
HOWARD M.,"MILITARY POWER AND INTERNATIONAL ORDER." FORCES
WOR+45 SOCIETY INT/ORG NAT/G BAL/PWR DOMIN COERCE ATTIT
NUC/PWR WEAPON PWR...NEW/IDEA 20. PAGE 68 A1400 WAR

S64
JACK H.,"NONALIGNMENT AND A TEST BAN AGREEMENT: THE PWR
ROLE OF THE NON-ALIGNED STATES." WOR+45 INT/ORG CONCPT
CONSULT DOMIN EDU/PROP LEGIT CHOOSE PEACE ATTIT NUC/PWR
DRIVE KNOWL ORD/FREE...TREND CHARTS GEN/LAWS UN
VAL/FREE 20. PAGE 72 A1471

S64
KARPOV P.V.,"PEACEFUL COEXISTENCE AND INTERNATIONAL COM
LAW." WOR+45 LAW SOCIETY INT/ORG VOL/ASSN FORCES ATTIT
CREATE CAP/ISM DIPLOM ADJUD NUC/PWR PEACE MORAL INT/LAW
ORD/FREE PWR MARXISM...MARXIST JURID CONCPT OBS USSR
TREND COLD/WAR MARX/KARL 20. PAGE 77 A1568

S64
KISSINGER H.A.,"COALITION DIPLOMACY IN A NUCLEAR CONSULT
AGE." COM EUR+WWI USA+45 WOR+45 INT/ORG NAT/G ATTIT
FORCES ACT/RES DOMIN LEGIT COERCE PERCEPT ALL/VALS DIPLOM
...POLICY TOT/POP 20. PAGE 80 A1644 NUC/PWR

S64
MAGGS P.B.,"SOVIET VIEWPOINT ON NUCLEAR WEAPONS IN COM
INTERNATIONAL LAW." USSR WOR+45 INT/ORG FORCES LAW
DIPLOM ARMS/CONT ATTIT ORD/FREE PWR...POLICY JURID INT/LAW
CONCPT OBS TREND CON/ANAL GEN/LAWS VAL/FREE 20. NUC/PWR
PAGE 93 A1905

B65
WHITE HOUSE CONFERENCE ON INTERNATIONAL R+D
COOPERATION(VOL.II). SPACE WOR+45 EXTR/IND INT/ORG CONFER
LABOR WORKER NUC/PWR PEACE AGE/Y...CENSUS ANTHOL 20 TEC/DEV
RESOURCE/N URBAN/RNWL PUB/TRANS. PAGE 3 A0071 DIPLOM

B65
PEACE RESEARCH ABSTRACTS. FUT WOR+45 R+D INT/ORG BIBLIOG/A
NAT/G PLAN TEC/DEV BAL/PWR DIPLOM FOR/AID NUC/PWR PEACE
HEALTH. PAGE 4 A0072 ARMS/CONT
WAR

B65
CORDIER A.W.,THE QUEST FOR PEACE. WOR+45 NAT/G PLAN PEACE
BAL/PWR ECO/TAC ARMS/CONT NUC/PWR PWR...ANTHOL UN DIPLOM
COLD/WAR. PAGE 30 A0617 POLICY
INT/ORG

B65
GRETTON P.,MARITIME STRATEGY - A STUDY OF DEFENSE FORCES
PROBLEMS. ASIA UK USSR DIPLOM COERCE DETER NUC/PWR PLAN
WEAPON...CONCPT NAT/COMP 20. PAGE 56 A1147 WAR
SEA

B65
HASSON J.A.,THE ECONOMICS OF NUCLEAR POWER. INDIA NUC/PWR
UK USA+45 WOR+45 INT/ORG TEC/DEV COST...SOC STAT INDUS
CHARTS 20 EURATOM. PAGE 63 A1286 ECO/DEV
METH

B65
HUSS P.J.,RED SPIES IN THE UN. CZECHOSLVK USA+45 PEACE
USSR COM/IND FORCES EDU/PROP NUC/PWR MARXISM 20 UN INT/ORG
COLD/WAR. PAGE 69 A1421 BAL/PWR
DIPLOM

B65
KAHN H.,ON ESCALATION; METAPHORS AND SCENARIOS. NUC/PWR
FORCES DIPLOM ARMS/CONT WAR CIVMIL/REL...INT/LAW ACT/RES
20. PAGE 76 A1548 INT/ORG
ORD/FREE

B65
LERCHE C.O.,THE COLD WAR AND AFTER. AFR COM S/ASIA DIPLOM
USA+45 USSR NUC/PWR SOVEREIGN MARXISM...TIME/SEQ BAL/PWR
TREND BIBLIOG 20 COLD/WAR. PAGE 87 A1784 IDEA/COMP

B65
LYONS G.M.,AMERICA: PURPOSE AND POWER. UK USA+45 PWR
FINAN INDUS MARKET WORKER TEC/DEV DIPLOM AUTOMAT PROB/SOLV
NUC/PWR WAR RACE/REL ORD/FREE 20 EEC CONGRESS ECO/DEV
SUPREME/CT CIV/RIGHTS. PAGE 92 A1881 TASK

B65
MIDDLETON D.,CRISIS IN THE WEST. EUR+WWI FUT WOR+45 INT/ORG
CHIEF PLAN ECO/TAC LEAD REGION NUC/PWR NAT/LISM DIPLOM
MARXISM 20 COLD/WAR NATO EEC. PAGE 101 A2068 NAT/G
POLICY

B65
MOSKOWITZ H.,US SECURITY, ARMS CONTROL, AND BIBLIOG/A
DISARMAMENT 1961-1965. FORCES DIPLOM DETER WAR ARMS/CONT
WEAPON...CHARTS 20 UN COLD/WAR NATO. PAGE 105 A2154 NUC/PWR
PEACE

B65
RANSOM H.H.,AN AMERICAN FOREIGN POLICY READER. NAT/G
USA+45 FORCES EDU/PROP COERCE NUC/PWR WAR PEACE DIPLOM
...DECISION 20. PAGE 119 A2443 POLICY

B65
RAPPAPORT A.,ISSUES IN AMERICAN DIPLOMACY: WORLD WAR
POWER AND LEADERSHIP SINCE 1895 (VOL. II). POLICY
CHINA/COM EUR+WWI L/A+17C USA+45 USA-45 NAT/G DIPLOM
ECO/TAC DOMIN CONFER LEAD NUC/PWR WEAPON...DECISION
19/20 WILSON/W ROOSEVLT/F CHINJAP. PAGE 119 A2447

B65
TREFOUSSE H.L.,THE COLD WAR: A BOOK OF DOCUMENTS. BAL/PWR
ASIA L/A+17C USSR WOR+45 WOR-45 ECO/TAC FOR/AID DIPLOM
ARMS/CONT NUC/PWR PEACE ORD/FREE...ANTHOL 20 MARXISM
COLD/WAR KENNEDY/JF EISNHWR/DD. PAGE 145 A2961

B65
UN,SPACE ACTIVITIES AND RESOURCES: REVIEW OF UNITED SPACE
NATION'S NATIONAL AND INTERNATIONAL PROGRAMS. NUC/PWR
INT/ORG LABOR PLAN TEC/DEV DIPLOM EFFICIENCY HEALTH FOR/AID
...GOV/COMP 20 UN. PAGE 146 A2995 PEACE

B65
US CONGRESS JT ATOM ENRGY COMM,ATOMIC ENERGY NUC/PWR
LEGISLATION THROUGH 89TH CONGRESS, 1ST SESSION. FORCES
USA+45 LAW INT/ORG DELIB/GP BUDGET DIPLOM 20 AEC PEACE
CONGRESS CASEBOOK EURATOM IAEA. PAGE 150 A3071 LEGIS

B65
US DEPARTMENT OF DEFENSE,US SECURITY ARMS CONTROL, BIBLIOG/A
AND DISARMAMENT 1961-1965 (PAMPHLET). CHINA/COM COM ARMS/CONT
GERMANY/W ISRAEL SPACE USA+45 USSR WOR+45 FORCES NUC/PWR
EDU/PROP DETER EQUILIB PEACE ALL/VALS...GOV/COMP 20 DIPLOM
NATO. PAGE 151 A3077

B65
US DEPARTMENT OF THE ARMY,NUCLEAR WEAPONS AND THE BIBLIOG/A
ATLANTIC ALLIANCE: A BIBLIOGRAPHIC SURVEY. ASIA COM ARMS/CONT
EUR+WWI USA+45 FORCES DIPLOM WEAPON...STAT 20 NATO. NUC/PWR
PAGE 152 A3108 BAL/PWR

C65
MARK M.,"BEYOND SOVEREIGNTY." WOR+45 WOR-45 NAT/LISM
ECO/UNDEV BAL/PWR INT/TRADE NUC/PWR REV WAR MARXISM NAT/G
NEW/LIB BIBLIOG. PAGE 95 A1942 DIPLOM
INTELL

C65
SCHWEBEL M.,"BEHAVIORAL SCIENCE AND HUMAN PEACE
SURVIVAL." FORCES ARMS/CONT COERCE NUC/PWR WAR ACT/RES
GP/REL NAT/LISM PERCEPT...POLICY PSY ANTHOL DIPLOM
BIBLIOG/A 20 COLD/WAR. PAGE 130 A2662 HEAL

C65
SEARA M.V.,"COSMIC INTERNATIONAL LAW." LAW ACADEM SPACE
ACT/RES DIPLOM COLONIAL CONTROL NUC/PWR SOVEREIGN INT/LAW
...GEN/LAWS BIBLIOG UN. PAGE 131 A2678 IDEA/COMP
INT/ORG

C65
US AIR FORCE ACADEMY,"AMERICAN DEFENSE POLICY." COM INT/ORG TEC/DEV FOR/AID ARMS/CONT DETER NUC/PWR ...POLICY DECISION CONCPT ANTHOL BIBLIOG/A 20 COLD/WAR NATO. PAGE 149 A3054 — PLAN FORCES WAR COERCE

B66
AMERICAN ASSEMBLY COLUMBIA U,A WORLD OF NUCLEAR POWERS? FUT WOR+45 ECO/DEV BAL/PWR ECO/TAC CONTROL RISK EFFICIENCY ATTIT PWR...METH/COMP ANTHOL 20. PAGE 7 A0137 — NUC/PWR DIPLOM TEC/DEV ARMS/CONT

B66
BEAUFRE A.,NATO AND EUROPE. WOR+45 PLAN CONFER EXEC NUC/PWR ATTIT...POLICY 20 NATO EUROPE. PAGE 12 A0243 — INT/ORG DETER DIPLOM ADMIN

B66
BERNSTEIN B.J.,THE TRUMAN ADMINISTRATION. WOR+45 LABOR POL/PAR LEGIS DIPLOM NUC/PWR WAR ATTIT ...POLICY 20 TRUMAN/HS. PAGE 14 A0279 — LEAD TOP/EX NAT/G

B66
BLOOMFIELD L.P.,KHRUSHCHEV AND THE ARMS RACE. USA+45 USSR ECO/DEV BAL/PWR EDU/PROP CONFER NUC/PWR ATTIT...CHARTS 20 KHRUSH/N. PAGE 16 A0321 — ARMS/CONT COM POLICY DIPLOM

B66
BUCHAN A.,A WORLD OF NUCLEAR POWERS? PEACE...ANTHOL 20. PAGE 21 A0423 — NUC/PWR BAL/PWR PROB/SOLV DIPLOM

B66
COYLE D.C.,THE UNITED NATIONS AND HOW IT WORKS. ECO/UNDEV DELIB/GP BAL/PWR EDU/PROP ARMS/CONT NUC/PWR WAR 20 UN. PAGE 32 A0648 — INT/ORG PEACE DIPLOM INT/TRADE

B66
CROWLEY D.W.,THE BACKGROUND TO CURRENT AFFAIRS. UK WOR+45 INT/ORG BAL/PWR NUC/PWR ATTIT ROLE 20 COLD/WAR. PAGE 33 A0665 — DIPLOM PWR POLICY

B66
DAENIKER G.,STRATEGIE DES KLEIN STAATS. SWITZERLND ACT/RES CREATE DIPLOM NEUTRAL DETER WAR WEAPON PWR SOVEREIGN...IDEA/COMP 20 COLD/WAR. PAGE 33 A0673 — NUC/PWR PLAN FORCES NAT/G

B66
ERICKSON J.,THE MILITARY-TECHNICAL REVOLUTION. USA+45 WOR+45 INT/ORG PLAN ATTIT...DECISION ANTHOL 20. PAGE 42 A0861 — DIPLOM DETER POLICY NUC/PWR

B66
FREIDEL F.,AMERICAN ISSUES IN THE TWENTIETH CENTURY. SOCIETY FINAN ECO/TAC FOR/AID CONTROL NUC/PWR WAR RACE/REL PEACE ATTIT...ANTHOL T 20 WILSON/W ROOSEVLT/F KENNEDY/JF TRUMAN/HS. PAGE 49 A0995 — DIPLOM POLICY NAT/G ORD/FREE

B66
FREUND L.,POLITISCHE WAFFEN. EUR+WWI GERMANY CONSULT FORCES CONFER NUC/PWR 20. PAGE 49 A1000 — EDU/PROP DIPLOM ATTIT

B66
GRAHAM I.C.C.,PUBLICATIONS OF THE SOCIAL SCIENCE DEPARTMENT, THE RAND CORPORATION, 1948-1966. USSR WOR+45 NAT/G ARMS/CONT DETER WAR NAT/LISM...SOC GOV/COMP. PAGE 55 A1127 — BIBLIOG DIPLOM NUC/PWR FORCES

B66
HALPERIN M.H.,CHINA AND NUCLEAR PROLIFERATION (PAMPHLET). CHINA/COM FUT INDIA USA+45 USSR ARMS/CONT WAR 20 CHINJAP. PAGE 60 A1239 — NUC/PWR FORCES POLICY DIPLOM

B66
HOLLINS E.J.,PEACE IS POSSIBLE: A READER FOR LAYMEN. WOR+45 CULTURE PLAN RISK AGE/Y ALL/VALS SOVEREIGN...PSY CONCPT TREND 20 UN JOHN/XXIII KENNAN/G MYRDAL/G. PAGE 67 A1370 — PEACE DIPLOM INT/ORG NUC/PWR

B66
HORELICK A.L.,STRATEGIC POWER AND SOVIET FOREIGN POLICY. CUBA USSR FORCES PLAN CIVMIL/REL...POLICY DECISION 20 COLD/WAR. PAGE 67 A1383 — DIPLOM BAL/PWR DETER NUC/PWR

B66
INTL ATOMIC ENERGY AGENCY,INTERNATIONAL CONVENTIONS ON CIVIL LIABILITY FOR NUCLEAR DAMAGE. FUT WOR+45 ADJUD WAR COST PEACE SOVEREIGN...JURID 20. PAGE 71 A1462 — DIPLOM INT/ORG DELIB/GP NUC/PWR

B66
KNORR K.E.,ON THE USES OF MILITARY POWER IN THE NUCLEAR AGE. WOR+45 INT/ORG TEC/DEV ADMIN CONTROL WAR COST 20. PAGE 81 A1656 — FORCES DIPLOM DETER NUC/PWR

B66
KUENNE R.E.,THE POLARIS MISSILE STRIKE* A GENERAL ECONOMIC SYSTEMS ANALYSIS. USA+45 USSR NAT/G BAL/PWR ARMS/CONT WAR...MATH PROBABIL COMPUT/IR CHARTS HYPO/EXP SIMUL. PAGE 82 A1689 — NUC/PWR FORCES DETER DIPLOM

B66
MAY E.R.,ANXIETY AND AFFLUENCE: 1945-1965. USA+45 DIPLOM FOR/AID ARMS/CONT RACE/REL CONSEN...ANTHOL 20 COLD/WAR KENNEDY/JF EISNHWR/DD TRUMAN/HS BERLIN/BLO. PAGE 97 A1982 — ANOMIE ECO/DEV NUC/PWR WEALTH

B66
MC LELLAN D.S.,THE COLD WAR IN TRANSITION. USSR WOR+45 CONTROL LEAD NUC/PWR NAT/LISM SOVEREIGN 20 COLD/WAR THIRD/WRLD. PAGE 97 A1994 — BAL/PWR DETER DIPLOM POLICY

B66
OBERMANN E.,VERTEIDIGUNG PER FREIHEIT. GERMANY/W WOR+45 INT/ORG COERCE NUC/PWR WEAPON MARXISM 20 UN NATO WARSAW/P TREATY. PAGE 111 A2273 — FORCES ORD/FREE WAR PEACE

B66
VON BORCH H.,FRIEDE TROTZ KRIEG. GERMANY USSR WOR+45 PEACE ANOMIE ATTIT 20. PAGE 112 A2305 — DIPLOM NUC/PWR WAR COERCE

B66
SALTER L.M.,RESOLUTION OF INTERNATIONAL CONFLICT. USA+45 INT/ORG SECT DIPLOM ECO/TAC FOR/AID DETER NUC/PWR WAR 20. PAGE 127 A2595 — PROB/SOLV PEACE INT/LAW POLICY

B66
SCHWARZ U.,AMERICAN STRATEGY: A NEW PERSPECTIVE. USA+45 USA-45 INT/ORG TEC/DEV BAL/PWR DIPLOM LEAD ARMS/CONT DETER NUC/PWR WAR 20 NATO. PAGE 130 A2659 — NAT/G POLICY FORCES PWR

B66
UNITED NATIONS,INTERNATIONAL SPACE BIBLIOGRAPHY. FUT INT/ORG TEC/DEV DIPLOM ARMS/CONT NUC/PWR ...JURID SOC UN. PAGE 149 A3037 — BIBLIOG SPACE PEACE R+D

B66
US DEPARTMENT OF THE ARMY,COMMUNIST CHINA: A STRATEGIC SURVEY: A BIBLIOGRAPHY (PAMPHLET NO. 20-67). CHINA/COM COM INDIA USSR NAT/G POL/PAR EX/STRUC FORCES NUC/PWR REV ATTIT...POLICY GEOG CHARTS. PAGE 152 A3109 — BIBLIOG/A MARXISM S/ASIA DIPLOM

B66
US SENATE COMM ON FOREIGN REL,UNITED STATES POLICY TOWARD EUROPE (AND RELATED MATTERS). COM EUR+WWI GERMANY PROB/SOLV REGION NUC/PWR WAR NAT/LISM PEACE PWR...NAT/COMP 20 NATO CONGRESS DEGAULLE/C. PAGE 156 A3184 — DIPLOM INT/ORG POLICY WOR+45

B66
WAINHOUSE D.W.,INTERNATIONAL PEACE OBSERVATION: A HISTORY AND FORECAST. INT/ORG PROB/SOLV BAL/PWR AGREE ARMS/CONT COERCE NUC/PWR...PREDICT METH/COMP 20 UN LEAGUE/NAT OAS TREATY. PAGE 160 A3261 — PEACE DIPLOM

B66
ZABLOCKI C.J.,SINO-SOVIET RIVALRY. AFR ASIA CHINA/COM CUBA EUR+WWI L/A+17C USA+45 USSR WOR+45 POL/PAR FORCES COERCE NUC/PWR...GOV/COMP IDEA/COMP 20 MAO KHRUSH/N. PAGE 169 A3442 — DIPLOM MARXISM COM

S66
DUROSELLE J.B.,"THE FUTURE OF THE ATLANTIC COMMUNITY." EUR+WWI USA+45 USSR NAT/G CAP/ISM REGION DETER NUC/PWR ATTIT MARXISM...INT/LAW 20 NATO. PAGE 40 A0811 — FUT DIPLOM MYTH POLICY

S66
ORVIK N.,"NATO: THE ROLE OF THE SMALL MEMBERS." EUR+WWI FUT USA+45 CONSULT FORCES PROB/SOLV ARMS/CONT DETER NUC/PWR PWR 20 NATO. PAGE 112 A2298 — NAT/G DIPLOM INT/ORG POLICY

S66
SHERMAN M.,"GUARANTEES AND NUCLEAR SPREAD." USA+45 WOR+45 INT/ORG PLAN DETER WAR ORD/FREE 20 NATO. PAGE 132 A2700 — DIPLOM POLICY NAT/G NUC/PWR

C66
KULSKI W.W.,"DEGAULLE AND THE WORLD: THE FOREIGN POLICY OF THE FIFTH FRENCH REPUBLIC." FRANCE ECO/UNDEV POL/PAR BAL/PWR DETER NUC/PWR ATTIT PWR ...RECORD BIBLIOG DEGAULLE NATO EEC. PAGE 83 A1694 — POLICY SOVEREIGN PERSON DIPLOM

B67
BURNS E.L.M.,MEGAMURDER. WOR+45 LAW INT/ORG NAT/G BAL/PWR DIPLOM DETER MURDER WEAPON CIVMIL/REL PEACE ...INT/LAW TREND 20. PAGE 22 A0444 — FORCES PLAN WAR NUC/PWR

B67
FINE S.,RECENT AMERICA* CONFLICTING INTERPRETATIONS OF THE GREAT ISSUES (2ND ED.). USA+45 USA-45 POL/PAR SECT CONFER NUC/PWR WAR ATTIT...POLICY TREND ANTHOL PRESIDENT 20. PAGE 46 A0931 — IDEA/COMP DIPLOM NAT/G

B67
GRIFFITH SB I.I.,THE CHINESE PEOPLE'S LIBERATION ARMY. CHINA/COM DIPLOM DOMIN GUERRILLA NUC/PWR REV ...CHARTS BIBLIOG 20. PAGE 57 A1163 — FORCES CIVMIL/REL NAT/LISM PWR

B67
HALPERIN M.H.,CONTEMPORARY MILITARY STRATEGY. ASIA CHINA/COM USA+45 USSR INT/ORG FORCES ACT/RES PLAN TEC/DEV BAL/PWR COERCE WAR...METH/COMP BIBLIOG 20 NATO. PAGE 60 A1240 — DIPLOM NUC/PWR DETER ARMS/CONT

B67
KAROL K.S.,CHINA, THE OTHER COMMUNISM (TRANS. BY — NAT/G

TOM BAISTOW). CHINA/COM CULTURE INDUS FORCES DIPLOM EDU/PROP CONTROL EXEC NUC/PWR ATTIT...SOC CHARTS 20. PAGE 77 A1567 — POL/PAR MARXISM INGP/REL

B67
MCBRIDE J.H.,THE TEST BAN TREATY: MILITARY, TECHNOLOGICAL, AND POLITICAL IMPLICATIONS. USA+45 USSR DELIB/GP FORCES LEGIS TEC/DEV BAL/PWR TREATY. PAGE 97 A1995 — ARMS/CONT DIPLOM NUC/PWR

B67
MCCLINTOCK R.,THE MEANING OF LIMITED WAR. FUT WOR+45 NAT/G FORCES GUERRILLA REV...POLICY SAMP/SIZ TREND NAT/COMP 45 COLD/WAR. PAGE 97 A1999 — WAR NUC/PWR BAL/PWR DIPLOM

B67
POGANY A.H.,POLITICAL SCIENCE AND INTERNATIONAL RELATIONS, BOOKS RECOMMENDED FOR AMERICAN CATHOLIC COLLEGE LIBRARIES. INT/ORG LOC/G NAT/G FORCES BAL/PWR ECO/TAC NUC/PWR...CATH INT/LAW TREATY 20. PAGE 117 A2393 — BIBLIOG DIPLOM

B67
US SENATE COMM ON FOREIGN REL,UNITED STATES ARMAMENT AND DISARMAMENT PROBLEMS. USA+45 AIR BAL/PWR DIPLOM FOR/AID NUC/PWR ORD/FREE SENATE TREATY. PAGE 156 A3190 — ARMS/CONT WEAPON FORCES PROB/SOLV

S67
"CHINESE STATEMENT ON NUCLEAR PROLIFERATION." CHINA/COM USA+45 USSR DOMIN COLONIAL PWR. PAGE 4 A0078 — NUC/PWR BAL/PWR ARMS/CONT DIPLOM

S67
APEL H.,"LES NOUVEAUX ASPECTS DE LA POLITIQUE ETRANGERE ALLEMANDE." EUR+WWI GERMANY POL/PAR BAL/PWR ECO/TAC INT/TRADE NUC/PWR NAT/LISM PEACE ...POLICY 20 EEC COLD/WAR. PAGE 8 A0168 — DIPLOM INT/ORG FEDERAL

S67
CARROLL K.J.,"SECOND STEP TOWARD ARMS CONTROL." WOR+45 INT/ORG VOL/ASSN FORCES PROB/SOLV RISK WEAPON 20 COLD/WAR. PAGE 25 A0503 — ARMS/CONT DIPLOM PLAN NUC/PWR

S67
D'AMATO D.,"LEGAL ASPECTS OF THE FRENCH NUCLEAR TESTS." FRANCE WOR+45 ACT/RES COLONIAL RISK GOV/REL EQUILIB ORD/FREE PWR DECISION. PAGE 33 A0672 — INT/LAW DIPLOM NUC/PWR ADJUD

S67
DEUTSCH K.W.,"ARMS CONTROL AND EUROPEAN UNITY* THE NEXT TEN YEARS." USA+45 ELITES NAT/G BAL/PWR DIPLOM NUC/PWR...INT KNO/TEST NATO EEC. PAGE 36 A0742 — ARMS/CONT PEACE REGION PLAN

S67
EISENDRATH C.,"THE OUTER SPACE TREATY." CHINA/COM COM USA+45 DIPLOM CONTROL NUC/PWR...INT/LAW 20 UN COLD/WAR TREATY. PAGE 41 A0831 — SPACE INT/ORG PEACE ARMS/CONT

S67
FELD B.T.,"A PLEDGE* NO FIRST USE." DELIB/GP BAL/PWR DOMIN DETER. PAGE 45 A0913 — ARMS/CONT NUC/PWR DIPLOM PEACE

S67
GRIFFITHS F.,"THE POLITICAL SIDE OF 'DISARMAMENT'." FUT WOR+45 NUC/PWR NAT/LISM PEACE...NEW/IDEA PREDICT METH/COMP GEN/LAWS 20. PAGE 57 A1164 — ARMS/CONT DIPLOM

S67
JACKSON W.G.F.,"NUCLEAR PROLIFERATION AND THE GREAT POWERS." FUT UK WOR+45 INT/ORG DOMIN ARMS/CONT DETER ORD/FREE PACIFIST. PAGE 72 A1480 — NUC/PWR ATTIT BAL/PWR NAT/LISM

S67
KAHN H.,"CRITERIA FOR LONG-RANGE NUCLEAR CONTROL POLICIES." WOR+45 INT/ORG TEC/DEV DOMIN DETER WAR WEAPON ISOLAT ORD/FREE POLICY. PAGE 76 A1549 — NUC/PWR ARMS/CONT BAL/PWR DIPLOM

S67
KRUSCHE H.,"THE STRIVING OF THE KIESINGER-STRAUS GOVERNMENT FOR NUCLEAR WEAPONS IS A THREAT TO EUROPEAN SECURITY." EUR+WWI GERMANY BAL/PWR SANCTION WEAPON PEACE ORD/FREE...MARXIST 20 NATO COLD/WAR. PAGE 82 A1688 — ARMS/CONT INT/ORG NUC/PWR DIPLOM

S67
REINTANZ G.,"THE SPACE TREATY." WOR+45 DIPLOM CONTROL ARMS/CONT NUC/PWR WAR...MARXIST 20 COLD/WAR UN TREATY. PAGE 120 A2461 — SPACE INT/LAW INT/ORG PEACE

S67
SHARP G.,"THE NEED OF A FUNCTIONAL SUBSTITUTE FOR WAR." FUT UNIV WOR+45 CULTURE SOCIETY INT/ORG CONSULT DELIB/GP ACT/RES CREATE BAL/PWR CONFER ARMS/CONT NUC/PWR 20. PAGE 132 A2696 — PEACE WAR DIPLOM PROB/SOLV

S67
SHULMAN M.D.,"'EUROPE' VERSUS 'DETENTE'." USA+45 USSR INT/ORG CONTROL ARMS/CONT DETER 20. PAGE 132 A2711 — DIPLOM BAL/PWR NUC/PWR

S67
STEEL R.,"BEYOND THE POWER BLOCS." USA+45 USSR ECO/UNDEV NEUTRAL NUC/PWR NAT/LISM ATTIT...GEOG NATO WARSAW/P COLD/WAR. PAGE 137 A2811 — DIPLOM TREND BAL/PWR PLAN

S67
SUINN R.M.,"THE DISARMAMENT FANTASY* PSYCHOLOGICAL FACTORS THAT MAY PRODUCE WARFARE." DIPLOM RISK ARMS/CONT DETER ANOMIE PERSON GAME. PAGE 140 A2860 — DECISION NUC/PWR WAR PSY

S67
WASHBURN A.M.,"NUCLEAR PROLIFERATION IN A REVOLUTIONARY INTERNATIONAL SYSTEM." WOR+45 NAT/G DELIB/GP PLAN TEC/DEV...POLICY 20. PAGE 161 A3287 — ARMS/CONT NUC/PWR DIPLOM CONFER

N67
US GOVERNMENT,TREATIES IN FORCE. NAT/G ECO/TAC FOR/AID INT/TRADE NUC/PWR 20. PAGE 153 A3117 — DIPLOM INT/ORG BAL/PWR

NUCLEAR POWER....SEE NUC/PWR

NUCLEAR WAR....SEE NUC/PWR+COERCE, WAR

NUMELIN R. A2260

NUMERICAL INDICES....SEE INDEX

NUNEZ JIMENEZ A. A2261

NUREMBERG....NUREMBERG WAR TRIALS; SEE ALSO WAR/TRIAL

B61
WECHSLER H.,PRINCIPLES, POLITICS AND FUNDAMENTAL LAW: SELECTED ESSAYS. USA+45 USA-45 LAW SOCIETY NAT/G PROVS DELIB/GP EX/STRUC ACT/RES LEGIT PERSON KNOWL PWR...JURID 20 NUREMBERG. PAGE 162 A3296 — CT/SYS CONSTN INT/LAW

NURTY K.S. A2262

NUSSBAUM D. A2263

NYASALAND....SEE MALAWI

B65
WALKER A.A.,THE RHODESIAS AND NYASALAND: A GUIDE TO OFFICIAL PUBLICATIONS. RHODESIA UK OP/RES PLAN PROB/SOLV DIPLOM...POLICY SOC CON/ANAL 19/20 NYASALAND. PAGE 160 A3263 — BIBLIOG NAT/G COLONIAL AFR

NYATURU....NYATURU, A TRIBE OF TANGANYIKA

NYC....NEW YORK CITY; SEE NEW YORK/C

NYE J.S. A2264

NYERERE J.K. A2265

O

O'BRIEN W. A2266

O'BRIEN W.V. A2267

O'CONNELL M.R. A2268

O'CONNOR A.M. A2269

O'LEARY M.K. A2270

OAKES J.B. A2271

OAS A2272

OAS....ORGANIZATION OF AMERICAN STATES; SEE ALSO INT/ORG, VOL/ASSN

N
COUNCIL ON FOREIGN RELATIONS,DOCUMENTS ON AMERICAN FOREIGN RELATIONS. INT/ORG ECO/TAC NUC/PWR WAR WEAPON...POLICY CON/ANAL CHARTS 20 OAS UN. PAGE 31 A0639 — BIBLIOG USA+45 USA-45 DIPLOM

N
OAS,DOCUMENTOS OFICIALES DE LA ORGANIZACION DE LOS ESTADOS AMERICANOS. L/A+17C ATTIT 20 OAS. PAGE 111 A2272 — BIBLIOG INT/ORG DIPLOM POLICY

B38
MATTHEWS M.A.,FEDERALISM: SELECT LIST OF REFERENCES ON FEDERAL GOVERNMENT REGIONALISM...EXAMPLES OF FEDERATIONS (PAMPHLET). WOR-45 CONSTN INT/ORG NAT/G 19/20 OAS LEAGUE/NAT. PAGE 96 A1976 — BIBLIOG/A FEDERAL REGION DIPLOM

B50
DAVIS E.P.,PERIODICALS OF INTERNATIONAL ORGANIZATIONS; PART I, THE UN AND SPECIALIZED AGENCIES; PART II, INTER-AMERICAN ORGS. CULTURE AGRI FINAN INDUS LABOR INT/TRADE...GEOG HEAL STAT 20 UN OAS UNESCO. PAGE 34 A0689 — BIBLIOG/A INT/ORG DIPLOM L/A+17C

L51
WHITAKER A.P.,"DEVELOPMENT OF AMERICAN REGIONALISM: THE ORGANIZATION OF AMERICAN STATES." L/A+17C — INT/ORG TIME/SEQ

USA+45 VOL/ASSN DELIB/GP FORCES TOP/EX ACT/RES ECO/TAC CT/SYS REGION PEACE ALL/VALS OAS 20. PAGE 163 A3330 — DETER

B54
US DEPARTMENT OF STATE,PUBLICATIONS OF THE DEPARTMENT OF STATE, OCTOBER 1,1929 TO JANUARY 1, 1953. AGRI INT/ORG FORCES FOR/AID EDU/PROP ARMS/CONT NUC/PWR ATTIT 20 DEPT/STATE OAS UN NATO. PAGE 151 A3089 — BIBLIOG DIPLOM

B54
WHITAKER A.P.,THE WESTERN HEMISPHERE IDEA. USA+45 USA-45 CONSTN INT/ORG NAT/G DIPLOM SOVEREIGN...GEOG TIME/SEQ OAS 19/20 MONROE/DOC. PAGE 164 A3331 — L/A+17C CONCPT REGION

B55
BURR R.N.,DOCUMENTS ON INTER-AMERICAN COOPERATION: VOL. I, 1810-1881; VOL. II, 1881-1948. DELIB/GP BAL/PWR INT/TRADE REPRESENT NAT/LISM PEACE HABITAT ORD/FREE PWR SOVEREIGN...INT/LAW 20 OAS. PAGE 22 A0445 — BIBLIOG DIPLOM INT/ORG L/A+17C

B55
TANNENBAUM F.,THE AMERICAN TRADITION IN FOREIGN POLICY. USA+45 USA-45 CONSTN INT/ORG NAT/G POL/PAR VOL/ASSN TOP/EX LEGIT DRIVE ORD/FREE PWR...CONCPT GEN/LAWS CONGRESS LEAGUE/NAT COLD/WAR OAS 18/20. PAGE 141 A2887 — TIME/SEQ

L55
KISER M.,"ORGANIZATION OF AMERICAN STATES." L/A+17C USA+45 ECO/UNDEV INT/ORG NAT/G PLAN TEC/DEV DIPLOM ECO/TAC INT/TRADE EDU/PROP ADMIN ALL/VALS...POLICY MGT RECORD ORG/CHARTS OAS 20. PAGE 80 A1639 — VOL/ASSN ECO/DEV REGION

B56
SOHN L.B.,BASIC DOCUMENTS OF THE UNITED NATIONS. WOR+45 LAW INT/ORG LEGIT EXEC ROUTINE CHOOSE PWR ...JURID CONCPT GEN/LAWS ANTHOL UN TOT/POP OAS FAO ILO 20. PAGE 135 A2761 — DELIB/GP CONSTN

B57
JENKS C.W.,THE INTERNATIONAL PROTECTION OF TRADE UNION FREEDOM. FUT WOR+45 WOR-45 VOL/ASSN DELIB/GP CT/SYS REGION ROUTINE...JURID METH/CNCPT RECORD TIME/SEQ CHARTS ILO WORK OAS 20. PAGE 73 A1504 — LABOR INT/ORG

B58
PAN AMERICAN UNION,REPERTORIO DE PUBLICACIONES PERIODICAS ACTUALES LATINO-AMERICANAS. CULTURE ECO/UNDEV ADMIN LEAD GOV/REL 20 OAS. PAGE 113 A2326 — BIBLIOG L/A+17C NAT/G DIPLOM

B58
US DEPARTMENT OF STATE,PUBLICATIONS OF THE DEPARTMENT OF STATE, JANUARY 1,1953 TO DECEMBER 31, 1957. AGRI INT/ORG FORCES FOR/AID EDU/PROP ARMS/CONT NUC/PWR ATTIT 20 DEPT/STATE OAS UN NATO. PAGE 151 A3092 — BIBLIOG DIPLOM

B59
PANAMERICAN UNION,PUBLICATIONS: PAU AND OFFICIAL RECORDS OF THE OAS, IN ENGLISH, SPANISH, PORTUGUESE, AND FRENCH, 1958-59. NAT/G ATTIT...SOC 20 OAS. PAGE 113 A2328 — BIBLIOG L/A+17C INT/LAW DIPLOM

S59
PLAZA G.,"FOR A REGIONAL MARKET IN LATIN AMERICA." FUT L/A+17C CULTURE INDUS NAT/G ECO/TAC INT/TRADE ATTIT WEALTH...NEW/IDEA TREND OAS 20. PAGE 116 A2389 — MARKET INT/ORG REGION

B60
CARNEGIE ENDOWMENT INT. PEACE,PERSPECTIVES ON PEACE - 1910-1960. WOR+45 WOR-45 INTELL INT/ORG CONSULT ACT/RES EDU/PROP ATTIT KNOWL ORD/FREE...TIME/SEQ TREND EEC OAS UNESCO NAZI 20. PAGE 24 A0489 — FUT CONCPT ARMS/CONT PEACE

B60
LIEUWEN E.,ARMS AND POLITICS IN LATIN AMERICA. FUT USA+45 USA-45 ECO/UNDEV INT/ORG NAT/G FORCES DIPLOM COERCE ATTIT ALL/VALS VAL/FREE OAS 20. PAGE 88 A1811 — L/A+17C FOR/AID

B60
PAN AMERICAN UNION,FIFTH MEETING OF CONSULTATION OF MINISTERS OF FOREIGN AFFAIRS OF AMERICAN STATES. L/A+17C FORCES PLAN PROB/SOLV ADJUD PEACE...POLICY INT/LAW 20 OAS. PAGE 113 A2327 — INT/ORG DIPLOM DELIB/GP ECO/UNDEV

S60
"THE EMERGING COMMON MARKETS IN LATIN AMERICA." FUT L/A+17C STRATA DIST/IND INDUS LABOR NAT/G LEGIS ECO/TAC ADMIN RIGID/FLEX HEALTH...NEW/IDEA TIME/SEQ OAS 20. PAGE 3 A0059 — FINAN ECO/UNDEV INT/TRADE

S60
FITZGIBBON R.H.,"DICTATORSHIP AND DEMOCRACY IN LATIN AMERICA." FUT ECO/DEV ECO/UNDEV INT/ORG LOC/G NAT/G TOP/EX PLAN TEC/DEV ECO/TAC CHOOSE ATTIT DRIVE PERSON ALL/VALS OAS TOT/POP 20. PAGE 46 A0943 — L/A+17C ACT/RES INT/TRADE

S60
KALUODA J.,"COMMUNIST STRATEGY IN LATIN AMERICA." L/A+17C USA+45 INT/ORG NAT/G POL/PAR DIPLOM ECO/TAC EDU/PROP COERCE WEALTH...CONCPT OAS COLD/WAR 20. PAGE 76 A1553 — COM PWR CUBA

S60
MORA J.A.,"THE ORGANIZATION OF AMERICAN STATES." USA+45 LAW ECO/UNDEV VOL/ASSN DELIB/GP PLAN BAL/PWR EDU/PROP ADMIN DRIVE RIGID/FLEX ORD/FREE WEALTH ...TIME/SEQ GEN/LAWS OAS 20. PAGE 103 A2126 — L/A+17C INT/ORG REGION

B61
BAGU S.,ARGENTINA EN EL MUNDO. L/A+17C INDUS INT/TRADE WAR ATTIT ROLE...TREND 19/20 ARGEN OAS. PAGE 10 A0202 — DIPLOM INT/ORG REGION ECO/UNDEV

B61
MECHAM J.L.,THE UNITED STATES AND INTER-AMERICAN SECURITY, 1889-1960. L/A+17C USA+45 USA-45 CONSTN FORCES INT/TRADE PEACE TOTALISM ATTIT...JURID 19/20 UN OAS. PAGE 99 A2030 — DIPLOM WAR ORD/FREE INT/ORG

B61
PEASLEE A.J.,INTERNATIONAL GOVERNMENTAL ORGANIZATIONS (2 VOLS.). CONSTN VOL/ASSN DIPLOM ...GP/COMP 20 UN OAS EEC EFTA ECSC. PAGE 114 A2345 — BIBLIOG INT/ORG INDEX LAW

S61
ANGLIN D.,"UNITED STATES OPPOSITION TO CANADIAN MEMBERSHIP IN THE PAN AMERICAN UNION: A CANADIAN VIEW." L/A+17C UK USA+45 VOL/ASSN DELIB/GP EX/STRUC PLAN DIPLOM DOMIN REGION ATTIT RIGID/FLEX PWR ...RELATIV CONCPT STERTYP CMN/WLTH OAS 20. PAGE 8 A0162 — INT/ORG CANADA

S61
BALL M.M.,"ISSUES FOR THE AMERICAS: NON-INTERVENTION VS HUMAN RIGHTS AND THE PRESERVATION OF DEMOCRATIC INSTITUTIONS." USA+45 INTELL INT/ORG NAT/G DIPLOM ECO/TAC LEGIT...TREND OAS TOT/POP 20. PAGE 11 A0213 — L/A+17C MORAL

B62
AIR FORCE ACADEMY LIBRARY,INTERNATIONAL ORGANIZATIONS AND MILITARY SECURITY SYSTEMS (PAMPHLET) (SPECIAL BIBLIOGRAPHY SERIES, NUMBER 25). DIPLOM FOR/AID INT/TRADE NUC/PWR PEACE 20 UN NATO OAS SEATO LEAGUE/NAT. PAGE 5 A0104 — BIBLIOG INT/ORG FORCES DETER

B62
ALEXANDROWICZ C.H.,WORLD ECONOMIC AGENCIES: LAW AND PRACTICE. WOR+45 DIST/IND FINAN LABOR CONSULT INT/TRADE TARIFFS REPRESENT HEALTH...JURID 20 UN GATT EEC OAS ECSC. PAGE 6 A0115 — INT/LAW INT/ORG DIPLOM ADJUD

B62
DREIER J.C.,THE ORGANIZATION OF AMERICAN STATES AND THE HEMISPHERE CRISIS. CUBA USA+45 CULTURE STRATA NAT/G VOL/ASSN CONSULT FORCES ACT/RES CREATE DIPLOM ECO/TAC FOR/AID ALL/VALS...POLICY OBS OAS 20. PAGE 38 A0786 — L/A+17C CONCPT

B62
DREIER J.C.,THE ALLIANCE FOR PROGRESS. L/A+17C USA+45 CULTURE ECO/DEV ECO/UNDEV NAT/G PLAN DIPLOM PWR 20 OAS. PAGE 39 A0787 — FOR/AID INT/ORG ECO/TAC POLICY

B62
SNYDER L.L.D.,THE IMPERIALISM READER. AFR ASIA CHINA/COM COM EUR+WWI FUT MOD/EUR USA+45 WOR+45 WOR-45 INT/ORG COLONIAL SOVEREIGN CMN/WLTH OAS 20. PAGE 134 A2751 — DOMIN PWR DIPLOM

L62
MALINOWSKI W.R.,"CENTRALIZATION AND DE-CENTRALIZATION IN THE UNITED NATIONS' ECONOMIC AND SOCIAL ACTIVITIES." WOR+45 CONSTN ECO/UNDEV INT/ORG VOL/ASSN DELIB/GP ECO/TAC EDU/PROP ADMIN RIGID/FLEX ...OBS CHARTS UNESCO UN EEC OAS OEEC 20. PAGE 93 A1913 — CREATE GEN/LAWS

S62
BERKES R.N.B.,"THE NEW FRONTIER IN THE UN." FUT USA+45 WOR+45 INT/ORG DELIB/GP NAT/LISM PERCEPT RESPECT UN OAS 20. PAGE 13 A0272 — GEN/LAWS DIPLOM

S62
FENWICK C.G.,"ISSUES AT PUNTA DEL ESTE: NON-INTERVENTION VS COLLECTIVE SECURITY." L/A+17C USA+45 VOL/ASSN DELIB/GP ECO/TAC LEGIT ADJUD REGION ORD/FREE OAS COLD/WAR 20. PAGE 45 A0917 — INT/ORG CUBA

B63
BOWETT D.W.,THE LAW OF INTERNATIONAL INSTITUTIONS. WOR+45 WOR-45 CONSTN DELIB/GP EX/STRUC JUDGE EDU/PROP LEGIT CT/SYS EXEC ROUTINE RIGID/FLEX ORD/FREE PWR...JURID CONCPT ORG/CHARTS GEN/METH LEAGUE/NAT OAS OEEC 20 UN. PAGE 17 A0354 — INT/ORG ADJUD DIPLOM

B63
MANGER W.,THE ALLIANCE FOR PROGRESS: A CRITICAL APPRAISAL. FUT L/A+17C USA+45 CULTURE ECO/UNDEV ACADEM NAT/G SCHOOL PLAN FOR/AID...POLICY OAS. PAGE 94 A1918 — DIPLOM INT/ORG ECO/TAC REGION

B63
PANAMERICAN UNION,DOCUMENTOS OFICIALES DE LA ORGANIZACION DE LOS ESTADOS AMERICANOS, INDICE Y LISTA (VOL. III, 1962). L/A+17C DELIB/GP INT/TRADE EDU/PROP REGION NUC/PWR...HEAL INT/LAW SOC/WK 20 OAS. PAGE 113 A2329 — BIBLIOG INT/ORG DIPLOM

S63
HOLBO P.S.,"COLD WAR DRIFT IN LATIN AMERICA." CUBA L/A+17C USA+45 USA-45 INT/ORG NAT/G NEIGH VOL/ASSN ACT/RES PLAN ECO/TAC ATTIT RIGID/FLEX ALL/VALS ...RECORD TIME/SEQ OAS LAFTA 20 COLD/WAR. PAGE 66 A1363 — DELIB/GP CREATE FOR/AID

S63
MANOLIU F.,"PERSPECTIVES D'UNE INTEGRATION — FINAN

ECONOMIQUE LATINOAMERICAINE." FUT L/A+17C STRUCT INT/ORG
MARKET LABOR POL/PAR VOL/ASSN PLAN RIGID/FLEX PWR PEACE
...METH/CNCPT OAS TOT/POP 20. PAGE 94 A1927

S63
WELLS H.,"THE OAS AND THE DOMINICAN ELECTIONS." CONSULT
L/A+17C INT/ORG NAT/G POL/PAR TEC/DEV ECO/TAC CHOOSE
EDU/PROP PERCEPT...TIME/SEQ OAS TOT/POP 20. DOMIN/REP
PAGE 163 A3317

B64
WYTHE G.,THE UNITED STATES AND INTER-AMERICAN ATTIT
RELATIONS: A CONTEMPORARY APPRAISAL. L/A+17C USA+45 ECO/TAC
ECO/UNDEV INT/ORG NAT/G VOL/ASSN INT/TRADE EDU/PROP FOR/AID
DRIVE...SOC TREND OAS UN 20. PAGE 168 A3425

L64
CLAUDE I.,"THE OAS, THE UN, AND THE UNITED STATES." INT/ORG
L/A+17C USA+45 CONSTN NAT/G DELIB/GP DOMIN EDU/PROP POLICY
LEGIT REGION COERCE ORD/FREE PWR...TIME/SEQ TREND
STERTYP OAS UN 20. PAGE 27 A0546

B65
AIR UNIVERSITY LIBRARY,LATIN AMERICA, SELECTED BIBLIOG
REFERENCES. ECO/UNDEV FORCES EDU/PROP MARXISM 20 L/A+17C
OAS. PAGE 5 A0106 NAT/G
DIPLOM

B65
SABLE M.H.,PERIODICALS FOR LATIN AMERICAN ECONOMIC BIBLIOG/A
DEVELOPMENT, TRADE, AND FINANCE: AN ANNOTATED L/A+17C
BIBLIOGRAPHY (A PAMPHLET). ECO/TAC PRODUC PROFIT ECO/UNDEV
...STAT NAT/COMP 20 OAS. PAGE 126 A2583 INT/TRADE

B65
STOETZER O.C.,THE ORGANIZATION OF AMERICAN STATES. INT/ORG
L/A+17C EX/STRUC FOR/AID CONFER PARL/PROC ORD/FREE REGION
SOVEREIGN...POLICY INT/LAW 20 OAS. PAGE 138 A2831 DIPLOM
BAL/PWR

S65
SCHNEIDER R.M.,"THE US IN LATIN AMERICA." L/A+17C VOL/ASSN
USA+45 NAT/G POL/PAR PLAN RIGID/FLEX ALL/VALS OAS ECO/UNDEV
20. PAGE 129 A2640 FOR/AID

B66
CONNEL-SMITH G.,THE INTERAMERICAN SYSTEM. CUBA DIPLOM
L/A+17C DELIB/GP FOR/AID COLONIAL PEACE PWR MARXISM INT/TRADE
...BIBLIOG 19/20 OAS. PAGE 29 A0586 REGION
INT/ORG

B66
US DEPARTMENT OF STATE,RESEARCH ON THE AMERICAN BIBLIOG/A
REPUBLICS (EXTERNAL RESEARCH LIST NO 6-25). CULTURE L/A+17C
SOCIETY POL/PAR DIPLOM EDU/PROP MARXISM WORSHIP 20 REGION
OAS. PAGE 152 A3095 NAT/G

B66
WAINHOUSE D.W.,INTERNATIONAL PEACE OBSERVATION: A PEACE
HISTORY AND FORECAST. INT/ORG PROB/SOLV BAL/PWR DIPLOM
AGREE ARMS/CONT COERCE NUC/PWR...PREDICT METH/COMP
20 UN LEAGUE/NAT OAS TREATY. PAGE 160 A3261

S66
JAVITS J.K.,"POLITICAL ACTION VITAL FOR LATIN L/A+17C
AMERICAN INTEGRATION." ECO/UNDEV INT/ORG POL/PAR ECO/TAC
VOL/ASSN PLAN PROB/SOLV INT/TRADE EFFICIENCY 20 OAS REGION
LAFTA. PAGE 73 A1500

B67
SABLE M.H.,A GUIDE TO LATIN AMERICAN STUDIES (2 BIBLIOG/A
VOLS). CONSTN FINAN INT/ORG LABOR MUNIC POL/PAR L/A+17C
FORCES CAP/ISM FOR/AID ADMIN MARXISM SOCISM OAS. DIPLOM
PAGE 126 A2584 NAT/LISM

L67
MACDONALD R.S.J.,"THE RESORT TO ECONOMIC COERCION INT/ORG
BY INTERNATIONAL POLITICAL ORGANIZATIONS." CUBA COERCE
ETHIOPIA RHODESIA SOUTH/AFR NAT/G FOR/AID INT/TRADE ECO/TAC
DOMIN CONTROL SANCTION...DECISION LEAGUE/NAT UN OAS DIPLOM
20. PAGE 92 A1887

OAU....ORGANIZATION FOR AFRICAN UNITY

N19
PROVISIONS SECTION OAU,ORGANIZATION OF AFRICAN CONSTN
UNITY: BASIC DOCUMENTS AND RESOLUTIONS (PAMPHLET). EX/STRUC
AFR CULTURE ECO/UNDEV DIPLOM ECO/TAC EDU/PROP SOVEREIGN
COLONIAL ARMS/CONT NUC/PWR RACE/REL DISCRIM INT/ORG
NAT/LISM 20 UN OAU. PAGE 118 A2415

S66
GREEN L.C.,"RHODESIAN OIL: BOOTLEGGERS OR PIRATES?" INT/TRADE
AFR RHODESIA UK WOR+45 INT/ORG NAT/G DIPLOM LEGIT SANCTION
COLONIAL SOVEREIGN 20 UN OAU. PAGE 55 A1139 INT/LAW
POLICY

OBAID A.H. A1941

OBERLIN....OBERLIN, OHIO

OBERMANN E. A2273

OBESITY....SEE HEALTH, EATING

OBJECTIVE....OBJECTIVE, OBJECTIVITY

S67
VAN DUSEN H.P.,"HAMMARSKOLD IN THE WORLD'S INT/ORG
SERVICE." DIPLOM CONFER LEAD PEACE STRANGE UTOPIA CONSULT
MORAL SKILL OBJECTIVE...INT/LAW SELF/OBS 20. TOP/EX
PAGE 158 A3211 NEUTRAL

OBLIGATION....SEE SUPEGO

OBS....OBSERVATION; SEE ALSO DIRECT OBSERVATION METHOD
INDEX, P. XIV

B00
MAINE H.S.,INTERNATIONAL LAW. MOD/EUR UNIV SOCIETY INT/ORG
STRUCT ACT/RES EXEC WAR ATTIT PERSON ALL/VALS LAW
...POLICY JURID CONCPT OBS TIME/SEQ TOT/POP. PEACE
PAGE 93 A1908 INT/LAW

B00
VOLPICELLI Z.,RUSSIA ON THE PACIFIC AND THE NAT/G
SIBERIAN RAILWAY. MOD/EUR ECO/UNDEV INT/ORG FORCES ACT/RES
PLAN DOMIN COLONIAL ROUTINE ATTIT ALL/VALS...OBS RUSSIA
HIST/WRIT TIME/SEQ TREND CON/ANAL AUD/VIS CHARTS
18/19. PAGE 159 A3248

B11
PHILLIPSON C.,THE INTERNATIONAL LAW AND CUSTOM OF INT/ORG
ANCIENT GREECE AND ROME. MEDIT-7 UNIV INTELL LAW
SOCIETY STRUCT NAT/G LEGIS EXEC PERSON...CONCPT OBS INT/LAW
CON/ANAL ROM/EMP. PAGE 116 A2377

B16
ROOT E.,THE MILITARY AND COLONIAL POLICY OF THE US. ACT/RES
L/A+17C USA-45 LAW SOCIETY STRATA STRUCT INT/ORG PLAN
NAT/G SCHOOL FORCES EDU/PROP ALL/VALS...OBS DIPLOM
VAL/FREE 19/20. PAGE 123 A2522 WAR

B17
UPTON E.,THE MILITARY POLICY OF THE US. USA-45 FORCES
STRUCT INT/ORG EXEC ATTIT PERCEPT...MGT CONCPT OBS SKILL
HIST/WRIT CHARTS CONGRESS 18/20. PAGE 149 A3049 WAR

S17
ROOT E.,"THE EFFECT OF DEMOCRACY ON INTERNATIONAL LEGIS
LAW." USA-45 WOR-45 INTELL SOCIETY INT/ORG NAT/G JURID
CONSULT ACT/RES CREATE PLAN EDU/PROP PEACE SKILL INT/LAW
...CONCPT METH/CNCPT OBS 20. PAGE 123 A2523

B19
KEYNES J.M.,THE ECONOMIC CONSEQUENCES OF THE PEACE. EUR+WWI
FUT GERMANY MOD/EUR RUSSIA UK USA-45 CULTURE SOCIETY
ECO/DEV FINAN INDUS INT/ORG TOP/EX ECO/TAC ROUTINE PEACE
WAR ATTIT PERCEPT ALL/VALS...OLD/LIB MYTH OBS
TIME/SEQ TREND 20 TREATY. PAGE 78 A1605

B19
SUTHERLAND G.,CONSTITUTIONAL POWER AND WORLD USA-45
AFFAIRS. CONSTN STRUCT INT/ORG NAT/G CHIEF LEGIS EXEC
ACT/RES PLAN GOV/REL ALL/VALS...OBS TIME/SEQ DIPLOM
CONGRESS VAL/FREE 20 PRESIDENT. PAGE 140 A2866

B21
STUART G.H.,FRENCH FOREIGN POLICY. CONSTN INT/ORG MOD/EUR
NAT/G POL/PAR EX/STRUC FORCES PLAN ECO/TAC DOMIN DIPLOM
EDU/PROP ADJUD COERCE ATTIT DRIVE RIGID/FLEX FRANCE
ALL/VALS...POLICY OBS RECORD BIOG TIME/SEQ TREND.
PAGE 139 A2852

B28
HALL W.P.,EMPIRE TO COMMONWEALTH. FUT WOR-45 CONSTN VOL/ASSN
ECO/DEV ECO/UNDEV INT/ORG PROVS PLAN DIPLOM NAT/G
EDU/PROP ADMIN COLONIAL PEACE PERSON ALL/VALS UK
...POLICY GEOG SOC OBS RECORD TREND CMN/WLTH
PARLIAMENT 19/20. PAGE 60 A1229

B29
DUNN F.,THE PRACTICE AND PROCEDURE OF INTERNATIONAL INT/ORG
CONFERENCES. WOR-45 NAT/G DELIB/GP BAL/PWR LEGIT DIPLOM
EXEC ROUTINE PEACE ORD/FREE RESPECT...JURID CONCPT
METH/CNCPT OBS RECORD TIME/SEQ 20. PAGE 39 A0799

B30
FLEMMING D.,THE TREATY VETO OF THE AMERICAN SENATE. LEGIS
FUT USA+45 USA-45 CONSTN INT/ORG NAT/G TOP/EX LEGIT RIGID/FLEX
GOV/REL PWR...POLICY MAJORIT CONCPT OBS TIME/SEQ
CONGRESS 20. PAGE 46 A0949

B31
STOWELL E.C.,INTERNATIONAL LAW. FUT UNIV WOR-45 INT/ORG
SOCIETY CONSULT EX/STRUC FORCES ACT/RES PLAN DIPLOM ROUTINE
EDU/PROP LEGIT DISPL PWR SKILL...POLICY CONCPT OBS INT/LAW
TREND TOT/POP 20. PAGE 139 A2839

B31
STUART G.H.,THE INTERNATIONAL CITY OF TANGIER. AFR LOC/G
EUR+WWI MOD/EUR MOROCCO CONSTN PROVS CREATE PLAN INT/ORG
LEGIT PEACE ORD/FREE PWR...INT/LAW OBS TIME/SEQ DIPLOM
CON/ANAL 20 TANGIER. PAGE 139 A2854 SOVEREIGN

B34
GRAHAM F.D.,PROTECTIVE TARIFFS. FUT USA+45 WOR-45 INT/ORG
INDUS MARKET VOL/ASSN PLAN CAP/ISM ECO/TAC PEACE TARIFFS
ATTIT DRIVE HEALTH ORD/FREE...OBS TREND GEN/LAWS
20. PAGE 55 A1124

B37
VINER J.,STUDIES IN THE THEORY OF INTERNATIONAL CAP/ISM
TRADE. WOR-45 CONSTN ECO/DEV AGRI INDUS MARKET INT/TRADE
INT/ORG LABOR NAT/G ECO/TAC TARIFFS COLONIAL ATTIT
WEALTH...POLICY CONCPT MATH STAT OBS SAMP TREND
GEN/LAWS MARX/KARL 20. PAGE 159 A3236

B38
RAPPARD W.E.,THE CRISIS OF DEMOCRACY. EUR+WWI UNIV NAT/G
WOR-45 CULTURE SOCIETY ECO/DEV INT/ORG POL/PAR CONCPT
ACT/RES EDU/PROP EXEC CHOOSE ATTIT ALL/VALS...SOC

OBS HIST/WRIT TIME/SEQ LEAGUE/NAT NAZI TOT/POP 20. PAGE 119 A2449

B39
ROBBINS L.,ECONOMIC CAUSES OF WAR. WOR-45 ECO/DEV ECO/UNDEV INT/ORG NAT/G TEC/DEV DIPLOM DOMIN COLONIAL ATTIT DRIVE PWR WEALTH...POLICY CONCPT OBS SAMP TREND CON/ANAL GEN/LAWS MARX/KARL 20. PAGE 122 A2493
COERCE ECO/TAC WAR

B39
ZIMMERN A.,MODERN POLITICAL DOCTRINE. WOR-45 CULTURE SOCIETY ECO/UNDEV DELIB/GP EX/STRUC CREATE DOMIN COERCE NAT/LISM ATTIT RIGID/FLEX ORD/FREE PWR WEALTH...POLICY CONCPT OBS TIME/SEQ TREND TOT/POP LEAGUE/NAT 20. PAGE 170 A3454
NAT/G ECO/TAC BAL/PWR INT/TRADE

L39
NEARING S.,"A WARLESS WORLD." FUT WOR-45 SOCIETY INT/ORG NAT/G EX/STRUC PLAN DOMIN WAR ATTIT DRIVE PWR...POLICY PSY CONCPT OBS TREND HYPO/EXP MARX/KARL 20 MARX/KARL LENIN/VI. PAGE 108 A2210
COERCE PEACE

B40
RAPPARD W.E.,THE QUEST FOR PEACE. UNIV USA-45 WOR-45 SOCIETY INT/ORG NAT/G PLAN EXEC ROUTINE WAR ATTIT DRIVE ALL/VALS...POLICY CONCPT OBS TIME/SEQ LEAGUE/NAT TOT/POP 20. PAGE 119 A2450
EUR+WWI ACT/RES PEACE

B41
YOUNG G.,FEDERALISM AND FREEDOM. EUR+WWI MOD/EUR RUSSIA USA-45 WOR-45 SOCIETY STRUCT ECO/DEV INT/ORG EXEC FEDERAL ATTIT PERSON ALL/VALS...OLD/LIB CONCPT OBS TREND LEAGUE/NAT TOT/POP. PAGE 169 A3435
NAT/G WAR

S42
TURNER F.J.,"AMERICAN SECTIONALISM AND WORLD ORGANIZATION." EUR+WWI UNIV USA-45 WOR-45 INTELL ECO/DEV TOP/EX ACT/RES PLAN EDU/PROP LEGIT ALL/VALS ...CONCPT NEW/IDEA OBS TREND LEAGUE/NAT TOT/POP 20. PAGE 146 A2981
INT/ORG DRIVE BAL/PWR

B44
DAVIS H.E.,PIONEERS IN WORLD ORDER. WOR-45 CONSTN ECO/TAC DOMIN EDU/PROP LEGIT ADJUD ADMIN ARMS/CONT CHOOSE KNOWL ORD/FREE...POLICY JURID SOC STAT OBS CENSUS TIME/SEQ ANTHOL LEAGUE/NAT 20. PAGE 34 A0691
INT/ORG ROUTINE

B44
PUTTKAMMER E.W.,WAR AND THE LAW. UNIV USA-45 CONSTN CULTURE SOCIETY NAT/G POL/PAR ROUTINE ALL/VALS ...JURID CONCPT OBS WORK VAL/FREE 20. PAGE 118 A2418
INT/ORG LAW WAR INT/LAW

L44
HAILEY,"THE FUTURE OF COLONIAL PEOPLES." WOR-45 CONSTN CULTURE ECO/UNDEV AGRI MARKET INT/ORG NAT/G SECT CONSULT ECO/TAC LEGIT ADMIN NAT/LISM ALL/VALS ...SOC OBS TREND STERTYP CMN/WLTH LEAGUE/NAT PARLIAMENT 20. PAGE 59 A1218
PLAN CONCPT DIPLOM UK

S44
WRIGHT Q.,"CONSTITUTIONAL PROCEDURES OF THE US FOR CARRYING OUT OBLIGATIONS FOR MILITARY SANCTIONS." EUR+WWI FUT USA-45 WOR-45 CONSTN INTELL NAT/G CONSULT EX/STRUC LEGIS ROUTINE DRIVE...POLICY JURID CONCPT OBS TREND TOT/POP 20. PAGE 167 A3406
TOP/EX FORCES INT/LAW WAR

B45
KANDELL I.L.,UNITED STATES ACTIVITIES IN INTERNATIONAL CULTURAL RELATIONS. INT/ORG NAT/G VOL/ASSN CREATE DIPLOM EDU/PROP ATTIT RIGID/FLEX KNOWL...PLURIST CONCPT OBS TREND GEN/LAWS TOT/POP UNESCO 20. PAGE 76 A1554
USA-45 CULTURE

B45
PASTUHOV V.D.,A GUIDE TO THE PRACTICE OF INTERNATIONAL CONFERENCES. WOR+45 PLAN LEGIT ORD/FREE...MGT OBS RECORD VAL/FREE ILO LEAGUE/NAT 20. PAGE 114 A2338
INT/ORG DELIB/GP

B47
GORDON D.L.,THE HIDDEN WEAPON: THE STORY OF ECONOMIC WARFARE. EUR+WWI USA-45 LAW FINAN INDUS NAT/G CONSULT FORCES PLAN DOMIN PWR WEALTH ...INT/LAW CONCPT OBS TOT/POP NAZI 20. PAGE 54 A1112
INT/ORG ECO/TAC INT/TRADE WAR

B48
VISSON A.,AS OTHERS SEE US. EUR+WWI FRANCE UK USA+45 CULTURE INTELL SOCIETY STRATA NAT/G POL/PAR FOR/AID ATTIT DRIVE LOVE ORD/FREE RESPECT WEALTH ...PLURIST SOC OBS TOT/POP 20. PAGE 159 A3244
USA-45 PERCEPT

B49
STETTINIUS E.R.,ROOSEVELT AND THE RUSSIANS: THE YALTA CONFERENCE. UK USSR WOR+45 WOR-45 INT/ORG VOL/ASSN TOP/EX ACT/RES EDU/PROP PEACE ATTIT DRIVE PERSON SUPEGO PWR...POLICY CONCPT MYTH OBS TIME/SEQ AUD/VIS COLD/WAR 20 CHURCHLL/W YALTA ROOSEVLT/F. PAGE 138 A2819
DIPLOM DELIB/GP BIOG

S49
KIRK G.,"MATTERIALS FOR THE STUDY OF INTERNATIONAL RELATIONS." FUT UNIV WOR+45 INTELL EDU/PROP ROUTINE PEACE ATTIT...INT/LAW JURID CONCPT OBS. PAGE 80 A1633
INT/ORG ACT/RES DIPLOM

B50
MACIVER R.M.,GREAT EXPRESSIONS OF HUMAN RIGHTS. LAW CONSTN CULTURE INTELL SOCIETY R+D INT/ORG ATTIT DRIVE...JURID OBS HIST/WRIT GEN/LAWS. PAGE 92 A1891
UNIV CONCPT

B51
MCKEON R.,DEMOCRACY IN A WORLD OF TENSION. UNIV LAW INTELL STRUCT R+D INT/ORG SCHOOL EDU/PROP LEGIT ATTIT DRIVE PERCEPT PERSON...POLICY JURID PSY SOC CONCPT METH/CNCPT OBS UNESCO TOT/POP VAL/FREE. PAGE 98 A2015
SOCIETY ALL/VALS ORD/FREE

B52
ALEXANDROWICZ C.H.,INTERNATIONAL ECONOMIC ORGANIZATION. WOR+45 ECO/DEV ECO/UNDEV DIST/IND FINAN MARKET PLAN ECO/TAC LEGIT DRIVE WEALTH ...POLICY CONCPT QUANT OBS TIME/SEQ GEN/LAWS WORK EEC ILO OEEC UNESCO 20. PAGE 6 A0114
INT/ORG INT/TRADE

B52
BARR S.,CITIZENS OF THE WORLD. USA+45 WOR+45 CULTURE FORCES LEGIS ACT/RES BAL/PWR LEGIT PEACE ATTIT ORD/FREE PWR...PLURIST CONCPT OBS TIME/SEQ COLD/WAR 20. PAGE 11 A0227
NAT/G INT/ORG DIPLOM

B52
ULAM A.B.,TITOISM AND THE COMINFORM. USSR WOR+45 STRUCT INT/ORG NAT/G ACT/RES PLAN EXEC ATTIT DRIVE ALL/VALS...CONCPT OBS VAL/FREE 20 COMINTERN TITO/MARSH. PAGE 146 A2993
COM POL/PAR TOTALISM YUGOSLAVIA

L52
THOMPSON K.W.,"THE STUDY OF INTERNATIONAL POLITICS: A SURVEY OF TRENDS AND DEVELOPMENTS." UNIV USA+45 WOR+45 WOR-45 SOCIETY ECO/DEV R+D ACT/RES PLAN ROUTINE ATTIT DRIVE PERCEPT PERSON...CONCPT OBS TREND GEN/LAWS TOT/POP. PAGE 143 A2928
INT/ORG BAL/PWR DIPLOM

B53
COUSINS N.,WHO SPEAKS FOR MAN. GERMANY KOREA WOR+45 SOCIETY INT/ORG NAT/G CREATE EDU/PROP HEALTH KNOWL LOVE MORAL...OBS SELF/OBS BIOG HYPO/EXP TOT/POP 20 CHINJAP. PAGE 32 A0642
ATTIT WAR PEACE

B54
MANGONE G.,A SHORT HISTORY OF INTERNATIONAL ORGANIZATION. MOD/EUR USA+45 USA-45 WOR+45 WOR-45 LAW LEGIS CREATE LEGIT ROUTINE RIGID/FLEX PWR ...JURID CONCPT OBS TIME/SEQ STERTYP GEN/LAWS UN TOT/POP VAL/FREE 18/20. PAGE 94 A1921
INT/ORG INT/LAW

L54
OPLER M.E.,"SOCIAL ASPECTS OF TECHNICAL ASSISTANCE IN OPERATION." WOR+45 VOL/ASSN CREATE PLAN TEC/DEV EDU/PROP ALL/VALS...METH/CNCPT OBS RECORD TREND UN 20. PAGE 112 A2292
INT/ORG CONSULT FOR/AID

B55
ALFIERI D.,DICTATORS FACE TO FACE. NAT/G TOP/EX DIPLOM EXEC COERCE ORD/FREE FASCISM...POLICY OBS 20 HITLER/A MUSSOLIN/B. PAGE 6 A0116
WAR CHIEF TOTALISM PERS/REL

B55
SNYDER R.C.,AMERICAN FOREIGN POLICY. USA+45 USA-45 WOR+45 WOR-45 CONSTN INT/ORG POL/PAR VOL/ASSN DELIB/GP LEGIS CREATE DOMIN EDU/PROP EXEC COERCE ATTIT DRIVE ORD/FREE PWR...MGT OBS RECORD TIME/SEQ TREND. PAGE 134 A2752
NAT/G DIPLOM

L55
ROSTOW W.W.,"RUSSIA AND CHINA UNDER COMMUNISM." CHINA/COM USSR INTELL STRUCT INT/ORG NAT/G POL/PAR TOP/EX ACT/RES PLAN ADMIN ATTIT ALL/VALS MARXISM ...CONCPT OBS TIME/SEQ TREND GOV/COMP VAL/FREE 20. PAGE 124 A2543
COM ASIA

S55
TORRE M.,"PSYCHIATRIC OBSERVATIONS OF INTERNATIONAL CONFERENCES." WOR+45 INT/ORG PROF/ORG VOL/ASSN CONSULT EDU/PROP ROUTINE ATTIT DRIVE KNOWL...PSY METH/CNCPT OBS/ENVIR STERTYP 20. PAGE 144 A2950
DELIB/GP OBS DIPLOM

B56
BROOK D.,THE UNITED NATIONS AND CHINA DILEMMA. CHINA/COM FUT WOR+45 ECO/UNDEV NAT/G DELIB/GP ACT/RES DIPLOM ROUTINE NAT/LISM TOTALISM ATTIT DRIVE...CONCPT OBS TIME/SEQ UN TOT/POP TIME UN 20. PAGE 19 A0390
ASIA INT/ORG BAL/PWR

B56
GEORGE A.L.,WOODROW WILSON AND COLONEL HOUSE. WOR-45 CONSTN FACE/GP INT/ORG NAT/G POL/PAR CONSULT LEGIT EXEC COERCE CHOOSE ATTIT DRIVE PERSON MORAL ORD/FREE PWR RESPECT...POLICY MGT PSY OBS RECORD INT LEAGUE/NAT. PAGE 52 A1060
USA-45 BIOG DIPLOM

B56
HOUSTON J.A.,LATIN AMERICA IN THE UNITED NATIONS. CONSULT DIPLOM LEGIT ROUTINE ATTIT ORD/FREE PWR ...JURID OBS RECORD TIME/SEQ CHARTS 20 UN. PAGE 68 A1395
L/A+17C INT/ORG INT/LAW REGION

B56
REITZEL W.,UNITED STATES FOREIGN POLICY, 1945-1955. USA+45 WOR+45 CONSTN INT/ORG EDU/PROP LEGIT EXEC COERCE NUC/PWR PEACE ATTIT ORD/FREE PWR...DECISION CONCPT OBS RECORD TIME/SEQ TREND COLD/WAR UN CONGRESS. PAGE 120 A2464
NAT/G POLICY DIPLOM

B57
ARON R.,L'UNIFICATION ECONOMIQUE DE L'EUROPE. EUR+WWI SWITZERLND UK INT/ORG NAT/G REGION NAT/LISM ORD/FREE PWR...CONCPT METH/CNCPT OBS TREND STERTYP GEN/LAWS EEC 20. PAGE 9 A0181
VOL/ASSN ECO/TAC

B57
BEAL J.R.,JOHN FOSTER DULLES, A BIOGRAPHY. USA+45
BIOG

USSR WOR+45 CONSTN INT/ORG NAT/G EX/STRUC LEGIT ADMIN NUC/PWR DISPL PERSON ORD/FREE PWR SKILL ...POLICY PSY OBS RECORD COLD/WAR UN 20 DULLES/JF. PAGE 12 A0237 DIPLOM

B57
BLOOMFIELD L.P.,EVOLUTION OR REVOLUTION: THE UNITED NATIONS AND THE PROBLEM OF PEACEFUL TERRITORIAL CHANGE. WOR+45 WOR-45 INT/ORG NAT/G DIPLOM ROUTINE REV ATTIT RIGID/FLEX PWR...CONCPT OBS HIST/WRIT UN LEAGUE/NAT 20. PAGE 15 A0315 ORD/FREE LEGIT

B57
KENNAN G.F.,RUSSIA, THE ATOM AND THE WEST. COM EUR+WWI FUT WOR+45 SOCIETY ECO/DEV FORCES DIPLOM ECO/TAC DOMIN EDU/PROP COERCE NUC/PWR ATTIT DRIVE ORD/FREE PWR...POLICY OBS TIME/SEQ TREND COLD/WAR NATO 20. PAGE 77 A1574 NAT/G INT/ORG USSR

B57
TRIFFIN R.,EUROPE AND THE MONEY MUDDLE. USA+45 INT/ORG NAT/G CONSULT PLAN ECO/TAC EXEC ROUTINE BAL/PAY WEALTH...METH/CNCPT OBS TREND CHARTS STERTYP GEN/METH EEC VAL/FREE ECSC. PAGE 145 A2962 EUR+WWI ECO/DEV REGION

B57
WASSENBERGH H.A.,POST-WAR INTERNATIONAL CIVIL AVIATION POLICY AND THE LAW OF THE AIR. WOR+45 AIR INT/ORG DOMIN LEGIT PEACE ORD/FREE...POLICY JURID NEW/IDEA OBS TIME/SEQ TREND CHARTS 20 TREATY. PAGE 162 A3290 COM/IND NAT/G INT/LAW

S57
ELDER R.E.,"THE PUBLIC STUDIES DIVISION OF THE DEPARTMENT OF STATE: PUBLIC OPINION ANALYSTS IN THE FORMULATION AND CONDUCT OF." INT/ORG CONSULT DOMIN EDU/PROP ADMIN ATTIT PWR...CONCPT OBS TIME/SEQ VAL/FREE 20. PAGE 41 A0836 USA+45 NAT/G DIPLOM

S57
SCHELLING T.C.,"BARGAINING COMMUNICATION, AND LIMITED WAR." UNIV WOR+45 FACE/GP INT/ORG NAT/G FORCES ACT/RES WAR PERCEPT ALL/VALS...PSY OBS PROJ/TEST CHARTS HYPO/EXP GEN/LAWS TOT/POP 20. PAGE 128 A2622 ROUTINE DECISION

B58
HENKIN L.,ARMS CONTROL AND INSPECTION IN AMERICAN LAW. LAW CONSTN INT/ORG LOC/G MUNIC NAT/G PROVS EDU/PROP LEGIT EXEC NUC/PWR KNOWL ORD/FREE...OBS TOT/POP CONGRESS 20. PAGE 64 A1315 USA+45 JURID ARMS/CONT

B58
MELMAN S.,INSPECTION FOR DISARMAMENT. USA+45 WOR+45 SOCIETY INT/ORG NAT/G CONSULT ACT/RES PLAN EDU/PROP CONTROL DETER PEACE ATTIT PERSON KNOWL...PSY STAT OBS CHARTS TOT/POP VAL/FREE 20. PAGE 99 A2035 FUT ORD/FREE ARMS/CONT NUC/PWR

B58
NOEL-BAKER D.,THE ARMS RACE. WOR+45 NAT/G DELIB/GP ACT/RES TEC/DEV EDU/PROP NUC/PWR ATTIT KNOWL PWR ...CONCPT OBS LEAGUE/NAT 20 COLD/WAR. PAGE 109 A2245 FUT INT/ORG ARMS/CONT PEACE

B58
RIGGS R.,POLITICS IN THE UNITED NATIONS: A STUDY OF UNITED STATES INFLUENCE IN THE GENERAL ASSEMBLY. USA+45 WOR+45 LEGIS TOP/EX CREATE BAL/PWR DIPLOM DOMIN EDU/PROP COLONIAL ROUTINE ATTIT RIGID/FLEX PWR...CONCPT OBS HIST/WRIT CHARTS STERTYP GEN/LAWS UN COLD/WAR 20. PAGE 121 A2480 INT/ORG

S58
BOURBON-BUSSET J.,"HOW DECISIONS ARE MADE IN FOREIGN POLITICS: PSYCHOLOGY IN INTERNATIONAL POLITICS." WOR+45 NAT/G SECT REGION WAR MORAL ...CONCPT OBS STERTYP GEN/LAWS TOT/POP COLD/WAR 20. PAGE 17 A0350 INT/ORG DELIB/GP DIPLOM

S58
BURNS A.L.,"THE INTERNATIONAL CONSEQUENCES OF EXPECTING SURPRISE." WOR+45 INT/ORG NAT/G FORCES DIPLOM COERCE NUC/PWR WAR CHOOSE ORD/FREE ...METH/CNCPT STYLE OBS STERTYP TOT/POP VAL/FREE. PAGE 22 A0440 PLAN PWR DETER

S58
DAVENPORT J.,"ARMS AND THE WELFARE STATE." INTELL STRUCT FORCES CREATE ECO/TAC FOR/AID DOMIN LEGIT ADMIN WAR ORD/FREE PWR...POLICY SOC CONCPT MYTH OBS TREND COLD/WAR TOT/POP 20. PAGE 34 A0685 USA+45 NAT/G USSR

B59
BALL M.M.,NATO AND THE EUROPEAN MOVEMENT. EUR+WWI USA+45 INT/ORG FORCES BAL/PWR EDU/PROP LEGIT REGION ATTIT ORD/FREE PWR...STAT OBS TIME/SEQ TREND CHARTS ORG/CHARTS STERTYP COLD/WAR EEC OEEC 20 NATO. PAGE 10 A0212 DELIB/GP STRUCT

B59
BOWLES C.,THE COMING POLITICAL BREAKTHROUGH. USA+45 ECO/DEV EX/STRUC ATTIT...CONCPT OBS 20. PAGE 18 A0360 DIPLOM CHOOSE PREDICT POL/PAR

B59
CHINA INSTITUTE OF AMERICA.,CHINA AND THE UNITED NATIONS. CHINA/COM FUT STRUCT EDU/PROP LEGIT ADMIN ATTIT KNOWL ORD/FREE PWR...OBS RECORD STAND/INT TIME/SEQ UN LEAGUE/NAT UNESCO 20. PAGE 26 A0531 ASIA INT/ORG

S59
BAILEY S.D.,"THE FUTURE COMPOSITION OF THE TRUSTEESHIP COUNCIL." FUT WOR+45 CONSTN VOL/ASSN ADMIN ATTIT PWR...OBS TREND CON/ANAL VAL/FREE UN 20. PAGE 10 A0203 INT/ORG NAT/LISM SOVEREIGN

S59
KINDLEBERGER C.P.,"UNITED STATES ECONOMIC FOREIGN POLICY: RESEARCH REQUIREMENTS FOR 1965." FUT USA+45 WOR+45 DIST/IND MARKET INT/ORG ECO/TAC INT/TRADE WEALTH...OBS TREND CON/ANAL GEN/LAWS VAL/FREE 20. PAGE 79 A1621 FINAN ECO/DEV FOR/AID

S59
KOHN L.Y.,"ISRAEL AND NEW NATION STATES OF ASIA AND AFRICA." AFR ASIA FUT S/ASIA VOL/ASSN TEC/DEV NAT/LISM RIGID/FLEX SKILL WEALTH...RELATIV OBS TREND CON/ANAL 20. PAGE 81 A1663 ECO/UNDEV ECO/TAC FOR/AID ISRAEL

S59
PADELFORD N.J.,"REGIONAL COOPERATION IN THE SOUTH PACIFIC: THE SOUTH PACIFIC COMMISSION." FUT NEW/ZEALND UK WOR+45 CULTURE ECO/UNDEV LOC/G VOL/ASSN...OBS CON/ANAL UNESCO VAL/FREE AUSTRAL 20. PAGE 112 A2308 INT/ORG ADMIN

S59
SOLDATI A.,"EOCNOMIC DISINTEGRATION IN EUROPE." EUR+WWI FUT WOR+45 INDUS INT/ORG NAT/G CAP/ISM WEALTH...NEW/IDEA OBS TREND CHARTS EEC 20. PAGE 135 A2764 FINAN ECO/TAC

S59
STOESSINGER J.G.,"THE INTERNATIONAL ATOMIC ENERGY AGENCY: THE FIRST PHASE." FUT WOR+45 NAT/G VOL/ASSN DELIB/GP BAL/PWR LEGIT ADMIN ROUTINE PWR...OBS CON/ANAL GEN/LAWS VAL/FREE 20 IAEA. PAGE 138 A2829 INT/ORG ECO/DEV FOR/AID NUC/PWR

B60
ALLEN H.C.,THE ANGLO-AMERICAN PREDICAMENT: THE BRITISH COMMONWEALTH, THE UNITED STATES AND EUROPEAN UNITY. EUR+WWI FUT UK USA+45 WOR+45 ECO/DEV NAT/G PLAN DETER...CONCPT OBS TIME/SEQ TREND COLD/WAR VAL/FREE CMN/WLTH 20. PAGE 6 A0123 INT/ORG PWR BAL/PWR

B60
FRANCK P.G.,AFGHANISTAN: BETWEEN EAST AND WEST. AFGHANISTN USA+45 USSR ECO/UNDEV PLAN ADMIN ROUTINE ATTIT PWR...STAT OBS CHARTS TOT/POP COLD/WAR 20. PAGE 48 A0978 ECO/TAC TREND FOR/AID

B60
JENNINGS R.,PROGRESS OF INTERNATIONAL LAW. FUT WOR+45 WOR-45 SOCIETY NAT/G VOL/ASSN DELIB/GP DIPLOM EDU/PROP LEGIT COERCE ATTIT DRIVE MORAL ORD/FREE...JURID CONCPT OBS TIME/SEQ TREND GEN/LAWS. PAGE 74 A1509 INT/ORG LAW INT/LAW

B60
PENTONY D.E.,THE UNDERDEVELOPED LANDS. FUT WOR+45 CULTURE AGRI FINAN INDUS MARKET INT/ORG LABOR NAT/G VOL/ASSN CONSULT TEC/DEV ECO/TAC EDU/PROP COLONIAL ATTIT WEALTH...OBS RECORD SAMP TREND GEN/METH WORK UN 20. PAGE 115 A2351 ECO/UNDEV POLICY FOR/AID INT/TRADE

B60
PLAMENATZ J.,ON ALIEN RULE AND SELF-GOVERNMENT. AFR FUT S/ASIA WOR+45 CULTURE SOCIETY ECO/UNDEV INT/ORG DOMIN EDU/PROP ATTIT RIGID/FLEX ALL/VALS...POLICY CONCPT OBS TREND CON/ANAL GEN/LAWS TOT/POP VAL/FREE. PAGE 116 A2386 NAT/G CONSTN NAT/LISM SOVEREIGN

L60
FERNBACH A.P.,"SOVIET COEXISTENCE STRATEGY." WOR+45 PROF/ORG VOL/ASSN DIPLOM DOMIN EDU/PROP ATTIT DRIVE PERSON PWR SKILL WEALTH...POLICY OBS SAMP TREND STERTYP ILO WORK COLD/WAR 420. PAGE 45 A0919 LABOR INT/ORG USSR

L60
MCCLELLAND C.A.,"THE FUNCTION OF THEORY IN INTERNATIONAL RELATIONS." WOR+45 PLAN EDU/PROP ROUTINE ORD/FREE...PHIL/SCI PSY SOC METH/CNCPT NEW/IDEA OBS TREND GEN/METH 20. PAGE 97 A1997 INT/ORG CONCPT DIPLOM

S60
BOWIE R.,"POLICY FORMATION IN AMERICAN FOREIGN POLICY." FUT USA+45 WOR+45 STRUCT ECO/DEV INT/ORG POL/PAR LEGIS ACT/RES EXEC ALL/VALS...POLICY OBS VAL/FREE 20. PAGE 17 A0355 PLAN DRIVE DIPLOM

S60
COHEN A.,"THE NEW AFRICA AND THE UN." FUT ECO/UNDEV NAT/G ECO/TAC INT/TRADE CHOOSE ATTIT ORD/FREE PWR ...POLICY METH/CNCPT OBS TREND CON/ANAL GEN/LAWS TOT/POP VAL/FREE UN 20. PAGE 27 A0558 AFR INT/ORG BAL/PWR FOR/AID

S60
HAVILAND H.F.,"PROBLEMS OF AMERICAN FOREIGN POLICY." ASIA COM USA+45 WOR+45 INT/ORG NAT/G CONSULT ECO/TAC FOR/AID DOMIN COERCE NUC/PWR ATTIT DRIVE ORD/FREE PWR RESPECT SKILL...POLICY GEOG OBS SAMP TREND GEN/METH METH COLD/WAR UN 20. PAGE 63 A1292 ECO/UNDEV FORCES DIPLOM

S60
KENNAN G.F.,"PEACEFUL CO-EXISTENCE: A WESTERN VIEW." COM EUR+WWI USA+45 USSR WOR+45 PLAN BAL/PWR DIPLOM INT/TRADE PWR...POLICY CONCPT OBS HIST/WRIT TREND GEN/LAWS COLD/WAR 20 KHRUSH/N. PAGE 78 A1589 ATTIT COERCE

S60
MAGATHAN W.,"SOME BASES OF WEST GERMAN MILITARY POLICY." EUR+WWI FUT INT/ORG TOP/EX ECO/TAC DOMIN DRIVE ORD/FREE PWR...TRADIT GEOG OBS TREND. PAGE 93 A1904 NAT/G FORCES GERMANY

S60
PETERSON E.N.,"HISTORICAL SCHOLARSHIP AND WORLD UNITY." FUT UNIV WOR-45 CULTURE INTELL INT/ORG NAT/G ACT/RES EDU/PROP ATTIT PERCEPT RIGID/FLEX ...NEW/IDEA OBS HIST/WRIT TREND COLD/WAR TOT/POP 20. PAGE 115 A2367 PLAN KNOWL NAT/LISM

B61
BARNES W.,THE FOREIGN SERVICE OF THE UNITED STATES. USA+45 USA-45 CONSTN INT/ORG POL/PAR CONSULT DELIB/GP LEGIS DOMIN EDU/PROP EXEC ATTIT RIGID/FLEX ORD/FREE PWR...POLICY CONCPT STAT OBS RECORD BIOG TIME/SEQ TREND. PAGE 11 A0224 NAT/G MGT DIPLOM

B61
EINZIG P.,A DYNAMIC THEORY OF FORWARD EXCHANGE. FUT WOR+45 WOR-45 INT/TRADE BAL/PAY WEALTH...OLD/LIB NEW/IDEA OBS TREND 20. PAGE 41 A0830 FINAN ECO/TAC

B61
HASAN H.S.,PAKISTAN AND THE UN. ISLAM WOR+45 ECO/DEV ECO/UNDEV NAT/G TOP/EX ECO/TAC FOR/AID EDU/PROP ADMIN DRIVE PERCEPT...OBS TIME/SEQ UN 20. PAGE 62 A1284 INT/ORG ATTIT PAKISTAN

B61
HAYTER W.,THE DIPLOMACY OF THE GREAT POWERS. FRANCE UK USSR WOR+45 EX/STRUC TOP/EX NUC/PWR PEACE...OBS 20. PAGE 63 A1296 DIPLOM POLICY NAT/G

B61
STILLMAN E.,THE NEW POLITICS: AMERICA AND THE END OF THE POSTWAR WORLD. FUT WOR+45 CULTURE SOCIETY ECO/UNDEV INT/ORG NAT/G FORCES TOP/EX ACT/RES DIPLOM EDU/PROP LEGIT ROUTINE DETER ATTIT ORD/FREE PWR...OBS STERTYP COLD/WAR TOT/POP VAL/FREE. PAGE 138 A2827 USA+45 PLAN

B61
STRAUSZ-HUPE R.,A FORWARD STRATEGY FOR AMERICA. FUT WOR+45 ECO/DEV INT/ORG NAT/G POL/PAR DELIB/GP FORCES ACT/RES CREATE ECO/TAC DOMIN EDU/PROP ATTIT DRIVE PWR...MAJORIT CONCPT STAT OBS TIME/SEQ TREND COLD/WAR TOT/POP. PAGE 139 A2848 USA+45 PLAN DIPLOM

B61
YDIT M.,INTERNATIONALISED TERRITORIES. FUT WOR+45 WOR-45 CONSTN VOL/ASSN CREATE PLAN LEGIT PEACE ORD/FREE...GEOG INT/LAW JURID SOC NEW/IDEA OBS RECORD SAMP TIME/SEQ TREND 19/20 BERLIN. PAGE 169 A3431 LOC/G INT/ORG DIPLOM SOVEREIGN

S61
DEUTSCH K.W.,"NATIONAL INDUSTRIALIZATION AND THE DECLINING SHARE OF THE INTERNATIONAL ECONOMIC SECTOR." EUR+WWI FUT WOR+45 WOR-45 MARKET PLAN EDU/PROP WEALTH...WELF/ST OBS TESTS 20. PAGE 36 A0740 DIST/IND ECO/DEV INT/TRADE

S61
JACKSON E.,"CONSTITUTIONAL DEVELOPMENTS OF THE UNITED NATIONS: THE GROWTH OF ITS EXECUTIVE CAPACITY." FUT WOR+45 CONSTN STRUCT ACT/RES PLAN ALL/VALS...NEW/IDEA OBS COLD/WAR UN 20. PAGE 72 A1475 INT/ORG EXEC

S61
MACHOWSKI K.,"SELECTED PROBLEMS OF NATIONAL SOVEREIGNTY WITH REFERENCE TO THE LAW OF OUTER SPACE." FUT WOR+45 AIR LAW INTELL SOCIETY ECO/DEV PLAN EDU/PROP DETER DRIVE PERCEPT SOVEREIGN ...POLICY INT/LAW OBS TREND TOT/POP 20. PAGE 92 A1889 UNIV ACT/RES NUC/PWR SPACE

S61
MILLER E.,"LEGAL ASPECTS OF UN ACTION IN THE CONGO." AFR CULTURE ADMIN PEACE DRIVE RIGID/FLEX ORD/FREE...WELF/ST JURID OBS UN CONGO 20. PAGE 101 A2076 INT/ORG LEGIT

B62
BELL C.,NEGOTIATION FROM STRENGTH. WOR+45 FACE/GP INT/ORG DELIB/GP FORCES PLAN DOMIN COERCE NUC/PWR PEACE DRIVE PWR...POLICY LOG OBS RECORD INT SAMP TREND COLD/WAR 20. PAGE 13 A0255 NAT/G CONCPT DIPLOM

B62
CARDOZA M.H.,DIPLOMATS IN INTERNATIONAL COOPERATION: STEPCHILDREN OF THE FOREIGN SERVICE. EUR+WWI USA+45 NAT/G CONSULT ACT/RES EDU/PROP ROUTINE RIGID/FLEX KNOWL SKILL...SOC OBS TIME/SEQ EEC OEEC NATO 20. PAGE 24 A0480 INT/ORG METH/CNCPT DIPLOM

B62
CLUBB O.E. JR.,THE UNITED STATES AND THE SINO-SOVIET BLOC IN SOUTHEAST ASIA. ASIA CHINA/COM COM USA+45 USSR ECO/UNDEV INT/ORG NAT/G FORCES TOP/EX PLAN ECO/TAC DOMIN COERCE GUERRILLA ATTIT RIGID/FLEX...POLICY OBS TREND 20. PAGE 27 A0553 S/ASIA PWR BAL/PWR DIPLOM

B62
DREIER J.C.,THE ORGANIZATION OF AMERICAN STATES AND THE HEMISPHERE CRISIS. CUBA USA+45 CULTURE STRATA NAT/G VOL/ASSN CONSULT FORCES ACT/RES CREATE DIPLOM ECO/TAC FOR/AID ALL/VALS...POLICY OBS OAS 20. PAGE 38 A0786 L/A+17C CONCPT

B62
DUTOIT B.,LA NEUTRALITE SUISSE A L'HEURE EUROPEENNE. EUR+WWI MOD/EUR INT/ORG NAT/G VOL/ASSN PLAN BAL/PWR LEGIT NEUTRAL REGION PEACE ORD/FREE SOVEREIGN...CONCPT OBS TIME/SEQ TREND STERTYP VAL/FREE LEAGUE/NAT UN 20. PAGE 40 A0812 ATTIT DIPLOM SWITZERLND

B62
FORBES H.W.,THE STRATEGY OF DISARMAMENT. FUT WOR+45 INT/ORG VOL/ASSN CONSULT ARMS/CONT COERCE NUC/PWR WAR DRIVE RIGID/FLEX ORD/FREE PWR...POLICY CONCPT OBS TREND STERTYP 20. PAGE 47 A0959 PLAN FORCES DIPLOM

B62
GUENA Y.,HISTORIQUE DE LA COMMUNAUTE. FUT ECO/UNDEV NAT/G PLAN EDU/PROP COLONIAL REGION NAT/LISM ALL/VALS SOVEREIGN...CONCPT OBS CHARTS 20. PAGE 58 A1186 AFR VOL/ASSN FOR/AID FRANCE

B62
KAHN H.,THINKING ABOUT THE UNTHINKABLE. FUT USA+45 LAW NAT/G CONSULT FORCES ACT/RES CREATE PLAN TEC/DEV BAL/PWR DIPLOM EDU/PROP ARMS/CONT DETER ATTIT...CONCPT OBS TREND COLD/WAR 20. PAGE 76 A1547 INT/ORG ORD/FREE NUC/PWR PEACE

B62
KING G.,THE UNITED NATIONS IN THE CONGO: A QUEST FOR PEACE. WOR+45 NAT/G CONSULT FORCES LEGIT COERCE WAR ORD/FREE...JURID METH/CNCPT OBS INT HIST/WRIT TIME/SEQ CONGO UN 20 COLD/WAR. PAGE 79 A1624 AFR INT/ORG

B62
KRAFT J.,THE GRAND DESIGN. EUR+WWI USA+45 AGRI FINAN INDUS MARKET INT/ORG NAT/G PLAN ECO/TAC TARIFFS REGION DRIVE ORD/FREE WEALTH...POLICY OBS TREND EEC 20. PAGE 82 A1674 VOL/ASSN ECO/DEV INT/TRADE

B62
MACKENTOSH J.M.,STRATEGY AND TACTICS OF SOVIET FOREIGN POLICY. CHINA/COM FUT USA+45 WOR+45 INT/ORG PLAN DOMIN LEGIT ROUTINE COERCE NUC/PWR WAR ATTIT DRIVE ORD/FREE PWR...CONCPT OBS TIME/SEQ TREND GEN/METH COLD/WAR 20. PAGE 92 A1894 COM POLICY DIPLOM USSR

B62
MOON P.,DIVIDE AND QUIT. INDIA PAKISTAN STRATA DELIB/GP PLAN DIPLOM REPRESENT GP/REL INGP/REL CONSEN DISCRIM...OBS 20. PAGE 103 A2119 WAR REGION ISOLAT SECT

B62
NEAL F.W.,WAR AND PEACE AND GERMANY. EUR+WWI USSR STRUCT INT/ORG NAT/G FORCES DOMIN EDU/PROP LEGIT EXEC COERCE ORD/FREE...HUM SOC NEW/IDEA OBS TIME/SEQ TOT/POP COLD/WAR 20 BERLIN. PAGE 108 A2208 USA+45 POLICY DIPLOM GERMANY

B62
ROSENNE S.,THE WORLD COURT: WHAT IT IS AND HOW IT WORKS. WOR+45 WOR-45 LAW CONSTN JUDGE EDU/PROP LEGIT ROUTINE CHOOSE PEACE ORD/FREE...JURID OBS TIME/SEQ CHARTS UN TOT/POP VAL/FREE 20. PAGE 124 A2538 INT/ORG ADJUD INT/LAW

B62
TRISKA J.F.,THE THEORY, LAW, AND POLICY OF SOVIET TREATIES. WOR+45 WOR-45 CONSTN INT/ORG NAT/G VOL/ASSN DOMIN LEGIT COERCE ATTIT PWR RESPECT ...POLICY JURID CONCPT OBS SAMP TIME/SEQ TREND GEN/LAWS 20. PAGE 145 A2966 COM LAW INT/LAW USSR

L62
MALINOWSKI W.R.,"CENTRALIZATION AND DE-CENTRALIZATION IN THE UNITED NATIONS' ECONOMIC AND SOCIAL ACTIVITIES." WOR+45 CONSTN ECO/UNDEV INT/ORG VOL/ASSN DELIB/GP ECO/TAC EDU/PROP ADMIN RIGID/FLEX ...OBS CHARTS UNESCO UN EEC OAS OEEC 20. PAGE 93 A1913 CREATE GEN/LAWS

L62
NIZARD L.,"CUBAN QUESTION AND SECURITY COUNCIL." L/A+17C USA+45 ECO/UNDEV NAT/G POL/PAR DELIB/GP ECO/TAC PWR...RELATIV OBS TIME/SEQ TREND GEN/LAWS UN 20 UN. PAGE 109 A2242 INT/ORG JURID DIPLOM CUBA

L62
STEIN E.,"MR HAMMARSKJOLD, THE CHARTER LAW AND THE FUTURE ROLE OF THE UNITED NATIONS SECRETARY-GENERAL." WOR+45 CONSTN INT/ORG DELIB/GP FORCES TOP/EX BAL/PWR LEGIT ROUTINE RIGID/FLEX PWR ...POLICY JURID OBS STERTYP UN COLD/WAR 20 HAMMARSK/D. PAGE 137 A2815 CONCPT BIOG

L62
WILCOX F.O.,"THE UN AND THE NON-ALIGNED NATIONS." AFR S/ASIA USA+45 ECO/UNDEV INT/ORG TEC/DEV EDU/PROP RIGID/FLEX ORD/FREE PWR...POLICY HUM CONCPT STAT OBS TIME/SEQ STERTYP GEN/METH UN 20. PAGE 164 A3345 ATTIT TREND

S62
CORET A.,"LE STATUT DE L'ILE CHRISTMAS DE L'OCEAN INDIEN." FUT S/ASIA ECO/DEV ECO/UNDEV VOL/ASSN DELIB/GP PLAN...RELATIV OBS TIME/SEQ TREND AUSTRAL 20. PAGE 30 A0619 NAT/G INT/ORG NEW/ZEALND

S62
DALLIN A.,"THE SOVIET VIEW OF THE UNITED NATIONS." WOR+45 VOL/ASSN TOP/EX DIPLOM DOMIN EDU/PROP LEGIT ATTIT RIGID/FLEX PWR...CONCPT OBS HIST/WRIT TIME/SEQ STERTYP GEN/LAWS COLD/WAR UN 20. PAGE 33 A0676 COM INT/ORG USSR

S62
FINKELSTEIN L.S.,"THE UNITED NATIONS AND ORGANIZATIONS FOR CONTROL OF ARMAMENT." FUT WOR+45 VOL/ASSN DELIB/GP TOP/EX CREATE EDU/PROP LEGIT ADJUD NUC/PWR ATTIT RIGID/FLEX ORD/FREE...POLICY DECISION CONCPT OBS TREND GEN/LAWS TOT/POP INT/ORG PWR ARMS/CONT

COLD/WAR. PAGE 46 A0933

S62
HOFFMANN S.,"RESTRAINTS AND CHOICES IN AMERICAN FOREIGN POLICY." USA-45 INT/ORG NAT/G PLAN ARMS/CONT ATTIT...POLICY CONCPT OBS TREND GEN/METH COLD/WAR 20. PAGE 66 A1356
USA+45 ORD/FREE DIPLOM

S62
JACOBSON H.K.,"THE UNITED NATIONS AND COLONIALISM: A TENTATIVE APPRAISAL." AFR FUT S/ASIA USA+45 USSR WOR+45 NAT/G DELIB/GP PLAN DIPLOM ECO/TAC DOMIN ADMIN ROUTINE COERCE ATTIT RIGID/FLEX ORD/FREE PWR ...OBS STERTYP UN 20. PAGE 73 A1486
INT/ORG CONCPT COLONIAL

S62
SCHACHTER O.,"DAG HAMMARSKJOLD AND THE RELATION OF LAW TO POLITICS." FUT WOR+45 INT/ORG CONSULT PLAN TEC/DEV BAL/PWR DIPLOM LEGIT ATTIT PERCEPT ORD/FREE ...POLICY JURID CONCPT OBS TESTS STERTYP GEN/LAWS 20 HAMMARSK/D. PAGE 128 A2616
ACT/RES ADJUD

S62
SCHILLING W.R.,"SCIENTISTS, FOREIGN POLICY AND POLITICS." WOR+45 WOR-45 INTELL INT/ORG CONSULT TOP/EX ACT/RES PLAN ADMIN KNOWL...CONCPT OBS TREND LEAGUE/NAT 20. PAGE 128 A2627
NAT/G TEC/DEV DIPLOM NUC/PWR

S62
SPENSER J.H.,"AFRICA AT THE UNITED NATIONS: SOME OBSERVATIONS." FUT ECO/UNDEV NAT/G CONSULT DELIB/GP PLAN BAL/PWR ECO/TAC EDU/PROP ATTIT RIGID/FLEX HEALTH ORD/FREE PWR WEALTH...POLICY CONCPT OBS TREND STERTYP GEN/METH UN VAL/FREE. PAGE 136 A2786
AFR INT/ORG REGION

S62
SPRINGER H.W.,"FEDERATION IN THE CARIBBEAN: AN ATTEMPT THAT FAILED." L/A+17C ECO/UNDEV INT/ORG POL/PAR PROVS LEGIS CREATE PLAN LEGIT ADMIN FEDERAL ATTIT DRIVE PERSON ORD/FREE PWR...POLICY GEOG PSY CONCPT OBS CARIBBEAN CMN/WLTH 20. PAGE 136 A2791
VOL/ASSN NAT/G REGION

S62
STRACHEY J.,"COMMUNIST INTENTIONS." ASIA USSR YUGOSLAVIA INT/ORG NAT/G FORCES DOMIN EDU/PROP COERCE NUC/PWR NAT/LISM PEACE RIGID/FLEX PWR MARXISM...CONCPT MYTH OBS TIME/SEQ TREND COLD/WAR TOT/POP 20. PAGE 139 A2843
COM ATTIT WAR

S62
THOMAS J.R.T.,"SOVIET BEHAVIOR IN THE QUEMOY CRISES OF 1958." CHINA/COM FUT USSR WOR+45 INT/ORG VOL/ASSN FORCES PLAN BAL/PWR DOMIN COERCE NUC/PWR REV WAR ATTIT DRIVE ORD/FREE...POLICY OBS RECORD COLD/WAR FOR/POL 20. PAGE 143 A2923
COM PWR

B63
LILIENTHAL D.E.,CHANGE, HOPE, AND THE BOMB. USA+45 WOR+45 R+D INT/ORG NAT/G DELIB/GP FORCES ACT/RES DETER RIGID/FLEX ORD/FREE...POLICY CONCPT OBS AEC 20. PAGE 89 A1815
ATTIT MYTH ARMS/CONT NUC/PWR

B63
PECQUET P.,THE DIPLOMACY OF THE CONFEDERATE CABINET OF RICHMOND AND ITS AGENTS ABROAD (LIMITED ED.). MOD/EUR USA-45 LEAD...OBS 19 CIVIL/WAR SOUTH/US. PAGE 114 A2347
DIPLOM WAR ORD/FREE

B63
QUAISON-SACKEY A.,AFRICA UNBOUND: REFLECTIONS OF AN AFRICAN STATESMAN. ISLAM CULTURE INTELL INT/ORG POL/PAR TOP/EX DOMIN EDU/PROP LEGIT ATTIT PERSON ...CONCPT OBS TIME/SEQ CHARTS STERTYP 20 UN. PAGE 118 A2423
AFR BIOG

B63
RIVKIN A.,THE AFRICAN PRESENCE IN WORLD AFFAIRS. ECO/UNDEV AGRI INT/ORG LOC/G NAT/LISM...OBS PREDICT GOV/COMP 20. PAGE 121 A2489
AFR NAT/G DIPLOM BAL/PWR

B63
TUCKER R.C.,THE SOVIET POLITICAL MIND. WOR+45 ELITES INT/ORG NAT/G POL/PAR PLAN DIPLOM ECO/TAC DOMIN ADMIN NUC/PWR REV DRIVE PERSON SUPEGO PWR WEALTH...POLICY MGT PSY CONCPT OBS BIOG TREND COLD/WAR MARX/KARL 20. PAGE 145 A2972
COM TOP/EX USSR

B63
WESTERFIELD H.,THE INSTRUMENTS OF AMERICA'S FOREIGN POLICY. WOR+45 ECO/DEV NAT/G CONSULT EX/STRUC LEGIS BAL/PWR FOR/AID INT/TRADE DOMIN EDU/PROP LEGIT ATTIT KNOWL ORD/FREE PWR WEALTH...OBS COLD/WAR TOT/POP VAL/FREE. PAGE 163 A3322
USA+45 INT/ORG DIPLOM

S63
HUMPHREY H.H.,"REGIONAL ARMS CONTROL AGREEMENTS." WOR+45 FORCES PLAN LEGIT COERCE ATTIT HEALTH ORD/FREE...HUM METH/CNCPT MYTH OBS INT TREND TOT/POP 20. PAGE 69 A1416
L/A+17C INT/ORG ARMS/CONT REGION

S63
MARTHELOT P.,"PROGRES DE LA REFORME AGRAIRE." INTELL ECO/DEV R+D FOR/AID ADMIN KNOWL...OBS VAL/FREE UN 20. PAGE 95 A1948
AGRI INT/ORG

S63
NYE J.S. JR.,"EAST AFRICAN ECONOMIC INTEGRATION." AFR UGANDA PROVS DELIB/GP PLAN ECO/TAC INT/TRADE ADMIN ROUTINE ORD/FREE PWR WEALTH...OBS TIME/SEQ VAL/FREE 20. PAGE 110 A2264
ECO/UNDEV INT/ORG

S63
WRIGHT Q.,"PROJECTED EUROPEAN UNION AND AMERICAN INTERNATIONAL PRESTIGE." EUR+WWI FRANCE GERMANY UK USA+45 INT/ORG NAT/G EDU/PROP ATTIT PERCEPT PWR ...CONCPT OBS EEC 20 UN. PAGE 168 A3417
FUT ORD/FREE REGION

B64
ADAMS V.,THE PEACE CORPS IN ACTION. USA+45 VOL/ASSN EX/STRUC GOV/REL PERCEPT ORD/FREE...OBS 20 KENNEDY/JF PEACE/CORP. PAGE 4 A0087
DIPLOM FOR/AID PERSON DRIVE

B64
IKLE F.C.,HOW NATIONS NEGOTIATE. COM EUR+WWI USA+45 INTELL INT/ORG VOL/ASSN DELIB/GP ACT/RES CREATE DOMIN EDU/PROP ADJUD ROUTINE ATTIT PERSON ORD/FREE RESPECT SKILL...PSY SOC OBS VAL/FREE. PAGE 70 A1433
NAT/G PWR POLICY

B64
LENSEN G.A.,REVELATIONS OF A RUSSIAN DIPLOMAT: THE MEMOIRS OF DMITRII I. ABRIKOSSOV. ASIA MOD/EUR RUSSIA USA-45 ELITES ACADEM CHIEF FORCES REV WAR PWR CONSERVE MARXISM 19/20 ABRIKSSV/D CHINJAP BOLSHEVISM. PAGE 87 A1775
DIPLOM POLICY OBS

L64
CARNEGIE ENDOWMENT INT. PEACE,"POLITICAL QUESTIONS (ISSUES BEFORE THE NINETEENTH GENERAL ASSEMBLY)." SPACE WOR+45 CONSTN FINAN NAT/G CONSULT DELIB/GP FORCES LEGIS TEC/DEV EDU/PROP LEGIT ARMS/CONT COERCE NUC/PWR ATTIT ALL/VALS...CONCPT OBS UN COLD/WAR 20. PAGE 24 A0490
INT/ORG PEACE

S64
CRANE R.D.,"BASIC PRINCIPLES IN SOVIET SPACE LAW." FUT WOR+45 AIR INT/ORG DIPLOM DOMIN ARMS/CONT COERCE NUC/PWR PEACE ATTIT DRIVE PWR...INT/LAW METH/CNCPT NEW/IDEA OBS TREND GEN/LAWS VAL/FREE MARX/KARL 20. PAGE 32 A0659
COM LAW USSR SPACE

S64
GARDNER R.N.,"THE SOVIET UNION AND THE UNITED NATIONS." WOR+45 FINAN POL/PAR VOL/ASSN FORCES ECO/TAC DOMIN EDU/PROP LEGIT ADJUD ADMIN ARMS/CONT COERCE ATTIT ALL/VALS...POLICY MAJORIT CONCPT OBS TIME/SEQ TREND STERTYP UN. PAGE 51 A1046
COM INT/ORG USSR

S64
GERBET P.,"LA MISE EN OEUVRE DU MARCHE COMMUN AGRICOLE." ECO/DEV MARKET INT/ORG NAT/G PLAN EDU/PROP NAT/LISM WEALTH...OBS EEC VAL/FREE 20. PAGE 52 A1064
EUR+WWI AGRI REGION

S64
GINSBURGS G.,"WARS OF NATIONAL LIBERATION - THE SOVIET THESIS." COM USSR WOR+45 WOR-45 LAW CULTURE INT/ORG DIPLOM LEGIT COLONIAL GUERRILLA WAR NAT/LISM ATTIT PERSON MORAL PWR...JURID OBS TREND MARX/KARL 20. PAGE 53 A1075
COERCE CONCPT INT/LAW REV

S64
GROSSER A.,"Y A-T-IL UN CONFLIT FRANCO-AMERICAIN." EUR+WWI USA+45 INT/ORG NAT/G PLAN BAL/PWR DIPLOM EDU/PROP NUC/PWR ATTIT DRIVE ORD/FREE PWR...CONCPT OBS TIME/SEQ TREND STERTYP VAL/FREE COLD/WAR. PAGE 57 A1179
VOL/ASSN NAT/LISM FRANCE

S64
GRZYBOWSKI K.,"INTERNATIONAL ORGANIZATIONS FROM THE SOVIET POINT OF VIEW." WOR+45 WOR-45 CULTURE ECO/DEV VOL/ASSN EDU/PROP ATTIT RIGID/FLEX KNOWL ...SOC OBS TIME/SEQ TREND GEN/LAWS VAL/FREE ILO UN 20. PAGE 58 A1184
COM INT/ORG DIPLOM USSR

S64
HOFFMANN S.,"CE QU'EN PENSENT LES AMERICAINS." EUR+WWI INT/ORG VOL/ASSN PLAN BAL/PWR DIPLOM DOMIN EDU/PROP REGION ARMS/CONT DRIVE ORD/FREE PWR ...POLICY CONCPT OBS TREND STERTYP COLD/WAR VAL/FREE 20. PAGE 66 A1357
USA+45 ATTIT FRANCE

S64
HOVET T. JR.,"THE ROLE OF AFRICA IN THE UNITED NATIONS." FUT WOR+45 NAT/G DELIB/GP DOMIN EDU/PROP LEGIT ORD/FREE PWR RESPECT SKILL...OBS TIME/SEQ TREND VAL/FREE UN 20. PAGE 68 A1398
AFR INT/ORG DIPLOM

S64
KARPOV P.V.,"PEACEFUL COEXISTENCE AND INTERNATIONAL LAW." WOR+45 LAW SOCIETY INT/ORG VOL/ASSN FORCES CREATE CAP/ISM DIPLOM ADJUD NUC/PWR PEACE MORAL ORD/FREE PWR MARXISM...MARXIST JURID CONCPT OBS TREND COLD/WAR MARX/KARL 20. PAGE 77 A1568
COM ATTIT INT/LAW USSR

S64
LIPSON L.,"PEACEFUL COEXISTENCE." COM USSR WOR+45 LAW INT/ORG DIPLOM LEGIT ADJUD ORD/FREE...CONCPT OBS TREND GEN/LAWS VAL/FREE COLD/WAR 20. PAGE 90 A1834
ATTIT JURID INT/LAW PEACE

S64
MAGGS P.B.,"SOVIET VIEWPOINT ON NUCLEAR WEAPONS IN INTERNATIONAL LAW." USSR WOR+45 INT/ORG FORCES DIPLOM ARMS/CONT ATTIT ORD/FREE PWR...POLICY JURID CONCPT OBS TREND CON/ANAL GEN/LAWS VAL/FREE 20. PAGE 93 A1905
COM LAW INT/LAW NUC/PWR

S64
MAZRUI A.A.,"THE UNITED NATIONS AND SOME AFRICAN POLITICAL ATTITUDES." ECO/TAC FOR/AID DOMIN ROUTINE CHOOSE ATTIT DRIVE MORAL PWR RESPECT WEALTH...PSY CONCPT OBS TREND UN VAL/FREE 20. PAGE 97 A1987
AFR INT/ORG SOVEREIGN

S64
SCHWELB E.,"OPERATION OF THE EUROPEAN CONVENTION ON
INT/ORG

HUMAN RIGHTS." EUR+WWI LAW SOCIETY CREATE EDU/PROP ADJUD ADMIN PEACE ATTIT ORD/FREE PWR...POLICY INT/LAW CONCPT OBS GEN/LAWS UN VAL/FREE ILO 20 ECHR. PAGE 130 A2665 — MORAL

S64
WOOD H.B.,"STRETCHING YOUR FOREIGN-AID DOLLAR." USA+45 WOR+45 CONSULT EDU/PROP ATTIT WEALTH...OBS TOT/POP CONGRESS 20. PAGE 166 A3390 — ECO/UNDEV MGT FOR/AID

B65
WHITE G.M.,THE USE OF EXPERTS BY INTERNATIONAL TRIBUNALS. WOR+45 WOR-45 INT/ORG NAT/G PAY ADJUD COST...OBS BIBLIOG 20. PAGE 164 A3334 — INT/LAW ROUTINE CONSULT CT/SYS

S65
AMRAM P.W.,"REPORT ON THE TENTH SESSION OF THE HAGUE CONFERENCE ON PRIVATE INTERNATIONAL LAW." USA+45 WOR+45 INT/ORG CREATE LEGIT ADJUD ALL/VALS ...JURID CONCPT METH/CNCPT OBS GEN/METH 20. PAGE 8 A0155 — VOL/ASSN DELIB/GP INT/LAW

S65
SPAAK P.H.,"THE SEARCH FOR CONSENSUS: A NEW EFFORT TO BUILD EUROPE." FRANCE GERMANY ECO/DEV NAT/G CONSULT FORCES PLAN EDU/PROP REGION CONSEN ATTIT ...SOC METH/CNCPT OBS TREND EEC NATO WORK 20. PAGE 135 A2770 — EUR+WWI INT/ORG

B66
FRIEDRICH C.J.,REVOLUTION: NOMOS VIII. NAT/G SOCISM ...OBS TREND IDEA/COMP ANTHOL 18/20. PAGE 49 A1007 — REV MARXISM CONCPT DIPLOM

B66
WHITAKER A.P.,NATIONALISM IN CONTEMPORARY LATIN AMERICA. AGRI NAT/G WEALTH...POLICY SOC CONCPT OBS TREND 20. PAGE 164 A3333 — NAT/LISM L/A+17C DIPLOM ECO/UNDEV

B67
SALISBURY H.E.,BEHIND THE LINES - HANOI. VIETNAM/N NAT/G GUERRILLA CIVMIL/REL NAT/LISM KNOWL 20. PAGE 126 A2592 — WAR PROB/SOLV DIPLOM OBS

B67
SALISBURY H.E.,ORBIT OF CHINA. ASIA CHINA/COM DIPLOM PEACE PWR 20. PAGE 126 A2593 — EDU/PROP OBS INT ARMS/CONT

L67
GALTUNG J.,"ON THE EFFECTS OF INTERNATIONAL ECONOMIC SANCTIONS, WITH EXAMPLES FROM THE CASE OF RHODESIA." NAT/G DIPLOM EDU/PROP ADJUST EFFICIENCY INT/TRADE MORAL...OBS CHARTS 20. PAGE 51 A1035 — SANCTION ECO/TAC INT/TRADE ECO/UNDEV

OBS/ENVIR....SOCIAL MILIEU OF AND RESISTANCES TO OBSERVATIONS

B24
POOLE D.C.,THE CONDUCT OF FOREIGN RELATIONS UNDER MODERN DEMOCRATIC CONDITIONS. EUR+WWI USA-45 INT/ORG PLAN LEGIT ADMIN KNOWL PWR...MAJORIT OBS/ENVIR HIST/WRIT GEN/LAWS 20. PAGE 117 A2395 — NAT/G EDU/PROP DIPLOM

B43
SERENI A.P.,THE ITALIAN CONCEPTION OF INTERNATIONAL LAW. EUR+WWI MOD/EUR INT/ORG NAT/G DOMIN COERCE ORD/FREE FASCISM...OBS/ENVIR TREND 20. PAGE 131 A2686 — LAW TIME/SEQ INT/LAW ITALY

S53
BOULDING K.E.,"ECONOMIC ISSUES IN INTERNATIONAL CONFLICT." WOR+45 ECO/DEV NAT/G TOP/EX DIPLOM ECO/TAC DOMIN ATTIT WEALTH...MAJORIT OBS/ENVIR TREND GEN/LAWS COLD/WAR TOT/POP 20. PAGE 17 A0345 — PWR FOR/AID

S55
TORRE M.,"PSYCHIATRIC OBSERVATIONS OF INTERNATIONAL CONFERENCES." WOR+45 INT/ORG PROF/ORG VOL/ASSN CONSULT EDU/PROP ROUTINE ATTIT DRIVE KNOWL...PSY METH/CNCPT OBS/ENVIR STERTYP 20. PAGE 144 A2950 — DELIB/GP OBS DIPLOM

B60
JAECKH A.,WELTSAAT; ERLEBTES UND ERSTREBTES. GERMANY WOR+45 WOR-45 PLAN WAR...POLICY OBS/ENVIR NAT/COMP PERS/COMP 20. PAGE 73 A1489 — BIOG NAT/G SELF/OBS DIPLOM

L60
DEUTSCH K.W.,"TOWARD AN INVENTORY OF BASIC TRENDS AND PATTERNS IN COMPARATIVE AND INTERNATIONAL POLITICS." UNIV WOR+45 SOCIETY STRUCT INT/ORG NAT/G CREATE PLAN EDU/PROP KNOWL...PHIL/SCI METH/CNCPT STAT SELF/OBS OBS/ENVIR SAMP TREND CON/ANAL CHARTS SOC/EXP GEN/METH 20. PAGE 36 A0739 — R+D PERCEPT

B65
ADENAUER K.,MEINE ERINNERUNGEN, 1945-53 (VOL. I), 1953-55 (VOL. II). EUR+WWI GERMANY CHIEF FORCES PROB/SOLV DIPLOM ARMS/CONT INGP/REL PEACE SOVEREIGN ...OBS/ENVIR RECORD 20. PAGE 4 A0089 — NAT/G BIOG SELF/OBS

OBSCENITY....OBSCENITY

OBSERVATION....SEE DIRECT-OBSERVATION METHOD INDEX, P. XIV

OBSOLESCNC....OBSOLESCENCE, PLANNED

OCAM....SEE UAM

OCCUPATION....SEE WORKER

OCEANIA....OCEANIA: AUSTRALIA, NEW ZEALAND, MALAYSIA, MELANESIA, MICRONESIA, AND POLYNESIA

OCHENG D. A2274,A2275

OCKERT R.A. A1190

ODA S. A2276

ODEGARD/P....PETER ODEGARD

ODINGA/O....OGINGA ODINGA

OECD A2277,A2278,A2279,A2280,A2281

OECD....ORGANIZATION FOR ECONOMIC COOPERATION AND DEVELOPMENT

B61
OECD,STATISTICS OF BALANCE OF PAYMENTS 1950-61. WOR+45 FINAN ECO/TAC INT/TRADE DEMAND WEALTH...STAT NAT/COMP 20 OEEC OECD. PAGE 111 A2278 — BAL/PAY ECO/DEV INT/ORG CHARTS

B64
OECD,DEVELOPMENT ASSISTANCE EFFORTS - POLICIES OF THE MEMBERS. AGRI INDUS BUDGET...GEOG NAT/COMP 20 OECD. PAGE 111 A2280 — INT/ORG FOR/AID ECO/UNDEV TEC/DEV

OEEC A2282

OEEC....ORGANIZATION FOR EUROPEAN ECONOMIC COOPERATION; SEE ALSO VOL/ASSN, INT/ORG

B49
BOYD A.,WESTERN UNION: A STUDY OF THE TREND TOWARD EUROPEAN UNITY. FUT REGION NAT/LISM...POLICY IDEA/COMP BIBLIOG 14/20 OEEC ERASMUS/D COUNCL/EUR FULBRGHT/J NATO. PAGE 18 A0363 — DIPLOM AGREE TREND INT/ORG

B52
ALEXANDROWICZ C.H.,INTERNATIONAL ECONOMIC ORGANIZATION. WOR+45 ECO/DEV ECO/UNDEV DIST/IND FINAN MARKET PLAN ECO/TAC LEGIT DRIVE WEALTH ...POLICY CONCPT QUANT OBS TIME/SEQ GEN/LAWS WORK EEC ILO OEEC UNESCO 20. PAGE 6 A0114 — INT/ORG INT/TRADE

B52
SCHUMAN F.,THE COMMONWEALTH OF MAN. WOR+45 WOR-45 LAW CULTURE ELITES SOCIETY FAM INT/ORG NAT/G VOL/ASSN TOP/EX PLAN BAL/PWR LEGIT ATTIT DISPL DRIVE...POLICY MYTH TREND TOT/POP ILO OEEC 20. PAGE 129 A2649 — CONCPT GEN/LAWS

B54
TINBERGEN J.,INTERNATIONAL ECONOMIC INTEGRATION. WOR+45 WOR-45 ECO/UNDEV NAT/G ECO/TAC BAL/PAY ...METH/CNCPT STAT TIME/SEQ GEN/METH OEEC 20. PAGE 144 A2941 — INT/ORG ECO/DEV INT/TRADE

S55
HALLETT D.,"THE HISTORY AND STRUCTURE OF OEEC." EUR+WWI USA+45 CONSTN INDUS INT/ORG NAT/G DELIB/GP ACT/RES PLAN ORD/FREE WEALTH...CONCPT OEEC 20 CMN/WLTH. PAGE 60 A1234 — VOL/ASSN ECO/DEV

B56
FOSTER J.G.,BRITAIN IN WESTERN EUROPE: WEU AND THE ATLANTIC ALLIANCE. EUR+WWI FRANCE GERMANY GERMANY/W ITALY UK STRATA NAT/G DELIB/GP ECO/TAC ORD/FREE PWR ...TRADIT TIME/SEQ TREND OEEC PARLIAMENT 20 EUROPE/W. PAGE 47 A0969 — INT/ORG FORCES WEAPON

S56
GORDON L.,"THE ORGANIZATION FOR EUROPEAN ECONOMIC COOPERATION." EUR+WWI INDUS INT/ORG NAT/G CONSULT DELIB/GP ACT/RES CREATE PLAN TEC/DEV EDU/PROP LEGIT WEALTH OEEC 20. PAGE 54 A1114 — VOL/ASSN ECO/DEV

B58
KINDLEBERGER C.P.,INTERNATIONAL ECONOMICS. WOR+45 WOR-45 ECO/DEV ECO/UNDEV FINAN VOL/ASSN ACT/RES DIPLOM ECO/TAC LEGIT REGION ATTIT DRIVE ORD/FREE WEALTH...POLICY STAT TREND GEN/LAWS EEC ECSC OEEC 20. PAGE 79 A1620 — INT/ORG BAL/PWR TARIFFS

B58
SCITOUSKY T.,ECONOMIC THEORY AND WESTERN EUROPEAN INTEGRATION. EUR+WWI INT/ORG ACT/RES INT/TRADE REGION BAL/PAY WEALTH...METH/CNCPT STAT CHARTS GEN/METH ECSC TOT/POP EEC OEEC 20. PAGE 130 A2668 — ECO/TAC

S58
ELKIN A.B.,"OEEC-ITS STRUCTURE AND POWERS." EUR+WWI CONSTN INDUS INT/ORG NAT/G VOL/ASSN DELIB/GP ACT/RES PLAN ORD/FREE WEALTH...CHARTS ORG/CHARTS OEEC 20. PAGE 41 A0839 — ECO/DEV EX/STRUC

B59
BALL M.M.,NATO AND THE EUROPEAN MOVEMENT. EUR+WWI — DELIB/GP

USA+45 INT/ORG FORCES BAL/PWR EDU/PROP LEGIT REGION ATTIT ORD/FREE PWR...STAT OBS TIME/SEQ TREND CHARTS ORG/CHARTS STERTYP COLD/WAR EEC OEEC 20 NATO. PAGE 10 A0212
STRUCT

B59
SANNWALD R.E.,ECONOMIC INTEGRATION: THEORETICAL ASSUMPTIONS AND CONSEQUENCES OF EUROPEAN UNIFICATION. EUR+WWI FUT FINAN INDUS VOL/ASSN ACT/RES ECO/TAC...PLURIST EEC OEEC 20. PAGE 127 A2601
INT/ORG
ECO/DEV
INT/TRADE

L59
MURPHY J.C.,"SOME IMPLICATIONS OF EUROPE'S COMMON MARKET. IN (COOK P. ECONOMIC DEVELOPMENT AND INTERNATIONAL TRADE.." EUR+WWI ECO/DEV DIST/IND INDUS NAT/G PLAN ECO/TAC INT/TRADE WEALTH...STAT TREND OEEC TOT/POP 20 EEC. PAGE 106 A2178
MARKET
INT/ORG
REGION

S59
BELOFF M.,"NATIONAL GOVERNMENT AND INTERNATIONAL GOVERNMENT." WOR+45 R+D DELIB/GP ACT/RES PLAN PWR ...GEN/METH VAL/FREE EEC OEEC 20. PAGE 13 A0259
NAT/G
INT/ORG
DIPLOM

L60
HAAS E.B.,"CONSENSUS FORMATION IN THE COUNCIL OF EUROPE." EUR+WWI NAT/G DELIB/GP DIPLOM REGION CHOOSE PWR SOVEREIGN...RELATIV NEW/IDEA QUANT CHARTS INDEX TOT/POP OEEC 20 COUNCL/EUR. PAGE 59 A1206
POL/PAR
INT/ORG
STAT

S60
KREININ M.E.,"THE 'OUTER-SEVEN' AND EUROPEAN INTEGRATION." EUR+WWI FRANCE GERMANY ITALY UK ECO/DEV DIST/IND INT/TRADE DRIVE WEALTH...MYTH CHARTS EEC OEEC 20. PAGE 82 A1682
ECO/TAC
GEN/LAWS

S60
NANES A.,"THE EUROPEAN COMMUNITY AND THE UNITED STATES: EVOLVING RELATIONS." EUR+WWI USA+45 WOR+45 ECO/UNDEV MARKET NAT/G DELIB/GP PLAN LEGIT ATTIT PWR WEALTH...CONCPT STAT TIME/SEQ CON/ANAL EEC OEEC 20 EURATOM. PAGE 107 A2194
INT/ORG
REGION

N60
ERDMAN P.E.,COMMON MARKETS AND FREE TRADE AREAS (PAMPHLET). USA+45 MARKET INT/ORG TEC/DEV DIPLOM UTIL...CON/ANAL CHARTS BIBLIOG 20 EEC OEEC. PAGE 42 A0859
TREND
PROB/SOLV
INT/TRADE
ECO/DEV

B61
OECD,STATISTICS OF BALANCE OF PAYMENTS 1950-61. WOR+45 FINAN ECO/TAC INT/TRADE DEMAND WEALTH...STAT NAT/COMP 20 OEEC OECD. PAGE 111 A2278
BAL/PAY
ECO/DEV
INT/ORG
CHARTS

B61
US CONGRESS JOINT ECO COMM,INTERNATIONAL PAYMENTS IMBALANCES AND NEED FOR STRENGTHENING INTERNATIONAL FINANCIAL ARRANGEMENTS. USA+45 WOR+45 DELIB/GP DIPLOM INT/TRADE...CHARTS 20 CONGRESS OEEC. PAGE 150 A3063
BAL/PAY
INT/ORG
FINAN
PROB/SOLV

S61
HAAS E.B.,"INTERNATIONAL INTEGRATION: THE EUROPEAN AND THE UNIVERSAL PROCESS." EUR+WWI FUT WOR+45 NAT/G EX/STRUC ATTIT DRIVE ORD/FREE PWR...CONCPT GEN/LAWS OEEC 20 NATO COUNCL/EUR. PAGE 59 A1207
INT/ORG
TREND
REGION

S61
RAY J.,"THE EUROPEAN FREE-TRADE ASSOCIATION AND ITS IMPACT ON INDIA'S TRADE." EUR+WWI FRANCE GERMANY INDIA S/ASIA UK NAT/G VOL/ASSN PLAN INT/TRADE ROUTINE WEALTH...STAT CHARTS CMN/WLTH EEC OEEC 20 EFTA. PAGE 120 A2453
ECO/DEV
ECO/TAC

B62
CARDOZA M.H.,DIPLOMATS IN INTERNATIONAL COOPERATION: STEPCHILDREN OF THE FOREIGN SERVICE. EUR+WWI USA+45 NAT/G CONSULT ACT/RES EDU/PROP ROUTINE RIGID/FLEX KNOWL SKILL...SOC OBS TIME/SEQ EEC OEEC NATO 20. PAGE 24 A0480
INT/ORG
METH/CNCPT
DIPLOM

B62
MEADE J.E.,CASE STUDIES IN EUROPEAN ECONOMIC UNION. BELGIUM EUR+WWI LUXEMBOURG NAT/G INT/TRADE REGION ROUTINE WEALTH...METH/CNCPT STAT CHARTS ECSC TOT/POP OEEC EEC 20. PAGE 99 A2028
INT/ORG
ECO/TAC

B62
US CONGRESS JOINT ECO COMM,FACTORS AFFECTING THE UNITED STATES BALANCE OF PAYMENTS. USA+45 DELIB/GP PLAN DIPLOM FOR/AID PRODUC WEALTH...CHARTS 20 CONGRESS OEEC. PAGE 150 A3064
BAL/PAY
INT/TRADE
ECO/TAC
FINAN

L62
MALINOWSKI W.R.,"CENTRALIZATION AND DE-CENTRALIZATION IN THE UNITED NATIONS' ECONOMIC AND SOCIAL ACTIVITIES." WOR+45 CONSTN ECO/UNDEV INT/ORG VOL/ASSN DELIB/GP ECO/TAC EDU/PROP ADMIN RIGID/FLEX ...OBS CHARTS UNESCO UN EEC OAS OEEC 20. PAGE 93 A1913
CREATE
GEN/LAWS

S62
ALBONETTI A.,"IL SECONDO PROGRAMMA QUINQUENNALE 1963-67 ED IL BILANCIO RICERCHE ED INVESTIMENTI PER IL 1963 DELL'ERATOM." EUR+WWI FUT ITALY WOR+45 ECO/DEV SERV/IND INT/ORG TEC/DEV ECO/TAC ATTIT SKILL WEALTH...MGT TIME/SEQ OEEC 20. PAGE 5 A0108
R+D
PLAN
NUC/PWR

S62
ORBAN M.,"L'EUROPE EN FORMATION ET SES PROBLEMES." EUR+WWI FUT WOR+45 WOR-45 INTELL STRUCT DELIB/GP ACT/RES FEDERAL RIGID/FLEX WEALTH...CONCPT TIME/SEQ OEEC 20. PAGE 112 A2295
INT/ORG
PLAN
REGION

B63
BELOFF M.,THE UNITED STATES AND THE UNITY OF EUROPE. EUR+WWI UK USA+45 WOR+45 VOL/ASSN DIPLOM REGION ATTIT PWR...CONCPT EEC OEEC 20 NATO. PAGE 13 A0261
ECO/DEV
INT/ORG

B63
BOWETT D.W.,THE LAW OF INTERNATIONAL INSTITUTIONS. WOR+45 WOR-45 CONSTN DELIB/GP EX/STRUC JUDGE EDU/PROP LEGIT CT/SYS EXEC ROUTINE RIGID/FLEX ORD/FREE PWR...JURID CONCPT ORG/CHARTS GEN/METH LEAGUE/NAT OAS OEEC 20 UN. PAGE 17 A0354
INT/ORG
ADJUD
DIPLOM

B63
KRAVIS I.B.,DOMESTIC INTERESTS AND INTERNATIONAL OBLIGATIONS: SAFEGUARDS IN INTERNATIONAL TRADE ORGANIZATIONS. EUR+WWI USA+45 WOR+45 FINAN DELIB/GP ATTIT RIGID/FLEX HEALTH...STAT EEC VAL/FREE OEEC ECSC 20. PAGE 82 A1680
INT/ORG
ECO/TAC
INT/TRADE

S63
HALLSTEIN W.,"THE EUROPEAN COMMUNITY AND ATLANTIC PARTNERSHIP." EUR+WWI USA+45 MARKET NAT/G VOL/ASSN DELIB/GP ARMS/CONT NUC/PWR ATTIT PWR...CONCPT STAT TIME/SEQ TREND OEEC 20 EEC. PAGE 60 A1235
INT/ORG
ECO/TAC
UK

S63
KAWALKOWSKI A.,"POUR UNE EUROPE INDEPENDENTE ET REUNIFIEE." EUR+WWI FUT USA+45 USSR WOR+45 ECO/DEV PROC/MFG INT/ORG NAT/G ACT/RES TEC/DEV FEDERAL RIGID/FLEX...CONCPT METH/CNCPT OEEC TOT/POP 20 DEGAULLE/C. PAGE 77 A1573
R+D
PLAN
NUC/PWR

S63
SCHOFLING J.A.,"EFTA: THE OTHER EUROPE." ECO/DEV MARKET CONSULT ECO/TAC WEALTH...TIME/SEQ EEC OEEC 20 EFTA. PAGE 129 A2642
EUR+WWI
INT/ORG
REGION

S63
SHWADRAN B.,"MIDDLE EAST OIL, 1962." ISLAM USSR ECO/DEV DIST/IND INDUS PLAN BAL/PWR DISPL DRIVE ...POLICY STAT TREND GEN/LAWS EEC OEEC 20 OIL. PAGE 132 A2712
MARKET
ECO/TAC
INT/TRADE

B64
ECONOMIDES C.P.,LE POUVOIR DE DECISION DES ORGANISATIONS INTERNATIONALES EUROPEENNES. DIPLOM DOMIN INGP/REL EFFICIENCY...INT/LAW JURID 20 NATO OEEC EEC COUNCL/EUR EURATOM. PAGE 40 A0821
INT/ORG
PWR
DECISION
GP/COMP

S64
BUCHAN A.,"THE MULTILATERAL FORCE." EUR+WWI FUT USA+45 NAT/G LEGIT PWR SKILL...CONCPT OEEC MLF 20. PAGE 21 A0422
INT/ORG
FORCES

B65
CASSELL F.,GOLD OR CREDIT? THE ECONOMICS AND POLITICS OF INTERNATIONAL MONEY. WOR+45 PLAN PROB/SOLV BAL/PAY SOVEREIGN WEALTH 20 OEEC GOLD/STAND. PAGE 25 A0506
FINAN
INT/ORG
DIPLOM
ECO/TAC

B65
SOPER T.,EVOLVING COMMONWEALTH. AFR CANADA INDIA IRELAND UK LAW CONSTN POL/PAR DOMIN CONTROL WAR PWR ...AUD/VIS 18/20 COMMONWLTH OEEC. PAGE 135 A2769
INT/ORG
COLONIAL
VOL/ASSN

B66
MEERHAEGHE M.,INTERNATIONAL ECONOMIC INSTITUTIONS. EUR+WWI FINAN INDUS MARKET PLAN TARIFFS BAL/PAY EQUILIB...POLICY BIBLIOG/A 20 GATT OEEC EEC IBRD EURCOALSTL. PAGE 99 A2032
ECO/TAC
ECO/DEV
INT/TRADE
INT/ORG

B66
SPINELLI A.,THE EUROCRATS; CONFLICT AND CRISIS IN THE EUROPEAN COMMUNITY (TRANS. BY C. GROVE HAINES). EUR+WWI MARKET POL/PAR ECO/TAC PARL/PROC EEC OEEC ECSC EURATOM. PAGE 136 A2789
INT/ORG
INGP/REL
CONSTN
ADMIN

B66
TRIFFIN R.,THE WORLD MONEY MAZE. INT/ORG ECO/TAC PRICE OPTIMAL WEALTH...METH/COMP 20 EEC OEEC GOLD/STAND SILVER. PAGE 145 A2964
BAL/PAY
FINAN
INT/TRADE
DIPLOM

OEO....OFFICE OF ECONOMIC OPPORTUNITY

OEP....OFFICE OF EMERGENCY PLANNING

OFFICE OF PRICE ADMINISTRATION....SEE OPA

OFFICE OF WAR INFORMATION....SEE OWI

OGBURN W. A2283

OGILVY-WEBB M. A2284

OHIO....OHIO

OHLIN B. A2285

OHLIN G. A2286

OHLIN/HECK....OHLIN-HECKSCHER THEORY OF COMMODITY TRADE

OIL

B47
FEIS H.,SEEN FROM E A, THREE INTERNATIONAL EPISODES. EUR+WWI ITALY USA-45 WOR-45 AGRI INT/ORG NAT/G INT/TRADE LEGIT EXEC ATTIT ORD/FREE...POLICY LEAGUE/NAT TOT/POP 20 OIL. PAGE 44 A0908
EXTR/IND ECO/TAC DIPLOM

S63
SHWADRAN B.,"MIDDLE EAST OIL, 1962." ISLAM USSR ECO/DEV DIST/IND INDUS PLAN BAL/PWR DISPL DRIVE ...POLICY STAT TREND GEN/LAWS EEC OEEC 20 OIL. PAGE 132 A2712
MARKET ECO/TAC INT/TRADE

OKELLO/J....JOHN OKELLO

OKINAWA....OKINAWA

OKINSHEVICH L.A. A2287

OKLAHOMA....OKLAHOMA

OLAS....ORGANIZATION FOR LATIN AMERICAN SOLIDARITY

OLD LIBERAL....SEE OLD/LIB

OLD/LIB....OLD LIBERAL

B19
KEYNES J.M.,THE ECONOMIC CONSEQUENCES OF THE PEACE. FUT GERMANY MOD/EUR RUSSIA UK USA-45 CULTURE ECO/DEV FINAN INDUS INT/ORG TOP/EX ECO/TAC ROUTINE WAR ATTIT PERCEPT ALL/VALS...OLD/LIB MYTH OBS TIME/SEQ TREND 20 TREATY. PAGE 78 A1605
EUR+WWI SOCIETY PEACE

B41
YOUNG G.,FEDERALISM AND FREEDOM. EUR+WWI MOD/EUR RUSSIA USA-45 WOR-45 SOCIETY STRUCT ECO/DEV INT/ORG EXEC FEDERAL ATTIT PERSON ALL/VALS...OLD/LIB CONCPT OBS TREND LEAGUE/NAT TOT/POP. PAGE 169 A3435
NAT/G WAR

S52
HAAS E.B.,"THE RECONCILIATION OF CONFLICT, COLONIAL POLICY AIMS: ACCEPTANCE OF THE LEAGUE OF NATIONS MANDATE SYSTEM." FRANCE GERMANY UK WOR+45 WOR-45 LEGIT ATTIT DRIVE ORD/FREE...OLD/LIB INT SYS/QU TIME/SEQ TREND LEAGUE/NAT 20. PAGE 58 A1201
INT/ORG COLONIAL

B56
UNDERHILL F.H.,THE BRITISH COMMONWEALTH: AN EXPERIMENT IN CO-OPERATION AMONG NATIONS. CANADA UK WOR+45 WOR-45 INT/ORG COLONIAL UTIL SOVEREIGN CONSERVE...OLD/LIB SOC/EXP BIBLIOG/A 19/20 CMN/WLTH. PAGE 147 A3007
VOL/ASSN NAT/LISM DIPLOM

B61
EINZIG P.,A DYNAMIC THEORY OF FORWARD EXCHANGE. FUT WOR+45 WOR-45 INT/TRADE BAL/PAY WEALTH...OLD/LIB NEW/IDEA OBS TREND 20. PAGE 41 A0830
FINAN ECO/TAC

B61
FRIEDMANN W.G.,JOINT INTERNATIONAL BUSINESS VENTURES. ASIA ISLAM L/A+17C ECO/DEV DIST/IND FINAN PROC/MFG FACE/GP LG/CO NAT/G VOL/ASSN CONSULT EX/STRUC PLAN ADMIN ROUTINE WEALTH...OLD/LIB WORK 20. PAGE 49 A1004
ECO/UNDEV INT/TRADE

B61
JENKS C.W.,INTERNATIONAL IMMUNITIES. PLAN EDU/PROP ADMIN PERCEPT...OLD/LIB JURID CONCPT TREND TOT/POP. PAGE 74 A1506
INT/ORG DIPLOM

B62
KING-HALL S.,POWER POLITICS IN THE NUCLEAR AGE: A POLICY FOR BRITAIN. UK WOR+45 PLAN ECO/TAC CONTROL RISK ARMS/CONT MORAL PWR RESPECT...OLD/LIB 20. PAGE 79 A1625
BAL/PWR NUC/PWR POLICY DIPLOM

B62
ROY P.A.,SOUTH WIND RED. L/A+17C USA+45 ECO/UNDEV NAT/G CAP/ISM MARXISM SOCISM...OLD/LIB GEOG RECORD INT CENSUS 20 COLD/WAR. PAGE 125 A2554
DIPLOM INDUS POLICY ECO/TAC

B96
SMITH A.,LECTURES ON JUSTICE, POLICE, REVENUE AND ARMS (1763). UK LAW FAM FORCES TARIFFS AGREE COERCE INCOME OWN WEALTH LAISSEZ...GEN/LAWS 17/18. PAGE 134 A2743
DIPLOM JURID OLD/LIB TAX

OLD/STOR....CONVENTIONAL INFORMATION-STORAGE SYSTEMS

OLDEROGGE D.A. A0687

OLIGARCHY....SEE ELITES

OLIN/MTHSN....OLIN MATHIESON

OLIVARES....OLIVARES, HEAD OF SPAIN DURING CATALAN REV., 1640

OLIVIER G. A2288

OLSON L. A2289

OLSON W.C. A2290

OMAN C. A2291

OMBUDSMAN....OMBUDSMAN; DOMESTIC GRIEVANCE ORGAN

ONTARIO....ONTARIO, CANADA

OP/RES....OPERATIONS RESEARCH; SEE ALSO CREATE

N
WORLD PEACE FOUNDATION,DOCUMENTS OF INTERNATIONAL ORGANIZATIONS: A SELECTED BIBLIOGRAPHY. WOR+45 WOR-45 AGRI FINAN ACT/RES OP/RES INT/TRADE ADMIN ...CON/ANAL 20 UN UNESCO LEAGUE/NAT. PAGE 167 A3396
BIBLIOG DIPLOM INT/ORG REGION

B05
GRIFFIN A.P.C.,LIST OF REFERENCES ON THE US CONSULAR SERVICE (PAMPHLET). FRANCE GERMANY SPAIN UK USA-45 WOR-45 OP/RES DOMIN ADMIN FEEDBACK ROUTINE GOV/REL...DECISION 19. PAGE 56 A1153
BIBLIOG/A NAT/G DIPLOM CONSULT

B35
CONOVER H.F.,A SELECTED LIST OF REFERENCES ON THE DIPLOMATIC & TRADE RELATIONS OF THE US WITH THE USSR, 1919-1935 (PAMPHLET). USA-45 USSR DELIB/GP LEGIS OP/RES PROB/SOLV BAL/PWR BARGAIN 20. PAGE 29 A0590
BIBLIOG DIPLOM INT/TRADE

B48
MORGENTHAL H.J.,POLITICS AMONG NATIONS: THE STRUGGLE FOR POWER AND PEACE. FUT WOR+45 INT/ORG OP/RES PROB/SOLV BAL/PWR CONTROL ATTIT MORAL ...INT/LAW BIBLIOG 20 COLD/WAR. PAGE 104 A2135
DIPLOM PEACE PWR POLICY

S49
FOX W.T.R.,"INTERWAR INTERNATIONAL RELATIONS RESEARCH: THE AMERICAN EXPERIENCE." USA+45 USA-45 INTELL INT/ORG VOL/ASSN OP/RES ATTIT SKILL ...TIME/SEQ LEAGUE/NAT 20. PAGE 48 A0973
ACT/RES CON/ANAL

N52
COORDINATING COMM DOC SOC SCI,INTERNATIONAL REPERTORY OF SOCIAL SCIENCE DOCUMENTATION CENTERS (PAMPHLET). ACT/RES OP/RES WRITING KNOWL...CON/ANAL METH. PAGE 30 A0610
BIBLIOG/A R+D NAT/G INT/ORG

B53
KANTOR H.,A BIBLIOGRAPHY OF UNPUBLISHED DOCTORAL DISSERTATIONS AND MASTERS' THESES DEALING WITH GOVTS, POL, INT REL OF LAT AM. L/A+17C INT/ORG POL/PAR ACT/RES OP/RES CONFER ATTIT...INT/LAW PHIL/SCI 20. PAGE 76 A1556
BIBLIOG ACADEM DIPLOM NAT/G

B53
LANDHEER B.,FUNDAMENTALS OF PUBLIC INTERNATIONAL LAW (SELECTIVE BIBLIOGRAPHIES OF THE LIBRARY OF THE PEACE PALACE, VOL. I; PAMPH). INT/ORG OP/RES PEACE ...IDEA/COMP 20. PAGE 84 A1715
BIBLIOG/A INT/LAW DIPLOM PHIL/SCI

C56
VAGTS A.,"DEFENSE AND DIPLOMACY: THE SOLDIER AND THE CONDUCT OF FOREIGN RELATIONS." OP/RES CONFER DETER WAR PEACE RESPECT...POLICY DECISION CONCPT BIBLIOG 17/20. PAGE 158 A3209
DIPLOM FORCES HIST/WRIT

B61
DIMOCK M.E.,BUSINESS AND GOVERNMENT (4TH ED.). AGRI FINAN OP/RES PLAN BUDGET DIPLOM LOBBY NUC/PWR NEW/LIB SOCISM...POLICY BIBLIOG 20. PAGE 37 A0765
NAT/G INDUS LABOR ECO/TAC

B61
ROSENAU J.N.,PUBLIC OPINION AND FOREIGN POLICY; AN OPERATIONAL FORMULA. USA+45 COM/IND OP/RES EDU/PROP LOBBY CROWD...CON/ANAL BIBLIOG 20. PAGE 124 A2532
ATTIT PRESS DIPLOM

B61
YUAN TUNG-LI,A GUIDE TO DOCTORAL DISSERTATIONS BY CHINESE STUDENTS IN AMERICA, 1905-1960. ASIA CULTURE SOCIETY ECO/UNDEV NAT/G PROB/SOLV DIPLOM LEAD ATTIT...HUM SOC STAT 20. PAGE 169 A3441
BIBLIOG ACADEM ACT/RES OP/RES

B63
THORELLI H.B.,INTOP: INTERNATIONAL OPERATIONS SIMULATION: PLAYER'S MANUAL. BRAZIL FINAN OP/RES ADMIN GP/REL INGP/REL PRODUC PERCEPT...DECISION MGT EEC. PAGE 144 A2935
GAME INT/TRADE EDU/PROP LG/CO

B64
HAMBRIDGE G.,DYNAMICS OF DEVELOPMENT. AGRI FINAN INDUS LABOR INT/TRADE EDU/PROP ADMIN LEAD OWN HEALTH...ANTHOL BIBLIOG 20. PAGE 61 A1245
ECO/UNDEV ECO/TAC OP/RES ACT/RES

B64
STEWART C.F.,A BIBLIOGRAPHY OF INTERNATIONAL BUSINESS. WOR+45 FINAN LG/CO NAT/G PLAN ECO/TAC TARIFFS...DECISION MGT GP/COMP NAT/COMP 20 EEC. PAGE 138 A2824
BIBLIOG INT/ORG OP/RES INT/TRADE

B65
THAYER F.C. JR.,AIR TRANSPORT POLICY AND NATIONAL SECURITY: A POLITICAL, ECONOMIC, AND MILITARY ANALYSIS. DIST/IND OP/RES PLAN TEC/DEV DIPLOM DETER WAR COST EFFICIENCY...POLICY BIBLIOG 20 DEPT/DEFEN FAA CAB. PAGE 142 A2908
AIR FORCES CIVMIL/REL ORD/FREE

B65
WALKER A.A.,THE RHODESIAS AND NYASALAND: A GUIDE TO OFFICIAL PUBLICATIONS. RHODESIA UK OP/RES PLAN PROB/SOLV DIPLOM...POLICY SOC CON/ANAL 19/20
BIBLIOG NAT/G COLONIAL

NYASALAND. PAGE 160 A3263 AFR

B65
WEAVER J.N.,THE INTERNATIONAL DEVELOPMENT ASSOCIATION: A NEW APPROACH TO FOREIGN AID. USA+45 NAT/G OP/RES PLAN PROB/SOLV WEALTH...CHARTS BIBLIOG 20 UN. PAGE 162 A3295
FOR/AID INT/ORG ECO/UNDEV FINAN

B65
WITHERELL J.W.,MADAGASCAR AND ADJACENT ISLANDS; A GUIDE TO OFFICIAL PUBLICATIONS (PAMPHLET). FRANCE MADAGASCAR S/ASIA UK LAW OP/RES PLAN DIPLOM ...POLICY CON/ANAL 19/20. PAGE 165 A3371
BIBLIOG COLONIAL LOC/G ADMIN

B66
FINKLE J.L.,POLITICAL DEVELOPMENT AND SOCIAL CHANGE. WOR+45 CULTURE NAT/G OP/RES PROB/SOLV DIPLOM ECO/TAC INGP/REL...METH/COMP ANTHOL 20. PAGE 46 A0934
ECO/UNDEV SOCIETY CREATE

C66
ZAWODNY J.K.,"GUIDE TO THE STUDY OF INTERNATIONAL RELATIONS." OP/RES PRESS...STAT INT 20. PAGE 169 A3449
BIBLIOG/A DIPLOM INT/LAW INT/ORG

B67
HIRSCHMAN A.O.,DEVELOPMENT PROJECTS OBSERVED. INDUS INT/ORG CONSULT EX/STRUC CREATE OP/RES ECO/TAC DEMAND...POLICY MGT METH/COMP 20 WORLD/BANK. PAGE 65 A1339
ECO/UNDEV R+D FINAN PLAN

B67
SCOTT A.M.,THE FUNCTIONING OF THE INTERNATIONAL POLITICAL SYSTEM. INT/ORG OP/RES PROB/SOLV COERCE WAR EQUILIB...METH/CNCPT BIBLIOG. PAGE 130 A2671
DIPLOM DECISION BAL/PWR

N67
US SENATE COMM ON FOREIGN REL,ARMS SALES AND FOREIGN POLICY (PAMPHLET). FINAN FOR/AID CONTROL 20. PAGE 156 A3187
ARMS/CONT ADMIN OP/RES DIPLOM

OPA....OFFICE OF PRICE ADMINISTRATION

OPEN/SPACE....OPEN SPACE - TOWN AND COUNTRY PLANNING

OPERATIONAL RESEARCH AND RELATED MANAGEMENT SCIENCE.... SEE OR/MS

OPERATIONS RESEARCH....SEE OP/RES

OPINION TESTS AND POLLS....SEE KNO/TEST

OPINIONS....SEE ATTIT

OPLER M.E. A2292

OPPENHEIM L. A2293,A2294

OPTIMAL....OPTIMALITY

C50
ELLSWORTH P.T.,"INTERNATIONAL ECONOMY." ECO/DEV ECO/UNDEV FINAN LABOR DIPLOM FOR/AID TARIFFS BAL/PAY EQUILIB NAT/LISM OPTIMAL...INT/LAW 20 ILO GATT. PAGE 41 A0843
BIBLIOG INT/TRADE ECO/TAC INT/ORG

B66
TRIFFIN R.,THE WORLD MONEY MAZE. INT/ORG ECO/TAC PRICE OPTIMAL WEALTH...METH/COMP 20 EEC OEEC GOLD/STAND SILVER. PAGE 145 A2964
BAL/PAY FINAN INT/TRADE DIPLOM

OR/MS....OPERATIONAL RESEARCH AND RELATED MANAGEMENT SCIENCE

ORANGE/STA....ORANGE FREE STATE

ORBAN M. A2295

ORD H.W. A2825

ORD/FREE....SECURITY, ORDER, RESTRAINT, LIBERTY, FREEDOM

N
INTERNATIONAL COMN JURISTS,AFRICAN CONFERENCE ON THE RULE OF LAW. AFR INT/ORG LEGIS DIPLOM CONFER COLONIAL ORD/FREE...CONCPT METH/COMP 20. PAGE 71 A1452
CT/SYS JURID DELIB/GP

N/R
FULBRIGHT J.W.,THE ARROGANCE OF POWER. USA+45 WOR+45 ECO/UNDEV ACADEM LEGIS ECO/TAC FOR/AID PEACE ROLE ORD/FREE PWR 20 COLD/WAR CONGRESS. PAGE 50 A1014
DIPLOM POLICY REV

B00
DARBY W.E.,INTERNATIONAL TRIBUNALS. WOR-45 NAT/G ECO/TAC DOMIN LEGIT CT/SYS COERCE ORD/FREE PWR SOVEREIGN JURID. PAGE 33 A0681
INT/ORG ADJUD PEACE INT/LAW

B00
HOLLAND T.E.,STUDIES IN INTERNATIONAL LAW. TURKEY USSR WOR-45 CONSTN NAT/G DIPLOM DOMIN LEGIT COERCE WAR PEACE ORD/FREE PWR SOVEREIGN...JURID CHARTS 20 PARLIAMENT SUEZ TREATY. PAGE 66 A1367
INT/ORG LAW INT/LAW

B00
LORIMER J.,THE INSTITUTES OF THE LAW OF NATIONS. WOR-45 CULTURE SOCIETY NAT/G VOL/ASSN DIPLOM LEGIT WAR PEACE DRIVE ORD/FREE SOVEREIGN...CONCPT RECORD INT TREND HYPO/EXP GEN/METH TOT/POP VAL/FREE 20. PAGE 91 A1863
INT/ORG LAW INT/LAW

B01
GRIFFIN A.P.C.,LIST OF BOOKS ON SAMOA (PAMPHLET). GERMANY S/ASIA UK USA-45 WOR-45 ECO/UNDEV REGION ALL/VALS ORD/FREE ALL/IDEOS...GEOG INT/LAW 19 SAMOA GUAM. PAGE 56 A1150
BIBLIOG/A COLONIAL DIPLOM

C05
DUNNING W.A.,"HISTORY OF POLITICAL THEORIES FROM LUTHER TO MONTESQUIEU." LAW NAT/G SECT DIPLOM REV WAR ORD/FREE SOVEREIGN CONSERVE...TRADIT BIBLIOG 16/18. PAGE 39 A0803
PHIL/SCI CONCPT GEN/LAWS

B13
BUTLER N.M.,THE INTERNATIONAL MIND. WOR-45 INT/ORG LEGIT PWR...JURID CONCPT 20. PAGE 22 A0452
ADJUD ORD/FREE INT/LAW

B17
SATOW E.,A GUIDE TO DIPLOMATIC PRACTICE. MOD/EUR INT/ORG BAL/PWR LEGIT ORD/FREE PWR SOVEREIGN ...POLICY GEN/METH 20. PAGE 127 A2607
GEN/LAWS DIPLOM

B17
VEBLEN T.B.,AN INQUIRY INTO THE NATURE OF PEACE AND THE TERMS OF ITS PERPETUATION. UNIV STRATA FINAN EDU/PROP PRICE COST DISCRIM NAT/LISM MORAL ORD/FREE PACIFIST 20 WORLDUNITY. PAGE 158 A3224
PEACE DIPLOM WAR NAT/G

N17
BURKE E.,THOUGHTS ON THE PROSPECT OF A REGICIDE PEACE (PAMPHLET). FRANCE UK SECT DOMIN MURDER PEACE ORD/FREE SOVEREIGN POPULISM...POLICY GOV/COMP IDEA/COMP 18 JACOBINISM COEXIST. PAGE 21 A0435
REV CHIEF NAT/G DIPLOM

B19
SUMNER W.G.,WAR AND OTHER ESSAYS. USA-45 DELIB/GP DIPLOM TARIFFS COLONIAL PEACE SOVEREIGN 20. PAGE 140 A2864
INT/TRADE ORD/FREE CAP/ISM ECO/TAC

B19
US DEPARTMENT OF STATE,A TENTATIVE LIST OF TREATY COLLECTIONS. WOR-45 BAL/PWR INT/TRADE TARIFFS WAR PEACE ORD/FREE 20. PAGE 151 A3080
ANTHOL DIPLOM DELIB/GP

N19
BARROS J.F.P.,THE INTERNATIONAL POLICE: THE USE OF FORCE IN THE STRUCTURE OF PEACE (PAMPHLET). BRAZIL WOR+45 WOR-45 FORCES DISCRIM NAT/LISM ORD/FREE SOVEREIGN...POLICY NEW/IDEA WORSHIP 20. PAGE 11 A0229
PEACE INT/ORG COERCE BAL/PWR

N19
FRANCK P.G.,AFGHANISTAN BETWEEN EAST AND WEST: THE ECONOMICS OF COMPETITIVE COEXISTENCE (PAMPHLET). AFGHANISTN USA+45 USA-45 USSR INDUS ECO/TAC INT/TRADE CONTROL NEUTRAL ORD/FREE MARXISM...GEOG 20 UN. PAGE 48 A0977
FOR/AID PLAN DIPLOM ECO/UNDEV

N19
FREEMAN H.A.,COERCION OF STATES IN FEDERAL UNIONS (PAMPHLET). WOR-45 DIPLOM CONTROL COERCE PEACE ORD/FREE...GOV/COMP METH/COMP NAT/COMP PACIFIST 20. PAGE 49 A0994
FEDERAL WAR INT/ORG PACIFISM

N19
HALPERN M.,THE MORALITY AND POLITICS OF INTERVENTION (PAMPHLET). USA+45 INT/ORG FORCES ECO/TAC MORAL ORD/FREE 20 INTERVENT CHRISTIAN. PAGE 61 A1243
POLICY DIPLOM SOVEREIGN DOMIN

N19
MEZERIK A.G.,COLONIALISM AND THE UNITED NATIONS (PAMPHLET). WOR+45 NAT/G ADMIN LEAD WAR CHOOSE EFFICIENCY PEACE ATTIT ORD/FREE...POLICY CHARTS UN COLD/WAR. PAGE 100 A2061
COLONIAL DIPLOM BAL/PWR INT/ORG

N19
VELYAMINOV G.,AFRICA AND THE COMMON MARKET (PAMPHLET). AFR MARKET VOL/ASSN ECO/TAC COLONIAL ORD/FREE...SOCIALIST 20 THIRD/WRLD. PAGE 158 A3227
INT/ORG INT/TRADE SOVEREIGN ECO/UNDEV

B20
HALDANE R.B.,BEFORE THE WAR. MOD/EUR SOCIETY INT/ORG NAT/G DELIB/GP PLAN DOMIN EDU/PROP LEGIT ADMIN COERCE ATTIT DRIVE MORAL ORD/FREE PWR...SOC CONCPT SELF/OBS RECORD BIOG TIME/SEQ. PAGE 60 A1223
POLICY DIPLOM UK

B21
OPPENHEIM L.,THE FUTURE OF INTERNATIONAL LAW. EUR+WWI MOD/EUR LAW LEGIS JUDGE LEGIT ORD/FREE ...JURID TIME/SEQ GEN/LAWS 20. PAGE 112 A2293
INT/ORG CT/SYS INT/LAW

B22
WALSH E.,THE HISTORY AND NATURE OF INTERNATIONAL RELATIONS. ASIA L/A+17C MOD/EUR USA-45 WOR-45 NAT/G FORCES TOP/EX BAL/PWR REGION ATTIT ORD/FREE RESPECT ...CONCPT HIST/WRIT TREND. PAGE 161 A3270
INT/ORG TIME/SEQ DIPLOM

B22
WRIGHT Q.,THE CONTROL OF AMERICAN FOREIGN RELATIONS. USA-45 WOR-45 CONSTN INT/ORG CONSULT LEGIS LEGIT ROUTINE ORD/FREE PWR...POLICY JURID
NAT/G EXEC DIPLOM

CONCPT METH/CNCPT RECORD LEAGUE/NAT 20. PAGE 167 A3402

S23
DEWEY J.,"ETHICS AND INTERNATIONAL RELATIONS." FUT WOR-45 SOCIETY INT/ORG VOL/ASSN DIPLOM LEGIT ORD/FREE...JURID CONCPT GEN/METH 20. PAGE 37 A0752
LAW MORAL

B24
HALL W.E.,A TREATISE ON INTERNATIONAL LAW. WOR-45 CONSTN INT/ORG NAT/G DIPLOM ORD/FREE LEAGUE/NAT 20 TREATY. PAGE 60 A1228
PWR JURID WAR INT/LAW

B24
NAVILLE A.,LIBERTE, EGALITE, SOLIDARITE: ESSAIS D'ANALYSE. STRATA FAM VOL/ASSN INT/TRADE GP/REL MORAL MARXISM SOCISM...PSY TREATY. PAGE 107 A2205
ORD/FREE SOC IDEA/COMP DIPLOM

L25
HUDSON M.,"THE PERMANENT COURT OF INTERNATIONAL JUSTICE AND THE QUESTION OF AMERICAN PARTICIPATION." WOR-45 LEGIT CT/SYS ORD/FREE ...JURID CONCPT TIME/SEQ GEN/LAWS VAL/FREE 20 ICJ. PAGE 68 A1406
INT/ORG ADJUD DIPLOM INT/LAW

B27
LAUTERPACHT H.,PRIVATE LAW SOURCES AND ANALOGIES OF INTERNATIONAL LAW. WOR-45 NAT/G DELIB/GP LEGIT COERCE ATTIT ORD/FREE PWR SOVEREIGN...JURID CONCPT HIST/WRIT TIME/SEQ GEN/METH LEAGUE/NAT 20. PAGE 85 A1748
INT/ORG ADJUD PEACE INT/LAW

B28
BUTLER G.,THE DEVELOPMENT OF INTERNATIONAL LAW. WOR-45 SOCIETY NAT/G KNOWL ORD/FREE PWR...JURID CONCPT HIST/WRIT GEN/LAWS. PAGE 22 A0451
LAW INT/LAW DIPLOM INT/ORG

B28
CORBETT P.E.,CANADA AND WORLD POLITICS. LAW CULTURE SOCIETY STRUCT MARKET INT/ORG FORCES ACT/RES PLAN ECO/TAC LEGIT ORD/FREE PWR RESPECT...SOC CONCPT TIME/SEQ TREND CMN/WLTH 20 LEAGUE/NAT. PAGE 30 A0612
NAT/G CANADA

B28
HOWARD-ELLIS C.,THE ORIGIN, STRUCTURE AND WORKING OF THE LEAGUE OF NATIONS. EUR+WWI MOD/EUR USA-45 CONSTN FORCES LEGIS ECO/TAC LEGIT COERCE ORD/FREE ...JURID SOC CONCPT LEAGUE/NAT 20 ILO ICJ. PAGE 68 A1401
INT/ORG ADJUD

B28
MAIR L.P.,THE PROTECTION OF MINORITIES. EUR+WWI WOR-45 CONSTN INT/ORG NAT/G LEGIT CT/SYS GP/REL RACE/REL DISCRIM ORD/FREE RESPECT...JURID CONCPT TIME/SEQ 20. PAGE 93 A1909
LAW SOVEREIGN

B29
BUELL R.,INTERNATIONAL RELATIONS. WOR+45 WOR-45 CONSTN STRATA FORCES TOP/EX ADMIN ATTIT DRIVE SUPEGO MORAL ORD/FREE PWR SOVEREIGN...JURID SOC CONCPT 20. PAGE 21 A0428
INT/ORG BAL/PWR DIPLOM

B29
DUNN F.,THE PRACTICE AND PROCEDURE OF INTERNATIONAL CONFERENCES. WOR-45 NAT/G DELIB/GP BAL/PWR LEGIT EXEC ROUTINE PEACE ORD/FREE RESPECT...JURID CONCPT METH/CNCPT OBS RECORD TIME/SEQ 20. PAGE 39 A0799
INT/ORG DIPLOM

B29
STURZO L.,THE INTERNATIONAL COMMUNITY AND THE RIGHT OF WAR (TRANS. BY BARBARA BARCLAY CARTER). CULTURE CREATE PROB/SOLV DIPLOM ADJUD CONTROL PEACE PERSON ORD/FREE...INT/LAW IDEA/COMP PACIFIST 20 LEAGUE/NAT. PAGE 140 A2858
INT/ORG PLAN WAR CONCPT

B30
SCHMITT B.E.,THE COMING OF THE WAR, 1914 (2 VOLS.). AUSTRIA FRANCE GERMANY MOD/EUR RUSSIA UK PLAN ROUTINE ORD/FREE. PAGE 128 A2633
WAR DIPLOM

B31
STUART G.H.,THE INTERNATIONAL CITY OF TANGIER. AFR EUR+WWI MOD/EUR MOROCCO CONSTN PROVS CREATE PLAN LEGIT PEACE ORD/FREE PWR...INT/LAW OBS TIME/SEQ CON/ANAL 20 TANGIER. PAGE 139 A2854
LOC/G INT/ORG DIPLOM SOVEREIGN

B32
BLUM L.,PEACE AND DISARMAMENT (TRANS. BY A. WERTH). NAT/G FORCES WORKER DIPLOM AGREE WAR ATTIT AUTHORIT ORD/FREE. PAGE 16 A0322
SOCIALIST PEACE INT/ORG ARMS/CONT

C32
MARRARO H.R.,"AMERICAN OPINION ON THE UNIFICATION OF ITALY." ITALY MOD/EUR USA-45 FORCES DIPLOM PRESS REV CATHISM...BIOG 19 PRESIDENT. PAGE 95 A1944
BIBLIOG/A NAT/LISM ATTIT ORD/FREE

B33
FERRERO G.,PEACE AND WAR (TRANS. BY BERTHA PRITCHARD). CULTURE FINAN SECT ATTIT SUPEGO MORAL ORD/FREE CONSERVE POPULISM SOCISM POLICY. PAGE 45 A0922
WAR PEACE DIPLOM PROB/SOLV

B33
LAUTERPACHT H.,THE FUNCTION OF LAW IN THE INTERNATIONAL COMMUNITY. WOR-45 NAT/G FORCES CREATE DOMIN LEGIT COERCE WAR PEACE ATTIT ORD/FREE PWR SOVEREIGN...JURID CONCPT METH/CNCPT TIME/SEQ GEN/LAWS GEN/METH LEAGUE/NAT TOT/POP VAL/FREE 20. PAGE 85 A1749
INT/ORG LAW INT/LAW

B33
REID H.D.,RECUEIL DES COURS; TOME 45: LES SERVITUDES INTERNATIONALES III. FRANCE CONSTN DELIB/GP PRESS CONTROL REV WAR CHOOSE PEACE MORAL MARITIME TREATY. PAGE 120 A2457
ORD/FREE DIPLOM LAW

B34
GRAHAM F.D.,PROTECTIVE TARIFFS. FUT USA+45 WOR-45 INDUS MARKET VOL/ASSN PLAN CAP/ISM ECO/TAC PEACE ATTIT DRIVE HEALTH ORD/FREE...OBS TREND GEN/LAWS 20. PAGE 55 A1124
INT/ORG TARIFFS

B35
HUDSON M.,BY PACIFIC MEANS. WOR-45 EDU/PROP ORD/FREE...CONCPT TIME/SEQ GEN/LAWS LEAGUE/NAT TOT/POP 20 TREATY. PAGE 68 A1407
INT/ORG CT/SYS PEACE

B35
MARRIOTT J.A.,DICTATORSHIP AND DEMOCRACY. GERMANY GREECE UK CHIEF DIPLOM DOMIN LEGIT PEACE ORD/FREE CONSERVE...TREND ROME HITLER/A. PAGE 95 A1946
TOTALISM POPULISM PLURIST NAT/G

B37
KOHN H.,FORCE OR REASON; ISSUES OF THE TWENTIETH CENTURY. WOR+45 NAT/G DIPLOM WAR DRIVE ORD/FREE ALL/IDEOS FASCISM PLURISM...POLICY IDEA/COMP 20. PAGE 81 A1660
COERCE DOMIN RATIONAL COLONIAL

B39
BENES E.,INTERNATIONAL SECURITY. GERMANY UK NAT/G DELIB/GP PLAN BAL/PWR ATTIT ORD/FREE PWR LEAGUE/NAT 20 TREATY. PAGE 13 A0267
EUR+WWI INT/ORG WAR

B39
BROWN J.F.,CONTEMPORARY WORLD POLITICS. WOR-45 NAT/G PLAN BAL/PWR EDU/PROP LEGIT REGION NAT/LISM ORD/FREE PWR SOVEREIGN...POLICY CONCPT HIST/WRIT TIME/SEQ GEN/LAWS LEAGUE/NAT. PAGE 20 A0403
INT/ORG DIPLOM PEACE

B39
MARRIOTT J.,COMMONWEALTH OR ANARCHY: A SURVEY OF PROJECTS OF PEACE. WOR-45 STRATA DOMIN ATTIT ORD/FREE PWR...TRADIT TIME/SEQ GEN/METH 16/20 CMN/WLTH. PAGE 95 A1945
FUT INT/ORG PEACE

B39
MAXWELL B.W.,INTERNATIONAL RELATIONS. EUR+WWI WOR-45 NAT/G CONSULT DIPLOM LEGIT ADJUD NAT/LISM ATTIT ORD/FREE SOVEREIGN...JURID LEAGUE/NAT TOT/POP VAL/FREE 20. PAGE 97 A1981
INT/ORG

B39
ZIMMERN A.,THE LEAGUE OF NATIONS AND THE RULE OF LAW. WOR-45 STRUCT NAT/G DELIB/GP EX/STRUC BAL/PWR DOMIN LEGIT COERCE ORD/FREE PWR...POLICY RECORD LEAGUE/NAT TOT/POP VAL/FREE 20 LEAGUE/NAT. PAGE 170 A3453
INT/ORG LAW DIPLOM

B39
ZIMMERN A.,MODERN POLITICAL DOCTRINE. WOR-45 CULTURE SOCIETY ECO/UNDEV DELIB/GP EX/STRUC CREATE DOMIN COERCE NAT/LISM ATTIT RIGID/FLEX ORD/FREE PWR WEALTH...POLICY CONCPT OBS TIME/SEQ TREND TOT/POP LEAGUE/NAT 20. PAGE 170 A3454
NAT/G ECO/TAC BAL/PWR INT/TRADE

B40
BOGGS S.W.,INTERNATIONAL BOUNDARIES. WOR-45 SOCIETY ECO/DEV INT/ORG NAT/G NEIGH LEGIT PERSON ORD/FREE PWR...POLICY GEOG MYTH LEAGUE/NAT 20. PAGE 16 A0329
ATTIT CONCPT NAT/LISM

B40
MIDDLEBUSH F.,ELEMENTS OF INTERNATIONAL RELATIONS. WOR-45 PROVS CONSULT EDU/PROP LEGIT WAR NAT/LISM ATTIT KNOWL MORAL ORD/FREE PWR...JURID LEAGUE/NAT TOT/POP VAL/FREE. PAGE 101 A2067
NAT/G INT/ORG PEACE DIPLOM

B41
BIRDSALL P.,VERSAILLES TWENTY YEARS AFTER. MOD/EUR POL/PAR CHIEF CONSULT FORCES LEGIS REPAR PEACE ORD/FREE...BIBLIOG 20 PRESIDENT TREATY. PAGE 14 A0290
DIPLOM NAT/LISM WAR

B41
MCCLURE W.,INTERNATIONAL EXECUTIVE AGREEMENTS. USA-45 WOR-45 INT/ORG NAT/G DELIB/GP ADJUD ROUTINE ORD/FREE PWR...TIME/SEQ TREND CON/ANAL. PAGE 97 A2000
TOP/EX DIPLOM

B41
NIEMEYER G.,LAW WITHOUT FORCE: THE FUNCTION OF POLITICS IN INTERNATIONAL LAW. PLAN INSPECT DIPLOM REPAR LEGIT ADJUD WAR ORD/FREE...IDEA/COMP METH/COMP GEN/LAWS 20. PAGE 109 A2240
COERCE LAW PWR INT/LAW

B41
WHITAKER A.P.,THE UNITED STATES AND THE INDEPENDENCE OF LATIN AMERICA, 1800-1830. PORTUGAL SPAIN USA-45 COLONIAL REGION SOVEREIGN...POLICY TIME/SEQ BIBLIOG/A 18/20. PAGE 163 A3329
DIPLOM L/A+17C CONCPT ORD/FREE

L41
COMM. STUDY ORGAN. PEACE,"PRELIMINARY REPORT." WOR-45 SOCIETY DELIB/GP PLAN LEGIT WAR ORD/FREE ...CONCPT TOT/POP 20. PAGE 28 A0574
INT/ORG ACT/RES PEACE

L41
COMM. STUDY ORGAN. PEACE,"ORGANIZATION OF PEACE." USA-45 WOR-45 STRATA NAT/G ACT/RES DIPLOM ECO/TAC EDU/PROP ADJUD ATTIT ORD/FREE PWR...SOC CONCPT ANTHOL LEAGUE/NAT 20. PAGE 28 A0575
INT/ORG PLAN PEACE

S41
WRIGHT Q.,"FUNDAMENTAL PROBLEMS OF INTERNATIONAL
INT/ORG

"ORGANIZATION." UNIV WOR-45 STRUCT FORCES ACT/RES CREATE DOMIN EDU/PROP LEGIT REGION NAT/LISM ORD/FREE PWR RESPECT SOVEREIGN...JURID SOC CONCPT METH/CNCPT TIME/SEQ 20. PAGE 167 A3405
ATTIT PEACE

B42
BONNET H.,THE UNITED NATIONS, WHAT THEY ARE, WHAT THEY MAY BECOME. FUT WOR-45 CREATE BAL/PWR ECO/TAC PWR...TREND GEN/LAWS 20. PAGE 16 A0335
INT/ORG ORD/FREE

B42
JACKSON M.V.,EUROPEAN POWERS AND SOUTH-EAST AFRICA: A STUDY OF INTERNATIONAL RELATIONS ON SOUTH-EAST COAST OF AFRICA, 1796-1856. AFR FRANCE PORTUGAL SOUTH/AFR UK USA-45 FORCES INT/TRADE PWR...CHARTS BIBLIOG 18/19 TREATY. PAGE 72 A1477
DOMIN POLICY ORD/FREE DIPLOM

B42
KELSEN H.,LAW AND PEACE IN INTERNATIONAL RELATIONS. FUT WOR-45 NAT/G DELIB/GP DIPLOM LEGIT RIGID/FLEX ORD/FREE SOVEREIGN...JURID CONCPT TREND STERTYP GEN/LAWS LEAGUE/NAT 20. PAGE 77 A1580
INT/ORG ADJUD PEACE INT/LAW

L42
SHOTWELL J.,"LESSON OF THE LAST WORLD WAR." EUR+WWI MOD/EUR USA-45 SOCIETY ECO/UNDEV INDUS VOL/ASSN CONSULT ACT/RES CREATE CAP/ISM INT/TRADE DRIVE ALL/VALS...CONCPT NEW/IDEA SELF/OBS GEN/LAWS LEAGUE/NAT NAZI 20. PAGE 132 A2708
INT/ORG ORD/FREE

B43
BEMIS S.F.,THE LATIN AMERICAN POLICY OF THE UNITED STATES: AN HISTORICAL INTERPRETATION. INT/ORG AGREE COLONIAL WAR PEACE ATTIT ORD/FREE...POLICY INT/LAW CHARTS 18/20 MEXIC/AMER WILSON/W MONROE/DOC. PAGE 13 A0265
DIPLOM SOVEREIGN USA-45 L/A+17C

B43
LIPPMANN W.,US FOREIGN POLICY: SHIELD OF THE REPUBLIC. USA-45 WOR-45 CULTURE INT/ORG POL/PAR CREATE BAL/PWR DOMIN EDU/PROP WAR ORD/FREE PWR ...PLURIST CONCPT TREND CON/ANAL 20. PAGE 89 A1827
NAT/G DIPLOM PEACE

B43
MC DOWELL R.B.,IRISH PUBLIC OPINION, 1750-1800. IRELAND CONSTN VOL/ASSN WORKER ORD/FREE CATHISM CONSERVE...POLICY IDEA/COMP BIBLIOG 18/ PARLIAMENT. PAGE 97 A1992
ATTIT NAT/G DIPLOM REV

B43
SERENI A.P.,THE ITALIAN CONCEPTION OF INTERNATIONAL LAW. EUR+WWI MOD/EUR INT/ORG NAT/G DOMIN COERCE ORD/FREE FASCISM...OBS/ENVIR TREND 20. PAGE 131 A2686
LAW TIME/SEQ INT/LAW ITALY

B43
WALKER E.A.,BRITAIN AND SOUTH AFRICA. SOUTH/AFR POL/PAR GP/REL RACE/REL ATTIT ORD/FREE 17/20. PAGE 160 A3264
COLONIAL WAR DIPLOM SOVEREIGN

C43
BENTHAM J.,"PRINCIPLES OF INTERNATIONAL LAW" IN J. BOWRING, ED., THE WORKS OF JEREMY BENTHAM." UNIV NAT/G PLAN PROB/SOLV DIPLOM CONTROL SANCTION MORAL ORD/FREE PWR SOVEREIGN 19. PAGE 13 A0270
INT/LAW JURID WAR PEACE

B44
ADLER M.J.,HOW TO THINK ABOUT WAR AND PEACE. WOR-45 LAW SOCIETY EX/STRUC DIPLOM KNOWL ORD/FREE...POLICY TREND GEN/LAWS 20. PAGE 4 A0092
INT/ORG CREATE ARMS/CONT PEACE

B44
BARTLETT R.J.,THE LEAGUE TO ENFORCE PEACE. FUT USA-45 NAT/G POL/PAR CREATE EDU/PROP ADMIN RIGID/FLEX PWR...CONCPT TREND GEN/METH LEAGUE/NAT 20. PAGE 11 A0231
INT/ORG ORD/FREE DIPLOM

B44
BRIERLY J.L.,THE OUTLOOK FOR INTERNATIONAL LAW. FUT WOR-45 CONSTN NAT/G VOL/ASSN FORCES ECO/TAC DOMIN LEGIT ADJUD ROUTINE PEACE ORD/FREE...INT/LAW JURID METH LEAGUE/NAT 20. PAGE 18 A0376
INT/ORG LAW

B44
DAVIS H.E.,PIONEERS IN WORLD ORDER. WOR-45 CONSTN ECO/TAC DOMIN EDU/PROP LEGIT ADJUD ADMIN ARMS/CONT CHOOSE KNOWL ORD/FREE...POLICY JURID SOC STAT OBS CENSUS TIME/SEQ ANTHOL LEAGUE/NAT 20. PAGE 34 A0691
INT/ORG ROUTINE

B44
FULLER G.H.,MILITARY GOVERNMENT: A LIST OF REFERENCES (A PAMPHLET). ITALY UK USA-45 WOR-45 LAW FORCES DOMIN ADMIN ARMS/CONT ORD/FREE PWR ...DECISION 20 CHINJAP. PAGE 50 A1023
BIBLIOG DIPLOM CIVMIL/REL SOVEREIGN

B44
HUDSON M.,INTERNATIONAL TRIBUNALS PAST AND FUTURE. FUT WOR-45 LAW EDU/PROP ADJUD ORD/FREE...CONCPT TIME/SEQ TREND GEN/LAWS TOT/POP VAL/FREE 18/20. PAGE 69 A1408
INT/ORG STRUCT INT/LAW

B44
LIPPMANN W.,US WAR AIMS. USA-45 DIPLOM ATTIT MORAL ORD/FREE PWR...CONCPT TIME/SEQ GEN/LAWS TOT/POP 20. PAGE 89 A1828
FUT INT/ORG PEACE WAR

B44
MACIVER R.M.,TOWARDS AN ABIDING PEACE. USA-45 ECO/TAC EDU/PROP DRIVE ORD/FREE PWR WEALTH...CONCPT TIME/SEQ GEN/METH TOT/POP 20. PAGE 92 A1890
INT/ORG PEACE INT/LAW

C44
SUAREZ F.,"ON WAR" (1621) IN SELECTIONS FROM THREE WORKS, VOL. I." NAT/G SECT CHIEF DIPLOM LEGIT MORAL PWR...POLICY INT/LAW 17. PAGE 140 A2859
WAR REV ORD/FREE CATH

B45
BEVERIDGE W.,THE PRICE OF PEACE. GERMANY UK WOR+45 WOR-45 NAT/G FORCES CREATE LEGIT REGION WAR ATTIT KNOWL ORD/FREE PWR...POLICY NEW/IDEA GEN/LAWS LEAGUE/NAT 20 TREATY. PAGE 14 A0284
INT/ORG TREND PEACE

B45
CARR E.H.,NATIONALISM AND AFTER. FUT WOR-45 NAT/G VOL/ASSN EX/STRUC PLAN ROUTINE TOTALISM ATTIT HEALTH ORD/FREE PWR...CONCPT 20. PAGE 25 A0499
INT/ORG TREND NAT/LISM REGION

B45
HILL N.,CLAIMS TO TERRITORY IN INTERNATIONAL LAW AND RELATIONS. WOR-45 NAT/G DOMIN EDU/PROP LEGIT REGION ROUTINE ORD/FREE PWR WEALTH...GEOG INT/LAW JURID 20. PAGE 65 A1332
INT/ORG ADJUD SOVEREIGN

B45
NELSON M.F.,KOREA AND THE OLD ORDERS IN EASTERN ASIA. ASIA FRANCE KOREA RUSSIA DELIB/GP INT/TRADE DOMIN CONTROL WAR ORD/FREE...POLICY BIBLIOG. PAGE 108 A2218
DIPLOM BAL/PWR ATTIT CONSERVE

B45
PASTUHOV V.D.,A GUIDE TO THE PRACTICE OF INTERNATIONAL CONFERENCES. WOR+45 PLAN LEGIT ORD/FREE...MGT OBS RECORD VAL/FREE ILO LEAGUE/NAT 20. PAGE 114 A2338
INT/ORG DELIB/GP

B45
RANSHOFFEN-WERTHEIMER EF,THE INTERNATIONAL SECRETARIAT: A GREAT EXPERIMENT IN INTERNATIONAL ADMINISTRATION. EUR+WWI FUT CONSTN FACE/GP CONSULT DELIB/GP ACT/RES ADMIN ROUTINE PEACE ORD/FREE...MGT RECORD ORG/CHARTS LEAGUE/NAT WORK 20. PAGE 119 A2442
INT/ORG EXEC

B45
TINGSTERN H.,PEACE AND SECURITY AFTER WW II. WOR-45 DELIB/GP TOP/EX LEGIT CT/SYS COERCE PEACE ATTIT PERCEPT...CONCPT LEAGUE/NAT 20. PAGE 144 A2943
INT/ORG ORD/FREE WAR INT/LAW

B45
WEST R.,CONSCIENCE AND SOCIETY: A STUDY OF THE PSYCHOLOGICAL PREREQUISITES OF LAW AND ORDER. FUT UNIV LAW SOCIETY STRUCT DIPLOM WAR PERS/REL SUPEGO ...SOC 20. PAGE 163 A3321
COERCE INT/LAW ORD/FREE PERSON

C45
NELSON M.F.,"KOREA AND THE OLD ORDERS IN EASTERN ASIA." KOREA WOR-45 DELIB/GP INT/TRADE DOMIN CONTROL WAR ATTIT ORD/FREE CONSERVE...POLICY TREATY. PAGE 108 A2217
BIBLIOG DIPLOM BAL/PWR ASIA

B46
BLUM L.,FOR ALL MANKIND (TRANS. BY W. PICKLES). FRANCE GERMANY USSR LAW SOCIETY STRUCT POL/PAR WORKER DIPLOM DOMIN CHOOSE ORD/FREE FASCISM 20. PAGE 16 A0323
POPULISM SOCIALIST NAT/G WAR

B46
BRODIE B.,THE OBSOLETE WEAPON: ATOMIC POWER AND WORLD ORDER. COM USA+45 USSR WOR+45 DELIB/GP PLAN ORD/FREE PWR...CONCPT TIME/SEQ TREND UN 20. PAGE 19 A0380
INT/ORG TEC/DEV ARMS/CONT NUC/PWR

B46
KEETON G.W.,MAKING INTERNATIONAL LAW WORK. FUT WOR-45 NAT/G DELIB/GP FORCES LEGIT COERCE PEACE ATTIT RIGID/FLEX ORD/FREE PWR...JURID CONCPT HIST/WRIT GEN/METH LEAGUE/NAT 20. PAGE 77 A1578
INT/ORG ADJUD INT/LAW

B46
LOWENSTEIN R.,POLITICAL RECONSTRUCTION. WOR+45 EX/STRUC EDU/PROP NAT/LISM ATTIT KNOWL ORD/FREE PWR ...SOCIALIST CONCPT GEN/LAWS TOT/POP 20. PAGE 91 A1869
FUT INT/ORG DIPLOM

B46
STURZO D.L.,NATIONALISM AND INTERNATIONALISM. WOR-45 INT/ORG LABOR NAT/G POL/PAR TOTALISM MORAL ORD/FREE FASCISM...MAJORIT 19/20 UN LEAGUE/NAT MUSSOLIN/B. PAGE 140 A2857
NAT/LISM DIPLOM WAR PEACE

B47
BROOKINGS INST.,MAJOR PROBLEMS OF UNITED STATES FOREIGN POLICY. USA+45 WOR+45 STRUCT ECO/DEV ECO/UNDEV INT/ORG NAT/G POL/PAR VOL/ASSN DELIB/GP FORCES ECO/TAC LEGIT COERCE ORD/FREE PWR WEALTH ...POLICY STAT TREND CHARTS TOT/POP. PAGE 19 A0392
ACT/RES DIPLOM

B47
FEIS H.,SEEN FROM E A, THREE INTERNATIONAL EPISODES. EUR+WWI ITALY USA-45 WOR-45 AGRI INT/ORG NAT/G INT/TRADE LEGIT EXEC ATTIT ORD/FREE...POLICY LEAGUE/NAT TOT/POP 20 OIL. PAGE 44 A0908
EXTR/IND ECO/TAC DIPLOM

B47
HEIMANN E.,FREEDOM AND ORDER: LESSONS FROM THE WAR. WOR-45 CONSTN FORCES CHOOSE CIVMIL/REL PERSON ALL/IDEOS SOCISM...SOC IDEA/COMP WORSHIP 20. PAGE 64 A1308
NAT/G SOCIETY ORD/FREE DIPLOM

B47
HYDE C.C.,INTERNATIONAL LAW, CHIEFLY AS INTERPRETED AND APPLIED BY THE UNITED STATES (3 VOLS., 2ND REV.
INT/LAW DIPLOM

ED.). USA-45 WOR+45 WOR-45 INT/ORG CT/SYS WAR NAT/LISM PEACE ORD/FREE...JURID 19/20 TREATY. PAGE 69 A1426 — NAT/G POLICY

B47
NIEBUHR R.,THE CHILDREN OF LIGHT AND THE CHILDREN OF DARKNESS: A VINDICATION OF DEMOCRACY AND CRITIQUE OF TRADITIONAL DEFENSE. UNIV STRUCT NAT/G SECT INGP/REL OWN PEACE ORD/FREE MARXISM ...IDEA/COMP GEN/LAWS 20 CHRISTIAN. PAGE 109 A2235 — POPULISM DIPLOM NEIGH GP/REL

L47
BRUNER J.S.,"TOWARD A COMMON GROUND-INTERNATIONAL SOCIAL SCIENCE." FUT WOR+45 INTELL R+D NAT/G VOL/ASSN CONSULT DELIB/GP ACT/RES CREATE PLAN TEC/DEV ATTIT ORD/FREE...PSY SOC CONCPT ANTHOL UNESCO 20. PAGE 20 A0410 — INT/ORG KNOWL

L47
COMM. STUDY ORGAN. PEACE,"SECURITY THROUGH THE UNITED NATIONS." COM FUT WOR+45 TOP/EX ACT/RES BAL/PWR ARMS/CONT NUC/PWR...CONCPT GEN/LAWS UN TOT/POP COLD/WAR 20. PAGE 28 A0577 — INT/ORG ORD/FREE PEACE

N47
FOX W.T.R.,UNITED STATES POLICY IN A TWO POWER WORLD. COM USA+45 USSR FORCES DOMIN AGREE NEUTRAL NUC/PWR ORD/FREE SOVEREIGN 20 COLD/WAR TREATY EUROPE/W INTERVENT. PAGE 48 A0972 — DIPLOM FOR/AID POLICY

B48
CHAMBERLAIN L.H.,AMERICAN FOREIGN POLICY. FUT USA+45 USA-45 WOR+45 WOR-45 NAT/G LEGIS TOP/EX ECO/TAC FOR/AID EDU/PROP EXEC ATTIT ORD/FREE ...JURID TREND TOT/POP 20. PAGE 25 A0517 — CONSTN DIPLOM

B48
CHURCHILL W.,THE GATHERING STORM. UK WOR-45 INT/ORG NAT/G FORCES TOP/EX DIPLOM ECO/TAC COERCE ATTIT ORD/FREE PWR WEALTH...POLICY SELF/OBS RECORD NAZI PARLIAMENT 20. PAGE 26 A0538 — BIOG

B48
COTTRELL L.S. JR.,AMERICAN PUBLIC OPINION ON WORLD AFFAIRS IN THE ATOMIC AGE. USA+45 CULTURE INT/ORG NAT/G DIPLOM EDU/PROP PEACE RIGID/FLEX ORD/FREE ...POLICY SOC CONCPT STAND/INT TOT/POP 20. PAGE 31 A0633 — SOCIETY ATTIT ARMS/CONT NUC/PWR

B48
VISSON A.,AS OTHERS SEE US. EUR+WWI FRANCE UK USA+45 CULTURE INTELL SOCIETY STRATA NAT/G POL/PAR FOR/AID ATTIT DRIVE LOVE ORD/FREE RESPECT WEALTH ...PLURIST SOC OBS TOT/POP 20. PAGE 159 A3244 — USA-45 PERCEPT

B49
KAFKA G.,FREIHEIT UND ANARCHIE. SECT COERCE DETER WAR ATTIT...IDEA/COMP 20 NATO. PAGE 75 A1545 — CONCPT ORD/FREE JURID INT/ORG

L49
COMM. STUDY ORGAN. PEACE,"A TEN YEAR RECORD, 1939-1949." FUT WOR+45 LAW R+D CONSULT DELIB/GP CREATE LEGIT ROUTINE ORD/FREE...TIME/SEQ UN 20. PAGE 28 A0578 — INT/ORG CONSTN PEACE

S49
DUNN F.,"THE PRESENT COURSE OF INTERNATIONAL RELATIONS RESEARCH." WOR+45 WOR-45 SOCIETY R+D INT/ORG WAR PERSON ORD/FREE...POLICY PSY SOC GEN/LAWS 20. PAGE 39 A0800 — CONCPT GEN/METH DIPLOM

B50
BROOKINGS INSTITUTION,MAJOR PROBLEMS OF UNITED STATES FOREIGN POLICY. AFR ASIA INDIA UK USA+45 USSR BAL/PWR FOR/AID WAR PEACE TOTALISM MARXISM SOCISM 20 CHINJAP COLD/WAR. PAGE 19 A0393 — DIPLOM POLICY ORD/FREE

B50
CHASE E.P.,THE UNITED NATIONS IN ACTION. WOR+45 CONSTN DELIB/GP LEGIT ROUTINE COERCE PEACE ORD/FREE PWR...CON/ANAL GEN/LAWS UN 20. PAGE 26 A0524 — INT/ORG STRUCT ARMS/CONT

B50
CHURCHILL W.,TRIUMPH AND TRAGEDY. UK WOR-45 INT/ORG NAT/G DELIB/GP FORCES TOP/EX DIPLOM COERCE CHOOSE ATTIT ORD/FREE PWR WEALTH...SELF/OBS CHARTS NAZI 20. PAGE 26 A0539 — BIOG PEACE WAR

B50
DE ARECHAGA E.J.,VOTING AND THE HANDLING OF DISPUTES IN THE SECURITY COUNCIL. WOR+45 CONSTN DIPLOM COERCE ORD/FREE...RECORD CON/ANAL GEN/METH COLD/WAR UN 20. PAGE 34 A0696 — INT/ORG PWR

B50
DE RUSETT A.,STRENGTHENING THE FRAMEWORK OF PEACE. WOR+45 VOL/ASSN FORCES CREATE INSPECT ADJUD CONTROL WAR EQUILIB FEDERAL ORD/FREE 20 UN EUROPE. PAGE 35 A0711 — INT/ORG DIPLOM PEACE METH/COMP

B50
DUCLOS P.,L'EVOLUTION DES RAPPORTS POLITIQUES DEPUIS 1750 (LIBERTE, INTEGRATION, UNITE). LAW INT/ORG FEDERAL TOTALISM ATTIT PWR...MAJORIT BIBLIOG 18/20 PARLIAMENT EUROPE. PAGE 39 A0792 — ORD/FREE DIPLOM NAT/G GOV/COMP

B50
DULLES J.F.,WAR OR PEACE. CHINA/COM USA+45 USSR INT/ORG SECT FORCES PLAN NUC/PWR WAR CENTRAL MARXISM...POLICY 20 UN ROOSEVLT/F STALIN/J. PAGE 39 A0797 — PEACE DIPLOM TREND ORD/FREE

B50
FEIS H.,THE ROAD TO PEARL HARBOR. USA-45 WOR-45 SOCIETY NAT/G FORCES WAR ORD/FREE 20 CHINJAP TREATY. PAGE 44 A0909 — DIPLOM POLICY ATTIT

B50
JIMENEZ E.,VOTING AND HANDLING OF DISPUTES IN THE SECURITY COUNCIL. WOR+45 CONSTN INT/ORG DIPLOM LEGIT DETER CHOOSE MORAL ORD/FREE PWR...JURID TIME/SEQ COLD/WAR UN 20. PAGE 74 A1517 — DELIB/GP ROUTINE

B50
LEVI W.,FUNDAMENTALS OF WORLD ORGANIZATION. WOR+45 WOR-45 CULTURE ECO/TAC GIVE RECEIVE PERSON WEALTH ...METH/COMP 19/20 UN LEAGUE/NAT. PAGE 88 A1793 — INT/ORG PEACE ORD/FREE DIPLOM

B50
LINCOLN G.,ECONOMICS OF NATIONAL SECURITY. USA+45 ELITES COM/IND DIST/IND INDUS NAT/G VOL/ASSN DELIB/GP EX/STRUC FOR/AID EDU/PROP COERCE NUC/PWR WAR ATTIT KNOWL ORD/FREE PWR COLD/WAR TOT/POP VAL/FREE 20. PAGE 89 A1818 — FORCES ECO/TAC

B50
ROSS A.,CONSTITUTION OF THE UNITED NATIONS. CONSTN CONSULT DELIB/GP ECO/TAC...INT/LAW JURID 20 UN LEAGUE/NAT. PAGE 124 A2540 — PEACE DIPLOM ORD/FREE INT/ORG

B51
BISSAINTHE M.,DICTIONNAIRE DE BIBLIOGRAPHIE HAITIENNE. HAITI ELITES AGRI LEGIS DIPLOM INT/TRADE WRITING ORD/FREE CATHISM...ART/METH GEOG 19/20 NEGRO TREATY. PAGE 15 A0295 — BIBLIOG L/A+17C SOCIETY NAT/G

B51
BROGAN D.W.,THE PRICE OF REVOLUTION. FRANCE USA+45 USA-45 USSR CONSTN NAT/G DIPLOM COLONIAL NAT/LISM ORD/FREE POPULISM...CONCPT 18/20 PRE/US/AM. PAGE 19 A0386 — REV METH/COMP COST MARXISM

B51
CARRINGTON C.E.,THE LIQUIDATION OF THE BRITISH EMPIRE. AFR NAT/G INT/TRADE COLONIAL RACE/REL ATTIT ORD/FREE...POLICY NAT/COMP 20 CMN/WLTH. PAGE 25 A0501 — SOVEREIGN NAT/LISM DIPLOM GP/REL

B51
HAVILAND H.F.,THE POLITICAL ROLE OF THE GENERAL ASSEMBLY. WOR+45 DELIB/GP EDU/PROP PEACE RIGID/FLEX PWR...CONCPT TIME/SEQ GEN/LAWS UN VAL/FREE 20. PAGE 63 A1290 — INT/ORG ORD/FREE DIPLOM

B51
HOLBORN H.,THE POLITICAL COLLAPSE OF EUROPE. EUR+WWI MOD/EUR USA-45 BAL/PWR PEACE POLICY. PAGE 66 A1364 — DIPLOM ORD/FREE WAR

B51
KELSEN H.,THE LAW OF THE UNITED NATIONS. WOR+45 STRUCT RIGID/FLEX ORD/FREE...INT/LAW JURID CONCPT CON/ANAL GEN/METH UN TOT/POP VAL/FREE 20. PAGE 77 A1581 — INT/ORG ADJUD

B51
MACLAURIN J.,THE UNITED NATIONS AND POWER POLITICS. WOR+45 CONSULT EDU/PROP LEGIT ADJUD EXEC MORAL ORD/FREE...HUM JURID CONCPT RECORD TIME/SEQ UN COLD/WAR 20. PAGE 93 A1896 — INT/ORG ROUTINE

B51
MCKEON R.,DEMOCRACY IN A WORLD OF TENSION. UNIV LAW INTELL STRUCT R+D INT/ORG SCHOOL EDU/PROP LEGIT ATTIT DRIVE PERCEPT PERSON...POLICY JURID PSY SOC CONCPT METH/CNCPT OBS UNESCO TOT/POP VAL/FREE. PAGE 98 A2015 — SOCIETY ALL/VALS ORD/FREE

B51
SWISHER C.B.,THE THEORY AND PRACTICE OF AMERICAN NATIONAL GOVERNMENT. CULTURE LEGIS DIPLOM ADJUD ADMIN WAR PEACE ORD/FREE...MAJORIT 17/20. PAGE 140 A2872 — CONSTN NAT/G GOV/REL GEN/LAWS

B51
YOUNG T.C.,NEAR EASTERN CULTURE AND SOCIETY. ISLAM ECO/UNDEV SECT WRITING ATTIT HABITAT ORD/FREE 20. PAGE 169 A3438 — CULTURE STRUCT REGION DIPLOM

L51
KELSEN H.,"RECENT TRENDS IN THE LAW OF THE UNITED NATIONS." KOREA WOR+45 CONSTN LEGIS DIPLOM LEGIT DETER WAR RIGID/FLEX HEALTH ORD/FREE RESPECT ...JURID CON/ANAL UN VAL/FREE 20 NATO. PAGE 77 A1582 — INT/ORG LAW INT/LAW

L51
LISSITZYN O.J.,"THE INTERNATIONAL COURT OF JUSTICE." WOR+45 INT/ORG LEGIT ORD/FREE...CONCPT TIME/SEQ TREND GEN/LAWS VAL/FREE 20 ICJ. PAGE 90 A1839 — ADJUD JURID INT/LAW

C51
LEONARD L.L.,"INTERNATIONAL ORGANIZATION (1ST ED.)" WOR+45 FINAN DELIB/GP ECO/TAC GIVE DOMIN SANCTION PEACE BIO/SOC ORD/FREE...INT/LAW 20 UN LEAGUE/NAT. PAGE 87 A1779 — BIBLIOG POLICY DIPLOM INT/ORG

B52
BARR S.,CITIZENS OF THE WORLD. USA+45 WOR+45 CULTURE FORCES LEGIS ACT/RES BAL/PWR LEGIT PEACE ATTIT ORD/FREE PWR...PLURIST CONCPT OBS TIME/SEQ COLD/WAR 20. PAGE 11 A0227 — NAT/G INT/ORG DIPLOM

B52
JACKSON E.,MEETING OF THE MINDS: A WAY TO PEACE THROUGH MEDIATION. WOR+45 INDUS INT/ORG NAT/G DELIB/GP DIPLOM EDU/PROP LEGIT ORD/FREE...NEW/IDEA SELF/OBS TIME/SEQ CHARTS GEN/LAWS TOT/POP 20 UN TREATY. PAGE 72 A1474
LABOR JUDGE

B52
KELSEN H.,PRINCIPLES OF INTERNATIONAL LAW. WOR+45 WOR-45 INT/ORG ORD/FREE...JURID GEN/LAWS TOT/POP 20. PAGE 77 A1583
ADJUD CONSTN INT/LAW

B52
U OF MICH SURVEY RESEARCH CTR,AMERICA'S ROLE IN WORLD AFFAIRS. ASIA COM EUR+WWI USA+45 USSR FOR/AID WAR AUTHORIT ORD/FREE...DEEP/QU 20. PAGE 146 A2986
DIPLOM NAT/G ROLE POLICY

L52
NIEBUHR R.,"THE MORAL IMPLICATIONS OF LOYALTY TO THE UNITED NATIONS." WOR+45 WOR-45 SOCIETY ECO/DEV INT/ORG VOL/ASSN PEACE ATTIT PERSON LOVE ORD/FREE PWR RESPECT...CONCPT UN TOT/POP COLD/WAR UNESCO 20. PAGE 109 A2236
SUPEGO GEN/LAWS

S52
HAAS E.B.,"THE RECONCILIATION OF CONFLICT, COLONIAL POLICY AIMS: ACCEPTANCE OF THE LEAGUE OF NATIONS MANDATE SYSTEM." FRANCE GERMANY UK WOR+45 WOR-45 LEGIT ATTIT DRIVE ORD/FREE...OLD/LIB INT SYS/QU TIME/SEQ TREND LEAGUE/NAT 20. PAGE 58 A1201
INT/ORG COLONIAL

B53
LANGER W.L.,THE UNDECLARED WAR, 1940-1941. EUR+WWI GERMANY USA-45 USSR AIR FORCES TEC/DEV CONFER CONTROL COERCE PERCEPT ORD/FREE PWR 20 CHINJAP EUROPE. PAGE 84 A1727
WAR POLICY DIPLOM

B53
MANSERGH N.,DOCUMENTS AND SPEECHES ON BRITISH COMMONWEALTH AFFAIRS 1931-1952. INDIA IRELAND PAKISTAN UK CONSTN POL/PAR CHIEF FORCES COLONIAL ORD/FREE SOVEREIGN...JURID 20 COMMONWLTH. PAGE 94 A1929
BIBLIOG/A DIPLOM ECO/TAC

B53
MARITAIN J.,L'HOMME ET L'ETAT. SECT DIPLOM GP/REL PEACE ORD/FREE...IDEA/COMP 17/20 CHURCH/STA NATURL/LAW. PAGE 95 A1940
CONCPT NAT/G SOVEREIGN COERCE

B53
OPPENHEIM L.,INTERNATIONAL LAW: A TREATISE (7TH ED., 2 VOLS.). LAW CONSTN PROB/SOLV INT/TRADE ADJUD AGREE NEUTRAL WAR ORD/FREE SOVEREIGN...BIBLIOG 20 LEAGUE/NAT UN ILO. PAGE 112 A2294
INT/LAW INT/ORG DIPLOM

B53
ROSCIO J.G.,OBRAS. L/A+17C SPAIN DIPLOM REV WAR NAT/LISM TOTALISM PWR SOVEREIGN 19. PAGE 123 A2527
ORD/FREE COLONIAL NAT/G PHIL/SCI

B53
STOUT H.M.,BRITISH GOVERNMENT. UK FINAN LOC/G POL/PAR DELIB/GP DIPLOM ADMIN COLONIAL CHOOSE ORD/FREE...JURID BIBLIOG 20 COMMONWLTH. PAGE 139 A2837
NAT/G PARL/PROC CONSTN NEW/LIB

B53
ZIMMERN A.,THE AMERICAN ROAD TO PEACE. USA+45 LAW INT/ORG NAT/G EX/STRUC TOP/EX EDU/PROP LEGIT COERCE PEACE ATTIT ORD/FREE PWR...CONCPT TIME/SEQ LEAGUE/NAT TOT/POP VAL/FREE 20 UN. PAGE 170 A3455
USA-45 DIPLOM

L53
UNESCO,"THE TECHNIQUE OF INTERNATIONAL CONFERENCES." WOR+45 INT/ORG VOL/ASSN EDU/PROP ROUTINE ATTIT DRIVE KNOWL ORD/FREE...SOC UNESCO 20. PAGE 148 A3016
DELIB/GP ACT/RES

C53
DEUTSCH K.W.,"NATIONALISM AND SOCIAL COMMUNICATION: AN INQUIRY INTO THE FOUNDATIONS OF NATIONALITY." CULTURE STRUCT DIPLOM DOMIN ATTIT ORD/FREE SOVEREIGN...SOC STAT CHARTS IDEA/COMP BIBLIOG. PAGE 36 A0735
NAT/LISM CONCPT PERCEPT STRATA

B54
BUCHANAN W.,AN INTERNATIONAL POLICE FORCE AND PUBLIC OPINION IN THE UNITED STATES, 1939-1953. USA+45 PROB/SOLV CONTROL ATTIT ORD/FREE...STAT TREND 20. PAGE 21 A0425
IDEA/COMP FORCES DIPLOM PLAN

B54
COOKSON J.,BEFORE THE AFRICAN STORM. BELGIUM CENTRL/AFR FRANCE UK ECO/UNDEV POL/PAR CREATE BAL/PWR RACE/REL NAT/LISM ORD/FREE CONSERVE MARXISM SOC/INTEG 20 CONGO/LEOP. PAGE 30 A0607
COLONIAL REV DISCRIM DIPLOM

B54
MILLARD E.L.,FREEDOM IN A FEDERAL WORLD. FUT WOR+45 VOL/ASSN TOP/EX LEGIT ROUTINE FEDERAL PEACE ATTIT DISPL ORD/FREE PWR...MAJORIT INT/LAW JURID TREND COLD/WAR 20. PAGE 101 A2073
INT/ORG CREATE ADJUD BAL/PWR

B54
NORTHROP F.S.C.,EUROPEAN UNION AND UNITED STATES FOREIGN POLICY: A STUDY IN SOCIOLOGICAL JURISPRUDENCE. EUR+WWI MOD/EUR USA+45 SOCIETY STRUCT NAT/G CREATE ECO/TAC DOMIN EDU/PROP REGION ATTIT RIGID/FLEX HEALTH ORD/FREE WEALTH ...METH/CNCPT TIME/SEQ TREND. PAGE 110 A2256
INT/ORG SOC DIPLOM

B54
SCHIFFER W.,THE LEGAL COMMUNITY OF MANKIND. UNIV WOR+45 WOR-45 SOCIETY NAT/G EDU/PROP LEGIT ATTIT PERSON ORD/FREE PWR...CONCPT HIST/WRIT TREND LEAGUE/NAT UN 20. PAGE 128 A2626
INT/ORG PHIL/SCI

B54
STREIT C.K.,FREEDOM AGAINST ITSELF. LAW SOCIETY DIPLOM UTOPIA PWR SOVEREIGN ALL/IDEOS 17/20 NATO UN. PAGE 139 A2850
ORD/FREE CREATE INT/ORG CONCPT

B54
WRIGHT Q.,PROBLEMS OF STABILITY AND PROGRESS IN INTERNATIONAL RELATIONSHIPS. FUT WOR+45 WOR-45 SOCIETY LEGIS CREATE TEC/DEV ECO/TAC EDU/PROP ADJUD WAR PEACE ORD/FREE PWR...KNO/TEST TREND GEN/LAWS 20. PAGE 167 A3409
INT/ORG CONCPT DIPLOM

S54
FOX W.T.R.,"CIVIL-MILITARY RELATIONS." USA+45 USA-45 R+D ACT/RES DIPLOM INT/TRADE EDU/PROP DETER DISPL DRIVE ORD/FREE...METH/CNCPT TREND COLD/WAR 20. PAGE 48 A0974
POLICY FORCES PLAN SOCIETY

B55
ALFIERI D.,DICTATORS FACE TO FACE. NAT/G TOP/EX DIPLOM EXEC COERCE ORD/FREE FASCISM...POLICY OBS 20 HITLER/A MUSSOLIN/B. PAGE 6 A0116
WAR CHIEF TOTALISM PERS/REL

B55
BURR R.N.,DOCUMENTS ON INTER-AMERICAN COOPERATION: VOL. I, 1810-1881; VOL. II, 1881-1948. DELIB/GP BAL/PWR INT/TRADE REPRESENT NAT/LISM PEACE HABITAT ORD/FREE PWR SOVEREIGN...INT/LAW 20 OAS. PAGE 22 A0445
BIBLIOG DIPLOM INT/ORG L/A+17C

B55
COTTRELL W.F.,ENERGY AND SOCIETY. FUT WOR+45 WOR-45 ECO/DEV ECO/UNDEV INT/ORG NAT/G DETER ORD/FREE PWR SKILL WEALTH...SOC TIME/SEQ TOT/POP VAL/FREE 20. PAGE 31 A0634
TEC/DEV BAL/PWR PEACE

B55
GOODRICH L.,THE UNITED NATIONS AND THE MAINTENANCE OF INTERNATIONAL PEACE AND SECURITY. WOR+45 CONSTN ACT/RES CREATE PLAN PERCEPT PWR...ORG/CHARTS GEN/LAWS UN 20. PAGE 54 A1102
INT/ORG ORD/FREE ARMS/CONT PEACE

B55
GULICK E.V.,EUROPE'S CLASSICAL BALANCE OF POWER: CASE HISTORY OF THEORY AND PRACTICE OF GREAT CONCEPTS OF EUROPEAN STATECRAFT. MOD/EUR INT/ORG VOL/ASSN FORCES ORD/FREE 18/19 TREATY. PAGE 58 A1192
IDEA/COMP BAL/PWR PWR DIPLOM

B55
HOGAN W.N.,INTERNATIONAL CONFLICT AND COLLECTIVE SECURITY: THE PRINCIPLE OF CONCERN IN INTERNATIONAL ORGANIZATION. CONSTN EX/STRUC BAL/PWR DIPLOM ADJUD CONTROL CENTRAL CONSEN PEACE...INT/LAW CONCPT METH/COMP 20 UN LEAGUE/NAT. PAGE 66 A1361
INT/ORG WAR ORD/FREE FORCES

B55
JOY C.T.,HOW COMMUNISTS NEGOTIATE. COM USA+45 CONSTN CULTURE ECO/UNDEV NAT/G CONSULT DELIB/GP FORCES PLAN ECO/TAC DOMIN EDU/PROP LEGIT EXEC ROUTINE COERCE WAR CHOOSE PEACE ATTIT RIGID/FLEX ORD/FREE PWR...POLICY 20. PAGE 75 A1539
ASIA INT/ORG DIPLOM

B55
MOCH J.,HUMAN FOLLY: DISARM OR PERISH. USA+45 WOR+45 SOCIETY INT/ORG NAT/G ACT/RES EDU/PROP ATTIT PERSON KNOWL ORD/FREE PWR...MAJORIT TOT/POP COLD/WAR 20. PAGE 102 A2093
FUT DELIB/GP ARMS/CONT NUC/PWR

B55
ROWE C.,VOLTAIRE AND THE STATE. FRANCE MOD/EUR BAL/PWR CONTROL TASK SUPEGO ORD/FREE PWR...CONCPT 18 VOLTAIRE. PAGE 125 A2553
NAT/G DIPLOM NAT/LISM ATTIT

B55
SEMJONOW J.M.,DIE FASCHISTISCHE GEOPOLITIK IM DIENSTE DES AMERIKANISCHEN IMPERIALISMUS. USA+45 USA-45 CAP/ISM PEACE ORD/FREE MARXISM SOCISM ...POLICY GEOG 20. PAGE 131 A2684
DIPLOM COERCE FASCISM WAR

B55
SNYDER R.C.,AMERICAN FOREIGN POLICY. USA+45 USA-45 WOR+45 WOR-45 CONSTN INT/ORG POL/PAR VOL/ASSN DELIB/GP LEGIS CREATE DOMIN EDU/PROP EXEC COERCE ATTIT DRIVE ORD/FREE PWR...MGT OBS RECORD TIME/SEQ TREND. PAGE 134 A2752
NAT/G DIPLOM

B55
SVARLIEN O.,AN INTRODUCTION TO THE LAW OF NATIONS. SEA AIR INT/ORG NAT/G CHIEF ADMIN AGREE WAR PRIVIL ORD/FREE SOVEREIGN...BIBLIOG 16/20. PAGE 140 A2868
INT/LAW DIPLOM

B55
TANNENBAUM F.,THE AMERICAN TRADITION IN FOREIGN POLICY. USA+45 USA-45 CONSTN INT/ORG NAT/G POL/PAR VOL/ASSN TOP/EX LEGIT DRIVE ORD/FREE PWR...CONCPT GEN/LAWS CONGRESS LEAGUE/NAT COLD/WAR OAS 18/20. PAGE 141 A2887
TIME/SEQ

B55
UN HEADQUARTERS LIBRARY,BIBLIOQRAPHIE DE LA CHARTE DES NATIONS UNIES. CHINA/COM KOREA WOR+45 VOL/ASSN CONFER ADMIN COERCE PEACE ATTIT ORD/FREE SOVEREIGN ...INT/LAW 20 UNESCO UN. PAGE 147 A3001
BIBLIOG/A INT/ORG DIPLOM

B55
WILCOX F.O.,PROPOSALS FOR CHANGES IN THE UNITED NATIONS. WOR+45 CONSTN ACT/RES CREATE LEGIT ATTIT ORD/FREE...CONCPT ORG/CHARTS UN TOT/POP 20. PAGE 164 A3344
INT/ORG STRUCT

S55
HALLETT D.,"THE HISTORY AND STRUCTURE OF OEEC." EUR+WWI USA+45 CONSTN INDUS INT/ORG NAT/G DELIB/GP ACT/RES PLAN ORD/FREE WEALTH...CONCPT OEEC 20 CMN/WLTH. PAGE 60 A1234
VOL/ASSN ECO/DEV

C55
APTER D.E.,"THE GOLD COAST IN TRANSITION." AFR CONSTN LOC/G LEGIS DIPLOM COLONIAL CONTROL GOV/REL ...CHARTS BIBLIOG 20 CMN/WLTH. PAGE 8 A0170
ORD/FREE REPRESENT PARL/PROC NAT/G

B56
BOWLES C.,AFRICA'S CHALLENGE TO AMERICA. USA+45 ECO/UNDEV NAT/G LEGIS COLONIAL CONTROL REV ORD/FREE SOVEREIGN 20 COLD/WAR. PAGE 18 A0358
AFR DIPLOM POLICY FOR/AID

B56
FIELD G.C.,POLITICAL THEORY. POL/PAR REPRESENT MORAL SOVEREIGN...JURID IDEA/COMP. PAGE 45 A0924
CONCPT NAT/G ORD/FREE DIPLOM

B56
FOSTER J.G.,BRITAIN IN WESTERN EUROPE: WEU AND THE ATLANTIC ALLIANCE. EUR+WWI FRANCE GERMANY GERMANY/W ITALY UK STRATA NAT/G DELIB/GP ECO/TAC ORD/FREE PWR ...TRADIT TIME/SEQ TREND OEEC PARLIAMENT 20 EUROPE/W. PAGE 47 A0969
INT/ORG FORCES WEAPON

B56
GEORGE A.L.,WOODROW WILSON AND COLONEL HOUSE. WOR-45 CONSTN FACE/GP INT/ORG NAT/G POL/PAR CONSULT LEGIT EXEC COERCE CHOOSE ATTIT DRIVE PERSON MORAL ORD/FREE PWR RESPECT...POLICY MGT PSY OBS RECORD INT LEAGUE/NAT. PAGE 52 A1060
USA-45 BIOG DIPLOM

B56
GILBERT R.,COMPETITIVE COEXISTENCE: THE NEW SOVIET CHALLENGE. WORKER DIPLOM WAR ORD/FREE 20 COLD/WAR. PAGE 52 A1071
NUC/PWR DOMIN MARXISM PEACE

B56
GREECE PRESBEIA U.S.,BRITISH OPINION ON CYPRUS. CYPRUS UK FORCES DIPLOM INT/TRADE DOMIN GOV/REL ORD/FREE SOVEREIGN...POLICY 20. PAGE 55 A1137
ATTIT COLONIAL LEGIS PRESS

B56
HOUSTON J.A.,LATIN AMERICA IN THE UNITED NATIONS. CONSULT DIPLOM LEGIT ROUTINE ATTIT ORD/FREE PWR ...JURID OBS RECORD TIME/SEQ CHARTS 20 UN. PAGE 68 A1395
L/A+17C INT/ORG INT/LAW REGION

B56
JAMESON J.F.,THE AMERICAN REVOLUTION CONSIDERED AS A SOCIAL MOVEMENT. USA-45 AGRI FINAN SECT INT/TRADE REPRESENT SUFF INGP/REL RACE/REL DISCRIM...MAJORIT 18/19 CHURCH/STA. PAGE 73 A1494
ORD/FREE REV FEDERAL CONSTN

B56
JESSUP P.C.,TRANSNATIONAL LAW. FUT WOR+45 JUDGE CREATE ADJUD ORD/FREE...CONCPT VAL/FREE 20. PAGE 74 A1515
LAW JURID INT/LAW

B56
REITZEL W.,UNITED STATES FOREIGN POLICY, 1945-1955. USA+45 WOR+45 CONSTN INT/ORG EDU/PROP LEGIT EXEC COERCE NUC/PWR PEACE ATTIT ORD/FREE PWR...DECISION CONCPT OBS RECORD TIME/SEQ TREND COLD/WAR UN CONGRESS. PAGE 120 A2464
NAT/G POLICY DIPLOM

B56
US DEPARTMENT OF STATE,THE SUEZ CANAL PROBLEM; JULY 26-SEPTEMBER 22, 1956. UAR WOR+45 BAL/PWR COERCE NAT/LISM ATTIT ORD/FREE SOVEREIGN 20 SUEZ. PAGE 151 A3091
DIPLOM CONFER INT/TRADE

B56
VON HARPE W.,DIE SOWJETUNION FINNLAND UND SKANDANAVIEN, 1945-1955. EUR+WWI FINLAND GERMANY USSR WAR INGP/REL ORD/FREE SOVEREIGN MARXISM ...POLICY GOV/COMP BIBLIOG 20 STALIN/J. PAGE 160 A3252
DIPLOM COM NEUTRAL BAL/PWR

B56
WOLFF R.L.,THE BALKANS IN OUR TIME. ALBANIA FUT MOD/EUR USSR YUGOSLAVIA CULTURE INT/ORG SECT DIPLOM EDU/PROP COERCE WAR ORD/FREE...CHARTS 4/20 BALKANS COMINFORM. PAGE 166 A3388
GEOG COM

S56
CUTLER R.,"THE DEVELOPMENT OF THE NATIONAL SECURITY COUNCIL." USA+45 INTELL CONSULT EX/STRUC DIPLOM LEAD 20 TRUMAN/HS EISNHWR/DD NSC. PAGE 33 A0670
ORD/FREE DELIB/GP PROB/SOLV NAT/G

B57
ARON R.,L'UNIFICATION ECONOMIQUE DE L'EUROPE. EUR+WWI SWITZERLND UK INT/ORG NAT/G REGION NAT/LISM ORD/FREE PWR...CONCPT METH/CNCPT OBS TREND STERTYP GEN/LAWS EEC 20. PAGE 9 A0181
VOL/ASSN ECO/TAC

B57
BEAL J.R.,JOHN FOSTER DULLES, A BIOGRAPHY. USA+45 USSR WOR+45 CONSTN INT/ORG NAT/G EX/STRUC LEGIT ADMIN NUC/PWR DISPL PERSON ORD/FREE PWR SKILL ...POLICY PSY OBS RECORD COLD/WAR UN 20 DULLES/JF. PAGE 12 A0237
BIOG DIPLOM

B57
BLOOMFIELD L.P.,EVOLUTION OR REVOLUTION: THE UNITED NATIONS AND THE PROBLEM OF PEACEFUL TERRITORIAL CHANGE. WOR+45 WOR-45 INT/ORG NAT/G DIPLOM ROUTINE REV ATTIT RIGID/FLEX PWR...CONCPT OBS HIST/WRIT UN LEAGUE/NAT 20. PAGE 15 A0315
ORD/FREE LEGIT

B57
BRODY H.,UN DIARY: THE SEARCH FOR PEACE. HUNGARY WOR+45 DELIB/GP ROUTINE REV WAR ORD/FREE...AUD/VIS 20 UN SUEZ. PAGE 19 A0382
INT/ORG PEACE DIPLOM POLICY

B57
COMM. STUDY ORGAN. PEACE,STRENGTHENING THE UNITED NATIONS. FUT USA+45 WOR+45 CONSTN NAT/G DELIB/GP FORCES LEGIS ECO/TAC LEGIT COERCE PEACE...JURID CONCPT UN COLD/WAR 20. PAGE 28 A0580
INT/ORG ORD/FREE

B57
DE VISSCHER C.,THEORY AND REALITY IN PUBLIC INTERNATIONAL LAW. WOR+45 WOR-45 SOCIETY NAT/G CT/SYS ATTIT MORAL ORD/FREE PWR...JURID CONCPT METH/CNCPT TIME/SEQ GEN/LAWS LEAGUE/NAT TOT/POP VAL/FREE COLD/WAR. PAGE 35 A0716
INT/ORG LAW INT/LAW

B57
DEUTSCH K.W.,POLITICAL COMMUNITY AND THE NORTH ATLANTIC AREA: INTERNATIONAL ORGANIZATION IN THE LIGHT OF HISTORICAL EXPERIENCE. MOD/EUR USA+45 USA-45 SOCIETY FORCES TOP/EX CREATE PLAN DIPLOM DOMIN EDU/PROP LEGIT ATTIT ORD/FREE PWR...SAMP/SIZ TIME/SEQ CHARTS TOT/POP. PAGE 36 A0736
EUR+WWI INT/ORG PEACE REGION

B57
INSTITUT DE DROIT INTL,TABLEAU GENERAL DES RESOLUTIONS (1873-1956). LAW NEUTRAL CRIME WAR MARRIAGE PEACE...JURID 19/20. PAGE 70 A1442
INT/LAW DIPLOM ORD/FREE ADJUD

B57
JASZI O.,AGAINST THE TYRANT. WOR+45 WOR-45 CONSTN DIPLOM CONTROL PARTIC REV WAR...CONCPT. PAGE 73 A1498
TOTALISM ORD/FREE CHIEF MURDER

B57
KENNAN G.F.,RUSSIA, THE ATOM AND THE WEST. COM EUR+WWI FUT WOR+45 SOCIETY ECO/DEV FORCES DIPLOM ECO/TAC DOMIN EDU/PROP COERCE NUC/PWR ATTIT DRIVE ORD/FREE PWR...POLICY OBS TIME/SEQ TREND COLD/WAR NATO 20. PAGE 77 A1574
NAT/G INT/ORG USSR

B57
LAVES W.H.C.,UNESCO. FUT WOR+45 NAT/G CONSULT DELIB/GP TEC/DEV ECO/TAC EDU/PROP PEACE ORD/FREE ...CONCPT TIME/SEQ TREND UNESCO VAL/FREE 20. PAGE 86 A1751
INT/ORG KNOWL

B57
LEVONTIN A.V.,THE MYTH OF INTERNATIONAL SECURITY: A JURIDICAL AND CRITICAL ANALYSIS. FUT WOR+45 WOR-45 LAW NAT/G VOL/ASSN ACT/RES BAL/PWR ATTIT ORD/FREE ...JURID METH/CNCPT TIME/SEQ TREND STERTYP 20. PAGE 88 A1797
INT/ORG INT/LAW SOVEREIGN MYTH

B57
LISKA G.,INTERNATIONAL EQUILIBRIUM. WOR+45 WOR-45 SOCIETY INT/ORG FORCES DETER ATTIT ORD/FREE PWR ...GEN/LAWS 19/20. PAGE 90 A1836
NAT/G BAL/PWR REGION DIPLOM

B57
NEUMANN F.,THE DEMOCRATIC AND THE AUTHORITARIAN STATE: ESSAYS IN POLITICAL AND LEGAL THEORY. USA+45 USA-45 CONTROL REV GOV/REL PEACE ALL/IDEOS ...INT/LAW CONCPT GEN/LAWS BIBLIOG 20. PAGE 108 A2221
DOMIN NAT/G ORD/FREE POLICY

B57
PETERSON H.C.,OPPONENTS OF WAR 1917-1918. USA-45 POL/PAR DOMIN ORD/FREE PWR PACIFISM SOCISM 20 IWW CONSCN/OBJ. PAGE 115 A2368
WAR PEACE ATTIT EDU/PROP

B57
REISS J.,GEORGE KENNANS POLITIK DER EINDAMMUNG. USSR NAT/G FORCES TOTALISM ATTIT ORD/FREE...POLICY 20 NATO TRUMAN/HS MARSHL/PLN KENNAN/G. PAGE 120 A2463
DIPLOM DETER PEACE

B57
US SENATE SPEC COMM FOR AID,COMPILATION OF STUDIES AND SURVEYS. AFR ASIA L/A+17C USA+45 ECO/UNDEV AGRI INT/ORG CONSULT TEC/DEV CONFER TOTALISM...NAT/COMP 20 CONGRESS. PAGE 157 A3197
FOR/AID DIPLOM ORD/FREE DELIB/GP

B57
US SENATE SPEC COMM FOR AID,HEARINGS BEFORE THE SPECIAL COMMITTEE TO STUDY THE FOREIGN AID PROGRAM. USA+45 USSR ECO/UNDEV INT/ORG FORCES WEAPON TOTALISM ATTIT SUPEGO...NAT/COMP CONGRESS. PAGE 157 A3198
FOR/AID DIPLOM ORD/FREE TEC/DEV

B57
WASSENBERGH H.A.,POST-WAR INTERNATIONAL CIVIL AVIATION POLICY AND THE LAW OF THE AIR. WOR+45 AIR INT/ORG DOMIN LEGIT PEACE ORD/FREE...POLICY JURID NEW/IDEA OBS TIME/SEQ TREND CHARTS 20 TREATY.
COM/IND NAT/G INT/LAW

PAGE 162 A3290

L57
FURNISS E.S.,"SOME PERSPECTIVES ON AMERICAN MILITARY ASSISTANCE." USA+45 WOR+45 ECO/UNDEV INT/ORG ECO/TAC ORD/FREE...GEOG TIME/SEQ TREND COLD/WAR 20. PAGE 50 A1028
FORCES FOR/AID WEAPON

L57
HAAS E.B.,"REGIONAL INTEGRATION AND NATIONAL POLICY." WOR+45 VOL/ASSN DELIB/GP EX/STRUC ECO/TAC DOMIN EDU/PROP LEGIT COERCE ATTIT PERCEPT KNOWL ...TIME/SEQ COLD/WAR 20 UN. PAGE 59 A1203
INT/ORG ORD/FREE REGION

S57
HOAG M.W.,"ECONOMIC PROBLEMS OF ALLIANCE." COM EUR+WWI WOR+45 ECO/DEV ECO/UNDEV NAT/G VOL/ASSN FORCES PLAN TEC/DEV DIPLOM COERCE ORD/FREE PWR WEALTH...DECISION GEN/LAWS NATO COLD/WAR. PAGE 65 A1345
INT/ORG ECO/TAC

S57
SPEIER H.,"SOVIET ATOMIC BLACKMAIL AND THE NORTH ATLANTIC ALLIANCE." EUR+WWI USA+45 USSR INT/ORG NAT/G FORCES DIPLOM DRIVE ORD/FREE PWR NATO VAL/FREE COLD/WAR 20. PAGE 136 A2781
COM COERCE NUC/PWR

S57
WRIGHT Q.,"THE VALUE OF CONFLICT RESOLUTION OF A GENERAL DISCIPLINE OF INTERNATIONAL RELATIONS." WOR+45 SOCIETY INT/ORG NAT/G FORCES TOP/EX PLAN TEC/DEV ECO/TAC DOMIN LEGIT COERCE ATTIT PWR ...GEN/METH COLD/WAR VAL/FREE. PAGE 168 A3412
ORD/FREE SOC DIPLOM

N57
US SENATE SPECIAL COMM FOR AFF,REPORT OF THE SPECIAL COMMITTEE TO STUDY THE FOREIGN AID PROGRAM (PAMPHLET). USA+45 CONSULT DELIB/GP LEGIS PLAN TEC/DEV CONFER SUPEGO CONGRESS. PAGE 157 A3199
FOR/AID ORD/FREE ECO/UNDEV DIPLOM

B58
ANGELL N.,DEFENCE AND THE ENGLISH-SPEAKING ROLE. CHINA/COM UK USSR INT/ORG FORCES EDU/PROP NEUTRAL NUC/PWR NAT/LISM PEACE TOTALISM 20 COLD/WAR COEXIST. PAGE 8 A0161
DIPLOM WAR MARXISM ORD/FREE

B58
BOWETT D.W.,SELF-DEFENSE IN INTERNATIONAL LAW. EUR+WWI MOD/EUR WOR+45 WOR-45 SOCIETY INT/ORG CONSULT DIPLOM LEGIT COERCE ATTIT ORD/FREE...JURID 20 UN. PAGE 17 A0353
ADJUD CONCPT WAR INT/LAW

B58
CAMPBELL J.C.,DEFENSE OF THE MIDDLE EAST: PROBLEMS OF AMERICAN POLICY. ISLAM USA+45 INT/ORG NAT/G EX/STRUC FORCES ECO/TAC DOMIN EDU/PROP LEGIT REGION COERCE...METH/CNCPT COLD/WAR TOT/POP 20. PAGE 23 A0474
TOP/EX ORD/FREE DIPLOM

B58
CRAIG G.A.,FROM BISMARCK TO ADENAUER: ASPECTS OF GERMAN STATECRAFT. GERMANY INTELL FORCES ECO/TAC CONFER COERCE WAR GP/REL ORD/FREE PWR CONSERVE 19/20 BISMARCK/O ADENAUER/K. PAGE 32 A0653
DIPLOM LEAD NAT/G

B58
GROBLER J.H.,AFRICA'S DESTINY. AFR EUR+WWI SOUTH/AFR UK USA+45 ELITES KIN LOC/G DIPLOM DISCRIM ATTIT CONSERVE MARXISM 20 ROOSEVLT/T NEGRO. PAGE 57 A1168
POLICY ORD/FREE COLONIAL CONSTN

B58
HAAS E.B.,THE UNITING OF EUROPE. EUR+WWI INT/ORG NAT/G POL/PAR TOP/EX ECO/TAC EDU/PROP LEGIT FEDERAL NAT/LISM DRIVE RIGID/FLEX ORD/FREE PWR PLURISM ...POLICY CONCPT INT GEN/LAWS ECSC EEC 20. PAGE 59 A1204
VOL/ASSN ECO/DEV

B58
HENKIN L.,ARMS CONTROL AND INSPECTION IN AMERICAN LAW. LAW CONSTN INT/ORG LOC/G MUNIC NAT/G PROVS EDU/PROP LEGIT EXEC NUC/PWR KNOWL ORD/FREE...OBS TOT/POP CONGRESS 20. PAGE 64 A1315
USA+45 JURID ARMS/CONT

B58
INDIAN COUNCIL WORLD AFFAIRS,DEFENCE AND SECURITY IN THE INDIAN OCEAN AREA. INDIA S/ASIA CULTURE CONSULT DELIB/GP FORCES PROB/SOLV DIPLOM INT/TRADE 20 CMN/WLTH. PAGE 70 A1438
GEOG HABITAT ECO/UNDEV ORD/FREE

B58
JAPANESE ASSOCIATION INT. LAW,JAPAN AND THE UNITED NATIONS. SOCIETY ROUTINE ATTIT DRIVE PERCEPT RIGID/FLEX ORD/FREE...METH/CNCPT CON/ANAL CHINJAP UN. PAGE 73 A1497
ASIA INT/ORG

B58
KINDLEBERGER C.P.,INTERNATIONAL ECONOMICS. WOR+45 WOR-45 ECO/DEV ECO/UNDEV FINAN VOL/ASSN ACT/RES DIPLOM ECO/TAC LEGIT REGION ATTIT DRIVE ORD/FREE WEALTH...POLICY STAT TREND GEN/LAWS EEC ECSC OEEC 20. PAGE 79 A1620
INT/ORG BAL/PWR TARIFFS

B58
MANSERGH N.,SURVEY OF BRITISH COMMONWEALTH AFFAIRS: PROBLEMS OF WARTIME CO-OPERATION AND POST-WAR CHANGE 1939-1952. INDIA IRELAND S/ASIA CONSTN INT/ORG BAL/PWR COLONIAL NEUTRAL WAR ADJUST PEACE ROLE ORD/FREE...CHARTS 20 CMN/WLTH NATO UN. PAGE 94 A1931
VOL/ASSN CONSEN PROB/SOLV INGP/REL

B58
MELMAN S.,INSPECTION FOR DISARMAMENT. USA+45 WOR+45 SOCIETY INT/ORG NAT/G CONSULT ACT/RES PLAN EDU/PROP CONTROL DETER PEACE ATTIT PERSON KNOWL...PSY STAT OBS CHARTS TOT/POP VAL/FREE 20. PAGE 99 A2035
FUT ORD/FREE ARMS/CONT NUC/PWR

B58
MILLIS W.,FOREIGN POLICY AND THE FREE SOCIETY. USA+45 WOR+45 SOCIETY NAT/G FORCES BAL/PWR FOR/AID EDU/PROP DETER ATTIT PWR 20 COLD/WAR. PAGE 102 A2084
DIPLOM POLICY ORD/FREE CONSULT

B58
MOORE B.T.,NATO AND THE FUTURE OF EUROPE. EUR+WWI FUT USA+45 ECO/DEV INDUS MARKET NAT/G VOL/ASSN FORCES DIPLOM NUC/PWR ORD/FREE...CONCPT CHARTS ORG/CHARTS CMN/WLTH 20 NATO. PAGE 103 A2122
INT/ORG REGION

B58
NATIONAL PLANNING ASSOCIATION,1970 WITHOUT ARMS CONTROL (PAMPHLET). WOR+45 PROB/SOLV TEC/DEV DIPLOM CONFER DETER NUC/PWR WAR...CHARTS 20 COLD/WAR. PAGE 107 A2204
ARMS/CONT ORD/FREE WEAPON PREDICT

B58
ORGANSKI A.F.K.,WORLD POLITICS. FUT WOR+45 SOCIETY STRUCT NAT/G BAL/PWR ECO/TAC DOMIN NAT/LISM ATTIT KNOWL ORD/FREE PWR...CONCPT METH/CNCPT TREND STERTYP GEN/LAWS TOT/POP 20. PAGE 112 A2297
INT/ORG DIPLOM

B58
PALMER E.E.,AMERICAN FOREIGN POLICY. USA+45 CULTURE ECO/UNDEV NAT/G PLAN GIVE BAL/PAY ORD/FREE WEALTH POPULISM...DECISION ANTHOL 20. PAGE 113 A2319
DIPLOM ECO/TAC POLICY

B58
PALMER E.E.,THE COMMUNIST CHALLENGE. COM USA+45 USA-45 ECO/DEV ECO/UNDEV NEUTRAL ORD/FREE POPULISM ...CONCPT NAT/COMP ANTHOL 19/20 LENIN/VI STALIN/J MAO MARX/KARL COM/PARTY. PAGE 113 A2320
MARXISM DIPLOM IDEA/COMP POLICY

B58
ROCKEFELLER BROTH FUND INC,INTERNATIONAL SECURITY - THE MILITARY ASPECT. USA+45 INT/ORG NAT/G BUDGET ARMS/CONT WAR WEAPON PEACE ORD/FREE 20 NATO. PAGE 123 A2511
NUC/PWR DETER FORCES DIPLOM

B58
RUSSELL R.B.,A HISTORY OF THE UNITED NATIONS CHARTER: THE ROLE OF THE UNITED STATES. SOCIETY NAT/G CONSULT DOMIN LEGIT ATTIT ORD/FREE PWR ...POLICY JURID CONCPT UN LEAGUE/NAT. PAGE 126 A2575
USA-45 INT/ORG CONSTN

B58
SCHUMAN F.,INTERNATIONAL POLITICS. WOR+45 WOR-45 INTELL NAT/G FORCES DOMIN LEGIT COERCE NUC/PWR ATTIT DISPL ORD/FREE PWR SOVEREIGN...POLICY CONCPT GEN/LAWS SUEZ 20. PAGE 129 A2650
FUT INT/ORG NAT/LISM DIPLOM

B58
SLICK T.,PERMANENT PEACE: A CHECK AND BALANCE PLAN. FUT WOR+45 NAT/G FORCES CREATE PLAN EDU/PROP LEGIT ADJUD COERCE NAT/LISM RIGID/FLEX MORAL...HUM CONCPT METH/CNCPT NEW/IDEA TREND CHARTS TOT/POP 20. PAGE 134 A2742
INT/ORG ORD/FREE PEACE ARMS/CONT

B58
SOC OF COMP LEGIS AND INT LAW,THE LAW OF THE SEA... (PAMPHLET). WOR+45 NAT/G INT/TRADE ADJUD CONTROL NUC/PWR WAR PEACE ATTIT ORD/FREE...JURID CHARTS 20 UN TREATY RESOURCE/N. PAGE 135 A2756
INT/LAW INT/ORG DIPLOM SEA

B58
STONE J.,AGGRESSION AND WORLD ORDER: A CRITIQUE OF UNITED NATIONS THEORIES OF AGGRESSION. LAW CONSTN DELIB/GP PROB/SOLV BAL/PWR DIPLOM DEBATE ADJUD CRIME PWR...POLICY IDEA/COMP 20 UN SUEZ LEAGUE/NAT. PAGE 138 A2835
ORD/FREE INT/ORG WAR CONCPT

B58
US HOUSE COMM GOVT OPERATIONS,HEARINGS BEFORE A SUBCOMMITTEE OF THE COMMITTEE ON GOVERNMENT OPERATIONS. CAMBODIA PHILIPPINE USA+45 CONSTRUC TEC/DEV ADMIN CONTROL WEAPON EFFICIENCY HOUSE/REP. PAGE 154 A3135
FOR/AID DIPLOM ORD/FREE ECO/UNDEV

S58
BURNS A.L.,"THE INTERNATIONAL CONSEQUENCES OF EXPECTING SURPRISE." WOR+45 INT/ORG NAT/G FORCES DIPLOM COERCE NUC/PWR WAR CHOOSE ORD/FREE ...METH/CNCPT STYLE OBS STERTYP TOT/POP VAL/FREE. PAGE 22 A0440
PLAN PWR DETER

S58
DAVENPORT J.,"ARMS AND THE WELFARE STATE." INTELL STRUCT FORCES CREATE ECO/TAC FOR/AID DOMIN LEGIT ADMIN WAR ORD/FREE PWR...POLICY SOC CONCPT MYTH OBS TREND COLD/WAR TOT/POP 20. PAGE 34 A0685
USA+45 NAT/G USSR

S58
ELKIN A.B.,"OEEC-ITS STRUCTURE AND POWERS." EUR+WWI CONSTN INDUS INT/ORG NAT/G VOL/ASSN DELIB/GP ACT/RES PLAN ORD/FREE WEALTH...CHARTS ORG/CHARTS OEEC 20. PAGE 41 A0839
ECO/DEV EX/STRUC

S58
MCDOUGAL M.S.,"PERSPECTIVES FOR A LAW OF OUTER SPACE." FUT WOR+45 AIR CONSULT DELIB/GP TEC/DEV CT/SYS ORD/FREE...POLICY JURID 20 UN. PAGE 98 A2004
INT/ORG SPACE INT/LAW

S58
STAAR R.F.,"ELECTIONS IN COMMUNIST POLAND." EUR+WWI SOCIETY INT/ORG NAT/G POL/PAR LEGIS ACT/RES ECO/TAC EDU/PROP ADJUD ADMIN ROUTINE COERCE TOTALISM ATTIT ORD/FREE PWR 20. PAGE 137 A2797
COM CHOOSE POLAND

S58
THOMPSON K.W.,"NATIONAL SECURITY IN A NUCLEAR AGE." USA+45 WOR+45 SOCIETY INT/ORG NAT/G TOP/EX DIPLOM DOMIN EDU/PROP LEGIT ARMS/CONT COERCE ORD/FREE ...TREND STERTYP TOT/POP VAL/FREE COLD/WAR 20. PAGE 143 A2929
FORCES PWR BAL/PWR

N58
US HOUSE COMM FOREIGN AFFAIRS,HEARINGS ON DRAFT LEGISLATION TO AMEND FURTHER THE MUTUAL SECURITY ACT OF 1954 (PAMPHLET). USA+45 CONSULT FORCES BUDGET DIPLOM DETER COST ORD/FREE...JURID 20 DEPT/DEFEN UN DEPT/STATE. PAGE 153 A3123
LEGIS DELIB/GP CONFER WEAPON

N58
US HOUSE COMM FOREIGN AFFAIRS,HEARINGS ON THE FAR EAST AND THE PACIFIC (PAMPHLET). LAOS USA+45 NAT/G CONSULT FORCES CONFER DEBATE ORD/FREE 20. PAGE 153 A3124
FOR/AID DIPLOM DELIB/GP LEGIS

B59
ARON R.,IMPERIALISM AND COLONIALISM (PAMPHLET). WOR+45 WOR-45 ECO/TAC CONTROL REV ORD/FREE 19/20. PAGE 9 A0183
COLONIAL DOMIN ECO/UNDEV DIPLOM

B59
BALL M.M.,NATO AND THE EUROPEAN MOVEMENT. EUR+WWI USA+45 INT/ORG FORCES BAL/PWR EDU/PROP LEGIT REGION ATTIT ORD/FREE PWR...STAT OBS TIME/SEQ TREND CHARTS ORG/CHARTS STERTYP COLD/WAR EEC OEEC 20 NATO. PAGE 10 A0212
DELIB/GP STRUCT

B59
BEMIS S.F.,A SHORT HISTORY OF AMERICAN FOREIGN POLICY AND DIPLOMACY. USA+45 USA-45 INT/ORG NEUTRAL REV WAR ISOLAT ORD/FREE...CHARTS T 18/20. PAGE 13 A0266
DIPLOM ATTIT

B59
CHINA INSTITUTE OF AMERICA.,CHINA AND THE UNITED NATIONS. CHINA/COM FUT STRUCT EDU/PROP LEGIT ADMIN ATTIT KNOWL ORD/FREE PWR...OBS RECORD STAND/INT TIME/SEQ UN LEAGUE/NAT UNESCO 20. PAGE 26 A0531
ASIA INT/ORG

B59
COMM. STUDY ORGAN. PEACE,ORGANIZING PEACE IN THE NUCLEAR AGE. FUT CONSULT DELIB/GP DOMIN ADJUD ROUTINE COERCE ORD/FREE...TECHNIC INT/LAW JURID NEW/IDEA UN COLD/WAR 20. PAGE 29 A0581
INT/ORG ACT/RES NUC/PWR

B59
CORBETT P.E.,LAW IN DIPLOMACY. UK USA+45 USSR CONSTN SOCIETY INT/ORG JUDGE LEGIT ATTIT ORD/FREE TOT/POP LEAGUE/NAT 20. PAGE 30 A0616
NAT/G ADJUD JURID DIPLOM

B59
COUDENHOVE-KALERGI,FROM WAR TO PEACE. USA+45 USSR WOR+45 WOR-45 LAW INT/ORG NAT/G LEGIT COERCE LOVE ...POLICY PLURIST METH/CNCPT STERTYP TOT/POP UN 20 NATO. PAGE 31 A0636
FUT ORD/FREE

B59
DIEBOLD W. JR.,THE SCHUMAN PLAN: A STUDY IN ECONOMIC COOPERATION, 1950-1959. EUR+WWI FRANCE GERMANY USA+45 EXTR/IND CONSULT DELIB/GP PLAN DIPLOM ECO/TAC INT/TRADE ROUTINE ORD/FREE WEALTH ...METH/CNCPT STAT CONT/OBS INT TIME/SEQ ECSC 20. PAGE 37 A0759
INT/ORG REGION

B59
EMME E.M.,THE IMPACT OF AIR POWER - NATIONAL SECURITY AND WORLD POLITICS. USA+45 USSR FORCES DIPLOM WEAPON PEACE TOTALISM...POLICY NAT/COMP 20 EUROPE. PAGE 42 A0850
DETER AIR WAR ORD/FREE

B59
GOODRICH L.,THE UNITED NATIONS. WOR+45 CONSTN STRUCT ACT/RES LEGIT COERCE KNOWL ORD/FREE PWR ...GEN/LAWS UN 20. PAGE 54 A1104
INT/ORG ROUTINE

B59
GORDENKER L.,THE UNITED NATIONS AND THE PEACEFUL UNIFICATION OF KOREA. ASIA LAW LOC/G CONSULT ACT/RES DIPLOM DOMIN LEGIT ADJUD ADMIN ORD/FREE SOVEREIGN...INT GEN/METH UN COLD/WAR 20. PAGE 54 A1109
DELIB/GP KOREA INT/ORG

B59
GOULD L.P.,THE PRICE OF SURVIVAL. EUR+WWI SPACE USA+45 FORCES ECO/TAC NUC/PWR WAR ORD/FREE MARXISM ...IDEA/COMP 20 COLD/WAR NATO. PAGE 54 A1117
POLICY PROB/SOLV DIPLOM PEACE

B59
HERZ J.H.,INTERNATIONAL POLITICS IN THE ATOMIC AGE. FUT USA+45 WOR+45 WOR-45 SOCIETY NAT/G FORCES PLAN COERCE DETER ATTIT DRIVE ORD/FREE PWR...TREND COLD/WAR 20. PAGE 64 A1319
INT/ORG ARMS/CONT NUC/PWR

B59
HUGHES E.M.,AMERICA THE VINCIBLE. USA+45 FOR/AID ARMS/CONT NUC/PWR PERS/REL RATIONAL ATTIT ALL/VALS 20 COLD/WAR. PAGE 69 A1413
ORD/FREE DIPLOM WAR

B59
JONES A.C.,NEW FABIAN COLONIAL ESSAYS. UK SOCIETY POL/PAR EDU/PROP ADMIN ORD/FREE SOVEREIGN SOCISM ...ANTHOL 20 CMN/WLTH LABOR/PAR. PAGE 75 A1530
COLONIAL INT/ORG INGP/REL DOMIN

B59
JOSEPH F.M.,AS OTHERS SEE US: THE UNITED STATES THROUGH FOREIGN EYES. AFR EUR+WWI ISLAM L/A+17C S/ASIA USA+45 CULTURE SOCIETY ECO/DEV ECO/UNDEV INT/ORG NAT/G DIPLOM ECO/TAC REV ATTIT RIGID/FLEX HEALTH ORD/FREE WEALTH 20. PAGE 75 A1537
RESPECT DOMIN NAT/LISM SOVEREIGN

B59
KARUNAKARAN K.P.,INDIA IN WORLD AFFAIRS, 1952-1958 (VOL. II). INDIA ECO/UNDEV SECT FOR/AID INT/TRADE ADJUD NEUTRAL REV WAR DISCRIM ORD/FREE MARXISM ...BIBLIOG 20. PAGE 77 A1569
DIPLOM INT/ORG S/ASIA COLONIAL

B59
KIRCHHEIMER O.,GEGENWARTSPROBLEME DER ASYLGEWAHRUNG. DOMIN GP/REL ATTIT...NAT/COMP 20. PAGE 79 A1630
DIPLOM INT/LAW JURID ORD/FREE

B59
KNIERIEM A.,THE NUREMBERG TRIALS. EUR+WWI GERMANY VOL/ASSN LEAD COERCE WAR INGP/REL TOTALISM SUPEGO ORD/FREE...CONCPT METH/COMP. PAGE 80 A1651
INT/LAW CRIME PARTIC JURID

B59
NIEBUHR R.,NATIONS AND EMPIRES. WOR+45 INT/ORG COLONIAL NUC/PWR TOTALISM UTOPIA ORD/FREE MARXISM WORSHIP 20 COLD/WAR PROTESTANT CHRISTIAN. PAGE 109 A2237
DIPLOM NAT/G POLICY PWR

B59
REIFF H.,THE UNITED STATES AND THE TREATY LAW OF THE SEA. USA+45 USA-45 SEA SOCIETY INT/ORG CONSULT DELIB/GP LEGIS DIPLOM LEGIT ATTIT ORD/FREE PWR WEALTH...GEOG JURID TOT/POP 20 TREATY. PAGE 120 A2459
ADJUD INT/LAW

B59
RICE E.A.,THE DIPLOMATIC RELATIONS BETWEEN THE UNITED STATES AND MEXICO 1925-1929. USA-45 NAT/G DOMIN PEACE ORD/FREE CATHISM 20 MEXIC/AMER. PAGE 121 A2472
DIPLOM SECT POLICY

B59
ROPKE W.,INTERNATIONAL ORDER AND ECONOMIC INTEGRATION. ECO/DEV ECO/UNDEV AGRI FINAN INDUS INT/ORG WAR PEACE ORD/FREE...SOC METH/COMP 20 EEC. PAGE 123 A2524
INT/TRADE DIPLOM BAL/PAY ALL/IDEOS

B59
SCHNEIDER J.,TREATY-MAKING POWER OF INTERNATIONAL ORGANIZATIONS. FUT WOR+45 WOR-45 LAW NAT/G JUDGE DIPLOM LEGIT CT/SYS ORD/FREE PWR...INT/LAW JURID GEN/LAWS TOT/POP UNESCO 20 TREATY. PAGE 129 A2639
INT/ORG ROUTINE

B59
SCHURZ W.L.,AMERICAN FOREIGN AFFAIRS: A GUIDE TO INTERNATIONAL AFFAIRS. USA+45 WOR+45 WOR-45 NAT/G FORCES LEGIS TOP/EX PLAN EDU/PROP LEGIT ADMIN ROUTINE ATTIT ORD/FREE PWR...SOC CONCPT STAT SAMP/SIZ CHARTS STERTYP 20. PAGE 129 A2653
INT/ORG SOCIETY DIPLOM

B59
SIMPSON J.L.,INTERNATIONAL ARBITRATION: LAW AND PRACTICE. WOR+45 WOR-45 INT/ORG DELIB/GP ADJUD PEACE MORAL ORD/FREE...METH 18/20. PAGE 133 A2720
INT/LAW DIPLOM CT/SYS CONSULT

B59
TARDIFF G.,LA LIBERTAD; LA LIBERTAD DE EXPRESION, IDEALES Y REALIDADES AMERICANAS. ISLAM INT/ORG PROB/SOLV PRESS CONFER PARTIC CATHISM...INT/LAW SOC/INTEG UN MID/EAST. PAGE 141 A2889
ORD/FREE ATTIT DIPLOM CONCPT

B59
THOMAS N.,THE PREREQUISITES FOR PEACE. ASIA EUR+WWI FUT ISLAM S/ASIA WOR+45 FORCES PLAN BAL/PWR EDU/PROP LEGIT ATTIT PWR...SOCIALIST CONCPT COLD/WAR 20 UN. PAGE 143 A2924
INT/ORG ORD/FREE ARMS/CONT PEACE

B59
TUNSTALL W.C.B.,THE COMMONWEALTH AND REGIONAL DEFENCE (PAMPHLET). UK LAW VOL/ASSN PLAN AGREE REGION WAR ORD/FREE 20 CMN/WLTH NATO SEATO TREATY. PAGE 146 A2977
INT/ORG FORCES DIPLOM

B59
US PRES COMM STUDY MIL ASSIST,COMPOSITE REPORT. USA+45 ECO/UNDEV PLAN BUDGET DIPLOM EFFICIENCY ...POLICY MGT 20. PAGE 155 A3164
FOR/AID FORCES WEAPON ORD/FREE

B59
VORSPAN A.,JUSTICE AND JUDAISM. FAM DIPLOM ECO/TAC EDU/PROP CRIME RACE/REL MARRIAGE ANOMIE ATTIT ORD/FREE...POLICY 20 UN. PAGE 160 A3254
SECT CULTURE ACT/RES GP/REL

L59
BEGUIN B.,"ILO AND THE TRIPARTITE SYSTEM." EUR+WWI WOR+45 WOR-45 CONSTN ECO/DEV ECO/UNDEV INDUS INT/ORG NAT/G VOL/ASSN DELIB/GP PLAN TEC/DEV LEGIT ORD/FREE WEALTH...CONCPT TIME/SEQ WORK ILO 20. PAGE 12 A0249
LABOR

L59
GRANDIN T.,"THE POLITICAL USE OF THE RADIO." EUR+WWI SOCIETY INT/ORG DIPLOM CONTROL ATTIT ORD/FREE...CONCPT STAT RECORD SAMP GEN/LAWS TOT/POP 20. PAGE 55 A1128
COM/IND EDU/PROP NAT/LISM

S59
CARLSTON K.S.,"NATIONALIZATION: AN ANALYTIC APPROACH." WOR+45 INT/ORG ECO/TAC DOMIN LEGIT ADJUD COERCE ORD/FREE PWR WEALTH SOCISM...JURID CONCPT
INDUS NAT/G NAT/LISM

TREND STERTYP TOT/POP VAL/FREE 20. PAGE 24 A0486 SOVEREIGN

S59

FISCHER L.,"THE SOVIET-AMERICAN ANTAGONISM: HOW WILL IT END." CONSTN CULTURE PLAN TEC/DEV RIGID/FLEX SUPEGO ORD/FREE...MARXIST DECISION PSY CONCPT CON/ANAL GEN/LAWS VAL/FREE 20 COLD/WAR. PAGE 46 A0936
USA+45 PWR DIPLOM USSR

S59

HARTT J.,"ANTARCTICA: ITS IMMEDIATE PRACTICALITIES." FUT USA+45 USSR WOR+45 INT/ORG NAT/G CREATE TEC/DEV REGION KNOWL WEALTH...GEOG 20 ANTARTICA. PAGE 62 A1276
VOL/ASSN ORD/FREE DIPLOM

S59

HARVEY M.F.,"THE PALESTINE REFUGEE PROBLEM: ELEMENTS OF A SOLUTION." ISLAM LAW INT/ORG DELIB/GP TOP/EX ECO/TAC ROUTINE DRIVE HEALTH LOVE ORD/FREE PWR WEALTH...MAJORIT FAO 20. PAGE 62 A1283
ACT/RES LEGIT PEACE ISRAEL

S59

KISSINGER H.A.,"THE SEARCH FOR STABILITY." COM GERMANY MOD/EUR USA+45 USA-45 USSR INT/ORG ARMS/CONT NUC/PWR ORD/FREE PWR COLD/WAR 20 NATO. PAGE 80 A1641
FUT ATTIT BAL/PWR

S59

PUGWASH CONFERENCE,"ON BIOLOGICAL AND CHEMICAL WARFARE." WOR+45 SOCIETY PROC/MFG INT/ORG FORCES EDU/PROP ADJUD RIGID/FLEX ORD/FREE PWR...DECISION PSY NEW/IDEA MATH VAL/FREE 20. PAGE 118 A2417
ACT/RES BIO/SOC WAR WEAPON

S59

QUIGLEY H.S.,"TOWARD REAPPRAISAL OF OUR CHINA POLICY." CHINA/COM USA+45 INT/ORG PLAN ECO/TAC PERCEPT ORD/FREE...DECISION PSY CON/ANAL GEN/METH VAL/FREE 20. PAGE 118 A2427
ASIA KNOWL DIPLOM

S59

REUBENS E.D.,"THE BASIS FOR REORIENATION OF AMERICAN FOREIGN AID POLICY." USA+45 USSR STRUCT INT/ORG CONSULT ECO/TAC ADMIN DRIVE MORAL ORD/FREE PWR WEALTH...RELATIV MATH STAT TREND GEN/LAWS VAL/FREE 20. PAGE 120 A2467
ECO/UNDEV PLAN FOR/AID DIPLOM

S59

SOHN L.B.,"THE DEFINITION OF AGGRESSION." FUT LAW FORCES LEGIT ADJUD ROUTINE COERCE ORD/FREE PWR ...MAJORIT JURID QUANT COLD/WAR 20. PAGE 135 A2762
INT/ORG CT/SYS DETER SOVEREIGN

S59

SUTTON F.X.,"REPRESENTATION AND THE NATURE OF POLITICAL SYSTEMS." UNIV WOR-45 CULTURE SOCIETY STRATA INT/ORG FORCES JUDGE DOMIN LEGIT EXEC REGION REPRESENT ATTIT ORD/FREE RESPECT...SOC HIST/WRIT TIME/SEQ. PAGE 140 A2867
NAT/G CONCPT

S59

TIPTON J.B.,"PARTICIPATION OF THE UNITED STATES IN THE INTERNATIONAL LABOR ORGANIZATION." USA+45 LAW STRUCT ECO/DEV ECO/UNDEV INDUS TEC/DEV ECO/TAC ADMIN PERCEPT ORD/FREE SKILL...STAT HIST/WRIT GEN/METH ILO WORK 20. PAGE 144 A2946
LABOR INT/ORG

N59

BRITISH COMMONWEALTH REL CONF,EXTRACTS FROM THE PROCEEDINGS OF THE SIXTH UNOFFICIAL CONFERENCE (PAMPHLET). GHANA INDIA RHODESIA UK FINAN FORCES DETER FEDERAL...LING 20 PARLIAMENT. PAGE 19 A0379
DIPLOM PARL/PROC INT/TRADE ORD/FREE

N59

US HOUSE COMM FOREIGN AFFAIRS,HEARINGS ON DRAFT LEGISLATION TO AMEND FURTHER THE MUTUAL SECURITY ACT OF 1954 (PAMPHLET). USA+45 USSR CONSULT DELIB/GP FORCES ECO/TAC CONFER...POLICY 20 CONGRESS. PAGE 153 A3126
DIPLOM FOR/AID ORD/FREE LEGIS

B60

ARMS CONTROL. FUT UNIV WOR+45 INTELL R+D INT/ORG NAT/G VOL/ASSN CONSULT CREATE EDU/PROP PEACE...HUM GEN/LAWS TOT/POP 20. PAGE 3 A0060
DELIB/GP ORD/FREE ARMS/CONT NUC/PWR

B60

BUCHAN A.,NATO IN THE 1960'S. EUR+WWI USA+45 WOR+45 INT/ORG ACT/RES PLAN LEGIT COERCE DETER ATTIT DRIVE RIGID/FLEX ORD/FREE...METH/CNCPT TIME/SEQ TREND GEN/LAWS COLD/WAR 20 NATO. PAGE 21 A0421
VOL/ASSN FORCES ARMS/CONT SOVEREIGN

B60

CARNEGIE ENDOWMENT INT. PEACE,PERSPECTIVES ON PEACE - 1910-1960. WOR+45 WOR-45 INTELL INT/ORG CONSULT ACT/RES EDU/PROP ATTIT KNOWL ORD/FREE...TIME/SEQ TREND EEC OAS UNESCO NAZI 20. PAGE 24 A0489
FUT CONCPT ARMS/CONT PEACE

B60

DAVIDS J.,AMERICA AND THE WORLD OF OUR TIME: UNITED STATES DIPLOMACY IN THE TWENTIETH CENTURY. USA-45 SOCIETY ECO/DEV INT/ORG NAT/G POL/PAR FORCES ECO/TAC DOMIN EDU/PROP EXEC COERCE WAR CHOOSE ATTIT PERSON ORD/FREE...CONCPT TIME/SEQ TOT/POP 20. PAGE 34 A0686
USA+45 PWR DIPLOM

B60

HAAS E.B.,THE COMPARATIVE STUDY OF THE UNITED NATIONS. WOR+45 NAT/G DOMIN LEGIT ROUTINE PEACE ORD/FREE PWR UN VAL/FREE 20. PAGE 59 A1205
INT/ORG DIPLOM

B60

HAHN W.F.,AMERICAN STRATEGY FOR THE NUCLEAR AGE. USA+45 NAT/G TEC/DEV ECO/TAC FOR/AID ARMS/CONT NUC/PWR ORD/FREE MARXISM...ANTHOL 20. PAGE 59 A1216
DIPLOM PLAN PEACE

B60

HANDLIN O.,AMERICAN PRINCIPLES AND ISSUES. USA+45 USA-45 DIPLOM WAR PERSON. PAGE 61 A1251
ORD/FREE NAT/LISM ATTIT

B60

JEFFRIES C.,TRANSFER OF POWER: PROBLEMS OF THE PASSAGE TO SELFGOVERNMENT. CEYLON GHANA MALAYSIA NIGERIA UK INT/ORG CONSULT DELIB/GP LEGIS DIPLOM CONFER PARL/PROC 20. PAGE 73 A1502
SOVEREIGN COLONIAL ORD/FREE NAT/G

B60

JENNINGS R.,PROGRESS OF INTERNATIONAL LAW. FUT WOR+45 WOR-45 SOCIETY NAT/G VOL/ASSN DELIB/GP DIPLOM EDU/PROP LEGIT COERCE ATTIT DRIVE MORAL ORD/FREE...JURID CONCPT OBS TIME/SEQ TREND GEN/LAWS. PAGE 74 A1509
INT/ORG LAW INT/LAW

B60

KENNEDY J.F.,THE STRATEGY OF PEACE. USA+45 WOR+45 BAL/PWR DIPLOM INGP/REL ORD/FREE...GOV/COMP NAT/COMP 20. PAGE 78 A1591
PEACE PLAN POLICY NAT/G

B60

KINGSTON-MCCLOUG E.,DEFENSE; POLICY AND STRATEGY. UK SEA AIR TEC/DEV DIPLOM ADMIN LEAD WAR ORD/FREE ...CHARTS 20. PAGE 79 A1627
FORCES PLAN POLICY DECISION

B60

LATIFI D.,INDIA AND UNITED STATES AID. ASIA INDIA UK USA+45 AGRI FINAN INDUS COLONIAL ORD/FREE SOVEREIGN WEALTH...METH/COMP 20. PAGE 85 A1743
FOR/AID DIPLOM ECO/UNDEV

B60

LINDSAY K.,EUROPEAN ASSEMBLIES: THE EXPERIMENTAL PERIOD 1949-1959. EUR+WWI ECO/DEV NAT/G POL/PAR LEGIS TOP/EX ACT/RES PLAN ECO/TAC DOMIN LEGIT ROUTINE ATTIT DRIVE ORD/FREE PWR SKILL...SOC CONCPT TREND CHARTS GEN/LAWS VAL/FREE. PAGE 89 A1823
VOL/ASSN INT/ORG REGION

B60

LISTER L.,EUROPE'S COAL AND STEEL COMMUNITY. FRANCE GERMANY STRUCT ECO/DEV EXTR/IND INDUS MARKET NAT/G DELIB/GP ECO/TAC INT/TRADE EDU/PROP ATTIT RIGID/FLEX ORD/FREE PWR WEALTH...CONCPT STAT TIME/SEQ CHARTS ECSC 20. PAGE 90 A1843
EUR+WWI INT/ORG REGION

B60

MENEZES A.J.,O BRASIL E O MUNDO ASIO-AFRICANO (REV. ED.). AFR ASIA BRAZIL WOR+45 INT/TRADE ORD/FREE PWR SOVEREIGN...POLICY 20. PAGE 99 A2040
DIPLOM BAL/PWR LEAD ECO/UNDEV

B60

MORAES F.,THE REVOLT IN TIBET. ASIA CHINA/COM INDIA CULTURE CONTROL COERCE WAR TOTALISM...POLICY SOC WORSHIP 20 TIBET INTERVENT. PAGE 104 A2127
COLONIAL FORCES DIPLOM ORD/FREE

B60

MUNRO L.,UNITED NATIONS, HOPE FOR A DIVIDED WORLD. FUT WOR+45 CONSTN DELIB/GP CREATE TEC/DEV DIPLOM EDU/PROP LEGIT PEACE ATTIT HEALTH ORD/FREE PWR ...CONCPT TREND UN VAL/FREE 20. PAGE 106 A2172
INT/ORG ROUTINE

B60

NURTY K.S.,STUDIES IN PROBLEMS OF PEACE. CHRIST-17C MOD/EUR S/ASIA WOR+45 WOR-45 INT/ORG NAT/G SECT COERCE REV NAT/LISM ALL/VALS...CONCPT MYTH TIME/SEQ. PAGE 110 A2262
POLICY PEACE PACIFISM ORD/FREE

B60

RITNER P.,THE DEATH OF AFRICA. USA+45 ECO/UNDEV DIPLOM ECO/TAC REGION RACE/REL NAT/LISM ORD/FREE ...POLICY 20 NEGRO. PAGE 121 A2485
AFR SOCIETY FUT TASK

B60

ROPKE W.,A HUMANE ECONOMY. CULTURE ECO/DEV FINAN INDUS GP/REL CENTRAL WEALTH...GEOG SOC IDEA/COMP 20 EEC. PAGE 123 A2525
ECO/TAC INT/ORG DIPLOM ORD/FREE

B60

SETON-WATSON H.,NEITHER WAR NOR PEACE. ASIA USSR WOR+45 ELITES INT/ORG NAT/G EX/STRUC FORCES BAL/PWR ECO/TAC EDU/PROP COERCE NAT/LISM ORD/FREE WEALTH TOT/POP 20. PAGE 131 A2688
ATTIT PWR DIPLOM TOTALISM

B60

STEVENSON A.E.,PUTTING FIRST THINGS FIRST. USA+45 INT/ORG NEIGH FOR/AID DISCRIM...ANTHOL 20. PAGE 138 A2822
DIPLOM ECO/UNDEV ORD/FREE EDU/PROP

B60

STRACHEY J.,THE END OF EMPIRE. UK WOR+45 WOR-45 DIPLOM INT/TRADE DOMIN ADJUST ORD/FREE WEALTH ...SOCIALIST GOV/COMP TIME COMMONWLTH. PAGE 139 A2841
COLONIAL ECO/DEV BAL/PWR LAISSEZ

B60

TAYLOR M.D.,THE UNCERTAIN TRUMPET. USA+45 USSR WOR+45 INT/ORG NAT/G CONSULT DOMIN COERCE NUC/PWR WAR ATTIT ORD/FREE PWR...POLICY CONCPT TREND GEN/METH COLD/WAR UN NATO 20. PAGE 142 A2900
PLAN FORCES DIPLOM

B60

THEOBALD R.,THE RICH AND THE POOR: A STUDY OF THE ECONOMICS OF RISING EXPECTATIONS. WOR+45 CONSTN ECO/DEV ECO/UNDEV INT/ORG NAT/G PLAN FOR/AID ROUTINE BAL/PAY ORD/FREE PWR WEALTH...GEOG TREND
ECO/TAC INT/TRADE

WORK 20. PAGE 142 A2912

B60
THOMPSON K.W.,POLITICAL REALISM AND THE CRISIS IN WORLD POLITICS. USA+45 USA-45 SOCIETY INT/ORG NAT/G LEGIS TOP/EX LEGIT DETER ATTIT ORD/FREE PWR ...GEN/LAWS TOT/POP 20. PAGE 143 A2931
PLAN HUM BAL/PWR DIPLOM

B60
US HOUSE COMM FOREIGN AFFAIRS,HEARINGS ON A BILL TO AMEND FURTHER THE MUTUAL SECURITY ACT OF 1954. USA+45 CONSULT FORCES BUDGET FOR/AID CONFER DETER ...CHARTS 20 DEPT/DEFEN DEPT/STATE UNEF. PAGE 153 A3127
DIPLOM ORD/FREE DELIB/GP LEGIS

B60
US HOUSE COMM. SCI. ASTRONAUT.,OCEAN SCIENCES AND NATIONAL SECURITY. FUT SEA ECO/DEV EXTR/IND INT/ORG NAT/G FORCES ACT/RES TEC/DEV ECO/TAC COERCE WAR BIO/SOC KNOWL PWR...CONCPT RECORD LAB/EXP 20. PAGE 154 A3141
R+D ORD/FREE

B60
WODDIS J.,AFRICA: THE ROOTS OF REVOLT. SOUTH/AFR WORKER INT/TRADE RACE/REL DISCRIM ORD/FREE 20. PAGE 166 A3374
COLONIAL SOVEREIGN WAR ECO/UNDEV

B60
WOETZEL R.K.,THE INTERNATIONAL CONTROL OF AIRSPACE AND OUTERSPACE. FUT WOR+45 AIR CONSTN STRUCT CONSULT PLAN TEC/DEV ADJUD RIGID/FLEX KNOWL ORD/FREE PWR...TECHNIC GEOG MGT NEW/IDEA TREND COMPUT/IR VAL/FREE 20 TREATY. PAGE 166 A3375
INT/ORG JURID SPACE INT/LAW

L60
DEAN A.W.,"SECOND GENEVA CONFERENCE OF THE LAW OF THE SEA: THE FIGHT FOR FREEDOM OF THE SEAS." FUT USA+45 USSR WOR+45 WOR-45 SEA CONSTN STRUCT PLAN INT/TRADE ADJUD ADMIN ORD/FREE...DECISION RECORD TREND GEN/LAWS 20 TREATY. PAGE 35 A0717
INT/ORG JURID INT/LAW

L60
HOLTON G.,"ARMS CONTROL." FUT WOR+45 CULTURE INT/ORG NAT/G FORCES TOP/EX PLAN EDU/PROP COERCE ATTIT RIGID/FLEX ORD/FREE...POLICY PHIL/SCI SOC TREND COLD/WAR. PAGE 67 A1377
ACT/RES CONSULT ARMS/CONT NUC/PWR

L60
LAUTERPACHT E.,"THE UNITED NATIONS EMERGENCY FORCE." R+D LEGIT ROUTINE COERCE KNOWL ORD/FREE SKILL...JURID UN 20. PAGE 85 A1746
INT/ORG FORCES

L60
MCCLELLAND C.A.,"THE FUNCTION OF THEORY IN INTERNATIONAL RELATIONS." WOR+45 PLAN EDU/PROP ROUTINE ORD/FREE...PHIL/SCI PSY SOC METH/CNCPT NEW/IDEA OBS TREND GEN/METH 20. PAGE 97 A1997
INT/ORG CONCPT DIPLOM

L60
NOGEE J.L.,"THE DIPLOMACY OF DISARMAMENT." WOR+45 INT/ORG NAT/G CONSULT DELIB/GP TOP/EX BAL/PWR DIPLOM EDU/PROP COERCE DETER WEAPON PEACE ATTIT ...RECORD TIME/SEQ TOT/POP VAL/FREE COLD/WAR 20. PAGE 109 A2246
PWR ORD/FREE ARMS/CONT NUC/PWR

S60
BOGARDUS E.S.,"THE SOCIOLOGY OF A STRUCTURED PEACE." FUT SOCIETY CREATE DIPLOM EDU/PROP ADJUD ROUTINE ATTIT RIGID/FLEX KNOWL ORD/FREE RESPECT ...POLICY INT/LAW JURID NEW/IDEA SELF/OBS TOT/POP 20 UN. PAGE 16 A0327
INT/ORG SOC NAT/LISM PEACE

S60
COHEN A.,"THE NEW AFRICA AND THE UN." FUT ECO/UNDEV NAT/G ECO/TAC INT/TRADE CHOOSE ATTIT ORD/FREE PWR ...POLICY METH/CNCPT OBS TREND CON/ANAL GEN/LAWS TOT/POP VAL/FREE UN 20. PAGE 27 A0558
AFR INT/ORG BAL/PWR FOR/AID

S60
DOUGHERTY J.E.,"KEY TO SECURITY: DISARMAMENT OR ARMS STABILITY." COM USA+45 USSR INT/ORG NAT/G CREATE EDU/PROP COERCE DETER ATTIT PWR...DECISION CONCPT MYTH NEW/IDEA TREND 20 COLD/WAR. PAGE 38 A0777
FORCES ORD/FREE ARMS/CONT NUC/PWR

S60
GRACIA-MORA M.R.,"INTERNATIONAL RESPONSIBILITY FOR SUBVERSIVE ACTIVITIES AND HOSTILE PROPAGANDA BY PRIVATE PERSONS AGAINST." COM EUR+WWI L/A+17C UK USA+45 USSR WOR-45 CONSTN NAT/G LEGIT ADJUD REV PEACE TOTALISM ORD/FREE...INT/LAW 20. PAGE 55 A1119
INT/ORG JURID SOVEREIGN

S60
HAVILAND H.F.,"PROBLEMS OF AMERICAN FOREIGN POLICY." ASIA COM USA+45 WOR+45 INT/ORG NAT/G CONSULT ECO/TAC FOR/AID DOMIN COERCE NUC/PWR ATTIT DRIVE ORD/FREE PWR RESPECT SKILL...POLICY GEOG OBS SAMP TREND GEN/METH METH COLD/WAR UN 20. PAGE 63 A1292
ECO/UNDEV FORCES DIPLOM

S60
IKLE F.C.,"NTH COUNTRIES AND DISARMAMENT." WOR+45 DELIB/GP ECO/TAC DOMIN EDU/PROP LEGIT ROUTINE COERCE RIGID/FLEX ORD/FREE...MARXIST TREND 20. PAGE 70 A1432
FUT INT/ORG ARMS/CONT NUC/PWR

S60
MAGATHAN W.,"SOME BASES OF WEST GERMAN MILITARY POLICY." EUR+WWI FUT INT/ORG TOP/EX ECO/TAC DOMIN DRIVE ORD/FREE PWR...TRADIT GEOG OBS TREND. PAGE 93 A1904
NAT/G FORCES GERMANY

S60
MORA J.A.,"THE ORGANIZATION OF AMERICAN STATES." USA+45 LAW ECO/UNDEV VOL/ASSN DELIB/GP PLAN BAL/PWR EDU/PROP ADMIN DRIVE RIGID/FLEX ORD/FREE WEALTH ...TIME/SEQ GEN/LAWS OAS 20. PAGE 103 A2126
L/A+17C INT/ORG REGION

S60
MORGENSTERN O.,"GOAL: AN ARMED, INSPECTED, OPEN WORLD." COM EUR+WWI USA+45 R+D INT/ORG NAT/G TEC/DEV BAL/PWR COERCE NUC/PWR ORD/FREE PWR...TREND 20. PAGE 104 A2133
FORCES CONCPT ARMS/CONT DETER

S60
MUNRO L.,"CAN THE UNITED NATIONS ENFORCE PEACE." WOR+45 LAW INT/ORG VOL/ASSN BAL/PWR LEGIT ARMS/CONT COERCE DETER PEACE PWR...CONCPT REC/INT TREND UN 20 HAMMARSK/D. PAGE 106 A2173
FORCES ORD/FREE

S60
OWEN C.F.,"US AND SOVIET RELATIONS WITH UNDERDEVELOPED COUNTRIES: LATIN AMERICA-A CASE STUDY." AFR COM L/A+17C USA+45 USSR EXTR/IND MARKET TEC/DEV DIPLOM ECO/TAC NAT/LISM ORD/FREE PWR ...TREND WORK 20. PAGE 112 A2303
ECO/UNDEV DRIVE INT/TRADE

S60
PADELFORD N.J.,"POLITICS AND CHANGE IN THE SECURITY COUNCIL." FUT WOR+45 CONSTN NAT/G EX/STRUC LEGIS ORD/FREE...CONCPT CHARTS UN 20. PAGE 113 A2309
INT/ORG DELIB/GP

S60
POTTER P.B.,"RELATIVE VALUES OF INTERNATIONAL RELATIONS, LAW, AND ORGANIZATIONS." WOR+45 NAT/G LEGIT ADJUD ORD/FREE...CONCPT TOT/POP COLD/WAR 20. PAGE 117 A2401
INT/ORG LEGIS DIPLOM INT/LAW

S60
RHYNE C.S.,"LAW AS AN INSTRUMENT FOR PEACE." FUT WOR+45 PLAN LEGIT ROUTINE ARMS/CONT NUC/PWR ATTIT ORD/FREE...JURID METH/CNCPT TREND CON/ANAL HYPO/EXP COLD/WAR 20. PAGE 120 A2471
ADJUD EDU/PROP INT/LAW PEACE

S60
THOMPSON K.W.,"MORAL PURPOSE IN FOREIGN POLICY: REALITIES AND ILLUSIONS." WOR+45 WOR-45 LAW CULTURE SOCIETY INT/ORG PLAN ADJUD ADMIN COERCE RIGID/FLEX SUPEGO KNOWL ORD/FREE PWR...SOC TREND SOC/EXP TOT/POP 20. PAGE 143 A2930
MORAL JURID DIPLOM

S60
WRIGHT Q.,"LEGAL ASPECTS OF THE U-2 INCIDENT." COM USA+45 USSR STRUCT NAT/G FORCES PLAN TEC/DEV ADJUD RIGID/FLEX MORAL ORD/FREE...DECISION INT/LAW JURID PSY TREND GEN/LAWS COLD/WAR VAL/FREE 20 U-2. PAGE 168 A3413
PWR POLICY SPACE

B61
ANAND R.P.,COMPULSORY JURISDICTION OF INTERNATIONAL COURT OF JUSTICE. FUT WOR+45 SOCIETY PLAN LEGIT ADJUD ATTIT DRIVE PERSON ORD/FREE...JURID CONCPT TREND 20 ICJ. PAGE 8 A0156
INT/ORG COERCE INT/LAW

B61
BARNES W.,THE FOREIGN SERVICE OF THE UNITED STATES. USA+45 USA-45 CONSTN INT/ORG POL/PAR CONSULT DELIB/GP LEGIS DOMIN EDU/PROP EXEC ATTIT RIGID/FLEX ORD/FREE PWR...POLICY CONCPT STAT OBS RECORD BIOG TIME/SEQ TREND. PAGE 11 A0224
NAT/G MGT DIPLOM

B61
BELOFF M.,NEW DIMENSIONS IN FOREIGN POLICY: A STUDY IN BRITISH ADMINISTRATION. UK NAT/G ATTIT RIGID/FLEX ORD/FREE...GEN/LAWS EUR+WWI CMN/WLTH EEC 20. PAGE 13 A0260
INT/ORG DIPLOM

B61
BONNEFOUS M.,EUROPE ET TIERS MONDE. EUR+WWI SOCIETY INT/ORG NAT/G VOL/ASSN ACT/RES TEC/DEV CAP/ISM ECO/TAC ATTIT ORD/FREE SOVEREIGN...POLICY CONCPT TREND 20. PAGE 16 A0334
AFR ECO/UNDEV FOR/AID INT/TRADE

B61
BRENNAN D.G.,ARMS CONTROL, DISARMAMENT, AND NATIONAL SECURITY. WOR+45 NAT/G FORCES CREATE PROB/SOLV PARTIC WAR PEACE...DECISION INT/LAW ANTHOL BIBLIOG 20. PAGE 18 A0372
ARMS/CONT ORD/FREE DIPLOM POLICY

B61
CAMERON J.,THE AFRICAN REVOLUTION. AFR UK ECO/UNDEV POL/PAR REGION RACE/REL DISCRIM PWR CONSERVE ...CONCPT SOC/INTEG 20 NEGRO. PAGE 23 A0472
REV COLONIAL ORD/FREE DIPLOM

B61
DEAN V.M.,BUILDERS OF EMERGING NATIONS. WOR+45 ECO/UNDEV ECO/TAC NEUTRAL TOTALISM ORD/FREE PWR ...BIOG AUD/VIS IDEA/COMP BIBLIOG 20 COLD/WAR. PAGE 35 A0719
NAT/G CHIEF POLICY DIPLOM

B61
DELZELL C.F.,MUSSOLINI'S ENEMIES - THE ITALIAN ANTI-FASCIST RESISTANCE. ITALY DIPLOM PRESS DETER WAR TOTALISM ORD/FREE MARXISM 20. PAGE 36 A0730
FASCISM GP/REL POL/PAR REV

B61
DIA M.,THE AFRICAN NATIONS AND WORLD SOLIDARITY. ISLAM CULTURE ELITES ECO/DEV ECO/UNDEV INT/ORG NAT/G PLAN ECO/TAC INT/TRADE EDU/PROP NAT/LISM ATTIT DRIVE ORD/FREE WEALTH...SOCIALIST CONCPT CON/ANAL GEN/LAWS TOT/POP 20. PAGE 37 A0753
AFR REGION SOCISM

B61
GALLOIS P.,THE BALANCE OF TERROR: STRATEGY FOR THE
PLAN

NUCLEAR AGE. FUT WOR+45 INT/ORG FORCES TOP/EX DETER WAR ATTIT RIGID/FLEX ORD/FREE PWR...HYPO/EXP 20. PAGE 50 A1032 — DECISION DIPLOM NUC/PWR

B61
GRAEBNER N.,THE NEW ISOLATIONISM: A STUDY IN POLITICS AND FOREIGN POLICY SINCE 1960. USA+45 INT/ORG LOC/G NAT/G POL/PAR LEGIS BAL/PWR EDU/PROP CHOOSE ATTIT PERSON ORD/FREE 20 TRUMAN/HS EISNHWR/DD. PAGE 55 A1120 — EXEC PWR DIPLOM

B61
GRAEBNER N.,AN UNCERTAIN TRADITION: AMERICAN SECRETARIES OF STATE IN THE 20TH CENTURY. USA+45 CONSTN INT/ORG NAT/G DELIB/GP TOP/EX BAL/PWR DOMIN LEGIT ADMIN ARMS/CONT ATTIT DRIVE PERSON SUPEGO ORD/FREE PWR...GEN/LAWS VAL/FREE CONGRESS. PAGE 55 A1121 — USA-45 BIOG DIPLOM

B61
HADDAD J.A.,REVOLUCAO CUBANA E REVOLUCAO BRASILEIRA. BRAZIL CUBA L/A+17C STRATA AGRI WORKER EDU/PROP REGION...POLICY NAT/COMP 20. PAGE 59 A1210 — REV ORD/FREE DIPLOM ECO/UNDEV

B61
JAKOBSON M.,THE DIPLOMACY OF THE WINTER WAR. EUR+WWI FINLAND GERMANY USSR INT/ORG NAT/G PEACE TOTALISM PWR...POLICY CONCPT 20 TREATY. PAGE 73 A1492 — WAR ORD/FREE DIPLOM

B61
KERTESZ S.D.,AMERICAN DIPLOMACY IN A NEW ERA. COM S/ASIA UK USA+45 FORCES PROB/SOLV BAL/PWR ECO/TAC ADMIN COLONIAL WAR PEACE ORD/FREE 20 NATO CONGRESS UN COLD/WAR. PAGE 78 A1601 — ANTHOL DIPLOM TREND

B61
KHAN A.W.,INDIA WINS FREEDOM: THE OTHER SIDE. INDIA PAKISTAN CULTURE LEGIS DIPLOM PARL/PROC REV WAR NAT/LISM 20. PAGE 78 A1607 — SOVEREIGN GP/REL RACE/REL ORD/FREE

B61
LERCHE C.O. JR.,FOREIGN POLICY OF THE AMERICAN PEOPLE (REV. ED.). USA+45 USSR FORCES TEC/DEV EDU/PROP WAR PRODUC ORD/FREE MARXISM...POLICY TREND BIBLIOG 20 COLD/WAR. PAGE 87 A1781 — DECISION PLAN PEACE DIPLOM

B61
LUKACS J.,A HISTORY OF THE COLD WAR. ASIA COM EUR+WWI USA+45 USA-45 INT/ORG NAT/G DELIB/GP ACT/RES BAL/PWR DIPLOM DOMIN EDU/PROP LEGIT DRIVE ORD/FREE...TREND COLD/WAR 20. PAGE 91 A1872 — PWR TIME/SEQ USSR

B61
MCDOUGAL M.S.,LAW AND MINIMUM WORLD PUBLIC ORDER. WOR+45 SOCIETY NAT/G DELIB/GP EDU/PROP LEGIT ADJUD COERCE ATTIT PERSON...JURID CONCPT RECORD TREND TOT/POP 20. PAGE 98 A2006 — INT/ORG ORD/FREE INT/LAW

B61
MECHAM J.L.,THE UNITED STATES AND INTER-AMERICAN SECURITY, 1889-1960. L/A+17C USA+45 USA-45 CONSTN FORCES INT/TRADE PEACE TOTALISM ATTIT...JURID 19/20 UN OAS. PAGE 99 A2030 — DIPLOM WAR ORD/FREE INT/ORG

B61
MILLIKAW M.F.,THE EMERGING NATIONS: THEIR GROWTH AND UNITED STATES POLICY. FUT USA+45 WOR+45 WOR-45 NAT/G PLAN TEC/DEV BAL/PWR GOV/REL PEACE ORD/FREE 20. PAGE 101 A2082 — ECO/UNDEV POLICY DIPLOM FOR/AID

B61
OAKES J.B.,THE EDGE OF FREEDOM. EUR+WWI USA+45 USSR ECO/UNDEV BAL/PWR DIPLOM DOMIN COLONIAL PWR MARXISM POPULISM...IDEA/COMP 20 COLD/WAR. PAGE 111 A2271 — AFR ORD/FREE SOVEREIGN NEUTRAL

B61
OEEC,LIBERALISATION OF CURRENT INVISIBLES AND CAPITAL MOVEMENTS BY THE OEEC (PAMPHLET). WOR+45 ECO/DEV BUDGET ECO/TAC ORD/FREE 20. PAGE 111 A2282 — FINAN INT/ORG INT/TRADE BAL/PAY

B61
PANIKKAR K.M.,THE VOICE OF FREEDOM: SELECTED SPEECHES OF PANDIT MOTILAL NEHRU. INDIA UK CONSTN FINAN FORCES LEGIS DIPLOM TAX COLONIAL...POLICY MAJORIT ANTHOL 20 NEHRU/PM. PAGE 114 A2331 — NAT/LISM ORD/FREE CHIEF NAT/G

B61
PERKINS D.,THE UNITED STATES AND LATIN AMERICAN. L/A+17C USA+45 USA-45 STRUCT COLONIAL REV ORD/FREE 19/20. PAGE 115 A2360 — DIPLOM INT/TRADE NAT/G

B61
ROBERTSON A.H.,THE LAW OF INTERNATIONAL INSTITUTIONS IN EUROPE. EUR+WWI MOD/EUR INT/ORG NAT/G VOL/ASSN DELIB/GP...JURID TIME/SEQ TOT/POP 20 TREATY. PAGE 122 A2497 — RIGID/FLEX ORD/FREE

B61
SCHMIDT H.,VERTEIDIGUNG ODER VERGELTUNG. COM CUBA GERMANY/W USSR FORCES DIPLOM ARMS/CONT DETER NUC/PWR...POLICY CHARTS HYPO/EXP SIMUL BIBLIOG 20 NATO COLD/WAR. PAGE 128 A2630 — PLAN WAR BAL/PWR ORD/FREE

B61
SCHNAPPER B.,LA POLITIQUE ET LE COMMERCE FRANCAIS DANS LE GOLFE DE GUINEE DE 1838 A 1871. FRANCE GUINEA UK SEA EXTR/IND NAT/G DELIB/GP LEGIS ADMIN ORD/FREE...POLICY GEOG CENSUS CHARTS BIBLIOG 19. PAGE 129 A2636 — COLONIAL INT/TRADE DOMIN AFR

B61
SCHONBRUNN G.,WELTKRIEGE UND REVOLUTIONEN 1914-1945. USSR DIPLOM TOTALISM ORD/FREE 20 TREATY WWI NAZI. PAGE 129 A2643 — WAR REV FASCISM SOCISM

B61
STILLMAN E.,THE NEW POLITICS: AMERICA AND THE END OF THE POSTWAR WORLD. FUT WOR+45 CULTURE SOCIETY ECO/UNDEV INT/ORG NAT/G FORCES TOP/EX ACT/RES DIPLOM EDU/PROP LEGIT ROUTINE DETER ATTIT ORD/FREE PWR...OBS STERTYP COLD/WAR TOT/POP VAL/FREE. PAGE 138 A2827 — USA+45 PLAN

B61
STONE J.,QUEST FOR SURVIVAL. WOR+45 NAT/G VOL/ASSN LEGIT ADMIN ARMS/CONT COERCE DISPL ORD/FREE PWR ...POLICY INT/LAW JURID COLD/WAR 20. PAGE 139 A2836 — INT/ORG ADJUD SOVEREIGN

B61
US SENATE COMM GOVT OPERATIONS,ORGANIZING FOR NATIONAL SECURITY. COM USA+45 BUDGET DIPLOM DETER NUC/PWR WAR WEAPON ORD/FREE...BIBLIOG 20 COLD/WAR. PAGE 156 A3172 — POLICY PLAN FORCES COERCE

B61
US SENATE COMM ON FOREIGN RELS,INTERNATIONAL DEVELOPMENT AND SECURITY: HEARINGS ON BILL (2 VOLS.). ECO/UNDEV FINAN FORCES REV COST WEALTH ...CHARTS 20 AID PRESIDENT. PAGE 157 A3191 — FOR/AID CIVMIL/REL ORD/FREE ECO/TAC

B61
WALLERSTEIN I.M.,AFRICA; THE POLITICS OF INDEPENDENCE. AFR SOCIETY STRUCT LEAD PARL/PROC PARTIC GP/REL...POLICY 20. PAGE 160 A3269 — ECO/UNDEV DIPLOM COLONIAL ORD/FREE

B61
YDIT M.,INTERNATIONALISED TERRITORIES. FUT WOR+45 WOR-45 CONSTN VOL/ASSN CREATE PLAN LEGIT PEACE ORD/FREE...GEOG INT/LAW JURID SOC NEW/IDEA OBS RECORD SAMP TIME/SEQ TREND 19/20 BERLIN. PAGE 169 A3431 — LOC/G INT/ORG DIPLOM SOVEREIGN

L61
CLAUDE I.,"THE UNITED NATIONS AND THE USE OF FORCE." FUT WOR+45 SOCIETY DIPLOM EDU/PROP LEGIT ADMIN ROUTINE COERCE WAR PEACE ORD/FREE...CONCPT TREND UN 20. PAGE 27 A0545 — INT/ORG FORCES

L61
HOYT E.C.,"UNITED STATES REACTION TO THE KOREAN ATTACK." COM KOREA USA+45 CONSTN DELIB/GP FORCES PLAN ECO/TAC DOMIN EDU/PROP LEGIT ROUTINE COERCE WAR ATTIT DISPL RIGID/FLEX ORD/FREE PWR...POLICY INT/LAW TREND UN 20. PAGE 68 A1402 — ASIA INT/ORG BAL/PWR DIPLOM

L61
TAUBENFELD H.J.,"A REGIME FOR OUTER SPACE." FUT UNIV R+D ACT/RES PLAN BAL/PWR LEGIT ARMS/CONT ORD/FREE...POLICY JURID TREND UN TOT/POP 20 COLD/WAR. PAGE 142 A2894 — INT/ORG ADJUD SPACE

L61
WRIGHT Q.,"STUDIES IN DETERRENCE: LIMITED WARS AND THE ROLE OF SEABORNE WEAPONS SYSTEMS." FUT USA+45 WOR+45 SEA INT/ORG NAT/G FORCES ACT/RES WAR WEAPON ORD/FREE TOT/POP 20. PAGE 168 A3415 — TEC/DEV SKILL BAL/PWR DETER

S61
HAAS E.B.,"INTERNATIONAL INTEGRATION: THE EUROPEAN AND THE UNIVERSAL PROCESS." EUR+WWI FUT WOR+45 NAT/G EX/STRUC ATTIT DRIVE ORD/FREE PWR...CONCPT GEN/LAWS OEEC 20 NATO COUNCL/EUR. PAGE 59 A1207 — INT/ORG TREND REGION

S61
MIKSCHE F.O.,"DEFENSE ORGANIZATION FOR WESTERN EUROPE." USA+45 INT/ORG NAT/G VOL/ASSN ACT/RES DOMIN LEGIT COERCE ORD/FREE PWR...RELATIV TREND 20 NATO. PAGE 101 A2071 — EUR+WWI FORCES WEAPON NUC/PWR

S61
MILLER E.,"LEGAL ASPECTS OF UN ACTION IN THE CONGO." AFR CULTURE ADMIN PEACE DRIVE RIGID/FLEX ORD/FREE...WELF/ST JURID OBS UN CONGO 20. PAGE 101 A2076 — INT/ORG LEGIT

S61
PADELFORD N.J.,"POLITICS AND THE FUTURE OF ECOSOC." AFR S/ASIA ECO/UNDEV INDUS NAT/G DELIB/GP ACT/RES ORD/FREE WEALTH...CONCPT CHARTS UN 20 ECOSOC. PAGE 113 A2310 — INT/ORG TEC/DEV

S61
ZAGORIA D.S.,"SINO-SOVIET FRICTION IN UNDERDEVELOPED AREAS." ASIA CHINA/COM COM ACT/RES PLAN ATTIT ORD/FREE PWR COLD/WAR 20. PAGE 169 A3443 — ECO/UNDEV ECO/TAC INT/TRADE USSR

B62
AMERICAN LAW INSTITUTE,FOREIGN RELATIONS LAW OF THE UNITED STATES: RESTATEMENT, SECOND. USA+45 NAT/G LEGIS ADJUD EXEC ROUTINE GOV/REL...INT/LAW JURID CONCPT 20 TREATY. PAGE 7 A0152 — PROF/ORG LAW DIPLOM ORD/FREE

B62
BLACKETT P.M.S.,STUDIES OF WAR: NUCLEAR AND CONVENTIONAL. EUR+WWI USA+45 DELIB/GP ACT/RES CREATE PLAN TEC/DEV LEGIT COERCE WAR ORD/FREE PWR ...POLICY TECHNIC TIME/SEQ 20. PAGE 15 A0300 — INT/ORG FORCES ARMS/CONT NUC/PWR

B62
BUCHMANN J.,L'AFRIQUE NOIRE INDEPENDANTE. POL/PAR DIPLOM COLONIAL PARTIC CHOOSE GP/REL ATTIT ORD/FREE — AFR NAT/LISM

WEALTH NEGRO. PAGE 21 A0426
DECISION

B62
CARLSTON K.S.,LAW AND ORGANIZATION IN WORLD SOCIETY. WOR+45 FINAN ECO/TAC DOMIN LEGIT CT/SYS ROUTINE COERCE ORD/FREE PWR WEALTH...PLURIST DECISION JURID MGT METH/CNCPT GEN/LAWS 20. PAGE 24 A0487
INT/ORG LAW

B62
COUNCIL ON WORLD TENSIONS,A STUDY OF WORLD TENSIONS AND DEVELOPMENT. WOR+45 ECO/DEV ECO/UNDEV INT/ORG PLAN DIPLOM ECO/TAC EDU/PROP ATTIT KNOWL ORD/FREE PWR WEALTH...CONCPT TREND CHARTS STERTYP COLD/WAR TOT/POP 20. PAGE 31 A0640
TEC/DEV SOC

B62
DAVAR F.C.,IRAN AND INDIA THROUGH THE AGES. INDIA IRAN ELITES SECT CREATE ORD/FREE...LING BIBLIOG. PAGE 34 A0683
NAT/COMP DIPLOM CULTURE

B62
DOUGLAS W.O.,DEMOCRACY'S MANIFESTO. COM USA+45 ECO/UNDEV INT/ORG FORCES PLAN NEUTRAL TASK MARXISM ...JURID 20 NATO SEATO. PAGE 38 A0779
DIPLOM POLICY NAT/G ORD/FREE

B62
DUROSELLE J.B.,HISTOIRE DIPLOMATIQUE DE 1919 A NOS JOURS (3RD ED.). FRANCE INT/ORG CHIEF FORCES CONFER ARMS/CONT WAR PEACE ORD/FREE...T TREATY 20 COLD/WAR. PAGE 39 A0807
DIPLOM WOR+45 WOR-45

B62
DUTOIT B.,LA NEUTRALITE SUISSE A L'HEURE EUROPEENNE. EUR+WWI MOD/EUR INT/ORG NAT/G VOL/ASSN PLAN BAL/PWR LEGIT NEUTRAL REGION PEACE ORD/FREE SOVEREIGN...CONCPT OBS TIME/SEQ TREND STERTYP VAL/FREE LEAGUE/NAT UN 20. PAGE 40 A0812
ATTIT DIPLOM SWITZERLND

B62
EBENSTEIN W.,TWO WAYS OF LIFE. USA+45 CULTURE ECO/DEV PLAN EDU/PROP CONTROL ORD/FREE...GOV/COMP IDEA/COMP T 20 MARX/KARL ENGELS/F LENIN/VI LOCKE/JOHN MILL/JS. PAGE 40 A0819
MARXISM POPULISM ECO/TAC DIPLOM

B62
ELLIOTT J.R.,THE APPEAL OF COMMUNISM IN THE UNDERDEVELOPED NATIONS. USSR WOR+45 INT/ORG NAT/G DIPLOM DOMIN EDU/PROP ROUTINE ATTIT RIGID/FLEX ORD/FREE PWR WEALTH MARXISM...POLICY SOC METH/CNCPT MYTH TOT/POP COLD/WAR 20. PAGE 41 A0842
COM ECO/UNDEV

B62
FORBES H.W.,THE STRATEGY OF DISARMAMENT. FUT WOR+45 INT/ORG VOL/ASSN CONSULT ARMS/CONT COERCE NUC/PWR WAR DRIVE RIGID/FLEX ORD/FREE PWR...POLICY CONCPT OBS TREND STERTYP 20. PAGE 47 A0959
PLAN FORCES DIPLOM

B62
GOLDWATER B.M.,WHY NOT VICTORY? A FRESH LOOK AT AMERICAN FOREIGN POLICY. USA+45 WOR+45 FOR/AID LEAD ARMS/CONT WAR PEACE ATTIT ORD/FREE PWR MARXISM ...INT/LAW 20 TREATY ECHR COUNCL/EUR. PAGE 53 A1092
DIPLOM POLICY CONSERVE NAT/LISM

B62
GRAEBNER N.,COLD WAR DIPLOMACY 1945-1960. WOR+45 INT/ORG ECO/TAC EDU/PROP COERCE ORD/FREE PWR WEALTH ...HIST/WRIT TOT/POP VAL/FREE COLD/WAR 20. PAGE 55 A1122
USA+45 DIPLOM

B62
HARARI M.,GOVERNMENT AND POLITICS OF THE MIDDLE EAST. ISLAM USA+45 NAT/G SECT CHIEF ADMIN ORD/FREE 20. PAGE 61 A1257
DIPLOM ECO/UNDEV TEC/DEV POLICY

B62
JORDAN A.A. JR.,FOREIGN AID AND THE DEFENSE OF SOUTHEAST ASIA. PAKISTAN VIETNAM/S FINAN PLAN BUDGET ECO/TAC DETER WAR ORD/FREE...POLICY DECISION CENSUS CHARTS BIBLIOG 20. PAGE 75 A1535
FOR/AID S/ASIA FORCES ECO/UNDEV

B62
KAHN H.,THINKING ABOUT THE UNTHINKABLE. FUT USA+45 LAW NAT/G CONSULT FORCES ACT/RES CREATE PLAN TEC/DEV BAL/PWR DIPLOM EDU/PROP ARMS/CONT DETER ATTIT...CONCPT OBS TREND COLD/WAR 20. PAGE 76 A1547
INT/ORG ORD/FREE NUC/PWR PEACE

B62
KENT R.K.,FROM MADAGASCAR TO THE MALAGASY REPUBLIC. FRANCE MADAGASCAR DIPLOM NAT/LISM ORD/FREE...MGT 18/20. PAGE 78 A1596
COLONIAL SOVEREIGN REV POL/PAR

B62
KING G.,THE UNITED NATIONS IN THE CONGO: A QUEST FOR PEACE. WOR+45 NAT/G CONSULT FORCES LEGIT COERCE WAR ORD/FREE...JURID METH/CNCPT OBS INT HIST/WRIT TIME/SEQ CONGO UN 20 COLD/WAR. PAGE 79 A1624
AFR INT/ORG

B62
KRAFT J.,THE GRAND DESIGN. EUR+WWI USA+45 AGRI FINAN INDUS MARKET INT/ORG NAT/G PLAN ECO/TAC TARIFFS REGION DRIVE ORD/FREE WEALTH...POLICY OBS TREND EEC 20. PAGE 82 A1674
VOL/ASSN ECO/DEV INT/TRADE

B62
LEFEVER E.W.,ARMS AND ARMS CONTROL. COM USA+45 INT/ORG TEC/DEV DIPLOM ORD/FREE 20. PAGE 86 A1763
ATTIT PWR ARMS/CONT BAL/PWR

B62
LEVY H.V.,LIBERDADE E JUSTICA SOCIAL (2ND ED.). BRAZIL COM L/A+17C USSR INT/ORG PARTIC GP/REL WEALTH 20 UN COM/PARTY. PAGE 88 A1798
ORD/FREE MARXISM CAP/ISM LAW

B62
MACKENTOSH J.M.,STRATEGY AND TACTICS OF SOVIET FOREIGN POLICY. CHINA/COM FUT USA+45 WOR+45 INT/ORG PLAN DOMIN LEGIT ROUTINE COERCE NUC/PWR WAR ATTIT DRIVE ORD/FREE PWR...CONCPT OBS TIME/SEQ TREND GEN/METH COLD/WAR 20. PAGE 92 A1894
COM POLICY DIPLOM USSR

B62
MANDER J.,BERLIN: HOSTAGE FOR THE WEST. FUT GERMANY WOR+45 FOR/AID RISK ATTIT ORD/FREE 20 BERLIN COLD/WAR. PAGE 93 A1916
DIPLOM BAL/PWR DOMIN DETER

B62
MCDOUGAL M.S.,THE PUBLIC ORDER OF THE OCEANS. WOR+45 WOR-45 SEA INT/ORG NAT/G CONSULT DELIB/GP DIPLOM LEGIT PEACE RIGID/FLEX...GEOG INT/LAW JURID RECORD TOT/POP 20 TREATY. PAGE 98 A2007
ADJUD ORD/FREE

B62
MODELSKI G.,SEATO-SIX STUDIES. ASIA CHINA/COM INDIA S/ASIA INT/ORG NAT/G ECO/TAC DETER ATTIT ORD/FREE PWR...TIME/SEQ COLD/WAR TOT/POP 20 SEATO. PAGE 102 A2098
MARKET ECO/UNDEV INT/TRADE

B62
MORGENSTERN O.,STRATEGIE - HEUTE (2ND ED.). USA+45 USSR ECO/DEV DELIB/GP WAR PEACE ORD/FREE...GOV/COMP NAT/COMP 20 COLD/WAR NATO. PAGE 104 A2134
NUC/PWR DIPLOM FORCES TEC/DEV

B62
MULLEY F.W.,THE POLITICS OF WESTERN DEFENSE. EUR+WWI USA-45 WOR+45 VOL/ASSN EX/STRUC FORCES COERCE DETER PEACE ATTIT ORD/FREE PWR...RECORD TIME/SEQ CHARTS COLD/WAR 20 NATO. PAGE 106 A2168
INT/ORG DELIB/GP NUC/PWR

B62
NEAL F.W.,WAR AND PEACE AND GERMANY. EUR+WWI USSR STRUCT INT/ORG NAT/G FORCES DOMIN EDU/PROP LEGIT EXEC COERCE ORD/FREE...HUM SOC NEW/IDEA OBS TIME/SEQ TOT/POP COLD/WAR 20 BERLIN. PAGE 108 A2208
USA+45 POLICY DIPLOM GERMANY

B62
NOBECOURT R.G.,LES SECRETS DE LA PROPAGANDE EN FRANCE OCCUPEE. FRANCE ELITES NAT/G DIPLOM GP/REL NAT/LISM TOTALISM ORD/FREE 20 VICHY VICHY. PAGE 109 A2244
METH/COMP EDU/PROP WAR CONTROL

B62
OSGOOD C.E.,AN ALTERNATIVE TO WAR OR SURRENDER. FUT UNIV CULTURE INTELL SOCIETY R+D INT/ORG CONSULT DELIB/GP ACT/RES PLAN CHOOSE ATTIT PERCEPT KNOWL ...PHIL/SCI PSY SOC TREND GEN/LAWS 20. PAGE 112 A2300
ORD/FREE EDU/PROP PEACE WAR

B62
OSGOOD R.E.,NATO: THE ENTANGLING ALLIANCE. USA+45 WOR+45 VOL/ASSN FORCES TOP/EX PLAN DETER WEAPON DRIVE RIGID/FLEX ORD/FREE PWR...TREND 20 NATO. PAGE 112 A2301
INT/ORG ARMS/CONT PEACE

B62
POSTON R.W.,DEMOCRACY SPEAKS MANY TONGUES. L/A+17C USA+45 ECO/UNDEV ACT/RES ECO/TAC ADMIN ORD/FREE ...METH/COMP 20. PAGE 117 A2397
FOR/AID DIPLOM CAP/ISM MARXISM

B62
ROSENNE S.,THE WORLD COURT: WHAT IT IS AND HOW IT WORKS. WOR+45 WOR-45 LAW CONSTN JUDGE EDU/PROP LEGIT ROUTINE CHOOSE PEACE ORD/FREE...JURID OBS TIME/SEQ CHARTS UN TOT/POP VAL/FREE 20. PAGE 124 A2538
INT/ORG ADJUD INT/LAW

B62
SCHRODER P.M.,METTERNICH'S DIPLOMACY AT ITS ZENITH, 1820-1823. MOD/EUR ELITES INT/ORG VOL/ASSN DELIB/GP ECO/TAC EDU/PROP DISPL PWR SOVEREIGN...POLICY CONCPT GEN/LAWS 19 METTRNCH/K. PAGE 129 A2647
ORD/FREE BIOG BAL/PWR DIPLOM

B62
SCHWARZENBERGER G.,THE FRONTIERS OF INTERNATIONAL LAW. WOR+45 WOR-45 NAT/G LEGIT CT/SYS ROUTINE MORAL ORD/FREE PWR...JURID SOC GEN/METH 20 COLD/WAR. PAGE 130 A2661
INT/ORG LAW INT/LAW

B62
SINGER J.D.,DETERRENCE, ARMS CONTROL AND DISARMAMENT: TOWARD A SYNTHESIS IN NATIONAL SECURITY POLICY. COM USA+45 INT/ORG BAL/PWR DETER ORD/FREE...POLICY COLD/WAR 20. PAGE 133 A2727
FUT ACT/RES ARMS/CONT

B62
SPANIER J.W.,THE POLITICS OF DISARMAMENT. COM USA+45 USSR EDU/PROP ATTIT ORD/FREE PWR RESPECT ...MYTH RECORD 20 COLD/WAR. PAGE 135 A2771
INT/ORG DELIB/GP ARMS/CONT

B62
STARR R.E.,POLAND 1944-1962: THE SOVIETIZATION OF A CAPTIVE PEOPLE. COM POLAND USSR POL/PAR SECT LEGIS DIPLOM DOMIN EDU/PROP CHOOSE ORD/FREE...POLICY CHARTS BIBLIOG 20. PAGE 137 A2808
MARXISM NAT/G TOTALISM NAT/COMP

B62
STRACHEY J.,ON THE PREVENTION OF WAR. FUT WOR+45 INT/ORG NAT/G ACT/RES PLAN BAL/PWR DOMIN EDU/PROP PEACE ATTIT...POLICY TREND TOT/POP COLD/WAR 20 UN. PAGE 139 A2842
FORCES ORD/FREE ARMS/CONT NUC/PWR

B62
TAYLOR D.,THE BRITISH IN AFRICA. UK CULTURE ECO/UNDEV INDUS DIPLOM INT/TRADE ADMIN WAR RACE/REL ORD/FREE SOVEREIGN...POLICY BIBLIOG 15/20 CMN/WLTH. PAGE 142 A2898 — AFR COLONIAL DOMIN

B62
UNIVERSITY OF TENNESSEE,GOVERNMENT AND WORLD CRISIS. USA+45 FOR/AID ORD/FREE...ANTHOL 20 UN. PAGE 149 A3048 — ECO/DEV DIPLOM NAT/G INT/ORG

B62
US SENATE COMM GOVT OPERATIONS,ADMINISTRATION OF NATIONAL SECURITY. USA+45 CHIEF PLAN PROB/SOLV TEC/DEV DIPLOM ATTIT...POLICY DECISION 20 KENNEDY/JF RUSK/D MCNAMARA/R BUNDY/M HERTER/C. PAGE 156 A3173 — ORD/FREE ADMIN NAT/G CONTROL

B62
US SENATE COMM ON JUDICIARY,CONSTITUTIONAL RIGHTS OF MILITARY PERSONNEL. USA+45 USA-45 FORCES DIPLOM WAR CONGRESS. PAGE 157 A3193 — CONSTN ORD/FREE JURID CT/SYS

B62
WOETZEL R.K.,THE NURENBERG TRIALS IN INTERNATIONAL LAW. CHRIST-17C MOD/EUR WOR+45 SOCIETY NAT/G DELIB/GP DOMIN LEGIT ROUTINE ATTIT DRIVE PERSON SUPEGO MORAL ORD/FREE...POLICY MAJORIT JURID PSY SOC SELF/OBS RECORD NAZI TOT/POP. PAGE 166 A3376 — INT/ORG ADJUD WAR

B62
WOLFERS A.,DISCORD AND COLLABORATION: ESSAYS ON INTERNATIONAL POLITICS. WOR+45 CULTURE SOCIETY INT/ORG NAT/G BAL/PWR DIPLOM DOMIN NAT/LISM PEACE PWR...POLICY CONCPT STYLE RECORD TREND GEN/LAWS 20. PAGE 166 A3385 — ATTIT ORD/FREE

B62
WRIGHT Q.,PREVENTING WORLD WAR THREE. FUT WOR+45 CULTURE INT/ORG NAT/G CONSULT FORCES ADMIN ARMS/CONT DRIVE RIGID/FLEX ORD/FREE SOVEREIGN ...POLICY CONCPT TREND STERTYP COLD/WAR 20. PAGE 168 A3416 — CREATE ATTIT

B62
YALEN R.,REGIONALISM AND WORLD ORDER. EUR+WWI WOR+45 WOR-45 INT/ORG VOL/ASSN DELIB/GP FORCES TOP/EX BAL/PWR DIPLOM DOMIN REGION ARMS/CONT PWR ...JURID HYPO/EXP COLD/WAR 20. PAGE 168 A3427 — ORD/FREE POLICY

L62
BAILEY S.D.,"THE TROIKA AND THE FUTURE OF THE UN." CONSTN CREATE LEGIT EXEC CHOOSE ORD/FREE PWR ...CONCPT NEW/IDEA UN COLD/WAR 20. PAGE 10 A0206 — FUT INT/ORG USSR

L62
PETKOFF D.K.,"RECOGNITION AND NON-RECOGNITION OF STATES AND GOVERNMENTS IN INTERNATIONAL LAW." ASIA COM USA+45 WOR+45 NAT/G ACT/RES DIPLOM DOMIN LEGIT COERCE ORD/FREE PWR...CONCPT GEN/LAWS 20. PAGE 115 A2369 — INT/ORG LAW INT/LAW

L62
WILCOX F.O.,"THE UN AND THE NON-ALIGNED NATIONS." AFR S/ASIA USA+45 ECO/UNDEV INT/ORG TEC/DEV EDU/PROP RIGID/FLEX ORD/FREE PWR...POLICY HUM CONCPT STAT OBS TIME/SEQ STERTYP GEN/METH UN 20. PAGE 164 A3345 — ATTIT TREND

S62
BLOOMFIELD L.P.,"THE UNITED NATIONS IN CRISIS: THE ROLE OF THE UN IN USA FOREIGN POLICY." FUT USA+45 WOR+45 ECO/UNDEV DIPLOM ATTIT ORD/FREE...CONCPT UN. PAGE 16 A0317 — INT/ORG TREND REV

S62
BOULDING K.E.,"THE PREVENTION OF WORLD WAR THREE." FUT WOR+45 INT/ORG PLAN BAL/PWR PEACE ORD/FREE PWR ...NEW/IDEA TREND TOT/POP COLD/WAR 20. PAGE 17 A0348 — VOL/ASSN NAT/G ARMS/CONT DIPLOM

S62
CRANE R.D.,"LAW AND STRATEGY IN SPACE." FUT USA+45 WOR+45 AIR LAW INT/ORG NAT/G FORCES ACT/RES PLAN BAL/PWR LEGIT ARMS/CONT COERCE ORD/FREE...POLICY INT/LAW JURID SOC/EXP 20 TREATY. PAGE 32 A0656 — CONCPT SPACE

S62
DRACHKOVITCH M.M.,"THE EMERGING PATTERN OF YUGOSLAV-SOVIET RELATIONS." COM FUT USSR WOR+45 INT/ORG ECO/TAC FOR/AID DOMIN COERCE ATTIT PERSON ORD/FREE PWR...TIME/SEQ 20 TITO/MARSH KHRUSH/N STALIN/J. PAGE 38 A0783 — TOP/EX DIPLOM YUGOSLAVIA

S62
FALK R.A.,"THE REALITY OF INTERNATIONAL LAW." WOR+45 NAT/G LEGIT COERCE DETER WAR MORAL ORD/FREE PWR SOVEREIGN...JURID CONCPT VAL/FREE COLD/WAR 20. PAGE 43 A0887 — INT/ORG ADJUD NUC/PWR INT/LAW

S62
FENWICK C.G.,"ISSUES AT PUNTA DEL ESTE: NON-INTERVENTION VS COLLECTIVE SECURITY." L/A+17C USA+45 VOL/ASSN DELIB/GP ECO/TAC LEGIT ADJUD REGION ORD/FREE OAS COLD/WAR 20. PAGE 45 A0917 — INT/ORG CUBA

S62
FINKELSTEIN L.S.,"THE UNITED NATIONS AND ORGANIZATIONS FOR CONTROL OF ARMAMENT." FUT WOR+45 VOL/ASSN DELIB/GP TOP/EX CREATE EDU/PROP LEGIT ADJUD NUC/PWR ATTIT RIGID/FLEX ORD/FREE...POLICY DECISION CONCPT OBS TREND GEN/LAWS TOT/POP COLD/WAR. PAGE 46 A0933 — INT/ORG PWR ARMS/CONT

S62
GAREAU F.H.,"BLOC POLITICS IN WEST AFRICA." AFR CONGO/BRAZ GHANA GUINEA MALI WOR+45 STRUCT ECO/UNDEV INT/ORG VOL/ASSN CHOOSE ORD/FREE PWR UN 20. PAGE 51 A1048 — NAT/G NAT/LISM

S62
GREEN L.C.,"POLITICAL OFFENSES, WAR CRIMES AND EXTRADITION." WOR+45 YUGOSLAVIA INT/ORG LEGIT ROUTINE WAR ORD/FREE SOVEREIGN...JURID NAZI 20 INTERPOL. PAGE 55 A1138 — LAW CONCPT INT/LAW

S62
GREENSPAN M.,"INTERNATIONAL LAW AND ITS PROTECTION FOR PARTICIPANTS IN UNCONVENTIONAL WARFARE." WOR+45 LAW INT/ORG NAT/G POL/PAR COERCE REV ORD/FREE ...INT/LAW TOT/POP 20. PAGE 56 A1143 — FORCES JURID GUERRILLA WAR

S62
HOFFMANN S.,"RESTRAINTS AND CHOICES IN AMERICAN FOREIGN POLICY." USA-45 INT/ORG NAT/G PLAN ARMS/CONT ATTIT...POLICY CONCPT OBS TREND GEN/METH COLD/WAR 20. PAGE 66 A1356 — USA+45 ORD/FREE DIPLOM

S62
JACOBSON H.K.,"THE UNITED NATIONS AND COLONIALISM: A TENTATIVE APPRAISAL." AFR FUT S/ASIA USA+45 USSR WOR+45 NAT/G DELIB/GP PLAN DIPLOM ECO/TAC DOMIN ADMIN ROUTINE COERCE ATTIT RIGID/FLEX ORD/FREE PWR ...OBS STERTYP UN 20. PAGE 73 A1486 — INT/ORG CONCPT COLONIAL

S62
JOHNSON O.H.,"THE ENGLISH TRADITION IN INTERNATIONAL LAW." CHRIST-17C MOD/EUR EDU/PROP LEGIT CT/SYS ORD/FREE...JURID CONCPT TIME/SEQ. PAGE 75 A1526 — LAW INT/LAW UK

S62
LISSITZYN O.J.,"SOME LEGAL IMPLICATIONS OF THE U-2 AND RB-47 INCIDENTS." FUT USA+45 USSR WOR+45 AIR NAT/G DIPLOM LEGIT MORAL ORD/FREE SOVEREIGN...JURID GEN/LAWS GEN/METH COLD/WAR 20 U-2. PAGE 90 A1840 — LAW CONCPT SPACE INT/LAW

S62
MCWHINNEY E.,"CO-EXISTENCE, THE CUBA CRISIS, AND COLD WAR-INTERNATIONAL WAR." CUBA USA+45 USSR WOR+45 NAT/G TOP/EX BAL/PWR DIPLOM DOMIN LEGIT PEACE RIGID/FLEX ORD/FREE...STERTYP COLD/WAR 20. PAGE 99 A2026 — CONCPT INT/LAW

S62
MORGENTHAU H.J.,"A POLITICAL THEORY OF FOREIGN AID." ECO/UNDEV NAT/G DELIB/GP PLAN ECO/TAC EDU/PROP EXEC ORD/FREE RESPECT WEALTH...METH/CNCPT TREND 20. PAGE 104 A2140 — USA+45 PHIL/SCI FOR/AID

S62
NANES A.,"DISARMAMENT: THE LAST SEVEN YEARS." COM EUR+WWI USA+45 USSR INT/ORG FORCES TOP/EX CREATE LEGIT NUC/PWR DISPL ORD/FREE...CONCPT TIME/SEQ CON/ANAL 20. PAGE 107 A2195 — DELIB/GP RIGID/FLEX ARMS/CONT

S62
PIQUEMAL M.,"LES PROBLEMES DES UNIONS D'ETATS EN AFRIQUE NOIRE." FRANCE SOCIETY INT/ORG NAT/G DELIB/GP PLAN LEGIT ADMIN COLONIAL ROUTINE ATTIT ORD/FREE PWR...GEOG METH/CNCPT 20. PAGE 116 A2382 — AFR ECO/UNDEV REGION

S62
RUSSETT B.M.,"CAUSE, SURPRISE, AND NO ESCAPE." FUT WOR-45 CULTURE SOCIETY INT/ORG FORCES TEC/DEV BAL/PWR EDU/PROP ARMS/CONT NUC/PWR WAR WEAPON PEACE KNOWL ORD/FREE PWR...POLICY CONCPT RECORD TIME/SEQ TREND GEN/LAWS 20 WWI. PAGE 126 A2578 — COERCE DIPLOM

S62
SCHACHTER O.,"DAG HAMMARSKJOLD AND THE RELATION OF LAW TO POLITICS." FUT WOR+45 INT/ORG CONSULT PLAN TEC/DEV BAL/PWR DIPLOM LEGIT ATTIT PERCEPT ORD/FREE ...POLICY JURID CONCPT OBS TESTS STERTYP GEN/LAWS 20 HAMMARSK/D. PAGE 128 A2616 — ACT/RES ADJUD

S62
SINGER J.D.,"STABLE DETERRENCE AND ITS LIMITS." FUT WOR+45 R+D INT/ORG CONSULT ACT/RES TEC/DEV ARMS/CONT COERCE DRIVE PERCEPT RIGID/FLEX ORD/FREE PWR...MYTH SIMUL TOT/POP 20. PAGE 133 A2728 — NAT/G FORCES DETER NUC/PWR

S62
SPENSER J.H.,"AFRICA AT THE UNITED NATIONS: SOME OBSERVATIONS." FUT ECO/UNDEV NAT/G CONSULT DELIB/GP PLAN BAL/PWR ECO/TAC EDU/PROP ATTIT RIGID/FLEX HEALTH ORD/FREE PWR WEALTH...POLICY CONCPT OBS TREND STERTYP GEN/METH UN VAL/FREE. PAGE 136 A2786 — AFR INT/ORG REGION

S62
SPRINGER H.W.,"FEDERATION IN THE CARIBBEAN: AN ATTEMPT THAT FAILED." L/A+17C ECO/UNDEV INT/ORG POL/PAR PROVS LEGIS CREATE PLAN LEGIT ADMIN FEDERAL ATTIT DRIVE PERSON ORD/FREE PWR...POLICY GEOG PSY CONCPT OBS CARIBBEAN CMN/WLTH 20. PAGE 136 A2791 — VOL/ASSN NAT/G REGION

S62
THOMAS J.R.T.,"SOVIET BEHAVIOR IN THE QUEMOY CRISES OF 1958." CHINA/COM FUT USSR WOR+45 INT/ORG VOL/ASSN FORCES PLAN BAL/PWR DOMIN COERCE NUC/PWR REV WAR ATTIT DRIVE ORD/FREE...POLICY OBS RECORD COLD/WAR FOR/POL 20. PAGE 143 A2923 — COM PWR

B63
ABSHIRE D.M.,NATIONAL SECURITY: POLITICAL, — FUT

MILITARY, AND ECONOMIC STRATEGIES IN THE DECADE AHEAD. ASIA COM USA+45 WOR+45 ECO/DEV ECO/UNDEV INT/ORG DELIB/GP FORCES ECO/TAC COERCE ATTIT RIGID/FLEX HEALTH ORD/FREE PWR WEALTH...POLICY STAT CHARTS ANTHOL COLD/WAR VAL/FREE. PAGE 4 A0083
ACT/RES BAL/PWR

B63
AFRICAN BIBLIOGRAPHIC CENTER,THE SCENE IS KENYA AND THE PERSONAGE IS TOM MBOYA: A SELECTED CURRENT READING LIST FROM 1956-1962 (PAMPHLET). ECO/UNDEV LABOR POL/PAR CHIEF COLONIAL CHOOSE NAT/LISM ORD/FREE 20. PAGE 5 A0096
BIBLIOG DIPLOM AFR NAT/G

B63
BOISSIER P.,HISTORIE DU COMITE INTERNATIONAL DE LA CROIX ROUGE. MOD/EUR WOR-45 CONSULT FORCES PLAN DIPLOM EDU/PROP ADMIN MORAL ORD/FREE...SOC CONCPT RECORD TIME/SEQ GEN/LAWS TOT/POP VAL/FREE 19/20. PAGE 16 A0332
INT/ORG HEALTH ARMS/CONT WAR

B63
BOWETT D.W.,THE LAW OF INTERNATIONAL INSTITUTIONS. WOR+45 WOR-45 CONSTN DELIB/GP EX/STRUC JUDGE EDU/PROP LEGIT CT/SYS EXEC ROUTINE RIGID/FLEX ORD/FREE PWR...JURID CONCPT ORG/CHARTS GEN/METH LEAGUE/NAT OAS OEEC 20 UN. PAGE 17 A0354
INT/ORG ADJUD DIPLOM

B63
BRECHER M.,THE NEW STATES OF ASIA. ASIA S/ASIA INT/ORG BAL/PWR COLONIAL NEUTRAL ORD/FREE PWR 20 UN. PAGE 18 A0369
NAT/G ECO/UNDEV DIPLOM POLICY

B63
BROEKMEIJER M.W.,DEVELOPING COUNTRIES AND NATO. USSR FORCES DIPLOM NUC/PWR WAR PEACE TOTALISM 20 NATO. PAGE 19 A0384
ECO/UNDEV FOR/AID ORD/FREE NAT/G

B63
BRZEZINSKI Z.K.,AFRICA AND THE COMMUNIST WORLD. AFR ASIA COM CULTURE SOCIETY INT/ORG DELIB/GP ACT/RES ECO/TAC COERCE ORD/FREE PWR WEALTH...STAT TOT/POP VAL/FREE 20. PAGE 21 A0418
ATTIT EDU/PROP DIPLOM USSR

B63
BURNS A.L.,PEACE-KEEPING BY U.N.FORCES - FROM SUEZ TO THE CONGO. AFR FUT ISLAM ISRAEL USSR WOR+45 NAT/G DELIB/GP BAL/PWR DOMIN LEGIT EXEC COERCE PEACE ATTIT PWR RESPECT SOVEREIGN...CONCPT UN 20. PAGE 22 A0441
INT/ORG FORCES ORD/FREE

B63
CONF ON FUTURE OF COMMONWEALTH,THE FUTURE OF THE COMMONWEALTH. UK ECO/UNDEV AGRI EDU/PROP ADMIN SOC/INTEG 20 COMMONWLTH. PAGE 29 A0583
DIPLOM RACE/REL ORD/FREE TEC/DEV

B63
DECOTTIGNIES R.,LES NATIONALITES AFRICAINES. AFR NAT/G PROB/SOLV DIPLOM COLONIAL ORD/FREE...CHARTS GOV/COMP 20. PAGE 35 A0721
NAT/LISM JURID LEGIS LAW

B63
ELLERT R.B.,NATO 'FAIR TRIAL' SAFEGUARDS: PRECURSOR TO AN INTERNATIONAL BILL OF PROCEDURAL RIGHTS. WOR+45 FORCES CRIME CIVMIL/REL ATTIT ORD/FREE 20 NATO. PAGE 41 A0841
JURID INT/LAW INT/ORG CT/SYS

B63
FALK R.A.,LAW, MORALITY, AND WAR IN THE CONTEMPORARY WORLD. WOR+45 LAW INT/ORG EX/STRUC FORCES EDU/PROP LEGIT DETER NUC/PWR MORAL ORD/FREE ...JURID TOT/POP 20. PAGE 43 A0888
ADJUD ARMS/CONT PEACE INT/LAW

B63
FIFIELD R.H.,SOUTHEAST ASIA IN UNITED STATES POLICY. S/ASIA USA+45 ECO/UNDEV NAT/G DIPLOM ECO/TAC ADMIN COERCE ORD/FREE...POLICY MAJORIT 20. PAGE 45 A0928
INT/ORG PWR

B63
FRANZ G.,TEILUNG UND WIEDERVEREINIGUNG. GERMANY IRELAND ITALY NETHERLAND POLAND CULTURE BAL/PWR CHOOSE NAT/LISM ORD/FREE SOVEREIGN 19/20. PAGE 48 A0987
DIPLOM WAR NAT/COMP ATTIT

B63
FULBRIGHT J.W.,PROSPECTS FOR THE WEST. COM USA+45 USSR INT/ORG NAT/G SCHOOL PROB/SOLV NUC/PWR WAR PEACE ORD/FREE...PREDICT METH/COMP 20 DEGAULLE/C. PAGE 50 A1015
DIPLOM BAL/PWR CONCPT POLICY

B63
GILBERT M.,THE APPEASERS. COM GERMANY UK PLAN ECO/TAC COLONIAL CONTROL EXEC ORD/FREE PWR FASCISM 20 PARLIAMENT. PAGE 52 A1068
DIPLOM WAR POLICY DECISION

B63
GORDON G.N.,THE IDEA INVADERS. USA+45 USSR CULTURE COM/IND DIPLOM PRESS TV TOTALISM MARXISM 20. PAGE 54 A1113
EDU/PROP ATTIT ORD/FREE CONTROL

B63
GRAEBNER N.A.,THE COLD WAR: IDEOLOGICAL CONFLICT OR POWER STRUGGLE? USSR WOR+45 WOR-45 PROB/SOLV EDU/PROP ARMS/CONT REV NAT/LISM PEACE ORD/FREE ...IDEA/COMP ANTHOL BIBLIOG/A 20 COLD/WAR. PAGE 55 A1123
DIPLOM BAL/PWR MARXISM

B63
HALEY A.G.,SPACE LAW AND GOVERNMENT. FUT USA+45 WOR+45 LEGIS ACT/RES CREATE ATTIT RIGID/FLEX ORD/FREE PWR SOVEREIGN...POLICY JURID CONCPT CHARTS VAL/FREE 20. PAGE 60 A1226
INT/ORG LAW SPACE

B63
HARTLEY A.,A STATE OF ENGLAND. UK ELITES SOCIETY ACADEM NAT/G SCHOOL INGP/REL CONSEN ORD/FREE NEW/LIB...POLICY 20. PAGE 62 A1275
DIPLOM ATTIT INTELL ECO/DEV

B63
HOVET T. JR.,AFRICA IN THE UNITED NATIONS. AFR DELIB/GP EDU/PROP LOBBY CHOOSE ORD/FREE PWR RESPECT SKILL...STAT TIME/SEQ CON/ANAL CHARTS STERTYP VAL/FREE 20 UN. PAGE 68 A1397
INT/ORG USSR

B63
JENNINGS W.I.,DEMOCRACY IN AFRICA. UK CULTURE STRUCT ECO/UNDEV DIPLOM COLONIAL GP/REL ADJUST NAT/LISM ORD/FREE...GOV/COMP 20 THIRD/WRLD. PAGE 74 A1512
PROB/SOLV AFR CONSTN POPULISM

B63
JUDD P.,AFRICAN INDEPENDENCE: THE EXPLODING EMERGENCE OF THE NEW AFRICAN NATIONS. AFR UK LAW CONSTN CULTURE KIN DIPLOM ATTIT...CHARTS BIBLIOG 20 UN DEGAULLE/C NEGRO THIRD/WRLD. PAGE 75 A1542
ORD/FREE POLICY DOMIN LOC/G

B63
LERCHE C.O. JR.,CONCEPTS OF INTERNATIONAL POLITICS. WOR+45 WOR-45 LAW DELIB/GP EX/STRUC TEC/DEV ECO/TAC INT/TRADE LEGIT ROUTINE COERCE ATTIT ORD/FREE PWR RESPECT...STERTYP GEN/LAWS VAL/FREE. PAGE 87 A1782
INT/ORG WAR

B63
LILIENTHAL D.E.,CHANGE, HOPE, AND THE BOMB. USA+45 WOR+45 R+D INT/ORG NAT/G DELIB/GP FORCES ACT/RES DETER RIGID/FLEX ORD/FREE...POLICY CONCPT OBS AEC 20. PAGE 89 A1815
ATTIT MYTH ARMS/CONT NUC/PWR

B63
MALIK C.,MAN IN THE STRUGGLE FOR PEACE. USSR WOR+45 CHIEF PLAN PROB/SOLV PARTIC NUC/PWR REV ORD/FREE ...IDEA/COMP METH/COMP 20 UN COLD/WAR. PAGE 93 A1912
PEACE MARXISM DIPLOM EDU/PROP

B63
MANSERGH N.,DOCUMENTS AND SPEECHES ON COMMONWEALTH AFFAIRS 1952-1962. CANADA INDIA PAKISTAN UK CONSTN FORCES ECO/TAC EDU/PROP COLONIAL DETER WAR ORD/FREE SOVEREIGN...POLICY 20 AUSTRAL. PAGE 94 A1932
BIBLIOG/A FEDERAL INT/TRADE DIPLOM

B63
MAYNE R.,THE COMMUNITY OF EUROPE. UK CONSTN NAT/G CONSULT DELIB/GP CREATE PLAN ECO/TAC LEGIT ADMIN ROUTINE ORD/FREE PWR WEALTH...CONCPT TIME/SEQ EEC EURATOM 20. PAGE 97 A1985
EUR+WWI INT/ORG REGION

B63
MCDOUGAL M.S.,LAW AND PUBLIC ORDER IN SPACE. FUT USA+45 ACT/RES TEC/DEV ADJUD...POLICY INT/LAW JURID 20. PAGE 98 A2009
SPACE ORD/FREE DIPLOM DECISION

B63
MENEZES A.J.,SUBDESENVOLVIMENTO E POLITICA INTERNACIONAL. BRAZIL WOR+45 PLAN CONTROL LEAD NAT/LISM ORD/FREE 20 THIRD/WRLD. PAGE 99 A2041
ECO/UNDEV DIPLOM POLICY BAL/PWR

B63
MONTER W.,THE GOVERNMENT OF GENEVA, 1536-1605 (DOCTORAL THESIS). SWITZERLND DIPLOM LEAD ORD/FREE SOVEREIGN 16/17 CALVIN/J ROME. PAGE 103 A2112
SECT FINAN LOC/G ADMIN

B63
MULLENBACH P.,CIVILIAN NUCLEAR POWER: ECONOMIC ISSUES AND POLICY FORMATION. FINAN INT/ORG DELIB/GP ACT/RES ECO/TAC ATTIT SUPEGO HEALTH ORD/FREE PWR ...POLICY CONCPT MATH STAT CHARTS VAL/FREE 20 COLD/WAR. PAGE 105 A2166
USA+45 ECO/DEV NUC/PWR

B63
MYRDAL G.,CHALLENGE TO AFFLUENCE. USA+45 WOR+45 FINAN INT/ORG NAT/G PLAN ECO/TAC INT/TRADE BAL/PAY ORD/FREE 20 EUROPE/W. PAGE 107 A2189
ECO/DEV WEALTH DIPLOM PRODUC

B63
PADELFORD N.J.,AFRICA AND WORLD ORDER. AFR COLONIAL SOVEREIGN...ANTHOL BIBLIOG 20 UN UNIFICA COMMONWLTH. PAGE 113 A2312
DIPLOM NAT/G ORD/FREE

B63
PECQUET P.,THE DIPLOMACY OF THE CONFEDERATE CABINET OF RICHMOND AND ITS AGENTS ABROAD (LIMITED ED.). MOD/EUR USA-45 LEAD...OBS 19 CIVIL/WAR SOUTH/US. PAGE 114 A2347
DIPLOM WAR ORD/FREE

B63
PERKINS B.,PROLOGUE TO THE WAR: ENGLAND AND THE UNITED STATES, 1805-1812. MOD/EUR UK USA-45 NAT/G ORD/FREE RESPECT SOVEREIGN...POLICY TREATY 19 WAR/1812. PAGE 115 A2358
WAR DIPLOM NEUTRAL

B63
ROBERTSON A.H.,HUMAN RIGHTS IN EUROPE. CONSTN SOCIETY INT/ORG NAT/G VOL/ASSN DELIB/GP ACT/RES PLAN ADJUD REGION ROUTINE ATTIT LOVE ORD/FREE RESPECT...JURID SOC CONCPT SOC/EXP UN 20. PAGE 122 A2498
EUR+WWI PERSON

B63
ROSECRANCE R.N.,ACTION AND REACTION IN WORLD POLITICS. FUT WOR-45 SOCIETY DELIB/GP ACT/RES CREATE DIPLOM ECO/TAC DOMIN EDU/PROP COERCE ATTIT PERSON SUPEGO ORD/FREE PWR...CHARTS SIMUL LEAGUE/NAT VAL/FREE UN 19/20. PAGE 123 A2529
WOR+45 INT/ORG BAL/PWR

B63
ROSNER G.,THE UNITED NATIONS EMERGENCY FORCE. FRANCE ISRAEL UAR UK WOR+45 CREATE WAR PEACE ORD/FREE PWR...INT/LAW JURID HIST/WRIT TIME/SEQ UN. PAGE 124 A2539
INT/ORG FORCES

B63
ROSS H.,THE COLD WAR: CONTAINMENT AND ITS CRITICSS. WOR+45 POL/PAR BAL/PWR ECO/TAC PEACE ORD/FREE ...POLICY IDEA/COMP ANTHOL T 20 COLD/WAR DULLES/JF TRUMAN/HS EISNHWR/DD. PAGE 124 A2541
MARXISM ARMS/CONT DIPLOM

B63
RUSK D.,THE WINDS OF FREEDOM. S/ASIA SOUTH/AFR INT/ORG FORCES NUC/PWR PEACE ORD/FREE 20 UN COLD/WAR. PAGE 125 A2569
DIPLOM FOR/AID INT/TRADE

B63
RUSSELL B.,UNARMED VICTORY. CHINA/COM CUBA INDIA USA+45 WAR MARXISM...POLICY IDEA/COMP 20 KHRUSH/N COLD/WAR. PAGE 125 A2573
DIPLOM ATTIT SOCISM ORD/FREE

B63
SMITH J.E.,THE DEFENSE OF BERLIN. COM GUATEMALA WOR+45 ECO/TAC ADMIN NEUTRAL ATTIT ORD/FREE SOVEREIGN...DECISION 20 DEPT/STATE. PAGE 134 A2747
DIPLOM FORCES BAL/PWR PLAN

B63
STROMBERG R.N.,COLLECTIVE SECURITY AND AMERICAN FOREIGN POLICY FROM THE LEAGUE OF NATIONS TO NATO. USA+45 USA-45 WOR-45 INT/ORG VOL/ASSN EX/STRUC FORCES LEGIT ROUTINE DRIVE...CONCPT TREND UN LEAGUE/NAT 20 NATO. PAGE 139 A2851
ORD/FREE TIME/SEQ DIPLOM

B63
SZULC T.,THE WINDS OF REVOLUTION; LATIN AMERICA TODAY - AND TOMORROW. L/A+17C ORD/FREE SOCISM ...PREDICT TREND 20. PAGE 141 A2880
REV INT/ORG MARXISM ECO/UNDEV

B63
THEOBALD R.,FREE MEN AND FREE MARKETS. USA+45 USA-45 ECO/DEV NAT/G TEC/DEV DIPLOM INT/TRADE INCOME ORD/FREE WEALTH...TREND 19/20 KEYNES/JM. PAGE 143 A2915
CONCPT ECO/TAC CAP/ISM MARKET

B63
US DEPARTMENT OF THE ARMY,US OVERSEAS BASES: PRESENT STATUS AND FUTURE PROSPECTS (PAMPHLET). USA+45 DIPLOM NUC/PWR ATTIT ORD/FREE...POLICY CHARTS 20. PAGE 152 A3107
BIBLIOG/A WAR BAL/PWR DETER

B63
US HOUSE COMM FOREIGN AFFAIRS,HEARINGS ON H.R. 5490 TO AMEND FURTHER THE FOREIGN ASSISTANCE ACT OF 1961. CUBA EUR+WWI INDIA INT/ORG DELIB/GP LEGIS DIPLOM CONFER ORD/FREE 20 DEPT/STATE DEPT/DEFEN UN. PAGE 153 A3129
FOR/AID INT/TRADE FORCES WEAPON

B63
US SENATE COMM ON FOREIGN REL,HEARINGS ON S 1276 A BILL TO AMEND FURTHER THE FOREIGN ASSISTANCE ACT OF 1961. USA+45 WOR+45 INDUS INT/ORG FORCES TAX WEAPON SUPEGO...NAT/COMP 20 UN CONGRESS PRESIDENT. PAGE 156 A3182
FOR/AID DIPLOM ECO/UNDEV ORD/FREE

B63
VAN SLYCK P.,PEACE: THE CONTROL OF NATIONAL POWER. CUBA WOR+45 FINAN NAT/G FORCES PROB/SOLV TEC/DEV BAL/PWR ADMIN CONTROL ORD/FREE...POLICY INT/LAW UN COLD/WAR TREATY. PAGE 158 A3214
ARMS/CONT PEACE INT/ORG DIPLOM

B63
VON HALLER A.,DIE LETZTEN WOLLEN DIE ERSTEN SEIN. AFR S/ASIA INT/TRADE REV ORD/FREE SOVEREIGN 20. PAGE 160 A3251
FOR/AID ECO/UNDEV MARXISM CAP/ISM

B63
VOSS E.H.,NUCLEAR AMBUSH: THE TEST-BAN TRAP. WOR+45 COM/IND INT/ORG NAT/G DELIB/GP FORCES LEGIS TOP/EX ACT/RES DOMIN EDU/PROP LEGIT ROUTINE COERCE ATTIT PERCEPT RIGID/FLEX HEALTH MORAL ORD/FREE PWR. PAGE 160 A3255
TEC/DEV HIST/WRIT ARMS/CONT NUC/PWR

B63
WELLESLEY COLLEGE,SYMPOSIUM ON LATIN AMERICA. FUT L/A+17C USA+45 INT/ORG ECO/TAC PARL/PROC REGION ANTHOL. PAGE 163 A3316
ECO/UNDEV CULTURE ORD/FREE DIPLOM

B63
WESTERFIELD H.,THE INSTRUMENTS OF AMERICA'S FOREIGN POLICY. WOR+45 ECO/DEV NAT/G CONSULT EX/STRUC LEGIS BAL/PWR FOR/AID INT/TRADE DOMIN EDU/PROP LEGIT ATTIT KNOWL ORD/FREE PWR WEALTH...OBS COLD/WAR TOT/POP VAL/FREE. PAGE 163 A3322
USA+45 INT/ORG DIPLOM

L63
CRANE R.D.,"THE CUBAN CRISIS: A STRATEGIC ANALYSIS OF AMERICAN AND SOVIET POLICY." CUBA USA+45 USSR BAL/PWR RISK DETER NUC/PWR PERCEPT ORD/FREE 20. PAGE 32 A0658
DIPLOM POLICY FORCES

L63
LISSITZYN O.J.,"INTERNATIONAL LAW IN A DIVIDED WORLD." FUT WOR+45 CONSTN CULTURE ECO/DEV ECO/UNDEV DIST/IND NAT/G FORCES ECO/TAC LEGIT ADJUD ADMIN COERCE ATTIT HEALTH MORAL ORD/FREE PWR RESPECT WEALTH VAL/FREE. PAGE 90 A1841
INT/ORG LAW

L63
PHELPS J.,"STUDIES IN DETERRENCE VIII: MILITARY STABILITARY AND ARMS CONTROL: A CRITICAL SURVEY." FUT WOR+45 INT/ORG ACT/RES EDU/PROP COERCE NUC/PWR WAR HEALTH PWR...POLICY TECHNIC TREND SIMUL TOT/POP 20. PAGE 116 A2373
FORCES ORD/FREE ARMS/CONT DETER

L63
SCHELLING T.C.,"STRATEGIC PROBLEMS OF AN INTERNATIONAL ARMED FORCE." WOR+45 ECO/DEV INT/ORG NAT/G PLAN BAL/PWR LEGIT ARMS/CONT COERCE DETER ORD/FREE PWR...POLICY CONCPT COLD/WAR 20. PAGE 128 A2624
CREATE FORCES

L63
SINGER J.D.,"WEAPONS MANAGEMENT IN WORLD POLITICS: PROCEEDINGS OF THE INTERNATIONAL ARMS CONTROL SYMPOSIUM, DECEMBER, 1962." FUT WOR+45 SOCIETY ECO/DEV INDUS INT/ORG DELIB/GP FORCES ACT/RES ECO/TAC EDU/PROP ARMS/CONT SUPEGO HEALTH ORD/FREE PWR SKILL...POLICY CHARTS SIMUL ANTHOL VAL/FREE 20. PAGE 133 A2729
CONSULT ATTIT DIPLOM NUC/PWR

S63
ALGER C.F.,"HYPOTHESES ON RELATIONSHIPS BETWEEN THE ORGANIZATION OF INTERNATIONAL SOCIETY AND INTERNATIONAL ORDER." WOR+45 WOR-45 ORD/FREE PWR ...JURID GEN/LAWS VAL/FREE 20. PAGE 6 A0119
INT/ORG LAW

S63
ALGER C.F.,"UNITED NATIONS PARTICIPATION AS A LEARNING EXPERIENCE." WOR+45 KNOWL ORD/FREE PWR ...INT VAL/FREE UN 20. PAGE 6 A0120
INT/ORG ATTIT

S63
ALPHAND H.,"FRANCE AND HER ALLIES." EUR+WWI UK USA+45 ECO/DEV INT/ORG NAT/G VOL/ASSN FORCES TOP/EX DIPLOM ECO/TAC LEGIT ATTIT DRIVE ORD/FREE PWR WEALTH...STAT EEC TOT/POP 20. PAGE 6 A0130
ACT/RES FRANCE

S63
BECHHOEFER B.G.,"UNITED NATIONS PROCEDURES IN CASE OF VIOLATIONS OF DISARMAMENT AGREEMENTS." COM USA+45 USSR LAW CONSTN NAT/G EX/STRUC FORCES LEGIS BAL/PWR EDU/PROP CT/SYS ARMS/CONT ORD/FREE PWR ...POLICY STERTYP UN VAL/FREE 20. PAGE 12 A0245
INT/ORG DELIB/GP

S63
BELOFF M.,"BRITAIN, EUROPE AND THE ATLANTIC COMMUNITY." EUR+WWI ELITES NAT/G VOL/ASSN TOP/EX ATTIT ORD/FREE PWR SOVEREIGN WEALTH EEC TOT/POP VAL/FREE CMN/WLTH 20. PAGE 13 A0262
INT/ORG ECO/DEV UK

S63
BLOOMFIELD L.P.,"INTERNATIONAL FORCE IN A DISARMING BUT REVOLUTIONARY WORLD." INT/ORG COERCE REV DRIVE PWR...CONCPT STERTYP GEN/LAWS 20. PAGE 16 A0318
FORCES ORD/FREE ARMS/CONT GUERRILLA

S63
BLOOMFIELD L.P.,"HEADQUARTERS-FIELD RELATIONS: SOME NOTES ON THE BEGINNING AND END OF ONUC." AFR INT/ORG ROUTINE COERCE WAR WEAPON UN CONGO 20. PAGE 16 A0319
FORCES ORD/FREE

S63
BOHN L.,"WHOSE NUCLEAR TEST: NON-PHYSICAL INSPECTION AND TEST BAN." WOR+45 R+D INT/ORG VOL/ASSN ORD/FREE...GEN/LAWS GEN/METH COLD/WAR 20. PAGE 16 A0331
ADJUD ARMS/CONT TEC/DEV NUC/PWR

S63
BULLOUGH V.L.,"THE ROMAN EMPIRE VS PERSIA, 363-502: A STUDY OF SUCCESSFUL DETERRENCE." NAT/G PLAN DIPLOM ORD/FREE PWR...TIME/SEQ COLD/WAR VAL/FREE 4/6 PERSIA ROM/EMP. PAGE 21 A0430
MEDIT-7 COERCE DETER

S63
EMERSON R.,"THE ATLANTIC COMMUNITY AND THE EMERGING COUNTRIES." FUT WOR+45 ECO/DEV ECO/UNDEV R+D NAT/G DELIB/GP BAL/PWR ECO/TAC EDU/PROP ROUTINE ORD/FREE PWR WEALTH...POLICY CONCPT TREND GEN/METH EEC 20 NATO. PAGE 42 A0848
ATTIT INT/TRADE

S63
ETZIONI A.,"EUROPEAN UNIFICATION: A STRATEGY OF CHANGE." EUR+WWI CULTURE ECO/DEV DELIB/GP ACT/RES ECO/TAC EDU/PROP ATTIT ORD/FREE PWR SKILL WEALTH ...STAT TIME/SEQ EEC TOT/POP VAL/FREE 20. PAGE 42 A0869
INT/ORG RIGID/FLEX

S63
ETZIONI A.,"EUROPEAN UNIFICATION AND PERSPECTIVES ON SOVEREIGNTY." EUR+WWI FUT DELIB/GP TEC/DEV ECO/TAC EDU/PROP DETER NUC/PWR ATTIT DRIVE ORD/FREE PWR WEALTH...CONCPT RECORD TIME/SEQ EEC VAL/FREE 20. PAGE 43 A0870
INT/ORG ECO/DEV SOVEREIGN

S63
FRIEDMANN W.G.,"THE USES OF 'GENERAL PRINCIPLES' IN THE DEVELOPMENT OF INTERNATIONAL LAW." WOR+45 NAT/G DIPLOM INT/TRADE LEGIT ROUTINE RIGID/FLEX ORD/FREE ...JURID CONCPT STERTYP GEN/METH 20. PAGE 49 A1005
LAW INT/LAW INT/ORG

S63
GROSS F.,"THE US NATIONAL INTEREST AND THE UN." FUT
USA+45

CONSTN NAT/G DELIB/GP CREATE DIPLOM RIGID/FLEX ORD/FREE...CONCPT GEN/LAWS 20 UN. PAGE 57 A1172
INT/ORG PEACE

S63
GROSSER A.,"FRANCE AND GERMANY IN THE ATLANTIC COMMUNITY." INT/ORG NAT/G TOP/EX DIPLOM REGION PEACE ATTIT ORD/FREE PWR...CONCPT RECORD TIME/SEQ GEN/LAWS VAL/FREE COLD/WAR 20. PAGE 57 A1178
EUR+WWI VOL/ASSN FRANCE GERMANY

S63
HORVATH J.,"MOSCOW'S AID PROGRAM: THE PERFORMANCE SO FAR." COM FUT USSR WOR+45 ECO/DEV FINAN PLAN TEC/DEV FOR/AID EDU/PROP ATTIT ORD/FREE PWR WEALTH ...POLICY STAT CHARTS VAL/FREE 20. PAGE 68 A1389
ECO/UNDEV ECO/TAC

S63
HUMPHREY H.H.,"REGIONAL ARMS CONTROL AGREEMENTS." WOR+45 FORCES PLAN LEGIT COERCE ATTIT HEALTH ORD/FREE...HUM METH/CNCPT MYTH OBS INT TREND TOT/POP 20. PAGE 69 A1416
L/A+17C INT/ORG ARMS/CONT REGION

S63
KINTNER W.R.,"THE PROJECTED EUROPEAN UNION AND AMERICAN RESPONSIBILITIES." EUR+WWI USA+45 STRATA INT/ORG NAT/G DOMIN DETER NUC/PWR ATTIT ORD/FREE PWR 20 NATO. PAGE 79 A1628
FUT FORCES DIPLOM REGION

S63
LERNER D.,"FRENCH ELITE PERSPECTIVES ON THE UNITED NATIONS." EUR+WWI INT/ORG HEALTH ORD/FREE PWR RESPECT...STAT INT SAMP/SIZ VAL/FREE UN 20. PAGE 87 A1786
ATTIT STERTYP ELITES FRANCE

S63
MAZRUI A.A.,"ON THE CONCEPT 'WE ARE ALL AFRICANS'." AFR CULTURE KIN LOC/G NAT/G DOMIN EDU/PROP LEGIT ATTIT PERCEPT PERSON KNOWL ORD/FREE...TIME/SEQ TOT/POP 20. PAGE 97 A1986
PROVS INT/ORG NAT/LISM

S63
MCDOUGAL M.S.,"THE SOVIET-CUBAN QUARANTINE AND SELF-DEFENSE." CUBA USA+45 USSR WOR+45 INT/ORG NAT/G BAL/PWR NUC/PWR ATTIT...JURID CONCPT. PAGE 98 A2008
ORD/FREE LEGIT SOVEREIGN

S63
MORGENTHAU H.J.,"THE POLITICAL CONDITIONS FOR AN INTERNATIONAL POLICE FORCE." FUT WOR+45 CREATE LEGIT ADMIN PEACE ORD/FREE 20. PAGE 104 A2141
INT/ORG FORCES ARMS/CONT DETER

S63
MURRAY J.N.,"UNITED NATIONS PEACE-KEEPING AND PROBLEMS OF POLITICAL CONTROL." FUT WOR+45 CONSTN DELIB/GP FORCES TOP/EX ACT/RES CREATE LEGIT PEACE PWR...METH/CNCPT CONGO UN 20. PAGE 106 A2182
INT/ORG ORD/FREE

S63
NYE J.S. JR.,"EAST AFRICAN ECONOMIC INTEGRATION." AFR UGANDA PROVS DELIB/GP PLAN ECO/TAC INT/TRADE ADMIN ROUTINE ORD/FREE PWR WEALTH...OBS TIME/SEQ VAL/FREE 20. PAGE 110 A2264
ECO/UNDEV INT/ORG

S63
PHELPS J.,"INFORMATION AND ARMS CONTROL." COM SPACE USA+45 USSR WOR+45 R+D INT/ORG NAT/G DELIB/GP DIPLOM ORD/FREE...CONCPT 20. PAGE 116 A2374
KNOWL ARMS/CONT NUC/PWR

S63
STANLEY T.W.,"DECENTRALIZING NUCLEAR CONTROL IN NATO." EUR+WWI USA+45 ELITES FORCES ACT/RES ATTIT ORD/FREE PWR...NEW/IDEA HYPO/EXP TOT/POP 20 NATO. PAGE 137 A2805
INT/ORG EX/STRUC NUC/PWR

S63
WRIGHT Q.,"PROJECTED EUROPEAN UNION AND AMERICAN INTERNATIONAL PRESTIGE." EUR+WWI FRANCE GERMANY UK USA+45 INT/ORG NAT/G EDU/PROP ATTIT PERCEPT PWR ...CONCPT OBS EEC 20 UN. PAGE 168 A3417
FUT ORD/FREE REGION

N63
US COMM STRENG SEC FREE WORLD,THE SCOPE AND DISTRIBUTION OF UNITED STATES MILITARY AND ECONOMIC ASSISTANCE PROGRAMS (PAMPHLET). USA+45 PLAN BAL/PWR BUDGET DIPLOM CONTROL CIVMIL/REL ATTIT. PAGE 150 A3059
DELIB/GP POLICY FOR/AID ORD/FREE

B64
ADAMS V.,THE PEACE CORPS IN ACTION. USA+45 VOL/ASSN EX/STRUC GOV/REL PERCEPT ORD/FREE...OBS 20 KENNEDY/JF PEACE/CORP. PAGE 4 A0087
DIPLOM FOR/AID PERSON DRIVE

B64
ALVIM J.C.,A REVOLUCAO SEM RUMO. BRAZIL NAT/G BAL/PWR DIPLOM INT/TRADE PARTIC WEALTH...POLICY SOC SOC/INTEG 20. PAGE 6 A0132
REV CIVMIL/REL ECO/UNDEV ORD/FREE

B64
ARNOLD G.,TOWARDS PEACE AND A MULTIRACIAL COMMONWEALTH. UK TEC/DEV BAL/PWR COLONIAL GP/REL NAT/LISM PEACE SOVEREIGN...POLICY SOC/INTEG 20 CMN/WLTH. PAGE 9 A0175
DIPLOM INT/TRADE FOR/AID ORD/FREE

B64
BLACKSTOCK P.W.,THE STRATEGY OF SUBVERSION. USA+45 FORCES EDU/PROP ADMIN COERCE GOV/REL...DECISION MGT 20 DEPT/DEFEN CIA DEPT/STATE. PAGE 15 A0301
ORD/FREE DIPLOM CONTROL

B64
BURKE F.G.,AFRICA'S QUEST FOR ORDER. AFR CULTURE KIN MUNIC NAT/G DIPLOM COLONIAL REV DISCRIM NAT/LISM AGE/Y 20. PAGE 21 A0437
ORD/FREE CONSEN RACE/REL LEAD

B64
CALDER R.,TWO-WAY PASSAGE. INT/ORG TEC/DEV WAR PERSON ORD/FREE 20. PAGE 23 A0467
FOR/AID ECO/UNDEV ECO/TAC DIPLOM

B64
CALVO SERER R.,LAS NUEVAS DEMOCRACIAS. AFR ASIA ISLAM USA+45 WOR+45 BAL/PWR DOMIN PARTIC INGP/REL AUTHORIT POPULISM...CONCPT 20 COM/PARTY. PAGE 23 A0469
ORD/FREE MARXISM DIPLOM POLICY

B64
CLAUDE I.,SWORDS INTO PLOWSHARES. FUT WOR+45 WOR-45 DELIB/GP EX/STRUC LEGIT ATTIT ORD/FREE...CONCPT TIME/SEQ TREND UN TOT/POP 20. PAGE 27 A0547
INT/ORG STRUCT

B64
COFFIN F.M.,WITNESS FOR AID. COM EUR+WWI USA+45 DIPLOM GP/REL CONSEN ORD/FREE MARXISM...NEW/IDEA 20 CONGRESS AID. PAGE 27 A0557
FOR/AID ECO/UNDEV DELIB/GP PLAN

B64
COTTRELL A.J.,THE POLITICS OF THE ATLANTIC ALLIANCE. EUR+WWI USA+45 INT/ORG NAT/G DELIB/GP EX/STRUC BAL/PWR DIPLOM REGION DETER ATTIT ORD/FREE ...CONCPT RECORD GEN/LAWS GEN/METH NATO 20. PAGE 31 A0632
VOL/ASSN FORCES

B64
COX R.,PAN-AFRICANISM IN PRACTICE. AFR DIPLOM CONFER RACE/REL ROLE SOVEREIGN...POLICY 20 PANAF/FREE. PAGE 32 A0645
ORD/FREE COLONIAL REGION NAT/LISM

B64
CZERNIN F.,VERSAILLES - 1919. EUR+WWI USA-45 FACE/GP POL/PAR VOL/ASSN DELIB/GP TOP/EX CREATE BAL/PWR DIPLOM LEGIT NAT/LISM PEACE ATTIT RIGID/FLEX ORD/FREE PWR...CON/ANAL LEAGUE/NAT 20 VERSAILLES. PAGE 33 A0671
INT/ORG STRUCT

B64
DALLIN A.,THE SOVIET UNION, ARMS CONTROL AND DISARMAMENT. COM INT/ORG VOL/ASSN EX/STRUC DIPLOM NUC/PWR ATTIT PWR TOT/POP COLD/WAR 20. PAGE 33 A0678
ORD/FREE ARMS/CONT USSR

B64
DUTT R.P.,THE INTERNATIONALE. COM WOR+45 WOR-45 WORKER CAP/ISM WAR ATTIT...TREND GEN/LAWS 18/20 COM/PARTY. PAGE 40 A0813
ALL/IDEOS INT/ORG MARXIST ORD/FREE

B64
ETZIONI A.,WINNING WITHOUT WAR. FUT MOD/EUR USA+45 WOR+45 ECO/DEV ECO/UNDEV INT/ORG NAT/G FORCES TOP/EX PLAN TEC/DEV ECO/TAC DOMIN EDU/PROP LEGIT COERCE CHOOSE ATTIT MORAL ORD/FREE RESPECT WEALTH MAJORIT. PAGE 43 A0871
PWR TREND DIPLOM USSR

B64
FISHER R.,INTERNATIONAL CONFLICT AND BEHAVIORAL SCIENCE: THE CRAIGVILLE PAPERS. COM FUT USA+45 WOR+45 NAT/G DELIB/GP EX/STRUC FORCES ECO/TAC DOMIN EDU/PROP LEGIT COERCE ATTIT PERCEPT ORD/FREE PWR RESPECT...PSY SOC VAL/FREE. PAGE 46 A0940
INT/ORG PLAN DIPLOM

B64
FRIEDMANN W.G.,THE CHANGING STRUCTURE OF INTERNATIONAL LAW. WOR+45 INT/ORG NAT/G PROVS LEGIT ORD/FREE PWR...JURID CONCPT GEN/LAWS TOT/POP UN 20. PAGE 49 A1006
ADJUD TREND INT/LAW

B64
FULBRIGHT J.W.,OLD MYTHS AND NEW REALITIES. USA+45 USSR LEGIS INT/TRADE DETER ATTIT...POLICY 20 COLD/WAR TREATY. PAGE 50 A1016
DIPLOM INT/ORG ORD/FREE

B64
GARDNER L.C.,ECONOMIC ASPECTS OF NEW DEAL DIPLOMACY. USA-45 WOR-45 LAW ECO/DEV INT/ORG NAT/G VOL/ASSN LEGIS TOP/EX EDU/PROP ORD/FREE PWR WEALTH ...POLICY TIME/SEQ VAL/FREE 20 ROOSEVLT/F. PAGE 51 A1043
ECO/TAC DIPLOM

B64
GIBSON J.S.,IDEOLOGY AND WORLD AFFAIRS. FUT WOR+45 ECO/UNDEV NAT/G CAP/ISM TOTALISM ORD/FREE FASCISM MARXISM 20. PAGE 52 A1067
ALL/IDEOS DIPLOM POLICY IDEA/COMP

B64
GREAT BRITAIN CENTRAL OFF INF,CONSTITUTIONAL DEVELOPMENT IN THE COMMONWEALTH. VOL/ASSN PLAN DIPLOM COLONIAL INGP/REL NAT/LISM ORD/FREE PWR 17/20 CMN/WLTH. PAGE 55 A1135
REGION CONSTN NAT/G SOVEREIGN

B64
GRODZINS M.,THE ATOMIC AGE: FORTY-FIVE SCIENTISTS AND SCHOLARS SPEAK ON NATIONAL AND WORLD AFFAIRS. FUT USA+45 WOR+45 R+D INT/ORG NAT/G CONSULT TEC/DEV EDU/PROP ATTIT PERSON ORD/FREE...HUM CONCPT TIME/SEQ CON/ANAL. PAGE 57 A1169
INTELL ARMS/CONT NUC/PWR

B64
HOROWITZ I.L.,REVOLUTION IN BRAZIL. BRAZIL L/A+17C ELITES STRATA NAT/G BAL/PWR PARTIC ATTIT 20. PAGE 68 A1388
ECO/UNDEV DIPLOM POLICY ORD/FREE

B64
IKLE F.C.,HOW NATIONS NEGOTIATE. COM EUR+WWI USA+45 NAT/G

INTELL INT/ORG VOL/ASSN DELIB/GP ACT/RES CREATE DOMIN EDU/PROP ADJUD ROUTINE ATTIT PERSON ORD/FREE RESPECT SKILL...PSY SOC OBS VAL/FREE. PAGE 70 A1433 PWR POLICY

B64
INTL INF CTR LOCAL CREDIT,GOVERNMENT MEASURES FOR THE PROMOTION OF REGIONAL ECONOMIC DEVELOPMENT. WOR+45 ECO/UNDEV FINAN INT/ORG DIPLOM ORD/FREE ...POLICY GEOG 20. PAGE 71 A1464 FOR/AID PLAN ECO/TAC REGION

B64
JOHNSON L.B.,MY HOPE FOR AMERICA. FUT USA+45 USSR LAW PLAN DIPLOM GIVE INCOME PEACE ATTIT ORD/FREE WEALTH 20 JOHNSON/LB PRESIDENT DEMOCRAT. PAGE 74 A1525 POLICY POL/PAR NAT/G GOV/REL

B64
KIMMINICH O.,RUSTUNG UND POLITISCHE SPANNUNG. INDUS ARMS/CONT COERCE NAT/LISM PEACE PERSON ORD/FREE ...POLICY GEOG 20. PAGE 79 A1619 DIPLOM FORCES WEAPON WAR

B64
KOLARZ W.,COMMUNISM AND COLONIALISM. AFR ASIA USSR DISCRIM ATTIT ORD/FREE SOVEREIGN SOC/INTEG 20. PAGE 81 A1668 EDU/PROP DIPLOM TOTALISM COLONIAL

B64
LEGGE J.D.,INDONESIA. INDONESIA ELITES ECO/UNDEV POL/PAR CHIEF FORCES INT/TRADE COERCE CHOOSE ORD/FREE...SOC CHARTS BIBLIOG 16/20 CHINJAP. PAGE 86 A1765 S/ASIA DOMIN NAT/LISM POLICY

B64
LENS S.,THE FUTILE CRUSADE. ASIA CHINA/COM L/A+17C USA+45 USSR WOR+45 ECO/DEV BAL/PWR DIPLOM NUC/PWR WAR NAT/LISM PEACE 20 COLD/WAR PRESIDENT CIA. PAGE 87 A1774 ORD/FREE ANOMIE COM MARXISM

B64
LIEVWEN E.,GENERALS VS PRESIDENTS: WEOMILITARISM IN LATIN AMERICA. L/A+17C FORCES DIPLOM FOR/AID LEAD ...NAT/COMP 20 PRESIDENT. PAGE 89 A1813 CIVMIL/REL REV CONSERVE ORD/FREE

B64
LOCKHART W.B.,CASES AND MATERIALS ON CONSTITUTIONAL RIGHTS AND LIBERTIES. USA+45 FORCES LEGIS DIPLOM PRESS CONTROL CRIME WAR PWR...AUD/VIS T WORSHIP 20 NEGRO. PAGE 90 A1849 ORD/FREE CONSTN NAT/G

B64
LUARD E.,THE COLD WAR: A RE-APPRAISAL. FUT USSR WOR+45 FORCES NUC/PWR NAT/LISM ORD/FREE SOVEREIGN ...INT 20 COLD/WAR STALIN/J TREATY UN. PAGE 91 A1870 DIPLOM WAR PEACE TOTALISM

B64
MARKHAM J.W.,THE COMMON MARKET: FRIEND OR COMPETITOR. EUR+WWI FUT USA+45 INT/ORG LG/CO NAT/G VOL/ASSN DELIB/GP EX/STRUC PLAN TARIFFS ORD/FREE PWR WEALTH...POLICY STAT TREND EEC VAL/FREE 20. PAGE 95 A1943 ECO/DEV ECO/TAC

B64
MAUD J.,AID FOR DEVELOPING COUNTRIES. COM EUR+WWI UK INT/TRADE ORD/FREE...GOV/COMP 20. PAGE 96 A1979 FOR/AID DIPLOM ECO/TAC ECO/UNDEV

B64
MEYER F.S.,WHAT IS CONSERVATISM? USA+45 NAT/G FORCES DIPLOM ORD/FREE IDEA/COMP. PAGE 100 A2048 CONSERVE CONCPT EDU/PROP CAP/ISM

B64
NICE R.W.,TREASURY OF LAW. WOR+45 WOR-45 SECT ADJUD MORAL ORD/FREE...INT/LAW JURID PHIL/SCI ANTHOL. PAGE 108 A2227 LAW WRITING PERS/REL DIPLOM

B64
NOVE A.,COMMUNISM AT THE CROSSROADS. USSR INT/ORG POL/PAR TOTALISM...POLICY CONCPT 20. PAGE 110 A2259 DIPLOM BAL/PWR MARXISM ORD/FREE

B64
OWEN W.,STRATEGY FOR MOBILITY. FUT WOR+45 WOR-45 DIST/IND INT/ORG NAT/G DELIB/GP PLAN TEC/DEV ECO/TAC ORD/FREE PWR WEALTH...STAT TIME/SEQ VAL/FREE 20. PAGE 112 A2304 COM/IND ECO/UNDEV

B64
PRAKASH B.,INDIA AND THE WORLD. INDIA INT/ORG CREATE ORD/FREE...POLICY TREND 20. PAGE 117 A2405 DIPLOM PEACE ATTIT

B64
ROCK V.P.,A STRATEGY OF INTERDEPENDENCE. COM USSR WOR+45 NAT/G FORCES PROB/SOLV TEC/DEV DETER WAR ORD/FREE...CONCPT NEW/IDEA METH/COMP 20. PAGE 122 A2509 DIPLOM NUC/PWR PEACE POLICY

B64
ROSECRANCE R.N.,THE DISPERSION OF NUCLEAR WEAPONS: STRATEGY AND POLITICS. ASIA COM FUT S/ASIA USA+45 INT/ORG NAT/G DELIB/GP FORCES ACT/RES TEC/DEV BAL/PWR COERCE DETER ATTIT RIGID/FLEX ORD/FREE ...POLICY CHARTS VAL/FREE. PAGE 123 A2530 EUR+WWI PWR PEACE

B64
RUBINSTEIN A.Z.,THE SOVIETS IN INTERNATIONAL ORGANIZATIONS: CHANGING POLICY TOWARD DEVELOPING COUNTRIES, 1953-1963. COM DELIB/GP ACT/RES ECO/TAC EDU/PROP ADMIN ATTIT ORD/FREE PWR...INT VAL/FREE UN 20. PAGE 125 A2563 ECO/UNDEV INT/ORG USSR

B64
RUSSELL R.B.,UNITED NATIONS EXPERIENCE WITH MILITARY FORCES: POLITICAL AND LEGAL ASPECTS. AFR KOREA WOR+45 LEGIS PROB/SOLV ADMIN CONTROL EFFICIENCY PEACE...POLICY INT/LAW BIBLIOG UN. PAGE 126 A2576 FORCES DIPLOM SANCTION ORD/FREE

B64
SCHWELB E.,HUMAN RIGHTS AND THE INTERNATIONAL COMMUNITY. WOR+45 WOR-45 NAT/G SECT DELIB/GP DIPLOM PEACE RESPECT TREATY 20 UN. PAGE 130 A2666 INT/ORG ORD/FREE INT/LAW

B64
STANKIEWICZ W.J.,POLITICAL THOUGHT SINCE WORLD WAR II. WOR+45 CAP/ISM DIPLOM COLONIAL COERCE REV REPRESENT ADJUST ANOMIE ALL/IDEOS 20. PAGE 137 A2804 IDEA/COMP DOMIN ORD/FREE AUTHORIT

B64
US HOUSE COMM FOREIGN AFFAIRS,HEARINGS ON H.R. 10502 TO AMEND FURTHER THE FOREIGN ASSISTANCE ACT OF 1961. AFR ASIA L/A+17C INT/ORG CONSULT DELIB/GP TEC/DEV ECO/TAC EDU/PROP CONFER 20 UN NATO CONGRESS AID. PAGE 153 A3130 FOR/AID DIPLOM ORD/FREE ECO/UNDEV

B64
US SENATE COMM GOVT OPERATIONS,ADMINISTRATION OF NATIONAL SECURITY. USA+45 CHIEF TOP/EX PLAN DIPLOM CONTROL PEACE...POLICY DECISION 20 PRESIDENT CONGRESS. PAGE 156 A3176 ADMIN FORCES ORD/FREE NAT/G

B64
WAINHOUSE D.W.,REMNANTS OF EMPIRE: THE UNITED NATIONS AND THE END OF COLONIALISM. FUT PORTUGAL WOR+45 NAT/G CONSULT DOMIN LEGIT ADMIN ROUTINE ATTIT ORD/FREE...POLICY JURID RECORD INT TIME/SEQ UN CMN/WLTH 20. PAGE 160 A3260 INT/ORG TREND COLONIAL

B64
WEINTRAUB S.,THE WAR IN THE WARDS. KOREA/N WOR+45 DIPLOM COERCE ORD/FREE SKILL 20 TREATY. PAGE 162 A3308 EDU/PROP PEACE CROWD PUB/INST

B64
WILLIAMS S.P.,TOWARD A GENUINE WORLD SECURITY SYSTEM (PAMPHLET). WOR+45 INT/ORG FORCES PLAN NUC/PWR ORD/FREE...INT/LAW CONCPT UN PRESIDENT. PAGE 165 A3353 BIBLIOG/A ARMS/CONT DIPLOM PEACE

L64
BARROS J.,"THE GREEK-BULGARIAN INCIDENT OF 1925: THE LEAGUE OF NATIONS AND THE GREAT POWERS." BULGARIA EUR+WWI NAT/G FORCES ECO/TAC EDU/PROP LEGIT ROUTINE COERCE WAR PEACE DRIVE PWR...JURID CONCPT METH/CNCPT GEN/LAWS GEN/METH LEAGUE/NAT TOT/POP 20. PAGE 11 A0228 INT/ORG ORD/FREE DIPLOM

L64
CLAUDE I.,"THE OAS, THE UN, AND THE UNITED STATES." L/A+17C USA+45 CONSTN NAT/G DELIB/GP DOMIN EDU/PROP LEGIT REGION COERCE ORD/FREE PWR...TIME/SEQ TREND STERTYP OAS UN 20. PAGE 27 A0546 INT/ORG POLICY

L64
HERZ J.H.,"THE RELEVANCY AND IRRELEVANCY OF APPEASEMENT." WOR+45 INT/ORG CONSULT TOP/EX LEGIT ATTIT SUPEGO ORD/FREE...POLICY SOC GEN/LAWS 20. PAGE 64 A1320 ACT/RES RIGID/FLEX

L64
POUNDS N.J.G.,"THE POLITICS OF PARTITION." AFR ASIA COM EUR+WWI FUT ISLAM S/ASIA USA-45 LAW ECO/DEV ECO/UNDEV AGRI INDUS INT/ORG POL/PAR PROVS SECT FORCES TOP/EX EDU/PROP LEGIT ATTIT MORAL ORD/FREE PWR RESPECT WEALTH. PAGE 117 A2402 NAT/G NAT/LISM

L64
SYMONDS R.,"REFLECTIONS IN LOCALISATION." AFR S/ASIA UK STRATA INT/ORG NAT/G SCHOOL EDU/PROP LEGIT KNOWL ORD/FREE PWR RESPECT CMN/WLTH 20. PAGE 140 A2874 ADMIN MGT COLONIAL

L64
WORLD PEACE FOUNDATION,"INTERNATIONAL ORGANIZATIONS: SUMMARY OF ACTIVITIES." INDIA PAKISTAN TURKEY WOR+45 CONSTN CONSULT EX/STRUC ECO/TAC EDU/PROP LEGIT ORD/FREE...JURID SOC UN 20 CYPRESS. PAGE 167 A3397 INT/ORG ROUTINE

S64
ASHRAF S.,"INDIA AND WORLD AFFAIRS: AN ANNUAL BIBLIOGRAPHY, 1962." WOR+45 LAW ECO/UNDEV INT/ORG FORCES PLAN ECO/TAC COERCE ORD/FREE PWR WEALTH ...HIST/WRIT VAL/FREE. PAGE 9 A0188 S/ASIA NAT/G

S64
BEIM D.,"THE COMMUNIST BLOC AND THE FOREIGN-AID GAME." WOR+45 NAT/G PLAN ROUTINE ATTIT KNOWL ORD/FREE...DECISION QUANT CONT/OBS TIME/SEQ CHARTS GAME SIMUL COLD/WAR 20. PAGE 12 A0252 COM ECO/UNDEV ECO/TAC FOR/AID

S64
CARNEGIE ENDOWMENT INT. PEACE,"HUMAN RIGHTS (ISSUES BEFORE THE NINETEENTH GENERAL ASSEMBLY)." AFR WOR+45 LAW CONSTN NAT/G EDU/PROP GP/REL DISCRIM PEACE ATTIT MORAL ORD/FREE...INT/LAW PSY CONCPT RECORD UN 20. PAGE 24 A0492 INT/ORG PERSON RACE/REL

S64
CARNEGIE ENDOWMENT INT. PEACE,"LEGAL QUESTIONS (ISSUES BEFORE THE NINETEENTH GENERAL ASSEMBLY)." WOR+45 CONSTN NAT/G DELIB/GP ADJUD PEACE MORAL ORD/FREE...RECORD UN 20 TREATY. PAGE 24 A0494 INT/ORG LAW INT/LAW

S64
COCHRANE J.D.,"US ATTITUDES TOWARD CENTRAL-AMERICAN INTEGRATION." L/A+17C USA+45 ECO/UNDEV FACE/GP VOL/ASSN DELIB/GP ECO/TAC INT/TRADE EDU/PROP RIGID/FLEX ORD/FREE WEALTH...TIME/SEQ TOT/POP 20. PAGE 27 A0555 NAT/G ATTIT REGION

S64
COFFEY J.,"THE SOVIET VIEW OF A DISARMED WORLD." COM USA+45 INT/ORG NAT/G EX/STRUC EDU/PROP COERCE PERCEPT ORD/FREE PWR...TREND STERTYP VAL/FREE 20 UN. PAGE 27 A0556 FORCES ATTIT ARMS/CONT USSR

S64
COHEN M.,"BASIC PRINCIPLES OF INTERNATIONAL LAW." UNIV WOR+45 WOR-45 BAL/PWR LEGIT ADJUD WAR ATTIT MORAL ORD/FREE PWR...JURID CONCPT MYTH TOT/POP 20. PAGE 27 A0560 INT/ORG INT/LAW

S64
FALK S.L.,"DISARMAMENT IN HISTORICAL PERSPECTIVE." WOR-45 NAT/G PLAN NUC/PWR PEACE ORD/FREE PWR ...TIME/SEQ AUD/VIS VAL/FREE LEAGUE/NAT 20. PAGE 44 A0892 INT/ORG COERCE ARMS/CONT

S64
GROSSER A.,"Y A-T-IL UN CONFLIT FRANCO-AMERICAIN." EUR+WWI USA+45 INT/ORG NAT/G PLAN BAL/PWR DIPLOM EDU/PROP NUC/PWR ATTIT DRIVE ORD/FREE PWR...CONCPT OBS TIME/SEQ TREND STERTYP VAL/FREE COLD/WAR. PAGE 57 A1179 VOL/ASSN NAT/LISM FRANCE

S64
HICKEY D.,"THE PHILOSOPHICAL ARGUMENT FOR WORLD GOVERNMENT." WOR+45 SOCIETY ACT/RES PLAN LEGIT ADJUD PEACE PERCEPT PERSON ORD/FREE...HUM JURID PHIL/SCI METH/CNCPT CON/ANAL STERTYP GEN/LAWS TOT/POP 20. PAGE 65 A1327 FUT INT/ORG

S64
HOFFMANN S.,"CE QU'EN PENSENT LES AMERICAINS." EUR+WWI INT/ORG VOL/ASSN PLAN BAL/PWR DIPLOM DOMIN EDU/PROP REGION ARMS/CONT DRIVE ORD/FREE PWR ...POLICY CONCPT OBS TREND STERTYP COLD/WAR VAL/FREE 20. PAGE 66 A1357 USA+45 ATTIT FRANCE

S64
HOSCH L.G.,"PUBLIC ADMINISTRATION ON THE INTERNATIONAL FRONTIER." WOR+45 R+D NAT/G EDU/PROP EXEC KNOWL ORD/FREE VAL/FREE 20 UN. PAGE 68 A1390 INT/ORG MGT

S64
HOSKYNS C.,"THE AFRICAN STATES AND THE UNITED NATIONS: 1958-1964." SOUTH/AFR NAT/G VOL/ASSN CONSULT BAL/PWR EDU/PROP MORAL ORD/FREE PWR ...CONCPT TREND UN 20. PAGE 68 A1393 AFR INT/ORG DIPLOM

S64
HOVET T. JR.,"THE ROLE OF AFRICA IN THE UNITED NATIONS." FUT WOR+45 NAT/G DELIB/GP DOMIN EDU/PROP LEGIT ORD/FREE PWR RESPECT SKILL...OBS TIME/SEQ TREND VAL/FREE UN 20. PAGE 68 A1398 AFR INT/ORG DIPLOM

S64
JACK H.,"NONALIGNMENT AND A TEST BAN AGREEMENT: THE ROLE OF THE NON-ALIGNED STATES." WOR+45 INT/ORG CONSULT DOMIN EDU/PROP LEGIT CHOOSE PEACE ATTIT DRIVE KNOWL ORD/FREE...TREND CHARTS GEN/LAWS UN VAL/FREE 20. PAGE 72 A1471 PWR CONCPT NUC/PWR

S64
KARPOV P.V.,"PEACEFUL COEXISTENCE AND INTERNATIONAL LAW." WOR+45 LAW SOCIETY INT/ORG VOL/ASSN FORCES CREATE CAP/ISM DIPLOM ADJUD NUC/PWR PEACE MORAL ORD/FREE PWR MARXISM...MARXIST JURID CONCPT OBS TREND COLD/WAR MARX/KARL 20. PAGE 77 A1568 COM ATTIT INT/LAW USSR

S64
KUNZ J.,"THE CHANGING SCIENCE OF INTERNATIONAL LAW." FUT WOR+45 WOR-45 INT/ORG LEGIT ORD/FREE ...JURID TIME/SEQ GEN/LAWS 20. PAGE 83 A1696 ADJUD CONCPT INT/LAW

S64
LIPSON L.,"PEACEFUL COEXISTENCE." COM USSR WOR+45 LAW INT/ORG DIPLOM LEGIT ADJUD ORD/FREE...CONCPT OBS TREND GEN/LAWS VAL/FREE COLD/WAR 20. PAGE 90 A1834 ATTIT JURID INT/LAW PEACE

S64
MAGGS P.B.,"SOVIET VIEWPOINT ON NUCLEAR WEAPONS IN INTERNATIONAL LAW." USSR WOR+45 INT/ORG FORCES DIPLOM ARMS/CONT ATTIT ORD/FREE PWR...POLICY JURID CONCPT OBS TREND CON/ANAL GEN/LAWS VAL/FREE 20. PAGE 93 A1905 COM LAW INT/LAW NUC/PWR

S64
MARTELLI G.,"PORTUGAL AND THE UNITED NATIONS." AFR EUR+WWI ELITES INT/ORG NAT/G PROVS PLAN DIPLOM ECO/TAC DOMIN COLONIAL RIGID/FLEX MORAL ORD/FREE PWR WEALTH...MYTH UN 20. PAGE 95 A1947 ATTIT PORTUGAL

S64
PADELFORD N.J.,"THE ORGANIZATION OF AFRICAN UNITY." ECO/UNDEV INT/ORG PLAN BAL/PWR DIPLOM ECO/TAC NAT/LISM ORD/FREE PWR WEALTH...CONCPT TREND STERTYP VAL/FREE COLD/WAR 20. PAGE 113 A2313 AFR VOL/ASSN REGION

S64
REIDY J.W.,"LATIN AMERICA AND THE ATLANTIC TRIANGLE." EUR+WWI FUT USA+45 INT/ORG NAT/G REGION COERCE ORD/FREE PWR...TIME/SEQ VAL/FREE 20. PAGE 120 A2458 L/A+17C WEALTH POLICY

S64
RUBINSTEIN A.Z.,"THE SOVIET IMAGE OF WESTERN EUROPE." COM EUR+WWI FRANCE GERMANY GERMANY/W USA+45 USSR INT/ORG NAT/G VOL/ASSN FORCES TOP/EX BAL/PWR EDU/PROP ORD/FREE PWR...MYTH RECORD NATO EEC 20. PAGE 125 A2564 RIGID/FLEX ATTIT

S64
SALVADORI M.,"EL CAPITALISMO EN LA EUROPA DE LA POSGUERRA." INT/ORG NAT/G POL/PAR PLAN ECO/TAC ATTIT ORD/FREE WEALTH...HIST/WRIT COLD/WAR EEC 20. PAGE 127 A2596 EUR+WWI ECO/DEV CAP/ISM

S64
SCHWELB E.,"OPERATION OF THE EUROPEAN CONVENTION ON HUMAN RIGHTS." EUR+WWI LAW SOCIETY CREATE EDU/PROP ADJUD ADMIN PEACE ATTIT ORD/FREE PWR...POLICY INT/LAW CONCPT OBS GEN/LAWS UN VAL/FREE ILO 20 ECHR. PAGE 130 A2665 INT/ORG MORAL

S64
TINKER H.,"POLITICS IN SOUTHEAST ASIA." INT/ORG NAT/G CREATE PLAN TEC/DEV GUERRILLA KNOWL ORD/FREE COLD/WAR. PAGE 144 A2944 S/ASIA ACT/RES REGION

S64
VANDENBOSCH A.,"THE SMALL STATES IN INTERNATIONAL POLITICS AND ORGANIZATION." EUR+WWI MOD/EUR WOR+45 WOR-45 CONSTN DELIB/GP COERCE ORD/FREE PWR ...TIME/SEQ GEN/LAWS VAL/FREE LEAGUE/NAT UN 19/20. PAGE 158 A3219 NAT/G INT/ORG DIPLOM

C64
EASTON S.C.,"THE RISE AND FALL OF WESTERN COLONIALISM." AFR ISLAM L/A+17C ECO/UNDEV REV NAT/LISM...CHARTS BIBLIOG 15/20. PAGE 40 A0817 COLONIAL DIPLOM ORD/FREE WAR

C64
SCHRAMM W.,"MASS MEDIA AND NATIONAL DEVELOPMENT: THE ROLE OF INFORMATION IN DEVELOPING COUNTRIES." FINAN R+D ACT/RES PLAN TEC/DEV DIPLOM CHOOSE SUPEGO ORD/FREE...BIBLIOG 20. PAGE 129 A2645 ECO/UNDEV COM/IND EDU/PROP MAJORIT

B65
COOMBS P.H.,EDUCATION AND FOREIGN AID. AFR USA+45 DIPLOM EFFICIENCY KNOWL ORD/FREE...ANTHOL 20 AID. PAGE 30 A0608 EDU/PROP FOR/AID SCHOOL ECO/UNDEV

B65
COOPER S.,BEHIND THE GOLDEN CURTAIN: A VIEW OF THE USA. UK USA+45 SECT EDU/PROP COERCE LEISURE ORD/FREE WEALTH 20. PAGE 30 A0609 SOCIETY DIPLOM ATTIT ACT/RES

B65
COX R.H.,THE STATE IN INTERNATIONAL RELATIONS. INT/ORG DIPLOM REV WAR PEACE MARXISM...CONCPT GOV/COMP. PAGE 32 A0647 SOVEREIGN NAT/G FASCISM ORD/FREE

B65
EISENHOWER D.D.,WAGING PEACE 1956-61: THE WHITE HOUSE YEARS. USA+45 DIPLOM LEAD INGP/REL RACE/REL PEACE ATTIT...TRADIT TIME/SEQ 20 EISNHWR/DD PRESIDENT COLD/WAR CIV/RIGHTS BERLIN. PAGE 41 A0833 TOP/EX BIOG ORD/FREE POLICY

B65
EMERSON R.,THE POLITICAL AWAKENING OF AFRICA. ECO/UNDEV INT/ORG COLONIAL RACE/REL ORD/FREE MARXISM...TREND ANTHOL 20. PAGE 42 A0849 AFR NAT/LISM DIPLOM POL/PAR

B65
GERASSI J.,THE GREAT FEAR IN LATIN AMERICA. L/A+17C USA+45 ELITES STRUCT INT/ORG REV ORD/FREE WEALTH 20 LAFTA. PAGE 52 A1063 SOCIETY FOR/AID DIPLOM

B65
INGRAM D.,COMMONWEALTH FOR A COLOUR-BLIND WORLD. AFR INDIA UK STRATA ECO/UNDEV VOL/ASSN CREATE PLAN CONFER COLONIAL ORD/FREE SOC/INTEG 20 COMMONWLTH. PAGE 70 A1441 RACE/REL INT/ORG INGP/REL PROB/SOLV

B65
KAHN H.,ON ESCALATION; METAPHORS AND SCENARIOS. FORCES DIPLOM ARMS/CONT WAR CIVMIL/REL...INT/LAW 20. PAGE 76 A1548 NUC/PWR ACT/RES INT/ORG ORD/FREE

B65
LARUS J.,FROM COLLECTIVE SECURITY TO PREVENTIVE DIPLOMACY. FUT FORCES PROB/SOLV DEBATE AGREE COERCE WAR PWR...ANTHOL 20 LEAGUE/NAT UN. PAGE 85 A1736 INT/ORG PEACE DIPLOM ORD/FREE

B65
LEVENSTEIN A.,FREEDOM'S ADVOCATE - A TWENTY-FIVE YEAR CHRONICLE. USA+45 POL/PAR LEGIS DIPLOM WAR PEACE TOTALISM DRIVE MARXISM 20 FREEDOM/HS. PAGE 87 A1791 ORD/FREE VOL/ASSN POLICY ATTIT

B65
LINDBLOM C.E.,THE INTELLIGENCE OF DEMOCRACY; DECISION MAKING THROUGH MUTUAL ADJUSTMENT. WOR+45 SOCIETY NAT/G PROB/SOLV DOMIN PARTIC GP/REL ORD/FREE...POLICY IDEA/COMP BIBLIOG 20. PAGE 89 PLURISM DECISION ADJUST DIPLOM

A1821

B65

LYONS G.M.,AMERICA: PURPOSE AND POWER. UK USA+45 FINAN INDUS MARKET WORKER TEC/DEV DIPLOM AUTOMAT NUC/PWR WAR RACE/REL ORD/FREE 20 EEC CONGRESS SUPREME/CT CIV/RIGHTS. PAGE 92 A1881
PWR PROB/SOLV ECO/DEV TASK

B65

MACDONALD R.W.,THE LEAGUE OF ARAB STATES: A STUDY IN THE DYNAMICS OF REGIONAL ORGANIZATION. ISRAEL UAR USSR FINAN INT/ORG DELIB/GP ECO/TAC AGREE NEUTRAL ORD/FREE PWR...DECISION BIBLIOG 20 TREATY UN. PAGE 92 A1888
ISLAM REGION DIPLOM ADMIN

B65

MENON K.P.S.,MANY WORLDS. INDIA BAL/PWR CAP/ISM COLONIAL REV ORD/FREE PWR MARXISM...POLICY 20 COLD/WAR. PAGE 100 A2042
BIOG DIPLOM NAT/G

B65

MOLNAR T.,AFRICA: A POLITICAL TRAVELOGUE. STRUCT ECO/UNDEV DIPLOM EDU/PROP LEAD RACE/REL MARXISM 20 INTERVENT EUROPE. PAGE 102 A2101
COLONIAL AFR ORD/FREE

B65

MONCONDUIT F.,LA COMMISSION EUROPEENNE DES DROITS DE L'HOMME. DIPLOM AGREE GP/REL ORD/FREE PWR ...BIBLIOG 20 TREATY. PAGE 102 A2103
INT/LAW INT/ORG ADJUD JURID

B65

MORRIS R.B.,THE PEACEMAKERS; THE GREAT POWERS AND AMERICAN INDEPENDENCE. BAL/PWR CONFER COLONIAL NEUTRAL PEACE ORD/FREE TREATY 18 PRE/US/AM. PAGE 105 A2149
SOVEREIGN REV DIPLOM

B65

NEWBURY C.W.,BRITISH POLICY TOWARDS WEST AFRICA: SELECT DOCUMENTS 1786-1874. AFR UK INT/TRADE DOMIN ADMIN COLONIAL CT/SYS COERCE ORD/FREE...BIBLIOG/A 18/19. PAGE 108 A2224
DIPLOM POLICY NAT/G WRITING

B65

RODRIGUES J.H.,BRAZIL AND AFRICA. AFR BRAZIL PORTUGAL UK USA+45 USA-45 CULTURE ECO/UNDEV INT/ORG INT/TRADE RACE/REL ORD/FREE 15/20 UN MISCEGEN. PAGE 123 A2513
DIPLOM COLONIAL POLICY ATTIT

B65

RUBINSTEIN A.,THE CHALLENGE OF POLITICS: IDEAS AND ISSUES. BAL/PWR COLONIAL WAR TOTALISM ORD/FREE PWR MARXISM SOCISM...INT/LAW 20. PAGE 125 A2561
NAT/G SOVEREIGN DIPLOM NAT/LISM

B65

RUBINSTEIN A.Z.,THE CHALLENGE OF POLITICS: IDEAS AND ISSUES (2ND ED.). UNIV ELITES SOCIETY EX/STRUC BAL/PWR PARL/PROC AUTHORIT...DECISION ANTHOL 20. PAGE 125 A2565
NAT/G DIPLOM GP/REL ORD/FREE

B65

STOETZER O.C.,THE ORGANIZATION OF AMERICAN STATES. L/A+17C EX/STRUC FOR/AID CONFER PARL/PROC ORD/FREE SOVEREIGN...POLICY INT/LAW 20 OAS. PAGE 138 A2831
INT/ORG REGION DIPLOM BAL/PWR

B65

THAYER F.C. JR.,AIR TRANSPORT POLICY AND NATIONAL SECURITY: A POLITICAL, ECONOMIC, AND MILITARY ANALYSIS. DIST/IND OP/RES PLAN TEC/DEV DIPLOM DETER WAR COST EFFICIENCY...POLICY BIBLIOG 20 DEPT/DEFEN FAA CAB. PAGE 142 A2908
AIR FORCES CIVMIL/REL ORD/FREE

B65

TREFOUSSE H.L.,THE COLD WAR: A BOOK OF DOCUMENTS. ASIA L/A+17C USSR WOR+45 WOR-45 ECO/TAC FOR/AID ARMS/CONT NUC/PWR PEACE ORD/FREE...ANTHOL 20 COLD/WAR KENNEDY/JF EISNHWR/DD. PAGE 145 A2961
BAL/PWR DIPLOM MARXISM

B65

US HOUSE COMM FOREIGN AFFAIRS,HEARINGS ON DRAFT BILL TO AMEND FURTHER THE FOREIGN ASSISTANCE ACT OF 1961. AFR ASIA L/A+17C USA+45 INT/ORG DELIB/GP TEC/DEV ECO/TAC CONFER TOTALISM 20 CONGRESS AID. PAGE 153 A3131
FOR/AID ECO/UNDEV DIPLOM ORD/FREE

B65

US SENATE COMM GOVT OPERATIONS,ADMINISTRATION OF NATIONAL SECURITY. USA+45 DELIB/GP ADMIN ROLE ...POLICY CHARTS SENATE. PAGE 156 A3177
NAT/G ORD/FREE DIPLOM PROB/SOLV

B65

US SENATE COMM ON FOREIGN REL,HEARINGS ON THE FOREIGN ASSISTANCE PROGRAM. AFR ASIA L/A+17C USA+45 WOR+45 FORCES TEC/DEV BUDGET CONTROL WEAPON ORD/FREE 20 UN CONGRESS SEC/STATE. PAGE 156 A3183
FOR/AID DIPLOM INT/ORG ECO/UNDEV

B65

US SENATE COMM ON JUDICIARY,REFUGEE PROBLEMS IN SOUTH VIETNAM AND LAOS: HEARINGS BEFORE SUBCOMMITTEE TO INVESTIGATE PROBLEMS OF REFUGEES, ESCAPEES. CHINA/COM LAOS USA+45 VIETNAM/S PROB/SOLV DIPLOM GOV/REL GP/REL EFFICIENCY ORD/FREE...POLICY GEOG 20 CONGRESS MIGRATION. PAGE 157 A3194
STRANGE HABITAT FOR/AID CIVMIL/REL

B65

WRESZIN M.,OSWALD GARRISON VILLARD: PACIFIST AT WAR. EDU/PROP MORAL ORD/FREE. PAGE 167 A3398
USA-45 NAT/G INT/ORG INTELL

L65

RUBIN A.P.,"UNITED STATES CONTEMPORARY PRACTICE RELATING TO INTERNATIONAL LAW." USA+45 WOR+45 CONSTN INT/ORG NAT/G DELIB/GP EX/STRUC DIPLOM DOMIN CT/SYS ROUTINE ORD/FREE...CONCPT COLD/WAR 20. PAGE 125 A2558
LAW LEGIT INT/LAW

S65

BROWN S.,"AN ALTERNATIVE TO THE GRAND DESIGN." EUR+WWI FUT USA+45 INT/ORG NAT/G EX/STRUC FORCES CREATE BAL/PWR DOMIN RIGID/FLEX ORD/FREE PWR ...NEW/IDEA RECORD EEC NATO 20. PAGE 20 A0407
VOL/ASSN CONCPT DIPLOM

S65

MAC CHESNEY B.,"SOME COMMENTS ON THE 'QUARANTINE' OF CUBA." USA+45 WOR+45 NAT/G BAL/PWR DIPLOM LEGIT ROUTINE ATTIT ORD/FREE...JURID METH/CNCPT 20. PAGE 92 A1883
INT/ORG LAW CUBA USSR

S65

MERRITT R.L.,"WOODROW WILSON AND THE 'GREAT AND SOLEMN REFERENDUM,' 1920." USA-45 SOCIETY NAT/G CONSULT LEGIS ACT/RES PLAN DOMIN EDU/PROP ROUTINE ATTIT DISPL DRIVE PERSON RIGID/FLEX MORAL ORD/FREE ...PSY SOC CONCPT MYTH LEAGUE/NAT. PAGE 100 A2044
INT/ORG TOP/EX DIPLOM

S65

PLISCHKE E.,"INTEGRATING BERLIN AND THE FEDERAL REPUBLIC OF GERMANY." EUR+WWI GERMANY/W LEGIS TEC/DEV DOMIN ORD/FREE PWR...JURID 20 BERLIN. PAGE 117 A2392
DIPLOM NAT/G MUNIC

S65

QUADE Q.L.,"THE TRUMAN ADMINISTRATION AND THE SEPARATION OF POWERS: THE CASE OF THE MARSHALL PLAN." SOCIETY INT/ORG NAT/G CONSULT DELIB/GP LEGIS PLAN ECO/TAC ROUTINE DRIVE PERCEPT RIGID/FLEX ORD/FREE PWR WEALTH...DECISION GEOG NEW/IDEA TREND 20 TRUMAN/HS. PAGE 118 A2422
USA+45 ECO/UNDEV DIPLOM

S65

TURNER F.C.,"THE IMPLICATIONS OF DEMOGRAPHIC CHANGE FOR NATIONALISM AND INTERNATIONALISM." FUT WOR+45 NAT/LISM AGE SEX CONCPT. PAGE 146 A2980
SOCIETY EDU/PROP DIPLOM ORD/FREE

C65

BURTON J.W.,"INTERNATIONAL RELATIONS: A GENERAL THEORY." WOR+45 NAT/G CREATE BAL/PWR NEUTRAL COERCE DETER ADJUST...TREND IDEA/COMP GEN/METH BIBLIOG. PAGE 22 A0447
DIPLOM GEN/LAWS ACT/RES ORD/FREE

B66

SUPPLEMENTAL FOREIGN ASSISTANCE FISCAL YEAR 1966: VIETNAM. CHINA/COM COM S/ASIA USA+45 VIETNAM EXTR/IND FINAN DIPLOM TAX GUERRILLA HABITAT ORD/FREE...STAT CHARTS 20 SENATE PRESIDENT. PAGE 4 A0077
CONFER LEGIS WAR FOR/AID

B66

AMERICAN FRIENDS SERVICE COMM,PEACE IN VIETNAM: A NEW APPROACH IN SOUTHEAST ASIA: A REPORT. ASIA S/ASIA USA+45 VIETNAM ORD/FREE 20 TREATY. PAGE 7 A0149
PEACE WAR NAT/LISM DIPLOM

B66

CANFIELD L.H.,THE PRESIDENCY OF WOODROW WILSON: PRELUDE TO A WORLD IN CRISIS. USA-45 ADJUD NEUTRAL WAR CHOOSE INGP/REL PEACE ORD/FREE 20 WILSON/W PRESIDENT TREATY LEAGUE/NAT. PAGE 24 A0477
PERSON POLICY DIPLOM GOV/REL

B66

COUNCIL OF EUROPE,EUROPEAN CONVENTION ON HUMAN RIGHTS - COLLECTED TEXTS (5TH ED.). EUR+WWI DIPLOM ADJUD CT/SYS...INT/LAW 20 ECHR. PAGE 31 A0638
ORD/FREE DELIB/GP INT/ORG JURID

B66

FREIDEL F.,AMERICAN ISSUES IN THE TWENTIETH CENTURY. SOCIETY FINAN ECO/TAC FOR/AID CONTROL NUC/PWR WAR RACE/REL PEACE ATTIT...ANTHOL T 20 WILSON/W ROOSEVLT/F KENNEDY/JF TRUMAN/HS. PAGE 49 A0995
DIPLOM POLICY NAT/G ORD/FREE

B66

GERARD-LIBOIS J.,KATANGA SECESSION. INT/ORG FORCES DIPLOM ADMIN CONTROL WAR CHOOSE PWR...CHARTS 20 KATANGA TSHOMBE/M UN. PAGE 52 A1062
NAT/G REGION ORD/FREE REV

B66

GRENVILLE J.A.S.,POLITICS, STRATEGY, AND AMERICAN DEMOCRACY: STUDIES IN FOREIGN POLICY, 1873-1917. CUBA PHILIPPINE SPAIN USA-45 VENEZUELA ELITES NAT/G CREATE PARTIC WAR RIGID/FLEX ORD/FREE...DECISION TREND 19/20 HAWAII. PAGE 56 A1146
DIPLOM COLONIAL POLICY

B66

KAREFA-SMART J.,AFRICA: PROGRESS THROUGH COOPERATION. AFR FINAN TEC/DEV DIPLOM FOR/AID EDU/PROP CONFER REGION GP/REL WEALTH...HEAL SOC/INTEG 20. PAGE 76 A1566
ORD/FREE ECO/UNDEV VOL/ASSN PLAN

B66

LATHAM E.,THE COMMUNIST CONTROVERSY IN WASHINGTON. USA+45 USA-45 DELIB/GP EX/STRUC LEGIS DIPLOM NAT/LISM MARXISM 20. PAGE 85 A1742
POL/PAR TOTALISM ORD/FREE NAT/G

B66

LUARD E.,THE EVOLUTION OF INTERNATIONAL ORGANIZATIONS. UK WOR+45 BUDGET INT/TRADE WAR BAL/PAY PEACE ORD/FREE...POLICY 19/20 EEC ILO LEAGUE/NAT UN. PAGE 91 A1871
INT/ORG EFFICIENCY CREATE TREND

B66
MCNAIR A.D.,THE LEGAL EFFECTS OF WAR. UK FINAN DIPLOM ORD/FREE 20 ENGLSH/LAW. PAGE 98 A2019
JURID WAR INT/TRADE LABOR

B66
MONTGOMERY J.D.,APPROACHES TO DEVELOPMENT: POLITICS, ADMINISTRATION AND CHANGE. USA+45 AGRI FOR/AID ORD/FREE...CONCPT IDEA/COMP METH/COMP ANTHOL. PAGE 103 A2116
ECO/UNDEV ADMIN POLICY ECO/TAC

B66
NIEDERGANG M.,LA REVOLUTION DE SAINT-DOMINGUE. DOMIN/REP INT/ORG NAT/G CONTROL LEAD GP/REL ORD/FREE MARXISM 20. PAGE 109 A2239
REV FORCES DIPLOM

B66
OBERMANN E.,VERTEIDIGUNG PER FREIHEIT. GERMANY/W WOR+45 INT/ORG COERCE NUC/PWR WEAPON MARXISM 20 UN NATO WARSAW/P TREATY. PAGE 111 A2273
FORCES ORD/FREE WAR PEACE

B66
POLLACK R.S.,THE INDIVIDUAL'S RIGHTS AND INTERNATIONAL ORGANIZATION. LAW INT/ORG DELIB/GP SUPEGO...JURID SOC/INTEG 20 TREATY UN. PAGE 117 A2394
INT/LAW ORD/FREE DIPLOM PERSON

B66
RISTIC D.N.,YUGOSLAVIA'S REVOLUTION OF 1941. EUR+WWI YUGOSLAVIA NAT/G WAR ORD/FREE...RECORD BIBLIOG 20 HITLER/A TREATY. PAGE 121 A2484
REV ATTIT FASCISM DIPLOM

B66
TYSON G.,NEHRU: THE YEARS OF POWER. INDIA UK STRATA ECO/UNDEV FINAN SECT TASK WAR ORD/FREE MARXISM ...POLICY BIBLIOG 20 NEHRU/J. PAGE 146 A2985
CHIEF PWR DIPLOM NAT/G

B66
US HOUSE COMM APPROPRIATIONS,HEARINGS ON FOREIGN OPERATIONS AND RELATED AGENCIES APPROPRIATIONS. CUBA USA+45 VOL/ASSN DELIB/GP DIPLOM CONFER ORD/FREE 20 CONGRESS MIGRATION INT/AM/DEV PEACE/CORP. PAGE 153 A3120
FOR/AID BUDGET ECO/UNDEV FORCES

B66
US HOUSE COMM FOREIGN AFFAIRS,HEARINGS ON HR 12449 A BILL TO AMEND FURTHER THE FOREIGN ASSISTANCE ACT OF 1961. AFR ASIA L/A+17C USA+45 VIETNAM INT/ORG TEC/DEV INT/TRADE ATTIT ORD/FREE 20 UN NATO CONGRESS AID. PAGE 154 A3132
FOR/AID ECO/TAC ECO/UNDEV DIPLOM

B66
US SENATE COMM ON FOREIGN REL,HEARINGS ON S 2859 AND S 2861. USA+45 WOR+45 FORCES BUDGET CAP/ISM ADMIN DETER WEAPON TOTALISM...NAT/COMP 20 UN CONGRESS. PAGE 156 A3185
FOR/AID DIPLOM ORD/FREE ECO/UNDEV

B66
ZEINE Z.N.,THE EMERGENCE OF ARAB NATIONALISM (REV. ED.). TURKEY UK NAT/G SECT TEC/DEV LEAD REV WAR AGE/Y ROLE ORD/FREE...TRADIT CHARTS BIBLIOG 20 ARABS OTTOMAN. PAGE 170 A3451
ISLAM NAT/LISM DIPLOM

S66
DINH TRANS V.A.N.,"VIETNAM: A THIRD WAY" S/ASIA USA+45 USSR VIETNAM VIETNAM/S NAT/G SECT FORCES CAP/ISM DIPLOM COLONIAL NEUTRAL MARXISM SOCISM 20 BUDDHISM UNIFICA. PAGE 38 A0766
WAR PLAN ORD/FREE SOCIALIST

S66
FRIEND A.,"THE MIDDLE EAST CRISIS" COM ISLAM ISRAEL SYRIA UAR USA+45 USSR FORCES PLAN FOR/AID CONTROL ORD/FREE PWR...SOCIALIST TIME/SEQ 20 NASSER/G. PAGE 49 A1009
WAR INT/ORG DIPLOM PEACE

S66
SHERMAN M.,"GUARANTEES AND NUCLEAR SPREAD." USA+45 WOR+45 INT/ORG PLAN DETER WAR ORD/FREE 20 NATO. PAGE 132 A2700
DIPLOM POLICY NAT/G NUC/PWR

C66
BLAISDELL D.C.,"INTERNATIONAL ORGANIZATION." FUT WOR+45 ECO/DEV DELIB/GP FORCES EFFICIENCY PEACE ORD/FREE...INT/LAW 20 UN LEAGUE/NAT NATO. PAGE 15 A0304
BIBLIOG INT/ORG DIPLOM ARMS/CONT

C66
TARLING N.,"A CONCISE HISTORY OF SOUTHEAST ASIA." BURMA CAMBODIA LAOS S/ASIA THAILAND VIETNAM ECO/UNDEV POL/PAR FORCES ADMIN REV WAR CIVMIL/REL ORD/FREE MARXISM SOCISM 13/20. PAGE 141 A2890
COLONIAL DOMIN INT/TRADE NAT/LISM

B67
BELL W.,THE DEMOCRATIC REVOLUTION IN THE WEST INDIES. WEST/IND WOR+45 DIPLOM RACE/REL NAT/LISM ...INT QU ANTHOL 20. PAGE 13 A0257
REGION ATTIT ORD/FREE ECO/UNDEV

B67
DE BLIJ H.J.,SYSTEMATIC POLITICAL GEOGRAPHY. WOR+45 STRUCT INT/ORG NAT/G EDU/PROP ADMIN COLONIAL ROUTINE ORD/FREE PWR...IDEA/COMP T 20. PAGE 34 A0697
GEOG CONCPT METH

B67
KIRK R.,THE POLITICAL PRINCIPLES OF ROBERT A. TAFT. USA+45 LABOR DIPLOM ADJUD ADJUST ORD/FREE TAFT/RA. PAGE 80 A1635
POL/PAR LEAD LEGIS ATTIT

B67
LAWYERS COMM AMER POLICY VIET,VIETNAM AND INTERNATIONAL LAW: AN ANALYSIS OF THE LEGALITY OF THE US MILITARY INVOLVEMENT. VIETNAM LAW INT/ORG COERCE WEAPON PEACE ORD/FREE 20 UN SEATO TREATY. PAGE 86 A1753
INT/LAW DIPLOM ADJUD WAR

B67
MAW B.,BREAKTHROUGH IN BURMA: MEMOIRS OF A REVOLUTION, 1939-1946. BURMA UK FORCES PROB/SOLV DIPLOM FOR/AID DOMIN LEAD...BIOG 20. PAGE 97 A1980
REV ORD/FREE NAT/LISM COLONIAL

B67
MEYNAUD J.,TRADE UNIONISM IN AFRICA; A STUDY OF ITS GROWTH AND ORIENTATION (TRANS. BY ANGELA BRENCH). INT/ORG PROB/SOLV COLONIAL PWR...TIME/SEQ TREND ILO. PAGE 100 A2055
LABOR AFR NAT/LISM ORD/FREE

B67
MURTY B.S.,PROPAGANDA AND WORLD PUBLIC ORDER. FUT WOR+45 COM/IND INT/ORG PROB/SOLV ATTIT KNOWL ORD/FREE...POLICY UN. PAGE 106 A2183
EDU/PROP DIPLOM CONTROL JURID

B67
NYERERE J.K.,FREEDOM AND UNITY/UHURU NA UMOJA: A SELECTION FROM WRITINGS AND SPEECHES, 1952-65. TANZANIA ELITES ECO/UNDEV INT/ORG NAT/G CREATE DIPLOM COLONIAL REGION RACE/REL...ANTHOL 20. PAGE 110 A2265
SOVEREIGN AFR TREND ORD/FREE

B67
PIKE F.B.,FREEDOM AND REFORM IN LATIN AMERICA. BRAZIL URUGUAY CONSTN CULTURE SECT DIPLOM EDU/PROP PARTIC DRIVE ALL/VALS CATHISM...GEOG ANTHOL BIBLIOG REFORMERS BOLIV. PAGE 116 A2379
L/A+17C ORD/FREE ECO/UNDEV REV

B67
SAYEED K.B.,THE POLITICAL SYSTEM OF PAKISTAN. PAKISTAN DIPLOM REGION CHOOSE ORD/FREE...BIBLIOG 20. PAGE 127 A2609
NAT/G POL/PAR CONSTN SECT

B67
STEVENS R.P.,LESOTHO, BATSWANA, AND SWAZILAND* THE FORMER HIGH COMMISSION TERRITORIES IN SOUTHERN AFRICA. ECO/DEV KIN POL/PAR HIST/WRIT. PAGE 138 A2821
COLONIAL DIPLOM ORD/FREE

B67
US DEPARTMENT OF THE ARMY,CIVILIAN IN PEACE, SOLDIER IN WAR: A BIBLIOGRAPHIC SURVEY OF THE ARMY AND AIR NATIONAL GUARD (PAMPHLET, NOS. 130-2). USA+45 USA-45 LOC/G NAT/G PROVS LEGIS PLAN ADMIN ATTIT ORD/FREE...POLICY 19/20. PAGE 152 A3111
BIBLIOG/A FORCES ROLE DIPLOM

B67
US SENATE COMM AERO SPACE SCI,TREATY ON PRINCIPLES GOVERNING ACTIVITIES OF STATES IN EXPLORATION AND USE OF OUTER SPACE, INCLUDING...BODIES. DELIB/GP FORCES LEGIS DIPLOM...JURID 20 DEPT/STATE NASA DEPT/DEFEN UN. PAGE 155 A3169
SPACE INT/LAW ORD/FREE PEACE

B67
US SENATE COMM ON FOREIGN REL,HUMAN RIGHTS CONVENTIONS. USA+45 LABOR VOL/ASSN DELIB/GP DOMIN ADJUD REPRESENT...INT/LAW MGT CONGRESS. PAGE 156 A3189
LEGIS ORD/FREE WORKER LOBBY

B67
US SENATE COMM ON FOREIGN REL,UNITED STATES ARMAMENT AND DISARMAMENT PROBLEMS. USA+45 AIR BAL/PWR DIPLOM FOR/AID NUC/PWR ORD/FREE SENATE TREATY. PAGE 156 A3190
ARMS/CONT WEAPON FORCES PROB/SOLV

B67
WILLIS F.R.,DE GAULLE: ANACHRONISM, REALIST, OR PROPHET? FRANCE POL/PAR FORCES DIPLOM WAR PEACE ROLE ORD/FREE...POLICY IDEA/COMP ANTHOL 20 DEGAULLE/C. PAGE 165 A3356
BIOG PERSON CHIEF LEAD

L67
"RESTRICTIVE SOVEREIGN IMMUNITY, THE STATE DEPARTMENT, AND THE COURTS." USA+45 USA-45 EX/STRUC DIPLOM ADJUD CONTROL GOV/REL 19/20 DEPT/STATE SUPREME/CT. PAGE 4 A0080
SOVEREIGN ORD/FREE PRIVIL CT/SYS

S67
ABT J.J.,"WORLD OF SENATOR FULBRIGHT." VIETNAM WOR+45 COERCE DETER REV ORD/FREE MARXISM...MARXIST 20. PAGE 4 A0084
DIPLOM PLAN PWR

S67
BATOR V.,"ONE WAR* TWO VIETNAMS." S/ASIA VIETNAM DIPLOM SUFF ATTIT ORD/FREE 20. PAGE 12 A0234
WAR BAL/PWR NAT/G STRUCT

S67
BREGMAN A.,"WHITHER RUSSIA?" COM RUSSIA INTELL POL/PAR DIPLOM PARTIC NAT/LISM TOTALISM ATTIT ORD/FREE 20. PAGE 18 A0370
MARXISM ELITES ADMIN CREATE

S67
BURNS E.B.,"TRADITIONS AND VARIATIONS IN BRAZILIAN FOREIGN POLICY." BRAZIL L/A+17C POL/PAR INT/TRADE COLONIAL INGP/REL ATTIT ORD/FREE PWR 20. PAGE 22 A0443
DIPLOM NAT/LISM CREATE

S67
COHN K.,"CRIMES AGAINST HUMANITY." GERMANY INT/ORG SANCTION ATTIT ORD/FREE...MARXIST CRIMLGY 20 UN.
WAR INT/LAW

PAGE 28 A0564 CRIME ADJUD

S67

D'AMATO D.,"LEGAL ASPECTS OF THE FRENCH NUCLEAR TESTS." FRANCE WOR+45 ACT/RES COLONIAL RISK GOV/REL EQUILIB ORD/FREE PWR DECISION. PAGE 33 A0672 INT/LAW DIPLOM NUC/PWR ADJUD

S67

FABREGA J.,"ANTECEDENTES EXTRANJEROS EN LA CONSTITUCION PANAMENA." CUBA L/A+17C PANAMA URUGUAY EX/STRUC LEGIS DIPLOM ORD/FREE 19/20 COLOMB MEXIC/AMER. PAGE 43 A0882 CONSTN JURID NAT/G PARL/PROC

S67

FOREIGN POLICY ASSOCIATION,"US CONCERN FOR WORLD LAW." USA+45 WOR+45 DELIB/GP JUDGE BAL/PWR CONFER PEACE ORD/FREE 20 UN. PAGE 47 A0962 INT/LAW INT/ORG DIPLOM ARMS/CONT

S67

JACKSON W.G.F.,"NUCLEAR PROLIFERATION AND THE GREAT POWERS." FUT UK WOR+45 INT/ORG DOMIN ARMS/CONT DETER ORD/FREE PACIFIST. PAGE 72 A1480 NUC/PWR ATTIT BAL/PWR NAT/LISM

S67

JOHNSTON D.M.,"LAW, TECHNOLOGY AND THE SEA." WOR+45 PLAN PROB/SOLV TEC/DEV CONFER ADJUD ORD/FREE ...POLICY JURID. PAGE 75 A1528 INT/LAW INT/ORG DIPLOM NEUTRAL

S67

KAHN H.,"CRITERIA FOR LONG-RANGE NUCLEAR CONTROL POLICIES." WOR+45 INT/ORG TEC/DEV DOMIN DETER WAR WEAPON ISOLAT ORD/FREE POLICY. PAGE 76 A1549 NUC/PWR ARMS/CONT BAL/PWR DIPLOM

S67

KIPP K.,"DIE POLITISCHE BEDEUTUNG DER 'GEGENKUSTE' DARGESTELLT AM BEISPIEL DER USA IM 20. JAHRHUNDERT" USA+45 USA-45 SEA NAT/G CONTROL COERCE WAR...POLICY GEOG 20. PAGE 79 A1629 FORCES ORD/FREE DIPLOM DETER

S67

KRUSCHE H.,"THE STRIVING OF THE KIESINGER-STRAUS GOVERNMENT FOR NUCLEAR WEAPONS IS A THREAT TO EUROPEAN SECURITY." EUR+WWI GERMANY BAL/PWR SANCTION WEAPON PEACE ORD/FREE...MARXIST 20 NATO COLD/WAR. PAGE 82 A1688 ARMS/CONT INT/ORG NUC/PWR DIPLOM

S67

MOBERG E.,"THE EFFECT OF SECURITY POLICY MEASURES: DISCUSSION RELATED TO SWEDEN'S SECURITY POLICY." SWEDEN PLAN PROB/SOLV DIPLOM GOV/REL MORAL...CHARTS 20. PAGE 102 A2092 POLICY ORD/FREE BUDGET FINAN

S67

PAUKER G.J.,"TOWARD A NEW ORDER IN INDONESIA." COM INDONESIA S/ASIA ECO/UNDEV POL/PAR EX/STRUC TOP/EX BAL/PWR ECO/TAC FOR/AID DOMIN NAT/LISM AUTHORIT ORD/FREE PWR 20. PAGE 114 A2342 REV NAT/G DIPLOM CIVMIL/REL

S67

ROGERS W.C.,"A COMPARISON OF INFORMED AND GENERAL PUBLIC OPINION ON US FOREIGN POLICY." USA+45 DIPLOM EDU/PROP ORD/FREE...POLICY SAMP IDEA/COMP 20. PAGE 123 A2515 KNOWL ATTIT GP/COMP ELITES

S67

VELIKONJA J.,"ITALIAN IMMIGRANTS IN THE UNITED STATES IN THE MID-SIXTIES" ITALY USA+45 KIN MUNIC NAT/G WORKER DIPLOM REGION GP/REL ADJUST...GEOG CHARTS SOC/INTEG 20. PAGE 158 A3226 HABITAT ORD/FREE TREND STAT

S67

WILLIAMS B.H.,"FREEDOM AS A SLOGAN IN INTERNATIONAL CONFLICT." VIETNAM DIPLOM COLONIAL. PAGE 164 A3351 EDU/PROP ORD/FREE WAR PWR

S67

YOUNG K.T.,"UNITED STATES POLICY AND VIETNAMESE POLITICAL VIABILITY 1954-1967." VIETNAM/S LOC/G MUNIC FOR/AID ORD/FREE...POLICY 20. PAGE 169 A3437 LEAD ADMIN GP/REL EFFICIENCY

B90

HOSMAR J.K.,A SHORT HISTORY OF ANGLO-SAXON FREEDOM. UK USA-45 ROMAN/EMP NAT/G EX/STRUC LEGIS COLONIAL REV NAT/LISM POPULISM PARLIAMENT ANGLO/SAX MAGNA/CART. PAGE 68 A1394 CONSTN ORD/FREE DIPLOM PARL/PROC

B96

DE VATTEL E.,THE LAW OF NATIONS. AGRI FINAN CHIEF DIPLOM INT/TRADE AGREE OWN ALL/VALS MORAL ORD/FREE SOVEREIGN...GEN/LAWS 18 NATURL/LAW WOLFF/C. PAGE 35 A0714 LAW CONCPT NAT/G INT/LAW

ORDER....SEE ORD/FREE

OREGON....OREGON

ORFIELD L.B. A2296

ORG/CHARTS....ORGANIZATIONAL CHARTS, BLUEPRINTS

ORGANIZATION FOR AFRICAN UNITY....SEE OAU

ORGANIZATION FOR ECONOMIC COOPERATION AND DEVELOPMENT.... SEE OECD

ORGANIZATION FOR EUROPEAN ECONOMIC COOPERATION....SEE OEEC

ORGANIZATION FOR LATIN AMERICAN SOLIDARITY....SEE OLAS

ORGANIZATION OF AFRICAN STATES.... SEE AFR/STATES

ORGANIZATION OF AMERICAN STATES....SEE OAS

ORGANIZATION, INTERNATIONAL....SEE INT/ORG

ORGANIZATION, LABOR....SEE LABOR

ORGANIZATION, POLITICAL....SEE POL/PAR

ORGANIZATION, PROFESSIONAL....SEE PROF/ORG

ORGANIZATION, VOLUNTARY....SEE VOL/ASSN

ORGANIZATIONAL BEHAVIOR, NONEXECUTIVE....SEE ADMIN

ORGANSKI A.F.K. A2297

ORTHO/GK....GREEK ORTHODOX CHURCH

ORTHO/RUSS....RUSSIAN ORTHODOX CATHOLIC

ORTHODOX EASTERN CHURCH....SEE ORTHO/GK

ORVIK N. A2298

ORWELL/G....GEORGE ORWELL

OSGOOD C.E. A2299,A2300

OSGOOD R.E. A2301

OSHOGBO....OSHOGBO, WEST AFRICA

OTTOMAN....OTTOMAN EMPIRE

B66

ZEINE Z.N.,THE EMERGENCE OF ARAB NATIONALISM (REV. ED.). TURKEY UK NAT/G SECT TEC/DEV LEAD REV WAR AGE/Y ROLE ORD/FREE...TRADIT CHARTS BIBLIOG 20 ARABS OTTOMAN. PAGE 170 A3451 ISLAM NAT/LISM DIPLOM

OUTER SPACE....SEE SPACE

OUTER/MONG....OUTER MONGOLIA

OVERSEAS DEVELOPMENT INSTITUTE....SEE OVRSEA/DEV

OVERSTREET B. A2302

OVERSTREET H. A2302

OVIMBUNDU....OVIMBUNDU PEOPLES OF ANGOLA

OVRSEA/DEV....OVERSEAS DEVELOPMENT INSTITUTE

B66

HAYER T.,FRENCH AID. AFR FRANCE AGRI FINAN BUDGET ADMIN WAR PRODUC...CHARTS 18/20 THIRD/WRLD OVRSEA/DEV. PAGE 63 A1295 TEC/DEV COLONIAL FOR/AID ECO/UNDEV

N66

BRITISH DEVELOPMENT POLICIES: 1966 (PAMPHLET). UK AGRI TARIFFS BAL/PAY...TREND CHARTS 20 OVRSEA/DEV. PAGE 4 A0076 WEALTH DIPLOM INT/TRADE FOR/AID

OWEN C.F. A2303

OWEN W. A2304

OWEN/RBT....ROBERT OWEN

OWI....OFFICE OF WAR INFORMATION

OWN....OWNERSHIP, OWNER

N

US SUPERINTENDENT OF DOCUMENTS,TARIFF AND TAXATION (PRICE LIST 37). USA+45 LAW INT/TRADE ADJUD ADMIN CT/SYS INCOME OWN...DECISION GATT. PAGE 157 A3204 BIBLIOG/A TAX TARIFFS NAT/G

B17

DE VICTORIA F.,DE INDIS ET DE JURE BELLI (1557) IN F. DE VICTORIA, DE INDIS ET DE JURE BELLI REFLECTIONES. UNIV NAT/G SECT CHIEF PARTIC COERCE PEACE MORAL...POLICY 16 INDIAN/AM CHRISTIAN CONSCN/OBJ. PAGE 35 A0715 WAR INT/LAW OWN

B20

VINOGRADOFF P.,OUTLINES OF HISTORICAL JURISPRUDENCE JURID

(2 VOLS.). GREECE MEDIT-7 LAW CONSTN FACE/GP FAM KIN MUNIC CRIME OWN...INT/LAW IDEA/COMP BIBLIOG. PAGE 159 A3241
METH

B31
BORCHARD E.H.,GUIDE TO THE LAW AND LEGAL LITERATURE OF FRANCE. FRANCE FINAN INDUS LABOR SECT LEGIS ADMIN COLONIAL CRIME OWN...INT/LAW 20. PAGE 17 A0337
BIBLIOG/A LAW CONSTN METH

B47
NIEBUHR R.,THE CHILDREN OF LIGHT AND THE CHILDREN OF DARKNESS: A VINDICATION OF DEMOCRACY AND CRITIQUE OF TRADITIONAL DEFENSE. UNIV STRUCT NAT/G SECT INGP/REL OWN PEACE ORD/FREE MARXISM ...IDEA/COMP GEN/LAWS 20 CHRISTIAN. PAGE 109 A2235
POPULISM DIPLOM NEIGH GP/REL

B59
HEWES T.,EQUALITY OF OPPORTUNITY - THE AMERICAN IDEAL AND KEY TO WORLD PEACE. USA+45 NAT/G OWN WEALTH ALL/IDEOS SOCISM...CONCPT 20. PAGE 64 A1323
POLICY PEACE ECO/TAC DIPLOM

B59
NUNEZ JIMENEZ A.,LA LIBERACION DE LAS ISLAS. CUBA L/A+17C USA+45 LAW CHIEF PLAN DIPLOM FOR/AID OWN WEALTH 20 CASTRO/F. PAGE 110 A2261
AGRI REV ECO/UNDEV NAT/G

B61
LARSON A.,WHEN NATIONS DISAGREE. USA+45 WOR+45 INT/ORG ADJUD COERCE CRIME OWN SOVEREIGN...POLICY JURID 20. PAGE 85 A1734
INT/LAW DIPLOM WAR

S61
OCHENG D.,"AN ECONOMIST LOOKS AT UGANDA'S FUTURE." FUT UGANDA AGRI INDUS PLAN PROB/SOLV INT/TRADE SOVEREIGN 20. PAGE 111 A2275
ECO/UNDEV INCOME ECO/TAC OWN

B62
US CONGRESS,COMMUNICATIONS SATELLITE LEGISLATION: HEARINGS BEFORE COMM ON AERON AND SPACE SCIENCES ON BILLS S2550 AND 2814. WOR+45 LAW VOL/ASSN PLAN DIPLOM CONTROL OWN PEACE...NEW/IDEA CONGRESS NASA. PAGE 150 A3062
SPACE COM/IND ADJUD GOV/REL

B64
DIAS R.W.M.,A BIBLIOGRAPHY OF JURISPRUDENCE (2ND ED.). VOL/ASSN LEGIS ADJUD CT/SYS OWN...INT/LAW 18/20. PAGE 37 A0754
BIBLIOG/A JURID LAW CONCPT

B64
HAMBRIDGE G.,DYNAMICS OF DEVELOPMENT. AGRI FINAN INDUS LABOR INT/TRADE EDU/PROP ADMIN LEAD OWN HEALTH...ANTHOL BIBLIOG 20. PAGE 61 A1245
ECO/UNDEV ECO/TAC OP/RES ACT/RES

B64
SZLADITS C.,BIBLIOGRAPHY ON FOREIGN AND COMPARATIVE LAW: BOOKS AND ARTICLES IN ENGLISH (SUPPLEMENT 1962). FINAN INDUS JUDGE LICENSE ADMIN CT/SYS PARL/PROC OWN...INT/LAW CLASSIF METH/COMP NAT/COMP 20. PAGE 141 A2877
BIBLIOG/A JURID ADJUD LAW

B64
US HOUSE COMM GOVT OPERATIONS,US OWNED FOREIGN CURRENCIES: HEARINGS (COMMITTEE ON GOVERNMENT OPERATIONS). INDIA ECO/DEV PLAN BUDGET TAX DEMAND EFFICIENCY 20 AID CONGRESS. PAGE 154 A3138
FINAN ECO/TAC FOR/AID OWN

B65
FALK R.A.,THE AFTERMATH OF SABBATINO: BACKGROUND PAPERS AND PROCEEDINGS OF SEVENTH HAMMARSKJOLD FORUM. USA+45 LAW ACT/RES ADJUD ROLE...BIBLIOG 20 EXPROPRIAT SABBATINO HARLAN/JM. PAGE 44 A0891
SOVEREIGN CT/SYS INT/LAW OWN

B65
LAFAVE W.R.,LAW AND SOVIET SOCIETY. EX/STRUC DIPLOM DOMIN EDU/PROP PRESS ADMIN CRIME OWN MARXISM 20 KHRUSH/N. PAGE 84 A1710
JURID CT/SYS ADJUD GOV/REL

B65
SILVA SOLAR J.,EL DESARROLLO DE LA NUEVA SOCIEDAD EN AMERICA. L/A+17C SOCIETY AGRI PROB/SOLV DIPLOM PARTIC GP/REL OWN...POLICY SOC 20 REFORMERS. PAGE 133 A2716
STRUCT ECO/UNDEV REGION CONTROL

B66
COPLIN W.D.,THE FUNCTIONS OF INTERNATIONAL LAW. WOR+45 ECO/DEV ECO/UNDEV ADJUD COLONIAL WAR OWN SOVEREIGN...POLICY GEN/LAWS 20. PAGE 30 A0611
INT/LAW DIPLOM INT/ORG

S67
RAMSEY J.A.,"THE STATUS OF INTERNATIONAL COPYRIGHTS." WOR+45 CREATE TEC/DEV DIPLOM CONFER CONTROL SANCTION OWN...POLICY JURID. PAGE 119 A2439
INT/LAW INT/ORG COM/IND PRESS

B96
DE VATTEL E.,THE LAW OF NATIONS. AGRI FINAN CHIEF DIPLOM INT/TRADE AGREE OWN ALL/VALS MORAL ORD/FREE SOVEREIGN...GEN/LAWS 18 NATURL/LAW WOLFF/C. PAGE 35 A0714
LAW CONCPT NAT/G INT/LAW

B96
SMITH A.,LECTURES ON JUSTICE, POLICE, REVENUE AND ARMS (1763). UK LAW FAM FORCES TARIFFS AGREE COERCE INCOME OWN WEALTH LAISSEZ...GEN/LAWS 17/18. PAGE 134 A2743
DIPLOM JURID OLD/LIB TAX

OXFORD/GRP....OXFORD GROUP

P

PACHTER H.M. A2307

PACIFIC/IS....PACIFIC ISLANDS: US TRUST TERRITORY OF THE PACIFIC ISLANDS - CAROLINE ISLANDS, MARSHALL ISLANDS, AND MARIANA ISLANDS

PACIFISM....SEE ALSO ARMS/CONT, PEACE

N
MONPIED E.,BIBLIOGRAPHIE FEDERALISTE: ARTICLES ET DOCUMENTS PUBLIES DANS LES PERIODIQUES PARUS EN FRANCE NOV. 1945-OCT. 1950. EUR+WWI WOR+45 ADMIN REGION ATTIT MARXISM PACIFISM 20 EEC. PAGE 103 A2108
BIBLIOG/A FEDERAL CENTRAL INT/ORG

N19
FREEMAN H.A.,COERCION OF STATES IN FEDERAL UNIONS (PAMPHLET). WOR-45 DIPLOM CONTROL COERCE PEACE ORD/FREE...GOV/COMP METH/COMP NAT/COMP PACIFIST 20. PAGE 49 A0994
FEDERAL WAR INT/ORG PACIFISM

B34
EINSTEIN A.,THE WORLD AS I SEE IT. WOR-45 INTELL R+D INT/ORG NAT/G SECT VOL/ASSN FORCES CREATE EDU/PROP LEGIT ARMS/CONT WAR WEAPON NAT/LISM ALL/VALS...POLICY CONCPT 20. PAGE 41 A0828
SOCIETY PHIL/SCI DIPLOM PACIFISM

B50
MONPIED E.,BIBLIOGRAPHIE FEDERALISTE: OUVRAGES CHOISIS (VOL. I, MIMEOGRAPHED PAPER). EUR+WWI DIPLOM ADMIN REGION ATTIT PACIFISM SOCISM...INT/LAW 19/20. PAGE 103 A2109
BIBLIOG/A FEDERAL CENTRAL INT/ORG

B55
VIGON J.,TEORIA DEL MILITARISMO. NAT/G DIPLOM COLONIAL COERCE GUERRILLA CIVMIL/REL NAT/LISM MORAL ALL/IDEOS PACIFISM 18/20. PAGE 159 A3234
FORCES PHIL/SCI WAR POLICY

B57
PETERSON H.C.,OPPONENTS OF WAR 1917-1918. USA-45 POL/PAR DOMIN ORD/FREE PWR PACIFISM SOCISM 20 IWW CONSCN/OBJ. PAGE 115 A2368
WAR PEACE ATTIT EDU/PROP

B60
NURTY K.S.,STUDIES IN PROBLEMS OF PEACE. CHRIST-17C MOD/EUR S/ASIA WOR+45 WOR-45 INT/ORG NAT/G SECT COERCE REV NAT/LISM ALL/VALS...CONCPT MYTH TIME/SEQ. PAGE 110 A2262
POLICY PEACE PACIFISM ORD/FREE

B63
WEINBERG A.,INSTEAD OF VIOLENCE: WRITINGS BY THE GREAT ADVOCATES OF PEACE AND NONVIOLENCE THROUGHOUT HISTORY. WOR+45 WOR-45 SOCIETY SECT PROB/SOLV DIPLOM GP/REL PERS/REL PEACE...ANTHOL PACIFIST. PAGE 162 A3304
PACIFISM WAR IDEA/COMP

B64
MARTIN J.J.,AMERICAN LIBERALISM AND WORLD POLITICS, 1931-41 (2 VOLS.). GERMANY USA-45 POL/PAR DISCRIM NAT/LISM PEACE RATIONAL ATTIT RIGID/FLEX MARXISM PACIFISM 20. PAGE 95 A1950
NEW/LIB DIPLOM NAT/G POLICY

B66
MAYER P.,THE PACIFIST CONSCIENCE. SECT CREATE ARMS/CONT WAR RACE/REL ATTIT LOVE...ANTHOL PACIFIST WORSHIP FREUD/S GANDHI/M LAO/TZU KING/MAR/L CONSCN/OBJ. PAGE 97 A1984
DIPLOM PACIFISM SUPEGO

PACIFIST....PACIFIST; SEE ALSO PEACE

B17
VEBLEN T.B.,AN INQUIRY INTO THE NATURE OF PEACE AND THE TERMS OF ITS PERPETUATION. UNIV STRATA FINAN EDU/PROP PRICE COST DISCRIM NAT/LISM MORAL ORD/FREE PACIFIST 20 WORLDUNITY. PAGE 158 A3224
PEACE DIPLOM WAR NAT/G

N19
FREEMAN H.A.,COERCION OF STATES IN FEDERAL UNIONS (PAMPHLET). WOR-45 DIPLOM CONTROL COERCE PEACE ORD/FREE...GOV/COMP METH/COMP NAT/COMP PACIFIST 20. PAGE 49 A0994
FEDERAL WAR INT/ORG PACIFISM

B29
STURZO L.,THE INTERNATIONAL COMMUNITY AND THE RIGHT OF WAR (TRANS. BY BARBARA BARCLAY CARTER). CULTURE CREATE PROB/SOLV DIPLOM ADJUD CONTROL PEACE PERSON ORD/FREE...INT/LAW IDEA/COMP PACIFIST 20 LEAGUE/NAT. PAGE 140 A2858
INT/ORG PLAN WAR CONCPT

B58
APPADORAI A.,THE USE OF FORCE IN INTERNATIONAL RELATIONS. WOR+45 CULTURE ECO/UNDEV CAP/ISM ARMS/CONT REV WAR ATTIT PERSON SOVEREIGN MARXISM ...INT/LAW PACIFIST 20 UN INTERVENT THIRD/WRLD COLD/WAR. PAGE 8 A0169
PEACE FEDERAL INT/ORG

B63
WEINBERG A.,INSTEAD OF VIOLENCE: WRITINGS BY THE GREAT ADVOCATES OF PEACE AND NONVIOLENCE THROUGHOUT HISTORY. WOR+45 WOR-45 SOCIETY SECT PROB/SOLV DIPLOM GP/REL PERS/REL PEACE...ANTHOL PACIFIST. PAGE 162 A3304
PACIFISM WAR IDEA/COMP

B66
MAYER P.,THE PACIFIST CONSCIENCE. SECT CREATE ARMS/CONT WAR RACE/REL ATTIT LOVE...ANTHOL PACIFIST WORSHIP FREUD/S GANDHI/M LAO/TZU KING/MAR/L CONSCN/OBJ. PAGE 97 A1984
DIPLOM PACIFISM SUPEGO

S67
JACKSON W.G.F.,"NUCLEAR PROLIFERATION AND THE GREAT POWERS." FUT UK WOR+45 INT/ORG DOMIN ARMS/CONT DETER ORD/FREE PACIFIST. PAGE 72 A1480
NUC/PWR ATTIT BAL/PWR NAT/LISM

PADELFORD N.J. A2308,A2309,A2310,A2311,A2312,A2313,A2314

PADOVER S.K. A2927

PAENSON I. A2315

PAGAN B. A2316

PAGINSKY P. A2317

PAIGE G.D. A2753

PAIN....SEE HEALTH

PAINE C.S. A1558

PAKISTAN....SEE ALSO S/ASIA

N19
MASON E.S.,THE DIPLOMACY OF ECONOMIC ASSISTANCE (PAMPHLET). INDIA PAKISTAN USA+45 ECO/UNDEV NAT/G BUDGET ATTIT...POLICY 20. PAGE 95 A1955
FOR/AID DIPLOM FINAN

B51
JENNINGS I.,THE COMMONWEALTH IN ASIA. CEYLON INDIA PAKISTAN CULTURE STRATA NAT/G LEGIS DIPLOM COLONIAL ATTIT...DECISION 20 CMN/WLTH. PAGE 74 A1507
CONSTN INT/ORG POLICY PLAN

B51
JENNINGS S.I.,THE COMMONWEALTH IN ASIA. CEYLON INDIA PAKISTAN S/ASIA UK CONSTN CULTURE SOCIETY STRATA STRUCT NAT/G POL/PAR EDU/PROP LEAD WAR 20 CMN/WLTH. PAGE 74 A1510
NAT/LISM REGION COLONIAL DIPLOM

B53
ELAHI K.N.,A GUIDE TO WORKS OF REFERENCE PUBLISHED IN PAKISTAN (PAMPHLET). PAKISTAN DIPLOM COLONIAL LEAD. PAGE 41 A0835
BIBLIOG S/ASIA NAT/G

B53
MANSERGH N.,DOCUMENTS AND SPEECHES ON BRITISH COMMONWEALTH AFFAIRS 1931-1952. INDIA IRELAND PAKISTAN UK CONSTN POL/PAR CHIEF FORCES COLONIAL ORD/FREE SOVEREIGN...JURID 20 COMMONWLTH. PAGE 94 A1929
BIBLIOG/A DIPLOM ECO/TAC

B56
WILSON P.,GOVERNMENT AND POLITICS OF INDIA AND PAKISTAN: 1885-1955; A BIBLIOGRAPHY OF WORKS IN WESTERN LANGUAGES. INDIA PAKISTAN CONSTN LOC/G POL/PAR FORCES DIPLOM ADMIN WAR CHOOSE...BIOG CON/ANAL 19/20. PAGE 165 A3361
BIBLIOG COLONIAL NAT/G S/ASIA

B57
WILSON P.,SOUTH ASIA; A SELECTED BIBLIOGRAPHY ON INDIA, PAKISTAN, CEYLON (PAMPHLET). CEYLON INDIA PAKISTAN LAW ECO/UNDEV PLAN DIPLOM 20. PAGE 165 A3362
BIBLIOG S/ASIA CULTURE NAT/G

B58
JENNINGS I.,PROBLEMS OF THE NEW COMMONWEALTH. CEYLON INDIA PAKISTAN S/ASIA ECO/UNDEV INT/ORG LOC/G DIPLOM ECO/TAC INT/TRADE COLONIAL RACE/REL DISCRIM 20 COMMONWLTH PARLIAMENT. PAGE 74 A1508
NAT/LISM NEUTRAL FOR/AID POL/PAR

B58
JENNINGS W.I.,PROBLEMS OF THE NEW COMMONWEALTH. CEYLON INDIA MALAYSIA PAKISTAN ECO/UNDEV VOL/ASSN RACE/REL NAT/LISM ROLE 20 CMN/WLTH. PAGE 74 A1511
GP/REL INGP/REL COLONIAL INT/ORG

B58
UNIV KARACHI INST PUB BUS ADM,PUBLICATIONS OF THE GOVERNMENT OF PAKISTAN 1947-1957. PAKISTAN S/ASIA DIPLOM COLONIAL ATTIT 20. PAGE 149 A3040
BIBLIOG NAT/G POLICY

N58
US HOUSE COMM FOREIGN AFFAIRS,HEARINGS ON REVIEW OF THE MUTUAL SECURITY PROGRAMS; EXAMINATION OF SELECTED PROJECTS IN FORMOSA AND PAKISTAN (PAMPHLET). ASIA PAKISTAN TAIWAN INDUS CONSULT DELIB/GP LEGIS BUDGET CONFER DEBATE 20. PAGE 153 A3125
FOR/AID ECO/UNDEV DIPLOM ECO/TAC

B61
HASAN H.S.,PAKISTAN AND THE UN. ISLAM WOR+45 ECO/DEV ECO/UNDEV NAT/G TOP/EX ECO/TAC FOR/AID EDU/PROP ADMIN DRIVE PERCEPT...OBS TIME/SEQ UN 20. PAGE 62 A1284
INT/ORG ATTIT PAKISTAN

B61
KHAN A.W.,INDIA WINS FREEDOM: THE OTHER SIDE. INDIA PAKISTAN CULTURE LEGIS DIPLOM PARL/PROC REV WAR NAT/LISM 20. PAGE 78 A1607
SOVEREIGN GP/REL RACE/REL ORD/FREE

B62
JORDAN A.A. JR.,FOREIGN AID AND THE DEFENSE OF SOUTHEAST ASIA. PAKISTAN VIETNAM/S FINAN PLAN BUDGET ECO/TAC DETER WAR ORD/FREE...POLICY DECISION CENSUS CHARTS BIBLIOG 20. PAGE 75 A1535
FOR/AID S/ASIA FORCES ECO/UNDEV

B62
MOON P.,DIVIDE AND QUIT. INDIA PAKISTAN STRATA DELIB/GP PLAN DIPLOM REPRESENT GP/REL INGP/REL CONSEN DISCRIM...OBS 20. PAGE 103 A2119
WAR REGION ISOLAT SECT

B62
PAKISTAN MINISTRY OF FINANCE,FOREIGN ECONOMIC AID: A REVIEW OF FOREIGN ECONOMIC AID TO PAKISTAN. EUR+WWI PAKISTAN UK USA+45 USSR ECO/UNDEV INT/ORG DELIB/GP DIPLOM ECO/TAC...CHARTS CMN/WLTH CHINJAP. PAGE 113 A2318
FOR/AID RECEIVE WEALTH FINAN

B63
BROWN W.N.,THE UNITED STATES AND INDIA AND PAKISTAN (REV. ED.). INDIA PAKISTAN S/ASIA WOR+45 POL/PAR SECT INT/TRADE COLONIAL COERCE DISCRIM. PAGE 20 A0408
DIPLOM ECO/UNDEV SOVEREIGN STRUCT

B63
KAHIN G.M.,MAJOR GOVERNMENTS OF ASIA (2ND ED.). ASIA INDIA INDONESIA PAKISTAN S/ASIA DIPLOM...SOC 20 CHINJAP. PAGE 75 A1546
GOV/COMP POL/PAR ELITES

B63
MANSERGH N.,DOCUMENTS AND SPEECHES ON COMMONWEALTH AFFAIRS 1952-1962. CANADA INDIA PAKISTAN UK CONSTN FORCES ECO/TAC EDU/PROP COLONIAL DETER WAR ORD/FREE SOVEREIGN...POLICY 20 AUSTRAL. PAGE 94 A1932
BIBLIOG/A FEDERAL INT/TRADE DIPLOM

B63
WILCOX W.A.,PAKISTAN; THE CONSOLIDATION OF A NATION. INDIA PAKISTAN CONSTN SECT PROB/SOLV COLONIAL PARTIC GP/REL FEDERAL...POLICY 19/20. PAGE 164 A3348
NAT/LISM ECO/UNDEV DIPLOM STRUCT

N63
PATEL H.M.,THE DEFENCE OF INDIA (PAMPHLET). CHINA/COM INDIA PAKISTAN WOR+45 TEC/DEV BAL/PWR DIPLOM CONTROL WAR. PAGE 114 A2340
FORCES POLICY SOVEREIGN DETER

B64
CASEY R.G.,THE FUTURE OF THE COMMONWEALTH. INDIA PAKISTAN UK ECO/UNDEV INT/ORG TEC/DEV COLONIAL SUPEGO 20 EEC AUSTRAL. PAGE 25 A0505
DIPLOM SOVEREIGN NAT/LISM FOR/AID

B64
DE SMITH S.A.,THE NEW COMMONWEALTH AND ITS CONSTITUTIONS. AFR CYPRUS PAKISTAN S/ASIA INT/ORG NAT/G LEGIS LEGIT RIGID/FLEX PWR...CONCPT TIME/SEQ CMN/WLTH 20. PAGE 35 A0713
EX/STRUC CONSTN SOVEREIGN

B64
MAHAR J.M.,INDIA: A CRITICAL BIBLIOGRAPHY. INDIA PAKISTAN CULTURE ECO/UNDEV LOC/G POL/PAR SECT PROB/SOLV DIPLOM ADMIN COLONIAL PARL/PROC ATTIT 20. PAGE 93 A1906
BIBLIOG/A S/ASIA NAT/G LEAD

L64
WORLD PEACE FOUNDATION,"INTERNATIONAL ORGANIZATIONS: SUMMARY OF ACTIVITIES." INDIA PAKISTAN TURKEY WOR+45 CONSTN CONSULT EX/STRUC ECO/TAC EDU/PROP LEGIT ORD/FREE...JURID SOC UN 20 CYPRESS. PAGE 167 A3397
INT/ORG ROUTINE

S64
"FURTHER READING." INDIA PAKISTAN SECT WAR PEACE ATTIT...POLICY 20. PAGE 3 A0067
BIBLIOG GP/REL DIPLOM NAT/G

S64
PRASAD B.,"SURVEY OF RECENT RESEARCH: STUDIES ON INDIA'S FOREIGN POLIC AND RELATIONS." ASIA INDIA PAKISTAN USA+45 NAT/G INT/TRADE GOV/REL 20 UN CMN/WLTH. PAGE 117 A2406
BIBLIOG DIPLOM ROLE POLICY

B65
NATIONAL BOOK CENTRE PAKISTAN,BOOKS ON PAKISTAN: A BIBLIOGRAPHY. PAKISTAN CULTURE DIPLOM ADMIN ATTIT ...MAJORIT SOC CONCPT 20. PAGE 107 A2201
BIBLIOG CONSTN S/ASIA NAT/G

B65
QURESHI I.H.,THE STRUGGLE FOR PAKISTAN. INDIA PAKISTAN UK CULTURE LEGIS DIPLOM EDU/PROP COLONIAL ATTIT SOVEREIGN 19/20 MUSLIM. PAGE 118 A2429
GP/REL RACE/REL WAR SECT

B66
GUPTA S.,KASHMIR - A STUDY IN INDIA-PAKISTAN RELATIONS. INDIA KASHMIR PAKISTAN CONSTN INT/ORG REV RACE/REL NAT/LISM 20 UN MUSLIM/LG. PAGE 58 A1194
DIPLOM GP/REL SOVEREIGN WAR

B66
SPICER K.,A SAMARITAN STATE? AFR CANADA INDIA PAKISTAN UK USA+45 FINAN INDUS PRODUC...CHARTS 20 NATO. PAGE 136 A2787
DIPLOM FOR/AID ECO/DEV ADMIN

B66
US DEPARTMENT OF THE ARMY,SOUTH ASIA: A STRATEGIC SURVEY (PAMPHLET NO. 550-3). AFGHANISTN INDIA NEPAL PAKISTAN ECO/UNDEV INT/ORG POL/PAR FORCES FOR/AID INT/TRADE LEAD WAR...POLICY SOC TREND 20. PAGE 152
BIBLIOG/A S/ASIA DIPLOM NAT/G

A3110

L66
BARMAN R.K.,"INDO-PAKISTANI RELATIONS 1947-1965: A SELECTED BIBLIOGRAPHY." INDIA PAKISTAN NAT/G 20. PAGE 11 A0223 BIBLIOG DIPLOM S/ASIA

S66
MANSERGH N.,"THE PARTITION OF INDIA IN RETROSPECT." INDIA PAKISTAN S/ASIA UK DIPLOM COLONIAL GP/REL PWR 20. PAGE 94 A1933 NAT/G PARL/PROC POLICY POL/PAR

B67
SAYEED K.B.,THE POLITICAL SYSTEM OF PAKISTAN. PAKISTAN DIPLOM REGION CHOOSE ORD/FREE...BIBLIOG 20. PAGE 127 A2609 NAT/G POL/PAR CONSTN SECT

S67
FELDMAN H.,"AID AS IMPERIALISM?" INDIA PAKISTAN UK USA+45 BAL/PWR CAP/ISM DIPLOM ECO/TAC DOMIN BAL/PAY WEALTH...POLICY 20. PAGE 45 A0914 COLONIAL FOR/AID S/ASIA ECO/UNDEV

PAKISTAN MINISTRY OF FINANCE A2318

PAKISTAN/E....EAST PAKISTAN

PALESTINE....PALESTINE (PRE-1948 ISRAEL); SEE ALSO ISRAEL

PALMER E.E. A2319,A2320

PALMER N.D. A2321,A2322,A2323

PALYI M. A2324

PAN S. A2325

PAN AFRICAN FREEDOM MOVEMENT....SEE PANAF/FREE

PAN AMERICAN UNION A2326,A2327

PANAF/FREE....PAN AFRICAN FREEDOM MOVEMENT

B64
COX R.,PAN-AFRICANISM IN PRACTICE. AFR DIPLOM CONFER RACE/REL ROLE SOVEREIGN...POLICY 20 PANAF/FREE. PAGE 32 A0645 ORD/FREE COLONIAL REGION NAT/LISM

PANAFR/ISM....PAN-AFRICANISM

PANAMA CANAL ZONE....SEE CANAL/ZONE

PANAMA....PANAMA

B40
BROWN A.D.,PANAMA CANAL AND PANAMA CANAL ZONE: A SELECTED LIST OF REFERENCES. PANAMA NAT/G SCHOOL DIPLOM HEALTH...GEOG SOC 20 CANAL/ZONE. PAGE 19 A0397 BIBLIOG/A ECO/UNDEV

B47
PERKINS D.,THE UNITED STATES AND THE CARIBBEAN. CUBA DOMIN/REP GUATEMALA HAITI PANAMA CULTURE ECO/UNDEV FOR/AID ADMIN COERCE HABITAT...POLICY 19/20. PAGE 115 A2359 DIPLOM L/A+17C USA-45

B60
DE HERRERA C.D.,LISTA BIBLIOGRAFICA DE LOS TRABAJOS DE GRADUACION Y TESIS PRESENTADOS EN LA UNIVERSIDAD, 1939-1960. PANAMA DIPLOM LEAD...SOC 20. PAGE 35 A0703 BIBLIOG L/A+17C NAT/G ACADEM

B64
DUBOIS J.,DANGER OVER PANAMA. FUT PANAMA SCHOOL PROB/SOLV EDU/PROP MARXISM...POLICY 19/20 TREATY INTERVENT CANAL/ZONE. PAGE 39 A0790 DIPLOM COERCE

S64
DELGADO J.,"EL MOMENTO POLITICO HISPANOAMERICA." CHINA/COM FUT PANAMA USA+45 USSR INT/ORG NAT/G POL/PAR FORCES DOMIN REGION COERCE ATTIT ALL/VALS ...TRADIT CONCPT COLD/WAR 20. PAGE 36 A0728 L/A+17C EDU/PROP NAT/LISM

S67
FABREGA J.,"ANTECEDENTES EXTRANJEROS EN LA CONSTITUCION PANAMENA." CUBA L/A+17C PANAMA URUGUAY EX/STRUC LEGIS DIPLOM ORD/FREE 19/20 COLOMB MEXIC/AMER. PAGE 43 A0882 CONSTN JURID NAT/G PARL/PROC

PANAMERICAN UNION A2328,A2329

PANHUYS H.F. A2330

PANIKKAR K.M. A2331,A2332

PAN-AFRICANISM....SEE PANAFR/ISM

PANJAB, PANJABI PEOPLE....SEE PUNJAB

PANJAB U EXTENSION LIBRARY A2333

PANT Y.P. A2334

PAPUA....PAPUA

PARAGUAY....SEE ALSO L/A+17C

B66
GARNER W.R.,THE CHACO DISPUTE; A STUDY OF PRESTIGE DIPLOMACY. L/A+17C PARAGUAY USA-45 INT/ORG AGREE PEACE...TIME/SEQ 20 BOLIV LEAGUE/NAT ARGEN CHACO/WAR. PAGE 51 A1050 WAR DIPLOM CONCPT PWR

PARETO/V....VILFREDO PARETO

PARIS....PARIS, FRANCE

PARISH H.C. A1958

PARITY....SEE ECO

PARK/R....ROBERT PARK

PARKER E.B. A3228

PARKER/H....HENRY PARKER

PARKFOREST....PARK FOREST, ILLINOIS

PARL/PROC....PARLIAMENTARY PROCESSES; SEE ALSO LEGIS

N
MCSPADDEN J.W.,THE AMERICAN STATESMAN'S YEARBOOK. WOR-45 LAW CONSTN AGRI FINAN DEBATE ADMIN PARL/PROC ...CHARTS BIBLIOG/A 20. PAGE 99 A2025 DIPLOM NAT/G PROVS LEGIS

B05
AMES J.G.,COMPREHENSIVE INDEX TO THE PUBLICATIONS OF THE UNITED STATES GOVERNMENT , 1881-1893. USA-45 CONSTN POL/PAR DELIB/GP TOP/EX DIPLOM PARL/PROC INGP/REL...INDEX 19 CONGRESS. PAGE 8 A0153 BIBLIOG/A LEGIS NAT/G GOV/REL

B26
LEWIN E.,RECENT PUBLICATIONS IN THE LIBRARY OF THE ROYAL COLONIAL INSTITUTE (PAMPHLET). CANADA UK EX/STRUC PARL/PROC NAT/LISM SOVEREIGN 20 CMN/WLTH PARLIAMENT. PAGE 88 A1799 BIBLIOG COLONIAL CONSTN DIPLOM

B27
GOOCH G.P.,ENGLISH DEMOCRATIC IDEAS IN THE SEVENTEENTH CENTURY (2ND ED.). UK LAW SECT FORCES DIPLOM LEAD PARL/PROC REV ATTIT AUTHORIT...ANARCH CONCPT 17 PARLIAMENT CMN/WLTH REFORMERS. PAGE 54 A1100 IDEA/COMP MAJORIT EX/STRUC CONSERVE

B35
KENNEDY W.P.,THE LAW AND CUSTOM OF THE SOUTH AFRICAN CONSTITUTION. AFR SOUTH/AFR KIN LOC/G PROVS DIPLOM ADJUD ADMIN EXEC 20. PAGE 78 A1594 CT/SYS CONSTN JURID PARL/PROC

B36
HUDSON M.O.,INTERNATIONAL LEGISLATION: 1929-1931. WOR-45 SEA AIR AGRI FINAN LABOR DIPLOM ECO/TAC REPAR CT/SYS ARMS/CONT WAR WEAPON...JURID 20 TREATY LEAGUE/NAT. PAGE 69 A1409 INT/LAW PARL/PROC ADJUD LAW

B39
THOMAS J.A.,THE HOUSE OF COMMONS, 1832-1901; A STUDY OF ITS ECONOMIC AND FUNCTIONAL CHARACTER. UK LAW STRATA FINAN DIPLOM CONTROL LEAD LOBBY REPRESENT WEALTH...POLICY STAT BIBLIOG 19/20 PARLIAMENT. PAGE 143 A2922 PARL/PROC LEGIS POL/PAR ECO/DEV

N45
INDIA QUARTERLY, A JOURNAL OF INTERNATIONAL AFFAIRS. INDIA LAW CONSTN ECO/UNDEV INT/ORG POL/PAR COLONIAL LEAD PARL/PROC WAR ATTIT...SOC 20 CMN/WLTH. PAGE 3 A0053 BIBLIOG/A S/ASIA DIPLOM NAT/G

B48
HOWARD J.E.,PARLIAMENT AND FOREIGN POLICY IN FRANCE. FRANCE CONSTN DELIB/GP BUDGET ADMIN PARL/PROC CHOOSE...BIBLIOG/A 20 PARLIAMENT. PAGE 68 A1399 LEGIS CONTROL DIPLOM ATTIT

B48
NEUBURGER O.,GUIDE TO OFFICIAL PUBLICATIONS OF THE OTHER AMERICAN REPUBLICS: VENEZUELA (VOL. XIX). VENEZUELA FINAN LEGIS PLAN BUDGET DIPLOM CT/SYS PARL/PROC 19/20. PAGE 108 A2219 BIBLIOG/A NAT/G CONSTN LAW

L49
HEINDEL R.H.,"THE NORTH ATLANTIC TREATY IN THE UNITED STATES SENATE." CONSTN POL/PAR CHIEF DEBATE LEAD ROUTINE WAR PEACE...CHARTS UN SENATE NATO. PAGE 64 A1309 DECISION PARL/PROC LEGIS INT/ORG

B53
STOUT H.M.,BRITISH GOVERNMENT. UK FINAN LOC/G POL/PAR DELIB/GP DIPLOM ADMIN COLONIAL CHOOSE ORD/FREE...JURID BIBLIOG 20 COMMONWLTH. PAGE 139 A2837 NAT/G PARL/PROC CONSTN NEW/LIB

C55
APTER D.E.,"THE GOLD COAST IN TRANSITION." AFR CONSTN LOC/G LEGIS DIPLOM COLONIAL CONTROL GOV/REL ...CHARTS BIBLIOG 20 CMN/WLTH. PAGE 8 A0170 ORD/FREE REPRESENT PARL/PROC NAT/G

C58
GOLAY J.F.,"THE FOUNDING OF THE FEDERAL REPUBLIC OF GERMANY." GERMANY/W CONSTN EX/STRUC DIPLOM ADMIN CHOOSE...DECISION BIBLIOG 20. PAGE 53 A1088
FEDERAL NAT/G PARL/PROC POL/PAR

C58
RAJAN M.S.,"UNITED NATIONS AND DOMESTIC JURISDICTION." WOR+45 WOR-45 PARL/PROC...IDEA/COMP BIBLIOG 20 UN. PAGE 119 A2434
INT/LAW DIPLOM CONSTN INT/ORG

C58
WILDING N.,"AN ENCYCLOPEDIA OF PARLIAMENT." UK LAW CONSTN CHIEF PROB/SOLV DIPLOM DEBATE WAR INGP/REL PRIVIL...BIBLIOG DICTIONARY 13/20 CMN/WLTH PARLIAMENT. PAGE 164 A3349
PARL/PROC POL/PAR NAT/G ADMIN

B59
BUNDESMIN FUR VERTRIEBENE,ZEITTAFEL DER VORGESCHICHTE UND DES ABLAUFS DER VERTREIBUNG SOWIE DER UNTERBRINGUNG UND EINGLIEDERUNG DER (2 VOLS.). GERMANY/E GERMANY/W NAT/G PROVS PROB/SOLV DIPLOM PARL/PROC ATTIT...BIBLIOG SOC/INTEG 20 MIGRATION PARLIAMENT. PAGE 21 A0431
JURID GP/REL INT/LAW

N59
BRITISH COMMONWEALTH REL CONF,EXTRACTS FROM THE PROCEEDINGS OF THE SIXTH UNOFFICIAL CONFERENCE (PAMPHLET). GHANA INDIA RHODESIA UK FINAN FORCES DETER FEDERAL...LING 20 PARLIAMENT. PAGE 19 A0379
DIPLOM PARL/PROC INT/TRADE ORD/FREE

B60
JEFFRIES C.,TRANSFER OF POWER: PROBLEMS OF THE PASSAGE TO SELFGOVERNMENT. CEYLON GHANA MALAYSIA NIGERIA UK INT/ORG CONSULT DELIB/GP LEGIS DIPLOM CONFER PARL/PROC 20. PAGE 73 A1502
SOVEREIGN COLONIAL ORD/FREE NAT/G

B61
BAINS J.S.,STUDIES IN POLITICAL SCIENCE. INDIA WOR+45 WOR-45 CONSTN BAL/PWR ADJUD ADMIN PARL/PROC SOVEREIGN...SOC METH/COMP ANTHOL 17/20 UN. PAGE 10 A0209
DIPLOM INT/LAW NAT/G

B61
KHAN A.W.,INDIA WINS FREEDOM: THE OTHER SIDE. INDIA PAKISTAN CULTURE LEGIS DIPLOM PARL/PROC REV WAR NAT/LISM 20. PAGE 78 A1607
SOVEREIGN GP/REL RACE/REL ORD/FREE

B61
WALLERSTEIN I.M.,AFRICA; THE POLITICS OF INDEPENDENCE. AFR SOCIETY STRUCT LEAD PARL/PROC PARTIC GP/REL...POLICY 20. PAGE 160 A3269
ECO/UNDEV DIPLOM COLONIAL ORD/FREE

B63
WELLESLEY COLLEGE,SYMPOSIUM ON LATIN AMERICA. FUT L/A+17C USA+45 INT/ORG ECO/TAC PARL/PROC REGION ANTHOL. PAGE 163 A3316
ECO/UNDEV CULTURE ORD/FREE DIPLOM

B64
BAILEY T.A.,A DIPLOMATIC HISTORY OF THE AMERICAN PEOPLE (7TH ED.). USA+45 USA-45 FOR/AID COLONIAL PARL/PROC WAR...CHARTS BIBLIOG/A T 18/20. PAGE 10 A0208
DIPLOM NAT/G

B64
GESELLSCHAFT RECHTSVERGLEICH,BIBLIOGRAPHIE DES DEUTSCHEN RECHTS (BIBLIOGRAPHY OF GERMAN LAW, TRANS. BY COURTLAND PETERSON). GERMANY FINAN INDUS LABOR SECT FORCES CT/SYS PARL/PROC CRIME...INT/LAW SOC NAT/COMP 20. PAGE 52 A1066
BIBLIOG/A JURID CONSTN ADMIN

B64
GJUPANOVIC H.,LEGAL SOURCES AND BIBLIOGRAPHY OF YUGOSLAVIA. COM YUGOSLAVIA LAW LEGIS DIPLOM ADMIN PARL/PROC REGION CRIME CENTRAL 20. PAGE 53 A1078
BIBLIOG/A JURID CONSTN ADJUD

B64
MAHAR J.M.,INDIA: A CRITICAL BIBLIOGRAPHY. INDIA PAKISTAN CULTURE ECO/UNDEV LOC/G POL/PAR SECT PROB/SOLV DIPLOM ADMIN COLONIAL PARL/PROC ATTIT 20. PAGE 93 A1906
BIBLIOG/A S/ASIA NAT/G LEAD

B64
NICOL D.,AFRICA - A SUBJECTIVE VIEW. AFR INT/ORG PLAN ADMIN COLONIAL PARL/PROC PARTIC REGION GOV/REL LITERACY ATTIT...BIBLIOG 20 CIVIL/SERV. PAGE 109 A2230
NAT/G LEAD CULTURE ACADEM

B64
QUIGG P.W.,AFRICA: A FOREIGN AFFAIRS READER. AFR FRANCE PORTUGAL UK DIPLOM LEAD PARL/PROC MARXISM ...MAJORIT METH/CNCPT GOV/COMP IDEA/COMP ANTHOL 19/20. PAGE 118 A2426
COLONIAL SOVEREIGN NAT/LISM RACE/REL

B64
SZLADITS C.,BIBLIOGRAPHY ON FOREIGN AND COMPARATIVE LAW: BOOKS AND ARTICLES IN ENGLISH (SUPPLEMENT 1962). FINAN INDUS JUDGE LICENSE ADMIN CT/SYS PARL/PROC OWN...INT/LAW CLASSIF METH/COMP NAT/COMP 20. PAGE 141 A2877
BIBLIOG/A JURID ADJUD LAW

B65
COWEN Z.,THE BRITISH COMMONWEALTH OF NATIONS IN A CHANGING WORLD. UK ECO/UNDEV INT/ORG ECO/TAC INT/TRADE COLONIAL WAR GP/REL RACE/REL SOVEREIGN SOC/INTEG 20 TREATY EEC COMMONWLTH. PAGE 32 A0644
JURID DIPLOM PARL/PROC NAT/LISM

B65
GEORGE M.,THE WARPED VISION. EUR+WWI UK NAT/G POL/PAR LEGIS PARL/PROC SANCTION COERCE WAR GOV/REL PEACE RESPECT 20 CONSRV/PAR. PAGE 52 A1061
LEAD ATTIT DIPLOM POLICY

B65
RUBINSTEIN A.Z.,THE CHALLENGE OF POLITICS: IDEAS AND ISSUES (2ND ED.). UNIV ELITES SOCIETY EX/STRUC BAL/PWR PARL/PROC AUTHORIT...DECISION ANTHOL 20. PAGE 125 A2565
NAT/G DIPLOM GP/REL ORD/FREE

B65
STOETZER O.C.,THE ORGANIZATION OF AMERICAN STATES. L/A+17C EX/STRUC FOR/AID CONFER PARL/PROC ORD/FREE SOVEREIGN...POLICY INT/LAW 20 OAS. PAGE 138 A2831
INT/ORG REGION DIPLOM BAL/PWR

B66
SPINELLI A.,THE EUROCRATS; CONFLICT AND CRISIS IN THE EUROPEAN COMMUNITY (TRANS. BY C. GROVE HAINES). EUR+WWI MARKET POL/PAR ECO/TAC PARL/PROC EEC OEEC ECSC EURATOM. PAGE 136 A2789
INT/ORG INGP/REL CONSTN ADMIN

B66
US HOUSE COMM FOREIGN AFFAIRS,UNITED STATES - SOUTH AFRICAN RELATIONS. SOUTH/AFR USA+45 NAT/G CONSULT DELIB/GP LEGIS CONFER SANCTION RACE/REL ATTIT 20 CONGRESS. PAGE 154 A3134
DISCRIM DIPLOM POLICY PARL/PROC

S66
MANSERGH N.,"THE PARTITION OF INDIA IN RETROSPECT." INDIA PAKISTAN S/ASIA UK DIPLOM COLONIAL GP/REL PWR 20. PAGE 94 A1933
NAT/G PARL/PROC POLICY POL/PAR

B67
O'LEARY M.K.,THE POLITICS OF AMERICAN FOREIGN AID. USA+45 POL/PAR CHIEF BUDGET EDU/PROP LOBBY CONGRESS. PAGE 111 A2270
FOR/AID DIPLOM PARL/PROC ATTIT

S67
FABREGA J.,"ANTECEDENTES EXTRANJEROS EN LA CONSTITUCION PANAMENA." CUBA L/A+17C PANAMA URUGUAY EX/STRUC LEGIS DIPLOM ORD/FREE 19/20 COLOMB MEXIC/AMER. PAGE 43 A0882
CONSTN JURID NAT/G PARL/PROC

S67
YEFROMEV A.,"THE TRUE FACE OF THE WEST GERMAN NATIONAL-DEMOCRATS." GERMANY/W NAT/G DOMIN LEAD SANCTION WAR ATTIT PERSON...MARXIST 20. PAGE 169 A3433
POL/PAR TOTALISM PARL/PROC DIPLOM

B90
HOSMAR J.K.,A SHORT HISTORY OF ANGLO-SAXON FREEDOM. UK USA-45 ROMAN/EMP NAT/G EX/STRUC LEGIS COLONIAL REV NAT/LISM POPULISM PARLIAMENT ANGLO/SAX MAGNA/CART. PAGE 68 A1394
CONSTN ORD/FREE DIPLOM PARL/PROC

B91
SIDGWICK H.,THE ELEMENTS OF POLITICS. LOC/G NAT/G LEGIS DIPLOM ADJUD CONTROL EXEC PARL/PROC REPRESENT GOV/REL SOVEREIGN ALL/IDEOS 19 MILL/JS BENTHAM/J. PAGE 132 A2713
POLICY LAW CONCPT

B96
LOWELL A.L.,GOVERNMENTS AND PARTIES IN CONTINENTAL EUROPE, VOL. II. AUSTRIA GERMANY HUNGARY MOD/EUR SWITZERLND SOCIETY EX/STRUC LEGIS DIPLOM AGREE LEAD PARL/PROC PWR...POLICY 19. PAGE 91 A1867
POL/PAR NAT/G GOV/REL ELITES

PARLIAMENTARY PROCESSES....SEE PARL/PROC

PARLIAMENT....PARLIAMENT (ALL NATIONS); SEE ALSO LEGIS

N
CANADIAN GOVERNMENT PUBLICATIONS (1955-). CANADA AGRI FINAN LABOR FORCES INT/TRADE HEALTH...JURID 20 PARLIAMENT. PAGE 1 A0007
BIBLIOG/A NAT/G DIPLOM INT/ORG

B00
HOLLAND T.E.,STUDIES IN INTERNATIONAL LAW. TURKEY USSR WOR-45 CONSTN NAT/G DIPLOM DOMIN LEGIT COERCE WAR PEACE ORD/FREE PWR SOVEREIGN...JURID CHARTS 20 PARLIAMENT SUEZ TREATY. PAGE 66 A1367
INT/ORG LAW INT/LAW

B02
SEELEY J.R.,THE EXPANSION OF ENGLAND. MOD/EUR S/ASIA UK CULTURE NAT/G FORCES PLAN DOMIN EDU/PROP COLONIAL ROUTINE ATTIT ALL/VALS SOVEREIGN...CONCPT HIST/WRIT PARLIAMENT 18 CMN/WLTH. PAGE 131 A2679
INT/ORG ACT/RES CAP/ISM INDIA

N19
HIGGINS R.,THE ADMINISTRATION OF UNITED KINGDOM FOREIGN POLICY THROUGH THE UNITED NATIONS (PAMPHLET). UK NAT/G ADMIN GOV/REL...CHARTS 20 UN PARLIAMENT. PAGE 65 A1329
DIPLOM POLICY INT/ORG

B26
LEWIN E.,RECENT PUBLICATIONS IN THE LIBRARY OF THE ROYAL COLONIAL INSTITUTE (PAMPHLET). CANADA UK EX/STRUC PARL/PROC NAT/LISM SOVEREIGN 20 CMN/WLTH PARLIAMENT. PAGE 88 A1799
BIBLIOG COLONIAL CONSTN DIPLOM

B27
GOOCH G.P.,ENGLISH DEMOCRATIC IDEAS IN THE SEVENTEENTH CENTURY (2ND ED.). UK LAW SECT FORCES DIPLOM LEAD PARL/PROC REV ATTIT AUTHORIT...ANARCH CONCPT 17 PARLIAMENT CMN/WLTH REFORMERS. PAGE 54 A1100
IDEA/COMP MAJORIT EX/STRUC CONSERVE

B28
HALL W.P.,EMPIRE TO COMMONWEALTH. FUT WOR-45 CONSTN VOL/ASSN

ECO/DEV ECO/UNDEV INT/ORG PROVS PLAN DIPLOM EDU/PROP ADMIN COLONIAL PEACE PERSON ALL/VALS ...POLICY GEOG SOC OBS RECORD TREND CMN/WLTH PARLIAMENT 19/20. PAGE 60 A1229 — NAT/G UK

C28
SCHNEIDER H.W.,"MAKING THE FASCIST STATE." ITALY CULTURE LABOR DIPLOM REV WAR NAT/LISM TOTALISM ATTIT DRIVE SOCISM...BIBLIOG PARLIAMENT 20. PAGE 129 A2638 — FASCISM POLICY POL/PAR

B39
THOMAS J.A.,THE HOUSE OF COMMONS, 1832-1901; A STUDY OF ITS ECONOMIC AND FUNCTIONAL CHARACTER. UK LAW STRATA FINAN DIPLOM CONTROL LEAD LOBBY REPRESENT WEALTH...POLICY STAT BIBLIOG 19/20 PARLIAMENT. PAGE 143 A2922 — PARL/PROC LEGIS POL/PAR ECO/DEV

B43
MC DOWELL R.B.,IRISH PUBLIC OPINION, 1750-1800. IRELAND CONSTN VOL/ASSN WORKER ORD/FREE CATHISM CONSERVE...POLICY IDEA/COMP BIBLIOG 18/ PARLIAMENT. PAGE 97 A1992 — ATTIT NAT/G DIPLOM REV

L44
HAILEY,"THE FUTURE OF COLONIAL PEOPLES." WOR-45 CONSTN CULTURE ECO/UNDEV AGRI MARKET INT/ORG NAT/G SECT CONSULT ECO/TAC LEGIT ADMIN NAT/LISM ALL/VALS ...SOC OBS TREND STERTYP CMN/WLTH LEAGUE/NAT PARLIAMENT 20. PAGE 59 A1218 — PLAN CONCPT DIPLOM UK

B48
CHURCHILL W.,THE GATHERING STORM. UK WOR-45 INT/ORG NAT/G FORCES TOP/EX DIPLOM ECO/TAC COERCE ATTIT ORD/FREE PWR WEALTH...POLICY SELF/OBS RECORD NAZI PARLIAMENT 20. PAGE 26 A0538 — BIOG

B48
HOWARD J.E.,PARLIAMENT AND FOREIGN POLICY IN FRANCE. FRANCE CONSTN DELIB/GP BUDGET ADMIN PARL/PROC CHOOSE...BIBLIOG/A 20 PARLIAMENT. PAGE 68 A1399 — LEGIS CONTROL DIPLOM ATTIT

B50
DUCLOS P.,L'EVOLUTION DES RAPPORTS POLITIQUES DEPUIS 1750 (LIBERTE, INTEGRATION, UNITE). LAW INT/ORG FEDERAL TOTALISM ATTIT PWR...MAJORIT BIBLIOG 18/20 PARLIAMENT EUROPE. PAGE 39 A0792 — ORD/FREE DIPLOM NAT/G GOV/COMP

B56
FOSTER J.G.,BRITAIN IN WESTERN EUROPE: WEU AND THE ATLANTIC ALLIANCE. EUR+WWI FRANCE GERMANY GERMANY/W ITALY UK STRATA NAT/G DELIB/GP ECO/TAC ORD/FREE PWR ...TRADIT TIME/SEQ TREND OEEC PARLIAMENT 20 EUROPE/W. PAGE 47 A0969 — INT/ORG FORCES WEAPON

B58
JENNINGS I.,PROBLEMS OF THE NEW COMMONWEALTH. CEYLON INDIA PAKISTAN S/ASIA ECO/UNDEV INT/ORG LOC/G DIPLOM ECO/TAC INT/TRADE COLONIAL RACE/REL DISCRIM 20 COMMONWLTH PARLIAMENT. PAGE 74 A1508 — NAT/LISM NEUTRAL FOR/AID POL/PAR

C58
WILDING N.,"AN ENCYCLOPEDIA OF PARLIAMENT." UK LAW CONSTN CHIEF PROB/SOLV DIPLOM DEBATE WAR INGP/REL PRIVIL...BIBLIOG DICTIONARY 13/20 CMN/WLTH PARLIAMENT. PAGE 164 A3349 — PARL/PROC POL/PAR NAT/G ADMIN

B59
BUNDESMIN FUR VERTRIEBENE,ZEITTAFEL DER VORGESCHICHTE UND DES ABLAUFS DER VERTREIBUNG SOWIE DER UNTERBRINGUNG UND EINGLIEDERUNG DER (2 VOLS.). GERMANY/E GERMANY/W NAT/G PROVS PROB/SOLV DIPLOM PARL/PROC ATTIT...BIBLIOG SOC/INTEG 20 MIGRATION PARLIAMENT. PAGE 21 A0431 — JURID GP/REL INT/LAW

N59
BRITISH COMMONWEALTH REL CONF,EXTRACTS FROM THE PROCEEDINGS OF THE SIXTH UNOFFICIAL CONFERENCE (PAMPHLET). GHANA INDIA RHODESIA UK FINAN FORCES DETER FEDERAL...LING 20 PARLIAMENT. PAGE 19 A0379 — DIPLOM PARL/PROC INT/TRADE ORD/FREE

S62
THOMPSON D.,"THE UNITED KINGDOM AND THE TREATY OF ROME." EUR+WWI INT/ORG NAT/G DELIB/GP LEGIS INT/TRADE RIGID/FLEX...CONCPT EEC PARLIAMENT CMN/WLTH 20. PAGE 143 A2925 — ADJUD JURID

B63
GILBERT M.,THE APPEASERS. COM GERMANY UK PLAN ECO/TAC COLONIAL CONTROL EXEC ORD/FREE PWR FASCISM 20 PARLIAMENT. PAGE 52 A1068 — DIPLOM WAR POLICY DECISION

B65
O'CONNELL M.R.,IRISH POLITICS AND SOCIAL CONFLICT IN THE AGE OF THE AMERICAN REVOLUTION. FRANCE IRELAND MOD/EUR STRATA SECT LEGIS DIPLOM INT/TRADE DOMIN REV WAR...BIBLIOG 18 PARLIAMENT. PAGE 111 A2268 — CATHISM ATTIT NAT/G DELIB/GP

B66
FRANK E.,LAWMAKERS IN A CHANGING WORLD. FRANCE UK USSR WOR+45 PARTIC EFFICIENCY ROLE ALL/IDEOS ...CHARTS ANTHOL PARLIAMENT 20 UN COLD/WAR. PAGE 48 A0979 — GOV/COMP LEGIS NAT/G DIPLOM

S67
MUDGE G.A.,"DOMESTIC POLICIES AND UN ACTIVITIES* THE CASE OF RHODESIA AND THE REPUBLIC OF SOUTH AFRICA." RHODESIA SOUTH/AFR POL/PAR LEAD SANCTION CHOOSE RACE/REL CONSEN DISCRIM ATTIT...INT/LAW UN PARLIAMENT 20. PAGE 105 A2163 — AFR NAT/G POLICY

S67
SENCOURT R.,"FOREIGN POLICY* AN HISTORIC RECTIFICATION." EUR+WWI UK DIPLOM EDU/PROP LEAD WAR CHOOSE PERS/REL...METH/COMP PARLIAMENT. PAGE 131 A2685 — POLICY POL/PAR NAT/G

B90
HOSMAR J.K.,A SHORT HISTORY OF ANGLO-SAXON FREEDOM. UK USA-45 ROMAN/EMP NAT/G EX/STRUC LEGIS COLONIAL REV NAT/LISM POPULISM PARLIAMENT ANGLO/SAX MAGNA/CART. PAGE 68 A1394 — CONSTN ORD/FREE DIPLOM PARL/PROC

PARMELEE M. A2335

PARNELL/CS....CHARLES STEWART PARNELL

PAROLE....SEE PUB/INST, ROUTINE, CRIME

PARRINGTON V.L. A2336

PARSONS/T....TALCOTT PARSONS

B51
STANTON A.H.,PERSONALITY AND POLITICAL CRISIS. WOR+45 WOR-45 STRUCT DIPLOM INGP/REL TOTALISM MORAL ...ANTHOL 20 LASSWELL/H PARSONS/T RIESMAN/D. PAGE 137 A2806 — EDU/PROP WAR PERSON PSY

PARTH/SASS....PARTHO-SASSANIAN EMPIRE

B63
JAIRAZBHOY R.A.,FOREIGN INFLUENCE IN ANCIENT INDIA. INDIA ELITES SECT DIPLOM EDU/PROP COLONIAL REGION GP/REL...ART/METH LING WORSHIP +/14 GRECO/ROMN MESOPOTAM PERSIA PARTH/SASS. PAGE 73 A1491 — CULTURE SOCIETY COERCE DOMIN

PARTIC....PARTICIPATION; CIVIC ACTIVITY AND NONACTIVITY

N
INTERNATIONAL STUDIES,"INDIA AND WORLD AFFAIRS: AN ANNUAL BIBLIOGRAPHY" INDIA INT/TRADE PARTIC GOV/REL 20. PAGE 71 A1461 — BIBLIOG POLICY DIPLOM ATTIT

B17
DE VICTORIA F.,DE INDIS ET DE JURE BELLI (1557) IN F. DE VICTORIA, DE INDIS ET DE JURE BELLI REFLECTIONES. UNIV NAT/G SECT CHIEF PARTIC COERCE PEACE MORAL...POLICY 16 INDIAN/AM CHRISTIAN CONSCN/OBJ. PAGE 35 A0715 — WAR INT/LAW OWN

N19
HANNA A.J.,EUROPEAN RULE IN AFRICA (PAMPHLET). BELGIUM FRANCE MOD/EUR UK WOR+45 WOR-45 ECO/UNDEV NAT/G PARTIC SOVEREIGN...NAT/COMP 19/20. PAGE 61 A1252 — DIPLOM COLONIAL AFR NAT/LISM

B40
NIEBUHR R.,CHRISTIANITY AND POWER POLITICS. WOR-45 SECT DIPLOM GP/REL SUPEGO ALL/IDEOS WORSHIP 20 CHRISTIAN. PAGE 109 A2234 — PARTIC PEACE MORAL

B45
HORN O.B.,BRITISH PUBLIC OPINION AND THE FIRST PARTITION OF POLAND. POLAND UK LEGIS PRESS RUMOR CONTROL PARTIC NAT/LISM SOVEREIGN 18/19. PAGE 67 A1385 — DIPLOM POLICY ATTIT NAT/G

B55
STILLMAN C.W.,AFRICA IN THE MODERN WORLD. AFR USA+45 WOR+45 INT/TRADE COLONIAL PARTIC REGION GOV/REL RACE/REL 20. PAGE 138 A2826 — ECO/UNDEV DIPLOM POLICY STRUCT

B57
DUDDEN A.P.,WOODROW WILSON AND THE WORLD OF TODAY. USA-45 NAT/G PROVS CONTROL PARTIC WAR ISOLAT PWR SKILL...PERS/COMP ANTHOL 19/20 WILSON/W UN LEAGUE/NAT WWI. PAGE 39 A0794 — CHIEF DIPLOM POL/PAR LEAD

B57
JASZI O.,AGAINST THE TYRANT. WOR+45 WOR-45 CONSTN DIPLOM CONTROL PARTIC REV WAR...CONCPT. PAGE 73 A1498 — TOTALISM ORD/FREE CHIEF MURDER

B58
ALMEYDA M.C.,REFLEXIONES POLITICAS. CHILE L/A+17C USA+45 INT/ORG POL/PAR ECO/TAC PARTIC ATTIT 20. PAGE 6 A0128 — ECO/UNDEV REGION DIPLOM INT/TRADE

B59
KNIERIEM A.,THE NUREMBERG TRIALS. EUR+WWI GERMANY VOL/ASSN LEAD COERCE WAR INGP/REL TOTALISM SUPEGO ORD/FREE...CONCPT METH/COMP. PAGE 80 A1651 — INT/LAW CRIME PARTIC JURID

B59
PAGAN B.,HISTORIA DE LOS PARTIDOS POLITICOS PUERTORRIQUENOS 1898-1956. PUERT/RICO PROVS DIPLOM DOMIN EDU/PROP PARTIC 20. PAGE 113 A2316 — POL/PAR CHOOSE COLONIAL PWR

B59
TARDIFF G.,LA LIBERTAD; LA LIBERTAD DE EXPRESION, IDEALES Y REALIDADES AMERICANAS. ISLAM INT/ORG PROB/SOLV PRESS CONFER PARTIC CATHISM...INT/LAW — ORD/FREE ATTIT DIPLOM

SOC/INTEG UN MID/EAST. PAGE 141 A2889 — CONCPT

B61
BRENNAN D.G.,ARMS CONTROL, DISARMAMENT, AND NATIONAL SECURITY. WOR+45 NAT/G FORCES CREATE PROB/SOLV PARTIC WAR PEACE...DECISION INT/LAW ANTHOL BIBLIOG 20. PAGE 18 A0372 — ARMS/CONT ORD/FREE DIPLOM POLICY

B61
EISENHOWER D.D.,PEACE WITH JUSTICE: SELECTED ADDRESSES. USSR PARTIC ARMS/CONT MORAL...TRADIT CONCPT GEN/LAWS ANTHOL 20 PRESIDENT COLD/WAR. PAGE 41 A0832 — PEACE DIPLOM EDU/PROP POLICY

B61
WALLERSTEIN I.M.,AFRICA; THE POLITICS OF INDEPENDENCE. AFR SOCIETY STRUCT LEAD PARL/PROC PARTIC GP/REL...POLICY 20. PAGE 160 A3269 — ECO/UNDEV DIPLOM COLONIAL ORD/FREE

B62
BUCHMANN J.,L'AFRIQUE NOIRE INDEPENDANTE. POL/PAR DIPLOM COLONIAL PARTIC CHOOSE GP/REL ATTIT ORD/FREE WEALTH NEGRO. PAGE 21 A0426 — AFR NAT/LISM DECISION

B62
LERNER M.,THE AGE OF OVERKILL: A PREFACE TO WORLD POLITICS. USA+45 USSR WOR+45 SOCIETY ECO/UNDEV BAL/PWR NEUTRAL PARTIC REV ALL/IDEOS MARXISM ...BIBLIOG/A 20. PAGE 87 A1787 — DIPLOM NUC/PWR PWR DEATH

B62
LEVY H.V.,LIBERDADE E JUSTICA SOCIAL (2ND ED.). BRAZIL COM L/A+17C USSR INT/ORG PARTIC GP/REL WEALTH 20 UN COM/PARTY. PAGE 88 A1798 — ORD/FREE MARXISM CAP/ISM LAW

B62
ROSAMOND R.,CRUSADE FOR PEACE: EISENHOWER'S PRESIDENTIAL LEGACY WITH THE PROGRAM FOR ACTION. USA+45 PARTIC ARMS/CONT MORAL MARXISM...TRADIT CONCPT CHARTS GEN/LAWS ANTHOL 20 PRESIDENT EISNHWR/DD. PAGE 123 A2526 — PEACE DIPLOM EDU/PROP POLICY

B63
MALIK C.,MAN IN THE STRUGGLE FOR PEACE. USSR WOR+45 CHIEF PLAN PROB/SOLV PARTIC NUC/PWR REV ORD/FREE ...IDEA/COMP METH/COMP 20 UN COLD/WAR. PAGE 93 A1912 — PEACE MARXISM DIPLOM EDU/PROP

B63
WILCOX W.A.,PAKISTAN; THE CONSOLIDATION OF A NATION. INDIA PAKISTAN CONSTN SECT PROB/SOLV COLONIAL PARTIC GP/REL FEDERAL...POLICY 19/20. PAGE 164 A3348 — NAT/LISM ECO/UNDEV DIPLOM STRUCT

B64
ALVIM J.C.,A REVOLUCAO SEM RUMO. BRAZIL NAT/G BAL/PWR DIPLOM INT/TRADE PARTIC WEALTH...POLICY SOC SOC/INTEG 20. PAGE 6 A0132 — REV CIVMIL/REL ECO/UNDEV ORD/FREE

B64
CALVO SERER R.,LAS NUEVAS DEMOCRACIAS. AFR ASIA ISLAM USA+45 WOR+45 BAL/PWR DOMIN PARTIC INGP/REL AUTHORIT POPULISM...CONCPT 20 COM/PARTY. PAGE 23 A0469 — ORD/FREE MARXISM DIPLOM POLICY

B64
HOROWITZ I.L.,REVOLUTION IN BRAZIL. BRAZIL L/A+17C ELITES STRATA NAT/G BAL/PWR PARTIC ATTIT 20. PAGE 68 A1388 — ECO/UNDEV DIPLOM POLICY ORD/FREE

B64
NICOL D.,AFRICA - A SUBJECTIVE VIEW. AFR INT/ORG PLAN ADMIN COLONIAL PARL/PROC PARTIC REGION GOV/REL LITERACY ATTIT...BIBLIOG 20 CIVIL/SERV. PAGE 109 A2230 — NAT/G LEAD CULTURE ACADEM

B65
BRACKETT R.D.,PATHWAYS TO PEACE. SECT VOL/ASSN GP/REL PERS/REL DISCRIM...LING 20 UN PEACE/CORP. PAGE 18 A0366 — PEACE INT/ORG EDU/PROP PARTIC

B65
LINDBLOM C.E.,THE INTELLIGENCE OF DEMOCRACY; DECISION MAKING THROUGH MUTUAL ADJUSTMENT. WOR+45 SOCIETY NAT/G PROB/SOLV DOMIN PARTIC GP/REL ORD/FREE...POLICY IDEA/COMP BIBLIOG 20. PAGE 89 A1821 — PLURISM DECISION ADJUST DIPLOM

B65
SILVA SOLAR J.,EL DESARROLLO DE LA NUEVA SOCIEDAD EN AMERICA. L/A+17C SOCIETY AGRI PROB/SOLV DIPLOM PARTIC GP/REL OWN...POLICY SOC 20 REFORMERS. PAGE 133 A2716 — STRUCT ECO/UNDEV REGION CONTROL

B65
WEIL G.L.,A HANDBOOK ON THE EUROPEAN ECONOMIC COMMUNITY. BELGIUM EUR+WWI FRANCE GERMANY/W ITALY CONSTN ECO/DEV CREATE PARTIC GP/REL...DECISION MGT CHARTS 20 EEC. PAGE 162 A3299 — INT/TRADE INT/ORG TEC/DEV INT/LAW

S65
GANGAL S.C.,"SURVEY OF RECENT RESEARCH: INDIA AND THE COMMONWEALTH" INDIA UK NAT/G INT/TRADE PARTIC GOV/REL ROLE 20 CMN/WLTH. PAGE 51 A1039 — BIBLIOG POLICY REGION DIPLOM

B66
FEHRENBACH T.R.,THIS KIND OF PEACE. WOR+45 LEAD PARTIC WAR EFFICIENCY ATTIT UN. PAGE 44 A0906 — PEACE DIPLOM INT/ORG BAL/PWR

B66
FRANK E.,LAWMAKERS IN A CHANGING WORLD. FRANCE UK USSR WOR+45 PARTIC EFFICIENCY ROLE ALL/IDEOS ...CHARTS ANTHOL PARLIAMENT 20 UN COLD/WAR. PAGE 48 A0979 — GOV/COMP LEGIS NAT/G DIPLOM

B66
GRENVILLE J.A.S.,POLITICS, STRATEGY, AND AMERICAN DEMOCRACY: STUDIES IN FOREIGN POLICY, 1873-1917. CUBA PHILIPPINE SPAIN USA-45 VENEZUELA ELITES NAT/G CREATE PARTIC WAR RIGID/FLEX ORD/FREE...DECISION TREND 19/20 HAWAII. PAGE 56 A1146 — DIPLOM COLONIAL POLICY

B66
HOROWITZ D.,HEMISPHERES NORTH AND SOUTH: ECONOMIC DISPARITY AMONG NATIONS. WOR+45 ECO/DEV ECO/UNDEV INT/ORG PLAN DIPLOM INT/TRADE GIVE PARTIC GP/REL ...WELF/ST 20. PAGE 67 A1387 — ECO/TAC FOR/AID STRATA WEALTH

L66
MCDOUGAL M.S.,"CHINESE PARTICIPATION IN THE UNITED NATIONS: THE LEGAL IMPERATIVES OF A NEGOTIATED SOLUTION" CHINA/COM WOR+45 VOL/ASSN DIPLOM PARTIC ...DECISION IDEA/COMP 20 UN. PAGE 98 A2010 — INT/ORG REPRESENT POLICY PROB/SOLV

B67
PIKE F.B.,FREEDOM AND REFORM IN LATIN AMERICA. BRAZIL URUGUAY CONSTN CULTURE SECT DIPLOM EDU/PROP PARTIC DRIVE ALL/VALS CATHISM...GEOG ANTHOL BIBLIOG REFORMERS BOLIV. PAGE 116 A2379 — L/A+17C ORD/FREE ECO/UNDEV REV

B67
ROSENAU J.N.,DOMESTIC SOURCES OF FOREIGN POLICY. WOR+45 STRATA COM/IND MUNIC POL/PAR LOBBY PARTIC REGION ATTIT...PSY SOC COLD/WAR. PAGE 124 A2534 — DIPLOM POLICY NAT/G CHOOSE

B67
SINGER D.,QUANTITATIVE INTERNATIONAL POLITICS* INSIGHTS AND EVIDENCE. WOR+45 WOR-45 PARTIC WAR INGP/REL ATTIT PERSON ROLE...PREDICT BIBLIOG 19/20 UN SENATE. PAGE 133 A2722 — DIPLOM NAT/G INT/ORG DECISION

S67
BENTLEY E.,"VIETNAM: THE STATE OF OUR FEELINGS." USA+45 VIETNAM PROB/SOLV DIPLOM GP/REL INGP/REL RACE/REL WEALTH. PAGE 13 A0271 — WAR PARTIC ATTIT PEACE

S67
BREGMAN A.,"WHITHER RUSSIA?" COM RUSSIA INTELL POL/PAR DIPLOM PARTIC NAT/LISM TOTALISM ATTIT ORD/FREE 20. PAGE 18 A0370 — MARXISM ELITES ADMIN CREATE

S67
KRAUS J.,"A MARXIST IN GHANA." GHANA ELITES CHIEF PROB/SOLV TEC/DEV DIPLOM ECO/TAC COLONIAL PARTIC PWR 20 NKRUMAH/K. PAGE 82 A1676 — MARXISM PLAN ATTIT CREATE

S67
RABIER J.-R.,"THE EUROPEAN IDEA AND NATIONAL PUBLIC OPINIONS." ACT/RES PLAN DIPLOM PARTIC CONSEN ATTIT PERCEPT...DECISION CHARTS. PAGE 118 A2430 — POLICY FEDERAL EUR+WWI PROB/SOLV

B91
DOLE C.F.,THE AMERICAN CITIZEN. USA-45 LAW PARTIC ATTIT...INT/LAW 19. PAGE 38 A0769 — NAT/G MORAL NAT/LISM MAJORITY

PARTIES, POLITICAL....SEE POL/PAR

PARTITION....PARTITIONS AND PARTITIONING - DIVISION OF AN EXISTING POLITICAL-GEOGRAPHICAL ENTITY INTO TWO OR MORE AUTONOMOUS ZONES

PASSIN H. A2337

PASSPORT....SEE LICENSE, TRAVEL

PASTUHOV V.D. A2338

PATAI R. A2339

PATEL H.M. A2340

PATENT....PATENT

PATENT/OFF....U.S. PATENT OFFICE

PATHAN....PATHAN PEOPLE (PAKISTAN, AFGHANISTAN)

PATHET/LAO....PATHET LAO

PATRA A.C. A2341

PATRIOTISM....SEE NAT/LISM

PAUKER G.J. A2342

PAULING/L....LINUS PAULING

PAULLIN O. A0994

PAY....EARNINGS; SEE ALSO INCOME

B60
KENEN P.B.,BRITISH MONETARY POLICY AND THE BALANCE OF PAYMENTS 1951-57. UK PLAN BUDGET ECO/TAC INT/TRADE PAY PRICE COST ATTIT 20. PAGE 77 A1585 BAL/PAY PROB/SOLV FINAN NAT/G

B63
GUIMARAES A.P.,INFLACAO E MONOPOLIO NO BRASIL. BRAZIL FINAN NAT/G PLAN PAY...METH/COMP 20. PAGE 58 A1189 ECO/UNDEV PRICE INT/TRADE BAL/PAY

B65
WHITE G.M.,THE USE OF EXPERTS BY INTERNATIONAL TRIBUNALS. WOR+45 WOR-45 INT/ORG NAT/G PAY ADJUD COST...OBS BIBLIOG 20. PAGE 164 A3334 INT/LAW ROUTINE CONSULT CT/SYS

PEACE OF WESTPHALIA....SEE WESTPHALIA

PEACE....SEE ALSO ORD/FREE

PEACE CORPS....SEE PEACE/CORP

PEACE/CORP....PEACE CORPS

B64
ADAMS V.,THE PEACE CORPS IN ACTION. USA+45 VOL/ASSN EX/STRUC GOV/REL PERCEPT ORD/FREE...OBS 20 KENNEDY/JF PEACE/CORP. PAGE 4 A0087 DIPLOM FOR/AID PERSON DRIVE

B64
RUBIN J.A.,YOUR HUNDRED BILLION DOLLARS. USA+45 USSR INDUS INT/ORG TEC/DEV ECO/TAC...METH/COMP 20 PEACE/CORP. PAGE 125 A2559 FOR/AID DIPLOM ECO/UNDEV

B65
BRACKETT R.D.,PATHWAYS TO PEACE. SECT VOL/ASSN GP/REL PERS/REL DISCRIM...LING 20 UN PEACE/CORP. PAGE 18 A0366 PEACE INT/ORG EDU/PROP PARTIC

B66
LENT H.B.,THE PEACE CORPS: AMBASSADORS OF GOOD WILL. USA+45 ECO/UNDEV...INT TESTS BIOG AUD/VIS SOC/INTEG 20 PEACE/CORP. PAGE 87 A1776 VOL/ASSN FOR/AID DIPLOM CONSULT

B66
ROBOCK S.H.,INTERNATIONAL DEVELOPMENT 1965. AGRI INDUS VOL/ASSN PLAN TEC/DEV EDU/PROP HEALTH...JURID 20 UN PEACE/CORP. PAGE 122 A2508 FOR/AID INT/ORG GEOG ECO/UNDEV

B66
US HOUSE COMM APPROPRIATIONS,HEARINGS ON FOREIGN OPERATIONS AND RELATED AGENCIES APPROPRIATIONS. CUBA USA+45 VOL/ASSN DELIB/GP DIPLOM CONFER ORD/FREE 20 CONGRESS MIGRATION INT/AM/DEV PEACE/CORP. PAGE 153 A3120 FOR/AID BUDGET ECO/UNDEV FORCES

PEACEFUL COEXISTENCE....SEE PEACE+COLD/WAR

PEARSON L.B. A2343

PEARSON/L....LESTER PEARSON

PEASLEE A.J. A2344,A2345

PEASNT/WAR....PEASANT WAR (1525)

PECKERT J. A2346

PECQUET P. A2347

PELCOVITS N.A. A2348

PENN/WM....WILLIAM PENN

PENICK J.L. JR. A2349

PENNOCK J.R. A2350

PENNSYLVAN....PENNSYLVANIA

PENOLOGY....SEE CRIME

PENTAGON....PENTAGON

PENTONY D.E. A2351,A2352

PEOPLE'S REPUBLIC OF CHINA....SEE CHINA/COM

PERAZA SARAUSA F. A2353

PERCEPT....PERCEPTION AND COGNITION

B
CURRENT THOUGHT ON PEACE AND WAR. WOR+45 INT/ORG FORCES PROB/SOLV DIPLOM NUC/PWR PERCEPT...POLICY SOC 20 UN NATO. PAGE 1 A0008 BIBLIOG/A PEACE ATTIT WAR

B00
GROTIUS H.,DE JURE BELLI AC PACIS. CHRIST-17C UNIV LAW SOCIETY PROVS LEGIT PEACE PERCEPT MORAL PWR ...CONCPT CON/ANAL GEN/LAWS. PAGE 57 A1180 JURID INT/LAW WAR

L16
WRIGHT Q.,"THE ENFORCEMENT OF INTERNATIONAL LAW THROUGH MUNICIPAL LAW IN THE US." USA-45 LOC/G NAT/G PUB/INST FORCES LEGIT CT/SYS PERCEPT ALL/VALS ...JURID 20. PAGE 167 A3401 INT/ORG LAW INT/LAW WAR

B17
UPTON E.,THE MILITARY POLICY OF THE US. USA-45 STRUCT INT/ORG EXEC ATTIT PERCEPT...MGT CONCPT OBS HIST/WRIT CHARTS CONGRESS 18/20. PAGE 149 A3049 FORCES SKILL WAR

B19
KEYNES J.M.,THE ECONOMIC CONSEQUENCES OF THE PEACE. FUT GERMANY MOD/EUR RUSSIA UK USA-45 CULTURE ECO/DEV FINAN INDUS INT/ORG TOP/EX ECO/TAC ROUTINE WAR ATTIT PERCEPT ALL/VALS...OLD/LIB MYTH OBS TIME/SEQ TREND 20 TREATY. PAGE 78 A1605 EUR+WWI SOCIETY PEACE

B22
POTTER P.B.,AN INTRODUCTION TO THE STUDY OF INTERNATIONAL ORGANIZATION. WOR-45 ACT/RES CREATE EDU/PROP ROUTINE PERCEPT KNOWL...CONT/OBS RECORD GEN/LAWS TOT/POP VAL/FREE 20. PAGE 117 A2398 INT/ORG CONCPT

B28
MILLER D.H.,THE DRAFTING OF THE COVENANT. UNIV WOR-45 INTELL NAT/G DELIB/GP PLAN ECO/TAC LEGIT WAR ATTIT PERCEPT...CONCPT TIME/SEQ LEAGUE/NAT TOT/POP 20. PAGE 101 A2074 INT/ORG STRUCT PEACE

B40
MILLER E.,THE NEUROSES OF WAR. UNIV INTELL SOCIETY INT/ORG NAT/G EDU/PROP DISPL DRIVE PERCEPT PERSON RIGID/FLEX...SOC TIME/SEQ 20. PAGE 101 A2075 HEALTH PSY WAR

B42
BORNSTEIN J.,ACTION AGAINST THE ENEMY'S MIND. EUR+WWI GERMANY USA-45 DIPLOM DOMIN PRESS LEAD GP/REL DISCRIM PERCEPT FASCISM MARXISM 20 JEWS NAZI ANTI/SEMIT. PAGE 17 A0343 EDU/PROP PSY WAR CONTROL

L44
WRIGHT Q.,"THE US AND INTERNATIONAL AGREEMENTS." FUT USA-45 CONSTN INTELL INT/ORG LOC/G NAT/G CHIEF CONSULT EX/STRUC DIPLOM LEGIT DRIVE PERCEPT PWR ...CONCPT CONGRESS 20. PAGE 167 A3407 DELIB/GP TOP/EX PEACE

B45
TINGSTERN H.,PEACE AND SECURITY AFTER WW II. WOR-45 DELIB/GP TOP/EX LEGIT CT/SYS COERCE PEACE ATTIT PERCEPT...CONCPT LEAGUE/NAT 20. PAGE 144 A2943 INT/ORG ORD/FREE WAR INT/LAW

B48
VISSON A.,AS OTHERS SEE US. EUR+WWI FRANCE UK USA+45 CULTURE INTELL SOCIETY STRATA NAT/G POL/PAR FOR/AID ATTIT DRIVE LOVE ORD/FREE RESPECT WEALTH ...PLURIST SOC OBS TOT/POP 20. PAGE 159 A3244 USA-45 PERCEPT

B49
MARITAIN J.,HUMAN RIGHTS: COMMENTS AND INTERPRETATIONS. COM UNIV WOR+45 LAW CONSTN CULTURE SOCIETY ECO/DEV ECO/UNDEV SCHOOL DELIB/GP EDU/PROP ATTIT PERCEPT ALL/VALS...HUM SOC TREND UNESCO 20. PAGE 95 A1939 INT/ORG CONCPT

B50
STONE J.,THE PROVINCE AND FUNCTION OF LAW. UNIV WOR+45 WOR-45 CULTURE INTELL SOCIETY ECO/DEV ECO/UNDEV NAT/G LEGIT ROUTINE ATTIT PERCEPT PERSON ...JURID CONCPT GEN/LAWS GEN/METH 20. PAGE 138 A2833 INT/ORG LAW

B51
MCKEON R.,DEMOCRACY IN A WORLD OF TENSION. UNIV LAW INTELL STRUCT R+D INT/ORG SCHOOL EDU/PROP LEGIT ATTIT DRIVE PERCEPT PERSON...POLICY JURID PSY SOC CONCPT METH/CNCPT OBS UNESCO TOT/POP VAL/FREE. PAGE 98 A2015 SOCIETY ALL/VALS ORD/FREE

B51
RAPPAPORT A.,THE BRITISH PRESS AND WILSONIAN NEUTRALITY. UK WOR-45 SEA POL/PAR WAR CHOOSE PEACE ATTIT PERCEPT...GEOG 20 WILSON/W. PAGE 119 A2446 PRESS DIPLOM NEUTRAL POLICY

S51
BUCHANAN W.,"STEREOTYPES AND TENSIONS AS REVEALED BY THE UNESCO INTERNATIONAL POLL." WOR+45 INT/ORG ATTIT DISPL PERCEPT RIGID/FLEX...INT TESTS SAMP 20. PAGE 21 A0424 R+D STERTYP

S51
CONNERY R.H.,"THE MUTUAL DEFENSE ASSISTANCE PROGRAM." COM EUR+WWI KOREA USA+45 NAT/G VOL/ASSN CREATE PLAN BAL/PWR EDU/PROP PERCEPT...POLICY DECISION CONCPT NATO 20. PAGE 29 A0587 INT/ORG FORCES FOR/AID

S51
ICHHEISER G.,"MISUNDERSTANDING IN INTERNATIONAL RELATIONS." UNIV SOCIETY FACE/GP INT/ORG SECT ATTIT PERSON RIGID/FLEX LOVE RESPECT...RELATIV PSY SOC CONCPT MYTH SOC/EXP GEN/LAWS. PAGE 70 A1431 PERCEPT STERTYP NAT/LISM DIPLOM

L52
HILSMAN R. JR.,"INTELLIGENCE AND POLICY MAKING IN FOREIGN AFFAIRS." USA+45 CONSULT ACT/RES DIPLOM PROF/ORG SIMUL

EDU/PROP ROUTINE PEACE PERCEPT PWR SKILL...POLICY MGT HYPO/EXP CONGRESS 20 CIA. PAGE 65 A1333 — WAR

L52
THOMPSON K.W.,"THE STUDY OF INTERNATIONAL POLITICS: A SURVEY OF TRENDS AND DEVELOPMENTS." UNIV USA+45 WOR+45 WOR-45 SOCIETY ECO/DEV R+D ACT/RES PLAN ROUTINE ATTIT DRIVE PERCEPT PERSON...CONCPT OBS TREND GEN/LAWS TOT/POP. PAGE 143 A2928 — INT/ORG BAL/PWR DIPLOM

B53
LANGER W.L.,THE UNDECLARED WAR, 1940-1941. EUR+WWI GERMANY USA-45 USSR AIR FORCES TEC/DEV CONFER CONTROL COERCE PERCEPT ORD/FREE PWR 20 CHINJAP EUROPE. PAGE 84 A1727 — WAR POLICY DIPLOM

S53
LINCOLN G.,"FACTORS DETERMINING ARMS AID." COM FUT USA+45 USSR WOR+45 ECO/DEV NAT/G CONSULT PLAN TEC/DEV DIPLOM DOMIN EDU/PROP PERCEPT PWR ...DECISION CONCPT TREND MARX/KARL 20. PAGE 89 A1819 — FORCES POLICY BAL/PWR FOR/AID

C53
DEUTSCH K.W.,"NATIONALISM AND SOCIAL COMMUNICATION: AN INQUIRY INTO THE FOUNDATIONS OF NATIONALITY." CULTURE STRUCT DIPLOM DOMIN ATTIT ORD/FREE SOVEREIGN...SOC STAT CHARTS IDEA/COMP BIBLIOG. PAGE 36 A0735 — NAT/LISM CONCPT PERCEPT STRATA

S54
DAWSON K.H.,"THE UNITED NATIONS IN A DISUNITED WORLD." WOR+45 WOR-45 LAW INTELL NAT/G PEACE ATTIT PERCEPT MORAL LEAGUE/NAT TOT/POP VAL/FREE 20 UN. PAGE 34 A0694 — INT/ORG LEGIT

B55
GOODRICH L.,THE UNITED NATIONS AND THE MAINTENANCE OF INTERNATIONAL PEACE AND SECURITY. WOR+45 CONSTN ACT/RES CREATE PLAN PERCEPT PWR...ORG/CHARTS GEN/LAWS UN 20. PAGE 54 A1102 — INT/ORG ORD/FREE ARMS/CONT PEACE

B57
BLOOMFIELD L.M.,EGYPT, ISRAEL AND THE GULF OF AQABA: IN INTERNATIONAL LAW. LAW NAT/G CONSULT FORCES PLAN ECO/TAC ROUTINE COERCE ATTIT DRIVE PERCEPT PERSON RIGID/FLEX LOVE PWR WEALTH...GEOG CONCPT MYTH TREND. PAGE 15 A0314 — ISLAM INT/LAW UAR

B57
HOLCOMBE A.N.,STRENGTHENING THE UNITED NATIONS. USA+45 ACT/RES CREATE PLAN EDU/PROP ATTIT PERCEPT PWR...METH/CNCPT CONT/OBS RECORD UN COLD/WAR 20. PAGE 66 A1365 — INT/ORG ROUTINE

B57
STRACHEY A.,THE UNCONSCIOUS MOTIVES OF WAR; A PSYCHO-ANALYTICAL CONTRIBUTION. UNIV SOCIETY DIPLOM DREAM GP/REL ADJUST ATTIT DISPL PERCEPT PERSON KNOWL MORAL. PAGE 139 A2840 — WAR DRIVE LOVE PSY

L57
HAAS E.B.,"REGIONAL INTEGRATION AND NATIONAL POLICY." WOR+45 VOL/ASSN DELIB/GP EX/STRUC ECO/TAC DOMIN EDU/PROP LEGIT COERCE ATTIT PERCEPT KNOWL ...TIME/SEQ COLD/WAR 20 UN. PAGE 59 A1203 — INT/ORG ORD/FREE REGION

S57
DEUTSCH K.W.,"MASS COMMUNICATIONS AND THE LOSS OF FREEDOM IN NATIONAL DECISION MAKING." FUT WOR+45 SOCIETY COM/IND INT/ORG NAT/G ACT/RES CREATE TEC/DEV EDU/PROP MAJORITY PERCEPT...METH/CNCPT 20. PAGE 36 A0737 — COERCE DECISION WAR

S57
SCHELLING T.C.,"BARGAINING COMMUNICATION, AND LIMITED WAR." UNIV WOR+45 FACE/GP INT/ORG NAT/G FORCES ACT/RES WAR PERCEPT ALL/VALS...PSY OBS PROJ/TEST CHARTS HYPO/EXP GEN/LAWS TOT/POP 20. PAGE 128 A2622 — ROUTINE DECISION

B58
JAPANESE ASSOCIATION INT. LAW,JAPAN AND THE UNITED NATIONS. SOCIETY ROUTINE ATTIT DRIVE PERCEPT RIGID/FLEX ORD/FREE...METH/CNCPT CON/ANAL CHINJAP UN. PAGE 73 A1497 — ASIA INT/ORG

S58
BOGART L.,"MEASURING THE EFFECTIVENESS OF AN OVERSEAS INFORMATION CAMPAIGN." EUR+WWI GREECE USA+45 INT/ORG MUNIC PLAN DIPLOM PEACE PERCEPT RIGID/FLEX KNOWL...TECHNIC PSY SOC NEW/IDEA CONT/OBS REC/INT STAND/INT SAMP/SIZ COLD/WAR 20. PAGE 16 A0328 — ATTIT EDU/PROP

S58
LASSWELL H.D.,"THE SCIENTIFIC STUDY OF INTERNATIONAL RELATIONS." USA+45 INT/ORG CREATE EDU/PROP DETER ATTIT PERCEPT PWR...DECISION CONCPT METH/CNCPT STYLE CON/ANAL 20. PAGE 85 A1740 — PHIL/SCI GEN/METH DIPLOM

S58
SINGER J.D.,"THREAT PERCEPTION AND THE ARMAMENT TENSION DILEMMA." WOR+45 WOR-45 ELITES INT/ORG NAT/G DELIB/GP PLAN LEGIT COERCE DETER ATTIT RIGID/FLEX PWR...DECISION PSY 20. PAGE 133 A2724 — PERCEPT ARMS/CONT BAL/PWR

B59
FREE L.A.,SIX ALLIES AND A NEUTRAL. ASIA COM EUR+WWI FRANCE GERMANY/W INDIA S/ASIA UK USA+45 INT/ORG NAT/G NUC/PWR PEACE ATTIT PERCEPT RIGID/FLEX ALL/VALS...STAT REC/INT COLD/WAR 20 CHINJAP. PAGE 48 A0992 — PSY DIPLOM

B59
STRAUSZ-HUPE R.,PROTRACTED CONFLICT. CHINA/COM KOREA WOR+45 INT/ORG FORCES ACT/RES ECO/TAC LEGIT COERCE DRIVE PERCEPT KNOWL PWR...PSY CONCPT RECORD GEN/METH COLD/WAR VAL/FREE 20. PAGE 139 A2847 — COM PLAN USSR

B59
SWIFT R.W.,WORLD AFFAIRS AND THE COLLEGE CURRICULUM. USA+45 PLAN EFFICIENCY PERCEPT...HUM METH/CNCPT. PAGE 140 A2871 — ACADEM DIPLOM METH/COMP EDU/PROP

S59
QUIGLEY H.S.,"TOWARD REAPPRAISAL OF OUR CHINA POLICY." CHINA/COM USA+45 INT/ORG PLAN ECO/TAC PERCEPT ORD/FREE...DECISION PSY CON/ANAL GEN/METH VAL/FREE 20. PAGE 118 A2427 — ASIA KNOWL DIPLOM

S59
SAYEGH F.,"ARAB NATIONALISM AND SOVIET-AMERICAN RELATIONS." ISLAM USA+45 ECO/UNDEV PLAN ECO/TAC LEGIT NAT/LISM DRIVE PERCEPT KNOWL PWR...DECISION CONCPT STAT RECORD TREND CON/ANAL VAL/FREE 20 COLD/WAR. PAGE 127 A2610 — DIPLOM USSR

S59
TIPTON J.B.,"PARTICIPATION OF THE UNITED STATES IN THE INTERNATIONAL LABOR ORGANIZATION." USA+45 LAW STRUCT ECO/DEV ECO/UNDEV INDUS TEC/DEV ECO/TAC ADMIN PERCEPT ORD/FREE SKILL...STAT HIST/WRIT GEN/METH ILO WORK 20. PAGE 144 A2946 — LABOR INT/ORG

B60
SCANLON D.G.,INTERNATIONAL EDUCATION: A DOCUMENTARY HISTORY. ADMIN CONTROL ATTIT PERCEPT...BIOG ANTHOL METH 20. PAGE 127 A2612 — EDU/PROP INT/ORG NAT/COMP DIPLOM

L60
DEUTSCH K.W.,"TOWARD AN INVENTORY OF BASIC TRENDS AND PATTERNS IN COMPARATIVE AND INTERNATIONAL POLITICS." UNIV WOR+45 SOCIETY STRUCT INT/ORG NAT/G CREATE PLAN EDU/PROP KNOWL...PHIL/SCI METH/CNCPT STAT SELF/OBS OBS/ENVIR SAMP TREND CON/ANAL CHARTS SOC/EXP GEN/METH 20. PAGE 36 A0739 — R+D PERCEPT

L60
RIGGS R.,"OVER-SELLING THE U.N. CHARTER, FACT AND MYTH." USA+45 SOCIETY NAT/G TOP/EX PLAN DIPLOM EDU/PROP PEACE ATTIT PERCEPT MORAL...POLICY SAMP UN 20. PAGE 121 A2481 — INT/ORG MYTH

S60
PETERSON E.N.,"HISTORICAL SCHOLARSHIP AND WORLD UNITY." FUT UNIV WOR-45 CULTURE INTELL INT/ORG NAT/G ACT/RES EDU/PROP ATTIT PERCEPT RIGID/FLEX ...NEW/IDEA OBS HIST/WRIT TREND COLD/WAR TOT/POP 20. PAGE 115 A2367 — PLAN KNOWL NAT/LISM

B61
HASAN H.S.,PAKISTAN AND THE UN. ISLAM WOR+45 ECO/DEV ECO/UNDEV NAT/G TOP/EX ECO/TAC FOR/AID EDU/PROP ADMIN DRIVE PERCEPT...OBS TIME/SEQ UN 20. PAGE 62 A1284 — INT/ORG ATTIT PAKISTAN

B61
JENKS C.W.,INTERNATIONAL IMMUNITIES. PLAN EDU/PROP ADMIN PERCEPT...OLD/LIB JURID CONCPT TREND TOT/POP. PAGE 74 A1506 — INT/ORG DIPLOM

B61
KAPLAN M.A.,THE POLITICAL FOUNDATIONS OF INTERNATIONAL LAW. WOR+45 WOR-45 CULTURE SOCIETY ECO/DEV DIPLOM PERCEPT...TECHNIC METH/CNCPT. PAGE 76 A1563 — INT/ORG LAW

B61
NOGEE J.L.,SOVIET POLICY TOWARD INTERNATIONAL CONTROL OF ATOMIC ENERGY. COM USA+45 WOR+45 INTELL NAT/G ACT/RES DIPLOM EDU/PROP NUC/PWR TOTALISM PERCEPT KNOWL PWR...TIME/SEQ COLD/WAR 20. PAGE 109 A2247 — INT/ORG ATTIT ARMS/CONT USSR

B61
SCHELLING T.C.,STRATEGY AND ARMS CONTROL. FUT UNIV WOR+45 INT/ORG PLAN TEC/DEV BAL/PWR LEGIT PERCEPT HEALTH...CONCPT VAL/FREE 20. PAGE 128 A2623 — ROUTINE POLICY ARMS/CONT

L61
HALPERIN M.H.,"NUCLEAR WEAPONS AND LIMITED WARS." FUT UNIV WOR+45 INTELL SOCIETY ECO/DEV ACT/RES DRIVE PERCEPT RIGID/FLEX...CONCPT TIME/SEQ TREND TOT/POP 20. PAGE 60 A1237 — PLAN COERCE NUC/PWR WAR

S61
CASTANEDA J.,"THE UNDERDEVELOPED NATIONS AND THE DEVELOPMENT OF INTERNATIONAL LAW." FUT UNIV LAW ACT/RES FOR/AID LEGIT PERCEPT SKILL...JURID METH/CNCPT TIME/SEQ TOT/POP 20 UN. PAGE 25 A0507 — INT/ORG ECO/UNDEV PEACE INT/LAW

S61
CLAUDE I.,"THE MANAGEMENT OF POWER IN THE CHANGING UNITED NATIONS." WOR+45 PERCEPT UN TOT/POP VAL/FREE 20. PAGE 27 A0544 — INT/ORG DELIB/GP BAL/PWR

S61
LEWY G.,"SUPERIOR ORDERS, NUCLEAR WARFARE AND THE DICTATES OF CONSCIENCE: THE DILEMMA OF MILITARY OBEDIENCE IN THE ATOMIC." FUT UNIV WOR+45 INTELL SOCIETY FORCES TOP/EX ACT/RES ADMIN ROUTINE NUC/PWR PERCEPT RIGID/FLEX ALL/VALS...POLICY CONCPT 20. PAGE 88 A1805 — DETER INT/ORG LAW INT/LAW

S61
MACHOWSKI K.,"SELECTED PROBLEMS OF NATIONAL SOVEREIGNTY WITH REFERENCE TO THE LAW OF OUTER SPACE." FUT WOR+45 AIR LAW INTELL SOCIETY ECO/DEV PLAN EDU/PROP DETER DRIVE PERCEPT SOVEREIGN ...POLICY INT/LAW OBS TREND TOT/POP 20. PAGE 92 A1889
UNIV ACT/RES NUC/PWR SPACE

S61
WEST F.J.,"THE NEW GUINEA QUESTION: AN AUSTRALIAN VIEW." WOR+45 INT/ORG VOL/ASSN LEGIT PERCEPT ...POLICY TIME/SEQ AUSTRAL VAL/FREE 20 CMN/WLTH. PAGE 163 A3320
S/ASIA ECO/UNDEV

B62
GILPIN R.,AMERICAN SCIENTISTS AND NUCLEAR WEAPONS POLICY. COM FUT USA+45 WOR+45 INT/ORG NAT/G PROF/ORG CONSULT FORCES CREATE TEC/DEV BAL/PWR EDU/PROP ARMS/CONT WAR PERCEPT KNOWL MORAL PWR ...PHIL/SCI SOC CONCPT GEN/LAWS 20. PAGE 52 A1073
INTELL ATTIT DETER NUC/PWR

B62
MANNING C.A.W.,THE NATURE OF INTERNATIONAL SOCIETY. FUT LAW NAT/G TOP/EX NAT/LISM PEACE PERCEPT PERSON ALL/VALS PLURISM...METH/CNCPT MYTH HYPO/EXP TOT/POP 20. PAGE 94 A1926
INT/ORG SOCIETY SIMUL DIPLOM

B62
NICHOLAS H.G.,THE UNITED NATIONS AS A POLITICAL INSTITUTION. WOR+45 CONSTN EX/STRUC ACT/RES LEGIT PERCEPT KNOWL PWR...CONCPT TIME/SEQ CON/ANAL ORG/CHARTS UN 20. PAGE 109 A2228
INT/ORG ROUTINE

B62
OSGOOD C.E.,AN ALTERNATIVE TO WAR OR SURRENDER. FUT UNIV CULTURE INTELL SOCIETY R+D INT/ORG CONSULT DELIB/GP ACT/RES PLAN CHOOSE ATTIT PERCEPT KNOWL ...PHIL/SCI PSY SOC TREND GEN/LAWS 20. PAGE 112 A2300
ORD/FREE EDU/PROP PEACE WAR

S62
BELSHAW C.,"TRAINING AND RECRUITMENT: SOME PRINCIPLES OF INTERNATIONAL AID." FUT WOR+45 SOCIETY INT/ORG NAT/G CREATE PLAN TEC/DEV ECO/TAC FOR/AID EDU/PROP ATTIT PERCEPT...HUM UN FAO ILO UNESCO 20. PAGE 13 A0263
VOL/ASSN ECO/UNDEV

S62
BERKES R.N.B.,"THE NEW FRONTIER IN THE UN." FUT USA+45 WOR+45 INT/ORG DELIB/GP NAT/LISM PERCEPT RESPECT UN OAS 20. PAGE 13 A0272
GEN/LAWS DIPLOM

S62
BRZEZINSKI Z.K.,"PEACEFUL ENGAGEMENT IN COMMUNIST DISUNITY." ASIA CHINA/COM USA+45 USSR NAT/G TOP/EX CREATE ECO/TAC FOR/AID DOMIN ATTIT PERCEPT RIGID/FLEX PWR...PSY 20. PAGE 20 A0417
COM DIPLOM TOTALISM

S62
FISCHER G.,"UNE NOUVELLE ORGANIZATION REGIONALE: L'ASA." S/ASIA WOR+45 ECO/UNDEV VOL/ASSN PERCEPT RIGID/FLEX...TIME/SEQ 20 ASA. PAGE 46 A0935
INT/ORG DRIVE REGION

S62
GRAVEN J.,"LE MOUVEAU DROIT PENAL INTERNATIONAL." UNIV STRUCT LEGIS ACT/RES CRIME ATTIT PERCEPT PERSON...JURID CONCPT 20. PAGE 55 A1132
CT/SYS PUB/INST INT/ORG INT/LAW

S62
LONDON K.,"SINO-SOVIET RELATIONS IN THE CONTEXT OF THE 'WORLD SOCIALIST SYSTEM'." ASIA CHINA/COM COM USSR INT/ORG NAT/G TOP/EX BAL/PWR DIPLOM DOMIN ATTIT PERCEPT RIGID/FLEX PWR MARXISM...METH/CNCPT TREND 20. PAGE 91 A1854
DELIB/GP CONCPT SOCISM

S62
MANGIN G.,"LES ACCORDS DE COOPERATION EN MATIERE DE JUSTICE ENTRE LA FRANCE ET LES ETATS AFRICAINS ET MALGACHE." AFR ISLAM WOR+45 STRUCT ECO/UNDEV NAT/G DELIB/GP PERCEPT ALL/VALS...JURID MGT TIME/SEQ 20. PAGE 94 A1919
INT/ORG LAW FRANCE

S62
MONNIER J.P.,"LA SUCCESSION D'ETATS EN MATIERE DE RESPONSABILITE INTERNATIONALE." UNIV CONSTN INTELL SOCIETY ADJUD ROUTINE PERCEPT SUPEGO...GEN/LAWS TOT/POP 20. PAGE 103 A2107
NAT/G JURID INT/LAW

S62
NORTH R.C.,"DECISION MAKING IN CRISIS: AN INTRODUCTION." WOR+45 WOR-45 NAT/G CONSULT DELIB/GP TEC/DEV PERCEPT KNOWL...POLICY DECISION PSY METH/CNCPT CONT/OBS TREND VAL/FREE 20. PAGE 110 A2251
INT/ORG ROUTINE DIPLOM

S62
SCHACHTER O.,"DAG HAMMARSKJOLD AND THE RELATION OF LAW TO POLITICS." FUT WOR+45 INT/ORG CONSULT PLAN TEC/DEV BAL/PWR DIPLOM LEGIT ATTIT PERCEPT ORD/FREE ...POLICY JURID CONCPT OBS TESTS STERTYP GEN/LAWS 20 HAMMARSK/D. PAGE 128 A2616
ACT/RES ADJUD

S62
SINGER J.D.,"STABLE DETERRENCE AND ITS LIMITS." FUT WOR+45 R+D INT/ORG CONSULT ACT/RES TEC/DEV ARMS/CONT COERCE DRIVE PERCEPT RIGID/FLEX ORD/FREE PWR...MYTH SIMUL TOT/POP 20. PAGE 133 A2728
NAT/G FORCES DETER NUC/PWR

S62
VASAK K.,"DE LA CONVENTION EUROPEENNE A LA CONVENTION AFRICAINE DES DROITS DE L'HOMME." AFR ISLAM WOR+45 LAW CONSTN ECO/UNDEV INT/ORG PERCEPT ALL/VALS 20. PAGE 158 A3223
DELIB/GP CONCPT COLONIAL

S62
VIGNES D.,"L'AUTORITE DES TRAITES INTERNATIONAUX EN DROIT INTERNE." EUR+WWI UNIV LAW CONSTN INTELL NAT/G POL/PAR DIPLOM ATTIT PERCEPT ALL/VALS ...POLICY INT/LAW JURID CONCPT TIME/SEQ 20 TREATY. PAGE 159 A3233
STRUCT LEGIT FRANCE

C62
ROBINSON J.A.,"CONGRESS AND FOREIGN POLICY-MAKING: A STUDY IN LEGISLATIVE INFLUENCE AND INITIATIVE." USA+45 CHIEF DELIB/GP CREATE CONTROL EXEC GOV/REL PERCEPT...TREND BIBLIOG 20 CONGRESS. PAGE 122 A2505
LEGIS DIPLOM POLICY DECISION

B63
JOYCE W.,THE PROPAGANDA GAP. USA+45 COM/IND ACADEM DOMIN FEEDBACK REV CIVMIL/REL...REALPOL COLD/WAR. PAGE 75 A1540
EDU/PROP PERCEPT BAL/PWR DIPLOM

B63
NORTH R.C.,CONTENT ANALYSIS: A HANDBOOK WITH APPLICATIONS FOR THE STUDY OF INTERNATIONAL CRISIS. ASIA COM EUR+WWI MOD/EUR INT/ORG TEC/DEV DOMIN EDU/PROP ROUTINE COERCE PERCEPT RIGID/FLEX ALL/VALS ...QUANT TESTS CON/ANAL SIMUL GEN/LAWS VAL/FREE. PAGE 110 A2252
METH/CNCPT COMPUT/IR USSR

B63
SCHMELTZ G.W.,LA POLITIQUE MONDIALE CONTEMPORAINE. SOCIETY ECO/UNDEV INDUS INT/ORG NAT/G POL/PAR CONSULT DELIB/GP PLAN TEC/DEV ECO/TAC DOMIN EDU/PROP ROUTINE COERCE PERCEPT PERSON LOVE SKILL ...SOC RECORD TOT/POP. PAGE 128 A2629
WOR+45 COLONIAL

B63
THORELLI H.B.,INTOP: INTERNATIONAL OPERATIONS SIMULATION: PLAYER'S MANUAL. BRAZIL FINAN OP/RES ADMIN GP/REL INGP/REL PRODUC PERCEPT...DECISION MGT EEC. PAGE 144 A2935
GAME INT/TRADE EDU/PROP LG/CO

B63
US DEPARTMENT OF STATE,POLITICAL BEHAVIOR--A LIST OF CURRENT STUDIES. USA+45 COM/IND DIPLOM LEAD PERS/REL DRIVE PERCEPT KNOWL...DECISION SIMUL METH. PAGE 151 A3093
BIBLIOG METH/COMP GP/REL ATTIT

B63
VOSS E.H.,NUCLEAR AMBUSH: THE TEST-BAN TRAP. WOR+45 COM/IND INT/ORG NAT/G DELIB/GP FORCES LEGIS TOP/EX ACT/RES DOMIN EDU/PROP LEGIT ROUTINE COERCE ATTIT PERCEPT RIGID/FLEX HEALTH MORAL ORD/FREE PWR. PAGE 160 A3255
TEC/DEV HIST/WRIT ARMS/CONT NUC/PWR

L63
CRANE R.D.,"THE CUBAN CRISIS: A STRATEGIC ANALYSIS OF AMERICAN AND SOVIET POLICY." CUBA USA+45 USSR BAL/PWR RISK DETER NUC/PWR PERCEPT ORD/FREE 20. PAGE 32 A0658
DIPLOM POLICY FORCES

S63
CAHIER P.,"LE DROIT INTERNE DES ORGANISATIONS INTERNATIONALES." UNIV CONSTN SOCIETY ECO/DEV R+D NAT/G TOP/EX LEGIT ATTIT PERCEPT...TIME/SEQ 19/20. PAGE 23 A0464
INT/ORG JURID DIPLOM INT/LAW

S63
DICKS H.V.,"NATIONAL LOYALTY, IDENTITY, AND THE INTERNATIONAL SOLDIER." FUT NAT/G COERCE ATTIT DRIVE PERCEPT PERSON RIGID/FLEX SUPEGO ALL/VALS ...PSY VAL/FREE. PAGE 37 A0758
INT/ORG FORCES

S63
MAZRUI A.A.,"ON THE CONCEPT 'WE ARE ALL AFRICANS'." AFR CULTURE KIN LOC/G NAT/G DOMIN EDU/PROP LEGIT ATTIT PERCEPT PERSON KNOWL ORD/FREE...TIME/SEQ TOT/POP 20. PAGE 97 A1986
PROVS INT/ORG NAT/LISM

S63
ROUGEMONT D.,"LES NOUVELLES CHANCES DE L'EUROPE." EUR+WWI FUT ECO/DEV INT/ORG NAT/G ACT/RES PLAN TEC/DEV EDU/PROP ADMIN COLONIAL FEDERAL ATTIT PWR SKILL...TREND 20. PAGE 124 A2549
ECO/UNDEV PERCEPT

S63
VEROFF J.,"AFRICAN STUDENTS IN THE UNITED STATES." AFR USA+45 CULTURE ACT/RES FOR/AID PEACE ATTIT KNOWL...SOC RECORD DEEP/QU SYS/QU CHARTS STERTYP TOT/POP 20. PAGE 159 A3230
PERCEPT RIGID/FLEX RACE/REL

S63
WALKER H.,"THE INTERNATIONAL LAW OF COMMODITY AGREEMENTS." FUT WOR+45 ECO/DEV ECO/UNDEV FINAN INT/ORG NAT/G CONSULT CREATE PLAN ECO/TAC ATTIT PERCEPT...CONCPT GEN/LAWS TOT/POP GATT 20. PAGE 160 A3265
MARKET VOL/ASSN INT/LAW INT/TRADE

S63
WEILLER J.,"UNIONS MONETAIRES ET RAPPORTS DE COOPERATION INTERNATIONALE DANS UN MONDE EN TRANSITION: L'EXAMPLE." AFR FUT UNIV WOR+45 SOCIETY ECO/UNDEV MARKET R+D NAT/G FOR/AID PERCEPT RIGID/FLEX...NEW/IDEA 20. PAGE 162 A3303
FINAN INT/ORG

S63
WEISSBERG G.,"MAPS AS EVIDENCE IN INTERNATIONAL BOUNDARY DISPUTES: A REAPPRAISAL." CHINA/COM EUR+WWI INDIA MOD/EUR S/ASIA INT/ORG NAT/G LEGIT PERCEPT...JURID CHARTS 20. PAGE 163 A3311
LAW GEOG SOVEREIGN

S63
WELLS H.,"THE OAS AND THE DOMINICAN ELECTIONS." L/A+17C INT/ORG NAT/G POL/PAR TEC/DEV ECO/TAC
CONSULT CHOOSE

EDU/PROP PERCEPT...TIME/SEQ OAS TOT/POP 20. PAGE 163 A3317 DOMIN/REP

S63
WENGLER W.,"LES CONFLITS DE LOIS ET LE PRINCIPE D'EGALITE." UNIV LAW SOCIETY ACT/RES LEGIT ATTIT PERCEPT 20. PAGE 163 A3318 JURID CONCPT INT/LAW

S63
WRIGHT Q.,"PROJECTED EUROPEAN UNION AND AMERICAN INTERNATIONAL PRESTIGE." EUR+WWI FRANCE GERMANY UK USA+45 INT/ORG NAT/G EDU/PROP ATTIT PERCEPT PWR ...CONCPT OBS EEC 20 UN. PAGE 168 A3417 FUT ORD/FREE REGION

B64
ADAMS V.,THE PEACE CORPS IN ACTION. USA+45 VOL/ASSN EX/STRUC GOV/REL PERCEPT ORD/FREE...OBS 20 KENNEDY/JF PEACE/CORP. PAGE 4 A0087 DIPLOM FOR/AID PERSON DRIVE

B64
APTER D.E.,IDEOLOGY AND DISCONTENT. FUT WOR+45 CONSTN CULTURE INTELL SOCIETY STRUCT INT/ORG NAT/G DELIB/GP LEGIS CREATE PLAN TEC/DEV EDU/PROP EXEC PERCEPT PERSON RIGID/FLEX ALL/VALS...POLICY TOT/POP. PAGE 8 A0171 ACT/RES ATTIT

B64
FISHER R.,INTERNATIONAL CONFLICT AND BEHAVIORAL SCIENCE: THE CRAIGVILLE PAPERS. COM FUT USA+45 WOR+45 NAT/G DELIB/GP EX/STRUC FORCES ECO/TAC DOMIN EDU/PROP LEGIT COERCE ATTIT PERCEPT ORD/FREE PWR RESPECT...PSY SOC VAL/FREE. PAGE 46 A0940 INT/ORG PLAN DIPLOM

B64
HARRISON H.V.,THE ROLE OF THEORY IN INTERNATIONAL RELATIONS. UNIV WOR+45 R+D INT/ORG NAT/G PERCEPT KNOWL...DECISION CONCPT GEN/METH METH 20. PAGE 62 A1270 METH/CNCPT HYPO/EXP DIPLOM

L64
WARD C.,"THE 'NEW MYTHS' AND 'OLD REALITIES' OF NUCLEAR WAR." COM FUT USA+45 USSR WOR+45 INT/ORG NAT/G DOMIN LEGIT EXEC ATTIT PERCEPT ALL/VALS ...POLICY RELATIV PSY MYTH TREND 20. PAGE 161 A3280 FORCES COERCE ARMS/CONT NUC/PWR

S64
COFFEY J.,"THE SOVIET VIEW OF A DISARMED WORLD." COM USA+45 INT/ORG NAT/G EX/STRUC EDU/PROP COERCE PERCEPT ORD/FREE PWR...TREND STERTYP VAL/FREE 20 UN. PAGE 27 A0556 FORCES ATTIT ARMS/CONT USSR

S64
HICKEY D.,"THE PHILOSOPHICAL ARGUMENT FOR WORLD GOVERNMENT." WOR+45 SOCIETY ACT/RES PLAN LEGIT ADJUD PEACE PERCEPT PERSON ORD/FREE...HUM JURID PHIL/SCI METH/CNCPT CON/ANAL STERTYP GEN/LAWS TOT/POP 20. PAGE 65 A1327 FUT INT/ORG

S64
JORDAN A.,"POLITICAL COMMUNICATION: THE THIRD DIMENSION OF STRATEGY." USA+45 WOR+45 INT/ORG NAT/G CONSULT FORCES PLAN LEGIT EXEC PERCEPT ALL/VALS ...POLICY RELATIV PSY NEW/IDEA AUD/VIS EXHIBIT TOT/POP 20. PAGE 75 A1534 EDU/PROP RIGID/FLEX ATTIT

S64
KISSINGER H.A.,"COALITION DIPLOMACY IN A NUCLEAR AGE." COM EUR+WWI USA+45 WOR+45 INT/ORG NAT/G FORCES ACT/RES DOMIN LEGIT COERCE PERCEPT ALL/VALS ...POLICY TOT/POP 20. PAGE 80 A1644 CONSULT ATTIT DIPLOM NUC/PWR

S64
RUBIN R.,"THE UN CORRESPONDENT." WOR+45 FACE/GP PROF/ORG EDU/PROP ROUTINE PERCEPT KNOWL...RECORD STAND/INT QU UN WORK TOT/POP VAL/FREE 20. PAGE 125 A2560 INT/ORG ATTIT DIPLOM

S64
WASKOW A.I.,"NEW ROADS TO A WORLD WITHOUT WAR." FUT WOR+45 CULTURE INTELL SOCIETY NAT/G DOMIN LEGIT EXEC COERCE PEACE ATTIT DISPL PERCEPT RIGID/FLEX ALL/VALS...POLICY RELATIV SOC NEW/IDEA 20. PAGE 161 A3288 INT/ORG FORCES

S65
KHOURI F.J.,"THE JORDON RIVER CONTROVERSY." LAW SOCIETY ECO/UNDEV AGRI FINAN INDUS SECT FORCES ACT/RES PLAN TEC/DEV ECO/TAC EDU/PROP COERCE ATTIT DRIVE PERCEPT RIGID/FLEX ALL/VALS...GEOG SOC MYTH WORK. PAGE 78 A1610 ISLAM INT/ORG ISRAEL JORDAN

S65
QUADE Q.L.,"THE TRUMAN ADMINISTRATION AND THE SEPARATION OF POWERS: THE CASE OF THE MARSHALL PLAN." SOCIETY INT/ORG NAT/G CONSULT DELIB/GP LEGIS PLAN ECO/TAC ROUTINE DRIVE PERCEPT RIGID/FLEX ORD/FREE PWR WEALTH...DECISION GEOG NEW/IDEA TREND 20 TRUMAN/HS. PAGE 118 A2422 USA+45 ECO/UNDEV DIPLOM

C65
SCHWEBEL M.,"BEHAVIORAL SCIENCE AND HUMAN SURVIVAL." FORCES ARMS/CONT COERCE NUC/PWR WAR GP/REL NAT/LISM PERCEPT...POLICY PSY ANTHOL BIBLIOG/A 20 COLD/WAR. PAGE 130 A2662 PEACE ACT/RES DIPLOM HEAL

B66
MORRIS B.S.,INTERNATIONAL COMMUNISM AND AMERICAN POLICY. CHINA/COM USA+45 USSR INT/ORG POL/PAR GP/REL NAT/LISM ATTIT PERCEPT 20. PAGE 105 A2147 DIPLOM POLICY MARXISM

S67
NORTH R.C.,"COMMUNICATION AS AN APPROACH TO POLITICS." UNIV INTELL DIPLOM PERCEPT PERSON ...CONCPT TIME. PAGE 110 A2254 PERS/REL GP/REL ACT/RES

S67
RABIER J.-R.,"THE EUROPEAN IDEA AND NATIONAL PUBLIC OPINIONS." ACT/RES PLAN DIPLOM PARTIC CONSEN ATTIT PERCEPT...DECISION CHARTS. PAGE 118 A2430 POLICY FEDERAL EUR+WWI PROB/SOLV

PERCEPTION....SEE PERCEPT

PERCY/CHAS....CHARLES PERCY

PEREZ ORTIZ R. A2354

PERF/ART....PERFORMING ARTS

B50
COUNCIL BRITISH NATIONAL BIB,BRITISH NATIONAL BIBLIOGRAPHY. UK AGRI CONSTRUC PERF/ART POL/PAR SECT CREATE INT/TRADE LEAD...HUM JURID PHIL/SCI 20. PAGE 31 A0637 BIBLIOG/A NAT/G TEC/DEV DIPLOM

B51
UNESCO,FREEDOM AND CULTURE. FUT WOR+45 CONSTN CULTURE PERF/ART VOL/ASSN EDU/PROP PEACE ATTIT ALL/VALS SOVEREIGN...POLICY MAJORIT CONCPT TREND STERTYP GEN/LAWS UN TOT/POP 20. PAGE 147 A3013 INT/ORG SOCIETY

L63
SZASZY E.,"L'EVOLUTION DES PRINCIPES GENERAUX DU DROIT INTERNATIONAL PRIVE DANS LES PAYS DE DEMOCRATIE POPULAIRE." COM FUT WOR+45 LAW ECO/DEV PERF/ART POL/PAR PROF/ORG ECO/TAC INT/TRADE EDU/PROP ATTIT RIGID/FLEX ALL/VALS SOCISM...JURID TREND GEN/LAWS WORK 20. PAGE 141 A2876 DIPLOM TOTALISM INT/LAW INT/ORG

B64
SPECTOR S.D.,A CHECKLIST OF PAPERBOUND BOOKS ON RUSSIA. USSR SECT DIPLOM EDU/PROP HEALTH...PHIL/SCI PSY SOC SOC/WK WORSHIP 20. PAGE 135 A2775 BIBLIOG COM PERF/ART

PERFORMING ARTS....SEE PERF/ART; ALSO ART/METH

PERHAM M. A2355,A2356

PERKINS B. A2357,A2358

PERKINS D. A2359,A2360,A2361,A2362

PERKINS H.C. A2321

PERLO V. A2363,A2364

PERON/JUAN....JUAN PERON

PERRE J. A2365

PERRY S.E. A2806

PERS/COMP....COMPARISON OF PERSONS

B57
DUDDEN A.P.,WOODROW WILSON AND THE WORLD OF TODAY. USA-45 NAT/G PROVS CONTROL PARTIC WAR ISOLAT PWR SKILL...PERS/COMP ANTHOL 19/20 WILSON/W UN LEAGUE/NAT WWI. PAGE 39 A0794 CHIEF DIPLOM POL/PAR LEAD

B60
JAECKH A.,WELTSAAT; ERLEBTES UND ERSTREBTES. GERMANY WOR+45 WOR-45 PLAN WAR...POLICY OBS/ENVIR NAT/COMP PERS/COMP 20. PAGE 73 A1489 BIOG NAT/G SELF/OBS DIPLOM

PERS/REL....RELATIONS BETWEEN PERSONS AND INTERPERSONAL COMMUNICATION

B42
TOLMAN E.C.,DRIVES TOWARD WAR. UNIV PLAN DIPLOM ECO/TAC COERCE PERS/REL ADJUST HAPPINESS BIO/SOC HEREDITY HEALTH KNOWL. PAGE 144 A2947 PSY WAR UTOPIA DRIVE

B45
WEST R.,CONSCIENCE AND SOCIETY: A STUDY OF THE PSYCHOLOGICAL PREREQUISITES OF LAW AND ORDER. FUT UNIV LAW SOCIETY STRUCT DIPLOM WAR PERS/REL SUPEGO ...SOC 20. PAGE 163 A3321 COERCE INT/LAW ORD/FREE PERSON

B53
MCNEILL W.H.,AMERICA, BRITAIN, AND RUSSIA; THEIR COOPERATION AND CONFLICT. UK USA-45 USSR ECO/DEV ECO/UNDEV FORCES PLAN ADMIN AGREE PERS/REL ...DECISION 20 TREATY. PAGE 98 A2021 WAR DIPLOM DOMIN

B55
ALFIERI D.,DICTATORS FACE TO FACE. NAT/G TOP/EX DIPLOM EXEC COERCE ORD/FREE FASCISM...POLICY OBS 20 HITLER/A MUSSOLIN/B. PAGE 6 A0116 WAR CHIEF TOTALISM PERS/REL

B56
BEARDSLEY S.W.,HUMAN RELATIONS IN INTERNATIONAL AFFAIRS: A GUIDE TO SIGNIFICANT INTERPRETATION AND RESEARCH. UNIV PERS/REL NAT/LISM DRIVE PERSON ...POLICY PSY SOC CON/ANAL IDEA/COMP 20. PAGE 12 BIBLIOG/A ATTIT CULTURE DIPLOM

A0241

B59
HUGHES E.M.,AMERICA THE VINCIBLE. USA+45 FOR/AID ARMS/CONT NUC/PWR PERS/REL RATIONAL ATTIT ALL/VALS 20 COLD/WAR. PAGE 69 A1413 — ORD/FREE DIPLOM WAR

B60
ENGELMAN F.L.,THE PEACE OF CHRISTMAS EVE. UK USA-45 NAT/G FORCES CONFER PERS/REL...AUD/VIS BIBLIOG 19 TREATY. PAGE 42 A0853 — WAR PEACE DIPLOM PERSON

B61
JAVITS B.A.,THE PEACE BY INVESTMENT CORPORATION. WOR+45 NAT/G LEGIS PROB/SOLV PERS/REL WEALTH ...POLICY 20. PAGE 73 A1499 — ECO/UNDEV DIPLOM FOR/AID PEACE

B63
LANGE O.,ECONOMIC DEVELOPMENT, PLANNING, AND INTERNATIONAL COOPERATION. UAR WOR+45 FINAN CAP/ISM PERS/REL 20. PAGE 84 A1722 — ECO/UNDEV DIPLOM INT/TRADE PLAN

B63
US DEPARTMENT OF STATE,POLITICAL BEHAVIOR--A LIST OF CURRENT STUDIES. USA+45 COM/IND DIPLOM LEAD PERS/REL DRIVE PERCEPT KNOWL...DECISION SIMUL METH. PAGE 151 A3093 — BIBLIOG METH/COMP GP/REL ATTIT

B63
WEINBERG A.,INSTEAD OF VIOLENCE: WRITINGS BY THE GREAT ADVOCATES OF PEACE AND NONVIOLENCE THROUGHOUT HISTORY. WOR+45 WOR-45 SOCIETY SECT PROB/SOLV DIPLOM GP/REL PERS/REL PEACE...ANTHOL PACIFIST. PAGE 162 A3304 — PACIFISM WAR IDEA/COMP

B64
EHRENBURG I.,THE WAR: 1941-1945 (VOL. V OF "MEN, YEARS - LIFE," TRANS. BY TATIANA SHEBUNINA). GERMANY USSR PRESS WRITING PERS/REL PEACE ANOMIE ATTIT PERSON...CONCPT RECORD BIOG 20 STALIN/J HITLER/A. PAGE 40 A0827 — WAR DIPLOM COM MARXIST

B64
NICE R.W.,TREASURY OF LAW. WOR+45 WOR-45 SECT ADJUD MORAL ORD/FREE...INT/LAW JURID PHIL/SCI ANTHOL. PAGE 108 A2227 — LAW WRITING PERS/REL DIPLOM

B64
REES D.,KOREA: THE LIMITED WAR. ASIA KOREA WOR+45 NAT/G CIVMIL/REL PERS/REL PERSON...POLICY CHARTS 20 UN TRUMAN/HS MACARTHR/D. PAGE 120 A2455 — DIPLOM WAR INT/ORG FORCES

B65
ADENAUER K.,MEMOIRS 1945-53. EUR+WWI GERMANY/W ECO/DEV CHIEF FORCES ECO/TAC WAR GOV/REL PWR SOVEREIGN 20 NATO ADENAUER/K. PAGE 4 A0088 — BIOG DIPLOM NAT/G PERS/REL

B65
BRACKETT R.D.,PATHWAYS TO PEACE. SECT VOL/ASSN GP/REL PERS/REL DISCRIM...LING 20 UN PEACE/CORP. PAGE 18 A0366 — PEACE INT/ORG EDU/PROP PARTIC

B65
DAVISON W.P.,INTERNATIONAL POLITICAL COMMUNICATION. COM USA+45 WOR+45 CULTURE ECO/UNDEV NAT/G PROB/SOLV PRESS TV ADMIN 20 FILM. PAGE 34 A0693 — EDU/PROP DIPLOM PERS/REL COM/IND

B65
HAIGHT D.E.,THE PRESIDENT; ROLES AND POWERS. USA+45 USA-45 POL/PAR PLAN DIPLOM CHOOSE PERS/REL PWR 18/20 PRESIDENT CONGRESS. PAGE 59 A1217 — CHIEF LEGIS TOP/EX EX/STRUC

B65
HART B.H.L.,THE MEMOIRS OF CAPTAIN LIDDELL HART (VOL. I). UK NAT/G PLAN TEC/DEV DIPLOM ADMIN WEAPON GOV/REL PERS/REL ATTIT PWR FASCISM...POLICY 20. PAGE 62 A1274 — FORCES BIOG LEAD WAR

B66
JACK H.A.,RELIGION AND PEACE: PAPERS FROM THE NATIONAL INTER-RELIGIOUS CONFERENCE ON PEACE, WASHINGTON, 1966. CHINA/COM USA+45 VIETNAM WOR+45 FORCES FOR/AID LEAD PERS/REL. PAGE 72 A1472 — PEACE SECT SUPEGO DIPLOM

B67
CECIL L.,ALBERT BALLIN; BUSINESS AND POLITICS IN IMPERIAL GERMANY 1888-1918. GERMANY UK INT/TRADE LEAD WAR PERS/REL ADJUST PWR WEALTH...MGT BIBLIOG 19/20. PAGE 25 A0510 — DIPLOM CONSTN ECO/DEV TOP/EX

B67
HOHENBERG J.,BETWEEN TWO WORLDS. ASIA S/ASIA USA+45 PRESS TV PERS/REL ISOLAT...INT CHARTS METH/COMP 20. PAGE 66 A1362 — COM/IND DIPLOM EFFICIENCY KNOWL

B67
US DEPARTMENT OF STATE,THE COUNTRY TEAM - AN ILLUSTRATED PROFILE OF OUR AMERICAN MISSIONS ABROAD. ECO/TAC FOR/AID EDU/PROP TASK PERS/REL ATTIT 20. PAGE 152 A3099 — DIPLOM NAT/G VOL/ASSN GOV/REL

S67
KELLY F.K.,"A PROPOSAL FOR AN ANNUAL REPORT ON THE STATE OF MANKIND." FUT INTELL COM/IND INT/ORG CREATE PROB/SOLV PERS/REL...CONCPT 20 UN. PAGE 77 A1579 — SOCIETY UNIV ATTIT NEW/IDEA

S67
NORTH R.C.,"COMMUNICATION AS AN APPROACH TO POLITICS." UNIV INTELL DIPLOM PERCEPT PERSON ...CONCPT TIME. PAGE 110 A2254 — PERS/REL GP/REL ACT/RES

S67
SENCOURT R.,"FOREIGN POLICY* AN HISTORIC RECTIFICATION." EUR+WWI UK DIPLOM EDU/PROP LEAD WAR CHOOSE PERS/REL...METH/COMP PARLIAMENT. PAGE 131 A2685 — POLICY POL/PAR NAT/G

S67
SPENCER R.,"GERMANY AFTER THE AUTUMN CRISIS." GERMANY CHOOSE GP/REL PERS/REL. PAGE 136 A2785 — DIPLOM POL/PAR PROB/SOLV

PERS/TEST....PERSONALITY TESTS

S58
ANDERSON N.,"INTERNATIONAL SEMINARS: AN ANALYSIS AND AN EVALUATION." WOR+45 R+D ACT/RES CREATE PLAN REGION ATTIT KNOWL SKILL...SOC REC/INT PERS/TEST CHARTS 20. PAGE 8 A0158 — INT/ORG DELIB/GP

PERSHAD A. A2331

PERSIA....PERSIA: ANCIENT IRAN

B58
SALETORE B.A.,INDIA'S DIPLOMATIC RELATIONS WITH THE WEST. GREECE INDIA CULTURE ETIQUET...IDEA/COMP 3 ROM/EMP PERSIA. PAGE 126 A2590 — DIPLOM CONCPT INT/TRADE

B60
SALETORE B.A.,INDIA'S DIPLOMATIC RELATIONS WITH THE EAST. ASIA CEYLON INDIA NEPAL S/ASIA CULTURE 7/14 PERSIA. PAGE 126 A2591 — DIPLOM NAT/COMP ETIQUET

B63
JAIRAZBHOY R.A.,FOREIGN INFLUENCE IN ANCIENT INDIA. INDIA ELITES SECT DIPLOM EDU/PROP COLONIAL REGION GP/REL...ART/METH LING WORSHIP +/14 GRECO/ROMN MESOPOTAM PERSIA PARTH/SASS. PAGE 73 A1491 — CULTURE SOCIETY COERCE DOMIN

S63
BULLOUGH V.L.,"THE ROMAN EMPIRE VS PERSIA, 363-502: A STUDY OF SUCCESSFUL DETERRENCE." NAT/G PLAN DIPLOM ORD/FREE PWR...TIME/SEQ COLD/WAR VAL/FREE 4/6 PERSIA ROM/EMP. PAGE 21 A0430 — MEDIT-7 COERCE DETER

PERSON....PERSONALITY AND HUMAN NATURE

N
JOURNAL OF INTERNATIONAL AFFAIRS. WOR+45 ECO/UNDEV POL/PAR ECO/TAC WAR PEACE PERSON ALL/IDEOS ...INT/LAW TREND. PAGE 1 A0015 — BIBLIOG DIPLOM INT/ORG NAT/G

N
BIBLIO, CATALOGUE DES OUVRAGES PARUS EN LANGUE FRANCAISE DANS LE MONDE ENTIER. FRANCE WOR+45 ADMIN LEAD PERSON...SOC 20. PAGE 2 A0029 — BIBLIOG NAT/G DIPLOM ECO/DEV

N
DEUTSCHE BUCHEREI,DEUTSCHES BUCHERVERZEICHNIS. GERMANY LAW CULTURE POL/PAR ADMIN LEAD ATTIT PERSON ...SOC 20. PAGE 37 A0746 — BIBLIOG NAT/G DIPLOM ECO/DEV

B00
MAINE H.S.,INTERNATIONAL LAW. MOD/EUR UNIV SOCIETY STRUCT ACT/RES EXEC WAR ATTIT PERSON ALL/VALS ...POLICY JURID CONCPT OBS TIME/SEQ TOT/POP. PAGE 93 A1908 — INT/ORG LAW PEACE INT/LAW

B00
OMAN C.,A HISTORY OF THE ART OF WAR: THE MIDDLE AGES FROM THE FOURTH TO THE FOURTEENTH CENTURY. CHRIST-17C MEDIT-7 CULTURE SOCIETY INT/ORG ROUTINE PERSON...CONT/OBS HIST/WRIT CHARTS VAL/FREE. PAGE 112 A2291 — FORCES SKILL WAR

B11
PHILLIPSON C.,THE INTERNATIONAL LAW AND CUSTOM OF ANCIENT GREECE AND ROME. MEDIT-7 UNIV INTELL SOCIETY STRUCT NAT/G LEGIS EXEC PERSON...CONCPT OBS CON/ANAL ROM/EMP. PAGE 116 A2377 — INT/ORG LAW INT/LAW

B16
PUFENDORF S.,LAW OF NATURE AND OF NATIONS (ABRIDGED). UNIV LAW NAT/G DIPLOM AGREE WAR PERSON ALL/VALS PWR...POLICY 18 DEITY NATURL/LAW. PAGE 118 A2416 — CONCPT INT/LAW SECT MORAL

B28
HALL W.P.,EMPIRE TO COMMONWEALTH. FUT WOR-45 CONSTN ECO/DEV ECO/UNDEV INT/ORG PROVS PLAN DIPLOM EDU/PROP ADMIN COLONIAL PEACE PERSON ALL/VALS ...POLICY GEOG SOC OBS RECORD TREND CMN/WLTH PARLIAMENT 19/20. PAGE 60 A1229 — VOL/ASSN NAT/G UK

B29
STURZO L.,THE INTERNATIONAL COMMUNITY AND THE RIGHT OF WAR (TRANS. BY BARBARA BARCLAY CARTER). CULTURE CREATE PROB/SOLV DIPLOM ADJUD CONTROL PEACE PERSON ORD/FREE...INT/LAW IDEA/COMP PACIFIST 20 LEAGUE/NAT. PAGE 140 A2858 — INT/ORG PLAN WAR CONCPT

B31
HODGES C.,THE BACKGROUND OF INTERNATIONAL RELATIONS. WOR-45 SOCIETY ECO/DEV ECO/UNDEV INT/ORG DIPLOM DOMIN EDU/PROP LEGIT WAR ATTIT DRIVE PERSON ALL/VALS...CONCPT METH/CNCPT TIME/SEQ CHARTS WORK LEAGUE/NAT 19/20. PAGE 66 A1350
NAT/G BAL/PWR

B38
DE MADARIAGA S.,THE WORLD'S DESIGN. WOR-45 SOCIETY STRUCT EDU/PROP PEACE ATTIT PERSON ALL/VALS ...SOCIALIST CONCPT TIME/SEQ TREND GEN/LAWS LEAGUE/NAT. PAGE 35 A0706
FUT INT/ORG DIPLOM

B39
DULLES J.,WAR, PEACE AND CHANGE. FRANCE ITALY UK USA-45 WOR-45 LAW INT/ORG NAT/G SECT VOL/ASSN FORCES TOP/EX DOMIN ARMS/CONT COERCE ATTIT PERSON RIGID/FLEX MORAL PWR...JURID STERTYP TOT/POP LEAGUE/NAT 20. PAGE 39 A0796
EDU/PROP TOTALISM WAR

B40
BOGGS S.W.,INTERNATIONAL BOUNDARIES. WOR-45 SOCIETY ECO/DEV INT/ORG NAT/G NEIGH LEGIT PERSON ORD/FREE PWR...POLICY GEOG MYTH LEAGUE/NAT 20. PAGE 16 A0329
ATTIT CONCPT NAT/LISM

B40
MILLER E.,THE NEUROSES OF WAR. UNIV INTELL SOCIETY INT/ORG NAT/G EDU/PROP DISPL DRIVE PERCEPT PERSON RIGID/FLEX...SOC TIME/SEQ 20. PAGE 101 A2075
HEALTH PSY WAR

B41
EVANS C.,AMERICAN BIBLIOGRAPHY... (12 VOLUMES). USA-45 LAW DIPLOM ADMIN PERSON...HUM SOC 17/18. PAGE 43 A0876
BIBLIOG NAT/G ALL/VALS ALL/IDEOS

B41
YOUNG G.,FEDERALISM AND FREEDOM. EUR+WWI MOD/EUR RUSSIA USA-45 WOR-45 SOCIETY STRUCT ECO/DEV INT/ORG EXEC FEDERAL ATTIT PERSON ALL/VALS...OLD/LIB CONCPT OBS TREND LEAGUE/NAT TOT/POP. PAGE 169 A3435
NAT/G WAR

B42
HAMBRO C.J.,HOW TO WIN THE PEACE. ECO/TAC EDU/PROP ADJUD PERSON ALL/VALS...SOCIALIST TREND GEN/LAWS 20. PAGE 61 A1246
FUT INT/ORG PEACE

B44
WEIGERT H.W.,COMPASS OF THE WORLD, A SYMPOSIUM ON POLITICAL GEOGRAPHY. EUR+WWI FUT MOD/EUR S/ASIA USA-45 WOR-45 SOCIETY AGRI INDUS MARKET ECO/TAC INT/TRADE PERSON 20. PAGE 162 A3298
TEC/DEV CAP/ISM RUSSIA GEOG

B45
WEST R.,CONSCIENCE AND SOCIETY: A STUDY OF THE PSYCHOLOGICAL PREREQUISITES OF LAW AND ORDER. FUT UNIV LAW SOCIETY STRUCT DIPLOM WAR PERS/REL SUPEGO ...SOC 20. PAGE 163 A3321
COERCE INT/LAW ORD/FREE PERSON

B46
GAULD W.A.,MAN, NATURE, AND TIME, AN INTRODUCTION TO WORLD STUDY. WOR-45 CULTURE CREATE DIPLOM GP/REL DRIVE...SOC LING CENSUS CHARTS TIME 18/20. PAGE 52 A1054
HABITAT PERSON

B47
HEIMANN E.,FREEDOM AND ORDER: LESSONS FROM THE WAR. WOR-45 CONSTN FORCES CHOOSE CIVMIL/REL PERSON ALL/IDEOS SOCISM...SOC IDEA/COMP WORSHIP 20. PAGE 64 A1308
NAT/G SOCIETY ORD/FREE DIPLOM

B48
DURBIN E.F.M.,THE POLITICS OF DEMOCRATIC SOCIALISM; AN ESSAY ON SOCIAL POLICY. STRATA POL/PAR PLAN COERCE DRIVE PERSON PWR MARXISM...CHARTS METH/COMP. PAGE 39 A0805
SOCIALIST POPULISM POLICY SOCIETY

B49
GORER G.,THE PEOPLE OF GREAT RUSSIA: A PSYCHOLOGICAL STUDY. RUSSIA USSR NAT/G DIPLOM LEAD AGE/C ANOMIE ATTIT DRIVE...POLICY 20. PAGE 54 A1116
ISOLAT PERSON PSY SOCIETY

B49
STETTINIUS E.R.,ROOSEVELT AND THE RUSSIANS: THE YALTA CONFERENCE. UK USSR WOR+45 WOR-45 INT/ORG VOL/ASSN TOP/EX ACT/RES EDU/PROP PEACE ATTIT DRIVE PERSON SUPEGO PWR...POLICY CONCPT MYTH OBS TIME/SEQ AUD/VIS COLD/WAR 20 CHURCHLL/W YALTA ROOSEVLT/F. PAGE 138 A2819
DIPLOM DELIB/GP BIOG

S49
DUNN F.,"THE PRESENT COURSE OF INTERNATIONAL RELATIONS RESEARCH." WOR+45 WOR-45 SOCIETY R+D INT/ORG WAR PERSON ORD/FREE...POLICY PSY SOC GEN/LAWS 20. PAGE 39 A0800
CONCPT GEN/METH DIPLOM

B50
ALMOND G.A.,THE AMERICAN PEOPLE AND FOREIGN POLICY. USA+45 USA-45 CULTURE SOCIETY STRUCT CONSEN PERSON PWR POPULISM...TIME/SEQ TREND 20 COLD/WAR. PAGE 6 A0129
ATTIT DIPLOM DECISION ELITES

B50
LAUTERPACHT H.,INTERNATIONAL LAW AND HUMAN RIGHTS. USA+45 CONSTN STRUCT INT/ORG ACT/RES EDU/PROP PEACE PERSON ALL/VALS...CONCPT CON/ANAL GEN/LAWS UN 20. PAGE 86 A1750
DELIB/GP LAW INT/LAW

B50
LEVI W.,FUNDAMENTALS OF WORLD ORGANIZATION. WOR+45 WOR-45 CULTURE ECO/TAC GIVE RECEIVE PERSON WEALTH ...METH/COMP 19/20 UN LEAGUE/NAT. PAGE 88 A1793
INT/ORG PEACE ORD/FREE DIPLOM

B50
STONE J.,THE PROVINCE AND FUNCTION OF LAW. UNIV WOR+45 WOR-45 CULTURE INTELL SOCIETY ECO/DEV ECO/UNDEV NAT/G LEGIT ROUTINE ATTIT PERCEPT PERSON ...JURID CONCPT GEN/LAWS GEN/METH 20. PAGE 138 A2833
INT/ORG LAW

S50
CORBETT P.E.,"OBJECTIVITY IN THE STUDY OF INTERNATIONAL AFFAIRS." WOR+45 SOCIETY ACT/RES EDU/PROP PERSON RIGID/FLEX KNOWL TOT/POP 20. PAGE 30 A0614
INT/ORG DIPLOM

B51
MCKEON R.,DEMOCRACY IN A WORLD OF TENSION. UNIV LAW INTELL STRUCT R+D INT/ORG SCHOOL EDU/PROP LEGIT ATTIT DRIVE PERCEPT PERSON...POLICY JURID PSY SOC CONCPT METH/CNCPT OBS UNESCO TOT/POP VAL/FREE. PAGE 98 A2015
SOCIETY ALL/VALS ORD/FREE

B51
STANTON A.H.,PERSONALITY AND POLITICAL CRISIS. WOR+45 WOR-45 STRUCT DIPLOM INGP/REL TOTALISM MORAL ...ANTHOL 20 LASSWELL/H PARSONS/T RIESMAN/D. PAGE 137 A2806
EDU/PROP WAR PERSON PSY

S51
ICHHEISER G.,"MISUNDERSTANDING IN INTERNATIONAL RELATIONS." UNIV SOCIETY FACE/GP INT/ORG SECT ATTIT PERSON RIGID/FLEX LOVE RESPECT...RELATIV PSY SOC CONCPT MYTH SOC/EXP GEN/LAWS. PAGE 70 A1431
PERCEPT STERTYP NAT/LISM DIPLOM

B52
UNESCO,CURRENT SOCIOLOGY (2 VOLS.). SOCIETY STRATA R+D GP/REL ATTIT PERSON 20 UN. PAGE 147 A3014
BIBLIOG SOC INT/ORG CULTURE

L52
NIEBUHR R.,"THE MORAL IMPLICATIONS OF LOYALTY TO THE UNITED NATIONS." WOR+45 WOR-45 SOCIETY ECO/DEV INT/ORG VOL/ASSN PEACE ATTIT PERSON LOVE ORD/FREE PWR RESPECT...CONCPT UN TOT/POP COLD/WAR UNESCO 20. PAGE 109 A2236
SUPEGO GEN/LAWS

L52
THOMPSON K.W.,"THE STUDY OF INTERNATIONAL POLITICS: A SURVEY OF TRENDS AND DEVELOPMENTS." UNIV USA+45 WOR+45 WOR-45 SOCIETY ECO/DEV R+D ACT/RES PLAN ROUTINE ATTIT DRIVE PERCEPT PERSON...CONCPT OBS TREND GEN/LAWS TOT/POP. PAGE 143 A2928
INT/ORG BAL/PWR DIPLOM

S52
SCHUMAN F.,"INTERNATIONAL IDEALS AND THE NATIONAL INTEREST." WOR+45 WOR-45 INT/ORG VOL/ASSN DELIB/GP CREATE BAL/PWR DOMIN PEACE PERSON MORAL PWR SOVEREIGN...POLICY GEN/LAWS TOT/POP LEAGUE/NAT 20. PAGE 129 A2648
ATTIT CONCPT

B53
BORGESE G.,FOUNDATIONS OF THE WORLD REPUBLIC. FUT SOCIETY NAT/G CREATE LEGIT PERSON MORAL...MAJORIT CON/ANAL LEAGUE/NAT TOT/POP 20. PAGE 17 A0340
INT/ORG CONSTN PEACE

B53
LENZ F.,DIE BEWEGUNGEN DER GROSSEN MACHTE. USA+45 USA-45 USSR SOCIETY STRATA STRUCT NAT/G PERSON MARXISM...CONCPT IDEA/COMP NAT/COMP 18/20. PAGE 87 A1777
BAL/PWR TREND DIPLOM HIST/WRIT

S53
CORY R.H. JR.,"FORGING A PUBLIC INFORMATION POLICY FOR THE UNITED NATIONS." FUT WOR+45 SOCIETY ADMIN PEACE ATTIT PERSON SKILL...CONCPT 20 UN. PAGE 31 A0628
INT/ORG EDU/PROP BAL/PWR

S53
MANNING C.A.W.,"THE PRETENTIONS OF INTERNATIONAL RELATIONS." WOR+45 SOCIETY CREATE EDU/PROP ATTIT PERSON KNOWL...GEN/LAWS TOT/POP VAL/FREE 20. PAGE 94 A1924
INT/ORG DIPLOM UK

B54
COOK T.,POWER THROUGH PURPOSE. USA+45 WOR+45 WOR-45 INT/ORG VOL/ASSN BAL/PWR DIPLOM EDU/PROP LEGIT PERSON...GEN/LAWS LEAGUE/NAT 20. PAGE 30 A0606
ATTIT CONCPT

B54
COUDENHOVE-KALERGI,AN IDEA CONQUERS THE WORLD. EUR+WWI MOD/EUR USA-45 CONSTN FAM CREATE EDU/PROP ATTIT PERSON KNOWL...CONCPT SELF/OBS TIME/SEQ. PAGE 31 A0635
INT/ORG BIOG DIPLOM

B54
SCHIFFER W.,THE LEGAL COMMUNITY OF MANKIND. UNIV WOR+45 WOR-45 SOCIETY NAT/G EDU/PROP LEGIT ATTIT PERSON ORD/FREE PWR...CONCPT HIST/WRIT TREND LEAGUE/NAT UN 20. PAGE 128 A2626
INT/ORG PHIL/SCI

B54
SHARMA J.S.,MAHATMA GANDHI: A DESCRIPTIVE BIBLIOGRAPHY. INDIA S/ASIA PROB/SOLV DIPLOM COLONIAL WAR NAT/LISM PEACE ATTIT PERSON SOVEREIGN ...CONCPT 20 GANDHI/M. PAGE 132 A2695
BIBLIOG/A BIOG CHIEF LEAD

B55
KROPOTKIN P.,MUTUAL AID, A FACTOR OF EVOLUTION (1902). UNIV ADJUST ATTIT HEREDITY PERSON LOVE DARWIN/C. PAGE 82 A1687
INGP/REL SOCIETY GEN/LAWS BIO/SOC

B55
MOCH J.,HUMAN FOLLY: DISARM OR PERISH. USA+45 WOR+45 SOCIETY INT/ORG NAT/G ACT/RES EDU/PROP ATTIT
FUT DELIB/GP

PERSON KNOWL ORD/FREE PWR...MAJORIT TOT/POP COLD/WAR 20. PAGE 102 A2093 — ARMS/CONT NUC/PWR

B56
BEALE H.K.,THEODORE ROOSEVELT AND THE RISE OF AMERICA TO WORLD POWER. USA-45 BAL/PWR COLONIAL DRIVE PERSON PWR...POLICY BIBLIOG 20 ROOSEVLT/T PRESIDENT. PAGE 12 A0238 — DIPLOM CHIEF BIOG

B56
BEARDSLEY S.W.,HUMAN RELATIONS IN INTERNATIONAL AFFAIRS: A GUIDE TO SIGNIFICANT INTERPRETATION AND RESEARCH. UNIV PERS/REL NAT/LISM DRIVE PERSON ...POLICY PSY SOC CON/ANAL IDEA/COMP 20. PAGE 12 A0241 — BIBLIOG/A ATTIT CULTURE DIPLOM

B56
GEORGE A.L.,WOODROW WILSON AND COLONEL HOUSE. WOR-45 CONSTN FACE/GP INT/ORG NAT/G POL/PAR CONSULT LEGIT EXEC COERCE CHOOSE ATTIT DRIVE PERSON MORAL ORD/FREE PWR RESPECT...POLICY MGT PSY OBS RECORD INT LEAGUE/NAT. PAGE 52 A1060 — USA-45 BIOG DIPLOM

B56
GUNTHER F.,BUCHERKUNDE ZUR WELTGESCHICHTE VON UNTERGANG DES ROMISCHEN WELTREICHES BIS ZUR GEGENWART. WOR+45 WOR-45 LEAD PERSON. PAGE 58 A1193 — BIBLIOG DIPLOM NAT/G TREND

B56
HAAS E.B.,DYNAMICS OF INTERNATIONAL RELATIONS. WOR-45 ELITES INT/ORG VOL/ASSN EX/STRUC FORCES ECO/TAC DOMIN LEGIT COERCE ATTIT PERSON PWR ...CONCPT TIME/SEQ CHARTS COLD/WAR 20. PAGE 58 A1202 — WOR+45 NAT/G DIPLOM

B56
SPROUT H.,MAN-MILIEU RELATIONSHIP HYPOTHESES IN THE CONTEXT OF INTERNATIONAL POLITICS. UNIV PROB/SOLV BIO/SOC PERSON...DECISION GEOG SOC METH/CNCPT PREDICT 20. PAGE 136 A2792 — HABITAT DIPLOM CONCPT DRIVE

B57
BEAL J.R.,JOHN FOSTER DULLES, A BIOGRAPHY. USA+45 USSR WOR+45 CONSTN INT/ORG NAT/G EX/STRUC LEGIT ADMIN NUC/PWR DISPL PERSON ORD/FREE PWR SKILL ...POLICY PSY OBS RECORD COLD/WAR UN 20 DULLES/JF. PAGE 12 A0237 — BIOG DIPLOM

B57
BLOOMFIELD L.M.,EGYPT, ISRAEL AND THE GULF OF AQABA: IN INTERNATIONAL LAW. LAW NAT/G CONSULT FORCES PLAN ECO/TAC ROUTINE COERCE ATTIT DRIVE PERCEPT PERSON RIGID/FLEX LOVE PWR WEALTH...GEOG CONCPT MYTH TREND. PAGE 15 A0314 — ISLAM INT/LAW UAR

B57
FRAZIER E.F.,RACE AND CULTURE CONTACTS IN THE MODERN WORLD. WOR+45 WOR-45 SOCIETY ECO/DEV AGRI INDUS INT/ORG LABOR NAT/G PERSON RIGID/FLEX ALL/VALS...SOC TIME/SEQ WORK 19/20. PAGE 48 A0991 — CULTURE RACE/REL

B57
KAPLAN M.A.,SYSTEM AND PROCESS OF INTERNATIONAL POLITICS. FUT WOR+45 WOR-45 SOCIETY PLAN BAL/PWR ADMIN ATTIT PERSON RIGID/FLEX PWR SOVEREIGN ...DECISION TREND VAL/FREE. PAGE 76 A1560 — INT/ORG DIPLOM

B57
STRACHEY A.,THE UNCONSCIOUS MOTIVES OF WAR; A PSYCHO-ANALYTICAL CONTRIBUTION. UNIV SOCIETY DIPLOM DREAM GP/REL ADJUST ATTIT DISPL PERCEPT PERSON KNOWL MORAL. PAGE 139 A2840 — WAR DRIVE LOVE PSY

B58
APPADORAI A.,THE USE OF FORCE IN INTERNATIONAL RELATIONS. WOR+45 CULTURE ECO/UNDEV CAP/ISM ARMS/CONT REV WAR ATTIT PERSON SOVEREIGN MARXISM ...INT/LAW PACIFIST 20 UN INTERVENT THIRD/WRLD COLD/WAR. PAGE 8 A0169 — PEACE FEDERAL INT/ORG

B58
ARON R.,ON WAR: ATOMIC WEAPONS AND GLOBAL DIPLOMACY (TRANS. BY TERENCE KILMARTIN). WOR+45 SOCIETY FORCES BAL/PWR WAR WEAPON PERSON...SOC 20. PAGE 9 A0182 — ARMS/CONT NUC/PWR COERCE DIPLOM

B58
MELMAN S.,INSPECTION FOR DISARMAMENT. USA+45 WOR+45 SOCIETY INT/ORG NAT/G CONSULT ACT/RES PLAN EDU/PROP CONTROL DETER PEACE ATTIT PERSON KNOWL...PSY STAT OBS CHARTS TOT/POP VAL/FREE 20. PAGE 99 A2035 — FUT ORD/FREE ARMS/CONT NUC/PWR

S58
SONDERMANN F.A.,"SOCIOLOGY AND INTERNATIONAL RELATIONS." WOR+45 CULTURE SOCIETY INT/ORG NAT/G CREATE ATTIT DRIVE PERSON RIGID/FLEX...PSY SOC 20. PAGE 135 A2767 — PLAN NEW/IDEA PEACE

B59
ALLEN R.L.,SOVIET INFLUENCE IN LATIN AMERICA. ECO/UNDEV FINAN PROC/MFG NAT/G TEC/DEV EDU/PROP EXEC ROUTINE ATTIT DRIVE PERSON ALL/VALS PWR...STAT CHARTS WORK 20. PAGE 6 A0125 — L/A+17C ECO/TAC INT/TRADE USSR

B59
GOLDWIN R.A.,READINGS IN RUSSIAN FOREIGN POLICY. HUNGARY USSR YUGOSLAVIA ELITES INT/ORG NAT/G REV WAR NAT/LISM PERSON SOCISM...CHARTS 20 MAPS BOLSHEVISM. PAGE 53 A1095 — COM MARXISM DIPLOM POLICY

B59
HALLE L.J.,DREAM AND REALITY: ASPECTS OF AMERICAN FOREIGN POLICY. USA+45 CONSTN CONSULT PROB/SOLV NAT/LISM PERSON. PAGE 60 A1230 — POLICY MYTH DIPLOM NAT/G

L59
WOLFERS A.,"ACTORS IN INTERNATIONAL POLITICS. IN (FOX,WTR. THEORETICAL ASPECTS OF INTERNATIONAL." FUT WOR+45 CONSTN INT/ORG NAT/G CREATE...CONCPT 20. PAGE 166 A3383 — PERSON PWR DIPLOM

S59
LASSWELL H.D.,"UNIVERSALITY IN PERSPECTIVE." FUT UNIV SOCIETY CONSULT TOP/EX PLAN EDU/PROP ADJUD ROUTINE ARMS/CONT COERCE PEACE ATTIT PERSON ALL/VALS. PAGE 85 A1741 — INT/ORG JURID TOTALISM

B60
DAVIDS J.,AMERICA AND THE WORLD OF OUR TIME: UNITED STATES DIPLOMACY IN THE TWENTIETH CENTURY. USA-45 SOCIETY ECO/DEV INT/ORG NAT/G POL/PAR FORCES ECO/TAC DOMIN EDU/PROP EXEC COERCE WAR CHOOSE ATTIT PERSON ORD/FREE...CONCPT TIME/SEQ TOT/POP 20. PAGE 34 A0686 — USA+45 PWR DIPLOM

B60
ENGEL-JANOSI F.,OSTERREICH UND DER VATIKAN (2 VOLS). AUSTRIA VATICAN NAT/LISM PEACE PERSON CATHISM 20. PAGE 42 A0852 — DIPLOM ATTIT WAR

B60
ENGELMAN F.L.,THE PEACE OF CHRISTMAS EVE. UK USA-45 NAT/G FORCES CONFER PERS/REL...AUD/VIS BIBLIOG 19 TREATY. PAGE 42 A0853 — WAR PEACE DIPLOM PERSON

B60
HAMADY S.,TEMPERAMENT AND CHARACTER OF THE ARABS. FAM NAT/G SECT DIPLOM NAT/LISM...POLICY 20 ARABS. PAGE 61 A1244 — NAT/COMP PERSON CULTURE ISLAM

B60
HANDLIN O.,AMERICAN PRINCIPLES AND ISSUES. USA+45 USA-45 DIPLOM WAR PERSON. PAGE 61 A1251 — ORD/FREE NAT/LISM ATTIT

B60
KHRUSHCHEV N.,FOR VICTORY IN PEACEFUL COMPETITION WITH CAPITALISM. COM FUT USSR WOR+45 CONSTN SOCIETY INDUS INT/ORG DELIB/GP PLAN BAL/PWR DIPLOM PERSON MARXISM...MARXIST WORK 20 COLD/WAR. PAGE 79 A1611 — TOP/EX PWR CAP/ISM SOCISM

B60
LANDHEER B.,ETHICAL VALUES IN INTERNATIONAL DECISION-MAKING. FUT LAW SOCIETY INT/ORG NAT/G DELIB/GP CREATE NAT/LISM ATTIT PERSON...DECISION CONCPT LEAGUE/NAT TOT/POP 20. PAGE 84 A1718 — HYPO/EXP POLICY PEACE

B60
PRITTIE T.,GERMANY DIVIDED: THE LEGACY OF THE NAZI ERA. EUR+WWI GERMANY RACE/REL SUPEGO...PSY AUD/VIS BIBLIOG/A 20 NAZI. PAGE 118 A2414 — STERTYP PERSON ATTIT DIPLOM

L60
FERNBACH A.P.,"SOVIET COEXISTENCE STRATEGY." WOR+45 PROF/ORG VOL/ASSN DIPLOM DOMIN EDU/PROP ATTIT DRIVE PERSON PWR SKILL WEALTH...POLICY OBS SAMP TREND STERTYP ILO WORK COLD/WAR 420. PAGE 45 A0919 — LABOR INT/ORG USSR

S60
FITZGIBBON R.H.,"DICTATORSHIP AND DEMOCRACY IN LATIN AMERICA." FUT ECO/DEV ECO/UNDEV INT/ORG LOC/G NAT/G TOP/EX PLAN TEC/DEV ECO/TAC CHOOSE ATTIT DRIVE PERSON ALL/VALS OAS TOT/POP 20. PAGE 46 A0943 — L/A+17C ACT/RES INT/TRADE

S60
OSGOOD C.E.,"COGNITIVE DYNAMICS IN THE CONDUCT OF HUMAN AFFAIRS." USA+45 INTELL INT/ORG CONSULT PLAN ATTIT PERSON...PSY CHARTS HYPO/EXP 20. PAGE 112 A2299 — R+D SOCIETY

B61
ANAND R.P.,COMPULSORY JURISDICTION OF INTERNATIONAL COURT OF JUSTICE. FUT WOR+45 SOCIETY PLAN LEGIT ADJUD ATTIT DRIVE PERSON ORD/FREE...JURID CONCPT TREND 20 ICJ. PAGE 8 A0156 — INT/ORG COERCE INT/LAW

B61
GRAEBNER N.,THE NEW ISOLATIONISM: A STUDY IN POLITICS AND FOREIGN POLICY SINCE 1960. USA+45 INT/ORG LOC/G NAT/G POL/PAR LEGIS BAL/PWR EDU/PROP CHOOSE ATTIT PERSON ORD/FREE 20 TRUMAN/HS EISNHWR/DD. PAGE 55 A1120 — EXEC PWR DIPLOM

B61
GRAEBNER N.,AN UNCERTAIN TRADITION: AMERICAN SECRETARIES OF STATE IN THE 20TH CENTURY. USA+45 CONSTN INT/ORG NAT/G DELIB/GP TOP/EX BAL/PWR DOMIN LEGIT ADMIN ARMS/CONT ATTIT DRIVE PERSON SUPEGO ORD/FREE PWR...GEN/LAWS VAL/FREE CONGRESS. PAGE 55 A1121 — USA-45 BIOG DIPLOM

B61
MCDOUGAL M.S.,LAW AND MINIMUM WORLD PUBLIC ORDER. WOR+45 SOCIETY NAT/G DELIB/GP EDU/PROP LEGIT ADJUD COERCE ATTIT PERSON...JURID CONCPT RECORD TREND TOT/POP 20. PAGE 98 A2006 — INT/ORG ORD/FREE INT/LAW

B61
MICHAEL D.N.,PROPOSED STUDIES ON THE IMPLICATIONS OF PEACEFUL SPACE ACTIVITIES FOR HUMAN AFFAIRS. COM/IND INDUS FORCES DIPLOM PEACE PERSON...PSY SOC 20. PAGE 101 A2066 — FUT SPACE ACT/RES PROB/SOLV

B61
WECHSLER H.,PRINCIPLES, POLITICS AND FUNDAMENTAL LAW: SELECTED ESSAYS. USA+45 USA-45 LAW SOCIETY NAT/G PROVS DELIB/GP EX/STRUC ACT/RES LEGIT PERSON KNOWL PWR...JURID 20 NUREMBERG. PAGE 162 A3296
CT/SYS CONSTN INT/LAW

S61
ZAGORIA D.S.,"THE FUTURE OF SINO-SOVIET RELATIONS." CHINA/COM INT/ORG NAT/G POL/PAR VOL/ASSN ACT/RES PLAN PERSON...METH/CNCPT TIME/SEQ TOT/POP VAL/FREE 20 MAO KHRUSH/N. PAGE 169 A3444
ASIA COM TOTALISM USSR

B62
HUNTINGTON S.P.,CHANGING PATTERNS OF MILITARY POLITICS. EUR+WWI L/A+17C S/ASIA USA+45 WOR+45 CULTURE INT/ORG NAT/G CONSULT PLAN DOMIN EDU/PROP LEGIT DETER WAR ATTIT PERSON PWR...DECISION CONCPT SIMUL GEN/LAWS ANTHOL COLD/WAR 20. PAGE 69 A1419
FORCES RIGID/FLEX

B62
MANNING C.A.W.,THE NATURE OF INTERNATIONAL SOCIETY. FUT LAW NAT/G TOP/EX NAT/LISM PEACE PERCEPT PERSON ALL/VALS PLURISM...METH/CNCPT MYTH HYPO/EXP TOT/POP 20. PAGE 94 A1926
INT/ORG SOCIETY SIMUL DIPLOM

B62
WOETZEL R.K.,THE NURENBERG TRIALS IN INTERNATIONAL LAW. CHRIST-17C MOD/EUR WOR+45 SOCIETY NAT/G DELIB/GP DOMIN LEGIT ROUTINE ATTIT DRIVE PERSON SUPEGO MORAL ORD/FREE...POLICY MAJORIT JURID PSY SOC SELF/OBS RECORD NAZI TOT/POP. PAGE 166 A3376
INT/ORG ADJUD WAR

L62
ULYSSES,"THE INTERNATIONAL AIMS AND POLICIES OF THE SOVIET UNION: THE NEW CONCEPTS AND STRATEGY OF KHRUSHCHEV." FUT USSR WOR+45 SOCIETY INT/ORG NAT/G POL/PAR FORCES TOP/EX PLAN DOMIN EDU/PROP COERCE ATTIT PERSON PWR...TREND COLD/WAR 20 KHRUSH/N. PAGE 146 A2994
COM POLICY BAL/PWR DIPLOM

S62
DRACHKOVITCH M.M.,"THE EMERGING PATTERN OF YUGOSLAV-SOVIET RELATIONS." COM FUT USSR WOR+45 INT/ORG ECO/TAC FOR/AID DOMIN COERCE ATTIT PERSON ORD/FREE PWR...TIME/SEQ 20 TITO/MARSH KHRUSH/N STALIN/J. PAGE 38 A0783
TOP/EX DIPLOM YUGOSLAVIA

S62
GRAVEN J.,"LE MOUVEAU DROIT PENAL INTERNATIONAL." UNIV STRUCT LEGIS ACT/RES CRIME ATTIT PERCEPT PERSON...JURID CONCPT 20. PAGE 55 A1132
CT/SYS PUB/INST INT/ORG INT/LAW

S62
SPRINGER H.W.,"FEDERATION IN THE CARIBBEAN: AN ATTEMPT THAT FAILED." L/A+17C ECO/UNDEV INT/ORG POL/PAR PROVS LEGIS CREATE PLAN LEGIT ADMIN FEDERAL ATTIT DRIVE PERSON ORD/FREE PWR...POLICY GEOG PSY CONCPT OBS CARIBBEAN CMN/WLTH 20. PAGE 136 A2791
VOL/ASSN NAT/G REGION

B63
ELIAS T.O.,GOVERNMENT AND POLITICS IN AFRICA. CONSTN CULTURE SOCIETY NAT/G POL/PAR DIPLOM REPRESENT PERSON...SOC TREND BIBLIOG 4/20. PAGE 41 A0837
AFR NAT/LISM COLONIAL LAW

B63
QUAISON-SACKEY A.,AFRICA UNBOUND: REFLECTIONS OF AN AFRICAN STATESMAN. ISLAM CULTURE INTELL INT/ORG POL/PAR TOP/EX DOMIN EDU/PROP LEGIT ATTIT PERSON ...CONCPT OBS TIME/SEQ CHARTS STERTYP 20 UN. PAGE 118 A2423
AFR BIOG

B63
ROBERTSON A.H.,HUMAN RIGHTS IN EUROPE. CONSTN SOCIETY INT/ORG NAT/G VOL/ASSN DELIB/GP ACT/RES PLAN ADJUD REGION ROUTINE ATTIT LOVE ORD/FREE RESPECT...JURID SOC CONCPT SOC/EXP UN 20. PAGE 122 A2498
EUR+WWI PERSON

B63
ROSECRANCE R.N.,ACTION AND REACTION IN WORLD POLITICS. FUT WOR-45 SOCIETY DELIB/GP ACT/RES CREATE DIPLOM ECO/TAC DOMIN EDU/PROP COERCE ATTIT PERSON SUPEGO ORD/FREE PWR...CHARTS SIMUL LEAGUE/NAT VAL/FREE UN 19/20. PAGE 123 A2529
WOR+45 INT/ORG BAL/PWR

B63
SCHMELTZ G.W.,LA POLITIQUE MONDIALE CONTEMPORAINE. SOCIETY ECO/UNDEV INDUS INT/ORG NAT/G POL/PAR CONSULT DELIB/GP PLAN TEC/DEV ECO/TAC DOMIN EDU/PROP ROUTINE COERCE PERCEPT PERSON LOVE SKILL ...SOC RECORD TOT/POP. PAGE 128 A2629
WOR+45 COLONIAL

B63
STEVENSON A.E.,LOOKING OUTWARD: YEARS OF CRISIS AT THE UNITED NATIONS. COM CUBA USA+45 WOR+45 SOCIETY NAT/G EX/STRUC ACT/RES LEGIT COLONIAL ATTIT PERSON SUPEGO ALL/VALS...POLICY HUM UN COLD/WAR CONGO 20. PAGE 138 A2823
INT/ORG CONCPT ARMS/CONT

B63
TUCKER R.C.,THE SOVIET POLITICAL MIND. WOR+45 ELITES INT/ORG NAT/G POL/PAR PLAN DIPLOM ECO/TAC DOMIN ADMIN NUC/PWR REV DRIVE PERSON SUPEGO PWR WEALTH...POLICY MGT PSY CONCPT OBS BIOG TREND COLD/WAR MARX/KARL 20. PAGE 145 A2972
COM TOP/EX USSR

S63
DICKS H.V.,"NATIONAL LOYALTY, IDENTITY, AND THE INTERNATIONAL SOLDIER." FUT NAT/G COERCE ATTIT DRIVE PERCEPT PERSON RIGID/FLEX SUPEGO ALL/VALS ...PSY VAL/FREE. PAGE 37 A0758
INT/ORG FORCES

S63
MAZRUI A.A.,"ON THE CONCEPT 'WE ARE ALL AFRICANS'." AFR CULTURE KIN LOC/G NAT/G DOMIN EDU/PROP LEGIT ATTIT PERCEPT PERSON KNOWL ORD/FREE...TIME/SEQ TOT/POP 20. PAGE 97 A1986
PROVS INT/ORG NAT/LISM

S63
NICHOLAS H.G.,"UN PEACE FORCES AND THE CHANGING GLOBE: THE LESSONS OF SUEZ AND CONGO." FUT WOR+45 CONSTN INT/ORG CONSULT DELIB/GP TOP/EX CREATE DIPLOM DOMIN LEGIT COERCE WAR PERSON RIGID/FLEX PWR UN SUEZ CONGO UNEF 20. PAGE 109 A2229
ACT/RES FORCES

B64
ADAMS V.,THE PEACE CORPS IN ACTION. USA+45 VOL/ASSN EX/STRUC GOV/REL PERCEPT ORD/FREE...OBS 20 KENNEDY/JF PEACE/CORP. PAGE 4 A0087
DIPLOM FOR/AID PERSON DRIVE

B64
APTER D.E.,IDEOLOGY AND DISCONTENT. FUT WOR+45 CONSTN CULTURE INTELL SOCIETY STRUCT INT/ORG NAT/G DELIB/GP LEGIS CREATE PLAN TEC/DEV EDU/PROP EXEC PERCEPT PERSON RIGID/FLEX ALL/VALS...POLICY TOT/POP. PAGE 8 A0171
ACT/RES ATTIT

B64
CALDER R.,TWO-WAY PASSAGE. INT/ORG TEC/DEV WAR PERSON ORD/FREE 20. PAGE 23 A0467
FOR/AID ECO/UNDEV ECO/TAC DIPLOM

B64
EHRENBURG I.,THE WAR: 1941-1945 (VOL. V OF "MEN, YEARS - LIFE," TRANS. BY TATIANA SHEBUNINA). GERMANY USSR PRESS WRITING PERS/REL PEACE ANOMIE ATTIT PERSON...CONCPT RECORD BIOG 20 STALIN/J HITLER/A. PAGE 40 A0827
WAR DIPLOM COM MARXIST

B64
GRODZINS M.,THE ATOMIC AGE: FORTY-FIVE SCIENTISTS AND SCHOLARS SPEAK ON NATIONAL AND WORLD AFFAIRS. FUT USA+45 WOR+45 R+D INT/ORG NAT/G CONSULT TEC/DEV EDU/PROP ATTIT PERSON ORD/FREE...HUM CONCPT TIME/SEQ CON/ANAL. PAGE 57 A1169
INTELL ARMS/CONT NUC/PWR

B64
HARPER F.,OUT OF CHINA. CHINA/COM ELITES STRATA ATTIT PERSON...BIOG 20 MAO HONG/KONG MIGRATION. PAGE 62 A1264
HABITAT DEEP/INT DIPLOM MARXISM

B64
IKLE F.C.,HOW NATIONS NEGOTIATE. COM EUR+WWI USA+45 INTELL INT/ORG VOL/ASSN DELIB/GP ACT/RES CREATE DOMIN EDU/PROP ADJUD ROUTINE ATTIT PERSON ORD/FREE RESPECT SKILL...PSY SOC OBS VAL/FREE. PAGE 70 A1433
NAT/G PWR POLICY

B64
JENSEN D.L.,DIPLOMACY AND DOGMATISM. FRANCE SPAIN REV WAR PERSON CATHISM...POLICY BIOG 16. PAGE 74 A1513
DIPLOM ATTIT SECT

B64
KIMMINICH O.,RUSTUNG UND POLITISCHE SPANNUNG. INDUS ARMS/CONT COERCE NAT/LISM PEACE PERSON ORD/FREE ...POLICY GEOG 20. PAGE 79 A1619
DIPLOM FORCES WEAPON WAR

B64
REES D.,KOREA: THE LIMITED WAR. ASIA KOREA WOR+45 NAT/G CIVMIL/REL PERS/REL PERSON...POLICY CHARTS 20 UN TRUMAN/HS MACARTHR/D. PAGE 120 A2455
DIPLOM WAR INT/ORG FORCES

B64
REMAK J.,THE GENTLE CRITIC: THEODOR FONTANE AND GERMAN POLITICS, 1848-1898. GERMANY PRUSSIA CULTURE ELITES BAL/PWR DIPLOM WRITING GOV/REL...HUM BIOG 19 BISMARCK/O JUNKER FONTANE/T. PAGE 120 A2465
PERSON SOCIETY WORKER CHIEF

B64
TAYLOR E.,RICHER BY ASIA. S/ASIA CULTURE VOL/ASSN ACT/RES ATTIT DISPL PERSON ALL/VALS...INT/LAW MYTH SELF/OBS 20. PAGE 142 A2899
SOCIETY RIGID/FLEX INDIA

B64
WARREN S.,THE PRESIDENT AS WORLD LEADER. USA+45 WOR+45 ELITES COM/IND INT/ORG NAT/G VOL/ASSN CHIEF EX/STRUC LEGIT COERCE ATTIT PERSON RIGID/FLEX...INT TIME/SEQ COLD/WAR 20 ROOSEVLT/F TRUMAN/HS EISNHWR/DD KENNEDY/JF. PAGE 161 A3286
TOP/EX PWR DIPLOM

L64
LLOYD W.B.,"PEACE REQUIRES PEACEMAKERS." AFR INDIA S/ASIA SWITZERLND WOR+45 INT/ORG VOL/ASSN PLAN PERSON PWR 20. PAGE 90 A1848
CONSULT PEACE

S64
CARNEGIE ENDOWMENT INT. PEACE,"HUMAN RIGHTS (ISSUES BEFORE THE NINETEENTH GENERAL ASSEMBLY)." AFR WOR+45 LAW CONSTN NAT/G EDU/PROP GP/REL DISCRIM PEACE ATTIT MORAL ORD/FREE...INT/LAW PSY CONCPT RECORD UN 20. PAGE 24 A0492
INT/ORG PERSON RACE/REL

S64
GINSBURGS G.,"WARS OF NATIONAL LIBERATION - THE SOVIET THESIS." COM USSR WOR+45 WOR-45 LAW CULTURE INT/ORG DIPLOM LEGIT COLONIAL GUERRILLA WAR NAT/LISM ATTIT PERSON MORAL PWR...JURID OBS TREND MARX/KARL 20. PAGE 53 A1075
COERCE CONCPT INT/LAW REV

S64
GREENBERG S.,"JUDAISM AND WORLD JUSTICE." MEDIT-7 WOR+45 LAW CULTURE SOCIETY INT/ORG NAT/G FORCES EDU/PROP ATTIT DRIVE PERSON SUPEGO ALL/VALS ...POLICY PSY CONCPT GEN/LAWS JEWS. PAGE 55 A1140 — SECT JURID PEACE

S64
HICKEY D.,"THE PHILOSOPHICAL ARGUMENT FOR WORLD GOVERNMENT." WOR+45 SOCIETY ACT/RES PLAN LEGIT ADJUD PEACE PERCEPT PERSON ORD/FREE...HUM JURID PHIL/SCI METH/CNCPT CON/ANAL STERTYP GEN/LAWS TOT/POP 20. PAGE 65 A1327 — FUT INT/ORG

S64
KHAN M.Z.,"ISLAM AND INTERNATIONAL RELATIONS." FUT WOR+45 LAW CULTURE SOCIETY NAT/G SECT DELIB/GP FORCES EDU/PROP ATTIT PERSON SUPEGO ALL/VALS ...POLICY PSY CONCPT MYTH HIST/WRIT GEN/LAWS. PAGE 78 A1608 — ISLAM INT/ORG DIPLOM

S64
MCCREARY E.A.,"THOSE AMERICAN MANAGERS DON'T IMPRESS EUROPE." EUR+WWI USA+45 CULTURE STRATA ECO/DEV TOP/EX INT/TRADE ATTIT DRIVE PERSON RIGID/FLEX...CONCPT 20. PAGE 98 A2003 — MARKET ACT/RES BAL/PAY CAP/ISM

S64
PESELT B.M.,"COMMUNIST ECONOMIC OFFENSIVE." WOR+45 SOCIETY INT/ORG PLAN ECO/TAC DOMIN EDU/PROP ATTIT PERSON PWR WEALTH...TREND CHARTS 20. PAGE 115 A2366 — COM ECO/UNDEV FOR/AID USSR

B65
LASKY V.,THE UGLY RUSSIAN. AFR ASIA USSR ECO/UNDEV NAT/LISM TOTALISM PERSON 20. PAGE 85 A1738 — FOR/AID ATTIT DIPLOM

B65
ROSENBERG A.,DEMOCRACY AND SOCIALISM. COM EUR+WWI FRANCE MOD/EUR STRUCT INT/ORG NAT/G POL/PAR TOP/EX EDU/PROP COERCE PERSON PWR FASCISM MARXISM...CONCPT TIME/SEQ MARX/KARL 19/20. PAGE 124 A2535 — ATTIT

S65
MERRITT R.L.,"WOODROW WILSON AND THE 'GREAT AND SOLEMN REFERENDUM,' 1920." USA-45 SOCIETY NAT/G CONSULT LEGIS ACT/RES PLAN DOMIN EDU/PROP ROUTINE ATTIT DISPL DRIVE PERSON RIGID/FLEX MORAL ORD/FREE ...PSY SOC CONCPT MYTH LEAGUE/NAT. PAGE 100 A2044 — INT/ORG TOP/EX DIPLOM

B66
CANFIELD L.H.,THE PRESIDENCY OF WOODROW WILSON: PRELUDE TO A WORLD IN CRISIS. USA-45 ADJUD NEUTRAL WAR CHOOSE INGP/REL PEACE ORD/FREE 20 WILSON/W PRESIDENT TREATY LEAGUE/NAT. PAGE 24 A0477 — PERSON POLICY DIPLOM GOV/REL

B66
DRACHOVITCH M.M.,THE COMINTERN HISTORICAL HIGHLIGHTS. USSR INT/ORG EX/STRUC LEGIT LEAD GUERRILLA...ANTHOL 20 COMINTERN LENIN/VI. PAGE 38 A0784 — DIPLOM REV MARXISM PERSON

B66
POLLACK R.S.,THE INDIVIDUAL'S RIGHTS AND INTERNATIONAL ORGANIZATION. LAW INT/ORG DELIB/GP SUPEGO...JURID SOC/INTEG 20 TREATY UN. PAGE 117 A2394 — INT/LAW ORD/FREE DIPLOM PERSON

B66
SINGER L.,ALLE LITTEN AN GROSSENWAHN: VON WOODROW WILSON BIS MAO TSE-TUNG. ASIA UK USSR INT/ORG DELIB/GP BAL/PWR DOMIN ATTIT PERSON 20 WILSON/W ROOSEVLT/F. PAGE 133 A2731 — DIPLOM TOTALISM WAR CHIEF

B66
SPEARS E.L.,TWO MEN WHO SAVED FRANCE: PETAIN AND DE GAULLE. FRANCE CONSTN FORCES DIPLOM WAR PERSON 20 WWI PETAIN/HP DEGAULLE/C. PAGE 135 A2773 — BIOG LEAD CHIEF NAT/G

C66
KULSKI W.W.,"DEGAULLE AND THE WORLD: THE FOREIGN POLICY OF THE FIFTH FRENCH REPUBLIC." FRANCE ECO/UNDEV POL/PAR BAL/PWR DETER NUC/PWR ATTIT PWR ...RECORD BIBLIOG DEGAULLE NATO EEC. PAGE 83 A1694 — POLICY SOVEREIGN PERSON DIPLOM

B67
KATZ R.,DEATH IN ROME. EUR+WWI ITALY POL/PAR DIPLOM LEAD ATTIT PERSON ROLE CATHISM. PAGE 77 A1570 — WAR MURDER FORCES DEATH

B67
SINGER D.,QUANTITATIVE INTERNATIONAL POLITICS* INSIGHTS AND EVIDENCE. WOR+45 WOR-45 PARTIC WAR INGP/REL ATTIT PERSON ROLE...PREDICT BIBLIOG 19/20 UN SENATE. PAGE 133 A2722 — DIPLOM NAT/G INT/ORG DECISION

B67
WILLIS F.R.,DE GAULLE: ANACHRONISM, REALIST, OR PROPHET? FRANCE POL/PAR FORCES DIPLOM WAR PEACE ROLE ORD/FREE...POLICY IDEA/COMP ANTHOL 20 DEGAULLE/C. PAGE 165 A3356 — BIOG PERSON CHIEF LEAD

L67
GRAUBARD S.R.,"TOWARD THE YEAR 2000: WORK IN PROGRESS." FUT ACADEM SECT DELIB/GP DIPLOM EDU/PROP AGE/Y PERSON ROLE...PSY ANTHOL. PAGE 55 A1131 — PREDICT PROB/SOLV SOCIETY CULTURE

S67
BELGION M.,"THE CASE FOR REHABILITATING MARSHAL PETAIN." EUR+WWI FRANCE NAT/G DIPLOM ATTIT PERSON MORAL PETAIN/HP. PAGE 12 A0253 — WAR FORCES LEAD

S67
GLENN N.D.,"ARE REGIONAL CULTURAL DIFFERENCES DIMINISHING?" USA+45 DIPLOM RACE/REL AGE/Y AGE/A PERSON MORAL...GP/COMP 20. PAGE 53 A1081 — SAMP ATTIT REGION CULTURE

S67
LIVNEH E.,"A NEW BEGINNING." ISRAEL USSR WOR+45 NAT/G DIPLOM INGP/REL FEDERAL HABITAT PWR...GEOG PSY JEWS. PAGE 90 A1847 — WAR PERSON PEACE PLAN

S67
NORTH R.C.,"COMMUNICATION AS AN APPROACH TO POLITICS." UNIV INTELL DIPLOM PERCEPT PERSON ...CONCPT TIME. PAGE 110 A2254 — PERS/REL GP/REL ACT/RES

S67
SUINN R.M.,"THE DISARMAMENT FANTASY* PSYCHOLOGICAL FACTORS THAT MAY PRODUCE WARFARE." DIPLOM RISK ARMS/CONT DETER ANOMIE PERSON GAME. PAGE 140 A2860 — DECISION NUC/PWR WAR PSY

S67
YEFROMEV A.,"THE TRUE FACE OF THE WEST GERMAN NATIONAL-DEMOCRATS." GERMANY/W NAT/G DOMIN LEAD SANCTION WAR ATTIT PERSON...MARXIST 20. PAGE 169 A3433 — POL/PAR TOTALISM PARL/PROC DIPLOM

PERSONAL RELATIONS....SEE PERS/REL

PERSONALITY....SEE PERSON, ALSO PERSONALITY INDEX, P. XIII

PERSONALITY TESTS....SEE PERS/TEST

PERSUASION....SEE LOBBY, EDU/PROP

PERU....SEE ALSO L/A+17C

B60
LEVIN J.V.,THE EXPORT ECONOMIES: THEIR PATTERN OF DEVELOPMENT IN HISTORICAL PERSPECTIVE. BURMA PERU AGRI WORKER COLONIAL COST DEMAND INCOME 20. PAGE 88 A1795 — INT/TRADE ECO/UNDEV BAL/PAY EXTR/IND

PESELT B.M. A2366

PETAIN/HP....H.P. PETAIN

B66
SPEARS E.L.,TWO MEN WHO SAVED FRANCE: PETAIN AND DE GAULLE. FRANCE CONSTN FORCES DIPLOM WAR PERSON 20 WWI PETAIN/HP DEGAULLE/C. PAGE 135 A2773 — BIOG LEAD CHIEF NAT/G

S67
BELGION M.,"THE CASE FOR REHABILITATING MARSHAL PETAIN." EUR+WWI FRANCE NAT/G DIPLOM ATTIT PERSON MORAL PETAIN/HP. PAGE 12 A0253 — WAR FORCES LEAD

PETERS....PETERS V. NEW YORK

PETERSON E.N. A2367

PETERSON H.C. A2368

PETKOFF D.K. A2369

PETTEE G.S. A2370

PEUKERT W. A2371

PFAFF W. A2827,A2828

PHADINIS U. A2372

PHALLE T.D. A0902

PHELPS J. A2373,A2374

PHIL/SCI....SCIENTIFIC METHOD AND PHILOSOPHY OF SCIENCE

N
AMERICAN DOCUMENTATION INST,DOCUMENTATION ABSTRACTS. WOR+45 NAT/G COMPUTER CREATE TEC/DEV DIPLOM EDU/PROP REGION KNOWL...PHIL/SCI CLASSIF LING. PAGE 7 A0143 — BIBLIOG/A AUTOMAT COMPUT/IR R+D

B
DEUTSCHE BIBLIOTH FRANKF A M,DEUTSCHE BIBLIOGRAPHIE. EUR+WWI GERMANY ECO/DEV FORCES DIPLOM LEAD...POLICY PHIL/SCI SOC 20. PAGE 36 A0743 — BIBLIOG LAW ADMIN NAT/G

N
AMERICAN POLITICAL SCIENCE REVIEW. USA+45 USA-45 WOR+45 WOR-45 INT/ORG ADMIN...INT/LAW PHIL/SCI CONCPT METH 20 UN. PAGE 1 A0003 — BIBLIOG/A DIPLOM NAT/G GOV/COMP

N
JOURNAL OF ASIAN STUDIES. CULTURE ECO/DEV SECT DIPLOM EDU/PROP WAR NAT/LISM...PHIL/SCI SOC 20. PAGE 1 A0013 — BIBLIOG ASIA S/ASIA

NAT/G

N
LITERATUR-VERZEICHNIS DER POLITISCHEN WISSENSCHAFTEN. GERMANY/W WOR+45 CONSTN SOCIETY ECO/DEV INT/ORG POL/PAR LEAD REPRESENT GOV/REL GP/REL...POLICY PHIL/SCI. PAGE 1 A0018
BIBLIOG EUR+WWI DIPLOM NAT/G

N
MIDDLE EAST JOURNAL. CULTURE SECT DIPLOM LEAD GOV/REL ATTIT...POLICY PHIL/SCI SOC LING BIOG 20. PAGE 1 A0019
BIBLIOG ISLAM NAT/G ECO/UNDEV

N
NEUE POLITISCHE LITERATUR. AFR ASIA EUR+WWI GERMANY RUSSIA SOCIETY ECO/DEV ECO/UNDEV PLAN PROB/SOLV LEAD MARXISM...PHIL/SCI CONCPT 20. PAGE 1 A0021
BIBLIOG DIPLOM COM NAT/G

N
REVIEW OF POLITICS. WOR+45 WOR-45 CONSTN LEGIS PROB/SOLV ADMIN LEAD ALL/IDEOS...PHIL/SCI 20. PAGE 2 A0024
BIBLIOG/A DIPLOM INT/ORG NAT/G

N
BIBLIOGRAPHIE DER SOZIALWISSENSCHAFTEN. WOR-45 CONSTN SOCIETY ECO/DEV ECO/UNDEV DIPLOM LEAD WAR PEACE...PHIL/SCI SOC 19/20. PAGE 2 A0030
BIBLIOG LAW CONCPT NAT/G

N
THE JAPAN SCIENCE REVIEW: LAW AND POLITICS: LIST OF BOOKS AND ARTICLES ON LAW AND POLITICS. CONSTN AGRI INDUS LABOR DIPLOM TAX ADMIN CRIME...INT/LAW SOC 20 CHINJAP. PAGE 2 A0042
BIBLIOG LAW S/ASIA PHIL/SCI

N
SCHOLARLY BOOKS IN AMERICA; A QUARTERLY BIBLIOGRAPHY OF UNIVERSITY PRESS PUBLICATIONS. WOR+45 AGRI COM/IND NAT/G HEALTH...GEOG PHIL/SCI PSY SOC LING 20. PAGE 3 A0046
BIBLIOG/A LAW MUNIC DIPLOM

N
AMER COUNCIL OF LEARNED SOCIET,THE ACLS CONSTITUENT SOCIETY JOURNAL PROJECT. FUT USA+45 LAW NAT/G PLAN DIPLOM PHIL/SCI. PAGE 7 A0134
BIBLIOG/A HUM COMPUT/IR COMPUTER

N
DEUTSCHE BUCHEREI,DEUTSCHE NATIONALBIBLIOGRAPHIE. GERMANY ECO/DEV DIPLOM AGE/Y ATTIT...PHIL/SCI SOC 20. PAGE 37 A0744
BIBLIOG NAT/G LEAD POLICY

C05
DUNNING W.A.,"HISTORY OF POLITICAL THEORIES FROM LUTHER TO MONTESQUIEU." LAW NAT/G SECT DIPLOM REV WAR ORD/FREE SOVEREIGN CONSERVE...TRADIT BIBLIOG 16/18. PAGE 39 A0803
PHIL/SCI CONCPT GEN/LAWS

B06
FOSTER J.W.,THE PRACTICE OF DIPLOMACY AS ILLUSTRATED IN THE FOREIGN RELATIONS OF THE UNITED STATES. MOD/EUR USA-45 NAT/G EX/STRUC ADMIN ...POLICY INT/LAW BIBLIOG 19/20. PAGE 47 A0970
DIPLOM ROUTINE PHIL/SCI

B21
BALFOUR A.J.,ESSAYS SPECULATIVE AND POLITICAL. SEA CULTURE CREATE WAR NAT/LISM PEACE LOVE...ART/METH INT/LAW CONCPT ANTHOL 20 JEWS. PAGE 10 A0211
PHIL/SCI SOCIETY DIPLOM

L21
HALDEMAN E.,"SERIALS OF AN INTERNATIONAL CHARACTER." WOR-45 DIPLOM...ART/METH GEOG HEAL HUM INT/LAW JURID PSY SOC. PAGE 60 A1224
BIBLIOG PHIL/SCI

B25
GODET M.,INDEX BIBLIOGRAPHICUS: INTERNATIONAL CATALOGUE OF SOURCES OF CURRENT BIBLIOGRAPHIC INFORMATION. EUR+WWI MOD/EUR SOCIETY SECT TAX ...JURID PHIL/SCI SOC MATH. PAGE 53 A1085
BIBLIOG/A DIPLOM EDU/PROP LAW

B26
INTERNATIONAL BIBLIOGRAPHY OF POLITICAL SCIENCE. WOR+45 NAT/G POL/PAR EX/STRUC LEGIS CT/SYS LEAD CHOOSE GOV/REL ATTIT...PHIL/SCI 20. PAGE 3 A0049
BIBLIOG DIPLOM CONCPT ADMIN

B34
EINSTEIN A.,THE WORLD AS I SEE IT. WOR-45 INTELL R+D INT/ORG NAT/G SECT VOL/ASSN FORCES CREATE EDU/PROP LEGIT ARMS/CONT WAR WEAPON NAT/LISM ALL/VALS...POLICY CONCPT 20. PAGE 41 A0828
SOCIETY PHIL/SCI DIPLOM PACIFISM

C39
SCOTT J.B.,"LAW, THESTATE, AND THE INTERNATIONAL COMMUNITY (2 VOLS.)" INTELL INT/ORG NAT/G SECT INT/TRADE WAR...INT/LAW GEN/LAWS BIBLIOG. PAGE 130 A2672
LAW PHIL/SCI DIPLOM CONCPT

B40
THE GUIDE TO CATHOLIC LITERATURE, 1888-1940. ALL/VALS...POLICY MYSTIC HUM PHIL/SCI 19/20. PAGE 3 A0051
BIBLIOG/A CATHISM DIPLOM CULTURE

B41
GRISMER R.,A NEW BIBLIOGRAPHY OF THE LITERATURES OF SPAIN AND SPANISH AMERICA. CHRIST-17C MOD/EUR PRE/AMER SPAIN CULTURE DIPLOM EDU/PROP...ART/METH GEOG HUM PHIL/SCI 20. PAGE 57 A1165
BIBLIOG LAW NAT/G ECO/UNDEV

B45
PERAZA SARAUSA F.,BIBLIOGRAFIAS CUBANAS. CUBA CULTURE ECO/UNDEV AGRI EDU/PROP PRESS CIVMIL/REL ...POLICY GEOG PHIL/SCI BIOG 19/20. PAGE 115 A2353
BIBLIOG/A L/A+17C NAT/G DIPLOM

B45
VANCE H.L.,GUIDE TO THE LAW AND LEGAL LITERATURE OF MEXICO. LAW CONSTN FINAN LABOR FORCES ADJUD ADMIN ...CRIMLGY PHIL/SCI CON/ANAL 20 MEXIC/AMER. PAGE 158 A3217
BIBLIOG/A INT/LAW JURID CT/SYS

B46
BIBLIOGRAFIIA DISSERTATSII: DOKTORSKIE DISSERTATSII ZA 19411944 (2 VOLS.). COM USSR LAW POL/PAR DIPLOM ADMIN LEAD...PHIL/SCI SOC 20. PAGE 3 A0054
BIBLIOG ACADEM KNOWL MARXIST

L46
MASTERS D.,"ONE WORLD OR NONE." FUT WOR+45 INTELL INT/ORG ACT/RES EDU/PROP DETER ATTIT RIGID/FLEX SUPEGO KNOWL...STAT TREND ORG/CHARTS 20. PAGE 96 A1960
POLICY PHIL/SCI ARMS/CONT NUC/PWR

B48
FLOREN LOZANO L.,BIBLIOGRAFIA DE LA BIBLIOGRAFIA DOMINICANA. DOMIN/REP NAT/G DIPLOM EDU/PROP CIVMIL/REL...POLICY ART/METH GEOG PHIL/SCI HIST/WRIT 20. PAGE 47 A0952
BIBLIOG/A BIOG L/A+17C CULTURE

B48
GRIFFITH E.S.,RESEARCH IN POLITICAL SCIENCE: THE WORK OF PANELS OF RESEARCH COMMITTEE, APSA. WOR+45 WOR-45 COM/IND R+D FORCES ACT/RES WAR...GOV/COMP ANTHOL 20. PAGE 56 A1160
BIBLIOG PHIL/SCI DIPLOM JURID

B49
HEADLAM-MORLEY,BIBLIOGRAPHY IN POLITICS FOR THE HONOUR SCHOOL OF PHILOSOPHY, POLITICS AND ECONOMICS (PAMPHLET). UK CONSTN LABOR MUNIC DIPLOM ADMIN 19/20. PAGE 64 A1305
BIBLIOG NAT/G PHIL/SCI GOV/REL

B50
COUNCIL BRITISH NATIONAL BIB,BRITISH NATIONAL BIBLIOGRAPHY. UK AGRI CONSTRUC PERF/ART POL/PAR SECT CREATE INT/TRADE LEAD...HUM JURID PHIL/SCI 20. PAGE 31 A0637
BIBLIOG/A NAT/G TEC/DEV DIPLOM

B53
KANTOR H.,A BIBLIOGRAPHY OF UNPUBLISHED DOCTORAL DISSERTATIONS AND MASTERS' THESES DEALING WITH GOVTS, POL, INT REL OF LAT AM. L/A+17C INT/ORG POL/PAR ACT/RES OP/RES CONFER ATTIT...INT/LAW PHIL/SCI 20. PAGE 76 A1556
BIBLIOG ACADEM DIPLOM NAT/G

B53
LANDHEER B.,FUNDAMENTALS OF PUBLIC INTERNATIONAL LAW (SELECTIVE BIBLIOGRAPHIES OF THE LIBRARY OF THE PEACE PALACE, VOL. I; PAMPH). INT/ORG OP/RES PEACE ...IDEA/COMP 20. PAGE 84 A1715
BIBLIOG/A INT/LAW DIPLOM PHIL/SCI

B53
ROSCIO J.G.,OBRAS. L/A+17C SPAIN DIPLOM REV WAR NAT/LISM TOTALISM PWR SOVEREIGN 19. PAGE 123 A2527
ORD/FREE COLONIAL NAT/G PHIL/SCI

B54
MANNING C.A.W.,THE UNIVERSITY TEACHING OF SOCIAL SCIENCES: INTERNATIONAL RELATIONS. WOR+45 INTELL STRATA R+D ACADEM INT/ORG NAT/G CONSULT DELIB/GP ACT/RES EDU/PROP NAT/LISM ATTIT...POLICY CONT/OBS HYPO/EXP VAL/FREE LEAGUE/NAT UNESCO 20. PAGE 94 A1925
KNOWL PHIL/SCI DIPLOM

B54
SCHIFFER W.,THE LEGAL COMMUNITY OF MANKIND. UNIV WOR+45 WOR-45 SOCIETY NAT/G EDU/PROP LEGIT ATTIT PERSON ORD/FREE PWR...CONCPT HIST/WRIT TREND LEAGUE/NAT UN 20. PAGE 128 A2626
INT/ORG PHIL/SCI

B55
JAPAN MOMBUSHO DAIGAKU GAKIYUT,BIBLIOGRAPHY OF THE STUDIES ON LAW AND POLITICS (PAMPHLET). CONSTN INDUS LABOR DIPLOM TAX ADMIN...CRIMLGY INT/LAW 20 CHINJAP. PAGE 73 A1496
BIBLIOG LAW PHIL/SCI

B55
STEPHENS O.,FACTS TO A CANDID WORLD. USA+45 WOR+45 COM/IND EX/STRUC PRESS ROUTINE EFFICIENCY ATTIT ...PSY 20. PAGE 138 A2817
EDU/PROP PHIL/SCI NAT/G DIPLOM

B55
VIGON J.,TEORIA DEL MILITARISMO. NAT/G DIPLOM COLONIAL COERCE GUERRILLA CIVMIL/REL NAT/LISM MORAL ALL/IDEOS PACIFISM 18/20. PAGE 159 A3234
FORCES PHIL/SCI WAR POLICY

S55
WRIGHT Q.,"THE PEACEFUL ADJUSTMENT OF INTERNATIONAL RELATIONS: PROBLEMS AND RESEARCH APPROACHES." UNIV INTELL EDU/PROP ADJUD ROUTINE KNOWL SKILL...INT/LAW JURID PHIL/SCI CLASSIF 20. PAGE 167 A3411
R+D METH/CNCPT PEACE

S57
KAPLAN M.,"BALANCE OF POWER, BIPOLARITY AND OTHER MODELS OF INTERNATIONAL SYSTEMS" (BMR)" ACT/RES BAL/PWR...PHIL/SCI METH 20. PAGE 76 A1559
DIPLOM GAME METH/CNCPT SIMUL

B58
MACLES L.M.,LES SOURCES DU TRAVAIL BIBLIOGRAPHIQUE (3 VOLS.). FRANCE WOR+45 DIPLOM...GEOG PHIL/SCI SOC 20. PAGE 93 A1897
BIBLIOG/A NAT/G HUM

B58
MASON H.L.,TOYNBEE'S APPROACH TO WORLD POLITICS. AFR USA+45 USSR LAW WAR NAT/LISM ALL/IDEOS...HUM BIBLIOG. PAGE 95 A1957
DIPLOM CONCPT PHIL/SCI SECT

B58
UNESCO,REPERTORIO DE PUBLICACIONES PERIODICAS ACTUALES LATINO AMERICANAS (VOL. VIII). LAW DIPLOM GP/REL...PHIL/SCI SOC 20 UNESCO. PAGE 148 A3021
BIBLIOG/A COM/IND L/A+17C

L58
HYVARINEN R.,"MONISTIC AND PLURALISTIC INTERPRETATIONS IN THE STUDY OF INTERNATIONAL POLITICS." COLONIAL REGION RACE/REL DISCRIM TOTALISM SOVEREIGN...INT/LAW PHIL/SCI CONCPT BIBLIOG 20. PAGE 70 A1429
DIPLOM PLURISM INT/ORG METH

S58
LASSWELL H.D.,"THE SCIENTIFIC STUDY OF INTERNATIONAL RELATIONS." USA+45 INT/ORG CREATE EDU/PROP DETER ATTIT PERCEPT PWR...DECISION CONCPT METH/CNCPT STYLE CON/ANAL 20. PAGE 85 A1740
PHIL/SCI GEN/METH DIPLOM

B59
MODELSKI G.,ATOMIC ENERGY IN THE COMMUNIST BLOC. FUT INT/ORG CONSULT FORCES ACT/RES PLAN KNOWL SKILL ...PHIL/SCI STAT CHARTS 20. PAGE 102 A2096
TEC/DEV NUC/PWR USSR COM

B59
STANFORD RESEARCH INSTITUTE,POSSIBLE NONMILITARY SCIENTIFIC DEVELOPMENTS AND THEIR POTENTIAL IMPACT ON FOREIGN POLICY PROBLEMS OF THE UNITED. FUT USA+45 INT/ORG PROF/ORG CONSULT ACT/RES CREATE PLAN PEACE KNOWL SKILL...TECHNIC PHIL/SCI NEW/IDEA UNESCO 20. PAGE 137 A2802
R+D TEC/DEV

B60
EINSTEIN A.,EINSTEIN ON PEACE. FUT WOR+45 WOR-45 SOCIETY NAT/G PLAN BAL/PWR CAP/ISM DIPLOM ARMS/CONT DETER NAT/LISM...POLICY RELATIV HUM PHIL/SCI CONCPT BIOG COLD/WAR LEAGUE/NAT NAZI. PAGE 41 A0829
INT/ORG ATTIT NUC/PWR PEACE

B60
HOFFMANN S.H.,CONTEMPORARY THEORY IN INTERNATIONAL RELATIONS. RATIONAL...SOC METH/CNCPT METH/COMP SIMUL ANTHOL 20. PAGE 66 A1359
DIPLOM METH PHIL/SCI DECISION

B60
MEYRIAT J.,LA SCIENCE POLITIQUE EN FRANCE, 1945-1958; BIBLIOGRAPHIES FRANCAISES DE SCIENCES SOCIALES (VOL. I). EUR+WWI FRANCE POL/PAR DIPLOM ADMIN CHOOSE ATTIT...IDEA/COMP METH/COMP NAT/COMP 20. PAGE 100 A2057
BIBLIOG/A NAT/G CONCPT PHIL/SCI

B60
UNITED WORLD FEDERALISTS,UNITED WORLD FEDERALISTS; PANORAMA OF RECENT BOOKS, FILMS, AND JOURNALS ON WORLD FEDERATION, THE UN, AND WORLD PEACE. CULTURE ECO/UNDEV PROB/SOLV FOR/AID ARMS/CONT NUC/PWR ...INT/LAW PHIL/SCI 20 UN. PAGE 149 A3039
BIBLIOG/A DIPLOM INT/ORG PEACE

L60
DEUTSCH K.W.,"TOWARD AN INVENTORY OF BASIC TRENDS AND PATTERNS IN COMPARATIVE AND INTERNATIONAL POLITICS." UNIV WOR+45 SOCIETY STRUCT INT/ORG NAT/G CREATE PLAN EDU/PROP KNOWL...PHIL/SCI METH/CNCPT STAT SELF/OBS OBS/ENVIR SAMP TREND CON/ANAL CHARTS SOC/EXP GEN/METH 20. PAGE 36 A0739
R+D PERCEPT

L60
HOLTON G.,"ARMS CONTROL." FUT WOR+45 CULTURE INT/ORG NAT/G FORCES TOP/EX PLAN EDU/PROP COERCE ATTIT RIGID/FLEX ORD/FREE...POLICY PHIL/SCI SOC TREND COLD/WAR. PAGE 67 A1377
ACT/RES CONSULT ARMS/CONT NUC/PWR

L60
MCCLELLAND C.A.,"THE FUNCTION OF THEORY IN INTERNATIONAL RELATIONS." WOR+45 PLAN EDU/PROP ROUTINE ORD/FREE...PHIL/SCI PSY SOC METH/CNCPT NEW/IDEA OBS TREND GEN/METH 20. PAGE 97 A1997
INT/ORG CONCPT DIPLOM

B61
WARD R.E.,JAPANESE POLITICAL SCIENCE: A GUIDE TO JAPANESE REFERENCE AND RESEARCH MATERIALS (2ND ED.). LAW CONSTN STRATA NAT/G POL/PAR DELIB/GP LEGIS ADMIN CHOOSE GP/REL...INT/LAW 19/20 CHINJAP. PAGE 161 A3282
BIBLIOG/A PHIL/SCI

B61
ZIMMERMAN I.,A GUIDE TO CURRENT LATIN AMERICAN PERIODICALS: HUMANITIES AND SOCIAL SCIENCES. LABOR SECT EDU/PROP...GEOG HUM SOC LING STAT NAT/COMP 20. PAGE 170 A3452
BIBLIOG/A DIPLOM L/A+17C PHIL/SCI

B62
COLLISON R.L.,BIBLIOGRAPHIES, SUBJECT AND NATIONAL: A GUIDE TO THEIR CONTENTS, ARRANGEMENT, AND USE (2ND REV. ED.). SECT DIPLOM...ART/METH GEOG HUM PHIL/SCI SOC MATH BIOG 20. PAGE 28 A0569
BIBLIOG/A CON/ANAL BIBLIOG

B62
GILPIN R.,AMERICAN SCIENTISTS AND NUCLEAR WEAPONS POLICY. COM FUT USA+45 WOR+45 INT/ORG NAT/G PROF/ORG CONSULT FORCES CREATE TEC/DEV BAL/PWR EDU/PROP ARMS/CONT WAR PERCEPT KNOWL MORAL PWR ...PHIL/SCI SOC CONCPT GEN/LAWS 20. PAGE 52 A1073
INTELL ATTIT DETER NUC/PWR

B62
OSGOOD C.E.,AN ALTERNATIVE TO WAR OR SURRENDER. FUT UNIV CULTURE INTELL SOCIETY R+D INT/ORG CONSULT DELIB/GP ACT/RES PLAN CHOOSE ATTIT PERCEPT KNOWL ...PHIL/SCI PSY SOC TREND GEN/LAWS 20. PAGE 112 A2300
ORD/FREE EDU/PROP PEACE WAR

B62
SCHWARTZ L.E.,INTERNATIONAL ORGANIZATIONS AND SPACE COOPERATION. VOL/ASSN CONSULT CREATE TEC/DEV SANCTION...POLICY INT/LAW PHIL/SCI 20 UN. PAGE 130 A2656
INT/ORG DIPLOM R+D SPACE

B62
THOMSON G.P.,NUCLEAR ENERGY IN BRITAIN DURING THE LAST WAR: THE CHERWELL SIMON LECTURE (MONOGRAPH). UK R+D CONSULT FORCES PLAN DIPLOM TASK CIVMIL/REL ROLE...PHIL/SCI NEW/IDEA LAB/EXP 20 MAUD. PAGE 143 A2934
CREATE TEC/DEV WAR NUC/PWR

B62
UNESCO,GENERAL CATALOGUE OF UNESCO PUBLICATIONS AND UNESCO SPONSORED PUBLICATIONS, 1946-1959. WOR+45 ...POLICY ART/METH HUM PHIL/SCI UN. PAGE 148 A3022
BIBLIOG INT/ORG ECO/UNDEV SOC

S62
MORGENTHAU H.J.,"A POLITICAL THEORY OF FOREIGN AID." ECO/UNDEV NAT/G DELIB/GP PLAN ECO/TAC EDU/PROP EXEC ORD/FREE RESPECT WEALTH...METH/CNCPT TREND 20. PAGE 104 A2140
USA+45 PHIL/SCI FOR/AID

B63
OECD,SCIENCE AND THE POLICIES OF GOVERNMENTS: THE IMPLICATIONS OF SCIENCE AND TECHNOLOGY FOR NATL AND INTL AFFAIRS. WOR+45 INT/ORG EDU/PROP AUTOMAT ...POLICY PHIL/SCI 20. PAGE 111 A2279
CREATE TEC/DEV DIPLOM NAT/G

B64
GOWING M.,BRITAIN AND ATOMIC ENERGY 1939-1945. FRANCE UK USA+45 USA-45 NAT/G CREATE...PHIL/SCI 20 AEA. PAGE 54 A1118
NUC/PWR DIPLOM TEC/DEV

B64
NICE R.W.,TREASURY OF LAW. WOR+45 WOR-45 SECT ADJUD MORAL ORD/FREE...INT/LAW JURID PHIL/SCI ANTHOL. PAGE 108 A2227
LAW WRITING PERS/REL DIPLOM

B64
SPECTOR S.D.,A CHECKLIST OF PAPERBOUND BOOKS ON RUSSIA. USSR SECT DIPLOM EDU/PROP HEALTH...PHIL/SCI PSY SOC SOC/WK WORSHIP 20. PAGE 135 A2775
BIBLIOG COM PERF/ART

S64
HICKEY D.,"THE PHILOSOPHICAL ARGUMENT FOR WORLD GOVERNMENT." WOR+45 SOCIETY ACT/RES PLAN LEGIT ADJUD PEACE PERCEPT PERSON ORD/FREE...HUM JURID PHIL/SCI METH/CNCPT CON/ANAL STERTYP GEN/LAWS TOT/POP 20. PAGE 65 A1327
FUT INT/ORG

B65
HALLE L.J.,THE SOCIETY OF MAN. WOR+45 WOR-45 EDU/PROP NAT/LISM MARXISM CONCPT. PAGE 60 A1231
DIPLOM PHIL/SCI CREATE SOCIETY

B65
INTERNATIONAL SOCIAL SCI COUN,SOCIAL SCIENCES IN THE USSR. USSR ECO/DEV AGRI FINAN INDUS PLAN CAP/ISM...INT/LAW PHIL/SCI PSY SOC 20. PAGE 71 A1460
BIBLIOG/A ACT/RES MARXISM JURID

B65
PENNICK JL J.R.,THE POLITICS OF AMERICAN SCIENCE, 1939 TO THE PRESENT. USA+45 USA-45 INTELL TEC/DEV DIPLOM NEW/LIB...ANTHOL 20 COLD/WAR. PAGE 114 A2349
POLICY ADMIN PHIL/SCI NAT/G

B65
UNIVERSAL REFERENCE SYSTEM,INTERNATIONAL AFFAIRS: VOLUME I IN THE POLITICAL SCIENCE, GOVERNMENT, AND PUBLIC POLICY SERIES....DECISION ECOMETRIC GEOG INT/LAW JURID MGT PHIL/SCI PSY SOC. PAGE 149 A3041
BIBLIOG/A GEN/METH COMPUT/IR DIPLOM

B65
WEISNER J.B.,WHERE SCIENCE AND POLITICS MEET. USA+45 ECO/DEV R+D FORCES PROB/SOLV DIPLOM FOR/AID CONTROL...PHIL/SCI PRESIDENT KENNEDY/JF JOHNSON/LB. PAGE 163 A3310
CHIEF NAT/G POLICY TEC/DEV

B66
OLSON W.C.,THE THEORY AND PRACTICE OF INTERNATIONAL RELATIONS (2ND ED.). WOR+45 LEAD SUPEGO...INT/LAW PHIL/SCI. PAGE 112 A2290
DIPLOM NAT/G INT/ORG POLICY

B67
UNESCO,PRINCIPLES AND PROBLEMS OF NATIONAL SCIENCE POLICIES. WOR+45 ECO/DEV ECO/UNDEV R+D INT/ORG PROB/SOLV CONFER...PHIL/SCI CHARTS 20 UNESCO UN. PAGE 148 A3026
NAT/COMP POLICY TEC/DEV CREATE

B67
US SUPERINTENDENT OF DOCUMENTS,LIBRARY OF CONGRESS (PRICE LIST 83). AFR ASIA EUR+WWI USA-45 USSR NAT/G DIPLOM CONFER CT/SYS WAR...DECISION PHIL/SCI CLASSIF 19/20 CONGRESS PRESIDENT. PAGE 157 A3205
BIBLIOG/A USA+45 AUTOMAT LAW

B82
POOLE W.F.,INDEX TO PERIODICAL LITERATURE. LOC/G NAT/G DIPLOM ADMIN...HUM PHIL/SCI SOC 19. PAGE 117 A2396
BIBLIOG USA-45 ALL/VALS SOCIETY

PHILADELPH....PHILADELPHIA, PENNSYLVANIA

PHILANTHROPY....SEE GIVE+WEALTH

PHILIP/J....JOHN PHILIP

PHILIPPINE STUDIES PROGRAM A2375

PHILIPPINE....PHILIPPINES; SEE ALSO S/ASIA

C51
GRUNDER G.A.,"THE PHILIPPINES AND THE UNITED STATES." PHILIPPINE S/ASIA USA-45 NAT/G POL/PAR ADMIN SOVEREIGN...TIME/SEQ BIBLIOG 20. PAGE 57 A1181
COLONIAL POLICY DIPLOM ECO/TAC

B52
US MUTUAL SECURITY AGENCY,U. S. TECHNICAL AND ECONOMIC ASSISTANCE IN THE FAR EAST (PAMPHLET). ASIA BURMA INDONESIA PHILIPPINE TAIWAN THAILAND USA+45 AGRI INDUS PLAN EDU/PROP ADMIN HEALTH. PAGE 155 A3161
FOR/AID TEC/DEV ECO/UNDEV BUDGET

B56
PHILIPPINE STUDIES PROGRAM,SELECTED BIBLIOGRAPHY ON THE PHILIPPINES, TOPICALLY ARRANGED AND ANNOTATED. PHILIPPINE SECT DIPLOM COLONIAL LEAD...SOC 18/20. PAGE 116 A2375
BIBLIOG/A S/ASIA NAT/G ECO/UNDEV

B58
US HOUSE COMM GOVT OPERATIONS,HEARINGS BEFORE A SUBCOMMITTEE OF THE COMMITTEE ON GOVERNMENT OPERATIONS. CAMBODIA PHILIPPINE USA+45 CONSTRUC TEC/DEV ADMIN CONTROL WEAPON EFFICIENCY HOUSE/REP. PAGE 154 A3135
FOR/AID DIPLOM ORD/FREE ECO/UNDEV

L59
WURFEL D.,"FOREIGN AID AND SOCIAL REFORM IN POLITICAL DEVELOPMENT" (BMR)" PHILIPPINE USA+45 WOR+45 SOCIETY POL/PAR ACT/RES TEC/DEV DIPLOM 20. PAGE 168 A3424
FOR/AID PROB/SOLV ECO/TAC ECO/UNDEV

B60
WOLF C.,FOREIGN AID: THEORY AND PRACTICE IN SOUTHERN ASIA. CEYLON INDONESIA PHILIPPINE S/ASIA CULTURE STRATA ECO/UNDEV PLAN EDU/PROP ATTIT ...METH/CNCPT MATH QUANT STAT CONT/OBS TIME/SEQ SIMUL TOT/POP 20. PAGE 166 A3378
ACT/RES ECO/TAC FOR/AID

B66
AMERICAN ASSEMBLY COLUMBIA U,THE UNITED STATES AND THE PHILIPPINES. PHILIPPINE S/ASIA USA+45 USA-45 SOCIETY FORCES INT/TRADE...POLICY 20. PAGE 7 A0138
COLONIAL DIPLOM NAT/LISM

B66
FARWELL G.,MASK OF ASIA: THE PHILIPPINES. PHILIPPINE SECT DIPLOM ATTIT...SOC RECORD PREDICT BIBLIOG 20. PAGE 44 A0901
S/ASIA CULTURE

B66
GRENVILLE J.A.S.,POLITICS, STRATEGY, AND AMERICAN DEMOCRACY: STUDIES IN FOREIGN POLICY, 1873-1917. CUBA PHILIPPINE SPAIN USA-45 VENEZUELA ELITES NAT/G CREATE PARTIC WAR RIGID/FLEX ORD/FREE...DECISION TREND 19/20 HAWAII. PAGE 56 A1146
DIPLOM COLONIAL POLICY

PHILLIP/IV....PHILLIP IV OF SPAIN

PHILLIPS J.F.V. A2376

PHILLIPS P.L. A1158

PHILLIPS/F....F. PHILLIPS - POLICE CHIEF, N.Y.C.

PHILLIPSON C. A2377

PHILOSOPHR....PHILOSOPHER

PHILOSOPHY....SEE GEN/LAWS. PHILOSOPHY OF SCIENCE....SEE PHIL/SCI

PHILOSOPHY OF SCIENCE....SEE PHIL/SCI

PHOTOGRAPHS....SEE AUD/VIS

PHS....PUBLIC HEALTH SERVICE

PIERCE/F....PRESIDENT FRANKLIN PIERCE

PIGOU/AC....ARTHUR CECIL PIGOU

PIKE F.B. A2378,A2379

PINCUS J. A2380

PINCUS/J....JOHN PINCUS

PIPER D.C. A2381

PIQUEMAL M. A2382,A2383

PIQUET H.S. A2384

PITTMAN J. A2385

PITTMAN M. A2385

PITTSBURGH....PITTSBURGH, PENNSYLVANIA

PLAMENATZ J. A2386

PLAN....PLANNING

N
INTERNATIONAL REVIEW OF ADMINISTRATIVE SCIENCES. WOR+45 WOR-45 STRATA ECO/DEV ECO/UNDEV CREATE PLAN PROB/SOLV DIPLOM CONTROL REPRESENT...MGT 20. PAGE 1 A0011
BIBLIOG/A ADMIN INT/ORG NAT/G

N
NEUE POLITISCHE LITERATUR. AFR ASIA EUR+WWI GERMANY RUSSIA SOCIETY ECO/DEV ECO/UNDEV PLAN PROB/SOLV LEAD MARXISM...PHIL/SCI CONCPT 20. PAGE 1 A0021
BIBLIOG DIPLOM COM NAT/G

N
INDIA: A REFERENCE ANNUAL. INDIA CULTURE COM/IND R+D FORCES PLAN RECEIVE EDU/PROP HEALTH...STAT CHARTS BIBLIOG 20. PAGE 2 A0036
CONSTN LABOR INT/ORG

N
AMER COUNCIL OF LEARNED SOCIET,THE ACLS CONSTITUENT SOCIETY JOURNAL PROJECT. FUT USA+45 LAW NAT/G PLAN DIPLOM PHIL/SCI. PAGE 7 A0134
BIBLIOG/A HUM COMPUT/IR COMPUTER

N
FOREIGN TRADE LIBRARY,NEW TITLES RECEIVED IN THE LIBRARY. WOR+45 ECO/UNDEV FINAN NAT/G PLAN TEC/DEV BUDGET ECO/TAC TARIFFS GOV/REL STAT. PAGE 47 A0964
BIBLIOG/A INT/TRADE INDUS ECO/DEV

N
US CONSOLATE GENERAL HONG KONG,REVIEW OF THE HONG KONG CHINESE PRESS. ECO/UNDEV LOC/G NAT/G PLAN DIPLOM EDU/PROP LEAD GP/REL MARXISM...POLICY INDEX 20. PAGE 150 A3073
BIBLIOG/A ASIA PRESS ATTIT

N
US CONSULATE GENERAL HONG KONG,CURRENT BACKGROUND. CHINA/COM ECO/UNDEV LOC/G NAT/G PLAN DIPLOM EDU/PROP LEAD REV ATTIT...POLICY INDEX 20. PAGE 151 A3074
BIBLIOG/A MARXIST ASIA PRESS

N
US CONSULATE GENERAL HONG KONG,SURVEY OF CHINA MAINLAND PRESS. CHINA/COM ECO/UNDEV LOC/G NAT/G PLAN DIPLOM EDU/PROP LEAD REV ATTIT...POLICY INDEX 20. PAGE 151 A3075
BIBLIOG/A MARXIST ASIA PRESS

N
US CONSULATE GENERAL HONG KONG,US CONSULATE GENERAL, HONG KONG, PRESS SUMMARIES. CHINA/COM ECO/UNDEV LOC/G NAT/G PLAN DIPLOM EDU/PROP LEAD REV ATTIT...POLICY INDEX 20. PAGE 151 A3076
BIBLIOG/A MARXIST ASIA PRESS

N
US LIBRARY OF CONGRESS,ACCESSIONS LIST - INDIA. INDIA CULTURE AGRI LOC/G POL/PAR PLAN PROB/SOLV TEC/DEV DIPLOM EDU/PROP LEAD GP/REL ATTIT 20. PAGE 154 A3142
BIBLIOG S/ASIA ECO/UNDEV NAT/G

N
US LIBRARY OF CONGRESS,ACCESSIONS LIST -- ISRAEL. ISRAEL CULTURE ECO/UNDEV POL/PAR PLAN PROB/SOLV TEC/DEV DIPLOM EDU/PROP LEAD WAR ATTIT 20 JEWS. PAGE 154 A3143
BIBLIOG ISLAM NAT/G GP/REL

NCO
CARRINGTON C.E.,THE COMMONWEALTH IN AFRICA (PAMPHLET). UK STRUCT NAT/G COLONIAL REPRESENT GOV/REL RACE/REL NAT/LISM...MAJORIT 20 EEC NEGRO COLD/WAR. PAGE 25 A0500
ECO/UNDEV AFR DIPLOM PLAN

B00
MORRIS H.C.,THE HISTORY OF COLONIZATION. WOR+45 WOR-45 ECO/DEV ECO/UNDEV INT/ORG ACT/RES PLAN ECO/TAC LEGIT ROUTINE COERCE ATTIT DRIVE ALL/VALS ...GEOG TREND 19. PAGE 105 A2148
DOMIN SOVEREIGN COLONIAL

B00
VOLPICELLI Z.,RUSSIA ON THE PACIFIC AND THE SIBERIAN RAILWAY. MOD/EUR ECO/UNDEV INT/ORG FORCES PLAN DOMIN COLONIAL ROUTINE ATTIT ALL/VALS...OBS HIST/WRIT TIME/SEQ TREND CON/ANAL AUD/VIS CHARTS 18/19. PAGE 159 A3248
NAT/G ACT/RES RUSSIA

B02
SEELEY J.R.,THE EXPANSION OF ENGLAND. MOD/EUR S/ASIA UK CULTURE NAT/G FORCES PLAN DOMIN EDU/PROP COLONIAL ROUTINE ATTIT ALL/VALS SOVEREIGN...CONCPT HIST/WRIT PARLIAMENT 18 CMN/WLTH. PAGE 131 A2679
INT/ORG ACT/RES CAP/ISM INDIA

B16
ROOT E.,THE MILITARY AND COLONIAL POLICY OF THE US. L/A+17C USA-45 LAW SOCIETY STRATA STRUCT INT/ORG NAT/G SCHOOL FORCES EDU/PROP ALL/VALS...OBS VAL/FREE 19/20. PAGE 123 A2522
ACT/RES PLAN DIPLOM WAR

S17
ROOT E.,"THE EFFECT OF DEMOCRACY ON INTERNATIONAL LAW." USA-45 WOR-45 INTELL SOCIETY INT/ORG NAT/G CONSULT ACT/RES CREATE PLAN EDU/PROP PEACE SKILL ...CONCPT METH/CNCPT OBS 20. PAGE 123 A2523
LEGIS JURID INT/LAW

B19
MEYER H.H.B.,SELECT LIST OF REFERENCES ON ECONOMIC RECONSTRUCTION: INCLUDING REPORTS OF THE BRITISH
BIBLIOG/A EUR+WWI

MINISTRY OF RECONSTRUCTION. UK LABOR PLAN PROB/SOLV ECO/TAC INT/TRADE WAR DEMAND PRODUC 20. PAGE 100 A2051
ECO/DEV WORKER

B19
ROUSSEAU J.J.,A LASTING PEACE. INT/ORG NAT/G CHIEF DIPLOM DETER WAR POLICY. PAGE 124 A2550
PLAN PEACE UTIL

B19
SUTHERLAND G.,CONSTITUTIONAL POWER AND WORLD AFFAIRS. CONSTN STRUCT INT/ORG NAT/G CHIEF LEGIS ACT/RES PLAN GOV/REL ALL/VALS...OBS TIME/SEQ CONGRESS VAL/FREE 20 PRESIDENT. PAGE 140 A2866
USA-45 EXEC DIPLOM

N19
ASIAN-AFRICAN CONFERENCE,SELECTED DOCUMENTS OF THE BANDUNG CONFERENCE (PAMPHLET). S/ASIA PLAN ECO/TAC CONFER REGION REV NAT/LISM 20. PAGE 9 A0191
NEUTRAL ECO/UNDEV COLONIAL DIPLOM

N19
FRANCK P.G.,AFGHANISTAN BETWEEN EAST AND WEST: THE ECONOMICS OF COMPETITIVE COEXISTENCE (PAMPHLET). AFGHANISTN USA+45 USA-45 USSR INDUS ECO/TAC INT/TRADE CONTROL NEUTRAL ORD/FREE MARXISM...GEOG 20 UN. PAGE 48 A0977
FOR/AID PLAN DIPLOM ECO/UNDEV

N19
HAJDA J.,THE COLD WAR VIEWED AS A SOCIOLOGICAL PROBLEM (PAMPHLET). COM CZECHOSLVK EUR+WWI SOCIETY PLAN EDU/PROP CONTROL TASK ATTIT MARXISM...POLICY 20 COLD/WAR MIGRATION. PAGE 59 A1220
DIPLOM LEAD PWR NAT/G

N19
HAUSER P.M.,WORLD POPULATION PROBLEMS (PAMPHLET). USA+45 WOR+45 ECO/DEV ECO/UNDEV FAM ACT/RES PLAN PROB/SOLV FOR/AID GIVE EATING...CHARTS 20 BIRTH/CON RESOURCE/N. PAGE 63 A1289
CONTROL CENSUS ATTIT PREDICT

N19
LANGE O.R.,"DISARMAMENT ECONOMIC GROWTH AND INTERNATIONAL CO-OPERATION" (PAMPHLET). WOR+45 DIST/IND PLAN INT/TRADE GIVE TASK DETER WEALTH SOCISM 18/19 BOLIVAR/S. PAGE 84 A1723
ARMS/CONT DIPLOM ECO/DEV ECO/UNDEV

N19
MARCUS W.,US PRIVATE INVESTMENT AND ECONOMIC AID IN UNDERDEVELOPED COUNTRIES (PAMPHLET). USA+45 LG/CO NAT/G CAP/ISM EDU/PROP 20. PAGE 94 A1937
FOR/AID ECO/UNDEV FINAN PLAN

N19
MEZERIK A.G.,U-2 AND OPEN SKIES (PAMPHLET). USA+45 USSR INT/ORG CHIEF FORCES PLAN EDU/PROP CONTROL SANCTION ARMS/CONT 20 UN EISNHWR/DD. PAGE 100 A2060
DIPLOM RISK DEBATE

N19
MORGENSTERN O.,THE COMMAND AND CONTROL STRUCTURE (PAMPHLET). USSR COM/IND INT/ORG WEAPON PEACE UTIL ...TREND 20 NATO. PAGE 104 A2132
CONTROL FORCES EFFICIENCY PLAN

N19
NATIONAL ACADEMY OF SCIENCES,THE GROWTH OF WORLD POPULATION: ANALYSIS OF THE PROBLEMS AND RECOMMENDATIONS FOR RESEARCH AND TRAINING (PAMPHLET). WOR+45 CULTURE ECO/UNDEV EDU/PROP MARRIAGE AGE HEALTH...ANTHOL 20 BIRTH/CON. PAGE 107 A2199
CENSUS PLAN FAM INT/ORG

N19
STEUBER F.A.,THE CONTRIBUTION OF SWITZERLAND TO THE ECONOMIC AND SOCIAL DEVELOPMENT OF LOW-INCOME COUNTRIES (PAMPHLET). SWITZERLND FINAN NAT/G VOL/ASSN INT/TRADE DRIVE...CHARTS 20. PAGE 138 A2820
FOR/AID ECO/UNDEV PLAN DIPLOM

B20
HALDANE R.B.,BEFORE THE WAR. MOD/EUR SOCIETY INT/ORG NAT/G DELIB/GP PLAN DOMIN EDU/PROP LEGIT ADMIN COERCE ATTIT DRIVE MORAL ORD/FREE PWR...SOC CONCPT SELF/OBS RECORD BIOG TIME/SEQ. PAGE 60 A1223
POLICY DIPLOM UK

B20
WOOLF L.,EMPIRE AND COMMERCE IN AFRICA. EUR+WWI MOD/EUR FINAN INDUS MARKET INT/ORG PLAN COERCE ATTIT DRIVE PWR WEALTH...CONCPT TIME/SEQ TREND CHARTS 20. PAGE 167 A3394
AFR DOMIN COLONIAL SOVEREIGN

B21
STUART G.H.,FRENCH FOREIGN POLICY. CONSTN INT/ORG NAT/G POL/PAR EX/STRUC FORCES PLAN ECO/TAC DOMIN EDU/PROP ADJUD COERCE ATTIT DRIVE RIGID/FLEX ALL/VALS...POLICY OBS RECORD BIOG TIME/SEQ TREND. PAGE 139 A2852
MOD/EUR DIPLOM FRANCE

B24
POOLE D.C.,THE CONDUCT OF FOREIGN RELATIONS UNDER MODERN DEMOCRATIC CONDITIONS. EUR+WWI USA-45 INT/ORG PLAN LEGIT ADMIN KNOWL PWR...MAJORIT OBS/ENVIR HIST/WRIT GEN/LAWS 20. PAGE 117 A2395
NAT/G EDU/PROP DIPLOM

B28
CORBETT P.E.,CANADA AND WORLD POLITICS. LAW CULTURE SOCIETY STRUCT MARKET INT/ORG FORCES ACT/RES PLAN ECO/TAC LEGIT ORD/FREE PWR RESPECT...SOC CONCPT TIME/SEQ TREND CMN/WLTH 20 LEAGUE/NAT. PAGE 30 A0612
NAT/G CANADA

B28
HALL W.P.,EMPIRE TO COMMONWEALTH. FUT WOR-45 CONSTN ECO/DEV ECO/UNDEV INT/ORG PROVS PLAN DIPLOM EDU/PROP ADMIN COLONIAL PEACE PERSON ALL/VALS ...POLICY GEOG SOC OBS RECORD TREND CMN/WLTH PARLIAMENT 19/20. PAGE 60 A1229
VOL/ASSN NAT/G UK

B28
MILLER D.H.,THE DRAFTING OF THE COVENANT. UNIV WOR-45 INTELL NAT/G DELIB/GP PLAN ECO/TAC LEGIT WAR ATTIT PERCEPT...CONCPT TIME/SEQ LEAGUE/NAT TOT/POP 20. PAGE 101 A2074
INT/ORG STRUCT PEACE

B28
STUART G.H.,LATIN AMERICA AND THE UNITED STATES. USA-45 ECO/UNDEV INT/ORG NAT/G POL/PAR PLAN DOMIN EDU/PROP COLONIAL REGION COERCE ATTIT ALL/VALS ...POLICY GEOG TREND 19/20. PAGE 139 A2853
L/A+17C DIPLOM

B29
STURZO L.,THE INTERNATIONAL COMMUNITY AND THE RIGHT OF WAR (TRANS. BY BARBARA BARCLAY CARTER). CULTURE CREATE PROB/SOLV DIPLOM ADJUD CONTROL PEACE PERSON ORD/FREE...INT/LAW IDEA/COMP PACIFIST 20 LEAGUE/NAT. PAGE 140 A2858
INT/ORG PLAN WAR CONCPT

B30
SCHMITT B.E.,THE COMING OF THE WAR, 1914 (2 VOLS.). AUSTRIA FRANCE GERMANY MOD/EUR RUSSIA UK PLAN ROUTINE ORD/FREE. PAGE 128 A2633
WAR DIPLOM

B31
BEALES A.C.,THE HISTORY OF PEACE. WOR-45 VOL/ASSN DELIB/GP CREATE PLAN EDU/PROP ATTIT MORAL ...TIME/SEQ VAL/FREE 19/20. PAGE 12 A0239
INT/ORG ARMS/CONT PEACE

B31
STOWELL E.C.,INTERNATIONAL LAW. FUT UNIV WOR-45 SOCIETY CONSULT EX/STRUC FORCES ACT/RES PLAN DIPLOM EDU/PROP LEGIT DISPL PWR SKILL...POLICY CONCPT OBS TREND TOT/POP 20. PAGE 139 A2839
INT/ORG ROUTINE INT/LAW

B31
STUART G.H.,THE INTERNATIONAL CITY OF TANGIER. AFR EUR+WWI MOD/EUR MOROCCO CONSTN PROVS CREATE PLAN LEGIT PEACE ORD/FREE PWR...INT/LAW OBS TIME/SEQ CON/ANAL 20 TANGIER. PAGE 139 A2854
LOC/G INT/ORG DIPLOM SOVEREIGN

B32
EAGLETON C.,INTERNATIONAL GOVERNMENT. BRAZIL FRANCE GERMANY ITALY UK USSR WOR-45 DELIB/GP TOP/EX PLAN ECO/TAC EDU/PROP LEGIT ADJUD REGION ARMS/CONT COERCE ATTIT PWR...GEOG MGT VAL/FREE LEAGUE/NAT 20. PAGE 40 A0816
INT/ORG JURID DIPLOM INT/LAW

B32
MORLEY F.,THE SOCIETY OF NATIONS. EUR+WWI UNIV WOR-45 LAW CONSTN ACT/RES PLAN EDU/PROP LEGIT ROUTINE...POLICY TIME/SEQ LEAGUE/NAT TOT/POP 20. PAGE 104 A2143
INT/ORG CONCPT

B32
WRIGHT Q.,GOLD AND MONETARY STABILIZATION. FUT USA+45 WOR-45 INTELL ECO/DEV INT/ORG NAT/G CONSULT PLAN ECO/TAC ADMIN ATTIT WEALTH...CONCPT TREND 20. PAGE 167 A3404
FINAN POLICY

B33
OHLIN B.,INTERREGIONAL AND INTERNATIONAL TRADE. USA-45 WOR-45 CULTURE FINAN MARKET CONSULT PLAN ECO/TAC ATTIT WEALTH...CONCPT MATH TOT/POP 20. PAGE 111 A2285
INT/ORG ECO/DEV INT/TRADE REGION

B34
GRAHAM F.D.,PROTECTIVE TARIFFS. FUT USA+45 WOR-45 INDUS MARKET VOL/ASSN PLAN CAP/ISM ECO/TAC PEACE ATTIT DRIVE HEALTH ORD/FREE...OBS TREND GEN/LAWS 20. PAGE 55 A1124
INT/ORG TARIFFS

B36
ROBINSON H.,DEVELOPMENT OF THE BRITISH EMPIRE. WOR-45 CULTURE SOCIETY STRUCT ECO/DEV ECO/UNDEV INT/ORG VOL/ASSN FORCES CREATE PLAN DOMIN EDU/PROP ADMIN COLONIAL PWR WEALTH...POLICY GEOG CHARTS CMN/WLTH 16/20. PAGE 122 A2503
NAT/G HIST/WRIT UK

B36
SHOTWELL J.,ON THE RIM OF THE ABYSS. EUR+WWI USA-45 STRUCT INT/ORG ACT/RES PLAN EDU/PROP EXEC ATTIT ALL/VALS...TIME/SEQ LEAGUE/NAT TOT/POP 20. PAGE 132 A2706
NAT/G BAL/PWR

B37
BOURNE H.E.,THE WORLD WAR: A LIST OF THE MORE IMPORTANT BOOKS PUBLISHED BEFORE 1937 (PAMPHLET). EUR+WWI NAT/G DIPLOM ATTIT SOC. PAGE 17 A0351
BIBLIOG/A WAR FORCES PLAN

B37
GALLOWAY G.B.,AMERICAN PAMPHLET LITERATURE OF PUBLIC AFFAIRS (PAMPHLET). USA-45 ECO/DEV LABOR ADMIN...MGT 20. PAGE 51 A1034
BIBLIOG/A PLAN DIPLOM NAT/G

B37
ROBBINS L.,ECONOMIC PLANNING AND INTERNATIONAL ORDER. WOR-45 SOCIETY FINAN INDUS NAT/G ECO/TAC ROUTINE WEALTH...SOC TIME/SEQ GEN/METH WORK 20 KEYNES/JM. PAGE 122 A2492
INT/ORG PLAN INT/TRADE

B37
ROYAL INST. INT. AFF.,THE COLONIAL PROBLEM. WOR-45 LAW ECO/DEV ECO/UNDEV NAT/G PLAN ECO/TAC EDU/PROP ADMIN ATTIT ALL/VALS...CONCPT 20. PAGE 125 A2556
INT/ORG ACT/RES SOVEREIGN COLONIAL

B38
COLBY C.C.,GEOGRAPHICAL ASPECTS OF INTERNATIONAL RELATIONS. WOR-45 ECO/DEV ECO/UNDEV AGRI EXTR/IND
PLAN GEOG

INDUS MARKET R+D INT/ORG NAT/G TEC/DEV ECO/TAC DIPLOM
INT/TRADE NAT/LISM WEALTH...METH/CNCPT CHARTS
GEN/LAWS 20. PAGE 28 A0565

B38
HARPER S.N.,THE GOVERNMENT OF THE SOVIET UNION. COM MARXISM
USSR LAW CONSTN ECO/DEV PLAN TEC/DEV DIPLOM NAT/G
INT/TRADE ADMIN REV NAT/LISM...POLICY 20. PAGE 62 LEAD
A1265 POL/PAR

B38
HOBSON J.A.,IMPERIALISM. MOD/EUR UK WOR-45 CULTURE DOMIN
ECO/UNDEV NAT/G VOL/ASSN PLAN EDU/PROP LEGIT REGION ECO/TAC
COERCE ATTIT PWR...POLICY PLURIST TIME/SEQ GEN/LAWS BAL/PWR
19/20. PAGE 66 A1348 COLONIAL

B38
PETTEE G.S.,THE PROCESS OF REVOLUTION. COM FRANCE COERCE
ITALY MOD/EUR RUSSIA SPAIN WOR-45 ELITES INTELL CONCPT
SOCIETY STRATA STRUCT INT/ORG NAT/G POL/PAR ACT/RES REV
PLAN EDU/PROP LEGIT EXEC...SOC MYTH TIME/SEQ
TOT/POP 18/20. PAGE 115 A2370

B39
BENES E.,INTERNATIONAL SECURITY. GERMANY UK NAT/G EUR+WWI
DELIB/GP PLAN BAL/PWR ATTIT ORD/FREE PWR LEAGUE/NAT INT/ORG
20 TREATY. PAGE 13 A0267 WAR

B39
BROWN J.F.,CONTEMPORARY WORLD POLITICS. WOR-45 INT/ORG
NAT/G PLAN BAL/PWR EDU/PROP LEGIT REGION NAT/LISM DIPLOM
ORD/FREE PWR SOVEREIGN...POLICY CONCPT HIST/WRIT PEACE
TIME/SEQ GEN/LAWS LEAGUE/NAT. PAGE 20 A0403

B39
FULLER G.H.,A SELECTED LIST OF REFERENCES ON THE BIBLIOG
EXPANSION OF THE US NAVY, 1933-1939 (PAMPHLET). FORCES
MOD/EUR USA-45 NAT/G PLAN DIPLOM DOMIN RISK WEAPON
ARMS/CONT EQUILIB PWR 20 NAVY. PAGE 50 A1019 WAR

B39
TAGGART F.J.,ROME AND CHINA. MEDIT-7 INT/ORG NAT/G ASIA
FORCES LEGIS TOP/EX PLAN PWR SOVEREIGN...CHARTS WAR
TOT/POP ROM/EMP. PAGE 141 A2883

L39
NEARING S.,"A WARLESS WORLD." FUT WOR-45 SOCIETY COERCE
INT/ORG NAT/G EX/STRUC PLAN DOMIN WAR ATTIT DRIVE PEACE
PWR...POLICY PSY CONCPT OBS TREND HYPO/EXP
MARX/KARL 20 MARX/KARL LENIN/VI. PAGE 108 A2210

B40
CONOVER H.F.,A BRIEF LIST OF REFERENCES ON WESTERN BIBLIOG
HEMISPHERE DEFENSE (PAMPHLET). USA-45 NAT/G CONSULT DIPLOM
DELIB/GP FORCES BAL/PWR CONFER DETER...PREDICT PLAN
CON/ANAL 20. PAGE 29 A0591 INT/ORG

B40
RAPPARD W.E.,THE QUEST FOR PEACE. UNIV USA-45 EUR+WWI
WOR-45 SOCIETY INT/ORG NAT/G PLAN EXEC ROUTINE WAR ACT/RES
ATTIT DRIVE ALL/VALS...POLICY CONCPT OBS TIME/SEQ PEACE
LEAGUE/NAT TOT/POP 20. PAGE 119 A2450

B40
WOLFERS A.,BRITAIN AND FRANCE BETWEEN TWO WORLD DIPLOM
WARS. FRANCE UK INT/ORG NAT/G PLAN BARGAIN ECO/TAC WAR
AGREE ISOLAT ALL/IDEOS...DECISION GEOG 20 TREATY POLICY
VERSAILLES INTERVENT. PAGE 166 A3380

B41
NIEMEYER G.,LAW WITHOUT FORCE: THE FUNCTION OF COERCE
POLITICS IN INTERNATIONAL LAW. PLAN INSPECT DIPLOM LAW
REPAR LEGIT ADJUD WAR ORD/FREE...IDEA/COMP PWR
METH/COMP GEN/LAWS 20. PAGE 109 A2240 INT/LAW

L41
COMM. STUDY ORGAN. PEACE,"PRELIMINARY REPORT." INT/ORG
WOR-45 SOCIETY DELIB/GP PLAN LEGIT WAR ORD/FREE ACT/RES
...CONCPT TOT/POP 20. PAGE 28 A0574 PEACE

L41
COMM. STUDY ORGAN. PEACE,"ORGANIZATION OF PEACE." INT/ORG
USA-45 WOR-45 STRATA NAT/G ACT/RES DIPLOM ECO/TAC PLAN
EDU/PROP ADJUD ATTIT ORD/FREE PWR...SOC CONCPT PEACE
ANTHOL LEAGUE/NAT 20. PAGE 28 A0575

B42
CORBETT P.E.,POST WAR WORLDS. ASIA EUR+WWI FUT WOR-45
S/ASIA USA-45 ECO/DEV ECO/UNDEV NAT/G DELIB/GP INT/ORG
FORCES PLAN ROUTINE ATTIT PWR 20. PAGE 30 A0613

B42
TOLMAN E.C.,DRIVES TOWARD WAR. UNIV PLAN DIPLOM PSY
ECO/TAC COERCE PERS/REL ADJUST HAPPINESS BIO/SOC WAR
HEREDITY HEALTH KNOWL. PAGE 144 A2947 UTOPIA
DRIVE

B42
US LIBRARY OF CONGRESS,ECONOMICS OF WAR (APRIL BIBLIOG/A
1941-MARCH 1942). WOR-45 FINAN INDUS LOC/G NAT/G INT/TRADE
PLAN BUDGET RATION COST DEMAND...POLICY 20. ECO/TAC
PAGE 154 A3146 WAR

B42
US LIBRARY OF CONGRESS,POSTWAR PLANNING AND BIBLIOG/A
RECONSTRUCTION: APRIL-DECEMBER 1942 (SUPPLEMENT 1). WAR
WOR+45 SOCIETY INT/ORG DIPLOM...SOC PREDICT 20 UN. PEACE
PAGE 154 A3147 PLAN

S42
TURNER F.J.,"AMERICAN SECTIONALISM AND WORLD INT/ORG
ORGANIZATION." EUR+WWI UNIV USA-45 WOR-45 INTELL DRIVE
ECO/DEV TOP/EX ACT/RES PLAN EDU/PROP LEGIT ALL/VALS BAL/PWR
...CONCPT NEW/IDEA OBS TREND LEAGUE/NAT TOT/POP 20.
PAGE 146 A2981

B43
FULLER G.F.,FOREIGN RELIEF AND REHABILITATION BIBLIOG/A
(PAMPHLET). FUT GERMANY UK USA-45 INT/ORG PROB/SOLV PLAN
DIPLOM FOR/AID ADMIN ADJUST PEACE ALL/VALS...SOC/WK GIVE
20 UN JEWS. PAGE 50 A1018 WAR

B43
GRIERSON P.,BOOKS ON SOVIET RUSSIA 1917-42: A BIBLIOG/A
BIBLIOGRAPHY AND A GUIDE TO READING. USSR CULTURE COM
ELITES NAT/G PLAN DIPLOM REV...GEOG 20. PAGE 56 MARXISM
A1148 LEAD

B43
VINER J.,TRADE RELATIONS BETWEEN FREE-MARKET AND INT/TRADE
CONTROLLED ECONOMIES. WOR-45 MARKET PLAN TARIFFS DIPLOM
DEMAND...POLICY STAT 20. PAGE 159 A3237 CONTROL
NAT/G

C43
BENTHAM J.,"PRINCIPLES OF INTERNATIONAL LAW" IN J. INT/LAW
BOWRING, ED., THE WORKS OF JEREMY BENTHAM." UNIV JURID
NAT/G PLAN PROB/SOLV DIPLOM CONTROL SANCTION MORAL WAR
ORD/FREE PWR SOVEREIGN 19. PAGE 13 A0270 PEACE

L44
HAILEY,"THE FUTURE OF COLONIAL PEOPLES." WOR-45 PLAN
CONSTN CULTURE ECO/UNDEV AGRI MARKET INT/ORG NAT/G CONCPT
SECT CONSULT ECO/TAC LEGIT ADMIN NAT/LISM ALL/VALS DIPLOM
...SOC OBS TREND STERTYP CMN/WLTH LEAGUE/NAT UK
PARLIAMENT 20. PAGE 59 A1218

B45
CARR E.H.,NATIONALISM AND AFTER. FUT WOR-45 NAT/G INT/ORG
VOL/ASSN EX/STRUC PLAN ROUTINE TOTALISM ATTIT TREND
HEALTH ORD/FREE PWR...CONCPT 20. PAGE 25 A0499 NAT/LISM
REGION

B45
GALLOWAY E.,ABSTRACTS OF POSTWAR LITERATURE (VOL. BIBLIOG/A
IV) JAN.-JULY, 1945 NOS. 901-1074. POLAND USA+45 NUC/PWR
USSR WOR+45 INDUS LABOR PLAN ECO/TAC INT/TRADE TAX NAT/G
EDU/PROP ADMIN COLONIAL INT/LAW. PAGE 51 A1033 DIPLOM

B45
PASTUHOV V.D.,A GUIDE TO THE PRACTICE OF INT/ORG
INTERNATIONAL CONFERENCES. WOR+45 PLAN LEGIT DELIB/GP
ORD/FREE...MGT OBS RECORD VAL/FREE ILO LEAGUE/NAT
20. PAGE 114 A2338

B46
BRODIE B.,THE OBSOLETE WEAPON: ATOMIC POWER AND INT/ORG
WORLD ORDER. COM USA+45 USSR WOR+45 DELIB/GP PLAN TEC/DEV
ORD/FREE PWR...CONCPT TIME/SEQ TREND UN 20. PAGE 19 ARMS/CONT
A0380 NUC/PWR

B46
MITRANY D.,A WORKING PEACE SYSTEM. WOR+45 WOR-45 VOL/ASSN
ECO/DEV INT/ORG NAT/G DELIB/GP ECO/TAC REGION ATTIT PLAN
RIGID/FLEX...TREND GEN/LAWS LEAGUE/NAT 20. PAGE 102 PEACE
A2091 SOVEREIGN

S46
DOUGLAS W.O.,"SYMPOSIUM ON WORLD ORGANIZATION." FUT INT/ORG
USA+45 WOR+45 CONSTN SOCIETY NAT/G PLAN EDU/PROP LAW
LEGIT RIGID/FLEX KNOWL...INT/LAW JURID STERTYP
TOT/POP 20. PAGE 38 A0778

B47
GORDON D.L.,THE HIDDEN WEAPON: THE STORY OF INT/ORG
ECONOMIC WARFARE. EUR+WWI USA-45 LAW FINAN INDUS ECO/TAC
NAT/G CONSULT FORCES PLAN DOMIN PWR WEALTH INT/TRADE
...INT/LAW CONCPT OBS TOT/POP NAZI 20. PAGE 54 WAR
A1112

B47
US LIBRARY OF CONGRESS,POSTWAR PLANNING AND BIBLIOG/A
RECONSTRUCTION: JANUARY-MARCH 1943. WOR+45 SOCIETY WAR
INT/ORG DIPLOM...SOC PREDICT 20. PAGE 154 A3149 PEACE
PLAN

L47
BRUNER J.S.,"TOWARD A COMMON GROUND-INTERNATIONAL INT/ORG
SOCIAL SCIENCE." FUT WOR+45 INTELL R+D NAT/G KNOWL
VOL/ASSN CONSULT DELIB/GP ACT/RES CREATE PLAN
TEC/DEV ATTIT ORD/FREE...PSY SOC CONCPT ANTHOL
UNESCO 20. PAGE 20 A0410

L47
HISS D.,"UNITED STATES PARTICIPATION IN THE UNITED INT/ORG
NATIONS." USA+45 EX/STRUC PLAN DIPLOM ROUTINE PWR
CHOOSE...PLURIST UN 20. PAGE 65 A1342

B48
DURBIN E.F.M.,THE POLITICS OF DEMOCRATIC SOCIALISM; SOCIALIST
AN ESSAY ON SOCIAL POLICY. STRATA POL/PAR PLAN POPULISM
COERCE DRIVE PERSON PWR MARXISM...CHARTS METH/COMP. POLICY
PAGE 39 A0805 SOCIETY

B48
GRAHAM F.D.,THE THEORY OF INTERNATIONAL VALUES. FUT NEW/IDEA
WOR+45 WOR-45 ECO/DEV FINAN INT/ORG PLAN TEC/DEV INT/TRADE
CAP/ISM DIPLOM ECO/TAC TARIFFS ROUTINE BAL/PAY
DRIVE PWR WEALTH SOCISM...POLICY STAT HYPO/EXP
GEN/LAWS 20. PAGE 55 A1125

B48
KULISCHER E.M.,EUROPE ON THE MOVE: WAR AND ECO/TAC
POPULATION CHANGES, 1917-1947. COM EUR+WWI FUT GEOG
GERMANY USSR DIST/IND PLAN INT/TRADE CONTROL WAR
DRIVE...CENSUS TREND COLD/WAR 20. PAGE 82 A1690

B48
LINEBARGER P.,PSYCHOLOGICAL WARFARE. NAT/G PLAN EDU/PROP
DIPLOM DOMIN ATTIT...POLICY CONCPT EXHIBIT 20 WWI. PSY

PAGE 89 A1824 — WAR COM/IND

B48
NEUBURGER O.,GUIDE TO OFFICIAL PUBLICATIONS OF THE OTHER AMERICAN REPUBLICS: VENEZUELA (VOL. XIX). VENEZUELA FINAN LEGIS PLAN BUDGET DIPLOM CT/SYS PARL/PROC 19/20. PAGE 108 A2219 — BIBLIOG/A NAT/G CONSTN LAW

B48
US DEPARTMENT OF STATE,FOREIGN AFFAIRS HIGHLIGHTS (NEWSLETTER). COM USA+45 INT/ORG PLAN BAL/PWR WAR PWR...BIBLIOG 20 COLD/WAR NATO UN DEPT/STATE. PAGE 151 A3083 — DIPLOM NAT/G POLICY

B48
WHEELER-BENNETT J.W.,MUNICH: PROLOGUE TO TRAGEDY. EUR+WWI FRANCE GERMANY UK PLAN PROB/SOLV SOVEREIGN ...POLICY DECISION 20 HITLER/A. PAGE 163 A3327 — DIPLOM WAR PEACE

B49
OGBURN W.,TECHNOLOGY AND INTERNATIONAL RELATIONS. WOR+45 WOR-45 ECO/DEV CREATE PLAN ECO/TAC EDU/PROP COERCE PWR SKILL WEALTH...TECHNIC PSY SOC NEW/IDEA CHARTS TOT/POP 20. PAGE 111 A2283 — TEC/DEV DIPLOM INT/ORG

B49
PARMELEE M.,GEO-ECONOMIC REGIONAL AND WORLD FEDERATION. FUT WOR+45 WOR-45 SOCIETY VOL/ASSN PLAN ...METH/CNCPT SIMUL GEN/METH TOT/POP 20. PAGE 114 A2335 — INT/ORG GEOG REGION

B49
ROSENHAUPT H.W.,HOW TO WAGE PEACE. USA+45 SOCIETY STRATA STRUCT R+D INT/ORG POL/PAR LEGIS ACT/RES CREATE PLAN EDU/PROP ADMIN EXEC ATTIT ALL/VALS ...TIME/SEQ TREND COLD/WAR 20. PAGE 124 A2536 — INTELL CONCPT DIPLOM

B49
SINGER K.,THE IDEA OF CONFLICT. UNIV INTELL INT/ORG NAT/G PLAN ROUTINE ATTIT DRIVE ALL/VALS...POLICY CONCPT TIME/SEQ. PAGE 133 A2730 — ACT/RES SOC

B49
STREIT C.,UNION NOW. UNIV USA-45 WOR-45 INTELL STRUCT INT/ORG NAT/G PLAN DIPLOM EXEC ATTIT ...CONCPT TIME/SEQ. PAGE 139 A2849 — SOCIETY ACT/RES WAR

B50
DULLES J.F.,WAR OR PEACE. CHINA/COM USA+45 USSR INT/ORG SECT FORCES PLAN NUC/PWR WAR CENTRAL MARXISM...POLICY 20 UN ROOSEVLT/F STALIN/J. PAGE 39 A0797 — PEACE DIPLOM TREND ORD/FREE

B50
MCCAMY J.,THE ADMINISTRATION OF AMERICAN FOREIGN AFFAIRS. USA+45 SOCIETY INT/ORG NAT/G ACT/RES PLAN INT/TRADE EDU/PROP ADJUD ALL/VALS...METH/CNCPT TIME/SEQ CONGRESS 20. PAGE 97 A1996 — EXEC STRUCT DIPLOM

B50
US DEPARTMENT OF STATE,POINT FOUR: COOPERATIVE PROGRAM FOR AID IN THE DEVELOPMENT OF ECONOMICALLY UNDERDEVELOPED AREAS. WOR+45 AGRI INDUS INT/ORG PLAN TEC/DEV DIPLOM EDU/PROP ADMIN PEACE PRODUC WEALTH 20 CONGRESS UN. PAGE 151 A3085 — ECO/UNDEV FOR/AID FINAN INT/TRADE

L50
US SENATE COMM. GOVT. OPER.,"REVISION OF THE UN CHARTER." FUT USA+45 WOR+45 CONSTN ECO/DEV ECO/UNDEV NAT/G DELIB/GP ACT/RES CREATE PLAN EXEC ROUTINE CHOOSE ALL/VALS...POLICY CONCPT CONGRESS UN TOT/POP 20 COLD/WAR. PAGE 157 A3196 — INT/ORG LEGIS PEACE

S50
UNESCO,"MEETING ON UNIVERSITY TEACHING OF INTERNATIONAL RELATIONS." FUT WOR+45 R+D VOL/ASSN CONSULT PLAN EDU/PROP ATTIT...CONCPT TREND 20. PAGE 147 A3012 — INT/ORG KNOWL DIPLOM

N50
SCHAPIRO J.S.,THE WORLD IN CRISES: POLITICAL AND SOCIAL MOVEMENTS IN THE TWENTIETH CENTURY. USA+45 INT/ORG LABOR PLAN CAP/ISM DIPLOM COLONIAL PEACE TOTALISM ATTIT LAISSEZ...BIBLIOG 20 COLD/WAR. PAGE 128 A2618 — NAT/LISM TEC/DEV REV WAR

B51
BORKENAU F.,EUROPEAN COMMUNISM. COM EUR+WWI GERMANY SPAIN USSR INT/ORG PLAN REV WAR ATTIT 20 STALIN/J HITLER/A. PAGE 17 A0342 — MARXISM POLICY DIPLOM NAT/G

B51
JENNINGS I.,THE COMMONWEALTH IN ASIA. CEYLON INDIA PAKISTAN CULTURE STRATA NAT/G LEGIS DIPLOM COLONIAL ATTIT...DECISION 20 CMN/WLTH. PAGE 74 A1507 — CONSTN INT/ORG POLICY PLAN

B51
PRICE D.K.,THE NEW DIMENSIONS OF DIPLOMACY: THE ORGANIZATION OF THE US GOVERNMENT FOR ITS NEW ROLE IN WORLD AFFAIRS (PAMPHLET). USA+45 WOR+45 INT/ORG VOL/ASSN CONSULT DELIB/GP PLAN PROB/SOLV 20 PRESIDENT. PAGE 117 A2411 — DIPLOM GP/REL NAT/G

B51
US DEPARTMENT OF STATE,POINT FOUR, NEAR EAST AND AFRICA, A SELECTED BIBLIOGRAPHY OF STUDIES ON ECONOMICALLY UNDERDEVELOPED COUNTRIES. AGRI COM/IND FINAN INDUS PLAN INT/TRADE...SOC TREND 20. PAGE 151 A3087 — BIBLIOG/A AFR S/ASIA ISLAM

L51
ULAM A.B.,"THE COMIMFORM AND THE PEOPLE'S DEMOCRACIES." EUR+WWI WOR+45 STRUCT NAT/G POL/PAR TOP/EX ACT/RES PLAN ECO/TAC DOMIN ATTIT ALL/VALS ...HIST/WRIT TIME/SEQ 20 COMINFORM. PAGE 146 A2992 — COM INT/ORG USSR TOTALISM

S51
CONNERY R.H.,"THE MUTUAL DEFENSE ASSISTANCE PROGRAM." COM EUR+WWI KOREA USA+45 NAT/G VOL/ASSN CREATE PLAN BAL/PWR EDU/PROP PERCEPT...POLICY DECISION CONCPT NATO 20. PAGE 29 A0587 — INT/ORG FORCES FOR/AID

B52
ALEXANDROWICZ C.H.,INTERNATIONAL ECONOMIC ORGANIZATION. WOR+45 ECO/DEV ECO/UNDEV DIST/IND FINAN MARKET PLAN ECO/TAC LEGIT DRIVE WEALTH ...POLICY CONCPT QUANT OBS TIME/SEQ GEN/LAWS WORK EEC ILO OEEC UNESCO 20. PAGE 6 A0114 — INT/ORG INT/TRADE

B52
HOSELITZ B.F.,THE PROGRESS OF UNDERDEVELOPED AREAS. FUT WOR+45 WOR-45 ECO/DEV ECO/TAC INT/TRADE WEALTH ...SOC TREND GEN/LAWS TOT/POP VAL/FREE COLD/WAR 20. PAGE 68 A1391 — ECO/UNDEV PLAN FOR/AID

B52
MANTOUX E.,THE CARTHAGINIAN PEACE. GERMANY WOR-45 SOCIETY FINAN INT/ORG DELIB/GP FORCES PLAN LEGIT ...CONCPT TIME/SEQ 20 KEYNES/JM HITLER/A. PAGE 94 A1935 — ECO/DEV INT/TRADE WAR

B52
SCHUMAN F.,THE COMMONWEALTH OF MAN. WOR+45 WOR-45 LAW CULTURE ELITES SOCIETY FAM INT/ORG NAT/G VOL/ASSN TOP/EX PLAN BAL/PWR LEGIT ATTIT DISPL DRIVE...POLICY MYTH TREND TOT/POP ILO OEEC 20. PAGE 129 A2649 — CONCPT GEN/LAWS

B52
SURANYI-UNGER T.,COMPARATIVE ECONOMIC SYSTEMS. FINAN MARKET DIPLOM PRICE WEALTH...GEOG SOC BIBLIOG METH T 20. PAGE 140 A2865 — LAISSEZ PLAN ECO/DEV IDEA/COMP

B52
ULAM A.B.,TITOISM AND THE COMINFORM. USSR WOR+45 STRUCT INT/ORG NAT/G ACT/RES PLAN EXEC ATTIT DRIVE ALL/VALS...CONCPT OBS VAL/FREE 20 COMINTERN TITO/MARSH. PAGE 146 A2993 — COM POL/PAR TOTALISM YUGOSLAVIA

B52
US MUTUAL SECURITY AGENCY,U. S. TECHNICAL AND ECONOMIC ASSISTANCE IN THE FAR EAST (PAMPHLET). ASIA BURMA INDONESIA PHILIPPINE TAIWAN THAILAND USA+45 AGRI INDUS PLAN EDU/PROP ADMIN HEALTH. PAGE 155 A3161 — FOR/AID TEC/DEV ECO/UNDEV BUDGET

B52
WALTERS F.P.,A HISTORY OF THE LEAGUE OF NATIONS. EUR+WWI CONSTN NAT/G LEGIS TOP/EX ACT/RES PLAN EDU/PROP LEGIT ROUTINE ATTIT...TREND LEAGUE/NAT 20 CHINJAP. PAGE 161 A3271 — INT/ORG TIME/SEQ NAT/LISM

L52
THOMPSON K.W.,"THE STUDY OF INTERNATIONAL POLITICS: A SURVEY OF TRENDS AND DEVELOPMENTS." UNIV USA+45 WOR+45 WOR-45 SOCIETY ECO/DEV R+D ACT/RES PLAN ROUTINE ATTIT DRIVE PERCEPT PERSON...CONCPT OBS TREND GEN/LAWS TOT/POP. PAGE 143 A2928 — INT/ORG BAL/PWR DIPLOM

B53
LARSEN K.,NATIONAL BIBLIOGRAPHIC SERVICES: THEIR CREATION AND OPERATION. WOR+45 COM/IND CREATE PLAN DIPLOM PRESS ADMIN ROUTINE...MGT UNESCO. PAGE 85 A1733 — BIBLIOG/A INT/ORG WRITING

B53
MATLOFF M.,STRATEGIC PLANNING FOR COALITION WARFARE. UK USA-45 CHIEF DIPLOM EXEC GOV/REL ...METH/COMP 20. PAGE 96 A1967 — WAR PLAN DECISION FORCES

B53
MCNEILL W.H.,AMERICA, BRITAIN, AND RUSSIA; THEIR COOPERATION AND CONFLICT. UK USA-45 USSR ECO/DEV ECO/UNDEV FORCES PLAN ADMIN AGREE PERS/REL ...DECISION 20 TREATY. PAGE 98 A2021 — WAR DIPLOM DOMIN

S53
LINCOLN G.,"FACTORS DETERMINING ARMS AID." COM FUT USA+45 USSR WOR+45 ECO/DEV NAT/G CONSULT PLAN TEC/DEV DIPLOM DOMIN EDU/PROP PERCEPT PWR ...DECISION CONCPT TREND MARX/KARL 20. PAGE 89 A1819 — FORCES POLICY BAL/PWR FOR/AID

B54
BINANI G.D.,INDIA AT A GLANCE (REV. ED.). INDIA COM/IND FINAN INDUS LABOR PROVS SCHOOL PLAN DIPLOM INT/TRADE ADMIN...JURID 20. PAGE 14 A0288 — INDEX CON/ANAL NAT/G ECO/UNDEV

B54
BUCHANAN W.,AN INTERNATIONAL POLICE FORCE AND PUBLIC OPINION IN THE UNITED STATES, 1939-1953. USA+45 PROB/SOLV CONTROL ATTIT ORD/FREE...STAT TREND 20. PAGE 21 A0425 — IDEA/COMP FORCES DIPLOM PLAN

B54
GERMANY FOREIGN MINISTRY,DOCUMENTS ON GERMAN FOREIGN POLICY 1918-1945, SERIES C (1933-1937) VOLS. I-V. GERMANY MOD/EUR FORCES PLAN ECO/TAC ...FASCIST CHARTS ANTHOL 20. PAGE 52 A1065 — NAT/G DIPLOM POLICY

B54
GROSS F.,FOREIGN POLICY ANALYSIS. USA+45 TOP/EX PLAN INGP/REL ATTIT TECHRACY...CONCPT 20. PAGE 57 — POLICY DIPLOM

A1171 DECISION EDU/PROP

B54
NATION ASSOCIATES,SECURITY AND THE MIDDLE EAST - THE PROBLEM AND ITS SOLUTION. ISRAEL JORDAN LEBANON SYRIA UAR FORCES FOR/AID GP/REL NAT/LISM PEACE TOTALISM...POLICY 20. PAGE 107 A2198 DIPLOM ECO/UNDEV WAR PLAN

B54
STALEY E.,THE FUTURE OF UNDERDEVELOPED COUNTRIES: POLITICAL IMPLICATIONS OF ECONOMIC DEVELOPMENT. COM FUT USA+45 SOCIETY ECO/UNDEV CREATE PLAN CAP/ISM ATTIT DRIVE MARXISM SOCISM...POLICY CONCPT CHARTS COLD/WAR 20. PAGE 137 A2801 EDU/PROP ECO/TAC FOR/AID

L54
OPLER M.E.,"SOCIAL ASPECTS OF TECHNICAL ASSISTANCE IN OPERATION." WOR+45 VOL/ASSN CREATE PLAN TEC/DEV EDU/PROP ALL/VALS...METH/CNCPT OBS RECORD TREND UN 20. PAGE 112 A2292 INT/ORG CONSULT FOR/AID

S54
DODD S.C.,"THE SCIENTIFIC MEASUREMENT OF FITNESS FOR SELF-GOVERNMENT." FUT CONSTN ECO/UNDEV INT/ORG PLAN PWR...CONCPT QUANT CON/ANAL SOC/EXP UN LEAGUE/NAT 20. PAGE 38 A0767 NAT/G STAT SOVEREIGN

S54
FOX W.T.R.,"CIVIL-MILITARY RELATIONS." USA+45 USA-45 R+D ACT/RES DIPLOM INT/TRADE EDU/PROP DETER DISPL DRIVE ORD/FREE...METH/CNCPT TREND COLD/WAR 20. PAGE 48 A0974 POLICY FORCES PLAN SOCIETY

B55
ARNOLD G.L.,THE PATTERN OF WORLD CONFLICT. USA+45 INT/ORG ECO/TAC INT/TRADE PEACE 20 EUROPE. PAGE 9 A0176 DIPLOM BAL/PWR NAT/LISM PLAN

B55
CHOWDHURI R.N.,INTERNATIONAL MANDATES AND TRUSTEESHIP SYSTEMS. WOR+45 STRUCT ECO/UNDEV INT/ORG LEGIS DOMIN EDU/PROP LEGIT ADJUD EXEC PWR ...CONCPT TIME/SEQ UN 20. PAGE 26 A0534 DELIB/GP PLAN SOVEREIGN

B55
COMM. STUDY ORGAN. PEACE,REPORTS. WOR-45 ECO/DEV ECO/UNDEV VOL/ASSN CONSULT FORCES PLAN TEC/DEV DOMIN EDU/PROP NUC/PWR ATTIT PWR WEALTH...JURID STERTYP FAO ILO 20 UN. PAGE 28 A0579 WOR+45 INT/ORG ARMS/CONT

B55
GOODRICH L.,THE UNITED NATIONS AND THE MAINTENANCE OF INTERNATIONAL PEACE AND SECURITY. WOR+45 CONSTN ACT/RES CREATE PLAN PERCEPT PWR...ORG/CHARTS GEN/LAWS UN 20. PAGE 54 A1102 INT/ORG ORD/FREE ARMS/CONT PEACE

B55
JOY C.T.,HOW COMMUNISTS NEGOTIATE. COM USA+45 CONSTN CULTURE ECO/UNDEV NAT/G CONSULT DELIB/GP FORCES PLAN ECO/TAC DOMIN EDU/PROP LEGIT EXEC ROUTINE COERCE WAR CHOOSE PEACE ATTIT RIGID/FLEX ORD/FREE PWR...POLICY 20. PAGE 75 A1539 ASIA INT/ORG DIPLOM

B55
MYRDAL A.R.,AMERICA'S ROLE IN INTERNATIONATIONAL SOCIAL WELFARE. FUT WOR+45 SOCIETY R+D VOL/ASSN ECO/TAC EDU/PROP HEALTH KNOWL WEALTH...SOC CHARTS ORG/CHARTS TOT/POP 20. PAGE 107 A2188 PLAN SKILL FOR/AID

B55
PANT Y.P.,PLANNING IN UNDERDEVELOPED ECONOMIES. INDIA NEPAL INT/TRADE COLONIAL SOVEREIGN ALL/IDEOS ...TIME/SEQ METH/COMP 20. PAGE 114 A2334 ECO/UNDEV PLAN ECO/TAC DIPLOM

B55
UN ECONOMIC AND SOCIAL COUNCIL,BIBLIOGRAPHY OF PUBLICATIONS OF THE UN AND SPECIALIZED AGENCIES IN THE SOCIAL WELFARE FIELD, 1946-1952. WOR+45 FAM INT/ORG MUNIC ACT/RES PLAN PROB/SOLV EDU/PROP AGE/C AGE/Y HABITAT...HEAL UN. PAGE 147 A3000 BIBLIOG/A SOC/WK ADMIN WEALTH

B55
VINSON J.C.,THE PARCHMENT PEACE: THE UNITED STATES SENATE AND THE WASHINGTON CONFERENCE, 1921-1922. USA-45 INT/ORG DELIB/GP PLAN ARMS/CONT GOV/REL ISOLAT PEACE ATTIT SOVEREIGN...INT/LAW BIBLIOG 20 SENATE PRESIDENT CONGRESS LEAGUE/NAT CHINJAP. PAGE 159 A3242 POLICY DIPLOM NAT/G LEGIS

L55
KISER M.,"ORGANIZATION OF AMERICAN STATES." L/A+17C USA+45 ECO/UNDEV INT/ORG NAT/G PLAN TEC/DEV DIPLOM ECO/TAC INT/TRADE EDU/PROP ADMIN ALL/VALS...POLICY MGT RECORD ORG/CHARTS OAS 20. PAGE 80 A1639 VOL/ASSN ECO/DEV REGION

L55
ROSTOW W.W.,"RUSSIA AND CHINA UNDER COMMUNISM." CHINA/COM USSR INTELL STRUCT INT/ORG NAT/G POL/PAR TOP/EX ACT/RES PLAN ADMIN ATTIT ALL/VALS MARXISM ...CONCPT OBS TIME/SEQ TREND GOV/COMP VAL/FREE 20. PAGE 124 A2543 COM ASIA

S55
HALLETT D.,"THE HISTORY AND STRUCTURE OF OEEC." EUR+WWI USA+45 CONSTN INDUS INT/ORG NAT/G DELIB/GP ACT/RES PLAN ORD/FREE WEALTH...CONCPT OEEC 20 CMN/WLTH. PAGE 60 A1234 VOL/ASSN ECO/DEV

B56
ESTEP R.,AN AIR POWER BIBLIOGRAPHY. USA+45 TEC/DEV BUDGET DIPLOM EDU/PROP DETER CIVMIL/REL...DECISION INT/LAW 20. PAGE 42 A0862 BIBLIOG/A FORCES WEAPON PLAN

B56
KNORR K.E.,RUBLE DIPLOMACY: CHALLENGE TO AMERICAN FOREIGN AID(PAMPHLET). CHINA/COM USA+45 USSR PLAN TEC/DEV CAP/ISM INT/TRADE DOMIN EDU/PROP CONTROL LEAD 20 COLD/WAR. PAGE 81 A1654 ECO/UNDEV COM DIPLOM FOR/AID

B56
SNELL J.L.,THE MEANING OF YALTA: BIG THREE DIPLOMACY AND THE NEW BALANCE OF POWER. EUR+WWI GERMANY USA-45 USSR FORCES PLAN BAL/PWR DIPLOM WAR CHOOSE PEACE...CHARTS BIBLIOG 20 UN CHINJAP ROOSEVLT/F. PAGE 134 A2749 CONFER CHIEF POLICY PROB/SOLV

B56
WOLFERS A.,THE ANGLO-AMERICAN TRADITION IN FOREIGN AFFAIRS. UK USA+45 WOR-45 CULTURE SOCIETY ECO/DEV INT/ORG NAT/G CREATE PLAN BAL/PWR ECO/TAC EDU/PROP PEACE DISPL DRIVE...TREND GEN/LAWS 20. PAGE 166 A3382 ATTIT CONCPT DIPLOM

S56
GORDON L.,"THE ORGANIZATION FOR EUROPEAN ECONOMIC COOPERATION." EUR+WWI INDUS INT/ORG NAT/G CONSULT DELIB/GP ACT/RES CREATE PLAN TEC/DEV EDU/PROP LEGIT WEALTH OEEC 20. PAGE 54 A1114 VOL/ASSN ECO/DEV

B57
ASHER R.E.,THE UNITED NATIONS AND THE PROMOTION OF THE GENERAL WELFARE. WOR+45 WOR-45 ECO/UNDEV EX/STRUC ACT/RES PLAN EDU/PROP ROUTINE HEALTH...HUM CONCPT CHARTS UNESCO UN ILO 20. PAGE 9 A0185 INT/ORG CONSULT

B57
ASHER R.E.,THE UNITED NATIONS AND ECONOMIC AND SOCIAL COOPERATION. ECO/UNDEV COM/IND DIST/IND FINAN PLAN PROB/SOLV INT/TRADE TASK WEALTH...SOC 20 UN. PAGE 9 A0186 INT/ORG DIPLOM FOR/AID

B57
BLOOMFIELD L.M.,EGYPT, ISRAEL AND THE GULF OF AQABA: IN INTERNATIONAL LAW. LAW NAT/G CONSULT FORCES PLAN ECO/TAC ROUTINE COERCE ATTIT DRIVE PERCEPT PERSON RIGID/FLEX LOVE PWR WEALTH...GEOG CONCPT MYTH TREND. PAGE 15 A0314 ISLAM INT/LAW UAR

B57
BURNS A.,IN DEFENCE OF COLONIES; BRITISH COLONIAL TERRITORIES IN INTERNATIONAL AFFAIRS. UK ECO/UNDEV PLAN DOMIN SOVEREIGN...MAJORIT 18/20 CMN/WLTH INTERVENT. PAGE 22 A0439 COLONIAL POLICY ATTIT DIPLOM

B57
DEUTSCH K.W.,POLITICAL COMMUNITY AND THE NORTH ATLANTIC AREA: INTERNATIONAL ORGANIZATION IN THE LIGHT OF HISTORICAL EXPERIENCE. MOD/EUR USA+45 USA-45 SOCIETY FORCES TOP/EX CREATE PLAN DIPLOM DOMIN EDU/PROP LEGIT ATTIT ORD/FREE PWR...SAMP/SIZ TIME/SEQ CHARTS TOT/POP. PAGE 36 A0736 EUR+WWI INT/ORG PEACE REGION

B57
FREUND G.,UNHOLY ALLIANCE. EUR+WWI GERMANY USSR FORCES ECO/TAC CONTROL WAR PWR...TREND TREATY. PAGE 49 A0999 DIPLOM PLAN POLICY

B57
HOLCOMBE A.N.,STRENGTHENING THE UNITED NATIONS. USA+45 ACT/RES CREATE PLAN EDU/PROP ATTIT PERCEPT PWR...METH/CNCPT CONT/OBS RECORD UN COLD/WAR 20. PAGE 66 A1365 INT/ORG ROUTINE

B57
KAPLAN M.A.,SYSTEM AND PROCESS OF INTERNATIONAL POLITICS. FUT WOR+45 WOR-45 SOCIETY PLAN BAL/PWR ADMIN ATTIT PERSON RIGID/FLEX PWR SOVEREIGN ...DECISION TREND VAL/FREE. PAGE 76 A1560 INT/ORG DIPLOM

B57
KISSINGER H.A.,NUCLEAR WEAPONS AND FOREIGN POLICY. FUT USA+45 WOR+45 INT/ORG FORCES ACT/RES TEC/DEV DIPLOM ARMS/CONT COERCE ATTIT KNOWL PWR...DECISION GEOG CHARTS 20. PAGE 80 A1640 PLAN DETER NUC/PWR

B57
MILLIKAN M.F.,A PROPOSAL: KEY TO AN EFFECTIVE FOREIGN POLICY. USA+45 AGRI FINAN DELIB/GP DIPLOM REPRESENT MAJORITY...NEW/IDEA CHARTS. PAGE 101 A2081 FOR/AID GIVE ECO/UNDEV PLAN

B57
NEHRU J.,MILITARY ALLIANCE (PAMPHLET). INDIA WOR+45 NAT/G PLAN DETER NUC/PWR WAR...POLICY ANTHOL NEHRU/J SEATO UN. PAGE 108 A2212 INT/ORG DIPLOM FORCES PEACE

B57
TRIFFIN R.,EUROPE AND THE MONEY MUDDLE. USA+45 INT/ORG NAT/G CONSULT PLAN ECO/TAC EXEC ROUTINE BAL/PAY WEALTH...METH/CNCPT OBS TREND CHARTS STERTYP GEN/METH EEC VAL/FREE ECSC. PAGE 145 A2962 EUR+WWI ECO/DEV REGION

B57
US COMMISSION GOVT SECURITY,RECOMMENDATIONS; AREA: IMMIGRANT PROGRAM. USA+45 LAW WORKER DIPLOM EDU/PROP WRITING ADMIN PEACE ATTIT...CONCPT ANTHOL 20 MIGRATION SUBVERT. PAGE 150 A3060 POLICY CONTROL PLAN NAT/G

B57
US PRES CITIZEN ADVISERS,REPORT TO THE PRESIDENT ON THE MUTUAL SECURITY PROGRAM. COM USA+45 WOR+45 FINAN INDUS PLAN BUDGET CAP/ISM DIPLOM FOR/AID INT/TRADE REGION 20 SECUR/PROG. PAGE 155 A3163 BAL/PWR FORCES INT/ORG ECO/TAC

B57
WILSON P.,SOUTH ASIA; A SELECTED BIBLIOGRAPHY ON INDIA, PAKISTAN, CEYLON (PAMPHLET). CEYLON INDIA PAKISTAN LAW ECO/UNDEV PLAN DIPLOM 20. PAGE 165 A3362
BIBLIOG S/ASIA CULTURE NAT/G

S57
HOAG M.W.,"ECONOMIC PROBLEMS OF ALLIANCE." COM EUR+WWI WOR+45 ECO/DEV ECO/UNDEV NAT/G VOL/ASSN FORCES PLAN TEC/DEV DIPLOM COERCE ORD/FREE PWR WEALTH...DECISION GEN/LAWS NATO COLD/WAR. PAGE 65 A1345
INT/ORG ECO/TAC

S57
WRIGHT Q.,"THE VALUE OF CONFLICT RESOLUTION OF A GENERAL DISCIPLINE OF INTERNATIONAL RELATIONS." WOR+45 SOCIETY INT/ORG NAT/G FORCES TOP/EX PLAN TEC/DEV ECO/TAC DOMIN LEGIT COERCE ATTIT PWR ...GEN/METH COLD/WAR VAL/FREE. PAGE 168 A3412
ORD/FREE SOC DIPLOM

N57
US SENATE SPECIAL COMM FOR AFF,REPORT OF THE SPECIAL COMMITTEE TO STUDY THE FOREIGN AID PROGRAM (PAMPHLET). USA+45 CONSULT DELIB/GP LEGIS PLAN TEC/DEV CONFER SUPEGO CONGRESS. PAGE 157 A3199
FOR/AID ORD/FREE ECO/UNDEV DIPLOM

B58
BERLINER J.S.,SOVIET ECONOMIC AID: THE AID AND TRADE POLICY IN UNDERDEVELOPED COUNTRIES. AFR COM ISLAM L/A+17C S/ASIA USSR ECO/DEV DIST/IND FINAN MARKET INT/ORG ACT/RES PLAN BAL/PWR WEAPON PWR WEALTH...CHARTS 20. PAGE 14 A0277
ECO/UNDEV ECO/TAC FOR/AID

B58
DUCLOUX L.,FROM BLACKMAIL TO TREASON. FRANCE PLAN DIPLOM EDU/PROP PRESS RUMOR NAT/LISM...CRIMLGY 20. PAGE 39 A0793
COERCE CRIME NAT/G PWR

B58
GAVIN J.M.,WAR AND PEACE IN THE SPACE AGE. SPACE USA+45 USSR FORCES PLAN TEC/DEV BAL/PWR DIPLOM ARMS/CONT WEAPON CIVMIL/REL...CHARTS GP/COMP 20 NATO COLD/WAR. PAGE 52 A1055
WAR DETER NUC/PWR PEACE

B58
HAUSER P.H.,POPULATION AND WORLD POLITICS. FUT WOR+45 WOR-45 AGRI DIST/IND INDUS INT/ORG PLAN ECO/TAC DISPL HEALTH COLD/WAR 20. PAGE 63 A1288
NAT/G ECO/UNDEV FOR/AID

B58
INSTITUTE MEDITERRANEAN AFF,THE PALESTINE REFUGEE PROBLEM. UAR WOR+45 INT/ORG PLAN PROB/SOLV PEACE ...POLICY GEOG STAT CHARTS 20 JEWS UN MIGRATION. PAGE 70 A1444
STRANGE HABITAT GP/REL INGP/REL

B58
ISLAM R.,INTERNATIONAL ECONOMIC COOPERATION AND THE UNITED NATIONS. FINAN PLAN EXEC TASK WAR PEACE ...SOC METH/CNCPT 20 UN LEAGUE/NAT. PAGE 72 A1470
INT/ORG DIPLOM ADMIN

B58
MELMAN S.,INSPECTION FOR DISARMAMENT. USA+45 WOR+45 SOCIETY INT/ORG NAT/G CONSULT ACT/RES PLAN EDU/PROP CONTROL DETER PEACE ATTIT PERSON KNOWL...PSY STAT OBS CHARTS TOT/POP VAL/FREE 20. PAGE 99 A2035
FUT ORD/FREE ARMS/CONT NUC/PWR

B58
MUNKMAN C.A.,AMERICAN AID TO GREECE. GREECE USA+45 AGRI FINAN PROB/SOLV WAR PWR...CHARTS 20 UN. PAGE 106 A2171
FOR/AID PLAN ECO/DEV INT/TRADE

B58
NEHRU J.,SPEECHES. INDIA ECO/UNDEV AGRI INDUS INT/ORG POL/PAR DIPLOM FOR/AID NAT/LISM...ANTHOL 20. PAGE 108 A2213
PLAN CHIEF COLONIAL NEUTRAL

B58
PALMER E.E.,AMERICAN FOREIGN POLICY. USA+45 CULTURE ECO/UNDEV NAT/G PLAN GIVE BAL/PAY ORD/FREE WEALTH POPULISM...DECISION ANTHOL 20. PAGE 113 A2319
DIPLOM ECO/TAC POLICY

B58
SLICK T.,PERMANENT PEACE: A CHECK AND BALANCE PLAN. FUT WOR+45 NAT/G FORCES CREATE PLAN EDU/PROP LEGIT ADJUD COERCE NAT/LISM RIGID/FLEX MORAL...HUM CONCPT METH/CNCPT NEW/IDEA TREND CHARTS TOT/POP 20. PAGE 134 A2742
INT/ORG ORD/FREE PEACE ARMS/CONT

B58
UN INTL CONF ON PEACEFUL USE,PROGRESS IN ATOMIC ENERGY (VOL. I). WOR+45 R+D PLAN TEC/DEV CONFER CONTROL PEACE SKILL...CHARTS ANTHOL 20 UN BAGHDAD. PAGE 147 A3003
NUC/PWR DIPLOM WORKER EDU/PROP

L58
HAVILAND H.F.,"FOREIGN AID AND THE POLICY PROCESS: 1957." USA+45 FACE/GP POL/PAR VOL/ASSN CHIEF DELIB/GP ACT/RES LEGIT EXEC GOV/REL ATTIT DRIVE PWR ...POLICY TESTS CONGRESS 20. PAGE 63 A1291
LEGIS PLAN FOR/AID

L58
TRAGER F.N.,"A SELECTED AND ANNOTATED BIBLIOGRAPHY ON ECONOMIC DEVELOPMENT, 1953-1957." WOR+45 AGRI FINAN INDUS MARKET LABOR MUNIC WORKER PLAN INT/TRADE PRODUC CENSUS. PAGE 145 A2958
BIBLIOG/A ECO/UNDEV ECO/DEV

S58
ANDERSON N.,"INTERNATIONAL SEMINARS: AN ANALYSIS AND AN EVALUATION." WOR+45 R+D ACT/RES CREATE PLAN REGION ATTIT KNOWL SKILL...SOC REC/INT PERS/TEST CHARTS 20. PAGE 8 A0158
INT/ORG DELIB/GP

S58
BLAISDELL D.C.,"PRESSURE GROUPS, FOREIGN POLICIES, AND INTERNATIONAL POLITICS." USA+45 WOR+45 INT/ORG PLAN DOMIN EDU/PROP LEGIT ADMIN ROUTINE CHOOSE ...DECISION MGT METH/CNCPT CON/ANAL 20. PAGE 15 A0303
PROF/ORG PWR

S58
BOGART L.,"MEASURING THE EFFECTIVENESS OF AN OVERSEAS INFORMATION CAMPAIGN." EUR+WWI GREECE USA+45 INT/ORG MUNIC PLAN DIPLOM PEACE PERCEPT RIGID/FLEX KNOWL...TECHNIC PSY SOC NEW/IDEA CONT/OBS REC/INT STAND/INT SAMP/SIZ COLD/WAR 20. PAGE 16 A0328
ATTIT EDU/PROP

S58
BURNS A.L.,"THE INTERNATIONAL CONSEQUENCES OF EXPECTING SURPRISE." WOR+45 INT/ORG NAT/G FORCES DIPLOM COERCE NUC/PWR WAR CHOOSE ORD/FREE ...METH/CNCPT STYLE OBS STERTYP TOT/POP VAL/FREE. PAGE 22 A0440
PLAN PWR DETER

S58
ELKIN A.B.,"OEEC-ITS STRUCTURE AND POWERS." EUR+WWI CONSTN INDUS INT/ORG NAT/G VOL/ASSN DELIB/GP ACT/RES PLAN ORD/FREE WEALTH...CHARTS ORG/CHARTS OEEC 20. PAGE 41 A0839
ECO/DEV EX/STRUC

S58
JORDAN A.,"MILITARY ASSISTANCE AND NATIONAL POLICY." ASIA FUT USA+45 WOR+45 ECO/DEV ECO/UNDEV INT/ORG NAT/G PLAN ECO/TAC ROUTINE WEAPON ATTIT RIGID/FLEX PWR...CONCPT TREND 20. PAGE 75 A1533
FORCES POLICY FOR/AID DIPLOM

S58
SINGER J.D.,"THREAT PERCEPTION AND THE ARMAMENT TENSION DILEMMA." WOR+45 WOR-45 ELITES INT/ORG NAT/G DELIB/GP PLAN LEGIT COERCE DETER ATTIT RIGID/FLEX PWR...DECISION PSY 20. PAGE 133 A2724
PERCEPT ARMS/CONT BAL/PWR

S58
SONDERMANN F.A.,"SOCIOLOGY AND INTERNATIONAL RELATIONS." WOR+45 CULTURE SOCIETY INT/ORG NAT/G CREATE ATTIT DRIVE PERSON RIGID/FLEX...PSY SOC 20. PAGE 135 A2767
PLAN NEW/IDEA PEACE

B59
AIR FORCE ACADEMY ASSEMBLY '59,INTERNATIONAL STABILITY AND PROGRESS (PAMPHLET). USA+45 USSR ECO/UNDEV PROB/SOLV BUDGET DIPLOM ADMIN DETER COST ATTIT...TREND 20. PAGE 5 A0103
FOR/AID FORCES WAR PLAN

B59
ALWAN M.,ALGERIA BEFORE THE UNITED NATIONS. AFR ASIA FRANCE ISLAM S/ASIA CONSTN SOCIETY STRUCT INT/ORG NAT/G ECO/TAC ADMIN COLONIAL NAT/LISM ATTIT PWR...DECISION TREND 420 UN. PAGE 7 A0133
PLAN RIGID/FLEX DIPLOM ALGERIA

B59
BRODIE B.,STRATEGY IN THE MISSILE AGE. FUT WOR+45 CONSULT PLAN COERCE DETER RIGID/FLEX PWR...CONCPT TIME/SEQ TREND 20. PAGE 19 A0381
ACT/RES FORCES ARMS/CONT NUC/PWR

B59
DIEBOLD W. JR.,THE SCHUMAN PLAN: A STUDY IN ECONOMIC COOPERATION, 1950-1959. EUR+WWI FRANCE GERMANY USA+45 EXTR/IND CONSULT DELIB/GP PLAN DIPLOM ECO/TAC INT/TRADE ROUTINE ORD/FREE WEALTH ...METH/CNCPT STAT CONT/OBS INT TIME/SEQ ECSC 20. PAGE 37 A0759
INT/ORG REGION

B59
ETSCHMANN R.,DIE WAHRUNGS- UND DEVISENPOLITIK DES OSTBLOCKS UND IHRE AUSWIRKUNGEN AUF DIE WIRTSCHAFTSBEZIEHUNGEN ZWISCHEN OST U WEST. BULGARIA CZECHOSLVK HUNGARY POLAND USSR MARKET NAT/G PLAN DIPLOM...NAT/COMP 20. PAGE 42 A0867
ECO/TAC FINAN POLICY INT/TRADE

B59
FERRELL R.H.,AMERICAN DIPLOMACY: A HISTORY. USA+45 USA-45 PLAN ROUTINE REV WAR PWR...T 18/20 EISNHWR/DD WWI. PAGE 45 A0921
DIPLOM NAT/G POLICY

B59
FOX W.T.R.,THEORETICAL ASPECTS OF INTERNATIONAL RELATIONS. WOR+45 INT/ORG NAT/G POL/PAR CONSULT PLAN ECO/TAC DOMIN EDU/PROP LEGIT EXEC COERCE PWR WEALTH...RELATIV CONCPT 20. PAGE 48 A0975
DELIB/GP ANTHOL

B59
HALEY A.G.,FIRST COLLOQUIUM ON THE LAW OF OUTER SPACE. WOR+45 INT/ORG ACT/RES PLAN BAL/PWR CONFER ATTIT PWR...POLICY JURID CHARTS ANTHOL 20. PAGE 60 A1225
SPACE LAW SOVEREIGN CONTROL

B59
HAZLEWOOD A.,THE ECONOMICS OF "UNDER-DEVELOPED" AREAS. WOR+45 DIST/IND EXTR/IND FINAN INDUS MARKET PLAN FOR/AID...GEOG 20. PAGE 63 A1302
BIBLIOG/A ECO/UNDEV AGRI INT/TRADE

B59
HERZ J.H.,INTERNATIONAL POLITICS IN THE ATOMIC AGE. FUT USA+45 WOR+45 WOR-45 SOCIETY NAT/G FORCES PLAN COERCE DETER ATTIT DRIVE ORD/FREE PWR...TREND COLD/WAR 20. PAGE 64 A1319
INT/ORG ARMS/CONT NUC/PWR

B59
KULSKI W.W.,PEACEFUL CO-EXISTENCE: AN ANALYSIS OF SOVIET FOREIGN POLICY. WOR+45 INTELL SOCIETY ECO/UNDEV POL/PAR EDU/PROP COERCE DRIVE RIGID/FLEX PWR SKILL...PSY CONCPT HIST/WRIT CON/ANAL GEN/METH
PLAN DIPLOM USSR

WORK VAL/FREE 20. PAGE 83 A1691

B59

MODELSKI G.,ATOMIC ENERGY IN THE COMMUNIST BLOC. FUT INT/ORG CONSULT FORCES ACT/RES PLAN KNOWL SKILL ...PHIL/SCI STAT CHARTS 20. PAGE 102 A2096 TEC/DEV NUC/PWR USSR COM

B59

NOVE A.,COMMUNIST ECONOMIC STRATEGY: SOVIET GROWTH AND CAPABILITIES. USSR AGRI LABOR PLAN TEC/DEV CAP/ISM INT/TRADE EFFICIENCY MARXISM 20 THIRD/WRLD. PAGE 110 A2257 FOR/AID ECO/TAC DIPLOM INDUS

B59

NUNEZ JIMENEZ A.,LA LIBERACION DE LAS ISLAS. CUBA L/A+17C USA+45 LAW CHIEF PLAN DIPLOM FOR/AID OWN WEALTH 20 CASTRO/F. PAGE 110 A2261 AGRI REV ECO/UNDEV NAT/G

B59

COLUMBIA U BUR APPL SOC RES,ATTITUDES OF PROMINENT AMERICANS TOWARD "WORLD PEACE THROUGH WORLD LAW" (SUPRA-NATL ORGANIZATION FOR WAR PREVENTION). USA+45 USSR ELITES FORCES PLAN PROB/SOLV CONTROL WAR PWR...POLICY SOC QU IDEA/COMP 20 UN. PAGE 117 A2403 ATTIT ACT/RES INT/LAW STAT

B59

SCHURZ W.L.,AMERICAN FOREIGN AFFAIRS: A GUIDE TO INTERNATIONAL AFFAIRS. USA+45 WOR+45 WOR-45 NAT/G FORCES LEGIS TOP/EX PLAN EDU/PROP LEGIT ADMIN ROUTINE ATTIT ORD/FREE PWR...SOC CONCPT STAT SAMP/SIZ CHARTS STERTYP 20. PAGE 129 A2653 INT/ORG SOCIETY DIPLOM

B59

STANFORD RESEARCH INSTITUTE,POSSIBLE NONMILITARY SCIENTIFIC DEVELOPMENTS AND THEIR POTENTIAL IMPACT ON FOREIGN POLICY PROBLEMS OF THE UNITED. FUT USA+45 INT/ORG PROF/ORG CONSULT ACT/RES CREATE PLAN PEACE KNOWL SKILL...TECHNIC PHIL/SCI NEW/IDEA UNESCO 20. PAGE 137 A2802 R+D TEC/DEV

B59

STERNBERG F.,THE MILITARY AND INDUSTRIAL REVOLUTION OF OUR TIME. USA+45 USSR WOR+45 WORKER COMPUTER PLAN TEC/DEV NUC/PWR GP/REL...POLICY NAT/COMP 20. PAGE 138 A2818 DIPLOM FORCES INDUS CIVMIL/REL

B59

STRAUSZ-HUPE R.,PROTRACTED CONFLICT. CHINA/COM KOREA WOR+45 INT/ORG FORCES ACT/RES ECO/TAC LEGIT COERCE DRIVE PERCEPT KNOWL PWR...PSY CONCPT RECORD GEN/METH COLD/WAR VAL/FREE 20. PAGE 139 A2847 COM PLAN USSR

B59

SWIFT R.W.,WORLD AFFAIRS AND THE COLLEGE CURRICULUM. USA+45 PLAN EFFICIENCY PERCEPT...HUM METH/CNCPT. PAGE 140 A2871 ACADEM DIPLOM METH/COMP EDU/PROP

B59

THOMAS N.,THE PREREQUISITES FOR PEACE. ASIA EUR+WWI FUT ISLAM S/ASIA WOR+45 FORCES PLAN BAL/PWR EDU/PROP LEGIT ATTIT PWR...SOCIALIST CONCPT COLD/WAR 20 UN. PAGE 143 A2924 INT/ORG ORD/FREE ARMS/CONT PEACE

B59

TUNSTALL W.C.B.,THE COMMONWEALTH AND REGIONAL DEFENCE (PAMPHLET). UK LAW VOL/ASSN PLAN AGREE REGION WAR ORD/FREE 20 CMN/WLTH NATO SEATO TREATY. PAGE 146 A2977 INT/ORG FORCES DIPLOM

B59

US GENERAL ACCOUNTING OFFICE,EXAM OF ECONOMIC AND TECHNICAL ASSISTANCE PROGRAM FOR INDIA INT'NAT'L COOP ADMIN REPORT TO CONGRESS 1955-1958. INDIA USA+45 ECO/UNDEV FINAN PLAN DIPLOM COST UTIL WEALTH ...CHARTS 20 CONGRESS AID. PAGE 153 A3114 FOR/AID EFFICIENCY ECO/TAC TEC/DEV

B59

US HOUSE COMM GOVT OPERATIONS,UNITED STATES AID OPERATIONS IN LAOS. LAOS USA+45 PLAN INSPECT HOUSE/REP. PAGE 154 A3136 FOR/AID ADMIN FORCES ECO/UNDEV

B59

US PRES COMM STUDY MIL ASSIST,COMPOSITE REPORT. USA+45 ECO/UNDEV PLAN BUDGET DIPLOM EFFICIENCY ...POLICY MGT 20. PAGE 155 A3164 FOR/AID FORCES WEAPON ORD/FREE

B59

WENTHOLT W.,SOME COMMENTS ON THE LIQUIDATION OF THE EUROPEAN PAYMENT UNION AND RELATED PROBLEMS (PAMPHLET). WOR+45 PLAN BUDGET PRICE CONTROL 20 EEC GOLD/STAND. PAGE 163 A3319 FINAN ECO/DEV INT/ORG ECO/TAC

L59

BEGUIN B.,"ILO AND THE TRIPARTITE SYSTEM." EUR+WWI WOR+45 WOR-45 CONSTN ECO/DEV ECO/UNDEV INDUS INT/ORG NAT/G VOL/ASSN DELIB/GP PLAN TEC/DEV LEGIT ORD/FREE WEALTH...CONCPT TIME/SEQ WORK ILO 20. PAGE 12 A0249 LABOR

L59

KAPLAN M.A.,"SOME PROBLEMS IN THE STRATEGIC ANALYSIS OF INTERNATIONAL POLITICS." UNIV R+D INT/ORG CREATE PLAN DIPLOM EDU/PROP COERCE DISPL PWR...METH/CNCPT NEW/IDEA HYPO/EXP TOT/POP 20. PAGE 76 A1561 DECISION BAL/PWR

L59

MURPHY J.C.,"SOME IMPLICATIONS OF EUROPE'S COMMON MARKET. IN (COOK P, ECONOMIC DEVELOPMENT AND INTERNATIONAL TRADE,." EUR+WWI ECO/DEV DIST/IND INDUS NAT/G PLAN ECO/TAC INT/TRADE WEALTH...STAT TREND OEEC TOT/POP 20 EEC. PAGE 106 A2178 MARKET INT/ORG REGION

S59

BELOFF M.,"NATIONAL GOVERNMENT AND INTERNATIONAL GOVERNMENT." WOR+45 R+D DELIB/GP ACT/RES PLAN PWR ...GEN/METH VAL/FREE EEC OEEC 20. PAGE 13 A0259 NAT/G INT/ORG DIPLOM

S59

FISCHER L.,"THE SOVIET-AMERICAN ANTAGONISM: HOW WILL IT END." CONSTN CULTURE PLAN TEC/DEV RIGID/FLEX SUPEGO ORD/FREE...MARXIST DECISION PSY CONCPT CON/ANAL GEN/LAWS VAL/FREE 20 COLD/WAR. PAGE 46 A0936 USA+45 PWR DIPLOM USSR

S59

FOX W.T.R.,"THE USES OF INTERNATIONAL RELATIONS THEORY. IN (FOX, THE THEORETICAL ASPECTS OF INTERNATIONAL RELATIONS,. WOR+45 INTELL SOCIETY STRATA INT/ORG CONSULT ACT/RES PWR...POLICY 20. PAGE 48 A0976 PLAN DIPLOM METH/CNCPT

S59

KRIPALANI A.J.B.,"FOR PRINCIPLED NEUTRALITY." CHINA/COM INDIA S/ASIA PLAN ECO/TAC RIGID/FLEX MORAL PWR...MYSTIC SOC RECORD 20 GANDHI/M. PAGE 82 A1684 ATTIT FOR/AID DIPLOM

S59

LASSWELL H.D.,"UNIVERSALITY IN PERSPECTIVE." FUT UNIV SOCIETY CONSULT TOP/EX PLAN EDU/PROP ADJUD ROUTINE ARMS/CONT COERCE PEACE ATTIT PERSON ALL/VALS. PAGE 85 A1741 INT/ORG JURID TOTALISM

S59

QUIGLEY H.S.,"TOWARD REAPPRAISAL OF OUR CHINA POLICY." CHINA/COM USA+45 INT/ORG PLAN ECO/TAC PERCEPT ORD/FREE...DECISION PSY CON/ANAL GEN/METH VAL/FREE 20. PAGE 118 A2427 ASIA KNOWL DIPLOM

S59

REUBENS E.D.,"THE BASIS FOR REORIENATION OF AMERICAN FOREIGN AID POLICY." USA+45 USSR STRUCT INT/ORG CONSULT ECO/TAC ADMIN DRIVE MORAL ORD/FREE PWR WEALTH...RELATIV MATH STAT TREND GEN/LAWS VAL/FREE 20. PAGE 120 A2467 ECO/UNDEV PLAN FOR/AID DIPLOM

S59

SAYEGH F.,"ARAB NATIONALISM AND SOVIET-AMERICAN RELATIONS." ISLAM USA+45 ECO/UNDEV PLAN ECO/TAC LEGIT NAT/LISM DRIVE PERCEPT KNOWL PWR...DECISION CONCPT STAT RECORD TREND CON/ANAL VAL/FREE 20 COLD/WAR. PAGE 127 A2610 DIPLOM USSR

S59

WARBURG J.P.,"THE CENTRAL EUROPEAN CRISIS: A PROPOSAL FOR WESTERN INITIATIVE." EUR+WWI INT/ORG NAT/G LEGIT DETER WAR...CONCPT BER/BLOC UN 20. PAGE 161 A3276 PLAN GERMANY

S59

ZAUBERMAN A.,"SOVIET BLOC ECONOMIC INTEGRATION." COM CULTURE INTELL ECO/DEV INDUS TOP/EX ACT/RES PLAN ECO/TAC INT/TRADE ROUTINE CHOOSE ATTIT ...TIME/SEQ 20. PAGE 169 A3448 MARKET INT/ORG USSR TOTALISM

B60

ALLEN H.C.,THE ANGLO-AMERICAN PREDICAMENT: THE BRITISH COMMONWEALTH, THE UNITED STATES AND EUROPEAN UNITY. EUR+WWI FUT UK USA+45 WOR+45 ECO/DEV NAT/G PLAN DETER...CONCPT OBS TIME/SEQ TREND COLD/WAR VAL/FREE CMN/WLTH 20. PAGE 6 A0123 INT/ORG PWR BAL/PWR

B60

ALLEN R.L.,SOVIET ECONOMIC WARFARE. USSR FINAN INDUS NAT/G PLAN TEC/DEV FOR/AID DETER WEALTH ...TREND GEN/LAWS 20. PAGE 6 A0126 COM ECO/TAC

B60

AMERICAN ASSEMBLY COLUMBIA U,THE SECRETARY OF STATE. USA+45 ELITES NAT/G PLAN ADMIN GOV/REL CENTRAL ATTIT...POLICY MGT 20 SEC/STATE CONGRESS PRESIDENT. PAGE 7 A0136 DELIB/GP EX/STRUC GP/REL DIPLOM

B60

APTHEKER H.,DISARMAMENT AND THE AMERICAN ECONOMY: A SYMPOSIUM. FUT USA+45 ECO/DEV DIST/IND FINAN INDUS PROC/MFG LABOR NAT/G POL/PAR CONSULT PLAN CAP/ISM INT/TRADE PEACE ATTIT MORAL WEALTH...TREND GEN/LAWS TOT/POP 20. PAGE 9 A0172 MARXIST ARMS/CONT

B60

BAILEY S.D.,THE GENERAL ASSEMBLY OF THE UNITED NATIONS. FUT WOR+45 STRUCT LEGIS ACT/RES PLAN EDU/PROP LEGIT ADMIN EXEC PEACE ATTIT HEALTH PWR ...CONCPT TREND CHARTS GEN/LAWS UN TOT/POP VAL/FREE COLD/WAR 20. PAGE 10 A0204 INT/ORG DELIB/GP DIPLOM

B60

BARNET R.,WHO WANTS DISARMAMENT. COM EUR+WWI USA+45 USSR INT/ORG NAT/G BAL/PWR DIPLOM EDU/PROP COERCE DETER NUC/PWR WAR WEAPON ATTIT PWR...TIME/SEQ COLD/WAR CONGRESS 20. PAGE 11 A0225 PLAN FORCES ARMS/CONT

B60

BLACK E.R.,THE DIPLOMACY OF ECONOMIC DEVELOPMENT. WOR+45 CONSULT PLAN TEC/DEV DIPLOM ECO/TAC FOR/AID ...CONCPT TREND 20. PAGE 15 A0297 ECO/UNDEV ACT/RES

B60

BUCHAN A.,NATO IN THE 1960'S. EUR+WWI USA+45 WOR+45 INT/ORG ACT/RES PLAN LEGIT COERCE DETER ATTIT DRIVE VOL/ASSN FORCES

RIGID/FLEX ORD/FREE...METH/CNCPT TIME/SEQ TREND GEN/LAWS COLD/WAR 20 NATO. PAGE 21 A0421 — ARMS/CONT SOVEREIGN

B60
EINSTEIN A.,EINSTEIN ON PEACE. FUT WOR+45 WOR-45 SOCIETY NAT/G PLAN BAL/PWR CAP/ISM DIPLOM ARMS/CONT DETER NAT/LISM...POLICY RELATIV HUM PHIL/SCI CONCPT BIOG COLD/WAR LEAGUE/NAT NAZI. PAGE 41 A0829 — INT/ORG ATTIT NUC/PWR PEACE

B60
FISCHER L.,RUSSIA, AMERICA, AND THE WORLD. FUT USA+45 USSR WOR+45 FORCES PLAN BAL/PWR ECO/TAC FOR/AID NEUTRAL TASK NUC/PWR PWR 20 COLD/WAR. PAGE 46 A0937 — DIPLOM POLICY MARXISM ECO/UNDEV

B60
FRANCK P.G.,AFGHANISTAN: BETWEEN EAST AND WEST. AFGHANISTN USA+45 USSR ECO/UNDEV PLAN ADMIN ROUTINE ATTIT PWR...STAT OBS CHARTS TOT/POP COLD/WAR 20. PAGE 48 A0978 — ECO/TAC TREND FOR/AID

B60
HAHN W.F.,AMERICAN STRATEGY FOR THE NUCLEAR AGE. USA+45 NAT/G TEC/DEV ECO/TAC FOR/AID ARMS/CONT NUC/PWR ORD/FREE MARXISM...ANTHOL 20. PAGE 59 A1216 — DIPLOM PLAN PEACE

B60
HYDE L.K.G.,THE US AND THE UN. WOR+45 STRUCT ECO/DEV ECO/UNDEV NAT/G ACT/RES PLAN DIPLOM EDU/PROP ADMIN ALL/VALS...CONCPT TIME/SEQ GEN/LAWS UN VAL/FREE 20. PAGE 70 A1428 — USA+45 INT/ORG FOR/AID

B60
JAECKH A.,WELTSAAT; ERLEBTES UND ERSTREBTES. GERMANY WOR+45 WOR-45 PLAN WAR...POLICY OBS/ENVIR NAT/COMP PERS/COMP 20. PAGE 73 A1489 — BIOG NAT/G SELF/OBS DIPLOM

B60
KENEN P.B.,GIANT AMONG NATIONS: PROBLEMS IN UNITED STATES FOREIGN ECONOMIC POLICY. USA+45 FINAN DIPLOM TARIFFS BAL/PAY WEALTH 20 COLD/WAR. PAGE 77 A1584 — FOR/AID ECO/UNDEV INT/TRADE PLAN

B60
KENEN P.B.,BRITISH MONETARY POLICY AND THE BALANCE OF PAYMENTS 1951-57. UK PLAN BUDGET ECO/TAC INT/TRADE PAY PRICE COST ATTIT 20. PAGE 77 A1585 — BAL/PAY PROB/SOLV FINAN NAT/G

B60
KENNEDY J.F.,THE STRATEGY OF PEACE. USA+45 WOR+45 BAL/PWR DIPLOM INGP/REL ORD/FREE...GOV/COMP NAT/COMP 20. PAGE 78 A1591 — PEACE PLAN POLICY NAT/G

B60
KHRUSHCHEV N.,FOR VICTORY IN PEACEFUL COMPETITION WITH CAPITALISM. COM FUT USSR WOR+45 CONSTN SOCIETY INDUS INT/ORG DELIB/GP PLAN BAL/PWR DIPLOM PERSON MARXISM...MARXIST WORK 20 COLD/WAR. PAGE 79 A1611 — TOP/EX PWR CAP/ISM SOCISM

B60
KINGSTON-MCCLOUG E.,DEFENSE; POLICY AND STRATEGY. UK SEA AIR TEC/DEV DIPLOM ADMIN LEAD WAR ORD/FREE ...CHARTS 20. PAGE 79 A1627 — FORCES PLAN POLICY DECISION

B60
LE GHAIT E.,NO CARTE BLANCHE TO CAPRICORN; THE FOLLY OF NUCLEAR WAR. WOR+45 INT/ORG BAL/PWR DIPLOM RISK COERCE...CENSUS 20 NATO. PAGE 86 A1754 — DETER NUC/PWR PLAN DECISION

B60
LERNER A.P.,THE ECONOMICS OF CONTROL. USA+45 ECO/UNDEV INT/ORG ACT/RES PLAN CAP/ISM INT/TRADE ATTIT WEALTH...SOC MATH STAT GEN/LAWS INDEX 20. PAGE 87 A1785 — ECO/DEV ROUTINE ECO/TAC SOCISM

B60
LINDSAY K.,EUROPEAN ASSEMBLIES: THE EXPERIMENTAL PERIOD 1949-1959. EUR+WWI ECO/DEV NAT/G POL/PAR LEGIS TOP/EX ACT/RES PLAN ECO/TAC DOMIN LEGIT ROUTINE ATTIT DRIVE ORD/FREE PWR SKILL...SOC CONCPT TREND CHARTS GEN/LAWS VAL/FREE. PAGE 89 A1823 — VOL/ASSN INT/ORG REGION

B60
MCKINNEY R.,REVIEW OF THE INTERNATIONAL ATOMIC POLICIES AND PROGRAMS OF THE UNITED STATES (5 VOLS.). COM FUT USA+45 ECO/DEV ECO/UNDEV INT/ORG DELIB/GP PLAN ADMIN 20 THIRD/WRLD. PAGE 98 A2016 — NUC/PWR PEACE DIPLOM POLICY

B60
NEALE A.D.,THE FLOW OF RESOURCES FROM RICH TO POOR. WOR+45 ECO/DEV ECO/UNDEV FINAN INDUS NAT/G PLAN EFFICIENCY WEALTH...POLICY NAT/COMP 20 RESOURCE/N. PAGE 108 A2209 — FOR/AID DIPLOM METH/CNCPT

B60
PAN AMERICAN UNION,FIFTH MEETING OF CONSULTATION OF MINISTERS OF FOREIGN AFFAIRS OF AMERICAN STATES. L/A+17C FORCES PLAN PROB/SOLV ADJUD PEACE...POLICY INT/LAW 20 OAS. PAGE 113 A2327 — INT/ORG DIPLOM DELIB/GP ECO/UNDEV

B60
RAO V.K.R.,INTERNATIONAL AID FOR ECONOMIC DEVELOPMENT - POSSIBILITIES AND LIMITATIONS. FINAN PLAN TEC/DEV ADMIN TASK EFFICIENCY...POLICY SOC METH/CNCPT CHARTS 20 UN. PAGE 119 A2444 — FOR/AID DIPLOM INT/ORG ECO/UNDEV

B60
SCHLESINGER J.R.,THE POLITICAL ECONOMY OF NATIONAL SECURITY. USA+45 USSR WOR+45 ECO/DEV ECO/UNDEV NAT/G DELIB/GP TOP/EX BAL/PWR DIPLOM INT/TRADE ATTIT PWR...STERTYP TOT/POP 20. PAGE 128 A2628 — PLAN ECO/TAC

B60
SHONFIELD A.,THE ATTACK ON WORLD POVERTY. WOR+45 ECO/DEV ECO/UNDEV FINAN VOL/ASSN PLAN EDU/PROP DRIVE KNOWL WEALTH...CONT/OBS STAND/INT ORG/CHARTS TOT/POP UNESCO 20. PAGE 132 A2704 — INT/ORG ECO/TAC FOR/AID INT/TRADE

B60
STEIN E.,AMERICAN ENTERPRISE IN THE EUROPEAN COMMON MARKET: A LEGAL PROFILE. EUR+WWI FUT USA+45 SOCIETY STRUCT ECO/DEV NAT/G VOL/ASSN CONSULT PLAN TEC/DEV ECO/TAC INT/TRADE ADMIN ATTIT RIGID/FLEX PWR...MGT NEW/IDEA STAT TREND COMPUT/IR SIMUL EEC 20. PAGE 137 A2814 — MARKET ADJUD INT/LAW

B60
TAYLOR M.D.,THE UNCERTAIN TRUMPET. USA+45 USSR WOR+45 INT/ORG NAT/G CONSULT DOMIN COERCE NUC/PWR WAR ATTIT ORD/FREE PWR...POLICY CONCPT TREND GEN/METH COLD/WAR UN NATO 20. PAGE 142 A2900 — PLAN FORCES DIPLOM

B60
THEOBALD R.,THE RICH AND THE POOR: A STUDY OF THE ECONOMICS OF RISING EXPECTATIONS. WOR+45 CONSTN ECO/DEV ECO/UNDEV INT/ORG NAT/G PLAN FOR/AID ROUTINE BAL/PAY ORD/FREE PWR WEALTH...GEOG TREND WORK 20. PAGE 142 A2912 — ECO/TAC INT/TRADE

B60
THOMPSON K.W.,POLITICAL REALISM AND THE CRISIS IN WORLD POLITICS. USA+45 USA-45 SOCIETY INT/ORG NAT/G LEGIS TOP/EX LEGIT DETER ATTIT ORD/FREE PWR ...GEN/LAWS TOT/POP 20. PAGE 143 A2931 — PLAN HUM BAL/PWR DIPLOM

B60
TURNER G.B.,NATIONAL SECURITY IN THE NUCLEAR AGE. KOREA USA+45 PLAN DIPLOM ARMS/CONT DETER WAR WEAPON ...BIBLIOG 20 COLD/WAR NATO. PAGE 146 A2982 — NAT/G POLICY FORCES NUC/PWR

B60
US HOUSE COMM GOVT OPERATIONS,OPERATIONS OF THE DEVELOPMENT LOAN FUND: HEARINGS (COMMITTEE ON GOVERNMENT OPERATIONS). USA+45 PLAN BUDGET DIPLOM GOV/REL COST...CHARTS 20 CONGRESS DEPT/STATE AID. PAGE 154 A3137 — FINAN FOR/AID ECO/TAC EFFICIENCY

B60
US SENATE COMM ON FOREIGN REL,SITUATION IN VIETNAM (2 VOLS.). USA+45 VIETNAM ECO/TAC COST SENATE DEPT/STATE. PAGE 156 A3181 — FOR/AID PLAN EFFICIENCY INSPECT

B60
VOGT W.,PEOPLE: CHALLENGE TO SURVIVAL. WOR+45 ECO/DEV ECO/UNDEV FAM INT/ORG NAT/G PLAN PROB/SOLV FOR/AID GIVE EATING 20 BIRTH/CON. PAGE 159 A3247 — CENSUS CONTROL ATTIT TEC/DEV

B60
WHITING A.S.,CHINA CROSSES THE YALU: THE DECISION TO ENTER THE KOREAN WAR. ASIA CHINA/COM KOREA ECO/UNDEV R+D INT/ORG TOP/EX ACT/RES BAL/PWR ATTIT PWR...GEN/METH 20. PAGE 164 A3338 — PLAN COERCE WAR

B60
WOETZEL R.K.,THE INTERNATIONAL CONTROL OF AIRSPACE AND OUTERSPACE. FUT WOR+45 AIR CONSTN STRUCT CONSULT PLAN TEC/DEV ADJUD RIGID/FLEX KNOWL ORD/FREE PWR...TECHNIC GEOG MGT NEW/IDEA TREND COMPUT/IR VAL/FREE 20 TREATY. PAGE 166 A3375 — INT/ORG JURID SPACE INT/LAW

B60
WOLF C.,FOREIGN AID: THEORY AND PRACTICE IN SOUTHERN ASIA. CEYLON INDONESIA PHILIPPINE S/ASIA CULTURE STRATA ECO/UNDEV PLAN EDU/PROP ATTIT ...METH/CNCPT MATH QUANT STAT CONT/OBS TIME/SEQ SIMUL TOT/POP 20. PAGE 166 A3378 — ACT/RES ECO/TAC FOR/AID

L60
BRENNAN D.G.,"SETTING AND GOALS OF ARMS CONTROL." FUT USA+45 USSR WOR+45 INTELL INT/ORG NAT/G VOL/ASSN CONSULT PLAN DIPLOM ECO/TAC ADMIN KNOWL PWR...POLICY CONCPT TREND COLD/WAR 20. PAGE 18 A0371 — FORCES COERCE ARMS/CONT DETER

L60
DEAN A.W.,"SECOND GENEVA CONFERENCE OF THE LAW OF THE SEA: THE FIGHT FOR FREEDOM OF THE SEAS." FUT USA+45 USSR WOR+45 WOR-45 SEA CONSTN STRUCT PLAN INT/TRADE ADJUD ADMIN ORD/FREE...DECISION RECORD TREND GEN/LAWS 20 TREATY. PAGE 35 A0717 — INT/ORG JURID INT/LAW

L60
DEUTSCH K.W.,"TOWARD AN INVENTORY OF BASIC TRENDS AND PATTERNS IN COMPARATIVE AND INTERNATIONAL POLITICS." UNIV WOR+45 SOCIETY STRUCT INT/ORG NAT/G CREATE PLAN EDU/PROP KNOWL...PHIL/SCI METH/CNCPT STAT SELF/OBS OBS/ENVIR SAMP TREND CON/ANAL CHARTS SOC/EXP GEN/METH 20. PAGE 36 A0739 — R+D PERCEPT

L60
HOLTON G.,"ARMS CONTROL." FUT WOR+45 CULTURE INT/ORG NAT/G FORCES TOP/EX PLAN EDU/PROP COERCE ATTIT RIGID/FLEX ORD/FREE...POLICY PHIL/SCI SOC TREND COLD/WAR. PAGE 67 A1377 — ACT/RES CONSULT ARMS/CONT NUC/PWR

L60
MCCLELLAND C.A.,"THE FUNCTION OF THEORY IN INTERNATIONAL RELATIONS." WOR+45 PLAN EDU/PROP ROUTINE ORD/FREE...PHIL/SCI PSY SOC METH/CNCPT NEW/IDEA OBS TREND GEN/METH 20. PAGE 97 A1997 — INT/ORG CONCPT DIPLOM

L60
RIGGS R.,"OVER-SELLING THE U.N. CHARTER, FACT AND MYTH." USA+45 SOCIETY NAT/G TOP/EX PLAN DIPLOM EDU/PROP PEACE ATTIT PERCEPT MORAL...POLICY SAMP UN 20. PAGE 121 A2481 — INT/ORG MYTH

S60
BOWIE R.,"POLICY FORMATION IN AMERICAN FOREIGN POLICY." FUT USA+45 WOR+45 STRUCT ECO/DEV INT/ORG POL/PAR LEGIS ACT/RES EXEC ALL/VALS...POLICY OBS VAL/FREE 20. PAGE 17 A0355 — PLAN DRIVE DIPLOM

S60
BRODY R.A.,"DETERRENCE STRATEGIES: AN ANNOTATED BIBLIOGRAPHY." WOR+45 PLAN ARMS/CONT NUC/PWR WAR WEAPON DECISION. PAGE 19 A0383 — BIBLIOG/A FORCES DETER DIPLOM

S60
DYSON F.J.,"THE FUTURE DEVELOPMENT OF NUCLEAR WEAPONS." FUT WOR+45 DELIB/GP ACT/RES PLAN DETER WEAPON ATTIT PWR...POLICY 20. PAGE 40 A0815 — INT/ORG ARMS/CONT NUC/PWR

S60
EFIMENCO N.M.,"CATEGORIES OF INTERNATIONAL INTEGRATION." UNIV WOR+45 INT/ORG NAT/G ACT/RES CREATE PEACE...CONCPT TREND 20. PAGE 40 A0824 — PLAN BAL/PWR SOVEREIGN

S60
FITZGIBBON R.H.,"DICTATORSHIP AND DEMOCRACY IN LATIN AMERICA." FUT ECO/DEV ECO/UNDEV INT/ORG LOC/G NAT/G TOP/EX PLAN TEC/DEV ECO/TAC CHOOSE ATTIT DRIVE PERSON ALL/VALS OAS TOT/POP 20. PAGE 46 A0943 — L/A+17C ACT/RES INT/TRADE

S60
FRANKEL S.H.,"ECONOMIC ASPECTS OF POLITICAL INDEPENDENCE IN AFRICA." AFR FUT SOCIETY ECO/UNDEV COM/IND FINAN LEGIS PLAN TEC/DEV CAP/ISM ECO/TAC INT/TRADE ADMIN ATTIT DRIVE RIGID/FLEX PWR WEALTH ...MGT NEW/IDEA MATH TIME/SEQ VAL/FREE 20. PAGE 48 A0984 — NAT/G FOR/AID

S60
GARNICK D.H.,"ON THE ECONOMIC FEASIBILITY OF A MIDDLE EASTERN COMMON MARKET." AFR ISLAM CULTURE INDUS NAT/G PLAN TEC/DEV ECO/TAC ADMIN ATTIT DRIVE RIGID/FLEX...PLURIST STAT TREND GEN/LAWS 20. PAGE 51 A1051 — MARKET INT/TRADE

S60
KAPLAN M.A.,"THEORETICAL ANALYSIS OF THE BALANCE OF POWER." FUT USA+45 WOR+45 INTELL ECO/DEV INT/ORG NAT/G CONSULT TOP/EX ACT/RES PLAN TEC/DEV ATTIT ALL/VALS...METH/CNCPT TOT/POP 20. PAGE 76 A1562 — CREATE NEW/IDEA DIPLOM NUC/PWR

S60
KENNAN G.F.,"PEACEFUL CO-EXISTENCE: A WESTERN VIEW." COM EUR+WWI USA+45 USSR WOR+45 PLAN BAL/PWR DIPLOM INT/TRADE PWR...POLICY CONCPT OBS HIST/WRIT TREND GEN/LAWS COLD/WAR 20 KHRUSH/N. PAGE 78 A1589 — ATTIT COERCE

S60
KISTIAKOWSKY G.B.,"SCIENCE AND FOREIGN AFFAIRS." FUT WOR+45 NAT/G PROF/ORG PLAN ECO/TAC EDU/PROP NUC/PWR...TREND COLD/WAR 20. PAGE 80 A1645 — CONSULT TEC/DEV FOR/AID DIPLOM

S60
MARTIN E.M.,"NEW TRENDS IN UNITED STATES ECONOMIC FOREIGN POLICY." USA+45 INTELL DELIB/GP FOR/AID INT/TRADE ROUTINE BAL/PAY...RELATIV 20. PAGE 95 A1949 — NAT/G PLAN DIPLOM

S60
MIKESELL R.F.,"AMERICA'S ECONOMIC RESPONSIBILITY AS A GREAT POWER." COM FUT USA+45 USSR WOR+45 INT/ORG PLAN ECO/TAC FOR/AID EDU/PROP CHOOSE WEALTH ...POLICY 20. PAGE 101 A2069 — ECO/UNDEV BAL/PWR CAP/ISM

S60
MODELSKI G.,"AUSTRALIA AND SEATO." S/ASIA USA+45 CULTURE INTELL ECO/DEV NAT/G PLAN DIPLOM ADMIN ROUTINE ATTIT SKILL...MGT TIME/SEQ AUSTRAL 20 SEATO. PAGE 102 A2097 — INT/ORG ACT/RES

S60
MORA J.A.,"THE ORGANIZATION OF AMERICAN STATES." USA+45 LAW ECO/UNDEV VOL/ASSN DELIB/GP PLAN BAL/PWR EDU/PROP ADMIN DRIVE RIGID/FLEX ORD/FREE WEALTH ...TIME/SEQ GEN/LAWS OAS 20. PAGE 103 A2126 — L/A+17C INT/ORG REGION

S60
NANES A.,"THE EUROPEAN COMMUNITY AND THE UNITED STATES: EVOLVING RELATIONS." EUR+WWI USA+45 WOR+45 ECO/UNDEV MARKET NAT/G DELIB/GP PLAN LEGIT ATTIT PWR WEALTH...CONCPT STAT TIME/SEQ CON/ANAL EEC OEEC 20 EURATOM. PAGE 107 A2194 — INT/ORG REGION

S60
OSGOOD C.E.,"COGNITIVE DYNAMICS IN THE CONDUCT OF HUMAN AFFAIRS." USA+45 INTELL INT/ORG CONSULT PLAN ATTIT PERSON...PSY CHARTS HYPO/EXP 20. PAGE 112 A2299 — R+D SOCIETY

S60
PETERSON E.N.,"HISTORICAL SCHOLARSHIP AND WORLD UNITY." FUT UNIV WOR-45 CULTURE INTELL INT/ORG NAT/G ACT/RES EDU/PROP ATTIT PERCEPT RIGID/FLEX ...NEW/IDEA OBS HIST/WRIT TREND COLD/WAR TOT/POP 20. PAGE 115 A2367 — PLAN KNOWL NAT/LISM

S60
PYE L.W.,"SOVIET AND AMERICAN STYLES IN FOREIGN AID." COM USA+45 USSR WOR+45 NAT/G PLAN ECO/TAC ROUTINE RIGID/FLEX...POLICY CONCPT TREND GEN/LAWS TOT/POP 20. PAGE 118 A2419 — ECO/UNDEV ATTIT FOR/AID

S60
RHYNE C.S.,"LAW AS AN INSTRUMENT FOR PEACE." FUT WOR+45 PLAN LEGIT ROUTINE ARMS/CONT NUC/PWR ATTIT ORD/FREE...JURID METH/CNCPT TREND CON/ANAL HYPO/EXP COLD/WAR 20. PAGE 120 A2471 — ADJUD EDU/PROP INT/LAW PEACE

S60
RICHTER J.H.,"TOWARDS AN INTERNATIONAL POLICY ON AGRICULTURAL TRADE." EUR+WWI USA+45 ECO/DEV NAT/G PLAN ECO/TAC ATTIT PWR WEALTH...CONCPT GEN/LAWS 20. PAGE 121 A2475 — AGRI INT/ORG

S60
RIVKIN A.,"AFRICAN ECONOMIC DEVELOPMENT: ADVANCED TECHNOLOGY AND THE STAGES OF GROWTH." CULTURE ECO/UNDEV AGRI COM/IND EXTR/IND PLAN ECO/TAC ATTIT DRIVE RIGID/FLEX SKILL WEALTH...MGT SOC GEN/LAWS WORK TOT/POP 20. PAGE 121 A2487 — AFR TEC/DEV FOR/AID

S60
SCHWELB E.,"INTERNATIONAL CONVENTIONS ON HUMAN RIGHTS." FUT WOR+45 LAW CONSTN CULTURE SOCIETY STRUCT VOL/ASSN DELIB/GP PLAN ADJUD SUPEGO LOVE MORAL...SOC CONCPT STAT RECORD HIST/WRIT TREND 20 UN. PAGE 130 A2664 — INT/ORG HUM

S60
THOMPSON K.W.,"MORAL PURPOSE IN FOREIGN POLICY: REALITIES AND ILLUSIONS." WOR+45 WOR-45 LAW CULTURE SOCIETY INT/ORG PLAN ADJUD ADMIN COERCE RIGID/FLEX SUPEGO KNOWL ORD/FREE PWR...SOC TREND SOC/EXP TOT/POP 20. PAGE 143 A2930 — MORAL JURID DIPLOM

S60
WRIGHT Q.,"LEGAL ASPECTS OF THE U-2 INCIDENT." COM USA+45 USSR STRUCT NAT/G FORCES PLAN TEC/DEV ADJUD RIGID/FLEX MORAL ORD/FREE...DECISION INT/LAW JURID PSY TREND GEN/LAWS COLD/WAR VAL/FREE 20 U-2. PAGE 168 A3413 — PWR POLICY SPACE

B61
ANAND R.P.,COMPULSORY JURISDICTION OF INTERNATIONAL COURT OF JUSTICE. FUT WOR+45 SOCIETY PLAN LEGIT ADJUD ATTIT DRIVE PERSON ORD/FREE...JURID CONCPT TREND 20 ICJ. PAGE 8 A0156 — INT/ORG COERCE INT/LAW

B61
AUBREY H.G.,COEXISTENCE: ECONOMIC CHALLENGE AND RESPONSE. USSR WOR+45 ACT/RES BAL/PWR CAP/ISM DIPLOM ECO/TAC FOR/AID INT/TRADE PEACE SOCISM ...METH/COMP NAT/COMP COLD/WAR. PAGE 10 A0196 — POLICY ECO/UNDEV PLAN COM

B61
BULL H.,THE CONTROL OF THE ARMS RACE. COM USA+45 INT/ORG NAT/G PLAN TEC/DEV DIPLOM ATTIT...RELATIV DECISION CONCPT SELF/OBS TREND CON/ANAL GEN/METH 20 COLD/WAR. PAGE 21 A0429 — FORCES PWR ARMS/CONT NUC/PWR

B61
DIA M.,THE AFRICAN NATIONS AND WORLD SOLIDARITY. ISLAM CULTURE ELITES ECO/DEV ECO/UNDEV INT/ORG NAT/G PLAN ECO/TAC INT/TRADE EDU/PROP NAT/LISM ATTIT DRIVE ORD/FREE WEALTH...SOCIALIST CONCPT CON/ANAL GEN/LAWS TOT/POP 20. PAGE 37 A0753 — AFR REGION SOCISM

B61
DIMOCK M.E.,BUSINESS AND GOVERNMENT (4TH ED.). AGRI FINAN OP/RES PLAN BUDGET DIPLOM LOBBY NUC/PWR NEW/LIB SOCISM...POLICY BIBLIOG 20. PAGE 37 A0765 — NAT/G INDUS LABOR ECO/TAC

B61
FRIEDMANN W.G.,JOINT INTERNATIONAL BUSINESS VENTURES. ASIA ISLAM L/A+17C ECO/DEV DIST/IND FINAN PROC/MFG FACE/GP LG/CO NAT/G VOL/ASSN CONSULT EX/STRUC PLAN ADMIN ROUTINE WEALTH...OLD/LIB WORK 20. PAGE 49 A1004 — ECO/UNDEV INT/TRADE

B61
FRISCH D.,ARMS REDUCTION: PROGRAM AND ISSUES. USA+45 INT/ORG NAT/G ACT/RES REGION NUC/PWR ATTIT PWR...POLICY 20. PAGE 49 A1010 — PLAN FORCES ARMS/CONT DIPLOM

B61
GALLOIS P.,THE BALANCE OF TERROR: STRATEGY FOR THE NUCLEAR AGE. FUT WOR+45 INT/ORG FORCES TOP/EX DETER WAR ATTIT RIGID/FLEX ORD/FREE PWR...HYPO/EXP 20. PAGE 50 A1032 — PLAN DECISION DIPLOM NUC/PWR

B61
GOLDWERT M.,CONSTABULARY IN THE DOMINICAN REPUBLIC AND NICARAGUA. DOMIN/REP L/A+17C NICARAGUA USA-45 NAT/G PLAN CONTROL TASK REV...POLICY 20 INTERVENT. PAGE 53 A1093 — DIPLOM PEACE FORCES

B61
HARRISON S.,INDIA AND THE UNITED STATES. FUT S/ASIA USA+45 WOR+45 INTELL ECO/DEV ECO/UNDEV AGRI INDUS INT/ORG NAT/G CONSULT EX/STRUC TOP/EX PLAN ECO/TAC NEUTRAL ALL/VALS...MGT TOT/POP 20. PAGE 62 A1272 — DELIB/GP ACT/RES FOR/AID INDIA

B61
JENKS C.W.,INTERNATIONAL IMMUNITIES. PLAN EDU/PROP ADMIN PERCEPT...OLD/LIB JURID CONCPT TREND TOT/POP. PAGE 74 A1506 — INT/ORG DIPLOM

B61
KISSINGER H.A.,THE NECESSITY FOR CHOICE. FUT USA+45 ECO/UNDEV NAT/G PLAN BAL/PWR ECO/TAC ARMS/CONT DETER NUC/PWR ATTIT...POLICY CONCPT RECORD GEN/LAWS — TOP/EX TREND DIPLOM

COLD/WAR 20. PAGE 80 A1642

B61
KITZINGER V.W.,THE CHALLENGE OF THE COMMON MARKET. EUR+WWI ECO/DEV DIST/IND PLAN ECO/TAC INT/TRADE LEGIT ATTIT PWR WEALTH...TIME/SEQ TREND CHARTS EEC 20. PAGE 80 A1647
MARKET INT/ORG UK

B61
KNORR K.E.,THE INTERNATIONAL SYSTEM. FUT SOCIETY INT/ORG NAT/G PLAN BAL/PWR DIPLOM WAR PWR ...DECISION METH/CNCPT CONT/OBS GAME METH UN 20. PAGE 81 A1655
ACT/RES SIMUL ECO/UNDEV

B61
LERCHE C.O. JR.,FOREIGN POLICY OF THE AMERICAN PEOPLE (REV. ED.). USA+45 USSR FORCES TEC/DEV EDU/PROP WAR PRODUC ORD/FREE MARXISM...POLICY TREND BIBLIOG 20 COLD/WAR. PAGE 87 A1781
DECISION PLAN PEACE DIPLOM

B61
MEZERIK A.G.,ECONOMIC DEVELOPMENT AIDS FOR UNDERDEVELOPED COUNTRIES. WOR+45 FINAN LEGIS PROB/SOLV TEC/DEV DIPLOM FOR/AID GIVE TASK WAR 20 UN. PAGE 101 A2062
ECO/UNDEV INT/ORG WEALTH PLAN

B61
MILLIKAW M.F.,THE EMERGING NATIONS: THEIR GROWTH AND UNITED STATES POLICY. FUT USA+45 WOR+45 WOR-45 NAT/G PLAN TEC/DEV BAL/PWR GOV/REL PEACE ORD/FREE 20. PAGE 101 A2082
ECO/UNDEV POLICY DIPLOM FOR/AID

B61
NATIONAL BANK OF LIBYA,INFLATION IN LIBYA (PAMPHLET). LIBYA SOCIETY NAT/G PLAN INT/TRADE ...STAT CHARTS 20 GOLD/STAND. PAGE 107 A2200
ECO/TAC ECO/UNDEV FINAN BUDGET

B61
NICOLSON H.G.,THE OLD DIPLOMACY AND THE NEW. NAT/G PLAN PROB/SOLV...METH 20. PAGE 109 A2233
DIPLOM POLICY INT/ORG

B61
RICE G.W.,THE SOVIET POSITION ON DEPENDENT TERRITORIES IN THE UNITED NATIONS (THESIS, OHIO STATE UNIVERSITY). USSR PLAN SOVEREIGN...POLICY 20 UN. PAGE 121 A2473
INT/ORG COM DIPLOM COLONIAL

B61
ROBINS D.B.,EVOLVING UNITED STATES POLICIES TOWARD THE EMERGING NATIONS OF ASIA AND AFRICA (PAMPHLET). ISLAM ECO/UNDEV INT/ORG CONSULT CREATE PLAN TEC/DEV FOR/AID CONFER ALL/VALS 20 KENNEDY/JF EISNHWR/DD UN AID. PAGE 122 A2501
AFR S/ASIA DIPLOM BIBLIOG

B61
SCHELLING T.C.,STRATEGY AND ARMS CONTROL. FUT UNIV WOR+45 INT/ORG PLAN TEC/DEV BAL/PWR LEGIT PERCEPT HEALTH...CONCPT VAL/FREE 20. PAGE 128 A2623
ROUTINE POLICY ARMS/CONT

B61
SCHMIDT H.,VERTEIDIGUNG ODER VERGELTUNG. COM CUBA GERMANY/W USSR FORCES DIPLOM ARMS/CONT DETER NUC/PWR...POLICY CHARTS HYPO/EXP SIMUL BIBLIOG 20 NATO COLD/WAR. PAGE 128 A2630
PLAN WAR BAL/PWR ORD/FREE

B61
SCOTT A.M.,POLITICS, USA; CASES ON THE AMERICAN DEMOCRATIC PROCESS. USA+45 CHIEF FORCES DIPLOM LOBBY CHOOSE RACE/REL FEDERAL ATTIT...JURID ANTHOL T 20 PRESIDENT CONGRESS CIVIL/LIB. PAGE 130 A2669
CT/SYS CONSTN NAT/G PLAN

B61
SHARP W.R.,FIELD ADMINISTRATION IN THE UNITED NATION SYSTEM: THE CONDUCT OF INTERNATIONAL ECONOMIC AND SOCIAL PROGRAMS. FUT WOR+45 CONSTN SOCIETY ECO/UNDEV R+D DELIB/GP ACT/RES PLAN TEC/DEV EDU/PROP EXEC ROUTINE HEALTH WEALTH...HUM CONCPT CHARTS METH ILO UNESCO VAL/FREE UN 20. PAGE 132 A2697
INT/ORG CONSULT

B61
SINGER J.D.,FINANCING INTERNATIONAL ORGANIZATION: THE UNITED NATIONS BUDGET PROCESS. WOR+45 FINAN ACT/RES CREATE PLAN BUDGET ECO/TAC ADMIN ROUTINE ATTIT KNOWL...DECISION METH/CNCPT TIME/SEQ UN 20. PAGE 133 A2726
INT/ORG MGT

B61
STILLMAN E.,THE NEW POLITICS: AMERICA AND THE END OF THE POSTWAR WORLD. FUT WOR+45 CULTURE SOCIETY ECO/UNDEV INT/ORG NAT/G FORCES TOP/EX ACT/RES DIPLOM EDU/PROP LEGIT ROUTINE DETER ATTIT ORD/FREE PWR...OBS STERTYP COLD/WAR TOT/POP VAL/FREE. PAGE 138 A2827
USA+45 PLAN

B61
STRAUSZ-HUPE R.,A FORWARD STRATEGY FOR AMERICA. FUT WOR+45 ECO/DEV INT/ORG NAT/G POL/PAR DELIB/GP FORCES ACT/RES CREATE ECO/TAC DOMIN EDU/PROP ATTIT DRIVE PWR...MAJORIT CONCPT STAT OBS TIME/SEQ TREND COLD/WAR TOT/POP. PAGE 139 A2848
USA+45 PLAN DIPLOM

B61
US SENATE COMM GOVT OPERATIONS,ORGANIZING FOR NATIONAL SECURITY. COM USA+45 BUDGET DIPLOM DETER NUC/PWR WAR WEAPON ORD/FREE...BIBLIOG 20 COLD/WAR. PAGE 156 A3172
POLICY PLAN FORCES COERCE

B61
WARD B.J.,INDIA AND THE WEST. INDIA UK USA+45 INT/TRADE GIVE COLONIAL ATTIT MARXISM 19/20. PAGE 161 A3279
PLAN ECO/UNDEV ECO/TAC FOR/AID

B61
WRINCH P.,THE MILITARY STRATEGY OF WINSTON CHURCHILL. UK WOR-45 SEA VOL/ASSN TEC/DEV BAL/PWR LEAD WAR PEACE ATTIT...POLICY 20 CHURCHLL/W. PAGE 168 A3421
CIVMIL/REL FORCES PLAN DIPLOM

B61
YDIT M.,INTERNATIONALISED TERRITORIES. FUT WOR+45 WOR-45 CONSTN VOL/ASSN CREATE PLAN LEGIT PEACE ORD/FREE...GEOG INT/LAW JURID SOC NEW/IDEA OBS RECORD SAMP TIME/SEQ TREND 19/20 BERLIN. PAGE 169 A3431
LOC/G INT/ORG DIPLOM SOVEREIGN

L61
HALPERIN M.H.,"NUCLEAR WEAPONS AND LIMITED WARS." FUT UNIV WOR+45 INTELL SOCIETY ECO/DEV ACT/RES DRIVE PERCEPT RIGID/FLEX...CONCPT TIME/SEQ TREND TOT/POP 20. PAGE 60 A1237
PLAN COERCE NUC/PWR WAR

L61
HOYT E.C.,"UNITED STATES REACTION TO THE KOREAN ATTACK." COM KOREA USA+45 CONSTN DELIB/GP FORCES PLAN ECO/TAC DOMIN EDU/PROP LEGIT ROUTINE COERCE WAR ATTIT DISPL RIGID/FLEX ORD/FREE PWR...POLICY INT/LAW TREND UN 20. PAGE 68 A1402
ASIA INT/ORG BAL/PWR DIPLOM

L61
SAND P.T.,"AN HISTORICAL SURVEY OF INTERNATIONAL AIR LAW SINCE 1944." USA+45 USA-45 WOR+45 WOR-45 SOCIETY ECO/DEV NAT/G CONSULT EX/STRUC ACT/RES PLAN LEGIT ROUTINE...JURID CONCPT METH/CNCPT TREND 20. PAGE 127 A2598
INT/ORG LAW INT/LAW SPACE

L61
TAUBENFELD H.J.,"A REGIME FOR OUTER SPACE." FUT UNIV R+D ACT/RES PLAN BAL/PWR LEGIT ARMS/CONT ORD/FREE...POLICY JURID TREND UN TOT/POP 20 COLD/WAR. PAGE 142 A2894
INT/ORG ADJUD SPACE

S61
"CRITERIA FOR ALLOCATING INVESTMENT RESOURCES AMONG VARIOUS FIELDS OF DEVELOPMENT IN UNDERDEVELOPED ECONOMIES." ASIA AGRI INT/ORG CAP/ISM BAL/PAY EFFICIENCY PROFIT WEALTH...STAT 20 UN. PAGE 3 A0061
BIBLIOG/A ECO/UNDEV PLAN TEC/DEV

S61
ALGER C.F.,"NON-RESOLUTION CONSEQUENCES OF THE UNITED NATIONS AND THEIR EFFECT ON INTERNATIONAL CONFLICT." WOR+45 CONSTN ECO/DEV NAT/G CONSULT DELIB/GP TOP/EX ACT/RES PLAN DIPLOM EDU/PROP ROUTINE ATTIT ALL/VALS...INT/LAW TOT/POP UN 20. PAGE 6 A0117
INT/ORG DRIVE BAL/PWR

S61
ANGLIN D.,"UNITED STATES OPPOSITION TO CANADIAN MEMBERSHIP IN THE PAN AMERICAN UNION: A CANADIAN VIEW." L/A+17C UK USA+45 VOL/ASSN DELIB/GP EX/STRUC PLAN DIPLOM DOMIN REGION ATTIT RIGID/FLEX PWR ...RELATIV CONCPT STERTYP CMN/WLTH OAS 20. PAGE 8 A0162
INT/ORG CANADA

S61
ASHFORD D.E.,"A CASE STUDY IN THE DIPLOMACY OF SOCIAL REVOLUTION." USA+45 WOR+45 DIPLOM ECO/TAC FOR/AID REV ALL/VALS VAL/FREE 20. PAGE 9 A0187
ECO/UNDEV PLAN

S61
BARALL M.,"THE UNITED STATES GOVERNMENT RESPONDS." L/A+17C USA+45 SOCIETY NAT/G CREATE PLAN DIPLOM ECO/TAC ATTIT DRIVE RIGID/FLEX KNOWL SKILL WEALTH ...METH/CNCPT TIME/SEQ GEN/METH 20. PAGE 11 A0217
ECO/UNDEV ACT/RES FOR/AID

S61
BARNET R.,"RUSSIA, CHINA, AND THE WORLD: THE SOVIET ATTITUDE ON DISARMAMENT (PART 3)." ASIA CHINA/COM FUT INT/ORG NAT/G POL/PAR VOL/ASSN ARMS/CONT ATTIT ...POLICY CONCPT TIME/SEQ TREND TOT/POP VAL/FREE 20. PAGE 11 A0226
COM PLAN TOTALISM USSR

S61
BURNET A.,"TOO MANY ALLIES." COM EUR+WWI UK WOR+45 WOR-45 ACT/RES PLAN DISPL PWR SKILL...TIME/SEQ 20 CMN/WLTH SEATO NATO CENTO. PAGE 22 A0438
VOL/ASSN INT/ORG DIPLOM

S61
CARLETON W.G.,"AMERICAN FOREIGN POLICY: MYTHS AND REALITIES." FUT USA+45 WOR+45 ECO/UNDEV INT/ORG EX/STRUC ARMS/CONT NUC/PWR WAR ATTIT...POLICY CONCPT CONT/OBS GEN/METH COLD/WAR TOT/POP 20. PAGE 24 A0484
PLAN MYTH DIPLOM

S61
DANIELS R.V.,"THE CHINESE REVOLUTION IN RUSSIAN PERSPECTIVE." ASIA CHINA/COM COM USSR INTELL INT/ORG TOP/EX REV TOTALISM PWR...POLICY WORK VAL/FREE 20. PAGE 33 A0680
POL/PAR PLAN

S61
DEUTSCH K.W.,"NATIONAL INDUSTRIALIZATION AND THE DECLINING SHARE OF THE INTERNATIONAL ECONOMIC SECTOR." EUR+WWI FUT WOR+45 WOR-45 MARKET PLAN EDU/PROP WEALTH...WELF/ST OBS TESTS 20. PAGE 36 A0740
DIST/IND ECO/DEV INT/TRADE

S61
HEILBRONER R.L.,"DYNAMICS OF FOREIGN AID: PROBLEMS OF UNDERDEVELOPED NATIONS PLAGUE ASSISTANCE PROGRAM." FUT USA+45 WOR+45 STRATA NAT/G PLAN TEC/DEV ATTIT DRIVE WEALTH WORK 20. PAGE 64 A1307
ECO/UNDEV ECO/TAC FOR/AID

S61
JACKSON E.,"CONSTITUTIONAL DEVELOPMENTS OF THE
INT/ORG

UNITED NATIONS: THE GROWTH OF ITS EXECUTIVE CAPACITY." FUT WOR+45 CONSTN STRUCT ACT/RES PLAN ALL/VALS...NEW/IDEA OBS COLD/WAR UN 20. PAGE 72 A1475
EXEC

S61
LANFALUSSY A.,"EUROPE'S PROGRESS: DUE TO COMMON MARKET." EUR+WWI ECO/DEV DELIB/GP PLAN ECO/TAC ROUTINE WEALTH...GEOG TREND EEC 20. PAGE 84 A1721
INT/ORG MARKET

S61
LIPSON L.,"AN ARGUMENT ON THE LEGALITY OF RECONNAISSANCE STATELLITES." COM USA+45 USSR WOR+45 AIR INTELL NAT/G CONSULT PLAN DIPLOM LEGIT ROUTINE ATTIT...INT/LAW JURID CONCPT METH/CNCPT TREND COLD/WAR 20. PAGE 90 A1833
INT/ORG LAW SPACE

S61
MACHOWSKI K.,"SELECTED PROBLEMS OF NATIONAL SOVEREIGNTY WITH REFERENCE TO THE LAW OF OUTER SPACE." FUT WOR+45 AIR LAW INTELL SOCIETY ECO/DEV PLAN EDU/PROP DETER DRIVE PERCEPT SOVEREIGN ...POLICY INT/LAW OBS TREND TOT/POP 20. PAGE 92 A1889
UNIV ACT/RES NUC/PWR SPACE

S61
MASTERS R.D.,"A MULTI-BLOC MODEL OF THE INTERNATIONAL SYSTEM." FUT UNIV WOR+45 SOCIETY ACT/RES PLAN...GEOG SOC TREND SIMUL TOT/POP 20. PAGE 96 A1963
INT/ORG CONCPT

S61
NOVE A.,"THE SOVIET MODEL AND UNDERDEVELOPED COUNTRIES." COM FUT USSR WOR+45 CULTURE ECO/DEV POL/PAR FOR/AID EDU/PROP ADMIN MORAL WEALTH ...POLICY RECORD HIST/WRIT 20. PAGE 110 A2258
ECO/UNDEV PLAN

S61
OCHENG D.,"AN ECONOMIST LOOKS AT UGANDA'S FUTURE." FUT UGANDA AGRI INDUS PLAN PROB/SOLV INT/TRADE SOVEREIGN 20. PAGE 111 A2275
ECO/UNDEV INCOME ECO/TAC OWN

S61
RAY J.,"THE EUROPEAN FREE-TRADE ASSOCIATION AND ITS IMPACT ON INDIA'S TRADE." EUR+WWI FRANCE GERMANY INDIA S/ASIA UK NAT/G VOL/ASSN PLAN INT/TRADE ROUTINE WEALTH...STAT CHARTS CMN/WLTH EEC OEEC 20 EFTA. PAGE 120 A2453
ECO/DEV ECO/TAC

S61
ROSTOW W.W.,"THE FUTURE OF FOREIGN AID." COM FUT WOR+45 ECO/DEV INDUS INT/ORG NAT/G CONSULT ACT/RES PLAN DOMIN LEGIT CHOOSE RIGID/FLEX ALL/VALS ...MAJORIT CONCPT TREND TOT/POP 20. PAGE 124 A2544
ECO/UNDEV ECO/TAC FOR/AID

S61
TAUBENFELD H.J.,"OUTER SPACE--PAST POLITICS AND FUTURE POLICY." FUT USA+45 USA-45 WOR+45 AIR INTELL STRUCT ECO/DEV NAT/G TOP/EX ACT/RES ADMIN ROUTINE NUC/PWR ATTIT DRIVE...CONCPT TIME/SEQ TREND TOT/POP 20. PAGE 141 A2892
PLAN SPACE INT/ORG

S61
TRAMPE G.,"DIE FORM DER DIPLOMATIC ALS POLITSCHE WAFFE." WOR+45 WOR-45 SOCIETY STRATA INT/ORG NAT/G ACT/RES PLAN ECO/TAC EDU/PROP COERCE WAR ATTIT RIGID/FLEX...DECISION CONCPT TREND. PAGE 145 A2959
CONSULT PWR DIPLOM

S61
VERNON R.,"A TRADE POLICY FOR THE 1960'S." COM FUT USA+45 WOR+45 ECO/DEV ECO/UNDEV FINAN TOP/EX ACT/RES...WELF/ST METH/CNCPT CONT/OBS TOT/POP 20. PAGE 159 A3229
PLAN INT/TRADE

S61
ZAGORIA D.S.,"SINO-SOVIET FRICTION IN UNDERDEVELOPED AREAS." ASIA CHINA/COM COM ACT/RES PLAN ATTIT ORD/FREE PWR COLD/WAR 20. PAGE 169 A3443
ECO/UNDEV ECO/TAC INT/TRADE USSR

S61
ZAGORIA D.S.,"THE FUTURE OF SINO-SOVIET RELATIONS." CHINA/COM INT/ORG NAT/G POL/PAR VOL/ASSN ACT/RES PLAN PERSON...METH/CNCPT TIME/SEQ TOT/POP VAL/FREE 20 MAO KHRUSH/N. PAGE 169 A3444
ASIA COM TOTALISM USSR

B62
ROUND TABLE ON EUROPE'S ROLE IN LATIN AMERICAN DEVELOPMENT. EUR+WWI L/A+17C PLAN BAL/PAY UTIL ROLE WEALTH...CHARTS ANTHOL 20 UN INT/AM/DEV. PAGE 3 A0063
ECO/UNDEV FINAN TEC/DEV FOR/AID

B62
BAILEY S.D.,THE SECRETARIAT OF THE UNITED NATIONS. FUT WOR+45 DELIB/GP PLAN BAL/PWR DOMIN EDU/PROP ADMIN PEACE ATTIT PWR...DECISION CONCPT TREND CON/ANAL CHARTS UN VAL/FREE COLD/WAR 20. PAGE 10 A0205
INT/ORG EXEC DIPLOM

B62
BEATON L.,THE SPREAD OF NUCLEAR WEAPONS. WOR+45 NAT/G PLAN PROB/SOLV DIPLOM ECO/TAC DETER...POLICY 20 COLD/WAR. PAGE 12 A0242
ARMS/CONT NUC/PWR TEC/DEV FUT

B62
BELL C.,NEGOTIATION FROM STRENGTH. WOR+45 FACE/GP INT/ORG DELIB/GP FORCES PLAN DOMIN COERCE NUC/PWR PEACE DRIVE PWR...POLICY LOG OBS RECORD INT SAMP TREND COLD/WAR 20. PAGE 13 A0255
NAT/G CONCPT DIPLOM

B62
BLACKETT P.M.S.,STUDIES OF WAR: NUCLEAR AND CONVENTIONAL. EUR+WWI USA+45 DELIB/GP ACT/RES CREATE PLAN TEC/DEV LEGIT COERCE WAR ORD/FREE PWR ...POLICY TECHNIC TIME/SEQ 20. PAGE 15 A0300
INT/ORG FORCES ARMS/CONT NUC/PWR

B62
BOUSCAREN A.T.,SOVIET FOREIGN POLICY: A PATTERN OF PERSISTANCE. WOR+45 WOR-45 SOCIETY STRUCT INT/ORG POL/PAR CREATE PLAN EDU/PROP ROUTINE ATTIT RIGID/FLEX...POLICY CONCPT RECORD HIST/WRIT TIME/SEQ MARX/KARL 20. PAGE 17 A0352
COM NAT/G DIPLOM USSR

B62
BURTON J.W.,PEACE THEORY: PRECONDITIONS OF DISARMAMENT. COM EUR+WWI USA+45 NAT/G FORCES BAL/PWR DIPLOM ECO/TAC EDU/PROP REGION COERCE DETER PEACE ATTIT PWR TOT/POP COLD/WAR 20. PAGE 22 A0446
INT/ORG PLAN ARMS/CONT

B62
CALDER R.,COMMON SENSE ABOUT A STARVING WORLD. WOR+45 STRATA ECO/DEV PLAN GP/REL BIO/SOC HABITAT ...POLICY GEOG STAT RECORD 20 UN BIRTH/CON. PAGE 23 A0466
FOR/AID CENSUS ECO/UNDEV AGRI

B62
CLUBB O.E. JR.,THE UNITED STATES AND THE SINO-SOVIET BLOC IN SOUTHEAST ASIA. ASIA CHINA/COM COM USA+45 USSR ECO/UNDEV INT/ORG NAT/G FORCES TOP/EX PLAN ECO/TAC DOMIN COERCE GUERRILLA ATTIT RIGID/FLEX...POLICY OBS TREND 20. PAGE 27 A0553
S/ASIA PWR BAL/PWR DIPLOM

B62
COUNCIL ON WORLD TENSIONS,A STUDY OF WORLD TENSIONS AND DEVELOPMENT. WOR+45 ECO/DEV ECO/UNDEV INT/ORG PLAN DIPLOM ECO/TAC EDU/PROP ATTIT KNOWL ORD/FREE PWR WEALTH...CONCPT TREND CHARTS STERTYP COLD/WAR TOT/POP 20. PAGE 31 A0640
TEC/DEV SOC

B62
COUNCIL ON WORLD TENSIONS,RESTLESS NATIONS. WOR+45 STRUCT INT/ORG NAT/G PLAN ECO/TAC...NAT/COMP ANTHOL 20. PAGE 32 A0641
ECO/UNDEV POLICY DIPLOM TASK

B62
DOUGLAS W.O.,DEMOCRACY'S MANIFESTO. COM USA+45 ECO/UNDEV INT/ORG FORCES PLAN NEUTRAL TASK MARXISM ...JURID 20 NATO SEATO. PAGE 38 A0779
DIPLOM POLICY NAT/G ORD/FREE

B62
DREIER J.C.,THE ALLIANCE FOR PROGRESS. L/A+17C USA+45 CULTURE ECO/DEV ECO/UNDEV NAT/G PLAN DIPLOM PWR 20 OAS. PAGE 39 A0787
FOR/AID INT/ORG ECO/TAC POLICY

B62
DUROSELLE J.B.,LES NOUVEAUX ETATS DANS LES RELATIONS INTERNATIONALES. AFR CHINA/COM FRANCE MOROCCO S/ASIA USSR ECO/UNDEV INT/ORG PLAN ECO/TAC EDU/PROP ATTIT DRIVE...TREND TOT/POP TUNIS 20. PAGE 39 A0806
NAT/G CONSTN DIPLOM

B62
DUTOIT B.,LA NEUTRALITE SUISSE A L'HEURE EUROPEENNE. EUR+WWI MOD/EUR INT/ORG NAT/G VOL/ASSN PLAN BAL/PWR LEGIT NEUTRAL REGION PEACE ORD/FREE SOVEREIGN...CONCPT OBS TIME/SEQ TREND STERTYP VAL/FREE LEAGUE/NAT UN 20. PAGE 40 A0812
ATTIT DIPLOM SWITZERLND

B62
EBENSTEIN W.,TWO WAYS OF LIFE. USA+45 CULTURE ECO/DEV PLAN EDU/PROP CONTROL ORD/FREE...GOV/COMP IDEA/COMP T 20 MARX/KARL ENGELS/F LENIN/VI LOCKE/JOHN MILL/JS. PAGE 40 A0819
MARXISM POPULISM ECO/TAC DIPLOM

B62
FORBES H.W.,THE STRATEGY OF DISARMAMENT. FUT WOR+45 INT/ORG VOL/ASSN CONSULT ARMS/CONT COERCE NUC/PWR WAR DRIVE RIGID/FLEX ORD/FREE PWR...POLICY CONCPT OBS TREND STERTYP 20. PAGE 47 A0959
PLAN FORCES DIPLOM

B62
GUENA Y.,HISTORIQUE DE LA COMMUNAUTE. FUT ECO/UNDEV NAT/G PLAN EDU/PROP COLONIAL REGION NAT/LISM ALL/VALS SOVEREIGN...CONCPT OBS CHARTS 20. PAGE 58 A1186
AFR VOL/ASSN FOR/AID FRANCE

B62
HATCH J.,AFRICA TODAY-AND TOMORROW: AN OUTLINE OF BASIC FACTS AND MAJOR PROBLEMS. AFR FUT ISLAM STRATA ECO/UNDEV INT/ORG NAT/G POL/PAR DELIB/GP TOP/EX EDU/PROP LEGIT CHOOSE ATTIT...TIME/SEQ TOT/POP COLD/WAR 20. PAGE 63 A1287
PLAN CONSTN NAT/LISM

B62
HUMPHREY D.D.,THE UNITED STATES AND THE COMMON MARKET. USA+45 INDUS MARKET INT/ORG PLAN EDU/PROP BAL/PAY DRIVE PWR WEALTH...TREND STERTYP EEC 20. PAGE 69 A1415
ATTIT ECO/TAC

B62
HUNTINGTON S.P.,CHANGING PATTERNS OF MILITARY POLITICS. EUR+WWI L/A+17C S/ASIA USA+45 WOR+45 CULTURE INT/ORG NAT/G CONSULT PLAN DOMIN EDU/PROP LEGIT DETER WAR ATTIT PERSON PWR...DECISION CONCPT SIMUL GEN/LAWS ANTHOL COLD/WAR 20. PAGE 69 A1419
FORCES RIGID/FLEX

B62
JORDAN A.A. JR.,FOREIGN AID AND THE DEFENSE OF SOUTHEAST ASIA. PAKISTAN VIETNAM/S FINAN PLAN BUDGET ECO/TAC DETER WAR ORD/FREE...POLICY DECISION CENSUS CHARTS BIBLIOG 20. PAGE 75 A1535
FOR/AID S/ASIA FORCES ECO/UNDEV

B62
KAHN H.,THINKING ABOUT THE UNTHINKABLE. FUT USA+45 LAW NAT/G CONSULT FORCES ACT/RES CREATE PLAN TEC/DEV BAL/PWR DIPLOM EDU/PROP ARMS/CONT DETER ATTIT...CONCPT OBS TREND COLD/WAR 20. PAGE 76 A1547
INT/ORG ORD/FREE NUC/PWR PEACE

B62
KING-HALL S.,POWER POLITICS IN THE NUCLEAR AGE: A POLICY FOR BRITAIN. UK WOR+45 PLAN ECO/TAC CONTROL RISK ARMS/CONT MORAL PWR RESPECT...OLD/LIB 20. PAGE 79 A1625
BAL/PWR NUC/PWR POLICY DIPLOM

B62
KLUCKHOHN F.L.,THE NAKED RISE OF COMMUNISM. CHINA/COM COM USSR WOR+45 CONSTN POL/PAR PLAN CONTROL LEAD NEUTRAL CONSERVE 20 STALIN/J EUROPE/E COM/PARTY. PAGE 80 A1650
MARXISM IDEA/COMP DIPLOM DOMIN

B62
KRAFT J.,THE GRAND DESIGN. EUR+WWI USA+45 AGRI FINAN INDUS MARKET INT/ORG NAT/G PLAN ECO/TAC TARIFFS REGION DRIVE ORD/FREE WEALTH...POLICY OBS TREND EEC 20. PAGE 82 A1674
VOL/ASSN ECO/DEV INT/TRADE

B62
LAQUEUR W.,THE FUTURE OF COMMUNIST SOCIETY. CHINA/COM USSR LAW ECO/DEV NAT/G POL/PAR PLAN PROB/SOLV DIPLOM LEAD...POLICY CONCPT IDEA/COMP ANTHOL 20. PAGE 85 A1731
MARXISM COM FUT SOCIETY

B62
LEWIS J.P.,QUIET CRISIS IN INDIA. INDIA USA+45 CULTURE ECO/UNDEV AGRI INDUS PROC/MFG NAT/G PLAN TEC/DEV DRIVE PWR SKILL WEALTH...MYTH 20. PAGE 88 A1801
S/ASIA ECO/TAC FOR/AID

B62
MACKENTOSH J.M.,STRATEGY AND TACTICS OF SOVIET FOREIGN POLICY. CHINA/COM FUT USA+45 WOR+45 INT/ORG PLAN DOMIN LEGIT ROUTINE COERCE NUC/PWR WAR ATTIT DRIVE ORD/FREE PWR...CONCPT OBS TIME/SEQ TREND GEN/METH COLD/WAR 20. PAGE 92 A1894
COM POLICY DIPLOM USSR

B62
MCKENNA J.,DIPLOMATIC PROTEST IN FOREIGN POLICY: ANALYSIS AND CASE STUDIES. COM USA+45 WOR+45 INT/ORG PUB/INST DELIB/GP TOP/EX ACT/RES PLAN LEGIT ATTIT 20. PAGE 98 A2014
NAT/G POLICY DIPLOM

B62
MONCRIEFF A.,THE STRATEGY OF SURVIVAL. UK FORCES BAL/PWR CONFER DETER WAR...ANTHOL 20 COLD/WAR. PAGE 102 A2104
PLAN DECISION DIPLOM ARMS/CONT

B62
MOON P.,DIVIDE AND QUIT. INDIA PAKISTAN STRATA DELIB/GP PLAN DIPLOM REPRESENT GP/REL INGP/REL CONSEN DISCRIM...OBS 20. PAGE 103 A2119
WAR REGION ISOLAT SECT

B62
MORGENTHAU H.J.,POLITICS IN THE TWENTIETH CENTURY: IMPASSE OF AMERICAN FOREIGN POLICY. FUT GERMANY USA+45 USSR WOR+45 INT/ORG NAT/G ACT/RES PLAN FOR/AID EDU/PROP LEGIT COERCE WAR PWR...TIME/SEQ TREND COLD/WAR 20. PAGE 104 A2138
SKILL DIPLOM

B62
MORGENTHAU H.J.,POLITICS IN THE 20TH CENTURY: RESTORATION OF AMERICAN POLITICS. ASIA GERMANY USA+45 USSR WOR+45 NAT/G PLAN EDU/PROP LEGIT NUC/PWR ATTIT PWR SKILL...CONCPT TREND COLD/WAR 20. PAGE 104 A2139
INT/ORG DIPLOM

B62
MORTON L.,STRATEGY AND COMMAND: THE FIRST TWO YEARS. USA-45 NAT/G CONTROL EXEC LEAD WEAPON CIVMIL/REL PWR...POLICY AUD/VIS CHARTS 20 CHINJAP. PAGE 105 A2150
WAR FORCES PLAN DIPLOM

B62
MOUSSA P.,THE UNDERPRIVILEGED NATIONS. FINAN INT/ORG PLAN PROB/SOLV CAP/ISM GIVE TASK WEALTH ...POLICY SOC 20. PAGE 105 A2159
ECO/UNDEV NAT/G DIPLOM FOR/AID

B62
OSGOOD C.E.,AN ALTERNATIVE TO WAR OR SURRENDER. FUT UNIV CULTURE INTELL SOCIETY R+D INT/ORG CONSULT DELIB/GP ACT/RES PLAN CHOOSE ATTIT PERCEPT KNOWL ...PHIL/SCI PSY SOC TREND GEN/LAWS 20. PAGE 112 A2300
ORD/FREE EDU/PROP PEACE WAR

B62
OSGOOD R.E.,NATO: THE ENTANGLING ALLIANCE. USA+45 WOR+45 VOL/ASSN FORCES TOP/EX PLAN DETER WEAPON DRIVE RIGID/FLEX ORD/FREE PWR...TREND 20 NATO. PAGE 112 A2301
INT/ORG ARMS/CONT PEACE

B62
RIMALOV V.V.,ECONOMIC COOPERATION BETWEEN USSR AND UNDERDEVELOPED COUNTRIES. USSR FINAN TEC/DEV INT/TRADE DOMIN EDU/PROP COLONIAL NAT/LISM DRIVE SOVEREIGN...AUD/VIS 20. PAGE 121 A2482
FOR/AID PLAN ECO/UNDEV DIPLOM

B62
RIVKIN A.,AFRICA AND THE WEST. AFR EUR+WWI FUT ISLAM ISRAEL USA+45 SOCIETY INT/ORG FORCES CREATE PLAN FOR/AID EDU/PROP ATTIT...CONCPT TREND EEC 20 CONGRESS UN. PAGE 121 A2488
ECO/UNDEV ECO/TAC

B62
ROBERTSON B.C.,REGIONAL DEVELOPMENT IN THE EUROPEAN ECONOMIC COMMUNITY. EUR+WWI FRANCE FUT ITALY UK ECO/UNDEV WORKER ACT/RES PROB/SOLV TEC/DEV ECO/TAC INT/TRADE EEC. PAGE 122 A2499
PLAN ECO/DEV INT/ORG REGION

B62
ROBINSON A.D.,DUTCH ORGANIZED AGRICULTURE IN INTERNATIONAL POLITICS, 1945-1960. EUR+WWI NETHERLAND STRUCT ECO/DEV NAT/G VOL/ASSN CONSULT DELIB/GP PLAN TEC/DEV INT/TRADE EDU/PROP ATTIT RIGID/FLEX ALL/VALS...NEW/IDEA TREND EEC 20. PAGE 122 A2502
AGRI INT/ORG

B62
SCHMITT H.A.,THE PATH TO EUROPEAN UNITY. EUR+WWI USA+45 PLAN TEC/DEV DIPLOM FOR/AID CONFER...INT/LAW 20 EEC EURCOALSTL MARSHL/PLN UNIFICA. PAGE 128 A2634
INT/ORG INT/TRADE REGION ECO/DEV

B62
STRACHEY J.,ON THE PREVENTION OF WAR. FUT WOR+45 INT/ORG NAT/G ACT/RES PLAN BAL/PWR DOMIN EDU/PROP PEACE ATTIT...POLICY TREND TOT/POP COLD/WAR 20 UN. PAGE 139 A2842
FORCES ORD/FREE ARMS/CONT NUC/PWR

B62
THANT U.,THE UNITED NATIONS' DEVELOPMENT DECADE: PROPOSALS FOR ACTION. WOR+45 SOCIETY ECO/UNDEV AGRI COM/IND FINAN R+D MUNIC SCHOOL VOL/ASSN CONSULT PLAN TEC/DEV ECO/TAC EDU/PROP ADMIN ROUTINE RIGID/FLEX...MGT SOC CONCPT UNESCO UN TOT/POP VAL/FREE. PAGE 142 A2906
INT/ORG ALL/VALS

B62
THEOBALD R.,NATIONAL DEVELOPMENT EFFORTS (PAMPHLET). WOR+45 AGRI BUDGET FOR/AID INT/TRADE TAX 20. PAGE 142 A2914
ECO/UNDEV PLAN BAL/PAY WEALTH

B62
THOMSON G.P.,NUCLEAR ENERGY IN BRITAIN DURING THE LAST WAR: THE CHERWELL SIMON LECTURE (MONOGRAPH). UK R+D CONSULT FORCES PLAN DIPLOM TASK CIVMIL/REL ROLE...PHIL/SCI NEW/IDEA LAB/EXP 20 MAUD. PAGE 143 A2934
CREATE TEC/DEV WAR NUC/PWR

B62
UNECA LIBRARY,BOOKS ON AFRICA IN THE UNECA LIBRARY. WOR+45 AGRI INT/ORG NAT/G PLAN WRITING REGION...SOC STAT UN. PAGE 147 A3008
BIBLIOG AFR ECO/UNDEV TEC/DEV

B62
UNECA LIBRARY,NEW ACQUISITIONS IN THE UNECA LIBRARY. LAW NAT/G PLAN PROB/SOLV TEC/DEV ADMIN REGION...GEOG SOC 20 UN. PAGE 147 A3009
BIBLIOG AFR ECO/UNDEV INT/ORG

B62
US CONGRESS,COMMUNICATIONS SATELLITE LEGISLATION: HEARINGS BEFORE COMM ON AERON AND SPACE SCIENCES ON BILLS S2550 AND 2814. WOR+45 LAW VOL/ASSN PLAN DIPLOM CONTROL OWN PEACE...NEW/IDEA CONGRESS NASA. PAGE 150 A3062
SPACE COM/IND ADJUD GOV/REL

B62
US CONGRESS JOINT ECO COMM,FACTORS AFFECTING THE UNITED STATES BALANCE OF PAYMENTS. USA+45 DELIB/GP PLAN DIPLOM FOR/AID PRODUC WEALTH...CHARTS 20 CONGRESS OEEC. PAGE 150 A3064
BAL/PAY INT/TRADE ECO/TAC FINAN

B62
US SENATE COMM GOVT OPERATIONS,ADMINISTRATION OF NATIONAL SECURITY. USA+45 CHIEF PLAN PROB/SOLV TEC/DEV DIPLOM ATTIT...POLICY DECISION 20 KENNEDY/JF RUSK/D MCNAMARA/R BUNDY/M HERTER/C. PAGE 156 A3173
ORD/FREE ADMIN NAT/G CONTROL

L62
MURACCIOLE L.,"LA LOI FONDAMENTALE DE LA REPUBLIQUE DU CONGO." WOR+45 SOCIETY ECO/UNDEV INT/ORG NAT/G LEGIS PLAN LEGIT ADJUD COLONIAL ROUTINE ATTIT SOVEREIGN 20 CONGO. PAGE 106 A2174
AFR CONSTN

L62
ULYSSES,"THE INTERNATIONAL AIMS AND POLICIES OF THE SOVIET UNION: THE NEW CONCEPTS AND STRATEGY OF KHRUSHCHEV." FUT USSR WOR+45 SOCIETY INT/ORG NAT/G POL/PAR FORCES TOP/EX PLAN DOMIN EDU/PROP COERCE ATTIT PERSON PWR...TREND COLD/WAR 20 KHRUSH/N. PAGE 146 A2994
COM POLICY BAL/PWR DIPLOM

S62
ALBONETTI A.,"IL SECONDO PROGRAMMA QUINQUENNALE 1963-67 ED IL BILANCIO RICERCHE ED INVESTIMENTI PER IL 1963 DELL'ERATOM." EUR+WWI FUT ITALY WOR+45 ECO/DEV SERV/IND INT/ORG TEC/DEV ECO/TAC ATTIT SKILL WEALTH...MGT TIME/SEQ OEEC 20. PAGE 5 A0108
R+D PLAN NUC/PWR

S62
BELSHAW C.,"TRAINING AND RECRUITMENT: SOME PRINCIPLES OF INTERNATIONAL AID." FUT WOR+45 SOCIETY INT/ORG NAT/G CREATE PLAN TEC/DEV ECO/TAC FOR/AID EDU/PROP ATTIT PERCEPT...HUM UN FAO ILO UNESCO 20. PAGE 13 A0263
VOL/ASSN ECO/UNDEV

S62
BOKOR-SZEGO H.,"LA CONVENTION DE BELGRADE ET LE REGIME DU DANUBE." COM EUR+WWI WOR+45 STRUCT POL/PAR VOL/ASSN PLAN EDU/PROP WEALTH...TIME/SEQ 20. PAGE 16 A0333
INT/ORG TOTALISM YUGOSLAVIA

S62
BOULDING K.E.,"THE PREVENTION OF WORLD WAR THREE."
VOL/ASSN

FUT WOR+45 INT/ORG PLAN BAL/PWR PEACE ORD/FREE PWR ...NEW/IDEA TREND TOT/POP COLD/WAR 20. PAGE 17 A0348
NAT/G ARMS/CONT DIPLOM

S62
CORET A.,"LE STATUT DE L'ILE CHRISTMAS DE L'OCEAN INDIEN." FUT S/ASIA ECO/DEV ECO/UNDEV VOL/ASSN DELIB/GP PLAN...RELATIV OBS TIME/SEQ TREND AUSTRAL 20. PAGE 30 A0619
NAT/G INT/ORG NEW/ZEALND

S62
CRANE R.D.,"LAW AND STRATEGY IN SPACE." FUT USA+45 WOR+45 AIR LAW INT/ORG NAT/G FORCES ACT/RES PLAN BAL/PWR LEGIT ARMS/CONT COERCE ORD/FREE...POLICY INT/LAW JURID SOC/EXP 20 TREATY. PAGE 32 A0656
CONCPT SPACE

S62
CROAN M.,"POLYCENTRISM: COMMUNIST INTERNATIONAL RELATIONS." ASIA STRUCT INT/ORG NAT/G POL/PAR CONSULT PLAN DOMIN EDU/PROP COERCE ATTIT RIGID/FLEX SOCISM...POLICY CONCPT TREND CON/ANAL GEN/LAWS MARX/KARL. PAGE 33 A0663
COM CREATE DIPLOM NAT/LISM

S62
DE MADARIAGA S.,"TOWARD THE UNITED STATES OF EUROPE." EUR+WWI PLAN DOMIN FEDERAL ATTIT PWR SOVEREIGN...GEOG TOT/POP 20. PAGE 35 A0707
FUT INT/ORG

S62
FOCSANEANU L.,"LES GRANDS TRAITES DE LA REPUBLIQUE POPULAIRE DE CHINE." ASIA CHINA/COM COM USSR WOR+45 INT/ORG NAT/G POL/PAR ACT/RES PLAN DIPLOM EDU/PROP ...CONCPT TIME/SEQ 20 TREATY. PAGE 47 A0957
VOL/ASSN TOTALISM

S62
FOSTER W.C.,"ARMS CONTROL AND DISARMAMENT IN A DIVIDED WORLD." COM FUT USA+45 USSR WOR+45 INTELL INT/ORG NAT/G VOL/ASSN CONSULT CREATE PLAN TEC/DEV EDU/PROP LEGIT NUC/PWR ATTIT RIGID/FLEX...CONCPT TREND TOT/POP 20 UN. PAGE 47 A0971
DELIB/GP POLICY ARMS/CONT DIPLOM

S62
GUETZKOW H.,"THE POTENTIAL OF CASE STUDY IN ANALYZING INTERNATIONAL CONFLICT." EUR+WWI FUT GERMANY INTELL SOCIETY STRUCT INT/ORG LOC/G NAT/G CONSULT CREATE PLAN CHOOSE ATTIT RIGID/FLEX ...POLICY SAAR 20. PAGE 58 A1188
EDU/PROP METH/CNCPT COERCE FRANCE

S62
HOFFMANN S.,"RESTRAINTS AND CHOICES IN AMERICAN FOREIGN POLICY." USA-45 INT/ORG NAT/G PLAN ARMS/CONT ATTIT...POLICY CONCPT OBS TREND GEN/METH COLD/WAR 20. PAGE 66 A1356
USA+45 ORD/FREE DIPLOM

S62
JACOBSON H.K.,"THE UNITED NATIONS AND COLONIALISM: A TENTATIVE APPRAISAL." AFR FUT S/ASIA USA+45 USSR WOR+45 NAT/G DELIB/GP PLAN DIPLOM ECO/TAC DOMIN ADMIN ROUTINE COERCE ATTIT RIGID/FLEX ORD/FREE PWR ...OBS STERTYP UN 20. PAGE 73 A1486
INT/ORG CONCPT COLONIAL

S62
KOLARZ W.,"THE IMPACT OF COMMUNISM ON WEST AFRICA." AFR FUT SOCIETY INT/ORG NAT/G CREATE PLAN DOMIN EDU/PROP COERCE NAT/LISM ATTIT RIGID/FLEX SOCISM ...POLICY CONCPT TREND MARX/KARL 20. PAGE 81 A1666
COM POL/PAR COLONIAL

S62
MARIAS J.,"A PROGRAM FOR EUROPE." EUR+WWI INT/ORG NAT/G PLAN DIPLOM DOMIN PWR...STERTYP TOT/POP 20. PAGE 95 A1938
VOL/ASSN CREATE REGION

S62
MILLIKEN M.,"NEW AND OLD CRITERIA FOR AID." WOR+45 ECO/DEV ECO/UNDEV ACT/RES PLAN ATTIT KNOWL...TREND CON/ANAL SIMUL GEN/METH 20. PAGE 102 A2083
USA+45 ECO/TAC FOR/AID

S62
MORGENTHAU H.J.,"A POLITICAL THEORY OF FOREIGN AID." ECO/UNDEV NAT/G DELIB/GP PLAN ECO/TAC EDU/PROP EXEC ORD/FREE RESPECT WEALTH...METH/CNCPT TREND 20. PAGE 104 A2140
USA+45 PHIL/SCI FOR/AID

S62
ORBAN M.,"L'EUROPE EN FORMATION ET SES PROBLEMES." EUR+WWI FUT WOR+45 WOR-45 INTELL STRUCT DELIB/GP ACT/RES FEDERAL RIGID/FLEX WEALTH...CONCPT TIME/SEQ OEEC 20. PAGE 112 A2295
INT/ORG PLAN REGION

S62
PIQUEMAL M.,"LES PROBLEMES DES UNIONS D'ETATS EN AFRIQUE NOIRE." FRANCE SOCIETY INT/ORG NAT/G DELIB/GP PLAN LEGIT ADMIN COLONIAL ROUTINE ATTIT ORD/FREE PWR...GEOG METH/CNCPT 20. PAGE 116 A2382
AFR ECO/UNDEV REGION

S62
RUBINSTEIN A.Z.,"RUSSIA AND THE UNCOMMITTED NATIONS." AFR INDIA ISLAM L/A+17C LAOS S/ASIA ELITES ECO/UNDEV INT/ORG KIN CREATE PLAN TEC/DEV NAT/LISM RIGID/FLEX PWR WEALTH...METH/CNCPT TIME/SEQ GEN/LAWS WORK. PAGE 125 A2562
ECO/TAC TREND COLONIAL USSR

S62
SCHACHTER O.,"DAG HAMMARSKJOLD AND THE RELATION OF LAW TO POLITICS." FUT WOR+45 INT/ORG CONSULT PLAN TEC/DEV BAL/PWR DIPLOM LEGIT ATTIT PERCEPT ORD/FREE ...POLICY JURID CONCPT OBS TESTS STERTYP GEN/LAWS 20 HAMMARSK/D. PAGE 128 A2616
ACT/RES ADJUD

S62
SCHILLING W.R.,"SCIENTISTS, FOREIGN POLICY AND POLITICS." WOR+45 WOR-45 INTELL INT/ORG CONSULT TOP/EX ACT/RES PLAN ADMIN KNOWL...CONCPT OBS TREND LEAGUE/NAT 20. PAGE 128 A2627
NAT/G TEC/DEV DIPLOM NUC/PWR

S62
SPENSER J.H.,"AFRICA AT THE UNITED NATIONS: SOME OBSERVATIONS." FUT ECO/UNDEV NAT/G CONSULT DELIB/GP PLAN BAL/PWR ECO/TAC EDU/PROP ATTIT RIGID/FLEX HEALTH ORD/FREE PWR WEALTH...POLICY CONCPT OBS TREND STERTYP GEN/METH UN VAL/FREE. PAGE 136 A2786
AFR INT/ORG REGION

S62
SPRINGER H.W.,"FEDERATION IN THE CARIBBEAN: AN ATTEMPT THAT FAILED." L/A+17C ECO/UNDEV INT/ORG POL/PAR PROVS LEGIS CREATE PLAN LEGIT ADMIN FEDERAL ATTIT DRIVE PERSON ORD/FREE PWR...POLICY GEOG PSY CONCPT OBS CARIBBEAN CMN/WLTH 20. PAGE 136 A2791
VOL/ASSN NAT/G REGION

S62
THOMAS J.R.T.,"SOVIET BEHAVIOR IN THE QUEMOY CRISES OF 1958." CHINA/COM FUT USSR WOR+45 INT/ORG VOL/ASSN FORCES PLAN BAL/PWR DOMIN COERCE NUC/PWR REV WAR ATTIT DRIVE ORD/FREE...POLICY OBS RECORD COLD/WAR FOR/POL 20. PAGE 143 A2923
COM PWR

S62
TOWSTER J.,"THE USSR AND THE USA: CHALLENGE AND RESPONSE." COM GERMANY USA+45 USSR WOR+45 ECO/UNDEV INT/ORG VOL/ASSN EX/STRUC FORCES TOP/EX CREATE PLAN TEC/DEV DIPLOM ECO/TAC EDU/PROP COLONIAL COERCE PWR ...GEN/METH COLD/WAR 20 KENNEDY/JF. PAGE 145 A2956
ACT/RES GEN/LAWS

B63
BOISSIER P.,HISTORIE DU COMITE INTERNATIONAL DE LA CROIX ROUGE. MOD/EUR WOR-45 CONSULT FORCES PLAN DIPLOM EDU/PROP ADMIN MORAL ORD/FREE...SOC CONCPT RECORD TIME/SEQ GEN/LAWS TOT/POP VAL/FREE 19/20. PAGE 16 A0332
INT/ORG HEALTH ARMS/CONT WAR

B63
CENTRO PARA EL DESARROLLO,LA ALIANZA PARA EL PROGRESO Y EL DESARROLLO SOCIAL DE AMERICA LATINA. L/A+17C INT/ORG DIPLOM ECO/TAC INT/TRADE ATTIT 20. PAGE 25 A0512
ECO/UNDEV FOR/AID PLAN REGION

B63
COLUMBIA U SCHOOL OF LAW,PUBLIC INTERNATIONAL DEVELOPMENT FINANCING IN SENEGAL. SENEGAL FINAN DELIB/GP GIVE EFFICIENCY...CHARTS GOV/COMP ANTHOL 20. PAGE 28 A0571
FOR/AID PLAN RECEIVE ECO/UNDEV

B63
CREMEANS C.,THE ARABS AND THE WORLD: NASSER'S ARAB NATIONALIST POLICY. FUT ISLAM UAR USA+45 SOCIETY STRATA NAT/G POL/PAR PLAN DIPLOM EDU/PROP LEGIT DRIVE ALL/VALS...INT TIME/SEQ CHARTS 20 NASSER/G. PAGE 33 A0662
TOP/EX ATTIT REGION NAT/LISM

B63
CROZIER B.,THE MORNING AFTER; A STUDY OF INDEPENDENCE. WOR+45 EX/STRUC PLAN BAL/PWR COLONIAL GP/REL 20 COLD/WAR. PAGE 33 A0666
SOVEREIGN NAT/LISM NAT/G DIPLOM

B63
DEENER D.R.,CANADA - UNITED STATES TREATY RELATIONS. CANADA USA+45 USA-45 NAT/G FORCES PLAN PROB/SOLV AGREE NUC/PWR...TREND 18/20 TREATY. PAGE 35 A0722
DIPLOM INT/LAW POLICY

B63
DUNN F.S.,PEACE-MAKING AND THE SETTLEMENT WITH JAPAN. ASIA USA+45 USA-45 FORCES BAL/PWR ECO/TAC CONFER WAR PWR SOVEREIGN 20 CHINJAP COLD/WAR TREATY. PAGE 39 A0802
POLICY PEACE PLAN DIPLOM

B63
EL-NAGGAR S.,FOREIGN AID TO UNITED ARAB REPUBLIC. UAR USA+45 USSR AGRI FINAN INDUS FORCES EATING DEMAND...CHARTS METH/COMP 20 RESOURCE/N AID. PAGE 41 A0838
FOR/AID ECO/UNDEV RECEIVE PLAN

B63
ERHARD L.,THE ECONOMICS OF SUCCESS. GERMANY/W WOR+45 LABOR CHIEF TAX REGION COST DEMAND ANTHOL. PAGE 42 A0860
ECO/DEV INT/TRADE PLAN DIPLOM

B63
FATEMI N.S.,THE DOLLAR CRISIS. USA+45 INDUS NAT/G LEGIS BUDGET TAX COST...CHARTS METH/COMP 20 EEC. PAGE 44 A0902
PROB/SOLV BAL/PAY FOR/AID PLAN

B63
FLORES E.,LAND REFORM AND THE ALLIANCE FOR PROGRESS (PAMPHLET). L/A+17C USA+45 STRUCT ECO/UNDEV NAT/G WORKER CREATE PLAN ECO/TAC COERCE REV 20. PAGE 47 A0953
AGRI INT/ORG DIPLOM POLICY

B63
FRANKEL J.,THE MAKING OF FOREIGN POLICY: AN ANALYSIS OF DECISION-MAKING. CHINA/COM EUR+WWI USA+45 ELITES INTELL FORCES LEGIS PLAN ATTIT ALL/VALS MORAL CONSERVE...GOV/COMP 20 PRESIDENT UN TREATY. PAGE 48 A0981
POLICY DECISION PROB/SOLV DIPLOM

B63
GILBERT M.,THE APPEASERS. COM GERMANY UK PLAN ECO/TAC COLONIAL CONTROL EXEC ORD/FREE PWR FASCISM 20 PARLIAMENT. PAGE 52 A1068
DIPLOM WAR POLICY DECISION

B63
GOLDWIN R.A.,FOREIGN AND MILITARY POLICY. COM USSR WOR+45 ECO/DEV INT/ORG FORCES PLAN ECO/TAC REGION ARMS/CONT MARXISM 20 UN. PAGE 54 A1097
DIPLOM POLICY PWR

NAT/G

B63
GORDON L.,A NEW DEAL FOR LATIN AMERICA. L/A+17C USA+45 CULTURE NAT/G TEC/DEV DIPLOM FOR/AID REGION TASK...POLICY 20 DEPT/STATE. PAGE 54 A1115
ECO/UNDEV ECO/TAC INT/ORG PLAN

B63
GREAT BRITAIN CENTRAL OFF INF,CONSULTATION AND CO-OPERATION IN THE COMMONWEALTH. LAW R+D FORCES PLAN EDU/PROP CONFER INGP/REL...GEOG CENSUS 19/20 CMN/WLTH. PAGE 55 A1133
DIPLOM DELIB/GP VOL/ASSN REGION

B63
GUIMARAES A.P.,INFLACAO E MONOPOLIO NO BRASIL. BRAZIL FINAN NAT/G PLAN PAY...METH/COMP 20. PAGE 58 A1189
ECO/UNDEV PRICE INT/TRADE BAL/PAY

B63
HALPERIN M.H.,LIMITED WAR IN A NUCLEAR AGE. CUBA KOREA USA+45 USSR INT/ORG FORCES PLAN DIPLOM DETER PWR...BIBLIOG/A 20. PAGE 60 A1238
WAR NUC/PWR CONTROL WEAPON

B63
HINSLEY F.H.,POWER AND THE PURSUIT OF PEACE. WOR+45 WOR-45 PLAN RIGID/FLEX ALL/VALS ALL/IDEOS...POLICY DECISION INT/LAW 12/20 ROUSSEAU/J KANT/I BENTHAM/J LEAGUE/NAT. PAGE 65 A1338
DIPLOM CONSTN PEACE COERCE

B63
INTERAMERICAN ECO AND SOC COUN,THE ALLIANCE FOR PROGRESS: ITS FIRST YEAR: 1961-1962. AGRI SCHOOL PLAN TEC/DEV INT/TRADE TAX GIVE ADMIN WEALTH...SOC 20 SOUTH/AMER. PAGE 71 A1449
INT/ORG PROB/SOLV ECO/TAC L/A+17C

B63
KATZ S.M.,A SELECTED LIST OF US READINGS ON DEVELOPMENT. AGRI COM/IND DIST/IND INDUS LABOR PLAN FOR/AID EDU/PROP HEALTH...POLICY SOC/WK 20. PAGE 77 A1571
BIBLIOG/A ECO/UNDEV TEC/DEV ACT/RES

B63
KLEIMAN R.,ATLANTIC CRISIS; AMERICAN DIPLOMACY CONFRONTS A RESURGENT EUROPE. EUR+WWI USA+45 ECO/DEV AGRI NAT/G CHIEF FORCES PLAN LEAD ATTIT ...CONCPT 20 NATO KENNEDY/JF DEGAULLE/C EEC JOHNSON/LB. PAGE 80 A1648
DIPLOM REGION POLICY

B63
LANGE O.,ECONOMIC DEVELOPMENT, PLANNING, AND INTERNATIONAL COOPERATION. UAR WOR+45 FINAN CAP/ISM PERS/REL 20. PAGE 84 A1722
ECO/UNDEV DIPLOM INT/TRADE PLAN

B63
LARY M.B.,PROBLEMS OF THE UNITED STATES AS WORLD TRADER AND BANKER. USA+45 NAT/G PLAN DIPLOM FOR/AID ...TREND CHARTS. PAGE 85 A1737
ECO/DEV FINAN BAL/PAY INT/TRADE

B63
LERCHE C.O. JR.,AMERICA IN WORLD AFFAIRS. COM UK USA+45 INT/ORG FORCES ECO/TAC INT/TRADE EDU/PROP WAR NAT/LISM PEACE...BIBLIOG 18/20 UN CONGRESS PRESIDENT COLD/WAR. PAGE 87 A1783
NAT/G DIPLOM PLAN

B63
MALIK C.,MAN IN THE STRUGGLE FOR PEACE. USSR WOR+45 CHIEF PLAN PROB/SOLV PARTIC NUC/PWR REV ORD/FREE ...IDEA/COMP METH/COMP 20 UN COLD/WAR. PAGE 93 A1912
PEACE MARXISM DIPLOM EDU/PROP

B63
MANGER W.,THE ALLIANCE FOR PROGRESS: A CRITICAL APPRAISAL. FUT L/A+17C USA+45 CULTURE ECO/UNDEV ACADEM NAT/G SCHOOL PLAN FOR/AID...POLICY OAS. PAGE 94 A1918
DIPLOM INT/ORG ECO/TAC REGION

B63
MARITANO N.,AN ALLIANCE FOR PROGRESS. FUT L/A+17C USA+45 CULTURE ECO/UNDEV NAT/G PLAN CONTROL POLICY. PAGE 95 A1941
DIPLOM INT/ORG ECO/TAC FOR/AID

B63
MAYNE R.,THE COMMUNITY OF EUROPE. UK CONSTN NAT/G CONSULT DELIB/GP CREATE PLAN ECO/TAC LEGIT ADMIN ROUTINE ORD/FREE PWR WEALTH...CONCPT TIME/SEQ EEC EURATOM 20. PAGE 97 A1985
EUR+WWI INT/ORG REGION

B63
MENEZES A.J.,SUBDESENVOLVIMENTO E POLITICA INTERNACIONAL. BRAZIL WOR+45 PLAN CONTROL LEAD NAT/LISM ORD/FREE 20 THIRD/WRLD. PAGE 99 A2041
ECO/UNDEV DIPLOM POLICY BAL/PWR

B63
MYRDAL G.,CHALLENGE TO AFFLUENCE. USA+45 WOR+45 FINAN INT/ORG NAT/G PLAN ECO/TAC INT/TRADE BAL/PAY ORD/FREE 20 EUROPE/W. PAGE 107 A2189
ECO/DEV WEALTH DIPLOM PRODUC

B63
ROBERTSON A.H.,HUMAN RIGHTS IN EUROPE. CONSTN SOCIETY INT/ORG NAT/G VOL/ASSN DELIB/GP ACT/RES PLAN ADJUD REGION ROUTINE ATTIT LOVE ORD/FREE RESPECT...JURID SOC CONCPT SOC/EXP UN 20. PAGE 122 A2498
EUR+WWI PERSON

B63
ROBOCK S.H.,OVERVIEW OF TOTAL BRAZILIAN SETTING, NEWER REGIONAL PATTERNS NING AND FOREIGN AID.
ECO/TAC REGION

BRAZIL ECO/UNDEV AGRI FINAN INDUS INT/ORG INCOME UTIL...CHARTS 20. PAGE 122 A2507
PLAN FOR/AID

B63
SCHMELTZ G.W.,LA POLITIQUE MONDIALE CONTEMPORAINE. SOCIETY ECO/UNDEV INDUS INT/ORG NAT/G POL/PAR CONSULT DELIB/GP PLAN TEC/DEV ECO/TAC DOMIN EDU/PROP ROUTINE COERCE PERCEPT PERSON LOVE SKILL ...SOC RECORD TOT/POP. PAGE 128 A2629
WOR+45 COLONIAL

B63
SCHRADER R.,SCIENCE AND POLICY. WOR+45 ECO/DEV ECO/UNDEV R+D FORCES PLAN DIPLOM GOV/REL TECHRACY BIBLIOG. PAGE 129 A2644
TEC/DEV NAT/G POLICY ADMIN

B63
SMITH J.E.,THE DEFENSE OF BERLIN. COM GUATEMALA WOR+45 ECO/TAC ADMIN NEUTRAL ATTIT ORD/FREE SOVEREIGN...DECISION 20 DEPT/STATE. PAGE 134 A2747
DIPLOM FORCES BAL/PWR PLAN

B63
SWEARER H.R.,CONTEMPORARY COMMUNISM: THEORY AND PRACTICE. COM USSR SOCIETY ECO/DEV POL/PAR FORCES PLAN ADMIN LEAD NAT/LISM...POLICY ANTHOL 20 LENIN/VI COM/PARTY. PAGE 140 A2869
MARXISM CONCPT DIPLOM NAT/G

B63
THUCYDIDES,THE PELOPONESIAN WARS. MEDIT-7 CULTURE INT/ORG NAT/G FORCES TOP/EX PLAN ROUTINE PWR ...CONCPT. PAGE 144 A2938
ATTIT COERCE WAR

B63
TUCKER R.C.,THE SOVIET POLITICAL MIND. WOR+45 ELITES INT/ORG NAT/G POL/PAR PLAN DIPLOM ECO/TAC DOMIN ADMIN NUC/PWR REV DRIVE PERSON SUPEGO PWR WEALTH...POLICY MGT PSY CONCPT OBS BIOG TREND COLD/WAR MARX/KARL 20. PAGE 145 A2972
COM TOP/EX USSR

B63
UN SECRETARY GENERAL,PLANNING FOR ECONOMIC DEVELOPMENT. ECO/UNDEV FINAN BUDGET INT/TRADE TARIFFS TAX ADMIN 20 UN. PAGE 147 A3005
PLAN ECO/TAC MGT NAT/COMP

B63
UNITED STATES GOVERNMENT,REPORT TO THE INTER-AMERICAN ECONOMIC AND SOCIAL COUNCIL. L/A+17C INDUS PLAN INT/TRADE TARIFFS CONFER...CHARTS 20 LAFTA. PAGE 149 A3038
FOR/AID ECO/TAC ECO/UNDEV DIPLOM

B63
US DEPARTMENT OF THE ARMY,SOVIET RUSSIA: STRATEGIC SURVEY (PAMPHLET). USSR POL/PAR PLAN DOMIN EDU/PROP ARMS/CONT GUERRILLA WAR WEAPON...TREND CHARTS ORG/CHARTS 20. PAGE 152 A3106
BIBLIOG/A MARXISM DIPLOM COERCE

B63
US ECON SURVEY TEAM INDONESIA,INDONESIA - PERSPECTIVE AND PROPOSALS FOR UNITED STATES ECONOMIC AID. INDONESIA AGRI MARKET TEC/DEV DIPLOM INT/TRADE EDU/PROP 20. PAGE 153 A3113
FOR/AID ECO/UNDEV PLAN INDUS

B63
US GOVERNMENT,REPORT TO INTER-AMERICAN ECONOMIC AND SOCIAL COUNCIL AT SECOND ANNUAL MEETING. L/A+17C USA+45 VOL/ASSN TEC/DEV DIPLOM TAX EATING EFFICIENCY HEALTH...STAT CHARTS 20 AID. PAGE 153 A3116
ECO/TAC FOR/AID FINAN PLAN

B63
US HOUSE COMM BANKING-CURR,RECENT CHANGES IN MONETARY POLICY AND BALANCE OF PAYMENTS PROBLEMS. USA+45 DELIB/GP PLAN DIPLOM...CHARTS 20 CONGRESS. PAGE 153 A3121
BAL/PAY FINAN ECO/TAC POLICY

B63
US SENATE COMM GOVT OPERATIONS,REPORT OF A STUDY OF US FOREIGN AID IN TEN MIDDLE EASTERN AND AFRICAN COUNTRIES. AFR ISLAM USA+45 FORCES PLAN BUDGET DIPLOM TAX DETER WEALTH...STAT CHARTS 20 CONGRESS AID MID/EAST. PAGE 156 A3174
FOR/AID EFFICIENCY ECO/TAC FINAN

B63
WALKER A.A.,OFFICIAL PUBLICATIONS OF SIERRA LEONE AND GAMBIA. GAMBIA SIER/LEONE UK LAW CONSTN LEGIS PLAN BUDGET DIPLOM...SOC SAMP CON/ANAL 20. PAGE 160 A3262
BIBLIOG NAT/G COLONIAL ADMIN

B63
WHITTON J.B.,PROPAGANDA AND THE COLD WAR. USA+45 USSR INDUS NAT/G PLAN WRITING EFFICIENCY...POLICY 20 COLD/WAR. PAGE 164 A3341
ATTIT EDU/PROP COM/IND DIPLOM

L63
PADELFORD N.J.,"FINANCIAL CRISIS AND THE UNITED NATIONS." FUT USSR WOR+45 LAW CONSTN FINAN INT/ORG DELIB/GP FORCES PLAN BUDGET DIPLOM COST WEALTH ...STAT CHARTS UN CONGO 20. PAGE 113 A2311
CREATE ECO/TAC

L63
PRINCETON UNIV. CONFERENCE,"ARAB DEVELOPMENT IN THE EMERGING INTERNATIONAL ECONOMY." FUT USA+45 DIST/IND FINAN DELIB/GP PLAN ECO/TAC WEALTH VAL/FREE 20. PAGE 118 A2413
ISLAM ECO/UNDEV FOR/AID INT/TRADE

L63
SCHELLING T.C.,"STRATEGIC PROBLEMS OF AN INTERNATIONAL ARMED FORCE." WOR+45 ECO/DEV INT/ORG NAT/G PLAN BAL/PWR LEGIT ARMS/CONT COERCE DETER ORD/FREE PWR...POLICY CONCPT COLD/WAR 20. PAGE 128 A2624
CREATE FORCES

S63
ANGUILE G.,"CIVILISATION DU PLAN DANS L'EUROPE ET L'AFRIQUE DE DEMAIN." AFR EUR+WWI GABON ECO/DEV FINAN MARKET DELIB/GP ECO/TAC WEALTH...TREND 20. PAGE 8 A0163 — ECO/UNDEV PLAN INT/TRADE

S63
BARTHELEMY G.,"LE NOUVEAU FRANC (CFA) ET LA BANQUE CENTRALE DES ETATS DE L'AFRIQUE DE L'OUEST." FUT STRUCT INT/ORG PLAN ATTIT ALL/VALS 20. PAGE 11 A0230 — AFR FINAN

S63
BRZEZINSKI Z.,"SOVIET QUIESCENCE." EUR+WWI USA+45 USSR FORCES CREATE PLAN COERCE DETER WAR ATTIT 20 TREATY EUROPE. PAGE 20 A0415 — DIPLOM ARMS/CONT NUC/PWR AGREE

S63
BULLOUGH V.L.,"THE ROMAN EMPIRE VS PERSIA, 363-502: A STUDY OF SUCCESSFUL DETERRENCE." NAT/G PLAN DIPLOM ORD/FREE PWR...TIME/SEQ COLD/WAR VAL/FREE 4/6 PERSIA ROM/EMP. PAGE 21 A0430 — MEDIT-7 COERCE DETER

S63
COSER L.,"AMERICA AND THE WORLD REVOLUTION." COM FUT USA+45 WOR+45 INTELL SOCIETY NAT/G ECO/TAC EDU/PROP ALL/VALS SOCISM...PSY GEN/LAWS TOT/POP 20 COLD/WAR. PAGE 31 A0629 — ECO/UNDEV PLAN FOR/AID DIPLOM

S63
DARLING F.C.,"THE GEOPOLITICS OF AMERICAN FOREIGN POLITICS IN ASIA." COM S/ASIA USA+45 USSR ECO/UNDEV NAT/G VOL/ASSN CONSULT PLAN GUERRILLA...STAT TOT/POP 20. PAGE 34 A0682 — FORCES ECO/TAC FOR/AID DIPLOM

S63
DIEBOLD W. JR.,"THE NEW SITUATION OF INTERNATIONAL TRADE POLICY." EUR+WWI FRANCE FUT UK USA+45 WOR+45 DIST/IND PLAN INT/TRADE EDU/PROP PWR WEALTH ...RECORD TREND GEN/LAWS EEC VAL/FREE 20. PAGE 37 A0760 — MARKET ECO/TAC

S63
GANDILHON J.,"LA SCIENCE ET LA TECHNIQUE A L'AIDE DES REGIONS PEU DEVELOPPEES." FRANCE FUT WOR+45 ECO/DEV R+D PROF/ORG ACT/RES PLAN...MGT TOT/POP VAL/FREE 20 UN. PAGE 51 A1037 — ECO/UNDEV TEC/DEV FOR/AID

S63
GORDON B.,"ECONOMIC IMPEDIMENTS TO REGIONALISM IN SOUTH EAST ASIA." BURMA FUT S/ASIA THAILAND USA+45 AGRI INDUS R+D NAT/G PLAN ECO/TAC WEALTH...STAT CONT/OBS 20. PAGE 54 A1110 — VOL/ASSN ECO/UNDEV INT/TRADE REGION

S63
HOLBO P.S.,"COLD WAR DRIFT IN LATIN AMERICA." CUBA L/A+17C USA+45 USA-45 INT/ORG NAT/G NEIGH VOL/ASSN ACT/RES PLAN ECO/TAC ATTIT RIGID/FLEX ALL/VALS ...RECORD TIME/SEQ OAS LAFTA 20 COLD/WAR. PAGE 66 A1363 — DELIB/GP CREATE FOR/AID

S63
HORVATH J.,"MOSCOW'S AID PROGRAM: THE PERFORMANCE SO FAR." COM FUT USSR WOR+45 ECO/DEV FINAN PLAN TEC/DEV FOR/AID EDU/PROP ATTIT ORD/FREE PWR WEALTH ...POLICY STAT CHARTS VAL/FREE 20. PAGE 68 A1389 — ECO/UNDEV ECO/TAC

S63
HUMPHREY H.H.,"REGIONAL ARMS CONTROL AGREEMENTS." WOR+45 FORCES PLAN LEGIT COERCE ATTIT HEALTH ORD/FREE...HUM METH/CNCPT MYTH OBS INT TREND TOT/POP 20. PAGE 69 A1416 — L/A+17C INT/ORG ARMS/CONT REGION

S63
KAWALKOWSKI A.,"POUR UNE EUROPE INDEPENDENTE ET REUNIFIEE." EUR+WWI FUT USA+45 USSR WOR+45 ECO/DEV PROC/MFG INT/ORG NAT/G ACT/RES TEC/DEV FEDERAL RIGID/FLEX...CONCPT METH/CNCPT OEEC TOT/POP 20 DEGAULLE/C. PAGE 77 A1573 — R+D PLAN NUC/PWR

S63
LEDUC G.,"L'AIDE INTERNATIONALE AU DEVELOPPEMENT." FUT WOR+45 ECO/DEV ECO/UNDEV R+D PROF/ORG TEC/DEV ECO/TAC ROUTINE ATTIT ALL/VALS...MGT TIME/SEQ TOT/POP 20. PAGE 86 A1758 — FINAN PLAN FOR/AID

S63
MANOLIU F.,"PERSPECTIVES D'UNE INTEGRATION ECONOMIQUE LATINOAMERICAINE." FUT L/A+17C STRUCT MARKET LABOR POL/PAR VOL/ASSN PLAN RIGID/FLEX PWR ...METH/CNCPT OAS TOT/POP 20. PAGE 94 A1927 — FINAN INT/ORG PEACE

S63
NADLER E.B.,"SOME ECONOMIC DISADVANTAGES OF THE ARMS RACE." USA+45 INDUS R+D FORCES PLAN TEC/DEV ECO/TAC FOR/AID EDU/PROP PWR WEALTH...TREND COLD/WAR 20. PAGE 107 A2190 — ECO/DEV MGT BAL/PAY

S63
NYE J.S. JR.,"EAST AFRICAN ECONOMIC INTEGRATION." AFR UGANDA PROVS DELIB/GP PLAN ECO/TAC INT/TRADE ADMIN ROUTINE ORD/FREE PWR WEALTH...OBS TIME/SEQ VAL/FREE 20. PAGE 110 A2264 — ECO/UNDEV INT/ORG

S63
ROUGEMONT D.,"LES NOUVELLES CHANCES DE L'EUROPE." EUR+WWI FUT ECO/DEV INT/ORG NAT/G ACT/RES PLAN TEC/DEV EDU/PROP ADMIN COLONIAL FEDERAL ATTIT PWR SKILL...TREND 20. PAGE 124 A2549 — ECO/UNDEV PERCEPT

S63
SCHMIDT W.E.,"THE CASE AGAINST COMMODITY AGREEMENTS." FUT L/A+17C STRATA CONSULT PLAN ECO/TAC EDU/PROP ATTIT DRIVE RIGID/FLEX WEALTH ...MYTH 20. PAGE 128 A2631 — ECO/UNDEV ACT/RES INT/TRADE

S63
SHONFIELD A.,"AFTER BRUSSELS." EUR+WWI FRANCE GERMANY UK ECO/DEV DIST/IND MARKET VOL/ASSN DELIB/GP CREATE INT/TRADE ATTIT RIGID/FLEX...RECORD TREND GEN/LAWS EEC CMN/WLTH 20. PAGE 132 A2705 — PLAN ECO/TAC

S63
SHWADRAN B.,"MIDDLE EAST OIL, 1962." ISLAM USSR ECO/DEV DIST/IND INDUS PLAN BAL/PWR DISPL DRIVE ...POLICY STAT TREND GEN/LAWS EEC OEEC 20 OIL. PAGE 132 A2712 — MARKET ECO/TAC INT/TRADE

S63
VINER J.,"REPORT OF THE CLAY COMMITTEE ON FOREIGN AID: A SYMPOSIUM." USA+45 WOR+45 NAT/G CONSULT PLAN BAL/PWR ATTIT WEALTH...MGT CONCPT TOT/POP 20. PAGE 159 A3240 — ACT/RES ECO/TAC FOR/AID

S63
WALKER H.,"THE INTERNATIONAL LAW OF COMMODITY AGREEMENTS." FUT WOR+45 ECO/DEV ECO/UNDEV FINAN INT/ORG NAT/G CONSULT CREATE PLAN ECO/TAC ATTIT PERCEPT...CONCPT GEN/LAWS TOT/POP GATT 20. PAGE 160 A3265 — MARKET VOL/ASSN INT/LAW INT/TRADE

N63
US AGENCY INTERNATIONAL DEV,PRINCIPLES OF FOREIGN ECONOMIC ASSISTANCE (PAMPHLET). USA+45 FINAN GP/REL BAL/PAY EFFICIENCY 20 AID. PAGE 149 A3051 — FOR/AID PLAN ECO/UNDEV ATTIT

N63
US COMM STRENG SEC FREE WORLD,THE SCOPE AND DISTRIBUTION OF UNITED STATES MILITARY AND ECONOMIC ASSISTANCE PROGRAMS (PAMPHLET). USA+45 PLAN BAL/PWR BUDGET DIPLOM CONTROL CIVMIL/REL ATTIT. PAGE 150 A3059 — DELIB/GP POLICY FOR/AID ORD/FREE

B64
APTER D.E.,IDEOLOGY AND DISCONTENT. FUT WOR+45 CONSTN CULTURE INTELL SOCIETY STRUCT INT/ORG NAT/G DELIB/GP LEGIS CREATE PLAN TEC/DEV EDU/PROP EXEC PERCEPT PERSON RIGID/FLEX ALL/VALS...POLICY TOT/POP. PAGE 8 A0171 — ACT/RES ATTIT

B64
BARKER A.J.,SUEZ: THE SEVEN DAY WAR. EUR+WWI ISLAM UAR INT/ORG NAT/G PLAN DIPLOM ECO/TAC DOMIN NAT/LISM DRIVE RIGID/FLEX PWR SOVEREIGN...POLICY JURID TREND CHARTS SUEZ UN 20. PAGE 11 A0221 — FORCES COERCE UK

B64
BELL C.,THE DEBATABLE ALLIANCE. COM UK USA+45 NAT/G FORCES PLAN BAL/PWR NUC/PWR WAR ATTIT...GOV/COMP 20. PAGE 13 A0256 — DIPLOM PWR PEACE POLICY

B64
BINDER L.,THE IDEOLOGICAL REVOLUTION IN THE MIDDLE EAST. ISLAM STRUCT INT/ORG KIN SECT EX/STRUC TOP/EX PLAN ATTIT DRIVE RIGID/FLEX PWR...MYTH TOT/POP 20. PAGE 14 A0289 — POL/PAR NAT/G NAT/LISM

B64
CEPEDE M.,POPULATION AND FOOD. USA+45 STRUCT ECO/UNDEV FAM PLAN TEC/DEV FOR/AID CONTROL...CATH SOC TREND 19/20. PAGE 25 A0513 — FUT GEOG AGRI CENSUS

B64
COFFIN F.M.,WITNESS FOR AID. COM EUR+WWI USA+45 DIPLOM GP/REL CONSEN ORD/FREE MARXISM...NEW/IDEA 20 CONGRESS AID. PAGE 27 A0557 — FOR/AID ECO/UNDEV DELIB/GP PLAN

B64
COLUMBIA U SCHOOL OF LAW,PUBLIC INTERNATIONAL DEVELOPMENT FINANCING IN INDIA. GERMANY/W INDIA UK USA+45 INDUS PLAN TEC/DEV DIPLOM ECO/TAC GIVE ADMIN UTIL ATTIT 20. PAGE 28 A0572 — ECO/UNDEV FINAN FOR/AID INT/ORG

B64
DAVIES U.P. JR.,FOREIGN AND OTHER AFFAIRS. EUR+WWI L/A+17C S/ASIA USA+45 ECO/UNDEV CHIEF PLAN ECO/TAC PWR MARXISM 20 KENNEDY/JF UN. PAGE 34 A0688 — DIPLOM NAT/G POLICY FOR/AID

B64
DEITCHMAN S.J.,LIMITED WAR AND AMERICAN DEFENSE POLICY. USA+45 WOR+45 INT/ORG NAT/G PLAN TEC/DEV COERCE NUC/PWR RIGID/FLEX PWR SKILL...DECISION METH/CNCPT TIME/SEQ TOT/POP COLD/WAR 20. PAGE 36 A0726 — FORCES WAR WEAPON

B64
ETZIONI A.,WINNING WITHOUT WAR. FUT MOD/EUR USA+45 WOR+45 ECO/DEV ECO/UNDEV INT/ORG NAT/G FORCES TOP/EX PLAN TEC/DEV ECO/TAC DOMIN EDU/PROP LEGIT COERCE CHOOSE ATTIT MORAL ORD/FREE RESPECT WEALTH MAJORIT. PAGE 43 A0871 — PWR TREND DIPLOM USSR

B64
FISHER R.,INTERNATIONAL CONFLICT AND BEHAVIORAL SCIENCE: THE CRAIGVILLE PAPERS. COM FUT USA+45 WOR+45 NAT/G DELIB/GP EX/STRUC FORCES ECO/TAC DOMIN EDU/PROP LEGIT COERCE ATTIT PERCEPT ORD/FREE PWR RESPECT...PSY SOC VAL/FREE. PAGE 46 A0940 — INT/ORG PLAN DIPLOM

B64
FREE L.A.,THE ATTITUDES, HOPES AND FEARS OF NIGERIANS. AFR NIGERIA ECO/UNDEV AGRI ACADEM PLAN — NAT/LISM SYS/QU

TASK...GEOG CHARTS METH 20. PAGE 49 A0993 DIPLOM

B64
FRYDENSBERG P.,PEACE-KEEPING: EXPERIENCE AND EVALUATION: THE OSLO PAPERS. NORWAY FORCES PLAN CONTROL...INT/LAW 20 UN. PAGE 49 A1012
INT/ORG DIPLOM PEACE COERCE

B64
GREAT BRITAIN CENTRAL OFF INF,CONSTITUTIONAL DEVELOPMENT IN THE COMMONWEALTH. VOL/ASSN PLAN DIPLOM COLONIAL INGP/REL NAT/LISM ORD/FREE PWR 17/20 CMN/WLTH. PAGE 55 A1135
REGION CONSTN NAT/G SOVEREIGN

B64
INTL INF CTR LOCAL CREDIT,GOVERNMENT MEASURES FOR THE PROMOTION OF REGIONAL ECONOMIC DEVELOPMENT. WOR+45 ECO/UNDEV FINAN INT/ORG DIPLOM ORD/FREE ...POLICY GEOG 20. PAGE 71 A1464
FOR/AID PLAN ECO/TAC REGION

B64
JACOB P.E.,THE INTEGRATION OF POLITICAL COMMUNITIES. USA+45 WOR+45 CULTURE LOC/G MUNIC NAT/G CREATE PLAN LEGIT REGION COERCE ALL/VALS ...POLICY GEOG PSY SOC TREND HYPO/EXP GEN/LAWS VAL/FREE 20. PAGE 72 A1483
INT/ORG METH/CNCPT SIMUL STAT

B64
JANOWITZ M.,THE MILITARY IN THE POLITICAL DEVELOPMENT OF NEW NATIONS: AN ESSAY IN COMPARATIVE ANALYSIS. AFR ASIA ISLAM L/A+17C S/ASIA USA+45 ECO/UNDEV INT/ORG NAT/G POL/PAR DELIB/GP PLAN ECO/TAC DOMIN LEGIT COERCE ATTIT DRIVE RESPECT ...SOC CONCPT CENSUS VAL/FREE. PAGE 73 A1495
FORCES PWR

B64
JOHNSON L.B.,MY HOPE FOR AMERICA. FUT USA+45 USSR LAW PLAN DIPLOM GIVE INCOME PEACE ATTIT ORD/FREE WEALTH 20 JOHNSON/LB PRESIDENT DEMOCRAT. PAGE 74 A1525
POLICY POL/PAR NAT/G GOV/REL

B64
KAUFMANN W.W.,THE MC NAMARA STRATEGY. TOP/EX INSPECT BAL/PWR DIPLOM CONTROL DETER GUERRILLA NUC/PWR WEAPON COST PWR...METH/COMP 20 MCNAMARA/R KENNEDY/JF JOHNSON/LB NATO DEPT/DEFEN. PAGE 77 A1572
FORCES WAR PLAN PROB/SOLV

B64
MARKHAM J.W.,THE COMMON MARKET: FRIEND OR COMPETITOR. EUR+WWI FUT USA+45 INT/ORG LG/CO NAT/G VOL/ASSN DELIB/GP EX/STRUC PLAN TARIFFS ORD/FREE PWR WEALTH...POLICY STAT TREND EEC VAL/FREE 20. PAGE 95 A1943
ECO/DEV ECO/TAC

B64
MYINT H.,THE ECONOMICS OF THE DEVELOPING COUNTRIES. WOR+45 AGRI PLAN COST...POLICY GEOG 20 MONEY. PAGE 107 A2187
ECO/UNDEV INT/TRADE EXTR/IND FINAN

B64
NICOL D.,AFRICA - A SUBJECTIVE VIEW. AFR INT/ORG PLAN ADMIN COLONIAL PARL/PROC PARTIC REGION GOV/REL LITERACY ATTIT...BIBLIOG 20 CIVIL/SERV. PAGE 109 A2230
NAT/G LEAD CULTURE ACADEM

B64
OWEN W.,STRATEGY FOR MOBILITY. FUT WOR+45 WOR-45 DIST/IND INT/ORG NAT/G DELIB/GP PLAN TEC/DEV ECO/TAC ORD/FREE PWR WEALTH...STAT TIME/SEQ VAL/FREE 20. PAGE 112 A2304
COM/IND ECO/UNDEV

B64
REGALA R.,WORLD PEACE THROUGH DIPLOMACY AND LAW. S/ASIA WOR+45 ECO/UNDEV INT/ORG FORCES PLAN PROB/SOLV FOR/AID NUC/PWR WAR...POLICY INT/LAW 20. PAGE 120 A2456
DIPLOM PEACE ADJUD

B64
REUSS H.S.,THE CRITICAL DECADE - AN ECONOMIC POLICY FOR AMERICA AND THE FREE WORLD. USA+45 FINAN POL/PAR WORKER PLAN DIPLOM ECO/TAC TARIFFS BAL/PAY ...POLICY 20 CONGRESS GOLD/STAND. PAGE 120 A2468
FOR/AID INT/TRADE LABOR LEGIS

B64
RICHARDSON I.L.,BIBLIOGRAFIA BRASILEIRA DE ADMINISTRACAO PUBLICA E ASSUNTOS CORRELATOS. BRAZIL CONSTN FINAN LOC/G NAT/G POL/PAR PLAN DIPLOM RECEIVE ATTIT...METH 20. PAGE 121 A2474
BIBLIOG MGT ADMIN LAW

B64
ROBERTS HL,FOREIGN AFFAIRS BIBLIOGRAPHY, 1952-1962. ECO/DEV SECT PLAN FOR/AID INT/TRADE ARMS/CONT NAT/LISM ATTIT...INT/LAW GOV/COMP IDEA/COMP 20. PAGE 122 A2495
BIBLIOG/A DIPLOM INT/ORG WAR

B64
SCHWARTZ M.D.,CONFERENCE ON SPACE SCIENCE AND SPACE LAW. FUT COM/IND NAT/G FORCES ACT/RES PLAN BUDGET DIPLOM NUC/PWR WEAPON...POLICY ANTHOL 20. PAGE 130 A2658
SPACE LAW PEACE TEC/DEV

B64
STANGER R.J.,ESSAYS ON INTERVENTION. PLAN PROB/SOLV BAL/PWR ADJUD COERCE WAR ROLE PWR...INT/LAW CONCPT 20 UN INTERVENT. PAGE 137 A2803
SOVEREIGN DIPLOM POLICY LEGIT

B64
STEWART C.F.,A BIBLIOGRAPHY OF INTERNATIONAL BUSINESS. WOR+45 FINAN LG/CO NAT/G PLAN ECO/TAC TARIFFS...DECISION MGT GP/COMP NAT/COMP 20 EEC. PAGE 138 A2824
BIBLIOG INT/ORG OP/RES INT/TRADE

B64
STILLMAN E.O.,THE POLITICS OF HYSTERIA: THE SOURCES OF TWENTIETH-CENTURY CONFLICT. WOR+45 WOR-45 CULTURE ECO/UNDEV PLAN CAP/ISM WAR MARXISM ...PREDICT BIBLIOG 20 COLD/WAR. PAGE 138 A2828
DIPLOM IDEA/COMP COLONIAL CONTROL

B64
SULLIVAN G.,THE STORY OF THE PEACE CORPS. USA+45 WOR+45 INTELL FACE/GP NAT/G SCHOOL VOL/ASSN CONSULT EX/STRUC PLAN EDU/PROP ADMIN ATTIT DRIVE ALL/VALS ...POLICY HEAL SOC CONCPT INT QU BIOG TREND SOC/EXP WORK. PAGE 140 A2861
INT/ORG ECO/UNDEV FOR/AID PEACE

B64
UN PUB. INFORM. ORGAN.,EVERY MAN'S UNITED NATIONS. UNIV WOR+45 CONSTN CULTURE SOCIETY ECO/DEV ECO/UNDEV NAT/G ACT/RES PLAN ECO/TAC INT/TRADE EDU/PROP LEGIT PEACE ATTIT ALL/VALS...POLICY HUM INT/LAW CONCPT CHARTS UN TOT/POP 20. PAGE 147 A3004
INT/ORG ROUTINE

B64
UNITED ARAB REPUBLIC,TOWARDS THE SECOND AFRICAN SUMMIT ASSEMBLY. AFR UAR CONSTN VOL/ASSN CHIEF PLAN DIPLOM AGREE 20 NASSER/G AFR/STATES. PAGE 148 A3030
CONFER DELIB/GP INT/ORG POLICY

B64
US HOUSE COMM GOVT OPERATIONS,US OWNED FOREIGN CURRENCIES: HEARINGS (COMMITTEE ON GOVERNMENT OPERATIONS). INDIA ECO/DEV PLAN BUDGET TAX DEMAND EFFICIENCY 20 AID CONGRESS. PAGE 154 A3138
FINAN ECO/TAC FOR/AID OWN

B64
US SENATE COMM GOVT OPERATIONS,THE SECRETARY OF STATE AND THE AMBASSADOR. USA+45 CHIEF CONSULT EX/STRUC FORCES PLAN ADMIN EXEC INGP/REL ROLE ...ANTHOL 20 PRESIDENT DEPT/STATE. PAGE 156 A3175
DIPLOM DELIB/GP NAT/G

B64
US SENATE COMM GOVT OPERATIONS,ADMINISTRATION OF NATIONAL SECURITY. USA+45 CHIEF TOP/EX PLAN DIPLOM CONTROL PEACE...POLICY DECISION 20 PRESIDENT CONGRESS. PAGE 156 A3176
ADMIN FORCES ORD/FREE NAT/G

B64
WILLIAMS S.P.,TOWARD A GENUINE WORLD SECURITY SYSTEM (PAMPHLET). WOR+45 INT/ORG FORCES PLAN NUC/PWR ORD/FREE...INT/LAW CONCPT UN PRESIDENT. PAGE 165 A3353
BIBLIOG/A ARMS/CONT DIPLOM PEACE

L64
BERKS R.N.,"THE US AND WEAPONS CONTROL." WOR+45 LAW INT/ORG NAT/G LEGIS EXEC COERCE PEACE ATTIT RIGID/FLEX ALL/VALS PWR...POLICY TOT/POP 20. PAGE 13 A0273
USA+45 PLAN ARMS/CONT

L64
CARNEGIE ENDOWMENT INT. PEACE,"ECONOMIC AND SOCIAL QUESTION (ISSUES BEFORE THE NINETEENTH GENERAL ASSEMBLY)." WOR+45 ECO/DEV ECO/UNDEV INDUS R+D DELIB/GP CREATE PLAN TEC/DEV ECO/TAC FOR/AID BAL/PAY...RECORD UN 20. PAGE 24 A0493
INT/ORG INT/TRADE

L64
CURTIS G.L.,"THE UNITED NATIONS OBSERVER GROUP IN LEBANON." ISLAM USA+45 NAT/G CONSULT ACT/RES PLAN BAL/PWR LEGIT ATTIT KNOWL...HIST/WRIT UN 20 UN. PAGE 33 A0669
INT/ORG FORCES DIPLOM LEBANON

L64
HAAS E.B.,"ECONOMICS AND DIFFERENTIAL PATTERNS OF POLITICAL INTEGRATION: PROJECTIONS ABOUT UNITY IN LATIN AMERICA." SOCIETY NAT/G DELIB/GP ACT/RES CREATE PLAN ECO/TAC REGION ROUTINE ATTIT DRIVE PWR WEALTH...CONCPT TREND CHARTS LAFTA 20. PAGE 59 A1208
L/A+17C INT/ORG MARKET

L64
LLOYD W.B.,"PEACE REQUIRES PEACEMAKERS." AFR INDIA S/ASIA SWITZERLND WOR+45 INT/ORG VOL/ASSN PLAN PERSON PWR 20. PAGE 90 A1848
CONSULT PEACE

L64
MILLIS W.,"THE DEMILITARIZED WORLD." COM USA+45 USSR WOR+45 CONSTN NAT/G EX/STRUC PLAN LEGIT ATTIT DRIVE...CONCPT TIME/SEQ STERTYP TOT/POP COLD/WAR 20. PAGE 102 A2085
FUT INT/ORG BAL/PWR PEACE

S64
ARMSTRONG J.A.,"THE SOVIET-AMERICAN CONFRONTATION: A NEW STAGE?" CUBA USA+45 USSR PLAN PROB/SOLV INT/TRADE CONTROL ARMS/CONT NUC/PWR MARXISM 20 COLD/WAR INTERVENT. PAGE 9 A0174
DIPLOM POLICY INSPECT

S64
ASHRAF S.,"INDIA AND WORLD AFFAIRS: AN ANNUAL BIBLIOGRAPHY, 1962." WOR+45 LAW ECO/UNDEV INT/ORG FORCES PLAN ECO/TAC COERCE ORD/FREE PWR WEALTH ...HIST/WRIT VAL/FREE. PAGE 9 A0188
S/ASIA NAT/G

S64
BEIM D.,"THE COMMUNIST BLOC AND THE FOREIGN-AID GAME." WOR+45 NAT/G PLAN ROUTINE ATTIT KNOWL ORD/FREE...DECISION QUANT CONT/OBS TIME/SEQ CHARTS GAME SIMUL COLD/WAR 20. PAGE 12 A0252
COM ECO/UNDEV ECO/TAC FOR/AID

S64
FALK S.L.,"DISARMAMENT IN HISTORICAL PERSPECTIVE." WOR-45 NAT/G PLAN NUC/PWR PEACE ORD/FREE PWR ...TIME/SEQ AUD/VIS VAL/FREE LEAGUE/NAT 20. PAGE 44 A0892
INT/ORG COERCE ARMS/CONT

S64
GARDNER R.N.,"GATT AND THE UNITED NATIONS
INT/ORG

CONFERENCE ON TRADE AND DEVELOPMENT." USA+45 WOR+45 SOCIETY ECO/UNDEV MARKET NAT/G DELIB/GP ACT/RES PLAN ECO/TAC TARIFFS EDU/PROP ROUTINE DRIVE RIGID/FLEX WEALTH...DECISION MGT TREND UN TOT/POP 20 GATT. PAGE 51 A1047 INT/TRADE

S64
GARMARNIKOW M.,"INFLUENCE-BUYING IN WEST AFRICA." COM FUT USSR INTELL NAT/G PLAN TEC/DEV ECO/TAC DOMIN EDU/PROP REGION NAT/LISM ATTIT DRIVE ALL/VALS SOVEREIGN...POLICY PSY SOC CONCPT TREND STERTYP WORK COLD/WAR 20. PAGE 51 A1049 AFR ECO/UNDEV FOR/AID SOCISM

S64
GERBET P.,"LA MISE EN OEUVRE DU MARCHE COMMUN AGRICOLE." ECO/DEV MARKET INT/ORG NAT/G PLAN EDU/PROP NAT/LISM WEALTH...OBS EEC VAL/FREE 20. PAGE 52 A1064 EUR+WWI AGRI REGION

S64
GROSSER A.,"Y A-T-IL UN CONFLIT FRANCO-AMERICAIN." EUR+WWI USA+45 INT/ORG NAT/G PLAN BAL/PWR DIPLOM EDU/PROP NUC/PWR ATTIT DRIVE ORD/FREE PWR...CONCPT OBS TIME/SEQ TREND STERTYP VAL/FREE COLD/WAR. PAGE 57 A1179 VOL/ASSN NAT/LISM FRANCE

S64
HICKEY D.,"THE PHILOSOPHICAL ARGUMENT FOR WORLD GOVERNMENT." WOR+45 SOCIETY ACT/RES PLAN LEGIT ADJUD PEACE PERCEPT PERSON ORD/FREE...HUM JURID PHIL/SCI METH/CNCPT CON/ANAL STERTYP GEN/LAWS TOT/POP 20. PAGE 65 A1327 FUT INT/ORG

S64
HOFFMANN S.,"CE QU'EN PENSENT LES AMERICAINS." EUR+WWI INT/ORG VOL/ASSN PLAN BAL/PWR DIPLOM DOMIN EDU/PROP REGION ARMS/CONT DRIVE ORD/FREE PWR ...POLICY CONCPT OBS TREND STERTYP COLD/WAR VAL/FREE 20. PAGE 66 A1357 USA+45 ATTIT FRANCE

S64
HUELIN D.,"ECONOMIC INTEGRATION IN LATIN AMERICAN: PROGRESS AND PROBLEMS." L/A+17C ECO/DEV AGRI DIST/IND FINAN INDUS NAT/G VOL/ASSN CONSULT DELIB/GP EX/STRUC ACT/RES PLAN TEC/DEV ECO/TAC ROUTINE BAL/PAY WEALTH WORK 20. PAGE 69 A1411 MARKET ECO/UNDEV INT/TRADE

S64
HUTCHINSON E.C.,"AMERICAN AID TO AFRICA." FUT USA+45 MARKET INT/ORG LOC/G NAT/G PUB/INST PLAN ECO/TAC ATTIT RIGID/FLEX...POLICY CONCPT TREND 20. PAGE 69 A1423 AFR ECO/UNDEV FOR/AID

S64
JORDAN A.,"POLITICAL COMMUNICATION: THE THIRD DIMENSION OF STRATEGY." USA+45 WOR+45 INT/ORG NAT/G CONSULT FORCES PLAN LEGIT EXEC PERCEPT ALL/VALS ...POLICY RELATIV PSY NEW/IDEA AUD/VIS EXHIBIT TOT/POP 20. PAGE 75 A1534 EDU/PROP RIGID/FLEX ATTIT

S64
KOTANI H.,"PEACE-KEEPING: PROBLEMS FOR SMALLER COUNTRIES." FUT WOR+45 NAT/G ACT/RES PLAN DOMIN EDU/PROP COERCE ALL/VALS...POLICY UN TOT/POP 20. PAGE 82 A1673 INT/ORG FORCES

S64
LERNER W.,"THE HISTORICAL ORIGINS OF THE SOVIET DOCTRINE OF PEACEFUL COEXISTENCE." COM USSR INT/ORG NAT/G VOL/ASSN PLAN PEACE ATTIT RIGID/FLEX PWR MARXISM...TIME/SEQ COLD/WAR 20. PAGE 87 A1788 EDU/PROP DIPLOM

S64
MARTELLI G.,"PORTUGAL AND THE UNITED NATIONS." AFR EUR+WWI ELITES INT/ORG NAT/G PROVS PLAN DIPLOM ECO/TAC DOMIN COLONIAL RIGID/FLEX MORAL ORD/FREE PWR WEALTH...MYTH UN 20. PAGE 95 A1947 ATTIT PORTUGAL

S64
NEISSER H.,"THE EXTERNAL EQUILIBRIUM OF THE UNITED STATES ECONOMY." FUT USA+45 NAT/G ACT/RES PLAN ECO/TAC ATTIT WEALTH...METH/CNCPT GEN/METH VAL/FREE 20. PAGE 108 A2216 FINAN ECO/DEV BAL/PAY INT/TRADE

S64
PADELFORD N.J.,"THE ORGANIZATION OF AFRICAN UNITY." ECO/UNDEV INT/ORG PLAN BAL/PWR DIPLOM ECO/TAC NAT/LISM ORD/FREE PWR WEALTH...CONCPT TREND STERTYP VAL/FREE COLD/WAR 20. PAGE 113 A2313 AFR VOL/ASSN REGION

S64
PESELT B.M.,"COMMUNIST ECONOMIC OFFENSIVE." WOR+45 SOCIETY INT/ORG PLAN ECO/TAC DOMIN EDU/PROP ATTIT PERSON PWR WEALTH...TREND CHARTS 20. PAGE 115 A2366 COM ECO/UNDEV FOR/AID USSR

S64
SAAB H.,"THE ARAB SEARCH FOR A FEDERAL UNION." SOCIETY INT/ORG NAT/G DELIB/GP FORCES ACT/RES TEC/DEV ECO/TAC DOMIN LEGIT REGION ROUTINE ATTIT DRIVE RIGID/FLEX ALL/VALS...SOC CONCPT NEW/IDEA TIME/SEQ TREND. PAGE 126 A2580 ISLAM PLAN

S64
SALVADORI M.,"EL CAPITALISMO EN LA EUROPA DE LA POSGUERRA." INT/ORG NAT/G POL/PAR PLAN ECO/TAC ATTIT ORD/FREE WEALTH...HIST/WRIT COLD/WAR EEC 20. PAGE 127 A2596 EUR+WWI ECO/DEV CAP/ISM

S64
TAUBENFELD R.K.,"INDEPENDENT REVENUE FOR THE UNITED NATIONS." WOR+45 SOCIETY STRUCT INDUS NAT/G CONSULT ACT/RES PLAN ECO/TAC LEGIT WEALTH...DECISION CON/ANAL GEN/METH UN 20. PAGE 142 A2896 INT/ORG FINAN

S64
TINKER H.,"POLITICS IN SOUTHEAST ASIA." INT/ORG NAT/G CREATE PLAN TEC/DEV GUERRILLA KNOWL ORD/FREE COLD/WAR. PAGE 144 A2944 S/ASIA ACT/RES REGION

C64
SCHRAMM W.,"MASS MEDIA AND NATIONAL DEVELOPMENT: THE ROLE OF INFORMATION IN DEVELOPING COUNTRIES." FINAN R+D ACT/RES PLAN TEC/DEV DIPLOM CHOOSE SUPEGO ORD/FREE...BIBLIOG 20. PAGE 129 A2645 ECO/UNDEV COM/IND EDU/PROP MAJORIT

N64
GREAT BRITAIN CENTRAL OFF INF,THE COLOMBO PLAN (PAMPHLET). ASIA S/ASIA USA+45 VOL/ASSN...CHARTS 20 COMMONWLTH RESOURCE/N. PAGE 55 A1134 FOR/AID PLAN INT/ORG ECO/UNDEV

B65
ANALYSIS AND ASSESSMENT OF THE ECONOMIC EFFECTS: PUBLIC LAW 480 TITLE I PROGRAM TURKEY. INDIA TURKEY USA+45 AGRI NAT/G PLAN BUDGET DIPLOM COST EFFICIENCY...CHARTS 20. PAGE 3 A0070 ECO/TAC FOR/AID FINAN ECO/UNDEV

B65
PEACE RESEARCH ABSTRACTS. FUT WOR+45 R+D INT/ORG NAT/G PLAN TEC/DEV BAL/PWR DIPLOM FOR/AID NUC/PWR HEALTH. PAGE 4 A0072 BIBLIOG/A PEACE ARMS/CONT WAR

B65
AMERICAN ECONOMIC ASSOCIATION,INDEX OF ECONOMIC JOURNALS 1886-1965 (7 VOLS.). UK USA+45 USA-45 AGRI FINAN PLAN ECO/TAC INT/TRADE ADMIN...STAT CENSUS 19/20. PAGE 7 A0145 BIBLIOG WRITING INDUS

B65
CASSELL F.,GOLD OR CREDIT? THE ECONOMICS AND POLITICS OF INTERNATIONAL MONEY. WOR+45 PLAN PROB/SOLV BAL/PAY SOVEREIGN WEALTH 20 OEEC GOLD/STAND. PAGE 25 A0506 FINAN INT/ORG DIPLOM ECO/TAC

B65
CBS,CONVERSATIONS WITH WALTER LIPPMANN. USA+45 INT/ORG NAT/G POL/PAR PLAN DIPLOM PWR ALL/IDEOS ...POLICY 20 LIPPMANN/W. PAGE 25 A0509 TV ATTIT INT

B65
CORDIER A.W.,THE QUEST FOR PEACE. WOR+45 NAT/G PLAN BAL/PWR ECO/TAC ARMS/CONT NUC/PWR PWR...ANTHOL UN COLD/WAR. PAGE 30 A0617 PEACE DIPLOM POLICY INT/ORG

B65
DEMAS W.G.,THE ECONOMICS OF DEVELOPMENT IN SMALL COUNTRIES WITH SPECIAL REFERENCE TO THE CARIBBEAN. WOR+45 BAL/PAY DEMAND EFFICIENCY PRODUC...GEOG CARIBBEAN. PAGE 36 A0731 ECO/UNDEV PLAN WEALTH INT/TRADE

B65
FORM W.H.,INDUSTRIAL RELATIONS AND SOCIAL CHANGE IN LATIN AMERICA. L/A+17C AGRI LABOR NAT/G PLAN PROB/SOLV DIPLOM...MGT SOC ANTHOL BIBLIOG/A METH 20. PAGE 47 A0966 INDUS GP/REL NAT/COMP ECO/UNDEV

B65
FRANKLAND N.,THE BOMBING OFFENSIVE AGAINST GERMANY. GERMANY UK TEC/DEV DIPLOM WAR...METH/COMP 20. PAGE 48 A0985 WEAPON PLAN DECISION FORCES

B65
GRETTON P.,MARITIME STRATEGY - A STUDY OF DEFENSE PROBLEMS. ASIA UK USSR DIPLOM COERCE DETER NUC/PWR WEAPON...CONCPT NAT/COMP 20. PAGE 56 A1147 FORCES PLAN WAR SEA

B65
HAIGHT D.E.,THE PRESIDENT; ROLES AND POWERS. USA+45 USA-45 POL/PAR PLAN DIPLOM CHOOSE PERS/REL PWR 18/20 PRESIDENT CONGRESS. PAGE 59 A1217 CHIEF LEGIS TOP/EX EX/STRUC

B65
HART B.H.L.,THE MEMOIRS OF CAPTAIN LIDDELL HART (VOL. I). UK NAT/G PLAN TEC/DEV DIPLOM ADMIN WEAPON GOV/REL PERS/REL ATTIT PWR FASCISM...POLICY 20. PAGE 62 A1274 FORCES BIOG LEAD WAR

B65
INGRAM D.,COMMONWEALTH FOR A COLOUR-BLIND WORLD. AFR INDIA UK STRATA ECO/UNDEV VOL/ASSN CREATE PLAN CONFER COLONIAL ORD/FREE SOC/INTEG 20 COMMONWLTH. PAGE 70 A1441 RACE/REL INT/ORG INGP/REL PROB/SOLV

B65
INTERNATIONAL SOCIAL SCI COUN,SOCIAL SCIENCES IN THE USSR. USSR ECO/DEV AGRI FINAN INDUS PLAN CAP/ISM...INT/LAW PHIL/SCI PSY SOC 20. PAGE 71 A1460 BIBLIOG/A ACT/RES MARXISM JURID

B65
JOHNSTON D.M.,THE INTERNATIONAL LAW OF FISHERIES: A FRAMEWORK FOR POLICYORIENTED INQUIRIES. WOR+45 ACT/RES PLAN PROB/SOLV CONTROL SOVEREIGN. PAGE 75 A1527 CONCPT EXTR/IND JURID DIPLOM

B65
KRAUSE W.,ECONOMIC DEVELOPMENT: THE UNDERDEVELOPED WORLD AND THE AMERICAN INTEREST. USA+45 AGRI PLAN MARXISM...CHARTS 20. PAGE 82 A1679 FOR/AID ECO/UNDEV FINAN PROB/SOLV

B65
MALLIN J.,FORTRESS CUBA; RUSSIA'S AMERICAN BASE. MARXISM

COM CUBA L/A+17C FORCES PLAN DIPLOM LEAD REV WAR ...POLICY 20 CASTRO/F GUEVARA/C INTERVENT. PAGE 93 A1914 — CHIEF GUERRILLA DOMIN

B65
MEAGHER R.F.,PUBLIC INTERNATIONAL DEVELOPMENT FINANCING IN SUDAN. SUDAN FINAN DELIB/GP GIVE ...CHARTS GOV/COMP 20. PAGE 99 A2029 — FOR/AID PLAN RECEIVE ECO/UNDEV

B65
MERKL P.H.,GERMANY: YESTERDAY AND TOMORROW. GERMANY POL/PAR PLAN DIPLOM LEAD FEDERAL 19/20. PAGE 100 A2043 — NAT/G FUT

B65
MEYERHOFF A.E.,THE STRATEGY OF PERSUASION: THE USE OF ADVERTISING SKILLS IN FIGHTING THE COLD WAR. USA+45 USSR PLAN ATTIT DRIVE...BIBLIOG 20 COLD/WAR. PAGE 100 A2054 — EDU/PROP SERV/IND METH/COMP DIPLOM

B65
MIDDLETON D.,CRISIS IN THE WEST. EUR+WWI FUT WOR+45 CHIEF PLAN ECO/TAC LEAD REGION NUC/PWR NAT/LISM MARXISM 20 COLD/WAR NATO EEC. PAGE 101 A2068 — INT/ORG DIPLOM NAT/G POLICY

B65
MONCRIEFF A.,SECOND THOUGHTS ON AID. WOR+45 ECO/UNDEV AGRI FINAN VOL/ASSN PLAN TEC/DEV GIVE EDU/PROP ROLE WEALTH 20. PAGE 102 A2105 — FOR/AID ECO/TAC INT/ORG IDEA/COMP

B65
MORGENTHAU H.,MORGENTHAU DIARY (CHINA) (2 VOLS.). ASIA USA+45 USA-45 LAW DELIB/GP EX/STRUC PLAN FOR/AID INT/TRADE CONFER WAR MARXISM 20 CHINJAP. PAGE 104 A2136 — DIPLOM ADMIN

B65
NATIONAL CENTRAL LIBRARY,LATIN AMERICAN ECONOMIC AND SOCIAL SERIALS. UK SOCIETY NAT/G PLAN PROB/SOLV ...SOC 20. PAGE 107 A2202 — BIBLIOG INT/TRADE ECO/UNDEV L/A+17C

B65
REQUA E.G.,THE DEVELOPING NATIONS: A GUIDE TO INFORMATION SOURCES CONCERNING THEIR ECON, POLIT, TECHNICAL, AND SOCIAL PROBLEMS. AFR ASIA ISLAM L/A+17C INDUS INT/ORG CONSULT PLAN PROB/SOLV...SOC 20 UN. PAGE 120 A2466 — BIBLIOG/A ECO/UNDEV FOR/AID TEC/DEV

B65
THAYER F.C. JR.,AIR TRANSPORT POLICY AND NATIONAL SECURITY: A POLITICAL, ECONOMIC, AND MILITARY ANALYSIS. DIST/IND OP/RES PLAN TEC/DEV DIPLOM DETER WAR COST EFFICIENCY...POLICY BIBLIOG 20 DEPT/DEFEN FAA CAB. PAGE 142 A2908 — AIR FORCES CIVMIL/REL ORD/FREE

B65
UN,SPACE ACTIVITIES AND RESOURCES: REVIEW OF UNITED NATION'S NATIONAL AND INTERNATIONAL PROGRAMS. INT/ORG LABOR PLAN TEC/DEV DIPLOM EFFICIENCY HEALTH ...GOV/COMP 20 UN. PAGE 146 A2995 — SPACE NUC/PWR FOR/AID PEACE

B65
US BUREAU EDUC CULTURAL AFF,RESOURCES SURVEY FOR LATIN AMERICAN COUNTRIES. L/A+17C USA+45 CULTURE INDUS INT/ORG SECT PLAN EDU/PROP POLICY. PAGE 150 A3056 — NAT/G ECO/UNDEV FOR/AID DIPLOM

B65
US CONGRESS JOINT ECO COMM,GUIDELINES FOR INTERNATIONAL MONETARY REFORM. USA+45 WOR+45 DELIB/GP BAL/PAY 20 CONGRESS IMF MONEY. PAGE 150 A3069 — DIPLOM FINAN PLAN INT/ORG

B65
US SENATE,US INTERNATIONAL SPACE PROGRAMS, 1959-65: STAFF REPORT FOR COMM ON AERONAUTICAL AND SPACE SCIENCES. WOR+45 VOL/ASSN CIVMIL/REL 20 CONGRESS NASA TREATY. PAGE 155 A3166 — SPACE DIPLOM PLAN GOV/REL

B65
US SENATE COMM AERO SPACE SCI,INTERNATIONAL COOPERATION AND ORGANIZATION FOR OUTER SPACE. FUT USA+45 WOR+45 PROF/ORG VOL/ASSN CONSULT DELIB/GP PLAN TEC/DEV ARMS/CONT GP/REL PEACE 20 UN NASA. PAGE 155 A3167 — DIPLOM SPACE R+D NAT/G

B65
WALKER A.A.,THE RHODESIAS AND NYASALAND: A GUIDE TO OFFICIAL PUBLICATIONS. RHODESIA UK OP/RES PLAN PROB/SOLV DIPLOM...POLICY SOC CON/ANAL 19/20 NYASALAND. PAGE 160 A3263 — BIBLIOG NAT/G COLONIAL AFR

B65
WEAVER J.N.,THE INTERNATIONAL DEVELOPMENT ASSOCIATION: A NEW APPROACH TO FOREIGN AID. USA+45 NAT/G OP/RES PLAN PROB/SOLV WEALTH...CHARTS BIBLIOG 20 UN. PAGE 162 A3295 — FOR/AID INT/ORG ECO/UNDEV FINAN

B65
WHITE J.,GERMAN AID. GERMANY/W FINAN PLAN TEC/DEV INT/TRADE ADMIN ATTIT...POLICY 20. PAGE 164 A3335 — FOR/AID ECO/UNDEV DIPLOM ECO/TAC

B65
WITHERELL J.W.,MADAGASCAR AND ADJACENT ISLANDS; A GUIDE TO OFFICIAL PUBLICATIONS (PAMPHLET). FRANCE MADAGASCAR S/ASIA UK LAW OP/RES PLAN DIPLOM ...POLICY CON/ANAL 19/20. PAGE 165 A3371 — BIBLIOG COLONIAL LOC/G ADMIN

L65
LOFTUS M.L.,"INTERNATIONAL MONETARY FUND, 1962-1965: A SELECTED BIBLIOGRAPHY." WOR+45 PLAN BUDGET INCOME PROFIT WEALTH. PAGE 90 A1852 — BIBLIOG FINAN INT/TRADE INT/ORG

L65
MATTHEWS D.G.,"LE TIERS MONDE: A SELECT AND PRELIMINARY BIBLIOGRAPHIC SURVEY OF MANPOWER IN DEVELOPING COUNTRIES, 1960-1964." AFR ISLAM L/A+17C INDUS PLAN PROB/SOLV TEC/DEV INT/TRADE EFFICIENCY WEALTH...STAT 20. PAGE 96 A1971 — BIBLIOG/A ECO/UNDEV LABOR WORKER

S65
KHOURI F.J.,"THE JORDON RIVER CONTROVERSY." LAW SOCIETY ECO/UNDEV AGRI FINAN INDUS SECT FORCES ACT/RES PLAN TEC/DEV ECO/TAC EDU/PROP COERCE ATTIT DRIVE PERCEPT RIGID/FLEX ALL/VALS...GEOG SOC MYTH WORK. PAGE 78 A1610 — ISLAM INT/ORG ISRAEL JORDAN

S65
MERRITT R.L.,"WOODROW WILSON AND THE 'GREAT AND SOLEMN REFERENDUM,' 1920." USA-45 SOCIETY NAT/G CONSULT LEGIS ACT/RES PLAN DOMIN EDU/PROP ROUTINE ATTIT DISPL DRIVE PERSON RIGID/FLEX MORAL ORD/FREE ...PSY SOC CONCPT MYTH LEAGUE/NAT. PAGE 100 A2044 — INT/ORG TOP/EX DIPLOM

S65
PRABHAKAR P.,"SURVEY OF RESEARCH AND SOURCE MATERIALS; THE SINO-INDIAN BORDER DISPUTE." CHINA/COM INDIA LAW NAT/G PLAN BAL/PWR WAR...POLICY 20 COLD/WAR. PAGE 117 A2404 — BIBLIOG ASIA S/ASIA DIPLOM

S65
QUADE Q.L.,"THE TRUMAN ADMINISTRATION AND THE SEPARATION OF POWERS: THE CASE OF THE MARSHALL PLAN." SOCIETY INT/ORG NAT/G CONSULT DELIB/GP LEGIS PLAN ECO/TAC ROUTINE DRIVE PERCEPT RIGID/FLEX ORD/FREE PWR WEALTH...DECISION GEOG NEW/IDEA TREND 20 TRUMAN/HS. PAGE 118 A2422 — USA+45 ECO/UNDEV DIPLOM

S65
SCHNEIDER R.M.,"THE US IN LATIN AMERICA." L/A+17C USA+45 NAT/G POL/PAR PLAN RIGID/FLEX ALL/VALS OAS 20. PAGE 129 A2640 — VOL/ASSN ECO/UNDEV FOR/AID

S65
SPAAK P.H.,"THE SEARCH FOR CONSENSUS: A NEW EFFORT TO BUILD EUROPE." FRANCE GERMANY ECO/DEV NAT/G CONSULT FORCES PLAN EDU/PROP REGION CONSEN ATTIT ...SOC METH/CNCPT OBS TREND EEC NATO WORK 20. PAGE 135 A2770 — EUR+WWI INT/ORG

C65
US AIR FORCE ACADEMY,"AMERICAN DEFENSE POLICY." COM INT/ORG TEC/DEV FOR/AID ARMS/CONT DETER NUC/PWR ...POLICY DECISION CONCPT ANTHOL BIBLIOG/A 20 COLD/WAR NATO. PAGE 149 A3054 — PLAN FORCES WAR COERCE

B66
BEAUFRE A.,NATO AND EUROPE. WOR+45 PLAN CONFER EXEC NUC/PWR ATTIT...POLICY 20 NATO EUROPE. PAGE 12 A0243 — INT/ORG DETER DIPLOM ADMIN

B66
ENTWICKLUNGSPOLITIK - HANDBUCH UND LEXIKON. MARKET SECT DIPLOM INT/TRADE EDU/PROP CATHISM 20. PAGE 14 A0283 — ECO/UNDEV FOR/AID ECO/TAC PLAN

B66
BROEKMEIJER M.W.J.,FICTION AND TRUTH ABOUT THE "DECADE OF DEVELOPMENT" WOR+45 AGRI FINAN INDUS NAT/G TEC/DEV DIPLOM EDU/PROP LEAD SKILL 20 THIRD/WRLD. PAGE 19 A0385 — FOR/AID POLICY ECO/UNDEV PLAN

B66
BROWN L.C.,STATE AND SOCIETY IN INDEPENDENT NORTH AFRICA. ALGERIA LIBYA MOROCCO AGRI INDUS INT/ORG POL/PAR SECT PLAN DIPLOM COLONIAL...LING NAT/COMP ANTHOL BIBLIOG 20 TUNIS MUSLIM. PAGE 20 A0406 — NAT/G SOCIETY CULTURE ECO/UNDEV

B66
CLARK G.,WORLD PEACE THROUGH WORLD LAW; TWO ALTERNATIVE PLANS. WOR+45 DELIB/GP FORCES TAX CONFER ADJUD SANCTION ARMS/CONT WAR CHOOSE PRIVIL 20 UN COLD/WAR. PAGE 27 A0541 — INT/LAW PEACE PLAN INT/ORG

B66
CLAUSEWITZ C.V.,ON WAR (VOL. III). UNIV EDU/PROP ...POLICY DECISION METH 18/20. PAGE 27 A0548 — WAR FORCES PLAN CIVMIL/REL

B66
COLE A.B.,SOCIALIST PARTIES IN POSTWAR JAPAN. STRATA AGRI LABOR PLAN DIPLOM ECO/TAC AGREE LEAD CHOOSE ATTIT...CHARTS 20 CHINJAP SOC/DEMPAR. PAGE 28 A0566 — POL/PAR POLICY SOCISM NAT/G

B66
CURRIE L.,ACCELERATING DEVELOPMENT: THE NECESSITY AND MEANS. COLOMBIA USA+45 INDUS DIPLOM EFFICIENCY WEALTH...METH/CNCPT NEW/IDEA 20. PAGE 33 A0668 — PLAN ECO/UNDEV FOR/AID TEC/DEV

B66
DAENIKER G.,STRATEGIE DES KLEIN STAATS. SWITZERLND ACT/RES CREATE DIPLOM NEUTRAL DETER WAR WEAPON PWR SOVEREIGN...IDEA/COMP 20 COLD/WAR. PAGE 33 A0673 — NUC/PWR PLAN FORCES NAT/G

B66
DAVIS V.,POSTWAR DEFENSE POLICY AND THE US NAVY, 1943-1946. USA+45 DIPLOM CONFER LEAD ATTIT...POLICY IDEA/COMP 20 NAVY. PAGE 34 A0692 — FORCES PLAN PROB/SOLV CIVMIL/REL

B66
ERICKSON J.,THE MILITARY-TECHNICAL REVOLUTION. USA+45 WOR+45 INT/ORG PLAN ATTIT...DECISION ANTHOL 20. PAGE 42 A0861 — DIPLOM DETER POLICY NUC/PWR

B66
EWING L.L.,THE REFERENCE HANDBOOK OF THE ARMED FORCES OF THE WORLD. WOR+45 ECO/TAC FOR/AID COERCE WAR PWR 20. PAGE 43 A0879 — FORCES STAT DIPLOM PLAN

B66
FELKER J.L.,SOVIET ECONOMIC CONTROVERSIES. USSR INDUS PLAN INT/TRADE GP/REL MARXISM SOCISM...POLICY 20. PAGE 45 A0915 — ECO/DEV MARKET PROFIT PRICE

B66
FISHER S.N.,NEW HORIZONS FOR THE UNITED STATES IN WORLD AFFAIRS. USA+45 FOR/AID...ANTHOL 20 UN. PAGE 46 A0941 — DIPLOM PLAN INT/ORG

B66
GLAZER M.,THE FEDERAL GOVERNMENT AND THE UNIVERSITY. CHILE PROB/SOLV DIPLOM GIVE ADMIN WAR ...POLICY SOC 20. PAGE 53 A1079 — BIBLIOG/A NAT/G PLAN ACADEM

B66
HANSON J.W.,EDUCATION AND THE DEVELOPMENT OF NATIONS. DIPLOM TASK ADJUST EFFICIENCY...POLICY ANTHOL 20. PAGE 61 A1256 — ECO/UNDEV EDU/PROP NAT/G PLAN

B66
HOLLINS E.J.,PEACE IS POSSIBLE: A READER FOR LAYMEN. WOR+45 CULTURE PLAN RISK AGE/Y ALL/VALS SOVEREIGN...PSY CONCPT TREND 20 UN JOHN/XXIII KENNAN/G MYRDAL/G. PAGE 67 A1370 — PEACE DIPLOM INT/ORG NUC/PWR

B66
HORELICK A.L.,STRATEGIC POWER AND SOVIET FOREIGN POLICY. CUBA USSR FORCES PLAN CIVMIL/REL...POLICY DECISION 20 COLD/WAR. PAGE 67 A1383 — DIPLOM BAL/PWR DETER NUC/PWR

B66
HOROWITZ D.,HEMISPHERES NORTH AND SOUTH: ECONOMIC DISPARITY AMONG NATIONS. WOR+45 ECO/DEV ECO/UNDEV INT/ORG PLAN DIPLOM INT/TRADE GIVE PARTIC GP/REL ...WELF/ST 20. PAGE 67 A1387 — ECO/TAC FOR/AID STRATA WEALTH

B66
KAREFA-SMART J.,AFRICA: PROGRESS THROUGH COOPERATION. AFR FINAN TEC/DEV DIPLOM FOR/AID EDU/PROP CONFER REGION GP/REL WEALTH...HEAL SOC/INTEG 20. PAGE 76 A1566 — ORD/FREE ECO/UNDEV VOL/ASSN PLAN

B66
KIRDAR U.,THE STRUCTURE OF UNITED NATIONS ECONOMIC AID TO UNDERDEVELOPED COUNTRIES. AGRI FINAN INDUS NAT/G EX/STRUC PLAN GIVE TASK...POLICY 20 UN. PAGE 79 A1631 — INT/ORG FOR/AID ECO/UNDEV ADMIN

B66
LEAGUE OF WOMEN VOTERS OF US,FOREIGN AID AT THE CROSSROADS. USA+45 WOR+45 DELIB/GP PROB/SOLV DIPLOM INT/TRADE RECEIVE BAL/PAY...CHARTS 20 UN. PAGE 86 A1756 — FOR/AID GIVE ECO/UNDEV PLAN

B66
MEERHAEGHE M.,INTERNATIONAL ECONOMIC INSTITUTIONS. EUR+WWI FINAN INDUS MARKET PLAN TARIFFS BAL/PAY EQUILIB...POLICY BIBLIOG/A 20 GATT OEEC EEC IBRD EURCOALSTL. PAGE 99 A2032 — ECO/TAC ECO/DEV INT/TRADE INT/ORG

B66
MOOMAW I.W.,THE CHALLENGE OF HUNGER. USA+45 PLAN ADMIN EATING 20. PAGE 103 A2118 — FOR/AID DIPLOM ECO/UNDEV ECO/TAC

B66
MURPHY G.G.,SOVIET MONGOLIA: A STUDY OF THE OLDEST POLITICAL SATELLITE. USSR STRATA STRUCT COST INCOME ATTIT SOCISM 20. PAGE 106 A2177 — DIPLOM ECO/TAC PLAN DOMIN

B66
NATIONAL COUN APPLIED ECO RES,DEVELOPMENT WITHOUT AID. INDIA FINAN TEC/DEV EFFICIENCY...ANTHOL 20. PAGE 107 A2203 — FOR/AID PLAN SOVEREIGN ECO/UNDEV

B66
OHLIN G.,FOREIGN AID POLICIES RECONSIDERED. ECO/DEV ECO/UNDEV VOL/ASSN CONSULT PLAN CONTROL ATTIT ...CONCPT CHARTS BIBLIOG 20. PAGE 111 A2286 — FOR/AID DIPLOM GIVE

B66
ROBOCK S.H.,INTERNATIONAL DEVELOPMENT 1965. AGRI INDUS VOL/ASSN PLAN TEC/DEV EDU/PROP HEALTH...JURID 20 UN PEACE/CORP. PAGE 122 A2508 — FOR/AID INT/ORG GEOG ECO/UNDEV

B66
SAPIN B.M.,THE MAKING OF UNITED STATES FOREIGN POLICY. USA+45 INT/ORG DELIB/GP FORCES PLAN ECO/TAC CIVMIL/REL PRESIDENT. PAGE 127 A2603 — DIPLOM EX/STRUC DECISION NAT/G

B66
SINGH L.P.,THE POLITICS OF ECONOMIC COOPERATION IN ASIA; A STUDY OF ASIAN INTERNATIONAL ORGANIZATIONS. ASIA INT/ORG ACT/RES PLAN GP/REL...POLICY GP/COMP BIBLIOG 20 UN SEATO. PAGE 133 A2733 — ECO/UNDEV ECO/TAC REGION DIPLOM

B66
SPULBER N.,THE STATE AND ECONOMIC DEVELOPMENT IN EASTERN EUROPE. BULGARIA COM CZECHOSLVK HUNGARY POLAND YUGOSLAVIA CULTURE PLAN CAP/ISM INT/TRADE CONTROL...POLICY CHARTS METH/COMP BIBLIOG/A 19/20. PAGE 136 A2793 — ECO/DEV ECO/UNDEV NAT/G TOTALISM

B66
STADLER K.R.,THE BIRTH OF THE AUSTRIAN REPUBLIC, 1918-1921. AUSTRIA PLAN TASK PEACE...POLICY DECISION 20. PAGE 137 A2798 — NAT/G DIPLOM WAR DELIB/GP

B66
THORNTON A.P.,THE IMPERIAL IDEA AND ITS ENEMIES. UK WOR+45 WOR-45 NAT/G PLAN DOMIN CONTROL WAR ATTIT PWR...TREND CHARTS 19/20 CMN/WLTH. PAGE 144 A2937 — COLONIAL DIPLOM

B66
UN ECAFE,ADMINISTRATIVE ASPECTS OF FAMILY PLANNING PROGRAMMES (PAMPHLET). ASIA THAILAND WOR+45 VOL/ASSN PROB/SOLV BUDGET FOR/AID EDU/PROP CONFER CONTROL GOV/REL TIME 20 UN BIRTH/CON. PAGE 147 A2999 — PLAN CENSUS FAM ADMIN

B66
US SENATE COMM AERO SPACE SCI,SOVIET SPACE PROGRAMS, 1962-65; GOALS AND PURPOSES, ACHIEVEMENTS, PLANS, AND INTERNATIONAL IMPLICATIONS. USA+45 USSR R+D FORCES PLAN EDU/PROP PRESS ADJUD ARMS/CONT ATTIT MARXISM. PAGE 155 A3168 — CONSULT SPACE FUT DIPLOM

B66
VYAS R.,DAWNING ON THE CAPITOL: US CONGRESS AND INDIA. INDIA S/ASIA USA+45 ELITES ECO/DEV ECO/UNDEV PLAN FOR/AID...BIBLIOG 20 CONGRESS. PAGE 160 A3256 — POLICY LEGIS NAT/G DIPLOM

B66
WARBURG J.P.,THE UNITED STATES IN THE POSTWAR WORLD. USA+45 ECO/TAC...POLICY 20 COLD/WAR. PAGE 161 A3277 — FOR/AID DIPLOM PLAN ADMIN

B66
WESTWOOD A.F.,FOREIGN AID IN A FOREIGN POLICY FRAMEWORK. AFR ASIA INDIA IRAN L/A+17C USA+45 USSR ECO/UNDEV AGRI FORCES LEGIS PLAN PROB/SOLV ...DECISION 20 COLD/WAR. PAGE 163 A3324 — FOR/AID DIPLOM POLICY ECO/TAC

B66
WILLIAMS P.,AID IN UGANDA - EDUCATION. UGANDA UK FINAN ACADEM INT/ORG SCHOOL PROB/SOLV ECO/TAC UTIL ...STAT CHARTS 20. PAGE 165 A3352 — PLAN EDU/PROP FOR/AID ECO/UNDEV

L66
AMERICAN ECONOMIC REVIEW,"SIXTY-THIRD LIST OF DOCTORAL DISSERTATIONS IN POLITICAL ECONOMY IN AMERICAN UNIVERSITIES AND COLLEGES." ECO/DEV AGRI FINAN LABOR WORKER PLAN BUDGET INT/TRADE ADMIN DEMAND...MGT STAT 20. PAGE 7 A0146 — BIBLIOG/A CONCPT ACADEM

S66
DINH TRANS V.A.N.,"VIETNAM: A THIRD WAY" S/ASIA USA+45 USSR VIETNAM VIETNAM/S NAT/G SECT FORCES CAP/ISM DIPLOM COLONIAL NEUTRAL MARXISM SOCISM 20 BUDDHISM UNIFICA. PAGE 38 A0766 — WAR PLAN ORD/FREE SOCIALIST

S66
FRIEND A.,"THE MIDDLE EAST CRISIS" COM ISLAM ISRAEL SYRIA UAR USA+45 USSR FORCES PLAN FOR/AID CONTROL ORD/FREE PWR...SOCIALIST TIME/SEQ 20 NASSER/G. PAGE 49 A1009 — WAR INT/ORG DIPLOM PEACE

S66
JAVITS J.K.,"POLITICAL ACTION VITAL FOR LATIN AMERICAN INTEGRATION." ECO/UNDEV INT/ORG POL/PAR VOL/ASSN PLAN PROB/SOLV INT/TRADE EFFICIENCY 20 OAS LAFTA. PAGE 73 A1500 — L/A+17C ECO/TAC REGION

S66
SHERMAN M.,"GUARANTEES AND NUCLEAR SPREAD." USA+45 WOR+45 INT/ORG PLAN DETER WAR ORD/FREE 20 NATO. PAGE 132 A2700 — DIPLOM POLICY NAT/G NUC/PWR

C66
DUROSELLE J.B.,"LE CONFLIT DE TRIESTE 1943-1954: ETUDES DE CAS DE CONFLITS INTERNATIONAUX III." ITALY USA+45 YUGOSLAVIA ELITES DELIB/GP PLAN ADJUST ...POLICY GEOG CHARTS IDEA/COMP TIME 20 TREATY UN COLD/WAR. PAGE 40 A0810 — BIBLIOG WAR DIPLOM GEN/LAWS

N66
EOMMITTEE ECONOMIC DEVELOPMENT,THE DOLLAR AND THE WORLD MONETARY SYSTEM: A STATEMENT ON NATIONAL POLICY (PAMPHLET). USA+45 NAT/G PLAN PROB/SOLV BUDGET ECO/TAC FOR/AID INCOME...POLICY 20 GOLD/STAND EUROPE. PAGE 42 A0854 — FINAN BAL/PAY DIPLOM ECO/DEV

N66
US HOUSE COMM FOREIGN AFFAIRS,UNITED STATES POLICY TOWARD ASIA (PAMPHLET). CHINA/COM USA+45 USSR VIETNAM INT/ORG NAT/G PWR MARXISM 20 UN. PAGE 154 — POLICY ASIA DIPLOM

A3133 — PLAN

B67
BLOOMFIELD L.,THE UNITED NATIONS AND US FOREIGN POLICY. USA+45 DIPLOM LEAD ARMS/CONT DETER PWR 20 UN. PAGE 15 A0313
INT/ORG PLAN CONFER IDEA/COMP

B67
BURNS E.L.M.,MEGAMURDER. WOR+45 LAW INT/ORG NAT/G BAL/PWR DIPLOM DETER MURDER WEAPON CIVMIL/REL PEACE ...INT/LAW TREND 20. PAGE 22 A0444
FORCES PLAN WAR NUC/PWR

B67
HALPERIN M.H.,CONTEMPORARY MILITARY STRATEGY. ASIA CHINA/COM USA+45 USSR INT/ORG FORCES ACT/RES PLAN TEC/DEV BAL/PWR COERCE WAR...METH/COMP BIBLIOG 20 NATO. PAGE 60 A1240
DIPLOM NUC/PWR DETER ARMS/CONT

B67
HIRSCHMAN A.O.,DEVELOPMENT PROJECTS OBSERVED. INDUS INT/ORG CONSULT EX/STRUC CREATE OP/RES ECO/TAC DEMAND...POLICY MGT METH/COMP 20 WORLD/BANK. PAGE 65 A1339
ECO/UNDEV R+D FINAN PLAN

B67
HOLLERMAN L.,JAPAN'S DEPENDENCE ON THE WORLD ECONOMY. INDUS MARKET LABOR NAT/G DIPLOM 20 CHINJAP. PAGE 67 A1369
PLAN ECO/DEV ECO/TAC INT/TRADE

B67
JAGAN C.,THE WEST ON TRIAL. GUYANA CONSTN ECO/UNDEV DIPLOM COERCE PWR SOVEREIGN...BIOG 20. PAGE 73 A1490
SOCISM CREATE PLAN COLONIAL

B67
JOHNSON D.G.,THE STRUGGLE AGAINST WORLD HUNGER (HEADLINE SERIES, NO. 184) (PAMPHLET). PLAN TEC/DEV FOR/AID...CHARTS 20 FAO MEXIC/AMER. PAGE 74 A1520
AGRI PROB/SOLV ECO/UNDEV HEALTH

B67
ROBINSON R.D.,INTERNATIONAL MANAGEMENT. USA+45 FINAN R+D PLAN PRODUC...DECISION T. PAGE 92 A1882
INT/TRADE MGT INT/LAW MARKET

B67
MEHDI M.T.,PEACE IN THE MIDDLE EAST. ISRAEL SOCIETY NAT/G PLAN EDU/PROP NAT/LISM DRIVE...IDEA/COMP 20 JEWS. PAGE 99 A2033
ISLAM DIPLOM GP/REL COERCE

B67
OLSON L.,JAPAN TODAY AND TOMORROW (PAMPHLET) (HEADLINE SERIES, NO. 181). PLAN DIPLOM NAT/LISM ATTIT...PREDICT 20 CHINJAP. PAGE 112 A2289
NAT/G CULTURE ECO/DEV

B67
US DEPARTMENT OF THE ARMY,CIVILIAN IN PEACE, SOLDIER IN WAR: A BIBLIOGRAPHIC SURVEY OF THE ARMY AND AIR NATIONAL GUARD (PAMPHLET, NOS. 130-2). USA+45 USA-45 LOC/G NAT/G PROVS LEGIS PLAN ADMIN ATTIT ORD/FREE...POLICY 19/20. PAGE 152 A3111
BIBLIOG/A FORCES ROLE DIPLOM

L67
"POLITICAL PARTIES ON FOREIGN POLICY IN THE INTER-ELECTION YEARS 1962-66." ASIA COM INDIA USA+45 PLAN ATTIT...DECISION 20. PAGE 4 A0079
POL/PAR DIPLOM POLICY

L67
BODENHEIMER S.J.,"THE 'POLITICAL UNION' DEBATE IN EUROPE* A CASE STUDY IN INTERGOVERNMENTAL DIPLOMACY." EUR+WWI FUT NAT/G FORCES PLAN DEBATE SOVEREIGN...CONCPT PREDICT EEC NATO. PAGE 16 A0326
DIPLOM REGION INT/ORG

L67
DEVADHAR Y.C.,"THE ROLE OF FOREIGN PRIVATE CAPITAL IN INDIA'S ECONOMIC DEVELOPMENT* ASSESSMENT OF POLICY AND PERFORMANCE." INDIA INDUS PLAN TEC/DEV BUDGET DIPLOM ECO/TAC BAL/PAY PRODUC WEALTH ...CHARTS 20. PAGE 37 A0750
CAP/ISM FOR/AID POLICY ACT/RES

S67
ABT J.J.,"WORLD OF SENATOR FULBRIGHT." VIETNAM WOR+45 COERCE DETER REV ORD/FREE MARXISM...MARXIST 20. PAGE 4 A0084
DIPLOM PLAN PWR

S67
BUTTINGER J.,"VIETNAM* FRAUD OF THE 'OTHER WAR'." VIETNAM/S ELITES STRUCT AGRI NAT/G FOR/AID RENT TREND. PAGE 22 A0456
PLAN WEALTH REV ECO/UNDEV

S67
CARROLL K.J.,"SECOND STEP TOWARD ARMS CONTROL." WOR+45 INT/ORG VOL/ASSN FORCES PROB/SOLV RISK WEAPON 20 COLD/WAR. PAGE 25 A0503
ARMS/CONT DIPLOM PLAN NUC/PWR

S67
CHAND A.,"INDIA AND TANZANIA." INDIA TANZANIA TEC/DEV ECO/TAC FOR/AID COLONIAL PEACE UTIL WEALTH ...GOV/COMP 20. PAGE 25 A0518
ECO/UNDEV NEUTRAL DIPLOM PLAN

S67
DAVIS H.B.,"LENIN AND NATIONALISM: THE REDIRECTION OF THE MARXIST THEORY OF NATIONALISM." COM MOD/EUR USSR STRATA INT/ORG PLAN DOMIN COLONIAL FEDERAL ...TREND 20. PAGE 34 A0690
NAT/LISM MARXISM ATTIT CENTRAL

S67
DEUTSCH K.W.,"ARMS CONTROL AND EUROPEAN UNITY* THE NEXT TEN YEARS." USA+45 ELITES NAT/G BAL/PWR DIPLOM NUC/PWR...INT KNO/TEST NATO EEC. PAGE 36 A0742
ARMS/CONT PEACE REGION PLAN

S67
FALKOWSKI M.,"SOCIALIST ECONOMISTS AND THE DEVELOPING COUNTRIES." COM PLAN TEC/DEV ROUTINE DEMAND EFFICIENCY PRODUC WEALTH...MARXIST TREND GEN/METH. PAGE 44 A0893
DIPLOM SOCISM ECO/UNDEV INDUS

S67
FRANKEL M.,"THE WAR IN VIETNAM." VIETNAM ECO/UNDEV DIPLOM CONFER INGP/REL PEACE PWR...POLICY PREDICT 20. PAGE 48 A0982
WAR COERCE PLAN GUERRILLA

S67
FRANKLIN W.O.,"CLAUSEWITZ ON LIMITED WAR." VIETNAM WOR+45 WOR-45 PROB/SOLV DIPLOM ECO/TAC DOMIN COLONIAL...METH/COMP 19/20. PAGE 48 A0986
COERCE WAR PLAN GUERRILLA

S67
GLOBERSON A.,"SOCIAL GROWTH IN THE DEVELOPING COUNTRIES." CULTURE SOCIETY CONSULT PROB/SOLV SOC. PAGE 53 A1082
ECO/UNDEV FOR/AID EDU/PROP PLAN

S67
HAZARD J.N.,"POST-DISARMAMENT INTERNATIONAL LAW." FUT USSR WOR+45 INT/ORG DELIB/GP FORCES DETER EQUILIB SOVEREIGN MARXISM 20 UN. PAGE 63 A1301
INT/LAW ARMS/CONT PWR PLAN

S67
HIBBERT R.A.,"THE MONGOLIAN PEOPLE'S REPUBLIC IN THE 1960'S." INT/ORG PLAN FOR/AID 20. PAGE 64 A1326
ASIA ECO/UNDEV PROB/SOLV DIPLOM

S67
HULL E.W.S.,"THE POLITICAL OCEAN." FUT UNIV WOR+45 EXTR/IND R+D VOL/ASSN PLAN BAL/PWR ECO/TAC PEACE WEALTH 20 UN. PAGE 69 A1414
DIPLOM ECO/UNDEV INT/ORG INT/LAW

S67
JOHNSTON D.M.,"LAW, TECHNOLOGY AND THE SEA." WOR+45 PLAN PROB/SOLV TEC/DEV CONFER ADJUD ORD/FREE ...POLICY JURID. PAGE 75 A1528
INT/LAW INT/ORG DIPLOM NEUTRAL

S67
KRAUS J.,"A MARXIST IN GHANA." GHANA ELITES CHIEF PROB/SOLV TEC/DEV DIPLOM ECO/TAC COLONIAL PARTIC PWR 20 NKRUMAH/K. PAGE 82 A1676
MARXISM PLAN ATTIT CREATE

S67
LIVNEH E.,"A NEW BEGINNING." ISRAEL USSR WOR+45 NAT/G DIPLOM INGP/REL FEDERAL HABITAT PWR...GEOG PSY JEWS. PAGE 90 A1847
WAR PERSON PEACE PLAN

S67
MOBERG E.,"THE EFFECT OF SECURITY POLICY MEASURES: DISCUSSION RELATED TO SWEDEN'S SECURITY POLICY." SWEDEN PLAN PROB/SOLV DIPLOM GOV/REL MORAL...CHARTS 20. PAGE 102 A2092
POLICY ORD/FREE BUDGET FINAN

S67
OLIVIER G.,"ASPECTS JURIDIQUES DE L'ADOPTION DU TRAITE CECA A LA CRISE CHARBONNIERE (SUITE ET FIN)" LAW DIST/IND PLAN DIPLOM RATION PRICE ADMIN COST DEMAND...POLICY CON/ANAL ECSC TREATY. PAGE 112 A2288
INT/TRADE INT/ORG EXTR/IND CONSTN

S67
RABIER J.-R.,"THE EUROPEAN IDEA AND NATIONAL PUBLIC OPINIONS." ACT/RES PLAN DIPLOM PARTIC CONSEN ATTIT PERCEPT...DECISION CHARTS. PAGE 118 A2430
POLICY FEDERAL EUR+WWI PROB/SOLV

S67
SCHACTER O.,"SCIENTIFIC ADVANCES AND INTERNATIONAL LAWMAKING." FUT R+D PLAN PROB/SOLV CONFER CONTROL ...POLICY PREDICT 20 UN. PAGE 128 A2617
TEC/DEV INT/LAW INT/ORG ACT/RES

S67
STEEL R.,"BEYOND THE POWER BLOCS." USA+45 USSR ECO/UNDEV NEUTRAL NUC/PWR NAT/LISM ATTIT...GEOG NATO WARSAW/P COLD/WAR. PAGE 137 A2811
DIPLOM TREND BAL/PWR PLAN

S67
TACKABERRY R.B.,"ORGANIZING AND TRAINING PEACE-KEEPING FORCES* THE CANADIAN VIEW." CANADA PLAN DIPLOM CONFER ADJUD ADMIN CIVMIL/REL 20 UN. PAGE 141 A2882
PEACE FORCES INT/ORG CONSULT

S67
VERBA S.,"PUBLIC OPINION AND THE WAR IN VIETNAM." USA+45 VIETNAM DIPLOM WAR...CORREL STAT QU CHARTS 20. PAGE 158 A3228
ATTIT KNO/TEST NAT/G PLAN

S67
WASHBURN A.M.,"NUCLEAR PROLIFERATION IN A REVOLUTIONARY INTERNATIONAL SYSTEM." WOR+45 NAT/G DELIB/GP PLAN TEC/DEV...POLICY 20. PAGE 161 A3287
ARMS/CONT NUC/PWR DIPLOM CONFER

S67
WILPERT C.,"A LOOK IN THE MIRROR AND OVER THE WALL." GERMANY POL/PAR...KNO/TEST COLD/WAR. PAGE 165 A3358 — NAT/G PLAN DIPLOM ATTIT

B68
ANTWERP-INST UNIVERSITAIRE,BIBLIOGRAPHIC COMPENDIUM: DEVELOPING COUNTRIES (ANTWERP-INST UNIVERSITAIRE DES TERRITOIRES D'OUTRE-MER). AFR EUR+WWI SOCIETY AGRI FINAN NEIGH VOL/ASSN PROB/SOLV TEC/DEV FOR/AID INT/TRADE 20. PAGE 8 A0166 — BIBLIOG ECO/UNDEV DIPLOM PLAN

PLAN/UNIT....PLANNED UNIT DEVELOPMENT

PLATO....PLATO

PLAYFAIR R.L. A2387

PLAYNE C.E. A2388

PLAZA G. A2389

PLEKHNV/GV....G.V. PLEKHANOV

PLISCHKE E. A2390,A2391,A2392

PLUNKITT/G....G.W. PLUNKITT, TAMMANY BOSS

PLURALISM....SEE PLURISM, PLURIST

PLURISM....PLURALISM, SOCIO-POLITICAL ORDER OF AUTONOMOUS GROUPS

C28
WARD P.W.,"SOVEREIGNTY: A STUDY OF A CONTEMPORARY POLITICAL NOTION." CONSTN NAT/G DIPLOM REPRESENT PLURISM...IDEA/COMP BIBLIOG. PAGE 161 A3281 — SOVEREIGN CONCPT NAT/LISM

B37
KOHN H.,FORCE OR REASON; ISSUES OF THE TWENTIETH CENTURY. WOR+45 NAT/G DIPLOM WAR DRIVE ORD/FREE ALL/IDEOS FASCISM PLURISM...POLICY IDEA/COMP 20. PAGE 81 A1660 — COERCE DOMIN RATIONAL COLONIAL

B39
FURNIVALL J.S.,NETHERLANDS INDIA. INDIA NETHERLAND CULTURE INDUS NAT/G DIPLOM ADMIN WEALTH...POLICY CHARTS 17/20. PAGE 50 A1029 — COLONIAL ECO/UNDEV SOVEREIGN PLURISM

B58
HAAS E.B.,THE UNITING OF EUROPE. EUR+WWI INT/ORG NAT/G POL/PAR TOP/EX ECO/TAC EDU/PROP LEGIT FEDERAL NAT/LISM DRIVE RIGID/FLEX ORD/FREE PWR PLURISM ...POLICY CONCPT INT GEN/LAWS ECSC EEC 20. PAGE 59 A1204 — VOL/ASSN ECO/DEV

L58
HYVARINEN R.,"MONISTIC AND PLURALISTIC INTERPRETATIONS IN THE STUDY OF INTERNATIONAL POLITICS." COLONIAL REGION RACE/REL DISCRIM TOTALISM SOVEREIGN...INT/LAW PHIL/SCI CONCPT BIBLIOG 20. PAGE 70 A1429 — DIPLOM PLURISM INT/ORG METH

B62
MANNING C.A.W.,THE NATURE OF INTERNATIONAL SOCIETY. FUT LAW NAT/G TOP/EX NAT/LISM PEACE PERCEPT PERSON ALL/VALS PLURISM...METH/CNCPT MYTH HYPO/EXP TOT/POP 20. PAGE 94 A1926 — INT/ORG SOCIETY SIMUL DIPLOM

B64
HORNE D.,THE LUCKY COUNTRY: AUSTRALIA TODAY. UK CULTURE STRATA ATTIT PWR PLURISM...GOV/COMP 20 AUSTRAL. PAGE 67 A1386 — RACE/REL DIPLOM NAT/G STRUCT

B65
LINDBLOM C.E.,THE INTELLIGENCE OF DEMOCRACY; DECISION MAKING THROUGH MUTUAL ADJUSTMENT. WOR+45 SOCIETY NAT/G PROB/SOLV DOMIN PARTIC GP/REL ORD/FREE...POLICY IDEA/COMP BIBLIOG 20. PAGE 89 A1821 — PLURISM DECISION ADJUST DIPLOM

S67
WEIL G.L.,"THE MERGER OF THE INSTITUTIONS OF THE EUROPEAN COMMUNITIES" EUR+WWI ECO/DEV INT/TRADE CONSEN PLURISM...DECISION MGT 20 EEC EURATOM ECSC TREATY. PAGE 162 A3300 — ECO/TAC INT/ORG CENTRAL INT/LAW

PLURIST....PLURALIST

B20
BURNS C.D.,INTERNATIONAL POLITICS. WOR-45 CULTURE SOCIETY ECO/UNDEV NAT/G VOL/ASSN DELIB/GP ACT/RES CREATE DOMIN EDU/PROP LEGIT ATTIT DRIVE RIGID/FLEX ALL/VALS...PLURIST PSY CONCPT TREND. PAGE 22 A0442 — INT/ORG PEACE SOVEREIGN

B22
BRYCE J.,INTERNATIONAL RELATIONS. CHRIST-17C EUR+WWI MOD/EUR CULTURE INTELL NAT/G DELIB/GP CREATE BAL/PWR DIPLOM ATTIT DRIVE RIGID/FLEX ALL/VALS...PLURIST JURID CONCPT TIME/SEQ GEN/LAWS TOT/POP. PAGE 20 A0412 — INT/ORG POLICY

B35
MARRIOTT J.A.,DICTATORSHIP AND DEMOCRACY. GERMANY GREECE UK CHIEF DIPLOM DOMIN LEGIT PEACE ORD/FREE CONSERVE...TREND ROME HITLER/A. PAGE 95 A1946 — TOTALISM POPULISM PLURIST NAT/G

B38
HOBSON J.A.,IMPERIALISM. MOD/EUR UK WOR-45 CULTURE ECO/UNDEV NAT/G VOL/ASSN PLAN EDU/PROP LEGIT REGION COERCE ATTIT PWR...POLICY PLURIST TIME/SEQ GEN/LAWS 19/20. PAGE 66 A1348 — DOMIN ECO/TAC BAL/PWR COLONIAL

B43
LIPPMANN W.,US FOREIGN POLICY: SHIELD OF THE REPUBLIC. USA-45 WOR-45 CULTURE INT/ORG POL/PAR CREATE BAL/PWR DOMIN EDU/PROP WAR ORD/FREE PWR ...PLURIST CONCPT TREND CON/ANAL 20. PAGE 89 A1827 — NAT/G DIPLOM PEACE

B45
KANDELL I.L.,UNITED STATES ACTIVITIES IN INTERNATIONAL CULTURAL RELATIONS. INT/ORG NAT/G VOL/ASSN CREATE DIPLOM EDU/PROP ATTIT RIGID/FLEX KNOWL...PLURIST CONCPT OBS TREND GEN/LAWS TOT/POP UNESCO 20. PAGE 76 A1554 — USA-45 CULTURE

L47
HISS D.,"UNITED STATES PARTICIPATION IN THE UNITED NATIONS." USA+45 EX/STRUC PLAN DIPLOM ROUTINE CHOOSE...PLURIST UN 20. PAGE 65 A1342 — INT/ORG PWR

B48
VISSON A.,AS OTHERS SEE US. EUR+WWI FRANCE UK USA+45 CULTURE INTELL SOCIETY STRATA NAT/G POL/PAR FOR/AID ATTIT DRIVE LOVE ORD/FREE RESPECT WEALTH ...PLURIST SOC OBS TOT/POP 20. PAGE 159 A3244 — USA-45 PERCEPT

B52
BARR S.,CITIZENS OF THE WORLD. USA+45 WOR+45 CULTURE FORCES LEGIS ACT/RES BAL/PWR LEGIT PEACE ATTIT ORD/FREE PWR...PLURIST CONCPT OBS TIME/SEQ COLD/WAR 20. PAGE 11 A0227 — NAT/G INT/ORG DIPLOM

B56
KIRK G.,THE CHANGING ENVIRONMENT OF INTERNATIONAL RELATIONS. ASIA S/ASIA USA+45 WOR+45 ECO/UNDEV INT/ORG NAT/G FOR/AID EDU/PROP PEACE KNOWL ...PLURIST COLD/WAR TOT/POP 20. PAGE 80 A1634 — FUT EXEC DIPLOM

B59
COUDENHOVE-KALERGI,FROM WAR TO PEACE. USA+45 USSR WOR+45 WOR-45 LAW INT/ORG NAT/G LEGIT COERCE LOVE ...POLICY PLURIST METH/CNCPT STERTYP TOT/POP UN 20 NATO. PAGE 31 A0636 — FUT ORD/FREE

B59
SANNWALD R.E.,ECONOMIC INTEGRATION: THEORETICAL ASSUMPTIONS AND CONSEQUENCES OF EUROPEAN UNIFICATION. EUR+WWI FUT FINAN INDUS VOL/ASSN ACT/RES ECO/TAC...PLURIST EEC OEEC 20. PAGE 127 A2601 — INT/ORG ECO/DEV INT/TRADE

B60
CONN S.,THE FRAMEWORK OF HEMISPHERE DEFENSE. CANADA L/A+17C USA-45 NAT/G FORCES BAL/PWR DOMIN WAR PEACE DISPL PWR RESPECT...PLURIST CONCPT HIST/WRIT HYPO/EXP MEXIC/AMER 20 ROOSEVLT/F. PAGE 29 A0585 — USA+45 INT/ORG DIPLOM

S60
GARNICK D.H.,"ON THE ECONOMIC FEASIBILITY OF A MIDDLE EASTERN COMMON MARKET." AFR ISLAM CULTURE INDUS NAT/G PLAN TEC/DEV ECO/TAC ADMIN ATTIT DRIVE RIGID/FLEX...PLURIST STAT TREND GEN/LAWS 20. PAGE 51 A1051 — MARKET INT/TRADE

S60
GULICK E.U.,"OUR BALANCE OF POWER SYSTEM IN PERSPECTIVE." FUT WOR+45 WOR-45 ECO/DEV DOMIN ROUTINE NUC/PWR PEACE PWR WEALTH...PLURIST CONCPT HIST/WRIT GEN/METH TOT/POP 20. PAGE 58 A1191 — INT/ORG TREND ARMS/CONT BAL/PWR

B62
BOULDING K.E.,CONFLICT AND DEFENSE: A GENERAL THEORY. FUT SOCIETY INT/ORG NAT/G CREATE BAL/PWR COERCE NAT/LISM DRIVE ALL/VALS...PLURIST DECISION CONCPT METH/CNCPT TREND HYPO/EXP TOT/POP 20. PAGE 17 A0347 — MATH SIMUL PEACE WAR

B62
CARLSTON K.S.,LAW AND ORGANIZATION IN WORLD SOCIETY. WOR+45 FINAN ECO/TAC DOMIN LEGIT CT/SYS ROUTINE COERCE ORD/FREE PWR WEALTH...PLURIST DECISION JURID MGT METH/CNCPT GEN/LAWS 20. PAGE 24 A0487 — INT/ORG LAW

POGANY A.H. A2393

POGANY H.L. A2393

POL....POLITICAL AND POWER PROCESS

POL/PAR....POLITICAL PARTIES

N
ANNALS OF THE AMERICAN ACADEMY OF POLITICAL AND SOCIAL SCIENCE. AFR ASIA S/ASIA WOR+45 POL/PAR DIPLOM CRIME REV...SOC BIOG 20. PAGE 1 A0004 — BIBLIOG/A NAT/G CULTURE ATTIT

N
JOURNAL OF INTERNATIONAL AFFAIRS. WOR+45 ECO/UNDEV POL/PAR ECO/TAC WAR PEACE PERSON ALL/IDEOS ...INT/LAW TREND. PAGE 1 A0015 — BIBLIOG DIPLOM INT/ORG NAT/G

N
JOURNAL OF POLITICS. USA+45 USA-45 CONSTN POL/PAR EX/STRUC LEGIS PROB/SOLV DIPLOM CT/SYS CHOOSE RACE/REL 20. PAGE 1 A0017
BIBLIOG/A NAT/G LAW LOC/G

N
LITERATUR-VERZEICHNIS DER POLITISCHEN WISSENSCHAFTEN. GERMANY/W WOR+45 CONSTN SOCIETY ECO/DEV INT/ORG POL/PAR LEAD REPRESENT GOV/REL GP/REL...POLICY PHIL/SCI. PAGE 1 A0018
BIBLIOG EUR+WWI DIPLOM NAT/G

N
MIDWEST JOURNAL OF POLITICAL SCIENCE. USA+45 CONSTN ECO/DEV LEGIS PROB/SOLV CT/SYS LEAD GOV/REL ATTIT POLICY. PAGE 1 A0020
BIBLIOG/A NAT/G DIPLOM POL/PAR

N
PEKING REVIEW. CHINA/COM CULTURE AGRI INDUS DIPLOM EDU/PROP GUERRILLA ATTIT MARXISM...BIBLIOG 20. PAGE 1 A0022
MARXIST NAT/G POL/PAR PRESS

N
POLITICAL SCIENCE QUARTERLY. USA+45 USA-45 LAW CONSTN ECO/DEV INT/ORG LOC/G POL/PAR LEGIS LEAD NUC/PWR...CONCPT 20. PAGE 1 A0023
BIBLIOG/A NAT/G DIPLOM POLICY

N
CHINA QUARTERLY. COM AGRI INDUS ACADEM POL/PAR INT/TRADE CONFER GOV/REL...TIME/SEQ CON/ANAL INDEX 20. PAGE 2 A0032
BIBLIOG/A ASIA DIPLOM POLICY

N
HANDBOOK OF LATIN AMERICAN STUDIES. LAW CULTURE ECO/UNDEV POL/PAR ADMIN LEAD...SOC 20. PAGE 2 A0035
BIBLIOG/A L/A+17C NAT/G DIPLOM

N
CORNELL UNIVERSITY LIBRARY,SOUTHEAST ASIA ACCESSIONS LIST. LAW SOCIETY STRUCT ECO/UNDEV POL/PAR TEC/DEV DIPLOM LEAD REGION. PAGE 31 A0626
BIBLIOG S/ASIA NAT/G CULTURE

N
DEUTSCHE BUCHEREI,DEUTSCHES BUCHERVERZEICHNIS. GERMANY LAW CULTURE POL/PAR ADMIN LEAD ATTIT PERSON ...SOC 20. PAGE 37 A0746
BIBLIOG NAT/G DIPLOM ECO/DEV

N
EUROPA PUBLICATIONS LIMITED,THE EUROPA YEAR BOOK. CONSTN FINAN INDUS POL/PAR DIPLOM TV CT/SYS...STAT BIOG CHARTS WORSHIP 20. PAGE 43 A0874
BIBLIOG NAT/G PRESS INT/ORG

N
INSTITUTE OF HISPANIC STUDIES,HISPANIC AMERICAN REPORT. EUR+WWI SPAIN LAW CONSTN ECO/UNDEV POL/PAR EX/STRUC LEGIS LEAD...HUM SOC 20. PAGE 70 A1445
BIBLIOG/A L/A+17C NAT/G DIPLOM

N
JOHNS HOPKINS UNIVERSITY LIB,RECENT ADDITIONS. WOR+45 ECO/UNDEV NAT/G POL/PAR FOR/AID INT/TRADE LEAD REGION ATTIT ALL/IDEOS TREND. PAGE 74 A1518
BIBLIOG DIPLOM INT/LAW INT/ORG

N
KYRIAK T.E.,CHINA: A BIBLIOGRAPHY. ASIA CHINA/COM AGRI FINAN INDUS NAT/G INT/TRADE PRESS...SOC 20. PAGE 83 A1700
BIBLIOG/A MARXISM TOP/EX POL/PAR

N
US DEPARTMENT OF STATE,ABSTRACTS OF COMPLETED DOCTORAL DISSERTATIONS FOR THE ACADEMIC YEAR 1950-1951. WOR+45 WOR-45 ACADEM POL/PAR ECO/TAC ...POLICY SOC 19/20. PAGE 151 A3078
BIBLIOG/A DIPLOM INT/ORG NAT/G

N
US LIBRARY OF CONGRESS,ACCESSIONS LIST - INDIA. INDIA CULTURE AGRI LOC/G POL/PAR PLAN PROB/SOLV TEC/DEV DIPLOM EDU/PROP LEAD GP/REL ATTIT 20. PAGE 154 A3142
BIBLIOG S/ASIA ECO/UNDEV NAT/G

N
US LIBRARY OF CONGRESS,ACCESSIONS LIST -- ISRAEL. ISRAEL CULTURE ECO/UNDEV POL/PAR PLAN PROB/SOLV TEC/DEV DIPLOM EDU/PROP LEAD WAR ATTIT 20 JEWS. PAGE 154 A3143
BIBLIOG ISLAM NAT/G GP/REL

B05
AMES J.G.,COMPREHENSIVE INDEX TO THE PUBLICATIONS OF THE UNITED STATES GOVERNMENT , 1881-1893. USA-45 CONSTN POL/PAR DELIB/GP TOP/EX DIPLOM PARL/PROC INGP/REL...INDEX 19 CONGRESS. PAGE 8 A0153
BIBLIOG/A LEGIS NAT/G GOV/REL

B08
ARON R.,WAR AND INDUSTRIAL SOCIETY. EUR+WWI MOD/EUR WOR+45 WOR-45 CONSTN SOCIETY INT/ORG POL/PAR VOL/ASSN DIPLOM INT/TRADE PEACE ATTIT...BIOG GEN/LAWS 19/20. PAGE 9 A0178
ECO/DEV WAR

B08
LABRIOLA A.,ESSAYS ON THE MATERIALISTIC CONCEPTION OF HISTORY. STRATA POL/PAR CAP/ISM DIPLOM INT/TRADE WAR 20. PAGE 83 A1706
MARXIST WORKER REV COLONIAL

B09
FREMANTLE H.E.S.,THE NEW NATION, A SURVEY OF THE CONDITION AND PROSPECTS OF SOUTH AFRICA. SOUTH/AFR CONSTN POL/PAR DIPLOM DOMIN COLONIAL WEALTH...SOC TREND 19. PAGE 49 A0996
NAT/LISM SOVEREIGN RACE/REL REGION

N19
GRANT N.,COMMUNIST PSYCHOLOGICAL OFFENSIVE: DISTORTION IN THE TRANSLATION OF OFFICIAL DOCUMENTS (PAMPHLET). USSR POL/PAR CHIEF FOR/AID PRESS WRITING COLONIAL LEAD WAR PEACE 20 KHRUSH/N. PAGE 55 A1129
MARXISM DIPLOM EDU/PROP

B21
STUART G.H.,FRENCH FOREIGN POLICY. CONSTN INT/ORG NAT/G POL/PAR EX/STRUC FORCES PLAN ECO/TAC DOMIN EDU/PROP ADJUD COERCE ATTIT DRIVE RIGID/FLEX ALL/VALS...POLICY OBS RECORD BIOG TIME/SEQ TREND. PAGE 139 A2852
MOD/EUR DIPLOM FRANCE

B26
INTERNATIONAL BIBLIOGRAPHY OF POLITICAL SCIENCE. WOR+45 NAT/G POL/PAR EX/STRUC LEGIS CT/SYS LEAD CHOOSE GOV/REL ATTIT...PHIL/SCI 20. PAGE 3 A0049
BIBLIOG DIPLOM CONCPT ADMIN

B27
PARRINGTON V.L.,MAIN CURRENTS IN AMERICAN THOUGHT (VOL.I). USA-45 AGRI POL/PAR DIPLOM TAX REGION REV 17/18 FRANKLIN/B JEFFERSN/T. PAGE 114 A2336
COLONIAL SECT FEEDBACK ALL/IDEOS

B27
SIEGFRIED A.,AMERICA COMES OF AGE: A FRENCH ANALYSIS (TRANS. BY H.H. HEMMING AND DORIS HEMMING). FRANCE UK POL/PAR WORKER TEC/DEV DIPLOM REGION RACE/REL ADJUST PRODUC HEREDITY...TIME/SEQ GP/COMP SOC/INTEG 20 DEMOCRAT REPUBLICAN KKK. PAGE 132 A2714
USA-45 CULTURE ECO/DEV SOC

B28
STUART G.H.,LATIN AMERICA AND THE UNITED STATES. USA-45 ECO/UNDEV INT/ORG NAT/G POL/PAR PLAN DOMIN EDU/PROP COLONIAL REGION COERCE ATTIT ALL/VALS ...POLICY GEOG TREND 19/20. PAGE 139 A2853
L/A+17C DIPLOM

C28
SCHNEIDER H.W.,"MAKING THE FASCIST STATE." ITALY CULTURE LABOR DIPLOM REV WAR NAT/LISM TOTALISM ATTIT DRIVE SOCISM...BIBLIOG PARLIAMENT 20. PAGE 129 A2638
FASCISM POLICY POL/PAR

B32
LENIN V.I.,THE WAR AND THE SECOND INTERNATIONAL. COM MOD/EUR USSR CAP/ISM DIPLOM NAT/LISM ATTIT MARXISM...CONCPT 20. PAGE 87 A1772
POL/PAR WAR SOCISM INT/ORG

B33
DAHLIN E.,FRENCH AND GERMAN PUBLIC OPINION ON DECLARED WAR AIMS 1914-1918. BELGIUM FRANCE GERMANY NAT/G POL/PAR DIPLOM COERCE REV WAR PEACE 20 WWI WILSON/W. PAGE 33 A0674
ATTIT EDU/PROP DOMIN NAT/COMP

B37
BORGESE G.A.,GOLIATH: THE MARCH OF FASCISM. GERMANY ITALY LAW POL/PAR SECT DIPLOM SOCISM...JURID MYTH 20 DANTE MACHIAVELL MUSSOLIN/B. PAGE 17 A0341
POLICY NAT/LISM FASCISM NAT/G

B37
TUPPER E.,JAPAN IN AMERICAN PUBLIC OPINION. USA-45 POL/PAR VOL/ASSN INT/TRADE DISCRIM...BIBLIOG 20 CHINJAP TREATY. PAGE 146 A2979
ATTIT IDEA/COMP DIPLOM PRESS

C37
TUPPER E.,"JAPAN IN AMERICAN PUBLIC OPINION." USA+45 POL/PAR VOL/ASSN INT/TRADE DISCRIM ...IDEA/COMP 20 CHINJAP. PAGE 146 A2978
BIBLIOG ATTIT DIPLOM PRESS

B38
HARPER S.N.,THE GOVERNMENT OF THE SOVIET UNION. COM USSR LAW CONSTN ECO/DEV PLAN TEC/DEV DIPLOM INT/TRADE ADMIN REV NAT/LISM...POLICY 20. PAGE 62 A1265
MARXISM NAT/G LEAD POL/PAR

B38
PETTEE G.S.,THE PROCESS OF REVOLUTION. COM FRANCE ITALY MOD/EUR RUSSIA SPAIN WOR-45 ELITES INTELL SOCIETY STRATA STRUCT INT/ORG NAT/G POL/PAR ACT/RES PLAN EDU/PROP LEGIT EXEC...SOC MYTH TIME/SEQ TOT/POP 18/20. PAGE 115 A2370
COERCE CONCPT REV

B38
RAPPARD W.E.,THE CRISIS OF DEMOCRACY. EUR+WWI UNIV WOR-45 CULTURE SOCIETY ECO/DEV INT/ORG POL/PAR ACT/RES EDU/PROP EXEC CHOOSE ATTIT ALL/VALS...SOC OBS HIST/WRIT TIME/SEQ LEAGUE/NAT NAZI TOT/POP 20. PAGE 119 A2449
NAT/G CONCPT

B39
THOMAS J.A.,THE HOUSE OF COMMONS, 1832-1901; A STUDY OF ITS ECONOMIC AND FUNCTIONAL CHARACTER. UK LAW STRATA FINAN DIPLOM CONTROL LEAD LOBBY REPRESENT WEALTH...POLICY STAT BIBLIOG 19/20 PARLIAMENT. PAGE 143 A2922
PARL/PROC LEGIS POL/PAR ECO/DEV

C39
REISCHAUER R.,"JAPAN'S GOVERNMENT--POLITICS." CONSTN STRATA POL/PAR FORCES LEGIS DIPLOM ADMIN EXEC CENTRAL...POLICY BIBLIOG 20 CHINJAP. PAGE 120
NAT/G S/ASIA CONCPT

A2462 — ROUTINE

C40
NORMAN E.H.,"JAPAN'S EMERGENCE AS A MODERN STATE: POLITICAL AND ECONOMIC PROBLEMS OF THE MEIJI PERIOD." CONSTN STRATA AGRI INDUS POL/PAR TEC/DEV CAP/ISM CIVMIL/REL...BIBLIOG 19/20 CHINJAP. PAGE 110 A2250
CENTRAL DIPLOM POLICY NAT/LISM

B41
BIRDSALL P.,VERSAILLES TWENTY YEARS AFTER. MOD/EUR POL/PAR CHIEF CONSULT FORCES LEGIS REPAR PEACE ORD/FREE...BIBLIOG 20 PRESIDENT TREATY. PAGE 14 A0290
DIPLOM NAT/LISM WAR

B42
JOSHI P.S.,THE TYRANNY OF COLOUR. INDIA SOUTH/AFR UK ECO/UNDEV NAT/G POL/PAR DIPLOM ECO/TAC WAR ...POLICY 19/20. PAGE 75 A1538
COLONIAL DISCRIM RACE/REL

B43
LIPPMANN W.,US FOREIGN POLICY: SHIELD OF THE REPUBLIC. USA-45 WOR-45 CULTURE INT/ORG POL/PAR CREATE BAL/PWR DOMIN EDU/PROP WAR ORD/FREE PWR ...PLURIST CONCPT TREND CON/ANAL 20. PAGE 89 A1827
NAT/G DIPLOM PEACE

B43
MICAUD C.A.,THE FRENCH RIGHT AND NAZI GERMANY 1933-1939: A STUDY OF PUBLIC OPINION. GERMANY UK USSR POL/PAR ARMS/CONT COERCE DETER PEACE RIGID/FLEX PWR MARXISM...FASCIST TREND 20 LEAGUE/NAT TREATY. PAGE 101 A2065
DIPLOM AGREE

B43
US DEPARTMENT OF STATE,NATIONAL SOCIALISM; BASIC PRINCIPLES, THEIR APPLICATION BY THE NAZI PARTY'S FOREIGN ORGANIZATION... GERMANY WOR-45 ECO/DEV LOC/G POL/PAR FORCES DIPLOM DOMIN COLONIAL ARMS/CONT COERCE NAT/LISM PWR 20 NAZI. PAGE 151 A3081
FASCISM SOCISM NAT/G TOTALISM

B43
US LIBRARY OF CONGRESS,POLITICAL DEVELOPMENTS AND THE WAR: APRIL-DECEMBER 1942 (SUPPLEMENT 1). WOR-45 CONSTN NAT/G POL/PAR CREATE RECEIVE EDU/PROP ATTIT 20. PAGE 154 A3148
BIBLIOG/A WAR DIPLOM

B43
WALKER E.A.,BRITAIN AND SOUTH AFRICA. SOUTH/AFR POL/PAR GP/REL RACE/REL ATTIT ORD/FREE 17/20. PAGE 160 A3264
COLONIAL WAR DIPLOM SOVEREIGN

B44
BARTLETT R.J.,THE LEAGUE TO ENFORCE PEACE. FUT USA-45 NAT/G POL/PAR CREATE EDU/PROP ADMIN RIGID/FLEX PWR...CONCPT TREND GEN/METH LEAGUE/NAT 20. PAGE 11 A0231
INT/ORG ORD/FREE DIPLOM

B44
PUTTKAMMER E.W.,WAR AND THE LAW. UNIV USA-45 CONSTN CULTURE SOCIETY NAT/G POL/PAR ROUTINE ALL/VALS ...JURID CONCPT OBS WORK VAL/FREE 20. PAGE 118 A2418
INT/ORG LAW WAR INT/LAW

B44
SHELBY C.,LATIN AMERICAN PERIODICALS CURRENTLY RECEIVED IN THE LIBRARY OF CONGRESS AND IN LIBRARY OF DEPARTMENT OF AGRICULTURE. SOCIETY AGRI INDUS LABOR POL/PAR INT/TRADE...GEOG SOC 20. PAGE 132 A2699
BIBLIOG ECO/UNDEV CULTURE L/A+17C

N45
INDIA QUARTERLY, A JOURNAL OF INTERNATIONAL AFFAIRS. INDIA LAW CONSTN ECO/UNDEV INT/ORG POL/PAR COLONIAL LEAD PARL/PROC WAR ATTIT...SOC 20 CMN/WLTH. PAGE 3 A0053
BIBLIOG/A S/ASIA DIPLOM NAT/G

B45
CLAGETT H.L.,COMMUNIST CHINA: RUTHLESS ENEMY OR PAPER TIGER (PAMPHLET). CHINA/COM ECO/UNDEV AGRI INDUS NAT/G POL/PAR ECO/TAC INT/TRADE GUERRILLA ATTIT...CHARTS NAT/COMP ORG/CHARTS 20. PAGE 26 A0540
BIBLIOG/A MARXISM DIPLOM COERCE

B45
CONOVER H.F.,THE GOVERNMENTS OF THE MAJOR FOREIGN POWERS: A BIBLIOGRAPHY. FRANCE GERMANY ITALY UK USSR CONSTN LOC/G POL/PAR EX/STRUC FORCES ADMIN CT/SYS CIVMIL/REL TOTALISM...POLICY 19/20. PAGE 29 A0598
BIBLIOG NAT/G DIPLOM

B45
CONOVER H.F.,ITALY: ECONOMICS, POLITICS AND MILITARY AFFAIRS, 1940-1945. ITALY ELITES NAT/G POL/PAR EX/STRUC TOP/EX DIPLOM DOMIN CONTROL COERCE WAR CIVMIL/REL EFFICIENCY 20. PAGE 29 A0599
BIBLIOG TOTALISM FORCES

B46
BIBLIOGRAFIIA DISSERTATSII: DOKTORSKIE DISSERTATSII ZA 19411944 (2 VOLS.). COM USSR LAW POL/PAR DIPLOM ADMIN LEAD...PHIL/SCI SOC 20. PAGE 3 A0054
BIBLIOG ACADEM KNOWL MARXIST

B46
BLUM L.,FOR ALL MANKIND (TRANS. BY W. PICKLES). FRANCE GERMANY USSR LAW SOCIETY STRUCT POL/PAR WORKER DIPLOM DOMIN CHOOSE ORD/FREE FASCISM 20. PAGE 16 A0323
POPULISM SOCIALIST NAT/G WAR

B46
STURZO D.L.,NATIONALISM AND INTERNATIONALISM. WOR-45 INT/ORG LABOR NAT/G POL/PAR TOTALISM MORAL ORD/FREE FASCISM...MAJORIT 19/20 UN LEAGUE/NAT
NAT/LISM DIPLOM WAR

MUSSOLIN/B. PAGE 140 A2857
PEACE

B47
BORGESE G.,COMMON CAUSE. LAW CONSTN SOCIETY STRATA ECO/DEV INT/ORG POL/PAR FORCES LEGIS TOP/EX CAP/ISM DIPLOM ADMIN EXEC ATTIT PWR 20. PAGE 17 A0339
WOR+45 NAT/G SOVEREIGN REGION

B47
BROOKINGS INST.,MAJOR PROBLEMS OF UNITED STATES FOREIGN POLICY. USA+45 WOR+45 STRUCT ECO/DEV ECO/UNDEV INT/ORG NAT/G POL/PAR VOL/ASSN DELIB/GP FORCES ECO/TAC LEGIT COERCE ORD/FREE PWR WEALTH ...POLICY STAT TREND CHARTS TOT/POP. PAGE 19 A0392
ACT/RES DIPLOM

B48
DURBIN E.F.M.,THE POLITICS OF DEMOCRATIC SOCIALISM; AN ESSAY ON SOCIAL POLICY. STRATA POL/PAR PLAN COERCE DRIVE PERSON PWR MARXISM...CHARTS METH/COMP. PAGE 39 A0805
SOCIALIST POPULISM POLICY SOCIETY

B48
VISSON A.,AS OTHERS SEE US. EUR+WWI FRANCE UK USA+45 CULTURE INTELL SOCIETY STRATA NAT/G POL/PAR FOR/AID ATTIT DRIVE LOVE ORD/FREE RESPECT WEALTH ...PLURIST SOC OBS TOT/POP 20. PAGE 159 A3244
USA-45 PERCEPT

B49
HINDEN R.,EMPIRE AND AFTER. UK POL/PAR BAL/PWR DIPLOM INT/TRADE WAR NAT/LISM PWR 17/20. PAGE 65 A1335
NAT/G COLONIAL ATTIT POLICY

B49
ROSENHAUPT H.W.,HOW TO WAGE PEACE. USA+45 SOCIETY STRATA STRUCT R+D INT/ORG POL/PAR LEGIS ACT/RES CREATE PLAN EDU/PROP ADMIN EXEC ATTIT ALL/VALS ...TIME/SEQ TREND COLD/WAR 20. PAGE 124 A2536
INTELL CONCPT DIPLOM

L49
HEINDEL R.H.,"THE NORTH ATLANTIC TREATY IN THE UNITED STATES SENATE." CONSTN POL/PAR CHIEF DEBATE LEAD ROUTINE WAR PEACE...CHARTS UN SENATE NATO. PAGE 64 A1309
DECISION PARL/PROC LEGIS INT/ORG

C49
YANAGA C.,"JAPAN SINCE PERRY." S/ASIA CULTURE ECO/DEV FORCES WAR 19/20 CHINJAP. PAGE 168 A3430
DIPLOM POL/PAR CIVMIL/REL NAT/LISM

B50
BERLE A.A.,NATURAL SELECTION OF POLITICAL FORCES. FUT WOR+45 WOR-45 CULTURE SOCIETY INT/ORG NAT/G FORCES EDU/PROP LEGIT COERCE...CONCPT HIST/WRIT TREND 20. PAGE 13 A0274
POL/PAR BAL/PWR DIPLOM

B50
COUNCIL BRITISH NATIONAL BIB,BRITISH NATIONAL BIBLIOGRAPHY. UK AGRI CONSTRUC PERF/ART POL/PAR SECT CREATE INT/TRADE LEAD...HUM JURID PHIL/SCI 20. PAGE 31 A0637
BIBLIOG/A NAT/G TEC/DEV DIPLOM

B50
GATZKE H.W.,GERMANY'S DRIVE TO THE WEST. BELGIUM GERMANY MOD/EUR AGRI INDUS POL/PAR FORCES DOMIN AGREE CONTROL REGION COERCE 20 TREATY WWI. PAGE 51 A1053
WAR POLICY NAT/G DIPLOM

B51
BLANSHARD P.,COMMUNISM, DEMOCRACY AND CATHOLIC POWER. USSR VATICAN WOR+45 WOR-45 CULTURE ELITES INTELL SOCIETY STRUCT INT/ORG POL/PAR EDU/PROP COERCE ATTIT KNOWL PWR MARXISM...CONCPT COLD/WAR 20. PAGE 15 A0308
COM SECT TOTALISM

B51
CHRISTENSEN A.N.,THE EVOLUTION OF LATIN AMERICAN GOVERNMENT: A BOOK OF READINGS. ECO/UNDEV INDUS LOC/G POL/PAR EX/STRUC LEGIS FOR/AID CT/SYS ...SOC/WK 20 SOUTH/AMER. PAGE 26 A0535
NAT/G CONSTN DIPLOM L/A+17C

B51
JENNINGS S.I.,THE COMMONWEALTH IN ASIA. CEYLON INDIA PAKISTAN S/ASIA UK CONSTN CULTURE SOCIETY STRATA STRUCT NAT/G POL/PAR EDU/PROP LEAD WAR 20 CMN/WLTH. PAGE 74 A1510
NAT/LISM REGION COLONIAL DIPLOM

B51
RAPPAPORT A.,THE BRITISH PRESS AND WILSONIAN NEUTRALITY. UK WOR-45 SEA POL/PAR WAR CHOOSE PEACE ATTIT PERCEPT...GEOG 20 WILSON/W. PAGE 119 A2446
PRESS DIPLOM NEUTRAL POLICY

B51
US LIBRARY OF CONGRESS,EAST EUROPEAN ACCESSIONS LIST (VOL. I). POL/PAR DIPLOM ADMIN LEAD 20. PAGE 155 A3152
BIBLIOG/A COM SOCIETY NAT/G

L51
ULAM A.B.,"THE COMIMFORM AND THE PEOPLE'S DEMOCRACIES." EUR+WWI WOR+45 STRUCT NAT/G POL/PAR TOP/EX ACT/RES PLAN ECO/TAC DOMIN ATTIT ALL/VALS ...HIST/WRIT TIME/SEQ 20 COMINFORM. PAGE 146 A2992
COM INT/ORG USSR TOTALISM

S51
BELKNAP G.,"POLITICAL PARTY IDENTIFICATION AND ATTITUDES TOWARD FOREIGN POLICY" (BMR)" USA+45 VOL/ASSN CONTROL CHOOSE...STAT INT CHARTS 20. PAGE 12 A0254
POL/PAR ATTIT POLICY DIPLOM

C51
GRUNDER G.A.,"THE PHILIPPINES AND THE UNITED STATES." PHILIPPINE S/ASIA USA-45 NAT/G POL/PAR
COLONIAL POLICY

ADMIN SOVEREIGN...TIME/SEQ BIBLIOG 20. PAGE 57 A1181
DIPLOM ECO/TAC

B52
FLECHTHEIM O.K.,FUNDAMENTALS OF POLITICAL SCIENCE. WOR+45 WOR-45 LAW POL/PAR EX/STRUC LEGIS ADJUD ATTIT PWR...INT/LAW. PAGE 46 A0945
NAT/G DIPLOM IDEA/COMP CONSTN

B52
RIGGS F.W.,FORMOSA UNDER CHINESE NATIONALIST RULE. CHINA/COM USA+45 CONSTN AGRI FINAN LABOR LOC/G NAT/G POL/PAR FORCES HEALTH KNOWL...STAT WORK VAL/FREE 20. PAGE 121 A2479
ASIA FOR/AID DIPLOM

B52
SHULIM J.I.,THE OLD DOMINION AND NAPOLEON BONAPARTE. POL/PAR DOMIN PRESS REV WAR 18/19 VIRGINIA. PAGE 132 A2710
ATTIT PROVS EDU/PROP DIPLOM

B52
SPENCER F.A.,WAR AND POSTWAR GREECE: AN ANALYSIS BASED ON GREEK WRITINGS. GREECE SOCIETY NAT/G POL/PAR FORCES CREATE DIPLOM LEAD MARXISM...SOC 20. PAGE 136 A2784
BIBLIOG/A WAR REV

B52
ULAM A.B.,TITOISM AND THE COMINFORM. USSR WOR+45 STRUCT INT/ORG NAT/G ACT/RES PLAN EXEC ATTIT DRIVE ALL/VALS...CONCPT OBS VAL/FREE 20 COMINTERN TITO/MARSH. PAGE 146 A2993
COM POL/PAR TOTALISM YUGOSLAVIA

B53
KANTOR H.,A BIBLIOGRAPHY OF UNPUBLISHED DOCTORAL DISSERTATIONS AND MASTERS' THESES DEALING WITH GOVTS, POL, INT REL OF LAT AM. L/A+17C INT/ORG POL/PAR ACT/RES OP/RES CONFER ATTIT...INT/LAW PHIL/SCI 20. PAGE 76 A1556
BIBLIOG ACADEM DIPLOM NAT/G

B53
MANSERGH N.,DOCUMENTS AND SPEECHES ON BRITISH COMMONWEALTH AFFAIRS 1931-1952. INDIA IRELAND PAKISTAN UK CONSTN POL/PAR CHIEF FORCES COLONIAL ORD/FREE SOVEREIGN...JURID 20 COMMONWLTH. PAGE 94 A1929
BIBLIOG/A DIPLOM ECO/TAC

B53
SHIRATO I.,JAPANESE SOURCES ON THE HISTORY OF THE CHINESE COMMUNIST MOVEMENT (PAMPHLET). CHINA/COM USSR CONSTRUC NAT/G POL/PAR FORCES DIPLOM DOMIN EDU/PROP CONTROL WAR TOTALISM SOCISM 20. PAGE 132 A2702
BIBLIOG/A MARXISM ECO/UNDEV

B53
STOUT H.M.,BRITISH GOVERNMENT. UK FINAN LOC/G POL/PAR DELIB/GP DIPLOM ADMIN COLONIAL CHOOSE ORD/FREE...JURID BIBLIOG 20 COMMONWLTH. PAGE 139 A2837
NAT/G PARL/PROC CONSTN NEW/LIB

B54
COOKSON J.,BEFORE THE AFRICAN STORM. BELGIUM CENTRL/AFR FRANCE UK ECO/UNDEV POL/PAR CREATE BAL/PWR RACE/REL NAT/LISM ORD/FREE CONSERVE MARXISM SOC/INTEG 20 CONGO/LEOP. PAGE 30 A0607
COLONIAL REV DISCRIM DIPLOM

B54
EPSTEIN L.D.,BRITAIN - UNEASY ALLY. KOREA UK USA+45 NAT/G POL/PAR ECO/TAC FOR/AID INT/TRADE WAR LABOR/PAR CONSRV/PAR. PAGE 42 A0857
DIPLOM ATTIT POLICY NAT/COMP

B54
REYNOLDS P.A.,BRITISH FOREIGN POLICY IN THE INTER-WAR YEARS. CZECHOSLVK GERMANY POLAND UK USA-45 POL/PAR FORCES ECO/TAC ARMS/CONT WAR ATTIT 20. PAGE 120 A2470
DIPLOM POLICY NAT/G

L54
CHARLESWORTH J.C.,"AMERICA AND A NEW ASIA." ASIA INDIA ISLAM S/ASIA USA+45 USA-45 ECO/UNDEV NAT/G POL/PAR FORCES FOR/AID DOMIN EDU/PROP COERCE DRIVE ALL/VALS MARXISM SOCISM TOT/POP 20. PAGE 26 A0522
ECO/TAC DIPLOM NAT/LISM

B55
SNYDER R.C.,AMERICAN FOREIGN POLICY. USA+45 USA-45 WOR+45 WOR-45 CONSTN INT/ORG POL/PAR VOL/ASSN DELIB/GP LEGIS CREATE DOMIN EDU/PROP EXEC COERCE ATTIT DRIVE ORD/FREE PWR...MGT OBS RECORD TIME/SEQ TREND. PAGE 134 A2752
NAT/G DIPLOM

B55
TAN C.C.,THE BOXER CATASTROPHE. ASIA UK USSR ELITES POL/PAR VOL/ASSN FORCES PROB/SOLV DIPLOM ADMIN COLONIAL NAT/LISM PEACE TREATY 19/20 BOXER/REBL. PAGE 141 A2885
REV NAT/G WAR

B55
TANNENBAUM F.,THE AMERICAN TRADITION IN FOREIGN POLICY. USA+45 USA-45 CONSTN INT/ORG NAT/G POL/PAR VOL/ASSN TOP/EX LEGIT DRIVE ORD/FREE PWR...CONCPT GEN/LAWS CONGRESS LEAGUE/NAT COLD/WAR OAS 18/20. PAGE 141 A2887
TIME/SEQ

L55
ROSTOW W.W.,"RUSSIA AND CHINA UNDER COMMUNISM." CHINA/COM USSR INTELL STRUCT INT/ORG NAT/G POL/PAR TOP/EX ACT/RES PLAN ADMIN ATTIT ALL/VALS MARXISM ...CONCPT OBS TIME/SEQ TREND GOV/COMP VAL/FREE 20. PAGE 124 A2543
COM ASIA

B56
BALL W.M.,NATIONALISM AND COMMUNISM IN EAST ASIA. ASIA BURMA EUR+WWI KOREA USA+45 ECO/UNDEV NAT/G POL/PAR DIPLOM ECO/TAC FOR/AID EDU/PROP COERCE RACE/REL NAT/LISM DRIVE SOVEREIGN...TREND 20 CHINJAP. PAGE 11 A0214
S/ASIA ATTIT

B56
DEGRAS J.,THE COMMUNIST INTERNATIONAL, 1919-1943: DOCUMENTS (3 VOLS.). EX/STRUC...ANTHOL BIBLIOG 20. PAGE 36 A0723
COM DIPLOM POLICY POL/PAR

B56
FIELD G.C.,POLITICAL THEORY. POL/PAR REPRESENT MORAL SOVEREIGN...JURID IDEA/COMP. PAGE 45 A0924
CONCPT NAT/G ORD/FREE DIPLOM

B56
GEORGE A.L.,WOODROW WILSON AND COLONEL HOUSE. WOR-45 CONSTN FACE/GP INT/ORG NAT/G POL/PAR CONSULT LEGIT EXEC COERCE CHOOSE ATTIT DRIVE PERSON MORAL ORD/FREE PWR RESPECT...POLICY MGT PSY OBS RECORD INT LEAGUE/NAT. PAGE 52 A1060
USA-45 BIOG DIPLOM

B56
KOENIG L.W.,THE TRUMAN ADMINISTRATION: ITS PRINCIPLES AND PRACTICE. USA+45 POL/PAR CHIEF LEGIS DIPLOM DEATH NUC/PWR WAR CIVMIL/REL PEACE ...DECISION 20 TRUMAN/HS PRESIDENT TREATY. PAGE 81 A1658
ADMIN POLICY EX/STRUC GOV/REL

B56
VON BECKERATH E.,HANDWORTERBUCH DER SOCIALWISSENSCHAFTEN (II VOLS.). EUR+WWI GERMANY POL/PAR WORKER DIPLOM LEAD CHOOSE SUFF WEALTH...SOC 20. PAGE 159 A3249
BIBLIOG INT/TRADE NAT/G ECO/DEV

B56
WHITAKER A.P.,ARGENTINE UPHEAVAL. STRUCT FORCES DIPLOM COERCE PWR 20 ARGEN. PAGE 164 A3332
REV POL/PAR STRATA NAT/G

B56
WILBUR C.M.,DOCUMENTS ON COMMUNISM, NATIONALISM, AND SOVIET ADVISERS IN CHINA, 1918-1927. CHINA/COM USSR STRUCT DIPLOM LEAD NAT/LISM...BIBLIOG/A 20. PAGE 164 A3343
REV POL/PAR MARXISM COM

B56
WILSON P.,GOVERNMENT AND POLITICS OF INDIA AND PAKISTAN: 1885-1955; A BIBLIOGRAPHY OF WORKS IN WESTERN LANGUAGES. INDIA PAKISTAN CONSTN LOC/G POL/PAR FORCES DIPLOM ADMIN WAR CHOOSE...BIOG CON/ANAL 19/20. PAGE 165 A3361
BIBLIOG COLONIAL NAT/G S/ASIA

B56
WU E.,LEADERS OF TWENTIETH-CENTURY CHINA; AN ANNOTATED BIBLIOGRAPHY OF SELECTED CHINESE BIOGRAPHICAL WORKS IN HOOVER LIBRARY. ASIA INDUS POL/PAR DIPLOM ADMIN REV WAR...HUM MGT 20. PAGE 168 A3422
BIBLIOG/A BIOG INTELL CHIEF

B57
ADLER S.,THE ISOLATIONIST IMPULSE: ITS TWENTIETH-CENTURY REACTION. USA+45 USA-45 POL/PAR WAR ISOLAT NAT/LISM 20. PAGE 5 A0093
DIPLOM POLICY ATTIT

B57
ALIGHIERI D.,ON WORLD GOVERNMENT. ROMAN/EMP LAW SOCIETY INT/ORG NAT/G POL/PAR ADJUD WAR GP/REL PEACE WORSHIP 15 WORLDUNITY DANTE. PAGE 6 A0121
POLICY CONCPT DIPLOM SECT

B57
CRABB C.,BIPARTISAN FOREIGN POLICY: MYTH OR REALITY. ASIA COM EUR+WWI ISLAM USA+45 USA-45 INT/ORG NAT/G LEGIS TOP/EX PWR CONGRESS 20. PAGE 32 A0649
POL/PAR ATTIT DIPLOM

B57
DUDDEN A.P.,WOODROW WILSON AND THE WORLD OF TODAY. USA-45 NAT/G PROVS CONTROL PARTIC WAR ISOLAT PWR SKILL...PERS/COMP ANTHOL 19/20 WILSON/W UN LEAGUE/NAT WWI. PAGE 39 A0794
CHIEF DIPLOM POL/PAR LEAD

B57
FRASER L.,PROPAGANDA. GERMANY USSR WOR+45 WOR-45 NAT/G POL/PAR CONTROL FEEDBACK LOBBY CROWD WAR CONSEN NAT/LISM 20. PAGE 48 A0988
EDU/PROP FASCISM MARXISM DIPLOM

B57
HODGKIN T.,NATIONALISM IN COLONIAL AFRICA. STRATA STRUCT MUNIC NAT/G POL/PAR LEGIS ATTIT SOVEREIGN ...POLICY TREND BIBLIOG 20. PAGE 66 A1351
AFR COLONIAL NAT/LISM DIPLOM

B57
PETERSON H.C.,OPPONENTS OF WAR 1917-1918. USA-45 POL/PAR DOMIN ORD/FREE PWR PACIFISM SOCISM 20 IWW CONSCN/OBJ. PAGE 115 A2368
WAR PEACE ATTIT EDU/PROP

B57
TOMASIC D.A.,NATIONAL COMMUNISM AND SOVIET STRATEGY. UK USSR YUGOSLAVIA NAT/G POL/PAR CHIEF CREATE DOMIN REV WAR PWR...BIOG TREND 20 TITO/MARSH STALIN/J. PAGE 144 A2948
COM NAT/LISM MARXISM DIPLOM

C57
TANG P.S.H.,"COMMUNIST CHINA TODAY: DOMESTIC AND FOREIGN POLICIES." CHINA/COM COM S/ASIA USSR STRATA FORCES DIPLOM EDU/PROP COERCE GOV/REL...POLICY MAJORIT BIBLIOG 20. PAGE 141 A2886
POL/PAR LEAD ADMIN CONSTN

B58
ALMEYDA M.C.,REFLEXIONES POLITICAS. CHILE L/A+17C USA+45 INT/ORG POL/PAR ECO/TAC PARTIC ATTIT 20. PAGE 6 A0128
ECO/UNDEV REGION DIPLOM INT/TRADE

B58
CARROLL H.N.,THE HOUSE OF REPRESENTATIVES AND FOREIGN AFFAIRS. USA+45 USA-45 NAT/G POL/PAR DIPLOM FOR/AID LEGIT ROUTINE PWR...TIME/SEQ CONGRESS. PAGE 25 A0502
DELIB/GP LEGIS

B58
HAAS E.B.,THE UNITING OF EUROPE. EUR+WWI INT/ORG NAT/G POL/PAR TOP/EX ECO/TAC EDU/PROP LEGIT FEDERAL NAT/LISM DRIVE RIGID/FLEX ORD/FREE PWR PLURISM ...POLICY CONCPT INT GEN/LAWS ECSC EEC 20. PAGE 59 A1204
VOL/ASSN ECO/DEV

B58
HOLT R.T.,RADIO FREE EUROPE. FUT USA+45 CULTURE ECO/DEV INT/ORG KIN POL/PAR SECT FORCES ACT/RES DIPLOM COERCE REV CHOOSE PEACE ATTIT PWR...MAJORIT CONCPT COLD/WAR WORK 20 RFE. PAGE 67 A1374
COM EDU/PROP COM/IND

B58
HUNT B.I.,BIPARTISANSHIP: A CASE STUDY OF THE FOREIGN ASSISTANCE PROGRAM, 1947-56 (DOCTORAL THESIS). USA+45 INT/ORG CONSULT LEGIS TEC/DEV ...BIBLIOG PRESIDENT TREATY NATO TRUMAN/HS EISNHWR/DD CONGRESS. PAGE 69 A1418
FOR/AID POL/PAR GP/REL DIPLOM

B58
JENNINGS I.,PROBLEMS OF THE NEW COMMONWEALTH. CEYLON INDIA PAKISTAN S/ASIA ECO/UNDEV INT/ORG LOC/G DIPLOM ECO/TAC INT/TRADE COLONIAL RACE/REL DISCRIM 20 COMMONWLTH PARLIAMENT. PAGE 74 A1508
NAT/LISM NEUTRAL FOR/AID POL/PAR

B58
NEAL F.W.,TITOISM IN ACTION. COM YUGOSLAVIA AGRI LOC/G DIPLOM TOTALISM...BIBLIOG 20 TITO/MARSH. PAGE 107 A2206
MARXISM POL/PAR CHIEF ADMIN

B58
NEHRU J.,SPEECHES. INDIA ECO/UNDEV AGRI INDUS INT/ORG POL/PAR DIPLOM FOR/AID NAT/LISM...ANTHOL 20. PAGE 108 A2213
PLAN CHIEF COLONIAL NEUTRAL

L58
HAVILAND H.F.,"FOREIGN AID AND THE POLICY PROCESS: 1957." USA+45 FACE/GP POL/PAR VOL/ASSN CHIEF DELIB/GP ACT/RES LEGIT EXEC GOV/REL ATTIT DRIVE PWR ...POLICY TESTS CONGRESS 20. PAGE 63 A1291
LEGIS PLAN FOR/AID

S58
STAAR R.F.,"ELECTIONS IN COMMUNIST POLAND." EUR+WWI SOCIETY INT/ORG NAT/G POL/PAR LEGIS ACT/RES ECO/TAC EDU/PROP ADJUD ADMIN ROUTINE COERCE TOTALISM ATTIT ORD/FREE PWR 20. PAGE 137 A2797
COM CHOOSE POLAND

C58
CARTER G.M.,"THE POLITICS OF INEQUALITY: SOUTH AFRICA SINCE 1948." SOUTH/AFR CONSTN DIPLOM EDU/PROP REPRESENT DISCRIM ATTIT...POLICY PREDICT CHARTS BIBLIOG 20. PAGE 25 A0504
RACE/REL POL/PAR CHOOSE DOMIN

C58
GOLAY J.F.,"THE FOUNDING OF THE FEDERAL REPUBLIC OF GERMANY." GERMANY/W CONSTN EX/STRUC DIPLOM ADMIN CHOOSE...DECISION BIBLIOG 20. PAGE 53 A1088
FEDERAL NAT/G PARL/PROC POL/PAR

C58
WILDING N.,"AN ENCYCLOPEDIA OF PARLIAMENT." UK LAW CONSTN CHIEF PROB/SOLV DIPLOM DEBATE WAR INGP/REL PRIVIL...BIBLIOG DICTIONARY 13/20 CMN/WLTH PARLIAMENT. PAGE 164 A3349
PARL/PROC POL/PAR NAT/G ADMIN

B59
BOWLES C.,THE COMING POLITICAL BREAKTHROUGH. USA+45 ECO/DEV EX/STRUC ATTIT...CONCPT OBS 20. PAGE 18 A0360
DIPLOM CHOOSE PREDICT POL/PAR

B59
CAREW-HUNT R.C.,BOOKS ON COMMUNISM. NAT/G POL/PAR DIPLOM REV...BIOG 19/20. PAGE 24 A0481
BIBLIOG/A MARXISM COM ASIA

B59
CHALUPA V.,RISE AND DEVELOPMENT OF A TOTALITARIAN STATE. CZECHOSLVK USSR STRUCT INT/ORG WORKER DIPLOM ECO/TAC COERCE NAT/LISM ATTIT...POLICY 20 COM/PARTY. PAGE 25 A0516
TOTALISM MARXISM REV POL/PAR

B59
FOX W.T.R.,THEORETICAL ASPECTS OF INTERNATIONAL RELATIONS. WOR+45 INT/ORG NAT/G POL/PAR CONSULT PLAN ECO/TAC DOMIN EDU/PROP LEGIT EXEC COERCE PWR WEALTH...RELATIV CONCPT 20. PAGE 48 A0975
DELIB/GP ANTHOL

B59
JONES A.C.,NEW FABIAN COLONIAL ESSAYS. UK SOCIETY POL/PAR EDU/PROP ADMIN ORD/FREE SOVEREIGN SOCISM ...ANTHOL 20 CMN/WLTH LABOR/PAR. PAGE 75 A1530
COLONIAL INT/ORG INGP/REL DOMIN

B59
KULSKI W.W.,PEACEFUL CO-EXISTENCE: AN ANALYSIS OF SOVIET FOREIGN POLICY. WOR+45 INTELL SOCIETY ECO/UNDEV POL/PAR EDU/PROP COERCE DRIVE RIGID/FLEX PWR SKILL...PSY CONCPT HIST/WRIT CON/ANAL GEN/METH WORK VAL/FREE 20. PAGE 83 A1691
PLAN DIPLOM USSR

B59
MATHISEN T.,METHODOLOGY IN THE STUDY OF INTERNATIONAL RELATIONS. FUT WOR+45 SOCIETY INT/ORG NAT/G POL/PAR WAR PEACE KNOWL PWR...RELATIV CONCPT METH/CNCPT TREND HYPO/EXP METH TOT/POP 20. PAGE 96 A1965
GEN/METH CON/ANAL DIPLOM CREATE

B59
PAGAN B.,HISTORIA DE LOS PARTIDOS POLITICOS PUERTORRIQUENOS 1898-1956. PUERT/RICO PROVS DIPLOM DOMIN EDU/PROP PARTIC 20. PAGE 113 A2316
POL/PAR CHOOSE COLONIAL PWR

B59
ROBINSON J.A.,THE MONRONEY RESOULUTION: CONGRESSIONAL INITIATIVE IN FOREIGN POLICY MAKING. USA+45 POL/PAR TOP/EX DIPLOM INT/TRADE 20 CONGRESS WORLD/BANK INTL/DEV. PAGE 122 A2504
LEGIS FINAN ECO/UNDEV CHIEF

B59
SHANNON D.A.,THE DECLINE OF AMERICAN COMMUNISM; A HISTORY OF THE COMMUNIST PARTY OF THE UNITED STATES SINCE 1945. USA+45 LAW SOCIETY LABOR NAT/G WORKER DIPLOM EDU/PROP LEAD...POLICY BIBLIOG 20 KHRUSH/N NEGRO AFL/CIO COLD/WAR COM/PARTY. PAGE 131 A2692
MARXISM POL/PAR ATTIT POPULISM

L59
WURFEL D.,"FOREIGN AID AND SOCIAL REFORM IN POLITICAL DEVELOPMENT" (BMR)" PHILIPPINE USA+45 WOR+45 SOCIETY POL/PAR ACT/RES TEC/DEV DIPLOM 20. PAGE 168 A3424
FOR/AID PROB/SOLV ECO/TAC ECO/UNDEV

C59
KULSKI W.W.,"PEACEFUL COEXISTENCE." USSR ECO/UNDEV INT/ORG POL/PAR EDU/PROP COLONIAL CONTROL REV NAT/LISM PEACE PWR MARXISM...BIBLIOG 20. PAGE 83 A1692
COM DIPLOM DOMIN

B60
APTHEKER H.,DISARMAMENT AND THE AMERICAN ECONOMY: A SYMPOSIUM. FUT USA+45 ECO/DEV DIST/IND FINAN INDUS PROC/MFG LABOR NAT/G POL/PAR CONSULT PLAN CAP/ISM INT/TRADE PEACE ATTIT MORAL WEALTH...TREND GEN/LAWS TOT/POP 20. PAGE 9 A0172
MARXIST ARMS/CONT

B60
DAVIDS J.,AMERICA AND THE WORLD OF OUR TIME: UNITED STATES DIPLOMACY IN THE TWENTIETH CENTURY. USA-45 SOCIETY ECO/DEV INT/ORG NAT/G POL/PAR FORCES ECO/TAC DOMIN EDU/PROP EXEC COERCE WAR CHOOSE ATTIT PERSON ORD/FREE...CONCPT TIME/SEQ TOT/POP 20. PAGE 34 A0686
USA+45 PWR DIPLOM

B60
DUMON F.,LA COMMUNAUTE FRANCO-AFRO-MALGACHE: SES ORIGINES, SES INSTITUTIONS, SON EVOLUTION. FRANCE MADAGASCAR POL/PAR DIPLOM ADMIN ATTIT...TREND T 20. PAGE 39 A0798
JURID INT/ORG AFR CONSTN

B60
JACOBSON H.K.,AMERICAN FOREIGN POLICY. COM EUR+WWI USA+45 USA-45 ECO/DEV ECO/UNDEV INT/ORG NAT/G INT/TRADE EDU/PROP COLONIAL CHOOSE MARXISM 20 NATO. PAGE 72 A1485
POL/PAR PWR DIPLOM

B60
LINDSAY K.,EUROPEAN ASSEMBLIES: THE EXPERIMENTAL PERIOD 1949-1959. EUR+WWI ECO/DEV NAT/G POL/PAR LEGIS TOP/EX ACT/RES PLAN ECO/TAC DOMIN LEGIT ROUTINE ATTIT DRIVE ORD/FREE PWR SKILL...SOC CONCPT TREND CHARTS GEN/LAWS VAL/FREE. PAGE 89 A1823
VOL/ASSN INT/ORG REGION

B60
MC CLELLAN G.S.,INDIA. CHINA/COM INDIA CONSTN ELITES STRATA AGRI POL/PAR FOR/AID ARMS/CONT REV MARXISM...CENSUS BIBLIOG 20 COLD/WAR GANDHI/M NEHRU/J. PAGE 97 A1990
DIPLOM NAT/G SOCIETY ECO/UNDEV

B60
MEYRIAT J.,LA SCIENCE POLITIQUE EN FRANCE, 1945-1958; BIBLIOGRAPHIES FRANCAISES DE SCIENCES SOCIALES (VOL. I). EUR+WWI FRANCE POL/PAR DIPLOM ADMIN CHOOSE ATTIT...IDEA/COMP METH/COMP NAT/COMP 20. PAGE 100 A2057
BIBLIOG/A NAT/G CONCPT PHIL/SCI

B60
MORISON E.E.,TURMOIL AND TRADITION: A STUDY OF THE LIFE AND TIMES OF HENRY L. STIMSON. USA+45 USA-45 POL/PAR CHIEF DELIB/GP FORCES BAL/PWR DIPLOM ARMS/CONT WAR PEACE 19/20 STIMSON/HL ROOSEVLT/F TAFT/WH HOOVER/H REPUBLICAN. PAGE 104 A2142
BIOG NAT/G EX/STRUC

B60
MUGRIDGE D.H.,A GUIDE TO THE STUDY OF THE UNITED STATES OF AMERICA: REPRESENTATIVE BOOKS REFLECTING THE DEVELOPMENT OF AMERICAN LIFE. USA+45 USA-45 CONSTN POL/PAR FORCES DIPLOM PRESS CHOOSE...SOC 17/20. PAGE 105 A2165
BIBLIOG/A CULTURE NAT/G POLICY

B60
PRINCETON U CONFERENCE,CURRENT PROBLEMS IN NORTH AFRICA. ALGERIA LIBYA MOROCCO USA+45 EXTR/IND POL/PAR PROB/SOLV DIPLOM ECO/TAC WAR...ANTHOL 20 TUNIS. PAGE 118 A2412
POLICY ECO/UNDEV NAT/G

B60
QUBAIN F.I.,INSIDE THE ARAB MIND: A BIBLIOGRAPHIC SURVEY OF LITERATURE IN ARABIC ON ARAB NATIONALISM AND UNITY. ISLAM POL/PAR SECT LEAD SOVEREIGN MARXISM SOCISM. PAGE 118 A2425
BIBLIOG/A FEDERAL DIPLOM NAT/LISM

B60
STOLPER W.F.,GERMANY BETWEEN EAST AND WEST: THE ECONOMICS OF COMPETITIVE COEXISTENCE. FUT GERMANY/E GERMANY/W WOR+45 FINAN POL/PAR BUDGET ECO/TAC FOR/AID INT/TRADE...STAT CHARTS METH/COMP 20 COLD/WAR. PAGE 138 A2832 — ECO/DEV DIPLOM GOV/COMP BAL/PWR

L60
HAAS E.B.,"CONSENSUS FORMATION IN THE COUNCIL OF EUROPE." EUR+WWI NAT/G DELIB/GP DIPLOM REGION CHOOSE PWR SOVEREIGN...RELATIV NEW/IDEA QUANT CHARTS INDEX TOT/POP OEEC 20 COUNCL/EUR. PAGE 59 A1206 — POL/PAR INT/ORG STAT

S60
BOWIE R.,"POLICY FORMATION IN AMERICAN FOREIGN POLICY." FUT USA+45 WOR+45 STRUCT ECO/DEV INT/ORG POL/PAR LEGIS ACT/RES EXEC ALL/VALS...POLICY OBS VAL/FREE 20. PAGE 17 A0355 — PLAN DRIVE DIPLOM

S60
KALUODA J.,"COMMUNIST STRATEGY IN LATIN AMERICA." L/A+17C USA+45 INT/ORG NAT/G POL/PAR DIPLOM ECO/TAC EDU/PROP COERCE WEALTH...CONCPT OAS COLD/WAR 20. PAGE 76 A1553 — COM PWR CUBA

C60
HAZARD J.N.,"THE SOVIET SYSTEM OF GOVERNMENT." USSR SOCIETY INDUS NAT/G POL/PAR DIPLOM CT/SYS...JURID CHARTS BIBLIOG/A 20. PAGE 63 A1298 — COM NAT/COMP STRUCT ADMIN

C60
WRIGGINS W.H.,"CEYLON: DILEMMAS OF A NEW NATION." ASIA CEYLON CONSTN STRUCT POL/PAR SECT FORCES DIPLOM GOV/REL NAT/LISM...CHARTS BIBLIOG 20. PAGE 167 A3399 — PROB/SOLV NAT/G ECO/UNDEV

B61
BARNES W.,THE FOREIGN SERVICE OF THE UNITED STATES. USA+45 USA-45 CONSTN INT/ORG POL/PAR CONSULT DELIB/GP LEGIS DOMIN EDU/PROP EXEC ATTIT RIGID/FLEX ORD/FREE PWR...POLICY CONCPT STAT OBS RECORD BIOG TIME/SEQ TREND. PAGE 11 A0224 — NAT/G MGT DIPLOM

B61
BISHOP D.G.,THE ADMINISTRATION OF BRITISH FOREIGN RELATIONS. EUR+WWI MOD/EUR INT/ORG NAT/G POL/PAR DELIB/GP LEGIS TOP/EX ECO/TAC DOMIN EDU/PROP ADMIN COERCE 20. PAGE 14 A0292 — ROUTINE PWR DIPLOM UK

B61
BURDETTE F.L.,POLITICAL SCIENCE: A SELECTED BIBLIOGRAPHY OF BOOKS IN PRINT, WITH ANNOTATIONS (PAMPHLET). LAW LOC/G NAT/G POL/PAR PROVS DIPLOM EDU/PROP ADMIN CHOOSE ATTIT 20. PAGE 21 A0432 — BIBLIOG/A GOV/COMP CONCPT ROUTINE

B61
CAMERON J.,THE AFRICAN REVOLUTION. AFR UK ECO/UNDEV POL/PAR REGION RACE/REL DISCRIM PWR CONSERVE ...CONCPT SOC/INTEG 20 NEGRO. PAGE 23 A0472 — REV COLONIAL ORD/FREE DIPLOM

B61
CARNELL F.,THE POLITICS OF THE NEW STATES: A SELECT ANNOTATED BIBLIOGRAPHY WITH SPECIAL REFERENCE TO THE COMMONWEALTH. CONSTN ELITES LABOR NAT/G POL/PAR EX/STRUC DIPLOM ADJUD ADMIN...GOV/COMP 20 COMMONWLTH. PAGE 24 A0496 — BIBLIOG/A AFR ASIA COLONIAL

B61
DELZELL C.F.,MUSSOLINI'S ENEMIES - THE ITALIAN ANTI-FASCIST RESISTANCE. ITALY DIPLOM PRESS DETER WAR TOTALISM ORD/FREE MARXISM 20. PAGE 36 A0730 — FASCISM GP/REL POL/PAR REV

B61
FUCHS G.,GEGEN HITLER UND HENLEIN. CZECHOSLVK GERMANY DIPLOM CHOOSE GP/REL TOTALISM SOVEREIGN 20 HITLER/A. PAGE 50 A1013 — FASCISM WORKER POL/PAR NAT/LISM

B61
GRAEBNER N.,THE NEW ISOLATIONISM: A STUDY IN POLITICS AND FOREIGN POLICY SINCE 1960. USA+45 INT/ORG LOC/G NAT/G POL/PAR LEGIS BAL/PWR EDU/PROP CHOOSE ATTIT PERSON ORD/FREE 20 TRUMAN/HS EISNHWR/DD. PAGE 55 A1120 — EXEC PWR DIPLOM

B61
HISTORICAL RESEARCH INSTITUTE,A SHORT BIBLIOGRAPHY OF INDO-MUSLIM HISTORY. INDIA S/ASIA DIPLOM EDU/PROP COLONIAL LEAD NAT/LISM ATTIT...BIOG 19/20. PAGE 65 A1343 — BIBLIOG NAT/G SECT POL/PAR

B61
LEGISLATIVE REFERENCE SERVICE,WORLD COMMUNIST MOVEMENT: SELECTIVE CHRONOLOGY, 1818-1957 (4 VOLS.). COM WOR+45 WOR-45 POL/PAR LEAD 19/20. PAGE 86 A1766 — BIBLIOG DIPLOM TIME/SEQ MARXISM

B61
NOLLAU G.,INTERNATIONAL COMMUNISM AND WORLD REVOLUTION: HISTORY AND METHODS. RUSSIA USSR INT/ORG NAT/G POL/PAR VOL/ASSN FORCES BAL/PWR DIPLOM EXEC REGION WAR ATTIT PWR MARXISM...CONCPT TIME/SEQ COLD/WAR 19/20. PAGE 102 A2100 — COM REV

B61
NOLLAU G.,INTERNATIONAL COMMUNISM AND WORLD REVOLUTION; HISTORY AND METHODS (TRANS. BY VICTOR ANDERSEN). COM WORKER DIPLOM CONFER INGP/REL ...CONCPT BIBLIOG 20 STALIN/J LENIN/VI COMINTERN COMINFORM WORLD/CONG. PAGE 110 A2249 — MARXISM POL/PAR INT/ORG REV

B61
OVERSTREET H.,THE WAR CALLED PEACE. USSR WOR+45 COM/IND INT/ORG POL/PAR BAL/PWR EDU/PROP PEACE ATTIT...CONCPT 20 KHRUSH/N. PAGE 112 A2302 — DIPLOM COM POLICY LEAD

B61
PALMER N.D.,THE INDIAN POLITICAL SYSTEM. INDIA ECO/UNDEV SECT CHIEF COLONIAL CHOOSE ALL/IDEOS SOCISM...CHARTS BIBLIOG/A 20. PAGE 113 A2322 — NAT/LISM POL/PAR NAT/G DIPLOM

B61
PANIKKAR K.M.,REVOLUTION IN AFRICA. AFR GUINEA ECO/UNDEV POL/PAR DIPLOM COLONIAL EXEC LEAD SOVEREIGN...CHARTS 20. PAGE 114 A2332 — NAT/LISM NAT/G CHIEF

B61
SCHWARTZ H.,THE RED PHOENIX: RUSSIA SINCE WORLD WAR II. USA+45 WOR+45 ELITES POL/PAR TEC/DEV ECO/TAC MARXISM. PAGE 130 A2655 — DIPLOM NAT/G ECO/DEV

B61
STRAUSZ-HUPE R.,A FORWARD STRATEGY FOR AMERICA. FUT WOR+45 ECO/DEV INT/ORG NAT/G POL/PAR DELIB/GP FORCES ACT/RES CREATE ECO/TAC DOMIN EDU/PROP ATTIT DRIVE PWR...MAJORIT CONCPT STAT OBS TIME/SEQ TREND COLD/WAR TOT/POP. PAGE 139 A2848 — USA+45 PLAN DIPLOM

B61
TETENS T.H.,THE NEW GERMANY AND THE OLD NAZIS. EUR+WWI GERMANY/W USA+45 NAT/G CRIME CHOOSE RACE/REL TOTALISM AGE/Y ATTIT 20 JEWS NAZI ADENAUER/K. PAGE 142 A2905 — FASCISM DIPLOM FOR/AID POL/PAR

B61
US LIBRARY OF CONGRESS,WORLD COMMUNIST MOVEMENT. USA+45 USSR WOR+45 INT/ORG DIPLOM REV ATTIT 19/20. PAGE 155 A3155 — BIBLIOG/A EDU/PROP MARXISM POL/PAR

B61
WARD R.E.,JAPANESE POLITICAL SCIENCE: A GUIDE TO JAPANESE REFERENCE AND RESEARCH MATERIALS (2ND ED.). LAW CONSTN STRATA NAT/G POL/PAR DELIB/GP LEGIS ADMIN CHOOSE GP/REL...INT/LAW 19/20 CHINJAP. PAGE 161 A3282 — BIBLIOG/A PHIL/SCI

L61
HILSMAN R. JR.,"THE NEW COMMUNIST TACTIC: PRECIS-INTERNAL WAR." COM FUT USA+45 ECO/UNDEV POL/PAR FOR/AID RIGID/FLEX ALL/VALS...TREND COLD/WAR 20. PAGE 65 A1334 — FORCES COERCE USSR GUERRILLA

S61
BARNET R.,"RUSSIA, CHINA, AND THE WORLD: THE SOVIET ATTITUDE ON DISARMAMENT (PART 3)." ASIA CHINA/COM FUT INT/ORG NAT/G POL/PAR VOL/ASSN ARMS/CONT ATTIT ...POLICY CONCPT TIME/SEQ TREND TOT/POP VAL/FREE 20. PAGE 11 A0226 — COM PLAN TOTALISM USSR

S61
DANIELS R.V.,"THE CHINESE REVOLUTION IN RUSSIAN PERSPECTIVE." ASIA CHINA/COM COM USSR INTELL INT/ORG TOP/EX REV TOTALISM PWR...POLICY WORK VAL/FREE 20. PAGE 33 A0680 — POL/PAR PLAN

S61
NOVE A.,"THE SOVIET MODEL AND UNDERDEVELOPED COUNTRIES." COM FUT USSR WOR+45 CULTURE ECO/DEV POL/PAR FOR/AID EDU/PROP ADMIN MORAL WEALTH ...POLICY RECORD HIST/WRIT 20. PAGE 110 A2258 — ECO/UNDEV PLAN

S61
ZAGORIA D.S.,"THE FUTURE OF SINO-SOVIET RELATIONS." CHINA/COM INT/ORG NAT/G POL/PAR VOL/ASSN ACT/RES PLAN PERSON...METH/CNCPT TIME/SEQ TOT/POP VAL/FREE 20 MAO KHRUSH/N. PAGE 169 A3444 — ASIA COM TOTALISM USSR

B62
APTHEKER H.,,AMERICAN FOREIGN POLICY AND THE COLD WAR. USA+45 NAT/G POL/PAR COLONIAL NAT/LISM SOVEREIGN MARXISM SOCISM 20 COLD/WAR MARX/KARL LENIN/VI INTERVENT. PAGE 8 A0167 — DIPLOM WAR PEACE

B62
BOUSCAREN A.T.,SOVIET FOREIGN POLICY: A PATTERN OF PERSISTANCE. WOR+45 WOR-45 SOCIETY STRUCT INT/ORG POL/PAR CREATE PLAN EDU/PROP ROUTINE ATTIT RIGID/FLEX...POLICY CONCPT RECORD HIST/WRIT TIME/SEQ MARX/KARL 20. PAGE 17 A0352 — COM NAT/G DIPLOM USSR

B62
BUCHMANN J.,L'AFRIQUE NOIRE INDEPENDANTE. POL/PAR DIPLOM COLONIAL PARTIC CHOOSE GP/REL ATTIT ORD/FREE WEALTH NEGRO. PAGE 21 A0426 — AFR NAT/LISM DECISION

B62
DELANEY R.F.,THE LITERATURE OF COMMUNISM IN AMERICA. COM USA+45 USA-45 INT/ORG LABOR NAT/G POL/PAR INGP/REL...MAJORIT 20. PAGE 36 A0727 — BIBLIOG/A MARXISM EDU/PROP IDEA/COMP

B62
GUTTMAN A.,THE WOUND IN THE HEART: AMERICA AND THE SPANISH CIVIL WAR. SPAIN USA-45 POL/PAR LEGIS ECO/TAC CHOOSE ANOMIE ATTIT MARXISM...POLICY ANARCH BIBLIOG 20 ROOSEVLT/F. PAGE 58 A1198 — ALL/IDEOS WAR DIPLOM CATHISM

B62
HATCH J.,AFRICA TODAY-AND TOMORROW: AN OUTLINE OF BASIC FACTS AND MAJOR PROBLEMS. AFR FUT ISLAM STRATA ECO/UNDEV INT/ORG NAT/G POL/PAR DELIB/GP — PLAN CONSTN NAT/LISM

TOP/EX EDU/PROP LEGIT CHOOSE ATTIT...TIME/SEQ TOT/POP COLD/WAR 20. PAGE 63 A1287

B62
HOOK S.,WORLD COMMUNISM: KEY DOCUMENTARY MATERIAL. CHINA/COM L/A+17C USA+45 USSR POL/PAR DIPLOM COLONIAL REV WAR...ANTHOL 20 MARX/KARL LENIN/VI COM/PARTY. PAGE 67 A1380 MARXISM COM GEN/LAWS NAT/G

B62
JEWELL M.E.,SENATORIAL POLITICS AND FOREIGN POLICY. NAT/G POL/PAR CHIEF DELIB/GP TOP/EX FOR/AID EDU/PROP ROUTINE ATTIT PWR SKILL...MAJORIT METH/CNCPT TIME/SEQ CONGRESS 20 PRESIDENT. PAGE 74 A1516 USA+45 LEGIS DIPLOM

B62
KENT R.K.,FROM MADAGASCAR TO THE MALAGASY REPUBLIC. FRANCE MADAGASCAR DIPLOM NAT/LISM ORD/FREE...MGT 18/20. PAGE 78 A1596 COLONIAL SOVEREIGN REV POL/PAR

B62
KLUCKHOHN F.L.,THE NAKED RISE OF COMMUNISM. CHINA/COM COM USSR WOR+45 CONSTN POL/PAR PLAN CONTROL LEAD NEUTRAL CONSERVE 20 STALIN/J EUROPE/E COM/PARTY. PAGE 80 A1650 MARXISM IDEA/COMP DIPLOM DOMIN

B62
KYRIAK T.E.,INTERNATIONAL COMMUNIST DEVELOPMENTS 1957-1961: INDEX TO TRANSLATIONS FROM AFRICA, ASIA, LATIN AMERICA, WEST EUROPE. COM WOR+45 NAT/G WORKER DIPLOM NAT/LISM. PAGE 83 A1704 BIBLIOG/A MARXISM LABOR POL/PAR

B62
LAQUEUR W.,THE FUTURE OF COMMUNIST SOCIETY. CHINA/COM USSR LAW ECO/DEV NAT/G POL/PAR PLAN PROB/SOLV DIPLOM LEAD...POLICY CONCPT IDEA/COMP ANTHOL 20. PAGE 85 A1731 MARXISM COM FUT SOCIETY

B62
MORRAY J.P.,THE SECOND REVOLUTION IN CUBA. CUBA AGRI LABOR POL/PAR DIPLOM FOR/AID GUERRILLA TOTALISM MARXISM 20. PAGE 104 A2146 REV MARXIST ECO/TAC NAT/LISM

B62
SCHMIDT-VOLKMAR E.,DER KULTURKAMPF IN DEUTSCHLAND 1871-1890. GERMANY PRUSSIA SOCIETY STRUCT SECT DIPLOM GP/REL NAT/LISM 19 CHURCH/STA BISMARCK/O. PAGE 128 A2632 POL/PAR CATHISM ATTIT NAT/G

B62
SELOSOEMARDJAN O.,SOCIAL CHANGES IN JOGJAKARTA. INDONESIA NETHERLAND ELITES STRATA STRUCT FAM POL/PAR CREATE DIPLOM INT/TRADE EDU/PROP ADMIN GOV/REL...SOC 20 JAVA CHINJAP. PAGE 131 A2683 ECO/UNDEV CULTURE REV COLONIAL

B62
STARR R.E.,POLAND 1944-1962: THE SOVIETIZATION OF A CAPTIVE PEOPLE. COM POLAND USSR POL/PAR SECT LEGIS DIPLOM DOMIN EDU/PROP CHOOSE ORD/FREE...POLICY CHARTS BIBLIOG 20. PAGE 137 A2808 MARXISM NAT/G TOTALISM NAT/COMP

B62
TOURE S.,THE INTERNATIONAL POLICY OF THE DEMOCRATIC PARTY OF GUINEA (VOL. VII). AFR ALGERIA GHANA GUINEA MALI CONSTN VOL/ASSN CHIEF WAR PEACE ATTIT ...WELF/ST 20 DEMOCRAT. PAGE 144 A2953 DIPLOM POLICY POL/PAR NEW/LIB

L62
NIZARD L.,"CUBAN QUESTION AND SECURITY COUNCIL." L/A+17C USA+45 ECO/UNDEV NAT/G POL/PAR DELIB/GP ECO/TAC PWR...RELATIV OBS TIME/SEQ TREND GEN/LAWS UN 20 UN. PAGE 109 A2242 INT/ORG JURID DIPLOM CUBA

L62
ULYSSES,"THE INTERNATIONAL AIMS AND POLICIES OF THE SOVIET UNION: THE NEW CONCEPTS AND STRATEGY OF KHRUSHCHEV." FUT USSR WOR+45 SOCIETY INT/ORG NAT/G POL/PAR FORCES TOP/EX PLAN DOMIN EDU/PROP COERCE ATTIT PERSON PWR...TREND COLD/WAR 20 KHRUSH/N. PAGE 146 A2994 COM POLICY BAL/PWR DIPLOM

S62
BOKOR-SZEGO H.,"LA CONVENTION DE BELGRADE ET LE REGIME DU DANUBE." COM EUR+WWI WOR+45 STRUCT POL/PAR VOL/ASSN PLAN EDU/PROP WEALTH...TIME/SEQ 20. PAGE 16 A0333 INT/ORG TOTALISM YUGOSLAVIA

S62
BROWN B.E.,"L'ONU ABANDONNE LA HONGRIE." COM USSR WOR+45 CONSTN NAT/G POL/PAR DELIB/GP ACT/RES TEC/DEV PWR...TIME/SEQ 20 UN. PAGE 20 A0400 INT/ORG TOTALISM HUNGARY POLICY

S62
CROAN M.,"POLYCENTRISM: COMMUNIST INTERNATIONAL RELATIONS." ASIA STRUCT INT/ORG NAT/G POL/PAR CONSULT PLAN DOMIN EDU/PROP COERCE ATTIT RIGID/FLEX SOCISM...POLICY CONCPT TREND CON/ANAL GEN/LAWS MARX/KARL. PAGE 33 A0663 COM CREATE DIPLOM NAT/LISM

S62
FOCSANEANU L.,"LES GRANDS TRAITES DE LA REPUBLIQUE POPULAIRE DE CHINE." ASIA CHINA/COM COM USSR WOR+45 INT/ORG NAT/G POL/PAR ACT/RES PLAN DIPLOM EDU/PROP ...CONCPT TIME/SEQ 20 TREATY. PAGE 47 A0957 VOL/ASSN TOTALISM

S62
GREENSPAN M.,"INTERNATIONAL LAW AND ITS PROTECTION FOR PARTICIPANTS IN UNCONVENTIONAL WARFARE." WOR+45 LAW INT/ORG NAT/G POL/PAR COERCE REV ORD/FREE ...INT/LAW TOT/POP 20. PAGE 56 A1143 FORCES JURID GUERRILLA WAR

S62
KOLARZ W.,"THE IMPACT OF COMMUNISM ON WEST AFRICA." AFR FUT SOCIETY INT/ORG NAT/G CREATE PLAN DOMIN EDU/PROP COERCE NAT/LISM ATTIT RIGID/FLEX SOCISM ...POLICY CONCPT TREND MARX/KARL 20. PAGE 81 A1666 COM POL/PAR COLONIAL

S62
SPRINGER H.W.,"FEDERATION IN THE CARIBBEAN: AN ATTEMPT THAT FAILED." L/A+17C ECO/UNDEV INT/ORG POL/PAR PROVS LEGIS CREATE PLAN LEGIT ADMIN FEDERAL ATTIT DRIVE PERSON ORD/FREE PWR...POLICY GEOG PSY CONCPT OBS CARIBBEAN CMN/WLTH 20. PAGE 136 A2791 VOL/ASSN NAT/G REGION

S62
TRUMAN D.,"THE DOMESTIC POLITICS OF FOREIGN AID." USA+45 WOR+45 NAT/G POL/PAR LEGIS DIPLOM ECO/TAC EDU/PROP ADMIN CHOOSE ATTIT PWR CONGRESS 20 CONGRESS. PAGE 145 A2970 ROUTINE FOR/AID

S62
VIGNES D.,"L'AUTORITE DES TRAITES INTERNATIONAUX EN DROIT INTERNE." EUR+WWI UNIV LAW CONSTN INTELL NAT/G POL/PAR DIPLOM ATTIT PERCEPT ALL/VALS ...POLICY INT/LAW JURID CONCPT TIME/SEQ 20 TREATY. PAGE 159 A3233 STRUCT LEGIT FRANCE

B63
AFRICAN BIBLIOGRAPHIC CENTER,THE SCENE IS GUINEA AND THE PERSONAGE IS SEKOU TOURE: A SELECTED CURRENT READING LIST, 1959-1962 (PAMPHLET). GUINEA ECO/UNDEV CHIEF FOR/AID COLONIAL...BIOG 20. PAGE 5 A0095 BIBLIOG AFR POL/PAR COM

B63
AFRICAN BIBLIOGRAPHIC CENTER,THE SCENE IS KENYA AND THE PERSONAGE IS TOM MBOYA: A SELECTED CURRENT READING LIST FROM 1956-1962 (PAMPHLET). ECO/UNDEV LABOR POL/PAR CHIEF COLONIAL CHOOSE NAT/LISM ORD/FREE 20. PAGE 5 A0096 BIBLIOG DIPLOM AFR NAT/G

B63
BROWN W.N.,THE UNITED STATES AND INDIA AND PAKISTAN (REV. ED.). INDIA PAKISTAN S/ASIA WOR+45 POL/PAR SECT INT/TRADE COLONIAL COERCE DISCRIM. PAGE 20 A0408 DIPLOM ECO/UNDEV SOVEREIGN STRUCT

B63
CREMEANS C.,THE ARABS AND THE WORLD: NASSER'S ARAB NATIONALIST POLICY. FUT ISLAM UAR USA+45 SOCIETY STRATA NAT/G POL/PAR PLAN DIPLOM EDU/PROP LEGIT DRIVE ALL/VALS...INT TIME/SEQ CHARTS 20 NASSER/G. PAGE 33 A0662 TOP/EX ATTIT REGION NAT/LISM

B63
DALLIN A.,DIVERSITY IN INTERNATIONAL COMMUNISM: A DOCUMENTARY RECORD, 1961-1963. CHINA/COM CHIEF PRESS WRITING DEBATE LEAD...POLICY ANTHOL 20. PAGE 33 A0677 COM DIPLOM POL/PAR CONFER

B63
ELIAS T.O.,GOVERNMENT AND POLITICS IN AFRICA. CONSTN CULTURE SOCIETY NAT/G POL/PAR DIPLOM REPRESENT PERSON...SOC TREND BIBLIOG 4/20. PAGE 41 A0837 AFR NAT/LISM COLONIAL LAW

B63
FABER K.,DIE NATIONALISTISCHE PUBLIZISTIK DEUTSCHLANDS VON 1866 BIS 1871 (2 VOLS.). EUR+WWI GERMANY DIPLOM EDU/PROP 19. PAGE 43 A0881 BIBLIOG/A NAT/G NAT/LISM POL/PAR

B63
GRIFFITH W.E.,ALBANIA AND THE SINO-SOVIET RIFT. ALBANIA CHINA/COM USSR POL/PAR CHIEF LEGIS DIPLOM DOMIN ATTIT PWR...POLICY 20 KHRUSH/N MAO. PAGE 57 A1161 EDU/PROP MARXISM NAT/LISM GOV/REL

B63
HAMM H.,ALBANIA - CHINA'S BEACHHEAD IN EUROPE. ALBANIA CHINA/COM USSR YUGOSLAVIA ELITES SOCIETY POL/PAR DELIB/GP FORCES ECO/TAC COERCE ISOLAT PEACE MARXISM...IDEA/COMP 20 MAO. PAGE 61 A1248 DIPLOM REV NAT/G POLICY

B63
HONEY P.J.,COMMUNISM IN NORTH VIETNAM: ITS ROLE IN THE SINO-SOVIET DISPUTE. CHINA/COM INDIA USSR VIETNAM/N AGRI POL/PAR LEGIS ECO/TAC WAR PEACE ATTIT...GEOG IDEA/COMP 20. PAGE 67 A1378 POLICY MARXISM CHIEF DIPLOM

B63
HYDE D.,THE PEACEFUL ASSAULT. COM UAR USSR ECO/DEV ECO/UNDEV NAT/G POL/PAR CAP/ISM PWR 20. PAGE 69 A1427 MARXISM CONTROL ECO/TAC DIPLOM

B63
KAHIN G.M.,MAJOR GOVERNMENTS OF ASIA (2ND ED.). ASIA INDIA INDONESIA PAKISTAN S/ASIA DIPLOM...SOC 20 CHINJAP. PAGE 75 A1546 GOV/COMP POL/PAR ELITES

B63
KHADDURI M.,MODERN LIBYA: A STUDY IN POLITICAL DEVELOPMENT. EUR+WWI ISLAM LIBYA ELITES INT/ORG POL/PAR FORCES DIPLOM FOR/AID DOMIN EDU/PROP LEGIT NAT/LISM DRIVE RIGID/FLEX SKILL...CONCPT TIME/SEQ TREND 20. PAGE 78 A1606 NAT/G STRUCT

B63
KHRUSHCHEV N.S.,THE NEW CONTENT OF PEACEFUL COEXISTENCE IN THE NUCLEAR AGE. GERMANY/E WORKER NUC/PWR REV SOCISM 20 COLD/WAR. PAGE 79 A1614 MARXISM POL/PAR PEACE DIPLOM

B63
MBOYA T.,FREEDOM AND AFTER. AFR LABOR POL/PAR DIPLOM EDU/PROP COERCE SOCISM 20. PAGE 97 A1989
COLONIAL ECO/UNDEV NAT/LISM INT/ORG

B63
MOSELY P.E.,THE SOVIET UNION, 1922-1962: A FOREIGN AFFAIRS READER. ASIA POLAND USSR CULTURE INTELL AGRI POL/PAR WORKER INT/TRADE DOMIN WAR NAT/LISM MARXISM SOCISM 20 KHRUSH/N. PAGE 105 A2152
PWR POLICY DIPLOM

B63
NORTH R.C.,M. N. ROY'S MISSION TO CHINA: THE COMMUNIST-KUOMINTANG SPLIT OF 1927. ASIA USSR STRATA LEGIS WORKER LEAD REV ATTIT ROLE SOCISM 20 ROY/MN COM/PARTY. PAGE 110 A2253
POL/PAR MARXISM DIPLOM

B63
QUAISON-SACKEY A.,AFRICA UNBOUND: REFLECTIONS OF AN AFRICAN STATESMAN. ISLAM CULTURE INTELL INT/ORG POL/PAR TOP/EX DOMIN EDU/PROP LEGIT ATTIT PERSON ...CONCPT OBS TIME/SEQ CHARTS STERTYP 20 UN. PAGE 118 A2423
AFR BIOG

B63
ROSS H.,THE COLD WAR: CONTAINMENT AND ITS CRITICSS. WOR+45 POL/PAR BAL/PWR ECO/TAC PEACE ORD/FREE ...POLICY IDEA/COMP ANTHOL T 20 COLD/WAR DULLES/JF TRUMAN/HS EISNHWR/DD. PAGE 124 A2541
MARXISM ARMS/CONT DIPLOM

B63
SCHMELTZ G.W.,LA POLITIQUE MONDIALE CONTEMPORAINE. SOCIETY ECO/UNDEV INDUS INT/ORG NAT/G POL/PAR CONSULT DELIB/GP PLAN TEC/DEV ECO/TAC DOMIN EDU/PROP ROUTINE COERCE PERCEPT PERSON LOVE SKILL ...SOC RECORD TOT/POP. PAGE 128 A2629
WOR+45 COLONIAL

B63
SWEARER H.R.,CONTEMPORARY COMMUNISM: THEORY AND PRACTICE. COM USSR SOCIETY ECO/DEV POL/PAR FORCES PLAN ADMIN LEAD NAT/LISM...POLICY ANTHOL 20 LENIN/VI COM/PARTY. PAGE 140 A2869
MARXISM CONCPT DIPLOM NAT/G

B63
TUCKER R.C.,THE SOVIET POLITICAL MIND. WOR+45 ELITES INT/ORG NAT/G POL/PAR PLAN DIPLOM ECO/TAC DOMIN ADMIN NUC/PWR REV DRIVE PERSON SUPEGO PWR WEALTH...POLICY MGT PSY CONCPT OBS BIOG TREND COLD/WAR MARX/KARL 20. PAGE 145 A2972
COM TOP/EX USSR

B63
US DEPARTMENT OF THE ARMY,SOVIET RUSSIA: STRATEGIC SURVEY (PAMPHLET). USSR POL/PAR PLAN DOMIN EDU/PROP ARMS/CONT GUERRILLA WAR WEAPON...TREND CHARTS ORG/CHARTS 20. PAGE 152 A3106
BIBLIOG/A MARXISM DIPLOM COERCE

B63
WATKINS K.W.,BRITAIN DIVIDED; THE EFFECT OF THE SPANISH CIVIL WAR ON BRITISH POLITICAL OPINION. SPAIN UK POL/PAR BAL/PWR LOBBY NEUTRAL 20. PAGE 162 A3293
EDU/PROP WAR POLICY DIPLOM

L63
MOUSKHELY M.,"LE BLOC COMMUNISTE ET LA COMMUNAUTE ECONOMIQUE EUROPEENNE." AFR COM EUR+WWI FUT USSR WOR+45 INTELL ECO/UNDEV LABOR POL/PAR NUC/PWR RIGID/FLEX...TIME/SEQ ORG/CHARTS EEC TOT/POP 20. PAGE 105 A2158
INT/ORG ECO/DEV

L63
RUSSETT B.M.,"TOWARD A MODEL OF COMPETITIVE INTERNATIONAL POLITICS." USA+45 WOR+45 INT/ORG NAT/G POL/PAR VOL/ASSN LEGIS BAL/PWR DIPLOM LEGIT PWR...CONCPT CONT/OBS STERTYP GEN/LAWS TOT/POP COLD/WAR 20 UN. PAGE 126 A2579
ATTIT EDU/PROP

L63
SZASZY E.,"L'EVOLUTION DES PRINCIPES GENERAUX DU DROIT INTERNATIONAL PRIVE DANS LES PAYS DE DEMOCRATIE POPULAIRE." COM FUT WOR+45 LAW ECO/DEV PERF/ART POL/PAR PROF/ORG ECO/TAC INT/TRADE EDU/PROP ATTIT RIGID/FLEX ALL/VALS SOCISM...JURID TREND GEN/LAWS WORK 20. PAGE 141 A2876
DIPLOM TOTALISM INT/LAW INT/ORG

S63
HINDLEY D.,"FOREIGN AID TO INDONESIA AND ITS POLITICAL IMPLICATIONS." INDONESIA POL/PAR ATTIT SOVEREIGN...CHARTS 20. PAGE 65 A1336
FOR/AID NAT/G WEALTH ECO/TAC

S63
MACWHINNEY E.,"LES CONCEPT SOVIETIQUE DE 'COEXISTENCE PACIFIQUE' ET LES RAPPORTS JURIDIQUES ENTRE L'URSS ET LES ETATS OCIDENTAUX." COM FUT WOR+45 LAW CULTURE INTELL POL/PAR ACT/RES BAL/PWR ...INT/LAW 20. PAGE 93 A1903
NAT/G CONCPT DIPLOM USSR

S63
MANOLIU F.,"PERSPECTIVES D'UNE INTEGRATION ECONOMIQUE LATINOAMERICAINE." FUT L/A+17C STRUCT MARKET LABOR POL/PAR VOL/ASSN PLAN RIGID/FLEX PWR ...METH/CNCPT OAS TOT/POP 20. PAGE 94 A1927
FINAN INT/ORG PEACE

S63
RAMERIE L.,"TENSION AU SEIN DU COMECON: LE CAS ROUMAIN." COM EUR+WWI USSR WOR+45 ECO/DEV DIST/IND NAT/G POL/PAR VOL/ASSN EDU/PROP TOTALISM ATTIT WEALTH...TIME/SEQ 20 COMECON. PAGE 119 A2438
INT/ORG ECO/TAC INT/TRADE ROMANIA

S63
WELLS H.,"THE OAS AND THE DOMINICAN ELECTIONS." L/A+17C INT/ORG NAT/G POL/PAR TEC/DEV ECO/TAC EDU/PROP PERCEPT...TIME/SEQ OAS TOT/POP 20. PAGE 163 A3317
CONSULT CHOOSE DOMIN/REP

C63
SCHMITT K.M.,"EVOLUTION OR CHAOS: DYNAMICS OF LATIN AMERICAN GOVERNMENT AND POLITICS." L/A+17C AGRI FINAN CAP/ISM EXEC LEAD BAL/PAY TOTALISM ATTIT ...TREND BIBLIOG 20. PAGE 129 A2635
DIPLOM POLICY POL/PAR LOBBY

B64
AFRO ASIAN SOLIDARITY AGAINST IMPERIALISM. AFR ISLAM S/ASIA ECO/UNDEV NAT/G POL/PAR TOP/EX PRESS ...INT ANTHOL 20 CHOU/ENLAI. PAGE 3 A0066
MARXISM DIPLOM EDU/PROP CHIEF

B64
BINDER L.,THE IDEOLOGICAL REVOLUTION IN THE MIDDLE EAST. ISLAM STRUCT INT/ORG KIN SECT EX/STRUC TOP/EX PLAN ATTIT DRIVE RIGID/FLEX PWR...MYTH TOT/POP 20. PAGE 14 A0289
POL/PAR NAT/G NAT/LISM

B64
CZERNIN F.,VERSAILLES - 1919. EUR+WWI USA-45 FACE/GP POL/PAR VOL/ASSN DELIB/GP TOP/EX CREATE BAL/PWR DIPLOM LEGIT NAT/LISM PEACE ATTIT RIGID/FLEX ORD/FREE PWR...CON/ANAL LEAGUE/NAT 20 VERSAILLES. PAGE 33 A0671
INT/ORG STRUCT

B64
GRIFFITH W.E.,COMMUNISM IN EUROPE (2 VOLS.). CZECHOSLVK USSR WOR+45 WOR-45 YUGOSLAVIA INGP/REL MARXISM SOCISM...ANTHOL 20 EUROPE/E. PAGE 57 A1162
COM POL/PAR DIPLOM GOV/COMP

B64
HALPERIN S.W.,MUSSOLINI AND ITALIAN FASCISM. ITALY NAT/G POL/PAR SECT ECO/TAC LEAD PWR SOCISM...POLICY 20 MUSSOLIN/B. PAGE 60 A1241
FASCISM NAT/LISM EDU/PROP CHIEF

B64
HARMON R.B.,BIBLIOGRAPHY OF BIBLIOGRAPHIES IN POLITICAL SCIENCE (MIMEOGRAPHED PAPER: LIMITED EDITION). WOR+45 WOR-45 INT/ORG POL/PAR GOV/REL ALL/IDEOS...INT/LAW JURID MGT 19/20. PAGE 61 A1260
BIBLIOG NAT/G DIPLOM LOC/G

B64
JANOWITZ M.,THE MILITARY IN THE POLITICAL DEVELOPMENT OF NEW NATIONS: AN ESSAY IN COMPARATIVE ANALYSIS. AFR ASIA ISLAM L/A+17C S/ASIA USA+45 ECO/UNDEV INT/ORG NAT/G POL/PAR DELIB/GP PLAN ECO/TAC DOMIN LEGIT COERCE ATTIT DRIVE RESPECT ...SOC CONCPT CENSUS VAL/FREE. PAGE 73 A1495
FORCES PWR

B64
JOHNSON L.B.,MY HOPE FOR AMERICA. FUT USA+45 USSR LAW PLAN DIPLOM GIVE INCOME PEACE ATTIT ORD/FREE WEALTH 20 JOHNSON/LB PRESIDENT DEMOCRAT. PAGE 74 A1525
POLICY POL/PAR NAT/G GOV/REL

B64
KEEP J.,CONTEMPORARY HISTORY IN THE SOVIET MIRROR. COM USSR POL/PAR CREATE DIPLOM AGREE WAR ATTIT ...MYTH TREND ANTHOL 20 COLD/WAR STALIN/J MARX/KARL LENIN/VI. PAGE 77 A1576
HIST/WRIT METH MARXISM IDEA/COMP

B64
KOLARZ W.,BOOKS ON COMMUNISM. USSR WOR+45 CULTURE NAT/G POL/PAR DIPLOM LEAD...CONCPT GOV/COMP IDEA/COMP. PAGE 81 A1667
BIBLIOG/A SOCIETY COM MARXISM

B64
LEGGE J.D.,INDONESIA. INDONESIA ELITES ECO/UNDEV POL/PAR CHIEF FORCES INT/TRADE COERCE CHOOSE ORD/FREE...SOC CHARTS BIBLIOG 16/20 CHINJAP. PAGE 86 A1765
S/ASIA DOMIN NAT/LISM POLICY

B64
LUTHULI A.,AFRICA'S FREEDOM. KIN LABOR POL/PAR SCHOOL DIPLOM NEUTRAL REGION REV NAT/LISM PWR WEALTH SOCISM SOC/INTEG 20. PAGE 92 A1874
AFR ECO/UNDEV COLONIAL

B64
MAHAR J.M.,INDIA: A CRITICAL BIBLIOGRAPHY. INDIA PAKISTAN CULTURE ECO/UNDEV LOC/G POL/PAR SECT PROB/SOLV DIPLOM ADMIN COLONIAL PARL/PROC ATTIT 20. PAGE 93 A1906
BIBLIOG/A S/ASIA NAT/G LEAD

B64
MAIER J.,POLITICS OF CHANGE IN LATIN AMERICA. BRAZIL L/A+17C STRATA INT/ORG NAT/G POL/PAR FOR/AID REV 20. PAGE 93 A1907
SOCIETY NAT/LISM DIPLOM REGION

B64
MARTIN J.J.,AMERICAN LIBERALISM AND WORLD POLITICS, 1931-41 (2 VOLS.). GERMANY USA-45 POL/PAR DISCRIM NAT/LISM PEACE RATIONAL ATTIT RIGID/FLEX MARXISM PACIFISM 20. PAGE 95 A1950
NEW/LIB DIPLOM NAT/G POLICY

B64
MORGAN T.,GOLDWATER EITHER/OR; A SELF-PORTRAIT BASED UPON HIS OWN WORDS. USA+45 CONSTN AGRI LABOR DIPLOM RACE/REL WEALTH POPULISM...POLICY MAJORIT 20 GOLDWATR/B REPUBLICAN. PAGE 104 A2131
LEAD POL/PAR CHOOSE ATTIT

B64
NOVE A.,COMMUNISM AT THE CROSSROADS. USSR INT/ORG POL/PAR TOTALISM...POLICY CONCPT 20. PAGE 110 A2259
DIPLOM BAL/PWR MARXISM ORD/FREE

B64
PENNOCK J.R.,SELF-GOVERNMENT IN MODERNIZING
ECO/UNDEV

NATIONS. AFR COM USA+45 ECO/DEV POL/PAR PROB/SOLV DIPLOM ECO/TAC COLONIAL REV POPULISM SOCISM 20. PAGE 114 A2350
POLICY · SOVEREIGN · NAT/G

B64
REUSS H.S.,THE CRITICAL DECADE - AN ECONOMIC POLICY FOR AMERICA AND THE FREE WORLD. USA+45 FINAN POL/PAR WORKER PLAN DIPLOM ECO/TAC TARIFFS BAL/PAY ...POLICY 20 CONGRESS GOLD/STAND. PAGE 120 A2468
FOR/AID · INT/TRADE · LABOR · LEGIS

B64
RICHARDSON I.L.,BIBLIOGRAFIA BRASILEIRA DE ADMINISTRACAO PUBLICA E ASSUNTOS CORRELATOS. BRAZIL CONSTN FINAN LOC/G NAT/G POL/PAR PLAN DIPLOM RECEIVE ATTIT...METH 20. PAGE 121 A2474
BIBLIOG · MGT · ADMIN · LAW

B64
SAKAI R.K.,STUDIES ON ASIA, 1964. ASIA CHINA/COM ISRAEL MALAYSIA S/ASIA USA+45 USSR ECO/UNDEV FAM POL/PAR SECT CONSULT NAT/LISM...POLICY SOC 20 CHINJAP. PAGE 126 A2588
PWR · DIPLOM

B64
SARROS P.P.,CONGRESS AND THE NEW DIPLOMACY: THE FORMULATION OF MUTUAL SECURITY POLICY: 1953-60 (THESIS). USA+45 CHIEF EX/STRUC REGION ROUTINE CHOOSE GOV/REL PEACE ROLE...POLICY 20 PRESIDENT CONGRESS. PAGE 127 A2606
DIPLOM · POL/PAR · NAT/G

L64
POUNDS N.J.G.,"THE POLITICS OF PARTITION." AFR ASIA COM EUR+WWI FUT ISLAM S/ASIA USA-45 LAW ECO/DEV ECO/UNDEV AGRI INDUS INT/ORG POL/PAR PROVS SECT FORCES TOP/EX EDU/PROP LEGIT ATTIT MORAL ORD/FREE PWR RESPECT WEALTH. PAGE 117 A2402
NAT/G · NAT/LISM

S64
DELGADO J.,"EL MOMENTO POLITICO HISPANOAMERICA." CHINA/COM FUT PANAMA USA+45 USSR INT/ORG NAT/G POL/PAR FORCES DOMIN REGION COERCE ATTIT ALL/VALS ...TRADIT CONCPT COLD/WAR 20. PAGE 36 A0728
L/A+17C · EDU/PROP · NAT/LISM

S64
DRAKE S.T.C.,"DEMOCRACY ON TRIAL IN AFRICA." EUR+WWI FUT USA+45 ECO/UNDEV INT/ORG NAT/G POL/PAR TOP/EX EDU/PROP LEGIT ATTIT ALL/VALS...POLICY TREND GEN/LAWS VAL/FREE 20. PAGE 38 A0785
AFR · STERTYP

S64
GARDNER R.N.,"THE SOVIET UNION AND THE UNITED NATIONS." WOR+45 FINAN POL/PAR VOL/ASSN FORCES ECO/TAC DOMIN EDU/PROP LEGIT ADJUD ADMIN ARMS/CONT COERCE ATTIT ALL/VALS...POLICY MAJORIT CONCPT OBS TIME/SEQ TREND STERTYP UN. PAGE 51 A1046
COM · INT/ORG · USSR

S64
HORECKY P.L.,"LIBRARY OF CONGRESS PUBLICATIONS IN AID OF USSR AND EAST EUROPEAN RESEARCH." BULGARIA CZECHOSLVK POLAND USSR YUGOSLAVIA NAT/G POL/PAR DIPLOM ADMIN GOV/REL...CLASSIF 20. PAGE 67 A1382
BIBLIOG/A · COM · MARXISM

S64
SALVADORI M.,"EL CAPITALISMO EN LA EUROPA DE LA POSGUERRA." INT/ORG NAT/G POL/PAR PLAN ECO/TAC ATTIT ORD/FREE WEALTH...HIST/WRIT COLD/WAR EEC 20. PAGE 127 A2596
EUR+WWI · ECO/DEV · CAP/ISM

S64
ZARTMAN I.W.,"LES RELATIONS ENTRE LA FRANCE ET L'ALGERIA DEPUIS LES ACCORDS D'EVIAN." EUR+WWI FUT ISLAM CULTURE AGRI EXTR/IND FINAN INDUS POL/PAR DIPLOM ECO/TAC FOR/AID PEACE ATTIT DRIVE ALL/VALS ...TIME/SEQ VAL/FREE 20. PAGE 169 A3446
ECO/UNDEV · ALGERIA · FRANCE

B65
CBS,CONVERSATIONS WITH WALTER LIPPMANN. USA+45 INT/ORG NAT/G POL/PAR PLAN DIPLOM PWR ALL/IDEOS ...POLICY 20 LIPPMANN/W. PAGE 25 A0509
TV · ATTIT · INT

B65
DOMENACH J.M.,LA PROPAGANDE POLITIQUE. COM/IND INT/ORG POL/PAR DOMIN RIGID/FLEX FASCISM MARXISM ...PSY 20. PAGE 38 A0770
ATTIT · EDU/PROP · TEC/DEV · MYTH

B65
EMERSON R.,THE POLITICAL AWAKENING OF AFRICA. ECO/UNDEV INT/ORG COLONIAL RACE/REL ORD/FREE MARXISM...TREND ANTHOL 20. PAGE 42 A0849
AFR · NAT/LISM · DIPLOM · POL/PAR

B65
GEORGE M.,THE WARPED VISION. EUR+WWI UK NAT/G POL/PAR LEGIS PARL/PROC SANCTION COERCE WAR GOV/REL PEACE RESPECT 20 CONSRV/PAR. PAGE 52 A1061
LEAD · ATTIT · DIPLOM · POLICY

B65
HAIGHT D.E.,THE PRESIDENT; ROLES AND POWERS. USA+45 USA-45 POL/PAR PLAN DIPLOM CHOOSE PERS/REL PWR 18/20 PRESIDENT CONGRESS. PAGE 59 A1217
CHIEF · LEGIS · TOP/EX · EX/STRUC

B65
HALPERIN E.,NATIONALISM AND COMMUNISM. CHILE L/A+17C CAP/ISM EDU/PROP CHOOSE DISCRIM SOCISM ...BIBLIOG 20 COM/PARTY. PAGE 60 A1236
NAT/LISM · MARXISM · POL/PAR · REV

B65
HARMON R.B.,POLITICAL SCIENCE: A BIBLIOGRAPHICAL GUIDE TO THE LITERATURE. WOR+45 WOR-45 R+D INT/ORG LOC/G NAT/G DIPLOM ADMIN...CONCPT METH. PAGE 61 A1261
BIBLIOG · POL/PAR · LAW · GOV/COMP

B65
LEVENSTEIN A.,FREEDOM'S ADVOCATE - A TWENTY-FIVE YEAR CHRONICLE. USA+45 POL/PAR LEGIS DIPLOM WAR PEACE TOTALISM DRIVE MARXISM 20 FREEDOM/HS. PAGE 87 A1791
ORD/FREE · VOL/ASSN · POLICY · ATTIT

B65
LEWIS W.A.,POLITICS IN WEST AFRICA. AFR BAL/PWR DIPLOM REPRESENT...POLICY 20. PAGE 88 A1804
POL/PAR · ELITES · NAT/G · ECO/UNDEV

B65
MEHROTRA S.R.,INDIA AND THE COMMONWEALTH 1885-1929. INDIA UK INT/ORG VOL/ASSN GP/REL ATTIT...POLICY BIBLIOG 19/20 CMN/WLTH. PAGE 99 A2034
DIPLOM · NAT/G · POL/PAR · NAT/LISM

B65
MERKL P.H.,GERMANY: YESTERDAY AND TOMORROW. GERMANY POL/PAR PLAN DIPLOM LEAD FEDERAL 19/20. PAGE 100 A2043
NAT/G · FUT

B65
MUNGER E.S.,NOTES ON THE FORMATION OF SOUTH AFRICAN FOREIGN POLICY. ACADEM POL/PAR SECT CHIEF DELIB/GP FORCES LEGIS PRESS ATTIT...TREND 20 NEGRO. PAGE 106 A2170
AFR · DOMIN · POLICY · DIPLOM

B65
ROSENBERG A.,DEMOCRACY AND SOCIALISM. COM EUR+WWI FRANCE MOD/EUR STRUCT INT/ORG NAT/G POL/PAR TOP/EX EDU/PROP COERCE PERSON PWR FASCISM MARXISM...CONCPT TIME/SEQ MARX/KARL 19/20. PAGE 124 A2535
ATTIT

B65
SABLE M.H.,MASTER DIRECTORY FOR LATIN AMERICA. AGRI COM/IND FINAN R+D ACADEM LABOR NAT/G POL/PAR VOL/ASSN INT/TRADE EDU/PROP 20. PAGE 126 A2582
INDEX · L/A+17C · INT/ORG · DIPLOM

B65
SOPER T.,EVOLVING COMMONWEALTH. AFR CANADA INDIA IRELAND UK LAW CONSTN POL/PAR DOMIN CONTROL WAR PWR ...AUD/VIS 18/20 COMMONWLTH OEEC. PAGE 135 A2769
INT/ORG · COLONIAL · VOL/ASSN

B65
WINT G.,COMMUNIST CHINA'S CRUSADE: MAO'S ROAD TO POWER AND THE NEW CAMPAIGN FOR WORLD REVOLUTION. ASIA CHINA/COM USA+45 USSR NAT/G POL/PAR DOMIN COERCE WAR PWR...POLICY CHARTS IDEA/COMP BIBLIOG 20 MAO. PAGE 165 A3364
DIPLOM · MARXISM · REV · COLONIAL

L65
MATTHEWS D.G.,"A CURRENT BIBLIOGRAPHY ON ETHIOPIAN AFFAIRS: A SELECT BIBLIOGRAPHY FROM 1950-1964." ETHIOPIA LAW CULTURE ECO/UNDEV INDUS LABOR SECT FORCES DIPLOM CIVMIL/REL RACE/REL...LING STAT 20. PAGE 96 A1969
BIBLIOG/A · ADMIN · POL/PAR · NAT/G

L65
MATTHEWS D.G.,"A CURRENT BIBLIOGRAPHY ON SUDANESE AFFAIRS; A SELECT BIBLIOGRAPHY FROM 1960-1964." SUDAN LAW CULTURE AGRI FINAN INDUS LABOR POL/PAR TEC/DEV FOR/AID RACE/REL LITERACY...LING 20. PAGE 96 A1970
BIBLIOG · ECO/UNDEV · NAT/G · DIPLOM

S65
RODNEY W.,"THE ENTENTE STATES OF WEST AFRICA." AFR FRANCE USA+45 POL/PAR SCHOOL FORCES ECO/TAC COLONIAL PWR 20 AFRICA/W. PAGE 123 A2512
DIPLOM · POLICY · NAT/G · ECO/UNDEV

S65
SCHNEIDER R.M.,"THE US IN LATIN AMERICA." L/A+17C USA+45 NAT/G POL/PAR PLAN RIGID/FLEX ALL/VALS OAS 20. PAGE 129 A2640
VOL/ASSN · ECO/UNDEV · FOR/AID

C65
WUORINEN J.H.,"SCANDINAVIA." DENMARK FINLAND ICELAND NORWAY SWEDEN SOCIETY AGRI POL/PAR DELIB/GP DIPLOM INT/TRADE NEUTRAL WAR...CHARTS TREATY 20. PAGE 168 A3423
BIBLIOG · NAT/G · POLICY

B66
BERNSTEIN B.J.,THE TRUMAN ADMINISTRATION. WOR+45 LABOR POL/PAR LEGIS DIPLOM NUC/PWR WAR ATTIT ...POLICY 20 TRUMAN/HS. PAGE 14 A0279
LEAD · TOP/EX · NAT/G

B66
BROWN J.F.,THE NEW EASTERN EUROPE. ALBANIA BULGARIA HUNGARY POLAND ROMANIA CULTURE AGRI POL/PAR WAR NAT/LISM MARXISM...CHARTS BIBLIOG 20. PAGE 20 A0404
DIPLOM · COM · NAT/G · ECO/UNDEV

B66
BROWN L.C.,STATE AND SOCIETY IN INDEPENDENT NORTH AFRICA. ALGERIA LIBYA MOROCCO AGRI INDUS INT/ORG POL/PAR SECT PLAN DIPLOM COLONIAL...LING NAT/COMP ANTHOL BIBLIOG 20 TUNIS MUSLIM. PAGE 20 A0406
NAT/G · SOCIETY · CULTURE · ECO/UNDEV

B66
COLE A.B.,SOCIALIST PARTIES IN POSTWAR JAPAN. STRATA AGRI LABOR PLAN DIPLOM ECO/TAC AGREE LEAD CHOOSE ATTIT...CHARTS 20 CHINJAP SOC/DEMPAR. PAGE 28 A0566
POL/PAR · POLICY · SOCISM · NAT/G

B66
EPSTEIN F.T.,THE AMERICAN BIBLIOGRAPHY OF RUSSIAN AND EAST EUROPEAN STUDIES FOR 1964. USSR LOC/G NAT/G POL/PAR FORCES ADMIN ARMS/CONT...JURID CONCPT 20 UN. PAGE 42 A0855
BIBLIOG · COM · MARXISM · DIPLOM

B66
EUDIN X.J.,SOVIET FOREIGN POLICY 1928-34: DOCUMENTS
DIPLOM

AND MATERIALS (VOL. I). ASIA USSR WOR-45 INT/ORG POL/PAR WORKER WAR PEACE...ANTHOL 20 TREATY LEAGUE/NAT INTERVENT. PAGE 43 A0873
POLICY GOV/REL MARXISM

B66
HARMON R.B.,SOURCES AND PROBLEMS OF BIBLIOGRAPHY IN POLITICAL SCIENCE (PAMPHLET). INT/ORG LOC/G MUNIC POL/PAR ADMIN GOV/REL ALL/IDEOS...JURID MGT CONCPT 19/20. PAGE 61 A1262
BIBLIOG DIPLOM INT/LAW NAT/G

B66
HENKYS R.,DEUTSCHLAND UND DIE OSTLICHEN NACHBARN. GERMANY POLAND NAT/G POL/PAR INGP/REL ATTIT 20 MIGRATION. PAGE 64 A1317
GP/REL JURID INT/LAW DIPLOM

B66
LATHAM E.,THE COMMUNIST CONTROVERSY IN WASHINGTON. USA+45 USA-45 DELIB/GP EX/STRUC LEGIS DIPLOM NAT/LISM MARXISM 20. PAGE 85 A1742
POL/PAR TOTALISM ORD/FREE NAT/G

B66
MOORE R.J.,SIR CHARLES WOOD'S INDIAN POLICY: 1853-66. INDIA POL/PAR CHIEF DELIB/GP DIPLOM CONTROL LEAD WOOD/CHAS. PAGE 103 A2124
COLONIAL ADMIN CONSULT DECISION

B66
MORRIS B.S.,INTERNATIONAL COMMUNISM AND AMERICAN POLICY. CHINA/COM USA+45 USSR INT/ORG POL/PAR GP/REL NAT/LISM ATTIT PERCEPT 20. PAGE 105 A2147
DIPLOM POLICY MARXISM

B66
NEUMANN R.G.,THE GOVERNMENT OF THE GERMAN FEDERAL REPUBLIC. EUR+WWI GERMANY/W LOC/G EX/STRUC LEGIS CT/SYS INGP/REL PWR...BIBLIOG 20 ADENAUER/K. PAGE 108 A2222
NAT/G POL/PAR DIPLOM CONSTN

B66
RIESELBACH L.N.,THE ROOTS OF ISOLATIONISM* CONGRESSIONAL VOTING AND PRESIDENTIAL LEADERSHIP IN FOREIGN POLICY. POL/PAR LEGIS DIPLOM EDU/PROP LEAD REGION REPRESENT...SOC STAT IDEA/COMP HYPO/EXP BIBLIOG 19/20 CONGRESS. PAGE 121 A2477
ISOLAT CHOOSE CHIEF POLICY

B66
SAGER P.,MOSKAUS HAND IN INDIEN. INDIA USSR DIPLOM DOMIN...PSY CONCPT 20 COM/PARTY. PAGE 126 A2586
PRESS EDU/PROP METH POL/PAR

B66
SPINELLI A.,THE EUROCRATS; CONFLICT AND CRISIS IN THE EUROPEAN COMMUNITY (TRANS. BY C. GROVE HAINES). EUR+WWI MARKET POL/PAR ECO/TAC PARL/PROC EEC OEEC ECSC EURATOM. PAGE 136 A2789
INT/ORG INGP/REL CONSTN ADMIN

B66
US DEPARTMENT OF STATE,RESEARCH ON AFRICA (EXTERNAL RESEARCH LIST NO 5-25). LAW CULTURE ECO/UNDEV POL/PAR DIPLOM EDU/PROP LEAD REGION MARXISM...GEOG LING WORSHIP 20. PAGE 152 A3094
BIBLIOG/A ASIA S/ASIA NAT/G

B66
US DEPARTMENT OF STATE,RESEARCH ON THE AMERICAN REPUBLICS (EXTERNAL RESEARCH LIST NO 6-25). CULTURE SOCIETY POL/PAR DIPLOM EDU/PROP MARXISM WORSHIP 20 OAS. PAGE 152 A3095
BIBLIOG/A L/A+17C REGION NAT/G

B66
US DEPARTMENT OF STATE,RESEARCH ON THE MIDDLE EAST (EXTERNAL RESEARCH LIST NO 4-25). GREECE ISRAEL SYRIA UAR YEMEN CULTURE SOCIETY POL/PAR SECT DIPLOM EDU/PROP WAR NAT/LISM...GEOG GOV/COMP 20. PAGE 152 A3096
BIBLIOG/A ISLAM NAT/G REGION

B66
US DEPARTMENT OF STATE,RESEARCH ON WESTERN EUROPE, GREAT BRITAIN, AND CANADA (EXTERNAL RESEARCH LIST NO 3-25). CANADA GERMANY/W UK LAW CULTURE NAT/G POL/PAR FORCES EDU/PROP REGION MARXISM...GEOG SOC WORSHIP 20 CMN/WLTH. PAGE 152 A3098
BIBLIOG/A EUR+WWI DIPLOM

B66
US DEPARTMENT OF THE ARMY,COMMUNIST CHINA: A STRATEGIC SURVEY: A BIBLIOGRAPHY (PAMPHLET NO. 20-67). CHINA/COM COM INDIA USSR NAT/G POL/PAR EX/STRUC FORCES NUC/PWR REV ATTIT...POLICY GEOG CHARTS. PAGE 152 A3109
BIBLIOG/A MARXISM S/ASIA DIPLOM

B66
US DEPARTMENT OF THE ARMY,SOUTH ASIA: A STRATEGIC SURVEY (PAMPHLET NO. 550-3). AFGHANISTN INDIA NEPAL PAKISTAN ECO/UNDEV INT/ORG POL/PAR FORCES FOR/AID INT/TRADE LEAD WAR...POLICY SOC TREND 20. PAGE 152 A3110
BIBLIOG/A S/ASIA DIPLOM NAT/G

B66
WELCH R.H.W.,THE NEW AMERICANISM, AND OTHER SPEECHES AND ESSAYS. USA+45 ACADEM POL/PAR SCHOOL VOL/ASSN FORCES CAP/ISM TAX REV DISCRIM 20 CIV/RIGHTS COLD/WAR BIRCH/SOC. PAGE 163 A3313
DIPLOM FASCISM MARXISM RACE/REL

B66
WESTIN A.F.,VIEWS OF AMERICA. COM USA+45 USSR SOCIETY ECO/UNDEV POL/PAR ECO/TAC GP/REL STRANGE MARXISM...MARXIST 20. PAGE 163 A3323
CONCPT ATTIT DIPLOM IDEA/COMP

B66
ZABLOCKI C.J.,SINO-SOVIET RIVALRY. AFR ASIA CHINA/COM CUBA EUR+WWI L/A+17C USA+45 USSR WOR+45 POL/PAR FORCES COERCE NUC/PWR...GOV/COMP IDEA/COMP 20 MAO KHRUSH/N. PAGE 169 A3442
DIPLOM MARXISM COM

S66
"RESEARCH WORK 1965-1966." NEW/ZEALND ELITES ACADEM LOC/G MUNIC POL/PAR PROVS DIPLOM COLONIAL...SOC 20 AUSTRAL. PAGE 4 A0073
BIBLIOG NAT/G CULTURE S/ASIA

S66
AFRICAN BIBLIOGRAPHIC CENTER,"A CURRENT VIEW OF AFRICANA: A SELECT AND ANNOTATED BIBLIOGRAPHICAL PUBLISHING GUIDE, 1965-1966." AFR CULTURE INDUS LABOR SECT FOR/AID ADMIN COLONIAL REV RACE/REL SOCISM...LING 20. PAGE 5 A0098
BIBLIOG/A NAT/G TEC/DEV POL/PAR

S66
GAMER R.E.,"URGENT SINGAPORE, PATIENT MALAYSIA." MALAYSIA S/ASIA ECO/UNDEV POL/PAR CHIEF TARIFFS TAX CONTROL LEAD REGION PWR 20 SINGAPORE. PAGE 51 A1036
DIPLOM NAT/G POLICY ECO/TAC

S66
JAVITS J.K.,"POLITICAL ACTION VITAL FOR LATIN AMERICAN INTEGRATION." ECO/UNDEV INT/ORG POL/PAR VOL/ASSN PLAN PROB/SOLV INT/TRADE EFFICIENCY 20 OAS LAFTA. PAGE 73 A1500
L/A+17C ECO/TAC REGION

S66
MANSERGH N.,"THE PARTITION OF INDIA IN RETROSPECT." INDIA PAKISTAN S/ASIA UK DIPLOM COLONIAL GP/REL PWR 20. PAGE 94 A1933
NAT/G PARL/PROC POLICY POL/PAR

S66
MATTHEWS D.G.,"ETHIOPIAN OUTLINE: A BIBLIOGRAPHIC RESEARCH GUIDE." ETHIOPIA LAW STRUCT ECO/UNDEV AGRI LABOR SECT CHIEF DELIB/GP EX/STRUC ADMIN...LING ORG/CHARTS 20. PAGE 96 A1972
BIBLIOG NAT/G DIPLOM POL/PAR

S66
MCNEAL R.H.,"THE LEGACY OF THE COMINTERN." USSR WOR+45 WOR-45 PROB/SOLV DIPLOM CONFER CONTROL LEAD WAR 20 STALIN/J COMINTERN. PAGE 98 A2020
MARXISM INT/ORG POL/PAR PWR

C66
KULSKI W.W.,"DEGAULLE AND THE WORLD: THE FOREIGN POLICY OF THE FIFTH FRENCH REPUBLIC." FRANCE ECO/UNDEV POL/PAR BAL/PWR DETER NUC/PWR ATTIT PWR ...RECORD BIBLIOG DEGAULLE NATO EEC. PAGE 83 A1694
POLICY SOVEREIGN PERSON DIPLOM

C66
TARLING N.,"A CONCISE HISTORY OF SOUTHEAST ASIA." BURMA CAMBODIA LAOS S/ASIA THAILAND VIETNAM ECO/UNDEV POL/PAR FORCES ADMIN REV WAR CIVMIL/REL ORD/FREE MARXISM SOCISM 13/20. PAGE 141 A2890
COLONIAL DOMIN INT/TRADE NAT/LISM

B67
ATTWOOD W.,THE REDS AND THE BLACKS. AFR POL/PAR CHOOSE GOV/REL RACE/REL NAT/LISM...BIOG 20. PAGE 10 A0195
DIPLOM PWR MARXISM

B67
BRZEZINSKI Z.K.,IDEOLOGY AND POWER IN SOVIET POLITICS. USSR NAT/G POL/PAR PWR...GEN/LAWS 19/20. PAGE 21 A0419
DIPLOM EX/STRUC MARXISM

B67
DOSSICK J.J.,DOCTORAL RESEARCH ON PUERTO RICO AND PUERTO RICANS. PUERT/RICO USA+45 USA-45 ADMIN 20. PAGE 38 A0776
BIBLIOG CONSTN POL/PAR DIPLOM

B67
FINE S.,RECENT AMERICA* CONFLICTING INTERPRETATIONS OF THE GREAT ISSUES (2ND ED.). USA+45 USA-45 POL/PAR SECT CONFER NUC/PWR WAR ATTIT...POLICY TREND ANTHOL PRESIDENT 20. PAGE 46 A0931
IDEA/COMP DIPLOM NAT/G

B67
KAROL K.S.,CHINA, THE OTHER COMMUNISM (TRANS. BY TOM BAISTOW). CHINA/COM CULTURE INDUS FORCES DIPLOM EDU/PROP CONTROL EXEC NUC/PWR ATTIT...SOC CHARTS 20. PAGE 77 A1567
NAT/G POL/PAR MARXISM INGP/REL

B67
KATZ R.,DEATH IN ROME. EUR+WWI ITALY POL/PAR DIPLOM LEAD ATTIT PERSON ROLE CATHISM. PAGE 77 A1570
WAR MURDER FORCES DEATH

B67
KIRK R.,THE POLITICAL PRINCIPLES OF ROBERT A. TAFT. USA+45 LABOR DIPLOM ADJUD ADJUST ORD/FREE TAFT/RA. PAGE 80 A1635
POL/PAR LEAD LEGIS ATTIT

B67
O'LEARY M.K.,THE POLITICS OF AMERICAN FOREIGN AID. USA+45 POL/PAR CHIEF BUDGET EDU/PROP LOBBY CONGRESS. PAGE 111 A2270
FOR/AID DIPLOM PARL/PROC ATTIT

B67
ROSENAU J.N.,DOMESTIC SOURCES OF FOREIGN POLICY. WOR+45 STRATA COM/IND MUNIC POL/PAR LOBBY PARTIC REGION ATTIT...PSY SOC COLD/WAR. PAGE 124 A2534
DIPLOM POLICY NAT/G CHOOSE

B67
SABLE M.H.,A GUIDE TO LATIN AMERICAN STUDIES (2 VOLS). CONSTN FINAN INT/ORG LABOR MUNIC POL/PAR FORCES CAP/ISM FOR/AID ADMIN MARXISM SOCISM OAS. PAGE 126 A2584
BIBLIOG/A L/A+17C DIPLOM NAT/LISM

B67
SACHS M.Y.,THE WORLDMARK ENCYCLOPEDIA OF THE NATIONS (5 VOLS.). ELITES SOCIETY STRATA ECO/DEV ECO/UNDEV AGRI EXTR/IND FINAN LABOR LOC/G NAT/G POL/PAR SECT INT/TRADE SOVEREIGN...SOC 20. PAGE 126 A2585 — WOR+45 INT/ORG BAL/PWR

B67
SAYEED K.B.,THE POLITICAL SYSTEM OF PAKISTAN. PAKISTAN DIPLOM REGION CHOOSE ORD/FREE...BIBLIOG 20. PAGE 127 A2609 — NAT/G POL/PAR CONSTN SECT

B67
SCHWARTZ M.A.,PUBLIC OPINION AND CANADIAN IDENTITY. CANADA SOCIETY LOC/G DIPLOM ADMIN LEAD REGION GP/REL SAMP. PAGE 130 A2657 — ATTIT NAT/G NAT/LISM POL/PAR

B67
STEVENS R.P.,LESOTHO, BATSWANA, AND SWAZILAND* THE FORMER HIGH COMMISSION TERRITORIES IN SOUTHERN AFRICA. ECO/DEV KIN POL/PAR HIST/WRIT. PAGE 138 A2821 — COLONIAL DIPLOM ORD/FREE

B67
THORNE C.,THE APPROACH OF WAR, 1938-1939. EUR+WWI POL/PAR CHIEF FORCES LEAD DRIVE PWR FASCISM ...BIBLIOG/A 20 HITLER/A. PAGE 144 A2936 — DIPLOM WAR ELITES

B67
WILLIS F.R.,DE GAULLE: ANACHRONISM, REALIST, OR PROPHET? FRANCE POL/PAR FORCES DIPLOM WAR PEACE ROLE ORD/FREE...POLICY IDEA/COMP ANTHOL 20 DEGAULLE/C. PAGE 165 A3356 — BIOG PERSON CHIEF LEAD

B67
YAMAMURA K.,ECONOMIC POLICY IN POSTWAR JAPAN. ASIA FINAN POL/PAR DIPLOM LEAD NAT/LISM ATTIT NEW/LIB POPULISM 20 CHINJAP. PAGE 168 A3429 — ECO/DEV POLICY NAT/G TEC/DEV

L67
"POLITICAL PARTIES ON FOREIGN POLICY IN THE INTER-ELECTION YEARS 1962-66." ASIA COM INDIA USA+45 PLAN ATTIT...DECISION 20. PAGE 4 A0079 — POL/PAR DIPLOM POLICY

S67
AFRICAN BIBLIOGRAPHIC CENTER,"THE SWORD AND GOVERNMENT: A PRELIMINARY AND SELECTED BIBLIOGRAPHICAL GUIDE TO AFRICAN MILITARY AFFAIRS; PART I." AFR USA+45 USSR INT/ORG POL/PAR FOR/AID COLONIAL ARMS/CONT PWR 20 UN. PAGE 5 A0101 — BIBLIOG/A FORCES CIVMIL/REL DIPLOM

S67
APEL H.,"LES NOUVEAUX ASPECTS DE LA POLITIQUE ETRANGERE ALLEMANDE." EUR+WWI GERMANY POL/PAR BAL/PWR ECO/TAC INT/TRADE NUC/PWR NAT/LISM PEACE ...POLICY 20 EEC COLD/WAR. PAGE 8 A0168 — DIPLOM INT/ORG FEDERAL

S67
BREGMAN A.,"WHITHER RUSSIA?" COM RUSSIA INTELL POL/PAR DIPLOM PARTIC NAT/LISM TOTALISM ATTIT ORD/FREE 20. PAGE 18 A0370 — MARXISM ELITES ADMIN CREATE

S67
BURNS E.B.,"TRADITIONS AND VARIATIONS IN BRAZILIAN FOREIGN POLICY." BRAZIL L/A+17C POL/PAR INT/TRADE COLONIAL INGP/REL ATTIT ORD/FREE PWR 20. PAGE 22 A0443 — DIPLOM NAT/LISM CREATE

S67
BUTT R.,"THE COMMON MARKET AND CONSERVATIVE POLITICS, 1961-2." UK CHIEF DIPLOM ECO/TAC INT/TRADE CONFER DEBATE REGION ATTIT...POLICY 20 EEC. PAGE 22 A0454 — EUR+WWI INT/ORG POL/PAR

S67
HEATH D.B.,"BOLIVIA UNDER BARRIENTOS." L/A+17C NAT/G CHIEF DIPLOM ECO/TAC...POLICY 20 BOLIV. PAGE 64 A1306 — ECO/UNDEV POL/PAR REV CONSTN

S67
JOHNSON J.,"THE UNITED STATES AND THE LATIN AMERICAN LEFT WINGS." L/A+17C STRATA POL/PAR INT/TRADE 20. PAGE 74 A1524 — ECO/UNDEV WORKER ECO/TAC REGION

S67
KIERNAN V.G.,"INDIA AND THE LABOUR PARTY." INDIA UK CAP/ISM GP/REL EFFICIENCY NAT/LISM PWR SOCISM ...SOCIALIST TIME/SEQ 20. PAGE 79 A1616 — COLONIAL DIPLOM POL/PAR ECO/UNDEV

S67
MUDGE G.A.,"DOMESTIC POLICIES AND UN ACTIVITIES* THE CASE OF RHODESIA AND THE REPUBLIC OF SOUTH AFRICA." RHODESIA SOUTH/AFR POL/PAR LEAD SANCTION CHOOSE RACE/REL CONSEN DISCRIM ATTIT...INT/LAW UN PARLIAMENT 20. PAGE 105 A2163 — AFR NAT/G POLICY

S67
PAUKER G.J.,"TOWARD A NEW ORDER IN INDONESIA." COM INDONESIA S/ASIA ECO/UNDEV POL/PAR EX/STRUC TOP/EX BAL/PWR ECO/TAC FOR/AID DOMIN NAT/LISM AUTHORIT ORD/FREE PWR 20. PAGE 114 A2342 — REV NAT/G DIPLOM CIVMIL/REL

S67
SENCOURT R.,"FOREIGN POLICY* AN HISTORIC RECTIFICATION." EUR+WWI UK DIPLOM EDU/PROP LEAD WAR CHOOSE PERS/REL...METH/COMP PARLIAMENT. PAGE 131 A2685 — POLICY POL/PAR NAT/G

S67
SOMMER T.,"BONN CHANGES COURSE." GERMANY/W NAT/G POL/PAR PROB/SOLV NAT/LISM 20 NATO BERLIN/BLO. PAGE 135 A2766 — DIPLOM BAL/PWR INT/ORG

S67
SPENCER R.,"GERMANY AFTER THE AUTUMN CRISIS." GERMANY CHOOSE GP/REL PERS/REL. PAGE 136 A2785 — DIPLOM POL/PAR PROB/SOLV

S67
WILPERT C.,"A LOOK IN THE MIRROR AND OVER THE WALL." GERMANY POL/PAR...KNO/TEST COLD/WAR. PAGE 165 A3358 — NAT/G PLAN DIPLOM ATTIT

S67
YEFROMEV A.,"THE TRUE FACE OF THE WEST GERMAN NATIONAL-DEMOCRATS." GERMANY/W NAT/G DOMIN LEAD SANCTION WAR ATTIT PERSON...MARXIST 20. PAGE 169 A3433 — POL/PAR TOTALISM PARL/PROC DIPLOM

C67
LING D.L.,"TUNISIA: FROM PROTECTORATE TO REPUBLIC." CULTURE NAT/G POL/PAR CHIEF DIPLOM COERCE WAR PWR ...BIBLIOG 19/20 TUNIS. PAGE 89 A1825 — AFR NAT/LISM COLONIAL PROB/SOLV

B96
LOWELL A.L.,GOVERNMENTS AND PARTIES IN CONTINENTAL EUROPE, VOL. II. AUSTRIA GERMANY HUNGARY MOD/EUR SWITZERLND SOCIETY EX/STRUC LEGIS DIPLOM AGREE LEAD PARL/PROC PWR...POLICY 19. PAGE 91 A1867 — POL/PAR NAT/G GOV/REL ELITES

POLAND....SEE ALSO COM

N
KYRIAK T.E.,EAST EUROPE: BIBLIOGRAPHY--INDEX TO US JPRS RESEARCH TRANSLATIONS. ALBANIA BULGARIA COM CZECHOSLVK HUNGARY POLAND ROMANIA AGRI EXTR/IND FINAN SERV/IND INT/TRADE WEAPON...GEOG MGT SOC 20. PAGE 83 A1701 — BIBLIOG/A PRESS MARXISM INDUS

B18
KERNER R.J.,SLAVIC EUROPE: A SELECTED BIBLIOGRAPHY IN THE WESTERN EUROPEAN LANGUAGES. BULGARIA CZECHOSLVK GERMANY/E POLAND RUSSIA YUGOSLAVIA NAT/G DIPLOM MARXISM...LING 19/20. PAGE 78 A1598 — BIBLIOG SOCIETY CULTURE COM

B45
GALLOWAY E.,ABSTRACTS OF POSTWAR LITERATURE (VOL. IV) JAN.-JULY, 1945 NOS. 901-1074. POLAND USA+45 USSR WOR+45 INDUS LABOR PLAN ECO/TAC INT/TRADE TAX EDU/PROP ADMIN COLONIAL INT/LAW. PAGE 51 A1033 — BIBLIOG/A NUC/PWR NAT/G DIPLOM

B45
HORN O.B.,BRITISH PUBLIC OPINION AND THE FIRST PARTITION OF POLAND. POLAND UK LEGIS PRESS RUMOR CONTROL PARTIC NAT/LISM SOVEREIGN 18/19. PAGE 67 A1385 — DIPLOM POLICY ATTIT NAT/G

B48
NAMIER L.B.,DIPLOMATIC PRELUDE 1938-1939. CZECHOSLVK EUR+WWI GERMANY POLAND UK FORCES DOMIN PWR 20 HITLER/A. PAGE 107 A2193 — WAR TOTALISM DIPLOM

B54
REYNOLDS P.A.,BRITISH FOREIGN POLICY IN THE INTER-WAR YEARS. CZECHOSLVK GERMANY POLAND UK USA-45 POL/PAR FORCES ECO/TAC ARMS/CONT WAR ATTIT 20. PAGE 120 A2470 — DIPLOM POLICY NAT/G

S58
STAAR R.F.,"ELECTIONS IN COMMUNIST POLAND." EUR+WWI SOCIETY INT/ORG NAT/G POL/PAR LEGIS ACT/RES ECO/TAC EDU/PROP ADJUD ADMIN ROUTINE COERCE TOTALISM ATTIT ORD/FREE PWR 20. PAGE 137 A2797 — COM CHOOSE POLAND

B59
ETSCHMANN R.,DIE WAHRUNGS- UND DEVISENPOLITIK DES OSTBLOCKS UND IHRE AUSWIRKUNGEN AUF DIE WIRTSCHAFTSBEZIEHUNGEN ZWISCHEN OST U WEST. BULGARIA CZECHOSLVK HUNGARY POLAND USSR MARKET NAT/G PLAN DIPLOM...NAT/COMP 20. PAGE 42 A0867 — ECO/TAC FINAN POLICY INT/TRADE

B61
FLEMING D.F.,THE COLD WAR AND ITS ORIGINS: 1950-1960 (VOL. II). ASIA FUT HUNGARY POLAND WOR+45 TEC/DEV DOMIN NUC/PWR REV PEACE...T 20 COLD/WAR EISNHWR/DD SUEZ. PAGE 46 A0946 — MARXISM DIPLOM BAL/PWR

B62
STARR R.E.,POLAND 1944-1962: THE SOVIETIZATION OF A CAPTIVE PEOPLE. COM POLAND USSR POL/PAR SECT LEGIS DIPLOM DOMIN EDU/PROP CHOOSE ORD/FREE...POLICY CHARTS BIBLIOG 20. PAGE 137 A2808 — MARXISM NAT/G TOTALISM NAT/COMP

B63
DRACHKOVITCH,UNITED STATES AID TO YUGOSLAVIA AND POLAND. POLAND USA+45 YUGOSLAVIA LEGIS EXEC TOTALISM MARXISM 20 CONGRESS. PAGE 38 A0782 — FOR/AID POLICY DIPLOM ATTIT

B63
FRANZ G.,TEILUNG UND WIEDERVEREINIGUNG. GERMANY IRELAND ITALY NETHERLAND POLAND CULTURE BAL/PWR CHOOSE NAT/LISM ORD/FREE SOVEREIGN 19/20. PAGE 48 A0987 — DIPLOM WAR NAT/COMP ATTIT

B63
KORBEL J.,POLAND BETWEEN EAST AND WEST: SOVIET AND GERMAN DIPLOMACY TOWARD POLAND 1919-1933. EUR+WWI GERMANY POLAND USSR FORCES AGREE WAR SOVEREIGN — BAL/PWR DIPLOM DOMIN

...BIBLIOG 20 TREATY. PAGE 81 A1670 NAT/LISM

B63
MOSELY P.E.,THE SOVIET UNION, 1922-1962: A FOREIGN AFFAIRS READER. ASIA POLAND USSR CULTURE INTELL AGRI POL/PAR WORKER INT/TRADE DOMIN WAR NAT/LISM MARXISM SOCISM 20 KHRUSH/N. PAGE 105 A2152 PWR POLICY DIPLOM

B63
RAVENS J.P.,STAAT UND KATHOLISCHE KIRCHE IN PREUSSENS POLNISCHEN TEILUNGSGEBIETEN. GERMANY POLAND PRUSSIA PROVS DIPLOM EDU/PROP DEBATE NAT/LISM...JURID 18 CHURCH/STA. PAGE 119 A2451 GP/REL CATHISM SECT NAT/G

S64
HORECKY P.L.,"LIBRARY OF CONGRESS PUBLICATIONS IN AID OF USSR AND EAST EUROPEAN RESEARCH." BULGARIA CZECHOSLVK POLAND USSR YUGOSLAVIA NAT/G POL/PAR DIPLOM ADMIN GOV/REL...CLASSIF 20. PAGE 67 A1382 BIBLIOG/A COM MARXISM

B65
SCHREIBER H.,TEUTON AND SLAV - THE STRUGGLE FOR CENTRAL EUROPE (TRANS. BY J. CLEUGH). GERMANY POLAND PRUSSIA USSR SOCIETY STRUCT SECT DIPLOM BALTIC. PAGE 129 A2646 GP/REL WAR RACE/REL NAT/LISM

B66
BROWN J.F.,THE NEW EASTERN EUROPE. ALBANIA BULGARIA HUNGARY POLAND ROMANIA CULTURE AGRI POL/PAR WAR NAT/LISM MARXISM...CHARTS BIBLIOG 20. PAGE 20 A0404 DIPLOM COM NAT/G ECO/UNDEV

B66
HENKYS R.,DEUTSCHLAND UND DIE OSTLICHEN NACHBARN. GERMANY POLAND NAT/G POL/PAR INGP/REL ATTIT 20 MIGRATION. PAGE 64 A1317 GP/REL JURID INT/LAW DIPLOM

B66
HERZ M.F.,BEGINNINGS OF THE COLD WAR. COM POLAND USA+45 USSR INT/ORG NAT/G CHIEF FOR/AID DOMIN CONFER AGREE WAR PEACE 20 STALIN/J COLD/WAR UN. PAGE 64 A1321 DIPLOM

B66
SPULBER N.,THE STATE AND ECONOMIC DEVELOPMENT IN EASTERN EUROPE. BULGARIA COM CZECHOSLVK HUNGARY POLAND YUGOSLAVIA CULTURE PLAN CAP/ISM INT/TRADE CONTROL...POLICY CHARTS METH/COMP BIBLIOG/A 19/20. PAGE 136 A2793 ECO/DEV ECO/UNDEV NAT/G TOTALISM

B67
BRZEZINSKI Z.K.,THE SOVIET BLOC: UNITY AND CONFLICT (2ND ED., REV., ENLARGED). COM POLAND USSR INTELL CHIEF EX/STRUC CONTROL EXEC GOV/REL PWR MARXISM ...TREND IDEA/COMP 20 LENIN/VI MARX/KARL STALIN/J. PAGE 21 A0420 NAT/G DIPLOM

L67
KOMESAR N.K.,"PRESIDENTIAL AMENDMENT & TERMINATION OF TREATIES* THE CASE OF THE WARSAW CONVENTION." POLAND USA+45 NAT/G CHIEF PROB/SOLV DIPLOM PWR 20 CONGRESS. PAGE 81 A1669 TOP/EX LEGIS CONSTN LICENSE

POLICE....SEE FORCES

POLICY....ETHICS OF PUBLIC POLICIES

POLIT/ACTN....POLITICAL ACTION COMMITTEE

POLITBURO....POLITBURO (U.S.S.R.)

POLITICAL BEHAVIOR....SEE POL

POLITICAL FINANCING....SEE POL+FINAN

POLITICAL MACHINE....SEE POL+ADMIN

POLITICAL MOVEMENT....SEE IDEOLOGICAL TOPIC INDEX

POLITICAL ORGANIZATION....SEE POL/PAR

POLITICAL PROCESS....SEE LEGIS, POL

POLITICAL SCIENCE....SEE POL

POLITICAL SYSTEMS....SEE IDEOLOGICAL TOPIC INDEX

POLITICAL SYSTEMS THEORY....SEE GEN/LAWS+NET/THEORY+POL

POLITICAL THEORY....SEE IDEOLOGICAL TOPIC INDEX

POLITICS....SEE POL

POLK/JAMES....PRESIDENT JAMES POLK

POLLACK N. A0995

POLLACK R.S. A2394

POLLACK/N....NORMAN POLLACK

POLLUTION....AIR OR WATER POLLUTION

POLYNESIA....POLYNESIA

POOLE D.C. A2395

POOLE W.F. A2396

POONA....POONA, INDIA

POPE....POPE

POPPER/K....KARL POPPER

POPULATION....SEE GEOG, CENSUS

POPULISM....MAJORITARIANISM

N17
BURKE E.,THOUGHTS ON THE PROSPECT OF A REGICIDE PEACE (PAMPHLET). FRANCE UK SECT DOMIN MURDER PEACE ORD/FREE SOVEREIGN POPULISM...POLICY GOV/COMP IDEA/COMP 18 JACOBINISM COEXIST. PAGE 21 A0435 REV CHIEF NAT/G DIPLOM

B33
FERRERO G.,PEACE AND WAR (TRANS. BY BERTHA PRITCHARD). CULTURE FINAN SECT ATTIT SUPEGO MORAL ORD/FREE CONSERVE POPULISM SOCISM POLICY. PAGE 45 A0922 WAR PEACE DIPLOM PROB/SOLV

B35
MARRIOTT J.A.,DICTATORSHIP AND DEMOCRACY. GERMANY GREECE UK CHIEF DIPLOM DOMIN LEGIT PEACE ORD/FREE CONSERVE...TREND ROME HITLER/A. PAGE 95 A1946 TOTALISM POPULISM PLURIST NAT/G

B46
BLUM L.,FOR ALL MANKIND (TRANS. BY W. PICKLES). FRANCE GERMANY USSR LAW SOCIETY STRUCT POL/PAR WORKER DIPLOM DOMIN CHOOSE ORD/FREE FASCISM 20. PAGE 16 A0323 POPULISM SOCIALIST NAT/G WAR

B47
NIEBUHR R.,THE CHILDREN OF LIGHT AND THE CHILDREN OF DARKNESS: A VINDICATION OF DEMOCRACY AND CRITIQUE OF TRADITIONAL DEFENSE. UNIV STRUCT NAT/G SECT INGP/REL OWN PEACE ORD/FREE MARXISM ...IDEA/COMP GEN/LAWS 20 CHRISTIAN. PAGE 109 A2235 POPULISM DIPLOM NEIGH GP/REL

B48
DURBIN E.F.M.,THE POLITICS OF DEMOCRATIC SOCIALISM; AN ESSAY ON SOCIAL POLICY. STRATA POL/PAR PLAN COERCE DRIVE PERSON PWR MARXISM...CHARTS METH/COMP. PAGE 39 A0805 SOCIALIST POPULISM POLICY SOCIETY

B50
ALMOND G.A.,THE AMERICAN PEOPLE AND FOREIGN POLICY. USA+45 USA-45 CULTURE SOCIETY STRUCT CONSEN PERSON PWR POPULISM...TIME/SEQ TREND 20 COLD/WAR. PAGE 6 A0129 ATTIT DIPLOM DECISION ELITES

B51
BROGAN D.W.,THE PRICE OF REVOLUTION. FRANCE USA+45 USA-45 USSR CONSTN NAT/G DIPLOM COLONIAL NAT/LISM ORD/FREE POPULISM...CONCPT 18/20 PRE/US/AM. PAGE 19 A0386 REV METH/COMP COST MARXISM

B54
STRAUSZ-HUPE R.,INTERNATIONAL RELATIONS IN THE AGE OF THE CONFLICT BETWEEN DEMOCRACY AND DICTATORSHIP (2ND ED.). INT/ORG BAL/PWR EDU/PROP ADMIN WAR PEACE PWR...CONCPT CHARTS BIBLIOG 20 COLD/WAR UN LEAGUE/NAT. PAGE 139 A2846 DIPLOM POPULISM MARXISM

B58
PALMER E.E.,AMERICAN FOREIGN POLICY. USA+45 CULTURE ECO/UNDEV NAT/G PLAN GIVE BAL/PAY ORD/FREE WEALTH POPULISM...DECISION ANTHOL 20. PAGE 113 A2319 DIPLOM ECO/TAC POLICY

B58
PALMER E.E.,THE COMMUNIST CHALLENGE. COM USA+45 USA-45 ECO/DEV ECO/UNDEV NEUTRAL ORD/FREE POPULISM ...CONCPT NAT/COMP ANTHOL 19/20 LENIN/VI STALIN/J MAO MARX/KARL COM/PARTY. PAGE 113 A2320 MARXISM DIPLOM IDEA/COMP POLICY

B59
SHANNON D.A.,THE DECLINE OF AMERICAN COMMUNISM; A HISTORY OF THE COMMUNIST PARTY OF THE UNITED STATES SINCE 1945. USA+45 LAW SOCIETY LABOR NAT/G WORKER DIPLOM EDU/PROP LEAD...POLICY BIBLIOG 20 KHRUSH/N NEGRO AFL/CIO COLD/WAR COM/PARTY. PAGE 131 A2692 MARXISM POL/PAR ATTIT POPULISM

B60
THEOBOLD R.,THE NEW NATIONS OF WEST AFRICA. GHANA NIGERIA CULTURE INT/ORG ECO/TAC FOR/AID COLONIAL RACE/REL POPULISM...ANTHOL BIBLIOG 20 UN. PAGE 143 A2916 AFR SOVEREIGN ECO/UNDEV DIPLOM

B61
OAKES J.B.,THE EDGE OF FREEDOM. EUR+WWI USA+45 USSR ECO/UNDEV BAL/PWR DIPLOM DOMIN COLONIAL PWR MARXISM POPULISM...IDEA/COMP 20 COLD/WAR. PAGE 111 A2271 AFR ORD/FREE SOVEREIGN NEUTRAL

B62
EBENSTEIN W.,TWO WAYS OF LIFE. USA+45 CULTURE ECO/DEV PLAN EDU/PROP CONTROL ORD/FREE...GOV/COMP IDEA/COMP T 20 MARX/KARL ENGELS/F LENIN/VI LOCKE/JOHN MILL/JS. PAGE 40 A0819 MARXISM POPULISM ECO/TAC DIPLOM

B62
HETHERINGTON H.,SOME ASPECTS OF THE BRITISH EXPERIMENT IN DEMOCRACY. UK DIPLOM COLONIAL ...CONCPT 20 CMN/WLTH. PAGE 64 A1322 EDU/PROP AFR POPULISM SOC/EXP

B63
JENNINGS W.I.,DEMOCRACY IN AFRICA. UK CULTURE STRUCT ECO/UNDEV DIPLOM COLONIAL GP/REL ADJUST NAT/LISM ORD/FREE...GOV/COMP 20 THIRD/WRLD. PAGE 74 A1512 — PROB/SOLV AFR CONSTN POPULISM

B64
CALVO SERER R.,LAS NUEVAS DEMOCRACIAS. AFR ASIA ISLAM USA+45 WOR+45 BAL/PWR DOMIN PARTIC INGP/REL AUTHORIT POPULISM...CONCPT 20 COM/PARTY. PAGE 23 A0469 — ORD/FREE MARXISM DIPLOM POLICY

B64
MORGAN T.,GOLDWATER EITHER/OR; A SELF-PORTRAIT BASED UPON HIS OWN WORDS. USA+45 CONSTN AGRI LABOR DIPLOM RACE/REL WEALTH POPULISM...POLICY MAJORIT 20 GOLDWATR/B REPUBLICAN. PAGE 104 A2131 — LEAD POL/PAR CHOOSE ATTIT

B64
PENNOCK J.R.,SELF-GOVERNMENT IN MODERNIZING NATIONS. AFR COM USA+45 ECO/DEV POL/PAR PROB/SOLV DIPLOM ECO/TAC COLONIAL REV POPULISM SOCISM 20. PAGE 114 A2350 — ECO/UNDEV POLICY SOVEREIGN NAT/G

B64
WRIGHT T.P. JR.,AMERICAN SUPPORT OF FREE ELECTIONS ABROAD. USA+45 USA-45 DOMIN LEAD NEUTRAL MARXISM ...POLICY TIME/SEQ BIBLIOG 19/20 COLD/WAR INTERVENT. PAGE 168 A3420 — DIPLOM CHOOSE L/A+17C POPULISM

B65
FAGG J.E.,CUBA, HAITI, AND THE DOMINICAN REPUBLIC. CUBA DOMIN/REP HAITI L/A+17C NAT/G DIPLOM ECO/TAC DOMIN CHOOSE AUTHORIT ROLE SOVEREIGN POPULISM 17/20. PAGE 43 A0883 — COLONIAL ECO/UNDEV REV GOV/COMP

B65
NKRUMAH K.,NEO-COLONIALISM: THE LAST STAGE OF IMPERIALISM. AFR INT/ORG WORKER FOR/AID INT/TRADE EDU/PROP GOV/REL NAT/LISM SOVEREIGN POPULISM SOCISM ...SOCIALIST 20 THIRD/WRLD INTRVN/ECO. PAGE 109 A2243 — COLONIAL DIPLOM ECO/UNDEV ECO/TAC

B66
BRACKMAN A.C.,SOUTHEAST ASIA'S SECOND FRONT: THE POWER STRUGGLE IN THE MALAY ARCHIPELAGO. CHINA/COM INDONESIA MALAYSIA ECO/UNDEV INT/ORG NAT/G FORCES DIPLOM EDU/PROP REGION COERCE GUERRILLA AUTHORIT POPULISM...MAJORIT 20 KENNEDY/JF SEATO. PAGE 18 A0367 — S/ASIA MARXISM REV

B67
KNOLES G.H.,THE RESPONSIBILITIES OF POWER, 1900-1929. USA-45 SOCIETY SECT JUDGE COLONIAL REPRESENT WEALTH POPULISM...IDEA/COMP ANTHOL PRESIDENT 20 LEAGUE/NAT. PAGE 81 A1653 — PWR DIPLOM NAT/LISM WAR

B67
YAMAMURA K.,ECONOMIC POLICY IN POSTWAR JAPAN. ASIA FINAN POL/PAR DIPLOM LEAD NAT/LISM ATTIT NEW/LIB POPULISM 20 CHINJAP. PAGE 168 A3429 — ECO/DEV POLICY NAT/G TEC/DEV

B90
HOSMAR J.K.,A SHORT HISTORY OF ANGLO-SAXON FREEDOM. UK USA-45 ROMAN/EMP NAT/G EX/STRUC LEGIS COLONIAL REV NAT/LISM POPULISM PARLIAMENT ANGLO/SAX MAGNA/CART. PAGE 68 A1394 — CONSTN ORD/FREE DIPLOM PARL/PROC

PORTUGAL....SEE ALSO APPROPRIATE TIME/SPACE/CULTURE INDEX

B14
HARRIS N.D.,INTERVENTION AND COLONIZATION IN AFRICA. BELGIUM FRANCE GERMANY MOD/EUR PORTUGAL UK ECO/UNDEV BAL/PWR DOMIN CONTROL PWR...GEOG 19/20. PAGE 62 A1267 — AFR COLONIAL DIPLOM

B17
DOS SANTOS M.,BIBLIOGRAPHIA GERAL, A DESCRIPCAO BIBLIOGRAFICA DE LIVROS TANTO DE AUTORES PORTUGUEZES COMO BRASILEIROS... BRAZIL PORTUGAL NAT/G LEAD GP/REL 15/20. PAGE 38 A0774 — BIBLIOG/A L/A+17C DIPLOM COLONIAL

B27
HARRIS N.D.,EUROPE AND AFRICA. BELGIUM FRANCE GERMANY MOD/EUR PORTUGAL UK ECO/UNDEV BAL/PWR PWR ...GEOG 19/20. PAGE 62 A1268 — AFR COLONIAL DIPLOM

B37
BLAKE J.W.,EUROPEAN BEGINNINGS IN WEST AFRICA 1454-1578. FRANCE GUINEA PORTUGAL UK PWR WEALTH 16/16 AFRICA/W. PAGE 15 A0305 — DIPLOM COLONIAL INT/TRADE DOMIN

B41
WHITAKER A.P.,THE UNITED STATES AND THE INDEPENDENCE OF LATIN AMERICA, 1800-1830. PORTUGAL SPAIN USA-45 COLONIAL REGION SOVEREIGN...POLICY TIME/SEQ BIBLIOG/A 18/20. PAGE 163 A3329 — DIPLOM L/A+17C CONCPT ORD/FREE

B42
JACKSON M.V.,EUROPEAN POWERS AND SOUTH-EAST AFRICA: A STUDY OF INTERNATIONAL RELATIONS ON SOUTH-EAST COAST OF AFRICA, 1796-1856. AFR FRANCE PORTUGAL SOUTH/AFR UK USA-45 FORCES INT/TRADE PWR...CHARTS BIBLIOG 18/19 TREATY. PAGE 72 A1477 — DOMIN POLICY ORD/FREE DIPLOM

B50
FIGANIERE J.C.,BIBLIOTHECA HISTORICA PORTUGUEZA. BRAZIL PORTUGAL SECT ADMIN. PAGE 45 A0929 — BIBLIOG NAT/G DIPLOM COLONIAL

B56
TOYNBEE A.,THE WAR AND THE NEUTRALS. L/A+17C PORTUGAL SPAIN SWEDEN SWITZERLND TURKEY WOR+45 WOR-45 ECO/TAC CONFER CONTROL REGION 20. PAGE 145 A2957 — NEUTRAL WAR INT/TRADE DIPLOM

B57
RUMEU DE ARMAS A.,ESPANA EEN EL AFRICA ATLANTICA. AFR CHRIST-17C PORTUGAL SPAIN DIPLOM ECO/TAC CONTROL 14/16 AFRICA/W. PAGE 125 A2568 — NAT/G COLONIAL CHIEF PWR

B62
BLANSHARD P.,FREEDOM AND CATHOLIC POWER IN SPAIN AND PORTUGAL: AN AMERICAN INTERPRETATION. AFR PORTUGAL SPAIN USA+45 LAW LABOR DIPLOM EDU/PROP DISCRIM ISOLAT TOTALISM 20 CHURCH/STA. PAGE 15 A0309 — GP/REL FASCISM CATHISM PWR

L62
CORET A.,"LES PROVINCES PORTUGALLES D'OUTREMER ET L'ONU." AFR PORTUGAL S/ASIA WOR+45 LOC/G NAT/G DOMIN...CONCPT TIME/SEQ UN 20 GOA. PAGE 31 A0620 — INT/ORG SOVEREIGN COLONIAL

C62
DUFFY J.,"PORTUGAL IN AFRICA." PORTUGAL SIER/LEONE INDUS WORKER INT/TRADE WAR CONSERVE...CATH GEOG TREND 16/20. PAGE 39 A0795 — BIBLIOG RACE/REL ECO/UNDEV COLONIAL

B64
QUIGG P.W.,AFRICA: A FOREIGN AFFAIRS READER. AFR FRANCE PORTUGAL UK DIPLOM LEAD PARL/PROC MARXISM ...MAJORIT METH/CNCPT GOV/COMP IDEA/COMP ANTHOL 19/20. PAGE 118 A2426 — COLONIAL SOVEREIGN NAT/LISM RACE/REL

B64
WAINHOUSE D.W.,REMNANTS OF EMPIRE: THE UNITED NATIONS AND THE END OF COLONIALISM. FUT PORTUGAL WOR+45 NAT/G CONSULT DOMIN LEGIT ADMIN ROUTINE ATTIT ORD/FREE...POLICY JURID RECORD INT TIME/SEQ UN CMN/WLTH 20. PAGE 160 A3260 — INT/ORG TREND COLONIAL

S64
MARTELLI G.,"PORTUGAL AND THE UNITED NATIONS." AFR EUR+WWI ELITES INT/ORG NAT/G PROVS PLAN DIPLOM ECO/TAC DOMIN COLONIAL RIGID/FLEX MORAL ORD/FREE PWR WEALTH...MYTH UN 20. PAGE 95 A1947 — ATTIT PORTUGAL

B65
HISPANIC SOCIETY OF AMERICA,CATALOGUE (10 VOLS.). PORTUGAL PRE/AMER SPAIN NAT/G ADMIN...POLICY SOC 15/20. PAGE 65 A1341 — BIBLIOG L/A+17C COLONIAL DIPLOM

B65
RODRIGUES J.H.,BRAZIL AND AFRICA. AFR BRAZIL PORTUGAL UK USA+45 USA-45 CULTURE ECO/UNDEV INT/ORG INT/TRADE RACE/REL ORD/FREE 15/20 UN MISCEGEN. PAGE 123 A2513 — DIPLOM COLONIAL POLICY ATTIT

B66
BIRMINGHAM D.,TRADE AND CONFLICT IN ANGOLA. PORTUGAL CULTURE FORCES DIPLOM GP/REL PROFIT HABITAT NAT/COMP. PAGE 14 A0291 — WAR INT/TRADE ECO/UNDEV COLONIAL

POSSONY S.T. A2846,A2848

POSTAL/SYS....POSTAL SYSTEMS

POSTOFFICE....POST OFFICE DEPARTMENT

POSTON R.W. A2397

POTSDAM....POTSDAM

B66
EUBANK K.,THE SUMMIT CONFERENCES. EUR+WWI USA+45 USA-45 MUNIC BAL/PWR WAR PEACE PWR...POLICY AUD/VIS 20 GENEVA/CON TEHERAN YALTA POTSDAM. PAGE 43 A0872 — CONFER NAT/G CHIEF DIPLOM

POTTER P.B. A2398,A2399,A2400,A2401

POUND/ROS....ROSCOE POUND

POUNDS N.J.G. A2402

POVERTY....SEE WEALTH, INCOME

POVRTY/WAR....WAR ON POVERTY; SEE ALSO JOHNSN/LB

POWELL/AC....ADAM CLAYTON POWELL

POWER....SEE PWR

PPBS....PLANNING-PROGRAMMING-BUDGETING SYSTEM

PRABHAKAR P. A2404

PRAGMATICS....SEE LOG

PRAKASH B. A2405

PRASAD B. A2406

PRATT G.N. A2598

PRATT I.A. A2407

PRATT R.C. A2408

PRE/AMER....PRE-EUROPEAN AMERICAS

N
DOHERTY D.K.,PRELIMINARY BIBLIOGRAPHY OF COLONIZATION AND SETTLEMENT IN LATIN AMERICA AND ANGLO-AMERICA. L/A+17C PRE/AMER USA-45 ECO/UNDEV NAT/G 15/20. PAGE 38 A0768
BIBLIOG COLONIAL ADMIN DIPLOM

B41
GRISMER R.,A NEW BIBLIOGRAPHY OF THE LITERATURES OF SPAIN AND SPANISH AMERICA. CHRIST-17C MOD/EUR PRE/AMER SPAIN CULTURE DIPLOM EDU/PROP...ART/METH GEOG HUM PHIL/SCI 20. PAGE 57 A1165
BIBLIOG LAW NAT/G ECO/UNDEV

B42
PAGINSKY P.,GERMAN WORKS RELATING TO AMERICA, 1493-1800; A LIST COMPILED FROM THE COLLECTIONS OF THE NEW YORK PUBLIC LIBRARY. GERMANY PRE/AMER CULTURE COLONIAL ATTIT...POLICY SOC 15/19. PAGE 113 A2317
BIBLIOG/A NAT/G L/A+17C DIPLOM

B62
DIAZ J.S.,MANUAL DE BIBLIOGRAFIA DE LA LITERATURA ESPANOLA. PRE/AMER SPAIN ECO/UNDEV DIPLOM LEAD ATTIT...SOC 15/20. PAGE 37 A0755
BIBLIOG L/A+17C NAT/G COLONIAL

B65
HISPANIC SOCIETY OF AMERICA,CATALOGUE (10 VOLS.). PORTUGAL PRE/AMER SPAIN NAT/G ADMIN...POLICY SOC 15/20. PAGE 65 A1341
BIBLIOG L/A+17C COLONIAL DIPLOM

PRE/US/AM....PRE-1776 UNITED STATES (THE COLONIES)

B01
HART A.B.,AMERICAN HISTORY TOLD BY CONTEMPORARIES. UK CULTURE FINAN SECT FORCES DIPLOM TAX RUMOR CT/SYS REV GOV/REL GP/REL...ANTHOL 17/18 PRE/US/AM FEDERALIST. PAGE 62 A1273
USA-45 COLONIAL SOVEREIGN

B07
GRIFFIN A.P.C.,LIST OF WORKS RELATING TO THE FRENCH ALLIANCE IN THE AMERICAN REVOLUTION. FRANCE FORCES DIPLOM 18 PRE/US/AM. PAGE 56 A1155
BIBLIOG/A REV WAR

B45
ELTON G.E.,IMPERIAL COMMONWEALTH. INDIA UK DIPLOM DOMIN WAR NAT/LISM SOVEREIGN...TRADIT CHARTS T 15/20 CMN/WLTH AUSTRAL PRE/US/AM. PAGE 41 A0844
REGION CONCPT COLONIAL

B51
BROGAN D.W.,THE PRICE OF REVOLUTION. FRANCE USA+45 USA-45 USSR CONSTN NAT/G DIPLOM COLONIAL NAT/LISM ORD/FREE POPULISM...CONCPT 18/20 PRE/US/AM. PAGE 19 A0386
REV METH/COMP COST MARXISM

B64
DONOUGHUE B.,BRITISH POLITICS AND THE AMERICAN REVOLUTION: THE PATH TO WAR 1773-75. UK USA-45 NAT/G LEGIS WAR 18 PRE/US/AM. PAGE 38 A0772
DIPLOM POLICY COLONIAL REV

B65
MORRIS R.B.,THE PEACEMAKERS; THE GREAT POWERS AND AMERICAN INDEPENDENCE. BAL/PWR CONFER COLONIAL NEUTRAL PEACE ORD/FREE TREATY 18 PRE/US/AM. PAGE 105 A2149
SOVEREIGN REV DIPLOM

C83
BURKE E.,"RESOLUTIONS FOR CONCILIATION WITH AMERICA" (1775), IN E. BURKE, COLLECTED WORKS, VOL. 2." UK USA-45 FORCES INT/TRADE TARIFFS TAX SANCTION PEACE...POLICY 18 PRE/US/AM. PAGE 21 A0436
COLONIAL WAR SOVEREIGN ECO/TAC

PREDICT....PREDICTION OF FUTURE EVENTS, SEE ALSO FUT

N
WEINTAL E.,FACING THE BRINK* AN INTIMATE STUDY OF CRISIS DIPLOMACY. CYPRUS FRANCE USA+45 USSR VIETNAM YEMEN INT/ORG NAT/G...POLICY DECISION PREDICT COLD/WAR PRESIDENT NATO 20. PAGE 162 A3307
DIPLOM

B00
MOCKLER-FERRYMAN A.,BRITISH WEST AFRICA. FRANCE GERMANY NIGER SIER/LEONE UK CULTURE DIPLOM WAR RACE/REL PRODUC PROFIT WEALTH...POLICY PREDICT 19. PAGE 102 A2095
AFR COLONIAL INT/TRADE CAP/ISM

B14
DE BLOCH J.,THE FUTURE OF WAR IN ITS TECHNICAL, ECONOMIC, AND POLITICAL RELATIONS (1899). MOD/EUR TEC/DEV BUDGET INT/TRADE DETER GUERRILLA WEAPON COST PEACE 20. PAGE 34 A0698
WAR BAL/PWR PREDICT FORCES

N19
BASCH A.,THE FUTURE OF FOREIGN LENDING FOR DEVELOPMENT (PAMPHLET). WOR+45 ECO/UNDEV FINAN INT/ORG ECO/TAC ATTIT...PREDICT 20. PAGE 11 A0232
FOR/AID ECO/DEV DIPLOM GIVE

N19
HAUSER P.M.,WORLD POPULATION PROBLEMS (PAMPHLET). USA+45 WOR+45 ECO/DEV ECO/UNDEV FAM ACT/RES PLAN PROB/SOLV FOR/AID GIVE EATING...CHARTS 20 BIRTH/CON RESOURCE/N. PAGE 63 A1289
CONTROL CENSUS ATTIT PREDICT

B40
CONOVER H.F.,A BRIEF LIST OF REFERENCES ON WESTERN HEMISPHERE DEFENSE (PAMPHLET). USA-45 NAT/G CONSULT DELIB/GP FORCES BAL/PWR CONFER DETER...PREDICT CON/ANAL 20. PAGE 29 A0591
BIBLIOG DIPLOM PLAN INT/ORG

B42
US LIBRARY OF CONGRESS,POSTWAR PLANNING AND RECONSTRUCTION: APRIL-DECEMBER 1942 (SUPPLEMENT 1). WOR+45 SOCIETY INT/ORG DIPLOM...SOC PREDICT 20 UN. PAGE 154 A3147
BIBLIOG/A WAR PEACE PLAN

B43
MAISEL A.Q.,AFRICA: FACTS AND FORECASTS. WOR+45 INT/ORG CONTROL RACE/REL SOVEREIGN...PREDICT CHARTS 20. PAGE 93 A1910
AFR WAR DIPLOM COLONIAL

B47
US LIBRARY OF CONGRESS,POSTWAR PLANNING AND RECONSTRUCTION: JANUARY-MARCH 1943. WOR+45 SOCIETY INT/ORG DIPLOM...SOC PREDICT 20. PAGE 154 A3149
BIBLIOG/A WAR PEACE PLAN

B53
SQUIRES J.D.,BRITISH PROPAGANDA AT HOME AND IN THE UNITED STATES FROM 1914 TO 1917. UK NAT/G PROB/SOLV DOMIN PRESS EFFICIENCY...PSY PREDICT 20 WWI INTERVENT PSY/WAR. PAGE 136 A2794
EDU/PROP CONTROL WAR DIPLOM

B56
SPROUT H.,MAN-MILIEU RELATIONSHIP HYPOTHESES IN THE CONTEXT OF INTERNATIONAL POLITICS. UNIV PROB/SOLV BIO/SOC PERSON...DECISION GEOG SOC METH/CNCPT PREDICT 20. PAGE 136 A2792
HABITAT DIPLOM CONCPT DRIVE

B58
NATIONAL PLANNING ASSOCIATION,1970 WITHOUT ARMS CONTROL (PAMPHLET). WOR+45 PROB/SOLV TEC/DEV DIPLOM CONFER DETER NUC/PWR WAR...CHARTS 20 COLD/WAR. PAGE 107 A2204
ARMS/CONT ORD/FREE WEAPON PREDICT

C58
CARTER G.M.,"THE POLITICS OF INEQUALITY: SOUTH AFRICA SINCE 1948." SOUTH/AFR CONSTN DIPLOM EDU/PROP REPRESENT DISCRIM ATTIT...POLICY PREDICT CHARTS BIBLIOG 20. PAGE 25 A0504
RACE/REL POL/PAR CHOOSE DOMIN

B59
BOWLES C.,THE COMING POLITICAL BREAKTHROUGH. USA+45 ECO/DEV EX/STRUC ATTIT...CONCPT OBS 20. PAGE 18 A0360
DIPLOM CHOOSE PREDICT POL/PAR

B60
MINIFIE J.M.,PEACEMAKER OR POWDER-MONKEY. CANADA INT/ORG NAT/G FORCES LEAD WAR...PREDICT 20. PAGE 102 A2086
DIPLOM POLICY NEUTRAL PEACE

B62
PERRE J.,LES MUTATIONS DE LA GUERRE MODERNE: DE LA REVOLUTION FRANCAISE A LA REVOLUTION NUCLEAIRE. DIPLOM ARMS/CONT DEATH REV WEAPON GP/REL PEACE ATTIT...STAT PREDICT BIBLIOG 18/20 WWI. PAGE 115 A2365
WAR FORCES NUC/PWR

B63
FULBRIGHT J.W.,PROSPECTS FOR THE WEST. COM USA+45 USSR INT/ORG NAT/G SCHOOL PROB/SOLV NUC/PWR WAR PEACE ORD/FREE...PREDICT METH/COMP 20 DEGAULLE/C. PAGE 50 A1015
DIPLOM BAL/PWR CONCPT POLICY

B63
LUNDBERG F.,THE COMING WORLD TRANSFORMATION. CULTURE SOCIETY ECO/DEV INT/ORG NAT/G DIPLOM ECO/TAC EDU/PROP 15/21. PAGE 91 A1873
PREDICT FUT WOR+45 TEC/DEV

B63
RIVKIN A.,THE AFRICAN PRESENCE IN WORLD AFFAIRS. ECO/UNDEV AGRI INT/ORG LOC/G NAT/LISM...OBS PREDICT GOV/COMP 20. PAGE 121 A2489
AFR NAT/G DIPLOM BAL/PWR

B63
SZULC T.,THE WINDS OF REVOLUTION; LATIN AMERICA TODAY - AND TOMORROW. L/A+17C ORD/FREE SOCISM ...PREDICT TREND 20. PAGE 141 A2880
REV INT/ORG MARXISM ECO/UNDEV

B63
US CONGRESS JOINT ECO COMM,THE UNITED STATES BALANCE OF PAYMENTS. USA+45 DELIB/GP CONFER...MATH PREDICT CHARTS 20 CONGRESS. PAGE 150 A3068
BAL/PAY ECO/TAC INT/TRADE CONSULT

B64
CHENG C.,ECONOMIC RELATIONS BETWEEN PEKING AND MOSCOW: 1949-63. ASIA CHINA/COM COM USSR FINAN INDUS CONSULT TEC/DEV INT/TRADE...PREDICT CHARTS BIBLIOG 20. PAGE 26 A0527
DIPLOM FOR/AID MARXISM

B64
STILLMAN E.O.,THE POLITICS OF HYSTERIA: THE SOURCES OF TWENTIETH-CENTURY CONFLICT. WOR+45 WOR-45 CULTURE ECO/UNDEV PLAN CAP/ISM WAR MARXISM
DIPLOM IDEA/COMP COLONIAL

...PREDICT BIBLIOG 20 COLD/WAR. PAGE 138 A2828 — CONTROL

B64
TAUBENFELD H.J.,SPACE AND SOCIETY. USA+45 LAW FORCES CREATE TEC/DEV ADJUD CONTROL COST PEACE ...PREDICT ANTHOL 20. PAGE 142 A2895 — SPACE SOCIETY ADJUST DIPLOM

B66
BLACK C.E.,THE DYNAMICS OF MODERNIZATION: A STUDY IN COMPARATIVE HISTORY. STRUCT ECO/DEV ECO/UNDEV NAT/G DIPLOM LEAD REV...PREDICT TIME/SEQ TREND SOC/INTEG 17/20. PAGE 15 A0296 — SOCIETY SOC NAT/COMP

B66
FARWELL G.,MASK OF ASIA: THE PHILIPPINES. PHILIPPINE SECT DIPLOM ATTIT...SOC RECORD PREDICT BIBLIOG 20. PAGE 44 A0901 — S/ASIA CULTURE

B66
WAINHOUSE D.W.,INTERNATIONAL PEACE OBSERVATION: A HISTORY AND FORECAST. INT/ORG PROB/SOLV BAL/PWR AGREE ARMS/CONT COERCE NUC/PWR...PREDICT METH/COMP 20 UN LEAGUE/NAT OAS TREATY. PAGE 160 A3261 — PEACE DIPLOM

B67
OLSON L.,JAPAN TODAY AND TOMORROW (PAMPHLET) (HEADLINE SERIES, NO. 181). PLAN DIPLOM NAT/LISM ATTIT...PREDICT 20 CHINJAP. PAGE 112 A2289 — NAT/G CULTURE ECO/DEV

B67
SINGER D.,QUANTITATIVE INTERNATIONAL POLITICS* INSIGHTS AND EVIDENCE. WOR+45 WOR-45 PARTIC WAR INGP/REL ATTIT PERSON ROLE...PREDICT BIBLIOG 19/20 UN SENATE. PAGE 133 A2722 — DIPLOM NAT/G INT/ORG DECISION

L67
BODENHEIMER S.J.,"THE 'POLITICAL UNION' DEBATE IN EUROPE* A CASE STUDY IN INTERGOVERNMENTAL DIPLOMACY." EUR+WWI FUT NAT/G FORCES PLAN DEBATE SOVEREIGN...CONCPT PREDICT EEC NATO. PAGE 16 A0326 — DIPLOM REGION INT/ORG

L67
GENEVEY P.,"LE DESARMEMENT APRES LE TRAITE DE VERSAILLES." EUR+WWI GERMANY INT/ORG PROB/SOLV CONFER WAR...POLICY PREDICT 20. PAGE 52 A1057 — ARMS/CONT PEACE DIPLOM FORCES

L67
GRAUBARD S.R.,"TOWARD THE YEAR 2000: WORK IN PROGRESS." FUT ACADEM SECT DELIB/GP DIPLOM EDU/PROP AGE/Y PERSON ROLE...PSY ANTHOL. PAGE 55 A1131 — PREDICT PROB/SOLV SOCIETY CULTURE

S67
DE ROUGEMENT D.,"THE CAMPAIGN OF THE EUROPEAN CONGRESSES." ELITES INTELL DIPLOM ECO/TAC CONFER PEACE...POLICY PREDICT. PAGE 35 A0710 — EUR+WWI REGION FEDERAL INT/ORG

S67
DOYLE S.E.,"COMMUNICATION SATELLITES* INTERNAL ORGANIZATION FOR DEVELOPMENT AND CONTROL." USA+45 R+D ACT/RES DIPLOM NAT/LISM...POLICY INT/LAW PREDICT UN. PAGE 38 A0781 — TEC/DEV SPACE COM/IND INT/ORG

S67
FRANKEL M.,"THE WAR IN VIETNAM." VIETNAM ECO/UNDEV DIPLOM CONFER INGP/REL PEACE PWR...POLICY PREDICT 20. PAGE 48 A0982 — WAR COERCE PLAN GUERRILLA

S67
GRIFFITHS F.,"THE POLITICAL SIDE OF 'DISARMAMENT'." FUT WOR+45 NUC/PWR NAT/LISM PEACE...NEW/IDEA PREDICT METH/COMP GEN/LAWS 20. PAGE 57 A1164 — ARMS/CONT DIPLOM

S67
HALLE L.J.,"DE GAULLE AND THE FUTURE OF EUROPE." FRANCE DIPLOM 20. PAGE 60 A1232 — NAT/LISM LEAD INT/ORG PREDICT

S67
KRISTENSEN T.,"THE SOUTH AS AN INDUSTRIAL POWER." FUT WOR+45 ECO/DEV AGRI INDUS TEC/DEV...CENSUS TREND CHARTS 20. PAGE 82 A1686 — DIPLOM ECO/UNDEV PREDICT PRODUC

S67
LACOUTRE J.,"HO CHI MINH." CHINA/COM USSR VIETNAM/N NAT/G CHIEF TOP/EX LEAD NEUTRAL...REALPOL PREDICT 20. PAGE 83 A1708 — NAT/LISM MARXISM REV DIPLOM

S67
MANN F.A.,"THE BRETTON WOODS AGREEMENT IN THE ENGLISH COURTS." UK JUDGE ADJUD CT/SYS...JURID PREDICT CON/ANAL 20. PAGE 94 A1923 — LAW INT/LAW CONSTN

S67
MEYER J.,"CUBA S'ENFERME DANS SA REVOLUTION." CHINA/COM CUBA USSR NAT/G TOP/EX DIPLOM LEAD ATTIT ...PREDICT 20. PAGE 100 A2053 — MARXISM REV CHIEF NAT/LISM

S67
SCHACTER O.,"SCIENTIFIC ADVANCES AND INTERNATIONAL LAWMAKING." FUT R+D PLAN PROB/SOLV CONFER CONTROL ...POLICY PREDICT 20 UN. PAGE 128 A2617 — TEC/DEV INT/LAW INT/ORG ACT/RES

S67
SHERSHNEV Y.,"THE KENNEDY ROUND* PLANS AND REALITY." EUR+WWI USA+45 INT/ORG DIPLOM TARIFFS DOMIN CONFER PWR...MARXIST PREDICT. PAGE 132 A2701 — ECO/TAC ECO/DEV INT/TRADE BAL/PWR

S67
VLASCIC I.A.,"THE SPACE TREATY* A PRELIMINARY EVALUATION." FUT USSR WOR+45 R+D ACT/RES TEC/DEV DIPLOM CONFER ARMS/CONT PEACE...PREDICT UN TREATY. PAGE 159 A3245 — SPACE INT/LAW INT/ORG NEUTRAL

S67
WALKER R.L.,"THE WEST AND THE 'NEW ASIA'." CHINA/COM ECO/UNDEV DIPLOM...PREDICT 20. PAGE 160 A3266 — ASIA INT/TRADE COLONIAL REGION

S67
WEIL G.L.,"THE EUROPEAN COMMUNITY* WHAT LIES BEYOND THE POINT OF NO RETURN?" VOL/ASSN PROB/SOLV DIPLOM REGION INGP/REL CENTRAL PWR 20 EEC. PAGE 162 A3301 — INT/ORG ECO/DEV INT/TRADE PREDICT

PREDICTION....SEE PREDICT, FUT

PREFECT....PREFECTS AND PREFECTORALISM

PREHIST....PREHISTORIC SOCIETY, PRIOR TO 3000 B.C.

PREJUDICE....SEE DISCRIM

PRENTICE E.S. A0859

PRESIDENT....PRESIDENCY (ALL NATIONS); SEE ALSO CHIEF

N
WEINTAL E.,FACING THE BRINK* AN INTIMATE STUDY OF CRISIS DIPLOMACY. CYPRUS FRANCE USA+45 USSR VIETNAM YEMEN INT/ORG NAT/G...POLICY DECISION PREDICT COLD/WAR PRESIDENT NATO 20. PAGE 162 A3307 — DIPLOM

N
US SUPERINTENDENT OF DOCUMENTS,MONTHLY CATALOG OF UNITED STATES GOVERNMENT PUBLICATIONS. USA+45 USA-45 AGRI LABOR FORCES INT/TRADE TARIFFS TAX EDU/PROP CT/SYS ARMS/CONT RACE/REL 19/20 CONGRESS PRESIDENT. PAGE 157 A3203 — BIBLIOG NAT/G VOL/ASSN POLICY

B17
MEYER H.H.B.,THE UNITED STATES AT WAR, ORGANIZATIONS AND LITERATURE. USA-45 AGRI FINAN INDUS CHIEF FORCES DIPLOM FOR/AID INT/TRADE...SOC 20 PRESIDENT. PAGE 100 A2050 — BIBLIOG/A WAR NAT/G VOL/ASSN

B19
SUTHERLAND G.,CONSTITUTIONAL POWER AND WORLD AFFAIRS. CONSTN STRUCT INT/ORG NAT/G CHIEF LEGIS ACT/RES PLAN GOV/REL ALL/VALS...OBS TIME/SEQ CONGRESS VAL/FREE 20 PRESIDENT. PAGE 140 A2866 — USA-45 EXEC DIPLOM

C32
MARRARO H.R.,"AMERICAN OPINION ON THE UNIFICATION OF ITALY." ITALY MOD/EUR USA-45 FORCES DIPLOM PRESS REV CATHISM...BIOG 19 PRESIDENT. PAGE 95 A1944 — BIBLIOG/A NAT/LISM ATTIT ORD/FREE

B41
BIRDSALL P.,VERSAILLES TWENTY YEARS AFTER. MOD/EUR POL/PAR CHIEF CONSULT FORCES LEGIS REPAR PEACE ORD/FREE...BIBLIOG 20 PRESIDENT TREATY. PAGE 14 A0290 — DIPLOM NAT/LISM WAR

B48
BELOFF M.,THOMAS JEFFERSON AND AMERICAN DEMOCRACY. USA-45 NAT/G DIPLOM GOV/REL PEACE 18/19 JEFFERSN/T PRESIDENT VIRGINIA. PAGE 13 A0258 — BIOG CHIEF REV

B51
PRICE D.K.,THE NEW DIMENSIONS OF DIPLOMACY: THE ORGANIZATION OF THE US GOVERNMENT FOR ITS NEW ROLE IN WORLD AFFAIRS (PAMPHLET). USA+45 WOR+45 INT/ORG VOL/ASSN CONSULT DELIB/GP PLAN PROB/SOLV 20 PRESIDENT. PAGE 117 A2411 — DIPLOM GP/REL NAT/G

B52
FIFIELD R.H.,WOODROW WILSON AND THE FAR EAST. ASIA CHIEF BAL/PWR CONFER COLONIAL ARMS/CONT WAR ...TIME/SEQ NAT/COMP BIBLIOG 19/20 WILSON/W LEAGUE/NAT PRESIDENT. PAGE 45 A0926 — DIPLOM DELIB/GP INT/ORG

B55
VINSON J.C.,THE PARCHMENT PEACE: THE UNITED STATES SENATE AND THE WASHINGTON CONFERENCE, 1921-1922. USA-45 INT/ORG DELIB/GP PLAN ARMS/CONT GOV/REL ISOLAT PEACE ATTIT SOVEREIGN...INT/LAW BIBLIOG 20 SENATE PRESIDENT CONGRESS LEAGUE/NAT CHINJAP. PAGE 159 A3242 — POLICY DIPLOM NAT/G LEGIS

B56
BEALE H.K.,THEODORE ROOSEVELT AND THE RISE OF AMERICA TO WORLD POWER. USA-45 BAL/PWR COLONIAL DRIVE PERSON PWR...POLICY BIBLIOG 20 ROOSEVLT/T PRESIDENT. PAGE 12 A0238 — DIPLOM CHIEF BIOG

B56
KOENIG L.W.,THE TRUMAN ADMINISTRATION: ITS PRINCIPLES AND PRACTICE. USA+45 POL/PAR CHIEF LEGIS DIPLOM DEATH NUC/PWR WAR CIVMIL/REL PEACE ...DECISION 20 TRUMAN/HS PRESIDENT TREATY. PAGE 81 A1658 — ADMIN POLICY EX/STRUC GOV/REL

B58
HUNT B.I.,BIPARTISANSHIP: A CASE STUDY OF THE FOREIGN ASSISTANCE PROGRAM, 1947-56 (DOCTORAL THESIS). USA+45 INT/ORG CONSULT LEGIS TEC/DEV ...BIBLIOG PRESIDENT TREATY NATO TRUMAN/HS EISNHWR/DD CONGRESS. PAGE 69 A1418
FOR/AID POL/PAR GP/REL DIPLOM

B58
KENNAN G.F.,THE DECISION TO INTERVENE: SOVIET-AMERICAN RELATIONS, 1917-1920 (VOL. II). CZECHOSLVK EUR+WWI USA-45 USSR ELITES NAT/G FORCES PROB/SOLV REV WAR TOTALISM PWR...CHARTS BIBLIOG 20 TREATY PRESIDENT CHINJAP. PAGE 78 A1588
DIPLOM POLICY ATTIT

B60
AMERICAN ASSEMBLY COLUMBIA U,THE SECRETARY OF STATE. USA+45 ELITES NAT/G PLAN ADMIN GOV/REL CENTRAL ATTIT...POLICY MGT 20 SEC/STATE CONGRESS PRESIDENT. PAGE 7 A0136
DELIB/GP EX/STRUC GP/REL DIPLOM

B61
EISENHOWER D.D.,PEACE WITH JUSTICE: SELECTED ADDRESSES. USSR PARTIC ARMS/CONT MORAL...TRADIT CONCPT GEN/LAWS ANTHOL 20 PRESIDENT COLD/WAR. PAGE 41 A0832
PEACE DIPLOM EDU/PROP POLICY

B61
SCOTT A.M.,POLITICS, USA; CASES ON THE AMERICAN DEMOCRATIC PROCESS. USA+45 CHIEF FORCES DIPLOM LOBBY CHOOSE RACE/REL FEDERAL ATTIT...JURID ANTHOL T 20 PRESIDENT CONGRESS CIVIL/LIB. PAGE 130 A2669
CT/SYS CONSTN NAT/G PLAN

B61
US SENATE COMM ON FOREIGN RELS,INTERNATIONAL DEVELOPMENT AND SECURITY: HEARINGS ON BILL (2 VOLS.). ECO/UNDEV FINAN FORCES REV COST WEALTH ...CHARTS 20 AID PRESIDENT. PAGE 157 A3191
FOR/AID CIVMIL/REL ORD/FREE ECO/TAC

B62
JEWELL M.E.,SENATORIAL POLITICS AND FOREIGN POLICY. NAT/G POL/PAR CHIEF DELIB/GP TOP/EX FOR/AID EDU/PROP ROUTINE ATTIT PWR SKILL...MAJORIT METH/CNCPT TIME/SEQ CONGRESS 20 PRESIDENT. PAGE 74 A1516
USA+45 LEGIS DIPLOM

B62
ROSAMOND R.,CRUSADE FOR PEACE: EISENHOWER'S PRESIDENTIAL LEGACY WITH THE PROGRAM FOR ACTION. USA+45 PARTIC ARMS/CONT MORAL MARXISM...TRADIT CONCPT CHARTS GEN/LAWS ANTHOL 20 PRESIDENT EISNHWR/DD. PAGE 123 A2526
PEACE DIPLOM EDU/PROP POLICY

B63
FRANKEL J.,THE MAKING OF FOREIGN POLICY: AN ANALYSIS OF DECISION-MAKING. CHINA/COM EUR+WWI USA+45 ELITES INTELL FORCES LEGIS PLAN ATTIT ALL/VALS MORAL CONSERVE...GOV/COMP 20 PRESIDENT UN TREATY. PAGE 48 A0981
POLICY DECISION PROB/SOLV DIPLOM

B63
LERCHE C.O. JR.,AMERICA IN WORLD AFFAIRS. COM UK USA+45 INT/ORG FORCES ECO/TAC INT/TRADE EDU/PROP WAR NAT/LISM PEACE...BIBLIOG 18/20 UN CONGRESS PRESIDENT COLD/WAR. PAGE 87 A1783
NAT/G DIPLOM PLAN

B63
US SENATE COMM ON FOREIGN REL,HEARINGS ON S 1276 A BILL TO AMEND FURTHER THE FOREIGN ASSISTANCE ACT OF 1961. USA+45 WOR+45 INDUS INT/ORG FORCES TAX WEAPON SUPEGO...NAT/COMP 20 UN CONGRESS PRESIDENT. PAGE 156 A3182
FOR/AID DIPLOM ECO/UNDEV ORD/FREE

B64
JOHNSON L.B.,MY HOPE FOR AMERICA. FUT USA+45 USSR LAW PLAN DIPLOM GIVE INCOME PEACE ATTIT ORD/FREE WEALTH 20 JOHNSON/LB PRESIDENT DEMOCRAT. PAGE 74 A1525
POLICY POL/PAR NAT/G GOV/REL

B64
KENNEDY J.F.,THE BURDEN AND THE GLORY. FUT USA+45 TEC/DEV ECO/TAC EDU/PROP ARMS/CONT MURDER RACE/REL PEACE...ANTHOL 20 KENNEDY/JF COLD/WAR NATO PRESIDENT. PAGE 78 A1593
ADMIN POLICY GOV/REL DIPLOM

B64
LENS S.,THE FUTILE CRUSADE. ASIA CHINA/COM L/A+17C USA+45 USSR WOR+45 ECO/DEV BAL/PWR DIPLOM NUC/PWR WAR NAT/LISM PEACE 20 COLD/WAR PRESIDENT CIA. PAGE 87 A1774
ORD/FREE ANOMIE COM MARXISM

B64
LIEVWEN E.,GENERALS VS PRESIDENTS: WEOMILITARISM IN LATIN AMERICA. L/A+17C FORCES DIPLOM FOR/AID LEAD ...NAT/COMP 20 PRESIDENT. PAGE 89 A1813
CIVMIL/REL REV CONSERVE ORD/FREE

B64
PERKINS D.,THE AMERICAN DEMOCRACY: ITS RISE TO POWER. ASIA USSR LAW CULTURE FINAN EDU/PROP COLONIAL CHOOSE...POLICY CHARTS BIBLIOG WORSHIP PRESIDENT 15/20 NEGRO. PAGE 115 A2362
LOC/G ECO/TAC WAR DIPLOM

B64
SARROS P.P.,CONGRESS AND THE NEW DIPLOMACY: THE FORMULATION OF MUTUAL SECURITY POLICY: 1953-60 (THESIS). USA+45 CHIEF EX/STRUC REGION ROUTINE CHOOSE GOV/REL PEACE ROLE...POLICY 20 PRESIDENT CONGRESS. PAGE 127 A2606
DIPLOM POL/PAR NAT/G

B64
US SENATE COMM GOVT OPERATIONS,THE SECRETARY OF STATE AND THE AMBASSADOR. USA+45 CHIEF CONSULT EX/STRUC FORCES PLAN ADMIN EXEC INGP/REL ROLE ...ANTHOL 20 PRESIDENT DEPT/STATE. PAGE 156 A3175
DIPLOM DELIB/GP NAT/G

B64
US SENATE COMM GOVT OPERATIONS,ADMINISTRATION OF NATIONAL SECURITY. USA+45 CHIEF TOP/EX PLAN DIPLOM CONTROL PEACE...POLICY DECISION 20 PRESIDENT CONGRESS. PAGE 156 A3176
ADMIN FORCES ORD/FREE NAT/G

B64
WILLIAMS S.P.,TOWARD A GENUINE WORLD SECURITY SYSTEM (PAMPHLET). WOR+45 INT/ORG FORCES PLAN NUC/PWR ORD/FREE...INT/LAW CONCPT UN PRESIDENT. PAGE 165 A3353
BIBLIOG/A ARMS/CONT DIPLOM PEACE

B65
EISENHOWER D.D.,WAGING PEACE 1956-61: THE WHITE HOUSE YEARS. USA+45 DIPLOM LEAD INGP/REL RACE/REL PEACE ATTIT...TRADIT TIME/SEQ 20 EISNHWR/DD PRESIDENT COLD/WAR CIV/RIGHTS BERLIN. PAGE 41 A0833
TOP/EX BIOG ORD/FREE POLICY

B65
HAIGHT D.E.,THE PRESIDENT; ROLES AND POWERS. USA+45 USA-45 POL/PAR PLAN DIPLOM CHOOSE PERS/REL PWR 18/20 PRESIDENT CONGRESS. PAGE 59 A1217
CHIEF LEGIS TOP/EX EX/STRUC

B65
JADOS S.S.,DOCUMENTS ON RUSSIAN-AMERICAN RELATIONS: WASHINGTON TO EISENHOWER. USA+45 USA-45 USSR INT/ORG LEGIS INT/TRADE WAR PEACE...ANTHOL BIBLIOG 18/20 PRESIDENT. PAGE 73 A1488
DIPLOM CHIEF CONTROL

B65
WEISNER J.B.,WHERE SCIENCE AND POLITICS MEET. USA+45 ECO/DEV R+D FORCES PROB/SOLV DIPLOM FOR/AID CONTROL...PHIL/SCI PRESIDENT KENNEDY/JF JOHNSON/LB. PAGE 163 A3310
CHIEF NAT/G POLICY TEC/DEV

B66
SUPPLEMENTAL FOREIGN ASSISTANCE FISCAL YEAR 1966: VIETNAM. CHINA/COM COM S/ASIA USA+45 VIETNAM EXTR/IND FINAN DIPLOM TAX GUERRILLA HABITAT ORD/FREE...STAT CHARTS 20 SENATE PRESIDENT. PAGE 4 A0077
CONFER LEGIS WAR FOR/AID

B66
CANFIELD L.H.,THE PRESIDENCY OF WOODROW WILSON: PRELUDE TO A WORLD IN CRISIS. USA-45 ADJUD NEUTRAL WAR CHOOSE INGP/REL PEACE ORD/FREE 20 WILSON/W PRESIDENT TREATY LEAGUE/NAT. PAGE 24 A0477
PERSON POLICY DIPLOM GOV/REL

B66
SAPIN B.M.,THE MAKING OF UNITED STATES FOREIGN POLICY. USA+45 INT/ORG DELIB/GP FORCES PLAN ECO/TAC CIVMIL/REL PRESIDENT. PAGE 127 A2603
DIPLOM EX/STRUC DECISION NAT/G

S66
"WORLD BANK CONVENTION ON INVESTMENT DISPUTES; A BIBLIOGRAPH ICAL NOTE." VOL/ASSN CONSULT CAP/ISM DIPLOM INT/TRADE 20 SENATE PRESIDENT. PAGE 4 A0074
BIBLIOG ADJUD FINAN INT/ORG

B67
FINE S.,RECENT AMERICA* CONFLICTING INTERPRETATIONS OF THE GREAT ISSUES (2ND ED.). USA+45 USA-45 POL/PAR SECT CONFER NUC/PWR WAR ATTIT...POLICY TREND ANTHOL PRESIDENT 20. PAGE 46 A0931
IDEA/COMP DIPLOM NAT/G

B67
KNOLES G.H.,THE RESPONSIBILITIES OF POWER, 1900-1929. USA-45 SOCIETY SECT JUDGE COLONIAL REPRESENT WEALTH POPULISM...IDEA/COMP ANTHOL PRESIDENT 20 LEAGUE/NAT. PAGE 81 A1653
PWR DIPLOM NAT/LISM WAR

B67
US SUPERINTENDENT OF DOCUMENTS,LIBRARY OF CONGRESS (PRICE LIST 83). AFR ASIA EUR+WWI USA-45 USSR NAT/G DIPLOM CONFER CT/SYS WAR...DECISION PHIL/SCI CLASSIF 19/20 CONGRESS PRESIDENT. PAGE 157 A3205
BIBLIOG/A USA+45 AUTOMAT LAW

PRESS....PRESS, OPERATIONS OF ALL PRINTED MEDIA, EXCEPT FILM AND TV (Q.V.), JOURNALISM; SEE ALSO COM/IND

N
AFRICANA NEWSLETTER. ECO/UNDEV ACADEM SECT DIPLOM PRESS COLONIAL NAT/LISM 20. PAGE 1 A0001
BIBLIOG/A AFR NAT/G

N
PEKING REVIEW. CHINA/COM CULTURE AGRI INDUS DIPLOM EDU/PROP GUERRILLA ATTIT MARXISM...BIBLIOG 20. PAGE 1 A0022
MARXIST NAT/G POL/PAR PRESS

N
AFRICAN RESEARCH BULLETIN. AFR CULTURE NAT/G COLONIAL...SOC 20. PAGE 2 A0026
BIBLIOG/A DIPLOM PRESS

N
DAILY SUMMARY OF THE JAPANESE PRESS. NAT/G DIPLOM LEAD 20 CHINJAP. PAGE 2 A0031
BIBLIOG PRESS ASIA ATTIT

N
LONDON TIMES OFFICIAL INDEX. UK LAW ECO/DEV NAT/G DIPLOM LEAD ATTIT 20. PAGE 2 A0038
BIBLIOG INDEX PRESS WRITING

N
"PROLOG",DIGEST OF THE SOVIET UKRANIAN PRESS. USSR
BIBLIOG/A

LAW AGRI INDUS PROVS SCHOOL DIPLOM GOV/REL ATTIT ...HUM LING 20. PAGE 4 A0081 — NAT/G PRESS COM

N
CARIBBEAN COMMISSION,CURRENT CARIBBEAN BIBLIOGRAPHY. FRANCE NETHERLAND UK CULTURE ECO/UNDEV PRESS LEAD ATTIT...GEOG SOC 20. PAGE 24 A0482 — BIBLIOG NAT/G L/A+17C DIPLOM

N
EUROPA PUBLICATIONS LIMITED,THE EUROPA YEAR BOOK. CONSTN FINAN INDUS POL/PAR DIPLOM TV CT/SYS...STAT BIOG CHARTS WORSHIP 20. PAGE 43 A0874 — BIBLIOG NAT/G PRESS INT/ORG

N
KYRIAK T.E.,CHINA: A BIBLIOGRAPHY. ASIA CHINA/COM AGRI FINAN INDUS NAT/G INT/TRADE PRESS...SOC 20. PAGE 83 A1700 — BIBLIOG/A MARXISM TOP/EX POL/PAR

N
KYRIAK T.E.,EAST EUROPE: BIBLIOGRAPHY--INDEX TO US JPRS RESEARCH TRANSLATIONS. ALBANIA BULGARIA COM CZECHOSLVK HUNGARY POLAND ROMANIA AGRI EXTR/IND FINAN SERV/IND INT/TRADE WEAPON...GEOG MGT SOC 20. PAGE 83 A1701 — BIBLIOG/A PRESS MARXISM INDUS

N
KYRIAK T.E.,SOVIET UNION: BIBLIOGRAPHY INDEX TO US JPRS RESEARCH TRANSLATIONS. USSR ECO/DEV AGRI COM/IND CONSTRUC DIST/IND EXTR/IND PROC/MFG R+D INT/TRADE...SOC 20. PAGE 83 A1703 — BIBLIOG/A INDUS MARXISM PRESS

N
UNIVERSITY MICROFILMS INC,DISSERTATION ABSTRACTS: ABSTRACTS OF DISSERTATIONS AND MONOGRAPHS IN MICROFILM. CANADA DIPLOM ADMIN...INDEX 20. PAGE 149 A3045 — BIBLIOG/A ACADEM PRESS WRITING

N
US CONSOLATE GENERAL HONG KONG,REVIEW OF THE HONG KONG CHINESE PRESS. ECO/UNDEV LOC/G NAT/G PLAN DIPLOM EDU/PROP LEAD GP/REL MARXISM...POLICY INDEX 20. PAGE 150 A3073 — BIBLIOG/A ASIA PRESS ATTIT

N
US CONSULATE GENERAL HONG KONG,CURRENT BACKGROUND. CHINA/COM ECO/UNDEV LOC/G NAT/G PLAN DIPLOM EDU/PROP LEAD REV ATTIT...POLICY INDEX 20. PAGE 151 A3074 — BIBLIOG/A MARXIST ASIA PRESS

N
US CONSULATE GENERAL HONG KONG,SURVEY OF CHINA MAINLAND PRESS. CHINA/COM ECO/UNDEV LOC/G NAT/G PLAN DIPLOM EDU/PROP LEAD REV ATTIT...POLICY INDEX 20. PAGE 151 A3075 — BIBLIOG/A MARXIST ASIA PRESS

N
US CONSULATE GENERAL HONG KONG,US CONSULATE GENERAL, HONG KONG, PRESS SUMMARIES. CHINA/COM ECO/UNDEV LOC/G NAT/G PLAN DIPLOM EDU/PROP LEAD REV ATTIT...POLICY INDEX 20. PAGE 151 A3076 — BIBLIOG/A MARXIST ASIA PRESS

N19
GRANT N.,COMMUNIST PSYCHOLOGICAL OFFENSIVE: DISTORTION IN THE TRANSLATION OF OFFICIAL DOCUMENTS (PAMPHLET). USSR POL/PAR CHIEF FOR/AID PRESS WRITING COLONIAL LEAD WAR PEACE 20 KHRUSH/N. PAGE 55 A1129 — MARXISM DIPLOM EDU/PROP

B23
KADEN E.H.,DER POLITISCHE CHARAKTER DER FRANZOSISCHEN KULTURPROPAGANDA AM RHEIN. FRANCE MOD/EUR DOMIN PRESS...GEOG METH/COMP 20. PAGE 75 A1544 — EDU/PROP ATTIT DIPLOM NAT/G

B28
CHILDS J.B.,FOREIGN GOVERNMENT PUBLICATIONS (PAMPHLET). LEGIS DIPLOM 19/20. PAGE 26 A0529 — BIBLIOG PRESS NAT/G

B28
HUBER G.,DIE FRANZOSISCHE PROPAGANDA IM WELTKRIEG GEGEN DEUTSCHLAND 1914 BIS 1918. FRANCE GERMANY MOD/EUR DIPLOM WAR...EXHIBIT 20 WWI. PAGE 68 A1403 — EDU/PROP ATTIT DOMIN PRESS

B28
PLAYNE C.E.,THE PRE-WAR MIND IN BRITAIN. GERMANY MOD/EUR UK STRATA SECT DIPLOM EDU/PROP CROWD SUFF ...POLICY ANARCH PSY SOC IDEA/COMP 20 WWI. PAGE 116 A2388 — PRESS WAR DOMIN ATTIT

C32
MARRARO H.R.,"AMERICAN OPINION ON THE UNIFICATION OF ITALY." ITALY MOD/EUR USA-45 FORCES DIPLOM PRESS REV CATHISM...BIOG 19 PRESIDENT. PAGE 95 A1944 — BIBLIOG/A NAT/LISM ATTIT ORD/FREE

B33
REID H.D.,RECUEIL DES COURS; TOME 45: LES SERVITUDES INTERNATIONALES III. FRANCE CONSTN DELIB/GP PRESS CONTROL REV WAR CHOOSE PEACE MORAL MARITIME TREATY. PAGE 120 A2457 — ORD/FREE DIPLOM LAW

B33
PUBLIC OPINION AND WORLD POLITICS. UNIV LAW CULTURE NAT/G PRESS REV GP/REL...MAJORIT METH/COMP ANTHOL 20. PAGE 167 A3400 — DIPLOM EDU/PROP ATTIT MAJORITY

B36
HUGENDUBEL P.,DIE KRIEGSMACHE DER FRANZOSISCHEN PRESSE. FRANCE GERMANY MOD/EUR COM/IND NAT/G DIPLOM DOMIN PWR 20. PAGE 69 A1412 — PRESS EDU/PROP WAR ATTIT

B36
METZ I.,DIE DEUTSCHE FLOTTE IN DER ENGLISCHEN PRESSE, DER NAVY SCARE VOM WINTER 1904/05. GERMANY UK FORCES DIPLOM WAR 20 NAVY. PAGE 100 A2047 — EDU/PROP ATTIT DOMIN PRESS

B37
TUPPER E.,JAPAN IN AMERICAN PUBLIC OPINION. USA-45 POL/PAR VOL/ASSN INT/TRADE DISCRIM...BIBLIOG 20 CHINJAP TREATY. PAGE 146 A2979 — ATTIT IDEA/COMP DIPLOM PRESS

C37
TUPPER E.,"JAPAN IN AMERICAN PUBLIC OPINION." USA+45 POL/PAR VOL/ASSN INT/TRADE DISCRIM ...IDEA/COMP 20 CHINJAP. PAGE 146 A2978 — BIBLIOG ATTIT DIPLOM PRESS

B40
FULLER G.H.,A LIST OF BIBLIOGRAPHIES ON PROPAGANDA (PAMPHLET). MOD/EUR USA-45 CONSULT ACT/RES PRESS FEEDBACK TASK WAR ATTIT PWR...CON/ANAL METH/COMP 20. PAGE 50 A1020 — BIBLIOG/A EDU/PROP DOMIN DIPLOM

B40
NAFZIGER R.O.,INTERNATIONAL NEWS AND THE PRESS: COMMUNICATIONS, ORGANIZATION OF NEWS-GATHERING INTERNATIONAL AFFAIRS AND FOREIGN... COM/IND FORCES WAR ATTIT...POLICY 20. PAGE 107 A2191 — BIBLIOG/A PRESS DIPLOM EDU/PROP

B40
WANDERSCHECK H.,FRANKREICHS PROPAGANDA GEGEN DEUTSCHLAND. FRANCE GERMANY MOD/EUR UK NAT/G DIPLOM WAR 20 JEWS. PAGE 161 A3273 — EDU/PROP ATTIT DOMIN PRESS

B41
BAUMANN G.,GRUNDLAGEN UND PRAXIS DER INTERNATIONALEN PROPAGANDA. FRANCE GERMANY UK CULTURE COM/IND PRESS PWR...PSY METH/COMP 20. PAGE 12 A0236 — EDU/PROP DOMIN ATTIT DIPLOM

B42
BORNSTEIN J.,ACTION AGAINST THE ENEMY'S MIND. EUR+WWI GERMANY USA-45 DIPLOM DOMIN PRESS LEAD GP/REL DISCRIM PERCEPT FASCISM MARXISM 20 JEWS NAZI ANTI/SEMIT. PAGE 17 A0343 — EDU/PROP PSY WAR CONTROL

B45
HORN O.B.,BRITISH PUBLIC OPINION AND THE FIRST PARTITION OF POLAND. POLAND UK LEGIS PRESS RUMOR CONTROL PARTIC NAT/LISM SOVEREIGN 18/19. PAGE 67 A1385 — DIPLOM POLICY ATTIT NAT/G

B45
PERAZA SARAUSA F.,BIBLIOGRAFIAS CUBANAS. CUBA CULTURE ECO/UNDEV AGRI EDU/PROP PRESS CIVMIL/REL ...POLICY GEOG PHIL/SCI BIOG 19/20. PAGE 115 A2353 — BIBLIOG/A L/A+17C NAT/G DIPLOM

B49
THE CURRENT DIGEST OF THE SOVIET PRESS. USSR WOR+45 LOC/G NAT/G DIPLOM EDU/PROP...MARXIST 20. PAGE 3 A0056 — BIBLIOG/A COM ATTIT PRESS

B50
BOHATTA H.,INTERNATIONALE BIBLIOGRAPHIE. WOR+45 LAW CULTURE PRESS. PAGE 16 A0330 — BIBLIOG DIPLOM NAT/G WRITING

B51
RAPPAPORT A.,THE BRITISH PRESS AND WILSONIAN NEUTRALITY. UK WOR-45 SEA POL/PAR WAR CHOOSE PEACE ATTIT PERCEPT...GEOG 20 WILSON/W. PAGE 119 A2446 — PRESS DIPLOM NEUTRAL POLICY

B52
SHULIM J.I.,THE OLD DOMINION AND NAPOLEON BONAPARTE. POL/PAR DOMIN PRESS REV WAR 18/19 VIRGINIA. PAGE 132 A2710 — ATTIT PROVS EDU/PROP DIPLOM

B53
GROPP A.E.,UNION LIST OF LATIN AMERICAN NEWSPAPERS IN LIBRARIES IN THE UNITED STATES. USA+45 DIPLOM ATTIT 20. PAGE 57 A1170 — BIBLIOG PRESS L/A+17C NAT/G

B53
LARSEN K.,NATIONAL BIBLIOGRAPHIC SERVICES: THEIR CREATION AND OPERATION. WOR+45 COM/IND CREATE PLAN DIPLOM PRESS ADMIN ROUTINE...MGT UNESCO. PAGE 85 A1733 — BIBLIOG/A INT/ORG WRITING

B53
SQUIRES J.D.,BRITISH PROPAGANDA AT HOME AND IN THE UNITED STATES FROM 1914 TO 1917. UK NAT/G PROB/SOLV DOMIN PRESS EFFICIENCY...PSY PREDICT 20 WWI INTERVENT PSY/WAR. PAGE 136 A2794 — EDU/PROP CONTROL WAR DIPLOM

B55
MALCLES L.N.,BIBLIOGRAPHICAL SERVICES THROUGHOUT THE WORLD (VOL. 4). WOR+45 INT/ORG VOL/ASSN DIPLOM PRESS WRITING 20 UNESCO. PAGE 93 A1911 — BIBLIOG ROUTINE COM/IND

B55
PLISCHKE E.,AMERICAN FOREIGN RELATIONS: A BIBLIOGRAPHY OF OFFICIAL SOURCES. USA+45 USA-45 INT/ORG FORCES PRESS WRITING DEBATE EXEC...POLICY — BIBLIOG/A DIPLOM NAT/G

INT/LAW 18/20 CONGRESS. PAGE 116 A2390

B55
STEPHENS O.,FACTS TO A CANDID WORLD. USA+45 WOR+45 COM/IND EX/STRUC PRESS ROUTINE EFFICIENCY ATTIT ...PSY 20. PAGE 138 A2817
EDU/PROP PHIL/SCI NAT/G DIPLOM

B56
GREECE PRESBEIA U.S.,BRITISH OPINION ON CYPRUS. CYPRUS UK FORCES DIPLOM INT/TRADE DOMIN GOV/REL ORD/FREE SOVEREIGN...POLICY 20. PAGE 55 A1137
ATTIT COLONIAL LEGIS PRESS

B56
US LIBRARY OF CONGRESS,UNITED STATES DIRECT ECONOMIC AID TO FOREIGN COUNTRIES: A COLLECTION OF EXCERPTS AND A BIBLIOGRAPHY (PAMPHLET). USA+45 PRESS DEBATE...ANTHOL BIBLIOG/A CONGRESS. PAGE 155 A3154
FOR/AID POLICY DIPLOM ECO/UNDEV

B58
DUCLOUX L.,FROM BLACKMAIL TO TREASON. FRANCE PLAN DIPLOM EDU/PROP PRESS RUMOR NAT/LISM...CRIMLGY 20. PAGE 39 A0793
COERCE CRIME NAT/G PWR

B59
LOPEZ M.M.,CATALOGOS DE PUBLICACIONES PERIODICAS MEXICANAS. L/A+17C CULTURE NAT/G DIPLOM 20 MEXIC/AMER. PAGE 91 A1861
BIBLIOG PRESS CON/ANAL

B59
TARDIFF G.,LA LIBERTAD; LA LIBERTAD DE EXPRESION, IDEALES Y REALIDADES AMERICANAS. ISLAM INT/ORG PROB/SOLV PRESS CONFER PARTIC CATHISM...INT/LAW SOC/INTEG UN MID/EAST. PAGE 141 A2889
ORD/FREE ATTIT DIPLOM CONCPT

B60
KHRUSHCHEV N.S.,KHRUSHCHEV IN AMERICA. USA+45 USSR INT/TRADE EDU/PROP PRESS PEACE...MARXIST RECORD INT 20 COLD/WAR KHRUSH/N. PAGE 79 A1613
MARXISM CHIEF DIPLOM

B60
MOUSKHELY M.,L'URSS ET LES PAYS DE L'EST. ASIA COM S/ASIA USSR PRESS...SOC 20. PAGE 105 A2156
BIBLIOG/A DIPLOM ATTIT

B60
MUGRIDGE D.H.,A GUIDE TO THE STUDY OF THE UNITED STATES OF AMERICA: REPRESENTATIVE BOOKS REFLECTING THE DEVELOPMENT OF AMERICAN LIFE. USA+45 USA-45 CONSTN POL/PAR FORCES DIPLOM PRESS CHOOSE...SOC 17/20. PAGE 105 A2165
BIBLIOG/A CULTURE NAT/G POLICY

B61
COLLISON R.L.,BIBLIOGRAPHICAL SERVICES THROUGHOUT THE WORLD: 1950-59 (VOL. 9). WOR+45 INT/ORG EDU/PROP PRESS WRITING ADMIN CENTRAL 20 UNESCO. PAGE 28 A0568
BIBLIOG COM/IND DIPLOM

B61
DELZELL C.F.,MUSSOLINI'S ENEMIES - THE ITALIAN ANTI-FASCIST RESISTANCE. ITALY DIPLOM PRESS DETER WAR TOTALISM ORD/FREE MARXISM 20. PAGE 36 A0730
FASCISM GP/REL POL/PAR REV

B61
HUDSON G.F.,THE SINO-SOVIET DISPUTE. CHINA/COM USSR INTELL INT/TRADE DEBATE REV...IDEA/COMP 20. PAGE 68 A1404
DIPLOM MARXISM PRESS ATTIT

B61
ROSENAU J.N.,PUBLIC OPINION AND FOREIGN POLICY; AN OPERATIONAL FORMULA. USA+45 COM/IND OP/RES EDU/PROP LOBBY CROWD...CON/ANAL BIBLIOG 20. PAGE 124 A2532
ATTIT PRESS DIPLOM

B62
ABOSCH H.,THE MENACE OF THE MIRACLE: GERMANY FROM HITLER TO ADENAUER. EUR+WWI GERMANY/W CULTURE FORCES PRESS NUC/PWR WAR CHOOSE 20 HITLER/A ADENAUER/K. PAGE 4 A0082
DIPLOM PEACE POLICY

B63
DALLIN A.,DIVERSITY IN INTERNATIONAL COMMUNISM: A DOCUMENTARY RECORD, 1961-1963. CHINA/COM COM CHIEF PRESS WRITING DEBATE LEAD...POLICY ANTHOL 20. PAGE 33 A0677
COM DIPLOM POL/PAR CONFER

B63
GALLAGHER M.P.,THE SOVIET HISTORY OF WORLD WAR II. EUR+WWI USSR DIPLOM DOMIN WRITING CONTROL WAR MARXISM...PSY TIME/SEQ 20 STALIN/J. PAGE 50 A1031
CIVMIL/REL EDU/PROP HIST/WRIT PRESS

B63
GORDON G.N.,THE IDEA INVADERS. USA+45 USSR CULTURE COM/IND DIPLOM PRESS TV TOTALISM MARXISM 20. PAGE 54 A1113
EDU/PROP ATTIT ORD/FREE CONTROL

B63
HONORD S.,PUBLIC RELATIONS IN ADMINISTRATION. WOR+45 NAT/G...SOC/WK BIBLIOG 20. PAGE 67 A1379
PRESS DIPLOM MGT METH/COMP

B64
AFRO ASIAN SOLIDARITY AGAINST IMPERIALISM. AFR ISLAM S/ASIA ECO/UNDEV NAT/G POL/PAR TOP/EX PRESS ...INT ANTHOL 20 CHOU/ENLAI. PAGE 3 A0066
MARXISM DIPLOM EDU/PROP CHIEF

B64
EHRENBURG I.,THE WAR: 1941-1945 (VOL. V OF "MEN, YEARS - LIFE," TRANS. BY TATIANA SHEBUNINA). GERMANY USSR PRESS WRITING PERS/REL PEACE ANOMIE ATTIT PERSON...CONCPT RECORD BIOG 20 STALIN/J HITLER/A. PAGE 40 A0827
WAR DIPLOM COM MARXIST

B64
LOCKHART W.B.,CASES AND MATERIALS ON CONSTITUTIONAL RIGHTS AND LIBERTIES. USA+45 FORCES LEGIS DIPLOM PRESS CONTROL CRIME WAR PWR...AUD/VIS T WORSHIP 20 NEGRO. PAGE 90 A1849
ORD/FREE CONSTN NAT/G

B64
MUSSO AMBROSI L.A.,BIBLIOGRAFIA DE BIBLIOGRAFIAS URUGUAYAS. URUGUAY DIPLOM ADMIN ATTIT...SOC 20. PAGE 106 A2185
BIBLIOG NAT/G L/A+17C PRESS

B64
UNESCO,WORLD COMMUNICATIONS: PRESS, RADIO, TELEVISION, FILM (4TH ED.). WOR+45 DIPLOM TV PEACE ...NAT/COMP SOC/INTEG 20 FILM. PAGE 148 A3023
COM/IND EDU/PROP PRESS TEC/DEV

B65
DAVISON W.P.,INTERNATIONAL POLITICAL COMMUNICATION. COM USA+45 WOR+45 CULTURE ECO/UNDEV NAT/G PROB/SOLV PRESS TV ADMIN 20 FILM. PAGE 34 A0693
EDU/PROP DIPLOM PERS/REL COM/IND

B65
LAFAVE W.R.,LAW AND SOVIET SOCIETY. EX/STRUC DIPLOM DOMIN EDU/PROP PRESS ADMIN CRIME OWN MARXISM 20 KHRUSH/N. PAGE 84 A1710
JURID CT/SYS ADJUD GOV/REL

B65
MCSHERRY J.E.,RUSSIA AND THE UNITED STATES UNDER EISENHOWER, KHRUSHCHEV, AND KENNEDY. USSR EX/STRUC TOP/EX PRESS WAR...POLICY TREND 20. PAGE 99 A2024
DIPLOM CHIEF NAT/G PEACE

B65
MOSTECKY V.,SOVIET LEGAL BIBLIOGRAPHY. USSR LEGIS PRESS WRITING CONFER ADJUD CT/SYS REV MARXISM ...INT/LAW JURID DICTIONARY 20. PAGE 105 A2155
BIBLIOG/A LAW COM CONSTN

B65
MUNGER E.S.,NOTES ON THE FORMATION OF SOUTH AFRICAN FOREIGN POLICY. ACADEM POL/PAR SECT CHIEF DELIB/GP FORCES LEGIS PRESS ATTIT...TREND 20 NEGRO. PAGE 106 A2170
AFR DOMIN POLICY DIPLOM

B65
PANJAB U EXTENSION LIBRARY,INDIAN NEWS INDEX. INDIA ECO/UNDEV INDUS INT/ORG SCHOOL FORCES ADJUD WAR ATTIT WEALTH 20. PAGE 114 A2333
BIBLIOG PRESS WRITING DIPLOM

B65
UNESCO,HANDBOOK OF INTERNATIONAL EXCHANGES. COM/IND R+D ACADEM PROF/ORG VOL/ASSN CREATE TEC/DEV EDU/PROP AGREE 20 TREATY. PAGE 148 A3025
INDEX INT/ORG DIPLOM PRESS

B66
MALLORY W.H.,POLITICAL HANDBOOK AND ATLAS OF THE WORLD: PARLIAMENTS, PARTIES AND PRESS AS OF JANUARY 1, 1966. WOR+45 LEGIS PRESS...GEOG 20. PAGE 93 A1915
CHARTS DIPLOM NAT/G

B66
SAGER P.,MOSKAUS HAND IN INDIEN. INDIA USSR DIPLOM DOMIN...PSY CONCPT 20 COM/PARTY. PAGE 126 A2586
PRESS EDU/PROP METH POL/PAR

B66
US SENATE COMM AERO SPACE SCI,SOVIET SPACE PROGRAMS, 1962-65; GOALS AND PURPOSES, ACHIEVEMENTS, PLANS, AND INTERNATIONAL IMPLICATIONS. USA+45 USSR R+D FORCES PLAN EDU/PROP PRESS ADJUD ARMS/CONT ATTIT MARXISM. PAGE 155 A3168
CONSULT SPACE FUT DIPLOM

C66
WINT G.,"ASIA: A HANDBOOK." ASIA S/ASIA INDUS LABOR SECT PRESS RACE/REL MARXISM...STAT CHARTS BIBLIOG 20. PAGE 165 A3366
ECO/UNDEV DIPLOM NAT/G SOCIETY

C66
ZAWODNY J.K.,"GUIDE TO THE STUDY OF INTERNATIONAL RELATIONS." OP/RES PRESS...STAT INT 20. PAGE 169 A3449
BIBLIOG/A DIPLOM INT/LAW INT/ORG

B67
ANDREATTA L.,VIETNAM, A CHECKLIST. S/ASIA VIETNAM PRESS PEACE ATTIT...POLICY 20. PAGE 8 A0159
BIBLIOG DIPLOM WAR

B67
FILENE P.G.,AMERICANS AND THE SOVIET EXPERIMENT, 1917-1933. USA-45 USSR INTELL NAT/G CAP/ISM DIPLOM EDU/PROP PRESS REV SOCISM...PSY 20. PAGE 45 A0930
ATTIT RIGID/FLEX MARXISM SOCIETY

B67
HOHENBERG J.,BETWEEN TWO WORLDS. ASIA S/ASIA USA+45 PRESS TV PERS/REL ISOLAT...INT CHARTS METH/COMP 20. PAGE 66 A1362
COM/IND DIPLOM EFFICIENCY KNOWL

S67
RAMSEY J.A.,"THE STATUS OF INTERNATIONAL
INT/LAW

COPYRIGHTS." WOR+45 CREATE TEC/DEV DIPLOM CONFER CONTROL SANCTION OWN...POLICY JURID. PAGE 119 A2439 INT/ORG COM/IND PRESS

PRESSURE GROUPS....SEE LOBBY

PRESTON W. A2409

PRICE D.K. A2410, A2411

PRICE F.W. A1768

PRICE CONTROL....SEE PRICE, COST, PLAN, RATION

PRICE....SEE ALSO COST

B17
VEBLEN T.B.,AN INQUIRY INTO THE NATURE OF PEACE AND THE TERMS OF ITS PERPETUATION. UNIV STRATA FINAN EDU/PROP PRICE COST DISCRIM NAT/LISM MORAL ORD/FREE PACIFIST 20 WORLDUNITY. PAGE 158 A3224 PEACE DIPLOM WAR NAT/G

B52
SURANYI-UNGER T.,COMPARATIVE ECONOMIC SYSTEMS. FINAN MARKET DIPLOM PRICE WEALTH...GEOG SOC BIBLIOG METH T 20. PAGE 140 A2865 LAISSEZ PLAN ECO/DEV IDEA/COMP

B53
NEISSER H.,NATIONAL INCOMES AND INTERNATIONAL TRADE. FRANCE GERMANY SWEDEN UK USA-45 EXTR/IND FINAN INDUS TEC/DEV PRICE BAL/PAY EQUILIB INCOME WEALTH...CHARTS METH 19 CHINJAP. PAGE 108 A2215 INT/TRADE PRODUC MARKET CON/ANAL

C54
BERLE A.A. JR.,"THE 20TH CENTURY CAPITALIST REVOLUTION." ECO/DEV NAT/G DIPLOM PRICE CONTROL ATTIT...BIBLIOG/A 20. PAGE 14 A0275 LG/CO CAP/ISM MGT PWR

B56
FORSTMANN A.,DIE GRUNDLAGEN DER AUSSENWIRTSCHAFTSTHEORIE. ECO/TAC TARIFFS PRICE WAR ...NAT/COMP 20. PAGE 47 A0967 INT/TRADE CONCPT DIPLOM ECO/DEV

B58
AVRAMOVIC D.,POSTWAR GROWTH IN INTERNATIONAL INDEBTEDNESS. WOR+45 AGRI INDUS CAP/ISM PRICE INCOME...NAT/COMP 20 GOLD/STAND SILVER. PAGE 10 A0199 INT/TRADE FINAN COST BAL/PAY

B59
LINK R.G.,ENGLISH THEORIES OF ECONOMIC FLUCTUATIONS: 1815-1848. FRANCE UK AGRI WORKER DIPLOM PRICE TASK WAR DEMAND PRODUC...POLICY BIBLIOG 18 MALTHUS MILL/JS WILSON/J. PAGE 89 A1826 IDEA/COMP ECO/DEV WEALTH EQUILIB

B59
STOVEL J.A.,CANADA IN THE WORLD ECONOMY. CANADA PRICE DEMAND...STAT CHARTS BIBLIOG 20 VINER/J. PAGE 139 A2838 INT/TRADE BAL/PAY FINAN ECO/TAC

B59
WENTHOLT W.,SOME COMMENTS ON THE LIQUIDATION OF THE EUROPEAN PAYMENT UNION AND RELATED PROBLEMS (PAMPHLET). WOR+45 PLAN BUDGET PRICE CONTROL 20 EEC GOLD/STAND. PAGE 163 A3319 FINAN ECO/DEV INT/ORG ECO/TAC

B60
KENEN P.B.,BRITISH MONETARY POLICY AND THE BALANCE OF PAYMENTS 1951-57. UK PLAN BUDGET ECO/TAC INT/TRADE PAY PRICE COST ATTIT 20. PAGE 77 A1585 BAL/PAY PROB/SOLV FINAN NAT/G

B61
BUSSCHAU W.J.,GOLD AND INTERNATIONAL LIQUIDITY. WOR+45 PRICE EQUILIB WEALTH...CHARTS 20 GOLD/STAND. PAGE 22 A0450 FINAN DIPLOM PROB/SOLV

B61
GURTOO D.H.N.,INDIA'S BALANCE OF PAYMENTS (1920-1960). INDIA FINAN DIPLOM FOR/AID INT/TRADE PRICE COLONIAL...CHARTS BIBLIOG 20. PAGE 58 A1197 BAL/PAY STAT ECO/TAC ECO/UNDEV

B61
HARRIS S.E.,THE DOLLAR IN CRISIS. USA+45 MARKET INT/ORG ECO/TAC PRICE CONTROL WEALTH...METH/COMP ANTHOL 20 GOLD/STAND. PAGE 62 A1269 BAL/PAY DIPLOM FINAN INT/TRADE

B61
TRIFFIN R.,GOLD AND THE DOLLAR CRISIS: THE FUTURE OF CONVERTIBILITY. USA+45 USA-45 INT/ORG PROB/SOLV BUDGET INT/TRADE PRICE...STAT CHARTS 19/20 GOLD/STAND. PAGE 145 A2963 FINAN ECO/DEV ECO/TAC BAL/PAY

B63
GUIMARAES A.P.,INFLACAO E MONOPOLIO NO BRASIL. BRAZIL FINAN NAT/G PLAN PAY...METH/COMP 20. PAGE 58 A1189 ECO/UNDEV PRICE INT/TRADE BAL/PAY

B63
US CONGRESS JOINT ECO COMM,DISCRIMINATORY OCEAN FREIGHT RATES AND BALANCE OF PAYMENTS. USA+45 SEA DELIB/GP DISCRIM...CHARTS 20 CONGRESS. PAGE 150 A3066 BAL/PAY DIST/IND PRICE INT/TRADE

B63
US CONGRESS JOINT ECO COMM,THE UNITED STATES BALANCE OF PAYMENTS. USA+45 DELIB/GP BUDGET PRICE PRODUC 20 CONGRESS GOLD/STAND MONEY. PAGE 150 A3067 BAL/PAY INT/TRADE FINAN ECO/TAC

B64
HANSEN B.,INTERNATIONAL LIQUIDITY. USA+45 INT/ORG ECO/TAC PRICE CONTROL WEALTH...POLICY 20. PAGE 61 A1254 BAL/PAY INT/TRADE DIPLOM FINAN

B64
ZEBOT C.A.,THE ECONOMICS OF COMPETITIVE COEXISTENCE. CHINA/COM USSR WOR+45 FINAN MARKET FOR/AID PRICE DEMAND EQUILIB WEALTH ALL/IDEOS 20. PAGE 169 A3450 TEC/DEV DIPLOM METH/COMP

B65
US SENATE COMM BANKING CURR,BALANCE OF PAYMENTS - 1965. USA+45 ECO/TAC PRICE WEALTH...CHARTS 20 CONGRESS GOLD/STAND. PAGE 156 A3171 BAL/PAY FINAN DIPLOM INT/TRADE

B66
FELKER J.L.,SOVIET ECONOMIC CONTROVERSIES. USSR INDUS PLAN INT/TRADE GP/REL MARXISM SOCISM...POLICY 20. PAGE 45 A0915 ECO/DEV MARKET PROFIT PRICE

B66
TRIFFIN R.,THE WORLD MONEY MAZE. INT/ORG ECO/TAC PRICE OPTIMAL WEALTH...METH/COMP 20 EEC OEEC GOLD/STAND SILVER. PAGE 145 A2964 BAL/PAY FINAN INT/TRADE DIPLOM

B66
TRIFFIN R.,THE BALANCE OF PAYMENTS AND THE FOREIGN INVESTMENT POSITION OF THE UNITED STATES. USA+45 INT/ORG INT/TRADE PRICE CONTROL...POLICY 20 GOLD/STAND. PAGE 145 A2965 BAL/PAY DIPLOM FINAN ECO/TAC

B67
RUEFF J.,BALANCE OF PAYMENTS. WOR+45 FINAN TEC/DEV DIPLOM TARIFFS PRICE CONTROL...POLICY CONCPT IDEA/COMP. PAGE 125 A2567 INT/TRADE BAL/PAY ECO/TAC NAT/COMP

S67
OLIVIER G.,"ASPECTS JURIDIQUES DE L'ADOPTION DU TRAITE CECA A LA CRISE CHARBONNIERE (SUITE ET FIN)" LAW DIST/IND PLAN DIPLOM RATION PRICE ADMIN COST DEMAND...POLICY CON/ANAL ECSC TREATY. PAGE 112 A2288 INT/TRADE INT/ORG EXTR/IND CONSTN

PRICING....SEE PRICE

PRIMARIES....ELECTORAL PRIMARIES

PRIME/MIN....PRIME MINISTER

PRINCETN/U....PRINCETON UNIVERSITY

PRINCETON U CONFERENCE A2412

PRINCETON UNIV. CONFERENCE A2413

PRISON....PRISONS; SEE ALSO PUB/INST

PRITTIE T. A2414

PRIVACY....PRIVACY AND ITS INVASION

PRIVIL....PRIVILEGED, AS CONDITION

B19
LONDON SCHOOL ECONOMICS-POL,ANNUAL DIGEST OF PUBLIC INTERNATIONAL LAW CASES. INT/ORG MUNIC NAT/G PROVS ADMIN NEUTRAL WAR GOV/REL PRIVIL 20. PAGE 91 A1858 BIBLIOG/A INT/LAW ADJUD DIPLOM

B55
SVARLIEN O.,AN INTRODUCTION TO THE LAW OF NATIONS. SEA AIR INT/ORG NAT/G CHIEF ADMIN AGREE WAR PRIVIL ORD/FREE SOVEREIGN...BIBLIOG 16/20. PAGE 140 A2868 INT/LAW DIPLOM

C58
WILDING N.,"AN ENCYCLOPEDIA OF PARLIAMENT." UK LAW CONSTN CHIEF PROB/SOLV DIPLOM DEBATE WAR INGP/REL PRIVIL...BIBLIOG DICTIONARY 13/20 CMN/WLTH PARLIAMENT. PAGE 164 A3349 PARL/PROC POL/PAR NAT/G ADMIN

B64
AHLUWALIA K.,THE LEGAL STATUS, PRIVILEGES AND IMMUNITIES OF SPECIALIZED AGENCIES OF UN AND CERTAIN OTHER INTERNATIONAL ORGANIZATIONS. WOR+45 LAW CONSULT DELIB/GP FORCES. PAGE 5 A0102 PRIVIL DIPLOM INT/ORG INT/LAW

B66
CLARK G.,WORLD PEACE THROUGH WORLD LAW; TWO ALTERNATIVE PLANS. WOR+45 DELIB/GP FORCES TAX CONFER ADJUD SANCTION ARMS/CONT WAR CHOOSE PRIVIL 20 UN COLD/WAR. PAGE 27 A0541 INT/LAW PEACE PLAN INT/ORG

B66
DOUMA J.,BIBLIOGRAPHY ON THE INTERNATIONAL COURT INCLUDING THE PERMANENT COURT, 1918-1964. WOR+45 WOR-45 DELIB/GP WAR PRIVIL...JURID NAT/COMP 20 UN BIBLIOG/A INT/ORG CT/SYS

LEAGUE/NAT. PAGE 38 A0780 DIPLOM

B66

LEE L.T.,VIENNA CONVENTION ON CONSULAR RELATIONS. WOR+45 LAW INT/ORG CONFER GP/REL PRIVIL...INT/LAW 20 TREATY VIENNA/CNV. PAGE 86 A1760
AGREE DIPLOM ADMIN

L67

"RESTRICTIVE SOVEREIGN IMMUNITY, THE STATE DEPARTMENT, AND THE COURTS." USA+45 USA-45 EX/STRUC DIPLOM ADJUD CONTROL GOV/REL 19/20 DEPT/STATE SUPREME/CT. PAGE 4 A0080
SOVEREIGN ORD/FREE PRIVIL CT/SYS

S67

FAWCETT J.E.S.,"GIBRALTAR* THE LEGAL ISSUES." SPAIN UK INT/ORG BAL/PWR LICENSE CONFER SANCTION PRIVIL ...JURID CHARTS 20. PAGE 44 A0905
INT/LAW DIPLOM COLONIAL ADJUD

PRIVILEGE....SEE PRIVIL

PROB/SOLV....PROBLEM SOLVING

N

CONOVER H.F.,WORLD GOVERNMENT: A LIST OF SELECTED REFERENCES (PAMPHLET). WOR+45 PROB/SOLV ARMS/CONT WAR PEACE 20 UN. PAGE 29 A0589
BIBLIOG/A NUC/PWR INT/ORG DIPLOM

B

CURRENT THOUGHT ON PEACE AND WAR. WOR+45 INT/ORG FORCES PROB/SOLV DIPLOM NUC/PWR PERCEPT...POLICY SOC 20 UN NATO. PAGE 1 A0008
BIBLIOG/A PEACE ATTIT WAR

N

BULLETIN ANALYTIQUE DE DOCUMENTATION POLITIQUE, ECONOMIQUE, ET SOCIAL CONTEMPORAIRE. FRANCE WOR+45 SOCIETY ECO/DEV ECO/UNDEV INT/ORG LOC/G PROB/SOLV FOR/AID LEAD REGION SOC. PAGE 1 A0006
BIBLIOG/A DIPLOM NAT/COMP NAT/G

N

INTERNATIONAL AFFAIRS. WOR+45 WOR-45 ECO/UNDEV INT/ORG NAT/G PROB/SOLV FOR/AID WAR...POLICY 20. PAGE 1 A0009
BIBLIOG/A DIPLOM INT/LAW INT/TRADE

N

INTERNATIONAL REVIEW OF ADMINISTRATIVE SCIENCES. WOR+45 WOR-45 STRATA ECO/DEV ECO/UNDEV CREATE PLAN PROB/SOLV DIPLOM CONTROL REPRESENT...MGT 20. PAGE 1 A0011
BIBLIOG/A ADMIN INT/ORG NAT/G

N

JOURNAL OF CONFLICT RESOLUTION. FUT WOR+45 INT/ORG NAT/G FORCES CREATE PROB/SOLV ARMS/CONT NUC/PWR WEAPON SOC. PAGE 1 A0014
BIBLIOG/A DIPLOM WAR

N

JOURNAL OF POLITICS. USA+45 USA-45 CONSTN POL/PAR EX/STRUC LEGIS PROB/SOLV DIPLOM CT/SYS CHOOSE RACE/REL 20. PAGE 1 A0017
BIBLIOG/A NAT/G LAW LOC/G

N

MIDWEST JOURNAL OF POLITICAL SCIENCE. USA+45 CONSTN ECO/DEV LEGIS PROB/SOLV CT/SYS LEAD GOV/REL ATTIT POLICY. PAGE 1 A0020
BIBLIOG/A NAT/G DIPLOM POL/PAR

N

NEUE POLITISCHE LITERATUR. AFR ASIA EUR+WWI GERMANY RUSSIA SOCIETY ECO/DEV ECO/UNDEV PLAN PROB/SOLV LEAD MARXISM...PHIL/SCI CONCPT 20. PAGE 1 A0021
BIBLIOG DIPLOM COM NAT/G

N

REVIEW OF POLITICS. WOR+45 WOR-45 CONSTN LEGIS PROB/SOLV ADMIN LEAD ALL/IDEOS...PHIL/SCI 20. PAGE 2 A0024
BIBLIOG/A DIPLOM INT/ORG NAT/G

N

PUBLISHERS' CIRCULAR, THE OFFICIAL ORGAN OF THE PUBLISHERS' ASSOCIATION OF GREAT BRITAIN AND IRELAND. EUR+WWI MOD/EUR UK LAW PROB/SOLV DIPLOM COLONIAL ATTIT...HUM 19/20 CMN/WLTH. PAGE 2 A0039
BIBLIOG NAT/G WRITING LEAD

N

LA DOCUMENTATION FRANCAISE,CHRONOLOGIE INTERNATIONAL. FRANCE WOR+45 CHIEF PROB/SOLV BAL/PWR CONFER LEAD...POLICY CON/ANAL 20. PAGE 83 A1705
BIBLIOG/A DIPLOM TIME/SEQ

N

UNESCO,INTERNATIONAL BIBLIOGRAPHY OF POLITICAL SCIENCE (VOLUMES 1-8). WOR+45 LAW NAT/G EX/STRUC LEGIS PROB/SOLV DIPLOM ADMIN GOV/REL 20 UNESCO. PAGE 147 A3010
BIBLIOG CONCPT IDEA/COMP

N

US LIBRARY OF CONGRESS,ACCESSIONS LIST - INDIA. INDIA CULTURE AGRI LOC/G POL/PAR PLAN PROB/SOLV TEC/DEV DIPLOM EDU/PROP LEAD GP/REL ATTIT 20. PAGE 154 A3142
BIBLIOG S/ASIA ECO/UNDEV NAT/G

N

US LIBRARY OF CONGRESS,ACCESSIONS LIST -- ISRAEL. ISRAEL CULTURE ECO/UNDEV POL/PAR PLAN PROB/SOLV TEC/DEV DIPLOM EDU/PROP LEAD WAR ATTIT 20 JEWS. PAGE 154 A3143
BIBLIOG ISLAM NAT/G GP/REL

B19

MEYER H.H.B.,SELECT LIST OF REFERENCES ON ECONOMIC RECONSTRUCTION: INCLUDING REPORTS OF THE BRITISH MINISTRY OF RECONSTRUCTION. UK LABOR PLAN PROB/SOLV ECO/TAC INT/TRADE WAR DEMAND PRODUC 20. PAGE 100 A2051
BIBLIOG/A EUR+WWI ECO/DEV WORKER

N19

HAUSER P.M.,WORLD POPULATION PROBLEMS (PAMPHLET). USA+45 WOR+45 ECO/DEV ECO/UNDEV FAM ACT/RES PLAN PROB/SOLV FOR/AID GIVE EATING...CHARTS 20 BIRTH/CON RESOURCE/N. PAGE 63 A1289
CONTROL CENSUS ATTIT PREDICT

N19

LISKA G.,THE GREATER MAGHREB: FROM INDEPENDENCE TO UNITY? (PAMPHLET). ALGERIA ISLAM MOROCCO PROB/SOLV BAL/PWR CONFER COLONIAL REPRESENT NAT/LISM 20 TUNIS. PAGE 90 A1835
ECO/UNDEV REGION DIPLOM DOMIN

N19

UNITED ARAB REPUBLIC,THE PROBLEM OF THE PALESTINIAN REFUGEES (PAMPHLET). ISRAEL UAR LAW PROB/SOLV EDU/PROP CONFER ADJUD CONTROL NAT/LISM HEALTH 20 JEWS UN MIGRATION. PAGE 148 A3029
STRANGE GP/REL INGP/REL DIPLOM

B29

STURZO L.,THE INTERNATIONAL COMMUNITY AND THE RIGHT OF WAR (TRANS. BY BARBARA BARCLAY CARTER). CULTURE CREATE PROB/SOLV DIPLOM ADJUD CONTROL PEACE PERSON ORD/FREE...INT/LAW IDEA/COMP PACIFIST 20 LEAGUE/NAT. PAGE 140 A2858
INT/ORG PLAN WAR CONCPT

B30

SMUTS J.C.,AFRICA AND SOME WORLD PROBLEMS. RHODESIA SOUTH/AFR CULTURE ECO/UNDEV INDUS INT/ORG SECT PROB/SOLV REGION GOV/REL DISCRIM ATTIT 19/20 LEAGUE/NAT LIVNGSTN/D NEGRO. PAGE 134 A2748
LEGIS AFR COLONIAL RACE/REL

B33

FERRERO G.,PEACE AND WAR (TRANS. BY BERTHA PRITCHARD). CULTURE FINAN SECT ATTIT SUPEGO MORAL ORD/FREE CONSERVE POPULISM SOCISM POLICY. PAGE 45 A0922
WAR PEACE DIPLOM PROB/SOLV

B35

BEMIS S.F.,GUIDE TO THE DIPLOMATIC HISTORY OF THE UNITED STATES, 17751921. NAT/G LEGIS TOP/EX PROB/SOLV CAP/ISM INT/TRADE TARIFFS ADJUD ...CON/ANAL 18/20. PAGE 13 A0264
BIBLIOG/A DIPLOM USA-45

B35

CONOVER H.F.,A SELECTED LIST OF REFERENCES ON THE DIPLOMATIC & TRADE RELATIONS OF THE US WITH THE USSR, 1919-1935 (PAMPHLET). USA-45 USSR DELIB/GP LEGIS OP/RES PROB/SOLV BAL/PWR BARGAIN 20. PAGE 29 A0590
BIBLIOG DIPLOM INT/TRADE

B36

BEARD C.A.,THE DEVIL THEORY OF WAR; AN INQUIRY INTO NATURE OF HISTORY AND THE POSSIBILITY OF KEEPING OUT OF WAR. USA-45 INT/ORG PROB/SOLV NEUTRAL ISOLAT ...CONCPT 20 LEAGUE/NAT WWI. PAGE 12 A0240
GEN/LAWS WAR POLICY DIPLOM

B37

KETCHAM E.H.,PRELIMINARY SELECT BIBLIOGRAPHY OF INTERNATIONAL LAW (PAMPHLET). WOR-45 LAW INT/ORG NAT/G PROB/SOLV CT/SYS NEUTRAL WAR 19/20. PAGE 78 A1602
BIBLIOG DIPLOM ADJUD INT/LAW

B42

CROWE S.E.,THE BERLIN WEST AFRICA CONFERENCE, 1884-85. GERMANY ELITES MARKET INT/ORG DELIB/GP FORCES PROB/SOLV BAL/PWR CAP/ISM DOMIN COLONIAL ...INT/LAW 19. PAGE 33 A0664
AFR CONFER INT/TRADE DIPLOM

B43

CONOVER H.F.,THE BALKANS: A SELECTED LIST OF REFERENCES. ALBANIA BULGARIA ROMANIA YUGOSLAVIA INT/ORG PROB/SOLV DIPLOM LEGIT CONFER ADJUD WAR NAT/LISM PEACE PWR 20 LEAGUE/NAT. PAGE 29 A0596
BIBLIOG EUR+WWI

B43

FULLER G.F.,FOREIGN RELIEF AND REHABILITATION (PAMPHLET). FUT GERMANY UK USA-45 INT/ORG PROB/SOLV DIPLOM FOR/AID ADMIN ADJUST PEACE ALL/VALS...SOC/WK 20 UN JEWS. PAGE 50 A1018
BIBLIOG/A PLAN GIVE WAR

C43

BENTHAM J.,"PRINCIPLES OF INTERNATIONAL LAW" IN J. BOWRING, ED., THE WORKS OF JEREMY BENTHAM." UNIV NAT/G PLAN PROB/SOLV DIPLOM CONTROL SANCTION MORAL ORD/FREE PWR SOVEREIGN 19. PAGE 13 A0270
INT/LAW JURID WAR PEACE

B47

DE HUSZAR G.B.,PERSISTENT INTERNATIONAL ISSUES. WOR+45 WOR-45 AGRI INDUS INT/ORG PROB/SOLV EFFICIENCY WEALTH...CON/ANAL ANTHOL UN. PAGE 35 A0704
DIPLOM PEACE ECO/TAC FOR/AID

B48

MORGENTHAU H.J.,POLITICS AMONG NATIONS: THE STRUGGLE FOR POWER AND PEACE. FUT WOR+45 INT/ORG OP/RES PROB/SOLV BAL/PWR CONTROL ATTIT MORAL ...INT/LAW BIBLIOG 20 COLD/WAR. PAGE 104 A2135
DIPLOM PEACE PWR POLICY

B48

WHEELER-BENNETT J.W.,MUNICH: PROLOGUE TO TRAGEDY. EUR+WWI FRANCE GERMANY UK PLAN PROB/SOLV SOVEREIGN ...POLICY DECISION 20 HITLER/A. PAGE 163 A3327
DIPLOM WAR PEACE

B50

BARGHOORN F.C.,THE SOVIET IMAGE OF THE UNITED STATES: A STUDY IN DISTORTION. COM USSR DOMIN WAR NAT/LISM TOTALISM SOCISM...PSY 20. PAGE 11 A0220
PROB/SOLV EDU/PROP DIPLOM ATTIT

B51
CORMACK M.,SELECTED PAMPHLETS ON THE UNITED NATIONS AND INTERNATIONAL RELATIONS (PAMPHLET). USA+45 R+D EX/STRUC PROB/SOLV ROUTINE...POLICY CON/ANAL 20 UN NATO. PAGE 31 A0624
BIBLIOG/A NAT/G INT/ORG DIPLOM

B51
PRICE D.K.,THE NEW DIMENSIONS OF DIPLOMACY: THE ORGANIZATION OF THE US GOVERNMENT FOR ITS NEW ROLE IN WORLD AFFAIRS (PAMPHLET). USA+45 WOR+45 INT/ORG VOL/ASSN CONSULT DELIB/GP PLAN PROB/SOLV 20 PRESIDENT. PAGE 117 A2411
DIPLOM GP/REL NAT/G

B52
ALBERTINI L.,THE ORIGINS OF THE WAR OF 1914 (3 VOLS.). AUSTRIA FRANCE GERMANY MOD/EUR RUSSIA UK PROB/SOLV NEUTRAL PWR...BIBLIOG 19/20. PAGE 5 A0107
WAR DIPLOM FORCES BAL/PWR

B52
US DEPARTMENT OF STATE,RESEARCH ON EASTERN EUROPE (EXCLUDING USSR). EUR+WWI LAW ECO/DEV NAT/G PROB/SOLV DIPLOM ADMIN LEAD MARXISM...TREND 19/20. PAGE 151 A3088
BIBLIOG R+D ACT/RES COM

B53
OPPENHEIM L.,INTERNATIONAL LAW: A TREATISE (7TH ED., 2 VOLS.). LAW CONSTN PROB/SOLV INT/TRADE ADJUD AGREE NEUTRAL WAR ORD/FREE SOVEREIGN...BIBLIOG 20 LEAGUE/NAT UN ILO. PAGE 112 A2294
INT/LAW INT/ORG DIPLOM

B53
SQUIRES J.D.,BRITISH PROPAGANDA AT HOME AND IN THE UNITED STATES FROM 1914 TO 1917. UK NAT/G PROB/SOLV DOMIN PRESS EFFICIENCY...PSY PREDICT 20 WWI INTERVENT PSY/WAR. PAGE 136 A2794
EDU/PROP CONTROL WAR DIPLOM

B54
BUCHANAN W.,AN INTERNATIONAL POLICE FORCE AND PUBLIC OPINION IN THE UNITED STATES, 1939-1953. USA+45 PROB/SOLV CONTROL ATTIT ORD/FREE...STAT TREND 20. PAGE 21 A0425
IDEA/COMP FORCES DIPLOM PLAN

B54
SAPIN B.M.,THE ROLE OF THE MILITARY IN AMERICAN FOREIGN POLICY. USA+45 INT/ORG PROB/SOLV DETER NUC/PWR ATTIT PWR...BIBLIOG 20 NATO. PAGE 127 A2602
DIPLOM POLICY CIVMIL/REL NAT/G

B54
SHARMA J.S.,MAHATMA GANDHI: A DESCRIPTIVE BIBLIOGRAPHY. INDIA S/ASIA PROB/SOLV DIPLOM COLONIAL WAR NAT/LISM PEACE ATTIT PERSON SOVEREIGN ...CONCPT 20 GANDHI/M. PAGE 132 A2695
BIBLIOG/A BIOG CHIEF LEAD

B55
JONES J.M.,THE FIFTEEN WEEKS (FEBRUARY 21-JUNE 5, 1947). EUR+WWI USA+45 PROB/SOLV BAL/PWR...POLICY TIME/SEQ 20 COLD/WAR MARSHL/PLN TRUMAN/HS WASHING/DC. PAGE 75 A1532
DIPLOM ECO/TAC FOR/AID

B55
QUAN K.L.,INTRODUCTION TO ASIA: A SELECTIVE GUIDE TO BACKGROUND READING. ECO/UNDEV NAT/G PROB/SOLV DIPLOM ATTIT 20. PAGE 118 A2424
BIBLIOG/A S/ASIA CULTURE ASIA

B55
TAN C.C.,THE BOXER CATASTROPHE. ASIA UK USSR ELITES POL/PAR VOL/ASSN FORCES PROB/SOLV DIPLOM ADMIN COLONIAL NAT/LISM PEACE TREATY 19/20 BOXER/REBL. PAGE 141 A2885
REV NAT/G WAR

B55
THOMPSON V.,MINORITY PROBLEMS IN SOUTHEAST ASIA. CAMBODIA CHINA/COM LAOS S/ASIA KIN NAT/G SECT PROB/SOLV EDU/PROP REGION GP/REL RACE/REL MARXISM ...SOC 20 BUDDHISM UN. PAGE 143 A2933
INGP/REL GEOG DIPLOM STRUCT

B55
UN ECONOMIC AND SOCIAL COUNCIL,BIBLIOGRAPHY OF PUBLICATIONS OF THE UN AND SPECIALIZED AGENCIES IN THE SOCIAL WELFARE FIELD, 1946-1952. WOR+45 FAM INT/ORG MUNIC ACT/RES PLAN PROB/SOLV EDU/PROP AGE/C AGE/Y HABITAT...HEAL UN. PAGE 147 A3000
BIBLIOG/A SOC/WK ADMIN WEALTH

B56
COMMONWEALTH OF WORLD CITIZENS,THE BIRTH OF A WORLD PEOPLE. WOR+45 CONSTN PROB/SOLV CONTROL TASK WAR GP/REL UTOPIA PWR...POLICY NEW/IDEA 20. PAGE 29 A0582
DIPLOM VOL/ASSN PEACE INT/ORG

B56
SNELL J.L.,THE MEANING OF YALTA: BIG THREE DIPLOMACY AND THE NEW BALANCE OF POWER. EUR+WWI GERMANY USA-45 USSR FORCES PLAN BAL/PWR DIPLOM WAR CHOOSE PEACE...CHARTS BIBLIOG 20 UN CHINJAP ROOSEVLT/F. PAGE 134 A2749
CONFER CHIEF POLICY PROB/SOLV

B56
SPROUT H.,MAN-MILIEU RELATIONSHIP HYPOTHESES IN THE CONTEXT OF INTERNATIONAL POLITICS. UNIV PROB/SOLV BIO/SOC PERSON...DECISION GEOG SOC METH/CNCPT PREDICT 20. PAGE 136 A2792
HABITAT DIPLOM CONCPT DRIVE

S56
CUTLER R.,"THE DEVELOPMENT OF THE NATIONAL SECURITY COUNCIL." USA+45 INTELL CONSULT EX/STRUC DIPLOM LEAD 20 TRUMAN/HS EISNHWR/DD NSC. PAGE 33 A0670
ORD/FREE DELIB/GP PROB/SOLV NAT/G

B57
ASHER R.E.,THE UNITED NATIONS AND ECONOMIC AND SOCIAL COOPERATION. ECO/UNDEV COM/IND DIST/IND FINAN PLAN PROB/SOLV INT/TRADE TASK WEALTH...SOC 20 UN. PAGE 9 A0186
INT/ORG DIPLOM FOR/AID

B57
CASTLE E.W.,THE GREAT GIVEAWAY: THE REALITIES OF FOREIGN AID. USA+45 DIPLOM EDU/PROP NEUTRAL ...DECISION 20. PAGE 25 A0508
FOR/AID GIVE ECO/UNDEV PROB/SOLV

B57
CONOVER H.F.,NORTH AND NORTHEAST AFRICA; A SELECTED ANNOTATED LIST OF WRITINGS. ALGERIA MOROCCO SUDAN UAR CULTURE INT/ORG PROB/SOLV ADJUD NAT/LISM PWR WEALTH...SOC 20 UN. PAGE 30 A0603
BIBLIOG/A DIPLOM AFR ECO/UNDEV

B57
HALD M.,A SELECTED BIBLIOGRAPHY ON ECONOMIC DEVELOPMENT AND FOREIGN AID. INT/ORG PROB/SOLV ...SOC 20. PAGE 59 A1222
BIBLIOG ECO/UNDEV TEC/DEV FOR/AID

B58
INDIAN COUNCIL WORLD AFFAIRS,DEFENCE AND SECURITY IN THE INDIAN OCEAN AREA. INDIA S/ASIA CULTURE CONSULT DELIB/GP FORCES PROB/SOLV DIPLOM INT/TRADE 20 CMN/WLTH. PAGE 70 A1438
GEOG HABITAT ECO/UNDEV ORD/FREE

B58
INSTITUTE MEDITERRANEAN AFF,THE PALESTINE REFUGEE PROBLEM. UAR WOR+45 INT/ORG PLAN PROB/SOLV PEACE ...POLICY GEOG STAT CHARTS 20 JEWS UN MIGRATION. PAGE 70 A1444
STRANGE HABITAT GP/REL INGP/REL

B58
KENNAN G.F.,THE DECISION TO INTERVENE: SOVIET-AMERICAN RELATIONS, 1917-1920 (VOL. II). CZECHOSLVK EUR+WWI USA-45 USSR ELITES NAT/G FORCES PROB/SOLV REV WAR TOTALISM PWR...CHARTS BIBLIOG 20 TREATY PRESIDENT CHINJAP. PAGE 78 A1588
DIPLOM POLICY ATTIT

B58
MANSERGH N.,SURVEY OF BRITISH COMMONWEALTH AFFAIRS: PROBLEMS OF WARTIME CO-OPERATION AND POST-WAR CHANGE 1939-1952. INDIA IRELAND S/ASIA CONSTN INT/ORG BAL/PWR COLONIAL NEUTRAL WAR ADJUST PEACE ROLE ORD/FREE...CHARTS 20 CMN/WLTH NATO UN. PAGE 94 A1931
VOL/ASSN CONSEN PROB/SOLV INGP/REL

B58
MUNKMAN C.A.,AMERICAN AID TO GREECE. GREECE USA+45 AGRI FINAN PROB/SOLV WAR PWR...CHARTS 20 UN. PAGE 106 A2171
FOR/AID PLAN ECO/DEV INT/TRADE

B58
NATIONAL PLANNING ASSOCIATION,1970 WITHOUT ARMS CONTROL (PAMPHLET). WOR+45 PROB/SOLV TEC/DEV DIPLOM CONFER DETER NUC/PWR WAR...CHARTS 20 COLD/WAR. PAGE 107 A2204
ARMS/CONT ORD/FREE WEAPON PREDICT

B58
STONE J.,AGGRESSION AND WORLD ORDER: A CRITIQUE OF UNITED NATIONS THEORIES OF AGGRESSION. LAW CONSTN DELIB/GP PROB/SOLV BAL/PWR DIPLOM DEBATE ADJUD CRIME PWR...POLICY IDEA/COMP 20 UN SUEZ LEAGUE/NAT. PAGE 138 A2835
ORD/FREE INT/ORG WAR CONCPT

B58
TILLION G.,ALGERIA: THE REALITIES. ALGERIA FRANCE ISLAM CULTURE STRATA PROB/SOLV DOMIN REV NAT/LISM WEALTH MARXISM...GEOG 20. PAGE 144 A2940
ECO/UNDEV SOC COLONIAL DIPLOM

B58
VARG P.A.,MISSIONARIES, CHINESE, AND DIPLOMATS: THE AMERICAN PROTESTANT MISSIONARY MOVEMENT IN CHINA, 1890-1952. ASIA ECO/UNDEV NAT/G PROB/SOLV CAP/ISM EDU/PROP COLONIAL NAT/LISM ATTIT MARXISM...NAT/COMP STERTYP 20 CHINJAP PROTESTANT MISSION. PAGE 158 A3221
CULTURE DIPLOM SECT

C58
WILDING N.,"AN ENCYCLOPEDIA OF PARLIAMENT." UK LAW CONSTN CHIEF PROB/SOLV DIPLOM DEBATE WAR INGP/REL PRIVIL...BIBLIOG DICTIONARY 13/20 CMN/WLTH PARLIAMENT. PAGE 164 A3349
PARL/PROC POL/PAR NAT/G ADMIN

B59
AIR FORCE ACADEMY ASSEMBLY '59,INTERNATIONAL STABILITY AND PROGRESS (PAMPHLET). USA+45 USSR ECO/UNDEV PROB/SOLV BUDGET DIPLOM ADMIN DETER COST ATTIT...TREND 20. PAGE 5 A0103
FOR/AID FORCES WAR PLAN

B59
BUNDESMIN FUR VERTRIEBENE,ZEITTAFEL DER VORGESCHICHTE UND DES ABLAUFS DER VERTREIBUNG SOWIE DER UNTERBRINGUNG UND EINGLIEDERUNG DER (2 VOLS.). GERMANY/E GERMANY/W NAT/G PROVS PROB/SOLV DIPLOM PARL/PROC ATTIT...BIBLIOG SOC/INTEG 20 MIGRATION PARLIAMENT. PAGE 21 A0431
JURID GP/REL INT/LAW

B59
CHANDLER E.H.S.,THE HIGH TOWER OF REFUGE: THE INSPIRING STORY OF REFUGEE RELIEF THROUGHOUT THE WORLD. WOR+45 NEIGH SECT WORKER PROB/SOLV DIPLOM ECO/TAC EDU/PROP COST HABITAT. PAGE 25 A0519
GIVE WEALTH STRANGE INT/ORG

B59
DAWSON R.H.,THE DECISION TO AID RUSSIA* FOREIGN POLICY AND DOMESTIC POLITICS. GERMANY USSR CHIEF EX/STRUC LEGIS TOP/EX PROB/SOLV WAR ATTIT...POLICY CONGRESS. PAGE 34 A0695
DECISION DELIB/GP DIPLOM FOR/AID

B59
GOULD L.P.,THE PRICE OF SURVIVAL. EUR+WWI SPACE USA+45 FORCES ECO/TAC NUC/PWR WAR ORD/FREE MARXISM ...IDEA/COMP 20 COLD/WAR NATO. PAGE 54 A1117 POLICY PROB/SOLV DIPLOM PEACE

B59
HALLE L.J.,DREAM AND REALITY: ASPECTS OF AMERICAN FOREIGN POLICY. USA+45 CONSTN CONSULT PROB/SOLV NAT/LISM PERSON. PAGE 60 A1230 POLICY MYTH DIPLOM NAT/G

B59
HARVARD UNIVERSITY LAW SCHOOL,INTERNATIONAL PROBLEMS OF FINANCIAL PROTECTION AGAINST NUCLEAR RISK. WOR+45 NAT/G DELIB/GP PROB/SOLV DIPLOM CONTROL ATTIT...POLICY INT/LAW MATH 20. PAGE 62 A1281 NUC/PWR ADJUD INDUS FINAN

B59
KAPLAN D.,THE ARAB REFUGEES: AN ABNORMAL PROBLEM. UAR WOR+45 PROB/SOLV DIPLOM GOV/REL ADJUST EFFICIENCY...POLICY GEOG INT/LAW 20 UN JEWS MIGRATION. PAGE 76 A1557 STRANGE HABITAT GP/REL INGP/REL

B59
COLUMBIA U BUR APPL SOC RES,ATTITUDES OF PROMINENT AMERICANS TOWARD "WORLD PEACE THROUGH WORLD LAW" (SUPRA-NATL ORGANIZATION FOR WAR PREVENTION). USA+45 USSR ELITES FORCES PLAN PROB/SOLV CONTROL WAR PWR...POLICY SOC QU IDEA/COMP 20 UN. PAGE 117 A2403 ATTIT ACT/RES INT/LAW STAT

B59
TARDIFF G.,LA LIBERTAD; LA LIBERTAD DE EXPRESION, IDEALES Y REALIDADES AMERICANAS. ISLAM INT/ORG PROB/SOLV PRESS CONFER PARTIC CATHISM...INT/LAW SOC/INTEG UN MID/EAST. PAGE 141 A2889 ORD/FREE ATTIT DIPLOM CONCPT

L59
WURFEL D.,"FOREIGN AID AND SOCIAL REFORM IN POLITICAL DEVELOPMENT" (BMR)" PHILIPPINE USA+45 WOR+45 SOCIETY POL/PAR ACT/RES TEC/DEV DIPLOM 20. PAGE 168 A3424 FOR/AID PROB/SOLV ECO/TAC ECO/UNDEV

B60
FEIS H.,BETWEEN WAR AND PEACE: THE POTSDAM CONFERENCE. EUR+WWI NAT/G DELIB/GP PROB/SOLV REPAR WAR CIVMIL/REL...BIBLIOG 20. PAGE 45 A0911 DIPLOM CONFER BAL/PWR

B60
KENEN P.B.,BRITISH MONETARY POLICY AND THE BALANCE OF PAYMENTS 1951-57. UK PLAN BUDGET ECO/TAC INT/TRADE PAY PRICE COST ATTIT 20. PAGE 77 A1585 BAL/PAY PROB/SOLV FINAN NAT/G

B60
PAN AMERICAN UNION,FIFTH MEETING OF CONSULTATION OF MINISTERS OF FOREIGN AFFAIRS OF AMERICAN STATES. L/A+17C FORCES PLAN PROB/SOLV ADJUD PEACE...POLICY INT/LAW 20 OAS. PAGE 113 A2327 INT/ORG DIPLOM DELIB/GP ECO/UNDEV

B60
PRINCETON U CONFERENCE,CURRENT PROBLEMS IN NORTH AFRICA. ALGERIA LIBYA MOROCCO USA+45 EXTR/IND POL/PAR PROB/SOLV DIPLOM ECO/TAC WAR...ANTHOL 20 TUNIS. PAGE 118 A2412 POLICY ECO/UNDEV NAT/G

B60
SOBEL R.,THE ORIGINS OF INTERVENTIONISM: THE UNITED STATES AND THE RUSSO-FINNISH WAR. FINLAND USA-45 USSR LEGIS ATTIT RIGID/FLEX...BIBLIOG 20 INTERVENT. PAGE 135 A2755 DIPLOM WAR PROB/SOLV NEUTRAL

B60
SPEER J.P.,FOR WHAT PURPOSE? CHINA/COM USSR CONSTN PROB/SOLV DIPLOM CONTROL TASK WAR NAT/LISM WORSHIP 20 UN. PAGE 136 A2778 PEACE SECT SUPEGO ALL/IDEOS

B60
UNITED WORLD FEDERALISTS,UNITED WORLD FEDERALISTS; PANORAMA OF RECENT BOOKS, FILMS, AND JOURNALS ON WORLD FEDERATION, THE UN, AND WORLD PEACE. CULTURE ECO/UNDEV PROB/SOLV FOR/AID ARMS/CONT NUC/PWR ...INT/LAW PHIL/SCI 20 UN. PAGE 149 A3039 BIBLIOG/A DIPLOM INT/ORG PEACE

B60
VOGT W.,PEOPLE: CHALLENGE TO SURVIVAL. WOR+45 ECO/DEV ECO/UNDEV FAM INT/ORG NAT/G PLAN PROB/SOLV FOR/AID GIVE EATING 20 BIRTH/CON. PAGE 159 A3247 CENSUS CONTROL ATTIT TEC/DEV

C60
WRIGGINS W.H.,"CEYLON: DILEMMAS OF A NEW NATION." ASIA CEYLON CONSTN STRUCT POL/PAR SECT FORCES DIPLOM GOV/REL NAT/LISM...CHARTS BIBLIOG 20. PAGE 167 A3399 PROB/SOLV NAT/G ECO/UNDEV

N60
ERDMAN P.E.,COMMON MARKETS AND FREE TRADE AREAS (PAMPHLET). USA+45 MARKET INT/ORG TEC/DEV DIPLOM UTIL...CON/ANAL CHARTS BIBLIOG 20 EEC OEEC. PAGE 42 A0859 TREND PROB/SOLV INT/TRADE ECO/DEV

B61
BRENNAN D.G.,ARMS CONTROL, DISARMAMENT, AND NATIONAL SECURITY. WOR+45 NAT/G FORCES CREATE PROB/SOLV PARTIC WAR PEACE...DECISION INT/LAW ANTHOL BIBLIOG 20. PAGE 18 A0372 ARMS/CONT ORD/FREE DIPLOM POLICY

B61
BUSSCHAU W.J.,GOLD AND INTERNATIONAL LIQUIDITY. WOR+45 PRICE EQUILIB WEALTH...CHARTS 20 GOLD/STAND. PAGE 22 A0450 FINAN DIPLOM PROB/SOLV

B61
FULLER J.F.C.,THE CONDUCT OF WAR, 1789-1961. FRANCE RUSSIA SOCIETY NAT/G FORCES PROB/SOLV AGREE NUC/PWR WEAPON PEACE...SOC 18/20 TREATY COLD/WAR. PAGE 50 A1025 WAR POLICY REV ROLE

B61
JAVITS B.A.,THE PEACE BY INVESTMENT CORPORATION. WOR+45 NAT/G LEGIS PROB/SOLV PERS/REL WEALTH ...POLICY 20. PAGE 73 A1499 ECO/UNDEV DIPLOM FOR/AID PEACE

B61
KERTESZ S.D.,AMERICAN DIPLOMACY IN A NEW ERA. COM S/ASIA UK USA+45 FORCES PROB/SOLV BAL/PWR ECO/TAC ADMIN COLONIAL WAR PEACE ORD/FREE 20 NATO CONGRESS UN COLD/WAR. PAGE 78 A1601 ANTHOL DIPLOM TREND

B61
MEZERIK A.G.,ECONOMIC DEVELOPMENT AIDS FOR UNDERDEVELOPED COUNTRIES. WOR+45 FINAN LEGIS PROB/SOLV TEC/DEV DIPLOM FOR/AID GIVE TASK WAR 20 UN. PAGE 101 A2062 ECO/UNDEV INT/ORG WEALTH PLAN

B61
MICHAEL D.N.,PROPOSED STUDIES ON THE IMPLICATIONS OF PEACEFUL SPACE ACTIVITIES FOR HUMAN AFFAIRS. COM/IND INDUS FORCES DIPLOM PEACE PERSON...PSY SOC 20. PAGE 101 A2066 FUT SPACE ACT/RES PROB/SOLV

B61
MILLER R.I.,DAG HAMMARSKJOLD AND CRISES DIPLOMACY. WOR+45 NAT/G PROB/SOLV LEAD ROLE...DECISION BIOG UN HAMMARSK/D. PAGE 101 A2079 DIPLOM INT/ORG CHIEF

B61
NEWMAN R.P.,RECOGNITION OF COMMUNIST CHINA? A STUDY IN ARGUMENT. CHINA/COM NAT/G PROB/SOLV RATIONAL ...INT/LAW LOG IDEA/COMP BIBLIOG 20. PAGE 108 A2226 MARXISM ATTIT DIPLOM POLICY

B61
NICOLSON H.G.,THE OLD DIPLOMACY AND THE NEW. NAT/G PLAN PROB/SOLV...METH 20. PAGE 109 A2233 DIPLOM POLICY INT/ORG

B61
SHAPP W.R.,FIELD ADMINISTRATION IN THE UNITED NATIONS SYSTEM. FINAN PROB/SOLV INSPECT DIPLOM EXEC REGION ROUTINE EFFICIENCY ROLE...INT CHARTS 20 UN. PAGE 131 A2694 INT/ORG ADMIN GP/REL FOR/AID

B61
THEOBALD R.,THE CHALLENGE OF ABUNDANCE. USA+45 WOR+45 MARKET DIPLOM FOR/AID REV PRODUC UTOPIA SUPEGO...POLICY TREND BIBLIOG/A 20. PAGE 142 A2913 WELF/ST ECO/UNDEV PROB/SOLV ECO/TAC

B61
TRIFFIN R.,GOLD AND THE DOLLAR CRISIS: THE FUTURE OF CONVERTIBILITY. USA+45 USA-45 INT/ORG PROB/SOLV BUDGET INT/TRADE PRICE...STAT CHARTS 19/20 GOLD/STAND. PAGE 145 A2963 FINAN ECO/DEV ECO/TAC BAL/PAY

B61
US CONGRESS JOINT ECO COMM,INTERNATIONAL PAYMENTS IMBALANCES AND NEED FOR STRENGTHENING INTERNATIONAL FINANCIAL ARRANGEMENTS. USA+45 WOR+45 DELIB/GP DIPLOM INT/TRADE...CHARTS 20 CONGRESS OEEC. PAGE 150 A3063 BAL/PAY INT/ORG FINAN PROB/SOLV

B61
YUAN TUNG-LI,A GUIDE TO DOCTORAL DISSERTATIONS BY CHINESE STUDENTS IN AMERICA, 1905-1960. ASIA CULTURE SOCIETY ECO/UNDEV NAT/G PROB/SOLV DIPLOM LEAD ATTIT...HUM SOC STAT 20. PAGE 169 A3441 BIBLIOG ACADEM ACT/RES OP/RES

S61
OCHENG D.,"AN ECONOMIST LOOKS AT UGANDA'S FUTURE." FUT UGANDA AGRI INDUS PLAN PROB/SOLV INT/TRADE SOVEREIGN 20. PAGE 111 A2275 ECO/UNDEV INCOME ECO/TAC OWN

S61
TUCKER R.C.,"TOWARDS A COMPARATIVE POLITICS OF MOVEMENT-REGIMES" (BMR)" USSR CONSTN NAT/G CREATE PROB/SOLV DIPLOM DOMIN REV...GP/COMP IDEA/COMP METH 20 STALIN/J BOLSHEVISM. PAGE 145 A2971 MARXISM POLICY GEN/LAWS PWR

B62
BEATON L.,THE SPREAD OF NUCLEAR WEAPONS. WOR+45 NAT/G PLAN PROB/SOLV DIPLOM ECO/TAC DETER...POLICY 20 COLD/WAR. PAGE 12 A0242 ARMS/CONT NUC/PWR TEC/DEV FUT

B62
BENNETT J.C.,NUCLEAR WEAPONS AND THE CONFLICT OF CONSCIENCE. WOR+45 PROB/SOLV DIPLOM WEAPON SUPEGO MORAL...ANTHOL WORSHIP 20. PAGE 13 A0268 POLICY NUC/PWR WAR

B62
BRIMMER B.,A GUIDE TO THE USE OF UNITED NATIONS DOCUMENTS. WOR+45 ECO/UNDEV AGRI EX/STRUC FORCES PROB/SOLV ADMIN WAR PEACE WEALTH...POLICY UN. PAGE 19 A0378 BIBLIOG/A INT/ORG DIPLOM

B62
LAQUEUR W.,THE FUTURE OF COMMUNIST SOCIETY. CHINA/COM USSR LAW ECO/DEV NAT/G POL/PAR PLAN PROB/SOLV DIPLOM LEAD...POLICY CONCPT IDEA/COMP ANTHOL 20. PAGE 85 A1731 MARXISM COM FUT SOCIETY

B62
LOWENSTEIN A.K.,BRUTAL MANDATE: A JOURNEY TO SOUTH AFR

WEST AFRICA. CULTURE INT/ORG NAT/G DIPLOM...GEOG 20 UN AFRICA/SW. PAGE 91 A1868 — POLICY RACE/REL PROB/SOLV

B62
LUTZ F.A.,THE PROBLEM OF INTERNATIONAL ECONOMIC EQUILIBRIUM. FINAN PRODUC WEALTH 20 MONEY. PAGE 92 A1876 — DIPLOM EQUILIB BAL/PAY PROB/SOLV

B62
MONTGOMERY J.D.,THE POLITICS OF FOREIGN AID: AMERICAN EXPERIENCE IN SOUTHEAST ASIA. S/ASIA USA+45 NAT/G PROB/SOLV COLONIAL 20. PAGE 103 A2115 — FOR/AID DIPLOM GOV/REL GIVE

B62
MOUSSA P.,THE UNDERPRIVILEGED NATIONS. FINAN INT/ORG PLAN PROB/SOLV CAP/ISM GIVE TASK WEALTH ...POLICY SOC 20. PAGE 105 A2159 — ECO/UNDEV NAT/G DIPLOM FOR/AID

B62
QUIRK R.E.,AN AFFAIR OF HONOR: WOODROW WILSON AND THE OCCUPATION OF VERACRUZ. L/A+17C USA-45 COLONIAL SUPEGO PWR 20 WILSON/W MEXIC/AMER. PAGE 118 A2428 — DOMIN DIPLOM COERCE PROB/SOLV

B62
ROBERTSON B.C.,REGIONAL DEVELOPMENT IN THE EUROPEAN ECONOMIC COMMUNITY. EUR+WWI FRANCE FUT ITALY UK ECO/UNDEV WORKER ACT/RES PROB/SOLV TEC/DEV ECO/TAC INT/TRADE EEC. PAGE 122 A2499 — PLAN ECO/DEV INT/ORG REGION

B62
ROOSEVELT J.,THE LIBERAL PAPERS. USA+45 WOR+45 ECO/DEV INT/ORG DELIB/GP ACT/RES PROB/SOLV DETER ATTIT...TREND IDEA/COMP ANTHOL. PAGE 123 A2520 — DIPLOM NEW/LIB POLICY FORCES

B62
SPIRO H.J.,POLITICS IN AFRICA: PROSPECTS SOUTH OF THE SAHARA. INT/ORG KIN FORCES LEGIS PROB/SOLV COERCE RACE/REL FEDERAL...TREND CHARTS BIBLIOG 20. PAGE 136 A2790 — AFR NAT/LISM DIPLOM

B62
UNECA LIBRARY,NEW ACQUISITIONS IN THE UNECA LIBRARY. LAW NAT/G PLAN PROB/SOLV TEC/DEV ADMIN REGION...GEOG SOC 20 UN. PAGE 147 A3009 — BIBLIOG AFR ECO/UNDEV INT/ORG

B62
US CONGRESS JOINT ECO COMM,ECONOMIC DEVELOPMENTS IN SOUTH AMERICA. USA+45 SOCIETY FINAN NAT/G PROB/SOLV TEC/DEV INT/TRADE TAX EFFICIENCY PRODUC ATTIT ...POLICY 20 CONGRESS SOUTH/AMER. PAGE 150 A3065 — L/A+17C ECO/UNDEV FOR/AID DIPLOM

B62
US SENATE COMM GOVT OPERATIONS,ADMINISTRATION OF NATIONAL SECURITY. USA+45 CHIEF PLAN PROB/SOLV TEC/DEV DIPLOM ATTIT...POLICY DECISION 20 KENNEDY/JF RUSK/D MCNAMARA/R BUNDY/M HERTER/C. PAGE 156 A3173 — ORD/FREE ADMIN NAT/G CONTROL

B62
WEIDNER E.W.,THE WORLD ROLE OF UNIVERSITIES. USA+45 WOR+45 SECT ACT/RES PROB/SOLV GIVE EFFICIENCY KNOWL ...LING CHARTS BIBLIOG 20. PAGE 162 A3297 — ACADEM EDU/PROP DIPLOM POLICY

C62
BACON F.,"OF EMPIRE" (1612) IN F. BACON, ESSAYS." ELITES NAT/G PROB/SOLV DIPLOM ADMIN CONTROL WEALTH 16/17 KING. PAGE 10 A0201 — PWR CHIEF DOMIN GEN/LAWS

C62
LILLICH R.B.,"INTERNATIONAL CLAIMS: THEIR ADJUDICATION BY NATIONAL COMMISSIONS." WOR+45 WOR-45 NAT/G ADJUD...JURID BIBLIOG 18/20. PAGE 89 A1817 — INT/LAW DIPLOM PROB/SOLV

B63
BAILEY S.D.,THE UNITED NATIONS: A SHORT POLITICAL GUIDE. FUT PROB/SOLV LEAD...INT/LAW 20 UN. PAGE 10 A0207 — INT/ORG PEACE DETER DIPLOM

B63
DECOTTIGNIES R.,LES NATIONALITES AFRICAINES. AFR NAT/G PROB/SOLV DIPLOM COLONIAL ORD/FREE...CHARTS GOV/COMP 20. PAGE 35 A0721 — NAT/LISM JURID LEGIS LAW

B63
DEENER D.R.,CANADA - UNITED STATES TREATY RELATIONS. CANADA USA+45 USA-45 NAT/G FORCES PLAN PROB/SOLV AGREE NUC/PWR...TREND 18/20 TREATY. PAGE 35 A0722 — DIPLOM INT/LAW POLICY

B63
FATEMI N.S.,THE DOLLAR CRISIS. USA+45 INDUS NAT/G LEGIS BUDGET TAX COST...CHARTS METH/COMP 20 EEC. PAGE 44 A0902 — PROB/SOLV BAL/PAY FOR/AID PLAN

B63
FRANKEL J.,THE MAKING OF FOREIGN POLICY: AN ANALYSIS OF DECISION-MAKING. CHINA/COM EUR+WWI USA+45 ELITES INTELL FORCES LEGIS PLAN ATTIT ALL/VALS MORAL CONSERVE...GOV/COMP 20 PRESIDENT UN TREATY. PAGE 48 A0981 — POLICY DECISION PROB/SOLV DIPLOM

B63
FULBRIGHT J.W.,PROSPECTS FOR THE WEST. COM USA+45 USSR INT/ORG NAT/G SCHOOL PROB/SOLV NUC/PWR WAR PEACE ORD/FREE...PREDICT METH/COMP 20 DEGAULLE/C. PAGE 50 A1015 — DIPLOM BAL/PWR CONCPT POLICY

B63
GRAEBNER N.A.,THE COLD WAR: IDEOLOGICAL CONFLICT OR POWER STRUGGLE? USSR WOR+45 WOR-45 PROB/SOLV EDU/PROP ARMS/CONT REV NAT/LISM PEACE ORD/FREE ...IDEA/COMP ANTHOL BIBLIOG/A 20 COLD/WAR. PAGE 55 A1123 — DIPLOM BAL/PWR MARXISM

B63
INTERAMERICAN ECO AND SOC COUN,THE ALLIANCE FOR PROGRESS: ITS FIRST YEAR: 1961-1962. AGRI SCHOOL PLAN TEC/DEV INT/TRADE TAX GIVE ADMIN WEALTH...SOC 20 SOUTH/AMER. PAGE 71 A1449 — INT/ORG PROB/SOLV ECO/TAC L/A+17C

B63
JENNINGS W.I.,DEMOCRACY IN AFRICA. UK CULTURE STRUCT ECO/UNDEV DIPLOM COLONIAL GP/REL ADJUST NAT/LISM ORD/FREE...GOV/COMP 20 THIRD/WRLD. PAGE 74 A1512 — PROB/SOLV AFR CONSTN POPULISM

B63
MALIK C.,MAN IN THE STRUGGLE FOR PEACE. USSR WOR+45 CHIEF PLAN PROB/SOLV PARTIC NUC/PWR REV ORD/FREE ...IDEA/COMP METH/COMP 20 UN COLD/WAR. PAGE 93 A1912 — PEACE MARXISM DIPLOM EDU/PROP

B63
RAO V.K.R.,FOREIGN AID AND INDIA'S ECONOMIC DEVELOPMENT. INDIA INT/ORG PROB/SOLV TEC/DEV ECO/TAC CONTROL WEALTH...TREND 20. PAGE 119 A2445 — FOR/AID ECO/UNDEV RECEIVE DIPLOM

B63
VAN SLYCK P.,PEACE: THE CONTROL OF NATIONAL POWER. CUBA WOR+45 FINAN NAT/G FORCES PROB/SOLV TEC/DEV BAL/PWR ADMIN CONTROL ORD/FREE...POLICY INT/LAW UN COLD/WAR TREATY. PAGE 158 A3214 — ARMS/CONT PEACE INT/ORG DIPLOM

B63
WEINBERG A.,INSTEAD OF VIOLENCE: WRITINGS BY THE GREAT ADVOCATES OF PEACE AND NONVIOLENCE THROUGHOUT HISTORY. WOR+45 WOR-45 SOCIETY SECT PROB/SOLV DIPLOM GP/REL PERS/REL PEACE...ANTHOL PACIFIST. PAGE 162 A3304 — PACIFISM WAR IDEA/COMP

B63
WILCOX W.A.,PAKISTAN; THE CONSOLIDATION OF A NATION. INDIA PAKISTAN CONSTN SECT PROB/SOLV COLONIAL PARTIC GP/REL FEDERAL...POLICY 19/20. PAGE 164 A3348 — NAT/LISM ECO/UNDEV DIPLOM STRUCT

S63
CLEVELAND H.,"CRISIS DIPLOMACY." USA+45 WOR+45 LAW FORCES TASK NUC/PWR PWR 20. PAGE 27 A0551 — DECISION DIPLOM PROB/SOLV POLICY

C63
CHARLETON W.G.,"THE REVOLUTION IN AMERICAN FOREIGN POLICY." COM PROB/SOLV FOR/AID DOMIN COLONIAL NEUTRAL DETER WAR ISOLAT NAT/LISM...BIBLIOG 19/20 UN COLD/WAR NATO. PAGE 26 A0523 — DIPLOM INT/ORG BAL/PWR

B64
DICKEY J.S.,THE UNITED STATES AND CANADA. CANADA USA+45...SOC 20. PAGE 37 A0756 — DIPLOM TREND GOV/COMP PROB/SOLV

B64
DUBOIS J.,DANGER OVER PANAMA. FUT PANAMA SCHOOL PROB/SOLV EDU/PROP MARXISM...POLICY 19/20 TREATY INTERVENT CANAL/ZONE. PAGE 39 A0790 — DIPLOM COERCE

B64
FINER H.,DULLES OVER SUEZ. FRANCE FUT UAR UK WOR+45 NAT/G PROB/SOLV CONTROL NUC/PWR WAR 20 DULLES/JF SUEZ. PAGE 46 A0932 — DIPLOM POLICY REC/INT

B64
KAUFMANN W.W.,THE MC NAMARA STRATEGY. TOP/EX INSPECT BAL/PWR DIPLOM CONTROL DETER GUERRILLA NUC/PWR WEAPON COST PWR...METH/COMP 20 MCNAMARA/R KENNEDY/JF JOHNSON/LB NATO DEPT/DEFEN. PAGE 77 A1572 — FORCES WAR PLAN PROB/SOLV

B64
LEGUM C.,SOUTH AFRICA: CRISIS FOR THE WEST. SOUTH/AFR COERCE DISCRIM ATTIT...TREND 20 INTERVENT. PAGE 86 A1767 — RACE/REL STRATA DIPLOM PROB/SOLV

B64
MAHAR J.M.,INDIA: A CRITICAL BIBLIOGRAPHY. INDIA PAKISTAN CULTURE ECO/UNDEV LOC/G POL/PAR SECT PROB/SOLV DIPLOM ADMIN COLONIAL PARL/PROC ATTIT 20. PAGE 93 A1906 — BIBLIOG/A S/ASIA NAT/G LEAD

B64
NASA,PROCEEDINGS OF CONFERENCE ON THE LAW OF SPACE AND OF SATELLITE COMMUNICATIONS: CHICAGO 1963. FUT WOR+45 DELIB/GP PROB/SOLV TEC/DEV CONFER ADJUD NUC/PWR...POLICY IDEA/COMP 20 NASA. PAGE 107 A2197 — SPACE COM/IND LAW DIPLOM

B64
NEHEMKIS P.,LATIN AMERICA: MYTH AND REALITY. INDUS INT/ORG MUNIC PROB/SOLV CAP/ISM DIPLOM REV...SOC 20. PAGE 108 A2211 — REGION MYTH L/A+17C ECO/UNDEV

B64
PENNOCK J.R.,SELF-GOVERNMENT IN MODERNIZING NATIONS. AFR COM USA+45 ECO/DEV POL/PAR PROB/SOLV DIPLOM ECO/TAC COLONIAL REV POPULISM SOCISM 20. PAGE 114 A2350
ECO/UNDEV POLICY SOVEREIGN NAT/G

B64
REGALA R.,WORLD PEACE THROUGH DIPLOMACY AND LAW. S/ASIA WOR+45 ECO/UNDEV INT/ORG FORCES PLAN PROB/SOLV FOR/AID NUC/PWR WAR...POLICY INT/LAW 20. PAGE 120 A2456
DIPLOM PEACE ADJUD

B64
ROCK V.P.,A STRATEGY OF INTERDEPENDENCE. COM USSR WOR+45 NAT/G FORCES PROB/SOLV TEC/DEV DETER WAR ORD/FREE...CONCPT NEW/IDEA METH/COMP 20. PAGE 122 A2509
DIPLOM NUC/PWR PEACE POLICY

B64
RUSSELL R.B.,UNITED NATIONS EXPERIENCE WITH MILITARY FORCES: POLITICAL AND LEGAL ASPECTS. AFR KOREA WOR+45 LEGIS PROB/SOLV ADMIN CONTROL EFFICIENCY PEACE...POLICY INT/LAW BIBLIOG UN. PAGE 126 A2576
FORCES DIPLOM SANCTION ORD/FREE

B64
STANGER R.J.,ESSAYS ON INTERVENTION. PLAN PROB/SOLV BAL/PWR ADJUD COERCE WAR ROLE PWR...INT/LAW CONCPT 20 UN INTERVENT. PAGE 137 A2803
SOVEREIGN DIPLOM POLICY LEGIT

B64
WRIGHT Q.,A STUDY OF WAR. LAW NAT/G PROB/SOLV BAL/PWR NAT/LISM PEACE ATTIT SOVEREIGN...CENSUS SOC/INTEG. PAGE 168 A3419
WAR CONCPT DIPLOM CONTROL

S64
ARMSTRONG J.A.,"THE SOVIET-AMERICAN CONFRONTATION: A NEW STAGE?" CUBA USA+45 USSR PLAN PROB/SOLV INT/TRADE CONTROL ARMS/CONT NUC/PWR MARXISM 20 COLD/WAR INTERVENT. PAGE 9 A0174
DIPLOM POLICY INSPECT

S64
MCGHEE G.C.,"EAST-WEST RELATIONS TODAY." WOR+45 PROB/SOLV BAL/PWR PEACE 20 COLD/WAR. PAGE 98 A2011
IDEA/COMP DIPLOM ADJUD

S64
RUSK D.,"THE MAKING OF FOREIGN POLICY" USA+45 CHIEF DELIB/GP WORKER PROB/SOLV ADMIN ATTIT PWR ...DECISION 20 DEPT/STATE RUSK/D GOLDMAN/E. PAGE 125 A2570
DIPLOM INT POLICY

B65
ADENAUER K.,MEINE ERINNERUNGEN, 1945-53 (VOL. I), 1953-55 (VOL. II). EUR+WWI GERMANY CHIEF FORCES PROB/SOLV DIPLOM ARMS/CONT INGP/REL PEACE SOVEREIGN ...OBS/ENVIR RECORD 20. PAGE 4 A0089
NAT/G BIOG SELF/OBS

B65
CASSELL F.,GOLD OR CREDIT? THE ECONOMICS AND POLITICS OF INTERNATIONAL MONEY. WOR+45 PLAN PROB/SOLV BAL/PAY SOVEREIGN WEALTH 20 OEEC GOLD/STAND. PAGE 25 A0506
FINAN INT/ORG DIPLOM ECO/TAC

B65
DAVISON W.P.,INTERNATIONAL POLITICAL COMMUNICATION. COM USA+45 WOR+45 CULTURE ECO/UNDEV NAT/G PROB/SOLV PRESS TV ADMIN 20 FILM. PAGE 34 A0693
EDU/PROP DIPLOM PERS/REL COM/IND

B65
FLYNN A.H.,WORLD UNDERSTANDING: A SELECTED BIBLIOGRAPHY. WOR+45 PROB/SOLV BAL/PWR DIPLOM EFFICIENCY PEACE UN. PAGE 47 A0956
BIBLIOG/A INT/ORG EDU/PROP ROUTINE

B65
FORM W.H.,INDUSTRIAL RELATIONS AND SOCIAL CHANGE IN LATIN AMERICA. L/A+17C AGRI LABOR NAT/G PLAN PROB/SOLV DIPLOM...MGT SOC ANTHOL BIBLIOG/A METH 20. PAGE 47 A0966
INDUS GP/REL NAT/COMP ECO/UNDEV

B65
FRIEDMANN W.,AN INTRODUCTION TO WORLD POLITICS (5TH ED.). WOR+45 ECO/UNDEV BAL/PWR FOR/AID INT/TRADE PEACE...STAT CENSUS CHARTS BIBLIOG T 20 COLD/WAR UN THIRD/WRLD. PAGE 49 A1003
DIPLOM INT/ORG PROB/SOLV

B65
INGRAM D.,COMMONWEALTH FOR A COLOUR-BLIND WORLD. AFR INDIA UK STRATA ECO/UNDEV VOL/ASSN CREATE PLAN CONFER COLONIAL ORD/FREE SOC/INTEG 20 COMMONWLTH. PAGE 70 A1441
RACE/REL INT/ORG INGP/REL PROB/SOLV

B65
JOHNSTON D.M.,THE INTERNATIONAL LAW OF FISHERIES: A FRAMEWORK FOR POLICYORIENTED INQUIRIES. WOR+45 ACT/RES PLAN PROB/SOLV CONTROL SOVEREIGN. PAGE 75 A1527
CONCPT EXTR/IND JURID DIPLOM

B65
KRAUSE W.,ECONOMIC DEVELOPMENT: THE UNDERDEVELOPED WORLD AND THE AMERICAN INTEREST. USA+45 AGRI PLAN MARXISM...CHARTS 20. PAGE 82 A1679
FOR/AID ECO/UNDEV FINAN PROB/SOLV

B65
LARUS J.,FROM COLLECTIVE SECURITY TO PREVENTIVE DIPLOMACY. FUT FORCES PROB/SOLV DEBATE AGREE COERCE WAR PWR...ANTHOL 20 LEAGUE/NAT UN. PAGE 85 A1736
INT/ORG PEACE DIPLOM ORD/FREE

B65
LINDBLOM C.E.,THE INTELLIGENCE OF DEMOCRACY; DECISION MAKING THROUGH MUTUAL ADJUSTMENT. WOR+45 SOCIETY NAT/G PROB/SOLV DOMIN PARTIC GP/REL ORD/FREE...POLICY IDEA/COMP BIBLIOG 20. PAGE 89 A1821
PLURISM DECISION ADJUST DIPLOM

B65
LYONS G.M.,AMERICA: PURPOSE AND POWER. UK USA+45 FINAN INDUS MARKET WORKER TEC/DEV DIPLOM AUTOMAT NUC/PWR WAR RACE/REL ORD/FREE 20 EEC CONGRESS SUPREME/CT CIV/RIGHTS. PAGE 92 A1881
PWR PROB/SOLV ECO/DEV TASK

B65
NATIONAL CENTRAL LIBRARY,LATIN AMERICAN ECONOMIC AND SOCIAL SERIALS. UK SOCIETY NAT/G PLAN PROB/SOLV ...SOC 20. PAGE 107 A2202
BIBLIOG INT/TRADE ECO/UNDEV L/A+17C

B65
REQUA E.G.,THE DEVELOPING NATIONS: A GUIDE TO INFORMATION SOURCES CONCERNING THEIR ECON, POLIT, TECHNICAL, AND SOCIAL PROBLEMS. AFR ASIA ISLAM L/A+17C INDUS INT/ORG CONSULT PLAN PROB/SOLV...SOC 20 UN. PAGE 120 A2466
BIBLIOG/A ECO/UNDEV FOR/AID TEC/DEV

B65
SILVA SOLAR J.,EL DESARROLLO DE LA NUEVA SOCIEDAD EN AMERICA. L/A+17C SOCIETY AGRI PROB/SOLV DIPLOM PARTIC GP/REL OWN...POLICY SOC 20 REFORMERS. PAGE 133 A2716
STRUCT ECO/UNDEV REGION CONTROL

B65
US BUREAU OF THE BUDGET,THE BALANCE OF PAYMENTS STATISTICS OF THE UNITED STATES: A REVIEW AND APPRAISAL. USA+45 FINAN NAT/G PROB/SOLV DIPLOM. PAGE 150 A3057
BAL/PAY STAT METH/COMP BUDGET

B65
US SENATE COMM GOVT OPERATIONS,ADMINISTRATION OF NATIONAL SECURITY. USA+45 DELIB/GP ADMIN ROLE ...POLICY CHARTS SENATE. PAGE 156 A3177
NAT/G ORD/FREE DIPLOM PROB/SOLV

B65
US SENATE COMM ON JUDICIARY,REFUGEE PROBLEMS IN SOUTH VIETNAM AND LAOS: HEARINGS BEFORE SUBCOMMITTEE TO INVESTIGATE PROBLEMS OF REFUGEES, ESCAPEES. CHINA/COM LAOS USA+45 VIETNAM/S PROB/SOLV DIPLOM GOV/REL GP/REL EFFICIENCY ORD/FREE...POLICY GEOG 20 CONGRESS MIGRATION. PAGE 157 A3194
STRANGE HABITAT FOR/AID CIVMIL/REL

B65
WALKER A.A.,THE RHODESIAS AND NYASALAND: A GUIDE TO OFFICIAL PUBLICATIONS. RHODESIA UK OP/RES PLAN PROB/SOLV DIPLOM...POLICY SOC CON/ANAL 19/20 NYASALAND. PAGE 160 A3263
BIBLIOG NAT/G COLONIAL AFR

B65
WASKOW A.I.,KEEPING THE WORLD DISARMED. AFR GERMANY/E DIPLOM CONTROL WAR 20 UN. PAGE 161 A3289
ARMS/CONT PEACE FORCES PROB/SOLV

B65
WEAVER J.N.,THE INTERNATIONAL DEVELOPMENT ASSOCIATION: A NEW APPROACH TO FOREIGN AID. USA+45 NAT/G OP/RES PLAN PROB/SOLV WEALTH...CHARTS BIBLIOG 20 UN. PAGE 162 A3295
FOR/AID INT/ORG ECO/UNDEV FINAN

B65
WEISNER J.B.,WHERE SCIENCE AND POLITICS MEET. USA+45 ECO/DEV R+D FORCES PROB/SOLV DIPLOM FOR/AID CONTROL...PHIL/SCI PRESIDENT KENNEDY/JF JOHNSON/LB. PAGE 163 A3310
CHIEF NAT/G POLICY TEC/DEV

L65
MATTHEWS D.G.,"LE TIERS MONDE: A SELECT AND PRELIMINARY BIBLIOGRAPHIC SURVEY OF MANPOWER IN DEVELOPING COUNTRIES, 1960-1964." AFR ISLAM L/A+17C INDUS PLAN PROB/SOLV TEC/DEV INT/TRADE EFFICIENCY WEALTH...STAT 20. PAGE 96 A1971
BIBLIOG/A ECO/UNDEV LABOR WORKER

B66
BOULDING K.E.,THE IMPACT OF THE SOCIAL SCIENCES. UNIV LAW SOCIETY CREATE PROB/SOLV...TREND WORSHIP. PAGE 17 A0349
SOC DIPLOM

B66
BUCHAN A.,A WORLD OF NUCLEAR POWERS? PEACE...ANTHOL 20. PAGE 21 A0423
NUC/PWR BAL/PWR PROB/SOLV DIPLOM

B66
DAVIS V.,POSTWAR DEFENSE POLICY AND THE US NAVY, 1943-1946. USA+45 DIPLOM CONFER LEAD ATTIT...POLICY IDEA/COMP 20 NAVY. PAGE 34 A0692
FORCES PLAN PROB/SOLV CIVMIL/REL

B66
FALL B.B.,VIET-NAM WITNESS, 1953-66. S/ASIA VIETNAM SECT PROB/SOLV COLONIAL GUERRILLA...CHARTS BIBLIOG 20. PAGE 44 A0895
MARXIST WAR DIPLOM

B66
FINKLE J.L.,POLITICAL DEVELOPMENT AND SOCIAL CHANGE. WOR+45 CULTURE NAT/G OP/RES PROB/SOLV DIPLOM ECO/TAC INGP/REL...METH/COMP ANTHOL 20. PAGE 46 A0934
ECO/UNDEV SOCIETY CREATE

B66
GILBERT M.,THE ROOTS OF APPEASEMENT. EUR+WWI GERMANY UK MUNIC BAL/PWR FASCISM...NEW/IDEA 20.
DIPLOM REPAR

PAGE 52 A1070 PROB/SOLV POLICY

B66
GLAZER M.,THE FEDERAL GOVERNMENT AND THE UNIVERSITY. CHILE PROB/SOLV DIPLOM GIVE ADMIN WAR ...POLICY SOC 20. PAGE 53 A1079 BIBLIOG/A NAT/G PLAN ACADEM

B66
GROSS F.,WORLD POLITICS AND TENSION AREAS. CHINA/COM SOMALIA VENEZUELA COERCE GP/REL RACE/REL ATTIT HABITAT 19/20 CASEBOOK NEWYORK/C. PAGE 57 A1173 DIPLOM WAR PROB/SOLV

B66
INTERNATIONAL ECO POLICY ASSN,THE UNITED STATES BALANCE OF PAYMENTS. INT/ORG NAT/G PROB/SOLV BUDGET DIPLOM INT/TRADE WEALTH 20. PAGE 71 A1454 BAL/PAY ECO/TAC POLICY FINAN

B66
LALL A.,MODERN INTERNATIONAL NEGOTIATION: PRINCIPLES AND PRACTICE. WOR+45 INT/ORG DELIB/GP PROB/SOLV DETER...INT/LAW TREATY. PAGE 84 A1712 DIPLOM ECO/TAC ATTIT

B66
LEAGUE OF WOMEN VOTERS OF US,FOREIGN AID AT THE CROSSROADS. USA+45 WOR+45 DELIB/GP PROB/SOLV DIPLOM INT/TRADE RECEIVE BAL/PAY...CHARTS 20 UN. PAGE 86 A1756 FOR/AID GIVE ECO/UNDEV PLAN

B66
LEWIS S.,TOWARDS INTERNATIONAL CO-OPERATION (1ST ED.). WOR+45 AGRI INDUS EDU/PROP RACE/REL ISOLAT NAT/LISM ATTIT HEALTH WEALTH...CHARTS WORSHIP 20 UN. PAGE 88 A1803 DIPLOM ANOMIE PROB/SOLV INT/ORG

B66
NANTWI E.K.,THE ENFORCEMENT OF INTERNATIONAL JUDICIAL DECISIONS AND ARBITAL AWARDS IN PUBLIC INTERNATIONAL LAW. WOR+45 WOR-45 JUDGE PROB/SOLV DIPLOM CT/SYS SUPEGO MORAL PWR RESPECT...METH/CNCPT 18/20 CASEBOOK. PAGE 107 A2196 INT/LAW ADJUD SOVEREIGN INT/ORG

B66
PIQUET H.S.,THE US BALANCE OF PAYMENTS AND INTERNATIONAL MONETARY RESERVES. USA+45 PROB/SOLV INT/TRADE GOV/REL EQUILIB...POLICY STAT CHARTS 20 GOLD/STAND. PAGE 116 A2384 BAL/PAY DIPLOM FINAN ECO/TAC

B66
SALTER L.M.,RESOLUTION OF INTERNATIONAL CONFLICT. USA+45 INT/ORG SECT DIPLOM ECO/TAC FOR/AID DETER NUC/PWR WAR 20. PAGE 127 A2595 PROB/SOLV PEACE INT/LAW POLICY

B66
THOMPSON J.H.,MODERNIZATION OF THE ARAB WORLD. FUT ISRAEL STRUCT ECO/UNDEV DIPLOM INGP/REL ATTIT ...CENSUS ANTHOL 20 ARABS. PAGE 143 A2926 ADJUST ISLAM PROB/SOLV NAT/COMP

B66
UN ECAFE,ADMINISTRATIVE ASPECTS OF FAMILY PLANNING PROGRAMMES (PAMPHLET). ASIA THAILAND WOR+45 VOL/ASSN PROB/SOLV BUDGET FOR/AID EDU/PROP CONFER CONTROL GOV/REL TIME 20 UN BIRTH/CON. PAGE 147 A2999 PLAN CENSUS FAM ADMIN

B66
US SENATE COMM GOVT OPERATIONS,POPULATION CRISIS. USA+45 ECO/DEV ECO/UNDEV AGRI SECT DELIB/GP PROB/SOLV FOR/AID REPRESENT ATTIT...GEOG CHARTS 20 CONGRESS DEPT/STATE DEPT/HEW BIRTH/CON. PAGE 156 A3178 CENSUS CONTROL LEGIS CONSULT

B66
US SENATE COMM ON FOREIGN REL,UNITED STATES POLICY TOWARD EUROPE (AND RELATED MATTERS). COM EUR+WWI GERMANY PROB/SOLV REGION NUC/PWR WAR NAT/LISM PEACE PWR...NAT/COMP 20 NATO CONGRESS DEGAULLE/C. PAGE 156 A3184 DIPLOM INT/ORG POLICY WOR+45

B66
WAINHOUSE D.W.,INTERNATIONAL PEACE OBSERVATION: A HISTORY AND FORECAST. INT/ORG PROB/SOLV BAL/PWR AGREE ARMS/CONT COERCE NUC/PWR...PREDICT METH/COMP 20 UN LEAGUE/NAT OAS TREATY. PAGE 160 A3261 PEACE DIPLOM

B66
WESTWOOD A.F.,FOREIGN AID IN A FOREIGN POLICY FRAMEWORK. AFR ASIA INDIA IRAN L/A+17C USA+45 USSR ECO/UNDEV AGRI FORCES LEGIS PLAN PROB/SOLV ...DECISION 20 COLD/WAR. PAGE 163 A3324 FOR/AID DIPLOM POLICY ECO/TAC

B66
WILLIAMS P.,AID IN UGANDA - EDUCATION. UGANDA UK FINAN ACADEM INT/ORG SCHOOL PROB/SOLV ECO/TAC UTIL ...STAT CHARTS 20. PAGE 165 A3352 PLAN EDU/PROP FOR/AID ECO/UNDEV

L66
MCDOUGAL M.S.,"CHINESE PARTICIPATION IN THE UNITED NATIONS: THE LEGAL IMPERATIVES OF A NEGOTIATED SOLUTION" CHINA/COM WOR+45 VOL/ASSN DIPLOM PARTIC ...DECISION IDEA/COMP 20 UN. PAGE 98 A2010 INT/ORG REPRESENT POLICY PROB/SOLV

S66
JAVITS J.K.,"POLITICAL ACTION VITAL FOR LATIN AMERICAN INTEGRATION." ECO/UNDEV INT/ORG POL/PAR VOL/ASSN PLAN PROB/SOLV INT/TRADE EFFICIENCY 20 OAS LAFTA. PAGE 73 A1500 L/A+17C ECO/TAC REGION

S66
MCNEAL R.H.,"THE LEGACY OF THE COMINTERN." USSR WOR+45 WOR-45 PROB/SOLV DIPLOM CONFER CONTROL LEAD WAR 20 STALIN/J COMINTERN. PAGE 98 A2020 MARXISM INT/ORG POL/PAR PWR

S66
ORVIK N.,"NATO: THE ROLE OF THE SMALL MEMBERS." EUR+WWI FUT USA+45 CONSULT FORCES PROB/SOLV ARMS/CONT DETER NUC/PWR PWR 20 NATO. PAGE 112 A2298 NAT/G DIPLOM INT/ORG POLICY

N66
EOMMITTEE ECONOMIC DEVELOPMENT,THE DOLLAR AND THE WORLD MONETARY SYSTEM: A STATEMENT ON NATIONAL POLICY (PAMPHLET). USA+45 NAT/G PLAN PROB/SOLV BUDGET ECO/TAC FOR/AID INCOME...POLICY 20 GOLD/STAND EUROPE. PAGE 42 A0854 FINAN BAL/PAY DIPLOM ECO/DEV

B67
AUBREY H.G.,ATLANTIC ECONOMIC COOPERATION. ECO/DEV INDUS VOL/ASSN PROB/SOLV DIPLOM INT/TRADE TARIFFS CONFER 20. PAGE 10 A0197 INT/ORG ECO/TAC TEC/DEV CAP/ISM

B67
BARANSON J.,TECHNOLOGY FOR UNDERDEVELOPED AREAS: AN ANNOTATED BIBLIOGRAPHY. FUT WOR+45 CULTURE INDUS INT/ORG CREATE PROB/SOLV INT/TRADE EDU/PROP AUTOMAT ...CONCPT METH. PAGE 11 A0218 BIBLIOG/A ECO/UNDEV TEC/DEV R+D

B67
CHO S.S.,KOREA IN WORLD POLITICS 1940-1950; AN EVALUATION OF AMERICAN RESPONSIBILITY. KOREA USA+45 USSR CONSTN INT/ORG NAT/G FORCES FOR/AID ANOMIE SUPEGO MARXISM...DECISION BIBLIOG 20. PAGE 26 A0533 POLICY DIPLOM PROB/SOLV WAR

B67
CLARK S.V.O.,CENTRAL BANK COOPERATION: 1924-31. WOR-45 PROB/SOLV ECO/TAC ADJUST BAL/PAY...TREND CHARTS METH/COMP 20. PAGE 27 A0542 FINAN EQUILIB DIPLOM POLICY

B67
JOHNSON D.G.,THE STRUGGLE AGAINST WORLD HUNGER (HEADLINE SERIES, NO. 184) (PAMPHLET). PLAN TEC/DEV FOR/AID...CHARTS 20 FAO MEXIC/AMER. PAGE 74 A1520 AGRI PROB/SOLV ECO/UNDEV HEALTH

B67
MAW B.,BREAKTHROUGH IN BURMA: MEMOIRS OF A REVOLUTION, 1939-1946. BURMA UK FORCES PROB/SOLV DIPLOM FOR/AID DOMIN LEAD...BIOG 20. PAGE 97 A1980 REV ORD/FREE NAT/LISM COLONIAL

B67
MAZRUI A.A.,TOWARDS A PAX AFRICANA. AFR STRUCT ECO/UNDEV NAT/G DIPLOM COLONIAL REGION WAR ATTIT 20. PAGE 97 A1988 PEACE FORCES PROB/SOLV SOVEREIGN

B67
MEYNAUD J.,TRADE UNIONISM IN AFRICA; A STUDY OF ITS GROWTH AND ORIENTATION (TRANS. BY ANGELA BRENCH). INT/ORG PROB/SOLV COLONIAL PWR...TIME/SEQ TREND ILO. PAGE 100 A2055 LABOR AFR NAT/LISM ORD/FREE

B67
MURTY B.S.,PROPAGANDA AND WORLD PUBLIC ORDER. FUT WOR+45 COM/IND INT/ORG PROB/SOLV ATTIT KNOWL ORD/FREE...POLICY UN. PAGE 106 A2183 EDU/PROP DIPLOM CONTROL JURID

B67
SALISBURY H.E.,BEHIND THE LINES - HANOI. VIETNAM/N NAT/G GUERRILLA CIVMIL/REL NAT/LISM KNOWL 20. PAGE 126 A2592 WAR PROB/SOLV DIPLOM OBS

B67
SCOTT A.M.,THE FUNCTIONING OF THE INTERNATIONAL POLITICAL SYSTEM. INT/ORG OP/RES PROB/SOLV COERCE WAR EQUILIB...METH/CNCPT BIBLIOG. PAGE 130 A2671 DIPLOM DECISION BAL/PWR

B67
UNESCO,PRINCIPLES AND PROBLEMS OF NATIONAL SCIENCE POLICIES. WOR+45 ECO/DEV ECO/UNDEV R+D INT/ORG PROB/SOLV CONFER...PHIL/SCI CHARTS 20 UNESCO UN. PAGE 148 A3026 NAT/COMP POLICY TEC/DEV CREATE

B67
US SENATE COMM ON FOREIGN REL,UNITED STATES ARMAMENT AND DISARMAMENT PROBLEMS. USA+45 AIR BAL/PWR DIPLOM FOR/AID NUC/PWR ORD/FREE SENATE TREATY. PAGE 156 A3190 ARMS/CONT WEAPON FORCES PROB/SOLV

L67
CAHIERS P.,"LE RECOURS EN CONSTATATION DE MANQUEMENTS DES ETATS MEMBRES DEVANT LA COUR DES COMMUNAUTES EUROPEENNES." LAW PROB/SOLV DIPLOM ADMIN CT/SYS SANCTION ATTIT...POLICY DECISION JURID ECSC EEC. PAGE 23 A0465 INT/ORG CONSTN ROUTINE ADJUD

L67
GENEVEY P.,"LE DESARMEMENT APRES LE TRAITE DE VERSAILLES." EUR+WWI GERMANY INT/ORG PROB/SOLV CONFER WAR...POLICY PREDICT 20. PAGE 52 A1057 ARMS/CONT PEACE DIPLOM FORCES

L67
GRAUBARD S.R.,"TOWARD THE YEAR 2000: WORK IN PROGRESS." FUT ACADEM SECT DELIB/GP DIPLOM EDU/PROP AGE/Y PERSON ROLE...PSY ANTHOL. PAGE 55 A1131 PREDICT PROB/SOLV SOCIETY CULTURE

KOMESAR N.K.,"PRESIDENTIAL AMENDMENT & TERMINATION OF TREATIES* THE CASE OF THE WARSAW CONVENTION." POLAND USA+45 NAT/G CHIEF PROB/SOLV DIPLOM PWR 20 CONGRESS. PAGE 81 A1669 — L67 TOP/EX LEGIS CONSTN LICENSE

BENTLEY E.,"VIETNAM: THE STATE OF OUR FEELINGS." USA+45 VIETNAM PROB/SOLV DIPLOM GP/REL INGP/REL RACE/REL WEALTH. PAGE 13 A0271 — S67 WAR PARTIC ATTIT PEACE

CARROLL K.J.,"SECOND STEP TOWARD ARMS CONTROL." WOR+45 INT/ORG VOL/ASSN FORCES PROB/SOLV RISK WEAPON 20 COLD/WAR. PAGE 25 A0503 — S67 ARMS/CONT DIPLOM PLAN NUC/PWR

CLINGHAM T.A. JR.,"LEGISLATIVE FLOTSAM AND INTERNATIONAL ACTION IN THE 'YARMOUTH CASTLE'S' WAKE." WOR+45 PROB/SOLV CONFER COST HEALTH...POLICY INT/LAW CONGRESS. PAGE 27 A0552 — S67 DIPLOM DIST/IND INT/ORG LAW

FRANK I.,"NEW PERSPECTIVES ON TRADE AND DEVELOPMENT." PROB/SOLV BARGAIN DIPLOM FOR/AID CONFER GP/REL WEALTH 20 UN GATT. PAGE 48 A0980 — S67 ECO/UNDEV INT/ORG INT/TRADE ECO/TAC

FRANKLIN W.O.,"CLAUSEWITZ ON LIMITED WAR." VIETNAM WOR+45 WOR-45 PROB/SOLV DIPLOM ECO/TAC DOMIN COLONIAL...METH/COMP 19/20. PAGE 48 A0986 — S67 COERCE WAR PLAN GUERRILLA

GLOBERSON A.,"SOCIAL GROWTH IN THE DEVELOPING COUNTRIES." CULTURE SOCIETY CONSULT PROB/SOLV SOC. PAGE 53 A1082 — S67 ECO/UNDEV FOR/AID EDU/PROP PLAN

HIBBERT R.A.,"THE MONGOLIAN PEOPLE'S REPUBLIC IN THE 1960'S." INT/ORG PLAN FOR/AID 20. PAGE 64 A1326 — S67 ASIA ECO/UNDEV PROB/SOLV DIPLOM

HUDSON R.,"WAS THIS WAR NECESSARY? THE UN AND THE MIDDLE EAST" WOR+45 STRUCT DIPLOM DOMIN CONTROL REPRESENT PWR...NEW/IDEA 20 UN MID/EAST. PAGE 69 A1410 — S67 DELIB/GP INT/ORG PROB/SOLV PEACE

INGLEHART R.,"AN END TO EUROPEAN INTEGRATION." PROB/SOLV BAL/PWR NAT/LISM...PSY SOC INT CHARTS GP/COMP 20. PAGE 70 A1440 — S67 DIPLOM EUR+WWI REGION ATTIT

JOHNSTON D.M.,"LAW, TECHNOLOGY AND THE SEA." WOR+45 PLAN PROB/SOLV TEC/DEV CONFER ADJUD ORD/FREE ...POLICY JURID. PAGE 75 A1528 — S67 INT/LAW INT/ORG DIPLOM NEUTRAL

KELLY F.K.,"A PROPOSAL FOR AN ANNUAL REPORT ON THE STATE OF MANKIND." FUT INTELL COM/IND INT/ORG CREATE PROB/SOLV PERS/REL...CONCPT 20 UN. PAGE 77 A1579 — S67 SOCIETY UNIV ATTIT NEW/IDEA

KRAUS J.,"A MARXIST IN GHANA." GHANA ELITES CHIEF PROB/SOLV TEC/DEV DIPLOM ECO/TAC COLONIAL PARTIC PWR 20 NKRUMAH/K. PAGE 82 A1676 — S67 MARXISM PLAN ATTIT CREATE

KYLE K.,"BACKGROUND TO THE CRISIS" ISLAM ISRAEL UAR UK USSR NAT/G PROB/SOLV LEGIT CONTROL REGION STRANGE MORAL 20 JEWS. PAGE 83 A1698 — S67 DIPLOM POLICY SOVEREIGN COERCE

MOBERG E.,"THE EFFECT OF SECURITY POLICY MEASURES: DISCUSSION RELATED TO SWEDEN'S SECURITY POLICY." SWEDEN PLAN PROB/SOLV DIPLOM GOV/REL MORAL...CHARTS 20. PAGE 102 A2092 — S67 POLICY ORD/FREE BUDGET FINAN

NIEBUHR R.,"THE SOCIAL MYTHS IN THE COLD WAR." USA+45 USSR VIETNAM PROB/SOLV BAL/PWR ARMS/CONT NAT/LISM PWR ALL/IDEOS CONCPT. PAGE 109 A2238 — S67 MYTH DIPLOM GOV/COMP

RABIER J.-R.,"THE EUROPEAN IDEA AND NATIONAL PUBLIC OPINIONS." ACT/RES PLAN DIPLOM PARTIC CONSEN ATTIT PERCEPT...DECISION CHARTS. PAGE 118 A2430 — S67 POLICY FEDERAL EUR+WWI PROB/SOLV

ROSE S.,"ASIAN NATIONALISM* THE SECOND STAGE." ASIA COM ECO/UNDEV NAT/G PROB/SOLV DIPLOM FOR/AID DOMIN NEUTRAL REGION TASK...METH/COMP 20. PAGE 123 A2528 — S67 NAT/LISM S/ASIA BAL/PWR COLONIAL

ROWAN C.T.,"NEW FRONTIERS IN RACE RELATIONS." USA+45 NAT/G DIPLOM 20. PAGE 124 A2551 — S67 RACE/REL DISCRIM POLICY PROB/SOLV

SCHACTER O.,"SCIENTIFIC ADVANCES AND INTERNATIONAL LAWMAKING." FUT R+D PLAN PROB/SOLV CONFER CONTROL ...POLICY PREDICT 20 UN. PAGE 128 A2617 — S67 TEC/DEV INT/LAW INT/ORG ACT/RES

SHARP G.,"THE NEED OF A FUNCTIONAL SUBSTITUTE FOR WAR." FUT UNIV WOR+45 CULTURE SOCIETY INT/ORG CONSULT DELIB/GP ACT/RES CREATE BAL/PWR CONFER ARMS/CONT NUC/PWR 20. PAGE 132 A2696 — S67 PEACE WAR DIPLOM PROB/SOLV

SOMMER T.,"BONN CHANGES COURSE." GERMANY/W NAT/G POL/PAR PROB/SOLV NAT/LISM 20 NATO BERLIN/BLO. PAGE 135 A2766 — S67 DIPLOM BAL/PWR INT/ORG

SPENCER R.,"GERMANY AFTER THE AUTUMN CRISIS." GERMANY CHOOSE GP/REL PERS/REL. PAGE 136 A2785 — S67 DIPLOM POL/PAR PROB/SOLV

WEIL G.L.,"THE EUROPEAN COMMUNITY* WHAT LIES BEYOND THE POINT OF NO RETURN?" VOL/ASSN PROB/SOLV DIPLOM REGION INGP/REL CENTRAL PWR 20 EEC. PAGE 162 A3301 — S67 INT/ORG ECO/DEV INT/TRADE PREDICT

WINTHROP H.,"CONTEMPORARY ECONOMIC DEHUMANIZATION* SOME DIFFICULTIES SURROUNDING ITS REDUCTION." USA+45 WOR+45 ACT/RES PROB/SOLV DIPLOM ROUTINE DEMAND UTIL. PAGE 165 A3368 — S67 TEC/DEV SOCIETY WEALTH

LING D.L.,"TUNISIA: FROM PROTECTORATE TO REPUBLIC." CULTURE NAT/G POL/PAR CHIEF DIPLOM COERCE WAR PWR ...BIBLIOG 19/20 TUNIS. PAGE 89 A1825 — C67 AFR NAT/LISM COLONIAL PROB/SOLV

ANTWERP-INST UNIVERSITAIRE,BIBLIOGRAPHIC COMPENDIUM: DEVELOPING COUNTRIES (ANTWERP-INST UNIVERSITAIRE DES TERRITOIRES D'OUTRE-MER). AFR EUR+WWI SOCIETY AGRI FINAN NEIGH VOL/ASSN PROB/SOLV TEC/DEV FOR/AID INT/TRADE 20. PAGE 8 A0166 — B68 BIBLIOG ECO/UNDEV DIPLOM PLAN

PROBABIL....PROBABILITY; SEE ALSO GAMBLE

KUENNE R.E.,THE POLARIS MISSILE STRIKE* A GENERAL ECONOMIC SYSTEMS ANALYSIS. USA+45 USSR NAT/G BAL/PWR ARMS/CONT WAR...MATH PROBABIL COMPUT/IR CHARTS HYPO/EXP SIMUL. PAGE 82 A1689 — B66 NUC/PWR FORCES DETER DIPLOM

PROBABILITY....SEE PROBABIL

PROBLEM SOLVING....SEE PROB/SOLV

PROC/MFG....PROCESSING OR MANUFACTURING INDUSTRIES

KYRIAK T.E.,SOVIET UNION: BIBLIOGRAPHY INDEX TO US JPRS RESEARCH TRANSLATIONS. USSR ECO/DEV AGRI COM/IND CONSTRUC DIST/IND EXTR/IND PROC/MFG R+D INT/TRADE...SOC 20. PAGE 83 A1703 — N BIBLIOG/A INDUS MARXISM PRESS

LEYPOLOT F.,AMERICAN CATALOGUE OF BOOKS, 1876-1910 (19 VOLS.). NAT/G DIPLOM...CON/ANAL 19/20. PAGE 88 A1806 — N BIBLIOG USA-45 PROF/ORG PROC/MFG

ALLEN R.L.,SOVIET INFLUENCE IN LATIN AMERICA. ECO/UNDEV FINAN PROC/MFG NAT/G TEC/DEV EDU/PROP EXEC ROUTINE ATTIT DRIVE PERSON ALL/VALS PWR...STAT CHARTS WORK 20. PAGE 6 A0125 — B59 L/A+17C ECO/TAC INT/TRADE USSR

PUGWASH CONFERENCE,"ON BIOLOGICAL AND CHEMICAL WARFARE." WOR+45 SOCIETY PROC/MFG INT/ORG FORCES EDU/PROP ADJUD RIGID/FLEX ORD/FREE PWR...DECISION PSY NEW/IDEA MATH VAL/FREE 20. PAGE 118 A2417 — S59 ACT/RES BIO/SOC WAR WEAPON

APTHEKER H.,DISARMAMENT AND THE AMERICAN ECONOMY: A SYMPOSIUM. FUT USA+45 ECO/DEV DIST/IND FINAN INDUS PROC/MFG LABOR NAT/G POL/PAR CONSULT PLAN CAP/ISM INT/TRADE PEACE ATTIT MORAL WEALTH...TREND GEN/LAWS TOT/POP 20. PAGE 9 A0172 — B60 MARXIST ARMS/CONT

FRIEDMANN W.G.,JOINT INTERNATIONAL BUSINESS VENTURES. ASIA ISLAM L/A+17C ECO/DEV DIST/IND FINAN PROC/MFG FACE/GP LG/CO NAT/G VOL/ASSN CONSULT EX/STRUC PLAN ADMIN ROUTINE WEALTH...OLD/LIB WORK 20. PAGE 49 A1004 — B61 ECO/UNDEV INT/TRADE

LEWIS J.P.,QUIET CRISIS IN INDIA. INDIA USA+45 CULTURE ECO/UNDEV AGRI INDUS PROC/MFG NAT/G PLAN TEC/DEV DRIVE PWR SKILL WEALTH...MYTH 20. PAGE 88 A1801 — B62 S/ASIA ECO/TAC FOR/AID

KAWALKOWSKI A.,"POUR UNE EUROPE INDEPENDENTE ET REUNIFIEE." EUR+WWI FUT USA+45 USSR WOR+45 ECO/DEV PROC/MFG INT/ORG NAT/G ACT/RES TEC/DEV FEDERAL RIGID/FLEX...CONCPT METH/CNCPT OEEC TOT/POP 20 DEGAULLE/C. PAGE 77 A1573 — S63 R+D PLAN NUC/PWR

B64
RAMAZANI R.K.,THE MIDDLE EAST AND THE EUROPEAN COMMON MARKET. EUR+WWI ISLAM ECO/DEV EXTR/IND MARKET PROC/MFG INT/ORG NAT/G TEC/DEV ECO/TAC REGION DRIVE WEALTH...STAT CHARTS EEC TOT/POP 20. PAGE 119 A2437
ECO/UNDEV ATTIT INT/TRADE

B65
MURUMBI J.,PROBLEMS OF ECONOMIC DEVELOPMENT IN EAST AFRICA. FINAN INDUS WORKER TEC/DEV INT/TRADE TAX DEMAND EFFICIENCY PRODUC SOCISM...TREND CHARTS 20 AFRICA/E. PAGE 106 A2184
AGRI ECO/TAC ECO/UNDEV PROC/MFG

PROCEDURAL SYSTEMS....SEE ROUTINE, ALSO PROCESSES AND PRACTICES INDEX

PROCESSING OR MANUFACTURING INDUSTRY....SEE PROC/MFG

PRODUC....PRODUCTIVITY; SEE ALSO PLAN

B00
MOCKLER-FERRYMAN A.,BRITISH WEST AFRICA. FRANCE GERMANY NIGER SIER/LEONE UK CULTURE DIPLOM WAR RACE/REL PRODUC PROFIT WEALTH...POLICY PREDICT 19. PAGE 102 A2095
AFR COLONIAL INT/TRADE CAP/ISM

B19
MEYER H.H.B.,SELECT LIST OF REFERENCES ON ECONOMIC RECONSTRUCTION: INCLUDING REPORTS OF THE BRITISH MINISTRY OF RECONSTRUCTION. UK LABOR PLAN PROB/SOLV ECO/TAC INT/TRADE WAR DEMAND PRODUC 20. PAGE 100 A2051
BIBLIOG/A EUR+WWI ECO/DEV WORKER

B27
SIEGFRIED A.,AMERICA COMES OF AGE: A FRENCH ANALYSIS (TRANS. BY H.H. HEMMING AND DORIS HEMMING). FRANCE UK POL/PAR WORKER TEC/DEV DIPLOM REGION RACE/REL ADJUST PRODUC HEREDITY...TIME/SEQ GP/COMP SOC/INTEG 20 DEMOCRAT REPUBLICAN KKK. PAGE 132 A2714
USA-45 CULTURE ECO/DEV SOC

B38
FRANKEL S.H.,CAPITAL INVESTMENT IN AFRICA. AFR EUR+WWI RHODESIA SOUTH/AFR UK FINAN FOR/AID COLONIAL DEMAND UTIL WEALTH...METH/CNCPT CHARTS 20 CONGO/LEOP. PAGE 48 A0983
ECO/UNDEV EXTR/IND DIPLOM PRODUC

B48
MINISTERE FINANCES ET ECO,BULLETIN BIBLIOGRAPHIQUE. AFR EUR+WWI FRANCE CULTURE STRUCT FINAN NAT/G ACT/RES INT/TRADE ADMIN REGION PRODUC STAT. PAGE 102 A2088
BIBLIOG/A ECO/UNDEV TEC/DEV COLONIAL

B50
US DEPARTMENT OF STATE,POINT FOUR: COOPERATIVE PROGRAM FOR AID IN THE DEVELOPMENT OF ECONOMICALLY UNDERDEVELOPED AREAS. WOR+45 AGRI INDUS INT/ORG PLAN TEC/DEV DIPLOM EDU/PROP ADMIN PEACE PRODUC WEALTH 20 CONGRESS UN. PAGE 151 A3085
ECO/UNDEV FOR/AID FINAN INT/TRADE

B53
NEISSER H.,NATIONAL INCOMES AND INTERNATIONAL TRADE. FRANCE GERMANY SWEDEN UK USA-45 EXTR/IND FINAN INDUS TEC/DEV PRICE BAL/PAY EQUILIB INCOME WEALTH...CHARTS METH 19 CHINJAP. PAGE 108 A2215
INT/TRADE PRODUC MARKET CON/ANAL

B54
GIRAUD A.,CIVILISATION ET PRODUCTIVITE. UNIV INDUS WORKER DIPLOM REV INCOME UTOPIA...GEOG 20. PAGE 53 A1076
SOCIETY PRODUC ROLE

B57
MCNEILL W.H.,GREECE: AMERICAN AID IN ACTION. GREECE UK USA+45 FINAN CAP/ISM INT/TRADE BAL/PAY PRODUC WEALTH...POLICY METH/COMP 20. PAGE 99 A2022
FOR/AID DIPLOM ECO/UNDEV

B58
PALYI M.,MANAGED MONEY AT THE CROSSROADS: THE EUROPEAN EXPERIENCE. WOR+45 WOR-45 TEC/DEV DIPLOM INT/TRADE DEMAND WEALTH...CHARTS BIBLIOG 19/20 EUROPE GOLD/STAND SILVER. PAGE 113 A2324
FINAN ECO/TAC ECO/DEV PRODUC

L58
TRAGER F.N.,"A SELECTED AND ANNOTATED BIBLIOGRAPHY ON ECONOMIC DEVELOPMENT, 1953-1957." WOR+45 AGRI FINAN INDUS MARKET LABOR MUNIC WORKER PLAN INT/TRADE PRODUC CENSUS. PAGE 145 A2958
BIBLIOG/A ECO/UNDEV ECO/DEV

B59
LINK R.G.,ENGLISH THEORIES OF ECONOMIC FLUCTUATIONS: 1815-1848. FRANCE UK AGRI WORKER DIPLOM PRICE TASK WAR DEMAND PRODUC...POLICY BIBLIOG 18 MALTHUS MILL/JS WILSON/J. PAGE 89 A1826
IDEA/COMP ECO/DEV WEALTH EQUILIB

B61
LERCHE C.O. JR.,FOREIGN POLICY OF THE AMERICAN PEOPLE (REV. ED.). USA+45 USSR FORCES TEC/DEV EDU/PROP WAR PRODUC ORD/FREE MARXISM...POLICY TREND BIBLIOG 20 COLD/WAR. PAGE 87 A1781
DECISION PLAN PEACE DIPLOM

B61
STARK H.,SOCIAL AND ECONOMIC FRONTIERS IN LATIN AMERICA (2ND ED.). CUBA FUT CULTURE AGRI INDUS ECO/TAC PRODUC ATTIT MARXISM...NAT/COMP BIBLIOG T 20. PAGE 137 A2807
L/A+17C SOCIETY DIPLOM ECO/UNDEV

B61
THEOBALD R.,THE CHALLENGE OF ABUNDANCE. USA+45 WOR+45 MARKET DIPLOM FOR/AID REV PRODUC UTOPIA SUPEGO...POLICY TREND BIBLIOG/A 20. PAGE 142 A2913
WELF/ST ECO/UNDEV PROB/SOLV ECO/TAC

B62
FAO,FOOD AND AGRICULTURE ORGANIZATION AFRICAN SURVEY. AFR CONGO/BRAZ GHANA STRATA AGRI INT/ORG TEC/DEV FOR/AID INT/TRADE RACE/REL DEMAND EFFICIENCY PRODUC...GEOG 20 UN CONGO/LEOP. PAGE 44 A0898
ECO/TAC WEALTH EXTR/IND ECO/UNDEV

B62
LUTZ F.A.,THE PROBLEM OF INTERNATIONAL ECONOMIC EQUILIBRIUM. FINAN PRODUC WEALTH 20 MONEY. PAGE 92 A1876
DIPLOM EQUILIB BAL/PAY PROB/SOLV

B62
US CONGRESS JOINT ECO COMM,FACTORS AFFECTING THE UNITED STATES BALANCE OF PAYMENTS. USA+45 DELIB/GP PLAN DIPLOM FOR/AID PRODUC WEALTH...CHARTS 20 CONGRESS OEEC. PAGE 150 A3064
BAL/PAY INT/TRADE ECO/TAC FINAN

B62
US CONGRESS JOINT ECO COMM,ECONOMIC DEVELOPMENTS IN SOUTH AMERICA. USA+45 SOCIETY FINAN NAT/G PROB/SOLV TEC/DEV INT/TRADE TAX EFFICIENCY PRODUC ATTIT ...POLICY 20 CONGRESS SOUTH/AMER. PAGE 150 A3065
L/A+17C ECO/UNDEV FOR/AID DIPLOM

B62
ZOOK P.D.,FOREIGN TRADE AND HUMAN CAPITAL. L/A+17C USA+45 FINAN DIPLOM ECO/TAC PRODUC...POLICY 20. PAGE 170 A3458
INT/TRADE ECO/UNDEV FOR/AID BAL/PAY

B63
FISCHER-GALATI S.,EASTERN EUROPE IN THE SIXTIES. ALBANIA USSR YUGOSLAVIA ECO/UNDEV AGRI MARKET LABOR WORKER DIPLOM INT/TRADE EDU/PROP GOV/REL PRODUC UTOPIA SOCISM 20. PAGE 46 A0939
MARXISM TEC/DEV BAL/PWR ECO/TAC

B63
MYRDAL G.,CHALLENGE TO AFFLUENCE. USA+45 WOR+45 FINAN INT/ORG NAT/G PLAN ECO/TAC INT/TRADE BAL/PAY ORD/FREE 20 EUROPE/W. PAGE 107 A2189
ECO/DEV WEALTH DIPLOM PRODUC

B63
PAENSON I.,SYSTEMATIC GLOSSARY ENGLISH, FRENCH, SPANISH, RUSSIAN OF SELECTED ECONOMIC AND SOCIAL TERMS. WOR+45 FINAN LABOR INT/TRADE DEMAND PRODUC 20. PAGE 113 A2315
DICTIONARY SOC LING

B63
SALENT W.S.,THE UNITED STATES BALANCE OF PAYMENTS IN 1968. EUR+WWI UK USA+45 AGRI R+D LABOR FORCES PRODUC...GEOG CONCPT CHARTS 20 CHINJAP EEC. PAGE 126 A2589
BAL/PAY DEMAND FINAN INT/TRADE

B63
THORELLI H.B.,INTOP: INTERNATIONAL OPERATIONS SIMULATION: PLAYER'S MANUAL. BRAZIL FINAN OP/RES ADMIN GP/REL INGP/REL PRODUC PERCEPT...DECISION MGT EEC. PAGE 144 A2935
GAME INT/TRADE EDU/PROP LG/CO

B63
US CONGRESS JOINT ECO COMM,THE UNITED STATES BALANCE OF PAYMENTS. USA+45 DELIB/GP BUDGET PRICE PRODUC 20 CONGRESS GOLD/STAND MONEY. PAGE 150 A3067
BAL/PAY INT/TRADE FINAN ECO/TAC

B65
DEMAS W.G.,THE ECONOMICS OF DEVELOPMENT IN SMALL COUNTRIES WITH SPECIAL REFERENCE TO THE CARIBBEAN. WOR+45 BAL/PAY DEMAND EFFICIENCY PRODUC...GEOG CARIBBEAN. PAGE 36 A0731
ECO/UNDEV PLAN WEALTH INT/TRADE

B65
JALEE P.,THE PILLAGE OF THE THIRD WORLD (TRANS. BY MARY KLOPPER). WOR+45 AGRI INDUS ECO/TAC FOR/AID COLONIAL CONTROL PRODUC PWR WEALTH...STAT CHARTS 20 RESOURCE/N. PAGE 73 A1493
ECO/UNDEV DOMIN INT/TRADE DIPLOM

B65
MCCOLL G.D.,THE AUSTRALIAN BALANCE OF PAYMENTS. UK USA+45 AGRI WORKER DIPLOM EQUILIB PRODUC...STAT TREND CHARTS BIBLIOG/A 20 AUSTRAL. PAGE 97 A2001
ECO/DEV BAL/PAY INT/TRADE COST

B65
MURUMBI J.,PROBLEMS OF ECONOMIC DEVELOPMENT IN EAST AFRICA. FINAN INDUS WORKER TEC/DEV INT/TRADE TAX DEMAND EFFICIENCY PRODUC SOCISM...TREND CHARTS 20 AFRICA/E. PAGE 106 A2184
AGRI ECO/TAC ECO/UNDEV PROC/MFG

B65
SABLE M.H.,PERIODICALS FOR LATIN AMERICAN ECONOMIC DEVELOPMENT, TRADE, AND FINANCE: AN ANNOTATED BIBLIOGRAPHY (A PAMPHLET). ECO/TAC PRODUC PROFIT ...STAT NAT/COMP 20 OAS. PAGE 126 A2583
BIBLIOG/A L/A+17C ECO/UNDEV INT/TRADE

B66
HAYER T.,FRENCH AID. AFR FRANCE AGRI FINAN BUDGET ADMIN WAR PRODUC...CHARTS 18/20 THIRD/WRLD OVRSEA/DEV. PAGE 63 A1295
TEC/DEV COLONIAL FOR/AID ECO/UNDEV

B66
SPICER K.,A SAMARITAN STATE? AFR CANADA INDIA PAKISTAN UK USA+45 FINAN INDUS PRODUC...CHARTS 20 NATO. PAGE 136 A2787
DIPLOM FOR/AID ECO/DEV ADMIN

L66
CHENERY H.B.,"FOREIGN ASSISTANCE AND ECONOMIC DEVELOPMENT" FUT WOR+45 NAT/G DIPLOM GIVE PRODUC ...METH/CNCPT CHARTS 20. PAGE 26 A0526
FOR/AID EFFICIENCY ECO/UNDEV TEC/DEV

B67
ROBINSON R.D.,INTERNATIONAL MANAGEMENT. USA+45 FINAN R+D PLAN PRODUC...DECISION T. PAGE 92 A1882 — INT/TRADE MGT INT/LAW MARKET

L67
DEVADHAR Y.C.,"THE ROLE OF FOREIGN PRIVATE CAPITAL IN INDIA'S ECONOMIC DEVELOPMENT* ASSESSMENT OF POLICY AND PERFORMANCE." INDIA INDUS PLAN TEC/DEV BUDGET DIPLOM ECO/TAC BAL/PAY PRODUC WEALTH ...CHARTS 20. PAGE 37 A0750 — CAP/ISM FOR/AID POLICY ACT/RES

S67
FALKOWSKI M.,"SOCIALIST ECONOMISTS AND THE DEVELOPING COUNTRIES." COM PLAN TEC/DEV ROUTINE DEMAND EFFICIENCY PRODUC WEALTH...MARXIST TREND GEN/METH. PAGE 44 A0893 — DIPLOM SOCISM ECO/UNDEV INDUS

S67
GOLDMAN M.I.,"SOVIET ECONOMIC GROWTH SINCE THE REVOLUTION." USSR WORKER INT/TRADE PRODUC MARXISM ...POLICY TIME/SEQ 20. PAGE 53 A1090 — ECO/DEV AGRI ECO/TAC INDUS

S67
KRISTENSEN T.,"THE SOUTH AS AN INDUSTRIAL POWER." FUT WOR+45 ECO/DEV AGRI INDUS TEC/DEV...CENSUS TREND CHARTS 20. PAGE 82 A1686 — DIPLOM ECO/UNDEV PREDICT PRODUC

S67
LEVI M.,"LES DIFFICULTES ECONOMIQUES DE LA GRANDE-BRETAGNE." UK INT/ORG TEC/DEV BARGAIN DIPLOM DOMIN REPRESENT DEMAND WEALTH...POLICY 20 EEC. PAGE 88 A1792 — BAL/PAY INT/TRADE PRODUC

PRODUCTIVITY....SEE PRODUC

PROF/ORG....PROFESSIONAL ORGANIZATIONS

N
KAPLAN L.,REVIEW INDEX. USA+45 USA-45 FINAN INDUS LABOR RACE/REL...GEOG PSY SOC 20. PAGE 76 A1558 — BIBLIOG PROF/ORG ECO/DEV DIPLOM

N
LEYPOLOT F.,AMERICAN CATALOGUE OF BOOKS, 1876-1910 (19 VOLS.). NAT/G DIPLOM...CON/ANAL 19/20. PAGE 88 A1806 — BIBLIOG USA-45 PROF/ORG PROC/MFG

B38
WARE E.E.,THE STUDY OF INTERNATIONAL RELATIONS IN THE UNITED STATES. USA+45 USA-45 WOR-45 INTELL SERV/IND INT/ORG NAT/G PROF/ORG SECT CONSULT INT/TRADE EDU/PROP ARMS/CONT...CONCPT 20. PAGE 161 A3283 — KNOWL DIPLOM

B39
STALEY E.,WORLD ECONOMY IN TRANSITION. WOR-45 SOCIETY INT/ORG PROF/ORG ECO/TAC ATTIT WEALTH ...METH/CNCPT TREND GEN/LAWS 20. PAGE 137 A2800 — TEC/DEV INT/TRADE

L52
HILSMAN R. JR.,"INTELLIGENCE AND POLICY MAKING IN FOREIGN AFFAIRS." USA+45 CONSULT ACT/RES DIPLOM EDU/PROP ROUTINE PEACE PERCEPT PWR SKILL...POLICY MGT HYPO/EXP CONGRESS 20 CIA. PAGE 65 A1333 — PROF/ORG SIMUL WAR

S55
TORRE M.,"PSYCHIATRIC OBSERVATIONS OF INTERNATIONAL CONFERENCES." WOR+45 INT/ORG PROF/ORG VOL/ASSN CONSULT EDU/PROP ROUTINE ATTIT DRIVE KNOWL...PSY METH/CNCPT OBS/ENVIR STERTYP 20. PAGE 144 A2950 — DELIB/GP OBS DIPLOM

B56
SPEECKAERT G.P.,INTERNATIONAL INSTITUTIONS AND INTERNATIONAL ORGANIZATIONS. PROF/ORG DELIB/GP KNOWL 19/20. PAGE 136 A2776 — BIBLIOG INT/ORG DIPLOM VOL/ASSN

S58
BLAISDELL D.C.,"PRESSURE GROUPS, FOREIGN POLICIES, AND INTERNATIONAL POLITICS." USA+45 WOR+45 INT/ORG PLAN DOMIN EDU/PROP LEGIT ADMIN ROUTINE CHOOSE ...DECISION MGT METH/CNCPT CON/ANAL 20. PAGE 15 A0303 — PROF/ORG PWR

B59
STANFORD RESEARCH INSTITUTE,POSSIBLE NONMILITARY SCIENTIFIC DEVELOPMENTS AND THEIR POTENTIAL IMPACT ON FOREIGN POLICY PROBLEMS OF THE UNITED. FUT USA+45 INT/ORG PROF/ORG CONSULT ACT/RES CREATE PLAN PEACE KNOWL SKILL...TECHNIC PHIL/SCI NEW/IDEA UNESCO 20. PAGE 137 A2802 — R+D TEC/DEV

L60
FERNBACH A.P.,"SOVIET COEXISTENCE STRATEGY." WOR+45 PROF/ORG VOL/ASSN DIPLOM DOMIN EDU/PROP ATTIT DRIVE PERSON PWR SKILL WEALTH...POLICY OBS SAMP TREND STERTYP ILO WORK COLD/WAR 420. PAGE 45 A0919 — LABOR INT/ORG USSR

S60
KISTIAKOWSKY G.B.,"SCIENCE AND FOREIGN AFFAIRS." FUT WOR+45 NAT/G PROF/ORG PLAN ECO/TAC EDU/PROP NUC/PWR...TREND COLD/WAR 20. PAGE 80 A1645 — CONSULT TEC/DEV FOR/AID DIPLOM

B61
ASIA SOCIETY,AMERICAN INSTITUTIONS ANS ORGANIZATIONS INTERESTED IN ASIA; A REFERENCE DIRECTORY (2ND ED.). ASIA USA+45 CULTURE SECT DIPLOM EDU/PROP...INDEX 20. PAGE 9 A0190 — VOL/ASSN ACADEM PROF/ORG

B62
AMERICAN LAW INSTITUTE,FOREIGN RELATIONS LAW OF THE UNITED STATES: RESTATEMENT, SECOND. USA+45 NAT/G LEGIS ADJUD EXEC ROUTINE GOV/REL...INT/LAW JURID CONCPT 20 TREATY. PAGE 7 A0152 — PROF/ORG LAW DIPLOM ORD/FREE

B62
GILPIN R.,AMERICAN SCIENTISTS AND NUCLEAR WEAPONS POLICY. COM FUT USA+45 WOR+45 INT/ORG NAT/G PROF/ORG CONSULT FORCES CREATE TEC/DEV BAL/PWR EDU/PROP ARMS/CONT WAR PERCEPT KNOWL MORAL PWR ...PHIL/SCI SOC CONCPT GEN/LAWS 20. PAGE 52 A1073 — INTELL ATTIT DETER NUC/PWR

L62
"HIGHER EDUCATION AND ECONOMIC AND SOCIAL DEVELOPMENT IN LATIN AMERICA: A BIBLIOGRAPHY." L/A+17C SOCIETY ECO/UNDEV PROF/ORG DIPLOM CONFER ...SOC 20. PAGE 3 A0062 — BIBLIOG/A ACADEM INTELL EDU/PROP

L63
SZASZY E.,"L'EVOLUTION DES PRINCIPES GENERAUX DU DROIT INTERNATIONAL PRIVE DANS LES PAYS DE DEMOCRATIE POPULAIRE." COM FUT WOR+45 LAW ECO/DEV PERF/ART POL/PAR PROF/ORG ECO/TAC INT/TRADE EDU/PROP ATTIT RIGID/FLEX ALL/VALS SOCISM...JURID TREND GEN/LAWS WORK 20. PAGE 141 A2876 — DIPLOM TOTALISM INT/LAW INT/ORG

S63
COUTY P.,"L'ASSISTANCE POUR LE DEVELOPPEMENT: POINT DE VUE SCANDINAVES." EUR+WWI FINLAND FUT SWEDEN WOR+45 ECO/DEV ECO/UNDEV COM/IND LABOR NAT/G PROF/ORG ACT/RES SKILL WEALTH TOT/POP 20. PAGE 32 A0643 — FINAN ROUTINE FOR/AID

S63
GANDILHON J.,"LA SCIENCE ET LA TECHNIQUE A L'AIDE DES REGIONS PEU DEVELOPPEES." FRANCE FUT WOR+45 ECO/DEV R+D PROF/ORG ACT/RES PLAN...MGT TOT/POP VAL/FREE 20 UN. PAGE 51 A1037 — ECO/UNDEV TEC/DEV FOR/AID

S63
LEDUC G.,"L'AIDE INTERNATIONALE AU DEVELOPPEMENT." FUT WOR+45 ECO/DEV ECO/UNDEV R+D PROF/ORG TEC/DEV ECO/TAC ROUTINE ATTIT ALL/VALS...MGT TIME/SEQ TOT/POP 20. PAGE 86 A1758 — FINAN PLAN FOR/AID

S64
RUBIN R.,"THE UN CORRESPONDENT." WOR+45 FACE/GP PROF/ORG EDU/PROP ROUTINE PERCEPT KNOWL...RECORD STAND/INT QU UN WORK TOT/POP VAL/FREE 20. PAGE 125 A2560 — INT/ORG ATTIT DIPLOM

B65
UNESCO,INTERNATIONAL ORGANIZATIONS IN THE SOCIAL SCIENCES(REV. ED.). LAW ADMIN ATTIT...CRIMLGY GEOG INT/LAW PSY SOC STAT 20 UNESCO. PAGE 148 A3024 — INT/ORG R+D PROF/ORG ACT/RES

B65
UNESCO,HANDBOOK OF INTERNATIONAL EXCHANGES. COM/IND R+D ACADEM PROF/ORG VOL/ASSN CREATE TEC/DEV EDU/PROP AGREE 20 TREATY. PAGE 148 A3025 — INDEX INT/ORG DIPLOM PRESS

B65
US LIBRARY OF CONGRESS,A DIRECTORY OF INFORMATION RESOURCES IN THE UNITED STATES: SOCIAL SCIENCES. USA+45 ACADEM INT/ORG LABOR PROF/ORG PUB/INST SCHOOL SECT 20. PAGE 155 A3159 — BIBLIOG R+D COMPUT/IR

B65
US SENATE COMM AERO SPACE SCI,INTERNATIONAL COOPERATION AND ORGANIZATION FOR OUTER SPACE. FUT USA+45 WOR+45 PROF/ORG VOL/ASSN CONSULT DELIB/GP PLAN TEC/DEV ARMS/CONT GP/REL PEACE 20 UN NASA. PAGE 155 A3167 — DIPLOM SPACE R+D NAT/G

S65
HAZARD J.N.,"CO-EXISTENCE LAW BOWS OUT." WOR+45 R+D INT/ORG VOL/ASSN CONSULT DELIB/GP ACT/RES CREATE PEACE KNOWL...JURID CONCPT COLD/WAR VAL/FREE 20. PAGE 63 A1300 — PROF/ORG ADJUD

PROFESSIONAL ORGANIZATION....SEE PROF/ORG

PROFIT....SEE ALSO ECO

B00
MOCKLER-FERRYMAN A.,BRITISH WEST AFRICA. FRANCE GERMANY NIGER SIER/LEONE UK CULTURE DIPLOM WAR RACE/REL PRODUC PROFIT WEALTH...POLICY PREDICT 19. PAGE 102 A2095 — AFR COLONIAL INT/TRADE CAP/ISM

S61
"CRITERIA FOR ALLOCATING INVESTMENT RESOURCES AMONG VARIOUS FIELDS OF DEVELOPMENT IN UNDERDEVELOPED ECONOMIES." ASIA AGRI INT/ORG CAP/ISM BAL/PAY EFFICIENCY PROFIT WEALTH...STAT 20 UN. PAGE 3 A0061 — BIBLIOG/A ECO/UNDEV PLAN TEC/DEV

B64
NEWCOMER H.A.,INTERNATIONAL AIDS TO OVERSEAS INVESTMENTS AND TRADE. ECO/UNDEV TARIFFS PROFIT ...BIBLIOG 20 GATT UN. PAGE 108 A2225 — INT/TRADE FINAN DIPLOM FOR/AID

B65
SABLE M.H.,PERIODICALS FOR LATIN AMERICAN ECONOMIC DEVELOPMENT, TRADE, AND FINANCE: AN ANNOTATED — BIBLIOG/A L/A+17C

BIBLIOGRAPHY (A PAMPHLET). ECO/TAC PRODUC PROFIT ...STAT NAT/COMP 20 OAS. PAGE 126 A2583 — ECO/UNDEV INT/TRADE

L65
LOFTUS M.L.,"INTERNATIONAL MONETARY FUND, 1962-1965: A SELECTED BIBLIOGRAPHY." WOR+45 PLAN BUDGET INCOME PROFIT WEALTH. PAGE 90 A1852 — BIBLIOG FINAN INT/TRADE INT/ORG

B66
BIRMINGHAM D.,TRADE AND CONFLICT IN ANGOLA. PORTUGAL CULTURE FORCES DIPLOM GP/REL PROFIT HABITAT NAT/COMP. PAGE 14 A0291 — WAR INT/TRADE ECO/UNDEV COLONIAL

B66
FELKER J.L.,SOVIET ECONOMIC CONTROVERSIES. USSR INDUS PLAN INT/TRADE GP/REL MARXISM SOCISM...POLICY 20. PAGE 45 A0915 — ECO/DEV MARKET PROFIT PRICE

PROFUMO/J....JOHN PROFUMO, THE PROFUMO AFFAIR

PROG/TEAC....PROGRAMMED INSTRUCTION

PROGRAMMING....SEE COMPUTER

PROGRSV/M....PROGRESSIVE MOVEMENT (ALL NATIONS)

PROJ/TEST....PROJECTIVE TESTS

S57
SCHELLING T.C.,"BARGAINING COMMUNICATION, AND LIMITED WAR." UNIV WOR+45 FACE/GP INT/ORG NAT/G FORCES ACT/RES WAR PERCEPT ALL/VALS...PSY OBS PROJ/TEST CHARTS HYPO/EXP GEN/LAWS TOT/POP 20. PAGE 128 A2622 — ROUTINE DECISION

PROJECTION....SEE DISPL

PROPAGANDA....SEE EDU/PROP

PROPERTY TAX....SEE PROPERTY/TX

PROPERTY/TX....PROPERTY TAX

PROSTITUTN....SEE ALSO SEX + CRIME

PROTECTNSM....PROTECTIONISM

PROTEST....SEE COERCE

PROTESTANT....PROTESTANTS, PROTESTANTISM

B58
VARG P.A.,MISSIONARIES, CHINESE, AND DIPLOMATS: THE AMERICAN PROTESTANT MISSIONARY MOVEMENT IN CHINA, 1890-1952. ASIA ECO/UNDEV NAT/G PROB/SOLV CAP/ISM EDU/PROP COLONIAL NAT/LISM ATTIT MARXISM...NAT/COMP STERTYP 20 CHINJAP PROTESTANT MISSION. PAGE 158 A3221 — CULTURE DIPLOM SECT

B59
NIEBUHR R.,NATIONS AND EMPIRES. WOR+45 INT/ORG COLONIAL NUC/PWR TOTALISM UTOPIA ORD/FREE MARXISM WORSHIP 20 COLD/WAR PROTESTANT CHRISTIAN. PAGE 109 A2237 — DIPLOM NAT/G POLICY PWR

PROUDHON/P....PIERRE JOSEPH PROUDHON

PROVISIONS SECTION OAU A2415

PROVS....STATE AND PROVINCES

N
"PROLOG",DIGEST OF THE SOVIET UKRANIAN PRESS. USSR LAW AGRI INDUS PROVS SCHOOL DIPLOM GOV/REL ATTIT ...HUM LING 20. PAGE 4 A0081 — BIBLIOG/A NAT/G PRESS COM

N
MCSPADDEN J.W.,THE AMERICAN STATESMAN'S YEARBOOK. WOR-45 LAW CONSTN AGRI FINAN DEBATE ADMIN PARL/PROC ...CHARTS BIBLIOG/A 20. PAGE 99 A2025 — DIPLOM NAT/G PROVS LEGIS

B00
GROTIUS H.,DE JURE BELLI AC PACIS. CHRIST-17C UNIV LAW SOCIETY PROVS LEGIT PEACE PERCEPT MORAL PWR ...CONCPT CON/ANAL GEN/LAWS. PAGE 57 A1180 — JURID INT/LAW WAR

B19
LONDON SCHOOL ECONOMICS-POL,ANNUAL DIGEST OF PUBLIC INTERNATIONAL LAW CASES. INT/ORG MUNIC NAT/G PROVS ADMIN NEUTRAL WAR GOV/REL PRIVIL 20. PAGE 91 A1858 — BIBLIOG/A INT/LAW ADJUD DIPLOM

B28
HALL W.P.,EMPIRE TO COMMONWEALTH. FUT WOR-45 CONSTN ECO/DEV ECO/UNDEV INT/ORG PROVS PLAN DIPLOM EDU/PROP ADMIN COLONIAL PEACE PERSON ALL/VALS ...POLICY GEOG SOC OBS RECORD TREND CMN/WLTH PARLIAMENT 19/20. PAGE 60 A1229 — VOL/ASSN NAT/G UK

B30
BYNKERSHOEK C.,QUAESTIONUM JURIS PUBLICI LIBRI DUO. CHRIST-17C MOD/EUR CONSTN ELITES SOCIETY NAT/G PROVS EX/STRUC FORCES TOP/EX BAL/PWR DIPLOM ATTIT MORAL...TRADIT CONCPT. PAGE 23 A0460 — INT/ORG LAW NAT/LISM INT/LAW

B31
STUART G.H.,THE INTERNATIONAL CITY OF TANGIER. AFR EUR+WWI MOD/EUR MOROCCO CONSTN PROVS CREATE PLAN LEGIT PEACE ORD/FREE PWR...INT/LAW OBS TIME/SEQ CON/ANAL 20 TANGIER. PAGE 139 A2854 — LOC/G INT/ORG DIPLOM SOVEREIGN

B35
KENNEDY W.P.,THE LAW AND CUSTOM OF THE SOUTH AFRICAN CONSTITUTION. AFR SOUTH/AFR KIN LOC/G PROVS DIPLOM ADJUD ADMIN EXEC 20. PAGE 78 A1594 — CT/SYS CONSTN JURID PARL/PROC

B40
MIDDLEBUSH F.,ELEMENTS OF INTERNATIONAL RELATIONS. WOR-45 PROVS CONSULT EDU/PROP LEGIT WAR NAT/LISM ATTIT KNOWL MORAL ORD/FREE PWR...JURID LEAGUE/NAT TOT/POP VAL/FREE. PAGE 101 A2067 — NAT/G INT/ORG PEACE DIPLOM

B50
BROWN E.S.,MANUAL OF GOVERNMENT PUBLICATIONS. WOR+45 WOR-45 CONSTN INT/ORG MUNIC PROVS DIPLOM ADMIN 20. PAGE 20 A0401 — BIBLIOG/A NAT/G LAW

B52
SHULIM J.I.,THE OLD DOMINION AND NAPOLEON BONAPARTE. POL/PAR DOMIN PRESS REV WAR 18/19 VIRGINIA. PAGE 132 A2710 — ATTIT PROVS EDU/PROP DIPLOM

B54
BINANI G.D.,INDIA AT A GLANCE (REV. ED.). INDIA COM/IND FINAN INDUS LABOR PROVS SCHOOL PLAN DIPLOM INT/TRADE ADMIN...JURID 20. PAGE 14 A0288 — INDEX CON/ANAL NAT/G ECO/UNDEV

B57
ALEXANDER L.M.,WORLD POLITICAL PATTERNS. NAT/G PROVS CAP/ISM DIPLOM COLONIAL NAT/LISM...POLICY GEOG CHARTS METH/COMP NAT/COMP 20. PAGE 5 A0111 — CONTROL METH GOV/COMP

B57
DUDDEN A.P.,WOODROW WILSON AND THE WORLD OF TODAY. USA-45 NAT/G PROVS CONTROL PARTIC WAR ISOLAT PWR SKILL...PERS/COMP ANTHOL 19/20 WILSON/W UN LEAGUE/NAT WWI. PAGE 39 A0794 — CHIEF DIPLOM POL/PAR LEAD

B58
HENKIN L.,ARMS CONTROL AND INSPECTION IN AMERICAN LAW. LAW CONSTN INT/ORG LOC/G MUNIC NAT/G PROVS EDU/PROP LEGIT EXEC NUC/PWR KNOWL ORD/FREE...OBS TOT/POP CONGRESS 20. PAGE 64 A1315 — USA+45 JURID ARMS/CONT

B59
BUNDESMIN FUR VERTRIEBENE,ZEITTAFEL DER VORGESCHICHTE UND DES ABLAUFS DER VERTREIBUNG SOWIE DER UNTERBRINGUNG UND EINGLIEDERUNG DER (2 VOLS.). GERMANY/E GERMANY/W NAT/G PROVS PROB/SOLV DIPLOM PARL/PROC ATTIT...BIBLIOG SOC/INTEG 20 MIGRATION PARLIAMENT. PAGE 21 A0431 — JURID GP/REL INT/LAW

B59
PAGAN B.,HISTORIA DE LOS PARTIDOS POLITICOS PUERTORRIQUENOS 1898-1956. PUERT/RICO PROVS DIPLOM DOMIN EDU/PROP PARTIC 20. PAGE 113 A2316 — POL/PAR CHOOSE COLONIAL PWR

S60
GINSBURGS G.,"PEKING-LHASA-NEW DELHI." CHINA/COM FUT INDIA S/ASIA KIN NAT/G PROVS SECT FORCES BAL/PWR ECO/TAC DOMIN EDU/PROP LEGIT ADMIN REGION GUERRILLA PWR...TREND TIBET 20. PAGE 52 A1074 — ASIA COERCE DIPLOM

B61
BURDETTE F.L.,POLITICAL SCIENCE: A SELECTED BIBLIOGRAPHY OF BOOKS IN PRINT, WITH ANNOTATIONS (PAMPHLET). LAW LOC/G NAT/G POL/PAR PROVS DIPLOM EDU/PROP ADMIN CHOOSE ATTIT 20. PAGE 21 A0432 — BIBLIOG/A GOV/COMP CONCPT ROUTINE

B61
WECHSLER H.,PRINCIPLES, POLITICS AND FUNDAMENTAL LAW: SELECTED ESSAYS. USA+45 USA-45 LAW SOCIETY NAT/G PROVS DELIB/GP EX/STRUC ACT/RES LEGIT PERSON KNOWL PWR...JURID 20 NUREMBERG. PAGE 162 A3296 — CT/SYS CONSTN INT/LAW

S62
SPRINGER H.W.,"FEDERATION IN THE CARIBBEAN: AN ATTEMPT THAT FAILED." L/A+17C ECO/UNDEV INT/ORG POL/PAR PROVS LEGIS CREATE PLAN LEGIT ADMIN FEDERAL ATTIT DRIVE PERSON ORD/FREE PWR...POLICY GEOG PSY CONCPT OBS CARIBBEAN CMN/WLTH 20. PAGE 136 A2791 — VOL/ASSN NAT/G REGION

B63
ADLER G.J.,BRITISH INDIA'S NORTHERN FRONTIER: 1865-95. AFGHANISTN RUSSIA UK PROVS COLONIAL COERCE PEACE...GEOG CHARTS BIBLIOG 19 TREATY. PAGE 4 A0091 — S/ASIA FORCES DIPLOM POLICY

B63
HAILEY L.,THE REPUBLIC OF SOUTH AFRICA AND THE HIGH COMMISSION TERRITORIES. AFR SOUTH/AFR UK INT/ORG NAT/G PROVS RACE/REL SOVEREIGN...CHARTS 19/20 COMMONWLTH. PAGE 59 A1219 — COLONIAL DIPLOM ATTIT

B63
LANOUE G.R.,A BIBLIOGRAPHY OF DOCTORAL — BIBLIOG

DISSERTATIONS ON POLITICS AND RELIGION. USA+45 NAT/G
USA-45 CONSTN PROVS DIPLOM CT/SYS MORAL...POLICY LOC/G
JURID CONCPT 20. PAGE 84 A1728 SECT

B63
RAVENS J.P.,STAAT UND KATHOLISCHE KIRCHE IN GP/REL
PREUSSENS POLNISCHEN TEILUNGSGEBIETEN. GERMANY CATHISM
POLAND PRUSSIA PROVS DIPLOM EDU/PROP DEBATE SECT
NAT/LISM...JURID 18 CHURCH/STA. PAGE 119 A2451 NAT/G

S63
MAZRUI A.A.,"ON THE CONCEPT 'WE ARE ALL AFRICANS'." PROVS
AFR CULTURE KIN LOC/G NAT/G DOMIN EDU/PROP LEGIT INT/ORG
ATTIT PERCEPT PERSON KNOWL ORD/FREE...TIME/SEQ NAT/LISM
TOT/POP 20. PAGE 97 A1986

S63
NYE J.S. JR.,"EAST AFRICAN ECONOMIC INTEGRATION." ECO/UNDEV
AFR UGANDA PROVS DELIB/GP PLAN ECO/TAC INT/TRADE INT/ORG
ADMIN ROUTINE ORD/FREE PWR WEALTH...OBS TIME/SEQ
VAL/FREE 20. PAGE 110 A2264

B64
FRIEDMANN W.G.,THE CHANGING STRUCTURE OF ADJUD
INTERNATIONAL LAW. WOR+45 INT/ORG NAT/G PROVS LEGIT TREND
ORD/FREE PWR...JURID CONCPT GEN/LAWS TOT/POP UN 20. INT/LAW
PAGE 49 A1006

L64
POUNDS N.J.G.,"THE POLITICS OF PARTITION." AFR ASIA NAT/G
COM EUR+WWI FUT ISLAM S/ASIA USA-45 LAW ECO/DEV NAT/LISM
ECO/UNDEV AGRI INDUS INT/ORG POL/PAR PROVS SECT
FORCES TOP/EX EDU/PROP LEGIT ATTIT MORAL ORD/FREE
PWR RESPECT WEALTH. PAGE 117 A2402

S64
MARTELLI G.,"PORTUGAL AND THE UNITED NATIONS." AFR ATTIT
EUR+WWI ELITES INT/ORG NAT/G PROVS PLAN DIPLOM PORTUGAL
ECO/TAC DOMIN COLONIAL RIGID/FLEX MORAL ORD/FREE
PWR WEALTH...MYTH UN 20. PAGE 95 A1947

S66
"RESEARCH WORK 1965-1966." NEW/ZEALND ELITES ACADEM BIBLIOG
LOC/G MUNIC POL/PAR PROVS DIPLOM COLONIAL...SOC 20 NAT/G
AUSTRAL. PAGE 4 A0073 CULTURE
S/ASIA

B67
US DEPARTMENT OF THE ARMY,CIVILIAN IN PEACE, BIBLIOG/A
SOLDIER IN WAR: A BIBLIOGRAPHIC SURVEY OF THE ARMY FORCES
AND AIR NATIONAL GUARD (PAMPHLET, NOS. 130-2). ROLE
USA+45 USA-45 LOC/G NAT/G PROVS LEGIS PLAN ADMIN DIPLOM
ATTIT ORD/FREE...POLICY 19/20. PAGE 152 A3111

PRUITT/DG....DEAN G. PRUITT

PRUSSIA....PRUSSIA

B22
FICHTE J.G.,ADDRESSES TO THE GERMAN NATION. GERMANY NAT/LISM
PRUSSIA ELITES NAT/G SECT CREATE INT/TRADE HEREDITY CULTURE
...ART/METH LING 19 FRANK/PARL. PAGE 45 A0923 EDU/PROP
REGION

B52
SKALWEIT S.,FRANKREICH UND FRIEDRICH DER GROSSE. ATTIT
FRANCE GERMANY PRUSSIA NAT/G DOMIN WAR 18 EDU/PROP
FREDERICK. PAGE 134 A2737 DIPLOM
SOC

B55
CRAIG G.A.,THE POLITICS OF THE PRUSSIAN ARMY FORCES
1640-1945. CHRIST-17C EUR+WWI MOD/EUR PRUSSIA NAT/G
STRUCT DIPLOM ADMIN REV WAR...SOC BIBLIOG 17/20. ROLE
PAGE 32 A0652 CHIEF

B62
SCHMIDT-VOLKMAR E.,DER KULTURKAMPF IN DEUTSCHLAND POL/PAR
1871-1890. GERMANY PRUSSIA SOCIETY STRUCT SECT CATHISM
DIPLOM GP/REL NAT/LISM 19 CHURCH/STA BISMARCK/O. ATTIT
PAGE 128 A2632 NAT/G

B63
RAVENS J.P.,STAAT UND KATHOLISCHE KIRCHE IN GP/REL
PREUSSENS POLNISCHEN TEILUNGSGEBIETEN. GERMANY CATHISM
POLAND PRUSSIA PROVS DIPLOM EDU/PROP DEBATE SECT
NAT/LISM...JURID 18 CHURCH/STA. PAGE 119 A2451 NAT/G

B64
REMAK J.,THE GENTLE CRITIC: THEODOR FONTANE AND PERSON
GERMAN POLITICS, 1848-1898. GERMANY PRUSSIA CULTURE SOCIETY
ELITES BAL/PWR DIPLOM WRITING GOV/REL...HUM BIOG 19 WORKER
BISMARCK/O JUNKER FONTANE/T. PAGE 120 A2465 CHIEF

B65
SCHREIBER H.,TEUTON AND SLAV - THE STRUGGLE FOR GP/REL
CENTRAL EUROPE (TRANS. BY J. CLEUGH). GERMANY WAR
POLAND PRUSSIA USSR SOCIETY STRUCT SECT DIPLOM RACE/REL
BALTIC. PAGE 129 A2646 NAT/LISM

B66
CRAIG G.A.,WAR, POLITICS, AND DIPLOMACY. PRUSSIA WAR
CONSTN FORCES CIVMIL/REL TOTALISM PWR 19/20 DIPLOM
BISMARCK/O DULLES/JF NAPOLEON/B. PAGE 32 A0654 BAL/PWR

PSY....PSYCHOLOGY

N
SCHOLARLY BOOKS IN AMERICA; A QUARTERLY BIBLIOG/A
BIBLIOGRAPHY OF UNIVERSITY PRESS PUBLICATIONS. LAW
WOR+45 AGRI COM/IND NAT/G HEALTH...GEOG PHIL/SCI MUNIC
PSY SOC LING 20. PAGE 3 A0046 DIPLOM

N
KAPLAN L.,REVIEW INDEX. USA+45 USA-45 FINAN INDUS BIBLIOG
LABOR RACE/REL...GEOG PSY SOC 20. PAGE 76 A1558 PROF/ORG
ECO/DEV
DIPLOM

N
US BUREAU OF THE CENSUS,BIBLIOGRAPHY OF SOCIAL BIBLIOG/A
SCIENCE PERIODICALS AND MONOGRAPH SERIES. WOR+45 CULTURE
LAW DIPLOM EDU/PROP HEALTH...PSY SOC LING STAT. NAT/G
PAGE 150 A3058 SOCIETY

B20
BURNS C.D.,INTERNATIONAL POLITICS. WOR-45 CULTURE INT/ORG
SOCIETY ECO/UNDEV NAT/G VOL/ASSN DELIB/GP ACT/RES PEACE
CREATE DOMIN EDU/PROP LEGIT ATTIT DRIVE RIGID/FLEX SOVEREIGN
ALL/VALS...PLURIST PSY CONCPT TREND. PAGE 22 A0442

L21
HALDEMAN E.,"SERIALS OF AN INTERNATIONAL BIBLIOG
CHARACTER." WOR-45 DIPLOM...ART/METH GEOG HEAL HUM PHIL/SCI
INT/LAW JURID PSY SOC. PAGE 60 A1224

B24
NAVILLE A.,LIBERTE, EGALITE, SOLIDARITE: ESSAIS ORD/FREE
D'ANALYSE. STRATA FAM VOL/ASSN INT/TRADE GP/REL SOC
MORAL MARXISM SOCISM...PSY TREATY. PAGE 107 A2205 IDEA/COMP
DIPLOM

B28
PLAYNE C.E.,THE PRE-WAR MIND IN BRITAIN. GERMANY PRESS
MOD/EUR UK STRATA SECT DIPLOM EDU/PROP CROWD SUFF WAR
...POLICY ANARCH PSY SOC IDEA/COMP 20 WWI. PAGE 116 DOMIN
A2388 ATTIT

B36
THWAITE D.,THE SEETHING AFRICAN POT: A STUDY OF NAT/LISM
BLACK NATIONALISM 1882-1935. ETHIOPIA SECT VOL/ASSN AFR
COERCE GUERRILLA MURDER DISCRIM MARXISM...PSY RACE/REL
TIME/SEQ 18/20 NEGRO. PAGE 144 A2939 DIPLOM

L39
NEARING S.,"A WARLESS WORLD." FUT WOR-45 SOCIETY COERCE
INT/ORG NAT/G EX/STRUC PLAN DOMIN WAR ATTIT DRIVE PEACE
PWR...POLICY PSY CONCPT OBS TREND HYPO/EXP
MARX/KARL 20 MARX/KARL LENIN/VI. PAGE 108 A2210

B40
MILLER E.,THE NEUROSES OF WAR. UNIV INTELL SOCIETY HEALTH
INT/ORG NAT/G EDU/PROP DISPL DRIVE PERCEPT PERSON PSY
RIGID/FLEX...SOC TIME/SEQ 20. PAGE 101 A2075 WAR

B41
BAUMANN G.,GRUNDLAGEN UND PRAXIS DER EDU/PROP
INTERNATIONALEN PROPAGANDA. FRANCE GERMANY UK DOMIN
CULTURE COM/IND PRESS PWR...PSY METH/COMP 20. ATTIT
PAGE 12 A0236 DIPLOM

B42
BORNSTEIN J.,ACTION AGAINST THE ENEMY'S MIND. EDU/PROP
EUR+WWI GERMANY USA-45 DIPLOM DOMIN PRESS LEAD PSY
GP/REL DISCRIM PERCEPT FASCISM MARXISM 20 JEWS NAZI WAR
ANTI/SEMIT. PAGE 17 A0343 CONTROL

B42
TOLMAN E.C.,DRIVES TOWARD WAR. UNIV PLAN DIPLOM PSY
ECO/TAC COERCE PERS/REL ADJUST HAPPINESS BIO/SOC WAR
HEREDITY HEALTH KNOWL. PAGE 144 A2947 UTOPIA
DRIVE

L47
BRUNER J.S.,"TOWARD A COMMON GROUND-INTERNATIONAL INT/ORG
SOCIAL SCIENCE." FUT WOR+45 INTELL R+D NAT/G KNOWL
VOL/ASSN CONSULT DELIB/GP ACT/RES CREATE PLAN
TEC/DEV ATTIT ORD/FREE...PSY SOC CONCPT ANTHOL
UNESCO 20. PAGE 20 A0410

S47
RADVANYI L.,"PROBLEMS OF INTERNATIONAL OPINION QU/SEMANT
SURVEYS." WOR+45 INT/ORG NAT/G CREATE ATTIT...PSY SAMP
SOC METH/CNCPT REC/INT KNO/TEST SAMP/SIZ METH DIPLOM
VAL/FREE 20. PAGE 118 A2431

B48
LINEBARGER P.,PSYCHOLOGICAL WARFARE. NAT/G PLAN EDU/PROP
DIPLOM DOMIN ATTIT...POLICY CONCPT EXHIBIT 20 WWI. PSY
PAGE 89 A1824 WAR
COM/IND

B49
FORD FOUNDATION,REPORT OF THE STUDY FOR THE FORD WEALTH
FOUNDATION ON POLICY AND PROGRAM. SOCIETY R+D GEN/LAWS
ACT/RES CAP/ISM FOR/AID EDU/PROP ADMIN KNOWL
...POLICY PSY SOC 20. PAGE 47 A0961

B49
GORER G.,THE PEOPLE OF GREAT RUSSIA: A ISOLAT
PSYCHOLOGICAL STUDY. RUSSIA USSR NAT/G DIPLOM LEAD PERSON
AGE/C ANOMIE ATTIT DRIVE...POLICY 20. PAGE 54 A1116 PSY
SOCIETY

B49
OGBURN W.,TECHNOLOGY AND INTERNATIONAL RELATIONS. TEC/DEV
WOR+45 WOR-45 ECO/DEV CREATE PLAN ECO/TAC EDU/PROP DIPLOM
COERCE PWR SKILL WEALTH...TECHNIC PSY SOC NEW/IDEA INT/ORG
CHARTS TOT/POP 20. PAGE 111 A2283

S49
DUNN F.,"THE PRESENT COURSE OF INTERNATIONAL CONCPT
RELATIONS RESEARCH." WOR+45 WOR-45 SOCIETY R+D GEN/METH
INT/ORG WAR PERSON ORD/FREE...POLICY PSY SOC DIPLOM
GEN/LAWS 20. PAGE 39 A0800

B50
BARGHOORN F.C.,THE SOVIET IMAGE OF THE UNITED STATES: A STUDY IN DISTORTION. COM USSR DOMIN WAR NAT/LISM TOTALISM SOCISM...PSY 20. PAGE 11 A0220
PROB/SOLV EDU/PROP DIPLOM ATTIT

B51
MCKEON R.,DEMOCRACY IN A WORLD OF TENSION. UNIV LAW INTELL STRUCT R+D INT/ORG SCHOOL EDU/PROP LEGIT ATTIT DRIVE PERCEPT PERSON...POLICY JURID PSY SOC CONCPT METH/CNCPT OBS UNESCO TOT/POP VAL/FREE. PAGE 98 A2015
SOCIETY ALL/VALS ORD/FREE

B51
STANTON A.H.,PERSONALITY AND POLITICAL CRISIS. WOR+45 WOR-45 STRUCT DIPLOM INGP/REL TOTALISM MORAL ...ANTHOL 20 LASSWELL/H PARSONS/T RIESMAN/D. PAGE 137 A2806
EDU/PROP WAR PERSON PSY

S51
ICHHEISER G.,"MISUNDERSTANDING IN INTERNATIONAL RELATIONS." UNIV SOCIETY FACE/GP INT/ORG SECT ATTIT PERSON RIGID/FLEX LOVE RESPECT...RELATIV PSY SOC CONCPT MYTH SOC/EXP GEN/LAWS. PAGE 70 A1431
PERCEPT STERTYP NAT/LISM DIPLOM

B52
UNESCO,THESES DE SCIENCES SOCIALES: CATALOGUE ANALYTIQUE INTERNATIONAL DE THESES INEDITES DE DOCTORAT, 1940-1950. INT/ORG DIPLOM EDU/PROP...GEOG INT/LAW MGT PSY SOC 20. PAGE 147 A3015
BIBLIOG ACADEM WRITING

B53
SQUIRES J.D.,BRITISH PROPAGANDA AT HOME AND IN THE UNITED STATES FROM 1914 TO 1917. UK NAT/G PROB/SOLV DOMIN PRESS EFFICIENCY...PSY PREDICT 20 WWI INTERVENT PSY/WAR. PAGE 136 A2794
EDU/PROP CONTROL WAR DIPLOM

B55
STEPHENS O.,FACTS TO A CANDID WORLD. USA+45 WOR+45 COM/IND EX/STRUC PRESS ROUTINE EFFICIENCY ATTIT ...PSY 20. PAGE 138 A2817
EDU/PROP PHIL/SCI NAT/G DIPLOM

S55
TORRE M.,"PSYCHIATRIC OBSERVATIONS OF INTERNATIONAL CONFERENCES." WOR+45 INT/ORG PROF/ORG VOL/ASSN CONSULT EDU/PROP ROUTINE ATTIT DRIVE KNOWL...PSY METH/CNCPT OBS/ENVIR STERTYP 20. PAGE 144 A2950
DELIB/GP OBS DIPLOM

B56
BEARDSLEY S.W.,HUMAN RELATIONS IN INTERNATIONAL AFFAIRS: A GUIDE TO SIGNIFICANT INTERPRETATION AND RESEARCH. UNIV PERS/REL NAT/LISM DRIVE PERSON ...POLICY PSY SOC CON/ANAL IDEA/COMP 20. PAGE 12 A0241
BIBLIOG/A ATTIT CULTURE DIPLOM

B56
GEORGE A.L.,WOODROW WILSON AND COLONEL HOUSE. WOR-45 CONSTN FACE/GP INT/ORG NAT/G POL/PAR CONSULT LEGIT EXEC COERCE CHOOSE ATTIT DRIVE PERSON MORAL ORD/FREE PWR RESPECT...POLICY MGT PSY OBS RECORD INT LEAGUE/NAT. PAGE 52 A1060
USA-45 BIOG DIPLOM

B56
US DEPARTMENT OF STATE,ECONOMIC PROBLEMS OF UNDERDEVELOPED AREAS (PAMPHLET). AFR ASIA ISLAM L/A+17C AGRI FINAN INDUS INT/ORG LABOR INT/TRADE ...PSY SOC 20. PAGE 151 A3090
BIBLIOG ECO/UNDEV TEC/DEV R+D

B57
BEAL J.R.,JOHN FOSTER DULLES, A BIOGRAPHY. USA+45 USSR WOR+45 CONSTN INT/ORG NAT/G EX/STRUC LEGIT ADMIN NUC/PWR DISPL PERSON ORD/FREE PWR SKILL ...POLICY PSY OBS RECORD COLD/WAR UN 20 DULLES/JF. PAGE 12 A0237
BIOG DIPLOM

B57
STRACHEY A.,THE UNCONSCIOUS MOTIVES OF WAR; A PSYCHO-ANALYTICAL CONTRIBUTION. UNIV SOCIETY DIPLOM DREAM GP/REL ADJUST ATTIT DISPL PERCEPT PERSON KNOWL MORAL. PAGE 139 A2840
WAR DRIVE LOVE PSY

B57
YAMADA H.,ANNALS OF THE SOCIAL SCIENCES. WOR+45 WOR-45 LAW CULTURE SOCIETY STRUCT DIPLOM...EPIST PSY CONCPT 15/20. PAGE 168 A3428
BIBLIOG/A TREND IDEA/COMP SOC

S57
SCHELLING T.C.,"BARGAINING COMMUNICATION, AND LIMITED WAR." UNIV WOR+45 FACE/GP INT/ORG NAT/G FORCES ACT/RES WAR PERCEPT ALL/VALS...PSY OBS PROJ/TEST CHARTS HYPO/EXP GEN/LAWS TOT/POP 20. PAGE 128 A2622
ROUTINE DECISION

B58
MELMAN S.,INSPECTION FOR DISARMAMENT. USA+45 WOR+45 SOCIETY INT/ORG NAT/G CONSULT ACT/RES PLAN EDU/PROP CONTROL DETER PEACE ATTIT PERSON KNOWL...PSY STAT OBS CHARTS TOT/POP VAL/FREE 20. PAGE 99 A2035
FUT ORD/FREE ARMS/CONT NUC/PWR

B58
REUTER P.,INTERNATIONAL INSTITUTIONS. WOR+45 WOR-45 CULTURE SOCIETY VOL/ASSN LEGIT ROUTINE GP/REL INGP/REL KNOWL...JURID METH/CNCPT TIME/SEQ 20. PAGE 120 A2469
INT/ORG PSY

S58
BOGART L.,"MEASURING THE EFFECTIVENESS OF AN OVERSEAS INFORMATION CAMPAIGN." EUR+WWI GREECE USA+45 INT/ORG MUNIC PLAN DIPLOM PEACE PERCEPT RIGID/FLEX KNOWL...TECHNIC PSY SOC NEW/IDEA CONT/OBS REC/INT STAND/INT SAMP/SIZ COLD/WAR 20. PAGE 16 A0328
ATTIT EDU/PROP

S58
SINGER J.D.,"THREAT PERCEPTION AND THE ARMAMENT TENSION DILEMMA." WOR+45 WOR-45 ELITES INT/ORG NAT/G DELIB/GP PLAN LEGIT COERCE DETER ATTIT RIGID/FLEX PWR...DECISION PSY 20. PAGE 133 A2724
PERCEPT ARMS/CONT BAL/PWR

S58
SONDERMANN F.A.,"SOCIOLOGY AND INTERNATIONAL RELATIONS." WOR+45 CULTURE SOCIETY INT/ORG NAT/G CREATE ATTIT DRIVE PERSON RIGID/FLEX...PSY SOC 20. PAGE 135 A2767
PLAN NEW/IDEA PEACE

B59
FREE L.A.,SIX ALLIES AND A NEUTRAL. ASIA COM EUR+WWI FRANCE GERMANY/W INDIA S/ASIA UK USA+45 INT/ORG NAT/G NUC/PWR PEACE ATTIT PERCEPT RIGID/FLEX ALL/VALS...STAT REC/INT COLD/WAR 20 CHINJAP. PAGE 48 A0992
PSY DIPLOM

B59
KULSKI W.W.,PEACEFUL CO-EXISTENCE: AN ANALYSIS OF SOVIET FOREIGN POLICY. WOR+45 INTELL SOCIETY ECO/UNDEV POL/PAR EDU/PROP COERCE DRIVE RIGID/FLEX PWR SKILL...PSY CONCPT HIST/WRIT CON/ANAL GEN/METH WORK VAL/FREE 20. PAGE 83 A1691
PLAN DIPLOM USSR

B59
STRAUSZ-HUPE R.,PROTRACTED CONFLICT. CHINA/COM KOREA WOR+45 INT/ORG FORCES ACT/RES ECO/TAC LEGIT COERCE DRIVE PERCEPT KNOWL PWR...PSY CONCPT RECORD GEN/METH COLD/WAR VAL/FREE 20. PAGE 139 A2847
COM PLAN USSR

S59
BROMKE A.,"DISENGAGEMENT IN EAST EUROPE." COM USSR INT/ORG DIPLOM EDU/PROP NEUTRAL NUC/PWR DRIVE RIGID/FLEX PWR...PSY CONCPT CON/ANAL GEN/METH VAL/FREE 20. PAGE 19 A0388
BAL/PWR

S59
FISCHER L.,"THE SOVIET-AMERICAN ANTAGONISM: HOW WILL IT END." CONSTN CULTURE PLAN TEC/DEV RIGID/FLEX SUPEGO ORD/FREE...MARXIST DECISION PSY CONCPT CON/ANAL GEN/LAWS VAL/FREE 20 COLD/WAR. PAGE 46 A0936
USA+45 PWR DIPLOM USSR

S59
PUGWASH CONFERENCE,"ON BIOLOGICAL AND CHEMICAL WARFARE." WOR+45 SOCIETY PROC/MFG INT/ORG FORCES EDU/PROP ADJUD RIGID/FLEX ORD/FREE PWR...DECISION PSY NEW/IDEA MATH VAL/FREE 20. PAGE 118 A2417
ACT/RES BIO/SOC WAR WEAPON

S59
QUIGLEY H.S.,"TOWARD REAPPRAISAL OF OUR CHINA POLICY." CHINA/COM USA+45 INT/ORG PLAN ECO/TAC PERCEPT ORD/FREE...DECISION PSY CON/ANAL GEN/METH VAL/FREE 20. PAGE 118 A2427
ASIA KNOWL DIPLOM

B60
HOLT R.T.,STRATEGIC PSYCHOLOGICAL OPERATIONS AND AMERICAN FOREIGN POLICY. ITALY USA+45 FOR/AID DOMIN RUMOR ADMIN TASK WAR CHOOSE ATTIT ALL/IDEOS...PSY COLD/WAR. PAGE 67 A1375
EDU/PROP ACT/RES DIPLOM POLICY

B60
PRITTIE T.,GERMANY DIVIDED: THE LEGACY OF THE NAZI ERA. EUR+WWI GERMANY RACE/REL SUPEGO...PSY AUD/VIS BIBLIOG/A 20 NAZI. PAGE 118 A2414
STERTYP PERSON ATTIT DIPLOM

L60
MCCLELLAND C.A.,"THE FUNCTION OF THEORY IN INTERNATIONAL RELATIONS." WOR+45 PLAN EDU/PROP ROUTINE ORD/FREE...PHIL/SCI PSY SOC METH/CNCPT NEW/IDEA OBS TREND GEN/METH 20. PAGE 97 A1997
INT/ORG CONCPT DIPLOM

S60
OSGOOD C.E.,"COGNITIVE DYNAMICS IN THE CONDUCT OF HUMAN AFFAIRS." USA+45 INTELL INT/ORG CONSULT PLAN ATTIT PERSON...PSY CHARTS HYPO/EXP 20. PAGE 112 A2299
R+D SOCIETY

S60
RUSSEL R.W.,"ROLES FOR PSYCHOLOGISTS IN THE MAINTENANCE OF PEACE." FUT USA+45 CULTURE INT/ORG DIPLOM FOR/AID EDU/PROP ATTIT KNOWL MORAL PWR ...POLICY SOC COLD/WAR 20. PAGE 125 A2572
PSY GEN/METH

S60
WRIGHT Q.,"LEGAL ASPECTS OF THE U-2 INCIDENT." COM USA+45 USSR STRUCT NAT/G FORCES PLAN TEC/DEV ADJUD RIGID/FLEX MORAL ORD/FREE...DECISION INT/LAW JURID PSY TREND GEN/LAWS COLD/WAR VAL/FREE 20 U-2. PAGE 168 A3413
PWR POLICY SPACE

B61
MICHAEL D.N.,PROPOSED STUDIES ON THE IMPLICATIONS OF PEACEFUL SPACE ACTIVITIES FOR HUMAN AFFAIRS. COM/IND INDUS FORCES DIPLOM PEACE PERSON...PSY SOC 20. PAGE 101 A2066
FUT SPACE ACT/RES PROB/SOLV

B61
SOCIAL SCIENCE SERIALS IN SPECIAL LIBRARIES IN THE NEW YORK AREA; A SELECTED LIST. R+D ACADEM EDU/PROP WRITING...PSY 20. PAGE 119 A2448
BIBLIOG DIPLOM SOC

B62
OSGOOD C.E.,AN ALTERNATIVE TO WAR OR SURRENDER. FUT UNIV CULTURE INTELL SOCIETY R+D INT/ORG CONSULT DELIB/GP ACT/RES PLAN CHOOSE ATTIT PERCEPT KNOWL ...PHIL/SCI PSY SOC TREND GEN/LAWS 20. PAGE 112 A2300
ORD/FREE EDU/PROP PEACE WAR

B62
WOETZEL R.K.,THE NURENBERG TRIALS IN INTERNATIONAL LAW. CHRIST-17C MOD/EUR WOR+45 SOCIETY NAT/G DELIB/GP DOMIN LEGIT ROUTINE ATTIT DRIVE PERSON SUPEGO MORAL ORD/FREE...POLICY MAJORIT JURID PSY SOC SELF/OBS RECORD NAZI TOT/POP. PAGE 166 A3376
INT/ORG ADJUD WAR

S62
BRZEZINSKI Z.K.,"PEACEFUL ENGAGEMENT IN COMMUNIST DISUNITY." ASIA CHINA/COM USA+45 USSR NAT/G TOP/EX CREATE ECO/TAC FOR/AID DOMIN ATTIT PERCEPT RIGID/FLEX PWR...PSY 20. PAGE 20 A0417
COM DIPLOM TOTALISM

S62
DEUTSCH K.W.,"TOWARDS WESTERN EUROPEAN INTEGRATION: AN INTERIM ASSESSMENT." EUR+WWI STRUCT ECO/DEV INT/ORG ECO/TAC INT/TRADE EDU/PROP PEACE ATTIT DRIVE PWR SOVEREIGN...PSY SOC TIME/SEQ CHARTS STERTYP 20. PAGE 36 A0741
VOL/ASSN RIGID/FLEX REGION

S62
NORTH R.C.,"DECISION MAKING IN CRISIS: AN INTRODUCTION." WOR+45 WOR-45 NAT/G CONSULT DELIB/GP TEC/DEV PERCEPT KNOWL...POLICY DECISION PSY METH/CNCPT CONT/OBS TREND VAL/FREE 20. PAGE 110 A2251
INT/ORG ROUTINE DIPLOM

S62
SPRINGER H.W.,"FEDERATION IN THE CARIBBEAN: AN ATTEMPT THAT FAILED." L/A+17C ECO/UNDEV INT/ORG POL/PAR PROVS LEGIS CREATE PLAN LEGIT ADMIN FEDERAL ATTIT DRIVE PERSON ORD/FREE PWR...POLICY GEOG PSY CONCPT OBS CARIBBEAN CMN/WLTH 20. PAGE 136 A2791
VOL/ASSN NAT/G REGION

B63
GALLAGHER M.P.,THE SOVIET HISTORY OF WORLD WAR II. EUR+WWI USSR DIPLOM DOMIN WRITING CONTROL WAR MARXISM...PSY TIME/SEQ 20 STALIN/J. PAGE 50 A1031
CIVMIL/REL EDU/PROP HIST/WRIT PRESS

B63
TUCKER R.C.,THE SOVIET POLITICAL MIND. WOR+45 ELITES INT/ORG NAT/G POL/PAR PLAN DIPLOM ECO/TAC DOMIN ADMIN NUC/PWR REV DRIVE PERSON SUPEGO PWR WEALTH...POLICY MGT PSY CONCPT OBS BIOG TREND COLD/WAR MARX/KARL 20. PAGE 145 A2972
COM TOP/EX USSR

S63
COSER L.,"AMERICA AND THE WORLD REVOLUTION." COM FUT USA+45 WOR+45 INTELL SOCIETY NAT/G ECO/TAC EDU/PROP ALL/VALS SOCISM...PSY GEN/LAWS TOT/POP 20 COLD/WAR. PAGE 31 A0629
ECO/UNDEV PLAN FOR/AID DIPLOM

S63
DICKS H.V.,"NATIONAL LOYALTY, IDENTITY, AND THE INTERNATIONAL SOLDIER." FUT NAT/G COERCE ATTIT DRIVE PERCEPT PERSON RIGID/FLEX SUPEGO ALL/VALS ...PSY VAL/FREE. PAGE 37 A0758
INT/ORG FORCES

S63
JORDAN N.,"INTERNATIONAL RELATIONS AND THE PSYCHOLOGIST." USA+45 WOR+45 DIPLOM...POLICY VAL/FREE 20. PAGE 75 A1536
KNOWL PSY

S63
KISSINGER H.A.,"STRAINS ON THE ALLIANCE." EUR+WWI FRANCE GERMANY GERMANY/W USA+45 ECO/DEV INT/ORG NAT/G TOP/EX EDU/PROP NUC/PWR ATTIT PWR...PSY TREND 20. PAGE 80 A1643
VOL/ASSN DRIVE DIPLOM

B64
DEUTSCHE GES AUSWARTIGE POL,STRATEGIE UND ABRUSTUNGSPOLITIK DER SOWJETUNION. USSR TEC/DEV DIPLOM COERCE DETER WEAPON...POLICY PSY 20 ABM/DEFSYS. PAGE 37 A0747
NUC/PWR WAR FORCES ARMS/CONT

B64
FISHER R.,INTERNATIONAL CONFLICT AND BEHAVIORAL SCIENCE: THE CRAIGVILLE PAPERS. COM FUT USA+45 WOR+45 NAT/G DELIB/GP EX/STRUC FORCES ECO/TAC DOMIN EDU/PROP LEGIT COERCE ATTIT PERCEPT ORD/FREE PWR RESPECT...PSY SOC VAL/FREE. PAGE 46 A0940
INT/ORG PLAN DIPLOM

B64
IKLE F.C.,HOW NATIONS NEGOTIATE. COM EUR+WWI USA+45 INTELL INT/ORG VOL/ASSN DELIB/GP ACT/RES CREATE DOMIN EDU/PROP ADJUD ROUTINE ATTIT PERSON ORD/FREE RESPECT SKILL...PSY SOC OBS VAL/FREE. PAGE 70 A1433
NAT/G PWR POLICY

B64
JACOB P.E.,THE INTEGRATION OF POLITICAL COMMUNITIES. USA+45 WOR+45 CULTURE LOC/G MUNIC NAT/G CREATE PLAN LEGIT REGION COERCE ALL/VALS ...POLICY GEOG PSY SOC TREND HYPO/EXP GEN/LAWS VAL/FREE 20. PAGE 72 A1483
INT/ORG METH/CNCPT SIMUL STAT

B64
SPECTOR S.D.,A CHECKLIST OF PAPERBOUND BOOKS ON RUSSIA. USSR SECT DIPLOM EDU/PROP HEALTH...PHIL/SCI PSY SOC SOC/WK WORSHIP 20. PAGE 135 A2775
BIBLIOG COM PERF/ART

L64
WARD C.,"THE 'NEW MYTHS' AND 'OLD REALITIES' OF NUCLEAR WAR." COM FUT USA+45 USSR WOR+45 INT/ORG NAT/G DOMIN LEGIT EXEC ATTIT PERCEPT ALL/VALS ...POLICY RELATIV PSY MYTH TREND 20. PAGE 161 A3280
FORCES COERCE ARMS/CONT NUC/PWR

S64
CARNEGIE ENDOWMENT INT. PEACE,"HUMAN RIGHTS (ISSUES BEFORE THE NINETEENTH GENERAL ASSEMBLY)." AFR WOR+45 LAW CONSTN NAT/G EDU/PROP GP/REL DISCRIM PEACE ATTIT MORAL ORD/FREE...INT/LAW PSY CONCPT RECORD UN 20. PAGE 24 A0492
INT/ORG PERSON RACE/REL

S64
GARMARNIKOW M.,"INFLUENCE-BUYING IN WEST AFRICA." COM FUT USSR INTELL NAT/G PLAN TEC/DEV ECO/TAC DOMIN EDU/PROP REGION NAT/LISM ATTIT DRIVE ALL/VALS SOVEREIGN...POLICY PSY SOC CONCPT TREND STERTYP WORK COLD/WAR 20. PAGE 51 A1049
AFR ECO/UNDEV FOR/AID SOCISM

S64
GREENBERG S.,"JUDAISM AND WORLD JUSTICE." MEDIT-7 WOR+45 LAW CULTURE SOCIETY INT/ORG NAT/G FORCES EDU/PROP ATTIT DRIVE PERSON SUPEGO ALL/VALS ...POLICY PSY CONCPT GEN/LAWS JEWS. PAGE 55 A1140
SECT JURID PEACE

S64
JORDAN A.,"POLITICAL COMMUNICATION: THE THIRD DIMENSION OF STRATEGY." USA+45 WOR+45 INT/ORG NAT/G CONSULT FORCES PLAN LEGIT EXEC PERCEPT ALL/VALS ...POLICY RELATIV PSY NEW/IDEA AUD/VIS EXHIBIT TOT/POP 20. PAGE 75 A1534
EDU/PROP RIGID/FLEX ATTIT

S64
KHAN M.Z.,"ISLAM AND INTERNATIONAL RELATIONS." FUT WOR+45 LAW CULTURE SOCIETY NAT/G SECT DELIB/GP FORCES EDU/PROP ATTIT PERSON SUPEGO ALL/VALS ...POLICY PSY CONCPT MYTH HIST/WRIT GEN/LAWS. PAGE 78 A1608
ISLAM INT/ORG DIPLOM

S64
MAZRUI A.A.,"THE UNITED NATIONS AND SOME AFRICAN POLITICAL ATTITUDES." ECO/TAC FOR/AID DOMIN ROUTINE CHOOSE ATTIT DRIVE MORAL PWR RESPECT WEALTH...PSY CONCPT OBS TREND UN VAL/FREE 20. PAGE 97 A1987
AFR INT/ORG SOVEREIGN

B65
DOMENACH J.M.,LA PROPAGANDE POLITIQUE. COM/IND INT/ORG POL/PAR DOMIN RIGID/FLEX FASCISM MARXISM ...PSY 20. PAGE 38 A0770
ATTIT EDU/PROP TEC/DEV MYTH

B65
INTERNATIONAL SOCIAL SCI COUN,SOCIAL SCIENCES IN THE USSR. USSR ECO/DEV AGRI FINAN INDUS PLAN CAP/ISM...INT/LAW PHIL/SCI PSY SOC 20. PAGE 71 A1460
BIBLIOG/A ACT/RES MARXISM JURID

B65
UNESCO,INTERNATIONAL ORGANIZATIONS IN THE SOCIAL SCIENCES(REV. ED.). LAW ADMIN ATTIT...CRIMLGY GEOG INT/LAW PSY SOC STAT 20 UNESCO. PAGE 148 A3024
INT/ORG R+D PROF/ORG ACT/RES

B65
UNIVERSAL REFERENCE SYSTEM,INTERNATIONAL AFFAIRS: VOLUME I IN THE POLITICAL SCIENCE, GOVERNMENT, AND PUBLIC POLICY SERIES....DECISION ECOMETRIC GEOG INT/LAW JURID MGT PHIL/SCI PSY SOC. PAGE 149 A3041
BIBLIOG/A GEN/METH COMPUT/IR DIPLOM

S65
MERRITT R.L.,"WOODROW WILSON AND THE 'GREAT AND SOLEMN REFERENDUM,' 1920." USA-45 SOCIETY NAT/G CONSULT LEGIS ACT/RES PLAN DOMIN EDU/PROP ROUTINE ATTIT DISPL DRIVE PERSON RIGID/FLEX MORAL ORD/FREE ...PSY SOC CONCPT MYTH LEAGUE/NAT. PAGE 100 A2044
INT/ORG TOP/EX DIPLOM

C65
SCHWEBEL M.,"BEHAVIORAL SCIENCE AND HUMAN SURVIVAL." FORCES ARMS/CONT COERCE NUC/PWR WAR GP/REL NAT/LISM PERCEPT...POLICY PSY ANTHOL BIBLIOG/A 20 COLD/WAR. PAGE 130 A2662
PEACE ACT/RES DIPLOM HEAL

B66
HOLLINS E.J.,PEACE IS POSSIBLE: A READER FOR LAYMEN. WOR+45 CULTURE PLAN RISK AGE/Y ALL/VALS SOVEREIGN...PSY CONCPT TREND 20 UN JOHN/XXIII KENNAN/G MYRDAL/G. PAGE 67 A1370
PEACE DIPLOM INT/ORG NUC/PWR

B66
SAGER P.,MOSKAUS HAND IN INDIEN. INDIA USSR DIPLOM DOMIN...PSY CONCPT 20 COM/PARTY. PAGE 126 A2586
PRESS EDU/PROP METH POL/PAR

B66
SOCIAL SCIENCE RESEARCH COUN,BIBLIOGRAPHY OF RESEARCH IN THE SOCIAL SCIENCES IN AUSTRALIA 1957-1960. LAW R+D DIPLOM 20 AUSTRAL. PAGE 135 A2758
BIBLIOG SOC PSY

B67
FILENE P.G.,AMERICANS AND THE SOVIET EXPERIMENT, 1917-1933. USA-45 USSR INTELL NAT/G CAP/ISM DIPLOM EDU/PROP PRESS REV SOCISM...PSY 20. PAGE 45 A0930
ATTIT RIGID/FLEX MARXISM SOCIETY

B67
ROSENAU J.N.,DOMESTIC SOURCES OF FOREIGN POLICY. WOR+45 STRATA COM/IND MUNIC POL/PAR LOBBY PARTIC REGION ATTIT...PSY SOC COLD/WAR. PAGE 124 A2534
DIPLOM POLICY NAT/G CHOOSE

B67
US DEPARTMENT OF STATE,FOREIGN AFFAIRS RESEARCH (PAMPHLET). USA+45 WOR+45 ACADEM NAT/G...PSY SOC CHARTS 20. PAGE 152 A3100
BIBLIOG INDEX R+D DIPLOM

L67
GRAUBARD S.R.,"TOWARD THE YEAR 2000: WORK IN PROGRESS." FUT ACADEM SECT DELIB/GP DIPLOM EDU/PROP AGE/Y PERSON ROLE...PSY ANTHOL. PAGE 55 A1131
PREDICT PROB/SOLV SOCIETY CULTURE

S67
INGLEHART R.,"AN END TO EUROPEAN INTEGRATION."
DIPLOM

PROB/SOLV BAL/PWR NAT/LISM...PSY SOC INT CHARTS EUR+WWI
GP/COMP 20. PAGE 70 A1440 REGION
ATTIT

S67
LIVNEH E.,"A NEW BEGINNING." ISRAEL USSR WOR+45 WAR
NAT/G DIPLOM INGP/REL FEDERAL HABITAT PWR...GEOG PERSON
PSY JEWS. PAGE 90 A1847 PEACE
PLAN

S67
SUINN R.M.,"THE DISARMAMENT FANTASY* PSYCHOLOGICAL DECISION
FACTORS THAT MAY PRODUCE WARFARE." DIPLOM RISK NUC/PWR
ARMS/CONT DETER ANOMIE PERSON GAME. PAGE 140 A2860 WAR
PSY

PSY/WAR....PSYCHOLOGICAL WARFARE; SEE ALSO PSY + EDU/PROP + WAR

B53
SQUIRES J.D.,BRITISH PROPAGANDA AT HOME AND IN THE EDU/PROP
UNITED STATES FROM 1914 TO 1917. UK NAT/G PROB/SOLV CONTROL
DOMIN PRESS EFFICIENCY...PSY PREDICT 20 WWI WAR
INTERVENT PSY/WAR. PAGE 136 A2794 DIPLOM

PSYCHIATRY....SEE PSY

PSYCHOANALYSIS....SEE BIOG, PSY

PSYCHO-DRAMA....SEE SELF/OBS

PSYCHOLOGICAL WARFARE....SEE PSY+EDU/PROP+WAR

PSYCHOLOGY....SEE PSY

PUB/INST....MENTAL, CORRECTIONAL, AND OTHER HABITATIONAL INSTITUTIONS

L16
WRIGHT Q.,"THE ENFORCEMENT OF INTERNATIONAL LAW INT/ORG
THROUGH MUNICIPAL LAW IN THE US." USA-45 LOC/G LAW
NAT/G PUB/INST FORCES LEGIT CT/SYS PERCEPT ALL/VALS INT/LAW
...JURID 20. PAGE 167 A3401 WAR

B37
UNION OF SOUTH AFRICA,REPORT CONCERNING NAT/G
ADMINISTRATION OF SOUTH WEST AFRICA (6 VOLS.). ADMIN
SOUTH/AFR INDUS PUB/INST FORCES LEGIS BUDGET DIPLOM COLONIAL
EDU/PROP ADJUD CT/SYS...GEOG CHARTS 20 AFRICA/SW CONSTN
LEAGUE/NAT. PAGE 148 A3028

B62
MCKENNA J.,DIPLOMATIC PROTEST IN FOREIGN POLICY: NAT/G
ANALYSIS AND CASE STUDIES. COM USA+45 WOR+45 POLICY
INT/ORG PUB/INST DELIB/GP TOP/EX ACT/RES PLAN LEGIT DIPLOM
ATTIT 20. PAGE 98 A2014

S62
GRAVEN J.,"LE MOUVEAU DROIT PENAL INTERNATIONAL." CT/SYS
UNIV STRUCT LEGIS ACT/RES CRIME ATTIT PERCEPT PUB/INST
PERSON...JURID CONCPT 20. PAGE 55 A1132 INT/ORG
INT/LAW

B64
WEINTRAUB S.,THE WAR IN THE WARDS. KOREA/N WOR+45 EDU/PROP
DIPLOM COERCE ORD/FREE SKILL 20 TREATY. PAGE 162 PEACE
A3308 CROWD
PUB/INST

S64
HUTCHINSON E.C.,"AMERICAN AID TO AFRICA." FUT AFR
USA+45 MARKET INT/ORG LOC/G NAT/G PUB/INST PLAN ECO/UNDEV
ECO/TAC ATTIT RIGID/FLEX...POLICY CONCPT TREND 20. FOR/AID
PAGE 69 A1423

B65
US LIBRARY OF CONGRESS,A DIRECTORY OF INFORMATION BIBLIOG
RESOURCES IN THE UNITED STATES: SOCIAL SCIENCES. R+D
USA+45 ACADEM INT/ORG LABOR PROF/ORG PUB/INST COMPUT/IR
SCHOOL SECT 20. PAGE 155 A3159

B67
BODENHEIMER E.,TREATISE ON JUSTICE. INT/ORG NAT/G ALL/VALS
PUB/INST ACT/RES RISK CRIME INGP/REL DISCRIM DRIVE STRUCT
LAISSEZ 20. PAGE 16 A0325 JURID
CONCPT

PUB/TRANS....PUBLIC TRANSPORTATION

B57
DRUCKER P.F.,AMERICA'S NEXT TWENTY YEARS. USA+45 WORKER
DIST/IND ACADEM MUNIC SCHOOL DIPLOM ECO/TAC AUTOMAT FOR/AID
HABITAT HEALTH...SOC/WK TREND 20 URBAN/RNWL CENSUS
PUB/TRANS. PAGE 39 A0788 GEOG

B65
WHITE HOUSE CONFERENCE ON INTERNATIONAL R+D
COOPERATION(VOL.II). SPACE WOR+45 EXTR/IND INT/ORG CONFER
LABOR WORKER NUC/PWR PEACE AGE/Y...CENSUS ANTHOL 20 TEC/DEV
RESOURCE/N URBAN/RNWL PUB/TRANS. PAGE 3 A0071 DIPLOM

PUBL/WORKS....PUBLIC WORKS

PUBLIC ADMINISTRATION....SEE ADMIN, NAT/G

PUBLIC POLICY....SEE NAT/G+PLAN

PUBLIC RELATIONS....SEE NAT/G+RELATIONS INDEX

PUBLIC WORKS....SEE PUBL/WORKS

PUBLIC/EDU....PUBLIC EDUCATION ASSOCIATION

PUBLIC/REL....PUBLIC RELATIONS; SEE ALSO NAT/G + RELATIONS INDEX

PUBLIC/USE....PUBLIC USE

PUEBLO....PUEBLO INCIDENT; SEE ALSO KOREA/N

PUERT/RICN....PUERTO RICAN

PUERT/RICO....PUERTO RICO; SEE ALSO L/A+17C

B59
PAGAN B.,HISTORIA DE LOS PARTIDOS POLITICOS POL/PAR
PUERTORRIQUENOS 1898-1956. PUERT/RICO PROVS DIPLOM CHOOSE
DOMIN EDU/PROP PARTIC 20. PAGE 113 A2316 COLONIAL
PWR

B67
DOSSICK J.J.,DOCTORAL RESEARCH ON PUERTO RICO AND BIBLIOG
PUERTO RICANS. PUERT/RICO USA+45 USA-45 ADMIN 20. CONSTN
PAGE 38 A0776 POL/PAR
DIPLOM

PUFENDORF S. A2416

PUGWASH CONFERENCE A2417

PULLMAN....PULLMAN, ILLINOIS

PUNISHMENT....SEE ADJUD, LAW, LEGIT, SANCTION

PUNJAB....THE PUNJAB AND ITS PEOPLES

PUNTA DEL ESTE....SEE PUNTA/ESTE

PUNTA/ESTE....PUNTA DEL ESTE

PURGE....PURGES

PURHAM/M....MARGERY PURHAM

PURITAN....PURITANS

PURSELL CW J.R. A2349

PUTIGNANO A. A2881

PUTTKAMMER E.W. A2418

PWR....POWER, PARTICIPATION IN DECISION-MAKING

PYE L.W. A2419,A2420

PYRAH G.B. A2421

Q

QU....QUESTIONNAIRES; SEE ALSO QUESTIONNAIRES INDEX, P. XIV

B47
SOCIAL SCIENCE RESEARCH COUN,PUBLIC REACTION TO THE ATTIT
ATOMIC BOMB AND WORLD AFFAIRS. SOCIETY CONFER NUC/PWR
ARMS/CONT...STAT QU SAMP CHARTS 20. PAGE 135 A2757 DIPLOM
WAR

B53
MURPHY G.,IN THE MINDS OF MEN: THE STUDY OF HUMAN SECT
BEHAVIOR AND SOCIAL TENSIONS IN INDIA. FUT S/ASIA STRATA
FAM INT/ORG NAT/G DIPLOM EDU/PROP GP/REL ATTIT INDIA
RIGID/FLEX ALL/VALS...SOC QU UNESCO 20. PAGE 106
A2176

B57
FULLER C.D.,TRAINING OF SPECIALISTS IN KNOWL
INTERNATIONAL RELATIONS. FUT USA+45 USA-45 INTELL DIPLOM
INT/ORG...MGT METH/CNCPT INT QU GEN/METH 20.
PAGE 50 A1017

B57
SPEIER H.,GERMAN REARMAMENT AND ATOMIC WAR: THE TOP/EX
VIEWS OF GERMAN MILITARY AND POLITICAL LEADERS. FUT FORCES
WOR+45 INT/ORG NAT/G WEAPON ATTIT PWR...INT QU NUC/PWR
TOT/POP VAL/FREE COLD/WAR 20. PAGE 136 A2780 GERMANY

B58
SCOTT W.A.,THE UNITED STATES AND THE UNITED ATTIT
NATIONS: THE PUBLIC VIEW 1945-1955. USA+45 EDU/PROP DIPLOM
...INT QU KNO/TEST SAMP GP/COMP 20 UN. PAGE 130 INT/ORG
A2674

B59
COLUMBIA U BUR APPL SOC RES,ATTITUDES OF ATTIT

PROMINENT AMERICANS TOWARD "WORLD PEACE THROUGH WORLD LAW" (SUPRA-NATL ORGANIZATION FOR WAR PREVENTION). USA+45 USSR ELITES FORCES PLAN PROB/SOLV CONTROL WAR PWR...POLICY SOC QU IDEA/COMP 20 UN. PAGE 117 A2403 — ACT/RES INT/LAW STAT

B64
SULLIVAN G.,THE STORY OF THE PEACE CORPS. USA+45 WOR+45 INTELL FACE/GP NAT/G SCHOOL VOL/ASSN CONSULT EX/STRUC PLAN EDU/PROP ADMIN ATTIT DRIVE ALL/VALS ...POLICY HEAL SOC CONCPT INT QU BIOG TREND SOC/EXP WORK. PAGE 140 A2861 — INT/ORG ECO/UNDEV FOR/AID PEACE

S64
RUBIN R.,"THE UN CORRESPONDENT." WOR+45 FACE/GP PROF/ORG EDU/PROP ROUTINE PERCEPT KNOWL...RECORD STAND/INT QU UN WORK TOT/POP VAL/FREE 20. PAGE 125 A2560 — INT/ORG ATTIT DIPLOM

B67
BELL W.,THE DEMOCRATIC REVOLUTION IN THE WEST INDIES. WEST/IND WOR+45 DIPLOM RACE/REL NAT/LISM ...INT QU ANTHOL 20. PAGE 13 A0257 — REGION ATTIT ORD/FREE ECO/UNDEV

S67
VERBA S.,"PUBLIC OPINION AND THE WAR IN VIETNAM." USA+45 VIETNAM DIPLOM WAR...CORREL STAT QU CHARTS 20. PAGE 158 A3228 — ATTIT KNO/TEST NAT/G PLAN

QU/SEMANT....SEMANTIC AND SOCIAL PROBLEMS OF QUESTIONNAIRES

S47
RADVANYI L.,"PROBLEMS OF INTERNATIONAL OPINION SURVEYS." WOR+45 INT/ORG NAT/G CREATE ATTIT...PSY SOC METH/CNCPT REC/INT KNO/TEST SAMP/SIZ METH VAL/FREE 20. PAGE 118 A2431 — QU/SEMANT SAMP DIPLOM

QUADE Q.L. A2422

QUAISON-SACKEY A. A2423

QUAKER....QUAKER

QUAN K.L. A2424

QUANDT R.E. A1562

QUANT....QUANTIFICATION

B52
ALEXANDROWICZ C.H.,INTERNATIONAL ECONOMIC ORGANIZATION. WOR+45 ECO/DEV ECO/UNDEV DIST/IND FINAN MARKET PLAN ECO/TAC LEGIT DRIVE WEALTH ...POLICY CONCPT QUANT OBS TIME/SEQ GEN/LAWS WORK EEC ILO OEEC UNESCO 20. PAGE 6 A0114 — INT/ORG INT/TRADE

S54
DODD S.C.,"THE SCIENTIFIC MEASUREMENT OF FITNESS FOR SELF-GOVERNMENT." FUT CONSTN ECO/UNDEV INT/ORG PLAN PWR...CONCPT QUANT CON/ANAL SOC/EXP UN LEAGUE/NAT 20. PAGE 38 A0767 — NAT/G STAT SOVEREIGN

B58
GANGE J.,UNIVERSITY RESEARCH ON INTERNATIONAL AFFAIRS. USA+45 ACADEM INT/ORG CONSULT CREATE EXEC ROUTINE...QUANT STAT INT STERTYP GEN/METH TOT/POP VAL/FREE 20. PAGE 51 A1040 — R+D MGT DIPLOM

L58
SNYDER R.N.,"THE UNITED STATES DECISION TO RESIST AGGRESSION IN KOREA." ASIA KOREA S/ASIA USA+45 USA-45 WOR+45 INT/ORG DELIB/GP BAL/PWR COERCE PWR ...CONCPT REC/INT RESIST/INT COLD/WAR 20. PAGE 134 A2753 — QUANT METH/CNCPT DIPLOM

S59
SOHN L.B.,"THE DEFINITION OF AGGRESSION." FUT LAW FORCES LEGIT ADJUD ROUTINE COERCE ORD/FREE PWR ...MAJORIT JURID QUANT COLD/WAR 20. PAGE 135 A2762 — INT/ORG CT/SYS DETER SOVEREIGN

B60
WOLF C.,FOREIGN AID: THEORY AND PRACTICE IN SOUTHERN ASIA. CEYLON INDONESIA PHILIPPINE S/ASIA CULTURE STRATA ECO/UNDEV PLAN EDU/PROP ATTIT ...METH/CNCPT MATH QUANT STAT CONT/OBS TIME/SEQ SIMUL TOT/POP 20. PAGE 166 A3378 — ACT/RES ECO/TAC FOR/AID

L60
HAAS E.B.,"CONSENSUS FORMATION IN THE COUNCIL OF EUROPE." EUR+WWI NAT/G DELIB/GP DIPLOM REGION CHOOSE PWR SOVEREIGN...RELATIV NEW/IDEA QUANT CHARTS INDEX TOT/POP OEEC 20 COUNCL/EUR. PAGE 59 A1206 — POL/PAR INT/ORG STAT

S60
RIESELBACH Z.N.,"QUANTITATIVE TECHNIQUES FOR STUDYING VOTING BEHAVIOR IN THE UNITED NATIONS GENERAL ASSEMBLY." FUT S/ASIA USA+45 INT/ORG BAL/PWR DIPLOM ECO/TAC FOR/AID ADMIN PWR...POLICY METH/CNCPT METH UN 20. PAGE 121 A2478 — QUANT CHOOSE

B63
NORTH R.C.,CONTENT ANALYSIS: A HANDBOOK WITH APPLICATIONS FOR THE STUDY OF INTERNATIONAL CRISIS. ASIA COM EUR+WWI MOD/EUR INT/ORG TEC/DEV DOMIN EDU/PROP ROUTINE COERCE PERCEPT RIGID/FLEX ALL/VALS ...QUANT TESTS CON/ANAL SIMUL GEN/LAWS VAL/FREE. PAGE 110 A2252 — METH/CNCPT COMPUT/IR USSR

S63
MATHUR P.N.,"GAINS IN ECONOMIC GROWTH FROM INTERNATIONAL TRADE." USA-45 ECO/DEV FINAN INDUS ATTIT WEALTH...MATH QUANT STAT BIOG TREND GEN/LAWS WORK 20. PAGE 96 A1966 — MARKET ECO/TAC CAP/ISM INT/TRADE

S64
BEIM D.,"THE COMMUNIST BLOC AND THE FOREIGN-AID GAME." WOR+45 NAT/G PLAN ROUTINE ATTIT KNOWL ORD/FREE...DECISION QUANT CONT/OBS TIME/SEQ CHARTS GAME SIMUL COLD/WAR 20. PAGE 12 A0252 — COM ECO/UNDEV ECO/TAC FOR/AID

QUANTIFICATION....SEE QUANT

QUANTITATIVE CONTENT ANALYSIS....SEE CON/ANAL

QUBAIN F.I. A2425

QUEBEC....QUEBEC, CANADA

QUESTIONNAIRES....SEE QU

QUIGG P.W. A2426

QUIGLEY H.S. A2427

QUIRK R.E. A2428

QURESHI I.H. A2429

R

R+D....RESEARCH AND DEVELOPMENT GROUP

N
AMERICAN DOCUMENTATION INST,DOCUMENTATION ABSTRACTS. WOR+45 NAT/G COMPUTER CREATE TEC/DEV DIPLOM EDU/PROP REGION KNOWL...PHIL/SCI CLASSIF LING. PAGE 7 A0143 — BIBLIOG/A AUTOMAT COMPUT/IR R+D

N
SOCIAL RESEARCH. WOR+45 WOR-45 R+D LEAD GP/REL ATTIT...SOC TREND 20. PAGE 2 A0025 — BIBLIOG/A DIPLOM NAT/G SOCIETY

N
INDIA: A REFERENCE ANNUAL. INDIA CULTURE COM/IND R+D FORCES PLAN RECEIVE EDU/PROP HEALTH...STAT CHARTS BIBLIOG 20. PAGE 2 A0036 — CONSTN LABOR INT/ORG

N
THE WORLD OF LEARNING. INTELL ACT/RES EDU/PROP 20 UNESCO. PAGE 2 A0045 — BIBLIOG/A ACADEM R+D INT/ORG

N
AMERICAN ECONOMIC ASSOCIATION,THE JOURNAL OF ECONOMIC ABSTRACTS. ECO/UNDEV MARKET LABOR DIPLOM ...MGT CONCPT METH 20. PAGE 7 A0144 — BIBLIOG/A R+D FINAN

N
CARNEGIE ENDOWMENT,CURRENT RESEARCH IN INTERNATIONAL AFFAIRS: SELECTED BIBLIOGRAPHY OF WORK IN PROGRESS BY PRIVATE RESEARCH AGENCIES. WOR+45 NAT/G ACT/RES GOV/COMP. PAGE 24 A0488 — BIBLIOG/A DIPLOM R+D

N
KYRIAK T.E.,SOVIET UNION: BIBLIOGRAPHY INDEX TO US JPRS RESEARCH TRANSLATIONS. USSR ECO/DEV AGRI COM/IND CONSTRUC DIST/IND EXTR/IND PROC/MFG R+D INT/TRADE...SOC 20. PAGE 83 A1703 — BIBLIOG/A INDUS MARXISM PRESS

B34
EINSTEIN A.,THE WORLD AS I SEE IT. WOR-45 INTELL R+D INT/ORG NAT/G SECT VOL/ASSN FORCES CREATE EDU/PROP LEGIT ARMS/CONT WAR WEAPON NAT/LISM ALL/VALS...POLICY CONCPT 20. PAGE 41 A0828 — SOCIETY PHIL/SCI DIPLOM PACIFISM

B38
COLBY C.C.,GEOGRAPHICAL ASPECTS OF INTERNATIONAL RELATIONS. WOR-45 ECO/DEV ECO/UNDEV AGRI EXTR/IND INDUS MARKET R+D INT/ORG NAT/G TEC/DEV ECO/TAC INT/TRADE NAT/LISM WEALTH...METH/CNCPT CHARTS GEN/LAWS 20. PAGE 28 A0565 — PLAN GEOG DIPLOM

S40
FLORIN J.,"BOLSHEVIST AND NATIONAL SOCIALIST DOCTRINES OF INTERNATIONAL LAW." EUR+WWI GERMANY USSR R+D INT/ORG NAT/G DIPLOM DOMIN EDU/PROP SOCISM ...CONCPT TIME/SEQ 20. PAGE 47 A0955 — LAW ATTIT TOTALISM INT/LAW

B47
KIRK G.,THE STUDY OF INTERNATIONAL RELATIONS. FUT USA-45 R+D ACADEM INT/ORG CONSULT DELIB/GP INT/TRADE EDU/PROP PEACE RIGID/FLEX KNOWL VAL/FREE 20. PAGE 80 A1632 — USA+45 DIPLOM

L47
BRUNER J.S.,"TOWARD A COMMON GROUND-INTERNATIONAL SOCIAL SCIENCE." FUT WOR+45 INTELL R+D NAT/G VOL/ASSN CONSULT DELIB/GP ACT/RES CREATE PLAN TEC/DEV ATTIT ORD/FREE...PSY SOC CONCPT ANTHOL UNESCO 20. PAGE 20 A0410 — INT/ORG KNOWL

B48
GRIFFITH E.S.,RESEARCH IN POLITICAL SCIENCE: THE — BIBLIOG

WORK OF PANELS OF RESEARCH COMMITTEE, APSA. WOR+45 WOR-45 COM/IND R+D FORCES ACT/RES WAR...GOV/COMP ANTHOL 20. PAGE 56 A1160 — PHIL/SCI DIPLOM JURID

B49
FORD FOUNDATION,REPORT OF THE STUDY FOR THE FORD FOUNDATION ON POLICY AND PROGRAM. SOCIETY R+D ACT/RES CAP/ISM FOR/AID EDU/PROP ADMIN KNOWL ...POLICY PSY SOC 20. PAGE 47 A0961 — WEALTH GEN/LAWS

B49
ROSENHAUPT H.W.,HOW TO WAGE PEACE. USA+45 SOCIETY STRATA STRUCT R+D INT/ORG POL/PAR LEGIS ACT/RES CREATE PLAN EDU/PROP ADMIN EXEC ATTIT ALL/VALS ...TIME/SEQ TREND COLD/WAR 20. PAGE 124 A2536 — INTELL CONCPT DIPLOM

L49
COMM. STUDY ORGAN. PEACE,"A TEN YEAR RECORD, 1939-1949." FUT WOR+45 LAW R+D CONSULT DELIB/GP CREATE LEGIT ROUTINE ORD/FREE...TIME/SEQ UN 20. PAGE 28 A0578 — INT/ORG CONSTN PEACE

S49
DUNN F.,"THE PRESENT COURSE OF INTERNATIONAL RELATIONS RESEARCH." WOR+45 WOR-45 SOCIETY R+D INT/ORG WAR PERSON ORD/FREE...POLICY PSY SOC GEN/LAWS 20. PAGE 39 A0800 — CONCPT GEN/METH DIPLOM

B50
MACIVER R.M.,GREAT EXPRESSIONS OF HUMAN RIGHTS. LAW CONSTN CULTURE INTELL SOCIETY R+D INT/ORG ATTIT DRIVE...JURID OBS HIST/WRIT GEN/LAWS. PAGE 92 A1891 — UNIV CONCPT

S50
UNESCO,"MEETING ON UNIVERSITY TEACHING OF INTERNATIONAL RELATIONS." FUT WOR+45 R+D VOL/ASSN CONSULT PLAN EDU/PROP ATTIT...CONCPT TREND 20. PAGE 147 A3012 — INT/ORG KNOWL DIPLOM

B51
CORMACK M.,SELECTED PAMPHLETS ON THE UNITED NATIONS AND INTERNATIONAL RELATIONS (PAMPHLET). USA+45 R+D EX/STRUC PROB/SOLV ROUTINE...POLICY CON/ANAL 20 UN NATO. PAGE 31 A0624 — BIBLIOG/A NAT/G INT/ORG DIPLOM

B51
MCKEON R.,DEMOCRACY IN A WORLD OF TENSION. UNIV LAW INTELL STRUCT R+D INT/ORG SCHOOL EDU/PROP LEGIT ATTIT DRIVE PERCEPT PERSON...POLICY JURID PSY SOC CONCPT METH/CNCPT OBS UNESCO TOT/POP VAL/FREE. PAGE 98 A2015 — SOCIETY ALL/VALS ORD/FREE

S51
BUCHANAN W.,"STEREOTYPES AND TENSIONS AS REVEALED BY THE UNESCO INTERNATIONAL POLL." WOR+45 INT/ORG ATTIT DISPL PERCEPT RIGID/FLEX...INT TESTS SAMP 20. PAGE 21 A0424 — R+D STERTYP

B52
SMITH C.M.,INTERNATIONAL COMMUNICATION AND POLITICAL WARFARE: AN ANNOTATED BIBLIOGRAPHY (A PAPER). WOR+45 INTELL R+D NAT/G FORCES ACT/RES DIPLOM COERCE ALL/IDEOS. PAGE 134 A2745 — BIBLIOG/A EDU/PROP WAR COM/IND

B52
UN DEPT. SOC. AFF.,PRELIMINARY REPORT ON THE WORLD SOCIAL SITUATION. ISLAM L/A+17C WOR+45 STRATA AGRI EXTR/IND INDUS INT/ORG SCHOOL ADMIN...GEOG SOC TREND UNESCO WORK FAO 20. PAGE 147 A2998 — R+D HEALTH FOR/AID

B52
UNESCO,CURRENT SOCIOLOGY (2 VOLS.). SOCIETY STRATA R+D GP/REL ATTIT PERSON 20 UN. PAGE 147 A3014 — BIBLIOG SOC INT/ORG CULTURE

B52
US DEPARTMENT OF STATE,RESEARCH ON EASTERN EUROPE (EXCLUDING USSR). EUR+WWI LAW ECO/DEV NAT/G PROB/SOLV DIPLOM ADMIN LEAD MARXISM...TREND 19/20. PAGE 151 A3088 — BIBLIOG R+D ACT/RES COM

L52
THOMPSON K.W.,"THE STUDY OF INTERNATIONAL POLITICS: A SURVEY OF TRENDS AND DEVELOPMENTS." UNIV USA+45 WOR+45 WOR-45 SOCIETY ECO/DEV R+D ACT/RES PLAN ROUTINE ATTIT DRIVE PERCEPT PERSON...CONCPT OBS TREND GEN/LAWS TOT/POP. PAGE 143 A2928 — INT/ORG BAL/PWR DIPLOM

N52
COORDINATING COMM DOC SOC SCI,INTERNATIONAL REPERTORY OF SOCIAL SCIENCE DOCUMENTATION CENTERS (PAMPHLET). ACT/RES OP/RES WRITING KNOWL...CON/ANAL METH. PAGE 30 A0610 — BIBLIOG/A R+D NAT/G INT/ORG

B54
MANNING C.A.W.,THE UNIVERSITY TEACHING OF SOCIAL SCIENCES: INTERNATIONAL RELATIONS. WOR+45 INTELL STRATA R+D ACADEM INT/ORG NAT/G CONSULT DELIB/GP ACT/RES EDU/PROP NAT/LISM ATTIT...POLICY CONT/OBS HYPO/EXP VAL/FREE LEAGUE/NAT UNESCO 20. PAGE 94 A1925 — KNOWL PHIL/SCI DIPLOM

S54
FOX W.T.R.,"CIVIL-MILITARY RELATIONS." USA+45 USA-45 R+D ACT/RES DIPLOM INT/TRADE EDU/PROP DETER DISPL DRIVE ORD/FREE...METH/CNCPT TREND COLD/WAR 20. PAGE 48 A0974 — POLICY FORCES PLAN SOCIETY

B55
MYRDAL A.R.,AMERICA'S ROLE IN INTERNATIONATIONAL SOCIAL WELFARE. FUT WOR+45 SOCIETY R+D VOL/ASSN ECO/TAC EDU/PROP HEALTH KNOWL WEALTH...SOC CHARTS ORG/CHARTS TOT/POP 20. PAGE 107 A2188 — PLAN SKILL FOR/AID

S55
WRIGHT Q.,"THE PEACEFUL ADJUSTMENT OF INTERNATIONAL RELATIONS: PROBLEMS AND RESEARCH APPROACHES." UNIV INTELL EDU/PROP ADJUD ROUTINE KNOWL SKILL...INT/LAW JURID PHIL/SCI CLASSIF 20. PAGE 167 A3411 — R+D METH/CNCPT PEACE

B56
CONOVER H.F.,A GUIDE TO BIBLIOGRAPHIC TOOLS FOR RESEARCH IN FOREIGN AFFAIRS. AFR ASIA COM EUR+WWI WOR+45 BAL/PWR CON/ANAL. PAGE 30 A0602 — BIBLIOG/A R+D DIPLOM INT/ORG

B56
UN HEADQUARTERS LIBRARY,BIBLIOGRAPHY OF INDUSTRIALIZATION IN UNDERDEVELOPED COUNTRIES (BIBLIOGRAPHICAL SERIES NO. 6). WOR+45 R+D ACADEM INT/ORG NAT/G. PAGE 147 A3002 — BIBLIOG ECO/UNDEV TEC/DEV

B56
UNITED NATIONS,BIBLIOGRAPHY ON INDUSTRIALIZATION IN UNDER-DEVELOPED COUNTRIES. WOR+45 R+D INT/ORG NAT/G FOR/AID ADMIN LEAD 20 UN. PAGE 149 A3036 — BIBLIOG ECO/UNDEV INDUS TEC/DEV

B56
US DEPARTMENT OF STATE,ECONOMIC PROBLEMS OF UNDERDEVELOPED AREAS (PAMPHLET). AFR ASIA ISLAM L/A+17C AGRI FINAN INDUS INT/ORG LABOR INT/TRADE ...PSY SOC 20. PAGE 151 A3090 — BIBLIOG ECO/UNDEV TEC/DEV R+D

B58
GANGE J.,UNIVERSITY RESEARCH ON INTERNATIONAL AFFAIRS. USA+45 ACADEM INT/ORG CONSULT CREATE EXEC ROUTINE...QUANT STAT INT STERTYP GEN/METH TOT/POP VAL/FREE 20. PAGE 51 A1040 — R+D MGT DIPLOM

B58
GARTHOFF R.L.,SOVIET STRATEGY IN THE NUCLEAR AGE. FUT USSR R+D INT/ORG NAT/G ACT/RES TEC/DEV DOMIN DETER WAR ATTIT PWR...RELATIV METH/CNCPT SELF/OBS TREND CON/ANAL STERTYP GEN/LAWS 20. PAGE 51 A1052 — COM FORCES BAL/PWR NUC/PWR

B58
UN INTL CONF ON PEACEFUL USE,PROGRESS IN ATOMIC ENERGY (VOL. I). WOR+45 R+D PLAN TEC/DEV CONFER CONTROL PEACE SKILL...CHARTS ANTHOL 20 UN BAGHDAD. PAGE 147 A3003 — NUC/PWR DIPLOM WORKER EDU/PROP

S58
ANDERSON N.,"INTERNATIONAL SEMINARS: AN ANALYSIS AND AN EVALUATION." WOR+45 R+D ACT/RES CREATE PLAN REGION ATTIT KNOWL SKILL...SOC REC/INT PERS/TEST CHARTS 20. PAGE 8 A0158 — INT/ORG DELIB/GP

B59
STANFORD RESEARCH INSTITUTE,POSSIBLE NONMILITARY SCIENTIFIC DEVELOPMENTS AND THEIR POTENTIAL IMPACT ON FOREIGN POLICY PROBLEMS OF THE UNITED. FUT USA+45 INT/ORG PROF/ORG CONSULT ACT/RES CREATE PLAN PEACE KNOWL SKILL...TECHNIC PHIL/SCI NEW/IDEA UNESCO 20. PAGE 137 A2802 — R+D TEC/DEV

L59
KAPLAN M.A.,"SOME PROBLEMS IN THE STRATEGIC ANALYSIS OF INTERNATIONAL POLITICS." UNIV R+D INT/ORG CREATE PLAN DIPLOM EDU/PROP COERCE DISPL PWR...METH/CNCPT NEW/IDEA HYPO/EXP TOT/POP 20. PAGE 76 A1561 — DECISION BAL/PWR

S59
BELOFF M.,"NATIONAL GOVERNMENT AND INTERNATIONAL GOVERNMENT." WOR+45 R+D DELIB/GP ACT/RES PLAN PWR ...GEN/METH VAL/FREE EEC OEEC 20. PAGE 13 A0259 — NAT/G INT/ORG DIPLOM

B60
ARMS CONTROL. FUT UNIV WOR+45 INTELL R+D INT/ORG NAT/G VOL/ASSN CONSULT CREATE EDU/PROP PEACE...HUM GEN/LAWS TOT/POP 20. PAGE 3 A0060 — DELIB/GP ORD/FREE ARMS/CONT NUC/PWR

B60
US HOUSE COMM. SCI. ASTRONAUT.,OCEAN SCIENCES AND NATIONAL SECURITY. FUT SEA ECO/DEV EXTR/IND INT/ORG NAT/G FORCES ACT/RES TEC/DEV ECO/TAC COERCE WAR BIO/SOC KNOWL PWR...CONCPT RECORD LAB/EXP 20. PAGE 154 A3141 — R+D ORD/FREE

B60
WHITING A.S.,CHINA CROSSES THE YALU: THE DECISION TO ENTER THE KOREAN WAR. ASIA CHINA/COM KOREA ECO/UNDEV R+D INT/ORG TOP/EX ACT/RES BAL/PWR ATTIT PWR...GEN/METH 20. PAGE 164 A3338 — PLAN COERCE WAR

L60
DEUTSCH K.W.,"TOWARD AN INVENTORY OF BASIC TRENDS AND PATTERNS IN COMPARATIVE AND INTERNATIONAL POLITICS." UNIV WOR+45 SOCIETY STRUCT INT/ORG NAT/G CREATE PLAN EDU/PROP KNOWL...PHIL/SCI METH/CNCPT STAT SELF/OBS OBS/ENVIR SAMP TREND CON/ANAL CHARTS SOC/EXP GEN/METH 20. PAGE 36 A0739 — R+D PERCEPT

L60
LAUTERPACHT E.,"THE UNITED NATIONS EMERGENCY FORCE." R+D LEGIT ROUTINE COERCE KNOWL ORD/FREE SKILL...JURID UN 20. PAGE 85 A1746 — INT/ORG FORCES

S60
HAYTON R.D.,"THE ANTARCTIC SETTLEMENT OF 1959." FUT USA+45 WOR+45 WOR-45 STRUCT R+D INT/ORG EX/STRUC CREATE TEC/DEV LEGIT PEACE ATTIT SOVEREIGN ...TIME/SEQ 20 TREATY IGY. PAGE 63 A1297 — DELIB/GP JURID DIPLOM REGION

S60
MORGENSTERN O.,"GOAL: AN ARMED, INSPECTED, OPEN — FORCES

WORLD." COM EUR+WWI USA+45 R+D INT/ORG NAT/G TEC/DEV BAL/PWR COERCE NUC/PWR ORD/FREE PWR...TREND 20. PAGE 104 A2133
CONCPT ARMS/CONT DETER

S60
OSGOOD C.E.,"COGNITIVE DYNAMICS IN THE CONDUCT OF HUMAN AFFAIRS." USA+45 INTELL INT/ORG CONSULT PLAN ATTIT PERSON...PSY CHARTS HYPO/EXP 20. PAGE 112 A2299
R+D SOCIETY

N60
INTERNATIONAL FEDN DOCUMENTTN,BIBLIOGRAPHY OF DIRECTORIES OF SOURCES OF INFORMATION (PAMPHLET). WOR+45 R+D INT/ORG NAT/G TEC/DEV DIPLOM. PAGE 71 A1456
BIBLIOG/A ECO/DEV ECO/UNDEV

B61
LANDSKROY W.A.,OFFICIAL SERIAL PUBLICATIONS RELATING TO ECONOMIC DEVELOPMENT IN AFRICA SOUTH OF THE SAHARA (PAMPHLET). AFR UK R+D ACT/RES 20 UN. PAGE 84 A1720
BIBLIOG ECO/UNDEV COLONIAL INT/ORG

B61
SOCIAL SCIENCE SERIALS IN SPECIAL LIBRARIES IN THE NEW YORK AREA; A SELECTED LIST. R+D ACADEM EDU/PROP WRITING...PSY 20. PAGE 119 A2448
BIBLIOG DIPLOM SOC

B61
SHARP W.R.,FIELD ADMINISTRATION IN THE UNITED NATION SYSTEM: THE CONDUCT OF INTERNATIONAL ECONOMIC AND SOCIAL PROGRAMS. FUT WOR+45 CONSTN SOCIETY ECO/UNDEV R+D DELIB/GP ACT/RES PLAN TEC/DEV EDU/PROP EXEC ROUTINE HEALTH WEALTH...HUM CONCPT CHARTS METH ILO UNESCO VAL/FREE UN 20. PAGE 132 A2697
INT/ORG CONSULT

L61
TAUBENFELD H.J.,"A TREATY FOR ANTARCTICA." FUT USA+45 INTELL INT/ORG LABOR 20 TREATY ANTARCTICA. PAGE 141 A2893
R+D ACT/RES DIPLOM

L61
TAUBENFELD H.J.,"A REGIME FOR OUTER SPACE." FUT UNIV R+D ACT/RES PLAN BAL/PWR LEGIT ARMS/CONT ORD/FREE...POLICY JURID TREND UN TOT/POP 20 COLD/WAR. PAGE 142 A2894
INT/ORG ADJUD SPACE

S61
SINGER J.D.,"THE LEVEL OF ANALYSIS: PROBLEMS IN INTERNATIONAL RELATIONS." FUT INTELL R+D INT/ORG CREATE EDU/PROP...METH/CNCPT HYPO/EXP GEN/METH METH VAL/FREE. PAGE 133 A2725
SOCIETY SOC DIPLOM

B62
OSGOOD C.E.,AN ALTERNATIVE TO WAR OR SURRENDER. FUT UNIV CULTURE INTELL SOCIETY R+D INT/ORG CONSULT DELIB/GP ACT/RES PLAN CHOOSE ATTIT PERCEPT KNOWL ...PHIL/SCI PSY SOC TREND GEN/LAWS 20. PAGE 112 A2300
ORD/FREE EDU/PROP PEACE WAR

B62
SAVORD R.,AMERICAN AGENCIES INTERESTED IN INTERNATIONAL AFFAIRS. USA+45 R+D NAT/G VOL/ASSN ACT/RES EDU/PROP KNOWL...CONCPT 20. PAGE 127 A2608
INT/ORG CONSULT DIPLOM

B62
SCHWARTZ L.E.,INTERNATIONAL ORGANIZATIONS AND SPACE COOPERATION. VOL/ASSN CONSULT CREATE TEC/DEV SANCTION...POLICY INT/LAW PHIL/SCI 20 UN. PAGE 130 A2656
INT/ORG DIPLOM R+D SPACE

B62
THANT U.,THE UNITED NATIONS' DEVELOPMENT DECADE: PROPOSALS FOR ACTION. WOR+45 SOCIETY ECO/UNDEV AGRI COM/IND FINAN R+D MUNIC SCHOOL VOL/ASSN CONSULT PLAN TEC/DEV ECO/TAC EDU/PROP ADMIN ROUTINE RIGID/FLEX...MGT SOC CONCPT UNESCO UN TOT/POP VAL/FREE. PAGE 142 A2906
INT/ORG ALL/VALS

B62
THOMSON G.P.,NUCLEAR ENERGY IN BRITAIN DURING THE LAST WAR: THE CHERWELL SIMON LECTURE (MONOGRAPH). UK R+D CONSULT FORCES PLAN DIPLOM TASK CIVMIL/REL ROLE...PHIL/SCI NEW/IDEA LAB/EXP 20 MAUD. PAGE 143 A2934
CREATE TEC/DEV WAR NUC/PWR

S62
ALBONETTI A.,"IL SECONDO PROGRAMMA QUINQUENNALE 1963-67 ED IL BILANCIO RICERCHE ED INVESTIMENTI PER IL 1963 DELL'ERATOM." EUR+WWI FUT ITALY WOR+45 ECO/DEV SERV/IND INT/ORG TEC/DEV ECO/TAC ATTIT SKILL WEALTH...MGT TIME/SEQ OEEC 20. PAGE 5 A0108
R+D PLAN NUC/PWR

S62
SINGER J.D.,"STABLE DETERRENCE AND ITS LIMITS." FUT WOR+45 R+D INT/ORG CONSULT ACT/RES TEC/DEV ARMS/CONT COERCE DRIVE PERCEPT RIGID/FLEX ORD/FREE PWR...MYTH SIMUL TOT/POP 20. PAGE 133 A2728
NAT/G FORCES DETER NUC/PWR

B63
GREAT BRITAIN CENTRAL OFF INF,CONSULTATION AND CO-OPERATION IN THE COMMONWEALTH. LAW R+D FORCES PLAN EDU/PROP CONFER INGP/REL...GEOG CENSUS 19/20 CMN/WLTH. PAGE 55 A1133
DIPLOM DELIB/GP VOL/ASSN REGION

B63
LILIENTHAL D.E.,CHANGE, HOPE, AND THE BOMB. USA+45 WOR+45 R+D INT/ORG NAT/G DELIB/GP FORCES ACT/RES DETER RIGID/FLEX ORD/FREE...POLICY CONCPT OBS AEC 20. PAGE 89 A1815
ATTIT MYTH ARMS/CONT NUC/PWR

B63
SALENT W.S.,THE UNITED STATES BALANCE OF PAYMENTS IN 1968. EUR+WWI UK USA+45 AGRI R+D LABOR FORCES PRODUC...GEOG CONCPT CHARTS 20 CHINJAP EEC. PAGE 126 A2589
BAL/PAY DEMAND FINAN INT/TRADE

B63
SCHRADER R.,SCIENCE AND POLICY. WOR+45 ECO/DEV ECO/UNDEV R+D FORCES PLAN DIPLOM GOV/REL TECHRACY BIBLIOG. PAGE 129 A2644
TEC/DEV NAT/G POLICY ADMIN

S63
BOHN L.,"WHOSE NUCLEAR TEST: NON-PHYSICAL INSPECTION AND TEST BAN." WOR+45 R+D INT/ORG VOL/ASSN ORD/FREE...GEN/LAWS GEN/METH COLD/WAR 20. PAGE 16 A0331
ADJUD ARMS/CONT TEC/DEV NUC/PWR

S63
CAHIER P.,"LE DROIT INTERNE DES ORGANISATIONS INTERNATIONALES." UNIV CONSTN SOCIETY ECO/DEV R+D NAT/G TOP/EX LEGIT ATTIT PERCEPT...TIME/SEQ 19/20. PAGE 23 A0464
INT/ORG JURID DIPLOM INT/LAW

S63
EMERSON R.,"THE ATLANTIC COMMUNITY AND THE EMERGING COUNTRIES." FUT WOR+45 ECO/DEV ECO/UNDEV R+D NAT/G DELIB/GP BAL/PWR ECO/TAC EDU/PROP ROUTINE ORD/FREE PWR WEALTH...POLICY CONCPT TREND GEN/METH EEC 20 NATO. PAGE 42 A0848
ATTIT INT/TRADE

S63
GANDILHON J.,"LA SCIENCE ET LA TECHNIQUE A L'AIDE DES REGIONS PEU DEVELOPPEES." FRANCE FUT WOR+45 ECO/DEV R+D PROF/ORG ACT/RES PLAN...MGT TOT/POP VAL/FREE 20 UN. PAGE 51 A1037
ECO/UNDEV TEC/DEV FOR/AID

S63
GORDON B.,"ECONOMIC IMPEDIMENTS TO REGIONALISM IN SOUTH EAST ASIA." BURMA FUT S/ASIA THAILAND USA+45 AGRI INDUS R+D NAT/G PLAN ECO/TAC WEALTH...STAT CONT/OBS 20. PAGE 54 A1110
VOL/ASSN ECO/UNDEV INT/TRADE REGION

S63
KAWALKOWSKI A.,"POUR UNE EUROPE INDEPENDENTE ET REUNIFIEE." EUR+WWI FUT USA+45 USSR WOR+45 ECO/DEV PROC/MFG INT/ORG NAT/G ACT/RES TEC/DEV FEDERAL RIGID/FLEX...CONCPT METH/CNCPT OEEC TOT/POP 20 DEGAULLE/C. PAGE 77 A1573
R+D PLAN NUC/PWR

S63
LEDUC G.,"L'AIDE INTERNATIONALE AU DEVELOPPEMENT." FUT WOR+45 ECO/DEV ECO/UNDEV R+D PROF/ORG TEC/DEV ECO/TAC ROUTINE ATTIT ALL/VALS...MGT TIME/SEQ TOT/POP 20. PAGE 86 A1758
FINAN PLAN FOR/AID

S63
MARTHELOT P.,"PROGRES DE LA REFORME AGRAIRE." INTELL ECO/DEV R+D FOR/AID ADMIN KNOWL...OBS VAL/FREE UN 20. PAGE 95 A1948
AGRI INT/ORG

S63
NADLER E.B.,"SOME ECONOMIC DISADVANTAGES OF THE ARMS RACE." USA+45 INDUS R+D FORCES PLAN TEC/DEV ECO/TAC FOR/AID EDU/PROP PWR WEALTH...TREND COLD/WAR 20. PAGE 107 A2190
ECO/DEV MGT BAL/PAY

S63
PHELPS J.,"INFORMATION AND ARMS CONTROL." COM SPACE USA+45 USSR WOR+45 R+D INT/ORG NAT/G DELIB/GP DIPLOM ORD/FREE...CONCPT 20. PAGE 116 A2374
KNOWL ARMS/CONT NUC/PWR

S63
WEILLER J.,"UNIONS MONETAIRES ET RAPPORTS DE COOPERATION INTERNATIONALE DANS UN MONDE EN TRANSITION: L'EXAMPLE." AFR FUT UNIV WOR+45 SOCIETY ECO/UNDEV MARKET R+D NAT/G FOR/AID PERCEPT RIGID/FLEX...NEW/IDEA 20. PAGE 162 A3303
FINAN INT/ORG

B64
GRODZINS M.,THE ATOMIC AGE: FORTY-FIVE SCIENTISTS AND SCHOLARS SPEAK ON NATIONAL AND WORLD AFFAIRS. FUT USA+45 WOR+45 R+D INT/ORG NAT/G CONSULT TEC/DEV EDU/PROP ATTIT PERSON ORD/FREE...HUM CONCPT TIME/SEQ CON/ANAL. PAGE 57 A1169
INTELL ARMS/CONT NUC/PWR

B64
HARRISON H.V.,THE ROLE OF THEORY IN INTERNATIONAL RELATIONS. UNIV WOR+45 R+D INT/ORG NAT/G PERCEPT KNOWL...DECISION CONCPT GEN/METH METH 20. PAGE 62 A1270
METH/CNCPT HYPO/EXP DIPLOM

L64
CARNEGIE ENDOWMENT INT. PEACE,"ECONOMIC AND SOCIAL QUESTION (ISSUES BEFORE THE NINETEENTH GENERAL ASSEMBLY)." WOR+45 ECO/DEV ECO/UNDEV INDUS R+D DELIB/GP CREATE PLAN TEC/DEV ECO/TAC FOR/AID BAL/PAY...RECORD UN 20. PAGE 24 A0493
INT/ORG INT/TRADE

S64
HOSCH L.G.,"PUBLIC ADMINISTRATION ON THE INTERNATIONAL FRONTIER." WOR+45 R+D NAT/G EDU/PROP EXEC KNOWL ORD/FREE VAL/FREE 20 UN. PAGE 68 A1390
INT/ORG MGT

C64
SCHRAMM W.,"MASS MEDIA AND NATIONAL DEVELOPMENT: THE ROLE OF INFORMATION IN DEVELOPING COUNTRIES." FINAN R+D ACT/RES PLAN TEC/DEV DIPLOM CHOOSE SUPEGO ORD/FREE...BIBLIOG 20. PAGE 129 A2645
ECO/UNDEV COM/IND EDU/PROP MAJORIT

B65
WHITE HOUSE CONFERENCE ON INTERNATIONAL COOPERATION(VOL.II). SPACE WOR+45 EXTR/IND INT/ORG LABOR WORKER NUC/PWR PEACE AGE/Y...CENSUS ANTHOL 20 RESOURCE/N URBAN/RNWL PUB/TRANS. PAGE 3 A0071
R+D CONFER TEC/DEV DIPLOM

B65
PEACE RESEARCH ABSTRACTS. FUT WOR+45 R+D INT/ORG
BIBLIOG/A

NAT/G PLAN TEC/DEV BAL/PWR DIPLOM FOR/AID NUC/PWR HEALTH. PAGE 4 A0072 PEACE ARMS/CONT WAR

B65
AUVADE R.,BIBLIOGRAPHIE CRITIQUE DES OEUVRES PARUES SUR L'INDOCHINE FRANCAISE: UN SIECLE D'HISTOIRE ET D'ENSEIGNEMENT. VIETNAM DIPLOM...SOC 20. PAGE 10 A0198 BIBLIOG/A R+D ACADEM COLONIAL

B65
HARMON R.B.,POLITICAL SCIENCE: A BIBLIOGRAPHICAL GUIDE TO THE LITERATURE. WOR+45 WOR-45 R+D INT/ORG LOC/G NAT/G DIPLOM ADMIN...CONCPT METH. PAGE 61 A1261 BIBLIOG POL/PAR LAW GOV/COMP

B65
SABLE M.H.,MASTER DIRECTORY FOR LATIN AMERICA. AGRI COM/IND FINAN R+D ACADEM LABOR NAT/G POL/PAR VOL/ASSN INT/TRADE EDU/PROP 20. PAGE 126 A2582 INDEX L/A+17C INT/ORG DIPLOM

B65
UNESCO,INTERNATIONAL ORGANIZATIONS IN THE SOCIAL SCIENCES(REV. ED.). LAW ADMIN ATTIT...CRIMLGY GEOG INT/LAW PSY SOC STAT 20 UNESCO. PAGE 148 A3024 INT/ORG R+D PROF/ORG ACT/RES

B65
UNESCO,HANDBOOK OF INTERNATIONAL EXCHANGES. COM/IND R+D ACADEM PROF/ORG VOL/ASSN CREATE TEC/DEV EDU/PROP AGREE 20 TREATY. PAGE 148 A3025 INDEX INT/ORG DIPLOM PRESS

B65
US LIBRARY OF CONGRESS,A DIRECTORY OF INFORMATION RESOURCES IN THE UNITED STATES: SOCIAL SCIENCES. USA+45 ACADEM INT/ORG LABOR PROF/ORG PUB/INST SCHOOL SECT 20. PAGE 155 A3159 BIBLIOG R+D COMPUT/IR

B65
US SENATE COMM AERO SPACE SCI,INTERNATIONAL COOPERATION AND ORGANIZATION FOR OUTER SPACE. FUT USA+45 WOR+45 PROF/ORG VOL/ASSN CONSULT DELIB/GP PLAN TEC/DEV ARMS/CONT GP/REL PEACE 20 UN NASA. PAGE 155 A3167 DIPLOM SPACE R+D NAT/G

B65
WEISNER J.B.,WHERE SCIENCE AND POLITICS MEET. USA+45 ECO/DEV R+D FORCES PROB/SOLV DIPLOM FOR/AID CONTROL...PHIL/SCI PRESIDENT KENNEDY/JF JOHNSON/LB. PAGE 163 A3310 CHIEF NAT/G POLICY TEC/DEV

S65
HAZARD J.N.,"CO-EXISTENCE LAW BOWS OUT." WOR+45 R+D INT/ORG VOL/ASSN CONSULT DELIB/GP ACT/RES CREATE PEACE KNOWL...JURID CONCPT COLD/WAR VAL/FREE 20. PAGE 63 A1300 PROF/ORG ADJUD

B66
MC CLELLAND C.A.,THEORY AND THE INTERNATIONAL SYSTEM. EDU/PROP PWR...DECISION SOC METH. PAGE 97 A1991 DIPLOM METH/CNCPT ACT/RES R+D

B66
SOCIAL SCIENCE RESEARCH COUN,BIBLIOGRAPHY OF RESEARCH IN THE SOCIAL SCIENCES IN AUSTRALIA 1957-1960. LAW R+D DIPLOM 20 AUSTRAL. PAGE 135 A2758 BIBLIOG SOC PSY

B66
UNITED NATIONS,INTERNATIONAL SPACE BIBLIOGRAPHY. FUT INT/ORG TEC/DEV DIPLOM ARMS/CONT NUC/PWR ...JURID SOC UN. PAGE 149 A3037 BIBLIOG SPACE PEACE R+D

B66
US SENATE COMM AERO SPACE SCI,SOVIET SPACE PROGRAMS, 1962-65; GOALS AND PURPOSES, ACHIEVEMENTS, PLANS, AND INTERNATIONAL IMPLICATIONS. USA+45 USSR R+D FORCES PLAN EDU/PROP PRESS ADJUD ARMS/CONT ATTIT MARXISM. PAGE 155 A3168 CONSULT SPACE FUT DIPLOM

S66
MERRITT R.L.,"SELECTED ARTICLES AND DOCUMENTS ON COMPARATIVE GOVERNMENT AND CROSS-NATIONAL RESEARCH." AFR ASIA EUR+WWI L/A+17C MOD/EUR ELITES R+D ACT/RES DIPLOM PWR...SOC CONCPT 18/20. PAGE 100 A2046 BIBLIOG GOV/COMP NAT/G GOV/REL

B67
BARANSON J.,TECHNOLOGY FOR UNDERDEVELOPED AREAS: AN ANNOTATED BIBLIOGRAPHY. FUT WOR+45 CULTURE INDUS INT/ORG CREATE PROB/SOLV INT/TRADE EDU/PROP AUTOMAT ...CONCPT METH. PAGE 11 A0218 BIBLIOG/A ECO/UNDEV TEC/DEV R+D

B67
CRABBS R.F.,UNITED STATES HIGHER EDUCATION AND WORLD AFFAIRS. WOR+45 R+D ACADEM...POLICY 20. PAGE 32 A0650 BIBLIOG/A NAT/G EDU/PROP DIPLOM

B67
HIRSCHMAN A.O.,DEVELOPMENT PROJECTS OBSERVED. INDUS INT/ORG CONSULT EX/STRUC CREATE OP/RES ECO/TAC DEMAND...POLICY MGT METH/COMP 20 WORLD/BANK. PAGE 65 A1339 ECO/UNDEV R+D FINAN PLAN

B67
ROBINSON R.D.,INTERNATIONAL MANAGEMENT. USA+45 FINAN R+D PLAN PRODUC...DECISION T. PAGE 92 A1882 INT/TRADE MGT INT/LAW MARKET

B67
UNESCO,PRINCIPLES AND PROBLEMS OF NATIONAL SCIENCE POLICIES. WOR+45 ECO/DEV ECO/UNDEV R+D INT/ORG PROB/SOLV CONFER...PHIL/SCI CHARTS 20 UNESCO UN. PAGE 148 A3026 NAT/COMP POLICY TEC/DEV CREATE

B67
US DEPARTMENT OF STATE,FOREIGN AFFAIRS RESEARCH (PAMPHLET). USA+45 WOR+45 ACADEM NAT/G...PSY SOC CHARTS 20. PAGE 152 A3100 BIBLIOG INDEX R+D DIPLOM

B67
ZUCKERMAN S.,SCIENTISTS AND WAR. ELITES INDUS DIPLOM CENTRAL EFFICIENCY KNOWL 20. PAGE 170 A3459 R+D CONSULT ACT/RES GP/REL

S67
DOYLE S.E.,"COMMUNICATION SATELLITES* INTERNAL ORGANIZATION FOR DEVELOPMENT AND CONTROL." USA+45 R+D ACT/RES DIPLOM NAT/LISM...POLICY INT/LAW PREDICT UN. PAGE 38 A0781 TEC/DEV SPACE COM/IND INT/ORG

S67
HULL E.W.S.,"THE POLITICAL OCEAN." FUT UNIV WOR+45 EXTR/IND R+D VOL/ASSN PLAN BAL/PWR ECO/TAC PEACE WEALTH 20 UN. PAGE 69 A1414 DIPLOM ECO/UNDEV INT/ORG INT/LAW

S67
KAISER R.G.,"THE TRUMAN DOCTRINE* HOW IT ALL BEGAN." COM EUR+WWI USA+45 R+D INT/ORG BAL/PWR ECO/TAC PEACE TRUMAN/DOC. PAGE 76 A1550 DIPLOM ECO/UNDEV FOR/AID

S67
MONTALVA E.F.,"THE ALLIANCE THAT LOST ITS WAY." L/A+17C USA+45 R+D BAL/PWR INT/TRADE RECEIVE REV PEACE...POLICY 20. PAGE 103 A2111 ECO/UNDEV DIPLOM FOR/AID INT/ORG

S67
SCHACTER O.,"SCIENTIFIC ADVANCES AND INTERNATIONAL LAWMAKING." FUT R+D PLAN PROB/SOLV CONFER CONTROL ...POLICY PREDICT 20 UN. PAGE 128 A2617 TEC/DEV INT/LAW INT/ORG ACT/RES

S67
VLASCIC I.A.,"THE SPACE TREATY* A PRELIMINARY EVALUATION." FUT USSR WOR+45 R+D ACT/RES TEC/DEV DIPLOM CONFER ARMS/CONT PEACE...PREDICT UN TREATY. PAGE 159 A3245 SPACE INT/LAW INT/ORG NEUTRAL

N67
US SUPERINTENDENT OF DOCUMENTS,SPACE: MISSILES, THE MOON, NASA, AND SATELLITES (PRICE LIST 79A). USA+45 COM/IND R+D NAT/G DIPLOM EDU/PROP ADMIN CONTROL HEALTH...POLICY SIMUL NASA CONGRESS. PAGE 157 A3206 BIBLIOG/A SPACE TEC/DEV PEACE

RABIER J.-R. A2430

RABINOWITCH E. A1169

RACE....SEE RACE/REL, KIN

RACE/REL....RACE RELATIONS; SEE ALSO DISCRIM, ISOLAT, KIN

N
JOURNAL OF POLITICS. USA+45 USA-45 CONSTN POL/PAR EX/STRUC LEGIS PROB/SOLV DIPLOM CT/SYS CHOOSE RACE/REL 20. PAGE 1 A0017 BIBLIOG/A NAT/G LAW LOC/G

N
HOOVER INSTITUTION,UNITED STATES AND CANADIAN PUBLICATIONS ON AFRICA. CULTURE ECO/UNDEV AGRI TEC/DEV EDU/PROP COLONIAL RACE/REL NAT/LISM ATTIT HEALTH...SOC SOC/WK 20. PAGE 67 A1381 BIBLIOG DIPLOM NAT/G AFR

N
KAPLAN L.,REVIEW INDEX. USA+45 USA-45 FINAN INDUS LABOR RACE/REL...GEOG PSY SOC 20. PAGE 76 A1558 BIBLIOG PROF/ORG ECO/DEV DIPLOM

N
US SUPERINTENDENT OF DOCUMENTS,MONTHLY CATALOG OF UNITED STATES GOVERNMENT PUBLICATIONS. USA+45 USA-45 AGRI LABOR FORCES INT/TRADE TARIFFS TAX EDU/PROP CT/SYS ARMS/CONT RACE/REL 19/20 CONGRESS PRESIDENT. PAGE 157 A3203 BIBLIOG NAT/G VOL/ASSN POLICY

NCO
CARRINGTON C.E.,THE COMMONWEALTH IN AFRICA (PAMPHLET). UK STRUCT NAT/G COLONIAL REPRESENT GOV/REL RACE/REL NAT/LISM...MAJORIT 20 EEC NEGRO COLD/WAR. PAGE 25 A0500 ECO/UNDEV AFR DIPLOM PLAN

B00
MOCKLER-FERRYMAN A.,BRITISH WEST AFRICA. FRANCE GERMANY NIGER SIER/LEONE UK CULTURE DIPLOM WAR RACE/REL PRODUC PROFIT WEALTH...POLICY PREDICT 19. PAGE 102 A2095 AFR COLONIAL INT/TRADE CAP/ISM

B02
MOREL E.D.,AFFAIRS OF WEST AFRICA. UK FINAN INDUS FAM KIN SECT CHIEF WORKER DIPLOM RACE/REL LITERACY HEALTH...CHARTS 18/20 AFRICA/W NEGRO. PAGE 104 A2129 COLONIAL ADMIN AFR

B03
GRIFFIN A.P.C.,LISTS PUBLISHED 1902-03: ANGLO-SAXON BIBLIOG

INTERESTS (PAMPHLET). UK USA-45 ELITES SOCIETY DIPLOM ISOLAT 19/20. PAGE 56 A1152
COLONIAL RACE/REL DOMIN

C06
MONTGOMERY H.,"A DICTIONARY OF POLITICAL PHRASES AND ILLUSIONS WITH A SHORT BIBLIOGRAPHY." EUR+WWI MOD/EUR UK AGRI LABOR LOC/G NAT/G COLONIAL CHOOSE RACE/REL. PAGE 103 A2114
BIBLIOG DICTIONARY POLICY DIPLOM

B09
FREMANTLE H.E.S.,THE NEW NATION, A SURVEY OF THE CONDITION AND PROSPECTS OF SOUTH AFRICA. SOUTH/AFR CONSTN POL/PAR DIPLOM DOMIN COLONIAL WEALTH...SOC TREND 19. PAGE 49 A0996
NAT/LISM SOVEREIGN RACE/REL REGION

B10
MENDELSSOHN S.,SOUTH AFRICAN BIBLIOGRAPHY (2 VOLS.). SOUTH/AFR EXTR/IND LABOR SECT DIPLOM INT/TRADE COLONIAL RACE/REL DISCRIM...GEOG 20. PAGE 99 A2038
BIBLIOG/A AFR NAT/G NAT/LISM

N19
FANI-KAYODE R.,BLACKISM (PAMPHLET). AFR WOR+45 INT/ORG BAL/PWR CONTROL CENTRAL...DECISION 20 UN. PAGE 44 A0896
RACE/REL ECO/UNDEV REGION DIPLOM

N19
PROVISIONS SECTION OAU,ORGANIZATION OF AFRICAN UNITY: BASIC DOCUMENTS AND RESOLUTIONS (PAMPHLET). AFR CULTURE ECO/UNDEV DIPLOM ECO/TAC EDU/PROP COLONIAL ARMS/CONT NUC/PWR RACE/REL DISCRIM NAT/LISM 20 UN OAU. PAGE 118 A2415
CONSTN EX/STRUC SOVEREIGN INT/ORG

B27
SIEGFRIED A.,AMERICA COMES OF AGE: A FRENCH ANALYSIS (TRANS. BY H.H. HEMMING AND DORIS HEMMING). FRANCE UK POL/PAR WORKER TEC/DEV DIPLOM REGION RACE/REL ADJUST PRODUC HEREDITY...TIME/SEQ GP/COMP SOC/INTEG 20 DEMOCRAT REPUBLICAN KKK. PAGE 132 A2714
USA-45 CULTURE ECO/DEV SOC

B28
MAIR L.P.,THE PROTECTION OF MINORITIES. EUR+WWI WOR-45 CONSTN INT/ORG NAT/G LEGIT CT/SYS GP/REL RACE/REL DISCRIM ORD/FREE RESPECT...JURID CONCPT TIME/SEQ 20. PAGE 93 A1909
LAW SOVEREIGN

B30
SMUTS J.C.,AFRICA AND SOME WORLD PROBLEMS. RHODESIA SOUTH/AFR CULTURE ECO/UNDEV INDUS INT/ORG SECT PROB/SOLV REGION GOV/REL DISCRIM ATTIT 19/20 LEAGUE/NAT LIVNGSTN/D NEGRO. PAGE 134 A2748
LEGIS AFR COLONIAL RACE/REL

B36
THWAITE D.,THE SEETHING AFRICAN POT: A STUDY OF BLACK NATIONALISM 1882-1935. ETHIOPIA SECT VOL/ASSN COERCE GUERRILLA MURDER DISCRIM MARXISM...PSY TIME/SEQ 18/20 NEGRO. PAGE 144 A2939
NAT/LISM AFR RACE/REL DIPLOM

B36
VARLEY D.H.,A BIBLIOGRAPHY OF ITALIAN COLONISATION IN AFRICA WITH A SECTION ON ABYSSINIA. AFR ETHIOPIA ITALY LIBYA SOMALIA AGRI FINAN LABOR TEC/DEV DIPLOM INT/TRADE RACE/REL DISCRIM 19/20. PAGE 158 A3222
BIBLIOG COLONIAL ADMIN LAW

B42
JOSHI P.S.,THE TYRANNY OF COLOUR. INDIA SOUTH/AFR UK ECO/UNDEV NAT/G POL/PAR DIPLOM ECO/TAC WAR ...POLICY 19/20. PAGE 75 A1538
COLONIAL DISCRIM RACE/REL

B43
MAISEL A.Q.,AFRICA: FACTS AND FORECASTS. WOR+45 INT/ORG CONTROL RACE/REL SOVEREIGN...PREDICT CHARTS 20. PAGE 93 A1910
AFR WAR DIPLOM COLONIAL

B43
WALKER E.A.,BRITAIN AND SOUTH AFRICA. SOUTH/AFR POL/PAR GP/REL RACE/REL ATTIT ORD/FREE 17/20. PAGE 160 A3264
COLONIAL WAR DIPLOM SOVEREIGN

C44
VAN VALKENBURG S.,"ELEMENTS OF POLITICAL GEOGRAPHY." FRANCE COM/IND INDUS NAT/G SECT RACE/REL...LING TREND GEN/LAWS BIBLIOG 20. PAGE 158 A3215
GEOG DIPLOM COLONIAL

B45
WOOLBERT R.G.,FOREIGN AFFAIRS BIBLIOGRAPHY, 1932-1942. INT/ORG SECT INT/TRADE COLONIAL RACE/REL NAT/LISM...GEOG INT/LAW GOV/COMP IDEA/COMP 20. PAGE 167 A3393
BIBLIOG/A DIPLOM WAR

B50
MUGRIDGE D.H.,AMERICAN HISTORY AND CIVILIZATION: LIST OF GUIDES AND ANNOTATED OR SELECTIVE BIBLIOGRAPHIES. NAT/G SECT DIPLOM RACE/REL DISCRIM ATTIT...ART/METH SOC 18/20. PAGE 105 A2164
BIBLIOG/A USA-45 SOCIETY

B51
CARRINGTON C.E.,THE LIQUIDATION OF THE BRITISH EMPIRE. AFR NAT/G INT/TRADE COLONIAL RACE/REL ATTIT ORD/FREE...POLICY NAT/COMP 20 CMN/WLTH. PAGE 25 A0501
SOVEREIGN NAT/LISM DIPLOM GP/REL

B53
SCHAAF R.W.,DOCUMENTS OF INTERNATIONAL MEETINGS. AGRI INDUS ACADEM DIPLOM NUC/PWR RACE/REL AGE/Y HEALTH...SOC 20. PAGE 127 A2614
BIBLIOG/A DELIB/GP INT/ORG POLICY

B54
COOKSON J.,BEFORE THE AFRICAN STORM. BELGIUM CENTRL/AFR FRANCE UK ECO/UNDEV POL/PAR CREATE BAL/PWR RACE/REL NAT/LISM ORD/FREE CONSERVE MARXISM SOC/INTEG 20 CONGO/LEOP. PAGE 30 A0607
COLONIAL REV DISCRIM DIPLOM

B55
PYRAH G.B.,IMPERIAL POLICY AND SOUTH AFRICA 1902-1910. SOUTH/AFR UK NAT/G WAR DISCRIM...CONCPT CHARTS BIBLIOG/A 19/20 CMN/WLTH. PAGE 118 A2421
DIPLOM COLONIAL POLICY RACE/REL

B55
STILLMAN C.W.,AFRICA IN THE MODERN WORLD. AFR USA+45 WOR+45 INT/TRADE COLONIAL PARTIC REGION GOV/REL RACE/REL 20. PAGE 138 A2826
ECO/UNDEV DIPLOM POLICY STRUCT

B55
THOMPSON V.,MINORITY PROBLEMS IN SOUTHEAST ASIA. CAMBODIA CHINA/COM LAOS S/ASIA KIN NAT/G SECT PROB/SOLV EDU/PROP REGION GP/REL RACE/REL MARXISM ...SOC 20 BUDDHISM UN. PAGE 143 A2933
INGP/REL GEOG DIPLOM STRUCT

B56
BALL W.M.,NATIONALISM AND COMMUNISM IN EAST ASIA. ASIA BURMA EUR+WWI KOREA USA+45 ECO/UNDEV NAT/G POL/PAR DIPLOM ECO/TAC FOR/AID EDU/PROP COERCE RACE/REL NAT/LISM DRIVE SOVEREIGN...TREND 20 CHINJAP. PAGE 11 A0214
S/ASIA ATTIT

B56
IRIKURA J.K.,SOUTHEAST ASIA: SELECTED ANNOTATED BIBLIOGRAPHY OF JAPANESE PUBLICATIONS. CULTURE ADMIN RACE/REL 20 CHINJAP. PAGE 71 A1466
BIBLIOG/A S/ASIA DIPLOM

B56
JAMESON J.F.,THE AMERICAN REVOLUTION CONSIDERED AS A SOCIAL MOVEMENT. USA-45 AGRI FINAN SECT INT/TRADE REPRESENT SUFF INGP/REL RACE/REL DISCRIM...MAJORIT 18/19 CHURCH/STA. PAGE 73 A1494
ORD/FREE REV FEDERAL CONSTN

B57
BYRNES R.F.,BIBLIOGRAPHY OF AMERICAN PUBLICATIONS ON EAST CENTRAL EUROPE, 1945-1957 (VOL. XXII). SECT DIPLOM EDU/PROP RACE/REL...ART/METH GEOG JURID SOC LING 20 JEWS. PAGE 23 A0462
BIBLIOG/A COM MARXISM NAT/G

B57
FRAZIER E.F.,RACE AND CULTURE CONTACTS IN THE MODERN WORLD. WOR+45 WOR-45 SOCIETY ECO/DEV AGRI INDUS INT/ORG LABOR NAT/G PERSON RIGID/FLEX ALL/VALS...SOC TIME/SEQ WORK 19/20. PAGE 48 A0991
CULTURE RACE/REL

B58
JENNINGS I.,PROBLEMS OF THE NEW COMMONWEALTH. CEYLON INDIA PAKISTAN S/ASIA ECO/UNDEV INT/ORG LOC/G DIPLOM ECO/TAC INT/TRADE COLONIAL RACE/REL DISCRIM 20 COMMONWLTH PARLIAMENT. PAGE 74 A1508
NAT/LISM NEUTRAL FOR/AID POL/PAR

B58
JENNINGS W.I.,PROBLEMS OF THE NEW COMMONWEALTH. CEYLON INDIA MALAYSIA PAKISTAN ECO/UNDEV VOL/ASSN RACE/REL NAT/LISM ROLE 20 CMN/WLTH. PAGE 74 A1511
GP/REL INGP/REL COLONIAL INT/ORG

L58
HYVARINEN R.,"MONISTIC AND PLURALISTIC INTERPRETATIONS IN THE STUDY OF INTERNATIONAL POLITICS." COLONIAL REGION RACE/REL DISCRIM TOTALISM SOVEREIGN...INT/LAW PHIL/SCI CONCPT BIBLIOG 20. PAGE 70 A1429
DIPLOM PLURISM INT/ORG METH

C58
CARTER G.M.,"THE POLITICS OF INEQUALITY: SOUTH AFRICA SINCE 1948." SOUTH/AFR CONSTN DIPLOM EDU/PROP REPRESENT DISCRIM ATTIT...POLICY PREDICT CHARTS BIBLIOG 20. PAGE 25 A0504
RACE/REL POL/PAR CHOOSE DOMIN

B59
BROOKES E.H.,THE COMMONWEALTH TODAY. UK ROMAN/EMP INT/ORG RACE/REL NAT/LISM SOVEREIGN...TREND SOC/INTEG 20. PAGE 19 A0391
FEDERAL DIPLOM JURID IDEA/COMP

B59
EGYPTIAN SOCIETY OF INT LAW,THE MONROVIA CONFERENCE (PAMPHLET). AFR ALGERIA FRANCE UAR CONFER REGION NUC/PWR WAR DISCRIM 20 SAHARA AFR/STATES. PAGE 40 A0826
COLONIAL SOVEREIGN RACE/REL DIPLOM

B59
VORSPAN A.,JUSTICE AND JUDAISM. FAM DIPLOM ECO/TAC EDU/PROP CRIME RACE/REL MARRIAGE ANOMIE ATTIT ORD/FREE...POLICY 20 UN. PAGE 160 A3254
SECT CULTURE ACT/RES GP/REL

B60
ASPREMONT-LYNDEN H.,RAPPORT SUR L'ADMINISTRATION BELGE DU RUANDA-URUNDI PENDANT L'ANNEE 1959. BELGIUM RWANDA AGRI INDUS DIPLOM ECO/TAC INT/TRADE DOMIN ADMIN RACE/REL...GEOG CENSUS 20 UN. PAGE 9 A0192
AFR COLONIAL ECO/UNDEV INT/ORG

B60
CENTRAL ASIAN RESEARCH CENTRE,RUSSIA LOOKS AT AFRICA (PAMPHLET). AFR USSR COLONIAL RACE/REL...HUM 19/20 STALIN/J. PAGE 25 A0511
BIBLIOG MARXISM TREND DIPLOM

B60
PHILLIPS J.F.V.,KWAME NKRUMAH AND THE FUTURE OF AFRICA. FUT GHANA ISLAM ECO/UNDEV CHIEF DIPLOM COLONIAL RACE/REL NAT/LISM...TREND IDEA/COMP
BIOG LEAD SOVEREIGN

BIBLIOG 20 NKRUMAH/K. PAGE 116 A2376
AFR

B60
PRITTIE T.,GERMANY DIVIDED: THE LEGACY OF THE NAZI ERA. EUR+WWI GERMANY RACE/REL SUPEGO...PSY AUD/VIS BIBLIOG/A 20 NAZI. PAGE 118 A2414
STERTYP PERSON ATTIT DIPLOM

B60
RITNER P.,THE DEATH OF AFRICA. USA+45 ECO/UNDEV DIPLOM ECO/TAC REGION RACE/REL NAT/LISM ORD/FREE ...POLICY 20 NEGRO. PAGE 121 A2485
AFR SOCIETY FUT TASK

B60
THE AFRICA 1960 COMMITTEE,MANDATE IN TRUST; THE PROBLEM OF SOUTH WEST AFRICA. GERMANY STRUCT REGION SANCTION CHOOSE DISCRIM...INT/LAW 20 AFRICA/SW UN LEAGUE/NAT TRUST/TERR. PAGE 142 A2910
NAT/G DIPLOM COLONIAL RACE/REL

B60
THEOBOLD R.,THE NEW NATIONS OF WEST AFRICA. GHANA NIGERIA CULTURE INT/ORG ECO/TAC FOR/AID COLONIAL RACE/REL POPULISM...ANTHOL BIBLIOG 20 UN. PAGE 143 A2916
AFR SOVEREIGN ECO/UNDEV DIPLOM

B60
WODDIS J.,AFRICA: THE ROOTS OF REVOLT. SOUTH/AFR WORKER INT/TRADE RACE/REL DISCRIM ORD/FREE 20. PAGE 166 A3374
COLONIAL SOVEREIGN WAR ECO/UNDEV

C60
FITZSIMMONS T.,"USSR: ITS PEOPLE, ITS SOCIETY, ITS CULTURE." USSR FAM SECT DIPLOM EDU/PROP ADMIN RACE/REL ATTIT...POLICY CHARTS BIBLIOG 20. PAGE 46 A0944
CULTURE STRUCT SOCIETY COM

B61
CALVOCORESSI P.,SOUTH AFRICA AND WORLD OPINION. SOUTH/AFR WOR+45 COM/IND INT/ORG 20. PAGE 23 A0470
ATTIT DISCRIM RACE/REL DIPLOM

B61
CAMERON J.,THE AFRICAN REVOLUTION. AFR UK ECO/UNDEV POL/PAR REGION RACE/REL DISCRIM PWR CONSERVE ...CONCPT SOC/INTEG 20 NEGRO. PAGE 23 A0472
REV COLONIAL ORD/FREE DIPLOM

B61
KHAN A.W.,INDIA WINS FREEDOM: THE OTHER SIDE. INDIA PAKISTAN CULTURE LEGIS DIPLOM PARL/PROC REV WAR NAT/LISM 20. PAGE 78 A1607
SOVEREIGN GP/REL RACE/REL ORD/FREE

B61
MACLURE M.,AFRICA: THE POLITICAL PATTERN. SOUTH/AFR CULTURE LEGIS DIPLOM COLONIAL RACE/REL 20. PAGE 93 A1898
AFR POLICY NAT/G

B61
PECKERT J.,DIE GROSSEN UND DIE KLEINEN MAECHTE. COM GERMANY/W ECO/DEV ECO/UNDEV NAT/G WAR RACE/REL PEACE...POLICY GP/COMP GOV/COMP 20 COLD/WAR. PAGE 114 A2346
DIPLOM ECO/TAC BAL/PWR

B61
SCHIEDER T.,DOCUMENTS ON THE EXPULSION OF THE GERMANS FROM EASTERN-CENTRAL-EUROPE (VOL. II/III). COM EUR+WWI GERMANY HUNGARY ROMANIA USSR DIPLOM RACE/REL 20 MIGRATION. PAGE 128 A2625
GEOG CULTURE

B61
SCOTT A.M.,POLITICS, USA; CASES ON THE AMERICAN DEMOCRATIC PROCESS. USA+45 CHIEF FORCES DIPLOM LOBBY CHOOSE RACE/REL FEDERAL ATTIT...JURID ANTHOL T 20 PRESIDENT CONGRESS CIVIL/LIB. PAGE 130 A2669
CT/SYS CONSTN NAT/G PLAN

B61
TETENS T.H.,THE NEW GERMANY AND THE OLD NAZIS. EUR+WWI GERMANY/W USA+45 NAT/G CRIME CHOOSE RACE/REL TOTALISM AGE/Y ATTIT 20 JEWS NAZI ADENAUER/K. PAGE 142 A2905
FASCISM DIPLOM FOR/AID POL/PAR

B62
FAO,FOOD AND AGRICULTURE ORGANIZATION AFRICAN SURVEY. AFR CONGO/BRAZ GHANA STRATA AGRI INT/ORG TEC/DEV FOR/AID INT/TRADE RACE/REL DEMAND EFFICIENCY PRODUC...GEOG 20 UN CONGO/LEOP. PAGE 44 A0898
ECO/TAC WEALTH EXTR/IND ECO/UNDEV

B62
LOWENSTEIN A.K.,BRUTAL MANDATE: A JOURNEY TO SOUTH WEST AFRICA. CULTURE INT/ORG NAT/G DIPLOM...GEOG 20 UN AFRICA/SW. PAGE 91 A1868
AFR POLICY RACE/REL PROB/SOLV

B62
SHAPIRO D.,A SELECT BIBLIOGRAPHY OF WORKS IN ENGLISH ON RUSSIAN HISTORY, 1801-1917. COM USSR STRATA FORCES EDU/PROP ADMIN REV RACE/REL ATTIT 19/20. PAGE 131 A2693
BIBLIOG DIPLOM COLONIAL

B62
SPIRO H.J.,POLITICS IN AFRICA: PROSPECTS SOUTH OF THE SAHARA. INT/ORG KIN FORCES LEGIS PROB/SOLV COERCE RACE/REL FEDERAL...TREND CHARTS BIBLIOG 20. PAGE 136 A2790
AFR NAT/LISM DIPLOM

B62
TAYLOR D.,THE BRITISH IN AFRICA. UK CULTURE ECO/UNDEV INDUS DIPLOM INT/TRADE ADMIN WAR RACE/REL ORD/FREE SOVEREIGN...POLICY BIBLIOG 15/20 CMN/WLTH. PAGE 142 A2898
AFR COLONIAL DOMIN

B62
US LIBRARY OF CONGRESS,UNITED STATES AND CANADIAN PUBLICATIONS ON AFRICA IN 1960. CANADA USA+45 CULTURE TEC/DEV DIPLOM FOR/AID RACE/REL...GEOG HUM SOC SOC/WK LING 20. PAGE 155 A3156
BIBLIOG/A AFR

C62
DUFFY J.,"PORTUGAL IN AFRICA." PORTUGAL SIER/LEONE INDUS WORKER INT/TRADE WAR CONSERVE...CATH GEOG TREND 16/20. PAGE 39 A0795
BIBLIOG RACE/REL ECO/UNDEV COLONIAL

B63
CONF ON FUTURE OF COMMONWEALTH,THE FUTURE OF THE COMMONWEALTH. UK ECO/UNDEV AGRI EDU/PROP ADMIN SOC/INTEG 20 COMMONWLTH. PAGE 29 A0583
DIPLOM RACE/REL ORD/FREE TEC/DEV

B63
ELLENDER A.J.,A REPORT ON UNITED STATES FOREIGN OPERATIONS IN AFRICA. SOUTH/AFR USA+45 STRATA EXTR/IND FORCES RACE/REL ISOLAT SOVEREIGN...CHARTS 20 NEGRO. PAGE 41 A0840
FOR/AID DIPLOM WEALTH ECO/UNDEV

B63
HAILEY L.,THE REPUBLIC OF SOUTH AFRICA AND THE HIGH COMMISSION TERRITORIES. AFR SOUTH/AFR UK INT/ORG NAT/G PROVS RACE/REL SOVEREIGN...CHARTS 19/20 COMMONWLTH. PAGE 59 A1219
COLONIAL DIPLOM ATTIT

B63
PRESTON W. JR.,ALIENS AND DISSENTERS: FEDERAL SUPPRESSION OF RADICALS 1903-1933. USA-45 DIPLOM ADJUD REPRESENT RACE/REL MAJORITY...BIBLIOG/A 19/20. PAGE 117 A2409
DISCRIM GP/REL INGP/REL ATTIT

B63
THIEN T.T.,INDIA AND SOUTHEAST ASIA 1947-1960. COM INDIA S/ASIA SECT DELIB/GP FOR/AID RACE/REL NAT/LISM SOCISM...CHARTS BIBLIOG 20 UN NEHRU/J TREATY. PAGE 143 A2917
DRIVE DIPLOM POLICY

S63
VEROFF J.,"AFRICAN STUDENTS IN THE UNITED STATES." AFR USA+45 CULTURE ACT/RES FOR/AID PEACE ATTIT KNOWL...SOC RECORD DEEP/QU SYS/QU CHARTS STERTYP TOT/POP 20. PAGE 159 A3230
PERCEPT RIGID/FLEX RACE/REL

B64
BURKE F.G.,AFRICA'S QUEST FOR ORDER. AFR CULTURE KIN MUNIC NAT/G DIPLOM COLONIAL REV DISCRIM NAT/LISM AGE/Y 20. PAGE 21 A0437
ORD/FREE CONSEN RACE/REL LEAD

B64
COX R.,PAN-AFRICANISM IN PRACTICE. AFR DIPLOM CONFER RACE/REL ROLE SOVEREIGN...POLICY 20 PANAF/FREE. PAGE 32 A0645
ORD/FREE COLONIAL REGION NAT/LISM

B64
DESHMUKH C.D.,THE COMMONWEALTH AS INDIA SEES IT. INDIA UK ECO/UNDEV TEC/DEV INT/TRADE GP/REL RACE/REL SOVEREIGN SOC/INTEG 19/20 COMMONWLTH. PAGE 36 A0733
DIPLOM COLONIAL NAT/LISM ATTIT

B64
HORNE D.,THE LUCKY COUNTRY: AUSTRALIA TODAY. UK CULTURE STRATA ATTIT PWR PLURISM...GOV/COMP 20 AUSTRAL. PAGE 67 A1386
RACE/REL DIPLOM NAT/G STRUCT

B64
KENNEDY J.F.,THE BURDEN AND THE GLORY. FUT USA+45 TEC/DEV ECO/TAC EDU/PROP ARMS/CONT MURDER RACE/REL PEACE...ANTHOL 20 KENNEDY/JF COLD/WAR NATO PRESIDENT. PAGE 78 A1593
ADMIN POLICY GOV/REL DIPLOM

B64
KITCHEN H.,A HANDBOOK OF AFRICAN AFFAIRS. ECO/UNDEV CREATE DIPLOM COLONIAL RACE/REL...ART/METH GEOG CHARTS 20. PAGE 80 A1646
AFR NAT/G INT/ORG FORCES

B64
LEGUM C.,SOUTH AFRICA: CRISIS FOR THE WEST. SOUTH/AFR COERCE DISCRIM ATTIT...TREND 20 INTERVENT. PAGE 86 A1767
RACE/REL STRATA DIPLOM PROB/SOLV

B64
MATTHEWS D.G.,A CURRENT VIEW OF AFRICANA (PAMPHLET). CULTURE ECO/UNDEV DIPLOM RACE/REL ATTIT 20. PAGE 96 A1968
BIBLIOG/A AFR NAT/G NAT/LISM

B64
MORGAN T.,GOLDWATER EITHER/OR; A SELF-PORTRAIT BASED UPON HIS OWN WORDS. USA+45 CONSTN AGRI LABOR DIPLOM RACE/REL WEALTH POPULISM...POLICY MAJORIT 20 GOLDWATR/B REPUBLICAN. PAGE 104 A2131
LEAD POL/PAR CHOOSE ATTIT

B64
QUIGG P.W.,AFRICA: A FOREIGN AFFAIRS READER. AFR FRANCE PORTUGAL UK DIPLOM LEAD PARL/PROC MARXISM ...MAJORIT METH/CNCPT GOV/COMP IDEA/COMP ANTHOL 19/20. PAGE 118 A2426
COLONIAL SOVEREIGN NAT/LISM RACE/REL

B64
SEGAL R.,SANCTIONS AGAINST SOUTH AFRICA. AFR SOUTH/AFR NAT/G INT/TRADE RACE/REL PEACE PWR ...INT/LAW ANTHOL 20 UN. PAGE 131 A2681
SANCTION DISCRIM ECO/TAC POLICY

B64
VOELKMANN K.,HERRSCHER VON MORGEN? BAL/PWR COLONIAL NEUTRAL REGION RACE/REL ALL/VALS SOVEREIGN...RECORD 20 COLD/WAR THIRD/WRLD. PAGE 159 A3246
DIPLOM ECO/UNDEV CONTROL NAT/COMP

S64
CARNEGIE ENDOWMENT INT. PEACE,"HUMAN RIGHTS (ISSUES BEFORE THE NINETEENTH GENERAL ASSEMBLY)." AFR WOR+45 LAW CONSTN NAT/G EDU/PROP GP/REL DISCRIM PEACE ATTIT MORAL ORD/FREE...INT/LAW PSY CONCPT RECORD UN 20. PAGE 24 A0492
INT/ORG PERSON RACE/REL

B65
COWEN Z.,THE BRITISH COMMONWEALTH OF NATIONS IN A CHANGING WORLD. UK ECO/UNDEV INT/ORG ECO/TAC INT/TRADE COLONIAL WAR GP/REL RACE/REL SOVEREIGN SOC/INTEG 20 TREATY EEC COMMONWLTH. PAGE 32 A0644
JURID DIPLOM PARL/PROC NAT/LISM

B65
EISENHOWER D.D.,WAGING PEACE 1956-61: THE WHITE HOUSE YEARS. USA+45 DIPLOM LEAD INGP/REL RACE/REL PEACE ATTIT...TRADIT TIME/SEQ 20 EISNHWR/DD PRESIDENT COLD/WAR CIV/RIGHTS BERLIN. PAGE 41 A0833
TOP/EX BIOG ORD/FREE POLICY

B65
EMERSON R.,THE POLITICAL AWAKENING OF AFRICA. ECO/UNDEV INT/ORG COLONIAL RACE/REL ORD/FREE MARXISM...TREND ANTHOL 20. PAGE 42 A0849
AFR NAT/LISM DIPLOM POL/PAR

B65
FANON F.,STUDIES IN A DYING COLONIALISM. ALGERIA FRANCE STRATA FAM DIPLOM DOMIN WAR RACE/REL DISCRIM HEALTH 20. PAGE 44 A0897
NAT/LISM COLONIAL REV SOVEREIGN

B65
INGRAM D.,COMMONWEALTH FOR A COLOUR-BLIND WORLD. AFR INDIA UK STRATA ECO/UNDEV VOL/ASSN CREATE PLAN CONFER COLONIAL ORD/FREE SOC/INTEG 20 COMMONWLTH. PAGE 70 A1441
RACE/REL INT/ORG INGP/REL PROB/SOLV

B65
LEISS A.C.,APARTHEID AND UNITED NATIONS COLLECTIVE MEASURES. SOUTH/AFR ECO/UNDEV EXTR/IND FORCES WORKER ECO/TAC FOR/AID INT/TRADE WEALTH...TREND CHARTS 20 UN NEGRO. PAGE 86 A1770
DISCRIM RACE/REL STRATA DIPLOM

B65
LYONS G.M.,AMERICA: PURPOSE AND POWER. UK USA+45 FINAN INDUS MARKET WORKER TEC/DEV DIPLOM AUTOMAT NUC/PWR WAR RACE/REL ORD/FREE 20 EEC CONGRESS SUPREME/CT CIV/RIGHTS. PAGE 92 A1881
PWR PROB/SOLV ECO/DEV TASK

B65
MOLNAR T.,AFRICA: A POLITICAL TRAVELOGUE. STRUCT ECO/UNDEV DIPLOM EDU/PROP LEAD RACE/REL MARXISM 20 INTERVENT EUROPE. PAGE 102 A2101
COLONIAL AFR ORD/FREE

B65
QURESHI I.H.,THE STRUGGLE FOR PAKISTAN. INDIA PAKISTAN UK CULTURE LEGIS DIPLOM EDU/PROP COLONIAL ATTIT SOVEREIGN 19/20 MUSLIM. PAGE 118 A2429
GP/REL RACE/REL WAR SECT

B65
RODRIGUES J.H.,BRAZIL AND AFRICA. AFR BRAZIL PORTUGAL UK USA+45 USA-45 CULTURE ECO/UNDEV INT/ORG INT/TRADE RACE/REL ORD/FREE 15/20 UN MISCEGEN. PAGE 123 A2513
DIPLOM COLONIAL POLICY ATTIT

B65
ROTBERG R.I.,A POLITICAL HISTORY OF TROPICAL AFRICA. EX/STRUC DIPLOM INT/TRADE DOMIN ADMIN RACE/REL NAT/LISM PWR SOVEREIGN...GEOG TIME/SEQ BIBLIOG 1/20. PAGE 124 A2545
AFR CULTURE COLONIAL

B65
SCHREIBER H.,TEUTON AND SLAV - THE STRUGGLE FOR CENTRAL EUROPE (TRANS. BY J. CLEUGH). GERMANY POLAND PRUSSIA USSR SOCIETY STRUCT SECT DIPLOM BALTIC. PAGE 129 A2646
GP/REL WAR RACE/REL NAT/LISM

B65
SPENCE J.E.,REPUBLIC UNDER PRESSURE: A STUDY OF SOUTH AFRICAN FOREIGN POLICY. SOUTH/AFR ADMIN COLONIAL GOV/REL RACE/REL DISCRIM NAT/LISM ATTIT ROLE...TREND 20 NEGRO. PAGE 136 A2783
DIPLOM POLICY AFR

B65
VAN DEN BERGHE P.L.,AFRICA: SOCIAL PROBLEMS OF CHANGE AND CONFLICT. ELITES STRATA ECO/UNDEV KIN MUNIC DIPLOM GP/REL RACE/REL NAT/LISM...ANTHOL BIBLIOG 20. PAGE 158 A3210
SOC CULTURE AFR STRUCT

L65
MATTHEWS D.G.,"A CURRENT BIBLIOGRAPHY ON ETHIOPIAN AFFAIRS: A SELECT BIBLIOGRAPHY FROM 1950-1964." ETHIOPIA LAW CULTURE ECO/UNDEV INDUS LABOR SECT FORCES DIPLOM CIVMIL/REL RACE/REL...LING STAT 20. PAGE 96 A1969
BIBLIOG/A ADMIN POL/PAR NAT/G

L65
MATTHEWS D.G.,"A CURRENT BIBLIOGRAPHY ON SUDANESE AFFAIRS; A SELECT BIBLIOGRAPHY FROM 1960-1964." SUDAN LAW CULTURE AGRI FINAN INDUS LABOR POL/PAR TEC/DEV FOR/AID RACE/REL LITERACY...LING 20. PAGE 96 A1970
BIBLIOG ECO/UNDEV NAT/G DIPLOM

B66
CLENDENON C.,AMERICANS IN AFRICA 1865-1900. AFR USA-45 ECO/UNDEV SECT REV RACE/REL CONSERVE ...TRADIT GEOG BIBLIOG 16/18. PAGE 27 A0549
DIPLOM COLONIAL INT/TRADE

B66
DAVIDSON A.B.,RUSSIA AND AFRICA. USSR AGRI INT/TRADE...GEOG BIBLIOG/A 18/20. PAGE 34 A0687
MARXISM COLONIAL RACE/REL DIPLOM

B66
FREIDEL F.,AMERICAN ISSUES IN THE TWENTIETH CENTURY. SOCIETY FINAN ECO/TAC FOR/AID CONTROL NUC/PWR WAR RACE/REL PEACE ATTIT...ANTHOL T 20 WILSON/W ROOSEVLT/F KENNEDY/JF TRUMAN/HS. PAGE 49 A0995
DIPLOM POLICY NAT/G ORD/FREE

B66
GROSS F.,WORLD POLITICS AND TENSION AREAS. CHINA/COM SOMALIA VENEZUELA COERCE GP/REL RACE/REL ATTIT HABITAT 19/20 CASEBOOK NEWYORK/C. PAGE 57 A1173
DIPLOM WAR PROB/SOLV

B66
GUPTA S.,KASHMIR - A STUDY IN INDIA-PAKISTAN RELATIONS. INDIA KASHMIR PAKISTAN CONSTN INT/ORG REV RACE/REL NAT/LISM 20 UN MUSLIM/LG. PAGE 58 A1194
DIPLOM GP/REL SOVEREIGN WAR

B66
KEENLEYSIDE H.L.,INTERNATIONAL AID: A SUMMARY. AFR INDIA S/ASIA UK STRATA EXTR/IND TEC/DEV ADMIN RACE/REL DEMAND NAT/LISM WEALTH...TREND CHINJAP. PAGE 77 A1575
ECO/UNDEV FOR/AID DIPLOM TASK

B66
KEYES J.G.,A BIBLIOGRAPHY OF WESTERN LANGUAGE PUBLICATIONS CONCERNING NORTH VIETNAM IN THE CORNELL LIBRARY. VIETNAM/N NAT/G FORCES TEC/DEV DIPLOM LEAD RACE/REL...GEOG SOC 20. PAGE 78 A1603
BIBLIOG/A CULTURE ECO/UNDEV S/ASIA

B66
LENGYEL E.,AFRICA: PAST, PRESENT, AND FUTURE. FUT SOUTH/AFR COLONIAL RACE/REL SOVEREIGN...GEOG AUD/VIS CHARTS T 20 CONGO/LEOP NEGRO. PAGE 87 A1771
AFR CONSTN ECO/UNDEV

B66
LEWIS S.,TOWARDS INTERNATIONAL CO-OPERATION (1ST ED.). WOR+45 AGRI INDUS EDU/PROP RACE/REL ISOLAT NAT/LISM ATTIT HEALTH WEALTH...CHARTS WORSHIP 20 UN. PAGE 88 A1803
DIPLOM ANOMIE PROB/SOLV INT/ORG

B66
MAY E.R.,ANXIETY AND AFFLUENCE: 1945-1965. USA+45 DIPLOM FOR/AID ARMS/CONT RACE/REL CONSEN...ANTHOL 20 COLD/WAR KENNEDY/JF EISNHWR/DD TRUMAN/HS BERLIN/BLO. PAGE 97 A1982
ANOMIE ECO/DEV NUC/PWR WEALTH

B66
MAYER P.,THE PACIFIST CONSCIENCE. SECT CREATE ARMS/CONT WAR RACE/REL ATTIT LOVE...ANTHOL PACIFIST WORSHIP FREUD/S GANDHI/M LAO/TZU KING/MAR/L CONSCN/OBJ. PAGE 97 A1984
DIPLOM PACIFISM SUPEGO

B66
MCKAY V.,AFRICAN DIPLOMACY STUDIES IN THE DETERMINANTS OF FOREIGN POLICY. AFR SOUTH/AFR CULTURE NEUTRAL REGION SOVEREIGN...INT/LAW GOV/COMP ANTHOL 20. PAGE 98 A2013
ECO/UNDEV RACE/REL CIVMIL/REL DIPLOM

B66
MULLER C.F.J.,A SELECT BIBLIOGRAPHY OF SOUTH AFRICAN HISTORY; A GUIDE FOR HISTORICAL RESEARCH. SOUTH/AFR UK LAW CONSTN SOCIETY STRUCT AGRI SECT DIPLOM COLONIAL LEAD RACE/REL...POLICY 17/20 NEGRO. PAGE 106 A2167
BIBLIOG AFR NAT/G

B66
US HOUSE COMM FOREIGN AFFAIRS,UNITED STATES - SOUTH AFRICAN RELATIONS. SOUTH/AFR USA+45 NAT/G CONSULT DELIB/GP LEGIS CONFER SANCTION RACE/REL ATTIT 20 CONGRESS. PAGE 154 A3134
DISCRIM DIPLOM POLICY PARL/PROC

B66
WELCH R.H.W.,THE NEW AMERICANISM, AND OTHER SPEECHES AND ESSAYS. USA+45 ACADEM POL/PAR SCHOOL VOL/ASSN FORCES CAP/ISM TAX REV DISCRIM 20 CIV/RIGHTS COLD/WAR BIRCH/SOC. PAGE 163 A3313
DIPLOM FASCISM MARXISM RACE/REL

S66
AFRICAN BIBLIOGRAPHIC CENTER,"A CURRENT VIEW OF AFRICANA: A SELECT AND ANNOTATED BIBLIOGRAPHICAL PUBLISHING GUIDE, 1965-1966." AFR CULTURE INDUS LABOR SECT FOR/AID ADMIN COLONIAL REV RACE/REL SOCISM...LING 20. PAGE 5 A0098
BIBLIOG/A NAT/G TEC/DEV POL/PAR

S66
AFRICAN BIBLIOGRAPHIC CENTER,"A DESCRIPTIVE STUDY OF CURRENT AFRICAN FOREIGN RELATIONS." COM CULTURE INT/ORG SECT RACE/REL DISCRIM ATTIT 20. PAGE 5 A0099
BIBLIOG DIPLOM AFR

S66
PRATT R.C.,"AFRICAN REACTIONS TO THE RHODESIAN CRISIS." RHODESIA UK LAW DIPLOM...POLICY 20. PAGE 117 A2408
ATTIT AFR COLONIAL RACE/REL

C66
WINT G.,"ASIA: A HANDBOOK." ASIA S/ASIA INDUS LABOR SECT PRESS RACE/REL MARXISM...STAT CHARTS BIBLIOG 20. PAGE 165 A3366
ECO/UNDEV DIPLOM NAT/G SOCIETY

B67
ATTWOOD W.,THE REDS AND THE BLACKS. AFR POL/PAR CHOOSE GOV/REL RACE/REL NAT/LISM...BIOG 20. PAGE 10 A0195
DIPLOM PWR MARXISM

B67
BELL W.,THE DEMOCRATIC REVOLUTION IN THE WEST INDIES. WEST/IND WOR+45 DIPLOM RACE/REL NAT/LISM ...INT QU ANTHOL 20. PAGE 13 A0257
REGION ATTIT ORD/FREE ECO/UNDEV

B67
NYERERE J.K.,FREEDOM AND UNITY/UHURU NA UMOJA: A SELECTION FROM WRITINGS AND SPEECHES, 1952-65. TANZANIA ELITES ECO/UNDEV INT/ORG NAT/G CREATE DIPLOM COLONIAL REGION RACE/REL...ANTHOL 20. PAGE 110 A2265
SOVEREIGN AFR TREND ORD/FREE

B67
RUSSELL B.,WAR CRIMES IN VIETNAM. USA+45 VIETNAM FORCES DIPLOM WEAPON RACE/REL DISCRIM ISOLAT BIO/SOC 20 COLD/WAR RUSSELL/B. PAGE 126 A2574
WAR CRIME ATTIT POLICY

S67
BENTLEY E.,"VIETNAM: THE STATE OF OUR FEELINGS." USA+45 VIETNAM PROB/SOLV DIPLOM GP/REL INGP/REL RACE/REL WEALTH. PAGE 13 A0271
WAR PARTIC ATTIT PEACE

S67
GLENN N.D.,"ARE REGIONAL CULTURAL DIFFERENCES DIMINISHING?" USA+45 DIPLOM RACE/REL AGE/Y AGE/A PERSON MORAL...GP/COMP 20. PAGE 53 A1081
SAMP ATTIT REGION CULTURE

S67
MUDGE G.A.,"DOMESTIC POLICIES AND UN ACTIVITIES* THE CASE OF RHODESIA AND THE REPUBLIC OF SOUTH AFRICA." RHODESIA SOUTH/AFR POL/PAR LEAD SANCTION CHOOSE RACE/REL CONSEN DISCRIM ATTIT...INT/LAW UN PARLIAMENT 20. PAGE 105 A2163
AFR NAT/G POLICY

S67
ROTBERG R.I.,"COLONIALISM AND AFTER: THE POLITICAL LITERATURE OF CENTRAL AFRICA - A BIBLIOGRAPHIC ESSAY." AFR CHIEF EX/STRUC REV INGP/REL RACE/REL SOVEREIGN 20. PAGE 124 A2546
BIBLIOG/A COLONIAL DIPLOM NAT/G

S67
ROWAN C.T.,"NEW FRONTIERS IN RACE RELATIONS." USA+45 NAT/G DIPLOM 20. PAGE 124 A2551
RACE/REL DISCRIM POLICY PROB/SOLV

RADIO FREE EUROPE....SEE RFE

RADVANYI L. A2431

RAF....ROYAL AIR FORCE

B60
GLUBB J.B.,WAR IN THE DESERT: AN R.A.F. FRONTIER CAMPAIGN. SAUDI/ARAB UK KIN SECT LEAD...GEOG 20 RAF. PAGE 53 A1083
COLONIAL WAR FORCES DIPLOM

RAGATZ L.J. A2432

RAGHAVAN M.D. A2433

RAHMAN/TA....TUNKU ABDUL RAHMAN

RAILROAD....RAILROADS AND RAILWAY SYSTEMS

RAJAN M.S. A2434

RAJARATAM/S....S. RAJARATAM

RAJASTHAN....RAJASTHAN

RALEIGH J.S. A2435

RALSTON D.B. A2436

RAMA RAO T.V. A0288

RAMAZANI R.K. A2437

RAMERIE L. A2438

RAMSEY J.A. A2439

RAND SCHOOL OF SOCIAL SCIENCE A2440

RANDOMNESS....SEE PROB/SOLV

RANIS G. A2441

RANKE/L....LEOPOLD VON RANKE

RANKOVIC/A....ALEXANDER RANKOVIC, YUGOSLAVIA'S FORMER VICE PRESIDENT

RANSHOFFEN-WERTHEIMER EF A2442

RANSOM H.H. A2443

RAO V.K.R. A2444,A2445

RAPPAPORT A. A2446,A2447

RAPPARD W.E. A2449,A2450

RATION....RATIONING

N
IMF AND IBRD, JOINT LIBRARY,LIST OF RECENT ADDITIONS. WOR+45 ECO/DEV ECO/UNDEV BUDGET FOR/AID RATION...CONCPT IDEA/COMP. PAGE 70 A1434
BIBLIOG INT/ORG INT/TRADE FINAN

N
IMF AND IBRD, JOINT LIBRARY,LIST OF RECENT PERIODICAL ARTICLES. WOR+45 ECO/DEV ECO/UNDEV BUDGET FOR/AID RATION...CONCPT IDEA/COMP. PAGE 70 A1435
BIBLIOG INT/ORG INT/TRADE FINAN

B42
US LIBRARY OF CONGRESS,ECONOMICS OF WAR (APRIL 1941-MARCH 1942). WOR-45 FINAN INDUS LOC/G NAT/G PLAN BUDGET RATION COST DEMAND...POLICY 20. PAGE 154 A3146
BIBLIOG/A INT/TRADE ECO/TAC WAR

B64
BLANCHARD C.H.,KOREAN WAR BIBLIOGRAPHY. KOREA FAM BAL/PWR RATION MURDER WEAPON MARXISM...CHARTS 20. PAGE 15 A0306
BIBLIOG/A WAR DIPLOM FORCES

B66
ZISCHKA A.,WAR ES EIN WUNDER? GERMANY/W ECO/DEV FINAN LG/CO BARGAIN CAP/ISM FOR/AID RATION 20 MARSHL/PLN. PAGE 170 A3456
ECO/TAC INT/TRADE INDUS WAR

S67
COSGROVE C.A.,"AGRICULTURE, FINANCE AND POLITICS IN THE EUROPEAN COMMUNITY." EUR+WWI DIST/IND MARKET INT/ORG VOL/ASSN DELIB/GP TEC/DEV BAL/PWR BARGAIN ECO/TAC RATION CONFER 20 EEC. PAGE 31 A0630
ECO/DEV DIPLOM AGRI INT/TRADE

S67
OLIVIER G.,"ASPECTS JURIDIQUES DE L'ADOPTION DU TRAITE CECA A LA CRISE CHARBONNIERE (SUITE ET FIN)" LAW DIST/IND PLAN DIPLOM RATION PRICE ADMIN COST DEMAND...POLICY CON/ANAL ECSC TREATY. PAGE 112 A2288
INT/TRADE INT/ORG EXTR/IND CONSTN

RATIONAL....RATIONALITY

B37
KOHN H.,FORCE OR REASON; ISSUES OF THE TWENTIETH CENTURY. WOR+45 NAT/G DIPLOM WAR DRIVE ORD/FREE ALL/IDEOS FASCISM PLURISM...POLICY IDEA/COMP 20. PAGE 81 A1660
COERCE DOMIN RATIONAL COLONIAL

B59
HUGHES E.M.,AMERICA THE VINCIBLE. USA+45 FOR/AID ARMS/CONT NUC/PWR PERS/REL RATIONAL ATTIT ALL/VALS 20 COLD/WAR. PAGE 69 A1413
ORD/FREE DIPLOM WAR

B60
HOFFMANN S.H.,CONTEMPORARY THEORY IN INTERNATIONAL RELATIONS. RATIONAL...SOC METH/CNCPT METH/COMP SIMUL ANTHOL 20. PAGE 66 A1359
DIPLOM METH PHIL/SCI DECISION

B61
NEWMAN R.P.,RECOGNITION OF COMMUNIST CHINA? A STUDY IN ARGUMENT. CHINA/COM NAT/G PROB/SOLV RATIONAL ...INT/LAW LOG IDEA/COMP BIBLIOG 20. PAGE 108 A2226
MARXISM ATTIT DIPLOM POLICY

B64
MARTIN J.J.,AMERICAN LIBERALISM AND WORLD POLITICS, 1931-41 (2 VOLS.). GERMANY USA-45 POL/PAR DISCRIM NAT/LISM PEACE RATIONAL ATTIT RIGID/FLEX MARXISM PACIFISM 20. PAGE 95 A1950
NEW/LIB DIPLOM NAT/G POLICY

B65
LARUS J.,COMPARATIVE WORLD POLITICS. ASIA INDIA WOR+45 WOR-45 BAL/PWR WAR PEACE RATIONAL MORAL PWR ...REALPOL INT/LAW MUSLIM. PAGE 85 A1735
GOV/COMP IDEA/COMP DIPLOM NAT/COMP

S67
THOMPSON K.W.,"THE EMPIRICAL, NORMATIVE, AND THEORETICAL FOUNDATIONS OF INTERNATIONAL STUDIES." WOR+45 INGP/REL RATIONAL...CONCPT RECORD IDEA/COMP. PAGE 143 A2932
DIPLOM INTELL METH/COMP KNOWL

RAVENS J.P. A2451

RAY H. A2452

RAY J. A2453

RAZAFIMBAHINY J. A2454

REAGAN/RON....RONALD REAGAN

REAL J. A0402

REALPOL....REALPOLITIK, PRACTICAL POLITICS

B60
DE GAULLE C.,THE EDGE OF THE SWORD. EUR+WWI FRANCE ELITES CHIEF DIPLOM ROLE...REALPOL TRADIT. PAGE 34 A0701
FORCES SUPEGO LEAD WAR

B63
JOYCE W.,THE PROPAGANDA GAP. USA+45 COM/IND ACADEM DOMIN FEEDBACK REV CIVMIL/REL...REALPOL COLD/WAR. PAGE 75 A1540
EDU/PROP PERCEPT BAL/PWR DIPLOM

B65
LARUS J.,COMPARATIVE WORLD POLITICS. ASIA INDIA WOR+45 WOR-45 BAL/PWR WAR PEACE RATIONAL MORAL PWR ...REALPOL INT/LAW MUSLIM. PAGE 85 A1735
GOV/COMP IDEA/COMP DIPLOM NAT/COMP

S67
LACOUTRE J.,"HO CHI MINH." CHINA/COM USSR VIETNAM/N NAT/G CHIEF TOP/EX LEAD NEUTRAL...REALPOL PREDICT 20. PAGE 83 A1708
NAT/LISM MARXISM REV DIPLOM

REALPOLITIK....SEE REALPOL

REC/INT....RECORDING OF INTERVIEWS

S47
RADVANYI L.,"PROBLEMS OF INTERNATIONAL OPINION SURVEYS." WOR+45 INT/ORG NAT/G CREATE ATTIT...PSY SOC METH/CNCPT REC/INT KNO/TEST SAMP/SIZ METH VAL/FREE 20. PAGE 118 A2431
QU/SEMANT SAMP DIPLOM

L58
SNYDER R.N.,"THE UNITED STATES DECISION TO RESIST AGGRESSION IN KOREA." ASIA KOREA S/ASIA USA+45 USA-45 WOR+45 INT/ORG DELIB/GP BAL/PWR COERCE PWR ...CONCPT REC/INT RESIST/INT COLD/WAR 20. PAGE 134 A2753
QUANT METH/CNCPT DIPLOM

S58
ANDERSON N.,"INTERNATIONAL SEMINARS: AN ANALYSIS AND AN EVALUATION." WOR+45 R+D ACT/RES CREATE PLAN REGION ATTIT KNOWL SKILL...SOC REC/INT PERS/TEST CHARTS 20. PAGE 8 A0158
INT/ORG DELIB/GP

S58
BOGART L.,"MEASURING THE EFFECTIVENESS OF AN OVERSEAS INFORMATION CAMPAIGN." EUR+WWI GREECE USA+45 INT/ORG MUNIC PLAN DIPLOM PEACE PERCEPT RIGID/FLEX KNOWL...TECHNIC PSY SOC NEW/IDEA CONT/OBS REC/INT STAND/INT SAMP/SIZ COLD/WAR 20. PAGE 16 A0328
ATTIT EDU/PROP

B59
FREE L.A.,SIX ALLIES AND A NEUTRAL. ASIA COM EUR+WWI FRANCE GERMANY/W INDIA S/ASIA UK USA+45 INT/ORG NAT/G NUC/PWR PEACE ATTIT PERCEPT RIGID/FLEX ALL/VALS...STAT REC/INT COLD/WAR 20 CHINJAP. PAGE 48 A0992
PSY DIPLOM

S60
MUNRO L.,"CAN THE UNITED NATIONS ENFORCE PEACE." WOR+45 LAW INT/ORG VOL/ASSN BAL/PWR LEGIT ARMS/CONT COERCE DETER PEACE PWR...CONCPT REC/INT TREND UN 20 HAMMARSK/D. PAGE 106 A2173
FORCES ORD/FREE

B64
FINER H.,DULLES OVER SUEZ. FRANCE FUT UAR UK WOR+45 NAT/G PROB/SOLV CONTROL NUC/PWR WAR 20 DULLES/JF SUEZ. PAGE 46 A0932
DIPLOM POLICY REC/INT

RECALL....RECALL PROCEDURE

RECEIVE....RECEIVING (IN WELFARE SENSE)

N
INDIA: A REFERENCE ANNUAL. INDIA CULTURE COM/IND R+D FORCES PLAN RECEIVE EDU/PROP HEALTH...STAT CHARTS BIBLIOG 20. PAGE 2 A0036
CONSTN LABOR INT/ORG

N
LATIN AMERICA IN PERIODICAL LITERATURE. LAW TEC/DEV DIPLOM RECEIVE EDU/PROP...GEOG HUM MGT 20. PAGE 2 A0037
BIBLIOG/A L/A+17C SOCIETY ECO/UNDEV

B43
US LIBRARY OF CONGRESS,POLITICAL DEVELOPMENTS AND THE WAR: APRIL-DECEMBER 1942 (SUPPLEMENT 1). WOR-45 CONSTN NAT/G POL/PAR CREATE RECEIVE EDU/PROP ATTIT 20. PAGE 154 A3148
BIBLIOG/A WAR DIPLOM

B50
LEVI W.,FUNDAMENTALS OF WORLD ORGANIZATION. WOR+45 WOR-45 CULTURE ECO/TAC GIVE RECEIVE PERSON WEALTH ...METH/COMP 19/20 UN LEAGUE/NAT. PAGE 88 A1793
INT/ORG PEACE ORD/FREE DIPLOM

B62
PAKISTAN MINISTRY OF FINANCE,FOREIGN ECONOMIC AID: A REVIEW OF FOREIGN ECONOMIC AID TO PAKISTAN. EUR+WWI PAKISTAN UK USA+45 USSR ECO/UNDEV INT/ORG DELIB/GP DIPLOM ECO/TAC...CHARTS CMN/WLTH CHINJAP. PAGE 113 A2318
FOR/AID RECEIVE WEALTH FINAN

B63
COLUMBIA U SCHOOL OF LAW,PUBLIC INTERNATIONAL DEVELOPMENT FINANCING IN SENEGAL. SENEGAL FINAN DELIB/GP GIVE EFFICIENCY...CHARTS GOV/COMP ANTHOL 20. PAGE 28 A0571
FOR/AID PLAN RECEIVE ECO/UNDEV

B63
EL-NAGGAR S.,FOREIGN AID TO UNITED ARAB REPUBLIC. UAR USA+45 USSR AGRI FINAN INDUS FORCES EATING DEMAND...CHARTS METH/COMP 20 RESOURCE/N AID. PAGE 41 A0838
FOR/AID ECO/UNDEV RECEIVE PLAN

B63
RAO V.K.R.,FOREIGN AID AND INDIA'S ECONOMIC DEVELOPMENT. INDIA INT/ORG PROB/SOLV TEC/DEV ECO/TAC CONTROL WEALTH...TREND 20. PAGE 119 A2445
FOR/AID ECO/UNDEV RECEIVE DIPLOM

B64
MC GOVERN G.S.,WAR AGAINST WANT. USA+45 AGRI DIPLOM INT/TRADE GIVE RECEIVE DEMAND HEALTH 20 KENNEDY/JF FOOD/PEACE. PAGE 97 A1993
FOR/AID ECO/DEV POLICY EATING

B64
RICHARDSON I.L.,BIBLIOGRAFIA BRASILEIRA DE ADMINISTRACAO PUBLICA E ASSUNTOS CORRELATOS. BRAZIL CONSTN FINAN LOC/G NAT/G POL/PAR PLAN DIPLOM RECEIVE ATTIT...METH 20. PAGE 121 A2474
BIBLIOG MGT ADMIN LAW

B65
MEAGHER R.F.,PUBLIC INTERNATIONAL DEVELOPMENT FINANCING IN SUDAN. SUDAN FINAN DELIB/GP GIVE ...CHARTS GOV/COMP 20. PAGE 99 A2029
FOR/AID PLAN RECEIVE ECO/UNDEV

B66
LEAGUE OF WOMEN VOTERS OF US,FOREIGN AID AT THE CROSSROADS. USA+45 WOR+45 DELIB/GP PROB/SOLV DIPLOM INT/TRADE RECEIVE BAL/PAY...CHARTS 20 UN. PAGE 86 A1756
FOR/AID GIVE ECO/UNDEV PLAN

S67
MONTALVA E.F.,"THE ALLIANCE THAT LOST ITS WAY." L/A+17C USA+45 R+D BAL/PWR INT/TRADE RECEIVE REV PEACE...POLICY 20. PAGE 103 A2111
ECO/UNDEV DIPLOM FOR/AID INT/ORG

RECIFE....RECIFE, BRAZIL

RECIPROCITY....SEE SANCTION

RECONSTRUCTION PERIOD....SEE CIVIL/WAR

RECORD....RECORDING OF DIRECT OBSERVATIONS

B00
LORIMER J.,THE INSTITUTES OF THE LAW OF NATIONS. WOR-45 CULTURE SOCIETY NAT/G VOL/ASSN DIPLOM LEGIT WAR PEACE DRIVE ORD/FREE SOVEREIGN...CONCPT RECORD INT TREND HYPO/EXP GEN/METH TOT/POP VAL/FREE 20. PAGE 91 A1863
INT/ORG LAW INT/LAW

B20
HALDANE R.B.,BEFORE THE WAR. MOD/EUR SOCIETY INT/ORG NAT/G DELIB/GP PLAN DOMIN EDU/PROP LEGIT ADMIN COERCE ATTIT DRIVE MORAL ORD/FREE PWR...SOC CONCPT SELF/OBS RECORD BIOG TIME/SEQ. PAGE 60 A1223
POLICY DIPLOM UK

B21
STUART G.H.,FRENCH FOREIGN POLICY. CONSTN INT/ORG NAT/G POL/PAR EX/STRUC FORCES PLAN ECO/TAC DOMIN EDU/PROP ADJUD COERCE ATTIT DRIVE RIGID/FLEX ALL/VALS...POLICY OBS RECORD BIOG TIME/SEQ TREND. PAGE 139 A2852
MOD/EUR DIPLOM FRANCE

B22
POTTER P.B.,AN INTRODUCTION TO THE STUDY OF INTERNATIONAL ORGANIZATION. WOR-45 ACT/RES CREATE EDU/PROP ROUTINE PERCEPT KNOWL...CONT/OBS RECORD GEN/LAWS TOT/POP VAL/FREE 20. PAGE 117 A2398
INT/ORG CONCPT

B22
WRIGHT Q.,THE CONTROL OF AMERICAN FOREIGN RELATIONS. USA-45 WOR-45 CONSTN INT/ORG CONSULT LEGIS LEGIT ROUTINE ORD/FREE PWR...POLICY JURID CONCPT METH/CNCPT RECORD LEAGUE/NAT 20. PAGE 167 A3402
NAT/G EXEC DIPLOM

B28
HALL W.P.,EMPIRE TO COMMONWEALTH. FUT WOR-45 CONSTN ECO/DEV ECO/UNDEV INT/ORG PROVS PLAN DIPLOM EDU/PROP ADMIN COLONIAL PEACE PERSON ALL/VALS ...POLICY GEOG SOC OBS RECORD TREND CMN/WLTH PARLIAMENT 19/20. PAGE 60 A1229
VOL/ASSN NAT/G UK

B29
DUNN F.,THE PRACTICE AND PROCEDURE OF INTERNATIONAL CONFERENCES. WOR-45 NAT/G DELIB/GP BAL/PWR LEGIT EXEC ROUTINE PEACE ORD/FREE RESPECT...JURID CONCPT METH/CNCPT OBS RECORD TIME/SEQ 20. PAGE 39 A0799
INT/ORG DIPLOM

B33
LANGER W.L.,FOREIGN AFFAIRS BIBLIOGRAPHY. WOR-45 INT/ORG CONSULT EDU/PROP ROUTINE NAT/LISM ATTIT SOVEREIGN...STAT RECORD GEN/METH LEAGUE/NAT TOT/POP. PAGE 84 A1725
KNOWL

B39
ZIMMERN A.,THE LEAGUE OF NATIONS AND THE RULE OF LAW. WOR-45 STRUCT NAT/G DELIB/GP EX/STRUC BAL/PWR DOMIN LEGIT COERCE ORD/FREE PWR...POLICY RECORD LEAGUE/NAT TOT/POP VAL/FREE 20 LEAGUE/NAT. PAGE 170 A3453
INT/ORG LAW DIPLOM

B45
PASTUHOV V.D.,A GUIDE TO THE PRACTICE OF INTERNATIONAL CONFERENCES. WOR+45 PLAN LEGIT ORD/FREE...MGT OBS RECORD VAL/FREE ILO LEAGUE/NAT 20. PAGE 114 A2338 — INT/ORG DELIB/GP

B45
RANSHOFFEN-WERTHEIMER EF,THE INTERNATIONAL SECRETARIAT: A GREAT EXPERIMENT IN INTERNATIONAL ADMINISTRATION. EUR+WWI FUT CONSTN FACE/GP CONSULT DELIB/GP ACT/RES ADMIN ROUTINE PEACE ORD/FREE...MGT RECORD ORG/CHARTS LEAGUE/NAT WORK 20. PAGE 119 A2442 — INT/ORG EXEC

B48
CHURCHILL W.,THE GATHERING STORM. UK WOR-45 INT/ORG NAT/G FORCES TOP/EX DIPLOM ECO/TAC COERCE ATTIT ORD/FREE PWR WEALTH...POLICY SELF/OBS RECORD NAZI PARLIAMENT 20. PAGE 26 A0538 — BIOG

B50
DE ARECHAGA E.J.,VOTING AND THE HANDLING OF DISPUTES IN THE SECURITY COUNCIL. WOR+45 CONSTN DIPLOM COERCE ORD/FREE...RECORD CON/ANAL GEN/METH COLD/WAR UN 20. PAGE 34 A0696 — INT/ORG PWR

B51
MACLAURIN J.,THE UNITED NATIONS AND POWER POLITICS. WOR+45 CONSULT EDU/PROP LEGIT ADJUD EXEC MORAL ORD/FREE...HUM JURID CONCPT RECORD TIME/SEQ UN COLD/WAR 20. PAGE 93 A1896 — INT/ORG ROUTINE

L54
OPLER M.E.,"SOCIAL ASPECTS OF TECHNICAL ASSISTANCE IN OPERATION." WOR+45 VOL/ASSN CREATE PLAN TEC/DEV EDU/PROP ALL/VALS...METH/CNCPT OBS RECORD TREND UN 20. PAGE 112 A2292 — INT/ORG CONSULT FOR/AID

B55
MACMAHON A.W.,FEDERALISM: MATURE AND EMERGENT. EUR+WWI FUT WOR+45 WOR-45 INT/ORG NAT/G REPRESENT FEDERAL...POLICY MGT RECORD TREND GEN/LAWS 20. PAGE 93 A1900 — STRUCT CONCPT

B55
SNYDER R.C.,AMERICAN FOREIGN POLICY. USA+45 USA-45 WOR+45 WOR-45 CONSTN INT/ORG POL/PAR VOL/ASSN DELIB/GP LEGIS CREATE DOMIN EDU/PROP EXEC COERCE ATTIT DRIVE ORD/FREE PWR...MGT OBS RECORD TIME/SEQ TREND. PAGE 134 A2752 — NAT/G DIPLOM

L55
KISER M.,"ORGANIZATION OF AMERICAN STATES." L/A+17C USA+45 ECO/UNDEV INT/ORG NAT/G PLAN TEC/DEV DIPLOM ECO/TAC INT/TRADE EDU/PROP ADMIN ALL/VALS...POLICY MGT RECORD ORG/CHARTS OAS 20. PAGE 80 A1639 — VOL/ASSN ECO/DEV REGION

B56
GEORGE A.L.,WOODROW WILSON AND COLONEL HOUSE. WOR-45 CONSTN FACE/GP INT/ORG NAT/G POL/PAR CONSULT LEGIT EXEC COERCE CHOOSE ATTIT DRIVE PERSON MORAL ORD/FREE PWR RESPECT...POLICY MGT PSY OBS RECORD INT LEAGUE/NAT. PAGE 52 A1060 — USA-45 BIOG DIPLOM

B56
HOUSTON J.A.,LATIN AMERICA IN THE UNITED NATIONS. CONSULT DIPLOM LEGIT ROUTINE ATTIT ORD/FREE PWR ...JURID OBS RECORD TIME/SEQ CHARTS 20 UN. PAGE 68 A1395 — L/A+17C INT/ORG INT/LAW REGION

B56
REITZEL W.,UNITED STATES FOREIGN POLICY, 1945-1955. USA+45 WOR+45 CONSTN INT/ORG EDU/PROP LEGIT EXEC COERCE NUC/PWR PEACE ATTIT ORD/FREE PWR...DECISION CONCPT OBS RECORD TIME/SEQ TREND COLD/WAR UN CONGRESS. PAGE 120 A2464 — NAT/G POLICY DIPLOM

B56
WEIS P.,NATIONALITY AND STATELESSNESS IN INTERNATIONAL LAW. UK WOR+45 WOR-45 LAW CONSTN NAT/G DIPLOM EDU/PROP LEGIT ROUTINE RIGID/FLEX ...JURID RECORD CMN/WLTH 20. PAGE 162 A3309 — INT/ORG SOVEREIGN INT/LAW

B57
BEAL J.R.,JOHN FOSTER DULLES, A BIOGRAPHY. USA+45 USSR WOR+45 CONSTN INT/ORG NAT/G EX/STRUC LEGIT ADMIN NUC/PWR DISPL PERSON ORD/FREE PWR SKILL ...POLICY PSY OBS RECORD COLD/WAR UN 20 DULLES/JF. PAGE 12 A0237 — BIOG DIPLOM

B57
HOLCOMBE A.N.,STRENGTHENING THE UNITED NATIONS. USA+45 ACT/RES CREATE PLAN EDU/PROP ATTIT PERCEPT PWR...METH/CNCPT CONT/OBS RECORD UN COLD/WAR 20. PAGE 66 A1365 — INT/ORG ROUTINE

B57
JENKS C.W.,THE INTERNATIONAL PROTECTION OF TRADE UNION FREEDOM. FUT WOR+45 WOR-45 VOL/ASSN DELIB/GP CT/SYS REGION ROUTINE...JURID METH/CNCPT RECORD TIME/SEQ CHARTS ILO WORK OAS 20. PAGE 73 A1504 — LABOR INT/ORG

B57
ROSENNE S.,THE INTERNATIONAL COURT OF JUSTICE. WOR+45 LAW DOMIN LEGIT PEACE PWR SOVEREIGN...JURID CONCPT RECORD TIME/SEQ CON/ANAL CHARTS UN TOT/POP VAL/FREE LEAGUE/NAT 20 ICJ. PAGE 124 A2537 — INT/ORG CT/SYS INT/LAW

B59
CHINA INSTITUTE OF AMERICA.,CHINA AND THE UNITED NATIONS. CHINA/COM FUT STRUCT EDU/PROP LEGIT ADMIN ATTIT KNOWL ORD/FREE PWR...OBS RECORD STAND/INT TIME/SEQ UN LEAGUE/NAT UNESCO 20. PAGE 26 A0531 — ASIA INT/ORG

B59
STRAUSZ-HUPE R.,PROTRACTED CONFLICT. CHINA/COM KOREA WOR+45 INT/ORG FORCES ACT/RES ECO/TAC LEGIT COERCE DRIVE PERCEPT KNOWL PWR...PSY CONCPT RECORD GEN/METH COLD/WAR VAL/FREE 20. PAGE 139 A2847 — COM PLAN USSR

L59
GRANDIN T.,"THE POLITICAL USE OF THE RADIO." EUR+WWI SOCIETY INT/ORG DIPLOM CONTROL ATTIT ORD/FREE...CONCPT STAT RECORD SAMP GEN/LAWS TOT/POP 20. PAGE 55 A1128 — COM/IND EDU/PROP NAT/LISM

S59
KRIPALANI A.J.B.,"FOR PRINCIPLED NEUTRALITY." CHINA/COM INDIA S/ASIA PLAN ECO/TAC RIGID/FLEX MORAL PWR...MYSTIC SOC RECORD 20 GANDHI/M. PAGE 82 A1684 — ATTIT FOR/AID DIPLOM

S59
SAYEGH F.,"ARAB NATIONALISM AND SOVIET-AMERICAN RELATIONS." ISLAM USA+45 ECO/UNDEV PLAN ECO/TAC LEGIT NAT/LISM DRIVE PERCEPT KNOWL PWR...DECISION CONCPT STAT RECORD TREND CON/ANAL VAL/FREE 20 COLD/WAR. PAGE 127 A2610 — DIPLOM USSR

B60
KHRUSHCHEV N.S.,KHRUSHCHEV IN AMERICA. USA+45 USSR INT/TRADE EDU/PROP PRESS PEACE...MARXIST RECORD INT 20 COLD/WAR KHRUSH/N. PAGE 79 A1613 — MARXISM CHIEF DIPLOM

B60
PENTONY D.E.,THE UNDERDEVELOPED LANDS. FUT WOR+45 CULTURE AGRI FINAN INDUS MARKET INT/ORG LABOR NAT/G VOL/ASSN CONSULT TEC/DEV ECO/TAC EDU/PROP COLONIAL ATTIT WEALTH...OBS RECORD SAMP TREND GEN/METH WORK UN 20. PAGE 115 A2351 — ECO/UNDEV POLICY FOR/AID INT/TRADE

B60
US HOUSE COMM. SCI. ASTRONAUT.,OCEAN SCIENCES AND NATIONAL SECURITY. FUT SEA ECO/DEV EXTR/IND INT/ORG NAT/G FORCES ACT/RES TEC/DEV ECO/TAC COERCE WAR BIO/SOC KNOWL PWR...CONCPT RECORD LAB/EXP 20. PAGE 154 A3141 — R+D ORD/FREE

L60
DEAN A.W.,"SECOND GENEVA CONFERENCE OF THE LAW OF THE SEA: THE FIGHT FOR FREEDOM OF THE SEAS." FUT USA+45 USSR WOR+45 WOR-45 SEA CONSTN STRUCT PLAN INT/TRADE ADJUD ADMIN ORD/FREE...DECISION RECORD TREND GEN/LAWS 20 TREATY. PAGE 35 A0717 — INT/ORG JURID INT/LAW

L60
JACOB P.E.,"THE DISARMAMENT CONSENSUS." USA+45 USSR WOR+45 INT/ORG NAT/G ACT/RES TEC/DEV BAL/PWR EDU/PROP ADMIN COERCE DETER NUC/PWR CONSEN RIGID/FLEX PWR...CONCPT RECORD CHARTS COLD/WAR 20. PAGE 72 A1482 — DELIB/GP ATTIT ARMS/CONT

L60
NOGEE J.L.,"THE DIPLOMACY OF DISARMAMENT." WOR+45 INT/ORG NAT/G CONSULT DELIB/GP TOP/EX BAL/PWR DIPLOM EDU/PROP COERCE DETER WEAPON PEACE ATTIT ...RECORD TIME/SEQ TOT/POP VAL/FREE COLD/WAR 20. PAGE 109 A2246 — PWR ORD/FREE ARMS/CONT NUC/PWR

S60
SCHWELB E.,"INTERNATIONAL CONVENTIONS ON HUMAN RIGHTS." FUT WOR+45 LAW CONSTN CULTURE SOCIETY STRUCT VOL/ASSN DELIB/GP PLAN ADJUD SUPEGO LOVE MORAL...SOC CONCPT STAT RECORD HIST/WRIT TREND 20 UN. PAGE 130 A2664 — INT/ORG HUM

B61
BARNES W.,THE FOREIGN SERVICE OF THE UNITED STATES. USA+45 USA-45 CONSTN INT/ORG POL/PAR CONSULT DELIB/GP LEGIS DOMIN EDU/PROP EXEC ATTIT RIGID/FLEX ORD/FREE PWR...POLICY CONCPT STAT OBS RECORD BIOG TIME/SEQ TREND. PAGE 11 A0224 — NAT/G MGT DIPLOM

B61
CHIDZERO B.T.G.,TANGANYIKA AND INTERNATIONAL TRUSTEESHIP. AFR WOR+45 WOR-45 ECO/DEV INT/ORG ECO/TAC DOMIN COLONIAL...RECORD CHARTS 20 TANGANYIKA CMN/WLTH. PAGE 26 A0528 — ECO/UNDEV CONSTN

B61
HENKIN L.,ARMS CONTROL: ISSUES FOR THE PUBLIC. EUR+WWI FUT USA+45 USSR INT/ORG NAT/G DIPLOM EDU/PROP DETER NUC/PWR ATTIT PWR...CONCPT RECORD HIST/WRIT TIME/SEQ TOT/POP COLD/WAR 20. PAGE 64 A1316 — WOR+45 DELIB/GP ARMS/CONT

B61
KISSINGER H.A.,THE NECESSITY FOR CHOICE. FUT USA+45 ECO/UNDEV NAT/G PLAN BAL/PWR ECO/TAC ARMS/CONT DETER NUC/PWR ATTIT...POLICY CONCPT RECORD GEN/LAWS COLD/WAR 20. PAGE 80 A1642 — TOP/EX TREND DIPLOM

B61
MCDOUGAL M.S.,LAW AND MINIMUM WORLD PUBLIC ORDER. WOR+45 SOCIETY NAT/G DELIB/GP EDU/PROP LEGIT ADJUD COERCE ATTIT PERSON...JURID CONCPT RECORD TREND TOT/POP 20. PAGE 98 A2006 — INT/ORG ORD/FREE INT/LAW

B61
YDIT M.,INTERNATIONALISED TERRITORIES. FUT WOR+45 WOR-45 CONSTN VOL/ASSN CREATE PLAN LEGIT PEACE ORD/FREE...GEOG INT/LAW JURID SOC NEW/IDEA OBS RECORD SAMP TIME/SEQ TREND 19/20 BERLIN. PAGE 169 A3431 — LOC/G INT/ORG DIPLOM SOVEREIGN

S61
NOVE A.,"THE SOVIET MODEL AND UNDERDEVELOPED — ECO/UNDEV

COUNTRIES." COM FUT USSR WOR+45 CULTURE ECO/DEV POL/PAR FOR/AID EDU/PROP ADMIN MORAL WEALTH ...POLICY RECORD HIST/WRIT 20. PAGE 110 A2258 PLAN

B62
BELL C.,NEGOTIATION FROM STRENGTH. WOR+45 FACE/GP INT/ORG DELIB/GP FORCES PLAN DOMIN COERCE NUC/PWR PEACE DRIVE PWR...POLICY LOG OBS RECORD INT SAMP TREND COLD/WAR 20. PAGE 13 A0255 NAT/G CONCPT DIPLOM

B62
BOUSCAREN A.T.,SOVIET FOREIGN POLICY: A PATTERN OF PERSISTANCE. WOR+45 WOR-45 SOCIETY STRUCT INT/ORG POL/PAR CREATE PLAN EDU/PROP ROUTINE ATTIT RIGID/FLEX...POLICY CONCPT RECORD HIST/WRIT TIME/SEQ MARX/KARL 20. PAGE 17 A0352 COM NAT/G DIPLOM USSR

B62
CALDER R.,COMMON SENSE ABOUT A STARVING WORLD. WOR+45 STRATA ECO/DEV PLAN GP/REL BIO/SOC HABITAT ...POLICY GEOG STAT RECORD 20 UN BIRTH/CON. PAGE 23 A0466 FOR/AID CENSUS ECO/UNDEV AGRI

B62
DALLIN A.,THE SOVIET UNION AT THE UNITED NATIONS: AN INQUIRY INTO SOVIET MOTIVES AND OBJECTIVES. ACT/RES EDU/PROP LEGIT ATTIT KNOWL PWR...POLICY RECORD HIST/WRIT TIME/SEQ TREND ORG/CHARTS GEN/METH COLD/WAR FAO 20 UN. PAGE 33 A0675 COM INT/ORG USSR

B62
MCDOUGAL M.S.,THE PUBLIC ORDER OF THE OCEANS. WOR+45 WOR-45 SEA INT/ORG NAT/G CONSULT DELIB/GP DIPLOM LEGIT PEACE RIGID/FLEX...GEOG INT/LAW JURID RECORD TOT/POP 20 TREATY. PAGE 98 A2007 ADJUD ORD/FREE

B62
MULLEY F.W.,THE POLITICS OF WESTERN DEFENSE. EUR+WWI USA-45 WOR+45 VOL/ASSN EX/STRUC FORCES COERCE DETER PEACE ATTIT ORD/FREE PWR...RECORD TIME/SEQ CHARTS COLD/WAR 20 NATO. PAGE 106 A2168 INT/ORG DELIB/GP NUC/PWR

B62
ROY P.A.,SOUTH WIND RED. L/A+17C USA+45 ECO/UNDEV NAT/G CAP/ISM MARXISM SOCISM...OLD/LIB GEOG RECORD INT CENSUS 20 COLD/WAR. PAGE 125 A2554 DIPLOM INDUS POLICY ECO/TAC

B62
SPANIER J.W.,THE POLITICS OF DISARMAMENT. COM USA+45 USSR EDU/PROP ATTIT ORD/FREE PWR RESPECT ...MYTH RECORD 20 COLD/WAR. PAGE 135 A2771 INT/ORG DELIB/GP ARMS/CONT

B62
WOETZEL R.K.,THE NURENBERG TRIALS IN INTERNATIONAL LAW. CHRIST-17C MOD/EUR WOR+45 SOCIETY NAT/G DELIB/GP DOMIN LEGIT ROUTINE ATTIT DRIVE PERSON SUPEGO MORAL ORD/FREE...POLICY MAJORIT JURID PSY SOC SELF/OBS RECORD NAZI TOT/POP. PAGE 166 A3376 INT/ORG ADJUD WAR

B62
WOLFERS A.,DISCORD AND COLLABORATION: ESSAYS ON INTERNATIONAL POLITICS. WOR+45 CULTURE SOCIETY INT/ORG NAT/G BAL/PWR DIPLOM DOMIN NAT/LISM PEACE PWR...POLICY CONCPT STYLE RECORD TREND GEN/LAWS 20. PAGE 166 A3385 ATTIT ORD/FREE

S62
RUSSETT B.M.,"CAUSE, SURPRISE, AND NO ESCAPE." FUT WOR-45 CULTURE SOCIETY INT/ORG FORCES TEC/DEV BAL/PWR EDU/PROP ARMS/CONT NUC/PWR WAR WEAPON PEACE KNOWL ORD/FREE PWR...POLICY CONCPT RECORD TIME/SEQ TREND GEN/LAWS 20 WWI. PAGE 126 A2578 COERCE DIPLOM

S62
THOMAS J.R.T.,"SOVIET BEHAVIOR IN THE QUEMOY CRISES OF 1958." CHINA/COM FUT USSR WOR+45 INT/ORG VOL/ASSN FORCES PLAN BAL/PWR DOMIN COERCE NUC/PWR REV WAR ATTIT DRIVE ORD/FREE...POLICY OBS RECORD COLD/WAR FOR/POL 20. PAGE 143 A2923 COM PWR

B63
BOISSIER P.,HISTORIE DU COMITE INTERNATIONAL DE LA CROIX ROUGE. MOD/EUR WOR-45 CONSULT FORCES PLAN DIPLOM EDU/PROP ADMIN MORAL ORD/FREE...SOC CONCPT RECORD TIME/SEQ GEN/LAWS TOT/POP VAL/FREE 19/20. PAGE 16 A0332 INT/ORG HEALTH ARMS/CONT WAR

B63
INTERNATIONAL BANK RECONST DEV,THE WORLD BANK GROUP IN ASIA. ASIA S/ASIA INDUS TEC/DEV ECO/TAC...RECORD 20 IBRD WORLD/BANK. PAGE 71 A1451 INT/ORG DIPLOM ECO/UNDEV FINAN

B63
SCHMELTZ G.W.,LA POLITIQUE MONDIALE CONTEMPORAINE. SOCIETY ECO/UNDEV INDUS INT/ORG NAT/G POL/PAR CONSULT DELIB/GP PLAN TEC/DEV ECO/TAC DOMIN EDU/PROP ROUTINE COERCE PERCEPT PERSON LOVE SKILL ...SOC RECORD TOT/POP. PAGE 128 A2629 WOR+45 COLONIAL

S63
ALEXANDER R.,"LATIN AMERICA AND THE COMMUNIST BLOC." ASIA COM CUBA L/A+17C USA+45 USSR NAT/G VOL/ASSN TEC/DEV FOR/AID LEGIT PWR WEALTH COLD/WAR 20. PAGE 6 A0112 ECO/UNDEV RECORD

S63
CHAKRAVARTI P.C.,"INDIAN NON-ALIGNMENT AND UNITED STATES POLICY." ASIA INDIA S/ASIA USA+45 CULTURE ECO/UNDEV NAT/G VOL/ASSN DELIB/GP TOP/EX FOR/AID NEUTRAL...POLICY HUM CONCPT RECORD GEN/LAWS 20. PAGE 25 A0515 ATTIT ALL/VALS COLONIAL DIPLOM

S63
DIEBOLD W. JR.,"THE NEW SITUATION OF INTERNATIONAL TRADE POLICY." EUR+WWI FRANCE FUT UK USA+45 WOR+45 DIST/IND PLAN INT/TRADE EDU/PROP PWR WEALTH ...RECORD TREND GEN/LAWS EEC VAL/FREE 20. PAGE 37 A0760 MARKET ECO/TAC

S63
ETZIONI A.,"EUROPEAN UNIFICATION AND PERSPECTIVES ON SOVEREIGNTY." EUR+WWI FUT DELIB/GP TEC/DEV ECO/TAC EDU/PROP DETER NUC/PWR ATTIT DRIVE ORD/FREE PWR WEALTH...CONCPT RECORD TIME/SEQ EEC VAL/FREE 20. PAGE 43 A0870 INT/ORG ECO/DEV SOVEREIGN

S63
GROSSER A.,"FRANCE AND GERMANY IN THE ATLANTIC COMMUNITY." INT/ORG NAT/G TOP/EX DIPLOM REGION PEACE ATTIT ORD/FREE PWR...CONCPT RECORD TIME/SEQ GEN/LAWS VAL/FREE COLD/WAR 20. PAGE 57 A1178 EUR+WWI VOL/ASSN FRANCE GERMANY

S63
GUPTA S.C.,"INDIA AND THE SOVIET UNION." CHINA/COM COM INDIA S/ASIA VOL/ASSN TOP/EX FOR/AID EDU/PROP PEACE PWR...RECORD COLD/WAR 20. PAGE 58 A1195 DISPL MYTH USSR

S63
HOLBO P.S.,"COLD WAR DRIFT IN LATIN AMERICA." CUBA L/A+17C USA+45 USA-45 INT/ORG NAT/G NEIGH VOL/ASSN ACT/RES PLAN ECO/TAC ATTIT RIGID/FLEX ALL/VALS ...RECORD TIME/SEQ OAS LAFTA 20 COLD/WAR. PAGE 66 A1363 DELIB/GP CREATE FOR/AID

S63
SHONFIELD A.,"AFTER BRUSSELS." EUR+WWI FRANCE GERMANY UK ECO/DEV DIST/IND MARKET VOL/ASSN DELIB/GP CREATE INT/TRADE ATTIT RIGID/FLEX...RECORD TREND GEN/LAWS EEC CMN/WLTH 20. PAGE 132 A2705 PLAN ECO/TAC

S63
VEROFF J.,"AFRICAN STUDENTS IN THE UNITED STATES." AFR USA+45 CULTURE ACT/RES FOR/AID PEACE ATTIT KNOWL...SOC RECORD DEEP/QU SYS/QU CHARTS STERTYP TOT/POP 20. PAGE 159 A3230 PERCEPT RIGID/FLEX RACE/REL

B64
COTTRELL A.J.,THE POLITICS OF THE ATLANTIC ALLIANCE. EUR+WWI USA+45 INT/ORG NAT/G DELIB/GP EX/STRUC BAL/PWR DIPLOM REGION DETER ATTIT ORD/FREE ...CONCPT RECORD GEN/LAWS GEN/METH NATO 20. PAGE 31 A0632 VOL/ASSN FORCES

B64
EHRENBURG I.,THE WAR: 1941-1945 (VOL. V OF "MEN, YEARS - LIFE," TRANS. BY TATIANA SHEBUNINA). GERMANY USSR PRESS WRITING PERS/REL PEACE ANOMIE ATTIT PERSON...CONCPT RECORD BIOG 20 STALIN/J HITLER/A. PAGE 40 A0827 WAR DIPLOM COM MARXIST

B64
EPSTEIN H.M.,REVOLT IN THE CONGO. AFR CONGO/BRAZ WOR+45 NAT/G FORCES DOMIN WAR CIVMIL/REL INGP/REL MARXISM...RECORD GP/COMP 20 CONGO/LEOP UN. PAGE 42 A0856 REV COLONIAL NAT/LISM DIPLOM

B64
VOELKMANN K.,HERRSCHER VON MORGEN? BAL/PWR COLONIAL NEUTRAL REGION RACE/REL ALL/VALS SOVEREIGN...RECORD 20 COLD/WAR THIRD/WRLD. PAGE 159 A3246 DIPLOM ECO/UNDEV CONTROL NAT/COMP

B64
WAINHOUSE D.W.,REMNANTS OF EMPIRE: THE UNITED NATIONS AND THE END OF COLONIALISM. FUT PORTUGAL WOR+45 NAT/G CONSULT DOMIN LEGIT ADMIN ROUTINE ATTIT ORD/FREE...POLICY JURID RECORD INT TIME/SEQ UN CMN/WLTH 20. PAGE 160 A3260 INT/ORG TREND COLONIAL

L64
CARNEGIE ENDOWMENT INT. PEACE,"ECONOMIC AND SOCIAL QUESTION (ISSUES BEFORE THE NINETEENTH GENERAL ASSEMBLY)." WOR+45 ECO/DEV ECO/UNDEV INDUS R+D DELIB/GP CREATE PLAN TEC/DEV ECO/TAC FOR/AID BAL/PAY...RECORD UN 20. PAGE 24 A0493 INT/ORG INT/TRADE

S64
CARNEGIE ENDOWMENT INT. PEACE,"COLONIAL COUNTRIES AND PEOPLES (ISSUES BEFORE THE NINETEENTH GENERAL ASSEMBLY)." AFR ISLAM L/A+17C WOR+45 DELIB/GP LEGIS ECO/TAC EDU/PROP NAT/LISM PEACE ALL/VALS...RECORD UN CMN/WLTH 20. PAGE 24 A0491 INT/ORG ECO/UNDEV COLONIAL

S64
CARNEGIE ENDOWMENT INT. PEACE,"HUMAN RIGHTS (ISSUES BEFORE THE NINETEENTH GENERAL ASSEMBLY)." AFR WOR+45 LAW CONSTN NAT/G EDU/PROP GP/REL DISCRIM PEACE ATTIT MORAL ORD/FREE...INT/LAW PSY CONCPT RECORD UN 20. PAGE 24 A0492 INT/ORG PERSON RACE/REL

S64
CARNEGIE ENDOWMENT INT. PEACE,"LEGAL QUESTIONS (ISSUES BEFORE THE NINETEENTH GENERAL ASSEMBLY)." WOR+45 CONSTN NAT/G DELIB/GP ADJUD PEACE MORAL ORD/FREE...RECORD UN 20 TREATY. PAGE 24 A0494 INT/ORG LAW INT/LAW

S64
CARNEGIE ENDOWMENT INT. PEACE,"ADMINISTRATION AND BUDGET (ISSUES BEFORE THE NINETEENTH GENERAL ASSEMBLY)." WOR+45 FINAN BUDGET ECO/TAC ROUTINE COST...STAT RECORD UN. PAGE 24 A0495 INT/ORG ADMIN

S64
LEVI W.,"CHINA AND THE UNITED NATIONS." ASIA CHINA CHINA/COM WOR+45 WOR-45 CONSTN NAT/G DELIB/GP INT/ORG ATTIT

EX/STRUC FORCES ACT/RES EDU/PROP PWR...POLICY RECORD TIME/SEQ GEN/LAWS UN COLD/WAR 20. PAGE 88 A1794 — NAT/LISM

S64
RUBIN R.,"THE UN CORRESPONDENT." WOR+45 FACE/GP PROF/ORG EDU/PROP ROUTINE PERCEPT KNOWL...RECORD STAND/INT QU UN WORK TOT/POP VAL/FREE 20. PAGE 125 A2560 — INT/ORG ATTIT DIPLOM

S64
RUBINSTEIN A.Z.,"THE SOVIET IMAGE OF WESTERN EUROPE." COM EUR+WWI FRANCE GERMANY GERMANY/W USA+45 USSR INT/ORG NAT/G VOL/ASSN FORCES TOP/EX BAL/PWR EDU/PROP ORD/FREE PWR...MYTH RECORD NATO EEC 20. PAGE 125 A2564 — RIGID/FLEX ATTIT

S64
TOUVAL S.,"THE SOMALI REPUBLIC." AFR ISLAM SOMALIA FAM KIN NAT/G CREATE FOR/AID LEGIT ATTIT ALL/VALS ...RECORD TREND 20. PAGE 144 A2954 — ECO/UNDEV RIGID/FLEX

B65
ADENAUER K.,MEINE ERINNERUNGEN, 1945-53 (VOL. I), 1953-55 (VOL. II). EUR+WWI GERMANY CHIEF FORCES PROB/SOLV DIPLOM ARMS/CONT INGP/REL PEACE SOVEREIGN ...OBS/ENVIR RECORD 20. PAGE 4 A0089 — NAT/G BIOG SELF/OBS

L65
KAPLAN M.A.,"OLD REALITIES AND NEW MYTHS." USA+45 WOR+45 INT/ORG NAT/G TOP/EX ACT/RES BAL/PWR ECO/TAC EDU/PROP LEGIT RIGID/FLEX ALL/VALS...RECORD COLD/WAR 20. PAGE 76 A1564 — ATTIT MYTH DIPLOM

S65
BROWN S.,"AN ALTERNATIVE TO THE GRAND DESIGN." EUR+WWI FUT USA+45 INT/ORG NAT/G EX/STRUC FORCES CREATE BAL/PWR DOMIN RIGID/FLEX ORD/FREE PWR ...NEW/IDEA RECORD EEC NATO 20. PAGE 20 A0407 — VOL/ASSN CONCPT DIPLOM

S65
FALK R.A.,"INTERNATIONAL LEGAL ORDER." USA+45 INTELL FACE/GP INT/ORG LEGIT KNOWL...CONCPT METH/CNCPT STYLE RECORD GEN/METH 20. PAGE 44 A0890 — ATTIT GEN/LAWS INT/LAW

C65
SCHEINGOLD S.A.,"THE RULE OF LAW IN EUROPEAN INTEGRATION: THE PATH OF THE SCHUMAN PLAN." EUR+WWI JUDGE ADJUD FEDERAL ATTIT PWR...RECORD INT BIBLIOG EEC ECSC. PAGE 128 A2621 — INT/LAW CT/SYS REGION CENTRAL

B66
FARWELL G.,MASK OF ASIA: THE PHILIPPINES. PHILIPPINE SECT DIPLOM ATTIT...SOC RECORD PREDICT BIBLIOG 20. PAGE 44 A0901 — S/ASIA CULTURE

B66
RISTIC D.N.,YUGOSLAVIA'S REVOLUTION OF 1941. EUR+WWI YUGOSLAVIA NAT/G WAR ORD/FREE...RECORD BIBLIOG 20 HITLER/A TREATY. PAGE 121 A2484 — REV ATTIT FASCISM DIPLOM

C66
KULSKI W.W.,"DEGAULLE AND THE WORLD: THE FOREIGN POLICY OF THE FIFTH FRENCH REPUBLIC." FRANCE ECO/UNDEV POL/PAR BAL/PWR DETER NUC/PWR ATTIT PWR ...RECORD BIBLIOG DEGAULLE NATO EEC. PAGE 83 A1694 — POLICY SOVEREIGN PERSON DIPLOM

S67
THOMPSON K.W.,"THE EMPIRICAL, NORMATIVE, AND THEORETICAL FOUNDATIONS OF INTERNATIONAL STUDIES." WOR+45 INGP/REL RATIONAL...CONCPT RECORD IDEA/COMP. PAGE 143 A2932 — DIPLOM INTELL METH/COMP KNOWL

RECORDING OF INTERVIEWS....SEE REC/INT

RECORDS....SEE OLD/STOR

RECTITUDE....SEE MORAL

RED/GUARD....RED GUARD

REDFIELD/R....ROBERT REDFIELD

REED/STAN....JUSTICE STANLEY REED

REES D. A2455

REFERENDUM....REFERENDUM; SEE ALSO PARTIC

REFORMERS....REFORMERS

B27
GOOCH G.P.,ENGLISH DEMOCRATIC IDEAS IN THE SEVENTEENTH CENTURY (2ND ED.). UK LAW SECT FORCES DIPLOM LEAD PARL/PROC REV ATTIT AUTHORIT...ANARCH CONCPT 17 PARLIAMENT CMN/WLTH REFORMERS. PAGE 54 A1100 — IDEA/COMP MAJORIT EX/STRUC CONSERVE

B65
SILVA SOLAR J.,EL DESARROLLO DE LA NUEVA SOCIEDAD EN AMERICA. L/A+17C SOCIETY AGRI PROB/SOLV DIPLOM PARTIC GP/REL OWN...POLICY SOC 20 REFORMERS. PAGE 133 A2716 — STRUCT ECO/UNDEV REGION CONTROL

B67
PIKE F.B.,FREEDOM AND REFORM IN LATIN AMERICA. BRAZIL URUGUAY CONSTN CULTURE SECT DIPLOM EDU/PROP PARTIC DRIVE ALL/VALS CATHISM...GEOG ANTHOL BIBLIOG REFORMERS BOLIV. PAGE 116 A2379 — L/A+17C ORD/FREE ECO/UNDEV REV

REGALA R. A2456

REGION....REGIONALISM

N
AMERICAN DOCUMENTATION INST,DOCUMENTATION ABSTRACTS. WOR+45 NAT/G COMPUTER CREATE TEC/DEV DIPLOM EDU/PROP REGION KNOWL...PHIL/SCI CLASSIF LING. PAGE 7 A0143 — BIBLIOG/A AUTOMAT COMPUT/IR R+D

N
MONPIED E.,BIBLIOGRAPHIE FEDERALISTE: ARTICLES ET DOCUMENTS PUBLIES DANS LES PERIODIQUES PARUS EN FRANCE NOV. 1945-OCT. 1950. EUR+WWI WOR+45 ADMIN REGION ATTIT MARXISM PACIFISM 20 EEC. PAGE 103 A2108 — BIBLIOG/A FEDERAL CENTRAL INT/ORG

N
BULLETIN ANALYTIQUE DE DOCUMENTATION POLITIQUE, ECONOMIQUE, ET SOCIAL CONTEMPORAIRE. FRANCE WOR+45 SOCIETY ECO/DEV ECO/UNDEV INT/ORG LOC/G PROB/SOLV FOR/AID LEAD REGION SOC. PAGE 1 A0006 — BIBLIOG/A DIPLOM NAT/COMP NAT/G

N
AFRICAN BIBLIOGRAPHIC CENTER,A CURRENT BIBLIOGRAPHY ON AFRICAN AFFAIRS. LAW CULTURE ECO/UNDEV LABOR SECT DIPLOM FOR/AID COLONIAL NAT/LISM...LING 20. PAGE 5 A0094 — BIBLIOG/A AFR NAT/G REGION

N
AIR UNIVERSITY LIBRARY,INDEX TO MILITARY PERIODICALS. FUT SPACE WOR+45 REGION ARMS/CONT NUC/PWR WAR PEACE INT/LAW. PAGE 5 A0105 — BIBLIOG/A FORCES NAT/G DIPLOM

N
ASIA FOUNDATION,LIBRARY NOTES. LAW CONSTN CULTURE SOCIETY ECO/UNDEV INT/ORG NAT/G COLONIAL LEAD REGION NAT/LISM ATTIT 20 UN. PAGE 9 A0189 — BIBLIOG/A ASIA S/ASIA DIPLOM

N
CORNELL UNIVERSITY LIBRARY,SOUTHEAST ASIA ACCESSIONS LIST. LAW SOCIETY STRUCT ECO/UNDEV POL/PAR TEC/DEV DIPLOM LEAD REGION. PAGE 31 A0626 — BIBLIOG S/ASIA NAT/G CULTURE

N
JOHNS HOPKINS UNIVERSITY LIB,RECENT ADDITIONS. WOR+45 ECO/UNDEV NAT/G POL/PAR FOR/AID INT/TRADE LEAD REGION ATTIT ALL/IDEOS TREND. PAGE 74 A1518 — BIBLIOG DIPLOM INT/LAW INT/ORG

N
WORLD PEACE FOUNDATION,DOCUMENTS OF INTERNATIONAL ORGANIZATIONS: A SELECTED BIBLIOGRAPHY. WOR+45 WOR-45 AGRI FINAN ACT/RES OP/RES INT/TRADE ADMIN ...CON/ANAL 20 UN UNESCO LEAGUE/NAT. PAGE 167 A3396 — BIBLIOG DIPLOM INT/ORG REGION

B00
GRIFFIN A.P.C.,LIST OF BOOKS RELATING TO THE THEORY OF COLONIZATION, GOVERNMENT OF DEPENDENCIES, PROTECTORATES, AND RELATED TOPICS. FRANCE GERMANY ITALY SPAIN UK USA-45 WOR-45 ECO/TAC ADMIN CONTROL REGION NAT/LISM ALL/VALS PWR...INT/LAW SOC 16/19. PAGE 56 A1149 — BIBLIOG/A COLONIAL GOV/REL DOMIN

B01
GRIFFIN A.P.C.,LIST OF BOOKS ON SAMOA (PAMPHLET). GERMANY S/ASIA UK USA-45 WOR-45 ECO/UNDEV REGION ALL/VALS ORD/FREE ALL/IDEOS...GEOG INT/LAW 19 SAMOA GUAM. PAGE 56 A1150 — BIBLIOG/A COLONIAL DIPLOM

B09
FREMANTLE H.E.S.,THE NEW NATION, A SURVEY OF THE CONDITION AND PROSPECTS OF SOUTH AFRICA. SOUTH/AFR CONSTN POL/PAR DIPLOM DOMIN COLONIAL WEALTH...SOC TREND 19. PAGE 49 A0996 — NAT/LISM SOVEREIGN RACE/REL REGION

N19
ASIAN-AFRICAN CONFERENCE,SELECTED DOCUMENTS OF THE BANDUNG CONFERENCE (PAMPHLET). S/ASIA PLAN ECO/TAC CONFER REGION REV NAT/LISM 20. PAGE 9 A0191 — NEUTRAL ECO/UNDEV COLONIAL DIPLOM

N19
FANI-KAYODE R.,BLACKISM (PAMPHLET). AFR WOR+45 INT/ORG BAL/PWR CONTROL CENTRAL...DECISION 20 UN. PAGE 44 A0896 — RACE/REL ECO/UNDEV REGION DIPLOM

N19
LISKA G.,THE GREATER MAGHREB: FROM INDEPENDENCE TO UNITY? (PAMPHLET). ALGERIA ISLAM MOROCCO PROB/SOLV BAL/PWR CONFER COLONIAL REPRESENT NAT/LISM 20 TUNIS. PAGE 90 A1835 — ECO/UNDEV REGION DIPLOM DOMIN

N19
TAYLOR T.G.,CANADA'S ROLE IN GEOPOLITICS (PAMPHLET). CANADA FUT USSR COLONIAL REGION WEALTH ...CHARTS 20. PAGE 142 A2901 — GEOG DIPLOM SOCIETY ECO/DEV

B22
FICHTE J.G.,ADDRESSES TO THE GERMAN NATION. GERMANY PRUSSIA ELITES NAT/G SECT CREATE INT/TRADE HEREDITY ...ART/METH LING 19 FRANK/PARL. PAGE 45 A0923 — NAT/LISM CULTURE EDU/PROP REGION

B22
WALSH E.,THE HISTORY AND NATURE OF INTERNATIONAL RELATIONS. ASIA L/A+17C MOD/EUR USA-45 WOR-45 NAT/G FORCES TOP/EX BAL/PWR REGION ATTIT ORD/FREE RESPECT — INT/ORG TIME/SEQ DIPLOM

...CONCPT HIST/WRIT TREND. PAGE 161 A3270

B27
PARRINGTON V.L.,MAIN CURRENTS IN AMERICAN THOUGHT (VOL.I). USA-45 AGRI POL/PAR DIPLOM TAX REGION REV 17/18 FRANKLIN/B JEFFERSN/T. PAGE 114 A2336
COLONIAL SECT FEEDBACK ALL/IDEOS

B27
SIEGFRIED A.,AMERICA COMES OF AGE: A FRENCH ANALYSIS (TRANS. BY H.H. HEMMING AND DORIS HEMMING). FRANCE UK POL/PAR WORKER TEC/DEV DIPLOM REGION RACE/REL ADJUST PRODUC HEREDITY...TIME/SEQ GP/COMP SOC/INTEG 20 DEMOCRAT REPUBLICAN KKK. PAGE 132 A2714
USA-45 CULTURE ECO/DEV SOC

B28
STUART G.H.,LATIN AMERICA AND THE UNITED STATES. USA-45 ECO/UNDEV INT/ORG NAT/G POL/PAR PLAN DOMIN EDU/PROP COLONIAL REGION COERCE ATTIT ALL/VALS ...POLICY GEOG TREND 19/20. PAGE 139 A2853
L/A+17C DIPLOM

B30
SMUTS J.C.,AFRICA AND SOME WORLD PROBLEMS. RHODESIA SOUTH/AFR CULTURE ECO/UNDEV INDUS INT/ORG SECT PROB/SOLV REGION GOV/REL DISCRIM ATTIT 19/20 LEAGUE/NAT LIVNGSTN/D NEGRO. PAGE 134 A2748
LEGIS AFR COLONIAL RACE/REL

B32
EAGLETON C.,INTERNATIONAL GOVERNMENT. BRAZIL FRANCE GERMANY ITALY UK USSR WOR-45 DELIB/GP TOP/EX PLAN ECO/TAC EDU/PROP LEGIT ADJUD REGION ARMS/CONT COERCE ATTIT PWR...GEOG MGT VAL/FREE LEAGUE/NAT 20. PAGE 40 A0816
INT/ORG JURID DIPLOM INT/LAW

B33
OHLIN B.,INTERREGIONAL AND INTERNATIONAL TRADE. USA-45 WOR-45 CULTURE FINAN MARKET CONSULT PLAN ECO/TAC ATTIT WEALTH...CONCPT MATH TOT/POP 20. PAGE 111 A2285
INT/ORG ECO/DEV INT/TRADE REGION

B37
SCHUSTER E.,GUIDE TO LAW AND LEGAL LITERATURE OF CENTRAL AMERICAN REPUBLICS. L/A+17C INT/ORG ADJUD SANCTION CRIME...JURID 19/20. PAGE 129 A2654
BIBLIOG/A REGION CT/SYS LAW

B38
HOBSON J.A.,IMPERIALISM. MOD/EUR UK WOR-45 CULTURE ECO/UNDEV NAT/G VOL/ASSN PLAN EDU/PROP LEGIT REGION COERCE ATTIT PWR...POLICY PLURIST TIME/SEQ GEN/LAWS 19/20. PAGE 66 A1348
DOMIN ECO/TAC BAL/PWR COLONIAL

B38
MATTHEWS M.A.,FEDERALISM: SELECT LIST OF REFERENCES ON FEDERAL GOVERNMENT REGIONALISM...EXAMPLES OF FEDERATIONS (PAMPHLET). WOR-45 CONSTN INT/ORG NAT/G 19/20 OAS LEAGUE/NAT. PAGE 96 A1976
BIBLIOG/A FEDERAL REGION DIPLOM

B39
BROWN J.F.,CONTEMPORARY WORLD POLITICS. WOR-45 NAT/G PLAN BAL/PWR EDU/PROP LEGIT REGION NAT/LISM ORD/FREE PWR SOVEREIGN...POLICY CONCPT HIST/WRIT TIME/SEQ GEN/LAWS LEAGUE/NAT. PAGE 20 A0403
INT/ORG DIPLOM PEACE

B41
WHITAKER A.P.,THE UNITED STATES AND THE INDEPENDENCE OF LATIN AMERICA, 1800-1830. PORTUGAL SPAIN USA-45 COLONIAL REGION SOVEREIGN...POLICY TIME/SEQ BIBLIOG/A 18/20. PAGE 163 A3329
DIPLOM L/A+17C CONCPT ORD/FREE

S41
WRIGHT Q.,"FUNDAMENTAL PROBLEMS OF INTERNATIONAL ORGANIZATION." UNIV WOR-45 STRUCT FORCES ACT/RES CREATE DOMIN EDU/PROP LEGIT REGION NAT/LISM ORD/FREE PWR RESPECT SOVEREIGN...JURID SOC CONCPT METH/CNCPT TIME/SEQ 20. PAGE 167 A3405
INT/ORG ATTIT PEACE

B45
BEVERIDGE W.,THE PRICE OF PEACE. GERMANY UK WOR+45 WOR-45 NAT/G FORCES CREATE LEGIT REGION WAR ATTIT KNOWL ORD/FREE PWR...POLICY NEW/IDEA GEN/LAWS LEAGUE/NAT 20 TREATY. PAGE 14 A0284
INT/ORG TREND PEACE

B45
CARR E.H.,NATIONALISM AND AFTER. FUT WOR-45 NAT/G VOL/ASSN EX/STRUC PLAN ROUTINE TOTALISM ATTIT HEALTH ORD/FREE PWR...CONCPT 20. PAGE 25 A0499
INT/ORG TREND NAT/LISM REGION

B45
ELTON G.E.,IMPERIAL COMMONWEALTH. INDIA UK DIPLOM DOMIN WAR NAT/LISM SOVEREIGN...TRADIT CHARTS T 15/20 CMN/WLTH AUSTRAL PRE/US/AM. PAGE 41 A0844
REGION CONCPT COLONIAL

B45
HILL N.,CLAIMS TO TERRITORY IN INTERNATIONAL LAW AND RELATIONS. WOR-45 NAT/G DOMIN EDU/PROP LEGIT REGION ROUTINE ORD/FREE PWR WEALTH...GEOG INT/LAW JURID 20. PAGE 65 A1332
INT/ORG ADJUD SOVEREIGN

B45
STRAUSZ-HUPE R.,THE BALANCE OF TOMORROW: POWER AND FOREIGN POLICY IN THE UNITED STATES. FUT USA+45 ECO/DEV EXTR/IND INT/ORG FORCES BAL/PWR REGION NUC/PWR...GEOG CHARTS 20 COLD/WAR EUROPE/W. PAGE 139 A2845
DIPLOM PWR POLICY WAR

B46
MITRANY D.,A WORKING PEACE SYSTEM. WOR+45 WOR-45 ECO/DEV INT/ORG NAT/G DELIB/GP ECO/TAC REGION ATTIT RIGID/FLEX...TREND GEN/LAWS LEAGUE/NAT 20. PAGE 102 A2091
VOL/ASSN PLAN PEACE SOVEREIGN

B47
BORGESE G.,COMMON CAUSE. LAW CONSTN SOCIETY STRATA ECO/DEV INT/ORG POL/PAR FORCES LEGIS TOP/EX CAP/ISM DIPLOM ADMIN EXEC ATTIT PWR 20. PAGE 17 A0339
WOR+45 NAT/G SOVEREIGN REGION

B48
FENWICK C.G.,INTERNATIONAL LAW. WOR+45 WOR-45 CONSTN NAT/G LEGIT CT/SYS REGION...CONCPT LEAGUE/NAT UN 20. PAGE 45 A0916
INT/ORG JURID INT/LAW

B48
MINISTERE FINANCES ET ECO,BULLETIN BIBLIOGRAPHIQUE. AFR EUR+WWI FRANCE CULTURE STRUCT FINAN NAT/G ACT/RES INT/TRADE ADMIN REGION PRODUC STAT. PAGE 102 A2088
BIBLIOG/A ECO/UNDEV TEC/DEV COLONIAL

B49
BOYD A.,WESTERN UNION: A STUDY OF THE TREND TOWARD EUROPEAN UNITY. FUT REGION NAT/LISM...POLICY IDEA/COMP BIBLIOG 14/20 OEEC ERASMUS/D COUNCL/EUR FULBRGHT/J NATO. PAGE 18 A0363
DIPLOM AGREE TREND INT/ORG

B49
PARMELEE M.,GEO-ECONOMIC REGIONAL AND WORLD FEDERATION. FUT WOR+45 WOR-45 SOCIETY VOL/ASSN PLAN ...METH/CNCPT SIMUL GEN/METH TOT/POP 20. PAGE 114 A2335
INT/ORG GEOG REGION

B50
GATZKE H.W.,GERMANY'S DRIVE TO THE WEST. BELGIUM GERMANY MOD/EUR AGRI INDUS POL/PAR FORCES DOMIN AGREE CONTROL REGION COERCE 20 TREATY WWI. PAGE 51 A1053
WAR POLICY NAT/G DIPLOM

B50
MONPIED E.,BIBLIOGRAPHIE FEDERALISTE: OUVRAGES CHOISIS (VOL. I, MIMEOGRAPHED PAPER). EUR+WWI DIPLOM ADMIN REGION ATTIT PACIFISM SOCISM...INT/LAW 19/20. PAGE 103 A2109
BIBLIOG/A FEDERAL CENTRAL INT/ORG

N51
MONPIED E.,FEDERALIST BIBLIOGRAPHY: ARTICLES AND DOCUMENTS PUBLISHED IN BRITISH PERIODICALS 1945-1951 (MIMEOGRAPHED). EUR+WWI UK WOR+45 DIPLOM REGION ATTIT SOCISM...INT/LAW 20. PAGE 103 A2110
BIBLIOG/A INT/ORG FEDERAL CENTRAL

B51
JENNINGS S.I.,THE COMMONWEALTH IN ASIA. CEYLON INDIA PAKISTAN S/ASIA UK CONSTN CULTURE SOCIETY STRATA STRUCT NAT/G POL/PAR EDU/PROP LEAD WAR 20 CMN/WLTH. PAGE 74 A1510
NAT/LISM REGION COLONIAL DIPLOM

B51
YOUNG T.C.,NEAR EASTERN CULTURE AND SOCIETY. ISLAM ECO/UNDEV SECT WRITING ATTIT HABITAT ORD/FREE 20. PAGE 169 A3438
CULTURE STRUCT REGION DIPLOM

L51
WHITAKER A.P.,"DEVELOPMENT OF AMERICAN REGIONALISM: THE ORGANIZATION OF AMERICAN STATES." L/A+17C USA+45 VOL/ASSN DELIB/GP FORCES TOP/EX ACT/RES ECO/TAC CT/SYS REGION PEACE ALL/VALS OAS 20. PAGE 163 A3330
INT/ORG TIME/SEQ DETER

B54
CHEEVER D.S.,ORGANIZING FOR PEACE. FUT WOR+45 WOR-45 STRATA STRUCT NAT/G CREATE DIPLOM LEGIT REGION COERCE DETER PEACE ATTIT DRIVE ALL/VALS ...TIME/SEQ TREND UN LEAGUE/NAT. PAGE 26 A0525
INT/ORG

B54
NORTHROP F.S.C.,EUROPEAN UNION AND UNITED STATES FOREIGN POLICY: A STUDY IN SOCIOLOGICAL JURISPRUDENCE. EUR+WWI MOD/EUR USA+45 SOCIETY STRUCT NAT/G CREATE ECO/TAC DOMIN EDU/PROP REGION ATTIT RIGID/FLEX HEALTH ORD/FREE WEALTH ...METH/CNCPT TIME/SEQ TREND. PAGE 110 A2256
INT/ORG SOC DIPLOM

B54
WHITAKER A.P.,THE WESTERN HEMISPHERE IDEA. USA+45 USA-45 CONSTN INT/ORG NAT/G DIPLOM SOVEREIGN...GEOG TIME/SEQ OAS 19/20 MONROE/DOC. PAGE 164 A3331
L/A+17C CONCPT REGION

B55
STILLMAN C.W.,AFRICA IN THE MODERN WORLD. AFR USA+45 WOR+45 INT/TRADE COLONIAL PARTIC REGION GOV/REL RACE/REL 20. PAGE 138 A2826
ECO/UNDEV DIPLOM POLICY STRUCT

B55
THOMPSON V.,MINORITY PROBLEMS IN SOUTHEAST ASIA. CAMBODIA CHINA/COM LAOS S/ASIA KIN NAT/G SECT PROB/SOLV EDU/PROP REGION GP/REL RACE/REL MARXISM ...SOC 20 BUDDHISM UN. PAGE 143 A2933
INGP/REL GEOG DIPLOM STRUCT

L55
KISER M.,"ORGANIZATION OF AMERICAN STATES." L/A+17C USA+45 ECO/UNDEV INT/ORG NAT/G PLAN TEC/DEV DIPLOM ECO/TAC INT/TRADE EDU/PROP ADMIN ALL/VALS...POLICY MGT RECORD ORG/CHARTS OAS 20. PAGE 80 A1639
VOL/ASSN ECO/DEV REGION

S55
DE SMITH S.A.,"CONSTITUTIONAL MONARCHY IN BURGANDA." AFR UGANDA UK STRUCT CHIEF REGION INGP/REL ADJUST NAT/LISM SOVEREIGN CONSERVE ...POLICY 19/20 BURGANDA. PAGE 35 A0712
NAT/G DIPLOM CONSTN COLONIAL

B56
CHANG C.J.,THE MINORITY GROUPS OF YUNN AN AND CHINESE POLITICAL EXPANSION INTO SOUTHEAST ASIA (DOCTORAL THESIS). ASIA CHINA/COM S/ASIA FORCES TEC/DEV DIPLOM EDU/PROP...GEOG BIBLIOG 20. PAGE 26
GP/REL REGION DOMIN MARXISM

A0520

B56
HOUSTON J.A.,LATIN AMERICA IN THE UNITED NATIONS. CONSULT DIPLOM LEGIT ROUTINE ATTIT ORD/FREE PWR ...JURID OBS RECORD TIME/SEQ CHARTS 20 UN. PAGE 68 A1395 — L/A+17C INT/ORG INT/LAW REGION

B56
TOYNBEE A.,THE WAR AND THE NEUTRALS. L/A+17C PORTUGAL SPAIN SWEDEN SWITZERLND TURKEY WOR+45 WOR-45 ECO/TAC CONFER CONTROL REGION 20. PAGE 145 A2957 — NEUTRAL WAR INT/TRADE DIPLOM

B57
ARON R.,L'UNIFICATION ECONOMIQUE DE L'EUROPE. EUR+WWI SWITZERLND UK INT/ORG NAT/G REGION NAT/LISM ORD/FREE PWR...CONCPT METH/CNCPT OBS TREND STERTYP GEN/LAWS EEC 20. PAGE 9 A0181 — VOL/ASSN ECO/TAC

B57
DEUTSCH K.W.,POLITICAL COMMUNITY AND THE NORTH ATLANTIC AREA: INTERNATIONAL ORGANIZATION IN THE LIGHT OF HISTORICAL EXPERIENCE. MOD/EUR USA+45 USA-45 SOCIETY FORCES TOP/EX CREATE PLAN DIPLOM DOMIN EDU/PROP LEGIT ATTIT ORD/FREE PWR...SAMP/SIZ TIME/SEQ CHARTS TOT/POP. PAGE 36 A0736 — EUR+WWI INT/ORG PEACE REGION

B57
JENKS C.W.,THE INTERNATIONAL PROTECTION OF TRADE UNION FREEDOM. FUT WOR+45 WOR-45 VOL/ASSN DELIB/GP CT/SYS REGION ROUTINE...JURID METH/CNCPT RECORD TIME/SEQ CHARTS ILO WORK OAS 20. PAGE 73 A1504 — LABOR INT/ORG

B57
LISKA G.,INTERNATIONAL EQUILIBRIUM. WOR+45 WOR-45 SOCIETY INT/ORG FORCES DETER ATTIT ORD/FREE PWR ...GEN/LAWS 19/20. PAGE 90 A1836 — NAT/G BAL/PWR REGION DIPLOM

B57
SEABURY P.,THE WANING OF SOUTHERN "INTERNATIONALISM" (PAMPHLET). USA+45 USA-45 INT/ORG LEGIS MAJORITY...TREND 20 SOUTH/US MIDWEST/US. PAGE 131 A2676 — DIPLOM REGION ATTIT ISOLAT

B57
TRIFFIN R.,EUROPE AND THE MONEY MUDDLE. USA+45 INT/ORG NAT/G CONSULT PLAN ECO/TAC EXEC ROUTINE BAL/PAY WEALTH...METH/CNCPT OBS TREND CHARTS STERTYP GEN/METH EEC VAL/FREE ECSC. PAGE 145 A2962 — EUR+WWI ECO/DEV REGION

B57
US PRES CITIZEN ADVISERS,REPORT TO THE PRESIDENT ON THE MUTUAL SECURITY PROGRAM. COM USA+45 WOR+45 FINAN INDUS PLAN BUDGET CAP/ISM DIPLOM FOR/AID INT/TRADE REGION 20 SECUR/PROG. PAGE 155 A3163 — BAL/PWR FORCES INT/ORG ECO/TAC

L57
HAAS E.B.,"REGIONAL INTEGRATION AND NATIONAL POLICY." WOR+45 VOL/ASSN DELIB/GP EX/STRUC ECO/TAC DOMIN EDU/PROP LEGIT COERCE ATTIT PERCEPT KNOWL ...TIME/SEQ COLD/WAR 20 UN. PAGE 59 A1203 — INT/ORG ORD/FREE REGION

B58
ALMEYDA M.C.,REFLEXIONES POLITICAS. CHILE L/A+17C USA+45 INT/ORG POL/PAR ECO/TAC PARTIC ATTIT 20. PAGE 6 A0128 — ECO/UNDEV REGION DIPLOM INT/TRADE

B58
CAMPBELL J.C.,DEFENSE OF THE MIDDLE EAST: PROBLEMS OF AMERICAN POLICY. ISLAM USA+45 INT/ORG NAT/G EX/STRUC FORCES ECO/TAC DOMIN EDU/PROP LEGIT REGION COERCE...METH/CNCPT COLD/WAR TOT/POP 20. PAGE 23 A0474 — TOP/EX ORD/FREE DIPLOM

B58
KINDLEBERGER C.P.,INTERNATIONAL ECONOMICS. WOR+45 WOR-45 ECO/DEV ECO/UNDEV FINAN VOL/ASSN ACT/RES DIPLOM ECO/TAC LEGIT REGION ATTIT DRIVE ORD/FREE WEALTH...POLICY STAT TREND GEN/LAWS EEC ECSC OEEC 20. PAGE 79 A1620 — INT/ORG BAL/PWR TARIFFS

B58
MOORE B.T.,NATO AND THE FUTURE OF EUROPE. EUR+WWI FUT USA+45 ECO/DEV INDUS MARKET NAT/G VOL/ASSN FORCES DIPLOM NUC/PWR ORD/FREE...CONCPT CHARTS ORG/CHARTS CMN/WLTH 20 NATO. PAGE 103 A2122 — INT/ORG REGION

B58
SCITOUSKY T.,ECONOMIC THEORY AND WESTERN EUROPEAN INTEGRATION. EUR+WWI INT/ORG ACT/RES INT/TRADE REGION BAL/PAY WEALTH...METH/CNCPT STAT CHARTS GEN/METH ECSC TOT/POP EEC OEEC 20. PAGE 130 A2668 — ECO/TAC

B58
WIGGINS J.W.,FOREIGN AID REEXAMINED: A CRITICAL APPRAISAL. CHINA/COM INDONESIA USA+45 FINAN INT/TRADE REGION NAT/LISM ATTIT...CENSUS 20. PAGE 164 A3342 — FOR/AID DIPLOM ECO/UNDEV SOVEREIGN

L58
HYVARINEN R.,"MONISTIC AND PLURALISTIC INTERPRETATIONS IN THE STUDY OF INTERNATIONAL POLITICS." COLONIAL REGION RACE/REL DISCRIM TOTALISM SOVEREIGN...INT/LAW PHIL/SCI CONCPT BIBLIOG 20. PAGE 70 A1429 — DIPLOM PLURISM INT/ORG METH

S58
ANDERSON N.,"INTERNATIONAL SEMINARS: AN ANALYSIS AND AN EVALUATION." WOR+45 R+D ACT/RES CREATE PLAN REGION ATTIT KNOWL SKILL...SOC REC/INT PERS/TEST CHARTS 20. PAGE 8 A0158 — INT/ORG DELIB/GP

S58
BOURBON-BUSSET J.,"HOW DECISIONS ARE MADE IN FOREIGN POLITICS: PSYCHOLOGY IN INTERNATIONAL POLITICS." WOR+45 NAT/G SECT REGION WAR MORAL ...CONCPT OBS STERTYP GEN/LAWS TOT/POP COLD/WAR 20. PAGE 17 A0350 — INT/ORG DELIB/GP DIPLOM

C58
FIFIELD R.H.,"THE DIPLOMACY OF SOUTHEAST ASIA: 1945-1958." INT/ORG NAT/G COLONIAL REGION...CHARTS BIBLIOG 20 UN. PAGE 45 A0927 — S/ASIA DIPLOM NAT/LISM

B59
BALL M.M.,NATO AND THE EUROPEAN MOVEMENT. EUR+WWI USA+45 INT/ORG FORCES BAL/PWR EDU/PROP LEGIT REGION ATTIT ORD/FREE PWR...STAT OBS TIME/SEQ TREND CHARTS ORG/CHARTS STERTYP COLD/WAR EEC OEEC 20 NATO. PAGE 10 A0212 — DELIB/GP STRUCT

B59
DIEBOLD W. JR.,THE SCHUMAN PLAN: A STUDY IN ECONOMIC COOPERATION, 1950-1959. EUR+WWI FRANCE GERMANY USA+45 EXTR/IND CONSULT DELIB/GP PLAN DIPLOM ECO/TAC INT/TRADE ROUTINE ORD/FREE WEALTH ...METH/CNCPT STAT CONT/OBS INT TIME/SEQ ECSC 20. PAGE 37 A0759 — INT/ORG REGION

B59
EGYPTIAN SOCIETY OF INT LAW,THE MONROVIA CONFERENCE (PAMPHLET). AFR ALGERIA FRANCE UAR CONFER REGION NUC/PWR WAR DISCRIM 20 SAHARA AFR/STATES. PAGE 40 A0826 — COLONIAL SOVEREIGN RACE/REL DIPLOM

B59
TUNSTALL W.C.B.,THE COMMONWEALTH AND REGIONAL DEFENCE (PAMPHLET). UK LAW VOL/ASSN PLAN AGREE REGION WAR ORD/FREE 20 CMN/WLTH NATO SEATO TREATY. PAGE 146 A2977 — INT/ORG FORCES DIPLOM

B59
YRARRAZAVAL E.,AMERICA LATINE EN LA GUERRA FRIA. EUR+WWI L/A+17C USA+45 USSR WOR+45 INDUS INT/ORG NAT/LISM...POLICY COLD/WAR. PAGE 169 A3439 — REGION DIPLOM ECO/UNDEV INT/TRADE

L59
MURPHY J.C.,"SOME IMPLICATIONS OF EUROPE'S COMMON MARKET. IN (COOK P, ECONOMIC DEVELOPMENT AND INTERNATIONAL TRADE.." EUR+WWI ECO/DEV DIST/IND INDUS NAT/G PLAN ECO/TAC INT/TRADE WEALTH...STAT TREND OEEC TOT/POP 20 EEC. PAGE 106 A2178 — MARKET INT/ORG REGION

S59
HARTT J.,"ANTARCTICA: ITS IMMEDIATE PRACTICALITIES." FUT USA+45 USSR WOR+45 INT/ORG NAT/G CREATE TEC/DEV REGION KNOWL WEALTH...GEOG 20 ANTARTICA. PAGE 62 A1276 — VOL/ASSN ORD/FREE DIPLOM

S59
PLAZA G.,"FOR A REGIONAL MARKET IN LATIN AMERICA." FUT L/A+17C CULTURE INDUS NAT/G ECO/TAC INT/TRADE ATTIT WEALTH...NEW/IDEA TREND OAS 20. PAGE 116 A2389 — MARKET INT/ORG REGION

S59
SUTTON F.X.,"REPRESENTATION AND THE NATURE OF POLITICAL SYSTEMS." UNIV WOR-45 CULTURE SOCIETY STRATA INT/ORG FORCES JUDGE DOMIN LEGIT EXEC REGION REPRESENT ATTIT ORD/FREE RESPECT...SOC HIST/WRIT TIME/SEQ. PAGE 140 A2867 — NAT/G CONCPT

B60
KRISTENSEN T.,THE ECONOMIC WORLD BALANCE. FUT WOR+45 CULTURE ECO/DEV BAL/PWR INT/TRADE REGION PWR WEALTH...STAT TREND CHARTS 20. PAGE 82 A1685 — ECO/UNDEV ECO/TAC FOR/AID

B60
LINDSAY K.,EUROPEAN ASSEMBLIES: THE EXPERIMENTAL PERIOD 1949-1959. EUR+WWI ECO/DEV NAT/G POL/PAR LEGIS TOP/EX ACT/RES PLAN ECO/TAC DOMIN LEGIT ROUTINE ATTIT DRIVE ORD/FREE PWR SKILL...SOC CONCPT TREND CHARTS GEN/LAWS VAL/FREE. PAGE 89 A1823 — VOL/ASSN INT/ORG REGION

B60
LISTER L.,EUROPE'S COAL AND STEEL COMMUNITY. FRANCE GERMANY STRUCT ECO/DEV EXTR/IND INDUS MARKET NAT/G DELIB/GP ECO/TAC INT/TRADE EDU/PROP ATTIT RIGID/FLEX ORD/FREE PWR WEALTH...CONCPT STAT TIME/SEQ CHARTS ECSC 20. PAGE 90 A1843 — EUR+WWI INT/ORG REGION

B60
RITNER P.,THE DEATH OF AFRICA. USA+45 ECO/UNDEV DIPLOM ECO/TAC REGION RACE/REL NAT/LISM ORD/FREE ...POLICY 20 NEGRO. PAGE 121 A2485 — AFR SOCIETY FUT TASK

B60
THE AFRICA 1960 COMMITTEE,MANDATE IN TRUST; THE PROBLEM OF SOUTH WEST AFRICA. GERMANY STRUCT REGION SANCTION CHOOSE DISCRIM...INT/LAW 20 AFRICA/SW UN LEAGUE/NAT TRUST/TERR. PAGE 142 A2910 — NAT/G DIPLOM COLONIAL RACE/REL

L60
HAAS E.B.,"CONSENSUS FORMATION IN THE COUNCIL OF EUROPE." EUR+WWI NAT/G DELIB/GP DIPLOM REGION CHOOSE PWR SOVEREIGN...RELATIV NEW/IDEA QUANT CHARTS INDEX TOT/POP OEEC 20 COUNCL/EUR. PAGE 59 A1206 — POL/PAR INT/ORG STAT

S60
GINSBURGS G.,"PEKING-LHASA-NEW DELHI." CHINA/COM FUT INDIA S/ASIA KIN NAT/G PROVS SECT FORCES BAL/PWR ECO/TAC DOMIN EDU/PROP LEGIT ADMIN REGION — ASIA COERCE DIPLOM

GUERRILLA PWR...TREND TIBET 20. PAGE 52 A1074

S60
HAYTON R.D.,"THE ANTARCTIC SETTLEMENT OF 1959." FUT USA+45 WOR+45 WOR-45 STRUCT R+D INT/ORG EX/STRUC CREATE TEC/DEV LEGIT PEACE ATTIT SOVEREIGN ...TIME/SEQ 20 TREATY IGY. PAGE 63 A1297
DELIB/GP JURID DIPLOM REGION

S60
MORA J.A.,"THE ORGANIZATION OF AMERICAN STATES." USA+45 LAW ECO/UNDEV VOL/ASSN DELIB/GP PLAN BAL/PWR EDU/PROP ADMIN DRIVE RIGID/FLEX ORD/FREE WEALTH ...TIME/SEQ GEN/LAWS OAS 20. PAGE 103 A2126
L/A+17C INT/ORG REGION

S60
MORALES C.J.,"TRADE AND ECONOMIC INTEGRATION IN LATIN AMERICA." FUT L/A+17C LAW STRATA ECO/UNDEV DIST/IND INDUS LABOR NAT/G LEGIS ECO/TAC ADMIN RIGID/FLEX WEALTH...CONCPT NEW/IDEA CONT/OBS TIME/SEQ WORK 20. PAGE 104 A2128
FINAN INT/TRADE REGION

S60
NANES A.,"THE EUROPEAN COMMUNITY AND THE UNITED STATES: EVOLVING RELATIONS." EUR+WWI USA+45 WOR+45 ECO/UNDEV MARKET NAT/G DELIB/GP PLAN LEGIT ATTIT PWR WEALTH...CONCPT STAT TIME/SEQ CON/ANAL EEC OEEC 20 EURATOM. PAGE 107 A2194
INT/ORG REGION

B61
ANSPRENGER F.,POLITIK IM SCHWARZEN AFRIKA. FRANCE NAT/G DIPLOM REGION REV NAT/LISM...CHARTS BIBLIOG 19/20. PAGE 8 A0164
AFR COLONIAL SOVEREIGN

B61
BAGU S.,ARGENTINA EN EL MUNDO. L/A+17C INDUS INT/TRADE WAR ATTIT ROLE...TREND 19/20 ARGEN OAS. PAGE 10 A0202
DIPLOM INT/ORG REGION ECO/UNDEV

B61
BECHHOEFER B.G.,POSTWAR NEGOTIATIONS FOR ARMS CONTROL. COM EUR+WWI USSR INT/ORG NAT/G ACT/RES BAL/PWR DIPLOM ECO/TAC EDU/PROP ADMIN REGION DETER NUC/PWR WAR WEAPON PEACE ATTIT PWR...POLICY TIME/SEQ COLD/WAR CONGRESS 20. PAGE 12 A0244
USA+45 ARMS/CONT

B61
CAMERON J.,THE AFRICAN REVOLUTION. AFR UK ECO/UNDEV POL/PAR REGION RACE/REL DISCRIM PWR CONSERVE ...CONCPT SOC/INTEG 20 NEGRO. PAGE 23 A0472
REV COLONIAL ORD/FREE DIPLOM

B61
DIA M.,THE AFRICAN NATIONS AND WORLD SOLIDARITY. ISLAM CULTURE ELITES ECO/DEV ECO/UNDEV INT/ORG NAT/G PLAN ECO/TAC INT/TRADE EDU/PROP NAT/LISM ATTIT DRIVE ORD/FREE WEALTH...SOCIALIST CONCPT CON/ANAL GEN/LAWS TOT/POP 20. PAGE 37 A0753
AFR REGION SOCISM

B61
FRISCH D.,ARMS REDUCTION: PROGRAM AND ISSUES. USA+45 INT/ORG NAT/G ACT/RES REGION NUC/PWR ATTIT PWR...POLICY 20. PAGE 49 A1010
PLAN FORCES ARMS/CONT DIPLOM

B61
HADDAD J.A.,REVOLUCAO CUBANA E REVOLUCAO BRASILEIRA. BRAZIL CUBA L/A+17C STRATA AGRI WORKER EDU/PROP REGION...POLICY NAT/COMP 20. PAGE 59 A1210
REV ORD/FREE DIPLOM ECO/UNDEV

B61
HOLDSWORTH M.,SOVIET AFRICAN STUDIES 1918-1959. USSR ACADEM NAT/G DIPLOM REGION KNOWL 20. PAGE 66 A1366
BIBLIOG/A AFR HABITAT NAT/COMP

B61
NOLLAU G.,INTERNATIONAL COMMUNISM AND WORLD REVOLUTION: HISTORY AND METHODS. RUSSIA USSR INT/ORG NAT/G POL/PAR VOL/ASSN FORCES BAL/PWR DIPLOM EXEC REGION WAR ATTIT PWR MARXISM...CONCPT TIME/SEQ COLD/WAR 19/20. PAGE 102 A2100
COM REV

B61
RIENOW R.,CONTEMPORARY INTERNATIONAL POLITICS. WOR+45 INT/ORG BAL/PWR EDU/PROP COLONIAL NEUTRAL REGION WAR PEACE...INT/LAW 20 COLD/WAR UN. PAGE 121 A2476
DIPLOM PWR POLICY NAT/G

B61
SHAPP W.R.,FIELD ADMINISTRATION IN THE UNITED NATIONS SYSTEM. FINAN PROB/SOLV INSPECT DIPLOM EXEC REGION ROUTINE EFFICIENCY ROLE...INT CHARTS 20 UN. PAGE 131 A2694
INT/ORG ADMIN GP/REL FOR/AID

S61
ANGLIN D.,"UNITED STATES OPPOSITION TO CANADIAN MEMBERSHIP IN THE PAN AMERICAN UNION: A CANADIAN VIEW." L/A+17C UK USA+45 VOL/ASSN DELIB/GP EX/STRUC PLAN DIPLOM DOMIN REGION ATTIT RIGID/FLEX PWR ...RELATIV CONCPT STERTYP CMN/WLTH OAS 20. PAGE 8 A0162
INT/ORG CANADA

S61
HAAS E.B.,"INTERNATIONAL INTEGRATION: THE EUROPEAN AND THE UNIVERSAL PROCESS." EUR+WWI FUT WOR+45 NAT/G EX/STRUC ATTIT DRIVE ORD/FREE PWR...CONCPT GEN/LAWS OEEC 20 NATO COUNCL/EUR. PAGE 59 A1207
INT/ORG TREND REGION

B62
BURTON J.W.,PEACE THEORY: PRECONDITIONS OF DISARMAMENT. COM EUR+WWI USA+45 NAT/G FORCES BAL/PWR DIPLOM ECO/TAC EDU/PROP REGION COERCE DETER PEACE ATTIT PWR TOT/POP COLD/WAR 20. PAGE 22 A0446
INT/ORG PLAN ARMS/CONT

B62
DUTOIT B.,LA NEUTRALITE SUISSE A L'HEURE EUROPEENNE. EUR+WWI MOD/EUR INT/ORG NAT/G VOL/ASSN PLAN BAL/PWR LEGIT NEUTRAL REGION PEACE ORD/FREE SOVEREIGN...CONCPT OBS TIME/SEQ TREND STERTYP VAL/FREE LEAGUE/NAT UN 20. PAGE 40 A0812
ATTIT DIPLOM SWITZERLND

B62
GUENA Y.,HISTORIQUE DE LA COMMUNAUTE. FUT ECO/UNDEV NAT/G PLAN EDU/PROP COLONIAL REGION NAT/LISM ALL/VALS SOVEREIGN...CONCPT OBS CHARTS 20. PAGE 58 A1186
AFR VOL/ASSN FOR/AID FRANCE

B62
KRAFT J.,THE GRAND DESIGN. EUR+WWI USA+45 AGRI FINAN INDUS MARKET INT/ORG NAT/G PLAN ECO/TAC TARIFFS REGION DRIVE ORD/FREE WEALTH...POLICY OBS TREND EEC 20. PAGE 82 A1674
VOL/ASSN ECO/DEV INT/TRADE

B62
LAWSON R.,INTERNATIONAL REGIONAL ORGANIZATIONS. WOR+45 NAT/G VOL/ASSN CONSULT LEGIS EDU/PROP LEGIT ADMIN EXEC ROUTINE HEALTH PWR WEALTH...JURID EEC COLD/WAR 20 UN. PAGE 86 A1752
INT/ORG DELIB/GP REGION

B62
MEADE J.E.,CASE STUDIES IN EUROPEAN ECONOMIC UNION. BELGIUM EUR+WWI LUXEMBOURG NAT/G INT/TRADE REGION ROUTINE WEALTH...METH/CNCPT STAT CHARTS ECSC TOT/POP OEEC EEC 20. PAGE 99 A2028
INT/ORG ECO/TAC

B62
MOON P.,DIVIDE AND QUIT. INDIA PAKISTAN STRATA DELIB/GP PLAN DIPLOM REPRESENT GP/REL INGP/REL CONSEN DISCRIM...OBS 20. PAGE 103 A2119
WAR REGION ISOLAT SECT

B62
ROBERTSON B.C.,REGIONAL DEVELOPMENT IN THE EUROPEAN ECONOMIC COMMUNITY. EUR+WWI FRANCE FUT ITALY UK ECO/UNDEV WORKER ACT/RES PROB/SOLV TEC/DEV ECO/TAC INT/TRADE EEC. PAGE 122 A2499
PLAN ECO/DEV INT/ORG REGION

B62
SCHMITT H.A.,THE PATH TO EUROPEAN UNITY. EUR+WWI USA+45 PLAN TEC/DEV DIPLOM FOR/AID CONFER...INT/LAW 20 EEC EURCOALSTL MARSHL/PLN UNIFICA. PAGE 128 A2634
INT/ORG INT/TRADE REGION ECO/DEV

B62
UNECA LIBRARY,BOOKS ON AFRICA IN THE UNECA LIBRARY. WOR+45 AGRI INT/ORG NAT/G PLAN WRITING REGION...SOC STAT UN. PAGE 147 A3008
BIBLIOG AFR ECO/UNDEV TEC/DEV

B62
UNECA LIBRARY,NEW ACQUISITIONS IN THE UNECA LIBRARY. LAW NAT/G PLAN PROB/SOLV TEC/DEV ADMIN REGION...GEOG SOC 20 UN. PAGE 147 A3009
BIBLIOG AFR ECO/UNDEV INT/ORG

B62
YALEN R.,REGIONALISM AND WORLD ORDER. EUR+WWI WOR+45 WOR-45 INT/ORG VOL/ASSN DELIB/GP FORCES TOP/EX BAL/PWR DIPLOM DOMIN REGION ARMS/CONT PWR ...JURID HYPO/EXP COLD/WAR 20. PAGE 168 A3427
ORD/FREE POLICY

S62
DEUTSCH K.W.,"TOWARDS WESTERN EUROPEAN INTEGRATION: AN INTERIM ASSESSMENT." EUR+WWI STRUCT ECO/DEV INT/ORG ECO/TAC INT/TRADE EDU/PROP PEACE ATTIT DRIVE PWR SOVEREIGN...PSY SOC TIME/SEQ CHARTS STERTYP 20. PAGE 36 A0741
VOL/ASSN RIGID/FLEX REGION

S62
FENWICK C.G.,"ISSUES AT PUNTA DEL ESTE: NON-INTERVENTION VS COLLECTIVE SECURITY." L/A+17C USA+45 VOL/ASSN DELIB/GP ECO/TAC LEGIT ADJUD REGION ORD/FREE OAS COLD/WAR 20. PAGE 45 A0917
INT/ORG CUBA

S62
FISCHER G.,"UNE NOUVELLE ORGANIZATION REGIONALE: L'ASA." S/ASIA WOR+45 ECO/UNDEV VOL/ASSN PERCEPT RIGID/FLEX...TIME/SEQ 20 ASA. PAGE 46 A0935
INT/ORG DRIVE REGION

S62
MARIAS J.,"A PROGRAM FOR EUROPE." EUR+WWI INT/ORG NAT/G PLAN DIPLOM DOMIN PWR...STERTYP TOT/POP 20. PAGE 95 A1938
VOL/ASSN CREATE REGION

S62
ORBAN M.,"L'EUROPE EN FORMATION ET SES PROBLEMES." EUR+WWI FUT WOR+45 WOR-45 INTELL STRUCT DELIB/GP ACT/RES FEDERAL RIGID/FLEX WEALTH...CONCPT TIME/SEQ OEEC 20. PAGE 112 A2295
INT/ORG PLAN REGION

S62
PIQUEMAL M.,"LES PROBLEMES DES UNIONS D'ETATS EN AFRIQUE NOIRE." FRANCE SOCIETY INT/ORG NAT/G DELIB/GP PLAN LEGIT ADMIN COLONIAL ROUTINE ATTIT ORD/FREE PWR...GEOG METH/CNCPT 20. PAGE 116 A2382
AFR ECO/UNDEV REGION

S62
SPECTOR I.,"SOVIET POLICY IN ASIA: A REAPPRAISAL." ASIA CHINA/COM COM INDIA INDONESIA ECO/UNDEV INT/ORG DOMIN EDU/PROP REGION RESPECT...CONCPT TREND TOT/POP COLD/WAR 20 CHINJAP. PAGE 135 A2774
S/ASIA PWR FOR/AID USSR

S62
SPENSER J.H.,"AFRICA AT THE UNITED NATIONS: SOME OBSERVATIONS." FUT ECO/UNDEV NAT/G CONSULT DELIB/GP PLAN BAL/PWR ECO/TAC EDU/PROP ATTIT RIGID/FLEX HEALTH ORD/FREE PWR WEALTH...POLICY CONCPT OBS
AFR INT/ORG REGION

TREND STERTYP GEN/METH UN VAL/FREE. PAGE 136 A2786

S62
SPRINGER H.W.,"FEDERATION IN THE CARIBBEAN: AN ATTEMPT THAT FAILED." L/A+17C ECO/UNDEV INT/ORG POL/PAR PROVS LEGIS CREATE PLAN LEGIT ADMIN FEDERAL ATTIT DRIVE PERSON ORD/FREE PWR...POLICY GEOG PSY CONCPT OBS CARIBBEAN CMN/WLTH 20. PAGE 136 A2791
VOL/ASSN NAT/G REGION

B63
BELOFF M.,THE UNITED STATES AND THE UNITY OF EUROPE. EUR+WWI UK USA+45 WOR+45 VOL/ASSN DIPLOM REGION ATTIT PWR...CONCPT EEC OEEC 20 NATO. PAGE 13 A0261
ECO/DEV INT/ORG

B63
CANELAS O.A.,RADIOGRAFIA DE LA ALIANZA PARA EL ATRASO. L/A+17C USA+45 ECO/TAC DOMIN COLONIAL NAT/LISM...SOCIALIST NAT/COMP 20. PAGE 23 A0476
REV DIPLOM ECO/UNDEV REGION

B63
CENTRO PARA EL DESARROLLO,LA ALIANZA PARA EL PROGRESO Y EL DESARROLLO SOCIAL DE AMERICA LATINA. L/A+17C INT/ORG DIPLOM ECO/TAC INT/TRADE ATTIT 20. PAGE 25 A0512
ECO/UNDEV FOR/AID PLAN REGION

B63
CERAMI C.A.,ALLIANCE BORN OF DANGER. EUR+WWI USA+45 USSR ECO/DEV INDUS VOL/ASSN ECO/TAC REGION ATTIT MARXISM ATLAN/ALL 20 NATO EEC. PAGE 25 A0514
DIPLOM INT/ORG NAT/G POLICY

B63
CREMEANS C.,THE ARABS AND THE WORLD: NASSER'S ARAB NATIONALIST POLICY. FUT ISLAM UAR USA+45 SOCIETY STRATA NAT/G POL/PAR PLAN DIPLOM EDU/PROP LEGIT DRIVE ALL/VALS...INT TIME/SEQ CHARTS 20 NASSER/G. PAGE 33 A0662
TOP/EX ATTIT REGION NAT/LISM

B63
ERHARD L.,THE ECONOMICS OF SUCCESS. GERMANY/W WOR+45 LABOR CHIEF TAX REGION COST DEMAND ANTHOL. PAGE 42 A0860
ECO/DEV INT/TRADE PLAN DIPLOM

B63
ETHIOPIAN MINISTRY INFORMATION,AFRICAN SUMMIT CONFERENCE ADDIS ABABA, ETHIOPIA, 1963. ETHIOPIA DELIB/GP COLONIAL NAT/LISM...POLICY DECISION 20. PAGE 42 A0865
AFR CONFER REGION DIPLOM

B63
GOLDWIN R.A.,FOREIGN AND MILITARY POLICY. COM USSR WOR+45 ECO/DEV INT/ORG FORCES PLAN ECO/TAC REGION ARMS/CONT MARXISM 20 UN. PAGE 54 A1097
DIPLOM POLICY PWR NAT/G

B63
GORDON L.,A NEW DEAL FOR LATIN AMERICA. L/A+17C USA+45 CULTURE NAT/G TEC/DEV DIPLOM FOR/AID REGION TASK...POLICY 20 DEPT/STATE. PAGE 54 A1115
ECO/UNDEV ECO/TAC INT/ORG PLAN

B63
GREAT BRITAIN CENTRAL OFF INF,CONSULTATION AND CO-OPERATION IN THE COMMONWEALTH. LAW R+D FORCES PLAN EDU/PROP CONFER INGP/REL...GEOG CENSUS 19/20 CMN/WLTH. PAGE 55 A1133
DIPLOM DELIB/GP VOL/ASSN REGION

B63
JAIRAZBHOY R.A.,FOREIGN INFLUENCE IN ANCIENT INDIA. INDIA ELITES SECT DIPLOM EDU/PROP COLONIAL REGION GP/REL...ART/METH LING WORSHIP +/14 GRECO/ROMN MESOPOTAM PERSIA PARTH/SASS. PAGE 73 A1491
CULTURE SOCIETY COERCE DOMIN

B63
KLEIMAN R.,ATLANTIC CRISIS; AMERICAN DIPLOMACY CONFRONTS A RESURGENT EUROPE. EUR+WWI USA+45 ECO/DEV AGRI NAT/G CHIEF FORCES PLAN LEAD ATTIT ...CONCPT 20 NATO KENNEDY/JF DEGAULLE/C EEC JOHNSON/LB. PAGE 80 A1648
DIPLOM REGION POLICY

B63
MANGER W.,THE ALLIANCE FOR PROGRESS: A CRITICAL APPRAISAL. FUT L/A+17C USA+45 CULTURE ECO/UNDEV ACADEM NAT/G SCHOOL PLAN FOR/AID...POLICY OAS. PAGE 94 A1918
DIPLOM INT/ORG ECO/TAC REGION

B63
MAYNE R.,THE COMMUNITY OF EUROPE. UK CONSTN NAT/G CONSULT DELIB/GP CREATE PLAN ECO/TAC LEGIT ADMIN ROUTINE ORD/FREE PWR WEALTH...CONCPT TIME/SEQ EEC EURATOM 20. PAGE 97 A1985
EUR+WWI INT/ORG REGION

B63
PANAMERICAN UNION,DOCUMENTOS OFICIALES DE LA ORGANIZACION DE LOS ESTADOS AMERICANOS, INDICE Y LISTA (VOL. III, 1962). L/A+17C DELIB/GP INT/TRADE EDU/PROP REGION NUC/PWR...HEAL INT/LAW SOC/WK 20 OAS. PAGE 113 A2329
BIBLIOG INT/ORG DIPLOM

B63
ROBERTSON A.H.,HUMAN RIGHTS IN EUROPE. CONSTN SOCIETY INT/ORG NAT/G VOL/ASSN DELIB/GP ACT/RES PLAN ADJUD REGION ROUTINE ATTIT LOVE ORD/FREE RESPECT...JURID SOC CONCPT SOC/EXP UN 20. PAGE 122 A2498
EUR+WWI PERSON

B63
ROBOCK S.H.,OVERVIEW OF TOTAL BRAZILIAN SETTING, NEWER REGIONAL PATTERNS NING AND FOREIGN AID. BRAZIL ECO/UNDEV AGRI FINAN INDUS INT/ORG INCOME UTIL...CHARTS 20. PAGE 122 A2507
ECO/TAC REGION PLAN FOR/AID

B63
WELLESLEY COLLEGE,SYMPOSIUM ON LATIN AMERICA. FUT L/A+17C USA+45 INT/ORG ECO/TAC PARL/PROC REGION ANTHOL. PAGE 163 A3316
ECO/UNDEV CULTURE ORD/FREE DIPLOM

L63
WILCOX F.O.,"THE ATLANTIC COMMUNITY: PROGRESS AND PROSPECTS." EUR+WWI FUT USA+45 WOR+45 SOCIETY CREATE ECO/TAC EDU/PROP LEGIT REGION ATTIT ALL/VALS ...POLICY ANTHOL VAL/FREE 20. PAGE 164 A3346
INT/ORG ACT/RES

S63
BANFIELD J.,"FEDERATION IN EAST-AFRICA." AFR UGANDA ELITES INT/ORG NAT/G VOL/ASSN LEGIS ECO/TAC FEDERAL ATTIT SOVEREIGN TOT/POP 20 TANGANYIKA. PAGE 11 A0216
EX/STRUC PWR REGION

S63
GORDON B.,"ECONOMIC IMPEDIMENTS TO REGIONALISM IN SOUTH EAST ASIA." BURMA FUT S/ASIA THAILAND USA+45 AGRI INDUS R+D NAT/G PLAN ECO/TAC WEALTH...STAT CONT/OBS 20. PAGE 54 A1110
VOL/ASSN ECO/UNDEV INT/TRADE REGION

S63
GROSSER A.,"FRANCE AND GERMANY IN THE ATLANTIC COMMUNITY." INT/ORG NAT/G TOP/EX DIPLOM REGION PEACE ATTIT ORD/FREE PWR...CONCPT RECORD TIME/SEQ GEN/LAWS VAL/FREE COLD/WAR 20. PAGE 57 A1178
EUR+WWI VOL/ASSN FRANCE GERMANY

S63
HUMPHREY H.H.,"REGIONAL ARMS CONTROL AGREEMENTS." WOR+45 FORCES PLAN LEGIT COERCE ATTIT HEALTH ORD/FREE...HUM METH/CNCPT MYTH OBS INT TREND TOT/POP 20. PAGE 69 A1416
L/A+17C INT/ORG ARMS/CONT REGION

S63
KINTNER W.R.,"THE PROJECTED EUROPEAN UNION AND AMERICAN RESPONSIBILITIES." EUR+WWI USA+45 STRATA INT/ORG NAT/G DOMIN DETER NUC/PWR ATTIT ORD/FREE PWR 20 NATO. PAGE 79 A1628
FUT FORCES DIPLOM REGION

S63
MULLEY F.W.,"NUCLEAR WEAPONS: CHALLENGE TO NATIONAL SOVEREIGNTY." EUR+WWI FRANCE UK USA+45 VOL/ASSN EX/STRUC FORCES TOP/EX ACT/RES REGION DRIVE PWR 20 NATO DEGAULLE/C. PAGE 106 A2169
INT/ORG ATTIT DIPLOM NUC/PWR

S63
SCHOFLING J.A.,"EFTA: THE OTHER EUROPE." ECO/DEV MARKET CONSULT ECO/TAC WEALTH...TIME/SEQ EEC OEEC 20 EFTA. PAGE 129 A2642
EUR+WWI INT/ORG REGION

S63
WRIGHT Q.,"PROJECTED EUROPEAN UNION AND AMERICAN INTERNATIONAL PRESTIGE." EUR+WWI FRANCE GERMANY UK USA+45 INT/ORG NAT/G EDU/PROP ATTIT PERCEPT PWR ...CONCPT OBS EEC 20 UN. PAGE 168 A3417
FUT ORD/FREE REGION

N63
LIBRARY HUNGARIAN ACADEMY SCI,HUNGARIAN PUBLICATIONS ON ASIA AND AFRICA, 1950-1962: A SELECTED BIBLIOGRAPHY (PAMPHLET). AFR ASIA HUNGARY S/ASIA ECO/UNDEV NAT/G EDU/PROP ATTIT 20 UNESCO. PAGE 88 A1807
BIBLIOG REGION DIPLOM WRITING

B64
AMERICAN ASSEMBLY,THE UNITED STATES AND THE MIDDLE EAST. ISRAEL USA+45 STRUCT ECO/DEV ECO/UNDEV INT/ORG NAT/G SCHOOL SECT VOL/ASSN EX/STRUC TEC/DEV NAT/LISM...SOC 20. PAGE 7 A0135
ISLAM DRIVE REGION

B64
BUTWELL R.,SOUTHEAST ASIA TODAY - AND TOMORROW. NAT/G COLONIAL LEAD REGION WAR CHOOSE WEALTH MARXISM 20. PAGE 23 A0458
S/ASIA DIPLOM ECO/UNDEV NAT/LISM

B64
COTTRELL A.J.,THE POLITICS OF THE ATLANTIC ALLIANCE. EUR+WWI USA+45 INT/ORG NAT/G DELIB/GP EX/STRUC BAL/PWR DIPLOM REGION DETER ATTIT ORD/FREE ...CONCPT RECORD GEN/LAWS GEN/METH NATO 20. PAGE 31 A0632
VOL/ASSN FORCES

B64
COX R.,PAN-AFRICANISM IN PRACTICE. AFR DIPLOM CONFER RACE/REL ROLE SOVEREIGN...POLICY 20 PANAF/FREE. PAGE 32 A0645
ORD/FREE COLONIAL REGION NAT/LISM

B64
GJUPANOVIC H.,LEGAL SOURCES AND BIBLIOGRAPHY OF YUGOSLAVIA. COM YUGOSLAVIA LAW LEGIS DIPLOM ADMIN PARL/PROC REGION CRIME CENTRAL 20. PAGE 53 A1078
BIBLIOG/A JURID CONSTN ADJUD

B64
GREAT BRITAIN CENTRAL OFF INF,CONSTITUTIONAL DEVELOPMENT IN THE COMMONWEALTH. VOL/ASSN PLAN DIPLOM COLONIAL INGP/REL NAT/LISM ORD/FREE PWR 17/20 CMN/WLTH. PAGE 55 A1135
REGION CONSTN NAT/G SOVEREIGN

B64
GRZYBOWSKI K.,THE SOCIALIST COMMONWEALTH OF NATIONS: ORGANIZATIONS AND INSTITUTIONS. FORCES DIPLOM INT/TRADE ADJUD ADMIN LEAD WAR MARXISM SOCISM...BIBLIOG 20 COMECON WARSAW/P. PAGE 58 A1185
INT/LAW COM REGION INT/ORG

B64
HEKHUIS D.J.,INTERNATIONAL STABILITY: MILITARY, ECONOMIC AND POLITICAL DIMENSIONS. FUT WOR+45 LAW ECO/UNDEV INT/ORG NAT/G VOL/ASSN FORCES ACT/RES BAL/PWR PWR WEALTH...STAT UN 20. PAGE 64 A1310
TEC/DEV DETER REGION

B64
HINSHAW R.,THE EUROPEAN COMMUNITY AND AMERICAN TRADE: A STUDY IN ATLANTIC ECONOMICS AND POLICY. EUR+WWI UK USA+45 ECO/DEV ECO/UNDEV AGRI INDUS INT/ORG NAT/G ECO/TAC TARIFFS REGION...STAT CHARTS EEC 20. PAGE 65 A1337
MARKET TREND INT/TRADE

B64
INTL INF CTR LOCAL CREDIT,GOVERNMENT MEASURES FOR THE PROMOTION OF REGIONAL ECONOMIC DEVELOPMENT. WOR+45 ECO/UNDEV FINAN INT/ORG DIPLOM ORD/FREE ...POLICY GEOG 20. PAGE 71 A1464
FOR/AID PLAN ECO/TAC REGION

B64
JACOB P.E.,THE INTEGRATION OF POLITICAL COMMUNITIES. USA+45 WOR+45 CULTURE LOC/G MUNIC NAT/G CREATE PLAN LEGIT REGION COERCE ALL/VALS ...POLICY GEOG PSY SOC TREND HYPO/EXP GEN/LAWS VAL/FREE 20. PAGE 72 A1483
INT/ORG METH/CNCPT SIMUL STAT

B64
KIS T.I.,LES PAYS DE L'EUROPE DE L'EST: LEURS RAPPORTS MUTUELS ET LE PROBLEME DE LEUR INTEGRATION DANS L'ORBITE DE L'USSR. EUR+WWI RUSSIA USSR INT/ORG NAT/G REV ATTIT...JURID SOC BIBLIOG WARSAW/P COMECON EUROPE/E. PAGE 80 A1638
DIPLOM COM MARXISM REGION

B64
KOHNSTAMM M.,THE EUROPEAN COMMUNITY AND ITS ROLE IN THE WORLD. FUT MOD/EUR UK USA+45 ECO/DEV 20. PAGE 81 A1664
INT/ORG NAT/G REGION DIPLOM

B64
KRAUSE L.B.,THE COMMON MARKET: PROGRESS AND CONTROVERSY. EUR+WWI UK ECO/DEV REGION...ANTHOL NATO EEC. PAGE 82 A1678
DIPLOM MARKET INT/TRADE INT/ORG

B64
LUTHULI A.,AFRICA'S FREEDOM. KIN LABOR POL/PAR SCHOOL DIPLOM NEUTRAL REGION REV NAT/LISM PWR WEALTH SOCISM SOC/INTEG 20. PAGE 92 A1874
AFR ECO/UNDEV COLONIAL

B64
MAIER J.,POLITICS OF CHANGE IN LATIN AMERICA. BRAZIL L/A+17C STRATA INT/ORG NAT/G POL/PAR FOR/AID REV 20. PAGE 93 A1907
SOCIETY NAT/LISM DIPLOM REGION

B64
NEHEMKIS P.,LATIN AMERICA: MYTH AND REALITY. INDUS INT/ORG MUNIC PROB/SOLV CAP/ISM DIPLOM REV...SOC 20. PAGE 108 A2211
REGION MYTH L/A+17C ECO/UNDEV

B64
NICOL D.,AFRICA - A SUBJECTIVE VIEW. AFR INT/ORG PLAN ADMIN COLONIAL PARL/PROC PARTIC REGION GOV/REL LITERACY ATTIT...BIBLIOG 20 CIVIL/SERV. PAGE 109 A2230
NAT/G LEAD CULTURE ACADEM

B64
PLISCHKE E.,SYSTEMS OF INTEGRATING THE INTERNATIONAL COMMUNITY. WOR+45 NAT/G VOL/ASSN ECO/TAC LEGIT PWR WEALTH...TIME/SEQ ANTHOL UN TOT/POP 20. PAGE 116 A2391
INT/ORG EX/STRUC REGION

B64
RAMAZANI R.K.,THE MIDDLE EAST AND THE EUROPEAN COMMON MARKET. EUR+WWI ISLAM ECO/DEV EXTR/IND MARKET PROC/MFG INT/ORG NAT/G TEC/DEV ECO/TAC REGION DRIVE WEALTH...STAT CHARTS EEC TOT/POP 20. PAGE 119 A2437
ECO/UNDEV ATTIT INT/TRADE

B64
SARROS P.P.,CONGRESS AND THE NEW DIPLOMACY: THE FORMULATION OF MUTUAL SECURITY POLICY: 1953-60 (THESIS). USA+45 CHIEF EX/STRUC REGION ROUTINE CHOOSE GOV/REL PEACE ROLE...POLICY 20 PRESIDENT CONGRESS. PAGE 127 A2606
DIPLOM POL/PAR NAT/G

B64
VOELKMANN K.,HERRSCHER VON MORGEN? BAL/PWR COLONIAL NEUTRAL REGION RACE/REL ALL/VALS SOVEREIGN...RECORD 20 COLD/WAR THIRD/WRLD. PAGE 159 A3246
DIPLOM ECO/UNDEV CONTROL NAT/COMP

L64
CLAUDE I.,"THE OAS, THE UN, AND THE UNITED STATES." L/A+17C USA+45 CONSTN NAT/G DELIB/GP DOMIN EDU/PROP LEGIT REGION COERCE ORD/FREE PWR...TIME/SEQ TREND STERTYP OAS UN 20. PAGE 27 A0546
INT/ORG POLICY

L64
HAAS E.B.,"ECONOMICS AND DIFFERENTIAL PATTERNS OF POLITICAL INTEGRATION: PROJECTIONS ABOUT UNITY IN LATIN AMERICA." SOCIETY NAT/G DELIB/GP ACT/RES CREATE PLAN ECO/TAC REGION ROUTINE ATTIT DRIVE PWR WEALTH...CONCPT TREND CHARTS LAFTA 20. PAGE 59 A1208
L/A+17C INT/ORG MARKET

S64
COCHRANE J.D.,"US ATTITUDES TOWARD CENTRAL-AMERICAN INTEGRATION." L/A+17C USA+45 ECO/UNDEV FACE/GP VOL/ASSN DELIB/GP ECO/TAC INT/TRADE EDU/PROP RIGID/FLEX ORD/FREE WEALTH...TIME/SEQ TOT/POP 20. PAGE 27 A0555
NAT/G ATTIT REGION

S64
DELGADO J.,"EL MOMENTO POLITICO HISPANOAMERICA." CHINA/COM FUT PANAMA USA+45 USSR INT/ORG NAT/G POL/PAR FORCES DOMIN REGION COERCE ATTIT ALL/VALS ...TRADIT CONCPT COLD/WAR 20. PAGE 36 A0728
L/A+17C EDU/PROP NAT/LISM

S64
GARMARNIKOW M.,"INFLUENCE-BUYING IN WEST AFRICA." COM FUT USSR INTELL NAT/G PLAN TEC/DEV ECO/TAC DOMIN EDU/PROP REGION NAT/LISM ATTIT DRIVE ALL/VALS SOVEREIGN...POLICY PSY SOC CONCPT TREND STERTYP WORK COLD/WAR 20. PAGE 51 A1049
AFR ECO/UNDEV FOR/AID SOCISM

S64
GERBET P.,"LA MISE EN OEUVRE DU MARCHE COMMUN AGRICOLE." ECO/DEV MARKET INT/ORG NAT/G PLAN EDU/PROP NAT/LISM WEALTH...OBS EEC VAL/FREE 20. PAGE 52 A1064
EUR+WWI AGRI REGION

S64
HOFFMANN S.,"CE QU'EN PENSENT LES AMERICAINS." EUR+WWI INT/ORG VOL/ASSN PLAN BAL/PWR DIPLOM DOMIN EDU/PROP REGION ARMS/CONT DRIVE ORD/FREE PWR ...POLICY CONCPT OBS TREND STERTYP COLD/WAR VAL/FREE 20. PAGE 66 A1357
USA+45 ATTIT FRANCE

S64
PADELFORD N.J.,"THE ORGANIZATION OF AFRICAN UNITY." ECO/UNDEV INT/ORG PLAN BAL/PWR DIPLOM ECO/TAC NAT/LISM ORD/FREE PWR WEALTH...CONCPT TREND STERTYP VAL/FREE COLD/WAR 20. PAGE 113 A2313
AFR VOL/ASSN REGION

S64
REIDY J.W.,"LATIN AMERICA AND THE ATLANTIC TRIANGLE." EUR+WWI FUT USA+45 INT/ORG NAT/G REGION COERCE ORD/FREE PWR...TIME/SEQ VAL/FREE 20. PAGE 120 A2458
L/A+17C WEALTH POLICY

S64
ROTHCHILD D.,"EAST AFRICAN FEDERATION." AFR TANZANIA UGANDA INDUS REGION 20. PAGE 124 A2547
INT/ORG DIPLOM ECO/UNDEV ECO/TAC

S64
SAAB H.,"THE ARAB SEARCH FOR A FEDERAL UNION." SOCIETY INT/ORG NAT/G DELIB/GP FORCES ACT/RES TEC/DEV ECO/TAC DOMIN LEGIT REGION ROUTINE ATTIT DRIVE RIGID/FLEX ALL/VALS...SOC CONCPT NEW/IDEA TIME/SEQ TREND. PAGE 126 A2580
ISLAM PLAN

S64
TINKER H.,"POLITICS IN SOUTHEAST ASIA." INT/ORG NAT/G CREATE PLAN TEC/DEV GUERRILLA KNOWL ORD/FREE COLD/WAR. PAGE 144 A2944
S/ASIA ACT/RES REGION

B65
BROMKE A.,THE COMMUNIST STATES AT THE CROSSROADS BETWEEN MOSCOW AND PEKING. CHINA/COM USSR INGP/REL NAT/LISM TOTALISM 20. PAGE 19 A0389
COM DIPLOM MARXISM REGION

B65
JOHNSON H.G.,THE WORLD ECONOMY AT THE CROSSROADS. COM WOR-45 ECO/DEV AGRI INDUS INT/TRADE REGION NAT/LISM 20. PAGE 74 A1523
FINAN DIPLOM INT/ORG ECO/UNDEV

B65
MACDONALD R.W.,THE LEAGUE OF ARAB STATES: A STUDY IN THE DYNAMICS OF REGIONAL ORGANIZATION. ISRAEL UAR USSR FINAN INT/ORG DELIB/GP ECO/TAC AGREE NEUTRAL ORD/FREE PWR...DECISION BIBLIOG 20 TREATY UN. PAGE 92 A1888
ISLAM REGION DIPLOM ADMIN

B65
MIDDLETON D.,CRISIS IN THE WEST. EUR+WWI FUT WOR+45 CHIEF PLAN ECO/TAC LEAD REGION NUC/PWR NAT/LISM MARXISM 20 COLD/WAR NATO EEC. PAGE 101 A2068
INT/ORG DIPLOM NAT/G POLICY

B65
SILVA SOLAR J.,EL DESARROLLO DE LA NUEVA SOCIEDAD EN AMERICA. L/A+17C SOCIETY AGRI PROB/SOLV DIPLOM PARTIC GP/REL OWN...POLICY SOC 20 REFORMERS. PAGE 133 A2716
STRUCT ECO/UNDEV REGION CONTROL

B65
SPEECKAERT G.P.,SELECT BIBLIOGRAPHY ON INTERNATIONAL ORGANIZATION, 1885-1964. WOR+45 WOR-45 EX/STRUC DIPLOM ADMIN REGION 19/20 UN. PAGE 136 A2777
BIBLIOG INT/ORG GEN/LAWS STRATA

B65
STOETZER O.C.,THE ORGANIZATION OF AMERICAN STATES. L/A+17C EX/STRUC FOR/AID CONFER PARL/PROC ORD/FREE SOVEREIGN...POLICY INT/LAW 20 OAS. PAGE 138 A2831
INT/ORG REGION DIPLOM BAL/PWR

B65
WEILER J.,L'ECONOMIE INTERNATIONALE DEPUIS 1950. WOR+45 DIPLOM TARIFFS CONFER...POLICY TREATY. PAGE 162 A3302
FINAN INT/TRADE REGION FOR/AID

B65
WILGUS A.C.,HISTORIES AND HISTORIANS OF HISPANIC AMERICA (REPRINT ED.). CHRIST-17C SECT DIPLOM REV 16/20. PAGE 164 A3350
BIBLIOG/A L/A+17C REGION COLONIAL

L65
WIONCZEK M.,"LATIN AMERICA FREE TRADE ASSOCIATION." AGRI DIST/IND FINAN INDUS INT/ORG LABOR NAT/G TEC/DEV ECO/TAC HEALTH SKILL WEALTH...POLICY RELATIV MGT LAFTA 20. PAGE 165 A3369
L/A+17C MARKET REGION

S65
GANGAL S.C.,"SURVEY OF RECENT RESEARCH: INDIA AND
BIBLIOG

THE COMMONWEALTH" INDIA UK NAT/G INT/TRADE PARTIC GOV/REL ROLE 20 CMN/WLTH. PAGE 51 A1039
POLICY REGION DIPLOM

S65
HOLSTI O.R.,"EAST-WEST CONFLICT AND SINO-SOVIET RELATIONS" CHINA/COM USSR COMPUTER REGION DECISION. PAGE 67 A1373
VOL/ASSN DIPLOM CON/ANAL COM

S65
SPAAK P.H.,"THE SEARCH FOR CONSENSUS: A NEW EFFORT TO BUILD EUROPE." FRANCE GERMANY ECO/DEV NAT/G CONSULT FORCES PLAN EDU/PROP REGION CONSEN ATTIT ...SOC METH/CNCPT OBS TREND EEC NATO WORK 20. PAGE 135 A2770
EUR+WWI INT/ORG

S65
STEIN E.,"TOWARD SUPREMACY OF TREATY-CONSTITUTION BY JUDICIAL FIAT: ON THE MARGIN OF THE COSTA CASE." EUR+WWI ITALY WOR+45 INT/ORG NAT/G LEGIT REGION NAT/LISM PWR...JURID CONCPT TREND TOT/POP VAL/FREE 20. PAGE 138 A2816
ADJUD CONSTN SOVEREIGN INT/LAW

C65
SCHEINGOLD S.A.,"THE RULE OF LAW IN EUROPEAN INTEGRATION: THE PATH OF THE SCHUMAN PLAN." EUR+WWI JUDGE ADJUD FEDERAL ATTIT PWR...RECORD INT BIBLIOG EEC ECSC. PAGE 128 A2621
INT/LAW CT/SYS REGION CENTRAL

B66
BRACKMAN A.C.,SOUTHEAST ASIA'S SECOND FRONT: THE POWER STRUGGLE IN THE MALAY ARCHIPELAGO. CHINA/COM INDONESIA MALAYSIA ECO/UNDEV INT/ORG NAT/G FORCES DIPLOM EDU/PROP REGION COERCE GUERRILLA AUTHORIT POPULISM...MAJORIT 20 KENNEDY/JF SEATO. PAGE 18 A0367
S/ASIA MARXISM REV

B66
CONNEL-SMITH G.,THE INTERAMERICAN SYSTEM. CUBA L/A+17C DELIB/GP FOR/AID COLONIAL PEACE PWR MARXISM ...BIBLIOG 19/20 OAS. PAGE 29 A0586
DIPLOM INT/TRADE REGION INT/ORG

B66
GERARD-LIBOIS J.,KATANGA SECESSION. INT/ORG FORCES DIPLOM ADMIN CONTROL WAR CHOOSE PWR...CHARTS 20 KATANGA TSHOMBE/M UN. PAGE 52 A1062
NAT/G REGION ORD/FREE REV

B66
GORDON B.K.,THE DIMENSIONS OF CONFLICT IN SOUTHEAST ASIA. S/ASIA FORCES ADJUD REGION...CHARTS 20. PAGE 54 A1111
DIPLOM NAT/COMP INT/ORG VOL/ASSN

B66
KAREFA-SMART J.,AFRICA: PROGRESS THROUGH COOPERATION. AFR FINAN TEC/DEV DIPLOM FOR/AID EDU/PROP CONFER REGION GP/REL WEALTH...HEAL SOC/INTEG 20. PAGE 76 A1566
ORD/FREE ECO/UNDEV VOL/ASSN PLAN

B66
MCKAY V.,AFRICAN DIPLOMACY STUDIES IN THE DETERMINANTS OF FOREIGN POLICY. AFR SOUTH/AFR CULTURE NEUTRAL REGION SOVEREIGN...INT/LAW GOV/COMP ANTHOL 20. PAGE 98 A2013
ECO/UNDEV RACE/REL CIVMIL/REL DIPLOM

B66
NIJHOFF M.,ANNUAIRE EUROPEEN (VOL. XII). INT/TRADE REGION PEACE 20 EFTA EEC ECSC EURATOM. PAGE 109 A2241
BIBLIOG INT/ORG EUR+WWI DIPLOM

B66
RIESELBACH L.N.,THE ROOTS OF ISOLATIONISM* CONGRESSIONAL VOTING AND PRESIDENTIAL LEADERSHIP IN FOREIGN POLICY. POL/PAR LEGIS DIPLOM EDU/PROP LEAD REGION REPRESENT...SOC STAT IDEA/COMP HYPO/EXP BIBLIOG 19/20 CONGRESS. PAGE 121 A2477
ISOLAT CHOOSE CHIEF POLICY

B66
SINGH L.P.,THE POLITICS OF ECONOMIC COOPERATION IN ASIA; A STUDY OF ASIAN INTERNATIONAL ORGANIZATIONS. ASIA INT/ORG ACT/RES PLAN GP/REL...POLICY GP/COMP BIBLIOG 20 UN SEATO. PAGE 133 A2733
ECO/UNDEV ECO/TAC REGION DIPLOM

B66
US DEPARTMENT OF STATE,RESEARCH ON AFRICA (EXTERNAL RESEARCH LIST NO 5-25). LAW CULTURE ECO/UNDEV POL/PAR DIPLOM EDU/PROP LEAD REGION MARXISM...GEOG LING WORSHIP 20. PAGE 152 A3094
BIBLIOG/A ASIA S/ASIA NAT/G

B66
US DEPARTMENT OF STATE,RESEARCH ON THE AMERICAN REPUBLICS (EXTERNAL RESEARCH LIST NO 6-25). CULTURE SOCIETY POL/PAR DIPLOM EDU/PROP MARXISM WORSHIP 20 OAS. PAGE 152 A3095
BIBLIOG/A L/A+17C REGION NAT/G

B66
US DEPARTMENT OF STATE,RESEARCH ON THE MIDDLE EAST (EXTERNAL RESEARCH LIST NO 4-25). GREECE ISRAEL SYRIA UAR YEMEN CULTURE SOCIETY POL/PAR SECT DIPLOM EDU/PROP WAR NAT/LISM...GEOG GOV/COMP 20. PAGE 152 A3096
BIBLIOG/A ISLAM NAT/G REGION

B66
US DEPARTMENT OF STATE,RESEARCH ON THE USSR AND EASTERN EUROPE (EXTERNAL RESEARCH LIST NO 1-25). USSR LAW CULTURE SOCIETY NAT/G TEC/DEV DIPLOM EDU/PROP REGION...GEOG LING. PAGE 152 A3097
BIBLIOG/A EUR+WWI COM MARXISM

B66
US DEPARTMENT OF STATE,RESEARCH ON WESTERN EUROPE, GREAT BRITAIN, AND CANADA (EXTERNAL RESEARCH LIST NO 3-25). CANADA GERMANY/W UK LAW CULTURE NAT/G POL/PAR FORCES EDU/PROP REGION MARXISM...GEOG SOC WORSHIP 20 CMN/WLTH. PAGE 152 A3098
BIBLIOG/A EUR+WWI DIPLOM

B66
US SENATE COMM ON FOREIGN REL,UNITED STATES POLICY TOWARD EUROPE (AND RELATED MATTERS). COM EUR+WWI GERMANY PROB/SOLV REGION NUC/PWR WAR NAT/LISM PEACE PWR...NAT/COMP 20 NATO CONGRESS DEGAULLE/C. PAGE 156 A3184
DIPLOM INT/ORG POLICY WOR+45

B66
WELCH C.E.,DREAM OF UNITY; PAN-AFRICANISM AND POLITICAL UNIFICATION IN WEST AFRICA. AFR ECO/UNDEV CONFER COLONIAL LEAD...INT/LAW 20. PAGE 163 A3312
INT/ORG REGION NAT/LISM DIPLOM

S66
DUROSELLE J.B.,"THE FUTURE OF THE ATLANTIC COMMUNITY." EUR+WWI USA+45 USSR NAT/G CAP/ISM REGION DETER NUC/PWR ATTIT MARXISM...INT/LAW 20 NATO. PAGE 40 A0811
FUT DIPLOM MYTH POLICY

S66
GAMER R.E.,"URGENT SINGAPORE, PATIENT MALAYSIA." MALAYSIA S/ASIA ECO/UNDEV POL/PAR CHIEF TARIFFS TAX CONTROL LEAD REGION PWR 20 SINGAPORE. PAGE 51 A1036
DIPLOM NAT/G POLICY ECO/TAC

S66
JAVITS J.K.,"POLITICAL ACTION VITAL FOR LATIN AMERICAN INTEGRATION." ECO/UNDEV INT/ORG POL/PAR VOL/ASSN PLAN PROB/SOLV INT/TRADE EFFICIENCY 20 OAS LAFTA. PAGE 73 A1500
L/A+17C ECO/TAC REGION

B67
ADAMS A.E.,AN ATLAS OF RUSSIAN AND EAST EUROPEAN HISTORY. CHRIST-17C COM MOD/EUR INDUS SECT FORCES DIPLOM COLONIAL REV WAR 4/20. PAGE 4 A0086
CHARTS REGION TREND

B67
BELL W.,THE DEMOCRATIC REVOLUTION IN THE WEST INDIES. WEST/IND WOR+45 DIPLOM RACE/REL NAT/LISM ...INT QU ANTHOL 20. PAGE 13 A0257
REGION ATTIT ORD/FREE ECO/UNDEV

B67
EUROPA-ARCHIV,DEUTSCHES AND AUSLANDISCHES SCHRIFTTUM ZU DEN REGIONALEN SICHERHEITSVEREINBARUNGEN 1945-1956. WOR+45 FORCES BAL/PWR REGION. PAGE 43 A0875
BIBLIOG INT/ORG PEACE DETER

B67
MAZRUI A.A.,TOWARDS A PAX AFRICANA. AFR STRUCT ECO/UNDEV NAT/G DIPLOM COLONIAL REGION WAR ATTIT 20. PAGE 97 A1988
PEACE FORCES PROB/SOLV SOVEREIGN

B67
NYERERE J.K.,FREEDOM AND UNITY/UHURU NA UMOJA: A SELECTION FROM WRITINGS AND SPEECHES, 1952-65. TANZANIA ELITES ECO/UNDEV INT/ORG NAT/G CREATE DIPLOM COLONIAL REGION RACE/REL...ANTHOL 20. PAGE 110 A2265
SOVEREIGN AFR TREND ORD/FREE

B67
PADELFORD N.J.,THE DYNAMICS OF INTERNATIONAL POLITICS (2ND ED.). WOR+45 LAW INT/ORG FORCES TEC/DEV REGION NAT/LISM PEACE ATTIT PWR ALL/IDEOS UN COLD/WAR NATO TREATY. PAGE 113 A2314
DIPLOM NAT/G POLICY DECISION

B67
ROACH J.R.,THE UNITED STATES AND THE ATLANTIC COMMUNITY; ISSUES AND PROSPECTS. WOR+45 TEC/DEV ECO/TAC COLONIAL REGION PEACE ROLE...ANTHOL NATO COLD/WAR EEC. PAGE 121 A2491
INT/ORG POLICY ADJUST DIPLOM

B67
ROSENAU J.N.,DOMESTIC SOURCES OF FOREIGN POLICY. WOR+45 STRATA COM/IND MUNIC POL/PAR LOBBY PARTIC REGION ATTIT...PSY SOC COLD/WAR. PAGE 124 A2534
DIPLOM POLICY NAT/G CHOOSE

B67
SAYEED K.B.,THE POLITICAL SYSTEM OF PAKISTAN. PAKISTAN DIPLOM REGION CHOOSE ORD/FREE...BIBLIOG 20. PAGE 127 A2609
NAT/G POL/PAR CONSTN SECT

B67
SCHWARTZ M.A.,PUBLIC OPINION AND CANADIAN IDENTITY. CANADA SOCIETY LOC/G DIPLOM ADMIN LEAD REGION GP/REL SAMP. PAGE 130 A2657
ATTIT NAT/G NAT/LISM POL/PAR

B67
WATERS M.,THE UNITED NATIONS* INTERNATIONAL ORGANIZATION AND ADMINISTRATION. WOR+45 EX/STRUC FORCES DIPLOM LEAD REGION ARMS/CONT REPRESENT INGP/REL ROLE...METH/COMP ANTHOL 20 UN LEAGUE/NAT. PAGE 162 A3291
CONSTN INT/ORG ADMIN ADJUD

L67
BODENHEIMER S.J.,"THE 'POLITICAL UNION' DEBATE IN EUROPE* A CASE STUDY IN INTERGOVERNMENTAL DIPLOMACY." EUR+WWI FUT NAT/G FORCES PLAN DEBATE SOVEREIGN...CONCPT PREDICT EEC NATO. PAGE 16 A0326
DIPLOM REGION INT/ORG

L67
SEGAL A.,"THE INTEGRATION OF DEVELOPING COUNTRIES: SOME THOUGHTS ON EAST AFRICA AND CENTRAL AMERICA." AFR L/A+17C INT/ORG NAT/G VOL/ASSN FOR/AID INT/TRADE EQUILIB NAT/LISM PWR 20. PAGE 131 A2680
ECO/UNDEV DIPLOM REGION

S67
BUTT R.,"THE COMMON MARKET AND CONSERVATIVE POLITICS, 1961-2." UK CHIEF DIPLOM ECO/TAC INT/TRADE CONFER DEBATE REGION ATTIT...POLICY 20 EEC. PAGE 22 A0454
EUR+WWI INT/ORG POL/PAR

S67
DE ROUGEMENT D.,"THE CAMPAIGN OF THE EUROPEAN CONGRESSES." ELITES INTELL DIPLOM ECO/TAC CONFER PEACE...POLICY PREDICT. PAGE 35 A0710
EUR+WWI REGION FEDERAL INT/ORG

S67
DEUTSCH K.W.,"ARMS CONTROL AND EUROPEAN UNITY* THE NEXT TEN YEARS." USA+45 ELITES NAT/G BAL/PWR DIPLOM NUC/PWR...INT KNO/TEST NATO EEC. PAGE 36 A0742
ARMS/CONT PEACE REGION PLAN

S67
GLENN N.D.,"ARE REGIONAL CULTURAL DIFFERENCES DIMINISHING?" USA+45 DIPLOM RACE/REL AGE/Y AGE/A PERSON MORAL...GP/COMP 20. PAGE 53 A1081
SAMP ATTIT REGION CULTURE

S67
HERRERA F.,"EUROPEAN PARTICIPATION IN THE LATIN AMERICAN REGIONAL INTEGRATION" EUR+WWI L/A+17C GP/REL INGP/REL 20. PAGE 64 A1318
DIPLOM REGION INT/ORG FINAN

S67
INGLEHART R.,"AN END TO EUROPEAN INTEGRATION." PROB/SOLV BAL/PWR NAT/LISM...PSY SOC INT CHARTS GP/COMP 20. PAGE 70 A1440
DIPLOM EUR+WWI REGION ATTIT

S67
JOHNSON J.,"THE UNITED STATES AND THE LATIN AMERICAN LEFT WINGS." L/A+17C STRATA POL/PAR INT/TRADE 20. PAGE 74 A1524
ECO/UNDEV WORKER ECO/TAC REGION

S67
KYLE K.,"BACKGROUND TO THE CRISIS" ISLAM ISRAEL UAR UK USSR NAT/G PROB/SOLV LEGIT CONTROL REGION STRANGE MORAL 20 JEWS. PAGE 83 A1698
DIPLOM POLICY SOVEREIGN COERCE

S67
NEUCHTERLEIN D.E.,"THAILAND* ANOTHER VIETNAM?" THAILAND ECO/UNDEV DIPLOM ADMIN REGION CENTRAL NAT/LISM...POLICY 20. PAGE 108 A2220
WAR GUERRILLA S/ASIA NAT/G

S67
ROSE S.,"ASIAN NATIONALISM* THE SECOND STAGE." ASIA COM ECO/UNDEV NAT/G PROB/SOLV DIPLOM FOR/AID DOMIN NEUTRAL REGION TASK...METH/COMP 20. PAGE 123 A2528
NAT/LISM S/ASIA BAL/PWR COLONIAL

S67
SAPP B.B.,"TRIBAL CULTURES AND COMMUNISM." AFR USA+45 STRATA DIPLOM FOR/AID REGION CENTRAL ATTIT AUTHORIT RIGID/FLEX KNOWL. PAGE 127 A2604
KIN MARXISM ECO/UNDEV STRUCT

S67
VELIKONJA J.,"ITALIAN IMMIGRANTS IN THE UNITED STATES IN THE MID-SIXTIES" ITALY USA+45 KIN MUNIC NAT/G WORKER DIPLOM REGION GP/REL ADJUST...GEOG CHARTS SOC/INTEG 20. PAGE 158 A3226
HABITAT ORD/FREE TREND STAT

S67
WALKER R.L.,"THE WEST AND THE 'NEW ASIA'." CHINA/COM ECO/UNDEV DIPLOM...PREDICT 20. PAGE 160 A3266
ASIA INT/TRADE COLONIAL REGION

S67
WEIL G.L.,"THE EUROPEAN COMMUNITY* WHAT LIES BEYOND THE POINT OF NO RETURN?" VOL/ASSN PROB/SOLV DIPLOM REGION INGP/REL CENTRAL PWR 20 EEC. PAGE 162 A3301
INT/ORG ECO/DEV INT/TRADE PREDICT

S67
ZARTMAN I.W.,"AFRICA AS A SUBORDINATE STATE SYSTEM IN INTERNATIONAL RELATIONS." LAW BAL/PWR REGION CENTRAL...GEOG 20. PAGE 169 A3447
DIPLOM INT/ORG CONSTN AFR

REGRESS....REGRESSION ANALYSIS; SEE ALSO CON/ANAL

REHABILITN....REHABILITATION

REID H.D. A2457

REIDY J.W. A2458

REIFF H. A2459

REINSCH P. A2460

REINTANZ G. A2461

REISCHAUER R. A2462

REISCHAUER R.D. A2926

REISS J. A2463

REITZEL W. A2464

RELATIONS AMONG GROUPS....SEE GP/REL

RELATISM....RELATIVISM

RELATIV....RELATIVITY

S51
ICHHEISER G.,"MISUNDERSTANDING IN INTERNATIONAL RELATIONS." UNIV SOCIETY FACE/GP INT/ORG SECT ATTIT PERSON RIGID/FLEX LOVE RESPECT...RELATIV PSY SOC CONCPT MYTH SOC/EXP GEN/LAWS. PAGE 70 A1431
PERCEPT STERTYP NAT/LISM DIPLOM

B56
BLACKETT P.M.S.,ATOMIC WEAPONS AND EAST-WEST RELATIONS. FUT WOR+45 INT/ORG DELIB/GP COERCE ATTIT RIGID/FLEX KNOWL...RELATIV HIST/WRIT TREND GEN/METH COLD/WAR 20. PAGE 15 A0299
FORCES PWR ARMS/CONT NUC/PWR

B57
DEAN V.M.,THE NATURE OF THE NON-WESTERN WORLD. AFR ASIA L/A+17C S/ASIA CULTURE SOCIETY STRATA ECO/DEV DIPLOM ECO/TAC FOR/AID ATTIT DRIVE ALL/VALS ...RELATIV SOC CONCPT TIME/SEQ TREND TOT/POP 20. PAGE 35 A0718
ECO/UNDEV STERTYP NAT/LISM

B58
GARTHOFF R.L.,SOVIET STRATEGY IN THE NUCLEAR AGE. FUT USSR R+D INT/ORG NAT/G ACT/RES TEC/DEV DOMIN DETER WAR ATTIT PWR...RELATIV METH/CNCPT SELF/OBS TREND CON/ANAL STERTYP GEN/LAWS 20. PAGE 51 A1052
COM FORCES BAL/PWR NUC/PWR

B59
FOX W.T.R.,THEORETICAL ASPECTS OF INTERNATIONAL RELATIONS. WOR+45 INT/ORG NAT/G POL/PAR CONSULT PLAN ECO/TAC DOMIN EDU/PROP LEGIT EXEC COERCE PWR WEALTH...RELATIV CONCPT 20. PAGE 48 A0975
DELIB/GP ANTHOL

B59
MATHISEN T.,METHODOLOGY IN THE STUDY OF INTERNATIONAL RELATIONS. FUT WOR+45 SOCIETY INT/ORG NAT/G POL/PAR WAR PEACE KNOWL PWR...RELATIV CONCPT METH/CNCPT TREND HYPO/EXP METH TOT/POP 20. PAGE 96 A1965
GEN/METH CON/ANAL DIPLOM CREATE

S59
KOHN L.Y.,"ISRAEL AND NEW NATION STATES OF ASIA AND AFRICA." AFR ASIA FUT S/ASIA VOL/ASSN TEC/DEV NAT/LISM RIGID/FLEX SKILL WEALTH...RELATIV OBS TREND CON/ANAL 20. PAGE 81 A1663
ECO/UNDEV ECO/TAC FOR/AID ISRAEL

S59
REUBENS E.D.,"THE BASIS FOR REORIENATION OF AMERICAN FOREIGN AID POLICY." USA+45 USSR STRUCT INT/ORG CONSULT ECO/TAC ADMIN DRIVE MORAL ORD/FREE PWR WEALTH...RELATIV MATH STAT TREND GEN/LAWS VAL/FREE 20. PAGE 120 A2467
ECO/UNDEV PLAN FOR/AID DIPLOM

B60
EINSTEIN A.,EINSTEIN ON PEACE. FUT WOR+45 WOR-45 SOCIETY NAT/G PLAN BAL/PWR CAP/ISM DIPLOM ARMS/CONT DETER NAT/LISM...POLICY RELATIV HUM PHIL/SCI CONCPT BIOG COLD/WAR LEAGUE/NAT NAZI. PAGE 41 A0829
INT/ORG ATTIT NUC/PWR PEACE

L60
HAAS E.B.,"CONSENSUS FORMATION IN THE COUNCIL OF EUROPE." EUR+WWI NAT/G DELIB/GP DIPLOM REGION CHOOSE PWR SOVEREIGN...RELATIV NEW/IDEA QUANT CHARTS INDEX TOT/POP OEEC 20 COUNCL/EUR. PAGE 59 A1206
POL/PAR INT/ORG STAT

S60
MARTIN E.M.,"NEW TRENDS IN UNITED STATES ECONOMIC FOREIGN POLICY." USA+45 INTELL DELIB/GP FOR/AID INT/TRADE ROUTINE BAL/PAY...RELATIV 20. PAGE 95 A1949
NAT/G PLAN DIPLOM

B61
BULL H.,THE CONTROL OF THE ARMS RACE. COM USA+45 INT/ORG NAT/G PLAN TEC/DEV DIPLOM ATTIT...RELATIV DECISION CONCPT SELF/OBS TREND CON/ANAL GEN/METH 20 COLD/WAR. PAGE 21 A0429
FORCES PWR ARMS/CONT NUC/PWR

S61
ANGLIN D.,"UNITED STATES OPPOSITION TO CANADIAN MEMBERSHIP IN THE PAN AMERICAN UNION: A CANADIAN VIEW." L/A+17C UK USA+45 VOL/ASSN DELIB/GP EX/STRUC PLAN DIPLOM DOMIN REGION ATTIT RIGID/FLEX PWR ...RELATIV CONCPT STERTYP CMN/WLTH OAS 20. PAGE 8 A0162
INT/ORG CANADA

S61
MIKSCHE F.O.,"DEFENSE ORGANIZATION FOR WESTERN EUROPE." USA+45 INT/ORG NAT/G VOL/ASSN ACT/RES DOMIN LEGIT COERCE ORD/FREE PWR...RELATIV TREND 20 NATO. PAGE 101 A2071
EUR+WWI FORCES WEAPON NUC/PWR

L62
NIZARD L.,"CUBAN QUESTION AND SECURITY COUNCIL." L/A+17C USA+45 ECO/UNDEV NAT/G POL/PAR DELIB/GP ECO/TAC PWR...RELATIV OBS TIME/SEQ TREND GEN/LAWS UN 20 UN. PAGE 109 A2242
INT/ORG JURID DIPLOM CUBA

S62
CORET A.,"LE STATUT DE L'ILE CHRISTMAS DE L'OCEAN INDIEN." FUT S/ASIA ECO/DEV ECO/UNDEV VOL/ASSN
NAT/G INT/ORG

DELIB/GP PLAN...RELATIV OBS TIME/SEQ TREND AUSTRAL NEW/ZEALND
20. PAGE 30 A0619

B64
FALK R.A.,THE ROLE OF DOMESTIC COURTS IN THE LAW
INTERNATIONAL LEGAL ORDER. FUT WOR+45 INT/ORG NAT/G INT/LAW
JUDGE EDU/PROP LEGIT CT/SYS...POLICY RELATIV JURID
CONCPT GEN/LAWS 20. PAGE 43 A0889

L64
ARMENGALD A.,"ECONOMIE ET COEXISTENCE." COM EUR+WWI MARKET
FUT USA+45 WOR+45 ECO/DEV ECO/UNDEV FINAN INT/ORG ECO/TAC
NAT/G EXEC CHOOSE ATTIT ALL/VALS...POLICY RELATIV CAP/ISM
DECISION TREND SOC/EXP COLD/WAR WORK 20. PAGE 9
A0173

L64
HOFFMANN S.,"EUROPE'S IDENTITY CRISIS: BETWEEN THE COERCE
PAST AND AMERICA." EUR+WWI FUT USA+45 INT/ORG NAT/G POLICY
LEGIT RIGID/FLEX ALL/VALS...RELATIV TOT/POP 20.
PAGE 66 A1358

L64
WARD C.,"THE 'NEW MYTHS' AND 'OLD REALITIES' OF FORCES
NUCLEAR WAR." COM FUT USA+45 USSR WOR+45 INT/ORG COERCE
NAT/G DOMIN LEGIT EXEC ATTIT PERCEPT ALL/VALS ARMS/CONT
...POLICY RELATIV PSY MYTH TREND 20. PAGE 161 A3280 NUC/PWR

S64
JORDAN A.,"POLITICAL COMMUNICATION: THE THIRD EDU/PROP
DIMENSION OF STRATEGY." USA+45 WOR+45 INT/ORG NAT/G RIGID/FLEX
CONSULT FORCES PLAN LEGIT EXEC PERCEPT ALL/VALS ATTIT
...POLICY RELATIV PSY NEW/IDEA AUD/VIS EXHIBIT
TOT/POP 20. PAGE 75 A1534

S64
WASKOW A.I.,"NEW ROADS TO A WORLD WITHOUT WAR." FUT INT/ORG
WOR+45 CULTURE INTELL SOCIETY NAT/G DOMIN LEGIT FORCES
EXEC COERCE PEACE ATTIT DISPL PERCEPT RIGID/FLEX
ALL/VALS...POLICY RELATIV SOC NEW/IDEA 20. PAGE 161
A3288

L65
WIONCZEK M.,"LATIN AMERICA FREE TRADE ASSOCIATION." L/A+17C
AGRI DIST/IND FINAN INDUS INT/ORG LABOR NAT/G MARKET
TEC/DEV ECO/TAC HEALTH SKILL WEALTH...POLICY REGION
RELATIV MGT LAFTA 20. PAGE 165 A3369

RELATIVISM....SEE RELATIV

RELATIVITY....SEE RELATIV

RELIABILITY....SEE METH/CNCPT

RELIGION....SEE SECT, WORSHIP

RELIGIOUS GROUP....SEE SECT

REMAK J. A2465

RENAISSAN....RENAISSANCE

RENT....RENTING

S67
BUTTINGER J.,"VIETNAM* FRAUD OF THE 'OTHER WAR'." PLAN
VIETNAM/S ELITES STRUCT AGRI NAT/G FOR/AID RENT WEALTH
TREND. PAGE 22 A0456 REV
ECO/UNDEV

REP/CONVEN....REPUBLICAN (PARTY - U.S.) NATIONAL CONVENTION

REPAR....REPARATIONS; SEE ALSO INT/REL, SANCTION

B10
GRIFFIN A.P.C.,LIST OF REFERENCES ON RECIPROCITY BIBLIOG/A
(2ND REV. ED.). CANADA CUBA UK USA-45 WOR-45 NAT/G VOL/ASSN
TARIFFS CONFER COLONIAL CONTROL SANCTION CONSEN DIPLOM
ALL/VALS...DECISION 19/20. PAGE 56 A1157 REPAR

B36
HUDSON M.O.,INTERNATIONAL LEGISLATION: 1929-1931. INT/LAW
WOR-45 SEA AIR AGRI FINAN LABOR DIPLOM ECO/TAC PARL/PROC
REPAR CT/SYS ARMS/CONT WAR WEAPON...JURID 20 TREATY ADJUD
LEAGUE/NAT. PAGE 69 A1409 LAW

B41
BIRDSALL P.,VERSAILLES TWENTY YEARS AFTER. MOD/EUR DIPLOM
POL/PAR CHIEF CONSULT FORCES LEGIS REPAR PEACE NAT/LISM
ORD/FREE...BIBLIOG 20 PRESIDENT TREATY. PAGE 14 WAR
A0290

B41
NIEMEYER G.,LAW WITHOUT FORCE: THE FUNCTION OF COERCE
POLITICS IN INTERNATIONAL LAW. PLAN INSPECT DIPLOM LAW
REPAR LEGIT ADJUD WAR ORD/FREE...IDEA/COMP PWR
METH/COMP GEN/LAWS 20. PAGE 109 A2240 INT/LAW

B44
RUDIN H.R.,ARMISTICE 1918. FRANCE GERMANY MOD/EUR AGREE
UK USA-45 NAT/G CHIEF DELIB/GP FORCES BAL/PWR REPAR WAR
ARMS/CONT 20 WILSON/W TREATY. PAGE 125 A2566 PEACE
DIPLOM

B49
JACKSON R.H.,INTERNATIONAL CONFERENCE ON MILITARY DIPLOM
TRIALS. FRANCE GERMANY UK USA+45 USSR VOL/ASSN INT/ORG
DELIB/GP REPAR ADJUD CT/SYS CRIME WAR 20 WAR/TRIAL. INT/LAW
PAGE 72 A1479 CIVMIL/REL

B60
FEIS H.,BETWEEN WAR AND PEACE: THE POTSDAM DIPLOM
CONFERENCE. EUR+WWI NAT/G DELIB/GP PROB/SOLV REPAR CONFER
WAR CIVMIL/REL...BIBLIOG 20. PAGE 45 A0911 BAL/PWR

B65
BRIDGMAN J.,GERMAN AFRICA: A SELECT ANNOTATED BIBLIOG/A
BIBLIOGRAPHY. AFR AGRI DIPLOM REPAR WAR FASCISM 20. COLONIAL
PAGE 18 A0374 NAT/G
EDU/PROP

B66
BROWNLIE I.,PRINCIPLES OF PUBLIC INTERNATIONAL LAW. INT/LAW
WOR+45 WOR-45 LAW JUDGE REPAR ADJUD SOVEREIGN DIPLOM
...JURID T. PAGE 20 A0409 INT/ORG

B66
GILBERT M.,THE ROOTS OF APPEASEMENT. EUR+WWI DIPLOM
GERMANY UK MUNIC BAL/PWR FASCISM...NEW/IDEA 20. REPAR
PAGE 52 A1070 PROB/SOLV
POLICY

S67
HALL M.,"GERMANY, EAST AND WEST* DANGER AT THE NAT/LISM
CROSSROADS." GERMANY ELITES CHIEF FORCES DIPLOM ATTIT
ECO/TAC REPAR ARMS/CONT...SOCIALIST 20. PAGE 60 FASCISM
A1227 WEAPON

S67
ODA S.,"THE NORMALIZATION OF RELATIONS BETWEEN DIPLOM
JAPAN AND THE REPUBLIC OF KOREA." NAT/G BAL/PWR LEGIS
REPAR INT/LAW. PAGE 111 A2276 DECISION

REPARATIONS....SEE REPAR

REPRESENT....REPRESENTATION; SEE ALSO LEGIS

N
INTERNATIONAL REVIEW OF ADMINISTRATIVE SCIENCES. BIBLIOG/A
WOR+45 WOR-45 STRATA ECO/DEV ECO/UNDEV CREATE PLAN ADMIN
PROB/SOLV DIPLOM CONTROL REPRESENT...MGT 20. PAGE 1 INT/ORG
A0011 NAT/G

N
LITERATUR-VERZEICHNIS DER POLITISCHEN BIBLIOG
WISSENSCHAFTEN. GERMANY/W WOR+45 CONSTN SOCIETY EUR+WWI
ECO/DEV INT/ORG POL/PAR LEAD REPRESENT GOV/REL DIPLOM
GP/REL...POLICY PHIL/SCI. PAGE 1 A0018 NAT/G

NCO
CARRINGTON C.E.,THE COMMONWEALTH IN AFRICA ECO/UNDEV
(PAMPHLET). UK STRUCT NAT/G COLONIAL REPRESENT AFR
GOV/REL RACE/REL NAT/LISM...MAJORIT 20 EEC NEGRO DIPLOM
COLD/WAR. PAGE 25 A0500 PLAN

N19
LISKA G.,THE GREATER MAGHREB: FROM INDEPENDENCE TO ECO/UNDEV
UNITY? (PAMPHLET). ALGERIA ISLAM MOROCCO PROB/SOLV REGION
BAL/PWR CONFER COLONIAL REPRESENT NAT/LISM 20 DIPLOM
TUNIS. PAGE 90 A1835 DOMIN

N19
MASSEY V.,CANADIANS AND THEIR COMMONWEALTH: THE ATTIT
ROMANES LECTURE DELIVERED IN THE SHELDONIAN THEATRE DIPLOM
JUNE 1, 1961 (PAMPHLET). CANADA UK CULTURE ECO/DEV NAT/G
REPRESENT NAT/LISM PEACE PWR CONSERVE 20 CMN/WLTH. SOVEREIGN
PAGE 96 A1959

C28
WARD P.W.,"SOVEREIGNTY: A STUDY OF A CONTEMPORARY SOVEREIGN
POLITICAL NOTION." CONSTN NAT/G DIPLOM REPRESENT CONCPT
PLURISM...IDEA/COMP BIBLIOG. PAGE 161 A3281 NAT/LISM

B39
THOMAS J.A.,THE HOUSE OF COMMONS, 1832-1901; A PARL/PROC
STUDY OF ITS ECONOMIC AND FUNCTIONAL CHARACTER. UK LEGIS
LAW STRATA FINAN DIPLOM CONTROL LEAD LOBBY POL/PAR
REPRESENT WEALTH...POLICY STAT BIBLIOG 19/20 ECO/DEV
PARLIAMENT. PAGE 143 A2922

B54
US SENATE COMM ON FOREIGN REL,REVIEW OF THE UNITED BIBLIOG
NATIONS CHARTER: A COLLECTION OF DOCUMENTS. LEGIS CONSTN
DIPLOM ADMIN ARMS/CONT WAR REPRESENT SOVEREIGN INT/ORG
...INT/LAW 20 UN. PAGE 156 A3180 DEBATE

B55
BURR R.N.,DOCUMENTS ON INTER-AMERICAN COOPERATION: BIBLIOG
VOL. I, 1810-1881; VOL. II, 1881-1948. DELIB/GP DIPLOM
BAL/PWR INT/TRADE REPRESENT NAT/LISM PEACE HABITAT INT/ORG
ORD/FREE PWR SOVEREIGN...INT/LAW 20 OAS. PAGE 22 L/A+17C
A0445

B55
MACMAHON A.W.,FEDERALISM: MATURE AND EMERGENT. STRUCT
EUR+WWI FUT WOR+45 WOR-45 INT/ORG NAT/G REPRESENT CONCPT
FEDERAL...POLICY MGT RECORD TREND GEN/LAWS 20.
PAGE 93 A1900

C55
APTER D.E.,"THE GOLD COAST IN TRANSITION." AFR ORD/FREE
CONSTN LOC/G LEGIS DIPLOM COLONIAL CONTROL GOV/REL REPRESENT
...CHARTS BIBLIOG 20 CMN/WLTH. PAGE 8 A0170 PARL/PROC
NAT/G

B56
FIELD G.C.,POLITICAL THEORY. POL/PAR REPRESENT CONCPT
MORAL SOVEREIGN...JURID IDEA/COMP. PAGE 45 A0924 NAT/G
ORD/FREE
DIPLOM

B56
JAMESON J.F.,THE AMERICAN REVOLUTION CONSIDERED AS A SOCIAL MOVEMENT. USA-45 AGRI FINAN SECT INT/TRADE REPRESENT SUFF INGP/REL RACE/REL DISCRIM...MAJORIT 18/19 CHURCH/STA. PAGE 73 A1494
ORD/FREE REV FEDERAL CONSTN

B57
MILLIKAN M.F.,A PROPOSAL: KEY TO AN EFFECTIVE FOREIGN POLICY. USA+45 AGRI FINAN DELIB/GP DIPLOM REPRESENT MAJORITY...NEW/IDEA CHARTS. PAGE 101 A2081
FOR/AID GIVE ECO/UNDEV PLAN

B57
US SENATE COMM ON JUDICIARY,HEARING BEFORE SUBCOMMITTEE ON COMMITTEE OF JUDICIARY, UNITED STATES SENATE: S. J. RES. 3. USA+45 NAT/G CONSULT DELIB/GP DIPLOM ADJUD LOBBY REPRESENT 20 CONGRESS TREATY. PAGE 157 A3192
LEGIS CONSTN CONFER AGREE

C58
CARTER G.M.,"THE POLITICS OF INEQUALITY: SOUTH AFRICA SINCE 1948." SOUTH/AFR CONSTN DIPLOM EDU/PROP REPRESENT DISCRIM ATTIT...POLICY PREDICT CHARTS BIBLIOG 20. PAGE 25 A0504
RACE/REL POL/PAR CHOOSE DOMIN

S59
SUTTON F.X.,"REPRESENTATION AND THE NATURE OF POLITICAL SYSTEMS." UNIV WOR-45 CULTURE SOCIETY STRATA INT/ORG FORCES JUDGE DOMIN LEGIT EXEC REGION REPRESENT ATTIT ORD/FREE RESPECT...SOC HIST/WRIT TIME/SEQ. PAGE 140 A2867
NAT/G CONCPT

B61
US HOUSE COMM FOREIGN AFFAIRS,THE INTERNATIONAL DEVELOPMENT AND SECURITY ACT: HEARINGS BEFORE COMMITTEE ON FOREIGN AFFAIRS, HOUSE OF REP: HR7372. USA+45 AGRI INT/ORG NAT/G CONSULT DELIB/GP DIPLOM ECO/TAC INT/TRADE LOBBY REPRESENT 20 MCNAMARA/R DILLON/D RUSK/D CONGRESS. PAGE 153 A3128
FOR/AID CONFER LEGIS ECO/UNDEV

B62
ALEXANDROWICZ C.H.,WORLD ECONOMIC AGENCIES: LAW AND PRACTICE. WOR+45 DIST/IND FINAN LABOR CONSULT INT/TRADE TARIFFS REPRESENT HEALTH...JURID 20 UN GATT EEC OAS ECSC. PAGE 6 A0115
INT/LAW INT/ORG DIPLOM ADJUD

B62
MOON P.,DIVIDE AND QUIT. INDIA PAKISTAN STRATA DELIB/GP PLAN DIPLOM REPRESENT GP/REL INGP/REL CONSEN DISCRIM...OBS 20. PAGE 103 A2119
WAR REGION ISOLAT SECT

B63
ELIAS T.O.,GOVERNMENT AND POLITICS IN AFRICA. CONSTN CULTURE SOCIETY NAT/G POL/PAR DIPLOM REPRESENT PERSON...SOC TREND BIBLIOG 4/20. PAGE 41 A0837
AFR NAT/LISM COLONIAL LAW

B63
PRESTON W. JR.,ALIENS AND DISSENTERS: FEDERAL SUPPRESSION OF RADICALS 1903-1933. USA-45 DIPLOM ADJUD REPRESENT RACE/REL MAJORITY...BIBLIOG/A 19/20. PAGE 117 A2409
DISCRIM GP/REL INGP/REL ATTIT

B64
STANKIEWICZ W.J.,POLITICAL THOUGHT SINCE WORLD WAR II. WOR+45 CAP/ISM DIPLOM COLONIAL COERCE REV REPRESENT ADJUST ANOMIE ALL/IDEOS 20. PAGE 137 A2804
IDEA/COMP DOMIN ORD/FREE AUTHORIT

B65
LEWIS W.A.,POLITICS IN WEST AFRICA. AFR BAL/PWR DIPLOM REPRESENT...POLICY 20. PAGE 88 A1804
POL/PAR ELITES NAT/G ECO/UNDEV

B66
RIESELBACH L.N.,THE ROOTS OF ISOLATIONISM* CONGRESSIONAL VOTING AND PRESIDENTIAL LEADERSHIP IN FOREIGN POLICY. POL/PAR LEGIS DIPLOM EDU/PROP LEAD REGION REPRESENT...SOC STAT IDEA/COMP HYPO/EXP BIBLIOG 19/20 CONGRESS. PAGE 121 A2477
ISOLAT CHOOSE CHIEF POLICY

B66
US SENATE COMM GOVT OPERATIONS,POPULATION CRISIS. USA+45 ECO/DEV ECO/UNDEV AGRI SECT DELIB/GP PROB/SOLV FOR/AID REPRESENT ATTIT...GEOG CHARTS 20 CONGRESS DEPT/STATE DEPT/HEW BIRTH/CON. PAGE 156 A3178
CENSUS CONTROL LEGIS CONSULT

L66
MCDOUGAL M.S.,"CHINESE PARTICIPATION IN THE UNITED NATIONS: THE LEGAL IMPERATIVES OF A NEGOTIATED SOLUTION" CHINA/COM WOR+45 VOL/ASSN DIPLOM PARTIC ...DECISION IDEA/COMP 20 UN. PAGE 98 A2010
INT/ORG REPRESENT POLICY PROB/SOLV

B67
KNOLES G.H.,THE RESPONSIBILITIES OF POWER, 1900-1929. USA-45 SOCIETY SECT JUDGE COLONIAL REPRESENT WEALTH POPULISM...IDEA/COMP ANTHOL PRESIDENT 20 LEAGUE/NAT. PAGE 81 A1653
PWR DIPLOM NAT/LISM WAR

B67
US SENATE COMM ON FOREIGN REL,HUMAN RIGHTS CONVENTIONS. USA+45 LABOR VOL/ASSN DELIB/GP DOMIN ADJUD REPRESENT...INT/LAW MGT CONGRESS. PAGE 156 A3189
LEGIS ORD/FREE WORKER LOBBY

B67
WATERS M.,THE UNITED NATIONS* INTERNATIONAL ORGANIZATION AND ADMINISTRATION. WOR+45 EX/STRUC FORCES DIPLOM LEAD REGION ARMS/CONT REPRESENT INGP/REL ROLE...METH/COMP ANTHOL 20 UN LEAGUE/NAT. PAGE 162 A3291
CONSTN INT/ORG ADMIN ADJUD

S67
BLUM Y.Z.,"INDONESIA'S RETURN TO THE UNITED NATIONS." INDONESIA ADJUD SANCTION REPRESENT ...JURID 20 UN. PAGE 16 A0324
CONSTN LAW DIPLOM INT/ORG

S67
HUDSON R.,"WAS THIS WAR NECESSARY? THE UN AND THE MIDDLE EAST" WOR+45 STRUCT DIPLOM DOMIN CONTROL REPRESENT PWR...NEW/IDEA 20 UN MID/EAST. PAGE 69 A1410
DELIB/GP INT/ORG PROB/SOLV PEACE

S67
LEVI M.,"LES DIFFICULTES ECONOMIQUES DE LA GRANDE-BRETAGNE." UK INT/ORG TEC/DEV BARGAIN DIPLOM DOMIN REPRESENT DEMAND WEALTH...POLICY 20 EEC. PAGE 88 A1792
BAL/PAY INT/TRADE PRODUC

S67
THIEN T.T.,"VIETNAM: A CASE OF SOCIAL ALIENATION." VIETNAM AGRI FORCES FOR/AID ADMIN REPRESENT INGP/REL PWR 19/20. PAGE 143 A2918
NAT/G ELITES WORKER STRANGE

B91
SIDGWICK H.,THE ELEMENTS OF POLITICS. LOC/G NAT/G LEGIS DIPLOM ADJUD CONTROL EXEC PARL/PROC REPRESENT GOV/REL SOVEREIGN ALL/IDEOS 19 MILL/JS BENTHAM/J. PAGE 132 A2713
POLICY LAW CONCPT

REPUBLIC OF CHINA....SEE TAIWAN

REPUBLICAN....REPUBLICAN PARTY (ALL NATIONS)

B27
SIEGFRIED A.,AMERICA COMES OF AGE: A FRENCH ANALYSIS (TRANS. BY H.H. HEMMING AND DORIS HEMMING). FRANCE UK POL/PAR WORKER TEC/DEV DIPLOM REGION RACE/REL ADJUST PRODUC HEREDITY...TIME/SEQ GP/COMP SOC/INTEG 20 DEMOCRAT REPUBLICAN KKK. PAGE 132 A2714
USA-45 CULTURE ECO/DEV SOC

B60
MORISON E.E.,TURMOIL AND TRADITION: A STUDY OF THE LIFE AND TIMES OF HENRY L. STIMSON. USA+45 USA-45 POL/PAR CHIEF DELIB/GP FORCES BAL/PWR DIPLOM ARMS/CONT WAR PEACE 19/20 STIMSON/HL ROOSEVLT/F TAFT/WH HOOVER/H REPUBLICAN. PAGE 104 A2142
BIOG NAT/G EX/STRUC

B64
MORGAN T.,GOLDWATER EITHER/OR; A SELF-PORTRAIT BASED UPON HIS OWN WORDS. USA+45 CONSTN AGRI LABOR DIPLOM RACE/REL WEALTH POPULISM...POLICY MAJORIT 20 GOLDWATR/B REPUBLICAN. PAGE 104 A2131
LEAD POL/PAR CHOOSE ATTIT

REQUA E.G. A2466

RESEARCH....SEE **OP/RES, R&D, CREATE**

RESEARCH AND DEVELOPMENT GROUP....SEE R+D

RESIST/INT....SOCIAL RESISTANCE TO INTERVIEWS

L58
SNYDER R.N.,"THE UNITED STATES DECISION TO RESIST AGGRESSION IN KOREA." ASIA KOREA S/ASIA USA+45 USA-45 WOR+45 INT/ORG DELIB/GP BAL/PWR COERCE PWR ...CONCPT REC/INT RESIST/INT COLD/WAR 20. PAGE 134 A2753
QUANT METH/CNCPT DIPLOM

RESOURCE/N....NATURAL RESOURCES; **SEE ALSO OIL.**

N19
HAUSER P.M.,WORLD POPULATION PROBLEMS (PAMPHLET). USA+45 WOR+45 ECO/DEV ECO/UNDEV FAM ACT/RES PLAN PROB/SOLV FOR/AID GIVE EATING...CHARTS 20 BIRTH/CON RESOURCE/N. PAGE 63 A1289
CONTROL CENSUS ATTIT PREDICT

B58
SOC OF COMP LEGIS AND INT LAW,THE LAW OF THE SEA... (PAMPHLET). WOR+45 NAT/G INT/TRADE ADJUD CONTROL NUC/PWR WAR PEACE ATTIT ORD/FREE...JURID CHARTS 20 UN TREATY RESOURCE/N. PAGE 135 A2756
INT/LAW INT/ORG DIPLOM SEA

B60
NEALE A.D.,THE FLOW OF RESOURCES FROM RICH TO POOR. WOR+45 ECO/DEV ECO/UNDEV FINAN INDUS NAT/G PLAN EFFICIENCY WEALTH...POLICY NAT/COMP 20 RESOURCE/N. PAGE 108 A2209
FOR/AID DIPLOM METH/CNCPT

B63
EL-NAGGAR S.,FOREIGN AID TO UNITED ARAB REPUBLIC. UAR USA+45 USSR AGRI FINAN INDUS FORCES EATING DEMAND...CHARTS METH/COMP 20 RESOURCE/N AID. PAGE 41 A0838
FOR/AID ECO/UNDEV RECEIVE PLAN

N64
GREAT BRITAIN CENTRAL OFF INF,THE COLOMBO PLAN (PAMPHLET). ASIA S/ASIA USA+45 VOL/ASSN...CHARTS 20 COMMONWLTH RESOURCE/N. PAGE 55 A1134
FOR/AID PLAN INT/ORG ECO/UNDEV

B65
WHITE HOUSE CONFERENCE ON INTERNATIONAL
R+D

COOPERATION(VOL.II). SPACE WOR+45 EXTR/IND INT/ORG LABOR WORKER NUC/PWR PEACE AGE/Y...CENSUS ANTHOL 20 RESOURCE/N URBAN/RNWL PUB/TRANS. PAGE 3 A0071 — CONFER TEC/DEV DIPLOM

B65
JALEE P.,THE PILLAGE OF THE THIRD WORLD (TRANS. BY MARY KLOPPER). WOR+45 AGRI INDUS ECO/TAC FOR/AID COLONIAL CONTROL PRODUC PWR WEALTH...STAT CHARTS 20 RESOURCE/N. PAGE 73 A1493 — ECO/UNDEV DOMIN INT/TRADE DIPLOM

RESPECT....RESPECT, SOCIAL CLASS, STRATIFICATION (CONTEMPT)

B22
WALSH E.,THE HISTORY AND NATURE OF INTERNATIONAL RELATIONS. ASIA L/A+17C MOD/EUR USA-45 WOR-45 NAT/G FORCES TOP/EX BAL/PWR REGION ATTIT ORD/FREE RESPECT ...CONCPT HIST/WRIT TREND. PAGE 161 A3270 — INT/ORG TIME/SEQ DIPLOM

B28
CORBETT P.E.,CANADA AND WORLD POLITICS. LAW CULTURE SOCIETY STRUCT MARKET INT/ORG FORCES ACT/RES PLAN ECO/TAC LEGIT ORD/FREE PWR RESPECT...SOC CONCPT TIME/SEQ TREND CMN/WLTH 20 LEAGUE/NAT. PAGE 30 A0612 — NAT/G CANADA

B28
MAIR L.P.,THE PROTECTION OF MINORITIES. EUR+WWI WOR-45 CONSTN INT/ORG NAT/G LEGIT CT/SYS GP/REL RACE/REL DISCRIM ORD/FREE RESPECT...JURID CONCPT TIME/SEQ 20. PAGE 93 A1909 — LAW SOVEREIGN

B29
DUNN F.,THE PRACTICE AND PROCEDURE OF INTERNATIONAL CONFERENCES. WOR-45 NAT/G DELIB/GP BAL/PWR LEGIT EXEC ROUTINE PEACE ORD/FREE RESPECT...JURID CONCPT METH/CNCPT OBS RECORD TIME/SEQ 20. PAGE 39 A0799 — INT/ORG DIPLOM

S41
WRIGHT Q.,"FUNDAMENTAL PROBLEMS OF INTERNATIONAL ORGANIZATION." UNIV WOR-45 STRUCT FORCES ACT/RES CREATE DOMIN EDU/PROP LEGIT REGION NAT/LISM ORD/FREE PWR RESPECT SOVEREIGN...JURID SOC CONCPT METH/CNCPT TIME/SEQ 20. PAGE 167 A3405 — INT/ORG ATTIT PEACE

B47
HILL M.,IMMUNITIES AND PRIVILEGES OF INTERNATIONAL OFFICIALS. CANADA EUR+WWI NETHERLAND SWITZERLND LAW LEGIS DIPLOM LEGIT RESPECT...TIME/SEQ LEAGUE/NAT UN VAL/FREE 20. PAGE 65 A1330 — INT/ORG ADMIN

B48
VISSON A.,AS OTHERS SEE US. EUR+WWI FRANCE UK USA+45 CULTURE INTELL SOCIETY STRATA NAT/G POL/PAR FOR/AID ATTIT DRIVE LOVE ORD/FREE RESPECT WEALTH ...PLURIST SOC OBS TOT/POP 20. PAGE 159 A3244 — USA-45 PERCEPT

L51
KELSEN H.,"RECENT TRENDS IN THE LAW OF THE UNITED NATIONS." KOREA WOR+45 CONSTN LEGIS DIPLOM LEGIT DETER WAR RIGID/FLEX HEALTH ORD/FREE RESPECT ...JURID CON/ANAL UN VAL/FREE 20 NATO. PAGE 77 A1582 — INT/ORG LAW INT/LAW

S51
ICHHEISER G.,"MISUNDERSTANDING IN INTERNATIONAL RELATIONS." UNIV SOCIETY FACE/GP INT/ORG SECT ATTIT PERSON RIGID/FLEX LOVE RESPECT...RELATIV PSY SOC CONCPT MYTH SOC/EXP GEN/LAWS. PAGE 70 A1431 — PERCEPT STERTYP NAT/LISM DIPLOM

L52
NIEBUHR R.,"THE MORAL IMPLICATIONS OF LOYALTY TO THE UNITED NATIONS." WOR+45 WOR-45 SOCIETY ECO/DEV INT/ORG VOL/ASSN PEACE ATTIT PERSON LOVE ORD/FREE PWR RESPECT...CONCPT UN TOT/POP COLD/WAR UNESCO 20. PAGE 109 A2236 — SUPEGO GEN/LAWS

B56
GEORGE A.L.,WOODROW WILSON AND COLONEL HOUSE. WOR-45 CONSTN FACE/GP INT/ORG NAT/G POL/PAR CONSULT LEGIT EXEC COERCE CHOOSE ATTIT DRIVE PERSON MORAL ORD/FREE PWR RESPECT...POLICY MGT PSY OBS RECORD INT LEAGUE/NAT. PAGE 52 A1060 — USA-45 BIOG DIPLOM

C56
VAGTS A.,"DEFENSE AND DIPLOMACY: THE SOLDIER AND THE CONDUCT OF FOREIGN RELATIONS." OP/RES CONFER DETER WAR PEACE RESPECT...POLICY DECISION CONCPT BIBLIOG 17/20. PAGE 158 A3209 — DIPLOM FORCES HIST/WRIT

B59
JOSEPH F.M.,AS OTHERS SEE US: THE UNITED STATES THROUGH FOREIGN EYES. AFR EUR+WWI ISLAM L/A+17C S/ASIA USA+45 CULTURE SOCIETY ECO/DEV ECO/UNDEV INT/ORG NAT/G DIPLOM ECO/TAC REV ATTIT RIGID/FLEX HEALTH ORD/FREE WEALTH 20. PAGE 75 A1537 — RESPECT DOMIN NAT/LISM SOVEREIGN

S59
SUTTON F.X.,"REPRESENTATION AND THE NATURE OF POLITICAL SYSTEMS." UNIV WOR-45 CULTURE SOCIETY STRATA INT/ORG FORCES JUDGE DOMIN LEGIT EXEC REGION REPRESENT ATTIT ORD/FREE RESPECT...SOC HIST/WRIT TIME/SEQ. PAGE 140 A2867 — NAT/G CONCPT

B60
CONN S.,THE FRAMEWORK OF HEMISPHERE DEFENSE. CANADA L/A+17C USA-45 NAT/G FORCES BAL/PWR DOMIN WAR PEACE DISPL PWR RESPECT...PLURIST CONCPT HIST/WRIT HYPO/EXP MEXIC/AMER 20 ROOSEVLT/F. PAGE 29 A0585 — USA+45 INT/ORG DIPLOM

S60
BOGARDUS E.S.,"THE SOCIOLOGY OF A STRUCTURED PEACE." FUT SOCIETY CREATE DIPLOM EDU/PROP ADJUD ROUTINE ATTIT RIGID/FLEX KNOWL ORD/FREE RESPECT ...POLICY INT/LAW JURID NEW/IDEA SELF/OBS TOT/POP 20 UN. PAGE 16 A0327 — INT/ORG SOC NAT/LISM PEACE

S60
HAVILAND H.F.,"PROBLEMS OF AMERICAN FOREIGN POLICY." ASIA COM USA+45 WOR+45 INT/ORG NAT/G CONSULT ECO/TAC FOR/AID DOMIN COERCE NUC/PWR ATTIT DRIVE ORD/FREE PWR RESPECT SKILL...POLICY GEOG OBS SAMP TREND GEN/METH METH COLD/WAR UN 20. PAGE 63 A1292 — ECO/UNDEV FORCES DIPLOM

B61
NEAL F.W.,US FOREIGN POLICY AND THE SOVIET UNION. USA+45 USSR INT/ORG ECO/TAC ARMS/CONT MAJORITY NAT/LISM ATTIT RESPECT MARXISM 20. PAGE 108 A2207 — DIPLOM POLICY PEACE

B62
KING-HALL S.,POWER POLITICS IN THE NUCLEAR AGE: A POLICY FOR BRITAIN. UK WOR+45 PLAN ECO/TAC CONTROL RISK ARMS/CONT MORAL PWR RESPECT...OLD/LIB 20. PAGE 79 A1625 — BAL/PWR NUC/PWR POLICY DIPLOM

B62
SPANIER J.W.,THE POLITICS OF DISARMAMENT. COM USA+45 USSR EDU/PROP ATTIT ORD/FREE PWR RESPECT ...MYTH RECORD 20 COLD/WAR. PAGE 135 A2771 — INT/ORG DELIB/GP ARMS/CONT

B62
TRISKA J.F.,THE THEORY, LAW, AND POLICY OF SOVIET TREATIES. WOR+45 WOR-45 CONSTN INT/ORG NAT/G VOL/ASSN DOMIN LEGIT COERCE ATTIT PWR RESPECT ...POLICY JURID CONCPT OBS SAMP TIME/SEQ TREND GEN/LAWS 20. PAGE 145 A2966 — COM LAW INT/LAW USSR

L62
GROSS L.,"IMMUNITIES AND PRIVILEGES OF DELIGATIONS TO THE UNITED NATIONS." USA+45 WOR+45 STRATA NAT/G VOL/ASSN CONSULT DIPLOM EDU/PROP ROUTINE RESPECT ...POLICY INT/LAW CONCPT UN 20. PAGE 57 A1176 — INT/ORG LAW ELITES

S62
BERKES R.N.B.,"THE NEW FRONTIER IN THE UN." FUT USA+45 WOR+45 INT/ORG DELIB/GP NAT/LISM PERCEPT RESPECT UN OAS 20. PAGE 13 A0272 — GEN/LAWS DIPLOM

S62
MORGENTHAU H.J.,"A POLITICAL THEORY OF FOREIGN AID." ECO/UNDEV NAT/G DELIB/GP PLAN ECO/TAC EDU/PROP EXEC ORD/FREE RESPECT WEALTH...METH/CNCPT TREND 20. PAGE 104 A2140 — USA+45 PHIL/SCI FOR/AID

S62
SPECTOR I.,"SOVIET POLICY IN ASIA: A REAPPRAISAL." ASIA CHINA/COM COM INDIA INDONESIA ECO/UNDEV INT/ORG DOMIN EDU/PROP REGION RESPECT...CONCPT TREND TOT/POP COLD/WAR 20 CHINJAP. PAGE 135 A2774 — S/ASIA PWR FOR/AID USSR

B63
BURNS A.L.,PEACE-KEEPING BY U.N.FORCES - FROM SUEZ TO THE CONGO. AFR FUT ISLAM ISRAEL USSR WOR+45 NAT/G DELIB/GP BAL/PWR DOMIN LEGIT EXEC COERCE PEACE ATTIT PWR RESPECT SOVEREIGN...CONCPT UN 20. PAGE 22 A0441 — INT/ORG FORCES ORD/FREE

B63
HOVET T. JR.,AFRICA IN THE UNITED NATIONS. AFR DELIB/GP EDU/PROP LOBBY CHOOSE ORD/FREE PWR RESPECT SKILL...STAT TIME/SEQ CON/ANAL CHARTS STERTYP VAL/FREE 20 UN. PAGE 68 A1397 — INT/ORG USSR

B63
LERCHE C.O. JR.,CONCEPTS OF INTERNATIONAL POLITICS. WOR+45 WOR-45 LAW DELIB/GP EX/STRUC TEC/DEV ECO/TAC INT/TRADE LEGIT ROUTINE COERCE ATTIT ORD/FREE PWR RESPECT...STERTYP GEN/LAWS VAL/FREE. PAGE 87 A1782 — INT/ORG WAR

B63
PERKINS B.,PROLOGUE TO THE WAR: ENGLAND AND THE UNITED STATES, 1805-1812. MOD/EUR UK USA-45 NAT/G ORD/FREE RESPECT SOVEREIGN...POLICY TREATY 19 WAR/1812. PAGE 115 A2358 — WAR DIPLOM NEUTRAL

B63
ROBERTSON A.H.,HUMAN RIGHTS IN EUROPE. CONSTN SOCIETY INT/ORG NAT/G VOL/ASSN DELIB/GP ACT/RES PLAN ADJUD REGION ROUTINE ATTIT LOVE ORD/FREE RESPECT...JURID SOC CONCPT SOC/EXP UN 20. PAGE 122 A2498 — EUR+WWI PERSON

L63
LISSITZYN O.J.,"INTERNATIONAL LAW IN A DIVIDED WORLD." FUT WOR+45 CONSTN CULTURE ECO/DEV ECO/UNDEV DIST/IND NAT/G FORCES ECO/TAC LEGIT ADJUD ADMIN COERCE ATTIT HEALTH MORAL ORD/FREE PWR RESPECT WEALTH VAL/FREE. PAGE 90 A1841 — INT/ORG LAW

S63
LERNER D.,"FRENCH ELITE PERSPECTIVES ON THE UNITED NATIONS." EUR+WWI INT/ORG HEALTH ORD/FREE PWR RESPECT...STAT INT SAMP/SIZ VAL/FREE UN 20. PAGE 87 A1786 — ATTIT STERTYP ELITES FRANCE

B64
BOYD J.P.,NUMBER 7: ALEXANDER HAMILTON'S SECRET ATTEMPTS TO CONTROL AMERICAN FOREIGN POLICY. AFR UK DIPLOM WAR RESPECT WEALTH...POLICY HIST/WRIT 18 HAMILTON/A. PAGE 18 A0364 — USA-45 NAT/G TOP/EX PWR

B64
ETZIONI A.,WINNING WITHOUT WAR. FUT MOD/EUR USA+45 WOR+45 ECO/DEV ECO/UNDEV INT/ORG NAT/G FORCES TOP/EX PLAN TEC/DEV ECO/TAC DOMIN EDU/PROP LEGIT COERCE CHOOSE ATTIT MORAL ORD/FREE RESPECT WEALTH — PWR TREND DIPLOM USSR

MAJORIT. PAGE 43 A0871

B64
FISHER R.,INTERNATIONAL CONFLICT AND BEHAVIORAL SCIENCE: THE CRAIGVILLE PAPERS. COM FUT USA+45 WOR+45 NAT/G DELIB/GP EX/STRUC FORCES ECO/TAC DOMIN EDU/PROP LEGIT COERCE ATTIT PERCEPT ORD/FREE PWR RESPECT...PSY SOC VAL/FREE. PAGE 46 A0940
INT/ORG PLAN DIPLOM

B64
IKLE F.C.,HOW NATIONS NEGOTIATE. COM EUR+WWI USA+45 INTELL INT/ORG VOL/ASSN DELIB/GP ACT/RES CREATE DOMIN EDU/PROP ADJUD ROUTINE ATTIT PERSON ORD/FREE RESPECT SKILL...PSY SOC OBS VAL/FREE. PAGE 70 A1433
NAT/G PWR POLICY

B64
JANOWITZ M.,THE MILITARY IN THE POLITICAL DEVELOPMENT OF NEW NATIONS: AN ESSAY IN COMPARATIVE ANALYSIS. AFR ASIA ISLAM L/A+17C S/ASIA USA+45 ECO/UNDEV INT/ORG NAT/G POL/PAR DELIB/GP PLAN ECO/TAC DOMIN LEGIT COERCE ATTIT DRIVE RESPECT ...SOC CONCPT CENSUS VAL/FREE. PAGE 73 A1495
FORCES PWR

B64
SCHWELB E.,HUMAN RIGHTS AND THE INTERNATIONAL COMMUNITY. WOR+45 WOR-45 NAT/G SECT DELIB/GP DIPLOM PEACE RESPECT TREATY 20 UN. PAGE 130 A2666
INT/ORG ORD/FREE INT/LAW

L64
POUNDS N.J.G.,"THE POLITICS OF PARTITION." AFR ASIA COM EUR+WWI FUT ISLAM S/ASIA USA-45 LAW ECO/DEV ECO/UNDEV AGRI INDUS INT/ORG POL/PAR PROVS SECT FORCES TOP/EX EDU/PROP LEGIT ATTIT MORAL ORD/FREE PWR RESPECT WEALTH. PAGE 117 A2402
NAT/G NAT/LISM

L64
SYMONDS R.,"REFLECTIONS IN LOCALISATION." AFR S/ASIA UK STRATA INT/ORG NAT/G SCHOOL EDU/PROP LEGIT KNOWL ORD/FREE PWR RESPECT CMN/WLTH 20. PAGE 140 A2874
ADMIN MGT COLONIAL

S64
HOVET T. JR.,"THE ROLE OF AFRICA IN THE UNITED NATIONS." FUT WOR+45 NAT/G DELIB/GP DOMIN EDU/PROP LEGIT ORD/FREE PWR RESPECT SKILL...OBS TIME/SEQ TREND VAL/FREE UN 20. PAGE 68 A1398
AFR INT/ORG DIPLOM

S64
KHAN M.Z.,"THE PRESIDENT OF THE GENERAL ASSEMBLY." WOR+45 CONSTN DELIB/GP EDU/PROP LEGIT ROUTINE PWR RESPECT SKILL...DECISION SOC BIOG TREND UN 20. PAGE 78 A1609
INT/ORG TOP/EX

S64
MAZRUI A.A.,"THE UNITED NATIONS AND SOME AFRICAN POLITICAL ATTITUDES." ECO/TAC FOR/AID DOMIN ROUTINE CHOOSE ATTIT DRIVE MORAL PWR RESPECT WEALTH...PSY CONCPT OBS TREND UN VAL/FREE 20. PAGE 97 A1987
AFR INT/ORG SOVEREIGN

B65
GEORGE M.,THE WARPED VISION. EUR+WWI UK NAT/G POL/PAR LEGIS PARL/PROC SANCTION COERCE WAR GOV/REL PEACE RESPECT 20 CONSRV/PAR. PAGE 52 A1061
LEAD ATTIT DIPLOM POLICY

B66
NANTWI E.K.,THE ENFORCEMENT OF INTERNATIONAL JUDICIAL DECISIONS AND ARBITAL AWARDS IN PUBLIC INTERNATIONAL LAW. WOR+45 WOR-45 JUDGE PROB/SOLV DIPLOM CT/SYS SUPEGO MORAL PWR RESPECT...METH/CNCPT 18/20 CASEBOOK. PAGE 107 A2196
INT/LAW ADJUD SOVEREIGN INT/ORG

RESPONSIBILITY....SEE SUPEGO, RESPECT

RESPONSIVENESS....SEE RIGID/FLEX

RESTRAINT....SEE ORD/FREE

RETAILING....SEE MARKET

RETIREMENT....SEE SENIOR, ADMIN

REUBENS E.D. A2467

REUSS H.S. A2468

REUTER P. A2469

REUTHER/W....WALTER REUTHER

REV....REVOLUTION; SEE ALSO WAR

N
ANNALS OF THE AMERICAN ACADEMY OF POLITICAL AND SOCIAL SCIENCE. AFR ASIA S/ASIA WOR+45 POL/PAR DIPLOM CRIME REV...SOC BIOG 20. PAGE 1 A0004
BIBLIOG/A NAT/G CULTURE ATTIT

N
US CONSULATE GENERAL HONG KONG,CURRENT BACKGROUND. CHINA/COM ECO/UNDEV LOC/G NAT/G PLAN DIPLOM EDU/PROP LEAD REV ATTIT...POLICY INDEX 20. PAGE 151 A3074
BIBLIOG/A MARXIST ASIA PRESS

N
US CONSULATE GENERAL HONG KONG,SURVEY OF CHINA MAINLAND PRESS. CHINA/COM ECO/UNDEV LOC/G NAT/G PLAN DIPLOM EDU/PROP LEAD REV ATTIT...POLICY INDEX 20. PAGE 151 A3075
BIBLIOG/A MARXIST ASIA PRESS

N
US CONSULATE GENERAL HONG KONG,US CONSULATE GENERAL, HONG KONG, PRESS SUMMARIES. CHINA/COM ECO/UNDEV LOC/G NAT/G PLAN DIPLOM EDU/PROP LEAD REV ATTIT...POLICY INDEX 20. PAGE 151 A3076
BIBLIOG/A MARXIST ASIA PRESS

N/R
FULBRIGHT J.W.,THE ARROGANCE OF POWER. USA+45 WOR+45 ECO/UNDEV ACADEM LEGIS ECO/TAC FOR/AID PEACE ROLE ORD/FREE PWR 20 COLD/WAR CONGRESS. PAGE 50 A1014
DIPLOM POLICY REV

B01
HART A.B.,AMERICAN HISTORY TOLD BY CONTEMPORARIES. UK CULTURE FINAN SECT FORCES DIPLOM TAX RUMOR CT/SYS REV GOV/REL GP/REL...ANTHOL 17/18 PRE/US/AM FEDERALIST. PAGE 62 A1273
USA-45 COLONIAL SOVEREIGN

C05
DUNNING W.A.,"HISTORY OF POLITICAL THEORIES FROM LUTHER TO MONTESQUIEU." LAW NAT/G SECT DIPLOM REV WAR ORD/FREE SOVEREIGN CONSERVE...TRADIT BIBLIOG 16/18. PAGE 39 A0803
PHIL/SCI CONCPT GEN/LAWS

B07
GRIFFIN A.P.C.,LIST OF WORKS RELATING TO THE FRENCH ALLIANCE IN THE AMERICAN REVOLUTION. FRANCE FORCES DIPLOM 18 PRE/US/AM. PAGE 56 A1155
BIBLIOG/A REV WAR

B08
LABRIOLA A.,ESSAYS ON THE MATERIALISTIC CONCEPTION OF HISTORY. STRATA POL/PAR CAP/ISM DIPLOM INT/TRADE WAR 20. PAGE 83 A1706
MARXIST WORKER REV COLONIAL

N17
BURKE E.,THOUGHTS ON THE PROSPECT OF A REGICIDE PEACE (PAMPHLET). FRANCE UK SECT DOMIN MURDER PEACE ORD/FREE SOVEREIGN POPULISM...POLICY GOV/COMP IDEA/COMP 18 JACOBINISM COEXIST. PAGE 21 A0435
REV CHIEF NAT/G DIPLOM

N19
ASIAN-AFRICAN CONFERENCE,SELECTED DOCUMENTS OF THE BANDUNG CONFERENCE (PAMPHLET). S/ASIA PLAN ECO/TAC CONFER REGION REV NAT/LISM 20. PAGE 9 A0191
NEUTRAL ECO/UNDEV COLONIAL DIPLOM

B27
GOOCH G.P.,ENGLISH DEMOCRATIC IDEAS IN THE SEVENTEENTH CENTURY (2ND ED.). UK LAW SECT FORCES DIPLOM LEAD PARL/PROC REV ATTIT AUTHORIT...ANARCH CONCPT 17 PARLIAMENT CMN/WLTH REFORMERS. PAGE 54 A1100
IDEA/COMP MAJORIT EX/STRUC CONSERVE

B27
PARRINGTON V.L.,MAIN CURRENTS IN AMERICAN THOUGHT (VOL.I). USA-45 AGRI POL/PAR DIPLOM TAX REGION REV 17/18 FRANKLIN/B JEFFERSN/T. PAGE 114 A2336
COLONIAL SECT FEEDBACK ALL/IDEOS

C28
SCHNEIDER H.W.,"MAKING THE FASCIST STATE." ITALY CULTURE LABOR DIPLOM REV WAR NAT/LISM TOTALISM ATTIT DRIVE SOCISM...BIBLIOG PARLIAMENT 20. PAGE 129 A2638
FASCISM POLICY POL/PAR

B29
DE REPARAZ G.,GEOGRAFIA Y POLITICA. CHILE SPAIN USSR NAT/G DIPLOM REV MARXISM...POLICY 19/20. PAGE 35 A0709
GEOG MOD/EUR

C32
MARRARO H.R.,"AMERICAN OPINION ON THE UNIFICATION OF ITALY." ITALY MOD/EUR USA-45 FORCES DIPLOM PRESS REV CATHISM...BIOG 19 PRESIDENT. PAGE 95 A1944
BIBLIOG/A NAT/LISM ATTIT ORD/FREE

B33
DAHLIN E.,FRENCH AND GERMAN PUBLIC OPINION ON DECLARED WAR AIMS 1914-1918. BELGIUM FRANCE GERMANY NAT/G POL/PAR DIPLOM COERCE REV WAR PEACE 20 WWI WILSON/W. PAGE 33 A0674
ATTIT EDU/PROP DOMIN NAT/COMP

B33
REID H.D.,RECUEIL DES COURS; TOME 45: LES SERVITUDES INTERNATIONALES III. FRANCE CONSTN DELIB/GP PRESS CONTROL REV WAR CHOOSE PEACE MORAL MARITIME TREATY. PAGE 120 A2457
ORD/FREE DIPLOM LAW

B33
PUBLIC OPINION AND WORLD POLITICS. UNIV LAW CULTURE NAT/G PRESS REV GP/REL...MAJORIT METH/COMP ANTHOL 20. PAGE 167 A3400
DIPLOM EDU/PROP ATTIT MAJORITY

B36
BOYCE A.N.,EUROPE AND SOUTH AFRICA. FRANCE GERMANY ITALY SOUTH/AFR UK INDUS NAT/G CONTROL REV WAR NAT/LISM...CONCPT HIST/WRIT 20. PAGE 18 A0362
COLONIAL GOV/COMP NAT/COMP DIPLOM

C37
ROWAN R.W.,"THE STORY OF THE SECRET SERVICE." WOR-45 REV...BIOG BIBLIOG. PAGE 124 A2552
WAR COERCE DIPLOM

B38
HARPER S.N.,THE GOVERNMENT OF THE SOVIET UNION. COM USSR LAW CONSTN ECO/DEV PLAN TEC/DEV DIPLOM INT/TRADE ADMIN REV NAT/LISM...POLICY 20. PAGE 62 A1265
MARXISM NAT/G LEAD POL/PAR

B38
PETTEE G.S.,THE PROCESS OF REVOLUTION. COM FRANCE ITALY MOD/EUR RUSSIA SPAIN WOR-45 ELITES INTELL
COERCE CONCPT

SOCIETY STRATA STRUCT INT/ORG NAT/G POL/PAR ACT/RES PLAN EDU/PROP LEGIT EXEC...SOC MYTH TIME/SEQ TOT/POP 18/20. PAGE 115 A2370 REV

B39
KOHN H.,REVOLUTIONS AND DICTATORSHIPS. COM EUR+WWI ISLAM MOD/EUR NAT/G CHIEF FORCES WAR CIVMIL/REL PWR MARXISM 18/20. PAGE 81 A1661 NAT/LISM TOTALISM REV FASCISM

B43
GRIERSON P.,BOOKS ON SOVIET RUSSIA 1917-42: A BIBLIOGRAPHY AND A GUIDE TO READING. USSR CULTURE ELITES NAT/G PLAN DIPLOM REV...GEOG 20. PAGE 56 A1148 BIBLIOG/A COM MARXISM LEAD

B43
MC DOWELL R.B.,IRISH PUBLIC OPINION, 1750-1800. IRELAND CONSTN VOL/ASSN WORKER ORD/FREE CATHISM CONSERVE...POLICY IDEA/COMP BIBLIOG 18/ PARLIAMENT. PAGE 97 A1992 ATTIT NAT/G DIPLOM REV

B43
ST LEGER A.,SELECTION OF WORKS FOR AN UNDERSTANDING OF WORLD AFFAIRS SINCE 1914. WOR-45 INT/ORG CREATE BAL/PWR REV ADJUST 20. PAGE 137 A2796 BIBLIOG/A WAR SOCIETY DIPLOM

C44
SUAREZ F.,"ON WAR" (1621) IN SELECTIONS FROM THREE WORKS, VOL. I." NAT/G SECT CHIEF DIPLOM LEGIT MORAL PWR...POLICY INT/LAW 17. PAGE 140 A2859 WAR REV ORD/FREE CATH

B48
BELOFF M.,THOMAS JEFFERSON AND AMERICAN DEMOCRACY. USA-45 NAT/G DIPLOM GOV/REL PEACE 18/19 JEFFERSN/T PRESIDENT VIRGINIA. PAGE 13 A0258 BIOG CHIEF REV

B50
GLEASON J.H.,THE GENESIS OF RUSSOPHOBIA IN GREAT BRITAIN: A STUDY OF THE INTERACTION OF POLICY AND OPINION. ASIA RUSSIA UK NAT/G AGREE CONTROL REV WAR LOVE PWR TREATY 19. PAGE 53 A1080 DIPLOM POLICY DOMIN COLONIAL

B50
PERHAM M.,COLONIAL GOVERNMENT: ANNOTATED READING LIST ON BRITISH COLONIAL GOVERNMENT. UK WOR+45 WOR-45 ECO/UNDEV INT/ORG LEGIS FOR/AID INT/TRADE DOMIN ADMIN REV 20. PAGE 115 A2356 BIBLIOG/A COLONIAL GOV/REL NAT/G

N50
SCHAPIRO J.S.,THE WORLD IN CRISES: POLITICAL AND SOCIAL MOVEMENTS IN THE TWENTIETH CENTURY. USA+45 INT/ORG LABOR PLAN CAP/ISM DIPLOM COLONIAL PEACE TOTALISM ATTIT LAISSEZ...BIBLIOG 20 COLD/WAR. PAGE 128 A2618 NAT/LISM TEC/DEV REV WAR

B51
BORKENAU F.,EUROPEAN COMMUNISM. COM EUR+WWI GERMANY SPAIN USSR INT/ORG PLAN REV WAR ATTIT 20 STALIN/J HITLER/A. PAGE 17 A0342 MARXISM POLICY DIPLOM NAT/G

B51
BROGAN D.W.,THE PRICE OF REVOLUTION. FRANCE USA+45 USA-45 USSR CONSTN NAT/G DIPLOM COLONIAL NAT/LISM ORD/FREE POPULISM...CONCPT 18/20 PRE/US/AM. PAGE 19 A0386 REV METH/COMP COST MARXISM

C51
BEST H.,"THE SOVIET STATE AND ITS INCEPTION." USSR CULTURE INDUS DIPLOM WEALTH...GEOG SOC BIBLIOG 20. PAGE 14 A0281 COM GEN/METH REV MARXISM

B52
SHULIM J.I.,THE OLD DOMINION AND NAPOLEON BONAPARTE. POL/PAR DOMIN PRESS REV WAR 18/19 VIRGINIA. PAGE 132 A2710 ATTIT PROVS EDU/PROP DIPLOM

B52
SPENCER F.A.,WAR AND POSTWAR GREECE: AN ANALYSIS BASED ON GREEK WRITINGS. GREECE SOCIETY NAT/G POL/PAR FORCES CREATE DIPLOM LEAD MARXISM...SOC 20. PAGE 136 A2784 BIBLIOG/A WAR REV

B53
FEIS H.,THE CHINA TANGLE. ASIA COM USA+45 USA-45 FORCES ECO/TAC REV ATTIT 20 INTERVENT. PAGE 45 A0910 POLICY DIPLOM WAR FOR/AID

B53
ROSCIO J.G.,OBRAS. L/A+17C SPAIN DIPLOM REV WAR NAT/LISM TOTALISM PWR SOVEREIGN 19. PAGE 123 A2527 ORD/FREE COLONIAL NAT/G PHIL/SCI

B54
COOKSON J.,BEFORE THE AFRICAN STORM. BELGIUM CENTRL/AFR FRANCE UK ECO/UNDEV POL/PAR CREATE BAL/PWR RACE/REL NAT/LISM ORD/FREE CONSERVE MARXISM SOC/INTEG 20 CONGO/LEOP. PAGE 30 A0607 COLONIAL REV DISCRIM DIPLOM

B54
GIRAUD A.,CIVILISATION ET PRODUCTIVITE. UNIV INDUS WORKER DIPLOM REV INCOME UTOPIA...GEOG 20. PAGE 53 A1076 SOCIETY PRODUC ROLE

B55
CRAIG G.A.,THE POLITICS OF THE PRUSSIAN ARMY 1640-1945. CHRIST-17C EUR+WWI MOD/EUR PRUSSIA STRUCT DIPLOM ADMIN REV WAR...SOC BIBLIOG 17/20. PAGE 32 A0652 FORCES NAT/G ROLE CHIEF

B55
JAPANESE STUDIES OF MODERN CHINA. ASIA DIPLOM LEAD REV MARXISM 19/20 CHINJAP. PAGE 43 A0885 BIBLIOG/A SOC

B55
KOHN H.,NATIONALISM: ITS MEANING AND HISTORY. GP/REL INGP/REL ATTIT...CONCPT NAT/COMP 16/20 MACHIAVELL. PAGE 81 A1662 NAT/LISM DIPLOM FASCISM REV

B55
TAN C.C.,THE BOXER CATASTROPHE. ASIA UK USSR ELITES POL/PAR VOL/ASSN FORCES PROB/SOLV DIPLOM ADMIN COLONIAL NAT/LISM PEACE TREATY 19/20 BOXER/REBL. PAGE 141 A2885 REV NAT/G WAR

B56
BOWLES C.,AFRICA'S CHALLENGE TO AMERICA. USA+45 ECO/UNDEV NAT/G LEGIS COLONIAL CONTROL REV ORD/FREE SOVEREIGN 20 COLD/WAR. PAGE 18 A0358 AFR DIPLOM POLICY FOR/AID

B56
JAMESON J.F.,THE AMERICAN REVOLUTION CONSIDERED AS A SOCIAL MOVEMENT. USA-45 AGRI FINAN SECT INT/TRADE REPRESENT SUFF INGP/REL RACE/REL DISCRIM...MAJORIT 18/19 CHURCH/STA. PAGE 73 A1494 ORD/FREE REV FEDERAL CONSTN

B56
WHITAKER A.P.,ARGENTINE UPHEAVAL. STRUCT FORCES DIPLOM COERCE PWR 20 ARGEN. PAGE 164 A3332 REV POL/PAR STRATA NAT/G

B56
WILBUR C.M.,DOCUMENTS ON COMMUNISM, NATIONALISM, AND SOVIET ADVISERS IN CHINA, 1918-1927. CHINA/COM USSR STRUCT DIPLOM LEAD NAT/LISM...BIBLIOG/A 20. PAGE 164 A3343 REV POL/PAR MARXISM COM

B56
WU E.,LEADERS OF TWENTIETH-CENTURY CHINA; AN ANNOTATED BIBLIOGRAPHY OF SELECTED CHINESE BIOGRAPHICAL WORKS IN HOOVER LIBRARY. ASIA INDUS POL/PAR DIPLOM ADMIN REV WAR...HUM MGT 20. PAGE 168 A3422 BIBLIOG/A BIOG INTELL CHIEF

B57
BLOOMFIELD L.P.,EVOLUTION OR REVOLUTION: THE UNITED NATIONS AND THE PROBLEM OF PEACEFUL TERRITORIAL CHANGE. WOR+45 WOR-45 INT/ORG NAT/G DIPLOM ROUTINE REV ATTIT RIGID/FLEX PWR...CONCPT OBS HIST/WRIT UN LEAGUE/NAT 20. PAGE 15 A0315 ORD/FREE LEGIT

B57
BRODY H.,UN DIARY: THE SEARCH FOR PEACE. HUNGARY WOR+45 DELIB/GP ROUTINE REV WAR ORD/FREE...AUD/VIS 20 UN SUEZ. PAGE 19 A0382 INT/ORG PEACE DIPLOM POLICY

B57
JASZI O.,AGAINST THE TYRANT. WOR+45 WOR-45 CONSTN DIPLOM CONTROL PARTIC REV WAR...CONCPT. PAGE 73 A1498 TOTALISM ORD/FREE CHIEF MURDER

B57
NEUMANN F.,THE DEMOCRATIC AND THE AUTHORITARIAN STATE: ESSAYS IN POLITICAL AND LEGAL THEORY. USA+45 USA-45 CONTROL REV GOV/REL PEACE ALL/IDEOS ...INT/LAW CONCPT GEN/LAWS BIBLIOG 20. PAGE 108 A2221 DOMIN NAT/G ORD/FREE POLICY

B57
TOMASIC D.A.,NATIONAL COMMUNISM AND SOVIET STRATEGY. UK USSR YUGOSLAVIA NAT/G POL/PAR CHIEF CREATE DOMIN REV WAR PWR...BIOG TREND 20 TITO/MARSH STALIN/J. PAGE 144 A2948 COM NAT/LISM MARXISM DIPLOM

B58
APPADORAI A.,THE USE OF FORCE IN INTERNATIONAL RELATIONS. WOR+45 CULTURE ECO/UNDEV CAP/ISM ARMS/CONT REV WAR ATTIT PERSON SOVEREIGN MARXISM ...INT/LAW PACIFIST 20 UN INTERVENT THIRD/WRLD COLD/WAR. PAGE 8 A0169 PEACE FEDERAL INT/ORG

B58
HOLT R.T.,RADIO FREE EUROPE. FUT USA+45 CULTURE ECO/DEV INT/ORG KIN POL/PAR SECT FORCES ACT/RES DIPLOM COERCE REV CHOOSE PEACE ATTIT PWR...MAJORIT CONCPT COLD/WAR WORK 20 RFE. PAGE 67 A1374 COM EDU/PROP COM/IND

B58
KENNAN G.F.,THE DECISION TO INTERVENE: SOVIET-AMERICAN RELATIONS, 1917-1920 (VOL. II). CZECHOSLVK EUR+WWI USA-45 USSR ELITES NAT/G FORCES PROB/SOLV REV WAR TOTALISM PWR...CHARTS BIBLIOG 20 TREATY PRESIDENT CHINJAP. PAGE 78 A1588 DIPLOM POLICY ATTIT

B58
TILLION G.,ALGERIA: THE REALITIES. ALGERIA FRANCE ISLAM CULTURE STRATA PROB/SOLV DOMIN REV NAT/LISM WEALTH MARXISM...GEOG 20. PAGE 144 A2940 ECO/UNDEV SOC COLONIAL DIPLOM

C58
BUTTINGER J.,"THE SMALLER DRAGON; A POLITICAL HISTORY OF VIETNAM." VIETNAM SECT DIPLOM CIVMIL/REL ISOLAT NAT/LISM...BIBLIOG/A 3/20. PAGE 22 A0455 COLONIAL DOMIN SOVEREIGN REV

B59
ARON R.,IMPERIALISM AND COLONIALISM (PAMPHLET). COLONIAL

WOR+45 WOR-45 ECO/TAC CONTROL REV ORD/FREE 19/20. PAGE 9 A0183 — DOMIN ECO/UNDEV DIPLOM

B59
BEMIS S.F.,A SHORT HISTORY OF AMERICAN FOREIGN POLICY AND DIPLOMACY. USA+45 USA-45 INT/ORG NEUTRAL REV WAR ISOLAT ORD/FREE...CHARTS T 18/20. PAGE 13 A0266 — DIPLOM ATTIT

B59
CAREW-HUNT R.C.,BOOKS ON COMMUNISM. NAT/G POL/PAR DIPLOM REV...BIOG 19/20. PAGE 24 A0481 — BIBLIOG/A MARXISM COM ASIA

B59
CHALUPA V.,RISE AND DEVELOPMENT OF A TOTALITARIAN STATE. CZECHOSLVK USSR STRUCT INT/ORG WORKER DIPLOM ECO/TAC COERCE NAT/LISM ATTIT...POLICY 20 COM/PARTY. PAGE 25 A0516 — TOTALISM MARXISM REV POL/PAR

B59
FERRELL R.H.,AMERICAN DIPLOMACY: A HISTORY. USA+45 USA-45 PLAN ROUTINE REV WAR PWR...T 18/20 EISNHWR/DD WWI. PAGE 45 A0921 — DIPLOM NAT/G POLICY

B59
GOLDWIN R.A.,READINGS IN RUSSIAN FOREIGN POLICY. HUNGARY USSR YUGOSLAVIA ELITES INT/ORG NAT/G REV WAR NAT/LISM PERSON SOCISM...CHARTS 20 MAPS BOLSHEVISM. PAGE 53 A1095 — COM MARXISM DIPLOM POLICY

B59
JOSEPH F.M.,AS OTHERS SEE US: THE UNITED STATES THROUGH FOREIGN EYES. AFR EUR+WWI ISLAM L/A+17C S/ASIA USA+45 CULTURE SOCIETY ECO/DEV ECO/UNDEV INT/ORG NAT/G DIPLOM ECO/TAC REV ATTIT RIGID/FLEX HEALTH ORD/FREE WEALTH 20. PAGE 75 A1537 — RESPECT DOMIN NAT/LISM SOVEREIGN

B59
KARUNAKARAN K.P.,INDIA IN WORLD AFFAIRS, 1952-1958 (VOL. II). INDIA ECO/UNDEV SECT FOR/AID INT/TRADE ADJUD NEUTRAL REV WAR DISCRIM ORD/FREE MARXISM ...BIBLIOG 20. PAGE 77 A1569 — DIPLOM INT/ORG S/ASIA COLONIAL

B59
NUNEZ JIMENEZ A.,LA LIBERACION DE LAS ISLAS. CUBA L/A+17C USA+45 LAW CHIEF PLAN DIPLOM FOR/AID OWN WEALTH 20 CASTRO/F. PAGE 110 A2261 — AGRI REV ECO/UNDEV NAT/G

B59
OKINSHEVICH L.A.,LATIN AMERICA IN SOVIET WRITINGS, 1945-1958: A BIBLIOGRAPHY. USSR LAW ECO/UNDEV LABOR DIPLOM EDU/PROP REV...GEOG SOC 20. PAGE 111 A2287 — BIBLIOG WRITING COM L/A+17C

C59
KULSKI W.W.,"PEACEFUL COEXISTENCE." USSR ECO/UNDEV INT/ORG POL/PAR EDU/PROP COLONIAL CONTROL REV NAT/LISM PEACE PWR MARXISM...BIBLIOG 20. PAGE 83 A1692 — COM DIPLOM DOMIN

B60
FISCHER L.,THE SOVIETS IN WORLD AFFAIRS. CHINA/COM COM EUR+WWI USSR INT/ORG CONFER LEAD ARMS/CONT REV PWR...CHARTS 20 TREATY VERSAILLES. PAGE 46 A0938 — DIPLOM NAT/G POLICY MARXISM

B60
FOOTMAN D.,INTERNATIONAL COMMUNISM. ASIA EUR+WWI FRANCE FUT GERMANY MOD/EUR S/ASIA USA-45 WOR+45 WOR-45 INTELL LABOR TOTALISM MARXISM WORK 20. PAGE 47 A0958 — COM INT/ORG STRUCT REV

B60
KENNAN G.F.,RUSSIA AND THE WEST. ASIA COM EUR+WWI GERMANY UK USA+45 USA-45 USSR INT/ORG NAT/G VOL/ASSN DOMIN REV WAR PWR...TIME/SEQ 20. PAGE 78 A1590 — EXEC DIPLOM

B60
MC CLELLAN G.S.,INDIA. CHINA/COM INDIA CONSTN ELITES STRATA AGRI POL/PAR FOR/AID ARMS/CONT REV MARXISM...CENSUS BIBLIOG 20 COLD/WAR GANDHI/M NEHRU/J. PAGE 97 A1990 — DIPLOM NAT/G SOCIETY ECO/UNDEV

B60
NURTY K.S.,STUDIES IN PROBLEMS OF PEACE. CHRIST-17C MOD/EUR S/ASIA WOR+45 WOR-45 INT/ORG NAT/G SECT COERCE REV NAT/LISM ALL/VALS...CONCPT MYTH TIME/SEQ. PAGE 110 A2262 — POLICY PEACE PACIFISM ORD/FREE

B60
SETHE P.,SCHICKSALSSTUNDEN DER WELTGESCHICHTE (6TH ED.). NAT/G BAL/PWR DOMIN REV PWR...NAT/COMP 16/20. PAGE 131 A2687 — DIPLOM WAR PEACE

B60
SZTARAY Z.,BIBLIOGRAPHY ON HUNGARY. HUNGARY MOD/EUR CULTURE INDUS SECT DIPLOM REV...ART/METH SOC LING 18/20. PAGE 141 A2879 — BIBLIOG NAT/G COM MARXISM

S60
GRACIA-MORA M.R.,"INTERNATIONAL RESPONSIBILITY FOR SUBVERSIVE ACTIVITIES AND HOSTILE PROPAGANDA BY PRIVATE PERSONS AGAINST." COM EUR+WWI L/A+17C UK USA+45 USSR WOR-45 CONSTN NAT/G LEGIT ADJUD REV PEACE TOTALISM ORD/FREE...INT/LAW 20. PAGE 55 A1119 — INT/ORG JURID SOVEREIGN

B61
ANSPRENGER F.,POLITIK IM SCHWARZEN AFRIKA. FRANCE NAT/G DIPLOM REGION REV NAT/LISM...CHARTS BIBLIOG 19/20. PAGE 8 A0164 — AFR COLONIAL SOVEREIGN

B61
CAMERON J.,THE AFRICAN REVOLUTION. AFR UK ECO/UNDEV POL/PAR REGION RACE/REL DISCRIM PWR CONSERVE ...CONCPT SOC/INTEG 20 NEGRO. PAGE 23 A0472 — REV COLONIAL ORD/FREE DIPLOM

B61
DELZELL C.F.,MUSSOLINI'S ENEMIES - THE ITALIAN ANTI-FASCIST RESISTANCE. ITALY DIPLOM PRESS DETER WAR TOTALISM ORD/FREE MARXISM 20. PAGE 36 A0730 — FASCISM GP/REL POL/PAR REV

B61
FLEMING D.F.,THE COLD WAR AND ITS ORIGINS: 1950-1960 (VOL. II). ASIA FUT HUNGARY POLAND WOR+45 TEC/DEV DOMIN NUC/PWR REV PEACE...T 20 COLD/WAR EISNHWR/DD SUEZ. PAGE 46 A0946 — MARXISM DIPLOM BAL/PWR

B61
FLEMING D.F.,THE COLD WAR AND ITS ORIGINS: 1917-1950 (VOL. I). ASIA USSR WOR+45 WOR-45 TEC/DEV FOR/AID NUC/PWR REV WAR PEACE FASCISM...T 20 COLD/WAR NATO BERLIN/BLO. PAGE 46 A0947 — DIPLOM MARXISM BAL/PWR

B61
FULLER J.F.C.,THE CONDUCT OF WAR, 1789-1961. FRANCE RUSSIA SOCIETY NAT/G FORCES PROB/SOLV AGREE NUC/PWR WEAPON PEACE...SOC 18/20 TREATY COLD/WAR. PAGE 50 A1025 — WAR POLICY REV ROLE

B61
GOLDWERT M.,CONSTABULARY IN THE DOMINICAN REPUBLIC AND NICARAGUA. DOMIN/REP L/A+17C NICARAGUA USA-45 NAT/G PLAN CONTROL TASK REV...POLICY 20 INTERVENT. PAGE 53 A1093 — DIPLOM PEACE FORCES

B61
HADDAD J.A.,REVOLUCAO CUBANA E REVOLUCAO BRASILEIRA. BRAZIL CUBA L/A+17C STRATA AGRI WORKER EDU/PROP REGION...POLICY NAT/COMP 20. PAGE 59 A1210 — REV ORD/FREE DIPLOM ECO/UNDEV

B61
HUDSON G.F.,THE SINO-SOVIET DISPUTE. CHINA/COM USSR INTELL INT/TRADE DEBATE REV...IDEA/COMP 20. PAGE 68 A1404 — DIPLOM MARXISM PRESS ATTIT

B61
KHAN A.W.,INDIA WINS FREEDOM: THE OTHER SIDE. INDIA PAKISTAN CULTURE LEGIS DIPLOM PARL/PROC REV WAR NAT/LISM 20. PAGE 78 A1607 — SOVEREIGN GP/REL RACE/REL ORD/FREE

B61
LIPPMANN W.,THE COMING TESTS WITH RUSSIA. COM CUBA GERMANY USSR FORCES CONTROL NEUTRAL COERCE NUC/PWR REV WAR PWR...INT 20 KHRUSH/N BERLIN. PAGE 89 A1830 — BAL/PWR DIPLOM MARXISM ARMS/CONT

B61
MATTHEWS T.,WAR IN ALGERIA. ALGERIA FRANCE CONTROL ATTIT SOVEREIGN 20. PAGE 96 A1978 — REV COLONIAL DIPLOM WAR

B61
NOLLAU G.,INTERNATIONAL COMMUNISM AND WORLD REVOLUTION: HISTORY AND METHODS. RUSSIA USSR INT/ORG NAT/G POL/PAR VOL/ASSN FORCES BAL/PWR DIPLOM EXEC REGION WAR ATTIT PWR MARXISM...CONCPT TIME/SEQ COLD/WAR 19/20. PAGE 102 A2100 — COM REV

B61
NOLLAU G.,INTERNATIONAL COMMUNISM AND WORLD REVOLUTION; HISTORY AND METHODS (TRANS. BY VICTOR ANDERSEN). COM WORKER DIPLOM CONFER INGP/REL ...CONCPT BIBLIOG 20 STALIN/J LENIN/VI COMINTERN COMINFORM WORLD/CONG. PAGE 110 A2249 — MARXISM POL/PAR INT/ORG REV

B61
PERKINS D.,THE UNITED STATES AND LATIN AMERICAN. L/A+17C USA+45 USA-45 STRUCT COLONIAL REV ORD/FREE 19/20. PAGE 115 A2360 — DIPLOM INT/TRADE NAT/G

B61
SCHONBRUNN G.,WELTKRIEGE UND REVOLUTIONEN 1914-1945. USSR DIPLOM TOTALISM ORD/FREE 20 TREATY WWI NAZI. PAGE 129 A2643 — WAR REV FASCISM SOCISM

B61
THEOBALD R.,THE CHALLENGE OF ABUNDANCE. USA+45 WOR+45 MARKET DIPLOM FOR/AID REV PRODUC UTOPIA SUPEGO...POLICY TREND BIBLIOG/A 20. PAGE 142 A2913 — WELF/ST ECO/UNDEV PROB/SOLV ECO/TAC

B61
UAR MINISTRY OF CULTURE,A BIBLIOGRAPHICAL LIST OF LIBYA. ISLAM LIBYA DIPLOM COLONIAL REV WAR 19/20. PAGE 146 A2988 — BIBLIOG GEOG SECT NAT/LISM

B61
US LIBRARY OF CONGRESS,WORLD COMMUNIST MOVEMENT. USA+45 USSR WOR+45 INT/ORG DIPLOM REV ATTIT 19/20. PAGE 155 A3155 — BIBLIOG/A EDU/PROP MARXISM POL/PAR

B61
US SENATE COMM ON FOREIGN RELS,INTERNATIONAL DEVELOPMENT AND SECURITY: HEARINGS ON BILL (2 VOLS.). ECO/UNDEV FINAN FORCES REV COST WEALTH — FOR/AID CIVMIL/REL ORD/FREE

...CHARTS 20 AID PRESIDENT. PAGE 157 A3191 ECO/TAC

B61
WARNER D.,HURRICANE FROM CHINA. ASIA CHINA/COM FUT L/A+17C USA+45 CULTURE NAT/G FORCES TOP/EX FOR/AID DRIVE PWR...CONCPT TIME/SEQ SEATO WORK 20. PAGE 161 A3284 ATTIT TREND REV

B61
WINTER R.C.,BLUEPRINTS FOR INDEPENDENCE. WOR+45 INT/ORG DIPLOM COLONIAL CONTROL REV WAR PWR ...BIBLIOG 20 UN. PAGE 165 A3367 NAT/G ECO/UNDEV SOVEREIGN CONSTN

S61
ASHFORD D.E.,"A CASE STUDY IN THE DIPLOMACY OF SOCIAL REVOLUTION." USA+45 WOR+45 DIPLOM ECO/TAC FOR/AID REV ALL/VALS VAL/FREE 20. PAGE 9 A0187 ECO/UNDEV PLAN

S61
DANIELS R.V.,"THE CHINESE REVOLUTION IN RUSSIAN PERSPECTIVE." ASIA CHINA/COM COM USSR INTELL INT/ORG TOP/EX REV TOTALISM PWR...POLICY WORK VAL/FREE 20. PAGE 33 A0680 POL/PAR PLAN

S61
TUCKER R.C.,"TOWARDS A COMPARATIVE POLITICS OF MOVEMENT-REGIMES" (BMR)" USSR CONSTN NAT/G CREATE PROB/SOLV DIPLOM DOMIN REV...GP/COMP IDEA/COMP METH 20 STALIN/J BOLSHEVISM. PAGE 145 A2971 MARXISM POLICY GEN/LAWS PWR

B62
BAULIN J.,THE ARAB ROLE IN AFRICA. AFR ALGERIA FUT ISLAM MOROCCO UAR COLONIAL NEUTRAL REV...SOC 20 TUNIS BOURGUIBA. PAGE 12 A0235 NAT/LISM DIPLOM NAT/G SECT

B62
GYORGY A.,PROBLEMS IN INTERNATIONAL RELATIONS. COM CT/SYS NUC/PWR ALL/IDEOS 20 UN EEC ECSC. PAGE 58 A1199 DIPLOM NEUTRAL BAL/PWR REV

B62
HOOK S.,WORLD COMMUNISM: KEY DOCUMENTARY MATERIAL. CHINA/COM L/A+17C USA+45 USSR POL/PAR DIPLOM COLONIAL REV WAR...ANTHOL 20 MARX/KARL LENIN/VI COM/PARTY. PAGE 67 A1380 MARXISM COM GEN/LAWS NAT/G

B62
KENT R.K.,FROM MADAGASCAR TO THE MALAGASY REPUBLIC. FRANCE MADAGASCAR DIPLOM NAT/LISM ORD/FREE...MGT 18/20. PAGE 78 A1596 COLONIAL SOVEREIGN REV POL/PAR

B62
LAUERHAUSS L.,COMMUNISM IN LATIN AMERICA: THE POST-WAR YEARS (1945 -1960) (PAPER). INTELL STRATA ECO/UNDEV AGRI WORKER FOR/AID INT/TRADE COLONIAL GUERRILLA 20. PAGE 85 A1745 BIBLIOG L/A+17C MARXISM REV

B62
LERNER M.,THE AGE OF OVERKILL: A PREFACE TO WORLD POLITICS. USA+45 USSR WOR+45 SOCIETY ECO/UNDEV BAL/PWR NEUTRAL PARTIC REV ALL/IDEOS MARXISM ...BIBLIOG/A 20. PAGE 87 A1787 DIPLOM NUC/PWR PWR DEATH

B62
MORRAY J.P.,THE SECOND REVOLUTION IN CUBA. CUBA AGRI LABOR POL/PAR DIPLOM FOR/AID GUERRILLA TOTALISM MARXISM 20. PAGE 104 A2146 REV MARXIST ECO/TAC NAT/LISM

B62
PERRE J.,LES MUTATIONS DE LA GUERRE MODERNE: DE LA REVOLUTION FRANCAISE A LA REVOLUTION NUCLEAIRE. DIPLOM ARMS/CONT DEATH REV WEAPON GP/REL PEACE ATTIT...STAT PREDICT BIBLIOG 18/20 WWI. PAGE 115 A2365 WAR FORCES NUC/PWR

B62
SELOSOEMARDJAN O.,SOCIAL CHANGES IN JOGJAKARTA. INDONESIA NETHERLAND ELITES STRATA STRUCT FAM POL/PAR CREATE DIPLOM INT/TRADE EDU/PROP ADMIN GOV/REL...SOC 20 JAVA CHINJAP. PAGE 131 A2683 ECO/UNDEV CULTURE REV COLONIAL

B62
SHAPIRO D.,A SELECT BIBLIOGRAPHY OF WORKS IN ENGLISH ON RUSSIAN HISTORY, 1801-1917. COM USSR STRATA FORCES EDU/PROP ADMIN REV RACE/REL ATTIT 19/20. PAGE 131 A2693 BIBLIOG DIPLOM COLONIAL

B62
WILLIAMS W.A.,THE UNITED STATES, CUBA, AND CASTRO: AN ESSAY ON THE DYNAMICS OF REVOLUTION AND THE DISSOLUTION OF EMPIRE. CUBA USA+45 AGRI VOL/ASSN DIPLOM ECO/TAC DOMIN COERCE...POLICY 20 EISNHWR/DD CIA KENNEDY/JF CASTRO/F. PAGE 165 A3354 REV CONSTN COM LEAD

S62
BLOOMFIELD L.P.,"THE UNITED NATIONS IN CRISIS: THE ROLE OF THE UN IN USA FOREIGN POLICY." FUT USA+45 WOR+45 ECO/UNDEV DIPLOM ATTIT ORD/FREE...CONCPT UN. PAGE 16 A0317 INT/ORG TREND REV

S62
GREENSPAN M.,"INTERNATIONAL LAW AND ITS PROTECTION FOR PARTICIPANTS IN UNCONVENTIONAL WARFARE." WOR+45 LAW INT/ORG NAT/G POL/PAR COERCE REV ORD/FREE ...INT/LAW TOT/POP 20. PAGE 56 A1143 FORCES JURID GUERRILLA WAR

S62
THOMAS J.R.T.,"SOVIET BEHAVIOR IN THE QUEMOY CRISES OF 1958." CHINA/COM FUT USSR WOR+45 INT/ORG VOL/ASSN FORCES PLAN BAL/PWR DOMIN COERCE NUC/PWR REV WAR ATTIT DRIVE ORD/FREE...POLICY OBS RECORD COLD/WAR FOR/POL 20. PAGE 143 A2923 COM PWR

B63
CANELAS O.A.,RADIOGRAFIA DE LA ALIANZA PARA EL ATRASO. L/A+17C USA+45 ECO/TAC DOMIN COLONIAL NAT/LISM...SOCIALIST NAT/COMP 20. PAGE 23 A0476 REV DIPLOM ECO/UNDEV REGION

B63
FLORES E.,LAND REFORM AND THE ALLIANCE FOR PROGRESS (PAMPHLET). L/A+17C USA+45 STRUCT ECO/UNDEV NAT/G WORKER CREATE PLAN ECO/TAC COERCE REV 20. PAGE 47 A0953 AGRI INT/ORG DIPLOM POLICY

B63
GRAEBNER N.A.,THE COLD WAR: IDEOLOGICAL CONFLICT OR POWER STRUGGLE? USSR WOR+45 WOR-45 PROB/SOLV EDU/PROP ARMS/CONT REV NAT/LISM PEACE ORD/FREE ...IDEA/COMP ANTHOL BIBLIOG/A 20 COLD/WAR. PAGE 55 A1123 DIPLOM BAL/PWR MARXISM

B63
HALASZ DE BEKY I.L.,A BIBLIOGRAPHY OF THE HUNGARIAN REVOLUTION 1956. COM HUNGARY USSR DIPLOM COERCE MARXISM...POLICY AUD/VIS 20 UN COLD/WAR. PAGE 59 A1221 BIBLIOG REV FORCES ATTIT

B63
HAMM H.,ALBANIA - CHINA'S BEACHHEAD IN EUROPE. ALBANIA CHINA/COM USSR YUGOSLAVIA ELITES SOCIETY POL/PAR DELIB/GP FORCES ECO/TAC COERCE ISOLAT PEACE MARXISM...IDEA/COMP 20 MAO. PAGE 61 A1248 DIPLOM REV NAT/G POLICY

B63
JOYCE W.,THE PROPAGANDA GAP. USA+45 COM/IND ACADEM DOMIN FEEDBACK REV CIVMIL/REL...REALPOL COLD/WAR. PAGE 75 A1540 EDU/PROP PERCEPT BAL/PWR DIPLOM

B63
KHRUSHCHEV N.S.,THE NEW CONTENT OF PEACEFUL COEXISTENCE IN THE NUCLEAR AGE. GERMANY/E WORKER NUC/PWR REV SOCISM 20 COLD/WAR. PAGE 79 A1614 MARXISM POL/PAR PEACE DIPLOM

B63
LEE C.,THE POLITICS OF KOREAN NATIONALISM. KOREA S/ASIA DIPLOM REV WAR 14/20 CHINJAP. PAGE 86 A1759 NAT/LISM SOVEREIGN COLONIAL

B63
MALIK C.,MAN IN THE STRUGGLE FOR PEACE. USSR WOR+45 CHIEF PLAN PROB/SOLV PARTIC NUC/PWR REV ORD/FREE ...IDEA/COMP METH/COMP 20 UN COLD/WAR. PAGE 93 A1912 PEACE MARXISM DIPLOM EDU/PROP

B63
MENDES C.,NACIONALISMO E DESENVOLVIMENTO. AFR ASIA L/A+17C STRATA INT/TRADE COLONIAL. PAGE 99 A2039 NAT/LISM ECO/UNDEV DIPLOM REV

B63
NORTH R.C.,M. N. ROY'S MISSION TO CHINA: THE COMMUNIST-KUOMINTANG SPLIT OF 1927. ASIA USSR STRATA LEGIS WORKER LEAD REV ATTIT ROLE SOCISM 20 ROY/MN COM/PARTY. PAGE 110 A2253 POL/PAR MARXISM DIPLOM

B63
SZULC T.,THE WINDS OF REVOLUTION; LATIN AMERICA TODAY - AND TOMORROW. L/A+17C ORD/FREE SOCISM ...PREDICT TREND 20. PAGE 141 A2880 REV INT/ORG MARXISM ECO/UNDEV

B63
TUCKER R.C.,THE SOVIET POLITICAL MIND. WOR+45 ELITES INT/ORG NAT/G POL/PAR PLAN DIPLOM ECO/TAC DOMIN ADMIN NUC/PWR REV DRIVE PERSON SUPEGO PWR WEALTH...POLICY MGT PSY CONCPT OBS BIOG TREND COLD/WAR MARX/KARL 20. PAGE 145 A2972 COM TOP/EX USSR

B63
VON HALLER A.,DIE LETZTEN WOLLEN DIE ERSTEN SEIN. AFR S/ASIA INT/TRADE REV ORD/FREE SOVEREIGN 20. PAGE 160 A3251 FOR/AID ECO/UNDEV MARXISM CAP/ISM

S63
BLOOMFIELD L.P.,"INTERNATIONAL FORCE IN A DISARMING BUT REVOLUTIONARY WORLD." INT/ORG COERCE REV DRIVE PWR...CONCPT STERTYP GEN/LAWS 20. PAGE 16 A0318 FORCES ORD/FREE ARMS/CONT GUERRILLA

B64
ALVIM J.C.,A REVOLUCAO SEM RUMO. BRAZIL NAT/G BAL/PWR DIPLOM INT/TRADE PARTIC WEALTH...POLICY SOC SOC/INTEG 20. PAGE 6 A0132 REV CIVMIL/REL ECO/UNDEV ORD/FREE

B64
BLOOMFIELD L.P.,INTERNATIONAL MILITARY FORCES: THE QUESTION OF PEACE-KEEPING IN AN ARMED AND DISARMING WORLD. WOR+45 ACADEM ARMS/CONT REV PEACE 20 UN. PAGE 16 A0320 INT/ORG FORCES FUT DIPLOM

B64
BURKE F.G.,AFRICA'S QUEST FOR ORDER. AFR CULTURE KIN MUNIC NAT/G DIPLOM COLONIAL REV DISCRIM NAT/LISM AGE/Y 20. PAGE 21 A0437 ORD/FREE CONSEN RACE/REL LEAD

B64
DONOUGHUE B.,BRITISH POLITICS AND THE AMERICAN REVOLUTION: THE PATH TO WAR 1773-75. UK USA-45 DIPLOM POLICY

NAT/G LEGIS WAR 18 PRE/US/AM. PAGE 38 A0772 — COLONIAL REV

B64
EPSTEIN H.M.,REVOLT IN THE CONGO. AFR CONGO/BRAZ WOR+45 NAT/G FORCES DOMIN WAR CIVMIL/REL INGP/REL MARXISM...RECORD GP/COMP 20 CONGO/LEOP UN. PAGE 42 A0856 — REV COLONIAL NAT/LISM DIPLOM

B64
FALL B.,STREET WITHOUT JOY. FRANCE USA+45 DIPLOM ECO/TAC FOR/AID GUERRILLA REV WEAPON...TREND 20. PAGE 44 A0894 — WAR S/ASIA FORCES COERCE

B64
IRISH M.D.,WORLD PRESSURES ON AMERICAN FOREIGN POLICY. ASIA COM L/A+17C SOUTH/AFR UK WOR+45 ECO/DEV ECO/UNDEV COLONIAL SANCTION COERCE REV TOTALISM...ANTHOL 20 COLD/WAR EUROPE/W INTERVENT. PAGE 72 A1467 — DIPLOM POLICY

B64
JENSEN D.L.,DIPLOMACY AND DOGMATISM. FRANCE SPAIN REV WAR PERSON CATHISM...POLICY BIOG 16. PAGE 74 A1513 — DIPLOM ATTIT SECT

B64
KIS T.I.,LES PAYS DE L'EUROPE DE L'EST: LEURS RAPPORTS MUTUELS ET LE PROBLEME DE LEUR INTEGRATION DANS L'ORBITE DE L'USSR. EUR+WWI RUSSIA USSR INT/ORG NAT/G REV ATTIT...JURID SOC BIBLIOG WARSAW/P COMECON EUROPE/E. PAGE 80 A1638 — DIPLOM COM MARXISM REGION

B64
LENSEN G.A.,REVELATIONS OF A RUSSIAN DIPLOMAT: THE MEMOIRS OF DMITRII I. ABRIKOSSOV. ASIA MOD/EUR RUSSIA USA-45 ELITES ACADEM CHIEF FORCES REV WAR PWR CONSERVE MARXISM 19/20 ABRIKSSV/D CHINJAP BOLSHEVISM. PAGE 87 A1775 — DIPLOM POLICY OBS

B64
LIEVWEN E.,GENERALS VS PRESIDENTS: WEOMILITARISM IN LATIN AMERICA. L/A+17C FORCES DIPLOM FOR/AID LEAD ...NAT/COMP 20 PRESIDENT. PAGE 89 A1813 — CIVMIL/REL REV CONSERVE ORD/FREE

B64
LUTHULI A.,AFRICA'S FREEDOM. KIN LABOR POL/PAR SCHOOL DIPLOM NEUTRAL REGION REV NAT/LISM PWR WEALTH SOCISM SOC/INTEG 20. PAGE 92 A1874 — AFR ECO/UNDEV COLONIAL

B64
MACKESY P.,THE WAR FOR AMERICA, 1775-1783. UK FORCES DIPLOM...POLICY 18. PAGE 93 A1895 — WAR COLONIAL LEAD REV

B64
MAIER J.,POLITICS OF CHANGE IN LATIN AMERICA. BRAZIL L/A+17C STRATA INT/ORG NAT/G POL/PAR FOR/AID REV 20. PAGE 93 A1907 — SOCIETY NAT/LISM DIPLOM REGION

B64
NEHEMKIS P.,LATIN AMERICA: MYTH AND REALITY. INDUS INT/ORG MUNIC PROB/SOLV CAP/ISM DIPLOM REV...SOC 20. PAGE 108 A2211 — REGION MYTH L/A+17C ECO/UNDEV

B64
PENNOCK J.R.,SELF-GOVERNMENT IN MODERNIZING NATIONS. AFR COM USA+45 ECO/DEV POL/PAR PROB/SOLV DIPLOM ECO/TAC COLONIAL REV POPULISM SOCISM 20. PAGE 114 A2350 — ECO/UNDEV POLICY SOVEREIGN NAT/G

B64
ROSENAU J.N.,INTERNATIONAL ASPECTS OF CIVIL STRIFE. CHINA/COM CUBA EUR+WWI USA+45 USSR BAL/PWR EDU/PROP NEUTRAL COERCE MORAL...NAT/COMP 20 COLD/WAR UN. PAGE 124 A2533 — POLICY DIPLOM REV WAR

B64
STANKIEWICZ W.J.,POLITICAL THOUGHT SINCE WORLD WAR II. WOR+45 CAP/ISM DIPLOM COLONIAL COERCE REV REPRESENT ADJUST ANOMIE ALL/IDEOS 20. PAGE 137 A2804 — IDEA/COMP DOMIN ORD/FREE AUTHORIT

S64
GINSBURGS G.,"WARS OF NATIONAL LIBERATION - THE SOVIET THESIS." COM USSR WOR+45 WOR-45 LAW CULTURE INT/ORG DIPLOM LEGIT COLONIAL GUERRILLA WAR NAT/LISM ATTIT PERSON MORAL PWR...JURID OBS TREND MARX/KARL 20. PAGE 53 A1075 — COERCE CONCPT INT/LAW REV

S64
MOORE W.E.,"PREDICTING DISCONTINUITIES IN SOCIAL CHANGE." UNIV WOR+45 ECO/DEV ECO/UNDEV INT/ORG NAT/G COERCE ALL/VALS...METH/CNCPT TIME/SEQ TREND TOT/POP VAL/FREE 20. PAGE 103 A2125 — SOCIETY GEN/LAWS REV

C64
EASTON S.C.,"THE RISE AND FALL OF WESTERN COLONIALISM." AFR ISLAM L/A+17C ECO/UNDEV REV NAT/LISM...CHARTS BIBLIOG 15/20. PAGE 40 A0817 — COLONIAL DIPLOM ORD/FREE WAR

B65
COLLINS H.,KARL MARX AND THE BRITISH LABOUR MOVEMENT; YEARS OF THE FIRST INTERNATIONAL. FRANCE SWITZERLND UK CAP/ISM WAR...MARXIST IDEA/COMP BIBLIOG 19. PAGE 28 A0567 — MARXISM LABOR INT/ORG REV

B65
COX R.H.,THE STATE IN INTERNATIONAL RELATIONS. INT/ORG DIPLOM REV WAR PEACE MARXISM...CONCPT GOV/COMP. PAGE 32 A0647 — SOVEREIGN NAT/G FASCISM ORD/FREE

B65
FAGG J.E.,CUBA, HAITI, AND THE DOMINICAN REPUBLIC. CUBA DOMIN/REP HAITI L/A+17C NAT/G DIPLOM ECO/TAC DOMIN CHOOSE AUTHORIT ROLE SOVEREIGN POPULISM 17/20. PAGE 43 A0883 — COLONIAL ECO/UNDEV REV GOV/COMP

B65
FANON F.,STUDIES IN A DYING COLONIALISM. ALGERIA FRANCE STRATA FAM DIPLOM DOMIN WAR RACE/REL DISCRIM HEALTH 20. PAGE 44 A0897 — NAT/LISM COLONIAL REV SOVEREIGN

B65
GERASSI J.,THE GREAT FEAR IN LATIN AMERICA. L/A+17C USA+45 ELITES STRUCT INT/ORG REV ORD/FREE WEALTH 20 LAFTA. PAGE 52 A1063 — SOCIETY FOR/AID DIPLOM

B65
GILBERT M.,THE EUROPEAN POWERS 1900-45. EUR+WWI ITALY MOD/EUR USSR REV WAR PWR ALL/IDEOS FASCISM ...AUD/VIS CHARTS BIBLIOG 20. PAGE 52 A1069 — DIPLOM NAT/G POLICY BAL/PWR

B65
HALPERIN E.,NATIONALISM AND COMMUNISM. CHILE L/A+17C CAP/ISM EDU/PROP CHOOSE DISCRIM SOCISM ...BIBLIOG 20 COM/PARTY. PAGE 60 A1236 — NAT/LISM MARXISM POL/PAR REV

B65
IRIYE A.,AFTER IMPERIALISM; THE SEARCH FOR A NEW ORDER IN THE FAR EAST 1921-1931. USA-45 USSR DOMIN AGREE COLONIAL REV PWR...BIBLIOG DICTIONARY 20 CHINJAP. PAGE 72 A1468 — DIPLOM ASIA SOVEREIGN

B65
LACOUTRE J.,VIETNAM: BETWEEN TWO TRUCES. USA+45 VIETNAM NAT/G REV 20. PAGE 83 A1707 — WAR ECO/UNDEV DIPLOM POLICY

B65
MALLIN J.,FORTRESS CUBA; RUSSIA'S AMERICAN BASE. COM CUBA L/A+17C FORCES PLAN DIPLOM LEAD REV WAR ...POLICY 20 CASTRO/F GUEVARA/C INTERVENT. PAGE 93 A1914 — MARXISM CHIEF GUERRILLA DOMIN

B65
MENON K.P.S.,MANY WORLDS. INDIA BAL/PWR CAP/ISM COLONIAL REV ORD/FREE PWR MARXISM...POLICY 20 COLD/WAR. PAGE 100 A2042 — BIOG DIPLOM NAT/G

B65
MORRIS R.B.,THE PEACEMAKERS; THE GREAT POWERS AND AMERICAN INDEPENDENCE. BAL/PWR CONFER COLONIAL NEUTRAL PEACE ORD/FREE TREATY 18 PRE/US/AM. PAGE 105 A2149 — SOVEREIGN REV DIPLOM

B65
MOSTECKY V.,SOVIET LEGAL BIBLIOGRAPHY. USSR LEGIS PRESS WRITING CONFER ADJUD CT/SYS REV MARXISM ...INT/LAW JURID DICTIONARY 20. PAGE 105 A2155 — BIBLIOG/A LAW COM CONSTN

B65
O'CONNELL M.R.,IRISH POLITICS AND SOCIAL CONFLICT IN THE AGE OF THE AMERICAN REVOLUTION. FRANCE IRELAND MOD/EUR STRATA SECT LEGIS DIPLOM INT/TRADE DOMIN REV WAR...BIBLIOG 18 PARLIAMENT. PAGE 111 A2268 — CATHISM ATTIT NAT/G DELIB/GP

B65
ROMEIN J.,THE ASIAN CENTURY. ASIA COM S/ASIA DIPLOM COLONIAL TIME 20. PAGE 123 A2519 — REV NAT/LISM CULTURE MARXISM

B65
WILGUS A.C.,HISTORIES AND HISTORIANS OF HISPANIC AMERICA (REPRINT ED.). CHRIST-17C SECT DIPLOM REV 16/20. PAGE 164 A3350 — BIBLIOG/A L/A+17C REGION COLONIAL

B65
WINT G.,COMMUNIST CHINA'S CRUSADE: MAO'S ROAD TO POWER AND THE NEW CAMPAIGN FOR WORLD REVOLUTION. ASIA CHINA/COM USA+45 USSR NAT/G POL/PAR DOMIN COERCE WAR PWR...POLICY CHARTS IDEA/COMP BIBLIOG 20 MAO. PAGE 165 A3364 — DIPLOM MARXISM REV COLONIAL

C65
MARK M.,"BEYOND SOVEREIGNTY." WOR+45 WOR-45 ECO/UNDEV BAL/PWR INT/TRADE NUC/PWR REV WAR MARXISM NEW/LIB BIBLIOG. PAGE 95 A1942 — NAT/LISM NAT/G DIPLOM INTELL

B66
BLACK C.E.,THE DYNAMICS OF MODERNIZATION: A STUDY IN COMPARATIVE HISTORY. STRUCT ECO/DEV ECO/UNDEV NAT/G DIPLOM LEAD REV...PREDICT TIME/SEQ TREND SOC/INTEG 17/20. PAGE 15 A0296 — SOCIETY SOC NAT/COMP

B66
BRACKMAN A.C.,SOUTHEAST ASIA'S SECOND FRONT: THE POWER STRUGGLE IN THE MALAY ARCHIPELAGO. CHINA/COM INDONESIA MALAYSIA ECO/UNDEV INT/ORG NAT/G FORCES DIPLOM EDU/PROP REGION COERCE GUERRILLA AUTHORIT POPULISM...MAJORIT 20 KENNEDY/JF SEATO. PAGE 18 A0367 — S/ASIA MARXISM REV

B66
CLENDENON C.,AMERICANS IN AFRICA 1865-1900. AFR USA-45 ECO/UNDEV SECT REV RACE/REL CONSERVE ...TRADIT GEOG BIBLIOG 16/18. PAGE 27 A0549
DIPLOM COLONIAL INT/TRADE

B66
DRACHOVITCH M.M.,THE COMINTERN HISTORICAL HIGHLIGHTS. USSR INT/ORG EX/STRUC LEGIT LEAD GUERRILLA...ANTHOL 20 COMINTERN LENIN/VI. PAGE 38 A0784
DIPLOM REV MARXISM PERSON

B66
FITZGERALD C.P.,THE BIRTH OF COMMUNIST CHINA (2ND ED.). ASIA CHINA/COM STRUCT BAL/PWR DIPLOM ECO/TAC INT/TRADE WEALTH 20. PAGE 46 A0942
REV MARXISM ECO/UNDEV

B66
FRIEDRICH C.J.,REVOLUTION: NOMOS VIII. NAT/G SOCISM ...OBS TREND IDEA/COMP ANTHOL 18/20. PAGE 49 A1007
REV MARXISM CONCPT DIPLOM

B66
GERARD-LIBOIS J.,KATANGA SECESSION. INT/ORG FORCES DIPLOM ADMIN CONTROL WAR CHOOSE PWR...CHARTS 20 KATANGA TSHOMBE/M UN. PAGE 52 A1062
NAT/G REGION ORD/FREE REV

B66
GUPTA S.,KASHMIR - A STUDY IN INDIA-PAKISTAN RELATIONS. INDIA KASHMIR PAKISTAN CONSTN INT/ORG REV RACE/REL NAT/LISM 20 UN MUSLIM/LG. PAGE 58 A1194
DIPLOM GP/REL SOVEREIGN WAR

B66
LAMBERG R.F.,PRAG UND DIE DRITTE WELT. AFR ASIA CZECHOSLVK L/A+17C MARKET TEC/DEV ECO/TAC REV ATTIT 20 TREATY. PAGE 84 A1713
DIPLOM ECO/UNDEV INT/TRADE FOR/AID

B66
NIEDERGANG M.,LA REVOLUTION DE SAINT-DOMINGUE. DOMIN/REP INT/ORG NAT/G CONTROL LEAD GP/REL ORD/FREE MARXISM 20. PAGE 109 A2239
REV FORCES DIPLOM

B66
RISTIC D.N.,YUGOSLAVIA'S REVOLUTION OF 1941. EUR+WWI YUGOSLAVIA NAT/G WAR ORD/FREE...RECORD BIBLIOG 20 HITLER/A TREATY. PAGE 121 A2484
REV ATTIT FASCISM DIPLOM

B66
SCHATTEN F.,COMMUNISM IN AFRICA. AFR GHANA GUINEA MALI CULTURE ECO/UNDEV LABOR SECT ECO/TAC EDU/PROP REV 20. PAGE 128 A2619
COLONIAL NAT/LISM MARXISM DIPLOM

B66
SOBEL L.A.,SOUTH VIETNAM: US-COMMUNIST CONFRONTATION IN SOUTHEAST ASIA 1961-65. VIETNAM FOR/AID CROWD DETER REV PEACE...GEOG 20 INTERVENT DIEM COLD/WAR. PAGE 134 A2754
WAR TIME/SEQ FORCES NAT/G

B66
TINKER H.,SOUTH ASIA. UK LAW ECO/UNDEV AGRI ACADEM SECT DIPLOM EDU/PROP REV WEALTH ALL/IDEOS...CHARTS BIBLIOG GANDHI/M NEHRU/J. PAGE 144 A2945
S/ASIA COLONIAL TREND

B66
US DEPARTMENT OF THE ARMY,COMMUNIST CHINA: A STRATEGIC SURVEY: A BIBLIOGRAPHY (PAMPHLET NO. 20-67). CHINA/COM COM INDIA USSR NAT/G POL/PAR EX/STRUC FORCES NUC/PWR REV ATTIT...POLICY GEOG CHARTS. PAGE 152 A3109
BIBLIOG/A MARXISM S/ASIA DIPLOM

B66
WELCH R.H.W.,THE NEW AMERICANISM, AND OTHER SPEECHES AND ESSAYS. USA+45 ACADEM POL/PAR SCHOOL VOL/ASSN FORCES CAP/ISM TAX REV DISCRIM 20 CIV/RIGHTS COLD/WAR BIRCH/SOC. PAGE 163 A3313
DIPLOM FASCISM MARXISM RACE/REL

B66
WOHL R.,FRENCH COMMUNISM IN THE MAKING 1914-1924. FRANCE USSR LEAD REV...IDEA/COMP 20 COM/PARTY. PAGE 166 A3377
MARXISM WORKER DIPLOM

B66
ZEINE Z.N.,THE EMERGENCE OF ARAB NATIONALISM (REV. ED.). TURKEY UK NAT/G SECT TEC/DEV LEAD REV WAR AGE/Y ROLE ORD/FREE...TRADIT CHARTS BIBLIOG 20 ARABS OTTOMAN. PAGE 170 A3451
ISLAM NAT/LISM DIPLOM

S66
AFRICAN BIBLIOGRAPHIC CENTER,"A CURRENT VIEW OF AFRICANA: A SELECT AND ANNOTATED BIBLIOGRAPHICAL PUBLISHING GUIDE, 1965-1966." AFR CULTURE INDUS LABOR SECT FOR/AID ADMIN COLONIAL REV RACE/REL SOCISM...LING 20. PAGE 5 A0098
BIBLIOG/A NAT/G TEC/DEV POL/PAR

C66
TARLING N.,"A CONCISE HISTORY OF SOUTHEAST ASIA." BURMA CAMBODIA LAOS S/ASIA THAILAND VIETNAM ECO/UNDEV POL/PAR FORCES ADMIN REV WAR CIVMIL/REL ORD/FREE MARXISM SOCISM 13/20. PAGE 141 A2890
COLONIAL DOMIN INT/TRADE NAT/LISM

B67
ADAMS A.E.,AN ATLAS OF RUSSIAN AND EAST EUROPEAN HISTORY. CHRIST-17C COM MOD/EUR INDUS SECT FORCES DIPLOM COLONIAL REV WAR 4/20. PAGE 4 A0086
CHARTS REGION TREND

B67
FILENE P.G.,AMERICANS AND THE SOVIET EXPERIMENT, 1917-1933. USA-45 USSR INTELL NAT/G CAP/ISM DIPLOM EDU/PROP PRESS REV SOCISM...PSY 20. PAGE 45 A0930
ATTIT RIGID/FLEX MARXISM SOCIETY

B67
GRIFFITH SB I.I.,THE CHINESE PEOPLE'S LIBERATION ARMY. CHINA/COM DIPLOM DOMIN GUERRILLA NUC/PWR REV ...CHARTS BIBLIOG 20. PAGE 57 A1163
FORCES CIVMIL/REL NAT/LISM PWR

B67
MAW B.,BREAKTHROUGH IN BURMA: MEMOIRS OF A REVOLUTION, 1939-1946. BURMA UK FORCES PROB/SOLV DIPLOM FOR/AID DOMIN LEAD...BIOG 20. PAGE 97 A1980
REV ORD/FREE NAT/LISM COLONIAL

B67
MCCLINTOCK R.,THE MEANING OF LIMITED WAR. FUT WOR+45 NAT/G FORCES GUERRILLA REV...POLICY SAMP/SIZ TREND NAT/COMP 45 COLD/WAR. PAGE 97 A1999
WAR NUC/PWR BAL/PWR DIPLOM

B67
MCNELLY T.,SOURCES IN MODERN EAST ASIAN HISTORY AND POLITICS. KOREA VIETNAM CULTURE DIPLOM COLONIAL REV WAR PWR ALL/IDEOS MARXISM...ANTHOL 20 CHINJAP. PAGE 99 A2023
NAT/COMP ASIA S/ASIA SOCIETY

B67
PIKE F.B.,FREEDOM AND REFORM IN LATIN AMERICA. BRAZIL URUGUAY CONSTN CULTURE SECT DIPLOM EDU/PROP PARTIC DRIVE ALL/VALS CATHISM...GEOG ANTHOL BIBLIOG REFORMERS BOLIV. PAGE 116 A2379
L/A+17C ORD/FREE ECO/UNDEV REV

B67
TEITELBAUM L.M.,WOODROW WILSON AND THE MEXICAN REVOLUTION 1913-1916: A HISTORY OF UNITED STATES-MEXICAN RELATIONS. USA-45 CHIEF TOP/EX WAR 20 MEXIC/AMER WILSON/W VILLA/P CARRANZA/V. PAGE 142 A2902
REV DIPLOM

B67
TROTSKY L.,PROBLEMS OF THE CHINESE REVOLUTION (3RD ED. TRANS. BY MAX SCHACTMAN). ASIA USSR DIPLOM MARXISM SOCISM...IDEA/COMP ANTHOL DICTIONARY 20 STALIN/J. PAGE 145 A2969
MARXIST REV

B67
WAELDER R.,PROGRESS AND REVOLUTION* A STUDY OF THE ISSUES OF OUR AGE. WOR+45 WOR-45 BAL/PWR DIPLOM COERCE ROLE MORAL ALL/IDEOS...IDEA/COMP NAT/COMP 19/20. PAGE 160 A3259
PWR NAT/G REV TEC/DEV

B67
WALLERSTEIN I.,AFRICA* THE POLITICS OF UNITY. AFR INT/ORG REV SOVEREIGN...HIST/WRIT 20. PAGE 160 A3268
TREND DIPLOM ATTIT

S67
ABT J.J.,"WORLD OF SENATOR FULBRIGHT." VIETNAM WOR+45 COERCE DETER REV ORD/FREE MARXISM...MARXIST 20. PAGE 4 A0084
DIPLOM PLAN PWR

S67
ADIE W.A.C.,"CHINA'S 'SECOND LIBERATION'." CHINA/COM SOCIETY WORKER DIPLOM TASK 20 MAO. PAGE 4 A0090
MARXISM REV INGP/REL ANOMIE

S67
BUTTINGER J.,"VIETNAM* FRAUD OF THE 'OTHER WAR'." VIETNAM/S ELITES STRUCT AGRI NAT/G FOR/AID RENT TREND. PAGE 22 A0456
PLAN WEALTH REV ECO/UNDEV

S67
GODUNSKY Y.,"'APOSTLES OF PEACE' IN LATIN AMERICA." L/A+17C USA+45 BAL/PWR DIPLOM FOR/AID DOMIN COLONIAL CIVMIL/REL MARXIST. PAGE 53 A1086
ECO/UNDEV REV VOL/ASSN EDU/PROP

S67
GRUNDY K.W.,"AFRICA IN THE WORLD ARENA." ECO/UNDEV BAL/PWR FOR/AID NEUTRAL REV NAT/LISM GOV/COMP. PAGE 58 A1183
AFR DIPLOM INT/ORG COLONIAL

S67
HEATH D.B.,"BOLIVIA UNDER BARRIENTOS." L/A+17C NAT/G CHIEF DIPLOM ECO/TAC...POLICY 20 BOLIV. PAGE 64 A1306
ECO/UNDEV POL/PAR REV CONSTN

S67
LACOUTRE J.,"HO CHI MINH." CHINA/COM USSR VIETNAM/N NAT/G CHIEF TOP/EX LEAD NEUTRAL...REALPOL PREDICT 20. PAGE 83 A1708
NAT/LISM MARXISM REV DIPLOM

S67
MEYER J.,"CUBA S'ENFERME DANS SA REVOLUTION." CHINA/COM CUBA USSR NAT/G TOP/EX DIPLOM LEAD ATTIT ...PREDICT 20. PAGE 100 A2053
MARXISM REV CHIEF NAT/LISM

S67
MONTALVA E.F.,"THE ALLIANCE THAT LOST ITS WAY." L/A+17C USA+45 R+D BAL/PWR INT/TRADE RECEIVE REV PEACE...POLICY 20. PAGE 103 A2111
ECO/UNDEV DIPLOM FOR/AID INT/ORG

S67
PAUKER G.J.,"TOWARD A NEW ORDER IN INDONESIA." COM INDONESIA S/ASIA ECO/UNDEV POL/PAR EX/STRUC TOP/EX BAL/PWR ECO/TAC FOR/AID DOMIN NAT/LISM AUTHORIT ORD/FREE PWR 20. PAGE 114 A2342
REV NAT/G DIPLOM CIVMIL/REL

S67
ROTBERG R.I.,"COLONIALISM AND AFTER: THE POLITICAL
BIBLIOG/A

LITERATURE OF CENTRAL AFRICA - A BIBLIOGRAPHIC ESSAY." AFR CHIEF EX/STRUC REV INGP/REL RACE/REL SOVEREIGN 20. PAGE 124 A2546 — COLONIAL DIPLOM NAT/G

S67
TERRILL R.,"THE SIEGE MENTALITY." CHINA/COM NAT/G FORCES DIPLOM REV EFFICIENCY NAT/LISM MARXISM ...TREND 20. PAGE 142 A2904 — EDU/PROP WAR DOMIN

S67
TUCKER R.C.,"THE DERADICALIZATION OF MARXIST MOVEMENTS." USSR SOCIETY DIPLOM 20. PAGE 145 A2973 — MARXISM ADJUST ATTIT REV

C67
SPANIER J.W.,"WORLD POLITICS IN AN AGE OF REVOLUTION." COM WOR+45 FORCES COERCE WAR NAT/LISM SOVEREIGN...POLICY BIBLIOG 20. PAGE 135 A2772 — DIPLOM TEC/DEV REV ECO/UNDEV

B90
HOSMAR J.K.,A SHORT HISTORY OF ANGLO-SAXON FREEDOM. UK USA-45 ROMAN/EMP NAT/G EX/STRUC LEGIS COLONIAL REV NAT/LISM POPULISM PARLIAMENT ANGLO/SAX MAGNA/CART. PAGE 68 A1394 — CONSTN ORD/FREE DIPLOM PARL/PROC

REVOLUTION....SEE REV

REWARD....SEE SANCTION

REYNOLDS P.A. A2470

RFE....RADIO FREE EUROPE

B58
HOLT R.T.,RADIO FREE EUROPE. FUT USA+45 CULTURE ECO/DEV INT/ORG KIN POL/PAR SECT FORCES ACT/RES DIPLOM COERCE REV CHOOSE PEACE ATTIT PWR...MAJORIT CONCPT COLD/WAR WORK 20 RFE. PAGE 67 A1374 — COM EDU/PROP COM/IND

RHODE/ISL....RHODE ISLAND

RHODES/C....CECIL RHODES

RHODESIA....SEE ALSO AFR

B30
SMUTS J.C.,AFRICA AND SOME WORLD PROBLEMS. RHODESIA SOUTH/AFR CULTURE ECO/UNDEV INDUS INT/ORG SECT PROB/SOLV REGION GOV/REL DISCRIM ATTIT 19/20 LEAGUE/NAT LIVNGSTN/D NEGRO. PAGE 134 A2748 — LEGIS AFR COLONIAL RACE/REL

B34
LOVELL R.I.,THE STRUGGLE FOR SOUTH AFRICA, 1875-1899. GERMANY RHODESIA SOUTH/AFR UK NAT/G ECO/TAC HABITAT WEALTH...POLICY 19. PAGE 91 A1866 — COLONIAL DIPLOM WAR GP/REL

B38
FRANKEL S.H.,CAPITAL INVESTMENT IN AFRICA. AFR EUR+WWI RHODESIA SOUTH/AFR UK FINAN FOR/AID COLONIAL DEMAND UTIL WEALTH...METH/CNCPT CHARTS 20 CONGO/LEOP. PAGE 48 A0983 — ECO/UNDEV EXTR/IND DIPLOM PRODUC

N59
BRITISH COMMONWEALTH REL CONF,EXTRACTS FROM THE PROCEEDINGS OF THE SIXTH UNOFFICIAL CONFERENCE (PAMPHLET). GHANA INDIA RHODESIA UK FINAN FORCES DETER FEDERAL...LING 20 PARLIAMENT. PAGE 19 A0379 — DIPLOM PARL/PROC INT/TRADE ORD/FREE

B65
WALKER A.A.,THE RHODESIAS AND NYASALAND: A GUIDE TO OFFICIAL PUBLICATIONS. RHODESIA UK OP/RES PLAN PROB/SOLV DIPLOM...POLICY SOC CON/ANAL 19/20 NYASALAND. PAGE 160 A3263 — BIBLIOG NAT/G COLONIAL AFR

S66
GREEN L.C.,"RHODESIAN OIL: BOOTLEGGERS OR PIRATES?" AFR RHODESIA UK WOR+45 INT/ORG NAT/G DIPLOM LEGIT COLONIAL SOVEREIGN 20 UN OAU. PAGE 55 A1139 — INT/TRADE SANCTION INT/LAW POLICY

S66
PRATT R.C.,"AFRICAN REACTIONS TO THE RHODESIAN CRISIS." RHODESIA UK LAW DIPLOM...POLICY 20. PAGE 117 A2408 — ATTIT AFR COLONIAL RACE/REL

L67
MACDONALD R.S.J.,"THE RESORT TO ECONOMIC COERCION BY INTERNATIONAL POLITICAL ORGANIZATIONS." CUBA ETHIOPIA RHODESIA SOUTH/AFR NAT/G FOR/AID INT/TRADE DOMIN CONTROL SANCTION...DECISION LEAGUE/NAT UN OAS 20. PAGE 92 A1887 — INT/ORG COERCE ECO/TAC DIPLOM

S67
MUDGE G.A.,"DOMESTIC POLICIES AND UN ACTIVITIES* THE CASE OF RHODESIA AND THE REPUBLIC OF SOUTH AFRICA." RHODESIA SOUTH/AFR POL/PAR LEAD SANCTION CHOOSE RACE/REL CONSEN DISCRIM ATTIT...INT/LAW UN PARLIAMENT 20. PAGE 105 A2163 — AFR NAT/G POLICY

S67
STEEL R.,"WHAT CAN THE UN DO?" RHODESIA ECO/UNDEV DIPLOM ECO/TAC SANCTION...INT/LAW UN. PAGE 137 A2810 — INT/ORG BAL/PWR PEACE FOR/AID

RHYNE C.S. A2471

RICARDO/D....DAVID RICARDO

RICE E.A. A2472

RICE G.W. A2473

RICHARD/H....HENRY RICHARD (WELSH POLITICIAN - 19TH CENTURY)

RICHARDSON I.L. A2474

RICHTER J.H. A2475

RICKMAN J. A1116

RIENOW R. A2476

RIESELBACH L.N. A2477,A2478

RIESMAN/D....DAVID RIESMAN

B51
STANTON A.H.,PERSONALITY AND POLITICAL CRISIS. WOR+45 WOR-45 STRUCT DIPLOM INGP/REL TOTALISM MORAL ...ANTHOL 20 LASSWELL/H PARSONS/T RIESMAN/D. PAGE 137 A2806 — EDU/PROP WAR PERSON PSY

RIGGS F.W. A2479

RIGGS R. A2480,A2481

RIGGS/FRED....FRED W. RIGGS

RIGHTS/MAN....RIGHTS OF MAN

RIGID/FLEX....DEGREE OF RESPONSIVENESS TO NEW IDEAS, METHODS, AND PEOPLE

B15
FARIES J.C.,THE RISE OF INTERNATIONALISM. ASIA MOD/EUR NAT/G VOL/ASSN DELIB/GP BAL/PWR EDU/PROP ARMS/CONT RIGID/FLEX TREND. PAGE 44 A0899 — INT/ORG DIPLOM PEACE

B20
BURNS C.D.,INTERNATIONAL POLITICS. WOR-45 CULTURE SOCIETY ECO/UNDEV NAT/G VOL/ASSN DELIB/GP ACT/RES CREATE DOMIN EDU/PROP LEGIT ATTIT DRIVE RIGID/FLEX ALL/VALS...PLURIST PSY CONCPT TREND. PAGE 22 A0442 — INT/ORG PEACE SOVEREIGN

B21
STUART G.H.,FRENCH FOREIGN POLICY. CONSTN INT/ORG NAT/G POL/PAR EX/STRUC FORCES PLAN ECO/TAC DOMIN EDU/PROP ADJUD COERCE ATTIT DRIVE RIGID/FLEX ALL/VALS...POLICY OBS RECORD BIOG TIME/SEQ TREND. PAGE 139 A2852 — MOD/EUR DIPLOM FRANCE

B22
BRYCE J.,INTERNATIONAL RELATIONS. CHRIST-17C EUR+WWI MOD/EUR CULTURE INTELL NAT/G DELIB/GP CREATE BAL/PWR DIPLOM ATTIT DRIVE RIGID/FLEX ALL/VALS...PLURIST JURID CONCPT TIME/SEQ GEN/LAWS TOT/POP. PAGE 20 A0412 — INT/ORG POLICY

B22
REINSCH P.,SECRET DIPLOMACY: HOW FAR CAN IT BE ELIMINATED. FUT WOR-45 CULTURE INT/ORG NAT/G EDU/PROP WAR...MYTH HIST/WRIT CON/ANAL 20. PAGE 120 A2460 — RIGID/FLEX PWR DIPLOM

B30
FLEMMING D.,THE TREATY VETO OF THE AMERICAN SENATE. FUT USA+45 USA-45 CONSTN INT/ORG NAT/G TOP/EX LEGIT GOV/REL PWR...POLICY MAJORIT CONCPT OBS TIME/SEQ CONGRESS 20. PAGE 46 A0949 — LEGIS RIGID/FLEX

B39
DULLES J.,WAR, PEACE AND CHANGE. FRANCE ITALY UK USA-45 WOR-45 LAW INT/ORG NAT/G SECT VOL/ASSN FORCES TOP/EX DOMIN ARMS/CONT COERCE ATTIT PERSON RIGID/FLEX MORAL PWR...JURID STERTYP TOT/POP LEAGUE/NAT 20. PAGE 39 A0796 — EDU/PROP TOTALISM WAR

B39
NICOLSON H.,CURZON: THE LAST PHASE, 1919-1925. UK NAT/G DELIB/GP TOP/EX ROUTINE WAR RIGID/FLEX ...METH/CNCPT 20 CURZON/GN. PAGE 109 A2231 — POLICY DIPLOM BIOG

B39
ZIMMERN A.,MODERN POLITICAL DOCTRINE. WOR-45 CULTURE SOCIETY ECO/UNDEV DELIB/GP EX/STRUC CREATE DOMIN COERCE NAT/LISM ATTIT RIGID/FLEX ORD/FREE PWR WEALTH...POLICY CONCPT OBS TIME/SEQ TREND TOT/POP LEAGUE/NAT 20. PAGE 170 A3454 — NAT/G ECO/TAC BAL/PWR INT/TRADE

B40
MILLER E.,THE NEUROSES OF WAR. UNIV INTELL SOCIETY INT/ORG NAT/G EDU/PROP DISPL DRIVE PERCEPT PERSON RIGID/FLEX...SOC TIME/SEQ 20. PAGE 101 A2075 — HEALTH PSY WAR

B41
BURTON M.E.,THE ASSEMBLY OF THE LEAGUE OF NATIONS. WOR-45 CONSTN SOCIETY STRUCT INT/ORG NAT/G CREATE ATTIT RIGID/FLEX PWR...POLICY TIME/SEQ LEAGUE/NAT — DELIB/GP EX/STRUC DIPLOM

20. PAGE 22 A0448

B42
KELSEN H.,LAW AND PEACE IN INTERNATIONAL RELATIONS. FUT WOR-45 NAT/G DELIB/GP DIPLOM LEGIT RIGID/FLEX ORD/FREE SOVEREIGN...JURID CONCPT TREND STERTYP GEN/LAWS LEAGUE/NAT 20. PAGE 77 A1580 INT/ORG ADJUD PEACE INT/LAW

B43
MICAUD C.A.,THE FRENCH RIGHT AND NAZI GERMANY 1933-1939: A STUDY OF PUBLIC OPINION. GERMANY UK USSR POL/PAR ARMS/CONT COERCE DETER PEACE RIGID/FLEX PWR MARXISM...FASCIST TREND 20 LEAGUE/NAT TREATY. PAGE 101 A2065 DIPLOM AGREE

B44
BARTLETT R.J.,THE LEAGUE TO ENFORCE PEACE. FUT USA-45 NAT/G POL/PAR CREATE EDU/PROP ADMIN RIGID/FLEX PWR...CONCPT TREND GEN/METH LEAGUE/NAT 20. PAGE 11 A0231 INT/ORG ORD/FREE DIPLOM

B45
KANDELL I.L.,UNITED STATES ACTIVITIES IN INTERNATIONAL CULTURAL RELATIONS. INT/ORG NAT/G VOL/ASSN CREATE DIPLOM EDU/PROP ATTIT RIGID/FLEX KNOWL...PLURIST CONCPT OBS TREND GEN/LAWS TOT/POP UNESCO 20. PAGE 76 A1554 USA-45 CULTURE

B46
KEETON G.W.,MAKING INTERNATIONAL LAW WORK. FUT WOR-45 NAT/G DELIB/GP FORCES LEGIT COERCE PEACE ATTIT RIGID/FLEX ORD/FREE PWR...JURID CONCPT HIST/WRIT GEN/METH LEAGUE/NAT 20. PAGE 77 A1578 INT/ORG ADJUD INT/LAW

B46
MITRANY D.,A WORKING PEACE SYSTEM. WOR+45 WOR-45 ECO/DEV INT/ORG NAT/G DELIB/GP ECO/TAC REGION ATTIT RIGID/FLEX...TREND GEN/LAWS LEAGUE/NAT 20. PAGE 102 A2091 VOL/ASSN PLAN PEACE SOVEREIGN

L46
MASTERS D.,"ONE WORLD OR NONE." FUT WOR+45 INTELL INT/ORG ACT/RES EDU/PROP DETER ATTIT RIGID/FLEX SUPEGO KNOWL...STAT TREND ORG/CHARTS 20. PAGE 96 A1960 POLICY PHIL/SCI ARMS/CONT NUC/PWR

S46
DOUGLAS W.O.,"SYMPOSIUM ON WORLD ORGANIZATION." FUT USA+45 WOR+45 CONSTN SOCIETY NAT/G PLAN EDU/PROP LEGIT RIGID/FLEX KNOWL...INT/LAW JURID STERTYP TOT/POP 20. PAGE 38 A0778 INT/ORG LAW

B47
KIRK G.,THE STUDY OF INTERNATIONAL RELATIONS. FUT USA-45 R+D ACADEM INT/ORG CONSULT DELIB/GP INT/TRADE EDU/PROP PEACE RIGID/FLEX KNOWL VAL/FREE 20. PAGE 80 A1632 USA+45 DIPLOM

B48
COTTRELL L.S. JR.,AMERICAN PUBLIC OPINION ON WORLD AFFAIRS IN THE ATOMIC AGE. USA+45 CULTURE INT/ORG NAT/G DIPLOM EDU/PROP PEACE RIGID/FLEX ORD/FREE ...POLICY SOC CONCPT STAND/INT TOT/POP 20. PAGE 31 A0633 SOCIETY ATTIT ARMS/CONT NUC/PWR

S50
CORBETT P.E.,"OBJECTIVITY IN THE STUDY OF INTERNATIONAL AFFAIRS." WOR+45 SOCIETY ACT/RES EDU/PROP PERSON RIGID/FLEX KNOWL TOT/POP 20. PAGE 30 A0614 INT/ORG DIPLOM

B51
HAVILAND H.F.,THE POLITICAL ROLE OF THE GENERAL ASSEMBLY. WOR+45 DELIB/GP EDU/PROP PEACE RIGID/FLEX PWR...CONCPT TIME/SEQ GEN/LAWS UN VAL/FREE 20. PAGE 63 A1290 INT/ORG ORD/FREE DIPLOM

B51
KELSEN H.,THE LAW OF THE UNITED NATIONS. WOR+45 STRUCT RIGID/FLEX ORD/FREE...INT/LAW JURID CONCPT CON/ANAL GEN/METH UN TOT/POP VAL/FREE 20. PAGE 77 A1581 INT/ORG ADJUD

L51
KELSEN H.,"RECENT TRENDS IN THE LAW OF THE UNITED NATIONS." KOREA WOR+45 CONSTN LEGIS DIPLOM LEGIT DETER WAR RIGID/FLEX HEALTH ORD/FREE RESPECT ...JURID CON/ANAL UN VAL/FREE 20 NATO. PAGE 77 A1582 INT/ORG LAW INT/LAW

S51
BUCHANAN W.,"STEREOTYPES AND TENSIONS AS REVEALED BY THE UNESCO INTERNATIONAL POLL." WOR+45 INT/ORG ATTIT DISPL PERCEPT RIGID/FLEX...INT TESTS SAMP 20. PAGE 21 A0424 R+D STERTYP

S51
ICHHEISER G.,"MISUNDERSTANDING IN INTERNATIONAL RELATIONS." UNIV SOCIETY FACE/GP INT/ORG SECT ATTIT PERSON RIGID/FLEX LOVE RESPECT...RELATIV PSY SOC CONCPT MYTH SOC/EXP GEN/LAWS. PAGE 70 A1431 PERCEPT STERTYP NAT/LISM DIPLOM

L52
WRIGHT Q.,"CONGRESS AND THE TREATY-MAKING POWER." USA+45 WOR+45 CONSTN INTELL NAT/G CHIEF CONSULT EX/STRUC LEGIS TOP/EX CREATE GOV/REL DISPL DRIVE RIGID/FLEX...TREND TOT/POP CONGRESS CONGRESS 20 TREATY. PAGE 167 A3408 ROUTINE DIPLOM INT/LAW DELIB/GP

B53
MACMAHON A.W.,ADMINISTRATION IN FOREIGN AFFAIRS. NAT/G CONSULT DELIB/GP LEGIS ACT/RES CREATE ADMIN EXEC RIGID/FLEX PWR...METH/CNCPT TIME/SEQ TOT/POP VAL/FREE 20. PAGE 93 A1899 USA+45 ROUTINE FOR/AID DIPLOM

B53
MURPHY G.,IN THE MINDS OF MEN: THE STUDY OF HUMAN BEHAVIOR AND SOCIAL TENSIONS IN INDIA. FUT S/ASIA FAM INT/ORG NAT/G DIPLOM EDU/PROP GP/REL ATTIT RIGID/FLEX ALL/VALS...SOC QU UNESCO 20. PAGE 106 A2176 SECT STRATA INDIA

B54
MANGONE G.,A SHORT HISTORY OF INTERNATIONAL ORGANIZATION. MOD/EUR USA+45 USA-45 WOR+45 WOR-45 LAW LEGIS CREATE LEGIT ROUTINE RIGID/FLEX PWR ...JURID CONCPT OBS TIME/SEQ STERTYP GEN/LAWS UN TOT/POP VAL/FREE 18/20. PAGE 94 A1921 INT/ORG INT/LAW

B54
NORTHROP F.S.C.,EUROPEAN UNION AND UNITED STATES FOREIGN POLICY: A STUDY IN SOCIOLOGICAL JURISPRUDENCE. EUR+WWI MOD/EUR USA+45 SOCIETY STRUCT NAT/G CREATE ECO/TAC DOMIN EDU/PROP REGION ATTIT RIGID/FLEX HEALTH ORD/FREE WEALTH ...METH/CNCPT TIME/SEQ TREND. PAGE 110 A2256 INT/ORG SOC DIPLOM

B55
JOY C.T.,HOW COMMUNISTS NEGOTIATE. COM USA+45 CONSTN CULTURE ECO/UNDEV NAT/G CONSULT DELIB/GP FORCES PLAN ECO/TAC DOMIN EDU/PROP LEGIT EXEC ROUTINE COERCE WAR CHOOSE PEACE ATTIT RIGID/FLEX ORD/FREE PWR...POLICY 20. PAGE 75 A1539 ASIA INT/ORG DIPLOM

B56
BLACKETT P.M.S.,ATOMIC WEAPONS AND EAST-WEST RELATIONS. FUT WOR+45 INT/ORG DELIB/GP COERCE ATTIT RIGID/FLEX KNOWL...RELATIV HIST/WRIT TREND GEN/METH COLD/WAR 20. PAGE 15 A0299 FORCES PWR ARMS/CONT NUC/PWR

B56
WEIS P.,NATIONALITY AND STATELESSNESS IN INTERNATIONAL LAW. UK WOR+45 WOR-45 LAW CONSTN NAT/G DIPLOM EDU/PROP LEGIT ROUTINE RIGID/FLEX ...JURID RECORD CMN/WLTH 20. PAGE 162 A3309 INT/ORG SOVEREIGN INT/LAW

B57
BLOOMFIELD L.M.,EGYPT, ISRAEL AND THE GULF OF AQABA: IN INTERNATIONAL LAW. LAW NAT/G CONSULT FORCES PLAN ECO/TAC ROUTINE COERCE ATTIT DRIVE PERCEPT PERSON RIGID/FLEX LOVE PWR WEALTH...GEOG CONCPT MYTH TREND. PAGE 15 A0314 ISLAM INT/LAW UAR

B57
BLOOMFIELD L.P.,EVOLUTION OR REVOLUTION: THE UNITED NATIONS AND THE PROBLEM OF PEACEFUL TERRITORIAL CHANGE. WOR+45 WOR-45 INT/ORG NAT/G DIPLOM ROUTINE REV ATTIT RIGID/FLEX PWR...CONCPT OBS HIST/WRIT UN LEAGUE/NAT 20. PAGE 15 A0315 ORD/FREE LEGIT

B57
FRAZIER E.F.,RACE AND CULTURE CONTACTS IN THE MODERN WORLD. WOR+45 WOR-45 SOCIETY ECO/DEV AGRI INDUS INT/ORG LABOR NAT/G PERSON RIGID/FLEX ALL/VALS...SOC TIME/SEQ WORK 19/20. PAGE 48 A0991 CULTURE RACE/REL

B57
KAPLAN M.A.,SYSTEM AND PROCESS OF INTERNATIONAL POLITICS. FUT WOR+45 WOR-45 SOCIETY PLAN BAL/PWR ADMIN ATTIT PERSON RIGID/FLEX PWR SOVEREIGN ...DECISION TREND VAL/FREE. PAGE 76 A1560 INT/ORG DIPLOM

B57
MATECKI B.,ESTABLISHMENT OF THE INTERNATIONAL FINANCE CORPORATION AND UNITED STATES POLICY. USA+45 WOR+45 CONSTN NAT/G CREATE RIGID/FLEX KNOWL ...METH/CNCPT TIME/SEQ SIMUL TOT/POP 20 INTL/FINAN. PAGE 96 A1964 FINAN INT/ORG DIPLOM

L57
WARREN S.,"FOREIGN AID AND FOREIGN POLICY." USA+45 WOR+45 WOR-45 DIST/IND INDUS MARKET CONSULT CREATE DIPLOM EDU/PROP LEGIT ATTIT RIGID/FLEX...TIME/SEQ GEN/LAWS WORK 20. PAGE 161 A3285 ECO/UNDEV ALL/VALS ECO/TAC FOR/AID

B58
HAAS E.B.,THE UNITING OF EUROPE. EUR+WWI INT/ORG NAT/G POL/PAR TOP/EX ECO/TAC EDU/PROP LEGIT FEDERAL NAT/LISM DRIVE RIGID/FLEX ORD/FREE PWR PLURISM ...POLICY CONCPT INT GEN/LAWS ECSC EEC 20. PAGE 59 A1204 VOL/ASSN ECO/DEV

B58
JAPANESE ASSOCIATION INT. LAW,JAPAN AND THE UNITED NATIONS. SOCIETY ROUTINE ATTIT DRIVE PERCEPT RIGID/FLEX ORD/FREE...METH/CNCPT CON/ANAL CHINJAP UN. PAGE 73 A1497 ASIA INT/ORG

B58
RIGGS R.,POLITICS IN THE UNITED NATIONS: A STUDY OF UNITED STATES INFLUENCE IN THE GENERAL ASSEMBLY. USA+45 WOR+45 LEGIS TOP/EX CREATE BAL/PWR DIPLOM DOMIN EDU/PROP COLONIAL ROUTINE ATTIT RIGID/FLEX PWR...CONCPT OBS HIST/WRIT CHARTS STERTYP GEN/LAWS UN COLD/WAR 20. PAGE 121 A2480 INT/ORG

B58
SLICK T.,PERMANENT PEACE: A CHECK AND BALANCE PLAN. FUT WOR+45 NAT/G FORCES CREATE PLAN EDU/PROP LEGIT ADJUD COERCE NAT/LISM RIGID/FLEX MORAL...HUM CONCPT METH/CNCPT NEW/IDEA TREND CHARTS TOT/POP 20. PAGE 134 A2742 INT/ORG ORD/FREE PEACE ARMS/CONT

L58
INT. SOC. SCI. BULL.,"TECHNIQUES OF MEDIATION AND CONCILIATION." EUR+WWI USA+45 SOCIETY INDUS INT/ORG LABOR NAT/G LEGIS DIPLOM EDU/PROP CHOOSE ATTIT VOL/ASSN DELIB/GP INT/LAW

RIGID/FLEX...JURID CONCPT GEN/LAWS 20. PAGE 70 A1447

S58
BOGART L.,"MEASURING THE EFFECTIVENESS OF AN OVERSEAS INFORMATION CAMPAIGN." EUR+WWI GREECE USA+45 INT/ORG MUNIC PLAN DIPLOM PEACE PERCEPT RIGID/FLEX KNOWL...TECHNIC PSY SOC NEW/IDEA CONT/OBS REC/INT STAND/INT SAMP/SIZ COLD/WAR 20. PAGE 16 A0328
ATTIT EDU/PROP

S58
JORDAN A.,"MILITARY ASSISTANCE AND NATIONAL POLICY." ASIA FUT USA+45 WOR+45 ECO/DEV ECO/UNDEV INT/ORG NAT/G PLAN ECO/TAC ROUTINE WEAPON ATTIT RIGID/FLEX PWR...CONCPT TREND 20. PAGE 75 A1533
FORCES POLICY FOR/AID DIPLOM

S58
SINGER J.D.,"THREAT PERCEPTION AND THE ARMAMENT TENSION DILEMMA." WOR+45 WOR-45 ELITES INT/ORG NAT/G DELIB/GP PLAN LEGIT COERCE DETER ATTIT RIGID/FLEX PWR...DECISION PSY 20. PAGE 133 A2724
PERCEPT ARMS/CONT BAL/PWR

S58
SONDERMANN F.A.,"SOCIOLOGY AND INTERNATIONAL RELATIONS." WOR+45 CULTURE SOCIETY INT/ORG NAT/G CREATE ATTIT DRIVE PERSON RIGID/FLEX...PSY SOC 20. PAGE 135 A2767
PLAN NEW/IDEA PEACE

B59
ALWAN M.,ALGERIA BEFORE THE UNITED NATIONS. AFR ASIA FRANCE ISLAM S/ASIA CONSTN SOCIETY STRUCT INT/ORG NAT/G ECO/TAC ADMIN COLONIAL NAT/LISM ATTIT PWR...DECISION TREND 420 UN. PAGE 7 A0133
PLAN RIGID/FLEX DIPLOM ALGERIA

B59
BRODIE B.,STRATEGY IN THE MISSILE AGE. FUT WOR+45 CONSULT PLAN COERCE DETER RIGID/FLEX PWR...CONCPT TIME/SEQ TREND 20. PAGE 19 A0381
ACT/RES FORCES ARMS/CONT NUC/PWR

B59
FREE L.A.,SIX ALLIES AND A NEUTRAL. ASIA COM EUR+WWI FRANCE GERMANY/W INDIA S/ASIA UK USA+45 INT/ORG NAT/G NUC/PWR PEACE ATTIT PERCEPT RIGID/FLEX ALL/VALS...STAT REC/INT COLD/WAR 20 CHINJAP. PAGE 48 A0992
PSY DIPLOM

B59
JOSEPH F.M.,AS OTHERS SEE US: THE UNITED STATES THROUGH FOREIGN EYES. AFR EUR+WWI ISLAM L/A+17C S/ASIA USA+45 CULTURE SOCIETY ECO/DEV ECO/UNDEV INT/ORG NAT/G DIPLOM ECO/TAC REV ATTIT RIGID/FLEX HEALTH ORD/FREE WEALTH 20. PAGE 75 A1537
RESPECT DOMIN NAT/LISM SOVEREIGN

B59
KULSKI W.W.,PEACEFUL CO-EXISTENCE: AN ANALYSIS OF SOVIET FOREIGN POLICY. WOR+45 INTELL SOCIETY ECO/UNDEV POL/PAR EDU/PROP COERCE DRIVE RIGID/FLEX PWR SKILL...PSY CONCPT HIST/WRIT CON/ANAL GEN/METH WORK VAL/FREE 20. PAGE 83 A1691
PLAN DIPLOM USSR

S59
BROMKE A.,"DISENGAGEMENT IN EAST EUROPE." COM USSR INT/ORG DIPLOM EDU/PROP NEUTRAL NUC/PWR DRIVE RIGID/FLEX PWR...PSY CONCPT CON/ANAL GEN/METH VAL/FREE 20. PAGE 19 A0388
BAL/PWR

S59
FISCHER L.,"THE SOVIET-AMERICAN ANTAGONISM: HOW WILL IT END." CONSTN CULTURE PLAN TEC/DEV RIGID/FLEX SUPEGO ORD/FREE...MARXIST DECISION PSY CONCPT CON/ANAL GEN/LAWS VAL/FREE 20 COLD/WAR. PAGE 46 A0936
USA+45 PWR DIPLOM USSR

S59
KOHN L.Y.,"ISRAEL AND NEW NATION STATES OF ASIA AND AFRICA." AFR ASIA FUT S/ASIA VOL/ASSN TEC/DEV NAT/LISM RIGID/FLEX SKILL WEALTH...RELATIV OBS TREND CON/ANAL 20. PAGE 81 A1663
ECO/UNDEV ECO/TAC FOR/AID ISRAEL

S59
KRIPALANI A.J.B.,"FOR PRINCIPLED NEUTRALITY." CHINA/COM INDIA S/ASIA PLAN ECO/TAC RIGID/FLEX MORAL PWR...MYSTIC SOC RECORD 20 GANDHI/M. PAGE 82 A1684
ATTIT FOR/AID DIPLOM

S59
PUGWASH CONFERENCE,"ON BIOLOGICAL AND CHEMICAL WARFARE." WOR+45 SOCIETY PROC/MFG INT/ORG FORCES EDU/PROP ADJUD RIGID/FLEX ORD/FREE PWR...DECISION PSY NEW/IDEA MATH VAL/FREE 20. PAGE 118 A2417
ACT/RES BIO/SOC WAR WEAPON

B60
BUCHAN A.,NATO IN THE 1960'S. EUR+WWI USA+45 WOR+45 INT/ORG ACT/RES PLAN LEGIT COERCE DETER ATTIT DRIVE RIGID/FLEX ORD/FREE...METH/CNCPT TIME/SEQ TREND GEN/LAWS COLD/WAR 20 NATO. PAGE 21 A0421
VOL/ASSN FORCES ARMS/CONT SOVEREIGN

B60
FURNIA A.H.,THE DIPLOMACY OF APPEASEMENT: ANGLO-FRENCH RELATIONS AND THE PRELUDE TO WORLD WAR II 1931-1938. FRANCE GERMANY UK ELITES NAT/G DELIB/GP FORCES WAR PEACE RIGID/FLEX 20. PAGE 50 A1026
DIPLOM BAL/PWR COERCE

B60
LISTER L.,EUROPE'S COAL AND STEEL COMMUNITY. FRANCE GERMANY STRUCT ECO/DEV EXTR/IND INDUS MARKET NAT/G DELIB/GP ECO/TAC INT/TRADE EDU/PROP ATTIT RIGID/FLEX ORD/FREE PWR WEALTH...CONCPT STAT TIME/SEQ CHARTS ECSC 20. PAGE 90 A1843
EUR+WWI INT/ORG REGION

B60
PLAMENATZ J.,ON ALIEN RULE AND SELF-GOVERNMENT. AFR FUT S/ASIA WOR+45 CULTURE SOCIETY ECO/UNDEV INT/ORG DOMIN EDU/PROP ATTIT RIGID/FLEX ALL/VALS...POLICY CONCPT OBS TREND CON/ANAL GEN/LAWS TOT/POP VAL/FREE. PAGE 116 A2386
NAT/G CONSTN NAT/LISM SOVEREIGN

B60
SOBEL R.,THE ORIGINS OF INTERVENTIONISM: THE UNITED STATES AND THE RUSSO-FINNISH WAR. FINLAND USA-45 USSR LEGIS ATTIT RIGID/FLEX...BIBLIOG 20 INTERVENT. PAGE 135 A2755
DIPLOM WAR PROB/SOLV NEUTRAL

B60
STEIN E.,AMERICAN ENTERPRISE IN THE EUROPEAN COMMON MARKET: A LEGAL PROFILE. EUR+WWI FUT USA+45 SOCIETY STRUCT ECO/DEV NAT/G VOL/ASSN CONSULT PLAN TEC/DEV ECO/TAC INT/TRADE ADMIN ATTIT RIGID/FLEX PWR...MGT NEW/IDEA STAT TREND COMPUT/IR SIMUL EEC 20. PAGE 137 A2814
MARKET ADJUD INT/LAW

B60
WOETZEL R.K.,THE INTERNATIONAL CONTROL OF AIRSPACE AND OUTERSPACE. FUT WOR+45 AIR CONSTN STRUCT CONSULT PLAN TEC/DEV ADJUD RIGID/FLEX KNOWL ORD/FREE PWR...TECHNIC GEOG MGT NEW/IDEA TREND COMPUT/IR VAL/FREE 20 TREATY. PAGE 166 A3375
INT/ORG JURID SPACE INT/LAW

L60
HOLTON G.,"ARMS CONTROL." FUT WOR+45 CULTURE INT/ORG NAT/G FORCES TOP/EX PLAN EDU/PROP COERCE ATTIT RIGID/FLEX ORD/FREE...POLICY PHIL/SCI SOC TREND COLD/WAR. PAGE 67 A1377
ACT/RES CONSULT ARMS/CONT NUC/PWR

L60
JACOB P.E.,"THE DISARMAMENT CONSENSUS." USA+45 USSR WOR+45 INT/ORG NAT/G ACT/RES TEC/DEV BAL/PWR EDU/PROP ADMIN COERCE DETER NUC/PWR CONSEN RIGID/FLEX PWR...CONCPT RECORD CHARTS COLD/WAR 20. PAGE 72 A1482
DELIB/GP ATTIT ARMS/CONT

S60
"THE EMERGING COMMON MARKETS IN LATIN AMERICA." FUT L/A+17C STRATA DIST/IND INDUS LABOR NAT/G LEGIS ECO/TAC ADMIN RIGID/FLEX HEALTH...NEW/IDEA TIME/SEQ OAS 20. PAGE 3 A0059
FINAN ECO/UNDEV INT/TRADE

S60
BOGARDUS E.S.,"THE SOCIOLOGY OF A STRUCTURED PEACE." FUT SOCIETY CREATE DIPLOM EDU/PROP ADJUD ROUTINE ATTIT RIGID/FLEX KNOWL ORD/FREE RESPECT ...POLICY INT/LAW JURID NEW/IDEA SELF/OBS TOT/POP 20 UN. PAGE 16 A0327
INT/ORG SOC NAT/LISM PEACE

S60
FRANKEL S.H.,"ECONOMIC ASPECTS OF POLITICAL INDEPENDENCE IN AFRICA." AFR FUT SOCIETY ECO/UNDEV COM/IND FINAN LEGIS PLAN TEC/DEV CAP/ISM ECO/TAC INT/TRADE ADMIN ATTIT DRIVE RIGID/FLEX PWR WEALTH ...MGT NEW/IDEA MATH TIME/SEQ VAL/FREE 20. PAGE 48 A0984
NAT/G FOR/AID

S60
GARNICK D.H.,"ON THE ECONOMIC FEASIBILITY OF A MIDDLE EASTERN COMMON MARKET." AFR ISLAM CULTURE INDUS NAT/G PLAN TEC/DEV ECO/TAC ADMIN ATTIT DRIVE RIGID/FLEX...PLURIST STAT TREND GEN/LAWS 20. PAGE 51 A1051
MARKET INT/TRADE

S60
GOODRICH L.,"GEOGRAPHICAL DISTRIBUTION OF THE STAFF OF THE UN SECRETARIAT." FUT WOR+45 CONSTN BAL/PWR DIPLOM EDU/PROP LEGIT ROUTINE RIGID/FLEX...CHARTS UN 20. PAGE 54 A1105
INT/ORG EX/STRUC

S60
IKLE F.C.,"NTH COUNTRIES AND DISARMAMENT." WOR+45 DELIB/GP ECO/TAC DOMIN EDU/PROP LEGIT ROUTINE COERCE RIGID/FLEX ORD/FREE...MARXIST TREND 20. PAGE 70 A1432
FUT INT/ORG ARMS/CONT NUC/PWR

S60
MORA J.A.,"THE ORGANIZATION OF AMERICAN STATES." USA+45 LAW ECO/UNDEV VOL/ASSN DELIB/GP PLAN BAL/PWR EDU/PROP ADMIN DRIVE RIGID/FLEX ORD/FREE WEALTH ...TIME/SEQ GEN/LAWS OAS 20. PAGE 103 A2126
L/A+17C INT/ORG REGION

S60
MORALES C.J.,"TRADE AND ECONOMIC INTEGRATION IN LATIN AMERICA." FUT L/A+17C LAW STRATA ECO/UNDEV DIST/IND INDUS LABOR NAT/G LEGIS ECO/TAC ADMIN RIGID/FLEX WEALTH...CONCPT NEW/IDEA CONT/OBS TIME/SEQ WORK 20. PAGE 104 A2128
FINAN INT/TRADE REGION

S60
PETERSON E.N.,"HISTORICAL SCHOLARSHIP AND WORLD UNITY." FUT UNIV WOR-45 CULTURE INTELL INT/ORG NAT/G ACT/RES EDU/PROP ATTIT PERCEPT RIGID/FLEX ...NEW/IDEA OBS HIST/WRIT TREND COLD/WAR TOT/POP 20. PAGE 115 A2367
PLAN KNOWL NAT/LISM

S60
PYE L.W.,"SOVIET AND AMERICAN STYLES IN FOREIGN AID." COM USA+45 USSR WOR+45 NAT/G PLAN ECO/TAC ROUTINE RIGID/FLEX...POLICY CONCPT TREND GEN/LAWS TOT/POP 20. PAGE 118 A2419
ECO/UNDEV ATTIT FOR/AID

S60
RIVKIN A.,"AFRICAN ECONOMIC DEVELOPMENT: ADVANCED TECHNOLOGY AND THE STAGES OF GROWTH." CULTURE ECO/UNDEV AGRI COM/IND EXTR/IND PLAN ECO/TAC ATTIT DRIVE RIGID/FLEX SKILL WEALTH...MGT SOC GEN/LAWS WORK TOT/POP 20. PAGE 121 A2487
AFR TEC/DEV FOR/AID

S60
SWIFT R.,"THE UNITED NATIONS AND ITS PUBLIC." WOR+45 CONSTN FINAN CONSULT DELIB/GP ACT/RES ADMIN ROUTINE RIGID/FLEX SKILL UN 20. PAGE 140 A2870 INT/ORG EDU/PROP

S60
THOMPSON K.W.,"MORAL PURPOSE IN FOREIGN POLICY: REALITIES AND ILLUSIONS." WOR+45 WOR-45 LAW CULTURE SOCIETY INT/ORG PLAN ADJUD ADMIN COERCE RIGID/FLEX SUPEGO KNOWL ORD/FREE PWR...SOC TREND SOC/EXP TOT/POP 20. PAGE 143 A2930 MORAL JURID DIPLOM

S60
WRIGHT Q.,"LEGAL ASPECTS OF THE U-2 INCIDENT." COM USA+45 USSR STRUCT NAT/G FORCES PLAN TEC/DEV ADJUD RIGID/FLEX MORAL ORD/FREE...DECISION INT/LAW JURID PSY TREND GEN/LAWS COLD/WAR VAL/FREE 20 U-2. PAGE 168 A3413 PWR POLICY SPACE

B61
BARNES W.,THE FOREIGN SERVICE OF THE UNITED STATES. USA+45 USA-45 CONSTN INT/ORG POL/PAR CONSULT DELIB/GP LEGIS DOMIN EDU/PROP EXEC ATTIT RIGID/FLEX ORD/FREE PWR...POLICY CONCPT STAT OBS RECORD BIOG TIME/SEQ TREND. PAGE 11 A0224 NAT/G MGT DIPLOM

B61
BELOFF M.,NEW DIMENSIONS IN FOREIGN POLICY: A STUDY IN BRITISH ADMINISTRATION. UK NAT/G ATTIT RIGID/FLEX ORD/FREE...GEN/LAWS EUR+WWI CMN/WLTH EEC 20. PAGE 13 A0260 INT/ORG DIPLOM

B61
GALLOIS P.,THE BALANCE OF TERROR: STRATEGY FOR THE NUCLEAR AGE. FUT WOR+45 INT/ORG FORCES TOP/EX DETER WAR ATTIT RIGID/FLEX ORD/FREE PWR...HYPO/EXP 20. PAGE 50 A1032 PLAN DECISION DIPLOM NUC/PWR

B61
ROBERTSON A.H.,THE LAW OF INTERNATIONAL INSTITUTIONS IN EUROPE. EUR+WWI MOD/EUR INT/ORG NAT/G VOL/ASSN DELIB/GP...JURID TIME/SEQ TOT/POP 20 TREATY. PAGE 122 A2497 RIGID/FLEX ORD/FREE

L61
HALPERIN M.H.,"NUCLEAR WEAPONS AND LIMITED WARS." FUT UNIV WOR+45 INTELL SOCIETY ECO/DEV ACT/RES DRIVE PERCEPT RIGID/FLEX...CONCPT TIME/SEQ TREND TOT/POP 20. PAGE 60 A1237 PLAN COERCE NUC/PWR WAR

L61
HILSMAN R. JR.,"THE NEW COMMUNIST TACTIC: PRECIS-INTERNAL WAR." COM FUT USA+45 ECO/UNDEV POL/PAR FOR/AID RIGID/FLEX ALL/VALS...TREND COLD/WAR 20. PAGE 65 A1334 FORCES COERCE USSR GUERRILLA

L61
HOYT E.C.,"UNITED STATES REACTION TO THE KOREAN ATTACK." COM KOREA USA+45 CONSTN DELIB/GP FORCES PLAN ECO/TAC DOMIN EDU/PROP LEGIT ROUTINE COERCE WAR ATTIT DISPL RIGID/FLEX ORD/FREE PWR...POLICY INT/LAW TREND UN 20. PAGE 68 A1402 ASIA INT/ORG BAL/PWR DIPLOM

S61
ANGLIN D.,"UNITED STATES OPPOSITION TO CANADIAN MEMBERSHIP IN THE PAN AMERICAN UNION: A CANADIAN VIEW." L/A+17C UK USA+45 VOL/ASSN DELIB/GP EX/STRUC PLAN DIPLOM DOMIN REGION ATTIT RIGID/FLEX PWR ...RELATIV CONCPT STERTYP CMN/WLTH OAS 20. PAGE 8 A0162 INT/ORG CANADA

S61
BARALL M.,"THE UNITED STATES GOVERNMENT RESPONDS." L/A+17C USA+45 SOCIETY NAT/G CREATE PLAN DIPLOM ECO/TAC ATTIT DRIVE RIGID/FLEX KNOWL SKILL WEALTH ...METH/CNCPT TIME/SEQ GEN/METH 20. PAGE 11 A0217 ECO/UNDEV ACT/RES FOR/AID

S61
JUVILER P.H.,"INTERPARLIAMENTARY CONTACTS IN SOVIET FOREIGN POLICY." COM FUT WOR+45 WOR-45 SOCIETY CONSULT ACT/RES DIPLOM ADMIN PEACE ATTIT RIGID/FLEX WEALTH...WELF/ST SOC TOT/POP CONGRESS 19/20. PAGE 75 A1543 INT/ORG DELIB/GP USSR

S61
LEWY G.,"SUPERIOR ORDERS, NUCLEAR WARFARE AND THE DICTATES OF CONSCIENCE: THE DILEMMA OF MILITARY OBEDIENCE IN THE ATOMIC." FUT UNIV WOR+45 INTELL SOCIETY FORCES TOP/EX ACT/RES ADMIN ROUTINE NUC/PWR PERCEPT RIGID/FLEX ALL/VALS...POLICY CONCPT 20. PAGE 88 A1805 DETER INT/ORG LAW INT/LAW

S61
MILLER E.,"LEGAL ASPECTS OF UN ACTION IN THE CONGO." AFR CULTURE ADMIN PEACE DRIVE RIGID/FLEX ORD/FREE...WELF/ST JURID OBS UN CONGO 20. PAGE 101 A2076 INT/ORG LEGIT

S61
ROSTOW W.W.,"THE FUTURE OF FOREIGN AID." COM FUT WOR+45 ECO/DEV INDUS INT/ORG NAT/G CONSULT ACT/RES PLAN DOMIN LEGIT CHOOSE RIGID/FLEX ALL/VALS ...MAJORIT CONCPT TREND TOT/POP 20. PAGE 124 A2544 ECO/UNDEV ECO/TAC FOR/AID

S61
TRAMPE G.,"DIE FORM DER DIPLOMATIC ALS POLITSCHE WAFFE." WOR+45 WOR-45 SOCIETY STRATA INT/ORG NAT/G ACT/RES PLAN ECO/TAC EDU/PROP COERCE WAR ATTIT RIGID/FLEX...DECISION CONCPT TREND. PAGE 145 A2959 CONSULT PWR DIPLOM

B62
ALIX C.,LE SAINT-SIEGE ET LES NATIONALISMES EN EUROPE 1870-1960. COM GERMANY IRELAND ITALY SOCIETY SECT TOTALISM RIGID/FLEX MORAL 19/20. PAGE 6 A0122 CATH NAT/LISM ATTIT DIPLOM

B62
BOUSCAREN A.T.,SOVIET FOREIGN POLICY: A PATTERN OF PERSISTANCE. WOR+45 WOR-45 SOCIETY STRUCT INT/ORG POL/PAR CREATE PLAN EDU/PROP ROUTINE ATTIT RIGID/FLEX...POLICY CONCPT RECORD HIST/WRIT TIME/SEQ MARX/KARL 20. PAGE 17 A0352 COM NAT/G DIPLOM USSR

B62
CARDOZA M.H.,DIPLOMATS IN INTERNATIONAL COOPERATION: STEPCHILDREN OF THE FOREIGN SERVICE. EUR+WWI USA+45 NAT/G CONSULT ACT/RES EDU/PROP ROUTINE RIGID/FLEX KNOWL SKILL...SOC OBS TIME/SEQ EEC OEEC NATO 20. PAGE 24 A0480 INT/ORG METH/CNCPT DIPLOM

B62
CLUBB O.E. JR.,THE UNITED STATES AND THE SINO-SOVIET BLOC IN SOUTHEAST ASIA. ASIA CHINA/COM COM USA+45 USSR ECO/UNDEV INT/ORG NAT/G FORCES TOP/EX PLAN ECO/TAC DOMIN COERCE GUERRILLA ATTIT RIGID/FLEX...POLICY OBS TREND 20. PAGE 27 A0553 S/ASIA PWR BAL/PWR DIPLOM

B62
ELLIOTT J.R.,THE APPEAL OF COMMUNISM IN THE UNDERDEVELOPED NATIONS. USSR WOR+45 INT/ORG NAT/G DIPLOM DOMIN EDU/PROP ROUTINE ATTIT RIGID/FLEX ORD/FREE PWR WEALTH MARXISM...POLICY SOC METH/CNCPT MYTH TOT/POP COLD/WAR 20. PAGE 41 A0842 COM ECO/UNDEV

B62
FORBES H.W.,THE STRATEGY OF DISARMAMENT. FUT WOR+45 INT/ORG VOL/ASSN CONSULT ARMS/CONT COERCE NUC/PWR WAR DRIVE RIGID/FLEX ORD/FREE PWR...POLICY CONCPT OBS TREND STERTYP 20. PAGE 47 A0959 PLAN FORCES DIPLOM

B62
HUNTINGTON S.P.,CHANGING PATTERNS OF MILITARY POLITICS. EUR+WWI L/A+17C S/ASIA USA+45 WOR+45 CULTURE INT/ORG NAT/G CONSULT PLAN DOMIN EDU/PROP LEGIT DETER WAR ATTIT PERSON PWR...DECISION CONCPT SIMUL GEN/LAWS ANTHOL COLD/WAR 20. PAGE 69 A1419 FORCES RIGID/FLEX

B62
MCDOUGAL M.S.,THE PUBLIC ORDER OF THE OCEANS. WOR+45 WOR-45 SEA INT/ORG NAT/G CONSULT DELIB/GP DIPLOM LEGIT PEACE RIGID/FLEX...GEOG INT/LAW JURID RECORD TOT/POP 20 TREATY. PAGE 98 A2007 ADJUD ORD/FREE

B62
OSGOOD R.E.,NATO: THE ENTANGLING ALLIANCE. USA+45 WOR+45 VOL/ASSN FORCES TOP/EX PLAN DETER WEAPON DRIVE RIGID/FLEX ORD/FREE PWR...TREND 20 NATO. PAGE 112 A2301 INT/ORG ARMS/CONT PEACE

B62
ROBINSON A.D.,DUTCH ORGANIZED AGRICULTURE IN INTERNATIONAL POLITICS, 1945-1960. EUR+WWI NETHERLAND STRUCT ECO/DEV NAT/G VOL/ASSN CONSULT DELIB/GP PLAN TEC/DEV INT/TRADE EDU/PROP ATTIT RIGID/FLEX ALL/VALS...NEW/IDEA TREND EEC 20. PAGE 122 A2502 AGRI INT/ORG

B62
THANT U.,THE UNITED NATIONS' DEVELOPMENT DECADE: PROPOSALS FOR ACTION. WOR+45 SOCIETY ECO/UNDEV AGRI COM/IND FINAN R+D MUNIC SCHOOL VOL/ASSN CONSULT PLAN TEC/DEV ECO/TAC EDU/PROP ADMIN ROUTINE RIGID/FLEX...MGT SOC CONCPT UNESCO UN TOT/POP VAL/FREE. PAGE 142 A2906 INT/ORG ALL/VALS

B62
WRIGHT Q.,PREVENTING WORLD WAR THREE. FUT WOR+45 CULTURE INT/ORG NAT/G CONSULT FORCES ADMIN ARMS/CONT DRIVE RIGID/FLEX ORD/FREE SOVEREIGN ...POLICY CONCPT TREND STERTYP COLD/WAR 20. PAGE 168 A3416 CREATE ATTIT

L62
MALINOWSKI W.R.,"CENTRALIZATION AND DE-CENTRALIZATION IN THE UNITED NATIONS' ECONOMIC AND SOCIAL ACTIVITIES." WOR+45 CONSTN ECO/UNDEV INT/ORG VOL/ASSN DELIB/GP ECO/TAC EDU/PROP ADMIN RIGID/FLEX ...OBS CHARTS UNESCO UN EEC OAS OEEC 20. PAGE 93 A1913 CREATE GEN/LAWS

L62
STEIN E.,"MR HAMMARSKJOLD, THE CHARTER LAW AND THE FUTURE ROLE OF THE UNITED NATIONS SECRETARY-GENERAL." WOR+45 CONSTN INT/ORG DELIB/GP FORCES TOP/EX BAL/PWR LEGIT ROUTINE RIGID/FLEX PWR ...POLICY JURID OBS STERTYP UN COLD/WAR 20 HAMMARSK/D. PAGE 137 A2815 CONCPT BIOG

L62
WILCOX F.O.,"THE UN AND THE NON-ALIGNED NATIONS." AFR S/ASIA USA+45 ECO/UNDEV INT/ORG TEC/DEV EDU/PROP RIGID/FLEX ORD/FREE PWR...POLICY HUM CONCPT STAT OBS TIME/SEQ STERTYP GEN/METH UN 20. PAGE 164 A3345 ATTIT TREND

S62
BIERZANECK R.,"LA NON-RECONAISSANCE ET LE DROIT INTERNATIONAL CONTEMPORAIN." EUR+WWI FUT WOR+45 LAW ECO/DEV ATTIT RIGID/FLEX...CONCPT TIME/SEQ TOT/POP 20. PAGE 14 A0286 EDU/PROP JURID DIPLOM INT/LAW

S62
BRZEZINSKI Z.K.,"PEACEFUL ENGAGEMENT IN COMMUNIST DISUNITY." ASIA CHINA/COM USA+45 USSR NAT/G TOP/EX CREATE ECO/TAC FOR/AID DOMIN ATTIT PERCEPT COM DIPLOM TOTALISM

RIGID/FLEX PWR...PSY 20. PAGE 20 A0417

S62
CROAN M.,"POLYCENTRISM: COMMUNIST INTERNATIONAL RELATIONS." ASIA STRUCT INT/ORG NAT/G POL/PAR CONSULT PLAN DOMIN EDU/PROP COERCE ATTIT RIGID/FLEX SOCISM...POLICY CONCPT TREND CON/ANAL GEN/LAWS MARX/KARL. PAGE 33 A0663
COM CREATE DIPLOM NAT/LISM

S62
DALLIN A.,"THE SOVIET VIEW OF THE UNITED NATIONS." WOR+45 VOL/ASSN TOP/EX DIPLOM DOMIN EDU/PROP LEGIT ATTIT RIGID/FLEX PWR...CONCPT OBS HIST/WRIT TIME/SEQ STERTYP GEN/LAWS COLD/WAR UN 20. PAGE 33 A0676
COM INT/ORG USSR

S62
DEUTSCH K.W.,"TOWARDS WESTERN EUROPEAN INTEGRATION: AN INTERIM ASSESSMENT." EUR+WWI STRUCT ECO/DEV INT/ORG ECO/TAC INT/TRADE EDU/PROP PEACE ATTIT DRIVE PWR SOVEREIGN...PSY SOC TIME/SEQ CHARTS STERTYP 20. PAGE 36 A0741
VOL/ASSN RIGID/FLEX REGION

S62
FINKELSTEIN L.S.,"THE UNITED NATIONS AND ORGANIZATIONS FOR CONTROL OF ARMAMENT." FUT WOR+45 VOL/ASSN DELIB/GP TOP/EX CREATE EDU/PROP LEGIT ADJUD NUC/PWR ATTIT RIGID/FLEX ORD/FREE...POLICY DECISION CONCPT OBS TREND GEN/LAWS TOT/POP COLD/WAR. PAGE 46 A0933
INT/ORG PWR ARMS/CONT

S62
FISCHER G.,"UNE NOUVELLE ORGANIZATION REGIONALE: L'ASA." S/ASIA WOR+45 ECO/UNDEV VOL/ASSN PERCEPT RIGID/FLEX...TIME/SEQ 20 ASA. PAGE 46 A0935
INT/ORG DRIVE REGION

S62
FOSTER W.C.,"ARMS CONTROL AND DISARMAMENT IN A DIVIDED WORLD." COM FUT USA+45 USSR WOR+45 INTELL INT/ORG NAT/G VOL/ASSN CONSULT CREATE PLAN TEC/DEV EDU/PROP LEGIT NUC/PWR ATTIT RIGID/FLEX...CONCPT TREND TOT/POP 20 UN. PAGE 47 A0971
DELIB/GP POLICY ARMS/CONT DIPLOM

S62
GUETZKOW H.,"THE POTENTIAL OF CASE STUDY IN ANALYZING INTERNATIONAL CONFLICT." EUR+WWI FUT GERMANY INTELL SOCIETY STRUCT INT/ORG LOC/G NAT/G CONSULT CREATE PLAN CHOOSE ATTIT RIGID/FLEX ...POLICY SAAR 20. PAGE 58 A1188
EDU/PROP METH/CNCPT COERCE FRANCE

S62
JACOBSON H.K.,"THE UNITED NATIONS AND COLONIALISM: A TENTATIVE APPRAISAL." AFR FUT S/ASIA USA+45 USSR WOR+45 NAT/G DELIB/GP PLAN DIPLOM ECO/TAC DOMIN ADMIN ROUTINE COERCE ATTIT RIGID/FLEX ORD/FREE PWR ...OBS STERTYP UN 20. PAGE 73 A1486
INT/ORG CONCPT COLONIAL

S62
KOLARZ W.,"THE IMPACT OF COMMUNISM ON WEST AFRICA." AFR FUT SOCIETY INT/ORG NAT/G CREATE PLAN DOMIN EDU/PROP COERCE NAT/LISM ATTIT RIGID/FLEX SOCISM ...POLICY CONCPT TREND MARX/KARL 20. PAGE 81 A1666
COM POL/PAR COLONIAL

S62
LONDON K.,"SINO-SOVIET RELATIONS IN THE CONTEXT OF THE 'WORLD SOCIALIST SYSTEM'." ASIA CHINA/COM COM USSR INT/ORG NAT/G TOP/EX BAL/PWR DIPLOM DOMIN ATTIT PERCEPT RIGID/FLEX PWR MARXISM...METH/CNCPT TREND 20. PAGE 91 A1854
DELIB/GP CONCPT SOCISM

S62
MCWHINNEY E.,"CO-EXISTENCE, THE CUBA CRISIS, AND COLD WAR-INTERNATIONAL WAR." CUBA USA+45 USSR WOR+45 NAT/G TOP/EX BAL/PWR DIPLOM DOMIN LEGIT PEACE RIGID/FLEX ORD/FREE...STERTYP COLD/WAR 20. PAGE 99 A2026
CONCPT INT/LAW

S62
MOUSKHELY M.,"LA NAISSANCE DES ETATS EN DROIT INTERNATIONAL PUBLIC." UNIV SOCIETY INT/ORG VOL/ASSN LEGIT ATTIT RIGID/FLEX...JURID TIME/SEQ 20. PAGE 105 A2157
NAT/G STRUCT INT/LAW

S62
NANES A.,"DISARMAMENT: THE LAST SEVEN YEARS." COM EUR+WWI USA+45 USSR INT/ORG FORCES TOP/EX CREATE LEGIT NUC/PWR DISPL ORD/FREE...CONCPT TIME/SEQ CON/ANAL 20. PAGE 107 A2195
DELIB/GP RIGID/FLEX ARMS/CONT

S62
ORBAN M.,"L'EUROPE EN FORMATION ET SES PROBLEMES." EUR+WWI FUT WOR+45 WOR-45 INTELL STRUCT DELIB/GP ACT/RES FEDERAL RIGID/FLEX WEALTH...CONCPT TIME/SEQ OEEC 20. PAGE 112 A2295
INT/ORG PLAN REGION

S62
RUBINSTEIN A.Z.,"RUSSIA AND THE UNCOMMITTED NATIONS." AFR INDIA ISLAM L/A+17C LAOS S/ASIA ELITES ECO/UNDEV INT/ORG KIN CREATE PLAN TEC/DEV NAT/LISM RIGID/FLEX PWR WEALTH...METH/CNCPT TIME/SEQ GEN/LAWS WORK. PAGE 125 A2562
ECO/TAC TREND COLONIAL USSR

S62
SINGER J.D.,"STABLE DETERRENCE AND ITS LIMITS." FUT WOR+45 R+D INT/ORG CONSULT ACT/RES TEC/DEV ARMS/CONT COERCE DRIVE PERCEPT RIGID/FLEX ORD/FREE PWR...MYTH SIMUL TOT/POP 20. PAGE 133 A2728
NAT/G FORCES DETER NUC/PWR

S62
SPENSER J.H.,"AFRICA AT THE UNITED NATIONS: SOME OBSERVATIONS." FUT ECO/UNDEV NAT/G CONSULT DELIB/GP PLAN BAL/PWR ECO/TAC EDU/PROP ATTIT RIGID/FLEX HEALTH ORD/FREE PWR WEALTH...POLICY CONCPT OBS TREND STERTYP GEN/METH UN VAL/FREE. PAGE 136 A2786
AFR INT/ORG REGION

S62
STRACHEY J.,"COMMUNIST INTENTIONS." ASIA USSR YUGOSLAVIA INT/ORG NAT/G FORCES DOMIN EDU/PROP COERCE NUC/PWR NAT/LISM PEACE RIGID/FLEX PWR MARXISM...CONCPT MYTH OBS TIME/SEQ TREND COLD/WAR TOT/POP 20. PAGE 139 A2843
COM ATTIT WAR

S62
THOMPSON D.,"THE UNITED KINGDOM AND THE TREATY OF ROME." EUR+WWI INT/ORG NAT/G DELIB/GP LEGIS INT/TRADE RIGID/FLEX...CONCPT EEC PARLIAMENT CMN/WLTH 20. PAGE 143 A2925
ADJUD JURID

B63
ABSHIRE D.M.,NATIONAL SECURITY: POLITICAL, MILITARY, AND ECONOMIC STRATEGIES IN THE DECADE AHEAD. ASIA COM USA+45 WOR+45 ECO/DEV ECO/UNDEV INT/ORG DELIB/GP FORCES ECO/TAC COERCE ATTIT RIGID/FLEX HEALTH ORD/FREE PWR WEALTH...POLICY STAT CHARTS ANTHOL COLD/WAR VAL/FREE. PAGE 4 A0083
FUT ACT/RES BAL/PWR

B63
BOWETT D.W.,THE LAW OF INTERNATIONAL INSTITUTIONS. WOR+45 WOR-45 CONSTN DELIB/GP EX/STRUC JUDGE EDU/PROP LEGIT CT/SYS EXEC ROUTINE RIGID/FLEX ORD/FREE PWR...JURID CONCPT ORG/CHARTS GEN/METH LEAGUE/NAT OAS OEEC 20 UN. PAGE 17 A0354
INT/ORG ADJUD DIPLOM

B63
HALEY A.G.,SPACE LAW AND GOVERNMENT. FUT USA+45 WOR+45 LEGIS ACT/RES CREATE ATTIT RIGID/FLEX ORD/FREE PWR SOVEREIGN...POLICY JURID CONCPT CHARTS VAL/FREE 20. PAGE 60 A1226
INT/ORG LAW SPACE

B63
HINSLEY F.H.,POWER AND THE PURSUIT OF PEACE. WOR+45 WOR-45 PLAN RIGID/FLEX ALL/VALS ALL/IDEOS...POLICY DECISION INT/LAW 12/20 ROUSSEAU/J KANT/I BENTHAM/J LEAGUE/NAT. PAGE 65 A1338
DIPLOM CONSTN PEACE COERCE

B63
JACOBSON H.K.,THE USSR AND THE UN'S ECONOMIC AND SOCIAL ACTIVITIES. COM WOR+45 DELIB/GP ACT/RES ECO/TAC EDU/PROP RIGID/FLEX SUPEGO HEALTH PWR SKILL ...POLICY CHARTS GEN/METH VAL/FREE UNESCO 20 UN. PAGE 73 A1487
INT/ORG ATTIT USSR

B63
KHADDURI M.,MODERN LIBYA: A STUDY IN POLITICAL DEVELOPMENT. EUR+WWI ISLAM LIBYA ELITES INT/ORG POL/PAR FORCES DIPLOM FOR/AID DOMIN EDU/PROP LEGIT NAT/LISM DRIVE RIGID/FLEX SKILL...CONCPT TIME/SEQ TREND 20. PAGE 78 A1606
NAT/G STRUCT

B63
KRAVIS I.B.,DOMESTIC INTERESTS AND INTERNATIONAL OBLIGATIONS: SAFEGUARDS IN INTERNATIONAL TRADE ORGANIZATIONS. EUR+WWI USA+45 WOR+45 FINAN DELIB/GP ATTIT RIGID/FLEX HEALTH...STAT EEC VAL/FREE OEEC ECSC 20. PAGE 82 A1680
INT/ORG ECO/TAC INT/TRADE

B63
LILIENTHAL D.E.,CHANGE, HOPE, AND THE BOMB. USA+45 WOR+45 R+D INT/ORG NAT/G DELIB/GP FORCES ACT/RES DETER RIGID/FLEX ORD/FREE...POLICY CONCPT OBS AEC 20. PAGE 89 A1815
ATTIT MYTH ARMS/CONT NUC/PWR

B63
NORTH R.C.,CONTENT ANALYSIS: A HANDBOOK WITH APPLICATIONS FOR THE STUDY OF INTERNATIONAL CRISIS. ASIA COM EUR+WWI MOD/EUR INT/ORG TEC/DEV DOMIN EDU/PROP ROUTINE COERCE PERCEPT RIGID/FLEX ALL/VALS ...QUANT TESTS CON/ANAL SIMUL GEN/LAWS VAL/FREE. PAGE 110 A2252
METH/CNCPT COMPUT/IR USSR

B63
VOSS E.H.,NUCLEAR AMBUSH: THE TEST-BAN TRAP. WOR+45 COM/IND INT/ORG NAT/G DELIB/GP FORCES LEGIS TOP/EX ACT/RES DOMIN EDU/PROP LEGIT ROUTINE COERCE ATTIT PERCEPT RIGID/FLEX HEALTH MORAL ORD/FREE PWR. PAGE 160 A3255
TEC/DEV HIST/WRIT ARMS/CONT NUC/PWR

L63
MOUSKHELY M.,"LE BLOC COMMUNISTE ET LA COMMUNAUTE ECONOMIQUE EUROPEENNE." AFR COM EUR+WWI FUT USSR WOR+45 INTELL ECO/UNDEV LABOR POL/PAR NUC/PWR RIGID/FLEX...TIME/SEQ ORG/CHARTS EEC TOT/POP 20. PAGE 105 A2158
INT/ORG ECO/DEV

L63
SZASZY E.,"L'EVOLUTION DES PRINCIPES GENERAUX DU DROIT INTERNATIONAL PRIVE DANS LES PAYS DE DEMOCRATIE POPULAIRE." COM FUT WOR+45 LAW ECO/DEV PERF/ART POL/PAR PROF/ORG ECO/TAC INT/TRADE EDU/PROP ATTIT RIGID/FLEX ALL/VALS SOCISM...JURID TREND GEN/LAWS WORK 20. PAGE 141 A2876
DIPLOM TOTALISM INT/LAW INT/ORG

S63
DICKS H.V.,"NATIONAL LOYALTY, IDENTITY, AND THE INTERNATIONAL SOLDIER." FUT NAT/G COERCE ATTIT DRIVE PERCEPT PERSON RIGID/FLEX SUPEGO ALL/VALS ...PSY VAL/FREE. PAGE 37 A0758
INT/ORG FORCES

S63
ETIENNE G.,"'LOIS OBJECTIVES' ET PROBLEMES DE DEVELOPPEMENT DANS LE CONTEXTE CHINE-URSS." ASIA CHINA/COM COM FUT STRUCT INT/ORG VOL/ASSN TOP/EX TEC/DEV ECO/TAC ATTIT RIGID/FLEX...GEOG MGT TIME/SEQ TOT/POP 20. PAGE 42 A0866
TOTALISM USSR

S63
ETZIONI A.,"EUROPEAN UNIFICATION: A STRATEGY OF CHANGE." EUR+WWI CULTURE ECO/DEV DELIB/GP ACT/RES ECO/TAC EDU/PROP ATTIT ORD/FREE PWR SKILL WEALTH ...STAT TIME/SEQ EEC TOT/POP VAL/FREE 20. PAGE 42 A0869
INT/ORG RIGID/FLEX

S63
FRIEDMANN W.G.,"THE USES OF 'GENERAL PRINCIPLES' IN THE DEVELOPMENT OF INTERNATIONAL LAW." WOR+45 NAT/G DIPLOM INT/TRADE LEGIT ROUTINE RIGID/FLEX ORD/FREE ...JURID CONCPT STERTYP GEN/METH 20. PAGE 49 A1005
LAW INT/LAW INT/ORG

S63
GIRAUD E.,"L'INTERDICTION DU RECOURS A LA FORCE, LA THEORIE ET LA PRATIQUE DES NATIONS UNIES." ALGERIA COM CUBA HUNGARY WOR+45 ADJUD TOTALISM ATTIT RIGID/FLEX PWR...POLICY JURID CONCPT UN 20 CONGO. PAGE 53 A1077
INT/ORG FORCES DIPLOM

S63
GROSS F.,"THE US NATIONAL INTEREST AND THE UN." FUT CONSTN NAT/G DELIB/GP CREATE DIPLOM RIGID/FLEX ORD/FREE...CONCPT GEN/LAWS 20 UN. PAGE 57 A1172
USA+45 INT/ORG PEACE

S63
HOLBO P.S.,"COLD WAR DRIFT IN LATIN AMERICA." CUBA L/A+17C USA+45 USA-45 INT/ORG NAT/G NEIGH VOL/ASSN ACT/RES PLAN ECO/TAC ATTIT RIGID/FLEX ALL/VALS ...RECORD TIME/SEQ OAS LAFTA 20 COLD/WAR. PAGE 66 A1363
DELIB/GP CREATE FOR/AID

S63
KAWALKOWSKI A.,"POUR UNE EUROPE INDEPENDENTE ET REUNIFIEE." EUR+WWI FUT USA+45 USSR WOR+45 ECO/DEV PROC/MFG INT/ORG NAT/G ACT/RES TEC/DEV FEDERAL RIGID/FLEX...CONCPT METH/CNCPT OEEC TOT/POP 20 DEGAULLE/C. PAGE 77 A1573
R+D PLAN NUC/PWR

S63
LOPEZIBOR J.,"L'EUROPE, FORME DE VIE." CHRIST-17C EUR+WWI FUT MOD/EUR SOCIETY INT/ORG SECT EDU/PROP ATTIT RIGID/FLEX ALL/VALS...POLICY HUM SOC TIME/SEQ TREND GEN/LAWS. PAGE 91 A1862
NAT/G CULTURE

S63
MANOLIU F.,"PERSPECTIVES D'UNE INTEGRATION ECONOMIQUE LATINOAMERICAINE." FUT L/A+17C STRUCT MARKET LABOR POL/PAR VOL/ASSN PLAN RIGID/FLEX PWR ...METH/CNCPT OAS TOT/POP 20. PAGE 94 A1927
FINAN INT/ORG PEACE

S63
NICHOLAS H.G.,"UN PEACE FORCES AND THE CHANGING GLOBE: THE LESSONS OF SUEZ AND CONGO." FUT WOR+45 CONSTN INT/ORG CONSULT DELIB/GP TOP/EX CREATE DIPLOM DOMIN LEGIT COERCE WAR PERSON RIGID/FLEX PWR UN SUEZ CONGO UNEF 20. PAGE 109 A2229
ACT/RES FORCES

S63
SCHMIDT W.E.,"THE CASE AGAINST COMMODITY AGREEMENTS." FUT L/A+17C STRATA CONSULT PLAN ECO/TAC EDU/PROP ATTIT DRIVE RIGID/FLEX WEALTH ...MYTH 20. PAGE 128 A2631
ECO/UNDEV ACT/RES INT/TRADE

S63
SHONFIELD A.,"AFTER BRUSSELS." EUR+WWI FRANCE GERMANY UK ECO/DEV DIST/IND MARKET VOL/ASSN DELIB/GP CREATE INT/TRADE ATTIT RIGID/FLEX...RECORD TREND GEN/LAWS EEC CMN/WLTH 20. PAGE 132 A2705
PLAN ECO/TAC

S63
TALLON D.,"L'ETUDE DU DROIT COMPARE COMME MOYEN DE RECHERCHER LES MATIERES SUSCEPTIBLES D'UNIFICATION INTERNATIONALE." WOR+45 LAW SOCIETY VOL/ASSN CONSULT LEGIT CT/SYS RIGID/FLEX KNOWL 20. PAGE 141 A2884
INT/ORG JURID INT/LAW

S63
VEROFF J.,"AFRICAN STUDENTS IN THE UNITED STATES." AFR USA+45 CULTURE ACT/RES FOR/AID PEACE ATTIT KNOWL...SOC RECORD DEEP/QU SYS/QU CHARTS STERTYP TOT/POP 20. PAGE 159 A3230
PERCEPT RIGID/FLEX RACE/REL

S63
WEILLER J.,"UNIONS MONETAIRES ET RAPPORTS DE COOPERATION INTERNATIONALE DANS UN MONDE EN TRANSITION: L'EXAMPLE." AFR FUT UNIV WOR+45 SOCIETY ECO/UNDEV MARKET R+D NAT/G FOR/AID PERCEPT RIGID/FLEX...NEW/IDEA 20. PAGE 162 A3303
FINAN INT/ORG

S63
WOLFERS A.,"INTEGRATION IN THE WEST: THE CONFLICT OF PERSPECTIVES." EUR+WWI USA+45 ECO/DEV INT/ORG DELIB/GP CREATE TEC/DEV DIPLOM ATTIT PWR...CONCPT HIST/WRIT TREND GEN/LAWS COLD/WAR EEC 20. PAGE 166 A3386
RIGID/FLEX ECO/TAC

B64
APTER D.E.,IDEOLOGY AND DISCONTENT. FUT WOR+45 CONSTN CULTURE INTELL SOCIETY STRUCT INT/ORG NAT/G DELIB/GP LEGIS CREATE PLAN TEC/DEV EDU/PROP EXEC PERCEPT PERSON RIGID/FLEX ALL/VALS...POLICY TOT/POP. PAGE 8 A0171
ACT/RES ATTIT

B64
BARKER A.J.,SUEZ: THE SEVEN DAY WAR. EUR+WWI ISLAM UAR INT/ORG NAT/G PLAN DIPLOM ECO/TAC DOMIN NAT/LISM DRIVE RIGID/FLEX PWR SOVEREIGN...POLICY JURID TREND CHARTS SUEZ UN 20. PAGE 11 A0221
FORCES COERCE UK

B64
BINDER L.,THE IDEOLOGICAL REVOLUTION IN THE MIDDLE EAST. ISLAM STRUCT INT/ORG KIN SECT EX/STRUC TOP/EX PLAN ATTIT DRIVE RIGID/FLEX PWR...MYTH TOT/POP 20. PAGE 14 A0289
POL/PAR NAT/G NAT/LISM

B64
CZERNIN F.,VERSAILLES - 1919. EUR+WWI USA-45 FACE/GP POL/PAR VOL/ASSN DELIB/GP TOP/EX CREATE BAL/PWR DIPLOM LEGIT NAT/LISM PEACE ATTIT RIGID/FLEX ORD/FREE PWR...CON/ANAL LEAGUE/NAT 20 VERSAILLES. PAGE 33 A0671
INT/ORG STRUCT

B64
DE SMITH S.A.,THE NEW COMMONWEALTH AND ITS CONSTITUTIONS. AFR CYPRUS PAKISTAN S/ASIA INT/ORG NAT/G LEGIS LEGIT RIGID/FLEX PWR...CONCPT TIME/SEQ CMN/WLTH 20. PAGE 35 A0713
EX/STRUC CONSTN SOVEREIGN

B64
DEITCHMAN S.J.,LIMITED WAR AND AMERICAN DEFENSE POLICY. USA+45 WOR+45 INT/ORG NAT/G PLAN TEC/DEV COERCE NUC/PWR RIGID/FLEX PWR SKILL...DECISION METH/CNCPT TIME/SEQ TOT/POP COLD/WAR 20. PAGE 36 A0726
FORCES WAR WEAPON

B64
MARTIN J.J.,AMERICAN LIBERALISM AND WORLD POLITICS, 1931-41 (2 VOLS.). GERMANY USA-45 POL/PAR DISCRIM NAT/LISM PEACE RATIONAL ATTIT RIGID/FLEX MARXISM PACIFISM 20. PAGE 95 A1950
NEW/LIB DIPLOM NAT/G POLICY

B64
MASON E.S.,FOREIGN AID AND FOREIGN POLICY. USA+45 AGRI INDUS NAT/G EX/STRUC ACT/RES RIGID/FLEX ALL/VALS...POLICY GEN/LAWS MARSHL/PLN CONGRESS 20. PAGE 95 A1956
ECO/UNDEV ECO/TAC FOR/AID DIPLOM

B64
ROSECRANCE R.N.,THE DISPERSION OF NUCLEAR WEAPONS: STRATEGY AND POLITICS. ASIA COM FUT S/ASIA USA+45 INT/ORG NAT/G DELIB/GP FORCES ACT/RES TEC/DEV BAL/PWR COERCE DETER ATTIT RIGID/FLEX ORD/FREE ...POLICY CHARTS VAL/FREE. PAGE 123 A2530
EUR+WWI PWR PEACE

B64
TAYLOR E.,RICHER BY ASIA. S/ASIA CULTURE VOL/ASSN ACT/RES ATTIT DISPL PERSON ALL/VALS...INT/LAW MYTH SELF/OBS 20. PAGE 142 A2899
SOCIETY RIGID/FLEX INDIA

B64
TEPASKE J.J.,EXPLOSIVE FORCES IN LATIN AMERICA. CULTURE INTELL ECO/UNDEV INT/ORG NAT/G SECT FORCES ECO/TAC EDU/PROP PWR WEALTH SOC. PAGE 142 A2903
L/A+17C RIGID/FLEX FOR/AID USSR

B64
WARREN S.,THE PRESIDENT AS WORLD LEADER. USA+45 WOR+45 ELITES COM/IND INT/ORG NAT/G VOL/ASSN CHIEF EX/STRUC LEGIT COERCE ATTIT PERSON RIGID/FLEX...INT TIME/SEQ COLD/WAR 20 ROOSEVLT/F TRUMAN/HS EISNHWR/DD KENNEDY/JF. PAGE 161 A3286
TOP/EX PWR DIPLOM

L64
BERKS R.N.,"THE US AND WEAPONS CONTROL." WOR+45 LAW INT/ORG NAT/G LEGIS EXEC COERCE PEACE ATTIT RIGID/FLEX ALL/VALS PWR...POLICY TOT/POP 20. PAGE 13 A0273
USA+45 PLAN ARMS/CONT

L64
HERZ J.H.,"THE RELEVANCY AND IRRELEVANCY OF APPEASEMENT." WOR+45 INT/ORG CONSULT TOP/EX LEGIT ATTIT SUPEGO ORD/FREE...POLICY SOC GEN/LAWS 20. PAGE 64 A1320
ACT/RES RIGID/FLEX

L64
HOFFMANN S.,"EUROPE'S IDENTITY CRISIS: BETWEEN THE PAST AND AMERICA." EUR+WWI FUT USA+45 INT/ORG NAT/G LEGIT RIGID/FLEX ALL/VALS...RELATIV TOT/POP 20. PAGE 66 A1358
COERCE POLICY

S64
COCHRANE J.D.,"US ATTITUDES TOWARD CENTRAL-AMERICAN INTEGRATION." L/A+17C USA+45 ECO/UNDEV FACE/GP VOL/ASSN DELIB/GP ECO/TAC INT/TRADE EDU/PROP RIGID/FLEX ORD/FREE WEALTH...TIME/SEQ TOT/POP 20. PAGE 27 A0555
NAT/G ATTIT REGION

S64
DEVILLERS P.H.,"L'URSS, LA CHINE ET LES ORIGINES DE LA GUERRE DE COREE." ASIA CHINA/COM USSR INT/ORG ECO/TAC EDU/PROP ATTIT RIGID/FLEX PWR...STAND/INT HIST/WRIT COLD/WAR 20. PAGE 37 A0751
WOR+45 KOREA

S64
GARDNER R.N.,"GATT AND THE UNITED NATIONS CONFERENCE ON TRADE AND DEVELOPMENT." USA+45 WOR+45 SOCIETY ECO/UNDEV MARKET NAT/G DELIB/GP ACT/RES PLAN ECO/TAC TARIFFS EDU/PROP ROUTINE DRIVE RIGID/FLEX WEALTH...DECISION MGT TREND UN TOT/POP 20 GATT. PAGE 51 A1047
INT/ORG INT/TRADE

S64
GRZYBOWSKI K.,"INTERNATIONAL ORGANIZATIONS FROM THE SOVIET POINT OF VIEW." WOR+45 WOR-45 CULTURE ECO/DEV VOL/ASSN EDU/PROP ATTIT RIGID/FLEX KNOWL ...SOC OBS TIME/SEQ TREND GEN/LAWS VAL/FREE ILO UN 20. PAGE 58 A1184
COM INT/ORG DIPLOM USSR

S64
HUTCHINSON E.C.,"AMERICAN AID TO AFRICA." FUT USA+45 MARKET INT/ORG LOC/G NAT/G PUB/INST PLAN ECO/TAC ATTIT RIGID/FLEX...POLICY CONCPT TREND 20. PAGE 69 A1423
AFR ECO/UNDEV FOR/AID

S64
JORDAN A.,"POLITICAL COMMUNICATION: THE THIRD
EDU/PROP

DIMENSION OF STRATEGY." USA+45 WOR+45 INT/ORG NAT/G CONSULT FORCES PLAN LEGIT EXEC PERCEPT ALL/VALS ...POLICY RELATIV PSY NEW/IDEA AUD/VIS EXHIBIT TOT/POP 20. PAGE 75 A1534 — RIGID/FLEX ATTIT

S64
LERNER W.,"THE HISTORICAL ORIGINS OF THE SOVIET DOCTRINE OF PEACEFUL COEXISTENCE." COM USSR INT/ORG NAT/G VOL/ASSN PLAN PEACE ATTIT RIGID/FLEX PWR MARXISM...TIME/SEQ COLD/WAR 20. PAGE 87 A1788 — EDU/PROP DIPLOM

S64
MARTELLI G.,"PORTUGAL AND THE UNITED NATIONS." AFR EUR+WWI ELITES INT/ORG NAT/G PROVS PLAN DIPLOM ECO/TAC DOMIN COLONIAL RIGID/FLEX MORAL ORD/FREE PWR WEALTH...MYTH UN 20. PAGE 95 A1947 — ATTIT PORTUGAL

S64
MCCREARY E.A.,"THOSE AMERICAN MANAGERS DON'T IMPRESS EUROPE." EUR+WWI USA+45 CULTURE STRATA ECO/DEV TOP/EX INT/TRADE ATTIT DRIVE PERSON RIGID/FLEX...CONCPT 20. PAGE 98 A2003 — MARKET ACT/RES BAL/PAY CAP/ISM

S64
RUBINSTEIN A.Z.,"THE SOVIET IMAGE OF WESTERN EUROPE." COM EUR+WWI FRANCE GERMANY GERMANY/W USA+45 USSR INT/ORG NAT/G VOL/ASSN FORCES TOP/EX BAL/PWR EDU/PROP ORD/FREE PWR...MYTH RECORD NATO EEC 20. PAGE 125 A2564 — RIGID/FLEX ATTIT

S64
SAAB H.,"THE ARAB SEARCH FOR A FEDERAL UNION." SOCIETY INT/ORG NAT/G DELIB/GP FORCES ACT/RES TEC/DEV ECO/TAC DOMIN LEGIT REGION ROUTINE ATTIT DRIVE RIGID/FLEX ALL/VALS...SOC CONCPT NEW/IDEA TIME/SEQ TREND. PAGE 126 A2580 — ISLAM PLAN

S64
TOUVAL S.,"THE SOMALI REPUBLIC." AFR ISLAM SOMALIA FAM KIN NAT/G CREATE FOR/AID LEGIT ATTIT ALL/VALS ...RECORD TREND 20. PAGE 144 A2954 — ECO/UNDEV RIGID/FLEX

S64
WASKOW A.I.,"NEW ROADS TO A WORLD WITHOUT WAR." FUT WOR+45 CULTURE INTELL SOCIETY NAT/G DOMIN LEGIT EXEC COERCE PEACE ATTIT DISPL PERCEPT RIGID/FLEX ALL/VALS...POLICY RELATIV SOC NEW/IDEA 20. PAGE 161 A3288 — INT/ORG FORCES

B65
DOMENACH J.M.,LA PROPAGANDE POLITIQUE. COM/IND INT/ORG POL/PAR DOMIN RIGID/FLEX FASCISM MARXISM ...PSY 20. PAGE 38 A0770 — ATTIT EDU/PROP TEC/DEV MYTH

B65
VONGLAHN G.,LAW AMONG NATIONS: AN INTRODUCTION TO PUBLIC INTERNATIONAL LAW. UNIV WOR+45 LAW INT/ORG NAT/G LEGIT EXEC RIGID/FLEX...CONCPT TIME/SEQ GEN/LAWS UN TOT/POP 20. PAGE 160 A3253 — CONSTN JURID INT/LAW

L65
KAPLAN M.A.,"OLD REALITIES AND NEW MYTHS." USA+45 WOR+45 INT/ORG NAT/G TOP/EX ACT/RES BAL/PWR ECO/TAC EDU/PROP LEGIT RIGID/FLEX ALL/VALS...RECORD COLD/WAR 20. PAGE 76 A1564 — ATTIT MYTH DIPLOM

S65
BROWN S.,"AN ALTERNATIVE TO THE GRAND DESIGN." EUR+WWI FUT USA+45 INT/ORG NAT/G EX/STRUC FORCES CREATE BAL/PWR DOMIN RIGID/FLEX ORD/FREE PWR ...NEW/IDEA RECORD EEC NATO 20. PAGE 20 A0407 — VOL/ASSN CONCPT DIPLOM

S65
GROSS L.,"PROBLEMS OF INTERNATIONAL ADJUDICATION AND COMPLIANCE WITH INTERNATIONAL LAW: SOME SIMPLE SOLUTIONS." WOR+45 SOCIETY NAT/G DOMIN LEGIT ADJUD CT/SYS RIGID/FLEX HEALTH PWR...JURID NEW/IDEA COLD/WAR 20. PAGE 57 A1177 — LAW METH/CNCPT INT/LAW

S65
HELMREICH E.C.,"KADAR'S HUNGARY." COM EUR+WWI HUNGARY USSR INTELL ECO/DEV AGRI INT/ORG TOP/EX DOMIN ALL/VALS WORK COLD/WAR 20. PAGE 64 A1311 — NAT/G RIGID/FLEX TOTALISM

S65
KHOURI F.J.,"THE JORDON RIVER CONTROVERSY." LAW SOCIETY ECO/UNDEV AGRI FINAN INDUS SECT FORCES ACT/RES PLAN TEC/DEV ECO/TAC EDU/PROP COERCE ATTIT DRIVE PERCEPT RIGID/FLEX ALL/VALS...GEOG SOC MYTH WORK. PAGE 78 A1610 — ISLAM INT/ORG ISRAEL JORDAN

S65
KORBONSKI A.,"USA POLICY IN EAST EUROPE." COM EUR+WWI GERMANY USA+45 CULTURE ECO/UNDEV EDU/PROP RIGID/FLEX WEALTH 20. PAGE 82 A1672 — ACT/RES ECO/TAC FOR/AID

S65
MERRITT R.L.,"WOODROW WILSON AND THE 'GREAT AND SOLEMN REFERENDUM,' 1920." USA-45 SOCIETY NAT/G CONSULT LEGIS ACT/RES PLAN DOMIN EDU/PROP ROUTINE ATTIT DISPL DRIVE PERSON RIGID/FLEX MORAL ORD/FREE ...PSY SOC CONCPT MYTH LEAGUE/NAT. PAGE 100 A2044 — INT/ORG TOP/EX DIPLOM

S65
QUADE Q.L.,"THE TRUMAN ADMINISTRATION AND THE SEPARATION OF POWERS: THE CASE OF THE MARSHALL PLAN." SOCIETY INT/ORG NAT/G CONSULT DELIB/GP LEGIS PLAN ECO/TAC ROUTINE DRIVE PERCEPT RIGID/FLEX ORD/FREE PWR WEALTH...DECISION GEOG NEW/IDEA TREND 20 TRUMAN/HS. PAGE 118 A2422 — USA+45 ECO/UNDEV DIPLOM

S65
RAY H.,"THE POLICY OF RUSSIA TOWARDS SINO-INDIAN CONFLICT." ASIA CHINA/COM COM INDIA USSR NAT/G TOP/EX FOR/AID EDU/PROP NEUTRAL COERCE PEACE RIGID/FLEX PWR...METH/CNCPT TIME/SEQ VAL/FREE 20. PAGE 120 A2452 — S/ASIA ATTIT DIPLOM WAR

S65
ROGGER H.,"EAST GERMANY: STABLE OR IMMOBILE." COM EUR+WWI GERMANY/E NAT/G INT/TRADE DOMIN EDU/PROP COERCE TOTALISM COLD/WAR 20. PAGE 123 A2516 — TOP/EX RIGID/FLEX GERMANY

S65
SCHNEIDER R.M.,"THE US IN LATIN AMERICA." L/A+17C USA+45 NAT/G POL/PAR PLAN RIGID/FLEX ALL/VALS OAS 20. PAGE 129 A2640 — VOL/ASSN ECO/UNDEV FOR/AID

B66
GRENVILLE J.A.S.,POLITICS, STRATEGY, AND AMERICAN DEMOCRACY: STUDIES IN FOREIGN POLICY, 1873-1917. CUBA PHILIPPINE SPAIN USA-45 VENEZUELA ELITES NAT/G CREATE PARTIC WAR RIGID/FLEX ORD/FREE...DECISION TREND 19/20 HAWAII. PAGE 56 A1146 — DIPLOM COLONIAL POLICY

B66
LONDON K.,EASTERN EUROPE IN TRANSITION. CHINA/COM USSR DOMIN COLONIAL CENTRAL RIGID/FLEX PWR...SOC ANTHOL 20. PAGE 91 A1855 — SOVEREIGN COM NAT/LISM DIPLOM

B67
FILENE P.G.,AMERICANS AND THE SOVIET EXPERIMENT, 1917-1933. USA-45 USSR INTELL NAT/G CAP/ISM DIPLOM EDU/PROP PRESS REV SOCISM...PSY 20. PAGE 45 A0930 — ATTIT RIGID/FLEX MARXISM SOCIETY

S67
SAPP B.B.,"TRIBAL CULTURES AND COMMUNISM." AFR USA+45 STRATA DIPLOM FOR/AID REGION CENTRAL ATTIT AUTHORIT RIGID/FLEX KNOWL. PAGE 127 A2604 — KIN MARXISM ECO/UNDEV STRUCT

RIMALOV V.V. A2482

RIO/PACT....RIO PACT

RIOT....RIOTS; SEE ALSO CROWD

RIPLEY R.B. A2483

RISK....SEE ALSO GAMBLE

N19
MEZERIK A.G.,U-2 AND OPEN SKIES (PAMPHLET). USA+45 USSR INT/ORG CHIEF FORCES PLAN EDU/PROP CONTROL SANCTION ARMS/CONT 20 UN EISNHWR/DD. PAGE 100 A2060 — DIPLOM RISK DEBATE

B37
THOMPSON J.W.,SECRET DIPLOMACY: A RECORD OF ESPIONAGE AND DOUBLE-DEALING: 1500-1815. CHRIST-17C MOD/EUR NAT/G WRITING RISK MORAL...ANTHOL BIBLIOG 16/19 ESPIONAGE. PAGE 143 A2927 — DIPLOM CRIME

B39
FULLER G.H.,A SELECTED LIST OF REFERENCES ON THE EXPANSION OF THE US NAVY, 1933-1939 (PAMPHLET). MOD/EUR USA-45 NAT/G PLAN DIPLOM DOMIN RISK ARMS/CONT EQUILIB PWR 20 NAVY. PAGE 50 A1019 — BIBLIOG FORCES WEAPON WAR

B60
LE GHAIT E.,NO CARTE BLANCHE TO CAPRICORN; THE FOLLY OF NUCLEAR WAR. WOR+45 INT/ORG BAL/PWR DIPLOM RISK COERCE...CENSUS 20 NATO. PAGE 86 A1754 — DETER NUC/PWR PLAN DECISION

B62
KING-HALL S.,POWER POLITICS IN THE NUCLEAR AGE: A POLICY FOR BRITAIN. UK WOR+45 PLAN ECO/TAC CONTROL RISK ARMS/CONT MORAL PWR RESPECT...OLD/LIB 20. PAGE 79 A1625 — BAL/PWR NUC/PWR POLICY DIPLOM

B62
MANDER J.,BERLIN: HOSTAGE FOR THE WEST. FUT GERMANY WOR+45 FOR/AID RISK ATTIT ORD/FREE 20 BERLIN COLD/WAR. PAGE 93 A1916 — DIPLOM BAL/PWR DOMIN DETER

L63
CRANE R.D.,"THE CUBAN CRISIS: A STRATEGIC ANALYSIS OF AMERICAN AND SOVIET POLICY." CUBA USA+45 USSR BAL/PWR RISK DETER NUC/PWR PERCEPT ORD/FREE 20. PAGE 32 A0658 — DIPLOM POLICY FORCES

B66
AMERICAN ASSEMBLY COLUMBIA U,A WORLD OF NUCLEAR POWERS? FUT WOR+45 ECO/DEV BAL/PWR ECO/TAC CONTROL RISK EFFICIENCY ATTIT PWR...METH/COMP ANTHOL 20. PAGE 7 A0137 — NUC/PWR DIPLOM TEC/DEV ARMS/CONT

B66
HOLLINS E.J.,PEACE IS POSSIBLE: A READER FOR LAYMEN. WOR+45 CULTURE PLAN RISK AGE/Y ALL/VALS SOVEREIGN...PSY CONCPT TREND 20 UN JOHN/XXIII KENNAN/G MYRDAL/G. PAGE 67 A1370 — PEACE DIPLOM INT/ORG NUC/PWR

B67
BODENHEIMER E.,TREATISE ON JUSTICE. INT/ORG NAT/G PUB/INST ACT/RES RISK CRIME INGP/REL DISCRIM DRIVE LAISSEZ 20. PAGE 16 A0325 — ALL/VALS STRUCT JURID CONCPT

S67
CARROLL K.J.,"SECOND STEP TOWARD ARMS CONTROL." WOR+45 INT/ORG VOL/ASSN FORCES PROB/SOLV RISK — ARMS/CONT DIPLOM

WEAPON 20 COLD/WAR. PAGE 25 A0503 — PLAN NUC/PWR

S67

D'AMATO D.,"LEGAL ASPECTS OF THE FRENCH NUCLEAR TESTS." FRANCE WOR+45 ACT/RES COLONIAL RISK GOV/REL EQUILIB ORD/FREE PWR DECISION. PAGE 33 A0672 — INT/LAW DIPLOM NUC/PWR ADJUD

S67

HODGE G.,"THE RISE AND DEMISE OF THE UN TECHNICAL ASSISTANCE ADMINISTRATION." RISK TASK INGP/REL CONSEN EFFICIENCY 20 UN. PAGE 66 A1349 — ADMIN TEC/DEV EX/STRUC INT/ORG

S67

SUINN R.M.,"THE DISARMAMENT FANTASY* PSYCHOLOGICAL FACTORS THAT MAY PRODUCE WARFARE." DIPLOM RISK ARMS/CONT DETER ANOMIE PERSON GAME. PAGE 140 A2860 — DECISION NUC/PWR WAR PSY

RISTIC D.N. A2484

RITCHIE/JM....JESS M. RITCHIE

RITNER P. A2485

RITSCHL/H....HANS RITSCHL

RITUAL....RITUALS AND SYMBOLIC CEREMONIES; SEE ALSO WORSHIP, SECT

RIVKIN A. A2486,A2487,A2488,A2489,A2490

RKFDV....REICHSKOMMISSARIAT FUR DIE FESTIGUNG DEUTSCHEN VOLKSTUMS

RKO....R.K.O.

ROACH J.R. A2491

ROBBINS L. A2492,A2493

ROBERTS H.L. A2080,A2494,A2495

ROBERTS J. A2154

ROBERTSON A.H. A1717,A2496,A2497,A2498

ROBERTSON B.C. A2499

ROBERTSON D.J. A2500

ROBESPR/M....MAXIMILIAN FRANCOIS ROBESPIERRE

ROBINS D.B. A2501

ROBINSN/JH....JAMES HARVEY ROBINSON

ROBINSON A.D. A2502

ROBINSON H. A2503

ROBINSON J.A. A2504,A2505

ROBINSON K. A1247

ROBINSON M.E. A2506
ROBINSON R.D. A1882
ROBINSON W.J. A3292

ROBINSON/H....HENRY ROBINSON

ROBOCK S.H. A2507,A2508

ROCK V.P. A2509

ROCKE J.R.M. A2510

ROCKEFELLER BROTHERS FUND INC.A2511

RODBRTUS/C....CARL RODBERTUS

RODNEY W. A2512

RODRIGUES J.H. A2513

ROGERS W.C. A2514,A2515

ROGGER H. A2516

ROLE....ROLE, REFERENCE GROUP, CROSS-PRESSURES

N/R

FULBRIGHT J.W.,THE ARROGANCE OF POWER. USA+45 WOR+45 ECO/UNDEV ACADEM LEGIS ECO/TAC FOR/AID PEACE ROLE ORD/FREE PWR 20 COLD/WAR CONGRESS. PAGE 50 A1014 — DIPLOM POLICY REV

N49

UN DEPARTMENT PUBLIC INF,SELECTED BIBLIOGRAPHY OF THE SPECIALIZED AGENCIES RELATED TO THE UNITED NATIONS (PAMPHLET). USA+45 ROLE 20 UN. PAGE 146 A2996 — BIBLIOG INT/ORG EX/STRUC ADMIN

B52

U OF MICH SURVEY RESEARCH CTR,AMERICA'S ROLE IN WORLD AFFAIRS. ASIA COM EUR+WWI USA+45 USSR FOR/AID WAR AUTHORIT ORD/FREE...DEEP/QU 20. PAGE 146 A2986 — DIPLOM NAT/G ROLE POLICY

B54

GIRAUD A.,CIVILISATION ET PRODUCTIVITE. UNIV INDUS WORKER DIPLOM REV INCOME UTOPIA...GEOG 20. PAGE 53 A1076 — SOCIETY PRODUC ROLE

B55

CRAIG G.A.,THE POLITICS OF THE PRUSSIAN ARMY 1640-1945. CHRIST-17C EUR+WWI MOD/EUR PRUSSIA STRUCT DIPLOM ADMIN REV WAR...SOC BIBLIOG 17/20. PAGE 32 A0652 — FORCES NAT/G ROLE CHIEF

B58

JENNINGS W.I.,PROBLEMS OF THE NEW COMMONWEALTH. CEYLON INDIA MALAYSIA PAKISTAN ECO/UNDEV VOL/ASSN RACE/REL NAT/LISM ROLE 20 CMN/WLTH. PAGE 74 A1511 — GP/REL INGP/REL COLONIAL INT/ORG

B58

MANSERGH N.,SURVEY OF BRITISH COMMONWEALTH AFFAIRS: PROBLEMS OF WARTIME CO-OPERATION AND POST-WAR CHANGE 1939-1952. INDIA IRELAND S/ASIA CONSTN INT/ORG BAL/PWR COLONIAL NEUTRAL WAR ADJUST PEACE ROLE ORD/FREE...CHARTS 20 CMN/WLTH NATO UN. PAGE 94 A1931 — VOL/ASSN CONSEN PROB/SOLV INGP/REL

B60

DE GAULLE C.,THE EDGE OF THE SWORD. EUR+WWI FRANCE ELITES CHIEF DIPLOM ROLE...REALPOL TRADIT. PAGE 34 A0701 — FORCES SUPEGO LEAD WAR

B61

BAGU S.,ARGENTINA EN EL MUNDO. L/A+17C INDUS INT/TRADE WAR ATTIT ROLE...TREND 19/20 ARGEN OAS. PAGE 10 A0202 — DIPLOM INT/ORG REGION ECO/UNDEV

B61

FULLER J.F.C.,THE CONDUCT OF WAR, 1789-1961. FRANCE RUSSIA SOCIETY NAT/G FORCES PROB/SOLV AGREE NUC/PWR WEAPON PEACE...SOC 18/20 TREATY COLD/WAR. PAGE 50 A1025 — WAR POLICY REV ROLE

B61

MILLER R.I.,DAG HAMMARSKJOLD AND CRISES DIPLOMACY. WOR+45 NAT/G PROB/SOLV LEAD ROLE...DECISION BIOG UN HAMMARSK/D. PAGE 101 A2079 — DIPLOM INT/ORG CHIEF

B61

ROBINSON M.E.,EDUCATION FOR SOCIAL CHANGE: ESTABLISHING INSTITUTES OF PUBLIC AND BUSINESS ADMINISTRATION ABROAD (PAMPHLET). WOR+45 SOCIETY ACADEM CONFER INGP/REL ROLE...SOC CHARTS BIBLIOG 20 ICA. PAGE 122 A2506 — FOR/AID EDU/PROP MGT ADJUST

B61

SHAPP W.R.,FIELD ADMINISTRATION IN THE UNITED NATIONS SYSTEM. FINAN PROB/SOLV INSPECT DIPLOM EXEC REGION ROUTINE EFFICIENCY ROLE...INT CHARTS 20 UN. PAGE 131 A2694 — INT/ORG ADMIN GP/REL FOR/AID

B62

ROUND TABLE ON EUROPE'S ROLE IN LATIN AMERICAN DEVELOPMENT. EUR+WWI L/A+17C PLAN BAL/PAY UTIL ROLE WEALTH...CHARTS ANTHOL 20 UN INT/AM/DEV. PAGE 3 A0063 — ECO/UNDEV FINAN TEC/DEV FOR/AID

B62

SHAW C.,LEGAL PROBLEMS IN INTERNATIONAL TRADE AND INVESTMENT. WOR+45 ECO/DEV ECO/UNDEV MARKET DIPLOM TAX INCOME ROLE...ANTHOL BIBLIOG 20 TREATY UN IMF GATT. PAGE 132 A2698 — INT/LAW INT/TRADE FINAN ECO/TAC

B62

THOMSON G.P.,NUCLEAR ENERGY IN BRITAIN DURING THE LAST WAR: THE CHERWELL SIMON LECTURE (MONOGRAPH). UK R+D CONSULT FORCES PLAN DIPLOM TASK CIVMIL/REL ROLE...PHIL/SCI NEW/IDEA LAB/EXP 20 MAUD. PAGE 143 A2934 — CREATE TEC/DEV WAR NUC/PWR

B63

NORTH R.C.,M. N. ROY'S MISSION TO CHINA: THE COMMUNIST-KUOMINTANG SPLIT OF 1927. ASIA USSR STRATA LEGIS WORKER LEAD REV ATTIT ROLE SOCISM 20 ROY/MN COM/PARTY. PAGE 110 A2253 — POL/PAR MARXISM DIPLOM

B64

COX R.,PAN-AFRICANISM IN PRACTICE. AFR DIPLOM CONFER RACE/REL ROLE SOVEREIGN...POLICY 20 PANAF/FREE. PAGE 32 A0645 — ORD/FREE COLONIAL REGION NAT/LISM

B64

DUROSELLE J.B.,LA COMMUNAUTE INTERNATIONALE FACE AUX JEUNES ETATS. CHINA/COM COM S/ASIA USSR INT/ORG ROLE...ANTHOL 20 UN SEATO THIRD/WRLD. PAGE 40 A0808 — DIPLOM COLONIAL ECO/UNDEV SOVEREIGN

B64
SARROS P.P.,CONGRESS AND THE NEW DIPLOMACY: THE FORMULATION OF MUTUAL SECURITY POLICY: 1953-60 (THESIS). USA+45 CHIEF EX/STRUC REGION ROUTINE CHOOSE GOV/REL PEACE ROLE...POLICY 20 PRESIDENT CONGRESS. PAGE 127 A2606
DIPLOM POL/PAR NAT/G

B64
SINGH N.,THE DEFENCE MECHANISM OF THE MODERN STATE. COM UK USA+45 CONSTN INT/ORG NUC/PWR WAR INGP/REL ROLE 20 DEPT/DEFEN COMMONWLTH. PAGE 134 A2735
FORCES TOP/EX NAT/G CIVMIL/REL

B64
STANGER R.J.,ESSAYS ON INTERVENTION. PLAN PROB/SOLV BAL/PWR ADJUD COERCE WAR ROLE PWR...INT/LAW CONCPT 20 UN INTERVENT. PAGE 137 A2803
SOVEREIGN DIPLOM POLICY LEGIT

B64
US SENATE COMM GOVT OPERATIONS,THE SECRETARY OF STATE AND THE AMBASSADOR. USA+45 CHIEF CONSULT EX/STRUC FORCES PLAN ADMIN EXEC INGP/REL ROLE ...ANTHOL 20 PRESIDENT DEPT/STATE. PAGE 156 A3175
DIPLOM DELIB/GP NAT/G

S64
PRASAD B.,"SURVEY OF RECENT RESEARCH: STUDIES ON INDIA'S FOREIGN POLIC AND RELATIONS." ASIA INDIA PAKISTAN USA+45 NAT/G INT/TRADE GOV/REL 20 UN CMN/WLTH. PAGE 117 A2406
BIBLIOG DIPLOM ROLE POLICY

B65
FAGG J.E.,CUBA, HAITI, AND THE DOMINICAN REPUBLIC. CUBA DOMIN/REP HAITI L/A+17C NAT/G DIPLOM ECO/TAC DOMIN CHOOSE AUTHORIT ROLE SOVEREIGN POPULISM 17/20. PAGE 43 A0883
COLONIAL ECO/UNDEV REV GOV/COMP

B65
FALK R.A.,THE AFTERMATH OF SABBATINO: BACKGROUND PAPERS AND PROCEEDINGS OF SEVENTH HAMMARSKJOLD FORUM. USA+45 LAW ACT/RES ADJUD ROLE...BIBLIOG 20 EXPROPRIAT SABBATINO HARLAN/JM. PAGE 44 A0891
SOVEREIGN CT/SYS INT/LAW OWN

B65
LEE M.,THE UNITED NATIONS AND WORLD REALITIES. ECO/UNDEV FORCES WAR PEACE ATTIT ROLE WEALTH 20 UN. PAGE 86 A1761
INT/ORG COLONIAL ARMS/CONT DIPLOM

B65
MONCRIEFF A.,SECOND THOUGHTS ON AID. WOR+45 ECO/UNDEV AGRI FINAN VOL/ASSN PLAN TEC/DEV GIVE EDU/PROP ROLE WEALTH 20. PAGE 102 A2105
FOR/AID ECO/TAC INT/ORG IDEA/COMP

B65
SPENCE J.E.,REPUBLIC UNDER PRESSURE: A STUDY OF SOUTH AFRICAN FOREIGN POLICY. SOUTH/AFR ADMIN COLONIAL GOV/REL RACE/REL DISCRIM NAT/LISM ATTIT ROLE...TREND 20 NEGRO. PAGE 136 A2783
DIPLOM POLICY AFR

B65
US SENATE COMM GOVT OPERATIONS,ADMINISTRATION OF NATIONAL SECURITY. USA+45 DELIB/GP ADMIN ROLE ...POLICY CHARTS SENATE. PAGE 156 A3177
NAT/G ORD/FREE DIPLOM PROB/SOLV

S65
GANGAL S.C.,"SURVEY OF RECENT RESEARCH: INDIA AND THE COMMONWEALTH" INDIA UK NAT/G INT/TRADE PARTIC GOV/REL ROLE 20 CMN/WLTH. PAGE 51 A1039
BIBLIOG POLICY REGION DIPLOM

B66
CROWLEY D.W.,THE BACKGROUND TO CURRENT AFFAIRS. UK WOR+45 INT/ORG BAL/PWR NUC/PWR ATTIT ROLE 20 COLD/WAR. PAGE 33 A0665
DIPLOM PWR POLICY

B66
FERKISS V.C.,AFRICA'S SEARCH FOR IDENTITY. AFR USA+45 CULTURE ECO/UNDEV INT/ORG NAT/G COLONIAL MARXISM 20. PAGE 45 A0918
NAT/LISM SOVEREIGN DIPLOM ROLE

B66
FRANK E.,LAWMAKERS IN A CHANGING WORLD. FRANCE UK USSR WOR+45 PARTIC EFFICIENCY ROLE ALL/IDEOS ...CHARTS ANTHOL PARLIAMENT 20 UN COLD/WAR. PAGE 48 A0979
GOV/COMP LEGIS NAT/G DIPLOM

B66
WILSON H.A.,THE IMPERIAL POLICY OF SIR ROBERT BORDEN. CANADA UK ELITES INT/ORG VOL/ASSN CONTROL LEAD WAR ROLE 20 CMN/WLTH BORDEN/R. PAGE 165 A3360
INGP/REL COLONIAL CONSTN CHIEF

B66
ZEINE Z.N.,THE EMERGENCE OF ARAB NATIONALISM (REV. ED.). TURKEY UK NAT/G SECT TEC/DEV LEAD REV WAR AGE/Y ROLE ORD/FREE...TRADIT CHARTS BIBLIOG 20 ARABS OTTOMAN. PAGE 170 A3451
ISLAM NAT/LISM DIPLOM

B67
KATZ R.,DEATH IN ROME. EUR+WWI ITALY POL/PAR DIPLOM LEAD ATTIT PERSON ROLE CATHISM. PAGE 77 A1570
WAR MURDER FORCES DEATH

B67
RALSTON D.B.,THE ARMY OF THE REPUBLIC; THE PLACE OF THE MILITARY IN THE POLITICAL EVOLUTION OF FRANCE 1871-1914. FRANCE MOD/EUR EX/STRUC LEGIS TOP/EX DIPLOM ADMIN WAR GP/REL ROLE...BIBLIOG 19/20. PAGE 119 A2436
FORCES NAT/G CIVMIL/REL POLICY

B67
ROACH J.R.,THE UNITED STATES AND THE ATLANTIC COMMUNITY; ISSUES AND PROSPECTS. WOR+45 TEC/DEV ECO/TAC COLONIAL REGION PEACE ROLE...ANTHOL NATO COLD/WAR EEC. PAGE 121 A2491
INT/ORG POLICY ADJUST DIPLOM

B67
SINGER D.,QUANTITATIVE INTERNATIONAL POLITICS* INSIGHTS AND EVIDENCE. WOR+45 WOR-45 PARTIC WAR INGP/REL ATTIT PERSON ROLE...PREDICT BIBLIOG 19/20 UN SENATE. PAGE 133 A2722
DIPLOM NAT/G INT/ORG DECISION

B67
US DEPARTMENT OF THE ARMY,CIVILIAN IN PEACE, SOLDIER IN WAR: A BIBLIOGRAPHIC SURVEY OF THE ARMY AND AIR NATIONAL GUARD (PAMPHLET, NOS. 130-2). USA+45 USA-45 LOC/G NAT/G PROVS LEGIS PLAN ADMIN ATTIT ORD/FREE...POLICY 19/20. PAGE 152 A3111
BIBLIOG/A FORCES ROLE DIPLOM

B67
WAELDER R.,PROGRESS AND REVOLUTION* A STUDY OF THE ISSUES OF OUR AGE. WOR+45 WOR-45 BAL/PWR DIPLOM COERCE ROLE MORAL ALL/IDEOS...IDEA/COMP NAT/COMP 19/20. PAGE 160 A3259
PWR NAT/G REV TEC/DEV

B67
WATERS M.,THE UNITED NATIONS* INTERNATIONAL ORGANIZATION AND ADMINISTRATION. WOR+45 EX/STRUC FORCES DIPLOM LEAD REGION ARMS/CONT REPRESENT INGP/REL ROLE...METH/COMP ANTHOL 20 UN LEAGUE/NAT. PAGE 162 A3291
CONSTN INT/ORG ADMIN ADJUD

B67
WILLIS F.R.,DE GAULLE: ANACHRONISM, REALIST, OR PROPHET? FRANCE POL/PAR FORCES DIPLOM WAR PEACE ROLE ORD/FREE...POLICY IDEA/COMP ANTHOL 20 DEGAULLE/C. PAGE 165 A3356
BIOG PERSON CHIEF LEAD

L67
GRAUBARD S.R.,"TOWARD THE YEAR 2000: WORK IN PROGRESS." FUT ACADEM SECT DELIB/GP DIPLOM EDU/PROP AGE/Y PERSON ROLE...PSY ANTHOL. PAGE 55 A1131
PREDICT PROB/SOLV SOCIETY CULTURE

ROLFE S.E. A2517

ROMAN CATHOLIC....SEE CATH, CATHISM

ROMAN/EMP....ROMAN EMPIRE

B11
PHILLIPSON C.,THE INTERNATIONAL LAW AND CUSTOM OF ANCIENT GREECE AND ROME. MEDIT-7 UNIV INTELL SOCIETY STRUCT NAT/G LEGIS EXEC PERSON...CONCPT OBS CON/ANAL ROM/EMP. PAGE 116 A2377
INT/ORG LAW INT/LAW

B39
TAGGART F.J.,ROME AND CHINA. MEDIT-7 INT/ORG NAT/G FORCES LEGIS TOP/EX PLAN PWR SOVEREIGN...CHARTS TOT/POP ROM/EMP. PAGE 141 A2883
ASIA WAR

B57
ALIGHIERI D.,ON WORLD GOVERNMENT. ROMAN/EMP LAW SOCIETY INT/ORG NAT/G POL/PAR ADJUD WAR GP/REL PEACE WORSHIP 15 WORLDUNITY DANTE. PAGE 6 A0121
POLICY CONCPT DIPLOM SECT

B58
SALETORE B.A.,INDIA'S DIPLOMATIC RELATIONS WITH THE WEST. GREECE INDIA CULTURE ETIQUET...IDEA/COMP 3 ROM/EMP PERSIA. PAGE 126 A2590
DIPLOM CONCPT INT/TRADE

B59
BROOKES E.H.,THE COMMONWEALTH TODAY. UK ROMAN/EMP INT/ORG RACE/REL NAT/LISM SOVEREIGN...TREND SOC/INTEG 20. PAGE 19 A0391
FEDERAL DIPLOM JURID IDEA/COMP

S63
BULLOUGH V.L.,"THE ROMAN EMPIRE VS PERSIA, 363-502: A STUDY OF SUCCESSFUL DETERRENCE." NAT/G PLAN DIPLOM ORD/FREE PWR...TIME/SEQ COLD/WAR VAL/FREE 4/6 PERSIA ROM/EMP. PAGE 21 A0430
MEDIT-7 COERCE DETER

B90
HOSMAR J.K.,A SHORT HISTORY OF ANGLO-SAXON FREEDOM. UK USA-45 ROMAN/EMP NAT/G EX/STRUC LEGIS COLONIAL REV NAT/LISM POPULISM PARLIAMENT ANGLO/SAX MAGNA/CART. PAGE 68 A1394
CONSTN ORD/FREE DIPLOM PARL/PROC

ROMAN/LAW....ROMAN LAW

ROMAN/REP....ROMAN REPUBLIC

ROMANIA....SEE ALSO COM

N
KYRIAK T.E.,EAST EUROPE: BIBLIOGRAPHY--INDEX TO US JPRS RESEARCH TRANSLATIONS. ALBANIA BULGARIA COM CZECHOSLVK HUNGARY POLAND ROMANIA AGRI EXTR/IND FINAN SERV/IND INT/TRADE WEAPON...GEOG MGT SOC 20. PAGE 83 A1701
BIBLIOG/A PRESS MARXISM INDUS

B43
CONOVER H.F.,THE BALKANS: A SELECTED LIST OF REFERENCES. ALBANIA BULGARIA ROMANIA YUGOSLAVIA
BIBLIOG EUR+WWI

INT/ORG PROB/SOLV DIPLOM LEGIT CONFER ADJUD WAR
NAT/LISM PEACE PWR 20 LEAGUE/NAT. PAGE 29 A0596

B61
SCHIEDER T.,DOCUMENTS ON THE EXPULSION OF THE GERMANS FROM EASTERN-CENTRAL-EUROPE (VOL. II/III). COM EUR+WWI GERMANY HUNGARY ROMANIA USSR DIPLOM RACE/REL 20 MIGRATION. PAGE 128 A2625
GEOG CULTURE

S63
RAMERIE L.,"TENSION AU SEIN DU COMECON: LE CAS ROUMAIN." COM EUR+WWI USSR WOR+45 ECO/DEV DIST/IND NAT/G POL/PAR VOL/ASSN EDU/PROP TOTALISM ATTIT WEALTH...TIME/SEQ 20 COMECON. PAGE 119 A2438
INT/ORG ECO/TAC INT/TRADE ROMANIA

B66
BROWN J.F.,THE NEW EASTERN EUROPE. ALBANIA BULGARIA HUNGARY POLAND ROMANIA CULTURE AGRI POL/PAR WAR NAT/LISM MARXISM...CHARTS BIBLIOG 20. PAGE 20 A0404
DIPLOM COM NAT/G ECO/UNDEV

S66
SKILLING H.G.,"THE RUMANIAN NATIONAL COURSE." COM EUR+WWI ROMANIA NAT/G ECO/TAC PWR 20. PAGE 134 A2739
NAT/LISM POLICY DIPLOM MARXISM

ROMANOVSKY S. A2518

ROME....ROME

B35
MARRIOTT J.A.,DICTATORSHIP AND DEMOCRACY. GERMANY GREECE UK CHIEF DIPLOM DOMIN LEGIT PEACE ORD/FREE CONSERVE...TREND ROME HITLER/A. PAGE 95 A1946
TOTALISM POPULISM PLURIST NAT/G

B63
MONTER W.,THE GOVERNMENT OF GENEVA, 1536-1605 (DOCTORAL THESIS). SWITZERLND DIPLOM LEAD ORD/FREE SOVEREIGN 16/17 CALVIN/J ROME. PAGE 103 A2112
SECT FINAN LOC/G ADMIN

ROME/ANC....ANCIENT ROME; SEE ALSO ROM/REP, **ROMAN/EMP**

ROMEIN J. A2519

ROMNEY/GEO....GEORGE ROMNEY

ROOSEVELT J. A2520

ROOSEVLT/F....PRESIDENT FRANKLIN D. ROOSEVELT

B38
GRISWOLD A.W.,THE FAR EASTERN POLICY OF THE UNITED STATES. ASIA S/ASIA USA-45 INT/ORG INT/TRADE WAR NAT/LISM...BIBLIOG 19/20 LEAGUE/NAT ROOSEVLT/T ROOSEVLT/F WILSON/W TREATY. PAGE 57 A1166
DIPLOM POLICY CHIEF

B49
STETTINIUS E.R.,ROOSEVELT AND THE RUSSIANS: THE YALTA CONFERENCE. UK USSR WOR+45 WOR-45 INT/ORG VOL/ASSN TOP/EX ACT/RES EDU/PROP PEACE ATTIT DRIVE PERSON SUPEGO PWR...POLICY CONCPT MYTH OBS TIME/SEQ AUD/VIS COLD/WAR 20 CHURCHLL/W YALTA ROOSEVLT/F. PAGE 138 A2819
DIPLOM DELIB/GP BIOG

B50
DULLES J.F.,WAR OR PEACE. CHINA/COM USA+45 USSR INT/ORG SECT FORCES PLAN NUC/PWR WAR CENTRAL MARXISM...POLICY 20 UN ROOSEVLT/F STALIN/J. PAGE 39 A0797
PEACE DIPLOM TREND ORD/FREE

B50
GUERRANT E.O.,ROOSEVELT'S GOOD NEIGHBOR POLICY. L/A+17C USA+45 USA-45 FOR/AID...IDEA/COMP 20 ROOSEVLT/F TRUMAN/HS. PAGE 58 A1187
DIPLOM NAT/G CHIEF POLICY

B56
SNELL J.L.,THE MEANING OF YALTA: BIG THREE DIPLOMACY AND THE NEW BALANCE OF POWER. EUR+WWI GERMANY USA-45 USSR FORCES PLAN BAL/PWR DIPLOM WAR CHOOSE PEACE...CHARTS BIBLIOG 20 UN CHINJAP ROOSEVLT/F. PAGE 134 A2749
CONFER CHIEF POLICY PROB/SOLV

B60
CONN S.,THE FRAMEWORK OF HEMISPHERE DEFENSE. CANADA L/A+17C USA-45 NAT/G FORCES BAL/PWR DOMIN WAR PEACE DISPL PWR RESPECT...PLURIST CONCPT HIST/WRIT HYPO/EXP MEXIC/AMER 20 ROOSEVLT/F. PAGE 29 A0585
USA+45 INT/ORG DIPLOM

B60
MORISON E.E.,TURMOIL AND TRADITION: A STUDY OF THE LIFE AND TIMES OF HENRY L. STIMSON. USA+45 USA-45 POL/PAR CHIEF DELIB/GP FORCES BAL/PWR DIPLOM ARMS/CONT WAR PEACE 19/20 STIMSON/HL ROOSEVLT/F TAFT/WH HOOVER/H REPUBLICAN. PAGE 104 A2142
BIOG NAT/G EX/STRUC

B62
GUTTMAN A.,THE WOUND IN THE HEART: AMERICA AND THE SPANISH CIVIL WAR. SPAIN USA-45 POL/PAR LEGIS ECO/TAC CHOOSE ANOMIE ATTIT MARXISM...POLICY ANARCH BIBLIOG 20 ROOSEVLT/F. PAGE 58 A1198
ALL/IDEOS WAR DIPLOM CATHISM

B64
GARDNER L.C.,ECONOMIC ASPECTS OF NEW DEAL DIPLOMACY. USA-45 WOR-45 LAW ECO/DEV INT/ORG NAT/G VOL/ASSN LEGIS TOP/EX EDU/PROP ORD/FREE PWR WEALTH ...POLICY TIME/SEQ VAL/FREE 20 ROOSEVLT/F. PAGE 51 A1043
ECO/TAC DIPLOM

B64
WARREN S.,THE PRESIDENT AS WORLD LEADER. USA+45 WOR+45 ELITES COM/IND INT/ORG NAT/G VOL/ASSN CHIEF EX/STRUC LEGIT COERCE ATTIT PERSON RIGID/FLEX...INT TIME/SEQ COLD/WAR 20 ROOSEVLT/F TRUMAN/HS EISNHWR/DD KENNEDY/JF. PAGE 161 A3286
TOP/EX PWR DIPLOM

B65
RAPPAPORT A.,ISSUES IN AMERICAN DIPLOMACY: WORLD POWER AND LEADERSHIP SINCE 1895 (VOL. II). CHINA/COM EUR+WWI L/A+17C USA+45 USA-45 NAT/G ECO/TAC DOMIN CONFER LEAD NUC/PWR WEAPON...DECISION 19/20 WILSON/W ROOSEVLT/F CHINJAP. PAGE 119 A2447
WAR POLICY DIPLOM

B66
FREIDEL F.,AMERICAN ISSUES IN THE TWENTIETH CENTURY. SOCIETY FINAN ECO/TAC FOR/AID CONTROL NUC/PWR WAR RACE/REL PEACE ATTIT...ANTHOL T 20 WILSON/W ROOSEVLT/F KENNEDY/JF TRUMAN/HS. PAGE 49 A0995
DIPLOM POLICY NAT/G ORD/FREE

B66
SINGER L.,ALLE LITTEN AN GROSSENWAHN: VON WOODROW WILSON BIS MAO TSE-TUNG. ASIA UK USSR INT/ORG DELIB/GP BAL/PWR DOMIN ATTIT PERSON 20 WILSON/W ROOSEVLT/F. PAGE 133 A2731
DIPLOM TOTALISM WAR CHIEF

ROOSEVLT/T....PRESIDENT THEODORE ROOSEVELT

B38
GRISWOLD A.W.,THE FAR EASTERN POLICY OF THE UNITED STATES. ASIA S/ASIA USA-45 INT/ORG INT/TRADE WAR NAT/LISM...BIBLIOG 19/20 LEAGUE/NAT ROOSEVLT/T ROOSEVLT/F WILSON/W TREATY. PAGE 57 A1166
DIPLOM POLICY CHIEF

B56
BEALE H.K.,THEODORE ROOSEVELT AND THE RISE OF AMERICA TO WORLD POWER. USA-45 BAL/PWR COLONIAL DRIVE PERSON PWR...POLICY BIBLIOG 20 ROOSEVLT/T PRESIDENT. PAGE 12 A0238
DIPLOM CHIEF BIOG

B58
GROBLER J.H.,AFRICA'S DESTINY. AFR EUR+WWI SOUTH/AFR UK USA+45 ELITES KIN LOC/G DIPLOM DISCRIM ATTIT CONSERVE MARXISM 20 ROOSEVLT/T NEGRO. PAGE 57 A1168
POLICY ORD/FREE COLONIAL CONSTN

ROOT E. A2521,A2522,A2523

ROPKE W. A2524,A2525

ROSAMOND R. A2526

ROSCIO J.G. A2527

ROSE S. A2528

ROSECRANCE R.N. A2529,A2530

ROSENAU J.N. A2531,A2532,A2533,A2534

ROSENBERG A. A2535

ROSENHAUPT H.W. A2536

ROSENNE S. A2537,A2538

ROSNER G. A2539

ROSS A. A2540

ROSS H. A2541

ROSS/EH....EDWARD H. ROSS

ROSSI M. A2542

ROSSMOOR....ROSSMOOR LEISURE WORLD, SEAL BEACH, CAL.

ROSTOW W.W. A2081,A2543,A2544

ROTBERG R.I. A2545,A2546

ROTHCHILD D. A2547

ROTHFELS H. A2548

ROUGEMONT D. A2549

ROUSCOS G. A2108

ROUSSEAU J.J. A2550

ROUSSEAU/J....JEAN JACQUES ROUSSEAU

B63
HINSLEY F.H.,POWER AND THE PURSUIT OF PEACE. WOR+45 WOR-45 PLAN RIGID/FLEX ALL/VALS ALL/IDEOS...POLICY DECISION INT/LAW 12/20 ROUSSEAU/J KANT/I BENTHAM/J
DIPLOM CONSTN PEACE

LEAGUE/NAT. PAGE 65 A1338 — COERCE

ROUSSOS G. A2110

ROUTINE....PROCEDURAL AND WORK SYSTEMS

N
REVUE FRANCAISE DE SCIENCE POLITIQUE. FRANCE UK ...BIBLIOG/A 20. PAGE 2 A0040 — NAT/G DIPLOM CONCPT ROUTINE

B00
MORRIS H.C.,THE HISTORY OF COLONIZATION. WOR+45 WOR-45 ECO/DEV ECO/UNDEV INT/ORG ACT/RES PLAN ECO/TAC LEGIT ROUTINE COERCE ATTIT DRIVE ALL/VALS ...GEOG TREND 19. PAGE 105 A2148 — DOMIN SOVEREIGN COLONIAL

B00
OMAN C.,A HISTORY OF THE ART OF WAR: THE MIDDLE AGES FROM THE FOURTH TO THE FOURTEENTH CENTURY. CHRIST-17C MEDIT-7 CULTURE SOCIETY INT/ORG ROUTINE PERSON...CONT/OBS HIST/WRIT CHARTS VAL/FREE. PAGE 112 A2291 — FORCES SKILL WAR

B00
VOLPICELLI Z.,RUSSIA ON THE PACIFIC AND THE SIBERIAN RAILWAY. MOD/EUR ECO/UNDEV INT/ORG FORCES PLAN DOMIN COLONIAL ROUTINE ATTIT ALL/VALS...OBS HIST/WRIT TIME/SEQ TREND CON/ANAL AUD/VIS CHARTS 18/19. PAGE 159 A3248 — NAT/G ACT/RES RUSSIA

B02
SEELEY J.R.,THE EXPANSION OF ENGLAND. MOD/EUR S/ASIA UK CULTURE NAT/G FORCES PLAN DOMIN EDU/PROP COLONIAL ROUTINE ATTIT ALL/VALS SOVEREIGN...CONCPT HIST/WRIT PARLIAMENT 18 CMN/WLTH. PAGE 131 A2679 — INT/ORG ACT/RES CAP/ISM INDIA

B05
GRIFFIN A.P.C.,LIST OF REFERENCES ON THE US CONSULAR SERVICE (PAMPHLET). FRANCE GERMANY SPAIN UK USA-45 WOR-45 OP/RES DOMIN ADMIN FEEDBACK ROUTINE GOV/REL...DECISION 19. PAGE 56 A1153 — BIBLIOG/A NAT/G DIPLOM CONSULT

B06
FOSTER J.W.,THE PRACTICE OF DIPLOMACY AS ILLUSTRATED IN THE FOREIGN RELATIONS OF THE UNITED STATES. MOD/EUR USA-45 NAT/G EX/STRUC ADMIN ...POLICY INT/LAW BIBLIOG 19/20. PAGE 47 A0970 — DIPLOM ROUTINE PHIL/SCI

B09
HOLLAND T.E.,LETTERS UPON WAR AND NEUTRALITY. WOR-45 NAT/G FORCES JUDGE ECO/TAC LEGIT CT/SYS NEUTRAL ROUTINE COERCE...JURID TIME/SEQ 20. PAGE 67 A1368 — LAW INT/LAW INT/ORG WAR

B19
KEYNES J.M.,THE ECONOMIC CONSEQUENCES OF THE PEACE. FUT GERMANY MOD/EUR RUSSIA UK USA-45 CULTURE ECO/DEV FINAN INDUS INT/ORG TOP/EX ECO/TAC ROUTINE WAR ATTIT PERCEPT ALL/VALS...OLD/LIB MYTH OBS TIME/SEQ TREND 20 TREATY. PAGE 78 A1605 — EUR+WWI SOCIETY PEACE

B22
POTTER P.B.,AN INTRODUCTION TO THE STUDY OF INTERNATIONAL ORGANIZATION. WOR-45 ACT/RES CREATE EDU/PROP ROUTINE PERCEPT KNOWL...CONT/OBS RECORD GEN/LAWS TOT/POP VAL/FREE 20. PAGE 117 A2398 — INT/ORG CONCPT

B22
WRIGHT Q.,THE CONTROL OF AMERICAN FOREIGN RELATIONS. USA-45 WOR-45 CONSTN INT/ORG CONSULT LEGIS LEGIT ROUTINE ORD/FREE PWR...POLICY JURID CONCPT METH/CNCPT RECORD LEAGUE/NAT 20. PAGE 167 A3402 — NAT/G EXEC DIPLOM

B29
CONWELL-EVANS T.P.,THE LEAGUE COUNCIL IN ACTION. EUR+WWI TURKEY UK USSR WOR-45 INT/ORG FORCES JUDGE ECO/TAC EDU/PROP LEGIT ROUTINE ARMS/CONT COERCE ATTIT PWR...MAJORIT GEOG JURID CONCPT LEAGUE/NAT TOT/POP VAL/FREE TUNIS 20. PAGE 30 A0605 — DELIB/GP INT/LAW

B29
DUNN F.,THE PRACTICE AND PROCEDURE OF INTERNATIONAL CONFERENCES. WOR-45 NAT/G DELIB/GP BAL/PWR LEGIT EXEC ROUTINE PEACE ORD/FREE RESPECT...JURID CONCPT METH/CNCPT OBS RECORD TIME/SEQ 20. PAGE 39 A0799 — INT/ORG DIPLOM

B30
SCHMITT B.E.,THE COMING OF THE WAR, 1914 (2 VOLS.). AUSTRIA FRANCE GERMANY MOD/EUR RUSSIA UK PLAN ROUTINE ORD/FREE. PAGE 128 A2633 — WAR DIPLOM

B31
GREAVES H.R.G.,THE LEAGUE COMMITTEES AND WORLD ORDER. WOR-45 DELIB/GP EX/STRUC EDU/PROP ALL/VALS LEAGUE/NAT VAL/FREE 20. PAGE 55 A1136 — INT/ORG DIPLOM ROUTINE

B31
STOWELL E.C.,INTERNATIONAL LAW. FUT UNIV WOR-45 SOCIETY CONSULT EX/STRUC FORCES ACT/RES PLAN DIPLOM EDU/PROP LEGIT DISPL PWR SKILL...POLICY CONCPT OBS TREND TOT/POP 20. PAGE 139 A2839 — INT/ORG ROUTINE INT/LAW

B32
MORLEY F.,THE SOCIETY OF NATIONS. EUR+WWI UNIV WOR-45 LAW CONSTN ACT/RES PLAN EDU/PROP LEGIT ROUTINE...POLICY TIME/SEQ LEAGUE/NAT TOT/POP 20. PAGE 104 A2143 — INT/ORG CONCPT

B33
LANGER W.L.,FOREIGN AFFAIRS BIBLIOGRAPHY. WOR-45 INT/ORG CONSULT EDU/PROP ROUTINE NAT/LISM ATTIT SOVEREIGN...STAT RECORD GEN/METH LEAGUE/NAT TOT/POP. PAGE 84 A1725 — KNOWL

B37
ROBBINS L.,ECONOMIC PLANNING AND INTERNATIONAL ORDER. WOR-45 SOCIETY FINAN INDUS NAT/G ECO/TAC ROUTINE WEALTH...SOC TIME/SEQ GEN/METH WORK 20 KEYNES/JM. PAGE 122 A2492 — INT/ORG PLAN INT/TRADE

B39
NICOLSON H.,CURZON: THE LAST PHASE, 1919-1925. UK NAT/G DELIB/GP TOP/EX ROUTINE WAR RIGID/FLEX ...METH/CNCPT 20 CURZON/GN. PAGE 109 A2231 — POLICY DIPLOM BIOG

C39
REISCHAUER R.,"JAPAN'S GOVERNMENT--POLITICS." CONSTN STRATA POL/PAR FORCES LEGIS DIPLOM ADMIN EXEC CENTRAL...POLICY BIBLIOG 20 CHINJAP. PAGE 120 A2462 — NAT/G S/ASIA CONCPT ROUTINE

B40
RAPPARD W.E.,THE QUEST FOR PEACE. UNIV USA-45 WOR-45 SOCIETY INT/ORG NAT/G PLAN EXEC ROUTINE WAR ATTIT DRIVE ALL/VALS...POLICY CONCPT OBS TIME/SEQ LEAGUE/NAT TOT/POP 20. PAGE 119 A2450 — EUR+WWI ACT/RES PEACE

B41
MCCLURE W.,INTERNATIONAL EXECUTIVE AGREEMENTS. USA-45 WOR-45 INT/ORG NAT/G DELIB/GP ADJUD ROUTINE ORD/FREE PWR...TIME/SEQ TREND CON/ANAL. PAGE 97 A2000 — TOP/EX DIPLOM

B42
CORBETT P.E.,POST WAR WORLDS. ASIA EUR+WWI FUT S/ASIA USA-45 ECO/DEV ECO/UNDEV NAT/G DELIB/GP FORCES PLAN ROUTINE ATTIT PWR 20. PAGE 30 A0613 — WOR-45 INT/ORG

B44
BRIERLY J.L.,THE OUTLOOK FOR INTERNATIONAL LAW. FUT WOR-45 CONSTN NAT/G VOL/ASSN FORCES ECO/TAC DOMIN LEGIT ADJUD ROUTINE PEACE ORD/FREE...INT/LAW JURID METH LEAGUE/NAT 20. PAGE 18 A0376 — INT/ORG LAW

B44
DAVIS H.E.,PIONEERS IN WORLD ORDER. WOR-45 CONSTN ECO/TAC DOMIN EDU/PROP LEGIT ADJUD ADMIN ARMS/CONT CHOOSE KNOWL ORD/FREE...POLICY JURID SOC STAT OBS CENSUS TIME/SEQ ANTHOL LEAGUE/NAT 20. PAGE 34 A0691 — INT/ORG ROUTINE

B44
PUTTKAMMER E.W.,WAR AND THE LAW. UNIV USA-45 CONSTN CULTURE SOCIETY NAT/G POL/PAR ROUTINE ALL/VALS ...JURID CONCPT OBS WORK VAL/FREE 20. PAGE 118 A2418 — INT/ORG LAW WAR INT/LAW

S44
WRIGHT Q.,"CONSTITUTIONAL PROCEDURES OF THE US FOR CARRYING OUT OBLIGATIONS FOR MILITARY SANCTIONS." EUR+WWI FUT USA-45 WOR-45 CONSTN INTELL NAT/G CONSULT EX/STRUC LEGIS ROUTINE DRIVE...POLICY JURID CONCPT OBS TREND TOT/POP 20. PAGE 167 A3406 — TOP/EX FORCES INT/LAW WAR

B45
CARR E.H.,NATIONALISM AND AFTER. FUT WOR-45 NAT/G VOL/ASSN EX/STRUC PLAN ROUTINE TOTALISM ATTIT HEALTH ORD/FREE PWR...CONCPT 20. PAGE 25 A0499 — INT/ORG TREND NAT/LISM REGION

B45
HILL N.,CLAIMS TO TERRITORY IN INTERNATIONAL LAW AND RELATIONS. WOR-45 NAT/G DOMIN EDU/PROP LEGIT REGION ROUTINE ORD/FREE PWR WEALTH...GEOG INT/LAW JURID 20. PAGE 65 A1332 — INT/ORG ADJUD SOVEREIGN

B45
RANSHOFFEN-WERTHEIMER EF,THE INTERNATIONAL SECRETARIAT: A GREAT EXPERIMENT IN INTERNATIONAL ADMINISTRATION. EUR+WWI FUT CONSTN FACE/GP CONSULT DELIB/GP ACT/RES ADMIN ROUTINE PEACE ORD/FREE...MGT RECORD ORG/CHARTS LEAGUE/NAT WORK 20. PAGE 119 A2442 — INT/ORG EXEC

L47
HISS D.,"UNITED STATES PARTICIPATION IN THE UNITED NATIONS." USA+45 EX/STRUC PLAN DIPLOM ROUTINE CHOOSE...PLURIST UN 20. PAGE 65 A1342 — INT/ORG PWR

B48
CHILDS J.R.,AMERICAN FOREIGN SERVICE. USA+45 SOCIETY NAT/G ROUTINE GOV/REL 20 DEPT/STATE CIVIL/SERV. PAGE 26 A0530 — DIPLOM ADMIN GP/REL

B48
GRAHAM F.D.,THE THEORY OF INTERNATIONAL VALUES. FUT WOR+45 WOR-45 ECO/DEV FINAN INT/ORG PLAN TEC/DEV CAP/ISM DIPLOM ECO/TAC TARIFFS ROUTINE BAL/PAY DRIVE PWR WEALTH SOCISM...POLICY STAT HYPO/EXP GEN/LAWS 20. PAGE 55 A1125 — NEW/IDEA INT/TRADE

B49
SINGER K.,THE IDEA OF CONFLICT. UNIV INTELL INT/ORG NAT/G PLAN ROUTINE ATTIT DRIVE ALL/VALS...POLICY CONCPT TIME/SEQ. PAGE 133 A2730 — ACT/RES SOC

L49
COMM. STUDY ORGAN. PEACE,"A TEN YEAR RECORD, 1939-1949." FUT WOR+45 LAW R+D CONSULT DELIB/GP CREATE LEGIT ROUTINE ORD/FREE...TIME/SEQ UN 20. PAGE 28 A0578 — INT/ORG CONSTN PEACE

L49
HEINDEL R.H.,"THE NORTH ATLANTIC TREATY IN THE UNITED STATES SENATE." CONSTN POL/PAR CHIEF DEBATE LEAD ROUTINE WAR PEACE...CHARTS UN SENATE NATO. — DECISION PARL/PROC LEGIS

PAGE 64 A1309 INT/ORG

S49
KIRK G.,"MATTERIALS FOR THE STUDY OF INTERNATIONAL RELATIONS." FUT UNIV WOR+45 INTELL EDU/PROP ROUTINE PEACE ATTIT...INT/LAW JURID CONCPT OBS. PAGE 80 A1633 INT/ORG ACT/RES DIPLOM

B50
CHASE E.P.,THE UNITED NATIONS IN ACTION. WOR+45 CONSTN DELIB/GP LEGIT ROUTINE COERCE PEACE ORD/FREE PWR...CON/ANAL GEN/LAWS UN 20. PAGE 26 A0524 INT/ORG STRUCT ARMS/CONT

B50
JIMENEZ E.,VOTING AND HANDLING OF DISPUTES IN THE SECURITY COUNCIL. WOR+45 CONSTN INT/ORG DIPLOM LEGIT DETER CHOOSE MORAL ORD/FREE PWR...JURID TIME/SEQ COLD/WAR UN 20. PAGE 74 A1517 DELIB/GP ROUTINE

B50
STONE J.,THE PROVINCE AND FUNCTION OF LAW. UNIV WOR+45 WOR-45 CULTURE INTELL SOCIETY ECO/DEV ECO/UNDEV NAT/G LEGIT ROUTINE ATTIT PERCEPT PERSON ...JURID CONCPT GEN/LAWS GEN/METH 20. PAGE 138 A2833 INT/ORG LAW

L50
US SENATE COMM. GOVT. OPER.,"REVISION OF THE UN CHARTER." FUT USA+45 WOR+45 CONSTN ECO/DEV ECO/UNDEV NAT/G DELIB/GP ACT/RES CREATE PLAN EXEC ROUTINE CHOOSE ALL/VALS...POLICY CONCPT CONGRESS UN TOT/POP 20 COLD/WAR. PAGE 157 A3196 INT/ORG LEGIS PEACE

B51
CORMACK M.,SELECTED PAMPHLETS ON THE UNITED NATIONS AND INTERNATIONAL RELATIONS (PAMPHLET). USA+45 R+D EX/STRUC PROB/SOLV ROUTINE...POLICY CON/ANAL 20 UN NATO. PAGE 31 A0624 BIBLIOG/A NAT/G INT/ORG DIPLOM

B51
MACLAURIN J.,THE UNITED NATIONS AND POWER POLITICS. WOR+45 CONSULT EDU/PROP LEGIT ADJUD EXEC MORAL ORD/FREE...HUM JURID CONCPT RECORD TIME/SEQ UN COLD/WAR 20. PAGE 93 A1896 INT/ORG ROUTINE

L51
MANGONE G.,"THE IDEA AND PRACTICE OF WORLD GOVERNMENT." FUT WOR+45 WOR-45 ECO/DEV LEGIS CREATE LEGIT ROUTINE ATTIT MORAL PWR WEALTH...CONCPT GEN/LAWS 20. PAGE 94 A1920 INT/ORG SOCIETY INT/LAW

B52
WALTERS F.P.,A HISTORY OF THE LEAGUE OF NATIONS. EUR+WWI CONSTN NAT/G LEGIS TOP/EX ACT/RES PLAN EDU/PROP LEGIT ROUTINE ATTIT...TREND LEAGUE/NAT 20 CHINJAP. PAGE 161 A3271 INT/ORG TIME/SEQ NAT/LISM

L52
HILSMAN R. JR.,"INTELLIGENCE AND POLICY MAKING IN FOREIGN AFFAIRS." USA+45 CONSULT ACT/RES DIPLOM EDU/PROP ROUTINE PEACE PERCEPT PWR SKILL...POLICY MGT HYPO/EXP CONGRESS 20 CIA. PAGE 65 A1333 PROF/ORG SIMUL WAR

L52
THOMPSON K.W.,"THE STUDY OF INTERNATIONAL POLITICS: A SURVEY OF TRENDS AND DEVELOPMENTS." UNIV USA+45 WOR+45 WOR-45 SOCIETY ECO/DEV R+D ACT/RES PLAN ROUTINE ATTIT DRIVE PERCEPT PERSON...CONCPT OBS TREND GEN/LAWS TOT/POP. PAGE 143 A2928 INT/ORG BAL/PWR DIPLOM

L52
WRIGHT Q.,"CONGRESS AND THE TREATY-MAKING POWER." USA+45 WOR+45 CONSTN INTELL NAT/G CHIEF CONSULT EX/STRUC LEGIS TOP/EX CREATE GOV/REL DISPL DRIVE RIGID/FLEX...TREND TOT/POP CONGRESS CONGRESS 20 TREATY. PAGE 167 A3408 ROUTINE DIPLOM INT/LAW DELIB/GP

B53
LARSEN K.,NATIONAL BIBLIOGRAPHIC SERVICES: THEIR CREATION AND OPERATION. WOR+45 COM/IND CREATE PLAN DIPLOM PRESS ADMIN ROUTINE...MGT UNESCO. PAGE 85 A1733 BIBLIOG/A INT/ORG WRITING

B53
MACMAHON A.W.,ADMINISTRATION IN FOREIGN AFFAIRS. NAT/G CONSULT DELIB/GP LEGIS ACT/RES CREATE ADMIN EXEC RIGID/FLEX PWR...METH/CNCPT TIME/SEQ TOT/POP VAL/FREE 20. PAGE 93 A1899 USA+45 ROUTINE FOR/AID DIPLOM

L53
UNESCO,"THE TECHNIQUE OF INTERNATIONAL CONFERENCES." WOR+45 INT/ORG VOL/ASSN EDU/PROP ROUTINE ATTIT DRIVE KNOWL ORD/FREE...SOC UNESCO 20. PAGE 148 A3016 DELIB/GP ACT/RES

B54
MANGONE G.,A SHORT HISTORY OF INTERNATIONAL ORGANIZATION. MOD/EUR USA+45 USA-45 WOR+45 WOR-45 LAW LEGIS CREATE LEGIT ROUTINE RIGID/FLEX PWR ...JURID CONCPT OBS TIME/SEQ STERTYP GEN/LAWS UN TOT/POP VAL/FREE 18/20. PAGE 94 A1921 INT/ORG INT/LAW

B54
MILLARD E.L.,FREEDOM IN A FEDERAL WORLD. FUT WOR+45 VOL/ASSN TOP/EX LEGIT ROUTINE FEDERAL PEACE ATTIT DISPL ORD/FREE PWR...MAJORIT INT/LAW JURID TREND COLD/WAR 20. PAGE 101 A2073 INT/ORG CREATE ADJUD BAL/PWR

S54
WOLFERS A.,"COLLECTIVE SECURITY AND THE WAR IN KOREA." ASIA KOREA USA+45 INT/ORG DIPLOM ROUTINE ...GEN/LAWS UN COLD/WAR 20. PAGE 166 A3381 ACT/RES LEGIT

B55
JOY C.T.,HOW COMMUNISTS NEGOTIATE. COM USA+45 CONSTN CULTURE ECO/UNDEV NAT/G CONSULT DELIB/GP FORCES PLAN ECO/TAC DOMIN EDU/PROP LEGIT EXEC ROUTINE COERCE WAR CHOOSE PEACE ATTIT RIGID/FLEX ORD/FREE PWR...POLICY 20. PAGE 75 A1539 ASIA INT/ORG DIPLOM

B55
MALCLES L.N.,BIBLIOGRAPHICAL SERVICES THROUGHOUT THE WORLD (VOL. 4). WOR+45 INT/ORG VOL/ASSN DIPLOM PRESS WRITING 20 UNESCO. PAGE 93 A1911 BIBLIOG ROUTINE COM/IND

B55
STEPHENS O.,FACTS TO A CANDID WORLD. USA+45 WOR+45 COM/IND EX/STRUC PRESS ROUTINE EFFICIENCY ATTIT ...PSY 20. PAGE 138 A2817 EDU/PROP PHIL/SCI NAT/G DIPLOM

S55
TORRE M.,"PSYCHIATRIC OBSERVATIONS OF INTERNATIONAL CONFERENCES." WOR+45 INT/ORG PROF/ORG VOL/ASSN CONSULT EDU/PROP ROUTINE ATTIT DRIVE KNOWL...PSY METH/CNCPT OBS/ENVIR STERTYP 20. PAGE 144 A2950 DELIB/GP OBS DIPLOM

S55
WRIGHT Q.,"THE PEACEFUL ADJUSTMENT OF INTERNATIONAL RELATIONS: PROBLEMS AND RESEARCH APPROACHES." UNIV INTELL EDU/PROP ADJUD ROUTINE KNOWL SKILL...INT/LAW JURID PHIL/SCI CLASSIF 20. PAGE 167 A3411 R+D METH/CNCPT PEACE

B56
BROOK D.,THE UNITED NATIONS AND CHINA DILEMMA. CHINA/COM FUT WOR+45 ECO/UNDEV NAT/G DELIB/GP ACT/RES DIPLOM ROUTINE NAT/LISM TOTALISM ATTIT DRIVE...CONCPT OBS TIME/SEQ UN TOT/POP TIME UN 20. PAGE 19 A0390 ASIA INT/ORG BAL/PWR

B56
HOUSTON J.A.,LATIN AMERICA IN THE UNITED NATIONS. CONSULT DIPLOM LEGIT ROUTINE ATTIT ORD/FREE PWR ...JURID OBS RECORD TIME/SEQ CHARTS 20 UN. PAGE 68 A1395 L/A+17C INT/ORG INT/LAW REGION

B56
LOVEDAY A.,REFLECTIONS ON INTERNATIONAL ADMINISTRATION. WOR+45 WOR-45 DELIB/GP ACT/RES ADMIN EXEC ROUTINE DRIVE...METH/CNCPT TIME/SEQ CON/ANAL SIMUL TOT/POP 20. PAGE 91 A1865 INT/ORG MGT

B56
SOHN L.B.,BASIC DOCUMENTS OF THE UNITED NATIONS. WOR+45 LAW INT/ORG LEGIT EXEC ROUTINE CHOOSE PWR ...JURID CONCPT GEN/LAWS ANTHOL UN TOT/POP OAS FAO ILO 20. PAGE 135 A2761 DELIB/GP CONSTN

B56
WEIS P.,NATIONALITY AND STATELESSNESS IN INTERNATIONAL LAW. UK WOR+45 WOR-45 LAW CONSTN NAT/G DIPLOM EDU/PROP LEGIT ROUTINE RIGID/FLEX ...JURID RECORD CMN/WLTH 20. PAGE 162 A3309 INT/ORG SOVEREIGN INT/LAW

C56
DUPUY R.E.,"MILITARY HERITAGE OF AMERICA." USA+45 USA-45 TEC/DEV DIPLOM ROUTINE...POLICY TREND CHARTS IDEA/COMP BIBLIOG COLD/WAR. PAGE 39 A0804 FORCES WAR CONCPT

B57
ASHER R.E.,THE UNITED NATIONS AND THE PROMOTION OF THE GENERAL WELFARE. WOR+45 WOR-45 ECO/UNDEV EX/STRUC ACT/RES PLAN EDU/PROP ROUTINE HEALTH...HUM CONCPT CHARTS UNESCO UN ILO 20. PAGE 9 A0185 INT/ORG CONSULT

B57
BLOOMFIELD L.M.,EGYPT, ISRAEL AND THE GULF OF AQABA: IN INTERNATIONAL LAW. LAW NAT/G CONSULT FORCES PLAN ECO/TAC ROUTINE COERCE ATTIT DRIVE PERCEPT PERSON RIGID/FLEX LOVE PWR WEALTH...GEOG CONCPT MYTH TREND. PAGE 15 A0314 ISLAM INT/LAW UAR

B57
BLOOMFIELD L.P.,EVOLUTION OR REVOLUTION: THE UNITED NATIONS AND THE PROBLEM OF PEACEFUL TERRITORIAL CHANGE. WOR+45 WOR-45 INT/ORG NAT/G DIPLOM ROUTINE REV ATTIT RIGID/FLEX PWR...CONCPT OBS HIST/WRIT UN LEAGUE/NAT 20. PAGE 15 A0315 ORD/FREE LEGIT

B57
BRODY H.,UN DIARY: THE SEARCH FOR PEACE. HUNGARY WOR+45 DELIB/GP ROUTINE REV WAR ORD/FREE...AUD/VIS 20 UN SUEZ. PAGE 19 A0382 INT/ORG PEACE DIPLOM POLICY

B57
HOLCOMBE A.N.,STRENGTHENING THE UNITED NATIONS. USA+45 ACT/RES CREATE PLAN EDU/PROP ATTIT PERCEPT PWR...METH/CNCPT CONT/OBS RECORD UN COLD/WAR 20. PAGE 66 A1365 INT/ORG ROUTINE

B57
JENKS C.W.,THE INTERNATIONAL PROTECTION OF TRADE UNION FREEDOM. FUT WOR+45 WOR-45 VOL/ASSN DELIB/GP CT/SYS REGION ROUTINE...JURID METH/CNCPT RECORD TIME/SEQ CHARTS ILO WORK OAS 20. PAGE 73 A1504 LABOR INT/ORG

B57
MURRAY J.N.,THE UNITED NATIONS TRUSTEESHIP SYSTEM. AFR WOR+45 CONSTN CONSULT LEGIS EDU/PROP LEGIT EXEC ROUTINE...INT TIME/SEQ SOMALI UN 20. PAGE 106 A2181 INT/ORG DELIB/GP

B57
TRIFFIN R.,EUROPE AND THE MONEY MUDDLE. USA+45 INT/ORG NAT/G CONSULT PLAN ECO/TAC EXEC ROUTINE BAL/PAY WEALTH...METH/CNCPT OBS TREND CHARTS STERTYP GEN/METH EEC VAL/FREE ECSC. PAGE 145 A2962 EUR+WWI ECO/DEV REGION

S57
SCHELLING T.C.,"BARGAINING COMMUNICATION, AND ROUTINE

LIMITED WAR." UNIV WOR+45 FACE/GP INT/ORG NAT/G FORCES ACT/RES WAR PERCEPT ALL/VALS...PSY OBS PROJ/TEST CHARTS HYPO/EXP GEN/LAWS TOT/POP 20. PAGE 128 A2622
DECISION

B58
CARROLL H.N.,THE HOUSE OF REPRESENTATIVES AND FOREIGN AFFAIRS. USA+45 USA-45 NAT/G POL/PAR DIPLOM FOR/AID LEGIT ROUTINE PWR...TIME/SEQ CONGRESS. PAGE 25 A0502
DELIB/GP
LEGIS

B58
GANGE J.,UNIVERSITY RESEARCH ON INTERNATIONAL AFFAIRS. USA+45 ACADEM INT/ORG CONSULT CREATE EXEC ROUTINE...QUANT STAT INT STERTYP GEN/METH TOT/POP VAL/FREE 20. PAGE 51 A1040
R+D
MGT
DIPLOM

B58
JAPANESE ASSOCIATION INT. LAW,JAPAN AND THE UNITED NATIONS. SOCIETY ROUTINE ATTIT DRIVE PERCEPT RIGID/FLEX ORD/FREE...METH/CNCPT CON/ANAL CHINJAP UN. PAGE 73 A1497
ASIA
INT/ORG

B58
REUTER P.,INTERNATIONAL INSTITUTIONS. WOR+45 WOR-45 CULTURE SOCIETY VOL/ASSN LEGIT ROUTINE GP/REL INGP/REL KNOWL...JURID METH/CNCPT TIME/SEQ 20. PAGE 120 A2469
INT/ORG
PSY

B58
RIGGS R.,POLITICS IN THE UNITED NATIONS: A STUDY OF UNITED STATES INFLUENCE IN THE GENERAL ASSEMBLY. USA+45 WOR+45 LEGIS TOP/EX CREATE BAL/PWR DIPLOM DOMIN EDU/PROP COLONIAL ROUTINE ATTIT RIGID/FLEX PWR...CONCPT OBS HIST/WRIT CHARTS STERTYP GEN/LAWS UN COLD/WAR 20. PAGE 121 A2480
INT/ORG

S58
BLAISDELL D.C.,"PRESSURE GROUPS, FOREIGN POLICIES, AND INTERNATIONAL POLITICS." USA+45 WOR+45 INT/ORG PLAN DOMIN EDU/PROP LEGIT ADMIN ROUTINE CHOOSE ...DECISION MGT METH/CNCPT CON/ANAL 20. PAGE 15 A0303
PROF/ORG
PWR

S58
JORDAN A.,"MILITARY ASSISTANCE AND NATIONAL POLICY." ASIA FUT USA+45 WOR+45 ECO/DEV ECO/UNDEV INT/ORG NAT/G PLAN ECO/TAC ROUTINE WEAPON ATTIT RIGID/FLEX PWR...CONCPT TREND 20. PAGE 75 A1533
FORCES
POLICY
FOR/AID
DIPLOM

S58
STAAR R.F.,"ELECTIONS IN COMMUNIST POLAND." EUR+WWI SOCIETY INT/ORG NAT/G POL/PAR LEGIS ACT/RES ECO/TAC EDU/PROP ADJUD ADMIN ROUTINE COERCE TOTALISM ATTIT ORD/FREE PWR 20. PAGE 137 A2797
COM
CHOOSE
POLAND

B59
ALLEN R.L.,SOVIET INFLUENCE IN LATIN AMERICA. ECO/UNDEV FINAN PROC/MFG NAT/G TEC/DEV EDU/PROP EXEC ROUTINE ATTIT DRIVE PERSON ALL/VALS PWR...STAT CHARTS WORK 20. PAGE 6 A0125
L/A+17C
ECO/TAC
INT/TRADE
USSR

B59
COMM. STUDY ORGAN. PEACE,ORGANIZING PEACE IN THE NUCLEAR AGE. FUT CONSULT DELIB/GP DOMIN ADJUD ROUTINE COERCE ORD/FREE...TECHNIC INT/LAW JURID NEW/IDEA UN COLD/WAR 20. PAGE 29 A0581
INT/ORG
ACT/RES
NUC/PWR

B59
DIEBOLD W. JR.,THE SCHUMAN PLAN: A STUDY IN ECONOMIC COOPERATION, 1950-1959. EUR+WWI FRANCE GERMANY USA+45 EXTR/IND CONSULT DELIB/GP PLAN DIPLOM ECO/TAC INT/TRADE ROUTINE ORD/FREE WEALTH ...METH/CNCPT STAT CONT/OBS INT TIME/SEQ ECSC 20. PAGE 37 A0759
INT/ORG
REGION

B59
FERRELL R.H.,AMERICAN DIPLOMACY: A HISTORY. USA+45 USA-45 PLAN ROUTINE REV WAR PWR...T 18/20 EISNHWR/DD WWI. PAGE 45 A0921
DIPLOM
NAT/G
POLICY

B59
GOODRICH L.,THE UNITED NATIONS. WOR+45 CONSTN STRUCT ACT/RES LEGIT COERCE KNOWL ORD/FREE PWR ...GEN/LAWS UN 20. PAGE 54 A1104
INT/ORG
ROUTINE

B59
SCHNEIDER J.,TREATY-MAKING POWER OF INTERNATIONAL ORGANIZATIONS. FUT WOR+45 WOR-45 LAW NAT/G JUDGE DIPLOM LEGIT CT/SYS ORD/FREE PWR...INT/LAW JURID GEN/LAWS TOT/POP UNESCO 20 TREATY. PAGE 129 A2639
INT/ORG
ROUTINE

B59
SCHURZ W.L.,AMERICAN FOREIGN AFFAIRS: A GUIDE TO INTERNATIONAL AFFAIRS. USA+45 WOR+45 WOR-45 NAT/G FORCES LEGIS TOP/EX PLAN EDU/PROP LEGIT ADMIN ROUTINE ATTIT ORD/FREE PWR...SOC CONCPT STAT SAMP/SIZ CHARTS STERTYP 20. PAGE 129 A2653
INT/ORG
SOCIETY
DIPLOM

S59
BOULDING K.E.,"NATIONAL IMAGES AND INTERNATIONAL SYSTEMS." FUT WOR+45 CULTURE INT/ORG TOP/EX ROUTINE ...METH/CNCPT MYTH CONT/OBS TREND HYPO/EXP GEN/METH TOT/POP 20. PAGE 17 A0346
NAT/G
DIPLOM

S59
HARVEY M.F.,"THE PALESTINE REFUGEE PROBLEM: ELEMENTS OF A SOLUTION." ISLAM LAW INT/ORG DELIB/GP TOP/EX ECO/TAC ROUTINE DRIVE HEALTH LOVE ORD/FREE PWR WEALTH...MAJORIT FAO 20. PAGE 62 A1283
ACT/RES
LEGIT
PEACE
ISRAEL

S59
HOFFMANN S.,"IMPLEMENTATION OF INTERNATIONAL INSTRUMENTS ON HUMAN RIGHTS." WOR+45 VOL/ASSN DELIB/GP JUDGE EDU/PROP LEGIT ROUTINE PEACE COLD/WAR 20. PAGE 66 A1355
INT/ORG
MORAL

S59
LASSWELL H.D.,"UNIVERSALITY IN PERSPECTIVE." FUT UNIV SOCIETY CONSULT TOP/EX PLAN EDU/PROP ADJUD ROUTINE ARMS/CONT COERCE PEACE ATTIT PERSON ALL/VALS. PAGE 85 A1741
INT/ORG
JURID
TOTALISM

S59
POTTER P.B.,"OBSTACLES AND ALTERNATIVES TO INTERNATIONAL LAW." WOR+45 NAT/G VOL/ASSN DELIB/GP BAL/PWR DOMIN ROUTINE...JURID VAL/FREE 20. PAGE 117 A2400
INT/ORG
LAW
DIPLOM
INT/LAW

S59
SOHN L.B.,"THE DEFINITION OF AGGRESSION." FUT LAW FORCES LEGIT ADJUD ROUTINE COERCE ORD/FREE PWR ...MAJORIT JURID QUANT COLD/WAR 20. PAGE 135 A2762
INT/ORG
CT/SYS
DETER
SOVEREIGN

S59
STOESSINGER J.G.,"THE INTERNATIONAL ATOMIC ENERGY AGENCY: THE FIRST PHASE." FUT WOR+45 NAT/G VOL/ASSN DELIB/GP BAL/PWR LEGIT ADMIN ROUTINE PWR...OBS CON/ANAL GEN/LAWS VAL/FREE 20 IAEA. PAGE 138 A2829
INT/ORG
ECO/DEV
FOR/AID
NUC/PWR

S59
ZAUBERMAN A.,"SOVIET BLOC ECONOMIC INTEGRATION." COM CULTURE INTELL ECO/DEV INDUS TOP/EX ACT/RES PLAN ECO/TAC INT/TRADE ROUTINE CHOOSE ATTIT ...TIME/SEQ 20. PAGE 169 A3448
MARKET
INT/ORG
USSR
TOTALISM

B60
FRANCK P.G.,AFGHANISTAN: BETWEEN EAST AND WEST. AFGHANISTN USA+45 USSR ECO/UNDEV PLAN ADMIN ROUTINE ATTIT PWR...STAT OBS CHARTS TOT/POP COLD/WAR 20. PAGE 48 A0978
ECO/TAC
TREND
FOR/AID

B60
HAAS E.B.,THE COMPARATIVE STUDY OF THE UNITED NATIONS. WOR+45 NAT/G DOMIN LEGIT ROUTINE PEACE ORD/FREE PWR UN VAL/FREE 20. PAGE 59 A1205
INT/ORG
DIPLOM

B60
LERNER A.P.,THE ECONOMICS OF CONTROL. USA+45 ECO/UNDEV INT/ORG ACT/RES PLAN CAP/ISM INT/TRADE ATTIT WEALTH...SOC MATH STAT GEN/LAWS INDEX 20. PAGE 87 A1785
ECO/DEV
ROUTINE
ECO/TAC
SOCISM

B60
LINDSAY K.,EUROPEAN ASSEMBLIES: THE EXPERIMENTAL PERIOD 1949-1959. EUR+WWI ECO/DEV NAT/G POL/PAR LEGIS TOP/EX ACT/RES PLAN ECO/TAC DOMIN LEGIT ROUTINE ATTIT DRIVE ORD/FREE PWR SKILL...SOC CONCPT TREND CHARTS GEN/LAWS VAL/FREE. PAGE 89 A1823
VOL/ASSN
INT/ORG
REGION

B60
MUNRO L.,UNITED NATIONS, HOPE FOR A DIVIDED WORLD. FUT WOR+45 CONSTN DELIB/GP CREATE TEC/DEV DIPLOM EDU/PROP LEGIT PEACE ATTIT HEALTH ORD/FREE PWR ...CONCPT TREND UN VAL/FREE 20. PAGE 106 A2172
INT/ORG
ROUTINE

B60
THEOBALD R.,THE RICH AND THE POOR: A STUDY OF THE ECONOMICS OF RISING EXPECTATIONS. WOR+45 CONSTN ECO/DEV ECO/UNDEV INT/ORG NAT/G PLAN FOR/AID ROUTINE BAL/PAY ORD/FREE PWR WEALTH...GEOG TREND WORK 20. PAGE 142 A2912
ECO/TAC
INT/TRADE

L60
LAUTERPACHT E.,"THE UNITED NATIONS EMERGENCY FORCE." R+D LEGIT ROUTINE COERCE KNOWL ORD/FREE SKILL...JURID UN 20. PAGE 85 A1746
INT/ORG
FORCES

L60
MCCLELLAND C.A.,"THE FUNCTION OF THEORY IN INTERNATIONAL RELATIONS." WOR+45 PLAN EDU/PROP ROUTINE ORD/FREE...PHIL/SCI PSY SOC METH/CNCPT NEW/IDEA OBS TREND GEN/METH 20. PAGE 97 A1997
INT/ORG
CONCPT
DIPLOM

S60
BOGARDUS E.S.,"THE SOCIOLOGY OF A STRUCTURED PEACE." FUT SOCIETY CREATE DIPLOM EDU/PROP ADJUD ROUTINE ATTIT RIGID/FLEX KNOWL ORD/FREE RESPECT ...POLICY INT/LAW JURID NEW/IDEA SELF/OBS TOT/POP 20 UN. PAGE 16 A0327
INT/ORG
SOC
NAT/LISM
PEACE

S60
GOODMAN E.,"THE CRY OF NATIONAL LIBERATION: RECENT SOVIET ATTITUDES TOWARDS NATIONAL SELF-DETERMINATION." COM INT/ORG LEGIS ROUTINE PWR ...TIME/SEQ CON/ANAL STERTYP GEN/LAWS 20 UN. PAGE 54 A1101
ATTIT
EDU/PROP
SOVEREIGN
USSR

S60
GOODRICH L.,"GEOGRAPHICAL DISTRIBUTION OF THE STAFF OF THE UN SECRETARIAT." FUT WOR+45 CONSTN BAL/PWR DIPLOM EDU/PROP LEGIT ROUTINE RIGID/FLEX...CHARTS UN 20. PAGE 54 A1105
INT/ORG
EX/STRUC

S60
GULICK E.U.,"OUR BALANCE OF POWER SYSTEM IN PERSPECTIVE." FUT WOR+45 WOR-45 ECO/DEV DOMIN ROUTINE NUC/PWR PEACE PWR WEALTH...PLURIST CONCPT HIST/WRIT GEN/METH TOT/POP 20. PAGE 58 A1191
INT/ORG
TREND
ARMS/CONT
BAL/PWR

S60
IKLE F.C.,"NTH COUNTRIES AND DISARMAMENT." WOR+45 DELIB/GP ECO/TAC DOMIN EDU/PROP LEGIT ROUTINE COERCE RIGID/FLEX ORD/FREE...MARXIST TREND 20. PAGE 70 A1432
FUT
INT/ORG
ARMS/CONT
NUC/PWR

S60
LEAR J.,"PEACE: SCIENCE'S NEXT GREAT EXPLORATION."
EX/STRUC

USA+45 INT/ORG TOP/EX TEC/DEV EDU/PROP ROUTINE PEACE KNOWL SKILL 20. PAGE 86 A1757
ARMS/CONT NUC/PWR

S60
MARTIN E.M.,"NEW TRENDS IN UNITED STATES ECONOMIC FOREIGN POLICY." USA+45 INTELL DELIB/GP FOR/AID INT/TRADE ROUTINE BAL/PAY...RELATIV 20. PAGE 95 A1949
NAT/G PLAN DIPLOM

S60
MODELSKI G.,"AUSTRALIA AND SEATO." S/ASIA USA+45 CULTURE INTELL ECO/DEV NAT/G PLAN DIPLOM ADMIN ROUTINE ATTIT SKILL...MGT TIME/SEQ AUSTRAL 20 SEATO. PAGE 102 A2097
INT/ORG ACT/RES

S60
PYE L.W.,"SOVIET AND AMERICAN STYLES IN FOREIGN AID." COM USA+45 USSR WOR+45 NAT/G PLAN ECO/TAC ROUTINE RIGID/FLEX...POLICY CONCPT TREND GEN/LAWS TOT/POP 20. PAGE 118 A2419
ECO/UNDEV ATTIT FOR/AID

S60
RHYNE C.S.,"LAW AS AN INSTRUMENT FOR PEACE." FUT WOR+45 PLAN LEGIT ROUTINE ARMS/CONT NUC/PWR ATTIT ORD/FREE...JURID METH/CNCPT TREND CON/ANAL HYPO/EXP COLD/WAR 20. PAGE 120 A2471
ADJUD EDU/PROP INT/LAW PEACE

S60
SCHACHTER O.,"THE ENFORCEMENT OF INTERNATIONAL JUDICIAL AND ARBITRAL DECISIONS." WOR+45 NAT/G ECO/TAC DOMIN LEGIT ROUTINE COERCE ATTIT DRIVE ALL/VALS PWR...METH/CNCPT TREND TOT/POP 20 UN. PAGE 128 A2615
INT/ORG ADJUD INT/LAW

S60
SWIFT R.,"THE UNITED NATIONS AND ITS PUBLIC." WOR+45 CONSTN FINAN CONSULT DELIB/GP ACT/RES ADMIN ROUTINE RIGID/FLEX SKILL UN 20. PAGE 140 A2870
INT/ORG EDU/PROP

B61
BISHOP D.G.,THE ADMINISTRATION OF BRITISH FOREIGN RELATIONS. EUR+WWI MOD/EUR INT/ORG NAT/G POL/PAR DELIB/GP LEGIS TOP/EX ECO/TAC DOMIN EDU/PROP ADMIN COERCE 20. PAGE 14 A0292
ROUTINE PWR DIPLOM UK

B61
BURDETTE F.L.,POLITICAL SCIENCE: A SELECTED BIBLIOGRAPHY OF BOOKS IN PRINT, WITH ANNOTATIONS (PAMPHLET). LAW LOC/G NAT/G POL/PAR PROVS DIPLOM EDU/PROP ADMIN CHOOSE ATTIT 20. PAGE 21 A0432
BIBLIOG/A GOV/COMP CONCPT ROUTINE

B61
FRIEDMANN W.G.,JOINT INTERNATIONAL BUSINESS VENTURES. ASIA ISLAM L/A+17C ECO/DEV DIST/IND FINAN PROC/MFG FACE/GP LG/CO NAT/G VOL/ASSN CONSULT EX/STRUC PLAN ADMIN ROUTINE WEALTH...OLD/LIB WORK 20. PAGE 49 A1004
ECO/UNDEV INT/TRADE

B61
PEASLEE A.J.,INTERNATIONAL GOVERNMENT ORGANIZATIONS, CONSTITUTIONAL DOCUMENTS. WOR+45 WOR-45 CONSTN VOL/ASSN DELIB/GP EX/STRUC ROUTINE KNOWL TOT/POP 20. PAGE 114 A2344
INT/ORG STRUCT

B61
SCHELLING T.C.,STRATEGY AND ARMS CONTROL. FUT UNIV WOR+45 INT/ORG PLAN TEC/DEV BAL/PWR LEGIT PERCEPT HEALTH...CONCPT VAL/FREE 20. PAGE 128 A2623
ROUTINE POLICY ARMS/CONT

B61
SHAPP W.R.,FIELD ADMINISTRATION IN THE UNITED NATIONS SYSTEM. FINAN PROB/SOLV INSPECT DIPLOM EXEC REGION ROUTINE EFFICIENCY ROLE...INT CHARTS 20 UN. PAGE 131 A2694
INT/ORG ADMIN GP/REL FOR/AID

B61
SHARP W.R.,FIELD ADMINISTRATION IN THE UNITED NATION SYSTEM: THE CONDUCT OF INTERNATIONAL ECONOMIC AND SOCIAL PROGRAMS. FUT WOR+45 CONSTN SOCIETY ECO/UNDEV R+D DELIB/GP ACT/RES PLAN TEC/DEV EDU/PROP EXEC ROUTINE HEALTH WEALTH...HUM CONCPT CHARTS METH ILO UNESCO VAL/FREE UN 20. PAGE 132 A2697
INT/ORG CONSULT

B61
SINGER J.D.,FINANCING INTERNATIONAL ORGANIZATION: THE UNITED NATIONS BUDGET PROCESS. WOR+45 FINAN ACT/RES CREATE PLAN BUDGET ECO/TAC ADMIN ROUTINE ATTIT KNOWL...DECISION METH/CNCPT TIME/SEQ UN 20. PAGE 133 A2726
INT/ORG MGT

B61
STILLMAN E.,THE NEW POLITICS: AMERICA AND THE END OF THE POSTWAR WORLD. FUT WOR+45 CULTURE SOCIETY ECO/UNDEV INT/ORG NAT/G FORCES TOP/EX ACT/RES DIPLOM EDU/PROP LEGIT ROUTINE DETER ATTIT ORD/FREE PWR...OBS STERTYP COLD/WAR TOT/POP VAL/FREE. PAGE 138 A2827
USA+45 PLAN

B61
WILLOUGHBY W.R.,THE ST LAWRENCE WATERWAY: A STUDY IN POLITICS AND DIPLOMACY. USA+45 ECO/DEV COM/IND INT/ORG CONSULT DELIB/GP ACT/RES TEC/DEV DIPLOM ECO/TAC ROUTINE...TIME/SEQ 20. PAGE 165 A3357
LEGIS INT/TRADE CANADA DIST/IND

L61
CLAUDE I.,"THE UNITED NATIONS AND THE USE OF FORCE." FUT WOR+45 SOCIETY DIPLOM EDU/PROP LEGIT ADMIN ROUTINE COERCE WAR PEACE ORD/FREE...CONCPT TREND UN 20. PAGE 27 A0545
INT/ORG FORCES

L61
HOYT E.C.,"UNITED STATES REACTION TO THE KOREAN ATTACK." COM KOREA USA+45 CONSTN DELIB/GP FORCES PLAN ECO/TAC DOMIN EDU/PROP LEGIT ROUTINE COERCE WAR ATTIT DISPL RIGID/FLEX ORD/FREE PWR...POLICY INT/LAW TREND UN 20. PAGE 68 A1402
ASIA INT/ORG BAL/PWR DIPLOM

L61
SAND P.T.,"AN HISTORICAL SURVEY OF INTERNATIONAL AIR LAW SINCE 1944." USA+45 USA-45 WOR+45 WOR-45 SOCIETY ECO/DEV NAT/G CONSULT EX/STRUC ACT/RES PLAN LEGIT ROUTINE...JURID CONCPT METH/CNCPT TREND 20. PAGE 127 A2598
INT/ORG LAW INT/LAW SPACE

S61
ALGER C.F.,"NON-RESOLUTION CONSEQUENCES OF THE UNITED NATIONS AND THEIR EFFECT ON INTERNATIONAL CONFLICT." WOR+45 CONSTN ECO/DEV NAT/G CONSULT DELIB/GP TOP/EX ACT/RES PLAN DIPLOM EDU/PROP ROUTINE ATTIT ALL/VALS...INT/LAW TOT/POP UN 20. PAGE 6 A0117
INT/ORG DRIVE BAL/PWR

S61
BRZEZINSKI Z.K.,"THE ORGANIZATION OF THE COMMUNIST CAMP." COM CZECHOSLVK COM/IND NAT/G DELIB/GP INT/TRADE DOMIN EDU/PROP EXEC ROUTINE COERCE ATTIT PWR...MGT CONCPT TIME/SEQ CHARTS VAL/FREE 20 TREATY. PAGE 20 A0416
VOL/ASSN DIPLOM USSR

S61
GALBRAITH J.K.,"A POSITIVE APPROACH TO ECONOMIC AID." FUT USA+45 INTELL NAT/G CONSULT ACT/RES DIPLOM ECO/TAC EDU/PROP ATTIT KNOWL PWR WEALTH ...SOC STERTYP 20. PAGE 50 A1030
ECO/UNDEV ROUTINE FOR/AID

S61
LANFALUSSY A.,"EUROPE'S PROGRESS: DUE TO COMMON MARKET." EUR+WWI ECO/DEV DELIB/GP PLAN ECO/TAC ROUTINE WEALTH...GEOG TREND EEC 20. PAGE 84 A1721
INT/ORG MARKET

S61
LEWY G.,"SUPERIOR ORDERS, NUCLEAR WARFARE AND THE DICTATES OF CONSCIENCE: THE DILEMMA OF MILITARY OBEDIENCE IN THE ATOMIC." FUT UNIV WOR+45 INTELL SOCIETY FORCES TOP/EX ACT/RES ADMIN ROUTINE NUC/PWR PERCEPT RIGID/FLEX ALL/VALS...POLICY CONCPT 20. PAGE 88 A1805
DETER INT/ORG LAW INT/LAW

S61
LIPSON L.,"AN ARGUMENT ON THE LEGALITY OF RECONNAISSANCE STATELLITES." COM USA+45 USSR WOR+45 AIR INTELL NAT/G CONSULT PLAN DIPLOM LEGIT ROUTINE ATTIT...INT/LAW JURID CONCPT METH/CNCPT TREND COLD/WAR 20. PAGE 90 A1833
INT/ORG LAW SPACE

S61
RAY J.,"THE EUROPEAN FREE-TRADE ASSOCIATION AND ITS IMPACT ON INDIA'S TRADE." EUR+WWI FRANCE GERMANY INDIA S/ASIA UK NAT/G VOL/ASSN PLAN INT/TRADE ROUTINE WEALTH...STAT CHARTS CMN/WLTH EEC OEEC 20 EFTA. PAGE 120 A2453
ECO/DEV ECO/TAC

S61
TAUBENFELD H.J.,"OUTER SPACE--PAST POLITICS AND FUTURE POLICY." FUT USA+45 USA-45 WOR+45 AIR INTELL STRUCT ECO/DEV NAT/G TOP/EX ACT/RES ADMIN ROUTINE NUC/PWR ATTIT DRIVE...CONCPT TIME/SEQ TREND TOT/POP 20. PAGE 141 A2892
PLAN SPACE INT/ORG

B62
AMERICAN LAW INSTITUTE,FOREIGN RELATIONS LAW OF THE UNITED STATES: RESTATEMENT, SECOND. USA+45 NAT/G LEGIS ADJUD EXEC ROUTINE GOV/REL...INT/LAW JURID CONCPT 20 TREATY. PAGE 7 A0152
PROF/ORG LAW DIPLOM ORD/FREE

B62
BOUSCAREN A.T.,SOVIET FOREIGN POLICY: A PATTERN OF PERSISTANCE. WOR+45 WOR-45 SOCIETY STRUCT INT/ORG POL/PAR CREATE PLAN EDU/PROP ROUTINE ATTIT RIGID/FLEX...POLICY CONCPT RECORD HIST/WRIT TIME/SEQ MARX/KARL 20. PAGE 17 A0352
COM NAT/G DIPLOM USSR

B62
CARDOZA M.H.,DIPLOMATS IN INTERNATIONAL COOPERATION: STEPCHILDREN OF THE FOREIGN SERVICE. EUR+WWI USA+45 NAT/G CONSULT ACT/RES EDU/PROP ROUTINE RIGID/FLEX KNOWL SKILL...SOC OBS TIME/SEQ EEC OEEC NATO 20. PAGE 24 A0480
INT/ORG METH/CNCPT DIPLOM

B62
CARLSTON K.S.,LAW AND ORGANIZATION IN WORLD SOCIETY. WOR+45 FINAN ECO/TAC DOMIN LEGIT CT/SYS ROUTINE COERCE ORD/FREE PWR WEALTH...PLURIST DECISION JURID MGT METH/CNCPT GEN/LAWS 20. PAGE 24 A0487
INT/ORG LAW

B62
ELLIOTT J.R.,THE APPEAL OF COMMUNISM IN THE UNDERDEVELOPED NATIONS. USSR WOR+45 INT/ORG NAT/G DIPLOM DOMIN EDU/PROP ROUTINE ATTIT RIGID/FLEX ORD/FREE PWR WEALTH MARXISM...POLICY SOC METH/CNCPT MYTH TOT/POP COLD/WAR 20. PAGE 41 A0842
COM ECO/UNDEV

B62
HADWEN J.G.,HOW UNITED NATIONS DECISIONS ARE MADE. WOR+45 LAW EDU/PROP LEGIT ADMIN PWR...DECISION SELF/OBS GEN/LAWS UN 20. PAGE 59 A1212
INT/ORG ROUTINE

B62
JEWELL M.E.,SENATORIAL POLITICS AND FOREIGN POLICY. NAT/G POL/PAR CHIEF DELIB/GP TOP/EX FOR/AID EDU/PROP ROUTINE ATTIT PWR SKILL...MAJORIT METH/CNCPT TIME/SEQ CONGRESS 20 PRESIDENT. PAGE 74 A1516
USA+45 LEGIS DIPLOM

B62
LAWSON R.,INTERNATIONAL REGIONAL ORGANIZATIONS. WOR+45 NAT/G VOL/ASSN CONSULT LEGIS EDU/PROP LEGIT ADMIN EXEC ROUTINE HEALTH PWR WEALTH...JURID EEC COLD/WAR 20 UN. PAGE 86 A1752
INT/ORG DELIB/GP REGION

B62
MACKENTOSH J.M.,STRATEGY AND TACTICS OF SOVIET FOREIGN POLICY. CHINA/COM FUT USA+45 WOR+45 INT/ORG PLAN DOMIN LEGIT ROUTINE COERCE NUC/PWR WAR ATTIT DRIVE ORD/FREE PWR...CONCPT OBS TIME/SEQ TREND GEN/METH COLD/WAR 20. PAGE 92 A1894
COM POLICY DIPLOM USSR

B62
MEADE J.E.,CASE STUDIES IN EUROPEAN ECONOMIC UNION. BELGIUM EUR+WWI LUXEMBOURG NAT/G INT/TRADE REGION ROUTINE WEALTH...METH/CNCPT STAT CHARTS ECSC TOT/POP OEEC EEC 20. PAGE 99 A2028
INT/ORG ECO/TAC

B62
NICHOLAS H.G.,THE UNITED NATIONS AS A POLITICAL INSTITUTION. WOR+45 CONSTN EX/STRUC ACT/RES LEGIT PERCEPT KNOWL PWR...CONCPT TIME/SEQ CON/ANAL ORG/CHARTS UN 20. PAGE 109 A2228
INT/ORG ROUTINE

B62
ROSENNE S.,THE WORLD COURT: WHAT IT IS AND HOW IT WORKS. WOR+45 WOR-45 LAW CONSTN JUDGE EDU/PROP LEGIT ROUTINE CHOOSE PEACE ORD/FREE...JURID OBS TIME/SEQ CHARTS UN TOT/POP VAL/FREE 20. PAGE 124 A2538
INT/ORG ADJUD INT/LAW

B62
SCHWARZENBERGER G.,THE FRONTIERS OF INTERNATIONAL LAW. WOR+45 WOR-45 NAT/G LEGIT CT/SYS ROUTINE MORAL ORD/FREE PWR...JURID SOC GEN/METH 20 COLD/WAR. PAGE 130 A2661
INT/ORG LAW INT/LAW

B62
THANT U.,THE UNITED NATIONS' DEVELOPMENT DECADE: PROPOSALS FOR ACTION. WOR+45 SOCIETY ECO/UNDEV AGRI COM/IND FINAN R+D MUNIC SCHOOL VOL/ASSN CONSULT PLAN TEC/DEV ECO/TAC EDU/PROP ADMIN ROUTINE RIGID/FLEX...MGT SOC CONCPT UNESCO UN TOT/POP VAL/FREE. PAGE 142 A2906
INT/ORG ALL/VALS

B62
WOETZEL R.K.,THE NURENBERG TRIALS IN INTERNATIONAL LAW. CHRIST-17C MOD/EUR WOR+45 SOCIETY NAT/G DELIB/GP DOMIN LEGIT ROUTINE ATTIT DRIVE PERSON SUPEGO MORAL ORD/FREE...POLICY MAJORIT JURID PSY SOC SELF/OBS RECORD NAZI TOT/POP. PAGE 166 A3376
INT/ORG ADJUD WAR

L62
GROSS L.,"IMMUNITIES AND PRIVILEGES OF DELIGATIONS TO THE UNITED NATIONS." USA+45 WOR+45 STRATA NAT/G VOL/ASSN CONSULT DIPLOM EDU/PROP ROUTINE RESPECT ...POLICY INT/LAW CONCPT UN 20. PAGE 57 A1176
INT/ORG LAW ELITES

L62
MURACCIOLE L.,"LA LOI FONDAMENTALE DE LA REPUBLIQUE DU CONGO." WOR+45 SOCIETY ECO/UNDEV INT/ORG NAT/G LEGIS PLAN LEGIT ADJUD COLONIAL ROUTINE ATTIT SOVEREIGN 20 CONGO. PAGE 106 A2174
AFR CONSTN

L62
MURACCIOLE L.,"LA BANQUE CENTRALE DES ETATS DE L'AFRIQUE DE L'OUEST." AFR LAW ECO/UNDEV INT/ORG NAT/G CONSULT ECO/TAC ROUTINE...CHARTS 20. PAGE 106 A2175
ISLAM FINAN INT/TRADE

L62
STEIN E.,"MR. HAMMARSKJOLD, THE CHARTER LAW AND THE FUTURE ROLE OF THE UNITED NATIONS SECRETARY-GENERAL." WOR+45 CONSTN INT/ORG DELIB/GP FORCES TOP/EX BAL/PWR LEGIT ROUTINE RIGID/FLEX PWR ...POLICY JURID OBS STERTYP UN COLD/WAR 20 HAMMARSK/D. PAGE 137 A2815
CONCPT BIOG

S62
CLEVELAND H.,"THE FUTURE ROLE OF THE UNITED STATES IN THE UNITED NATIONS." USA+45 ECO/UNDEV INT/ORG EX/STRUC DIPLOM FOR/AID ROUTINE SKILL SOVEREIGN WEALTH UN 20. PAGE 27 A0550
FUT ATTIT

S62
GREEN L.C.,"POLITICAL OFFENSES, WAR CRIMES AND EXTRADITION." WOR+45 YUGOSLAVIA INT/ORG LEGIT ROUTINE WAR ORD/FREE SOVEREIGN...JURID NAZI 20 INTERPOL. PAGE 55 A1138
LAW CONCPT INT/LAW

S62
JACOBSON H.K.,"THE UNITED NATIONS AND COLONIALISM: A TENTATIVE APPRAISAL." AFR FUT S/ASIA USA+45 USSR WOR+45 NAT/G DELIB/GP PLAN DIPLOM ECO/TAC DOMIN ADMIN ROUTINE COERCE ATTIT RIGID/FLEX ORD/FREE PWR ...OBS STERTYP UN 20. PAGE 73 A1486
INT/ORG CONCPT COLONIAL

S62
MONNIER J.P.,"LA SUCCESSION D'ETATS EN MATIERE DE RESPONSABILITE INTERNATIONALE." UNIV CONSTN INTELL SOCIETY ADJUD ROUTINE PERCEPT SUPEGO...GEN/LAWS TOT/POP 20. PAGE 103 A2107
NAT/G JURID INT/LAW

S62
NORTH R.C.,"DECISION MAKING IN CRISIS: AN INTRODUCTION." WOR+45 WOR-45 NAT/G CONSULT DELIB/GP TEC/DEV PERCEPT KNOWL...POLICY DECISION PSY METH/CNCPT CONT/OBS TREND VAL/FREE 20. PAGE 110 A2251
INT/ORG ROUTINE DIPLOM

S62
PIQUEMAL M.,"LES PROBLEMES DES UNIONS D'ETATS EN AFRIQUE NOIRE." FRANCE SOCIETY INT/ORG NAT/G DELIB/GP PLAN LEGIT ADMIN COLONIAL ROUTINE ATTIT ORD/FREE PWR...GEOG METH/CNCPT 20. PAGE 116 A2382
AFR ECO/UNDEV REGION

S62
PYE L.W.,"THE POLITICAL IMPULSES AND FANTASIES BEHIND FOREIGN AID." FUT USA+45 ECO/UNDEV DIPLOM ECO/TAC ROUTINE DRIVE KNOWL...SOC METH/CNCPT NEW/IDEA TREND HYPO/EXP STERTYP GEN/METH 20. PAGE 118 A2420
ACT/RES ATTIT FOR/AID

S62
TRUMAN D.,"THE DOMESTIC POLITICS OF FOREIGN AID." USA+45 WOR+45 NAT/G POL/PAR LEGIS DIPLOM ECO/TAC EDU/PROP ADMIN CHOOSE ATTIT PWR CONGRESS 20 CONGRESS. PAGE 145 A2970
ROUTINE FOR/AID

B63
BOWETT D.W.,THE LAW OF INTERNATIONAL INSTITUTIONS. WOR+45 WOR-45 CONSTN DELIB/GP EX/STRUC JUDGE EDU/PROP LEGIT CT/SYS EXEC ROUTINE RIGID/FLEX ORD/FREE PWR...JURID CONCPT ORG/CHARTS GEN/METH LEAGUE/NAT OAS OEEC 20 UN. PAGE 17 A0354
INT/ORG ADJUD DIPLOM

B63
LERCHE C.O. JR.,CONCEPTS OF INTERNATIONAL POLITICS. WOR+45 WOR-45 LAW DELIB/GP EX/STRUC TEC/DEV ECO/TAC INT/TRADE LEGIT ROUTINE COERCE ATTIT ORD/FREE PWR RESPECT...STERTYP GEN/LAWS VAL/FREE. PAGE 87 A1782
INT/ORG WAR

B63
MAYNE R.,THE COMMUNITY OF EUROPE. UK CONSTN NAT/G CONSULT DELIB/GP CREATE PLAN ECO/TAC LEGIT ADMIN ROUTINE ORD/FREE PWR WEALTH...CONCPT TIME/SEQ EEC EURATOM 20. PAGE 97 A1985
EUR+WWI INT/ORG REGION

B63
NORTH R.C.,CONTENT ANALYSIS: A HANDBOOK WITH APPLICATIONS FOR THE STUDY OF INTERNATIONAL CRISIS. ASIA COM EUR+WWI MOD/EUR INT/ORG TEC/DEV DOMIN EDU/PROP ROUTINE COERCE PERCEPT RIGID/FLEX ALL/VALS ...QUANT TESTS CON/ANAL SIMUL GEN/LAWS VAL/FREE. PAGE 110 A2252
METH/CNCPT COMPUT/IR USSR

B63
ROBERTSON A.H.,HUMAN RIGHTS IN EUROPE. CONSTN SOCIETY INT/ORG NAT/G VOL/ASSN DELIB/GP ACT/RES PLAN ADJUD REGION ROUTINE ATTIT LOVE ORD/FREE RESPECT...JURID SOC CONCPT SOC/EXP UN 20. PAGE 122 A2498
EUR+WWI PERSON

B63
SCHMELTZ G.W.,LA POLITIQUE MONDIALE CONTEMPORAINE. SOCIETY ECO/UNDEV INDUS INT/ORG NAT/G POL/PAR CONSULT DELIB/GP PLAN TEC/DEV ECO/TAC DOMIN EDU/PROP ROUTINE COERCE PERCEPT PERSON LOVE SKILL ...SOC RECORD TOT/POP. PAGE 128 A2629
WOR+45 COLONIAL

B63
STROMBERG R.N.,COLLECTIVE SECURITY AND AMERICAN FOREIGN POLICY FROM THE LEAGUE OF NATIONS TO NATO. USA+45 USA-45 WOR-45 INT/ORG VOL/ASSN EX/STRUC FORCES LEGIT ROUTINE DRIVE...CONCPT TREND UN LEAGUE/NAT 20 NATO. PAGE 139 A2851
ORD/FREE TIME/SEQ DIPLOM

B63
THUCYDIDES,THE PELOPONESIAN WARS. MEDIT-7 CULTURE INT/ORG NAT/G FORCES TOP/EX PLAN ROUTINE PWR ...CONCPT. PAGE 144 A2938
ATTIT COERCE WAR

B63
VOSS E.H.,NUCLEAR AMBUSH: THE TEST-BAN TRAP. WOR+45 COM/IND INT/ORG NAT/G DELIB/GP FORCES LEGIS TOP/EX ACT/RES DOMIN EDU/PROP LEGIT ROUTINE COERCE ATTIT PERCEPT RIGID/FLEX HEALTH MORAL ORD/FREE PWR. PAGE 160 A3255
TEC/DEV HIST/WRIT ARMS/CONT NUC/PWR

S63
BALOGH T.,"L'INFLUENCE DES INSTITUTIONS MONETAIRES ET COMMERCIALES SUR LA STRUCTURE ECONOMIQUE AFRICAIN." AFR EUR+WWI FUT USA+45 USA-45 WOR+45 SERV/IND INT/ORG NAT/G TOP/EX ROUTINE...INDEX EEC 20. PAGE 11 A0215
FINAN

S63
BLOOMFIELD L.P.,"HEADQUARTERS-FIELD RELATIONS: SOME NOTES ON THE BEGINNING AND END OF ONUC." AFR INT/ORG ROUTINE COERCE WAR WEAPON UN CONGO 20. PAGE 16 A0319
FORCES ORD/FREE

S63
COUTY P.,"L'ASSISTANCE POUR LE DEVELOPPEMENT: POINT DE VUE SCANDINAVES." EUR+WWI FINLAND FUT SWEDEN WOR+45 ECO/DEV ECO/UNDEV COM/IND LABOR NAT/G PROF/ORG ACT/RES SKILL WEALTH TOT/POP 20. PAGE 32 A0643
FINAN ROUTINE FOR/AID

S63
DAVEE R.,"POUR UN FONDS DE DEVELOPPEMENT SOCIAL." FUT WOR+45 INTELL SOCIETY ECO/DEV FINAN TEC/DEV ROUTINE WEALTH...TREND TOT/POP VAL/FREE UN 20. PAGE 34 A0684
INT/ORG SOC FOR/AID

S63
EMERSON R.,"THE ATLANTIC COMMUNITY AND THE EMERGING COUNTRIES." FUT WOR+45 ECO/DEV ECO/UNDEV R+D NAT/G DELIB/GP BAL/PWR ECO/TAC EDU/PROP ROUTINE ORD/FREE PWR WEALTH...POLICY CONCPT TREND GEN/METH EEC 20 NATO. PAGE 42 A0848
ATTIT INT/TRADE

S63
FRIEDMANN W.G.,"THE USES OF 'GENERAL PRINCIPLES' IN THE DEVELOPMENT OF INTERNATIONAL LAW." WOR+45 NAT/G
LAW INT/LAW

DIPLOM INT/TRADE LEGIT ROUTINE RIGID/FLEX ORD/FREE ...JURID CONCPT STERTYP GEN/METH 20. PAGE 49 A1005 — INT/ORG

S63
HAVILAND H.F.,"BUILDING A POLITICAL COMMUNITY." EUR+WWI FUT UK USA+45 ECO/DEV ECO/UNDEV INT/ORG NAT/G DELIB/GP BAL/PWR ECO/TAC NEUTRAL ROUTINE ATTIT PWR WEALTH...CONCPT COLD/WAR TOT/POP 20. PAGE 63 A1293 — VOL/ASSN DIPLOM

S63
LEDUC G.,"L'AIDE INTERNATIONALE AU DEVELOPPEMENT." FUT WOR+45 ECO/DEV ECO/UNDEV R+D PROF/ORG TEC/DEV ECO/TAC ROUTINE ATTIT ALL/VALS...MGT TIME/SEQ TOT/POP 20. PAGE 86 A1758 — FINAN PLAN FOR/AID

S63
MANGONE G.,"THE UNITED NATIONS AND UNITED STATES FOREIGN POLICY." USA+45 WOR+45 ECO/UNDEV NAT/G DIPLOM LEGIT ROUTINE ATTIT DRIVE...TIME/SEQ UN COLD/WAR 20. PAGE 94 A1922 — INT/ORG ECO/TAC FOR/AID

S63
NYE J.S. JR.,"EAST AFRICAN ECONOMIC INTEGRATION." AFR UGANDA PROVS DELIB/GP PLAN ECO/TAC INT/TRADE ADMIN ROUTINE ORD/FREE PWR WEALTH...OBS TIME/SEQ VAL/FREE 20. PAGE 110 A2264 — ECO/UNDEV INT/ORG

B64
IKLE F.C.,HOW NATIONS NEGOTIATE. COM EUR+WWI USA+45 INTELL INT/ORG VOL/ASSN DELIB/GP ACT/RES CREATE DOMIN EDU/PROP ADJUD ROUTINE ATTIT PERSON ORD/FREE RESPECT SKILL...PSY SOC OBS VAL/FREE. PAGE 70 A1433 — NAT/G PWR POLICY

B64
SARROS P.P.,CONGRESS AND THE NEW DIPLOMACY: THE FORMULATION OF MUTUAL SECURITY POLICY: 1953-60 (THESIS). USA+45 CHIEF EX/STRUC REGION ROUTINE CHOOSE GOV/REL PEACE ROLE...POLICY 20 PRESIDENT CONGRESS. PAGE 127 A2606 — DIPLOM POL/PAR NAT/G

B64
UN PUB. INFORM. ORGAN.,EVERY MAN'S UNITED NATIONS. UNIV WOR+45 CONSTN CULTURE SOCIETY ECO/DEV ECO/UNDEV NAT/G ACT/RES PLAN ECO/TAC INT/TRADE EDU/PROP LEGIT PEACE ATTIT ALL/VALS...POLICY HUM INT/LAW CONCPT CHARTS UN TOT/POP 20. PAGE 147 A3004 — INT/ORG ROUTINE

B64
WAINHOUSE D.W.,REMNANTS OF EMPIRE: THE UNITED NATIONS AND THE END OF COLONIALISM. FUT PORTUGAL WOR+45 NAT/G CONSULT DOMIN LEGIT ADMIN ROUTINE ATTIT ORD/FREE...POLICY JURID RECORD INT TIME/SEQ UN CMN/WLTH 20. PAGE 160 A3260 — INT/ORG TREND COLONIAL

L64
BARROS J.,"THE GREEK-BULGARIAN INCIDENT OF 1925: THE LEAGUE OF NATIONS AND THE GREAT POWERS." BULGARIA EUR+WWI NAT/G FORCES ECO/TAC EDU/PROP LEGIT ROUTINE COERCE WAR PEACE DRIVE PWR...JURID CONCPT METH/CNCPT GEN/LAWS GEN/METH LEAGUE/NAT TOT/POP 20. PAGE 11 A0228 — INT/ORG ORD/FREE DIPLOM

L64
HAAS E.B.,"ECONOMICS AND DIFFERENTIAL PATTERNS OF POLITICAL INTEGRATION: PROJECTIONS ABOUT UNITY IN LATIN AMERICA." SOCIETY NAT/G DELIB/GP ACT/RES CREATE PLAN ECO/TAC REGION ROUTINE ATTIT DRIVE PWR WEALTH...CONCPT TREND CHARTS LAFTA 20. PAGE 59 A1208 — L/A+17C INT/ORG MARKET

L64
RIPLEY R.B.,"INTERAGENCY COMMITTEES AND INCREMENTALISM: THE CASE OF AID TO INDIA." INDIA USA+45 INTELL NAT/G DELIB/GP ACT/RES DIPLOM ROUTINE NAT/LISM ATTIT PWR...SOC CONCPT NEW/IDEA TIME/SEQ CON/ANAL VAL/FREE 20. PAGE 121 A2483 — EXEC MGT FOR/AID

L64
WORLD PEACE FOUNDATION,"INTERNATIONAL ORGANIZATIONS: SUMMARY OF ACTIVITIES." INDIA PAKISTAN TURKEY WOR+45 CONSTN CONSULT EX/STRUC ECO/TAC EDU/PROP LEGIT ORD/FREE...JURID SOC UN 20 CYPRESS. PAGE 167 A3397 — INT/ORG ROUTINE

S64
BEIM D.,"THE COMMUNIST BLOC AND THE FOREIGN-AID GAME." WOR+45 NAT/G PLAN ROUTINE ATTIT KNOWL ORD/FREE...DECISION QUANT CONT/OBS TIME/SEQ CHARTS GAME SIMUL COLD/WAR 20. PAGE 12 A0252 — COM ECO/UNDEV ECO/TAC FOR/AID

S64
CARNEGIE ENDOWMENT INT. PEACE,"ADMINISTRATION AND BUDGET (ISSUES BEFORE THE NINETEENTH GENERAL ASSEMBLY)." WOR+45 FINAN BUDGET ECO/TAC ROUTINE COST...STAT RECORD UN. PAGE 24 A0495 — INT/ORG ADMIN

S64
GARDNER R.N.,"GATT AND THE UNITED NATIONS CONFERENCE ON TRADE AND DEVELOPMENT." USA+45 WOR+45 SOCIETY ECO/UNDEV MARKET NAT/G DELIB/GP ACT/RES PLAN ECO/TAC TARIFFS EDU/PROP ROUTINE DRIVE RIGID/FLEX WEALTH...DECISION MGT TREND UN TOT/POP 20 GATT. PAGE 51 A1047 — INT/ORG INT/TRADE

S64
GROSS J.A.,"WHITEHALL AND THE COMMONWEALTH." EUR+WWI MOD/EUR INT/ORG NAT/G CONSULT DELIB/GP LEGIS DOMIN ADMIN COLONIAL ROUTINE PWR CMN/WLTH 19/20. PAGE 57 A1174 — EX/STRUC ATTIT TREND

S64
HUELIN D.,"ECONOMIC INTEGRATION IN LATIN AMERICAN: PROGRESS AND PROBLEMS." L/A+17C ECO/DEV AGRI DIST/IND FINAN INDUS NAT/G VOL/ASSN CONSULT DELIB/GP EX/STRUC ACT/RES PLAN TEC/DEV ECO/TAC ROUTINE BAL/PAY WEALTH WORK 20. PAGE 69 A1411 — MARKET ECO/UNDEV INT/TRADE

S64
KHAN M.Z.,"THE PRESIDENT OF THE GENERAL ASSEMBLY." WOR+45 CONSTN DELIB/GP EDU/PROP LEGIT ROUTINE PWR RESPECT SKILL...DECISION SOC BIOG TREND UN 20. PAGE 78 A1609 — INT/ORG TOP/EX

S64
MAZRUI A.A.,"THE UNITED NATIONS AND SOME AFRICAN POLITICAL ATTITUDES." ECO/TAC FOR/AID DOMIN ROUTINE CHOOSE ATTIT DRIVE MORAL PWR RESPECT WEALTH...PSY CONCPT OBS TREND UN VAL/FREE 20. PAGE 97 A1987 — AFR INT/ORG SOVEREIGN

S64
MOWER A.G.,"THE OFFICIAL PRESSURE GROUP OF THE COUNCIL OF EUROPE'S CONSULATIVE ASSEMBLY." EUR+WWI SOCIETY STRUCT FINAN CONSULT ECO/TAC ADMIN ROUTINE ATTIT PWR WEALTH...STAT CHARTS 20 COUNCL/EUR. PAGE 105 A2160 — INT/ORG EDU/PROP

S64
RUBIN R.,"THE UN CORRESPONDENT." WOR+45 FACE/GP PROF/ORG EDU/PROP ROUTINE PERCEPT KNOWL...RECORD STAND/INT QU UN WORK TOT/POP VAL/FREE 20. PAGE 125 A2560 — INT/ORG ATTIT DIPLOM

S64
SAAB H.,"THE ARAB SEARCH FOR A FEDERAL UNION." SOCIETY INT/ORG NAT/G DELIB/GP FORCES ACT/RES TEC/DEV ECO/TAC DOMIN LEGIT REGION ROUTINE ATTIT DRIVE RIGID/FLEX ALL/VALS...SOC CONCPT NEW/IDEA TIME/SEQ TREND. PAGE 126 A2580 — ISLAM PLAN

B65
FLYNN A.H.,WORLD UNDERSTANDING: A SELECTED BIBLIOGRAPHY. WOR+45 PROB/SOLV BAL/PWR DIPLOM EFFICIENCY PEACE UN. PAGE 47 A0956 — BIBLIOG/A INT/ORG EDU/PROP ROUTINE

B65
SCOTT A.M.,THE REVOLUTION IN STATECRAFT: INFORMAL PENETRATION. WOR+45 WOR-45 CULTURE INT/ORG FORCES ECO/TAC ROUTINE...BIBLIOG 20. PAGE 130 A2670 — DIPLOM EDU/PROP FOR/AID

B65
WHITE G.M.,THE USE OF EXPERTS BY INTERNATIONAL TRIBUNALS. WOR+45 WOR-45 INT/ORG NAT/G PAY ADJUD COST...OBS BIBLIOG 20. PAGE 164 A3334 — INT/LAW ROUTINE CONSULT CT/SYS

L65
RUBIN A.P.,"UNITED STATES CONTEMPORARY PRACTICE RELATING TO INTERNATIONAL LAW." USA+45 WOR+45 CONSTN INT/ORG NAT/G DELIB/GP EX/STRUC DIPLOM DOMIN CT/SYS ROUTINE ORD/FREE...CONCPT COLD/WAR 20. PAGE 125 A2558 — LAW LEGIT INT/LAW

S65
MAC CHESNEY B.,"SOME COMMENTS ON THE 'QUARANTINE' OF CUBA." USA+45 WOR+45 NAT/G BAL/PWR DIPLOM LEGIT ROUTINE ATTIT ORD/FREE...JURID METH/CNCPT 20. PAGE 92 A1883 — INT/ORG LAW CUBA USSR

S65
MERRITT R.L.,"WOODROW WILSON AND THE 'GREAT AND SOLEMN REFERENDUM,' 1920." USA-45 SOCIETY NAT/G CONSULT LEGIS ACT/RES PLAN DOMIN EDU/PROP ROUTINE ATTIT DISPL DRIVE PERSON RIGID/FLEX MORAL ORD/FREE ...PSY SOC CONCPT MYTH LEAGUE/NAT. PAGE 100 A2044 — INT/ORG TOP/EX DIPLOM

S65
QUADE Q.L.,"THE TRUMAN ADMINISTRATION AND THE SEPARATION OF POWERS: THE CASE OF THE MARSHALL PLAN." SOCIETY INT/ORG NAT/G CONSULT DELIB/GP LEGIS PLAN ECO/TAC ROUTINE DRIVE PERCEPT RIGID/FLEX ORD/FREE PWR WEALTH...DECISION GEOG NEW/IDEA TREND 20 TRUMAN/HS. PAGE 118 A2422 — USA+45 ECO/UNDEV DIPLOM

B66
MARTIN L.W.,DIPLOMACY IN MODERN EUROPEAN HISTORY. EUR+WWI MOD/EUR INT/ORG NAT/G EX/STRUC ROUTINE WAR PEACE TOTALISM PWR 15/20 COLD/WAR EUROPE/W. PAGE 95 A1953 — DIPLOM POLICY

B67
DE BLIJ H.J.,SYSTEMATIC POLITICAL GEOGRAPHY. WOR+45 STRUCT INT/ORG NAT/G EDU/PROP ADMIN COLONIAL ROUTINE ORD/FREE PWR...IDEA/COMP T 20. PAGE 34 A0697 — GEOG CONCPT METH

L67
CAHIERS P.,"LE RECOURS EN CONSTATATION DE MANQUEMENTS DES ETATS MEMBRES DEVANT LA COUR DES COMMUNAUTES EUROPEENNES." LAW PROB/SOLV DIPLOM ADMIN CT/SYS SANCTION ATTIT...POLICY DECISION JURID ECSC EEC. PAGE 23 A0465 — INT/ORG CONSTN ROUTINE ADJUD

S67
FALKOWSKI M.,"SOCIALIST ECONOMISTS AND THE DEVELOPING COUNTRIES." COM PLAN TEC/DEV ROUTINE DEMAND EFFICIENCY PRODUC WEALTH...MARXIST TREND GEN/METH. PAGE 44 A0893 — DIPLOM SOCISM ECO/UNDEV INDUS

S67
WINTHROP H.,"CONTEMPORARY ECONOMIC DEHUMANIZATION* SOME DIFFICULTIES SURROUNDING ITS REDUCTION." USA+45 WOR+45 ACT/RES PROB/SOLV DIPLOM ROUTINE DEMAND UTIL. PAGE 165 A3368 — TEC/DEV SOCIETY WEALTH

ROWAN C.T. A2551

ROWAN R.W. A2552

ROWE C. A2553

ROY P.A. A2554

ROY/MN....M.N. ROY

B63
NORTH R.C.,M. N. ROY'S MISSION TO CHINA: THE COMMUNIST-KUOMINTANG SPLIT OF 1927. ASIA USSR STRATA LEGIS WORKER LEAD REV ATTIT ROLE SOCISM 20 ROY/MN COM/PARTY. PAGE 110 A2253
POL/PAR MARXISM DIPLOM

ROYAL AIR FORCE....SEE RAF

ROYAL GEOGRAPHICAL SOCIETY A2555

ROYAL INSTITUTE INTL AFFAIRS A2556,A2557

RUBIN A.P. A2558

RUBIN J.A. A2559

RUBIN R. A2560

RUBINSTEIN A.Z. A2561, A2562, A2563, A2564, A2565

RUDIN H.R. A2566

RUEF/ABE....ABRAHAM RUEF

RUEFF J. A2567

RULES/COMM....RULES COMMITTEES OF CONGRESS

RUMEU DE ARMAS A. A2568

RUMOR....SEE ALSO PERS/REL

B01
HART A.B.,AMERICAN HISTORY TOLD BY CONTEMPORARIES. UK CULTURE FINAN SECT FORCES DIPLOM TAX RUMOR CT/SYS REV GOV/REL GP/REL...ANTHOL 17/18 PRE/US/AM FEDERALIST. PAGE 62 A1273
USA-45 COLONIAL SOVEREIGN

B45
HORN O.B.,BRITISH PUBLIC OPINION AND THE FIRST PARTITION OF POLAND. POLAND UK LEGIS PRESS RUMOR CONTROL PARTIC NAT/LISM SOVEREIGN 18/19. PAGE 67 A1385
DIPLOM POLICY ATTIT NAT/G

B58
DUCLOUX L.,FROM BLACKMAIL TO TREASON. FRANCE PLAN DIPLOM EDU/PROP PRESS RUMOR NAT/LISM...CRIMLGY 20. PAGE 39 A0793
COERCE CRIME NAT/G PWR

B60
HOLT R.T.,STRATEGIC PSYCHOLOGICAL OPERATIONS AND AMERICAN FOREIGN POLICY. ITALY USA+45 FOR/AID DOMIN RUMOR ADMIN TASK WAR CHOOSE ATTIT ALL/IDEOS...PSY COLD/WAR. PAGE 67 A1375
EDU/PROP ACT/RES DIPLOM POLICY

RURAL....RURAL AREAS, PEOPLE, ETC.

RUSH M. A1383

RUSK D. A2188,A2569,A2570

RUSK/DEAN....DEAN RUSK

B61
US HOUSE COMM FOREIGN AFFAIRS,THE INTERNATIONAL DEVELOPMENT AND SECURITY ACT: HEARINGS BEFORE COMMITTEE ON FOREIGN AFFAIRS, HOUSE OF REP: HR7372. USA+45 AGRI INT/ORG NAT/G CONSULT DELIB/GP DIPLOM ECO/TAC INT/TRADE LOBBY REPRESENT 20 MCNAMARA/R DILLON/D RUSK/D CONGRESS. PAGE 153 A3128
FOR/AID CONFER LEGIS ECO/UNDEV

B62
US SENATE COMM GOVT OPERATIONS,ADMINISTRATION OF NATIONAL SECURITY. USA+45 CHIEF PLAN PROB/SOLV TEC/DEV DIPLOM ATTIT...POLICY DECISION 20 KENNEDY/JF RUSK/D MCNAMARA/R BUNDY/M HERTER/C. PAGE 156 A3173
ORD/FREE ADMIN NAT/G CONTROL

S64
RUSK D.,"THE MAKING OF FOREIGN POLICY" USA+45 CHIEF DELIB/GP WORKER PROB/SOLV ADMIN ATTIT PWR ...DECISION 20 DEPT/STATE RUSK/D GOLDMAN/E. PAGE 125 A2570
DIPLOM INT POLICY

RUSKIN/J....JOHN RUSKIN

RUSSEL F.M. A2571

RUSSEL R.W. A2572

RUSSELL B. A2573,A2574

RUSSELL R.B. A2575,A2576

RUSSELL/B....BERTRAND RUSSELL

B67
RUSSELL B.,WAR CRIMES IN VIETNAM. USA+45 VIETNAM FORCES DIPLOM WEAPON RACE/REL DISCRIM ISOLAT BIO/SOC 20 COLD/WAR RUSSELL/B. PAGE 126 A2574
WAR CRIME ATTIT POLICY

RUSSETT B.M. A2577,A2578,A2579

RUSSIA....PRE-REVOLUTIONARY RUSSIA; SEE ALSO APPROPRIATE TIME/SPACE/CULTURE INDEX

N
NEUE POLITISCHE LITERATUR. AFR ASIA EUR+WWI GERMANY RUSSIA SOCIETY ECO/DEV ECO/UNDEV PLAN PROB/SOLV LEAD MARXISM...PHIL/SCI CONCPT 20. PAGE 1 A0021
BIBLIOG DIPLOM COM NAT/G

NLO
WHITE J.A.,THE DIPLOMACY OF THE RUSSO-JAPANESE WAR. ASIA KOREA RUSSIA FORCES CONFER CONTROL PEACE ...BIBLIOG 19 CHINJAP. PAGE 164 A3336
DIPLOM WAR BAL/PWR

B00
VOLPICELLI Z.,RUSSIA ON THE PACIFIC AND THE SIBERIAN RAILWAY. MOD/EUR ECO/UNDEV INT/ORG FORCES PLAN DOMIN COLONIAL ROUTINE ATTIT ALL/VALS...OBS HIST/WRIT TIME/SEQ TREND CON/ANAL AUD/VIS CHARTS 18/19. PAGE 159 A3248
NAT/G ACT/RES RUSSIA

B18
KERNER R.J.,SLAVIC EUROPE: A SELECTED BIBLIOGRAPHY IN THE WESTERN EUROPEAN LANGUAGES. BULGARIA CZECHOSLVK GERMANY/E POLAND RUSSIA YUGOSLAVIA NAT/G DIPLOM MARXISM...LING 19/20. PAGE 78 A1598
BIBLIOG SOCIETY CULTURE COM

B19
KEYNES J.M.,THE ECONOMIC CONSEQUENCES OF THE PEACE. FUT GERMANY MOD/EUR RUSSIA UK USA-45 CULTURE ECO/DEV FINAN INDUS INT/ORG TOP/EX ECO/TAC ROUTINE WAR ATTIT PERCEPT ALL/VALS...OLD/LIB MYTH OBS TIME/SEQ TREND 20 TREATY. PAGE 78 A1605
EUR+WWI SOCIETY PEACE

B30
SCHMITT B.E.,THE COMING OF THE WAR, 1914 (2 VOLS.). AUSTRIA FRANCE GERMANY MOD/EUR RUSSIA UK PLAN ROUTINE ORD/FREE. PAGE 128 A2633
WAR DIPLOM

B38
PETTEE G.S.,THE PROCESS OF REVOLUTION. COM FRANCE ITALY MOD/EUR RUSSIA SPAIN WOR-45 ELITES INTELL SOCIETY STRATA STRUCT INT/ORG NAT/G POL/PAR ACT/RES PLAN EDU/PROP LEGIT EXEC...SOC MYTH TIME/SEQ TOT/POP 18/20. PAGE 115 A2370
COERCE CONCPT REV

B39
KERNER R.J.,NORTHEAST ASIA: A SELECTED BIBLIOGRAPHY (2 VOLS.). KOREA RUSSIA NAT/G DIPLOM...GEOG 19/20 CHINJAP. PAGE 78 A1599
BIBLIOG ASIA SOCIETY CULTURE

B41
YOUNG G.,FEDERALISM AND FREEDOM. EUR+WWI MOD/EUR RUSSIA USA-45 WOR-45 SOCIETY STRUCT ECO/DEV INT/ORG EXEC FEDERAL ATTIT PERSON ALL/VALS...OLD/LIB CONCPT OBS TREND LEAGUE/NAT TOT/POP. PAGE 169 A3435
NAT/G WAR

B44
WEIGERT H.W.,COMPASS OF THE WORLD, A SYMPOSIUM ON POLITICAL GEOGRAPHY. EUR+WWI FUT MOD/EUR S/ASIA USA-45 WOR-45 SOCIETY AGRI INDUS MARKET ECO/TAC INT/TRADE PERSON 20. PAGE 162 A3298
TEC/DEV CAP/ISM RUSSIA GEOG

B45
NELSON M.F.,KOREA AND THE OLD ORDERS IN EASTERN ASIA. ASIA FRANCE KOREA RUSSIA DELIB/GP INT/TRADE DOMIN CONTROL WAR ORD/FREE...POLICY BIBLIOG. PAGE 108 A2218
DIPLOM BAL/PWR ATTIT CONSERVE

B49
GORER G.,THE PEOPLE OF GREAT RUSSIA: A PSYCHOLOGICAL STUDY. RUSSIA USSR NAT/G DIPLOM LEAD AGE/C ANOMIE ATTIT DRIVE...POLICY 20. PAGE 54 A1116
ISOLAT PERSON PSY SOCIETY

B50
GLEASON J.H.,THE GENESIS OF RUSSOPHOBIA IN GREAT BRITAIN: A STUDY OF THE INTERACTION OF POLICY AND OPINION. ASIA RUSSIA UK NAT/G AGREE CONTROL REV WAR LOVE PWR TREATY 19. PAGE 53 A1080
DIPLOM POLICY DOMIN COLONIAL

S50
WITTFOGEL K.A.,"RUSSIA AND ASIA: PROBLEMS OF CONTEMPORARY AREA STUDIES AND INTERNATIONAL RELATIONS." ASIA COM USA+45 SOCIETY NAT/G DIPLOM ECO/TAC FOR/AID EDU/PROP KNOWL...HIST/WRIT TOT/POP
ECO/DEV ADMIN RUSSIA USSR

20. PAGE 166 A3373

B52

ALBERTINI L.,THE ORIGINS OF THE WAR OF 1914 (3 VOLS.). AUSTRIA FRANCE GERMANY MOD/EUR RUSSIA UK PROB/SOLV NEUTRAL PWR...BIBLIOG 19/20. PAGE 5 A0107
WAR DIPLOM FORCES BAL/PWR

B61

FULLER J.F.C.,THE CONDUCT OF WAR, 1789-1961. FRANCE RUSSIA SOCIETY NAT/G FORCES PROB/SOLV AGREE NUC/PWR WEAPON PEACE...SOC 18/20 TREATY COLD/WAR. PAGE 50 A1025
WAR POLICY REV ROLE

B61

NOLLAU G.,INTERNATIONAL COMMUNISM AND WORLD REVOLUTION: HISTORY AND METHODS. RUSSIA USSR INT/ORG NAT/G POL/PAR VOL/ASSN FORCES BAL/PWR DIPLOM EXEC REGION WAR ATTIT PWR MARXISM...CONCPT TIME/SEQ COLD/WAR 19/20. PAGE 102 A2100
COM REV

B62

JELAVICH C.,TSARIST RUSSIA AND BALKAN NATIONALISM. BULGARIA MOD/EUR RUSSIA DOMIN GOV/REL...GEOG 19 SERBIA. PAGE 73 A1503
NAT/LISM DIPLOM WAR

B63

ADLER G.J.,BRITISH INDIA'S NORTHERN FRONTIER: 1865-95. AFGHANISTN RUSSIA UK PROVS COLONIAL COERCE PEACE...GEOG CHARTS BIBLIOG 19 TREATY. PAGE 4 A0091
S/ASIA FORCES DIPLOM POLICY

B63

MONGER G.W.,THE END OF ISOLATION. FRANCE MOD/EUR RUSSIA UK NAT/G LEGIS TOP/EX GOV/REL PWR 20 TREATY CHINJAP. PAGE 103 A2106
DIPLOM POLICY WAR

B64

KIS T.I.,LES PAYS DE L'EUROPE DE L'EST: LEURS RAPPORTS MUTUELS ET LE PROBLEME DE LEUR INTEGRATION DANS L'ORBITE DE L'USSR. EUR+WWI RUSSIA USSR INT/ORG NAT/G REV ATTIT...JURID SOC BIBLIOG WARSAW/P COMECON EUROPE/E. PAGE 80 A1638
DIPLOM COM MARXISM REGION

B64

LENSEN G.A.,REVELATIONS OF A RUSSIAN DIPLOMAT: THE MEMOIRS OF DMITRII I. ABRIKOSSOV. ASIA MOD/EUR RUSSIA USA-45 ELITES ACADEM CHIEF FORCES REV WAR PWR CONSERVE MARXISM 19/20 ABRIKSSV/D CHINJAP BOLSHEVISM. PAGE 87 A1775
DIPLOM POLICY OBS

S67

BREGMAN A.,"WHITHER RUSSIA?" COM RUSSIA INTELL POL/PAR DIPLOM PARTIC NAT/LISM TOTALISM ATTIT ORD/FREE 20. PAGE 18 A0370
MARXISM ELITES ADMIN CREATE

RWANDA....SEE ALSO AFR

B60

ASPREMONT-LYNDEN H.,RAPPORT SUR L'ADMINISTRATION BELGE DU RUANDA-URUNDI PENDANT L'ANNEE 1959. BELGIUM RWANDA AGRI INDUS DIPLOM ECO/TAC INT/TRADE DOMIN ADMIN RACE/REL...GEOG CENSUS 20 UN. PAGE 9 A0192
AFR COLONIAL ECO/UNDEV INT/ORG

S

S/ASIA....SOUTHEAST ASIA; SEE ALSO APPROPRIATE NATIONS

N

INDIAN COUNCIL WORLD AFFAIRS,SELECT ARTICLES ON CURRENT AFFAIRS (BIBLIOGRAPHICAL SERIES: 7). AFR ASIA COM EUR+WWI S/ASIA UK COLONIAL NUC/PWR PEACE ATTIT...INT/LAW SOC 20. PAGE 70 A1437
BIBLIOG DIPLOM INT/ORG ECO/UNDEV

N

ANNALS OF THE AMERICAN ACADEMY OF POLITICAL AND SOCIAL SCIENCE. AFR ASIA S/ASIA WOR+45 POL/PAR DIPLOM CRIME REV...SOC BIOG 20. PAGE 1 A0004
BIBLIOG/A NAT/G CULTURE ATTIT

N

INTERNATIONAL STUDIES. ASIA S/ASIA WOR+45 ECO/UNDEV INT/ORG NAT/G LEAD ATTIT WEALTH...SOC 20. PAGE 1 A0012
BIBLIOG/A DIPLOM INT/LAW INT/TRADE

N

JOURNAL OF ASIAN STUDIES. CULTURE ECO/DEV SECT DIPLOM EDU/PROP WAR NAT/LISM...PHIL/SCI SOC 20. PAGE 1 A0013
BIBLIOG ASIA S/ASIA NAT/G

N

THE JAPAN SCIENCE REVIEW: LAW AND POLITICS: LIST OF BOOKS AND ARTICLES ON LAW AND POLITICS. CONSTN AGRI INDUS LABOR DIPLOM TAX ADMIN CRIME...INT/LAW SOC 20 CHINJAP. PAGE 2 A0042
BIBLIOG LAW S/ASIA PHIL/SCI

N

AMERICAN BIBLIOGRAPHIC SERVICE,INTERNATIONAL GUIDE TO INDIC STUDIES - A QUARTERLY INDEX TO PERIODICAL LITERATURE. INDIA CULTURE NAT/G DIPLOM...EPIST SOC BIOG 20. PAGE 7 A0140
BIBLIOG S/ASIA CON/ANAL

N

AMERICAN BIBLIOGRAPHIC SERVICE,QUARTERLY CHECKLIST OF ORIENTAL STUDIES. CULTURE LOC/G NAT/G DIPLOM ...HIST/WRIT CON/ANAL 20. PAGE 7 A0141
BIBLIOG S/ASIA ASIA

N

ASIA FOUNDATION,LIBRARY NOTES. LAW CONSTN CULTURE SOCIETY ECO/UNDEV INT/ORG NAT/G COLONIAL LEAD REGION NAT/LISM ATTIT 20 UN. PAGE 9 A0189
BIBLIOG/A ASIA S/ASIA DIPLOM

N

CORNELL UNIVERSITY LIBRARY,SOUTHEAST ASIA ACCESSIONS LIST. LAW SOCIETY STRUCT ECO/UNDEV POL/PAR TEC/DEV DIPLOM LEAD REGION. PAGE 31 A0626
BIBLIOG S/ASIA NAT/G CULTURE

N

KYRIAK T.E.,ASIAN DEVELOPMENTS: A BIBLIOGRAPHY. INDONESIA KOREA/N VIETNAM/N CULTURE SOCIETY ECO/UNDEV NAT/G DIPLOM...SOC TREND 20 MONGOLIA. PAGE 83 A1699
BIBLIOG/A ALL/IDEOS S/ASIA ASIA

N

US LIBRARY OF CONGRESS,ACCESSIONS LIST - INDIA. INDIA CULTURE AGRI LOC/G POL/PAR PLAN PROB/SOLV TEC/DEV DIPLOM EDU/PROP LEAD GP/REL ATTIT 20. PAGE 154 A3142
BIBLIOG S/ASIA ECO/UNDEV NAT/G

B01

GRIFFIN A.P.C.,LIST OF BOOKS ON SAMOA (PAMPHLET). GERMANY S/ASIA UK USA-45 WOR-45 ECO/UNDEV REGION ALL/VALS ORD/FREE ALL/IDEOS...GEOG INT/LAW 19 SAMOA GUAM. PAGE 56 A1150
BIBLIOG/A COLONIAL DIPLOM

B02

SEELEY J.R.,THE EXPANSION OF ENGLAND. MOD/EUR S/ASIA UK CULTURE NAT/G FORCES PLAN DOMIN EDU/PROP COLONIAL ROUTINE ATTIT ALL/VALS SOVEREIGN...CONCPT HIST/WRIT PARLIAMENT 18 CMN/WLTH. PAGE 131 A2679
INT/ORG ACT/RES CAP/ISM INDIA

N19

ASIAN-AFRICAN CONFERENCE,SELECTED DOCUMENTS OF THE BANDUNG CONFERENCE (PAMPHLET). S/ASIA PLAN ECO/TAC CONFER REGION REV NAT/LISM 20. PAGE 9 A0191
NEUTRAL ECO/UNDEV COLONIAL DIPLOM

B29

BOUDET P.,BIBLIOGRAPHIE DE L'INDOCHINE FRANCAISE. S/ASIA VIETNAM SECT...GEOG LING 20. PAGE 17 A0344
BIBLIOG ADMIN COLONIAL DIPLOM

B38

GRISWOLD A.W.,THE FAR EASTERN POLICY OF THE UNITED STATES. ASIA S/ASIA USA-45 INT/ORG INT/TRADE WAR NAT/LISM...BIBLIOG 19/20 LEAGUE/NAT ROOSEVLT/T ROOSEVLT/F WILSON/W TREATY. PAGE 57 A1166
DIPLOM POLICY CHIEF

C39

REISCHAUER R.,"JAPAN'S GOVERNMENT--POLITICS." CONSTN STRATA POL/PAR FORCES LEGIS DIPLOM ADMIN EXEC CENTRAL...POLICY BIBLIOG 20 CHINJAP. PAGE 120 A2462
NAT/G S/ASIA CONCPT ROUTINE

B42

CONOVER H.F.,NEW ZEALAND: A SELECTED LIST OF REFERENCES (PAMPHLET). NEW/ZEALND ECO/UNDEV AGRI INDUS LABOR NAT/G SCHOOL FORCES DIPLOM COLONIAL WAR ...HUM 20. PAGE 29 A0595
BIBLIOG/A S/ASIA CULTURE

B42

CORBETT P.E.,POST WAR WORLDS. ASIA EUR+WWI FUT S/ASIA USA-45 ECO/DEV ECO/UNDEV NAT/G DELIB/GP FORCES PLAN ROUTINE ATTIT PWR 20. PAGE 30 A0613
WOR-45 INT/ORG

B44

WEIGERT H.W.,COMPASS OF THE WORLD, A SYMPOSIUM ON POLITICAL GEOGRAPHY. EUR+WWI FUT MOD/EUR S/ASIA USA-45 WOR-45 SOCIETY AGRI INDUS MARKET ECO/TAC INT/TRADE PERSON 20. PAGE 162 A3298
TEC/DEV CAP/ISM RUSSIA GEOG

N45

INDIA QUARTERLY, A JOURNAL OF INTERNATIONAL AFFAIRS. INDIA LAW CONSTN ECO/UNDEV INT/ORG POL/PAR COLONIAL LEAD PARL/PROC WAR ATTIT...SOC 20 CMN/WLTH. PAGE 3 A0053
BIBLIOG/A S/ASIA DIPLOM NAT/G

B45

HARVARD WIDENER LIBRARY,INDOCHINA: A SELECTED LIST OF REFERENCES. CAMBODIA FRANCE S/ASIA VIETNAM COLONIAL...POLICY 19/20. PAGE 62 A1282
BIBLIOG/A ACADEM DIPLOM NAT/G

N46

HOBBS C.C.,SOUTHEAST ASIA, 1935-45: A SELECTED LIST OF REFERENCE BOOKS (PAMPHLET). S/ASIA AGRI INDUS NAT/G SECT DIPLOM WAR...ART/METH GEOG SOC LING 20. PAGE 65 A1346
BIBLIOG/A CULTURE HABITAT

C49

YANAGA C.,"JAPAN SINCE PERRY." S/ASIA CULTURE ECO/DEV FORCES WAR 19/20 CHINJAP. PAGE 168 A3430
DIPLOM POL/PAR CIVMIL/REL NAT/LISM

B50

CORNELL U DEPT ASIAN STUDIES,SOUTHEAST ASIA PROGRAM DATA PAPER. BURMA CAMBODIA INDONESIA MALAYSIA VIETNAM SOCIETY STRUCT NAT/G SECT DIPLOM FOR/AID PWR WEALTH...SOC 20. PAGE 31 A0625
BIBLIOG/A CULTURE S/ASIA ECO/UNDEV

B51

JENNINGS W.I.,THE COMMONWEALTH IN ASIA. CEYLON INDIA PAKISTAN S/ASIA UK CONSTN CULTURE SOCIETY STRATA STRUCT NAT/G POL/PAR EDU/PROP LEAD WAR 20 CMN/WLTH. PAGE 74 A1510
NAT/LISM REGION COLONIAL DIPLOM

B51

US DEPARTMENT OF STATE,POINT FOUR, NEAR EAST AND AFRICA, A SELECTED BIBLIOGRAPHY OF STUDIES ON ECONOMICALLY UNDERDEVELOPED COUNTRIES. AGRI COM/IND FINAN INDUS PLAN INT/TRADE...SOC TREND 20. PAGE 151 A3087
BIBLIOG/A AFR S/ASIA ISLAM

B51
US HOUSE COMM APPROPRIATIONS,MUTUAL SECURITY PROGRAM APPROPRIATIONS FOR 1952: HEARINGS BEFORE A SUBCOMMITTEE OF THE COMMITTEE ON APPROPRIATIONS. KOREA L/A+17C ECO/DEV ECO/UNDEV INT/ORG INSPECT BAL/PWR DIPLOM DEBATE WAR...POLICY STAT ASIA/S 20 CONGRESS NATO COLD/WAR MID/EAST. PAGE 153 A3118
LEGIS FORCES BUDGET FOR/AID

C51
GRUNDER G.A.,"THE PHILIPPINES AND THE UNITED STATES." PHILIPPINE S/ASIA USA-45 NAT/G POL/PAR ADMIN SOVEREIGN...TIME/SEQ BIBLIOG 20. PAGE 57 A1181
COLONIAL POLICY DIPLOM ECO/TAC

B53
ELAHI K.N.,A GUIDE TO WORKS OF REFERENCE PUBLISHED IN PAKISTAN (PAMPHLET). PAKISTAN DIPLOM COLONIAL LEAD. PAGE 41 A0835
BIBLIOG S/ASIA NAT/G

B53
KALIJARVI T.V.,MODERN WORLD POLITICS (3RD ED.). AFR L/A+17C MOD/EUR S/ASIA UK USSR WOR+45 INT/ORG BAL/PWR WAR PWR 20. PAGE 76 A1552
DIPLOM INT/LAW PEACE

B53
MURPHY G.,IN THE MINDS OF MEN: THE STUDY OF HUMAN BEHAVIOR AND SOCIAL TENSIONS IN INDIA. FUT S/ASIA FAM INT/ORG NAT/G DIPLOM EDU/PROP GP/REL ATTIT RIGID/FLEX ALL/VALS...SOC QU UNESCO 20. PAGE 106 A2176
SECT STRATA INDIA

B53
THAYER P.W.,SOUTHEAST ASIA IN THE COMING WORLD. ASIA S/ASIA USA+45 USA-45 SOCIETY INT/ORG ACT/RES ECO/TAC EDU/PROP COERCE TOTALISM ALL/VALS...JURID 20. PAGE 142 A2909
ECO/UNDEV ATTIT FOR/AID DIPLOM

B54
NUSSBAUM D.,A CONCISE HISTORY OF THE LAW OF NATIONS. ASIA CHRIST-17C EUR+WWI ISLAM MEDIT-7 MOD/EUR S/ASIA UNIV WOR+45 WOR-45 SOCIETY STRUCT EXEC ATTIT ALL/VALS...CONCPT HIST/WRIT TIME/SEQ. PAGE 110 A2263
INT/ORG LAW PEACE INT/LAW

B54
SHARMA J.S.,MAHATMA GANDHI: A DESCRIPTIVE BIBLIOGRAPHY. INDIA S/ASIA PROB/SOLV DIPLOM COLONIAL WAR NAT/LISM PEACE ATTIT PERSON SOVEREIGN ...CONCPT 20 GANDHI/M. PAGE 132 A2695
BIBLIOG/A BIOG CHIEF LEAD

L54
CHARLESWORTH J.C.,"AMERICA AND A NEW ASIA." ASIA INDIA ISLAM S/ASIA USA+45 USA-45 ECO/UNDEV NAT/G POL/PAR FORCES FOR/AID DOMIN EDU/PROP COERCE DRIVE ALL/VALS MARXISM SOCISM TOT/POP 20. PAGE 26 A0522
ECO/TAC DIPLOM NAT/LISM

B55
QUAN K.L.,INTRODUCTION TO ASIA: A SELECTIVE GUIDE TO BACKGROUND READING. ECO/UNDEV NAT/G PROB/SOLV DIPLOM ATTIT 20. PAGE 118 A2424
BIBLIOG/A S/ASIA CULTURE ASIA

B55
THOMPSON V.,MINORITY PROBLEMS IN SOUTHEAST ASIA. CAMBODIA CHINA/COM LAOS S/ASIA KIN NAT/G SECT PROB/SOLV EDU/PROP REGION GP/REL RACE/REL MARXISM ...SOC 20 BUDDHISM UN. PAGE 143 A2933
INGP/REL GEOG DIPLOM STRUCT

B56
BALL W.M.,NATIONALISM AND COMMUNISM IN EAST ASIA. ASIA BURMA EUR+WWI KOREA USA+45 ECO/UNDEV NAT/G POL/PAR DIPLOM ECO/TAC FOR/AID EDU/PROP COERCE RACE/REL NAT/LISM DRIVE SOVEREIGN...TREND 20 CHINJAP. PAGE 11 A0214
S/ASIA ATTIT

B56
CHANG C.J.,THE MINORITY GROUPS OF YUNN AN AND CHINESE POLITICAL EXPANSION INTO SOUTHEAST ASIA (DOCTORAL THESIS). ASIA CHINA/COM S/ASIA FORCES TEC/DEV DIPLOM EDU/PROP...GEOG BIBLIOG 20. PAGE 26 A0520
GP/REL REGION DOMIN MARXISM

B56
IRIKURA J.K.,SOUTHEAST ASIA: SELECTED ANNOTATED BIBLIOGRAPHY OF JAPANESE PUBLICATIONS. CULTURE ADMIN RACE/REL 20 CHINJAP. PAGE 71 A1466
BIBLIOG/A S/ASIA DIPLOM

B56
KIRK G.,THE CHANGING ENVIRONMENT OF INTERNATIONAL RELATIONS. ASIA S/ASIA USA+45 WOR+45 ECO/UNDEV INT/ORG NAT/G FOR/AID EDU/PROP PEACE KNOWL ...PLURIST COLD/WAR TOT/POP 20. PAGE 80 A1634
FUT EXEC DIPLOM

B56
PHILIPPINE STUDIES PROGRAM,SELECTED BIBLIOGRAPHY ON THE PHILIPPINES, TOPICALLY ARRANGED AND ANNOTATED. PHILIPPINE SECT DIPLOM COLONIAL LEAD...SOC 18/20. PAGE 116 A2375
BIBLIOG/A S/ASIA NAT/G ECO/UNDEV

B56
ROBERTS H.L.,RUSSIA AND AMERICA. CHINA/COM S/ASIA USSR FORCES TEC/DEV FOR/AID NUC/PWR ALL/IDEOS ...MAJORIT TREND NAT/COMP 20 COLD/WAR UN NATO. PAGE 122 A2494
DIPLOM INT/ORG BAL/PWR TOTALISM

B56
WILSON P.,GOVERNMENT AND POLITICS OF INDIA AND PAKISTAN: 1885-1955; A BIBLIOGRAPHY OF WORKS IN WESTERN LANGUAGES. INDIA PAKISTAN CONSTN LOC/G POL/PAR FORCES DIPLOM ADMIN WAR CHOOSE...BIOG CON/ANAL 19/20. PAGE 165 A3361
BIBLIOG COLONIAL NAT/G S/ASIA

B57
DEAN V.M.,THE NATURE OF THE NON-WESTERN WORLD. AFR ASIA L/A+17C S/ASIA CULTURE SOCIETY STRATA ECO/DEV DIPLOM ECO/TAC FOR/AID ATTIT DRIVE ALL/VALS ...RELATIV SOC CONCPT TIME/SEQ TREND TOT/POP 20. PAGE 35 A0718
ECO/UNDEV STERTYP NAT/LISM

B57
WILSON P.,SOUTH ASIA; A SELECTED BIBLIOGRAPHY ON INDIA, PAKISTAN, CEYLON (PAMPHLET). CEYLON INDIA PAKISTAN LAW ECO/UNDEV PLAN DIPLOM 20. PAGE 165 A3362
BIBLIOG S/ASIA CULTURE NAT/G

C57
TANG P.S.H.,"COMMUNIST CHINA TODAY: DOMESTIC AND FOREIGN POLICIES." CHINA/COM COM S/ASIA USSR STRATA FORCES DIPLOM EDU/PROP COERCE GOV/REL...POLICY MAJORIT BIBLIOG 20. PAGE 141 A2886
POL/PAR LEAD ADMIN CONSTN

B58
ALEXANDROWICZ,A BIBLIOGRAPHY OF INDIAN LAW. INDIA S/ASIA CONSTN CT/SYS...INT/LAW 19/20. PAGE 6 A0113
BIBLIOG LAW ADJUD JURID

B58
BERLINER J.S.,SOVIET ECONOMIC AID: THE AID AND TRADE POLICY IN UNDERDEVELOPED COUNTRIES. AFR COM ISLAM L/A+17C S/ASIA USSR ECO/DEV DIST/IND FINAN MARKET INT/ORG ACT/RES PLAN BAL/PWR WEAPON PWR WEALTH...CHARTS 20. PAGE 14 A0277
ECO/UNDEV ECO/TAC FOR/AID

B58
INDIAN COUNCIL WORLD AFFAIRS,DEFENCE AND SECURITY IN THE INDIAN OCEAN AREA. INDIA S/ASIA CULTURE CONSULT DELIB/GP FORCES PROB/SOLV DIPLOM INT/TRADE 20 CMN/WLTH. PAGE 70 A1438
GEOG HABITAT ECO/UNDEV ORD/FREE

B58
JENNINGS I.,PROBLEMS OF THE NEW COMMONWEALTH. CEYLON INDIA PAKISTAN S/ASIA ECO/UNDEV INT/ORG LOC/G DIPLOM ECO/TAC INT/TRADE COLONIAL RACE/REL DISCRIM 20 COMMONWLTH PARLIAMENT. PAGE 74 A1508
NAT/LISM NEUTRAL FOR/AID POL/PAR

B58
MANSERGH N.,SURVEY OF BRITISH COMMONWEALTH AFFAIRS: PROBLEMS OF WARTIME CO-OPERATION AND POST-WAR CHANGE 1939-1952. INDIA IRELAND S/ASIA CONSTN INT/ORG BAL/PWR COLONIAL NEUTRAL WAR ADJUST PEACE ROLE ORD/FREE...CHARTS 20 CMN/WLTH NATO UN. PAGE 94 A1931
VOL/ASSN CONSEN PROB/SOLV INGP/REL

B58
MASON J.B.,THAILAND BIBLIOGRAPHY. S/ASIA THAILAND CULTURE EDU/PROP ADMIN...GEOG SOC LING 20. PAGE 95 A1958
BIBLIOG/A ECO/UNDEV DIPLOM NAT/G

B58
UNIV KARACHI INST PUB BUS ADM,PUBLICATIONS OF THE GOVERNMENT OF PAKISTAN 1947-1957. PAKISTAN S/ASIA DIPLOM COLONIAL ATTIT 20. PAGE 149 A3040
BIBLIOG NAT/G POLICY

L58
SNYDER R.N.,"THE UNITED STATES DECISION TO RESIST AGGRESSION IN KOREA." ASIA KOREA S/ASIA USA+45 USA-45 WOR+45 INT/ORG DELIB/GP BAL/PWR COERCE PWR ...CONCPT REC/INT RESIST/INT COLD/WAR 20. PAGE 134 A2753
QUANT METH/CNCPT DIPLOM

C58
BLANCHARD W.,"THAILAND." THAILAND CULTURE AGRI FINAN INDUS FAM LABOR INT/TRADE ATTIT...GEOG HEAL SOC BIBLIOG 20. PAGE 15 A0307
NAT/G DIPLOM ECO/UNDEV S/ASIA

C58
FIFIELD R.H.,"THE DIPLOMACY OF SOUTHEAST ASIA: 1945-1958." INT/ORG NAT/G COLONIAL REGION...CHARTS BIBLIOG 20 UN. PAGE 45 A0927
S/ASIA DIPLOM NAT/LISM

B59
ALWAN M.,ALGERIA BEFORE THE UNITED NATIONS. AFR ASIA FRANCE ISLAM S/ASIA CONSTN SOCIETY STRUCT INT/ORG NAT/G ECO/TAC ADMIN COLONIAL NAT/LISM ATTIT PWR...DECISION TREND 420 UN. PAGE 7 A0133
PLAN RIGID/FLEX DIPLOM ALGERIA

B59
FREE L.A.,SIX ALLIES AND A NEUTRAL. ASIA COM EUR+WWI FRANCE GERMANY/W INDIA S/ASIA UK USA+45 INT/ORG NAT/G NUC/PWR PEACE ATTIT PERCEPT RIGID/FLEX ALL/VALS...STAT REC/INT COLD/WAR 20 CHINJAP. PAGE 48 A0992
PSY DIPLOM

B59
JOSEPH F.M.,AS OTHERS SEE US: THE UNITED STATES THROUGH FOREIGN EYES. AFR EUR+WWI ISLAM L/A+17C S/ASIA USA+45 CULTURE SOCIETY ECO/DEV ECO/UNDEV INT/ORG NAT/G DIPLOM ECO/TAC REV ATTIT RIGID/FLEX HEALTH ORD/FREE WEALTH 20. PAGE 75 A1537
RESPECT DOMIN NAT/LISM SOVEREIGN

B59
KARUNAKARAN K.P.,INDIA IN WORLD AFFAIRS, 1952-1958 (VOL. II). INDIA ECO/UNDEV SECT FOR/AID INT/TRADE ADJUD NEUTRAL REV WAR DISCRIM ORD/FREE MARXISM ...BIBLIOG 20. PAGE 77 A1569
DIPLOM INT/ORG S/ASIA COLONIAL

B59
THOMAS N.,THE PREREQUISITES FOR PEACE. ASIA EUR+WWI FUT ISLAM S/ASIA WOR+45 FORCES PLAN BAL/PWR EDU/PROP LEGIT ATTIT PWR...SOCIALIST CONCPT COLD/WAR 20 UN. PAGE 143 A2924
INT/ORG ORD/FREE ARMS/CONT PEACE

B59
VINACKE H.M.,A HISTORY OF THE FAR EAST IN MODERN TIMES (6TH ED.). KOREA S/ASIA USSR CONSTN CULTURE STRATA ECO/UNDEV NAT/G CHIEF FOR/AID INT/TRADE
STRUCT ASIA

GP/REL...SOC NAT/COMP 19/20 CHINJAP. PAGE 159 A3235

S59
KOHN L.Y.,"ISRAEL AND NEW NATION STATES OF ASIA AND AFRICA." AFR ASIA FUT S/ASIA VOL/ASSN TEC/DEV NAT/LISM RIGID/FLEX SKILL WEALTH...RELATIV OBS TREND CON/ANAL 20. PAGE 81 A1663 ECO/UNDEV ECO/TAC FOR/AID ISRAEL

S59
KRIPALANI A.J.B.,"FOR PRINCIPLED NEUTRALITY." CHINA/COM INDIA S/ASIA PLAN ECO/TAC RIGID/FLEX MORAL PWR...MYSTIC SOC RECORD 20 GANDHI/M. PAGE 82 A1684 ATTIT FOR/AID DIPLOM

B60
EMERSON R.,FROM EMPIRE TO NATION: THE RISE TO SELF-ASSERTION OF ASIAN AND AFRICAN PEOPLES. S/ASIA CULTURE NAT/G SECT DIPLOM ATTIT SOVEREIGN MARXISM ...POLICY BIBLIOG 19/20. PAGE 41 A0847 NAT/LISM COLONIAL AFR ASIA

B60
FOOTMAN D.,INTERNATIONAL COMMUNISM. ASIA EUR+WWI FRANCE FUT GERMANY MOD/EUR S/ASIA USA-45 WOR+45 WOR-45 INTELL LABOR TOTALISM MARXISM WORK 20. PAGE 47 A0958 COM INT/ORG STRUCT REV

B60
MOUSKHELY M.,L'URSS ET LES PAYS DE L'EST. ASIA COM S/ASIA USSR PRESS...SOC 20. PAGE 105 A2156 BIBLIOG/A DIPLOM ATTIT

B60
NURTY K.S.,STUDIES IN PROBLEMS OF PEACE. CHRIST-17C MOD/EUR S/ASIA WOR+45 WOR-45 INT/ORG NAT/G SECT COERCE REV NAT/LISM ALL/VALS...CONCPT MYTH TIME/SEQ. PAGE 110 A2262 POLICY PEACE PACIFISM ORD/FREE

B60
PLAMENATZ J.,ON ALIEN RULE AND SELF-GOVERNMENT. AFR FUT S/ASIA WOR+45 CULTURE SOCIETY ECO/UNDEV INT/ORG DOMIN EDU/PROP ATTIT RIGID/FLEX ALL/VALS...POLICY CONCPT OBS TREND CON/ANAL GEN/LAWS TOT/POP VAL/FREE. PAGE 116 A2386 NAT/G CONSTN NAT/LISM SOVEREIGN

B60
SALETORE B.A.,INDIA'S DIPLOMATIC RELATIONS WITH THE EAST. ASIA CEYLON INDIA NEPAL S/ASIA CULTURE 7/14 PERSIA. PAGE 126 A2591 DIPLOM NAT/COMP ETIQUET

B60
WOLF C.,FOREIGN AID: THEORY AND PRACTICE IN SOUTHERN ASIA. CEYLON INDONESIA PHILIPPINE S/ASIA CULTURE STRATA ECO/UNDEV PLAN EDU/PROP ATTIT ...METH/CNCPT MATH QUANT STAT CONT/OBS TIME/SEQ SIMUL TOT/POP 20. PAGE 166 A3378 ACT/RES ECO/TAC FOR/AID

S60
GINSBURGS G.,"PEKING-LHASA-NEW DELHI." CHINA/COM FUT INDIA S/ASIA KIN NAT/G PROVS SECT FORCES BAL/PWR ECO/TAC DOMIN EDU/PROP LEGIT ADMIN REGION GUERRILLA PWR...TREND TIBET 20. PAGE 52 A1074 ASIA COERCE DIPLOM

S60
KEYFITZ N.,"WESTERN PERSPECTIVES AND ASIAN PROBLEMS." ASIA EUR+WWI S/ASIA SOCIETY FOR/AID ...POLICY SOC CONCPT STERTYP WORK TOT/POP 20. PAGE 78 A1604 CULTURE ATTIT

S60
MODELSKI G.,"AUSTRALIA AND SEATO." S/ASIA USA+45 CULTURE INTELL ECO/DEV NAT/G PLAN DIPLOM ADMIN ROUTINE ATTIT SKILL...MGT TIME/SEQ AUSTRAL 20 SEATO. PAGE 102 A2097 INT/ORG ACT/RES

S60
RIESELBACH Z.N.,"QUANTITATIVE TECHNIQUES FOR STUDYING VOTING BEHAVIOR IN THE UNITED NATIONS GENERAL ASSEMBLY." FUT S/ASIA USA+45 INT/ORG BAL/PWR DIPLOM ECO/TAC FOR/AID ADMIN PWR...POLICY METH/CNCPT METH UN 20. PAGE 121 A2478 QUANT CHOOSE

B61
HARRISON S.,INDIA AND THE UNITED STATES. FUT S/ASIA USA+45 WOR+45 INTELL ECO/DEV ECO/UNDEV AGRI INDUS INT/ORG NAT/G CONSULT EX/STRUC TOP/EX PLAN ECO/TAC NEUTRAL ALL/VALS...MGT TOT/POP 20. PAGE 62 A1272 DELIB/GP ACT/RES FOR/AID INDIA

B61
HISTORICAL RESEARCH INSTITUTE,A SHORT BIBLIOGRAPHY OF INDO-MUSLIM HISTORY. INDIA S/ASIA DIPLOM EDU/PROP COLONIAL LEAD NAT/LISM ATTIT...BIOG 19/20. PAGE 65 A1343 BIBLIOG NAT/G SECT POL/PAR

B61
KERTESZ S.D.,AMERICAN DIPLOMACY IN A NEW ERA. COM S/ASIA UK USA+45 FORCES PROB/SOLV BAL/PWR ECO/TAC ADMIN COLONIAL WAR PEACE ORD/FREE 20 NATO CONGRESS UN COLD/WAR. PAGE 78 A1601 ANTHOL DIPLOM TREND

B61
ROBINS D.B.,EVOLVING UNITED STATES POLICIES TOWARD THE EMERGING NATIONS OF ASIA AND AFRICA (PAMPHLET). ISLAM ECO/UNDEV INT/ORG CONSULT CREATE PLAN TEC/DEV FOR/AID CONFER ALL/VALS 20 KENNEDY/JF EISNHWR/DD UN AID. PAGE 122 A2501 AFR S/ASIA DIPLOM BIBLIOG

B61
SYATAUW J.J.G.,SOME NEWLY ESTABLISHED ASIAN STATES AND THE DEVELOPMENT OF INTERNATIONAL LAW. BURMA CEYLON INDIA INDONESIA ECO/UNDEV COLONIAL NEUTRAL WAR PEACE SOVEREIGN...CHARTS 19/20. PAGE 140 A2873 INT/LAW ADJUST SOCIETY S/ASIA

S61
PADELFORD N.J.,"POLITICS AND THE FUTURE OF ECOSOC." AFR S/ASIA ECO/UNDEV INDUS NAT/G DELIB/GP ACT/RES ORD/FREE WEALTH...CONCPT CHARTS UN 20 ECOSOC. PAGE 113 A2310 INT/ORG TEC/DEV

S61
RAY J.,"THE EUROPEAN FREE-TRADE ASSOCIATION AND ITS IMPACT ON INDIA'S TRADE." EUR+WWI FRANCE GERMANY INDIA S/ASIA UK NAT/G VOL/ASSN PLAN INT/TRADE ROUTINE WEALTH...STAT CHARTS CMN/WLTH EEC OEEC 20 EFTA. PAGE 120 A2453 ECO/DEV ECO/TAC

S61
WEST F.J.,"THE NEW GUINEA QUESTION: AN AUSTRALIAN VIEW." WOR+45 INT/ORG VOL/ASSN LEGIT PERCEPT ...POLICY TIME/SEQ AUSTRAL VAL/FREE 20 CMN/WLTH. PAGE 163 A3320 S/ASIA ECO/UNDEV

B62
CALVOCORESSI P.,WORLD ORDER AND NEW STATES: PROBLEMS OF KEEPING THE PEACE. AFR EUR+WWI S/ASIA ELITES NAT/G ECO/TAC FOR/AID EDU/PROP COERCE ATTIT DRIVE ALL/VALS...GEN/LAWS COLD/WAR 20 UN. PAGE 23 A0471 INT/ORG PEACE

B62
CLUBB O.E. JR.,THE UNITED STATES AND THE SINO-SOVIET BLOC IN SOUTHEAST ASIA. ASIA CHINA/COM COM USA+45 USSR ECO/UNDEV INT/ORG NAT/G FORCES TOP/EX PLAN ECO/TAC DOMIN COERCE GUERRILLA ATTIT RIGID/FLEX...POLICY OBS TREND 20. PAGE 27 A0553 S/ASIA PWR BAL/PWR DIPLOM

B62
DUROSELLE J.B.,LES NOUVEAUX ETATS DANS LES RELATIONS INTERNATIONALES. AFR CHINA/COM FRANCE MOROCCO S/ASIA USSR ECO/UNDEV INT/ORG PLAN ECO/TAC EDU/PROP ATTIT DRIVE...TREND TOT/POP TUNIS 20. PAGE 39 A0806 NAT/G CONSTN DIPLOM

B62
GOLDWIN R.A.,WHY FOREIGN AID? - TWO MESSAGES BY PRESIDENT KENNEDY AND ESSAYS. S/ASIA USA+45 ECO/UNDEV 20 KENNEDY/JF THIRD/WRLD. PAGE 54 A1096 DIPLOM FOR/AID POLICY

B62
HUNTINGTON S.P.,CHANGING PATTERNS OF MILITARY POLITICS. EUR+WWI L/A+17C S/ASIA USA+45 WOR+45 CULTURE INT/ORG NAT/G CONSULT PLAN DOMIN EDU/PROP LEGIT DETER WAR ATTIT PERSON PWR...DECISION CONCPT SIMUL GEN/LAWS ANTHOL COLD/WAR 20. PAGE 69 A1419 FORCES RIGID/FLEX

B62
HUTTENBACK R.A.,BRITISH RELATIONS WITH THE SIND, 1799-1843. FRANCE INDIA UK FORCES...POLICY CHARTS BIBLIOG 18/19 SIND. PAGE 69 A1425 COLONIAL DIPLOM DOMIN S/ASIA

B62
JORDAN A.A. JR.,FOREIGN AID AND THE DEFENSE OF SOUTHEAST ASIA. PAKISTAN VIETNAM/S FINAN PLAN BUDGET ECO/TAC DETER WAR ORD/FREE...POLICY DECISION CENSUS CHARTS BIBLIOG 20. PAGE 75 A1535 FOR/AID S/ASIA FORCES ECO/UNDEV

B62
LEWIS J.P.,QUIET CRISIS IN INDIA. INDIA USA+45 CULTURE ECO/UNDEV AGRI INDUS PROC/MFG NAT/G PLAN TEC/DEV DRIVE PWR SKILL WEALTH...MYTH 20. PAGE 88 A1801 S/ASIA ECO/TAC FOR/AID

B62
MODELSKI G.,SEATO-SIX STUDIES. ASIA CHINA/COM INDIA S/ASIA INT/ORG NAT/G ECO/TAC DETER ATTIT ORD/FREE PWR...TIME/SEQ COLD/WAR TOT/POP 20 SEATO. PAGE 102 A2098 MARKET ECO/UNDEV INT/TRADE

B62
MONTGOMERY J.D.,THE POLITICS OF FOREIGN AID: AMERICAN EXPERIENCE IN SOUTHEAST ASIA. S/ASIA USA+45 NAT/G PROB/SOLV COLONIAL 20. PAGE 103 A2115 FOR/AID DIPLOM GOV/REL GIVE

B62
US DEPARTMENT OF THE ARMY,GUIDE TO JAPANESE MONOGRAPHS AND JAPANESE STUDIES ON MANCHURIA: 1945-1960. CHINA/COM NAT/G DIPLOM LEAD COERCE WAR ...CHARTS 19/20 CHINJAP. PAGE 152 A3105 BIBLIOG/A FORCES ASIA S/ASIA

L62
CORET A.,"LES PROVINCES PORTUGALLES D'OUTREMER ET L'ONU." AFR PORTUGAL S/ASIA WOR+45 LOC/G NAT/G DOMIN...CONCPT TIME/SEQ UN 20 GOA. PAGE 31 A0620 INT/ORG SOVEREIGN COLONIAL

L62
CORET A.,"L'INDEPENDANCE DU SAMOA OCCIDENTAL." S/ASIA LAW INT/ORG EXEC ALL/VALS SAMOA UN 20. PAGE 31 A0622 NAT/G STRUCT SOVEREIGN

L62
WILCOX F.O.,"THE UN AND THE NON-ALIGNED NATIONS." AFR S/ASIA USA+45 ECO/UNDEV INT/ORG TEC/DEV EDU/PROP RIGID/FLEX ORD/FREE PWR...POLICY HUM CONCPT STAT OBS TIME/SEQ STERTYP GEN/METH UN 20. PAGE 164 A3345 ATTIT TREND

S62
CORET A.,"LE STATUT DE L'ILE CHRISTMAS DE L'OCEAN INDIEN." FUT S/ASIA ECO/DEV ECO/UNDEV VOL/ASSN DELIB/GP PLAN...RELATIV OBS TIME/SEQ TREND AUSTRAL 20. PAGE 30 A0619 NAT/G INT/ORG NEW/ZEALND

S62
CORET A.,"LA DECLARATION DE L'ASSEMBLEE GENERAL DE L'ONU SUR L'OCTROI DE L'INDEPENDENCE AUX PAYS ET AUX PEUPLES." AFR ASIA ISLAM NIGERIA S/ASIA USSR WOR+45 ECO/UNDEV NAT/G DELIB/GP COLONIAL ALL/VALS ...CONCPT TIME/SEQ TREND UN TOT/POP 20 MEXIC/AMER. INT/ORG STRUCT SOVEREIGN

PAGE 31 A0621

S62
DIHN N.Q.,"L'INTERNATIONALISATION DU MEKONG." CAMBODIA LAOS VIETNAM WOR+45 INT/ORG NAT/G VOL/ASSN PEACE HEALTH...CONCPT TIME/SEQ CHARTS METH VAL/FREE 20. PAGE 37 A0761
S/ASIA DELIB/GP

S62
FISCHER G.,"UNE NOUVELLE ORGANIZATION REGIONALE: L'ASA." S/ASIA WOR+45 ECO/UNDEV VOL/ASSN PERCEPT RIGID/FLEX...TIME/SEQ 20 ASA. PAGE 46 A0935
INT/ORG DRIVE REGION

S62
JACOBSON H.K.,"THE UNITED NATIONS AND COLONIALISM: A TENTATIVE APPRAISAL." AFR FUT S/ASIA USA+45 USSR WOR+45 NAT/G DELIB/GP PLAN DIPLOM ECO/TAC DOMIN ADMIN ROUTINE COERCE ATTIT RIGID/FLEX ORD/FREE PWR ...OBS STERTYP UN 20. PAGE 73 A1486
INT/ORG CONCPT COLONIAL

S62
RUBINSTEIN A.Z.,"RUSSIA AND THE UNCOMMITTED NATIONS." AFR INDIA ISLAM L/A+17C LAOS S/ASIA ELITES ECO/UNDEV INT/ORG KIN CREATE PLAN TEC/DEV NAT/LISM RIGID/FLEX PWR WEALTH...METH/CNCPT TIME/SEQ GEN/LAWS WORK. PAGE 125 A2562
ECO/TAC TREND COLONIAL USSR

S62
SPECTOR I.,"SOVIET POLICY IN ASIA: A REAPPRAISAL." ASIA CHINA/COM COM INDIA INDONESIA ECO/UNDEV INT/ORG DOMIN EDU/PROP REGION RESPECT...CONCPT TREND TOT/POP COLD/WAR 20 CHINJAP. PAGE 135 A2774
S/ASIA PWR FOR/AID USSR

B63
ADLER G.J.,BRITISH INDIA'S NORTHERN FRONTIER: 1865-95. AFGHANISTN RUSSIA UK PROVS COLONIAL COERCE PEACE...GEOG CHARTS BIBLIOG 19 TREATY. PAGE 4 A0091
S/ASIA FORCES DIPLOM POLICY

B63
BRECHER M.,THE NEW STATES OF ASIA. ASIA S/ASIA INT/ORG BAL/PWR COLONIAL NEUTRAL ORD/FREE PWR 20 UN. PAGE 18 A0369
NAT/G ECO/UNDEV DIPLOM POLICY

B63
BROWN W.N.,THE UNITED STATES AND INDIA AND PAKISTAN (REV. ED.). INDIA PAKISTAN S/ASIA WOR+45 POL/PAR SECT INT/TRADE COLONIAL COERCE DISCRIM. PAGE 20 A0408
DIPLOM ECO/UNDEV SOVEREIGN STRUCT

B63
FIFIELD R.H.,SOUTHEAST ASIA IN UNITED STATES POLICY. S/ASIA USA+45 ECO/UNDEV NAT/G DIPLOM ECO/TAC ADMIN COERCE ORD/FREE...POLICY MAJORIT 20. PAGE 45 A0928
INT/ORG PWR

B63
HENDERSON W.,SOUTHEAST ASIA: PROBLEMS OF UNITED STATES POLICY. COM S/ASIA CULTURE STRATA ECO/UNDEV INT/ORG DELIB/GP ACT/RES ECO/TAC DOMIN EDU/PROP LEGIT COERCE ATTIT ALL/VALS...STAT TIME/SEQ ANTHOL VAL/FREE 20. PAGE 64 A1313
ASIA USA+45 DIPLOM

B63
INTERNATIONAL BANK RECONST DEV,THE WORLD BANK GROUP IN ASIA. ASIA S/ASIA INDUS TEC/DEV ECO/TAC...RECORD 20 IBRD WORLD/BANK. PAGE 71 A1451
INT/ORG DIPLOM ECO/UNDEV FINAN

B63
KAHIN G.M.,MAJOR GOVERNMENTS OF ASIA (2ND ED.). ASIA INDIA INDONESIA PAKISTAN S/ASIA DIPLOM...SOC 20 CHINJAP. PAGE 75 A1546
GOV/COMP POL/PAR ELITES

B63
LEE C.,THE POLITICS OF KOREAN NATIONALISM. KOREA S/ASIA DIPLOM REV WAR 14/20 CHINJAP. PAGE 86 A1759
NAT/LISM SOVEREIGN COLONIAL

B63
RUSK D.,THE WINDS OF FREEDOM. S/ASIA SOUTH/AFR INT/ORG FORCES NUC/PWR PEACE ORD/FREE 20 UN COLD/WAR. PAGE 125 A2569
DIPLOM FOR/AID INT/TRADE

B63
THIEN T.T.,INDIA AND SOUTHEAST ASIA 1947-1960. COM INDIA S/ASIA SECT DELIB/GP FOR/AID RACE/REL NAT/LISM SOCISM...CHARTS BIBLIOG 20 UN NEHRU/J TREATY. PAGE 143 A2917
DRIVE DIPLOM POLICY

B63
VON HALLER A.,DIE LETZTEN WOLLEN DIE ERSTEN SEIN. AFR S/ASIA INT/TRADE REV ORD/FREE SOVEREIGN 20. PAGE 160 A3251
FOR/AID ECO/UNDEV MARXISM CAP/ISM

S63
CHAKRAVARTI P.C.,"INDIAN NON-ALIGNMENT AND UNITED STATES POLICY." ASIA INDIA S/ASIA USA+45 CULTURE ECO/UNDEV NAT/G VOL/ASSN DELIB/GP TOP/EX FOR/AID NEUTRAL...POLICY HUM CONCPT RECORD GEN/LAWS 20. PAGE 25 A0515
ATTIT ALL/VALS COLONIAL DIPLOM

S63
DARLING F.C.,"THE GEOPOLITICS OF AMERICAN FOREIGN POLITICS IN ASIA." COM S/ASIA USA+45 USSR ECO/UNDEV NAT/G VOL/ASSN CONSULT PLAN GUERRILLA...STAT TOT/POP 20. PAGE 34 A0682
FORCES ECO/TAC FOR/AID DIPLOM

S63
GORDON B.,"ECONOMIC IMPEDIMENTS TO REGIONALISM IN SOUTH EAST ASIA." BURMA FUT S/ASIA THAILAND USA+45 AGRI INDUS R+D NAT/G PLAN ECO/TAC WEALTH...STAT CONT/OBS 20. PAGE 54 A1110
VOL/ASSN ECO/UNDEV INT/TRADE REGION

S63
GUPTA S.C.,"INDIA AND THE SOVIET UNION." CHINA/COM COM INDIA S/ASIA VOL/ASSN TOP/EX FOR/AID EDU/PROP PEACE PWR...RECORD COLD/WAR 20. PAGE 58 A1195
DISPL MYTH USSR

S63
WEISSBERG G.,"MAPS AS EVIDENCE IN INTERNATIONAL BOUNDARY DISPUTES: A REAPPRAISAL." CHINA/COM EUR+WWI INDIA MOD/EUR S/ASIA INT/ORG NAT/G LEGIT PERCEPT...JURID CHARTS 20. PAGE 163 A3311
LAW GEOG SOVEREIGN

S63
WYZNER E.,"NIEKTORE ASPEKTY PRAWNE FINANSOWANIA OPERACJI ONZ W KONGO I NA BEIZKIM WSCHODZIE." S/ASIA CONSTN FINAN INT/ORG TOP/EX...TIME/SEQ UN 20 CONGRESS. PAGE 168 A3426
FORCES JURID DIPLOM

N63
LIBRARY HUNGARIAN ACADEMY SCI,HUNGARIAN PUBLICATIONS ON ASIA AND AFRICA, 1950-1962: A SELECTED BIBLIOGRAPHY (PAMPHLET). AFR ASIA HUNGARY S/ASIA ECO/UNDEV NAT/G EDU/PROP ATTIT 20 UNESCO. PAGE 88 A1807
BIBLIOG REGION DIPLOM WRITING

B64
AFRO ASIAN SOLIDARITY AGAINST IMPERIALISM. AFR ISLAM S/ASIA ECO/UNDEV NAT/G POL/PAR TOP/EX PRESS ...INT ANTHOL 20 CHOU/ENLAI. PAGE 3 A0066
MARXISM DIPLOM EDU/PROP CHIEF

B64
BUTWELL R.,SOUTHEAST ASIA TODAY - AND TOMORROW. NAT/G COLONIAL LEAD REGION WAR CHOOSE WEALTH MARXISM 20. PAGE 23 A0458
S/ASIA DIPLOM ECO/UNDEV NAT/LISM

B64
DAVIES U.P. JR.,FOREIGN AND OTHER AFFAIRS. EUR+WWI L/A+17C S/ASIA USA+45 ECO/UNDEV CHIEF PLAN ECO/TAC PWR MARXISM 20 KENNEDY/JF UN. PAGE 34 A0688
DIPLOM NAT/G POLICY FOR/AID

B64
DE SMITH S.A.,THE NEW COMMONWEALTH AND ITS CONSTITUTIONS. AFR CYPRUS PAKISTAN S/ASIA INT/ORG NAT/G LEGIS LEGIT RIGID/FLEX PWR...CONCPT TIME/SEQ CMN/WLTH 20. PAGE 35 A0713
EX/STRUC CONSTN SOVEREIGN

B64
DUROSELLE J.B.,LA COMMUNAUTE INTERNATIONALE FACE AUX JEUNES ETATS. CHINA/COM COM S/ASIA USSR INT/ORG ROLE...ANTHOL 20 UN SEATO THIRD/WRLD. PAGE 40 A0808
DIPLOM COLONIAL ECO/UNDEV SOVEREIGN

B64
EMBREE A.T.,A GUIDE TO PAPERBACKS ON ASIA; SELECTED AND ANNOTATED (PAMPHLET). CULTURE SOCIETY ECO/UNDEV SECT DIPLOM COLONIAL MARXISM...SOC 20. PAGE 41 A0845
BIBLIOG/A ASIA S/ASIA NAT/G

B64
ESTHUS R.A.,FROM ENMITY TO ALLIANCE: US AUSTRALIAN RELATIONS. S/ASIA DIST/IND VOL/ASSN FORCES ATTIT 20 AUSTRAL TREATY CMN/WLTH. PAGE 42 A0863
DIPLOM WAR INT/TRADE FOR/AID

B64
FALL B.,STREET WITHOUT JOY. FRANCE USA+45 DIPLOM ECO/TAC FOR/AID GUERRILLA REV WEAPON...TREND 20. PAGE 44 A0894
WAR S/ASIA FORCES COERCE

B64
JANOWITZ M.,THE MILITARY IN THE POLITICAL DEVELOPMENT OF NEW NATIONS: AN ESSAY IN COMPARATIVE ANALYSIS. AFR ASIA ISLAM L/A+17C S/ASIA USA+45 ECO/UNDEV INT/ORG NAT/G POL/PAR DELIB/GP PLAN ECO/TAC DOMIN LEGIT COERCE ATTIT DRIVE RESPECT ...SOC CONCPT CENSUS VAL/FREE. PAGE 73 A1495
FORCES PWR

B64
LEGGE J.D.,INDONESIA. INDONESIA ELITES ECO/UNDEV POL/PAR CHIEF FORCES INT/TRADE COERCE CHOOSE ORD/FREE...SOC CHARTS BIBLIOG 16/20 CHINJAP. PAGE 86 A1765
S/ASIA DOMIN NAT/LISM POLICY

B64
MAHAR J.M.,INDIA: A CRITICAL BIBLIOGRAPHY. INDIA PAKISTAN CULTURE ECO/UNDEV LOC/G POL/PAR SECT PROB/SOLV DIPLOM ADMIN COLONIAL PARL/PROC ATTIT 20. PAGE 93 A1906
BIBLIOG/A S/ASIA NAT/G LEAD

B64
RAGHAVAN M.D.,INDIA IN CEYLONESE HISTORY, SOCIETY AND CULTURE. CEYLON INDIA S/ASIA LAW SOCIETY INT/TRADE ATTIT...ART/METH JURID SOC LING 20. PAGE 119 A2433
DIPLOM CULTURE SECT STRUCT

B64
REGALA R.,WORLD PEACE THROUGH DIPLOMACY AND LAW. S/ASIA WOR+45 ECO/UNDEV INT/ORG FORCES PLAN PROB/SOLV FOR/AID NUC/PWR WAR...POLICY INT/LAW 20. PAGE 120 A2456
DIPLOM PEACE ADJUD

B64
ROSECRANCE R.N.,THE DISPERSION OF NUCLEAR WEAPONS: STRATEGY AND POLITICS. ASIA COM FUT S/ASIA USA+45 INT/ORG NAT/G DELIB/GP FORCES ACT/RES TEC/DEV BAL/PWR COERCE DETER ATTIT RIGID/FLEX ORD/FREE ...POLICY CHARTS VAL/FREE. PAGE 123 A2530
EUR+WWI PWR PEACE

B64
SAKAI R.K.,STUDIES ON ASIA, 1964. ASIA CHINA/COM ISRAEL MALAYSIA S/ASIA USA+45 USSR ECO/UNDEV FAM
PWR DIPLOM

POL/PAR SECT CONSULT NAT/LISM...POLICY SOC 20 CHINJAP. PAGE 126 A2588

B64
TAYLOR E.,RICHER BY ASIA. S/ASIA CULTURE VOL/ASSN ACT/RES ATTIT DISPL PERSON ALL/VALS...INT/LAW MYTH SELF/OBS 20. PAGE 142 A2899 — SOCIETY RIGID/FLEX INDIA

L64
LLOYD W.B.,"PEACE REQUIRES PEACEMAKERS." AFR INDIA S/ASIA SWITZERLND WOR+45 INT/ORG VOL/ASSN PLAN PERSON PWR 20. PAGE 90 A1848 — CONSULT PEACE

L64
POUNDS N.J.G.,"THE POLITICS OF PARTITION." AFR ASIA COM EUR+WWI FUT ISLAM S/ASIA USA-45 LAW ECO/DEV ECO/UNDEV AGRI INDUS INT/ORG POL/PAR PROVS SECT FORCES TOP/EX EDU/PROP LEGIT ATTIT MORAL ORD/FREE PWR RESPECT WEALTH. PAGE 117 A2402 — NAT/G NAT/LISM

L64
SYMONDS R.,"REFLECTIONS IN LOCALISATION." AFR S/ASIA UK STRATA INT/ORG NAT/G SCHOOL EDU/PROP LEGIT KNOWL ORD/FREE PWR RESPECT CMN/WLTH 20. PAGE 140 A2874 — ADMIN MGT COLONIAL

S64
ASHRAF S.,"INDIA AND WORLD AFFAIRS: AN ANNUAL BIBLIOGRAPHY, 1962." WOR+45 LAW ECO/UNDEV INT/ORG FORCES PLAN ECO/TAC COERCE ORD/FREE PWR WEALTH ...HIST/WRIT VAL/FREE. PAGE 9 A0188 — S/ASIA NAT/G

S64
PALMER N.D.,"INDIA AS A FACTOR IN UNITED STATES FOREIGN POLICY." INDIA USA+45 USA-45 ECO/UNDEV NAT/G TOP/EX ECO/TAC EDU/PROP...METH/CNCPT TIME/SEQ 20. PAGE 113 A2323 — S/ASIA ATTIT FOR/AID DIPLOM

S64
SINGH N.,"THE CONTEMPORARY PRACTICE OF INDIA IN THE FIELD OF INTERNATIONAL LAW." INDIA S/ASIA INT/ORG NAT/G DOMIN EDU/PROP LEGIT KNOWL...CONCPT TOT/POP 20. PAGE 133 A2734 — LAW ATTIT DIPLOM INT/LAW

S64
TINKER H.,"POLITICS IN SOUTHEAST ASIA." INT/ORG NAT/G CREATE PLAN TEC/DEV GUERRILLA KNOWL ORD/FREE COLD/WAR. PAGE 144 A2944 — S/ASIA ACT/RES REGION

N64
GREAT BRITAIN CENTRAL OFF INF,THE COLOMBO PLAN (PAMPHLET). ASIA S/ASIA USA+45 VOL/ASSN...CHARTS 20 COMMONWLTH RESOURCE/N. PAGE 55 A1134 — FOR/AID PLAN INT/ORG ECO/UNDEV

B65
LERCHE C.O.,THE COLD WAR AND AFTER. AFR COM S/ASIA USA+45 USSR NUC/PWR SOVEREIGN MARXISM...TIME/SEQ TREND BIBLIOG 20 COLD/WAR. PAGE 87 A1784 — DIPLOM BAL/PWR IDEA/COMP

B65
NATIONAL BOOK CENTRE PAKISTAN,BOOKS ON PAKISTAN: A BIBLIOGRAPHY. PAKISTAN CULTURE DIPLOM ADMIN ATTIT ...MAJORIT SOC CONCPT 20. PAGE 107 A2201 — BIBLIOG CONSTN S/ASIA NAT/G

B65
ROMEIN J.,THE ASIAN CENTURY. ASIA COM S/ASIA DIPLOM COLONIAL TIME 20. PAGE 123 A2519 — REV NAT/LISM CULTURE MARXISM

B65
WARBEY W.,VIETNAM: THE TRUTH. FRANCE S/ASIA USA+45 VIETNAM CULTURE INT/ORG NAT/G DIPLOM FOR/AID EDU/PROP ARMS/CONT PEACE 20 TREATY NLF UN. PAGE 161 A3274 — WAR AGREE

B65
WITHERELL J.W.,MADAGASCAR AND ADJACENT ISLANDS; A GUIDE TO OFFICIAL PUBLICATIONS (PAMPHLET). FRANCE MADAGASCAR S/ASIA UK LAW OP/RES PLAN DIPLOM ...POLICY CON/ANAL 19/20. PAGE 165 A3371 — BIBLIOG COLONIAL LOC/G ADMIN

S65
PRABHAKAR P.,"SURVEY OF RESEARCH AND SOURCE MATERIALS; THE SINO-INDIAN BORDER DISPUTE." CHINA/COM INDIA LAW NAT/G PLAN BAL/PWR WAR...POLICY 20 COLD/WAR. PAGE 117 A2404 — BIBLIOG ASIA S/ASIA DIPLOM

S65
RAY H.,"THE POLICY OF RUSSIA TOWARDS SINO-INDIAN CONFLICT." ASIA CHINA/COM COM INDIA USSR NAT/G TOP/EX FOR/AID EDU/PROP NEUTRAL COERCE PEACE RIGID/FLEX PWR...METH/CNCPT TIME/SEQ VAL/FREE 20. PAGE 120 A2452 — S/ASIA ATTIT DIPLOM WAR

B66
SUPPLEMENTAL FOREIGN ASSISTANCE FISCAL YEAR 1966: VIETNAM. CHINA/COM COM S/ASIA USA+45 VIETNAM EXTR/IND FINAN DIPLOM TAX GUERRILLA HABITAT ORD/FREE...STAT CHARTS 20 SENATE PRESIDENT. PAGE 4 A0077 — CONFER LEGIS WAR FOR/AID

B66
AMERICAN ASSEMBLY COLUMBIA U,THE UNITED STATES AND THE PHILIPPINES. PHILIPPINE S/ASIA USA+45 USA-45 SOCIETY FORCES INT/TRADE...POLICY 20. PAGE 7 A0138 — COLONIAL DIPLOM NAT/LISM

B66
AMERICAN FRIENDS SERVICE COMM,PEACE IN VIETNAM: A NEW APPROACH IN SOUTHEAST ASIA: A REPORT. ASIA S/ASIA USA+45 VIETNAM ORD/FREE 20 TREATY. PAGE 7 A0149 — PEACE WAR NAT/LISM DIPLOM

B66
BRACKMAN A.C.,SOUTHEAST ASIA'S SECOND FRONT: THE POWER STRUGGLE IN THE MALAY ARCHIPELAGO. CHINA/COM INDONESIA MALAYSIA ECO/UNDEV INT/ORG NAT/G FORCES DIPLOM EDU/PROP REGION COERCE GUERRILLA AUTHORIT POPULISM...MAJORIT 20 KENNEDY/JF SEATO. PAGE 18 A0367 — S/ASIA MARXISM REV

B66
EMBREE A.T.,ASIA: A GUIDE TO BASIC BOOKS (PAMPHLET). ECO/UNDEV SECT FORCES DIPLOM ALL/IDEOS ...SOC 20. PAGE 41 A0846 — BIBLIOG/A ASIA S/ASIA NAT/G

B66
FALL B.B.,VIET-NAM WITNESS, 1953-66. S/ASIA VIETNAM SECT PROB/SOLV COLONIAL GUERRILLA...CHARTS BIBLIOG 20. PAGE 44 A0895 — MARXIST WAR DIPLOM

B66
FARWELL G.,MASK OF ASIA: THE PHILIPPINES. PHILIPPINE SECT DIPLOM ATTIT...SOC RECORD PREDICT BIBLIOG 20. PAGE 44 A0901 — S/ASIA CULTURE

B66
GORDON B.K.,THE DIMENSIONS OF CONFLICT IN SOUTHEAST ASIA. S/ASIA FORCES ADJUD REGION...CHARTS 20. PAGE 54 A1111 — DIPLOM NAT/COMP INT/ORG VOL/ASSN

B66
HANSEN G.H.,AFRO-ASIA AND NON-ALIGNMENT. AFR ASIA S/ASIA NEUTRAL MORAL 20. PAGE 61 A1255 — DIPLOM CONFER POLICY NAT/LISM

B66
HUTTENBACK R.A.,BRITISH IMPERIAL EXPERIENCE. S/ASIA UK WOR-45 INT/ORG TEC/DEV...CHARTS 16/20 COMMONWLTH MERCANTLST. PAGE 69 A1424 — COLONIAL TIME/SEQ INT/TRADE

B66
KEENLEYSIDE H.L.,INTERNATIONAL AID: A SUMMARY. AFR INDIA S/ASIA UK STRATA EXTR/IND TEC/DEV ADMIN RACE/REL DEMAND NAT/LISM WEALTH...TREND CHINJAP. PAGE 77 A1575 — ECO/UNDEV FOR/AID DIPLOM TASK

B66
KEYES J.G.,A BIBLIOGRAPHY OF WESTERN LANGUAGE PUBLICATIONS CONCERNING NORTH VIETNAM IN THE CORNELL LIBRARY. VIETNAM/N NAT/G FORCES TEC/DEV DIPLOM LEAD RACE/REL...GEOG SOC 20. PAGE 78 A1603 — BIBLIOG/A CULTURE ECO/UNDEV S/ASIA

B66
LEIGH M.B.,CHECK LIST OF HOLDINGS ON BORNEO IN THE CORNELL UNIVERSITY LIBRARIES (PAMPHLET). BORNEO MALAYSIA LAW CONSTN GP/REL SOC. PAGE 86 A1769 — BIBLIOG S/ASIA DIPLOM NAT/G

B66
TINKER H.,SOUTH ASIA. UK LAW ECO/UNDEV AGRI ACADEM SECT DIPLOM EDU/PROP REV WEALTH ALL/IDEOS...CHARTS BIBLIOG GANDHI/M NEHRU/J. PAGE 144 A2945 — S/ASIA COLONIAL TREND

B66
US DEPARTMENT OF STATE,RESEARCH ON AFRICA (EXTERNAL RESEARCH LIST NO 5-25). LAW CULTURE ECO/UNDEV POL/PAR DIPLOM EDU/PROP LEAD REGION MARXISM...GEOG LING WORSHIP 20. PAGE 152 A3094 — BIBLIOG/A ASIA S/ASIA NAT/G

B66
US DEPARTMENT OF THE ARMY,COMMUNIST CHINA: A STRATEGIC SURVEY: A BIBLIOGRAPHY (PAMPHLET NO. 20-67). CHINA/COM COM INDIA USSR NAT/G POL/PAR EX/STRUC FORCES NUC/PWR REV ATTIT...POLICY GEOG CHARTS. PAGE 152 A3109 — BIBLIOG/A MARXISM S/ASIA DIPLOM

B66
US DEPARTMENT OF THE ARMY,SOUTH ASIA: A STRATEGIC SURVEY (PAMPHLET NO. 550-3). AFGHANISTN INDIA NEPAL PAKISTAN ECO/UNDEV INT/ORG POL/PAR FORCES FOR/AID INT/TRADE LEAD WAR...POLICY SOC TREND 20. PAGE 152 A3110 — BIBLIOG/A S/ASIA DIPLOM NAT/G

B66
US SENATE COMM ON FOREIGN REL,ASIAN DEVELOPMENT BANK ACT. USA+45 LAW DIPLOM...CHARTS 20 BLACK/EUG S/EASTASIA. PAGE 156 A3186 — FOR/AID FINAN ECO/UNDEV S/ASIA

B66
VYAS R.,DAWNING ON THE CAPITOL: US CONGRESS AND INDIA. INDIA S/ASIA USA+45 ELITES ECO/DEV ECO/UNDEV PLAN FOR/AID...BIBLIOG 20 CONGRESS. PAGE 160 A3256 — POLICY LEGIS NAT/G DIPLOM

L66
BARMAN R.K.,"INDO-PAKISTANI RELATIONS 1947-1965: A SELECTED BIBLIOGRAPHY." INDIA PAKISTAN NAT/G 20. PAGE 11 A0223 — BIBLIOG DIPLOM S/ASIA

S66
"RESEARCH WORK 1965-1966." NEW/ZEALND ELITES ACADEM LOC/G MUNIC POL/PAR PROVS DIPLOM COLONIAL...SOC 20 AUSTRAL. PAGE 4 A0073 — BIBLIOG NAT/G CULTURE S/ASIA

S66
DINH TRANS V.A.N.,"VIETNAM: A THIRD WAY" S/ASIA USA+45 USSR VIETNAM VIETNAM/S NAT/G SECT FORCES CAP/ISM DIPLOM COLONIAL NEUTRAL MARXISM SOCISM 20 BUDDHISM UNIFICA. PAGE 38 A0766 — WAR PLAN ORD/FREE SOCIALIST

S66
GAMER R.E.,"URGENT SINGAPORE, PATIENT MALAYSIA." — DIPLOM

MALAYSIA S/ASIA ECO/UNDEV POL/PAR CHIEF TARIFFS TAX CONTROL LEAD REGION PWR 20 SINGAPORE. PAGE 51 A1036 NAT/G POLICY ECO/TAC

S66
MANSERGH N.,"THE PARTITION OF INDIA IN RETROSPECT." INDIA PAKISTAN S/ASIA UK DIPLOM COLONIAL GP/REL PWR 20. PAGE 94 A1933 NAT/G PARL/PROC POLICY POL/PAR

C66
TARLING N.,"A CONCISE HISTORY OF SOUTHEAST ASIA." BURMA CAMBODIA LAOS S/ASIA THAILAND VIETNAM ECO/UNDEV POL/PAR FORCES ADMIN REV WAR CIVMIL/REL ORD/FREE MARXISM SOCISM 13/20. PAGE 141 A2890 COLONIAL DOMIN INT/TRADE NAT/LISM

C66
WINT G.,"ASIA: A HANDBOOK." ASIA S/ASIA INDUS LABOR SECT PRESS RACE/REL MARXISM...STAT CHARTS BIBLIOG 20. PAGE 165 A3366 ECO/UNDEV DIPLOM NAT/G SOCIETY

B67
ANDREATTA L.,VIETNAM, A CHECKLIST. S/ASIA VIETNAM PRESS PEACE ATTIT...POLICY 20. PAGE 8 A0159 BIBLIOG DIPLOM WAR

B67
HOHENBERG J.,BETWEEN TWO WORLDS. ASIA S/ASIA USA+45 PRESS TV PERS/REL ISOLAT...INT CHARTS METH/COMP 20. PAGE 66 A1362 COM/IND DIPLOM EFFICIENCY KNOWL

B67
MCNELLY T.,SOURCES IN MODERN EAST ASIAN HISTORY AND POLITICS. KOREA VIETNAM CULTURE DIPLOM COLONIAL REV WAR PWR ALL/IDEOS MARXISM...ANTHOL 20 CHINJAP. PAGE 99 A2023 NAT/COMP ASIA S/ASIA SOCIETY

B67
MILLER J.D.B.,THE POLITICS OF THE THIRD WORLD. AFR S/ASIA 20 UN. PAGE 101 A2078 INT/ORG DIPLOM COLONIAL SOVEREIGN

B67
US AGENCY INTERNATIONAL DEV,PROPOSED FOREIGN AID PROGRAM FOR 1968: SUMMARY PRESENTATION TO THE CONGRESS. AFR S/ASIA USA+45 AGRI TEC/DEV DIPLOM ECO/TAC BAL/PAY COST HEALTH KNOWL SKILL 20 AID CONGRESS. PAGE 149 A3053 ECO/UNDEV BUDGET FOR/AID STAT

S67
BATOR V.,"ONE WAR* TWO VIETNAMS." S/ASIA VIETNAM DIPLOM SUFF ATTIT ORD/FREE 20. PAGE 12 A0234 WAR BAL/PWR NAT/G STRUCT

S67
FELDMAN H.,"AID AS IMPERIALISM?" INDIA PAKISTAN UK USA+45 BAL/PWR CAP/ISM DIPLOM ECO/TAC DOMIN BAL/PAY WEALTH...POLICY 20. PAGE 45 A0914 COLONIAL FOR/AID S/ASIA ECO/UNDEV

S67
NEUCHTERLEIN D.E.,"THAILAND* ANOTHER VIETNAM?" THAILAND ECO/UNDEV DIPLOM ADMIN REGION CENTRAL NAT/LISM...POLICY 20. PAGE 108 A2220 WAR GUERRILLA S/ASIA NAT/G

S67
PAUKER G.J.,"TOWARD A NEW ORDER IN INDONESIA." COM INDONESIA S/ASIA ECO/UNDEV POL/PAR EX/STRUC TOP/EX BAL/PWR ECO/TAC FOR/AID DOMIN NAT/LISM AUTHORIT ORD/FREE PWR 20. PAGE 114 A2342 REV NAT/G DIPLOM CIVMIL/REL

S67
ROSE S.,"ASIAN NATIONALISM* THE SECOND STAGE." ASIA COM ECO/UNDEV NAT/G PROB/SOLV DIPLOM FOR/AID DOMIN NEUTRAL REGION TASK...METH/COMP 20. PAGE 123 A2528 NAT/LISM S/ASIA BAL/PWR COLONIAL

C67
HUDSON G.F.,"THE HARD AND BITTER PEACE; WORLD POLITICS SINCE 1945." ASIA COM S/ASIA USSR WOR+45 COLONIAL WAR...TREND BIBLIOG/A 20 COLD/WAR UN. PAGE 68 A1405 DIPLOM INT/ORG ARMS/CONT BAL/PWR

S/EASTASIA....SOUTHEAST ASIA: CAMBODIA, LAOS, NORTH AND SOUTH VIETNAM, AND THAILAND

B66
US SENATE COMM ON FOREIGN REL,ASIAN DEVELOPMENT BANK ACT. USA+45 LAW DIPLOM...CHARTS 20 BLACK/EUG S/EASTASIA. PAGE 156 A3186 FOR/AID FINAN ECO/UNDEV S/ASIA

SAAB H. A2580

SAAR....SAAR VALLEY (GERMANY)

S62
GUETZKOW H.,"THE POTENTIAL OF CASE STUDY IN ANALYZING INTERNATIONAL CONFLICT." EUR+WWI FUT GERMANY INTELL SOCIETY STRUCT INT/ORG LOC/G NAT/G CONSULT CREATE PLAN CHOOSE ATTIT RIGID/FLEX ...POLICY SAAR 20. PAGE 58 A1188 EDU/PROP METH/CNCPT COERCE FRANCE

SABAH....SABAH, MALAYSIA

SABBATINO....SABBATINO CASE

B65
FALK R.A.,THE AFTERMATH OF SABBATINO: BACKGROUND PAPERS AND PROCEEDINGS OF SEVENTH HAMMARSKJOLD FORUM. USA+45 LAW ACT/RES ADJUD ROLE...BIBLIOG 20 EXPROPRIAT SABBATINO HARLAN/JM. PAGE 44 A0891 SOVEREIGN CT/SYS INT/LAW OWN

SABIN J. A2581

SABLE M.H. A2582,A2583,A2584

SACHS M.Y. A2585

SAGER P. A2586

SAHARA

B59
EGYPTIAN SOCIETY OF INT LAW,THE MONROVIA CONFERENCE (PAMPHLET). AFR ALGERIA FRANCE UAR CONFER REGION NUC/PWR WAR DISCRIM 20 SAHARA AFR/STATES. PAGE 40 A0826 COLONIAL SOVEREIGN RACE/REL DIPLOM

SAID A.A. A1782

SAINT AUGUSTINE....SEE AUGUSTINE

SAINT/PIER....JACQUES SAINT-PIERRE

SAINT-PIERRE C.I. A2587

SAINTSIMON....COMTE DE SAINT-SIMON

SAKAI R.K. A2588

SALARY....SEE WORKER, WEALTH, ROUTINE

SALAZAR/A....ANTONIO DE OLIVERA SALAZAR

B61
ACHESON D.,SKETCHES FROM LIFE. WOR+45 20 CHURCHLL/W EDEN/A ADENAUER/K SALAZAR/A. PAGE 4 A0085 BIOG LEAD CHIEF DIPLOM

SALANT W.S. A2589

SALETORE B.A. A2590,A2591

SALIENCE....SALIENCE

SALINGER/P....PIERRE SALINGER

SALISBURY H.E. A2592,A2593

SALKEVER L.R. A2594

SALO....SALO REPUBLIC

SALTER L.M. A2595

SALVADORI M. A2596

SALVEMINI G. A2597

SAMBURU....SAMBURU TRIBE OF EAST AFRICA

SAMOA....SEE ALSO WEST/SAMOA

B01
GRIFFIN A.P.C.,LIST OF BOOKS ON SAMOA (PAMPHLET). GERMANY S/ASIA UK USA-45 WOR-45 ECO/UNDEV REGION ALL/VALS ORD/FREE ALL/IDEOS...GEOG INT/LAW 19 SAMOA GUAM. PAGE 56 A1150 BIBLIOG/A COLONIAL DIPLOM

L62
CORET A.,"L'INDEPENDANCE DU SAMOA OCCIDENTAL." S/ASIA LAW INT/ORG EXEC ALL/VALS SAMOA UN 20. PAGE 31 A0622 NAT/G STRUCT SOVEREIGN

SAMP....SAMPLE SURVEY

B37
VINER J.,STUDIES IN THE THEORY OF INTERNATIONAL TRADE. WOR-45 CONSTN ECO/DEV AGRI INDUS MARKET INT/ORG LABOR NAT/G ECO/TAC TARIFFS COLONIAL ATTIT WEALTH...POLICY CONCPT MATH STAT OBS SAMP TREND GEN/LAWS MARX/KARL 20. PAGE 159 A3236 CAP/ISM INT/TRADE

B39
ROBBINS L.,ECONOMIC CAUSES OF WAR. WOR-45 ECO/DEV ECO/UNDEV INT/ORG NAT/G TEC/DEV DIPLOM DOMIN COLONIAL ATTIT DRIVE PWR WEALTH...POLICY CONCPT OBS SAMP TREND CON/ANAL GEN/LAWS MARX/KARL 20. PAGE 122 A2493 COERCE ECO/TAC WAR

B47
SOCIAL SCIENCE RESEARCH COUN,PUBLIC REACTION TO THE ATOMIC BOMB AND WORLD AFFAIRS. SOCIETY CONFER ARMS/CONT...STAT QU SAMP CHARTS 20. PAGE 135 A2757 — ATTIT NUC/PWR DIPLOM WAR

S47
RADVANYI L.,"PROBLEMS OF INTERNATIONAL OPINION SURVEYS." WOR+45 INT/ORG NAT/G CREATE ATTIT...PSY SOC METH/CNCPT REC/INT KNO/TEST SAMP/SIZ METH VAL/FREE 20. PAGE 118 A2431 — QU/SEMANT SAMP DIPLOM

S51
BUCHANAN W.,"STEREOTYPES AND TENSIONS AS REVEALED BY THE UNESCO INTERNATIONAL POLL." WOR+45 INT/ORG ATTIT DISPL PERCEPT RIGID/FLEX...INT TESTS SAMP 20. PAGE 21 A0424 — R+D STERTYP

S51
GYR J.,"ANALYSIS OF COMMITTEE MEMBER BEHAVIOUR IN FOUR CULTURES." ASIA ISLAM L/A+17C USA+45 INT/ORG VOL/ASSN LEGIT ATTIT...INT DEEP/QU SAMP CHARTS 20. PAGE 58 A1200 — DELIB/GP CULTURE

B58
SCOTT W.A.,THE UNITED STATES AND THE UNITED NATIONS: THE PUBLIC VIEW 1945-1955. USA+45 EDU/PROP ...INT QU KNO/TEST SAMP GP/COMP 20 UN. PAGE 130 A2674 — ATTIT DIPLOM INT/ORG

L59
GRANDIN T.,"THE POLITICAL USE OF THE RADIO." EUR+WWI SOCIETY INT/ORG DIPLOM CONTROL ATTIT ORD/FREE...CONCPT STAT RECORD SAMP GEN/LAWS TOT/POP 20. PAGE 55 A1128 — COM/IND EDU/PROP NAT/LISM

B60
PENTONY D.E.,THE UNDERDEVELOPED LANDS. FUT WOR+45 CULTURE AGRI FINAN INDUS MARKET INT/ORG LABOR NAT/G VOL/ASSN CONSULT TEC/DEV ECO/TAC EDU/PROP COLONIAL ATTIT WEALTH...OBS RECORD SAMP TREND GEN/METH WORK UN 20. PAGE 115 A2351 — ECO/UNDEV POLICY FOR/AID INT/TRADE

L60
DEUTSCH K.W.,"TOWARD AN INVENTORY OF BASIC TRENDS AND PATTERNS IN COMPARATIVE AND INTERNATIONAL POLITICS." UNIV WOR+45 SOCIETY STRUCT INT/ORG NAT/G CREATE PLAN EDU/PROP KNOWL...PHIL/SCI METH/CNCPT STAT SELF/OBS OBS/ENVIR SAMP TREND CON/ANAL CHARTS SOC/EXP GEN/METH 20. PAGE 36 A0739 — R+D PERCEPT

L60
FERNBACH A.P.,"SOVIET COEXISTENCE STRATEGY." WOR+45 PROF/ORG VOL/ASSN DIPLOM DOMIN EDU/PROP ATTIT DRIVE PERSON PWR SKILL WEALTH...POLICY OBS SAMP TREND STERTYP ILO WORK COLD/WAR 420. PAGE 45 A0919 — LABOR INT/ORG USSR

L60
RIGGS R.,"OVER-SELLING THE U.N. CHARTER, FACT AND MYTH." USA+45 SOCIETY NAT/G TOP/EX PLAN DIPLOM EDU/PROP PEACE ATTIT PERCEPT MORAL...POLICY SAMP UN 20. PAGE 121 A2481 — INT/ORG MYTH

S60
HAVILAND H.F.,"PROBLEMS OF AMERICAN FOREIGN POLICY." ASIA COM USA+45 WOR+45 INT/ORG NAT/G CONSULT ECO/TAC FOR/AID DOMIN COERCE NUC/PWR ATTIT DRIVE ORD/FREE PWR RESPECT SKILL...POLICY GEOG OBS SAMP TREND GEN/METH METH COLD/WAR UN 20. PAGE 63 A1292 — ECO/UNDEV FORCES DIPLOM

B61
YDIT M.,INTERNATIONALISED TERRITORIES. FUT WOR+45 WOR-45 CONSTN VOL/ASSN CREATE PLAN LEGIT PEACE ORD/FREE...GEOG INT/LAW JURID SOC NEW/IDEA OBS RECORD SAMP TIME/SEQ TREND 19/20 BERLIN. PAGE 169 A3431 — LOC/G INT/ORG DIPLOM SOVEREIGN

B62
BELL C.,NEGOTIATION FROM STRENGTH. WOR+45 FACE/GP INT/ORG DELIB/GP FORCES PLAN DOMIN COERCE NUC/PWR PEACE DRIVE PWR...POLICY LOG OBS RECORD INT SAMP TREND COLD/WAR 20. PAGE 13 A0255 — NAT/G CONCPT DIPLOM

B62
TRISKA J.F.,THE THEORY, LAW, AND POLICY OF SOVIET TREATIES. WOR+45 WOR-45 CONSTN INT/ORG NAT/G VOL/ASSN DOMIN LEGIT COERCE ATTIT PWR RESPECT ...POLICY JURID CONCPT OBS SAMP TIME/SEQ TREND GEN/LAWS 20. PAGE 145 A2966 — COM LAW INT/LAW USSR

B63
WALKER A.A.,OFFICIAL PUBLICATIONS OF SIERRA LEONE AND GAMBIA. GAMBIA SIER/LEONE UK LAW CONSTN LEGIS PLAN BUDGET DIPLOM...SOC SAMP CON/ANAL 20. PAGE 160 A3262 — BIBLIOG NAT/G COLONIAL ADMIN

S64
TRISKA J.F.,"SOVIET TREATY LAW: A QUANTITATIVE ANALYSIS." WOR+45 LAW ECO/UNDEV AGRI COM/IND INDUS CREATE TEC/DEV DIPLOM ATTIT PWR WEALTH...JURID SAMP TIME/SEQ TREND CHARTS VAL/FREE 20 TREATY. PAGE 145 A2967 — COM ECO/TAC INT/LAW USSR

B67
SCHWARTZ M.A.,PUBLIC OPINION AND CANADIAN IDENTITY. CANADA SOCIETY LOC/G DIPLOM ADMIN LEAD REGION GP/REL SAMP. PAGE 130 A2657 — ATTIT NAT/G NAT/LISM POL/PAR

S67
GLENN N.D.,"ARE REGIONAL CULTURAL DIFFERENCES DIMINISHING?" USA+45 DIPLOM RACE/REL AGE/Y AGE/A PERSON MORAL...GP/COMP 20. PAGE 53 A1081 — SAMP ATTIT REGION CULTURE

S67
ROGERS W.C.,"A COMPARISON OF INFORMED AND GENERAL PUBLIC OPINION ON US FOREIGN POLICY." USA+45 DIPLOM EDU/PROP ORD/FREE...POLICY SAMP IDEA/COMP 20. PAGE 123 A2515 — KNOWL ATTIT GP/COMP ELITES

SAMP/SIZ....SIZES AND TECHNIQUES OF SAMPLING

S47
RADVANYI L.,"PROBLEMS OF INTERNATIONAL OPINION SURVEYS." WOR+45 INT/ORG NAT/G CREATE ATTIT...PSY SOC METH/CNCPT REC/INT KNO/TEST SAMP/SIZ METH VAL/FREE 20. PAGE 118 A2431 — QU/SEMANT SAMP DIPLOM

B57
DEUTSCH K.W.,POLITICAL COMMUNITY AND THE NORTH ATLANTIC AREA: INTERNATIONAL ORGANIZATION IN THE LIGHT OF HISTORICAL EXPERIENCE. MOD/EUR USA+45 USA-45 SOCIETY FORCES TOP/EX CREATE PLAN DIPLOM DOMIN EDU/PROP LEGIT ATTIT ORD/FREE PWR...SAMP/SIZ TIME/SEQ CHARTS TOT/POP. PAGE 36 A0736 — EUR+WWI INT/ORG PEACE REGION

S58
BOGART L.,"MEASURING THE EFFECTIVENESS OF AN OVERSEAS INFORMATION CAMPAIGN." EUR+WWI GREECE USA+45 INT/ORG MUNIC PLAN DIPLOM PEACE PERCEPT RIGID/FLEX KNOWL...TECHNIC PSY SOC NEW/IDEA CONT/OBS REC/INT STAND/INT SAMP/SIZ COLD/WAR 20. PAGE 16 A0328 — ATTIT EDU/PROP

B59
SCHURZ W.L.,AMERICAN FOREIGN AFFAIRS: A GUIDE TO INTERNATIONAL AFFAIRS. USA+45 WOR+45 WOR-45 NAT/G FORCES LEGIS TOP/EX PLAN EDU/PROP LEGIT ADMIN ROUTINE ATTIT ORD/FREE PWR...SOC CONCPT STAT SAMP/SIZ CHARTS STERTYP 20. PAGE 129 A2653 — INT/ORG SOCIETY DIPLOM

S63
LERNER D.,"FRENCH ELITE PERSPECTIVES ON THE UNITED NATIONS." EUR+WWI INT/ORG HEALTH ORD/FREE PWR RESPECT...STAT INT SAMP/SIZ VAL/FREE UN 20. PAGE 87 A1786 — ATTIT STERTYP ELITES FRANCE

B67
MCCLINTOCK R.,THE MEANING OF LIMITED WAR. FUT WOR+45 NAT/G FORCES GUERRILLA REV...POLICY SAMP/SIZ TREND NAT/COMP 45 COLD/WAR. PAGE 97 A1999 — WAR NUC/PWR BAL/PWR DIPLOM

SAMPLE....SEE SAMP

SAMPLE AND SAMPLING....SEE UNIVERSES AND SAMPLING INDEX, P. XIV

SAMUELSN/P....PAUL SAMUELSON

SAN/FRAN....SAN FRANCISCO

SAN/MARINO....SAN MARINO

SAN/MARTIN....JOSE DE SAN MARTIN

SAN/QUENTN....SAN QUENTIN PRISON

SANCTION....SANCTION OF LAW AND SEMI-LEGAL PRIVATE ASSOCIATIONS AND SOCIAL GROUPS

B10
GRIFFIN A.P.C.,LIST OF REFERENCES ON RECIPROCITY (2ND REV. ED.). CANADA CUBA UK USA-45 WOR-45 NAT/G TARIFFS CONFER COLONIAL CONTROL SANCTION CONSEN ALL/VALS...DECISION 19/20. PAGE 56 A1157 — BIBLIOG/A VOL/ASSN DIPLOM REPAR

N19
MEZERIK A.G.,U-2 AND OPEN SKIES (PAMPHLET). USA+45 USSR INT/ORG CHIEF FORCES PLAN EDU/PROP CONTROL SANCTION ARMS/CONT 20 UN EISNHWR/DD. PAGE 100 A2060 — DIPLOM RISK DEBATE

B33
WAMBAUCH S.,PLEBISCITES SINCE THE WORLD WAR: WITH A COLLECTION OF OFFICIAL DOCUMENTS. WOR-45 COLONIAL SANCTION...MAJORIT DECISION CHARTS BIBLIOG 19/20 WWI. PAGE 161 A3272 — DIPLOM CONSTN NAT/G CHOOSE

B37
SCHUSTER E.,GUIDE TO LAW AND LEGAL LITERATURE OF CENTRAL AMERICAN REPUBLICS. L/A+17C INT/ORG ADJUD SANCTION CRIME...JURID 19/20. PAGE 129 A2654 — BIBLIOG/A REGION CT/SYS LAW

C43
BENTHAM J.,"PRINCIPLES OF INTERNATIONAL LAW" IN J. BOWRING, ED., THE WORKS OF JEREMY BENTHAM." UNIV NAT/G PLAN PROB/SOLV DIPLOM CONTROL SANCTION MORAL ORD/FREE PWR SOVEREIGN 19. PAGE 13 A0270 — INT/LAW JURID WAR PEACE

C51
LEONARD L.L.,"INTERNATIONAL ORGANIZATION (1ST ED.)" WOR+45 FINAN DELIB/GP ECO/TAC GIVE DOMIN SANCTION PEACE BIO/SOC ORD/FREE...INT/LAW 20 UN LEAGUE/NAT. PAGE 87 A1779 — BIBLIOG POLICY DIPLOM INT/ORG

B52
BASSETT R.,DEMOCRACY AND FOREIGN POLICY: A CASE HISTORY, THE SINOJAPANESE DISPUTE, 1931-1933. ASIA UK 20 CHINJAP. PAGE 11 A0233
DIPLOM WAR INT/ORG SANCTION

B54
LANDHEER B.,RECOGNITION IN INTERNATIONAL LAW (SELECTIVE BIBLIOGRAPHIES OF THE LIBRARY OF THE PEACE PALACE, VOL. II; PAMPHLET). NAT/G LEGIT SANCTION 20. PAGE 84 A1716
BIBLIOG/A INT/LAW INT/ORG DIPLOM

B60
THE AFRICA 1960 COMMITTEE,MANDATE IN TRUST; THE PROBLEM OF SOUTH WEST AFRICA. GERMANY STRUCT REGION SANCTION CHOOSE DISCRIM...INT/LAW 20 AFRICA/SW UN LEAGUE/NAT TRUST/TERR. PAGE 142 A2910
NAT/G DIPLOM COLONIAL RACE/REL

B62
SCHWARTZ L.E.,INTERNATIONAL ORGANIZATIONS AND SPACE COOPERATION. VOL/ASSN CONSULT CREATE TEC/DEV SANCTION...POLICY INT/LAW PHIL/SCI 20 UN. PAGE 130 A2656
INT/ORG DIPLOM R+D SPACE

B64
IRISH M.D.,WORLD PRESSURES ON AMERICAN FOREIGN POLICY. ASIA COM L/A+17C SOUTH/AFR UK WOR+45 ECO/DEV ECO/UNDEV COLONIAL SANCTION COERCE REV TOTALISM...ANTHOL 20 COLD/WAR EUROPE/W INTERVENT. PAGE 72 A1467
DIPLOM POLICY

B64
RUSSELL R.B.,UNITED NATIONS EXPERIENCE WITH MILITARY FORCES: POLITICAL AND LEGAL ASPECTS. AFR KOREA WOR+45 LEGIS PROB/SOLV ADMIN CONTROL EFFICIENCY PEACE...POLICY INT/LAW BIBLIOG UN. PAGE 126 A2576
FORCES DIPLOM SANCTION ORD/FREE

B64
SEGAL R.,SANCTIONS AGAINST SOUTH AFRICA. AFR SOUTH/AFR NAT/G INT/TRADE RACE/REL PEACE PWR ...INT/LAW ANTHOL 20 UN. PAGE 131 A2681
SANCTION DISCRIM ECO/TAC POLICY

B65
GEORGE M.,THE WARPED VISION. EUR+WWI UK NAT/G POL/PAR LEGIS PARL/PROC SANCTION COERCE WAR GOV/REL PEACE RESPECT 20 CONSRV/PAR. PAGE 52 A1061
LEAD ATTIT DIPLOM POLICY

B65
SHUKRI A.,THE CONCEPT OF SELF-DETERMINATION IN THE UNITED NATIONS. WOR+45 DIPLOM INT/TRADE SANCTION NAT/LISM...BIBLIOG 20 UN. PAGE 132 A2709
COLONIAL INT/ORG INT/LAW SOVEREIGN

B66
CLARK G.,WORLD PEACE THROUGH WORLD LAW; TWO ALTERNATIVE PLANS. WOR+45 DELIB/GP FORCES TAX CONFER ADJUD SANCTION ARMS/CONT WAR CHOOSE PRIVIL 20 UN COLD/WAR. PAGE 27 A0541
INT/LAW PEACE PLAN INT/ORG

B66
SANDERS R.E.,SPAIN AND THE UNITED NATIONS 1945-1950. SPAIN CHIEF DIPLOM CONFER SANCTION ATTIT ...POLICY 20 UN COLD/WAR. PAGE 127 A2599
INT/ORG FASCISM GP/REL STRANGE

B66
US HOUSE COMM FOREIGN AFFAIRS,UNITED STATES - SOUTH AFRICAN RELATIONS. SOUTH/AFR USA+45 NAT/G CONSULT DELIB/GP LEGIS CONFER SANCTION RACE/REL ATTIT 20 CONGRESS. PAGE 154 A3134
DISCRIM DIPLOM POLICY PARL/PROC

S66
GREEN L.C.,"RHODESIAN OIL: BOOTLEGGERS OR PIRATES?" AFR RHODESIA UK WOR+45 INT/ORG NAT/G DIPLOM LEGIT COLONIAL SOVEREIGN 20 UN OAU. PAGE 55 A1139
INT/TRADE SANCTION INT/LAW POLICY

L67
ANAND R.P.,"SOVEREIGN EQUALITY OF STATES IN INTERNATIONAL LAW." UNIV DIPLOM DOMIN CONFER DEBATE SANCTION ATTIT UN. PAGE 8 A0157
INT/LAW INT/ORG CONCPT POLICY

L67
CAHIERS P.,"LE RECOURS EN CONSTATATION DE MANQUEMENTS DES ETATS MEMBRES DEVANT LA COUR DES COMMUNAUTES EUROPEENNES." LAW PROB/SOLV DIPLOM ADMIN CT/SYS SANCTION ATTIT...POLICY DECISION JURID ECSC EEC. PAGE 23 A0465
INT/ORG CONSTN ROUTINE ADJUD

L67
GALTUNG J.,"ON THE EFFECTS OF INTERNATIONAL ECONOMIC SANCTIONS, WITH EXAMPLES FROM THE CASE OF RHODESIA." NAT/G DIPLOM EDU/PROP ADJUST EFFICIENCY ATTIT MORAL...OBS CHARTS 20. PAGE 51 A1035
SANCTION ECO/TAC INT/TRADE ECO/UNDEV

L67
MACDONALD R.S.J.,"THE RESORT TO ECONOMIC COERCION BY INTERNATIONAL POLITICAL ORGANIZATIONS." CUBA ETHIOPIA RHODESIA SOUTH/AFR NAT/G FOR/AID INT/TRADE DOMIN CONTROL SANCTION...DECISION LEAGUE/NAT UN OAS 20. PAGE 92 A1887
INT/ORG COERCE ECO/TAC DIPLOM

S67
BLUM Y.Z.,"INDONESIA'S RETURN TO THE UNITED NATIONS." INDONESIA ADJUD SANCTION REPRESENT ...JURID 20 UN. PAGE 16 A0324
CONSTN LAW DIPLOM INT/ORG

S67
COHN K.,"CRIMES AGAINST HUMANITY." GERMANY INT/ORG SANCTION ATTIT ORD/FREE...MARXIST CRIMLGY 20 UN. PAGE 28 A0564
WAR INT/LAW CRIME ADJUD

S67
FAWCETT J.E.S.,"GIBRALTAR* THE LEGAL ISSUES." SPAIN UK INT/ORG BAL/PWR LICENSE CONFER SANCTION PRIVIL ...JURID CHARTS 20. PAGE 44 A0905
INT/LAW DIPLOM COLONIAL ADJUD

S67
KRUSCHE H.,"THE STRIVING OF THE KIESINGER-STRAUS GOVERNMENT FOR NUCLEAR WEAPONS IS A THREAT TO EUROPEAN SECURITY." EUR+WWI GERMANY BAL/PWR SANCTION WEAPON PEACE ORD/FREE...MARXIST 20 NATO COLD/WAR. PAGE 82 A1688
ARMS/CONT INT/ORG NUC/PWR DIPLOM

S67
MUDGE G.A.,"DOMESTIC POLICIES AND UN ACTIVITIES* THE CASE OF RHODESIA AND THE REPUBLIC OF SOUTH AFRICA." RHODESIA SOUTH/AFR POL/PAR LEAD SANCTION CHOOSE RACE/REL CONSEN DISCRIM ATTIT...INT/LAW UN PARLIAMENT 20. PAGE 105 A2163
AFR NAT/G POLICY

S67
PEUKERT W.,"WEST GERMANY'S 'RED TRADE'." COM GERMANY INDUS CAP/ISM DOMIN SANCTION DEMAND PEACE UTIL...MARXIST 20 COLD/WAR. PAGE 115 A2371
DIPLOM ECO/TAC INT/TRADE

S67
RAMSEY J.A.,"THE STATUS OF INTERNATIONAL COPYRIGHTS." WOR+45 CREATE TEC/DEV DIPLOM CONFER CONTROL SANCTION OWN...POLICY JURID. PAGE 119 A2439
INT/LAW INT/ORG COM/IND PRESS

S67
STEEL R.,"WHAT CAN THE UN DO?" RHODESIA ECO/UNDEV DIPLOM ECO/TAC SANCTION...INT/LAW UN. PAGE 137 A2810
INT/ORG BAL/PWR PEACE FOR/AID

S67
YEFROMEV A.,"THE TRUE FACE OF THE WEST GERMAN NATIONAL-DEMOCRATS." GERMANY/W NAT/G DOMIN LEAD SANCTION WAR ATTIT PERSON...MARXIST 20. PAGE 169 A3433
POL/PAR TOTALISM PARL/PROC DIPLOM

C83
BURKE E.,"RESOLUTIONS FOR CONCILIATION WITH AMERICA" (1775), IN E. BURKE, COLLECTED WORKS, VOL. 2." UK USA-45 FORCES INT/TRADE TARIFFS TAX SANCTION PEACE...POLICY 18 PRE/US/AM. PAGE 21 A0436
COLONIAL WAR SOVEREIGN ECO/TAC

SAND P.T. A2598

SANDERS R.E. A2599

SANDERSON G.N. A2600

SANNWALD R.E. A2601

SANTAYAN/G....GEORGE SANTAYANA

SAO/PAULO....SAO PAULO, BRAZIL

SAPIN B.M. A2602,A2603

SAPIR/EDW....EDWARD SAPIR

SAPP B.B. A2604

SARAWAK....SARAWAK, MALAYSIA

SARBADHIKARI P. A2605

SARROS P.P. A2606

SARTRE/J....JEAN-PAUL SARTRE

SARVODAYA....SARVODAYA - GANDHIAN SOCIALIST POLITICAL IDEAL OF UNIVERSAL MATERIAL AND SPIRITUAL WELFARE; SEE ALSO GANDHI/M

SASKATCH....SASKATCHEWAN, CANADA

SATELLITE....SPACE SATELLITES

SATISFACTION....SEE HAPPINESS

SATOW E. A2607

SAUDI/ARAB....SAUDI ARABIA; SEE ALSO ISLAM

B60
GLUBB J.B.,WAR IN THE DESERT: AN R.A.F. FRONTIER CAMPAIGN. SAUDI/ARAB UK KIN SECT LEAD...GEOG 20 RAF. PAGE 53 A1083
COLONIAL WAR FORCES DIPLOM

B63
UAR MINISTRY OF CULTURE,A BIBLIOGRAPHICAL LIST OF ARABIAN PENINSULA. ISLAM SAUDI/ARAB YEMEN FINAN NAT/G DIPLOM 19/20. PAGE 146 A2990
BIBLIOG GEOG INDUS

SECT

SCHOOL....SCHOOLS, EXCEPT UNIVERSITIES

N
"PROLOG",DIGEST OF THE SOVIET UKRANIAN PRESS. USSR LAW AGRI INDUS PROVS SCHOOL DIPLOM GOV/REL ATTIT ...HUM LING 20. PAGE 4 A0081
BIBLIOG/A NAT/G PRESS COM

N
MURRA R.O.,POST-WAR PROBLEMS: A CURRENT LIST OF UNITED STATES GOVERNMENT PUBLICATIONS (PAMPHLET). WOR+45 SOCIETY FINAN INT/ORG SCHOOL WORKER TEC/DEV ECO/TAC...SOC 20. PAGE 106 A2180
BIBLIOG/A ADJUST AGRI INDUS

B16
ROOT E.,THE MILITARY AND COLONIAL POLICY OF THE US. L/A+17C USA-45 LAW SOCIETY STRATA STRUCT INT/ORG NAT/G SCHOOL FORCES EDU/PROP ALL/VALS...OBS VAL/FREE 19/20. PAGE 123 A2522
ACT/RES PLAN DIPLOM WAR

N19
SALKEVER L.R.,SUB-SAHARA AFRICA (PAMPHLET). AFR USSR EXTR/IND NAT/G SCHOOL DIPLOM COLONIAL WEALTH ...GEOG CHARTS 16/20. PAGE 127 A2594
ECO/UNDEV TEC/DEV TASK INT/TRADE

B40
BROWN A.D.,PANAMA CANAL AND PANAMA CANAL ZONE: A SELECTED LIST OF REFERENCES. PANAMA NAT/G SCHOOL DIPLOM HEALTH...GEOG SOC 20 CANAL/ZONE. PAGE 19 A0397
BIBLIOG/A ECO/UNDEV

B42
CONOVER H.F.,NEW ZEALAND: A SELECTED LIST OF REFERENCES (PAMPHLET). NEW/ZEALND ECO/UNDEV AGRI INDUS LABOR NAT/G SCHOOL FORCES DIPLOM COLONIAL WAR ...HUM 20. PAGE 29 A0595
BIBLIOG/A S/ASIA CULTURE

B49
BEHRENDT R.F.,MODERN LATIN AMERICA IN SOCIAL SCIENCE LITERATURE. STRUCT ECO/UNDEV SCHOOL DIPLOM INT/TRADE EDU/PROP...GEOG 20. PAGE 12 A0250
BIBLIOG/A SOC L/A+17C

B49
MARITAIN J.,HUMAN RIGHTS: COMMENTS AND INTERPRETATIONS. COM UNIV WOR+45 LAW CONSTN CULTURE SOCIETY ECO/DEV ECO/UNDEV SCHOOL DELIB/GP EDU/PROP ATTIT PERCEPT ALL/VALS...HUM SOC TREND UNESCO 20. PAGE 95 A1939
INT/ORG CONCPT

L49
UNESCO,"SOME SUGGESTIONS ON TEACHING ABOUT THE UN AND ITS SPECIALIZED AGENCIES." UNIV WOR+45 SOCIETY STRATA SCHOOL WAR ALL/VALS KNOWL...SOC CONCPT UNESCO 20 UN. PAGE 147 A3011
INT/ORG EDU/PROP

B50
BEHRENDT R.F.,MODERN LATIN AMERICA IN SOCIAL SCIENCE LITERATURE (SUPPLEMENTS I AND II). STRUCT ECO/UNDEV SCHOOL DIPLOM INT/TRADE...GEOG 20. PAGE 12 A0251
BIBLIOG/A SOC L/A+17C

B51
MCKEON R.,DEMOCRACY IN A WORLD OF TENSION. UNIV LAW INTELL STRUCT R+D INT/ORG SCHOOL EDU/PROP LEGIT ATTIT DRIVE PERCEPT PERSON...POLICY JURID PSY SOC CONCPT METH/CNCPT OBS UNESCO TOT/POP VAL/FREE. PAGE 98 A2015
SOCIETY ALL/VALS ORD/FREE

B52
UN DEPT. SOC. AFF.,PRELIMINARY REPORT ON THE WORLD SOCIAL SITUATION. ISLAM L/A+17C WOR+45 STRATA AGRI EXTR/IND INDUS INT/ORG SCHOOL ADMIN...GEOG SOC TREND UNESCO WORK FAO 20. PAGE 147 A2998
R+D HEALTH FOR/AID

B54
BINANI G.D.,INDIA AT A GLANCE (REV. ED.). INDIA COM/IND FINAN INDUS LABOR PROVS SCHOOL PLAN DIPLOM INT/TRADE ADMIN...JURID 20. PAGE 14 A0288
INDEX CON/ANAL NAT/G ECO/UNDEV

B57
DRUCKER P.F.,AMERICA'S NEXT TWENTY YEARS. USA+45 DIST/IND ACADEM MUNIC SCHOOL DIPLOM ECO/TAC AUTOMAT HABITAT HEALTH...SOC/WK TREND 20 URBAN/RNWL PUB/TRANS. PAGE 39 A0788
WORKER FOR/AID CENSUS GEOG

B62
THANT U.,THE UNITED NATIONS' DEVELOPMENT DECADE: PROPOSALS FOR ACTION. WOR+45 SOCIETY ECO/UNDEV AGRI COM/IND FINAN R+D MUNIC SCHOOL VOL/ASSN CONSULT PLAN TEC/DEV ECO/TAC EDU/PROP ADMIN ROUTINE RIGID/FLEX...MGT SOC CONCPT UNESCO UN TOT/POP VAL/FREE. PAGE 142 A2906
INT/ORG ALL/VALS

B63
BRITISH AID. UK AGRI DIST/IND INDUS SCHOOL TEC/DEV INT/TRADE COLONIAL DEMAND...TREND CHARTS 20. PAGE 3 A0064
FOR/AID ECO/UNDEV NAT/G FINAN

B63
BUTTS R.F.,AMERICAN EDUCATION IN INTERNATIONAL DEVELOPMENT. USA+45 WOR+45 INTELL SCHOOL DIPLOM EDU/PROP...BIBLIOG 20. PAGE 23 A0457
ACADEM FOR/AID CONSULT ECO/UNDEV

B63
FULBRIGHT J.W.,PROSPECTS FOR THE WEST. COM USA+45 USSR INT/ORG NAT/G SCHOOL PROB/SOLV NUC/PWR WAR PEACE ORD/FREE...PREDICT METH/COMP 20 DEGAULLE/C. PAGE 50 A1015
DIPLOM BAL/PWR CONCPT POLICY

B63
HARTLEY A.,A STATE OF ENGLAND. UK ELITES SOCIETY ACADEM NAT/G SCHOOL INGP/REL CONSEN ORD/FREE NEW/LIB...POLICY 20. PAGE 62 A1275 DIPLOM ATTIT INTELL ECO/DEV

B63
INTERAMERICAN ECO AND SOC COUN,THE ALLIANCE FOR PROGRESS: ITS FIRST YEAR: 1961-1962. AGRI SCHOOL PLAN TEC/DEV INT/TRADE TAX GIVE ADMIN WEALTH...SOC 20 SOUTH/AMER. PAGE 71 A1449 INT/ORG PROB/SOLV ECO/TAC L/A+17C

B63
MANGER W.,THE ALLIANCE FOR PROGRESS: A CRITICAL APPRAISAL. FUT L/A+17C USA+45 CULTURE ECO/UNDEV ACADEM NAT/G SCHOOL PLAN FOR/AID...POLICY OAS. PAGE 94 A1918 DIPLOM INT/ORG ECO/TAC REGION

B64
THE SPECIAL COMMONWEALTH AFRICAN ASSISTANCE PLAN. AFR CANADA INDIA NIGERIA UK FINAN SCHOOL...CHARTS 20 COMMONWLTH. PAGE 3 A0065 ECO/UNDEV TREND FOR/AID ADMIN

B64
AMERICAN ASSEMBLY,THE UNITED STATES AND THE MIDDLE EAST. ISRAEL USA+45 STRUCT ECO/DEV ECO/UNDEV INT/ORG NAT/G SCHOOL SECT VOL/ASSN EX/STRUC TEC/DEV NAT/LISM...SOC 20. PAGE 7 A0135 ISLAM DRIVE REGION

B64
DUBOIS J.,DANGER OVER PANAMA. FUT PANAMA SCHOOL PROB/SOLV EDU/PROP MARXISM...POLICY 19/20 TREATY INTERVENT CANAL/ZONE. PAGE 39 A0790 DIPLOM COERCE

B64
LUTHULI A.,AFRICA'S FREEDOM. KIN LABOR POL/PAR SCHOOL DIPLOM NEUTRAL REGION REV NAT/LISM PWR WEALTH SOCISM SOC/INTEG 20. PAGE 92 A1874 AFR ECO/UNDEV COLONIAL

B64
SULLIVAN G.,THE STORY OF THE PEACE CORPS. USA+45 WOR+45 INTELL FACE/GP NAT/G SCHOOL VOL/ASSN CONSULT EX/STRUC PLAN EDU/PROP ADMIN ATTIT DRIVE ALL/VALS ...POLICY HEAL SOC CONCPT INT QU BIOG TREND SOC/EXP WORK. PAGE 140 A2861 INT/ORG ECO/UNDEV FOR/AID PEACE

L64
SYMONDS R.,"REFLECTIONS IN LOCALISATION." AFR S/ASIA UK STRATA INT/ORG NAT/G SCHOOL EDU/PROP LEGIT KNOWL ORD/FREE PWR RESPECT CMN/WLTH 20. PAGE 140 A2874 ADMIN MGT COLONIAL

B65
COOMBS P.H.,EDUCATION AND FOREIGN AID. AFR USA+45 DIPLOM EFFICIENCY KNOWL ORD/FREE...ANTHOL 20 AID. PAGE 30 A0608 EDU/PROP FOR/AID SCHOOL ECO/UNDEV

B65
PANJAB U EXTENSION LIBRARY,INDIAN NEWS INDEX. INDIA ECO/UNDEV INDUS INT/ORG SCHOOL FORCES ADJUD WAR ATTIT WEALTH 20. PAGE 114 A2333 BIBLIOG PRESS WRITING DIPLOM

B65
US LIBRARY OF CONGRESS,A DIRECTORY OF INFORMATION RESOURCES IN THE UNITED STATES: SOCIAL SCIENCES. USA+45 ACADEM INT/ORG LABOR PROF/ORG PUB/INST SCHOOL SECT 20. PAGE 155 A3159 BIBLIOG R+D COMPUT/IR

S65
RODNEY W.,"THE ENTENTE STATES OF WEST AFRICA." AFR FRANCE USA+45 POL/PAR SCHOOL FORCES ECO/TAC COLONIAL PWR 20 AFRICA/W. PAGE 123 A2512 DIPLOM POLICY NAT/G ECO/UNDEV

B66
HOFMANN L.,UNITED STATES AND CANADIAN PUBLICATIONS ON AFRICA IN 1964. LAW AGRI INDUS SCHOOL...HUM SOC 20. PAGE 66 A1360 BIBLIOG AFR DIPLOM

B66
WELCH R.H.W.,THE NEW AMERICANISM, AND OTHER SPEECHES AND ESSAYS. USA+45 ACADEM POL/PAR SCHOOL VOL/ASSN FORCES CAP/ISM TAX REV DISCRIM 20 CIV/RIGHTS COLD/WAR BIRCH/SOC. PAGE 163 A3313 DIPLOM FASCISM MARXISM RACE/REL

B66
WILLIAMS P.,AID IN UGANDA - EDUCATION. UGANDA UK FINAN ACADEM INT/ORG SCHOOL PROB/SOLV ECO/TAC UTIL ...STAT CHARTS 20. PAGE 165 A3352 PLAN EDU/PROP FOR/AID ECO/UNDEV

SCHRADER A. A2813

SCHRADER R. A2644

SCHRAMM W. A2645

SCHREIBER H. A2646

SCHRODER P.M. A2647

SCHUMAN F.L. A2648, A2649, A2650, A2651

SCHUMANN H. A2652

SCHUMCHR/K....KURT SCHUMACHER

SCHUMPTR/J....JOSEPH SCHUMPETER

SCHURZ W.L. A2653

SCHUSTER E. A2654

SCHWARTZ H. A2655

SCHWARTZ L.E. A2656

SCHWARTZ M.A. A2657

SCHWARTZ M.D. A2658

SCHWARZ U. A2659

SCHWARZENBERGER G. A1578,A2660,A2661

SCHWEBEL M. A2662

SCHWEBEL S.M. A2663

SCHWELB E. A2664,A2665,A2666

SCHWERIN K. A2667

SCHWINN....ARNOLD, SCHWINN + COMPANY

SCI/ADVSRY....SCIENCE ADVISORY COMMISSION

SCIENCE....SEE PHIL/SCI, CREATE

SCIENTIFIC METHOD....SEE PHIL/SCI

SCITOUSKY T. A2668

SCOT/YARD....SCOTLAND YARD - LONDON POLICE HEADQUARTERS AND DETECTIVE BUREAU

B66
HOEVELER H.J.,INTERNATIONALE BEKAMPFUNG DES VERBRECHENS. AUSTRIA SWITZERLND WOR+45 INT/ORG CONTROL BIO/SOC...METH/COMP NAT/COMP 20 MAFIA SCOT/YARD FBI. PAGE 66 A1352 CRIMLGY CRIME DIPLOM INT/LAW

SCOTLAND....SCOTLAND

SCOTT A.M. A2669,A2670,A2671

SCOTT G.B. A0715

SCOTT J.B. A1059,A2672,A2673

SCOTT W.A. A2674

SCOTT W.E. A2675

SCREENING AND SELECTION....SEE CHOOSE, SAMP

SDR....SPECIAL DRAWING RIGHTS

SDS....STUDENTS FOR A DEMOCRATIC SOCIETY

SEA....LOCALE OF SUBJECT ACTIVITY IS AQUATIC

B21
BALFOUR A.J.,ESSAYS SPECULATIVE AND POLITICAL. SEA CULTURE CREATE WAR NAT/LISM PEACE LOVE...ART/METH INT/LAW CONCPT ANTHOL 20 JEWS. PAGE 10 A0211 PHIL/SCI SOCIETY DIPLOM

B36
HUDSON M.O.,INTERNATIONAL LEGISLATION: 1929-1931. WOR-45 SEA AIR AGRI FINAN LABOR DIPLOM ECO/TAC REPAR CT/SYS ARMS/CONT WAR WEAPON...JURID 20 TREATY LEAGUE/NAT. PAGE 69 A1409 INT/LAW PARL/PROC ADJUD LAW

B51
RAPPAPORT A.,THE BRITISH PRESS AND WILSONIAN NEUTRALITY. UK WOR-45 SEA POL/PAR WAR CHOOSE PEACE ATTIT PERCEPT...GEOG 20 WILSON/W. PAGE 119 A2446 PRESS DIPLOM NEUTRAL POLICY

B55
SVARLIEN O.,AN INTRODUCTION TO THE LAW OF NATIONS. SEA AIR INT/ORG NAT/G CHIEF ADMIN AGREE WAR PRIVIL ORD/FREE SOVEREIGN...BIBLIOG 16/20. PAGE 140 A2868 INT/LAW DIPLOM

B58
SOC OF COMP LEGIS AND INT LAW,THE LAW OF THE SEA... (PAMPHLET). WOR+45 NAT/G INT/TRADE ADJUD CONTROL NUC/PWR WAR PEACE ATTIT ORD/FREE...JURID CHARTS 20 UN TREATY RESOURCE/N. PAGE 135 A2756 INT/LAW INT/ORG DIPLOM SEA

B59
REIFF H.,THE UNITED STATES AND THE TREATY LAW OF THE SEA. USA+45 USA-45 SEA SOCIETY INT/ORG CONSULT DELIB/GP LEGIS DIPLOM LEGIT ATTIT ORD/FREE PWR WEALTH...GEOG JURID TOT/POP 20 TREATY. PAGE 120 A2459 ADJUD INT/LAW

B60
KINGSTON-MCCLOUG E.,DEFENSE; POLICY AND STRATEGY. UK SEA AIR TEC/DEV DIPLOM ADMIN LEAD WAR ORD/FREE ...CHARTS 20. PAGE 79 A1627
FORCES PLAN POLICY DECISION

B60
US HOUSE COMM. SCI. ASTRONAUT.,OCEAN SCIENCES AND NATIONAL SECURITY. FUT SEA ECO/DEV EXTR/IND INT/ORG NAT/G FORCES ACT/RES TEC/DEV ECO/TAC COERCE WAR BIO/SOC KNOWL PWR...CONCPT RECORD LAB/EXP 20. PAGE 154 A3141
R+D ORD/FREE

L60
DEAN A.W.,"SECOND GENEVA CONFERENCE OF THE LAW OF THE SEA: THE FIGHT FOR FREEDOM OF THE SEAS." FUT USA+45 USSR WOR+45 WOR-45 SEA CONSTN STRUCT PLAN INT/TRADE ADJUD ADMIN ORD/FREE...DECISION RECORD TREND GEN/LAWS 20 TREATY. PAGE 35 A0717
INT/ORG JURID INT/LAW

B61
SCHNAPPER B.,LA POLITIQUE ET LE COMMERCE FRANCAIS DANS LE GOLFE DE GUINEE DE 1838 A 1871. FRANCE GUINEA UK SEA EXTR/IND NAT/G DELIB/GP LEGIS ADMIN ORD/FREE...POLICY GEOG CENSUS CHARTS BIBLIOG 19. PAGE 129 A2636
COLONIAL INT/TRADE DOMIN AFR

B61
SOKOL A.E.,SEAPOWER IN THE NUCLEAR AGE. USA+45 USSR DIST/IND FORCES INT/TRADE DETER WAR...POLICY NAT/COMP BIBLIOG COLD/WAR. PAGE 135 A2763
SEA PWR WEAPON NUC/PWR

B61
WRINCH P.,THE MILITARY STRATEGY OF WINSTON CHURCHILL. UK WOR-45 SEA VOL/ASSN TEC/DEV BAL/PWR LEAD WAR PEACE ATTIT...POLICY 20 CHURCHLL/W. PAGE 168 A3421
CIVMIL/REL FORCES PLAN DIPLOM

L61
WRIGHT Q.,"STUDIES IN DETERRENCE: LIMITED WARS AND THE ROLE OF SEABORNE WEAPONS SYSTEMS." FUT USA+45 WOR+45 SEA INT/ORG NAT/G FORCES ACT/RES WAR WEAPON ORD/FREE TOT/POP 20. PAGE 168 A3415
TEC/DEV SKILL BAL/PWR DETER

B62
COLOMBOS C.J.,THE INTERNATIONAL LAW OF THE SEA. WOR+45 EXTR/IND DIPLOM INT/TRADE TARIFFS AGREE WAR ...TIME/SEQ 20 TREATY. PAGE 28 A0570
INT/LAW SEA JURID ADJUD

B62
MCDOUGAL M.S.,THE PUBLIC ORDER OF THE OCEANS. WOR+45 WOR-45 SEA INT/ORG NAT/G CONSULT DELIB/GP DIPLOM LEGIT PEACE RIGID/FLEX...GEOG INT/LAW JURID RECORD TOT/POP 20 TREATY. PAGE 98 A2007
ADJUD ORD/FREE

B63
US CONGRESS JOINT ECO COMM,DISCRIMINATORY OCEAN FREIGHT RATES AND BALANCE OF PAYMENTS. USA+45 SEA DELIB/GP DISCRIM...CHARTS 20 CONGRESS. PAGE 150 A3066
BAL/PAY DIST/IND PRICE INT/TRADE

B65
GRAHAM G.S.,THE POLITICS OF NAVAL SUPREMACY; STUDIES IN BRITISH MARITIME ASCENDANCY. UK SEA NAT/G BAL/PWR LEAD WAR WEAPON PEACE...POLICY 18/19 COMMONWLTH. PAGE 55 A1126
FORCES PWR COLONIAL DIPLOM

B65
GRETTON P.,MARITIME STRATEGY - A STUDY OF DEFENSE PROBLEMS. ASIA UK USSR DIPLOM COERCE DETER NUC/PWR WEAPON...CONCPT NAT/COMP 20. PAGE 56 A1147
FORCES PLAN WAR SEA

B66
SMITH D.M.,AMERICAN INTERVENTION, 1917. GERMANY UK USA-45 SEA FORCES DIPLOM INT/TRADE EDU/PROP COERCE WEAPON PEACE 20 WILSON/W WWI. PAGE 134 A2746
WAR ATTIT POLICY NEUTRAL

S67
KIPP K.,"DIE POLITISCHE BEDEUTUNG DER 'GEGENKUSTE' DARGESTELLT AM BEISPIEL DER USA IM 20. JAHRHUNDERT" USA+45 USA-45 SEA NAT/G CONTROL COERCE WAR...POLICY GEOG 20. PAGE 79 A1629
FORCES ORD/FREE DIPLOM DETER

SEABURY P. A2676,A2677

SEARA M.V. A2678

SEARCH FOR EDUCATION, ELEVATION, AND KNOWLEDGE....SEE SEEK

SEATO....SOUTH EAST ASIA TREATY ORGANIZATION; SEE ALSO INT/ORG, VOL/ASSN, FORCES, DETER

B57
NEHRU J.,MILITARY ALLIANCE (PAMPHLET). INDIA WOR+45 NAT/G PLAN DETER NUC/PWR WAR...POLICY ANTHOL NEHRU/J SEATO UN. PAGE 108 A2212
INT/ORG DIPLOM FORCES PEACE

B59
TUNSTALL W.C.B.,THE COMMONWEALTH AND REGIONAL DEFENCE (PAMPHLET). UK LAW VOL/ASSN PLAN AGREE REGION WAR ORD/FREE 20 CMN/WLTH NATO SEATO TREATY. PAGE 146 A2977
INT/ORG FORCES DIPLOM

S60
MODELSKI G.,"AUSTRALIA AND SEATO." S/ASIA USA+45 CULTURE INTELL ECO/DEV NAT/G PLAN DIPLOM ADMIN ROUTINE ATTIT SKILL...MGT TIME/SEQ AUSTRAL 20 SEATO. PAGE 102 A2097
INT/ORG ACT/RES

B61
WARNER D.,HURRICANE FROM CHINA. ASIA CHINA/COM FUT L/A+17C USA+45 CULTURE NAT/G FORCES TOP/EX FOR/AID DRIVE PWR...CONCPT TIME/SEQ SEATO WORK 20. PAGE 161 A3284
ATTIT TREND REV

S61
BURNET A.,"TOO MANY ALLIES." COM EUR+WWI UK WOR+45 WOR-45 ACT/RES PLAN DISPL PWR SKILL...TIME/SEQ 20 CMN/WLTH SEATO NATO CENTO. PAGE 22 A0438
VOL/ASSN INT/ORG DIPLOM

B62
AIR FORCE ACADEMY LIBRARY,INTERNATIONAL ORGANIZATIONS AND MILITARY SECURITY SYSTEMS (PAMPHLET) (SPECIAL BIBLIOGRAPHY SERIES, NUMBER 25). DIPLOM FOR/AID INT/TRADE NUC/PWR PEACE 20 UN NATO OAS SEATO LEAGUE/NAT. PAGE 5 A0104
BIBLIOG INT/ORG FORCES DETER

B62
DOUGLAS W.O.,DEMOCRACY'S MANIFESTO. COM USA+45 ECO/UNDEV INT/ORG FORCES PLAN NEUTRAL TASK MARXISM ...JURID 20 NATO SEATO. PAGE 38 A0779
DIPLOM POLICY NAT/G ORD/FREE

B62
MODELSKI G.,SEATO-SIX STUDIES. ASIA CHINA/COM INDIA S/ASIA INT/ORG NAT/G ECO/TAC DETER ATTIT ORD/FREE PWR...TIME/SEQ COLD/WAR TOT/POP 20 SEATO. PAGE 102 A2098
MARKET ECO/UNDEV INT/TRADE

B64
DUROSELLE J.B.,LA COMMUNAUTE INTERNATIONALE FACE AUX JEUNES ETATS. CHINA/COM COM S/ASIA USSR INT/ORG ROLE...ANTHOL 20 UN SEATO THIRD/WRLD. PAGE 40 A0808
DIPLOM COLONIAL ECO/UNDEV SOVEREIGN

B66
BRACKMAN A.C.,SOUTHEAST ASIA'S SECOND FRONT: THE POWER STRUGGLE IN THE MALAY ARCHIPELAGO. CHINA/COM INDONESIA MALAYSIA ECO/UNDEV INT/ORG NAT/G FORCES DIPLOM EDU/PROP REGION COERCE GUERRILLA AUTHORIT POPULISM...MAJORIT 20 KENNEDY/JF SEATO. PAGE 18 A0367
S/ASIA MARXISM REV

B66
SINGH L.P.,THE POLITICS OF ECONOMIC COOPERATION IN ASIA; A STUDY OF ASIAN INTERNATIONAL ORGANIZATIONS. ASIA INT/ORG ACT/RES PLAN GP/REL...POLICY GP/COMP BIBLIOG 20 UN SEATO. PAGE 133 A2733
ECO/UNDEV ECO/TAC REGION DIPLOM

B67
LAWYERS COMM AMER POLICY VIET,VIETNAM AND INTERNATIONAL LAW: AN ANALYSIS OF THE LEGALITY OF THE US MILITARY INVOLVEMENT. VIETNAM LAW INT/ORG COERCE WEAPON PEACE ORD/FREE 20 UN SEATO TREATY. PAGE 86 A1753
INT/LAW DIPLOM ADJUD WAR

SEATTLE....SEATTLE, WASHINGTON

SEC/EXCHNG....SECURITY EXCHANGE COMMISSION

SEC/REFORM....SECOND REFORM ACT OF 1867 (U.K.)

SEC/STATE....U.S. SECRETARY OF STATE

B60
AMERICAN ASSEMBLY COLUMBIA U,THE SECRETARY OF STATE. USA+45 ELITES NAT/G PLAN ADMIN GOV/REL CENTRAL ATTIT...POLICY MGT 20 SEC/STATE CONGRESS PRESIDENT. PAGE 7 A0136
DELIB/GP EX/STRUC GP/REL DIPLOM

B65
US SENATE COMM ON FOREIGN REL,HEARINGS ON THE FOREIGN ASSISTANCE PROGRAM. AFR ASIA L/A+17C USA+45 WOR+45 FORCES TEC/DEV BUDGET CONTROL WEAPON ORD/FREE 20 UN CONGRESS SEC/STATE. PAGE 156 A3183
FOR/AID DIPLOM INT/ORG ECO/UNDEV

SECOND REFORM ACT OF 1867 (U.K.)....SEE SEC/REFORM

SECRETARY OF STATE (U.S.)....SEE SEC/STATE

SECT....CHURCH, SECT, RELIGIOUS GROUP

N
AFRICANA NEWSLETTER. ECO/UNDEV ACADEM SECT DIPLOM PRESS COLONIAL NAT/LISM 20. PAGE 1 A0001
BIBLIOG/A AFR NAT/G

N
JOURNAL OF ASIAN STUDIES. CULTURE ECO/DEV SECT DIPLOM EDU/PROP WAR NAT/LISM...PHIL/SCI SOC 20. PAGE 1 A0013
BIBLIOG ASIA S/ASIA NAT/G

N
MIDDLE EAST JOURNAL. CULTURE SECT DIPLOM LEAD GOV/REL ATTIT...POLICY PHIL/SCI SOC LING BIOG 20. PAGE 1 A0019
BIBLIOG ISLAM NAT/G ECO/UNDEV

N
AFRICAN BIBLIOGRAPHIC CENTER,A CURRENT BIBLIOGRAPHY ON AFRICAN AFFAIRS. LAW CULTURE ECO/UNDEV LABOR SECT DIPLOM FOR/AID COLONIAL NAT/LISM...LING 20. PAGE 5 A0094
BIBLIOG/A AFR NAT/G REGION

N
CORDIER H.,BIBLIOTECA SINICA. SOCIETY STRUCT SECT DIPLOM COLONIAL...GEOG SOC CON/ANAL. PAGE 30 A0618
BIBLIOG/A NAT/G CULTURE ASIA

B01
HART A.B.,AMERICAN HISTORY TOLD BY CONTEMPORARIES. UK CULTURE FINAN SECT FORCES DIPLOM TAX RUMOR CT/SYS REV GOV/REL GP/REL...ANTHOL 17/18 PRE/US/AM FEDERALIST. PAGE 62 A1273
USA-45 COLONIAL SOVEREIGN

B02
MOREL E.D.,AFFAIRS OF WEST AFRICA. UK FINAN INDUS FAM KIN SECT CHIEF WORKER DIPLOM RACE/REL LITERACY HEALTH...CHARTS 18/20 AFRICA/W NEGRO. PAGE 104 A2129
COLONIAL ADMIN AFR

C05
DUNNING W.A.,"HISTORY OF POLITICAL THEORIES FROM LUTHER TO MONTESQUIEU." LAW NAT/G SECT DIPLOM REV WAR ORD/FREE SOVEREIGN CONSERVE...TRADIT BIBLIOG 16/18. PAGE 39 A0803
PHIL/SCI CONCPT GEN/LAWS

B10
MENDELSSOHN S.,SOUTH AFRICAN BIBLIOGRAPHY (2 VOLS.). SOUTH/AFR EXTR/IND LABOR SECT DIPLOM INT/TRADE COLONIAL RACE/REL DISCRIM...GEOG 20. PAGE 99 A2038
BIBLIOG/A AFR NAT/G NAT/LISM

B16
PUFENDORF S.,LAW OF NATURE AND OF NATIONS (ABRIDGED). UNIV LAW NAT/G DIPLOM AGREE WAR PERSON ALL/VALS PWR...POLICY 18 DEITY NATURL/LAW. PAGE 118 A2416
CONCPT INT/LAW SECT MORAL

B17
DE VICTORIA F.,DE INDIS ET DE JURE BELLI (1557) IN F. DE VICTORIA, DE INDIS ET DE JURE BELLI REFLECTIONES. UNIV NAT/G SECT CHIEF PARTIC COERCE PEACE MORAL...POLICY 16 INDIAN/AM CHRISTIAN CONSCN/OBJ. PAGE 35 A0715
WAR INT/LAW OWN

N17
BURKE E.,THOUGHTS ON THE PROSPECT OF A REGICIDE PEACE (PAMPHLET). FRANCE UK SECT DOMIN MURDER PEACE ORD/FREE SOVEREIGN POPULISM...POLICY GOV/COMP IDEA/COMP 18 JACOBINISM COEXIST. PAGE 21 A0435
REV CHIEF NAT/G DIPLOM

B19
VANDERPOL A.,LA DOCTRINE SCOLASTIQUE DU DROIT DE GUERRE. CHRIST-17C FORCES DIPLOM LEGIT SUPEGO MORAL ...BIOG AQUINAS/T SUAREZ/F CHRISTIAN. PAGE 158 A3220
WAR SECT INT/LAW

B22
FICHTE J.G.,ADDRESSES TO THE GERMAN NATION. GERMANY PRUSSIA ELITES NAT/G SECT CREATE INT/TRADE HEREDITY ...ART/METH LING 19 FRANK/PARL. PAGE 45 A0923
NAT/LISM CULTURE EDU/PROP REGION

B24
GENTILI A.,DE LEGATIONIBUS. CHRIST-17C NAT/G SECT CONSULT LEGIT...POLICY CATH JURID CONCPT MYTH. PAGE 52 A1058
DIPLOM INT/LAW INT/ORG LAW

B25
GODET M.,INDEX BIBLIOGRAPHICUS: INTERNATIONAL CATALOGUE OF SOURCES OF CURRENT BIBLIOGRAPHIC INFORMATION. EUR+WWI MOD/EUR SOCIETY SECT TAX ...JURID PHIL/SCI SOC MATH. PAGE 53 A1085
BIBLIOG/A DIPLOM EDU/PROP LAW

B27
GOOCH G.P.,ENGLISH DEMOCRATIC IDEAS IN THE SEVENTEENTH CENTURY (2ND ED.). UK LAW SECT FORCES DIPLOM LEAD PARL/PROC REV ATTIT AUTHORIT...ANARCH CONCPT 17 PARLIAMENT CMN/WLTH REFORMERS. PAGE 54 A1100
IDEA/COMP MAJORIT EX/STRUC CONSERVE

B27
PARRINGTON V.L.,MAIN CURRENTS IN AMERICAN THOUGHT (VOL.I). USA-45 AGRI POL/PAR DIPLOM TAX REGION REV 17/18 FRANKLIN/B JEFFERSN/T. PAGE 114 A2336
COLONIAL SECT FEEDBACK ALL/IDEOS

B28
PLAYNE C.E.,THE PRE-WAR MIND IN BRITAIN. GERMANY MOD/EUR UK STRATA SECT DIPLOM EDU/PROP CROWD SUFF ...POLICY ANARCH PSY SOC IDEA/COMP 20 WWI. PAGE 116 A2388
PRESS WAR DOMIN ATTIT

B29
BOUDET P.,BIBLIOGRAPHIE DE L'INDOCHINE FRANCAISE. S/ASIA VIETNAM SECT...GEOG LING 20. PAGE 17 A0344
BIBLIOG ADMIN COLONIAL DIPLOM

B30
SMUTS J.C.,AFRICA AND SOME WORLD PROBLEMS. RHODESIA SOUTH/AFR CULTURE ECO/UNDEV INDUS INT/ORG SECT PROB/SOLV REGION GOV/REL DISCRIM ATTIT 19/20 LEAGUE/NAT LIVNGSTN/D NEGRO. PAGE 134 A2748
LEGIS AFR COLONIAL RACE/REL

B31
BORCHARD E.H.,GUIDE TO THE LAW AND LEGAL LITERATURE OF FRANCE. FRANCE FINAN INDUS LABOR SECT LEGIS ADMIN COLONIAL CRIME OWN...INT/LAW 20. PAGE 17 A0337
BIBLIOG/A LAW CONSTN METH

B32
BRYCE J.,THE HOLY ROMAN EMPIRE. GERMANY ITALY MOD/EUR CULTURE SOCIETY STRUCT INT/ORG NAT/G SECT DIPLOM DOMIN WAR SUPEGO ALL/VALS SOVEREIGN...GEOG SOC TIME/SEQ CHARTS STERTYP. PAGE 20 A0413
CHRIST-17C NAT/LISM

B33
AMERICAN FOREIGN LAW ASSN,BIOGRAPHICAL NOTES ON THE LAWS AND LEGAL LITERATURE OF URUGUAY AND CURACAO. URUGUAY CONSTN FINAN SECT FORCES JUDGE DIPLOM INT/TRADE ADJUD CT/SYS CRIME 20. PAGE 7 A0147
BIBLIOG/A LAW JURID ADMIN

B33
FERRERO G.,PEACE AND WAR (TRANS. BY BERTHA PRITCHARD). CULTURE FINAN SECT ATTIT SUPEGO MORAL ORD/FREE CONSERVE POPULISM SOCISM POLICY. PAGE 45 A0922
WAR PEACE DIPLOM PROB/SOLV

B34
EINSTEIN A.,THE WORLD AS I SEE IT. WOR-45 INTELL R+D INT/ORG NAT/G SECT VOL/ASSN FORCES CREATE EDU/PROP LEGIT ARMS/CONT WAR WEAPON NAT/LISM ALL/VALS...POLICY CONCPT 20. PAGE 41 A0828
SOCIETY PHIL/SCI DIPLOM PACIFISM

B36
THWAITE D.,THE SEETHING AFRICAN POT: A STUDY OF BLACK NATIONALISM 1882-1935. ETHIOPIA SECT VOL/ASSN COERCE GUERRILLA MURDER DISCRIM MARXISM...PSY TIME/SEQ 18/20 NEGRO. PAGE 144 A2939
NAT/LISM AFR RACE/REL DIPLOM

B37
BORGESE G.A.,GOLIATH: THE MARCH OF FASCISM. GERMANY ITALY LAW POL/PAR SECT DIPLOM SOCISM...JURID MYTH 20 DANTE MACHIAVELL MUSSOLIN/B. PAGE 17 A0341
POLICY NAT/LISM FASCISM NAT/G

B38
WARE E.E.,THE STUDY OF INTERNATIONAL RELATIONS IN THE UNITED STATES. USA+45 USA-45 WOR-45 INTELL SERV/IND INT/ORG NAT/G PROF/ORG SECT CONSULT INT/TRADE EDU/PROP ARMS/CONT...CONCPT 20. PAGE 161 A3283
KNOWL DIPLOM

B39
DULLES J.,WAR, PEACE AND CHANGE. FRANCE ITALY UK USA-45 WOR-45 LAW INT/ORG NAT/G SECT VOL/ASSN FORCES TOP/EX DOMIN ARMS/CONT COERCE ATTIT PERSON RIGID/FLEX MORAL PWR...JURID STERTYP TOT/POP LEAGUE/NAT 20. PAGE 39 A0796
EDU/PROP TOTALISM WAR

C39
SCOTT J.B.,"LAW, THESTATE, AND THE INTERNATIONAL COMMUNITY (2 VOLS.)" INTELL INT/ORG NAT/G SECT INT/TRADE WAR...INT/LAW GEN/LAWS BIBLIOG. PAGE 130 A2672
LAW PHIL/SCI DIPLOM CONCPT

B40
NIEBUHR R.,CHRISTIANITY AND POWER POLITICS. WOR-45 SECT DIPLOM GP/REL SUPEGO ALL/IDEOS WORSHIP 20 CHRISTIAN. PAGE 109 A2234
PARTIC PEACE MORAL

B41
KEESING F.M.,THE SOUTH SEAS IN THE MODERN WORLD. INDONESIA STRUCT FAM SECT EDU/PROP LEAD INCOME WEALTH...HEAL SOC 20. PAGE 77 A1577
CULTURE ECO/UNDEV GOV/COMP DIPLOM

B42
CONOVER H.F.,FRENCH COLONIES IN AFRICA: A LIST OF REFERENCES. ALGERIA FRANCE MOROCCO SOMALIA SUDAN CULTURE AGRI LOC/G SECT FORCES DIPLOM INT/TRADE NAT/LISM HEALTH...CON/ANAL 20. PAGE 29 A0594
BIBLIOG AFR ECO/UNDEV COLONIAL

B43
BROWN A.D.,GREECE: SELECTED LIST OF REFERENCES. GREECE ECO/UNDEV AGRI FINAN INDUS LABOR SECT TEC/DEV INT/TRADE LEAD...SOC 20. PAGE 20 A0399
BIBLIOG/A WAR DIPLOM NAT/G

L44
HAILEY,"THE FUTURE OF COLONIAL PEOPLES." WOR-45 CONSTN CULTURE ECO/UNDEV AGRI MARKET INT/ORG NAT/G SECT CONSULT ECO/TAC LEGIT ADMIN NAT/LISM ALL/VALS ...SOC OBS TREND STERTYP CMN/WLTH LEAGUE/NAT PARLIAMENT 20. PAGE 59 A1218
PLAN CONCPT DIPLOM UK

C44
SUAREZ F.,"ON WAR" (1621) IN SELECTIONS FROM THREE WORKS, VOL. I." NAT/G SECT CHIEF DIPLOM LEGIT MORAL PWR...POLICY INT/LAW 17. PAGE 140 A2859
WAR REV ORD/FREE CATH

C44
VAN VALKENBURG S.,"ELEMENTS OF POLITICAL GEOGRAPHY." FRANCE COM/IND INDUS NAT/G SECT RACE/REL...LING TREND GEN/LAWS BIBLIOG 20. PAGE 158 A3215
GEOG DIPLOM COLONIAL

B45
CONOVER H.F.,THE NAZI STATE: WAR CRIMES AND WAR CRIMINALS. GERMANY CULTURE NAT/G SECT FORCES DIPLOM INT/TRADE EDU/PROP...INT/LAW BIOG HIST/WRIT TIME/SEQ 20. PAGE 30 A0600
BIBLIOG WAR CRIME

B45
WOOLBERT R.G.,FOREIGN AFFAIRS BIBLIOGRAPHY, 1932-1942. INT/ORG SECT INT/TRADE COLONIAL RACE/REL NAT/LISM...GEOG INT/LAW GOV/COMP IDEA/COMP 20. PAGE 167 A3393
BIBLIOG/A DIPLOM WAR

N46
HOBBS C.C.,SOUTHEAST ASIA, 1935-45: A SELECTED LIST OF REFERENCE BOOKS (PAMPHLET). S/ASIA AGRI INDUS NAT/G SECT DIPLOM WAR...ART/METH GEOG SOC LING 20. PAGE 65 A1346
BIBLIOG/A CULTURE HABITAT

B47
NIEBUHR R.,THE CHILDREN OF LIGHT AND THE CHILDREN OF DARKNESS: A VINDICATION OF DEMOCRACY AND
POPULISM DIPLOM

CRITIQUE OF TRADITIONAL DEFENSE. UNIV STRUCT NAT/G SECT INGP/REL OWN PEACE ORD/FREE MARXISM ...IDEA/COMP GEN/LAWS 20 CHRISTIAN. PAGE 109 A2235
NEIGH GP/REL

B49
KAFKA G.,FREIHEIT UND ANARCHIE. SECT COERCE DETER WAR ATTIT...IDEA/COMP 20 NATO. PAGE 75 A1545
CONCPT ORD/FREE JURID INT/ORG

B50
CORNELL U DEPT ASIAN STUDIES,SOUTHEAST ASIA PROGRAM DATA PAPER. BURMA CAMBODIA INDONESIA MALAYSIA VIETNAM SOCIETY STRUCT NAT/G SECT DIPLOM FOR/AID PWR WEALTH...SOC 20. PAGE 31 A0625
BIBLIOG/A CULTURE S/ASIA ECO/UNDEV

B50
COUNCIL BRITISH NATIONAL BIB,BRITISH NATIONAL BIBLIOGRAPHY. UK AGRI CONSTRUC PERF/ART POL/PAR SECT CREATE INT/TRADE LEAD...HUM JURID PHIL/SCI 20. PAGE 31 A0637
BIBLIOG/A NAT/G TEC/DEV DIPLOM

B50
DULLES J.F.,WAR OR PEACE. CHINA/COM USA+45 USSR INT/ORG SECT FORCES PLAN NUC/PWR WAR CENTRAL MARXISM...POLICY 20 UN ROOSEVLT/F STALIN/J. PAGE 39 A0797
PEACE DIPLOM TREND ORD/FREE

B50
FIGANIERE J.C.,BIBLIOTHECA HISTORICA PORTUGUEZA. BRAZIL PORTUGAL SECT ADMIN. PAGE 45 A0929
BIBLIOG NAT/G DIPLOM COLONIAL

B50
MUGRIDGE D.H.,AMERICAN HISTORY AND CIVILIZATION: LIST OF GUIDES AND ANNOTATED OR SELECTIVE BIBLIOGRAPHIES. NAT/G SECT DIPLOM RACE/REL DISCRIM ATTIT...ART/METH SOC 18/20. PAGE 105 A2164
BIBLIOG/A USA-45 SOCIETY

B51
BLANSHARD P.,COMMUNISM, DEMOCRACY AND CATHOLIC POWER. USSR VATICAN WOR+45 WOR-45 CULTURE ELITES INTELL SOCIETY STRUCT INT/ORG POL/PAR EDU/PROP COERCE ATTIT KNOWL PWR MARXISM...CONCPT COLD/WAR 20. PAGE 15 A0308
COM SECT TOTALISM

B51
US DEPARTMENT OF STATE,LIVRES AMERICAINS TRADUITS EN FRANCAIS ET LIVRES FRANCAIS SUR LES ETATS-UNIS D'AMERIQUE (2ND ED.). FRANCE USA+45 SECT DIPLOM EDU/PROP LEISURE...ART/METH GEOG HUM 20. PAGE 151 A3086
BIBLIOG/A SOC

B51
YOUNG T.C.,NEAR EASTERN CULTURE AND SOCIETY. ISLAM ECO/UNDEV SECT WRITING ATTIT HABITAT ORD/FREE 20. PAGE 169 A3438
CULTURE STRUCT REGION DIPLOM

S51
ICHHEISER G.,"MISUNDERSTANDING IN INTERNATIONAL RELATIONS." UNIV SOCIETY FACE/GP INT/ORG SECT ATTIT PERSON RIGID/FLEX LOVE RESPECT...RELATIV PSY SOC CONCPT MYTH SOC/EXP GEN/LAWS. PAGE 70 A1431
PERCEPT STERTYP NAT/LISM DIPLOM

B53
MARITAIN J.,L'HOMME ET L'ETAT. SECT DIPLOM GP/REL PEACE ORD/FREE...IDEA/COMP 17/20 CHURCH/STA NATURL/LAW. PAGE 95 A1940
CONCPT NAT/G SOVEREIGN COERCE

B53
MURPHY G.,IN THE MINDS OF MEN: THE STUDY OF HUMAN BEHAVIOR AND SOCIAL TENSIONS IN INDIA. FUT S/ASIA FAM INT/ORG NAT/G DIPLOM EDU/PROP GP/REL ATTIT RIGID/FLEX ALL/VALS...SOC QU UNESCO 20. PAGE 106 A2176
SECT STRATA INDIA

B55
THOMPSON V.,MINORITY PROBLEMS IN SOUTHEAST ASIA. CAMBODIA CHINA/COM LAOS S/ASIA KIN NAT/G SECT PROB/SOLV EDU/PROP REGION GP/REL RACE/REL MARXISM ...SOC 20 BUDDHISM UN. PAGE 143 A2933
INGP/REL GEOG DIPLOM STRUCT

B55
TROTIER A.H.,DOCTORAL DISSERTATIONS ACCEPTED BY AMERICAN UNIVERSITIES 1954-55. SECT DIPLOM HEALTH ...ART/METH GEOG INT/LAW SOC LING CHARTS 20. PAGE 145 A2968
BIBLIOG ACADEM USA+45 WRITING

B56
JAMESON J.F.,THE AMERICAN REVOLUTION CONSIDERED AS A SOCIAL MOVEMENT. USA-45 AGRI FINAN SECT INT/TRADE REPRESENT SUFF INGP/REL RACE/REL DISCRIM...MAJORIT 18/19 CHURCH/STA. PAGE 73 A1494
ORD/FREE REV FEDERAL CONSTN

B56
PHILIPPINE STUDIES PROGRAM,SELECTED BIBLIOGRAPHY ON THE PHILIPPINES, TOPICALLY ARRANGED AND ANNOTATED. PHILIPPINE SECT DIPLOM COLONIAL LEAD...SOC 18/20. PAGE 116 A2375
BIBLIOG/A S/ASIA NAT/G ECO/UNDEV

B56
WOLFF R.L.,THE BALKANS IN OUR TIME. ALBANIA FUT MOD/EUR USSR YUGOSLAVIA CULTURE INT/ORG SECT DIPLOM EDU/PROP COERCE WAR ORD/FREE...CHARTS 4/20 BALKANS COMINFORM. PAGE 166 A3388
GEOG COM

B57
ALIGHIERI D.,ON WORLD GOVERNMENT. ROMAN/EMP LAW SOCIETY INT/ORG NAT/G POL/PAR ADJUD WAR GP/REL PEACE WORSHIP 15 WORLDUNITY DANTE. PAGE 6 A0121
POLICY CONCPT DIPLOM SECT

B57
BYRNES R.F.,BIBLIOGRAPHY OF AMERICAN PUBLICATIONS ON EAST CENTRAL EUROPE, 1945-1957 (VOL. XXII). SECT DIPLOM EDU/PROP RACE/REL...ART/METH GEOG JURID SOC LING 20 JEWS. PAGE 23 A0462
BIBLIOG/A COM MARXISM NAT/G

B57
MOYER K.E.,FROM IRAN TO MORROCCO; FROM TURKEY TO THE SUDAN: A SELECTED AND ANNOTATED BIBLIOGRAPHY OF NORTH AFRICA AND NEAR EAST... ISLAM DIPLOM EDU/PROP 20. PAGE 105 A2162
BIBLIOG/A ECO/UNDEV SECT NAT/G

B58
HOLT R.T.,RADIO FREE EUROPE. FUT USA+45 CULTURE ECO/DEV INT/ORG KIN POL/PAR SECT FORCES ACT/RES DIPLOM COERCE REV CHOOSE PEACE ATTIT PWR...MAJORIT CONCPT COLD/WAR WORK 20 RFE. PAGE 67 A1374
COM EDU/PROP COM/IND

B58
MASON H.L.,TOYNBEE'S APPROACH TO WORLD POLITICS. AFR USA+45 USSR LAW WAR NAT/LISM ALL/IDEOS...HUM BIBLIOG. PAGE 95 A1957
DIPLOM CONCPT PHIL/SCI SECT

B58
VARG P.A.,MISSIONARIES, CHINESE, AND DIPLOMATS: THE AMERICAN PROTESTANT MISSIONARY MOVEMENT IN CHINA, 1890-1952. ASIA ECO/UNDEV NAT/G PROB/SOLV CAP/ISM EDU/PROP COLONIAL NAT/LISM ATTIT MARXISM...NAT/COMP STERTYP 20 CHINJAP PROTESTANT MISSION. PAGE 158 A3221
CULTURE DIPLOM SECT

B58
YUAN TUNG-LI,CHINA IN WESTERN LITERATURE. SECT DIPLOM...ART/METH GEOG JURID SOC BIOG CON/ANAL. PAGE 169 A3440
BIBLIOG ASIA CULTURE HUM

S58
BOURBON-BUSSET J.,"HOW DECISIONS ARE MADE IN FOREIGN POLITICS: PSYCHOLOGY IN INTERNATIONAL POLITICS." WOR+45 NAT/G SECT REGION WAR MORAL ...CONCPT OBS STERTYP GEN/LAWS TOT/POP COLD/WAR 20. PAGE 17 A0350
INT/ORG DELIB/GP DIPLOM

C58
BUTTINGER J.,"THE SMALLER DRAGON; A POLITICAL HISTORY OF VIETNAM." VIETNAM SECT DIPLOM CIVMIL/REL ISOLAT NAT/LISM...BIBLIOG/A 3/20. PAGE 22 A0455
COLONIAL DOMIN SOVEREIGN REV

B59
CHANDLER E.H.S.,THE HIGH TOWER OF REFUGE: THE INSPIRING STORY OF REFUGEE RELIEF THROUGHOUT THE WORLD. WOR+45 NEIGH SECT WORKER PROB/SOLV DIPLOM ECO/TAC EDU/PROP COST HABITAT. PAGE 25 A0519
GIVE WEALTH STRANGE INT/ORG

B59
GILBERT R.,GENOCIDE IN TIBET. ASIA SECT CHIEF DIPLOM 20. PAGE 52 A1072
MARXISM MURDER WAR GP/REL

B59
KARUNAKARAN K.P.,INDIA IN WORLD AFFAIRS, 1952-1958 (VOL. II). INDIA ECO/UNDEV SECT FOR/AID INT/TRADE ADJUD NEUTRAL REV WAR DISCRIM ORD/FREE MARXISM ...BIBLIOG 20. PAGE 77 A1569
DIPLOM INT/ORG S/ASIA COLONIAL

B59
RICE E.A.,THE DIPLOMATIC RELATIONS BETWEEN THE UNITED STATES AND MEXICO 1925-1929. USA-45 NAT/G DOMIN PEACE ORD/FREE CATHISM 20 MEXIC/AMER. PAGE 121 A2472
DIPLOM SECT POLICY

B59
VORSPAN A.,JUSTICE AND JUDAISM. FAM DIPLOM ECO/TAC EDU/PROP CRIME RACE/REL MARRIAGE ANOMIE ATTIT ORD/FREE...POLICY 20 UN. PAGE 160 A3254
SECT CULTURE ACT/RES GP/REL

B60
EMERSON R.,FROM EMPIRE TO NATION: THE RISE TO SELF-ASSERTION OF ASIAN AND AFRICAN PEOPLES. S/ASIA CULTURE NAT/G SECT DIPLOM ATTIT SOVEREIGN MARXISM ...POLICY BIBLIOG 19/20. PAGE 41 A0847
NAT/LISM COLONIAL AFR ASIA

B60
GLUBB J.B.,WAR IN THE DESERT: AN R.A.F. FRONTIER CAMPAIGN. SAUDI/ARAB UK KIN SECT LEAD...GEOG 20 RAF. PAGE 53 A1083
COLONIAL WAR FORCES DIPLOM

B60
HAMADY S.,TEMPERAMENT AND CHARACTER OF THE ARABS. FAM NAT/G SECT DIPLOM NAT/LISM...POLICY 20 ARABS. PAGE 61 A1244
NAT/COMP PERSON CULTURE ISLAM

B60
NURTY K.S.,STUDIES IN PROBLEMS OF PEACE. CHRIST-17C MOD/EUR S/ASIA WOR+45 WOR-45 INT/ORG NAT/G SECT COERCE REV NAT/LISM ALL/VALS...CONCPT MYTH TIME/SEQ. PAGE 110 A2262
POLICY PEACE PACIFISM ORD/FREE

B60
QUBAIN F.I.,INSIDE THE ARAB MIND: A BIBLIOGRAPHIC SURVEY OF LITERATURE IN ARABIC ON ARAB NATIONALISM AND UNITY. ISLAM POL/PAR SECT LEAD SOVEREIGN MARXISM SOCISM. PAGE 118 A2425
BIBLIOG/A FEDERAL DIPLOM NAT/LISM

B60
SPEER J.P.,FOR WHAT PURPOSE? CHINA/COM USSR CONSTN PROB/SOLV DIPLOM CONTROL TASK WAR NAT/LISM WORSHIP
PEACE SECT

20 UN. PAGE 136 A2778
SUPEGO ALL/IDEOS

B60
SZTARAY Z.,BIBLIOGRAPHY ON HUNGARY. HUNGARY MOD/EUR CULTURE INDUS SECT DIPLOM REV...ART/METH SOC LING 18/20. PAGE 141 A2879
BIBLIOG NAT/G COM MARXISM

S60
GINSBURGS G.,"PEKING-LHASA-NEW DELHI." CHINA/COM FUT INDIA S/ASIA KIN NAT/G PROVS SECT FORCES BAL/PWR ECO/TAC DOMIN EDU/PROP LEGIT ADMIN REGION GUERRILLA PWR...TREND TIBET 20. PAGE 52 A1074
ASIA COERCE DIPLOM

C60
FITZSIMMONS T.,"USSR: ITS PEOPLE, ITS SOCIETY, ITS CULTURE." USSR FAM SECT DIPLOM EDU/PROP ADMIN RACE/REL ATTIT...POLICY CHARTS BIBLIOG 20. PAGE 46 A0944
CULTURE STRUCT SOCIETY COM

C60
WRIGGINS W.H.,"CEYLON: DILEMMAS OF A NEW NATION." ASIA CEYLON CONSTN STRUCT POL/PAR SECT FORCES DIPLOM GOV/REL NAT/LISM...CHARTS BIBLIOG 20. PAGE 167 A3399
PROB/SOLV NAT/G ECO/UNDEV

B61
ASIA SOCIETY,AMERICAN INSTITUTIONS ANS ORGANIZATIONS INTERESTED IN ASIA; A REFERENCE DIRECTORY (2ND ED.). ASIA USA+45 CULTURE SECT DIPLOM EDU/PROP...INDEX 20. PAGE 9 A0190
VOL/ASSN ACADEM PROF/ORG

B61
HISTORICAL RESEARCH INSTITUTE,A SHORT BIBLIOGRAPHY OF INDO-MUSLIM HISTORY. INDIA S/ASIA DIPLOM EDU/PROP COLONIAL LEAD NAT/LISM ATTIT...BIOG 19/20. PAGE 65 A1343
BIBLIOG NAT/G SECT POL/PAR

B61
PALMER N.D.,THE INDIAN POLITICAL SYSTEM. INDIA ECO/UNDEV SECT CHIEF COLONIAL CHOOSE ALL/IDEOS SOCISM...CHARTS BIBLIOG/A 20. PAGE 113 A2322
NAT/LISM POL/PAR NAT/G DIPLOM

B61
UAR MINISTRY OF CULTURE,A BIBLIOGRAPHICAL LIST OF AL MAGHRIB. ALGERIA ISLAM MOROCCO UAR SECT INT/TRADE COLONIAL 19/20 TUNIS. PAGE 146 A2987
BIBLIOG DIPLOM GEOG

B61
UAR MINISTRY OF CULTURE,A BIBLIOGRAPHICAL LIST OF LIBYA. ISLAM LIBYA DIPLOM COLONIAL REV WAR 19/20. PAGE 146 A2988
BIBLIOG GEOG SECT NAT/LISM

B61
UAR MINISTRY OF CULTURE,A BIBLIOGRAPHICAL LIST OF TUNISIA. ISLAM CULTURE NAT/G EDU/PROP COLONIAL ...GEOG 19/20 TUNIS. PAGE 146 A2989
BIBLIOG DIPLOM SECT

B61
ZIMMERMAN I.,A GUIDE TO CURRENT LATIN AMERICAN PERIODICALS: HUMANITIES AND SOCIAL SCIENCES. LABOR SECT EDU/PROP...GEOG HUM SOC LING STAT NAT/COMP 20. PAGE 170 A3452
BIBLIOG/A DIPLOM L/A+17C PHIL/SCI

B62
ALIX C.,LE SAINT-SIEGE ET LES NATIONALISMES EN EUROPE 1870-1960. COM GERMANY IRELAND ITALY SOCIETY SECT TOTALISM RIGID/FLEX MORAL 19/20. PAGE 6 A0122
CATH NAT/LISM ATTIT DIPLOM

B62
BAULIN J.,THE ARAB ROLE IN AFRICA. AFR ALGERIA FUT ISLAM MOROCCO UAR COLONIAL NEUTRAL REV...SOC 20 TUNIS BOURGUIBA. PAGE 12 A0235
NAT/LISM DIPLOM NAT/G SECT

B62
CADWELL R.,COMMUNISM IN THE MODERN WORLD. USSR WOR+45 SOCIETY AGRI INDUS INT/ORG SECT EDU/PROP COLONIAL PEACE...SOC 20. PAGE 23 A0463
COM DIPLOM POLICY CONCPT

B62
COLLISON R.L.,BIBLIOGRAPHIES, SUBJECT AND NATIONAL: A GUIDE TO THEIR CONTENTS, ARRANGEMENT, AND USE (2ND REV. ED.). SECT DIPLOM...ART/METH GEOG HUM PHIL/SCI SOC MATH BIOG 20. PAGE 28 A0569
BIBLIOG/A CON/ANAL BIBLIOG

B62
DAVAR F.C.,IRAN AND INDIA THROUGH THE AGES. INDIA IRAN ELITES SECT CREATE ORD/FREE...LING BIBLIOG. PAGE 34 A0683
NAT/COMP DIPLOM CULTURE

B62
HARARI M.,GOVERNMENT AND POLITICS OF THE MIDDLE EAST. ISLAM USA+45 NAT/G SECT CHIEF ADMIN ORD/FREE 20. PAGE 61 A1257
DIPLOM ECO/UNDEV TEC/DEV POLICY

B62
KIDDER F.E.,THESES ON PAN AMERICAN TOPICS. LAW CULTURE NAT/G SECT DIPLOM HEALTH...ART/METH GEOG SOC 13/20. PAGE 79 A1615
BIBLIOG CHRIST-17C L/A+17C SOCIETY

B62
MOON P.,DIVIDE AND QUIT. INDIA PAKISTAN STRATA DELIB/GP PLAN DIPLOM REPRESENT GP/REL INGP/REL CONSEN DISCRIM...OBS 20. PAGE 103 A2119
WAR REGION ISOLAT SECT

B62
SCHMIDT-VOLKMAR E.,DER KULTURKAMPF IN DEUTSCHLAND 1871-1890. GERMANY PRUSSIA SOCIETY STRUCT SECT DIPLOM GP/REL NAT/LISM 19 CHURCH/STA BISMARCK/O. PAGE 128 A2632
POL/PAR CATHISM ATTIT NAT/G

B62
STARR R.E.,POLAND 1944-1962: THE SOVIETIZATION OF A CAPTIVE PEOPLE. COM POLAND USSR POL/PAR SECT LEGIS DIPLOM DOMIN EDU/PROP CHOOSE ORD/FREE...POLICY CHARTS BIBLIOG 20. PAGE 137 A2808
MARXISM NAT/G TOTALISM NAT/COMP

B62
US LIBRARY OF CONGRESS,A LIST OF AMERICAN DOCTORAL DISSERTATIONS ON AFRICA. SOCIETY SECT DIPLOM EDU/PROP ADMIN...GEOG 19/20. PAGE 155 A3157
BIBLIOG AFR ACADEM CULTURE

B62
WEIDNER E.W.,THE WORLD ROLE OF UNIVERSITIES. USA+45 WOR+45 SECT ACT/RES PROB/SOLV GIVE EFFICIENCY KNOWL ...LING CHARTS BIBLIOG 20. PAGE 162 A3297
ACADEM EDU/PROP DIPLOM POLICY

B63
BROWN W.N.,THE UNITED STATES AND INDIA AND PAKISTAN (REV. ED.). INDIA PAKISTAN S/ASIA WOR+45 POL/PAR SECT INT/TRADE COLONIAL COERCE DISCRIM. PAGE 20 A0408
DIPLOM ECO/UNDEV SOVEREIGN STRUCT

B63
JAIRAZBHOY R.A.,FOREIGN INFLUENCE IN ANCIENT INDIA. INDIA ELITES SECT DIPLOM EDU/PROP COLONIAL REGION GP/REL...ART/METH LING WORSHIP +/14 GRECO/ROMN MESOPOTAM PERSIA PARTH/SASS. PAGE 73 A1491
CULTURE SOCIETY COERCE DOMIN

B63
LANOUE G.R.,A BIBLIOGRAPHY OF DOCTORAL DISSERTATIONS ON POLITICS AND RELIGION. USA+45 USA-45 CONSTN PROVS DIPLOM CT/SYS MORAL...POLICY JURID CONCPT 20. PAGE 84 A1728
BIBLIOG NAT/G LOC/G SECT

B63
LIU K.C.,AMERICANS AND CHINESE: A HISTORICAL ESSAY AND BIBLIOGRAPHY. ASIA USA+45 USA-45 SOCIETY SECT 18/20. PAGE 90 A1845
BIBLIOG/A GP/REL DIPLOM ATTIT

B63
LYONS F.S.L.,INTERNATIONALISM IN EUROPE 1815-1914. LAW AGRI COM/IND DIST/IND LABOR SECT INT/TRADE TARIFFS...BIBLIOG 19/20. PAGE 92 A1880
DIPLOM MOD/EUR INT/ORG

B63
MONTER W.,THE GOVERNMENT OF GENEVA, 1536-1605 (DOCTORAL THESIS). SWITZERLND DIPLOM LEAD ORD/FREE SOVEREIGN 16/17 CALVIN/J ROME. PAGE 103 A2112
SECT FINAN LOC/G ADMIN

B63
RAVENS J.P.,STAAT UND KATHOLISCHE KIRCHE IN PREUSSENS POLNISCHEN TEILUNGSGEBIETEN. GERMANY POLAND PRUSSIA PROVS DIPLOM EDU/PROP DEBATE NAT/LISM...JURID 18 CHURCH/STA. PAGE 119 A2451
GP/REL CATHISM SECT NAT/G

B63
THIEN T.T.,INDIA AND SOUTHEAST ASIA 1947-1960. COM INDIA S/ASIA SECT DELIB/GP FOR/AID RACE/REL NAT/LISM SOCISM...CHARTS BIBLIOG 20 UN NEHRU/J TREATY. PAGE 143 A2917
DRIVE DIPLOM POLICY

B63
UAR MINISTRY OF CULTURE,A BIBLIOGRAPHICAL LIST OF ARABIAN PENINSULA. ISLAM SAUDI/ARAB YEMEN FINAN NAT/G DIPLOM 19/20. PAGE 146 A2990
BIBLIOG GEOG INDUS SECT

B63
WEINBERG A.,INSTEAD OF VIOLENCE: WRITINGS BY THE GREAT ADVOCATES OF PEACE AND NONVIOLENCE THROUGHOUT HISTORY. WOR+45 WOR-45 SOCIETY SECT PROB/SOLV DIPLOM GP/REL PERS/REL PEACE...ANTHOL PACIFIST. PAGE 162 A3304
PACIFISM WAR IDEA/COMP

B63
WILCOX W.A.,PAKISTAN; THE CONSOLIDATION OF A NATION. INDIA PAKISTAN CONSTN SECT PROB/SOLV COLONIAL PARTIC GP/REL FEDERAL...POLICY 19/20. PAGE 164 A3348
NAT/LISM ECO/UNDEV DIPLOM STRUCT

S63
LOPEZIBOR J.,"L'EUROPE, FORME DE VIE." CHRIST-17C EUR+WWI FUT MOD/EUR SOCIETY INT/ORG SECT EDU/PROP ATTIT RIGID/FLEX ALL/VALS...POLICY HUM SOC TIME/SEQ TREND GEN/LAWS. PAGE 91 A1862
NAT/G CULTURE

B64
AMERICAN ASSEMBLY,THE UNITED STATES AND THE MIDDLE EAST. ISRAEL USA+45 STRUCT ECO/DEV ECO/UNDEV INT/ORG NAT/G SCHOOL SECT VOL/ASSN EX/STRUC TEC/DEV NAT/LISM...SOC 20. PAGE 7 A0135
ISLAM DRIVE REGION

B64
ANDREWS D.H.,LATIN AMERICA: A BIBLIOGRAPHY OF PAPERBACK BOOKS. SECT INT/TRADE EDU/PROP WAR GOV/REL ADJUST NAT/LISM ATTIT...ART/METH LING BIOG 20. PAGE 8 A0160
BIBLIOG L/A+17C CULTURE NAT/G

B64
BINDER L.,THE IDEOLOGICAL REVOLUTION IN THE MIDDLE EAST. ISLAM STRUCT INT/ORG KIN SECT EX/STRUC TOP/EX PLAN ATTIT DRIVE RIGID/FLEX PWR...MYTH TOT/POP 20. PAGE 14 A0289
POL/PAR NAT/G NAT/LISM

B64
EMBREE A.T.,A GUIDE TO PAPERBACKS ON ASIA; SELECTED AND ANNOTATED (PAMPHLET). CULTURE SOCIETY ECO/UNDEV
BIBLIOG/A ASIA

SECT DIPLOM COLONIAL MARXISM...SOC 20. PAGE 41 A0845 S/ASIA NAT/G

B64
FREUD A.,OF HUMAN SOVEREIGNTY. WOR+45 INDUS SECT ECO/TAC CRIME CHOOSE ATTIT MORAL MARXISM...POLICY BIBLIOG 20. PAGE 49 A0998 NAT/LISM DIPLOM WAR PEACE

B64
GESELLSCHAFT RECHTSVERGLEICH,BIBLIOGRAPHIE DES DEUTSCHEN RECHTS (BIBLIOGRAPHY OF GERMAN LAW. TRANS. BY COURTLAND PETERSON). GERMANY FINAN INDUS LABOR SECT FORCES CT/SYS PARL/PROC CRIME...INT/LAW SOC NAT/COMP 20. PAGE 52 A1066 BIBLIOG/A JURID CONSTN ADMIN

B64
HALPERIN S.W.,MUSSOLINI AND ITALIAN FASCISM. ITALY NAT/G POL/PAR SECT ECO/TAC LEAD PWR SOCISM...POLICY 20 MUSSOLIN/B. PAGE 60 A1241 FASCISM NAT/LISM EDU/PROP CHIEF

B64
JENSEN D.L.,DIPLOMACY AND DOGMATISM. FRANCE SPAIN REV WAR PERSON CATHISM...POLICY BIOG 16. PAGE 74 A1513 DIPLOM ATTIT SECT

B64
MAHAR J.M.,INDIA: A CRITICAL BIBLIOGRAPHY. INDIA PAKISTAN CULTURE ECO/UNDEV LOC/G POL/PAR SECT PROB/SOLV DIPLOM ADMIN COLONIAL PARL/PROC ATTIT 20. PAGE 93 A1906 BIBLIOG/A S/ASIA NAT/G LEAD

B64
NICE R.W.,TREASURY OF LAW. WOR+45 WOR-45 SECT ADJUD MORAL ORD/FREE...INT/LAW JURID PHIL/SCI ANTHOL. PAGE 108 A2227 LAW WRITING PERS/REL DIPLOM

B64
RAGHAVAN M.D.,INDIA IN CEYLONESE HISTORY, SOCIETY AND CULTURE. CEYLON INDIA S/ASIA LAW SOCIETY INT/TRADE ATTIT...ART/METH JURID SOC LING 20. PAGE 119 A2433 DIPLOM CULTURE SECT STRUCT

B64
ROBERTS HL,FOREIGN AFFAIRS BIBLIOGRAPHY, 1952-1962. ECO/DEV SECT PLAN FOR/AID INT/TRADE ARMS/CONT NAT/LISM ATTIT...INT/LAW GOV/COMP IDEA/COMP 20. PAGE 122 A2495 BIBLIOG/A DIPLOM INT/ORG WAR

B64
SAKAI R.K.,STUDIES ON ASIA, 1964. ASIA CHINA/COM ISRAEL MALAYSIA S/ASIA USA+45 USSR ECO/UNDEV FAM POL/PAR SECT CONSULT NAT/LISM...POLICY SOC 20 CHINJAP. PAGE 126 A2588 PWR DIPLOM

B64
SCHWELB E.,HUMAN RIGHTS AND THE INTERNATIONAL COMMUNITY. WOR+45 WOR-45 NAT/G SECT DELIB/GP DIPLOM PEACE RESPECT TREATY 20 UN. PAGE 130 A2666 INT/ORG ORD/FREE INT/LAW

B64
SPECTOR S.D.,A CHECKLIST OF PAPERBOUND BOOKS ON RUSSIA. USSR SECT DIPLOM EDU/PROP HEALTH...PHIL/SCI PSY SOC SOC/WK WORSHIP 20. PAGE 135 A2775 BIBLIOG COM PERF/ART

B64
TEPASKE J.J.,EXPLOSIVE FORCES IN LATIN AMERICA. CULTURE INTELL ECO/UNDEV INT/ORG NAT/G SECT FORCES ECO/TAC EDU/PROP PWR WEALTH SOC. PAGE 142 A2903 L/A+17C RIGID/FLEX FOR/AID USSR

B64
UAR NATIONAL LIBRARY,A BIBLIOGRAPHICAL LIST OF WORKS ABOUT PALESTINE AND JORDAN (2ND ED.). ISRAEL JORDAN SECT DIPLOM...SOC 20 JEWS. PAGE 146 A2991 BIBLIOG ISLAM

L64
POUNDS N.J.G.,"THE POLITICS OF PARTITION." AFR ASIA COM EUR+WWI FUT ISLAM S/ASIA USA-45 LAW ECO/DEV ECO/UNDEV AGRI INDUS INT/ORG POL/PAR PROVS SECT FORCES TOP/EX EDU/PROP LEGIT ATTIT MORAL ORD/FREE PWR RESPECT WEALTH. PAGE 117 A2402 NAT/G NAT/LISM

S64
"FURTHER READING." INDIA PAKISTAN SECT WAR PEACE ATTIT...POLICY 20. PAGE 3 A0067 BIBLIOG GP/REL DIPLOM NAT/G

S64
GREENBERG S.,"JUDAISM AND WORLD JUSTICE." MEDIT-7 WOR+45 LAW CULTURE SOCIETY INT/ORG NAT/G FORCES EDU/PROP ATTIT DRIVE PERSON SUPEGO ALL/VALS ...POLICY PSY CONCPT GEN/LAWS JEWS. PAGE 55 A1140 SECT JURID PEACE

S64
KHAN M.Z.,"ISLAM AND INTERNATIONAL RELATIONS." FUT WOR+45 LAW CULTURE SOCIETY NAT/G SECT DELIB/GP FORCES EDU/PROP ATTIT PERSON SUPEGO ALL/VALS ...POLICY PSY CONCPT MYTH HIST/WRIT GEN/LAWS. PAGE 78 A1608 ISLAM INT/ORG DIPLOM

B65
BRACKETT R.D.,PATHWAYS TO PEACE. SECT VOL/ASSN GP/REL PERS/REL DISCRIM...LING 20 UN PEACE/CORP. PAGE 18 A0366 PEACE INT/ORG EDU/PROP PARTIC

B65
COOPER S.,BEHIND THE GOLDEN CURTAIN: A VIEW OF THE USA. UK USA+45 SECT EDU/PROP COERCE LEISURE ORD/FREE WEALTH 20. PAGE 30 A0609 SOCIETY DIPLOM ATTIT ACT/RES

B65
MUNGER E.S.,NOTES ON THE FORMATION OF SOUTH AFRICAN FOREIGN POLICY. ACADEM POL/PAR SECT CHIEF DELIB/GP FORCES LEGIS PRESS ATTIT...TREND 20 NEGRO. PAGE 106 A2170 AFR DOMIN POLICY DIPLOM

B65
O'CONNELL M.R.,IRISH POLITICS AND SOCIAL CONFLICT IN THE AGE OF THE AMERICAN REVOLUTION. FRANCE IRELAND MOD/EUR STRATA SECT LEGIS DIPLOM INT/TRADE DOMIN REV WAR...BIBLIOG 18 PARLIAMENT. PAGE 111 A2268 CATHISM ATTIT NAT/G DELIB/GP

B65
QURESHI I.H.,THE STRUGGLE FOR PAKISTAN. INDIA PAKISTAN UK CULTURE LEGIS DIPLOM EDU/PROP COLONIAL ATTIT SOVEREIGN 19/20 MUSLIM. PAGE 118 A2429 GP/REL RACE/REL WAR SECT

B65
SCHREIBER H.,TEUTON AND SLAV - THE STRUGGLE FOR CENTRAL EUROPE (TRANS. BY J. CLEUGH). GERMANY POLAND PRUSSIA USSR SOCIETY STRUCT SECT DIPLOM BALTIC. PAGE 129 A2646 GP/REL WAR RACE/REL NAT/LISM

B65
US BUREAU EDUC CULTURAL AFF,RESOURCES SURVEY FOR LATIN AMERICAN COUNTRIES. L/A+17C USA+45 CULTURE INDUS INT/ORG SECT PLAN EDU/PROP POLICY. PAGE 150 A3056 NAT/G ECO/UNDEV FOR/AID DIPLOM

B65
US LIBRARY OF CONGRESS,RARE BOOKS DIVISION: GUIDE TO ITS COLLECTION AND SERVICES. LOC/G SECT WAR. PAGE 155 A3158 BIBLIOG/A NAT/G DIPLOM

B65
US LIBRARY OF CONGRESS,A DIRECTORY OF INFORMATION RESOURCES IN THE UNITED STATES: SOCIAL SCIENCES. USA+45 ACADEM INT/ORG LABOR PROF/ORG PUB/INST SCHOOL SECT 20. PAGE 155 A3159 BIBLIOG R+D COMPUT/IR

B65
WILGUS A.C.,HISTORIES AND HISTORIANS OF HISPANIC AMERICA (REPRINT ED.). CHRIST-17C SECT DIPLOM REV 16/20. PAGE 164 A3350 BIBLIOG/A L/A+17C REGION COLONIAL

L65
MATTHEWS D.G.,"A CURRENT BIBLIOGRAPHY ON ETHIOPIAN AFFAIRS: A SELECT BIBLIOGRAPHY FROM 1950-1964." ETHIOPIA LAW CULTURE ECO/UNDEV INDUS LABOR SECT FORCES DIPLOM CIVMIL/REL RACE/REL...LING STAT 20. PAGE 96 A1969 BIBLIOG/A ADMIN POL/PAR NAT/G

S65
KHOURI F.J.,"THE JORDON RIVER CONTROVERSY." LAW SOCIETY ECO/UNDEV AGRI FINAN INDUS SECT FORCES ACT/RES PLAN TEC/DEV ECO/TAC EDU/PROP COERCE ATTIT DRIVE PERCEPT RIGID/FLEX ALL/VALS...GEOG SOC MYTH WORK. PAGE 78 A1610 ISLAM INT/ORG ISRAEL JORDAN

B66
ENTWICKLUNGSPOLITIK - HANDBUCH UND LEXIKON. MARKET SECT DIPLOM INT/TRADE EDU/PROP CATHISM 20. PAGE 14 A0283 ECO/UNDEV FOR/AID ECO/TAC PLAN

B66
BROWN L.C.,STATE AND SOCIETY IN INDEPENDENT NORTH AFRICA. ALGERIA LIBYA MOROCCO AGRI INDUS INT/ORG POL/PAR SECT PLAN DIPLOM COLONIAL...LING NAT/COMP ANTHOL BIBLIOG 20 TUNIS MUSLIM. PAGE 20 A0406 NAT/G SOCIETY CULTURE ECO/UNDEV

B66
CLENDENON C.,AMERICANS IN AFRICA 1865-1900. AFR USA-45 ECO/UNDEV SECT REV RACE/REL CONSERVE ...TRADIT GEOG BIBLIOG 16/18. PAGE 27 A0549 DIPLOM COLONIAL INT/TRADE

B66
EMBREE A.T.,ASIA: A GUIDE TO BASIC BOOKS (PAMPHLET). ECO/UNDEV SECT FORCES DIPLOM ALL/IDEOS ...SOC 20. PAGE 41 A0846 BIBLIOG/A ASIA S/ASIA NAT/G

B66
FALL B.B.,VIET-NAM WITNESS, 1953-66. S/ASIA VIETNAM SECT PROB/SOLV COLONIAL GUERRILLA...CHARTS BIBLIOG 20. PAGE 44 A0895 MARXIST WAR DIPLOM

B66
FARWELL G.,MASK OF ASIA: THE PHILIPPINES. PHILIPPINE SECT DIPLOM ATTIT...SOC RECORD PREDICT BIBLIOG 20. PAGE 44 A0901 S/ASIA CULTURE

B66
JACK H.A.,RELIGION AND PEACE: PAPERS FROM THE NATIONAL INTER-RELIGIOUS CONFERENCE ON PEACE, WASHINGTON, 1966. CHINA/COM USA+45 VIETNAM WOR+45 FORCES FOR/AID LEAD PERS/REL. PAGE 72 A1472 PEACE SECT SUPEGO DIPLOM

B66
MAYER P.,THE PACIFIST CONSCIENCE. SECT CREATE ARMS/CONT WAR RACE/REL ATTIT LOVE...ANTHOL PACIFIST WORSHIP FREUD/S GANDHI/M LAO/TZU KING/MAR/L CONSCN/OBJ. PAGE 97 A1984 DIPLOM PACIFISM SUPEGO

B66
MULLER C.F.J.,A SELECT BIBLIOGRAPHY OF SOUTH AFRICAN HISTORY; A GUIDE FOR HISTORICAL RESEARCH. SOUTH/AFR UK LAW CONSTN SOCIETY STRUCT AGRI SECT DIPLOM COLONIAL LEAD RACE/REL...POLICY 17/20 NEGRO. PAGE 106 A2167 BIBLIOG AFR NAT/G

B66
SALTER L.M.,RESOLUTION OF INTERNATIONAL CONFLICT. USA+45 INT/ORG SECT DIPLOM ECO/TAC FOR/AID DETER NUC/PWR WAR 20. PAGE 127 A2595
PROB/SOLV PEACE INT/LAW POLICY

B66
SCHATTEN F.,COMMUNISM IN AFRICA. AFR GHANA GUINEA MALI CULTURE ECO/UNDEV LABOR SECT ECO/TAC EDU/PROP REV 20. PAGE 128 A2619
COLONIAL NAT/LISM MARXISM DIPLOM

B66
TINKER H.,SOUTH ASIA. UK LAW ECO/UNDEV AGRI ACADEM SECT DIPLOM EDU/PROP REV WEALTH ALL/IDEOS...CHARTS BIBLIOG GANDHI/M NEHRU/J. PAGE 144 A2945
S/ASIA COLONIAL TREND

B66
TYSON G.,NEHRU: THE YEARS OF POWER. INDIA UK STRATA ECO/UNDEV FINAN SECT TASK WAR ORD/FREE MARXISM ...POLICY BIBLIOG 20 NEHRU/J. PAGE 146 A2985
CHIEF PWR DIPLOM NAT/G

B66
US DEPARTMENT OF STATE,RESEARCH ON THE MIDDLE EAST (EXTERNAL RESEARCH LIST NO 4-25). GREECE ISRAEL SYRIA UAR YEMEN CULTURE SOCIETY POL/PAR SECT DIPLOM EDU/PROP WAR NAT/LISM...GEOG GOV/COMP 20. PAGE 152 A3096
BIBLIOG/A ISLAM NAT/G REGION

B66
US SENATE COMM GOVT OPERATIONS,POPULATION CRISIS. USA+45 ECO/DEV ECO/UNDEV AGRI SECT DELIB/GP PROB/SOLV FOR/AID REPRESENT ATTIT...GEOG CHARTS 20 CONGRESS DEPT/STATE DEPT/HEW BIRTH/CON. PAGE 156 A3178
CENSUS CONTROL LEGIS CONSULT

B66
ZEINE Z.N.,THE EMERGENCE OF ARAB NATIONALISM (REV. ED.). TURKEY UK NAT/G SECT TEC/DEV LEAD REV WAR AGE/Y ROLE ORD/FREE...TRADIT CHARTS BIBLIOG 20 ARABS OTTOMAN. PAGE 170 A3451
ISLAM NAT/LISM DIPLOM

S66
AFRICAN BIBLIOGRAPHIC CENTER,"A CURRENT VIEW OF AFRICANA: A SELECT AND ANNOTATED BIBLIOGRAPHICAL PUBLISHING GUIDE, 1965-1966." AFR CULTURE INDUS LABOR SECT FOR/AID ADMIN COLONIAL REV RACE/REL SOCISM...LING 20. PAGE 5 A0098
BIBLIOG/A NAT/G TEC/DEV POL/PAR

S66
AFRICAN BIBLIOGRAPHIC CENTER,"A DESCRIPTIVE STUDY OF CURRENT AFRICAN FOREIGN RELATIONS." COM CULTURE INT/ORG SECT RACE/REL DISCRIM ATTIT 20. PAGE 5 A0099
BIBLIOG DIPLOM AFR

S66
DINH TRANS V.A.N.,"VIETNAM: A THIRD WAY" S/ASIA USA+45 USSR VIETNAM VIETNAM/S NAT/G SECT FORCES CAP/ISM DIPLOM COLONIAL NEUTRAL MARXISM SOCISM 20 BUDDHISM UNIFICA. PAGE 38 A0766
WAR PLAN ORD/FREE SOCIALIST

S66
MATTHEWS D.G.,"ETHIOPIAN OUTLINE: A BIBLIOGRAPHIC RESEARCH GUIDE." ETHIOPIA LAW STRUCT ECO/UNDEV AGRI LABOR SECT CHIEF DELIB/GP EX/STRUC ADMIN...LING ORG/CHARTS 20. PAGE 96 A1972
BIBLIOG NAT/G DIPLOM POL/PAR

C66
WINT G.,"ASIA: A HANDBOOK." ASIA S/ASIA INDUS LABOR SECT PRESS RACE/REL MARXISM...STAT CHARTS BIBLIOG 20. PAGE 165 A3366
ECO/UNDEV DIPLOM NAT/G SOCIETY

B67
ADAMS A.E.,AN ATLAS OF RUSSIAN AND EAST EUROPEAN HISTORY. CHRIST-17C COM MOD/EUR INDUS SECT FORCES DIPLOM COLONIAL REV WAR 4/20. PAGE 4 A0086
CHARTS REGION TREND

B67
FINE S.,RECENT AMERICA* CONFLICTING INTERPRETATIONS OF THE GREAT ISSUES (2ND ED.). USA+45 USA-45 POL/PAR SECT CONFER NUC/PWR WAR ATTIT...POLICY TREND ANTHOL PRESIDENT 20. PAGE 46 A0931
IDEA/COMP DIPLOM NAT/G

B67
KNOLES G.H.,THE RESPONSIBILITIES OF POWER, 1900-1929. USA-45 SOCIETY SECT JUDGE COLONIAL REPRESENT WEALTH POPULISM...IDEA/COMP ANTHOL PRESIDENT 20 LEAGUE/NAT. PAGE 81 A1653
PWR DIPLOM NAT/LISM WAR

B67
LANDEN R.G.,OMAN SINCE 1856: DISRUPTIVE MODERNIZATION IN A TRADITIONAL ARAB SOCIETY. UK DIST/IND EXTR/IND SECT DIPLOM INT/TRADE...SOC LING CHARTS BIBLIOG 19/20. PAGE 84 A1714
ISLAM CULTURE ECO/UNDEV NAT/G

B67
PIKE F.B.,FREEDOM AND REFORM IN LATIN AMERICA. BRAZIL URUGUAY CONSTN CULTURE SECT DIPLOM EDU/PROP PARTIC DRIVE ALL/VALS CATHISM...GEOG ANTHOL BIBLIOG REFORMERS BOLIV. PAGE 116 A2379
L/A+17C ORD/FREE ECO/UNDEV REV

B67
SACHS M.Y.,THE WORLDMARK ENCYCLOPEDIA OF THE NATIONS (5 VOLS.). ELITES SOCIETY STRATA ECO/DEV ECO/UNDEV AGRI EXTR/IND FINAN LABOR LOC/G NAT/G POL/PAR SECT INT/TRADE SOVEREIGN...SOC 20. PAGE 126 A2585
WOR+45 INT/ORG BAL/PWR

B67
SAYEED K.B.,THE POLITICAL SYSTEM OF PAKISTAN. PAKISTAN DIPLOM REGION CHOOSE ORD/FREE...BIBLIOG 20. PAGE 127 A2609
NAT/G POL/PAR CONSTN

SECT

L67
GRAUBARD S.R.,"TOWARD THE YEAR 2000: WORK IN PROGRESS." FUT ACADEM SECT DELIB/GP DIPLOM EDU/PROP AGE/Y PERSON ROLE...PSY ANTHOL. PAGE 55 A1131
PREDICT PROB/SOLV SOCIETY CULTURE

S67
ECKHARDT A.R.,"SILENCE IN THE CHURCHES." ISRAEL WOR+45 CONSTN GP/REL DISCRIM DRIVE JEWS. PAGE 40 A0820
SECT ATTIT DIPLOM ISLAM

B86
MAS LATRIE L.,RELATIONS ET COMMERCE DE L'AFRIQUE SEPTENTRIONALE OU MAGREB AVEC LES NATIONS CHRETIENNES AU MOYEN AGE. CULTURE CHIEF FORCES WAR ...SOC CENSUS TREATY 10/16. PAGE 95 A1954
ISLAM SECT DIPLOM INT/TRADE

SECUR/COUN....UNITED NATIONS SECURITY COUNCIL

SECUR/PROG....SECURITY PROGRAM

B57
US PRES CITIZEN ADVISERS,REPORT TO THE PRESIDENT ON THE MUTUAL SECURITY PROGRAM. COM USA+45 WOR+45 FINAN INDUS PLAN BUDGET CAP/ISM DIPLOM FOR/AID INT/TRADE REGION 20 SECUR/PROG. PAGE 155 A3163
BAL/PWR FORCES INT/ORG ECO/TAC

SECURITIES....SEE FINAN

SECURITY....SEE ORD/FREE

SECURITY COUNCIL....SEE UN+DELIB/GP

SECURITY PROGRAM....SEE SECUR/PROG

SEDITION....SEDITION

SEEK....SEARCH FOR EDUCATION, ELEVATION, AND KNOWLEDGE

SEELEY J.R. A2679

SEGAL A. A2680

SEGAL R. A2681

SEGREGATION....SEE NEGRO, SOUTH/US, RACE/REL, SOC/INTEG, CIV/RIGHTS, DISCRIM, MISCEGEN, ISOLAT, SCHOOL, STRANGE, ANOMIE

SEGUNDO-SANCHEZ M. A2682

SELASSIE/H....HAILE SELASSIE

SELBORNE/W....WILLIAM SELBORNE

SELEC/SERV....SELECTIVE SERVICE

SELF/OBS....SELF/OBSERVATION

B20
HALDANE R.B.,BEFORE THE WAR. MOD/EUR SOCIETY INT/ORG NAT/G DELIB/GP PLAN DOMIN EDU/PROP LEGIT ADMIN COERCE ATTIT DRIVE MORAL ORD/FREE PWR...SOC CONCPT SELF/OBS RECORD BIOG TIME/SEQ. PAGE 60 A1223
POLICY DIPLOM UK

L42
SHOTWELL J.,"LESSON OF THE LAST WORLD WAR." EUR+WWI MOD/EUR USA-45 SOCIETY ECO/UNDEV INDUS VOL/ASSN CONSULT ACT/RES CREATE CAP/ISM INT/TRADE DRIVE ALL/VALS...CONCPT NEW/IDEA SELF/OBS GEN/LAWS LEAGUE/NAT NAZI 20. PAGE 132 A2708
INT/ORG ORD/FREE

B48
CHURCHILL W.,THE GATHERING STORM. UK WOR-45 INT/ORG NAT/G FORCES TOP/EX DIPLOM ECO/TAC COERCE ATTIT ORD/FREE PWR WEALTH...POLICY SELF/OBS RECORD NAZI PARLIAMENT 20. PAGE 26 A0538
BIOG

B50
CHURCHILL W.,TRIUMPH AND TRAGEDY. UK WOR-45 INT/ORG NAT/G DELIB/GP FORCES TOP/EX DIPLOM COERCE CHOOSE ATTIT ORD/FREE PWR WEALTH...SELF/OBS CHARTS NAZI 20. PAGE 26 A0539
BIOG PEACE WAR

B52
JACKSON E.,MEETING OF THE MINDS: A WAY TO PEACE THROUGH MEDIATION. WOR+45 INDUS INT/ORG NAT/G DELIB/GP DIPLOM EDU/PROP LEGIT ORD/FREE...NEW/IDEA SELF/OBS TIME/SEQ CHARTS GEN/LAWS TOT/POP 20 UN TREATY. PAGE 72 A1474
LABOR JUDGE

B53
COUSINS N.,WHO SPEAKS FOR MAN. GERMANY KOREA WOR+45 SOCIETY INT/ORG NAT/G CREATE EDU/PROP HEALTH KNOWL LOVE MORAL...OBS SELF/OBS BIOG HYPO/EXP TOT/POP 20 CHINJAP. PAGE 32 A0642
ATTIT WAR PEACE

B54
COUDENHOVE-KALERGI,AN IDEA CONQUERS THE WORLD. EUR+WWI MOD/EUR USA-45 CONSTN FAM CREATE EDU/PROP
INT/ORG BIOG

ATTIT PERSON KNOWL...CONCPT SELF/OBS TIME/SEQ. PAGE 31 A0635 DIPLOM

B58
GARTHOFF R.L.,SOVIET STRATEGY IN THE NUCLEAR AGE. FUT USSR R+D INT/ORG NAT/G ACT/RES TEC/DEV DOMIN DETER WAR ATTIT PWR...RELATIV METH/CNCPT SELF/OBS TREND CON/ANAL STERTYP GEN/LAWS 20. PAGE 51 A1052 COM FORCES BAL/PWR NUC/PWR

B60
JAECKH A.,WELTSAAT; ERLEBTES UND ERSTREBTES. GERMANY WOR+45 WOR-45 PLAN WAR...POLICY OBS/ENVIR NAT/COMP PERS/COMP 20. PAGE 73 A1489 BIOG NAT/G SELF/OBS DIPLOM

L60
DEUTSCH K.W.,"TOWARD AN INVENTORY OF BASIC TRENDS AND PATTERNS IN COMPARATIVE AND INTERNATIONAL POLITICS." UNIV WOR+45 SOCIETY STRUCT INT/ORG NAT/G CREATE PLAN EDU/PROP KNOWL...PHIL/SCI METH/CNCPT STAT SELF/OBS OBS/ENVIR SAMP TREND CON/ANAL CHARTS SOC/EXP GEN/METH 20. PAGE 36 A0739 R+D PERCEPT

S60
BOGARDUS E.S.,"THE SOCIOLOGY OF A STRUCTURED PEACE." FUT SOCIETY CREATE DIPLOM EDU/PROP ADJUD ROUTINE ATTIT RIGID/FLEX KNOWL ORD/FREE RESPECT ...POLICY INT/LAW JURID NEW/IDEA SELF/OBS TOT/POP 20 UN. PAGE 16 A0327 INT/ORG SOC NAT/LISM PEACE

B61
BULL H.,THE CONTROL OF THE ARMS RACE. COM USA+45 INT/ORG NAT/G PLAN TEC/DEV DIPLOM ATTIT...RELATIV DECISION CONCPT SELF/OBS TREND CON/ANAL GEN/METH 20 COLD/WAR. PAGE 21 A0429 FORCES PWR ARMS/CONT NUC/PWR

B62
HADWEN J.G.,HOW UNITED NATIONS DECISIONS ARE MADE. WOR+45 LAW EDU/PROP LEGIT ADMIN PWR...DECISION SELF/OBS GEN/LAWS UN 20. PAGE 59 A1212 INT/ORG ROUTINE

B62
WOETZEL R.K.,THE NURENBERG TRIALS IN INTERNATIONAL LAW. CHRIST-17C MOD/EUR WOR+45 SOCIETY NAT/G DELIB/GP DOMIN LEGIT ROUTINE ATTIT DRIVE PERSON SUPEGO MORAL ORD/FREE...POLICY MAJORIT JURID PSY SOC SELF/OBS RECORD NAZI TOT/POP. PAGE 166 A3376 INT/ORG ADJUD WAR

B64
TAYLOR E.,RICHER BY ASIA. S/ASIA CULTURE VOL/ASSN ACT/RES ATTIT DISPL PERSON ALL/VALS...INT/LAW MYTH SELF/OBS 20. PAGE 142 A2899 SOCIETY RIGID/FLEX INDIA

B65
ADENAUER K.,MEINE ERINNERUNGEN, 1945-53 (VOL. I), 1953-55 (VOL. II). EUR+WWI GERMANY CHIEF FORCES PROB/SOLV DIPLOM ARMS/CONT INGP/REL PEACE SOVEREIGN ...OBS/ENVIR RECORD 20. PAGE 4 A0089 NAT/G BIOG SELF/OBS

S67
VAN DUSEN H.P.,"HAMMARSKOLD IN THE WORLD'S SERVICE." DIPLOM CONFER LEAD PEACE STRANGE UTOPIA MORAL SKILL OBJECTIVE...INT/LAW SELF/OBS 20. PAGE 158 A3211 INT/ORG CONSULT TOP/EX NEUTRAL

SELIVANOV V. A1086

SELLERS R.C. A0879

SELOSOEMARDJAN O. A2683

SEMANTICS...SEE LOG

SEMJONOW J.M. A2684

SEN/SPACE....UNITED STATES SENATE SPECIAL COMMITTEE ON SPACE ASTRONAUTICS

SENATE SPECIAL COMMITTEE ON SPACE ASTRONAUTICS....SEE SEN/SPACE

SENATE....SENATE (ALL NATIONS); SEE ALSO CONGRESS, LEGIS

L49
HEINDEL R.H.,"THE NORTH ATLANTIC TREATY IN THE UNITED STATES SENATE." CONSTN POL/PAR CHIEF DEBATE LEAD ROUTINE WAR PEACE...CHARTS UN SENATE NATO. PAGE 64 A1309 DECISION PARL/PROC LEGIS INT/ORG

B55
VINSON J.C.,THE PARCHMENT PEACE: THE UNITED STATES SENATE AND THE WASHINGTON CONFERENCE, 1921-1922. USA-45 INT/ORG DELIB/GP PLAN ARMS/CONT GOV/REL ISOLAT PEACE ATTIT SOVEREIGN...INT/LAW BIBLIOG 20 SENATE PRESIDENT CONGRESS LEAGUE/NAT CHINJAP. PAGE 159 A3242 POLICY DIPLOM NAT/G LEGIS

B60
BYRD E.M. JR.,TREATIES AND EXECUTIVE AGREEMENTS IN THE UNITED STATES: THEIR SEPARATE ROLES AND LIMITATIONS. USA+45 USA-45 EX/STRUC TARIFFS CT/SYS GOV/REL FEDERAL...IDEA/COMP BIBLIOG SUPREME/CT SENATE CONGRESS. PAGE 23 A0461 CHIEF INT/LAW DIPLOM

B60
FOREIGN POLICY CLEARING HOUSE,STRATEGY FOR THE 60'S. FUT USA+45 WOR+45 ECO/UNDEV FORCES BAL/PWR TASK ARMS/CONT DETER PWR MARXISM 20 SENATE. PAGE 47 A0963 DIPLOM NAT/G POLICY ACT/RES

B60
US SENATE COMM ON FOREIGN REL,SITUATION IN VIETNAM (2 VOLS.). USA+45 VIETNAM ECO/TAC COST SENATE DEPT/STATE. PAGE 156 A3181 FOR/AID PLAN EFFICIENCY INSPECT

B65
US SENATE COMM GOVT OPERATIONS,ADMINISTRATION OF NATIONAL SECURITY. USA+45 DELIB/GP ADMIN ROLE ...POLICY CHARTS SENATE. PAGE 156 A3177 NAT/G ORD/FREE DIPLOM PROB/SOLV

B66
SUPPLEMENTAL FOREIGN ASSISTANCE FISCAL YEAR 1966: VIETNAM. CHINA/COM COM S/ASIA USA+45 VIETNAM EXTR/IND FINAN DIPLOM TAX GUERRILLA HABITAT ORD/FREE...STAT CHARTS 20 SENATE PRESIDENT. PAGE 4 A0077 CONFER LEGIS WAR FOR/AID

S66
"WORLD BANK CONVENTION ON INVESTMENT DISPUTES; A BIBLIOGRAPH ICAL NOTE." VOL/ASSN CONSULT CAP/ISM DIPLOM INT/TRADE 20 SENATE PRESIDENT. PAGE 4 A0074 BIBLIOG ADJUD FINAN INT/ORG

B67
SINGER D.,QUANTITATIVE INTERNATIONAL POLITICS* INSIGHTS AND EVIDENCE. WOR+45 WOR-45 PARTIC WAR INGP/REL ATTIT PERSON ROLE...PREDICT BIBLIOG 19/20 UN SENATE. PAGE 133 A2722 DIPLOM NAT/G INT/ORG DECISION

B67
US CONGRESS SENATE,SURVEY OF THE ALLIANCE FOR PROGRESS; INFLATION IN LATIN AMERICA (PAMPHLET). USA+45 MARKET INT/ORG DIPLOM INT/TRADE BAL/PAY SENATE. PAGE 150 A3072 L/A+17C FINAN POLICY FOR/AID

B67
US SENATE COMM ON FOREIGN REL,BACKGROUND INFORMATION RELATING TO SOUTHEAST ASIA AND VIETNAM (3RD REV. ED.). USA+45 VIETNAM/S VIETNAM/N...CHARTS 20 SENATE UN. PAGE 156 A3188 DIPLOM WAR FOR/AID

B67
US SENATE COMM ON FOREIGN REL,UNITED STATES ARMAMENT AND DISARMAMENT PROBLEMS. USA+45 AIR BAL/PWR DIPLOM FOR/AID NUC/PWR ORD/FREE SENATE TREATY. PAGE 156 A3190 ARMS/CONT WEAPON FORCES PROB/SOLV

SENCOURT R. A2685

SENEGAL....SEE ALSO AFR

B63
COLUMBIA U SCHOOL OF LAW,PUBLIC INTERNATIONAL DEVELOPMENT FINANCING IN SENEGAL. SENEGAL FINAN DELIB/GP GIVE EFFICIENCY...CHARTS GOV/COMP ANTHOL 20. PAGE 28 A0571 FOR/AID PLAN RECEIVE ECO/UNDEV

SENIOR....SENIORITY; SEE ALSO ADMIN, ROUTINE

SENSENIG B. A2732

SEPARATION....SEE ISOLAT, DISCRIM, RACE/REL

SERBIA....SERBIA

B62
JELAVICH C.,TSARIST RUSSIA AND BALKAN NATIONALISM. BULGARIA MOD/EUR RUSSIA DOMIN GOV/REL...GEOG 19 SERBIA. PAGE 73 A1503 NAT/LISM DIPLOM WAR

SERENI A.P. A2686

SERV/IND....SERVICE INDUSTRY

B
UN DEPARTMENT SOCIAL AFFAIRS,SOCIAL WELFARE INFORMATION SERIES: CURRENT LITERATURE AND NATIONAL CONFERENCES. WOR+45 INDUS SERV/IND INT/ORG CONSULT ACT/RES WEALTH...HEAL UN. PAGE 147 A2997 BIBLIOG/A SOC/WK DIPLOM ADMIN

N
KYRIAK T.E.,EAST EUROPE: BIBLIOGRAPHY--INDEX TO US JPRS RESEARCH TRANSLATIONS. ALBANIA BULGARIA COM CZECHOSLVK HUNGARY POLAND ROMANIA AGRI EXTR/IND FINAN SERV/IND INT/TRADE WEAPON...GEOG MGT SOC 20. PAGE 83 A1701 BIBLIOG/A PRESS MARXISM INDUS

B38
WARE E.E.,THE STUDY OF INTERNATIONAL RELATIONS IN THE UNITED STATES. USA+45 USA-45 WOR-45 INTELL SERV/IND INT/ORG NAT/G PROF/ORG SECT CONSULT INT/TRADE EDU/PROP ARMS/CONT...CONCPT 20. PAGE 161 A3283 KNOWL DIPLOM

B55
OECD,MARSHALL PLAN IN TURKEY. TURKEY USA+45 COM/IND CONSTRUC SERV/IND FORCES BUDGET...STAT 20 MARSHL/PLN. PAGE 111 A2277 FOR/AID ECO/UNDEV AGRI INDUS

S62
ALBONETTI A.,"IL SECONDO PROGRAMMA QUINQUENNALE 1963-67 ED IL BILANCIO RICERCHE ED INVESTIMENTI PER IL 1963 DELL'ERATOM." EUR+WWI FUT ITALY WOR+45 ECO/DEV SERV/IND INT/ORG TEC/DEV ECO/TAC ATTIT R+D PLAN NUC/PWR

SKILL WEALTH...MGT TIME/SEQ OEEC 20. PAGE 5 A0108

S63
BALOGH T.,"L'INFLUENCE DES INSTITUTIONS MONETAIRES ET COMMERCIALES SUR LA STRUCTURE ECONOMIQUE AFRICAIN." AFR EUR+WWI FUT USA+45 USA-45 WOR+45 SERV/IND INT/ORG NAT/G TOP/EX ROUTINE...INDEX EEC 20. PAGE 11 A0215 — FINAN

B65
MEYERHOFF A.E.,THE STRATEGY OF PERSUASION: THE USE OF ADVERTISING SKILLS IN FIGHTING THE COLD WAR. USA+45 USSR PLAN ATTIT DRIVE...BIBLIOG 20 COLD/WAR. PAGE 100 A2054 — EDU/PROP SERV/IND METH/COMP DIPLOM

SERVAN/JJ....JEAN JACQUES SERVAN-SCHREIBER

SERVAN-SCHREIBER, JEAN-JACQUES....SEE SERVAN/JJ

SERVICE INDUSTRY....SEE SERV/IND

SET THEORY....SEE CLASSIF

SETHE P. A2687

SETON-WATSON H. A2688

SEVENTHDAY....SEVENTH DAY ADVENTISTS

SEX DIFFERENCES....SEE SEX

SEX....SEE ALSO BIO/SOC

S65
TURNER F.C.,"THE IMPLICATIONS OF DEMOGRAPHIC CHANGE FOR NATIONALISM AND INTERNATIONALISM." FUT WOR+45 NAT/LISM AGE SEX CONCPT. PAGE 146 A2980 — SOCIETY EDU/PROP DIPLOM ORD/FREE

SEXUAL BEHAVIOR....SEE SEX, PERSON

SEYID MUHAMMAD V.A. A2689

SEYLER W.C. A2690

SHAFFER H.G. A2691

SHANGHAI....SHANGHAI

SHANNON D.A. A2692

SHAPIRO D. A2693

SHAPP W.R. A2694

SHARMA J.S. A2695

SHARP G. A2696

SHARP W.R. A2697

SHASTRI/LB....LAL BAHADUR SHASTRI

SHAW C. A2698

SHELBY C. A2699

SHEPPARD/S....SAMUEL SHEPPARD

SHERMAN M. A2700

SHERMN/ACT....SHERMAN ANTI-TRUST ACT

SHERSHNEV Y. A2701

SHIRATO I. A2702

SHOEMAKER R.L. A2703

SHONFIELD A. A2704,A2705

SHORT TAKE-OFF AND LANDING AIRCRAFT....SEE STOL

SHOTWELL J. A2706,A2707,A2708

SHOUP/C....C. SHOUP

SHRIVER/S....SARGENT SHRIVER

SHUKRI A. A2709

SHULIM J.I. A2710

SHULMAN M.D. A2080,A2711

SHWADRAN B. A2712

SIBERIA....SIBERIA

SIBRON....SIBRON V. NEW YORK

SICILY....SICILY

SICKNESS....SEE HEALTH

SIDDIQUI A.H. A0835

SIDGWICK H. A2713

SIDGWICK/H....HENRY SIDGWICK

SIEGFRIED A. A2714

SIER/LEONE....SIERRA LEONE; SEE ALSO AFR

B00
MOCKLER-FERRYMAN A.,BRITISH WEST AFRICA. FRANCE GERMANY NIGER SIER/LEONE UK CULTURE DIPLOM WAR RACE/REL PRODUC PROFIT WEALTH...POLICY PREDICT 19. PAGE 102 A2095 — AFR COLONIAL INT/TRADE CAP/ISM

C62
DUFFY J.,"PORTUGAL IN AFRICA." PORTUGAL SIER/LEONE INDUS WORKER INT/TRADE WAR CONSERVE...CATH GEOG TREND 16/20. PAGE 39 A0795 — BIBLIOG RACE/REL ECO/UNDEV COLONIAL

B63
WALKER A.A.,OFFICIAL PUBLICATIONS OF SIERRA LEONE AND GAMBIA. GAMBIA SIER/LEONE UK LAW CONSTN LEGIS PLAN BUDGET DIPLOM...SOC SAMP CON/ANAL 20. PAGE 160 A3262 — BIBLIOG NAT/G COLONIAL ADMIN

SIFFIN W.J. A2116

SIHANOUK....NORODOM SIHANOUK

SIKKIM....SEE ALSO S/ASIA

SILBERNER E. A2715

SILVA SOLAR J. A2716

SILVER....SILVER STANDARD AND POLICIES RELATING TO SILVER

B58
AVRAMOVIC D.,POSTWAR GROWTH IN INTERNATIONAL INDEBTEDNESS. WOR+45 AGRI INDUS CAP/ISM PRICE INCOME...NAT/COMP 20 GOLD/STAND SILVER. PAGE 10 A0199 — INT/TRADE FINAN COST BAL/PAY

B58
PALYI M.,MANAGED MONEY AT THE CROSSROADS: THE EUROPEAN EXPERIENCE. WOR+45 WOR-45 TEC/DEV DIPLOM INT/TRADE DEMAND WEALTH...CHARTS BIBLIOG 19/20 EUROPE GOLD/STAND SILVER. PAGE 113 A2324 — FINAN ECO/TAC ECO/DEV PRODUC

B66
TRIFFIN R.,THE WORLD MONEY MAZE. INT/ORG ECO/TAC PRICE OPTIMAL WEALTH...METH/COMP 20 EEC OEEC GOLD/STAND SILVER. PAGE 145 A2964 — BAL/PAY FINAN INT/TRADE DIPLOM

SIMMEL/G....GEORG SIMMEL

SIMMONS G.B. A2824

SIMMONS J.G. A1081

SIMOES DOS REIS A. A2717

SIMONDS F.H. A2718

SIMONS H. A2719

SIMPSON J.L. A2720

SIMPSON....SIMPSON V. UNION OIL COMPANY

SIMUL....SCIENTIFIC MODELS

B49
PARMELEE M.,GEO-ECONOMIC REGIONAL AND WORLD FEDERATION. FUT WOR+45 WOR-45 SOCIETY VOL/ASSN PLAN ...METH/CNCPT SIMUL GEN/METH TOT/POP 20. PAGE 114 A2335 — INT/ORG GEOG REGION

L52
HILSMAN R. JR.,"INTELLIGENCE AND POLICY MAKING IN FOREIGN AFFAIRS." USA+45 CONSULT ACT/RES DIPLOM EDU/PROP ROUTINE PEACE PERCEPT PWR SKILL...POLICY MGT HYPO/EXP CONGRESS 20 CIA. PAGE 65 A1333 — PROF/ORG SIMUL WAR

B56
LOVEDAY A.,REFLECTIONS ON INTERNATIONAL ADMINISTRATION. WOR+45 WOR-45 DELIB/GP ACT/RES ADMIN EXEC ROUTINE DRIVE...METH/CNCPT TIME/SEQ CON/ANAL SIMUL TOT/POP 20. PAGE 91 A1865 — INT/ORG MGT

B57
MATECKI B.,ESTABLISHMENT OF THE INTERNATIONAL FINANCE CORPORATION AND UNITED STATES POLICY. — FINAN INT/ORG

USA+45 WOR+45 CONSTN NAT/G CREATE RIGID/FLEX KNOWL ...METH/CNCPT TIME/SEQ SIMUL TOT/POP 20 INTL/FINAN. PAGE 96 A1964 — DIPLOM

S57
KAPLAN M.,"BALANCE OF POWER, BIPOLARITY AND OTHER MODELS OF INTERNATIONAL SYSTEMS" (BMR)" ACT/RES BAL/PWR...PHIL/SCI METH 20. PAGE 76 A1559 — DIPLOM GAME METH/CNCPT SIMUL

B60
HOFFMANN S.H.,CONTEMPORARY THEORY IN INTERNATIONAL RELATIONS. RATIONAL...SOC METH/CNCPT METH/COMP SIMUL ANTHOL 20. PAGE 66 A1359 — DIPLOM METH PHIL/SCI DECISION

B60
STEIN E.,AMERICAN ENTERPRISE IN THE EUROPEAN COMMON MARKET: A LEGAL PROFILE. EUR+WWI FUT USA+45 SOCIETY STRUCT ECO/DEV NAT/G VOL/ASSN CONSULT PLAN TEC/DEV ECO/TAC INT/TRADE ADMIN ATTIT RIGID/FLEX PWR...MGT NEW/IDEA STAT TREND COMPUT/IR SIMUL EEC 20. PAGE 137 A2814 — MARKET ADJUD INT/LAW

B60
WOLF C.,FOREIGN AID: THEORY AND PRACTICE IN SOUTHERN ASIA. CEYLON INDONESIA PHILIPPINE S/ASIA CULTURE STRATA ECO/UNDEV PLAN EDU/PROP ATTIT ...METH/CNCPT MATH QUANT STAT CONT/OBS TIME/SEQ SIMUL TOT/POP 20. PAGE 166 A3378 — ACT/RES ECO/TAC FOR/AID

B61
KNORR K.E.,THE INTERNATIONAL SYSTEM. FUT SOCIETY INT/ORG NAT/G PLAN BAL/PWR DIPLOM WAR PWR ...DECISION METH/CNCPT CONT/OBS GAME METH UN 20. PAGE 81 A1655 — ACT/RES SIMUL ECO/UNDEV

B61
ROSENAU J.N.,INTERNATIONAL POLITICS AND FOREIGN POLICY: A READER IN RESEARCH AND THEORY. ELITES ATTIT SOVEREIGN...DECISION CHARTS HYPO/EXP GAME SIMUL ANTHOL BIBLIOG METH 20. PAGE 124 A2531 — ACT/RES DIPLOM CONCPT POLICY

B61
SCHMIDT H.,VERTEIDIGUNG ODER VERGELTUNG. COM CUBA GERMANY/W USSR FORCES DIPLOM ARMS/CONT DETER NUC/PWR...POLICY CHARTS HYPO/EXP SIMUL BIBLIOG 20 NATO COLD/WAR. PAGE 128 A2630 — PLAN WAR BAL/PWR ORD/FREE

S61
MASTERS R.D.,"A MULTI-BLOC MODEL OF THE INTERNATIONAL SYSTEM." FUT UNIV WOR+45 SOCIETY ACT/RES PLAN...GEOG SOC TREND SIMUL TOT/POP 20. PAGE 96 A1963 — INT/ORG CONCPT

B62
BOULDING K.E.,CONFLICT AND DEFENSE: A GENERAL THEORY. FUT SOCIETY INT/ORG NAT/G CREATE BAL/PWR COERCE NAT/LISM DRIVE ALL/VALS...PLURIST DECISION CONCPT METH/CNCPT TREND HYPO/EXP TOT/POP 20. PAGE 17 A0347 — MATH SIMUL PEACE WAR

B62
HUNTINGTON S.P.,CHANGING PATTERNS OF MILITARY POLITICS. EUR+WWI L/A+17C S/ASIA USA+45 WOR+45 CULTURE INT/ORG NAT/G CONSULT PLAN DOMIN EDU/PROP LEGIT DETER WAR ATTIT PERSON PWR...DECISION CONCPT SIMUL GEN/LAWS ANTHOL COLD/WAR 20. PAGE 69 A1419 — FORCES RIGID/FLEX

B62
MANNING C.A.W.,THE NATURE OF INTERNATIONAL SOCIETY. FUT LAW NAT/G TOP/EX NAT/LISM PEACE PERCEPT PERSON ALL/VALS PLURISM...METH/CNCPT MYTH HYPO/EXP TOT/POP 20. PAGE 94 A1926 — INT/ORG SOCIETY SIMUL DIPLOM

S62
MILLIKEN M.,"NEW AND OLD CRITERIA FOR AID." WOR+45 ECO/DEV ECO/UNDEV ACT/RES PLAN ATTIT KNOWL...TREND CON/ANAL SIMUL GEN/METH 20. PAGE 102 A2083 — USA+45 ECO/TAC FOR/AID

S62
SINGER J.D.,"STABLE DETERRENCE AND ITS LIMITS." FUT WOR+45 R+D INT/ORG CONSULT ACT/RES TEC/DEV ARMS/CONT COERCE DRIVE PERCEPT RIGID/FLEX ORD/FREE PWR...MYTH SIMUL TOT/POP 20. PAGE 133 A2728 — NAT/G FORCES DETER NUC/PWR

B63
NORTH R.C.,CONTENT ANALYSIS: A HANDBOOK WITH APPLICATIONS FOR THE STUDY OF INTERNATIONAL CRISIS. ASIA COM EUR+WWI MOD/EUR INT/ORG TEC/DEV DOMIN EDU/PROP ROUTINE COERCE PERCEPT RIGID/FLEX ALL/VALS ...QUANT TESTS CON/ANAL SIMUL GEN/LAWS VAL/FREE. PAGE 110 A2252 — METH/CNCPT COMPUT/IR USSR

B63
ROSECRANCE R.N.,ACTION AND REACTION IN WORLD POLITICS. FUT WOR-45 SOCIETY DELIB/GP ACT/RES CREATE DIPLOM ECO/TAC DOMIN EDU/PROP COERCE ATTIT PERSON SUPEGO ORD/FREE PWR...CHARTS SIMUL LEAGUE/NAT VAL/FREE UN 19/20. PAGE 123 A2529 — WOR+45 INT/ORG BAL/PWR

B63
US DEPARTMENT OF STATE,POLITICAL BEHAVIOR--A LIST OF CURRENT STUDIES. USA+45 COM/IND DIPLOM LEAD PERS/REL DRIVE PERCEPT KNOWL...DECISION SIMUL METH. PAGE 151 A3093 — BIBLIOG METH/COMP GP/REL ATTIT

L63
PHELPS J.,"STUDIES IN DETERRENCE VIII: MILITARY STABILITARY AND ARMS CONTROL: A CRITICAL SURVEY." FUT WOR+45 INT/ORG ACT/RES EDU/PROP COERCE NUC/PWR WAR HEALTH PWR...POLICY TECHNIC TREND SIMUL TOT/POP 20. PAGE 116 A2373 — FORCES ORD/FREE ARMS/CONT DETER

L63
SINGER J.D.,"WEAPONS MANAGEMENT IN WORLD POLITICS: PROCEEDINGS OF THE INTERNATIONAL ARMS CONTROL SYMPOSIUM, DECEMBER, 1962." FUT WOR+45 SOCIETY ECO/DEV INDUS INT/ORG DELIB/GP FORCES ACT/RES ECO/TAC EDU/PROP ARMS/CONT SUPEGO HEALTH ORD/FREE PWR SKILL...POLICY CHARTS SIMUL ANTHOL VAL/FREE 20. PAGE 133 A2729 — CONSULT ATTIT DIPLOM NUC/PWR

S63
SINGER M.R.,"ELECTIONS WITHIN THE UNITED NATIONS: AN EXPERIMENTAL STUDY UTILIZING STATISTICAL ANALYSIS." USA+45 WOR+45 DIPLOM ECO/TAC COERCE PWR WEALTH...STAT CHARTS SIMUL GEN/LAWS COLD/WAR VAL/FREE UN 20. PAGE 133 A2732 — INT/ORG CHOOSE

B64
JACOB P.E.,THE INTEGRATION OF POLITICAL COMMUNITIES. USA+45 WOR+45 CULTURE LOC/G MUNIC NAT/G CREATE PLAN LEGIT REGION COERCE ALL/VALS ...POLICY GEOG PSY SOC TREND HYPO/EXP GEN/LAWS VAL/FREE 20. PAGE 72 A1483 — INT/ORG METH/CNCPT SIMUL STAT

S64
BEIM D.,"THE COMMUNIST BLOC AND THE FOREIGN-AID GAME." WOR+45 NAT/G PLAN ROUTINE ATTIT KNOWL ORD/FREE...DECISION QUANT CONT/OBS TIME/SEQ CHARTS GAME SIMUL COLD/WAR 20. PAGE 12 A0252 — COM ECO/UNDEV ECO/TAC FOR/AID

B66
KUENNE R.E.,THE POLARIS MISSILE STRIKE* A GENERAL ECONOMIC SYSTEMS ANALYSIS. USA+45 USSR NAT/G BAL/PWR ARMS/CONT WAR...MATH PROBABIL COMPUT/IR CHARTS HYPO/EXP SIMUL. PAGE 82 A1689 — NUC/PWR FORCES DETER DIPLOM

N67
US SUPERINTENDENT OF DOCUMENTS,SPACE: MISSILES, THE MOON, NASA, AND SATELLITES (PRICE LIST 79A). USA+45 COM/IND R+D NAT/G DIPLOM EDU/PROP ADMIN CONTROL HEALTH...POLICY SIMUL NASA CONGRESS. PAGE 157 A3206 — BIBLIOG/A SPACE TEC/DEV PEACE

SIMULATION....SEE SIMUL, MODELS INDEX

SINAI....SINAI

SIND....SIND - REGION OF PAKISTAN

B62
HUTTENBACK R.A.,BRITISH RELATIONS WITH THE SIND, 1799-1843. FRANCE INDIA UK FORCES...POLICY CHARTS BIBLIOG 18/19 SIND. PAGE 69 A1425 — COLONIAL DIPLOM DOMIN S/ASIA

SINEY M.C. A2721

SINGAPORE....SINGAPORE; SEE ALSO MALAYSIA

S66
GAMER R.E.,"URGENT SINGAPORE, PATIENT MALAYSIA." MALAYSIA S/ASIA ECO/UNDEV POL/PAR CHIEF TARIFFS TAX CONTROL LEAD REGION PWR 20 SINGAPORE. PAGE 51 A1036 — DIPLOM NAT/G POLICY ECO/TAC

SINGER D. A2722

SINGER H.W. A2723

SINGER J.D. A2724,A2725,A2726,A2727,A2728,A2729

SINGER K. A2730

SINGER L. A2731

SINGER M.R. A2732

SINGH D. A0223

SINGH L.P. A2733

SINGH N. A2734,A2735

SINO/SOV....SINO-SOVIET RELATIONSHIPS

SINO-SOVIET RELATIONS....SEE SINO/SOV

SINYAVSK/A....ANDREY SINYAVSKY

SIPKOV I. A2736

SIRS....SALARY INFORMATION RETRIEVAL SYSTEM

SKALWEIT S. A2737

SKILL....DEXTERITY

B00
OMAN C.,A HISTORY OF THE ART OF WAR: THE MIDDLE AGES FROM THE FOURTH TO THE FOURTEENTH CENTURY. CHRIST-17C MEDIT-7 CULTURE SOCIETY INT/ORG ROUTINE PERSON...CONT/OBS HIST/WRIT CHARTS VAL/FREE. PAGE 112 A2291 — FORCES SKILL WAR

B14
BERNHARDI F.,ON THE WAR OF TODAY. MOD/EUR INT/ORG NAT/G TOP/EX PWR CHARTS. PAGE 14 A0278
FORCES SKILL WAR

B17
UPTON E.,THE MILITARY POLICY OF THE US. USA-45 STRUCT INT/ORG EXEC ATTIT PERCEPT...MGT CONCPT OBS HIST/WRIT CHARTS CONGRESS 18/20. PAGE 149 A3049
FORCES SKILL WAR

S17
ROOT E.,"THE EFFECT OF DEMOCRACY ON INTERNATIONAL LAW." USA-45 WOR-45 INTELL SOCIETY INT/ORG NAT/G CONSULT ACT/RES CREATE PLAN EDU/PROP PEACE SKILL ...CONCPT METH/CNCPT OBS 20. PAGE 123 A2523
LEGIS JURID INT/LAW

B31
STOWELL E.C.,INTERNATIONAL LAW. FUT UNIV WOR-45 SOCIETY CONSULT EX/STRUC FORCES ACT/RES PLAN DIPLOM EDU/PROP LEGIT DISPL PWR SKILL...POLICY CONCPT OBS TREND TOT/POP 20. PAGE 139 A2839
INT/ORG ROUTINE INT/LAW

S35
MCMAHON A.H.,"INTERNATIONAL BOUNDARIES." WOR-45 INT/ORG NAT/G LEGIT SKILL...CHARTS GEN/LAWS 20. PAGE 98 A2017
GEOG VOL/ASSN INT/LAW

B44
COMM. STUDY ORGAN. PEACE,UNITED NATIONS GUARDS AND TECHNICAL FIELD SERVICES. WOR+45 DELIB/GP EDU/PROP DRIVE PWR SKILL...CONCPT GEN/LAWS UN TOT/POP 20. PAGE 28 A0576
INT/ORG FORCES PEACE

B49
OGBURN W.,TECHNOLOGY AND INTERNATIONAL RELATIONS. WOR+45 WOR-45 ECO/DEV CREATE PLAN ECO/TAC EDU/PROP COERCE PWR SKILL WEALTH...TECHNIC PSY SOC NEW/IDEA CHARTS TOT/POP 20. PAGE 111 A2283
TEC/DEV DIPLOM INT/ORG

S49
FOX W.T.R.,"INTERWAR INTERNATIONAL RELATIONS RESEARCH: THE AMERICAN EXPERIENCE." USA+45 USA-45 INTELL INT/ORG VOL/ASSN OP/RES ATTIT SKILL ...TIME/SEQ LEAGUE/NAT 20. PAGE 48 A0973
ACT/RES CON/ANAL

L52
HILSMAN R. JR.,"INTELLIGENCE AND POLICY MAKING IN FOREIGN AFFAIRS." USA+45 CONSULT ACT/RES DIPLOM EDU/PROP ROUTINE PEACE PERCEPT PWR SKILL...POLICY MGT HYPO/EXP CONGRESS 20 CIA. PAGE 65 A1333
PROF/ORG SIMUL WAR

S53
CORY R.H. JR.,"FORGING A PUBLIC INFORMATION POLICY FOR THE UNITED NATIONS." FUT WOR+45 SOCIETY ADMIN PEACE ATTIT PERSON SKILL...CONCPT 20 UN. PAGE 31 A0628
INT/ORG EDU/PROP BAL/PWR

B55
COTTRELL W.F.,ENERGY AND SOCIETY. FUT WOR+45 WOR-45 ECO/DEV ECO/UNDEV INT/ORG NAT/G DETER ORD/FREE PWR SKILL WEALTH...SOC TIME/SEQ TOT/POP VAL/FREE 20. PAGE 31 A0634
TEC/DEV BAL/PWR PEACE

B55
MYRDAL A.R.,AMERICA'S ROLE IN INTERNATIONATIONAL SOCIAL WELFARE. FUT WOR+45 SOCIETY R+D VOL/ASSN ECO/TAC EDU/PROP HEALTH KNOWL WEALTH...SOC CHARTS ORG/CHARTS TOT/POP 20. PAGE 107 A2188
PLAN SKILL FOR/AID

S55
WRIGHT Q.,"THE PEACEFUL ADJUSTMENT OF INTERNATIONAL RELATIONS: PROBLEMS AND RESEARCH APPROACHES." UNIV INTELL EDU/PROP ADJUD ROUTINE KNOWL SKILL...INT/LAW JURID PHIL/SCI CLASSIF 20. PAGE 167 A3411
R+D METH/CNCPT PEACE

B57
BEAL J.R.,JOHN FOSTER DULLES, A BIOGRAPHY. USA+45 USSR WOR+45 CONSTN INT/ORG NAT/G EX/STRUC LEGIT ADMIN NUC/PWR DISPL PERSON ORD/FREE PWR SKILL ...POLICY PSY OBS RECORD COLD/WAR UN 20 DULLES/JF. PAGE 12 A0237
BIOG DIPLOM

B57
DUDDEN A.P.,WOODROW WILSON AND THE WORLD OF TODAY. USA-45 NAT/G PROVS CONTROL PARTIC WAR ISOLAT PWR SKILL...PERS/COMP ANTHOL 19/20 WILSON/W UN LEAGUE/NAT WWI. PAGE 39 A0794
CHIEF DIPLOM POL/PAR LEAD

S57
ALLEN R.L.,"UNITED NATIONS TECHNICAL ASSISTANCE: SOVIET AND EAST-EUROPEAN PARTICIPATION." COM WOR+45 AGRI INDUS INT/ORG NAT/G FOR/AID SKILL UN 20. PAGE 6 A0124
ECO/UNDEV TEC/DEV USSR

B58
UN INTL CONF ON PEACEFUL USE,PROGRESS IN ATOMIC ENERGY (VOL. I). WOR+45 R+D PLAN TEC/DEV CONFER CONTROL PEACE SKILL...CHARTS ANTHOL 20 UN BAGHDAD. PAGE 147 A3003
NUC/PWR DIPLOM WORKER EDU/PROP

S58
ANDERSON N.,"INTERNATIONAL SEMINARS: AN ANALYSIS AND AN EVALUATION." WOR+45 R+D ACT/RES CREATE PLAN REGION ATTIT KNOWL SKILL...SOC REC/INT PERS/TEST CHARTS 20. PAGE 8 A0158
INT/ORG DELIB/GP

B59
KULSKI W.W.,PEACEFUL CO-EXISTENCE: AN ANALYSIS OF SOVIET FOREIGN POLICY. WOR+45 INTELL SOCIETY ECO/UNDEV POL/PAR EDU/PROP COERCE DRIVE RIGID/FLEX PWR SKILL...PSY CONCPT HIST/WRIT CON/ANAL GEN/METH WORK VAL/FREE 20. PAGE 83 A1691
PLAN DIPLOM USSR

B59
MODELSKI G.,ATOMIC ENERGY IN THE COMMUNIST BLOC. FUT INT/ORG CONSULT FORCES ACT/RES PLAN KNOWL SKILL ...PHIL/SCI STAT CHARTS 20. PAGE 102 A2096
TEC/DEV NUC/PWR USSR COM

B59
STANFORD RESEARCH INSTITUTE,POSSIBLE NONMILITARY SCIENTIFIC DEVELOPMENTS AND THEIR POTENTIAL IMPACT ON FOREIGN POLICY PROBLEMS OF THE UNITED. FUT USA+45 INT/ORG PROF/ORG CONSULT ACT/RES CREATE PLAN PEACE KNOWL SKILL...TECHNIC PHIL/SCI NEW/IDEA UNESCO 20. PAGE 137 A2802
R+D TEC/DEV

S59
KOHN L.Y.,"ISRAEL AND NEW NATION STATES OF ASIA AND AFRICA." AFR ASIA FUT S/ASIA VOL/ASSN TEC/DEV NAT/LISM RIGID/FLEX SKILL WEALTH...RELATIV OBS TREND CON/ANAL 20. PAGE 81 A1663
ECO/UNDEV ECO/TAC FOR/AID ISRAEL

S59
SIMONS H.,"WORLD-WIDE CAPABILITIES FOR PRODUCTION AND CONTROL OF NUCLEAR WEAPONS." FUT WOR+45 INDUS INT/ORG NAT/G ECO/TAC ATTIT PWR SKILL...TREND CHARTS VAL/FREE 20. PAGE 133 A2719
TEC/DEV ARMS/CONT NUC/PWR

S59
TIPTON J.B.,"PARTICIPATION OF THE UNITED STATES IN THE INTERNATIONAL LABOR ORGANIZATION." USA+45 LAW STRUCT ECO/DEV ECO/UNDEV INDUS TEC/DEV ECO/TAC ADMIN PERCEPT ORD/FREE SKILL...STAT HIST/WRIT GEN/METH ILO WORK 20. PAGE 144 A2946
LABOR INT/ORG

B60
DUCHACEK I.D.,CONFLICT AND COOPERATION AMONG NATIONS. WOR+45 WOR-45 SOCIETY NAT/G DOMIN DETER PWR SKILL COLD/WAR 20. PAGE 39 A0791
INT/ORG BAL/PWR DIPLOM

B60
LINDSAY K.,EUROPEAN ASSEMBLIES: THE EXPERIMENTAL PERIOD 1949-1959. EUR+WWI ECO/DEV NAT/G POL/PAR LEGIS TOP/EX ACT/RES PLAN ECO/TAC DOMIN LEGIT ROUTINE ATTIT DRIVE ORD/FREE PWR SKILL...SOC CONCPT TREND CHARTS GEN/LAWS VAL/FREE. PAGE 89 A1823
VOL/ASSN INT/ORG REGION

B60
PRICE D.,THE SECRETARY OF STATE. USA+45 CONSTN ELITES INTELL CHIEF EX/STRUC TOP/EX LEGIT ATTIT PWR SKILL...DECISION 20 CONGRESS. PAGE 117 A2410
CONSULT DIPLOM INT/LAW

L60
FERNBACH A.P.,"SOVIET COEXISTENCE STRATEGY." WOR+45 PROF/ORG VOL/ASSN DIPLOM DOMIN EDU/PROP ATTIT DRIVE PERSON PWR SKILL WEALTH...POLICY OBS SAMP TREND STERTYP ILO WORK COLD/WAR 420. PAGE 45 A0919
LABOR INT/ORG USSR

L60
LAUTERPACHT E.,"THE UNITED NATIONS EMERGENCY FORCE." R+D LEGIT ROUTINE COERCE KNOWL ORD/FREE SKILL...JURID UN 20. PAGE 85 A1746
INT/ORG FORCES

S60
CLARK W.,"NEW FORCES IN THE UN." FUT UK WOR+45 CONSTN BAL/PWR DIPLOM DRIVE PWR SKILL...CONCPT TREND UN TOT/POP 20. PAGE 27 A0543
INT/ORG ECO/UNDEV SOVEREIGN

S60
HAVILAND H.F.,"PROBLEMS OF AMERICAN FOREIGN POLICY." ASIA COM USA+45 WOR+45 INT/ORG NAT/G CONSULT ECO/TAC FOR/AID DOMIN COERCE NUC/PWR ATTIT DRIVE ORD/FREE PWR RESPECT SKILL...POLICY GEOG OBS SAMP TREND GEN/METH METH COLD/WAR UN 20. PAGE 63 A1292
ECO/UNDEV FORCES DIPLOM

S60
LEAR J.,"PEACE: SCIENCE'S NEXT GREAT EXPLORATION." USA+45 INT/ORG TOP/EX TEC/DEV EDU/PROP ROUTINE PEACE KNOWL SKILL 20. PAGE 86 A1757
EX/STRUC ARMS/CONT NUC/PWR

S60
MODELSKI G.,"AUSTRALIA AND SEATO." S/ASIA USA+45 CULTURE INTELL ECO/DEV NAT/G PLAN DIPLOM ADMIN ROUTINE ATTIT SKILL...MGT TIME/SEQ AUSTRAL 20 SEATO. PAGE 102 A2097
INT/ORG ACT/RES

S60
RIVKIN A.,"AFRICAN ECONOMIC DEVELOPMENT: ADVANCED TECHNOLOGY AND THE STAGES OF GROWTH." CULTURE ECO/UNDEV AGRI COM/IND EXTR/IND PLAN ECO/TAC ATTIT DRIVE RIGID/FLEX SKILL WEALTH...MGT SOC GEN/LAWS WORK TOT/POP 20. PAGE 121 A2487
AFR TEC/DEV FOR/AID

S60
SWIFT R.,"THE UNITED NATIONS AND ITS PUBLIC." WOR+45 CONSTN FINAN CONSULT DELIB/GP ACT/RES ADMIN ROUTINE RIGID/FLEX SKILL UN 20. PAGE 140 A2870
INT/ORG EDU/PROP

L61
WRIGHT Q.,"STUDIES IN DETERRENCE: LIMITED WARS AND THE ROLE OF SEABORNE WEAPONS SYSTEMS." FUT USA+45 WOR+45 SEA INT/ORG NAT/G FORCES ACT/RES WAR WEAPON ORD/FREE TOT/POP 20. PAGE 168 A3415
TEC/DEV SKILL BAL/PWR DETER

S61
BARALL M.,"THE UNITED STATES GOVERNMENT RESPONDS." L/A+17C USA+45 SOCIETY NAT/G CREATE PLAN DIPLOM ECO/TAC ATTIT DRIVE RIGID/FLEX KNOWL SKILL WEALTH ...METH/CNCPT TIME/SEQ GEN/METH 20. PAGE 11 A0217
ECO/UNDEV ACT/RES FOR/AID

S61
BURNET A.,"TOO MANY ALLIES." COM EUR+WWI UK WOR+45 WOR-45 ACT/RES PLAN DISPL PWR SKILL...TIME/SEQ 20 CMN/WLTH SEATO NATO CENTO. PAGE 22 A0438
VOL/ASSN INT/ORG DIPLOM

S61
CASTANEDA J.,"THE UNDERDEVELOPED NATIONS AND THE DEVELOPMENT OF INTERNATIONAL LAW." FUT UNIV LAW
INT/ORG ECO/UNDEV

ACT/RES FOR/AID LEGIT PERCEPT SKILL...JURID METH/CNCPT TIME/SEQ TOT/POP 20 UN. PAGE 25 A0507 PEACE INT/LAW

S61
WHELAN J.G.,"KHRUSHCHEV AND THE BALANCE OF WORLD POWER." FUT WOR+45 INT/ORG VOL/ASSN CAP/ISM DIPLOM SKILL...POLICY COLD/WAR 20 KHRUSH/N. PAGE 163 A3328 COM PWR BAL/PWR USSR

B62
CARDOZA M.H.,DIPLOMATS IN INTERNATIONAL COOPERATION: STEPCHILDREN OF THE FOREIGN SERVICE. EUR+WWI USA+45 NAT/G CONSULT ACT/RES EDU/PROP ROUTINE RIGID/FLEX KNOWL SKILL...SOC OBS TIME/SEQ EEC OEEC NATO 20. PAGE 24 A0480 INT/ORG METH/CNCPT DIPLOM

B62
JEWELL M.E.,SENATORIAL POLITICS AND FOREIGN POLICY. NAT/G POL/PAR CHIEF DELIB/GP TOP/EX FOR/AID EDU/PROP ROUTINE ATTIT PWR SKILL...MAJORIT METH/CNCPT TIME/SEQ CONGRESS 20 PRESIDENT. PAGE 74 A1516 USA+45 LEGIS DIPLOM

B62
LEWIS J.P.,QUIET CRISIS IN INDIA. INDIA USA+45 CULTURE ECO/UNDEV AGRI INDUS PROC/MFG NAT/G PLAN TEC/DEV DRIVE PWR SKILL WEALTH...MYTH 20. PAGE 88 A1801 S/ASIA ECO/TAC FOR/AID

B62
MORGENTHAU H.J.,POLITICS IN THE TWENTIETH CENTURY: IMPASSE OF AMERICAN FOREIGN POLICY. FUT GERMANY USA+45 USSR WOR+45 INT/ORG NAT/G ACT/RES PLAN FOR/AID EDU/PROP LEGIT COERCE WAR PWR...TIME/SEQ TREND COLD/WAR 20. PAGE 104 A2138 SKILL DIPLOM

B62
MORGENTHAU H.J.,POLITICS IN THE 20TH CENTURY: RESTORATION OF AMERICAN POLITICS. ASIA GERMANY USA+45 USSR WOR+45 NAT/G PLAN EDU/PROP LEGIT NUC/PWR ATTIT PWR SKILL...CONCPT TREND COLD/WAR 20. PAGE 104 A2139 INT/ORG DIPLOM

S62
ALBONETTI A.,"IL SECONDO PROGRAMMA QUINQUENNALE 1963-67 ED IL BILANCIO RICERCHE ED INVESTIMENTI PER IL 1963 DELL'ERATOM." EUR+WWI FUT ITALY WOR+45 ECO/DEV SERV/IND INT/ORG TEC/DEV ECO/TAC ATTIT SKILL WEALTH...MGT TIME/SEQ OEEC 20. PAGE 5 A0108 R+D PLAN NUC/PWR

S62
CLEVELAND H.,"THE FUTURE ROLE OF THE UNITED STATES IN THE UNITED NATIONS." USA+45 ECO/UNDEV INT/ORG EX/STRUC DIPLOM FOR/AID ROUTINE SKILL SOVEREIGN WEALTH UN 20. PAGE 27 A0550 FUT ATTIT

B63
HOVET T. JR.,AFRICA IN THE UNITED NATIONS. AFR DELIB/GP EDU/PROP LOBBY CHOOSE ORD/FREE PWR RESPECT SKILL...STAT TIME/SEQ CON/ANAL CHARTS STERTYP VAL/FREE 20 UN. PAGE 68 A1397 INT/ORG USSR

B63
JACOBSON H.K.,THE USSR AND THE UN'S ECONOMIC AND SOCIAL ACTIVITIES. COM WOR+45 DELIB/GP ACT/RES ECO/TAC EDU/PROP RIGID/FLEX SUPEGO HEALTH PWR SKILL ...POLICY CHARTS GEN/METH VAL/FREE UNESCO 20 UN. PAGE 73 A1487 INT/ORG ATTIT USSR

B63
KHADDURI M.,MODERN LIBYA: A STUDY IN POLITICAL DEVELOPMENT. EUR+WWI ISLAM LIBYA ELITES INT/ORG POL/PAR FORCES DIPLOM FOR/AID DOMIN EDU/PROP LEGIT NAT/LISM DRIVE RIGID/FLEX SKILL...CONCPT TIME/SEQ TREND 20. PAGE 78 A1606 NAT/G STRUCT

B63
SCHMELTZ G.W.,LA POLITIQUE MONDIALE CONTEMPORAINE. SOCIETY ECO/UNDEV INDUS INT/ORG NAT/G POL/PAR CONSULT DELIB/GP PLAN TEC/DEV ECO/TAC DOMIN EDU/PROP ROUTINE COERCE PERCEPT PERSON LOVE SKILL ...SOC RECORD TOT/POP. PAGE 128 A2629 WOR+45 COLONIAL

B63
US SENATE COMM APPROPRIATIONS,PERSONNEL ADMINISTRATION AND OPERATIONS OF AGENCY FOR INTERNATIONAL DEVELOPMENT: SPECIAL HEARING. FINAN LEAD COST UTIL SKILL...CHARTS 20 CONGRESS AID CIVIL/SERV. PAGE 155 A3170 ADMIN FOR/AID EFFICIENCY DIPLOM

L63
SINGER J.D.,"WEAPONS MANAGEMENT IN WORLD POLITICS: PROCEEDINGS OF THE INTERNATIONAL ARMS CONTROL SYMPOSIUM, DECEMBER, 1962." FUT WOR+45 SOCIETY ECO/DEV INDUS INT/ORG DELIB/GP FORCES ACT/RES ECO/TAC EDU/PROP ARMS/CONT SUPEGO HEALTH ORD/FREE PWR SKILL...POLICY CHARTS SIMUL ANTHOL VAL/FREE 20. PAGE 133 A2729 CONSULT ATTIT DIPLOM NUC/PWR

S63
COUTY P.,"L'ASSISTANCE POUR LE DEVELOPPEMENT: POINT DE VUE SCANDINAVES." EUR+WWI FINLAND FUT SWEDEN WOR+45 ECO/DEV ECO/UNDEV COM/IND LABOR NAT/G PROF/ORG ACT/RES SKILL WEALTH TOT/POP 20. PAGE 32 A0643 FINAN ROUTINE FOR/AID

S63
ETZIONI A.,"EUROPEAN UNIFICATION: A STRATEGY OF CHANGE." EUR+WWI CULTURE ECO/DEV DELIB/GP ACT/RES ECO/TAC EDU/PROP ATTIT ORD/FREE PWR SKILL WEALTH ...STAT TIME/SEQ EEC TOT/POP VAL/FREE 20. PAGE 42 A0869 INT/ORG RIGID/FLEX

S63
MODELSKI G.,"STUDY OF ALLIANCES." WOR+45 WOR-45 INT/ORG NAT/G FORCES LEGIT ADMIN CHOOSE ALL/VALS PWR SKILL...INT/LAW CONCPT GEN/LAWS 20 TREATY. PAGE 102 A2099 VOL/ASSN CON/ANAL DIPLOM

S63
ROUGEMONT D.,"LES NOUVELLES CHANCES DE L'EUROPE." EUR+WWI FUT ECO/DEV INT/ORG NAT/G ACT/RES PLAN TEC/DEV EDU/PROP ADMIN COLONIAL FEDERAL ATTIT PWR SKILL...TREND 20. PAGE 124 A2549 ECO/UNDEV PERCEPT

B64
DEITCHMAN S.J.,LIMITED WAR AND AMERICAN DEFENSE POLICY. USA+45 WOR+45 INT/ORG NAT/G PLAN TEC/DEV COERCE NUC/PWR RIGID/FLEX PWR SKILL...DECISION METH/CNCPT TIME/SEQ TOT/POP COLD/WAR 20. PAGE 36 A0726 FORCES WAR WEAPON

B64
IKLE F.C.,HOW NATIONS NEGOTIATE. COM EUR+WWI USA+45 INTELL INT/ORG VOL/ASSN DELIB/GP ACT/RES CREATE DOMIN EDU/PROP ADJUD ROUTINE ATTIT PERSON ORD/FREE RESPECT SKILL...PSY SOC OBS VAL/FREE. PAGE 70 A1433 NAT/G PWR POLICY

B64
WEINTRAUB S.,THE WAR IN THE WARDS. KOREA/N WOR+45 DIPLOM COERCE ORD/FREE SKILL 20 TREATY. PAGE 162 A3308 EDU/PROP PEACE CROWD PUB/INST

S64
BUCHAN A.,"THE MULTILATERAL FORCE." EUR+WWI FUT USA+45 NAT/G LEGIT PWR SKILL...CONCPT OEEC MLF 20. PAGE 21 A0422 INT/ORG FORCES

S64
HOVET T. JR.,"THE ROLE OF AFRICA IN THE UNITED NATIONS." FUT WOR+45 NAT/G DELIB/GP DOMIN EDU/PROP LEGIT ORD/FREE PWR RESPECT SKILL...OBS TIME/SEQ TREND VAL/FREE UN 20. PAGE 68 A1398 AFR INT/ORG DIPLOM

S64
KHAN M.Z.,"THE PRESIDENT OF THE GENERAL ASSEMBLY." WOR+45 CONSTN DELIB/GP EDU/PROP LEGIT ROUTINE PWR RESPECT SKILL...DECISION SOC BIOG TREND UN 20. PAGE 78 A1609 INT/ORG TOP/EX

L65
WIONCZEK M.,"LATIN AMERICA FREE TRADE ASSOCIATION." AGRI DIST/IND FINAN INDUS INT/ORG LABOR NAT/G TEC/DEV ECO/TAC HEALTH SKILL WEALTH...POLICY RELATIV MGT LAFTA 20. PAGE 165 A3369 L/A+17C MARKET REGION

B66
BROEKMEIJER M.W.J.,FICTION AND TRUTH ABOUT THE "DECADE OF DEVELOPMENT" WOR+45 AGRI FINAN INDUS NAT/G TEC/DEV DIPLOM EDU/PROP LEAD SKILL 20 THIRD/WRLD. PAGE 19 A0385 FOR/AID POLICY ECO/UNDEV PLAN

B67
MACRIDIS R.C.,FOREIGN POLICY IN WORLD POLITICS (3RD ED.). EX/STRUC BAL/PWR COLONIAL NAT/LISM SKILL SOVEREIGN WEALTH...CONCPT TIME/SEQ ANTHOL 20 COLD/WAR. PAGE 93 A1902 DIPLOM POLICY NAT/G IDEA/COMP

B67
US AGENCY INTERNATIONAL DEV,PROPOSED FOREIGN AID PROGRAM FOR 1968: SUMMARY PRESENTATION TO THE CONGRESS. AFR S/ASIA USA+45 AGRI TEC/DEV DIPLOM ECO/TAC BAL/PAY COST HEALTH KNOWL SKILL 20 AID CONGRESS. PAGE 149 A3053 ECO/UNDEV BUDGET FOR/AID STAT

S67
VAN DUSEN H.P.,"HAMMARSKOLD IN THE WORLD'S SERVICE." DIPLOM CONFER LEAD PEACE STRANGE UTOPIA MORAL SKILL OBJECTIVE...INT/LAW SELF/OBS 20. PAGE 158 A3211 INT/ORG CONSULT TOP/EX NEUTRAL

SKILLING H.G. A2738,A2739

SKUBISZEWSKI K. A2740

SLAV/MACED....SLAVO-MACEDONIANS

SLAVERY....SEE ORD/FREE, DOMIN

SLAVS....SLAVS - PERTAINING TO THE SLAVIC PEOPLE AND SLAVOPHILISM

SLEEP....SLEEPING AND FATIGUE

SLESSOR J. A2741

SLICK T. A2742

SLUMS....SLUMS

SLUSSER R.M. A0873,A2966

SMITH A. A2743

SMITH A.A. A0612

SMITH A.L. A2744

SMITH C.M. A2745

SMITH D.M. A2746

SMITH J.E. A2747

SMITH/ACT....SMITH ACT

SMITH/ADAM....ADAM SMITH

SMITH/ALF....ALFRED E. SMITH

SMITH/IAN....IAN SMITH

SMITH/JOS....JOSEPH SMITH

SMITH/LEVR....SMITH-LEVER ACT

SML/CO....SMALL COMPANY

L61
LEVINE R.A.,"THE ANTHROPOLOGY OF CONFLICT." FUT SOCIETY
CULTURE INTELL FAM INT/ORG LG/CO SML/CO ATTIT KNOWL ACT/RES
...METH/CNCPT VAL/FREE 20. PAGE 88 A1796

SMUTS J.C. A2748

SMUTS/JAN....JAN CHRISTIAN SMUTS

SNCC....STUDENT NONVIOLENT COORDINATING COMMITTEE

SNELL E.M. A1967

SNELL J.L. A2749

SNOW J.H. A2750

SNYDER L.L.D. A2751

SNYDER R.C. A2602,A2752

SNYDER R.N. A2753

SOBEL L.A. A2754

SOBEL R. A2755

SOC....SOCIOLOGY

N
INDIAN COUNCIL WORLD AFFAIRS,SELECT ARTICLES ON BIBLIOG
CURRENT AFFAIRS (BIBLIOGRAPHICAL SERIES: 7). AFR DIPLOM
ASIA COM EUR+WWI S/ASIA UK COLONIAL NUC/PWR PEACE INT/ORG
ATTIT...INT/LAW SOC 20. PAGE 70 A1437 ECO/UNDEV

N
LIBRARY INTERNATIONAL REL,INTERNATIONAL INFORMATION BIBLIOG/A
SERVICE. WOR+45 CULTURE INT/ORG FORCES...GEOG HUM DIPLOM
SOC. PAGE 88 A1808 INT/TRADE
INT/LAW

N
SABIN J.,BIBLIOTHECA AMERICANA: A DICTIONARY OF BIBLIOG
BOOKS RELATING TO AMERICA, FROM ITS DISCOVERY TO L/A+17C
THE PRESENT TIME(29 VOLS.). CONSTN CULTURE SOCIETY DIPLOM
ECO/DEV LOC/G EDU/PROP NAT/LISM...POLICY GEOG SOC NAT/G
19. PAGE 126 A2581

N
UNIVERSITY OF FLORIDA LIBRARY,DOORS TO LATIN BIBLIOG/A
AMERICA; RECENT BOOKS AND PAMPHLETS. CONSTN CULTURE L/A+17C
SOCIETY ECO/UNDEV COLONIAL LEAD GOV/REL NAT/LISM DIPLOM
ATTIT...HUM SOC 20. PAGE 149 A3047 NAT/G

B
CURRENT THOUGHT ON PEACE AND WAR. WOR+45 INT/ORG BIBLIOG/A
FORCES PROB/SOLV DIPLOM NUC/PWR PERCEPT...POLICY PEACE
SOC 20 UN NATO. PAGE 1 A0008 ATTIT
WAR

B
DEUTSCHE BIBLIOTH FRANKF A M,DEUTSCHE BIBLIOG
BIBLIOGRAPHIE. EUR+WWI GERMANY ECO/DEV FORCES LAW
DIPLOM LEAD...POLICY PHIL/SCI SOC 20. PAGE 36 A0743 ADMIN
NAT/G

N
ANNALS OF THE AMERICAN ACADEMY OF POLITICAL AND BIBLIOG/A
SOCIAL SCIENCE. AFR ASIA S/ASIA WOR+45 POL/PAR NAT/G
DIPLOM CRIME REV...SOC BIOG 20. PAGE 1 A0004 CULTURE
ATTIT

N
BULLETIN ANALYTIQUE DE DOCUMENTATION POLITIQUE, BIBLIOG/A
ECONOMIQUE, ET SOCIAL CONTEMPORAIRE. FRANCE WOR+45 DIPLOM
SOCIETY ECO/DEV ECO/UNDEV INT/ORG LOC/G PROB/SOLV NAT/COMP
FOR/AID LEAD REGION SOC. PAGE 1 A0006 NAT/G

N
INTERNATIONAL STUDIES. ASIA S/ASIA WOR+45 ECO/UNDEV BIBLIOG/A
INT/ORG NAT/G LEAD ATTIT WEALTH...SOC 20. PAGE 1 DIPLOM
A0012 INT/LAW
INT/TRADE

N
JOURNAL OF ASIAN STUDIES. CULTURE ECO/DEV SECT BIBLIOG
DIPLOM EDU/PROP WAR NAT/LISM...PHIL/SCI SOC 20. ASIA
PAGE 1 A0013 S/ASIA
NAT/G

N
JOURNAL OF CONFLICT RESOLUTION. FUT WOR+45 INT/ORG BIBLIOG/A
NAT/G FORCES CREATE PROB/SOLV ARMS/CONT NUC/PWR DIPLOM
WEAPON SOC. PAGE 1 A0014 WAR

N
MIDDLE EAST JOURNAL. CULTURE SECT DIPLOM LEAD BIBLIOG
GOV/REL ATTIT...POLICY PHIL/SCI SOC LING BIOG 20. ISLAM
PAGE 1 A0019 NAT/G
ECO/UNDEV

N
SOCIAL RESEARCH. WOR+45 WOR-45 R+D LEAD GP/REL BIBLIOG/A
ATTIT...SOC TREND 20. PAGE 2 A0025 DIPLOM
NAT/G
SOCIETY

N
AFRICAN RESEARCH BULLETIN. AFR CULTURE NAT/G BIBLIOG/A
COLONIAL...SOC 20. PAGE 2 A0026 DIPLOM
PRESS

N
AUSTRALIAN PUBLIC AFFAIRS INFORMATION SERVICE. LAW BIBLIOG
...HEAL HUM MGT SOC CON/ANAL 20 AUSTRAL. PAGE 2 NAT/G
A0028 CULTURE
DIPLOM

N
BIBLIO, CATALOGUE DES OUVRAGES PARUS EN LANGUE BIBLIOG
FRANCAISE DANS LE MONDE ENTIER. FRANCE WOR+45 ADMIN NAT/G
LEAD PERSON...SOC 20. PAGE 2 A0029 DIPLOM
ECO/DEV

N
BIBLIOGRAPHIE DER SOZIALWISSENSCHAFTEN. WOR-45 BIBLIOG
CONSTN SOCIETY ECO/DEV ECO/UNDEV DIPLOM LEAD WAR LAW
PEACE...PHIL/SCI SOC 19/20. PAGE 2 A0030 CONCPT
NAT/G

N
DOCUMENTATION ECONOMIQUE: REVUE BIBLIOGRAPHIQUE DE BIBLIOG/A
SYNTHESE. WOR+45 COM/IND FINAN BUDGET DIPLOM...GEOG SOC
20. PAGE 2 A0033

N
HANDBOOK OF LATIN AMERICAN STUDIES. LAW CULTURE BIBLIOG/A
ECO/UNDEV POL/PAR ADMIN LEAD...SOC 20. PAGE 2 A0035 L/A+17C
NAT/G
DIPLOM

N
THE JAPAN SCIENCE REVIEW: LAW AND POLITICS: LIST OF BIBLIOG
BOOKS AND ARTICLES ON LAW AND POLITICS. CONSTN AGRI LAW
INDUS LABOR DIPLOM TAX ADMIN CRIME...INT/LAW SOC 20 S/ASIA
CHINJAP. PAGE 2 A0042 PHIL/SCI

N
SCHOLARLY BOOKS IN AMERICA; A QUARTERLY BIBLIOG/A
BIBLIOGRAPHY OF UNIVERSITY PRESS PUBLICATIONS. LAW
WOR+45 AGRI COM/IND NAT/G HEALTH...GEOG PHIL/SCI MUNIC
PSY SOC LING 20. PAGE 3 A0046 DIPLOM

N
AMERICAN BIBLIOGRAPHIC SERVICE,INTERNATIONAL GUIDE BIBLIOG
TO INDIC STUDIES - A QUARTERLY INDEX TO PERIODICAL S/ASIA
LITERATURE. INDIA CULTURE NAT/G DIPLOM...EPIST SOC CON/ANAL
BIOG 20. PAGE 7 A0140

N
ATLANTIC INSTITUTE,ATLANTIC STUDIES. COM EUR+WWI BIBLIOG/A
USA+45 CULTURE STRUCT ECO/DEV FORCES LEAD ARMS/CONT DIPLOM
...INT/LAW JURID SOC. PAGE 10 A0193 POLICY
GOV/REL

N
CARIBBEAN COMMISSION,CURRENT CARIBBEAN BIBLIOG
BIBLIOGRAPHY. FRANCE NETHERLAND UK CULTURE NAT/G
ECO/UNDEV PRESS LEAD ATTIT...GEOG SOC 20. PAGE 24 L/A+17C
A0482 DIPLOM

N
CORDIER H.,BIBLIOTECA SINICA. SOCIETY STRUCT SECT BIBLIOG/A
DIPLOM COLONIAL...GEOG SOC CON/ANAL. PAGE 30 A0618 NAT/G
CULTURE
ASIA

N
DEUTSCHE BUCHEREI,DEUTSCHE NATIONALBIBLIOGRAPHIE. BIBLIOG
GERMANY ECO/DEV DIPLOM AGE/Y ATTIT...PHIL/SCI SOC NAT/G
20. PAGE 37 A0744 LEAD
POLICY

N
DEUTSCHE BUCHEREI,JAHRESVERZEICHNIS DES DEUTSCHEN BIBLIOG
SCHRIFTUMS. AUSTRIA EUR+WWI GERMANY SWITZERLND LAW WRITING
LOC/G DIPLOM ADMIN...MGT SOC 19/20. PAGE 37 A0745 NAT/G

N
DEUTSCHE BUCHEREI,DEUTSCHES BUCHERVERZEICHNIS. BIBLIOG
GERMANY LAW CULTURE POL/PAR ADMIN LEAD ATTIT PERSON NAT/G
...SOC 20. PAGE 37 A0746 DIPLOM
ECO/DEV

N
HOOVER INSTITUTION,UNITED STATES AND CANADIAN BIBLIOG
PUBLICATIONS ON AFRICA. CULTURE ECO/UNDEV AGRI DIPLOM
TEC/DEV EDU/PROP COLONIAL RACE/REL NAT/LISM ATTIT NAT/G
HEALTH...SOC SOC/WK 20. PAGE 67 A1381 AFR

N
INSTITUTE OF HISPANIC STUDIES,HISPANIC AMERICAN REPORT. EUR+WWI SPAIN LAW CONSTN ECO/UNDEV POL/PAR EX/STRUC LEGIS LEAD...HUM SOC 20. PAGE 70 A1445
BIBLIOG/A L/A+17C NAT/G DIPLOM

N
KAPLAN L.,REVIEW INDEX. USA+45 USA-45 FINAN INDUS LABOR RACE/REL...GEOG PSY SOC 20. PAGE 76 A1558
BIBLIOG PROF/ORG ECO/DEV DIPLOM

N
KYRIAK T.E.,ASIAN DEVELOPMENTS: A BIBLIOGRAPHY. INDONESIA KOREA/N VIETNAM/N CULTURE SOCIETY ECO/UNDEV NAT/G DIPLOM...SOC TREND 20 MONGOLIA. PAGE 83 A1699
BIBLIOG/A ALL/IDEOS S/ASIA ASIA

N
KYRIAK T.E.,CHINA: A BIBLIOGRAPHY. ASIA CHINA/COM AGRI FINAN INDUS NAT/G INT/TRADE PRESS...SOC 20. PAGE 83 A1700
BIBLIOG/A MARXISM TOP/EX POL/PAR

N
KYRIAK T.E.,EAST EUROPE: BIBLIOGRAPHY--INDEX TO US JPRS RESEARCH TRANSLATIONS. ALBANIA BULGARIA COM CZECHOSLVK HUNGARY POLAND ROMANIA AGRI EXTR/IND FINAN SERV/IND INT/TRADE WEAPON...GEOG MGT SOC 20. PAGE 83 A1701
BIBLIOG/A PRESS MARXISM INDUS

N
KYRIAK T.E.,SOVIET UNION: BIBLIOGRAPHY INDEX TO US JPRS RESEARCH TRANSLATIONS. USSR ECO/DEV AGRI COM/IND CONSTRUC DIST/IND EXTR/IND PROC/MFG R+D INT/TRADE...SOC 20. PAGE 83 A1703
BIBLIOG/A INDUS MARXISM PRESS

N
LONDON LIBRARY ASSOCIATION,ATHENAEUM SUBJECT INDEX. 1915-1918. NAT/G DIPLOM NAT/LISM 20. PAGE 91 A1857
BIBLIOG CON/ANAL SOC

N
MINISTERE DE L'EDUC NATIONALE,CATALOGUE DES THESES DE DOCTORAT SOUTENNES DEVANT LES UNIVERSITAIRES FRANCAISES. FRANCE LAW DIPLOM ADMIN...HUM SOC 20. PAGE 102 A2087
BIBLIOG ACADEM KNOWL NAT/G

N
MURRA R.O.,POST-WAR PROBLEMS: A CURRENT LIST OF UNITED STATES GOVERNMENT PUBLICATIONS (PAMPHLET). WOR+45 SOCIETY FINAN INT/ORG SCHOOL WORKER TEC/DEV ECO/TAC...SOC 20. PAGE 106 A2180
BIBLIOG/A ADJUST AGRI INDUS

N
UNITED NATIONS,OFFICIAL RECORDS OF THE ECONOMIC AND SOCIAL COUNCIL OF THE UNITED NATIONS. WOR+45 DIPLOM INT/TRADE CONFER...SOC SOC/WK 20 UN UNESCO. PAGE 148 A3031
INT/ORG DELIB/GP WRITING

N
US BUREAU OF THE CENSUS,BIBLIOGRAPHY OF SOCIAL SCIENCE PERIODICALS AND MONOGRAPH SERIES. WOR+45 LAW DIPLOM EDU/PROP HEALTH...PSY SOC LING STAT. PAGE 150 A3058
BIBLIOG/A CULTURE NAT/G SOCIETY

N
US DEPARTMENT OF STATE,ABSTRACTS OF COMPLETED DOCTORAL DISSERTATIONS FOR THE ACADEMIC YEAR 1950-1951. WOR+45 WOR-45 ACADEM POL/PAR ECO/TAC ...POLICY SOC 19/20. PAGE 151 A3078
BIBLIOG/A DIPLOM INT/ORG NAT/G

N
US DEPARTMENT OF STATE,BIBLIOGRAPHY (PAMPHLETS). AGRI INDUS INT/ORG FOR/AID EDU/PROP WAR MARXISM ...SOC GOV/COMP METH/COMP 20. PAGE 151 A3079
BIBLIOG DIPLOM ECO/DEV NAT/G

B00
GRIFFIN A.P.C.,LIST OF BOOKS RELATING TO THE THEORY OF COLONIZATION, GOVERNMENT OF DEPENDENCIES, PROTECTORATES, AND RELATED TOPICS. FRANCE GERMANY ITALY SPAIN UK USA-45 WOR-45 ECO/TAC ADMIN CONTROL REGION NAT/LISM ALL/VALS PWR...INT/LAW SOC 16/19. PAGE 56 A1149
BIBLIOG/A COLONIAL GOV/REL DOMIN

L00
HISTORICUS,"LETTERS AND SOME QUESTIONS OF INTERNATIONAL LAW." FRANCE NETHERLAND UK USA-45 WOR-45 LAW NAT/G COERCE...SOC CONCPT GEN/LAWS TOT/POP 19 CIVIL/WAR. PAGE 65 A1344
WEALTH JURID WAR INT/LAW

B09
FREMANTLE H.E.S.,THE NEW NATION, A SURVEY OF THE CONDITION AND PROSPECTS OF SOUTH AFRICA. SOUTH/AFR CONSTN POL/PAR DIPLOM DOMIN COLONIAL WEALTH...SOC TREND 19. PAGE 49 A0996
NAT/LISM SOVEREIGN RACE/REL REGION

B17
MEYER H.H.B.,THE UNITED STATES AT WAR, ORGANIZATIONS AND LITERATURE. USA-45 AGRI FINAN INDUS CHIEF FORCES DIPLOM FOR/AID INT/TRADE...SOC 20 PRESIDENT. PAGE 100 A2050
BIBLIOG/A WAR NAT/G VOL/ASSN

B20
HALDANE R.B.,BEFORE THE WAR. MOD/EUR SOCIETY INT/ORG NAT/G DELIB/GP PLAN DOMIN EDU/PROP LEGIT ADMIN COERCE ATTIT DRIVE MORAL ORD/FREE PWR...SOC CONCPT SELF/OBS RECORD BIOG TIME/SEQ. PAGE 60 A1223
POLICY DIPLOM UK

L21
HALDEMAN E.,"SERIALS OF AN INTERNATIONAL CHARACTER." WOR-45 DIPLOM...ART/METH GEOG HEAL HUM INT/LAW JURID PSY SOC. PAGE 60 A1224
BIBLIOG PHIL/SCI

B24
NAVILLE A.,LIBERTE, EGALITE, SOLIDARITE: ESSAIS D'ANALYSE. STRATA FAM VOL/ASSN INT/TRADE GP/REL MORAL MARXISM SOCISM...PSY TREATY. PAGE 107 A2205
ORD/FREE SOC IDEA/COMP DIPLOM

B25
GODET M.,INDEX BIBLIOGRAPHICUS: INTERNATIONAL CATALOGUE OF SOURCES OF CURRENT BIBLIOGRAPHIC INFORMATION. EUR+WWI MOD/EUR SOCIETY SECT TAX ...JURID PHIL/SCI SOC MATH. PAGE 53 A1085
BIBLIOG/A DIPLOM EDU/PROP LAW

B27
SIEGFRIED A.,AMERICA COMES OF AGE: A FRENCH ANALYSIS (TRANS. BY H.H. HEMMING AND DORIS HEMMING). FRANCE UK POL/PAR WORKER TEC/DEV DIPLOM REGION RACE/REL ADJUST PRODUC HEREDITY...TIME/SEQ GP/COMP SOC/INTEG 20 DEMOCRAT REPUBLICAN KKK. PAGE 132 A2714
USA-45 CULTURE ECO/DEV SOC

B28
CORBETT P.E.,CANADA AND WORLD POLITICS. LAW CULTURE SOCIETY STRUCT MARKET INT/ORG FORCES ACT/RES PLAN ECO/TAC LEGIT ORD/FREE PWR RESPECT...SOC CONCPT TIME/SEQ TREND CMN/WLTH 20 LEAGUE/NAT. PAGE 30 A0612
NAT/G CANADA

B28
HALL W.P.,EMPIRE TO COMMONWEALTH. FUT WOR-45 CONSTN ECO/DEV ECO/UNDEV INT/ORG PROVS PLAN DIPLOM EDU/PROP ADMIN COLONIAL PEACE PERSON ALL/VALS ...POLICY GEOG SOC OBS RECORD TREND CMN/WLTH PARLIAMENT 19/20. PAGE 60 A1229
VOL/ASSN NAT/G UK

B28
HOWARD-ELLIS C.,THE ORIGIN, STRUCTURE AND WORKING OF THE LEAGUE OF NATIONS. EUR+WWI MOD/EUR USA-45 CONSTN FORCES LEGIS ECO/TAC LEGIT COERCE ORD/FREE ...JURID SOC CONCPT LEAGUE/NAT 20 ILO ICJ. PAGE 68 A1401
INT/ORG ADJUD

B28
PLAYNE C.E.,THE PRE-WAR MIND IN BRITAIN. GERMANY MOD/EUR UK STRATA SECT DIPLOM EDU/PROP CROWD SUFF ...POLICY ANARCH PSY SOC IDEA/COMP 20 WWI. PAGE 116 A2388
PRESS WAR DOMIN ATTIT

B29
BUELL R.,INTERNATIONAL RELATIONS. WOR+45 WOR-45 CONSTN STRATA FORCES TOP/EX ADMIN ATTIT DRIVE SUPEGO MORAL ORD/FREE PWR SOVEREIGN...JURID SOC CONCPT 20. PAGE 21 A0428
INT/ORG BAL/PWR DIPLOM

B29
PRATT I.A.,MODERN EGYPT: A LIST OF REFERENCES TO MATERIAL IN THE NEW YORK PUBLIC LIBRARY. UAR ECO/UNDEV...GEOG JURID SOC LING 20. PAGE 117 A2407
BIBLIOG ISLAM DIPLOM NAT/G

B32
BRYCE J.,THE HOLY ROMAN EMPIRE. GERMANY ITALY MOD/EUR CULTURE SOCIETY STRUCT INT/ORG NAT/G SECT DIPLOM DOMIN WAR SUPEGO ALL/VALS SOVEREIGN...GEOG SOC TIME/SEQ CHARTS STERTYP. PAGE 20 A0413
CHRIST-17C NAT/LISM

B37
BOURNE H.E.,THE WORLD WAR: A LIST OF THE MORE IMPORTANT BOOKS PUBLISHED BEFORE 1937 (PAMPHLET). EUR+WWI NAT/G DIPLOM ATTIT SOC. PAGE 17 A0351
BIBLIOG/A WAR FORCES PLAN

B37
DE KIEWIET C.W.,THE IMPERIAL FACTOR IN SOUTH AFRICA. AFR SOUTH/AFR UK WAR...POLICY SOC 19. PAGE 35 A0705
DIPLOM COLONIAL CULTURE

B37
ROBBINS L.,ECONOMIC PLANNING AND INTERNATIONAL ORDER. WOR-45 SOCIETY FINAN INDUS NAT/G ECO/TAC ROUTINE WEALTH...SOC TIME/SEQ GEN/METH WORK 20 KEYNES/JM. PAGE 122 A2492
INT/ORG PLAN INT/TRADE

B38
PETTEE G.S.,THE PROCESS OF REVOLUTION. COM FRANCE ITALY MOD/EUR RUSSIA SPAIN WOR-45 ELITES INTELL SOCIETY STRATA STRUCT INT/ORG NAT/G POL/PAR ACT/RES PLAN EDU/PROP LEGIT EXEC...SOC MYTH TIME/SEQ TOT/POP 18/20. PAGE 115 A2370
COERCE CONCPT REV

B38
RAPPARD W.E.,THE CRISIS OF DEMOCRACY. EUR+WWI UNIV WOR-45 CULTURE SOCIETY ECO/DEV INT/ORG POL/PAR ACT/RES EDU/PROP EXEC CHOOSE ATTIT ALL/VALS...SOC OBS HIST/WRIT TIME/SEQ LEAGUE/NAT NAZI TOT/POP 20. PAGE 119 A2449
NAT/G CONCPT

B40
BROWN A.D.,PANAMA CANAL AND PANAMA CANAL ZONE: A SELECTED LIST OF REFERENCES. PANAMA NAT/G SCHOOL DIPLOM HEALTH...GEOG SOC 20 CANAL/ZONE. PAGE 19 A0397
BIBLIOG/A ECO/UNDEV

B40
CONOVER H.F.,JAPAN-ECONOMIC DEVELOPMENT AND FOREIGN POLICY, A SELECTED LIST OF REFERENCES (PAMPHLET). CULTURE FINAN INDUS NAT/G FORCES INT/TRADE WAR ...SOC TREND 20 CHINJAP. PAGE 29 A0593
BIBLIOG ASIA ECO/DEV DIPLOM

B40
MILLER E.,THE NEUROSES OF WAR. UNIV INTELL SOCIETY INT/ORG NAT/G EDU/PROP DISPL DRIVE PERCEPT PERSON RIGID/FLEX...SOC TIME/SEQ 20. PAGE 101 A2075
HEALTH PSY WAR

B41
EVANS C.,AMERICAN BIBLIOGRAPHY... (12 VOLUMES). USA-45 LAW DIPLOM ADMIN PERSON...HUM SOC 17/18. PAGE 43 A0876
BIBLIOG NAT/G ALL/VALS ALL/IDEOS

B41
KEESING F.M.,THE SOUTH SEAS IN THE MODERN WORLD. INDONESIA STRUCT FAM SECT EDU/PROP LEAD INCOME WEALTH...HEAL SOC 20. PAGE 77 A1577
CULTURE ECO/UNDEV GOV/COMP DIPLOM

L41
COMM. STUDY ORGAN. PEACE,"ORGANIZATION OF PEACE." USA-45 WOR-45 STRATA NAT/G ACT/RES DIPLOM ECO/TAC EDU/PROP ADJUD ATTIT ORD/FREE PWR...SOC CONCPT ANTHOL LEAGUE/NAT 20. PAGE 28 A0575
INT/ORG PLAN PEACE

S41
WRIGHT Q.,"FUNDAMENTAL PROBLEMS OF INTERNATIONAL ORGANIZATION." UNIV WOR-45 STRUCT FORCES ACT/RES CREATE DOMIN EDU/PROP LEGIT REGION NAT/LISM ORD/FREE PWR RESPECT SOVEREIGN...JURID SOC CONCPT METH/CNCPT TIME/SEQ 20. PAGE 167 A3405
INT/ORG ATTIT PEACE

B42
FULLER G.H.,AUSTRALIA: A SELECT LIST OF REFERENCES. FORCES DIPLOM WAR 20 AUSTRAL. PAGE 50 A1022
BIBLIOG SOC

B42
PAGINSKY P.,GERMAN WORKS RELATING TO AMERICA, 1493-1800; A LIST COMPILED FROM THE COLLECTIONS OF THE NEW YORK PUBLIC LIBRARY. GERMANY PRE/AMER CULTURE COLONIAL ATTIT...POLICY SOC 15/19. PAGE 113 A2317
BIBLIOG/A NAT/G L/A+17C DIPLOM

B42
US LIBRARY OF CONGRESS,POSTWAR PLANNING AND RECONSTRUCTION: APRIL-DECEMBER 1942 (SUPPLEMENT 1). WOR+45 SOCIETY INT/ORG DIPLOM...SOC PREDICT 20 UN. PAGE 154 A3147
BIBLIOG/A WAR PEACE PLAN

B43
BROWN A.D.,GREECE: SELECTED LIST OF REFERENCES. GREECE ECO/UNDEV AGRI FINAN INDUS LABOR SECT TEC/DEV INT/TRADE LEAD...SOC 20. PAGE 20 A0399
BIBLIOG/A WAR DIPLOM NAT/G

B44
DAVIS H.E.,PIONEERS IN WORLD ORDER. WOR-45 CONSTN ECO/TAC DOMIN EDU/PROP LEGIT ADJUD ADMIN ARMS/CONT CHOOSE KNOWL ORD/FREE...POLICY JURID SOC STAT OBS CENSUS TIME/SEQ ANTHOL LEAGUE/NAT 20. PAGE 34 A0691
INT/ORG ROUTINE

B44
FULLER G.H.,TURKEY: A SELECTED LIST OF REFERENCES. ISLAM TURKEY CULTURE ECO/UNDEV AGRI DIPLOM NAT/LISM CONSERVE...GEOG HUM INT/LAW SOC 7/20 MAPS. PAGE 50 A1024
BIBLIOG/A ALL/VALS

B44
SHELBY C.,LATIN AMERICAN PERIODICALS CURRENTLY RECEIVED IN THE LIBRARY OF CONGRESS AND IN LIBRARY OF DEPARTMENT OF AGRICULTURE. SOCIETY AGRI INDUS LABOR POL/PAR INT/TRADE...GEOG SOC 20. PAGE 132 A2699
BIBLIOG ECO/UNDEV CULTURE L/A+17C

B44
WHITTON J.B.,THE SECOND CHANCE: AMERICA AND THE PEACE. EUR+WWI USA-45 SOCIETY STRUCT INT/ORG NAT/G LEGIT EXEC WAR ALL/VALS...SOC CONCPT TIME/SEQ TREND CONGRESS 20. PAGE 164 A3340
LEGIS PEACE

L44
HAILEY,"THE FUTURE OF COLONIAL PEOPLES." WOR-45 CONSTN CULTURE ECO/UNDEV AGRI MARKET INT/ORG NAT/G SECT CONSULT ECO/TAC LEGIT ADMIN NAT/LISM ALL/VALS ...SOC OBS TREND STERTYP CMN/WLTH LEAGUE/NAT PARLIAMENT 20. PAGE 59 A1218
PLAN CONCPT DIPLOM UK

N45
INDIA QUARTERLY, A JOURNAL OF INTERNATIONAL AFFAIRS. INDIA LAW CONSTN ECO/UNDEV INT/ORG POL/PAR COLONIAL LEAD PARL/PROC WAR ATTIT...SOC 20 CMN/WLTH. PAGE 3 A0053
BIBLIOG/A S/ASIA DIPLOM NAT/G

B45
WEST R.,CONSCIENCE AND SOCIETY: A STUDY OF THE PSYCHOLOGICAL PREREQUISITES OF LAW AND ORDER. FUT UNIV LAW SOCIETY STRUCT DIPLOM WAR PERS/REL SUPEGO ...SOC 20. PAGE 163 A3321
COERCE INT/LAW ORD/FREE PERSON

B46
BIBLIOGRAFIIA DISSERTATSII: DOKTORSKIE DISSERTATSII ZA 19411944 (2 VOLS.). COM USSR LAW POL/PAR DIPLOM ADMIN LEAD...PHIL/SCI SOC 20. PAGE 3 A0054
BIBLIOG ACADEM KNOWL MARXIST

B46
GAULD W.A.,MAN, NATURE, AND TIME, AN INTRODUCTION TO WORLD STUDY. WOR-45 CULTURE CREATE DIPLOM GP/REL DRIVE...SOC LING CENSUS CHARTS TIME 18/20. PAGE 52 A1054
HABITAT PERSON

N46
HOBBS C.C.,SOUTHEAST ASIA, 1935-45: A SELECTED LIST OF REFERENCE BOOKS (PAMPHLET). S/ASIA AGRI INDUS NAT/G SECT DIPLOM WAR...ART/METH GEOG SOC LING 20. PAGE 65 A1346
BIBLIOG/A CULTURE HABITAT

B47
CONOVER H.F.,NON-SELF-GOVERNING AREAS. BELGIUM FRANCE ITALY UK WOR+45 CULTURE ECO/UNDEV INT/ORG LOC/G NAT/G ECO/TAC INT/TRADE ADMIN HEALTH...SOC UN. PAGE 30 A0601
BIBLIOG/A COLONIAL DIPLOM

B47
HEIMANN E.,FREEDOM AND ORDER: LESSONS FROM THE WAR. WOR-45 CONSTN FORCES CHOOSE CIVMIL/REL PERSON ALL/IDEOS SOCISM...SOC IDEA/COMP WORSHIP 20. PAGE 64 A1308
NAT/G SOCIETY ORD/FREE DIPLOM

B47
HIRSHBERG H.S.,SUBJECT GUIDE TO UNITED STATES GOVERNMENT PUBLICATIONS. USA+45 USA-45 LAW ADMIN ...SOC 20. PAGE 65 A1340
BIBLIOG NAT/G DIPLOM LOC/G

B47
US LIBRARY OF CONGRESS,POSTWAR PLANNING AND RECONSTRUCTION: JANUARY-MARCH 1943. WOR+45 SOCIETY INT/ORG DIPLOM...SOC PREDICT 20. PAGE 154 A3149
BIBLIOG/A WAR PEACE PLAN

L47
BRUNER J.S.,"TOWARD A COMMON GROUND-INTERNATIONAL SOCIAL SCIENCE." FUT WOR+45 INTELL R+D NAT/G VOL/ASSN CONSULT DELIB/GP ACT/RES CREATE PLAN TEC/DEV ATTIT ORD/FREE...PSY SOC CONCPT ANTHOL UNESCO 20. PAGE 20 A0410
INT/ORG KNOWL

S47
RADVANYI L.,"PROBLEMS OF INTERNATIONAL OPINION SURVEYS." WOR+45 INT/ORG NAT/G CREATE ATTIT...PSY SOC METH/CNCPT REC/INT KNO/TEST SAMP/SIZ METH VAL/FREE 20. PAGE 118 A2431
QU/SEMANT SAMP DIPLOM

B48
COTTRELL L.S. JR.,AMERICAN PUBLIC OPINION ON WORLD AFFAIRS IN THE ATOMIC AGE. USA+45 CULTURE INT/ORG NAT/G DIPLOM EDU/PROP PEACE RIGID/FLEX ORD/FREE ...POLICY SOC CONCPT STAND/INT TOT/POP 20. PAGE 31 A0633
SOCIETY ATTIT ARMS/CONT NUC/PWR

B48
VISSON A.,AS OTHERS SEE US. EUR+WWI FRANCE UK USA+45 CULTURE INTELL SOCIETY STRATA NAT/G POL/PAR FOR/AID ATTIT DRIVE LOVE ORD/FREE RESPECT WEALTH ...PLURIST SOC OBS TOT/POP 20. PAGE 159 A3244
USA-45 PERCEPT

B49
BEHRENDT R.F.,MODERN LATIN AMERICA IN SOCIAL SCIENCE LITERATURE. STRUCT ECO/UNDEV SCHOOL DIPLOM INT/TRADE EDU/PROP...GEOG 20. PAGE 12 A0250
BIBLIOG/A SOC L/A+17C

B49
BORBA DE MORAES R.,MANUAL BIBLIOGRAFICO DE ESTUDOS BRASILEIROS. BRAZIL DIPLOM ADMIN LEAD...SOC 20. PAGE 17 A0336
BIBLIOG L/A+17C NAT/G ECO/UNDEV

B49
FORD FOUNDATION,REPORT OF THE STUDY FOR THE FORD FOUNDATION ON POLICY AND PROGRAM. SOCIETY R+D ACT/RES CAP/ISM FOR/AID EDU/PROP ADMIN KNOWL ...POLICY PSY SOC 20. PAGE 47 A0961
WEALTH GEN/LAWS

B49
MARITAIN J.,HUMAN RIGHTS: COMMENTS AND INTERPRETATIONS. COM UNIV WOR+45 LAW CONSTN CULTURE SOCIETY ECO/DEV ECO/UNDEV SCHOOL DELIB/GP EDU/PROP ATTIT PERCEPT ALL/VALS...HUM SOC TREND UNESCO 20. PAGE 95 A1939
INT/ORG CONCPT

B49
OGBURN W.,TECHNOLOGY AND INTERNATIONAL RELATIONS. WOR+45 WOR-45 ECO/DEV CREATE PLAN ECO/TAC EDU/PROP COERCE PWR SKILL WEALTH...TECHNIC PSY SOC NEW/IDEA CHARTS TOT/POP 20. PAGE 111 A2283
TEC/DEV DIPLOM INT/ORG

B49
SINGER K.,THE IDEA OF CONFLICT. UNIV INTELL INT/ORG NAT/G PLAN ROUTINE ATTIT DRIVE ALL/VALS...POLICY CONCPT TIME/SEQ. PAGE 133 A2730
ACT/RES SOC

L49
UNESCO,"SOME SUGGESTIONS ON TEACHING ABOUT THE UN AND ITS SPECIALIZED AGENCIES." UNIV WOR+45 SOCIETY STRATA SCHOOL WAR ALL/VALS KNOWL...SOC CONCPT UNESCO 20 UN. PAGE 147 A3011
INT/ORG EDU/PROP

S49
DUNN F.,"THE PRESENT COURSE OF INTERNATIONAL RELATIONS RESEARCH." WOR+45 WOR-45 SOCIETY R+D INT/ORG WAR PERSON ORD/FREE...POLICY PSY SOC GEN/LAWS 20. PAGE 39 A0800
CONCPT GEN/METH DIPLOM

B50
BEHRENDT R.F.,MODERN LATIN AMERICA IN SOCIAL SCIENCE LITERATURE (SUPPLEMENTS I AND II). STRUCT ECO/UNDEV SCHOOL DIPLOM INT/TRADE...GEOG 20. PAGE 12 A0251
BIBLIOG/A SOC L/A+17C

B50
CORNELL U DEPT ASIAN STUDIES,SOUTHEAST ASIA PROGRAM DATA PAPER. BURMA CAMBODIA INDONESIA MALAYSIA VIETNAM SOCIETY STRUCT NAT/G SECT DIPLOM FOR/AID PWR WEALTH...SOC 20. PAGE 31 A0625
BIBLIOG/A CULTURE S/ASIA ECO/UNDEV

B50
MUGRIDGE D.H.,AMERICAN HISTORY AND CIVILIZATION: LIST OF GUIDES AND ANNOTATED OR SELECTIVE BIBLIOGRAPHIES. NAT/G SECT DIPLOM RACE/REL DISCRIM ATTIT...ART/METH SOC 18/20. PAGE 105 A2164
BIBLIOG/A USA-45 SOCIETY

B50
US LIBRARY OF CONGRESS,THE UNITED STATES AND EUROPE: BIBLIOGRAPHY OF THOUGHT EXPRESSED IN AMERICAN PUBLICATIONS DURING 1950. EUR+WWI GERMANY
BIBLIOG/A SOC ATTIT

USA+45 USSR INT/ORG DIPLOM COLONIAL SOVEREIGN ...POLICY 20 COLD/WAR UN BERLIN/BLO. PAGE 154 A3150

B51
CATALOGO GENERAL DE LA LIBRERIA ESPANOLA E HISPANOAMERICANA 1901-1930; AUTORES (5 VOLS., 1932-1951). SPAIN COLONIAL GOV/REL...SOC 20. PAGE 3 A0058
BIBLIOG L/A+17C DIPLOM NAT/G

B51
MCKEON R.,DEMOCRACY IN A WORLD OF TENSION. UNIV LAW INTELL STRUCT R+D INT/ORG SCHOOL EDU/PROP LEGIT ATTIT DRIVE PERCEPT PERSON...POLICY JURID PSY SOC CONCPT METH/CNCPT OBS UNESCO TOT/POP VAL/FREE. PAGE 98 A2015
SOCIETY ALL/VALS ORD/FREE

B51
US DEPARTMENT OF STATE,LIVRES AMERICAINS TRADUITS EN FRANCAIS ET LIVRES FRANCAIS SUR LES ETATS-UNIS D'AMERIQUE (2ND ED.). FRANCE USA+45 SECT DIPLOM EDU/PROP LEISURE...ART/METH GEOG HUM 20. PAGE 151 A3086
BIBLIOG/A SOC

B51
US DEPARTMENT OF STATE,POINT FOUR, NEAR EAST AND AFRICA, A SELECTED BIBLIOGRAPHY OF STUDIES ON ECONOMICALLY UNDERDEVELOPED COUNTRIES. AGRI COM/IND FINAN INDUS PLAN INT/TRADE...SOC TREND 20. PAGE 151 A3087
BIBLIOG/A AFR S/ASIA ISLAM

S51
ICHHEISER G.,"MISUNDERSTANDING IN INTERNATIONAL RELATIONS." UNIV SOCIETY FACE/GP INT/ORG SECT ATTIT PERSON RIGID/FLEX LOVE RESPECT...RELATIV PSY SOC CONCPT MYTH SOC/EXP GEN/LAWS. PAGE 70 A1431
PERCEPT STERTYP NAT/LISM DIPLOM

C51
BEST H.,"THE SOVIET STATE AND ITS INCEPTION." USSR CULTURE INDUS DIPLOM WEALTH...GEOG SOC BIBLIOG 20. PAGE 14 A0281
COM GEN/METH REV MARXISM

B52
DILLON D.R.,LATIN AMERICA, 1935-1949; A SELECTED BIBLIOGRAPHY. LAW EDU/PROP...SOC 20. PAGE 37 A0764
BIBLIOG L/A+17C NAT/G DIPLOM

B52
HOSELITZ B.F.,THE PROGRESS OF UNDERDEVELOPED AREAS. FUT WOR+45 WOR-45 ECO/DEV ECO/TAC INT/TRADE WEALTH ...SOC TREND GEN/LAWS TOT/POP VAL/FREE COLD/WAR 20. PAGE 68 A1391
ECO/UNDEV PLAN FOR/AID

B52
SKALWEIT S.,FRANKREICH UND FRIEDRICH DER GROSSE. FRANCE GERMANY PRUSSIA NAT/G DOMIN WAR 18 FREDERICK. PAGE 134 A2737
ATTIT EDU/PROP DIPLOM SOC

B52
SPENCER F.A.,WAR AND POSTWAR GREECE: AN ANALYSIS BASED ON GREEK WRITINGS. GREECE SOCIETY NAT/G POL/PAR FORCES CREATE DIPLOM LEAD MARXISM...SOC 20. PAGE 136 A2784
BIBLIOG/A WAR REV

B52
SURANYI-UNGER T.,COMPARATIVE ECONOMIC SYSTEMS. FINAN MARKET DIPLOM PRICE WEALTH...GEOG SOC BIBLIOG METH T 20. PAGE 140 A2865
LAISSEZ PLAN ECO/DEV IDEA/COMP

B52
UN DEPT. SOC. AFF.,PRELIMINARY REPORT ON THE WORLD SOCIAL SITUATION. ISLAM L/A+17C WOR+45 STRATA AGRI EXTR/IND INDUS INT/ORG SCHOOL ADMIN...GEOG SOC TREND UNESCO WORK FAO 20. PAGE 147 A2998
R+D HEALTH FOR/AID

B52
UNESCO,CURRENT SOCIOLOGY (2 VOLS.). SOCIETY STRATA R+D GP/REL ATTIT PERSON 20 UN. PAGE 147 A3014
BIBLIOG SOC INT/ORG CULTURE

B52
UNESCO,THESES DE SCIENCES SOCIALES: CATALOGUE ANALYTIQUE INTERNATIONAL DE THESES INEDITES DE DOCTORAT, 1940-1950. INT/ORG DIPLOM EDU/PROP...GEOG INT/LAW MGT PSY SOC 20. PAGE 147 A3015
BIBLIOG ACADEM WRITING

B53
MURPHY G.,IN THE MINDS OF MEN: THE STUDY OF HUMAN BEHAVIOR AND SOCIAL TENSIONS IN INDIA. FUT S/ASIA FAM INT/ORG NAT/G DIPLOM EDU/PROP GP/REL ATTIT RIGID/FLEX ALL/VALS...SOC QU UNESCO 20. PAGE 106 A2176
SECT STRATA INDIA

B53
SCHAAF R.W.,DOCUMENTS OF INTERNATIONAL MEETINGS. AGRI INDUS ACADEM DIPLOM NUC/PWR RACE/REL AGE/Y HEALTH...SOC 20. PAGE 127 A2614
BIBLIOG/A DELIB/GP INT/ORG POLICY

L53
UNESCO,"THE TECHNIQUE OF INTERNATIONAL CONFERENCES." WOR+45 INT/ORG VOL/ASSN EDU/PROP ROUTINE ATTIT DRIVE KNOWL ORD/FREE...SOC UNESCO 20. PAGE 148 A3016
DELIB/GP ACT/RES

C53
DEUTSCH K.W.,"NATIONALISM AND SOCIAL COMMUNICATION: AN INQUIRY INTO THE FOUNDATIONS OF NATIONALITY." CULTURE STRUCT DIPLOM DOMIN ATTIT ORD/FREE SOVEREIGN...SOC STAT CHARTS IDEA/COMP BIBLIOG. PAGE 36 A0735
NAT/LISM CONCPT PERCEPT STRATA

B54
NORTHROP F.S.C.,EUROPEAN UNION AND UNITED STATES FOREIGN POLICY: A STUDY IN SOCIOLOGICAL JURISPRUDENCE. EUR+WWI MOD/EUR USA+45 SOCIETY STRUCT NAT/G CREATE ECO/TAC DOMIN EDU/PROP REGION ATTIT RIGID/FLEX HEALTH ORD/FREE WEALTH ...METH/CNCPT TIME/SEQ TREND. PAGE 110 A2256
INT/ORG SOC DIPLOM

B54
TOTOK W.,HANDBUCH DER BIBLIOGRAPHISCHEN NACHSCHLAGEWERKE. GERMANY LAW CULTURE ADMIN...SOC 20. PAGE 144 A2952
BIBLIOG/A NAT/G DIPLOM POLICY

B55
BUSS C.,THE FAR EAST: A HISTORY OF RECENT AND CONTEMPORARY INTERNATIONAL RELATIONS IN EAST ASIA. WOR+45 WOR-45 CONSTN INT/ORG NAT/G BAL/PWR ATTIT PWR SOVEREIGN...GEOG JURID SOC CONCPT METH/CNCPT 19/20. PAGE 22 A0449
ASIA DIPLOM

B55
COTTRELL W.F.,ENERGY AND SOCIETY. FUT WOR+45 WOR-45 ECO/DEV ECO/UNDEV INT/ORG NAT/G DETER ORD/FREE PWR SKILL WEALTH...SOC TIME/SEQ TOT/POP VAL/FREE 20. PAGE 31 A0634
TEC/DEV BAL/PWR PEACE

B55
CRAIG G.A.,THE POLITICS OF THE PRUSSIAN ARMY 1640-1945. CHRIST-17C EUR+WWI MOD/EUR PRUSSIA STRUCT DIPLOM ADMIN REV WAR...SOC BIBLIOG 17/20. PAGE 32 A0652
FORCES NAT/G ROLE CHIEF

B55
JAPANESE STUDIES OF MODERN CHINA. ASIA DIPLOM LEAD REV MARXISM 19/20 CHINJAP. PAGE 43 A0885
BIBLIOG/A SOC

B55
MYRDAL A.R.,AMERICA'S ROLE IN INTERNATIONATIONAL SOCIAL WELFARE. FUT WOR+45 SOCIETY R+D VOL/ASSN ECO/TAC EDU/PROP HEALTH KNOWL WEALTH...SOC CHARTS ORG/CHARTS TOT/POP 20. PAGE 107 A2188
PLAN SKILL FOR/AID

B55
THOMPSON V.,MINORITY PROBLEMS IN SOUTHEAST ASIA. CAMBODIA CHINA/COM LAOS S/ASIA KIN NAT/G SECT PROB/SOLV EDU/PROP REGION GP/REL RACE/REL MARXISM ...SOC 20 BUDDHISM UN. PAGE 143 A2933
INGP/REL GEOG DIPLOM STRUCT

B55
TROTIER A.H.,DOCTORAL DISSERTATIONS ACCEPTED BY AMERICAN UNIVERSITIES 1954-55. SECT DIPLOM HEALTH ...ART/METH GEOG INT/LAW SOC LING CHARTS 20. PAGE 145 A2968
BIBLIOG ACADEM USA+45 WRITING

B56
BEARDSLEY S.W.,HUMAN RELATIONS IN INTERNATIONAL AFFAIRS: A GUIDE TO SIGNIFICANT INTERPRETATION AND RESEARCH. UNIV PERS/REL NAT/LISM DRIVE PERSON ...POLICY PSY SOC CON/ANAL IDEA/COMP 20. PAGE 12 A0241
BIBLIOG/A ATTIT CULTURE DIPLOM

B56
JUAN T.L.,ECONOMIC AND SOCIAL DEVELOPMENT OF MODERN CHINA: A BIBLIOGRAPHICAL GUIDE. ASIA AGRI COM/IND DIST/IND FINAN INDUS DIPLOM...STAT 20. PAGE 75 A1541
BIBLIOG SOC

B56
PHILIPPINE STUDIES PROGRAM,SELECTED BIBLIOGRAPHY ON THE PHILIPPINES, TOPICALLY ARRANGED AND ANNOTATED. PHILIPPINE SECT DIPLOM COLONIAL LEAD...SOC 18/20. PAGE 116 A2375
BIBLIOG/A S/ASIA NAT/G ECO/UNDEV

B56
SPROUT H.,MAN-MILIEU RELATIONSHIP HYPOTHESES IN THE CONTEXT OF INTERNATIONAL POLITICS. UNIV PROB/SOLV BIO/SOC PERSON...DECISION GEOG SOC METH/CNCPT PREDICT 20. PAGE 136 A2792
HABITAT DIPLOM CONCPT DRIVE

B56
US DEPARTMENT OF STATE,ECONOMIC PROBLEMS OF UNDERDEVELOPED AREAS (PAMPHLET). AFR ASIA ISLAM L/A+17C AGRI FINAN INDUS INT/ORG LABOR INT/TRADE ...PSY SOC 20. PAGE 151 A3090
BIBLIOG ECO/UNDEV TEC/DEV R+D

B56
VON BECKERATH E.,HANDWORTERBUCH DER SOCIALWISSENSCHAFTEN (II VOLS.). EUR+WWI GERMANY POL/PAR WORKER DIPLOM LEAD CHOOSE SUFF WEALTH...SOC 20. PAGE 159 A3249
BIBLIOG INT/TRADE NAT/G ECO/DEV

B57
ASHER R.E.,THE UNITED NATIONS AND ECONOMIC AND SOCIAL COOPERATION. ECO/UNDEV COM/IND DIST/IND FINAN PLAN PROB/SOLV INT/TRADE TASK WEALTH...SOC 20 UN. PAGE 9 A0186
INT/ORG DIPLOM FOR/AID

B57
BYRNES R.F.,BIBLIOGRAPHY OF AMERICAN PUBLICATIONS ON EAST CENTRAL EUROPE, 1945-1957 (VOL. XXII). SECT DIPLOM EDU/PROP RACE/REL...ART/METH GEOG JURID SOC LING 20 JEWS. PAGE 23 A0462
BIBLIOG/A COM MARXISM NAT/G

B57
CARIBBEAN COMMISSION,A CATALOGUE OF CARIBBEAN COMMISSION PUBLICATIONS (PAMPHLET). WEST/IND CULTURE ECO/UNDEV LOC/G DIPLOM SOC. PAGE 24 A0483
BIBLIOG L/A+17C INT/ORG NAT/G

B57
CONOVER H.F.,NORTH AND NORTHEAST AFRICA; A SELECTED ANNOTATED LIST OF WRITINGS. ALGERIA MOROCCO SUDAN
BIBLIOG/A DIPLOM

UAR CULTURE INT/ORG PROB/SOLV ADJUD NAT/LISM PWR WEALTH...SOC 20 UN. PAGE 30 A0603 — AFR ECO/UNDEV

B57
DEAN V.M.,THE NATURE OF THE NON-WESTERN WORLD. AFR ASIA L/A+17C S/ASIA CULTURE SOCIETY STRATA ECO/DEV DIPLOM ECO/TAC FOR/AID ATTIT DRIVE ALL/VALS ...RELATIV SOC CONCPT TIME/SEQ TREND TOT/POP 20. PAGE 35 A0718 — ECO/UNDEV STERTYP NAT/LISM

B57
FRAZIER E.F.,RACE AND CULTURE CONTACTS IN THE MODERN WORLD. WOR+45 WOR-45 SOCIETY ECO/DEV AGRI INDUS INT/ORG LABOR NAT/G PERSON RIGID/FLEX ALL/VALS...SOC TIME/SEQ WORK 19/20. PAGE 48 A0991 — CULTURE RACE/REL

B57
HALD M.,A SELECTED BIBLIOGRAPHY ON ECONOMIC DEVELOPMENT AND FOREIGN AID. INT/ORG PROB/SOLV ...SOC 20. PAGE 59 A1222 — BIBLIOG ECO/UNDEV TEC/DEV FOR/AID

B57
UNESCO,WORLD LIST OF SOCIAL SCIENCE PERIODICALS (2ND ED.). WOR+45 20 UN. PAGE 148 A3020 — BIBLIOG SOC INT/ORG

B57
YAMADA H.,ANNALS OF THE SOCIAL SCIENCES. WOR+45 WOR-45 LAW CULTURE SOCIETY STRUCT DIPLOM...EPIST PSY CONCPT 15/20. PAGE 168 A3428 — BIBLIOG/A TREND IDEA/COMP SOC

S57
WRIGHT Q.,"THE VALUE OF CONFLICT RESOLUTION OF A GENERAL DISCIPLINE OF INTERNATIONAL RELATIONS." WOR+45 SOCIETY INT/ORG NAT/G FORCES TOP/EX PLAN TEC/DEV ECO/TAC DOMIN LEGIT COERCE ATTIT PWR ...GEN/METH COLD/WAR VAL/FREE. PAGE 168 A3412 — ORD/FREE SOC DIPLOM

B58
ARON R.,ON WAR: ATOMIC WEAPONS AND GLOBAL DIPLOMACY (TRANS. BY TERENCE KILMARTIN). WOR+45 SOCIETY FORCES BAL/PWR WAR WEAPON PERSON...SOC 20. PAGE 9 A0182 — ARMS/CONT NUC/PWR COERCE DIPLOM

B58
ISLAM R.,INTERNATIONAL ECONOMIC COOPERATION AND THE UNITED NATIONS. FINAN PLAN EXEC TASK WAR PEACE ...SOC METH/CNCPT 20 UN LEAGUE/NAT. PAGE 72 A1470 — INT/ORG DIPLOM ADMIN

B58
MACLES L.M.,LES SOURCES DU TRAVAIL BIBLIOGRAPHIQUE (3 VOLS.). FRANCE WOR+45 DIPLOM...GEOG PHIL/SCI SOC 20. PAGE 93 A1897 — BIBLIOG/A NAT/G HUM

B58
MASON J.B.,THAILAND BIBLIOGRAPHY. S/ASIA THAILAND CULTURE EDU/PROP ADMIN...GEOG SOC LING 20. PAGE 95 A1958 — BIBLIOG/A ECO/UNDEV DIPLOM NAT/G

B58
TILLION G.,ALGERIA: THE REALITIES. ALGERIA FRANCE ISLAM CULTURE STRATA PROB/SOLV DOMIN REV NAT/LISM WEALTH MARXISM...GEOG 20. PAGE 144 A2940 — ECO/UNDEV SOC COLONIAL DIPLOM

B58
UNESCO,REPERTORIO DE PUBLICACIONES PERIODICAS ACTUALES LATINO AMERICANAS (VOL. VIII). LAW DIPLOM GP/REL...PHIL/SCI SOC 20 UNESCO. PAGE 148 A3021 — BIBLIOG/A COM/IND L/A+17C

B58
YUAN TUNG-LI,CHINA IN WESTERN LITERATURE. SECT DIPLOM...ART/METH GEOG JURID SOC BIOG CON/ANAL. PAGE 169 A3440 — BIBLIOG ASIA CULTURE HUM

S58
ANDERSON N.,"INTERNATIONAL SEMINARS: AN ANALYSIS AND AN EVALUATION." WOR+45 R+D ACT/RES CREATE PLAN REGION ATTIT KNOWL SKILL...SOC REC/INT PERS/TEST CHARTS 20. PAGE 8 A0158 — INT/ORG DELIB/GP

S58
BOGART L.,"MEASURING THE EFFECTIVENESS OF AN OVERSEAS INFORMATION CAMPAIGN." EUR+WWI GREECE USA+45 INT/ORG MUNIC PLAN DIPLOM PEACE PERCEPT RIGID/FLEX KNOWL...TECHNIC PSY SOC NEW/IDEA CONT/OBS REC/INT STAND/INT SAMP/SIZ COLD/WAR 20. PAGE 16 A0328 — ATTIT EDU/PROP

S58
DAVENPORT J.,"ARMS AND THE WELFARE STATE." INTELL STRUCT FORCES CREATE ECO/TAC FOR/AID DOMIN LEGIT ADMIN WAR ORD/FREE PWR...POLICY SOC CONCPT MYTH OBS TREND COLD/WAR TOT/POP 20. PAGE 34 A0685 — USA+45 NAT/G USSR

S58
SONDERMANN F.A.,"SOCIOLOGY AND INTERNATIONAL RELATIONS." WOR+45 CULTURE SOCIETY INT/ORG NAT/G CREATE ATTIT DRIVE PERSON RIGID/FLEX...PSY SOC 20. PAGE 135 A2767 — PLAN NEW/IDEA PEACE

C58
BLANCHARD W.,"THAILAND." THAILAND CULTURE AGRI FINAN INDUS FAM LABOR INT/TRADE ATTIT...GEOG HEAL SOC BIBLIOG 20. PAGE 15 A0307 — NAT/G DIPLOM ECO/UNDEV S/ASIA

B59
INTERAMERICAN CULTURAL COUN,LISTA DE LIBROS REPRESENTAVOS DE AMERICA. CULTURE DIPLOM ADMIN 20. PAGE 71 A1448 — BIBLIOG/A NAT/G L/A+17C

SOC

B59
MAC MILLAN W.M.,THE ROAD TO SELF-RULE. SOUTH/AFR UK CULTURE SOCIETY AGRI LABOR NAT/G INT/TRADE CONTROL GP/REL...SOC 19/20. PAGE 92 A1884 — AFR COLONIAL SOVEREIGN POLICY

B59
OKINSHEVICH L.A.,LATIN AMERICA IN SOVIET WRITINGS, 1945-1958: A BIBLIOGRAPHY. USSR LAW ECO/UNDEV LABOR DIPLOM EDU/PROP REV...GEOG SOC 20. PAGE 111 A2287 — BIBLIOG WRITING COM L/A+17C

B59
PANAMERICAN UNION,PUBLICATIONS: PAU AND OFFICIAL RECORDS OF THE OAS, IN ENGLISH, SPANISH, PORTUGUESE, AND FRENCH, 1958-59. NAT/G ATTIT...SOC 20 OAS. PAGE 113 A2328 — BIBLIOG L/A+17C INT/LAW DIPLOM

B59
PHADINIS U.,DOCUMENTS ON ASIAN AFFAIRS: A SELECT BIBLIOGRAPHY. ASIA...SOC 20. PAGE 116 A2372 — BIBLIOG NAT/G DIPLOM

B59
COLUMBIA U BUR APPL SOC RES,ATTITUDES OF PROMINENT AMERICANS TOWARD "WORLD PEACE THROUGH WORLD LAW" (SUPRA-NATL ORGANIZATION FOR WAR PREVENTION). USA+45 USSR ELITES FORCES PLAN PROB/SOLV CONTROL WAR PWR...POLICY SOC QU IDEA/COMP 20 UN. PAGE 117 A2403 — ATTIT ACT/RES INT/LAW STAT

B59
ROPKE W.,INTERNATIONAL ORDER AND ECONOMIC INTEGRATION. ECO/DEV ECO/UNDEV AGRI FINAN INDUS INT/ORG WAR PEACE ORD/FREE...SOC METH/COMP 20 EEC. PAGE 123 A2524 — INT/TRADE DIPLOM BAL/PAY ALL/IDEOS

B59
SCHURZ W.L.,AMERICAN FOREIGN AFFAIRS: A GUIDE TO INTERNATIONAL AFFAIRS. USA+45 WOR+45 WOR-45 NAT/G FORCES LEGIS TOP/EX PLAN EDU/PROP LEGIT ADMIN ROUTINE ATTIT ORD/FREE PWR...SOC CONCPT STAT SAMP/SIZ CHARTS STERTYP 20. PAGE 129 A2653 — INT/ORG SOCIETY DIPLOM

B59
VINACKE H.M.,A HISTORY OF THE FAR EAST IN MODERN TIMES (6TH ED.). KOREA S/ASIA USSR CONSTN CULTURE STRATA ECO/UNDEV NAT/G CHIEF FOR/AID INT/TRADE GP/REL...SOC NAT/COMP 19/20 CHINJAP. PAGE 159 A3235 — STRUCT ASIA

S59
KRIPALANI A.J.B.,"FOR PRINCIPLED NEUTRALITY." CHINA/COM INDIA S/ASIA PLAN ECO/TAC RIGID/FLEX MORAL PWR...MYSTIC SOC RECORD 20 GANDHI/M. PAGE 82 A1684 — ATTIT FOR/AID DIPLOM

S59
SUTTON F.X.,"REPRESENTATION AND THE NATURE OF POLITICAL SYSTEMS." UNIV WOR-45 CULTURE SOCIETY STRATA INT/ORG FORCES JUDGE DOMIN LEGIT EXEC REGION REPRESENT ATTIT ORD/FREE RESPECT...SOC HIST/WRIT TIME/SEQ. PAGE 140 A2867 — NAT/G CONCPT

B60
DE HERRERA C.D.,LISTA BIBLIOGRAFICA DE LOS TRABAJOS DE GRADUACION Y TESIS PRESENTADOS EN LA UNIVERSIDAD, 1939-1960. PANAMA DIPLOM LEAD...SOC 20. PAGE 35 A0703 — BIBLIOG L/A+17C NAT/G ACADEM

B60
FLORES R.H.,CATALOGO DE TESIS DOCTORALES DE LAS FACULTADES DE LA UNIVERSIDAD DE EL SALVADOR. EL/SALVADR LAW DIPLOM ADMIN LEAD GOV/REL...SOC 19/20. PAGE 47 A0954 — BIBLIOG ACADEM L/A+17C NAT/G

B60
HOFFMANN S.H.,CONTEMPORARY THEORY IN INTERNATIONAL RELATIONS. RATIONAL...SOC METH/CNCPT METH/COMP SIMUL ANTHOL 20. PAGE 66 A1359 — DIPLOM METH PHIL/SCI DECISION

B60
LERNER A.P.,THE ECONOMICS OF CONTROL. USA+45 ECO/UNDEV INT/ORG ACT/RES PLAN CAP/ISM INT/TRADE ATTIT WEALTH...SOC MATH STAT GEN/LAWS INDEX 20. PAGE 87 A1785 — ECO/DEV ROUTINE ECO/TAC SOCISM

B60
LEWIS P.R.,LITERATURE OF THE SOCIAL SCIENCES: AN INTRODUCTORY SURVEY AND GUIDE. UK LAW INDUS DIPLOM INT/TRADE ADMIN...MGT 19/20. PAGE 88 A1802 — BIBLIOG/A SOC

B60
LINDSAY K.,EUROPEAN ASSEMBLIES: THE EXPERIMENTAL PERIOD 1949-1959. EUR+WWI ECO/DEV NAT/G POL/PAR LEGIS TOP/EX ACT/RES PLAN ECO/TAC DOMIN LEGIT ROUTINE ATTIT DRIVE ORD/FREE PWR SKILL...SOC CONCPT TREND CHARTS GEN/LAWS VAL/FREE. PAGE 89 A1823 — VOL/ASSN INT/ORG REGION

B60
MORAES F.,THE REVOLT IN TIBET. ASIA CHINA/COM INDIA CULTURE CONTROL COERCE WAR TOTALISM...POLICY SOC WORSHIP 20 TIBET INTERVENT. PAGE 104 A2127 — COLONIAL FORCES DIPLOM ORD/FREE

B60
MOUSKHELY M.,L'URSS ET LES PAYS DE L'EST. ASIA COM S/ASIA USSR PRESS...SOC 20. PAGE 105 A2156 — BIBLIOG/A DIPLOM ATTIT

B60
MUGRIDGE D.H.,A GUIDE TO THE STUDY OF THE UNITED STATES OF AMERICA: REPRESENTATIVE BOOKS REFLECTING — BIBLIOG/A CULTURE

THE DEVELOPMENT OF AMERICAN LIFE. USA+45 USA-45 CONSTN POL/PAR FORCES DIPLOM PRESS CHOOSE...SOC 17/20. PAGE 105 A2165 — NAT/G POLICY

B60
RAO V.K.R.,INTERNATIONAL AID FOR ECONOMIC DEVELOPMENT - POSSIBILITIES AND LIMITATIONS. FINAN PLAN TEC/DEV ADMIN TASK EFFICIENCY...POLICY SOC METH/CNCPT CHARTS 20 UN. PAGE 119 A2444 — FOR/AID DIPLOM INT/ORG ECO/UNDEV

B60
ROPKE W.,A HUMANE ECONOMY. CULTURE ECO/DEV FINAN INDUS GP/REL CENTRAL WEALTH...GEOG SOC IDEA/COMP 20 EEC. PAGE 123 A2525 — ECO/TAC INT/ORG DIPLOM ORD/FREE

B60
SZTARAY Z.,BIBLIOGRAPHY ON HUNGARY. HUNGARY MOD/EUR CULTURE INDUS SECT DIPLOM REV...ART/METH SOC LING 18/20. PAGE 141 A2879 — BIBLIOG NAT/G COM MARXISM

L60
HOLTON G.,"ARMS CONTROL." FUT WOR+45 CULTURE INT/ORG NAT/G FORCES TOP/EX PLAN EDU/PROP COERCE ATTIT RIGID/FLEX ORD/FREE...POLICY PHIL/SCI SOC TREND COLD/WAR. PAGE 67 A1377 — ACT/RES CONSULT ARMS/CONT NUC/PWR

L60
MCCLELLAND C.A.,"THE FUNCTION OF THEORY IN INTERNATIONAL RELATIONS." WOR+45 PLAN EDU/PROP ROUTINE ORD/FREE...PHIL/SCI PSY SOC METH/CNCPT NEW/IDEA OBS TREND GEN/METH 20. PAGE 97 A1997 — INT/ORG CONCPT DIPLOM

S60
BOGARDUS E.S.,"THE SOCIOLOGY OF A STRUCTURED PEACE." FUT SOCIETY CREATE DIPLOM EDU/PROP ADJUD ROUTINE ATTIT RIGID/FLEX KNOWL ORD/FREE RESPECT ...POLICY INT/LAW JURID NEW/IDEA SELF/OBS TOT/POP 20 UN. PAGE 16 A0327 — INT/ORG SOC NAT/LISM PEACE

S60
KEYFITZ N.,"WESTERN PERSPECTIVES AND ASIAN PROBLEMS." ASIA EUR+WWI S/ASIA SOCIETY FOR/AID ...POLICY SOC CONCPT STERTYP WORK TOT/POP 20. PAGE 78 A1604 — CULTURE ATTIT

S60
RIVKIN A.,"AFRICAN ECONOMIC DEVELOPMENT: ADVANCED TECHNOLOGY AND THE STAGES OF GROWTH." CULTURE ECO/UNDEV AGRI COM/IND EXTR/IND PLAN ECO/TAC ATTIT DRIVE RIGID/FLEX SKILL WEALTH...MGT SOC GEN/LAWS WORK TOT/POP 20. PAGE 121 A2487 — AFR TEC/DEV FOR/AID

S60
RUSSEL R.W.,"ROLES FOR PSYCHOLOGISTS IN THE MAINTENANCE OF PEACE." FUT USA+45 CULTURE INT/ORG DIPLOM FOR/AID EDU/PROP ATTIT KNOWL MORAL PWR ...POLICY SOC COLD/WAR 20. PAGE 125 A2572 — PSY GEN/METH

S60
SCHWELB E.,"INTERNATIONAL CONVENTIONS ON HUMAN RIGHTS." FUT WOR+45 LAW CONSTN CULTURE SOCIETY STRUCT VOL/ASSN DELIB/GP PLAN ADJUD SUPEGO LOVE MORAL...SOC CONCPT STAT RECORD HIST/WRIT TREND 20 UN. PAGE 130 A2664 — INT/ORG HUM

S60
THOMPSON K.W.,"MORAL PURPOSE IN FOREIGN POLICY: REALITIES AND ILLUSIONS." WOR+45 WOR-45 LAW CULTURE SOCIETY INT/ORG PLAN ADJUD ADMIN COERCE RIGID/FLEX SUPEGO KNOWL ORD/FREE PWR...SOC TREND SOC/EXP TOT/POP 20. PAGE 143 A2930 — MORAL JURID DIPLOM

B61
BAINS J.S.,STUDIES IN POLITICAL SCIENCE. INDIA WOR+45 WOR-45 CONSTN BAL/PWR ADJUD ADMIN PARL/PROC SOVEREIGN...SOC METH/COMP ANTHOL 17/20 UN. PAGE 10 A0209 — DIPLOM INT/LAW NAT/G

B61
CONOVER H.F.,SERIALS FOR AFRICAN STUDIES. ECO/UNDEV DIPLOM LEAD NAT/LISM ATTIT...SOC 20. PAGE 30 A0604 — BIBLIOG AFR NAT/G

B61
DETHINE P.,BIBLIOGRAPHIE DES ASPECTS ECONOMIQUES ET SOCIAUX DE L'INDUSTRIALISATION EN AFRIQUE. AFR FINAN LABOR FOR/AID...SOC 20. PAGE 36 A0734 — BIBLIOG/A ECO/UNDEV INDUS TEC/DEV

B61
FULLER J.F.C.,THE CONDUCT OF WAR, 1789-1961. FRANCE RUSSIA SOCIETY NAT/G FORCES PROB/SOLV AGREE NUC/PWR WEAPON PEACE...SOC 18/20 TREATY COLD/WAR. PAGE 50 A1025 — WAR POLICY REV ROLE

B61
GRASES P.,ESTUDIOS BIBLIOGRAFICOS. VENEZUELA...SOC 20. PAGE 55 A1130 — BIBLIOG NAT/G DIPLOM L/A+17C

B61
MICHAEL D.N.,PROPOSED STUDIES ON THE IMPLICATIONS OF PEACEFUL SPACE ACTIVITIES FOR HUMAN AFFAIRS. COM/IND INDUS FORCES DIPLOM PEACE PERSON...PSY SOC 20. PAGE 101 A2066 — FUT SPACE ACT/RES PROB/SOLV

B61
PATAI R.,CULTURES IN CONFLICT; AN INQUIRY INTO THE SOCIO-CULTURAL PROBLEMS OF ISRAEL AND HER NEIGHBORS (2ND REV. ED.). ISLAM ISRAEL SOCIETY STRUCT DIPLOM GP/REL ALL/VALS...SOC 20 JEWS ARABS. PAGE 114 A2339 — NAT/COMP CULTURE GP/COMP ATTIT

B61
SOCIAL SCIENCE SERIALS IN SPECIAL LIBRARIES IN THE NEW YORK AREA; A SELECTED LIST. R+D ACADEM EDU/PROP WRITING...PSY 20. PAGE 119 A2448 — BIBLIOG DIPLOM SOC

B61
ROBINSON M.E.,EDUCATION FOR SOCIAL CHANGE: ESTABLISHING INSTITUTES OF PUBLIC AND BUSINESS ADMINISTRATION ABROAD (PAMPHLET). WOR+45 SOCIETY ACADEM CONFER INGP/REL ROLE...SOC CHARTS BIBLIOG 20 ICA. PAGE 122 A2506 — FOR/AID EDU/PROP MGT ADJUST

B61
SSU-YU T.,JAPANESE STUDIES ON JAPAN AND THE FAR EAST: A SHORT BIOGRAPHICAL AND BIBLIOGRAPHICAL INTRODUCTION. ASIA CULTURE ECO/UNDEV NAT/G DIPLOM 20 CHINJAP. PAGE 136 A2795 — BIBLIOG SOC

B61
YDIT M.,INTERNATIONALISED TERRITORIES. FUT WOR+45 WOR-45 CONSTN VOL/ASSN CREATE PLAN LEGIT PEACE ORD/FREE...GEOG INT/LAW JURID SOC NEW/IDEA OBS RECORD SAMP TIME/SEQ TREND 19/20 BERLIN. PAGE 169 A3431 — LOC/G INT/ORG DIPLOM SOVEREIGN

B61
YUAN TUNG-LI,A GUIDE TO DOCTORAL DISSERTATIONS BY CHINESE STUDENTS IN AMERICA, 1905-1960. ASIA CULTURE SOCIETY ECO/UNDEV NAT/G PROB/SOLV DIPLOM LEAD ATTIT...HUM SOC STAT 20. PAGE 169 A3441 — BIBLIOG ACADEM ACT/RES OP/RES

B61
ZIMMERMAN I.,A GUIDE TO CURRENT LATIN AMERICAN PERIODICALS: HUMANITIES AND SOCIAL SCIENCES. LABOR SECT EDU/PROP...GEOG HUM SOC LING STAT NAT/COMP 20. PAGE 170 A3452 — BIBLIOG/A DIPLOM L/A+17C PHIL/SCI

S61
DELLA PORT G.,"PROBLEMI E PROSPETTIVE DI COESISTENZA FRA ORIENTE ED OCCIDENTE, (PART 3)." COM FUT WOR+45 NAT/G BAL/PWR FOR/AID BAL/PAY PWR WEALTH...SOC CONCPT GEN/LAWS COLD/WAR 20. PAGE 36 A0729 — INT/TRADE

S61
GALBRAITH J.K.,"A POSITIVE APPROACH TO ECONOMIC AID." FUT USA+45 INTELL NAT/G CONSULT ACT/RES DIPLOM ECO/TAC EDU/PROP ATTIT KNOWL PWR WEALTH ...SOC STERTYP 20. PAGE 50 A1030 — ECO/UNDEV ROUTINE FOR/AID

S61
JUVILER P.H.,"INTERPARLIAMENTARY CONTACTS IN SOVIET FOREIGN POLICY." COM FUT WOR+45 WOR-45 SOCIETY CONSULT ACT/RES DIPLOM ADMIN PEACE ATTIT RIGID/FLEX WEALTH...WELF/ST SOC TOT/POP CONGRESS 19/20. PAGE 75 A1543 — INT/ORG DELIB/GP USSR

S61
MASTERS R.D.,"A MULTI-BLOC MODEL OF THE INTERNATIONAL SYSTEM." FUT UNIV WOR+45 SOCIETY ACT/RES PLAN...GEOG SOC TREND SIMUL TOT/POP 20. PAGE 96 A1963 — INT/ORG CONCPT

S61
SINGER J.D.,"THE LEVEL OF ANALYSIS: PROBLEMS IN INTERNATIONAL RELATIONS." FUT INTELL R+D INT/ORG CREATE EDU/PROP...METH/CNCPT HYPO/EXP GEN/METH METH VAL/FREE. PAGE 133 A2725 — SOCIETY SOC DIPLOM

B62
BAULIN J.,THE ARAB ROLE IN AFRICA. AFR ALGERIA FUT ISLAM MOROCCO UAR COLONIAL NEUTRAL REV...SOC 20 TUNIS BOURGUIBA. PAGE 12 A0235 — NAT/LISM DIPLOM NAT/G SECT

B62
CADWELL R.,COMMUNISM IN THE MODERN WORLD. USSR WOR+45 SOCIETY AGRI INDUS INT/ORG SECT EDU/PROP COLONIAL PEACE...SOC 20. PAGE 23 A0463 — COM DIPLOM POLICY CONCPT

B62
CARDOZA M.H.,DIPLOMATS IN INTERNATIONAL COOPERATION: STEPCHILDREN OF THE FOREIGN SERVICE. EUR+WWI USA+45 NAT/G CONSULT ACT/RES EDU/PROP ROUTINE RIGID/FLEX KNOWL SKILL...SOC OBS TIME/SEQ EEC OEEC NATO 20. PAGE 24 A0480 — INT/ORG METH/CNCPT DIPLOM

B62
COLLISON R.L.,BIBLIOGRAPHIES, SUBJECT AND NATIONAL: A GUIDE TO THEIR CONTENTS, ARRANGEMENT, AND USE (2ND REV. ED.). SECT DIPLOM...ART/METH GEOG HUM PHIL/SCI SOC MATH BIOG 20. PAGE 28 A0569 — BIBLIOG/A CON/ANAL BIBLIOG

B62
COSTA RICA UNIVERSIDAD BIBL,LISTA DE TESIS DE GRADO DE LA UNIVERSIDAD DE COSTA RICA. COSTA/RICA LAW LOC/G ADMIN LEAD...SOC 20. PAGE 31 A0631 — BIBLIOG/A NAT/G DIPLOM ECO/UNDEV

B62
COUNCIL ON WORLD TENSIONS,A STUDY OF WORLD TENSIONS AND DEVELOPMENT. WOR+45 ECO/DEV ECO/UNDEV INT/ORG PLAN DIPLOM ECO/TAC EDU/PROP ATTIT KNOWL ORD/FREE PWR WEALTH...CONCPT TREND CHARTS STERTYP COLD/WAR TOT/POP 20. PAGE 31 A0640 — TEC/DEV SOC

B62
DIAZ J.S.,MANUAL DE BIBLIOGRAFIA DE LA LITERATURA ESPANOLA. PRE/AMER SPAIN ECO/UNDEV DIPLOM LEAD ATTIT...SOC 15/20. PAGE 37 A0755 — BIBLIOG L/A+17C NAT/G COLONIAL

B62
ELLIOTT J.R.,THE APPEAL OF COMMUNISM IN THE UNDERDEVELOPED NATIONS. USSR WOR+45 INT/ORG NAT/G DIPLOM DOMIN EDU/PROP ROUTINE ATTIT RIGID/FLEX ORD/FREE PWR WEALTH MARXISM...POLICY SOC METH/CNCPT MYTH TOT/POP COLD/WAR 20. PAGE 41 A0842
COM ECO/UNDEV

B62
GILPIN R.,AMERICAN SCIENTISTS AND NUCLEAR WEAPONS POLICY. COM FUT USA+45 WOR+45 INT/ORG NAT/G PROF/ORG CONSULT FORCES CREATE TEC/DEV BAL/PWR EDU/PROP ARMS/CONT WAR PERCEPT KNOWL MORAL PWR ...PHIL/SCI SOC CONCPT GEN/LAWS 20. PAGE 52 A1073
INTELL ATTIT DETER NUC/PWR

B62
INGHAM K.,A HISTORY OF EAST AFRICA. NAT/G DIPLOM ADMIN WAR NAT/LISM...SOC BIOG BIBLIOG. PAGE 70 A1439
AFR CONSTN COLONIAL

B62
KIDDER F.E.,THESES ON PAN AMERICAN TOPICS. LAW CULTURE NAT/G SECT DIPLOM HEALTH...ART/METH GEOG SOC 13/20. PAGE 79 A1615
BIBLIOG CHRIST-17C L/A+17C SOCIETY

B62
MOUSSA P.,THE UNDERPRIVILEGED NATIONS. FINAN INT/ORG PLAN PROB/SOLV CAP/ISM GIVE TASK WEALTH ...POLICY SOC 20. PAGE 105 A2159
ECO/UNDEV NAT/G DIPLOM FOR/AID

B62
NEAL F.W.,WAR AND PEACE AND GERMANY. EUR+WWI USSR STRUCT INT/ORG NAT/G FORCES DOMIN EDU/PROP LEGIT EXEC COERCE ORD/FREE...HUM SOC NEW/IDEA OBS TIME/SEQ TOT/POP COLD/WAR 20 BERLIN. PAGE 108 A2208
USA+45 POLICY DIPLOM GERMANY

B62
OSGOOD C.E.,AN ALTERNATIVE TO WAR OR SURRENDER. FUT UNIV CULTURE INTELL SOCIETY R+D INT/ORG CONSULT DELIB/GP ACT/RES PLAN CHOOSE ATTIT PERCEPT KNOWL ...PHIL/SCI PSY SOC TREND GEN/LAWS 20. PAGE 112 A2300
ORD/FREE EDU/PROP PEACE WAR

B62
SCHWARZENBERGER G.,THE FRONTIERS OF INTERNATIONAL LAW. WOR+45 WOR-45 NAT/G LEGIT CT/SYS ROUTINE MORAL ORD/FREE PWR...JURID SOC GEN/METH 20 COLD/WAR. PAGE 130 A2661
INT/ORG LAW INT/LAW

B62
SELOSOEMARDJAN O.,SOCIAL CHANGES IN JOGJAKARTA. INDONESIA NETHERLAND ELITES STRATA STRUCT FAM POL/PAR CREATE DIPLOM INT/TRADE EDU/PROP ADMIN GOV/REL...SOC 20 JAVA CHINJAP. PAGE 131 A2683
ECO/UNDEV CULTURE REV COLONIAL

B62
THANT U.,THE UNITED NATIONS' DEVELOPMENT DECADE: PROPOSALS FOR ACTION. WOR+45 SOCIETY ECO/UNDEV AGRI COM/IND FINAN R+D MUNIC SCHOOL VOL/ASSN CONSULT PLAN TEC/DEV ECO/TAC EDU/PROP ADMIN ROUTINE RIGID/FLEX...MGT SOC CONCPT UNESCO UN TOT/POP VAL/FREE. PAGE 142 A2906
INT/ORG ALL/VALS

B62
UNECA LIBRARY,BOOKS ON AFRICA IN THE UNECA LIBRARY. WOR+45 AGRI INT/ORG NAT/G PLAN WRITING REGION...SOC STAT UN. PAGE 147 A3008
BIBLIOG AFR ECO/UNDEV TEC/DEV

B62
UNECA LIBRARY,NEW ACQUISITIONS IN THE UNECA LIBRARY. LAW NAT/G PLAN PROB/SOLV TEC/DEV ADMIN REGION...GEOG SOC 20 UN. PAGE 147 A3009
BIBLIOG AFR ECO/UNDEV INT/ORG

B62
UNESCO,GENERAL CATALOGUE OF UNESCO PUBLICATIONS AND UNESCO SPONSORED PUBLICATIONS, 1946-1959. WOR+45 ...POLICY ART/METH HUM PHIL/SCI UN. PAGE 148 A3022
BIBLIOG INT/ORG ECO/UNDEV SOC

B62
US LIBRARY OF CONGRESS,UNITED STATES AND CANADIAN PUBLICATIONS ON AFRICA IN 1960. CANADA USA+45 CULTURE TEC/DEV DIPLOM FOR/AID RACE/REL...GEOG HUM SOC SOC/WK LING 20. PAGE 155 A3156
BIBLIOG/A AFR

B62
WOETZEL R.K.,THE NURENBERG TRIALS IN INTERNATIONAL LAW. CHRIST-17C MOD/EUR WOR+45 SOCIETY NAT/G DELIB/GP DOMIN LEGIT ROUTINE ATTIT DRIVE PERSON SUPEGO MORAL ORD/FREE...POLICY MAJORIT JURID PSY SOC SELF/OBS RECORD NAZI TOT/POP. PAGE 166 A3376
INT/ORG ADJUD WAR

L62
"HIGHER EDUCATION AND ECONOMIC AND SOCIAL DEVELOPMENT IN LATIN AMERICA: A BIBLIOGRAPHY." L/A+17C SOCIETY ECO/UNDEV PROF/ORG DIPLOM CONFER ...SOC 20. PAGE 3 A0062
BIBLIOG/A ACADEM INTELL EDU/PROP

S62
ALGER C.F.,"THE EXTERNAL BUREAUCRACY IN UNITED STATES FOREIGN AFFAIRS." USA+45 WOR+45 SOCIETY COM/IND INT/ORG NAT/G CONSULT EX/STRUC ACT/RES ...MGT SOC CONCPT TREND 20. PAGE 6 A0118
ADMIN ATTIT DIPLOM

S62
DEUTSCH K.W.,"TOWARDS WESTERN EUROPEAN INTEGRATION: AN INTERIM ASSESSMENT." EUR+WWI STRUCT ECO/DEV INT/ORG ECO/TAC INT/TRADE EDU/PROP PEACE ATTIT DRIVE PWR SOVEREIGN...PSY SOC TIME/SEQ CHARTS STERTYP 20. PAGE 36 A0741
VOL/ASSN RIGID/FLEX REGION

S62
PYE L.W.,"THE POLITICAL IMPULSES AND FANTASIES BEHIND FOREIGN AID." FUT USA+45 ECO/UNDEV DIPLOM ECO/TAC ROUTINE DRIVE KNOWL...SOC METH/CNCPT NEW/IDEA TREND HYPO/EXP STERTYP GEN/METH 20. PAGE 118 A2420
ACT/RES ATTIT FOR/AID

B63
BOISSIER P.,HISTORIE DU COMITE INTERNATIONAL DE LA CROIX ROUGE. MOD/EUR WOR-45 CONSULT FORCES PLAN DIPLOM EDU/PROP ADMIN MORAL ORD/FREE...SOC CONCPT RECORD TIME/SEQ GEN/LAWS TOT/POP VAL/FREE 19/20. PAGE 16 A0332
INT/ORG HEALTH ARMS/CONT WAR

B63
COMISION DE HISTORIO,GUIA DE LOS DOCUMENTOS MICROFOTOGRAFIADOS POR LA UNIDAD MOVIL DE LA UNESCO. SOCIETY ECO/UNDEV INT/ORG ADMIN...SOC 20 UNESCO. PAGE 28 A0573
BIBLIOG NAT/G L/A+17C DIPLOM

B63
ELIAS T.O.,GOVERNMENT AND POLITICS IN AFRICA. CONSTN CULTURE SOCIETY NAT/G POL/PAR DIPLOM REPRESENT PERSON...SOC TREND BIBLIOG 4/20. PAGE 41 A0837
AFR NAT/LISM COLONIAL LAW

B63
GOLDSCHMIDT W.,THE UNITED STATES AND AFRICA. USA+45 CULTURE ECO/TAC INT/TRADE GOV/REL...SOC ANTHOL 20 INTERVENT. PAGE 53 A1091
AFR ECO/UNDEV DIPLOM

B63
INTERAMERICAN ECO AND SOC COUN,THE ALLIANCE FOR PROGRESS: ITS FIRST YEAR: 1961-1962. AGRI SCHOOL PLAN TEC/DEV INT/TRADE TAX GIVE ADMIN WEALTH...SOC 20 SOUTH/AMER. PAGE 71 A1449
INT/ORG PROB/SOLV ECO/TAC L/A+17C

B63
KAHIN G.M.,MAJOR GOVERNMENTS OF ASIA (2ND ED.). ASIA INDIA INDONESIA PAKISTAN S/ASIA DIPLOM...SOC 20 CHINJAP. PAGE 75 A1546
GOV/COMP POL/PAR ELITES

B63
PAENSON I.,SYSTEMATIC GLOSSARY ENGLISH, FRENCH, SPANISH, RUSSIAN OF SELECTED ECONOMIC AND SOCIAL TERMS. WOR+45 FINAN LABOR INT/TRADE DEMAND PRODUC 20. PAGE 113 A2315
DICTIONARY SOC LING

B63
PEREZ ORTIZ R.,ANUARIO BIBLIOGRAFICO COLOMBIANO, 1961. AGRI...INT/LAW JURID SOC LING 20 COLOMB. PAGE 115 A2354
BIBLIOG L/A+17C NAT/G

B63
ROBERTSON A.H.,HUMAN RIGHTS IN EUROPE. CONSTN SOCIETY INT/ORG NAT/G VOL/ASSN DELIB/GP ACT/RES PLAN ADJUD REGION ROUTINE ATTIT LOVE ORD/FREE RESPECT...JURID SOC CONCPT SOC/EXP UN 20. PAGE 122 A2498
EUR+WWI PERSON

B63
SCHMELTZ G.W.,LA POLITIQUE MONDIALE CONTEMPORAINE. SOCIETY ECO/UNDEV INDUS INT/ORG NAT/G POL/PAR CONSULT DELIB/GP PLAN TEC/DEV ECO/TAC DOMIN EDU/PROP ROUTINE COERCE PERCEPT PERSON LOVE SKILL ...SOC RECORD TOT/POP. PAGE 128 A2629
WOR+45 COLONIAL

B63
WALKER A.A.,OFFICIAL PUBLICATIONS OF SIERRA LEONE AND GAMBIA. GAMBIA SIER/LEONE UK LAW CONSTN LEGIS PLAN BUDGET DIPLOM...SOC SAMP CON/ANAL 20. PAGE 160 A3262
BIBLIOG NAT/G COLONIAL ADMIN

S63
DAVEE R.,"POUR UN FONDS DE DEVELOPPEMENT SOCIAL." FUT WOR+45 INTELL SOCIETY ECO/DEV FINAN TEC/DEV ROUTINE WEALTH...TREND TOT/POP VAL/FREE UN 20. PAGE 34 A0684
INT/ORG SOC FOR/AID

S63
LOPEZIBOR J.,"L'EUROPE, FORME DE VIE." CHRIST-17C EUR+WWI FUT MOD/EUR SOCIETY INT/ORG SECT EDU/PROP ATTIT RIGID/FLEX ALL/VALS...POLICY HUM SOC TIME/SEQ TREND GEN/LAWS. PAGE 91 A1862
NAT/G CULTURE

S63
VEROFF J.,"AFRICAN STUDENTS IN THE UNITED STATES." AFR USA+45 CULTURE ACT/RES FOR/AID PEACE ATTIT KNOWL...SOC RECORD DEEP/QU SYS/QU CHARTS STERTYP TOT/POP 20. PAGE 159 A3230
PERCEPT RIGID/FLEX RACE/REL

B64
ALVIM J.C.,A REVOLUCAO SEM RUMO. BRAZIL NAT/G BAL/PWR DIPLOM INT/TRADE PARTIC WEALTH...POLICY SOC SOC/INTEG 20. PAGE 6 A0132
REV CIVMIL/REL ECO/UNDEV ORD/FREE

B64
AMERICAN ASSEMBLY,THE UNITED STATES AND THE MIDDLE EAST. ISRAEL USA+45 STRUCT ECO/DEV ECO/UNDEV INT/ORG NAT/G SCHOOL SECT VOL/ASSN EX/STRUC TEC/DEV NAT/LISM...SOC 20. PAGE 7 A0135
ISLAM DRIVE REGION

B64
CEPEDE M.,POPULATION AND FOOD. USA+45 STRUCT ECO/UNDEV FAM PLAN TEC/DEV FOR/AID CONTROL...CATH SOC TREND 19/20. PAGE 25 A0513
FUT GEOG AGRI CENSUS

B64
CORFO,CHILE, A SELECTED BIBLIOGRAPHY IN ENGLISH (PAMPHLET). CHILE DIPLOM...SOC 20. PAGE 31 A0623
BIBLIOG NAT/G POLICY L/A+17C

B64
DICKEY J.S.,THE UNITED STATES AND CANADA. CANADA USA+45...SOC 20. PAGE 37 A0756 DIPLOM TREND GOV/COMP PROB/SOLV

B64
EMBREE A.T.,A GUIDE TO PAPERBACKS ON ASIA; SELECTED AND ANNOTATED (PAMPHLET). CULTURE SOCIETY ECO/UNDEV SECT DIPLOM COLONIAL MARXISM...SOC 20. PAGE 41 A0845 BIBLIOG/A ASIA S/ASIA NAT/G

B64
FEIS H.,FOREIGN AID AND FOREIGN POLICY. USA+45 WOR+45 NAT/G VOL/ASSN ACT/RES TEC/DEV ATTIT HEALTH WEALTH...SOC GEN/LAWS 20. PAGE 45 A0912 ECO/UNDEV ECO/TAC FOR/AID DIPLOM

B64
FISHER R.,INTERNATIONAL CONFLICT AND BEHAVIORAL SCIENCE: THE CRAIGVILLE PAPERS. COM FUT USA+45 WOR+45 NAT/G DELIB/GP EX/STRUC FORCES ECO/TAC DOMIN EDU/PROP LEGIT COERCE ATTIT PERCEPT ORD/FREE PWR RESPECT...PSY SOC VAL/FREE. PAGE 46 A0940 INT/ORG PLAN DIPLOM

B64
GESELLSCHAFT RECHTSVERGLEICH,BIBLIOGRAPHIE DES DEUTSCHEN RECHTS (BIBLIOGRAPHY OF GERMAN LAW, TRANS. BY COURTLAND PETERSON). GERMANY FINAN INDUS LABOR SECT FORCES CT/SYS PARL/PROC CRIME...INT/LAW SOC NAT/COMP 20. PAGE 52 A1066 BIBLIOG/A JURID CONSTN ADMIN

B64
HALPERN J.M.,GOVERNMENT, POLITICS, AND SOCIAL STRUCTURE IN LAOS. LAOS CULTURE SOCIETY STRATA STRUCT FAM DIPLOM DOMIN MARXISM...INT GOV/COMP WORSHIP SOC/INTEG 20. PAGE 60 A1242 NAT/G SOC LOC/G

B64
IBERO-AMERICAN INSTITUTES,IBEROAMERICANA. STRUCT ADMIN SOC. PAGE 70 A1430 BIBLIOG L/A+17C NAT/G DIPLOM

B64
IKLE F.C.,HOW NATIONS NEGOTIATE. COM EUR+WWI USA+45 INTELL INT/ORG VOL/ASSN DELIB/GP ACT/RES CREATE DOMIN EDU/PROP ADJUD ROUTINE ATTIT PERSON ORD/FREE RESPECT SKILL...PSY SOC OBS VAL/FREE. PAGE 70 A1433 NAT/G PWR POLICY

B64
JACKSON W.V.,LIBRARY GUIDE FOR BRAZILIAN STUDIES. BRAZIL USA+45 STRUCT DIPLOM ADMIN...SOC 20. PAGE 72 A1481 BIBLIOG L/A+17C NAT/G LOC/G

B64
JACOB P.E.,THE INTEGRATION OF POLITICAL COMMUNITIES. USA+45 WOR+45 CULTURE LOC/G MUNIC NAT/G CREATE PLAN LEGIT REGION COERCE ALL/VALS ...POLICY GEOG PSY SOC TREND HYPO/EXP GEN/LAWS VAL/FREE 20. PAGE 72 A1483 INT/ORG METH/CNCPT SIMUL STAT

B64
JANOWITZ M.,THE MILITARY IN THE POLITICAL DEVELOPMENT OF NEW NATIONS: AN ESSAY IN COMPARATIVE ANALYSIS. AFR ASIA ISLAM L/A+17C S/ASIA USA+45 ECO/UNDEV INT/ORG NAT/G POL/PAR DELIB/GP PLAN ECO/TAC DOMIN LEGIT COERCE ATTIT DRIVE RESPECT ...SOC CONCPT CENSUS VAL/FREE. PAGE 73 A1495 FORCES PWR

B64
JOHNSON E.A.J.,THE DIMENSIONS OF DIPLOMACY. INT/ORG FORCES TEC/DEV WAR PEACE PWR...SOC ANTHOL 20. PAGE 74 A1522 DIPLOM POLICY METH

B64
KIS T.I.,LES PAYS DE L'EUROPE DE L'EST: LEURS RAPPORTS MUTUELS ET LE PROBLEME DE LEUR INTEGRATION DANS L'ORBITE DE L'USSR. EUR+WWI RUSSIA USSR INT/ORG NAT/G REV ATTIT...JURID SOC BIBLIOG WARSAW/P COMECON EUROPE/E. PAGE 80 A1638 DIPLOM COM MARXISM REGION

B64
LEGGE J.D.,INDONESIA. INDONESIA ELITES ECO/UNDEV POL/PAR CHIEF FORCES INT/TRADE COERCE CHOOSE ORD/FREE...SOC CHARTS BIBLIOG 16/20 CHINJAP. PAGE 86 A1765 S/ASIA DOMIN NAT/LISM POLICY

B64
MUSSO AMBROSI L.A.,BIBLIOGRAFIA DE BIBLIOGRAFIAS URUGUAYAS. URUGUAY DIPLOM ADMIN ATTIT...SOC 20. PAGE 106 A2185 BIBLIOG NAT/G L/A+17C PRESS

B64
NEHEMKIS P.,LATIN AMERICA: MYTH AND REALITY. INDUS INT/ORG MUNIC PROB/SOLV CAP/ISM DIPLOM REV...SOC 20. PAGE 108 A2211 REGION MYTH L/A+17C ECO/UNDEV

B64
RAGHAVAN M.D.,INDIA IN CEYLONESE HISTORY, SOCIETY AND CULTURE. CEYLON INDIA S/ASIA LAW SOCIETY INT/TRADE ATTIT...ART/METH JURID SOC LING 20. PAGE 119 A2433 DIPLOM CULTURE SECT STRUCT

B64
SAKAI R.K.,STUDIES ON ASIA, 1964. ASIA CHINA/COM ISRAEL MALAYSIA S/ASIA USA+45 USSR ECO/UNDEV FAM POL/PAR SECT CONSULT NAT/LISM...POLICY SOC 20 CHINJAP. PAGE 126 A2588 PWR DIPLOM

B64
SPECTOR S.D.,A CHECKLIST OF PAPERBOUND BOOKS ON RUSSIA. USSR SECT DIPLOM EDU/PROP HEALTH...PHIL/SCI PSY SOC SOC/WK WORSHIP 20. PAGE 135 A2775 BIBLIOG COM PERF/ART

B64
SULLIVAN G.,THE STORY OF THE PEACE CORPS. USA+45 WOR+45 INTELL FACE/GP NAT/G SCHOOL VOL/ASSN CONSULT EX/STRUC PLAN EDU/PROP ADMIN ATTIT DRIVE ALL/VALS ...POLICY HEAL SOC CONCPT INT QU BIOG TREND SOC/EXP WORK. PAGE 140 A2861 INT/ORG ECO/UNDEV FOR/AID PEACE

B64
TEPASKE J.J.,EXPLOSIVE FORCES IN LATIN AMERICA. CULTURE INTELL ECO/UNDEV INT/ORG NAT/G SECT FORCES ECO/TAC EDU/PROP PWR WEALTH SOC. PAGE 142 A2903 L/A+17C RIGID/FLEX FOR/AID USSR

B64
TURNER M.C.,LIBROS EN VENTA EN HISPANOAMERICA Y ESPANA. SPAIN LAW CONSTN CULTURE ADMIN LEAD...HUM SOC 20. PAGE 146 A2983 BIBLIOG L/A+17C NAT/G DIPLOM

B64
UAR NATIONAL LIBRARY,A BIBLIOGRAPHICAL LIST OF WORKS ABOUT PALESTINE AND JORDAN (2ND ED.). ISRAEL JORDAN SECT DIPLOM...SOC 20 JEWS. PAGE 146 A2991 BIBLIOG ISLAM

B64
WYTHE G.,THE UNITED STATES AND INTER-AMERICAN RELATIONS: A CONTEMPORARY APPRAISAL. L/A+17C USA+45 ECO/UNDEV INT/ORG NAT/G VOL/ASSN INT/TRADE EDU/PROP DRIVE...SOC TREND OAS UN 20. PAGE 168 A3425 ATTIT ECO/TAC FOR/AID

L64
HERZ J.H.,"THE RELEVANCY AND IRRELEVANCY OF APPEASEMENT." WOR+45 INT/ORG CONSULT TOP/EX LEGIT ATTIT SUPEGO ORD/FREE...POLICY SOC GEN/LAWS 20. PAGE 64 A1320 ACT/RES RIGID/FLEX

L64
RIPLEY R.B.,"INTERAGENCY COMMITTEES AND INCREMENTALISM: THE CASE OF AID TO INDIA." INDIA USA+45 INTELL NAT/G DELIB/GP ACT/RES DIPLOM ROUTINE NAT/LISM ATTIT PWR...SOC CONCPT NEW/IDEA TIME/SEQ CON/ANAL VAL/FREE 20. PAGE 121 A2483 EXEC MGT FOR/AID

L64
WORLD PEACE FOUNDATION,"INTERNATIONAL ORGANIZATIONS: SUMMARY OF ACTIVITIES." INDIA PAKISTAN TURKEY WOR+45 CONSTN CONSULT EX/STRUC ECO/TAC EDU/PROP LEGIT ORD/FREE...JURID SOC UN 20 CYPRESS. PAGE 167 A3397 INT/ORG ROUTINE

S64
GARMARNIKOW M.,"INFLUENCE-BUYING IN WEST AFRICA." COM FUT USSR INTELL NAT/G PLAN TEC/DEV ECO/TAC DOMIN EDU/PROP REGION NAT/LISM ATTIT DRIVE ALL/VALS SOVEREIGN...POLICY PSY SOC CONCPT TREND STERTYP WORK COLD/WAR 20. PAGE 51 A1049 AFR ECO/UNDEV FOR/AID SOCISM

S64
GRZYBOWSKI K.,"INTERNATIONAL ORGANIZATIONS FROM THE SOVIET POINT OF VIEW." WOR+45 WOR-45 CULTURE ECO/DEV VOL/ASSN EDU/PROP ATTIT RIGID/FLEX KNOWL ...SOC OBS TIME/SEQ TREND GEN/LAWS VAL/FREE ILO UN 20. PAGE 58 A1184 COM INT/ORG DIPLOM USSR

S64
KHAN M.Z.,"THE PRESIDENT OF THE GENERAL ASSEMBLY." WOR+45 CONSTN DELIB/GP EDU/PROP LEGIT ROUTINE PWR RESPECT SKILL...DECISION SOC BIOG TREND UN 20. PAGE 78 A1609 INT/ORG TOP/EX

S64
SAAB H.,"THE ARAB SEARCH FOR A FEDERAL UNION." SOCIETY INT/ORG NAT/G DELIB/GP FORCES ACT/RES TEC/DEV ECO/TAC DOMIN LEGIT REGION ROUTINE ATTIT DRIVE RIGID/FLEX ALL/VALS...SOC CONCPT NEW/IDEA TIME/SEQ TREND. PAGE 126 A2580 ISLAM PLAN

S64
WASKOW A.I.,"NEW ROADS TO A WORLD WITHOUT WAR." FUT WOR+45 CULTURE INTELL SOCIETY NAT/G DOMIN LEGIT EXEC COERCE PEACE ATTIT DISPL PERCEPT RIGID/FLEX ALL/VALS...POLICY RELATIV SOC NEW/IDEA 20. PAGE 161 A3288 INT/ORG FORCES

B65
AUVADE R.,BIBLIOGRAPHIE CRITIQUE DES OEUVRES PARUES SUR L'INDOCHINE FRANCAISE: UN SIECLE D'HISTOIRE ET D'ENSEIGNEMENT. VIETNAM DIPLOM...SOC 20. PAGE 10 A0198 BIBLIOG/A R+D ACADEM COLONIAL

B65
CHUNG Y.S.,KOREA: A SELECTED BIBLIOGRAPHY 1959-1963. ASIA KOREA NAT/G DIPLOM 20. PAGE 26 A0537 BIBLIOG/A SOC

B65
FORM W.H.,INDUSTRIAL RELATIONS AND SOCIAL CHANGE IN LATIN AMERICA. L/A+17C AGRI LABOR NAT/G PLAN PROB/SOLV DIPLOM...MGT SOC ANTHOL BIBLIOG/A METH 20. PAGE 47 A0966 INDUS GP/REL NAT/COMP ECO/UNDEV

B65
HASSON J.A.,THE ECONOMICS OF NUCLEAR POWER. INDIA UK USA+45 WOR+45 INT/ORG TEC/DEV COST...SOC STAT CHARTS 20 EURATOM. PAGE 63 A1286 NUC/PWR INDUS ECO/DEV METH

B65
HISPANIC SOCIETY OF AMERICA,CATALOGUE (10 VOLS.). BIBLIOG

PORTUGAL PRE/AMER SPAIN NAT/G ADMIN...POLICY SOC 15/20. PAGE 65 A1341 — L/A+17C COLONIAL DIPLOM

B65
INTERNATIONAL SOCIAL SCI COUN,SOCIAL SCIENCES IN THE USSR. USSR ECO/DEV AGRI FINAN INDUS PLAN CAP/ISM...INT/LAW PHIL/SCI PSY SOC 20. PAGE 71 A1460 — BIBLIOG/A ACT/RES MARXISM JURID

B65
NATIONAL BOOK CENTRE PAKISTAN,BOOKS ON PAKISTAN: A BIBLIOGRAPHY. PAKISTAN CULTURE DIPLOM ADMIN ATTIT ...MAJORIT SOC CONCPT 20. PAGE 107 A2201 — BIBLIOG CONSTN S/ASIA NAT/G

B65
NATIONAL CENTRAL LIBRARY,LATIN AMERICAN ECONOMIC AND SOCIAL SERIALS. UK SOCIETY NAT/G PLAN PROB/SOLV ...SOC 20. PAGE 107 A2202 — BIBLIOG INT/TRADE ECO/UNDEV L/A+17C

B65
REQUA E.G.,THE DEVELOPING NATIONS: A GUIDE TO INFORMATION SOURCES CONCERNING THEIR ECON, POLIT, TECHNICAL, AND SOCIAL PROBLEMS. AFR ASIA ISLAM L/A+17C INDUS INT/ORG CONSULT PLAN PROB/SOLV...SOC 20 UN. PAGE 120 A2466 — BIBLIOG/A ECO/UNDEV FOR/AID TEC/DEV

B65
SILVA SOLAR J.,EL DESARROLLO DE LA NUEVA SOCIEDAD EN AMERICA. L/A+17C SOCIETY AGRI PROB/SOLV DIPLOM PARTIC GP/REL OWN...POLICY SOC 20 REFORMERS. PAGE 133 A2716 — STRUCT ECO/UNDEV REGION CONTROL

B65
UNESCO,INTERNATIONAL ORGANIZATIONS IN THE SOCIAL SCIENCES(REV. ED.). LAW ADMIN ATTIT...CRIMLGY GEOG INT/LAW PSY SOC STAT 20 UNESCO. PAGE 148 A3024 — INT/ORG R+D PROF/ORG ACT/RES

B65
UNIVERSAL REFERENCE SYSTEM,INTERNATIONAL AFFAIRS: VOLUME I IN THE POLITICAL SCIENCE, GOVERNMENT, AND PUBLIC POLICY SERIES....DECISION ECOMETRIC GEOG INT/LAW JURID MGT PHIL/SCI PSY SOC. PAGE 149 A3041 — BIBLIOG/A GEN/METH COMPUT/IR DIPLOM

B65
VAN DEN BERGHE P.L.,AFRICA: SOCIAL PROBLEMS OF CHANGE AND CONFLICT. ELITES STRATA ECO/UNDEV KIN MUNIC DIPLOM GP/REL RACE/REL NAT/LISM...ANTHOL BIBLIOG 20. PAGE 158 A3210 — SOC CULTURE AFR STRUCT

B65
WALKER A.A.,THE RHODESIAS AND NYASALAND: A GUIDE TO OFFICIAL PUBLICATIONS. RHODESIA UK OP/RES PLAN PROB/SOLV DIPLOM...POLICY SOC CON/ANAL 19/20 NYASALAND. PAGE 160 A3263 — BIBLIOG NAT/G COLONIAL AFR

B65
WINT G.,ASIA: A HANDBOOK. ASIA COM INDIA USSR CULTURE INTELL NAT/G...GEOG STAT CENSUS NAT/COMP WORSHIP 20 TREATY CHINJAP. PAGE 165 A3365 — DIPLOM SOC

S65
DOSSICK J.J.,"DOCTORAL DISSERTATIONS ON RUSSIA, THE SOVIET UNION, AND EASTERN EUROPE." USSR ACADEM DIPLOM EDU/PROP MARXISM 19/20 COLD/WAR. PAGE 38 A0775 — BIBLIOG HUM SOC

S65
KHOURI F.J.,"THE JORDON RIVER CONTROVERSY." LAW SOCIETY ECO/UNDEV AGRI FINAN INDUS SECT FORCES ACT/RES PLAN TEC/DEV ECO/TAC EDU/PROP COERCE ATTIT DRIVE PERCEPT RIGID/FLEX ALL/VALS...GEOG SOC MYTH WORK. PAGE 78 A1610 — ISLAM INT/ORG ISRAEL JORDAN

S65
MERRITT R.L.,"WOODROW WILSON AND THE 'GREAT AND SOLEMN REFERENDUM,' 1920." USA-45 SOCIETY NAT/G CONSULT LEGIS ACT/RES PLAN DOMIN EDU/PROP ROUTINE ATTIT DISPL DRIVE PERSON RIGID/FLEX MORAL ORD/FREE ...PSY SOC CONCPT MYTH LEAGUE/NAT. PAGE 100 A2044 — INT/ORG TOP/EX DIPLOM

S65
SPAAK P.H.,"THE SEARCH FOR CONSENSUS: A NEW EFFORT TO BUILD EUROPE." FRANCE GERMANY ECO/DEV NAT/G CONSULT FORCES PLAN EDU/PROP REGION CONSEN ATTIT ...SOC METH/CNCPT OBS TREND EEC NATO WORK 20. PAGE 135 A2770 — EUR+WWI INT/ORG

B66
BLACK C.E.,THE DYNAMICS OF MODERNIZATION: A STUDY IN COMPARATIVE HISTORY. STRUCT ECO/DEV ECO/UNDEV NAT/G DIPLOM LEAD REV...PREDICT TIME/SEQ TREND SOC/INTEG 17/20. PAGE 15 A0296 — SOCIETY SOC NAT/COMP

B66
BOULDING K.E.,THE IMPACT OF THE SOCIAL SCIENCES. UNIV LAW SOCIETY CREATE PROB/SOLV...TREND WORSHIP. PAGE 17 A0349 — SOC DIPLOM

B66
CANNING HOUSE LIBRARY,AUTHOR AND SUBJECT CATALOGUES OF THE CANNING HOUSE LIBRARY (5 VOLS.). UK CULTURE LEAD...SOC 19/20. PAGE 24 A0478 — BIBLIOG L/A+17C NAT/G DIPLOM

B66
EMBREE A.T.,ASIA: A GUIDE TO BASIC BOOKS (PAMPHLET). ECO/UNDEV SECT FORCES DIPLOM ALL/IDEOS ...SOC 20. PAGE 41 A0846 — BIBLIOG/A ASIA S/ASIA NAT/G

B66
FARWELL G.,MASK OF ASIA: THE PHILIPPINES. PHILIPPINE SECT DIPLOM ATTIT...SOC RECORD PREDICT BIBLIOG 20. PAGE 44 A0901 — S/ASIA CULTURE

B66
GLAZER M.,THE FEDERAL GOVERNMENT AND THE UNIVERSITY. CHILE PROB/SOLV DIPLOM GIVE ADMIN WAR ...POLICY SOC 20. PAGE 53 A1079 — BIBLIOG/A NAT/G PLAN ACADEM

B66
GRAHAM I.C.C.,PUBLICATIONS OF THE SOCIAL SCIENCE DEPARTMENT, THE RAND CORPORATION, 1948-1966. USSR WOR+45 NAT/G ARMS/CONT DETER WAR NAT/LISM...SOC GOV/COMP. PAGE 55 A1127 — BIBLIOG DIPLOM NUC/PWR FORCES

B66
HOFMANN L.,UNITED STATES AND CANADIAN PUBLICATIONS ON AFRICA IN 1964. LAW AGRI INDUS SCHOOL...HUM SOC 20. PAGE 66 A1360 — BIBLIOG AFR DIPLOM

B66
HOLT R.T.,THE POLITICAL BASIS OF ECONOMIC DEVELOPMENT. STRATA STRUCT NAT/G DIPLOM ADMIN...SOC NAT/COMP BIBLIOG 20. PAGE 67 A1376 — ECO/TAC GOV/COMP CONSTN EX/STRUC

B66
KEYES J.G.,A BIBLIOGRAPHY OF WESTERN LANGUAGE PUBLICATIONS CONCERNING NORTH VIETNAM IN THE CORNELL LIBRARY. VIETNAM/N NAT/G FORCES TEC/DEV DIPLOM LEAD RACE/REL...GEOG SOC 20. PAGE 78 A1603 — BIBLIOG/A CULTURE ECO/UNDEV S/ASIA

B66
LEIGH M.B.,CHECK LIST OF HOLDINGS ON BORNEO IN THE CORNELL UNIVERSITY LIBRARIES (PAMPHLET). BORNEO MALAYSIA LAW CONSTN GP/REL SOC. PAGE 86 A1769 — BIBLIOG S/ASIA DIPLOM NAT/G

B66
LONDON K.,EASTERN EUROPE IN TRANSITION. CHINA/COM USSR DOMIN COLONIAL CENTRAL RIGID/FLEX PWR...SOC ANTHOL 20. PAGE 91 A1855 — SOVEREIGN COM NAT/LISM DIPLOM

B66
MC CLELLAND C.A.,THEORY AND THE INTERNATIONAL SYSTEM. EDU/PROP PWR...DECISION SOC METH. PAGE 97 A1991 — DIPLOM METH/CNCPT ACT/RES R+D

B66
RIESELBACH L.N.,THE ROOTS OF ISOLATIONISM* CONGRESSIONAL VOTING AND PRESIDENTIAL LEADERSHIP IN FOREIGN POLICY. POL/PAR LEGIS DIPLOM EDU/PROP LEAD REGION REPRESENT...SOC STAT IDEA/COMP HYPO/EXP BIBLIOG 19/20 CONGRESS. PAGE 121 A2477 — ISOLAT CHOOSE CHIEF POLICY

B66
SOCIAL SCIENCE RESEARCH COUN,BIBLIOGRAPHY OF RESEARCH IN THE SOCIAL SCIENCES IN AUSTRALIA 1957-1960. LAW R+D DIPLOM 20 AUSTRAL. PAGE 135 A2758 — BIBLIOG SOC PSY

B66
UNITED NATIONS,INTERNATIONAL SPACE BIBLIOGRAPHY. FUT INT/ORG TEC/DEV DIPLOM ARMS/CONT NUC/PWR ...JURID SOC UN. PAGE 149 A3037 — BIBLIOG SPACE PEACE R+D

B66
US DEPARTMENT OF STATE,RESEARCH ON WESTERN EUROPE, GREAT BRITAIN, AND CANADA (EXTERNAL RESEARCH LIST NO 3-25). CANADA GERMANY/W UK LAW CULTURE NAT/G POL/PAR FORCES EDU/PROP REGION MARXISM...GEOG SOC WORSHIP 20 CMN/WLTH. PAGE 152 A3098 — BIBLIOG/A EUR+WWI DIPLOM

B66
US DEPARTMENT OF THE ARMY,SOUTH ASIA: A STRATEGIC SURVEY (PAMPHLET NO. 550-3). AFGHANISTN INDIA NEPAL PAKISTAN ECO/UNDEV INT/ORG POL/PAR FORCES FOR/AID INT/TRADE LEAD WAR...POLICY SOC TREND 20. PAGE 152 A3110 — BIBLIOG/A S/ASIA DIPLOM NAT/G

B66
WHITAKER A.P.,NATIONALISM IN CONTEMPORARY LATIN AMERICA. AGRI NAT/G WEALTH...POLICY SOC CONCPT OBS TREND 20. PAGE 164 A3333 — NAT/LISM L/A+17C DIPLOM ECO/UNDEV

S66
"RESEARCH WORK 1965-1966." NEW/ZEALND ELITES ACADEM LOC/G MUNIC POL/PAR PROVS DIPLOM COLONIAL...SOC 20 AUSTRAL. PAGE 4 A0073 — BIBLIOG NAT/G CULTURE S/ASIA

S66
MERRITT R.L.,"SELECTED ARTICLES AND DOCUMENTS ON COMPARATIVE GOVERNMENT AND CROSS-NATIONAL RESEARCH." AFR ASIA EUR+WWI L/A+17C MOD/EUR ELITES R+D ACT/RES DIPLOM PWR...SOC CONCPT 18/20. PAGE 100 A2046 — BIBLIOG GOV/COMP NAT/G GOV/REL

B67
KAROL K.S.,CHINA, THE OTHER COMMUNISM (TRANS. BY TOM BAISTOW). CHINA/COM CULTURE INDUS FORCES DIPLOM EDU/PROP CONTROL EXEC NUC/PWR ATTIT...SOC CHARTS 20. PAGE 77 A1567 — NAT/G POL/PAR MARXISM INGP/REL

B67
LANDEN R.G.,OMAN SINCE 1856: DISRUPTIVE MODERNIZATION IN A TRADITIONAL ARAB SOCIETY. UK DIST/IND EXTR/IND SECT DIPLOM INT/TRADE...SOC LING — ISLAM CULTURE ECO/UNDEV

CHARTS BIBLIOG 19/20. PAGE 84 A1714 NAT/G

B67
ROSENAU J.N.,DOMESTIC SOURCES OF FOREIGN POLICY. WOR+45 STRATA COM/IND MUNIC POL/PAR LOBBY PARTIC REGION ATTIT...PSY SOC COLD/WAR. PAGE 124 A2534
DIPLOM POLICY NAT/G CHOOSE

B67
SACHS M.Y.,THE WORLDMARK ENCYCLOPEDIA OF THE NATIONS (5 VOLS.). ELITES SOCIETY STRATA ECO/DEV ECO/UNDEV AGRI EXTR/IND FINAN LABOR LOC/G NAT/G POL/PAR SECT INT/TRADE SOVEREIGN...SOC 20. PAGE 126 A2585
WOR+45 INT/ORG BAL/PWR

B67
UNIVERSAL REFERENCE SYSTEM,BIBLIOGRAPHY OF BIBLIOGRAPHIES IN POLITICAL SCIENCE, GOVERNMENT, AND PUBLIC POLICY (VOLUME III). WOR+45 WOR-45 LAW ADMIN...SOC CON/ANAL COMPUT/IR GEN/METH. PAGE 149 A3042
BIBLIOG/A NAT/G DIPLOM POLICY

B67
US DEPARTMENT OF STATE,FOREIGN AFFAIRS RESEARCH (PAMPHLET). USA+45 WOR+45 ACADEM NAT/G...PSY SOC CHARTS 20. PAGE 152 A3100
BIBLIOG INDEX R+D DIPLOM

S67
GLOBERSON A.,"SOCIAL GROWTH IN THE DEVELOPING COUNTRIES." CULTURE SOCIETY CONSULT PROB/SOLV SOC. PAGE 53 A1082
ECO/UNDEV FOR/AID EDU/PROP PLAN

S67
INGLEHART R.,"AN END TO EUROPEAN INTEGRATION." PROB/SOLV BAL/PWR NAT/LISM...PSY SOC INT CHARTS GP/COMP 20. PAGE 70 A1440
DIPLOM EUR+WWI REGION ATTIT

S67
LOSMAN D.L.,"FOREIGN AID, SOCIALISM AND THE EMERGING COUNTRIES" WOR+45 ADMIN CONTROL PWR 20. PAGE 91 A1864
ECO/UNDEV FOR/AID SOC

S67
SCHUMANN H.,"IMPERIALISMUS-KRITIK UND KOLONIALISMUS-FORSCHUNG." GERMANY/E DIPLOM SOVEREIGN...SOC HIST/WRIT 20. PAGE 129 A2652
COLONIAL ATTIT DOMIN CAP/ISM

B82
POOLE W.F.,INDEX TO PERIODICAL LITERATURE. LOC/G NAT/G DIPLOM ADMIN...HUM PHIL/SCI SOC 19. PAGE 117 A2396
BIBLIOG USA-45 ALL/VALS SOCIETY

B86
MAS LATRIE L.,RELATIONS ET COMMERCE DE L'AFRIQUE SEPTENTRIONALE OU MAGREB AVEC LES NATIONS CHRETIENNES AU MOYEN AGE. CULTURE CHIEF FORCES WAR ...SOC CENSUS TREATY 10/16. PAGE 95 A1954
ISLAM SECT DIPLOM INT/TRADE

C93
PLAYFAIR R.L.,"A BIBLIOGRAPHY OF MOROCCO." MOROCCO CULTURE AGRI FORCES DIPLOM WAR HEALTH...GEOG JURID SOC CHARTS. PAGE 116 A2387
BIBLIOG ISLAM MEDIT-7

B98
GRIFFIN A.P.C.,LIST OF BOOKS RELATING TO CUBA (PAMPHLET). CUBA L/A+17C USA-45 INT/TRADE DOMIN WAR GP/REL ALL/VALS...GEOG SOC CHARTS 19/20. PAGE 56 A1158
BIBLIOG/A NAT/G COLONIAL

SOC OF COMP LEGIS AND INT LAW A2756

SOC/DEMPAR....SOCIAL DEMOCRATIC PARTY (USE WITH SPECIFIC NATION)

B66
COLE A.B.,SOCIALIST PARTIES IN POSTWAR JAPAN. STRATA AGRI LABOR PLAN DIPLOM ECO/TAC AGREE LEAD CHOOSE ATTIT...CHARTS 20 CHINJAP SOC/DEMPAR. PAGE 28 A0566
POL/PAR POLICY SOCISM NAT/G

SOC/EXP...."SOCIAL" EXPERIMENTATION UNDER UNCONTROLLED CONDITIONS

S51
ICHHEISER G.,"MISUNDERSTANDING IN INTERNATIONAL RELATIONS." UNIV SOCIETY FACE/GP INT/ORG SECT ATTIT PERSON RIGID/FLEX LOVE RESPECT...RELATIV PSY SOC CONCPT MYTH SOC/EXP GEN/LAWS. PAGE 70 A1431
PERCEPT STERTYP NAT/LISM DIPLOM

S54
DODD S.C.,"THE SCIENTIFIC MEASUREMENT OF FITNESS FOR SELF-GOVERNMENT." FUT CONSTN ECO/UNDEV INT/ORG PLAN PWR...CONCPT QUANT CON/ANAL SOC/EXP UN LEAGUE/NAT 20. PAGE 38 A0767
NAT/G STAT SOVEREIGN

B56
UNDERHILL F.H.,THE BRITISH COMMONWEALTH: AN EXPERIMENT IN CO-OPERATION AMONG NATIONS. CANADA UK WOR+45 WOR-45 INT/ORG COLONIAL UTIL SOVEREIGN CONSERVE...OLD/LIB SOC/EXP BIBLIOG/A 19/20 CMN/WLTH. PAGE 147 A3007
VOL/ASSN NAT/LISM DIPLOM

L60
DEUTSCH K.W.,"TOWARD AN INVENTORY OF BASIC TRENDS AND PATTERNS IN COMPARATIVE AND INTERNATIONAL POLITICS." UNIV WOR+45 SOCIETY STRUCT INT/ORG NAT/G CREATE PLAN EDU/PROP KNOWL...PHIL/SCI METH/CNCPT STAT SELF/OBS OBS/ENVIR SAMP TREND CON/ANAL CHARTS SOC/EXP GEN/METH 20. PAGE 36 A0739
R+D PERCEPT

S60
THOMPSON K.W.,"MORAL PURPOSE IN FOREIGN POLICY: REALITIES AND ILLUSIONS." WOR+45 WOR-45 LAW CULTURE SOCIETY INT/ORG PLAN ADJUD ADMIN COERCE RIGID/FLEX SUPEGO KNOWL ORD/FREE PWR...SOC TREND SOC/EXP TOT/POP 20. PAGE 143 A2930
MORAL JURID DIPLOM

B62
HETHERINGTON H.,SOME ASPECTS OF THE BRITISH EXPERIMENT IN DEMOCRACY. UK DIPLOM COLONIAL ...CONCPT 20 CMN/WLTH. PAGE 64 A1322
EDU/PROP AFR POPULISM SOC/EXP

S62
CRANE R.D.,"LAW AND STRATEGY IN SPACE." FUT USA+45 WOR+45 AIR LAW INT/ORG NAT/G FORCES ACT/RES PLAN BAL/PWR LEGIT ARMS/CONT COERCE ORD/FREE...POLICY INT/LAW JURID SOC/EXP 20 TREATY. PAGE 32 A0656
CONCPT SPACE

B63
ROBERTSON A.H.,HUMAN RIGHTS IN EUROPE. CONSTN SOCIETY INT/ORG NAT/G VOL/ASSN DELIB/GP ACT/RES PLAN ADJUD REGION ROUTINE ATTIT LOVE ORD/FREE RESPECT...JURID SOC CONCPT SOC/EXP UN 20. PAGE 122 A2498
EUR+WWI PERSON

B64
SULLIVAN G.,THE STORY OF THE PEACE CORPS. USA+45 WOR+45 INTELL FACE/GP NAT/G SCHOOL VOL/ASSN CONSULT EX/STRUC PLAN EDU/PROP ADMIN ATTIT DRIVE ALL/VALS ...POLICY HEAL SOC CONCPT INT QU BIOG TREND SOC/EXP WORK. PAGE 140 A2861
INT/ORG ECO/UNDEV FOR/AID PEACE

L64
ARMENGALD A.,"ECONOMIE ET COEXISTENCE." COM EUR+WWI FUT USA+45 WOR+45 ECO/DEV ECO/UNDEV FINAN INT/ORG NAT/G EXEC CHOOSE ATTIT ALL/VALS...POLICY RELATIV DECISION TREND SOC/EXP COLD/WAR WORK 20. PAGE 9 A0173
MARKET ECO/TAC CAP/ISM

SOC/INTEG....SOCIAL INTEGRATION; SEE ALSO CONSEN, RACE/REL

B27
SIEGFRIED A.,AMERICA COMES OF AGE: A FRENCH ANALYSIS (TRANS. BY H.H. HEMMING AND DORIS HEMMING). FRANCE UK POL/PAR WORKER TEC/DEV DIPLOM REGION RACE/REL ADJUST PRODUC HEREDITY...TIME/SEQ GP/COMP SOC/INTEG 20 DEMOCRAT REPUBLICAN KKK. PAGE 132 A2714
USA-45 CULTURE ECO/DEV SOC

B54
COOKSON J.,BEFORE THE AFRICAN STORM. BELGIUM CENTRL/AFR FRANCE UK ECO/UNDEV POL/PAR CREATE BAL/PWR RACE/REL NAT/LISM ORD/FREE CONSERVE MARXISM SOC/INTEG 20 CONGO/LEOP. PAGE 30 A0607
COLONIAL REV DISCRIM DIPLOM

B59
BROOKES E.H.,THE COMMONWEALTH TODAY. UK ROMAN/EMP INT/ORG RACE/REL NAT/LISM SOVEREIGN...TREND SOC/INTEG 20. PAGE 19 A0391
FEDERAL DIPLOM JURID IDEA/COMP

B59
BUNDESMIN FUR VERTRIEBENE,ZEITTAFEL DER VORGESCHICHTE UND DES ABLAUFS DER VERTREIBUNG SOWIE DER UNTERBRINGUNG UND EINGLIEDERUNG DER (2 VOLS.). GERMANY/E GERMANY/W NAT/G PROVS PROB/SOLV DIPLOM PARL/PROC ATTIT...BIBLIOG SOC/INTEG 20 MIGRATION PARLIAMENT. PAGE 21 A0431
JURID GP/REL INT/LAW

B59
TARDIFF G.,LA LIBERTAD; LA LIBERTAD DE EXPRESION, IDEALES Y REALIDADES AMERICANAS. ISLAM INT/ORG PROB/SOLV PRESS CONFER PARTIC CATHISM...INT/LAW SOC/INTEG UN MID/EAST. PAGE 141 A2889
ORD/FREE ATTIT DIPLOM CONCPT

B61
CAMERON J.,THE AFRICAN REVOLUTION. AFR UK ECO/UNDEV POL/PAR REGION RACE/REL DISCRIM PWR CONSERVE ...CONCPT SOC/INTEG 20 NEGRO. PAGE 23 A0472
REV COLONIAL ORD/FREE DIPLOM

B61
LIEFMANN-KEIL E.,OKONOMISCHE THEORIE DER SOZIALPOLITIK. INT/ORG LABOR WORKER COST INCOME NEW/LIB...CONCPT SOC/INTEG 20. PAGE 88 A1810
ECO/DEV INDUS NAT/G SOC/WK

B63
CONF ON FUTURE OF COMMONWEALTH,THE FUTURE OF THE COMMONWEALTH. UK ECO/UNDEV AGRI EDU/PROP ADMIN SOC/INTEG 20 COMMONWLTH. PAGE 29 A0583
DIPLOM RACE/REL ORD/FREE TEC/DEV

B64
ALVIM J.C.,A REVOLUCAO SEM RUMO. BRAZIL NAT/G BAL/PWR DIPLOM INT/TRADE PARTIC WEALTH...POLICY SOC SOC/INTEG 20. PAGE 6 A0132
REV CIVMIL/REL ECO/UNDEV ORD/FREE

B64
ARNOLD G.,TOWARDS PEACE AND A MULTIRACIAL COMMONWEALTH. UK TEC/DEV BAL/PWR COLONIAL GP/REL NAT/LISM PEACE SOVEREIGN...POLICY SOC/INTEG 20 CMN/WLTH. PAGE 9 A0175
DIPLOM INT/TRADE FOR/AID ORD/FREE

B64
CURRIE D.P.,FEDERALISM AND THE NEW NATIONS OF
FEDERAL

AFRICA. CANADA USA+45 INT/TRADE TAX GP/REL ...NAT/COMP SOC/INTEG 20. PAGE 33 A0667 — AFR ECO/UNDEV INT/LAW

B64
DESHMUKH C.D.,THE COMMONWEALTH AS INDIA SEES IT. INDIA UK ECO/UNDEV TEC/DEV INT/TRADE GP/REL RACE/REL SOVEREIGN SOC/INTEG 19/20 COMMONWLTH. PAGE 36 A0733 — DIPLOM COLONIAL NAT/LISM ATTIT

B64
HALPERN J.M.,GOVERNMENT, POLITICS, AND SOCIAL STRUCTURE IN LAOS. LAOS CULTURE SOCIETY STRATA STRUCT FAM DIPLOM DOMIN MARXISM...INT GOV/COMP WORSHIP SOC/INTEG 20. PAGE 60 A1242 — NAT/G SOC LOC/G

B64
KOLARZ W.,COMMUNISM AND COLONIALISM. AFR ASIA USSR DISCRIM ATTIT ORD/FREE SOVEREIGN SOC/INTEG 20. PAGE 81 A1668 — EDU/PROP DIPLOM TOTALISM COLONIAL

B64
LUTHULI A.,AFRICA'S FREEDOM. KIN LABOR POL/PAR SCHOOL DIPLOM NEUTRAL REGION REV NAT/LISM PWR WEALTH SOCISM SOC/INTEG 20. PAGE 92 A1874 — AFR ECO/UNDEV COLONIAL

B64
UNESCO,WORLD COMMUNICATIONS: PRESS, RADIO, TELEVISION, FILM (4TH ED.). WOR+45 DIPLOM TV PEACE ...NAT/COMP SOC/INTEG 20 FILM. PAGE 148 A3023 — COM/IND EDU/PROP PRESS TEC/DEV

B64
WRIGHT Q.,A STUDY OF WAR. LAW NAT/G PROB/SOLV BAL/PWR NAT/LISM PEACE ATTIT SOVEREIGN...CENSUS SOC/INTEG. PAGE 168 A3419 — WAR CONCPT DIPLOM CONTROL

B65
COWEN Z.,THE BRITISH COMMONWEALTH OF NATIONS IN A CHANGING WORLD. UK ECO/UNDEV INT/ORG ECO/TAC INT/TRADE COLONIAL WAR GP/REL RACE/REL SOVEREIGN SOC/INTEG 20 TREATY EEC COMMONWLTH. PAGE 32 A0644 — JURID DIPLOM PARL/PROC NAT/LISM

B65
INGRAM D.,COMMONWEALTH FOR A COLOUR-BLIND WORLD. AFR INDIA UK STRATA ECO/UNDEV VOL/ASSN CREATE PLAN CONFER COLONIAL ORD/FREE SOC/INTEG 20 COMMONWLTH. PAGE 70 A1441 — RACE/REL INT/ORG INGP/REL PROB/SOLV

B66
BLACK C.E.,THE DYNAMICS OF MODERNIZATION: A STUDY IN COMPARATIVE HISTORY. STRUCT ECO/DEV ECO/UNDEV NAT/G DIPLOM LEAD REV...PREDICT TIME/SEQ TREND SOC/INTEG 17/20. PAGE 15 A0296 — SOCIETY SOC NAT/COMP

B66
KANET R.E.,THE SOVIET UNION AND SUB-SAHARAN AFRICA: COMMUNIST POLICY TOWARD AFRICA, 1917-1965. AFR USSR ECO/UNDEV TEC/DEV EDU/PROP TASK DISCRIM PEACE WEALTH ALL/IDEOS...CHARTS BIBLIOG SOC/INTEG 19/20 NEGRO UN INTERVENT. PAGE 76 A1555 — DIPLOM ECO/TAC MARXISM

B66
KAREFA-SMART J.,AFRICA: PROGRESS THROUGH COOPERATION. AFR FINAN TEC/DEV DIPLOM FOR/AID EDU/PROP CONFER REGION GP/REL WEALTH...HEAL SOC/INTEG 20. PAGE 76 A1566 — ORD/FREE ECO/UNDEV VOL/ASSN PLAN

B66
LENT H.B.,THE PEACE CORPS: AMBASSADORS OF GOOD WILL. USA+45 ECO/UNDEV...INT TESTS BIOG AUD/VIS SOC/INTEG 20 PEACE/CORP. PAGE 87 A1776 — VOL/ASSN FOR/AID DIPLOM CONSULT

B66
POLLACK R.S.,THE INDIVIDUAL'S RIGHTS AND INTERNATIONAL ORGANIZATION. LAW INT/ORG DELIB/GP SUPEGO...JURID SOC/INTEG 20 TREATY UN. PAGE 117 A2394 — INT/LAW ORD/FREE DIPLOM PERSON

S67
VELIKONJA J.,"ITALIAN IMMIGRANTS IN THE UNITED STATES IN THE MID-SIXTIES" ITALY USA+45 KIN MUNIC NAT/G WORKER DIPLOM REGION GP/REL ADJUST...GEOG CHARTS SOC/INTEG 20. PAGE 158 A3226 — HABITAT ORD/FREE TREND STAT

SOC/PAR....SOCIALIST PARTY (USE WITH SPECIFIC NATION)

SOC/REVPAR....SOCIALIST REVOLUTIONARY PARTY (USE WITH SPECIFIC NATION)

SOC/SECUR....SOCIAL SECURITY

SOC/WK....SOCIAL WORK, SOCIAL SERVICE ORGANIZATION

B
UN DEPARTMENT SOCIAL AFFAIRS,SOCIAL WELFARE INFORMATION SERIES: CURRENT LITERATURE AND NATIONAL CONFERENCES. WOR+45 INDUS SERV/IND INT/ORG CONSULT ACT/RES WEALTH...HEAL UN. PAGE 147 A2997 — BIBLIOG/A SOC/WK DIPLOM ADMIN

N
INTERNATIONAL BOOK NEWS, 1928-1934. ECO/UNDEV FINAN INDUS LABOR INT/TRADE CONFER ADJUD COLONIAL...HEAL SOC/WK CHARTS 20 LEAGUE/NAT. PAGE 1 A0010 — BIBLIOG/A DIPLOM INT/LAW INT/ORG

N
HOOVER INSTITUTION,UNITED STATES AND CANADIAN PUBLICATIONS ON AFRICA. CULTURE ECO/UNDEV AGRI TEC/DEV EDU/PROP COLONIAL RACE/REL NAT/LISM ATTIT HEALTH...SOC SOC/WK 20. PAGE 67 A1381 — BIBLIOG DIPLOM NAT/G AFR

N
UNITED NATIONS,OFFICIAL RECORDS OF THE ECONOMIC AND SOCIAL COUNCIL OF THE UNITED NATIONS. WOR+45 DIPLOM INT/TRADE CONFER...SOC SOC/WK 20 UN UNESCO. PAGE 148 A3031 — INT/ORG DELIB/GP WRITING

B43
FULLER G.F.,FOREIGN RELIEF AND REHABILITATION (PAMPHLET). FUT GERMANY UK USA-45 INT/ORG PROB/SOLV DIPLOM FOR/AID ADMIN ADJUST PEACE ALL/VALS...SOC/WK 20 UN JEWS. PAGE 50 A1018 — BIBLIOG/A PLAN GIVE WAR

B45
UNCIO CONFERENCE LIBRARY,SHORT TITLE CLASSIFIED CATALOG. WOR-45 DOMIN COLONIAL WAR...SOC/WK 20 LEAGUE/NAT UN. PAGE 147 A3006 — BIBLIOG DIPLOM INT/ORG INT/LAW

B51
CHRISTENSEN A.N.,THE EVOLUTION OF LATIN AMERICAN GOVERNMENT: A BOOK OF READINGS. ECO/UNDEV INDUS LOC/G POL/PAR EX/STRUC LEGIS FOR/AID CT/SYS ...SOC/WK 20 SOUTH/AMER. PAGE 26 A0535 — NAT/G CONSTN DIPLOM L/A+17C

B51
LEONARD L.L.,INTERNATIONAL ORGANIZATION. WOR+45 WOR-45 EX/STRUC FORCES LEGIS ECO/TAC INT/TRADE COLONIAL ARMS/CONT...SOC/WK GOV/COMP BIBLIOG. PAGE 87 A1778 — NAT/G DIPLOM INT/ORG DELIB/GP

B55
UN ECONOMIC AND SOCIAL COUNCIL,BIBLIOGRAPHY OF PUBLICATIONS OF THE UN AND SPECIALIZED AGENCIES IN THE SOCIAL WELFARE FIELD, 1946-1952. WOR+45 FAM INT/ORG MUNIC ACT/RES PLAN PROB/SOLV EDU/PROP AGE/C AGE/Y HABITAT...HEAL UN. PAGE 147 A3000 — BIBLIOG/A SOC/WK ADMIN WEALTH

B57
DRUCKER P.F.,AMERICA'S NEXT TWENTY YEARS. USA+45 DIST/IND ACADEM MUNIC SCHOOL DIPLOM ECO/TAC AUTOMAT HABITAT HEALTH...SOC/WK TREND 20 URBAN/RNWL PUB/TRANS. PAGE 39 A0788 — WORKER FOR/AID CENSUS GEOG

B61
LIEFMANN-KEIL E.,OKONOMISCHE THEORIE DER SOZIALPOLITIK. INT/ORG LABOR WORKER COST INCOME NEW/LIB...CONCPT SOC/INTEG 20. PAGE 88 A1810 — ECO/DEV INDUS NAT/G SOC/WK

B62
US LIBRARY OF CONGRESS,UNITED STATES AND CANADIAN PUBLICATIONS ON AFRICA IN 1960. CANADA USA+45 CULTURE TEC/DEV DIPLOM FOR/AID RACE/REL...GEOG HUM SOC SOC/WK LING 20. PAGE 155 A3156 — BIBLIOG/A AFR

B63
HONORD S.,PUBLIC RELATIONS IN ADMINISTRATION. WOR+45 NAT/G...SOC/WK BIBLIOG 20. PAGE 67 A1379 — PRESS DIPLOM MGT METH/COMP

B63
KATZ S.M.,A SELECTED LIST OF US READINGS ON DEVELOPMENT. AGRI COM/IND DIST/IND INDUS LABOR PLAN FOR/AID EDU/PROP HEALTH...POLICY SOC/WK 20. PAGE 77 A1571 — BIBLIOG/A ECO/UNDEV TEC/DEV ACT/RES

B63
PANAMERICAN UNION,DOCUMENTOS OFICIALES DE LA ORGANIZACION DE LOS ESTADOS AMERICANOS, INDICE Y LISTA (VOL. III, 1962). L/A+17C DELIB/GP INT/TRADE EDU/PROP REGION NUC/PWR...HEAL INT/LAW SOC/WK 20 OAS. PAGE 113 A2329 — BIBLIOG INT/ORG DIPLOM

B64
SPECTOR S.D.,A CHECKLIST OF PAPERBOUND BOOKS ON RUSSIA. USSR SECT DIPLOM EDU/PROP HEALTH...PHIL/SCI PSY SOC SOC/WK WORSHIP 20. PAGE 135 A2775 — BIBLIOG COM PERF/ART

SOCIAL ANALYSIS....SEE SOC

SOCIAL DEMOCRATIC PARTY (ALL NATIONS)....SEE SOC/DEMPAR

SOCIAL CLASS....SEE STRATA

SOCIAL INSTITUTIONS....SEE INSTITUTIONAL INDEX

SOCIAL MOBILITY....SEE STRATA

SOCIAL PSYCHOLOGY (GROUPS)....SEE SOC

SOCIAL PSYCHOLOGY (INDIVIDUALS)....SEE PSY

SOCIAL STRUCTURE....SEE STRUCT

SOCIAL WORK....SEE SOC/WK

SOCIAL REVOLUTIONARY PARTY (ALL NATIONS)....SEE SOC/REVPAR

SOCIAL STRUCTURE....SEE STRUCT, STRATA

SOCIAL SCIENCE RESEARCH COUN A2757,A2758

SOCIALISM....SEE SOCISM, SOCIALIST

SOCIALIST....NON-COMMUNIST SOCIALIST; SEE ALSO SOCISM

B15
HOBSON J.A.,TOWARDS INTERNATIONAL GOVERNMENT. MOD/EUR STRUCT ECO/TAC EDU/PROP ADJUD ALL/VALS ...SOCIALIST CONCPT GEN/LAWS TOT/POP 20. PAGE 65 A1347 FUT INT/ORG CENTRAL

N19
DEANE H.,THE WAR IN VIETNAM (PAMPHLET). CHINA/COM VIETNAM BAL/PWR DIPLOM ECO/TAC SOCISM INTERVENT COLD/WAR INTERVENT COLD/WAR. PAGE 35 A0720 WAR SOCIALIST MORAL CAP/ISM

N19
VELYAMINOV G.,AFRICA AND THE COMMON MARKET (PAMPHLET). AFR MARKET VOL/ASSN ECO/TAC COLONIAL ORD/FREE...SOCIALIST 20 THIRD/WRLD. PAGE 158 A3227 INT/ORG INT/TRADE SOVEREIGN ECO/UNDEV

B32
BLUM L.,PEACE AND DISARMAMENT (TRANS. BY A. WERTH). NAT/G FORCES WORKER DIPLOM AGREE WAR ATTIT AUTHORIT ORD/FREE. PAGE 16 A0322 SOCIALIST PEACE INT/ORG ARMS/CONT

B38
DE MADARIAGA S.,THE WORLD'S DESIGN. WOR-45 SOCIETY STRUCT EDU/PROP PEACE ATTIT PERSON ALL/VALS ...SOCIALIST CONCPT TIME/SEQ TREND GEN/LAWS LEAGUE/NAT. PAGE 35 A0706 FUT INT/ORG DIPLOM

B42
HAMBRO C.J.,HOW TO WIN THE PEACE. ECO/TAC EDU/PROP ADJUD PERSON ALL/VALS...SOCIALIST TREND GEN/LAWS 20. PAGE 61 A1246 FUT INT/ORG PEACE

B46
BLUM L.,FOR ALL MANKIND (TRANS. BY W. PICKLES). FRANCE GERMANY USSR LAW SOCIETY STRUCT POL/PAR WORKER DIPLOM DOMIN CHOOSE ORD/FREE FASCISM 20. PAGE 16 A0323 POPULISM SOCIALIST NAT/G WAR

B46
LOWENSTEIN R.,POLITICAL RECONSTRUCTION. WOR+45 EX/STRUC EDU/PROP NAT/LISM ATTIT KNOWL ORD/FREE PWR ...SOCIALIST CONCPT GEN/LAWS TOT/POP 20. PAGE 91 A1869 FUT INT/ORG DIPLOM

B48
DURBIN E.F.M.,THE POLITICS OF DEMOCRATIC SOCIALISM; AN ESSAY ON SOCIAL POLICY. STRATA POL/PAR PLAN COERCE DRIVE PERSON PWR MARXISM...CHARTS METH/COMP. PAGE 39 A0805 SOCIALIST POPULISM POLICY SOCIETY

B59
THOMAS N.,THE PREREQUISITES FOR PEACE. ASIA EUR+WWI FUT ISLAM S/ASIA WOR+45 FORCES PLAN BAL/PWR EDU/PROP LEGIT ATTIT PWR...SOCIALIST CONCPT COLD/WAR 20 UN. PAGE 143 A2924 INT/ORG ORD/FREE ARMS/CONT PEACE

B60
STRACHEY J.,THE END OF EMPIRE. UK WOR+45 WOR-45 DIPLOM INT/TRADE DOMIN ADJUST ORD/FREE WEALTH ...SOCIALIST GOV/COMP TIME COMMONWLTH. PAGE 139 A2841 COLONIAL ECO/DEV BAL/PWR LAISSEZ

B61
DIA M.,THE AFRICAN NATIONS AND WORLD SOLIDARITY. ISLAM CULTURE ELITES ECO/DEV ECO/UNDEV INT/ORG NAT/G PLAN ECO/TAC INT/TRADE EDU/PROP NAT/LISM ATTIT DRIVE ORD/FREE WEALTH...SOCIALIST CONCPT CON/ANAL GEN/LAWS TOT/POP 20. PAGE 37 A0753 AFR REGION SOCISM

B61
PERLO V.,EL IMPERIALISMO NORTHEAMERICANO. USA+45 USA-45 FINAN CAP/ISM DIPLOM DOMIN CONTROL DISCRIM 19/20. PAGE 115 A2363 SOCIALIST ECO/DEV INT/TRADE ECO/TAC

B63
BLACK J.E.,FOREIGN POLICIES IN A WORLD OF CHANGE. FUT INT/ORG ALL/VALS...POLICY MAJORIT MARXIST SOCIALIST TRADIT TIME/SEQ TREND ANTHOL 20. PAGE 15 A0298 WOR+45 NAT/G DIPLOM

B63
CANELAS O.A.,RADIOGRAFIA DE LA ALIANZA PARA EL ATRASO. L/A+17C USA+45 ECO/TAC DOMIN COLONIAL NAT/LISM...SOCIALIST NAT/COMP 20. PAGE 23 A0476 REV DIPLOM ECO/UNDEV REGION

B65
NKRUMAH K.,NEO-COLONIALISM: THE LAST STAGE OF IMPERIALISM. AFR INT/ORG WORKER FOR/AID INT/TRADE EDU/PROP GOV/REL NAT/LISM SOVEREIGN POPULISM SOCISM ...SOCIALIST 20 THIRD/WRLD INTRVN/ECO. PAGE 109 A2243 COLONIAL DIPLOM ECO/UNDEV ECO/TAC

S66
DINH TRANS V.A.N.,"VIETNAM: A THIRD WAY" S/ASIA USA+45 USSR VIETNAM VIETNAM/S NAT/G SECT FORCES CAP/ISM DIPLOM COLONIAL NEUTRAL MARXISM SOCISM 20 BUDDHISM UNIFICA. PAGE 38 A0766 WAR PLAN ORD/FREE SOCIALIST

S66
FRIEND A.,"THE MIDDLE EAST CRISIS" COM ISLAM ISRAEL SYRIA UAR USA+45 USSR FORCES PLAN FOR/AID CONTROL ORD/FREE PWR...SOCIALIST TIME/SEQ 20 NASSER/G. PAGE 49 A1009 WAR INT/ORG DIPLOM PEACE

S67
HALL M.,"GERMANY, EAST AND WEST* DANGER AT THE CROSSROADS." GERMANY ELITES CHIEF FORCES DIPLOM ECO/TAC REPAR ARMS/CONT...SOCIALIST 20. PAGE 60 A1227 NAT/LISM ATTIT FASCISM WEAPON

S67
KIERNAN V.G.,"INDIA AND THE LABOUR PARTY." INDIA UK CAP/ISM GP/REL EFFICIENCY NAT/LISM PWR SOCISM ...SOCIALIST TIME/SEQ 20. PAGE 79 A1616 COLONIAL DIPLOM POL/PAR ECO/UNDEV

S67
PERLO V.,"NEW DIMENSIONS IN EAST-WEST TRADE." UK USA+45 USSR WOR+45 ECO/DEV NAT/G CAP/ISM PEACE WEALTH LAISSEZ...SOCIALIST MGT 20. PAGE 115 A2364 BAL/PWR ECO/TAC INT/TRADE

SOCIALIZATION....SEE ADJUST

SOCIETE DES NATIONS A2759

SOCIETY....SOCIETY AS A WHOLE

SOCIOLOGY....SEE SOC

SOCIOLOGY OF KNOWLEDGE....SEE EPIST

SOCIOMETRY, AS THEORY....SEE GEN/METH

SOCISM....SOCIALISM; SEE ALSO SOCIALIST

N19
DEANE H.,THE WAR IN VIETNAM (PAMPHLET). CHINA/COM VIETNAM BAL/PWR DIPLOM ECO/TAC SOCISM INTERVENT COLD/WAR INTERVENT COLD/WAR. PAGE 35 A0720 WAR SOCIALIST MORAL CAP/ISM

N19
LANGE O.R.,"DISARMAMENT ECONOMIC GROWTH AND INTERNATIONAL CO-OPERATION" (PAMPHLET). WOR+45 DIST/IND PLAN INT/TRADE GIVE TASK DETER WEALTH SOCISM 18/19 BOLIVAR/S. PAGE 84 A1723 ARMS/CONT DIPLOM ECO/DEV ECO/UNDEV

B24
NAVILLE A.,LIBERTE, EGALITE, SOLIDARITE: ESSAIS D'ANALYSE. STRATA FAM VOL/ASSN INT/TRADE GP/REL MORAL MARXISM SOCISM...PSY TREATY. PAGE 107 A2205 ORD/FREE SOC IDEA/COMP DIPLOM

C28
SCHNEIDER H.W.,"MAKING THE FASCIST STATE." ITALY CULTURE LABOR DIPLOM REV WAR NAT/LISM TOTALISM ATTIT DRIVE SOCISM...BIBLIOG PARLIAMENT 20. PAGE 129 A2638 FASCISM POLICY POL/PAR

B32
HANSEN A.H.,ECONOMIC STABILIZATION IN AN UNBALANCED WORLD. COM EUR+WWI USA-45 WOR-45 AGRI FINAN INDUS MARKET INT/ORG LABOR VOL/ASSN EDU/PROP ATTIT HEALTH KNOWL WEALTH...HIST/WRIT TREND VAL/FREE 20. PAGE 61 A1253 NAT/G ECO/DEV CAP/ISM SOCISM

B32
LENIN V.I.,THE WAR AND THE SECOND INTERNATIONAL. COM MOD/EUR USSR CAP/ISM DIPLOM NAT/LISM ATTIT MARXISM...CONCPT 20. PAGE 87 A1772 POL/PAR WAR SOCISM INT/ORG

B33
FERRERO G.,PEACE AND WAR (TRANS. BY BERTHA PRITCHARD). CULTURE FINAN SECT ATTIT SUPEGO MORAL ORD/FREE CONSERVE POPULISM SOCISM POLICY. PAGE 45 A0922 WAR PEACE DIPLOM PROB/SOLV

B37
BORGESE G.A.,GOLIATH: THE MARCH OF FASCISM. GERMANY ITALY LAW POL/PAR SECT DIPLOM SOCISM...JURID MYTH 20 DANTE MACHIAVELL MUSSOLIN/B. PAGE 17 A0341 POLICY NAT/LISM FASCISM NAT/G

B39
LENIN V.I.,IMPERIALISM: THE HIGHEST STAGE OF CAPITALISM. USSR WOR-45 DIST/IND INT/TRADE ATTIT MARXISM SOCISM...CHARTS 20. PAGE 87 A1773 MARXIST CAP/ISM COLONIAL DOMIN

S40
FLORIN J.,"BOLSHEVIST AND NATIONAL SOCIALIST DOCTRINES OF INTERNATIONAL LAW." EUR+WWI GERMANY USSR R+D INT/ORG NAT/G DIPLOM DOMIN EDU/PROP SOCISM ...CONCPT TIME/SEQ 20. PAGE 47 A0955 LAW ATTIT TOTALISM INT/LAW

B43
US DEPARTMENT OF STATE,NATIONAL SOCIALISM; BASIC PRINCIPLES, THEIR APPLICATION BY THE NAZI PARTY'S FOREIGN ORGANIZATION... GERMANY WOR-45 ECO/DEV LOC/G POL/PAR FORCES DIPLOM DOMIN COLONIAL ARMS/CONT COERCE NAT/LISM PWR 20 NAZI. PAGE 151 A3081 FASCISM SOCISM NAT/G TOTALISM

B47
HEIMANN E.,FREEDOM AND ORDER: LESSONS FROM THE WAR. WOR-45 CONSTN FORCES CHOOSE CIVMIL/REL PERSON ALL/IDEOS SOCISM...SOC IDEA/COMP WORSHIP 20. PAGE 64 A1308 NAT/G SOCIETY ORD/FREE DIPLOM

B48
GRAHAM F.D.,THE THEORY OF INTERNATIONAL VALUES. FUT WOR+45 WOR-45 ECO/DEV FINAN INT/ORG PLAN TEC/DEV CAP/ISM DIPLOM ECO/TAC TARIFFS ROUTINE BAL/PAY DRIVE PWR WEALTH SOCISM...POLICY STAT HYPO/EXP GEN/LAWS 20. PAGE 55 A1125 NEW/IDEA INT/TRADE

B50
BARGHOORN F.C.,THE SOVIET IMAGE OF THE UNITED STATES: A STUDY IN DISTORTION. COM USSR DOMIN WAR PROB/SOLV EDU/PROP

NAT/LISM TOTALISM SOCISM...PSY 20. PAGE 11 A0220 — DIPLOM ATTIT

B50
BROOKINGS INSTITUTION,MAJOR PROBLEMS OF UNITED STATES FOREIGN POLICY. AFR ASIA INDIA UK USA+45 USSR BAL/PWR FOR/AID WAR PEACE TOTALISM MARXISM SOCISM 20 CHINJAP COLD/WAR. PAGE 19 A0393 — DIPLOM POLICY ORD/FREE

B50
MONPIED E.,BIBLIOGRAPHIE FEDERALISTE: OUVRAGES CHOISIS (VOL. I, MIMEOGRAPHED PAPER). EUR+WWI DIPLOM ADMIN REGION ATTIT PACIFISM SOCISM...INT/LAW 19/20. PAGE 103 A2109 — BIBLIOG/A FEDERAL CENTRAL INT/ORG

N51
MONPIED E.,FEDERALIST BIBLIOGRAPHY: ARTICLES AND DOCUMENTS PUBLISHED IN BRITISH PERIODICALS 1945-1951 (MIMEOGRAPHED). EUR+WWI UK WOR+45 DIPLOM REGION ATTIT SOCISM...INT/LAW 20. PAGE 103 A2110 — BIBLIOG/A INT/ORG FEDERAL CENTRAL

B52
MACARTHUR D.,REVITALIZING A NATION. ASIA COM FUT KOREA WOR+45 NAT/G FOR/AID TAX GIVE WAR ATTIT SOCISM 20 CHINJAP EUROPE. PAGE 92 A1885 — LEAD FORCES TOP/EX POLICY

B53
SHIRATO I.,JAPANESE SOURCES ON THE HISTORY OF THE CHINESE COMMUNIST MOVEMENT (PAMPHLET). CHINA/COM USSR CONSTRUC NAT/G POL/PAR FORCES DIPLOM DOMIN EDU/PROP CONTROL WAR TOTALISM SOCISM 20. PAGE 132 A2702 — BIBLIOG/A MARXISM ECO/UNDEV

B54
STALEY E.,THE FUTURE OF UNDERDEVELOPED COUNTRIES: POLITICAL IMPLICATIONS OF ECONOMIC DEVELOPMENT. COM FUT USA+45 SOCIETY ECO/UNDEV CREATE PLAN CAP/ISM ATTIT DRIVE MARXISM SOCISM...POLICY CONCPT CHARTS COLD/WAR 20. PAGE 137 A2801 — EDU/PROP ECO/TAC FOR/AID

L54
CHARLESWORTH J.C.,"AMERICA AND A NEW ASIA." ASIA INDIA ISLAM S/ASIA USA+45 USA-45 ECO/UNDEV NAT/G POL/PAR FORCES FOR/AID DOMIN EDU/PROP COERCE DRIVE ALL/VALS MARXISM SOCISM TOT/POP 20. PAGE 26 A0522 — ECO/TAC DIPLOM NAT/LISM

B55
O3HEVSS E.,WIRTSCHAFTSSYSTEME UND INTERNATIONALER HANDEL. ECO/DEV FINAN MARKET DIPLOM ECO/TAC COST ...METH/COMP NAT/COMP 20. PAGE 112 A2306 — CAP/ISM SOCISM INT/TRADE IDEA/COMP

B55
SEMJONOW J.M.,DIE FASCHISTISCHE GEOPOLITIK IM DIENSTE DES AMERIKANISCHEN IMPERIALISMUS. USA+45 USA-45 CAP/ISM PEACE ORD/FREE MARXISM SOCISM ...POLICY GEOG 20. PAGE 131 A2684 — DIPLOM COERCE FASCISM WAR

B57
PETERSON H.C.,OPPONENTS OF WAR 1917-1918. USA-45 POL/PAR DOMIN ORD/FREE PWR PACIFISM SOCISM 20 IWW CONSCN/OBJ. PAGE 115 A2368 — WAR PEACE ATTIT EDU/PROP

B59
GOLDWIN R.A.,READINGS IN RUSSIAN FOREIGN POLICY. HUNGARY USSR YUGOSLAVIA ELITES INT/ORG NAT/G REV WAR NAT/LISM PERSON SOCISM...CHARTS 20 MAPS BOLSHEVISM. PAGE 53 A1095 — COM MARXISM DIPLOM POLICY

B59
HEWES T.,EQUALITY OF OPPORTUNITY - THE AMERICAN IDEAL AND KEY TO WORLD PEACE. USA+45 NAT/G OWN WEALTH ALL/IDEOS SOCISM...CONCPT 20. PAGE 64 A1323 — POLICY PEACE ECO/TAC DIPLOM

B59
JONES A.C.,NEW FABIAN COLONIAL ESSAYS. UK SOCIETY POL/PAR EDU/PROP ADMIN ORD/FREE SOVEREIGN SOCISM ...ANTHOL 20 CMN/WLTH LABOR/PAR. PAGE 75 A1530 — COLONIAL INT/ORG INGP/REL DOMIN

S59
CARLSTON K.S.,"NATIONALIZATION: AN ANALYTIC APPROACH." WOR+45 INT/ORG ECO/TAC DOMIN LEGIT ADJUD COERCE ORD/FREE PWR WEALTH SOCISM...JURID CONCPT TREND STERTYP TOT/POP VAL/FREE 20. PAGE 24 A0486 — INDUS NAT/G NAT/LISM SOVEREIGN

B60
KHRUSHCHEV N.,FOR VICTORY IN PEACEFUL COMPETITION WITH CAPITALISM. COM FUT USSR WOR+45 CONSTN SOCIETY INDUS INT/ORG DELIB/GP PLAN BAL/PWR DIPLOM PERSON MARXISM...MARXIST WORK 20 COLD/WAR. PAGE 79 A1611 — TOP/EX PWR CAP/ISM SOCISM

B60
LERNER A.P.,THE ECONOMICS OF CONTROL. USA+45 ECO/UNDEV INT/ORG ACT/RES PLAN CAP/ISM INT/TRADE ATTIT WEALTH...SOC MATH STAT GEN/LAWS INDEX 20. PAGE 87 A1785 — ECO/DEV ROUTINE ECO/TAC SOCISM

B60
QUBAIN F.I.,INSIDE THE ARAB MIND: A BIBLIOGRAPHIC SURVEY OF LITERATURE IN ARABIC ON ARAB NATIONALISM AND UNITY. ISLAM POL/PAR SECT LEAD SOVEREIGN MARXISM SOCISM. PAGE 118 A2425 — BIBLIOG/A FEDERAL DIPLOM NAT/LISM

B61
AUBREY H.G.,COEXISTENCE: ECONOMIC CHALLENGE AND RESPONSE. USSR WOR+45 ACT/RES BAL/PWR CAP/ISM DIPLOM ECO/TAC FOR/AID INT/TRADE PEACE SOCISM ...METH/COMP NAT/COMP COLD/WAR. PAGE 10 A0196 — POLICY ECO/UNDEV PLAN COM

B61
DIA M.,THE AFRICAN NATIONS AND WORLD SOLIDARITY. ISLAM CULTURE ELITES ECO/DEV ECO/UNDEV INT/ORG NAT/G PLAN ECO/TAC INT/TRADE EDU/PROP NAT/LISM ATTIT DRIVE ORD/FREE WEALTH...SOCIALIST CONCPT CON/ANAL GEN/LAWS TOT/POP 20. PAGE 37 A0753 — AFR REGION SOCISM

B61
DIMOCK M.E.,BUSINESS AND GOVERNMENT (4TH ED.). AGRI FINAN OP/RES PLAN BUDGET DIPLOM LOBBY NUC/PWR NEW/LIB SOCISM...POLICY BIBLIOG 20. PAGE 37 A0765 — NAT/G INDUS LABOR ECO/TAC

B61
PALMER N.D.,THE INDIAN POLITICAL SYSTEM. INDIA ECO/UNDEV SECT CHIEF COLONIAL CHOOSE ALL/IDEOS SOCISM...CHARTS BIBLIOG/A 20. PAGE 113 A2322 — NAT/LISM POL/PAR NAT/G DIPLOM

B61
SCHONBRUNN G.,WELTKRIEGE UND REVOLUTIONEN 1914-1945. USSR DIPLOM TOTALISM ORD/FREE 20 TREATY WWI NAZI. PAGE 129 A2643 — WAR REV FASCISM SOCISM

B62
APATHEKER H.,AMERICAN FOREIGN POLICY AND THE COLD WAR. USA+45 NAT/G POL/PAR COLONIAL NAT/LISM SOVEREIGN MARXISM SOCISM 20 COLD/WAR MARX/KARL LENIN/VI INTERVENT. PAGE 8 A0167 — DIPLOM WAR PEACE

B62
EVANS M.S.,THE FRINGE ON TOP. USSR EX/STRUC FORCES DIPLOM ECO/TAC PEACE CONSERVE SOCISM...TREND 20 KENNEDY/JF. PAGE 43 A0877 — NAT/G PWR CENTRAL POLICY

B62
ROY P.A.,SOUTH WIND RED. L/A+17C USA+45 ECO/UNDEV NAT/G CAP/ISM MARXISM SOCISM...OLD/LIB GEOG RECORD INT CENSUS 20 COLD/WAR. PAGE 125 A2554 — DIPLOM INDUS POLICY ECO/TAC

S62
CROAN M.,"POLYCENTRISM: COMMUNIST INTERNATIONAL RELATIONS." ASIA STRUCT INT/ORG NAT/G POL/PAR CONSULT PLAN DOMIN EDU/PROP COERCE ATTIT RIGID/FLEX SOCISM...POLICY CONCPT TREND CON/ANAL GEN/LAWS MARX/KARL. PAGE 33 A0663 — COM CREATE DIPLOM NAT/LISM

S62
KOLARZ W.,"THE IMPACT OF COMMUNISM ON WEST AFRICA." AFR FUT SOCIETY INT/ORG NAT/G CREATE PLAN DOMIN EDU/PROP COERCE NAT/LISM ATTIT RIGID/FLEX SOCISM ...POLICY CONCPT TREND MARX/KARL 20. PAGE 81 A1666 — COM POL/PAR COLONIAL

S62
LONDON K.,"SINO-SOVIET RELATIONS IN THE CONTEXT OF THE 'WORLD SOCIALIST SYSTEM'." ASIA CHINA/COM COM USSR INT/ORG NAT/G TOP/EX BAL/PWR DIPLOM DOMIN ATTIT PERCEPT RIGID/FLEX PWR MARXISM...METH/CNCPT TREND 20. PAGE 91 A1854 — DELIB/GP CONCPT SOCISM

B63
FISCHER-GALATI S.,EASTERN EUROPE IN THE SIXTIES. ALBANIA USSR YUGOSLAVIA ECO/UNDEV AGRI MARKET LABOR WORKER DIPLOM INT/TRADE EDU/PROP GOV/REL PRODUC UTOPIA SOCISM 20. PAGE 46 A0939 — MARXISM TEC/DEV BAL/PWR ECO/TAC

B63
KHRUSHCHEV N.S.,THE NEW CONTENT OF PEACEFUL COEXISTENCE IN THE NUCLEAR AGE. GERMANY/E WORKER NUC/PWR REV SOCISM 20 COLD/WAR. PAGE 79 A1614 — MARXISM POL/PAR PEACE DIPLOM

B63
MBOYA T.,FREEDOM AND AFTER. AFR LABOR POL/PAR DIPLOM EDU/PROP COERCE SOCISM 20. PAGE 97 A1989 — COLONIAL ECO/UNDEV NAT/LISM INT/ORG

B63
MOSELY P.E.,THE SOVIET UNION, 1922-1962: A FOREIGN AFFAIRS READER. ASIA POLAND USSR CULTURE INTELL AGRI POL/PAR WORKER INT/TRADE DOMIN WAR NAT/LISM MARXISM SOCISM 20 KHRUSH/N. PAGE 105 A2152 — PWR POLICY DIPLOM

B63
NORTH R.C.,M. N. ROY'S MISSION TO CHINA: THE COMMUNIST-KUOMINTANG SPLIT OF 1927. ASIA USSR STRATA LEGIS WORKER LEAD REV ATTIT ROLE SOCISM 20 ROY/MN COM/PARTY. PAGE 110 A2253 — POL/PAR MARXISM DIPLOM

B63
RUSSELL B.,UNARMED VICTORY. CHINA/COM CUBA INDIA USA+45 WAR MARXISM...POLICY IDEA/COMP 20 KHRUSH/N COLD/WAR. PAGE 125 A2573 — DIPLOM ATTIT SOCISM ORD/FREE

B63
SZULC T.,THE WINDS OF REVOLUTION; LATIN AMERICA TODAY - AND TOMORROW. L/A+17C ORD/FREE SOCISM ...PREDICT TREND 20. PAGE 141 A2880 — REV INT/ORG MARXISM ECO/UNDEV

B63
THIEN T.T.,INDIA AND SOUTHEAST ASIA 1947-1960. COM INDIA S/ASIA SECT DELIB/GP FOR/AID RACE/REL NAT/LISM SOCISM...CHARTS BIBLIOG 20 UN NEHRU/J TREATY. PAGE 143 A2917 — DRIVE DIPLOM POLICY

L63
SZASZY E.,"L'EVOLUTION DES PRINCIPES GENERAUX DU DROIT INTERNATIONAL PRIVE DANS LES PAYS DE DEMOCRATIE POPULAIRE." COM FUT WOR+45 LAW ECO/DEV PERF/ART POL/PAR PROF/ORG ECO/TAC INT/TRADE — DIPLOM TOTALISM INT/LAW INT/ORG

EDU/PROP ATTIT RIGID/FLEX ALL/VALS SOCISM...JURID TREND GEN/LAWS WORK 20. PAGE 141 A2876

S63
COSER L.,"AMERICA AND THE WORLD REVOLUTION." COM FUT USA+45 WOR+45 INTELL SOCIETY NAT/G ECO/TAC EDU/PROP ALL/VALS SOCISM...PSY GEN/LAWS TOT/POP 20 COLD/WAR. PAGE 31 A0629
ECO/UNDEV PLAN FOR/AID DIPLOM

B64
GRIFFITH W.E.,COMMUNISM IN EUROPE (2 VOLS.). CZECHOSLVK USSR WOR+45 WOR-45 YUGOSLAVIA INGP/REL MARXISM SOCISM...ANTHOL 20 EUROPE/E. PAGE 57 A1162
COM POL/PAR DIPLOM GOV/COMP

B64
GRZYBOWSKI K.,THE SOCIALIST COMMONWEALTH OF NATIONS: ORGANIZATIONS AND INSTITUTIONS. FORCES DIPLOM INT/TRADE ADJUD ADMIN LEAD WAR MARXISM SOCISM...BIBLIOG 20 COMECON WARSAW/P. PAGE 58 A1185
INT/LAW COM REGION INT/ORG

B64
HALPERIN S.W.,MUSSOLINI AND ITALIAN FASCISM. ITALY NAT/G POL/PAR SECT ECO/TAC LEAD PWR SOCISM...POLICY 20 MUSSOLIN/B. PAGE 60 A1241
FASCISM NAT/LISM EDU/PROP CHIEF

B64
LUTHULI A.,AFRICA'S FREEDOM. KIN LABOR POL/PAR SCHOOL DIPLOM NEUTRAL REGION REV NAT/LISM PWR WEALTH SOCISM SOC/INTEG 20. PAGE 92 A1874
AFR ECO/UNDEV COLONIAL

B64
PENNOCK J.R.,SELF-GOVERNMENT IN MODERNIZING NATIONS. AFR COM USA+45 ECO/DEV POL/PAR PROB/SOLV DIPLOM ECO/TAC COLONIAL REV POPULISM SOCISM 20. PAGE 114 A2350
ECO/UNDEV POLICY SOVEREIGN NAT/G

B64
WITHERS W.,THE ECONOMIC CRISIS IN LATIN AMERICA. BRAZIL CHILE STRATA AGRI DIPLOM FOR/AID PWR SOCISM ...POLICY 20 MEXIC/AMER ARGEN. PAGE 166 A3372
L/A+17C ECO/UNDEV CAP/ISM ALL/IDEOS

S64
GARMARNIKOW M.,"INFLUENCE-BUYING IN WEST AFRICA." COM FUT USSR INTELL NAT/G PLAN TEC/DEV ECO/TAC DOMIN EDU/PROP REGION NAT/LISM ATTIT DRIVE ALL/VALS SOVEREIGN...POLICY PSY SOC CONCPT TREND STERTYP WORK COLD/WAR 20. PAGE 51 A1049
AFR ECO/UNDEV FOR/AID SOCISM

B65
DU BOIS W.E.B.,THE WORLD AND AFRICA. USA+45 CAP/ISM DISCRIM STRANGE SOCISM...TIME/SEQ TREND IDEA/COMP 19/20 NEGRO. PAGE 39 A0789
AFR DIPLOM COLONIAL CULTURE

B65
HALPERIN E.,NATIONALISM AND COMMUNISM. CHILE L/A+17C CAP/ISM EDU/PROP CHOOSE DISCRIM SOCISM ...BIBLIOG 20 COM/PARTY. PAGE 60 A1236
NAT/LISM MARXISM POL/PAR REV

B65
MURUMBI J.,PROBLEMS OF ECONOMIC DEVELOPMENT IN EAST AFRICA. FINAN INDUS WORKER TEC/DEV INT/TRADE TAX DEMAND EFFICIENCY PRODUC SOCISM...TREND CHARTS 20 AFRICA/E. PAGE 106 A2184
AGRI ECO/TAC ECO/UNDEV PROC/MFG

B65
NKRUMAH K.,NEO-COLONIALISM: THE LAST STAGE OF IMPERIALISM. AFR INT/ORG WORKER FOR/AID INT/TRADE EDU/PROP GOV/REL NAT/LISM SOVEREIGN POPULISM SOCISM ...SOCIALIST 20 THIRD/WRLD INTRVN/ECO. PAGE 109 A2243
COLONIAL DIPLOM ECO/UNDEV ECO/TAC

B65
RUBINSTEIN A.,THE CHALLENGE OF POLITICS: IDEAS AND ISSUES. BAL/PWR COLONIAL WAR TOTALISM ORD/FREE PWR MARXISM SOCISM...INT/LAW 20. PAGE 125 A2561
NAT/G SOVEREIGN DIPLOM NAT/LISM

S65
"FURTHER READING." INDIA USSR FORCES ATTIT SOCISM 20. PAGE 3 A0068
BIBLIOG DIPLOM MARXISM

B66
COLE A.B.,SOCIALIST PARTIES IN POSTWAR JAPAN. STRATA AGRI LABOR PLAN DIPLOM ECO/TAC AGREE LEAD CHOOSE ATTIT...CHARTS 20 CHINJAP SOC/DEMPAR. PAGE 28 A0566
POL/PAR POLICY SOCISM NAT/G

B66
FELKER J.L.,SOVIET ECONOMIC CONTROVERSIES. USSR INDUS PLAN INT/TRADE GP/REL MARXISM SOCISM...POLICY 20. PAGE 45 A0915
ECO/DEV MARKET PROFIT PRICE

B66
FRIEDRICH C.J.,REVOLUTION: NOMOS VIII. NAT/G SOCISM ...OBS TREND IDEA/COMP ANTHOL 18/20. PAGE 49 A1007
REV MARXISM CONCPT DIPLOM

B66
MURPHY G.G.,SOVIET MONGOLIA: A STUDY OF THE OLDEST POLITICAL SATELLITE. USSR STRATA STRUCT COST INCOME ATTIT SOCISM 20. PAGE 106 A2177
DIPLOM ECO/TAC PLAN DOMIN

B66
SKILLING H.G.,THE GOVERNMENTS OF COMMUNIST EAST EUROPE. COM EUR+WWI ELITES FORCES DIPLOM ECO/TAC CONTROL HABITAT SOCISM...DECISION BIBLIOG 20 EUROPE/E COM/PARTY. PAGE 134 A2738
MARXISM NAT/COMP GP/COMP DOMIN

S66
AFRICAN BIBLIOGRAPHIC CENTER,"A CURRENT VIEW OF AFRICANA: A SELECT AND ANNOTATED BIBLIOGRAPHICAL PUBLISHING GUIDE, 1965-1966." AFR CULTURE INDUS LABOR SECT FOR/AID ADMIN COLONIAL REV RACE/REL SOCISM...LING 20. PAGE 5 A0098
BIBLIOG/A NAT/G TEC/DEV POL/PAR

S66
DINH TRANS V.A.N.,"VIETNAM: A THIRD WAY" S/ASIA USA+45 USSR VIETNAM VIETNAM/S NAT/G SECT FORCES CAP/ISM DIPLOM COLONIAL NEUTRAL MARXISM SOCISM 20 BUDDHISM UNIFICA. PAGE 38 A0766
WAR PLAN ORD/FREE SOCIALIST

S66
O'BRIEN W.V.,"EVENTS AND TRENDS: PATTERNS OF AFRICAN INTERNATIONAL POLITICAL BEHAVIOR." CULTURE SOCIETY NAT/G NAT/LISM SOCISM. PAGE 111 A2267
BIBLIOG/A AFR TREND DIPLOM

C66
TARLING N.,"A CONCISE HISTORY OF SOUTHEAST ASIA." BURMA CAMBODIA LAOS S/ASIA THAILAND VIETNAM ECO/UNDEV POL/PAR FORCES ADMIN REV WAR CIVMIL/REL ORD/FREE MARXISM SOCISM 13/20. PAGE 141 A2890
COLONIAL DOMIN INT/TRADE NAT/LISM

B67
FILENE P.G.,AMERICANS AND THE SOVIET EXPERIMENT, 1917-1933. USA-45 USSR INTELL NAT/G CAP/ISM DIPLOM EDU/PROP PRESS REV SOCISM...PSY 20. PAGE 45 A0930
ATTIT RIGID/FLEX MARXISM SOCIETY

B67
JAGAN C.,THE WEST ON TRIAL. GUYANA CONSTN ECO/UNDEV DIPLOM COERCE PWR SOVEREIGN...BIOG 20. PAGE 73 A1490
SOCISM CREATE PLAN COLONIAL

B67
MACDONALD D.F.,THE AGE OF TRANSITION: BRITAIN IN THE NINETEENTH & TWENTIETH CENTURIES. UK ECO/DEV LEGIS DIPLOM NEW/LIB...POLICY 19/20. PAGE 92 A1886
TREND INDUS SOCISM

B67
SABLE M.H.,A GUIDE TO LATIN AMERICAN STUDIES (2 VOLS). CONSTN FINAN INT/ORG LABOR MUNIC POL/PAR FORCES CAP/ISM FOR/AID ADMIN MARXISM SOCISM OAS. PAGE 126 A2584
BIBLIOG/A L/A+17C DIPLOM NAT/LISM

B67
SHAFFER H.G.,THE COMMUNIST WORLD: MARXIST AND NON-MARXIST VIEWS. WOR+45 SOCIETY DIPLOM ECO/TAC CONTROL SOCISM...MARXIST ANTHOL BIBLIOG/A 20. PAGE 131 A2691
MARXISM NAT/COMP IDEA/COMP COM

B67
TROTSKY L.,PROBLEMS OF THE CHINESE REVOLUTION (3RD ED. TRANS. BY MAX SCHACTMAN). ASIA USSR DIPLOM MARXISM SOCISM...IDEA/COMP ANTHOL DICTIONARY 20 STALIN/J. PAGE 145 A2969
MARXIST REV

S67
FALKOWSKI M.,"SOCIALIST ECONOMISTS AND THE DEVELOPING COUNTRIES." COM PLAN TEC/DEV ROUTINE DEMAND EFFICIENCY PRODUC WEALTH...MARXIST TREND GEN/METH. PAGE 44 A0893
DIPLOM SOCISM ECO/UNDEV INDUS

S67
KIERNAN V.G.,"INDIA AND THE LABOUR PARTY." INDIA UK CAP/ISM GP/REL EFFICIENCY NAT/LISM PWR SOCISM ...SOCIALIST TIME/SEQ 20. PAGE 79 A1616
COLONIAL DIPLOM POL/PAR ECO/UNDEV

SOCRATES....SOCRATES

SOHN L.B. A0541,A2760,A2761,A2762

SOKOL A.E. A2763

SOLDATI A. A2764

SOLODOVNIKOV V.G. A0687

SOLOMON L.M. A2508

SOLOMONS....THE SOLOMON ISLANDS

SOMALI

B57
MURRAY J.N.,THE UNITED NATIONS TRUSTEESHIP SYSTEM. AFR WOR+45 CONSTN CONSULT LEGIS EDU/PROP LEGIT EXEC ROUTINE...INT TIME/SEQ SOMALI UN 20. PAGE 106 A2181
INT/ORG DELIB/GP

SOMALIA....SOMALIA; SEE ALSO AFR

B36
VARLEY D.H.,A BIBLIOGRAPHY OF ITALIAN COLONISATION IN AFRICA WITH A SECTION ON ABYSSINIA. AFR ETHIOPIA ITALY LIBYA SOMALIA AGRI FINAN LABOR TEC/DEV DIPLOM INT/TRADE RACE/REL DISCRIM 19/20. PAGE 158 A3222
BIBLIOG COLONIAL ADMIN LAW

B42
CONOVER H.F.,FRENCH COLONIES IN AFRICA: A LIST OF REFERENCES. ALGERIA FRANCE MOROCCO SOMALIA SUDAN CULTURE AGRI LOC/G SECT FORCES DIPLOM INT/TRADE NAT/LISM HEALTH...CON/ANAL 20. PAGE 29 A0594
BIBLIOG AFR ECO/UNDEV COLONIAL

S64
TOUVAL S.,"THE SOMALI REPUBLIC." AFR ISLAM SOMALIA FAM KIN NAT/G CREATE FOR/AID LEGIT ATTIT ALL/VALS ...RECORD TREND 20. PAGE 144 A2954
ECO/UNDEV RIGID/FLEX

B66
GROSS F.,WORLD POLITICS AND TENSION AREAS. CHINA/COM SOMALIA VENEZUELA COERCE GP/REL RACE/REL ATTIT HABITAT 19/20 CASEBOOK NEWYORK/C. PAGE 57 A1173
DIPLOM WAR PROB/SOLV

SOMMER T. A2765,A2766

SONDERMANN F.A. A2290,A2767

SONGAI....SONGAI EMPIRES (AFRICA)

SONNENFELDT H. A2768

SOPER T. A2769

SOREL/G....GEORGES SOREL

SOUPHANGOU....PRINCE SOUPHANGOU-VONG (LEADER OF PATHET LAO)

SOUTH AFRICA....SEE S/AFR

SOUTH KOREA....SEE KOREA/S

SOUTH VIETNAM....SEE VIETNAM/S

SOUTH WEST AFRICA....SEE AFRICA/SW

SOUTH/AFR....UNION OF SOUTH AFRICA

B09
FREMANTLE H.E.S.,THE NEW NATION, A SURVEY OF THE CONDITION AND PROSPECTS OF SOUTH AFRICA. SOUTH/AFR CONSTN POL/PAR DIPLOM DOMIN COLONIAL WEALTH...SOC TREND 19. PAGE 49 A0996
NAT/LISM SOVEREIGN RACE/REL REGION

B10
MENDELSSOHN S.,SOUTH AFRICAN BIBLIOGRAPHY (2 VOLS.). SOUTH/AFR EXTR/IND LABOR SECT DIPLOM INT/TRADE COLONIAL RACE/REL DISCRIM...GEOG 20. PAGE 99 A2038
BIBLIOG/A AFR NAT/G NAT/LISM

B30
SMUTS J.C.,AFRICA AND SOME WORLD PROBLEMS. RHODESIA SOUTH/AFR CULTURE ECO/UNDEV INDUS INT/ORG SECT PROB/SOLV REGION GOV/REL DISCRIM ATTIT 19/20 LEAGUE/NAT LIVNGSTN/D NEGRO. PAGE 134 A2748
LEGIS AFR COLONIAL RACE/REL

B34
LOVELL R.I.,THE STRUGGLE FOR SOUTH AFRICA, 1875-1899. GERMANY RHODESIA SOUTH/AFR UK NAT/G ECO/TAC HABITAT WEALTH...POLICY 19. PAGE 91 A1866
COLONIAL DIPLOM WAR GP/REL

B35
KENNEDY W.P.,THE LAW AND CUSTOM OF THE SOUTH AFRICAN CONSTITUTION. AFR SOUTH/AFR KIN LOC/G PROVS DIPLOM ADJUD ADMIN EXEC 20. PAGE 78 A1594
CT/SYS CONSTN JURID PARL/PROC

B36
BOYCE A.N.,EUROPE AND SOUTH AFRICA. FRANCE GERMANY ITALY SOUTH/AFR UK INDUS NAT/G CONTROL REV WAR NAT/LISM...CONCPT HIST/WRIT 20. PAGE 18 A0362
COLONIAL GOV/COMP NAT/COMP DIPLOM

B37
DE KIEWIET C.W.,THE IMPERIAL FACTOR IN SOUTH AFRICA. AFR SOUTH/AFR UK WAR...POLICY SOC 19. PAGE 35 A0705
DIPLOM COLONIAL CULTURE

B37
UNION OF SOUTH AFRICA,REPORT CONCERNING ADMINISTRATION OF SOUTH WEST AFRICA (6 VOLS.). SOUTH/AFR INDUS PUB/INST FORCES LEGIS BUDGET DIPLOM EDU/PROP ADJUD CT/SYS...GEOG CHARTS 20 AFRICA/SW LEAGUE/NAT. PAGE 148 A3028
NAT/G ADMIN COLONIAL CONSTN

B38
FRANKEL S.H.,CAPITAL INVESTMENT IN AFRICA. AFR EUR+WWI RHODESIA SOUTH/AFR UK FINAN FOR/AID COLONIAL DEMAND UTIL WEALTH...METH/CNCPT CHARTS 20 CONGO/LEOP. PAGE 48 A0983
ECO/UNDEV EXTR/IND DIPLOM PRODUC

B42
JACKSON M.V.,EUROPEAN POWERS AND SOUTH-EAST AFRICA: A STUDY OF INTERNATIONAL RELATIONS ON SOUTH-EAST COAST OF AFRICA, 1796-1856. AFR FRANCE PORTUGAL SOUTH/AFR UK USA-45 FORCES INT/TRADE PWR...CHARTS BIBLIOG 18/19 TREATY. PAGE 72 A1477
DOMIN POLICY ORD/FREE DIPLOM

B42
JOSHI P.S.,THE TYRANNY OF COLOUR. INDIA SOUTH/AFR UK ECO/UNDEV NAT/G POL/PAR DIPLOM ECO/TAC WAR ...POLICY 19/20. PAGE 75 A1538
COLONIAL DISCRIM RACE/REL

B43
WALKER E.A.,BRITAIN AND SOUTH AFRICA. SOUTH/AFR POL/PAR GP/REL RACE/REL ATTIT ORD/FREE 17/20. PAGE 160 A3264
COLONIAL WAR DIPLOM SOVEREIGN

B50
MOCKFORD J.,SOUTH-WEST AFRICA AND THE INTERNATIONAL COURT (PAMPHLET). AFR GERMANY SOUTH/AFR UK ECO/UNDEV DIPLOM CONTROL DISCRIM...DECISION JURID 20 AFRICA/SW. PAGE 102 A2094
COLONIAL SOVEREIGN INT/LAW DOMIN

B55
PYRAH G.B.,IMPERIAL POLICY AND SOUTH AFRICA 1902-1910. SOUTH/AFR UK NAT/G WAR DISCRIM...CONCPT CHARTS BIBLIOG/A 19/20 CMN/WLTH. PAGE 118 A2421
DIPLOM COLONIAL POLICY RACE/REL

B58
GROBLER J.H.,AFRICA'S DESTINY. AFR EUR+WWI SOUTH/AFR UK USA+45 ELITES KIN LOC/G DIPLOM DISCRIM ATTIT CONSERVE MARXISM 20 ROOSEVLT/T NEGRO. PAGE 57 A1168
POLICY ORD/FREE COLONIAL CONSTN

C58
CARTER G.M.,"THE POLITICS OF INEQUALITY: SOUTH AFRICA SINCE 1948." SOUTH/AFR CONSTN DIPLOM EDU/PROP REPRESENT DISCRIM ATTIT...POLICY PREDICT CHARTS BIBLIOG 20. PAGE 25 A0504
RACE/REL POL/PAR CHOOSE DOMIN

B59
MAC MILLAN W.M.,THE ROAD TO SELF-RULE. SOUTH/AFR UK CULTURE SOCIETY AGRI LABOR NAT/G INT/TRADE CONTROL GP/REL...SOC 19/20. PAGE 92 A1884
AFR COLONIAL SOVEREIGN POLICY

B60
WODDIS J.,AFRICA: THE ROOTS OF REVOLT. SOUTH/AFR WORKER INT/TRADE RACE/REL DISCRIM ORD/FREE 20. PAGE 166 A3374
COLONIAL SOVEREIGN WAR ECO/UNDEV

B61
CALVOCORESSI P.,SOUTH AFRICA AND WORLD OPINION. SOUTH/AFR WOR+45 COM/IND INT/ORG 20. PAGE 23 A0470
ATTIT DISCRIM RACE/REL DIPLOM

B61
MACLURE M.,AFRICA: THE POLITICAL PATTERN. SOUTH/AFR CULTURE LEGIS DIPLOM COLONIAL RACE/REL 20. PAGE 93 A1898
AFR POLICY NAT/G

B63
ELLENDER A.J.,A REPORT ON UNITED STATES FOREIGN OPERATIONS IN AFRICA. SOUTH/AFR USA+45 STRATA EXTR/IND FORCES RACE/REL ISOLAT SOVEREIGN...CHARTS 20 NEGRO. PAGE 41 A0840
FOR/AID DIPLOM WEALTH ECO/UNDEV

B63
HAILEY L.,THE REPUBLIC OF SOUTH AFRICA AND THE HIGH COMMISSION TERRITORIES. AFR SOUTH/AFR UK INT/ORG NAT/G PROVS RACE/REL SOVEREIGN...CHARTS 19/20 COMMONWLTH. PAGE 59 A1219
COLONIAL DIPLOM ATTIT

B63
RUSK D.,THE WINDS OF FREEDOM. S/ASIA SOUTH/AFR INT/ORG FORCES NUC/PWR PEACE ORD/FREE 20 UN COLD/WAR. PAGE 125 A2569
DIPLOM FOR/AID INT/TRADE

S63
HARNETTY P.,"CANADA, SOUTH AFRICA AND THE COMMONWEALTH." CANADA SOUTH/AFR LAW INT/ORG VOL/ASSN DELIB/GP LEGIS TOP/EX ECO/TAC LEGIT DRIVE MORAL...CONCPT CMN/WLTH 20. PAGE 62 A1263
AFR ATTIT

B64
IRISH M.D.,WORLD PRESSURES ON AMERICAN FOREIGN POLICY. ASIA COM L/A+17C SOUTH/AFR UK WOR+45 ECO/DEV ECO/UNDEV COLONIAL SANCTION COERCE REV TOTALISM...ANTHOL 20 COLD/WAR EUROPE/W INTERVENT. PAGE 72 A1467
DIPLOM POLICY

B64
LEGUM C.,SOUTH AFRICA: CRISIS FOR THE WEST. SOUTH/AFR COERCE DISCRIM ATTIT...TREND 20 INTERVENT. PAGE 86 A1767
RACE/REL STRATA DIPLOM PROB/SOLV

B64
SEGAL R.,SANCTIONS AGAINST SOUTH AFRICA. AFR SOUTH/AFR NAT/G INT/TRADE RACE/REL PEACE PWR ...INT/LAW ANTHOL 20 UN. PAGE 131 A2681
SANCTION DISCRIM ECO/TAC POLICY

S64
HOSKYNS C.,"THE AFRICAN STATES AND THE UNITED NATIONS: 1958-1964." SOUTH/AFR NAT/G VOL/ASSN CONSULT BAL/PWR EDU/PROP MORAL ORD/FREE PWR ...CONCPT TREND UN 20. PAGE 68 A1393
AFR INT/ORG DIPLOM

B65
LEISS A.C.,APARTHEID AND UNITED NATIONS COLLECTIVE MEASURES. SOUTH/AFR ECO/UNDEV EXTR/IND FORCES WORKER ECO/TAC FOR/AID INT/TRADE WEALTH...TREND CHARTS 20 UN NEGRO. PAGE 86 A1770
DISCRIM RACE/REL STRATA DIPLOM

B65
SPENCE J.E.,REPUBLIC UNDER PRESSURE: A STUDY OF SOUTH AFRICAN FOREIGN POLICY. SOUTH/AFR ADMIN COLONIAL GOV/REL RACE/REL DISCRIM NAT/LISM ATTIT ROLE...TREND 20 NEGRO. PAGE 136 A2783
DIPLOM POLICY AFR

B66
EDWARDS C.D.,TRADE REGULATIONS OVERSEAS. IRELAND NEW/ZEALND SOUTH/AFR NAT/G CAP/ISM TARIFFS CONTROL ...POLICY JURID 20 EEC CHINJAP. PAGE 40 A0823
INT/TRADE DIPLOM INT/LAW ECO/TAC

B66
LENGYEL E.,AFRICA: PAST, PRESENT, AND FUTURE. FUT
AFR

SOUTH/AFR COLONIAL RACE/REL SOVEREIGN...GEOG AUD/VIS CHARTS T 20 CONGO/LEOP NEGRO. PAGE 87 A1771 CONSTN ECO/UNDEV

B66
MCKAY V.,AFRICAN DIPLOMACY STUDIES IN THE DETERMINANTS OF FOREIGN POLICY. AFR SOUTH/AFR CULTURE NEUTRAL REGION SOVEREIGN...INT/LAW GOV/COMP ANTHOL 20. PAGE 98 A2013 ECO/UNDEV RACE/REL CIVMIL/REL DIPLOM

B66
MULLER C.F.J.,A SELECT BIBLIOGRAPHY OF SOUTH AFRICAN HISTORY; A GUIDE FOR HISTORICAL RESEARCH. SOUTH/AFR UK LAW CONSTN SOCIETY STRUCT AGRI SECT DIPLOM COLONIAL LEAD RACE/REL...POLICY 17/20 NEGRO. PAGE 106 A2167 BIBLIOG AFR NAT/G

B66
US HOUSE COMM FOREIGN AFFAIRS,UNITED STATES - SOUTH AFRICAN RELATIONS. SOUTH/AFR USA+45 NAT/G CONSULT DELIB/GP LEGIS CONFER SANCTION RACE/REL ATTIT 20 CONGRESS. PAGE 154 A3134 DISCRIM DIPLOM POLICY PARL/PROC

L67
LANDIS E.S.,"THE SOUTH WEST AFRICA CASES* REMAND TO THE UNITED NATIONS." ETHIOPIA LIBERIA SOUTH/AFR BAL/PWR 20 UN. PAGE 84 A1719 INT/LAW INT/ORG DIPLOM ADJUD

L67
MACDONALD R.S.J.,"THE RESORT TO ECONOMIC COERCION BY INTERNATIONAL POLITICAL ORGANIZATIONS." CUBA ETHIOPIA RHODESIA SOUTH/AFR NAT/G FOR/AID INT/TRADE DOMIN CONTROL SANCTION...DECISION LEAGUE/NAT UN OAS 20. PAGE 92 A1887 INT/ORG COERCE ECO/TAC DIPLOM

S67
JOHNSON D.H.N.,"THE SOUTH-WEST AFRICA CASES." AFR ETHIOPIA LIBERIA SOUTH/AFR CONSULT JUDGE BAL/PWR 20. PAGE 74 A1521 INT/LAW DIPLOM INT/ORG ADJUD

S67
MUDGE G.A.,"DOMESTIC POLICIES AND UN ACTIVITIES* THE CASE OF RHODESIA AND THE REPUBLIC OF SOUTH AFRICA." RHODESIA SOUTH/AFR POL/PAR LEAD SANCTION CHOOSE RACE/REL CONSEN DISCRIM ATTIT...INT/LAW UN PARLIAMENT 20. PAGE 105 A2163 AFR NAT/G POLICY

B99
BROOKS S.,BRITAIN AND THE BOERS. AFR SOUTH/AFR UK CULTURE INSPECT LEGIT...INT/LAW 19/20 BOER/WAR. PAGE 19 A0396 WAR DIPLOM NAT/G

SOUTH/AMER....SOUTH AMERICA

B51
CHRISTENSEN A.N.,THE EVOLUTION OF LATIN AMERICAN GOVERNMENT: A BOOK OF READINGS. ECO/UNDEV INDUS LOC/G POL/PAR EX/STRUC LEGIS FOR/AID CT/SYS ...SOC/WK 20 SOUTH/AMER. PAGE 26 A0535 NAT/G CONSTN DIPLOM L/A+17C

B62
US CONGRESS JOINT ECO COMM,ECONOMIC DEVELOPMENTS IN SOUTH AMERICA. USA+45 SOCIETY FINAN NAT/G PROB/SOLV TEC/DEV INT/TRADE TAX EFFICIENCY PRODUC ATTIT ...POLICY 20 CONGRESS SOUTH/AMER. PAGE 150 A3065 L/A+17C ECO/UNDEV FOR/AID DIPLOM

B63
INTERAMERICAN ECO AND SOC COUN,THE ALLIANCE FOR PROGRESS: ITS FIRST YEAR: 1961-1962. AGRI SCHOOL PLAN TEC/DEV INT/TRADE TAX GIVE ADMIN WEALTH...SOC 20 SOUTH/AMER. PAGE 71 A1449 INT/ORG PROB/SOLV ECO/TAC L/A+17C

SOUTH/CAR....SOUTH CAROLINA

SOUTH/DAK....SOUTH DAKOTA

SOUTH/US....SOUTH (UNITED STATES)

B57
SEABURY P.,THE WANING OF SOUTHERN "INTERNATIONALISM" (PAMPHLET). USA+45 USA-45 INT/ORG LEGIS MAJORITY...TREND 20 SOUTH/US MIDWEST/US. PAGE 131 A2676 DIPLOM REGION ATTIT ISOLAT

B63
PECQUET P.,THE DIPLOMACY OF THE CONFEDERATE CABINET OF RICHMOND AND ITS AGENTS ABROAD (LIMITED ED.). MOD/EUR USA-45 LEAD...OBS 19 CIVIL/WAR SOUTH/US. PAGE 114 A2347 DIPLOM WAR ORD/FREE

SOUTHEAST ASIA....SEE S/EASTASIA, S/ASIA

SOUTHEAST ASIA TREATY ORGANIZATION....SEE SEATO

SOUTHERN RHODESIA....SEE RHODESIA, COMMONWLTH

SOVEREIGN....SOVEREIGNTY

N
SEMINAR: THE MONTHLY SYMPOSIUM. INDIA ACT/RES TEC/DEV DIPLOM ATTIT...BIBLIOG 20. PAGE 2 A0041 NAT/G ECO/UNDEV SOVEREIGN POLICY

B00
DARBY W.E.,INTERNATIONAL TRIBUNALS. WOR-45 NAT/G ECO/TAC DOMIN LEGIT CT/SYS COERCE ORD/FREE PWR SOVEREIGN JURID. PAGE 33 A0681 INT/ORG ADJUD PEACE INT/LAW

B00
HOLLAND T.E.,STUDIES IN INTERNATIONAL LAW. TURKEY USSR WOR-45 CONSTN NAT/G DIPLOM DOMIN LEGIT COERCE WAR PEACE ORD/FREE PWR SOVEREIGN...JURID CHARTS 20 PARLIAMENT SUEZ TREATY. PAGE 66 A1367 INT/ORG LAW INT/LAW

B00
LORIMER J.,THE INSTITUTES OF THE LAW OF NATIONS. WOR-45 CULTURE SOCIETY NAT/G VOL/ASSN DIPLOM LEGIT WAR PEACE DRIVE ORD/FREE SOVEREIGN...CONCPT RECORD INT TREND HYPO/EXP GEN/METH TOT/POP VAL/FREE 20. PAGE 91 A1863 INT/ORG LAW INT/LAW

B00
MORRIS H.C.,THE HISTORY OF COLONIZATION. WOR+45 WOR-45 ECO/DEV ECO/UNDEV INT/ORG ACT/RES PLAN ECO/TAC LEGIT ROUTINE COERCE ATTIT DRIVE ALL/VALS ...GEOG TREND 19. PAGE 105 A2148 DOMIN SOVEREIGN COLONIAL

B01
HART A.B.,AMERICAN HISTORY TOLD BY CONTEMPORARIES. UK CULTURE FINAN SECT FORCES DIPLOM TAX RUMOR CT/SYS REV GOV/REL GP/REL...ANTHOL 17/18 PRE/US/AM FEDERALIST. PAGE 62 A1273 USA-45 COLONIAL SOVEREIGN

B02
SEELEY J.R.,THE EXPANSION OF ENGLAND. MOD/EUR S/ASIA UK CULTURE NAT/G FORCES PLAN DOMIN EDU/PROP COLONIAL ROUTINE ATTIT ALL/VALS SOVEREIGN...CONCPT HIST/WRIT PARLIAMENT 18 CMN/WLTH. PAGE 131 A2679 INT/ORG ACT/RES CAP/ISM INDIA

C05
DUNNING W.A.,"HISTORY OF POLITICAL THEORIES FROM LUTHER TO MONTESQUIEU." LAW NAT/G SECT DIPLOM REV WAR ORD/FREE SOVEREIGN CONSERVE...TRADIT BIBLIOG 16/18. PAGE 39 A0803 PHIL/SCI CONCPT GEN/LAWS

B08
GRIFFIN A.P.C.,LIST OF REFERENCES ON INTERNATIONAL ARBITRATION. FRANCE L/A+17C USA-45 WOR-45 DIPLOM CONFER COLONIAL ARMS/CONT BAL/PAY EQUILIB SOVEREIGN ...DECISION 19/20 MEXIC/AMER. PAGE 56 A1156 BIBLIOG/A INT/ORG INT/LAW DELIB/GP

B09
FREMANTLE H.E.S.,THE NEW NATION, A SURVEY OF THE CONDITION AND PROSPECTS OF SOUTH AFRICA. SOUTH/AFR CONSTN POL/PAR DIPLOM DOMIN COLONIAL WEALTH...SOC TREND 19. PAGE 49 A0996 NAT/LISM SOVEREIGN RACE/REL REGION

B17
SATOW E.,A GUIDE TO DIPLOMATIC PRACTICE. MOD/EUR INT/ORG BAL/PWR LEGIT ORD/FREE PWR SOVEREIGN ...POLICY GEN/METH 20. PAGE 127 A2607 GEN/LAWS DIPLOM

N17
BURKE E.,THOUGHTS ON THE PROSPECT OF A REGICIDE PEACE (PAMPHLET). FRANCE UK SECT DOMIN MURDER PEACE ORD/FREE SOVEREIGN POPULISM...POLICY GOV/COMP IDEA/COMP 18 JACOBINISM COEXIST. PAGE 21 A0435 REV CHIEF NAT/G DIPLOM

B19
SUMNER W.G.,WAR AND OTHER ESSAYS. USA-45 DELIB/GP DIPLOM TARIFFS COLONIAL PEACE SOVEREIGN 20. PAGE 140 A2864 INT/TRADE ORD/FREE CAP/ISM ECO/TAC

N19
BARROS J.F.P.,THE INTERNATIONAL POLICE: THE USE OF FORCE IN THE STRUCTURE OF PEACE (PAMPHLET). BRAZIL WOR+45 WOR-45 FORCES DISCRIM NAT/LISM ORD/FREE SOVEREIGN...POLICY NEW/IDEA WORSHIP 20. PAGE 11 A0229 PEACE INT/ORG COERCE BAL/PWR

N19
BENTHAM J.,A PLAN FOR AN UNIVERSAL AND PERPETUAL PEACE (1838) (PAMPHLET). NAT/G FORCES BAL/PWR INT/TRADE ADMIN AGREE CT/SYS ARMS/CONT SOVEREIGN WEALTH GEN/LAWS. PAGE 13 A0269 INT/ORG INT/LAW PEACE COLONIAL

N19
HALPERN M.,THE MORALITY AND POLITICS OF INTERVENTION (PAMPHLET). USA+45 INT/ORG FORCES ECO/TAC MORAL ORD/FREE 20 INTERVENT CHRISTIAN. PAGE 61 A1243 POLICY DIPLOM SOVEREIGN DOMIN

N19
HANNA A.J.,EUROPEAN RULE IN AFRICA (PAMPHLET). BELGIUM FRANCE MOD/EUR UK WOR+45 WOR-45 ECO/UNDEV NAT/G PARTIC SOVEREIGN...NAT/COMP 19/20. PAGE 61 A1252 DIPLOM COLONIAL AFR NAT/LISM

N19
JACKSON R.G.A.,THE CASE FOR AN INTERNATIONAL DEVELOPMENT AUTHORITY (PAMPHLET). WOR+45 ECO/DEV DIPLOM GIVE CONTROL GP/REL EFFICIENCY NAT/LISM SOVEREIGN 20. PAGE 72 A1478 FOR/AID INT/ORG ECO/UNDEV ADMIN

N19
MASSEY V.,CANADIANS AND THEIR COMMONWEALTH: THE ROMANES LECTURE DELIVERED IN THE SHELDONIAN THEATRE JUNE 1, 1961 (PAMPHLET). CANADA UK CULTURE ECO/DEV REPRESENT NAT/LISM PEACE PWR CONSERVE 20 CMN/WLTH. PAGE 96 A1959 ATTIT DIPLOM NAT/G SOVEREIGN

N19
MEZERIK AG,OUTER SPACE: UN, US, USSR (PAMPHLET). USSR DELIB/GP FORCES DETER NUC/PWR SOVEREIGN ...POLICY 20 UN TREATY. PAGE 101 A2063 SPACE CONTROL DIPLOM INT/ORG

N19
PROVISIONS SECTION OAU,ORGANIZATION OF AFRICAN CONSTN

UNITY: BASIC DOCUMENTS AND RESOLUTIONS (PAMPHLET). AFR CULTURE ECO/UNDEV DIPLOM ECO/TAC EDU/PROP COLONIAL ARMS/CONT NUC/PWR RACE/REL DISCRIM NAT/LISM 20 UN OAU. PAGE 118 A2415
EX/STRUC SOVEREIGN INT/ORG

N19
VELYAMINOV G.,AFRICA AND THE COMMON MARKET (PAMPHLET). AFR MARKET VOL/ASSN ECO/TAC COLONIAL ORD/FREE...SOCIALIST 20 THIRD/WRLD. PAGE 158 A3227
INT/ORG INT/TRADE SOVEREIGN ECO/UNDEV

B20
BURNS C.D.,INTERNATIONAL POLITICS. WOR-45 CULTURE SOCIETY ECO/UNDEV NAT/G VOL/ASSN DELIB/GP ACT/RES CREATE DOMIN EDU/PROP LEGIT ATTIT DRIVE RIGID/FLEX ALL/VALS...PLURIST PSY CONCPT TREND. PAGE 22 A0442
INT/ORG PEACE SOVEREIGN

B20
DICKINSON E.,THE EQUALITY OF STATES IN INTERNATIONAL LAW. WOR-45 INT/ORG NAT/G DIPLOM EDU/PROP LEGIT PEACE ATTIT ALL/VALS...JURID TIME/SEQ LEAGUE/NAT. PAGE 37 A0757
LAW CONCPT SOVEREIGN

B20
WOOLF L.,EMPIRE AND COMMERCE IN AFRICA. EUR+WWI MOD/EUR FINAN INDUS MARKET INT/ORG PLAN COERCE ATTIT DRIVE PWR WEALTH...CONCPT TIME/SEQ TREND CHARTS 20. PAGE 167 A3394
AFR DOMIN COLONIAL SOVEREIGN

B22
MYERS D.P.,MANUAL OF COLLECTIONS OF TREATIES AND OF COLLECTIONS RELATING TO TREATIES. MOD/EUR INT/ORG LEGIS WRITING ADMIN SOVEREIGN...INT/LAW 19/20. PAGE 106 A2186
BIBLIOG/A DIPLOM CONFER

B26
LEWIN E.,RECENT PUBLICATIONS IN THE LIBRARY OF THE ROYAL COLONIAL INSTITUTE (PAMPHLET). CANADA UK EX/STRUC PARL/PROC NAT/LISM SOVEREIGN 20 CMN/WLTH PARLIAMENT. PAGE 88 A1799
BIBLIOG COLONIAL CONSTN DIPLOM

B27
LAUTERPACHT H.,PRIVATE LAW SOURCES AND ANALOGIES OF INTERNATIONAL LAW. WOR-45 NAT/G DELIB/GP LEGIT COERCE ATTIT ORD/FREE PWR SOVEREIGN...JURID CONCPT HIST/WRIT TIME/SEQ GEN/METH LEAGUE/NAT 20. PAGE 85 A1748
INT/ORG ADJUD PEACE INT/LAW

B28
HURST C.,GREAT BRITAIN AND THE DOMINIONS. EUR+WWI CULTURE ECO/DEV INT/ORG NAT/G DIPLOM ECO/TAC COLONIAL ATTIT PWR SOVEREIGN...TIME/SEQ GEN/LAWS TOT/POP VAL/FREE 20 CMN/WLTH. PAGE 69 A1420
VOL/ASSN DOMIN UK

B28
MAIR L.P.,THE PROTECTION OF MINORITIES. EUR+WWI WOR-45 CONSTN INT/ORG NAT/G LEGIT CT/SYS GP/REL RACE/REL DISCRIM ORD/FREE RESPECT...JURID CONCPT TIME/SEQ 20. PAGE 93 A1909
LAW SOVEREIGN

C28
WARD P.W.,"SOVEREIGNTY: A STUDY OF A CONTEMPORARY POLITICAL NOTION." CONSTN NAT/G DIPLOM REPRESENT PLURISM...IDEA/COMP BIBLIOG. PAGE 161 A3281
SOVEREIGN CONCPT NAT/LISM

B29
BUELL R.,INTERNATIONAL RELATIONS. WOR+45 WOR-45 CONSTN STRATA FORCES TOP/EX ADMIN ATTIT DRIVE SUPEGO MORAL ORD/FREE PWR SOVEREIGN...JURID SOC CONCPT 20. PAGE 21 A0428
INT/ORG BAL/PWR DIPLOM

B31
STUART G.H.,THE INTERNATIONAL CITY OF TANGIER. AFR EUR+WWI MOD/EUR MOROCCO CONSTN PROVS CREATE PLAN LEGIT PEACE ORD/FREE PWR...INT/LAW OBS TIME/SEQ CON/ANAL 20 TANGIER. PAGE 139 A2854
LOC/G INT/ORG DIPLOM SOVEREIGN

B32
BRYCE J.,THE HOLY ROMAN EMPIRE. GERMANY ITALY MOD/EUR CULTURE SOCIETY STRUCT INT/ORG NAT/G SECT DIPLOM DOMIN WAR SUPEGO ALL/VALS SOVEREIGN...GEOG SOC TIME/SEQ CHARTS STERTYP. PAGE 20 A0413
CHRIST-17C NAT/LISM

B32
FLEMMING D.,THE UNITED STATES AND THE LEAGUE OF NATIONS, 1918-1920. FUT USA-45 NAT/G LEGIS TOP/EX DEBATE CHOOSE PEACE ATTIT SOVEREIGN...TIME/SEQ CON/ANAL CONGRESS LEAGUE/NAT 20 TREATY. PAGE 46 A0950
INT/ORG EDU/PROP

B33
GENTILI A.,DE JURE BELLI, LIBRI TRES (1612) (VOL. 2). FORCES DIPLOM AGREE PEACE SOVEREIGN. PAGE 52 A1059
WAR INT/LAW MORAL SUPEGO

B33
LANGER W.L.,FOREIGN AFFAIRS BIBLIOGRAPHY. WOR-45 INT/ORG CONSULT EDU/PROP ROUTINE NAT/LISM ATTIT SOVEREIGN...STAT RECORD GEN/METH LEAGUE/NAT TOT/POP. PAGE 84 A1725
KNOWL

B33
LAUTERPACHT H.,THE FUNCTION OF LAW IN THE INTERNATIONAL COMMUNITY. WOR-45 NAT/G FORCES CREATE DOMIN LEGIT COERCE WAR PEACE ATTIT ORD/FREE PWR SOVEREIGN...JURID CONCPT METH/CNCPT TIME/SEQ GEN/LAWS GEN/METH LEAGUE/NAT TOT/POP VAL/FREE 20. PAGE 85 A1749
INT/ORG LAW INT/LAW

B35
LANGER W.L.,THE DIPLOMACY OF IMPERIALISM 1890-1902. FRANCE GERMANY ITALY UK WOR-45 BAL/PWR INT/TRADE LEGIT ADJUD CONTROL WAR PWR SOVEREIGN...CHARTS BIBLIOG/A 19/20. PAGE 84 A1726
DIPLOM COLONIAL DOMIN

B36
RUSSEL F.M.,THEORIES OF INTERNATIONAL RELATIONS. EUR+WWI FUT MOD/EUR USA-45 INT/ORG DIPLOM...JURID CONCPT. PAGE 125 A2571
PWR POLICY BAL/PWR SOVEREIGN

B37
ROYAL INST. INT. AFF.,THE COLONIAL PROBLEM. WOR-45 LAW ECO/DEV ECO/UNDEV NAT/G PLAN ECO/TAC EDU/PROP ADMIN ATTIT ALL/VALS...CONCPT 20. PAGE 125 A2556
INT/ORG ACT/RES SOVEREIGN COLONIAL

B38
SAINT-PIERRE C.I.,SCHEME FOR LASTING PEACE (TRANS. BY H. BELLOT). INDUS NAT/G CHIEF FORCES INT/TRADE CT/SYS WAR PWR SOVEREIGN WEALTH...POLICY 18. PAGE 126 A2587
INT/ORG PEACE AGREE INT/LAW

B39
BROWN J.F.,CONTEMPORARY WORLD POLITICS. WOR-45 NAT/G PLAN BAL/PWR EDU/PROP LEGIT REGION NAT/LISM ORD/FREE PWR SOVEREIGN...POLICY CONCPT HIST/WRIT TIME/SEQ GEN/LAWS LEAGUE/NAT. PAGE 20 A0403
INT/ORG DIPLOM PEACE

B39
FURNIVALL J.S.,NETHERLANDS INDIA. INDIA NETHERLAND CULTURE INDUS NAT/G DIPLOM ADMIN WEALTH...POLICY CHARTS 17/20. PAGE 50 A1029
COLONIAL ECO/UNDEV SOVEREIGN PLURISM

B39
MAXWELL B.W.,INTERNATIONAL RELATIONS. EUR+WWI WOR-45 NAT/G CONSULT DIPLOM LEGIT ADJUD NAT/LISM ATTIT ORD/FREE SOVEREIGN...JURID LEAGUE/NAT TOT/POP VAL/FREE 20. PAGE 97 A1981
INT/ORG

B39
TAGGART F.J.,ROME AND CHINA. MEDIT-7 INT/ORG NAT/G FORCES LEGIS TOP/EX PLAN PWR SOVEREIGN...CHARTS TOT/POP ROM/EMP. PAGE 141 A2883
ASIA WAR

C40
FAHS C.B.,"GOVERNMENT IN JAPAN." FINAN FORCES LEGIS TOP/EX BUDGET INT/TRADE EDU/PROP SOVEREIGN ...CON/ANAL BIBLIOG/A 20 CHINJAP. PAGE 43 A0884
ASIA DIPLOM NAT/G ADMIN

B41
WHITAKER A.P.,THE UNITED STATES AND THE INDEPENDENCE OF LATIN AMERICA, 1800-1830. PORTUGAL SPAIN USA-45 COLONIAL REGION SOVEREIGN...POLICY TIME/SEQ BIBLIOG/A 18/20. PAGE 163 A3329
DIPLOM L/A+17C CONCPT ORD/FREE

S41
WRIGHT Q.,"FUNDAMENTAL PROBLEMS OF INTERNATIONAL ORGANIZATION." UNIV WOR-45 STRUCT FORCES ACT/RES CREATE DOMIN EDU/PROP LEGIT REGION NAT/LISM ORD/FREE PWR RESPECT SOVEREIGN...JURID SOC CONCPT METH/CNCPT TIME/SEQ 20. PAGE 167 A3405
INT/ORG ATTIT PEACE

B42
KELSEN H.,LAW AND PEACE IN INTERNATIONAL RELATIONS. FUT WOR-45 NAT/G DELIB/GP DIPLOM LEGIT RIGID/FLEX ORD/FREE SOVEREIGN...JURID CONCPT TREND STERTYP GEN/LAWS LEAGUE/NAT 20. PAGE 77 A1580
INT/ORG ADJUD PEACE INT/LAW

S42
SHOTWELL J.,"AFTER THE WAR." COM EUR+WWI USA+45 USA-45 NAT/G DIPLOM INT/TRADE ARMS/CONT SOVEREIGN ...CONCPT LEAGUE/NAT TOT/POP FAO 20. PAGE 132 A2707
FUT INT/ORG PEACE

B43
BEMIS S.F.,THE LATIN AMERICAN POLICY OF THE UNITED STATES: AN HISTORICAL INTERPRETATION. INT/ORG AGREE COLONIAL WAR PEACE ATTIT ORD/FREE...POLICY INT/LAW CHARTS 18/20 MEXIC/AMER WILSON/W MONROE/DOC. PAGE 13 A0265
DIPLOM SOVEREIGN USA-45 L/A+17C

B43
MAISEL A.Q.,AFRICA: FACTS AND FORECASTS. WOR+45 INT/ORG CONTROL RACE/REL SOVEREIGN...PREDICT CHARTS 20. PAGE 93 A1910
AFR WAR DIPLOM COLONIAL

B43
WALKER E.A.,BRITAIN AND SOUTH AFRICA. SOUTH/AFR POL/PAR GP/REL RACE/REL ATTIT ORD/FREE 17/20. PAGE 160 A3264
COLONIAL WAR DIPLOM SOVEREIGN

C43
BENTHAM J.,"PRINCIPLES OF INTERNATIONAL LAW" IN J. BOWRING, ED., THE WORKS OF JEREMY BENTHAM." UNIV NAT/G PLAN PROB/SOLV DIPLOM CONTROL SANCTION MORAL ORD/FREE PWR SOVEREIGN 19. PAGE 13 A0270
INT/LAW JURID WAR PEACE

B44
FULLER G.H.,MILITARY GOVERNMENT: A LIST OF REFERENCES (A PAMPHLET). ITALY UK USA-45 WOR-45 LAW FORCES DOMIN ADMIN ARMS/CONT ORD/FREE PWR ...DECISION 20 CHINJAP. PAGE 50 A1023
BIBLIOG DIPLOM CIVMIL/REL SOVEREIGN

L44
CORWIN E.S.,"THE CONSTITUTION AND WORLD ORGANIZATION." FUT USA+45 USA-45 NAT/G EX/STRUC LEGIS PEACE KNOWL...CON/ANAL UN 20. PAGE 31 A0627
INT/ORG CONSTN SOVEREIGN

B45
ELTON G.E.,IMPERIAL COMMONWEALTH. INDIA UK DIPLOM DOMIN WAR NAT/LISM SOVEREIGN...TRADIT CHARTS T 15/20 CMN/WLTH AUSTRAL PRE/US/AM. PAGE 41 A0844
REGION CONCPT COLONIAL

B45
HILL N.,CLAIMS TO TERRITORY IN INTERNATIONAL LAW
INT/ORG

AND RELATIONS. WOR-45 NAT/G DOMIN EDU/PROP LEGIT REGION ROUTINE ORD/FREE PWR WEALTH...GEOG INT/LAW JURID 20. PAGE 65 A1332 ADJUD SOVEREIGN

B45
HORN O.B.,BRITISH PUBLIC OPINION AND THE FIRST PARTITION OF POLAND. POLAND UK LEGIS PRESS RUMOR CONTROL PARTIC NAT/LISM SOVEREIGN 18/19. PAGE 67 A1385 DIPLOM POLICY ATTIT NAT/G

B46
GRIFFIN G.G.,A GUIDE TO MANUSCRIPTS RELATING TO AMERICAN HISTORY IN BRITISH DEPOSITORIES. CANADA IRELAND MOD/EUR UK USA-45 LAW DIPLOM ADMIN COLONIAL WAR NAT/LISM SOVEREIGN...GEOG INT/LAW 15/19 CMN/WLTH. PAGE 56 A1159 BIBLIOG/A ALL/VALS NAT/G

B46
MITRANY D.,A WORKING PEACE SYSTEM. WOR+45 WOR-45 ECO/DEV INT/ORG NAT/G DELIB/GP ECO/TAC REGION ATTIT RIGID/FLEX...TREND GEN/LAWS LEAGUE/NAT 20. PAGE 102 A2091 VOL/ASSN PLAN PEACE SOVEREIGN

B47
BORGESE G.,COMMON CAUSE. LAW CONSTN SOCIETY STRATA ECO/DEV INT/ORG POL/PAR FORCES LEGIS TOP/EX CAP/ISM DIPLOM ADMIN EXEC ATTIT PWR 20. PAGE 17 A0339 WOR+45 NAT/G SOVEREIGN REGION

N47
FOX W.T.R.,UNITED STATES POLICY IN A TWO POWER WORLD. COM USA+45 USSR FORCES DOMIN AGREE NEUTRAL NUC/PWR ORD/FREE SOVEREIGN 20 COLD/WAR TREATY EUROPE/W INTERVENT. PAGE 48 A0972 DIPLOM FOR/AID POLICY

B48
PELCOVITS N.A.,OLD CHINA HANDS AND THE FOREIGN OFFICE. ASIA BURMA UK ECO/UNDEV NAT/G ECO/TAC FOR/AID TARIFFS DOMIN COLONIAL GOV/REL SOVEREIGN 19 HONG/KONG TREATY. PAGE 114 A2348 INT/TRADE ATTIT DIPLOM

B48
WHEELER-BENNETT J.W.,MUNICH: PROLOGUE TO TRAGEDY. EUR+WWI FRANCE GERMANY UK PLAN PROB/SOLV SOVEREIGN ...POLICY DECISION 20 HITLER/A. PAGE 163 A3327 DIPLOM WAR PEACE

B50
MOCKFORD J.,SOUTH-WEST AFRICA AND THE INTERNATIONAL COURT (PAMPHLET). AFR GERMANY SOUTH/AFR UK ECO/UNDEV DIPLOM CONTROL DISCRIM...DECISION JURID 20 AFRICA/SW. PAGE 102 A2094 COLONIAL SOVEREIGN INT/LAW DOMIN

B50
US LIBRARY OF CONGRESS,THE UNITED STATES AND EUROPE: BIBLIOGRAPHY OF THOUGHT EXPRESSED IN AMERICAN PUBLICATIONS DURING 1950. EUR+WWI GERMANY USA+45 USSR INT/ORG DIPLOM COLONIAL SOVEREIGN ...POLICY 20 COLD/WAR UN BERLIN/BLO. PAGE 154 A3150 BIBLIOG/A SOC ATTIT

B51
CARRINGTON C.E.,THE LIQUIDATION OF THE BRITISH EMPIRE. AFR NAT/G INT/TRADE COLONIAL RACE/REL ATTIT ORD/FREE...POLICY NAT/COMP 20 CMN/WLTH. PAGE 25 A0501 SOVEREIGN NAT/LISM DIPLOM GP/REL

B51
UNESCO,FREEDOM AND CULTURE. FUT WOR+45 CONSTN CULTURE PERF/ART VOL/ASSN EDU/PROP PEACE ATTIT ALL/VALS SOVEREIGN...POLICY MAJORIT CONCPT TREND STERTYP GEN/LAWS UN TOT/POP 20. PAGE 147 A3013 INT/ORG SOCIETY

C51
GRUNDER G.A.,"THE PHILIPPINES AND THE UNITED STATES." PHILIPPINE S/ASIA USA-45 NAT/G POL/PAR ADMIN SOVEREIGN...TIME/SEQ BIBLIOG 20. PAGE 57 A1181 COLONIAL POLICY DIPLOM ECO/TAC

B52
LIPPMANN W.,ISOLATION AND ALLIANCES: AN AMERICAN SPEAKS TO THE BRITISH. USA+45 USA-45 INT/ORG AGREE COERCE DETER WAR PEACE MORAL 20 TREATY INTERVENT. PAGE 89 A1829 DIPLOM SOVEREIGN COLONIAL ATTIT

S52
SCHUMAN F.,"INTERNATIONAL IDEALS AND THE NATIONAL INTEREST." WOR+45 WOR-45 INT/ORG VOL/ASSN DELIB/GP CREATE BAL/PWR DOMIN PEACE PERSON MORAL PWR SOVEREIGN...POLICY GEN/LAWS TOT/POP LEAGUE/NAT 20. PAGE 129 A2648 ATTIT CONCPT

B53
MANSERGH N.,DOCUMENTS AND SPEECHES ON BRITISH COMMONWEALTH AFFAIRS 1931-1952. INDIA IRELAND PAKISTAN UK CONSTN POL/PAR CHIEF FORCES COLONIAL ORD/FREE SOVEREIGN...JURID 20 COMMONWLTH. PAGE 94 A1929 BIBLIOG/A DIPLOM ECO/TAC

B53
MARITAIN J.,L'HOMME ET L'ETAT. SECT DIPLOM GP/REL PEACE ORD/FREE...IDEA/COMP 17/20 CHURCH/STA NATURL/LAW. PAGE 95 A1940 CONCPT NAT/G SOVEREIGN COERCE

B53
OPPENHEIM L.,INTERNATIONAL LAW: A TREATISE (7TH ED., 2 VOLS.). LAW CONSTN PROB/SOLV INT/TRADE ADJUD AGREE NEUTRAL WAR ORD/FREE SOVEREIGN...BIBLIOG 20 LEAGUE/NAT UN ILO. PAGE 112 A2294 INT/LAW INT/ORG DIPLOM

B53
ROSCIO J.G.,OBRAS. L/A+17C SPAIN DIPLOM REV WAR NAT/LISM TOTALISM PWR SOVEREIGN 19. PAGE 123 A2527 ORD/FREE COLONIAL NAT/G PHIL/SCI

C53
DEUTSCH K.W.,"NATIONALISM AND SOCIAL COMMUNICATION: AN INQUIRY INTO THE FOUNDATIONS OF NATIONALITY." CULTURE STRUCT DIPLOM DOMIN ATTIT ORD/FREE SOVEREIGN...SOC STAT CHARTS IDEA/COMP BIBLIOG. PAGE 36 A0735 NAT/LISM CONCPT PERCEPT STRATA

B54
SHARMA J.S.,MAHATMA GANDHI: A DESCRIPTIVE BIBLIOGRAPHY. INDIA S/ASIA PROB/SOLV DIPLOM COLONIAL WAR NAT/LISM PEACE ATTIT PERSON SOVEREIGN ...CONCPT 20 GANDHI/M. PAGE 132 A2695 BIBLIOG/A BIOG CHIEF LEAD

B54
STONE J.,LEGAL CONTROLS OF INTERNATIONAL CONFLICT: A TREATISE ON THE DYNAMICS OF DISPUTES AND WAR LAW. WOR+45 WOR-45 NAT/G DIPLOM CT/SYS SOVEREIGN...JURID CONCPT METH/CNCPT GEN/LAWS TOT/POP VAL/FREE COLD/WAR LEAGUE/NAT 20. PAGE 138 A2834 INT/ORG LAW WAR INT/LAW

B54
STREIT C.K.,FREEDOM AGAINST ITSELF. LAW SOCIETY DIPLOM UTOPIA PWR SOVEREIGN ALL/IDEOS 17/20 NATO UN. PAGE 139 A2850 ORD/FREE CREATE INT/ORG CONCPT

B54
US SENATE COMM ON FOREIGN REL,REVIEW OF THE UNITED NATIONS CHARTER: A COLLECTION OF DOCUMENTS. LEGIS DIPLOM ADMIN ARMS/CONT WAR REPRESENT SOVEREIGN ...INT/LAW 20 UN. PAGE 156 A3180 BIBLIOG CONSTN INT/ORG DEBATE

B54
WHITAKER A.P.,THE WESTERN HEMISPHERE IDEA. USA+45 USA-45 CONSTN INT/ORG NAT/G DIPLOM SOVEREIGN...GEOG TIME/SEQ OAS 19/20 MONROE/DOC. PAGE 164 A3331 L/A+17C CONCPT REGION

S54
DODD S.C.,"THE SCIENTIFIC MEASUREMENT OF FITNESS FOR SELF-GOVERNMENT." FUT CONSTN ECO/UNDEV INT/ORG PLAN PWR...CONCPT QUANT CON/ANAL SOC/EXP UN LEAGUE/NAT 20. PAGE 38 A0767 NAT/G STAT SOVEREIGN

B55
BURR R.N.,DOCUMENTS ON INTER-AMERICAN COOPERATION: VOL. I, 1810-1881; VOL. II, 1881-1948. DELIB/GP BAL/PWR INT/TRADE REPRESENT NAT/LISM PEACE HABITAT ORD/FREE PWR SOVEREIGN...INT/LAW 20 OAS. PAGE 22 A0445 BIBLIOG DIPLOM INT/ORG L/A+17C

B55
BUSS C.,THE FAR EAST: A HISTORY OF RECENT AND CONTEMPORARY INTERNATIONAL RELATIONS IN EAST ASIA. WOR+45 WOR-45 CONSTN INT/ORG NAT/G BAL/PWR ATTIT PWR SOVEREIGN...GEOG JURID SOC CONCPT METH/CNCPT 19/20. PAGE 22 A0449 ASIA DIPLOM

B55
CHOWDHURI R.N.,INTERNATIONAL MANDATES AND TRUSTEESHIP SYSTEMS. WOR+45 STRUCT ECO/UNDEV INT/ORG LEGIS DOMIN EDU/PROP LEGIT ADJUD EXEC PWR ...CONCPT TIME/SEQ UN 20. PAGE 26 A0534 DELIB/GP PLAN SOVEREIGN

B55
PANT Y.P.,PLANNING IN UNDERDEVELOPED ECONOMIES. INDIA NEPAL INT/TRADE COLONIAL SOVEREIGN ALL/IDEOS ...TIME/SEQ METH/COMP 20. PAGE 114 A2334 ECO/UNDEV PLAN ECO/TAC DIPLOM

B55
SVARLIEN O.,AN INTRODUCTION TO THE LAW OF NATIONS. SEA AIR INT/ORG NAT/G CHIEF ADMIN AGREE WAR PRIVIL ORD/FREE SOVEREIGN...BIBLIOG 16/20. PAGE 140 A2868 INT/LAW DIPLOM

B55
UN HEADQUARTERS LIBRARY,BIBLIOQRAPHIE DE LA CHARTE DES NATIONS UNIES. CHINA/COM KOREA WOR+45 VOL/ASSN CONFER ADMIN COERCE PEACE ATTIT ORD/FREE SOVEREIGN ...INT/LAW 20 UNESCO UN. PAGE 147 A3001 BIBLIOG/A INT/ORG DIPLOM

B55
VINSON J.C.,THE PARCHMENT PEACE: THE UNITED STATES SENATE AND THE WASHINGTON CONFERENCE, 1921-1922. USA-45 INT/ORG DELIB/GP PLAN ARMS/CONT GOV/REL ISOLAT PEACE ATTIT SOVEREIGN...INT/LAW BIBLIOG 20 SENATE PRESIDENT CONGRESS LEAGUE/NAT CHINJAP. PAGE 159 A3242 POLICY DIPLOM NAT/G LEGIS

S55
DE SMITH S.A.,"CONSTITUTIONAL MONARCHY IN BURGANDA." AFR UGANDA UK STRUCT CHIEF REGION INGP/REL ADJUST NAT/LISM SOVEREIGN CONSERVE ...POLICY 19/20 BURGANDA. PAGE 35 A0712 NAT/G DIPLOM CONSTN COLONIAL

B56
BALL W.M.,NATIONALISM AND COMMUNISM IN EAST ASIA. ASIA BURMA EUR+WWI KOREA USA+45 ECO/UNDEV NAT/G POL/PAR DIPLOM ECO/TAC FOR/AID EDU/PROP COERCE RACE/REL NAT/LISM DRIVE SOVEREIGN...TREND 20 CHINJAP. PAGE 11 A0214 S/ASIA ATTIT

B56
BOWLES C.,AFRICA'S CHALLENGE TO AMERICA. USA+45 ECO/UNDEV NAT/G LEGIS COLONIAL CONTROL REV ORD/FREE SOVEREIGN 20 COLD/WAR. PAGE 18 A0358 AFR DIPLOM POLICY FOR/AID

B56
FIELD G.C.,POLITICAL THEORY. POL/PAR REPRESENT MORAL SOVEREIGN...JURID IDEA/COMP. PAGE 45 A0924 CONCPT NAT/G ORD/FREE DIPLOM

B56
GREECE PRESBEIA U.S.,BRITISH OPINION ON CYPRUS. CYPRUS UK FORCES DIPLOM INT/TRADE DOMIN GOV/REL ORD/FREE SOVEREIGN...POLICY 20. PAGE 55 A1137 — ATTIT COLONIAL LEGIS PRESS

B56
UNDERHILL F.H.,THE BRITISH COMMONWEALTH: AN EXPERIMENT IN CO-OPERATION AMONG NATIONS. CANADA UK WOR+45 WOR-45 INT/ORG COLONIAL UTIL SOVEREIGN CONSERVE...OLD/LIB SOC/EXP BIBLIOG/A 19/20 CMN/WLTH. PAGE 147 A3007 — VOL/ASSN NAT/LISM DIPLOM

B56
US DEPARTMENT OF STATE,THE SUEZ CANAL PROBLEM; JULY 26-SEPTEMBER 22, 1956. UAR WOR+45 BAL/PWR COERCE NAT/LISM ATTIT ORD/FREE SOVEREIGN 20 SUEZ. PAGE 151 A3091 — DIPLOM CONFER INT/TRADE

B56
VON HARPE W.,DIE SOWJETUNION FINNLAND UND SKANDANAVIEN, 1945-1955. EUR+WWI FINLAND GERMANY USSR WAR INGP/REL ORD/FREE SOVEREIGN MARXISM ...POLICY GOV/COMP BIBLIOG 20 STALIN/J. PAGE 160 A3252 — DIPLOM COM NEUTRAL BAL/PWR

B56
WEIS P.,NATIONALITY AND STATELESSNESS IN INTERNATIONAL LAW. UK WOR+45 WOR-45 LAW CONSTN NAT/G DIPLOM EDU/PROP LEGIT ROUTINE RIGID/FLEX ...JURID RECORD CMN/WLTH 20. PAGE 162 A3309 — INT/ORG SOVEREIGN INT/LAW

B57
BROMBERGER M.,LES SECRETS DE L'EXPEDITION D'EGYPTE. FRANCE ISLAM UAR UK USA+45 USSR WOR+45 INT/ORG NAT/G FORCES BAL/PWR ECO/TAC DOMIN WAR NAT/LISM ATTIT PWR SOVEREIGN...MAJORIT TIME/SEQ CHARTS SUEZ COLD/WAR 20. PAGE 19 A0387 — COERCE DIPLOM

B57
BURNS A.,IN DEFENCE OF COLONIES; BRITISH COLONIAL TERRITORIES IN INTERNATIONAL AFFAIRS. UK ECO/UNDEV PLAN DOMIN SOVEREIGN...MAJORIT 18/20 CMN/WLTH INTERVENT. PAGE 22 A0439 — COLONIAL POLICY ATTIT DIPLOM

B57
HODGKIN T.,NATIONALISM IN COLONIAL AFRICA. STRATA STRUCT MUNIC NAT/G POL/PAR LEGIS ATTIT SOVEREIGN ...POLICY TREND BIBLIOG 20. PAGE 66 A1351 — AFR COLONIAL NAT/LISM DIPLOM

B57
KAPLAN M.A.,SYSTEM AND PROCESS OF INTERNATIONAL POLITICS. FUT WOR+45 WOR-45 SOCIETY PLAN BAL/PWR ADMIN ATTIT PERSON RIGID/FLEX PWR SOVEREIGN ...DECISION TREND VAL/FREE. PAGE 76 A1560 — INT/ORG DIPLOM

B57
LEVONTIN A.V.,THE MYTH OF INTERNATIONAL SECURITY: A JURIDICAL AND CRITICAL ANALYSIS. FUT WOR+45 WOR-45 LAW NAT/G VOL/ASSN ACT/RES BAL/PWR ATTIT ORD/FREE ...JURID METH/CNCPT TIME/SEQ TREND STERTYP 20. PAGE 88 A1797 — INT/ORG INT/LAW SOVEREIGN MYTH

B57
PALMER N.D.,INTERNATIONAL RELATIONS. WOR+45 INT/ORG NAT/G ECO/TAC EDU/PROP COLONIAL WAR PWR SOVEREIGN ...POLICY T 20 TREATY. PAGE 113 A2321 — DIPLOM BAL/PWR NAT/COMP

B57
ROSENNE S.,THE INTERNATIONAL COURT OF JUSTICE. WOR+45 LAW DOMIN LEGIT PEACE PWR SOVEREIGN...JURID CONCPT RECORD TIME/SEQ CON/ANAL CHARTS UN TOT/POP VAL/FREE LEAGUE/NAT 20 ICJ. PAGE 124 A2537 — INT/ORG CT/SYS INT/LAW

B58
APPADORAI A.,THE USE OF FORCE IN INTERNATIONAL RELATIONS. WOR+45 CULTURE ECO/UNDEV CAP/ISM ARMS/CONT REV WAR ATTIT PERSON SOVEREIGN MARXISM ...INT/LAW PACIFIST 20 UN INTERVENT THIRD/WRLD COLD/WAR. PAGE 8 A0169 — PEACE FEDERAL INT/ORG

B58
BRIERLY J.L.,THE BASIS OF OBLIGATION IN INTERNATIONAL LAW, AND OTHER PAPERS. WOR+45 WOR-45 LEGIS...JURID CONCPT NAT/COMP ANTHOL 20. PAGE 19 A0377 — INT/LAW DIPLOM ADJUD SOVEREIGN

B58
JENKS C.W.,THE COMMON LAW OF MANKIND. EUR+WWI MOD/EUR SPACE WOR+45 INT/ORG BAL/PWR ARMS/CONT COERCE SUPEGO MORAL...TREND 20. PAGE 73 A1505 — JURID SOVEREIGN

B58
MANSERGH N.,COMMONWEALTH PERSPECTIVES. GHANA UK LAW VOL/ASSN CONFER HEALTH SOVEREIGN...GEOG CHARTS ANTHOL 20 CMN/WLTH AUSTRAL. PAGE 94 A1930 — DIPLOM COLONIAL INT/ORG INGP/REL

B58
SCHUMAN F.,INTERNATIONAL POLITICS. WOR+45 WOR-45 INTELL NAT/G FORCES DOMIN LEGIT COERCE NUC/PWR ATTIT DISPL ORD/FREE PWR SOVEREIGN...POLICY CONCPT GEN/LAWS SUEZ 20. PAGE 129 A2650 — FUT INT/ORG NAT/LISM DIPLOM

B58
WIGGINS J.W.,FOREIGN AID REEXAMINED: A CRITICAL APPRAISAL. CHINA/COM INDONESIA USA+45 FINAN INT/TRADE REGION NAT/LISM ATTIT...CENSUS 20. PAGE 164 A3342 — FOR/AID DIPLOM ECO/UNDEV SOVEREIGN

L58
HYVARINEN R.,"MONISTIC AND PLURALISTIC INTERPRETATIONS IN THE STUDY OF INTERNATIONAL POLITICS." COLONIAL REGION RACE/REL DISCRIM TOTALISM SOVEREIGN...INT/LAW PHIL/SCI CONCPT BIBLIOG 20. PAGE 70 A1429 — DIPLOM PLURISM INT/ORG METH

C58
BUTTINGER J.,"THE SMALLER DRAGON; A POLITICAL HISTORY OF VIETNAM." VIETNAM SECT DIPLOM CIVMIL/REL ISOLAT NAT/LISM...BIBLIOG/A 3/20. PAGE 22 A0455 — COLONIAL DOMIN SOVEREIGN REV

B59
BROOKES E.H.,THE COMMONWEALTH TODAY. UK ROMAN/EMP INT/ORG RACE/REL NAT/LISM SOVEREIGN...TREND SOC/INTEG 20. PAGE 19 A0391 — FEDERAL DIPLOM JURID IDEA/COMP

B59
DEHIO L.,GERMANY AND WORLD POLITICS IN THE TWENTIETH CENTURY. EUR+WWI FRANCE GERMANY MOD/EUR UK USSR NAT/G CHIEF BAL/PWR DOMIN COLONIAL CONTROL LEAD...IDEA/COMP 20 VERSAILLES. PAGE 36 A0724 — DIPLOM WAR NAT/LISM SOVEREIGN

B59
EGYPTIAN SOCIETY OF INT LAW,THE MONROVIA CONFERENCE (PAMPHLET). AFR ALGERIA FRANCE UAR CONFER REGION NUC/PWR WAR DISCRIM 20 SAHARA AFR/STATES. PAGE 40 A0826 — COLONIAL SOVEREIGN RACE/REL DIPLOM

B59
GORDENKER L.,THE UNITED NATIONS AND THE PEACEFUL UNIFICATION OF KOREA. ASIA LAW LOC/G CONSULT ACT/RES DIPLOM DOMIN LEGIT ADJUD ADMIN ORD/FREE SOVEREIGN...INT GEN/METH UN COLD/WAR 20. PAGE 54 A1109 — DELIB/GP KOREA INT/ORG

B59
HALEY A.G.,FIRST COLLOQUIUM ON THE LAW OF OUTER SPACE. WOR+45 INT/ORG ACT/RES PLAN BAL/PWR CONFER ATTIT PWR...POLICY JURID CHARTS ANTHOL 20. PAGE 60 A1225 — SPACE LAW SOVEREIGN CONTROL

B59
JONES A.C.,NEW FABIAN COLONIAL ESSAYS. UK SOCIETY POL/PAR EDU/PROP ADMIN ORD/FREE SOVEREIGN SOCISM ...ANTHOL 20 CMN/WLTH LABOR/PAR. PAGE 75 A1530 — COLONIAL INT/ORG INGP/REL DOMIN

B59
JOSEPH F.M.,AS OTHERS SEE US: THE UNITED STATES THROUGH FOREIGN EYES. AFR EUR+WWI ISLAM L/A+17C S/ASIA USA+45 CULTURE SOCIETY ECO/DEV ECO/UNDEV INT/ORG NAT/G DIPLOM ECO/TAC REV ATTIT RIGID/FLEX HEALTH ORD/FREE WEALTH 20. PAGE 75 A1537 — RESPECT DOMIN NAT/LISM SOVEREIGN

B59
MAC MILLAN W.M.,THE ROAD TO SELF-RULE. SOUTH/AFR UK CULTURE SOCIETY AGRI LABOR NAT/G INT/TRADE CONTROL GP/REL...SOC 19/20. PAGE 92 A1884 — AFR COLONIAL SOVEREIGN POLICY

S59
BAILEY S.D.,"THE FUTURE COMPOSITION OF THE TRUSTEESHIP COUNCIL." FUT WOR+45 CONSTN VOL/ASSN ADMIN ATTIT PWR...OBS TREND CON/ANAL VAL/FREE UN 20. PAGE 10 A0203 — INT/ORG NAT/LISM SOVEREIGN

S59
CARLSTON K.S.,"NATIONALIZATION: AN ANALYTIC APPROACH." WOR+45 INT/ORG ECO/TAC DOMIN LEGIT ADJUD COERCE ORD/FREE PWR WEALTH SOCISM...JURID CONCPT TREND STERTYP TOT/POP VAL/FREE 20. PAGE 24 A0486 — INDUS NAT/G NAT/LISM SOVEREIGN

S59
SOHN L.B.,"THE DEFINITION OF AGGRESSION." FUT LAW FORCES LEGIT ADJUD ROUTINE COERCE ORD/FREE PWR ...MAJORIT JURID QUANT COLD/WAR 20. PAGE 135 A2762 — INT/ORG CT/SYS DETER SOVEREIGN

B60
BUCHAN A.,NATO IN THE 1960'S. EUR+WWI USA+45 WOR+45 INT/ORG ACT/RES PLAN LEGIT COERCE DETER ATTIT DRIVE RIGID/FLEX ORD/FREE...METH/CNCPT TIME/SEQ TREND GEN/LAWS COLD/WAR 20 NATO. PAGE 21 A0421 — VOL/ASSN FORCES ARMS/CONT SOVEREIGN

B60
EMERSON R.,FROM EMPIRE TO NATION: THE RISE TO SELF-ASSERTION OF ASIAN AND AFRICAN PEOPLES. S/ASIA CULTURE NAT/G SECT DIPLOM ATTIT SOVEREIGN MARXISM ...POLICY BIBLIOG 19/20. PAGE 41 A0847 — NAT/LISM COLONIAL AFR ASIA

B60
HEYSE T.,PROBLEMS FONCIERS ET REGIME DES TERRES (ASPECTS ECONOMIQUES, JURIDIQUES ET SOCIAUX). AFR CONGO/BRAZ INT/ORG DIPLOM SOVEREIGN...GEOG TREATY 20. PAGE 64 A1325 — BIBLIOG AGRI ECO/UNDEV LEGIS

B60
JEFFRIES C.,TRANSFER OF POWER: PROBLEMS OF THE PASSAGE TO SELFGOVERNMENT. CEYLON GHANA MALAYSIA NIGERIA UK INT/ORG CONSULT DELIB/GP LEGIS DIPLOM CONFER PARL/PROC 20. PAGE 73 A1502 — SOVEREIGN COLONIAL ORD/FREE NAT/G

B60
LATIFI D.,INDIA AND UNITED STATES AID. ASIA INDIA UK USA+45 AGRI FINAN INDUS COLONIAL ORD/FREE SOVEREIGN WEALTH...METH/COMP 20. PAGE 85 A1743 — FOR/AID DIPLOM ECO/UNDEV

B60
MENEZES A.J.,O BRASIL E O MUNDO ASIO-AFRICANO (REV. ED.). AFR ASIA BRAZIL WOR+45 INT/TRADE ORD/FREE PWR SOVEREIGN...POLICY 20. PAGE 99 A2040 — DIPLOM BAL/PWR LEAD ECO/UNDEV

B60
PHILLIPS J.F.V.,KWAME NKRUMAH AND THE FUTURE OF — BIOG

AFRICA. FUT GHANA ISLAM ECO/UNDEV CHIEF DIPLOM COLONIAL RACE/REL NAT/LISM...TREND IDEA/COMP BIBLIOG 20 NKRUMAH/K. PAGE 116 A2376
LEAD SOVEREIGN AFR

B60
PLAMENATZ J.,ON ALIEN RULE AND SELF-GOVERNMENT. AFR FUT S/ASIA WOR+45 CULTURE SOCIETY ECO/UNDEV INT/ORG DOMIN EDU/PROP ATTIT RIGID/FLEX ALL/VALS...POLICY CONCPT OBS TREND CON/ANAL GEN/LAWS TOT/POP VAL/FREE. PAGE 116 A2386
NAT/G CONSTN NAT/LISM SOVEREIGN

B60
QUBAIN F.I.,INSIDE THE ARAB MIND: A BIBLIOGRAPHIC SURVEY OF LITERATURE IN ARABIC ON ARAB NATIONALISM AND UNITY. ISLAM POL/PAR SECT LEAD SOVEREIGN MARXISM SOCISM. PAGE 118 A2425
BIBLIOG/A FEDERAL DIPLOM NAT/LISM

B60
THEOBOLD R.,THE NEW NATIONS OF WEST AFRICA. GHANA NIGERIA CULTURE INT/ORG ECO/TAC FOR/AID COLONIAL RACE/REL POPULISM...ANTHOL BIBLIOG 20 UN. PAGE 143 A2916
AFR SOVEREIGN ECO/UNDEV DIPLOM

B60
VAN HOOGSTRATE D.J.,AMERICAN FOREIGN POLICY: REALISTS AND IDEALISTS: A CATHOLIC INTERPRETATION. BAL/PWR FOR/AID ARMS/CONT GOV/REL PEACE LOVE MORAL SOVEREIGN CATHISM...BIBLIOG 20. PAGE 158 A3213
CATH DIPLOM POLICY IDEA/COMP

B60
WHEARE K.C.,THE CONSTITUTIONAL STRUCTURE OF THE COMMONWEALTH. UK EX/STRUC DIPLOM DOMIN ADMIN COLONIAL CONTROL LEAD INGP/REL SUPEGO 20 CMN/WLTH. PAGE 163 A3325
CONSTN INT/ORG VOL/ASSN SOVEREIGN

B60
WODDIS J.,AFRICA: THE ROOTS OF REVOLT. SOUTH/AFR WORKER INT/TRADE RACE/REL DISCRIM ORD/FREE 20. PAGE 166 A3374
COLONIAL SOVEREIGN WAR ECO/UNDEV

L60
HAAS E.B.,"CONSENSUS FORMATION IN THE COUNCIL OF EUROPE." EUR+WWI NAT/G DELIB/GP DIPLOM REGION CHOOSE PWR SOVEREIGN...RELATIV NEW/IDEA QUANT CHARTS INDEX TOT/POP OEEC 20 COUNCL/EUR. PAGE 59 A1206
POL/PAR INT/ORG STAT

S60
CLARK W.,"NEW FORCES IN THE UN." FUT UK WOR+45 CONSTN BAL/PWR DIPLOM DRIVE PWR SKILL...CONCPT TREND UN TOT/POP 20. PAGE 27 A0543
INT/ORG ECO/UNDEV SOVEREIGN

S60
EFIMENCO N.M.,"CATEGORIES OF INTERNATIONAL INTEGRATION." UNIV WOR+45 INT/ORG NAT/G ACT/RES CREATE PEACE...CONCPT TREND 20. PAGE 40 A0824
PLAN BAL/PWR SOVEREIGN

S60
GOODMAN E.,"THE CRY OF NATIONAL LIBERATION: RECENT SOVIET ATTITUDES TOWARDS NATIONAL SELF-DETERMINATION." COM INT/ORG LEGIS ROUTINE PWR ...TIME/SEQ CON/ANAL STERTYP GEN/LAWS 20 UN. PAGE 54 A1101
ATTIT EDU/PROP SOVEREIGN USSR

S60
GRACIA-MORA M.R.,"INTERNATIONAL RESPONSIBILITY FOR SUBVERSIVE ACTIVITIES AND HOSTILE PROPAGANDA BY PRIVATE PERSONS AGAINST." COM EUR+WWI L/A+17C UK USA+45 USSR WOR-45 CONSTN NAT/G LEGIT ADJUD REV PEACE TOTALISM ORD/FREE...INT/LAW 20. PAGE 55 A1119
INT/ORG JURID SOVEREIGN

S60
HAYTON R.D.,"THE ANTARCTIC SETTLEMENT OF 1959." FUT USA+45 WOR+45 WOR-45 STRUCT R+D INT/ORG EX/STRUC CREATE TEC/DEV LEGIT PEACE ATTIT SOVEREIGN ...TIME/SEQ 20 TREATY IGY. PAGE 63 A1297
DELIB/GP JURID DIPLOM REGION

B61
ANSPRENGER F.,POLITIK IM SCHWARZEN AFRIKA. FRANCE NAT/G DIPLOM REGION REV NAT/LISM...CHARTS BIBLIOG 19/20. PAGE 8 A0164
AFR COLONIAL SOVEREIGN

B61
BAINS J.S.,STUDIES IN POLITICAL SCIENCE. INDIA WOR+45 WOR-45 CONSTN BAL/PWR ADJUD ADMIN PARL/PROC SOVEREIGN...SOC METH/COMP ANTHOL 17/20 UN. PAGE 10 A0209
DIPLOM INT/LAW NAT/G

B61
BONNEFOUS M.,EUROPE ET TIERS MONDE. EUR+WWI SOCIETY INT/ORG NAT/G VOL/ASSN ACT/RES TEC/DEV CAP/ISM ECO/TAC ATTIT ORD/FREE SOVEREIGN...POLICY CONCPT TREND 20. PAGE 16 A0334
AFR ECO/UNDEV FOR/AID INT/TRADE

B61
FUCHS G.,GEGEN HITLER UND HENLEIN. CZECHOSLVK GERMANY DIPLOM CHOOSE GP/REL TOTALISM SOVEREIGN 20 HITLER/A. PAGE 50 A1013
FASCISM WORKER POL/PAR NAT/LISM

B61
KHAN A.W.,INDIA WINS FREEDOM: THE OTHER SIDE. INDIA PAKISTAN CULTURE LEGIS DIPLOM PARL/PROC REV WAR NAT/LISM 20. PAGE 78 A1607
SOVEREIGN GP/REL RACE/REL ORD/FREE

B61
LARSON A.,WHEN NATIONS DISAGREE. USA+45 WOR+45 INT/ORG ADJUD COERCE CRIME OWN SOVEREIGN...POLICY JURID 20. PAGE 85 A1734
INT/LAW DIPLOM WAR

B61
MATTHEWS T.,WAR IN ALGERIA. ALGERIA FRANCE CONTROL ATTIT SOVEREIGN 20. PAGE 96 A1978
REV COLONIAL DIPLOM WAR

B61
OAKES J.B.,THE EDGE OF FREEDOM. EUR+WWI USA+45 USSR ECO/UNDEV BAL/PWR DIPLOM DOMIN COLONIAL PWR MARXISM POPULISM...IDEA/COMP 20 COLD/WAR. PAGE 111 A2271
AFR ORD/FREE SOVEREIGN NEUTRAL

B61
PANIKKAR K.M.,REVOLUTION IN AFRICA. AFR GUINEA ECO/UNDEV POL/PAR DIPLOM COLONIAL EXEC LEAD SOVEREIGN...CHARTS 20. PAGE 114 A2332
NAT/LISM NAT/G CHIEF

B61
RICE G.W.,THE SOVIET POSITION ON DEPENDENT TERRITORIES IN THE UNITED NATIONS (THESIS, OHIO STATE UNIVERSITY). USSR PLAN SOVEREIGN...POLICY 20 UN. PAGE 121 A2473
INT/ORG COM DIPLOM COLONIAL

B61
ROSENAU J.N.,INTERNATIONAL POLITICS AND FOREIGN POLICY: A READER IN RESEARCH AND THEORY. ELITES ATTIT SOVEREIGN...DECISION CHARTS HYPO/EXP GAME SIMUL ANTHOL BIBLIOG METH 20. PAGE 124 A2531
ACT/RES DIPLOM CONCPT POLICY

B61
STONE J.,QUEST FOR SURVIVAL. WOR+45 NAT/G VOL/ASSN LEGIT ADMIN ARMS/CONT COERCE DISPL ORD/FREE PWR ...POLICY INT/LAW JURID COLD/WAR 20. PAGE 139 A2836
INT/ORG ADJUD SOVEREIGN

B61
SYATAUW J.J.G.,SOME NEWLY ESTABLISHED ASIAN STATES AND THE DEVELOPMENT OF INTERNATIONAL LAW. BURMA CEYLON INDIA INDONESIA ECO/UNDEV COLONIAL NEUTRAL WAR PEACE SOVEREIGN...CHARTS 19/20. PAGE 140 A2873
INT/LAW ADJUST SOCIETY S/ASIA

B61
WINTER R.C.,BLUEPRINTS FOR INDEPENDENCE. WOR+45 INT/ORG DIPLOM COLONIAL CONTROL REV WAR PWR ...BIBLIOG 20 UN. PAGE 165 A3367
NAT/G ECO/UNDEV SOVEREIGN CONSTN

B61
YDIT M.,INTERNATIONALISED TERRITORIES. FUT WOR+45 WOR-45 CONSTN VOL/ASSN CREATE PLAN LEGIT PEACE ORD/FREE...GEOG INT/LAW JURID SOC NEW/IDEA OBS RECORD SAMP TIME/SEQ TREND 19/20 BERLIN. PAGE 169 A3431
LOC/G INT/ORG DIPLOM SOVEREIGN

S61
MACHOWSKI K.,"SELECTED PROBLEMS OF NATIONAL SOVEREIGNTY WITH REFERENCE TO THE LAW OF OUTER SPACE." FUT WOR+45 AIR LAW INTELL SOCIETY ECO/DEV PLAN EDU/PROP DETER DRIVE PERCEPT SOVEREIGN ...POLICY INT/LAW OBS TREND TOT/POP 20. PAGE 92 A1889
UNIV ACT/RES NUC/PWR SPACE

S61
OCHENG D.,"ECONOMIC FORCES AND UGANDA'S FOREIGN POLICY." AFR UGANDA INT/TRADE TARIFFS INCOME SOVEREIGN WEALTH 20 EACM EEC TANGANYIKA. PAGE 111 A2274
ECO/TAC DIPLOM ECO/UNDEV INT/ORG

S61
OCHENG D.,"AN ECONOMIST LOOKS AT UGANDA'S FUTURE." FUT UGANDA AGRI INDUS PLAN PROB/SOLV INT/TRADE SOVEREIGN 20. PAGE 111 A2275
ECO/UNDEV INCOME ECO/TAC OWN

B62
ALTHING F.A.M.,EUROPEAN ORGANIZATIONS AND FOREIGN RELATIONS OF STATES: A COMPARATIVE ANALYSIS OF DECISION-MAKING. EUR+WWI CONSTN ELITES BAL/PWR INT/TRADE SOVEREIGN TREATY. PAGE 6 A0131
DELIB/GP INT/ORG DECISION DIPLOM

B62
APATHEKER H.,AMERICAN FOREIGN POLICY AND THE COLD WAR. USA+45 NAT/G POL/PAR COLONIAL NAT/LISM SOVEREIGN MARXISM SOCISM 20 COLD/WAR MARX/KARL LENIN/VI INTERVENT. PAGE 8 A0167
DIPLOM WAR PEACE

B62
BRYANT A.,A CHOICE FOR DESTINY: COMMONWEALTH AND THE COMMON MARKET. EUR+WWI FUT UK INT/TRADE COLONIAL ATTIT SOVEREIGN 20 CMN/WLTH EEC. PAGE 20 A0411
INT/ORG VOL/ASSN DIPLOM CHOOSE

B62
DUTOIT B.,LA NEUTRALITE SUISSE A L'HEURE EUROPEENNE. EUR+WWI MOD/EUR INT/ORG NAT/G VOL/ASSN PLAN BAL/PWR LEGIT NEUTRAL REGION PEACE ORD/FREE SOVEREIGN...CONCPT OBS TIME/SEQ TREND STERTYP VAL/FREE LEAGUE/NAT UN 20. PAGE 40 A0812
ATTIT DIPLOM SWITZERLND

B62
GUENA Y.,HISTORIQUE DE LA COMMUNAUTE. FUT ECO/UNDEV NAT/G PLAN EDU/PROP COLONIAL REGION NAT/LISM ALL/VALS SOVEREIGN...CONCPT OBS CHARTS 20. PAGE 58 A1186
AFR VOL/ASSN FOR/AID FRANCE

B62
KENT R.K.,FROM MADAGASCAR TO THE MALAGASY REPUBLIC. FRANCE MADAGASCAR DIPLOM NAT/LISM ORD/FREE...MGT 18/20. PAGE 78 A1596
COLONIAL SOVEREIGN REV POL/PAR

B62
LAQUEUR W.,POLYCENTRISM. CHINA/COM COM USSR WOR+45 INT/ORG NAT/G ECO/TAC DOMIN LEAD ATTIT PWR SOVEREIGN...ANTHOL 20. PAGE 85 A1732
MARXISM DIPLOM BAL/PWR POLICY

B62
RIMALOV V.V.,ECONOMIC COOPERATION BETWEEN USSR AND
FOR/AID

UNDERDEVELOPED COUNTRIES. USSR FINAN TEC/DEV INT/TRADE DOMIN EDU/PROP COLONIAL NAT/LISM DRIVE SOVEREIGN...AUD/VIS 20. PAGE 121 A2482
PLAN ECO/UNDEV DIPLOM

B62
SCHRODER P.M.,METTERNICH'S DIPLOMACY AT ITS ZENITH, 1820-1823. MOD/EUR ELITES INT/ORG VOL/ASSN DELIB/GP ECO/TAC EDU/PROP DISPL PWR SOVEREIGN...POLICY CONCPT GEN/LAWS 19 METTRNCH/K. PAGE 129 A2647
ORD/FREE BIOG BAL/PWR DIPLOM

B62
SNYDER L.L.D.,THE IMPERIALISM READER. AFR ASIA CHINA/COM COM EUR+WWI FUT MOD/EUR USA+45 WOR+45 WOR-45 INT/ORG COLONIAL SOVEREIGN CMN/WLTH OAS 20. PAGE 134 A2751
DOMIN PWR DIPLOM

B62
TAYLOR D.,THE BRITISH IN AFRICA. UK CULTURE ECO/UNDEV INDUS DIPLOM INT/TRADE ADMIN WAR RACE/REL ORD/FREE SOVEREIGN...POLICY BIBLIOG 15/20 CMN/WLTH. PAGE 142 A2898
AFR COLONIAL DOMIN

B62
US DEPARTMENT OF THE ARMY,AFRICA: ITS PROBLEMS AND PROSPECTS. CHINA/COM USSR INT/ORG FOR/AID COLONIAL LEAD FEDERAL DRIVE SOVEREIGN MARXISM...GEOG 20 COLD/WAR. PAGE 152 A3104
BIBLIOG/A AFR NAT/LISM DIPLOM

B62
WRIGHT Q.,PREVENTING WORLD WAR THREE. FUT WOR+45 CULTURE INT/ORG NAT/G CONSULT FORCES ADMIN ARMS/CONT DRIVE RIGID/FLEX ORD/FREE SOVEREIGN ...POLICY CONCPT TREND STERTYP COLD/WAR 20. PAGE 168 A3416
CREATE ATTIT

L62
CORET A.,"LES PROVINCES PORTUGALLES D'OUTREMER ET L'ONU." AFR PORTUGAL S/ASIA WOR+45 LOC/G NAT/G DOMIN...CONCPT TIME/SEQ UN 20 GOA. PAGE 31 A0620
INT/ORG SOVEREIGN COLONIAL

L62
CORET A.,"L'INDEPENDANCE DU SAMOA OCCIDENTAL." S/ASIA LAW INT/ORG EXEC ALL/VALS SAMOA UN 20. PAGE 31 A0622
NAT/G STRUCT SOVEREIGN

L62
MURACCIOLE L.,"LA LOI FONDAMENTALE DE LA REPUBLIQUE DU CONGO." WOR+45 SOCIETY ECO/UNDEV INT/ORG NAT/G LEGIS PLAN LEGIT ADJUD COLONIAL ROUTINE ATTIT SOVEREIGN 20 CONGO. PAGE 106 A2174
AFR CONSTN

S62
CLEVELAND H.,"THE FUTURE ROLE OF THE UNITED STATES IN THE UNITED NATIONS." USA+45 ECO/UNDEV INT/ORG EX/STRUC DIPLOM FOR/AID ROUTINE SKILL SOVEREIGN WEALTH UN 20. PAGE 27 A0550
FUT ATTIT

S62
CORET A.,"LA DECLARATION DE L'ASSEMBLEE GENERAL DE L'ONU SUR L'OCTROI DE L'INDEPENDENCE AUX PAYS ET AUX PEUPLES." AFR ASIA ISLAM NIGERIA S/ASIA USSR WOR+45 ECO/UNDEV NAT/G DELIB/GP COLONIAL ALL/VALS ...CONCPT TIME/SEQ TREND UN TOT/POP 20 MEXIC/AMER. PAGE 31 A0621
INT/ORG STRUCT SOVEREIGN

S62
DE MADARIAGA S.,"TOWARD THE UNITED STATES OF EUROPE." EUR+WWI PLAN DOMIN FEDERAL ATTIT PWR SOVEREIGN...GEOG TOT/POP 20. PAGE 35 A0707
FUT INT/ORG

S62
DEUTSCH K.W.,"TOWARDS WESTERN EUROPEAN INTEGRATION: AN INTERIM ASSESSMENT." EUR+WWI STRUCT ECO/DEV INT/ORG ECO/TAC INT/TRADE EDU/PROP PEACE ATTIT DRIVE PWR SOVEREIGN...PSY SOC TIME/SEQ CHARTS STERTYP 20. PAGE 36 A0741
VOL/ASSN RIGID/FLEX REGION

S62
FALK R.A.,"THE REALITY OF INTERNATIONAL LAW." WOR+45 NAT/G LEGIT COERCE DETER WAR MORAL ORD/FREE PWR SOVEREIGN...JURID CONCPT VAL/FREE COLD/WAR 20. PAGE 43 A0887
INT/ORG ADJUD NUC/PWR INT/LAW

S62
GREEN L.C.,"POLITICAL OFFENSES, WAR CRIMES AND EXTRADITION." WOR+45 YUGOSLAVIA INT/ORG LEGIT ROUTINE WAR ORD/FREE SOVEREIGN...JURID NAZI 20 INTERPOL. PAGE 55 A1138
LAW CONCPT INT/LAW

S62
LISSITZYN O.J.,"SOME LEGAL IMPLICATIONS OF THE U-2 AND RB-47 INCIDENTS." FUT USA+45 USSR WOR+45 AIR NAT/G DIPLOM LEGIT MORAL ORD/FREE SOVEREIGN...JURID GEN/LAWS GEN/METH COLD/WAR 20 U-2. PAGE 90 A1840
LAW CONCPT SPACE INT/LAW

B63
BROWN W.N.,THE UNITED STATES AND INDIA AND PAKISTAN (REV. ED.). INDIA PAKISTAN S/ASIA WOR+45 POL/PAR SECT INT/TRADE COLONIAL COERCE DISCRIM. PAGE 20 A0408
DIPLOM ECO/UNDEV SOVEREIGN STRUCT

B63
BURNS A.L.,PEACE-KEEPING BY U.N.FORCES - FROM SUEZ TO THE CONGO. AFR FUT ISLAM ISRAEL USSR WOR+45 NAT/G DELIB/GP BAL/PWR DOMIN LEGIT EXEC COERCE PEACE ATTIT PWR RESPECT SOVEREIGN...CONCPT UN 20. PAGE 22 A0441
INT/ORG FORCES ORD/FREE

B63
CROZIER B.,THE MORNING AFTER; A STUDY OF INDEPENDENCE. WOR+45 EX/STRUC PLAN BAL/PWR COLONIAL GP/REL 20 COLD/WAR. PAGE 33 A0666
SOVEREIGN NAT/LISM NAT/G DIPLOM

B63
DUNN F.S.,PEACE-MAKING AND THE SETTLEMENT WITH JAPAN. ASIA USA+45 USA-45 FORCES BAL/PWR ECO/TAC CONFER WAR PWR SOVEREIGN 20 CHINJAP COLD/WAR TREATY. PAGE 39 A0802
POLICY PEACE PLAN DIPLOM

B63
ELLENDER A.J.,A REPORT ON UNITED STATES FOREIGN OPERATIONS IN AFRICA. SOUTH/AFR USA+45 STRATA EXTR/IND FORCES RACE/REL ISOLAT SOVEREIGN...CHARTS 20 NEGRO. PAGE 41 A0840
FOR/AID DIPLOM WEALTH ECO/UNDEV

B63
FRANZ G.,TEILUNG UND WIEDERVEREINIGUNG. GERMANY IRELAND ITALY NETHERLAND POLAND CULTURE BAL/PWR CHOOSE NAT/LISM ORD/FREE SOVEREIGN 19/20. PAGE 48 A0987
DIPLOM WAR NAT/COMP ATTIT

B63
GARDINIER D.E.,CAMEROON: UNITED NATIONS CHALLENGE TO FRENCH POLICY. AFR CAMEROON FRANCE NAT/G LEGIS CONTROL SOVEREIGN 20 UN. PAGE 51 A1042
DIPLOM POLICY INT/ORG COLONIAL

B63
HAILEY L.,THE REPUBLIC OF SOUTH AFRICA AND THE HIGH COMMISSION TERRITORIES. AFR SOUTH/AFR UK INT/ORG NAT/G PROVS RACE/REL SOVEREIGN...CHARTS 19/20 COMMONWLTH. PAGE 59 A1219
COLONIAL DIPLOM ATTIT

B63
HALEY A.G.,SPACE LAW AND GOVERNMENT. FUT USA+45 WOR+45 LEGIS ACT/RES CREATE ATTIT RIGID/FLEX ORD/FREE PWR SOVEREIGN...POLICY JURID CONCPT CHARTS VAL/FREE 20. PAGE 60 A1226
INT/ORG LAW SPACE

B63
HUSSEY W.D.,THE BRITISH EMPIRE AND COMMONWEALTH 1500 TO 1961. UK USA-45 SOCIETY ECO/UNDEV NAT/G VOL/ASSN INT/TRADE DOMIN CONTROL WAR PWR ...DICTIONARY 16/20 COMMONWLTH TRUST/TERR. PAGE 69 A1422
COLONIAL SOVEREIGN INT/ORG

B63
KORBEL J.,POLAND BETWEEN EAST AND WEST: SOVIET AND GERMAN DIPLOMACY TOWARD POLAND 1919-1933. EUR+WWI GERMANY POLAND USSR FORCES AGREE WAR SOVEREIGN ...BIBLIOG 20 TREATY. PAGE 81 A1670
BAL/PWR DIPLOM DOMIN NAT/LISM

B63
LAFEBER W.,THE NEW EMPIRE: AN INTERPRETATION OF AMERICAN EXPANSION, 1860-1898. USA-45 CONSTN NAT/LISM SOVEREIGN...TREND BIBLIOG 19/20. PAGE 84 A1711
INDUS NAT/G DIPLOM CAP/ISM

B63
LEE C.,THE POLITICS OF KOREAN NATIONALISM. KOREA S/ASIA DIPLOM REV WAR 14/20 CHINJAP. PAGE 86 A1759
NAT/LISM SOVEREIGN COLONIAL

B63
MANSERGH N.,DOCUMENTS AND SPEECHES ON COMMONWEALTH AFFAIRS 1952-1962. CANADA INDIA PAKISTAN UK CONSTN FORCES ECO/TAC EDU/PROP COLONIAL DETER WAR ORD/FREE SOVEREIGN...POLICY 20 AUSTRAL. PAGE 94 A1932
BIBLIOG/A FEDERAL INT/TRADE DIPLOM

B63
MONTER W.,THE GOVERNMENT OF GENEVA, 1536-1605 (DOCTORAL THESIS). SWITZERLND DIPLOM LEAD ORD/FREE SOVEREIGN 16/17 CALVIN/J ROME. PAGE 103 A2112
SECT FINAN LOC/G ADMIN

B63
PADELFORD N.J.,AFRICA AND WORLD ORDER. AFR COLONIAL SOVEREIGN...ANTHOL BIBLIOG 20 UN UNIFICA COMMONWLTH. PAGE 113 A2312
DIPLOM NAT/G ORD/FREE

B63
PERKINS B.,PROLOGUE TO THE WAR: ENGLAND AND THE UNITED STATES, 1805-1812. MOD/EUR UK USA-45 NAT/G ORD/FREE RESPECT SOVEREIGN...POLICY TREATY 19 WAR/1812. PAGE 115 A2358
WAR DIPLOM NEUTRAL

B63
RIUKIN A.,THE AFRICAN PRESENCE IN WORLD AFFAIRS. AFR WOR+45 ECO/UNDEV AGRI INT/ORG BAL/PWR ECO/TAC COLONIAL NEUTRAL NAT/LISM PEACE SOVEREIGN 20 UN. PAGE 121 A2486
DIPLOM NAT/G POLICY PWR

B63
SMITH J.E.,THE DEFENSE OF BERLIN. COM GUATEMALA WOR+45 ECO/TAC ADMIN NEUTRAL ATTIT ORD/FREE SOVEREIGN...DECISION 20 DEPT/STATE. PAGE 134 A2747
DIPLOM FORCES BAL/PWR PLAN

B63
VON HALLER A.,DIE LETZTEN WOLLEN DIE ERSTEN SEIN. AFR S/ASIA INT/TRADE REV ORD/FREE SOVEREIGN 20. PAGE 160 A3251
FOR/AID ECO/UNDEV MARXISM CAP/ISM

S63
BANFIELD J.,"FEDERATION IN EAST-AFRICA." AFR UGANDA ELITES INT/ORG NAT/G VOL/ASSN LEGIS ECO/TAC FEDERAL ATTIT SOVEREIGN TOT/POP 20 TANGANYIKA. PAGE 11 A0216
EX/STRUC PWR REGION

S63
BELOFF M.,"BRITAIN, EUROPE AND THE ATLANTIC COMMUNITY." EUR+WWI ELITES NAT/G VOL/ASSN TOP/EX ATTIT ORD/FREE PWR SOVEREIGN WEALTH EEC TOT/POP VAL/FREE CMN/WLTH 20. PAGE 13 A0262
INT/ORG ECO/DEV UK

S63
ETZIONI A.,"EUROPEAN UNIFICATION AND PERSPECTIVES
INT/ORG

ON SOVEREIGNTY." EUR+WWI FUT DELIB/GP TEC/DEV ECO/TAC EDU/PROP DETER NUC/PWR ATTIT DRIVE ORD/FREE PWR WEALTH...CONCPT RECORD TIME/SEQ EEC VAL/FREE 20. PAGE 43 A0870
ECO/DEV SOVEREIGN

S63
HINDLEY D.,"FOREIGN AID TO INDONESIA AND ITS POLITICAL IMPLICATIONS." INDONESIA POL/PAR ATTIT SOVEREIGN...CHARTS 20. PAGE 65 A1336
FOR/AID NAT/G WEALTH ECO/TAC

S63
MCDOUGAL M.S.,"THE SOVIET-CUBAN QUARANTINE AND SELF-DEFENSE." CUBA USA+45 USSR WOR+45 INT/ORG NAT/G BAL/PWR NUC/PWR ATTIT...JURID CONCPT. PAGE 98 A2008
ORD/FREE LEGIT SOVEREIGN

S63
WEISSBERG G.,"MAPS AS EVIDENCE IN INTERNATIONAL BOUNDARY DISPUTES: A REAPPRAISAL." CHINA/COM EUR+WWI INDIA MOD/EUR S/ASIA INT/ORG NAT/G LEGIT PERCEPT...JURID CHARTS 20. PAGE 163 A3311
LAW GEOG SOVEREIGN

N63
PATEL H.M.,THE DEFENCE OF INDIA (PAMPHLET). CHINA/COM INDIA PAKISTAN WOR+45 TEC/DEV BAL/PWR DIPLOM CONTROL WAR. PAGE 114 A2340
FORCES POLICY SOVEREIGN DETER

B64
ARNOLD G.,TOWARDS PEACE AND A MULTIRACIAL COMMONWEALTH. UK TEC/DEV BAL/PWR COLONIAL GP/REL NAT/LISM PEACE SOVEREIGN...POLICY SOC/INTEG 20 CMN/WLTH. PAGE 9 A0175
DIPLOM INT/TRADE FOR/AID ORD/FREE

B64
BARKER A.J.,SUEZ: THE SEVEN DAY WAR. EUR+WWI ISLAM UAR INT/ORG NAT/G PLAN DIPLOM ECO/TAC DOMIN NAT/LISM DRIVE RIGID/FLEX PWR SOVEREIGN...POLICY JURID TREND CHARTS SUEZ UN 20. PAGE 11 A0221
FORCES COERCE UK

B64
CASEY R.G.,THE FUTURE OF THE COMMONWEALTH. INDIA PAKISTAN UK ECO/UNDEV INT/ORG TEC/DEV COLONIAL SUPEGO 20 EEC AUSTRAL. PAGE 25 A0505
DIPLOM SOVEREIGN NAT/LISM FOR/AID

B64
COX R.,PAN-AFRICANISM IN PRACTICE. AFR DIPLOM CONFER RACE/REL ROLE SOVEREIGN...POLICY 20 PANAF/FREE. PAGE 32 A0645
ORD/FREE COLONIAL REGION NAT/LISM

B64
DE SMITH S.A.,THE NEW COMMONWEALTH AND ITS CONSTITUTIONS. AFR CYPRUS PAKISTAN S/ASIA INT/ORG NAT/G LEGIS LEGIT RIGID/FLEX PWR...CONCPT TIME/SEQ CMN/WLTH 20. PAGE 35 A0713
EX/STRUC CONSTN SOVEREIGN

B64
DESHMUKH C.D.,THE COMMONWEALTH AS INDIA SEES IT. INDIA UK ECO/UNDEV TEC/DEV INT/TRADE GP/REL RACE/REL SOVEREIGN SOC/INTEG 19/20 COMMONWLTH. PAGE 36 A0733
DIPLOM COLONIAL NAT/LISM ATTIT

B64
DUROSELLE J.B.,LA COMMUNAUTE INTERNATIONALE FACE AUX JEUNES ETATS. CHINA/COM COM S/ASIA USSR INT/ORG ROLE...ANTHOL 20 UN SEATO THIRD/WRLD. PAGE 40 A0808
DIPLOM COLONIAL ECO/UNDEV SOVEREIGN

B64
EAYRS J.,THE COMMONWEALTH AND SUEZ: A DOCUMENTARY SURVEY. FRANCE ISLAM VOL/ASSN FORCES CONFER COLONIAL WAR INGP/REL 20 CMN/WLTH SUEZ UN. PAGE 40 A0818
DIPLOM NAT/LISM DIST/IND SOVEREIGN

B64
GREAT BRITAIN CENTRAL OFF INF,CONSTITUTIONAL DEVELOPMENT IN THE COMMONWEALTH. VOL/ASSN PLAN DIPLOM COLONIAL INGP/REL NAT/LISM ORD/FREE PWR 17/20 CMN/WLTH. PAGE 55 A1135
REGION CONSTN NAT/G SOVEREIGN

B64
KOLARZ W.,COMMUNISM AND COLONIALISM. AFR ASIA USSR DISCRIM ATTIT ORD/FREE SOVEREIGN SOC/INTEG 20. PAGE 81 A1668
EDU/PROP DIPLOM TOTALISM COLONIAL

B64
LUARD E.,THE COLD WAR: A RE-APPRAISAL. FUT USSR WOR+45 FORCES NUC/PWR NAT/LISM ORD/FREE SOVEREIGN ...INT 20 COLD/WAR STALIN/J TREATY UN. PAGE 91 A1870
DIPLOM WAR PEACE TOTALISM

B64
NEWBURY C.W.,THE WEST AFRICAN COMMONWEALTH. CONSTN INTELL ECO/UNDEV VOL/ASSN CHIEF DELIB/GP LEGIS INT/TRADE COLONIAL FEDERAL ATTIT 20 COMMONWLTH AFRICA/W. PAGE 108 A2223
INT/ORG SOVEREIGN GOV/REL AFR

B64
PENNOCK J.R.,SELF-GOVERNMENT IN MODERNIZING NATIONS. AFR COM USA+45 ECO/DEV POL/PAR PROB/SOLV DIPLOM ECO/TAC COLONIAL REV POPULISM SOCISM 20. PAGE 114 A2350
ECO/UNDEV POLICY SOVEREIGN NAT/G

B64
QUIGG P.W.,AFRICA: A FOREIGN AFFAIRS READER. AFR FRANCE PORTUGAL UK DIPLOM LEAD PARL/PROC MARXISM ...MAJORIT METH/CNCPT GOV/COMP IDEA/COMP ANTHOL 19/20. PAGE 118 A2426
COLONIAL SOVEREIGN NAT/LISM RACE/REL

B64
SCHECHTER A.H.,INTERPRETATION OF AMBIGUOUS DOCUMENTS BY INTERNATIONAL ADMINISTRATIVE TRIBUNALS. WOR+45 EX/STRUC INT/TRADE CT/SYS SOVEREIGN 20 UN ILO EURCT/JUST. PAGE 128 A2620
INT/LAW DIPLOM INT/ORG ADJUD

B64
STANGER R.J.,ESSAYS ON INTERVENTION. PLAN PROB/SOLV BAL/PWR ADJUD COERCE WAR ROLE PWR...INT/LAW CONCPT 20 UN INTERVENT. PAGE 137 A2803
SOVEREIGN DIPLOM POLICY LEGIT

B64
THANT U.,TOWARD WORLD PEACE. DELIB/GP TEC/DEV EDU/PROP WAR SOVEREIGN...INT/LAW 20 UN MID/EAST. PAGE 142 A2907
DIPLOM BIOG PEACE COERCE

B64
VECCHIO G.D.,L'ETAT ET LE DROIT. ITALY CONSTN EX/STRUC LEGIS DIPLOM CT/SYS...JURID 20 UN. PAGE 158 A3225
NAT/G SOVEREIGN CONCPT INT/LAW

B64
VOELKMANN K.,HERRSCHER VON MORGEN? BAL/PWR COLONIAL NEUTRAL REGION RACE/REL ALL/VALS SOVEREIGN...RECORD 20 COLD/WAR THIRD/WRLD. PAGE 159 A3246
DIPLOM ECO/UNDEV CONTROL NAT/COMP

B64
WOODHOUSE C.M.,THE NEW CONCERT OF NATIONS. WOR+45 ECO/DEV ECO/UNDEV NAT/G BAL/PWR ECO/TAC NAT/LISM PWR SOVEREIGN ALL/IDEOS 20 UN COLD/WAR. PAGE 166 A3391
DIPLOM MORAL FOR/AID COLONIAL

B64
WRIGHT Q.,A STUDY OF WAR. LAW NAT/G PROB/SOLV BAL/PWR NAT/LISM PEACE ATTIT SOVEREIGN...CENSUS SOC/INTEG. PAGE 168 A3419
WAR CONCPT DIPLOM CONTROL

S64
GARMARNIKOW M.,"INFLUENCE-BUYING IN WEST AFRICA." COM FUT USSR INTELL NAT/G PLAN TEC/DEV ECO/TAC DOMIN EDU/PROP REGION NAT/LISM ATTIT DRIVE ALL/VALS SOVEREIGN...POLICY PSY SOC CONCPT TREND STERTYP WORK COLD/WAR 20. PAGE 51 A1049
AFR ECO/UNDEV FOR/AID SOCISM

S64
MAZRUI A.A.,"THE UNITED NATIONS AND SOME AFRICAN POLITICAL ATTITUDES." ECO/TAC FOR/AID DOMIN ROUTINE CHOOSE ATTIT DRIVE MORAL PWR RESPECT WEALTH...PSY CONCPT OBS TREND UN VAL/FREE 20. PAGE 97 A1987
AFR INT/ORG SOVEREIGN

B65
ADENAUER K.,MEMOIRS 1945-53. EUR+WWI GERMANY/W ECO/DEV CHIEF FORCES ECO/TAC WAR GOV/REL PWR SOVEREIGN 20 NATO ADENAUER/K. PAGE 4 A0088
BIOG DIPLOM NAT/G PERS/REL

B65
ADENAUER K.,MEINE ERINNERUNGEN, 1945-53 (VOL. I), 1953-55 (VOL. II). EUR+WWI GERMANY CHIEF FORCES PROB/SOLV DIPLOM ARMS/CONT INGP/REL PEACE SOVEREIGN ...OBS/ENVIR RECORD 20. PAGE 4 A0089
NAT/G BIOG SELF/OBS

B65
CALLEO D.P.,EUROPE'S FUTURE: THE GRAND ALTERNATIVES. UK INT/ORG DIPLOM PWR SOVEREIGN ...CONCPT IDEA/COMP NAT/COMP BIBLIOG 20 EEC EUROPE DEGAULLE/C NATO. PAGE 23 A0468
FUT EUR+WWI FEDERAL NAT/LISM

B65
CASSELL F.,GOLD OR CREDIT? THE ECONOMICS AND POLITICS OF INTERNATIONAL MONEY. WOR+45 PLAN PROB/SOLV BAL/PAY SOVEREIGN WEALTH 20 OEEC GOLD/STAND. PAGE 25 A0506
FINAN INT/ORG DIPLOM ECO/TAC

B65
COWEN Z.,THE BRITISH COMMONWEALTH OF NATIONS IN A CHANGING WORLD. UK ECO/UNDEV INT/ORG ECO/TAC INT/TRADE COLONIAL WAR GP/REL RACE/REL SOVEREIGN SOC/INTEG 20 TREATY EEC COMMONWLTH. PAGE 32 A0644
JURID DIPLOM PARL/PROC NAT/LISM

B65
COX R.H.,THE STATE IN INTERNATIONAL RELATIONS. INT/ORG DIPLOM REV WAR PEACE MARXISM...CONCPT GOV/COMP. PAGE 32 A0647
SOVEREIGN NAT/G FASCISM ORD/FREE

B65
FAGG J.E.,CUBA, HAITI, AND THE DOMINICAN REPUBLIC. CUBA DOMIN/REP HAITI L/A+17C NAT/G DIPLOM ECO/TAC DOMIN CHOOSE AUTHORIT ROLE SOVEREIGN POPULISM 17/20. PAGE 43 A0883
COLONIAL ECO/UNDEV REV GOV/COMP

B65
FALK R.A.,THE AFTERMATH OF SABBATINO: BACKGROUND PAPERS AND PROCEEDINGS OF SEVENTH HAMMARSKJOLD FORUM. USA+45 LAW ACT/RES ADJUD ROLE...BIBLIOG 20 EXPROPRIAT SABBATINO HARLAN/JM. PAGE 44 A0891
SOVEREIGN CT/SYS INT/LAW OWN

B65
FANON F.,STUDIES IN A DYING COLONIALISM. ALGERIA FRANCE STRATA FAM DIPLOM DOMIN WAR RACE/REL DISCRIM HEALTH 20. PAGE 44 A0897
NAT/LISM COLONIAL REV SOVEREIGN

B65
IRIYE A.,AFTER IMPERIALISM; THE SEARCH FOR A NEW ORDER IN THE FAR EAST 1921-1931. USA-45 USSR DOMIN AGREE COLONIAL REV PWR...BIBLIOG DICTIONARY 20 CHINJAP. PAGE 72 A1468
DIPLOM ASIA SOVEREIGN

B65
JOHNSTON D.M.,THE INTERNATIONAL LAW OF FISHERIES: A CONCPT

FRAMEWORK FOR POLICYORIENTED INQUIRIES. WOR+45 ACT/RES PLAN PROB/SOLV CONTROL SOVEREIGN. PAGE 75 A1527
EXTR/IND JURID DIPLOM

B65
JOHNSTONE A.,UNITED STATES DIRECT INVESTMENT IN FRANCE: AN INVESTIGATION OF THE FRENCH CHARGES. FRANCE USA+45 ECO/DEV INDUS LG/CO NAT/G ECO/TAC CONTROL WEALTH...BIBLIOG 20 INTERVENT. PAGE 75 A1529
FINAN DIPLOM POLICY SOVEREIGN

B65
KIRKWOOD K.,BRITAIN AND AFRICA. AFR UK ECO/UNDEV ECO/TAC WAR NAT/LISM SOVEREIGN 19/20. PAGE 80 A1636
NAT/G DIPLOM POLICY COLONIAL

B65
LERCHE C.O.,THE COLD WAR AND AFTER. AFR COM S/ASIA USA+45 USSR NUC/PWR SOVEREIGN MARXISM...TIME/SEQ TREND BIBLIOG 20 COLD/WAR. PAGE 87 A1784
DIPLOM BAL/PWR IDEA/COMP

B65
LOEWENHEIM F.L.,PEACE OR APPEASEMENT? HITLER, CHAMBERLAIN AND THE MUNICH CRISIS. MUNIC DELIB/GP WAR TOTALISM ATTIT SOVEREIGN...TIME/SEQ ANTHOL BIBLIOG 20 HITLER/A CHAMBRLN/N. PAGE 90 A1851
DIPLOM LEAD PEACE

B65
MANSFIELD P.,NASSER'S EGYPT. AFR ISLAM UAR ECO/UNDEV AGRI COLONIAL SOVEREIGN...CHARTS 20 NASSER/G MID/EAST. PAGE 94 A1934
CHIEF ECO/TAC DIPLOM POLICY

B65
MILLER J.D.B.,THE COMMONWEALTH IN THE WORLD (3RD ED.). CONSTN COLONIAL PWR SOVEREIGN 20 CMN/WLTH. PAGE 101 A2077
VOL/ASSN INT/ORG INGP/REL DIPLOM

B65
MORRIS R.B.,THE PEACEMAKERS; THE GREAT POWERS AND AMERICAN INDEPENDENCE. BAL/PWR CONFER COLONIAL NEUTRAL PEACE ORD/FREE TREATY 18 PRE/US/AM. PAGE 105 A2149
SOVEREIGN REV DIPLOM

B65
NKRUMAH K.,NEO-COLONIALISM: THE LAST STAGE OF IMPERIALISM. AFR INT/ORG WORKER FOR/AID INT/TRADE EDU/PROP GOV/REL NAT/LISM SOVEREIGN POPULISM SOCISM ...SOCIALIST 20 THIRD/WRLD INTRVN/ECO. PAGE 109 A2243
COLONIAL DIPLOM ECO/UNDEV ECO/TAC

B65
QURESHI I.H.,THE STRUGGLE FOR PAKISTAN. INDIA PAKISTAN UK CULTURE LEGIS DIPLOM EDU/PROP COLONIAL ATTIT SOVEREIGN 19/20 MUSLIM. PAGE 118 A2429
GP/REL RACE/REL WAR SECT

B65
ROTBERG R.I.,A POLITICAL HISTORY OF TROPICAL AFRICA. EX/STRUC DIPLOM INT/TRADE DOMIN ADMIN RACE/REL NAT/LISM PWR SOVEREIGN...GEOG TIME/SEQ BIBLIOG 1/20. PAGE 124 A2545
AFR CULTURE COLONIAL

B65
RUBINSTEIN A.,THE CHALLENGE OF POLITICS: IDEAS AND ISSUES. BAL/PWR COLONIAL WAR TOTALISM ORD/FREE PWR MARXISM SOCISM...INT/LAW 20. PAGE 125 A2561
NAT/G SOVEREIGN DIPLOM NAT/LISM

B65
SHUKRI A.,THE CONCEPT OF SELF-DETERMINATION IN THE UNITED NATIONS. WOR+45 DIPLOM INT/TRADE SANCTION NAT/LISM...BIBLIOG 20 UN. PAGE 132 A2709
COLONIAL INT/ORG INT/LAW SOVEREIGN

B65
STOETZER O.C.,THE ORGANIZATION OF AMERICAN STATES. L/A+17C EX/STRUC FOR/AID CONFER PARL/PROC ORD/FREE SOVEREIGN...POLICY INT/LAW 20 OAS. PAGE 138 A2831
INT/ORG REGION DIPLOM BAL/PWR

B65
SULZBERGER C.L.,UNFINISHED REVOLUTION. USA+45 WOR+45 INT/ORG TEC/DEV BAL/PWR FOR/AID COLONIAL NEUTRAL PWR SOVEREIGN MARXISM 20. PAGE 140 A2863
DIPLOM ECO/UNDEV POLICY NAT/G

B65
WILLIAMSON J.A.,GREAT BRITAIN AND THE COMMONWEALTH. UK DOMIN COLONIAL INGP/REL...POLICY 18/20 CMN/WLTH. PAGE 165 A3355
NAT/G DIPLOM INT/ORG SOVEREIGN

S65
STEIN E.,"TOWARD SUPREMACY OF TREATY-CONSTITUTION BY JUDICIAL FIAT: ON THE MARGIN OF THE COSTA CASE." EUR+WWI ITALY WOR+45 INT/ORG NAT/G LEGIT REGION NAT/LISM PWR...JURID CONCPT TREND TOT/POP VAL/FREE 20. PAGE 138 A2816
ADJUD CONSTN SOVEREIGN INT/LAW

C65
SEARA M.V.,"COSMIC INTERNATIONAL LAW." LAW ACADEM ACT/RES DIPLOM COLONIAL CONTROL NUC/PWR SOVEREIGN ...GEN/LAWS BIBLIOG UN. PAGE 131 A2678
SPACE INT/LAW IDEA/COMP INT/ORG

B66
BROWNLIE I.,PRINCIPLES OF PUBLIC INTERNATIONAL LAW. WOR+45 WOR-45 LAW JUDGE REPAR ADJUD SOVEREIGN ...JURID T. PAGE 20 A0409
INT/LAW DIPLOM INT/ORG

B66
COPLIN W.D.,THE FUNCTIONS OF INTERNATIONAL LAW. WOR+45 ECO/DEV ECO/UNDEV ADJUD COLONIAL WAR OWN SOVEREIGN...POLICY GEN/LAWS 20. PAGE 30 A0611
INT/LAW DIPLOM INT/ORG

B66
DAENIKER G.,STRATEGIE DES KLEIN STAATS. SWITZERLND ACT/RES CREATE DIPLOM NEUTRAL DETER WAR WEAPON PWR SOVEREIGN...IDEA/COMP 20 COLD/WAR. PAGE 33 A0673
NUC/PWR PLAN FORCES NAT/G

B66
ESTHUS R.A.,THEODORE ROOSEVELT AND JAPAN. ASIA USA-45 FORCES CONFER WAR SOVEREIGN...BIBLIOG 20 CHINJAP. PAGE 42 A0864
DIPLOM DELIB/GP

B66
FERKISS V.C.,AFRICA'S SEARCH FOR IDENTITY. AFR USA+45 CULTURE ECO/UNDEV INT/ORG NAT/G COLONIAL MARXISM 20. PAGE 45 A0918
NAT/LISM SOVEREIGN DIPLOM ROLE

B66
GUPTA S.,KASHMIR - A STUDY IN INDIA-PAKISTAN RELATIONS. INDIA KASHMIR PAKISTAN CONSTN INT/ORG REV RACE/REL NAT/LISM 20 UN MUSLIM/LG. PAGE 58 A1194
DIPLOM GP/REL SOVEREIGN WAR

B66
HAY P.,FEDERALISM AND SUPRANATIONAL ORGANIZATIONS: PATTERNS FOR NEW LEGAL STRUCTURES. EUR+WWI LAW NAT/G VOL/ASSN DIPLOM PWR...NAT/COMP TREATY EEC. PAGE 63 A1294
SOVEREIGN FEDERAL INT/ORG INT/LAW

B66
HOLLINS E.J.,PEACE IS POSSIBLE: A READER FOR LAYMEN. WOR+45 CULTURE PLAN RISK AGE/Y ALL/VALS SOVEREIGN...PSY CONCPT TREND 20 UN JOHN/XXIII KENNAN/G MYRDAL/G. PAGE 67 A1370
PEACE DIPLOM INT/ORG NUC/PWR

B66
INTL ATOMIC ENERGY AGENCY,INTERNATIONAL CONVENTIONS ON CIVIL LIABILITY FOR NUCLEAR DAMAGE. FUT WOR+45 ADJUD WAR COST PEACE SOVEREIGN...JURID 20. PAGE 71 A1462
DIPLOM INT/ORG DELIB/GP NUC/PWR

B66
INTL CONF ON WORLD POLITICS-5,EASTERN EUROPE IN TRANSITION. EUR+WWI USSR ECO/TAC NAT/LISM ATTIT SOVEREIGN...CHARTS ANTHOL 20 TREATY WARSAW/P. PAGE 71 A1463
COM NAT/COMP MARXISM DIPLOM

B66
LENGYEL E.,AFRICA: PAST, PRESENT, AND FUTURE. FUT SOUTH/AFR COLONIAL RACE/REL SOVEREIGN...GEOG AUD/VIS CHARTS T 20 CONGO/LEOP NEGRO. PAGE 87 A1771
AFR CONSTN ECO/UNDEV

B66
LONDON K.,EASTERN EUROPE IN TRANSITION. CHINA/COM USSR DOMIN COLONIAL CENTRAL RIGID/FLEX PWR...SOC ANTHOL 20. PAGE 91 A1855
SOVEREIGN COM NAT/LISM DIPLOM

B66
LYND S.,THE OTHER SIDE. USA+45 VIETNAM/N NAT/G PEACE SOVEREIGN 20. PAGE 92 A1877
WAR POLICY MORAL DIPLOM

B66
MC LELLAN D.S.,THE COLD WAR IN TRANSITION. USSR WOR+45 CONTROL LEAD NUC/PWR NAT/LISM SOVEREIGN 20 COLD/WAR THIRD/WRLD. PAGE 97 A1994
BAL/PWR DETER DIPLOM POLICY

B66
MCINTYRE W.D.,COLONIES INTO COMMONWEALTH. UK CONSTN VOL/ASSN DOMIN CONTROL...BIBLIOG 18/20 CMN/WLTH. PAGE 98 A2012
DIPLOM INT/ORG COLONIAL SOVEREIGN

B66
MCKAY V.,AFRICAN DIPLOMACY STUDIES IN THE DETERMINANTS OF FOREIGN POLICY. AFR SOUTH/AFR CULTURE NEUTRAL REGION SOVEREIGN...INT/LAW GOV/COMP ANTHOL 20. PAGE 98 A2013
ECO/UNDEV RACE/REL CIVMIL/REL DIPLOM

B66
NANTWI E.K.,THE ENFORCEMENT OF INTERNATIONAL JUDICIAL DECISIONS AND ARBITAL AWARDS IN PUBLIC INTERNATIONAL LAW. WOR+45 WOR-45 JUDGE PROB/SOLV DIPLOM CT/SYS SUPEGO MORAL PWR RESPECT...METH/CNCPT 18/20 CASEBOOK. PAGE 107 A2196
INT/LAW ADJUD SOVEREIGN INT/ORG

B66
NATIONAL COUN APPLIED ECO RES,DEVELOPMENT WITHOUT AID. INDIA FINAN TEC/DEV EFFICIENCY...ANTHOL 20. PAGE 107 A2203
FOR/AID PLAN SOVEREIGN ECO/UNDEV

B66
VAN DYKE V.,INTERNATIONAL POLITICS. WOR+45 ECO/DEV ECO/UNDEV INT/ORG BAL/PWR AGREE ARMS/CONT NAT/LISM PEACE PWR...INT/LAW 20 TREATY UN. PAGE 158 A3212
DIPLOM NAT/G WAR SOVEREIGN

S66
GREEN L.C.,"RHODESIAN OIL: BOOTLEGGERS OR PIRATES?" AFR RHODESIA UK WOR+45 INT/ORG NAT/G DIPLOM LEGIT COLONIAL SOVEREIGN 20 UN OAU. PAGE 55 A1139
INT/TRADE SANCTION INT/LAW POLICY

C66
KULSKI W.W.,"DEGAULLE AND THE WORLD: THE FOREIGN POLICY OF THE FIFTH FRENCH REPUBLIC." FRANCE ECO/UNDEV POL/PAR BAL/PWR DETER NUC/PWR ATTIT PWR ...RECORD BIBLIOG DEGAULLE NATO EEC. PAGE 83 A1694
POLICY SOVEREIGN PERSON DIPLOM

B67
JAGAN C.,THE WEST ON TRIAL. GUYANA CONSTN ECO/UNDEV DIPLOM COERCE PWR SOVEREIGN...BIOG 20. PAGE 73 A1490 SOCISM CREATE PLAN COLONIAL

B67
MACRIDIS R.C.,FOREIGN POLICY IN WORLD POLITICS (3RD ED.). EX/STRUC BAL/PWR COLONIAL NAT/LISM SKILL SOVEREIGN WEALTH...CONCPT TIME/SEQ ANTHOL 20 COLD/WAR. PAGE 93 A1902 DIPLOM POLICY NAT/G IDEA/COMP

B67
MAZRUI A.A.,TOWARDS A PAX AFRICANA. AFR STRUCT ECO/UNDEV NAT/G DIPLOM COLONIAL REGION WAR ATTIT 20. PAGE 97 A1988 PEACE FORCES PROB/SOLV SOVEREIGN

B67
MILLER J.D.B.,THE POLITICS OF THE THIRD WORLD. AFR S/ASIA 20 UN. PAGE 101 A2078 INT/ORG DIPLOM COLONIAL SOVEREIGN

B67
NYERERE J.K.,FREEDOM AND UNITY/UHURU NA UMOJA: A SELECTION FROM WRITINGS AND SPEECHES, 1952-65. TANZANIA ELITES ECO/UNDEV INT/ORG NAT/G CREATE DIPLOM COLONIAL REGION RACE/REL...ANTHOL 20. PAGE 110 A2265 SOVEREIGN AFR TREND ORD/FREE

B67
SACHS M.Y.,THE WORLDMARK ENCYCLOPEDIA OF THE NATIONS (5 VOLS.). ELITES SOCIETY STRATA ECO/DEV ECO/UNDEV AGRI EXTR/IND FINAN LABOR LOC/G NAT/G POL/PAR SECT INT/TRADE SOVEREIGN...SOC 20. PAGE 126 A2585 WOR+45 INT/ORG BAL/PWR

B67
WALLERSTEIN I.,AFRICA* THE POLITICS OF UNITY. AFR INT/ORG REV SOVEREIGN...HIST/WRIT 20. PAGE 160 A3268 TREND DIPLOM ATTIT

L67
"RESTRICTIVE SOVEREIGN IMMUNITY, THE STATE DEPARTMENT, AND THE COURTS." USA+45 USA-45 EX/STRUC DIPLOM ADJUD CONTROL GOV/REL 19/20 DEPT/STATE SUPREME/CT. PAGE 4 A0080 SOVEREIGN ORD/FREE PRIVIL CT/SYS

L67
BODENHEIMER S.J.,"THE 'POLITICAL UNION' DEBATE IN EUROPE* A CASE STUDY IN INTERGOVERNMENTAL DIPLOMACY." EUR+WWI FUT NAT/G FORCES PLAN DEBATE SOVEREIGN...CONCPT PREDICT EEC NATO. PAGE 16 A0326 DIPLOM REGION INT/ORG

S67
CONNOR W.,"SELF-DETERMINATION: THE NEW PHASE." WOR+45 WOR-45 CULTURE INT/ORG COLONIAL 19/20. PAGE 29 A0588 NAT/LISM SOVEREIGN INGP/REL GP/REL

S67
HAZARD J.N.,"POST-DISARMAMENT INTERNATIONAL LAW." FUT USSR WOR+45 INT/ORG DELIB/GP FORCES DETER EQUILIB SOVEREIGN MARXISM 20 UN. PAGE 63 A1301 INT/LAW ARMS/CONT PWR PLAN

S67
KYLE K.,"BACKGROUND TO THE CRISIS" ISLAM ISRAEL UAR UK USSR NAT/G PROB/SOLV LEGIT CONTROL REGION STRANGE MORAL 20 JEWS. PAGE 83 A1698 DIPLOM POLICY SOVEREIGN COERCE

S67
ROTBERG R.I.,"COLONIALISM AND AFTER: THE POLITICAL LITERATURE OF CENTRAL AFRICA - A BIBLIOGRAPHIC ESSAY." AFR CHIEF EX/STRUC REV INGP/REL RACE/REL SOVEREIGN 20. PAGE 124 A2546 BIBLIOG/A COLONIAL DIPLOM NAT/G

S67
SCHUMANN H.,"IMPERIALISMUS-KRITIK UND KOLONIALISMUS-FORSCHUNG." GERMANY/E DIPLOM SOVEREIGN...SOC HIST/WRIT 20. PAGE 129 A2652 COLONIAL ATTIT DOMIN CAP/ISM

C67
SPANIER J.W.,"WORLD POLITICS IN AN AGE OF REVOLUTION." COM WOR+45 FORCES COERCE WAR NAT/LISM SOVEREIGN...POLICY BIBLIOG 20. PAGE 135 A2772 DIPLOM TEC/DEV REV ECO/UNDEV

C83
BURKE E.,"RESOLUTIONS FOR CONCILIATION WITH AMERICA" (1775), IN E. BURKE, COLLECTED WORKS, VOL. 2." UK USA-45 FORCES INT/TRADE TARIFFS TAX SANCTION PEACE...POLICY 18 PRE/US/AM. PAGE 21 A0436 COLONIAL WAR SOVEREIGN ECO/TAC

B91
SIDGWICK H.,THE ELEMENTS OF POLITICS. LOC/G NAT/G LEGIS DIPLOM ADJUD CONTROL EXEC PARL/PROC REPRESENT GOV/REL SOVEREIGN ALL/IDEOS 19 MILL/JS BENTHAM/J. PAGE 132 A2713 POLICY LAW CONCPT

B96
DE VATTEL E.,THE LAW OF NATIONS. AGRI FINAN CHIEF DIPLOM INT/TRADE AGREE OWN ALL/VALS MORAL ORD/FREE SOVEREIGN...GEN/LAWS 18 NATURL/LAW WOLFF/C. PAGE 35 A0714 LAW CONCPT NAT/G INT/LAW

SOVEREIGNTY....SEE SOVEREIGN

SOVIET UNION....SEE USSR

SPAAK P.H. A2770

SPACE....OUTER SPACE, SPACE LAW

N
FOREIGN AFFAIRS. SPACE WOR+45 WOR-45 CULTURE ECO/UNDEV FINAN NAT/G TEC/DEV INT/TRADE ARMS/CONT NUC/PWR...POLICY 20 UN EURATOM ECSC EEC. PAGE 2 A0034 BIBLIOG DIPLOM INT/ORG INT/LAW

N
AIR UNIVERSITY LIBRARY,INDEX TO MILITARY PERIODICALS. FUT SPACE WOR+45 REGION ARMS/CONT NUC/PWR WAR PEACE INT/LAW. PAGE 5 A0105 BIBLIOG/A FORCES NAT/G DIPLOM

N19
MEZERIK AG,OUTER SPACE: UN, US, USSR (PAMPHLET). USSR DELIB/GP FORCES DETER NUC/PWR SOVEREIGN ...POLICY 20 UN TREATY. PAGE 101 A2063 SPACE CONTROL DIPLOM INT/ORG

N19
ZLOTNICK M.,WEAPONS IN SPACE (PAMPHLET). FUT WOR+45 TEC/DEV DIPLOM ARMS/CONT CIVMIL/REL PEACE HABITAT ...CONCPT NEW/IDEA CHARTS. PAGE 170 A3457 SPACE WEAPON NUC/PWR WAR

B58
GAVIN J.M.,WAR AND PEACE IN THE SPACE AGE. SPACE USA+45 USSR FORCES PLAN TEC/DEV BAL/PWR DIPLOM ARMS/CONT WEAPON CIVMIL/REL...CHARTS GP/COMP 20 NATO COLD/WAR. PAGE 52 A1055 WAR DETER NUC/PWR PEACE

B58
JENKS C.W.,THE COMMON LAW OF MANKIND. EUR+WWI MOD/EUR SPACE WOR+45 INT/ORG BAL/PWR ARMS/CONT COERCE SUPEGO MORAL...TREND 20. PAGE 73 A1505 JURID SOVEREIGN

S58
MCDOUGAL M.S.,"PERSPECTIVES FOR A LAW OF OUTER SPACE." FUT WOR+45 AIR CONSULT DELIB/GP TEC/DEV CT/SYS ORD/FREE...POLICY JURID 20 UN. PAGE 98 A2004 INT/ORG SPACE INT/LAW

B59
GOULD L.P.,THE PRICE OF SURVIVAL. EUR+WWI SPACE USA+45 FORCES ECO/TAC NUC/PWR WAR ORD/FREE MARXISM ...IDEA/COMP 20 COLD/WAR NATO. PAGE 54 A1117 POLICY PROB/SOLV DIPLOM PEACE

B59
HALEY A.G.,FIRST COLLOQUIUM ON THE LAW OF OUTER SPACE. WOR+45 INT/ORG ACT/RES PLAN BAL/PWR CONFER ATTIT PWR...POLICY JURID CHARTS ANTHOL 20. PAGE 60 A1225 SPACE LAW SOVEREIGN CONTROL

B60
WOETZEL R.K.,THE INTERNATIONAL CONTROL OF AIRSPACE AND OUTERSPACE. FUT WOR+45 AIR CONSTN STRUCT CONSULT PLAN TEC/DEV ADJUD RIGID/FLEX KNOWL ORD/FREE PWR...TECHNIC GEOG MGT NEW/IDEA TREND COMPUT/IR VAL/FREE 20 TREATY. PAGE 166 A3375 INT/ORG JURID SPACE INT/LAW

S60
WRIGHT Q.,"LEGAL ASPECTS OF THE U-2 INCIDENT." COM USA+45 USSR STRUCT NAT/G FORCES PLAN TEC/DEV ADJUD RIGID/FLEX MORAL ORD/FREE...DECISION INT/LAW JURID PSY TREND GEN/LAWS COLD/WAR VAL/FREE 20 U-2. PAGE 168 A3413 PWR POLICY SPACE

B61
MICHAEL D.N.,PROPOSED STUDIES ON THE IMPLICATIONS OF PEACEFUL SPACE ACTIVITIES FOR HUMAN AFFAIRS. COM/IND INDUS FORCES DIPLOM PEACE PERSON...PSY SOC 20. PAGE 101 A2066 FUT SPACE ACT/RES PROB/SOLV

L61
SAND P.T.,"AN HISTORICAL SURVEY OF INTERNATIONAL AIR LAW SINCE 1944." USA+45 USA-45 WOR+45 WOR-45 SOCIETY ECO/DEV NAT/G CONSULT EX/STRUC ACT/RES PLAN LEGIT ROUTINE...JURID CONCPT METH/CNCPT TREND 20. PAGE 127 A2598 INT/ORG LAW INT/LAW SPACE

L61
TAUBENFELD H.J.,"A REGIME FOR OUTER SPACE." FUT UNIV R+D ACT/RES PLAN BAL/PWR LEGIT ARMS/CONT ORD/FREE...POLICY JURID TREND UN TOT/POP 20 COLD/WAR. PAGE 142 A2894 INT/ORG ADJUD SPACE

S61
LIPSON L.,"AN ARGUMENT ON THE LEGALITY OF RECONNAISSANCE STATELLITES." COM USA+45 USSR WOR+45 AIR INTELL NAT/G CONSULT PLAN DIPLOM LEGIT ROUTINE ATTIT...INT/LAW JURID CONCPT METH/CNCPT TREND COLD/WAR 20. PAGE 90 A1833 INT/ORG LAW SPACE

S61
MACHOWSKI K.,"SELECTED PROBLEMS OF NATIONAL SOVEREIGNTY WITH REFERENCE TO THE LAW OF OUTER SPACE." FUT WOR+45 AIR LAW INTELL SOCIETY ECO/DEV PLAN EDU/PROP DETER DRIVE PERCEPT SOVEREIGN ...POLICY INT/LAW OBS TREND TOT/POP 20. PAGE 92 A1889 UNIV ACT/RES NUC/PWR SPACE

S61
TAUBENFELD H.J.,"OUTER SPACE--PAST POLITICS AND FUTURE POLICY." FUT USA+45 USA-45 WOR+45 AIR INTELL STRUCT ECO/DEV NAT/G TOP/EX ACT/RES ADMIN ROUTINE NUC/PWR ATTIT DRIVE...CONCPT TIME/SEQ TREND TOT/POP 20. PAGE 141 A2892 PLAN SPACE INT/ORG

B62
KENNEDY J.F.,TO TURN THE TIDE. SPACE AGRI INT/ORG DIPLOM

FORCES TEC/DEV ADMIN NUC/PWR PEACE WEALTH...ANTHOL 20 KENNEDY/JF CIV/RIGHTS. PAGE 78 A1592 — CHIEF POLICY NAT/G

B62
SCHWARTZ L.E.,INTERNATIONAL ORGANIZATIONS AND SPACE COOPERATION. VOL/ASSN CONSULT CREATE TEC/DEV SANCTION...POLICY INT/LAW PHIL/SCI 20 UN. PAGE 130 A2656 — INT/ORG DIPLOM R+D SPACE

B62
US CONGRESS,COMMUNICATIONS SATELLITE LEGISLATION: HEARINGS BEFORE COMM ON AERON AND SPACE SCIENCES ON BILLS S2550 AND 2814. WOR+45 LAW VOL/ASSN PLAN DIPLOM CONTROL OWN PEACE...NEW/IDEA CONGRESS NASA. PAGE 150 A3062 — SPACE COM/IND ADJUD GOV/REL

S62
CRANE R.D.,"LAW AND STRATEGY IN SPACE." FUT USA+45 WOR+45 AIR LAW INT/ORG NAT/G FORCES ACT/RES PLAN BAL/PWR LEGIT ARMS/CONT COERCE ORD/FREE...POLICY INT/LAW JURID SOC/EXP 20 TREATY. PAGE 32 A0656 — CONCPT SPACE

S62
CRANE R.D.,"SOVIET ATTITUDE TOWARD INTERNATIONAL SPACE LAW." COM FUT USA+45 USSR AIR CONSTN DELIB/GP DOMIN PWR...JURID TREND TOT/POP 20. PAGE 32 A0657 — LAW ATTIT INT/LAW SPACE

S62
LISSITZYN O.J.,"SOME LEGAL IMPLICATIONS OF THE U-2 AND RB-47 INCIDENTS." FUT USA+45 USSR WOR+45 AIR NAT/G DIPLOM LEGIT MORAL ORD/FREE SOVEREIGN...JURID GEN/LAWS GEN/METH COLD/WAR 20 U-2. PAGE 90 A1840 — LAW CONCPT SPACE INT/LAW

B63
HALEY A.G.,SPACE LAW AND GOVERNMENT. FUT USA+45 WOR+45 LEGIS ACT/RES CREATE ATTIT RIGID/FLEX ORD/FREE PWR SOVEREIGN...POLICY JURID CONCPT CHARTS VAL/FREE 20. PAGE 60 A1226 — INT/ORG LAW SPACE

B63
MCDOUGAL M.S.,LAW AND PUBLIC ORDER IN SPACE. FUT USA+45 ACT/RES TEC/DEV ADJUD...POLICY INT/LAW JURID 20. PAGE 98 A2009 — SPACE ORD/FREE DIPLOM DECISION

B63
US SENATE,DOCUMENTS ON INTERNATIONAL AS"ECTS OF EXPLORATION AND USE OF OUTER SPACE, 1954-62: STAFF REPORT FOR COMM AERON SPACE SCI. USA+45 USSR LEGIS LEAD CIVMIL/REL PEACE...POLICY INT/LAW ANTHOL 20 CONGRESS NASA KHRUSH/N. PAGE 155 A3165 — SPACE UTIL GOV/REL DIPLOM

S63
GARDNER R.N.,"COOPERATION IN OUTER SPACE." FUT USSR WOR+45 AIR LAW COM/IND CONSULT DELIB/GP CREATE KNOWL 20 TREATY. PAGE 51 A1045 — INT/ORG ACT/RES PEACE SPACE

S63
PHELPS J.,"INFORMATION AND ARMS CONTROL." COM SPACE USA+45 USSR WOR+45 R+D INT/ORG NAT/G DELIB/GP DIPLOM ORD/FREE...CONCPT 20. PAGE 116 A2374 — KNOWL ARMS/CONT NUC/PWR

B64
COHEN M.,LAW AND POLITICS IN SPACE: SPECIFIC AND URGENT PROBLEMS IN THE LAW OF OUTER SPACE. CHINA/COM COM USA+45 USSR WOR+45 COM/IND INT/ORG NAT/G LEGIT NUC/PWR ATTIT BIO/SOC...JURID CONCPT CONGRESS 20 STALIN/J. PAGE 28 A0561 — DELIB/GP LAW INT/LAW SPACE

B64
NASA,PROCEEDINGS OF CONFERENCE ON THE LAW OF SPACE AND OF SATELLITE COMMUNICATIONS: CHICAGO 1963. FUT WOR+45 DELIB/GP PROB/SOLV TEC/DEV CONFER ADJUD NUC/PWR...POLICY IDEA/COMP 20 NASA. PAGE 107 A2197 — SPACE COM/IND LAW DIPLOM

B64
SCHWARTZ M.D.,CONFERENCE ON SPACE SCIENCE AND SPACE LAW. FUT COM/IND NAT/G FORCES ACT/RES PLAN BUDGET DIPLOM NUC/PWR WEAPON...POLICY ANTHOL 20. PAGE 130 A2658 — SPACE LAW PEACE TEC/DEV

B64
TAUBENFELD H.J.,SPACE AND SOCIETY. USA+45 LAW FORCES CREATE TEC/DEV ADJUD CONTROL COST PEACE ...PREDICT ANTHOL 20. PAGE 142 A2895 — SPACE SOCIETY ADJUST DIPLOM

B64
US AIR FORCE ACADEMY ASSEMBLY,OUTER SPACE: FINAL REPORT APRIL 1-4, 1964. FUT USA+45 WOR+45 LAW DELIB/GP CONFER ARMS/CONT WAR PEACE ATTIT MORAL ...ANTHOL 20 NASA. PAGE 150 A3055 — SPACE CIVMIL/REL NUC/PWR DIPLOM

L64
CARNEGIE ENDOWMENT INT. PEACE,"POLITICAL QUESTIONS (ISSUES BEFORE THE NINETEENTH GENERAL ASSEMBLY)." SPACE WOR+45 CONSTN FINAN NAT/G CONSULT DELIB/GP FORCES LEGIS TEC/DEV EDU/PROP LEGIT ARMS/CONT COERCE NUC/PWR ATTIT ALL/VALS...CONCPT OBS UN COLD/WAR 20. PAGE 24 A0490 — INT/ORG PEACE

S64
CRANE R.D.,"BASIC PRINCIPLES IN SOVIET SPACE LAW." FUT WOR+45 AIR INT/ORG DIPLOM DOMIN ARMS/CONT COERCE NUC/PWR PEACE ATTIT DRIVE PWR...INT/LAW METH/CNCPT NEW/IDEA OBS TREND GEN/LAWS VAL/FREE MARX/KARL 20. PAGE 32 A0659 — COM LAW USSR SPACE

B65
WHITE HOUSE CONFERENCE ON INTERNATIONAL COOPERATION(VOL.II). SPACE WOR+45 EXTR/IND INT/ORG LABOR WORKER NUC/PWR PEACE AGE/Y...CENSUS ANTHOL 20 RESOURCE/N URBAN/RNWL PUB/TRANS. PAGE 3 A0071 — R+D CONFER TEC/DEV DIPLOM

B65
FRUTKIN A.W.,SPACE AND THE INTERNATIONAL COOPERATION YEAR: A NATIONAL CHALLENGE (PAMPHLET). EUR+WWI USA+45 FINAN TEC/DEV BUDGET...MGT 20 NASA. PAGE 49 A1011 — SPACE INDUS NAT/G DIPLOM

B65
UN,SPACE ACTIVITIES AND RESOURCES: REVIEW OF UNITED NATION'S NATIONAL AND INTERNATIONAL PROGRAMS. INT/ORG LABOR PLAN TEC/DEV DIPLOM EFFICIENCY HEALTH ...GOV/COMP 20 UN. PAGE 146 A2995 — SPACE NUC/PWR FOR/AID PEACE

B65
US DEPARTMENT OF DEFENSE,US SECURITY ARMS CONTROL, AND DISARMAMENT 1961-1965 (PAMPHLET). CHINA/COM COM GERMANY/W ISRAEL SPACE USA+45 USSR WOR+45 FORCES EDU/PROP DETER EQUILIB PEACE ALL/VALS...GOV/COMP 20 NATO. PAGE 151 A3077 — BIBLIOG/A ARMS/CONT NUC/PWR DIPLOM

B65
US SENATE,US INTERNATIONAL SPACE PROGRAMS, 1959-65: STAFF REPORT FOR COMM ON AERONAUTICAL AND SPACE SCIENCES. WOR+45 VOL/ASSN CIVMIL/REL 20 CONGRESS NASA TREATY. PAGE 155 A3166 — SPACE DIPLOM PLAN GOV/REL

B65
US SENATE COMM AERO SPACE SCI,INTERNATIONAL COOPERATION AND ORGANIZATION FOR OUTER SPACE. FUT USA+45 WOR+45 PROF/ORG VOL/ASSN CONSULT DELIB/GP PLAN TEC/DEV ARMS/CONT GP/REL PEACE 20 UN NASA. PAGE 155 A3167 — DIPLOM SPACE R+D NAT/G

C65
SEARA M.V.,"COSMIC INTERNATIONAL LAW." LAW ACADEM ACT/RES DIPLOM COLONIAL CONTROL NUC/PWR SOVEREIGN ...GEN/LAWS BIBLIOG UN. PAGE 131 A2678 — SPACE INT/LAW IDEA/COMP INT/ORG

B66
UNITED NATIONS,INTERNATIONAL SPACE BIBLIOGRAPHY. FUT INT/ORG TEC/DEV DIPLOM ARMS/CONT NUC/PWR ...JURID SOC UN. PAGE 149 A3037 — BIBLIOG SPACE PEACE R+D

B66
US SENATE COMM AERO SPACE SCI,SOVIET SPACE PROGRAMS, 1962-65; GOALS AND PURPOSES, ACHIEVEMENTS, PLANS, AND INTERNATIONAL IMPLICATIONS. USA+45 USSR R+D FORCES PLAN EDU/PROP PRESS ADJUD ARMS/CONT ATTIT MARXISM. PAGE 155 A3168 — CONSULT SPACE FUT DIPLOM

B67
US SENATE COMM AERO SPACE SCI,TREATY ON PRINCIPLES GOVERNING ACTIVITIES OF STATES IN EXPLORATION AND USE OF OUTER SPACE, INCLUDING...BODIES. DELIB/GP FORCES LEGIS DIPLOM...JURID 20 DEPT/STATE NASA DEPT/DEFEN UN. PAGE 155 A3169 — SPACE INT/LAW ORD/FREE PEACE

S67
DOYLE S.E.,"COMMUNICATION SATELLITES* INTERNAL ORGANIZATION FOR DEVELOPMENT AND CONTROL." USA+45 R+D ACT/RES DIPLOM NAT/LISM...POLICY INT/LAW PREDICT UN. PAGE 38 A0781 — TEC/DEV SPACE COM/IND INT/ORG

S67
EISENDRATH C.,"THE OUTER SPACE TREATY." CHINA/COM COM USA+45 DIPLOM CONTROL NUC/PWR...INT/LAW 20 UN COLD/WAR TREATY. PAGE 41 A0831 — SPACE INT/ORG PEACE ARMS/CONT

S67
REINTANZ G.,"THE SPACE TREATY." WOR+45 DIPLOM CONTROL ARMS/CONT NUC/PWR WAR...MARXIST 20 COLD/WAR UN TREATY. PAGE 120 A2461 — SPACE INT/LAW INT/ORG PEACE

S67
VLASCIC I.A.,"THE SPACE TREATY* A PRELIMINARY EVALUATION." FUT USSR WOR+45 R+D ACT/RES TEC/DEV DIPLOM CONFER ARMS/CONT PEACE...PREDICT UN TREATY. PAGE 159 A3245 — SPACE INT/LAW INT/ORG NEUTRAL

N67
US SUPERINTENDENT OF DOCUMENTS,SPACE: MISSILES, THE MOON, NASA, AND SATELLITES (PRICE LIST 79A). USA+45 COM/IND R+D NAT/G DIPLOM EDU/PROP ADMIN CONTROL HEALTH...POLICY SIMUL NASA CONGRESS. PAGE 157 A3206 — BIBLIOG/A SPACE TEC/DEV PEACE

SPAIN....SPAIN

N
INSTITUTE OF HISPANIC STUDIES,HISPANIC AMERICAN REPORT. EUR+WWI SPAIN LAW CONSTN ECO/UNDEV POL/PAR EX/STRUC LEGIS LEAD...HUM SOC 20. PAGE 70 A1445 — BIBLIOG/A L/A+17C NAT/G DIPLOM

B00
GRIFFIN A.P.C.,LIST OF BOOKS RELATING TO THE THEORY OF COLONIZATION, GOVERNMENT OF DEPENDENCIES, PROTECTORATES, AND RELATED TOPICS. FRANCE GERMANY ITALY SPAIN UK USA-45 WOR-45 ECO/TAC ADMIN CONTROL REGION NAT/LISM ALL/VALS PWR...INT/LAW SOC 16/19. PAGE 56 A1149 — BIBLIOG/A COLONIAL GOV/REL DOMIN

B05
GRIFFIN A.P.C.,LIST OF REFERENCES ON THE US CONSULAR SERVICE (PAMPHLET). FRANCE GERMANY SPAIN UK USA-45 WOR-45 OP/RES DOMIN ADMIN FEEDBACK ROUTINE GOV/REL...DECISION 19. PAGE 56 A1153 — BIBLIOG/A NAT/G DIPLOM CONSULT

B29
DE REPARAZ G.,GEOGRAFIA Y POLITICA. CHILE SPAIN USSR NAT/G DIPLOM REV MARXISM...POLICY 19/20. PAGE 35 A0709 — GEOG MOD/EUR

B38
PETTEE G.S.,THE PROCESS OF REVOLUTION. COM FRANCE ITALY MOD/EUR RUSSIA SPAIN WOR-45 ELITES INTELL SOCIETY STRATA STRUCT INT/ORG NAT/G POL/PAR ACT/RES PLAN EDU/PROP LEGIT EXEC...SOC MYTH TIME/SEQ TOT/POP 18/20. PAGE 115 A2370 — COERCE CONCPT REV

B41
GRISMER R.,A NEW BIBLIOGRAPHY OF THE LITERATURES OF SPAIN AND SPANISH AMERICA. CHRIST-17C MOD/EUR PRE/AMER SPAIN CULTURE DIPLOM EDU/PROP...ART/METH GEOG HUM PHIL/SCI 20. PAGE 57 A1165 — BIBLIOG LAW NAT/G ECO/UNDEV

B41
WHITAKER A.P.,THE UNITED STATES AND THE INDEPENDENCE OF LATIN AMERICA, 1800-1830. PORTUGAL SPAIN USA-45 COLONIAL REGION SOVEREIGN...POLICY TIME/SEQ BIBLIOG/A 18/20. PAGE 163 A3329 — DIPLOM L/A+17C CONCPT ORD/FREE

B51
CATALOGO GENERAL DE LA LIBRERIA ESPANOLA E HISPANOAMERICANA 1901-1930; AUTORES (5 VOLS., 1932-1951). SPAIN COLONIAL GOV/REL...SOC 20. PAGE 3 A0058 — BIBLIOG L/A+17C DIPLOM NAT/G

B51
BORKENAU F.,EUROPEAN COMMUNISM. COM EUR+WWI GERMANY SPAIN USSR INT/ORG PLAN REV WAR ATTIT 20 STALIN/J HITLER/A. PAGE 17 A0342 — MARXISM POLICY DIPLOM NAT/G

B53
ROSCIO J.G.,OBRAS. L/A+17C SPAIN DIPLOM REV WAR NAT/LISM TOTALISM PWR SOVEREIGN 19. PAGE 123 A2527 — ORD/FREE COLONIAL NAT/G PHIL/SCI

B56
TOYNBEE A.,THE WAR AND THE NEUTRALS. L/A+17C PORTUGAL SPAIN SWEDEN SWITZERLND TURKEY WOR+45 WOR-45 ECO/TAC CONFER CONTROL REGION 20. PAGE 145 A2957 — NEUTRAL WAR INT/TRADE DIPLOM

B57
RUMEU DE ARMAS A.,ESPANA EEN EL AFRICA ATLANTICA. AFR CHRIST-17C PORTUGAL SPAIN DIPLOM ECO/TAC CONTROL 14/16 AFRICA/W. PAGE 125 A2568 — NAT/G COLONIAL CHIEF PWR

B62
BLANSHARD P.,FREEDOM AND CATHOLIC POWER IN SPAIN AND PORTUGAL: AN AMERICAN INTERPRETATION. AFR PORTUGAL SPAIN USA+45 LAW LABOR DIPLOM EDU/PROP DISCRIM ISOLAT TOTALISM 20 CHURCH/STA. PAGE 15 A0309 — GP/REL FASCISM CATHISM PWR

B62
DEHIO L.,THE PRECARIOUS BALANCE: FOUR CENTURIES OF THE EUROPEAN POWER STRUGGLE. FRANCE GERMANY SPAIN NAT/G DOMIN PWR...GOV/COMP 8/20. PAGE 36 A0725 — BAL/PWR WAR DIPLOM COERCE

B62
DIAZ J.S.,MANUAL DE BIBLIOGRAFIA DE LA LITERATURA ESPANOLA. PRE/AMER SPAIN ECO/UNDEV DIPLOM LEAD ATTIT...SOC 15/20. PAGE 37 A0755 — BIBLIOG L/A+17C NAT/G COLONIAL

B62
GUTTMAN A.,THE WOUND IN THE HEART: AMERICA AND THE SPANISH CIVIL WAR. SPAIN USA-45 POL/PAR LEGIS ECO/TAC CHOOSE ANOMIE ATTIT MARXISM...POLICY ANARCH BIBLIOG 20 ROOSEVLT/F. PAGE 58 A1198 — ALL/IDEOS WAR DIPLOM CATHISM

B63
LOOMIE A.J.,THE SPANISH ELIZABETHANS: THE ENGLISH EXILES AT THE COURT OF PHILIP II. SPAIN UK WAR INGP/REL DRIVE HABITAT CATHISM...BIOG 16/17 MIGRATION. PAGE 91 A1860 — NAT/G STRANGE POLICY DIPLOM

B63
WATKINS K.W.,BRITAIN DIVIDED; THE EFFECT OF THE SPANISH CIVIL WAR ON BRITISH POLITICAL OPINION. SPAIN UK POL/PAR BAL/PWR LOBBY NEUTRAL 20. PAGE 162 A3293 — EDU/PROP WAR POLICY DIPLOM

B64
JENSEN D.L.,DIPLOMACY AND DOGMATISM. FRANCE SPAIN REV WAR PERSON CATHISM...POLICY BIOG 16. PAGE 74 A1513 — DIPLOM ATTIT SECT

B64
TURNER M.C.,LIBROS EN VENTA EN HISPANOAMERICA Y ESPANA. SPAIN LAW CONSTN CULTURE ADMIN LEAD...HUM SOC 20. PAGE 146 A2983 — BIBLIOG L/A+17C NAT/G DIPLOM

B65
HISPANIC SOCIETY OF AMERICA,CATALOGUE (10 VOLS.). PORTUGAL PRE/AMER SPAIN NAT/G ADMIN...POLICY SOC 15/20. PAGE 65 A1341 — BIBLIOG L/A+17C COLONIAL DIPLOM

B66
GRENVILLE J.A.S.,POLITICS, STRATEGY, AND AMERICAN DEMOCRACY: STUDIES IN FOREIGN POLICY, 1873-1917. CUBA PHILIPPINE SPAIN USA-45 VENEZUELA ELITES NAT/G CREATE PARTIC WAR RIGID/FLEX ORD/FREE...DECISION TREND 19/20 HAWAII. PAGE 56 A1146 — DIPLOM COLONIAL POLICY

B66
SANDERS R.E.,SPAIN AND THE UNITED NATIONS 1945-1950. SPAIN CHIEF DIPLOM CONFER SANCTION ATTIT ...POLICY 20 UN COLD/WAR. PAGE 127 A2599 — INT/ORG FASCISM GP/REL STRANGE

S67
FAWCETT J.E.S.,"GIBRALTAR* THE LEGAL ISSUES." SPAIN UK INT/ORG BAL/PWR LICENSE CONFER SANCTION PRIVIL ...JURID CHARTS 20. PAGE 44 A0905 — INT/LAW DIPLOM COLONIAL ADJUD

SPAN/AMER....SPANISH-AMERICAN CULTURE

SPANIER J.W. A2771,A2772

SPEAKER OF THE HOUSE....SEE CONGRESS, HOUSE/REP, LEGIS, PARLIAMENT

SPEAR/BRWN....SPEARMAN BROWN PREDICTION FORMULA

SPEARS E.L. A2773

SPECIALIZATION....SEE TASK, SKILL

SPECTOR I. A2774

SPECTOR S.D. A2775

SPECULATION....SEE GAMBLE, RISK

SPEECKAERT G.P. A2776,A2777

SPEER J.P. A2778

SPEIER H. A2779,A2780,A2781,A2782

SPENCE J.E. A2783

SPENCER F.A. A2784

SPENCER R. A2785

SPENCER/H....HERBERT SPENCER

SPENGLER/O....OSWALD SPENGLER

SPENSER J.H. A2786

SPICER K. A2787

SPINELLI A. A2788,A2789

SPINOZA/B....BARUCH (OR BENEDICT) SPINOZA

SPIRO H.J. A2790

SPOCK/B....BENJAMIN SPOCK

SPORTS....SPORTS AND ATHLETIC COMPETITIONS

SPRINGER H.W. A2791

SPRINGER M. A1544

SPROUT H. A2792

SPROUT M. A2792

SPULBER N. A2793

SQUIRES J.D. A2794

SRAFFA/P....PIERO SRAFFA

SST....SUPERSONIC TRANSPORT

ST LEGER A. A2796

ST/LOUIS....ST. LOUIS, MO.

ST/PAUL....SAINT PAUL, MINNESOTA

STAAR R.F. A2797

STADLER K.R. A2798

STAGES....SEE TIME/SEQ

STALEY E. A2799,A2800,A2801

STALIN/J....JOSEPH STALIN

B50
DULLES J.F.,WAR OR PEACE. CHINA/COM USA+45 USSR INT/ORG SECT FORCES PLAN NUC/PWR WAR CENTRAL MARXISM...POLICY 20 UN ROOSEVLT/F STALIN/J. PAGE 39 A0797 — PEACE DIPLOM TREND ORD/FREE

B51
BORKENAU F.,EUROPEAN COMMUNISM. COM EUR+WWI GERMANY SPAIN USSR INT/ORG PLAN REV WAR ATTIT 20 STALIN/J HITLER/A. PAGE 17 A0342 — MARXISM POLICY DIPLOM NAT/G

B56
VON HARPE W.,DIE SOWJETUNION FINNLAND UND SKANDANAVIEN, 1945-1955. EUR+WWI FINLAND GERMANY USSR WAR INGP/REL ORD/FREE SOVEREIGN MARXISM ...POLICY GOV/COMP BIBLIOG 20 STALIN/J. PAGE 160 A3252 — DIPLOM COM NEUTRAL BAL/PWR

B57
TOMASIC D.A.,NATIONAL COMMUNISM AND SOVIET STRATEGY. UK USSR YUGOSLAVIA NAT/G POL/PAR CHIEF CREATE DOMIN REV WAR PWR...BIOG TREND 20 TITO/MARSH STALIN/J. PAGE 144 A2948 — COM NAT/LISM MARXISM DIPLOM

B58
PALMER E.E.,THE COMMUNIST CHALLENGE. COM USA+45 USA-45 ECO/DEV ECO/UNDEV NEUTRAL ORD/FREE POPULISM ...CONCPT NAT/COMP ANTHOL 19/20 LENIN/VI STALIN/J MAO MARX/KARL COM/PARTY. PAGE 113 A2320 — MARXISM DIPLOM IDEA/COMP POLICY

B59
HARRIMAN A.,PEACE WITH RUSSIA? USA+45 USSR SOCIETY ECO/TAC CONTROL TOTALISM ATTIT MARXISM...POLICY 20 STALIN/J KHRUSH/N. PAGE 62 A1266 — DIPLOM PEACE NAT/G TASK

B60
CENTRAL ASIAN RESEARCH CENTRE,RUSSIA LOOKS AT AFRICA (PAMPHLET). AFR USSR COLONIAL RACE/REL...HUM 19/20 STALIN/J. PAGE 25 A0511 — BIBLIOG MARXISM TREND DIPLOM

B60
MOSELY P.E.,THE KREMLIN AND WORLD POLITICS. EUR+WWI GERMANY USA+45 USSR CHIEF TOP/EX BAL/PWR DOMIN PEACE PWR...METH 20 COLD/WAR STALIN/J EUROPE/E. PAGE 105 A2151 — COM DIPLOM POLICY WAR

B61
NOLLAU G.,INTERNATIONAL COMMUNISM AND WORLD REVOLUTION; HISTORY AND METHODS (TRANS. BY VICTOR ANDERSEN). COM WORKER DIPLOM CONFER INGP/REL ...CONCPT BIBLIOG 20 STALIN/J LENIN/VI COMINTERN COMINFORM WORLD/CONG. PAGE 110 A2249 — MARXISM POL/PAR INT/ORG REV

S61
TUCKER R.C.,"TOWARDS A COMPARATIVE POLITICS OF MOVEMENT-REGIMES" (BMR)" USSR CONSTN NAT/G CREATE PROB/SOLV DIPLOM DOMIN REV...GP/COMP IDEA/COMP METH 20 STALIN/J BOLSHEVISM. PAGE 145 A2971 — MARXISM POLICY GEN/LAWS PWR

B62
KLUCKHOHN F.L.,THE NAKED RISE OF COMMUNISM. CHINA/COM COM USSR WOR+45 CONSTN POL/PAR PLAN CONTROL LEAD NEUTRAL CONSERVE 20 STALIN/J EUROPE/E COM/PARTY. PAGE 80 A1650 — MARXISM IDEA/COMP DIPLOM DOMIN

S62
DRACHKOVITCH M.M.,"THE EMERGING PATTERN OF YUGOSLAV-SOVIET RELATIONS." COM FUT USSR WOR+45 INT/ORG ECO/TAC FOR/AID DOMIN COERCE ATTIT PERSON ORD/FREE PWR...TIME/SEQ 20 TITO/MARSH KHRUSH/N STALIN/J. PAGE 38 A0783 — TOP/EX DIPLOM YUGOSLAVIA

B63
GALLAGHER M.P.,THE SOVIET HISTORY OF WORLD WAR II. EUR+WWI USSR DIPLOM DOMIN WRITING CONTROL WAR MARXISM...PSY TIME/SEQ 20 STALIN/J. PAGE 50 A1031 — CIVMIL/REL EDU/PROP HIST/WRIT PRESS

B63
MILLER W.J.,THE MEANING OF COMMUNISM. USSR SOCIETY ECO/DEV EX/STRUC WORKER TEC/DEV ADMIN TOTALISM ...POLICY CONCPT CHARTS BIBLIOG T 20 COLD/WAR LENIN/VI STALIN/J. PAGE 101 A2080 — MARXISM TRADIT DIPLOM NAT/G

B63
WHITNEY T.P.,KHRUSHCHEV SPEAKS. USSR AGRI LEAD ...BIOG ANTHOL 20 KHRUSH/N STALIN/J ESPIONAGE. PAGE 164 A3339 — DIPLOM MARXISM CHIEF

B64
COHEN M.,LAW AND POLITICS IN SPACE: SPECIFIC AND URGENT PROBLEMS IN THE LAW OF OUTER SPACE. CHINA/COM COM USA+45 USSR WOR+45 COM/IND INT/ORG NAT/G LEGIT NUC/PWR ATTIT BIO/SOC...JURID CONCPT CONGRESS 20 STALIN/J. PAGE 28 A0561 — DELIB/GP LAW INT/LAW SPACE

B64
EHRENBURG I.,THE WAR: 1941-1945 (VOL. V OF "MEN, YEARS - LIFE," TRANS. BY TATIANA SHEBUNINA). GERMANY USSR PRESS WRITING PERS/REL PEACE ANOMIE ATTIT PERSON...CONCPT RECORD BIOG 20 STALIN/J HITLER/A. PAGE 40 A0827 — WAR DIPLOM COM MARXIST

B64
KEEP J.,CONTEMPORARY HISTORY IN THE SOVIET MIRROR. COM USSR POL/PAR CREATE DIPLOM AGREE WAR ATTIT ...MYTH TREND ANTHOL 20 COLD/WAR STALIN/J MARX/KARL LENIN/VI. PAGE 77 A1576 — HIST/WRIT METH MARXISM IDEA/COMP

B64
LUARD E.,THE COLD WAR: A RE-APPRAISAL. FUT USSR WOR+45 FORCES NUC/PWR NAT/LISM ORD/FREE SOVEREIGN ...INT 20 COLD/WAR STALIN/J TREATY UN. PAGE 91 A1870 — DIPLOM WAR PEACE TOTALISM

B66
HERZ M.F.,BEGINNINGS OF THE COLD WAR. COM POLAND USA+45 USSR INT/ORG NAT/G CHIEF FOR/AID DOMIN CONFER AGREE WAR PEACE 20 STALIN/J COLD/WAR UN. PAGE 64 A1321 — DIPLOM

S66
MCNEAL R.H.,"THE LEGACY OF THE COMINTERN." USSR WOR+45 WOR-45 PROB/SOLV DIPLOM CONFER CONTROL LEAD WAR 20 STALIN/J COMINTERN. PAGE 98 A2020 — MARXISM INT/ORG POL/PAR PWR

B67
BRZEZINSKI Z.K.,THE SOVIET BLOC: UNITY AND CONFLICT (2ND ED., REV., ENLARGED). COM POLAND USSR INTELL CHIEF EX/STRUC CONTROL EXEC GOV/REL PWR MARXISM ...TREND IDEA/COMP 20 LENIN/VI MARX/KARL STALIN/J. PAGE 21 A0420 — NAT/G DIPLOM

B67
TROTSKY L.,PROBLEMS OF THE CHINESE REVOLUTION (3RD ED. TRANS. BY MAX SCHACTMAN). ASIA USSR DIPLOM MARXISM SOCISM...IDEA/COMP ANTHOL DICTIONARY 20 STALIN/J. PAGE 145 A2969 — MARXIST REV

STAMMLER/R....RUDOLF STAMMLER

STAND/INT....STANDARDIZED INTERVIEWS

B48
COTTRELL L.S. JR.,AMERICAN PUBLIC OPINION ON WORLD AFFAIRS IN THE ATOMIC AGE. USA+45 CULTURE INT/ORG NAT/G DIPLOM EDU/PROP PEACE RIGID/FLEX ORD/FREE ...POLICY SOC CONCPT STAND/INT TOT/POP 20. PAGE 31 A0633 — SOCIETY ATTIT ARMS/CONT NUC/PWR

S58
BOGART L.,"MEASURING THE EFFECTIVENESS OF AN OVERSEAS INFORMATION CAMPAIGN." EUR+WWI GREECE USA+45 INT/ORG MUNIC PLAN DIPLOM PEACE PERCEPT RIGID/FLEX KNOWL...TECHNIC PSY SOC NEW/IDEA CONT/OBS REC/INT STAND/INT SAMP/SIZ COLD/WAR 20. PAGE 16 A0328 — ATTIT EDU/PROP

B59
CHINA INSTITUTE OF AMERICA.,CHINA AND THE UNITED NATIONS. CHINA/COM FUT STRUCT EDU/PROP LEGIT ADMIN ATTIT KNOWL ORD/FREE PWR...OBS RECORD STAND/INT TIME/SEQ UN LEAGUE/NAT UNESCO 20. PAGE 26 A0531 — ASIA INT/ORG

B60
SHONFIELD A.,THE ATTACK ON WORLD POVERTY. WOR+45 ECO/DEV ECO/UNDEV FINAN VOL/ASSN PLAN EDU/PROP DRIVE KNOWL WEALTH...CONT/OBS STAND/INT ORG/CHARTS TOT/POP UNESCO 20. PAGE 132 A2704 — INT/ORG ECO/TAC FOR/AID INT/TRADE

S64
DEVILLERS P.H.,"L'URSS, LA CHINE ET LES ORIGINES DE LA GUERRE DE COREE." ASIA CHINA/COM USSR INT/ORG ECO/TAC EDU/PROP ATTIT RIGID/FLEX PWR...STAND/INT HIST/WRIT COLD/WAR 20. PAGE 37 A0751 — WOR+45 KOREA

S64
RUBIN R.,"THE UN CORRESPONDENT." WOR+45 FACE/GP PROF/ORG EDU/PROP ROUTINE PERCEPT KNOWL...RECORD STAND/INT QU UN WORK TOT/POP VAL/FREE 20. PAGE 125 A2560 — INT/ORG ATTIT DIPLOM

STANDARDIZED INTERVIEWS....SEE STAND/INT

STANFORD RESEARCH INSTITUTE A2802

STANFORD/U....STANFORD UNIVERSITY

B65
EDUCATION AND WORLD AFFAIRS,THE UNIVERSITY LOOKS ABROAD: APPROACHES TO WORLD AFFAIRS AT SIX AMERICAN UNIVERSITIES. USA+45 CREATE EDU/PROP CONFER LEAD KNOWL 20 CORNELL/U MICH/STA/U STANFORD/U TULANE/U WISCONSN/U. PAGE 40 A0822 — ACADEM DIPLOM ATTIT GP/COMP

STANGER R.J. A2803

STANKIEW/W....W.J. STANKIEWICZ

STANKIEWICZ W.J. A2804

STANKIEWICZ, W.J.....SEE STANKIEW/W

STANLEY T.W. A2805

STANTON A.H. A2806

STAR/CARR....STAR-CARR, A PREHISTORIC SOCIETY

STARK H. A2807

STARR R.E. A2808

STAT....STATISTICS

N
INDIA: A REFERENCE ANNUAL. INDIA CULTURE COM/IND R+D FORCES PLAN RECEIVE EDU/PROP HEALTH...STAT CHARTS BIBLIOG 20. PAGE 2 A0036
CONSTN LABOR INT/ORG

N
THE MIDDLE EAST AND NORTH AFRICA. AFR ISLAM CULTURE ECO/UNDEV AGRI NAT/G TEC/DEV FOR/AID INT/TRADE EDU/PROP...CHARTS 20. PAGE 2 A0043
INDEX INDUS FINAN STAT

N
EUROPA PUBLICATIONS LIMITED,THE EUROPA YEAR BOOK. CONSTN FINAN INDUS POL/PAR DIPLOM TV CT/SYS...STAT BIOG CHARTS WORSHIP 20. PAGE 43 A0874
BIBLIOG NAT/G PRESS INT/ORG

N
FOREIGN TRADE LIBRARY,NEW TITLES RECEIVED IN THE LIBRARY. WOR+45 ECO/UNDEV FINAN NAT/G PLAN TEC/DEV BUDGET ECO/TAC TARIFFS GOV/REL STAT. PAGE 47 A0964
BIBLIOG/A INT/TRADE INDUS ECO/DEV

N
MINISTRY OF OVERSEAS DEVELOPME,TECHNICAL CO-OPERATION -- A BIBLIOGRAPHY. UK LAW SOCIETY DIPLOM ECO/TAC FOR/AID...STAT 20 CMN/WLTH. PAGE 102 A2089
BIBLIOG TEC/DEV ECO/DEV NAT/G

N
UNIVERSITY OF CALIFORNIA,STATISTICAL ABSTRACT OF LATIN AMERICA. L/A+17C DIPLOM 20. PAGE 149 A3046
BIBLIOG NAT/G ECO/UNDEV STAT

N
US BUREAU OF THE CENSUS,BIBLIOGRAPHY OF SOCIAL SCIENCE PERIODICALS AND MONOGRAPH SERIES. WOR+45 LAW DIPLOM EDU/PROP HEALTH...PSY SOC LING STAT. PAGE 150 A3058
BIBLIOG/A CULTURE NAT/G SOCIETY

B33
LANGER W.L.,FOREIGN AFFAIRS BIBLIOGRAPHY. WOR-45 INT/ORG CONSULT EDU/PROP ROUTINE NAT/LISM ATTIT SOVEREIGN...STAT RECORD GEN/METH LEAGUE/NAT TOT/POP. PAGE 84 A1725
KNOWL

B37
VINER J.,STUDIES IN THE THEORY OF INTERNATIONAL TRADE. WOR-45 CONSTN ECO/DEV AGRI INDUS MARKET INT/ORG LABOR NAT/G ECO/TAC TARIFFS COLONIAL ATTIT WEALTH...POLICY CONCPT MATH STAT OBS SAMP TREND GEN/LAWS MARX/KARL 20. PAGE 159 A3236
CAP/ISM INT/TRADE

B39
THOMAS J.A.,THE HOUSE OF COMMONS, 1832-1901; A STUDY OF ITS ECONOMIC AND FUNCTIONAL CHARACTER. UK LAW STRATA FINAN DIPLOM CONTROL LEAD LOBBY REPRESENT WEALTH...POLICY STAT BIBLIOG 19/20 PARLIAMENT. PAGE 143 A2922
PARL/PROC LEGIS POL/PAR ECO/DEV

B43
VINER J.,TRADE RELATIONS BETWEEN FREE-MARKET AND CONTROLLED ECONOMIES. WOR-45 MARKET PLAN TARIFFS DEMAND...POLICY STAT 20. PAGE 159 A3237
INT/TRADE DIPLOM CONTROL NAT/G

B44
DAVIS H.E.,PIONEERS IN WORLD ORDER. WOR-45 CONSTN ECO/TAC DOMIN EDU/PROP LEGIT ADJUD ADMIN ARMS/CONT CHOOSE KNOWL ORD/FREE...POLICY JURID SOC STAT OBS CENSUS TIME/SEQ ANTHOL LEAGUE/NAT 20. PAGE 34 A0691
INT/ORG ROUTINE

L46
MASTERS D.,"ONE WORLD OR NONE." FUT WOR+45 INTELL INT/ORG ACT/RES EDU/PROP DETER ATTIT RIGID/FLEX SUPEGO KNOWL...STAT TREND ORG/CHARTS 20. PAGE 96 A1960
POLICY PHIL/SCI ARMS/CONT NUC/PWR

B47
BROOKINGS INST.,MAJOR PROBLEMS OF UNITED STATES FOREIGN POLICY. USA+45 WOR+45 STRUCT ECO/DEV ECO/UNDEV INT/ORG NAT/G POL/PAR VOL/ASSN DELIB/GP FORCES ECO/TAC LEGIT COERCE ORD/FREE PWR WEALTH ...POLICY STAT TREND CHARTS TOT/POP. PAGE 19 A0392
ACT/RES DIPLOM

B47
SOCIAL SCIENCE RESEARCH COUN,PUBLIC REACTION TO THE ATOMIC BOMB AND WORLD AFFAIRS. SOCIETY CONFER ARMS/CONT...STAT QU SAMP CHARTS 20. PAGE 135 A2757
ATTIT NUC/PWR DIPLOM WAR

B48
GRAHAM F.D.,THE THEORY OF INTERNATIONAL VALUES. FUT WOR+45 WOR-45 ECO/DEV FINAN INT/ORG PLAN TEC/DEV CAP/ISM DIPLOM ECO/TAC TARIFFS ROUTINE BAL/PAY DRIVE PWR WEALTH SOCISM...POLICY STAT HYPO/EXP GEN/LAWS 20. PAGE 55 A1125
NEW/IDEA INT/TRADE

B48
MINISTERE FINANCES ET ECO,BULLETIN BIBLIOGRAPHIQUE. AFR EUR+WWI FRANCE CULTURE STRUCT FINAN NAT/G ACT/RES INT/TRADE ADMIN REGION PRODUC STAT. PAGE 102 A2088
BIBLIOG/A ECO/UNDEV TEC/DEV COLONIAL

B50
DAVIS E.P.,PERIODICALS OF INTERNATIONAL ORGANIZATIONS; PART I, THE UN AND SPECIALIZED AGENCIES; PART II, INTER-AMERICAN ORGS. CULTURE AGRI FINAN INDUS LABOR INT/TRADE...GEOG HEAL STAT 20 UN OAS UNESCO. PAGE 34 A0689
BIBLIOG/A INT/ORG DIPLOM L/A+17C

B51
US HOUSE COMM APPROPRIATIONS,MUTUAL SECURITY PROGRAM APPROPRIATIONS FOR 1952: HEARINGS BEFORE A SUBCOMMITTEE OF THE COMMITTEE ON APPROPRIATIONS. KOREA L/A+17C ECO/DEV ECO/UNDEV INT/ORG INSPECT BAL/PWR DIPLOM DEBATE WAR...POLICY STAT ASIA/S 20 CONGRESS NATO COLD/WAR MID/EAST. PAGE 153 A3118
LEGIS FORCES BUDGET FOR/AID

B51
US TARIFF COMMISSION,LIST OF PUBLICATIONS OF THE TARIFF COMMISSION (PAMPHLET). USA+45 USA-45 AGRI EXTR/IND INDUS INT/TRADE...STAT 20. PAGE 157 A3207
BIBLIOG TARIFFS NAT/G ADMIN

S51
BELKNAP G.,"POLITICAL PARTY IDENTIFICATION AND ATTITUDES TOWARD FOREIGN POLICY" (BMR)" USA+45 VOL/ASSN CONTROL CHOOSE...STAT INT CHARTS 20. PAGE 12 A0254
POL/PAR ATTIT POLICY DIPLOM

B52
RIGGS F.W.,FORMOSA UNDER CHINESE NATIONALIST RULE. CHINA/COM USA+45 CONSTN AGRI FINAN LABOR LOC/G NAT/G POL/PAR FORCES HEALTH KNOWL...STAT WORK VAL/FREE 20. PAGE 121 A2479
ASIA FOR/AID DIPLOM

B53
MACK R.T.,RAISING THE WORLDS STANDARD OF LIVING. IRAN INT/ORG VOL/ASSN EX/STRUC ECO/TAC WEALTH...MGT METH/CNCPT STAT CONT/OBS INT TOT/POP VAL/FREE 20 UN. PAGE 92 A1893
WOR+45 FOR/AID INT/TRADE

C53
DEUTSCH K.W.,"NATIONALISM AND SOCIAL COMMUNICATION: AN INQUIRY INTO THE FOUNDATIONS OF NATIONALITY." CULTURE STRUCT DIPLOM DOMIN ATTIT ORD/FREE SOVEREIGN...SOC STAT CHARTS IDEA/COMP BIBLIOG. PAGE 36 A0735
NAT/LISM CONCPT PERCEPT STRATA

B54
BUCHANAN W.,AN INTERNATIONAL POLICE FORCE AND PUBLIC OPINION IN THE UNITED STATES, 1939-1953. USA+45 PROB/SOLV CONTROL ATTIT ORD/FREE...STAT TREND 20. PAGE 21 A0425
IDEA/COMP FORCES DIPLOM PLAN

B54
TINBERGEN J.,INTERNATIONAL ECONOMIC INTEGRATION. WOR+45 WOR-45 ECO/UNDEV NAT/G ECO/TAC BAL/PAY ...METH/CNCPT STAT TIME/SEQ GEN/METH OEEC 20. PAGE 144 A2941
INT/ORG ECO/DEV INT/TRADE

S54
DODD S.C.,"THE SCIENTIFIC MEASUREMENT OF FITNESS FOR SELF-GOVERNMENT." FUT CONSTN ECO/UNDEV INT/ORG PLAN PWR...CONCPT QUANT CON/ANAL SOC/EXP UN LEAGUE/NAT 20. PAGE 38 A0767
NAT/G STAT SOVEREIGN

B55
OECD,MARSHALL PLAN IN TURKEY. TURKEY USA+45 COM/IND CONSTRUC SERV/IND FORCES BUDGET...STAT 20 MARSHL/PLN. PAGE 111 A2277
FOR/AID ECO/UNDEV AGRI INDUS

B56
JUAN T.L.,ECONOMIC AND SOCIAL DEVELOPMENT OF MODERN CHINA: A BIBLIOGRAPHICAL GUIDE. ASIA AGRI COM/IND DIST/IND FINAN INDUS DIPLOM...STAT 20. PAGE 75 A1541
BIBLIOG SOC

B56
US HOUSE COMM FOREIGN AFFAIRS,SURVEY OF ACTIVITIES OF THE COMMITTEE ON FOREIGN AFFAIRS HOUSE OF REPRESENTATIVES: 84TH THROUGH 86TH CONGRESS. USA+45 LAW ADJUD...POLICY STAT CHARTS 20 CONGRESS HOUSE/REP. PAGE 153 A3122
LEGIS DELIB/GP NAT/G DIPLOM

B58
GANGE J.,UNIVERSITY RESEARCH ON INTERNATIONAL AFFAIRS. USA+45 ACADEM INT/ORG CONSULT CREATE EXEC ROUTINE...QUANT STAT INT STERTYP GEN/METH TOT/POP VAL/FREE 20. PAGE 51 A1040
R+D MGT DIPLOM

B58
IMLAH A.H.,ECONOMIC ELEMENTS IN THE PAX BRITANNICA. MOD/EUR USA+45 USA-45 ECO/DEV INT/ORG NAT/G BAL/PWR ECO/TAC PEACE ATTIT PWR WEALTH...STAT CHARTS VAL/FREE 19. PAGE 70 A1436
MARKET UK

B58
INSTITUTE MEDITERRANEAN AFF,THE PALESTINE REFUGEE PROBLEM. UAR WOR+45 INT/ORG PLAN PROB/SOLV PEACE ...POLICY GEOG STAT CHARTS 20 JEWS UN MIGRATION. PAGE 70 A1444
STRANGE HABITAT GP/REL INGP/REL

B58
KINDLEBERGER C.P.,INTERNATIONAL ECONOMICS. WOR+45 WOR-45 ECO/DEV ECO/UNDEV FINAN VOL/ASSN ACT/RES DIPLOM ECO/TAC LEGIT REGION ATTIT DRIVE ORD/FREE WEALTH...POLICY STAT TREND GEN/LAWS EEC ECSC OEEC 20. PAGE 79 A1620
INT/ORG BAL/PWR TARIFFS

B58
MELMAN S.,INSPECTION FOR DISARMAMENT. USA+45 WOR+45 SOCIETY INT/ORG NAT/G CONSULT ACT/RES PLAN EDU/PROP CONTROL DETER PEACE ATTIT PERSON KNOWL...PSY STAT OBS CHARTS TOT/POP VAL/FREE 20. PAGE 99 A2035
FUT ORD/FREE ARMS/CONT NUC/PWR

B58
SCITOUSKY T.,ECONOMIC THEORY AND WESTERN EUROPEAN INTEGRATION. EUR+WWI INT/ORG ACT/RES INT/TRADE REGION BAL/PAY WEALTH...METH/CNCPT STAT CHARTS GEN/METH ECSC TOT/POP EEC OEEC 20. PAGE 130 A2668
ECO/TAC

B58
US OPERATIONS MISSION TO VIET,BUILDING ECONOMIC STRENGTH (PAMPHLET). USA+45 VIETNAM/S INDUS TEC/DEV
FOR/AID ECO/UNDEV

BUDGET ADMIN EATING HEALTH...STAT 20. PAGE 155 A3162 — AGRI EDU/PROP

B59
ALLEN R.L.,SOVIET INFLUENCE IN LATIN AMERICA. ECO/UNDEV FINAN PROC/MFG NAT/G TEC/DEV EDU/PROP EXEC ROUTINE ATTIT DRIVE PERSON ALL/VALS PWR...STAT CHARTS WORK 20. PAGE 6 A0125 — L/A+17C ECO/TAC INT/TRADE USSR

B59
BALL M.M.,NATO AND THE EUROPEAN MOVEMENT. EUR+WWI USA+45 INT/ORG FORCES BAL/PWR EDU/PROP LEGIT REGION ATTIT ORD/FREE PWR...STAT OBS TIME/SEQ TREND CHARTS ORG/CHARTS STERTYP COLD/WAR EEC OEEC 20 NATO. PAGE 10 A0212 — DELIB/GP STRUCT

B59
DIEBOLD W. JR.,THE SCHUMAN PLAN: A STUDY IN ECONOMIC COOPERATION, 1950-1959. EUR+WWI FRANCE GERMANY USA+45 EXTR/IND CONSULT DELIB/GP PLAN DIPLOM ECO/TAC INT/TRADE ROUTINE ORD/FREE WEALTH ...METH/CNCPT STAT CONT/OBS INT TIME/SEQ ECSC 20. PAGE 37 A0759 — INT/ORG REGION

B59
FREE L.A.,SIX ALLIES AND A NEUTRAL. ASIA COM EUR+WWI FRANCE GERMANY/W INDIA S/ASIA UK USA+45 INT/ORG NAT/G NUC/PWR PEACE ATTIT PERCEPT RIGID/FLEX ALL/VALS...STAT REC/INT COLD/WAR 20 CHINJAP. PAGE 48 A0992 — PSY DIPLOM

B59
MODELSKI G.,ATOMIC ENERGY IN THE COMMUNIST BLOC. FUT INT/ORG CONSULT FORCES ACT/RES PLAN KNOWL SKILL ...PHIL/SCI STAT CHARTS 20. PAGE 102 A2096 — TEC/DEV NUC/PWR USSR COM

B59
COLUMBIA U BUR APPL SOC RES,ATTITUDES OF PROMINENT AMERICANS TOWARD "WORLD PEACE THROUGH WORLD LAW" (SUPRA-NATL ORGANIZATION FOR WAR PREVENTION). USA+45 USSR ELITES FORCES PLAN PROB/SOLV CONTROL WAR PWR...POLICY SOC QU IDEA/COMP 20 UN. PAGE 117 A2403 — ATTIT ACT/RES INT/LAW STAT

B59
SCHURZ W.L.,AMERICAN FOREIGN AFFAIRS: A GUIDE TO INTERNATIONAL AFFAIRS. USA+45 WOR+45 WOR-45 NAT/G FORCES LEGIS TOP/EX PLAN EDU/PROP LEGIT ADMIN ROUTINE ATTIT ORD/FREE PWR...SOC CONCPT STAT SAMP/SIZ CHARTS STERTYP 20. PAGE 129 A2653 — INT/ORG SOCIETY DIPLOM

B59
STOVEL J.A.,CANADA IN THE WORLD ECONOMY. CANADA PRICE DEMAND...STAT CHARTS BIBLIOG 20 VINER/J. PAGE 139 A2838 — INT/TRADE BAL/PAY FINAN ECO/TAC

L59
GRANDIN T.,"THE POLITICAL USE OF THE RADIO." EUR+WWI SOCIETY INT/ORG DIPLOM CONTROL ATTIT ORD/FREE...CONCPT STAT RECORD SAMP GEN/LAWS TOT/POP 20. PAGE 55 A1128 — COM/IND EDU/PROP NAT/LISM

L59
MURPHY J.C.,"SOME IMPLICATIONS OF EUROPE'S COMMON MARKET. IN (COOK P, ECONOMIC DEVELOPMENT AND INTERNATIONAL TRADE,." EUR+WWI ECO/DEV DIST/IND INDUS NAT/G PLAN ECO/TAC INT/TRADE WEALTH...STAT TREND OEEC TOT/POP 20 EEC. PAGE 106 A2178 — MARKET INT/ORG REGION

S59
REUBENS E.D.,"THE BASIS FOR REORIENATION OF AMERICAN FOREIGN AID POLICY." USA+45 USSR STRUCT INT/ORG CONSULT ECO/TAC ADMIN DRIVE MORAL ORD/FREE PWR WEALTH...RELATIV MATH STAT TREND GEN/LAWS VAL/FREE 20. PAGE 120 A2467 — ECO/UNDEV PLAN FOR/AID DIPLOM

S59
SAYEGH F.,"ARAB NATIONALISM AND SOVIET-AMERICAN RELATIONS." ISLAM USA+45 ECO/UNDEV PLAN ECO/TAC LEGIT NAT/LISM DRIVE PERCEPT KNOWL PWR...DECISION CONCPT STAT RECORD TREND CON/ANAL VAL/FREE 20 COLD/WAR. PAGE 127 A2610 — DIPLOM USSR

S59
TIPTON J.B.,"PARTICIPATION OF THE UNITED STATES IN THE INTERNATIONAL LABOR ORGANIZATION." USA+45 LAW STRUCT ECO/DEV ECO/UNDEV INDUS TEC/DEV ECO/TAC ADMIN PERCEPT ORD/FREE SKILL...STAT HIST/WRIT GEN/METH ILO WORK 20. PAGE 144 A2946 — LABOR INT/ORG

B60
FRANCK P.G.,AFGHANISTAN: BETWEEN EAST AND WEST. AFGHANISTN USA+45 USSR ECO/UNDEV PLAN ADMIN ROUTINE ATTIT PWR...STAT OBS CHARTS TOT/POP COLD/WAR 20. PAGE 48 A0978 — ECO/TAC TREND FOR/AID

B60
HOVET T. JR.,BLOC POLITICS IN THE UNITED NATIONS. WOR+45...POLICY STAT CHARTS METH UN. PAGE 68 A1396 — LOBBY INT/ORG DIPLOM CHOOSE

B60
KRISTENSEN T.,THE ECONOMIC WORLD BALANCE. FUT WOR+45 CULTURE ECO/DEV BAL/PWR INT/TRADE REGION PWR WEALTH...STAT TREND CHARTS 20. PAGE 82 A1685 — ECO/UNDEV ECO/TAC FOR/AID

B60
LERNER A.P.,THE ECONOMICS OF CONTROL. USA+45 ECO/UNDEV INT/ORG ACT/RES PLAN CAP/ISM INT/TRADE ATTIT WEALTH...SOC MATH STAT GEN/LAWS INDEX 20. PAGE 87 A1785 — ECO/DEV ROUTINE ECO/TAC SOCISM

B60
LISTER L.,EUROPE'S COAL AND STEEL COMMUNITY. FRANCE GERMANY STRUCT ECO/DEV EXTR/IND INDUS MARKET NAT/G DELIB/GP ECO/TAC INT/TRADE EDU/PROP ATTIT RIGID/FLEX ORD/FREE PWR WEALTH...CONCPT STAT TIME/SEQ CHARTS ECSC 20. PAGE 90 A1843 — EUR+WWI INT/ORG REGION

B60
STEIN E.,AMERICAN ENTERPRISE IN THE EUROPEAN COMMON MARKET: A LEGAL PROFILE. EUR+WWI FUT USA+45 SOCIETY STRUCT ECO/DEV NAT/G VOL/ASSN CONSULT PLAN TEC/DEV ECO/TAC INT/TRADE ADMIN ATTIT RIGID/FLEX PWR...MGT NEW/IDEA STAT TREND COMPUT/IR SIMUL EEC 20. PAGE 137 A2814 — MARKET ADJUD INT/LAW

B60
STOLPER W.F.,GERMANY BETWEEN EAST AND WEST: THE ECONOMICS OF COMPETITIVE COEXISTENCE. FUT GERMANY/E GERMANY/W WOR+45 FINAN POL/PAR BUDGET ECO/TAC FOR/AID INT/TRADE...STAT CHARTS METH/COMP 20 COLD/WAR. PAGE 138 A2832 — ECO/DEV DIPLOM GOV/COMP BAL/PWR

B60
THE ECONOMIST (LONDON),THE COMMONWEALTH AND EUROPE. EUR+WWI WOR+45 AGRI FINAN INCOME...STAT CENSUS CHARTS CMN/WLTH EEC. PAGE 142 A2911 — INT/TRADE INDUS INT/ORG NAT/COMP

B60
WOLF C.,FOREIGN AID: THEORY AND PRACTICE IN SOUTHERN ASIA. CEYLON INDONESIA PHILIPPINE S/ASIA CULTURE STRATA ECO/UNDEV PLAN EDU/PROP ATTIT ...METH/CNCPT MATH QUANT STAT CONT/OBS TIME/SEQ SIMUL TOT/POP 20. PAGE 166 A3378 — ACT/RES ECO/TAC FOR/AID

L60
DEUTSCH K.W.,"TOWARD AN INVENTORY OF BASIC TRENDS AND PATTERNS IN COMPARATIVE AND INTERNATIONAL POLITICS." UNIV WOR+45 SOCIETY STRUCT INT/ORG NAT/G CREATE PLAN EDU/PROP KNOWL...PHIL/SCI METH/CNCPT STAT SELF/OBS OBS/ENVIR SAMP TREND CON/ANAL CHARTS SOC/EXP GEN/METH 20. PAGE 36 A0739 — R+D PERCEPT

L60
HAAS E.B.,"CONSENSUS FORMATION IN THE COUNCIL OF EUROPE." EUR+WWI NAT/G DELIB/GP DIPLOM REGION CHOOSE PWR SOVEREIGN...RELATIV NEW/IDEA QUANT CHARTS INDEX TOT/POP OEEC 20 COUNCL/EUR. PAGE 59 A1206 — POL/PAR INT/ORG STAT

S60
GARNICK D.H.,"ON THE ECONOMIC FEASIBILITY OF A MIDDLE EASTERN COMMON MARKET." AFR ISLAM CULTURE INDUS NAT/G PLAN TEC/DEV ECO/TAC ADMIN ATTIT DRIVE RIGID/FLEX...PLURIST STAT TREND GEN/LAWS 20. PAGE 51 A1051 — MARKET INT/TRADE

S60
NANES A.,"THE EUROPEAN COMMUNITY AND THE UNITED STATES: EVOLVING RELATIONS." EUR+WWI USA+45 WOR+45 ECO/UNDEV MARKET NAT/G DELIB/GP PLAN LEGIT ATTIT PWR WEALTH...CONCPT STAT TIME/SEQ CON/ANAL EEC OEEC 20 EURATOM. PAGE 107 A2194 — INT/ORG REGION

S60
SCHWELB E.,"INTERNATIONAL CONVENTIONS ON HUMAN RIGHTS." FUT WOR+45 LAW CONSTN CULTURE SOCIETY STRUCT VOL/ASSN DELIB/GP PLAN ADJUD SUPEGO LOVE MORAL...SOC CONCPT STAT RECORD HIST/WRIT TREND 20 UN. PAGE 130 A2664 — INT/ORG HUM

B61
BARNES W.,THE FOREIGN SERVICE OF THE UNITED STATES. USA+45 USA-45 CONSTN INT/ORG POL/PAR CONSULT DELIB/GP LEGIS DOMIN EDU/PROP EXEC ATTIT RIGID/FLEX ORD/FREE PWR...POLICY CONCPT STAT OBS RECORD BIOG TIME/SEQ TREND. PAGE 11 A0224 — NAT/G MGT DIPLOM

B61
GURTOO D.H.N.,INDIA'S BALANCE OF PAYMENTS (1920-1960). INDIA FINAN DIPLOM FOR/AID INT/TRADE PRICE COLONIAL...CHARTS BIBLIOG 20. PAGE 58 A1197 — BAL/PAY STAT ECO/TAC ECO/UNDEV

B61
NATIONAL BANK OF LIBYA,INFLATION IN LIBYA (PAMPHLET). LIBYA SOCIETY NAT/G PLAN INT/TRADE ...STAT CHARTS 20 GOLD/STAND. PAGE 107 A2200 — ECO/TAC ECO/UNDEV FINAN BUDGET

B61
OECD,STATISTICS OF BALANCE OF PAYMENTS 1950-61. WOR+45 FINAN ECO/TAC INT/TRADE DEMAND WEALTH...STAT NAT/COMP 20 OEEC OECD. PAGE 111 A2278 — BAL/PAY ECO/DEV INT/ORG CHARTS

B61
STRAUSZ-HUPE R.,A FORWARD STRATEGY FOR AMERICA. FUT WOR+45 ECO/DEV INT/ORG NAT/G POL/PAR DELIB/GP FORCES ACT/RES CREATE ECO/TAC DOMIN EDU/PROP ATTIT DRIVE PWR...MAJORIT CONCPT STAT OBS TIME/SEQ TREND COLD/WAR TOT/POP. PAGE 139 A2848 — USA+45 PLAN DIPLOM

B61
TRIFFIN R.,GOLD AND THE DOLLAR CRISIS: THE FUTURE OF CONVERTIBILITY. USA+45 USA-45 INT/ORG PROB/SOLV BUDGET INT/TRADE PRICE...STAT CHARTS 19/20 GOLD/STAND. PAGE 145 A2963 — FINAN ECO/DEV ECO/TAC BAL/PAY

B61
YUAN TUNG-LI,A GUIDE TO DOCTORAL DISSERTATIONS BY — BIBLIOG

CHINESE STUDENTS IN AMERICA, 1905-1960. ASIA CULTURE SOCIETY ECO/UNDEV NAT/G PROB/SOLV DIPLOM LEAD ATTIT...HUM SOC STAT 20. PAGE 169 A3441
ACADEM ACT/RES OP/RES

B61
ZIMMERMAN I.,A GUIDE TO CURRENT LATIN AMERICAN PERIODICALS: HUMANITIES AND SOCIAL SCIENCES. LABOR SECT EDU/PROP...GEOG HUM SOC LING STAT NAT/COMP 20. PAGE 170 A3452
BIBLIOG/A DIPLOM L/A+17C PHIL/SCI

S61
"CRITERIA FOR ALLOCATING INVESTMENT RESOURCES AMONG VARIOUS FIELDS OF DEVELOPMENT IN UNDERDEVELOPED ECONOMIES." ASIA AGRI INT/ORG CAP/ISM BAL/PAY EFFICIENCY PROFIT WEALTH...STAT 20 UN. PAGE 3 A0061
BIBLIOG/A ECO/UNDEV PLAN TEC/DEV

S61
RAY J.,"THE EUROPEAN FREE-TRADE ASSOCIATION AND ITS IMPACT ON INDIA'S TRADE." EUR+WWI FRANCE GERMANY INDIA S/ASIA UK NAT/G VOL/ASSN PLAN INT/TRADE ROUTINE WEALTH...STAT CHARTS CMN/WLTH EEC OEEC 20 EFTA. PAGE 120 A2453
ECO/DEV ECO/TAC

B62
CALDER R.,COMMON SENSE ABOUT A STARVING WORLD. WOR+45 STRATA ECO/DEV PLAN GP/REL BIO/SOC HABITAT ...POLICY GEOG STAT RECORD 20 UN BIRTH/CON. PAGE 23 A0466
FOR/AID CENSUS ECO/UNDEV AGRI

B62
FORD A.G.,THE GOLD STANDARD 1880-1914: BRITAIN AND ARGENTINA. UK ECO/UNDEV INT/TRADE ADMIN GOV/REL DEMAND EFFICIENCY...STAT CHARTS 19/20 ARGEN GOLD/STAND. PAGE 47 A0960
FINAN ECO/TAC BUDGET BAL/PAY

B62
MEADE J.E.,CASE STUDIES IN EUROPEAN ECONOMIC UNION. BELGIUM EUR+WWI LUXEMBOURG NAT/G INT/TRADE REGION ROUTINE WEALTH...METH/CNCPT STAT CHARTS ECSC TOT/POP OEEC EEC 20. PAGE 99 A2028
INT/ORG ECO/TAC

B62
PERRE J.,LES MUTATIONS DE LA GUERRE MODERNE: DE LA REVOLUTION FRANCAISE A LA REVOLUTION NUCLEAIRE. DIPLOM ARMS/CONT DEATH REV WEAPON GP/REL PEACE ATTIT...STAT PREDICT BIBLIOG 18/20 WWI. PAGE 115 A2365
WAR FORCES NUC/PWR

B62
UNECA LIBRARY,BOOKS ON AFRICA IN THE UNECA LIBRARY. WOR+45 AGRI INT/ORG NAT/G PLAN WRITING REGION...SOC STAT UN. PAGE 147 A3008
BIBLIOG AFR ECO/UNDEV TEC/DEV

L62
SCHWERIN K.,"LAW LIBRARIES AND FOREIGN LAW COLLECTION IN THE USA." USA+45 USA-45...INT/LAW STAT 20. PAGE 130 A2667
BIBLIOG LAW ACADEM ADMIN

L62
WILCOX F.O.,"THE UN AND THE NON-ALIGNED NATIONS." AFR S/ASIA USA+45 ECO/UNDEV INT/ORG TEC/DEV EDU/PROP RIGID/FLEX ORD/FREE PWR...POLICY HUM CONCPT STAT OBS TIME/SEQ STERTYP GEN/METH UN 20. PAGE 164 A3345
ATTIT TREND

B63
ABSHIRE D.M.,NATIONAL SECURITY: POLITICAL, MILITARY, AND ECONOMIC STRATEGIES IN THE DECADE AHEAD. ASIA COM USA+45 WOR+45 ECO/DEV ECO/UNDEV INT/ORG DELIB/GP FORCES ECO/TAC COERCE ATTIT RIGID/FLEX HEALTH ORD/FREE PWR WEALTH...POLICY STAT CHARTS ANTHOL COLD/WAR VAL/FREE. PAGE 4 A0083
FUT ACT/RES BAL/PWR

B63
BRZEZINSKI Z.K.,AFRICA AND THE COMMUNIST WORLD. AFR ASIA COM CULTURE SOCIETY INT/ORG DELIB/GP ACT/RES ECO/TAC COERCE ORD/FREE PWR WEALTH...STAT TOT/POP VAL/FREE 20. PAGE 21 A0418
ATTIT EDU/PROP DIPLOM USSR

B63
HENDERSON W.,SOUTHEAST ASIA: PROBLEMS OF UNITED STATES POLICY. COM S/ASIA CULTURE STRATA ECO/UNDEV INT/ORG DELIB/GP ACT/RES ECO/TAC DOMIN EDU/PROP LEGIT COERCE ATTIT ALL/VALS...STAT TIME/SEQ ANTHOL VAL/FREE 20. PAGE 64 A1313
ASIA USA+45 DIPLOM

B63
HOVET T. JR.,AFRICA IN THE UNITED NATIONS. AFR DELIB/GP EDU/PROP LOBBY CHOOSE ORD/FREE PWR RESPECT SKILL...STAT TIME/SEQ CON/ANAL CHARTS STERTYP VAL/FREE 20 UN. PAGE 68 A1397
INT/ORG USSR

B63
KRAVIS I.B.,DOMESTIC INTERESTS AND INTERNATIONAL OBLIGATIONS: SAFEGUARDS IN INTERNATIONAL TRADE ORGANIZATIONS. EUR+WWI USA+45 WOR+45 FINAN DELIB/GP ATTIT RIGID/FLEX HEALTH...STAT EEC VAL/FREE OEEC ECSC 20. PAGE 82 A1680
INT/ORG ECO/TAC INT/TRADE

B63
MULLENBACH P.,CIVILIAN NUCLEAR POWER: ECONOMIC ISSUES AND POLICY FORMATION. FINAN INT/ORG DELIB/GP ACT/RES ECO/TAC ATTIT SUPEGO HEALTH ORD/FREE PWR ...POLICY CONCPT MATH STAT CHARTS VAL/FREE 20 COLD/WAR. PAGE 105 A2166
USA+45 ECO/DEV NUC/PWR

B63
US AGENCY INTERNATIONAL DEV,US FOREIGN ASSISTANCE AND ASSISTANCE FROM INTERNATIONAL ORGANIZATIONS. USA+45 WOR+45 ECO/UNDEV AGRI NAT/G TEC/DEV BUDGET. PAGE 149 A3050
FOR/AID INT/ORG CHARTS STAT

B63
US GOVERNMENT,REPORT TO INTER-AMERICAN ECONOMIC AND SOCIAL COUNCIL AT SECOND ANNUAL MEETING. L/A+17C USA+45 VOL/ASSN TEC/DEV DIPLOM TAX EATING EFFICIENCY HEALTH...STAT CHARTS 20 AID. PAGE 153 A3116
ECO/TAC FOR/AID FINAN PLAN

B63
US SENATE COMM GOVT OPERATIONS,REPORT OF A STUDY OF US FOREIGN AID IN TEN MIDDLE EASTERN AND AFRICAN COUNTRIES. AFR ISLAM USA+45 FORCES PLAN BUDGET DIPLOM TAX DETER WEALTH...STAT CHARTS 20 CONGRESS AID MID/EAST. PAGE 156 A3174
FOR/AID EFFICIENCY ECO/TAC FINAN

L63
PADELFORD N.J.,"FINANCIAL CRISIS AND THE UNITED NATIONS." FUT USSR WOR+45 LAW CONSTN FINAN INT/ORG DELIB/GP FORCES PLAN BUDGET DIPLOM COST WEALTH ...STAT CHARTS UN CONGO 20. PAGE 113 A2311
CREATE ECO/TAC

S63
ALPHAND H.,"FRANCE AND HER ALLIES." EUR+WWI UK USA+45 ECO/DEV INT/ORG NAT/G VOL/ASSN FORCES TOP/EX DIPLOM ECO/TAC LEGIT ATTIT DRIVE ORD/FREE PWR WEALTH...STAT EEC TOT/POP 20. PAGE 6 A0130
ACT/RES FRANCE

S63
DARLING F.C.,"THE GEOPOLITICS OF AMERICAN FOREIGN POLITICS IN ASIA." COM S/ASIA USA+45 USSR ECO/UNDEV NAT/G VOL/ASSN CONSULT PLAN GUERRILLA...STAT TOT/POP 20. PAGE 34 A0682
FORCES ECO/TAC FOR/AID DIPLOM

S63
ETZIONI A.,"EUROPEAN UNIFICATION: A STRATEGY OF CHANGE." EUR+WWI CULTURE ECO/DEV DELIB/GP ACT/RES ECO/TAC EDU/PROP ATTIT ORD/FREE PWR SKILL WEALTH ...STAT TIME/SEQ EEC TOT/POP VAL/FREE 20. PAGE 42 A0869
INT/ORG RIGID/FLEX

S63
GORDON B.,"ECONOMIC IMPEDIMENTS TO REGIONALISM IN SOUTH EAST ASIA." BURMA FUT S/ASIA THAILAND USA+45 AGRI INDUS R+D NAT/G PLAN ECO/TAC WEALTH...STAT CONT/OBS 20. PAGE 54 A1110
VOL/ASSN ECO/UNDEV INT/TRADE REGION

S63
HALLSTEIN W.,"THE EUROPEAN COMMUNITY AND ATLANTIC PARTNERSHIP." EUR+WWI USA+45 MARKET NAT/G VOL/ASSN DELIB/GP ARMS/CONT NUC/PWR ATTIT PWR...CONCPT STAT TIME/SEQ TREND OEEC 20 EEC. PAGE 60 A1235
INT/ORG ECO/TAC UK

S63
HORVATH J.,"MOSCOW'S AID PROGRAM: THE PERFORMANCE SO FAR." COM FUT USSR WOR+45 ECO/DEV FINAN PLAN TEC/DEV FOR/AID EDU/PROP ATTIT ORD/FREE PWR WEALTH ...POLICY STAT CHARTS VAL/FREE 20. PAGE 68 A1389
ECO/UNDEV ECO/TAC

S63
KRAVIS I.B.,"THE POLITICAL ARITHMETIC OF INTERNATIONAL BURDENSHARING." FUT USA+45 WOR+45 FINAN DELIB/GP ACT/RES CREATE TEC/DEV ATTIT PWR WEALTH...POLICY MATH STAT VAL/FREE 20. PAGE 82 A1681
INT/ORG ECO/TAC

S63
LERNER D.,"FRENCH ELITE PERSPECTIVES ON THE UNITED NATIONS." EUR+WWI INT/ORG HEALTH ORD/FREE PWR RESPECT...STAT INT SAMP/SIZ VAL/FREE UN 20. PAGE 87 A1786
ATTIT STERTYP ELITES FRANCE

S63
LIPSHART A.,"THE ANALYSIS OF BLOC VOTING IN THE GENERAL ASSEMBLY." L/A+17C WOR+45 ACT/RES INGP/REL ...POLICY DECISION NEW/IDEA STAT IDEA/COMP UN. PAGE 90 A1832
CHOOSE INT/ORG DELIB/GP

S63
MATHUR P.N.,"GAINS IN ECONOMIC GROWTH FROM INTERNATIONAL TRADE." USA-45 ECO/DEV FINAN INDUS ATTIT WEALTH...MATH QUANT STAT BIOG TREND GEN/LAWS WORK 20. PAGE 96 A1966
MARKET ECO/TAC CAP/ISM INT/TRADE

S63
PINCUS J.,"THE COST OF FOREIGN AID." WOR+45 ECO/DEV FINAN NAT/G VOL/ASSN CREATE ECO/TAC EDU/PROP WEALTH ...METH/CNCPT STAT CHARTS HYPO/EXP TOT/POP VAL/FREE 20. PAGE 116 A2380
USA+45 ECO/UNDEV FOR/AID

S63
SHWADRAN B.,"MIDDLE EAST OIL, 1962." ISLAM USSR ECO/DEV DIST/IND INDUS PLAN BAL/PWR DISPL DRIVE ...POLICY STAT TREND GEN/LAWS EEC OEEC 20 OIL. PAGE 132 A2712
MARKET ECO/TAC INT/TRADE

S63
SINGER M.R.,"ELECTIONS WITHIN THE UNITED NATIONS: AN EXPERIMENTAL STUDY UTILIZING STATISTICAL ANALYSIS." USA+45 WOR+45 DIPLOM ECO/TAC COERCE PWR WEALTH...STAT CHARTS SIMUL GEN/LAWS COLD/WAR VAL/FREE UN 20. PAGE 133 A2732
INT/ORG CHOOSE

B64
HEKHUIS D.J.,INTERNATIONAL STABILITY: MILITARY, ECONOMIC AND POLITICAL DIMENSIONS. FUT WOR+45 LAW ECO/UNDEV INT/ORG NAT/G VOL/ASSN FORCES ACT/RES BAL/PWR PWR WEALTH...STAT UN 20. PAGE 64 A1310
TEC/DEV DETER REGION

B64
HINSHAW R.,THE EUROPEAN COMMUNITY AND AMERICAN TRADE: A STUDY IN ATLANTIC ECONOMICS AND POLICY. EUR+WWI UK USA+45 ECO/DEV ECO/UNDEV AGRI INDUS INT/ORG NAT/G ECO/TAC TARIFFS REGION...STAT CHARTS EEC 20. PAGE 65 A1337
MARKET TREND INT/TRADE

B64
JACOB P.E.,THE INTEGRATION OF POLITICAL COMMUNITIES. USA+45 WOR+45 CULTURE LOC/G MUNIC NAT/G CREATE PLAN LEGIT REGION COERCE ALL/VALS ...POLICY GEOG PSY SOC TREND HYPO/EXP GEN/LAWS VAL/FREE 20. PAGE 72 A1483 — INT/ORG METH/CNCPT SIMUL STAT

B64
MARKHAM J.W.,THE COMMON MARKET: FRIEND OR COMPETITOR. EUR+WWI FUT USA+45 INT/ORG LG/CO NAT/G VOL/ASSN DELIB/GP EX/STRUC PLAN TARIFFS ORD/FREE PWR WEALTH...POLICY STAT TREND EEC VAL/FREE 20. PAGE 95 A1943 — ECO/DEV ECO/TAC

B64
OECD,THE FLOW OF FINANCIAL RESOURCES TO LESS DEVELOPED COUNTRIES 1956-1963. WOR+45 FINAN CAP/ISM ...POLICY STAT 20. PAGE 111 A2281 — FOR/AID BUDGET INT/ORG ECO/UNDEV

B64
OWEN W.,STRATEGY FOR MOBILITY. FUT WOR+45 WOR-45 DIST/IND INT/ORG NAT/G DELIB/GP PLAN TEC/DEV ECO/TAC ORD/FREE PWR WEALTH...STAT TIME/SEQ VAL/FREE 20. PAGE 112 A2304 — COM/IND ECO/UNDEV

B64
RAMAZANI R.K.,THE MIDDLE EAST AND THE EUROPEAN COMMON MARKET. EUR+WWI ISLAM ECO/DEV EXTR/IND MARKET PROC/MFG INT/ORG NAT/G TEC/DEV ECO/TAC REGION DRIVE WEALTH...STAT CHARTS EEC TOT/POP 20. PAGE 119 A2437 — ECO/UNDEV ATTIT INT/TRADE

B64
RUSSET B.M.,WORLD HANDBOOK OF POLITICAL AND SOCIAL INDICATORS. WOR+45 COM/IND ADMIN WEALTH...GEOG 20. PAGE 126 A2577 — DIPLOM STAT NAT/G NAT/COMP

B64
SINGER H.W.,INTERNATIONAL DEVELOPMENT: GROWTH AND CHANGE. AFR BRAZIL L/A+17C WOR+45 CULTURE AGRI INDUS NAT/G ACT/RES ECO/TAC EDU/PROP WEALTH...GEOG CONCPT METH/CNCPT STAT HYPO/EXP WORK TOT/POP 20. PAGE 133 A2723 — FINAN ECO/UNDEV FOR/AID INT/TRADE

B64
STOESSINGER J.G.,FINANCING THE UNITED NATIONS SYSTEM. FUT WOR+45 CONSTN NAT/G VOL/ASSN DELIB/GP EX/STRUC ECO/TAC LEGIT CT/SYS PWR WEALTH...STAT TIME/SEQ TREND CHARTS VAL/FREE. PAGE 138 A2830 — FINAN INT/ORG

S64
CARNEGIE ENDOWMENT INT. PEACE,"ADMINISTRATION AND BUDGET (ISSUES BEFORE THE NINETEENTH GENERAL ASSEMBLY)." WOR+45 FINAN BUDGET ECO/TAC ROUTINE COST...STAT RECORD UN. PAGE 24 A0495 — INT/ORG ADMIN

S64
KOJIMA K.,"THE PATTERN OF INTERNATIONAL TRADE AMONG ADVANCED COUNTRIES." EUR+WWI UK USA+45 WOR+45 MARKET NAT/G ECO/TAC WEALTH...MATH STAT CON/ANAL CHARTS EEC CHINJAP 20 CHINJAP. PAGE 81 A1665 — ECO/DEV TREND INT/TRADE

S64
MOWER A.G.,"THE OFFICIAL PRESSURE GROUP OF THE COUNCIL OF EUROPE'S CONSULATIVE ASSEMBLY." EUR+WWI SOCIETY STRUCT FINAN CONSULT ECO/TAC ADMIN ROUTINE ATTIT PWR WEALTH...STAT CHARTS 20 COUNCL/EUR. PAGE 105 A2160 — INT/ORG EDU/PROP

B65
AMERICAN ECONOMIC ASSOCIATION,INDEX OF ECONOMIC JOURNALS 1886-1965 (7 VOLS.). UK USA+45 USA-45 AGRI FINAN PLAN ECO/TAC INT/TRADE ADMIN...STAT CENSUS 19/20. PAGE 7 A0145 — BIBLIOG WRITING INDUS

B65
FRIEDMANN W.,AN INTRODUCTION TO WORLD POLITICS (5TH ED.). WOR+45 ECO/UNDEV BAL/PWR FOR/AID INT/TRADE PEACE...STAT CENSUS CHARTS BIBLIOG T 20 COLD/WAR UN THIRD/WRLD. PAGE 49 A1003 — DIPLOM INT/ORG PROB/SOLV

B65
HASSON J.A.,THE ECONOMICS OF NUCLEAR POWER. INDIA UK USA+45 WOR+45 INT/ORG TEC/DEV COST...SOC STAT CHARTS 20 EURATOM. PAGE 63 A1286 — NUC/PWR INDUS ECO/DEV METH

B65
HOSELITZ B.F.,ECONOMICS AND THE IDEA OF MANKIND. UNIV ECO/DEV ECO/UNDEV DIST/IND INDUS INT/ORG NAT/G ACT/RES ECO/TAC WEALTH...CONCPT STAT. PAGE 68 A1392 — CREATE INT/TRADE

B65
JALEE P.,THE PILLAGE OF THE THIRD WORLD (TRANS. BY MARY KLOPPER). WOR+45 AGRI INDUS ECO/TAC FOR/AID COLONIAL CONTROL PRODUC PWR WEALTH...STAT CHARTS 20 RESOURCE/N. PAGE 73 A1493 — ECO/UNDEV DOMIN INT/TRADE DIPLOM

B65
MCCOLL G.D.,THE AUSTRALIAN BALANCE OF PAYMENTS. UK USA+45 AGRI WORKER DIPLOM EQUILIB PRODUC...STAT TREND CHARTS BIBLIOG/A 20 AUSTRAL. PAGE 97 A2001 — ECO/DEV BAL/PAY INT/TRADE COST

B65
SABLE M.H.,PERIODICALS FOR LATIN AMERICAN ECONOMIC DEVELOPMENT, TRADE, AND FINANCE: AN ANNOTATED BIBLIOGRAPHY (A PAMPHLET). ECO/TAC PRODUC PROFIT ...STAT NAT/COMP 20 OAS. PAGE 126 A2583 — BIBLIOG/A L/A+17C ECO/UNDEV INT/TRADE

B65
UNESCO,INTERNATIONAL ORGANIZATIONS IN THE SOCIAL SCIENCES(REV. ED.). LAW ADMIN ATTIT...CRIMLGY GEOG INT/LAW PSY SOC STAT 20 UNESCO. PAGE 148 A3024 — INT/ORG R+D PROF/ORG ACT/RES

B65
US BUREAU OF THE BUDGET,THE BALANCE OF PAYMENTS STATISTICS OF THE UNITED STATES: A REVIEW AND APPRAISAL. USA+45 FINAN NAT/G PROB/SOLV DIPLOM. PAGE 150 A3057 — BAL/PAY STAT METH/COMP BUDGET

B65
US DEPARTMENT OF THE ARMY,NUCLEAR WEAPONS AND THE ATLANTIC ALLIANCE: A BIBLIOGRAPHIC SURVEY. ASIA COM EUR+WWI USA+45 FORCES DIPLOM WEAPON...STAT 20 NATO. PAGE 152 A3108 — BIBLIOG/A ARMS/CONT NUC/PWR BAL/PWR

B65
WINT G.,ASIA: A HANDBOOK. ASIA COM INDIA USSR CULTURE INTELL NAT/G...GEOG STAT CENSUS NAT/COMP WORSHIP 20 TREATY CHINJAP. PAGE 165 A3365 — DIPLOM SOC

L65
MATTHEWS D.G.,"A CURRENT BIBLIOGRAPHY ON ETHIOPIAN AFFAIRS: A SELECT BIBLIOGRAPHY FROM 1950-1964." ETHIOPIA LAW CULTURE ECO/UNDEV INDUS LABOR SECT FORCES DIPLOM CIVMIL/REL RACE/REL...LING STAT 20. PAGE 96 A1969 — BIBLIOG/A ADMIN POL/PAR NAT/G

L65
MATTHEWS D.G.,"LE TIERS MONDE: A SELECT AND PRELIMINARY BIBLIOGRAPHIC SURVEY OF MANPOWER IN DEVELOPING COUNTRIES, 1960-1964." AFR ISLAM L/A+17C INDUS PLAN PROB/SOLV TEC/DEV INT/TRADE EFFICIENCY WEALTH...STAT 20. PAGE 96 A1971 — BIBLIOG/A ECO/UNDEV LABOR WORKER

B66
SUPPLEMENTAL FOREIGN ASSISTANCE FISCAL YEAR 1966: VIETNAM. CHINA/COM COM S/ASIA USA+45 VIETNAM EXTR/IND FINAN DIPLOM TAX GUERRILLA HABITAT ORD/FREE...STAT CHARTS 20 SENATE PRESIDENT. PAGE 4 A0077 — CONFER LEGIS WAR FOR/AID

B66
EWING L.L.,THE REFERENCE HANDBOOK OF THE ARMED FORCES OF THE WORLD. WOR+45 ECO/TAC FOR/AID COERCE WAR PWR 20. PAGE 43 A0879 — FORCES STAT DIPLOM PLAN

B66
PIQUET H.S.,THE US BALANCE OF PAYMENTS AND INTERNATIONAL MONETARY RESERVES. USA+45 PROB/SOLV INT/TRADE GOV/REL EQUILIB...POLICY STAT CHARTS 20 GOLD/STAND. PAGE 116 A2384 — BAL/PAY DIPLOM FINAN ECO/TAC

B66
RIESELBACH L.N.,THE ROOTS OF ISOLATIONISM* CONGRESSIONAL VOTING AND PRESIDENTIAL LEADERSHIP IN FOREIGN POLICY. POL/PAR LEGIS DIPLOM EDU/PROP LEAD REGION REPRESENT...SOC STAT IDEA/COMP HYPO/EXP BIBLIOG 19/20 CONGRESS. PAGE 121 A2477 — ISOLAT CHOOSE CHIEF POLICY

B66
WILLIAMS P.,AID IN UGANDA - EDUCATION. UGANDA UK FINAN ACADEM INT/ORG SCHOOL PROB/SOLV ECO/TAC UTIL ...STAT CHARTS 20. PAGE 165 A3352 — PLAN EDU/PROP FOR/AID ECO/UNDEV

B66
WOOLLEY H.B.,MEASURING TRANSACTIONS BETWEEN WORLD AREAS. WOR+45 FINAN...STAT NET/THEORY CHARTS DICTIONARY 20 GOLD/STAND. PAGE 167 A3395 — INT/TRADE BAL/PAY DIPLOM ECOMETRIC

L66
AMERICAN ECONOMIC REVIEW,"SIXTY-THIRD LIST OF DOCTORAL DISSERTATIONS IN POLITICAL ECONOMY IN AMERICAN UNIVERSITIES AND COLLEGES." ECO/DEV AGRI FINAN LABOR WORKER PLAN BUDGET INT/TRADE ADMIN DEMAND...MGT STAT 20. PAGE 7 A0146 — BIBLIOG/A CONCPT ACADEM

C66
WINT G.,"ASIA: A HANDBOOK." ASIA S/ASIA INDUS LABOR SECT PRESS RACE/REL MARXISM...STAT CHARTS BIBLIOG 20. PAGE 165 A3366 — ECO/UNDEV DIPLOM NAT/G SOCIETY

C66
ZAWODNY J.K.,"GUIDE TO THE STUDY OF INTERNATIONAL RELATIONS." OP/RES PRESS...STAT INT 20. PAGE 169 A3449 — BIBLIOG/A DIPLOM INT/LAW INT/ORG

B67
US AGENCY INTERNATIONAL DEV,PROPOSED FOREIGN AID PROGRAM FOR 1968: SUMMARY PRESENTATION TO THE CONGRESS. AFR S/ASIA USA+45 AGRI TEC/DEV DIPLOM ECO/TAC BAL/PAY COST HEALTH KNOWL SKILL 20 AID CONGRESS. PAGE 149 A3053 — ECO/UNDEV BUDGET FOR/AID STAT

S67
VELIKONJA J.,"ITALIAN IMMIGRANTS IN THE UNITED STATES IN THE MID-SIXTIES" ITALY USA+45 KIN MUNIC NAT/G WORKER DIPLOM REGION GP/REL ADJUST...GEOG CHARTS SOC/INTEG 20. PAGE 158 A3226 — HABITAT ORD/FREE TREND STAT

S67
VERBA S.,"PUBLIC OPINION AND THE WAR IN VIETNAM." USA+45 VIETNAM DIPLOM WAR...CORREL STAT QU CHARTS 20. PAGE 158 A3228 — ATTIT KNO/TEST NAT/G PLAN

STATE GOVERNMENT....SEE PROVS

STATE DEPARTMENT....SEE DEPT/STATE

STATHAM J. A2466

STATISTICS....SEE STAT, ALSO LOGIC, MATHEMATICS, AND LANGUAGE INDEX, P. XIV

STEEL R. A2809,A2810,A2811

STEELE R. A2812

STEGER H.S. A2813

STEIN E. A2814,A2815,A2816

STEPHENS O. A2817

STEREOTYPE....SEE STERTYP

STERN/GANG....STERN GANG (PALESTINE)

STERNBERG F. A2818

STERTYP....STEREOTYPE

B32
BRYCE J.,THE HOLY ROMAN EMPIRE. GERMANY ITALY MOD/EUR CULTURE SOCIETY STRUCT INT/ORG NAT/G SECT DIPLOM DOMIN WAR SUPEGO ALL/VALS SOVEREIGN...GEOG SOC TIME/SEQ CHARTS STERTYP. PAGE 20 A0413
CHRIST-17C NAT/LISM

B39
DULLES J.,WAR, PEACE AND CHANGE. FRANCE ITALY UK USA-45 WOR-45 LAW INT/ORG NAT/G SECT VOL/ASSN FORCES TOP/EX DOMIN ARMS/CONT COERCE ATTIT PERSON RIGID/FLEX MORAL PWR...JURID STERTYP TOT/POP LEAGUE/NAT 20. PAGE 39 A0796
EDU/PROP TOTALISM WAR

B42
KELSEN H.,LAW AND PEACE IN INTERNATIONAL RELATIONS. FUT WOR-45 NAT/G DELIB/GP DIPLOM LEGIT RIGID/FLEX ORD/FREE SOVEREIGN...JURID CONCPT TREND STERTYP GEN/LAWS LEAGUE/NAT 20. PAGE 77 A1580
INT/ORG ADJUD PEACE INT/LAW

L44
HAILEY,"THE FUTURE OF COLONIAL PEOPLES." WOR-45 CONSTN CULTURE ECO/UNDEV AGRI MARKET INT/ORG NAT/G SECT CONSULT ECO/TAC LEGIT ADMIN NAT/LISM ALL/VALS ...SOC OBS TREND STERTYP CMN/WLTH LEAGUE/NAT PARLIAMENT 20. PAGE 59 A1218
PLAN CONCPT DIPLOM UK

S46
DOUGLAS W.O.,"SYMPOSIUM ON WORLD ORGANIZATION." FUT USA+45 WOR+45 CONSTN SOCIETY NAT/G PLAN EDU/PROP LEGIT RIGID/FLEX KNOWL...INT/LAW JURID STERTYP TOT/POP 20. PAGE 38 A0778
INT/ORG LAW

B51
UNESCO,FREEDOM AND CULTURE. FUT WOR+45 CONSTN CULTURE PERF/ART VOL/ASSN EDU/PROP PEACE ATTIT ALL/VALS SOVEREIGN...POLICY MAJORIT CONCPT TREND STERTYP GEN/LAWS UN TOT/POP 20. PAGE 147 A3013
INT/ORG SOCIETY

S51
BUCHANAN W.,"STEREOTYPES AND TENSIONS AS REVEALED BY THE UNESCO INTERNATIONAL POLL." WOR+45 INT/ORG ATTIT DISPL PERCEPT RIGID/FLEX...INT TESTS SAMP 20. PAGE 21 A0424
R+D STERTYP

S51
ICHHEISER G.,"MISUNDERSTANDING IN INTERNATIONAL RELATIONS." UNIV SOCIETY FACE/GP INT/ORG SECT ATTIT PERSON RIGID/FLEX LOVE RESPECT...RELATIV PSY SOC CONCPT MYTH SOC/EXP GEN/LAWS. PAGE 70 A1431
PERCEPT STERTYP NAT/LISM DIPLOM

S52
MASTERS R.D.,"RUSSIA AND THE UNITED NATIONS." FUT USA+45 USSR WOR+45 CONSTN VOL/ASSN DELIB/GP TOP/EX CREATE DIPLOM ADMIN...TREND STERTYP UN 20. PAGE 96 A1962
INT/ORG PWR

B54
MANGONE G.,A SHORT HISTORY OF INTERNATIONAL ORGANIZATION. MOD/EUR USA+45 USA-45 WOR+45 WOR-45 LAW LEGIS CREATE LEGIT ROUTINE RIGID/FLEX PWR ...JURID CONCPT OBS TIME/SEQ STERTYP GEN/LAWS UN TOT/POP VAL/FREE 18/20. PAGE 94 A1921
INT/ORG INT/LAW

B55
COMM. STUDY ORGAN. PEACE,REPORTS. WOR-45 ECO/DEV ECO/UNDEV VOL/ASSN CONSULT FORCES PLAN TEC/DEV DOMIN EDU/PROP NUC/PWR ATTIT PWR WEALTH...JURID STERTYP FAO ILO 20 UN. PAGE 28 A0579
WOR+45 INT/ORG ARMS/CONT

S55
TORRE M.,"PSYCHIATRIC OBSERVATIONS OF INTERNATIONAL CONFERENCES." WOR+45 INT/ORG PROF/ORG VOL/ASSN CONSULT EDU/PROP ROUTINE ATTIT DRIVE KNOWL...PSY METH/CNCPT OBS/ENVIR STERTYP 20. PAGE 144 A2950
DELIB/GP OBS DIPLOM

B57
ARON R.,L'UNIFICATION ECONOMIQUE DE L'EUROPE. EUR+WWI SWITZERLND UK INT/ORG NAT/G REGION NAT/LISM ORD/FREE PWR...CONCPT METH/CNCPT OBS TREND STERTYP GEN/LAWS EEC 20. PAGE 9 A0181
VOL/ASSN ECO/TAC

B57
BERLE A.A.,TIDES OF CRISIS: A PRIMER OF FOREIGN RELATIONS. USA+45 WOR+45 DOMIN NUC/PWR NAT/LISM PWR ...CONCPT STERTYP GEN/LAWS 20 UN. PAGE 14 A0276
INT/ORG TREND PEACE

B57
DEAN V.M.,THE NATURE OF THE NON-WESTERN WORLD. AFR ASIA L/A+17C S/ASIA CULTURE SOCIETY STRATA ECO/DEV DIPLOM ECO/TAC FOR/AID ATTIT DRIVE ALL/VALS ...RELATIV SOC CONCPT TIME/SEQ TREND TOT/POP 20. PAGE 35 A0718
ECO/UNDEV STERTYP NAT/LISM

B57
LEVONTIN A.V.,THE MYTH OF INTERNATIONAL SECURITY: A JURIDICAL AND CRITICAL ANALYSIS. FUT WOR+45 WOR-45 LAW NAT/G VOL/ASSN ACT/RES BAL/PWR ATTIT ORD/FREE ...JURID METH/CNCPT TIME/SEQ TREND STERTYP 20. PAGE 88 A1797
INT/ORG INT/LAW SOVEREIGN MYTH

B57
TRIFFIN R.,EUROPE AND THE MONEY MUDDLE. USA+45 INT/ORG NAT/G CONSULT PLAN ECO/TAC EXEC ROUTINE BAL/PAY WEALTH...METH/CNCPT OBS TREND CHARTS STERTYP GEN/METH EEC VAL/FREE ECSC. PAGE 145 A2962
EUR+WWI ECO/DEV REGION

B58
GANGE J.,UNIVERSITY RESEARCH ON INTERNATIONAL AFFAIRS. USA+45 ACADEM INT/ORG CONSULT CREATE EXEC ROUTINE...QUANT STAT INT STERTYP GEN/METH TOT/POP VAL/FREE 20. PAGE 51 A1040
R+D MGT DIPLOM

B58
GARTHOFF R.L.,SOVIET STRATEGY IN THE NUCLEAR AGE. FUT USSR R+D INT/ORG NAT/G ACT/RES TEC/DEV DOMIN DETER WAR ATTIT PWR...RELATIV METH/CNCPT SELF/OBS TREND CON/ANAL STERTYP GEN/LAWS 20. PAGE 51 A1052
COM FORCES BAL/PWR NUC/PWR

B58
ORGANSKI A.F.K.,WORLD POLITICS. FUT WOR+45 SOCIETY STRUCT NAT/G BAL/PWR ECO/TAC DOMIN NAT/LISM ATTIT KNOWL ORD/FREE PWR...CONCPT METH/CNCPT TREND STERTYP GEN/LAWS TOT/POP 20. PAGE 112 A2297
INT/ORG DIPLOM

B58
RIGGS R.,POLITICS IN THE UNITED NATIONS: A STUDY OF UNITED STATES INFLUENCE IN THE GENERAL ASSEMBLY. USA+45 WOR+45 LEGIS TOP/EX CREATE BAL/PWR DIPLOM DOMIN EDU/PROP COLONIAL ROUTINE ATTIT RIGID/FLEX PWR...CONCPT OBS HIST/WRIT CHARTS STERTYP GEN/LAWS UN COLD/WAR 20. PAGE 121 A2480
INT/ORG

B58
VARG P.A.,MISSIONARIES, CHINESE, AND DIPLOMATS: THE AMERICAN PROTESTANT MISSIONARY MOVEMENT IN CHINA, 1890-1952. ASIA ECO/UNDEV NAT/G PROB/SOLV CAP/ISM EDU/PROP COLONIAL NAT/LISM ATTIT MARXISM...NAT/COMP STERTYP 20 CHINJAP PROTESTANT MISSION. PAGE 158 A3221
CULTURE DIPLOM SECT

S58
BOURBON-BUSSET J.,"HOW DECISIONS ARE MADE IN FOREIGN POLITICS: PSYCHOLOGY IN INTERNATIONAL POLITICS." WOR+45 NAT/G SECT REGION WAR MORAL ...CONCPT OBS STERTYP GEN/LAWS TOT/POP COLD/WAR 20. PAGE 17 A0350
INT/ORG DELIB/GP DIPLOM

S58
BURNS A.L.,"THE INTERNATIONAL CONSEQUENCES OF EXPECTING SURPRISE." WOR+45 INT/ORG NAT/G FORCES DIPLOM COERCE NUC/PWR WAR CHOOSE ORD/FREE ...METH/CNCPT STYLE OBS STERTYP TOT/POP VAL/FREE. PAGE 22 A0440
PLAN PWR DETER

S58
THOMPSON K.W.,"NATIONAL SECURITY IN A NUCLEAR AGE." USA+45 WOR+45 SOCIETY INT/ORG NAT/G TOP/EX DIPLOM DOMIN EDU/PROP LEGIT ARMS/CONT COERCE ORD/FREE ...TREND STERTYP TOT/POP VAL/FREE COLD/WAR 20. PAGE 143 A2929
FORCES PWR BAL/PWR

B59
BALL M.M.,NATO AND THE EUROPEAN MOVEMENT. EUR+WWI USA+45 INT/ORG FORCES BAL/PWR EDU/PROP LEGIT REGION ATTIT ORD/FREE PWR...STAT OBS TIME/SEQ TREND CHARTS ORG/CHARTS STERTYP COLD/WAR EEC OEEC 20 NATO. PAGE 10 A0212
DELIB/GP STRUCT

B59
COUDENHOVE-KALERGI,FROM WAR TO PEACE. USA+45 USSR WOR+45 WOR-45 LAW INT/ORG NAT/G LEGIT COERCE LOVE ...POLICY PLURIST METH/CNCPT STERTYP TOT/POP UN 20 NATO. PAGE 31 A0636
FUT ORD/FREE

B59
GREENSPAN M.,THE MODERN LAW OF LAND WARFARE. WOR+45 INT/ORG NAT/G DELIB/GP FORCES ATTIT...POLICY HYPO/EXP STERTYP 20. PAGE 56 A1142
ADJUD PWR WAR

B59
SCHURZ W.L.,AMERICAN FOREIGN AFFAIRS: A GUIDE TO INTERNATIONAL AFFAIRS. USA+45 WOR+45 WOR-45 NAT/G FORCES LEGIS TOP/EX PLAN EDU/PROP LEGIT ADMIN ROUTINE ATTIT ORD/FREE PWR...SOC CONCPT STAT SAMP/SIZ CHARTS STERTYP 20. PAGE 129 A2653
INT/ORG SOCIETY DIPLOM

S59
CARLSTON K.S.,"NATIONALIZATION: AN ANALYTIC APPROACH." WOR+45 INT/ORG ECO/TAC DOMIN LEGIT ADJUD COERCE ORD/FREE PWR WEALTH SOCISM...JURID CONCPT TREND STERTYP TOT/POP VAL/FREE 20. PAGE 24 A0486
INDUS NAT/G NAT/LISM SOVEREIGN

B60
CAMPAIGNE J.G.,AMERICAN MIGHT AND SOVIET MYTH. COM
USA+45

EUR+WWI ECO/DEV ECO/UNDEV INT/ORG NAT/G CAP/ISM ECO/TAC FOR/AID EDU/PROP ATTIT PWR WEALTH...POLICY CONCPT MYTH TREND STERTYP GEN/LAWS COLD/WAR. PAGE 23 A0473 — DOMIN DIPLOM USSR

B60
PRITTIE T.,GERMANY DIVIDED: THE LEGACY OF THE NAZI ERA. EUR+WWI GERMANY RACE/REL SUPEGO...PSY AUD/VIS BIBLIOG/A 20 NAZI. PAGE 118 A2414 — STERTYP PERSON ATTIT DIPLOM

B60
SCHLESINGER J.R.,THE POLITICAL ECONOMY OF NATIONAL SECURITY. USA+45 USSR WOR+45 ECO/DEV ECO/UNDEV NAT/G DELIB/GP TOP/EX BAL/PWR DIPLOM INT/TRADE ATTIT PWR...STERTYP TOT/POP 20. PAGE 128 A2628 — PLAN ECO/TAC

L60
FERNBACH A.P.,"SOVIET COEXISTENCE STRATEGY." WOR+45 PROF/ORG VOL/ASSN DIPLOM DOMIN EDU/PROP ATTIT DRIVE PERSON PWR SKILL WEALTH...POLICY OBS SAMP TREND STERTYP ILO WORK COLD/WAR 420. PAGE 45 A0919 — LABOR INT/ORG USSR

S60
GOODMAN E.,"THE CRY OF NATIONAL LIBERATION: RECENT SOVIET ATTITUDES TOWARDS NATIONAL SELF-DETERMINATION." COM INT/ORG LEGIS ROUTINE PWR ...TIME/SEQ CON/ANAL STERTYP GEN/LAWS 20 UN. PAGE 54 A1101 — ATTIT EDU/PROP SOVEREIGN USSR

S60
KEYFITZ N.,"WESTERN PERSPECTIVES AND ASIAN PROBLEMS." ASIA EUR+WWI S/ASIA SOCIETY FOR/AID ...POLICY SOC CONCPT STERTYP WORK TOT/POP 20. PAGE 78 A1604 — CULTURE ATTIT

S60
O'BRIEN W.,"THE ROLE OF FORCE IN THE INTERNATIONAL JURIDICAL ORDER." WOR+45 NAT/G FORCES DOMIN ADJUD ARMS/CONT DETER NUC/PWR WAR ATTIT PWR...CATH INT/LAW JURID CONCPT TREND STERTYP GEN/LAWS 20. PAGE 110 A2266 — INT/ORG COERCE

B61
STILLMAN E.,THE NEW POLITICS: AMERICA AND THE END OF THE POSTWAR WORLD. FUT WOR+45 CULTURE SOCIETY ECO/UNDEV INT/ORG NAT/G FORCES TOP/EX ACT/RES DIPLOM EDU/PROP LEGIT ROUTINE DETER ATTIT ORD/FREE PWR...OBS STERTYP COLD/WAR TOT/POP VAL/FREE. PAGE 138 A2827 — USA+45 PLAN

S61
ANGLIN D.,"UNITED STATES OPPOSITION TO CANADIAN MEMBERSHIP IN THE PAN AMERICAN UNION: A CANADIAN VIEW." L/A+17C UK USA+45 VOL/ASSN DELIB/GP EX/STRUC PLAN DIPLOM DOMIN REGION ATTIT RIGID/FLEX PWR ...RELATIV CONCPT STERTYP CMN/WLTH OAS 20. PAGE 8 A0162 — INT/ORG CANADA

S61
GALBRAITH J.K.,"A POSITIVE APPROACH TO ECONOMIC AID." FUT USA+45 INTELL NAT/G CONSULT ACT/RES DIPLOM ECO/TAC EDU/PROP ATTIT KNOWL PWR WEALTH ...SOC STERTYP 20. PAGE 50 A1030 — ECO/UNDEV ROUTINE FOR/AID

B62
ARNOLD H.J.P.,AID FOR DEVELOPING COUNTRIES. COM EUR+WWI USA+45 USSR WOR+45 EDU/PROP ATTIT DRIVE PWR WEALTH...TREND CHARTS STERTYP NAT/ 20. PAGE 9 A0177 — ECO/UNDEV ECO/TAC FOR/AID

B62
COUNCIL ON WORLD TENSIONS,A STUDY OF WORLD TENSIONS AND DEVELOPMENT. WOR+45 ECO/DEV ECO/UNDEV INT/ORG PLAN DIPLOM ECO/TAC EDU/PROP ATTIT KNOWL ORD/FREE PWR WEALTH...CONCPT TREND CHARTS STERTYP COLD/WAR TOT/POP 20. PAGE 31 A0640 — TEC/DEV SOC

B62
DUTOIT B.,LA NEUTRALITE SUISSE A L'HEURE EUROPEENNE. EUR+WWI MOD/EUR INT/ORG NAT/G VOL/ASSN PLAN BAL/PWR LEGIT NEUTRAL REGION PEACE ORD/FREE SOVEREIGN...CONCPT OBS TIME/SEQ TREND STERTYP VAL/FREE LEAGUE/NAT UN 20. PAGE 40 A0812 — ATTIT DIPLOM SWITZERLND

B62
FORBES H.W.,THE STRATEGY OF DISARMAMENT. FUT WOR+45 INT/ORG VOL/ASSN CONSULT ARMS/CONT COERCE NUC/PWR WAR DRIVE RIGID/FLEX ORD/FREE PWR...POLICY CONCPT OBS TREND STERTYP 20. PAGE 47 A0959 — PLAN FORCES DIPLOM

B62
HUMPHREY D.D.,THE UNITED STATES AND THE COMMON MARKET. USA+45 INDUS MARKET INT/ORG PLAN EDU/PROP BAL/PAY DRIVE PWR WEALTH...TREND STERTYP EEC 20. PAGE 69 A1415 — ATTIT ECO/TAC

B62
WRIGHT Q.,PREVENTING WORLD WAR THREE. FUT WOR+45 CULTURE INT/ORG NAT/G CONSULT FORCES ADMIN ARMS/CONT DRIVE RIGID/FLEX ORD/FREE SOVEREIGN ...POLICY CONCPT TREND STERTYP COLD/WAR 20. PAGE 168 A3416 — CREATE ATTIT

L62
STEIN E.,"MR HAMMARSKJOLD, THE CHARTER LAW AND THE FUTURE ROLE OF THE UNITED NATIONS SECRETARY-GENERAL." WOR+45 CONSTN INT/ORG DELIB/GP FORCES TOP/EX BAL/PWR LEGIT ROUTINE RIGID/FLEX PWR ...POLICY JURID OBS STERTYP UN COLD/WAR 20 HAMMARSK/D. PAGE 137 A2815 — CONCPT BIOG

L62
WILCOX F.O.,"THE UN AND THE NON-ALIGNED NATIONS." AFR S/ASIA USA+45 ECO/UNDEV INT/ORG TEC/DEV EDU/PROP RIGID/FLEX ORD/FREE PWR...POLICY HUM CONCPT STAT OBS TIME/SEQ STERTYP GEN/METH UN 20. PAGE 164 A3345 — ATTIT TREND

S62
DALLIN A.,"THE SOVIET VIEW OF THE UNITED NATIONS." WOR+45 VOL/ASSN TOP/EX DIPLOM DOMIN EDU/PROP LEGIT ATTIT RIGID/FLEX PWR...CONCPT OBS HIST/WRIT TIME/SEQ STERTYP GEN/LAWS COLD/WAR UN 20. PAGE 33 A0676 — COM INT/ORG USSR

S62
DEUTSCH K.W.,"TOWARDS WESTERN EUROPEAN INTEGRATION: AN INTERIM ASSESSMENT." EUR+WWI STRUCT ECO/DEV INT/ORG ECO/TAC INT/TRADE EDU/PROP PEACE ATTIT DRIVE PWR SOVEREIGN...PSY SOC TIME/SEQ CHARTS STERTYP 20. PAGE 36 A0741 — VOL/ASSN RIGID/FLEX REGION

S62
JACOBSON H.K.,"THE UNITED NATIONS AND COLONIALISM: A TENTATIVE APPRAISAL." AFR FUT S/ASIA USA+45 USSR WOR+45 NAT/G DELIB/GP PLAN DIPLOM ECO/TAC DOMIN ADMIN ROUTINE COERCE ATTIT RIGID/FLEX ORD/FREE PWR ...OBS STERTYP UN 20. PAGE 73 A1486 — INT/ORG CONCPT COLONIAL

S62
MARIAS J.,"A PROGRAM FOR EUROPE." EUR+WWI INT/ORG NAT/G PLAN DIPLOM DOMIN PWR...STERTYP TOT/POP 20. PAGE 95 A1938 — VOL/ASSN CREATE REGION

S62
MCWHINNEY E.,"CO-EXISTENCE, THE CUBA CRISIS, AND COLD WAR-INTERNATIONAL WAR." CUBA USA+45 USSR WOR+45 NAT/G TOP/EX BAL/PWR DIPLOM DOMIN LEGIT PEACE RIGID/FLEX ORD/FREE...STERTYP COLD/WAR 20. PAGE 99 A2026 — CONCPT INT/LAW

S62
PYE L.W.,"THE POLITICAL IMPULSES AND FANTASIES BEHIND FOREIGN AID." FUT USA+45 ECO/UNDEV DIPLOM ECO/TAC ROUTINE DRIVE KNOWL...SOC METH/CNCPT NEW/IDEA TREND HYPO/EXP STERTYP GEN/METH 20. PAGE 118 A2420 — ACT/RES ATTIT FOR/AID

S62
SCHACHTER O.,"DAG HAMMARSKJOLD AND THE RELATION OF LAW TO POLITICS." FUT WOR+45 INT/ORG CONSULT PLAN TEC/DEV BAL/PWR DIPLOM LEGIT ATTIT PERCEPT ORD/FREE ...POLICY JURID CONCPT OBS TESTS STERTYP GEN/LAWS 20 HAMMARSK/D. PAGE 128 A2616 — ACT/RES ADJUD

S62
SPENSER J.H.,"AFRICA AT THE UNITED NATIONS: SOME OBSERVATIONS." FUT ECO/UNDEV NAT/G CONSULT DELIB/GP PLAN BAL/PWR ECO/TAC EDU/PROP ATTIT RIGID/FLEX HEALTH ORD/FREE PWR WEALTH...POLICY CONCPT OBS TREND STERTYP GEN/METH UN VAL/FREE. PAGE 136 A2786 — AFR INT/ORG REGION

B63
HOVET T. JR.,AFRICA IN THE UNITED NATIONS. AFR DELIB/GP EDU/PROP LOBBY CHOOSE ORD/FREE PWR RESPECT SKILL...STAT TIME/SEQ CON/ANAL CHARTS STERTYP VAL/FREE 20 UN. PAGE 68 A1397 — INT/ORG USSR

B63
LERCHE C.O. JR.,CONCEPTS OF INTERNATIONAL POLITICS. WOR+45 WOR-45 LAW DELIB/GP EX/STRUC TEC/DEV ECO/TAC INT/TRADE LEGIT ROUTINE COERCE ATTIT ORD/FREE PWR RESPECT...STERTYP GEN/LAWS VAL/FREE. PAGE 87 A1782 — INT/ORG WAR

B63
QUAISON-SACKEY A.,AFRICA UNBOUND: REFLECTIONS OF AN AFRICAN STATESMAN. ISLAM CULTURE INTELL INT/ORG POL/PAR TOP/EX DOMIN EDU/PROP LEGIT ATTIT PERSON ...CONCPT OBS TIME/SEQ CHARTS STERTYP 20 UN. PAGE 118 A2423 — AFR BIOG

L63
RUSSETT B.M.,"TOWARD A MODEL OF COMPETITIVE INTERNATIONAL POLITICS." USA+45 WOR+45 INT/ORG NAT/G POL/PAR VOL/ASSN LEGIS BAL/PWR DIPLOM LEGIT PWR...CONCPT CONT/OBS STERTYP GEN/LAWS TOT/POP COLD/WAR 20 UN. PAGE 126 A2579 — ATTIT EDU/PROP

S63
BECHHOEFER B.G.,"UNITED NATIONS PROCEDURES IN CASE OF VIOLATIONS OF DISARMAMENT AGREEMENTS." COM USA+45 USSR LAW CONSTN NAT/G EX/STRUC FORCES LEGIS BAL/PWR EDU/PROP CT/SYS ARMS/CONT ORD/FREE PWR ...POLICY STERTYP UN VAL/FREE 20. PAGE 12 A0245 — INT/ORG DELIB/GP

S63
BLOOMFIELD L.P.,"INTERNATIONAL FORCE IN A DISARMING BUT REVOLUTIONARY WORLD." INT/ORG COERCE REV DRIVE PWR...CONCPT STERTYP GEN/LAWS 20. PAGE 16 A0318 — FORCES ORD/FREE ARMS/CONT GUERRILLA

S63
FRIEDMANN W.G.,"THE USES OF 'GENERAL PRINCIPLES' IN THE DEVELOPMENT OF INTERNATIONAL LAW." WOR+45 NAT/G DIPLOM INT/TRADE LEGIT ROUTINE RIGID/FLEX ORD/FREE ...JURID CONCPT STERTYP GEN/METH 20. PAGE 49 A1005 — LAW INT/LAW INT/ORG

S63
LERNER D.,"FRENCH ELITE PERSPECTIVES ON THE UNITED NATIONS." EUR+WWI INT/ORG HEALTH ORD/FREE PWR RESPECT...STAT INT SAMP/SIZ VAL/FREE UN 20. PAGE 87 A1786 — ATTIT STERTYP ELITES FRANCE

S63
NOGEE J.L.,"PROPOGANDA AND NEGOTIATION: THE CASE OF THE TEN NATION DISARMAMENT COMMITTEE." COM EUR+WWI — INT/ORG EDU/PROP

USA+45 VOL/ASSN DELIB/GP FORCES DIPLOM DOMIN LEGIT PWR...METH/CNCPT STERTYP COLD/WAR VAL/FREE 20. PAGE 110 A2248 — ARMS/CONT

S63
VEROFF J.,"AFRICAN STUDENTS IN THE UNITED STATES." AFR USA+45 CULTURE ACT/RES FOR/AID PEACE ATTIT KNOWL...SOC RECORD DEEP/QU SYS/QU CHARTS STERTYP TOT/POP 20. PAGE 159 A3230 — PERCEPT RIGID/FLEX RACE/REL

L64
CLAUDE I.,"THE OAS, THE UN, AND THE UNITED STATES." L/A+17C USA+45 CONSTN NAT/G DELIB/GP DOMIN EDU/PROP LEGIT REGION COERCE ORD/FREE PWR...TIME/SEQ TREND STERTYP OAS UN 20. PAGE 27 A0546 — INT/ORG POLICY

L64
MILLIS W.,"THE DEMILITARIZED WORLD." COM USA+45 USSR WOR+45 CONSTN NAT/G EX/STRUC PLAN LEGIT ATTIT DRIVE...CONCPT TIME/SEQ STERTYP TOT/POP COLD/WAR 20. PAGE 102 A2085 — FUT INT/ORG BAL/PWR PEACE

S64
COFFEY J.,"THE SOVIET VIEW OF A DISARMED WORLD." COM USA+45 INT/ORG NAT/G EX/STRUC EDU/PROP COERCE PERCEPT ORD/FREE PWR...TREND STERTYP VAL/FREE 20 UN. PAGE 27 A0556 — FORCES ATTIT ARMS/CONT USSR

S64
DRAKE S.T.C.,"DEMOCRACY ON TRIAL IN AFRICA." EUR+WWI FUT USA+45 ECO/UNDEV INT/ORG NAT/G POL/PAR TOP/EX EDU/PROP LEGIT ATTIT ALL/VALS...POLICY TREND GEN/LAWS VAL/FREE 20. PAGE 38 A0785 — AFR STERTYP

S64
GARDNER R.N.,"THE SOVIET UNION AND THE UNITED NATIONS." WOR+45 FINAN POL/PAR VOL/ASSN FORCES ECO/TAC DOMIN EDU/PROP LEGIT ADJUD ADMIN ARMS/CONT COERCE ATTIT ALL/VALS...POLICY MAJORIT CONCPT OBS TIME/SEQ TREND STERTYP UN. PAGE 51 A1046 — COM INT/ORG USSR

S64
GARMARNIKOW M.,"INFLUENCE-BUYING IN WEST AFRICA." COM FUT USSR INTELL NAT/G PLAN TEC/DEV ECO/TAC DOMIN EDU/PROP REGION NAT/LISM ATTIT DRIVE ALL/VALS SOVEREIGN...POLICY PSY SOC CONCPT TREND STERTYP WORK COLD/WAR 20. PAGE 51 A1049 — AFR ECO/UNDEV FOR/AID SOCISM

S64
GROSSER A.,"Y A-T-IL UN CONFLIT FRANCO-AMERICAIN." EUR+WWI USA+45 INT/ORG NAT/G PLAN BAL/PWR DIPLOM EDU/PROP NUC/PWR ATTIT DRIVE ORD/FREE PWR...CONCPT OBS TIME/SEQ TREND STERTYP VAL/FREE COLD/WAR. PAGE 57 A1179 — VOL/ASSN NAT/LISM FRANCE

S64
HICKEY D.,"THE PHILOSOPHICAL ARGUMENT FOR WORLD GOVERNMENT." WOR+45 SOCIETY ACT/RES PLAN LEGIT ADJUD PEACE PERCEPT PERSON ORD/FREE...HUM JURID PHIL/SCI METH/CNCPT CON/ANAL STERTYP GEN/LAWS TOT/POP 20. PAGE 65 A1327 — FUT INT/ORG

S64
HOFFMANN S.,"CE QU'EN PENSENT LES AMERICAINS." EUR+WWI INT/ORG VOL/ASSN PLAN BAL/PWR DIPLOM DOMIN EDU/PROP REGION ARMS/CONT DRIVE ORD/FREE PWR ...POLICY CONCPT OBS TREND STERTYP COLD/WAR VAL/FREE 20. PAGE 66 A1357 — USA+45 ATTIT FRANCE

S64
PADELFORD N.J.,"THE ORGANIZATION OF AFRICAN UNITY." ECO/UNDEV INT/ORG PLAN BAL/PWR DIPLOM ECO/TAC NAT/LISM ORD/FREE PWR WEALTH...CONCPT TREND STERTYP VAL/FREE COLD/WAR 20. PAGE 113 A2313 — AFR VOL/ASSN REGION

STETTINIUS E.R. A2819

STEUBER F.A. A2820

STEVENS R.P. A2821

STEVENSN/A....ADLAI STEVENSON

STEVENSON A.E. A2822,A2823

STEWARD/JH....JULIAN H. STEWARD

STEWART C.F. A2824

STEWART I.G. A2825

STILLMAN C.W. A2826

STILLMAN E.O. A2827, A2828

STIMSON/HL....HENRY L. STIMSON

B60
MORISON E.E.,TURMOIL AND TRADITION: A STUDY OF THE LIFE AND TIMES OF HENRY L. STIMSON. USA+45 USA-45 POL/PAR CHIEF DELIB/GP FORCES BAL/PWR DIPLOM ARMS/CONT WAR PEACE 19/20 STIMSON/HL ROOSEVLT/F TAFT/WH HOOVER/H REPUBLICAN. PAGE 104 A2142 — BIOG NAT/G EX/STRUC

STOCHASTIC PROCESSES....SEE PROB/SOLV, MODELS INDEX

STOCKHOLM....STOCKHOLM

STOESSINGER J.G. A2829,A2830

STOETZER O.C. A2831

STOHLER J. A2601

STOKES/CB....CARL B. STOKES

STOL....SHORT TAKE-OFF AND LANDING AIRCRAFT

STOLPER W.F. A2832

STONE J. A2833,A2834,A2835,A2836

STONE/HF....HARLAN FISKE STONE

STONE/IF....I.F. STONE

STORING/HJ....H.J. STORING

STOURZH G. A1094,A1095

STOUT H.M. A2837

STOVEL J.A. A2838

STOWELL E.C. A2839

STRACHEY A. A2840

STRACHEY J. A2841,A2842,A2843

STRANGE....ESTRANGEMENT, ALIENATION, IMPERSONALITY

N19
UNITED ARAB REPUBLIC,THE PROBLEM OF THE PALESTINIAN REFUGEES (PAMPHLET). ISRAEL UAR LAW PROB/SOLV EDU/PROP CONFER ADJUD CONTROL NAT/LISM HEALTH 20 JEWS UN MIGRATION. PAGE 148 A3029 — STRANGE GP/REL INGP/REL DIPLOM

C50
NUMELIN R.,"THE BEGINNINGS OF DIPLOMACY." INT/TRADE WAR GP/REL PEACE STRANGE ATTIT...INT/LAW CONCPT BIBLIOG. PAGE 110 A2260 — DIPLOM KIN CULTURE LAW

B58
INSTITUTE MEDITERRANEAN AFF,THE PALESTINE REFUGEE PROBLEM. UAR WOR+45 INT/ORG PLAN PROB/SOLV PEACE ...POLICY GEOG STAT CHARTS 20 JEWS UN MIGRATION. PAGE 70 A1444 — STRANGE HABITAT GP/REL INGP/REL

B59
CHANDLER E.H.S.,THE HIGH TOWER OF REFUGE: THE INSPIRING STORY OF REFUGEE RELIEF THROUGHOUT THE WORLD. WOR+45 NEIGH SECT WORKER PROB/SOLV DIPLOM ECO/TAC EDU/PROP COST HABITAT. PAGE 25 A0519 — GIVE WEALTH STRANGE INT/ORG

B59
KAPLAN D.,THE ARAB REFUGEES: AN ABNORMAL PROBLEM. UAR WOR+45 PROB/SOLV DIPLOM GOV/REL ADJUST EFFICIENCY...POLICY GEOG INT/LAW 20 UN JEWS MIGRATION. PAGE 76 A1557 — STRANGE HABITAT GP/REL INGP/REL

B59
PANHUYS H.F.,THE ROLE OF NATIONALITY IN INTERNATIONAL LAW. ADJUD CRIME WAR STRANGE...JURID TREND. PAGE 114 A2330 — INT/LAW NAT/LISM INGP/REL

B63
LOOMIE A.J.,THE SPANISH ELIZABETHANS: THE ENGLISH EXILES AT THE COURT OF PHILIP II. SPAIN UK WAR INGP/REL DRIVE HABITAT CATHISM...BIOG 16/17 MIGRATION. PAGE 91 A1860 — NAT/G STRANGE POLICY DIPLOM

B64
US HOUSE COMM ON JUDICIARY,IMMIGRATION HEARINGS. DELIB/GP STRANGE HABITAT...GEOG JURID 20 CONGRESS MIGRATION. PAGE 154 A3140 — NAT/G POLICY DIPLOM NAT/LISM

B65
DU BOIS W.E.B.,THE WORLD AND AFRICA. USA+45 CAP/ISM DISCRIM STRANGE SOCISM...TIME/SEQ TREND IDEA/COMP 19/20 NEGRO. PAGE 39 A0789 — AFR DIPLOM COLONIAL CULTURE

B65
SMITH A.L. JR.,THE DEUTSCHTUM OF NAZI GERMANY AND THE UNITED STATES. GERMANY USA-45 DIPLOM ATTIT FASCISM...BIBLIOG 20 MIGRATION NAZI. PAGE 134 A2744 — INGP/REL NAT/LISM STRANGE DELIB/GP

B65
US SENATE COMM ON JUDICIARY,REFUGEE PROBLEMS IN SOUTH VIETNAM AND LAOS: HEARINGS BEFORE SUBCOMMITTEE TO INVESTIGATE PROBLEMS OF REFUGEES, ESCAPEES. CHINA/COM LAOS USA+45 VIETNAM/S PROB/SOLV DIPLOM GOV/REL GP/REL EFFICIENCY ORD/FREE...POLICY GEOG 20 CONGRESS MIGRATION. PAGE 157 A3194 — STRANGE HABITAT FOR/AID CIVMIL/REL

B66
SANDERS R.E.,SPAIN AND THE UNITED NATIONS 1945-1950. SPAIN CHIEF DIPLOM CONFER SANCTION ATTIT ...POLICY 20 UN COLD/WAR. PAGE 127 A2599 — INT/ORG FASCISM GP/REL

STRANGE

B66
WESTIN A.F.,VIEWS OF AMERICA. COM USA+45 USSR SOCIETY ECO/UNDEV POL/PAR ECO/TAC GP/REL STRANGE MARXISM...MARXIST 20. PAGE 163 A3323
CONCPT ATTIT DIPLOM IDEA/COMP

S67
KYLE K.,"BACKGROUND TO THE CRISIS" ISLAM ISRAEL UAR UK USSR NAT/G PROB/SOLV LEGIT CONTROL REGION STRANGE MORAL 20 JEWS. PAGE 83 A1698
DIPLOM POLICY SOVEREIGN COERCE

S67
THIEN T.T.,"VIETNAM: A CASE OF SOCIAL ALIENATION." VIETNAM AGRI FORCES FOR/AID ADMIN REPRESENT INGP/REL PWR 19/20. PAGE 143 A2918
NAT/G ELITES WORKER STRANGE

S67
VAN DUSEN H.P.,"HAMMARSKOLD IN THE WORLD'S SERVICE." DIPLOM CONFER LEAD PEACE STRANGE UTOPIA MORAL SKILL OBJECTIVE...INT/LAW SELF/OBS 20. PAGE 158 A3211
INT/ORG CONSULT TOP/EX NEUTRAL

STRASBOURG....STRASBOURG PLAN

STRATA....SOCIAL STRATA, CLASS DIVISION

N
INTERNATIONAL REVIEW OF ADMINISTRATIVE SCIENCES. WOR+45 WOR-45 STRATA ECO/DEV ECO/UNDEV CREATE PLAN PROB/SOLV DIPLOM CONTROL REPRESENT...MGT 20. PAGE 1 A0011
BIBLIOG/A ADMIN INT/ORG NAT/G

B08
LABRIOLA A.,ESSAYS ON THE MATERIALISTIC CONCEPTION OF HISTORY. STRATA POL/PAR CAP/ISM DIPLOM INT/TRADE WAR 20. PAGE 83 A1706
MARXIST WORKER REV COLONIAL

B16
ROOT E.,THE MILITARY AND COLONIAL POLICY OF THE US. L/A+17C USA-45 LAW SOCIETY STRATA STRUCT INT/ORG NAT/G SCHOOL FORCES EDU/PROP ALL/VALS...OBS VAL/FREE 19/20. PAGE 123 A2522
ACT/RES PLAN DIPLOM WAR

B17
VEBLEN T.B.,AN INQUIRY INTO THE NATURE OF PEACE AND THE TERMS OF ITS PERPETUATION. UNIV STRATA FINAN EDU/PROP PRICE COST DISCRIM NAT/LISM MORAL ORD/FREE PACIFIST 20 WORLDUNITY. PAGE 158 A3224
PEACE DIPLOM WAR NAT/G

B24
NAVILLE A.,LIBERTE, EGALITE, SOLIDARITE: ESSAIS D'ANALYSE. STRATA FAM VOL/ASSN INT/TRADE GP/REL MORAL MARXISM SOCISM...PSY TREATY. PAGE 107 A2205
ORD/FREE SOC IDEA/COMP DIPLOM

B28
PLAYNE C.E.,THE PRE-WAR MIND IN BRITAIN. GERMANY MOD/EUR UK STRATA SECT DIPLOM EDU/PROP CROWD SUFF ...POLICY ANARCH PSY SOC IDEA/COMP 20 WWI. PAGE 116 A2388
PRESS WAR DOMIN ATTIT

B29
BUELL R.,INTERNATIONAL RELATIONS. WOR+45 WOR-45 CONSTN STRATA FORCES TOP/EX ADMIN ATTIT DRIVE SUPEGO MORAL ORD/FREE PWR SOVEREIGN...JURID SOC CONCPT 20. PAGE 21 A0428
INT/ORG BAL/PWR DIPLOM

B32
MASTERS R.D.,INTERNATIONAL LAW IN INTERNATIONAL COURTS. BELGIUM EUR+WWI FRANCE GERMANY MOD/EUR SWITZERLND WOR-45 SOCIETY STRATA STRUCT LEGIT EXEC ALL/VALS...JURID HIST/WRIT TIME/SEQ TREND GEN/LAWS 20. PAGE 96 A1961
INT/ORG LAW INT/LAW

B38
PETTEE G.S.,THE PROCESS OF REVOLUTION. COM FRANCE ITALY MOD/EUR RUSSIA SPAIN WOR-45 ELITES INTELL SOCIETY STRATA STRUCT INT/ORG NAT/G POL/PAR ACT/RES PLAN EDU/PROP LEGIT EXEC...SOC MYTH TIME/SEQ TOT/POP 18/20. PAGE 115 A2370
COERCE CONCPT REV

B39
MARRIOTT J.,COMMONWEALTH OR ANARCHY: A SURVEY OF PROJECTS OF PEACE. WOR-45 STRATA DOMIN ATTIT ORD/FREE PWR...TRADIT TIME/SEQ GEN/METH 16/20 CMN/WLTH. PAGE 95 A1945
FUT INT/ORG PEACE

B39
THOMAS J.A.,THE HOUSE OF COMMONS, 1832-1901; A STUDY OF ITS ECONOMIC AND FUNCTIONAL CHARACTER. UK LAW STRATA FINAN DIPLOM CONTROL LEAD LOBBY REPRESENT WEALTH...POLICY STAT BIBLIOG 19/20 PARLIAMENT. PAGE 143 A2922
PARL/PROC LEGIS POL/PAR ECO/DEV

C39
REISCHAUER R.,"JAPAN'S GOVERNMENT--POLITICS." CONSTN STRATA POL/PAR FORCES LEGIS DIPLOM ADMIN EXEC CENTRAL...POLICY BIBLIOG 20 CHINJAP. PAGE 120 A2462
NAT/G S/ASIA CONCPT ROUTINE

C40
NORMAN E.H.,"JAPAN'S EMERGENCE AS A MODERN STATE: POLITICAL AND ECONOMIC PROBLEMS OF THE MEIJI PERIOD." CONSTN STRATA AGRI INDUS POL/PAR TEC/DEV CAP/ISM CIVMIL/REL...BIBLIOG 19/20 CHINJAP. PAGE 110 A2250
CENTRAL DIPLOM POLICY NAT/LISM

L41
COMM. STUDY ORGAN. PEACE,"ORGANIZATION OF PEACE." USA-45 WOR-45 STRATA NAT/G ACT/RES DIPLOM ECO/TAC EDU/PROP ADJUD ATTIT ORD/FREE PWR...SOC CONCPT ANTHOL LEAGUE/NAT 20. PAGE 28 A0575
INT/ORG PLAN PEACE

B47
BORGESE G.,COMMON CAUSE. LAW CONSTN SOCIETY STRATA ECO/DEV INT/ORG POL/PAR FORCES LEGIS TOP/EX CAP/ISM DIPLOM ADMIN EXEC ATTIT PWR 20. PAGE 17 A0339
WOR+45 NAT/G SOVEREIGN REGION

B48
DURBIN E.F.M.,THE POLITICS OF DEMOCRATIC SOCIALISM; AN ESSAY ON SOCIAL POLICY. STRATA POL/PAR PLAN COERCE DRIVE PERSON PWR MARXISM...CHARTS METH/COMP. PAGE 39 A0805
SOCIALIST POPULISM POLICY SOCIETY

B48
VISSON A.,AS OTHERS SEE US. EUR+WWI FRANCE UK USA+45 CULTURE INTELL SOCIETY STRATA NAT/G POL/PAR FOR/AID ATTIT DRIVE LOVE ORD/FREE RESPECT WEALTH ...PLURIST SOC OBS TOT/POP 20. PAGE 159 A3244
USA-45 PERCEPT

B49
ROSENHAUPT H.W.,HOW TO WAGE PEACE. USA+45 SOCIETY STRATA STRUCT R+D INT/ORG POL/PAR LEGIS ACT/RES CREATE PLAN EDU/PROP ADMIN EXEC ATTIT ALL/VALS ...TIME/SEQ TREND COLD/WAR 20. PAGE 124 A2536
INTELL CONCPT DIPLOM

L49
UNESCO,"SOME SUGGESTIONS ON TEACHING ABOUT THE UN AND ITS SPECIALIZED AGENCIES." UNIV WOR+45 SOCIETY STRATA SCHOOL WAR ALL/VALS KNOWL...SOC CONCPT UNESCO 20 UN. PAGE 147 A3011
INT/ORG EDU/PROP

B51
JENNINGS I.,THE COMMONWEALTH IN ASIA. CEYLON INDIA PAKISTAN CULTURE STRATA NAT/G LEGIS DIPLOM COLONIAL ATTIT...DECISION 20 CMN/WLTH. PAGE 74 A1507
CONSTN INT/ORG POLICY PLAN

B51
JENNINGS S.I.,THE COMMONWEALTH IN ASIA. CEYLON INDIA PAKISTAN S/ASIA UK CONSTN CULTURE SOCIETY STRATA STRUCT NAT/G POL/PAR EDU/PROP LEAD WAR 20 CMN/WLTH. PAGE 74 A1510
NAT/LISM REGION COLONIAL DIPLOM

B52
UN DEPT. SOC. AFF.,PRELIMINARY REPORT ON THE WORLD SOCIAL SITUATION. ISLAM L/A+17C WOR+45 STRATA AGRI EXTR/IND INDUS INT/ORG SCHOOL ADMIN...GEOG SOC TREND UNESCO WORK FAO 20. PAGE 147 A2998
R+D HEALTH FOR/AID

B52
UNESCO,CURRENT SOCIOLOGY (2 VOLS.). SOCIETY STRATA R+D GP/REL ATTIT PERSON 20 UN. PAGE 147 A3014
BIBLIOG SOC INT/ORG CULTURE

B53
LENZ F.,DIE BEWEGUNGEN DER GROSSEN MACHTE. USA+45 USA-45 USSR SOCIETY STRATA STRUCT NAT/G PERSON MARXISM...CONCPT IDEA/COMP NAT/COMP 18/20. PAGE 87 A1777
BAL/PWR TREND DIPLOM HIST/WRIT

B53
MURPHY G.,IN THE MINDS OF MEN: THE STUDY OF HUMAN BEHAVIOR AND SOCIAL TENSIONS IN INDIA. FUT S/ASIA FAM INT/ORG NAT/G DIPLOM EDU/PROP GP/REL ATTIT RIGID/FLEX ALL/VALS...SOC QU UNESCO 20. PAGE 106 A2176
SECT STRATA INDIA

C53
DEUTSCH K.W.,"NATIONALISM AND SOCIAL COMMUNICATION: AN INQUIRY INTO THE FOUNDATIONS OF NATIONALITY." CULTURE STRUCT DIPLOM DOMIN ATTIT ORD/FREE SOVEREIGN...SOC STAT CHARTS IDEA/COMP BIBLIOG. PAGE 36 A0735
NAT/LISM CONCPT PERCEPT STRATA

B54
CHEEVER D.S.,ORGANIZING FOR PEACE. FUT WOR+45 WOR-45 STRATA STRUCT NAT/G CREATE DIPLOM LEGIT REGION COERCE DETER PEACE ATTIT DRIVE ALL/VALS ...TIME/SEQ TREND UN LEAGUE/NAT. PAGE 26 A0525
INT/ORG

B54
MANNING C.A.W.,THE UNIVERSITY TEACHING OF SOCIAL SCIENCES: INTERNATIONAL RELATIONS. WOR+45 INTELL STRATA R+D ACADEM INT/ORG NAT/G CONSULT DELIB/GP ACT/RES EDU/PROP NAT/LISM ATTIT...POLICY CONT/OBS HYPO/EXP VAL/FREE LEAGUE/NAT UNESCO 20. PAGE 94 A1925
KNOWL PHIL/SCI DIPLOM

B56
FOSTER J.G.,BRITAIN IN WESTERN EUROPE: WEU AND THE ATLANTIC ALLIANCE. EUR+WWI FRANCE GERMANY GERMANY/W ITALY UK STRATA NAT/G DELIB/GP ECO/TAC ORD/FREE PWR ...TRADIT TIME/SEQ TREND OEEC PARLIAMENT 20 EUROPE/W. PAGE 47 A0969
INT/ORG FORCES WEAPON

B56
WHITAKER A.P.,ARGENTINE UPHEAVAL. STRUCT FORCES DIPLOM COERCE PWR 20 ARGEN. PAGE 164 A3332
REV POL/PAR STRATA NAT/G

B57
DEAN V.M.,THE NATURE OF THE NON-WESTERN WORLD. AFR ASIA L/A+17C S/ASIA CULTURE SOCIETY STRATA ECO/DEV DIPLOM ECO/TAC FOR/AID ATTIT DRIVE ALL/VALS ...RELATIV SOC CONCPT TIME/SEQ TREND TOT/POP 20. PAGE 35 A0718
ECO/UNDEV STERTYP NAT/LISM

B57
HODGKIN T.,NATIONALISM IN COLONIAL AFRICA. STRATA STRUCT MUNIC NAT/G POL/PAR LEGIS ATTIT SOVEREIGN ...POLICY TREND BIBLIOG 20. PAGE 66 A1351
AFR COLONIAL NAT/LISM DIPLOM

C57
TANG P.S.H.,"COMMUNIST CHINA TODAY: DOMESTIC AND FOREIGN POLICIES." CHINA/COM COM S/ASIA USSR STRATA FORCES DIPLOM EDU/PROP COERCE GOV/REL...POLICY MAJORIT BIBLIOG 20. PAGE 141 A2886
POL/PAR LEAD ADMIN CONSTN

B58
TILLION G.,ALGERIA: THE REALITIES. ALGERIA FRANCE ISLAM CULTURE STRATA PROB/SOLV DOMIN REV NAT/LISM WEALTH MARXISM...GEOG 20. PAGE 144 A2940
ECO/UNDEV SOC COLONIAL DIPLOM

B59
VINACKE H.M.,A HISTORY OF THE FAR EAST IN MODERN TIMES (6TH ED.). KOREA S/ASIA USSR CONSTN CULTURE STRATA ECO/UNDEV NAT/G CHIEF FOR/AID INT/TRADE GP/REL...SOC NAT/COMP 19/20 CHINJAP. PAGE 159 A3235
STRUCT ASIA

S59
FOX W.T.R.,"THE USES OF INTERNATIONAL RELATIONS THEORY. IN (FOX, THE THEORETICAL ASPECTS OF INTERNATIONAL RELATIONS,. WOR+45 INTELL SOCIETY STRATA INT/ORG CONSULT ACT/RES PWR...POLICY 20. PAGE 48 A0976
PLAN DIPLOM METH/CNCPT

S59
SUTTON F.X.,"REPRESENTATION AND THE NATURE OF POLITICAL SYSTEMS." UNIV WOR-45 CULTURE SOCIETY STRATA INT/ORG FORCES JUDGE DOMIN LEGIT EXEC REGION REPRESENT ATTIT ORD/FREE RESPECT...SOC HIST/WRIT TIME/SEQ. PAGE 140 A2867
NAT/G CONCPT

B60
ENGEL J.,THE SECURITY OF THE FREE WORLD. USSR WOR+45 STRATA STRUCT ECO/DEV ECO/UNDEV INT/ORG DELIB/GP FORCES DOMIN LEGIT ADJUD EXEC ARMS/CONT COERCE...POLICY CONCPT NEW/IDEA TIME/SEQ GEN/LAWS COLD/WAR WORK UN 20 NATO. PAGE 42 A0851
COM TREND DIPLOM

B60
MC CLELLAN G.S.,INDIA. CHINA/COM INDIA CONSTN ELITES STRATA AGRI POL/PAR FOR/AID ARMS/CONT REV MARXISM...CENSUS BIBLIOG 20 COLD/WAR GANDHI/M NEHRU/J. PAGE 97 A1990
DIPLOM NAT/G SOCIETY ECO/UNDEV

B60
WOLF C.,FOREIGN AID: THEORY AND PRACTICE IN SOUTHERN ASIA. CEYLON INDONESIA PHILIPPINE S/ASIA CULTURE STRATA ECO/UNDEV PLAN EDU/PROP ATTIT ...METH/CNCPT MATH QUANT STAT CONT/OBS TIME/SEQ SIMUL TOT/POP 20. PAGE 166 A3378
ACT/RES ECO/TAC FOR/AID

S60
"THE EMERGING COMMON MARKETS IN LATIN AMERICA." FUT L/A+17C STRATA DIST/IND INDUS LABOR NAT/G LEGIS ECO/TAC ADMIN RIGID/FLEX HEALTH...NEW/IDEA TIME/SEQ OAS 20. PAGE 3 A0059
FINAN ECO/UNDEV INT/TRADE

S60
MORALES C.J.,"TRADE AND ECONOMIC INTEGRATION IN LATIN AMERICA." FUT L/A+17C LAW STRATA ECO/UNDEV DIST/IND INDUS LABOR NAT/G LEGIS ECO/TAC ADMIN RIGID/FLEX WEALTH...CONCPT NEW/IDEA CONT/OBS TIME/SEQ WORK 20. PAGE 104 A2128
FINAN INT/TRADE REGION

B61
HADDAD J.A.,REVOLUCAO CUBANA E REVOLUCAO BRASILEIRA. BRAZIL CUBA L/A+17C STRATA AGRI WORKER EDU/PROP REGION...POLICY NAT/COMP 20. PAGE 59 A1210
REV ORD/FREE DIPLOM ECO/UNDEV

B61
WARD R.E.,JAPANESE POLITICAL SCIENCE: A GUIDE TO JAPANESE REFERENCE AND RESEARCH MATERIALS (2ND ED.). LAW CONSTN STRATA NAT/G POL/PAR DELIB/GP LEGIS ADMIN CHOOSE GP/REL...INT/LAW 19/20 CHINJAP. PAGE 161 A3282
BIBLIOG/A PHIL/SCI

S61
HEILBRONER R.L.,"DYNAMICS OF FOREIGN AID: PROBLEMS OF UNDERDEVELOPED NATIONS PLAGUE ASSISTANCE PROGRAM." FUT USA+45 WOR+45 STRATA NAT/G PLAN TEC/DEV ATTIT DRIVE WEALTH WORK 20. PAGE 64 A1307
ECO/UNDEV ECO/TAC FOR/AID

S61
TRAMPE G.,"DIE FORM DER DIPLOMATIC ALS POLITSCHE WAFFE." WOR+45 WOR-45 SOCIETY STRATA INT/ORG NAT/G ACT/RES PLAN ECO/TAC EDU/PROP COERCE WAR ATTIT RIGID/FLEX...DECISION CONCPT TREND. PAGE 145 A2959
CONSULT PWR DIPLOM

B62
CALDER R.,COMMON SENSE ABOUT A STARVING WORLD. WOR+45 STRATA ECO/DEV PLAN GP/REL BIO/SOC HABITAT ...POLICY GEOG STAT RECORD 20 UN BIRTH/CON. PAGE 23 A0466
FOR/AID CENSUS ECO/UNDEV AGRI

B62
DREIER J.C.,THE ORGANIZATION OF AMERICAN STATES AND THE HEMISPHERE CRISIS. CUBA USA+45 CULTURE STRATA NAT/G VOL/ASSN CONSULT FORCES ACT/RES CREATE DIPLOM ECO/TAC FOR/AID ALL/VALS...POLICY OBS OAS 20. PAGE 38 A0786
L/A+17C CONCPT

B62
FAO,FOOD AND AGRICULTURE ORGANIZATION AFRICAN SURVEY. AFR CONGO/BRAZ GHANA STRATA AGRI INT/ORG TEC/DEV FOR/AID INT/TRADE RACE/REL DEMAND EFFICIENCY PRODUC...GEOG 20 UN CONGO/LEOP. PAGE 44 A0898
ECO/TAC WEALTH EXTR/IND ECO/UNDEV

B62
HATCH J.,AFRICA TODAY-AND TOMORROW: AN OUTLINE OF BASIC FACTS AND MAJOR PROBLEMS. AFR FUT ISLAM STRATA ECO/UNDEV INT/ORG NAT/G POL/PAR DELIB/GP TOP/EX EDU/PROP LEGIT CHOOSE ATTIT...TIME/SEQ TOT/POP COLD/WAR 20. PAGE 63 A1287
PLAN CONSTN NAT/LISM

B62
LAUERHAUSS L.,COMMUNISM IN LATIN AMERICA: THE POST-WAR YEARS (1945 -1960) (PAPER). INTELL STRATA ECO/UNDEV AGRI WORKER FOR/AID INT/TRADE COLONIAL GUERRILLA 20. PAGE 85 A1745
BIBLIOG L/A+17C MARXISM REV

B62
MOON P.,DIVIDE AND QUIT. INDIA PAKISTAN STRATA DELIB/GP PLAN DIPLOM REPRESENT GP/REL INGP/REL CONSEN DISCRIM...OBS 20. PAGE 103 A2119
WAR REGION ISOLAT SECT

B62
SELOSOEMARDJAN O.,SOCIAL CHANGES IN JOGJAKARTA. INDONESIA NETHERLAND ELITES STRATA STRUCT FAM POL/PAR CREATE DIPLOM INT/TRADE EDU/PROP ADMIN GOV/REL...SOC 20 JAVA CHINJAP. PAGE 131 A2683
ECO/UNDEV CULTURE REV COLONIAL

B62
SHAPIRO D.,A SELECT BIBLIOGRAPHY OF WORKS IN ENGLISH ON RUSSIAN HISTORY, 1801-1917. COM USSR STRATA FORCES EDU/PROP ADMIN REV RACE/REL ATTIT 19/20. PAGE 131 A2693
BIBLIOG DIPLOM COLONIAL

L62
GROSS L.,"IMMUNITIES AND PRIVILEGES OF DELIGATIONS TO THE UNITED NATIONS." USA+45 WOR+45 STRATA NAT/G VOL/ASSN CONSULT DIPLOM EDU/PROP ROUTINE RESPECT ...POLICY INT/LAW CONCPT UN 20. PAGE 57 A1176
INT/ORG LAW ELITES

B63
CREMEANS C.,THE ARABS AND THE WORLD: NASSER'S ARAB NATIONALIST POLICY. FUT ISLAM UAR USA+45 SOCIETY STRATA NAT/G POL/PAR PLAN DIPLOM EDU/PROP LEGIT DRIVE ALL/VALS...INT TIME/SEQ CHARTS 20 NASSER/G. PAGE 33 A0662
TOP/EX ATTIT REGION NAT/LISM

B63
ELLENDER A.J.,A REPORT ON UNITED STATES FOREIGN OPERATIONS IN AFRICA. SOUTH/AFR USA+45 STRATA EXTR/IND FORCES RACE/REL ISOLAT SOVEREIGN...CHARTS 20 NEGRO. PAGE 41 A0840
FOR/AID DIPLOM WEALTH ECO/UNDEV

B63
HENDERSON W.,SOUTHEAST ASIA: PROBLEMS OF UNITED STATES POLICY. COM S/ASIA CULTURE STRATA ECO/UNDEV INT/ORG DELIB/GP ACT/RES ECO/TAC DOMIN EDU/PROP LEGIT COERCE ATTIT ALL/VALS...STAT TIME/SEQ ANTHOL VAL/FREE 20. PAGE 64 A1313
ASIA USA+45 DIPLOM

B63
MENDES C.,NACIONALISMO E DESENVOLVIMENTO. AFR ASIA L/A+17C STRATA INT/TRADE COLONIAL. PAGE 99 A2039
NAT/LISM ECO/UNDEV DIPLOM REV

B63
NORTH R.C.,M. N. ROY'S MISSION TO CHINA: THE COMMUNIST-KUOMINTANG SPLIT OF 1927. ASIA USSR STRATA LEGIS WORKER LEAD REV ATTIT ROLE SOCISM 20 ROY/MN COM/PARTY. PAGE 110 A2253
POL/PAR MARXISM DIPLOM

B63
PIKE F.B.,CHILE AND THE UNITED STATES 1880-1962: THE EMERGENCE OF CHILE'S CRISIS AND THE CHALLENGE TO US DIPLOMACY. CHILE COM USA+45 USA-45 SOCIETY STRATA ECO/UNDEV...MYTH 19/20. PAGE 116 A2378
FOR/AID DIPLOM ATTIT STRUCT

S63
KINTNER W.R.,"THE PROJECTED EUROPEAN UNION AND AMERICAN RESPONSIBILITIES." EUR+WWI USA+45 STRATA INT/ORG NAT/G DOMIN DETER NUC/PWR ATTIT ORD/FREE PWR 20 NATO. PAGE 79 A1628
FUT FORCES DIPLOM REGION

S63
SCHMIDT W.E.,"THE CASE AGAINST COMMODITY AGREEMENTS." FUT L/A+17C STRATA CONSULT PLAN ECO/TAC EDU/PROP ATTIT DRIVE RIGID/FLEX WEALTH ...MYTH 20. PAGE 128 A2631
ECO/UNDEV ACT/RES INT/TRADE

B64
HALPERN J.M.,GOVERNMENT, POLITICS, AND SOCIAL STRUCTURE IN LAOS. LAOS CULTURE SOCIETY STRATA STRUCT FAM DIPLOM DOMIN MARXISM...INT GOV/COMP WORSHIP SOC/INTEG 20. PAGE 60 A1242
NAT/G SOC LOC/G

B64
HARPER F.,OUT OF CHINA. CHINA/COM ELITES STRATA ATTIT PERSON...BIOG 20 MAO HONG/KONG MIGRATION. PAGE 62 A1264
HABITAT DEEP/INT DIPLOM MARXISM

B64
HORNE D.,THE LUCKY COUNTRY: AUSTRALIA TODAY. UK CULTURE STRATA ATTIT PWR PLURISM...GOV/COMP 20 AUSTRAL. PAGE 67 A1386
RACE/REL DIPLOM NAT/G STRUCT

B64
HOROWITZ I.L.,REVOLUTION IN BRAZIL. BRAZIL L/A+17C ELITES STRATA NAT/G BAL/PWR PARTIC ATTIT 20. PAGE 68 A1388
ECO/UNDEV DIPLOM POLICY ORD/FREE

B64
LEGUM C.,SOUTH AFRICA: CRISIS FOR THE WEST. SOUTH/AFR COERCE DISCRIM ATTIT...TREND 20 INTERVENT. PAGE 86 A1767
RACE/REL STRATA DIPLOM PROB/SOLV

B64
MAIER J.,POLITICS OF CHANGE IN LATIN AMERICA. BRAZIL L/A+17C STRATA INT/ORG NAT/G POL/PAR FOR/AID REV 20. PAGE 93 A1907
SOCIETY NAT/LISM DIPLOM REGION

B64
WITHERS W.,THE ECONOMIC CRISIS IN LATIN AMERICA. BRAZIL CHILE STRATA AGRI DIPLOM FOR/AID PWR SOCISM ...POLICY 20 MEXIC/AMER ARGEN. PAGE 166 A3372
L/A+17C ECO/UNDEV CAP/ISM ALL/IDEOS

L64
SYMONDS R.,"REFLECTIONS IN LOCALISATION." AFR S/ASIA UK STRATA INT/ORG NAT/G SCHOOL EDU/PROP LEGIT KNOWL ORD/FREE PWR RESPECT CMN/WLTH 20. PAGE 140 A2874
ADMIN MGT COLONIAL

S64
MCCREARY E.A.,"THOSE AMERICAN MANAGERS DON'T IMPRESS EUROPE." EUR+WWI USA+45 CULTURE STRATA ECO/DEV TOP/EX INT/TRADE ATTIT DRIVE PERSON RIGID/FLEX...CONCPT 20. PAGE 98 A2003
MARKET ACT/RES BAL/PAY CAP/ISM

B65
FANON F.,STUDIES IN A DYING COLONIALISM. ALGERIA FRANCE STRATA FAM DIPLOM DOMIN WAR RACE/REL DISCRIM HEALTH 20. PAGE 44 A0897
NAT/LISM COLONIAL REV SOVEREIGN

B65
INGRAM D.,COMMONWEALTH FOR A COLOUR-BLIND WORLD. AFR INDIA UK STRATA ECO/UNDEV VOL/ASSN CREATE PLAN CONFER COLONIAL ORD/FREE SOC/INTEG 20 COMMONWLTH. PAGE 70 A1441
RACE/REL INT/ORG INGP/REL PROB/SOLV

B65
LEISS A.C.,APARTHEID AND UNITED NATIONS COLLECTIVE MEASURES. SOUTH/AFR ECO/UNDEV EXTR/IND FORCES WORKER ECO/TAC FOR/AID INT/TRADE WEALTH...TREND CHARTS 20 UN NEGRO. PAGE 86 A1770
DISCRIM RACE/REL STRATA DIPLOM

B65
O'CONNELL M.R.,IRISH POLITICS AND SOCIAL CONFLICT IN THE AGE OF THE AMERICAN REVOLUTION. FRANCE IRELAND MOD/EUR STRATA SECT LEGIS DIPLOM INT/TRADE DOMIN REV WAR...BIBLIOG 18 PARLIAMENT. PAGE 111 A2268
CATHISM ATTIT NAT/G DELIB/GP

B65
SPEECKAERT G.P.,SELECT BIBLIOGRAPHY ON INTERNATIONAL ORGANIZATION, 1885-1964. WOR+45 WOR-45 EX/STRUC DIPLOM ADMIN REGION 19/20 UN. PAGE 136 A2777
BIBLIOG INT/ORG GEN/LAWS STRATA

B65
VAN DEN BERGHE P.L.,AFRICA: SOCIAL PROBLEMS OF CHANGE AND CONFLICT. ELITES STRATA ECO/UNDEV KIN MUNIC DIPLOM GP/REL RACE/REL NAT/LISM...ANTHOL BIBLIOG 20. PAGE 158 A3210
SOC CULTURE AFR STRUCT

B66
BRYNES A.,WE GIVE TO CONQUER. USA+45 USSR STRATA ECO/UNDEV INT/ORG NAT/G DIPLOM DRIVE...TREND IDEA/COMP 20. PAGE 20 A0414
FOR/AID CONTROL GIVE WAR

B66
COLE A.B.,SOCIALIST PARTIES IN POSTWAR JAPAN. STRATA AGRI LABOR PLAN DIPLOM ECO/TAC AGREE LEAD CHOOSE ATTIT...CHARTS 20 CHINJAP SOC/DEMPAR. PAGE 28 A0566
POL/PAR POLICY SOCISM NAT/G

B66
HOLT R.T.,THE POLITICAL BASIS OF ECONOMIC DEVELOPMENT. STRATA STRUCT NAT/G DIPLOM ADMIN...SOC NAT/COMP BIBLIOG 20. PAGE 67 A1376
ECO/TAC GOV/COMP CONSTN EX/STRUC

B66
HOROWITZ D.,HEMISPHERES NORTH AND SOUTH: ECONOMIC DISPARITY AMONG NATIONS. WOR+45 ECO/DEV ECO/UNDEV INT/ORG PLAN DIPLOM INT/TRADE GIVE PARTIC GP/REL ...WELF/ST 20. PAGE 67 A1387
ECO/TAC FOR/AID STRATA WEALTH

B66
KEENLEYSIDE H.L.,INTERNATIONAL AID: A SUMMARY. AFR INDIA S/ASIA UK STRATA EXTR/IND TEC/DEV ADMIN RACE/REL DEMAND NAT/LISM WEALTH...TREND CHINJAP. PAGE 77 A1575
ECO/UNDEV FOR/AID DIPLOM TASK

B66
KOH S.J.,STAGES OF INDUSTRIAL DEVELOPMENT IN ASIA. ASIA INDIA KOREA STRATA STRUCT NAT/G INT/TRADE ...CHARTS 19/20 CHINJAP. PAGE 81 A1659
INDUS ECO/UNDEV ECO/DEV LABOR

B66
MURPHY G.G.,SOVIET MONGOLIA: A STUDY OF THE OLDEST POLITICAL SATELLITE. USSR STRATA STRUCT COST INCOME ATTIT SOCISM 20. PAGE 106 A2177
DIPLOM ECO/TAC PLAN DOMIN

B66
TYSON G.,NEHRU: THE YEARS OF POWER. INDIA UK STRATA ECO/UNDEV FINAN SECT TASK WAR ORD/FREE MARXISM ...POLICY BIBLIOG 20 NEHRU/J. PAGE 146 A2985
CHIEF PWR DIPLOM NAT/G

B67
ROSENAU J.N.,DOMESTIC SOURCES OF FOREIGN POLICY. WOR+45 STRATA COM/IND MUNIC POL/PAR LOBBY PARTIC REGION ATTIT...PSY SOC COLD/WAR. PAGE 124 A2534
DIPLOM POLICY NAT/G CHOOSE

B67
SACHS M.Y.,THE WORLDMARK ENCYCLOPEDIA OF THE NATIONS (5 VOLS.). ELITES SOCIETY STRATA ECO/DEV ECO/UNDEV AGRI EXTR/IND FINAN LABOR LOC/G NAT/G POL/PAR SECT INT/TRADE SOVEREIGN...SOC 20. PAGE 126 A2585
WOR+45 INT/ORG BAL/PWR

S67
DAVIS H.B.,"LENIN AND NATIONALISM: THE REDIRECTION OF THE MARXIST THEORY OF NATIONALISM." COM MOD/EUR USSR STRATA INT/ORG PLAN DOMIN COLONIAL FEDERAL ...TREND 20. PAGE 34 A0690
NAT/LISM MARXISM ATTIT CENTRAL

S67
JOHNSON J.,"THE UNITED STATES AND THE LATIN AMERICAN LEFT WINGS." L/A+17C STRATA POL/PAR INT/TRADE 20. PAGE 74 A1524
ECO/UNDEV WORKER ECO/TAC REGION

S67
SAPP B.B.,"TRIBAL CULTURES AND COMMUNISM." AFR USA+45 STRATA DIPLOM FOR/AID REGION CENTRAL ATTIT AUTHORIT RIGID/FLEX KNOWL. PAGE 127 A2604
KIN MARXISM ECO/UNDEV STRUCT

STRATEGY....SEE PLAN, DECISION

STRATIFICATION....SEE STRATA

STRAUSS L.L. A2844

STRAUSZ-HUPE R. A2845,A2846,A2847,A2848

STREIT C.K. A2849, A2850

STRESEMANN, GUSTAV....SEE STRESEMN/G

STRESEMN/G....GUSTAV STRESEMANN

B53
BRETTON H.L.,STRESEMANN AND THE REVISION OF VERSAILLES: A FIGHT FOR REASON. EUR+WWI GERMANY FORCES BUDGET ARMS/CONT WAR SUPEGO...BIBLIOG 20 TREATY VERSAILLES STRESEMN/G. PAGE 18 A0373
POLICY DIPLOM BIOG

STRESS....SEE PERSON, DRIVE

STRIKE....STRIKE OF WORKERS

STRIKES....SEE LABOR, GP/REL, FINAN

STROMBERG R.N. A2851

STROUT A.M. A0526

STRUC/FUNC....STRUCTURAL-FUNCTIONAL THEORY

STRUCT...SOCIAL STRUCTURE

N
ATLANTIC INSTITUTE,ATLANTIC STUDIES. COM EUR+WWI USA+45 CULTURE STRUCT ECO/DEV FORCES LEAD ARMS/CONT ...INT/LAW JURID SOC. PAGE 10 A0193
BIBLIOG/A DIPLOM POLICY GOV/REL

N
CORDIER H.,BIBLIOTECA SINICA. SOCIETY STRUCT SECT DIPLOM COLONIAL...GEOG SOC CON/ANAL. PAGE 30 A0618
BIBLIOG/A NAT/G CULTURE ASIA

N
CORNELL UNIVERSITY LIBRARY,SOUTHEAST ASIA ACCESSIONS LIST. LAW SOCIETY STRUCT ECO/UNDEV POL/PAR TEC/DEV DIPLOM LEAD REGION. PAGE 31 A0626
BIBLIOG S/ASIA NAT/G CULTURE

NCO
CARRINGTON C.E.,THE COMMONWEALTH IN AFRICA (PAMPHLET). UK STRUCT NAT/G COLONIAL REPRESENT GOV/REL RACE/REL NAT/LISM...MAJORIT 20 EEC NEGRO COLD/WAR. PAGE 25 A0500
ECO/UNDEV AFR DIPLOM PLAN

B00
MAINE H.S.,INTERNATIONAL LAW. MOD/EUR UNIV SOCIETY STRUCT ACT/RES EXEC WAR ATTIT PERSON ALL/VALS ...POLICY JURID CONCPT OBS TIME/SEQ TOT/POP. PAGE 93 A1908
INT/ORG LAW PEACE INT/LAW

B11
PHILLIPSON C.,THE INTERNATIONAL LAW AND CUSTOM OF ANCIENT GREECE AND ROME. MEDIT-7 UNIV INTELL SOCIETY STRUCT NAT/G LEGIS EXEC PERSON...CONCPT OBS CON/ANAL ROM/EMP. PAGE 116 A2377
INT/ORG LAW INT/LAW

B15
HOBSON J.A.,TOWARDS INTERNATIONAL GOVERNMENT. MOD/EUR STRUCT ECO/TAC EDU/PROP ADJUD ALL/VALS
FUT INT/ORG

...SOCIALIST CONCPT GEN/LAWS TOT/POP 20. PAGE 65 A1347 — CENTRAL

B16

ROOT E.,THE MILITARY AND COLONIAL POLICY OF THE US. L/A+17C USA-45 LAW SOCIETY STRATA STRUCT INT/ORG NAT/G SCHOOL FORCES EDU/PROP ALL/VALS...OBS VAL/FREE 19/20. PAGE 123 A2522 — ACT/RES PLAN DIPLOM WAR

B17

UPTON E.,THE MILITARY POLICY OF THE US. USA-45 STRUCT INT/ORG EXEC ATTIT PERCEPT...MGT CONCPT OBS HIST/WRIT CHARTS CONGRESS 18/20. PAGE 149 A3049 — FORCES SKILL WAR

B19

SUTHERLAND G.,CONSTITUTIONAL POWER AND WORLD AFFAIRS. CONSTN STRUCT INT/ORG NAT/G CHIEF LEGIS ACT/RES PLAN GOV/REL ALL/VALS...OBS TIME/SEQ CONGRESS VAL/FREE 20 PRESIDENT. PAGE 140 A2866 — USA-45 EXEC DIPLOM

B28

CORBETT P.E.,CANADA AND WORLD POLITICS. LAW CULTURE SOCIETY STRUCT MARKET INT/ORG FORCES ACT/RES PLAN ECO/TAC LEGIT ORD/FREE PWR RESPECT...SOC CONCPT TIME/SEQ TREND CMN/WLTH 20 LEAGUE/NAT. PAGE 30 A0612 — NAT/G CANADA

B28

MILLER D.H.,THE DRAFTING OF THE COVENANT. UNIV WOR-45 INTELL NAT/G DELIB/GP PLAN ECO/TAC LEGIT WAR ATTIT PERCEPT...CONCPT TIME/SEQ LEAGUE/NAT TOT/POP 20. PAGE 101 A2074 — INT/ORG STRUCT PEACE

B32

BRYCE J.,THE HOLY ROMAN EMPIRE. GERMANY ITALY MOD/EUR CULTURE SOCIETY STRUCT INT/ORG NAT/G SECT DIPLOM DOMIN WAR SUPEGO ALL/VALS SOVEREIGN...GEOG SOC TIME/SEQ CHARTS STERTYP. PAGE 20 A0413 — CHRIST-17C NAT/LISM

B32

MASTERS R.D.,INTERNATIONAL LAW IN INTERNATIONAL COURTS. BELGIUM EUR+WWI FRANCE GERMANY MOD/EUR SWITZERLND WOR-45 SOCIETY STRATA STRUCT LEGIT EXEC ALL/VALS...JURID HIST/WRIT TIME/SEQ TREND GEN/LAWS 20. PAGE 96 A1961 — INT/ORG LAW INT/LAW

B36

ROBINSON H.,DEVELOPMENT OF THE BRITISH EMPIRE. WOR-45 CULTURE SOCIETY STRUCT ECO/DEV ECO/UNDEV INT/ORG VOL/ASSN FORCES CREATE PLAN DOMIN EDU/PROP ADMIN COLONIAL PWR WEALTH...POLICY GEOG CHARTS CMN/WLTH 16/20. PAGE 122 A2503 — NAT/G HIST/WRIT UK

B36

SHOTWELL J.,ON THE RIM OF THE ABYSS. EUR+WWI USA-45 STRUCT INT/ORG ACT/RES PLAN EDU/PROP EXEC ATTIT ALL/VALS...TIME/SEQ LEAGUE/NAT TOT/POP 20. PAGE 132 A2706 — NAT/G BAL/PWR

B38

DE MADARIAGA S.,THE WORLD'S DESIGN. WOR-45 SOCIETY STRUCT EDU/PROP PEACE ATTIT PERSON ALL/VALS ...SOCIALIST CONCPT TIME/SEQ TREND GEN/LAWS LEAGUE/NAT. PAGE 35 A0706 — FUT INT/ORG DIPLOM

B38

PETTEE G.S.,THE PROCESS OF REVOLUTION. COM FRANCE ITALY MOD/EUR RUSSIA SPAIN WOR-45 ELITES INTELL SOCIETY STRATA STRUCT INT/ORG NAT/G POL/PAR ACT/RES PLAN EDU/PROP LEGIT EXEC...SOC MYTH TIME/SEQ TOT/POP 18/20. PAGE 115 A2370 — COERCE CONCPT REV

B39

ZIMMERN A.,THE LEAGUE OF NATIONS AND THE RULE OF LAW. WOR-45 STRUCT NAT/G DELIB/GP EX/STRUC BAL/PWR DOMIN LEGIT COERCE ORD/FREE PWR...POLICY RECORD LEAGUE/NAT TOT/POP VAL/FREE 20 LEAGUE/NAT. PAGE 170 A3453 — INT/ORG LAW DIPLOM

B41

BURTON M.E.,THE ASSEMBLY OF THE LEAGUE OF NATIONS. WOR-45 CONSTN SOCIETY STRUCT INT/ORG NAT/G CREATE ATTIT RIGID/FLEX PWR...POLICY TIME/SEQ LEAGUE/NAT 20. PAGE 22 A0448 — DELIB/GP EX/STRUC DIPLOM

B41

KEESING F.M.,THE SOUTH SEAS IN THE MODERN WORLD. INDONESIA STRUCT FAM SECT EDU/PROP LEAD INCOME WEALTH...HEAL SOC 20. PAGE 77 A1577 — CULTURE ECO/UNDEV GOV/COMP DIPLOM

B41

YOUNG G.,FEDERALISM AND FREEDOM. EUR+WWI MOD/EUR RUSSIA USA-45 WOR-45 SOCIETY STRUCT ECO/DEV INT/ORG EXEC FEDERAL ATTIT PERSON ALL/VALS...OLD/LIB CONCPT OBS TREND LEAGUE/NAT TOT/POP. PAGE 169 A3435 — NAT/G WAR

S41

WRIGHT Q.,"FUNDAMENTAL PROBLEMS OF INTERNATIONAL ORGANIZATION." UNIV WOR-45 STRUCT FORCES ACT/RES CREATE DOMIN EDU/PROP LEGIT REGION NAT/LISM ORD/FREE PWR RESPECT SOVEREIGN...JURID SOC CONCPT METH/CNCPT TIME/SEQ 20. PAGE 167 A3405 — INT/ORG ATTIT PEACE

B44

HUDSON M.,INTERNATIONAL TRIBUNALS PAST AND FUTURE. FUT WOR-45 LAW EDU/PROP ADJUD ORD/FREE...CONCPT TIME/SEQ TREND GEN/LAWS TOT/POP VAL/FREE 18/20. PAGE 69 A1408 — INT/ORG STRUCT INT/LAW

B44

WHITTON J.B.,THE SECOND CHANCE: AMERICA AND THE PEACE. EUR+WWI USA-45 SOCIETY STRUCT INT/ORG NAT/G LEGIT EXEC WAR ALL/VALS...SOC CONCPT TIME/SEQ TREND CONGRESS 20. PAGE 164 A3340 — LEGIS PEACE

B45

WEST R.,CONSCIENCE AND SOCIETY: A STUDY OF THE PSYCHOLOGICAL PREREQUISITES OF LAW AND ORDER. FUT UNIV LAW SOCIETY STRUCT DIPLOM WAR PERS/REL SUPEGO ...SOC 20. PAGE 163 A3321 — COERCE INT/LAW ORD/FREE PERSON

B46

BLUM L.,FOR ALL MANKIND (TRANS. BY W. PICKLES). FRANCE GERMANY USSR LAW SOCIETY STRUCT POL/PAR WORKER DIPLOM DOMIN CHOOSE ORD/FREE FASCISM 20. PAGE 16 A0323 — POPULISM SOCIALIST NAT/G WAR

B47

BROOKINGS INST.,MAJOR PROBLEMS OF UNITED STATES FOREIGN POLICY. USA+45 WOR+45 STRUCT ECO/DEV ECO/UNDEV INT/ORG NAT/G POL/PAR VOL/ASSN DELIB/GP FORCES ECO/TAC LEGIT COERCE ORD/FREE PWR WEALTH ...POLICY STAT TREND CHARTS TOT/POP. PAGE 19 A0392 — ACT/RES DIPLOM

B47

NIEBUHR R.,THE CHILDREN OF LIGHT AND THE CHILDREN OF DARKNESS: A VINDICATION OF DEMOCRACY AND CRITIQUE OF TRADITIONAL DEFENSE. UNIV STRUCT NAT/G SECT INGP/REL OWN PEACE ORD/FREE MARXISM ...IDEA/COMP GEN/LAWS 20 CHRISTIAN. PAGE 109 A2235 — POPULISM DIPLOM NEIGH GP/REL

B48

MINISTERE FINANCES ET ECO,BULLETIN BIBLIOGRAPHIQUE. AFR EUR+WWI FRANCE CULTURE STRUCT FINAN NAT/G ACT/RES INT/TRADE ADMIN REGION PRODUC STAT. PAGE 102 A2088 — BIBLIOG/A ECO/UNDEV TEC/DEV COLONIAL

B49

BEHRENDT R.F.,MODERN LATIN AMERICA IN SOCIAL SCIENCE LITERATURE. STRUCT ECO/UNDEV SCHOOL DIPLOM INT/TRADE EDU/PROP...GEOG 20. PAGE 12 A0250 — BIBLIOG/A SOC L/A+17C

B49

ROSENHAUPT H.W.,HOW TO WAGE PEACE. USA+45 SOCIETY STRATA STRUCT R+D INT/ORG POL/PAR LEGIS ACT/RES CREATE PLAN EDU/PROP ADMIN EXEC ATTIT ALL/VALS ...TIME/SEQ TREND COLD/WAR 20. PAGE 124 A2536 — INTELL CONCPT DIPLOM

B49

STREIT C.,UNION NOW. UNIV USA-45 WOR-45 INTELL STRUCT INT/ORG NAT/G PLAN DIPLOM EXEC ATTIT ...CONCPT TIME/SEQ. PAGE 139 A2849 — SOCIETY ACT/RES WAR

B50

ALMOND G.A.,THE AMERICAN PEOPLE AND FOREIGN POLICY. USA+45 USA-45 CULTURE SOCIETY STRUCT CONSEN PERSON PWR POPULISM...TIME/SEQ TREND 20 COLD/WAR. PAGE 6 A0129 — ATTIT DIPLOM DECISION ELITES

B50

BEHRENDT R.F.,MODERN LATIN AMERICA IN SOCIAL SCIENCE LITERATURE (SUPPLEMENTS I AND II). STRUCT ECO/UNDEV SCHOOL DIPLOM INT/TRADE...GEOG 20. PAGE 12 A0251 — BIBLIOG/A SOC L/A+17C

B50

CHASE E.P.,THE UNITED NATIONS IN ACTION. WOR+45 CONSTN DELIB/GP LEGIT ROUTINE COERCE PEACE ORD/FREE PWR...CON/ANAL GEN/LAWS UN 20. PAGE 26 A0524 — INT/ORG STRUCT ARMS/CONT

B50

CORNELL U DEPT ASIAN STUDIES,SOUTHEAST ASIA PROGRAM DATA PAPER. BURMA CAMBODIA INDONESIA MALAYSIA VIETNAM SOCIETY STRUCT NAT/G SECT DIPLOM FOR/AID PWR WEALTH...SOC 20. PAGE 31 A0625 — BIBLIOG/A CULTURE S/ASIA ECO/UNDEV

B50

LAUTERPACHT H.,INTERNATIONAL LAW AND HUMAN RIGHTS. USA+45 CONSTN STRUCT INT/ORG ACT/RES EDU/PROP PEACE PERSON ALL/VALS...CONCPT CON/ANAL GEN/LAWS UN 20. PAGE 86 A1750 — DELIB/GP LAW INT/LAW

B50

MCCAMY J.,THE ADMINISTRATION OF AMERICAN FOREIGN AFFAIRS. USA+45 SOCIETY INT/ORG NAT/G ACT/RES PLAN INT/TRADE EDU/PROP ADJUD ALL/VALS...METH/CNCPT TIME/SEQ CONGRESS 20. PAGE 97 A1996 — EXEC STRUCT DIPLOM

B50

NORTHROP F.S.C.,THE TAMING OF THE NATIONS. KOREA USA+45 USSR WOR+45 STRUCT ECO/UNDEV INT/ORG NAT/G TOP/EX NUC/PWR ATTIT ALL/VALS...TIME/SEQ 20 HIROSHIMA. PAGE 110 A2255 — CONCPT BAL/PWR

B51

BLANSHARD P.,COMMUNISM, DEMOCRACY AND CATHOLIC POWER. USSR VATICAN WOR+45 WOR-45 CULTURE ELITES INTELL SOCIETY STRUCT INT/ORG POL/PAR EDU/PROP COERCE ATTIT KNOWL PWR MARXISM...CONCPT COLD/WAR 20. PAGE 15 A0308 — COM SECT TOTALISM

B51

JENNINGS W.I.,THE COMMONWEALTH IN ASIA. CEYLON INDIA PAKISTAN S/ASIA UK CONSTN CULTURE SOCIETY STRATA STRUCT NAT/G POL/PAR EDU/PROP LEAD WAR 20 CMN/WLTH. PAGE 74 A1510 — NAT/LISM REGION COLONIAL DIPLOM

B51

KELSEN H.,THE LAW OF THE UNITED NATIONS. WOR+45 STRUCT RIGID/FLEX ORD/FREE...INT/LAW JURID CONCPT CON/ANAL GEN/METH UN TOT/POP VAL/FREE 20. PAGE 77 A1581 — INT/ORG ADJUD

B51

MCKEON R.,DEMOCRACY IN A WORLD OF TENSION. UNIV LAW INTELL STRUCT R+D INT/ORG SCHOOL EDU/PROP LEGIT ATTIT DRIVE PERCEPT PERSON...POLICY JURID PSY SOC CONCPT METH/CNCPT OBS UNESCO TOT/POP VAL/FREE. — SOCIETY ALL/VALS ORD/FREE

PAGE 98 A2015

B51
STANTON A.H.,PERSONALITY AND POLITICAL CRISIS. WOR+45 WOR-45 STRUCT DIPLOM INGP/REL TOTALISM MORAL ...ANTHOL 20 LASSWELL/H PARSONS/T RIESMAN/D. PAGE 137 A2806 — EDU/PROP WAR PERSON PSY

B51
WELLES S.,SEVEN DECISIONS THAT SHAPED HISTORY. ASIA FRANCE FUT USA+45 WOR+45 WOR-45 CONSTN STRUCT INT/ORG NAT/G ACT/RES EDU/PROP DRIVE...POLICY CONCPT TIME/SEQ TREND TOT/POP UN 20 CHINJAP. PAGE 163 A3315 — USA-45 DIPLOM WAR

B51
YOUNG T.C.,NEAR EASTERN CULTURE AND SOCIETY. ISLAM ECO/UNDEV SECT WRITING ATTIT HABITAT ORD/FREE 20. PAGE 169 A3438 — CULTURE STRUCT REGION DIPLOM

L51
ULAM A.B.,"THE COMIMFORM AND THE PEOPLE'S DEMOCRACIES." EUR+WWI WOR+45 STRUCT NAT/G POL/PAR TOP/EX ACT/RES PLAN ECO/TAC DOMIN ATTIT ALL/VALS ...HIST/WRIT TIME/SEQ 20 COMINFORM. PAGE 146 A2992 — COM INT/ORG USSR TOTALISM

B52
ULAM A.B.,TITOISM AND THE COMINFORM. USSR WOR+45 STRUCT INT/ORG NAT/G ACT/RES PLAN EXEC ATTIT DRIVE ALL/VALS...CONCPT OBS VAL/FREE 20 COMINTERN TITO/MARSH. PAGE 146 A2993 — COM POL/PAR TOTALISM YUGOSLAVIA

B52
VANDENBOSCH A.,THE UN: BACKGROUND, ORGANIZATION, FUNCTIONS, ACTIVITIES. WOR+45 LAW CONSTN STRUCT INT/ORG CONSULT BAL/PWR EDU/PROP EXEC ALL/VALS ...POLICY CONCPT UN 20. PAGE 158 A3218 — DELIB/GP TIME/SEQ PEACE

B53
LENZ F.,DIE BEWEGUNGEN DER GROSSEN MACHTE. USA+45 USA-45 USSR SOCIETY STRATA STRUCT NAT/G PERSON MARXISM...CONCPT IDEA/COMP NAT/COMP 18/20. PAGE 87 A1777 — BAL/PWR TREND DIPLOM HIST/WRIT

C53
DEUTSCH K.W.,"NATIONALISM AND SOCIAL COMMUNICATION: AN INQUIRY INTO THE FOUNDATIONS OF NATIONALITY." CULTURE STRUCT DIPLOM DOMIN ATTIT ORD/FREE SOVEREIGN...SOC STAT CHARTS IDEA/COMP BIBLIOG. PAGE 36 A0735 — NAT/LISM CONCPT PERCEPT STRATA

B54
CHEEVER D.S.,ORGANIZING FOR PEACE. FUT WOR+45 WOR-45 STRATA STRUCT NAT/G CREATE DIPLOM LEGIT REGION COERCE DETER PEACE ATTIT DRIVE ALL/VALS ...TIME/SEQ TREND UN LEAGUE/NAT. PAGE 26 A0525 — INT/ORG

B54
NORTHROP F.S.C.,EUROPEAN UNION AND UNITED STATES FOREIGN POLICY: A STUDY IN SOCIOLOGICAL JURISPRUDENCE. EUR+WWI MOD/EUR USA+45 SOCIETY STRUCT NAT/G CREATE ECO/TAC DOMIN EDU/PROP REGION ATTIT RIGID/FLEX HEALTH ORD/FREE WEALTH ...METH/CNCPT TIME/SEQ TREND. PAGE 110 A2256 — INT/ORG SOC DIPLOM

B54
NUSSBAUM D.,A CONCISE HISTORY OF THE LAW OF NATIONS. ASIA CHRIST-17C EUR+WWI ISLAM MEDIT-7 MOD/EUR S/ASIA UNIV WOR+45 WOR-45 SOCIETY STRUCT EXEC ATTIT ALL/VALS...CONCPT HIST/WRIT TIME/SEQ. PAGE 110 A2263 — INT/ORG LAW PEACE INT/LAW

B55
CHOWDHURI R.N.,INTERNATIONAL MANDATES AND TRUSTEESHIP SYSTEMS. WOR+45 STRUCT ECO/UNDEV INT/ORG LEGIS DOMIN EDU/PROP LEGIT ADJUD EXEC PWR ...CONCPT TIME/SEQ UN 20. PAGE 26 A0534 — DELIB/GP PLAN SOVEREIGN

B55
CRAIG G.A.,THE POLITICS OF THE PRUSSIAN ARMY 1640-1945. CHRIST-17C EUR+WWI MOD/EUR PRUSSIA STRUCT DIPLOM ADMIN REV WAR...SOC BIBLIOG 17/20. PAGE 32 A0652 — FORCES NAT/G ROLE CHIEF

B55
MACMAHON A.W.,FEDERALISM: MATURE AND EMERGENT. EUR+WWI FUT WOR+45 WOR-45 INT/ORG NAT/G REPRESENT FEDERAL...POLICY MGT RECORD TREND GEN/LAWS 20. PAGE 93 A1900 — STRUCT CONCPT

B55
STILLMAN C.W.,AFRICA IN THE MODERN WORLD. AFR USA+45 WOR+45 INT/TRADE COLONIAL PARTIC REGION GOV/REL RACE/REL 20. PAGE 138 A2826 — ECO/UNDEV DIPLOM POLICY STRUCT

B55
THOMPSON V.,MINORITY PROBLEMS IN SOUTHEAST ASIA. CAMBODIA CHINA/COM LAOS S/ASIA KIN NAT/G SECT PROB/SOLV EDU/PROP REGION GP/REL RACE/REL MARXISM ...SOC 20 BUDDHISM UN. PAGE 143 A2933 — INGP/REL GEOG DIPLOM STRUCT

B55
WILCOX F.O.,PROPOSALS FOR CHANGES IN THE UNITED NATIONS. WOR+45 CONSTN ACT/RES CREATE LEGIT ATTIT ORD/FREE...CONCPT ORG/CHARTS UN TOT/POP 20. PAGE 164 A3344 — INT/ORG STRUCT

L55
ROSTOW W.W.,"RUSSIA AND CHINA UNDER COMMUNISM." CHINA/COM USSR INTELL STRUCT INT/ORG NAT/G POL/PAR TOP/EX ACT/RES PLAN ADMIN ATTIT ALL/VALS MARXISM ...CONCPT OBS TIME/SEQ TREND GOV/COMP VAL/FREE 20. PAGE 124 A2543 — COM ASIA

S55
DE SMITH S.A.,"CONSTITUTIONAL MONARCHY IN BURGANDA." AFR UGANDA UK STRUCT CHIEF REGION INGP/REL ADJUST NAT/LISM SOVEREIGN CONSERVE ...POLICY 19/20 BURGANDA. PAGE 35 A0712 — NAT/G DIPLOM CONSTN COLONIAL

B56
GOODRICH L.,KOREA: A STUDY OF US POLICY IN THE UNITED NATIONS. ASIA USA+45 STRUCT CONSULT DELIB/GP ATTIT DRIVE PWR...JURID GEN/LAWS COLD/WAR 20 UN. PAGE 54 A1103 — INT/ORG DIPLOM KOREA

B56
WHITAKER A.P.,ARGENTINE UPHEAVAL. STRUCT FORCES DIPLOM COERCE PWR 20 ARGEN. PAGE 164 A3332 — REV POL/PAR STRATA NAT/G

B56
WILBUR C.M.,DOCUMENTS ON COMMUNISM, NATIONALISM, AND SOVIET ADVISERS IN CHINA, 1918-1927. CHINA/COM USSR STRUCT DIPLOM LEAD NAT/LISM...BIBLIOG/A 20. PAGE 164 A3343 — REV POL/PAR MARXISM COM

B57
HODGKIN T.,NATIONALISM IN COLONIAL AFRICA. STRATA STRUCT MUNIC NAT/G POL/PAR LEGIS ATTIT SOVEREIGN ...POLICY TREND BIBLIOG 20. PAGE 66 A1351 — AFR COLONIAL NAT/LISM DIPLOM

B57
YAMADA H.,ANNALS OF THE SOCIAL SCIENCES. WOR+45 WOR-45 LAW CULTURE SOCIETY STRUCT DIPLOM...EPIST PSY CONCPT 15/20. PAGE 168 A3428 — BIBLIOG/A TREND IDEA/COMP SOC

B58
ORGANSKI A.F.K.,WORLD POLITICS. FUT WOR+45 SOCIETY STRUCT NAT/G BAL/PWR ECO/TAC DOMIN NAT/LISM ATTIT KNOWL ORD/FREE PWR...CONCPT METH/CNCPT TREND STERTYP GEN/LAWS TOT/POP 20. PAGE 112 A2297 — INT/ORG DIPLOM

S58
DAVENPORT J.,"ARMS AND THE WELFARE STATE." INTELL STRUCT FORCES CREATE ECO/TAC FOR/AID DOMIN LEGIT ADMIN WAR ORD/FREE PWR...POLICY SOC CONCPT MYTH OBS TREND COLD/WAR TOT/POP 20. PAGE 34 A0685 — USA+45 NAT/G USSR

B59
ALWAN M.,ALGERIA BEFORE THE UNITED NATIONS. AFR ASIA FRANCE ISLAM S/ASIA CONSTN SOCIETY STRUCT INT/ORG NAT/G ECO/TAC ADMIN COLONIAL NAT/LISM ATTIT PWR...DECISION TREND 420 UN. PAGE 7 A0133 — PLAN RIGID/FLEX DIPLOM ALGERIA

B59
BALL M.M.,NATO AND THE EUROPEAN MOVEMENT. EUR+WWI USA+45 INT/ORG FORCES BAL/PWR EDU/PROP LEGIT REGION ATTIT ORD/FREE PWR...STAT OBS TIME/SEQ TREND CHARTS ORG/CHARTS STERTYP COLD/WAR EEC OEEC 20 NATO. PAGE 10 A0212 — DELIB/GP STRUCT

B59
CHALUPA V.,RISE AND DEVELOPMENT OF A TOTALITARIAN STATE. CZECHOSLVK USSR STRUCT INT/ORG WORKER DIPLOM ECO/TAC COERCE NAT/LISM ATTIT...POLICY 20 COM/PARTY. PAGE 25 A0516 — TOTALISM MARXISM REV POL/PAR

B59
CHINA INSTITUTE OF AMERICA.,CHINA AND THE UNITED NATIONS. CHINA/COM FUT STRUCT EDU/PROP LEGIT ADMIN ATTIT KNOWL ORD/FREE PWR...OBS RECORD STAND/INT TIME/SEQ UN LEAGUE/NAT UNESCO 20. PAGE 26 A0531 — ASIA INT/ORG

B59
GOODRICH L.,THE UNITED NATIONS. WOR+45 CONSTN STRUCT ACT/RES LEGIT COERCE KNOWL ORD/FREE PWR ...GEN/LAWS UN 20. PAGE 54 A1104 — INT/ORG ROUTINE

B59
VINACKE H.M.,A HISTORY OF THE FAR EAST IN MODERN TIMES (6TH ED.). KOREA S/ASIA USSR CONSTN CULTURE STRATA ECO/UNDEV NAT/G CHIEF FOR/AID INT/TRADE GP/REL...SOC NAT/COMP 19/20 CHINJAP. PAGE 159 A3235 — STRUCT ASIA

B59
WARD B.,5 IDEAS THAT CHANGE THE WORLD. WOR+45 WOR-45 SOCIETY STRUCT AGRI INDUS INT/ORG NAT/G FORCES ACT/RES ARMS/CONT TOTALISM ATTIT DRIVE GEN/LAWS. PAGE 161 A3278 — ECO/UNDEV ALL/VALS NAT/LISM COLONIAL

S59
REUBENS E.D.,"THE BASIS FOR REORIENATION OF AMERICAN FOREIGN AID POLICY." USA+45 USSR STRUCT INT/ORG CONSULT ECO/TAC ADMIN DRIVE MORAL ORD/FREE PWR WEALTH...RELATIV MATH STAT TREND GEN/LAWS VAL/FREE 20. PAGE 120 A2467 — ECO/UNDEV PLAN FOR/AID DIPLOM

S59
TIPTON J.B.,"PARTICIPATION OF THE UNITED STATES IN THE INTERNATIONAL LABOR ORGANIZATION." USA+45 LAW STRUCT ECO/DEV ECO/UNDEV INDUS TEC/DEV ECO/TAC ADMIN PERCEPT ORD/FREE SKILL...STAT HIST/WRIT GEN/METH ILO WORK 20. PAGE 144 A2946 — LABOR INT/ORG

B60
BAILEY S.D.,THE GENERAL ASSEMBLY OF THE UNITED NATIONS. FUT WOR+45 STRUCT LEGIS ACT/RES PLAN EDU/PROP LEGIT ADMIN EXEC PEACE ATTIT HEALTH PWR ...CONCPT TREND CHARTS GEN/LAWS UN TOT/POP VAL/FREE COLD/WAR 20. PAGE 10 A0204 — INT/ORG DELIB/GP DIPLOM

B60
ENGEL J.,THE SECURITY OF THE FREE WORLD. USSR — COM

WOR+45 STRATA STRUCT ECO/DEV ECO/UNDEV INT/ORG DELIB/GP FORCES DOMIN LEGIT ADJUD EXEC ARMS/CONT COERCE...POLICY CONCPT NEW/IDEA TIME/SEQ GEN/LAWS COLD/WAR WORK UN 20 NATO. PAGE 42 A0851
TREND DIPLOM

B60
FOOTMAN D.,INTERNATIONAL COMMUNISM. ASIA EUR+WWI FRANCE FUT GERMANY MOD/EUR S/ASIA USA-45 WOR+45 WOR-45 INTELL LABOR TOTALISM MARXISM WORK 20. PAGE 47 A0958
COM INT/ORG STRUCT REV

B60
HYDE L.K.G.,THE US AND THE UN. WOR+45 STRUCT ECO/DEV ECO/UNDEV NAT/G ACT/RES PLAN DIPLOM EDU/PROP ADMIN ALL/VALS...CONCPT TIME/SEQ GEN/LAWS UN VAL/FREE 20. PAGE 70 A1428
USA+45 INT/ORG FOR/AID

B60
LISTER L.,EUROPE'S COAL AND STEEL COMMUNITY. FRANCE GERMANY STRUCT ECO/DEV EXTR/IND INDUS MARKET NAT/G DELIB/GP ECO/TAC INT/TRADE EDU/PROP ATTIT RIGID/FLEX ORD/FREE PWR WEALTH...CONCPT STAT TIME/SEQ CHARTS ECSC 20. PAGE 90 A1843
EUR+WWI INT/ORG REGION

B60
STEIN E.,AMERICAN ENTERPRISE IN THE EUROPEAN COMMON MARKET: A LEGAL PROFILE. EUR+WWI FUT USA+45 SOCIETY STRUCT ECO/DEV NAT/G VOL/ASSN CONSULT PLAN TEC/DEV ECO/TAC INT/TRADE ADMIN ATTIT RIGID/FLEX PWR...MGT NEW/IDEA STAT TREND COMPUT/IR SIMUL EEC 20. PAGE 137 A2814
MARKET ADJUD INT/LAW

B60
THE AFRICA 1960 COMMITTEE,MANDATE IN TRUST; THE PROBLEM OF SOUTH WEST AFRICA. GERMANY STRUCT REGION SANCTION CHOOSE DISCRIM...INT/LAW 20 AFRICA/SW UN LEAGUE/NAT TRUST/TERR. PAGE 142 A2910
NAT/G DIPLOM COLONIAL RACE/REL

B60
WOETZEL R.K.,THE INTERNATIONAL CONTROL OF AIRSPACE AND OUTERSPACE. FUT WOR+45 AIR CONSTN STRUCT CONSULT PLAN TEC/DEV ADJUD RIGID/FLEX KNOWL ORD/FREE PWR...TECHNIC GEOG MGT NEW/IDEA TREND COMPUT/IR VAL/FREE 20 TREATY. PAGE 166 A3375
INT/ORG JURID SPACE INT/LAW

L60
DEAN A.W.,"SECOND GENEVA CONFERENCE OF THE LAW OF THE SEA: THE FIGHT FOR FREEDOM OF THE SEAS." FUT USA+45 USSR WOR+45 WOR-45 SEA CONSTN STRUCT PLAN INT/TRADE ADJUD ADMIN ORD/FREE...DECISION RECORD TREND GEN/LAWS 20 TREATY. PAGE 35 A0717
INT/ORG JURID INT/LAW

L60
DEUTSCH K.W.,"TOWARD AN INVENTORY OF BASIC TRENDS AND PATTERNS IN COMPARATIVE AND INTERNATIONAL POLITICS." UNIV WOR+45 SOCIETY STRUCT INT/ORG NAT/G CREATE PLAN EDU/PROP KNOWL...PHIL/SCI METH/CNCPT STAT SELF/OBS OBS/ENVIR SAMP TREND CON/ANAL CHARTS SOC/EXP GEN/METH 20. PAGE 36 A0739
R+D PERCEPT

S60
BOWIE R.,"POLICY FORMATION IN AMERICAN FOREIGN POLICY." FUT USA+45 WOR+45 STRUCT ECO/DEV INT/ORG POL/PAR LEGIS ACT/RES EXEC ALL/VALS...POLICY OBS VAL/FREE 20. PAGE 17 A0355
PLAN DRIVE DIPLOM

S60
HAYTON R.D.,"THE ANTARCTIC SETTLEMENT OF 1959." FUT USA+45 WOR+45 WOR-45 STRUCT R+D INT/ORG EX/STRUC CREATE TEC/DEV LEGIT PEACE ATTIT SOVEREIGN ...TIME/SEQ 20 TREATY IGY. PAGE 63 A1297
DELIB/GP JURID DIPLOM REGION

S60
JACOBSON H.K.,"THE USSR AND ILO." COM STRUCT ECO/DEV ECO/UNDEV CONSULT DELIB/GP ECO/TAC ILO WORK COLD/WAR 20. PAGE 72 A1484
INT/ORG LABOR USSR

S60
SCHWELB E.,"INTERNATIONAL CONVENTIONS ON HUMAN RIGHTS." FUT WOR+45 LAW CONSTN CULTURE SOCIETY STRUCT VOL/ASSN DELIB/GP PLAN ADJUD SUPEGO LOVE MORAL...SOC CONCPT STAT RECORD HIST/WRIT TREND 20 UN. PAGE 130 A2664
INT/ORG HUM

S60
WRIGHT Q.,"LEGAL ASPECTS OF THE U-2 INCIDENT." COM USA+45 USSR STRUCT NAT/G FORCES PLAN TEC/DEV ADJUD RIGID/FLEX MORAL ORD/FREE...DECISION INT/LAW JURID PSY TREND GEN/LAWS COLD/WAR VAL/FREE 20 U-2. PAGE 168 A3413
PWR POLICY SPACE

C60
FITZSIMMONS T.,"USSR: ITS PEOPLE, ITS SOCIETY, ITS CULTURE." USSR FAM SECT DIPLOM EDU/PROP ADMIN RACE/REL ATTIT...POLICY CHARTS BIBLIOG 20. PAGE 46 A0944
CULTURE STRUCT SOCIETY COM

C60
HAZARD J.N.,"THE SOVIET SYSTEM OF GOVERNMENT." USSR SOCIETY INDUS NAT/G POL/PAR DIPLOM CT/SYS...JURID CHARTS BIBLIOG/A 20. PAGE 63 A1298
COM NAT/COMP STRUCT ADMIN

C60
WRIGGINS W.H.,"CEYLON: DILEMMAS OF A NEW NATION." ASIA CEYLON CONSTN STRUCT POL/PAR SECT FORCES DIPLOM GOV/REL NAT/LISM...CHARTS BIBLIOG 20. PAGE 167 A3399
PROB/SOLV NAT/G ECO/UNDEV

B61
PATAI R.,CULTURES IN CONFLICT; AN INQUIRY INTO THE SOCIO-CULTURAL PROBLEMS OF ISRAEL AND HER NEIGHBORS (2ND REV. ED.). ISLAM ISRAEL SOCIETY STRUCT DIPLOM GP/REL ALL/VALS...SOC 20 JEWS ARABS. PAGE 114 A2339
NAT/COMP CULTURE GP/COMP ATTIT

B61
PEASLEE A.J.,INTERNATIONAL GOVERNMENT ORGANIZATIONS, CONSTITUTIONAL DOCUMENTS. WOR+45 WOR-45 CONSTN VOL/ASSN DELIB/GP EX/STRUC ROUTINE KNOWL TOT/POP 20. PAGE 114 A2344
INT/ORG STRUCT

B61
PERKINS D.,THE UNITED STATES AND LATIN AMERICAN. L/A+17C USA+45 USA-45 STRUCT COLONIAL REV ORD/FREE 19/20. PAGE 115 A2360
DIPLOM INT/TRADE NAT/G

B61
WALLERSTEIN I.M.,AFRICA; THE POLITICS OF INDEPENDENCE. AFR SOCIETY STRUCT LEAD PARL/PROC PARTIC GP/REL...POLICY 20. PAGE 160 A3269
ECO/UNDEV DIPLOM COLONIAL ORD/FREE

S61
JACKSON E.,"CONSTITUTIONAL DEVELOPMENTS OF THE UNITED NATIONS: THE GROWTH OF ITS EXECUTIVE CAPACITY." FUT WOR+45 CONSTN STRUCT ACT/RES PLAN ALL/VALS...NEW/IDEA OBS COLD/WAR UN 20. PAGE 72 A1475
INT/ORG EXEC

S61
TAUBENFELD H.J.,"OUTER SPACE--PAST POLITICS AND FUTURE POLICY." FUT USA+45 USA-45 WOR+45 AIR INTELL STRUCT ECO/DEV NAT/G TOP/EX ACT/RES ADMIN ROUTINE NUC/PWR ATTIT DRIVE...CONCPT TIME/SEQ TREND TOT/POP 20. PAGE 141 A2892
PLAN SPACE INT/ORG

B62
BOUSCAREN A.T.,SOVIET FOREIGN POLICY: A PATTERN OF PERSISTANCE. WOR+45 WOR-45 SOCIETY STRUCT INT/ORG POL/PAR CREATE PLAN EDU/PROP ROUTINE ATTIT RIGID/FLEX...POLICY CONCPT RECORD HIST/WRIT TIME/SEQ MARX/KARL 20. PAGE 17 A0352
COM NAT/G DIPLOM USSR

B62
BOWLES C.,THE CONSCIENCE OF A LIBERAL. COM USA+45 WOR+45 STRUCT LOC/G NAT/G FORCES LEGIS GOV/REL DISCRIM 20 UN CIV/RIGHTS. PAGE 18 A0361
DIPLOM POLICY

B62
COUNCIL ON WORLD TENSIONS,RESTLESS NATIONS. WOR+45 STRUCT INT/ORG NAT/G PLAN ECO/TAC...NAT/COMP ANTHOL 20. PAGE 32 A0641
ECO/UNDEV POLICY DIPLOM TASK

B62
KIRPICEVA I.K.,HANDBUCH DER RUSSISCHEN UND SOWJETISCHEN BIBLIOGRAPHIEN (5 VOLS.). USSR STRUCT ECO/DEV DIPLOM LEAD ATTIT 18/20. PAGE 80 A1637
BIBLIOG/A NAT/G MARXISM COM

B62
NEAL F.W.,WAR AND PEACE AND GERMANY. EUR+WWI USSR STRUCT INT/ORG NAT/G FORCES DOMIN EDU/PROP LEGIT EXEC COERCE ORD/FREE...HUM SOC NEW/IDEA OBS TIME/SEQ TOT/POP COLD/WAR 20 BERLIN. PAGE 108 A2208
USA+45 POLICY DIPLOM GERMANY

B62
ROBINSON A.D.,DUTCH ORGANIZED AGRICULTURE IN INTERNATIONAL POLITICS, 1945-1960. EUR+WWI NETHERLAND STRUCT ECO/DEV NAT/G VOL/ASSN CONSULT DELIB/GP PLAN TEC/DEV INT/TRADE EDU/PROP ATTIT RIGID/FLEX ALL/VALS...NEW/IDEA TREND EEC 20. PAGE 122 A2502
AGRI INT/ORG

B62
SCHMIDT-VOLKMAR E.,DER KULTURKAMPF IN DEUTSCHLAND 1871-1890. GERMANY PRUSSIA SOCIETY STRUCT SECT DIPLOM GP/REL NAT/LISM 19 CHURCH/STA BISMARCK/O. PAGE 128 A2632
POL/PAR CATHISM ATTIT NAT/G

B62
SELOSOEMARDJAN O.,SOCIAL CHANGES IN JOGJAKARTA. INDONESIA NETHERLAND ELITES STRATA STRUCT FAM POL/PAR CREATE DIPLOM INT/TRADE EDU/PROP ADMIN GOV/REL...SOC 20 JAVA CHINJAP. PAGE 131 A2683
ECO/UNDEV CULTURE REV COLONIAL

L62
CORET A.,"L'INDEPENDANCE DU SAMOA OCCIDENTAL." S/ASIA LAW INT/ORG EXEC ALL/VALS SAMOA UN 20. PAGE 31 A0622
NAT/G STRUCT SOVEREIGN

S62
BOKOR-SZEGO H.,"LA CONVENTION DE BELGRADE ET LE REGIME DU DANUBE." COM EUR+WWI WOR+45 STRUCT POL/PAR VOL/ASSN PLAN EDU/PROP WEALTH...TIME/SEQ 20. PAGE 16 A0333
INT/ORG TOTALISM YUGOSLAVIA

S62
CORET A.,"LA DECLARATION DE L'ASSEMBLEE GENERAL DE L'ONU SUR L'OCTROI DE L'INDEPENDANCE AUX PAYS ET AUX PEUPLES." AFR ASIA ISLAM NIGERIA S/ASIA USSR WOR+45 ECO/UNDEV NAT/G DELIB/GP COLONIAL ALL/VALS ...CONCPT TIME/SEQ TREND UN TOT/POP 20 MEXIC/AMER. PAGE 31 A0621
INT/ORG STRUCT SOVEREIGN

S62
CROAN M.,"POLYCENTRISM: COMMUNIST INTERNATIONAL RELATIONS." ASIA STRUCT INT/ORG NAT/G POL/PAR CONSULT PLAN DOMIN EDU/PROP COERCE ATTIT RIGID/FLEX SOCISM...POLICY CONCPT TREND CON/ANAL GEN/LAWS MARX/KARL. PAGE 33 A0663
COM CREATE DIPLOM NAT/LISM

S62
DEUTSCH K.W.,"TOWARDS WESTERN EUROPEAN INTEGRATION: AN INTERIM ASSESSMENT." EUR+WWI STRUCT ECO/DEV INT/ORG ECO/TAC INT/TRADE EDU/PROP PEACE ATTIT DRIVE PWR SOVEREIGN...PSY SOC TIME/SEQ CHARTS
VOL/ASSN RIGID/FLEX REGION

STERTYP 20. PAGE 36 A0741

S62
GAREAU F.H.,"BLOC POLITICS IN WEST AFRICA." AFR CONGO/BRAZ GHANA GUINEA MALI WOR+45 STRUCT ECO/UNDEV INT/ORG VOL/ASSN CHOOSE ORD/FREE PWR UN 20. PAGE 51 A1048
NAT/G NAT/LISM

S62
GRAVEN J.,"LE MOUVEAU DROIT PENAL INTERNATIONAL." UNIV STRUCT LEGIS ACT/RES CRIME ATTIT PERCEPT PERSON...JURID CONCPT 20. PAGE 55 A1132
CT/SYS PUB/INST INT/ORG INT/LAW

S62
GUETZKOW H.,"THE POTENTIAL OF CASE STUDY IN ANALYZING INTERNATIONAL CONFLICT." EUR+WWI FUT GERMANY INTELL SOCIETY STRUCT INT/ORG LOC/G NAT/G CONSULT CREATE PLAN CHOOSE ATTIT RIGID/FLEX ...POLICY SAAR 20. PAGE 58 A1188
EDU/PROP METH/CNCPT COERCE FRANCE

S62
MANGIN G.,"LES ACCORDS DE COOPERATION EN MATIERE DE JUSTICE ENTRE LA FRANCE ET LES ETATS AFRICAINS ET MALGACHE." AFR ISLAM WOR+45 STRUCT ECO/UNDEV NAT/G DELIB/GP PERCEPT ALL/VALS...JURID MGT TIME/SEQ 20. PAGE 94 A1919
INT/ORG LAW FRANCE

S62
MILLAR T.B.,"THE COMMONWEALTH AND THE UNITED NATIONS." FUT WOR+45 STRUCT NAT/G VOL/ASSN CONSULT DELIB/GP EDU/PROP LEGIT ATTIT...POLICY CONCPT TREND CMN/WLTH UN 20. PAGE 101 A2072
INT/ORG

S62
MOUSKHELY M.,"LA NAISSANCE DES ETATS EN DROIT INTERNATIONAL PUBLIC." UNIV SOCIETY INT/ORG VOL/ASSN LEGIT ATTIT RIGID/FLEX...JURID TIME/SEQ 20. PAGE 105 A2157
NAT/G STRUCT INT/LAW

S62
ORBAN M.,"L'EUROPE EN FORMATION ET SES PROBLEMES." EUR+WWI FUT WOR+45 WOR-45 INTELL STRUCT DELIB/GP ACT/RES FEDERAL RIGID/FLEX WEALTH...CONCPT TIME/SEQ OEEC 20. PAGE 112 A2295
INT/ORG PLAN REGION

S62
VIGNES D.,"L'AUTORITE DES TRAITES INTERNATIONAUX EN DROIT INTERNE." EUR+WWI UNIV LAW CONSTN INTELL NAT/G POL/PAR DIPLOM ATTIT PERCEPT ALL/VALS ...POLICY INT/LAW JURID CONCPT TIME/SEQ 20 TREATY. PAGE 159 A3233
STRUCT LEGIT FRANCE

B63
BROWN W.N.,THE UNITED STATES AND INDIA AND PAKISTAN (REV. ED.). INDIA PAKISTAN S/ASIA WOR+45 POL/PAR SECT INT/TRADE COLONIAL COERCE DISCRIM. PAGE 20 A0408
DIPLOM ECO/UNDEV SOVEREIGN STRUCT

B63
FLORES E.,LAND REFORM AND THE ALLIANCE FOR PROGRESS (PAMPHLET). L/A+17C USA+45 STRUCT ECO/UNDEV NAT/G WORKER CREATE PLAN ECO/TAC COERCE REV 20. PAGE 47 A0953
AGRI INT/ORG DIPLOM POLICY

B63
JENNINGS W.I.,DEMOCRACY IN AFRICA. UK CULTURE STRUCT ECO/UNDEV DIPLOM COLONIAL GP/REL ADJUST NAT/LISM ORD/FREE...GOV/COMP 20 THIRD/WRLD. PAGE 74 A1512
PROB/SOLV AFR CONSTN POPULISM

B63
KHADDURI M.,MODERN LIBYA: A STUDY IN POLITICAL DEVELOPMENT. EUR+WWI ISLAM LIBYA ELITES INT/ORG POL/PAR FORCES DIPLOM FOR/AID DOMIN EDU/PROP LEGIT NAT/LISM DRIVE RIGID/FLEX SKILL...CONCPT TIME/SEQ TREND 20. PAGE 78 A1606
NAT/G STRUCT

B63
PIKE F.B.,CHILE AND THE UNITED STATES 1880-1962: THE EMERGENCE OF CHILE'S CRISIS AND THE CHALLENGE TO US DIPLOMACY. CHILE COM USA+45 USA-45 SOCIETY STRATA ECO/UNDEV...MYTH 19/20. PAGE 116 A2378
FOR/AID DIPLOM ATTIT STRUCT

B63
WILCOX W.A.,PAKISTAN; THE CONSOLIDATION OF A NATION. INDIA PAKISTAN CONSTN SECT PROB/SOLV COLONIAL PARTIC GP/REL FEDERAL...POLICY 19/20. PAGE 164 A3348
NAT/LISM ECO/UNDEV DIPLOM STRUCT

S63
BARTHELEMY G.,"LE NOUVEAU FRANC (CFA) ET LA BANQUE CENTRALE DES ETATS DE L'AFRIQUE DE L'OUEST." FUT STRUCT INT/ORG PLAN ATTIT ALL/VALS 20. PAGE 11 A0230
AFR FINAN

S63
ETIENNE G.,"'LOIS OBJECTIVES' ET PROBLEMES DE DEVELOPPEMENT DANS LE CONTEXTE CHINE-URSS." ASIA CHINA/COM COM FUT STRUCT INT/ORG VOL/ASSN TOP/EX TEC/DEV ECO/TAC ATTIT RIGID/FLEX...GEOG MGT TIME/SEQ TOT/POP 20. PAGE 42 A0866
TOTALISM USSR

S63
MANOLIU F.,"PERSPECTIVES D'UNE INTEGRATION ECONOMIQUE LATINOAMERICAINE." FUT L/A+17C STRUCT MARKET LABOR POL/PAR VOL/ASSN PLAN RIGID/FLEX PWR ...METH/CNCPT OAS TOT/POP 20. PAGE 94 A1927
FINAN INT/ORG PEACE

B64
AMERICAN ASSEMBLY,THE UNITED STATES AND THE MIDDLE EAST. ISRAEL USA+45 STRUCT ECO/DEV ECO/UNDEV INT/ORG NAT/G SCHOOL SECT VOL/ASSN EX/STRUC TEC/DEV NAT/LISM...SOC 20. PAGE 7 A0135
ISLAM DRIVE REGION

B64
APTER D.E.,IDEOLOGY AND DISCONTENT. FUT WOR+45 CONSTN CULTURE INTELL SOCIETY STRUCT INT/ORG NAT/G DELIB/GP LEGIS CREATE PLAN TEC/DEV EDU/PROP EXEC PERCEPT PERSON RIGID/FLEX ALL/VALS...POLICY TOT/POP. PAGE 8 A0171
ACT/RES ATTIT

B64
BINDER L.,THE IDEOLOGICAL REVOLUTION IN THE MIDDLE EAST. ISLAM STRUCT INT/ORG KIN SECT EX/STRUC TOP/EX PLAN ATTIT DRIVE RIGID/FLEX PWR...MYTH TOT/POP 20. PAGE 14 A0289
POL/PAR NAT/G NAT/LISM

B64
CEPEDE M.,POPULATION AND FOOD. USA+45 STRUCT ECO/UNDEV FAM PLAN TEC/DEV FOR/AID CONTROL...CATH SOC TREND 19/20. PAGE 25 A0513
FUT GEOG AGRI CENSUS

B64
CLAUDE I.,SWORDS INTO PLOWSHARES. FUT WOR+45 WOR-45 DELIB/GP EX/STRUC LEGIT ATTIT ORD/FREE...CONCPT TIME/SEQ TREND UN TOT/POP 20. PAGE 27 A0547
INT/ORG STRUCT

B64
CZERNIN F.,VERSAILLES - 1919. EUR+WWI USA-45 FACE/GP POL/PAR VOL/ASSN DELIB/GP TOP/EX CREATE BAL/PWR DIPLOM LEGIT NAT/LISM PEACE ATTIT RIGID/FLEX ORD/FREE PWR...CON/ANAL LEAGUE/NAT 20 VERSAILLES. PAGE 33 A0671
INT/ORG STRUCT

B64
HALPERN J.M.,GOVERNMENT, POLITICS, AND SOCIAL STRUCTURE IN LAOS. LAOS CULTURE SOCIETY STRATA STRUCT FAM DIPLOM DOMIN MARXISM...INT GOV/COMP WORSHIP SOC/INTEG 20. PAGE 60 A1242
NAT/G SOC LOC/G

B64
HORNE D.,THE LUCKY COUNTRY: AUSTRALIA TODAY. UK CULTURE STRATA ATTIT PWR PLURISM...GOV/COMP 20 AUSTRAL. PAGE 67 A1386
RACE/REL DIPLOM NAT/G STRUCT

B64
IBERO-AMERICAN INSTITUTES,IBEROAMERICANA. STRUCT ADMIN SOC. PAGE 70 A1430
BIBLIOG L/A+17C NAT/G DIPLOM

B64
JACKSON W.V.,LIBRARY GUIDE FOR BRAZILIAN STUDIES. BRAZIL USA+45 STRUCT DIPLOM ADMIN...SOC 20. PAGE 72 A1481
BIBLIOG L/A+17C NAT/G LOC/G

B64
KRETZSCHMAR W.W.,AUSLANDSHILFE ALS MITTEL DER AUSSENWIRTSCHAFTS- UND AUSSENPOLITIK. ASIA GERMANY/W UK USA+45 SOCIETY STRUCT ECO/UNDEV LOBBY EFFICIENCY 20. PAGE 82 A1683
FOR/AID DIPLOM AGRI DIST/IND

B64
RAGHAVAN M.D.,INDIA IN CEYLONESE HISTORY, SOCIETY AND CULTURE. CEYLON INDIA S/ASIA LAW SOCIETY INT/TRADE ATTIT...ART/METH JURID SOC LING 20. PAGE 119 A2433
DIPLOM CULTURE SECT STRUCT

L64
CAMPBELL J.C.,"THE MIDDLE EAST IN THE MUTED COLD WAR." COM EUR+WWI UAR USA+45 USSR STRUCT ECO/UNDEV NAT/G VOL/ASSN EX/STRUC TOP/EX DIPLOM ECO/TAC EDU/PROP...TIME/SEQ COLD/WAR 20. PAGE 23 A0475
ISLAM FOR/AID NAT/LISM

S64
MOWER A.G.,"THE OFFICIAL PRESSURE GROUP OF THE COUNCIL OF EUROPE'S CONSULATIVE ASSEMBLY." EUR+WWI SOCIETY STRUCT FINAN CONSULT ECO/TAC ADMIN ROUTINE ATTIT PWR WEALTH...STAT CHARTS 20 COUNCL/EUR. PAGE 105 A2160
INT/ORG EDU/PROP

S64
TAUBENFELD R.K.,"INDEPENDENT REVENUE FOR THE UNITED NATIONS." WOR+45 SOCIETY STRUCT INDUS NAT/G CONSULT ACT/RES PLAN ECO/TAC LEGIT WEALTH...DECISION CON/ANAL GEN/METH UN 20. PAGE 142 A2896
INT/ORG FINAN

B65
GERASSI J.,THE GREAT FEAR IN LATIN AMERICA. L/A+17C USA+45 ELITES STRUCT INT/ORG REV ORD/FREE WEALTH 20 LAFTA. PAGE 52 A1063
SOCIETY FOR/AID DIPLOM

B65
MOLNAR T.,AFRICA: A POLITICAL TRAVELOGUE. STRUCT ECO/UNDEV DIPLOM EDU/PROP LEAD RACE/REL MARXISM 20 INTERVENT EUROPE. PAGE 102 A2101
COLONIAL AFR ORD/FREE

B65
ROSENBERG A.,DEMOCRACY AND SOCIALISM. COM EUR+WWI FRANCE MOD/EUR STRUCT INT/ORG NAT/G POL/PAR TOP/EX EDU/PROP COERCE PERSON PWR FASCISM MARXISM...CONCPT TIME/SEQ MARX/KARL 19/20. PAGE 124 A2535
ATTIT

B65
SCHREIBER H.,TEUTON AND SLAV - THE STRUGGLE FOR CENTRAL EUROPE (TRANS. BY J. CLEUGH). GERMANY POLAND PRUSSIA USSR SOCIETY STRUCT SECT DIPLOM BALTIC. PAGE 129 A2646
GP/REL WAR RACE/REL NAT/LISM

B65
SILVA SOLAR J.,EL DESARROLLO DE LA NUEVA SOCIEDAD EN AMERICA. L/A+17C SOCIETY AGRI PROB/SOLV DIPLOM PARTIC GP/REL OWN...POLICY SOC 20 REFORMERS. PAGE 133 A2716
STRUCT ECO/UNDEV REGION CONTROL

B65
VAN DEN BERGHE P.L.,AFRICA: SOCIAL PROBLEMS OF CHANGE AND CONFLICT. ELITES STRATA ECO/UNDEV KIN MUNIC DIPLOM GP/REL RACE/REL NAT/LISM...ANTHOL BIBLIOG 20. PAGE 158 A3210 — SOC CULTURE AFR STRUCT

B66
BESSON W.,DIE GROSSEN MACHTE - STRUKTURFRAGEN DER GEGENWARTIGEN WELTPOLITIK. ASIA USSR WOR+45 ATTIT ...IDEA/COMP 20 KENNEDY/JF. PAGE 14 A0280 — NAT/COMP DIPLOM STRUCT

B66
BLACK C.E.,THE DYNAMICS OF MODERNIZATION: A STUDY IN COMPARATIVE HISTORY. STRUCT ECO/DEV ECO/UNDEV NAT/G DIPLOM LEAD REV...PREDICT TIME/SEQ TREND SOC/INTEG 17/20. PAGE 15 A0296 — SOCIETY SOC NAT/COMP

B66
FITZGERALD C.P.,THE BIRTH OF COMMUNIST CHINA (2ND ED.). ASIA CHINA/COM STRUCT BAL/PWR DIPLOM ECO/TAC INT/TRADE WEALTH 20. PAGE 46 A0942 — REV MARXISM ECO/UNDEV

B66
HOLT R.T.,THE POLITICAL BASIS OF ECONOMIC DEVELOPMENT. STRATA STRUCT NAT/G DIPLOM ADMIN...SOC NAT/COMP BIBLIOG 20. PAGE 67 A1376 — ECO/TAC GOV/COMP CONSTN EX/STRUC

B66
KOH S.J.,STAGES OF INDUSTRIAL DEVELOPMENT IN ASIA. ASIA INDIA KOREA STRATA STRUCT NAT/G INT/TRADE ...CHARTS 19/20 CHINJAP. PAGE 81 A1659 — INDUS ECO/UNDEV ECO/DEV LABOR

B66
MULLER C.F.J.,A SELECT BIBLIOGRAPHY OF SOUTH AFRICAN HISTORY; A GUIDE FOR HISTORICAL RESEARCH. SOUTH/AFR UK LAW CONSTN SOCIETY STRUCT AGRI SECT DIPLOM COLONIAL LEAD RACE/REL...POLICY 17/20 NEGRO. PAGE 106 A2167 — BIBLIOG AFR NAT/G

B66
MURPHY G.G.,SOVIET MONGOLIA: A STUDY OF THE OLDEST POLITICAL SATELLITE. USSR STRATA STRUCT COST INCOME ATTIT SOCISM 20. PAGE 106 A2177 — DIPLOM ECO/TAC PLAN DOMIN

B66
THOMPSON J.H.,MODERNIZATION OF THE ARAB WORLD. FUT ISRAEL STRUCT ECO/UNDEV DIPLOM INGP/REL ATTIT ...CENSUS ANTHOL 20 ARABS. PAGE 143 A2926 — ADJUST ISLAM PROB/SOLV NAT/COMP

S66
MATTHEWS D.G.,"ETHIOPIAN OUTLINE: A BIBLIOGRAPHIC RESEARCH GUIDE." ETHIOPIA LAW STRUCT ECO/UNDEV AGRI LABOR SECT CHIEF DELIB/GP EX/STRUC ADMIN...LING ORG/CHARTS 20. PAGE 96 A1972 — BIBLIOG NAT/G DIPLOM POL/PAR

B67
BODENHEIMER E.,TREATISE ON JUSTICE. INT/ORG NAT/G PUB/INST ACT/RES RISK CRIME INGP/REL DISCRIM DRIVE LAISSEZ 20. PAGE 16 A0325 — ALL/VALS STRUCT JURID CONCPT

B67
DE BLIJ H.J.,SYSTEMATIC POLITICAL GEOGRAPHY. WOR+45 STRUCT INT/ORG NAT/G EDU/PROP ADMIN COLONIAL ROUTINE ORD/FREE PWR...IDEA/COMP T 20. PAGE 34 A0697 — GEOG CONCPT METH

B67
MAZRUI A.A.,TOWARDS A PAX AFRICANA. AFR STRUCT ECO/UNDEV NAT/G DIPLOM COLONIAL REGION WAR ATTIT 20. PAGE 97 A1988 — PEACE FORCES PROB/SOLV SOVEREIGN

S67
BATOR V.,"ONE WAR* TWO VIETNAMS." S/ASIA VIETNAM DIPLOM SUFF ATTIT ORD/FREE 20. PAGE 12 A0234 — WAR BAL/PWR NAT/G STRUCT

S67
BUTTINGER J.,"VIETNAM* FRAUD OF THE 'OTHER WAR'." VIETNAM/S ELITES STRUCT AGRI NAT/G FOR/AID RENT TREND. PAGE 22 A0456 — PLAN WEALTH REV ECO/UNDEV

S67
HUDSON R.,"WAS THIS WAR NECESSARY? THE UN AND THE MIDDLE EAST" WOR+45 STRUCT DIPLOM DOMIN CONTROL REPRESENT PWR...NEW/IDEA 20 UN MID/EAST. PAGE 69 A1410 — DELIB/GP INT/ORG PROB/SOLV PEACE

S67
SAPP B.B.,"TRIBAL CULTURES AND COMMUNISM." AFR USA+45 STRATA DIPLOM FOR/AID REGION CENTRAL ATTIT AUTHORIT RIGID/FLEX KNOWL. PAGE 127 A2604 — KIN MARXISM ECO/UNDEV STRUCT

B93
ROYAL GEOGRAPHIC SOCIETY,BIBLIOGRAPHY OF BARBARY STATES (4 SUPPLEMENTARY PAPERS). ALGERIA LIBYA MOROCCO SOCIETY STRUCT DIPLOM LEAD 14/19 TUNIS. PAGE 125 A2555 — BIBLIOG ISLAM NAT/G COLONIAL

STRUVE/P....PETER STRUVE

STUART G.H. A2852,A2853,A2854,A2855,A2856

STUART DYNASTY....SEE STUART/DYN

STUART/DYN....THE STUART DYNASTY

STUDNT/PWR....STUDENT POWER: STUDENT PROTESTS AND PROTEST MOVEMENTS

STUHLER B. A2515

STUMBERG G.W. A0337

STURZO L. A2857, A2858

STYLE....STYLES OF SCIENTIFIC COMMUNICATION

B49
GROB F.,THE RELATIVITY OF WAR AND PEACE: A STUDY IN LAW, HISTORY, AND POLLTICS. WOR+45 WOR-45 LAW DIPLOM DEBATE...CONCPT LING IDEA/COMP BIBLIOG 18/20. PAGE 57 A1167 — WAR PEACE INT/LAW STYLE

S58
BURNS A.L.,"THE INTERNATIONAL CONSEQUENCES OF EXPECTING SURPRISE." WOR+45 INT/ORG NAT/G FORCES DIPLOM COERCE NUC/PWR WAR CHOOSE ORD/FREE ...METH/CNCPT STYLE OBS STERTYP TOT/POP VAL/FREE. PAGE 22 A0440 — PLAN PWR DETER

S58
LASSWELL H.D.,"THE SCIENTIFIC STUDY OF INTERNATIONAL RELATIONS." USA+45 INT/ORG CREATE EDU/PROP DETER ATTIT PERCEPT PWR...DECISION CONCPT METH/CNCPT STYLE CON/ANAL 20. PAGE 85 A1740 — PHIL/SCI GEN/METH DIPLOM

B62
WOLFERS A.,DISCORD AND COLLABORATION: ESSAYS ON INTERNATIONAL POLITICS. WOR+45 CULTURE SOCIETY INT/ORG NAT/G BAL/PWR DIPLOM DOMIN NAT/LISM PEACE PWR...POLICY CONCPT STYLE RECORD TREND GEN/LAWS 20. PAGE 166 A3385 — ATTIT ORD/FREE

S65
FALK R.A.,"INTERNATIONAL LEGAL ORDER." USA+45 INTELL FACE/GP INT/ORG LEGIT KNOWL...CONCPT METH/CNCPT STYLE RECORD GEN/METH 20. PAGE 44 A0890 — ATTIT GEN/LAWS INT/LAW

SUAREZ F. A2859

SUAREZ/F....FRANCISCO SUAREZ

B19
VANDERPOL A.,LA DOCTRINE SCOLASTIQUE DU DROIT DE GUERRE. CHRIST-17C FORCES DIPLOM LEGIT SUPEGO MORAL ...BIOG AQUINAS/T SUAREZ/F CHRISTIAN. PAGE 158 A3220 — WAR SECT INT/LAW

SUBMARINE....SUBMARINES AND SUBMARINE WARFARE

SUBSIDIES....SEE FINAN

SUBURBS....SUBURBS

SUBVERT....SUBVERSION

B57
US COMMISSION GOVT SECURITY,RECOMMENDATIONS; AREA: IMMIGRANT PROGRAM. USA+45 LAW WORKER DIPLOM EDU/PROP WRITING ADMIN PEACE ATTIT...CONCPT ANTHOL 20 MIGRATION SUBVERT. PAGE 150 A3060 — POLICY CONTROL PLAN NAT/G

SUCCESSION....SUCCESSION (POLITICAL)

SUDAN....SEE ALSO AFR

B42
CONOVER H.F.,FRENCH COLONIES IN AFRICA: A LIST OF REFERENCES. ALGERIA FRANCE MOROCCO SOMALIA SUDAN CULTURE AGRI LOC/G SECT FORCES DIPLOM INT/TRADE NAT/LISM HEALTH...CON/ANAL 20. PAGE 29 A0594 — BIBLIOG AFR ECO/UNDEV COLONIAL

B52
US LIBRARY OF CONGRESS,EGYPT AND THE ANGLO-EGYPTIAN SUDAN: A SELECTIVE GUIDE TO BACKGROUND READING (PAMPHLET). SUDAN UAR UK DIPLOM...POLICY 20. PAGE 155 A3153 — BIBLIOG/A COLONIAL ISLAM NAT/G

B57
CONOVER H.F.,NORTH AND NORTHEAST AFRICA; A SELECTED ANNOTATED LIST OF WRITINGS. ALGERIA MOROCCO SUDAN UAR CULTURE INT/ORG PROB/SOLV ADJUD NAT/LISM PWR WEALTH...SOC 20 UN. PAGE 30 A0603 — BIBLIOG/A DIPLOM AFR ECO/UNDEV

B65
MEAGHER R.F.,PUBLIC INTERNATIONAL DEVELOPMENT FINANCING IN SUDAN. SUDAN FINAN DELIB/GP GIVE ...CHARTS GOV/COMP 20. PAGE 99 A2029 — FOR/AID PLAN RECEIVE

ECO/UNDEV

L65
MATTHEWS D.G.,"A CURRENT BIBLIOGRAPHY ON SUDANESE AFFAIRS; A SELECT BIBLIOGRAPHY FROM 1960-1964." SUDAN LAW CULTURE AGRI FINAN INDUS LABOR POL/PAR TEC/DEV FOR/AID RACE/REL LITERACY...LING 20. PAGE 96 A1970
BIBLIOG ECO/UNDEV NAT/G DIPLOM

SUDETENLND....SUDETENLAND

SUEZ CRISIS....SEE NAT/LISM+COERCE, ALSO INDIVIDUAL NATIONS, SUEZ

SUEZ....SUEZ CANAL

B00
HOLLAND T.E.,STUDIES IN INTERNATIONAL LAW. TURKEY USSR WOR-45 CONSTN NAT/G DIPLOM DOMIN LEGIT COERCE WAR PEACE ORD/FREE PWR SOVEREIGN...JURID CHARTS 20 PARLIAMENT SUEZ TREATY. PAGE 66 A1367
INT/ORG LAW INT/LAW

B56
US DEPARTMENT OF STATE,THE SUEZ CANAL PROBLEM; JULY 26-SEPTEMBER 22, 1956. UAR WOR+45 BAL/PWR COERCE NAT/LISM ATTIT ORD/FREE SOVEREIGN 20 SUEZ. PAGE 151 A3091
DIPLOM CONFER INT/TRADE

B56
WATT D.C.,BRITAIN AND THE SUEZ CANAL. COM UAR UK ...INT/LAW 20 SUEZ TREATY. PAGE 162 A3294
DIPLOM INT/TRADE DIST/IND NAT/G

B57
BRODY H.,UN DIARY: THE SEARCH FOR PEACE. HUNGARY WOR+45 DELIB/GP ROUTINE REV WAR ORD/FREE...AUD/VIS 20 UN SUEZ. PAGE 19 A0382
INT/ORG PEACE DIPLOM POLICY

B57
BROMBERGER M.,LES SECRETS DE L'EXPEDITION D'EGYPTE. FRANCE ISLAM UAR UK USA+45 USSR WOR+45 INT/ORG NAT/G FORCES BAL/PWR ECO/TAC DOMIN WAR NAT/LISM ATTIT PWR SOVEREIGN...MAJORIT TIME/SEQ CHARTS SUEZ COLD/WAR 20. PAGE 19 A0387
COERCE DIPLOM

B58
SCHUMAN F.,INTERNATIONAL POLITICS. WOR+45 WOR-45 INTELL NAT/G FORCES DOMIN LEGIT COERCE NUC/PWR ATTIT DISPL ORD/FREE PWR SOVEREIGN...POLICY CONCPT GEN/LAWS SUEZ 20. PAGE 129 A2650
FUT INT/ORG NAT/LISM DIPLOM

B58
STONE J.,AGGRESSION AND WORLD ORDER: A CRITIQUE OF UNITED NATIONS THEORIES OF AGGRESSION. LAW CONSTN DELIB/GP PROB/SOLV BAL/PWR DIPLOM DEBATE ADJUD CRIME PWR...POLICY IDEA/COMP 20 UN SUEZ LEAGUE/NAT. PAGE 138 A2835
ORD/FREE INT/ORG WAR CONCPT

L60
LAUTERPACHT E.,"THE SUEZ CANAL SETTLEMENT." FRANCE ISLAM ISRAEL UAR UK BAL/PWR DIPLOM LEGIT...JURID GEN/LAWS ANTHOL SUEZ VAL/FREE 20. PAGE 85 A1747
INT/ORG LAW

B61
FLEMING D.F.,THE COLD WAR AND ITS ORIGINS: 1950-1960 (VOL. II). ASIA FUT HUNGARY POLAND WOR+45 TEC/DEV DOMIN NUC/PWR REV PEACE...T 20 COLD/WAR EISNHWR/DD SUEZ. PAGE 46 A0946
MARXISM DIPLOM BAL/PWR

S63
NICHOLAS H.G.,"UN PEACE FORCES AND THE CHANGING GLOBE: THE LESSONS OF SUEZ AND CONGO." FUT WOR+45 CONSTN INT/ORG CONSULT DELIB/GP TOP/EX CREATE DIPLOM DOMIN LEGIT COERCE WAR PERSON RIGID/FLEX PWR UN SUEZ CONGO UNEF 20. PAGE 109 A2229
ACT/RES FORCES

C63
ATTIA G.E.O.,"LES FORCES ARMEES DES NATIONS UNIES EN COREE ET AU MOYENORIENT." KOREA CONSTN DELIB/GP LEGIS PWR...IDEA/COMP NAT/COMP BIBLIOG UN SUEZ. PAGE 10 A0194
FORCES NAT/G INT/LAW

B64
BARKER A.J.,SUEZ: THE SEVEN DAY WAR. EUR+WWI ISLAM UAR INT/ORG NAT/G PLAN DIPLOM ECO/TAC DOMIN NAT/LISM DRIVE RIGID/FLEX PWR SOVEREIGN...POLICY JURID TREND CHARTS SUEZ UN 20. PAGE 11 A0221
FORCES COERCE UK

B64
EAYRS J.,THE COMMONWEALTH AND SUEZ: A DOCUMENTARY SURVEY. FRANCE ISLAM VOL/ASSN FORCES CONFER COLONIAL WAR INGP/REL 20 CMN/WLTH SUEZ UN. PAGE 40 A0818
DIPLOM NAT/LISM DIST/IND SOVEREIGN

B64
FINER H.,DULLES OVER SUEZ. FRANCE FUT UAR UK WOR+45 NAT/G PROB/SOLV CONTROL NUC/PWR WAR 20 DULLES/JF SUEZ. PAGE 46 A0932
DIPLOM POLICY REC/INT

SUFF....SUFFRAGE; SEE ALSO CHOOSE

B28
PLAYNE C.E.,THE PRE-WAR MIND IN BRITAIN. GERMANY MOD/EUR UK STRATA SECT DIPLOM EDU/PROP CROWD SUFF ...POLICY ANARCH PSY SOC IDEA/COMP 20 WWI. PAGE 116 A2388
PRESS WAR DOMIN ATTIT

B56
JAMESON J.F.,THE AMERICAN REVOLUTION CONSIDERED AS A SOCIAL MOVEMENT. USA-45 AGRI FINAN SECT INT/TRADE REPRESENT SUFF INGP/REL RACE/REL DISCRIM...MAJORIT 18/19 CHURCH/STA. PAGE 73 A1494
ORD/FREE REV FEDERAL CONSTN

B56
VON BECKERATH E.,HANDWORTERBUCH DER SOCIALWISSENSCHAFTEN (II VOLS.). EUR+WWI GERMANY POL/PAR WORKER DIPLOM LEAD CHOOSE SUFF WEALTH...SOC 20. PAGE 159 A3249
BIBLIOG INT/TRADE NAT/G ECO/DEV

S67
BATOR V.,"ONE WAR* TWO VIETNAMS." S/ASIA VIETNAM DIPLOM SUFF ATTIT ORD/FREE 20. PAGE 12 A0234
WAR BAL/PWR NAT/G STRUCT

SUFFRAGE....SEE SUFF

SUICIDE....SUICIDE AND RELATED SELF-DESTRUCTIVENESS

SUINN R.M. A2860

SUKARNO/A....ACHMED SUKARNO

SULLIVAN G. A2861

SULZBACH W. A2862

SULZBERGER C.L. A2863

SUMATRA....SUMATRA

SUMER....SUMER, A PRE- OR EARLY HISTORIC SOCIETY

SUMNER W.G. A2864

SUN/YAT....SUN YAT SEN

SUPEGO....CONSCIENCE, SUPEREGO, RESPONSIBILITY

B19
VANDERPOL A.,LA DOCTRINE SCOLASTIQUE DU DROIT DE GUERRE. CHRIST-17C FORCES DIPLOM LEGIT SUPEGO MORAL ...BIOG AQUINAS/T SUAREZ/F CHRISTIAN. PAGE 158 A3220
WAR SECT INT/LAW

B29
BUELL R.,INTERNATIONAL RELATIONS. WOR+45 WOR-45 CONSTN STRATA FORCES TOP/EX ADMIN ATTIT DRIVE SUPEGO MORAL ORD/FREE PWR SOVEREIGN...JURID SOC CONCPT 20. PAGE 21 A0428
INT/ORG BAL/PWR DIPLOM

B32
BRYCE J.,THE HOLY ROMAN EMPIRE. GERMANY ITALY MOD/EUR CULTURE SOCIETY STRUCT INT/ORG NAT/G SECT DIPLOM DOMIN WAR SUPEGO ALL/VALS SOVEREIGN...GEOG SOC TIME/SEQ CHARTS STERTYP. PAGE 20 A0413
CHRIST-17C NAT/LISM

B33
FERRERO G.,PEACE AND WAR (TRANS. BY BERTHA PRITCHARD). CULTURE FINAN SECT ATTIT SUPEGO MORAL ORD/FREE CONSERVE POPULISM SOCISM POLICY. PAGE 45 A0922
WAR PEACE DIPLOM PROB/SOLV

B33
GENTILI A.,DE JURE BELLI, LIBRI TRES (1612) (VOL. 2). FORCES DIPLOM AGREE PEACE SOVEREIGN. PAGE 52 A1059
WAR INT/LAW MORAL SUPEGO

B40
NIEBUHR R.,CHRISTIANITY AND POWER POLITICS. WOR-45 SECT DIPLOM GP/REL SUPEGO ALL/IDEOS WORSHIP 20 CHRISTIAN. PAGE 109 A2234
PARTIC PEACE MORAL

B45
WEST R.,CONSCIENCE AND SOCIETY: A STUDY OF THE PSYCHOLOGICAL PREREQUISITES OF LAW AND ORDER. FUT UNIV LAW SOCIETY STRUCT DIPLOM WAR PERS/REL SUPEGO ...SOC 20. PAGE 163 A3321
COERCE INT/LAW ORD/FREE PERSON

L46
MASTERS D.,"ONE WORLD OR NONE." FUT WOR+45 INTELL INT/ORG ACT/RES EDU/PROP DETER ATTIT RIGID/FLEX SUPEGO KNOWL...STAT TREND ORG/CHARTS 20. PAGE 96 A1960
POLICY PHIL/SCI ARMS/CONT NUC/PWR

B49
STETTINIUS E.R.,ROOSEVELT AND THE RUSSIANS: THE YALTA CONFERENCE. UK USSR WOR+45 WOR-45 INT/ORG VOL/ASSN TOP/EX ACT/RES EDU/PROP PEACE ATTIT DRIVE PERSON SUPEGO PWR...POLICY CONCPT MYTH OBS TIME/SEQ AUD/VIS COLD/WAR 20 CHURCHLL/W YALTA ROOSEVLT/F. PAGE 138 A2819
DIPLOM DELIB/GP BIOG

L52
NIEBUHR R.,"THE MORAL IMPLICATIONS OF LOYALTY TO THE UNITED NATIONS." WOR+45 WOR-45 SOCIETY ECO/DEV INT/ORG VOL/ASSN PEACE ATTIT PERSON LOVE ORD/FREE PWR RESPECT...CONCPT UN TOT/POP COLD/WAR UNESCO 20. PAGE 109 A2236
SUPEGO GEN/LAWS

B53
BRETTON H.L.,STRESEMANN AND THE REVISION OF VERSAILLES: A FIGHT FOR REASON. EUR+WWI GERMANY FORCES BUDGET ARMS/CONT WAR SUPEGO...BIBLIOG 20 TREATY VERSAILLES STRESEMN/G. PAGE 18 A0373
POLICY DIPLOM BIOG

B55
ROWE C.,VOLTAIRE AND THE STATE. FRANCE MOD/EUR BAL/PWR CONTROL TASK SUPEGO ORD/FREE PWR...CONCPT 18 VOLTAIRE. PAGE 125 A2553
NAT/G DIPLOM NAT/LISM ATTIT

B57
US SENATE SPEC COMM FOR AID,HEARINGS BEFORE THE SPECIAL COMMITTEE TO STUDY THE FOREIGN AID PROGRAM. USA+45 USSR ECO/UNDEV INT/ORG FORCES WEAPON TOTALISM ATTIT SUPEGO...NAT/COMP CONGRESS. PAGE 157 A3198
FOR/AID DIPLOM ORD/FREE TEC/DEV

N57
US SENATE SPECIAL COMM FOR AFF,REPORT OF THE SPECIAL COMMITTEE TO STUDY THE FOREIGN AID PROGRAM (PAMPHLET). USA+45 CONSULT DELIB/GP LEGIS PLAN TEC/DEV CONFER SUPEGO CONGRESS. PAGE 157 A3199
FOR/AID ORD/FREE ECO/UNDEV DIPLOM

B58
JENKS C.W.,THE COMMON LAW OF MANKIND. EUR+WWI MOD/EUR SPACE WOR+45 INT/ORG BAL/PWR ARMS/CONT COERCE SUPEGO MORAL...TREND 20. PAGE 73 A1505
JURID SOVEREIGN

B59
KNIERIEM A.,THE NUREMBERG TRIALS. EUR+WWI GERMANY VOL/ASSN LEAD COERCE WAR INGP/REL TOTALISM SUPEGO ORD/FREE...CONCPT METH/COMP. PAGE 80 A1651
INT/LAW CRIME PARTIC JURID

S59
FISCHER L.,"THE SOVIET-AMERICAN ANTAGONISM: HOW WILL IT END." CONSTN CULTURE PLAN TEC/DEV RIGID/FLEX SUPEGO ORD/FREE...MARXIST DECISION PSY CONCPT CON/ANAL GEN/LAWS VAL/FREE 20 COLD/WAR. PAGE 46 A0936
USA+45 PWR DIPLOM USSR

B60
DE GAULLE C.,THE EDGE OF THE SWORD. EUR+WWI FRANCE ELITES CHIEF DIPLOM ROLE...REALPOL TRADIT. PAGE 34 A0701
FORCES SUPEGO LEAD WAR

B60
PRITTIE T.,GERMANY DIVIDED: THE LEGACY OF THE NAZI ERA. EUR+WWI GERMANY RACE/REL SUPEGO...PSY AUD/VIS BIBLIOG/A 20 NAZI. PAGE 118 A2414
STERTYP PERSON ATTIT DIPLOM

B60
SPEER J.P.,FOR WHAT PURPOSE? CHINA/COM USSR CONSTN PROB/SOLV DIPLOM CONTROL TASK WAR NAT/LISM WORSHIP 20 UN. PAGE 136 A2778
PEACE SECT SUPEGO ALL/IDEOS

B60
WHEARE K.C.,THE CONSTITUTIONAL STRUCTURE OF THE COMMONWEALTH. UK EX/STRUC DIPLOM DOMIN ADMIN COLONIAL CONTROL LEAD INGP/REL SUPEGO 20 CMN/WLTH. PAGE 163 A3325
CONSTN INT/ORG VOL/ASSN SOVEREIGN

S60
SCHWELB E.,"INTERNATIONAL CONVENTIONS ON HUMAN RIGHTS." FUT WOR+45 LAW CONSTN CULTURE SOCIETY STRUCT VOL/ASSN DELIB/GP PLAN ADJUD SUPEGO LOVE MORAL...SOC CONCPT STAT RECORD HIST/WRIT TREND 20 UN. PAGE 130 A2664
INT/ORG HUM

S60
THOMPSON K.W.,"MORAL PURPOSE IN FOREIGN POLICY: REALITIES AND ILLUSIONS." WOR+45 WOR-45 LAW CULTURE SOCIETY INT/ORG PLAN ADJUD ADMIN COERCE RIGID/FLEX SUPEGO KNOWL ORD/FREE PWR...SOC TREND SOC/EXP TOT/POP 20. PAGE 143 A2930
MORAL JURID DIPLOM

B61
GRAEBNER N.,AN UNCERTAIN TRADITION: AMERICAN SECRETARIES OF STATE IN THE 20TH CENTURY. USA+45 CONSTN INT/ORG NAT/G DELIB/GP TOP/EX BAL/PWR DOMIN LEGIT ADMIN ARMS/CONT ATTIT DRIVE PERSON SUPEGO ORD/FREE PWR...GEN/LAWS VAL/FREE CONGRESS. PAGE 55 A1121
USA-45 BIOG DIPLOM

B61
THEOBALD R.,THE CHALLENGE OF ABUNDANCE. USA+45 WOR+45 MARKET DIPLOM FOR/AID REV PRODUC UTOPIA SUPEGO...POLICY TREND BIBLIOG/A 20. PAGE 142 A2913
WELF/ST ECO/UNDEV PROB/SOLV ECO/TAC

B62
BENNETT J.C.,NUCLEAR WEAPONS AND THE CONFLICT OF CONSCIENCE. WOR+45 PROB/SOLV DIPLOM WEAPON SUPEGO MORAL...ANTHOL WORSHIP 20. PAGE 13 A0268
POLICY NUC/PWR WAR

B62
QUIRK R.E.,AN AFFAIR OF HONOR: WOODROW WILSON AND THE OCCUPATION OF VERACRUZ. L/A+17C USA-45 COLONIAL SUPEGO PWR 20 WILSON/W MEXIC/AMER. PAGE 118 A2428
DOMIN DIPLOM COERCE PROB/SOLV

B62
WOETZEL R.K.,THE NURENBERG TRIALS IN INTERNATIONAL LAW. CHRIST-17C MOD/EUR WOR+45 SOCIETY NAT/G DELIB/GP DOMIN LEGIT ROUTINE ATTIT DRIVE PERSON SUPEGO MORAL ORD/FREE...POLICY MAJORIT JURID PSY SOC SELF/OBS RECORD NAZI TOT/POP. PAGE 166 A3376
INT/ORG ADJUD WAR

S62
MONNIER J.P.,"LA SUCCESSION D'ETATS EN MATIERE DE RESPONSABILITE INTERNATIONALE." UNIV CONSTN INTELL SOCIETY ADJUD ROUTINE PERCEPT SUPEGO...GEN/LAWS TOT/POP 20. PAGE 103 A2107
NAT/G JURID INT/LAW

B63
JACOBSON H.K.,THE USSR AND THE UN'S ECONOMIC AND SOCIAL ACTIVITIES. COM WOR+45 DELIB/GP ACT/RES ECO/TAC EDU/PROP RIGID/FLEX SUPEGO HEALTH PWR SKILL ...POLICY CHARTS GEN/METH VAL/FREE UNESCO 20 UN. PAGE 73 A1487
INT/ORG ATTIT USSR

B63
MULLENBACH P.,CIVILIAN NUCLEAR POWER: ECONOMIC ISSUES AND POLICY FORMATION. FINAN INT/ORG DELIB/GP ACT/RES ECO/TAC ATTIT SUPEGO HEALTH ORD/FREE PWR ...POLICY CONCPT MATH STAT CHARTS VAL/FREE 20 COLD/WAR. PAGE 105 A2166
USA+45 ECO/DEV NUC/PWR

B63
ROSECRANCE R.N.,ACTION AND REACTION IN WORLD POLITICS. FUT WOR-45 SOCIETY DELIB/GP ACT/RES CREATE DIPLOM ECO/TAC DOMIN EDU/PROP COERCE ATTIT PERSON SUPEGO ORD/FREE PWR...CHARTS SIMUL LEAGUE/NAT VAL/FREE UN 19/20. PAGE 123 A2529
WOR+45 INT/ORG BAL/PWR

B63
STEVENSON A.E.,LOOKING OUTWARD: YEARS OF CRISIS AT THE UNITED NATIONS. COM CUBA USA+45 WOR+45 SOCIETY NAT/G EX/STRUC ACT/RES LEGIT COLONIAL ATTIT PERSON SUPEGO ALL/VALS...POLICY HUM UN COLD/WAR CONGO 20. PAGE 138 A2823
INT/ORG CONCPT ARMS/CONT

B63
TUCKER R.C.,THE SOVIET POLITICAL MIND. WOR+45 ELITES INT/ORG NAT/G POL/PAR PLAN DIPLOM ECO/TAC DOMIN ADMIN NUC/PWR REV DRIVE PERSON SUPEGO PWR WEALTH...POLICY MGT PSY CONCPT OBS BIOG TREND COLD/WAR MARX/KARL 20. PAGE 145 A2972
COM TOP/EX USSR

B63
US SENATE COMM ON FOREIGN REL,HEARINGS ON S 1276 A BILL TO AMEND FURTHER THE FOREIGN ASSISTANCE ACT OF 1961. USA+45 WOR+45 INDUS INT/ORG FORCES TAX WEAPON SUPEGO...NAT/COMP 20 UN CONGRESS PRESIDENT. PAGE 156 A3182
FOR/AID DIPLOM ECO/UNDEV ORD/FREE

L63
SINGER J.D.,"WEAPONS MANAGEMENT IN WORLD POLITICS: PROCEEDINGS OF THE INTERNATIONAL ARMS CONTROL SYMPOSIUM, DECEMBER, 1962." FUT WOR+45 SOCIETY ECO/DEV INDUS INT/ORG DELIB/GP FORCES ACT/RES ECO/TAC EDU/PROP ARMS/CONT SUPEGO HEALTH ORD/FREE PWR SKILL...POLICY CHARTS SIMUL ANTHOL VAL/FREE 20. PAGE 133 A2729
CONSULT ATTIT DIPLOM NUC/PWR

S63
DICKS H.V.,"NATIONAL LOYALTY, IDENTITY, AND THE INTERNATIONAL SOLDIER." FUT NAT/G COERCE ATTIT DRIVE PERCEPT PERSON RIGID/FLEX SUPEGO ALL/VALS ...PSY VAL/FREE. PAGE 37 A0758
INT/ORG FORCES

B64
CASEY R.G.,THE FUTURE OF THE COMMONWEALTH. INDIA PAKISTAN UK ECO/UNDEV INT/ORG TEC/DEV COLONIAL SUPEGO 20 EEC AUSTRAL. PAGE 25 A0505
DIPLOM SOVEREIGN NAT/LISM FOR/AID

L64
HERZ J.H.,"THE RELEVANCY AND IRRELEVANCY OF APPEASEMENT." WOR+45 INT/ORG CONSULT TOP/EX LEGIT ATTIT SUPEGO ORD/FREE...POLICY SOC GEN/LAWS 20. PAGE 64 A1320
ACT/RES RIGID/FLEX

S64
GREENBERG S.,"JUDAISM AND WORLD JUSTICE." MEDIT-7 WOR+45 LAW CULTURE SOCIETY INT/ORG NAT/G FORCES EDU/PROP ATTIT DRIVE PERSON SUPEGO ALL/VALS ...POLICY PSY CONCPT GEN/LAWS JEWS. PAGE 55 A1140
SECT JURID PEACE

S64
KHAN M.Z.,"ISLAM AND INTERNATIONAL RELATIONS." FUT WOR+45 LAW CULTURE SOCIETY NAT/G SECT DELIB/GP FORCES EDU/PROP ATTIT PERSON SUPEGO ALL/VALS ...POLICY PSY CONCPT MYTH HIST/WRIT GEN/LAWS. PAGE 78 A1608
ISLAM INT/ORG DIPLOM

C64
SCHRAMM W.,"MASS MEDIA AND NATIONAL DEVELOPMENT: THE ROLE OF INFORMATION IN DEVELOPING COUNTRIES." FINAN R+D ACT/RES PLAN TEC/DEV DIPLOM CHOOSE SUPEGO ORD/FREE...BIBLIOG 20. PAGE 129 A2645
ECO/UNDEV COM/IND EDU/PROP MAJORIT

B66
JACK H.A.,RELIGION AND PEACE: PAPERS FROM THE NATIONAL INTER-RELIGIOUS CONFERENCE ON PEACE, WASHINGTON, 1966. CHINA/COM USA+45 VIETNAM WOR+45 FORCES FOR/AID LEAD PERS/REL. PAGE 72 A1472
PEACE SECT SUPEGO DIPLOM

B66
MAYER P.,THE PACIFIST CONSCIENCE. SECT CREATE ARMS/CONT WAR RACE/REL ATTIT LOVE...ANTHOL PACIFIST WORSHIP FREUD/S GANDHI/M LAO/TZU KING/MAR/L CONSCN/OBJ. PAGE 97 A1984
DIPLOM PACIFISM SUPEGO

B66
NANTWI E.K.,THE ENFORCEMENT OF INTERNATIONAL JUDICIAL DECISIONS AND ARBITAL AWARDS IN PUBLIC INTERNATIONAL LAW. WOR+45 WOR-45 JUDGE PROB/SOLV DIPLOM CT/SYS SUPEGO MORAL PWR RESPECT...METH/CNCPT 18/20 CASEBOOK. PAGE 107 A2196
INT/LAW ADJUD SOVEREIGN INT/ORG

B66
OLSON W.C.,THE THEORY AND PRACTICE OF INTERNATIONAL RELATIONS (2ND ED.). WOR+45 LEAD SUPEGO...INT/LAW PHIL/SCI. PAGE 112 A2290
DIPLOM NAT/G INT/ORG POLICY

B66
POLLACK R.S.,THE INDIVIDUAL'S RIGHTS AND INTERNATIONAL ORGANIZATION. LAW INT/ORG DELIB/GP SUPEGO...JURID SOC/INTEG 20 TREATY UN. PAGE 117 A2394 — INT/LAW ORD/FREE DIPLOM PERSON

B67
CHO S.S.,KOREA IN WORLD POLITICS 1940-1950; AN EVALUATION OF AMERICAN RESPONSIBILITY. KOREA USA+45 USSR CONSTN INT/ORG NAT/G FORCES FOR/AID ANOMIE SUPEGO MARXISM...DECISION BIBLIOG 20. PAGE 26 A0533 — POLICY DIPLOM PROB/SOLV WAR

SUPERVISION....SEE EXEC, CONTROL, LEAD, TASK

SUPPLE B.E. A1519

SUPREME/CT....SUPREME COURT (ALL NATIONS)

B60
BYRD E.M. JR.,TREATIES AND EXECUTIVE AGREEMENTS IN THE UNITED STATES: THEIR SEPARATE ROLES AND LIMITATIONS. USA+45 USA-45 EX/STRUC TARIFFS CT/SYS GOV/REL FEDERAL...IDEA/COMP BIBLIOG SUPREME/CT SENATE CONGRESS. PAGE 23 A0461 — CHIEF INT/LAW DIPLOM

B65
LYONS G.M.,AMERICA: PURPOSE AND POWER. UK USA+45 FINAN INDUS MARKET WORKER TEC/DEV DIPLOM AUTOMAT NUC/PWR WAR RACE/REL ORD/FREE 20 EEC CONGRESS SUPREME/CT CIV/RIGHTS. PAGE 92 A1881 — PWR PROB/SOLV ECO/DEV TASK

B66
AMERICAN JOURNAL COMP LAW,THE AMERICAN JOURNAL OF COMPARATIVE LAW READER. EUR+WWI USA+45 USA-45 LAW CONSTN LOC/G MUNIC NAT/G DIPLOM...ANTHOL 20 SUPREME/CT EURCT/JUST. PAGE 7 A0151 — IDEA/COMP JURID INT/LAW CT/SYS

L67
"RESTRICTIVE SOVEREIGN IMMUNITY, THE STATE DEPARTMENT, AND THE COURTS." USA+45 USA-45 EX/STRUC DIPLOM ADJUD CONTROL GOV/REL 19/20 DEPT/STATE SUPREME/CT. PAGE 4 A0080 — SOVEREIGN ORD/FREE PRIVIL CT/SYS

SURANYI-UNGER T. A2865

SURPLUS....SEE DEMAND,PLAN

SURVEY ANALYSIS....SEE SAMP/SIZ

SUTHERLAND G. A2866

SUTTON F.X. A2867

SVARLIEN O. A2868

SWATANTRA....SWATANTRA - COALITION RIGHT-WING PARTY IN INDIA

SWEARER H.R. A2869

SWEDEN....SEE ALSO APPROPRIATE TIME/SPACE/CULTURE INDEX

B53
NEISSER H.,NATIONAL INCOMES AND INTERNATIONAL TRADE. FRANCE GERMANY SWEDEN UK USA-45 EXTR/IND FINAN INDUS TEC/DEV PRICE BAL/PAY EQUILIB INCOME WEALTH...CHARTS METH 19 CHINJAP. PAGE 108 A2215 — INT/TRADE PRODUC MARKET CON/ANAL

B53
ORFIELD L.B.,THE GROWTH OF SCANDINAVIAN LAW. DENMARK ICELAND NORWAY SWEDEN LAW DIPLOM...BIBLIOG 9/20. PAGE 112 A2296 — JURID CT/SYS NAT/G

B56
TOYNBEE A.,THE WAR AND THE NEUTRALS. L/A+17C PORTUGAL SPAIN SWEDEN SWITZERLND TURKEY WOR+45 WOR-45 ECO/TAC CONFER CONTROL REGION 20. PAGE 145 A2957 — NEUTRAL WAR INT/TRADE DIPLOM

S63
COUTY P.,"L'ASSISTANCE POUR LE DEVELOPPEMENT: POINT DE VUE SCANDINAVES." EUR+WWI FINLAND FUT SWEDEN WOR+45 ECO/DEV ECO/UNDEV COM/IND LABOR NAT/G PROF/ORG ACT/RES SKILL WEALTH TOT/POP 20. PAGE 32 A0643 — FINAN ROUTINE FOR/AID

C65
WUORINEN J.H.,"SCANDINAVIA." DENMARK FINLAND ICELAND NORWAY SWEDEN SOCIETY AGRI POL/PAR DELIB/GP DIPLOM INT/TRADE NEUTRAL WAR...CHARTS TREATY 20. PAGE 168 A3423 — BIBLIOG NAT/G POLICY

S67
MOBERG E.,"THE EFFECT OF SECURITY POLICY MEASURES: DISCUSSION RELATED TO SWEDEN'S SECURITY POLICY." SWEDEN PLAN PROB/SOLV DIPLOM GOV/REL MORAL...CHARTS 20. PAGE 102 A2092 — POLICY ORD/FREE BUDGET FINAN

SWIFT R.N. A2870, A2871

SWISHER C.B. A2872

SWITZERLND....SWITZERLAND; SEE ALSO APPROPRIATE TIME/SPACE/CULTURE INDEX

N
DEUTSCHE BUCHEREI,JAHRESVERZEICHNIS DES DEUTSCHEN SCHRIFTUMS. AUSTRIA EUR+WWI GERMANY SWITZERLND LAW LOC/G DIPLOM ADMIN...MGT SOC 19/20. PAGE 37 A0745 — BIBLIOG WRITING NAT/G

N19
STEUBER F.A.,THE CONTRIBUTION OF SWITZERLAND TO THE ECONOMIC AND SOCIAL DEVELOPMENT OF LOW-INCOME COUNTRIES (PAMPHLET). SWITZERLND FINAN NAT/G VOL/ASSN INT/TRADE DRIVE...CHARTS 20. PAGE 138 A2820 — FOR/AID ECO/UNDEV PLAN DIPLOM

B32
MASTERS R.D.,INTERNATIONAL LAW IN INTERNATIONAL COURTS. BELGIUM EUR+WWI FRANCE GERMANY MOD/EUR SWITZERLND WOR-45 SOCIETY STRATA STRUCT LEGIT EXEC ALL/VALS...JURID HIST/WRIT TIME/SEQ TREND GEN/LAWS 20. PAGE 96 A1961 — INT/ORG LAW INT/LAW

B47
HILL M.,IMMUNITIES AND PRIVILEGES OF INTERNATIONAL OFFICIALS. CANADA EUR+WWI NETHERLAND SWITZERLND LAW LEGIS DIPLOM LEGIT RESPECT...TIME/SEQ LEAGUE/NAT UN VAL/FREE 20. PAGE 65 A1330 — INT/ORG ADMIN

B47
INTERNATIONAL COURT OF JUSTICE,CHARTER OF THE UNITED NATIONS, STATUTE AND RULES OF COURT AND OTHER CONSTITUTIONAL DOCUMENTS. SWITZERLND LAW ADJUD INGP/REL...JURID 20 ICJ UN. PAGE 71 A1453 — INT/LAW INT/ORG CT/SYS DIPLOM

B56
TOYNBEE A.,THE WAR AND THE NEUTRALS. L/A+17C PORTUGAL SPAIN SWEDEN SWITZERLND TURKEY WOR+45 WOR-45 ECO/TAC CONFER CONTROL REGION 20. PAGE 145 A2957 — NEUTRAL WAR INT/TRADE DIPLOM

B57
ARON R.,L'UNIFICATION ECONOMIQUE DE L'EUROPE. EUR+WWI SWITZERLND UK INT/ORG NAT/G REGION NAT/LISM ORD/FREE PWR...CONCPT METH/CNCPT OBS TREND STERTYP GEN/LAWS EEC 20. PAGE 9 A0181 — VOL/ASSN ECO/TAC

B62
DUTOIT B.,LA NEUTRALITE SUISSE A L'HEURE EUROPEENNE. EUR+WWI MOD/EUR INT/ORG NAT/G VOL/ASSN PLAN BAL/PWR LEGIT NEUTRAL REGION PEACE ORD/FREE SOVEREIGN...CONCPT OBS TIME/SEQ TREND STERTYP VAL/FREE LEAGUE/NAT UN 20. PAGE 40 A0812 — ATTIT DIPLOM SWITZERLND

B63
MONTER W.,THE GOVERNMENT OF GENEVA, 1536-1605 (DOCTORAL THESIS). SWITZERLND DIPLOM LEAD ORD/FREE SOVEREIGN 16/17 CALVIN/J ROME. PAGE 103 A2112 — SECT FINAN LOC/G ADMIN

L64
LLOYD W.B.,"PEACE REQUIRES PEACEMAKERS." AFR INDIA S/ASIA SWITZERLND WOR+45 INT/ORG VOL/ASSN PLAN PERSON PWR 20. PAGE 90 A1848 — CONSULT PEACE

B65
COLLINS H.,KARL MARX AND THE BRITISH LABOUR MOVEMENT; YEARS OF THE FIRST INTERNATIONAL. FRANCE SWITZERLND UK CAP/ISM WAR...MARXIST IDEA/COMP BIBLIOG 19. PAGE 28 A0567 — MARXISM LABOR INT/ORG REV

B66
DAENIKER G.,STRATEGIE DES KLEIN STAATS. SWITZERLND ACT/RES CREATE DIPLOM NEUTRAL DETER WAR WEAPON PWR SOVEREIGN...IDEA/COMP 20 COLD/WAR. PAGE 33 A0673 — NUC/PWR PLAN FORCES NAT/G

B66
HOEVELER H.J.,INTERNATIONALE BEKAMPFUNG DES VERBRECHENS. AUSTRIA SWITZERLND WOR+45 INT/ORG CONTROL BIO/SOC...METH/COMP NAT/COMP 20 MAFIA SCOT/YARD FBI. PAGE 66 A1352 — CRIMLGY CRIME DIPLOM INT/LAW

B96
LOWELL A.L.,GOVERNMENTS AND PARTIES IN CONTINENTAL EUROPE, VOL. II. AUSTRIA GERMANY HUNGARY MOD/EUR SWITZERLND SOCIETY EX/STRUC LEGIS DIPLOM AGREE LEAD PARL/PROC PWR...POLICY 19. PAGE 91 A1867 — POL/PAR NAT/G GOV/REL ELITES

SYATAUW J.J.G. A2873

SYMONDS R. A2874

SYNANON....SYNANON: COMMUNITY OF FORMER DRUG ADDICTS AND CRIMINALS

SYNTAX....SEE LOG

SYRIA....SEE ALSO UAR

B54
NATION ASSOCIATES,SECURITY AND THE MIDDLE EAST - THE PROBLEM AND ITS SOLUTION. ISRAEL JORDAN LEBANON SYRIA UAR FORCES FOR/AID GP/REL NAT/LISM PEACE TOTALISM...POLICY 20. PAGE 107 A2198 — DIPLOM ECO/UNDEV WAR PLAN

B66
US DEPARTMENT OF STATE,RESEARCH ON THE MIDDLE EAST (EXTERNAL RESEARCH LIST NO 4-25). GREECE ISRAEL SYRIA UAR YEMEN CULTURE SOCIETY POL/PAR SECT DIPLOM EDU/PROP WAR NAT/LISM...GEOG GOV/COMP 20. PAGE 152 — BIBLIOG/A ISLAM NAT/G REGION

A3096

S66
FRIEND A.,"THE MIDDLE EAST CRISIS" COM ISLAM ISRAEL SYRIA UAR USA+45 USSR FORCES PLAN FOR/AID CONTROL ORD/FREE PWR...SOCIALIST TIME/SEQ 20 NASSER/G. PAGE 49 A1009
WAR INT/ORG DIPLOM PEACE

SYRKIN M. A2875

SYS/QU....SYSTEMATIZING AND ANALYZING QUESTIONNAIRES

S52
HAAS E.B.,"THE RECONCILIATION OF CONFLICT, COLONIAL POLICY AIMS: ACCEPTANCE OF THE LEAGUE OF NATIONS MANDATE SYSTEM." FRANCE GERMANY UK WOR+45 WOR-45 LEGIT ATTIT DRIVE ORD/FREE...OLD/LIB INT SYS/QU TIME/SEQ TREND LEAGUE/NAT 20. PAGE 58 A1201
INT/ORG COLONIAL

S63
VEROFF J.,"AFRICAN STUDENTS IN THE UNITED STATES." AFR USA+45 CULTURE ACT/RES FOR/AID PEACE ATTIT KNOWL...SOC RECORD DEEP/QU SYS/QU CHARTS STERTYP TOT/POP 20. PAGE 159 A3230
PERCEPT RIGID/FLEX RACE/REL

B64
FREE L.A.,THE ATTITUDES, HOPES AND FEARS OF NIGERIANS. AFR NIGERIA ECO/UNDEV AGRI ACADEM PLAN TASK...GEOG CHARTS METH 20. PAGE 49 A0993
NAT/LISM SYS/QU DIPLOM

SYSTEMS....SEE ROUTINE, COMPUTER

SZASZ/T....THOMAS SZASZ

SZASZY E. A2876

SZLADITS C. A2877,A2878

SZTARAY Z. A2879

SZULC T. A2880

T

T....TEXTBOOK

C25
MOON P.T.,"SYLLABUS ON INTERNATIONAL RELATIONS." EUR+WWI MOD/EUR USA-45 FORCES COLONIAL WAR WEAPON NAT/LISM...POLICY BIBLIOG T 19/20. PAGE 103 A2120
INT/ORG DIPLOM NAT/G

C39
HADDOW A.,"POLITICAL SCIENCE IN AMERICAN COLLEGES AND UNIVERSITIES 1636-1900." CONSTN MORAL...POLICY INT/LAW CON/ANAL BIBLIOG T 17/20. PAGE 59 A1211
USA-45 LAW ACADEM KNOWL

B45
ELTON G.E.,IMPERIAL COMMONWEALTH. INDIA UK DIPLOM DOMIN WAR NAT/LISM SOVEREIGN...TRADIT CHARTS T 15/20 CMN/WLTH AUSTRAL PRE/US/AM. PAGE 41 A0844
REGION CONCPT COLONIAL

B52
SURANYI-UNGER T.,COMPARATIVE ECONOMIC SYSTEMS. FINAN MARKET DIPLOM PRICE WEALTH...GEOG SOC BIBLIOG METH T 20. PAGE 140 A2865
LAISSEZ PLAN ECO/DEV IDEA/COMP

B55
STUART G.H.,LATIN AMERICA AND THE UNITED STATES (5TH ED.). L/A+17C USA+45 USA-45 INT/TRADE COLONIAL ...POLICY CHARTS T 19/20. PAGE 140 A2856
NAT/G DIPLOM

B57
PALMER N.D.,INTERNATIONAL RELATIONS. WOR+45 INT/ORG NAT/G ECO/TAC EDU/PROP COLONIAL WAR PWR SOVEREIGN ...POLICY T 20 TREATY. PAGE 113 A2321
DIPLOM BAL/PWR NAT/COMP

B59
BEMIS S.F.,A SHORT HISTORY OF AMERICAN FOREIGN POLICY AND DIPLOMACY. USA+45 USA-45 INT/ORG NEUTRAL REV WAR ISOLAT ORD/FREE...CHARTS T 18/20. PAGE 13 A0266
DIPLOM ATTIT

B59
FERRELL R.H.,AMERICAN DIPLOMACY: A HISTORY. USA+45 USA-45 PLAN ROUTINE REV WAR PWR...T 18/20 EISNHWR/DD WWI. PAGE 45 A0921
DIPLOM NAT/G POLICY

B60
DUMON F.,LA COMMUNAUTE FRANCO-AFRO-MALGACHE: SES ORIGINES, SES INSTITUTIONS, SON EVOLUTION. FRANCE MADAGASCAR POL/PAR DIPLOM ADMIN ATTIT...TREND T 20. PAGE 39 A0798
JURID INT/ORG AFR CONSTN

B61
FLEMING D.F.,THE COLD WAR AND ITS ORIGINS: 1950-1960 (VOL. II). ASIA FUT HUNGARY POLAND WOR+45 TEC/DEV DOMIN NUC/PWR REV PEACE...T 20 COLD/WAR EISNHWR/DD SUEZ. PAGE 46 A0946
MARXISM DIPLOM BAL/PWR

B61
FLEMING D.F.,THE COLD WAR AND ITS ORIGINS: 1917-1950 (VOL. I). ASIA USSR WOR+45 WOR-45 TEC/DEV FOR/AID NUC/PWR REV WAR PEACE FASCISM...T 20 COLD/WAR NATO BERLIN/BLO. PAGE 46 A0947
DIPLOM MARXISM BAL/PWR

B61
SCOTT A.M.,POLITICS, USA; CASES ON THE AMERICAN DEMOCRATIC PROCESS. USA+45 CHIEF FORCES DIPLOM LOBBY CHOOSE RACE/REL FEDERAL ATTIT...JURID ANTHOL T 20 PRESIDENT CONGRESS CIVIL/LIB. PAGE 130 A2669
CT/SYS CONSTN NAT/G PLAN

B61
STARK H.,SOCIAL AND ECONOMIC FRONTIERS IN LATIN AMERICA (2ND ED.). CUBA FUT CULTURE AGRI INDUS ECO/TAC PRODUC ATTIT MARXISM...NAT/COMP BIBLIOG T 20. PAGE 137 A2807
L/A+17C SOCIETY DIPLOM ECO/UNDEV

B62
DUROSELLE J.B.,HISTOIRE DIPLOMATIQUE DE 1919 A NOS JOURS (3RD ED.). FRANCE INT/ORG CHIEF FORCES CONFER ARMS/CONT WAR PEACE ORD/FREE...T TREATY 20 COLD/WAR. PAGE 39 A0807
DIPLOM WOR+45 WOR-45

B62
EBENSTEIN W.,TWO WAYS OF LIFE. USA+45 CULTURE ECO/DEV PLAN EDU/PROP CONTROL ORD/FREE...GOV/COMP IDEA/COMP T 20 MARX/KARL ENGELS/F LENIN/VI LOCKE/JOHN MILL/JS. PAGE 40 A0819
MARXISM POPULISM ECO/TAC DIPLOM

B62
LEOPOLD R.W.,THE GROWTH OF AMERICAN FOREIGN POLICY: A HISTORY. USA+45 USA-45 EX/STRUC LEGIS INT/TRADE WAR...CHARTS BIBLIOG/A T 18/20. PAGE 87 A1780
NAT/G DIPLOM POLICY

B62
WELLEQUET J.,LE CONGO BELGE ET LA WELTPOLITIK (1894-1914. GERMANY DOMIN EDU/PROP WAR ATTIT ...BIBLIOG T CONGO/LEOP. PAGE 163 A3314
ADMIN DIPLOM GP/REL COLONIAL

B63
MILLER W.J.,THE MEANING OF COMMUNISM. USSR SOCIETY ECO/DEV EX/STRUC WORKER TEC/DEV ADMIN TOTALISM ...POLICY CONCPT CHARTS BIBLIOG T 20 COLD/WAR LENIN/VI STALIN/J. PAGE 101 A2080
MARXISM TRADIT DIPLOM NAT/G

B63
ROSS H.,THE COLD WAR: CONTAINMENT AND ITS CRITICSS. WOR+45 POL/PAR BAL/PWR ECO/TAC PEACE ORD/FREE ...POLICY IDEA/COMP ANTHOL T 20 COLD/WAR DULLES/JF TRUMAN/HS EISNHWR/DD. PAGE 124 A2541
MARXISM ARMS/CONT DIPLOM

B64
BAILEY T.A.,A DIPLOMATIC HISTORY OF THE AMERICAN PEOPLE (7TH ED.). USA+45 USA-45 FOR/AID COLONIAL PARL/PROC WAR...CHARTS BIBLIOG/A T 18/20. PAGE 10 A0208
DIPLOM NAT/G

B64
LOCKHART W.B.,CASES AND MATERIALS ON CONSTITUTIONAL RIGHTS AND LIBERTIES. USA+45 FORCES LEGIS DIPLOM PRESS CONTROL CRIME WAR PWR...AUD/VIS T WORSHIP 20 NEGRO. PAGE 90 A1849
ORD/FREE CONSTN NAT/G

B65
FRIEDMANN W.,AN INTRODUCTION TO WORLD POLITICS (5TH ED.). WOR+45 ECO/UNDEV BAL/PWR FOR/AID INT/TRADE PEACE...STAT CENSUS CHARTS BIBLIOG T 20 COLD/WAR UN THIRD/WRLD. PAGE 49 A1003
DIPLOM INT/ORG PROB/SOLV

B66
BROWNLIE I.,PRINCIPLES OF PUBLIC INTERNATIONAL LAW. WOR+45 WOR-45 LAW JUDGE REPAR ADJUD SOVEREIGN ...JURID T. PAGE 20 A0409
INT/LAW DIPLOM INT/ORG

B66
FREIDEL F.,AMERICAN ISSUES IN THE TWENTIETH CENTURY. SOCIETY FINAN ECO/TAC FOR/AID CONTROL NUC/PWR WAR RACE/REL PEACE ATTIT...ANTHOL T 20 WILSON/W ROOSEVLT/F KENNEDY/JF TRUMAN/HS. PAGE 49 A0995
DIPLOM POLICY NAT/G ORD/FREE

B66
LENGYEL E.,AFRICA: PAST, PRESENT, AND FUTURE. FUT SOUTH/AFR COLONIAL RACE/REL SOVEREIGN...GEOG AUD/VIS CHARTS T 20 CONGO/LEOP NEGRO. PAGE 87 A1771
AFR CONSTN ECO/UNDEV

B67
DE BLIJ H.J.,SYSTEMATIC POLITICAL GEOGRAPHY. WOR+45 STRUCT INT/ORG NAT/G EDU/PROP ADMIN COLONIAL ROUTINE ORD/FREE PWR...IDEA/COMP T 20. PAGE 34 A0697
GEOG CONCPT METH

B67
M)½(*ROBINSON R.D.,INTERNATIONAL MANAGEMENT. USA+45 FINAN R+D PLAN PRODUC...DECISION T. PAGE 92 A1882
INT/TRADE MGT INT/LAW MARKET

TABORN P. A2881

TACKABERRY R.B. A2882

TAFT/HART....TAFT-HARTLEY ACT

TAFT/RA....ROBERT A. TAFT

B67
KIRK R.,THE POLITICAL PRINCIPLES OF ROBERT A. TAFT. USA+45 LABOR DIPLOM ADJUD ADJUST ORD/FREE TAFT/RA. PAGE 80 A1635
POL/PAR LEAD LEGIS ATTIT

TAFT/WH....PRESIDENT WILLIAM HOWARD TAFT

B60
MORISON E.E.,TURMOIL AND TRADITION: A STUDY OF THE LIFE AND TIMES OF HENRY L. STIMSON. USA+45 USA-45 POL/PAR CHIEF DELIB/GP FORCES BAL/PWR DIPLOM
BIOG NAT/G EX/STRUC

ARMS/CONT WAR PEACE 19/20 STIMSON/HL ROOSEVLT/F TAFT/WH HOOVER/H REPUBLICAN. PAGE 104 A2142

TAGGART F.J. A2883

TAHITI....TAHITI

TAIWAN....TAIWAN AND REPUBLIC OF CHINA

B52
US MUTUAL SECURITY AGENCY,U. S. TECHNICAL AND ECONOMIC ASSISTANCE IN THE FAR EAST (PAMPHLET). ASIA BURMA INDONESIA PHILIPPINE TAIWAN THAILAND USA+45 AGRI INDUS PLAN EDU/PROP ADMIN HEALTH. PAGE 155 A3161
FOR/AID TEC/DEV ECO/UNDEV BUDGET

N58
US HOUSE COMM FOREIGN AFFAIRS,HEARINGS ON REVIEW OF THE MUTUAL SECURITY PROGRAMS; EXAMINATION OF SELECTED PROJECTS IN FORMOSA AND PAKISTAN (PAMPHLET). ASIA PAKISTAN TAIWAN INDUS CONSULT DELIB/GP LEGIS BUDGET CONFER DEBATE 20. PAGE 153 A3125
FOR/AID ECO/UNDEV DIPLOM ECO/TAC

S66
KLEIN S.,"A SURVEY OF SINO-JAPANESE TRADE, 1950-1966" TAIWAN EDU/PROP 20 CHINJAP. PAGE 80 A1649
INT/TRADE DIPLOM MARXISM

TALLON D. A2884

TAMMANY....TAMMANY HALL

TAN C.C. A2885

TANDON J.C. A0223

TANG P.S.H. A2886

TANGANYIKA....SEE ALSO TANZANIA

B61
CHIDZERO B.T.G.,TANGANYIKA AND INTERNATIONAL TRUSTEESHIP. AFR WOR+45 WOR-45 ECO/DEV INT/ORG ECO/TAC DOMIN COLONIAL...RECORD CHARTS 20 TANGANYIKA CMN/WLTH. PAGE 26 A0528
ECO/UNDEV CONSTN

S61
OCHENG D.,"ECONOMIC FORCES AND UGANDA'S FOREIGN POLICY." AFR UGANDA INT/TRADE TARIFFS INCOME SOVEREIGN WEALTH 20 EACM EEC TANGANYIKA. PAGE 111 A2274
ECO/TAC DIPLOM ECO/UNDEV INT/ORG

S63
BANFIELD J.,"FEDERATION IN EAST-AFRICA." AFR UGANDA ELITES INT/ORG NAT/G VOL/ASSN LEGIS ECO/TAC FEDERAL ATTIT SOVEREIGN TOT/POP 20 TANGANYIKA. PAGE 11 A0216
EX/STRUC PWR REGION

TANGIER

B31
STUART G.H.,THE INTERNATIONAL CITY OF TANGIER. AFR EUR+WWI MOD/EUR MOROCCO CONSTN PROVS CREATE PLAN LEGIT PEACE ORD/FREE PWR...INT/LAW OBS TIME/SEQ CON/ANAL 20 TANGIER. PAGE 139 A2854
LOC/G INT/ORG DIPLOM SOVEREIGN

TANNENBAUM F. A2887,A2888

TANZANIA....TANZANIA; SEE ALSO AFR, TANGANYIKA

S64
ROTHCHILD D.,"EAST AFRICAN FEDERATION." AFR TANZANIA UGANDA INDUS REGION 20. PAGE 124 A2547
INT/ORG DIPLOM ECO/UNDEV ECO/TAC

B66
O'CONNER A.M.,AN ECONOMIC GEOGRAPHY OF EAST AFRICA. AFR TANZANIA UGANDA AGRI WORKER INT/TRADE COLONIAL GOV/REL...CHARTS METH/COMP 20 AFRICA/E. PAGE 111 A2269
ECO/UNDEV EXTR/IND GEOG HABITAT

B67
NYERERE J.K.,FREEDOM AND UNITY/UHURU NA UMOJA: A SELECTION FROM WRITINGS AND SPEECHES, 1952-65. TANZANIA ELITES ECO/UNDEV INT/ORG NAT/G CREATE DIPLOM COLONIAL REGION RACE/REL...ANTHOL 20. PAGE 110 A2265
SOVEREIGN AFR TREND ORD/FREE

S67
CHAND A.,"INDIA AND TANZANIA." INDIA TANZANIA TEC/DEV ECO/TAC FOR/AID COLONIAL PEACE UTIL WEALTH ...GOV/COMP 20. PAGE 25 A0518
ECO/UNDEV NEUTRAL DIPLOM PLAN

TARDIFF G. A2889

TARIFFS....SEE ALSO ECO, INT/TRADE, GATT

N
FOREIGN TRADE LIBRARY,NEW TITLES RECEIVED IN THE LIBRARY. WOR+45 ECO/UNDEV FINAN NAT/G PLAN TEC/DEV BUDGET ECO/TAC TARIFFS GOV/REL STAT. PAGE 47 A0964
BIBLIOG/A INT/TRADE INDUS ECO/DEV

N
US SUPERINTENDENT OF DOCUMENTS,MONTHLY CATALOG OF UNITED STATES GOVERNMENT PUBLICATIONS. USA+45 USA-45 AGRI LABOR FORCES INT/TRADE TARIFFS TAX EDU/PROP CT/SYS ARMS/CONT RACE/REL 19/20 CONGRESS PRESIDENT. PAGE 157 A3203
BIBLIOG NAT/G VOL/ASSN POLICY

N
US SUPERINTENDENT OF DOCUMENTS,TARIFF AND TAXATION (PRICE LIST 37). USA+45 LAW INT/TRADE ADJUD ADMIN CT/SYS INCOME OWN...DECISION GATT. PAGE 157 A3204
BIBLIOG/A TAX TARIFFS NAT/G

B06
GRIFFIN A.P.C.,SELECT LIST OF REFERENCES ON THE BRITISH TARIFF MOVEMENT. MOD/EUR UK BAL/PWR BARGAIN ECO/TAC LAISSEZ 20. PAGE 56 A1154
BIBLIOG/A INT/TRADE TARIFFS COLONIAL

B10
GRIFFIN A.P.C.,LIST OF REFERENCES ON RECIPROCITY (2ND REV. ED.). CANADA CUBA UK USA-45 WOR-45 NAT/G TARIFFS CONFER COLONIAL CONTROL SANCTION CONSEN ALL/VALS...DECISION 19/20. PAGE 56 A1157
BIBLIOG/A VOL/ASSN DIPLOM REPAR

B19
SUMNER W.G.,WAR AND OTHER ESSAYS. USA-45 DELIB/GP DIPLOM TARIFFS COLONIAL PEACE SOVEREIGN 20. PAGE 140 A2864
INT/TRADE ORD/FREE CAP/ISM ECO/TAC

B19
US DEPARTMENT OF STATE,A TENTATIVE LIST OF TREATY COLLECTIONS. WOR-45 BAL/PWR INT/TRADE TARIFFS WAR PEACE ORD/FREE 20. PAGE 151 A3080
ANTHOL DIPLOM DELIB/GP

B34
GRAHAM F.D.,PROTECTIVE TARIFFS. FUT USA+45 WOR-45 INDUS MARKET VOL/ASSN PLAN CAP/ISM ECO/TAC PEACE ATTIT DRIVE HEALTH ORD/FREE...OBS TREND GEN/LAWS 20. PAGE 55 A1124
INT/ORG TARIFFS

B34
US TARIFF COMMISSION,THE TARIFF; A BIBLIOGRAPHY: A SELECT LIST OF REFERENCES. USA-45 LAW DIPLOM TAX ADMIN...POLICY TREATY 20. PAGE 157 A3208
BIBLIOG/A TARIFFS ECO/TAC

B35
BEMIS S.F.,GUIDE TO THE DIPLOMATIC HISTORY OF THE UNITED STATES, 17751921. NAT/G LEGIS TOP/EX PROB/SOLV CAP/ISM INT/TRADE TARIFFS ADJUD ...CON/ANAL 18/20. PAGE 13 A0264
BIBLIOG/A DIPLOM USA-45

B36
HARVARD BUREAU ECO RES LAT AM,THE ECONOMIC LITERATURE OF LATIN AMERICA: A TENTATIVE BIBLIOGRAPHY. NAT/G TARIFFS CENTRAL COST DEMAND 20. PAGE 62 A1277
BIBLIOG ECO/UNDEV L/A+17C INT/TRADE

B37
VINER J.,STUDIES IN THE THEORY OF INTERNATIONAL TRADE. WOR-45 CONSTN ECO/DEV AGRI INDUS MARKET INT/ORG LABOR NAT/G ECO/TAC TARIFFS COLONIAL ATTIT WEALTH...POLICY CONCPT MATH STAT OBS SAMP TREND GEN/LAWS MARX/KARL 20. PAGE 159 A3236
CAP/ISM INT/TRADE

B40
CONOVER H.F.,FOREIGN RELATIONS OF THE UNITED STATES: A LIST OF RECENT BOOKS (PAMPHLET). ASIA CANADA L/A+17C UK INT/ORG INT/TRADE TARIFFS NEUTRAL WAR PEACE...INT/LAW CON/ANAL 20 CHINJAP. PAGE 29 A0592
BIBLIOG/A USA-45 DIPLOM

B43
VINER J.,TRADE RELATIONS BETWEEN FREE-MARKET AND CONTROLLED ECONOMIES. WOR-45 MARKET PLAN TARIFFS DEMAND...POLICY STAT 20. PAGE 159 A3237
INT/TRADE DIPLOM CONTROL NAT/G

B48
GRAHAM F.D.,THE THEORY OF INTERNATIONAL VALUES. FUT WOR+45 WOR-45 ECO/DEV FINAN INT/ORG PLAN TEC/DEV CAP/ISM DIPLOM ECO/TAC TARIFFS ROUTINE BAL/PAY DRIVE PWR WEALTH SOCISM...POLICY STAT HYPO/EXP GEN/LAWS 20. PAGE 55 A1125
NEW/IDEA INT/TRADE

B48
PELCOVITS N.A.,OLD CHINA HANDS AND THE FOREIGN OFFICE. ASIA BURMA UK ECO/UNDEV NAT/G ECO/TAC FOR/AID TARIFFS DOMIN COLONIAL GOV/REL SOVEREIGN 19 HONG/KONG TREATY. PAGE 114 A2348
INT/TRADE ATTIT DIPLOM

C50
ELLSWORTH P.T.,"INTERNATIONAL ECONOMY." ECO/DEV ECO/UNDEV FINAN LABOR DIPLOM FOR/AID TARIFFS BAL/PAY EQUILIB NAT/LISM OPTIMAL...INT/LAW 20 ILO GATT. PAGE 41 A0843
BIBLIOG INT/TRADE ECO/TAC INT/ORG

B51
US TARIFF COMMISSION,LIST OF PUBLICATIONS OF THE TARIFF COMMISSION (PAMPHLET). USA+45 USA-45 AGRI EXTR/IND INDUS INT/TRADE...STAT 20. PAGE 157 A3207
BIBLIOG TARIFFS NAT/G ADMIN

B56
FORSTMANN A.,DIE GRUNDLAGEN DER AUSSENWIRTSCHAFTSTHEORIE. ECO/TAC TARIFFS PRICE WAR ...NAT/COMP 20. PAGE 47 A0967
INT/TRADE CONCPT DIPLOM

ECO/DEV

B56
KRAUS O.,THEORIE DER ZWISCHENSTAATLICHEN WIRTSCHAFTSBEZIEHUNGEN. TARIFFS WAR COST 20. PAGE 82 A1677
INT/TRADE DIPLOM BAL/PAY ECO/TAC

B58
KINDLEBERGER C.P.,INTERNATIONAL ECONOMICS. WOR+45 WOR-45 ECO/DEV ECO/UNDEV FINAN VOL/ASSN ACT/RES DIPLOM ECO/TAC LEGIT REGION ATTIT DRIVE ORD/FREE WEALTH...POLICY STAT TREND GEN/LAWS EEC ECSC OEEC 20. PAGE 79 A1620
INT/ORG BAL/PWR TARIFFS

B58
SEYID MUHAMMAD V.A.,THE LEGAL FRAMEWORK OF WORLD TRADE. WOR+45 INT/ORG DIPLOM CONTROL...BIBLIOG 20 TREATY UN IMF GATT. PAGE 131 A2689
INT/LAW VOL/ASSN INT/TRADE TARIFFS

B59
ROBERTSON A.H.,EUROPEAN INSTITUTIONS: COOPERATION, INTEGRATION, UNIFICATION. EUR+WWI FINAN INT/ORG FORCES INT/TRADE TARIFFS 20 EEC EURATOM ECSC NATO TREATY. PAGE 122 A2496
ECO/DEV DIPLOM INDUS ECO/TAC

B60
BYRD E.M. JR.,TREATIES AND EXECUTIVE AGREEMENTS IN THE UNITED STATES: THEIR SEPARATE ROLES AND LIMITATIONS. USA+45 USA-45 EX/STRUC TARIFFS CT/SYS GOV/REL FEDERAL...IDEA/COMP BIBLIOG SUPREME/CT SENATE CONGRESS. PAGE 23 A0461
CHIEF INT/LAW DIPLOM

B60
KENEN P.B.,GIANT AMONG NATIONS: PROBLEMS IN UNITED STATES FOREIGN ECONOMIC POLICY. USA+45 FINAN DIPLOM TARIFFS BAL/PAY WEALTH 20 COLD/WAR. PAGE 77 A1584
FOR/AID ECO/UNDEV INT/TRADE PLAN

S61
OCHENG D.,"ECONOMIC FORCES AND UGANDA'S FOREIGN POLICY." AFR UGANDA INT/TRADE TARIFFS INCOME SOVEREIGN WEALTH 20 EACM EEC TANGANYIKA. PAGE 111 A2274
ECO/TAC DIPLOM ECO/UNDEV INT/ORG

S61
VINER J.,"ECONOMIC FOREIGN POLICY ON THE NEW FRONTIER." USA+45 ECO/UNDEV AGRI FINAN INDUS MARKET INT/ORG NAT/G FOR/AID INT/TRADE ADMIN ATTIT PWR 20 KENNEDY/JF. PAGE 159 A3239
TOP/EX ECO/TAC BAL/PAY TARIFFS

B62
ALEXANDROWICZ C.H.,WORLD ECONOMIC AGENCIES: LAW AND PRACTICE. WOR+45 DIST/IND FINAN LABOR CONSULT INT/TRADE TARIFFS REPRESENT HEALTH...JURID 20 UN GATT EEC OAS ECSC. PAGE 6 A0115
INT/LAW INT/ORG DIPLOM ADJUD

B62
COLOMBOS C.J.,THE INTERNATIONAL LAW OF THE SEA. WOR+45 EXTR/IND DIPLOM INT/TRADE TARIFFS AGREE WAR ...TIME/SEQ 20 TREATY. PAGE 28 A0570
INT/LAW SEA JURID ADJUD

B62
KRAFT J.,THE GRAND DESIGN. EUR+WWI USA+45 AGRI FINAN INDUS MARKET INT/ORG NAT/G PLAN ECO/TAC TARIFFS REGION DRIVE ORD/FREE WEALTH...POLICY OBS TREND EEC 20. PAGE 82 A1674
VOL/ASSN ECO/DEV INT/TRADE

B63
LYONS F.S.L.,INTERNATIONALISM IN EUROPE 1815-1914. LAW AGRI COM/IND DIST/IND LABOR SECT INT/TRADE TARIFFS...BIBLIOG 19/20. PAGE 92 A1880
DIPLOM MOD/EUR INT/ORG

B63
UN SECRETARY GENERAL,PLANNING FOR ECONOMIC DEVELOPMENT. ECO/UNDEV FINAN BUDGET INT/TRADE TARIFFS TAX ADMIN 20 UN. PAGE 147 A3005
PLAN ECO/TAC MGT NAT/COMP

B63
UNITED STATES GOVERNMENT,REPORT TO THE INTER-AMERICAN ECONOMIC AND SOCIAL COUNCIL. L/A+17C INDUS PLAN INT/TRADE TARIFFS CONFER...CHARTS 20 LAFTA. PAGE 149 A3038
FOR/AID ECO/TAC ECO/UNDEV DIPLOM

B64
HINSHAW R.,THE EUROPEAN COMMUNITY AND AMERICAN TRADE: A STUDY IN ATLANTIC ECONOMICS AND POLICY. EUR+WWI UK USA+45 ECO/DEV ECO/UNDEV AGRI INDUS INT/ORG NAT/G ECO/TAC TARIFFS REGION...STAT CHARTS EEC 20. PAGE 65 A1337
MARKET TREND INT/TRADE

B64
LISKA G.,EUROPE ASCENDANT. EUR+WWI ECO/DEV FORCES INT/TRADE MARXISM 20 EEC. PAGE 90 A1838
DIPLOM BAL/PWR TARIFFS CENTRAL

B64
MARKHAM J.W.,THE COMMON MARKET: FRIEND OR COMPETITOR. EUR+WWI FUT USA+45 INT/ORG LG/CO NAT/G VOL/ASSN DELIB/GP EX/STRUC PLAN TARIFFS ORD/FREE PWR WEALTH...POLICY STAT TREND EEC VAL/FREE 20. PAGE 95 A1943
ECO/DEV ECO/TAC

B64
NEWCOMER H.A.,INTERNATIONAL AIDS TO OVERSEAS INVESTMENTS AND TRADE. ECO/UNDEV TARIFFS PROFIT ...BIBLIOG 20 GATT UN. PAGE 108 A2225
INT/TRADE FINAN DIPLOM FOR/AID

B64
REUSS H.S.,THE CRITICAL DECADE - AN ECONOMIC POLICY FOR AMERICA AND THE FREE WORLD. USA+45 FINAN POL/PAR WORKER PLAN DIPLOM ECO/TAC TARIFFS BAL/PAY ...POLICY 20 CONGRESS GOLD/STAND. PAGE 120 A2468
FOR/AID INT/TRADE LABOR LEGIS

B64
RIVKIN A.,AFRICA AND THE EUROPEAN COMMON MARKET (PAMPHLET). AFR MOD/EUR WOR+45 TEC/DEV FOR/AID TARIFFS BAL/PAY...POLICY 20 EEC. PAGE 121 A2490
INT/ORG INT/TRADE ECO/TAC ECO/UNDEV

B64
STEWART C.F.,A BIBLIOGRAPHY OF INTERNATIONAL BUSINESS. WOR+45 FINAN LG/CO NAT/G PLAN ECO/TAC TARIFFS...DECISION MGT GP/COMP NAT/COMP 20 EEC. PAGE 138 A2824
BIBLIOG INT/ORG OP/RES INT/TRADE

S64
GARDNER R.N.,"GATT AND THE UNITED NATIONS CONFERENCE ON TRADE AND DEVELOPMENT." USA+45 WOR+45 SOCIETY ECO/UNDEV MARKET NAT/G DELIB/GP ACT/RES PLAN ECO/TAC TARIFFS EDU/PROP ROUTINE DRIVE RIGID/FLEX WEALTH...DECISION MGT TREND UN TOT/POP 20 GATT. PAGE 51 A1047
INT/ORG INT/TRADE

B65
WEILER J.,L'ECONOMIE INTERNATIONALE DEPUIS 1950. WOR+45 DIPLOM TARIFFS CONFER...POLICY TREATY. PAGE 162 A3302
FINAN INT/TRADE REGION FOR/AID

B66
EDWARDS C.D.,TRADE REGULATIONS OVERSEAS. IRELAND NEW/ZEALND SOUTH/AFR NAT/G CAP/ISM TARIFFS CONTROL ...POLICY JURID 20 EEC CHINJAP. PAGE 40 A0823
INT/TRADE DIPLOM INT/LAW ECO/TAC

B66
MEERHAEGHE M.,INTERNATIONAL ECONOMIC INSTITUTIONS. EUR+WWI FINAN INDUS MARKET PLAN TARIFFS BAL/PAY EQUILIB...POLICY BIBLIOG/A 20 GATT OEEC EEC IBRD EURCOALSTL. PAGE 99 A2032
ECO/TAC ECO/DEV INT/TRADE INT/ORG

S66
GAMER R.E.,"URGENT SINGAPORE, PATIENT MALAYSIA." MALAYSIA S/ASIA ECO/UNDEV POL/PAR CHIEF TARIFFS TAX CONTROL LEAD REGION PWR 20 SINGAPORE. PAGE 51 A1036
DIPLOM NAT/G POLICY ECO/TAC

N66
BRITISH DEVELOPMENT POLICIES: 1966 (PAMPHLET). UK AGRI TARIFFS BAL/PAY...TREND CHARTS 20 OVRSEA/DEV. PAGE 4 A0076
WEALTH DIPLOM INT/TRADE FOR/AID

B67
AUBREY H.G.,ATLANTIC ECONOMIC COOPERATION. ECO/DEV INDUS VOL/ASSN PROB/SOLV DIPLOM INT/TRADE TARIFFS CONFER 20. PAGE 10 A0197
INT/ORG ECO/TAC TEC/DEV CAP/ISM

B67
RUEFF J.,BALANCE OF PAYMENTS. WOR+45 FINAN TEC/DEV DIPLOM TARIFFS PRICE CONTROL...POLICY CONCPT IDEA/COMP. PAGE 125 A2567
INT/TRADE BAL/PAY ECO/TAC NAT/COMP

S67
LEFF N.H.,"EXPORT STAGNATION AND AUTARKIC DEVELOPMENT IN BRAZIL, 19471962." BRAZIL ECO/TAC TARIFFS 20. PAGE 86 A1764
BAL/PAY INT/TRADE WEALTH DIPLOM

S67
SHERSHNEV Y.,"THE KENNEDY ROUND* PLANS AND REALITY." EUR+WWI USA+45 INT/ORG DIPLOM TARIFFS DOMIN CONFER PWR...MARXIST PREDICT. PAGE 132 A2701
ECO/TAC ECO/DEV INT/TRADE BAL/PWR

C83
BURKE E.,"RESOLUTIONS FOR CONCILIATION WITH AMERICA" (1775), IN E. BURKE, COLLECTED WORKS, VOL. 2." UK USA-45 FORCES INT/TRADE TARIFFS TAX SANCTION PEACE...POLICY 18 PRE/US/AM. PAGE 21 A0436
COLONIAL WAR SOVEREIGN ECO/TAC

B96
SMITH A.,LECTURES ON JUSTICE, POLICE, REVENUE AND ARMS (1763). UK LAW FAM FORCES TARIFFS AGREE COERCE INCOME OWN WEALTH LAISSEZ...GEN/LAWS 17/18. PAGE 134 A2743
DIPLOM JURID OLD/LIB TAX

TARLING N. A2890

TARTARS....TARTARS

TASK....SPECIFIC SELF-ASSIGNED OR OTHER ASSIGNED OPERATIONS

N19
HAJDA J.,THE COLD WAR VIEWED AS A SOCIOLOGICAL PROBLEM (PAMPHLET). COM CZECHOSLVK EUR+WWI SOCIETY PLAN EDU/PROP CONTROL TASK ATTIT MARXISM...POLICY 20 COLD/WAR MIGRATION. PAGE 59 A1220
DIPLOM LEAD PWR NAT/G

N19
LANGE O.R.,"DISARMAMENT ECONOMIC GROWTH AND INTERNATIONAL CO-OPERATION" (PAMPHLET). WOR+45 DIST/IND PLAN INT/TRADE GIVE TASK DETER WEALTH SOCISM 18/19 BOLIVAR/S. PAGE 84 A1723
ARMS/CONT DIPLOM ECO/DEV ECO/UNDEV

N19
SALKEVER L.R.,SUB-SAHARA AFRICA (PAMPHLET). AFR USSR EXTR/IND NAT/G SCHOOL DIPLOM COLONIAL WEALTH ...GEOG CHARTS 16/20. PAGE 127 A2594
ECO/UNDEV TEC/DEV TASK

INT/TRADE

B40
FULLER G.H.,A LIST OF BIBLIOGRAPHIES ON PROPAGANDA (PAMPHLET). MOD/EUR USA-45 CONSULT ACT/RES PRESS FEEDBACK TASK WAR ATTIT PWR...CON/ANAL METH/COMP 20. PAGE 50 A1020
BIBLIOG/A EDU/PROP DOMIN DIPLOM

B54
BECKEL G.,WORKSHOPS FOR THE WORLD; THE SPECIALIZED AGENCIES OF THE UN. WOR+45 AGRI DIST/IND CREATE TEC/DEV BUDGET CONTROL TASK WEALTH...CHARTS ORG/CHARTS 20 UN CASEBOOK. PAGE 12 A0246
INT/ORG DIPLOM PEACE CON/ANAL

B55
ROWE C.,VOLTAIRE AND THE STATE. FRANCE MOD/EUR BAL/PWR CONTROL TASK SUPEGO ORD/FREE PWR...CONCPT 18 VOLTAIRE. PAGE 125 A2553
NAT/G DIPLOM NAT/LISM ATTIT

B56
COMMONWEALTH OF WORLD CITIZENS,THE BIRTH OF A WORLD PEOPLE. WOR+45 CONSTN PROB/SOLV CONTROL TASK WAR GP/REL UTOPIA PWR...POLICY NEW/IDEA 20. PAGE 29 A0582
DIPLOM VOL/ASSN PEACE INT/ORG

B57
ASHER R.E.,THE UNITED NATIONS AND ECONOMIC AND SOCIAL COOPERATION. ECO/UNDEV COM/IND DIST/IND FINAN PLAN PROB/SOLV INT/TRADE TASK WEALTH...SOC 20 UN. PAGE 9 A0186
INT/ORG DIPLOM FOR/AID

B58
BOWLES C.,IDEAS, PEOPLE AND PEACE. ASIA CHINA/COM FUT INDIA USA+45 USSR ECO/UNDEV INT/ORG LEAD TASK MARXISM 20 NATO UN COLD/WAR. PAGE 18 A0359
PEACE POLICY NAT/G DIPLOM

B58
ISLAM R.,INTERNATIONAL ECONOMIC COOPERATION AND THE UNITED NATIONS. FINAN PLAN EXEC TASK WAR PEACE ...SOC METH/CNCPT 20 UN LEAGUE/NAT. PAGE 72 A1470
INT/ORG DIPLOM ADMIN

B59
HARRIMAN A.,PEACE WITH RUSSIA? USA+45 USSR SOCIETY ECO/TAC CONTROL TOTALISM ATTIT MARXISM...POLICY 20 STALIN/J KHRUSH/N. PAGE 62 A1266
DIPLOM PEACE NAT/G TASK

B59
LINK R.G.,ENGLISH THEORIES OF ECONOMIC FLUCTUATIONS: 1815-1848. FRANCE UK AGRI WORKER DIPLOM PRICE TASK WAR DEMAND PRODUC...POLICY BIBLIOG 18 MALTHUS MILL/JS WILSON/J. PAGE 89 A1826
IDEA/COMP ECO/DEV WEALTH EQUILIB

B60
FISCHER L.,RUSSIA, AMERICA, AND THE WORLD. FUT USA+45 USSR WOR+45 FORCES PLAN BAL/PWR ECO/TAC FOR/AID NEUTRAL TASK NUC/PWR PWR 20 COLD/WAR. PAGE 46 A0937
DIPLOM POLICY MARXISM ECO/UNDEV

B60
FOREIGN POLICY CLEARING HOUSE,STRATEGY FOR THE 60'S. FUT USA+45 WOR+45 ECO/UNDEV FORCES BAL/PWR TASK ARMS/CONT DETER PWR MARXISM 20 SENATE. PAGE 47 A0963
DIPLOM NAT/G POLICY ACT/RES

B60
HOLT R.T.,STRATEGIC PSYCHOLOGICAL OPERATIONS AND AMERICAN FOREIGN POLICY. ITALY USA+45 FOR/AID DOMIN RUMOR ADMIN TASK WAR CHOOSE ATTIT ALL/IDEOS...PSY COLD/WAR. PAGE 67 A1375
EDU/PROP ACT/RES DIPLOM POLICY

B60
RAO V.K.R.,INTERNATIONAL AID FOR ECONOMIC DEVELOPMENT - POSSIBILITIES AND LIMITATIONS. FINAN PLAN TEC/DEV ADMIN TASK EFFICIENCY...POLICY SOC METH/CNCPT CHARTS 20 UN. PAGE 119 A2444
FOR/AID DIPLOM INT/ORG ECO/UNDEV

B60
RITNER P.,THE DEATH OF AFRICA. USA+45 ECO/UNDEV DIPLOM ECO/TAC REGION RACE/REL NAT/LISM ORD/FREE ...POLICY 20 NEGRO. PAGE 121 A2485
AFR SOCIETY FUT TASK

B60
SPEER J.P.,FOR WHAT PURPOSE? CHINA/COM USSR CONSTN PROB/SOLV DIPLOM CONTROL TASK WAR NAT/LISM WORSHIP 20 UN. PAGE 136 A2778
PEACE SECT SUPEGO ALL/IDEOS

B61
GOLDWERT M.,CONSTABULARY IN THE DOMINICAN REPUBLIC AND NICARAGUA. DOMIN/REP L/A+17C NICARAGUA USA-45 NAT/G PLAN CONTROL TASK REV...POLICY 20 INTERVENT. PAGE 53 A1093
DIPLOM PEACE FORCES

B61
MEZERIK A.G.,ECONOMIC DEVELOPMENT AIDS FOR UNDERDEVELOPED COUNTRIES. WOR+45 FINAN LEGIS PROB/SOLV TEC/DEV DIPLOM FOR/AID GIVE TASK WAR 20 UN. PAGE 101 A2062
ECO/UNDEV INT/ORG WEALTH PLAN

B62
COUNCIL ON WORLD TENSIONS,RESTLESS NATIONS. WOR+45 STRUCT INT/ORG NAT/G PLAN ECO/TAC...NAT/COMP ANTHOL 20. PAGE 32 A0641
ECO/UNDEV POLICY DIPLOM TASK

B62
DOUGLAS W.O.,DEMOCRACY'S MANIFESTO. COM USA+45 ECO/UNDEV INT/ORG FORCES PLAN NEUTRAL TASK MARXISM ...JURID 20 NATO SEATO. PAGE 38 A0779
DIPLOM POLICY NAT/G ORD/FREE

B62
MOUSSA P.,THE UNDERPRIVILEGED NATIONS. FINAN INT/ORG PLAN PROB/SOLV CAP/ISM GIVE TASK WEALTH ...POLICY SOC 20. PAGE 105 A2159
ECO/UNDEV NAT/G DIPLOM FOR/AID

B62
THOMSON G.P.,NUCLEAR ENERGY IN BRITAIN DURING THE LAST WAR: THE CHERWELL SIMON LECTURE (MONOGRAPH). UK R+D CONSULT FORCES PLAN DIPLOM TASK CIVMIL/REL ROLE...PHIL/SCI NEW/IDEA LAB/EXP 20 MAUD. PAGE 143 A2934
CREATE TEC/DEV WAR NUC/PWR

B63
GORDON L.,A NEW DEAL FOR LATIN AMERICA. L/A+17C USA+45 CULTURE NAT/G TEC/DEV DIPLOM FOR/AID REGION TASK...POLICY 20 DEPT/STATE. PAGE 54 A1115
ECO/UNDEV ECO/TAC INT/ORG PLAN

S63
CLEVELAND H.,"CRISIS DIPLOMACY." USA+45 WOR+45 LAW FORCES TASK NUC/PWR PWR 20. PAGE 27 A0551
DECISION DIPLOM PROB/SOLV POLICY

B64
FREE L.A.,THE ATTITUDES, HOPES AND FEARS OF NIGERIANS. AFR NIGERIA ECO/UNDEV AGRI ACADEM PLAN TASK...GEOG CHARTS METH 20. PAGE 49 A0993
NAT/LISM SYS/QU DIPLOM

B65
LYONS G.M.,AMERICA: PURPOSE AND POWER. UK USA+45 FINAN INDUS MARKET WORKER TEC/DEV DIPLOM AUTOMAT NUC/PWR WAR RACE/REL ORD/FREE 20 EEC CONGRESS SUPREME/CT CIV/RIGHTS. PAGE 92 A1881
PWR PROB/SOLV ECO/DEV TASK

B66
HANSON J.W.,EDUCATION AND THE DEVELOPMENT OF NATIONS. DIPLOM TASK ADJUST EFFICIENCY...POLICY ANTHOL 20. PAGE 61 A1256
ECO/UNDEV EDU/PROP NAT/G PLAN

B66
KANET R.E.,THE SOVIET UNION AND SUB-SAHARAN AFRICA: COMMUNIST POLICY TOWARD AFRICA, 1917-1965. AFR USSR ECO/UNDEV TEC/DEV EDU/PROP TASK DISCRIM PEACE WEALTH ALL/IDEOS...CHARTS BIBLIOG SOC/INTEG 19/20 NEGRO UN INTERVENT. PAGE 76 A1555
DIPLOM ECO/TAC MARXISM

B66
KEENLEYSIDE H.L.,INTERNATIONAL AID: A SUMMARY. AFR INDIA S/ASIA UK STRATA EXTR/IND TEC/DEV ADMIN RACE/REL DEMAND NAT/LISM WEALTH...TREND CHINJAP. PAGE 77 A1575
ECO/UNDEV FOR/AID DIPLOM TASK

B66
KIRDAR U.,THE STRUCTURE OF UNITED NATIONS ECONOMIC AID TO UNDERDEVELOPED COUNTRIES. AGRI FINAN INDUS NAT/G EX/STRUC PLAN GIVE TASK...POLICY 20 UN. PAGE 79 A1631
INT/ORG FOR/AID ECO/UNDEV ADMIN

B66
STADLER K.R.,THE BIRTH OF THE AUSTRIAN REPUBLIC, 1918-1921. AUSTRIA PLAN TASK PEACE...POLICY DECISION 20. PAGE 137 A2798
NAT/G DIPLOM WAR DELIB/GP

B66
TYSON G.,NEHRU: THE YEARS OF POWER. INDIA UK STRATA ECO/UNDEV FINAN SECT TASK WAR ORD/FREE MARXISM ...POLICY BIBLIOG 20 NEHRU/J. PAGE 146 A2985
CHIEF PWR DIPLOM NAT/G

B67
US DEPARTMENT OF STATE,THE COUNTRY TEAM - AN ILLUSTRATED PROFILE OF OUR AMERICAN MISSIONS ABROAD. ECO/TAC FOR/AID EDU/PROP TASK PERS/REL ATTIT 20. PAGE 152 A3099
DIPLOM NAT/G VOL/ASSN GOV/REL

S67
ADIE W.A.C.,"CHINA'S 'SECOND LIBERATION'." CHINA/COM SOCIETY WORKER DIPLOM TASK 20 MAO. PAGE 4 A0090
MARXISM REV INGP/REL ANOMIE

S67
HODGE G.,"THE RISE AND DEMISE OF THE UN TECHNICAL ASSISTANCE ADMINISTRATION." RISK TASK INGP/REL CONSEN EFFICIENCY 20 UN. PAGE 66 A1349
ADMIN TEC/DEV EX/STRUC INT/ORG

S67
ROSE S.,"ASIAN NATIONALISM* THE SECOND STAGE." ASIA COM ECO/UNDEV NAT/G PROB/SOLV DIPLOM FOR/AID DOMIN NEUTRAL REGION TASK...METH/COMP 20. PAGE 123 A2528
NAT/LISM S/ASIA BAL/PWR COLONIAL

TATOMIR N. A2891

TAUBENFELD H.J. A2892,A2893,A2894,A2895,A2896

TAUBENFELD R.K. A2896

TAX....TAXING, TAXATION

N
THE JAPAN SCIENCE REVIEW: LAW AND POLITICS: LIST OF BOOKS AND ARTICLES ON LAW AND POLITICS. CONSTN AGRI INDUS LABOR DIPLOM TAX ADMIN CRIME...INT/LAW SOC 20 CHINJAP. PAGE 2 A0042
BIBLIOG LAW S/ASIA PHIL/SCI

N
US SUPERINTENDENT OF DOCUMENTS,MONTHLY CATALOG OF UNITED STATES GOVERNMENT PUBLICATIONS. USA+45 USA-45 AGRI LABOR FORCES INT/TRADE TARIFFS TAX EDU/PROP CT/SYS ARMS/CONT RACE/REL 19/20 CONGRESS PRESIDENT. PAGE 157 A3203 — BIBLIOG NAT/G VOL/ASSN POLICY

N
US SUPERINTENDENT OF DOCUMENTS,TARIFF AND TAXATION (PRICE LIST 37). USA+45 LAW INT/TRADE ADJUD ADMIN CT/SYS INCOME OWN...DECISION GATT. PAGE 157 A3204 — BIBLIOG/A TAX TARIFFS NAT/G

B01
HART A.B.,AMERICAN HISTORY TOLD BY CONTEMPORARIES. UK CULTURE FINAN SECT FORCES DIPLOM TAX RUMOR CT/SYS REV GOV/REL GP/REL...ANTHOL 17/18 PRE/US/AM FEDERALIST. PAGE 62 A1273 — USA-45 COLONIAL SOVEREIGN

B25
GODET M.,INDEX BIBLIOGRAPHICUS: INTERNATIONAL CATALOGUE OF SOURCES OF CURRENT BIBLIOGRAPHIC INFORMATION. EUR+WWI MOD/EUR SOCIETY SECT TAX ...JURID PHIL/SCI SOC MATH. PAGE 53 A1085 — BIBLIOG/A DIPLOM EDU/PROP LAW

B27
PARRINGTON V.L.,MAIN CURRENTS IN AMERICAN THOUGHT (VOL.I). USA-45 AGRI POL/PAR DIPLOM TAX REGION REV 17/18 FRANKLIN/B JEFFERSN/T. PAGE 114 A2336 — COLONIAL SECT FEEDBACK ALL/IDEOS

B34
US TARIFF COMMISSION,THE TARIFF; A BIBLIOGRAPHY: A SELECT LIST OF REFERENCES. USA-45 LAW DIPLOM TAX ADMIN...POLICY TREATY 20. PAGE 157 A3208 — BIBLIOG/A TARIFFS ECO/TAC

B45
GALLOWAY E.,ABSTRACTS OF POSTWAR LITERATURE (VOL. IV) JAN.-JULY, 1945 NOS. 901-1074. POLAND USA+45 USSR WOR+45 INDUS LABOR PLAN ECO/TAC INT/TRADE TAX EDU/PROP ADMIN COLONIAL INT/LAW. PAGE 51 A1033 — BIBLIOG/A NUC/PWR NAT/G DIPLOM

B52
MACARTHUR D.,REVITALIZING A NATION. ASIA COM FUT KOREA WOR+45 NAT/G FOR/AID TAX GIVE WAR ATTIT SOCISM 20 CHINJAP EUROPE. PAGE 92 A1885 — LEAD FORCES TOP/EX POLICY

B55
JAPAN MOMBUSHO DAIGAKU GAKIYUT,BIBLIOGRAPHY OF THE STUDIES ON LAW AND POLITICS (PAMPHLET). CONSTN INDUS LABOR DIPLOM TAX ADMIN...CRIMLGY INT/LAW 20 CHINJAP. PAGE 73 A1496 — BIBLIOG LAW PHIL/SCI

B61
INTERNATIONAL BANK RECONST DEV,THE WORLD BANK IN AFRICA: SUMMARY OF ACTIVITIES. AGRI COM/IND DIST/IND EXTR/IND INDUS TAX COST...CHARTS 20. PAGE 71 A1450 — FINAN ECO/UNDEV INT/ORG AFR

B61
PANIKKAR K.M.,THE VOICE OF FREEDOM: SELECTED SPEECHES OF PANDIT MOTILAL NEHRU. INDIA UK CONSTN FINAN FORCES LEGIS DIPLOM TAX COLONIAL...POLICY MAJORIT ANTHOL 20 NEHRU/PM. PAGE 114 A2331 — NAT/LISM ORD/FREE CHIEF NAT/G

B62
SHAW C.,LEGAL PROBLEMS IN INTERNATIONAL TRADE AND INVESTMENT. WOR+45 ECO/DEV ECO/UNDEV MARKET DIPLOM TAX INCOME ROLE...ANTHOL BIBLIOG 20 TREATY UN IMF GATT. PAGE 132 A2698 — INT/LAW INT/TRADE FINAN ECO/TAC

B62
SNOW J.H.,GOVERNMENT BY TREASON. USA+45 USA-45 LEGIS DIPLOM FOR/AID GIVE CONTROL WEALTH MARXISM ...MAJORIT 20 CONGRESS COLD/WAR. PAGE 134 A2750 — FINAN TAX PWR POLICY

B62
THEOBALD R.,NATIONAL DEVELOPMENT EFFORTS (PAMPHLET). WOR+45 AGRI BUDGET FOR/AID INT/TRADE TAX 20. PAGE 142 A2914 — ECO/UNDEV PLAN BAL/PAY WEALTH

B62
US CONGRESS,LEGISLATIVE HISTORY OF UNITED STATES TAX CONVENTIONS(VOL. 1). USA+45 USA-45 DELIB/GP WEALTH...CHARTS 20 CONGRESS. PAGE 150 A3061 — TAX LEGIS LAW DIPLOM

B62
US CONGRESS JOINT ECO COMM,ECONOMIC DEVELOPMENTS IN SOUTH AMERICA. USA+45 SOCIETY FINAN NAT/G PROB/SOLV TEC/DEV INT/TRADE TAX EFFICIENCY PRODUC ATTIT ...POLICY 20 CONGRESS SOUTH/AMER. PAGE 150 A3065 — L/A+17C ECO/UNDEV FOR/AID DIPLOM

B63
ERHARD L.,THE ECONOMICS OF SUCCESS. GERMANY/W WOR+45 LABOR CHIEF TAX REGION COST DEMAND ANTHOL. PAGE 42 A0860 — ECO/DEV INT/TRADE PLAN DIPLOM

B63
FATEMI N.S.,THE DOLLAR CRISIS. USA+45 INDUS NAT/G LEGIS BUDGET TAX COST...CHARTS METH/COMP 20 EEC. PAGE 44 A0902 — PROB/SOLV BAL/PAY FOR/AID PLAN

B63
INTERAMERICAN ECO AND SOC COUN,THE ALLIANCE FOR PROGRESS: ITS FIRST YEAR: 1961-1962. AGRI SCHOOL PLAN TEC/DEV INT/TRADE TAX GIVE ADMIN WEALTH...SOC 20 SOUTH/AMER. PAGE 71 A1449 — INT/ORG PROB/SOLV ECO/TAC L/A+17C

B63
LIVNEH E.,ISRAEL LEGAL BIBLIOGRAPHY IN EUROPEAN LANGUAGES. ISRAEL LOC/G JUDGE TAX...INT/LAW 20. PAGE 90 A1846 — BIBLIOG LAW NAT/G CONSTN

B63
UN SECRETARY GENERAL,PLANNING FOR ECONOMIC DEVELOPMENT. ECO/UNDEV FINAN BUDGET INT/TRADE TARIFFS TAX ADMIN 20 UN. PAGE 147 A3005 — PLAN ECO/TAC MGT NAT/COMP

B63
US GOVERNMENT,REPORT TO INTER-AMERICAN ECONOMIC AND SOCIAL COUNCIL AT SECOND ANNUAL MEETING. L/A+17C USA+45 VOL/ASSN TEC/DEV DIPLOM TAX EATING EFFICIENCY HEALTH...STAT CHARTS 20 AID. PAGE 153 A3116 — ECO/TAC FOR/AID FINAN PLAN

B63
US SENATE COMM GOVT OPERATIONS,REPORT OF A STUDY OF US FOREIGN AID IN TEN MIDDLE EASTERN AND AFRICAN COUNTRIES. AFR ISLAM USA+45 FORCES PLAN BUDGET DIPLOM TAX DETER WEALTH...STAT CHARTS 20 CONGRESS AID MID/EAST. PAGE 156 A3174 — FOR/AID EFFICIENCY ECO/TAC FINAN

B63
US SENATE COMM ON FOREIGN REL,HEARINGS ON S 1276 A BILL TO AMEND FURTHER THE FOREIGN ASSISTANCE ACT OF 1961. USA+45 WOR+45 INDUS INT/ORG FORCES TAX WEAPON SUPEGO...NAT/COMP 20 UN CONGRESS PRESIDENT. PAGE 156 A3182 — FOR/AID DIPLOM ECO/UNDEV ORD/FREE

B64
CURRIE D.P.,FEDERALISM AND THE NEW NATIONS OF AFRICA. CANADA USA+45 INT/TRADE TAX GP/REL ...NAT/COMP SOC/INTEG 20. PAGE 33 A0667 — FEDERAL AFR ECO/UNDEV INT/LAW

B64
KNOX V.H.,PUBLIC FINANCE: INFORMATION SOURCES. USA+45 DIPLOM ADMIN GOV/REL COST...POLICY 20. PAGE 81 A1657 — BIBLIOG/A FINAN TAX BUDGET

B64
US HOUSE COMM GOVT OPERATIONS,US OWNED FOREIGN CURRENCIES: HEARINGS (COMMITTEE ON GOVERNMENT OPERATIONS). INDIA ECO/DEV PLAN BUDGET TAX DEMAND EFFICIENCY 20 AID CONGRESS. PAGE 154 A3138 — FINAN ECO/TAC FOR/AID OWN

B65
BROOKINGS INSTITUTION,BROOKINGS PAPERS ON PUBLIC POLICY. USA+45 ECO/UNDEV LEGIS CAP/ISM ECO/TAC TAX EDU/PROP CONTROL APPORT 20. PAGE 19 A0395 — DIPLOM FOR/AID POLICY FINAN

B65
MURUMBI J.,PROBLEMS OF ECONOMIC DEVELOPMENT IN EAST AFRICA. FINAN INDUS WORKER TEC/DEV INT/TRADE TAX DEMAND EFFICIENCY PRODUC SOCISM...TREND CHARTS 20 AFRICA/E. PAGE 106 A2184 — AGRI ECO/TAC ECO/UNDEV PROC/MFG

B66
SUPPLEMENTAL FOREIGN ASSISTANCE FISCAL YEAR 1966: VIETNAM. CHINA/COM COM S/ASIA USA+45 VIETNAM EXTR/IND FINAN DIPLOM TAX GUERRILLA HABITAT ORD/FREE...STAT CHARTS 20 SENATE PRESIDENT. PAGE 4 A0077 — CONFER LEGIS WAR FOR/AID

B66
CLARK G.,WORLD PEACE THROUGH WORLD LAW; TWO ALTERNATIVE PLANS. WOR+45 DELIB/GP FORCES TAX CONFER ADJUD SANCTION ARMS/CONT WAR CHOOSE PRIVIL 20 UN COLD/WAR. PAGE 27 A0541 — INT/LAW PEACE PLAN INT/ORG

B66
ROBERTSON D.J.,THE BRITISH BALANCE OF PAYMENTS. UK WOR+45 INDUS BUDGET TAX ADJUST...CHARTS ANTHOL 20. PAGE 122 A2500 — FINAN BAL/PAY ECO/DEV INT/TRADE

B66
WELCH R.H.W.,THE NEW AMERICANISM, AND OTHER SPEECHES AND ESSAYS. USA+45 ACADEM POL/PAR SCHOOL VOL/ASSN FORCES CAP/ISM TAX REV DISCRIM 20 CIV/RIGHTS COLD/WAR BIRCH/SOC. PAGE 163 A3313 — DIPLOM FASCISM MARXISM RACE/REL

S66
GAMER R.E.,"URGENT SINGAPORE, PATIENT MALAYSIA." MALAYSIA S/ASIA ECO/UNDEV POL/PAR CHIEF TARIFFS TAX CONTROL LEAD REGION PWR 20 SINGAPORE. PAGE 51 A1036 — DIPLOM NAT/G POLICY ECO/TAC

C83
BURKE E.,"RESOLUTIONS FOR CONCILIATION WITH AMERICA" (1775), IN E. BURKE, COLLECTED WORKS, VOL. 2." UK USA-45 FORCES INT/TRADE TARIFFS TAX SANCTION PEACE...POLICY 18 PRE/US/AM. PAGE 21 A0436 — COLONIAL WAR SOVEREIGN ECO/TAC

B96
SMITH A.,LECTURES ON JUSTICE, POLICE, REVENUE AND ARMS (1763). UK LAW FAM FORCES TARIFFS AGREE COERCE INCOME OWN WEALTH LAISSEZ...GEN/LAWS 17/18. PAGE 134 A2743 — DIPLOM JURID OLD/LIB TAX

TAYLOR A.J.P. A2897

TAYLOR D. A2898

TAYLOR E. A2899

TAYLOR M.D. A2900

TAYLOR T.G. A2901

TAYLOR/AJP....A.J.P. TAYLOR

TAYLOR/Z....PRESIDENT ZACHARY TAYLOR

TCHAD....SEE CHAD

TEC/DEV....DEVELOPMENT OF TECHNIQUES

N
AMERICAN DOCUMENTATION INST,DOCUMENTATION ABSTRACTS. WOR+45 NAT/G COMPUTER CREATE TEC/DEV DIPLOM EDU/PROP REGION KNOWL...PHIL/SCI CLASSIF LING. PAGE 7 A0143
BIBLIOG/A AUTOMAT COMPUT/IR R+D

N
FOREIGN AFFAIRS. SPACE WOR+45 WOR-45 CULTURE ECO/UNDEV FINAN NAT/G TEC/DEV INT/TRADE ARMS/CONT NUC/PWR...POLICY 20 UN EURATOM ECSC EEC. PAGE 2 A0034
BIBLIOG DIPLOM INT/ORG INT/LAW

N
LATIN AMERICA IN PERIODICAL LITERATURE. LAW TEC/DEV DIPLOM RECEIVE EDU/PROP...GEOG HUM MGT 20. PAGE 2 A0037
BIBLIOG/A L/A+17C SOCIETY ECO/UNDEV

N
SEMINAR: THE MONTHLY SYMPOSIUM. INDIA ACT/RES TEC/DEV DIPLOM ATTIT...BIBLIOG 20. PAGE 2 A0041
NAT/G ECO/UNDEV SOVEREIGN POLICY

N
THE MIDDLE EAST AND NORTH AFRICA. AFR ISLAM CULTURE ECO/UNDEV AGRI NAT/G TEC/DEV FOR/AID INT/TRADE EDU/PROP...CHARTS 20. PAGE 2 A0043
INDEX INDUS FINAN STAT

N
CORNELL UNIVERSITY LIBRARY,SOUTHEAST ASIA ACCESSIONS LIST. LAW SOCIETY STRUCT ECO/UNDEV POL/PAR TEC/DEV DIPLOM LEAD REGION. PAGE 31 A0626
BIBLIOG S/ASIA NAT/G CULTURE

N
FOREIGN TRADE LIBRARY,NEW TITLES RECEIVED IN THE LIBRARY. WOR+45 ECO/UNDEV FINAN NAT/G PLAN TEC/DEV BUDGET ECO/TAC TARIFFS GOV/REL STAT. PAGE 47 A0964
BIBLIOG/A INT/TRADE INDUS ECO/DEV

N
HOOVER INSTITUTION,UNITED STATES AND CANADIAN PUBLICATIONS ON AFRICA. CULTURE ECO/UNDEV AGRI TEC/DEV EDU/PROP COLONIAL RACE/REL NAT/LISM ATTIT HEALTH...SOC SOC/WK 20. PAGE 67 A1381
BIBLIOG DIPLOM NAT/G AFR

N
MINISTRY OF OVERSEAS DEVELOPME,TECHNICAL CO-OPERATION -- A BIBLIOGRAPHY. UK LAW SOCIETY DIPLOM ECO/TAC FOR/AID...STAT 20 CMN/WLTH. PAGE 102 A2089
BIBLIOG TEC/DEV ECO/DEV NAT/G

N
MURRA R.O.,POST-WAR PROBLEMS: A CURRENT LIST OF UNITED STATES GOVERNMENT PUBLICATIONS (PAMPHLET). WOR+45 SOCIETY FINAN INT/ORG SCHOOL WORKER TEC/DEV ECO/TAC...SOC 20. PAGE 106 A2180
BIBLIOG/A ADJUST AGRI INDUS

N
UNITED NATIONS,OFFICIAL RECORDS OF THE UNITED NATIONS' ATOMIC ENERGY COMMISSION - DISARMAMENT COMMISSION. WOR+45 TEC/DEV DIPLOM WRITING NUC/PWR 20 UN. PAGE 148 A3032
ARMS/CONT INT/ORG DELIB/GP CONFER

N
US LIBRARY OF CONGRESS,ACCESSIONS LIST - INDIA. INDIA CULTURE AGRI LOC/G POL/PAR PLAN PROB/SOLV TEC/DEV DIPLOM EDU/PROP LEAD GP/REL ATTIT 20. PAGE 154 A3142
BIBLIOG S/ASIA ECO/UNDEV NAT/G

N
US LIBRARY OF CONGRESS,ACCESSIONS LIST -- ISRAEL. ISRAEL CULTURE ECO/UNDEV POL/PAR PLAN PROB/SOLV TEC/DEV DIPLOM EDU/PROP LEAD WAR ATTIT 20 JEWS. PAGE 154 A3143
BIBLIOG ISLAM NAT/G GP/REL

B14
DE BLOCH J.,THE FUTURE OF WAR IN ITS TECHNICAL, ECONOMIC, AND POLITICAL RELATIONS (1899). MOD/EUR TEC/DEV BUDGET INT/TRADE DETER GUERRILLA WEAPON COST PEACE 20. PAGE 34 A0698
WAR BAL/PWR PREDICT FORCES

N19
SALKEVER L.R.,SUB-SAHARA AFRICA (PAMPHLET). AFR USSR EXTR/IND NAT/G SCHOOL DIPLOM COLONIAL WEALTH ...GEOG CHARTS 16/20. PAGE 127 A2594
ECO/UNDEV TEC/DEV TASK INT/TRADE

N19
ZLOTNICK M.,WEAPONS IN SPACE (PAMPHLET). FUT WOR+45 TEC/DEV DIPLOM ARMS/CONT CIVMIL/REL PEACE HABITAT ...CONCPT NEW/IDEA CHARTS. PAGE 170 A3457
SPACE WEAPON NUC/PWR WAR

B27
SIEGFRIED A.,AMERICA COMES OF AGE: A FRENCH ANALYSIS (TRANS. BY H.H. HEMMING AND DORIS HEMMING). FRANCE UK POL/PAR WORKER TEC/DEV DIPLOM REGION RACE/REL ADJUST PRODUC HEREDITY...TIME/SEQ GP/COMP SOC/INTEG 20 DEMOCRAT REPUBLICAN KKK. PAGE 132 A2714
USA-45 CULTURE ECO/DEV SOC

B36
VARLEY D.H.,A BIBLIOGRAPHY OF ITALIAN COLONISATION IN AFRICA WITH A SECTION ON ABYSSINIA. AFR ETHIOPIA ITALY LIBYA SOMALIA AGRI FINAN LABOR TEC/DEV DIPLOM INT/TRADE RACE/REL DISCRIM 19/20. PAGE 158 A3222
BIBLIOG COLONIAL ADMIN LAW

B38
COLBY C.C.,GEOGRAPHICAL ASPECTS OF INTERNATIONAL RELATIONS. WOR-45 ECO/DEV ECO/UNDEV AGRI EXTR/IND INDUS MARKET R+D INT/ORG NAT/G TEC/DEV ECO/TAC INT/TRADE NAT/LISM WEALTH...METH/CNCPT CHARTS GEN/LAWS 20. PAGE 28 A0565
PLAN GEOG DIPLOM

B38
HARPER S.N.,THE GOVERNMENT OF THE SOVIET UNION. COM USSR LAW CONSTN ECO/DEV PLAN TEC/DEV DIPLOM INT/TRADE ADMIN REV NAT/LISM...POLICY 20. PAGE 62 A1265
MARXISM NAT/G LEAD POL/PAR

B39
ROBBINS L.,ECONOMIC CAUSES OF WAR. WOR-45 ECO/DEV ECO/UNDEV INT/ORG NAT/G TEC/DEV DIPLOM DOMIN COLONIAL ATTIT DRIVE PWR WEALTH...POLICY CONCPT OBS SAMP TREND CON/ANAL GEN/LAWS MARX/KARL 20. PAGE 122 A2493
COERCE ECO/TAC WAR

B39
SPEIER H.,WAR IN OUR TIME. WOR-45 AGRI FINAN FORCES TEC/DEV BAL/PWR EDU/PROP WEAPON PEACE PWR...ANTHOL 20. PAGE 136 A2779
FASCISM WAR DIPLOM NAT/G

B39
STALEY E.,WORLD ECONOMY IN TRANSITION. WOR-45 SOCIETY INT/ORG PROF/ORG ECO/TAC ATTIT WEALTH ...METH/CNCPT TREND GEN/LAWS 20. PAGE 137 A2800
TEC/DEV INT/TRADE

C40
NORMAN E.H.,"JAPAN'S EMERGENCE AS A MODERN STATE: POLITICAL AND ECONOMIC PROBLEMS OF THE MEIJI PERIOD." CONSTN STRATA AGRI INDUS POL/PAR TEC/DEV CAP/ISM CIVMIL/REL...BIBLIOG 19/20 CHINJAP. PAGE 110 A2250
CENTRAL DIPLOM POLICY NAT/LISM

B43
BROWN A.D.,GREECE: SELECTED LIST OF REFERENCES. GREECE ECO/UNDEV AGRI FINAN INDUS LABOR SECT TEC/DEV INT/TRADE LEAD...SOC 20. PAGE 20 A0399
BIBLIOG/A WAR DIPLOM NAT/G

B43
CONOVER H.F.,SOVIET RUSSIA: SELECTED LIST OF REFERENCES. USSR CULTURE INDUS NAT/G TOP/EX TEC/DEV BUDGET WAR CIVMIL/REL EFFICIENCY MARXISM 20. PAGE 29 A0597
BIBLIOG ECO/DEV COM DIPLOM

B43
LEWIN E.,ROYAL EMPIRE SOCIETY BIBLIOGRAPHIES NO. 9: SUB-SAHARA AFRICA. ECO/UNDEV TEC/DEV DIPLOM ADMIN COLONIAL LEAD 20. PAGE 88 A1800
BIBLIOG AFR NAT/G SOCIETY

B44
WEIGERT H.W.,COMPASS OF THE WORLD, A SYMPOSIUM ON POLITICAL GEOGRAPHY. EUR+WWI FUT MOD/EUR S/ASIA USA-45 WOR-45 SOCIETY AGRI INDUS MARKET ECO/TAC INT/TRADE PERSON 20. PAGE 162 A3298
TEC/DEV CAP/ISM RUSSIA GEOG

B46
BRODIE B.,THE OBSOLETE WEAPON: ATOMIC POWER AND WORLD ORDER. COM USA+45 USSR WOR+45 DELIB/GP PLAN ORD/FREE PWR...CONCPT TIME/SEQ TREND UN 20. PAGE 19 A0380
INT/ORG TEC/DEV ARMS/CONT NUC/PWR

L47
BRUNER J.S.,"TOWARD A COMMON GROUND-INTERNATIONAL SOCIAL SCIENCE." FUT WOR+45 INTELL R+D NAT/G VOL/ASSN CONSULT DELIB/GP ACT/RES CREATE PLAN TEC/DEV ATTIT ORD/FREE...PSY SOC CONCPT ANTHOL UNESCO 20. PAGE 20 A0410
INT/ORG KNOWL

B48
GRAHAM F.D.,THE THEORY OF INTERNATIONAL VALUES. FUT WOR+45 WOR-45 ECO/DEV FINAN INT/ORG PLAN TEC/DEV CAP/ISM DIPLOM ECO/TAC TARIFFS ROUTINE BAL/PAY DRIVE PWR WEALTH SOCISM...POLICY STAT HYPO/EXP GEN/LAWS 20. PAGE 55 A1125
NEW/IDEA INT/TRADE

B48
MINISTERE FINANCES ET ECO,BULLETIN BIBLIOGRAPHIQUE. AFR EUR+WWI FRANCE CULTURE STRUCT FINAN NAT/G ACT/RES INT/TRADE ADMIN REGION PRODUC STAT. PAGE 102 A2088
BIBLIOG/A ECO/UNDEV TEC/DEV COLONIAL

B49
OGBURN W.,TECHNOLOGY AND INTERNATIONAL RELATIONS. WOR+45 WOR-45 ECO/DEV CREATE PLAN ECO/TAC EDU/PROP COERCE PWR SKILL WEALTH...TECHNIC PSY SOC NEW/IDEA CHARTS TOT/POP 20. PAGE 111 A2283
TEC/DEV DIPLOM INT/ORG

B50
COUNCIL BRITISH NATIONAL BIB,BRITISH NATIONAL BIBLIOGRAPHY. UK AGRI CONSTRUC PERF/ART POL/PAR SECT CREATE INT/TRADE LEAD...HUM JURID PHIL/SCI 20. PAGE 31 A0637
BIBLIOG/A NAT/G TEC/DEV DIPLOM

B50
US DEPARTMENT OF STATE,POINT FOUR: COOPERATIVE PROGRAM FOR AID IN THE DEVELOPMENT OF ECONOMICALLY UNDERDEVELOPED AREAS. WOR+45 AGRI INDUS INT/ORG
ECO/UNDEV FOR/AID FINAN

PLAN TEC/DEV DIPLOM EDU/PROP ADMIN PEACE PRODUC WEALTH 20 CONGRESS UN. PAGE 151 A3085 INT/TRADE

N50
SCHAPIRO J.S.,THE WORLD IN CRISES: POLITICAL AND SOCIAL MOVEMENTS IN THE TWENTIETH CENTURY. USA+45 INT/ORG LABOR PLAN CAP/ISM DIPLOM COLONIAL PEACE TOTALISM ATTIT LAISSEZ...BIBLIOG 20 COLD/WAR. PAGE 128 A2618 NAT/LISM TEC/DEV REV WAR

B52
US MUTUAL SECURITY AGENCY,U. S. TECHNICAL AND ECONOMIC ASSISTANCE IN THE FAR EAST (PAMPHLET). ASIA BURMA INDONESIA PHILIPPINE TAIWAN THAILAND USA+45 AGRI INDUS PLAN EDU/PROP ADMIN HEALTH. PAGE 155 A3161 FOR/AID TEC/DEV ECO/UNDEV BUDGET

B53
LANGER W.L.,THE UNDECLARED WAR, 1940-1941. EUR+WWI GERMANY USA-45 USSR AIR FORCES TEC/DEV CONFER CONTROL COERCE PERCEPT ORD/FREE PWR 20 CHINJAP EUROPE. PAGE 84 A1727 WAR POLICY DIPLOM

B53
NEISSER H.,NATIONAL INCOMES AND INTERNATIONAL TRADE. FRANCE GERMANY SWEDEN UK USA-45 EXTR/IND FINAN INDUS TEC/DEV PRICE BAL/PAY EQUILIB INCOME WEALTH...CHARTS METH 19 CHINJAP. PAGE 108 A2215 INT/TRADE PRODUC MARKET CON/ANAL

S53
LINCOLN G.,"FACTORS DETERMINING ARMS AID." COM FUT USA+45 USSR WOR+45 ECO/DEV NAT/G CONSULT PLAN TEC/DEV DIPLOM DOMIN EDU/PROP PERCEPT PWR ...DECISION CONCPT TREND MARX/KARL 20. PAGE 89 A1819 FORCES POLICY BAL/PWR FOR/AID

B54
BECKEL G.,WORKSHOPS FOR THE WORLD; THE SPECIALIZED AGENCIES OF THE UN. WOR+45 AGRI DIST/IND CREATE TEC/DEV BUDGET CONTROL TASK WEALTH...CHARTS ORG/CHARTS 20 UN CASEBOOK. PAGE 12 A0246 INT/ORG DIPLOM PEACE CON/ANAL

B54
WRIGHT Q.,PROBLEMS OF STABILITY AND PROGRESS IN INTERNATIONAL RELATIONSHIPS. FUT WOR+45 WOR-45 SOCIETY LEGIS CREATE TEC/DEV ECO/TAC EDU/PROP ADJUD WAR PEACE ORD/FREE PWR...KNO/TEST TREND GEN/LAWS 20. PAGE 167 A3409 INT/ORG CONCPT DIPLOM

L54
OPLER M.E.,"SOCIAL ASPECTS OF TECHNICAL ASSISTANCE IN OPERATION." WOR+45 VOL/ASSN CREATE PLAN TEC/DEV EDU/PROP ALL/VALS...METH/CNCPT OBS RECORD TREND UN 20. PAGE 112 A2292 INT/ORG CONSULT FOR/AID

B55
COMM. STUDY ORGAN. PEACE,REPORTS. WOR-45 ECO/DEV ECO/UNDEV VOL/ASSN CONSULT FORCES PLAN TEC/DEV DOMIN EDU/PROP NUC/PWR ATTIT PWR WEALTH...JURID STERTYP FAO ILO 20 UN. PAGE 28 A0579 WOR+45 INT/ORG ARMS/CONT

B55
COTTRELL W.F.,ENERGY AND SOCIETY. FUT WOR+45 WOR-45 ECO/DEV ECO/UNDEV INT/ORG NAT/G DETER ORD/FREE PWR SKILL WEALTH...SOC TIME/SEQ TOT/POP VAL/FREE 20. PAGE 31 A0634 TEC/DEV BAL/PWR PEACE

L55
KISER M.,"ORGANIZATION OF AMERICAN STATES." L/A+17C USA+45 ECO/UNDEV INT/ORG NAT/G PLAN TEC/DEV DIPLOM ECO/TAC INT/TRADE EDU/PROP ADMIN ALL/VALS...POLICY MGT RECORD ORG/CHARTS OAS 20. PAGE 80 A1639 VOL/ASSN ECO/DEV REGION

B56
CHANG C.J.,THE MINORITY GROUPS OF YUNN AN AND CHINESE POLITICAL EXPANSION INTO SOUTHEAST ASIA (DOCTORAL THESIS). ASIA CHINA/COM S/ASIA FORCES TEC/DEV DIPLOM EDU/PROP...GEOG BIBLIOG 20. PAGE 26 A0520 GP/REL REGION DOMIN MARXISM

B56
ESTEP R.,AN AIR POWER BIBLIOGRAPHY. USA+45 TEC/DEV BUDGET DIPLOM EDU/PROP DETER CIVMIL/REL...DECISION INT/LAW 20. PAGE 42 A0862 BIBLIOG/A FORCES WEAPON PLAN

B56
KNORR K.E.,RUBLE DIPLOMACY: CHALLENGE TO AMERICAN FOREIGN AID(PAMPHLET). CHINA/COM USA+45 USSR PLAN TEC/DEV CAP/ISM INT/TRADE DOMIN EDU/PROP CONTROL LEAD 20 COLD/WAR. PAGE 81 A1654 ECO/UNDEV COM DIPLOM FOR/AID

B56
ROBERTS H.L.,RUSSIA AND AMERICA. CHINA/COM S/ASIA USSR FORCES TEC/DEV FOR/AID NUC/PWR ALL/IDEOS ...MAJORIT TREND NAT/COMP 20 COLD/WAR UN NATO. PAGE 122 A2494 DIPLOM INT/ORG BAL/PWR TOTALISM

B56
UN HEADQUARTERS LIBRARY,BIBLIOGRAPHY OF INDUSTRIALIZATION IN UNDERDEVELOPED COUNTRIES (BIBLIOGRAPHICAL SERIES NO. 6). WOR+45 R+D ACADEM INT/ORG NAT/G. PAGE 147 A3002 BIBLIOG ECO/UNDEV TEC/DEV

B56
UNITED NATIONS,BIBLIOGRAPHY ON INDUSTRIALIZATION IN UNDER-DEVELOPED COUNTRIES. WOR+45 R+D INT/ORG NAT/G FOR/AID ADMIN LEAD 20 UN. PAGE 149 A3036 BIBLIOG ECO/UNDEV INDUS TEC/DEV

B56
US DEPARTMENT OF STATE,ECONOMIC PROBLEMS OF UNDERDEVELOPED AREAS (PAMPHLET). AFR ASIA ISLAM L/A+17C AGRI FINAN INDUS INT/ORG LABOR INT/TRADE ...PSY SOC 20. PAGE 151 A3090 BIBLIOG ECO/UNDEV TEC/DEV R+D

S56
GORDON L.,"THE ORGANIZATION FOR EUROPEAN ECONOMIC COOPERATION." EUR+WWI INDUS INT/ORG NAT/G CONSULT DELIB/GP ACT/RES CREATE PLAN TEC/DEV EDU/PROP LEGIT WEALTH OEEC 20. PAGE 54 A1114 VOL/ASSN ECO/DEV

C56
DUPUY R.E.,"MILITARY HERITAGE OF AMERICA." USA+45 USA-45 TEC/DEV DIPLOM ROUTINE...POLICY TREND CHARTS IDEA/COMP BIBLIOG COLD/WAR. PAGE 39 A0804 FORCES WAR CONCPT

B57
HALD M.,A SELECTED BIBLIOGRAPHY ON ECONOMIC DEVELOPMENT AND FOREIGN AID. INT/ORG PROB/SOLV ...SOC 20. PAGE 59 A1222 BIBLIOG ECO/UNDEV TEC/DEV FOR/AID

B57
KISSINGER H.A.,NUCLEAR WEAPONS AND FOREIGN POLICY. FUT USA+45 WOR+45 INT/ORG FORCES ACT/RES TEC/DEV DIPLOM ARMS/CONT COERCE ATTIT KNOWL PWR...DECISION GEOG CHARTS 20. PAGE 80 A1640 PLAN DETER NUC/PWR

B57
LAVES W.H.C.,UNESCO. FUT WOR+45 NAT/G CONSULT DELIB/GP TEC/DEV ECO/TAC EDU/PROP PEACE ORD/FREE ...CONCPT TIME/SEQ TREND UNESCO VAL/FREE 20. PAGE 86 A1751 INT/ORG KNOWL

B57
US SENATE SPEC COMM FOR AID,COMPILATION OF STUDIES AND SURVEYS. AFR ASIA L/A+17C USA+45 ECO/UNDEV AGRI INT/ORG CONSULT TEC/DEV CONFER TOTALISM...NAT/COMP 20 CONGRESS. PAGE 157 A3197 FOR/AID DIPLOM ORD/FREE DELIB/GP

B57
US SENATE SPEC COMM FOR AID,HEARINGS BEFORE THE SPECIAL COMMITTEE TO STUDY THE FOREIGN AID PROGRAM. USA+45 USSR ECO/UNDEV INT/ORG FORCES WEAPON TOTALISM ATTIT SUPEGO...NAT/COMP CONGRESS. PAGE 157 A3198 FOR/AID DIPLOM ORD/FREE TEC/DEV

S57
ALLEN R.L.,"UNITED NATIONS TECHNICAL ASSISTANCE: SOVIET AND EAST-EUROPEAN PARTICIPATION." COM WOR+45 AGRI INDUS INT/ORG NAT/G FOR/AID SKILL UN 20. PAGE 6 A0124 ECO/UNDEV TEC/DEV USSR

S57
DEUTSCH K.W.,"MASS COMMUNICATIONS AND THE LOSS OF FREEDOM IN NATIONAL DECISION MAKING." FUT WOR+45 SOCIETY COM/IND INT/ORG NAT/G ACT/RES CREATE TEC/DEV EDU/PROP MAJORITY PERCEPT...METH/CNCPT 20. PAGE 36 A0737 COERCE DECISION WAR

S57
HOAG M.W.,"ECONOMIC PROBLEMS OF ALLIANCE." COM EUR+WWI WOR+45 ECO/DEV ECO/UNDEV NAT/G VOL/ASSN FORCES PLAN TEC/DEV DIPLOM COERCE ORD/FREE PWR WEALTH...DECISION GEN/LAWS NATO COLD/WAR. PAGE 65 A1345 INT/ORG ECO/TAC

S57
WRIGHT Q.,"THE VALUE OF CONFLICT RESOLUTION OF A GENERAL DISCIPLINE OF INTERNATIONAL RELATIONS." WOR+45 SOCIETY INT/ORG NAT/G FORCES TOP/EX PLAN TEC/DEV ECO/TAC DOMIN LEGIT COERCE ATTIT PWR ...GEN/METH COLD/WAR VAL/FREE. PAGE 168 A3412 ORD/FREE SOC DIPLOM

N57
US SENATE SPECIAL COMM FOR AFF,REPORT OF THE SPECIAL COMMITTEE TO STUDY THE FOREIGN AID PROGRAM (PAMPHLET). USA+45 CONSULT DELIB/GP LEGIS PLAN TEC/DEV CONFER SUPEGO CONGRESS. PAGE 157 A3199 FOR/AID ORD/FREE ECO/UNDEV DIPLOM

B58
GARTHOFF R.L.,SOVIET STRATEGY IN THE NUCLEAR AGE. FUT USSR R+D INT/ORG NAT/G ACT/RES TEC/DEV DOMIN DETER WAR ATTIT PWR...RELATIV METH/CNCPT SELF/OBS TREND CON/ANAL STERTYP GEN/LAWS 20. PAGE 51 A1052 COM FORCES BAL/PWR NUC/PWR

B58
GAVIN J.M.,WAR AND PEACE IN THE SPACE AGE. SPACE USA+45 USSR FORCES PLAN TEC/DEV BAL/PWR DIPLOM ARMS/CONT WEAPON CIVMIL/REL...CHARTS GP/COMP 20 NATO COLD/WAR. PAGE 52 A1055 WAR DETER NUC/PWR PEACE

B58
HUNT B.I.,BIPARTISANSHIP: A CASE STUDY OF THE FOREIGN ASSISTANCE PROGRAM, 1947-56 (DOCTORAL THESIS). USA+45 INT/ORG CONSULT LEGIS TEC/DEV ...BIBLIOG PRESIDENT TREATY NATO TRUMAN/HS EISNHWR/DD CONGRESS. PAGE 69 A1418 FOR/AID POL/PAR GP/REL DIPLOM

B58
NATIONAL PLANNING ASSOCIATION,1970 WITHOUT ARMS CONTROL (PAMPHLET). WOR+45 PROB/SOLV TEC/DEV DIPLOM CONFER DETER NUC/PWR WAR...CHARTS 20 COLD/WAR. PAGE 107 A2204 ARMS/CONT ORD/FREE WEAPON PREDICT

B58
NOEL-BAKER D.,THE ARMS RACE. WOR+45 NAT/G DELIB/GP ACT/RES TEC/DEV EDU/PROP NUC/PWR ATTIT KNOWL PWR ...CONCPT OBS LEAGUE/NAT 20 COLD/WAR. PAGE 109 A2245 FUT INT/ORG ARMS/CONT PEACE

B58
PALYI M.,MANAGED MONEY AT THE CROSSROADS: THE EUROPEAN EXPERIENCE. WOR+45 WOR-45 TEC/DEV DIPLOM INT/TRADE DEMAND WEALTH...CHARTS BIBLIOG 19/20 EUROPE GOLD/STAND SILVER. PAGE 113 A2324 FINAN ECO/TAC ECO/DEV PRODUC

B58
UN INTL CONF ON PEACEFUL USE,PROGRESS IN ATOMIC ENERGY (VOL. I). WOR+45 R+D PLAN TEC/DEV CONFER CONTROL PEACE SKILL...CHARTS ANTHOL 20 UN BAGHDAD. PAGE 147 A3003
NUC/PWR DIPLOM WORKER EDU/PROP

B58
US HOUSE COMM GOVT OPERATIONS,HEARINGS BEFORE A SUBCOMMITTEE OF THE COMMITTEE ON GOVERNMENT OPERATIONS. CAMBODIA PHILIPPINE USA+45 CONSTRUC TEC/DEV ADMIN CONTROL WEAPON EFFICIENCY HOUSE/REP. PAGE 154 A3135
FOR/AID DIPLOM ORD/FREE ECO/UNDEV

B58
US OPERATIONS MISSION TO VIET,BUILDING ECONOMIC STRENGTH (PAMPHLET). USA+45 VIETNAM/S INDUS TEC/DEV BUDGET ADMIN EATING HEALTH...STAT 20. PAGE 155 A3162
FOR/AID ECO/UNDEV AGRI EDU/PROP

S58
MCDOUGAL M.S.,"PERSPECTIVES FOR A LAW OF OUTER SPACE." FUT WOR+45 AIR CONSULT DELIB/GP TEC/DEV CT/SYS ORD/FREE...POLICY JURID 20 UN. PAGE 98 A2004
INT/ORG SPACE INT/LAW

B59
ALLEN R.L.,SOVIET INFLUENCE IN LATIN AMERICA. ECO/UNDEV FINAN PROC/MFG NAT/G TEC/DEV EDU/PROP EXEC ROUTINE ATTIT DRIVE PERSON ALL/VALS PWR...STAT CHARTS WORK 20. PAGE 6 A0125
L/A+17C ECO/TAC INT/TRADE USSR

B59
MODELSKI G.,ATOMIC ENERGY IN THE COMMUNIST BLOC. FUT INT/ORG CONSULT FORCES ACT/RES PLAN KNOWL SKILL ...PHIL/SCI STAT CHARTS 20. PAGE 102 A2096
TEC/DEV NUC/PWR USSR COM

B59
NOVE A.,COMMUNIST ECONOMIC STRATEGY: SOVIET GROWTH AND CAPABILITIES. USSR AGRI LABOR PLAN TEC/DEV CAP/ISM INT/TRADE EFFICIENCY MARXISM 20 THIRD/WRLD. PAGE 110 A2257
FOR/AID ECO/TAC DIPLOM INDUS

B59
STANFORD RESEARCH INSTITUTE,POSSIBLE NONMILITARY SCIENTIFIC DEVELOPMENTS AND THEIR POTENTIAL IMPACT ON FOREIGN POLICY PROBLEMS OF THE UNITED. FUT USA+45 INT/ORG PROF/ORG CONSULT ACT/RES CREATE PLAN PEACE KNOWL SKILL...TECHNIC PHIL/SCI NEW/IDEA UNESCO 20. PAGE 137 A2802
R+D TEC/DEV

B59
STERNBERG F.,THE MILITARY AND INDUSTRIAL REVOLUTION OF OUR TIME. USA+45 USSR WOR+45 WORKER COMPUTER PLAN TEC/DEV NUC/PWR GP/REL...POLICY NAT/COMP 20. PAGE 138 A2818
DIPLOM FORCES INDUS CIVMIL/REL

B59
US GENERAL ACCOUNTING OFFICE,EXAM OF ECONOMIC AND TECHNICAL ASSISTANCE PROGRAM FOR INDIA INT'NAT'L COOP ADMIN REPORT TO CONGRESS 1955-1958. INDIA USA+45 ECO/UNDEV FINAN PLAN DIPLOM COST UTIL WEALTH ...CHARTS 20 CONGRESS AID. PAGE 153 A3114
FOR/AID EFFICIENCY ECO/TAC TEC/DEV

L59
BEGUIN B.,"ILO AND THE TRIPARTITE SYSTEM." EUR+WWI WOR+45 WOR-45 CONSTN ECO/DEV ECO/UNDEV INDUS INT/ORG NAT/G VOL/ASSN DELIB/GP PLAN TEC/DEV LEGIT ORD/FREE WEALTH...CONCPT TIME/SEQ WORK ILO 20. PAGE 12 A0249
LABOR

L59
WURFEL D.,"FOREIGN AID AND SOCIAL REFORM IN POLITICAL DEVELOPMENT" (BMR)" PHILIPPINE USA+45 WOR+45 SOCIETY POL/PAR ACT/RES TEC/DEV DIPLOM 20. PAGE 168 A3424
FOR/AID PROB/SOLV ECO/TAC ECO/UNDEV

S59
FISCHER L.,"THE SOVIET-AMERICAN ANTAGONISM: HOW WILL IT END." CONSTN CULTURE PLAN TEC/DEV RIGID/FLEX SUPEGO ORD/FREE...MARXIST DECISION PSY CONCPT CON/ANAL GEN/LAWS VAL/FREE 20 COLD/WAR. PAGE 46 A0936
USA+45 PWR DIPLOM USSR

S59
HARTT J.,"ANTARCTICA: ITS IMMEDIATE PRACTICALITIES." FUT USA+45 USSR WOR+45 INT/ORG NAT/G CREATE TEC/DEV REGION KNOWL WEALTH...GEOG 20 ANTARTICA. PAGE 62 A1276
VOL/ASSN ORD/FREE DIPLOM

S59
KOHN L.Y.,"ISRAEL AND NEW NATION STATES OF ASIA AND AFRICA." AFR ASIA FUT S/ASIA VOL/ASSN TEC/DEV NAT/LISM RIGID/FLEX SKILL WEALTH...RELATIV OBS TREND CON/ANAL 20. PAGE 81 A1663
ECO/UNDEV ECO/TAC FOR/AID ISRAEL

S59
SIMONS H.,"WORLD-WIDE CAPABILITIES FOR PRODUCTION AND CONTROL OF NUCLEAR WEAPONS." FUT WOR+45 INDUS INT/ORG NAT/G ECO/TAC ATTIT PWR SKILL...TREND CHARTS VAL/FREE 20. PAGE 133 A2719
TEC/DEV ARMS/CONT NUC/PWR

S59
TIPTON J.B.,"PARTICIPATION OF THE UNITED STATES IN THE INTERNATIONAL LABOR ORGANIZATION." USA+45 LAW STRUCT ECO/DEV ECO/UNDEV INDUS TEC/DEV ECO/TAC ADMIN PERCEPT ORD/FREE SKILL...STAT HIST/WRIT GEN/METH ILO WORK 20. PAGE 144 A2946
LABOR INT/ORG

B60
ALLEN R.L.,SOVIET ECONOMIC WARFARE. USSR FINAN INDUS NAT/G PLAN TEC/DEV FOR/AID DETER WEALTH ...TREND GEN/LAWS 20. PAGE 6 A0126
COM ECO/TAC

B60
BILLERBECK K.,SOVIET BLOC FOREIGN AID TO UNDERDEVELOPED COUNTRIES. COM FUT USSR FINAN FORCES TEC/DEV DIPLOM INT/TRADE EDU/PROP NUC/PWR...TREND 20. PAGE 14 A0287
FOR/AID ECO/UNDEV ECO/TAC MARXISM

B60
BLACK E.R.,THE DIPLOMACY OF ECONOMIC DEVELOPMENT. WOR+45 CONSULT PLAN TEC/DEV DIPLOM ECO/TAC FOR/AID ...CONCPT TREND 20. PAGE 15 A0297
ECO/UNDEV ACT/RES

B60
BROWN H.,COMMUNITY OF FEAR. FORCES TEC/DEV ARMS/CONT COERCE PEACE 20. PAGE 20 A0402
NUC/PWR WAR DIPLOM DETER

B60
HAHN W.F.,AMERICAN STRATEGY FOR THE NUCLEAR AGE. USA+45 NAT/G TEC/DEV ECO/TAC FOR/AID ARMS/CONT NUC/PWR ORD/FREE MARXISM...ANTHOL 20. PAGE 59 A1216
DIPLOM PLAN PEACE

B60
HOFFMANN P.G.,ONE HUNDRED COUNTRIES, ONE AND ONE QUARTER BILLION PEOPLE. MARKET INT/ORG TEC/DEV CAP/ISM...GEOG CHARTS METH/COMP 20 UN. PAGE 66 A1354
FOR/AID ECO/TAC ECO/UNDEV INT/TRADE

B60
KINGSTON-MCCLOUG E.,DEFENSE; POLICY AND STRATEGY. UK SEA AIR TEC/DEV DIPLOM ADMIN LEAD WAR ORD/FREE ...CHARTS 20. PAGE 79 A1627
FORCES PLAN POLICY DECISION

B60
MUNRO L.,UNITED NATIONS, HOPE FOR A DIVIDED WORLD. FUT WOR+45 CONSTN DELIB/GP CREATE TEC/DEV DIPLOM EDU/PROP LEGIT PEACE ATTIT HEALTH ORD/FREE PWR ...CONCPT TREND UN VAL/FREE 20. PAGE 106 A2172
INT/ORG ROUTINE

B60
PENTONY D.E.,THE UNDERDEVELOPED LANDS. FUT WOR+45 CULTURE AGRI FINAN INDUS MARKET INT/ORG LABOR NAT/G VOL/ASSN CONSULT TEC/DEV ECO/TAC EDU/PROP COLONIAL ATTIT WEALTH...OBS RECORD SAMP TREND GEN/METH WORK UN 20. PAGE 115 A2351
ECO/UNDEV POLICY FOR/AID INT/TRADE

B60
RAO V.K.R.,INTERNATIONAL AID FOR ECONOMIC DEVELOPMENT - POSSIBILITIES AND LIMITATIONS. FINAN PLAN TEC/DEV ADMIN TASK EFFICIENCY...POLICY SOC METH/CNCPT CHARTS 20 UN. PAGE 119 A2444
FOR/AID DIPLOM INT/ORG ECO/UNDEV

B60
STEIN E.,AMERICAN ENTERPRISE IN THE EUROPEAN COMMON MARKET: A LEGAL PROFILE. EUR+WWI FUT USA+45 SOCIETY STRUCT ECO/DEV NAT/G VOL/ASSN CONSULT PLAN TEC/DEV ECO/TAC INT/TRADE ADMIN ATTIT RIGID/FLEX PWR...MGT NEW/IDEA STAT TREND COMPUT/IR SIMUL EEC 20. PAGE 137 A2814
MARKET ADJUD INT/LAW

B60
US HOUSE COMM. SCI. ASTRONAUT.,OCEAN SCIENCES AND NATIONAL SECURITY. FUT SEA ECO/DEV EXTR/IND INT/ORG NAT/G FORCES ACT/RES TEC/DEV ECO/TAC COERCE WAR BIO/SOC KNOWL PWR...CONCPT RECORD LAB/EXP 20. PAGE 154 A3141
R+D ORD/FREE

B60
VOGT W.,PEOPLE: CHALLENGE TO SURVIVAL. WOR+45 ECO/DEV ECO/UNDEV FAM INT/ORG NAT/G PLAN PROB/SOLV FOR/AID GIVE EATING 20 BIRTH/CON. PAGE 159 A3247
CENSUS CONTROL ATTIT TEC/DEV

B60
WOETZEL R.K.,THE INTERNATIONAL CONTROL OF AIRSPACE AND OUTERSPACE. FUT WOR+45 AIR CONSTN STRUCT CONSULT PLAN TEC/DEV ADJUD RIGID/FLEX KNOWL ORD/FREE PWR...TECHNIC GEOG MGT NEW/IDEA TREND COMPUT/IR VAL/FREE 20 TREATY. PAGE 166 A3375
INT/ORG JURID SPACE INT/LAW

L60
JACOB P.E.,"THE DISARMAMENT CONSENSUS." USA+45 USSR WOR+45 INT/ORG NAT/G ACT/RES TEC/DEV BAL/PWR EDU/PROP ADMIN COERCE DETER NUC/PWR CONSEN RIGID/FLEX PWR...CONCPT RECORD CHARTS COLD/WAR 20. PAGE 72 A1482
DELIB/GP ATTIT ARMS/CONT

S60
FITZGIBBON R.H.,"DICTATORSHIP AND DEMOCRACY IN LATIN AMERICA." FUT ECO/DEV ECO/UNDEV INT/ORG LOC/G NAT/G TOP/EX PLAN TEC/DEV ECO/TAC CHOOSE ATTIT DRIVE PERSON ALL/VALS OAS TOT/POP 20. PAGE 46 A0943
L/A+17C ACT/RES INT/TRADE

S60
FRANKEL S.H.,"ECONOMIC ASPECTS OF POLITICAL INDEPENDENCE IN AFRICA." AFR FUT SOCIETY ECO/UNDEV COM/IND FINAN LEGIS PLAN TEC/DEV CAP/ISM ECO/TAC INT/TRADE ADMIN ATTIT DRIVE RIGID/FLEX PWR WEALTH ...MGT NEW/IDEA MATH TIME/SEQ VAL/FREE 20. PAGE 48 A0984
NAT/G FOR/AID

S60
GARNICK D.H.,"ON THE ECONOMIC FEASIBILITY OF A MIDDLE EASTERN COMMON MARKET." AFR ISLAM CULTURE INDUS NAT/G PLAN TEC/DEV ECO/TAC ADMIN ATTIT DRIVE RIGID/FLEX...PLURIST STAT TREND GEN/LAWS 20. PAGE 51 A1051
MARKET INT/TRADE

S60
HAYTON R.D.,"THE ANTARCTIC SETTLEMENT OF 1959." FUT USA+45 WOR+45 WOR-45 STRUCT R+D INT/ORG EX/STRUC CREATE TEC/DEV LEGIT PEACE ATTIT SOVEREIGN
DELIB/GP JURID DIPLOM

...TIME/SEQ 20 TREATY IGY. PAGE 63 A1297 REGION

S60
KAPLAN M.A.,"THEORETICAL ANALYSIS OF THE BALANCE OF POWER." FUT USA+45 WOR+45 INTELL ECO/DEV INT/ORG NAT/G CONSULT TOP/EX ACT/RES PLAN TEC/DEV ATTIT ALL/VALS...METH/CNCPT TOT/POP 20. PAGE 76 A1562
CREATE NEW/IDEA DIPLOM NUC/PWR

S60
KISTIAKOWSKY G.B.,"SCIENCE AND FOREIGN AFFAIRS." FUT WOR+45 NAT/G PROF/ORG PLAN ECO/TAC EDU/PROP NUC/PWR...TREND COLD/WAR 20. PAGE 80 A1645
CONSULT TEC/DEV FOR/AID DIPLOM

S60
LEAR J.,"PEACE: SCIENCE'S NEXT GREAT EXPLORATION." USA+45 INT/ORG TOP/EX TEC/DEV EDU/PROP ROUTINE PEACE KNOWL SKILL 20. PAGE 86 A1757
EX/STRUC ARMS/CONT NUC/PWR

S60
MORGENSTERN O.,"GOAL: AN ARMED, INSPECTED, OPEN WORLD." COM EUR+WWI USA+45 R+D INT/ORG NAT/G TEC/DEV BAL/PWR COERCE NUC/PWR ORD/FREE PWR...TREND 20. PAGE 104 A2133
FORCES CONCPT ARMS/CONT DETER

S60
OWEN C.F.,"US AND SOVIET RELATIONS WITH UNDERDEVELOPED COUNTRIES: LATIN AMERICA-A CASE STUDY." AFR COM L/A+17C USA+45 USSR EXTR/IND MARKET TEC/DEV DIPLOM ECO/TAC NAT/LISM ORD/FREE PWR ...TREND WORK 20. PAGE 112 A2303
ECO/UNDEV DRIVE INT/TRADE

S60
RIVKIN A.,"AFRICAN ECONOMIC DEVELOPMENT: ADVANCED TECHNOLOGY AND THE STAGES OF GROWTH." CULTURE ECO/UNDEV AGRI COM/IND EXTR/IND PLAN ECO/TAC ATTIT DRIVE RIGID/FLEX SKILL WEALTH...MGT SOC GEN/LAWS WORK TOT/POP 20. PAGE 121 A2487
AFR TEC/DEV FOR/AID

S60
WRIGHT Q.,"LEGAL ASPECTS OF THE U-2 INCIDENT." COM USA+45 USSR STRUCT NAT/G FORCES PLAN TEC/DEV ADJUD RIGID/FLEX MORAL ORD/FREE...DECISION INT/LAW JURID PSY TREND GEN/LAWS COLD/WAR VAL/FREE 20 U-2. PAGE 168 A3413
PWR POLICY SPACE

N60
ERDMAN P.E.,COMMON MARKETS AND FREE TRADE AREAS (PAMPHLET). USA+45 MARKET INT/ORG TEC/DEV DIPLOM UTIL...CON/ANAL CHARTS BIBLIOG 20 EEC OEEC. PAGE 42 A0859
TREND PROB/SOLV INT/TRADE ECO/DEV

N60
INTERNATIONAL FEDN DOCUMENTTN,BIBLIOGRAPHY OF DIRECTORIES OF SOURCES OF INFORMATION (PAMPHLET). WOR+45 R+D INT/ORG NAT/G TEC/DEV DIPLOM. PAGE 71 A1456
BIBLIOG/A ECO/DEV ECO/UNDEV

B61
BONNEFOUS M.,EUROPE ET TIERS MONDE. EUR+WWI SOCIETY INT/ORG NAT/G VOL/ASSN ACT/RES TEC/DEV CAP/ISM ECO/TAC ATTIT ORD/FREE SOVEREIGN...POLICY CONCPT TREND 20. PAGE 16 A0334
AFR ECO/UNDEV FOR/AID INT/TRADE

B61
BULL H.,THE CONTROL OF THE ARMS RACE. COM USA+45 INT/ORG NAT/G PLAN TEC/DEV DIPLOM ATTIT...RELATIV DECISION CONCPT SELF/OBS TREND CON/ANAL GEN/METH 20 COLD/WAR. PAGE 21 A0429
FORCES PWR ARMS/CONT NUC/PWR

B61
DETHINE P.,BIBLIOGRAPHIE DES ASPECTS ECONOMIQUES ET SOCIAUX DE L'INDUSTRIALISATION EN AFRIQUE. AFR FINAN LABOR FOR/AID...SOC 20. PAGE 36 A0734
BIBLIOG/A ECO/UNDEV INDUS TEC/DEV

B61
FLEMING D.F.,THE COLD WAR AND ITS ORIGINS: 1950-1960 (VOL. II). ASIA FUT HUNGARY POLAND WOR+45 TEC/DEV DOMIN NUC/PWR REV PEACE...T 20 COLD/WAR EISNHWR/DD SUEZ. PAGE 46 A0946
MARXISM DIPLOM BAL/PWR

B61
FLEMING D.F.,THE COLD WAR AND ITS ORIGINS: 1917-1950 (VOL. I). ASIA USSR WOR+45 WOR-45 TEC/DEV FOR/AID NUC/PWR REV WAR PEACE FASCISM...T 20 COLD/WAR NATO BERLIN/BLO. PAGE 46 A0947
DIPLOM MARXISM BAL/PWR

B61
LERCHE C.O. JR.,FOREIGN POLICY OF THE AMERICAN PEOPLE (REV. ED.). USA+45 USSR FORCES TEC/DEV EDU/PROP WAR PRODUC ORD/FREE MARXISM...POLICY TREND BIBLIOG 20 COLD/WAR. PAGE 87 A1781
DECISION PLAN PEACE DIPLOM

B61
MEZERIK A.G.,ECONOMIC DEVELOPMENT AIDS FOR UNDERDEVELOPED COUNTRIES. WOR+45 FINAN LEGIS PROB/SOLV TEC/DEV DIPLOM FOR/AID GIVE TASK WAR 20 UN. PAGE 101 A2062
ECO/UNDEV INT/ORG WEALTH PLAN

B61
MILLIKAW M.F.,THE EMERGING NATIONS: THEIR GROWTH AND UNITED STATES POLICY. FUT USA+45 WOR+45 WOR-45 NAT/G PLAN TEC/DEV BAL/PWR GOV/REL PEACE ORD/FREE 20. PAGE 101 A2082
ECO/UNDEV POLICY DIPLOM FOR/AID

B61
MORLEY L.,THE PATCHWORK HISTORY OF FOREIGN AID. KOREA/S USA+45 USSR LAW FINAN INT/ORG TEC/DEV BAL/PWR GIVE 20 COLD/WAR NATO. PAGE 104 A2144
FOR/AID ECO/UNDEV FORCES DIPLOM

B61
ROBINS D.B.,EVOLVING UNITED STATES POLICIES TOWARD THE EMERGING NATIONS OF ASIA AND AFRICA (PAMPHLET).
AFR S/ASIA

ISLAM ECO/UNDEV INT/ORG CONSULT CREATE PLAN TEC/DEV FOR/AID CONFER ALL/VALS 20 KENNEDY/JF EISNHWR/DD UN AID. PAGE 122 A2501
DIPLOM BIBLIOG

B61
SCHELLING T.C.,STRATEGY AND ARMS CONTROL. FUT UNIV WOR+45 INT/ORG PLAN TEC/DEV BAL/PWR LEGIT PERCEPT HEALTH...CONCPT VAL/FREE 20. PAGE 128 A2623
ROUTINE POLICY ARMS/CONT

B61
SCHWARTZ H.,THE RED PHOENIX: RUSSIA SINCE WORLD WAR II. USA+45 WOR+45 ELITES POL/PAR TEC/DEV ECO/TAC MARXISM. PAGE 130 A2655
DIPLOM NAT/G ECO/DEV

B61
SHARP W.R.,FIELD ADMINISTRATION IN THE UNITED NATION SYSTEM: THE CONDUCT OF INTERNATIONAL ECONOMIC AND SOCIAL PROGRAMS. FUT WOR+45 CONSTN SOCIETY ECO/UNDEV R+D DELIB/GP ACT/RES PLAN TEC/DEV EDU/PROP EXEC ROUTINE HEALTH WEALTH...HUM CONCPT CHARTS METH ILO UNESCO VAL/FREE UN 20. PAGE 132 A2697
INT/ORG CONSULT

B61
US GENERAL ACCOUNTING OFFICE,EXAMINATION OF ECONOMIC AND TECHNICAL ASSISTANCE PROGRAM FOR IRAN. IRAN USA+45 AGRI INDUS DIPLOM CONTROL COST 20. PAGE 153 A3115
FOR/AID ADMIN TEC/DEV ECO/UNDEV

B61
WILLOUGHBY W.R.,THE ST LAWRENCE WATERWAY: A STUDY IN POLITICS AND DIPLOMACY. USA+45 ECO/DEV COM/IND INT/ORG CONSULT DELIB/GP ACT/RES TEC/DEV DIPLOM ECO/TAC ROUTINE...TIME/SEQ 20. PAGE 165 A3357
LEGIS INT/TRADE CANADA DIST/IND

B61
WRINCH P.,THE MILITARY STRATEGY OF WINSTON CHURCHILL. UK WOR-45 SEA VOL/ASSN TEC/DEV BAL/PWR LEAD WAR PEACE ATTIT...POLICY 20 CHURCHLL/W. PAGE 168 A3421
CIVMIL/REL FORCES PLAN DIPLOM

L61
WRIGHT Q.,"STUDIES IN DETERRENCE: LIMITED WARS AND THE ROLE OF SEABORNE WEAPONS SYSTEMS." FUT USA+45 WOR+45 SEA INT/ORG NAT/G FORCES ACT/RES WAR WEAPON ORD/FREE TOT/POP 20. PAGE 168 A3415
TEC/DEV SKILL BAL/PWR DETER

S61
"CRITERIA FOR ALLOCATING INVESTMENT RESOURCES AMONG VARIOUS FIELDS OF DEVELOPMENT IN UNDERDEVELOPED ECONOMIES." ASIA AGRI INT/ORG CAP/ISM BAL/PAY EFFICIENCY PROFIT WEALTH...STAT 20 UN. PAGE 3 A0061
BIBLIOG/A ECO/UNDEV PLAN TEC/DEV

S61
HAZARD J.N.,"CODIFYING PEACEFUL COEXISTANCE." FUT INTELL INT/ORG TEC/DEV PEACE HEALTH...INT/LAW CONT/OBS 20. PAGE 63 A1299
VOL/ASSN JURID

S61
HEILBRONER R.L.,"DYNAMICS OF FOREIGN AID: PROBLEMS OF UNDERDEVELOPED NATIONS PLAGUE ASSISTANCE PROGRAM." FUT USA+45 WOR+45 STRATA NAT/G PLAN TEC/DEV ATTIT DRIVE WEALTH WORK 20. PAGE 64 A1307
ECO/UNDEV ECO/TAC FOR/AID

S61
PADELFORD N.J.,"POLITICS AND THE FUTURE OF ECOSOC." AFR S/ASIA ECO/UNDEV INDUS NAT/G DELIB/GP ACT/RES ORD/FREE WEALTH...CONCPT CHARTS UN 20 ECOSOC. PAGE 113 A2310
INT/ORG TEC/DEV

B62
ROUND TABLE ON EUROPE'S ROLE IN LATIN AMERICAN DEVELOPMENT. EUR+WWI L/A+17C PLAN BAL/PAY UTIL ROLE WEALTH...CHARTS ANTHOL 20 UN INT/AM/DEV. PAGE 3 A0063
ECO/UNDEV FINAN TEC/DEV FOR/AID

B62
BEATON L.,THE SPREAD OF NUCLEAR WEAPONS. WOR+45 NAT/G PLAN PROB/SOLV DIPLOM ECO/TAC DETER...POLICY 20 COLD/WAR. PAGE 12 A0242
ARMS/CONT NUC/PWR TEC/DEV FUT

B62
BLACKETT P.M.S.,STUDIES OF WAR: NUCLEAR AND CONVENTIONAL. EUR+WWI USA+45 DELIB/GP ACT/RES CREATE PLAN TEC/DEV LEGIT COERCE WAR ORD/FREE PWR ...POLICY TECHNIC TIME/SEQ 20. PAGE 15 A0300
INT/ORG FORCES ARMS/CONT NUC/PWR

B62
COUNCIL ON WORLD TENSIONS,A STUDY OF WORLD TENSIONS AND DEVELOPMENT. WOR+45 ECO/DEV ECO/UNDEV INT/ORG PLAN DIPLOM ECO/TAC EDU/PROP ATTIT KNOWL ORD/FREE PWR WEALTH...CONCPT TREND CHARTS STERTYP COLD/WAR TOT/POP 20. PAGE 31 A0640
TEC/DEV SOC

B62
FAO,FOOD AND AGRICULTURE ORGANIZATION AFRICAN SURVEY. AFR CONGO/BRAZ GHANA STRATA AGRI INT/ORG TEC/DEV FOR/AID INT/TRADE RACE/REL DEMAND EFFICIENCY PRODUC...GEOG 20 UN CONGO/LEOP. PAGE 44 A0898
ECO/TAC WEALTH EXTR/IND ECO/UNDEV

B62
FRIEDMANN W.,METHODS AND POLICIES OF PRINCIPAL DONOR COUNTRIES IN PUBLIC INTERNATIONAL DEVELOPMENT FINANCING: PRELIMINARY APPRAISAL. FRANCE GERMANY/W UK USA+45 USSR WOR+45 FINAN TEC/DEV CAP/ISM DIPLOM ECO/TAC ATTIT 20 EEC. PAGE 49 A1002
INT/ORG FOR/AID NAT/COMP ADMIN

B62
FRIEDRICH-EBERT-STIFTUNG,THE SOVIET BLOC AND DEVELOPING COUNTRIES. CHINA/COM COM GERMANY/E USSR WOR+45 ECO/UNDEV INT/ORG NAT/G TEC/DEV NEUTRAL PWR ...POLICY 20. PAGE 49 A1008
MARXISM DIPLOM ECO/TAC FOR/AID

B62
GILPIN R.,AMERICAN SCIENTISTS AND NUCLEAR WEAPONS POLICY. COM FUT USA+45 WOR+45 INT/ORG NAT/G PROF/ORG CONSULT FORCES CREATE TEC/DEV BAL/PWR EDU/PROP ARMS/CONT WAR PERCEPT KNOWL MORAL PWR ...PHIL/SCI SOC CONCPT GEN/LAWS 20. PAGE 52 A1073
INTELL ATTIT DETER NUC/PWR

B62
HARARI M.,GOVERNMENT AND POLITICS OF THE MIDDLE EAST. ISLAM USA+45 NAT/G SECT CHIEF ADMIN ORD/FREE 20. PAGE 61 A1257
DIPLOM ECO/UNDEV TEC/DEV POLICY

B62
KAHN H.,THINKING ABOUT THE UNTHINKABLE. FUT USA+45 LAW NAT/G CONSULT FORCES ACT/RES CREATE PLAN TEC/DEV BAL/PWR DIPLOM EDU/PROP ARMS/CONT DETER ATTIT...CONCPT OBS TREND COLD/WAR 20. PAGE 76 A1547
INT/ORG ORD/FREE NUC/PWR PEACE

B62
KENNEDY J.F.,TO TURN THE TIDE. SPACE AGRI INT/ORG FORCES TEC/DEV ADMIN NUC/PWR PEACE WEALTH...ANTHOL 20 KENNEDY/JF CIV/RIGHTS. PAGE 78 A1592
DIPLOM CHIEF POLICY NAT/G

B62
LEFEVER E.W.,ARMS AND ARMS CONTROL. COM USA+45 INT/ORG TEC/DEV DIPLOM ORD/FREE 20. PAGE 86 A1763
ATTIT PWR ARMS/CONT BAL/PWR

B62
LEWIS J.P.,QUIET CRISIS IN INDIA. INDIA USA+45 CULTURE ECO/UNDEV AGRI INDUS PROC/MFG NAT/G PLAN TEC/DEV DRIVE PWR SKILL WEALTH...MYTH 20. PAGE 88 A1801
S/ASIA ECO/TAC FOR/AID

B62
MORGENSTERN O.,STRATEGIE - HEUTE (2ND ED.). USA+45 USSR ECO/DEV DELIB/GP WAR PEACE ORD/FREE...GOV/COMP NAT/COMP 20 COLD/WAR NATO. PAGE 104 A2134
NUC/PWR DIPLOM FORCES TEC/DEV

B62
RIMALOV V.V.,ECONOMIC COOPERATION BETWEEN USSR AND UNDERDEVELOPED COUNTRIES. USSR FINAN TEC/DEV INT/TRADE DOMIN EDU/PROP COLONIAL NAT/LISM DRIVE SOVEREIGN...AUD/VIS 20. PAGE 121 A2482
FOR/AID PLAN ECO/UNDEV DIPLOM

B62
ROBERTSON B.C.,REGIONAL DEVELOPMENT IN THE EUROPEAN ECONOMIC COMMUNITY. EUR+WWI FRANCE FUT ITALY UK ECO/UNDEV WORKER ACT/RES PROB/SOLV TEC/DEV ECO/TAC INT/TRADE EEC. PAGE 122 A2499
PLAN ECO/DEV INT/ORG REGION

B62
ROBINSON A.D.,DUTCH ORGANIZED AGRICULTURE IN INTERNATIONAL POLITICS, 1945-1960. EUR+WWI NETHERLAND STRUCT ECO/DEV NAT/G VOL/ASSN CONSULT DELIB/GP PLAN TEC/DEV INT/TRADE EDU/PROP ATTIT RIGID/FLEX ALL/VALS...NEW/IDEA TREND EEC 20. PAGE 122 A2502
AGRI INT/ORG

B62
SCHMITT H.A.,THE PATH TO EUROPEAN UNITY. EUR+WWI USA+45 PLAN TEC/DEV DIPLOM FOR/AID CONFER...INT/LAW 20 EEC EURCOALSTL MARSHL/PLN UNIFICA. PAGE 128 A2634
INT/ORG INT/TRADE REGION ECO/DEV

B62
SCHUMAN F.L.,THE COLD WAR: RETROSPECT AND PROSPECT. FUT USA+45 USSR WOR+45 BAL/PWR EDU/PROP ARMS/CONT ATTIT...MAJORIT IDEA/COMP ANTHOL BIBLIOG 20 COLD/WAR. PAGE 129 A2651
MARXISM TEC/DEV DIPLOM NUC/PWR

B62
SCHWARTZ L.E.,INTERNATIONAL ORGANIZATIONS AND SPACE COOPERATION. VOL/ASSN CONSULT CREATE TEC/DEV SANCTION...POLICY INT/LAW PHIL/SCI 20 UN. PAGE 130 A2656
INT/ORG DIPLOM R+D SPACE

B62
THANT U.,THE UNITED NATIONS' DEVELOPMENT DECADE: PROPOSALS FOR ACTION. WOR+45 SOCIETY ECO/UNDEV AGRI COM/IND FINAN R+D MUNIC SCHOOL VOL/ASSN CONSULT PLAN TEC/DEV ECO/TAC EDU/PROP ADMIN ROUTINE RIGID/FLEX...MGT SOC CONCPT UNESCO UN TOT/POP VAL/FREE. PAGE 142 A2906
INT/ORG ALL/VALS

B62
THOMSON G.P.,NUCLEAR ENERGY IN BRITAIN DURING THE LAST WAR: THE CHERWELL SIMON LECTURE (MONOGRAPH). UK R+D CONSULT FORCES PLAN DIPLOM TASK CIVMIL/REL ROLE...PHIL/SCI NEW/IDEA LAB/EXP 20 MAUD. PAGE 143 A2934
CREATE TEC/DEV WAR NUC/PWR

B62
UNECA LIBRARY,BOOKS ON AFRICA IN THE UNECA LIBRARY. WOR+45 AGRI INT/ORG NAT/G PLAN WRITING REGION...SOC STAT UN. PAGE 147 A3008
BIBLIOG AFR ECO/UNDEV TEC/DEV

B62
UNECA LIBRARY,NEW ACQUISITIONS IN THE UNECA LIBRARY. LAW NAT/G PLAN PROB/SOLV TEC/DEV ADMIN REGION...GEOG SOC 20 UN. PAGE 147 A3009
BIBLIOG AFR ECO/UNDEV INT/ORG

B62
US CONGRESS JOINT ECO COMM,ECONOMIC DEVELOPMENTS IN SOUTH AMERICA. USA+45 SOCIETY FINAN NAT/G PROB/SOLV TEC/DEV INT/TRADE TAX EFFICIENCY PRODUC ATTIT ...POLICY 20 CONGRESS SOUTH/AMER. PAGE 150 A3065
L/A+17C ECO/UNDEV FOR/AID DIPLOM

B62
US LIBRARY OF CONGRESS,UNITED STATES AND CANADIAN PUBLICATIONS ON AFRICA IN 1960. CANADA USA+45 CULTURE TEC/DEV DIPLOM FOR/AID RACE/REL...GEOG HUM SOC SOC/WK LING 20. PAGE 155 A3156
BIBLIOG/A AFR

B62
US SENATE COMM GOVT OPERATIONS,ADMINISTRATION OF NATIONAL SECURITY. USA+45 CHIEF PLAN PROB/SOLV TEC/DEV DIPLOM ATTIT...POLICY DECISION 20 KENNEDY/JF RUSK/D MCNAMARA/R BUNDY/M HERTER/C. PAGE 156 A3173
ORD/FREE ADMIN NAT/G CONTROL

B62
VIET J.,INTERNATIONAL COOPERATION AND PROGRAMMES OF ECONOMIC AND SOCIAL DEVELOPMENT. TEC/DEV FOR/AID DOMIN COLONIAL PEACE WEALTH 20 UNESCO. PAGE 159 A3232
BIBLIOG/A INT/ORG DIPLOM ECO/UNDEV

B62
WADSWORTH J.J.,THE PRICE OF PEACE. WOR+45 TEC/DEV CONTROL NUC/PWR PEACE ATTIT TREATY 20. PAGE 160 A3258
DIPLOM INT/ORG ARMS/CONT POLICY

L62
WILCOX F.O.,"THE UN AND THE NON-ALIGNED NATIONS." AFR S/ASIA USA+45 ECO/UNDEV INT/ORG TEC/DEV EDU/PROP RIGID/FLEX ORD/FREE PWR...POLICY HUM CONCPT STAT OBS TIME/SEQ STERTYP GEN/METH UN 20. PAGE 164 A3345
ATTIT TREND

S62
ALBONETTI A.,"IL SECONDO PROGRAMMA QUINQUENNALE 1963-67 ED IL BILANCIO RICERCHE ED INVESTIMENTI PER IL 1963 DELL'ERATOM." EUR+WWI FUT ITALY WOR+45 ECO/DEV SERV/IND INT/ORG TEC/DEV ECO/TAC ATTIT SKILL WEALTH...MGT TIME/SEQ OEEC 20. PAGE 5 A0108
R+D PLAN NUC/PWR

S62
BELSHAW C.,"TRAINING AND RECRUITMENT: SOME PRINCIPLES OF INTERNATIONAL AID." FUT WOR+45 SOCIETY INT/ORG NAT/G CREATE PLAN TEC/DEV ECO/TAC FOR/AID EDU/PROP ATTIT PERCEPT...HUM UN FAO ILO UNESCO 20. PAGE 13 A0263
VOL/ASSN ECO/UNDEV

S62
BROWN B.E.,"L'ONU ABANDONNE LA HONGRIE." COM USSR WOR+45 CONSTN NAT/G POL/PAR DELIB/GP ACT/RES TEC/DEV PWR...TIME/SEQ 20 UN. PAGE 20 A0400
INT/ORG TOTALISM HUNGARY POLICY

S62
FOSTER W.C.,"ARMS CONTROL AND DISARMAMENT IN A DIVIDED WORLD." COM FUT USA+45 USSR WOR+45 INTELL INT/ORG NAT/G VOL/ASSN CONSULT CREATE PLAN TEC/DEV EDU/PROP LEGIT NUC/PWR ATTIT RIGID/FLEX...CONCPT TREND TOT/POP 20 UN. PAGE 47 A0971
DELIB/GP POLICY ARMS/CONT DIPLOM

S62
NORTH R.C.,"DECISION MAKING IN CRISIS: AN INTRODUCTION." WOR+45 WOR-45 NAT/G CONSULT DELIB/GP TEC/DEV PERCEPT KNOWL...POLICY DECISION PSY METH/CNCPT CONT/OBS TREND VAL/FREE 20. PAGE 110 A2251
INT/ORG ROUTINE DIPLOM

S62
RUBINSTEIN A.Z.,"RUSSIA AND THE UNCOMMITTED NATIONS." AFR INDIA ISLAM L/A+17C LAOS S/ASIA ELITES ECO/UNDEV INT/ORG KIN CREATE PLAN TEC/DEV NAT/LISM RIGID/FLEX PWR WEALTH...METH/CNCPT TIME/SEQ GEN/LAWS WORK. PAGE 125 A2562
ECO/TAC TREND COLONIAL USSR

S62
RUSSETT B.M.,"CAUSE, SURPRISE, AND NO ESCAPE." FUT WOR-45 CULTURE SOCIETY INT/ORG FORCES TEC/DEV BAL/PWR EDU/PROP ARMS/CONT NUC/PWR WAR WEAPON PEACE KNOWL ORD/FREE PWR...POLICY CONCPT RECORD TIME/SEQ TREND GEN/LAWS 20 WWI. PAGE 126 A2578
COERCE DIPLOM

S62
SCHACHTER O.,"DAG HAMMARSKJOLD AND THE RELATION OF LAW TO POLITICS." FUT WOR+45 INT/ORG CONSULT PLAN TEC/DEV BAL/PWR DIPLOM LEGIT ATTIT PERCEPT ORD/FREE ...POLICY JURID CONCPT OBS TESTS STERTYP GEN/LAWS 20 HAMMARSK/D. PAGE 128 A2616
ACT/RES ADJUD

S62
SCHILLING W.R.,"SCIENTISTS, FOREIGN POLICY AND POLITICS." WOR+45 WOR-45 INTELL INT/ORG CONSULT TOP/EX ACT/RES PLAN ADMIN KNOWL...CONCPT OBS TREND LEAGUE/NAT 20. PAGE 128 A2627
NAT/G TEC/DEV DIPLOM NUC/PWR

S62
SINGER J.D.,"STABLE DETERRENCE AND ITS LIMITS." FUT WOR+45 R+D INT/ORG CONSULT ACT/RES TEC/DEV ARMS/CONT COERCE DRIVE PERCEPT RIGID/FLEX ORD/FREE PWR...MYTH SIMUL TOT/POP 20. PAGE 133 A2728
NAT/G FORCES DETER NUC/PWR

S62
TOWSTER J.,"THE USSR AND THE USA: CHALLENGE AND RESPONSE." COM GERMANY USA+45 USSR WOR+45 ECO/UNDEV INT/ORG VOL/ASSN EX/STRUC FORCES TOP/EX CREATE PLAN TEC/DEV DIPLOM ECO/TAC EDU/PROP COLONIAL COERCE PWR ...GEN/METH COLD/WAR 20 KENNEDY/JF. PAGE 145 A2956
ACT/RES GEN/LAWS

B63
BRITISH AID. UK AGRI DIST/IND INDUS SCHOOL TEC/DEV INT/TRADE COLONIAL DEMAND...TREND CHARTS 20. PAGE 3 A0064
FOR/AID ECO/UNDEV NAT/G FINAN

B63
CONF ON FUTURE OF COMMONWEALTH,THE FUTURE OF THE COMMONWEALTH. UK ECO/UNDEV AGRI EDU/PROP ADMIN SOC/INTEG 20 COMMONWLTH. PAGE 29 A0583
DIPLOM RACE/REL ORD/FREE TEC/DEV

B63
FISCHER-GALATI S.,EASTERN EUROPE IN THE SIXTIES. ALBANIA USSR YUGOSLAVIA ECO/UNDEV AGRI MARKET LABOR WORKER DIPLOM INT/TRADE EDU/PROP GOV/REL PRODUC UTOPIA SOCISM 20. PAGE 46 A0939
MARXISM TEC/DEV BAL/PWR ECO/TAC

B63
GORDON L.,A NEW DEAL FOR LATIN AMERICA. L/A+17C USA+45 CULTURE NAT/G TEC/DEV DIPLOM FOR/AID REGION TASK...POLICY 20 DEPT/STATE. PAGE 54 A1115
ECO/UNDEV ECO/TAC INT/ORG PLAN

B63
INTERAMERICAN ECO AND SOC COUN,THE ALLIANCE FOR PROGRESS: ITS FIRST YEAR: 1961-1962. AGRI SCHOOL PLAN TEC/DEV INT/TRADE TAX GIVE ADMIN WEALTH...SOC 20 SOUTH/AMER. PAGE 71 A1449
INT/ORG PROB/SOLV ECO/TAC L/A+17C

B63
INTERNATIONAL BANK RECONST DEV,THE WORLD BANK GROUP IN ASIA. ASIA S/ASIA INDUS TEC/DEV ECO/TAC...RECORD 20 IBRD WORLD/BANK. PAGE 71 A1451
INT/ORG DIPLOM ECO/UNDEV FINAN

B63
KATZ S.M.,A SELECTED LIST OF US READINGS ON DEVELOPMENT. AGRI COM/IND DIST/IND INDUS LABOR PLAN FOR/AID EDU/PROP HEALTH...POLICY SOC/WK 20. PAGE 77 A1571
BIBLIOG/A ECO/UNDEV TEC/DEV ACT/RES

B63
LERCHE C.O. JR.,CONCEPTS OF INTERNATIONAL POLITICS. WOR+45 WOR-45 LAW DELIB/GP EX/STRUC TEC/DEV ECO/TAC INT/TRADE LEGIT ROUTINE COERCE ATTIT ORD/FREE PWR RESPECT...STERTYP GEN/LAWS VAL/FREE. PAGE 87 A1782
INT/ORG WAR

B63
LUNDBERG F.,THE COMING WORLD TRANSFORMATION. CULTURE SOCIETY ECO/DEV INT/ORG NAT/G DIPLOM ECO/TAC EDU/PROP 15/21. PAGE 91 A1873
PREDICT FUT WOR+45 TEC/DEV

B63
MCDOUGAL M.S.,LAW AND PUBLIC ORDER IN SPACE. FUT USA+45 ACT/RES TEC/DEV ADJUD...POLICY INT/LAW JURID 20. PAGE 98 A2009
SPACE ORD/FREE DIPLOM DECISION

B63
MILLER W.J.,THE MEANING OF COMMUNISM. USSR SOCIETY ECO/DEV EX/STRUC WORKER TEC/DEV ADMIN TOTALISM ...POLICY CONCPT CHARTS BIBLIOG T 20 COLD/WAR LENIN/VI STALIN/J. PAGE 101 A2080
MARXISM TRADIT DIPLOM NAT/G

B63
NORTH R.C.,CONTENT ANALYSIS: A HANDBOOK WITH APPLICATIONS FOR THE STUDY OF INTERNATIONAL CRISIS. ASIA COM EUR+WWI MOD/EUR INT/ORG TEC/DEV DOMIN EDU/PROP ROUTINE COERCE PERCEPT RIGID/FLEX ALL/VALS ...QUANT TESTS CON/ANAL SIMUL GEN/LAWS VAL/FREE. PAGE 110 A2252
METH/CNCPT COMPUT/IR USSR

B63
OECD,SCIENCE AND THE POLICIES OF GOVERNMENTS: THE IMPLICATIONS OF SCIENCE AND TECHNOLOGY FOR NATL AND INTL AFFAIRS. WOR+45 INT/ORG EDU/PROP AUTOMAT ...POLICY PHIL/SCI 20. PAGE 111 A2279
CREATE TEC/DEV DIPLOM NAT/G

B63
RAO V.K.R.,FOREIGN AID AND INDIA'S ECONOMIC DEVELOPMENT. INDIA INT/ORG PROB/SOLV TEC/DEV ECO/TAC CONTROL WEALTH...TREND 20. PAGE 119 A2445
FOR/AID ECO/UNDEV RECEIVE DIPLOM

B63
SCHMELTZ G.W.,LA POLITIQUE MONDIALE CONTEMPORAINE. SOCIETY ECO/UNDEV INDUS INT/ORG NAT/G POL/PAR CONSULT DELIB/GP PLAN TEC/DEV ECO/TAC DOMIN EDU/PROP ROUTINE COERCE PERCEPT PERSON LOVE SKILL ...SOC RECORD TOT/POP. PAGE 128 A2629
WOR+45 COLONIAL

B63
SCHRADER R.,SCIENCE AND POLICY. WOR+45 ECO/DEV ECO/UNDEV R+D FORCES PLAN DIPLOM GOV/REL TECHRACY BIBLIOG. PAGE 129 A2644
TEC/DEV NAT/G POLICY ADMIN

B63
THEOBALD R.,FREE MEN AND FREE MARKETS. USA+45 USA-45 ECO/DEV NAT/G TEC/DEV DIPLOM INT/TRADE INCOME ORD/FREE WEALTH...TREND 19/20 KEYNES/JM. PAGE 143 A2915
CONCPT ECO/TAC CAP/ISM MARKET

B63
US AGENCY INTERNATIONAL DEV,US FOREIGN ASSISTANCE AND ASSISTANCE FROM INTERNATIONAL ORGANIZATIONS. USA+45 WOR+45 ECO/UNDEV AGRI NAT/G TEC/DEV BUDGET. PAGE 149 A3050
FOR/AID INT/ORG CHARTS STAT

B63
US ECON SURVEY TEAM INDONESIA,INDONESIA - PERSPECTIVE AND PROPOSALS FOR UNITED STATES ECONOMIC AID. INDONESIA AGRI MARKET TEC/DEV DIPLOM INT/TRADE EDU/PROP 20. PAGE 153 A3113
FOR/AID ECO/UNDEV PLAN INDUS

B63
US GOVERNMENT,REPORT TO INTER-AMERICAN ECONOMIC AND SOCIAL COUNCIL AT SECOND ANNUAL MEETING. L/A+17C USA+45 VOL/ASSN TEC/DEV DIPLOM TAX EATING EFFICIENCY HEALTH...STAT CHARTS 20 AID. PAGE 153 A3116
ECO/TAC FOR/AID FINAN PLAN

B63
VAN SLYCK P.,PEACE: THE CONTROL OF NATIONAL POWER. CUBA WOR+45 FINAN NAT/G FORCES PROB/SOLV TEC/DEV BAL/PWR ADMIN CONTROL ORD/FREE...POLICY INT/LAW UN COLD/WAR TREATY. PAGE 158 A3214
ARMS/CONT PEACE INT/ORG DIPLOM

B63
VOSS E.H.,NUCLEAR AMBUSH: THE TEST-BAN TRAP. WOR+45 COM/IND INT/ORG NAT/G DELIB/GP FORCES LEGIS TOP/EX ACT/RES DOMIN EDU/PROP LEGIT ROUTINE COERCE ATTIT PERCEPT RIGID/FLEX HEALTH MORAL ORD/FREE PWR. PAGE 160 A3255
TEC/DEV HIST/WRIT ARMS/CONT NUC/PWR

S63
ALEXANDER R.,"LATIN AMERICA AND THE COMMUNIST BLOC." ASIA COM CUBA L/A+17C USA+45 USSR NAT/G VOL/ASSN TEC/DEV FOR/AID LEGIT PWR WEALTH COLD/WAR 20. PAGE 6 A0112
ECO/UNDEV RECORD

S63
BOHN L.,"WHOSE NUCLEAR TEST: NON-PHYSICAL INSPECTION AND TEST BAN." WOR+45 R+D INT/ORG VOL/ASSN ORD/FREE...GEN/LAWS GEN/METH COLD/WAR 20. PAGE 16 A0331
ADJUD ARMS/CONT TEC/DEV NUC/PWR

S63
DAVEE R.,"POUR UN FONDS DE DEVELOPPEMENT SOCIAL." FUT WOR+45 INTELL SOCIETY ECO/DEV FINAN TEC/DEV ROUTINE WEALTH...TREND TOT/POP VAL/FREE UN 20. PAGE 34 A0684
INT/ORG SOC FOR/AID

S63
ETIENNE G.,"'LOIS OBJECTIVES' ET PROBLEMES DE DEVELOPPEMENT DANS LE CONTEXTE CHINE-URSS." ASIA CHINA/COM COM FUT STRUCT INT/ORG VOL/ASSN TOP/EX TEC/DEV ECO/TAC ATTIT RIGID/FLEX...GEOG MGT TIME/SEQ TOT/POP 20. PAGE 42 A0866
TOTALISM USSR

S63
ETZIONI A.,"EUROPEAN UNIFICATION AND PERSPECTIVES ON SOVEREIGNTY." EUR+WWI FUT DELIB/GP TEC/DEV ECO/TAC EDU/PROP DETER NUC/PWR ATTIT DRIVE ORD/FREE PWR WEALTH...CONCPT RECORD TIME/SEQ EEC VAL/FREE 20. PAGE 43 A0870
INT/ORG ECO/DEV SOVEREIGN

S63
GANDILHON J.,"LA SCIENCE ET LA TECHNIQUE A L'AIDE DES REGIONS PEU DEVELOPPEES." FRANCE FUT WOR+45 ECO/DEV R+D PROF/ORG ACT/RES PLAN...MGT TOT/POP VAL/FREE 20 UN. PAGE 51 A1037
ECO/UNDEV TEC/DEV FOR/AID

S63
HORVATH J.,"MOSCOW'S AID PROGRAM: THE PERFORMANCE SO FAR." COM FUT USSR WOR+45 ECO/DEV FINAN PLAN TEC/DEV FOR/AID EDU/PROP ATTIT ORD/FREE PWR WEALTH ...POLICY STAT CHARTS VAL/FREE 20. PAGE 68 A1389
ECO/UNDEV ECO/TAC

S63
KAWALKOWSKI A.,"POUR UNE EUROPE INDEPENDENTE ET REUNIFIEE." EUR+WWI FUT USA+45 USSR WOR+45 ECO/DEV PROC/MFG INT/ORG NAT/G ACT/RES TEC/DEV FEDERAL RIGID/FLEX...CONCPT METH/CNCPT OEEC TOT/POP 20 DEGAULLE/C. PAGE 77 A1573
R+D PLAN NUC/PWR

S63
KRAVIS I.B.,"THE POLITICAL ARITHMETIC OF INTERNATIONAL BURDENSHARING." FUT USA+45 WOR+45 FINAN DELIB/GP ACT/RES CREATE TEC/DEV ATTIT PWR WEALTH...POLICY MATH STAT VAL/FREE 20. PAGE 82 A1681
INT/ORG ECO/TAC

S63
LEDUC G.,"L'AIDE INTERNATIONALE AU DEVELOPPEMENT." FUT WOR+45 ECO/DEV ECO/UNDEV R+D PROF/ORG TEC/DEV ECO/TAC ROUTINE ATTIT ALL/VALS...MGT TIME/SEQ TOT/POP 20. PAGE 86 A1758
FINAN PLAN FOR/AID

S63
NADLER E.B.,"SOME ECONOMIC DISADVANTAGES OF THE ARMS RACE." USA+45 INDUS R+D FORCES PLAN TEC/DEV ECO/TAC FOR/AID EDU/PROP PWR WEALTH...TREND COLD/WAR 20. PAGE 107 A2190
ECO/DEV MGT BAL/PAY

S63
ROUGEMONT D.,"LES NOUVELLES CHANCES DE L'EUROPE." EUR+WWI FUT ECO/DEV INT/ORG NAT/G ACT/RES PLAN TEC/DEV EDU/PROP ADMIN COLONIAL FEDERAL ATTIT PWR SKILL...TREND 20. PAGE 124 A2549
ECO/UNDEV PERCEPT

S63
WELLS H.,"THE OAS AND THE DOMINICAN ELECTIONS." L/A+17C INT/ORG NAT/G POL/PAR TEC/DEV ECO/TAC EDU/PROP PERCEPT...TIME/SEQ OAS TOT/POP 20. PAGE 163 A3317
CONSULT CHOOSE DOMIN/REP

S63
WOLFERS A.,"INTEGRATION IN THE WEST: THE CONFLICT OF PERSPECTIVES." EUR+WWI USA+45 ECO/DEV INT/ORG DELIB/GP CREATE TEC/DEV DIPLOM ATTIT PWR...CONCPT HIST/WRIT TREND GEN/LAWS COLD/WAR EEC 20. PAGE 166 A3386
RIGID/FLEX ECO/TAC

S63
WRIGHT Q.,"DECLINE OF CLASSIC DIPLOMACY." CHRIST-17C EUR+WWI MOD/EUR WOR+45 WOR-45 INT/ORG NAT/G DELIB/GP BAL/PWR ATTIT PWR...HIST/WRIT LEAGUE/NAT. PAGE 168 A3418
TEC/DEV CONCPT DIPLOM

N63
PATEL H.M.,THE DEFENCE OF INDIA (PAMPHLET).
FORCES

CHINA/COM INDIA PAKISTAN WOR+45 TEC/DEV BAL/PWR DIPLOM CONTROL WAR. PAGE 114 A2340 — POLICY SOVEREIGN DETER

B64
AMERICAN ASSEMBLY,THE UNITED STATES AND THE MIDDLE EAST. ISRAEL USA+45 STRUCT ECO/DEV ECO/UNDEV INT/ORG NAT/G SCHOOL SECT VOL/ASSN EX/STRUC TEC/DEV NAT/LISM...SOC 20. PAGE 7 A0135 — ISLAM DRIVE REGION

B64
APTER D.E.,IDEOLOGY AND DISCONTENT. FUT WOR+45 CONSTN CULTURE INTELL SOCIETY STRUCT INT/ORG NAT/G DELIB/GP LEGIS CREATE PLAN TEC/DEV EDU/PROP EXEC PERCEPT PERSON RIGID/FLEX ALL/VALS...POLICY TOT/POP. PAGE 8 A0171 — ACT/RES ATTIT

B64
ARNOLD G.,TOWARDS PEACE AND A MULTIRACIAL COMMONWEALTH. UK TEC/DEV BAL/PWR COLONIAL GP/REL NAT/LISM PEACE SOVEREIGN...POLICY SOC/INTEG 20 CMN/WLTH. PAGE 9 A0175 — DIPLOM INT/TRADE FOR/AID ORD/FREE

B64
CALDER R.,TWO-WAY PASSAGE. INT/ORG TEC/DEV WAR PERSON ORD/FREE 20. PAGE 23 A0467 — FOR/AID ECO/UNDEV ECO/TAC DIPLOM

B64
CASEY R.G.,THE FUTURE OF THE COMMONWEALTH. INDIA PAKISTAN UK ECO/UNDEV INT/ORG TEC/DEV COLONIAL SUPEGO 20 EEC AUSTRAL. PAGE 25 A0505 — DIPLOM SOVEREIGN NAT/LISM FOR/AID

B64
CEPEDE M.,POPULATION AND FOOD. USA+45 STRUCT ECO/UNDEV FAM PLAN TEC/DEV FOR/AID CONTROL...CATH SOC TREND 19/20. PAGE 25 A0513 — FUT GEOG AGRI CENSUS

B64
CHENG C.,ECONOMIC RELATIONS BETWEEN PEKING AND MOSCOW: 1949-63. ASIA CHINA/COM COM USSR FINAN INDUS CONSULT TEC/DEV INT/TRADE...PREDICT CHARTS BIBLIOG 20. PAGE 26 A0527 — DIPLOM FOR/AID MARXISM

B64
COLUMBIA U SCHOOL OF LAW,PUBLIC INTERNATIONAL DEVELOPMENT FINANCING IN INDIA. GERMANY/W INDIA UK USA+45 INDUS PLAN TEC/DEV DIPLOM ECO/TAC GIVE ADMIN UTIL ATTIT 20. PAGE 28 A0572 — ECO/UNDEV FINAN FOR/AID INT/ORG

B64
DEITCHMAN S.J.,LIMITED WAR AND AMERICAN DEFENSE POLICY. USA+45 WOR+45 INT/ORG NAT/G PLAN TEC/DEV COERCE NUC/PWR RIGID/FLEX PWR SKILL...DECISION METH/CNCPT TIME/SEQ TOT/POP COLD/WAR 20. PAGE 36 A0726 — FORCES WAR WEAPON

B64
DESHMUKH C.D.,THE COMMONWEALTH AS INDIA SEES IT. INDIA UK ECO/UNDEV TEC/DEV INT/TRADE GP/REL RACE/REL SOVEREIGN SOC/INTEG 19/20 COMMONWLTH. PAGE 36 A0733 — DIPLOM COLONIAL NAT/LISM ATTIT

B64
DEUTSCHE GES AUSWARTIGE POL,STRATEGIE UND ABRUSTUNGSPOLITIK DER SOWJETUNION. USSR TEC/DEV DIPLOM COERCE DETER WEAPON...POLICY PSY 20 ABM/DEFSYS. PAGE 37 A0747 — NUC/PWR WAR FORCES ARMS/CONT

B64
ETZIONI A.,WINNING WITHOUT WAR. FUT MOD/EUR USA+45 WOR+45 ECO/DEV ECO/UNDEV INT/ORG NAT/G FORCES TOP/EX PLAN TEC/DEV ECO/TAC DOMIN EDU/PROP LEGIT COERCE CHOOSE ATTIT MORAL ORD/FREE RESPECT WEALTH MAJORIT. PAGE 43 A0871 — PWR TREND DIPLOM USSR

B64
FEIS H.,FOREIGN AID AND FOREIGN POLICY. USA+45 WOR+45 NAT/G VOL/ASSN ACT/RES TEC/DEV ATTIT HEALTH WEALTH...SOC GEN/LAWS 20. PAGE 45 A0912 — ECO/UNDEV ECO/TAC FOR/AID DIPLOM

B64
GOWING M.,BRITAIN AND ATOMIC ENERGY 1939-1945. FRANCE UK USA+45 USA-45 NAT/G CREATE...PHIL/SCI 20 AEA. PAGE 54 A1118 — NUC/PWR DIPLOM TEC/DEV

B64
GRODZINS M.,THE ATOMIC AGE: FORTY-FIVE SCIENTISTS AND SCHOLARS SPEAK ON NATIONAL AND WORLD AFFAIRS. FUT USA+45 WOR+45 R+D INT/ORG NAT/G CONSULT TEC/DEV EDU/PROP ATTIT PERSON ORD/FREE...HUM CONCPT TIME/SEQ CON/ANAL. PAGE 57 A1169 — INTELL ARMS/CONT NUC/PWR

B64
HAZLEWOOD A.,THE ECONOMICS OF DEVELOPMENT: AN ANNOTATED LIST OF BOOKS AND ARTICLES PUBLISHED 1958-1962. AGRI FINAN INDUS LABOR NAT/G DIPLOM INT/TRADE INCOME...MGT 20. PAGE 63 A1303 — BIBLIOG/A ECO/UNDEV TEC/DEV

B64
HEKHUIS D.J.,INTERNATIONAL STABILITY: MILITARY, ECONOMIC AND POLITICAL DIMENSIONS. FUT WOR+45 LAW ECO/UNDEV INT/ORG NAT/G VOL/ASSN FORCES ACT/RES BAL/PWR PWR WEALTH...STAT UN 20. PAGE 64 A1310 — TEC/DEV DETER REGION

B64
JOHNSON E.A.J.,THE DIMENSIONS OF DIPLOMACY. INT/ORG FORCES TEC/DEV WAR PEACE PWR...SOC ANTHOL 20. PAGE 74 A1522 — DIPLOM POLICY METH

B64
KENNEDY J.F.,THE BURDEN AND THE GLORY. FUT USA+45 TEC/DEV ECO/TAC EDU/PROP ARMS/CONT MURDER RACE/REL PEACE...ANTHOL 20 KENNEDY/JF COLD/WAR NATO PRESIDENT. PAGE 78 A1593 — ADMIN POLICY GOV/REL DIPLOM

B64
LITTLE I.M.D.,AID TO AFRICA. AFR UK TEC/DEV DIPLOM ECO/TAC INCOME WEALTH 20. PAGE 90 A1844 — FOR/AID ECO/UNDEV ADMIN POLICY

B64
NASA,PROCEEDINGS OF CONFERENCE ON THE LAW OF SPACE AND OF SATELLITE COMMUNICATIONS: CHICAGO 1963. FUT WOR+45 DELIB/GP PROB/SOLV TEC/DEV CONFER ADJUD NUC/PWR...POLICY IDEA/COMP 20 NASA. PAGE 107 A2197 — SPACE COM/IND LAW DIPLOM

B64
OECD,DEVELOPMENT ASSISTANCE EFFORTS - POLICIES OF THE MEMBERS. AGRI INDUS BUDGET...GEOG NAT/COMP 20 OECD. PAGE 111 A2280 — INT/ORG FOR/AID ECO/UNDEV TEC/DEV

B64
OWEN W.,STRATEGY FOR MOBILITY. FUT WOR+45 WOR-45 DIST/IND INT/ORG NAT/G DELIB/GP PLAN TEC/DEV ECO/TAC ORD/FREE PWR WEALTH...STAT TIME/SEQ VAL/FREE 20. PAGE 112 A2304 — COM/IND ECO/UNDEV

B64
RAMAZANI R.K.,THE MIDDLE EAST AND THE EUROPEAN COMMON MARKET. EUR+WWI ISLAM ECO/DEV EXTR/IND MARKET PROC/MFG INT/ORG NAT/G TEC/DEV ECO/TAC REGION DRIVE WEALTH...STAT CHARTS EEC TOT/POP 20. PAGE 119 A2437 — ECO/UNDEV ATTIT INT/TRADE

B64
RANIS G.,THE UNITED STATES AND THE DEVELOPING ECONOMIES. COM USA+45 AGRI FINAN TEC/DEV CAP/ISM ECO/TAC INT/TRADE...POLICY METH/COMP ANTHOL 20 AID. PAGE 119 A2441 — ECO/UNDEV DIPLOM FOR/AID

B64
RIVKIN A.,AFRICA AND THE EUROPEAN COMMON MARKET (PAMPHLET). AFR MOD/EUR WOR+45 TEC/DEV FOR/AID TARIFFS BAL/PAY...POLICY 20 EEC. PAGE 121 A2490 — INT/ORG INT/TRADE ECO/TAC ECO/UNDEV

B64
ROCK V.P.,A STRATEGY OF INTERDEPENDENCE. COM USSR WOR+45 NAT/G FORCES PROB/SOLV TEC/DEV DETER WAR ORD/FREE...CONCPT NEW/IDEA METH/COMP 20. PAGE 122 A2509 — DIPLOM NUC/PWR PEACE POLICY

B64
ROSECRANCE R.N.,THE DISPERSION OF NUCLEAR WEAPONS: STRATEGY AND POLITICS. ASIA COM FUT S/ASIA USA+45 INT/ORG NAT/G DELIB/GP FORCES ACT/RES TEC/DEV BAL/PWR COERCE DETER ATTIT RIGID/FLEX ORD/FREE ...POLICY CHARTS VAL/FREE. PAGE 123 A2530 — EUR+WWI PWR PEACE

B64
RUBIN J.A.,YOUR HUNDRED BILLION DOLLARS. USA+45 USSR INDUS INT/ORG TEC/DEV ECO/TAC...METH/COMP 20 PEACE/CORP. PAGE 125 A2559 — FOR/AID DIPLOM ECO/UNDEV

B64
SCHWARTZ M.D.,CONFERENCE ON SPACE SCIENCE AND SPACE LAW. FUT COM/IND NAT/G FORCES ACT/RES PLAN BUDGET DIPLOM NUC/PWR WEAPON...POLICY ANTHOL 20. PAGE 130 A2658 — SPACE LAW PEACE TEC/DEV

B64
TAUBENFELD H.J.,SPACE AND SOCIETY. USA+45 LAW FORCES CREATE TEC/DEV ADJUD CONTROL COST PEACE ...PREDICT ANTHOL 20. PAGE 142 A2895 — SPACE SOCIETY ADJUST DIPLOM

B64
THANT U.,TOWARD WORLD PEACE. DELIB/GP TEC/DEV EDU/PROP WAR SOVEREIGN...INT/LAW 20 UN MID/EAST. PAGE 142 A2907 — DIPLOM BIOG PEACE COERCE

B64
UNESCO,WORLD COMMUNICATIONS: PRESS, RADIO, TELEVISION, FILM (4TH ED.). WOR+45 DIPLOM TV PEACE ...NAT/COMP SOC/INTEG 20 FILM. PAGE 148 A3023 — COM/IND EDU/PROP PRESS TEC/DEV

B64
US AGENCY INTERNATIONAL DEV,REPORT TO CONGRESS ON THE FOREIGN ASSISTANCE PROGRAM. AFR ASIA L/A+17C USA+45 INT/ORG VOL/ASSN FORCES CAP/ISM ADMIN WEAPON. PAGE 149 A3052 — FOR/AID ECO/UNDEV TEC/DEV BUDGET

B64
US HOUSE COMM FOREIGN AFFAIRS,HEARINGS ON H.R. 10502 TO AMEND FURTHER THE FOREIGN ASSISTANCE ACT OF 1961. AFR ASIA L/A+17C INT/ORG CONSULT DELIB/GP TEC/DEV ECO/TAC EDU/PROP CONFER 20 UN NATO CONGRESS AID. PAGE 153 A3130 — FOR/AID DIPLOM ORD/FREE ECO/UNDEV

B64
ZEBOT C.A.,THE ECONOMICS OF COMPETITIVE COEXISTENCE. CHINA/COM USSR WOR+45 FINAN MARKET FOR/AID PRICE DEMAND EQUILIB WEALTH ALL/IDEOS 20. PAGE 169 A3450 — TEC/DEV DIPLOM METH/COMP

L64
CARNEGIE ENDOWMENT INT. PEACE,"POLITICAL QUESTIONS (ISSUES BEFORE THE NINETEENTH GENERAL ASSEMBLY)." SPACE WOR+45 CONSTN FINAN NAT/G CONSULT DELIB/GP — INT/ORG PEACE

FORCES LEGIS TEC/DEV EDU/PROP LEGIT ARMS/CONT COERCE NUC/PWR ATTIT ALL/VALS...CONCPT OBS UN COLD/WAR 20. PAGE 24 A0490

L64
CARNEGIE ENDOWMENT INT. PEACE,"ECONOMIC AND SOCIAL QUESTION (ISSUES BEFORE THE NINETEENTH GENERAL ASSEMBLY)." WOR+45 ECO/DEV ECO/UNDEV INDUS R+D DELIB/GP CREATE PLAN TEC/DEV ECO/TAC FOR/AID BAL/PAY...RECORD UN 20. PAGE 24 A0493
INT/ORG INT/TRADE

S64
GARMARNIKOW M.,"INFLUENCE-BUYING IN WEST AFRICA." COM FUT USSR INTELL NAT/G PLAN TEC/DEV ECO/TAC DOMIN EDU/PROP REGION NAT/LISM ATTIT DRIVE ALL/VALS SOVEREIGN...POLICY PSY SOC CONCPT TREND STERTYP WORK COLD/WAR 20. PAGE 51 A1049
AFR ECO/UNDEV FOR/AID SOCISM

S64
HUELIN D.,"ECONOMIC INTEGRATION IN LATIN AMERICAN: PROGRESS AND PROBLEMS." L/A+17C ECO/DEV AGRI DIST/IND FINAN INDUS NAT/G VOL/ASSN CONSULT DELIB/GP EX/STRUC ACT/RES PLAN TEC/DEV ECO/TAC ROUTINE BAL/PAY WEALTH WORK 20. PAGE 69 A1411
MARKET ECO/UNDEV INT/TRADE

S64
SAAB H.,"THE ARAB SEARCH FOR A FEDERAL UNION." SOCIETY INT/ORG NAT/G DELIB/GP FORCES ACT/RES TEC/DEV ECO/TAC DOMIN LEGIT REGION ROUTINE ATTIT DRIVE RIGID/FLEX ALL/VALS...SOC CONCPT NEW/IDEA TIME/SEQ TREND. PAGE 126 A2580
ISLAM PLAN

S64
TINKER H.,"POLITICS IN SOUTHEAST ASIA." INT/ORG NAT/G CREATE PLAN TEC/DEV GUERRILLA KNOWL ORD/FREE COLD/WAR. PAGE 144 A2944
S/ASIA ACT/RES REGION

S64
TRISKA J.F.,"SOVIET TREATY LAW: A QUANTITATIVE ANALYSIS." WOR+45 LAW ECO/UNDEV AGRI COM/IND INDUS CREATE TEC/DEV DIPLOM ATTIT PWR WEALTH...JURID SAMP TIME/SEQ TREND CHARTS VAL/FREE 20 TREATY. PAGE 145 A2967
COM ECO/TAC INT/LAW USSR

C64
SCHRAMM W.,"MASS MEDIA AND NATIONAL DEVELOPMENT: THE ROLE OF INFORMATION IN DEVELOPING COUNTRIES." FINAN R+D ACT/RES PLAN TEC/DEV DIPLOM CHOOSE SUPEGO ORD/FREE...BIBLIOG 20. PAGE 129 A2645
ECO/UNDEV COM/IND EDU/PROP MAJORIT

B65
WHITE HOUSE CONFERENCE ON INTERNATIONAL COOPERATION(VOL.II). SPACE WOR+45 EXTR/IND INT/ORG LABOR WORKER NUC/PWR PEACE AGE/Y...CENSUS ANTHOL 20 RESOURCE/N URBAN/RNWL PUB/TRANS. PAGE 3 A0071
R+D CONFER TEC/DEV DIPLOM

B65
PEACE RESEARCH ABSTRACTS. FUT WOR+45 R+D INT/ORG NAT/G PLAN TEC/DEV BAL/PWR DIPLOM FOR/AID NUC/PWR HEALTH. PAGE 4 A0072
BIBLIOG/A PEACE ARMS/CONT WAR

B65
DOMENACH J.M.,LA PROPAGANDE POLITIQUE. COM/IND INT/ORG POL/PAR DOMIN RIGID/FLEX FASCISM MARXISM ...PSY 20. PAGE 38 A0770
ATTIT EDU/PROP TEC/DEV MYTH

B65
FRANKLAND N.,THE BOMBING OFFENSIVE AGAINST GERMANY. GERMANY UK TEC/DEV DIPLOM WAR...METH/COMP 20. PAGE 48 A0985
WEAPON PLAN DECISION FORCES

B65
FRUTKIN A.W.,SPACE AND THE INTERNATIONAL COOPERATION YEAR: A NATIONAL CHALLENGE (PAMPHLET). EUR+WWI USA+45 FINAN TEC/DEV BUDGET...MGT 20 NASA. PAGE 49 A1011
SPACE INDUS NAT/G DIPLOM

B65
HAGRAS K.M.,UNITED NATIONS CONFERENCE ON TRADE AND DEVELOPMENT: A CASE STUDY OF UN DIPLOMACY. CONSULT ACT/RES TEC/DEV FOR/AID INT/TRADE...BIBLIOG 20 UN LEAGUE/NAT UNCTAD. PAGE 59 A1213
INT/ORG ADMIN DELIB/GP DIPLOM

B65
HART B.H.L.,THE MEMOIRS OF CAPTAIN LIDDELL HART (VOL. I). UK NAT/G PLAN TEC/DEV DIPLOM ADMIN WEAPON GOV/REL PERS/REL ATTIT PWR FASCISM...POLICY 20. PAGE 62 A1274
FORCES BIOG LEAD WAR

B65
HASSON J.A.,THE ECONOMICS OF NUCLEAR POWER. INDIA UK USA+45 WOR+45 INT/ORG TEC/DEV COST...SOC STAT CHARTS 20 EURATOM. PAGE 63 A1286
NUC/PWR INDUS ECO/DEV METH

B65
LYONS G.M.,AMERICA: PURPOSE AND POWER. UK USA+45 FINAN INDUS MARKET WORKER TEC/DEV DIPLOM AUTOMAT NUC/PWR WAR RACE/REL ORD/FREE 20 EEC CONGRESS SUPREME/CT CIV/RIGHTS. PAGE 92 A1881
PWR PROB/SOLV ECO/DEV TASK

B65
MONCRIEFF A.,SECOND THOUGHTS ON AID. WOR+45 ECO/UNDEV AGRI FINAN VOL/ASSN PLAN TEC/DEV GIVE EDU/PROP ROLE WEALTH 20. PAGE 102 A2105
FOR/AID ECO/TAC INT/ORG IDEA/COMP

B65
MOWRY G.E.,THE URBAN NATION 1920-1960. USA+45 USA-45 SOCIETY ECO/DEV MUNIC FOR/AID INT/TRADE AUTOMAT...BIBLIOG/A 20. PAGE 105 A2161
TEC/DEV NAT/G TOTALISM

DIPLOM

B65
MURUMBI J.,PROBLEMS OF ECONOMIC DEVELOPMENT IN EAST AFRICA. FINAN INDUS WORKER TEC/DEV INT/TRADE TAX DEMAND EFFICIENCY PRODUC SOCISM...TREND CHARTS 20 AFRICA/E. PAGE 106 A2184
AGRI ECO/TAC ECO/UNDEV PROC/MFG

B65
PENNICK JL J.R.,THE POLITICS OF AMERICAN SCIENCE, 1939 TO THE PRESENT. USA+45 USA-45 INTELL TEC/DEV DIPLOM NEW/LIB...ANTHOL 20 COLD/WAR. PAGE 114 A2349
POLICY ADMIN PHIL/SCI NAT/G

B65
REQUA E.G.,THE DEVELOPING NATIONS: A GUIDE TO INFORMATION SOURCES CONCERNING THEIR ECON, POLIT, TECHNICAL, AND SOCIAL PROBLEMS. AFR ASIA ISLAM L/A+17C INDUS INT/ORG CONSULT PLAN PROB/SOLV...SOC 20 UN. PAGE 120 A2466
BIBLIOG/A ECO/UNDEV FOR/AID TEC/DEV

B65
SULZBERGER C.L.,UNFINISHED REVOLUTION. USA+45 WOR+45 INT/ORG TEC/DEV BAL/PWR FOR/AID COLONIAL NEUTRAL PWR SOVEREIGN MARXISM 20. PAGE 140 A2863
DIPLOM ECO/UNDEV POLICY NAT/G

B65
THAYER F.C. JR.,AIR TRANSPORT POLICY AND NATIONAL SECURITY: A POLITICAL, ECONOMIC, AND MILITARY ANALYSIS. DIST/IND OP/RES PLAN TEC/DEV DIPLOM DETER WAR COST EFFICIENCY...POLICY BIBLIOG 20 DEPT/DEFEN FAA CAB. PAGE 142 A2908
AIR FORCES CIVMIL/REL ORD/FREE

B65
UN,SPACE ACTIVITIES AND RESOURCES: REVIEW OF UNITED NATION'S NATIONAL AND INTERNATIONAL PROGRAMS. INT/ORG LABOR PLAN TEC/DEV DIPLOM EFFICIENCY HEALTH ...GOV/COMP 20 UN. PAGE 146 A2995
SPACE NUC/PWR FOR/AID PEACE

B65
UNESCO,HANDBOOK OF INTERNATIONAL EXCHANGES. COM/IND R+D ACADEM PROF/ORG VOL/ASSN CREATE TEC/DEV EDU/PROP AGREE 20 TREATY. PAGE 148 A3025
INDEX INT/ORG DIPLOM PRESS

B65
US HOUSE COMM FOREIGN AFFAIRS,HEARINGS ON DRAFT BILL TO AMEND FURTHER THE FOREIGN ASSISTANCE ACT OF 1961. AFR ASIA L/A+17C USA+45 INT/ORG DELIB/GP TEC/DEV ECO/TAC CONFER TOTALISM 20 CONGRESS AID. PAGE 153 A3131
FOR/AID ECO/UNDEV DIPLOM ORD/FREE

B65
US SENATE COMM AERO SPACE SCI,INTERNATIONAL COOPERATION AND ORGANIZATION FOR OUTER SPACE. FUT USA+45 WOR+45 PROF/ORG VOL/ASSN CONSULT DELIB/GP PLAN TEC/DEV ARMS/CONT GP/REL PEACE 20 UN NASA. PAGE 155 A3167
DIPLOM SPACE R+D NAT/G

B65
US SENATE COMM ON FOREIGN REL,HEARINGS ON THE FOREIGN ASSISTANCE PROGRAM. AFR ASIA L/A+17C USA+45 WOR+45 FORCES TEC/DEV BUDGET CONTROL WEAPON ORD/FREE 20 UN CONGRESS SEC/STATE. PAGE 156 A3183
FOR/AID DIPLOM INT/ORG ECO/UNDEV

B65
WEIL G.L.,A HANDBOOK ON THE EUROPEAN ECONOMIC COMMUNITY. BELGIUM EUR+WWI FRANCE GERMANY/W ITALY CONSTN ECO/DEV CREATE PARTIC GP/REL...DECISION MGT CHARTS 20 EEC. PAGE 162 A3299
INT/TRADE INT/ORG TEC/DEV INT/LAW

B65
WEISNER J.B.,WHERE SCIENCE AND POLITICS MEET. USA+45 ECO/DEV R+D FORCES PROB/SOLV DIPLOM FOR/AID CONTROL...PHIL/SCI PRESIDENT KENNEDY/JF JOHNSON/LB. PAGE 163 A3310
CHIEF NAT/G POLICY TEC/DEV

B65
WHITE J.,GERMAN AID. GERMANY/W FINAN PLAN TEC/DEV INT/TRADE ADMIN ATTIT...POLICY 20. PAGE 164 A3335
FOR/AID ECO/UNDEV DIPLOM ECO/TAC

L65
MATTHEWS D.G.,"A CURRENT BIBLIOGRAPHY ON SUDANESE AFFAIRS; A SELECT BIBLIOGRAPHY FROM 1960-1964." SUDAN LAW CULTURE AGRI FINAN INDUS LABOR POL/PAR TEC/DEV FOR/AID RACE/REL LITERACY...LING 20. PAGE 96 A1970
BIBLIOG ECO/UNDEV NAT/G DIPLOM

L65
MATTHEWS D.G.,"LE TIERS MONDE: A SELECT AND PRELIMINARY BIBLIOGRAPHIC SURVEY OF MANPOWER IN DEVELOPING COUNTRIES, 1960-1964." AFR ISLAM L/A+17C INDUS PLAN PROB/SOLV TEC/DEV INT/TRADE EFFICIENCY WEALTH...STAT 20. PAGE 96 A1971
BIBLIOG/A ECO/UNDEV LABOR WORKER

L65
WIONCZEK M.,"LATIN AMERICA FREE TRADE ASSOCIATION." AGRI DIST/IND FINAN INDUS INT/ORG LABOR NAT/G TEC/DEV ECO/TAC HEALTH SKILL WEALTH...POLICY RELATIV MGT LAFTA 20. PAGE 165 A3369
L/A+17C MARKET REGION

S65
AFRICAN BIBLIOGRAPHIC CENTER,"US TREATIES AND AGREEMENTS WITH COUNTRIES IN AFRICA, 1957 TO MID-1963." AFR USA+45 AGRI FINAN FORCES TEC/DEV CAP/ISM FOR/AID 20. PAGE 5 A0097
BIBLIOG DIPLOM INT/ORG INT/TRADE

S65
KHOURI F.J.,"THE JORDON RIVER CONTROVERSY." LAW SOCIETY ECO/UNDEV AGRI FINAN INDUS SECT FORCES ACT/RES PLAN TEC/DEV ECO/TAC EDU/PROP COERCE ATTIT
ISLAM INT/ORG ISRAEL

DRIVE PERCEPT RIGID/FLEX ALL/VALS...GEOG SOC MYTH WORK. PAGE 78 A1610 — JORDAN

S65
PLISCHKE E.,"INTEGRATING BERLIN AND THE FEDERAL REPUBLIC OF GERMANY." EUR+WWI GERMANY/W LEGIS TEC/DEV DOMIN ORD/FREE PWR...JURID 20 BERLIN. PAGE 117 A2392 — DIPLOM NAT/G MUNIC

C65
US AIR FORCE ACADEMY,"AMERICAN DEFENSE POLICY." COM INT/ORG TEC/DEV FOR/AID ARMS/CONT DETER NUC/PWR ...POLICY DECISION CONCPT ANTHOL BIBLIOG/A 20 COLD/WAR NATO. PAGE 149 A3054 — PLAN FORCES WAR COERCE

B66
AMERICAN ASSEMBLY COLUMBIA U,A WORLD OF NUCLEAR POWERS? FUT WOR+45 ECO/DEV BAL/PWR ECO/TAC CONTROL RISK EFFICIENCY ATTIT PWR...METH/COMP ANTHOL 20. PAGE 7 A0137 — NUC/PWR DIPLOM TEC/DEV ARMS/CONT

B66
BROEKMEIJER M.W.J.,FICTION AND TRUTH ABOUT THE "DECADE OF DEVELOPMENT" WOR+45 AGRI FINAN INDUS NAT/G TEC/DEV DIPLOM EDU/PROP LEAD SKILL 20 THIRD/WRLD. PAGE 19 A0385 — FOR/AID POLICY ECO/UNDEV PLAN

B66
CURRIE L.,ACCELERATING DEVELOPMENT: THE NECESSITY AND MEANS. COLOMBIA USA+45 INDUS DIPLOM EFFICIENCY WEALTH...METH/CNCPT NEW/IDEA 20. PAGE 33 A0668 — PLAN ECO/UNDEV FOR/AID TEC/DEV

B66
HAYER T.,FRENCH AID. AFR FRANCE AGRI FINAN BUDGET ADMIN WAR PRODUC...CHARTS 18/20 THIRD/WRLD OVRSEA/DEV. PAGE 63 A1295 — TEC/DEV COLONIAL FOR/AID ECO/UNDEV

B66
HUTTENBACK R.A.,BRITISH IMPERIAL EXPERIENCE. S/ASIA UK WOR-45 INT/ORG TEC/DEV...CHARTS 16/20 COMMONWLTH MERCANTLST. PAGE 69 A1424 — COLONIAL TIME/SEQ INT/TRADE

B66
KANET R.E.,THE SOVIET UNION AND SUB-SAHARAN AFRICA: COMMUNIST POLICY TOWARD AFRICA, 1917-1965. AFR USSR ECO/UNDEV TEC/DEV EDU/PROP TASK DISCRIM PEACE WEALTH ALL/IDEOS...CHARTS BIBLIOG SOC/INTEG 19/20 NEGRO UN INTERVENT. PAGE 76 A1555 — DIPLOM ECO/TAC MARXISM

B66
KAREFA-SMART J.,AFRICA: PROGRESS THROUGH COOPERATION. AFR FINAN TEC/DEV DIPLOM FOR/AID EDU/PROP CONFER REGION GP/REL WEALTH...HEAL SOC/INTEG 20. PAGE 76 A1566 — ORD/FREE ECO/UNDEV VOL/ASSN PLAN

B66
KEENLEYSIDE H.L.,INTERNATIONAL AID: A SUMMARY. AFR INDIA S/ASIA UK STRATA EXTR/IND TEC/DEV ADMIN RACE/REL DEMAND NAT/LISM WEALTH...TREND CHINJAP. PAGE 77 A1575 — ECO/UNDEV FOR/AID DIPLOM TASK

B66
KEYES J.G.,A BIBLIOGRAPHY OF WESTERN LANGUAGE PUBLICATIONS CONCERNING NORTH VIETNAM IN THE CORNELL LIBRARY. VIETNAM/N NAT/G FORCES TEC/DEV DIPLOM LEAD RACE/REL...GEOG SOC 20. PAGE 78 A1603 — BIBLIOG/A CULTURE ECO/UNDEV S/ASIA

B66
KNORR K.E.,ON THE USES OF MILITARY POWER IN THE NUCLEAR AGE. WOR+45 INT/ORG TEC/DEV ADMIN CONTROL WAR COST 20. PAGE 81 A1656 — FORCES DIPLOM DETER NUC/PWR

B66
LAMBERG R.F.,PRAG UND DIE DRITTE WELT. AFR ASIA CZECHOSLVK L/A+17C MARKET TEC/DEV ECO/TAC REV ATTIT 20 TREATY. PAGE 84 A1713 — DIPLOM ECO/UNDEV INT/TRADE FOR/AID

B66
NATIONAL COUN APPLIED ECO RES,DEVELOPMENT WITHOUT AID. INDIA FINAN TEC/DEV EFFICIENCY...ANTHOL 20. PAGE 107 A2203 — FOR/AID PLAN SOVEREIGN ECO/UNDEV

B66
ROBOCK S.H.,INTERNATIONAL DEVELOPMENT 1965. AGRI INDUS VOL/ASSN PLAN TEC/DEV EDU/PROP HEALTH...JURID 20 UN PEACE/CORP. PAGE 122 A2508 — FOR/AID INT/ORG GEOG ECO/UNDEV

B66
SCHWARZ U.,AMERICAN STRATEGY: A NEW PERSPECTIVE. USA+45 USA-45 INT/ORG TEC/DEV BAL/PWR DIPLOM LEAD ARMS/CONT DETER NUC/PWR WAR 20 NATO. PAGE 130 A2659 — NAT/G POLICY FORCES PWR

B66
UNITED NATIONS,INTERNATIONAL SPACE BIBLIOGRAPHY. FUT INT/ORG TEC/DEV DIPLOM ARMS/CONT NUC/PWR ...JURID SOC UN. PAGE 149 A3037 — BIBLIOG SPACE PEACE R+D

B66
US DEPARTMENT OF STATE,RESEARCH ON THE USSR AND EASTERN EUROPE (EXTERNAL RESEARCH LIST NO 1-25). USSR LAW CULTURE SOCIETY NAT/G TEC/DEV DIPLOM EDU/PROP REGION...GEOG LING. PAGE 152 A3097 — BIBLIOG/A EUR+WWI COM MARXISM

B66
US HOUSE COMM FOREIGN AFFAIRS,HEARINGS ON HR 12449 A BILL TO AMEND FURTHER THE FOREIGN ASSISTANCE ACT OF 1961. AFR ASIA L/A+17C USA+45 VIETNAM INT/ORG TEC/DEV INT/TRADE ATTIT ORD/FREE 20 UN NATO CONGRESS AID. PAGE 154 A3132 — FOR/AID ECO/TAC ECO/UNDEV DIPLOM

B66
ZEINE Z.N.,THE EMERGENCE OF ARAB NATIONALISM (REV. ED.). TURKEY UK NAT/G SECT TEC/DEV LEAD REV WAR AGE/Y ROLE ORD/FREE...TRADIT CHARTS BIBLIOG 20 ARABS OTTOMAN. PAGE 170 A3451 — ISLAM NAT/LISM DIPLOM

L66
CHENERY H.B.,"FOREIGN ASSISTANCE AND ECONOMIC DEVELOPMENT" FUT WOR+45 NAT/G DIPLOM GIVE PRODUC ...METH/CNCPT CHARTS 20. PAGE 26 A0526 — FOR/AID EFFICIENCY ECO/UNDEV TEC/DEV

S66
AFRICAN BIBLIOGRAPHIC CENTER,"A CURRENT VIEW OF AFRICANA: A SELECT AND ANNOTATED BIBLIOGRAPHICAL PUBLISHING GUIDE, 1965-1966." AFR CULTURE INDUS LABOR SECT FOR/AID ADMIN COLONIAL REV RACE/REL SOCISM...LING 20. PAGE 5 A0098 — BIBLIOG/A NAT/G TEC/DEV POL/PAR

S66
AFRICAN BIBLIOGRAPHIC CENTER,"THE NEW AFRO-ASIAN STATES IN PERSPECTIVE, 1960-1963: A SELECT BIBLIOGRAPHY." AFR ASIA CULTURE SOCIETY INT/ORG LABOR TEC/DEV LITERACY 20 UN. PAGE 5 A0100 — BIBLIOG DIPLOM FOR/AID INT/TRADE

B67
AUBREY H.G.,ATLANTIC ECONOMIC COOPERATION. ECO/DEV INDUS VOL/ASSN PROB/SOLV DIPLOM INT/TRADE TARIFFS CONFER 20. PAGE 10 A0197 — INT/ORG ECO/TAC TEC/DEV CAP/ISM

B67
BARANSON J.,TECHNOLOGY FOR UNDERDEVELOPED AREAS: AN ANNOTATED BIBLIOGRAPHY. FUT WOR+45 CULTURE INDUS INT/ORG CREATE PROB/SOLV INT/TRADE EDU/PROP AUTOMAT ...CONCPT METH. PAGE 11 A0218 — BIBLIOG/A ECO/UNDEV TEC/DEV R+D

B67
HALPERIN M.H.,CONTEMPORARY MILITARY STRATEGY. ASIA CHINA/COM USA+45 USSR INT/ORG FORCES ACT/RES PLAN TEC/DEV BAL/PWR COERCE WAR...METH/COMP BIBLIOG 20 NATO. PAGE 60 A1240 — DIPLOM NUC/PWR DETER ARMS/CONT

B67
JOHNSON D.G.,THE STRUGGLE AGAINST WORLD HUNGER (HEADLINE SERIES, NO. 184) (PAMPHLET). PLAN TEC/DEV FOR/AID...CHARTS 20 FAO MEXIC/AMER. PAGE 74 A1520 — AGRI PROB/SOLV ECO/UNDEV HEALTH

B67
MCBRIDE J.H.,THE TEST BAN TREATY: MILITARY, TECHNOLOGICAL, AND POLITICAL IMPLICATIONS. USA+45 USSR DELIB/GP FORCES LEGIS TEC/DEV BAL/PWR TREATY. PAGE 97 A1995 — ARMS/CONT DIPLOM NUC/PWR

B67
PADELFORD N.J.,THE DYNAMICS OF INTERNATIONAL POLITICS (2ND ED.). WOR+45 LAW INT/ORG FORCES TEC/DEV REGION NAT/LISM PEACE ATTIT PWR ALL/IDEOS UN COLD/WAR NATO TREATY. PAGE 113 A2314 — DIPLOM NAT/G POLICY DECISION

B67
ROACH J.R.,THE UNITED STATES AND THE ATLANTIC COMMUNITY; ISSUES AND PROSPECTS. WOR+45 TEC/DEV ECO/TAC COLONIAL REGION PEACE ROLE...ANTHOL NATO COLD/WAR EEC. PAGE 121 A2491 — INT/ORG POLICY ADJUST DIPLOM

B67
RUEFF J.,BALANCE OF PAYMENTS. WOR+45 FINAN TEC/DEV DIPLOM TARIFFS PRICE CONTROL...POLICY CONCPT IDEA/COMP. PAGE 125 A2567 — INT/TRADE BAL/PAY ECO/TAC NAT/COMP

B67
UNESCO,PRINCIPLES AND PROBLEMS OF NATIONAL SCIENCE POLICIES. WOR+45 ECO/DEV ECO/UNDEV R+D INT/ORG PROB/SOLV CONFER...PHIL/SCI CHARTS 20 UNESCO UN. PAGE 148 A3026 — NAT/COMP POLICY TEC/DEV CREATE

B67
UNIVERSAL REFERENCE SYSTEM,ECONOMIC REGULATION, BUSINESS, AND GOVERNMENT (VOLUME VIII). WOR+45 WOR-45 ECO/DEV ECO/UNDEV FINAN LABOR TEC/DEV ECO/TAC INT/TRADE GOV/REL...POLICY COMPUT/IR. PAGE 149 A3043 — BIBLIOG/A CONTROL NAT/G

B67
US AGENCY INTERNATIONAL DEV,PROPOSED FOREIGN AID PROGRAM FOR 1968: SUMMARY PRESENTATION TO THE CONGRESS. AFR S/ASIA USA+45 AGRI TEC/DEV DIPLOM ECO/TAC BAL/PAY COST HEALTH KNOWL SKILL 20 AID CONGRESS. PAGE 149 A3053 — ECO/UNDEV BUDGET FOR/AID STAT

B67
WAELDER R.,PROGRESS AND REVOLUTION* A STUDY OF THE ISSUES OF OUR AGE. WOR+45 WOR-45 BAL/PWR DIPLOM COERCE ROLE MORAL ALL/IDEOS...IDEA/COMP NAT/COMP 19/20. PAGE 160 A3259 — PWR NAT/G REV TEC/DEV

B67
YAMAMURA K.,ECONOMIC POLICY IN POSTWAR JAPAN. ASIA FINAN POL/PAR DIPLOM LEAD NAT/LISM ATTIT NEW/LIB POPULISM 20 CHINJAP. PAGE 168 A3429 — ECO/DEV POLICY NAT/G TEC/DEV

L67
DEVADHAR Y.C.,"THE ROLE OF FOREIGN PRIVATE CAPITAL IN INDIA'S ECONOMIC DEVELOPMENT* ASSESSMENT OF POLICY AND PERFORMANCE." INDIA INDUS PLAN TEC/DEV BUDGET DIPLOM ECO/TAC BAL/PAY PRODUC WEALTH ...CHARTS 20. PAGE 37 A0750 — CAP/ISM FOR/AID POLICY ACT/RES

S67
CHAND A.,"INDIA AND TANZANIA." INDIA TANZANIA TEC/DEV ECO/TAC FOR/AID COLONIAL PEACE UTIL WEALTH ...GOV/COMP 20. PAGE 25 A0518
ECO/UNDEV NEUTRAL DIPLOM PLAN

S67
COSGROVE C.A.,"AGRICULTURE, FINANCE AND POLITICS IN THE EUROPEAN COMMUNITY." EUR+WWI DIST/IND MARKET INT/ORG VOL/ASSN DELIB/GP TEC/DEV BAL/PWR BARGAIN ECO/TAC RATION CONFER 20 EEC. PAGE 31 A0630
ECO/DEV DIPLOM AGRI INT/TRADE

S67
DOYLE S.E.,"COMMUNICATION SATELLITES* INTERNAL ORGANIZATION FOR DEVELOPMENT AND CONTROL." USA+45 R+D ACT/RES DIPLOM NAT/LISM...POLICY INT/LAW PREDICT UN. PAGE 38 A0781
TEC/DEV SPACE COM/IND INT/ORG

S67
FALKOWSKI M.,"SOCIALIST ECONOMISTS AND THE DEVELOPING COUNTRIES." COM PLAN TEC/DEV ROUTINE DEMAND EFFICIENCY PRODUC WEALTH...MARXIST TREND GEN/METH. PAGE 44 A0893
DIPLOM SOCISM ECO/UNDEV INDUS

S67
HODGE G.,"THE RISE AND DEMISE OF THE UN TECHNICAL ASSISTANCE ADMINISTRATION." RISK TASK INGP/REL CONSEN EFFICIENCY 20 UN. PAGE 66 A1349
ADMIN TEC/DEV EX/STRUC INT/ORG

S67
JOHNSTON D.M.,"LAW, TECHNOLOGY AND THE SEA." WOR+45 PLAN PROB/SOLV TEC/DEV CONFER ADJUD ORD/FREE ...POLICY JURID. PAGE 75 A1528
INT/LAW INT/ORG DIPLOM NEUTRAL

S67
KAHN H.,"CRITERIA FOR LONG-RANGE NUCLEAR CONTROL POLICIES." WOR+45 INT/ORG TEC/DEV DOMIN DETER WAR WEAPON ISOLAT ORD/FREE POLICY. PAGE 76 A1549
NUC/PWR ARMS/CONT BAL/PWR DIPLOM

S67
KINGSLEY R.E.,"THE US BUSINESS IMAGE IN LATIN AMERICA." L/A+17C USA+45 NAT/G TEC/DEV CAP/ISM FOR/AID DOMIN EDU/PROP...CONCPT LING IDEA/COMP 20. PAGE 79 A1626
ATTIT LOVE DIPLOM ECO/UNDEV

S67
KRAUS J.,"A MARXIST IN GHANA." GHANA ELITES CHIEF PROB/SOLV TEC/DEV DIPLOM ECO/TAC COLONIAL PARTIC PWR 20 NKRUMAH/K. PAGE 82 A1676
MARXISM PLAN ATTIT CREATE

S67
KRISTENSEN T.,"THE SOUTH AS AN INDUSTRIAL POWER." FUT WOR+45 ECO/DEV AGRI INDUS TEC/DEV...CENSUS TREND CHARTS 20. PAGE 82 A1686
DIPLOM ECO/UNDEV PREDICT PRODUC

S67
LEVI M.,"LES DIFFICULTES ECONOMIQUES DE LA GRANDE-BRETAGNE." UK INT/ORG TEC/DEV BARGAIN DIPLOM DOMIN REPRESENT DEMAND WEALTH...POLICY 20 EEC. PAGE 88 A1792
BAL/PAY INT/TRADE PRODUC

S67
RAMSEY J.A.,"THE STATUS OF INTERNATIONAL COPYRIGHTS." WOR+45 CREATE TEC/DEV DIPLOM CONFER CONTROL SANCTION OWN...POLICY JURID. PAGE 119 A2439
INT/LAW INT/ORG COM/IND PRESS

S67
SCHACTER O.,"SCIENTIFIC ADVANCES AND INTERNATIONAL LAWMAKING." FUT R+D PLAN PROB/SOLV CONFER CONTROL ...POLICY PREDICT 20 UN. PAGE 128 A2617
TEC/DEV INT/LAW INT/ORG ACT/RES

S67
SHOEMAKER R.L.,"JAPANESE ARMY AND THE WEST." ASIA ELITES EX/STRUC DIPLOM DOMIN EDU/PROP COERCE ATTIT AUTHORIT PWR 1/20 CHINJAP. PAGE 132 A2703
FORCES TEC/DEV WAR TOTALISM

S67
VLASCIC I.A.,"THE SPACE TREATY* A PRELIMINARY EVALUATION." FUT USSR WOR+45 R+D ACT/RES TEC/DEV DIPLOM CONFER ARMS/CONT PEACE...PREDICT UN TREATY. PAGE 159 A3245
SPACE INT/LAW INT/ORG NEUTRAL

S67
WASHBURN A.M.,"NUCLEAR PROLIFERATION IN A REVOLUTIONARY INTERNATIONAL SYSTEM." WOR+45 NAT/G DELIB/GP PLAN TEC/DEV...POLICY 20. PAGE 161 A3287
ARMS/CONT NUC/PWR DIPLOM CONFER

S67
WINTHROP H.,"CONTEMPORARY ECONOMIC DEHUMANIZATION* SOME DIFFICULTIES SURROUNDING ITS REDUCTION." USA+45 WOR+45 ACT/RES PROB/SOLV DIPLOM ROUTINE DEMAND UTIL. PAGE 165 A3368
TEC/DEV SOCIETY WEALTH

C67
SPANIER J.W.,"WORLD POLITICS IN AN AGE OF REVOLUTION." COM WOR+45 FORCES COERCE WAR NAT/LISM SOVEREIGN...POLICY BIBLIOG 20. PAGE 135 A2772
DIPLOM TEC/DEV REV ECO/UNDEV

N67
US SUPERINTENDENT OF DOCUMENTS,SPACE: MISSILES, THE MOON, NASA, AND SATELLITES (PRICE LIST 79A). USA+45 COM/IND R+D NAT/G DIPLOM EDU/PROP ADMIN CONTROL HEALTH...POLICY SIMUL NASA CONGRESS. PAGE 157 A3206
BIBLIOG/A SPACE TEC/DEV PEACE

B68
ANTWERP-INST UNIVERSITAIRE,BIBLIOGRAPHIC COMPENDIUM: DEVELOPING COUNTRIES (ANTWERP-INST UNIVERSITAIRE DES TERRITOIRES D'OUTRE-MER). AFR EUR+WWI SOCIETY AGRI FINAN NEIGH VOL/ASSN PROB/SOLV TEC/DEV FOR/AID INT/TRADE 20. PAGE 8 A0166
BIBLIOG ECO/UNDEV DIPLOM PLAN

TECHNIC....TECHNOCRATIC

B49
OGBURN W.,TECHNOLOGY AND INTERNATIONAL RELATIONS. WOR+45 WOR-45 ECO/DEV CREATE PLAN ECO/TAC EDU/PROP COERCE PWR SKILL WEALTH...TECHNIC PSY SOC NEW/IDEA CHARTS TOT/POP 20. PAGE 111 A2283
TEC/DEV DIPLOM INT/ORG

S58
BOGART L.,"MEASURING THE EFFECTIVENESS OF AN OVERSEAS INFORMATION CAMPAIGN." EUR+WWI GREECE USA+45 INT/ORG MUNIC PLAN DIPLOM PEACE PERCEPT RIGID/FLEX KNOWL...TECHNIC PSY SOC NEW/IDEA CONT/OBS REC/INT STAND/INT SAMP/SIZ COLD/WAR 20. PAGE 16 A0328
ATTIT EDU/PROP

B59
COMM. STUDY ORGAN. PEACE,ORGANIZING PEACE IN THE NUCLEAR AGE. FUT CONSULT DELIB/GP DOMIN ADJUD ROUTINE COERCE ORD/FREE...TECHNIC INT/LAW JURID NEW/IDEA UN COLD/WAR 20. PAGE 29 A0581
INT/ORG ACT/RES NUC/PWR

B59
STANFORD RESEARCH INSTITUTE,POSSIBLE NONMILITARY SCIENTIFIC DEVELOPMENTS AND THEIR POTENTIAL IMPACT ON FOREIGN POLICY PROBLEMS OF THE UNITED. FUT USA+45 INT/ORG PROF/ORG CONSULT ACT/RES CREATE PLAN PEACE KNOWL SKILL...TECHNIC PHIL/SCI NEW/IDEA UNESCO 20. PAGE 137 A2802
R+D TEC/DEV

B60
WOETZEL R.K.,THE INTERNATIONAL CONTROL OF AIRSPACE AND OUTERSPACE. FUT WOR+45 AIR CONSTN STRUCT CONSULT PLAN TEC/DEV ADJUD RIGID/FLEX KNOWL ORD/FREE PWR...TECHNIC GEOG MGT NEW/IDEA TREND COMPUT/IR VAL/FREE 20 TREATY. PAGE 166 A3375
INT/ORG JURID SPACE INT/LAW

B61
KAPLAN M.A.,THE POLITICAL FOUNDATIONS OF INTERNATIONAL LAW. WOR+45 WOR-45 CULTURE SOCIETY ECO/DEV DIPLOM PERCEPT...TECHNIC METH/CNCPT. PAGE 76 A1563
INT/ORG LAW

B62
BLACKETT P.M.S.,STUDIES OF WAR: NUCLEAR AND CONVENTIONAL. EUR+WWI USA+45 DELIB/GP ACT/RES CREATE PLAN TEC/DEV LEGIT COERCE WAR ORD/FREE PWR ...POLICY TECHNIC TIME/SEQ 20. PAGE 15 A0300
INT/ORG FORCES ARMS/CONT NUC/PWR

L63
PHELPS J.,"STUDIES IN DETERRENCE VIII: MILITARY STABILITARY AND ARMS CONTROL: A CRITICAL SURVEY." FUT WOR+45 INT/ORG ACT/RES EDU/PROP COERCE NUC/PWR WAR HEALTH PWR...POLICY TECHNIC TREND SIMUL TOT/POP 20. PAGE 116 A2373
FORCES ORD/FREE ARMS/CONT DETER

TECHNIQUES....SEE TEC/DEV, METHODOLOGICAL INDEXES, PP. XIII-XIV

TECHNOCRACY....SEE TECHRACY, TECHNIC

TECHNOLOGY....SEE COMPUTER, TECHNIC, TEC/DEV

TECHRACY....SOCIO-POLITICAL ORDER DOMINATED BY TECHNICIANS

B54
GROSS F.,FOREIGN POLICY ANALYSIS. USA+45 TOP/EX PLAN INGP/REL ATTIT TECHRACY...CONCPT 20. PAGE 57 A1171
POLICY DIPLOM DECISION EDU/PROP

B63
SCHRADER R.,SCIENCE AND POLICY. WOR+45 ECO/DEV ECO/UNDEV R+D FORCES PLAN DIPLOM GOV/REL TECHRACY BIBLIOG. PAGE 129 A2644
TEC/DEV NAT/G POLICY ADMIN

TEHERAN....TEHERAN CONFERENCE

B66
EUBANK K.,THE SUMMIT CONFERENCES. EUR+WWI USA+45 USA-45 MUNIC BAL/PWR WAR PEACE PWR...POLICY AUD/VIS 20 GENEVA/CON TEHERAN YALTA POTSDAM. PAGE 43 A0872
CONFER NAT/G CHIEF DIPLOM

TEITELBAUM L.M. A2902

TEMPERANCE....TEMPERANCE MOVEMENTS

TENG SSU-YU A2795

TENNESSEE VALLEY AUTHORITY....SEE TVA

TENNESSEE....TENNESSEE

TENNEY F. A0460

TEPASKE J.J. A2903

TERRELL/G....GLENN TERRELL

TERRILL R. A2904

TERRY V. OHIO....SEE TERRY

TERRY....TERRY V. OHIO

TESTS....THEORY AND USES OF TESTS AND SCALES; SEE ALSO TESTS AND SCALES INDEX, P. XIV

S51
BUCHANAN W.,"STEREOTYPES AND TENSIONS AS REVEALED BY THE UNESCO INTERNATIONAL POLL." WOR+45 INT/ORG ATTIT DISPL PERCEPT RIGID/FLEX...INT TESTS SAMP 20. PAGE 21 A0424
R+D STERTYP

L58
HAVILAND H.F.,"FOREIGN AID AND THE POLICY PROCESS: 1957." USA+45 FACE/GP POL/PAR VOL/ASSN CHIEF DELIB/GP ACT/RES LEGIT EXEC GOV/REL ATTIT DRIVE PWR ...POLICY TESTS CONGRESS 20. PAGE 63 A1291
LEGIS PLAN FOR/AID

S61
DEUTSCH K.W.,"NATIONAL INDUSTRIALIZATION AND THE DECLINING SHARE OF THE INTERNATIONAL ECONOMIC SECTOR." EUR+WWI FUT WOR+45 WOR-45 MARKET PLAN EDU/PROP WEALTH...WELF/ST OBS TESTS 20. PAGE 36 A0740
DIST/IND ECO/DEV INT/TRADE

S62
SCHACHTER O.,"DAG HAMMARSKJOLD AND THE RELATION OF LAW TO POLITICS." FUT WOR+45 INT/ORG CONSULT PLAN TEC/DEV BAL/PWR DIPLOM LEGIT ATTIT PERCEPT ORD/FREE ...POLICY JURID CONCPT OBS TESTS STERTYP GEN/LAWS 20 HAMMARSK/D. PAGE 128 A2616
ACT/RES ADJUD

B63
NORTH R.C.,CONTENT ANALYSIS: A HANDBOOK WITH APPLICATIONS FOR THE STUDY OF INTERNATIONAL CRISIS. ASIA COM EUR+WWI MOD/EUR INT/ORG TEC/DEV DOMIN EDU/PROP ROUTINE COERCE PERCEPT RIGID/FLEX ALL/VALS ...QUANT TESTS CON/ANAL SIMUL GEN/LAWS VAL/FREE. PAGE 110 A2252
METH/CNCPT COMPUT/IR USSR

B66
LENT H.B.,THE PEACE CORPS: AMBASSADORS OF GOOD WILL. USA+45 ECO/UNDEV...INT TESTS BIOG AUD/VIS SOC/INTEG 20 PEACE/CORP. PAGE 87 A1776
VOL/ASSN FOR/AID DIPLOM CONSULT

TETENS T.H. A2905

TEXAS....TEXAS

THAILAND....THAILAND; SEE ALSO S/ASIA

B52
US MUTUAL SECURITY AGENCY,U. S. TECHNICAL AND ECONOMIC ASSISTANCE IN THE FAR EAST (PAMPHLET). ASIA BURMA INDONESIA PHILIPPINE TAIWAN THAILAND USA+45 AGRI INDUS PLAN EDU/PROP ADMIN HEALTH. PAGE 155 A3161
FOR/AID TEC/DEV ECO/UNDEV BUDGET

B58
MASON J.B.,THAILAND BIBLIOGRAPHY. S/ASIA THAILAND CULTURE EDU/PROP ADMIN...GEOG SOC LING 20. PAGE 95 A1958
BIBLIOG/A ECO/UNDEV DIPLOM NAT/G

C58
BLANCHARD W.,"THAILAND." THAILAND CULTURE AGRI FINAN INDUS FAM LABOR INT/TRADE ATTIT...GEOG HEAL SOC BIBLIOG 20. PAGE 15 A0307
NAT/G DIPLOM ECO/UNDEV S/ASIA

S63
GORDON B.,"ECONOMIC IMPEDIMENTS TO REGIONALISM IN SOUTH EAST ASIA." BURMA FUT S/ASIA THAILAND USA+45 AGRI INDUS R+D NAT/G PLAN ECO/TAC WEALTH...STAT CONT/OBS 20. PAGE 54 A1110
VOL/ASSN ECO/UNDEV INT/TRADE REGION

B66
UN ECAFE,ADMINISTRATIVE ASPECTS OF FAMILY PLANNING PROGRAMMES (PAMPHLET). ASIA THAILAND WOR+45 VOL/ASSN PROB/SOLV BUDGET FOR/AID EDU/PROP CONFER CONTROL GOV/REL TIME 20 UN BIRTH/CON. PAGE 147 A2999
PLAN CENSUS FAM ADMIN

C66
TARLING N.,"A CONCISE HISTORY OF SOUTHEAST ASIA." BURMA CAMBODIA LAOS S/ASIA THAILAND VIETNAM ECO/UNDEV POL/PAR FORCES ADMIN REV WAR CIVMIL/REL ORD/FREE MARXISM SOCISM 13/20. PAGE 141 A2890
COLONIAL DOMIN INT/TRADE NAT/LISM

S67
NEUCHTERLEIN D.E.,"THAILAND* ANOTHER VIETNAM?" THAILAND ECO/UNDEV DIPLOM ADMIN REGION CENTRAL NAT/LISM...POLICY 20. PAGE 108 A2220
WAR GUERRILLA S/ASIA NAT/G

THANT U. A2906,A2907

THAYER F.C. A2908

THAYER P.W. A2909

THE AFRICA 1960 COMMITTEE A2910

THE ECONOMIST (LONDON) A2911

THEOBALD R. A2912,A2913,A2914,A2915,A2916

THERAPY....SEE SPECIFICS, SUCH AS PROJ/TEST, DEEP/INT, SOC/EXP; ALSO SEE DIFFERENT VALUES (E.G., LOVE) AND TOPICAL TERMS (E.G., PRESS)

THIEN T.T. A2917,A2918

THING/STOR....ARTIFACTS AND MATERIAL EVIDENCE

THIRD/WRLD....THIRD WORLD - NONALIGNED NATIONS

N19
VELYAMINOV G.,AFRICA AND THE COMMON MARKET (PAMPHLET). AFR MARKET VOL/ASSN ECO/TAC COLONIAL ORD/FREE...SOCIALIST 20 THIRD/WRLD. PAGE 158 A3227
INT/ORG INT/TRADE SOVEREIGN ECO/UNDEV

B58
APPADORAI A.,THE USE OF FORCE IN INTERNATIONAL RELATIONS. WOR+45 CULTURE ECO/UNDEV CAP/ISM ARMS/CONT REV WAR ATTIT PERSON SOVEREIGN MARXISM ...INT/LAW PACIFIST 20 UN INTERVENT THIRD/WRLD COLD/WAR. PAGE 8 A0169
PEACE FEDERAL INT/ORG

B59
NOVE A.,COMMUNIST ECONOMIC STRATEGY: SOVIET GROWTH AND CAPABILITIES. USSR AGRI LABOR PLAN TEC/DEV CAP/ISM INT/TRADE EFFICIENCY MARXISM 20 THIRD/WRLD. PAGE 110 A2257
FOR/AID ECO/TAC DIPLOM INDUS

B60
MCKINNEY R.,REVIEW OF THE INTERNATIONAL ATOMIC POLICIES AND PROGRAMS OF THE UNITED STATES (5 VOLS.). COM FUT USA+45 ECO/DEV ECO/UNDEV INT/ORG DELIB/GP PLAN ADMIN 20 THIRD/WRLD. PAGE 98 A2016
NUC/PWR PEACE DIPLOM POLICY

B62
GOLDWIN R.A.,WHY FOREIGN AID? - TWO MESSAGES BY PRESIDENT KENNEDY AND ESSAYS. S/ASIA USA+45 ECO/UNDEV 20 KENNEDY/JF THIRD/WRLD. PAGE 54 A1096
DIPLOM FOR/AID POLICY

B63
JENNINGS W.I.,DEMOCRACY IN AFRICA. UK CULTURE STRUCT ECO/UNDEV DIPLOM COLONIAL GP/REL ADJUST NAT/LISM ORD/FREE...GOV/COMP 20 THIRD/WRLD. PAGE 74 A1512
PROB/SOLV AFR CONSTN POPULISM

B63
JUDD P.,AFRICAN INDEPENDENCE: THE EXPLODING EMERGENCE OF THE NEW AFRICAN NATIONS. AFR UK LAW CONSTN CULTURE KIN DIPLOM ATTIT...CHARTS BIBLIOG 20 UN DEGAULLE/C NEGRO THIRD/WRLD. PAGE 75 A1542
ORD/FREE POLICY DOMIN LOC/G

B63
MENEZES A.J.,SUBDESENVOLVIMENTO E POLITICA INTERNACIONAL. BRAZIL WOR+45 PLAN CONTROL LEAD NAT/LISM ORD/FREE 20 THIRD/WRLD. PAGE 99 A2041
ECO/UNDEV DIPLOM POLICY BAL/PWR

B63
ROSSI M.,THE THIRD WORLD. FUT WOR+45 INT/ORG NAT/G CAP/ISM COLONIAL PEACE PWR MARXISM 20 UN THIRD/WRLD. PAGE 124 A2542
ECO/UNDEV DIPLOM BAL/PWR NEUTRAL

B64
DUROSELLE J.B.,LA COMMUNAUTE INTERNATIONALE FACE AUX JEUNES ETATS. CHINA/COM COM S/ASIA USSR INT/ORG ROLE...ANTHOL 20 UN SEATO THIRD/WRLD. PAGE 40 A0808
DIPLOM COLONIAL ECO/UNDEV SOVEREIGN

B64
VOELKMANN K.,HERRSCHER VON MORGEN? BAL/PWR COLONIAL NEUTRAL REGION RACE/REL ALL/VALS SOVEREIGN...RECORD 20 COLD/WAR THIRD/WRLD. PAGE 159 A3246
DIPLOM ECO/UNDEV CONTROL NAT/COMP

B65
FRIEDMANN W.,AN INTRODUCTION TO WORLD POLITICS (5TH ED.). WOR+45 ECO/UNDEV BAL/PWR FOR/AID INT/TRADE PEACE...STAT CENSUS CHARTS BIBLIOG T 20 COLD/WAR UN THIRD/WRLD. PAGE 49 A1003
DIPLOM INT/ORG PROB/SOLV

B65
NKRUMAH K.,NEO-COLONIALISM: THE LAST STAGE OF IMPERIALISM. AFR INT/ORG WORKER FOR/AID INT/TRADE EDU/PROP GOV/REL NAT/LISM SOVEREIGN POPULISM SOCISM ...SOCIALIST 20 THIRD/WRLD INTRVN/ECO. PAGE 109 A2243
COLONIAL DIPLOM ECO/UNDEV ECO/TAC

B66
BROEKMEIJER M.W.J.,FICTION AND TRUTH ABOUT THE "DECADE OF DEVELOPMENT" WOR+45 AGRI FINAN INDUS NAT/G TEC/DEV DIPLOM EDU/PROP LEAD SKILL 20 THIRD/WRLD. PAGE 19 A0385
FOR/AID POLICY ECO/UNDEV PLAN

B66
HAYER T.,FRENCH AID. AFR FRANCE AGRI FINAN BUDGET ADMIN WAR PRODUC...CHARTS 18/20 THIRD/WRLD OVRSEA/DEV. PAGE 63 A1295
TEC/DEV COLONIAL FOR/AID ECO/UNDEV

B66
MC LELLAN D.S.,THE COLD WAR IN TRANSITION. USSR
BAL/PWR

WOR+45 CONTROL LEAD NUC/PWR NAT/LISM SOVEREIGN 20 COLD/WAR THIRD/WRLD. PAGE 97 A1994 — DETER DIPLOM POLICY

THOM J.M. A2919

THOMAS A.J. A2920

THOMAS A.V. A2920

THOMAS D.H. A2921

THOMAS J.A. A2922

THOMAS J.R.T. A2923

THOMAS N. A2924

THOMAS/FA....F.A. THOMAS

THOMAS/N....NORMAN THOMAS

THOMAS/TK....TREVOR K. THOMAS

THOMPSON D. A2925

THOMPSON J.H. A2926

THOMPSON J.W. A2927

THOMPSON K.W. A0298,A2928,A2929,A2930,A2931,A2932

THOMPSON V. A2933

THOMSON C.A. A1751

THOMSON G.P. A2934

THOREAU/H....HENRY THOREAU

THORELLI H.B. A2935

THORNE C. A2936

THORNTN/WT....WILLIAM T. THORNTON

THORNTON A.P. A2937

THUCYDIDES A2938

THUCYDIDES....THUCYDIDES

THUMM G.W. A2561,A2565

THURSTON/L....LOUIS LEON THURSTONE

THWAITE D. A2939

TIBET....TIBET; SEE ALSO ASIA, CHINA

B60
MORAES F.,THE REVOLT IN TIBET. ASIA CHINA/COM INDIA CULTURE CONTROL COERCE WAR TOTALISM...POLICY SOC WORSHIP 20 TIBET INTERVENT. PAGE 104 A2127 — COLONIAL FORCES DIPLOM ORD/FREE

S60
GINSBURGS G.,"PEKING-LHASA-NEW DELHI." CHINA/COM FUT INDIA S/ASIA KIN NAT/G PROVS SECT FORCES BAL/PWR ECO/TAC DOMIN EDU/PROP LEGIT ADMIN REGION GUERRILLA PWR...TREND TIBET 20. PAGE 52 A1074 — ASIA COERCE DIPLOM

TILLICH/P....PAUL TILLICH

TILLION G. A2940

TIME....TIMING, TIME FACTOR; SEE ALSO ANALYSIS OF TEMPORAL SEQUENCES INDEX, P. XIV

B46
GAULD W.A.,MAN, NATURE, AND TIME, AN INTRODUCTION TO WORLD STUDY. WOR-45 CULTURE CREATE DIPLOM GP/REL DRIVE...SOC LING CENSUS CHARTS TIME 18/20. PAGE 52 A1054 — HABITAT PERSON

B56
BROOK D.,THE UNITED NATIONS AND CHINA DILEMMA. CHINA/COM FUT WOR+45 ECO/UNDEV NAT/G DELIB/GP ACT/RES DIPLOM ROUTINE NAT/LISM TOTALISM ATTIT DRIVE...CONCPT OBS TIME/SEQ UN TOT/POP TIME UN 20. PAGE 19 A0390 — ASIA INT/ORG BAL/PWR

B60
STRACHEY J.,THE END OF EMPIRE. UK WOR+45 WOR-45 DIPLOM INT/TRADE DOMIN ADJUST ORD/FREE WEALTH ...SOCIALIST GOV/COMP TIME COMMONWLTH. PAGE 139 A2841 — COLONIAL ECO/DEV BAL/PWR LAISSEZ

B65
ROMEIN J.,THE ASIAN CENTURY. ASIA COM S/ASIA DIPLOM COLONIAL TIME 20. PAGE 123 A2519 — REV NAT/LISM CULTURE MARXISM

B66
UN ECAFE,ADMINISTRATIVE ASPECTS OF FAMILY PLANNING PROGRAMMES (PAMPHLET). ASIA THAILAND WOR+45 VOL/ASSN PROB/SOLV BUDGET FOR/AID EDU/PROP CONFER CONTROL GOV/REL TIME 20 UN BIRTH/CON. PAGE 147 A2999 — PLAN CENSUS FAM ADMIN

C66
DUROSELLE J.B.,"LE CONFLIT DE TRIESTE 1943-1954: ETUDES DE CAS DE CONFLITS INTERNATIONAUX III." ITALY USA+45 YUGOSLAVIA ELITES DELIB/GP PLAN ADJUST ...POLICY GEOG CHARTS IDEA/COMP TIME 20 TREATY UN COLD/WAR. PAGE 40 A0810 — BIBLIOG WAR DIPLOM GEN/LAWS

S67
NORTH R.C.,"COMMUNICATION AS AN APPROACH TO POLITICS." UNIV INTELL DIPLOM PERCEPT PERSON ...CONCPT TIME. PAGE 110 A2254 — PERS/REL GP/REL ACT/RES

TIME/SEQ....CHRONOLOGY AND GENETIC SERIES

N
JOURNAL OF MODERN HISTORY. WOR+45 WOR-45 LEAD WAR ...TIME/SEQ TREND NAT/COMP 20. PAGE 1 A0016 — BIBLIOG/A DIPLOM NAT/G

N
CHINA QUARTERLY. COM AGRI INDUS ACADEM POL/PAR INT/TRADE CONFER GOV/REL...TIME/SEQ CON/ANAL INDEX 20. PAGE 2 A0032 — BIBLIOG/A ASIA DIPLOM POLICY

N
LA DOCUMENTATION FRANCAISE,CHRONOLOGIE INTERNATIONAL. FRANCE WOR+45 CHIEF PROB/SOLV BAL/PWR CONFER LEAD...POLICY CON/ANAL 20. PAGE 83 A1705 — BIBLIOG/A DIPLOM TIME/SEQ

B00
MAINE H.S.,INTERNATIONAL LAW. MOD/EUR UNIV SOCIETY STRUCT ACT/RES EXEC WAR ATTIT PERSON ALL/VALS ...POLICY JURID CONCPT OBS TIME/SEQ TOT/POP. PAGE 93 A1908 — INT/ORG LAW PEACE INT/LAW

B00
VOLPICELLI Z.,RUSSIA ON THE PACIFIC AND THE SIBERIAN RAILWAY. MOD/EUR ECO/UNDEV INT/ORG FORCES PLAN DOMIN COLONIAL ROUTINE ATTIT ALL/VALS...OBS HIST/WRIT TIME/SEQ TREND CON/ANAL AUD/VIS CHARTS 18/19. PAGE 159 A3248 — NAT/G ACT/RES RUSSIA

B09
HOLLAND T.E.,LETTERS UPON WAR AND NEUTRALITY. WOR-45 NAT/G FORCES JUDGE ECO/TAC LEGIT CT/SYS NEUTRAL ROUTINE COERCE...JURID TIME/SEQ 20. PAGE 67 A1368 — LAW INT/LAW INT/ORG WAR

B19
KEYNES J.M.,THE ECONOMIC CONSEQUENCES OF THE PEACE. FUT GERMANY MOD/EUR RUSSIA UK USA-45 CULTURE ECO/DEV FINAN INDUS INT/ORG TOP/EX ECO/TAC ROUTINE WAR ATTIT PERCEPT ALL/VALS...OLD/LIB MYTH OBS TIME/SEQ TREND 20 TREATY. PAGE 78 A1605 — EUR+WWI SOCIETY PEACE

B19
SUTHERLAND G.,CONSTITUTIONAL POWER AND WORLD AFFAIRS. CONSTN STRUCT INT/ORG NAT/G CHIEF LEGIS ACT/RES PLAN GOV/REL ALL/VALS...OBS TIME/SEQ CONGRESS VAL/FREE 20 PRESIDENT. PAGE 140 A2866 — USA-45 EXEC DIPLOM

B20
DICKINSON E.,THE EQUALITY OF STATES IN INTERNATIONAL LAW. WOR-45 INT/ORG NAT/G DIPLOM EDU/PROP LEGIT PEACE ATTIT ALL/VALS...JURID TIME/SEQ LEAGUE/NAT. PAGE 37 A0757 — LAW CONCPT SOVEREIGN

B20
HALDANE R.B.,BEFORE THE WAR. MOD/EUR SOCIETY INT/ORG NAT/G DELIB/GP PLAN DOMIN EDU/PROP LEGIT ADMIN COERCE ATTIT DRIVE MORAL ORD/FREE PWR...SOC CONCPT SELF/OBS RECORD BIOG TIME/SEQ. PAGE 60 A1223 — POLICY DIPLOM UK

B20
MEYER H.H.B.,LIST OF REFERENCES ON THE TREATY-MAKING POWER. USA-45 CONTROL PWR...INT/LAW TIME/SEQ 18/20 TREATY. PAGE 100 A2052 — BIBLIOG DIPLOM CONSTN

B20
WOOLF L.,EMPIRE AND COMMERCE IN AFRICA. EUR+WWI MOD/EUR FINAN INDUS MARKET INT/ORG PLAN COERCE ATTIT DRIVE PWR WEALTH...CONCPT TIME/SEQ TREND CHARTS 20. PAGE 167 A3394 — AFR DOMIN COLONIAL SOVEREIGN

B21
OPPENHEIM L.,THE FUTURE OF INTERNATIONAL LAW. EUR+WWI MOD/EUR LAW LEGIS JUDGE LEGIT ORD/FREE ...JURID TIME/SEQ GEN/LAWS 20. PAGE 112 A2293 — INT/ORG CT/SYS INT/LAW

B21
STUART G.H.,FRENCH FOREIGN POLICY. CONSTN INT/ORG NAT/G POL/PAR EX/STRUC FORCES PLAN ECO/TAC DOMIN EDU/PROP ADJUD COERCE ATTIT DRIVE RIGID/FLEX ALL/VALS...POLICY OBS RECORD BIOG TIME/SEQ TREND. PAGE 139 A2852 — MOD/EUR DIPLOM FRANCE

B22
BRYCE J.,INTERNATIONAL RELATIONS. CHRIST-17C — INT/ORG

EUR+WWI MOD/EUR CULTURE INTELL NAT/G DELIB/GP POLICY
CREATE BAL/PWR DIPLOM ATTIT DRIVE RIGID/FLEX
ALL/VALS...PLURIST JURID CONCPT TIME/SEQ GEN/LAWS
TOT/POP. PAGE 20 A0412

B22
WALSH E.,THE HISTORY AND NATURE OF INTERNATIONAL INT/ORG
RELATIONS. ASIA L/A+17C MOD/EUR USA-45 WOR-45 NAT/G TIME/SEQ
FORCES TOP/EX BAL/PWR REGION ATTIT ORD/FREE RESPECT DIPLOM
...CONCPT HIST/WRIT TREND. PAGE 161 A3270

L25
HUDSON M.,"THE PERMANENT COURT OF INTERNATIONAL INT/ORG
JUSTICE AND THE QUESTION OF AMERICAN ADJUD
PARTICIPATION." WOR-45 LEGIT CT/SYS ORD/FREE DIPLOM
...JURID CONCPT TIME/SEQ GEN/LAWS VAL/FREE 20 ICJ. INT/LAW
PAGE 68 A1406

B27
LAUTERPACHT H.,PRIVATE LAW SOURCES AND ANALOGIES OF INT/ORG
INTERNATIONAL LAW. WOR-45 NAT/G DELIB/GP LEGIT ADJUD
COERCE ATTIT ORD/FREE PWR SOVEREIGN...JURID CONCPT PEACE
HIST/WRIT TIME/SEQ GEN/METH LEAGUE/NAT 20. PAGE 85 INT/LAW
A1748

B27
SIEGFRIED A.,AMERICA COMES OF AGE: A FRENCH USA-45
ANALYSIS (TRANS. BY H.H. HEMMING AND DORIS CULTURE
HEMMING). FRANCE UK POL/PAR WORKER TEC/DEV DIPLOM ECO/DEV
REGION RACE/REL ADJUST PRODUC HEREDITY...TIME/SEQ SOC
GP/COMP SOC/INTEG 20 DEMOCRAT REPUBLICAN KKK.
PAGE 132 A2714

B28
CORBETT P.E.,CANADA AND WORLD POLITICS. LAW CULTURE NAT/G
SOCIETY STRUCT MARKET INT/ORG FORCES ACT/RES PLAN CANADA
ECO/TAC LEGIT ORD/FREE PWR RESPECT...SOC CONCPT
TIME/SEQ TREND CMN/WLTH 20 LEAGUE/NAT. PAGE 30
A0612

B28
HURST C.,GREAT BRITAIN AND THE DOMINIONS. EUR+WWI VOL/ASSN
CULTURE ECO/DEV INT/ORG NAT/G DIPLOM ECO/TAC DOMIN
COLONIAL ATTIT PWR SOVEREIGN...TIME/SEQ GEN/LAWS UK
TOT/POP VAL/FREE 20 CMN/WLTH. PAGE 69 A1420

B28
MAIR L.P.,THE PROTECTION OF MINORITIES. EUR+WWI LAW
WOR-45 CONSTN INT/ORG NAT/G LEGIT CT/SYS GP/REL SOVEREIGN
RACE/REL DISCRIM ORD/FREE RESPECT...JURID CONCPT
TIME/SEQ 20. PAGE 93 A1909

B28
MILLER D.H.,THE DRAFTING OF THE COVENANT. UNIV INT/ORG
WOR-45 INTELL NAT/G DELIB/GP PLAN ECO/TAC LEGIT WAR STRUCT
ATTIT PERCEPT...CONCPT TIME/SEQ LEAGUE/NAT TOT/POP PEACE
20. PAGE 101 A2074

B29
DUNN F.,THE PRACTICE AND PROCEDURE OF INTERNATIONAL INT/ORG
CONFERENCES. WOR-45 NAT/G DELIB/GP BAL/PWR LEGIT DIPLOM
EXEC ROUTINE PEACE ORD/FREE RESPECT...JURID CONCPT
METH/CNCPT OBS RECORD TIME/SEQ 20. PAGE 39 A0799

B29
LANGER W.L.,THE FRANCO-RUSSIAN ALLIANCE: 1890-1894. DIPLOM
FRANCE MOD/EUR UK USSR NAT/G CHIEF FORCES BAL/PWR
AGREE WAR PEACE PWR...TIME/SEQ TREATY 19
BISMARCK/O. PAGE 84 A1724

B30
FLEMMING D.,THE TREATY VETO OF THE AMERICAN SENATE. LEGIS
FUT USA+45 USA-45 CONSTN INT/ORG NAT/G TOP/EX LEGIT RIGID/FLEX
GOV/REL PWR...POLICY MAJORIT CONCPT OBS TIME/SEQ
CONGRESS 20. PAGE 46 A0949

B31
BEALES A.C.,THE HISTORY OF PEACE. WOR-45 VOL/ASSN INT/ORG
DELIB/GP CREATE PLAN EDU/PROP ATTIT MORAL ARMS/CONT
...TIME/SEQ VAL/FREE 19/20. PAGE 12 A0239 PEACE

B31
HILL N.,INTERNATIONAL ADMINISTRATION. WOR-45 INT/ORG
DELIB/GP DIPLOM EDU/PROP ALL/VALS...MGT TIME/SEQ ADMIN
LEAGUE/NAT TOT/POP VAL/FREE 20. PAGE 65 A1331

B31
HODGES C.,THE BACKGROUND OF INTERNATIONAL NAT/G
RELATIONS. WOR-45 SOCIETY ECO/DEV ECO/UNDEV INT/ORG BAL/PWR
DIPLOM DOMIN EDU/PROP LEGIT WAR ATTIT DRIVE PERSON
ALL/VALS...CONCPT METH/CNCPT TIME/SEQ CHARTS WORK
LEAGUE/NAT 19/20. PAGE 66 A1350

B31
STUART G.H.,THE INTERNATIONAL CITY OF TANGIER. AFR LOC/G
EUR+WWI MOD/EUR MOROCCO CONSTN PROVS CREATE PLAN INT/ORG
LEGIT PEACE ORD/FREE PWR...INT/LAW OBS TIME/SEQ DIPLOM
CON/ANAL 20 TANGIER. PAGE 139 A2854 SOVEREIGN

B32
BRYCE J.,THE HOLY ROMAN EMPIRE. GERMANY ITALY CHRIST-17C
MOD/EUR CULTURE SOCIETY STRUCT INT/ORG NAT/G SECT NAT/LISM
DIPLOM DOMIN WAR SUPEGO ALL/VALS SOVEREIGN...GEOG
SOC TIME/SEQ CHARTS STERTYP. PAGE 20 A0413

B32
FLEMMING D.,THE UNITED STATES AND THE LEAGUE OF INT/ORG
NATIONS, 1918-1920. FUT USA-45 NAT/G LEGIS TOP/EX EDU/PROP
DEBATE CHOOSE PEACE ATTIT SOVEREIGN...TIME/SEQ
CON/ANAL CONGRESS LEAGUE/NAT 20 TREATY. PAGE 46
A0950

B32
MASTERS R.D.,INTERNATIONAL LAW IN INTERNATIONAL INT/ORG
COURTS. BELGIUM EUR+WWI FRANCE GERMANY MOD/EUR LAW
SWITZERLND WOR-45 SOCIETY STRATA STRUCT LEGIT EXEC INT/LAW
ALL/VALS...JURID HIST/WRIT TIME/SEQ TREND GEN/LAWS
20. PAGE 96 A1961

B32
MORLEY F.,THE SOCIETY OF NATIONS. EUR+WWI UNIV INT/ORG
WOR-45 LAW CONSTN ACT/RES PLAN EDU/PROP LEGIT CONCPT
ROUTINE...POLICY TIME/SEQ LEAGUE/NAT TOT/POP 20.
PAGE 104 A2143

B33
LAUTERPACHT H.,THE FUNCTION OF LAW IN THE INT/ORG
INTERNATIONAL COMMUNITY. WOR-45 NAT/G FORCES CREATE LAW
DOMIN LEGIT COERCE WAR PEACE ATTIT ORD/FREE PWR INT/LAW
SOVEREIGN...JURID CONCPT METH/CNCPT TIME/SEQ
GEN/LAWS GEN/METH LEAGUE/NAT TOT/POP VAL/FREE 20.
PAGE 85 A1749

B35
HUDSON M.,BY PACIFIC MEANS. WOR-45 EDU/PROP INT/ORG
ORD/FREE...CONCPT TIME/SEQ GEN/LAWS LEAGUE/NAT CT/SYS
TOT/POP 20 TREATY. PAGE 68 A1407 PEACE

B35
STALEY E.,WAR AND THE PRIVATE INVESTOR. UNIV WOR-45 FINAN
INTELL SOCIETY INT/ORG NAT/G TOP/EX CAP/ISM ECO/TAC INT/TRADE
WAR ATTIT ALL/VALS...INT TIME/SEQ TREND CON/ANAL DIPLOM
WORK TOT/POP 20. PAGE 137 A2799

B36
SHOTWELL J.,ON THE RIM OF THE ABYSS. EUR+WWI USA-45 NAT/G
STRUCT INT/ORG ACT/RES PLAN EDU/PROP EXEC ATTIT BAL/PWR
ALL/VALS...TIME/SEQ LEAGUE/NAT TOT/POP 20. PAGE 132
A2706

B36
THWAITE D.,THE SEETHING AFRICAN POT: A STUDY OF NAT/LISM
BLACK NATIONALISM 1882-1935. ETHIOPIA SECT VOL/ASSN AFR
COERCE GUERRILLA MURDER DISCRIM MARXISM...PSY RACE/REL
TIME/SEQ 18/20 NEGRO. PAGE 144 A2939 DIPLOM

B37
ROBBINS L.,ECONOMIC PLANNING AND INTERNATIONAL INT/ORG
ORDER. WOR-45 SOCIETY FINAN INDUS NAT/G ECO/TAC PLAN
ROUTINE WEALTH...SOC TIME/SEQ GEN/METH WORK 20 INT/TRADE
KEYNES/JM. PAGE 122 A2492

B38
DE MADARIAGA S.,THE WORLD'S DESIGN. WOR-45 SOCIETY FUT
STRUCT EDU/PROP PEACE ATTIT PERSON ALL/VALS INT/ORG
...SOCIALIST CONCPT TIME/SEQ TREND GEN/LAWS DIPLOM
LEAGUE/NAT. PAGE 35 A0706

B38
FLEMMING D.,THE UNITED STATES AND WORLD USA-45
ORGANIZATION, 1920-1933. ASIA FUT WOR-45 NAT/G INT/ORG
TOP/EX DIPLOM ECO/TAC EDU/PROP LEGIT COERCE WAR PEACE
...TIME/SEQ LEAGUE/NAT 20 CHINJAP. PAGE 47 A0951

B38
HOBSON J.A.,IMPERIALISM. MOD/EUR UK WOR-45 CULTURE DOMIN
ECO/UNDEV NAT/G VOL/ASSN PLAN EDU/PROP LEGIT REGION ECO/TAC
COERCE ATTIT PWR...POLICY PLURIST TIME/SEQ GEN/LAWS BAL/PWR
19/20. PAGE 66 A1348 COLONIAL

B38
PETTEE G.S.,THE PROCESS OF REVOLUTION. COM FRANCE COERCE
ITALY MOD/EUR RUSSIA SPAIN WOR-45 ELITES INTELL CONCPT
SOCIETY STRATA STRUCT INT/ORG NAT/G POL/PAR ACT/RES REV
PLAN EDU/PROP LEGIT EXEC...SOC MYTH TIME/SEQ
TOT/POP 18/20. PAGE 115 A2370

B38
RAPPARD W.E.,THE CRISIS OF DEMOCRACY. EUR+WWI UNIV NAT/G
WOR-45 CULTURE SOCIETY ECO/DEV INT/ORG POL/PAR CONCPT
ACT/RES EDU/PROP EXEC CHOOSE ATTIT ALL/VALS...SOC
OBS HIST/WRIT TIME/SEQ LEAGUE/NAT NAZI TOT/POP 20.
PAGE 119 A2449

B39
BROWN J.F.,CONTEMPORARY WORLD POLITICS. WOR-45 INT/ORG
NAT/G PLAN BAL/PWR EDU/PROP LEGIT REGION NAT/LISM DIPLOM
ORD/FREE PWR SOVEREIGN...POLICY CONCPT HIST/WRIT PEACE
TIME/SEQ GEN/LAWS LEAGUE/NAT. PAGE 20 A0403

B39
MARRIOTT J.,COMMONWEALTH OR ANARCHY: A SURVEY OF FUT
PROJECTS OF PEACE. WOR-45 STRATA DOMIN ATTIT INT/ORG
ORD/FREE PWR...TRADIT TIME/SEQ GEN/METH 16/20 PEACE
CMN/WLTH. PAGE 95 A1945

B39
WILSON G.G.,HANDBOOK OF INTERNATIONAL LAW. FUT UNIV INT/ORG
USA-45 WOR-45 SOCIETY LEGIT ATTIT DISPL DRIVE LAW
ALL/VALS...INT/LAW TIME/SEQ TREND. PAGE 165 A3359 CONCPT
WAR

B39
ZIMMERN A.,MODERN POLITICAL DOCTRINE. WOR-45 NAT/G
CULTURE SOCIETY ECO/UNDEV DELIB/GP EX/STRUC CREATE ECO/TAC
DOMIN COERCE NAT/LISM ATTIT RIGID/FLEX ORD/FREE PWR BAL/PWR
WEALTH...POLICY CONCPT OBS TIME/SEQ TREND TOT/POP INT/TRADE
LEAGUE/NAT 20. PAGE 170 A3454

B40
CARR E.H.,THE TWENTY YEARS' CRISIS 1919-1939. FUT INT/ORG
WOR-45 BAL/PWR ECO/TAC LEGIT TOTALISM ATTIT DIPLOM
ALL/VALS...POLICY JURID CONCPT TIME/SEQ TREND PEACE
GEN/LAWS TOT/POP 20. PAGE 24 A0498

B40
MILLER E.,THE NEUROSES OF WAR. UNIV INTELL SOCIETY HEALTH
INT/ORG NAT/G EDU/PROP DISPL DRIVE PERCEPT PERSON PSY

RIGID/FLEX...SOC TIME/SEQ 20. PAGE 101 A2075 WAR

B40
RAPPARD W.E.,THE QUEST FOR PEACE. UNIV USA-45 WOR-45 SOCIETY INT/ORG NAT/G PLAN EXEC ROUTINE WAR ATTIT DRIVE ALL/VALS...POLICY CONCPT OBS TIME/SEQ LEAGUE/NAT TOT/POP 20. PAGE 119 A2450 EUR+WWI ACT/RES PEACE

S40
FLORIN J.,"BOLSHEVIST AND NATIONAL SOCIALIST DOCTRINES OF INTERNATIONAL LAW." EUR+WWI GERMANY USSR R+D INT/ORG NAT/G DIPLOM DOMIN EDU/PROP SOCISM ...CONCPT TIME/SEQ 20. PAGE 47 A0955 LAW ATTIT TOTALISM INT/LAW

B41
BURTON M.E.,THE ASSEMBLY OF THE LEAGUE OF NATIONS. WOR-45 CONSTN SOCIETY STRUCT INT/ORG NAT/G CREATE ATTIT RIGID/FLEX PWR...POLICY TIME/SEQ LEAGUE/NAT 20. PAGE 22 A0448 DELIB/GP EX/STRUC DIPLOM

B41
MCCLURE W.,INTERNATIONAL EXECUTIVE AGREEMENTS. USA-45 WOR-45 INT/ORG NAT/G DELIB/GP ADJUD ROUTINE ORD/FREE PWR...TIME/SEQ TREND CON/ANAL. PAGE 97 A2000 TOP/EX DIPLOM

B41
WHITAKER A.P.,THE UNITED STATES AND THE INDEPENDENCE OF LATIN AMERICA, 1800-1830. PORTUGAL SPAIN USA-45 COLONIAL REGION SOVEREIGN...POLICY TIME/SEQ BIBLIOG/A 18/20. PAGE 163 A3329 DIPLOM L/A+17C CONCPT ORD/FREE

S41
WRIGHT Q.,"FUNDAMENTAL PROBLEMS OF INTERNATIONAL ORGANIZATION." UNIV WOR-45 STRUCT FORCES ACT/RES CREATE DOMIN EDU/PROP LEGIT REGION NAT/LISM ORD/FREE PWR RESPECT SOVEREIGN...JURID SOC CONCPT METH/CNCPT TIME/SEQ 20. PAGE 167 A3405 INT/ORG ATTIT PEACE

B43
HEMLEBEN S.J.,PLANS FOR WORLD PEACE THROUGH SIX CENTURIES. WOR-45 EDU/PROP DRIVE PWR...CONCPT TIME/SEQ GEN/LAWS TOT/POP LEAGUE/NAT 14/20. PAGE 64 A1312 INT/ORG PEACE

B43
SERENI A.P.,THE ITALIAN CONCEPTION OF INTERNATIONAL LAW. EUR+WWI MOD/EUR INT/ORG NAT/G DOMIN COERCE ORD/FREE FASCISM...OBS/ENVIR TREND 20. PAGE 131 A2686 LAW TIME/SEQ INT/LAW ITALY

B44
DAVIS H.E.,PIONEERS IN WORLD ORDER. WOR-45 CONSTN ECO/TAC DOMIN EDU/PROP LEGIT ADJUD ADMIN ARMS/CONT CHOOSE KNOWL ORD/FREE...POLICY JURID SOC STAT OBS CENSUS TIME/SEQ ANTHOL LEAGUE/NAT 20. PAGE 34 A0691 INT/ORG ROUTINE

B44
HUDSON M.,INTERNATIONAL TRIBUNALS PAST AND FUTURE. FUT WOR-45 LAW EDU/PROP ADJUD ORD/FREE...CONCPT TIME/SEQ TREND GEN/LAWS TOT/POP VAL/FREE 18/20. PAGE 69 A1408 INT/ORG STRUCT INT/LAW

B44
LIPPMANN W.,US WAR AIMS. USA-45 DIPLOM ATTIT MORAL ORD/FREE PWR...CONCPT TIME/SEQ GEN/LAWS TOT/POP 20. PAGE 89 A1828 FUT INT/ORG PEACE WAR

B44
MACIVER R.M.,TOWARDS AN ABIDING PEACE. USA-45 ECO/TAC EDU/PROP DRIVE ORD/FREE PWR WEALTH...CONCPT TIME/SEQ GEN/METH TOT/POP 20. PAGE 92 A1890 INT/ORG PEACE INT/LAW

B44
WHITTON J.B.,THE SECOND CHANCE: AMERICA AND THE PEACE. EUR+WWI USA-45 SOCIETY STRUCT INT/ORG NAT/G LEGIT EXEC WAR ALL/VALS...SOC CONCPT TIME/SEQ TREND CONGRESS 20. PAGE 164 A3340 LEGIS PEACE

B45
CONOVER H.F.,THE NAZI STATE: WAR CRIMES AND WAR CRIMINALS. GERMANY CULTURE NAT/G SECT FORCES DIPLOM INT/TRADE EDU/PROP...INT/LAW BIOG HIST/WRIT TIME/SEQ 20. PAGE 30 A0600 BIBLIOG WAR CRIME

B46
BRODIE B.,THE OBSOLETE WEAPON: ATOMIC POWER AND WORLD ORDER. COM USA+45 USSR WOR+45 DELIB/GP PLAN ORD/FREE PWR...CONCPT TIME/SEQ TREND UN 20. PAGE 19 A0380 INT/ORG TEC/DEV ARMS/CONT NUC/PWR

B47
HILL M.,IMMUNITIES AND PRIVILEGES OF INTERNATIONAL OFFICIALS. CANADA EUR+WWI NETHERLAND SWITZERLND LAW LEGIS DIPLOM LEGIT RESPECT...TIME/SEQ LEAGUE/NAT UN VAL/FREE 20. PAGE 65 A1330 INT/ORG ADMIN

B47
MANDER L.,FOUNDATIONS OF MODERN WORLD SOCIETY. WOR+45 DELIB/GP ECO/TAC INT/TRADE EDU/PROP ALL/VALS ...TIME/SEQ GEN/LAWS TOT/POP VAL/FREE ILO 20. PAGE 94 A1917 INT/ORG EX/STRUC DIPLOM

B47
TOWLE L.W.,INTERNATIONAL TRADE AND COMMERCIAL POLICY. WOR+45 LAW ECO/DEV FINAN INDUS NAT/G ECO/TAC WEALTH...TIME/SEQ ILO 20. PAGE 144 A2955 MARKET INT/ORG INT/TRADE

B48
JESSUP P.C.,A MODERN LAW OF NATIONS. FUT WOR+45 WOR-45 SOCIETY NAT/G DELIB/GP LEGIS BAL/PWR EDU/PROP LEGIT PWR...INT/LAW JURID TIME/SEQ LEAGUE/NAT 20. PAGE 74 A1514 INT/ORG ADJUD

B49
ROSENHAUPT H.W.,HOW TO WAGE PEACE. USA+45 SOCIETY STRATA STRUCT R+D INT/ORG POL/PAR LEGIS ACT/RES CREATE PLAN EDU/PROP ADMIN EXEC ATTIT ALL/VALS ...TIME/SEQ TREND COLD/WAR 20. PAGE 124 A2536 INTELL CONCPT DIPLOM

B49
SINGER K.,THE IDEA OF CONFLICT. UNIV INTELL INT/ORG NAT/G PLAN ROUTINE ATTIT DRIVE ALL/VALS...POLICY CONCPT TIME/SEQ. PAGE 133 A2730 ACT/RES SOC

B49
STETTINIUS E.R.,ROOSEVELT AND THE RUSSIANS: THE YALTA CONFERENCE. UK USSR WOR+45 WOR-45 INT/ORG VOL/ASSN TOP/EX ACT/RES EDU/PROP PEACE ATTIT DRIVE PERSON SUPEGO PWR...POLICY CONCPT MYTH OBS TIME/SEQ AUD/VIS COLD/WAR 20 CHURCHLL/W YALTA ROOSEVLT/F. PAGE 138 A2819 DIPLOM DELIB/GP BIOG

B49
STREIT C.,UNION NOW. UNIV USA-45 WOR-45 INTELL STRUCT INT/ORG NAT/G PLAN DIPLOM EXEC ATTIT ...CONCPT TIME/SEQ. PAGE 139 A2849 SOCIETY ACT/RES WAR

L49
COMM. STUDY ORGAN. PEACE,"A TEN YEAR RECORD, 1939-1949." FUT WOR+45 LAW R+D CONSULT DELIB/GP CREATE LEGIT ROUTINE ORD/FREE...TIME/SEQ UN 20. PAGE 28 A0578 INT/ORG CONSTN PEACE

S49
FOX W.T.R.,"INTERWAR INTERNATIONAL RELATIONS RESEARCH: THE AMERICAN EXPERIENCE." USA+45 USA-45 INTELL INT/ORG VOL/ASSN OP/RES ATTIT SKILL ...TIME/SEQ LEAGUE/NAT 20. PAGE 48 A0973 ACT/RES CON/ANAL

B50
ALMOND G.A.,THE AMERICAN PEOPLE AND FOREIGN POLICY. USA+45 USA-45 CULTURE SOCIETY STRUCT CONSEN PERSON PWR POPULISM...TIME/SEQ TREND 20 COLD/WAR. PAGE 6 A0129 ATTIT DIPLOM DECISION ELITES

B50
JIMENEZ E.,VOTING AND HANDLING OF DISPUTES IN THE SECURITY COUNCIL. WOR+45 CONSTN INT/ORG DIPLOM LEGIT DETER CHOOSE MORAL ORD/FREE PWR...JURID TIME/SEQ COLD/WAR UN 20. PAGE 74 A1517 DELIB/GP ROUTINE

B50
MCCAMY J.,THE ADMINISTRATION OF AMERICAN FOREIGN AFFAIRS. USA+45 SOCIETY INT/ORG NAT/G ACT/RES PLAN INT/TRADE EDU/PROP ADJUD ALL/VALS...METH/CNCPT TIME/SEQ CONGRESS 20. PAGE 97 A1996 EXEC STRUCT DIPLOM

B50
NORTHROP F.S.C.,THE TAMING OF THE NATIONS. KOREA USA+45 USSR WOR+45 STRUCT ECO/UNDEV INT/ORG NAT/G TOP/EX NUC/PWR ATTIT ALL/VALS...TIME/SEQ 20 HIROSHIMA. PAGE 110 A2255 CONCPT BAL/PWR

B51
HAVILAND H.F.,THE POLITICAL ROLE OF THE GENERAL ASSEMBLY. WOR+45 DELIB/GP EDU/PROP PEACE RIGID/FLEX PWR...CONCPT TIME/SEQ GEN/LAWS UN VAL/FREE 20. PAGE 63 A1290 INT/ORG ORD/FREE DIPLOM

B51
MACLAURIN J.,THE UNITED NATIONS AND POWER POLITICS. WOR+45 CONSULT EDU/PROP LEGIT ADJUD EXEC MORAL ORD/FREE...HUM JURID CONCPT RECORD TIME/SEQ UN COLD/WAR 20. PAGE 93 A1896 INT/ORG ROUTINE

B51
VINER J.,INTERNATIONAL ECONOMICS. USA-45 WOR-45 ECO/DEV INDUS NAT/G ECO/TAC ALL/VALS...TIME/SEQ 20. PAGE 159 A3238 FINAN INT/ORG WAR INT/TRADE

B51
WELLES S.,SEVEN DECISIONS THAT SHAPED HISTORY. ASIA FRANCE FUT USA+45 WOR+45 WOR-45 CONSTN STRUCT INT/ORG NAT/G ACT/RES EDU/PROP DRIVE...POLICY CONCPT TIME/SEQ TREND TOT/POP UN 20 CHINJAP. PAGE 163 A3315 USA-45 DIPLOM WAR

L51
LISSITZYN O.J.,"THE INTERNATIONAL COURT OF JUSTICE." WOR+45 INT/ORG LEGIT ORD/FREE...CONCPT TIME/SEQ TREND GEN/LAWS VAL/FREE 20 ICJ. PAGE 90 A1839 ADJUD JURID INT/LAW

L51
ULAM A.B.,"THE COMIMFORM AND THE PEOPLE'S DEMOCRACIES." EUR+WWI WOR+45 STRUCT NAT/G POL/PAR TOP/EX ACT/RES PLAN ECO/TAC DOMIN ATTIT ALL/VALS ...HIST/WRIT TIME/SEQ 20 COMINFORM. PAGE 146 A2992 COM INT/ORG USSR TOTALISM

L51
WHITAKER A.P.,"DEVELOPMENT OF AMERICAN REGIONALISM: THE ORGANIZATION OF AMERICAN STATES." L/A+17C USA+45 VOL/ASSN DELIB/GP FORCES TOP/EX ACT/RES ECO/TAC CT/SYS REGION PEACE ALL/VALS OAS 20. PAGE 163 A3330 INT/ORG TIME/SEQ DETER

C51
GRUNDER G.A.,"THE PHILIPPINES AND THE UNITED STATES." PHILIPPINE S/ASIA USA-45 NAT/G POL/PAR ADMIN SOVEREIGN...TIME/SEQ BIBLIOG 20. PAGE 57 A1181 COLONIAL POLICY DIPLOM ECO/TAC

B52
ALEXANDROWICZ C.H.,INTERNATIONAL ECONOMIC ORGANIZATION. WOR+45 ECO/DEV ECO/UNDEV DIST/IND FINAN MARKET PLAN ECO/TAC LEGIT DRIVE WEALTH INT/ORG INT/TRADE

...POLICY CONCPT QUANT OBS TIME/SEQ GEN/LAWS WORK EEC ILO OEEC UNESCO 20. PAGE 6 A0114

B52
BARR S.,CITIZENS OF THE WORLD. USA+45 WOR+45 CULTURE FORCES LEGIS ACT/RES BAL/PWR LEGIT PEACE ATTIT ORD/FREE PWR...PLURIST CONCPT OBS TIME/SEQ COLD/WAR 20. PAGE 11 A0227 — NAT/G INT/ORG DIPLOM

B52
FIFIELD R.H.,WOODROW WILSON AND THE FAR EAST. ASIA CHIEF BAL/PWR CONFER COLONIAL ARMS/CONT WAR ...TIME/SEQ NAT/COMP BIBLIOG 19/20 WILSON/W LEAGUE/NAT PRESIDENT. PAGE 45 A0926 — DIPLOM DELIB/GP INT/ORG

B52
JACKSON E.,MEETING OF THE MINDS: A WAY TO PEACE THROUGH MEDIATION. WOR+45 INDUS INT/ORG NAT/G DELIB/GP DIPLOM EDU/PROP LEGIT ORD/FREE...NEW/IDEA SELF/OBS TIME/SEQ CHARTS GEN/LAWS TOT/POP 20 UN TREATY. PAGE 72 A1474 — LABOR JUDGE

B52
MANTOUX E.,THE CARTHAGINIAN PEACE. GERMANY WOR-45 SOCIETY FINAN INT/ORG DELIB/GP FORCES PLAN LEGIT ...CONCPT TIME/SEQ 20 KEYNES/JM HITLER/A. PAGE 94 A1935 — ECO/DEV INT/TRADE WAR

B52
VANDENBOSCH A.,THE UN: BACKGROUND, ORGANIZATION, FUNCTIONS, ACTIVITIES. WOR+45 LAW CONSTN STRUCT INT/ORG CONSULT BAL/PWR EDU/PROP EXEC ALL/VALS ...POLICY CONCPT UN 20. PAGE 158 A3218 — DELIB/GP TIME/SEQ PEACE

B52
WALTERS F.P.,A HISTORY OF THE LEAGUE OF NATIONS. EUR+WWI CONSTN NAT/G LEGIS TOP/EX ACT/RES PLAN EDU/PROP LEGIT ROUTINE ATTIT...TREND LEAGUE/NAT 20 CHINJAP. PAGE 161 A3271 — INT/ORG TIME/SEQ NAT/LISM

S52
HAAS E.B.,"THE RECONCILIATION OF CONFLICT, COLONIAL POLICY AIMS: ACCEPTANCE OF THE LEAGUE OF NATIONS MANDATE SYSTEM." FRANCE GERMANY UK WOR+45 WOR-45 LEGIT ATTIT DRIVE ORD/FREE...OLD/LIB INT SYS/QU TIME/SEQ TREND LEAGUE/NAT 20. PAGE 58 A1201 — INT/ORG COLONIAL

C52
FIFIELD R.H.,"WOODROW WILSON AND THE FAR EAST." ASIA CHIEF DELIB/GP BAL/PWR CONFER COLONIAL ARMS/CONT WAR...TIME/SEQ NAT/COMP 19/20 WILSON/W LEAGUE/NAT. PAGE 45 A0925 — BIBLIOG DIPLOM INT/ORG

B53
COHEN B.C.,CITIZEN EDUCATION IN WORLD AFFAIRS. USA+45 INT/ORG VOL/ASSN CONSULT ATTIT PWR...INT TIME/SEQ 20. PAGE 27 A0559 — KNOWL EDU/PROP DIPLOM

B53
MACMAHON A.W.,ADMINISTRATION IN FOREIGN AFFAIRS. NAT/G CONSULT DELIB/GP LEGIS ACT/RES CREATE ADMIN EXEC RIGID/FLEX PWR...METH/CNCPT TIME/SEQ TOT/POP VAL/FREE 20. PAGE 93 A1899 — USA+45 ROUTINE FOR/AID DIPLOM

B53
ZIMMERN A.,THE AMERICAN ROAD TO PEACE. USA+45 LAW INT/ORG NAT/G EX/STRUC TOP/EX EDU/PROP LEGIT COERCE PEACE ATTIT ORD/FREE PWR...CONCPT TIME/SEQ LEAGUE/NAT TOT/POP VAL/FREE 20 UN. PAGE 170 A3455 — USA-45 DIPLOM

B54
ARON R.,CENTURY OF TOTAL WAR. FUT WOR+45 WOR-45 SOCIETY INT/ORG NAT/G FORCES TOP/EX CREATE BAL/PWR DOMIN EDU/PROP COERCE DETER PEACE TOTALISM PWR ...TIME/SEQ TREND COLD/WAR TOT/POP VAL/FREE LEAGUE/NAT 20. PAGE 9 A0179 — ATTIT WAR

B54
CHEEVER D.S.,ORGANIZING FOR PEACE. FUT WOR+45 WOR-45 STRATA STRUCT NAT/G CREATE DIPLOM LEGIT REGION COERCE DETER PEACE ATTIT DRIVE ALL/VALS ...TIME/SEQ TREND UN LEAGUE/NAT. PAGE 26 A0525 — INT/ORG

B54
COUDENHOVE-KALERGI,AN IDEA CONQUERS THE WORLD. EUR+WWI MOD/EUR USA-45 CONSTN FAM CREATE EDU/PROP ATTIT PERSON KNOWL...CONCPT SELF/OBS TIME/SEQ. PAGE 31 A0635 — INT/ORG BIOG DIPLOM

B54
MANGONE G.,A SHORT HISTORY OF INTERNATIONAL ORGANIZATION. MOD/EUR USA+45 USA-45 WOR+45 WOR-45 LAW LEGIS CREATE LEGIT ROUTINE RIGID/FLEX PWR ...JURID CONCPT OBS TIME/SEQ STERTYP GEN/LAWS UN TOT/POP VAL/FREE 18/20. PAGE 94 A1921 — INT/ORG INT/LAW

B54
NORTHROP F.S.C.,EUROPEAN UNION AND UNITED STATES FOREIGN POLICY: A STUDY IN SOCIOLOGICAL JURISPRUDENCE. EUR+WWI MOD/EUR USA+45 SOCIETY STRUCT NAT/G CREATE ECO/TAC DOMIN EDU/PROP REGION ATTIT RIGID/FLEX HEALTH ORD/FREE WEALTH ...METH/CNCPT TIME/SEQ TREND. PAGE 110 A2256 — INT/ORG SOC DIPLOM

B54
NUSSBAUM D.,A CONCISE HISTORY OF THE LAW OF NATIONS. ASIA CHRIST-17C EUR+WWI ISLAM MEDIT-7 MOD/EUR S/ASIA UNIV WOR+45 WOR-45 SOCIETY STRUCT EXEC ATTIT ALL/VALS...CONCPT HIST/WRIT TIME/SEQ. PAGE 110 A2263 — INT/ORG LAW PEACE INT/LAW

B54
TINBERGEN J.,INTERNATIONAL ECONOMIC INTEGRATION. WOR+45 WOR-45 ECO/UNDEV NAT/G ECO/TAC BAL/PAY ...METH/CNCPT STAT TIME/SEQ GEN/METH OEEC 20. PAGE 144 A2941 — INT/ORG ECO/DEV INT/TRADE

B54
WHITAKER A.P.,THE WESTERN HEMISPHERE IDEA. USA+45 USA-45 CONSTN INT/ORG NAT/G DIPLOM SOVEREIGN...GEOG TIME/SEQ OAS 19/20 MONROE/DOC. PAGE 164 A3331 — L/A+17C CONCPT REGION

B55
CHOWDHURI R.N.,INTERNATIONAL MANDATES AND TRUSTEESHIP SYSTEMS. WOR+45 STRUCT ECO/UNDEV INT/ORG LEGIS DOMIN EDU/PROP LEGIT ADJUD EXEC PWR ...CONCPT TIME/SEQ UN 20. PAGE 26 A0534 — DELIB/GP PLAN SOVEREIGN

B55
COTTRELL W.F.,ENERGY AND SOCIETY. FUT WOR+45 WOR-45 ECO/DEV ECO/UNDEV INT/ORG NAT/G DETER ORD/FREE PWR SKILL WEALTH...SOC TIME/SEQ TOT/POP VAL/FREE 20. PAGE 31 A0634 — TEC/DEV BAL/PWR PEACE

B55
JONES J.M.,THE FIFTEEN WEEKS (FEBRUARY 21-JUNE 5, 1947). EUR+WWI USA+45 PROB/SOLV BAL/PWR...POLICY TIME/SEQ 20 COLD/WAR MARSHL/PLN TRUMAN/HS WASHING/DC. PAGE 75 A1532 — DIPLOM ECO/TAC FOR/AID

B55
PANT Y.P.,PLANNING IN UNDERDEVELOPED ECONOMIES. INDIA NEPAL INT/TRADE COLONIAL SOVEREIGN ALL/IDEOS ...TIME/SEQ METH/COMP 20. PAGE 114 A2334 — ECO/UNDEV PLAN ECO/TAC DIPLOM

B55
SNYDER R.C.,AMERICAN FOREIGN POLICY. USA+45 USA-45 WOR+45 WOR-45 CONSTN INT/ORG POL/PAR VOL/ASSN DELIB/GP LEGIS CREATE DOMIN EDU/PROP EXEC COERCE ATTIT DRIVE ORD/FREE PWR...MGT OBS RECORD TIME/SEQ TREND. PAGE 134 A2752 — NAT/G DIPLOM

B55
TANNENBAUM F.,THE AMERICAN TRADITION IN FOREIGN POLICY. USA+45 USA-45 CONSTN INT/ORG NAT/G POL/PAR VOL/ASSN TOP/EX LEGIT DRIVE ORD/FREE PWR...CONCPT GEN/LAWS CONGRESS LEAGUE/NAT COLD/WAR OAS 18/20. PAGE 141 A2887 — TIME/SEQ

L55
ROSTOW W.W.,"RUSSIA AND CHINA UNDER COMMUNISM." CHINA/COM USSR INTELL STRUCT INT/ORG NAT/G POL/PAR TOP/EX ACT/RES PLAN ADMIN ATTIT ALL/VALS MARXISM ...CONCPT OBS TIME/SEQ TREND GOV/COMP VAL/FREE 20. PAGE 124 A2543 — COM ASIA

B56
BROOK D.,THE UNITED NATIONS AND CHINA DILEMMA. CHINA/COM FUT WOR+45 ECO/UNDEV NAT/G DELIB/GP ACT/RES DIPLOM ROUTINE NAT/LISM TOTALISM ATTIT DRIVE...CONCPT OBS TIME/SEQ UN TOT/POP TIME UN 20. PAGE 19 A0390 — ASIA INT/ORG BAL/PWR

B56
FOSTER J.G.,BRITAIN IN WESTERN EUROPE: WEU AND THE ATLANTIC ALLIANCE. EUR+WWI FRANCE GERMANY GERMANY/W ITALY UK STRATA NAT/G DELIB/GP ECO/TAC ORD/FREE PWR ...TRADIT TIME/SEQ TREND OEEC PARLIAMENT 20 EUROPE/W. PAGE 47 A0969 — INT/ORG FORCES WEAPON

B56
HAAS E.B.,DYNAMICS OF INTERNATIONAL RELATIONS. WOR-45 ELITES INT/ORG VOL/ASSN EX/STRUC FORCES ECO/TAC DOMIN LEGIT COERCE ATTIT PERSON PWR ...CONCPT TIME/SEQ CHARTS COLD/WAR 20. PAGE 58 A1202 — WOR+45 NAT/G DIPLOM

B56
HOUSTON J.A.,LATIN AMERICA IN THE UNITED NATIONS. CONSULT DIPLOM LEGIT ROUTINE ATTIT ORD/FREE PWR ...JURID OBS RECORD TIME/SEQ CHARTS 20 UN. PAGE 68 A1395 — L/A+17C INT/ORG INT/LAW REGION

B56
LOVEDAY A.,REFLECTIONS ON INTERNATIONAL ADMINISTRATION. WOR+45 WOR-45 DELIB/GP ACT/RES ADMIN EXEC ROUTINE DRIVE...METH/CNCPT TIME/SEQ CON/ANAL SIMUL TOT/POP 20. PAGE 91 A1865 — INT/ORG MGT

B56
REITZEL W.,UNITED STATES FOREIGN POLICY, 1945-1955. USA+45 WOR+45 CONSTN INT/ORG EDU/PROP LEGIT EXEC COERCE NUC/PWR PEACE ATTIT ORD/FREE PWR...DECISION CONCPT OBS RECORD TIME/SEQ TREND COLD/WAR UN CONGRESS. PAGE 120 A2464 — NAT/G POLICY DIPLOM

B57
BEERS H.P.,THE FRENCH IN NORTH AMERICA. FRANCE USA-45...TIME/SEQ BIBLIOG. PAGE 12 A0247 — HIST/WRIT DIPLOM BIOG WRITING

B57
BROMBERGER M.,LES SECRETS DE L'EXPEDITION D'EGYPTE. FRANCE ISLAM UAR UK USA+45 USSR WOR+45 INT/ORG NAT/G FORCES BAL/PWR ECO/TAC DOMIN WAR NAT/LISM ATTIT PWR SOVEREIGN...MAJORIT TIME/SEQ CHARTS SUEZ COLD/WAR 20. PAGE 19 A0387 — COERCE DIPLOM

B57
DE VISSCHER C.,THEORY AND REALITY IN PUBLIC INTERNATIONAL LAW. WOR+45 WOR-45 SOCIETY NAT/G CT/SYS ATTIT MORAL ORD/FREE PWR...JURID CONCPT METH/CNCPT TIME/SEQ GEN/LAWS LEAGUE/NAT TOT/POP VAL/FREE COLD/WAR. PAGE 35 A0716 — INT/ORG LAW INT/LAW

B57
DEAN V.M.,THE NATURE OF THE NON-WESTERN WORLD. AFR ASIA L/A+17C S/ASIA CULTURE SOCIETY STRATA ECO/DEV DIPLOM ECO/TAC FOR/AID ATTIT DRIVE ALL/VALS ...RELATIV SOC CONCPT TIME/SEQ TREND TOT/POP 20. PAGE 35 A0718
ECO/UNDEV STERTYP NAT/LISM

B57
DEUTSCH K.W.,POLITICAL COMMUNITY AND THE NORTH ATLANTIC AREA: INTERNATIONAL ORGANIZATION IN THE LIGHT OF HISTORICAL EXPERIENCE. MOD/EUR USA+45 USA-45 SOCIETY FORCES TOP/EX CREATE PLAN DIPLOM DOMIN EDU/PROP LEGIT ATTIT ORD/FREE PWR...SAMP/SIZ TIME/SEQ CHARTS TOT/POP. PAGE 36 A0736
EUR+WWI INT/ORG PEACE REGION

B57
FRAZIER E.F.,RACE AND CULTURE CONTACTS IN THE MODERN WORLD. WOR+45 WOR-45 SOCIETY ECO/DEV AGRI INDUS INT/ORG LABOR NAT/G PERSON RIGID/FLEX ALL/VALS...SOC TIME/SEQ WORK 19/20. PAGE 48 A0991
CULTURE RACE/REL

B57
JENKS C.W.,THE INTERNATIONAL PROTECTION OF TRADE UNION FREEDOM. FUT WOR+45 WOR-45 VOL/ASSN DELIB/GP CT/SYS REGION ROUTINE...JURID METH/CNCPT RECORD TIME/SEQ CHARTS ILO WORK OAS 20. PAGE 73 A1504
LABOR INT/ORG

B57
KENNAN G.F.,RUSSIA, THE ATOM AND THE WEST. COM EUR+WWI FUT WOR+45 SOCIETY ECO/DEV FORCES DIPLOM ECO/TAC DOMIN EDU/PROP COERCE NUC/PWR ATTIT DRIVE ORD/FREE PWR...POLICY OBS TIME/SEQ TREND COLD/WAR NATO 20. PAGE 77 A1574
NAT/G INT/ORG USSR

B57
LAVES W.H.C.,UNESCO. FUT WOR+45 NAT/G CONSULT DELIB/GP TEC/DEV ECO/TAC EDU/PROP PEACE ORD/FREE ...CONCPT TIME/SEQ TREND UNESCO VAL/FREE 20. PAGE 86 A1751
INT/ORG KNOWL

B57
LEVONTIN A.V.,THE MYTH OF INTERNATIONAL SECURITY: A JURIDICAL AND CRITICAL ANALYSIS. FUT WOR+45 WOR-45 LAW NAT/G VOL/ASSN ACT/RES BAL/PWR ATTIT ORD/FREE ...JURID METH/CNCPT TIME/SEQ TREND STERTYP 20. PAGE 88 A1797
INT/ORG INT/LAW SOVEREIGN MYTH

B57
MATECKI B.,ESTABLISHMENT OF THE INTERNATIONAL FINANCE CORPORATION AND UNITED STATES POLICY. USA+45 WOR+45 CONSTN NAT/G CREATE RIGID/FLEX KNOWL ...METH/CNCPT TIME/SEQ SIMUL TOT/POP 20 INTL/FINAN. PAGE 96 A1964
FINAN INT/ORG DIPLOM

B57
MURRAY J.N.,THE UNITED NATIONS TRUSTEESHIP SYSTEM. AFR WOR+45 CONSTN CONSULT LEGIS EDU/PROP LEGIT EXEC ROUTINE...INT TIME/SEQ SOMALI UN 20. PAGE 106 A2181
INT/ORG DELIB/GP

B57
ROSENNE S.,THE INTERNATIONAL COURT OF JUSTICE. WOR+45 LAW DOMIN LEGIT PEACE PWR SOVEREIGN...JURID CONCPT RECORD TIME/SEQ CON/ANAL CHARTS UN TOT/POP VAL/FREE LEAGUE/NAT 20 ICJ. PAGE 124 A2537
INT/ORG CT/SYS INT/LAW

B57
WASSENBERGH H.A.,POST-WAR INTERNATIONAL CIVIL AVIATION POLICY AND THE LAW OF THE AIR. WOR+45 AIR INT/ORG DOMIN LEGIT PEACE ORD/FREE...POLICY JURID NEW/IDEA OBS TIME/SEQ TREND CHARTS 20 TREATY. PAGE 162 A3290
COM/IND NAT/G INT/LAW

L57
FURNISS E.S.,"SOME PERSPECTIVES ON AMERICAN MILITARY ASSISTANCE." USA+45 WOR+45 ECO/UNDEV INT/ORG ECO/TAC ORD/FREE...GEOG TIME/SEQ TREND COLD/WAR 20. PAGE 50 A1028
FORCES FOR/AID WEAPON

L57
HAAS E.B.,"REGIONAL INTEGRATION AND NATIONAL POLICY." WOR+45 VOL/ASSN DELIB/GP EX/STRUC ECO/TAC DOMIN EDU/PROP LEGIT COERCE ATTIT PERCEPT KNOWL ...TIME/SEQ COLD/WAR 20 UN. PAGE 59 A1203
INT/ORG ORD/FREE REGION

L57
WARREN S.,"FOREIGN AID AND FOREIGN POLICY." USA+45 WOR+45 WOR-45 DIST/IND INDUS MARKET CONSULT CREATE DIPLOM EDU/PROP LEGIT ATTIT RIGID/FLEX...TIME/SEQ GEN/LAWS WORK 20. PAGE 161 A3285
ECO/UNDEV ALL/VALS ECO/TAC FOR/AID

S57
ELDER R.E.,"THE PUBLIC STUDIES DIVISION OF THE DEPARTMENT OF STATE: PUBLIC OPINION ANALYSTS IN THE FORMULATION AND CONDUCT OF." INT/ORG CONSULT DOMIN EDU/PROP ADMIN ATTIT PWR...CONCPT OBS TIME/SEQ VAL/FREE 20. PAGE 41 A0836
USA+45 NAT/G DIPLOM

B58
CARROLL H.N.,THE HOUSE OF REPRESENTATIVES AND FOREIGN AFFAIRS. USA+45 USA-45 NAT/G POL/PAR DIPLOM FOR/AID LEGIT ROUTINE PWR...TIME/SEQ CONGRESS. PAGE 25 A0502
DELIB/GP LEGIS

B58
REUTER P.,INTERNATIONAL INSTITUTIONS. WOR+45 WOR-45 CULTURE SOCIETY VOL/ASSN LEGIT ROUTINE GP/REL INGP/REL KNOWL...JURID METH/CNCPT TIME/SEQ 20. PAGE 120 A2469
INT/ORG PSY

B59
BALL M.M.,NATO AND THE EUROPEAN MOVEMENT. EUR+WWI USA+45 INT/ORG FORCES BAL/PWR EDU/PROP LEGIT REGION ATTIT ORD/FREE PWR...STAT OBS TIME/SEQ TREND CHARTS ORG/CHARTS STERTYP COLD/WAR EEC OEEC 20 NATO. PAGE 10 A0212
DELIB/GP STRUCT

B59
BRODIE B.,STRATEGY IN THE MISSILE AGE. FUT WOR+45 CONSULT PLAN COERCE DETER RIGID/FLEX PWR...CONCPT TIME/SEQ TREND 20. PAGE 19 A0381
ACT/RES FORCES ARMS/CONT NUC/PWR

B59
CHINA INSTITUTE OF AMERICA.,CHINA AND THE UNITED NATIONS. CHINA/COM FUT STRUCT EDU/PROP LEGIT ADMIN ATTIT KNOWL ORD/FREE PWR...OBS RECORD STAND/INT TIME/SEQ UN LEAGUE/NAT UNESCO 20. PAGE 26 A0531
ASIA INT/ORG

B59
DIEBOLD W. JR.,THE SCHUMAN PLAN: A STUDY IN ECONOMIC COOPERATION, 1950-1959. EUR+WWI FRANCE GERMANY USA+45 EXTR/IND CONSULT DELIB/GP PLAN DIPLOM ECO/TAC INT/TRADE ROUTINE ORD/FREE WEALTH ...METH/CNCPT STAT CONT/OBS INT TIME/SEQ ECSC 20. PAGE 37 A0759
INT/ORG REGION

B59
LAQUER W.Z.,THE SOVIET UNION AND THE MIDDLE EAST. COM UAR USSR ECO/UNDEV NAT/G VOL/ASSN ECO/TAC EDU/PROP COLONIAL EXEC PWR...TIME/SEQ TREND COLD/WAR 20. PAGE 85 A1730
ISLAM DRIVE FOR/AID NAT/LISM

L59
BEGUIN B.,"ILO AND THE TRIPARTITE SYSTEM." EUR+WWI WOR+45 WOR-45 CONSTN ECO/DEV ECO/UNDEV INDUS INT/ORG NAT/G VOL/ASSN DELIB/GP PLAN TEC/DEV LEGIT ORD/FREE WEALTH...CONCPT TIME/SEQ WORK ILO 20. PAGE 12 A0249
LABOR

S59
SUTTON F.X.,"REPRESENTATION AND THE NATURE OF POLITICAL SYSTEMS." UNIV WOR-45 CULTURE SOCIETY STRATA INT/ORG FORCES JUDGE DOMIN LEGIT EXEC REGION REPRESENT ATTIT ORD/FREE RESPECT...SOC HIST/WRIT TIME/SEQ. PAGE 140 A2867
NAT/G CONCPT

S59
ZAUBERMAN A.,"SOVIET BLOC ECONOMIC INTEGRATION." COM CULTURE INTELL ECO/DEV INDUS TOP/EX ACT/RES PLAN ECO/TAC INT/TRADE ROUTINE CHOOSE ATTIT ...TIME/SEQ 20. PAGE 169 A3448
MARKET INT/ORG USSR TOTALISM

B60
ALLEN H.C.,THE ANGLO-AMERICAN PREDICAMENT: THE BRITISH COMMONWEALTH, THE UNITED STATES AND EUROPEAN UNITY. EUR+WWI FUT UK USA+45 WOR+45 ECO/DEV NAT/G PLAN DETER...CONCPT OBS TIME/SEQ TREND COLD/WAR VAL/FREE CMN/WLTH 20. PAGE 6 A0123
INT/ORG PWR BAL/PWR

B60
BARNET R.,WHO WANTS DISARMAMENT. COM EUR+WWI USA+45 USSR INT/ORG NAT/G BAL/PWR DIPLOM EDU/PROP COERCE DETER NUC/PWR WAR WEAPON ATTIT PWR...TIME/SEQ COLD/WAR CONGRESS 20. PAGE 11 A0225
PLAN FORCES ARMS/CONT

B60
BUCHAN A.,NATO IN THE 1960'S. EUR+WWI USA+45 WOR+45 INT/ORG ACT/RES PLAN LEGIT COERCE DETER ATTIT DRIVE RIGID/FLEX ORD/FREE...METH/CNCPT TIME/SEQ TREND GEN/LAWS COLD/WAR 20 NATO. PAGE 21 A0421
VOL/ASSN FORCES ARMS/CONT SOVEREIGN

B60
CARNEGIE ENDOWMENT INT. PEACE,PERSPECTIVES ON PEACE - 1910-1960. WOR+45 WOR-45 INTELL INT/ORG CONSULT ACT/RES EDU/PROP ATTIT KNOWL ORD/FREE...TIME/SEQ TREND EEC OAS UNESCO NAZI 20. PAGE 24 A0489
FUT CONCPT ARMS/CONT PEACE

B60
DAVIDS J.,AMERICA AND THE WORLD OF OUR TIME: UNITED STATES DIPLOMACY IN THE TWENTIETH CENTURY. USA-45 SOCIETY ECO/DEV INT/ORG NAT/G POL/PAR FORCES ECO/TAC DOMIN EDU/PROP EXEC COERCE WAR CHOOSE ATTIT PERSON ORD/FREE...CONCPT TIME/SEQ TOT/POP 20. PAGE 34 A0686
USA+45 PWR DIPLOM

B60
ENGEL J.,THE SECURITY OF THE FREE WORLD. USSR WOR+45 STRATA STRUCT ECO/DEV ECO/UNDEV INT/ORG DELIB/GP FORCES DOMIN LEGIT ADJUD EXEC ARMS/CONT COERCE...POLICY CONCPT NEW/IDEA TIME/SEQ GEN/LAWS COLD/WAR WORK UN 20 NATO. PAGE 42 A0851
COM TREND DIPLOM

B60
HYDE L.K.G.,THE US AND THE UN. WOR+45 STRUCT ECO/DEV ECO/UNDEV NAT/G ACT/RES PLAN DIPLOM EDU/PROP ADMIN ALL/VALS...CONCPT TIME/SEQ GEN/LAWS UN VAL/FREE 20. PAGE 70 A1428
USA+45 INT/ORG FOR/AID

B60
JENNINGS R.,PROGRESS OF INTERNATIONAL LAW. FUT WOR+45 WOR-45 SOCIETY NAT/G VOL/ASSN DELIB/GP DIPLOM EDU/PROP LEGIT COERCE ATTIT DRIVE MORAL ORD/FREE...JURID CONCPT OBS TIME/SEQ TREND GEN/LAWS. PAGE 74 A1509
INT/ORG LAW INT/LAW

B60
KENNAN G.F.,RUSSIA AND THE WEST. ASIA COM EUR+WWI GERMANY UK USA+45 USA-45 USSR INT/ORG NAT/G VOL/ASSN DOMIN REV WAR PWR...TIME/SEQ 20. PAGE 78 A1590
EXEC DIPLOM

B60
LISTER L.,EUROPE'S COAL AND STEEL COMMUNITY. FRANCE GERMANY STRUCT ECO/DEV EXTR/IND INDUS MARKET NAT/G DELIB/GP ECO/TAC INT/TRADE EDU/PROP ATTIT RIGID/FLEX ORD/FREE PWR WEALTH...CONCPT STAT
EUR+WWI INT/ORG REGION

TIME/SEQ CHARTS ECSC 20. PAGE 90 A1843

B60
NURTY K.S.,STUDIES IN PROBLEMS OF PEACE. CHRIST-17C MOD/EUR S/ASIA WOR+45 WOR-45 INT/ORG NAT/G SECT COERCE REV NAT/LISM ALL/VALS...CONCPT MYTH TIME/SEQ. PAGE 110 A2262
POLICY PEACE PACIFISM ORD/FREE

B60
WOLF C.,FOREIGN AID: THEORY AND PRACTICE IN SOUTHERN ASIA. CEYLON INDONESIA PHILIPPINE S/ASIA CULTURE STRATA ECO/UNDEV PLAN EDU/PROP ATTIT ...METH/CNCPT MATH QUANT STAT CONT/OBS TIME/SEQ SIMUL TOT/POP 20. PAGE 166 A3378
ACT/RES ECO/TAC FOR/AID

L60
KUNZ J.,"SANCTIONS IN INTERNATIONAL LAW." WOR+45 WOR-45 LEGIT ARMS/CONT COERCE PEACE ATTIT ...METH/CNCPT TIME/SEQ TREND 20. PAGE 83 A1695
INT/ORG ADJUD INT/LAW

L60
NOGEE J.L.,"THE DIPLOMACY OF DISARMAMENT." WOR+45 INT/ORG NAT/G CONSULT DELIB/GP TOP/EX BAL/PWR DIPLOM EDU/PROP COERCE DETER WEAPON PEACE ATTIT ...RECORD TIME/SEQ TOT/POP VAL/FREE COLD/WAR 20. PAGE 109 A2246
PWR ORD/FREE ARMS/CONT NUC/PWR

S60
"THE EMERGING COMMON MARKETS IN LATIN AMERICA." FUT L/A+17C STRATA DIST/IND INDUS LABOR NAT/G LEGIS ECO/TAC ADMIN RIGID/FLEX HEALTH...NEW/IDEA TIME/SEQ OAS 20. PAGE 3 A0059
FINAN ECO/UNDEV INT/TRADE

S60
FRANKEL S.H.,"ECONOMIC ASPECTS OF POLITICAL INDEPENDENCE IN AFRICA." AFR FUT SOCIETY ECO/UNDEV COM/IND FINAN LEGIS PLAN TEC/DEV CAP/ISM ECO/TAC INT/TRADE ADMIN ATTIT DRIVE RIGID/FLEX PWR WEALTH ...MGT NEW/IDEA MATH TIME/SEQ VAL/FREE 20. PAGE 48 A0984
NAT/G FOR/AID

S60
GOODMAN E.,"THE CRY OF NATIONAL LIBERATION: RECENT SOVIET ATTITUDES TOWARDS NATIONAL SELF-DETERMINATION." COM INT/ORG LEGIS ROUTINE PWR ...TIME/SEQ CON/ANAL STERTYP GEN/LAWS 20 UN. PAGE 54 A1101
ATTIT EDU/PROP SOVEREIGN USSR

S60
HAYTON R.D.,"THE ANTARCTIC SETTLEMENT OF 1959." FUT USA+45 WOR+45 WOR-45 STRUCT R+D INT/ORG EX/STRUC CREATE TEC/DEV LEGIT PEACE ATTIT SOVEREIGN ...TIME/SEQ 20 TREATY IGY. PAGE 63 A1297
DELIB/GP JURID DIPLOM REGION

S60
LYON P.,"NEUTRALITY AND THE EMERGENCE OF THE CONCEPT OF NEUTRALISM." WOR+45 WOR-45 INT/ORG NAT/G BAL/PWR NEUTRAL ATTIT PWR...POLICY TIME/SEQ TREND COLD/WAR TOT/POP VAL/FREE 20 UN. PAGE 92 A1878
CONCPT

S60
MODELSKI G.,"AUSTRALIA AND SEATO." S/ASIA USA+45 CULTURE INTELL ECO/DEV NAT/G PLAN DIPLOM ADMIN ROUTINE ATTIT SKILL...MGT TIME/SEQ AUSTRAL 20 SEATO. PAGE 102 A2097
INT/ORG ACT/RES

S60
MORA J.A.,"THE ORGANIZATION OF AMERICAN STATES." USA+45 LAW ECO/UNDEV VOL/ASSN DELIB/GP PLAN BAL/PWR EDU/PROP ADMIN DRIVE RIGID/FLEX ORD/FREE WEALTH ...TIME/SEQ GEN/LAWS OAS 20. PAGE 103 A2126
L/A+17C INT/ORG REGION

S60
MORALES C.J.,"TRADE AND ECONOMIC INTEGRATION IN LATIN AMERICA." FUT L/A+17C LAW STRATA ECO/UNDEV DIST/IND INDUS LABOR NAT/G LEGIS ECO/TAC ADMIN RIGID/FLEX WEALTH...CONCPT NEW/IDEA CONT/OBS TIME/SEQ WORK 20. PAGE 104 A2128
FINAN INT/TRADE REGION

S60
NANES A.,"THE EUROPEAN COMMUNITY AND THE UNITED STATES: EVOLVING RELATIONS." EUR+WWI USA+45 WOR+45 ECO/UNDEV MARKET NAT/G DELIB/GP PLAN LEGIT ATTIT PWR WEALTH...CONCPT STAT TIME/SEQ CON/ANAL EEC OEEC 20 EURATOM. PAGE 107 A2194
INT/ORG REGION

B61
BARNES W.,THE FOREIGN SERVICE OF THE UNITED STATES. USA+45 USA-45 CONSTN INT/ORG POL/PAR CONSULT DELIB/GP LEGIS DOMIN EDU/PROP EXEC ATTIT RIGID/FLEX ORD/FREE PWR...POLICY CONCPT STAT OBS RECORD BIOG TIME/SEQ TREND. PAGE 11 A0224
NAT/G MGT DIPLOM

B61
BECHHOEFER B.G.,POSTWAR NEGOTIATIONS FOR ARMS CONTROL. COM EUR+WWI USSR INT/ORG NAT/G ACT/RES BAL/PWR DIPLOM ECO/TAC EDU/PROP ADMIN REGION DETER NUC/PWR WAR WEAPON PEACE ATTIT PWR...POLICY TIME/SEQ COLD/WAR CONGRESS 20. PAGE 12 A0244
USA+45 ARMS/CONT

B61
HASAN H.S.,PAKISTAN AND THE UN. ISLAM WOR+45 ECO/DEV ECO/UNDEV NAT/G TOP/EX ECO/TAC FOR/AID EDU/PROP ADMIN DRIVE PERCEPT...OBS TIME/SEQ UN 20. PAGE 62 A1284
INT/ORG ATTIT PAKISTAN

B61
HENKIN L.,ARMS CONTROL: ISSUES FOR THE PUBLIC. EUR+WWI FUT USA+45 USSR INT/ORG NAT/G DIPLOM EDU/PROP DETER NUC/PWR ATTIT PWR...CONCPT RECORD HIST/WRIT TIME/SEQ TOT/POP COLD/WAR 20. PAGE 64 A1316
WOR+45 DELIB/GP ARMS/CONT

B61
KITZINGER V.W.,THE CHALLENGE OF THE COMMON MARKET. EUR+WWI ECO/DEV DIST/IND PLAN ECO/TAC INT/TRADE LEGIT ATTIT PWR WEALTH...TIME/SEQ TREND CHARTS EEC 20. PAGE 80 A1647
MARKET INT/ORG UK

B61
LEGISLATIVE REFERENCE SERVICE,WORLD COMMUNIST MOVEMENT: SELECTIVE CHRONOLOGY, 1818-1957 (4 VOLS.). COM WOR+45 WOR-45 POL/PAR LEAD 19/20. PAGE 86 A1766
BIBLIOG DIPLOM TIME/SEQ MARXISM

B61
LUKACS J.,A HISTORY OF THE COLD WAR. ASIA COM EUR+WWI USA+45 USA-45 INT/ORG NAT/G DELIB/GP ACT/RES BAL/PWR DIPLOM DOMIN EDU/PROP LEGIT DRIVE ORD/FREE...TREND COLD/WAR 20. PAGE 91 A1872
PWR TIME/SEQ USSR

B61
NOLLAU G.,INTERNATIONAL COMMUNISM AND WORLD REVOLUTION: HISTORY AND METHODS. RUSSIA USSR INT/ORG NAT/G POL/PAR VOL/ASSN FORCES BAL/PWR DIPLOM EXEC REGION WAR ATTIT PWR MARXISM...CONCPT TIME/SEQ COLD/WAR 19/20. PAGE 102 A2100
COM REV

B61
NOGEE J.L.,SOVIET POLICY TOWARD INTERNATIONAL CONTROL OF ATOMIC ENERGY. COM USA+45 WOR+45 INTELL NAT/G ACT/RES DIPLOM EDU/PROP NUC/PWR TOTALISM PERCEPT KNOWL PWR...TIME/SEQ COLD/WAR 20. PAGE 109 A2247
INT/ORG ATTIT ARMS/CONT USSR

B61
ROBERTSON A.H.,THE LAW OF INTERNATIONAL INSTITUTIONS IN EUROPE. EUR+WWI MOD/EUR INT/ORG NAT/G VOL/ASSN DELIB/GP...JURID TIME/SEQ TOT/POP 20 TREATY. PAGE 122 A2497
RIGID/FLEX ORD/FREE

B61
SINGER J.D.,FINANCING INTERNATIONAL ORGANIZATION: THE UNITED NATIONS BUDGET PROCESS. WOR+45 FINAN ACT/RES CREATE PLAN BUDGET ECO/TAC ADMIN ROUTINE ATTIT KNOWL...DECISION METH/CNCPT TIME/SEQ UN 20. PAGE 133 A2726
INT/ORG MGT

B61
STRAUSZ-HUPE R.,A FORWARD STRATEGY FOR AMERICA. FUT WOR+45 ECO/DEV INT/ORG NAT/G POL/PAR DELIB/GP FORCES ACT/RES CREATE ECO/TAC DOMIN EDU/PROP ATTIT DRIVE PWR...MAJORIT CONCPT STAT OBS TIME/SEQ TREND COLD/WAR TOT/POP. PAGE 139 A2848
USA+45 PLAN DIPLOM

B61
WARNER D.,HURRICANE FROM CHINA. ASIA CHINA/COM FUT L/A+17C USA+45 CULTURE NAT/G FORCES TOP/EX FOR/AID DRIVE PWR...CONCPT TIME/SEQ SEATO WORK 20. PAGE 161 A3284
ATTIT TREND REV

B61
WILLOUGHBY W.R.,THE ST LAWRENCE WATERWAY: A STUDY IN POLITICS AND DIPLOMACY. USA+45 ECO/DEV COM/IND INT/ORG CONSULT DELIB/GP ACT/RES TEC/DEV DIPLOM ECO/TAC ROUTINE...TIME/SEQ 20. PAGE 165 A3357
LEGIS INT/TRADE CANADA DIST/IND

B61
WRIGHT Q.,THE ROLE OF INTERNATIONAL LAW IN THE ELIMINATION OF WAR. FUT WOR+45 WOR-45 NAT/G BAL/PWR DIPLOM DOMIN LEGIT PWR...POLICY INT/LAW JURID CONCPT TIME/SEQ TREND GEN/LAWS COLD/WAR 20. PAGE 168 A3414
INT/ORG ADJUD ARMS/CONT

B61
YDIT M.,INTERNATIONALISED TERRITORIES. FUT WOR+45 WOR-45 CONSTN VOL/ASSN CREATE PLAN LEGIT PEACE ORD/FREE...GEOG INT/LAW JURID SOC NEW/IDEA OBS RECORD SAMP TIME/SEQ TREND 19/20 BERLIN. PAGE 169 A3431
LOC/G INT/ORG DIPLOM SOVEREIGN

L61
HALPERIN M.H.,"NUCLEAR WEAPONS AND LIMITED WARS." FUT UNIV WOR+45 INTELL SOCIETY ECO/DEV ACT/RES DRIVE PERCEPT RIGID/FLEX...CONCPT TIME/SEQ TREND TOT/POP 20. PAGE 60 A1237
PLAN COERCE NUC/PWR WAR

S61
BARALL M.,"THE UNITED STATES GOVERNMENT RESPONDS." L/A+17C USA+45 SOCIETY NAT/G CREATE PLAN DIPLOM ECO/TAC ATTIT DRIVE RIGID/FLEX KNOWL SKILL WEALTH ...METH/CNCPT TIME/SEQ GEN/METH 20. PAGE 11 A0217
ECO/UNDEV ACT/RES FOR/AID

S61
BARNET R.,"RUSSIA, CHINA, AND THE WORLD: THE SOVIET ATTITUDE ON DISARMAMENT (PART 3)." ASIA CHINA/COM FUT INT/ORG NAT/G POL/PAR VOL/ASSN ARMS/CONT ATTIT ...POLICY CONCPT TIME/SEQ TREND TOT/POP VAL/FREE 20. PAGE 11 A0226
COM PLAN TOTALISM USSR

S61
BRZEZINSKI Z.K.,"THE ORGANIZATION OF THE COMMUNIST CAMP." COM CZECHOSLVK COM/IND NAT/G DELIB/GP INT/TRADE DOMIN EDU/PROP EXEC ROUTINE COERCE ATTIT PWR...MGT CONCPT TIME/SEQ CHARTS VAL/FREE 20 TREATY. PAGE 20 A0416
VOL/ASSN DIPLOM USSR

S61
BURNET A.,"TOO MANY ALLIES." COM EUR+WWI UK WOR+45 WOR-45 ACT/RES PLAN DISPL PWR SKILL...TIME/SEQ 20 CMN/WLTH SEATO NATO CENTO. PAGE 22 A0438
VOL/ASSN INT/ORG DIPLOM

S61
CASTANEDA J.,"THE UNDERDEVELOPED NATIONS AND THE DEVELOPMENT OF INTERNATIONAL LAW." FUT UNIV LAW ACT/RES FOR/AID LEGIT PERCEPT SKILL...JURID
INT/ORG ECO/UNDEV PEACE

METH/CNCPT TIME/SEQ TOT/POP 20 UN. PAGE 25 A0507 INT/LAW

S61
TAUBENFELD H.J.,"OUTER SPACE--PAST POLITICS AND FUTURE POLICY." FUT USA+45 USA-45 WOR+45 AIR INTELL STRUCT ECO/DEV NAT/G TOP/EX ACT/RES ADMIN ROUTINE NUC/PWR ATTIT DRIVE...CONCPT TIME/SEQ TREND TOT/POP 20. PAGE 141 A2892 PLAN SPACE INT/ORG

S61
WEST F.J.,"THE NEW GUINEA QUESTION: AN AUSTRALIAN VIEW." WOR+45 INT/ORG VOL/ASSN LEGIT PERCEPT ...POLICY TIME/SEQ AUSTRAL VAL/FREE 20 CMN/WLTH. PAGE 163 A3320 S/ASIA ECO/UNDEV

S61
ZAGORIA D.S.,"THE FUTURE OF SINO-SOVIET RELATIONS." CHINA/COM INT/ORG NAT/G POL/PAR VOL/ASSN ACT/RES PLAN PERSON...METH/CNCPT TIME/SEQ TOT/POP VAL/FREE 20 MAO KHRUSH/N. PAGE 169 A3444 ASIA COM TOTALISM USSR

B62
BLACKETT P.M.S.,STUDIES OF WAR: NUCLEAR AND CONVENTIONAL. EUR+WWI USA+45 DELIB/GP ACT/RES CREATE PLAN TEC/DEV LEGIT COERCE WAR ORD/FREE PWR ...POLICY TECHNIC TIME/SEQ 20. PAGE 15 A0300 INT/ORG FORCES ARMS/CONT NUC/PWR

B62
BOUSCAREN A.T.,SOVIET FOREIGN POLICY: A PATTERN OF PERSISTANCE. WOR+45 WOR-45 SOCIETY STRUCT INT/ORG POL/PAR CREATE PLAN EDU/PROP ROUTINE ATTIT RIGID/FLEX...POLICY CONCPT RECORD HIST/WRIT TIME/SEQ MARX/KARL 20. PAGE 17 A0352 COM NAT/G DIPLOM USSR

B62
CARDOZA M.H.,DIPLOMATS IN INTERNATIONAL COOPERATION: STEPCHILDREN OF THE FOREIGN SERVICE. EUR+WWI USA+45 NAT/G CONSULT ACT/RES EDU/PROP ROUTINE RIGID/FLEX KNOWL SKILL...SOC OBS TIME/SEQ EEC OEEC NATO 20. PAGE 24 A0480 INT/ORG METH/CNCPT DIPLOM

B62
COLOMBOS C.J.,THE INTERNATIONAL LAW OF THE SEA. WOR+45 EXTR/IND DIPLOM INT/TRADE TARIFFS AGREE WAR ...TIME/SEQ 20 TREATY. PAGE 28 A0570 INT/LAW SEA JURID ADJUD

B62
DALLIN A.,THE SOVIET UNION AT THE UNITED NATIONS: AN INQUIRY INTO SOVIET MOTIVES AND OBJECTIVES. ACT/RES EDU/PROP LEGIT ATTIT KNOWL PWR...POLICY RECORD HIST/WRIT TIME/SEQ TREND ORG/CHARTS GEN/METH COLD/WAR FAO 20 UN. PAGE 33 A0675 COM INT/ORG USSR

B62
DUTOIT B.,LA NEUTRALITE SUISSE A L'HEURE EUROPEENNE. EUR+WWI MOD/EUR INT/ORG NAT/G VOL/ASSN PLAN BAL/PWR LEGIT NEUTRAL REGION PEACE ORD/FREE SOVEREIGN...CONCPT OBS TIME/SEQ TREND STERTYP VAL/FREE LEAGUE/NAT UN 20. PAGE 40 A0812 ATTIT DIPLOM SWITZERLND

B62
HATCH J.,AFRICA TODAY-AND TOMORROW: AN OUTLINE OF BASIC FACTS AND MAJOR PROBLEMS. AFR FUT ISLAM STRATA ECO/UNDEV INT/ORG NAT/G POL/PAR DELIB/GP TOP/EX EDU/PROP LEGIT CHOOSE ATTIT...TIME/SEQ TOT/POP COLD/WAR 20. PAGE 63 A1287 PLAN CONSTN NAT/LISM

B62
HIGGANS B.,UNITED NATIONS AND U.S. FOREIGN ECONOMIC POLICY. FUT USA+45 WOR+45 ECO/DEV ECO/UNDEV NAT/G ECO/TAC WEALTH...TIME/SEQ TOT/POP UN 20. PAGE 65 A1328 INT/ORG ACT/RES FOR/AID DIPLOM

B62
JEWELL M.E.,SENATORIAL POLITICS AND FOREIGN POLICY. NAT/G POL/PAR CHIEF DELIB/GP TOP/EX FOR/AID EDU/PROP ROUTINE ATTIT PWR SKILL...MAJORIT METH/CNCPT TIME/SEQ CONGRESS 20 PRESIDENT. PAGE 74 A1516 USA+45 LEGIS DIPLOM

B62
KING G.,THE UNITED NATIONS IN THE CONGO: A QUEST FOR PEACE. WOR+45 NAT/G CONSULT FORCES LEGIT COERCE WAR ORD/FREE...JURID METH/CNCPT OBS INT HIST/WRIT TIME/SEQ CONGO UN 20 COLD/WAR. PAGE 79 A1624 AFR INT/ORG

B62
MACKENTOSH J.M.,STRATEGY AND TACTICS OF SOVIET FOREIGN POLICY. CHINA/COM FUT USA+45 WOR+45 INT/ORG PLAN DOMIN LEGIT ROUTINE COERCE NUC/PWR WAR ATTIT DRIVE ORD/FREE PWR...CONCPT OBS TIME/SEQ TREND GEN/METH COLD/WAR 20. PAGE 92 A1894 COM POLICY DIPLOM USSR

B62
MODELSKI G.,SEATO-SIX STUDIES. ASIA CHINA/COM INDIA S/ASIA INT/ORG NAT/G ECO/TAC DETER ATTIT ORD/FREE PWR...TIME/SEQ COLD/WAR TOT/POP 20 SEATO. PAGE 102 A2098 MARKET ECO/UNDEV INT/TRADE

B62
MORGENTHAU H.J.,POLITICS IN THE TWENTIETH CENTURY: IMPASSE OF AMERICAN FOREIGN POLICY. FUT GERMANY USA+45 USSR WOR+45 INT/ORG NAT/G ACT/RES PLAN FOR/AID EDU/PROP LEGIT COERCE WAR PWR...TIME/SEQ TREND COLD/WAR 20. PAGE 104 A2138 SKILL DIPLOM

B62
MULLEY F.W.,THE POLITICS OF WESTERN DEFENSE. EUR+WWI USA-45 WOR+45 VOL/ASSN EX/STRUC FORCES COERCE DETER PEACE ATTIT ORD/FREE PWR...RECORD TIME/SEQ CHARTS COLD/WAR 20 NATO. PAGE 106 A2168 INT/ORG DELIB/GP NUC/PWR

B62
NEAL F.W.,WAR AND PEACE AND GERMANY. EUR+WWI USSR STRUCT INT/ORG NAT/G FORCES DOMIN EDU/PROP LEGIT EXEC COERCE ORD/FREE...HUM SOC NEW/IDEA OBS TIME/SEQ TOT/POP COLD/WAR 20 BERLIN. PAGE 108 A2208 USA+45 POLICY DIPLOM GERMANY

B62
NICHOLAS H.G.,THE UNITED NATIONS AS A POLITICAL INSTITUTION. WOR+45 CONSTN EX/STRUC ACT/RES LEGIT PERCEPT KNOWL PWR...CONCPT TIME/SEQ CON/ANAL ORG/CHARTS UN 20. PAGE 109 A2228 INT/ORG ROUTINE

B62
ROSENNE S.,THE WORLD COURT: WHAT IT IS AND HOW IT WORKS. WOR+45 WOR-45 LAW CONSTN JUDGE EDU/PROP LEGIT ROUTINE CHOOSE PEACE ORD/FREE...JURID OBS TIME/SEQ CHARTS UN TOT/POP VAL/FREE 20. PAGE 124 A2538 INT/ORG ADJUD INT/LAW

B62
TRISKA J.F.,THE THEORY, LAW, AND POLICY OF SOVIET TREATIES. WOR+45 WOR-45 CONSTN INT/ORG NAT/G VOL/ASSN DOMIN LEGIT COERCE ATTIT PWR RESPECT ...POLICY JURID CONCPT OBS SAMP TIME/SEQ TREND GEN/LAWS 20. PAGE 145 A2966 COM LAW INT/LAW USSR

L62
CORET A.,"LES PROVINCES PORTUGALLES D'OUTREMER ET L'ONU." AFR PORTUGAL S/ASIA WOR+45 LOC/G NAT/G DOMIN...CONCPT TIME/SEQ UN 20 GOA. PAGE 31 A0620 INT/ORG SOVEREIGN COLONIAL

L62
NIZARD L.,"CUBAN QUESTION AND SECURITY COUNCIL." L/A+17C USA+45 ECO/UNDEV NAT/G POL/PAR DELIB/GP ECO/TAC PWR...RELATIV OBS TIME/SEQ TREND GEN/LAWS UN 20 UN. PAGE 109 A2242 INT/ORG JURID DIPLOM CUBA

L62
WILCOX F.O.,"THE UN AND THE NON-ALIGNED NATIONS." AFR S/ASIA USA+45 ECO/UNDEV INT/ORG TEC/DEV EDU/PROP RIGID/FLEX ORD/FREE PWR...POLICY HUM CONCPT STAT OBS TIME/SEQ STERTYP GEN/METH UN 20. PAGE 164 A3345 ATTIT TREND

S62
ALBONETTI A.,"IL SECONDO PROGRAMMA QUINQUENNALE 1963-67 ED IL BILANCIO RICERCHE ED INVESTIMENTI PER IL 1963 DELL'ERATOM." EUR+WWI FUT ITALY WOR+45 ECO/DEV SERV/IND INT/ORG TEC/DEV ECO/TAC ATTIT SKILL WEALTH...MGT TIME/SEQ OEEC 20. PAGE 5 A0108 R+D PLAN NUC/PWR

S62
BIERZANECK R.,"LA NON-RECONAISSANCE ET LE DROIT INTERNATIONAL CONTEMPORAIN." EUR+WWI FUT WOR+45 LAW ECO/DEV ATTIT RIGID/FLEX...CONCPT TIME/SEQ TOT/POP 20. PAGE 14 A0286 EDU/PROP JURID DIPLOM INT/LAW

S62
BOKOR-SZEGO H.,"LA CONVENTION DE BELGRADE ET LE REGIME DU DANUBE." COM EUR+WWI WOR+45 STRUCT POL/PAR VOL/ASSN PLAN EDU/PROP WEALTH...TIME/SEQ 20. PAGE 16 A0333 INT/ORG TOTALISM YUGOSLAVIA

S62
BROWN B.E.,"L'ONU ABANDONNE LA HONGRIE." COM USSR WOR+45 CONSTN NAT/G POL/PAR DELIB/GP ACT/RES TEC/DEV PWR...TIME/SEQ 20 UN. PAGE 20 A0400 INT/ORG TOTALISM HUNGARY POLICY

S62
CORET A.,"LE STATUT DE L'ILE CHRISTMAS DE L'OCEAN INDIEN." FUT S/ASIA ECO/DEV ECO/UNDEV VOL/ASSN DELIB/GP PLAN...RELATIV OBS TIME/SEQ TREND AUSTRAL 20. PAGE 30 A0619 NAT/G INT/ORG NEW/ZEALND

S62
CORET A.,"LA DECLARATION DE L'ASSEMBLEE GENERAL DE L'ONU SUR L'OCTROI DE L'INDEPENDENCE AUX PAYS ET AUX PEUPLES." AFR ASIA ISLAM NIGERIA S/ASIA USSR WOR+45 ECO/UNDEV NAT/G DELIB/GP COLONIAL ALL/VALS ...CONCPT TIME/SEQ TREND UN TOT/POP 20 MEXIC/AMER. PAGE 31 A0621 INT/ORG STRUCT SOVEREIGN

S62
DALLIN A.,"THE SOVIET VIEW OF THE UNITED NATIONS." WOR+45 VOL/ASSN TOP/EX DIPLOM DOMIN EDU/PROP LEGIT ATTIT RIGID/FLEX PWR...CONCPT OBS HIST/WRIT TIME/SEQ STERTYP GEN/LAWS COLD/WAR UN 20. PAGE 33 A0676 COM INT/ORG USSR

S62
DEUTSCH K.W.,"TOWARDS WESTERN EUROPEAN INTEGRATION: AN INTERIM ASSESSMENT." EUR+WWI STRUCT ECO/DEV INT/ORG ECO/TAC INT/TRADE EDU/PROP PEACE ATTIT DRIVE PWR SOVEREIGN...PSY SOC TIME/SEQ CHARTS STERTYP 20. PAGE 36 A0741 VOL/ASSN RIGID/FLEX REGION

S62
DIHN N.Q.,"L'INTERNATIONALISATION DU MEKONG." CAMBODIA LAOS VIETNAM WOR+45 INT/ORG NAT/G VOL/ASSN PEACE HEALTH...CONCPT TIME/SEQ CHARTS METH VAL/FREE 20. PAGE 37 A0761 S/ASIA DELIB/GP

S62
DRACHKOVITCH M.M.,"THE EMERGING PATTERN OF YUGOSLAV-SOVIET RELATIONS." COM FUT USSR WOR+45 INT/ORG ECO/TAC FOR/AID DOMIN COERCE ATTIT PERSON ORD/FREE PWR...TIME/SEQ 20 TITO/MARSH KHRUSH/N STALIN/J. PAGE 38 A0783 TOP/EX DIPLOM YUGOSLAVIA

S62
FISCHER G.,"UNE NOUVELLE ORGANIZATION REGIONALE: L'ASA." S/ASIA WOR+45 ECO/UNDEV VOL/ASSN PERCEPT INT/ORG DRIVE

VOL. 1

RIGID/FLEX...TIME/SEQ 20 ASA. PAGE 46 A0935 REGION

S62
FOCSANEANU L.,"LES GRANDS TRAITES DE LA REPUBLIQUE POPULAIRE DE CHINE." ASIA CHINA/COM COM USSR WOR+45 INT/ORG NAT/G POL/PAR ACT/RES PLAN DIPLOM EDU/PROP ...CONCPT TIME/SEQ 20 TREATY. PAGE 47 A0957 VOL/ASSN TOTALISM

S62
JOHNSON O.H.,"THE ENGLISH TRADITION IN INTERNATIONAL LAW." CHRIST-17C MOD/EUR EDU/PROP LEGIT CT/SYS ORD/FREE...JURID CONCPT TIME/SEQ. PAGE 75 A1526 LAW INT/LAW UK

S62
MANGIN G.,"LES ACCORDS DE COOPERATION EN MATIERE DE JUSTICE ENTRE LA FRANCE ET LES ETATS AFRICAINS ET MALGACHE." AFR ISLAM WOR+45 STRUCT ECO/UNDEV NAT/G DELIB/GP PERCEPT ALL/VALS...JURID MGT TIME/SEQ 20. PAGE 94 A1919 INT/ORG LAW FRANCE

S62
MOUSKHELY M.,"LA NAISSANCE DES ETATS EN DROIT INTERNATIONAL PUBLIC." UNIV SOCIETY INT/ORG VOL/ASSN LEGIT ATTIT RIGID/FLEX...JURID TIME/SEQ 20. PAGE 105 A2157 NAT/G STRUCT INT/LAW

S62
NANES A.,"DISARMAMENT: THE LAST SEVEN YEARS." COM EUR+WWI USA+45 USSR INT/ORG FORCES TOP/EX CREATE LEGIT NUC/PWR DISPL ORD/FREE...CONCPT TIME/SEQ CON/ANAL 20. PAGE 107 A2195 DELIB/GP RIGID/FLEX ARMS/CONT

S62
ORBAN M.,"L'EUROPE EN FORMATION ET SES PROBLEMES." EUR+WWI FUT WOR+45 WOR-45 INTELL STRUCT DELIB/GP ACT/RES FEDERAL RIGID/FLEX WEALTH...CONCPT TIME/SEQ OEEC 20. PAGE 112 A2295 INT/ORG PLAN REGION

S62
RAZAFIMBAHINY J.,"L'ORGANISATION AFRICAINE ET MALGACHE DE COOPERATION ECONOMIQUE." AFR ISLAM MADAGASCAR NAT/G ACT/RES ECO/TAC ALL/VALS ...TIME/SEQ 20. PAGE 120 A2454 INT/ORG ECO/UNDEV

S62
RUBINSTEIN A.Z.,"RUSSIA AND THE UNCOMMITTED NATIONS." AFR INDIA ISLAM L/A+17C LAOS S/ASIA ELITES ECO/UNDEV INT/ORG KIN CREATE PLAN TEC/DEV NAT/LISM RIGID/FLEX PWR WEALTH...METH/CNCPT TIME/SEQ GEN/LAWS WORK. PAGE 125 A2562 ECO/TAC TREND COLONIAL USSR

S62
RUSSETT B.M.,"CAUSE, SURPRISE, AND NO ESCAPE." FUT WOR-45 CULTURE SOCIETY INT/ORG FORCES TEC/DEV BAL/PWR EDU/PROP ARMS/CONT NUC/PWR WAR WEAPON PEACE KNOWL ORD/FREE PWR...POLICY CONCPT RECORD TIME/SEQ TREND GEN/LAWS 20 WWI. PAGE 126 A2578 COERCE DIPLOM

S62
STRACHEY J.,"COMMUNIST INTENTIONS." ASIA USSR YUGOSLAVIA INT/ORG NAT/G FORCES DOMIN EDU/PROP COERCE NUC/PWR NAT/LISM PEACE RIGID/FLEX PWR MARXISM...CONCPT MYTH OBS TIME/SEQ TREND COLD/WAR TOT/POP 20. PAGE 139 A2843 COM ATTIT WAR

S62
VIGNES D.,"L'AUTORITE DES TRAITES INTERNATIONAUX EN DROIT INTERNE." EUR+WWI UNIV LAW CONSTN INTELL NAT/G POL/PAR DIPLOM ATTIT PERCEPT ALL/VALS ...POLICY INT/LAW JURID CONCPT TIME/SEQ 20 TREATY. PAGE 159 A3233 STRUCT LEGIT FRANCE

B63
BLACK J.E.,FOREIGN POLICIES IN A WORLD OF CHANGE. FUT INT/ORG ALL/VALS...POLICY MAJORIT MARXIST SOCIALIST TRADIT TIME/SEQ TREND ANTHOL 20. PAGE 15 A0298 WOR+45 NAT/G DIPLOM

B63
BOISSIER P.,HISTORIE DU COMITE INTERNATIONAL DE LA CROIX ROUGE. MOD/EUR WOR-45 CONSULT FORCES PLAN DIPLOM EDU/PROP ADMIN MORAL ORD/FREE...SOC CONCPT RECORD TIME/SEQ GEN/LAWS TOT/POP VAL/FREE 19/20. PAGE 16 A0332 INT/ORG HEALTH ARMS/CONT WAR

B63
CREMEANS C.,THE ARABS AND THE WORLD: NASSER'S ARAB NATIONALIST POLICY. FUT ISLAM UAR USA+45 SOCIETY STRATA NAT/G POL/PAR PLAN DIPLOM EDU/PROP LEGIT DRIVE ALL/VALS...INT TIME/SEQ CHARTS 20 NASSER/G. PAGE 33 A0662 TOP/EX ATTIT REGION NAT/LISM

B63
GALLAGHER M.P.,THE SOVIET HISTORY OF WORLD WAR II. EUR+WWI USSR DIPLOM DOMIN WRITING CONTROL WAR MARXISM...PSY TIME/SEQ 20 STALIN/J. PAGE 50 A1031 CIVMIL/REL EDU/PROP HIST/WRIT PRESS

B63
HENDERSON W.,SOUTHEAST ASIA: PROBLEMS OF UNITED STATES POLICY. COM S/ASIA CULTURE STRATA ECO/UNDEV INT/ORG DELIB/GP ACT/RES ECO/TAC DOMIN EDU/PROP LEGIT COERCE ATTIT ALL/VALS...STAT TIME/SEQ ANTHOL VAL/FREE 20. PAGE 64 A1313 ASIA USA+45 DIPLOM

B63
HOVET T. JR.,AFRICA IN THE UNITED NATIONS. AFR DELIB/GP EDU/PROP LOBBY CHOOSE ORD/FREE PWR RESPECT SKILL...STAT TIME/SEQ CON/ANAL CHARTS STERTYP VAL/FREE 20 UN. PAGE 68 A1397 INT/ORG USSR

B63
KHADDURI M.,MODERN LIBYA: A STUDY IN POLITICAL DEVELOPMENT. EUR+WWI ISLAM LIBYA ELITES INT/ORG POL/PAR FORCES DIPLOM FOR/AID DOMIN EDU/PROP LEGIT NAT/LISM DRIVE RIGID/FLEX SKILL...CONCPT TIME/SEQ TREND 20. PAGE 78 A1606 NAT/G STRUCT

B63
MAYNE R.,THE COMMUNITY OF EUROPE. UK CONSTN NAT/G CONSULT DELIB/GP CREATE PLAN ECO/TAC LEGIT ADMIN ROUTINE ORD/FREE PWR WEALTH...CONCPT TIME/SEQ EEC EURATOM 20. PAGE 97 A1985 EUR+WWI INT/ORG REGION

B63
QUAISON-SACKEY A.,AFRICA UNBOUND: REFLECTIONS OF AN AFRICAN STATESMAN. ISLAM CULTURE INTELL INT/ORG POL/PAR TOP/EX DOMIN EDU/PROP LEGIT ATTIT PERSON ...CONCPT OBS TIME/SEQ CHARTS STERTYP 20 UN. PAGE 118 A2423 AFR BIOG

B63
ROSNER G.,THE UNITED NATIONS EMERGENCY FORCE. FRANCE ISRAEL UAR UK WOR+45 CREATE WAR PEACE ORD/FREE PWR...INT/LAW JURID HIST/WRIT TIME/SEQ UN. PAGE 124 A2539 INT/ORG FORCES

B63
STROMBERG R.N.,COLLECTIVE SECURITY AND AMERICAN FOREIGN POLICY FROM THE LEAGUE OF NATIONS TO NATO. USA+45 USA-45 WOR-45 INT/ORG VOL/ASSN EX/STRUC FORCES LEGIT ROUTINE DRIVE...CONCPT TREND UN LEAGUE/NAT 20 NATO. PAGE 139 A2851 ORD/FREE TIME/SEQ DIPLOM

L63
MOUSKHELY M.,"LE BLOC COMMUNISTE ET LA COMMUNAUTE ECONOMIQUE EUROPEENNE." AFR COM EUR+WWI FUT USSR WOR+45 INTELL ECO/UNDEV LABOR POL/PAR NUC/PWR RIGID/FLEX...TIME/SEQ ORG/CHARTS EEC TOT/POP 20. PAGE 105 A2158 INT/ORG ECO/DEV

L63
ZARTMAN I.W.,"THE SAHARA--BRIDGE OR BARRIER." ISLAM CULTURE SOCIETY NAT/G DELIB/GP DOMIN EDU/PROP LEGIT ATTIT...HIST/WRIT TIME/SEQ CHARTS TOT/POP VAL/FREE 20. PAGE 169 A3445 INT/ORG PWR NAT/LISM

S63
BULLOUGH V.L.,"THE ROMAN EMPIRE VS PERSIA, 363-502: A STUDY OF SUCCESSFUL DETERRENCE." NAT/G PLAN DIPLOM ORD/FREE PWR...TIME/SEQ COLD/WAR VAL/FREE 4/6 PERSIA ROM/EMP. PAGE 21 A0430 MEDIT-7 COERCE DETER

S63
CAHIER P.,"LE DROIT INTERNE DES ORGANISATIONS INTERNATIONALES." UNIV CONSTN SOCIETY ECO/DEV R+D NAT/G TOP/EX LEGIT ATTIT PERCEPT...TIME/SEQ 19/20. PAGE 23 A0464 INT/ORG JURID DIPLOM INT/LAW

S63
ETIENNE G.,"'LOIS OBJECTIVES' ET PROBLEMES DE DEVELOPPEMENT DANS LE CONTEXTE CHINE-URSS." ASIA CHINA/COM COM FUT STRUCT INT/ORG VOL/ASSN TOP/EX TEC/DEV ECO/TAC ATTIT RIGID/FLEX...GEOG MGT TIME/SEQ TOT/POP 20. PAGE 42 A0866 TOTALISM USSR

S63
ETZIONI A.,"EUROPEAN UNIFICATION: A STRATEGY OF CHANGE." EUR+WWI CULTURE ECO/DEV DELIB/GP ACT/RES ECO/TAC EDU/PROP ATTIT ORD/FREE PWR SKILL WEALTH ...STAT TIME/SEQ EEC TOT/POP VAL/FREE 20. PAGE 42 A0869 INT/ORG RIGID/FLEX

S63
ETZIONI A.,"EUROPEAN UNIFICATION AND PERSPECTIVES ON SOVEREIGNTY." EUR+WWI FUT DELIB/GP TEC/DEV ECO/TAC EDU/PROP DETER NUC/PWR ATTIT DRIVE ORD/FREE PWR WEALTH...CONCPT RECORD TIME/SEQ EEC VAL/FREE 20. PAGE 43 A0870 INT/ORG ECO/DEV SOVEREIGN

S63
GROSSER A.,"FRANCE AND GERMANY IN THE ATLANTIC COMMUNITY." INT/ORG NAT/G TOP/EX DIPLOM REGION PEACE ATTIT ORD/FREE PWR...CONCPT RECORD TIME/SEQ GEN/LAWS VAL/FREE COLD/WAR 20. PAGE 57 A1178 EUR+WWI VOL/ASSN FRANCE GERMANY

S63
HALLSTEIN W.,"THE EUROPEAN COMMUNITY AND ATLANTIC PARTNERSHIP." EUR+WWI USA+45 MARKET NAT/G VOL/ASSN DELIB/GP ARMS/CONT NUC/PWR ATTIT PWR...CONCPT STAT TIME/SEQ TREND OEEC 20 EEC. PAGE 60 A1235 INT/ORG ECO/TAC UK

S63
HOLBO P.S.,"COLD WAR DRIFT IN LATIN AMERICA." CUBA L/A+17C USA+45 USA-45 INT/ORG NAT/G NEIGH VOL/ASSN ACT/RES PLAN ECO/TAC ATTIT RIGID/FLEX ALL/VALS ...RECORD TIME/SEQ OAS LAFTA 20 COLD/WAR. PAGE 66 A1363 DELIB/GP CREATE FOR/AID

S63
LEDUC G.,"L'AIDE INTERNATIONALE AU DEVELOPPEMENT." FUT WOR+45 ECO/DEV ECO/UNDEV R+D PROF/ORG TEC/DEV ECO/TAC ROUTINE ATTIT ALL/VALS...MGT TIME/SEQ TOT/POP 20. PAGE 86 A1758 FINAN PLAN FOR/AID

S63
LIGOT M.,"LA COOPERATION MILITAIRE DANS LES ACCORDS, PASSES ENTRE LA FRANCE ET LES ETATS AFRICAINS ET MALGACHE D'EXPRESSION." ECO/UNDEV INT/ORG NAT/G VOL/ASSN...CONCPT TIME/SEQ 20. PAGE 89 A1814 AFR FORCES FOR/AID FRANCE

S63
LOPEZIBOR J.,"L'EUROPE, FORME DE VIE." CHRIST-17C EUR+WWI FUT MOD/EUR SOCIETY INT/ORG SECT EDU/PROP ATTIT RIGID/FLEX ALL/VALS...POLICY HUM SOC TIME/SEQ NAT/G CULTURE

TREND GEN/LAWS. PAGE 91 A1862

S63
MANGONE G.,"THE UNITED NATIONS AND UNITED STATES FOREIGN POLICY." USA+45 WOR+45 ECO/UNDEV NAT/G DIPLOM LEGIT ROUTINE ATTIT DRIVE...TIME/SEQ UN COLD/WAR 20. PAGE 94 A1922 INT/ORG ECO/TAC FOR/AID

S63
MAZRUI A.A.,"ON THE CONCEPT 'WE ARE ALL AFRICANS'." AFR CULTURE KIN LOC/G NAT/G DOMIN EDU/PROP LEGIT ATTIT PERCEPT PERSON KNOWL ORD/FREE...TIME/SEQ TOT/POP 20. PAGE 97 A1986 PROVS INT/ORG NAT/LISM

S63
NYE J.S. JR.,"EAST AFRICAN ECONOMIC INTEGRATION." AFR UGANDA PROVS DELIB/GP PLAN ECO/TAC INT/TRADE ADMIN ROUTINE ORD/FREE PWR WEALTH...OBS TIME/SEQ VAL/FREE 20. PAGE 110 A2264 ECO/UNDEV INT/ORG

S63
RAMERIE L.,"TENSION AU SEIN DU COMECON: LE CAS ROUMAIN." COM EUR+WWI USSR WOR+45 ECO/DEV DIST/IND NAT/G POL/PAR VOL/ASSN EDU/PROP TOTALISM ATTIT WEALTH...TIME/SEQ 20 COMECON. PAGE 119 A2438 INT/ORG ECO/TAC INT/TRADE ROMANIA

S63
SCHOFLING J.A.,"EFTA: THE OTHER EUROPE." ECO/DEV MARKET CONSULT ECO/TAC WEALTH...TIME/SEQ EEC OEEC 20 EFTA. PAGE 129 A2642 EUR+WWI INT/ORG REGION

S63
WELLS H.,"THE OAS AND THE DOMINICAN ELECTIONS." L/A+17C INT/ORG NAT/G POL/PAR TEC/DEV ECO/TAC EDU/PROP PERCEPT...TIME/SEQ OAS TOT/POP 20. PAGE 163 A3317 CONSULT CHOOSE DOMIN/REP

S63
WYZNER E.,"NIEKTORE ASPEKTY PRAWNE FINANSOWANIA OPERACJI ONZ W KONGO I NA BEIZKIM WSCHODZIE." S/ASIA CONSTN FINAN INT/ORG TOP/EX...TIME/SEQ UN 20 CONGRESS. PAGE 168 A3426 FORCES JURID DIPLOM

B64
CLAUDE I.,SWORDS INTO PLOWSHARES. FUT WOR+45 WOR-45 DELIB/GP EX/STRUC LEGIT ATTIT ORD/FREE...CONCPT TIME/SEQ TREND UN TOT/POP 20. PAGE 27 A0547 INT/ORG STRUCT

B64
DE SMITH S.A.,THE NEW COMMONWEALTH AND ITS CONSTITUTIONS. AFR CYPRUS PAKISTAN S/ASIA INT/ORG NAT/G LEGIS LEGIT RIGID/FLEX PWR...CONCPT TIME/SEQ CMN/WLTH 20. PAGE 35 A0713 EX/STRUC CONSTN SOVEREIGN

B64
DEITCHMAN S.J.,LIMITED WAR AND AMERICAN DEFENSE POLICY. USA+45 WOR+45 INT/ORG NAT/G PLAN TEC/DEV COERCE NUC/PWR RIGID/FLEX PWR SKILL...DECISION METH/CNCPT TIME/SEQ TOT/POP COLD/WAR 20. PAGE 36 A0726 FORCES WAR WEAPON

B64
GARDNER L.C.,ECONOMIC ASPECTS OF NEW DEAL DIPLOMACY. USA-45 WOR-45 LAW ECO/DEV INT/ORG NAT/G VOL/ASSN LEGIS TOP/EX EDU/PROP ORD/FREE PWR WEALTH ...POLICY TIME/SEQ VAL/FREE 20 ROOSEVLT/F. PAGE 51 A1043 ECO/TAC DIPLOM

B64
GRODZINS M.,THE ATOMIC AGE: FORTY-FIVE SCIENTISTS AND SCHOLARS SPEAK ON NATIONAL AND WORLD AFFAIRS. FUT USA+45 WOR+45 R+D INT/ORG NAT/G CONSULT TEC/DEV EDU/PROP ATTIT PERSON ORD/FREE...HUM CONCPT TIME/SEQ CON/ANAL. PAGE 57 A1169 INTELL ARMS/CONT NUC/PWR

B64
OWEN W.,STRATEGY FOR MOBILITY. FUT WOR+45 WOR-45 DIST/IND INT/ORG NAT/G DELIB/GP PLAN TEC/DEV ECO/TAC ORD/FREE PWR WEALTH...STAT TIME/SEQ VAL/FREE 20. PAGE 112 A2304 COM/IND ECO/UNDEV

B64
PLISCHKE E.,SYSTEMS OF INTEGRATING THE INTERNATIONAL COMMUNITY. WOR+45 NAT/G VOL/ASSN ECO/TAC LEGIT PWR WEALTH...TIME/SEQ ANTHOL UN TOT/POP 20. PAGE 116 A2391 INT/ORG EX/STRUC REGION

B64
STOESSINGER J.G.,FINANCING THE UNITED NATIONS SYSTEM. FUT WOR+45 CONSTN NAT/G VOL/ASSN DELIB/GP EX/STRUC ECO/TAC LEGIT CT/SYS PWR WEALTH...STAT TIME/SEQ TREND CHARTS VAL/FREE. PAGE 138 A2830 FINAN INT/ORG

B64
WAINHOUSE D.W.,REMNANTS OF EMPIRE: THE UNITED NATIONS AND THE END OF COLONIALISM. FUT PORTUGAL WOR+45 NAT/G CONSULT DOMIN LEGIT ADMIN ROUTINE ATTIT ORD/FREE...POLICY JURID RECORD INT TIME/SEQ UN CMN/WLTH 20. PAGE 160 A3260 INT/ORG TREND COLONIAL

B64
WARREN S.,THE PRESIDENT AS WORLD LEADER. USA+45 WOR+45 ELITES COM/IND INT/ORG NAT/G VOL/ASSN CHIEF EX/STRUC LEGIT COERCE ATTIT PERSON RIGID/FLEX...INT TIME/SEQ COLD/WAR 20 ROOSEVLT/F TRUMAN/HS EISNHWR/DD KENNEDY/JF. PAGE 161 A3286 TOP/EX PWR DIPLOM

B64
WRIGHT T.P. JR.,AMERICAN SUPPORT OF FREE ELECTIONS ABROAD. USA+45 USA-45 DOMIN LEAD NEUTRAL MARXISM ...POLICY TIME/SEQ BIBLIOG 19/20 COLD/WAR INTERVENT. PAGE 168 A3420 DIPLOM CHOOSE L/A+17C POPULISM

L64
CAMPBELL J.C.,"THE MIDDLE EAST IN THE MUTED COLD WAR." COM EUR+WWI UAR USA+45 USSR STRUCT ECO/UNDEV NAT/G VOL/ASSN EX/STRUC TOP/EX DIPLOM ECO/TAC EDU/PROP...TIME/SEQ COLD/WAR 20. PAGE 23 A0475 ISLAM FOR/AID NAT/LISM

L64
CLAUDE I.,"THE OAS, THE UN, AND THE UNITED STATES." L/A+17C USA+45 CONSTN NAT/G DELIB/GP DOMIN EDU/PROP LEGIT REGION COERCE ORD/FREE PWR...TIME/SEQ TREND STERTYP OAS UN 20. PAGE 27 A0546 INT/ORG POLICY

L64
MILLIS W.,"THE DEMILITARIZED WORLD." COM USA+45 USSR WOR+45 CONSTN NAT/G EX/STRUC PLAN LEGIT ATTIT DRIVE...CONCPT TIME/SEQ STERTYP TOT/POP COLD/WAR 20. PAGE 102 A2085 FUT INT/ORG BAL/PWR PEACE

L64
RIPLEY R.B.,"INTERAGENCY COMMITTEES AND INCREMENTALISM: THE CASE OF AID TO INDIA." INDIA USA+45 INTELL NAT/G DELIB/GP ACT/RES DIPLOM ROUTINE NAT/LISM ATTIT PWR...SOC CONCPT NEW/IDEA TIME/SEQ CON/ANAL VAL/FREE 20. PAGE 121 A2483 EXEC MGT FOR/AID

S64
BEIM D.,"THE COMMUNIST BLOC AND THE FOREIGN-AID GAME." WOR+45 NAT/G PLAN ROUTINE ATTIT KNOWL ORD/FREE...DECISION QUANT CONT/OBS TIME/SEQ CHARTS GAME SIMUL COLD/WAR 20. PAGE 12 A0252 COM ECO/UNDEV ECO/TAC FOR/AID

S64
COCHRANE J.D.,"US ATTITUDES TOWARD CENTRAL-AMERICAN INTEGRATION." L/A+17C USA+45 ECO/UNDEV FACE/GP VOL/ASSN DELIB/GP ECO/TAC INT/TRADE EDU/PROP RIGID/FLEX ORD/FREE WEALTH...TIME/SEQ TOT/POP 20. PAGE 27 A0555 NAT/G ATTIT REGION

S64
DERWINSKI E.J.,"THE COST OF THE INTERNATIONAL COFFEE AGREEMENT." L/A+17C USA+45 WOR+45 ECO/UNDEV NAT/G VOL/ASSN LEGIS DIPLOM ECO/TAC FOR/AID LEGIT ATTIT...TIME/SEQ CONGRESS 20 TREATY. PAGE 36 A0732 MARKET DELIB/GP INT/TRADE

S64
FALK S.L.,"DISARMAMENT IN HISTORICAL PERSPECTIVE." WOR-45 NAT/G PLAN NUC/PWR PEACE ORD/FREE PWR ...TIME/SEQ AUD/VIS VAL/FREE LEAGUE/NAT 20. PAGE 44 A0892 INT/ORG COERCE ARMS/CONT

S64
GARDNER R.N.,"THE SOVIET UNION AND THE UNITED NATIONS." WOR+45 FINAN POL/PAR VOL/ASSN FORCES ECO/TAC DOMIN EDU/PROP LEGIT ADJUD ADMIN ARMS/CONT COERCE ATTIT ALL/VALS...POLICY MAJORIT CONCPT OBS TIME/SEQ TREND STERTYP UN. PAGE 51 A1046 COM INT/ORG USSR

S64
GROSSER A.,"Y A-T-IL UN CONFLIT FRANCO-AMERICAIN." EUR+WWI USA+45 INT/ORG NAT/G PLAN BAL/PWR DIPLOM EDU/PROP NUC/PWR ATTIT DRIVE ORD/FREE PWR...CONCPT OBS TIME/SEQ TREND STERTYP VAL/FREE COLD/WAR. PAGE 57 A1179 VOL/ASSN NAT/LISM FRANCE

S64
GRZYBOWSKI K.,"INTERNATIONAL ORGANIZATIONS FROM THE SOVIET POINT OF VIEW." WOR+45 WOR-45 CULTURE ECO/DEV VOL/ASSN EDU/PROP ATTIT RIGID/FLEX KNOWL ...SOC OBS TIME/SEQ TREND GEN/LAWS VAL/FREE ILO UN 20. PAGE 58 A1184 COM INT/ORG DIPLOM USSR

S64
HABERLER G.,"INTEGRATION AND GROWTH OF THE WORLD ECONOMY IN HISTORICAL PERSPECTIVE." FUT WOR+45 WOR-45 ECO/DEV ECO/UNDEV...TIME/SEQ TREND VAL/FREE 20. PAGE 59 A1209 WEALTH INT/TRADE

S64
HOVET T. JR.,"THE ROLE OF AFRICA IN THE UNITED NATIONS." FUT WOR+45 NAT/G DELIB/GP DOMIN EDU/PROP LEGIT ORD/FREE PWR RESPECT SKILL...OBS TIME/SEQ TREND VAL/FREE UN 20. PAGE 68 A1398 AFR INT/ORG DIPLOM

S64
KUNZ J.,"THE CHANGING SCIENCE OF INTERNATIONAL LAW." FUT WOR+45 WOR-45 INT/ORG LEGIT ORD/FREE ...JURID TIME/SEQ GEN/LAWS 20. PAGE 83 A1696 ADJUD CONCPT INT/LAW

S64
LERNER W.,"THE HISTORICAL ORIGINS OF THE SOVIET DOCTRINE OF PEACEFUL COEXISTENCE." COM USSR INT/ORG NAT/G VOL/ASSN PLAN PEACE ATTIT RIGID/FLEX PWR MARXISM...TIME/SEQ COLD/WAR 20. PAGE 87 A1788 EDU/PROP DIPLOM

S64
LEVI W.,"CHINA AND THE UNITED NATIONS." ASIA CHINA CHINA/COM WOR+45 WOR-45 CONSTN NAT/G DELIB/GP EX/STRUC FORCES ACT/RES EDU/PROP PWR...POLICY RECORD TIME/SEQ GEN/LAWS UN COLD/WAR 20. PAGE 88 A1794 INT/ORG ATTIT NAT/LISM

S64
MOORE W.E.,"PREDICTING DISCONTINUITIES IN SOCIAL CHANGE." UNIV WOR+45 ECO/DEV ECO/UNDEV INT/ORG NAT/G COERCE ALL/VALS...METH/CNCPT TIME/SEQ TREND TOT/POP VAL/FREE 20. PAGE 103 A2125 SOCIETY GEN/LAWS REV

S64
PALMER N.D.,"INDIA AS A FACTOR IN UNITED STATES FOREIGN POLICY." INDIA USA+45 USA-45 ECO/UNDEV NAT/G TOP/EX ECO/TAC EDU/PROP...METH/CNCPT TIME/SEQ 20. PAGE 113 A2323 S/ASIA ATTIT FOR/AID DIPLOM

S64
REIDY J.W.,"LATIN AMERICA AND THE ATLANTIC TRIANGLE." EUR+WWI FUT USA+45 INT/ORG NAT/G REGION L/A+17C WEALTH

COERCE ORD/FREE PWR...TIME/SEQ VAL/FREE 20. PAGE 120 A2458 POLICY

S64
SAAB H.,"THE ARAB SEARCH FOR A FEDERAL UNION." SOCIETY INT/ORG NAT/G DELIB/GP FORCES ACT/RES TEC/DEV ECO/TAC DOMIN LEGIT REGION ROUTINE ATTIT DRIVE RIGID/FLEX ALL/VALS...SOC CONCPT NEW/IDEA TIME/SEQ TREND. PAGE 126 A2580 ISLAM PLAN

S64
TRISKA J.F.,"SOVIET TREATY LAW: A QUANTITATIVE ANALYSIS." WOR+45 LAW ECO/UNDEV AGRI COM/IND INDUS CREATE TEC/DEV DIPLOM ATTIT PWR WEALTH...JURID SAMP TIME/SEQ TREND CHARTS VAL/FREE 20 TREATY. PAGE 145 A2967 COM ECO/TAC INT/LAW USSR

S64
VANDENBOSCH A.,"THE SMALL STATES IN INTERNATIONAL POLITICS AND ORGANIZATION." EUR+WWI MOD/EUR WOR+45 WOR-45 CONSTN DELIB/GP COERCE ORD/FREE PWR ...TIME/SEQ GEN/LAWS VAL/FREE LEAGUE/NAT UN 19/20. PAGE 158 A3219 NAT/G INT/ORG DIPLOM

S64
ZARTMAN I.W.,"LES RELATIONS ENTRE LA FRANCE ET L'ALGERIA DEPUIS LES ACCORDS D'EVIAN." EUR+WWI FUT ISLAM CULTURE AGRI EXTR/IND FINAN INDUS POL/PAR DIPLOM ECO/TAC FOR/AID PEACE ATTIT DRIVE ALL/VALS ...TIME/SEQ VAL/FREE 20. PAGE 169 A3446 ECO/UNDEV ALGERIA FRANCE

B65
DU BOIS W.E.B.,THE WORLD AND AFRICA. USA+45 CAP/ISM DISCRIM STRANGE SOCISM...TIME/SEQ TREND IDEA/COMP 19/20 NEGRO. PAGE 39 A0789 AFR DIPLOM COLONIAL CULTURE

B65
EISENHOWER D.D.,WAGING PEACE 1956-61: THE WHITE HOUSE YEARS. USA+45 DIPLOM LEAD INGP/REL RACE/REL PEACE ATTIT...TRADIT TIME/SEQ 20 EISNHWR/DD PRESIDENT COLD/WAR CIV/RIGHTS BERLIN. PAGE 41 A0833 TOP/EX BIOG ORD/FREE POLICY

B65
LERCHE C.O.,THE COLD WAR AND AFTER. AFR COM S/ASIA USA+45 USSR NUC/PWR SOVEREIGN MARXISM...TIME/SEQ TREND BIBLIOG 20 COLD/WAR. PAGE 87 A1784 DIPLOM BAL/PWR IDEA/COMP

B65
LOEWENHEIM F.L.,PEACE OR APPEASEMENT? HITLER, CHAMBERLAIN AND THE MUNICH CRISIS. MUNIC DELIB/GP WAR TOTALISM ATTIT SOVEREIGN...TIME/SEQ ANTHOL BIBLIOG 20 HITLER/A CHAMBRLN/N. PAGE 90 A1851 DIPLOM LEAD PEACE

B65
ROSENBERG A.,DEMOCRACY AND SOCIALISM. COM EUR+WWI FRANCE MOD/EUR STRUCT INT/ORG NAT/G POL/PAR TOP/EX EDU/PROP COERCE PERSON PWR FASCISM MARXISM...CONCPT TIME/SEQ MARX/KARL 19/20. PAGE 124 A2535 ATTIT

B65
ROTBERG R.I.,A POLITICAL HISTORY OF TROPICAL AFRICA. EX/STRUC DIPLOM INT/TRADE DOMIN ADMIN RACE/REL NAT/LISM PWR SOVEREIGN...GEOG TIME/SEQ BIBLIOG 1/20. PAGE 124 A2545 AFR CULTURE COLONIAL

B65
VONGLAHN G.,LAW AMONG NATIONS: AN INTRODUCTION TO PUBLIC INTERNATIONAL LAW. UNIV WOR+45 LAW INT/ORG NAT/G LEGIT EXEC RIGID/FLEX...CONCPT TIME/SEQ GEN/LAWS UN TOT/POP 20. PAGE 160 A3253 CONSTN JURID INT/LAW

S65
RAY H.,"THE POLICY OF RUSSIA TOWARDS SINO-INDIAN CONFLICT." ASIA CHINA/COM COM INDIA USSR NAT/G TOP/EX FOR/AID EDU/PROP NEUTRAL COERCE PEACE RIGID/FLEX PWR...METH/CNCPT TIME/SEQ VAL/FREE 20. PAGE 120 A2452 S/ASIA ATTIT DIPLOM WAR

B66
BLACK C.E.,THE DYNAMICS OF MODERNIZATION: A STUDY IN COMPARATIVE HISTORY. STRUCT ECO/DEV ECO/UNDEV NAT/G DIPLOM LEAD REV...PREDICT TIME/SEQ TREND SOC/INTEG 17/20. PAGE 15 A0296 SOCIETY SOC NAT/COMP

B66
FABAR R.,THE VISION AND THE NEED: LATE VICTORIAN IMPERIALIST AIMS. MOD/EUR UK WOR-45 CULTURE NAT/G DIPLOM...TIME/SEQ METH/COMP 19 KIPLING/R COMMONWLTH. PAGE 43 A0880 COLONIAL CONCPT ADMIN ATTIT

B66
GARNER W.R.,THE CHACO DISPUTE; A STUDY OF PRESTIGE DIPLOMACY. L/A+17C PARAGUAY USA-45 INT/ORG AGREE PEACE...TIME/SEQ 20 BOLIV LEAGUE/NAT ARGEN CHACO/WAR. PAGE 51 A1050 WAR DIPLOM CONCPT PWR

B66
HUTTENBACK R.A.,BRITISH IMPERIAL EXPERIENCE. S/ASIA UK WOR-45 INT/ORG TEC/DEV...CHARTS 16/20 COMMONWLTH MERCANTLST. PAGE 69 A1424 COLONIAL TIME/SEQ INT/TRADE

B66
MIKESELL R.F.,PUBLIC INTERNATIONAL LENDING FOR DEVELOPMENT. WOR+45 WOR-45 DELIB/GP...TIME/SEQ CHARTS BIBLIOG 20. PAGE 101 A2070 INT/ORG FOR/AID ECO/UNDEV FINAN

B66
SOBEL L.A.,SOUTH VIETNAM: US-COMMUNIST CONFRONTATION IN SOUTHEAST ASIA 1961-65. VIETNAM FOR/AID CROWD DETER REV PEACE...GEOG 20 INTERVENT DIEM COLD/WAR. PAGE 134 A2754 WAR TIME/SEQ FORCES NAT/G

S66
FRIEND A.,"THE MIDDLE EAST CRISIS" COM ISLAM ISRAEL SYRIA UAR USA+45 USSR FORCES PLAN FOR/AID CONTROL ORD/FREE PWR...SOCIALIST TIME/SEQ 20 NASSER/G. PAGE 49 A1009 WAR INT/ORG DIPLOM PEACE

B67
MACRIDIS R.C.,FOREIGN POLICY IN WORLD POLITICS (3RD ED.). EX/STRUC BAL/PWR COLONIAL NAT/LISM SKILL SOVEREIGN WEALTH...CONCPT TIME/SEQ ANTHOL 20 COLD/WAR. PAGE 93 A1902 DIPLOM POLICY NAT/G IDEA/COMP

B67
MEYNAUD J.,TRADE UNIONISM IN AFRICA; A STUDY OF ITS GROWTH AND ORIENTATION (TRANS. BY ANGELA BRENCH). INT/ORG PROB/SOLV COLONIAL PWR...TIME/SEQ TREND ILO. PAGE 100 A2055 LABOR AFR NAT/LISM ORD/FREE

S67
GOLDMAN M.I.,"SOVIET ECONOMIC GROWTH SINCE THE REVOLUTION." USSR WORKER INT/TRADE PRODUC MARXISM ...POLICY TIME/SEQ 20. PAGE 53 A1090 ECO/DEV AGRI ECO/TAC INDUS

S67
KIERNAN V.G.,"INDIA AND THE LABOUR PARTY." INDIA UK CAP/ISM GP/REL EFFICIENCY NAT/LISM PWR SOCISM ...SOCIALIST TIME/SEQ 20. PAGE 79 A1616 COLONIAL DIPLOM POL/PAR ECO/UNDEV

TIMING....SEE TIME

TINBERGEN J. A2941,A2942

TINGSTERN H. A2943

TINKER H. A2944,A2945

TIPTON J.B. A2946

TITO/MARSH....JOSIP BROZ TITO

B52
ULAM A.B.,TITOISM AND THE COMINFORM. USSR WOR+45 STRUCT INT/ORG NAT/G ACT/RES PLAN EXEC ATTIT DRIVE ALL/VALS...CONCPT OBS VAL/FREE 20 COMINTERN TITO/MARSH. PAGE 146 A2993 COM POL/PAR TOTALISM YUGOSLAVIA

B57
TOMASIC D.A.,NATIONAL COMMUNISM AND SOVIET STRATEGY. UK USSR YUGOSLAVIA NAT/G POL/PAR CHIEF CREATE DOMIN REV WAR PWR...BIOG TREND 20 TITO/MARSH STALIN/J. PAGE 144 A2948 COM NAT/LISM MARXISM DIPLOM

B58
NEAL F.W.,TITOISM IN ACTION. COM YUGOSLAVIA AGRI LOC/G DIPLOM TOTALISM...BIBLIOG 20 TITO/MARSH. PAGE 107 A2206 MARXISM POL/PAR CHIEF ADMIN

S62
DRACHKOVITCH M.M.,"THE EMERGING PATTERN OF YUGOSLAV-SOVIET RELATIONS." COM FUT USSR WOR+45 INT/ORG ECO/TAC FOR/AID DOMIN COERCE ATTIT PERSON ORD/FREE PWR...TIME/SEQ 20 TITO/MARSH KHRUSH/N STALIN/J. PAGE 38 A0783 TOP/EX DIPLOM YUGOSLAVIA

TIZARD/H....HENRY TIZARD

TOCQUEVILL....ALEXIS DE TOCQUEVILLE

TOGO....SEE ALSO AFR

B64
WITHERELL J.W.,OFFICIAL PUBLICATIONS OF FRENCH EQUATORIAL AFRICA, FRENCH CAMEROONS, AND TOGO, 1946-1958 (PAMPHLET). CAMEROON CHAD FRANCE GABON TOGO LAW ECO/UNDEV EXTR/IND INT/TRADE...GEOG HEAL 20. PAGE 165 A3370 BIBLIOG/A AFR NAT/G ADMIN

TOLEDO/O....TOLEDO, OHIO

TOLMAN E.C. A2947

TOMASIC D.A. A2948

TONG T. A2949

TONGA....TONGA

TOP/EX....TOP EXECUTIVES

N
KYRIAK T.E.,CHINA: A BIBLIOGRAPHY. ASIA CHINA/COM AGRI FINAN INDUS NAT/G INT/TRADE PRESS...SOC 20. PAGE 83 A1700 BIBLIOG/A MARXISM TOP/EX POL/PAR

B03
GRIFFIN A.P.C.,SELECT LIST OF REFERENCES ON THE MONROE DOCTRINE (PAMPHLET). L/A+17C NAT/G TOP/EX 19/20. PAGE 56 A1151 BIBLIOG DIPLOM COLONIAL

B05
AMES J.G.,COMPREHENSIVE INDEX TO THE PUBLICATIONS OF THE UNITED STATES GOVERNMENT , 1881-1893. USA-45 CONSTN POL/PAR DELIB/GP TOP/EX DIPLOM PARL/PROC INGP/REL...INDEX 19 CONGRESS. PAGE 8 A0153
BIBLIOG/A LEGIS NAT/G GOV/REL

B14
BERNHARDI F.,ON THE WAR OF TODAY. MOD/EUR INT/ORG NAT/G TOP/EX PWR CHARTS. PAGE 14 A0278
FORCES SKILL WAR

B19
DE CALLIERES F.,THE PRACTICE OF DIPLOMACY. MOD/EUR INT/ORG NAT/G DELIB/GP LEGIS TOP/EX DOMIN ATTIT KNOWL LEAGUE/NAT 20. PAGE 34 A0699
CONSULT ACT/RES DIPLOM INT/LAW

B19
KEYNES J.M.,THE ECONOMIC CONSEQUENCES OF THE PEACE. FUT GERMANY MOD/EUR RUSSIA UK USA-45 CULTURE ECO/DEV FINAN INDUS INT/ORG TOP/EX ECO/TAC ROUTINE WAR ATTIT PERCEPT ALL/VALS...OLD/LIB MYTH OBS TIME/SEQ TREND 20 TREATY. PAGE 78 A1605
EUR+WWI SOCIETY PEACE

B22
WALSH E.,THE HISTORY AND NATURE OF INTERNATIONAL RELATIONS. ASIA L/A+17C MOD/EUR USA-45 WOR-45 NAT/G FORCES TOP/EX BAL/PWR REGION ATTIT ORD/FREE RESPECT ...CONCPT HIST/WRIT TREND. PAGE 161 A3270
INT/ORG TIME/SEQ DIPLOM

B29
BUELL R.,INTERNATIONAL RELATIONS. WOR+45 WOR-45 CONSTN STRATA FORCES TOP/EX ADMIN ATTIT DRIVE SUPEGO MORAL ORD/FREE PWR SOVEREIGN...JURID SOC CONCPT 20. PAGE 21 A0428
INT/ORG BAL/PWR DIPLOM

B30
BYNKERSHOEK C.,QUAESTIONUM JURIS PUBLICI LIBRI DUO. CHRIST-17C MOD/EUR CONSTN ELITES SOCIETY NAT/G PROVS EX/STRUC FORCES TOP/EX BAL/PWR DIPLOM ATTIT MORAL...TRADIT CONCPT. PAGE 23 A0460
INT/ORG LAW NAT/LISM INT/LAW

B30
FLEMMING D.,THE TREATY VETO OF THE AMERICAN SENATE. FUT USA+45 USA-45 CONSTN INT/ORG NAT/G TOP/EX LEGIT GOV/REL PWR...POLICY MAJORIT CONCPT OBS TIME/SEQ CONGRESS 20. PAGE 46 A0949
LEGIS RIGID/FLEX

B30
WRIGHT Q.,MANDATES UNDER THE LEAGUE OF NATIONS. WOR-45 CONSTN ECO/DEV ECO/UNDEV NAT/G DELIB/GP TOP/EX LEGIT ALL/VALS...JURID CONCPT LEAGUE/NAT 20. PAGE 167 A3403
INT/ORG LAW INT/LAW

B32
EAGLETON C.,INTERNATIONAL GOVERNMENT. BRAZIL FRANCE GERMANY ITALY UK USSR WOR-45 DELIB/GP TOP/EX PLAN ECO/TAC EDU/PROP LEGIT ADJUD REGION ARMS/CONT COERCE ATTIT PWR...GEOG MGT VAL/FREE LEAGUE/NAT 20. PAGE 40 A0816
INT/ORG JURID DIPLOM INT/LAW

B32
FLEMMING D.,THE UNITED STATES AND THE LEAGUE OF NATIONS, 1918-1920. FUT USA-45 NAT/G LEGIS TOP/EX DEBATE CHOOSE PEACE ATTIT SOVEREIGN...TIME/SEQ CON/ANAL CONGRESS LEAGUE/NAT 20 TREATY. PAGE 46 A0950
INT/ORG EDU/PROP

B35
BEMIS S.F.,GUIDE TO THE DIPLOMATIC HISTORY OF THE UNITED STATES, 17751921. NAT/G LEGIS TOP/EX PROB/SOLV CAP/ISM INT/TRADE TARIFFS ADJUD ...CON/ANAL 18/20. PAGE 13 A0264
BIBLIOG/A DIPLOM USA-45

B35
STALEY E.,WAR AND THE PRIVATE INVESTOR. UNIV WOR-45 INTELL SOCIETY INT/ORG NAT/G TOP/EX CAP/ISM ECO/TAC WAR ATTIT ALL/VALS...INT TIME/SEQ TREND CON/ANAL WORK TOT/POP 20. PAGE 137 A2799
FINAN INT/TRADE DIPLOM

B38
FLEMMING D.,THE UNITED STATES AND WORLD ORGANIZATION, 1920-1933. ASIA FUT WOR-45 NAT/G TOP/EX DIPLOM ECO/TAC EDU/PROP LEGIT COERCE WAR ...TIME/SEQ LEAGUE/NAT 20 CHINJAP. PAGE 47 A0951
USA-45 INT/ORG PEACE

B39
DULLES J.,WAR, PEACE AND CHANGE. FRANCE ITALY UK USA-45 WOR-45 LAW INT/ORG NAT/G SECT VOL/ASSN FORCES TOP/EX DOMIN ARMS/CONT COERCE ATTIT PERSON RIGID/FLEX MORAL PWR...JURID STERTYP TOT/POP LEAGUE/NAT 20. PAGE 39 A0796
EDU/PROP TOTALISM WAR

B39
NICOLSON H.,CURZON: THE LAST PHASE, 1919-1925. UK NAT/G DELIB/GP TOP/EX ROUTINE WAR RIGID/FLEX ...METH/CNCPT 20 CURZON/GN. PAGE 109 A2231
POLICY DIPLOM BIOG

B39
TAGGART F.J.,ROME AND CHINA. MEDIT-7 INT/ORG NAT/G FORCES LEGIS TOP/EX PLAN PWR SOVEREIGN...CHARTS TOT/POP ROM/EMP. PAGE 141 A2883
ASIA WAR

B39
WHEELER-BENNET J.W.,THE FORGOTTEN PEACE: BREST-LITOVSK. COM GERMANY USSR TOP/EX AGREE WAR PWR ...BIBLIOG 20 TREATY LENIN/VI UKRAINE. PAGE 163 A3326
PEACE DIPLOM CONFER

C40
FAHS C.B.,"GOVERNMENT IN JAPAN." FINAN FORCES LEGIS TOP/EX BUDGET INT/TRADE EDU/PROP SOVEREIGN ...CON/ANAL BIBLIOG/A 20 CHINJAP. PAGE 43 A0884
ASIA DIPLOM NAT/G ADMIN

B41
MCCLURE W.,INTERNATIONAL EXECUTIVE AGREEMENTS. USA-45 WOR-45 INT/ORG NAT/G DELIB/GP ADJUD ROUTINE ORD/FREE PWR...TIME/SEQ TREND CON/ANAL. PAGE 97 A2000
TOP/EX DIPLOM

S42
TURNER F.J.,"AMERICAN SECTIONALISM AND WORLD ORGANIZATION." EUR+WWI UNIV USA-45 WOR-45 INTELL ECO/DEV TOP/EX ACT/RES PLAN EDU/PROP LEGIT ALL/VALS ...CONCPT NEW/IDEA OBS TREND LEAGUE/NAT TOT/POP 20. PAGE 146 A2981
INT/ORG DRIVE BAL/PWR

B43
CONOVER H.F.,SOVIET RUSSIA: SELECTED LIST OF REFERENCES. USSR CULTURE INDUS NAT/G TOP/EX TEC/DEV BUDGET WAR CIVMIL/REL EFFICIENCY MARXISM 20. PAGE 29 A0597
BIBLIOG ECO/DEV COM DIPLOM

L44
WRIGHT Q.,"THE US AND INTERNATIONAL AGREEMENTS." FUT USA-45 CONSTN INTELL INT/ORG LOC/G NAT/G CHIEF CONSULT EX/STRUC DIPLOM LEGIT DRIVE PERCEPT PWR ...CONCPT CONGRESS 20. PAGE 167 A3407
DELIB/GP TOP/EX PEACE

S44
WRIGHT Q.,"CONSTITUTIONAL PROCEDURES OF THE US FOR CARRYING OUT OBLIGATIONS FOR MILITARY SANCTIONS." EUR+WWI FUT USA-45 CONSTN INTELL NAT/G CONSULT EX/STRUC LEGIS ROUTINE DRIVE...POLICY JURID CONCPT OBS TREND TOT/POP 20. PAGE 167 A3406
TOP/EX FORCES INT/LAW WAR

B45
CONOVER H.F.,ITALY: ECONOMICS, POLITICS AND MILITARY AFFAIRS, 1940-1945. ITALY ELITES NAT/G POL/PAR EX/STRUC TOP/EX DIPLOM DOMIN CONTROL COERCE WAR CIVMIL/REL EFFICIENCY 20. PAGE 29 A0599
BIBLIOG TOTALISM FORCES

B45
TINGSTERN H.,PEACE AND SECURITY AFTER WW II. WOR-45 DELIB/GP TOP/EX LEGIT CT/SYS COERCE PEACE ATTIT PERCEPT...CONCPT LEAGUE/NAT 20. PAGE 144 A2943
INT/ORG ORD/FREE WAR INT/LAW

B47
BORGESE G.,COMMON CAUSE. LAW CONSTN SOCIETY STRATA ECO/DEV INT/ORG POL/PAR FORCES LEGIS TOP/EX CAP/ISM DIPLOM ADMIN EXEC ATTIT PWR 20. PAGE 17 A0339
WOR+45 NAT/G SOVEREIGN REGION

L47
COMM. STUDY ORGAN. PEACE,"SECURITY THROUGH THE UNITED NATIONS." COM FUT WOR+45 TOP/EX ACT/RES BAL/PWR ARMS/CONT NUC/PWR...CONCPT GEN/LAWS UN TOT/POP COLD/WAR 20. PAGE 28 A0577
INT/ORG ORD/FREE PEACE

B48
CHAMBERLAIN L.H.,AMERICAN FOREIGN POLICY. FUT USA+45 USA-45 WOR+45 WOR-45 NAT/G LEGIS TOP/EX ECO/TAC FOR/AID EDU/PROP EXEC ATTIT ORD/FREE ...JURID TREND TOT/POP 20. PAGE 25 A0517
CONSTN DIPLOM

B48
CHURCHILL W.,THE GATHERING STORM. UK WOR-45 INT/ORG NAT/G FORCES TOP/EX DIPLOM ECO/TAC COERCE ATTIT ORD/FREE PWR WEALTH...POLICY SELF/OBS RECORD NAZI PARLIAMENT 20. PAGE 26 A0538
BIOG

B49
STETTINIUS E.R.,ROOSEVELT AND THE RUSSIANS: THE YALTA CONFERENCE. UK USSR WOR+45 WOR-45 INT/ORG VOL/ASSN TOP/EX ACT/RES EDU/PROP PEACE ATTIT DRIVE PERSON SUPEGO PWR...POLICY CONCPT MYTH OBS TIME/SEQ AUD/VIS COLD/WAR 20 CHURCHLL/W YALTA ROOSEVLT/F. PAGE 138 A2819
DIPLOM DELIB/GP BIOG

B50
CHURCHILL W.,TRIUMPH AND TRAGEDY. UK WOR-45 INT/ORG NAT/G DELIB/GP FORCES TOP/EX DIPLOM COERCE CHOOSE ATTIT ORD/FREE PWR WEALTH...SELF/OBS CHARTS NAZI 20. PAGE 26 A0539
BIOG PEACE WAR

B50
NORTHROP F.S.C.,THE TAMING OF THE NATIONS. KOREA USA+45 USSR WOR+45 STRUCT ECO/UNDEV INT/ORG NAT/G TOP/EX NUC/PWR ATTIT ALL/VALS...TIME/SEQ 20 HIROSHIMA. PAGE 110 A2255
CONCPT BAL/PWR

L51
ULAM A.B.,"THE COMIMFORM AND THE PEOPLE'S DEMOCRACIES." EUR+WWI WOR+45 STRUCT NAT/G POL/PAR TOP/EX ACT/RES PLAN ECO/TAC DOMIN ATTIT ALL/VALS ...HIST/WRIT TIME/SEQ 20 COMINFORM. PAGE 146 A2992
COM INT/ORG USSR TOTALISM

L51
WHITAKER A.P.,"DEVELOPMENT OF AMERICAN REGIONALISM: THE ORGANIZATION OF AMERICAN STATES." L/A+17C USA+45 VOL/ASSN DELIB/GP FORCES TOP/EX ACT/RES ECO/TAC CT/SYS REGION PEACE ALL/VALS OAS 20. PAGE 163 A3330
INT/ORG TIME/SEQ DETER

B52
MACARTHUR D.,REVITALIZING A NATION. ASIA COM FUT KOREA WOR+45 NAT/G FOR/AID TAX GIVE WAR ATTIT SOCISM 20 CHINJAP EUROPE. PAGE 92 A1885
LEAD FORCES TOP/EX POLICY

B52
SCHUMAN F.,THE COMMONWEALTH OF MAN. WOR+45 WOR-45 LAW CULTURE ELITES SOCIETY FAM INT/ORG NAT/G VOL/ASSN TOP/EX PLAN BAL/PWR LEGIT ATTIT DISPL DRIVE...POLICY MYTH TREND TOT/POP ILO OEEC 20. PAGE 129 A2649
CONCPT GEN/LAWS

B52
WALTERS F.P.,A HISTORY OF THE LEAGUE OF NATIONS. EUR+WWI CONSTN NAT/G LEGIS TOP/EX ACT/RES PLAN EDU/PROP LEGIT ROUTINE ATTIT...TREND LEAGUE/NAT 20 CHINJAP. PAGE 161 A3271 INT/ORG TIME/SEQ NAT/LISM

L52
WRIGHT Q.,"CONGRESS AND THE TREATY-MAKING POWER." USA+45 WOR+45 CONSTN INTELL NAT/G CHIEF CONSULT EX/STRUC LEGIS TOP/EX CREATE GOV/REL DISPL DRIVE RIGID/FLEX...TREND TOT/POP CONGRESS CONGRESS 20 TREATY. PAGE 167 A3408 ROUTINE DIPLOM INT/LAW DELIB/GP

S52
MASTERS R.D.,"RUSSIA AND THE UNITED NATIONS." FUT USA+45 USSR WOR+45 CONSTN VOL/ASSN DELIB/GP TOP/EX CREATE DIPLOM ADMIN...TREND STERTYP UN 20. PAGE 96 A1962 INT/ORG PWR

S52
SCHWEBEL S.M.,"THE SECRETARY-GENERAL OF THE UN." FUT INTELL CONSULT DELIB/GP ADMIN PEACE ATTIT ...JURID MGT CONCPT TREND UN CONGRESS 20. PAGE 130 A2663 INT/ORG TOP/EX

B53
ZIMMERN A.,THE AMERICAN ROAD TO PEACE. USA+45 LAW INT/ORG NAT/G EX/STRUC TOP/EX EDU/PROP LEGIT COERCE PEACE ATTIT ORD/FREE PWR...CONCPT TIME/SEQ LEAGUE/NAT TOT/POP VAL/FREE 20 UN. PAGE 170 A3455 USA-45 DIPLOM

S53
BOULDING K.E.,"ECONOMIC ISSUES IN INTERNATIONAL CONFLICT." WOR+45 ECO/DEV NAT/G TOP/EX DIPLOM ECO/TAC DOMIN ATTIT WEALTH...MAJORIT OBS/ENVIR TREND GEN/LAWS COLD/WAR TOT/POP 20. PAGE 17 A0345 PWR FOR/AID

B54
ARON R.,CENTURY OF TOTAL WAR. FUT WOR+45 WOR-45 SOCIETY INT/ORG NAT/G FORCES TOP/EX CREATE BAL/PWR DOMIN EDU/PROP COERCE DETER PEACE TOTALISM PWR ...TIME/SEQ TREND COLD/WAR TOT/POP VAL/FREE LEAGUE/NAT 20. PAGE 9 A0179 ATTIT WAR

B54
GROSS F.,FOREIGN POLICY ANALYSIS. USA+45 TOP/EX PLAN INGP/REL ATTIT TECHRACY...CONCPT 20. PAGE 57 A1171 POLICY DIPLOM DECISION EDU/PROP

B54
MILLARD E.L.,FREEDOM IN A FEDERAL WORLD. FUT WOR+45 VOL/ASSN TOP/EX LEGIT ROUTINE FEDERAL PEACE ATTIT DISPL ORD/FREE PWR...MAJORIT INT/LAW JURID TREND COLD/WAR 20. PAGE 101 A2073 INT/ORG CREATE ADJUD BAL/PWR

B55
ALFIERI D.,DICTATORS FACE TO FACE. NAT/G TOP/EX DIPLOM EXEC COERCE ORD/FREE FASCISM...POLICY OBS 20 HITLER/A MUSSOLIN/B. PAGE 6 A0116 WAR CHIEF TOTALISM PERS/REL

B55
TANNENBAUM F.,THE AMERICAN TRADITION IN FOREIGN POLICY. USA+45 USA-45 CONSTN INT/ORG NAT/G POL/PAR VOL/ASSN TOP/EX LEGIT DRIVE ORD/FREE PWR...CONCPT GEN/LAWS CONGRESS LEAGUE/NAT COLD/WAR OAS 18/20. PAGE 141 A2887 TIME/SEQ

L55
ROSTOW W.W.,"RUSSIA AND CHINA UNDER COMMUNISM." CHINA/COM USSR INTELL STRUCT INT/ORG NAT/G POL/PAR TOP/EX ACT/RES PLAN ADMIN ATTIT ALL/VALS MARXISM ...CONCPT OBS TIME/SEQ TREND GOV/COMP VAL/FREE 20. PAGE 124 A2543 COM ASIA

B57
BUCK P.W.,CONTOL OF FOREIGN RELATIONS IN MODERN NATIONS. FRANCE L/A+17C NETHERLAND USSR WOR+45 INT/ORG TOP/EX BAL/PWR DOMIN EDU/PROP COERCE PEACE ATTIT...CONCPT TREND 20 CMN/WLTH. PAGE 21 A0427 NAT/G PWR DIPLOM

B57
CRABB C.,BIPARTISAN FOREIGN POLICY: MYTH OR REALITY. ASIA COM EUR+WWI ISLAM USA+45 USA-45 INT/ORG NAT/G LEGIS TOP/EX PWR CONGRESS 20. PAGE 32 A0649 POL/PAR ATTIT DIPLOM

B57
DEUTSCH K.W.,POLITICAL COMMUNITY AND THE NORTH ATLANTIC AREA: INTERNATIONAL ORGANIZATION IN THE LIGHT OF HISTORICAL EXPERIENCE. MOD/EUR USA+45 USA-45 SOCIETY FORCES TOP/EX CREATE PLAN DIPLOM DOMIN EDU/PROP LEGIT ATTIT ORD/FREE PWR...SAMP/SIZ TIME/SEQ CHARTS TOT/POP. PAGE 36 A0736 EUR+WWI INT/ORG PEACE REGION

B57
SPEIER H.,GERMAN REARMAMENT AND ATOMIC WAR: THE VIEWS OF GERMAN MILITARY AND POLITICAL LEADERS. FUT WOR+45 INT/ORG NAT/G WEAPON ATTIT PWR...INT QU TOT/POP VAL/FREE COLD/WAR 20. PAGE 136 A2780 TOP/EX FORCES NUC/PWR GERMANY

S57
WRIGHT Q.,"THE VALUE OF CONFLICT RESOLUTION OF A GENERAL DISCIPLINE OF INTERNATIONAL RELATIONS." WOR+45 SOCIETY INT/ORG NAT/G FORCES TOP/EX PLAN TEC/DEV ECO/TAC DOMIN LEGIT COERCE ATTIT PWR ...GEN/METH COLD/WAR VAL/FREE. PAGE 168 A3412 ORD/FREE SOC DIPLOM

B58
CAMPBELL J.C.,DEFENSE OF THE MIDDLE EAST: PROBLEMS OF AMERICAN POLICY. ISLAM USA+45 INT/ORG NAT/G EX/STRUC FORCES ECO/TAC DOMIN EDU/PROP LEGIT REGION COERCE...METH/CNCPT COLD/WAR TOT/POP 20. PAGE 23 A0474 TOP/EX ORD/FREE DIPLOM

B58
HAAS E.B.,THE UNITING OF EUROPE. EUR+WWI INT/ORG NAT/G POL/PAR TOP/EX ECO/TAC EDU/PROP LEGIT FEDERAL NAT/LISM DRIVE RIGID/FLEX ORD/FREE PWR PLURISM ...POLICY CONCPT INT GEN/LAWS ECSC EEC 20. PAGE 59 A1204 VOL/ASSN ECO/DEV

B58
RIGGS R.,POLITICS IN THE UNITED NATIONS: A STUDY OF UNITED STATES INFLUENCE IN THE GENERAL ASSEMBLY. USA+45 WOR+45 LEGIS TOP/EX CREATE BAL/PWR DIPLOM DOMIN EDU/PROP COLONIAL ROUTINE ATTIT RIGID/FLEX PWR...CONCPT OBS HIST/WRIT CHARTS STERTYP GEN/LAWS UN COLD/WAR 20. PAGE 121 A2480 INT/ORG

S58
THOMPSON K.W.,"NATIONAL SECURITY IN A NUCLEAR AGE." USA+45 WOR+45 SOCIETY INT/ORG NAT/G TOP/EX DIPLOM DOMIN EDU/PROP LEGIT ARMS/CONT COERCE ORD/FREE ...TREND STERTYP TOT/POP VAL/FREE COLD/WAR 20. PAGE 143 A2929 FORCES PWR BAL/PWR

B59
DAWSON R.H.,THE DECISION TO AID RUSSIA* FOREIGN POLICY AND DOMESTIC POLITICS. GERMANY USSR CHIEF EX/STRUC LEGIS TOP/EX PROB/SOLV WAR ATTIT...POLICY CONGRESS. PAGE 34 A0695 DECISION DELIB/GP DIPLOM FOR/AID

B59
ROBINSON J.A.,THE MONRONEY RESOULUTION: CONGRESSIONAL INITIATIVE IN FOREIGN POLICY MAKING. USA+45 POL/PAR TOP/EX DIPLOM INT/TRADE 20 CONGRESS WORLD/BANK INTL/DEV. PAGE 122 A2504 LEGIS FINAN ECO/UNDEV CHIEF

B59
SCHURZ W.L.,AMERICAN FOREIGN AFFAIRS: A GUIDE TO INTERNATIONAL AFFAIRS. USA+45 WOR+45 WOR-45 NAT/G FORCES LEGIS TOP/EX PLAN EDU/PROP LEGIT ADMIN ROUTINE ATTIT ORD/FREE PWR...SOC CONCPT STAT SAMP/SIZ CHARTS STERTYP 20. PAGE 129 A2653 INT/ORG SOCIETY DIPLOM

S59
BOULDING K.E.,"NATIONAL IMAGES AND INTERNATIONAL SYSTEMS." FUT WOR+45 CULTURE INT/ORG TOP/EX ROUTINE ...METH/CNCPT MYTH CONT/OBS TREND HYPO/EXP GEN/METH TOT/POP 20. PAGE 17 A0346 NAT/G DIPLOM

S59
HARVEY M.F.,"THE PALESTINE REFUGEE PROBLEM: ELEMENTS OF A SOLUTION." ISLAM LAW INT/ORG DELIB/GP TOP/EX ECO/TAC ROUTINE DRIVE HEALTH LOVE ORD/FREE PWR WEALTH...MAJORIT FAO 20. PAGE 62 A1283 ACT/RES LEGIT PEACE ISRAEL

S59
LASSWELL H.D.,"UNIVERSALITY IN PERSPECTIVE." FUT UNIV SOCIETY CONSULT TOP/EX PLAN EDU/PROP ADJUD ROUTINE ARMS/CONT COERCE PEACE ATTIT PERSON ALL/VALS. PAGE 85 A1741 INT/ORG JURID TOTALISM

S59
ZAUBERMAN A.,"SOVIET BLOC ECONOMIC INTEGRATION." COM CULTURE INTELL ECO/DEV INDUS TOP/EX ACT/RES PLAN ECO/TAC INT/TRADE ROUTINE CHOOSE ATTIT ...TIME/SEQ 20. PAGE 169 A3448 MARKET INT/ORG USSR TOTALISM

B60
KHRUSHCHEV N.,FOR VICTORY IN PEACEFUL COMPETITION WITH CAPITALISM. COM FUT USSR WOR+45 CONSTN SOCIETY INDUS INT/ORG DELIB/GP PLAN BAL/PWR DIPLOM PERSON MARXISM...MARXIST WORK 20 COLD/WAR. PAGE 79 A1611 TOP/EX PWR CAP/ISM SOCISM

B60
LINDSAY K.,EUROPEAN ASSEMBLIES: THE EXPERIMENTAL PERIOD 1949-1959. EUR+WWI ECO/DEV NAT/G POL/PAR LEGIS TOP/EX ACT/RES PLAN ECO/TAC DOMIN LEGIT ROUTINE ATTIT DRIVE ORD/FREE PWR SKILL...SOC CONCPT TREND CHARTS GEN/LAWS VAL/FREE. PAGE 89 A1823 VOL/ASSN INT/ORG REGION

B60
MOSELY P.E.,THE KREMLIN AND WORLD POLITICS. EUR+WWI GERMANY USA+45 USSR CHIEF TOP/EX BAL/PWR DOMIN PEACE PWR...METH 20 COLD/WAR STALIN/J EUROPE/E. PAGE 105 A2151 COM DIPLOM POLICY WAR

B60
PRICE D.,THE SECRETARY OF STATE. USA+45 CONSTN ELITES INTELL CHIEF EX/STRUC TOP/EX LEGIT ATTIT PWR SKILL...DECISION 20 CONGRESS. PAGE 117 A2410 CONSULT DIPLOM INT/LAW

B60
SCHLESINGER J.R.,THE POLITICAL ECONOMY OF NATIONAL SECURITY. USA+45 USSR WOR+45 ECO/DEV ECO/UNDEV NAT/G DELIB/GP TOP/EX BAL/PWR DIPLOM INT/TRADE ATTIT PWR...STERTYP TOT/POP 20. PAGE 128 A2628 PLAN ECO/TAC

B60
SPEIER H.,DIVIDED BERLIN: THE ANATOMY OF SOVIET POLITICAL BLACKMAIL. COM GERMANY USA+45 USSR WOR+45 NAT/G TOP/EX DOMIN EDU/PROP ALL/VALS...POLICY CONCPT COLD/WAR 20 U-2. PAGE 136 A2782 INT/ORG ACT/RES DIPLOM

B60
THOMPSON K.W.,POLITICAL REALISM AND THE CRISIS IN WORLD POLITICS. USA+45 USA-45 SOCIETY INT/ORG NAT/G LEGIS TOP/EX LEGIT DETER ATTIT ORD/FREE PWR ...GEN/LAWS TOT/POP 20. PAGE 143 A2931 PLAN HUM BAL/PWR DIPLOM

B60
WHITING A.S.,CHINA CROSSES THE YALU: THE DECISION TO ENTER THE KOREAN WAR. ASIA CHINA/COM KOREA ECO/UNDEV R+D INT/ORG TOP/EX ACT/RES BAL/PWR ATTIT PLAN COERCE WAR

PWR...GEN/METH 20. PAGE 164 A3338

L60
HOLTON G.,"ARMS CONTROL." FUT WOR+45 CULTURE INT/ORG NAT/G FORCES TOP/EX PLAN EDU/PROP COERCE ATTIT RIGID/FLEX ORD/FREE...POLICY PHIL/SCI SOC TREND COLD/WAR. PAGE 67 A1377
ACT/RES CONSULT ARMS/CONT NUC/PWR

L60
NOGEE J.L.,"THE DIPLOMACY OF DISARMAMENT." WOR+45 INT/ORG NAT/G CONSULT DELIB/GP TOP/EX BAL/PWR DIPLOM EDU/PROP COERCE DETER WEAPON PEACE ATTIT ...RECORD TIME/SEQ TOT/POP VAL/FREE COLD/WAR 20. PAGE 109 A2246
PWR ORD/FREE ARMS/CONT NUC/PWR

L60
RIGGS R.,"OVER-SELLING THE U.N. CHARTER, FACT AND MYTH." USA+45 SOCIETY NAT/G TOP/EX PLAN DIPLOM EDU/PROP PEACE ATTIT PERCEPT MORAL...POLICY SAMP UN 20. PAGE 121 A2481
INT/ORG MYTH

S60
FITZGIBBON R.H.,"DICTATORSHIP AND DEMOCRACY IN LATIN AMERICA." FUT ECO/DEV ECO/UNDEV INT/ORG LOC/G NAT/G TOP/EX PLAN TEC/DEV ECO/TAC CHOOSE ATTIT DRIVE PERSON ALL/VALS OAS TOT/POP 20. PAGE 46 A0943
L/A+17C ACT/RES INT/TRADE

S60
KAPLAN M.A.,"THEORETICAL ANALYSIS OF THE BALANCE OF POWER." FUT USA+45 WOR+45 INTELL ECO/DEV INT/ORG NAT/G CONSULT TOP/EX ACT/RES PLAN TEC/DEV ATTIT ALL/VALS...METH/CNCPT TOT/POP 20. PAGE 76 A1562
CREATE NEW/IDEA DIPLOM NUC/PWR

S60
LEAR J.,"PEACE: SCIENCE'S NEXT GREAT EXPLORATION." USA+45 INT/ORG TOP/EX TEC/DEV EDU/PROP ROUTINE PEACE KNOWL SKILL 20. PAGE 86 A1757
EX/STRUC ARMS/CONT NUC/PWR

S60
MAGATHAN W.,"SOME BASES OF WEST GERMAN MILITARY POLICY." EUR+WWI FUT INT/ORG TOP/EX ECO/TAC DOMIN DRIVE ORD/FREE PWR...TRADIT GEOG OBS TREND. PAGE 93 A1904
NAT/G FORCES GERMANY

B61
BISHOP D.G.,THE ADMINISTRATION OF BRITISH FOREIGN RELATIONS. EUR+WWI MOD/EUR INT/ORG NAT/G POL/PAR DELIB/GP LEGIS TOP/EX ECO/TAC DOMIN EDU/PROP ADMIN COERCE 20. PAGE 14 A0292
ROUTINE PWR DIPLOM UK

B61
DALLIN D.J.,SOVIET FOREIGN POLICY AFTER STALIN. ASIA CHINA/COM EUR+WWI GERMANY IRAN UK YUGOSLAVIA INT/ORG NAT/G VOL/ASSN FORCES TOP/EX BAL/PWR DOMIN EDU/PROP COERCE ATTIT PWR 20. PAGE 33 A0679
COM DIPLOM USSR

B61
GALLOIS P.,THE BALANCE OF TERROR: STRATEGY FOR THE NUCLEAR AGE. FUT WOR+45 INT/ORG FORCES TOP/EX DETER WAR ATTIT RIGID/FLEX ORD/FREE PWR...HYPO/EXP 20. PAGE 50 A1032
PLAN DECISION DIPLOM NUC/PWR

B61
GRAEBNER N.,AN UNCERTAIN TRADITION: AMERICAN SECRETARIES OF STATE IN THE 20TH CENTURY. USA+45 CONSTN INT/ORG NAT/G DELIB/GP TOP/EX BAL/PWR DOMIN LEGIT ADMIN ARMS/CONT ATTIT DRIVE PERSON SUPEGO ORD/FREE PWR...GEN/LAWS VAL/FREE CONGRESS. PAGE 55 A1121
USA-45 BIOG DIPLOM

B61
HARRISON S.,INDIA AND THE UNITED STATES. FUT S/ASIA USA+45 WOR+45 INTELL ECO/DEV ECO/UNDEV AGRI INDUS INT/ORG NAT/G CONSULT EX/STRUC TOP/EX PLAN ECO/TAC NEUTRAL ALL/VALS...MGT TOT/POP 20. PAGE 62 A1272
DELIB/GP ACT/RES FOR/AID INDIA

B61
HASAN H.S.,PAKISTAN AND THE UN. ISLAM WOR+45 ECO/DEV ECO/UNDEV NAT/G TOP/EX ECO/TAC FOR/AID EDU/PROP ADMIN DRIVE PERCEPT...OBS TIME/SEQ UN 20. PAGE 62 A1284
INT/ORG ATTIT PAKISTAN

B61
HAYTER W.,THE DIPLOMACY OF THE GREAT POWERS. FRANCE UK USSR WOR+45 EX/STRUC TOP/EX NUC/PWR PEACE...OBS 20. PAGE 63 A1296
DIPLOM POLICY NAT/G

B61
KISSINGER H.A.,THE NECESSITY FOR CHOICE. FUT USA+45 ECO/UNDEV NAT/G PLAN BAL/PWR ECO/TAC ARMS/CONT DETER NUC/PWR ATTIT...POLICY CONCPT RECORD GEN/LAWS COLD/WAR 20. PAGE 80 A1642
TOP/EX TREND DIPLOM

B61
STILLMAN E.,THE NEW POLITICS: AMERICA AND THE END OF THE POSTWAR WORLD. FUT WOR+45 CULTURE SOCIETY ECO/UNDEV INT/ORG NAT/G FORCES TOP/EX ACT/RES DIPLOM EDU/PROP LEGIT ROUTINE DETER ATTIT ORD/FREE PWR...OBS STERTYP COLD/WAR TOT/POP VAL/FREE. PAGE 138 A2827
USA+45 PLAN

B61
WARNER D.,HURRICANE FROM CHINA. ASIA CHINA/COM FUT L/A+17C USA+45 CULTURE NAT/G FORCES TOP/EX FOR/AID DRIVE PWR...CONCPT TIME/SEQ SEATO WORK 20. PAGE 161 A3284
ATTIT TREND REV

S61
ALGER C.F.,"NON-RESOLUTION CONSEQUENCES OF THE UNITED NATIONS AND THEIR EFFECT ON INTERNATIONAL CONFLICT." WOR+45 CONSTN ECO/DEV NAT/G CONSULT DELIB/GP TOP/EX ACT/RES PLAN DIPLOM EDU/PROP ROUTINE ATTIT ALL/VALS...INT/LAW TOT/POP UN 20. PAGE 6 A0117
INT/ORG DRIVE BAL/PWR

S61
DANIELS R.V.,"THE CHINESE REVOLUTION IN RUSSIAN PERSPECTIVE." ASIA CHINA/COM COM USSR INTELL INT/ORG TOP/EX REV TOTALISM PWR...POLICY WORK VAL/FREE 20. PAGE 33 A0680
POL/PAR PLAN

S61
GOODWIN G.L.,"THE EXPANDING UNITED NATIONS: 2- DIPLOMATIC PRESSURES AND TECHNIQUES." COM ECO/UNDEV TOP/EX BAL/PWR DIPLOM DOMIN...POLICY CONCPT UN COLD/WAR 20. PAGE 54 A1108
INT/ORG PWR

S61
LEWY G.,"SUPERIOR ORDERS, NUCLEAR WARFARE AND THE DICTATES OF CONSCIENCE: THE DILEMMA OF MILITARY OBEDIENCE IN THE ATOMIC." FUT UNIV WOR+45 INTELL SOCIETY FORCES TOP/EX ACT/RES ADMIN ROUTINE NUC/PWR PERCEPT RIGID/FLEX ALL/VALS...POLICY CONCPT 20. PAGE 88 A1805
DETER INT/ORG LAW INT/LAW

S61
TAUBENFELD H.J.,"OUTER SPACE--PAST POLITICS AND FUTURE POLICY." FUT USA+45 USA-45 WOR+45 AIR INTELL STRUCT ECO/DEV NAT/G TOP/EX ACT/RES ADMIN ROUTINE NUC/PWR ATTIT DRIVE...CONCPT TIME/SEQ TREND TOT/POP 20. PAGE 141 A2892
PLAN SPACE INT/ORG

S61
VERNON R.,"A TRADE POLICY FOR THE 1960'S." COM FUT USA+45 WOR+45 ECO/DEV ECO/UNDEV FINAN TOP/EX ACT/RES...WELF/ST METH/CNCPT CONT/OBS TOT/POP 20. PAGE 159 A3229
PLAN INT/TRADE

S61
VINER J.,"ECONOMIC FOREIGN POLICY ON THE NEW FRONTIER." USA+45 ECO/UNDEV AGRI FINAN INDUS MARKET INT/ORG NAT/G FOR/AID INT/TRADE ADMIN ATTIT PWR 20 KENNEDY/JF. PAGE 159 A3239
TOP/EX ECO/TAC BAL/PAY TARIFFS

S61
VIRALLY M.,"VERS UNE REFORME DU SECRETARIAT DES NATIONS UNIES." FUT WOR+45 CONSTN ECO/DEV TOP/EX BAL/PWR ADMIN ALL/VALS...CONCPT BIOG UN VAL/FREE 20. PAGE 159 A3243
INT/ORG INTELL DIPLOM

B62
CLUBB O.E. JR.,THE UNITED STATES AND THE SINO-SOVIET BLOC IN SOUTHEAST ASIA. ASIA CHINA/COM COM USA+45 USSR ECO/UNDEV INT/ORG NAT/G FORCES TOP/EX PLAN ECO/TAC DOMIN COERCE GUERRILLA ATTIT RIGID/FLEX...POLICY OBS TREND 20. PAGE 27 A0553
S/ASIA PWR BAL/PWR DIPLOM

B62
HATCH J.,AFRICA TODAY-AND TOMORROW: AN OUTLINE OF BASIC FACTS AND MAJOR PROBLEMS. AFR FUT ISLAM STRATA ECO/UNDEV INT/ORG NAT/G POL/PAR DELIB/GP TOP/EX EDU/PROP LEGIT CHOOSE ATTIT...TIME/SEQ TOT/POP COLD/WAR 20. PAGE 63 A1287
PLAN CONSTN NAT/LISM

B62
JEWELL M.E.,SENATORIAL POLITICS AND FOREIGN POLICY. NAT/G POL/PAR CHIEF DELIB/GP TOP/EX FOR/AID EDU/PROP ROUTINE ATTIT PWR SKILL...MAJORIT METH/CNCPT TIME/SEQ CONGRESS 20 PRESIDENT. PAGE 74 A1516
USA+45 LEGIS DIPLOM

B62
MANNING C.A.W.,THE NATURE OF INTERNATIONAL SOCIETY. FUT LAW NAT/G TOP/EX NAT/LISM PEACE PERCEPT PERSON ALL/VALS PLURISM...METH/CNCPT MYTH HYPO/EXP TOT/POP 20. PAGE 94 A1926
INT/ORG SOCIETY SIMUL DIPLOM

B62
MCKENNA J.,DIPLOMATIC PROTEST IN FOREIGN POLICY: ANALYSIS AND CASE STUDIES. COM USA+45 WOR+45 INT/ORG PUB/INST DELIB/GP TOP/EX ACT/RES PLAN LEGIT ATTIT 20. PAGE 98 A2014
NAT/G POLICY DIPLOM

B62
OSGOOD R.E.,NATO: THE ENTANGLING ALLIANCE. USA+45 WOR+45 VOL/ASSN FORCES TOP/EX PLAN DETER WEAPON DRIVE RIGID/FLEX ORD/FREE PWR...TREND 20 NATO. PAGE 112 A2301
INT/ORG ARMS/CONT PEACE

B62
STRAUSS L.L.,MEN AND DECISIONS. USA+45 USA-45 USSR CONSULT FORCES TOP/EX WAR PEACE 20. PAGE 139 A2844
DECISION PWR NUC/PWR DIPLOM

B62
YALEN R.,REGIONALISM AND WORLD ORDER. EUR+WWI WOR+45 WOR-45 INT/ORG VOL/ASSN DELIB/GP FORCES TOP/EX BAL/PWR DIPLOM DOMIN REGION ARMS/CONT PWR ...JURID HYPO/EXP COLD/WAR 20. PAGE 168 A3427
ORD/FREE POLICY

L62
STEIN E.,"MR HAMMARSKJOLD, THE CHARTER LAW AND THE FUTURE ROLE OF THE UNITED NATIONS SECRETARY-GENERAL." WOR+45 CONSTN INT/ORG DELIB/GP FORCES TOP/EX BAL/PWR LEGIT ROUTINE RIGID/FLEX PWR ...POLICY JURID OBS STERTYP UN COLD/WAR 20 HAMMARSK/D. PAGE 137 A2815
CONCPT BIOG

L62
ULYSSES,"THE INTERNATIONAL AIMS AND POLICIES OF THE SOVIET UNION: THE NEW CONCEPTS AND STRATEGY OF KHRUSHCHEV." FUT USSR WOR+45 SOCIETY INT/ORG NAT/G POL/PAR FORCES TOP/EX PLAN DOMIN EDU/PROP COERCE ATTIT PERSON PWR...TREND COLD/WAR 20 KHRUSH/N. PAGE 146 A2994
COM POLICY BAL/PWR DIPLOM

S62
BRZEZINSKI Z.K.,"PEACEFUL ENGAGEMENT IN COMMUNIST DISUNITY." ASIA CHINA/COM USA+45 USSR NAT/G TOP/EX CREATE ECO/TAC FOR/AID DOMIN ATTIT PERCEPT RIGID/FLEX PWR...PSY 20. PAGE 20 A0417 — COM DIPLOM TOTALISM

S62
DALLIN A.,"THE SOVIET VIEW OF THE UNITED NATIONS." WOR+45 VOL/ASSN TOP/EX DIPLOM DOMIN EDU/PROP LEGIT ATTIT RIGID/FLEX PWR...CONCPT OBS HIST/WRIT TIME/SEQ STERTYP GEN/LAWS COLD/WAR UN 20. PAGE 33 A0676 — COM INT/ORG USSR

S62
DRACHKOVITCH M.M.,"THE EMERGING PATTERN OF YUGOSLAV-SOVIET RELATIONS." COM FUT USSR WOR+45 INT/ORG ECO/TAC FOR/AID DOMIN COERCE ATTIT PERSON ORD/FREE PWR...TIME/SEQ 20 TITO/MARSH KHRUSH/N STALIN/J. PAGE 38 A0783 — TOP/EX DIPLOM YUGOSLAVIA

S62
FINKELSTEIN L.S.,"THE UNITED NATIONS AND ORGANIZATIONS FOR CONTROL OF ARMAMENT." FUT WOR+45 VOL/ASSN DELIB/GP TOP/EX CREATE EDU/PROP LEGIT ADJUD NUC/PWR ATTIT RIGID/FLEX ORD/FREE...POLICY DECISION CONCPT OBS TREND GEN/LAWS TOT/POP COLD/WAR. PAGE 46 A0933 — INT/ORG PWR ARMS/CONT

S62
LONDON K.,"SINO-SOVIET RELATIONS IN THE CONTEXT OF THE 'WORLD SOCIALIST SYSTEM'." ASIA CHINA/COM COM USSR INT/ORG NAT/G TOP/EX BAL/PWR DIPLOM DOMIN ATTIT PERCEPT RIGID/FLEX PWR MARXISM...METH/CNCPT TREND 20. PAGE 91 A1854 — DELIB/GP CONCPT SOCISM

S62
MCWHINNEY E.,"CO-EXISTENCE, THE CUBA CRISIS, AND COLD WAR-INTERNATIONAL WAR." CUBA USA+45 USSR WOR+45 NAT/G TOP/EX BAL/PWR DIPLOM DOMIN LEGIT PEACE RIGID/FLEX ORD/FREE...STERTYP COLD/WAR 20. PAGE 99 A2026 — CONCPT INT/LAW

S62
NANES A.,"DISARMAMENT: THE LAST SEVEN YEARS." COM EUR+WWI USA+45 USSR INT/ORG FORCES TOP/EX CREATE LEGIT NUC/PWR DISPL ORD/FREE...CONCPT TIME/SEQ CON/ANAL 20. PAGE 107 A2195 — DELIB/GP RIGID/FLEX ARMS/CONT

S62
PIQUEMAL M.,"LA COOPERATION FINANCIERE ENTRE LA FRANCE ET LES ETATS AFRICAINS ET MALGACHE." ISLAM INT/ORG TOP/EX ECO/TAC...JURID CHARTS 20. PAGE 116 A2383 — AFR FINAN FRANCE MADAGASCAR

S62
SCHILLING W.R.,"SCIENTISTS, FOREIGN POLICY AND POLITICS." WOR+45 WOR-45 INTELL INT/ORG CONSULT TOP/EX ACT/RES PLAN ADMIN KNOWL...CONCPT OBS TREND LEAGUE/NAT 20. PAGE 128 A2627 — NAT/G TEC/DEV DIPLOM NUC/PWR

S62
TOWSTER J.,"THE USSR AND THE USA: CHALLENGE AND RESPONSE." COM GERMANY USA+45 USSR WOR+45 ECO/UNDEV INT/ORG VOL/ASSN EX/STRUC FORCES TOP/EX CREATE PLAN TEC/DEV DIPLOM ECO/TAC EDU/PROP COLONIAL COERCE PWR ...GEN/METH COLD/WAR 20 KENNEDY/JF. PAGE 145 A2956 — ACT/RES GEN/LAWS

B63
CREMEANS C.,THE ARABS AND THE WORLD: NASSER'S ARAB NATIONALIST POLICY. FUT ISLAM UAR USA+45 SOCIETY STRATA NAT/G POL/PAR PLAN DIPLOM EDU/PROP LEGIT DRIVE ALL/VALS...INT TIME/SEQ CHARTS 20 NASSER/G. PAGE 33 A0662 — TOP/EX ATTIT REGION NAT/LISM

B63
MONGER G.W.,THE END OF ISOLATION. FRANCE MOD/EUR RUSSIA UK NAT/G LEGIS TOP/EX GOV/REL PWR 20 TREATY CHINJAP. PAGE 103 A2106 — DIPLOM POLICY WAR

B63
QUAISON-SACKEY A.,AFRICA UNBOUND: REFLECTIONS OF AN AFRICAN STATESMAN. ISLAM CULTURE INTELL INT/ORG POL/PAR TOP/EX DOMIN EDU/PROP LEGIT ATTIT PERSON ...CONCPT OBS TIME/SEQ CHARTS STERTYP 20 UN. PAGE 118 A2423 — AFR BIOG

B63
THUCYDIDES,THE PELOPONESIAN WARS. MEDIT-7 CULTURE INT/ORG NAT/G FORCES TOP/EX PLAN ROUTINE PWR ...CONCPT. PAGE 144 A2938 — ATTIT COERCE WAR

B63
TUCKER R.C.,THE SOVIET POLITICAL MIND. WOR+45 ELITES INT/ORG NAT/G POL/PAR PLAN DIPLOM ECO/TAC DOMIN ADMIN NUC/PWR REV DRIVE PERSON SUPEGO PWR WEALTH...POLICY MGT PSY CONCPT OBS BIOG TREND COLD/WAR MARX/KARL 20. PAGE 145 A2972 — COM TOP/EX USSR

B63
VOSS E.H.,NUCLEAR AMBUSH: THE TEST-BAN TRAP. WOR+45 COM/IND INT/ORG NAT/G DELIB/GP FORCES LEGIS TOP/EX ACT/RES DOMIN EDU/PROP LEGIT ROUTINE COERCE ATTIT PERCEPT RIGID/FLEX HEALTH MORAL ORD/FREE PWR. PAGE 160 A3255 — TEC/DEV HIST/WRIT ARMS/CONT NUC/PWR

S63
ALPHAND H.,"FRANCE AND HER ALLIES." EUR+WWI UK USA+45 ECO/DEV INT/ORG NAT/G VOL/ASSN FORCES TOP/EX DIPLOM ECO/TAC LEGIT ATTIT DRIVE ORD/FREE PWR WEALTH...STAT EEC TOT/POP 20. PAGE 6 A0130 — ACT/RES FRANCE

S63
BALOGH T.,"L'INFLUENCE DES INSTITUTIONS MONETAIRES ET COMMERCIALES SUR LA STRUCTURE ECONOMIQUE AFRICAIN." AFR EUR+WWI FUT USA+45 USA-45 WOR+45 SERV/IND INT/ORG NAT/G TOP/EX ROUTINE...INDEX EEC 20. PAGE 11 A0215 — FINAN

S63
BELOFF M.,"BRITAIN, EUROPE AND THE ATLANTIC COMMUNITY." EUR+WWI ELITES NAT/G VOL/ASSN TOP/EX ATTIT ORD/FREE PWR SOVEREIGN WEALTH EEC TOT/POP VAL/FREE CMN/WLTH 20. PAGE 13 A0262 — INT/ORG ECO/DEV UK

S63
CAHIER P.,"LE DROIT INTERNE DES ORGANISATIONS INTERNATIONALES." UNIV CONSTN SOCIETY ECO/DEV R+D NAT/G TOP/EX LEGIT ATTIT PERCEPT...TIME/SEQ 19/20. PAGE 23 A0464 — INT/ORG JURID DIPLOM INT/LAW

S63
CHAKRAVARTI P.C.,"INDIAN NON-ALIGNMENT AND UNITED STATES POLICY." ASIA INDIA S/ASIA USA+45 CULTURE ECO/UNDEV NAT/G VOL/ASSN DELIB/GP TOP/EX FOR/AID NEUTRAL...POLICY HUM CONCPT RECORD GEN/LAWS 20. PAGE 25 A0515 — ATTIT ALL/VALS COLONIAL DIPLOM

S63
ETIENNE G.,"'LOIS OBJECTIVES' ET PROBLEMES DE DEVELOPPEMENT DANS LE CONTEXTE CHINE-URSS." ASIA CHINA/COM COM FUT STRUCT INT/ORG VOL/ASSN TOP/EX TEC/DEV ECO/TAC ATTIT RIGID/FLEX...GEOG MGT TIME/SEQ TOT/POP 20. PAGE 42 A0866 — TOTALISM USSR

S63
GROSSER A.,"FRANCE AND GERMANY IN THE ATLANTIC COMMUNITY." INT/ORG NAT/G TOP/EX DIPLOM REGION PEACE ATTIT ORD/FREE PWR...CONCPT RECORD TIME/SEQ GEN/LAWS VAL/FREE COLD/WAR 20. PAGE 57 A1178 — EUR+WWI VOL/ASSN FRANCE GERMANY

S63
GUPTA S.C.,"INDIA AND THE SOVIET UNION." CHINA/COM COM INDIA S/ASIA VOL/ASSN TOP/EX FOR/AID EDU/PROP PEACE PWR...RECORD COLD/WAR 20. PAGE 58 A1195 — DISPL MYTH USSR

S63
HARNETTY P.,"CANADA, SOUTH AFRICA AND THE COMMONWEALTH." CANADA SOUTH/AFR LAW INT/ORG VOL/ASSN DELIB/GP LEGIS TOP/EX ECO/TAC LEGIT DRIVE MORAL...CONCPT CMN/WLTH 20. PAGE 62 A1263 — AFR ATTIT

S63
KISSINGER H.A.,"STRAINS ON THE ALLIANCE." EUR+WWI FRANCE GERMANY GERMANY/W USA+45 ECO/DEV INT/ORG NAT/G TOP/EX EDU/PROP NUC/PWR ATTIT PWR...PSY TREND 20. PAGE 80 A1643 — VOL/ASSN DRIVE DIPLOM

S63
MULLEY F.W.,"NUCLEAR WEAPONS: CHALLENGE TO NATIONAL SOVEREIGNTY." EUR+WWI FRANCE UK USA+45 VOL/ASSN EX/STRUC FORCES TOP/EX ACT/RES REGION DRIVE PWR 20 NATO DEGAULLE/C. PAGE 106 A2169 — INT/ORG ATTIT DIPLOM NUC/PWR

S63
MURRAY J.N.,"UNITED NATIONS PEACE-KEEPING AND PROBLEMS OF POLITICAL CONTROL." FUT WOR+45 CONSTN DELIB/GP FORCES TOP/EX ACT/RES CREATE LEGIT PEACE PWR...METH/CNCPT CONGO UN 20. PAGE 106 A2182 — INT/ORG ORD/FREE

S63
NICHOLAS H.G.,"UN PEACE FORCES AND THE CHANGING GLOBE: THE LESSONS OF SUEZ AND CONGO." FUT WOR+45 CONSTN INT/ORG CONSULT DELIB/GP TOP/EX CREATE DIPLOM DOMIN LEGIT COERCE WAR PERSON RIGID/FLEX PWR UN SUEZ CONGO UNEF 20. PAGE 109 A2229 — ACT/RES FORCES

S63
WYZNER E.,"NIEKTORE ASPEKTY PRAWNE FINANSOWANIA OPERACJI ONZ W KONGO I NA BEIZKIM WSCHODZIE." S/ASIA CONSTN FINAN INT/ORG TOP/EX...TIME/SEQ UN 20 CONGRESS. PAGE 168 A3426 — FORCES JURID DIPLOM

B64
AFRO ASIAN SOLIDARITY AGAINST IMPERIALISM. AFR ISLAM S/ASIA ECO/UNDEV NAT/G POL/PAR TOP/EX PRESS ...INT ANTHOL 20 CHOU/ENLAI. PAGE 3 A0066 — MARXISM DIPLOM EDU/PROP CHIEF

B64
BINDER L.,THE IDEOLOGICAL REVOLUTION IN THE MIDDLE EAST. ISLAM STRUCT INT/ORG KIN SECT EX/STRUC TOP/EX PLAN ATTIT DRIVE RIGID/FLEX PWR...MYTH TOT/POP 20. PAGE 14 A0289 — POL/PAR NAT/G NAT/LISM

B64
BOYD J.P.,NUMBER 7: ALEXANDER HAMILTON'S SECRET ATTEMPTS TO CONTROL AMERICAN FOREIGN POLICY. AFR UK DIPLOM WAR RESPECT WEALTH...POLICY HIST/WRIT 18 HAMILTON/A. PAGE 18 A0364 — USA-45 NAT/G TOP/EX PWR

B64
CZERNIN F.,VERSAILLES - 1919. EUR+WWI USA-45 FACE/GP POL/PAR VOL/ASSN DELIB/GP TOP/EX CREATE BAL/PWR DIPLOM LEGIT NAT/LISM PEACE ATTIT RIGID/FLEX ORD/FREE PWR...CON/ANAL LEAGUE/NAT 20 VERSAILLES. PAGE 33 A0671 — INT/ORG STRUCT

B64
ETZIONI A.,WINNING WITHOUT WAR. FUT MOD/EUR USA+45 WOR+45 ECO/DEV ECO/UNDEV INT/ORG NAT/G FORCES TOP/EX PLAN TEC/DEV ECO/TAC DOMIN EDU/PROP LEGIT COERCE CHOOSE ATTIT MORAL ORD/FREE RESPECT WEALTH MAJORIT. PAGE 43 A0871 — PWR TREND DIPLOM USSR

B64
GARDNER L.C.,ECONOMIC ASPECTS OF NEW DEAL DIPLOMACY. USA-45 WOR-45 LAW ECO/DEV INT/ORG NAT/G — ECO/TAC DIPLOM

VOL/ASSN LEGIS TOP/EX EDU/PROP ORD/FREE PWR WEALTH ...POLICY TIME/SEQ VAL/FREE 20 ROOSEVLT/F. PAGE 51 A1043

B64
KAUFMANN W.W.,THE MC NAMARA STRATEGY. TOP/EX INSPECT BAL/PWR DIPLOM CONTROL DETER GUERRILLA NUC/PWR WEAPON COST PWR...METH/COMP 20 MCNAMARA/R KENNEDY/JF JOHNSON/LB NATO DEPT/DEFEN. PAGE 77 A1572
FORCES WAR PLAN PROB/SOLV

B64
SINGH N.,THE DEFENCE MECHANISM OF THE MODERN STATE. COM UK USA+45 CONSTN INT/ORG NUC/PWR WAR INGP/REL ROLE 20 DEPT/DEFEN COMMONWLTH. PAGE 134 A2735
FORCES TOP/EX NAT/G CIVMIL/REL

B64
US SENATE COMM GOVT OPERATIONS,ADMINISTRATION OF NATIONAL SECURITY. USA+45 CHIEF TOP/EX PLAN DIPLOM CONTROL PEACE...POLICY DECISION 20 PRESIDENT CONGRESS. PAGE 156 A3176
ADMIN FORCES ORD/FREE NAT/G

B64
WARREN S.,THE PRESIDENT AS WORLD LEADER. USA+45 WOR+45 ELITES COM/IND INT/ORG NAT/G VOL/ASSN CHIEF EX/STRUC LEGIT COERCE ATTIT PERSON RIGID/FLEX...INT TIME/SEQ COLD/WAR 20 ROOSEVLT/F TRUMAN/HS EISNHWR/DD KENNEDY/JF. PAGE 161 A3286
TOP/EX PWR DIPLOM

L64
CAMPBELL J.C.,"THE MIDDLE EAST IN THE MUTED COLD WAR." COM EUR+WWI UAR USA+45 USSR STRUCT ECO/UNDEV NAT/G VOL/ASSN EX/STRUC TOP/EX DIPLOM ECO/TAC EDU/PROP...TIME/SEQ COLD/WAR 20. PAGE 23 A0475
ISLAM FOR/AID NAT/LISM

L64
HERZ J.H.,"THE RELEVANCY AND IRRELEVANCY OF APPEASEMENT." WOR+45 INT/ORG CONSULT TOP/EX LEGIT ATTIT SUPEGO ORD/FREE...POLICY SOC GEN/LAWS 20. PAGE 64 A1320
ACT/RES RIGID/FLEX

L64
MANZER R.A.,"THE UNITED NATIONS SPECIAL FUND." WOR+45 CONSTN ECO/UNDEV NAT/G TOP/EX LEGIT WEALTH ...CHARTS UN 20. PAGE 94 A1936
FINAN INT/ORG

L64
POUNDS N.J.G.,"THE POLITICS OF PARTITION." AFR ASIA COM EUR+WWI FUT ISLAM S/ASIA USA-45 LAW ECO/DEV ECO/UNDEV AGRI INDUS INT/ORG POL/PAR PROVS SECT FORCES TOP/EX EDU/PROP LEGIT ATTIT MORAL ORD/FREE PWR RESPECT WEALTH. PAGE 117 A2402
NAT/G NAT/LISM

S64
DE GAULLE C.,"FRENCH WORLD VIEW." AFR ASIA CHINA/COM EUR+WWI ISLAM ECO/UNDEV INT/ORG NAT/G VOL/ASSN ACT/RES DIPLOM ECO/TAC EDU/PROP ATTIT DRIVE WEALTH 20. PAGE 35 A0702
TOP/EX PWR FOR/AID FRANCE

S64
DRAKE S.T.C.,"DEMOCRACY ON TRIAL IN AFRICA." EUR+WWI FUT USA+45 ECO/UNDEV INT/ORG NAT/G POL/PAR TOP/EX EDU/PROP LEGIT ATTIT ALL/VALS...POLICY TREND GEN/LAWS VAL/FREE 20. PAGE 38 A0785
AFR STERTYP

S64
KHAN M.Z.,"THE PRESIDENT OF THE GENERAL ASSEMBLY." WOR+45 CONSTN DELIB/GP EDU/PROP LEGIT ROUTINE PWR RESPECT SKILL...DECISION SOC BIOG TREND UN 20. PAGE 78 A1609
INT/ORG TOP/EX

S64
MCCREARY E.A.,"THOSE AMERICAN MANAGERS DON'T IMPRESS EUROPE." EUR+WWI USA+45 CULTURE STRATA ECO/DEV TOP/EX INT/TRADE ATTIT DRIVE PERSON RIGID/FLEX...CONCPT 20. PAGE 98 A2003
MARKET ACT/RES BAL/PAY CAP/ISM

S64
PALMER N.D.,"INDIA AS A FACTOR IN UNITED STATES FOREIGN POLICY." INDIA USA+45 USA-45 ECO/UNDEV NAT/G TOP/EX ECO/TAC EDU/PROP...METH/CNCPT TIME/SEQ 20. PAGE 113 A2323
S/ASIA ATTIT FOR/AID DIPLOM

S64
RUBINSTEIN A.Z.,"THE SOVIET IMAGE OF WESTERN EUROPE." COM EUR+WWI FRANCE GERMANY GERMANY/W USA+45 USSR INT/ORG NAT/G VOL/ASSN FORCES TOP/EX BAL/PWR EDU/PROP ORD/FREE PWR...MYTH RECORD NATO EEC 20. PAGE 125 A2564
RIGID/FLEX ATTIT

B65
EISENHOWER D.D.,WAGING PEACE 1956-61: THE WHITE HOUSE YEARS. USA+45 DIPLOM LEAD INGP/REL RACE/REL PEACE ATTIT...TRADIT TIME/SEQ 20 EISNHWR/DD PRESIDENT COLD/WAR CIV/RIGHTS BERLIN. PAGE 41 A0833
TOP/EX BIOG ORD/FREE POLICY

B65
HAIGHT D.E.,THE PRESIDENT; ROLES AND POWERS. USA+45 USA-45 POL/PAR PLAN DIPLOM CHOOSE PERS/REL PWR 18/20 PRESIDENT CONGRESS. PAGE 59 A1217
CHIEF LEGIS TOP/EX EX/STRUC

B65
MCSHERRY J.E.,RUSSIA AND THE UNITED STATES UNDER EISENHOWER, KHRUSHCHEV, AND KENNEDY. USSR EX/STRUC TOP/EX PRESS WAR...POLICY TREND 20. PAGE 99 A2024
DIPLOM CHIEF NAT/G PEACE

B65
ROSENBERG A.,DEMOCRACY AND SOCIALISM. COM EUR+WWI FRANCE MOD/EUR STRUCT INT/ORG NAT/G POL/PAR TOP/EX EDU/PROP COERCE PERSON PWR FASCISM MARXISM...CONCPT TIME/SEQ MARX/KARL 19/20. PAGE 124 A2535
ATTIT

L65
KAPLAN M.A.,"OLD REALITIES AND NEW MYTHS." USA+45 WOR+45 INT/ORG NAT/G TOP/EX ACT/RES BAL/PWR ECO/TAC EDU/PROP LEGIT RIGID/FLEX ALL/VALS...RECORD COLD/WAR 20. PAGE 76 A1564
ATTIT MYTH DIPLOM

S65
HELMREICH E.C.,"KADAR'S HUNGARY." COM EUR+WWI HUNGARY USSR INTELL ECO/DEV AGRI INT/ORG TOP/EX DOMIN ALL/VALS WORK COLD/WAR 20. PAGE 64 A1311
NAT/G RIGID/FLEX TOTALISM

S65
MERRITT R.L.,"WOODROW WILSON AND THE 'GREAT AND SOLEMN REFERENDUM,' 1920." USA-45 SOCIETY NAT/G CONSULT LEGIS ACT/RES PLAN DOMIN EDU/PROP ROUTINE ATTIT DISPL DRIVE PERSON RIGID/FLEX MORAL ORD/FREE ...PSY SOC CONCPT MYTH LEAGUE/NAT. PAGE 100 A2044
INT/ORG TOP/EX DIPLOM

S65
RAY H.,"THE POLICY OF RUSSIA TOWARDS SINO-INDIAN CONFLICT." ASIA CHINA/COM COM INDIA USSR NAT/G TOP/EX FOR/AID EDU/PROP NEUTRAL COERCE PEACE RIGID/FLEX PWR...METH/CNCPT TIME/SEQ VAL/FREE 20. PAGE 120 A2452
S/ASIA ATTIT DIPLOM WAR

S65
ROGGER H.,"EAST GERMANY: STABLE OR IMMOBILE." COM EUR+WWI GERMANY/E NAT/G INT/TRADE DOMIN EDU/PROP COERCE TOTALISM COLD/WAR 20. PAGE 123 A2516
TOP/EX RIGID/FLEX GERMANY

B66
BERNSTEIN B.J.,THE TRUMAN ADMINISTRATION. WOR+45 LABOR POL/PAR LEGIS DIPLOM NUC/PWR WAR ATTIT ...POLICY 20 TRUMAN/HS. PAGE 14 A0279
LEAD TOP/EX NAT/G

B67
CECIL L.,ALBERT BALLIN; BUSINESS AND POLITICS IN IMPERIAL GERMANY 1888-1918. GERMANY UK INT/TRADE LEAD WAR PERS/REL ADJUST PWR WEALTH...MGT BIBLIOG 19/20. PAGE 25 A0510
DIPLOM CONSTN ECO/DEV TOP/EX

B67
RALSTON D.B.,THE ARMY OF THE REPUBLIC; THE PLACE OF THE MILITARY IN THE POLITICAL EVOLUTION OF FRANCE 1871-1914. FRANCE MOD/EUR EX/STRUC LEGIS TOP/EX DIPLOM ADMIN WAR GP/REL ROLE...BIBLIOG 19/20. PAGE 119 A2436
FORCES NAT/G CIVMIL/REL POLICY

B67
TEITELBAUM L.M.,WOODROW WILSON AND THE MEXICAN REVOLUTION 1913-1916: A HISTORY OF UNITED STATES-MEXICAN RELATIONS. USA-45 CHIEF TOP/EX WAR 20 MEXIC/AMER WILSON/W VILLA/P CARRANZA/V. PAGE 142 A2902
REV DIPLOM

L67
KOMESAR N.K.,"PRESIDENTIAL AMENDMENT & TERMINATION OF TREATIES* THE CASE OF THE WARSAW CONVENTION." POLAND USA+45 NAT/G CHIEF PROB/SOLV DIPLOM PWR 20 CONGRESS. PAGE 81 A1669
TOP/EX LEGIS CONSTN LICENSE

S67
LACOUTRE J.,"HO CHI MINH." CHINA/COM USSR VIETNAM/N NAT/G CHIEF TOP/EX LEAD NEUTRAL...REALPOL PREDICT 20. PAGE 83 A1708
NAT/LISM MARXISM REV DIPLOM

S67
MEYER J.,"CUBA S'ENFERME DANS SA REVOLUTION." CHINA/COM CUBA USSR NAT/G TOP/EX DIPLOM LEAD ATTIT ...PREDICT 20. PAGE 100 A2053
MARXISM REV CHIEF NAT/LISM

S67
PAUKER G.J.,"TOWARD A NEW ORDER IN INDONESIA." COM INDONESIA S/ASIA ECO/UNDEV POL/PAR EX/STRUC TOP/EX BAL/PWR ECO/TAC FOR/AID DOMIN NAT/LISM AUTHORIT ORD/FREE PWR 20. PAGE 114 A2342
REV NAT/G DIPLOM CIVMIL/REL

S67
VAN DUSEN H.P.,"HAMMARSKOLD IN THE WORLD'S SERVICE." DIPLOM CONFER LEAD PEACE STRANGE UTOPIA MORAL SKILL OBJECTIVE...INT/LAW SELF/OBS 20. PAGE 158 A3211
INT/ORG CONSULT TOP/EX NEUTRAL

TORONTO....TORONTO, ONTARIO

TORRE M. A2950

TORY/PARTY....TORY PARTY

TOSCANO J.V. A1483

TOSCANO M. A2951

TOTALISM....TOTALITARIANISM

C28
SCHNEIDER H.W.,"MAKING THE FASCIST STATE." ITALY CULTURE LABOR DIPLOM REV WAR NAT/LISM TOTALISM ATTIT DRIVE SOCISM...BIBLIOG PARLIAMENT 20. PAGE 129 A2638
FASCISM POLICY POL/PAR

B35
MARRIOTT J.A.,DICTATORSHIP AND DEMOCRACY. GERMANY GREECE UK CHIEF DIPLOM DOMIN LEGIT PEACE ORD/FREE CONSERVE...TREND ROME HITLER/A. PAGE 95 A1946
TOTALISM POPULISM PLURIST NAT/G

B39
DULLES J.,WAR, PEACE AND CHANGE. FRANCE ITALY UK
EDU/PROP

USA-45 WOR-45 LAW INT/ORG NAT/G SECT VOL/ASSN FORCES TOP/EX DOMIN ARMS/CONT COERCE ATTIT PERSON RIGID/FLEX MORAL PWR...JURID STERTYP TOT/POP LEAGUE/NAT 20. PAGE 39 A0796
TOTALISM WAR

B39
KOHN H.,REVOLUTIONS AND DICTATORSHIPS. COM EUR+WWI ISLAM MOD/EUR NAT/G CHIEF FORCES WAR CIVMIL/REL PWR MARXISM 18/20. PAGE 81 A1661
NAT/LISM TOTALISM REV FASCISM

B40
CARR E.H.,THE TWENTY YEARS' CRISIS 1919-1939. FUT WOR-45 BAL/PWR ECO/TAC LEGIT TOTALISM ATTIT ALL/VALS...POLICY JURID CONCPT TIME/SEQ TREND GEN/LAWS TOT/POP 20. PAGE 24 A0498
INT/ORG DIPLOM PEACE

S40
FLORIN J.,"BOLSHEVIST AND NATIONAL SOCIALIST DOCTRINES OF INTERNATIONAL LAW." EUR+WWI GERMANY USSR R+D INT/ORG NAT/G DIPLOM DOMIN EDU/PROP SOCISM ...CONCPT TIME/SEQ 20. PAGE 47 A0955
LAW ATTIT TOTALISM INT/LAW

B43
US DEPARTMENT OF STATE,NATIONAL SOCIALISM; BASIC PRINCIPLES, THEIR APPLICATION BY THE NAZI PARTY'S FOREIGN ORGANIZATION... GERMANY WOR-45 ECO/DEV LOC/G POL/PAR FORCES DIPLOM DOMIN COLONIAL ARMS/CONT COERCE NAT/LISM PWR 20 NAZI. PAGE 151 A3081
FASCISM SOCISM NAT/G TOTALISM

B45
CARR E.H.,NATIONALISM AND AFTER. FUT WOR-45 NAT/G VOL/ASSN EX/STRUC PLAN ROUTINE TOTALISM ATTIT HEALTH ORD/FREE PWR...CONCPT 20. PAGE 25 A0499
INT/ORG TREND NAT/LISM REGION

B45
CONOVER H.F.,THE GOVERNMENTS OF THE MAJOR FOREIGN POWERS: A BIBLIOGRAPHY. FRANCE GERMANY ITALY UK USSR CONSTN LOC/G POL/PAR EX/STRUC FORCES ADMIN CT/SYS CIVMIL/REL TOTALISM...POLICY 19/20. PAGE 29 A0598
BIBLIOG NAT/G DIPLOM

B45
CONOVER H.F.,ITALY: ECONOMICS, POLITICS AND MILITARY AFFAIRS, 1940-1945. ITALY ELITES NAT/G POL/PAR EX/STRUC TOP/EX DIPLOM DOMIN CONTROL COERCE WAR CIVMIL/REL EFFICIENCY 20. PAGE 29 A0599
BIBLIOG TOTALISM FORCES

B46
STURZO D.L.,NATIONALISM AND INTERNATIONALISM. WOR-45 INT/ORG LABOR NAT/G POL/PAR TOTALISM MORAL ORD/FREE FASCISM...MAJORIT 19/20 UN LEAGUE/NAT MUSSOLIN/B. PAGE 140 A2857
NAT/LISM DIPLOM WAR PEACE

B48
NAMIER L.B.,DIPLOMATIC PRELUDE 1938-1939. CZECHOSLVK EUR+WWI GERMANY POLAND UK FORCES DOMIN PWR 20 HITLER/A. PAGE 107 A2193
WAR TOTALISM DIPLOM

B50
BARGHOORN F.C.,THE SOVIET IMAGE OF THE UNITED STATES: A STUDY IN DISTORTION. COM USSR DOMIN WAR NAT/LISM TOTALISM SOCISM...PSY 20. PAGE 11 A0220
PROB/SOLV EDU/PROP DIPLOM ATTIT

B50
BROOKINGS INSTITUTION,MAJOR PROBLEMS OF UNITED STATES FOREIGN POLICY. AFR ASIA INDIA UK USA+45 USSR BAL/PWR FOR/AID WAR PEACE TOTALISM MARXISM SOCISM 20 CHINJAP COLD/WAR. PAGE 19 A0393
DIPLOM POLICY ORD/FREE

B50
DUCLOS P.,L'EVOLUTION DES RAPPORTS POLITIQUES DEPUIS 1750 (LIBERTE, INTEGRATION, UNITE). LAW INT/ORG FEDERAL TOTALISM ATTIT PWR...MAJORIT BIBLIOG 18/20 PARLIAMENT EUROPE. PAGE 39 A0792
ORD/FREE DIPLOM NAT/G GOV/COMP

N50
SCHAPIRO J.S.,THE WORLD IN CRISES: POLITICAL AND SOCIAL MOVEMENTS IN THE TWENTIETH CENTURY. USA+45 INT/ORG LABOR PLAN CAP/ISM DIPLOM COLONIAL PEACE TOTALISM ATTIT LAISSEZ...BIBLIOG 20 COLD/WAR. PAGE 128 A2618
NAT/LISM TEC/DEV REV WAR

B51
BLANSHARD P.,COMMUNISM, DEMOCRACY AND CATHOLIC POWER. USSR VATICAN WOR+45 WOR-45 CULTURE ELITES INTELL SOCIETY STRUCT INT/ORG POL/PAR EDU/PROP COERCE ATTIT KNOWL PWR MARXISM...CONCPT COLD/WAR 20. PAGE 15 A0308
COM SECT TOTALISM

B51
STANTON A.H.,PERSONALITY AND POLITICAL CRISIS. WOR+45 WOR-45 STRUCT DIPLOM INGP/REL TOTALISM MORAL ...ANTHOL 20 LASSWELL/H PARSONS/T RIESMAN/D. PAGE 137 A2806
EDU/PROP WAR PERSON PSY

L51
ULAM A.B.,"THE COMIMFORM AND THE PEOPLE'S DEMOCRACIES." EUR+WWI WOR+45 STRUCT NAT/G POL/PAR TOP/EX ACT/RES PLAN ECO/TAC DOMIN ATTIT ALL/VALS ...HIST/WRIT TIME/SEQ 20 COMINFORM. PAGE 146 A2992
COM INT/ORG USSR TOTALISM

B52
GURLAND A.R.L.,POLITICAL SCIENCE IN WESTERN GERMANY: THOUGHTS AND WRITINGS, 1950-1952 (PAMPHLET). EUR+WWI GERMANY/W ELITES SOCIETY NAT/G NAT/LISM TOTALISM 20. PAGE 58 A1196
BIBLIOG/A DIPLOM CIVMIL/REL FASCISM

B52
ULAM A.B.,TITOISM AND THE COMINFORM. USSR WOR+45 STRUCT INT/ORG NAT/G ACT/RES PLAN EXEC ATTIT DRIVE ALL/VALS...CONCPT OBS VAL/FREE 20 COMINTERN TITO/MARSH. PAGE 146 A2993
COM POL/PAR TOTALISM YUGOSLAVIA

B53
ROSCIO J.G.,OBRAS. L/A+17C SPAIN DIPLOM REV WAR NAT/LISM TOTALISM PWR SOVEREIGN 19. PAGE 123 A2527
ORD/FREE COLONIAL NAT/G PHIL/SCI

B53
SHIRATO I.,JAPANESE SOURCES ON THE HISTORY OF THE CHINESE COMMUNIST MOVEMENT (PAMPHLET). CHINA/COM USSR CONSTRUC NAT/G POL/PAR FORCES DIPLOM DOMIN EDU/PROP CONTROL WAR TOTALISM SOCISM 20. PAGE 132 A2702
BIBLIOG/A MARXISM ECO/UNDEV

B53
THAYER P.W.,SOUTHEAST ASIA IN THE COMING WORLD. ASIA S/ASIA USA+45 USA-45 SOCIETY INT/ORG ACT/RES ECO/TAC EDU/PROP COERCE TOTALISM ALL/VALS...JURID 20. PAGE 142 A2909
ECO/UNDEV ATTIT FOR/AID DIPLOM

B54
ARON R.,CENTURY OF TOTAL WAR. FUT WOR+45 WOR-45 SOCIETY INT/ORG NAT/G FORCES TOP/EX CREATE BAL/PWR DOMIN EDU/PROP COERCE DETER PEACE TOTALISM PWR ...TIME/SEQ TREND COLD/WAR TOT/POP VAL/FREE LEAGUE/NAT 20. PAGE 9 A0179
ATTIT WAR

B54
KENNAN G.F.,REALITIES OF AMERICAN FOREIGN POLICY. USA+45 INT/ORG NUC/PWR TOTALISM 20 COLD/WAR. PAGE 77 A1586
DIPLOM BAL/PWR DECISION DETER

B54
NATION ASSOCIATES,SECURITY AND THE MIDDLE EAST - THE PROBLEM AND ITS SOLUTION. ISRAEL JORDAN LEBANON SYRIA UAR FORCES FOR/AID GP/REL NAT/LISM PEACE TOTALISM...POLICY 20. PAGE 107 A2198
DIPLOM ECO/UNDEV WAR PLAN

B54
SALVEMINI G.,PRELUDE TO WORLD WAR II. ITALY MOD/EUR INT/ORG BAL/PWR EDU/PROP CONTROL TOTALISM...TREND NAT/COMP BIBLIOG 19 HITLER/A LEAGUE/NAT MUSSOLIN/B. PAGE 127 A2597
WAR FASCISM LEAD PWR

B55
ALFIERI D.,DICTATORS FACE TO FACE. NAT/G TOP/EX DIPLOM EXEC COERCE ORD/FREE FASCISM...POLICY OBS 20 HITLER/A MUSSOLIN/B. PAGE 6 A0116
WAR CHIEF TOTALISM PERS/REL

B56
BROOK D.,THE UNITED NATIONS AND CHINA DILEMMA. CHINA/COM FUT WOR+45 ECO/UNDEV NAT/G DELIB/GP ACT/RES DIPLOM ROUTINE NAT/LISM TOTALISM ATTIT DRIVE...CONCPT OBS TIME/SEQ UN TOT/POP TIME UN 20. PAGE 19 A0390
ASIA INT/ORG BAL/PWR

B56
ROBERTS H.L.,RUSSIA AND AMERICA. CHINA/COM S/ASIA USSR FORCES TEC/DEV FOR/AID NUC/PWR ALL/IDEOS ...MAJORIT TREND NAT/COMP 20 COLD/WAR UN NATO. PAGE 122 A2494
DIPLOM INT/ORG BAL/PWR TOTALISM

B56
SIPKOV I.,LEGAL SOURCES AND BIBLIOGRAPHY OF BULGARIA. BULGARIA COM LEGIS WRITING ADJUD CT/SYS ...INT/LAW TREATY 20. PAGE 134 A2736
BIBLIOG LAW TOTALISM MARXISM

B57
JASZI O.,AGAINST THE TYRANT. WOR+45 WOR-45 CONSTN DIPLOM CONTROL PARTIC REV WAR...CONCPT. PAGE 73 A1498
TOTALISM ORD/FREE CHIEF MURDER

B57
REISS J.,GEORGE KENNANS POLITIK DER EINDAMMUNG. USSR NAT/G FORCES TOTALISM ATTIT ORD/FREE...POLICY 20 NATO TRUMAN/HS MARSHL/PLN KENNAN/G. PAGE 120 A2463
DIPLOM DETER PEACE

B57
US SENATE SPEC COMM FOR AID,COMPILATION OF STUDIES AND SURVEYS. AFR ASIA L/A+17C USA+45 ECO/UNDEV AGRI INT/ORG CONSULT TEC/DEV CONFER TOTALISM...NAT/COMP 20 CONGRESS. PAGE 157 A3197
FOR/AID DIPLOM ORD/FREE DELIB/GP

B57
US SENATE SPEC COMM FOR AID,HEARINGS BEFORE THE SPECIAL COMMITTEE TO STUDY THE FOREIGN AID PROGRAM. USA+45 USSR ECO/UNDEV INT/ORG FORCES WEAPON TOTALISM ATTIT SUPEGO...NAT/COMP CONGRESS. PAGE 157 A3198
FOR/AID DIPLOM ORD/FREE TEC/DEV

B58
ANGELL N.,DEFENCE AND THE ENGLISH-SPEAKING ROLE. CHINA/COM UK USSR INT/ORG FORCES EDU/PROP NEUTRAL NUC/PWR NAT/LISM PEACE TOTALISM 20 COLD/WAR COEXIST. PAGE 8 A0161
DIPLOM WAR MARXISM ORD/FREE

B58
KENNAN G.F.,THE DECISION TO INTERVENE: SOVIET-AMERICAN RELATIONS, 1917-1920 (VOL. II). CZECHOSLVK EUR+WWI USA-45 USSR ELITES NAT/G FORCES PROB/SOLV REV WAR TOTALISM PWR...CHARTS BIBLIOG 20 TREATY PRESIDENT CHINJAP. PAGE 78 A1588
DIPLOM POLICY ATTIT

B58
NEAL F.W.,TITOISM IN ACTION. COM YUGOSLAVIA AGRI LOC/G DIPLOM TOTALISM...BIBLIOG 20 TITO/MARSH. PAGE 107 A2206
MARXISM POL/PAR CHIEF

ADMIN

L58
HYVARINEN R.,"MONISTIC AND PLURALISTIC INTERPRETATIONS IN THE STUDY OF INTERNATIONAL POLITICS." COLONIAL REGION RACE/REL DISCRIM TOTALISM SOVEREIGN...INT/LAW PHIL/SCI CONCPT BIBLIOG 20. PAGE 70 A1429
DIPLOM PLURISM INT/ORG METH

S58
STAAR R.F.,"ELECTIONS IN COMMUNIST POLAND." EUR+WWI SOCIETY INT/ORG NAT/G POL/PAR LEGIS ACT/RES ECO/TAC EDU/PROP ADJUD ADMIN ROUTINE COERCE TOTALISM ATTIT ORD/FREE PWR 20. PAGE 137 A2797
COM CHOOSE POLAND

B59
CHALUPA V.,RISE AND DEVELOPMENT OF A TOTALITARIAN STATE. CZECHOSLVK USSR STRUCT INT/ORG WORKER DIPLOM ECO/TAC COERCE NAT/LISM ATTIT...POLICY 20 COM/PARTY. PAGE 25 A0516
TOTALISM MARXISM REV POL/PAR

B59
EMME E.M.,THE IMPACT OF AIR POWER - NATIONAL SECURITY AND WORLD POLITICS. USA+45 USSR FORCES DIPLOM WEAPON PEACE TOTALISM...POLICY NAT/COMP 20 EUROPE. PAGE 42 A0850
DETER AIR WAR ORD/FREE

B59
HARRIMAN A.,PEACE WITH RUSSIA? USA+45 USSR SOCIETY ECO/TAC CONTROL TOTALISM ATTIT MARXISM...POLICY 20 STALIN/J KHRUSH/N. PAGE 62 A1266
DIPLOM PEACE NAT/G TASK

B59
KNIERIEM A.,THE NUREMBERG TRIALS. EUR+WWI GERMANY VOL/ASSN LEAD COERCE WAR INGP/REL TOTALISM SUPEGO ORD/FREE...CONCPT METH/COMP. PAGE 80 A1651
INT/LAW CRIME PARTIC JURID

B59
NIEBUHR R.,NATIONS AND EMPIRES. WOR+45 INT/ORG COLONIAL NUC/PWR TOTALISM UTOPIA ORD/FREE MARXISM WORSHIP 20 COLD/WAR PROTESTANT CHRISTIAN. PAGE 109 A2237
DIPLOM NAT/G POLICY PWR

B59
WARD B.,5 IDEAS THAT CHANGE THE WORLD. WOR+45 WOR-45 SOCIETY STRUCT AGRI INDUS INT/ORG NAT/G FORCES ACT/RES ARMS/CONT TOTALISM ATTIT DRIVE GEN/LAWS. PAGE 161 A3278
ECO/UNDEV ALL/VALS NAT/LISM COLONIAL

S59
LASSWELL H.D.,"UNIVERSALITY IN PERSPECTIVE." FUT UNIV SOCIETY CONSULT TOP/EX PLAN EDU/PROP ADJUD ROUTINE ARMS/CONT COERCE PEACE ATTIT PERSON ALL/VALS. PAGE 85 A1741
INT/ORG JURID TOTALISM

S59
ZAUBERMAN A.,"SOVIET BLOC ECONOMIC INTEGRATION." COM CULTURE INTELL ECO/DEV INDUS TOP/EX ACT/RES PLAN ECO/TAC INT/TRADE ROUTINE CHOOSE ATTIT ...TIME/SEQ 20. PAGE 169 A3448
MARKET INT/ORG USSR TOTALISM

B60
FOOTMAN D.,INTERNATIONAL COMMUNISM. ASIA EUR+WWI FRANCE FUT GERMANY MOD/EUR S/ASIA USA-45 WOR+45 WOR-45 INTELL LABOR TOTALISM MARXISM WORK 20. PAGE 47 A0958
COM INT/ORG STRUCT REV

B60
MORAES F.,THE REVOLT IN TIBET. ASIA CHINA/COM INDIA CULTURE CONTROL COERCE WAR TOTALISM...POLICY SOC WORSHIP 20 TIBET INTERVENT. PAGE 104 A2127
COLONIAL FORCES DIPLOM ORD/FREE

B60
SETON-WATSON H.,NEITHER WAR NOR PEACE. ASIA USSR WOR+45 ELITES INT/ORG NAT/G EX/STRUC FORCES BAL/PWR ECO/TAC EDU/PROP COERCE NAT/LISM ORD/FREE WEALTH TOT/POP 20. PAGE 131 A2688
ATTIT PWR DIPLOM TOTALISM

S60
GRACIA-MORA M.R.,"INTERNATIONAL RESPONSIBILITY FOR SUBVERSIVE ACTIVITIES AND HOSTILE PROPAGANDA BY PRIVATE PERSONS AGAINST." COM EUR+WWI L/A+17C UK USA+45 USSR WOR-45 CONSTN NAT/G LEGIT ADJUD REV PEACE TOTALISM ORD/FREE...INT/LAW 20. PAGE 55 A1119
INT/ORG JURID SOVEREIGN

B61
DEAN V.M.,BUILDERS OF EMERGING NATIONS. WOR+45 ECO/UNDEV ECO/TAC NEUTRAL TOTALISM ORD/FREE PWR ...BIOG AUD/VIS IDEA/COMP BIBLIOG 20 COLD/WAR. PAGE 35 A0719
NAT/G CHIEF POLICY DIPLOM

B61
DELZELL C.F.,MUSSOLINI'S ENEMIES - THE ITALIAN ANTI-FASCIST RESISTANCE. ITALY DIPLOM PRESS DETER WAR TOTALISM ORD/FREE MARXISM 20. PAGE 36 A0730
FASCISM GP/REL POL/PAR REV

B61
FUCHS G.,GEGEN HITLER UND HENLEIN. CZECHOSLVK GERMANY DIPLOM CHOOSE GP/REL TOTALISM SOVEREIGN 20 HITLER/A. PAGE 50 A1013
FASCISM WORKER POL/PAR NAT/LISM

B61
JAKOBSON M.,THE DIPLOMACY OF THE WINTER WAR. EUR+WWI FINLAND GERMANY USSR INT/ORG NAT/G PEACE TOTALISM PWR...POLICY CONCPT 20 TREATY. PAGE 73 A1492
WAR ORD/FREE DIPLOM

B61
MECHAM J.L.,THE UNITED STATES AND INTER-AMERICAN SECURITY, 1889-1960. L/A+17C USA+45 USA-45 CONSTN FORCES INT/TRADE PEACE TOTALISM ATTIT...JURID 19/20 UN OAS. PAGE 99 A2030
DIPLOM WAR ORD/FREE INT/ORG

B61
NOGEE J.L.,SOVIET POLICY TOWARD INTERNATIONAL CONTROL OF ATOMIC ENERGY. COM USA+45 WOR+45 INTELL NAT/G ACT/RES DIPLOM EDU/PROP NUC/PWR TOTALISM PERCEPT KNOWL PWR...TIME/SEQ COLD/WAR 20. PAGE 109 A2247
INT/ORG ATTIT ARMS/CONT USSR

B61
SCHONBRUNN G.,WELTKRIEGE UND REVOLUTIONEN 1914-1945. USSR DIPLOM TOTALISM ORD/FREE 20 TREATY WWI NAZI. PAGE 129 A2643
WAR REV FASCISM SOCISM

B61
TETENS T.H.,THE NEW GERMANY AND THE OLD NAZIS. EUR+WWI GERMANY/W USA+45 NAT/G CRIME CHOOSE RACE/REL TOTALISM AGE/Y ATTIT 20 JEWS NAZI ADENAUER/K. PAGE 142 A2905
FASCISM DIPLOM FOR/AID POL/PAR

S61
BARNET R.,"RUSSIA, CHINA, AND THE WORLD: THE SOVIET ATTITUDE ON DISARMAMENT (PART 3)." ASIA CHINA/COM FUT INT/ORG NAT/G POL/PAR VOL/ASSN ARMS/CONT ATTIT ...POLICY CONCPT TIME/SEQ TREND TOT/POP VAL/FREE 20. PAGE 11 A0226
COM PLAN TOTALISM USSR

S61
DANIELS R.V.,"THE CHINESE REVOLUTION IN RUSSIAN PERSPECTIVE." ASIA CHINA/COM COM USSR INTELL INT/ORG TOP/EX REV TOTALISM PWR...POLICY WORK VAL/FREE 20. PAGE 33 A0680
POL/PAR PLAN

S61
KRANNHALS H.V.,"COMMAND INTEGRATION WITHIN THE WARSAW PACT." COM USSR WOR+45 DELIB/GP EDU/PROP ...CONCPT AUD/VIS CHARTS COLD/WAR TOT/POP VAL/FREE 20 TREATY WARSAW/P. PAGE 82 A1675
INT/ORG FORCES TOTALISM

S61
ZAGORIA D.S.,"THE FUTURE OF SINO-SOVIET RELATIONS." CHINA/COM INT/ORG NAT/G POL/PAR VOL/ASSN ACT/RES PLAN PERSON...METH/CNCPT TIME/SEQ TOT/POP VAL/FREE 20 MAO KHRUSH/N. PAGE 169 A3444
ASIA COM TOTALISM USSR

B62
ALIX C.,LE SAINT-SIEGE ET LES NATIONALISMES EN EUROPE 1870-1960. COM GERMANY IRELAND ITALY SOCIETY SECT TOTALISM RIGID/FLEX MORAL 19/20. PAGE 6 A0122
CATH NAT/LISM ATTIT DIPLOM

B62
BLANSHARD P.,FREEDOM AND CATHOLIC POWER IN SPAIN AND PORTUGAL: AN AMERICAN INTERPRETATION. AFR PORTUGAL SPAIN USA+45 LAW LABOR DIPLOM EDU/PROP DISCRIM ISOLAT TOTALISM 20 CHURCH/STA. PAGE 15 A0309
GP/REL FASCISM CATHISM PWR

B62
MORRAY J.P.,THE SECOND REVOLUTION IN CUBA. CUBA AGRI LABOR POL/PAR DIPLOM FOR/AID GUERRILLA TOTALISM MARXISM 20. PAGE 104 A2146
REV MARXIST ECO/TAC NAT/LISM

B62
NOBECOURT R.G.,LES SECRETS DE LA PROPAGANDE EN FRANCE OCCUPEE. FRANCE ELITES NAT/G DIPLOM GP/REL NAT/LISM TOTALISM ORD/FREE 20 VICHY VICHY. PAGE 109 A2244
METH/COMP EDU/PROP WAR CONTROL

B62
SCOTT W.E.,ALLIANCE AGAINST HITLER. EUR+WWI FRANCE GERMANY USSR BAL/PWR LEAD TOTALISM PWR FASCISM MARXISM...POLICY BIBLIOG 20 HITLER/A. PAGE 131 A2675
WAR DIPLOM FORCES

B62
SOMMER T.,DEUTSCHLAND UND JAPAN ZWISCHEN DEN MACHTEN. GERMANY DELIB/GP BAL/PWR AGREE COERCE TOTALISM PWR 20 CHINJAP TREATY. PAGE 135 A2765
DIPLOM WAR ATTIT

B62
STARR R.E.,POLAND 1944-1962: THE SOVIETIZATION OF A CAPTIVE PEOPLE. COM POLAND USSR POL/PAR SECT LEGIS DIPLOM DOMIN EDU/PROP CHOOSE ORD/FREE...POLICY CHARTS BIBLIOG 20. PAGE 137 A2808
MARXISM NAT/G TOTALISM NAT/COMP

S62
BOKOR-SZEGO H.,"LA CONVENTION DE BELGRADE ET LE REGIME DU DANUBE." COM EUR+WWI WOR+45 STRUCT POL/PAR VOL/ASSN PLAN EDU/PROP WEALTH...TIME/SEQ 20. PAGE 16 A0333
INT/ORG TOTALISM YUGOSLAVIA

S62
BROWN B.E.,"L'ONU ABANDONNE LA HONGRIE." COM USSR WOR+45 CONSTN NAT/G POL/PAR DELIB/GP ACT/RES TEC/DEV PWR...TIME/SEQ 20 UN. PAGE 20 A0400
INT/ORG TOTALISM HUNGARY POLICY

S62
BRZEZINSKI Z.K.,"PEACEFUL ENGAGEMENT IN COMMUNIST DISUNITY." ASIA CHINA/COM COM USA+45 USSR NAT/G TOP/EX CREATE ECO/TAC FOR/AID DOMIN ATTIT PERCEPT RIGID/FLEX PWR...PSY 20. PAGE 20 A0417
COM DIPLOM TOTALISM

S62
FOCSANEANU L.,"LES GRANDS TRAITES DE LA REPUBLIQUE POPULAIRE DE CHINE." ASIA CHINA/COM COM USSR WOR+45 INT/ORG NAT/G POL/PAR ACT/RES PLAN DIPLOM EDU/PROP ...CONCPT TIME/SEQ 20 TREATY. PAGE 47 A0957
VOL/ASSN TOTALISM

B63
BROEKMEIJER M.W.,DEVELOPING COUNTRIES AND NATO.
ECO/UNDEV

USSR FORCES DIPLOM NUC/PWR WAR PEACE TOTALISM 20 NATO. PAGE 19 A0384
FOR/AID ORD/FREE NAT/G

B63
DRACHKOVITCH,UNITED STATES AID TO YUGOSLAVIA AND POLAND. POLAND USA+45 YUGOSLAVIA LEGIS EXEC TOTALISM MARXISM 20 CONGRESS. PAGE 38 A0782
FOR/AID POLICY DIPLOM ATTIT

B63
GORDON G.N.,THE IDEA INVADERS. USA+45 USSR CULTURE COM/IND DIPLOM PRESS TV TOTALISM MARXISM 20. PAGE 54 A1113
EDU/PROP ATTIT ORD/FREE CONTROL

B63
MILLER W.J.,THE MEANING OF COMMUNISM. USSR SOCIETY ECO/DEV EX/STRUC WORKER TEC/DEV ADMIN TOTALISM ...POLICY CONCPT CHARTS BIBLIOG T 20 COLD/WAR LENIN/VI STALIN/J. PAGE 101 A2080
MARXISM TRADIT DIPLOM NAT/G

L63
SZASZY E.,"L'EVOLUTION DES PRINCIPES GENERAUX DU DROIT INTERNATIONAL PRIVE DANS LES PAYS DE DEMOCRATIE POPULAIRE." COM FUT WOR+45 LAW ECO/DEV PERF/ART POL/PAR PROF/ORG ECO/TAC INT/TRADE EDU/PROP ATTIT RIGID/FLEX ALL/VALS SOCISM...JURID TREND GEN/LAWS WORK 20. PAGE 141 A2876
DIPLOM TOTALISM INT/LAW INT/ORG

S63
ETIENNE G.,"'LOIS OBJECTIVES' ET PROBLEMES DE DEVELOPPEMENT DANS LE CONTEXTE CHINE-URSS." ASIA CHINA/COM COM FUT STRUCT INT/ORG VOL/ASSN TOP/EX TEC/DEV ECO/TAC ATTIT RIGID/FLEX...GEOG MGT TIME/SEQ TOT/POP 20. PAGE 42 A0866
TOTALISM USSR

S63
GIRAUD E.,"L'INTERDICTION DU RECOURS A LA FORCE, LA THEORIE ET LA PRATIQUE DES NATIONS UNIES." ALGERIA COM CUBA HUNGARY WOR+45 ADJUD TOTALISM ATTIT RIGID/FLEX PWR...POLICY JURID CONCPT UN 20 CONGO. PAGE 53 A1077
INT/ORG FORCES DIPLOM

S63
RAMERIE L.,"TENSION AU SEIN DU COMECON: LE CAS ROUMAIN." COM EUR+WWI USSR WOR+45 ECO/DEV DIST/IND NAT/G POL/PAR VOL/ASSN EDU/PROP TOTALISM ATTIT WEALTH...TIME/SEQ 20 COMECON. PAGE 119 A2438
INT/ORG ECO/TAC INT/TRADE ROMANIA

S63
SPINELLI A.,"IL TRATTATO DI MOSCA E I PROBLEMI DELLA COESISTENZA PACIFICA." CHINA/COM COM FRANCE FUT WOR+45 INT/ORG VOL/ASSN PEACE...POLICY MYTH 20. PAGE 136 A2788
ATTIT ARMS/CONT TOTALISM

C63
SCHMITT K.M.,"EVOLUTION OR CHAOS: DYNAMICS OF LATIN AMERICAN GOVERNMENT AND POLITICS." L/A+17C AGRI FINAN CAP/ISM EXEC LEAD BAL/PAY TOTALISM ATTIT ...TREND BIBLIOG 20. PAGE 129 A2635
DIPLOM POLICY POL/PAR LOBBY

B64
GIBSON J.S.,IDEOLOGY AND WORLD AFFAIRS. FUT WOR+45 ECO/UNDEV NAT/G CAP/ISM TOTALISM ORD/FREE FASCISM MARXISM 20. PAGE 52 A1067
ALL/IDEOS DIPLOM POLICY IDEA/COMP

B64
IRISH M.D.,WORLD PRESSURES ON AMERICAN FOREIGN POLICY. ASIA COM L/A+17C SOUTH/AFR UK WOR+45 ECO/DEV ECO/UNDEV COLONIAL SANCTION COERCE REV TOTALISM...ANTHOL 20 COLD/WAR EUROPE/W INTERVENT. PAGE 72 A1467
DIPLOM POLICY

B64
KOLARZ W.,COMMUNISM AND COLONIALISM. AFR ASIA USSR DISCRIM ATTIT ORD/FREE SOVEREIGN SOC/INTEG 20. PAGE 81 A1668
EDU/PROP DIPLOM TOTALISM COLONIAL

B64
LUARD E.,THE COLD WAR: A RE-APPRAISAL. FUT USSR WOR+45 FORCES NUC/PWR NAT/LISM ORD/FREE SOVEREIGN ...INT 20 COLD/WAR STALIN/J TREATY UN. PAGE 91 A1870
DIPLOM WAR PEACE TOTALISM

B64
NOVE A.,COMMUNISM AT THE CROSSROADS. USSR INT/ORG POL/PAR TOTALISM...POLICY CONCPT 20. PAGE 110 A2259
DIPLOM BAL/PWR MARXISM ORD/FREE

B64
TREADGOLD D.W.,THE DEVELOPMENT OF THE USSR. COM USSR ECO/DEV CREATE BAL/PWR DEBATE COLONIAL TOTALISM...HUM ANTHOL BIBLIOG 19/20. PAGE 145 A2960
MARXISM CONSERVE DIPLOM DOMIN

B65
BROMKE A.,THE COMMUNIST STATES AT THE CROSSROADS BETWEEN MOSCOW AND PEKING. CHINA/COM USSR INGP/REL NAT/LISM TOTALISM 20. PAGE 19 A0389
COM DIPLOM MARXISM REGION

B65
LASKY V.,THE UGLY RUSSIAN. AFR ASIA USSR ECO/UNDEV NAT/LISM TOTALISM PERSON 20. PAGE 85 A1738
FOR/AID ATTIT DIPLOM

B65
LEVENSTEIN A.,FREEDOM'S ADVOCATE - A TWENTY-FIVE YEAR CHRONICLE. USA+45 POL/PAR LEGIS DIPLOM WAR PEACE TOTALISM DRIVE MARXISM 20 FREEDOM/HS. PAGE 87 A1791
ORD/FREE VOL/ASSN POLICY ATTIT

B65
LOEWENHEIM F.L.,PEACE OR APPEASEMENT? HITLER, CHAMBERLAIN AND THE MUNICH CRISIS. MUNIC DELIB/GP WAR TOTALISM ATTIT SOVEREIGN...TIME/SEQ ANTHOL BIBLIOG 20 HITLER/A CHAMBRLN/N. PAGE 90 A1851
DIPLOM LEAD PEACE

B65
MOWRY G.E.,THE URBAN NATION 1920-1960. USA+45 USA-45 SOCIETY ECO/DEV MUNIC FOR/AID INT/TRADE AUTOMAT...BIBLIOG/A 20. PAGE 105 A2161
TEC/DEV NAT/G TOTALISM DIPLOM

B65
RUBINSTEIN A.,THE CHALLENGE OF POLITICS: IDEAS AND ISSUES. BAL/PWR COLONIAL WAR TOTALISM ORD/FREE PWR MARXISM SOCISM...INT/LAW 20. PAGE 125 A2561
NAT/G SOVEREIGN DIPLOM NAT/LISM

B65
US HOUSE COMM FOREIGN AFFAIRS,HEARINGS ON DRAFT BILL TO AMEND FURTHER THE FOREIGN ASSISTANCE ACT OF 1961. AFR ASIA L/A+17C USA+45 INT/ORG DELIB/GP TEC/DEV ECO/TAC CONFER TOTALISM 20 CONGRESS AID. PAGE 153 A3131
FOR/AID ECO/UNDEV DIPLOM ORD/FREE

S65
HELMREICH E.C.,"KADAR'S HUNGARY." COM EUR+WWI HUNGARY USSR INTELL ECO/DEV AGRI INT/ORG TOP/EX DOMIN ALL/VALS WORK COLD/WAR 20. PAGE 64 A1311
NAT/G RIGID/FLEX TOTALISM

S65
ROGGER H.,"EAST GERMANY: STABLE OR IMMOBILE." COM EUR+WWI GERMANY/E NAT/G INT/TRADE DOMIN EDU/PROP COERCE TOTALISM COLD/WAR 20. PAGE 123 A2516
TOP/EX RIGID/FLEX GERMANY

B66
CRAIG G.A.,WAR, POLITICS, AND DIPLOMACY. PRUSSIA CONSTN FORCES CIVMIL/REL TOTALISM PWR 19/20 BISMARCK/O DULLES/JF NAPOLEON/B. PAGE 32 A0654
WAR DIPLOM BAL/PWR

B66
LATHAM E.,THE COMMUNIST CONTROVERSY IN WASHINGTON. USA+45 USA-45 DELIB/GP EX/STRUC LEGIS DIPLOM NAT/LISM MARXISM 20. PAGE 85 A1742
POL/PAR TOTALISM ORD/FREE NAT/G

B66
MARTIN L.W.,DIPLOMACY IN MODERN EUROPEAN HISTORY. EUR+WWI MOD/EUR INT/ORG NAT/G EX/STRUC ROUTINE WAR PEACE TOTALISM PWR 15/20 COLD/WAR EUROPE/W. PAGE 95 A1953
DIPLOM POLICY

B66
SINGER L.,ALLE LITTEN AN GROSSENWAHN: VON WOODROW WILSON BIS MAO TSE-TUNG. ASIA UK USSR INT/ORG DELIB/GP BAL/PWR DOMIN ATTIT PERSON 20 WILSON/W ROOSEVLT/F. PAGE 133 A2731
DIPLOM TOTALISM WAR CHIEF

B66
SPULBER N.,THE STATE AND ECONOMIC DEVELOPMENT IN EASTERN EUROPE. BULGARIA COM CZECHOSLVK HUNGARY POLAND YUGOSLAVIA CULTURE PLAN CAP/ISM INT/TRADE CONTROL...POLICY CHARTS METH/COMP BIBLIOG/A 19/20. PAGE 136 A2793
ECO/DEV ECO/UNDEV NAT/G TOTALISM

B66
US SENATE COMM ON FOREIGN REL,HEARINGS ON S 2859 AND S 2861. USA+45 WOR+45 FORCES BUDGET CAP/ISM ADMIN DETER WEAPON TOTALISM...NAT/COMP 20 UN CONGRESS. PAGE 156 A3185
FOR/AID DIPLOM ORD/FREE ECO/UNDEV

S67
BREGMAN A.,"WHITHER RUSSIA?" COM RUSSIA INTELL POL/PAR DIPLOM PARTIC NAT/LISM TOTALISM ATTIT ORD/FREE 20. PAGE 18 A0370
MARXISM ELITES ADMIN CREATE

S67
EGBERT D.D.,"POLITICS AND ART IN COMMUNIST BULGARIA" BULGARIA COM USSR CULTURE DIPLOM INGP/REL TOTALISM...TREND 20. PAGE 40 A0825
CREATE ART/METH CONTROL MARXISM

S67
MCCORD W.,"ARMIES AND POLITICS; A PROBLEM IN THE THIRD WORLD." AFR ISLAM USA+45 ECO/UNDEV TOTALISM 20. PAGE 98 A2002
FOR/AID POLICY NAT/G FORCES

S67
SARBADHIKARI P.,"A NOTE ON THE DOMESTIC CRISIS OF NON-ALIGNMENT." ELITES INTELL ECO/UNDEV FOR/AID DOMIN. PAGE 127 A2605
NEUTRAL WEALTH TOTALISM BAL/PWR

S67
SHOEMAKER R.L.,"JAPANESE ARMY AND THE WEST." ASIA ELITES EX/STRUC DIPLOM DOMIN EDU/PROP COERCE ATTIT AUTHORIT PWR 1/20 CHINJAP. PAGE 132 A2703
FORCES TEC/DEV WAR TOTALISM

S67
YEFROMEV A.,"THE TRUE FACE OF THE WEST GERMAN NATIONAL-DEMOCRATS." GERMANY/W NAT/G DOMIN LEAD SANCTION WAR ATTIT PERSON...MARXIST 20. PAGE 169 A3433
POL/PAR TOTALISM PARL/PROC DIPLOM

TOTALITARIANISM....SEE TOTALISM

TOTOK W. A2952

TOTTEN G.O. A0566

TOURE S. A2953

TOUSSAIN/P....PIERRE DOMINIQUE TOUSSAINT L'OUVERTURE

TOUVAL S. A2954

TOWLE L.W. A2955

TOWNS....SEE MUNIC

TOWNSD/PLN....TOWNSEND PLAN

TOWNSEND PLAN....SEE TOWNSD/PLN

TOWSTER J. A2956

TOYNBEE A. A2957

TOYNBEE V.M. A2957

TOYNBEE/A....ARNOLD TOYNBEE

TRADE, INTERNATIONAL....SEE INT/TRADE

TRADIT....TRADITIONAL AND ARISTOCRATIC

C05
DUNNING W.A.,"HISTORY OF POLITICAL THEORIES FROM LUTHER TO MONTESQUIEU." LAW NAT/G SECT DIPLOM REV WAR ORD/FREE SOVEREIGN CONSERVE...TRADIT BIBLIOG 16/18. PAGE 39 A0803
PHIL/SCI CONCPT GEN/LAWS

B30
BYNKERSHOEK C.,QUAESTIONUM JURIS PUBLICI LIBRI DUO. CHRIST-17C MOD/EUR CONSTN ELITES SOCIETY NAT/G PROVS EX/STRUC FORCES TOP/EX BAL/PWR DIPLOM ATTIT MORAL...TRADIT CONCPT. PAGE 23 A0460
INT/ORG LAW NAT/LISM INT/LAW

B39
MARRIOTT J.,COMMONWEALTH OR ANARCHY: A SURVEY OF PROJECTS OF PEACE. WOR-45 STRATA DOMIN ATTIT ORD/FREE PWR...TRADIT TIME/SEQ GEN/METH 16/20 CMN/WLTH. PAGE 95 A1945
FUT INT/ORG PEACE

B45
ELTON G.E.,IMPERIAL COMMONWEALTH. INDIA UK DIPLOM DOMIN WAR NAT/LISM SOVEREIGN...TRADIT CHARTS T 15/20 CMN/WLTH AUSTRAL PRE/US/AM. PAGE 41 A0844
REGION CONCPT COLONIAL

B56
FOSTER J.G.,BRITAIN IN WESTERN EUROPE: WEU AND THE ATLANTIC ALLIANCE. EUR+WWI FRANCE GERMANY GERMANY/W ITALY UK STRATA NAT/G DELIB/GP ECO/TAC ORD/FREE PWR ...TRADIT TIME/SEQ TREND OEEC PARLIAMENT 20 EUROPE/W. PAGE 47 A0969
INT/ORG FORCES WEAPON

B60
DE GAULLE C.,THE EDGE OF THE SWORD. EUR+WWI FRANCE ELITES CHIEF DIPLOM ROLE...REALPOL TRADIT. PAGE 34 A0701
FORCES SUPEGO LEAD WAR

S60
MAGATHAN W.,"SOME BASES OF WEST GERMAN MILITARY POLICY." EUR+WWI FUT INT/ORG TOP/EX ECO/TAC DOMIN DRIVE ORD/FREE PWR...TRADIT GEOG OBS TREND. PAGE 93 A1904
NAT/G FORCES GERMANY

B61
EISENHOWER D.D.,PEACE WITH JUSTICE: SELECTED ADDRESSES. USSR PARTIC ARMS/CONT MORAL...TRADIT CONCPT GEN/LAWS ANTHOL 20 PRESIDENT COLD/WAR. PAGE 41 A0832
PEACE DIPLOM EDU/PROP POLICY

B62
ROSAMOND R.,CRUSADE FOR PEACE: EISENHOWER'S PRESIDENTIAL LEGACY WITH THE PROGRAM FOR ACTION. USA+45 PARTIC ARMS/CONT MORAL MARXISM...TRADIT CONCPT CHARTS GEN/LAWS ANTHOL 20 PRESIDENT EISNHWR/DD. PAGE 123 A2526
PEACE DIPLOM EDU/PROP POLICY

B63
BLACK J.E.,FOREIGN POLICIES IN A WORLD OF CHANGE. FUT INT/ORG ALL/VALS...POLICY MAJORIT MARXIST SOCIALIST TRADIT TIME/SEQ TREND ANTHOL 20. PAGE 15 A0298
WOR+45 NAT/G DIPLOM

B63
MILLER W.J.,THE MEANING OF COMMUNISM. USSR SOCIETY ECO/DEV EX/STRUC WORKER TEC/DEV ADMIN TOTALISM ...POLICY CONCPT CHARTS BIBLIOG T 20 COLD/WAR LENIN/VI STALIN/J. PAGE 101 A2080
MARXISM TRADIT DIPLOM NAT/G

S64
DELGADO J.,"EL MOMENTO POLITICO HISPANOAMERICA." CHINA/COM FUT PANAMA USA+45 USSR INT/ORG NAT/G POL/PAR FORCES DOMIN REGION COERCE ATTIT ALL/VALS ...TRADIT CONCPT COLD/WAR 20. PAGE 36 A0728
L/A+17C EDU/PROP NAT/LISM

B65
EISENHOWER D.D.,WAGING PEACE 1956-61: THE WHITE HOUSE YEARS. USA+45 DIPLOM LEAD INGP/REL RACE/REL PEACE ATTIT...TRADIT TIME/SEQ 20 EISNHWR/DD PRESIDENT COLD/WAR CIV/RIGHTS BERLIN. PAGE 41 A0833
TOP/EX BIOG ORD/FREE POLICY

B66
CLENDENON C.,AMERICANS IN AFRICA 1865-1900. AFR USA-45 ECO/UNDEV SECT REV RACE/REL CONSERVE ...TRADIT GEOG BIBLIOG 16/18. PAGE 27 A0549
DIPLOM COLONIAL INT/TRADE

B66
ZEINE Z.N.,THE EMERGENCE OF ARAB NATIONALISM (REV. ED.). TURKEY UK NAT/G SECT TEC/DEV LEAD REV WAR AGE/Y ROLE ORD/FREE...TRADIT CHARTS BIBLIOG 20 ARABS OTTOMAN. PAGE 170 A3451
ISLAM NAT/LISM DIPLOM

TRADITIONAL....SEE CONSERVE, TRADIT

TRAGER F.N. A2958

TRAINING....SEE SCHOOL, ACADEM, SKILL, EDU/PROP

TRAMPE G. A2959

TRANSFER....TRANSFER

TRANSITIVITY OF CHOICE....SEE DECISION

TRANSKEI....TRANSKEI

TRANSPORTATION....SEE DIST/IND

TRAVEL....TRAVEL AND TOURISM

TREADGOLD D.W. A2960

TREATY....TREATIES; INTERNATIONAL AGREEMENTS

N
TOSCANO M.,THE HISTORY OF TREATIES AND INTERNATIONAL POLITICS (REV. ED.). WOR-45 AGREE WAR ...BIOG 19/20 TREATY WWI. PAGE 144 A2951
DIPLOM INT/ORG

N
DE MARTENS G.F.,RECUEIL GENERALE DE TRAITES ET AUTRES ACTES RELATIFS AUX RAPPORTS DE DROIT INTERNATIONAL (41 VOLS.). EUR+WWI MOD/EUR USA-45 ...INDEX TREATY 18/20. PAGE 35 A0708
BIBLIOG INT/LAW DIPLOM

N
SOCIETE DES NATIONS,TRAITES INTERNATIONAUX ET ACTES LEGISLATIFS. WOR-45 INT/ORG NAT/G...INT/LAW JURID 20 LEAGUE/NAT TREATY. PAGE 135 A2759
BIBLIOG DIPLOM LEGIS ADJUD

B00
HOLLAND T.E.,STUDIES IN INTERNATIONAL LAW. TURKEY USSR WOR-45 CONSTN NAT/G DIPLOM DOMIN LEGIT COERCE WAR PEACE ORD/FREE PWR SOVEREIGN...JURID CHARTS 20 PARLIAMENT SUEZ TREATY. PAGE 66 A1367
INT/ORG LAW INT/LAW

B04
CRANDALL S.B.,TREATIES: THEIR MAKING AND ENFORCEMENT. MOD/EUR USA-45 CONSTN INT/ORG NAT/G LEGIS EDU/PROP LEGIT EXEC PEACE KNOWL MORAL...JURID CONGRESS 19/20 TREATY. PAGE 32 A0655
LAW

B19
KEYNES J.M.,THE ECONOMIC CONSEQUENCES OF THE PEACE. FUT GERMANY MOD/EUR RUSSIA UK USA-45 CULTURE ECO/DEV FINAN INDUS INT/ORG TOP/EX ECO/TAC ROUTINE WAR ATTIT PERCEPT ALL/VALS...OLD/LIB MYTH OBS TIME/SEQ TREND 20 TREATY. PAGE 78 A1605
EUR+WWI SOCIETY PEACE

N19
MEZERIK A.G.,ATOM TESTS AND RADIATION HAZARDS (PAMPHLET). WOR+45 INT/ORG DIPLOM DETER 20 UN TREATY. PAGE 100 A2059
NUC/PWR ARMS/CONT CONFER HEALTH

N19
MEZERIK AG,OUTER SPACE: UN, US, USSR (PAMPHLET). USSR DELIB/GP FORCES DETER NUC/PWR SOVEREIGN ...POLICY 20 UN TREATY. PAGE 101 A2063
SPACE CONTROL DIPLOM INT/ORG

B20
MEYER H.H.B.,LIST OF REFERENCES ON THE TREATY-MAKING POWER. USA-45 CONTROL PWR...INT/LAW TIME/SEQ 18/20 TREATY. PAGE 100 A2052
BIBLIOG DIPLOM CONSTN

B24
HALL W.E.,A TREATISE ON INTERNATIONAL LAW. WOR-45 CONSTN INT/ORG NAT/G DIPLOM ORD/FREE LEAGUE/NAT 20 TREATY. PAGE 60 A1228
PWR JURID WAR INT/LAW

B24
NAVILLE A.,LIBERTE, EGALITE, SOLIDARITE: ESSAIS D'ANALYSE. STRATA FAM VOL/ASSN INT/TRADE GP/REL MORAL MARXISM SOCISM...PSY TREATY. PAGE 107 A2205
ORD/FREE SOC IDEA/COMP DIPLOM

B26
INSTITUT INTERMEDIAIRE INTL,REPERTOIRE GENERAL DES TRAITES ET AUTRES ACTES DIPLOMATIQUES CONCLUS DEPUIS 1895 JUSQU'EN 1920. MOD/EUR WOR-45 INT/ORG VOL/ASSN DELIB/GP INT/TRADE WAR TREATY 19/20. PAGE 70 A1443
BIBLIOG DIPLOM

B27
BRANDENBURG E.,FROM BISMARCK TO THE WORLD WAR; A HISTORY OF GERMAN FOREIGN POLICY, 1870-1914 (TRANS. BY ANNIE ELIZABETH ADAMS). GERMANY MOD/EUR FORCES
DIPLOM POLICY WAR

AGREE PWR 19/20 TREATY CHAMBRLN/J WWI BISMARCK/O. PAGE 18 A0368

B29
LANGER W.L.,THE FRANCO-RUSSIAN ALLIANCE: 1890-1894. FRANCE MOD/EUR UK USSR NAT/G CHIEF FORCES BAL/PWR AGREE WAR PEACE PWR...TIME/SEQ TREATY 19 BISMARCK/O. PAGE 84 A1724
DIPLOM

B32
FLEMMING D.,THE UNITED STATES AND THE LEAGUE OF NATIONS, 1918-1920. FUT USA-45 NAT/G LEGIS TOP/EX DEBATE CHOOSE PEACE ATTIT SOVEREIGN...TIME/SEQ CON/ANAL CONGRESS LEAGUE/NAT 20 TREATY. PAGE 46 A0950
INT/ORG EDU/PROP

B33
REID H.D.,RECUEIL DES COURS; TOME 45: LES SERVITUDES INTERNATIONALES III. FRANCE CONSTN DELIB/GP PRESS CONTROL REV WAR CHOOSE PEACE MORAL MARITIME TREATY. PAGE 120 A2457
ORD/FREE DIPLOM LAW

B34
US TARIFF COMMISSION,THE TARIFF; A BIBLIOGRAPHY: A SELECT LIST OF REFERENCES. USA-45 LAW DIPLOM TAX ADMIN...POLICY TREATY 20. PAGE 157 A3208
BIBLIOG/A TARIFFS ECO/TAC

B35
HUDSON M.,BY PACIFIC MEANS. WOR-45 EDU/PROP ORD/FREE...CONCPT TIME/SEQ GEN/LAWS LEAGUE/NAT TOT/POP 20 TREATY. PAGE 68 A1407
INT/ORG CT/SYS PEACE

B36
BRIERLY J.L.,THE LAW OF NATIONS (2ND ED.). WOR+45 WOR-45 INT/ORG AGREE CONTROL COERCE WAR NAT/LISM PEACE PWR 16/20 TREATY LEAGUE/NAT. PAGE 18 A0375
DIPLOM INT/LAW NAT/G

B36
HUDSON M.O.,INTERNATIONAL LEGISLATION: 1929-1931. WOR-45 SEA AIR AGRI FINAN LABOR DIPLOM ECO/TAC REPAR CT/SYS ARMS/CONT WAR WEAPON...JURID 20 TREATY LEAGUE/NAT. PAGE 69 A1409
INT/LAW PARL/PROC ADJUD LAW

B37
TUPPER E.,JAPAN IN AMERICAN PUBLIC OPINION. USA-45 POL/PAR VOL/ASSN INT/TRADE DISCRIM...BIBLIOG 20 CHINJAP TREATY. PAGE 146 A2979
ATTIT IDEA/COMP DIPLOM PRESS

B38
GRISWOLD A.W.,THE FAR EASTERN POLICY OF THE UNITED STATES. ASIA S/ASIA USA-45 INT/ORG INT/TRADE WAR NAT/LISM...BIBLIOG 19/20 LEAGUE/NAT ROOSEVLT/T ROOSEVLT/F WILSON/W TREATY. PAGE 57 A1166
DIPLOM POLICY CHIEF

B38
MCNAIR A.D.,THE LAW OF TREATIES: BRITISH PRACTICE AND OPINIONS. UK CREATE DIPLOM LEGIT WRITING ADJUD WAR...INT/LAW JURID TREATY. PAGE 98 A2018
AGREE LAW CT/SYS NAT/G

B39
BENES E.,INTERNATIONAL SECURITY. GERMANY UK NAT/G DELIB/GP PLAN BAL/PWR ATTIT ORD/FREE PWR LEAGUE/NAT 20 TREATY. PAGE 13 A0267
EUR+WWI INT/ORG WAR

B39
CARR E.H.,PROPAGANDA IN INTERNATIONAL POLITICS (PAMPHLET). EUR+WWI GERMANY MOD/EUR NAT/G AGREE WAR MORAL...POLICY 20 TREATY. PAGE 24 A0497
DIPLOM EDU/PROP CONTROL ATTIT

B39
WHEELER-BENNET J.W.,THE FORGOTTEN PEACE: BREST-LITOVSK. COM GERMANY USSR TOP/EX AGREE WAR PWR ...BIBLIOG 20 TREATY LENIN/VI UKRAINE. PAGE 163 A3326
PEACE DIPLOM CONFER

B40
WOLFERS A.,BRITAIN AND FRANCE BETWEEN TWO WORLD WARS. FRANCE UK INT/ORG NAT/G PLAN BARGAIN ECO/TAC AGREE ISOLAT ALL/IDEOS...DECISION GEOG 20 TREATY VERSAILLES INTERVENT. PAGE 166 A3380
DIPLOM WAR POLICY

B41
BIRDSALL P.,VERSAILLES TWENTY YEARS AFTER. MOD/EUR POL/PAR CHIEF CONSULT FORCES LEGIS REPAR PEACE ORD/FREE...BIBLIOG 20 PRESIDENT TREATY. PAGE 14 A0290
DIPLOM NAT/LISM WAR

B42
JACKSON M.V.,EUROPEAN POWERS AND SOUTH-EAST AFRICA: A STUDY OF INTERNATIONAL RELATIONS ON SOUTH-EAST COAST OF AFRICA, 1796-1856. AFR FRANCE PORTUGAL SOUTH/AFR UK USA-45 FORCES INT/TRADE PWR...CHARTS BIBLIOG 18/19 TREATY. PAGE 72 A1477
DOMIN POLICY ORD/FREE DIPLOM

B43
MICAUD C.A.,THE FRENCH RIGHT AND NAZI GERMANY 1933-1939: A STUDY OF PUBLIC OPINION. GERMANY UK USSR POL/PAR ARMS/CONT COERCE DETER PEACE RIGID/FLEX PWR MARXISM...FASCIST TREND 20 LEAGUE/NAT TREATY. PAGE 101 A2065
DIPLOM AGREE

B44
RUDIN H.R.,ARMISTICE 1918. FRANCE GERMANY MOD/EUR UK USA-45 NAT/G CHIEF DELIB/GP FORCES BAL/PWR REPAR ARMS/CONT 20 WILSON/W TREATY. PAGE 125 A2566
AGREE WAR PEACE DIPLOM

B45
BEVERIDGE W.,THE PRICE OF PEACE. GERMANY UK WOR+45 WOR-45 NAT/G FORCES CREATE LEGIT REGION WAR ATTIT KNOWL ORD/FREE PWR...POLICY NEW/IDEA GEN/LAWS LEAGUE/NAT 20 TREATY. PAGE 14 A0284
INT/ORG TREND PEACE

C45
NELSON M.F.,"KOREA AND THE OLD ORDERS IN EASTERN ASIA." KOREA WOR-45 DELIB/GP INT/TRADE DOMIN CONTROL WAR ATTIT ORD/FREE CONSERVE...POLICY TREATY. PAGE 108 A2217
BIBLIOG DIPLOM BAL/PWR ASIA

B47
HYDE C.C.,INTERNATIONAL LAW, CHIEFLY AS INTERPRETED AND APPLIED BY THE UNITED STATES (3 VOLS., 2ND REV. ED.). USA-45 WOR+45 WOR-45 INT/ORG CT/SYS WAR NAT/LISM PEACE ORD/FREE...JURID 19/20 TREATY. PAGE 69 A1426
INT/LAW DIPLOM NAT/G POLICY

N47
FOX W.T.R.,UNITED STATES POLICY IN A TWO POWER WORLD. COM USA+45 USSR FORCES DOMIN AGREE NEUTRAL NUC/PWR ORD/FREE SOVEREIGN 20 COLD/WAR TREATY EUROPE/W INTERVENT. PAGE 48 A0972
DIPLOM FOR/AID POLICY

B48
PELCOVITS N.A.,OLD CHINA HANDS AND THE FOREIGN OFFICE. ASIA BURMA UK ECO/UNDEV NAT/G ECO/TAC FOR/AID TARIFFS DOMIN COLONIAL GOV/REL SOVEREIGN 19 HONG/KONG TREATY. PAGE 114 A2348
INT/TRADE ATTIT DIPLOM

S48
GROSS L.,"THE PEACE OF WESTPHALIA, 1648-1948." WOR+45 WOR-45 CONSTN BAL/PWR FEDERAL 17/20 TREATY WESTPHALIA. PAGE 57 A1175
INT/LAW AGREE CONCPT DIPLOM

S48
MORGENTHAU H.J.,"THE TWILIGHT OF INTERNATIONAL MORALITY" (BMR)" WOR+45 WOR-45 BAL/PWR WAR NAT/LISM PEACE...POLICY INT/LAW IDEA/COMP 15/20 TREATY INTERVENT. PAGE 104 A2137
MORAL DIPLOM NAT/G

B49
MANSERGH N.,THE COMING OF THE FIRST WORLD WAR: A STUDY IN EUROPEAN BALANCE, 1878-1914. GERMANY MOD/EUR VOL/ASSN COLONIAL CONTROL PWR 19/20 TREATY. PAGE 94 A1928
DIPLOM WAR BAL/PWR

B50
FEIS H.,THE ROAD TO PEARL HARBOR. USA-45 WOR-45 SOCIETY NAT/G FORCES WAR ORD/FREE 20 CHINJAP TREATY. PAGE 44 A0909
DIPLOM POLICY ATTIT

B50
GATZKE H.W.,GERMANY'S DRIVE TO THE WEST. BELGIUM GERMANY MOD/EUR AGRI INDUS POL/PAR FORCES DOMIN AGREE CONTROL REGION COERCE 20 TREATY WWI. PAGE 51 A1053
WAR POLICY NAT/G DIPLOM

B50
GLEASON J.H.,THE GENESIS OF RUSSOPHOBIA IN GREAT BRITAIN: A STUDY OF THE INTERACTION OF POLICY AND OPINION. ASIA RUSSIA UK NAT/G AGREE CONTROL REV WAR LOVE PWR TREATY 19. PAGE 53 A1080
DIPLOM POLICY DOMIN COLONIAL

B51
BISSAINTHE M.,DICTIONNAIRE DE BIBLIOGRAPHIE HAITIENNE. HAITI ELITES AGRI LEGIS DIPLOM INT/TRADE WRITING ORD/FREE CATHISM...ART/METH GEOG 19/20 NEGRO TREATY. PAGE 15 A0295
BIBLIOG L/A+17C SOCIETY NAT/G

B51
CORBETT P.E.,LAW AND SOCIETY IN THE RELATIONS OF STATES. FUT WOR+45 WOR-45 CONTROL WAR PEACE PWR ...POLICY JURID 16/20 TREATY. PAGE 30 A0615
INT/LAW DIPLOM INT/ORG

B52
DUNN F.S.,CURRENT RESEARCH IN INTERNATIONAL AFFAIRS. UK USA+45...POLICY TREATY. PAGE 39 A0801
BIBLIOG/A DIPLOM INT/LAW

B52
FERRELL R.H.,PEACE IN THEIR TIME. FRANCE UK USA-45 INT/ORG NAT/G FORCES CREATE AGREE ARMS/CONT COERCE WAR TREATY 20 WILSON/W LEAGUE/NAT BRIAND/A. PAGE 45 A0920
PEACE DIPLOM

B52
JACKSON E.,MEETING OF THE MINDS: A WAY TO PEACE THROUGH MEDIATION. WOR+45 INDUS INT/ORG NAT/G DELIB/GP DIPLOM EDU/PROP LEGIT ORD/FREE...NEW/IDEA SELF/OBS TIME/SEQ CHARTS GEN/LAWS TOT/POP 20 UN TREATY. PAGE 72 A1474
LABOR JUDGE

B52
LIPPMANN W.,ISOLATION AND ALLIANCES: AN AMERICAN SPEAKS TO THE BRITISH. USA+45 USA-45 INT/ORG AGREE COERCE DETER WAR PEACE MORAL 20 TREATY INTERVENT. PAGE 89 A1829
DIPLOM SOVEREIGN COLONIAL ATTIT

L52
WRIGHT Q.,"CONGRESS AND THE TREATY-MAKING POWER." USA+45 WOR+45 CONSTN INTELL NAT/G CHIEF CONSULT EX/STRUC LEGIS TOP/EX CREATE GOV/REL DISPL DRIVE RIGID/FLEX...TREND TOT/POP CONGRESS CONGRESS 20 TREATY. PAGE 167 A3408
ROUTINE DIPLOM INT/LAW DELIB/GP

B53
BRETTON H.L.,STRESEMANN AND THE REVISION OF VERSAILLES: A FIGHT FOR REASON. EUR+WWI GERMANY FORCES BUDGET ARMS/CONT WAR SUPEGO...BIBLIOG 20 TREATY VERSAILLES STRESEMN/G. PAGE 18 A0373
POLICY DIPLOM BIOG

B53
MCNEILL W.H.,AMERICA, BRITAIN, AND RUSSIA; THEIR COOPERATION AND CONFLICT. UK USA-45 USSR ECO/DEV ECO/UNDEV FORCES PLAN ADMIN AGREE PERS/REL ...DECISION 20 TREATY. PAGE 98 A2021
WAR DIPLOM DOMIN

B54
BUTOW R.J.C.,JAPAN'S DECISION TO SURRENDER. USA-45 USSR CHIEF FORCES DOMIN NUC/PWR...BIBLIOG 20 TREATY CHINJAP. PAGE 22 A0453 ELITES DIPLOM WAR PEACE

B54
TAYLOR A.J.P.,THE STRUGGLE FOR MASTERY IN EUROPE 1848-1918. MOD/EUR VOL/ASSN FORCES BAL/PWR DOMIN CONTROL PEACE MORAL 19/20 TREATY EUROPE WWI. PAGE 142 A2897 DIPLOM WAR PWR

B55
GULICK E.V.,EUROPE'S CLASSICAL BALANCE OF POWER: CASE HISTORY OF THEORY AND PRACTICE OF GREAT CONCEPTS OF EUROPEAN STATECRAFT. MOD/EUR INT/ORG VOL/ASSN FORCES ORD/FREE 18/19 TREATY. PAGE 58 A1192 IDEA/COMP BAL/PWR PWR DIPLOM

B55
TAN C.C.,THE BOXER CATASTROPHE. ASIA UK USSR ELITES POL/PAR VOL/ASSN FORCES PROB/SOLV DIPLOM ADMIN COLONIAL NAT/LISM PEACE TREATY 19/20 BOXER/REBL. PAGE 141 A2885 REV NAT/G WAR

B56
KOENIG L.W.,THE TRUMAN ADMINISTRATION: ITS PRINCIPLES AND PRACTICE. USA+45 POL/PAR CHIEF LEGIS DIPLOM DEATH NUC/PWR WAR CIVMIL/REL PEACE ...DECISION 20 TRUMAN/HS PRESIDENT TREATY. PAGE 81 A1658 ADMIN POLICY EX/STRUC GOV/REL

B56
SIPKOV I.,LEGAL SOURCES AND BIBLIOGRAPHY OF BULGARIA. BULGARIA COM LEGIS WRITING ADJUD CT/SYS ...INT/LAW TREATY 20. PAGE 134 A2736 BIBLIOG LAW TOTALISM MARXISM

B56
WATT D.C.,BRITAIN AND THE SUEZ CANAL. COM UAR UK ...INT/LAW 20 SUEZ TREATY. PAGE 162 A3294 DIPLOM INT/TRADE DIST/IND NAT/G

B57
FREUND G.,UNHOLY ALLIANCE. EUR+WWI GERMANY USSR FORCES ECO/TAC CONTROL WAR PWR...TREND TREATY. PAGE 49 A0999 DIPLOM PLAN POLICY

B57
PALMER N.D.,INTERNATIONAL RELATIONS. WOR+45 INT/ORG NAT/G ECO/TAC EDU/PROP COLONIAL WAR PWR SOVEREIGN ...POLICY T 20 TREATY. PAGE 113 A2321 DIPLOM BAL/PWR NAT/COMP

B57
US SENATE COMM ON JUDICIARY,HEARING BEFORE SUBCOMMITTEE ON COMMITTEE OF JUDICIARY, UNITED STATES SENATE: S. J. RES. 3. USA+45 NAT/G CONSULT DELIB/GP DIPLOM ADJUD LOBBY REPRESENT 20 CONGRESS TREATY. PAGE 157 A3192 LEGIS CONSTN CONFER AGREE

B57
WASSENBERGH H.A.,POST-WAR INTERNATIONAL CIVIL AVIATION POLICY AND THE LAW OF THE AIR. WOR+45 AIR INT/ORG DOMIN LEGIT PEACE ORD/FREE...POLICY JURID NEW/IDEA OBS TIME/SEQ TREND CHARTS 20 TREATY. PAGE 162 A3290 COM/IND NAT/G INT/LAW

B58
HUNT B.I.,BIPARTISANSHIP: A CASE STUDY OF THE FOREIGN ASSISTANCE PROGRAM, 1947-56 (DOCTORAL THESIS). USA+45 INT/ORG CONSULT LEGIS TEC/DEV ...BIBLIOG PRESIDENT TREATY NATO TRUMAN/HS EISNHWR/DD CONGRESS. PAGE 69 A1418 FOR/AID POL/PAR GP/REL DIPLOM

B58
KENNAN G.F.,THE DECISION TO INTERVENE: SOVIET-AMERICAN RELATIONS, 1917-1920 (VOL. II). CZECHOSLVK EUR+WWI USA-45 USSR ELITES NAT/G FORCES PROB/SOLV REV WAR TOTALISM PWR...CHARTS BIBLIOG 20 TREATY PRESIDENT CHINJAP. PAGE 78 A1588 DIPLOM POLICY ATTIT

B58
SCHOEDER P.W.,THE AXIS ALLIANCE AND JAPANESE-AMERICAN RELATIONS 1941. ASIA GERMANY UK USA-45 PEACE ATTIT...POLICY BIBLIOG 20 CHINJAP TREATY. PAGE 129 A2641 AGREE DIPLOM WAR

B58
SEYID MUHAMMAD V.A.,THE LEGAL FRAMEWORK OF WORLD TRADE. WOR+45 INT/ORG DIPLOM CONTROL...BIBLIOG 20 TREATY UN IMF GATT. PAGE 131 A2689 INT/LAW VOL/ASSN INT/TRADE TARIFFS

B58
SOC OF COMP LEGIS AND INT LAW,THE LAW OF THE SEA... (PAMPHLET). WOR+45 NAT/G INT/TRADE ADJUD CONTROL NUC/PWR WAR PEACE ATTIT ORD/FREE...JURID CHARTS 20 UN TREATY RESOURCE/N. PAGE 135 A2756 INT/LAW INT/ORG DIPLOM SEA

B59
REIFF H.,THE UNITED STATES AND THE TREATY LAW OF THE SEA. USA+45 USA-45 SEA SOCIETY INT/ORG CONSULT DELIB/GP LEGIS DIPLOM LEGIT ATTIT ORD/FREE PWR WEALTH...GEOG JURID TOT/POP 20 TREATY. PAGE 120 A2459 ADJUD INT/LAW

B59
ROBERTSON A.H.,EUROPEAN INSTITUTIONS: COOPERATION, INTEGRATION, UNIFICATION. EUR+WWI FINAN INT/ORG FORCES INT/TRADE TARIFFS 20 EEC EURATOM ECSC NATO TREATY. PAGE 122 A2496 ECO/DEV DIPLOM INDUS ECO/TAC

B59
SCHNEIDER J.,TREATY-MAKING POWER OF INTERNATIONAL ORGANIZATIONS. FUT WOR+45 WOR-45 LAW NAT/G JUDGE DIPLOM LEGIT CT/SYS ORD/FREE PWR...INT/LAW JURID GEN/LAWS TOT/POP UNESCO 20 TREATY. PAGE 129 A2639 INT/ORG ROUTINE

B59
TUNSTALL W.C.B.,THE COMMONWEALTH AND REGIONAL DEFENCE (PAMPHLET). UK LAW VOL/ASSN PLAN AGREE REGION WAR ORD/FREE 20 CMN/WLTH NATO SEATO TREATY. PAGE 146 A2977 INT/ORG FORCES DIPLOM

B60
ALBRECHT-CARRIE R.,FRANCE, EUROPE AND THE TWO WORLD WARS. EUR+WWI FRANCE GERMANY MOD/EUR UK ECO/DEV NAT/G FORCES BAL/PWR DOMIN ARMS/CONT PEACE PWR 20 TREATY EUROPE. PAGE 5 A0109 DIPLOM WAR

B60
ENGELMAN F.L.,THE PEACE OF CHRISTMAS EVE. UK USA-45 NAT/G FORCES CONFER PERS/REL...AUD/VIS BIBLIOG 19 TREATY. PAGE 42 A0853 WAR PEACE DIPLOM PERSON

B60
FISCHER L.,THE SOVIETS IN WORLD AFFAIRS. CHINA/COM COM EUR+WWI USSR INT/ORG CONFER LEAD ARMS/CONT REV PWR...CHARTS 20 TREATY VERSAILLES. PAGE 46 A0938 DIPLOM NAT/G POLICY MARXISM

B60
HEYSE T.,PROBLEMS FONCIERS ET REGIME DES TERRES (ASPECTS ECONOMIQUES, JURIDIQUES ET SOCIAUX). AFR CONGO/BRAZ INT/ORG DIPLOM SOVEREIGN...GEOG TREATY 20. PAGE 64 A1325 BIBLIOG AGRI ECO/UNDEV LEGIS

B60
WOETZEL R.K.,THE INTERNATIONAL CONTROL OF AIRSPACE AND OUTERSPACE. FUT WOR+45 AIR CONSTN STRUCT CONSULT PLAN TEC/DEV ADJUD RIGID/FLEX KNOWL ORD/FREE PWR...TECHNIC GEOG MGT NEW/IDEA TREND COMPUT/IR VAL/FREE 20 TREATY. PAGE 166 A3375 INT/ORG JURID SPACE INT/LAW

L60
DEAN A.W.,"SECOND GENEVA CONFERENCE OF THE LAW OF THE SEA: THE FIGHT FOR FREEDOM OF THE SEAS." FUT USA+45 USSR WOR+45 WOR-45 SEA CONSTN STRUCT PLAN INT/TRADE ADJUD ADMIN ORD/FREE...DECISION RECORD TREND GEN/LAWS 20 TREATY. PAGE 35 A0717 INT/ORG JURID INT/LAW

S60
HAYTON R.D.,"THE ANTARCTIC SETTLEMENT OF 1959." FUT USA+45 WOR+45 WOR-45 STRUCT R+D INT/ORG EX/STRUC CREATE TEC/DEV LEGIT PEACE ATTIT SOVEREIGN ...TIME/SEQ 20 TREATY IGY. PAGE 63 A1297 DELIB/GP JURID DIPLOM REGION

B61
AMORY J.F.,AROUND THE EDGE OF WAR: A NEW APPROACH TO THE PROBLEMS OF AMERICAN FOREIGN POLICY. COM L/A+17C USA+45 USSR FOR/AID EDU/PROP AGREE CONTROL ARMS/CONT NUC/PWR WAR PWR...IDEA/COMP 20 TREATY ESPIONAGE. PAGE 8 A0154 NAT/G DIPLOM POLICY

B61
FULLER J.F.C.,THE CONDUCT OF WAR, 1789-1961. FRANCE RUSSIA SOCIETY NAT/G FORCES PROB/SOLV AGREE NUC/PWR WEAPON PEACE...SOC 18/20 TREATY COLD/WAR. PAGE 50 A1025 WAR POLICY REV ROLE

B61
JAKOBSON M.,THE DIPLOMACY OF THE WINTER WAR. EUR+WWI FINLAND GERMANY USSR INT/ORG NAT/G PEACE TOTALISM PWR...POLICY CONCPT 20 TREATY. PAGE 73 A1492 WAR ORD/FREE DIPLOM

B61
ROBERTSON A.H.,THE LAW OF INTERNATIONAL INSTITUTIONS IN EUROPE. EUR+WWI MOD/EUR INT/ORG NAT/G VOL/ASSN DELIB/GP...JURID TIME/SEQ TOT/POP 20 TREATY. PAGE 122 A2497 RIGID/FLEX ORD/FREE

B61
SCHONBRUNN G.,WELTKRIEGE UND REVOLUTIONEN 1914-1945. USSR DIPLOM TOTALISM ORD/FREE 20 TREATY WWI NAZI. PAGE 129 A2643 WAR REV FASCISM SOCISM

L61
TAUBENFELD H.J.,"A TREATY FOR ANTARCTICA." FUT USA+45 INTELL INT/ORG LABOR 20 TREATY ANTARCTICA. PAGE 141 A2893 R+D ACT/RES DIPLOM

S61
BRZEZINSKI Z.K.,"THE ORGANIZATION OF THE COMMUNIST CAMP." COM CZECHOSLVK COM/IND NAT/G DELIB/GP INT/TRADE DOMIN EDU/PROP EXEC ROUTINE COERCE ATTIT PWR...MGT CONCPT TIME/SEQ CHARTS VAL/FREE 20 TREATY. PAGE 20 A0416 VOL/ASSN DIPLOM USSR

S61
KRANNHALS H.V.,"COMMAND INTEGRATION WITHIN THE WARSAW PACT." COM USSR WOR+45 DELIB/GP EDU/PROP ...CONCPT AUD/VIS CHARTS COLD/WAR TOT/POP VAL/FREE 20 TREATY WARSAW/P. PAGE 82 A1675 INT/ORG FORCES TOTALISM

B62
ALTHING F.A.M.,EUROPEAN ORGANIZATIONS AND FOREIGN RELATIONS OF STATES: A COMPARATIVE ANALYSIS OF DECISION-MAKING. EUR+WWI CONSTN ELITES BAL/PWR INT/TRADE SOVEREIGN TREATY. PAGE 6 A0131 DELIB/GP INT/ORG DECISION DIPLOM

B62
AMERICAN LAW INSTITUTE,FOREIGN RELATIONS LAW OF THE UNITED STATES: RESTATEMENT, SECOND. USA+45 NAT/G PROF/ORG LAW

LEGIS ADJUD EXEC ROUTINE GOV/REL...INT/LAW JURID CONCPT 20 TREATY. PAGE 7 A0152
DIPLOM ORD/FREE

B62
COLOMBOS C.J.,THE INTERNATIONAL LAW OF THE SEA. WOR+45 EXTR/IND DIPLOM INT/TRADE TARIFFS AGREE WAR ...TIME/SEQ 20 TREATY. PAGE 28 A0570
INT/LAW SEA JURID ADJUD

B62
DUROSELLE J.B.,HISTOIRE DIPLOMATIQUE DE 1919 A NOS JOURS (3RD ED.). FRANCE INT/ORG CHIEF FORCES CONFER ARMS/CONT WAR PEACE ORD/FREE...T TREATY 20 COLD/WAR. PAGE 39 A0807
DIPLOM WOR+45 WOR-45

B62
FATOUROS A.A.,GOVERNMENT GUARANTEES TO FOREIGN INVESTORS. WOR+45 ECO/UNDEV INDUS WORKER ADJUD ...NAT/COMP BIBLIOG TREATY. PAGE 44 A0903
NAT/G FINAN INT/TRADE ECO/DEV

B62
GOLDWATER B.M.,WHY NOT VICTORY? A FRESH LOOK AT AMERICAN FOREIGN POLICY. USA+45 WOR+45 FOR/AID LEAD ARMS/CONT WAR PEACE ATTIT ORD/FREE PWR MARXISM ...INT/LAW 20 TREATY ECHR COUNCL/EUR. PAGE 53 A1092
DIPLOM POLICY CONSERVE NAT/LISM

B62
MCDOUGAL M.S.,THE PUBLIC ORDER OF THE OCEANS. WOR+45 WOR-45 SEA INT/ORG NAT/G CONSULT DELIB/GP DIPLOM LEGIT PEACE RIGID/FLEX...GEOG INT/LAW JURID RECORD TOT/POP 20 TREATY. PAGE 98 A2007
ADJUD ORD/FREE

B62
PERKINS D.,AMERICA'S QUEST FOR PEACE. USA+45 WOR+45 DIPLOM CONFER NAT/LISM ATTIT 20 UN TREATY. PAGE 115 A2361
INT/LAW INT/ORG ARMS/CONT PEACE

B62
SHAW C.,LEGAL PROBLEMS IN INTERNATIONAL TRADE AND INVESTMENT. WOR+45 ECO/DEV ECO/UNDEV MARKET DIPLOM TAX INCOME ROLE...ANTHOL BIBLIOG 20 TREATY UN IMF GATT. PAGE 132 A2698
INT/LAW INT/TRADE FINAN ECO/TAC

B62
SOMMER T.,DEUTSCHLAND UND JAPAN ZWISCHEN DEN MACHTEN. GERMANY DELIB/GP BAL/PWR AGREE COERCE TOTALISM PWR 20 CHINJAP TREATY. PAGE 135 A2765
DIPLOM WAR ATTIT

B62
WADSWORTH J.J.,THE PRICE OF PEACE. WOR+45 TEC/DEV CONTROL NUC/PWR PEACE ATTIT TREATY 20. PAGE 160 A3258
DIPLOM INT/ORG ARMS/CONT POLICY

S62
CRANE R.D.,"LAW AND STRATEGY IN SPACE." FUT USA+45 WOR+45 AIR LAW INT/ORG NAT/G FORCES ACT/RES PLAN BAL/PWR LEGIT ARMS/CONT COERCE ORD/FREE...POLICY INT/LAW JURID SOC/EXP 20 TREATY. PAGE 32 A0656
CONCPT SPACE

S62
FOCSANEANU L.,"LES GRANDS TRAITES DE LA REPUBLIQUE POPULAIRE DE CHINE." ASIA CHINA/COM COM USSR WOR+45 INT/ORG NAT/G POL/PAR ACT/RES PLAN DIPLOM EDU/PROP ...CONCPT TIME/SEQ 20 TREATY. PAGE 47 A0957
VOL/ASSN TOTALISM

S62
VIGNES D.,"L'AUTORITE DES TRAITES INTERNATIONAUX EN DROIT INTERNE." EUR+WWI UNIV LAW CONSTN INTELL NAT/G POL/PAR DIPLOM ATTIT PERCEPT ALL/VALS ...POLICY INT/LAW JURID CONCPT TIME/SEQ 20 TREATY. PAGE 159 A3233
STRUCT LEGIT FRANCE

C62
BACON F.,"OF THE TRUE GREATNESS OF KINGDOMS AND ESTATES" (1612) IN F. BACON, ESSAYS." ELITES FORCES DOMIN EDU/PROP LEGIT...POLICY GEN/LAWS 16/17 TREATY. PAGE 10 A0200
WAR PWR DIPLOM CONSTN

B63
ADLER G.J.,BRITISH INDIA'S NORTHERN FRONTIER: 1865-95. AFGHANISTN RUSSIA UK PROVS COLONIAL COERCE PEACE...GEOG CHARTS BIBLIOG 19 TREATY. PAGE 4 A0091
S/ASIA FORCES DIPLOM POLICY

B63
DEENER D.R.,CANADA - UNITED STATES TREATY RELATIONS. CANADA USA+45 USA-45 NAT/G FORCES PLAN PROB/SOLV AGREE NUC/PWR...TREND 18/20 TREATY. PAGE 35 A0722
DIPLOM INT/LAW POLICY

B63
DUNN F.S.,PEACE-MAKING AND THE SETTLEMENT WITH JAPAN. ASIA USA+45 USA-45 FORCES BAL/PWR ECO/TAC CONFER WAR PWR SOVEREIGN 20 CHINJAP COLD/WAR TREATY. PAGE 39 A0802
POLICY PEACE PLAN DIPLOM

B63
FRANKEL J.,THE MAKING OF FOREIGN POLICY: AN ANALYSIS OF DECISION-MAKING. CHINA/COM EUR+WWI USA+45 ELITES INTELL FORCES LEGIS PLAN ATTIT ALL/VALS MORAL CONSERVE...GOV/COMP 20 PRESIDENT UN TREATY. PAGE 48 A0981
POLICY DECISION PROB/SOLV DIPLOM

B63
KORBEL J.,POLAND BETWEEN EAST AND WEST: SOVIET AND GERMAN DIPLOMACY TOWARD POLAND 1919-1933. EUR+WWI GERMANY POLAND USSR FORCES AGREE WAR SOVEREIGN ...BIBLIOG 20 TREATY. PAGE 81 A1670
BAL/PWR DIPLOM DOMIN NAT/LISM

B63
MONGER G.W.,THE END OF ISOLATION. FRANCE MOD/EUR RUSSIA UK NAT/G LEGIS TOP/EX GOV/REL PWR 20 TREATY CHINJAP. PAGE 103 A2106
DIPLOM POLICY WAR

B63
PERKINS B.,PROLOGUE TO THE WAR: ENGLAND AND THE UNITED STATES, 1805-1812. MOD/EUR UK USA-45 NAT/G ORD/FREE RESPECT SOVEREIGN...POLICY TREATY 19 WAR/1812. PAGE 115 A2358
WAR DIPLOM NEUTRAL

B63
THIEN T.T.,INDIA AND SOUTHEAST ASIA 1947-1960. COM INDIA S/ASIA SECT DELIB/GP FOR/AID RACE/REL NAT/LISM SOCISM...CHARTS BIBLIOG 20 UN NEHRU/J TREATY. PAGE 143 A2917
DRIVE DIPLOM POLICY

B63
VAN SLYCK P.,PEACE: THE CONTROL OF NATIONAL POWER. CUBA WOR+45 FINAN NAT/G FORCES PROB/SOLV TEC/DEV BAL/PWR ADMIN CONTROL ORD/FREE...POLICY INT/LAW UN COLD/WAR TREATY. PAGE 158 A3214
ARMS/CONT PEACE INT/ORG DIPLOM

S63
BRZEZINSKI Z.,"SOVIET QUIESCENCE." EUR+WWI USA+45 USSR FORCES CREATE PLAN COERCE DETER WAR ATTIT 20 TREATY EUROPE. PAGE 20 A0415
DIPLOM ARMS/CONT NUC/PWR AGREE

S63
GARDNER R.N.,"COOPERATION IN OUTER SPACE." FUT USSR WOR+45 AIR LAW COM/IND CONSULT DELIB/GP CREATE KNOWL 20 TREATY. PAGE 51 A1045
INT/ORG ACT/RES PEACE SPACE

S63
MODELSKI G.,"STUDY OF ALLIANCES." WOR+45 WOR-45 INT/ORG NAT/G FORCES LEGIT ADMIN CHOOSE ALL/VALS PWR SKILL...INT/LAW CONCPT GEN/LAWS 20 TREATY. PAGE 102 A2099
VOL/ASSN CON/ANAL DIPLOM

B64
DUBOIS J.,DANGER OVER PANAMA. FUT PANAMA SCHOOL PROB/SOLV EDU/PROP MARXISM...POLICY 19/20 TREATY INTERVENT CANAL/ZONE. PAGE 39 A0790
DIPLOM COERCE

B64
ESTHUS R.A.,FROM ENMITY TO ALLIANCE: US AUSTRALIAN RELATIONS. S/ASIA DIST/IND VOL/ASSN FORCES ATTIT 20 AUSTRAL TREATY CMN/WLTH. PAGE 42 A0863
DIPLOM WAR INT/TRADE FOR/AID

B64
FULBRIGHT J.W.,OLD MYTHS AND NEW REALITIES. USA+45 USSR LEGIS INT/TRADE DETER ATTIT...POLICY 20 COLD/WAR TREATY. PAGE 50 A1016
DIPLOM INT/ORG ORD/FREE

B64
LUARD E.,THE COLD WAR: A RE-APPRAISAL. FUT USSR WOR+45 FORCES NUC/PWR NAT/LISM ORD/FREE SOVEREIGN ...INT 20 COLD/WAR STALIN/J TREATY UN. PAGE 91 A1870
DIPLOM WAR PEACE TOTALISM

B64
SCHWELB E.,HUMAN RIGHTS AND THE INTERNATIONAL COMMUNITY. WOR+45 WOR-45 NAT/G SECT DELIB/GP DIPLOM PEACE RESPECT TREATY 20 UN. PAGE 130 A2666
INT/ORG ORD/FREE INT/LAW

B64
TONG T.,UNITED STATES DIPLOMACY IN CHINA, 1844-1860. ASIA USA-45 ECO/UNDEV ECO/TAC COERCE GP/REL...INT/LAW 19 TREATY. PAGE 144 A2949
DIPLOM INT/TRADE COLONIAL

B64
WEINTRAUB S.,THE WAR IN THE WARDS. KOREA/N WOR+45 DIPLOM COERCE ORD/FREE SKILL 20 TREATY. PAGE 162 A3308
EDU/PROP PEACE CROWD PUB/INST

S64
CARNEGIE ENDOWMENT INT. PEACE,"LEGAL QUESTIONS (ISSUES BEFORE THE NINETEENTH GENERAL ASSEMBLY)." WOR+45 CONSTN NAT/G DELIB/GP ADJUD PEACE MORAL ORD/FREE...RECORD UN 20 TREATY. PAGE 24 A0494
INT/ORG LAW INT/LAW

S64
DERWINSKI E.J.,"THE COST OF THE INTERNATIONAL COFFEE AGREEMENT." L/A+17C USA+45 WOR+45 ECO/UNDEV NAT/G VOL/ASSN LEGIS DIPLOM ECO/TAC FOR/AID LEGIT ATTIT...TIME/SEQ CONGRESS 20 TREATY. PAGE 36 A0732
MARKET DELIB/GP INT/TRADE

S64
TRISKA J.F.,"SOVIET TREATY LAW: A QUANTITATIVE ANALYSIS." WOR+45 LAW ECO/UNDEV AGRI COM/IND INDUS CREATE TEC/DEV DIPLOM ATTIT PWR WEALTH...JURID SAMP TIME/SEQ TREND CHARTS VAL/FREE 20 TREATY. PAGE 145 A2967
COM ECO/TAC INT/LAW USSR

B65
COWEN Z.,THE BRITISH COMMONWEALTH OF NATIONS IN A CHANGING WORLD. UK ECO/UNDEV INT/ORG ECO/TAC INT/TRADE COLONIAL WAR GP/REL RACE/REL SOVEREIGN SOC/INTEG 20 TREATY EEC COMMONWLTH. PAGE 32 A0644
JURID DIPLOM PARL/PROC NAT/LISM

B65
MACDONALD R.W.,THE LEAGUE OF ARAB STATES: A STUDY IN THE DYNAMICS OF REGIONAL ORGANIZATION. ISRAEL UAR USSR FINAN INT/ORG DELIB/GP ECO/TAC AGREE NEUTRAL ORD/FREE PWR...DECISION BIBLIOG 20 TREATY UN. PAGE 92 A1888
ISLAM REGION DIPLOM ADMIN

B65
MONCONDUIT F.,LA COMMISSION EUROPEENNE DES DROITS DE L'HOMME. DIPLOM AGREE GP/REL ORD/FREE PWR ...BIBLIOG 20 TREATY. PAGE 102 A2103
INT/LAW INT/ORG ADJUD JURID

B65
MORRIS R.B.,THE PEACEMAKERS; THE GREAT POWERS AND
SOVEREIGN

AMERICAN INDEPENDENCE. BAL/PWR CONFER COLONIAL NEUTRAL PEACE ORD/FREE TREATY 18 PRE/US/AM. PAGE 105 A2149
REV DIPLOM

B65
UNESCO,HANDBOOK OF INTERNATIONAL EXCHANGES. COM/IND R+D ACADEM PROF/ORG VOL/ASSN CREATE TEC/DEV EDU/PROP AGREE 20 TREATY. PAGE 148 A3025
INDEX INT/ORG DIPLOM PRESS

B65
US SENATE,US INTERNATIONAL SPACE PROGRAMS, 1959-65: STAFF REPORT FOR COMM ON AERONAUTICAL AND SPACE SCIENCES. WOR+45 VOL/ASSN CIVMIL/REL 20 CONGRESS NASA TREATY. PAGE 155 A3166
SPACE DIPLOM PLAN GOV/REL

B65
WARBEY W.,VIETNAM: THE TRUTH. FRANCE S/ASIA USA+45 VIETNAM CULTURE INT/ORG NAT/G DIPLOM FOR/AID EDU/PROP ARMS/CONT PEACE 20 TREATY NLF UN. PAGE 161 A3274
WAR AGREE

B65
WEILER J.,L'ECONOMIE INTERNATIONALE DEPUIS 1950. WOR+45 DIPLOM TARIFFS CONFER...POLICY TREATY. PAGE 162 A3302
FINAN INT/TRADE REGION FOR/AID

B65
WINT G.,ASIA: A HANDBOOK. ASIA COM INDIA USSR CULTURE INTELL NAT/G...GEOG STAT CENSUS NAT/COMP WORSHIP 20 TREATY CHINJAP. PAGE 165 A3365
DIPLOM SOC

C65
WUORINEN J.H.,"SCANDINAVIA." DENMARK FINLAND ICELAND NORWAY SWEDEN SOCIETY AGRI POL/PAR DELIB/GP DIPLOM INT/TRADE NEUTRAL WAR...CHARTS TREATY 20. PAGE 168 A3423
BIBLIOG NAT/G POLICY

B66
AMERICAN FRIENDS SERVICE COMM,PEACE IN VIETNAM: A NEW APPROACH IN SOUTHEAST ASIA: A REPORT. ASIA S/ASIA USA+45 VIETNAM ORD/FREE 20 TREATY. PAGE 7 A0149
PEACE WAR NAT/LISM DIPLOM

B66
CANFIELD L.H.,THE PRESIDENCY OF WOODROW WILSON: PRELUDE TO A WORLD IN CRISIS. USA-45 ADJUD NEUTRAL WAR CHOOSE INGP/REL PEACE ORD/FREE 20 WILSON/W PRESIDENT TREATY LEAGUE/NAT. PAGE 24 A0477
PERSON POLICY DIPLOM GOV/REL

B66
DYCK H.V.,WEIMAR GERMANY AND SOVIET RUSSIA 1926-1933. EUR+WWI GERMANY UK USSR ECO/TAC INT/TRADE NEUTRAL WAR ATTIT 20 WEIMAR/REP TREATY. PAGE 40 A0814
DIPLOM GOV/REL POLICY

B66
EUDIN X.J.,SOVIET FOREIGN POLICY 1928-34: DOCUMENTS AND MATERIALS (VOL. I). ASIA USSR WOR-45 INT/ORG POL/PAR WORKER WAR PEACE...ANTHOL 20 TREATY LEAGUE/NAT INTERVENT. PAGE 43 A0873
DIPLOM POLICY GOV/REL MARXISM

B66
HAY P.,FEDERALISM AND SUPRANATIONAL ORGANIZATIONS: PATTERNS FOR NEW LEGAL STRUCTURES. EUR+WWI LAW NAT/G VOL/ASSN DIPLOM PWR...NAT/COMP TREATY EEC. PAGE 63 A1294
SOVEREIGN FEDERAL INT/ORG INT/LAW

B66
INTL CONF ON WORLD POLITICS-5,EASTERN EUROPE IN TRANSITION. EUR+WWI USSR ECO/TAC NAT/LISM ATTIT SOVEREIGN...CHARTS ANTHOL 20 TREATY WARSAW/P. PAGE 71 A1463
COM NAT/COMP MARXISM DIPLOM

B66
LALL A.,MODERN INTERNATIONAL NEGOTIATION: PRINCIPLES AND PRACTICE. WOR+45 INT/ORG DELIB/GP PROB/SOLV DETER...INT/LAW TREATY. PAGE 84 A1712
DIPLOM ECO/TAC ATTIT

B66
LAMBERG R.F.,PRAG UND DIE DRITTE WELT. AFR ASIA CZECHOSLVK L/A+17C MARKET TEC/DEV ECO/TAC REV ATTIT 20 TREATY. PAGE 84 A1713
DIPLOM ECO/UNDEV INT/TRADE FOR/AID

B66
LEE L.T.,VIENNA CONVENTION ON CONSULAR RELATIONS. WOR+45 LAW INT/ORG CONFER GP/REL PRIVIL...INT/LAW 20 TREATY VIENNA/CNV. PAGE 86 A1760
AGREE DIPLOM ADMIN

B66
OBERMANN E.,VERTEIDIGUNG PER FREIHEIT. GERMANY/W WOR+45 INT/ORG COERCE NUC/PWR WEAPON MARXISM 20 UN NATO WARSAW/P TREATY. PAGE 111 A2273
FORCES ORD/FREE WAR PEACE

B66
PASSIN H.,THE UNITED STATES AND JAPAN. USA+45 INDUS CAP/ISM...TREND 20 CHINJAP TREATY. PAGE 114 A2337
DIPLOM INT/TRADE ECO/DEV ECO/TAC

B66
POLLACK R.S.,THE INDIVIDUAL'S RIGHTS AND INTERNATIONAL ORGANIZATION. LAW INT/ORG DELIB/GP SUPEGO...JURID SOC/INTEG 20 TREATY UN. PAGE 117 A2394
INT/LAW ORD/FREE DIPLOM PERSON

B66
RISTIC D.N.,YUGOSLAVIA'S REVOLUTION OF 1941. EUR+WWI YUGOSLAVIA NAT/G WAR ORD/FREE...RECORD BIBLIOG 20 HITLER/A TREATY. PAGE 121 A2484
REV ATTIT FASCISM DIPLOM

B66
VAN DYKE V.,INTERNATIONAL POLITICS. WOR+45 ECO/DEV ECO/UNDEV INT/ORG BAL/PWR AGREE ARMS/CONT NAT/LISM PEACE PWR...INT/LAW 20 TREATY UN. PAGE 158 A3212
DIPLOM NAT/G WAR SOVEREIGN

B66
WAINHOUSE D.W.,INTERNATIONAL PEACE OBSERVATION: A HISTORY AND FORECAST. INT/ORG PROB/SOLV BAL/PWR AGREE ARMS/CONT COERCE NUC/PWR...PREDICT METH/COMP 20 UN LEAGUE/NAT OAS TREATY. PAGE 160 A3261
PEACE DIPLOM

B66
WEINSTEIN F.B.,VIETNAM'S UNHELD ELECTIONS: THE FAILURE TO CARRY OUT THE 1956 REUNIFICATION ELECTIONS... (MONOGRAPH). VIETNAM/S VIETNAM/N LEGIT CONFER ADJUD WAR PEACE 20 TREATY GENEVA/CON UNIFICA. PAGE 162 A3306
AGREE NAT/G CHOOSE DIPLOM

C66
DUROSELLE J.B.,"LE CONFLIT DE TRIESTE 1943-1954: ETUDES DE CAS DE CONFLITS INTERNATIONAUX III." ITALY USA+45 YUGOSLAVIA ELITES DELIB/GP PLAN ADJUST ...POLICY GEOG CHARTS IDEA/COMP TIME 20 TREATY UN COLD/WAR. PAGE 40 A0810
BIBLIOG WAR DIPLOM GEN/LAWS

B67
LAWYERS COMM AMER POLICY VIET,VIETNAM AND INTERNATIONAL LAW: AN ANALYSIS OF THE LEGALITY OF THE US MILITARY INVOLVEMENT. VIETNAM LAW INT/ORG COERCE WEAPON PEACE ORD/FREE 20 UN SEATO TREATY. PAGE 86 A1753
INT/LAW DIPLOM ADJUD WAR

B67
MCBRIDE J.H.,THE TEST BAN TREATY: MILITARY, TECHNOLOGICAL, AND POLITICAL IMPLICATIONS. USA+45 USSR DELIB/GP FORCES LEGIS TEC/DEV BAL/PWR TREATY. PAGE 97 A1995
ARMS/CONT DIPLOM NUC/PWR

B67
PADELFORD N.J.,THE DYNAMICS OF INTERNATIONAL POLITICS (2ND ED.). WOR+45 LAW INT/ORG FORCES TEC/DEV REGION NAT/LISM PEACE ATTIT PWR ALL/IDEOS UN COLD/WAR NATO TREATY. PAGE 113 A2314
DIPLOM NAT/G POLICY DECISION

B67
POGANY A.H.,POLITICAL SCIENCE AND INTERNATIONAL RELATIONS, BOOKS RECOMMENDED FOR AMERICAN CATHOLIC COLLEGE LIBRARIES. INT/ORG LOC/G NAT/G FORCES BAL/PWR ECO/TAC NUC/PWR...CATH INT/LAW TREATY 20. PAGE 117 A2393
BIBLIOG DIPLOM

B67
US DEPARTMENT OF STATE,TREATIES IN FORCE. USA+45 WOR+45 AGREE WAR PEACE 20 TREATY. PAGE 152 A3101
BIBLIOG DIPLOM INT/ORG DETER

B67
US SENATE COMM ON FOREIGN REL,UNITED STATES ARMAMENT AND DISARMAMENT PROBLEMS. USA+45 AIR BAL/PWR DIPLOM FOR/AID NUC/PWR ORD/FREE SENATE TREATY. PAGE 156 A3190
ARMS/CONT WEAPON FORCES PROB/SOLV

S67
EISENDRATH C.,"THE OUTER SPACE TREATY." CHINA/COM COM USA+45 DIPLOM CONTROL NUC/PWR...INT/LAW 20 UN COLD/WAR TREATY. PAGE 41 A0831
SPACE INT/ORG PEACE ARMS/CONT

S67
OLIVIER G.,"ASPECTS JURIDIQUES DE L'ADOPTION DU TRAITE CECA A LA CRISE CHARBONNIERE (SUITE ET FIN)" LAW DIST/IND PLAN DIPLOM RATION PRICE ADMIN COST DEMAND...POLICY CON/ANAL ECSC TREATY. PAGE 112 A2288
INT/TRADE INT/ORG EXTR/IND CONSTN

S67
REINTANZ G.,"THE SPACE TREATY." WOR+45 DIPLOM CONTROL ARMS/CONT NUC/PWR WAR...MARXIST 20 COLD/WAR UN TREATY. PAGE 120 A2461
SPACE INT/LAW INT/ORG PEACE

S67
VLASCIC I.A.,"THE SPACE TREATY* A PRELIMINARY EVALUATION." FUT USSR WOR+45 R+D ACT/RES TEC/DEV DIPLOM CONFER ARMS/CONT PEACE...PREDICT UN TREATY. PAGE 159 A3245
SPACE INT/LAW INT/ORG NEUTRAL

S67
WEIL G.L.,"THE MERGER OF THE INSTITUTIONS OF THE EUROPEAN COMMUNITIES" EUR+WWI ECO/DEV INT/TRADE CONSEN PLURISM...DECISION MGT 20 EEC EURATOM ECSC TREATY. PAGE 162 A3300
ECO/TAC INT/ORG CENTRAL INT/LAW

B86
MAS LATRIE L.,RELATIONS ET COMMERCE DE L'AFRIQUE SEPTENTRIONALE OU MAGREB AVEC LES NATIONS CHRETIENNES AU MOYEN AGE. CULTURE CHIEF FORCES WAR ...SOC CENSUS TREATY 10/16. PAGE 95 A1954
ISLAM SECT DIPLOM INT/TRADE

TREFOUSSE H.L. A2961

TREND....PROJECTION OF HISTORICAL TRENDS

N
JOURNAL OF INTERNATIONAL AFFAIRS. WOR+45 ECO/UNDEV POL/PAR ECO/TAC WAR PEACE PERSON ALL/IDEOS ...INT/LAW TREND. PAGE 1 A0015
BIBLIOG DIPLOM INT/ORG NAT/G

N
JOURNAL OF MODERN HISTORY. WOR+45 WOR-45 LEAD WAR ...TIME/SEQ TREND NAT/COMP 20. PAGE 1 A0016
BIBLIOG/A DIPLOM NAT/G

N
SOCIAL RESEARCH. WOR+45 WOR-45 R+D LEAD GP/REL ATTIT...SOC TREND 20. PAGE 2 A0025
BIBLIOG/A DIPLOM NAT/G SOCIETY

N
THE WORLD IN FOCUS. WOR+45 LEAD ATTIT...POLICY TREND. PAGE 2 A0044
BIBLIOG INT/ORG INT/LAW DIPLOM

N
JAHRBUCH DER DISSERTATIONEN. GERMANY/W WOR+45 ...TREND 20. PAGE 3 A0048
BIBLIOG/A NAT/G ACADEM DIPLOM

N
AMERICAN HISTORICAL SOCIETY,LIST OF DOCTORAL DISSERTATIONS IN HISTORY IN PROGRESS OR COMPLETED IN COLLEGES AND UNIVERSITIES IN THE UNITED STATES. WOR+45 WOR-45 CULTURE SOCIETY NAT/G DIPLOM LEAD TREND. PAGE 7 A0150
BIBLIOG ACADEM INTELL

N
JOHNS HOPKINS UNIVERSITY LIB,RECENT ADDITIONS. WOR+45 ECO/UNDEV NAT/G POL/PAR FOR/AID INT/TRADE LEAD REGION ATTIT ALL/IDEOS TREND. PAGE 74 A1518
BIBLIOG DIPLOM INT/LAW INT/ORG

N
KYRIAK T.E.,ASIAN DEVELOPMENTS: A BIBLIOGRAPHY. INDONESIA KOREA/N VIETNAM/N CULTURE SOCIETY ECO/UNDEV NAT/G DIPLOM...SOC TREND 20 MONGOLIA. PAGE 83 A1699
BIBLIOG/A ALL/IDEOS S/ASIA ASIA

B00
LORIMER J.,THE INSTITUTES OF THE LAW OF NATIONS. WOR-45 CULTURE SOCIETY NAT/G VOL/ASSN DIPLOM LEGIT WAR PEACE DRIVE ORD/FREE SOVEREIGN...CONCPT RECORD INT TREND HYPO/EXP GEN/METH TOT/POP VAL/FREE 20. PAGE 91 A1863
INT/ORG LAW INT/LAW

B00
MORRIS H.C.,THE HISTORY OF COLONIZATION. WOR+45 WOR-45 ECO/DEV ECO/UNDEV INT/ORG ACT/RES PLAN ECO/TAC LEGIT ROUTINE COERCE ATTIT DRIVE ALL/VALS ...GEOG TREND 19. PAGE 105 A2148
DOMIN SOVEREIGN COLONIAL

B00
VOLPICELLI Z.,RUSSIA ON THE PACIFIC AND THE SIBERIAN RAILWAY. MOD/EUR ECO/UNDEV INT/ORG FORCES PLAN DOMIN COLONIAL ROUTINE ATTIT ALL/VALS...OBS HIST/WRIT TIME/SEQ TREND CON/ANAL AUD/VIS CHARTS 18/19. PAGE 159 A3248
NAT/G ACT/RES RUSSIA

B09
FREMANTLE H.E.S.,THE NEW NATION, A SURVEY OF THE CONDITION AND PROSPECTS OF SOUTH AFRICA. SOUTH/AFR CONSTN POL/PAR DIPLOM DOMIN COLONIAL WEALTH...SOC TREND 19. PAGE 49 A0996
NAT/LISM SOVEREIGN RACE/REL REGION

B15
FARIES J.C.,THE RISE OF INTERNATIONALISM. ASIA MOD/EUR NAT/G VOL/ASSN DELIB/GP BAL/PWR EDU/PROP ARMS/CONT RIGID/FLEX TREND. PAGE 44 A0899
INT/ORG DIPLOM PEACE

B19
KEYNES J.M.,THE ECONOMIC CONSEQUENCES OF THE PEACE. FUT GERMANY MOD/EUR RUSSIA UK USA-45 CULTURE ECO/DEV FINAN INDUS INT/ORG TOP/EX ECO/TAC ROUTINE WAR ATTIT PERCEPT ALL/VALS...OLD/LIB MYTH OBS TIME/SEQ TREND 20 TREATY. PAGE 78 A1605
EUR+WWI SOCIETY PEACE

N19
MORGENSTERN O.,THE COMMAND AND CONTROL STRUCTURE (PAMPHLET). USSR COM/IND INT/ORG WEAPON PEACE UTIL ...TREND 20 NATO. PAGE 104 A2132
CONTROL FORCES EFFICIENCY PLAN

B20
BURNS C.D.,INTERNATIONAL POLITICS. WOR-45 CULTURE SOCIETY ECO/UNDEV NAT/G VOL/ASSN DELIB/GP ACT/RES CREATE DOMIN EDU/PROP LEGIT ATTIT DRIVE RIGID/FLEX ALL/VALS...PLURIST PSY CONCPT TREND. PAGE 22 A0442
INT/ORG PEACE SOVEREIGN

B20
WOOLF L.,EMPIRE AND COMMERCE IN AFRICA. EUR+WWI MOD/EUR FINAN INDUS MARKET INT/ORG PLAN COERCE ATTIT DRIVE PWR WEALTH...CONCPT TIME/SEQ TREND CHARTS 20. PAGE 167 A3394
AFR DOMIN COLONIAL SOVEREIGN

B21
STUART G.H.,FRENCH FOREIGN POLICY. CONSTN INT/ORG NAT/G POL/PAR EX/STRUC FORCES PLAN ECO/TAC DOMIN EDU/PROP ADJUD COERCE ATTIT DRIVE RIGID/FLEX ALL/VALS...POLICY OBS RECORD BIOG TIME/SEQ TREND. PAGE 139 A2852
MOD/EUR DIPLOM FRANCE

B22
WALSH E.,THE HISTORY AND NATURE OF INTERNATIONAL RELATIONS. ASIA L/A+17C MOD/EUR USA-45 WOR-45 NAT/G FORCES TOP/EX BAL/PWR REGION ATTIT ORD/FREE RESPECT ...CONCPT HIST/WRIT TREND. PAGE 161 A3270
INT/ORG TIME/SEQ DIPLOM

B28
CORBETT P.E.,CANADA AND WORLD POLITICS. LAW CULTURE SOCIETY STRUCT MARKET INT/ORG FORCES ACT/RES PLAN ECO/TAC LEGIT ORD/FREE PWR RESPECT...SOC CONCPT TIME/SEQ TREND CMN/WLTH 20 LEAGUE/NAT. PAGE 30 A0612
NAT/G CANADA

B28
HALL W.P.,EMPIRE TO COMMONWEALTH. FUT WOR-45 CONSTN ECO/DEV ECO/UNDEV INT/ORG PROVS PLAN DIPLOM EDU/PROP ADMIN COLONIAL PEACE PERSON ALL/VALS ...POLICY GEOG SOC OBS RECORD TREND CMN/WLTH PARLIAMENT 19/20. PAGE 60 A1229
VOL/ASSN NAT/G UK

B28
STUART G.H.,LATIN AMERICA AND THE UNITED STATES. USA-45 ECO/UNDEV INT/ORG NAT/G POL/PAR PLAN DOMIN EDU/PROP COLONIAL REGION COERCE ATTIT ALL/VALS ...POLICY GEOG TREND 19/20. PAGE 139 A2853
L/A+17C DIPLOM

B31
STOWELL E.C.,INTERNATIONAL LAW. FUT UNIV WOR-45 SOCIETY CONSULT EX/STRUC FORCES ACT/RES PLAN DIPLOM EDU/PROP LEGIT DISPL PWR SKILL...POLICY CONCPT OBS TREND TOT/POP 20. PAGE 139 A2839
INT/ORG ROUTINE INT/LAW

B32
HANSEN A.H.,ECONOMIC STABILIZATION IN AN UNBALANCED WORLD. COM EUR+WWI USA-45 WOR-45 AGRI FINAN INDUS MARKET INT/ORG LABOR VOL/ASSN EDU/PROP ATTIT HEALTH KNOWL WEALTH...HIST/WRIT TREND VAL/FREE 20. PAGE 61 A1253
NAT/G ECO/DEV CAP/ISM SOCISM

B32
MASTERS R.D.,INTERNATIONAL LAW IN INTERNATIONAL COURTS. BELGIUM EUR+WWI FRANCE GERMANY MOD/EUR SWITZERLND WOR-45 SOCIETY STRATA STRUCT LEGIT EXEC ALL/VALS...JURID HIST/WRIT TIME/SEQ TREND GEN/LAWS 20. PAGE 96 A1961
INT/ORG LAW INT/LAW

B32
WRIGHT Q.,GOLD AND MONETARY STABILIZATION. FUT USA-45 WOR-45 INTELL ECO/DEV INT/ORG NAT/G CONSULT PLAN ECO/TAC ADMIN ATTIT WEALTH...CONCPT TREND 20. PAGE 167 A3404
FINAN POLICY

B34
GRAHAM F.D.,PROTECTIVE TARIFFS. FUT USA+45 WOR-45 INDUS MARKET VOL/ASSN PLAN CAP/ISM ECO/TAC PEACE ATTIT DRIVE HEALTH ORD/FREE...OBS TREND GEN/LAWS 20. PAGE 55 A1124
INT/ORG TARIFFS

B35
MARRIOTT J.A.,DICTATORSHIP AND DEMOCRACY. GERMANY GREECE UK CHIEF DIPLOM DOMIN LEGIT PEACE ORD/FREE CONSERVE...TREND ROME HITLER/A. PAGE 95 A1946
TOTALISM POPULISM PLURIST NAT/G

B35
STALEY E.,WAR AND THE PRIVATE INVESTOR. UNIV WOR-45 INTELL SOCIETY INT/ORG NAT/G TOP/EX CAP/ISM ECO/TAC WAR ATTIT ALL/VALS...INT TIME/SEQ TREND CON/ANAL WORK TOT/POP 20. PAGE 137 A2799
FINAN INT/TRADE DIPLOM

B37
VINER J.,STUDIES IN THE THEORY OF INTERNATIONAL TRADE. WOR-45 CONSTN ECO/DEV AGRI INDUS MARKET INT/ORG LABOR NAT/G ECO/TAC TARIFFS COLONIAL ATTIT WEALTH...POLICY CONCPT MATH STAT OBS SAMP TREND GEN/LAWS MARX/KARL 20. PAGE 159 A3236
CAP/ISM INT/TRADE

B38
DE MADARIAGA S.,THE WORLD'S DESIGN. WOR-45 SOCIETY STRUCT EDU/PROP PEACE ATTIT PERSON ALL/VALS ...SOCIALIST CONCPT TIME/SEQ TREND GEN/LAWS LEAGUE/NAT. PAGE 35 A0706
FUT INT/ORG DIPLOM

B39
ROBBINS L.,ECONOMIC CAUSES OF WAR. WOR-45 ECO/DEV ECO/UNDEV INT/ORG NAT/G TEC/DEV DIPLOM DOMIN COLONIAL ATTIT DRIVE PWR WEALTH...POLICY CONCPT OBS SAMP TREND CON/ANAL GEN/LAWS MARX/KARL 20. PAGE 122 A2493
COERCE ECO/TAC WAR

B39
STALEY E.,WORLD ECONOMY IN TRANSITION. WOR-45 SOCIETY INT/ORG PROF/ORG ECO/TAC ATTIT WEALTH ...METH/CNCPT TREND GEN/LAWS 20. PAGE 137 A2800
TEC/DEV INT/TRADE

B39
WILSON G.G.,HANDBOOK OF INTERNATIONAL LAW. FUT UNIV USA-45 WOR-45 SOCIETY LEGIT ATTIT DISPL DRIVE ALL/VALS...INT/LAW TIME/SEQ TREND. PAGE 165 A3359
INT/ORG LAW CONCPT WAR

B39
ZIMMERN A.,MODERN POLITICAL DOCTRINE. WOR-45 CULTURE SOCIETY ECO/UNDEV DELIB/GP EX/STRUC CREATE DOMIN COERCE NAT/LISM ATTIT RIGID/FLEX ORD/FREE PWR WEALTH...POLICY CONCPT OBS TIME/SEQ TREND TOT/POP LEAGUE/NAT 20. PAGE 170 A3454
NAT/G ECO/TAC BAL/PWR INT/TRADE

L39
NEARING S.,"A WARLESS WORLD." FUT WOR-45 SOCIETY INT/ORG NAT/G EX/STRUC PLAN DOMIN WAR ATTIT DRIVE PWR...POLICY PSY CONCPT OBS TREND HYPO/EXP MARX/KARL 20 MARX/KARL LENIN/VI. PAGE 108 A2210
COERCE PEACE

B40
CARR E.H.,THE TWENTY YEARS' CRISIS 1919-1939. FUT WOR-45 BAL/PWR ECO/TAC LEGIT TOTALISM ATTIT ALL/VALS...POLICY JURID CONCPT TIME/SEQ TREND GEN/LAWS TOT/POP 20. PAGE 24 A0498
INT/ORG DIPLOM PEACE

B40
CONOVER H.F.,JAPAN-ECONOMIC DEVELOPMENT AND FOREIGN POLICY, A SELECTED LIST OF REFERENCES (PAMPHLET).
BIBLIOG ASIA

CULTURE FINAN INDUS NAT/G FORCES INT/TRADE WAR ...SOC TREND 20 CHINJAP. PAGE 29 A0593 — ECO/DEV DIPLOM

B41
MCCLURE W.,INTERNATIONAL EXECUTIVE AGREEMENTS. USA-45 WOR-45 INT/ORG NAT/G DELIB/GP ADJUD ROUTINE ORD/FREE PWR...TIME/SEQ TREND CON/ANAL. PAGE 97 A2000 — TOP/EX DIPLOM

B41
YOUNG G.,FEDERALISM AND FREEDOM. EUR+WWI MOD/EUR RUSSIA USA-45 WOR-45 SOCIETY STRUCT ECO/DEV INT/ORG EXEC FEDERAL ATTIT PERSON ALL/VALS...OLD/LIB CONCPT OBS TREND LEAGUE/NAT TOT/POP. PAGE 169 A3435 — NAT/G WAR

B42
BONNET H.,THE UNITED NATIONS, WHAT THEY ARE, WHAT THEY MAY BECOME. FUT WOR-45 CREATE BAL/PWR ECO/TAC PWR...TREND GEN/LAWS 20. PAGE 16 A0335 — INT/ORG ORD/FREE

B42
HAMBRO C.J.,HOW TO WIN THE PEACE. ECO/TAC EDU/PROP ADJUD PERSON ALL/VALS...SOCIALIST TREND GEN/LAWS 20. PAGE 61 A1246 — FUT INT/ORG PEACE

B42
KELSEN H.,LAW AND PEACE IN INTERNATIONAL RELATIONS. FUT WOR-45 NAT/G DELIB/GP DIPLOM LEGIT RIGID/FLEX ORD/FREE SOVEREIGN...JURID CONCPT TREND STERTYP GEN/LAWS LEAGUE/NAT 20. PAGE 77 A1580 — INT/ORG ADJUD PEACE INT/LAW

S42
TURNER F.J.,"AMERICAN SECTIONALISM AND WORLD ORGANIZATION." EUR+WWI UNIV USA-45 WOR-45 INTELL ECO/DEV TOP/EX ACT/RES PLAN EDU/PROP LEGIT ALL/VALS ...CONCPT NEW/IDEA OBS TREND LEAGUE/NAT TOT/POP 20. PAGE 146 A2981 — INT/ORG DRIVE BAL/PWR

B43
LIPPMANN W.,US FOREIGN POLICY: SHIELD OF THE REPUBLIC. USA-45 WOR-45 CULTURE INT/ORG POL/PAR CREATE BAL/PWR DOMIN EDU/PROP WAR ORD/FREE PWR ...PLURIST CONCPT TREND CON/ANAL 20. PAGE 89 A1827 — NAT/G DIPLOM PEACE

B43
MICAUD C.A.,THE FRENCH RIGHT AND NAZI GERMANY 1933-1939: A STUDY OF PUBLIC OPINION. GERMANY UK USSR POL/PAR ARMS/CONT COERCE DETER PEACE RIGID/FLEX PWR MARXISM...FASCIST TREND 20 LEAGUE/NAT TREATY. PAGE 101 A2065 — DIPLOM AGREE

B43
SERENI A.P.,THE ITALIAN CONCEPTION OF INTERNATIONAL LAW. EUR+WWI MOD/EUR INT/ORG NAT/G DOMIN COERCE ORD/FREE FASCISM...OBS/ENVIR TREND 20. PAGE 131 A2686 — LAW TIME/SEQ INT/LAW ITALY

B43
SULZBACH W.,NATIONAL CONSCIOUSNESS. FUT WOR-45 INT/ORG PEACE MORAL FASCISM MARXISM...MAJORIT TREND WORSHIP 19/20 LEAGUE/NAT INTERVENT WWI. PAGE 140 A2862 — NAT/LISM NAT/G DIPLOM WAR

B44
ADLER M.J.,HOW TO THINK ABOUT WAR AND PEACE. WOR-45 LAW SOCIETY EX/STRUC DIPLOM KNOWL ORD/FREE...POLICY TREND GEN/LAWS 20. PAGE 4 A0092 — INT/ORG CREATE ARMS/CONT PEACE

B44
BARTLETT R.J.,THE LEAGUE TO ENFORCE PEACE. FUT USA-45 NAT/G POL/PAR CREATE EDU/PROP ADMIN RIGID/FLEX PWR...CONCPT TREND GEN/METH LEAGUE/NAT 20. PAGE 11 A0231 — INT/ORG ORD/FREE DIPLOM

B44
HUDSON M.,INTERNATIONAL TRIBUNALS PAST AND FUTURE. FUT WOR-45 LAW EDU/PROP ADJUD ORD/FREE...CONCPT TIME/SEQ TREND GEN/LAWS TOT/POP VAL/FREE 18/20. PAGE 69 A1408 — INT/ORG STRUCT INT/LAW

B44
WHITTON J.B.,THE SECOND CHANCE: AMERICA AND THE PEACE. EUR+WWI USA-45 SOCIETY STRUCT INT/ORG NAT/G LEGIT EXEC WAR ALL/VALS...SOC CONCPT TIME/SEQ TREND CONGRESS 20. PAGE 164 A3340 — LEGIS PEACE

L44
HAILEY,"THE FUTURE OF COLONIAL PEOPLES." WOR-45 CONSTN CULTURE ECO/UNDEV AGRI MARKET INT/ORG NAT/G SECT CONSULT ECO/TAC LEGIT ADMIN NAT/LISM ALL/VALS ...SOC OBS TREND STERTYP CMN/WLTH LEAGUE/NAT PARLIAMENT 20. PAGE 59 A1218 — PLAN CONCPT DIPLOM UK

S44
WRIGHT Q.,"CONSTITUTIONAL PROCEDURES OF THE US FOR CARRYING OUT OBLIGATIONS FOR MILITARY SANCTIONS." EUR+WWI FUT USA-45 WOR-45 CONSTN INTELL NAT/G CONSULT EX/STRUC LEGIS ROUTINE DRIVE...POLICY JURID CONCPT OBS TREND TOT/POP 20. PAGE 167 A3406 — TOP/EX FORCES INT/LAW WAR

C44
VAN VALKENBURG S.,"ELEMENTS OF POLITICAL GEOGRAPHY." FRANCE COM/IND INDUS NAT/G SECT RACE/REL...LING TREND GEN/LAWS BIBLIOG 20. PAGE 158 A3215 — GEOG DIPLOM COLONIAL

B45
BEVERIDGE W.,THE PRICE OF PEACE. GERMANY UK WOR+45 WOR-45 NAT/G FORCES CREATE LEGIT REGION WAR ATTIT KNOWL ORD/FREE PWR...POLICY NEW/IDEA GEN/LAWS LEAGUE/NAT 20 TREATY. PAGE 14 A0284 — INT/ORG TREND PEACE

B45
CARR E.H.,NATIONALISM AND AFTER. FUT WOR-45 NAT/G VOL/ASSN EX/STRUC PLAN ROUTINE TOTALISM ATTIT HEALTH ORD/FREE PWR...CONCPT 20. PAGE 25 A0499 — INT/ORG TREND NAT/LISM REGION

B45
KANDELL I.L.,UNITED STATES ACTIVITIES IN INTERNATIONAL CULTURAL RELATIONS. INT/ORG NAT/G VOL/ASSN CREATE DIPLOM EDU/PROP ATTIT RIGID/FLEX KNOWL...PLURIST CONCPT OBS TREND GEN/LAWS TOT/POP UNESCO 20. PAGE 76 A1554 — USA-45 CULTURE

B46
BRODIE B.,THE OBSOLETE WEAPON: ATOMIC POWER AND WORLD ORDER. COM USA+45 USSR WOR+45 DELIB/GP PLAN ORD/FREE PWR...CONCPT TIME/SEQ TREND UN 20. PAGE 19 A0380 — INT/ORG TEC/DEV ARMS/CONT NUC/PWR

B46
MITRANY D.,A WORKING PEACE SYSTEM. WOR+45 WOR-45 ECO/DEV INT/ORG NAT/G DELIB/GP ECO/TAC REGION ATTIT RIGID/FLEX...TREND GEN/LAWS LEAGUE/NAT 20. PAGE 102 A2091 — VOL/ASSN PLAN PEACE SOVEREIGN

L46
MASTERS D.,"ONE WORLD OR NONE." FUT WOR+45 INTELL INT/ORG ACT/RES EDU/PROP DETER ATTIT RIGID/FLEX SUPEGO KNOWL...STAT TREND ORG/CHARTS 20. PAGE 96 A1960 — POLICY PHIL/SCI ARMS/CONT NUC/PWR

B47
BROOKINGS INST.,MAJOR PROBLEMS OF UNITED STATES FOREIGN POLICY. USA+45 WOR+45 STRUCT ECO/DEV ECO/UNDEV INT/ORG NAT/G POL/PAR VOL/ASSN DELIB/GP FORCES ECO/TAC LEGIT COERCE ORD/FREE PWR WEALTH ...POLICY STAT TREND CHARTS TOT/POP. PAGE 19 A0392 — ACT/RES DIPLOM

B48
CHAMBERLAIN L.H.,AMERICAN FOREIGN POLICY. FUT USA+45 USA-45 WOR+45 WOR-45 NAT/G LEGIS TOP/EX ECO/TAC FOR/AID EDU/PROP EXEC ATTIT ORD/FREE ...JURID TREND TOT/POP 20. PAGE 25 A0517 — CONSTN DIPLOM

B48
KULISCHER E.M.,EUROPE ON THE MOVE: WAR AND POPULATION CHANGES, 1917-1947. COM EUR+WWI FUT GERMANY USSR DIST/IND PLAN INT/TRADE CONTROL WAR DRIVE...CENSUS TREND COLD/WAR 20. PAGE 82 A1690 — ECO/TAC GEOG

B49
BOYD A.,WESTERN UNION: A STUDY OF THE TREND TOWARD EUROPEAN UNITY. FUT REGION NAT/LISM...POLICY IDEA/COMP BIBLIOG 14/20 OEEC ERASMUS/D COUNCL/EUR FULBRGHT/J NATO. PAGE 18 A0363 — DIPLOM AGREE TREND INT/ORG

B49
MARITAIN J.,HUMAN RIGHTS: COMMENTS AND INTERPRETATIONS. COM UNIV WOR+45 LAW CONSTN CULTURE SOCIETY ECO/DEV ECO/UNDEV SCHOOL DELIB/GP EDU/PROP ATTIT PERCEPT ALL/VALS...HUM SOC TREND UNESCO 20. PAGE 95 A1939 — INT/ORG CONCPT

B49
ROSENHAUPT H.W.,HOW TO WAGE PEACE. USA+45 SOCIETY STRATA STRUCT R+D INT/ORG POL/PAR LEGIS ACT/RES CREATE PLAN EDU/PROP ADMIN EXEC ATTIT ALL/VALS ...TIME/SEQ TREND COLD/WAR 20. PAGE 124 A2536 — INTELL CONCPT DIPLOM

B50
ALMOND G.A.,THE AMERICAN PEOPLE AND FOREIGN POLICY. USA+45 USA-45 CULTURE SOCIETY STRUCT CONSEN PERSON PWR POPULISM...TIME/SEQ TREND 20 COLD/WAR. PAGE 6 A0129 — ATTIT DIPLOM DECISION ELITES

B50
BERLE A.A.,NATURAL SELECTION OF POLITICAL FORCES. FUT WOR+45 WOR-45 CULTURE SOCIETY INT/ORG NAT/G FORCES EDU/PROP LEGIT COERCE...CONCPT HIST/WRIT TREND 20. PAGE 13 A0274 — POL/PAR BAL/PWR DIPLOM

B50
DULLES J.F.,WAR OR PEACE. CHINA/COM USA+45 USSR INT/ORG SECT FORCES PLAN NUC/PWR WAR CENTRAL MARXISM...POLICY 20 UN ROOSEVLT/F STALIN/J. PAGE 39 A0797 — PEACE DIPLOM TREND ORD/FREE

S50
UNESCO,"MEETING ON UNIVERSITY TEACHING OF INTERNATIONAL RELATIONS." FUT WOR+45 R+D VOL/ASSN CONSULT PLAN EDU/PROP ATTIT...CONCPT TREND 20. PAGE 147 A3012 — INT/ORG KNOWL DIPLOM

B51
UNESCO,FREEDOM AND CULTURE. FUT WOR+45 CONSTN CULTURE PERF/ART VOL/ASSN EDU/PROP PEACE ATTIT ALL/VALS SOVEREIGN...POLICY MAJORIT CONCPT TREND STERTYP GEN/LAWS UN TOT/POP 20. PAGE 147 A3013 — INT/ORG SOCIETY

B51
US DEPARTMENT OF STATE,POINT FOUR. NEAR EAST AND AFRICA. A SELECTED BIBLIOGRAPHY OF STUDIES ON ECONOMICALLY UNDERDEVELOPED COUNTRIES. AGRI COM/IND FINAN INDUS PLAN INT/TRADE...SOC TREND 20. PAGE 151 A3087 — BIBLIOG/A AFR S/ASIA ISLAM

B51
WELLES S.,SEVEN DECISIONS THAT SHAPED HISTORY. ASIA FRANCE FUT USA+45 WOR+45 WOR-45 CONSTN STRUCT INT/ORG NAT/G ACT/RES EDU/PROP DRIVE...POLICY CONCPT TIME/SEQ TREND TOT/POP UN 20 CHINJAP. PAGE 163 A3315 — USA-45 DIPLOM WAR

L51
LISSITZYN O.J.,"THE INTERNATIONAL COURT OF JUSTICE." WOR+45 INT/ORG LEGIT ORD/FREE...CONCPT — ADJUD JURID

TIME/SEQ TREND GEN/LAWS VAL/FREE 20 ICJ. PAGE 90 A1839
INT/LAW

B52
HOSELITZ B.F.,THE PROGRESS OF UNDERDEVELOPED AREAS. FUT WOR+45 WOR-45 ECO/DEV ECO/TAC INT/TRADE WEALTH ...SOC TREND GEN/LAWS TOT/POP VAL/FREE COLD/WAR 20. PAGE 68 A1391
ECO/UNDEV / PLAN / FOR/AID

B52
SCHUMAN F.,THE COMMONWEALTH OF MAN. WOR+45 WOR-45 LAW CULTURE ELITES SOCIETY FAM INT/ORG NAT/G VOL/ASSN TOP/EX PLAN BAL/PWR LEGIT ATTIT DISPL DRIVE...POLICY MYTH TREND TOT/POP ILO OEEC 20. PAGE 129 A2649
CONCPT / GEN/LAWS

B52
UN DEPT. SOC. AFF.,PRELIMINARY REPORT ON THE WORLD SOCIAL SITUATION. ISLAM L/A+17C WOR+45 STRATA AGRI EXTR/IND INDUS INT/ORG SCHOOL ADMIN...GEOG SOC TREND UNESCO WORK FAO 20. PAGE 147 A2998
R+D / HEALTH / FOR/AID

B52
US DEPARTMENT OF STATE,RESEARCH ON EASTERN EUROPE (EXCLUDING USSR). EUR+WWI LAW ECO/DEV NAT/G PROB/SOLV DIPLOM ADMIN LEAD MARXISM...TREND 19/20. PAGE 151 A3088
BIBLIOG / R+D / ACT/RES / COM

B52
WALTERS F.P.,A HISTORY OF THE LEAGUE OF NATIONS. EUR+WWI CONSTN NAT/G LEGIS TOP/EX ACT/RES PLAN EDU/PROP LEGIT ROUTINE ATTIT...TREND LEAGUE/NAT 20 CHINJAP. PAGE 161 A3271
INT/ORG / TIME/SEQ / NAT/LISM

L52
THOMPSON K.W.,"THE STUDY OF INTERNATIONAL POLITICS: A SURVEY OF TRENDS AND DEVELOPMENTS." UNIV USA+45 WOR+45 WOR-45 SOCIETY ECO/DEV R+D ACT/RES PLAN ROUTINE ATTIT DRIVE PERCEPT PERSON...CONCPT OBS TREND GEN/LAWS TOT/POP. PAGE 143 A2928
INT/ORG / BAL/PWR / DIPLOM

L52
WRIGHT Q.,"CONGRESS AND THE TREATY-MAKING POWER." USA+45 WOR+45 CONSTN INTELL NAT/G CHIEF CONSULT EX/STRUC LEGIS TOP/EX CREATE GOV/REL DISPL DRIVE RIGID/FLEX...TREND TOT/POP CONGRESS CONGRESS 20 TREATY. PAGE 167 A3408
ROUTINE / DIPLOM / INT/LAW / DELIB/GP

S52
HAAS E.B.,"THE RECONCILIATION OF CONFLICT, COLONIAL POLICY AIMS: ACCEPTANCE OF THE LEAGUE OF NATIONS MANDATE SYSTEM." FRANCE GERMANY UK WOR+45 WOR-45 LEGIT ATTIT DRIVE ORD/FREE...OLD/LIB INT SYS/QU TIME/SEQ TREND LEAGUE/NAT 20. PAGE 58 A1201
INT/ORG / COLONIAL

S52
MASTERS R.D.,"RUSSIA AND THE UNITED NATIONS." FUT USA+45 USSR WOR+45 CONSTN VOL/ASSN DELIB/GP TOP/EX CREATE DIPLOM ADMIN...TREND STERTYP UN 20. PAGE 96 A1962
INT/ORG / PWR

S52
SCHWEBEL S.M.,"THE SECRETARY-GENERAL OF THE UN." FUT INTELL CONSULT DELIB/GP ADMIN PEACE ATTIT ...JURID MGT CONCPT TREND UN CONGRESS 20. PAGE 130 A2663
INT/ORG / TOP/EX

B53
LENZ F.,DIE BEWEGUNGEN DER GROSSEN MACHTE. USA+45 USA-45 USSR SOCIETY STRATA STRUCT NAT/G PERSON MARXISM...CONCPT IDEA/COMP NAT/COMP 18/20. PAGE 87 A1777
BAL/PWR / TREND / DIPLOM / HIST/WRIT

B53
MENDE T.,WORLD POWER IN THE BALANCE. FUT USA+45 USSR WOR-45 ECO/DEV ECO/TAC INT/TRADE EDU/PROP UTOPIA ATTIT...HUM CONCPT TREND COLD/WAR TOT/POP 20. PAGE 99 A2036
WOR+45 / PWR / BAL/PWR

S53
BOULDING K.E.,"ECONOMIC ISSUES IN INTERNATIONAL CONFLICT." WOR+45 ECO/DEV NAT/G TOP/EX DIPLOM ECO/TAC DOMIN ATTIT WEALTH...MAJORIT OBS/ENVIR TREND GEN/LAWS COLD/WAR TOT/POP 20. PAGE 17 A0345
PWR / FOR/AID

S53
LINCOLN G.,"FACTORS DETERMINING ARMS AID." COM FUT USA+45 USSR WOR+45 ECO/DEV NAT/G CONSULT PLAN TEC/DEV DIPLOM DOMIN EDU/PROP PERCEPT PWR ...DECISION CONCPT TREND MARX/KARL 20. PAGE 89 A1819
FORCES / POLICY / BAL/PWR / FOR/AID

B54
ARON R.,CENTURY OF TOTAL WAR. FUT WOR+45 WOR-45 SOCIETY INT/ORG NAT/G FORCES TOP/EX CREATE BAL/PWR DOMIN EDU/PROP COERCE DETER PEACE TOTALISM PWR ...TIME/SEQ TREND COLD/WAR TOT/POP VAL/FREE LEAGUE/NAT 20. PAGE 9 A0179
ATTIT / WAR

B54
BUCHANAN W.,AN INTERNATIONAL POLICE FORCE AND PUBLIC OPINION IN THE UNITED STATES, 1939-1953. USA+45 PROB/SOLV CONTROL ATTIT ORD/FREE...STAT TREND 20. PAGE 21 A0425
IDEA/COMP / FORCES / DIPLOM / PLAN

B54
CHEEVER D.S.,ORGANIZING FOR PEACE. FUT WOR+45 WOR-45 STRATA STRUCT NAT/G CREATE DIPLOM LEGIT REGION COERCE DETER PEACE ATTIT DRIVE ALL/VALS ...TIME/SEQ TREND UN LEAGUE/NAT. PAGE 26 A0525
INT/ORG

B54
MILLARD E.L.,FREEDOM IN A FEDERAL WORLD. FUT WOR+45 VOL/ASSN TOP/EX LEGIT ROUTINE FEDERAL PEACE ATTIT DISPL ORD/FREE PWR...MAJORIT INT/LAW JURID TREND COLD/WAR 20. PAGE 101 A2073
INT/ORG / CREATE / ADJUD / BAL/PWR

B54
NORTHROP F.S.C.,EUROPEAN UNION AND UNITED STATES FOREIGN POLICY: A STUDY IN SOCIOLOGICAL JURISPRUDENCE. EUR+WWI MOD/EUR USA+45 SOCIETY STRUCT NAT/G CREATE ECO/TAC DOMIN EDU/PROP REGION ATTIT RIGID/FLEX HEALTH ORD/FREE WEALTH ...METH/CNCPT TIME/SEQ TREND. PAGE 110 A2256
INT/ORG / SOC / DIPLOM

B54
SALVEMINI G.,PRELUDE TO WORLD WAR II. ITALY MOD/EUR INT/ORG BAL/PWR EDU/PROP CONTROL TOTALISM...TREND NAT/COMP BIBLIOG 19 HITLER/A LEAGUE/NAT MUSSOLIN/B. PAGE 127 A2597
WAR / FASCISM / LEAD / PWR

B54
SCHIFFER W.,THE LEGAL COMMUNITY OF MANKIND. UNIV WOR+45 WOR-45 SOCIETY NAT/G EDU/PROP LEGIT ATTIT PERSON ORD/FREE PWR...CONCPT HIST/WRIT TREND LEAGUE/NAT UN 20. PAGE 128 A2626
INT/ORG / PHIL/SCI

B54
WRIGHT Q.,PROBLEMS OF STABILITY AND PROGRESS IN INTERNATIONAL RELATIONSHIPS. FUT WOR+45 WOR-45 SOCIETY LEGIS CREATE TEC/DEV ECO/TAC EDU/PROP ADJUD WAR PEACE ORD/FREE PWR...KNO/TEST TREND GEN/LAWS 20. PAGE 167 A3409
INT/ORG / CONCPT / DIPLOM

L54
OPLER M.E.,"SOCIAL ASPECTS OF TECHNICAL ASSISTANCE IN OPERATION." WOR+45 VOL/ASSN CREATE PLAN TEC/DEV EDU/PROP ALL/VALS...METH/CNCPT OBS RECORD TREND UN 20. PAGE 112 A2292
INT/ORG / CONSULT / FOR/AID

S54
FOX W.T.R.,"CIVIL-MILITARY RELATIONS." USA+45 USA-45 R+D ACT/RES DIPLOM INT/TRADE EDU/PROP DETER DISPL DRIVE ORD/FREE...METH/CNCPT TREND COLD/WAR 20. PAGE 48 A0974
POLICY / FORCES / PLAN / SOCIETY

B55
INSTITUTE POLITISCHE WISSEN,POLITISCHE LITERATUR (3 VOLS.). INT/ORG LEAD WAR PEACE...CONCPT TREND NAT/COMP 20. PAGE 70 A1446
BIBLIOG/A / NAT/G / DIPLOM / POLICY

B55
MACMAHON A.W.,FEDERALISM: MATURE AND EMERGENT. EUR+WWI FUT WOR+45 WOR-45 INT/ORG NAT/G REPRESENT FEDERAL...POLICY MGT RECORD TREND GEN/LAWS 20. PAGE 93 A1900
STRUCT / CONCPT

B55
SNYDER R.C.,AMERICAN FOREIGN POLICY. USA+45 USA-45 WOR+45 WOR-45 CONSTN INT/ORG POL/PAR VOL/ASSN DELIB/GP LEGIS CREATE DOMIN EDU/PROP EXEC COERCE ATTIT DRIVE ORD/FREE PWR...MGT OBS RECORD TIME/SEQ TREND. PAGE 134 A2752
NAT/G / DIPLOM

L55
ROSTOW W.W.,"RUSSIA AND CHINA UNDER COMMUNISM." CHINA/COM USSR INTELL STRUCT INT/ORG NAT/G POL/PAR TOP/EX ACT/RES PLAN ADMIN ATTIT ALL/VALS MARXISM ...CONCPT OBS TIME/SEQ TREND GOV/COMP VAL/FREE 20. PAGE 124 A2543
COM / ASIA

B56
BALL W.M.,NATIONALISM AND COMMUNISM IN EAST ASIA. ASIA BURMA EUR+WWI KOREA USA+45 ECO/UNDEV NAT/G POL/PAR DIPLOM ECO/TAC FOR/AID EDU/PROP COERCE RACE/REL NAT/LISM DRIVE SOVEREIGN...TREND 20 CHINJAP. PAGE 11 A0214
S/ASIA / ATTIT

B56
BLACKETT P.M.S.,ATOMIC WEAPONS AND EAST-WEST RELATIONS. FUT WOR+45 INT/ORG DELIB/GP COERCE ATTIT RIGID/FLEX KNOWL...RELATIV HIST/WRIT TREND GEN/METH COLD/WAR 20. PAGE 15 A0299
FORCES / PWR / ARMS/CONT / NUC/PWR

B56
FOSTER J.G.,BRITAIN IN WESTERN EUROPE: WEU AND THE ATLANTIC ALLIANCE. EUR+WWI FRANCE GERMANY GERMANY/W ITALY UK STRATA NAT/G DELIB/GP ECO/TAC ORD/FREE PWR ...TRADIT TIME/SEQ TREND OEEC PARLIAMENT 20 EUROPE/W. PAGE 47 A0969
INT/ORG / FORCES / WEAPON

B56
GUNTHER F.,BUCHERKUNDE ZUR WELTGESCHICHTE VON UNTERGANG DES ROMISCHEN WELTREICHES BIS ZUR GEGENWART. WOR+45 WOR-45 LEAD PERSON. PAGE 58 A1193
BIBLIOG / DIPLOM / NAT/G / TREND

B56
REITZEL W.,UNITED STATES FOREIGN POLICY, 1945-1955. USA+45 WOR+45 CONSTN INT/ORG EDU/PROP LEGIT EXEC COERCE NUC/PWR PEACE ATTIT ORD/FREE PWR...DECISION CONCPT OBS RECORD TIME/SEQ TREND COLD/WAR UN CONGRESS. PAGE 120 A2464
NAT/G / POLICY / DIPLOM

B56
ROBERTS H.L.,RUSSIA AND AMERICA. CHINA/COM S/ASIA USSR FORCES TEC/DEV FOR/AID NUC/PWR ALL/IDEOS ...MAJORIT TREND NAT/COMP 20 COLD/WAR UN NATO. PAGE 122 A2494
DIPLOM / INT/ORG / BAL/PWR / TOTALISM

B56
WOLFERS A.,THE ANGLO-AMERICAN TRADITION IN FOREIGN AFFAIRS. UK USA+45 WOR-45 CULTURE SOCIETY ECO/DEV INT/ORG NAT/G CREATE PLAN BAL/PWR ECO/TAC EDU/PROP PEACE DISPL DRIVE...TREND GEN/LAWS 20. PAGE 166 A3382
ATTIT / CONCPT / DIPLOM

C56
DUPUY R.E.,"MILITARY HERITAGE OF AMERICA." USA+45 USA-45 TEC/DEV DIPLOM ROUTINE...POLICY TREND CHARTS IDEA/COMP BIBLIOG COLD/WAR. PAGE 39 A0804
FORCES
WAR
CONCPT

B57
ARON R.,L'UNIFICATION ECONOMIQUE DE L'EUROPE. EUR+WWI SWITZERLND UK INT/ORG NAT/G REGION NAT/LISM ORD/FREE PWR...CONCPT METH/CNCPT OBS TREND STERTYP GEN/LAWS EEC 20. PAGE 9 A0181
VOL/ASSN
ECO/TAC

B57
BERLE A.A.,TIDES OF CRISIS: A PRIMER OF FOREIGN RELATIONS. USA+45 WOR+45 DOMIN NUC/PWR NAT/LISM PWR ...CONCPT STERTYP GEN/LAWS 20 UN. PAGE 14 A0276
INT/ORG
TREND
PEACE

B57
BLOOMFIELD L.M.,EGYPT, ISRAEL AND THE GULF OF AQABA: IN INTERNATIONAL LAW. LAW NAT/G CONSULT FORCES PLAN ECO/TAC ROUTINE COERCE ATTIT DRIVE PERCEPT PERSON RIGID/FLEX LOVE PWR WEALTH...GEOG CONCPT MYTH TREND. PAGE 15 A0314
ISLAM
INT/LAW
UAR

B57
BUCK P.W.,CONTOL OF FOREIGN RELATIONS IN MODERN NATIONS. FRANCE L/A+17C NETHERLAND USSR WOR+45 INT/ORG TOP/EX BAL/PWR DOMIN EDU/PROP COERCE PEACE ATTIT...CONCPT TREND 20 CMN/WLTH. PAGE 21 A0427
NAT/G
PWR
DIPLOM

B57
DEAN V.M.,THE NATURE OF THE NON-WESTERN WORLD. AFR ASIA L/A+17C S/ASIA CULTURE SOCIETY STRATA ECO/DEV DIPLOM ECO/TAC FOR/AID ATTIT DRIVE ALL/VALS ...RELATIV SOC CONCPT TIME/SEQ TREND TOT/POP 20. PAGE 35 A0718
ECO/UNDEV
STERTYP
NAT/LISM

B57
DRUCKER P.F.,AMERICA'S NEXT TWENTY YEARS. USA+45 DIST/IND ACADEM MUNIC SCHOOL DIPLOM ECO/TAC AUTOMAT HABITAT HEALTH...SOC/WK TREND 20 URBAN/RNWL PUB/TRANS. PAGE 39 A0788
WORKER
FOR/AID
CENSUS
GEOG

B57
FREUND G.,UNHOLY ALLIANCE. EUR+WWI GERMANY USSR FORCES ECO/TAC CONTROL WAR PWR...TREND TREATY. PAGE 49 A0999
DIPLOM
PLAN
POLICY

B57
HODGKIN T.,NATIONALISM IN COLONIAL AFRICA. STRATA STRUCT MUNIC NAT/G POL/PAR LEGIS ATTIT SOVEREIGN ...POLICY TREND BIBLIOG 20. PAGE 66 A1351
AFR
COLONIAL
NAT/LISM
DIPLOM

B57
KAPLAN M.A.,SYSTEM AND PROCESS OF INTERNATIONAL POLITICS. FUT WOR+45 WOR-45 SOCIETY PLAN BAL/PWR ADMIN ATTIT PERSON RIGID/FLEX PWR SOVEREIGN ...DECISION TREND VAL/FREE. PAGE 76 A1560
INT/ORG
DIPLOM

B57
KENNAN G.F.,RUSSIA, THE ATOM AND THE WEST. COM EUR+WWI FUT WOR+45 SOCIETY ECO/DEV FORCES DIPLOM ECO/TAC DOMIN EDU/PROP COERCE NUC/PWR ATTIT DRIVE ORD/FREE PWR...POLICY OBS TIME/SEQ TREND COLD/WAR NATO 20. PAGE 77 A1574
NAT/G
INT/ORG
USSR

B57
LAVES W.H.C.,UNESCO. FUT WOR+45 NAT/G CONSULT DELIB/GP TEC/DEV ECO/TAC EDU/PROP PEACE ORD/FREE ...CONCPT TIME/SEQ TREND UNESCO VAL/FREE 20. PAGE 86 A1751
INT/ORG
KNOWL

B57
LEFEVER E.W.,ETHICS AND UNITED STATUS FOREIGN POLICY. SOCIETY INT/ORG NAT/G ACT/RES DIPLOM EDU/PROP COERCE ATTIT MORAL...TREND GEN/LAWS COLD/WAR 20. PAGE 86 A1762
USA+45
CULTURE
CONCPT
POLICY

B57
LEVONTIN A.V.,THE MYTH OF INTERNATIONAL SECURITY: A JURIDICAL AND CRITICAL ANALYSIS. FUT WOR+45 WOR-45 LAW NAT/G VOL/ASSN ACT/RES BAL/PWR ATTIT ORD/FREE ...JURID METH/CNCPT TIME/SEQ TREND STERTYP 20. PAGE 88 A1797
INT/ORG
INT/LAW
SOVEREIGN
MYTH

B57
SEABURY P.,THE WANING OF SOUTHERN "INTERNATIONALISM" (PAMPHLET). USA+45 USA-45 INT/ORG LEGIS MAJORITY...TREND 20 SOUTH/US MIDWEST/US. PAGE 131 A2676
DIPLOM
REGION
ATTIT
ISOLAT

B57
TOMASIC D.A.,NATIONAL COMMUNISM AND SOVIET STRATEGY. UK USSR YUGOSLAVIA NAT/G POL/PAR CHIEF CREATE DOMIN REV WAR PWR...BIOG TREND 20 TITO/MARSH STALIN/J. PAGE 144 A2948
COM
NAT/LISM
MARXISM
DIPLOM

B57
TRIFFIN R.,EUROPE AND THE MONEY MUDDLE. USA+45 INT/ORG NAT/G CONSULT PLAN ECO/TAC EXEC ROUTINE BAL/PAY WEALTH...METH/CNCPT OBS TREND CHARTS STERTYP GEN/METH EEC VAL/FREE ECSC. PAGE 145 A2962
EUR+WWI
ECO/DEV
REGION

B57
WASSENBERGH H.A.,POST-WAR INTERNATIONAL CIVIL AVIATION POLICY AND THE LAW OF THE AIR. WOR+45 AIR INT/ORG DOMIN LEGIT PEACE ORD/FREE...POLICY JURID NEW/IDEA OBS TIME/SEQ TREND CHARTS 20 TREATY. PAGE 162 A3290
COM/IND
NAT/G
INT/LAW

B57
YAMADA H.,ANNALS OF THE SOCIAL SCIENCES. WOR+45 WOR-45 LAW CULTURE SOCIETY STRUCT DIPLOM...EPIST PSY CONCPT 15/20. PAGE 168 A3428
BIBLIOG/A
TREND
IDEA/COMP

SOC

L57
FURNISS E.S.,"SOME PERSPECTIVES ON AMERICAN MILITARY ASSISTANCE." USA+45 WOR+45 ECO/UNDEV INT/ORG ECO/TAC ORD/FREE...GEOG TIME/SEQ TREND COLD/WAR 20. PAGE 50 A1028
FORCES
FOR/AID
WEAPON

B58
GARTHOFF R.L.,SOVIET STRATEGY IN THE NUCLEAR AGE. FUT USSR R+D INT/ORG NAT/G ACT/RES TEC/DEV DOMIN DETER WAR ATTIT PWR...RELATIV METH/CNCPT SELF/OBS TREND CON/ANAL STERTYP GEN/LAWS 20. PAGE 51 A1052
COM
FORCES
BAL/PWR
NUC/PWR

B58
JENKS C.W.,THE COMMON LAW OF MANKIND. EUR+WWI MOD/EUR SPACE WOR+45 INT/ORG BAL/PWR ARMS/CONT COERCE SUPEGO MORAL...TREND 20. PAGE 73 A1505
JURID
SOVEREIGN

B58
KINDLEBERGER C.P.,INTERNATIONAL ECONOMICS. WOR+45 WOR-45 ECO/DEV ECO/UNDEV FINAN VOL/ASSN ACT/RES DIPLOM ECO/TAC LEGIT REGION ATTIT DRIVE ORD/FREE WEALTH...POLICY STAT TREND GEN/LAWS EEC ECSC OEEC 20. PAGE 79 A1620
INT/ORG
BAL/PWR
TARIFFS

B58
ORGANSKI A.F.K.,WORLD POLITICS. FUT WOR+45 SOCIETY STRUCT NAT/G BAL/PWR ECO/TAC DOMIN NAT/LISM ATTIT KNOWL ORD/FREE PWR...CONCPT METH/CNCPT TREND STERTYP GEN/LAWS TOT/POP 20. PAGE 112 A2297
INT/ORG
DIPLOM

B58
SLICK T.,PERMANENT PEACE: A CHECK AND BALANCE PLAN. FUT WOR+45 NAT/G FORCES CREATE PLAN EDU/PROP LEGIT ADJUD COERCE NAT/LISM RIGID/FLEX MORAL...HUM CONCPT METH/CNCPT NEW/IDEA TREND CHARTS TOT/POP 20. PAGE 134 A2742
INT/ORG
ORD/FREE
PEACE
ARMS/CONT

S58
DAVENPORT J.,"ARMS AND THE WELFARE STATE." INTELL STRUCT FORCES CREATE ECO/TAC FOR/AID DOMIN LEGIT ADMIN WAR ORD/FREE PWR...POLICY SOC CONCPT MYTH OBS TREND COLD/WAR TOT/POP 20. PAGE 34 A0685
USA+45
NAT/G
USSR

S58
JORDAN A.,"MILITARY ASSISTANCE AND NATIONAL POLICY." ASIA FUT USA+45 WOR+45 ECO/DEV ECO/UNDEV INT/ORG NAT/G PLAN ECO/TAC ROUTINE WEAPON ATTIT RIGID/FLEX PWR...CONCPT TREND 20. PAGE 75 A1533
FORCES
POLICY
FOR/AID
DIPLOM

S58
THOMPSON K.W.,"NATIONAL SECURITY IN A NUCLEAR AGE." USA+45 WOR+45 SOCIETY INT/ORG NAT/G TOP/EX DIPLOM DOMIN EDU/PROP LEGIT ARMS/CONT COERCE ORD/FREE ...TREND STERTYP TOT/POP VAL/FREE COLD/WAR 20. PAGE 143 A2929
FORCES
PWR
BAL/PWR

B59
AIR FORCE ACADEMY ASSEMBLY '59,INTERNATIONAL STABILITY AND PROGRESS (PAMPHLET). USA+45 USSR ECO/UNDEV PROB/SOLV BUDGET DIPLOM ADMIN DETER COST ATTIT...TREND 20. PAGE 5 A0103
FOR/AID
FORCES
WAR
PLAN

B59
ALWAN M.,ALGERIA BEFORE THE UNITED NATIONS. AFR ASIA FRANCE ISLAM S/ASIA CONSTN SOCIETY STRUCT INT/ORG NAT/G ECO/TAC ADMIN COLONIAL NAT/LISM ATTIT PWR...DECISION TREND 420 UN. PAGE 7 A0133
PLAN
RIGID/FLEX
DIPLOM
ALGERIA

B59
BALL M.M.,NATO AND THE EUROPEAN MOVEMENT. EUR+WWI USA+45 INT/ORG FORCES BAL/PWR EDU/PROP LEGIT REGION ATTIT ORD/FREE PWR...STAT OBS TIME/SEQ TREND CHARTS ORG/CHARTS STERTYP COLD/WAR EEC OEEC 20 NATO. PAGE 10 A0212
DELIB/GP
STRUCT

B59
BLOOMFIELD L.P.,WESTERN EUROPE AND THE UN - TRENDS AND PROSPECTS. EUR+WWI BAL/PWR DIPLOM ECO/TAC COLONIAL ATTIT PWR...POLICY 20 UN EUROPE/W. PAGE 16 A0316
INT/ORG
TREND
FUT
NAT/G

B59
BRODIE B.,STRATEGY IN THE MISSILE AGE. FUT WOR+45 CONSULT PLAN COERCE DETER RIGID/FLEX PWR...CONCPT TIME/SEQ TREND 20. PAGE 19 A0381
ACT/RES
FORCES
ARMS/CONT
NUC/PWR

B59
BROOKES E.H.,THE COMMONWEALTH TODAY. UK ROMAN/EMP INT/ORG RACE/REL NAT/LISM SOVEREIGN...TREND SOC/INTEG 20. PAGE 19 A0391
FEDERAL
DIPLOM
JURID
IDEA/COMP

B59
HERZ J.H.,INTERNATIONAL POLITICS IN THE ATOMIC AGE. FUT USA+45 WOR+45 WOR-45 SOCIETY NAT/G FORCES PLAN COERCE DETER ATTIT DRIVE ORD/FREE PWR...TREND COLD/WAR 20. PAGE 64 A1319
INT/ORG
ARMS/CONT
NUC/PWR

B59
LAQUER W.Z.,THE SOVIET UNION AND THE MIDDLE EAST. COM UAR USSR ECO/UNDEV NAT/G VOL/ASSN ECO/TAC EDU/PROP COLONIAL EXEC PWR...TIME/SEQ TREND COLD/WAR 20. PAGE 85 A1730
ISLAM
DRIVE
FOR/AID
NAT/LISM

B59
MATHISEN T.,METHODOLOGY IN THE STUDY OF INTERNATIONAL RELATIONS. FUT WOR+45 SOCIETY INT/ORG NAT/G POL/PAR WAR PEACE KNOWL PWR...RELATIV CONCPT METH/CNCPT TREND HYPO/EXP METH TOT/POP 20. PAGE 96 A1965
GEN/METH
CON/ANAL
DIPLOM
CREATE

B59
MAYER A.J.,"POLITICAL ORIGINS OF THE NEW DIPLOMACY, 1917-1918. EUR+WWI MOD/EUR USA-45 WAR PWR...POLICY INT/LAW BIBLIOG. PAGE 97 A1983
TREND DIPLOM

B59
PANHUYS H.F.,THE ROLE OF NATIONALITY IN INTERNATIONAL LAW. ADJUD CRIME WAR STRANGE...JURID TREND. PAGE 114 A2330
INT/LAW NAT/LISM INGP/REL

B59
PEARSON L.B.,DIPLOMACY IN THE NUCLEAR AGE. USA+45 USSR INT/ORG PWR...TREND 20 NATO UN. PAGE 114 A2343
NUC/PWR PEACE POLICY DIPLOM

L59
MURPHY J.C.,"SOME IMPLICATIONS OF EUROPE'S COMMON MARKET. IN (COOK P, ECONOMIC DEVELOPMENT AND INTERNATIONAL TRADE,." EUR+WWI ECO/DEV DIST/IND INDUS NAT/G PLAN ECO/TAC INT/TRADE WEALTH...STAT TREND OEEC TOT/POP 20 EEC. PAGE 106 A2178
MARKET INT/ORG REGION

S59
BAILEY S.D.,"THE FUTURE COMPOSITION OF THE TRUSTEESHIP COUNCIL." FUT WOR+45 CONSTN VOL/ASSN ADMIN ATTIT PWR...OBS TREND CON/ANAL VAL/FREE UN 20. PAGE 10 A0203
INT/ORG NAT/LISM SOVEREIGN

S59
BOULDING K.E.,"NATIONAL IMAGES AND INTERNATIONAL SYSTEMS." FUT WOR+45 CULTURE INT/ORG TOP/EX ROUTINE ...METH/CNCPT MYTH CONT/OBS TREND HYPO/EXP GEN/METH TOT/POP 20. PAGE 17 A0346
NAT/G DIPLOM

S59
CARLSTON K.S.,"NATIONALIZATION: AN ANALYTIC APPROACH." WOR+45 INT/ORG ECO/TAC DOMIN LEGIT ADJUD COERCE ORD/FREE PWR WEALTH SOCISM...JURID CONCPT TREND STERTYP TOT/POP VAL/FREE 20. PAGE 24 A0486
INDUS NAT/G NAT/LISM SOVEREIGN

S59
KINDLEBERGER C.P.,"UNITED STATES ECONOMIC FOREIGN POLICY: RESEARCH REQUIREMENTS FOR 1965." FUT USA+45 WOR+45 DIST/IND MARKET INT/ORG ECO/TAC INT/TRADE WEALTH...OBS TREND CON/ANAL GEN/LAWS VAL/FREE 20. PAGE 79 A1621
FINAN ECO/DEV FOR/AID

S59
KOHN L.Y.,"ISRAEL AND NEW NATION STATES OF ASIA AND AFRICA." AFR ASIA FUT S/ASIA VOL/ASSN TEC/DEV NAT/LISM RIGID/FLEX SKILL WEALTH...RELATIV OBS TREND CON/ANAL 20. PAGE 81 A1663
ECO/UNDEV ECO/TAC FOR/AID ISRAEL

S59
PLAZA G.,"FOR A REGIONAL MARKET IN LATIN AMERICA." FUT L/A+17C CULTURE INDUS NAT/G ECO/TAC INT/TRADE ATTIT WEALTH...NEW/IDEA TREND OAS 20. PAGE 116 A2389
MARKET INT/ORG REGION

S59
REUBENS E.D.,"THE BASIS FOR REORIENATION OF AMERICAN FOREIGN AID POLICY." USA+45 USSR STRUCT INT/ORG CONSULT ECO/TAC ADMIN DRIVE MORAL ORD/FREE PWR WEALTH...RELATIV MATH STAT TREND GEN/LAWS VAL/FREE 20. PAGE 120 A2467
ECO/UNDEV PLAN FOR/AID DIPLOM

S59
SAYEGH F.,"ARAB NATIONALISM AND SOVIET-AMERICAN RELATIONS." ISLAM USA+45 ECO/UNDEV PLAN ECO/TAC LEGIT NAT/LISM DRIVE PERCEPT KNOWL PWR...DECISION CONCPT STAT RECORD TREND CON/ANAL VAL/FREE 20 COLD/WAR. PAGE 127 A2610
DIPLOM USSR

S59
SIMONS H.,"WORLD-WIDE CAPABILITIES FOR PRODUCTION AND CONTROL OF NUCLEAR WEAPONS." FUT WOR+45 INDUS INT/ORG NAT/G ECO/TAC ATTIT PWR SKILL...TREND CHARTS VAL/FREE 20. PAGE 133 A2719
TEC/DEV ARMS/CONT NUC/PWR

S59
SOLDATI A.,"EOCNOMIC DISINTEGRATION IN EUROPE." EUR+WWI FUT WOR+45 INDUS INT/ORG NAT/G CAP/ISM WEALTH...NEW/IDEA OBS TREND CHARTS EEC 20. PAGE 135 A2764
FINAN ECO/TAC

B60
ALLEN H.C.,THE ANGLO-AMERICAN PREDICAMENT: THE BRITISH COMMONWEALTH, THE UNITED STATES AND EUROPEAN UNITY. EUR+WWI FUT UK USA+45 WOR+45 ECO/DEV NAT/G PLAN DETER...CONCPT OBS TIME/SEQ TREND COLD/WAR VAL/FREE CMN/WLTH 20. PAGE 6 A0123
INT/ORG PWR BAL/PWR

B60
ALLEN R.L.,SOVIET ECONOMIC WARFARE. USSR FINAN INDUS NAT/G PLAN TEC/DEV FOR/AID DETER WEALTH ...TREND GEN/LAWS 20. PAGE 6 A0126
COM ECO/TAC

B60
APTHEKER H.,DISARMAMENT AND THE AMERICAN ECONOMY: A SYMPOSIUM. FUT USA+45 ECO/DEV DIST/IND FINAN INDUS PROC/MFG LABOR NAT/G POL/PAR CONSULT PLAN CAP/ISM INT/TRADE PEACE ATTIT MORAL WEALTH...TREND GEN/LAWS TOT/POP 20. PAGE 9 A0172
MARXIST ARMS/CONT

B60
BAILEY S.D.,THE GENERAL ASSEMBLY OF THE UNITED NATIONS. FUT WOR+45 STRUCT LEGIS ACT/RES PLAN EDU/PROP LEGIT ADMIN EXEC PEACE ATTIT HEALTH PWR ...CONCPT TREND CHARTS GEN/LAWS UN TOT/POP VAL/FREE COLD/WAR 20. PAGE 10 A0204
INT/ORG DELIB/GP DIPLOM

B60
BILLERBECK K.,SOVIET BLOC FOREIGN AID TO UNDERDEVELOPED COUNTRIES. COM FUT USSR FINAN FORCES TEC/DEV DIPLOM INT/TRADE EDU/PROP NUC/PWR...TREND 20. PAGE 14 A0287
FOR/AID ECO/UNDEV ECO/TAC MARXISM

B60
BLACK E.R.,THE DIPLOMACY OF ECONOMIC DEVELOPMENT. WOR+45 CONSULT PLAN TEC/DEV DIPLOM ECO/TAC FOR/AID ...CONCPT TREND 20. PAGE 15 A0297
ECO/UNDEV ACT/RES

B60
BUCHAN A.,NATO IN THE 1960'S. EUR+WWI USA+45 WOR+45 INT/ORG ACT/RES PLAN LEGIT COERCE DETER ATTIT DRIVE RIGID/FLEX ORD/FREE...METH/CNCPT TIME/SEQ TREND GEN/LAWS COLD/WAR 20 NATO. PAGE 21 A0421
VOL/ASSN FORCES ARMS/CONT SOVEREIGN

B60
CAMPAIGNE J.G.,AMERICAN MIGHT AND SOVIET MYTH. COM EUR+WWI ECO/DEV ECO/UNDEV INT/ORG NAT/G CAP/ISM ECO/TAC FOR/AID EDU/PROP ATTIT PWR WEALTH...POLICY CONCPT MYTH TREND STERTYP GEN/LAWS COLD/WAR. PAGE 23 A0473
USA+45 DOMIN DIPLOM USSR

B60
CARNEGIE ENDOWMENT INT. PEACE,PERSPECTIVES ON PEACE - 1910-1960. WOR+45 WOR-45 INTELL INT/ORG CONSULT ACT/RES EDU/PROP ATTIT KNOWL ORD/FREE...TIME/SEQ TREND EEC OAS UNESCO NAZI 20. PAGE 24 A0489
FUT CONCPT ARMS/CONT PEACE

B60
CENTRAL ASIAN RESEARCH CENTRE,RUSSIA LOOKS AT AFRICA (PAMPHLET). AFR USSR COLONIAL RACE/REL...HUM 19/20 STALIN/J. PAGE 25 A0511
BIBLIOG MARXISM TREND DIPLOM

B60
DUMON F.,LA COMMUNAUTE FRANCO-AFRO-MALGACHE: SES ORIGINES, SES INSTITUTIONS, SON EVOLUTION. FRANCE MADAGASCAR POL/PAR DIPLOM ADMIN ATTIT...TREND T 20. PAGE 39 A0798
JURID INT/ORG AFR CONSTN

B60
ENGEL J.,THE SECURITY OF THE FREE WORLD. USSR WOR+45 STRATA STRUCT ECO/DEV ECO/UNDEV INT/ORG DELIB/GP FORCES DOMIN LEGIT ADJUD EXEC ARMS/CONT COERCE...POLICY CONCPT NEW/IDEA TIME/SEQ GEN/LAWS COLD/WAR WORK UN 20 NATO. PAGE 42 A0851
COM TREND DIPLOM

B60
FRANCK P.G.,AFGHANISTAN: BETWEEN EAST AND WEST. AFGHANISTN USA+45 USSR ECO/UNDEV PLAN ADMIN ROUTINE ATTIT PWR...STAT OBS CHARTS TOT/POP COLD/WAR 20. PAGE 48 A0978
ECO/TAC TREND FOR/AID

B60
JENNINGS R.,PROGRESS OF INTERNATIONAL LAW. FUT WOR+45 WOR-45 SOCIETY NAT/G VOL/ASSN DELIB/GP DIPLOM EDU/PROP LEGIT COERCE ATTIT DRIVE MORAL ORD/FREE...JURID CONCPT OBS TIME/SEQ TREND GEN/LAWS. PAGE 74 A1509
INT/ORG LAW INT/LAW

B60
KRISTENSEN T.,THE ECONOMIC WORLD BALANCE. FUT WOR+45 CULTURE ECO/DEV BAL/PWR INT/TRADE REGION PWR WEALTH...STAT TREND CHARTS 20. PAGE 82 A1685
ECO/UNDEV ECO/TAC FOR/AID

B60
LINDSAY K.,EUROPEAN ASSEMBLIES: THE EXPERIMENTAL PERIOD 1949-1959. EUR+WWI ECO/DEV NAT/G POL/PAR LEGIS TOP/EX ACT/RES PLAN ECO/TAC DOMIN LEGIT ROUTINE ATTIT DRIVE ORD/FREE PWR SKILL...SOC CONCPT TREND CHARTS GEN/LAWS VAL/FREE. PAGE 89 A1823
VOL/ASSN INT/ORG REGION

B60
LISKA G.,THE NEW STATECRAFT. WOR+45 WOR-45 LEGIS DIPLOM ADMIN ATTIT PWR WEALTH...HIST/WRIT TREND COLD/WAR 20. PAGE 90 A1837
ECO/TAC CONCPT FOR/AID

B60
MUNRO L.,UNITED NATIONS, HOPE FOR A DIVIDED WORLD. FUT WOR+45 CONSTN DELIB/GP CREATE TEC/DEV DIPLOM EDU/PROP LEGIT PEACE ATTIT HEALTH ORD/FREE PWR ...CONCPT TREND UN VAL/FREE 20. PAGE 106 A2172
INT/ORG ROUTINE

B60
PENTONY D.E.,THE UNDERDEVELOPED LANDS. FUT WOR+45 CULTURE AGRI FINAN INDUS MARKET INT/ORG LABOR NAT/G VOL/ASSN CONSULT TEC/DEV ECO/TAC EDU/PROP COLONIAL ATTIT WEALTH...OBS RECORD SAMP TREND GEN/METH WORK UN 20. PAGE 115 A2351
ECO/UNDEV POLICY FOR/AID INT/TRADE

B60
PHILLIPS J.F.V.,KWAME NKRUMAH AND THE FUTURE OF AFRICA. FUT GHANA ISLAM ECO/UNDEV CHIEF DIPLOM COLONIAL RACE/REL NAT/LISM...TREND IDEA/COMP BIBLIOG 20 NKRUMAH/K. PAGE 116 A2376
BIOG LEAD SOVEREIGN AFR

B60
PLAMENATZ J.,ON ALIEN RULE AND SELF-GOVERNMENT. AFR FUT S/ASIA WOR+45 CULTURE SOCIETY ECO/UNDEV INT/ORG DOMIN EDU/PROP ATTIT RIGID/FLEX ALL/VALS...POLICY CONCPT OBS TREND CON/ANAL GEN/LAWS TOT/POP VAL/FREE. PAGE 116 A2386
NAT/G CONSTN NAT/LISM SOVEREIGN

B60
STEIN E.,AMERICAN ENTERPRISE IN THE EUROPEAN COMMON MARKET: A LEGAL PROFILE. EUR+WWI FUT USA+45 SOCIETY STRUCT ECO/DEV NAT/G VOL/ASSN CONSULT PLAN TEC/DEV ECO/TAC INT/TRADE ADMIN ATTIT RIGID/FLEX PWR...MGT NEW/IDEA STAT TREND COMPUT/IR SIMUL EEC 20. PAGE 137 A2814
MARKET ADJUD INT/LAW

B60
TAYLOR M.D.,THE UNCERTAIN TRUMPET. USA+45 USSR WOR+45 INT/ORG NAT/G CONSULT DOMIN COERCE NUC/PWR
PLAN FORCES

WAR ATTIT ORD/FREE PWR...POLICY CONCPT TREND GEN/METH COLD/WAR UN NATO 20. PAGE 142 A2900
DIPLOM

B60
THEOBALD R.,THE RICH AND THE POOR: A STUDY OF THE ECONOMICS OF RISING EXPECTATIONS. WOR+45 CONSTN ECO/DEV ECO/UNDEV INT/ORG NAT/G PLAN FOR/AID ROUTINE BAL/PAY ORD/FREE PWR WEALTH...GEOG TREND WORK 20. PAGE 142 A2912
ECO/TAC
INT/TRADE

B60
WOETZEL R.K.,THE INTERNATIONAL CONTROL OF AIRSPACE AND OUTERSPACE. FUT WOR+45 AIR CONSTN STRUCT CONSULT PLAN TEC/DEV ADJUD RIGID/FLEX KNOWL ORD/FREE PWR...TECHNIC GEOG MGT NEW/IDEA TREND COMPUT/IR VAL/FREE 20 TREATY. PAGE 166 A3375
INT/ORG
JURID
SPACE
INT/LAW

L60
BRENNAN D.G.,"SETTING AND GOALS OF ARMS CONTROL." FUT USA+45 USSR WOR+45 INTELL INT/ORG NAT/G VOL/ASSN CONSULT PLAN DIPLOM ECO/TAC ADMIN KNOWL PWR...POLICY CONCPT TREND COLD/WAR 20. PAGE 18 A0371
FORCES
COERCE
ARMS/CONT
DETER

L60
DEAN A.W.,"SECOND GENEVA CONFERENCE OF THE LAW OF THE SEA: THE FIGHT FOR FREEDOM OF THE SEAS." FUT USA+45 USSR WOR+45 WOR-45 SEA CONSTN STRUCT PLAN INT/TRADE ADJUD ADMIN ORD/FREE...DECISION RECORD TREND GEN/LAWS 20 TREATY. PAGE 35 A0717
INT/ORG
JURID
INT/LAW

L60
DEUTSCH K.W.,"TOWARD AN INVENTORY OF BASIC TRENDS AND PATTERNS IN COMPARATIVE AND INTERNATIONAL POLITICS." UNIV WOR+45 SOCIETY STRUCT INT/ORG NAT/G CREATE PLAN EDU/PROP KNOWL...PHIL/SCI METH/CNCPT STAT SELF/OBS OBS/ENVIR SAMP TREND CON/ANAL CHARTS SOC/EXP GEN/METH 20. PAGE 36 A0739
R+D
PERCEPT

L60
FERNBACH A.P.,"SOVIET COEXISTENCE STRATEGY." WOR+45 PROF/ORG VOL/ASSN DIPLOM DOMIN EDU/PROP ATTIT DRIVE PERSON PWR SKILL WEALTH...POLICY OBS SAMP TREND STERTYP ILO WORK COLD/WAR 420. PAGE 45 A0919
LABOR
INT/ORG
USSR

L60
HOLTON G.,"ARMS CONTROL." FUT WOR+45 CULTURE INT/ORG NAT/G FORCES TOP/EX PLAN EDU/PROP COERCE ATTIT RIGID/FLEX ORD/FREE...POLICY PHIL/SCI SOC TREND COLD/WAR. PAGE 67 A1377
ACT/RES
CONSULT
ARMS/CONT
NUC/PWR

L60
KUNZ J.,"SANCTIONS IN INTERNATIONAL LAW." WOR+45 WOR-45 LEGIT ARMS/CONT COERCE PEACE ATTIT ...METH/CNCPT TIME/SEQ TREND 20. PAGE 83 A1695
INT/ORG
ADJUD
INT/LAW

L60
MCCLELLAND C.A.,"THE FUNCTION OF THEORY IN INTERNATIONAL RELATIONS." WOR+45 PLAN EDU/PROP ROUTINE ORD/FREE...PHIL/SCI PSY SOC METH/CNCPT NEW/IDEA OBS TREND GEN/METH 20. PAGE 97 A1997
INT/ORG
CONCPT
DIPLOM

S60
CLARK W.,"NEW FORCES IN THE UN." FUT UK WOR+45 CONSTN BAL/PWR DIPLOM DRIVE PWR SKILL...CONCPT TREND UN TOT/POP 20. PAGE 27 A0543
INT/ORG
ECO/UNDEV
SOVEREIGN

S60
COHEN A.,"THE NEW AFRICA AND THE UN." FUT ECO/UNDEV NAT/G ECO/TAC INT/TRADE CHOOSE ATTIT ORD/FREE PWR ...POLICY METH/CNCPT OBS TREND CON/ANAL GEN/LAWS TOT/POP VAL/FREE UN 20. PAGE 27 A0558
AFR
INT/ORG
BAL/PWR
FOR/AID

S60
DOUGHERTY J.E.,"KEY TO SECURITY: DISARMAMENT OR ARMS STABILITY." COM USA+45 USSR INT/ORG NAT/G CREATE EDU/PROP COERCE DETER ATTIT PWR...DECISION CONCPT MYTH NEW/IDEA TREND 20 COLD/WAR. PAGE 38 A0777
FORCES
ORD/FREE
ARMS/CONT
NUC/PWR

S60
EFIMENCO N.M.,"CATEGORIES OF INTERNATIONAL INTEGRATION." UNIV WOR+45 INT/ORG NAT/G ACT/RES CREATE PEACE...CONCPT TREND 20. PAGE 40 A0824
PLAN
BAL/PWR
SOVEREIGN

S60
GARNICK D.H.,"ON THE ECONOMIC FEASIBILITY OF A MIDDLE EASTERN COMMON MARKET." AFR ISLAM CULTURE INDUS NAT/G PLAN TEC/DEV ECO/TAC ADMIN ATTIT DRIVE RIGID/FLEX...PLURIST STAT TREND GEN/LAWS 20. PAGE 51 A1051
MARKET
INT/TRADE

S60
GINSBURGS G.,"PEKING-LHASA-NEW DELHI." CHINA/COM FUT INDIA S/ASIA KIN NAT/G PROVS SECT FORCES BAL/PWR ECO/TAC DOMIN EDU/PROP LEGIT ADMIN REGION GUERRILLA PWR...TREND TIBET 20. PAGE 52 A1074
ASIA
COERCE
DIPLOM

S60
GULICK E.V.,"OUR BALANCE OF POWER SYSTEM IN PERSPECTIVE." FUT WOR+45 WOR-45 ECO/DEV DOMIN ROUTINE NUC/PWR PEACE PWR WEALTH...PLURIST CONCPT HIST/WRIT GEN/METH TOT/POP 20. PAGE 58 A1191
INT/ORG
TREND
ARMS/CONT
BAL/PWR

S60
HAVILAND H.F.,"PROBLEMS OF AMERICAN FOREIGN POLICY." ASIA COM USA+45 WOR+45 INT/ORG NAT/G CONSULT ECO/TAC FOR/AID DOMIN COERCE NUC/PWR ATTIT DRIVE ORD/FREE PWR RESPECT SKILL...POLICY GEOG OBS SAMP TREND GEN/METH METH COLD/WAR UN 20. PAGE 63 A1292
ECO/UNDEV
FORCES
DIPLOM

S60
IKLE F.C.,"NTH COUNTRIES AND DISARMAMENT." WOR+45
FUT

DELIB/GP ECO/TAC DOMIN EDU/PROP LEGIT ROUTINE COERCE RIGID/FLEX ORD/FREE...MARXIST TREND 20. PAGE 70 A1432
INT/ORG
ARMS/CONT
NUC/PWR

S60
KENNAN G.F.,"PEACEFUL CO-EXISTENCE: A WESTERN VIEW." COM EUR+WWI USA+45 USSR WOR+45 PLAN BAL/PWR DIPLOM INT/TRADE PWR...POLICY CONCPT OBS HIST/WRIT TREND GEN/LAWS COLD/WAR 20 KHRUSH/N. PAGE 78 A1589
ATTIT
COERCE

S60
KISTIAKOWSKY G.B.,"SCIENCE AND FOREIGN AFFAIRS." FUT WOR+45 NAT/G PROF/ORG PLAN ECO/TAC EDU/PROP NUC/PWR...TREND COLD/WAR 20. PAGE 80 A1645
CONSULT
TEC/DEV
FOR/AID
DIPLOM

S60
LYON P.,"NEUTRALITY AND THE EMERGENCE OF THE CONCEPT OF NEUTRALISM." WOR+45 WOR-45 INT/ORG NAT/G BAL/PWR NEUTRAL ATTIT PWR...POLICY TIME/SEQ TREND COLD/WAR TOT/POP VAL/FREE 20 UN. PAGE 92 A1878
CONCPT

S60
MAGATHAN W.,"SOME BASES OF WEST GERMAN MILITARY POLICY." EUR+WWI FUT INT/ORG TOP/EX ECO/TAC DOMIN DRIVE ORD/FREE PWR...TRADIT GEOG OBS TREND. PAGE 93 A1904
NAT/G
FORCES
GERMANY

S60
MORGENSTERN O.,"GOAL: AN ARMED, INSPECTED, OPEN WORLD." COM EUR+WWI USA+45 R+D INT/ORG NAT/G TEC/DEV BAL/PWR COERCE NUC/PWR ORD/FREE PWR...TREND 20. PAGE 104 A2133
FORCES
CONCPT
ARMS/CONT
DETER

S60
MUNRO L.,"CAN THE UNITED NATIONS ENFORCE PEACE." WOR+45 LAW INT/ORG VOL/ASSN BAL/PWR LEGIT ARMS/CONT COERCE DETER PEACE PWR...CONCPT REC/INT TREND UN 20 HAMMARSK/D. PAGE 106 A2173
FORCES
ORD/FREE

S60
O'BRIEN W.,"THE ROLE OF FORCE IN THE INTERNATIONAL JURIDICAL ORDER." WOR+45 NAT/G FORCES DOMIN ADJUD ARMS/CONT DETER NUC/PWR WAR ATTIT PWR...CATH INT/LAW JURID CONCPT TREND STERTYP GEN/LAWS 20. PAGE 110 A2266
INT/ORG
COERCE

S60
OWEN C.F.,"US AND SOVIET RELATIONS WITH UNDERDEVELOPED COUNTRIES: LATIN AMERICA-A CASE STUDY." AFR COM L/A+17C USA+45 USSR EXTR/IND MARKET TEC/DEV DIPLOM ECO/TAC NAT/LISM ORD/FREE PWR ...TREND WORK 20. PAGE 112 A2303
ECO/UNDEV
DRIVE
INT/TRADE

S60
PETERSON E.N.,"HISTORICAL SCHOLARSHIP AND WORLD UNITY." FUT UNIV WOR-45 CULTURE INTELL INT/ORG NAT/G ACT/RES EDU/PROP ATTIT PERCEPT RIGID/FLEX ...NEW/IDEA OBS HIST/WRIT TREND COLD/WAR TOT/POP 20. PAGE 115 A2367
PLAN
KNOWL
NAT/LISM

S60
PYE L.W.,"SOVIET AND AMERICAN STYLES IN FOREIGN AID." COM USA+45 USSR WOR+45 NAT/G PLAN ECO/TAC ROUTINE RIGID/FLEX...POLICY CONCPT TREND GEN/LAWS TOT/POP 20. PAGE 118 A2419
ECO/UNDEV
ATTIT
FOR/AID

S60
RHYNE C.S.,"LAW AS AN INSTRUMENT FOR PEACE." FUT WOR+45 PLAN LEGIT ROUTINE ARMS/CONT NUC/PWR ATTIT ORD/FREE...JURID METH/CNCPT TREND CON/ANAL HYPO/EXP COLD/WAR 20. PAGE 120 A2471
ADJUD
EDU/PROP
INT/LAW
PEACE

S60
SCHACHTER O.,"THE ENFORCEMENT OF INTERNATIONAL JUDICIAL AND ARBITRAL DECISIONS." WOR+45 NAT/G ECO/TAC DOMIN LEGIT ROUTINE COERCE ATTIT DRIVE ALL/VALS PWR...METH/CNCPT TREND TOT/POP 20 UN. PAGE 128 A2615
INT/ORG
ADJUD
INT/LAW

S60
SCHWELB E.,"INTERNATIONAL CONVENTIONS ON HUMAN RIGHTS." FUT WOR+45 LAW CONSTN CULTURE SOCIETY STRUCT VOL/ASSN DELIB/GP PLAN ADJUD SUPEGO LOVE MORAL...SOC CONCPT STAT RECORD HIST/WRIT TREND 20 UN. PAGE 130 A2664
INT/ORG
HUM

S60
THOMPSON K.W.,"MORAL PURPOSE IN FOREIGN POLICY: REALITIES AND ILLUSIONS." WOR+45 WOR-45 LAW CULTURE SOCIETY INT/ORG PLAN ADJUD ADMIN COERCE RIGID/FLEX SUPEGO KNOWL ORD/FREE PWR...SOC TREND SOC/EXP TOT/POP 20. PAGE 143 A2930
MORAL
JURID
DIPLOM

S60
WRIGHT Q.,"LEGAL ASPECTS OF THE U-2 INCIDENT." COM USA+45 USSR STRUCT NAT/G FORCES PLAN TEC/DEV ADJUD RIGID/FLEX MORAL ORD/FREE...DECISION INT/LAW JURID PSY TREND GEN/LAWS COLD/WAR VAL/FREE 20 U-2. PAGE 168 A3413
PWR
POLICY
SPACE

N60
ERDMAN P.E.,COMMON MARKETS AND FREE TRADE AREAS (PAMPHLET). USA+45 MARKET INT/ORG TEC/DEV DIPLOM UTIL...CON/ANAL CHARTS BIBLIOG 20 EEC OEEC. PAGE 42 A0859
TREND
PROB/SOLV
INT/TRADE
ECO/DEV

B61
ANAND R.P.,COMPULSORY JURISDICTION OF INTERNATIONAL COURT OF JUSTICE. FUT WOR+45 SOCIETY PLAN LEGIT ADJUD ATTIT DRIVE PERSON ORD/FREE...JURID CONCPT TREND 20 ICJ. PAGE 8 A0156
INT/ORG
COERCE
INT/LAW

B61
BAGU S.,ARGENTINA EN EL MUNDO. L/A+17C INDUS INT/TRADE WAR ATTIT ROLE...TREND 19/20 ARGEN OAS. PAGE 10 A0202
DIPLOM INT/ORG REGION ECO/UNDEV

B61
BARNES W.,THE FOREIGN SERVICE OF THE UNITED STATES. USA+45 USA-45 CONSTN INT/ORG POL/PAR CONSULT DELIB/GP LEGIS DOMIN EDU/PROP EXEC ATTIT RIGID/FLEX ORD/FREE PWR...POLICY CONCPT STAT OBS RECORD BIOG TIME/SEQ TREND. PAGE 11 A0224
NAT/G MGT DIPLOM

B61
BONNEFOUS M.,EUROPE ET TIERS MONDE. EUR+WWI SOCIETY INT/ORG NAT/G VOL/ASSN ACT/RES TEC/DEV CAP/ISM ECO/TAC ATTIT ORD/FREE SOVEREIGN...POLICY CONCPT TREND 20. PAGE 16 A0334
AFR ECO/UNDEV FOR/AID INT/TRADE

B61
BULL H.,THE CONTROL OF THE ARMS RACE. COM USA+45 INT/ORG NAT/G PLAN TEC/DEV DIPLOM ATTIT...RELATIV DECISION CONCPT SELF/OBS TREND CON/ANAL GEN/METH 20 COLD/WAR. PAGE 21 A0429
FORCES PWR ARMS/CONT NUC/PWR

B61
EINZIG P.,A DYNAMIC THEORY OF FORWARD EXCHANGE. FUT WOR+45 WOR-45 INT/TRADE BAL/PAY WEALTH...OLD/LIB NEW/IDEA OBS TREND 20. PAGE 41 A0830
FINAN ECO/TAC

B61
HANCOCK W.K.,FOUR STUDIES OF WAR AND PEACE IN THIS CENTURY. FUT WOR+45 WOR-45 ACT/RES LEGIT DETER HEALTH...TREND ANTHOL TOT/POP VAL/FREE UN 20. PAGE 61 A1250
INT/ORG POLICY ARMS/CONT

B61
JENKS C.W.,INTERNATIONAL IMMUNITIES. PLAN EDU/PROP ADMIN PERCEPT...OLD/LIB JURID CONCPT TREND TOT/POP. PAGE 74 A1506
INT/ORG DIPLOM

B61
KERTESZ S.D.,AMERICAN DIPLOMACY IN A NEW ERA. COM S/ASIA UK USA+45 FORCES PROB/SOLV BAL/PWR ECO/TAC ADMIN COLONIAL WAR PEACE ORD/FREE 20 NATO CONGRESS UN COLD/WAR. PAGE 78 A1601
ANTHOL DIPLOM TREND

B61
KISSINGER H.A.,THE NECESSITY FOR CHOICE. FUT USA+45 ECO/UNDEV NAT/G PLAN BAL/PWR ECO/TAC ARMS/CONT DETER NUC/PWR ATTIT...POLICY CONCPT RECORD GEN/LAWS COLD/WAR 20. PAGE 80 A1642
TOP/EX TREND DIPLOM

B61
KITZINGER V.W.,THE CHALLENGE OF THE COMMON MARKET. EUR+WWI ECO/DEV DIST/IND PLAN ECO/TAC INT/TRADE LEGIT ATTIT PWR WEALTH...TIME/SEQ TREND CHARTS EEC 20. PAGE 80 A1647
MARKET INT/ORG UK

B61
LERCHE C.O. JR.,FOREIGN POLICY OF THE AMERICAN PEOPLE (REV. ED.). USA+45 USSR FORCES TEC/DEV EDU/PROP WAR PRODUC ORD/FREE MARXISM...POLICY TREND BIBLIOG 20 COLD/WAR. PAGE 87 A1781
DECISION PLAN PEACE DIPLOM

B61
LUKACS J.,A HISTORY OF THE COLD WAR. ASIA COM EUR+WWI USA+45 INT/ORG NAT/G DELIB/GP ACT/RES BAL/PWR DIPLOM DOMIN EDU/PROP LEGIT DRIVE ORD/FREE...TREND COLD/WAR 20. PAGE 91 A1872
PWR TIME/SEQ USSR

B61
MCDOUGAL M.S.,LAW AND MINIMUM WORLD PUBLIC ORDER. WOR+45 SOCIETY NAT/G DELIB/GP EDU/PROP LEGIT ADJUD COERCE ATTIT PERSON...JURID CONCPT RECORD TREND TOT/POP 20. PAGE 98 A2006
INT/ORG ORD/FREE INT/LAW

B61
SLESSOR J.,WHAT PRICE COEXISTENCE? COM INT/ORG NAT/G FORCES COLONIAL ARMS/CONT WAR...POLICY TREND 20 NATO COLD/WAR. PAGE 134 A2741
DIPLOM PEACE WOR+45 NUC/PWR

B61
STRAUSZ-HUPE R.,A FORWARD STRATEGY FOR AMERICA. FUT WOR+45 ECO/DEV INT/ORG NAT/G POL/PAR DELIB/GP FORCES ACT/RES CREATE ECO/TAC DOMIN EDU/PROP ATTIT DRIVE PWR...MAJORIT CONCPT STAT OBS TIME/SEQ TREND COLD/WAR TOT/POP. PAGE 139 A2848
USA+45 PLAN DIPLOM

B61
THEOBALD R.,THE CHALLENGE OF ABUNDANCE. USA+45 WOR+45 MARKET DIPLOM FOR/AID REV PRODUC UTOPIA SUPEGO...POLICY TREND BIBLIOG/A 20. PAGE 142 A2913
WELF/ST ECO/UNDEV PROB/SOLV ECO/TAC

B61
WARNER D.,HURRICANE FROM CHINA. ASIA CHINA/COM FUT L/A+17C USA+45 CULTURE NAT/G FORCES TOP/EX FOR/AID DRIVE PWR...CONCPT TIME/SEQ SEATO WORK 20. PAGE 161 A3284
ATTIT TREND REV

B61
WRIGHT Q.,THE ROLE OF INTERNATIONAL LAW IN THE ELIMINATION OF WAR. FUT WOR+45 WOR-45 NAT/G BAL/PWR DIPLOM DOMIN LEGIT PWR...POLICY INT/LAW JURID CONCPT TIME/SEQ TREND GEN/LAWS COLD/WAR 20. PAGE 168 A3414
INT/ORG ADJUD ARMS/CONT

B61
YDIT M.,INTERNATIONALISED TERRITORIES. FUT WOR+45 WOR-45 CONSTN VOL/ASSN CREATE PLAN LEGIT PEACE ORD/FREE...GEOG INT/LAW JURID SOC NEW/IDEA OBS RECORD SAMP TIME/SEQ TREND 19/20 BERLIN. PAGE 169 A3431
LOC/G INT/ORG DIPLOM SOVEREIGN

L61
CLAUDE I.,"THE UNITED NATIONS AND THE USE OF FORCE." FUT WOR+45 SOCIETY DIPLOM EDU/PROP LEGIT ADMIN ROUTINE COERCE WAR PEACE ORD/FREE...CONCPT TREND UN 20. PAGE 27 A0545
INT/ORG FORCES

L61
HALPERIN M.H.,"NUCLEAR WEAPONS AND LIMITED WARS." FUT UNIV WOR+45 INTELL SOCIETY ECO/DEV ACT/RES DRIVE PERCEPT RIGID/FLEX...CONCPT TIME/SEQ TREND TOT/POP 20. PAGE 60 A1237
PLAN COERCE NUC/PWR WAR

L61
HILSMAN R. JR.,"THE NEW COMMUNIST TACTIC: PRECIS-INTERNAL WAR." COM FUT USA+45 ECO/UNDEV POL/PAR FOR/AID RIGID/FLEX ALL/VALS...TREND COLD/WAR 20. PAGE 65 A1334
FORCES COERCE USSR GUERRILLA

L61
HOYT E.C.,"UNITED STATES REACTION TO THE KOREAN ATTACK." COM KOREA USA+45 CONSTN DELIB/GP FORCES PLAN ECO/TAC DOMIN EDU/PROP LEGIT ROUTINE COERCE WAR ATTIT DISPL RIGID/FLEX ORD/FREE PWR...POLICY INT/LAW TREND UN 20. PAGE 68 A1402
ASIA INT/ORG BAL/PWR DIPLOM

L61
SAND P.T.,"AN HISTORICAL SURVEY OF INTERNATIONAL AIR LAW SINCE 1944." USA+45 USA-45 WOR+45 WOR-45 SOCIETY ECO/DEV NAT/G CONSULT EX/STRUC ACT/RES PLAN LEGIT ROUTINE...JURID CONCPT METH/CNCPT TREND 20. PAGE 127 A2598
INT/ORG LAW INT/LAW SPACE

L61
TAUBENFELD H.J.,"A REGIME FOR OUTER SPACE." FUT UNIV R+D ACT/RES PLAN BAL/PWR LEGIT ARMS/CONT ORD/FREE...POLICY JURID TREND UN TOT/POP 20 COLD/WAR. PAGE 142 A2894
INT/ORG ADJUD SPACE

S61
BALL M.M.,"ISSUES FOR THE AMERICAS: NON-INTERVENTION VS HUMAN RIGHTS AND THE PRESERVATION OF DEMOCRATIC INSTITUTIONS." USA+45 INTELL INT/ORG NAT/G DIPLOM ECO/TAC LEGIT...TREND OAS TOT/POP 20. PAGE 11 A0213
L/A+17C MORAL

S61
BARNET R.,"RUSSIA, CHINA, AND THE WORLD: THE SOVIET ATTITUDE ON DISARMAMENT (PART 3)." ASIA CHINA/COM FUT INT/ORG NAT/G POL/PAR VOL/ASSN ARMS/CONT ATTIT ...POLICY CONCPT TIME/SEQ TREND TOT/POP VAL/FREE 20. PAGE 11 A0226
COM PLAN TOTALISM USSR

S61
HAAS E.B.,"INTERNATIONAL INTEGRATION: THE EUROPEAN AND THE UNIVERSAL PROCESS." EUR+WWI FUT WOR+45 NAT/G EX/STRUC ATTIT DRIVE ORD/FREE PWR...CONCPT GEN/LAWS OEEC 20 NATO COUNCL/EUR. PAGE 59 A1207
INT/ORG TREND REGION

S61
LANFALUSSY A.,"EUROPE'S PROGRESS: DUE TO COMMON MARKET." EUR+WWI ECO/DEV DELIB/GP PLAN ECO/TAC ROUTINE WEALTH...GEOG TREND EEC 20. PAGE 84 A1721
INT/ORG MARKET

S61
LIPSON L.,"AN ARGUMENT ON THE LEGALITY OF RECONNAISSANCE STATELLITES." COM USA+45 USSR WOR+45 AIR INTELL NAT/G CONSULT PLAN DIPLOM LEGIT ROUTINE ATTIT...INT/LAW JURID CONCPT METH/CNCPT TREND COLD/WAR 20. PAGE 90 A1833
INT/ORG LAW SPACE

S61
MACHOWSKI K.,"SELECTED PROBLEMS OF NATIONAL SOVEREIGNTY WITH REFERENCE TO THE LAW OF OUTER SPACE." FUT WOR+45 AIR LAW INTELL SOCIETY ECO/DEV PLAN EDU/PROP DETER DRIVE PERCEPT SOVEREIGN ...POLICY INT/LAW OBS TREND TOT/POP 20. PAGE 92 A1889
UNIV ACT/RES NUC/PWR SPACE

S61
MASTERS R.D.,"A MULTI-BLOC MODEL OF THE INTERNATIONAL SYSTEM." FUT UNIV WOR+45 SOCIETY ACT/RES PLAN...GEOG SOC TREND SIMUL TOT/POP 20. PAGE 96 A1963
INT/ORG CONCPT

S61
MIKSCHE F.O.,"DEFENSE ORGANIZATION FOR WESTERN EUROPE." USA+45 INT/ORG NAT/G VOL/ASSN ACT/RES DOMIN LEGIT COERCE ORD/FREE PWR...RELATIV TREND 20 NATO. PAGE 101 A2071
EUR+WWI FORCES WEAPON NUC/PWR

S61
RALEIGH J.S.,"THE MIDDLE EAST IN 1960: A POLITICAL SURVEY." FUT ISLAM INTELL KIN BAL/PWR EDU/PROP NAT/LISM...TREND VAL/FREE 20. PAGE 119 A2435
INT/ORG EX/STRUC

S61
ROSTOW W.W.,"THE FUTURE OF FOREIGN AID." COM FUT WOR+45 ECO/DEV INDUS INT/ORG NAT/G CONSULT ACT/RES PLAN DOMIN LEGIT CHOOSE RIGID/FLEX ALL/VALS ...MAJORIT CONCPT TREND TOT/POP 20. PAGE 124 A2544
ECO/UNDEV ECO/TAC FOR/AID

S61
TAUBENFELD H.J.,"OUTER SPACE--PAST POLITICS AND FUTURE POLICY." FUT USA+45 USA-45 WOR+45 AIR INTELL STRUCT ECO/DEV NAT/G TOP/EX ACT/RES ADMIN ROUTINE NUC/PWR ATTIT DRIVE...CONCPT TIME/SEQ TREND TOT/POP 20. PAGE 141 A2892
PLAN SPACE INT/ORG

S61
TRAMPE G.,"DIE FORM DER DIPLOMATIC ALS POLITSCHE WAFFE." WOR+45 WOR-45 SOCIETY STRATA INT/ORG NAT/G ACT/RES PLAN ECO/TAC EDU/PROP COERCE WAR ATTIT
CONSULT PWR DIPLOM

RIGID/FLEX...DECISION CONCPT TREND. PAGE 145 A2959

B62
ARNOLD H.J.P.,AID FOR DEVELOPING COUNTRIES. COM EUR+WWI USA+45 USSR WOR+45 EDU/PROP ATTIT DRIVE PWR WEALTH...TREND CHARTS STERTYP NAT/ 20. PAGE 9 A0177 ECO/UNDEV ECO/TAC FOR/AID

B62
BAILEY S.D.,THE SECRETARIAT OF THE UNITED NATIONS. FUT WOR+45 DELIB/GP PLAN BAL/PWR DOMIN EDU/PROP ADMIN PEACE ATTIT PWR...DECISION CONCPT TREND CON/ANAL CHARTS UN VAL/FREE COLD/WAR 20. PAGE 10 A0205 INT/ORG EXEC DIPLOM

B62
BELL C.,NEGOTIATION FROM STRENGTH. WOR+45 FACE/GP INT/ORG DELIB/GP FORCES PLAN DOMIN COERCE NUC/PWR PEACE DRIVE PWR...POLICY LOG OBS RECORD INT SAMP TREND COLD/WAR 20. PAGE 13 A0255 NAT/G CONCPT DIPLOM

B62
BOULDING K.E.,CONFLICT AND DEFENSE: A GENERAL THEORY. FUT SOCIETY INT/ORG NAT/G CREATE BAL/PWR COERCE NAT/LISM DRIVE ALL/VALS...PLURIST DECISION CONCPT METH/CNCPT TREND HYPO/EXP TOT/POP 20. PAGE 17 A0347 MATH SIMUL PEACE WAR

B62
CLUBB O.E. JR.,THE UNITED STATES AND THE SINO-SOVIET BLOC IN SOUTHEAST ASIA. ASIA CHINA/COM COM USA+45 USSR ECO/UNDEV INT/ORG NAT/G FORCES TOP/EX PLAN ECO/TAC DOMIN COERCE GUERRILLA ATTIT RIGID/FLEX...POLICY OBS TREND 20. PAGE 27 A0553 S/ASIA PWR BAL/PWR DIPLOM

B62
COUNCIL ON WORLD TENSIONS,A STUDY OF WORLD TENSIONS AND DEVELOPMENT. WOR+45 ECO/DEV ECO/UNDEV INT/ORG PLAN DIPLOM ECO/TAC EDU/PROP ATTIT KNOWL ORD/FREE PWR WEALTH...CONCPT TREND CHARTS STERTYP COLD/WAR TOT/POP 20. PAGE 31 A0640 TEC/DEV SOC

B62
DALLIN A.,THE SOVIET UNION AT THE UNITED NATIONS: AN INQUIRY INTO SOVIET MOTIVES AND OBJECTIVES. ACT/RES EDU/PROP LEGIT ATTIT KNOWL PWR...POLICY RECORD HIST/WRIT TIME/SEQ TREND ORG/CHARTS GEN/METH COLD/WAR FAO 20 UN. PAGE 33 A0675 COM INT/ORG USSR

B62
DUROSELLE J.B.,LES NOUVEAUX ETATS DANS LES RELATIONS INTERNATIONALES. AFR CHINA/COM FRANCE MOROCCO S/ASIA USSR ECO/UNDEV INT/ORG PLAN ECO/TAC EDU/PROP ATTIT DRIVE...TREND TOT/POP TUNIS 20. PAGE 39 A0806 NAT/G CONSTN DIPLOM

B62
DUTOIT B.,LA NEUTRALITE SUISSE A L'HEURE EUROPEENNE. EUR+WWI MOD/EUR INT/ORG NAT/G VOL/ASSN PLAN BAL/PWR LEGIT NEUTRAL REGION PEACE ORD/FREE SOVEREIGN...CONCPT OBS TIME/SEQ TREND STERTYP VAL/FREE LEAGUE/NAT UN 20. PAGE 40 A0812 ATTIT DIPLOM SWITZERLND

B62
EVANS M.S.,THE FRINGE ON TOP. USSR EX/STRUC FORCES DIPLOM ECO/TAC PEACE CONSERVE SOCISM...TREND 20 KENNEDY/JF. PAGE 43 A0877 NAT/G PWR CENTRAL POLICY

B62
FORBES H.W.,THE STRATEGY OF DISARMAMENT. FUT WOR+45 INT/ORG VOL/ASSN CONSULT ARMS/CONT COERCE NUC/PWR WAR DRIVE RIGID/FLEX ORD/FREE PWR...POLICY CONCPT OBS TREND STERTYP 20. PAGE 47 A0959 PLAN FORCES DIPLOM

B62
HOFFMAN P.,WORLD WITHOUT WANT. FUT WOR+45 ECO/UNDEV INT/ORG HEALTH KNOWL...TREND TOT/POP FAO 20. PAGE 66 A1353 CONCPT POLICY FOR/AID

B62
HUMPHREY D.D.,THE UNITED STATES AND THE COMMON MARKET. USA+45 INDUS MARKET INT/ORG PLAN EDU/PROP BAL/PAY DRIVE PWR WEALTH...TREND STERTYP EEC 20. PAGE 69 A1415 ATTIT ECO/TAC

B62
KAHN H.,THINKING ABOUT THE UNTHINKABLE. FUT USA+45 LAW NAT/G CONSULT FORCES ACT/RES CREATE PLAN TEC/DEV BAL/PWR DIPLOM EDU/PROP ARMS/CONT DETER ATTIT...CONCPT OBS TREND COLD/WAR 20. PAGE 76 A1547 INT/ORG ORD/FREE NUC/PWR PEACE

B62
KRAFT J.,THE GRAND DESIGN. EUR+WWI USA+45 AGRI FINAN INDUS MARKET INT/ORG NAT/G PLAN ECO/TAC TARIFFS REGION DRIVE ORD/FREE WEALTH...POLICY OBS TREND EEC 20. PAGE 82 A1674 VOL/ASSN ECO/DEV INT/TRADE

B62
MACKENTOSH J.M.,STRATEGY AND TACTICS OF SOVIET FOREIGN POLICY. CHINA/COM FUT USA+45 WOR+45 INT/ORG PLAN DOMIN LEGIT ROUTINE COERCE NUC/PWR WAR ATTIT DRIVE ORD/FREE PWR...CONCPT OBS TIME/SEQ TREND GEN/METH COLD/WAR 20. PAGE 92 A1894 COM POLICY DIPLOM USSR

B62
MORGENTHAU H.J.,POLITICS IN THE TWENTIETH CENTURY: IMPASSE OF AMERICAN FOREIGN POLICY. FUT GERMANY USA+45 USSR WOR+45 INT/ORG NAT/G ACT/RES PLAN FOR/AID EDU/PROP LEGIT COERCE WAR PWR...TIME/SEQ TREND COLD/WAR 20. PAGE 104 A2138 SKILL DIPLOM

B62
MORGENTHAU H.J.,POLITICS IN THE 20TH CENTURY: RESTORATION OF AMERICAN POLITICS. ASIA GERMANY USA+45 USSR WOR+45 NAT/G PLAN EDU/PROP LEGIT NUC/PWR ATTIT PWR SKILL...CONCPT TREND COLD/WAR 20. PAGE 104 A2139 INT/ORG DIPLOM

B62
OSGOOD C.E.,AN ALTERNATIVE TO WAR OR SURRENDER. FUT UNIV CULTURE INTELL SOCIETY R+D INT/ORG CONSULT DELIB/GP ACT/RES PLAN CHOOSE ATTIT PERCEPT KNOWL ...PHIL/SCI PSY SOC TREND GEN/LAWS 20. PAGE 112 A2300 ORD/FREE EDU/PROP PEACE WAR

B62
OSGOOD R.E.,NATO: THE ENTANGLING ALLIANCE. USA+45 WOR+45 VOL/ASSN FORCES TOP/EX PLAN DETER WEAPON DRIVE RIGID/FLEX ORD/FREE PWR...TREND 20 NATO. PAGE 112 A2301 INT/ORG ARMS/CONT PEACE

B62
RIVKIN A.,AFRICA AND THE WEST. AFR EUR+WWI FUT ISLAM ISRAEL USA+45 SOCIETY INT/ORG FORCES CREATE PLAN FOR/AID EDU/PROP ATTIT...CONCPT TREND EEC 20 CONGRESS UN. PAGE 121 A2488 ECO/UNDEV ECO/TAC

B62
ROBINSON A.D.,DUTCH ORGANIZED AGRICULTURE IN INTERNATIONAL POLITICS, 1945-1960. EUR+WWI NETHERLAND STRUCT ECO/DEV NAT/G VOL/ASSN CONSULT DELIB/GP PLAN TEC/DEV INT/TRADE EDU/PROP ATTIT RIGID/FLEX ALL/VALS...NEW/IDEA TREND EEC 20. PAGE 122 A2502 AGRI INT/ORG

B62
ROOSEVELT J.,THE LIBERAL PAPERS. USA+45 WOR+45 ECO/DEV INT/ORG DELIB/GP ACT/RES PROB/SOLV DETER ATTIT...TREND IDEA/COMP ANTHOL. PAGE 123 A2520 DIPLOM NEW/LIB POLICY FORCES

B62
SPIRO H.J.,POLITICS IN AFRICA: PROSPECTS SOUTH OF THE SAHARA. INT/ORG KIN FORCES LEGIS PROB/SOLV COERCE RACE/REL FEDERAL...TREND CHARTS BIBLIOG 20. PAGE 136 A2790 AFR NAT/LISM DIPLOM

B62
STRACHEY J.,ON THE PREVENTION OF WAR. FUT WOR+45 INT/ORG NAT/G ACT/RES PLAN BAL/PWR DOMIN EDU/PROP PEACE ATTIT...POLICY TREND TOT/POP COLD/WAR 20 UN. PAGE 139 A2842 FORCES ORD/FREE ARMS/CONT NUC/PWR

B62
TRISKA J.F.,THE THEORY, LAW, AND POLICY OF SOVIET TREATIES. WOR+45 WOR-45 CONSTN INT/ORG NAT/G VOL/ASSN DOMIN LEGIT COERCE ATTIT PWR RESPECT ...POLICY JURID CONCPT OBS SAMP TIME/SEQ TREND GEN/LAWS 20. PAGE 145 A2966 COM LAW INT/LAW USSR

B62
WOLFERS A.,DISCORD AND COLLABORATION: ESSAYS ON INTERNATIONAL POLITICS. WOR+45 CULTURE SOCIETY INT/ORG NAT/G BAL/PWR DIPLOM DOMIN NAT/LISM PEACE PWR...POLICY CONCPT STYLE RECORD TREND GEN/LAWS 20. PAGE 166 A3385 ATTIT ORD/FREE

B62
WRIGHT Q.,PREVENTING WORLD WAR THREE. FUT WOR+45 CULTURE INT/ORG NAT/G CONSULT FORCES ADMIN ARMS/CONT DRIVE RIGID/FLEX ORD/FREE SOVEREIGN ...POLICY CONCPT TREND STERTYP COLD/WAR 20. PAGE 168 A3416 CREATE ATTIT

L62
NIZARD L.,"CUBAN QUESTION AND SECURITY COUNCIL." L/A+17C USA+45 ECO/UNDEV NAT/G POL/PAR DELIB/GP ECO/TAC PWR...RELATIV OBS TIME/SEQ TREND GEN/LAWS UN 20 UN. PAGE 109 A2242 INT/ORG JURID DIPLOM CUBA

L62
ULYSSES,"THE INTERNATIONAL AIMS AND POLICIES OF THE SOVIET UNION: THE NEW CONCEPTS AND STRATEGY OF KHRUSHCHEV." FUT USSR WOR+45 SOCIETY INT/ORG NAT/G POL/PAR FORCES TOP/EX PLAN DOMIN EDU/PROP COERCE ATTIT PERSON PWR...TREND COLD/WAR 20 KHRUSH/N. PAGE 146 A2994 COM POLICY BAL/PWR DIPLOM

L62
WILCOX F.O.,"THE UN AND THE NON-ALIGNED NATIONS." AFR S/ASIA USA+45 ECO/UNDEV INT/ORG TEC/DEV EDU/PROP RIGID/FLEX ORD/FREE PWR...POLICY HUM CONCPT STAT OBS TIME/SEQ STERTYP GEN/METH UN 20. PAGE 164 A3345 ATTIT TREND

S62
ALGER C.F.,"THE EXTERNAL BUREAUCRACY IN UNITED STATES FOREIGN AFFAIRS." USA+45 WOR+45 SOCIETY COM/IND INT/ORG NAT/G CONSULT EX/STRUC ACT/RES ...MGT SOC CONCPT TREND 20. PAGE 6 A0118 ADMIN ATTIT DIPLOM

S62
BLOOMFIELD L.P.,"THE UNITED NATIONS IN CRISIS: THE ROLE OF THE UN IN USA FOREIGN POLICY." FUT USA+45 WOR+45 ECO/UNDEV DIPLOM ATTIT ORD/FREE...CONCPT UN. PAGE 16 A0317 INT/ORG TREND REV

S62
BOULDING K.E.,"THE PREVENTION OF WORLD WAR THREE." FUT WOR+45 INT/ORG PLAN BAL/PWR PEACE ORD/FREE PWR ...NEW/IDEA TREND TOT/POP COLD/WAR 20. PAGE 17 A0348 VOL/ASSN NAT/G ARMS/CONT DIPLOM

S62
CORET A.,"LE STATUT DE L'ILE CHRISTMAS DE L'OCEAN INDIEN." FUT S/ASIA ECO/DEV ECO/UNDEV VOL/ASSN DELIB/GP PLAN...RELATIV OBS TIME/SEQ TREND AUSTRAL NAT/G INT/ORG NEW/ZEALND

20. PAGE 30 A0619

S62
CORET A.,"LA DECLARATION DE L'ASSEMBLEE GENERAL DE L'ONU SUR L'OCTROI DE L'INDEPENDENCE AUX PAYS ET AUX PEUPLES." AFR ASIA ISLAM NIGERIA S/ASIA USSR WOR+45 ECO/UNDEV NAT/G DELIB/GP COLONIAL ALL/VALS ...CONCPT TIME/SEQ TREND UN TOT/POP 20 MEXIC/AMER. PAGE 31 A0621
INT/ORG STRUCT SOVEREIGN

S62
CRANE R.D.,"SOVIET ATTITUDE TOWARD INTERNATIONAL SPACE LAW." COM FUT USA+45 USSR AIR CONSTN DELIB/GP DOMIN PWR...JURID TREND TOT/POP 20. PAGE 32 A0657
LAW ATTIT INT/LAW SPACE

S62
CROAN M.,"POLYCENTRISM: COMMUNIST INTERNATIONAL RELATIONS." ASIA STRUCT INT/ORG NAT/G POL/PAR CONSULT PLAN DOMIN EDU/PROP COERCE ATTIT RIGID/FLEX SOCISM...POLICY CONCPT TREND CON/ANAL GEN/LAWS MARX/KARL. PAGE 33 A0663
COM CREATE DIPLOM NAT/LISM

S62
FINKELSTEIN L.S.,"THE UNITED NATIONS AND ORGANIZATIONS FOR CONTROL OF ARMAMENT." FUT WOR+45 VOL/ASSN DELIB/GP TOP/EX CREATE EDU/PROP LEGIT ADJUD NUC/PWR ATTIT RIGID/FLEX ORD/FREE...POLICY DECISION CONCPT OBS TREND GEN/LAWS TOT/POP COLD/WAR. PAGE 46 A0933
INT/ORG PWR ARMS/CONT

S62
FOSTER W.C.,"ARMS CONTROL AND DISARMAMENT IN A DIVIDED WORLD." COM FUT USA+45 USSR WOR+45 INTELL INT/ORG NAT/G VOL/ASSN CONSULT CREATE PLAN TEC/DEV EDU/PROP LEGIT NUC/PWR ATTIT RIGID/FLEX...CONCPT TREND TOT/POP 20 UN. PAGE 47 A0971
DELIB/GP POLICY ARMS/CONT DIPLOM

S62
HOFFMANN S.,"RESTRAINTS AND CHOICES IN AMERICAN FOREIGN POLICY." USA-45 INT/ORG NAT/G PLAN ARMS/CONT ATTIT...POLICY CONCPT OBS TREND GEN/METH COLD/WAR 20. PAGE 66 A1356
USA+45 ORD/FREE DIPLOM

S62
KOLARZ W.,"THE IMPACT OF COMMUNISM ON WEST AFRICA." AFR FUT SOCIETY INT/ORG NAT/G CREATE PLAN DOMIN EDU/PROP COERCE NAT/LISM ATTIT RIGID/FLEX SOCISM ...POLICY CONCPT TREND MARX/KARL 20. PAGE 81 A1666
COM POL/PAR COLONIAL

S62
LONDON K.,"SINO-SOVIET RELATIONS IN THE CONTEXT OF THE 'WORLD SOCIALIST SYSTEM'." ASIA CHINA/COM COM USSR INT/ORG NAT/G TOP/EX BAL/PWR DIPLOM DOMIN ATTIT PERCEPT RIGID/FLEX PWR MARXISM...METH/CNCPT TREND 20. PAGE 91 A1854
DELIB/GP CONCPT SOCISM

S62
MILLAR T.B.,"THE COMMONWEALTH AND THE UNITED NATIONS." FUT WOR+45 STRUCT NAT/G VOL/ASSN CONSULT DELIB/GP EDU/PROP LEGIT ATTIT...POLICY CONCPT TREND CMN/WLTH UN 20. PAGE 101 A2072
INT/ORG

S62
MILLIKEN M.,"NEW AND OLD CRITERIA FOR AID." WOR+45 ECO/DEV ECO/UNDEV ACT/RES PLAN ATTIT KNOWL...TREND CON/ANAL SIMUL GEN/METH 20. PAGE 102 A2083
USA+45 ECO/TAC FOR/AID

S62
MORGENTHAU H.J.,"A POLITICAL THEORY OF FOREIGN AID." ECO/UNDEV NAT/G DELIB/GP PLAN ECO/TAC EDU/PROP EXEC ORD/FREE RESPECT WEALTH...METH/CNCPT TREND 20. PAGE 104 A2140
USA+45 PHIL/SCI FOR/AID

S62
NORTH R.C.,"DECISION MAKING IN CRISIS: AN INTRODUCTION." WOR+45 WOR-45 NAT/G CONSULT DELIB/GP TEC/DEV PERCEPT KNOWL...POLICY DECISION PSY METH/CNCPT CONT/OBS TREND VAL/FREE 20. PAGE 110 A2251
INT/ORG ROUTINE DIPLOM

S62
PYE L.W.,"THE POLITICAL IMPULSES AND FANTASIES BEHIND FOREIGN AID." FUT USA+45 ECO/UNDEV DIPLOM ECO/TAC ROUTINE DRIVE KNOWL...SOC METH/CNCPT NEW/IDEA TREND HYPO/EXP STERTYP GEN/METH 20. PAGE 118 A2420
ACT/RES ATTIT FOR/AID

S62
RUBINSTEIN A.Z.,"RUSSIA AND THE UNCOMMITTED NATIONS." AFR INDIA ISLAM L/A+17C LAOS S/ASIA ELITES ECO/UNDEV INT/ORG KIN CREATE PLAN TEC/DEV NAT/LISM RIGID/FLEX PWR WEALTH...METH/CNCPT TIME/SEQ GEN/LAWS WORK. PAGE 125 A2562
ECO/TAC TREND COLONIAL USSR

S62
RUSSETT B.M.,"CAUSE, SURPRISE, AND NO ESCAPE." FUT WOR-45 CULTURE SOCIETY INT/ORG FORCES TEC/DEV BAL/PWR EDU/PROP ARMS/CONT NUC/PWR WAR WEAPON PEACE KNOWL ORD/FREE PWR...POLICY CONCPT RECORD TIME/SEQ TREND GEN/LAWS 20 WWI. PAGE 126 A2578
COERCE DIPLOM

S62
SCHILLING W.R.,"SCIENTISTS, FOREIGN POLICY AND POLITICS." WOR+45 WOR-45 INTELL INT/ORG CONSULT TOP/EX ACT/RES PLAN ADMIN KNOWL...CONCPT OBS TREND LEAGUE/NAT 20. PAGE 128 A2627
NAT/G TEC/DEV DIPLOM NUC/PWR

S62
SCOTT J.B.,"ANGLO-SOVIET TRADE AND ITS EFFECTS ON THE COMMONWEALTH." COM FUT UK USSR WOR+45 ECO/DEV MARKET INT/ORG CONSULT WEALTH...POLICY TREND CMN/WLTH 20. PAGE 130 A2673
NAT/G ECO/TAC

S62
SPECTOR I.,"SOVIET POLICY IN ASIA: A REAPPRAISAL." ASIA CHINA/COM COM INDIA INDONESIA ECO/UNDEV INT/ORG DOMIN EDU/PROP REGION RESPECT...CONCPT TREND TOT/POP COLD/WAR 20 CHINJAP. PAGE 135 A2774
S/ASIA PWR FOR/AID USSR

S62
SPENSER J.H.,"AFRICA AT THE UNITED NATIONS: SOME OBSERVATIONS." FUT ECO/UNDEV NAT/G CONSULT DELIB/GP PLAN BAL/PWR ECO/TAC EDU/PROP ATTIT RIGID/FLEX HEALTH ORD/FREE PWR WEALTH...POLICY CONCPT OBS TREND STERTYP GEN/METH UN VAL/FREE. PAGE 136 A2786
AFR INT/ORG REGION

S62
STRACHEY J.,"COMMUNIST INTENTIONS." ASIA USSR YUGOSLAVIA INT/ORG NAT/G FORCES DOMIN EDU/PROP COERCE NUC/PWR NAT/LISM PEACE RIGID/FLEX PWR MARXISM...CONCPT MYTH OBS TIME/SEQ TREND COLD/WAR TOT/POP 20. PAGE 139 A2843
COM ATTIT WAR

C62
DUFFY J.,"PORTUGAL IN AFRICA." PORTUGAL SIER/LEONE INDUS WORKER INT/TRADE WAR CONSERVE...CATH GEOG TREND 16/20. PAGE 39 A0795
BIBLIOG RACE/REL ECO/UNDEV COLONIAL

C62
ROBINSON J.A.,"CONGRESS AND FOREIGN POLICY-MAKING: A STUDY IN LEGISLATIVE INFLUENCE AND INITIATIVE." USA+45 CHIEF DELIB/GP CREATE CONTROL EXEC GOV/REL PERCEPT...TREND BIBLIOG 20 CONGRESS. PAGE 122 A2505
LEGIS DIPLOM POLICY DECISION

B63
BRITISH AID. UK AGRI DIST/IND INDUS SCHOOL TEC/DEV INT/TRADE COLONIAL DEMAND...TREND CHARTS 20. PAGE 3 A0064
FOR/AID ECO/UNDEV NAT/G FINAN

B63
BLACK J.E.,FOREIGN POLICIES IN A WORLD OF CHANGE. FUT INT/ORG ALL/VALS...POLICY MAJORIT MARXIST SOCIALIST TRADIT TIME/SEQ TREND ANTHOL 20. PAGE 15 A0298
WOR+45 NAT/G DIPLOM

B63
DEENER D.R.,CANADA - UNITED STATES TREATY RELATIONS. CANADA USA+45 USA-45 NAT/G FORCES PLAN PROB/SOLV AGREE NUC/PWR...TREND 18/20 TREATY. PAGE 35 A0722
DIPLOM INT/LAW POLICY

B63
ELIAS T.O.,GOVERNMENT AND POLITICS IN AFRICA. CONSTN CULTURE SOCIETY NAT/G POL/PAR DIPLOM REPRESENT PERSON...SOC TREND BIBLIOG 4/20. PAGE 41 A0837
AFR NAT/LISM COLONIAL LAW

B63
INTERNATIONAL MONETARY FUND,COMPENSATORY FINANCING OF EXPORT FLUCTUATIONS (PAMPHLET). WOR+45 ECO/DEV ECO/UNDEV INT/ORG WEALTH...TREND 20 IMF MONEY. PAGE 71 A1459
BAL/PAY FINAN BUDGET INT/TRADE

B63
KHADDURI M.,MODERN LIBYA: A STUDY IN POLITICAL DEVELOPMENT. EUR+WWI ISLAM LIBYA ELITES INT/ORG POL/PAR FORCES DIPLOM FOR/AID DOMIN EDU/PROP LEGIT NAT/LISM DRIVE RIGID/FLEX SKILL...CONCPT TIME/SEQ TREND 20. PAGE 78 A1606
NAT/G STRUCT

B63
LAFEBER W.,THE NEW EMPIRE: AN INTERPRETATION OF AMERICAN EXPANSION, 1860-1898. USA-45 CONSTN NAT/LISM SOVEREIGN...TREND BIBLIOG 19/20. PAGE 84 A1711
INDUS NAT/G DIPLOM CAP/ISM

B63
LARY M.B.,PROBLEMS OF THE UNITED STATES AS WORLD TRADER AND BANKER. USA+45 NAT/G PLAN DIPLOM FOR/AID ...TREND CHARTS. PAGE 85 A1737
ECO/DEV FINAN BAL/PAY INT/TRADE

B63
RAO V.K.R.,FOREIGN AID AND INDIA'S ECONOMIC DEVELOPMENT. INDIA INT/ORG PROB/SOLV TEC/DEV ECO/TAC CONTROL WEALTH...TREND 20. PAGE 119 A2445
FOR/AID ECO/UNDEV RECEIVE DIPLOM

B63
STROMBERG R.N.,COLLECTIVE SECURITY AND AMERICAN FOREIGN POLICY FROM THE LEAGUE OF NATIONS TO NATO. USA+45 USA-45 WOR-45 INT/ORG VOL/ASSN EX/STRUC FORCES LEGIT ROUTINE DRIVE...CONCPT TREND UN LEAGUE/NAT 20 NATO. PAGE 139 A2851
ORD/FREE TIME/SEQ DIPLOM

B63
SZULC T.,THE WINDS OF REVOLUTION; LATIN AMERICA TODAY - AND TOMORROW. L/A+17C ORD/FREE SOCISM ...PREDICT TREND 20. PAGE 141 A2880
REV INT/ORG MARXISM ECO/UNDEV

B63
THEOBALD R.,FREE MEN AND FREE MARKETS. USA+45 USA-45 ECO/DEV NAT/G TEC/DEV DIPLOM INT/TRADE INCOME ORD/FREE WEALTH...TREND 19/20 KEYNES/JM. PAGE 143 A2915
CONCPT ECO/TAC CAP/ISM MARKET

B63
TUCKER R.C.,THE SOVIET POLITICAL MIND. WOR+45 ELITES INT/ORG NAT/G POL/PAR PLAN DIPLOM ECO/TAC DOMIN ADMIN NUC/PWR REV DRIVE PERSON SUPEGO PWR WEALTH...POLICY MGT PSY CONCPT OBS BIOG TREND COLD/WAR MARX/KARL 20. PAGE 145 A2972
COM TOP/EX USSR

B63
US DEPARTMENT OF THE ARMY,SOVIET RUSSIA: STRATEGIC SURVEY (PAMPHLET). USSR POL/PAR PLAN DOMIN EDU/PROP ARMS/CONT GUERRILLA WAR WEAPON...TREND CHARTS ORG/CHARTS 20. PAGE 152 A3106
BIBLIOG/A MARXISM DIPLOM COERCE

L63
PHELPS J.,"STUDIES IN DETERRENCE VIII: MILITARY STABILITARY AND ARMS CONTROL: A CRITICAL SURVEY." FUT WOR+45 INT/ORG ACT/RES EDU/PROP COERCE NUC/PWR WAR HEALTH PWR...POLICY TECHNIC TREND SIMUL TOT/POP 20. PAGE 116 A2373
FORCES ORD/FREE ARMS/CONT DETER

L63
SZASZY E.,"L'EVOLUTION DES PRINCIPES GENERAUX DU DROIT INTERNATIONAL PRIVE DANS LES PAYS DE DEMOCRATIE POPULAIRE." COM FUT WOR+45 LAW ECO/DEV PERF/ART POL/PAR PROF/ORG ECO/TAC INT/TRADE EDU/PROP ATTIT RIGID/FLEX ALL/VALS SOCISM...JURID TREND GEN/LAWS WORK 20. PAGE 141 A2876
DIPLOM TOTALISM INT/LAW INT/ORG

S63
ANGUILE G.,"CIVILISATION DU PLAN DANS L'EUROPE ET L'AFRIQUE DE DEMAIN." AFR EUR+WWI GABON ECO/DEV FINAN MARKET DELIB/GP ECO/TAC WEALTH...TREND 20. PAGE 8 A0163
ECO/UNDEV PLAN INT/TRADE

S63
DAVEE R.,"POUR UN FONDS DE DEVELOPPEMENT SOCIAL." FUT WOR+45 INTELL SOCIETY ECO/DEV FINAN TEC/DEV ROUTINE WEALTH...TREND TOT/POP VAL/FREE UN 20. PAGE 34 A0684
INT/ORG SOC FOR/AID

S63
DIEBOLD W. JR.,"THE NEW SITUATION OF INTERNATIONAL TRADE POLICY." EUR+WWI FRANCE FUT UK USA+45 WOR+45 DIST/IND PLAN INT/TRADE EDU/PROP PWR WEALTH ...RECORD TREND GEN/LAWS EEC VAL/FREE 20. PAGE 37 A0760
MARKET ECO/TAC

S63
EMERSON R.,"THE ATLANTIC COMMUNITY AND THE EMERGING COUNTRIES." FUT WOR+45 ECO/DEV ECO/UNDEV R+D NAT/G DELIB/GP BAL/PWR ECO/TAC EDU/PROP ROUTINE ORD/FREE PWR WEALTH...POLICY CONCPT TREND GEN/METH EEC 20 NATO. PAGE 42 A0848
ATTIT INT/TRADE

S63
HALLSTEIN W.,"THE EUROPEAN COMMUNITY AND ATLANTIC PARTNERSHIP." EUR+WWI USA+45 MARKET NAT/G VOL/ASSN DELIB/GP ARMS/CONT NUC/PWR ATTIT PWR...CONCPT STAT TIME/SEQ TREND OEEC 20 EEC. PAGE 60 A1235
INT/ORG ECO/TAC UK

S63
HUMPHREY H.H.,"REGIONAL ARMS CONTROL AGREEMENTS." WOR+45 FORCES PLAN LEGIT COERCE ATTIT HEALTH ORD/FREE...HUM METH/CNCPT MYTH OBS INT TREND TOT/POP 20. PAGE 69 A1416
L/A+17C INT/ORG ARMS/CONT REGION

S63
KISSINGER H.A.,"STRAINS ON THE ALLIANCE." EUR+WWI FRANCE GERMANY GERMANY/W USA+45 ECO/DEV INT/ORG NAT/G TOP/EX EDU/PROP NUC/PWR ATTIT PWR...PSY TREND 20. PAGE 80 A1643
VOL/ASSN DRIVE DIPLOM

S63
LOPEZIBOR J.,"L'EUROPE, FORME DE VIE." CHRIST-17C EUR+WWI FUT MOD/EUR SOCIETY INT/ORG SECT EDU/PROP ATTIT RIGID/FLEX ALL/VALS...POLICY HUM SOC TIME/SEQ TREND GEN/LAWS. PAGE 91 A1862
NAT/G CULTURE

S63
MATHUR P.N.,"GAINS IN ECONOMIC GROWTH FROM INTERNATIONAL TRADE." USA-45 ECO/DEV FINAN INDUS ATTIT WEALTH...MATH QUANT STAT BIOG TREND GEN/LAWS WORK 20. PAGE 96 A1966
MARKET ECO/TAC CAP/ISM INT/TRADE

S63
NADLER E.B.,"SOME ECONOMIC DISADVANTAGES OF THE ARMS RACE." USA+45 INDUS R+D FORCES PLAN TEC/DEV ECO/TAC FOR/AID EDU/PROP PWR WEALTH...TREND COLD/WAR 20. PAGE 107 A2190
ECO/DEV MGT BAL/PAY

S63
ROUGEMONT D.,"LES NOUVELLES CHANCES DE L'EUROPE." EUR+WWI FUT ECO/DEV INT/ORG NAT/G ACT/RES PLAN TEC/DEV EDU/PROP ADMIN COLONIAL FEDERAL ATTIT PWR SKILL...TREND 20. PAGE 124 A2549
ECO/UNDEV PERCEPT

S63
SHONFIELD A.,"AFTER BRUSSELS." EUR+WWI FRANCE GERMANY UK ECO/DEV DIST/IND MARKET VOL/ASSN DELIB/GP CREATE INT/TRADE ATTIT RIGID/FLEX...RECORD TREND GEN/LAWS EEC CMN/WLTH 20. PAGE 132 A2705
PLAN ECO/TAC

S63
SHWADRAN B.,"MIDDLE EAST OIL, 1962." ISLAM USSR ECO/DEV DIST/IND INDUS PLAN BAL/PWR DISPL DRIVE ...POLICY STAT TREND GEN/LAWS EEC OEEC 20 OIL. PAGE 132 A2712
MARKET ECO/TAC INT/TRADE

S63
WOLF C.,"SOME ASPECTS OF THE 'VALUE' OF LESS-DEVELOPED COUNTRIES TO THE UNITED STATES." ASIA CHINA/COM COM USA+45 USSR ECO/UNDEV BAL/PWR ECO/TAC FOR/AID DOMIN EDU/PROP ATTIT PWR...POLICY METH/CNCPT CONT/OBS TREND CHARTS 20. PAGE 166 A3379
CONCPT GEN/LAWS DIPLOM

S63
WOLFERS A.,"INTEGRATION IN THE WEST: THE CONFLICT OF PERSPECTIVES." EUR+WWI USA+45 ECO/DEV INT/ORG DELIB/GP CREATE TEC/DEV DIPLOM ATTIT PWR...CONCPT HIST/WRIT TREND GEN/LAWS COLD/WAR EEC 20. PAGE 166 A3386
RIGID/FLEX ECO/TAC

C63
SCHMITT K.M.,"EVOLUTION OR CHAOS: DYNAMICS OF LATIN AMERICAN GOVERNMENT AND POLITICS." L/A+17C AGRI FINAN CAP/ISM EXEC LEAD BAL/PAY TOTALISM ATTIT ...TREND BIBLIOG 20. PAGE 129 A2635
DIPLOM POLICY POL/PAR LOBBY

B64
THE SPECIAL COMMONWEALTH AFRICAN ASSISTANCE PLAN. AFR CANADA INDIA NIGERIA UK FINAN SCHOOL...CHARTS 20 COMMONWLTH. PAGE 3 A0065
ECO/UNDEV TREND FOR/AID ADMIN

B64
BARKER A.J.,SUEZ: THE SEVEN DAY WAR. EUR+WWI ISLAM UAR INT/ORG NAT/G PLAN DIPLOM ECO/TAC DOMIN NAT/LISM DRIVE RIGID/FLEX PWR SOVEREIGN...POLICY JURID TREND CHARTS SUEZ UN 20. PAGE 11 A0221
FORCES COERCE UK

B64
CEPEDE M.,POPULATION AND FOOD. USA+45 STRUCT ECO/UNDEV FAM PLAN TEC/DEV FOR/AID CONTROL...CATH SOC TREND 19/20. PAGE 25 A0513
FUT GEOG AGRI CENSUS

B64
CLAUDE I.,SWORDS INTO PLOWSHARES. FUT WOR+45 WOR-45 DELIB/GP EX/STRUC LEGIT ATTIT ORD/FREE...CONCPT TIME/SEQ TREND UN TOT/POP 20. PAGE 27 A0547
INT/ORG STRUCT

B64
DICKEY J.S.,THE UNITED STATES AND CANADA. CANADA USA+45...SOC 20. PAGE 37 A0756
DIPLOM TREND GOV/COMP PROB/SOLV

B64
DUTT R.P.,THE INTERNATIONALE. COM WOR+45 WOR-45 WORKER CAP/ISM WAR ATTIT...TREND GEN/LAWS 18/20 COM/PARTY. PAGE 40 A0813
ALL/IDEOS INT/ORG MARXIST ORD/FREE

B64
ETZIONI A.,WINNING WITHOUT WAR. FUT MOD/EUR USA+45 WOR+45 ECO/DEV ECO/UNDEV INT/ORG NAT/G FORCES TOP/EX PLAN TEC/DEV ECO/TAC DOMIN EDU/PROP LEGIT COERCE CHOOSE ATTIT MORAL ORD/FREE RESPECT WEALTH MAJORIT. PAGE 43 A0871
PWR TREND DIPLOM USSR

B64
FALL B.,STREET WITHOUT JOY. FRANCE USA+45 DIPLOM ECO/TAC FOR/AID GUERRILLA REV WEAPON...TREND 20. PAGE 44 A0894
WAR S/ASIA FORCES COERCE

B64
FRIEDMANN W.G.,THE CHANGING STRUCTURE OF INTERNATIONAL LAW. WOR+45 INT/ORG NAT/G PROVS LEGIT ORD/FREE PWR...JURID CONCPT GEN/LAWS TOT/POP UN 20. PAGE 49 A1006
ADJUD TREND INT/LAW

B64
HINSHAW R.,THE EUROPEAN COMMUNITY AND AMERICAN TRADE: A STUDY IN ATLANTIC ECONOMICS AND POLICY. EUR+WWI UK USA+45 ECO/DEV ECO/UNDEV AGRI INDUS INT/ORG NAT/G ECO/TAC TARIFFS REGION...STAT CHARTS EEC 20. PAGE 65 A1337
MARKET TREND INT/TRADE

B64
JACOB P.E.,THE INTEGRATION OF POLITICAL COMMUNITIES. USA+45 WOR+45 CULTURE LOC/G MUNIC NAT/G CREATE PLAN LEGIT REGION COERCE ALL/VALS ...POLICY GEOG PSY SOC TREND HYPO/EXP GEN/LAWS VAL/FREE 20. PAGE 72 A1483
INT/ORG METH/CNCPT SIMUL STAT

B64
KEEP J.,CONTEMPORARY HISTORY IN THE SOVIET MIRROR. COM USSR POL/PAR CREATE DIPLOM AGREE WAR ATTIT ...MYTH TREND ANTHOL 20 COLD/WAR STALIN/J MARX/KARL LENIN/VI. PAGE 77 A1576
HIST/WRIT METH MARXISM IDEA/COMP

B64
LEGUM C.,SOUTH AFRICA: CRISIS FOR THE WEST. SOUTH/AFR COERCE DISCRIM ATTIT...TREND 20 INTERVENT. PAGE 86 A1767
RACE/REL STRATA DIPLOM PROB/SOLV

B64
MARKHAM J.W.,THE COMMON MARKET: FRIEND OR COMPETITOR. EUR+WWI FUT USA+45 INT/ORG LG/CO NAT/G VOL/ASSN DELIB/GP EX/STRUC PLAN TARIFFS ORD/FREE PWR WEALTH...POLICY STAT TREND EEC VAL/FREE 20. PAGE 95 A1943
ECO/DEV ECO/TAC

B64
PRAKASH B.,INDIA AND THE WORLD. INDIA INT/ORG CREATE ORD/FREE...POLICY TREND 20. PAGE 117 A2405
DIPLOM PEACE ATTIT

B64
STOESSINGER J.G.,FINANCING THE UNITED NATIONS SYSTEM. FUT WOR+45 CONSTN NAT/G VOL/ASSN DELIB/GP EX/STRUC ECO/TAC LEGIT CT/SYS PWR WEALTH...STAT TIME/SEQ TREND CHARTS VAL/FREE. PAGE 138 A2830
FINAN INT/ORG

B64
SULLIVAN G.,THE STORY OF THE PEACE CORPS. USA+45 WOR+45 INTELL FACE/GP NAT/G SCHOOL VOL/ASSN CONSULT EX/STRUC PLAN EDU/PROP ADMIN ATTIT DRIVE ALL/VALS ...POLICY HEAL SOC CONCPT INT QU BIOG TREND SOC/EXP WORK. PAGE 140 A2861
INT/ORG ECO/UNDEV FOR/AID PEACE

B64
WAINHOUSE D.W.,REMNANTS OF EMPIRE: THE UNITED
INT/ORG

NATIONS AND THE END OF COLONIALISM. FUT PORTUGAL WOR+45 NAT/G CONSULT DOMIN LEGIT ADMIN ROUTINE ATTIT ORD/FREE...POLICY JURID RECORD INT TIME/SEQ UN CMN/WLTH 20. PAGE 160 A3260 TREND COLONIAL

B64
WYTHE G.,THE UNITED STATES AND INTER-AMERICAN RELATIONS: A CONTEMPORARY APPRAISAL. L/A+17C USA+45 ECO/UNDEV INT/ORG NAT/G VOL/ASSN INT/TRADE EDU/PROP DRIVE...SOC TREND OAS UN 20. PAGE 168 A3425 ATTIT ECO/TAC FOR/AID

L64
ARMENGALD A.,"ECONOMIE ET COEXISTENCE." COM EUR+WWI FUT USA+45 WOR+45 ECO/DEV ECO/UNDEV FINAN INT/ORG NAT/G EXEC CHOOSE ATTIT ALL/VALS...POLICY RELATIV DECISION TREND SOC/EXP COLD/WAR WORK 20. PAGE 9 A0173 MARKET ECO/TAC CAP/ISM

L64
CLAUDE I.,"THE OAS, THE UN, AND THE UNITED STATES." L/A+17C USA+45 CONSTN NAT/G DELIB/GP DOMIN EDU/PROP LEGIT REGION COERCE ORD/FREE PWR...TIME/SEQ TREND STERTYP OAS UN 20. PAGE 27 A0546 INT/ORG POLICY

L64
HAAS E.B.,"ECONOMICS AND DIFFERENTIAL PATTERNS OF POLITICAL INTEGRATION: PROJECTIONS ABOUT UNITY IN LATIN AMERICA." SOCIETY NAT/G DELIB/GP ACT/RES CREATE PLAN ECO/TAC REGION ROUTINE ATTIT DRIVE PWR WEALTH...CONCPT TREND CHARTS LAFTA 20. PAGE 59 A1208 L/A+17C INT/ORG MARKET

L64
WARD C.,"THE 'NEW MYTHS' AND 'OLD REALITIES' OF NUCLEAR WAR." COM FUT USA+45 USSR WOR+45 INT/ORG NAT/G DOMIN LEGIT EXEC ATTIT PERCEPT ALL/VALS ...POLICY RELATIV PSY MYTH TREND 20. PAGE 161 A3280 FORCES COERCE ARMS/CONT NUC/PWR

S64
COFFEY J.,"THE SOVIET VIEW OF A DISARMED WORLD." COM USA+45 INT/ORG NAT/G EX/STRUC EDU/PROP COERCE PERCEPT ORD/FREE PWR...TREND STERTYP VAL/FREE 20 UN. PAGE 27 A0556 FORCES ATTIT ARMS/CONT USSR

S64
CRANE R.D.,"BASIC PRINCIPLES IN SOVIET SPACE LAW." FUT WOR+45 AIR INT/ORG DIPLOM DOMIN ARMS/CONT COERCE NUC/PWR PEACE ATTIT DRIVE PWR...INT/LAW METH/CNCPT NEW/IDEA OBS TREND GEN/LAWS VAL/FREE MARX/KARL 20. PAGE 32 A0659 COM LAW USSR SPACE

S64
DRAKE S.T.C.,"DEMOCRACY ON TRIAL IN AFRICA." EUR+WWI FUT USA+45 ECO/UNDEV INT/ORG NAT/G POL/PAR TOP/EX EDU/PROP LEGIT ATTIT ALL/VALS...POLICY TREND GEN/LAWS VAL/FREE 20. PAGE 38 A0785 AFR STERTYP

S64
GARDNER R.N.,"THE SOVIET UNION AND THE UNITED NATIONS." WOR+45 FINAN POL/PAR VOL/ASSN FORCES ECO/TAC DOMIN EDU/PROP LEGIT ADJUD ADMIN ARMS/CONT COERCE ATTIT ALL/VALS...POLICY MAJORIT CONCPT OBS TIME/SEQ TREND STERTYP UN. PAGE 51 A1046 COM INT/ORG USSR

S64
GARDNER R.N.,"GATT AND THE UNITED NATIONS CONFERENCE ON TRADE AND DEVELOPMENT." USA+45 WOR+45 SOCIETY ECO/UNDEV MARKET NAT/G DELIB/GP ACT/RES PLAN ECO/TAC TARIFFS EDU/PROP ROUTINE DRIVE RIGID/FLEX WEALTH...DECISION MGT TREND UN TOT/POP 20 GATT. PAGE 51 A1047 INT/ORG INT/TRADE

S64
GARMARNIKOW M.,"INFLUENCE-BUYING IN WEST AFRICA." COM FUT USSR INTELL NAT/G PLAN TEC/DEV ECO/TAC DOMIN EDU/PROP REGION NAT/LISM ATTIT DRIVE ALL/VALS SOVEREIGN...POLICY PSY SOC CONCPT TREND STERTYP WORK COLD/WAR 20. PAGE 51 A1049 AFR ECO/UNDEV FOR/AID SOCISM

S64
GINSBURGS G.,"WARS OF NATIONAL LIBERATION - THE SOVIET THESIS." COM USSR WOR+45 WOR-45 LAW CULTURE INT/ORG DIPLOM LEGIT COLONIAL GUERRILLA WAR NAT/LISM ATTIT PERSON MORAL PWR...JURID OBS TREND MARX/KARL 20. PAGE 53 A1075 COERCE CONCPT INT/LAW REV

S64
GROSS J.A.,"WHITEHALL AND THE COMMONWEALTH." EUR+WWI MOD/EUR INT/ORG NAT/G CONSULT DELIB/GP LEGIS DOMIN ADMIN COLONIAL ROUTINE PWR CMN/WLTH 19/20. PAGE 57 A1174 EX/STRUC ATTIT TREND

S64
GROSSER A.,"Y A-T-IL UN CONFLIT FRANCO-AMERICAIN." EUR+WWI USA+45 INT/ORG NAT/G PLAN BAL/PWR DIPLOM EDU/PROP NUC/PWR ATTIT DRIVE ORD/FREE PWR...CONCPT OBS TIME/SEQ TREND STERTYP VAL/FREE COLD/WAR. PAGE 57 A1179 VOL/ASSN NAT/LISM FRANCE

S64
GRZYBOWSKI K.,"INTERNATIONAL ORGANIZATIONS FROM THE SOVIET POINT OF VIEW." WOR+45 WOR-45 CULTURE ECO/DEV VOL/ASSN EDU/PROP ATTIT RIGID/FLEX KNOWL ...SOC OBS TIME/SEQ TREND GEN/LAWS VAL/FREE ILO UN 20. PAGE 58 A1184 COM INT/ORG DIPLOM USSR

S64
HABERLER G.,"INTEGRATION AND GROWTH OF THE WORLD ECONOMY IN HISTORICAL PERSPECTIVE." FUT WOR+45 WOR-45 ECO/DEV ECO/UNDEV...TIME/SEQ TREND VAL/FREE 20. PAGE 59 A1209 WEALTH INT/TRADE

S64
HOFFMANN S.,"CE QU'EN PENSENT LES AMERICAINS." EUR+WWI INT/ORG VOL/ASSN PLAN BAL/PWR DIPLOM DOMIN EDU/PROP REGION ARMS/CONT DRIVE ORD/FREE PWR ...POLICY CONCPT OBS TREND STERTYP COLD/WAR VAL/FREE 20. PAGE 66 A1357 USA+45 ATTIT FRANCE

S64
HOSKYNS C.,"THE AFRICAN STATES AND THE UNITED NATIONS: 1958-1964." SOUTH/AFR NAT/G VOL/ASSN CONSULT BAL/PWR EDU/PROP MORAL ORD/FREE PWR ...CONCPT TREND UN 20. PAGE 68 A1393 AFR INT/ORG DIPLOM

S64
HOVET T. JR.,"THE ROLE OF AFRICA IN THE UNITED NATIONS." FUT WOR+45 NAT/G DELIB/GP DOMIN EDU/PROP LEGIT ORD/FREE PWR RESPECT SKILL...OBS TIME/SEQ TREND VAL/FREE UN 20. PAGE 68 A1398 AFR INT/ORG DIPLOM

S64
HUTCHINSON E.C.,"AMERICAN AID TO AFRICA." FUT USA+45 MARKET INT/ORG LOC/G NAT/G PUB/INST PLAN ECO/TAC ATTIT RIGID/FLEX...POLICY CONCPT TREND 20. PAGE 69 A1423 AFR ECO/UNDEV FOR/AID

S64
JACK H.,"NONALIGNMENT AND A TEST BAN AGREEMENT: THE ROLE OF THE NON-ALIGNED STATES." WOR+45 INT/ORG CONSULT DOMIN EDU/PROP LEGIT CHOOSE PEACE ATTIT DRIVE KNOWL ORD/FREE...TREND CHARTS GEN/LAWS UN VAL/FREE 20. PAGE 72 A1471 PWR CONCPT NUC/PWR

S64
KARPOV P.V.,"PEACEFUL COEXISTENCE AND INTERNATIONAL LAW." WOR+45 LAW SOCIETY INT/ORG VOL/ASSN FORCES CREATE CAP/ISM DIPLOM ADJUD NUC/PWR PEACE MORAL ORD/FREE PWR MARXISM...MARXIST JURID CONCPT OBS TREND COLD/WAR MARX/KARL 20. PAGE 77 A1568 COM ATTIT INT/LAW USSR

S64
KHAN M.Z.,"THE PRESIDENT OF THE GENERAL ASSEMBLY." WOR+45 CONSTN DELIB/GP EDU/PROP LEGIT ROUTINE PWR RESPECT SKILL...DECISION SOC BIOG TREND UN 20. PAGE 78 A1609 INT/ORG TOP/EX

S64
KOJIMA K.,"THE PATTERN OF INTERNATIONAL TRADE AMONG ADVANCED COUNTRIES." EUR+WWI UK USA+45 WOR+45 MARKET NAT/G ECO/TAC WEALTH...MATH STAT CON/ANAL CHARTS EEC CHINJAP 20 CHINJAP. PAGE 81 A1665 ECO/DEV TREND INT/TRADE

S64
LIPSON L.,"PEACEFUL COEXISTENCE." COM USSR WOR+45 LAW INT/ORG DIPLOM LEGIT ADJUD ORD/FREE...CONCPT OBS TREND GEN/LAWS VAL/FREE COLD/WAR 20. PAGE 90 A1834 ATTIT JURID INT/LAW PEACE

S64
MAGGS P.B.,"SOVIET VIEWPOINT ON NUCLEAR WEAPONS IN INTERNATIONAL LAW." USSR WOR+45 INT/ORG FORCES DIPLOM ARMS/CONT ATTIT ORD/FREE PWR...POLICY JURID CONCPT OBS TREND CON/ANAL GEN/LAWS VAL/FREE 20. PAGE 93 A1905 COM LAW INT/LAW NUC/PWR

S64
MAZRUI A.A.,"THE UNITED NATIONS AND SOME AFRICAN POLITICAL ATTITUDES." ECO/TAC FOR/AID DOMIN ROUTINE CHOOSE ATTIT DRIVE MORAL PWR RESPECT WEALTH...PSY CONCPT OBS TREND UN VAL/FREE 20. PAGE 97 A1987 AFR INT/ORG SOVEREIGN

S64
MOORE W.E.,"PREDICTING DISCONTINUITIES IN SOCIAL CHANGE." UNIV WOR+45 ECO/DEV ECO/UNDEV INT/ORG NAT/G COERCE ALL/VALS...METH/CNCPT TIME/SEQ TREND TOT/POP VAL/FREE 20. PAGE 103 A2125 SOCIETY GEN/LAWS REV

S64
PADELFORD N.J.,"THE ORGANIZATION OF AFRICAN UNITY." ECO/UNDEV INT/ORG PLAN BAL/PWR DIPLOM ECO/TAC NAT/LISM ORD/FREE PWR WEALTH...CONCPT TREND STERTYP VAL/FREE COLD/WAR 20. PAGE 113 A2313 AFR VOL/ASSN REGION

S64
PESELT B.M.,"COMMUNIST ECONOMIC OFFENSIVE." WOR+45 SOCIETY INT/ORG PLAN ECO/TAC DOMIN EDU/PROP ATTIT PERSON PWR WEALTH...TREND CHARTS 20. PAGE 115 A2366 COM ECO/UNDEV FOR/AID USSR

S64
SAAB H.,"THE ARAB SEARCH FOR A FEDERAL UNION." SOCIETY INT/ORG NAT/G DELIB/GP FORCES ACT/RES TEC/DEV ECO/TAC DOMIN LEGIT REGION ROUTINE ATTIT DRIVE RIGID/FLEX ALL/VALS...SOC CONCPT NEW/IDEA TIME/SEQ TREND. PAGE 126 A2580 ISLAM PLAN

S64
SKUBISZEWSKI K.,"FORMS OF PARTICIPATION OF INTERNATIONAL ORGANIZATION IN THE LAW MAKING PROCESS." FUT WOR+45 NAT/G DELIB/GP DOMIN LEGIT KNOWL PWR...JURID TREND 20. PAGE 134 A2740 INT/ORG LAW INT/LAW

S64
TOUVAL S.,"THE SOMALI REPUBLIC." AFR ISLAM SOMALIA FAM KIN NAT/G CREATE FOR/AID LEGIT ATTIT ALL/VALS ...RECORD TREND 20. PAGE 144 A2954 ECO/UNDEV RIGID/FLEX

S64
TRISKA J.F.,"SOVIET TREATY LAW: A QUANTITATIVE ANALYSIS." WOR+45 LAW ECO/UNDEV AGRI COM/IND INDUS CREATE TEC/DEV DIPLOM ATTIT PWR WEALTH...JURID SAMP TIME/SEQ TREND CHARTS VAL/FREE 20 TREATY. PAGE 145 A2967 COM ECO/TAC INT/LAW USSR

B65
DU BOIS W.E.B.,THE WORLD AND AFRICA. USA+45 CAP/ISM DISCRIM STRANGE SOCISM...TIME/SEQ TREND IDEA/COMP 19/20 NEGRO. PAGE 39 A0789
AFR DIPLOM COLONIAL CULTURE

B65
EMERSON R.,THE POLITICAL AWAKENING OF AFRICA. ECO/UNDEV INT/ORG COLONIAL RACE/REL ORD/FREE MARXISM...TREND ANTHOL 20. PAGE 42 A0849
AFR NAT/LISM DIPLOM POL/PAR

B65
LEISS A.C.,APARTHEID AND UNITED NATIONS COLLECTIVE MEASURES. SOUTH/AFR ECO/UNDEV EXTR/IND FORCES WORKER ECO/TAC FOR/AID INT/TRADE WEALTH...TREND CHARTS 20 UN NEGRO. PAGE 86 A1770
DISCRIM RACE/REL STRATA DIPLOM

B65
LERCHE C.O.,THE COLD WAR AND AFTER. AFR COM S/ASIA USA+45 USSR NUC/PWR SOVEREIGN MARXISM...TIME/SEQ TREND BIBLIOG 20 COLD/WAR. PAGE 87 A1784
DIPLOM BAL/PWR IDEA/COMP

B65
MCCOLL G.D.,THE AUSTRALIAN BALANCE OF PAYMENTS. UK USA+45 AGRI WORKER DIPLOM EQUILIB PRODUC...STAT TREND CHARTS BIBLIOG/A 20 AUSTRAL. PAGE 97 A2001
ECO/DEV BAL/PAY INT/TRADE COST

B65
MCSHERRY J.E.,RUSSIA AND THE UNITED STATES UNDER EISENHOWER, KHRUSHCHEV, AND KENNEDY. USSR EX/STRUC TOP/EX PRESS WAR...POLICY TREND 20. PAGE 99 A2024
DIPLOM CHIEF NAT/G PEACE

B65
MUNGER E.S.,NOTES ON THE FORMATION OF SOUTH AFRICAN FOREIGN POLICY. ACADEM POL/PAR SECT CHIEF DELIB/GP FORCES LEGIS PRESS ATTIT...TREND 20 NEGRO. PAGE 106 A2170
AFR DOMIN POLICY DIPLOM

B65
MURUMBI J.,PROBLEMS OF ECONOMIC DEVELOPMENT IN EAST AFRICA. FINAN INDUS WORKER TEC/DEV INT/TRADE TAX DEMAND EFFICIENCY PRODUC SOCISM...TREND CHARTS 20 AFRICA/E. PAGE 106 A2184
AGRI ECO/TAC ECO/UNDEV PROC/MFG

B65
SPENCE J.E.,REPUBLIC UNDER PRESSURE: A STUDY OF SOUTH AFRICAN FOREIGN POLICY. SOUTH/AFR ADMIN COLONIAL GOV/REL RACE/REL DISCRIM NAT/LISM ATTIT ROLE...TREND 20 NEGRO. PAGE 136 A2783
DIPLOM POLICY AFR

B65
VON GLAHN G.,LAW AMONG NATIONS: AN INTRODUCTION TO PUBLIC INTERNATIONAL LAW. WOR+45 WOR-45 INT/ORG NAT/G CREATE ADJUD WAR...GEOG CLASSIF TREND BIBLIOG. PAGE 160 A3250
ACADEM INT/LAW GEN/LAWS LAW

S65
QUADE Q.L.,"THE TRUMAN ADMINISTRATION AND THE SEPARATION OF POWERS: THE CASE OF THE MARSHALL PLAN." SOCIETY INT/ORG NAT/G CONSULT DELIB/GP LEGIS PLAN ECO/TAC ROUTINE DRIVE PERCEPT RIGID/FLEX ORD/FREE PWR WEALTH...DECISION GEOG NEW/IDEA TREND 20 TRUMAN/HS. PAGE 118 A2422
USA+45 ECO/UNDEV DIPLOM

S65
SPAAK P.H.,"THE SEARCH FOR CONSENSUS: A NEW EFFORT TO BUILD EUROPE." FRANCE GERMANY ECO/DEV NAT/G CONSULT FORCES PLAN EDU/PROP REGION CONSEN ATTIT ...SOC METH/CNCPT OBS TREND EEC NATO WORK 20. PAGE 135 A2770
EUR+WWI INT/ORG

S65
STEIN E.,"TOWARD SUPREMACY OF TREATY-CONSTITUTION BY JUDICIAL FIAT: ON THE MARGIN OF THE COSTA CASE." EUR+WWI ITALY WOR+45 INT/ORG NAT/G LEGIT REGION NAT/LISM PWR...JURID CONCPT TREND TOT/POP VAL/FREE 20. PAGE 138 A2816
ADJUD CONSTN SOVEREIGN INT/LAW

C65
BURTON J.W.,"INTERNATIONAL RELATIONS: A GENERAL THEORY." WOR+45 NAT/G CREATE BAL/PWR NEUTRAL COERCE DETER ADJUST...TREND IDEA/COMP GEN/METH BIBLIOG. PAGE 22 A0447
DIPLOM GEN/LAWS ACT/RES ORD/FREE

B66
BLACK C.E.,THE DYNAMICS OF MODERNIZATION: A STUDY IN COMPARATIVE HISTORY. STRUCT ECO/DEV ECO/UNDEV NAT/G DIPLOM LEAD REV...PREDICT TIME/SEQ TREND SOC/INTEG 17/20. PAGE 15 A0296
SOCIETY SOC NAT/COMP

B66
BOULDING K.E.,THE IMPACT OF THE SOCIAL SCIENCES. UNIV LAW SOCIETY CREATE PROB/SOLV...TREND WORSHIP. PAGE 17 A0349
SOC DIPLOM

B66
BRYNES A.,WE GIVE TO CONQUER. USA+45 USSR STRATA ECO/UNDEV INT/ORG NAT/G DIPLOM DRIVE...TREND IDEA/COMP 20. PAGE 20 A0414
FOR/AID CONTROL GIVE WAR

B66
FRIEDRICH C.J.,REVOLUTION: NOMOS VIII. NAT/G SOCISM ...OBS TREND IDEA/COMP ANTHOL 18/20. PAGE 49 A1007
REV MARXISM CONCPT DIPLOM

B66
GRENVILLE J.A.S.,POLITICS, STRATEGY, AND AMERICAN DEMOCRACY: STUDIES IN FOREIGN POLICY, 1873-1917. CUBA PHILIPPINE SPAIN USA-45 VENEZUELA ELITES NAT/G CREATE PARTIC WAR RIGID/FLEX ORD/FREE...DECISION TREND 19/20 HAWAII. PAGE 56 A1146
DIPLOM COLONIAL POLICY

B66
HALLET R.,PEOPLE AND PROGRESS IN WEST AFRICA: AN INTRODUCTION TO THE PROBLEMS OF DEVELOPMENT. COM/IND INDUS KIN DIPLOM FOR/AID INT/TRADE HEALTH ...GEOG TREND CHARTS BIBLIOG/A 20 AFRICA/W. PAGE 60 A1233
AFR SOCIETY ECO/UNDEV ECO/TAC

B66
HOLLINS E.J.,PEACE IS POSSIBLE: A READER FOR LAYMEN. WOR+45 CULTURE PLAN RISK AGE/Y ALL/VALS SOVEREIGN...PSY CONCPT TREND 20 UN JOHN/XXIII KENNAN/G MYRDAL/G. PAGE 67 A1370
PEACE DIPLOM INT/ORG NUC/PWR

B66
INTERNATIONAL ECONOMIC ASSN,STABILITY AND PROGRESS IN THE WORLD ECONOMY: THE FIRST CONGRESS OF THE INTERNATIONAL ECONOMIC ASSOCIATION. WOR+45 ECO/DEV ECO/UNDEV DELIB/GP FOR/AID BAL/PAY...TREND CMN/WLTH 20. PAGE 71 A1455
INT/TRADE

B66
KEENLEYSIDE H.L.,INTERNATIONAL AID: A SUMMARY. AFR INDIA S/ASIA UK STRATA EXTR/IND TEC/DEV ADMIN RACE/REL DEMAND NAT/LISM WEALTH...TREND CHINJAP. PAGE 77 A1575
ECO/UNDEV FOR/AID DIPLOM TASK

B66
LUARD E.,THE EVOLUTION OF INTERNATIONAL ORGANIZATIONS. UK WOR+45 BUDGET INT/TRADE WAR BAL/PAY PEACE ORD/FREE...POLICY 19/20 EEC ILO LEAGUE/NAT UN. PAGE 91 A1871
INT/ORG EFFICIENCY CREATE TREND

B66
PASSIN H.,THE UNITED STATES AND JAPAN. USA+45 INDUS CAP/ISM...TREND 20 CHINJAP TREATY. PAGE 114 A2337
DIPLOM INT/TRADE ECO/DEV ECO/TAC

B66
THORNTON A.P.,THE IMPERIAL IDEA AND ITS ENEMIES. UK WOR+45 WOR-45 NAT/G PLAN DOMIN CONTROL WAR ATTIT PWR...TREND CHARTS 19/20 CMN/WLTH. PAGE 144 A2937
COLONIAL DIPLOM

B66
TINKER H.,SOUTH ASIA. UK LAW ECO/UNDEV AGRI ACADEM SECT DIPLOM EDU/PROP REV WEALTH ALL/IDEOS...CHARTS BIBLIOG GANDHI/M NEHRU/J. PAGE 144 A2945
S/ASIA COLONIAL TREND

B66
US DEPARTMENT OF THE ARMY,SOUTH ASIA: A STRATEGIC SURVEY (PAMPHLET NO. 550-3). AFGHANISTN INDIA NEPAL PAKISTAN ECO/UNDEV INT/ORG POL/PAR FORCES FOR/AID INT/TRADE LEAD WAR...POLICY SOC TREND 20. PAGE 152 A3110
BIBLIOG/A S/ASIA DIPLOM NAT/G

B66
WHITAKER A.P.,NATIONALISM IN CONTEMPORARY LATIN AMERICA. AGRI NAT/G WEALTH...POLICY SOC CONCPT OBS TREND 20. PAGE 164 A3333
NAT/LISM L/A+17C DIPLOM ECO/UNDEV

S66
O'BRIEN W.V.,"EVENTS AND TRENDS: PATTERNS OF AFRICAN INTERNATIONAL POLITICAL BEHAVIOR." CULTURE SOCIETY NAT/G NAT/LISM SOCISM. PAGE 111 A2267
BIBLIOG/A AFR TREND DIPLOM

N66
BRITISH DEVELOPMENT POLICIES: 1966 (PAMPHLET). UK AGRI TARIFFS BAL/PAY...TREND CHARTS 20 OVRSEA/DEV. PAGE 4 A0076
WEALTH DIPLOM INT/TRADE FOR/AID

B67
ADAMS A.E.,AN ATLAS OF RUSSIAN AND EAST EUROPEAN HISTORY. CHRIST-17C COM MOD/EUR INDUS SECT FORCES DIPLOM COLONIAL REV WAR 4/20. PAGE 4 A0086
CHARTS REGION TREND

B67
BRZEZINSKI Z.K.,THE SOVIET BLOC: UNITY AND CONFLICT (2ND ED., REV., ENLARGED). COM POLAND USSR INTELL CHIEF EX/STRUC CONTROL EXEC GOV/REL PWR MARXISM ...TREND IDEA/COMP 20 LENIN/VI MARX/KARL STALIN/J. PAGE 21 A0420
NAT/G DIPLOM

B67
BURNS E.L.M.,MEGAMURDER. WOR+45 LAW INT/ORG NAT/G BAL/PWR DIPLOM DETER MURDER WEAPON CIVMIL/REL PEACE ...INT/LAW TREND 20. PAGE 22 A0444
FORCES PLAN WAR NUC/PWR

B67
CLARK S.V.O.,CENTRAL BANK COOPERATION: 1924-31. WOR-45 PROB/SOLV ECO/TAC ADJUST BAL/PAY...TREND CHARTS METH/COMP 20. PAGE 27 A0542
FINAN EQUILIB DIPLOM POLICY

B67
FINE S.,RECENT AMERICA* CONFLICTING INTERPRETATIONS OF THE GREAT ISSUES (2ND ED.). USA+45 USA-45 POL/PAR SECT CONFER NUC/PWR WAR ATTIT...POLICY TREND ANTHOL PRESIDENT 20. PAGE 46 A0931
IDEA/COMP DIPLOM NAT/G

B67
MACDONALD D.F.,THE AGE OF TRANSITION: BRITAIN IN THE NINETEENTH & TWENTIETH CENTURIES. UK ECO/DEV LEGIS DIPLOM NEW/LIB...POLICY 19/20. PAGE 92 A1886
TREND INDUS SOCISM

B67
MCCLINTOCK R.,THE MEANING OF LIMITED WAR. FUT WOR+45 NAT/G FORCES GUERRILLA REV...POLICY SAMP/SIZ TREND NAT/COMP 45 COLD/WAR. PAGE 97 A1999
WAR NUC/PWR BAL/PWR

DIPLOM

B67
MEYNAUD J.,TRADE UNIONISM IN AFRICA; A STUDY OF ITS GROWTH AND ORIENTATION (TRANS. BY ANGELA BRENCH). INT/ORG PROB/SOLV COLONIAL PWR...TIME/SEQ TREND ILO. PAGE 100 A2055
LABOR AFR NAT/LISM ORD/FREE

B67
NYERERE J.K.,FREEDOM AND UNITY/UHURU NA UMOJA: A SELECTION FROM WRITINGS AND SPEECHES, 1952-65. TANZANIA ELITES ECO/UNDEV INT/ORG NAT/G CREATE DIPLOM COLONIAL REGION RACE/REL...ANTHOL 20. PAGE 110 A2265
SOVEREIGN AFR TREND ORD/FREE

B67
WALLERSTEIN I.,AFRICA* THE POLITICS OF UNITY. AFR INT/ORG REV SOVEREIGN...HIST/WRIT 20. PAGE 160 A3268
TREND DIPLOM ATTIT

S67
BUTTINGER J.,"VIETNAM* FRAUD OF THE 'OTHER WAR'." VIETNAM/S ELITES STRUCT AGRI NAT/G FOR/AID RENT TREND. PAGE 22 A0456
PLAN WEALTH REV ECO/UNDEV

S67
DAVIS H.B.,"LENIN AND NATIONALISM: THE REDIRECTION OF THE MARXIST THEORY OF NATIONALISM." COM MOD/EUR USSR STRATA INT/ORG PLAN DOMIN COLONIAL FEDERAL ...TREND 20. PAGE 34 A0690
NAT/LISM MARXISM ATTIT CENTRAL

S67
EGBERT D.D.,"POLITICS AND ART IN COMMUNIST BULGARIA" BULGARIA COM USSR CULTURE DIPLOM INGP/REL TOTALISM...TREND 20. PAGE 40 A0825
CREATE ART/METH CONTROL MARXISM

S67
FALKOWSKI M.,"SOCIALIST ECONOMISTS AND THE DEVELOPING COUNTRIES." COM PLAN TEC/DEV ROUTINE DEMAND EFFICIENCY PRODUC WEALTH...MARXIST TREND GEN/METH. PAGE 44 A0893
DIPLOM SOCISM ECO/UNDEV INDUS

S67
KRISTENSEN T.,"THE SOUTH AS AN INDUSTRIAL POWER." FUT WOR+45 ECO/DEV AGRI INDUS TEC/DEV...CENSUS TREND CHARTS 20. PAGE 82 A1686
DIPLOM ECO/UNDEV PREDICT PRODUC

S67
STEEL R.,"BEYOND THE POWER BLOCS." USA+45 USSR ECO/UNDEV NEUTRAL NUC/PWR NAT/LISM ATTIT...GEOG NATO WARSAW/P COLD/WAR. PAGE 137 A2811
DIPLOM TREND BAL/PWR PLAN

S67
STEELE R.,"A TASTE FOR INTERVENTION." USA+45 FOR/AID INT/TRADE EDU/PROP COLONIAL WAR PWR...TREND 20 COLD/WAR. PAGE 137 A2812
POLICY DIPLOM DOMIN ATTIT

S67
TERRILL R.,"THE SIEGE MENTALITY." CHINA/COM NAT/G FORCES DIPLOM REV EFFICIENCY NAT/LISM MARXISM ...TREND 20. PAGE 142 A2904
EDU/PROP WAR DOMIN

S67
VELIKONJA J.,"ITALIAN IMMIGRANTS IN THE UNITED STATES IN THE MID-SIXTIES" ITALY USA+45 KIN MUNIC NAT/G WORKER DIPLOM REGION GP/REL ADJUST...GEOG CHARTS SOC/INTEG 20. PAGE 158 A3226
HABITAT ORD/FREE TREND STAT

C67
HUDSON G.F.,"THE HARD AND BITTER PEACE; WORLD POLITICS SINCE 1945." ASIA COM S/ASIA USSR WOR+45 COLONIAL WAR...TREND BIBLIOG/A 20 COLD/WAR UN. PAGE 68 A1405
DIPLOM INT/ORG ARMS/CONT BAL/PWR

TRIBAL....SEE KIN

TRIBUTE....FORMAL PAYMENTS TO DOMINANT POWER BY MINOR POWER GROUP; SEE ALSO SANCTION

TRIESTE....TRIESTE

TRIFFIN R. A2962,A2963,A2964,A2965

TRINIDAD....TRINIDAD AND TOBAGO; SEE ALSO L/A+17C

TRISKA J.F. A2966,A2967

TROBRIAND....TROBRIAND ISLANDS AND ISLANDERS

TROTIER A.H. A2968

TROTSKY L. A2969

TROTSKY/L....LEON TROTSKY

TRUJILLO/R....RAFAEL TRUJILLO

TRUMAN D. A2970

TRUMAN DOCTRINE....SEE TRUMAN/DOC

TRUMAN/DOC....TRUMAN DOCTRINE

S67
KAISER R.G.,"THE TRUMAN DOCTRINE* HOW IT ALL BEGAN." COM EUR+WWI USA+45 R+D INT/ORG BAL/PWR ECO/TAC PEACE TRUMAN/DOC. PAGE 76 A1550
DIPLOM ECO/UNDEV FOR/AID

TRUMAN/HS....PRESIDENT HARRY S. TRUMAN

B50
GUERRANT E.O.,ROOSEVELT'S GOOD NEIGHBOR POLICY. L/A+17C USA+45 USA-45 FOR/AID...IDEA/COMP 20 ROOSEVLT/F TRUMAN/HS. PAGE 58 A1187
DIPLOM NAT/G CHIEF POLICY

B55
JONES J.M.,THE FIFTEEN WEEKS (FEBRUARY 21-JUNE 5, 1947). EUR+WWI USA+45 PROB/SOLV BAL/PWR...POLICY TIME/SEQ 20 COLD/WAR MARSHL/PLN TRUMAN/HS WASHING/DC. PAGE 75 A1532
DIPLOM ECO/TAC FOR/AID

B56
KOENIG L.W.,THE TRUMAN ADMINISTRATION: ITS PRINCIPLES AND PRACTICE. USA+45 POL/PAR CHIEF LEGIS DIPLOM DEATH NUC/PWR WAR CIVMIL/REL PEACE ...DECISION 20 TRUMAN/HS PRESIDENT TREATY. PAGE 81 A1658
ADMIN POLICY EX/STRUC GOV/REL

S56
CUTLER R.,"THE DEVELOPMENT OF THE NATIONAL SECURITY COUNCIL." USA+45 INTELL CONSULT EX/STRUC DIPLOM LEAD 20 TRUMAN/HS EISNHWR/DD NSC. PAGE 33 A0670
ORD/FREE DELIB/GP PROB/SOLV NAT/G

B57
REISS J.,GEORGE KENNANS POLITIK DER EINDAMMUNG. USSR NAT/G FORCES TOTALISM ATTIT ORD/FREE...POLICY 20 NATO TRUMAN/HS MARSHL/PLN KENNAN/G. PAGE 120 A2463
DIPLOM DETER PEACE

B58
HUNT B.I.,BIPARTISANSHIP: A CASE STUDY OF THE FOREIGN ASSISTANCE PROGRAM, 1947-56 (DOCTORAL THESIS). USA+45 INT/ORG CONSULT LEGIS TEC/DEV ...BIBLIOG PRESIDENT TREATY NATO TRUMAN/HS EISNHWR/DD CONGRESS. PAGE 69 A1418
FOR/AID POL/PAR GP/REL DIPLOM

B61
GRAEBNER N.,THE NEW ISOLATIONISM: A STUDY IN POLITICS AND FOREIGN POLICY SINCE 1960. USA+45 INT/ORG LOC/G NAT/G POL/PAR LEGIS BAL/PWR EDU/PROP CHOOSE ATTIT PERSON ORD/FREE 20 TRUMAN/HS EISNHWR/DD. PAGE 55 A1120
EXEC PWR DIPLOM

B63
ROSS H.,THE COLD WAR: CONTAINMENT AND ITS CRITICSS. WOR+45 POL/PAR BAL/PWR ECO/TAC PEACE ORD/FREE ...POLICY IDEA/COMP ANTHOL T 20 COLD/WAR DULLES/JF TRUMAN/HS EISNHWR/DD. PAGE 124 A2541
MARXISM ARMS/CONT DIPLOM

B64
REES D.,KOREA: THE LIMITED WAR. ASIA KOREA WOR+45 NAT/G CIVMIL/REL PERS/REL PERSON...POLICY CHARTS 20 UN TRUMAN/HS MACARTHR/D. PAGE 120 A2455
DIPLOM WAR INT/ORG FORCES

B64
WARREN S.,THE PRESIDENT AS WORLD LEADER. USA+45 WOR+45 ELITES COM/IND INT/ORG NAT/G VOL/ASSN CHIEF EX/STRUC LEGIT COERCE ATTIT PERSON RIGID/FLEX...INT TIME/SEQ COLD/WAR 20 ROOSEVLT/F TRUMAN/HS EISNHWR/DD KENNEDY/JF. PAGE 161 A3286
TOP/EX PWR DIPLOM

S65
QUADE Q.L.,"THE TRUMAN ADMINISTRATION AND THE SEPARATION OF POWERS: THE CASE OF THE MARSHALL PLAN." SOCIETY INT/ORG NAT/G CONSULT DELIB/GP LEGIS PLAN ECO/TAC ROUTINE DRIVE PERCEPT RIGID/FLEX ORD/FREE PWR WEALTH...DECISION GEOG NEW/IDEA TREND 20 TRUMAN/HS. PAGE 118 A2422
USA+45 ECO/UNDEV DIPLOM

B66
BERNSTEIN B.J.,THE TRUMAN ADMINISTRATION. WOR+45 LABOR POL/PAR LEGIS DIPLOM NUC/PWR WAR ATTIT ...POLICY 20 TRUMAN/HS. PAGE 14 A0279
LEAD TOP/EX NAT/G

B66
FREIDEL F.,AMERICAN ISSUES IN THE TWENTIETH CENTURY. SOCIETY FINAN ECO/TAC FOR/AID CONTROL NUC/PWR WAR RACE/REL PEACE ATTIT...ANTHOL T 20 WILSON/W ROOSEVLT/F KENNEDY/JF TRUMAN/HS. PAGE 49 A0995
DIPLOM POLICY NAT/G ORD/FREE

B66
MAY E.R.,ANXIETY AND AFFLUENCE: 1945-1965. USA+45 DIPLOM FOR/AID ARMS/CONT RACE/REL CONSEN...ANTHOL 20 COLD/WAR KENNEDY/JF EISNHWR/DD TRUMAN/HS BERLIN/BLO. PAGE 97 A1982
ANOMIE ECO/DEV NUC/PWR WEALTH

TRUST, PERSONAL....SEE RESPECT, SUPEGO

TRUST/TERR....TRUST TERRITORY

B60
THE AFRICA 1960 COMMITTEE,MANDATE IN TRUST; THE PROBLEM OF SOUTH WEST AFRICA. GERMANY STRUCT REGION SANCTION CHOOSE DISCRIM...INT/LAW 20 AFRICA/SW UN LEAGUE/NAT TRUST/TERR. PAGE 142 A2910
NAT/G DIPLOM COLONIAL RACE/REL

B63
HUSSEY W.D.,THE BRITISH EMPIRE AND COMMONWEALTH 1500 TO 1961. UK USA-45 SOCIETY ECO/UNDEV NAT/G
COLONIAL SOVEREIGN

VOL/ASSN INT/TRADE DOMIN CONTROL WAR PWR ...DICTIONARY 16/20 COMMONWLTH TRUST/TERR. PAGE 69 A1422 — INT/ORG

TSHOMBE/M....MOISE TSHOMBE

B66
GERARD-LIBOIS J.,KATANGA SECESSION. INT/ORG FORCES DIPLOM ADMIN CONTROL WAR CHOOSE PWR...CHARTS 20 KATANGA TSHOMBE/M UN. PAGE 52 A1062 — NAT/G REGION ORD/FREE REV

TUCKER R.C. A2971,A2972,A2973

TUCKER R.W. A2974,A2975

TULANE/U....TULANE UNIVERSITY

B65
EDUCATION AND WORLD AFFAIRS,THE UNIVERSITY LOOKS ABROAD: APPROACHES TO WORLD AFFAIRS AT SIX AMERICAN UNIVERSITIES. USA+45 CREATE EDU/PROP CONFER LEAD KNOWL 20 CORNELL/U MICH/STA/U STANFORD/U TULANE/U WISCONSN/U. PAGE 40 A0822 — ACADEM DIPLOM ATTIT GP/COMP

TULLY A. A2976

TUNISIA....SEE ALSO ISLAM, AFR

N19
LISKA G.,THE GREATER MAGHREB: FROM INDEPENDENCE TO UNITY? (PAMPHLET). ALGERIA ISLAM MOROCCO PROB/SOLV BAL/PWR CONFER COLONIAL REPRESENT NAT/LISM 20 TUNIS. PAGE 90 A1835 — ECO/UNDEV REGION DIPLOM DOMIN

B29
CONWELL-EVANS T.P.,THE LEAGUE COUNCIL IN ACTION. EUR+WWI TURKEY UK USSR WOR-45 INT/ORG FORCES JUDGE ECO/TAC EDU/PROP LEGIT ROUTINE ARMS/CONT COERCE ATTIT PWR...MAJORIT GEOG JURID CONCPT LEAGUE/NAT TOT/POP VAL/FREE TUNIS 20. PAGE 30 A0605 — DELIB/GP INT/LAW

B60
PRINCETON U CONFERENCE,CURRENT PROBLEMS IN NORTH AFRICA. ALGERIA LIBYA MOROCCO USA+45 EXTR/IND POL/PAR PROB/SOLV DIPLOM ECO/TAC WAR...ANTHOL 20 TUNIS. PAGE 118 A2412 — POLICY ECO/UNDEV NAT/G

B61
UAR MINISTRY OF CULTURE,A BIBLIOGRAPHICAL LIST OF AL MAGHRIB. ALGERIA ISLAM MOROCCO UAR SECT INT/TRADE COLONIAL 19/20 TUNIS. PAGE 146 A2987 — BIBLIOG DIPLOM GEOG

B61
UAR MINISTRY OF CULTURE,A BIBLIOGRAPHICAL LIST OF TUNISIA. ISLAM CULTURE NAT/G EDU/PROP COLONIAL ...GEOG 19/20 TUNIS. PAGE 146 A2989 — BIBLIOG DIPLOM SECT

B62
BAULIN J.,THE ARAB ROLE IN AFRICA. AFR ALGERIA FUT ISLAM MOROCCO UAR COLONIAL NEUTRAL REV...SOC 20 TUNIS BOURGUIBA. PAGE 12 A0235 — NAT/LISM DIPLOM NAT/G SECT

B62
DUROSELLE J.B.,LES NOUVEAUX ETATS DANS LES RELATIONS INTERNATIONALES. AFR CHINA/COM FRANCE MOROCCO S/ASIA USSR ECO/UNDEV INT/ORG PLAN ECO/TAC EDU/PROP ATTIT DRIVE...TREND TOT/POP TUNIS 20. PAGE 39 A0806 — NAT/G CONSTN DIPLOM

B66
BROWN L.C.,STATE AND SOCIETY IN INDEPENDENT NORTH AFRICA. ALGERIA LIBYA MOROCCO AGRI INDUS INT/ORG POL/PAR SECT PLAN DIPLOM COLONIAL...LING NAT/COMP ANTHOL BIBLIOG 20 TUNIS MUSLIM. PAGE 20 A0406 — NAT/G SOCIETY CULTURE ECO/UNDEV

C67
LING D.L.,"TUNISIA: FROM PROTECTORATE TO REPUBLIC." CULTURE NAT/G POL/PAR CHIEF DIPLOM COERCE WAR PWR ...BIBLIOG 19/20 TUNIS. PAGE 89 A1825 — AFR NAT/LISM COLONIAL PROB/SOLV

B93
ROYAL GEOGRAPHIC SOCIETY,BIBLIOGRAPHY OF BARBARY STATES (4 SUPPLEMENTARY PAPERS). ALGERIA LIBYA MOROCCO SOCIETY STRUCT DIPLOM LEAD 14/19 TUNIS. PAGE 125 A2555 — BIBLIOG ISLAM NAT/G COLONIAL

TUNSTALL W.C.B. A2977

TUPPER E. A2978,A2979

TURKESTAN....TURKESTAN

TURKEY....TURKEY; SEE ALSO ISLAM

B00
HOLLAND T.E.,STUDIES IN INTERNATIONAL LAW. TURKEY USSR WOR-45 CONSTN NAT/G DIPLOM DOMIN LEGIT COERCE WAR PEACE ORD/FREE PWR SOVEREIGN...JURID CHARTS 20 PARLIAMENT SUEZ TREATY. PAGE 66 A1367 — INT/ORG LAW INT/LAW

B29
CONWELL-EVANS T.P.,THE LEAGUE COUNCIL IN ACTION. EUR+WWI TURKEY UK USSR WOR-45 INT/ORG FORCES JUDGE ECO/TAC EDU/PROP LEGIT ROUTINE ARMS/CONT COERCE ATTIT PWR...MAJORIT GEOG JURID CONCPT LEAGUE/NAT TOT/POP VAL/FREE TUNIS 20. PAGE 30 A0605 — DELIB/GP INT/LAW

B44
FULLER G.H.,TURKEY: A SELECTED LIST OF REFERENCES. ISLAM TURKEY CULTURE ECO/UNDEV AGRI DIPLOM NAT/LISM CONSERVE...GEOG HUM INT/LAW SOC 7/20 MAPS. PAGE 50 A1024 — BIBLIOG/A ALL/VALS

B55
OECD,MARSHALL PLAN IN TURKEY. TURKEY USA+45 COM/IND CONSTRUC SERV/IND FORCES BUDGET...STAT 20 MARSHL/PLN. PAGE 111 A2277 — FOR/AID ECO/UNDEV AGRI INDUS

B56
TOYNBEE A.,THE WAR AND THE NEUTRALS. L/A+17C PORTUGAL SPAIN SWEDEN SWITZERLND TURKEY WOR+45 WOR-45 ECO/TAC CONFER CONTROL REGION 20. PAGE 145 A2957 — NEUTRAL WAR INT/TRADE DIPLOM

L64
WORLD PEACE FOUNDATION,"INTERNATIONAL ORGANIZATIONS: SUMMARY OF ACTIVITIES." INDIA PAKISTAN TURKEY WOR+45 CONSTN CONSULT EX/STRUC ECO/TAC EDU/PROP LEGIT ORD/FREE...JURID SOC UN 20 CYPRESS. PAGE 167 A3397 — INT/ORG ROUTINE

B65
ANALYSIS AND ASSESSMENT OF THE ECONOMIC EFFECTS: PUBLIC LAW 480 TITLE I PROGRAM TURKEY. INDIA TURKEY USA+45 AGRI NAT/G PLAN BUDGET DIPLOM COST EFFICIENCY...CHARTS 20. PAGE 3 A0070 — ECO/TAC FOR/AID FINAN ECO/UNDEV

B66
ZEINE Z.N.,THE EMERGENCE OF ARAB NATIONALISM (REV. ED.). TURKEY UK NAT/G SECT TEC/DEV LEAD REV WAR AGE/Y ROLE ORD/FREE...TRADIT CHARTS BIBLIOG 20 ARABS OTTOMAN. PAGE 170 A3451 — ISLAM NAT/LISM DIPLOM

S67
ANTHEM T.,"CYPRUS* WHAT NOW?" CYPRUS GREECE TURKEY NAT/G BUDGET MAJORITY 20 NATO. PAGE 8 A0165 — DIPLOM COERCE INT/TRADE ADJUD

TURKIC....TURKIC PEOPLES

TURNER F.C. A2980

TURNER F.J. A2981

TURNER G.B. A2982

TURNER J.E. A1376

TURNER M.C. A2983

TURNER R.K. A2984

TUSKEGEE....TUSKEGEE, ALABAMA

TV....TELEVISION; SEE ALSO PRESS, COM/IND

N
EUROPA PUBLICATIONS LIMITED,THE EUROPA YEAR BOOK. CONSTN FINAN INDUS POL/PAR DIPLOM TV CT/SYS...STAT BIOG CHARTS WORSHIP 20. PAGE 43 A0874 — BIBLIOG NAT/G PRESS INT/ORG

B63
GORDON G.N.,THE IDEA INVADERS. USA+45 USSR CULTURE COM/IND DIPLOM PRESS TV TOTALISM MARXISM 20. PAGE 54 A1113 — EDU/PROP ATTIT ORD/FREE CONTROL

B64
UNESCO,WORLD COMMUNICATIONS: PRESS, RADIO, TELEVISION, FILM (4TH ED.). WOR+45 DIPLOM TV PEACE ...NAT/COMP SOC/INTEG 20 FILM. PAGE 148 A3023 — COM/IND EDU/PROP PRESS TEC/DEV

B65
CBS,CONVERSATIONS WITH WALTER LIPPMANN. USA+45 INT/ORG NAT/G POL/PAR PLAN DIPLOM PWR ALL/IDEOS ...POLICY 20 LIPPMANN/W. PAGE 25 A0509 — TV ATTIT INT

B65
DAVISON W.P.,INTERNATIONAL POLITICAL COMMUNICATION. COM USA+45 WOR+45 CULTURE ECO/UNDEV NAT/G PROB/SOLV PRESS TV ADMIN 20 FILM. PAGE 34 A0693 — EDU/PROP DIPLOM PERS/REL COM/IND

B67
HOHENBERG J.,BETWEEN TWO WORLDS. ASIA S/ASIA USA+45 PRESS TV PERS/REL ISOLAT...INT CHARTS METH/COMP 20. PAGE 66 A1362 — COM/IND DIPLOM EFFICIENCY KNOWL

TVA....TENNESSEE VALLEY AUTHORITY

TWAIN/MARK....MARK TWAIN (SAMUEL CLEMENS)

TYLER/JOHN....PRESIDENT JOHN TYLER

TYPOLOGY....SEE CLASSIF

TYSON G. A2985

U

U OF MICH SURVEY RESEARCH CTR A2986

U/THANT....U THANT

UA/PAR....UNITED AUSTRALIAN PARTY

UAM....UNION AFRICAINE ET MALGACHE

UAR....UNITED ARAB REPUBLIC (EGYPT AND SYRIA 1958-1961, EGYPT AFTER 1958); SEE ALSO EGYPT, ISLAM

N
US SUPERINTENDENT OF DOCUMENTS,FOREIGN RELATIONS OF THE UNITED STATES; PUBLICATIONS RELATING TO FOREIGN COUNTRIES (PRICE LIST 65). UAR USA+45 VIETNAM ECO/UNDEV VOL/ASSN FOR/AID EDU/PROP ARMS/CONT HEALTH MARXISM...POLICY INT/LAW UN NATO. PAGE 157 A3201
BIBLIOG/A DIPLOM INT/ORG NAT/G

N19
KUWAIT ARABIA,KUWAIT FUND FOR ARAB ECONOMIC DEVELOPMENT (PAMPHLET). ISLAM KUWAIT UAR ECO/UNDEV LEGIS ECO/TAC WEALTH 20. PAGE 83 A1697
FOR/AID DIPLOM FINAN ADMIN

N19
UNITED ARAB REPUBLIC,THE PROBLEM OF THE PALESTINIAN REFUGEES (PAMPHLET). ISRAEL UAR LAW PROB/SOLV EDU/PROP CONFER ADJUD CONTROL NAT/LISM HEALTH 20 JEWS UN MIGRATION. PAGE 148 A3029
STRANGE GP/REL INGP/REL DIPLOM

B29
PRATT I.A.,MODERN EGYPT: A LIST OF REFERENCES TO MATERIAL IN THE NEW YORK PUBLIC LIBRARY. UAR ECO/UNDEV...GEOG JURID SOC LING 20. PAGE 117 A2407
BIBLIOG ISLAM DIPLOM NAT/G

B52
US LIBRARY OF CONGRESS,EGYPT AND THE ANGLO-EGYPTIAN SUDAN: A SELECTIVE GUIDE TO BACKGROUND READING (PAMPHLET). SUDAN UAR UK DIPLOM...POLICY 20. PAGE 155 A3153
BIBLIOG/A COLONIAL ISLAM NAT/G

B54
NATION ASSOCIATES,SECURITY AND THE MIDDLE EAST - THE PROBLEM AND ITS SOLUTION. ISRAEL JORDAN LEBANON SYRIA UAR FORCES FOR/AID GP/REL NAT/LISM PEACE TOTALISM...POLICY 20. PAGE 107 A2198
DIPLOM ECO/UNDEV WAR PLAN

B56
US DEPARTMENT OF STATE,THE SUEZ CANAL PROBLEM; JULY 26-SEPTEMBER 22, 1956. UAR WOR+45 BAL/PWR COERCE NAT/LISM ATTIT ORD/FREE SOVEREIGN 20 SUEZ. PAGE 151 A3091
DIPLOM CONFER INT/TRADE

B56
WATT D.C.,BRITAIN AND THE SUEZ CANAL. COM UAR UK ...INT/LAW 20 SUEZ TREATY. PAGE 162 A3294
DIPLOM INT/TRADE DIST/IND NAT/G

B57
BLOOMFIELD L.M.,EGYPT, ISRAEL AND THE GULF OF AQABA: IN INTERNATIONAL LAW. LAW NAT/G CONSULT FORCES PLAN ECO/TAC ROUTINE COERCE ATTIT DRIVE PERCEPT PERSON RIGID/FLEX LOVE PWR WEALTH...GEOG CONCPT MYTH TREND. PAGE 15 A0314
ISLAM INT/LAW UAR

B57
BROMBERGER M.,LES SECRETS DE L'EXPEDITION D'EGYPTE. FRANCE ISLAM UAR UK USA+45 USSR WOR+45 INT/ORG NAT/G FORCES BAL/PWR ECO/TAC DOMIN WAR NAT/LISM ATTIT PWR SOVEREIGN...MAJORIT TIME/SEQ CHARTS SUEZ COLD/WAR 20. PAGE 19 A0387
COERCE DIPLOM

B57
CONOVER H.F.,NORTH AND NORTHEAST AFRICA; A SELECTED ANNOTATED LIST OF WRITINGS. ALGERIA MOROCCO SUDAN UAR CULTURE INT/ORG PROB/SOLV ADJUD NAT/LISM PWR WEALTH...SOC 20 UN. PAGE 30 A0603
BIBLIOG/A DIPLOM AFR ECO/UNDEV

B58
INSTITUTE MEDITERRANEAN AFF,THE PALESTINE REFUGEE PROBLEM. UAR WOR+45 INT/ORG PLAN PROB/SOLV PEACE ...POLICY GEOG STAT CHARTS 20 JEWS UN MIGRATION. PAGE 70 A1444
STRANGE HABITAT GP/REL INGP/REL

B59
EGYPTIAN SOCIETY OF INT LAW,THE MONROVIA CONFERENCE (PAMPHLET). AFR ALGERIA FRANCE UAR CONFER REGION NUC/PWR WAR DISCRIM 20 SAHARA AFR/STATES. PAGE 40 A0826
COLONIAL SOVEREIGN RACE/REL DIPLOM

B59
KAPLAN D.,THE ARAB REFUGEES: AN ABNORMAL PROBLEM. UAR WOR+45 PROB/SOLV DIPLOM GOV/REL ADJUST EFFICIENCY...POLICY GEOG INT/LAW 20 UN JEWS MIGRATION. PAGE 76 A1557
STRANGE HABITAT GP/REL INGP/REL

B59
LAQUER W.Z.,THE SOVIET UNION AND THE MIDDLE EAST. COM UAR USSR ECO/UNDEV NAT/G VOL/ASSN ECO/TAC EDU/PROP COLONIAL EXEC PWR...TIME/SEQ TREND COLD/WAR 20. PAGE 85 A1730
ISLAM DRIVE FOR/AID NAT/LISM

L60
LAUTERPACHT E.,"THE SUEZ CANAL SETTLEMENT." FRANCE ISLAM ISRAEL UAR UK BAL/PWR DIPLOM LEGIT...JURID GEN/LAWS ANTHOL SUEZ VAL/FREE 20. PAGE 85 A1747
INT/ORG LAW

B61
UAR MINISTRY OF CULTURE,A BIBLIOGRAPHICAL LIST OF AL MAGHRIB. ALGERIA ISLAM MOROCCO UAR SECT INT/TRADE COLONIAL 19/20 TUNIS. PAGE 146 A2987
BIBLIOG DIPLOM GEOG

B62
BAULIN J.,THE ARAB ROLE IN AFRICA. AFR ALGERIA FUT ISLAM MOROCCO UAR COLONIAL NEUTRAL REV...SOC 20 TUNIS BOURGUIBA. PAGE 12 A0235
NAT/LISM DIPLOM NAT/G SECT

B63
CREMEANS C.,THE ARABS AND THE WORLD: NASSER'S ARAB NATIONALIST POLICY. FUT ISLAM UAR USA+45 SOCIETY STRATA NAT/G POL/PAR PLAN DIPLOM EDU/PROP LEGIT DRIVE ALL/VALS...INT TIME/SEQ CHARTS 20 NASSER/G. PAGE 33 A0662
TOP/EX ATTIT REGION NAT/LISM

B63
EL-NAGGAR S.,FOREIGN AID TO UNITED ARAB REPUBLIC. UAR USA+45 USSR AGRI FINAN INDUS FORCES EATING DEMAND...CHARTS METH/COMP 20 RESOURCE/N AID. PAGE 41 A0838
FOR/AID ECO/UNDEV RECEIVE PLAN

B63
HYDE D.,THE PEACEFUL ASSAULT. COM UAR USSR ECO/DEV ECO/UNDEV NAT/G POL/PAR CAP/ISM PWR 20. PAGE 69 A1427
MARXISM CONTROL ECO/TAC DIPLOM

B63
LANGE O.,ECONOMIC DEVELOPMENT, PLANNING, AND INTERNATIONAL COOPERATION. UAR WOR+45 FINAN CAP/ISM PERS/REL 20. PAGE 84 A1722
ECO/UNDEV DIPLOM INT/TRADE PLAN

B63
ROSNER G.,THE UNITED NATIONS EMERGENCY FORCE. FRANCE ISRAEL UAR UK WOR+45 CREATE WAR PEACE ORD/FREE PWR...INT/LAW JURID HIST/WRIT TIME/SEQ UN. PAGE 124 A2539
INT/ORG FORCES

B64
BARKER A.J.,SUEZ: THE SEVEN DAY WAR. EUR+WWI ISLAM UAR INT/ORG NAT/G PLAN DIPLOM ECO/TAC DOMIN NAT/LISM DRIVE RIGID/FLEX PWR SOVEREIGN...POLICY JURID TREND CHARTS SUEZ UN 20. PAGE 11 A0221
FORCES COERCE UK

B64
FINER H.,DULLES OVER SUEZ. FRANCE FUT UAR UK WOR+45 NAT/G PROB/SOLV CONTROL NUC/PWR WAR 20 DULLES/JF SUEZ. PAGE 46 A0932
DIPLOM POLICY REC/INT

B64
UNITED ARAB REPUBLIC,TOWARDS THE SECOND AFRICAN SUMMIT ASSEMBLY. AFR UAR CONSTN VOL/ASSN CHIEF PLAN DIPLOM AGREE 20 NASSER/G AFR/STATES. PAGE 148 A3030
CONFER DELIB/GP INT/ORG POLICY

L64
CAMPBELL J.C.,"THE MIDDLE EAST IN THE MUTED COLD WAR." COM EUR+WWI UAR USA+45 USSR STRUCT ECO/UNDEV NAT/G VOL/ASSN EX/STRUC TOP/EX DIPLOM ECO/TAC EDU/PROP...TIME/SEQ COLD/WAR 20. PAGE 23 A0475
ISLAM FOR/AID NAT/LISM

B65
MACDONALD R.W.,THE LEAGUE OF ARAB STATES: A STUDY IN THE DYNAMICS OF REGIONAL ORGANIZATION. ISRAEL UAR USSR FINAN INT/ORG DELIB/GP ECO/TAC AGREE NEUTRAL ORD/FREE PWR...DECISION BIBLIOG 20 TREATY UN. PAGE 92 A1888
ISLAM REGION DIPLOM ADMIN

B65
MANSFIELD P.,NASSER'S EGYPT. AFR ISLAM UAR ECO/UNDEV AGRI COLONIAL SOVEREIGN...CHARTS 20 NASSER/G MID/EAST. PAGE 94 A1934
CHIEF ECO/TAC DIPLOM POLICY

B65
SANDERSON G.N.,ENGLAND, EUROPE, AND THE UPPER NILE 1882-1899. ISLAM MOD/EUR UAR UK CHIEF...POLICY CHARTS BIBLIOG/A 19 ARABS NEGRO. PAGE 127 A2600
AFR DIPLOM COLONIAL

B66
US DEPARTMENT OF STATE,RESEARCH ON THE MIDDLE EAST (EXTERNAL RESEARCH LIST NO 4-25). GREECE ISRAEL SYRIA UAR YEMEN CULTURE SOCIETY POL/PAR SECT DIPLOM EDU/PROP WAR NAT/LISM...GEOG GOV/COMP 20. PAGE 152 A3096
BIBLIOG/A ISLAM NAT/G REGION

S66
FRIEND A.,"THE MIDDLE EAST CRISIS" COM ISLAM ISRAEL SYRIA UAR USA+45 USSR FORCES PLAN FOR/AID CONTROL ORD/FREE PWR...SOCIALIST TIME/SEQ 20 NASSER/G. PAGE 49 A1009
WAR INT/ORG DIPLOM PEACE

S67
KYLE K.,"BACKGROUND TO THE CRISIS" ISLAM ISRAEL UAR UK USSR NAT/G PROB/SOLV LEGIT CONTROL REGION STRANGE MORAL 20 JEWS. PAGE 83 A1698
DIPLOM POLICY SOVEREIGN COERCE

UAR MINISTRY OF CULTURE A2987,A2988,A2989,A2990

UAR NATIONAL LIBRARY A2991

UAW....UNITED AUTO WORKERS

UDR....UNION POUR LA DEFENSE DE LA REPUBLIQUE (FRANCE)

UGANDA....SEE ALSO AFR

B54
MITCHELL P.,AFRICAN AFTERTHOUGHTS. UGANDA CONSTN NAT/G ADJUD COERCE WAR 20 WWI MAU/MAU. PAGE 102 A2090
BIOG
CHIEF
COLONIAL
DOMIN

S55
DE SMITH S.A.,"CONSTITUTIONAL MONARCHY IN BURGANDA." AFR UGANDA UK STRUCT CHIEF REGION INGP/REL ADJUST NAT/LISM SOVEREIGN CONSERVE ...POLICY 19/20 BURGANDA. PAGE 35 A0712
NAT/G
DIPLOM
CONSTN
COLONIAL

S61
OCHENG D.,"ECONOMIC FORCES AND UGANDA'S FOREIGN POLICY." AFR UGANDA INT/TRADE TARIFFS INCOME SOVEREIGN WEALTH 20 EACM EEC TANGANYIKA. PAGE 111 A2274
ECO/TAC
DIPLOM
ECO/UNDEV
INT/ORG

S61
OCHENG D.,"AN ECONOMIST LOOKS AT UGANDA'S FUTURE." FUT UGANDA AGRI INDUS PLAN PROB/SOLV INT/TRADE SOVEREIGN 20. PAGE 111 A2275
ECO/UNDEV
INCOME
ECO/TAC
OWN

S63
BANFIELD J.,"FEDERATION IN EAST-AFRICA." AFR UGANDA ELITES INT/ORG NAT/G VOL/ASSN LEGIS ECO/TAC FEDERAL ATTIT SOVEREIGN TOT/POP 20 TANGANYIKA. PAGE 11 A0216
EX/STRUC
PWR
REGION

S63
NYE J.S. JR.,"EAST AFRICAN ECONOMIC INTEGRATION." AFR UGANDA PROVS DELIB/GP PLAN ECO/TAC INT/TRADE ADMIN ROUTINE ORD/FREE PWR WEALTH...OBS TIME/SEQ VAL/FREE 20. PAGE 110 A2264
ECO/UNDEV
INT/ORG

S64
ROTHCHILD D.,"EAST AFRICAN FEDERATION." AFR TANZANIA UGANDA INDUS REGION 20. PAGE 124 A2547
INT/ORG
DIPLOM
ECO/UNDEV
ECO/TAC

B66
O'CONNER A.M.,AN ECONOMIC GEOGRAPHY OF EAST AFRICA. AFR TANZANIA UGANDA AGRI WORKER INT/TRADE COLONIAL GOV/REL...CHARTS METH/COMP 20 AFRICA/E. PAGE 111 A2269
ECO/UNDEV
EXTR/IND
GEOG
HABITAT

B66
WILLIAMS P.,AID IN UGANDA - EDUCATION. UGANDA UK FINAN ACADEM INT/ORG SCHOOL PROB/SOLV ECO/TAC UTIL ...STAT CHARTS 20. PAGE 165 A3352
PLAN
EDU/PROP
FOR/AID
ECO/UNDEV

U-2....INTELLIGENCE AIRCRAFT

B60
SPEIER H.,DIVIDED BERLIN: THE ANATOMY OF SOVIET POLITICAL BLACKMAIL. COM GERMANY USA+45 USSR WOR+45 NAT/G TOP/EX DOMIN EDU/PROP ALL/VALS...POLICY CONCPT COLD/WAR 20 U-2. PAGE 136 A2782
INT/ORG
ACT/RES
DIPLOM

S60
WRIGHT Q.,"LEGAL ASPECTS OF THE U-2 INCIDENT." COM USA+45 USSR STRUCT NAT/G FORCES PLAN TEC/DEV ADJUD RIGID/FLEX MORAL ORD/FREE...DECISION INT/LAW JURID PSY TREND GEN/LAWS COLD/WAR VAL/FREE 20 U-2. PAGE 168 A3413
PWR
POLICY
SPACE

S62
LISSITZYN O.J.,"SOME LEGAL IMPLICATIONS OF THE U-2 AND RB-47 INCIDENTS." FUT USA+45 USSR WOR+45 AIR NAT/G DIPLOM LEGIT MORAL ORD/FREE SOVEREIGN...JURID GEN/LAWS GEN/METH COLD/WAR 20 U-2. PAGE 90 A1840
LAW
CONCPT
SPACE
INT/LAW

UK....UNITED KINGDOM; SEE ALSO APPROPRIATE TIME/SPACE/ CULTURE INDEX, COMMONWLTH

N
INDIAN COUNCIL WORLD AFFAIRS,SELECT ARTICLES ON CURRENT AFFAIRS (BIBLIOGRAPHICAL SERIES: 7). AFR ASIA COM EUR+WWI S/ASIA UK COLONIAL NUC/PWR PEACE ATTIT...INT/LAW SOC 20. PAGE 70 A1437
BIBLIOG
DIPLOM
INT/ORG
ECO/UNDEV

N
LONDON TIMES OFFICIAL INDEX. UK LAW ECO/DEV NAT/G DIPLOM LEAD ATTIT 20. PAGE 2 A0038
BIBLIOG
INDEX
PRESS
WRITING

N
PUBLISHERS' CIRCULAR, THE OFFICIAL ORGAN OF THE PUBLISHERS' ASSOCIATION OF GREAT BRITAIN AND IRELAND. EUR+WWI MOD/EUR UK LAW PROB/SOLV DIPLOM COLONIAL ATTIT...HUM 19/20 CMN/WLTH. PAGE 2 A0039
BIBLIOG
NAT/G
WRITING
LEAD

N
REVUE FRANCAISE DE SCIENCE POLITIQUE. FRANCE UK ...BIBLIOG/A 20. PAGE 2 A0040
NAT/G
DIPLOM
CONCPT
ROUTINE

N
CARIBBEAN COMMISSION,CURRENT CARIBBEAN BIBLIOGRAPHY. FRANCE NETHERLAND UK CULTURE ECO/UNDEV PRESS LEAD ATTIT...GEOG SOC 20. PAGE 24 A0482
BIBLIOG
NAT/G
L/A+17C
DIPLOM

N
MINISTRY OF OVERSEAS DEVELOPME,TECHNICAL CO-OPERATION -- A BIBLIOGRAPHY. UK LAW SOCIETY DIPLOM ECO/TAC FOR/AID...STAT 20 CMN/WLTH. PAGE 102 A2089
BIBLIOG
TEC/DEV
ECO/DEV
NAT/G

NCO
CARRINGTON C.E.,THE COMMONWEALTH IN AFRICA (PAMPHLET). UK STRUCT NAT/G COLONIAL REPRESENT GOV/REL RACE/REL NAT/LISM...MAJORIT 20 EEC NEGRO COLD/WAR. PAGE 25 A0500
ECO/UNDEV
AFR
DIPLOM
PLAN

B00
GRIFFIN A.P.C.,LIST OF BOOKS RELATING TO THE THEORY OF COLONIZATION, GOVERNMENT OF DEPENDENCIES, PROTECTORATES, AND RELATED TOPICS. FRANCE GERMANY ITALY SPAIN UK USA-45 WOR-45 ECO/TAC ADMIN CONTROL REGION NAT/LISM ALL/VALS PWR...INT/LAW SOC 16/19. PAGE 56 A1149
BIBLIOG/A
COLONIAL
GOV/REL
DOMIN

B00
MOCKLER-FERRYMAN A.,BRITISH WEST AFRICA. FRANCE GERMANY NIGER SIER/LEONE UK CULTURE DIPLOM WAR RACE/REL PRODUC PROFIT WEALTH...POLICY PREDICT 19. PAGE 102 A2095
AFR
COLONIAL
INT/TRADE
CAP/ISM

L00
HISTORICUS,"LETTERS AND SOME QUESTIONS OF INTERNATIONAL LAW." FRANCE NETHERLAND UK USA-45 WOR-45 LAW NAT/G COERCE...SOC CONCPT GEN/LAWS TOT/POP 19 CIVIL/WAR. PAGE 65 A1344
WEALTH
JURID
WAR
INT/LAW

B01
GRIFFIN A.P.C.,LIST OF BOOKS ON SAMOA (PAMPHLET). GERMANY S/ASIA UK USA-45 WOR-45 ECO/UNDEV REGION ALL/VALS ORD/FREE ALL/IDEOS...GEOG INT/LAW 19 SAMOA GUAM. PAGE 56 A1150
BIBLIOG/A
COLONIAL
DIPLOM

B01
HART A.B.,AMERICAN HISTORY TOLD BY CONTEMPORARIES. UK CULTURE FINAN SECT FORCES DIPLOM TAX RUMOR CT/SYS REV GOV/REL GP/REL...ANTHOL 17/18 PRE/US/AM FEDERALIST. PAGE 62 A1273
USA-45
COLONIAL
SOVEREIGN

B02
MOREL E.D.,AFFAIRS OF WEST AFRICA. UK FINAN INDUS FAM KIN SECT CHIEF WORKER DIPLOM RACE/REL LITERACY HEALTH...CHARTS 18/20 AFRICA/W NEGRO. PAGE 104 A2129
COLONIAL
ADMIN
AFR

B02
SEELEY J.R.,THE EXPANSION OF ENGLAND. MOD/EUR S/ASIA UK CULTURE NAT/G FORCES PLAN DOMIN EDU/PROP COLONIAL ROUTINE ATTIT ALL/VALS SOVEREIGN...CONCPT HIST/WRIT PARLIAMENT 18 CMN/WLTH. PAGE 131 A2679
INT/ORG
ACT/RES
CAP/ISM
INDIA

B03
FORTESCUE G.K.,SUBJECT INDEX OF THE MODERN WORKS ADDED TO THE LIBRARY OF THE BRITISH MUSEUM IN THE YEARS 1881-1900 (3 VOLS.). UK LAW CONSTN FINAN NAT/G FORCES INT/TRADE COLONIAL 19. PAGE 47 A0968
BIBLIOG
INDEX
WRITING

B03
GRIFFIN A.P.C.,LISTS PUBLISHED 1902-03: ANGLO-SAXON INTERESTS (PAMPHLET). UK USA-45 ELITES SOCIETY DIPLOM ISOLAT 19/20. PAGE 56 A1152
BIBLIOG
COLONIAL
RACE/REL
DOMIN

B03
MOREL E.D.,THE BRITISH CASE IN FRENCH CONGO. CONGO/BRAZ FRANCE UK COERCE MORAL WEALTH...POLICY INT/LAW 20 CONGO/LEOP. PAGE 104 A2130
DIPLOM
INT/TRADE
COLONIAL
AFR

B05
GRIFFIN A.P.C.,LIST OF REFERENCES ON THE US CONSULAR SERVICE (PAMPHLET). FRANCE GERMANY SPAIN UK USA-45 OP/RES DOMIN ADMIN FEEDBACK ROUTINE GOV/REL...DECISION 19. PAGE 56 A1153
BIBLIOG/A
NAT/G
DIPLOM
CONSULT

B06
GRIFFIN A.P.C.,SELECT LIST OF REFERENCES ON THE BRITISH TARIFF MOVEMENT. MOD/EUR UK BAL/PWR BARGAIN ECO/TAC LAISSEZ 20. PAGE 56 A1154
BIBLIOG/A
INT/TRADE
TARIFFS
COLONIAL

C06
MONTGOMERY H.,"A DICTIONARY OF POLITICAL PHRASES AND ILLUSIONS WITH A SHORT BIBLIOGRAPHY." EUR+WWI MOD/EUR UK AGRI LABOR LOC/G NAT/G COLONIAL CHOOSE RACE/REL. PAGE 103 A2114
BIBLIOG
DICTIONARY
POLICY
DIPLOM

B10
GRIFFIN A.P.C.,LIST OF REFERENCES ON RECIPROCITY (2ND REV. ED.). CANADA CUBA UK USA-45 WOR-45 NAT/G TARIFFS CONFER COLONIAL CONTROL SANCTION CONSEN ALL/VALS...DECISION 19/20. PAGE 56 A1157
BIBLIOG/A
VOL/ASSN
DIPLOM
REPAR

B13
BORCHARD E.M.,BIBLIOGRAPHY OF INTERNATIONAL LAW AND CONTINENTAL LAW. EUR+WWI MOD/EUR UK LAW INT/TRADE WAR PEACE...GOV/COMP NAT/COMP 19/20. PAGE 17 A0338
BIBLIOG
INT/LAW
JURID
DIPLOM

B14
HARRIS N.D.,INTERVENTION AND COLONIZATION IN AFRICA. BELGIUM FRANCE GERMANY MOD/EUR PORTUGAL UK ECO/UNDEV BAL/PWR DOMIN CONTROL PWR...GEOG 19/20. PAGE 62 A1267
AFR
COLONIAL
DIPLOM

N17
BURKE E.,THOUGHTS ON THE PROSPECT OF A REGICIDE PEACE (PAMPHLET). FRANCE UK SECT DOMIN MURDER PEACE
REV
CHIEF

ORD/FREE SOVEREIGN POPULISM...POLICY GOV/COMP IDEA/COMP 18 JACOBINISM COEXIST. PAGE 21 A0435
NAT/G DIPLOM

B19
KEYNES J.M.,THE ECONOMIC CONSEQUENCES OF THE PEACE. FUT GERMANY MOD/EUR RUSSIA UK USA-45 CULTURE ECO/DEV FINAN INDUS INT/ORG TOP/EX ECO/TAC ROUTINE WAR ATTIT PERCEPT ALL/VALS...OLD/LIB MYTH OBS TIME/SEQ TREND 20 TREATY. PAGE 78 A1605
EUR+WWI SOCIETY PEACE

B19
MEYER H.H.B.,SELECT LIST OF REFERENCES ON ECONOMIC RECONSTRUCTION: INCLUDING REPORTS OF THE BRITISH MINISTRY OF RECONSTRUCTION. UK LABOR PLAN PROB/SOLV ECO/TAC INT/TRADE WAR DEMAND PRODUC 20. PAGE 100 A2051
BIBLIOG/A EUR+WWI ECO/DEV WORKER

N19
HANNA A.J.,EUROPEAN RULE IN AFRICA (PAMPHLET). BELGIUM FRANCE MOD/EUR UK WOR+45 WOR-45 ECO/UNDEV NAT/G PARTIC SOVEREIGN...NAT/COMP 19/20. PAGE 61 A1252
DIPLOM COLONIAL AFR NAT/LISM

N19
HIGGINS R.,THE ADMINISTRATION OF UNITED KINGDOM FOREIGN POLICY THROUGH THE UNITED NATIONS (PAMPHLET). UK NAT/G ADMIN GOV/REL...CHARTS 20 UN PARLIAMENT. PAGE 65 A1329
DIPLOM POLICY INT/ORG

N19
MASSEY V.,CANADIANS AND THEIR COMMONWEALTH: THE ROMANES LECTURE DELIVERED IN THE SHELDONIAN THEATRE JUNE 1, 1961 (PAMPHLET). CANADA UK CULTURE ECO/DEV REPRESENT NAT/LISM PEACE PWR CONSERVE 20 CMN/WLTH. PAGE 96 A1959
ATTIT DIPLOM NAT/G SOVEREIGN

B20
HALDANE R.B.,BEFORE THE WAR. MOD/EUR SOCIETY INT/ORG NAT/G DELIB/GP PLAN DOMIN EDU/PROP LEGIT ADMIN COERCE ATTIT DRIVE MORAL ORD/FREE PWR...SOC CONCPT SELF/OBS RECORD BIOG TIME/SEQ. PAGE 60 A1223
POLICY DIPLOM UK

B23
HEADICAR B.M.,CATALOGUE OF THE BOOKS, PAMPHLETS, AND OTHER DOCUMENTS IN THE EDWARD FRY LIBRARY OF INTERNATIONAL LAW... UK INT/ORG 20. PAGE 63 A1304
BIBLIOG INT/LAW DIPLOM

B26
LEWIN E.,RECENT PUBLICATIONS IN THE LIBRARY OF THE ROYAL COLONIAL INSTITUTE (PAMPHLET). CANADA UK EX/STRUC PARL/PROC NAT/LISM SOVEREIGN 20 CMN/WLTH PARLIAMENT. PAGE 88 A1799
BIBLIOG COLONIAL CONSTN DIPLOM

B27
GOOCH G.P.,ENGLISH DEMOCRATIC IDEAS IN THE SEVENTEENTH CENTURY (2ND ED.). UK LAW SECT FORCES DIPLOM LEAD PARL/PROC REV ATTIT AUTHORIT...ANARCH CONCPT 17 PARLIAMENT CMN/WLTH REFORMERS. PAGE 54 A1100
IDEA/COMP MAJORIT EX/STRUC CONSERVE

B27
HARRIS N.D.,EUROPE AND AFRICA. BELGIUM FRANCE GERMANY MOD/EUR PORTUGAL UK ECO/UNDEV BAL/PWR PWR ...GEOG 19/20. PAGE 62 A1268
AFR COLONIAL DIPLOM

B27
SIEGFRIED A.,AMERICA COMES OF AGE: A FRENCH ANALYSIS (TRANS. BY H.H. HEMMING AND DORIS HEMMING). FRANCE UK POL/PAR WORKER TEC/DEV DIPLOM REGION RACE/REL ADJUST PRODUC HEREDITY...TIME/SEQ GP/COMP SOC/INTEG 20 DEMOCRAT REPUBLICAN KKK. PAGE 132 A2714
USA-45 CULTURE ECO/DEV SOC

B28
HALL W.P.,EMPIRE TO COMMONWEALTH. FUT WOR-45 CONSTN ECO/DEV ECO/UNDEV INT/ORG PROVS PLAN DIPLOM EDU/PROP ADMIN COLONIAL PEACE PERSON ALL/VALS ...POLICY GEOG SOC OBS RECORD TREND CMN/WLTH PARLIAMENT 19/20. PAGE 60 A1229
VOL/ASSN NAT/G UK

B28
HURST C.,GREAT BRITAIN AND THE DOMINIONS. EUR+WWI CULTURE ECO/DEV INT/ORG NAT/G DIPLOM ECO/TAC COLONIAL ATTIT PWR SOVEREIGN...TIME/SEQ GEN/LAWS TOT/POP VAL/FREE 20 CMN/WLTH. PAGE 69 A1420
VOL/ASSN DOMIN UK

B28
PLAYNE C.E.,THE PRE-WAR MIND IN BRITAIN. GERMANY MOD/EUR UK STRATA SECT DIPLOM EDU/PROP CROWD SUFF ...POLICY ANARCH PSY SOC IDEA/COMP 20 WWI. PAGE 116 A2388
PRESS WAR DOMIN ATTIT

B29
CONWELL-EVANS T.P.,THE LEAGUE COUNCIL IN ACTION. EUR+WWI TURKEY UK USSR WOR-45 INT/ORG FORCES JUDGE ECO/TAC EDU/PROP LEGIT ROUTINE ARMS/CONT COERCE ATTIT PWR...MAJORIT GEOG JURID CONCPT LEAGUE/NAT TOT/POP VAL/FREE TUNIS 20. PAGE 30 A0605
DELIB/GP INT/LAW

B29
LANGER W.L.,THE FRANCO-RUSSIAN ALLIANCE: 1890-1894. FRANCE MOD/EUR UK USSR NAT/G CHIEF FORCES BAL/PWR AGREE WAR PEACE PWR...TIME/SEQ TREATY 19 BISMARCK/O. PAGE 84 A1724
DIPLOM

B30
SCHMITT B.E.,THE COMING OF THE WAR, 1914 (2 VOLS.). AUSTRIA FRANCE GERMANY MOD/EUR RUSSIA UK PLAN ROUTINE ORD/FREE. PAGE 128 A2633
WAR DIPLOM

B32
CARDINALL AW,A BIBLIOGRAPHY OF THE GOLD COAST. AFR UK NAT/G EX/STRUC ATTIT...POLICY 19/20. PAGE 24 A0479
BIBLIOG ADMIN COLONIAL DIPLOM

B32
EAGLETON C.,INTERNATIONAL GOVERNMENT. BRAZIL FRANCE GERMANY ITALY UK USSR WOR-45 DELIB/GP TOP/EX PLAN ECO/TAC EDU/PROP LEGIT ADJUD REGION ARMS/CONT COERCE ATTIT PWR...GEOG MGT VAL/FREE LEAGUE/NAT 20. PAGE 40 A0816
INT/ORG JURID DIPLOM INT/LAW

B34
LOVELL R.I.,THE STRUGGLE FOR SOUTH AFRICA, 1875-1899. GERMANY RHODESIA SOUTH/AFR UK NAT/G ECO/TAC HABITAT WEALTH...POLICY 19. PAGE 91 A1866
COLONIAL DIPLOM WAR GP/REL

B35
LANGER W.L.,THE DIPLOMACY OF IMPERIALISM 1890-1902. FRANCE GERMANY ITALY UK WOR-45 BAL/PWR INT/TRADE LEGIT ADJUD CONTROL WAR PWR SOVEREIGN...CHARTS BIBLIOG/A 19/20. PAGE 84 A1726
DIPLOM COLONIAL DOMIN

B35
MARRIOTT J.A.,DICTATORSHIP AND DEMOCRACY. GERMANY GREECE UK CHIEF DIPLOM DOMIN LEGIT PEACE ORD/FREE CONSERVE...TREND ROME HITLER/A. PAGE 95 A1946
TOTALISM POPULISM PLURIST NAT/G

B35
SIMONDS F.H.,THE GREAT POWERS IN WORLD POLITICS. FRANCE GERMANY UK WOR-45 INT/ORG NAT/G ARMS/CONT PEACE FASCISM...POLICY GEOG 20 DEPRESSION NAZI. PAGE 133 A2718
DIPLOM WEALTH WAR

B36
BOYCE A.N.,EUROPE AND SOUTH AFRICA. FRANCE GERMANY ITALY SOUTH/AFR UK INDUS NAT/G CONTROL REV WAR NAT/LISM...CONCPT HIST/WRIT 20. PAGE 18 A0362
COLONIAL GOV/COMP NAT/COMP DIPLOM

B36
METZ I.,DIE DEUTSCHE FLOTTE IN DER ENGLISCHEN PRESSE, DER NAVY SCARE VOM WINTER 1904/05. GERMANY UK FORCES DIPLOM WAR 20 NAVY. PAGE 100 A2047
EDU/PROP ATTIT DOMIN PRESS

B36
ROBINSON H.,DEVELOPMENT OF THE BRITISH EMPIRE. WOR-45 CULTURE SOCIETY STRUCT ECO/DEV ECO/UNDEV INT/ORG VOL/ASSN FORCES CREATE PLAN DOMIN EDU/PROP ADMIN COLONIAL PWR WEALTH...POLICY GEOG CHARTS CMN/WLTH 16/20. PAGE 122 A2503
NAT/G HIST/WRIT UK

B37
BLAKE J.W.,EUROPEAN BEGINNINGS IN WEST AFRICA 1454-1578. FRANCE GUINEA PORTUGAL UK PWR WEALTH 16/16 AFRICA/W. PAGE 15 A0305
DIPLOM COLONIAL INT/TRADE DOMIN

B37
DE KIEWIET C.W.,THE IMPERIAL FACTOR IN SOUTH AFRICA. AFR SOUTH/AFR UK WAR...POLICY SOC 19. PAGE 35 A0705
DIPLOM COLONIAL CULTURE

B38
FRANKEL S.H.,CAPITAL INVESTMENT IN AFRICA. AFR EUR+WWI RHODESIA SOUTH/AFR UK FINAN FOR/AID COLONIAL DEMAND UTIL WEALTH...METH/CNCPT CHARTS 20 CONGO/LEOP. PAGE 48 A0983
ECO/UNDEV EXTR/IND DIPLOM PRODUC

B38
HOBSON J.A.,IMPERIALISM. MOD/EUR UK WOR-45 CULTURE ECO/UNDEV NAT/G VOL/ASSN PLAN EDU/PROP LEGIT REGION COERCE ATTIT PWR...POLICY PLURIST TIME/SEQ GEN/LAWS 19/20. PAGE 66 A1348
DOMIN ECO/TAC BAL/PWR COLONIAL

B38
MCNAIR A.D.,THE LAW OF TREATIES: BRITISH PRACTICE AND OPINIONS. UK CREATE DIPLOM LEGIT WRITING ADJUD WAR...INT/LAW JURID TREATY. PAGE 98 A2018
AGREE LAW CT/SYS NAT/G

B39
BENES E.,INTERNATIONAL SECURITY. GERMANY UK NAT/G DELIB/GP PLAN BAL/PWR ATTIT ORD/FREE PWR LEAGUE/NAT 20 TREATY. PAGE 13 A0267
EUR+WWI INT/ORG WAR

B39
DULLES J.,WAR, PEACE AND CHANGE. FRANCE ITALY UK USA-45 WOR-45 LAW INT/ORG NAT/G SECT VOL/ASSN FORCES TOP/EX DOMIN ARMS/CONT COERCE ATTIT PERSON RIGID/FLEX MORAL PWR...JURID STERTYP TOT/POP LEAGUE/NAT 20. PAGE 39 A0796
EDU/PROP TOTALISM WAR

B39
NICOLSON H.,CURZON: THE LAST PHASE, 1919-1925. UK NAT/G DELIB/GP TOP/EX ROUTINE WAR RIGID/FLEX ...METH/CNCPT 20 CURZON/GN. PAGE 109 A2231
POLICY DIPLOM BIOG

B39
THOMAS J.A.,THE HOUSE OF COMMONS, 1832-1901; A STUDY OF ITS ECONOMIC AND FUNCTIONAL CHARACTER. UK LAW STRATA FINAN DIPLOM CONTROL LEAD LOBBY REPRESENT WEALTH...POLICY STAT BIBLIOG 19/20 PARLIAMENT. PAGE 143 A2922
PARL/PROC LEGIS POL/PAR ECO/DEV

B40
CONOVER H.F.,FOREIGN RELATIONS OF THE UNITED STATES: A LIST OF RECENT BOOKS (PAMPHLET). ASIA CANADA L/A+17C UK INT/ORG INT/TRADE TARIFFS NEUTRAL WAR PEACE...INT/LAW CON/ANAL 20 CHINJAP. PAGE 29 A0592
BIBLIOG/A USA-45 DIPLOM

B40
WANDERSCHECK H.,FRANKREICHS PROPAGANDA GEGEN DEUTSCHLAND. FRANCE GERMANY MOD/EUR UK NAT/G DIPLOM
EDU/PROP ATTIT

WAR 20 JEWS. PAGE 161 A3273
DOMIN PRESS

B40
WOLFERS A.,BRITAIN AND FRANCE BETWEEN TWO WORLD WARS. FRANCE UK INT/ORG NAT/G PLAN BARGAIN ECO/TAC AGREE ISOLAT ALL/IDEOS...DECISION GEOG 20 TREATY VERSAILLES INTERVENT. PAGE 166 A3380
DIPLOM WAR POLICY

B41
BAUMANN G.,GRUNDLAGEN UND PRAXIS DER INTERNATIONALEN PROPAGANDA. FRANCE GERMANY UK CULTURE COM/IND PRESS PWR...PSY METH/COMP 20. PAGE 12 A0236
EDU/PROP DOMIN ATTIT DIPLOM

B41
PERHAM M.,AFRICANS AND BRITISH RULE. AFR UK ECO/TAC CONTROL GP/REL ATTIT 20. PAGE 115 A2355
DIPLOM COLONIAL ADMIN ECO/UNDEV

B42
FULLER G.H.,DEFENSE FINANCING: A SUPPLEMENTARY LIST OF REFERENCES (PAMPHLET). CANADA UK USA-45 ECO/DEV NAT/G DELIB/GP BUDGET ADJUD ARMS/CONT WEAPON COST PEACE PWR 20 AUSTRAL CHINJAP CONGRESS. PAGE 50 A1021
BIBLIOG/A FINAN FORCES DIPLOM

B42
JACKSON M.V.,EUROPEAN POWERS AND SOUTH-EAST AFRICA: A STUDY OF INTERNATIONAL RELATIONS ON SOUTH-EAST COAST OF AFRICA, 1796-1856. AFR FRANCE PORTUGAL SOUTH/AFR UK USA-45 FORCES INT/TRADE PWR...CHARTS BIBLIOG 18/19 TREATY. PAGE 72 A1477
DOMIN POLICY ORD/FREE DIPLOM

B42
JOSHI P.S.,THE TYRANNY OF COLOUR. INDIA SOUTH/AFR UK ECO/UNDEV NAT/G POL/PAR DIPLOM ECO/TAC WAR ...POLICY 19/20. PAGE 75 A1538
COLONIAL DISCRIM RACE/REL

B43
BROWN A.D.,BRITISH POSSESSIONS IN THE CARIBBEAN AREA: A SELECTED LIST OF REFERENCES. UK NAT/G DIPLOM...GEOG 20 CARIBBEAN. PAGE 20 A0398
BIBLIOG COLONIAL ECO/UNDEV L/A+17C

B43
FULLER G.F.,FOREIGN RELIEF AND REHABILITATION (PAMPHLET). FUT GERMANY UK USA-45 INT/ORG PROB/SOLV DIPLOM FOR/AID ADMIN ADJUST PEACE ALL/VALS...SOC/WK 20 UN JEWS. PAGE 50 A1018
BIBLIOG/A PLAN GIVE WAR

B43
MICAUD C.A.,THE FRENCH RIGHT AND NAZI GERMANY 1933-1939: A STUDY OF PUBLIC OPINION. GERMANY UK USSR POL/PAR ARMS/CONT COERCE DETER PEACE RIGID/FLEX PWR MARXISM...FASCIST TREND 20 LEAGUE/NAT TREATY. PAGE 101 A2065
DIPLOM AGREE

B44
FULLER G.H.,MILITARY GOVERNMENT: A LIST OF REFERENCES (A PAMPHLET). ITALY UK USA-45 WOR-45 LAW FORCES DOMIN ADMIN ARMS/CONT ORD/FREE PWR ...DECISION 20 CHINJAP. PAGE 50 A1023
BIBLIOG DIPLOM CIVMIL/REL SOVEREIGN

B44
RUDIN H.R.,ARMISTICE 1918. FRANCE GERMANY MOD/EUR UK USA-45 NAT/G CHIEF DELIB/GP FORCES BAL/PWR REPAR ARMS/CONT 20 WILSON/W TREATY. PAGE 125 A2566
AGREE WAR PEACE DIPLOM

L44
HAILEY,"THE FUTURE OF COLONIAL PEOPLES." WOR-45 CONSTN CULTURE ECO/UNDEV AGRI MARKET INT/ORG NAT/G SECT CONSULT ECO/TAC LEGIT ADMIN NAT/LISM ALL/VALS ...SOC OBS TREND STERTYP CMN/WLTH LEAGUE/NAT PARLIAMENT 20. PAGE 59 A1218
PLAN CONCPT DIPLOM UK

B45
BEVERIDGE W.,THE PRICE OF PEACE. GERMANY UK WOR+45 WOR-45 NAT/G FORCES CREATE LEGIT REGION WAR ATTIT KNOWL ORD/FREE PWR...POLICY NEW/IDEA GEN/LAWS LEAGUE/NAT 20 TREATY. PAGE 14 A0284
INT/ORG TREND PEACE

B45
CONOVER H.F.,THE GOVERNMENTS OF THE MAJOR FOREIGN POWERS: A BIBLIOGRAPHY. FRANCE GERMANY ITALY UK USSR CONSTN LOC/G POL/PAR EX/STRUC FORCES ADMIN CT/SYS CIVMIL/REL TOTALISM...POLICY 19/20. PAGE 29 A0598
BIBLIOG NAT/G DIPLOM

B45
ELTON G.E.,IMPERIAL COMMONWEALTH. INDIA UK DIPLOM DOMIN WAR NAT/LISM SOVEREIGN...TRADIT CHARTS T 15/20 CMN/WLTH AUSTRAL PRE/US/AM. PAGE 41 A0844
REGION CONCPT COLONIAL

B45
HORN O.B.,BRITISH PUBLIC OPINION AND THE FIRST PARTITION OF POLAND. POLAND UK LEGIS PRESS RUMOR CONTROL PARTIC NAT/LISM SOVEREIGN 18/19. PAGE 67 A1385
DIPLOM POLICY ATTIT NAT/G

B45
MACMINN N.,BIBLIOGRAPHY OF THE PUBLISHED WRITINGS OF JOHN STUART MILL. MOD/EUR UK CAP/ISM DIPLOM KNOWL...EPIST CONCPT 19 MILL/JS. PAGE 93 A1901
BIBLIOG/A SOCIETY INGP/REL LAISSEZ

B45
WING D.,SHORT-TITLE CATALOGUE OF BOOKS PRINTED IN THE BRITISH ISLES, AND OF ENGLISH BOOKS PRINTED OVERSEAS; 1641-1700 (3 VOLS.). UK USA-45 LAW DIPLOM ADMIN COLONIAL LEAD ATTIT 17. PAGE 165 A3363
BIBLIOG MOD/EUR NAT/G

B46
GRIFFIN G.G.,A GUIDE TO MANUSCRIPTS RELATING TO AMERICAN HISTORY IN BRITISH DEPOSITORIES. CANADA IRELAND MOD/EUR UK USA-45 LAW DIPLOM ADMIN COLONIAL WAR NAT/LISM SOVEREIGN...GEOG INT/LAW 15/19 CMN/WLTH. PAGE 56 A1159
BIBLIOG/A ALL/VALS NAT/G

B47
CONOVER H.F.,NON-SELF-GOVERNING AREAS. BELGIUM FRANCE ITALY UK WOR+45 CULTURE ECO/UNDEV INT/ORG LOC/G NAT/G ECO/TAC INT/TRADE ADMIN HEALTH...SOC UN. PAGE 30 A0601
BIBLIOG/A COLONIAL DIPLOM

B48
CHURCHILL W.,THE GATHERING STORM. UK WOR-45 INT/ORG NAT/G FORCES TOP/EX DIPLOM ECO/TAC COERCE ATTIT ORD/FREE PWR WEALTH...POLICY SELF/OBS RECORD NAZI PARLIAMENT 20. PAGE 26 A0538
BIOG

B48
NAMIER L.B.,DIPLOMATIC PRELUDE 1938-1939. CZECHOSLVK EUR+WWI GERMANY POLAND UK FORCES DOMIN PWR 20 HITLER/A. PAGE 107 A2193
WAR TOTALISM DIPLOM

B48
PELCOVITS N.A.,OLD CHINA HANDS AND THE FOREIGN OFFICE. ASIA BURMA UK ECO/UNDEV NAT/G ECO/TAC FOR/AID TARIFFS DOMIN COLONIAL GOV/REL SOVEREIGN 19 HONG/KONG TREATY. PAGE 114 A2348
INT/TRADE ATTIT DIPLOM

B48
VISSON A.,AS OTHERS SEE US. EUR+WWI FRANCE UK USA+45 CULTURE INTELL SOCIETY STRATA NAT/G POL/PAR FOR/AID ATTIT DRIVE LOVE ORD/FREE RESPECT WEALTH ...PLURIST SOC OBS TOT/POP 20. PAGE 159 A3244
USA-45 PERCEPT

B48
WHEELER-BENNETT J.W.,MUNICH: PROLOGUE TO TRAGEDY. EUR+WWI FRANCE GERMANY UK PLAN PROB/SOLV SOVEREIGN ...POLICY DECISION 20 HITLER/A. PAGE 163 A3327
DIPLOM WAR PEACE

B49
HEADLAM-MORLEY,BIBLIOGRAPHY IN POLITICS FOR THE HONOUR SCHOOL OF PHILOSOPHY, POLITICS AND ECONOMICS (PAMPHLET). UK CONSTN LABOR MUNIC DIPLOM ADMIN 19/20. PAGE 64 A1305
BIBLIOG NAT/G PHIL/SCI GOV/REL

B49
HINDEN R.,EMPIRE AND AFTER. UK POL/PAR BAL/PWR DIPLOM INT/TRADE WAR NAT/LISM PWR 17/20. PAGE 65 A1335
NAT/G COLONIAL ATTIT POLICY

B49
JACKSON R.H.,INTERNATIONAL CONFERENCE ON MILITARY TRIALS. FRANCE GERMANY UK USA+45 USSR VOL/ASSN DELIB/GP REPAR ADJUD CT/SYS CRIME WAR 20 WAR/TRIAL. PAGE 72 A1479
DIPLOM INT/ORG INT/LAW CIVMIL/REL

B49
STETTINIUS E.R.,ROOSEVELT AND THE RUSSIANS: THE YALTA CONFERENCE. UK USSR WOR+45 WOR-45 INT/ORG VOL/ASSN TOP/EX ACT/RES EDU/PROP PEACE ATTIT DRIVE PERSON SUPEGO PWR...POLICY CONCPT MYTH OBS TIME/SEQ AUD/VIS COLD/WAR 20 CHURCHLL/W YALTA ROOSEVLT/F. PAGE 138 A2819
DIPLOM DELIB/GP BIOG

B50
BROOKINGS INSTITUTION,MAJOR PROBLEMS OF UNITED STATES FOREIGN POLICY. AFR ASIA INDIA UK USA+45 USSR BAL/PWR FOR/AID WAR PEACE TOTALISM MARXISM SOCISM 20 CHINJAP COLD/WAR. PAGE 19 A0393
DIPLOM POLICY ORD/FREE

B50
CHURCHILL W.,TRIUMPH AND TRAGEDY. UK WOR-45 INT/ORG NAT/G DELIB/GP FORCES TOP/EX DIPLOM COERCE CHOOSE ATTIT ORD/FREE PWR WEALTH...SELF/OBS CHARTS NAZI 20. PAGE 26 A0539
BIOG PEACE WAR

B50
COUNCIL BRITISH NATIONAL BIB,BRITISH NATIONAL BIBLIOGRAPHY. UK AGRI CONSTRUC PERF/ART POL/PAR SECT CREATE INT/TRADE LEAD...HUM JURID PHIL/SCI 20. PAGE 31 A0637
BIBLIOG/A NAT/G TEC/DEV DIPLOM

B50
GLEASON J.H.,THE GENESIS OF RUSSOPHOBIA IN GREAT BRITAIN: A STUDY OF THE INTERACTION OF POLICY AND OPINION. ASIA RUSSIA UK NAT/G AGREE CONTROL REV WAR LOVE PWR TREATY 19. PAGE 53 A1080
DIPLOM POLICY DOMIN COLONIAL

B50
MOCKFORD J.,SOUTH-WEST AFRICA AND THE INTERNATIONAL COURT (PAMPHLET). AFR GERMANY SOUTH/AFR UK ECO/UNDEV DIPLOM CONTROL DISCRIM...DECISION JURID 20 AFRICA/SW. PAGE 102 A2094
COLONIAL SOVEREIGN INT/LAW DOMIN

B50
PERHAM M.,COLONIAL GOVERNMENT: ANNOTATED READING LIST ON BRITISH COLONIAL GOVERNMENT. UK WOR+45 WOR-45 ECO/UNDEV INT/ORG LEGIS FOR/AID INT/TRADE DOMIN ADMIN REV 20. PAGE 115 A2356
BIBLIOG/A COLONIAL GOV/REL NAT/G

N51
MONPIED E.,FEDERALIST BIBLIOGRAPHY: ARTICLES AND DOCUMENTS PUBLISHED IN BRITISH PERIODICALS 1945-1951 (MIMEOGRAPHED). EUR+WWI UK WOR+45 DIPLOM REGION ATTIT SOCISM...INT/LAW 20. PAGE 103 A2110
BIBLIOG/A INT/ORG FEDERAL CENTRAL

B51
JENNINGS S.I.,THE COMMONWEALTH IN ASIA. CEYLON INDIA PAKISTAN S/ASIA UK CONSTN CULTURE SOCIETY STRATA STRUCT NAT/G POL/PAR EDU/PROP LEAD WAR 20 CMN/WLTH. PAGE 74 A1510
NAT/LISM REGION COLONIAL DIPLOM

B51
RAPPAPORT A.,THE BRITISH PRESS AND WILSONIAN NEUTRALITY. UK WOR-45 SEA POL/PAR WAR CHOOSE PEACE ATTIT PERCEPT...GEOG 20 WILSON/W. PAGE 119 A2446
PRESS DIPLOM NEUTRAL POLICY

B52
ALBERTINI L.,THE ORIGINS OF THE WAR OF 1914 (3 VOLS.). AUSTRIA FRANCE GERMANY MOD/EUR RUSSIA UK PROB/SOLV NEUTRAL PWR...BIBLIOG 19/20. PAGE 5 A0107
WAR DIPLOM FORCES BAL/PWR

B52
BASSETT R.,DEMOCRACY AND FOREIGN POLICY: A CASE HISTORY, THE SINOJAPANESE DISPUTE, 1931-1933. ASIA UK 20 CHINJAP. PAGE 11 A0233
DIPLOM WAR INT/ORG SANCTION

B52
DUNN F.S.,CURRENT RESEARCH IN INTERNATIONAL AFFAIRS. UK USA+45...POLICY TREATY. PAGE 39 A0801
BIBLIOG/A DIPLOM INT/LAW

B52
FERRELL R.H.,PEACE IN THEIR TIME. FRANCE UK USA-45 INT/ORG NAT/G FORCES CREATE AGREE ARMS/CONT COERCE WAR TREATY 20 WILSON/W LEAGUE/NAT BRIAND/A. PAGE 45 A0920
PEACE DIPLOM

B52
US LIBRARY OF CONGRESS,EGYPT AND THE ANGLO-EGYPTIAN SUDAN: A SELECTIVE GUIDE TO BACKGROUND READING (PAMPHLET). SUDAN UAR UK DIPLOM...POLICY 20. PAGE 155 A3153
BIBLIOG/A COLONIAL ISLAM NAT/G

S52
HAAS E.B.,"THE RECONCILIATION OF CONFLICT, COLONIAL POLICY AIMS: ACCEPTANCE OF THE LEAGUE OF NATIONS MANDATE SYSTEM." FRANCE GERMANY UK WOR+45 WOR-45 LEGIT ATTIT DRIVE ORD/FREE...OLD/LIB INT SYS/QU TIME/SEQ TREND LEAGUE/NAT 20. PAGE 58 A1201
INT/ORG COLONIAL

B53
KALIJARVI T.V.,MODERN WORLD POLITICS (3RD ED.). AFR L/A+17C MOD/EUR S/ASIA UK USSR WOR+45 INT/ORG BAL/PWR WAR PWR 20. PAGE 76 A1552
DIPLOM INT/LAW PEACE

B53
MANSERGH N.,DOCUMENTS AND SPEECHES ON BRITISH COMMONWEALTH AFFAIRS 1931-1952. INDIA IRELAND PAKISTAN UK CONSTN POL/PAR CHIEF FORCES COLONIAL ORD/FREE SOVEREIGN...JURID 20 COMMONWLTH. PAGE 94 A1929
BIBLIOG/A DIPLOM ECO/TAC

B53
MATLOFF M.,STRATEGIC PLANNING FOR COALITION WARFARE. UK USA-45 CHIEF DIPLOM EXEC GOV/REL ...METH/COMP 20. PAGE 96 A1967
WAR PLAN DECISION FORCES

B53
MCNEILL W.H.,AMERICA, BRITAIN, AND RUSSIA; THEIR COOPERATION AND CONFLICT. UK USA-45 USSR ECO/DEV ECO/UNDEV FORCES PLAN ADMIN AGREE PERS/REL ...DECISION 20 TREATY. PAGE 98 A2021
WAR DIPLOM DOMIN

B53
NEISSER H.,NATIONAL INCOMES AND INTERNATIONAL TRADE. FRANCE GERMANY SWEDEN UK USA-45 EXTR/IND FINAN INDUS TEC/DEV PRICE BAL/PAY EQUILIB INCOME WEALTH...CHARTS METH 19 CHINJAP. PAGE 108 A2215
INT/TRADE PRODUC MARKET CON/ANAL

B53
SQUIRES J.D.,BRITISH PROPAGANDA AT HOME AND IN THE UNITED STATES FROM 1914 TO 1917. UK NAT/G PROB/SOLV DOMIN PRESS EFFICIENCY...PSY PREDICT 20 WWI INTERVENT PSY/WAR. PAGE 136 A2794
EDU/PROP CONTROL WAR DIPLOM

B53
STOUT H.M.,BRITISH GOVERNMENT. UK FINAN LOC/G POL/PAR DELIB/GP DIPLOM ADMIN COLONIAL CHOOSE ORD/FREE...JURID BIBLIOG 20 COMMONWLTH. PAGE 139 A2837
NAT/G PARL/PROC CONSTN NEW/LIB

S53
MANNING C.A.W.,"THE PRETENTIONS OF INTERNATIONAL RELATIONS." WOR+45 SOCIETY CREATE EDU/PROP ATTIT PERSON KNOWL...GEN/LAWS TOT/POP VAL/FREE 20. PAGE 94 A1924
INT/ORG DIPLOM UK

B54
COOKSON J.,BEFORE THE AFRICAN STORM. BELGIUM CENTRL/AFR FRANCE UK ECO/UNDEV POL/PAR CREATE BAL/PWR RACE/REL NAT/LISM ORD/FREE CONSERVE MARXISM SOC/INTEG 20 CONGO/LEOP. PAGE 30 A0607
COLONIAL REV DISCRIM DIPLOM

B54
EPSTEIN L.D.,BRITAIN - UNEASY ALLY. KOREA UK USA+45 NAT/G POL/PAR ECO/TAC FOR/AID INT/TRADE WAR LABOR/PAR CONSRV/PAR. PAGE 42 A0857
DIPLOM ATTIT POLICY NAT/COMP

B54
REYNOLDS P.A.,BRITISH FOREIGN POLICY IN THE INTER-WAR YEARS. CZECHOSLVK GERMANY POLAND UK USA-45 POL/PAR FORCES ECO/TAC ARMS/CONT WAR ATTIT 20. PAGE 120 A2470
DIPLOM POLICY NAT/G

B55
GULICK C.A.,HISTORY AND THEORIES OF WORKING-CLASS MOVEMENTS: A SELECT BIBLIOGRAPHY. EUR+WWI MOD/EUR UK USA-45 INT/ORG. PAGE 58 A1190
BIBLIOG WORKER LABOR ADMIN

B55
PERKINS B.,THE FIRST RAPPROCHEMENTS: ENGLAND AND THE UNITED STATES, 1795-1805. UK USA-45 ATTIT ...HIST/WRIT BIBLIOG 18/19 MADISON/J WAR/1812. PAGE 115 A2357
DIPLOM COLONIAL WAR

B55
PYRAH G.B.,IMPERIAL POLICY AND SOUTH AFRICA 1902-1910. SOUTH/AFR UK NAT/G WAR DISCRIM...CONCPT CHARTS BIBLIOG/A 19/20 CMN/WLTH. PAGE 118 A2421
DIPLOM COLONIAL POLICY RACE/REL

B55
TAN C.C.,THE BOXER CATASTROPHE. ASIA UK USSR ELITES POL/PAR VOL/ASSN FORCES PROB/SOLV DIPLOM ADMIN COLONIAL NAT/LISM PEACE TREATY 19/20 BOXER/REBL. PAGE 141 A2885
REV NAT/G WAR

B55
WOODWARD E.L.,DOCUMENTS ON BRITISH FOREIGN POLICY 1919-39 (9 VOLS.). EUR+WWI UK WOR-45 INT/ORG WAR 20. PAGE 167 A3392
BIBLIOG DIPLOM

S55
DE SMITH S.A.,"CONSTITUTIONAL MONARCHY IN BURGANDA." AFR UGANDA UK STRUCT CHIEF REGION INGP/REL ADJUST NAT/LISM SOVEREIGN CONSERVE ...POLICY 19/20 BURGANDA. PAGE 35 A0712
NAT/G DIPLOM CONSTN COLONIAL

B56
FOSTER J.G.,BRITAIN IN WESTERN EUROPE: WEU AND THE ATLANTIC ALLIANCE. EUR+WWI FRANCE GERMANY GERMANY/W ITALY UK STRATA NAT/G DELIB/GP ECO/TAC ORD/FREE PWR ...TRADIT TIME/SEQ TREND OEEC PARLIAMENT 20 EUROPE/W. PAGE 47 A0969
INT/ORG FORCES WEAPON

B56
GREECE PRESBEIA U.S.,BRITISH OPINION ON CYPRUS. CYPRUS UK FORCES DIPLOM INT/TRADE DOMIN GOV/REL ORD/FREE SOVEREIGN...POLICY 20. PAGE 55 A1137
ATTIT COLONIAL LEGIS PRESS

B56
UNDERHILL F.H.,THE BRITISH COMMONWEALTH: AN EXPERIMENT IN CO-OPERATION AMONG NATIONS. CANADA UK WOR+45 WOR-45 INT/ORG COLONIAL UTIL SOVEREIGN CONSERVE...OLD/LIB SOC/EXP BIBLIOG/A 19/20 CMN/WLTH. PAGE 147 A3007
VOL/ASSN NAT/LISM DIPLOM

B56
WATT D.C.,BRITAIN AND THE SUEZ CANAL. COM UAR UK ...INT/LAW 20 SUEZ TREATY. PAGE 162 A3294
DIPLOM INT/TRADE DIST/IND NAT/G

B56
WEIS P.,NATIONALITY AND STATELESSNESS IN INTERNATIONAL LAW. UK WOR+45 WOR-45 LAW CONSTN NAT/G DIPLOM EDU/PROP LEGIT ROUTINE RIGID/FLEX ...JURID RECORD CMN/WLTH 20. PAGE 162 A3309
INT/ORG SOVEREIGN INT/LAW

B56
WOLFERS A.,THE ANGLO-AMERICAN TRADITION IN FOREIGN AFFAIRS. UK USA+45 WOR-45 CULTURE SOCIETY ECO/DEV INT/ORG NAT/G CREATE PLAN BAL/PWR ECO/TAC EDU/PROP PEACE DISPL DRIVE...TREND GEN/LAWS 20. PAGE 166 A3382
ATTIT CONCPT DIPLOM

B57
ARON R.,L'UNIFICATION ECONOMIQUE DE L'EUROPE. EUR+WWI SWITZERLND UK INT/ORG NAT/G REGION NAT/LISM ORD/FREE PWR...CONCPT METH/CNCPT OBS TREND STERTYP GEN/LAWS EEC 20. PAGE 9 A0181
VOL/ASSN ECO/TAC

B57
BISHOP O.B.,PUBLICATIONS OF THE GOVERNMENTS OF NOVA SCOTIA, PRINCE EDWARD ISLAND, NEW BRUNSWICK 1758-1952. CANADA UK ADMIN COLONIAL LEAD...POLICY 18/20. PAGE 14 A0293
BIBLIOG NAT/G DIPLOM

B57
BROMBERGER M.,LES SECRETS DE L'EXPEDITION D'EGYPTE. FRANCE ISLAM UAR UK USA+45 USSR WOR+45 INT/ORG NAT/G FORCES BAL/PWR ECO/TAC DOMIN WAR NAT/LISM ATTIT PWR SOVEREIGN...MAJORIT TIME/SEQ CHARTS SUEZ COLD/WAR 20. PAGE 19 A0387
COERCE DIPLOM

B57
BURNS A.,IN DEFENCE OF COLONIES; BRITISH COLONIAL TERRITORIES IN INTERNATIONAL AFFAIRS. UK ECO/UNDEV PLAN DOMIN SOVEREIGN...MAJORIT 18/20 CMN/WLTH INTERVENT. PAGE 22 A0439
COLONIAL POLICY ATTIT DIPLOM

B57
MCNEILL W.H.,GREECE: AMERICAN AID IN ACTION. GREECE UK USA+45 FINAN CAP/ISM INT/TRADE BAL/PAY PRODUC WEALTH...POLICY METH/COMP 20. PAGE 99 A2022
FOR/AID DIPLOM ECO/UNDEV

B57
TOMASIC D.A.,NATIONAL COMMUNISM AND SOVIET STRATEGY. UK USSR YUGOSLAVIA NAT/G POL/PAR CHIEF CREATE DOMIN REV WAR PWR...BIOG TREND 20 TITO/MARSH STALIN/J. PAGE 144 A2948
COM NAT/LISM MARXISM DIPLOM

B58
ANGELL N.,DEFENCE AND THE ENGLISH-SPEAKING ROLE. CHINA/COM UK USSR INT/ORG FORCES EDU/PROP NEUTRAL NUC/PWR NAT/LISM PEACE TOTALISM 20 COLD/WAR COEXIST. PAGE 8 A0161
DIPLOM WAR MARXISM ORD/FREE

B58
GROBLER J.H.,AFRICA'S DESTINY. AFR EUR+WWI SOUTH/AFR UK USA+45 ELITES KIN LOC/G DIPLOM DISCRIM ATTIT CONSERVE MARXISM 20 ROOSEVLT/T NEGRO. PAGE 57
POLICY ORD/FREE COLONIAL

A1168 CONSTN

B58
IMLAH A.H.,ECONOMIC ELEMENTS IN THE PAX BRITANNICA. MOD/EUR USA+45 USA-45 ECO/DEV INT/ORG NAT/G BAL/PWR ECO/TAC PEACE ATTIT PWR WEALTH...STAT CHARTS VAL/FREE 19. PAGE 70 A1436
MARKET UK

B58
MANSERGH N.,COMMONWEALTH PERSPECTIVES. GHANA UK LAW VOL/ASSN CONFER HEALTH SOVEREIGN...GEOG CHARTS ANTHOL 20 CMN/WLTH AUSTRAL. PAGE 94 A1930
DIPLOM COLONIAL INT/ORG INGP/REL

B58
MARTIN L.J.,INTERNATIONAL PROPAGANDA: ITS LEGAL AND DIPLOMATIC CONTROL. UK USA+45 USSR CONSULT DELIB/GP DOMIN CONTROL 20. PAGE 95 A1951
EDU/PROP DIPLOM INT/LAW ATTIT

B58
SCHOEDER P.W.,THE AXIS ALLIANCE AND JAPANESE-AMERICAN RELATIONS 1941. ASIA GERMANY UK USA-45 PEACE ATTIT...POLICY BIBLIOG 20 CHINJAP TREATY. PAGE 129 A2641
AGREE DIPLOM WAR

C58
WILDING N.,"AN ENCYCLOPEDIA OF PARLIAMENT." UK LAW CONSTN CHIEF PROB/SOLV DIPLOM DEBATE WAR INGP/REL PRIVIL...BIBLIOG DICTIONARY 13/20 CMN/WLTH PARLIAMENT. PAGE 164 A3349
PARL/PROC POL/PAR NAT/G ADMIN

B59
BROOKES E.H.,THE COMMONWEALTH TODAY. UK ROMAN/EMP INT/ORG RACE/REL NAT/LISM SOVEREIGN...TREND SOC/INTEG 20. PAGE 19 A0391
FEDERAL DIPLOM JURID IDEA/COMP

B59
CORBETT P.E.,LAW IN DIPLOMACY. UK USA+45 USSR CONSTN SOCIETY INT/ORG JUDGE LEGIT ATTIT ORD/FREE TOT/POP LEAGUE/NAT 20. PAGE 30 A0616
NAT/G ADJUD JURID DIPLOM

B59
DEHIO L.,GERMANY AND WORLD POLITICS IN THE TWENTIETH CENTURY. EUR+WWI FRANCE GERMANY MOD/EUR UK USSR NAT/G CHIEF BAL/PWR DOMIN COLONIAL CONTROL LEAD...IDEA/COMP 20 VERSAILLES. PAGE 36 A0724
DIPLOM WAR NAT/LISM SOVEREIGN

B59
FREE L.A.,SIX ALLIES AND A NEUTRAL. ASIA COM EUR+WWI FRANCE GERMANY/W INDIA S/ASIA UK USA+45 INT/ORG NAT/G NUC/PWR PEACE ATTIT PERCEPT RIGID/FLEX ALL/VALS...STAT REC/INT COLD/WAR 20 CHINJAP. PAGE 48 A0992
PSY DIPLOM

B59
JONES A.C.,NEW FABIAN COLONIAL ESSAYS. UK SOCIETY POL/PAR EDU/PROP ADMIN ORD/FREE SOVEREIGN SOCISM ...ANTHOL 20 CMN/WLTH LABOR/PAR. PAGE 75 A1530
COLONIAL INT/ORG INGP/REL DOMIN

B59
LINK R.G.,ENGLISH THEORIES OF ECONOMIC FLUCTUATIONS: 1815-1848. FRANCE UK AGRI WORKER DIPLOM PRICE TASK WAR DEMAND PRODUC...POLICY BIBLIOG 18 MALTHUS MILL/JS WILSON/J. PAGE 89 A1826
IDEA/COMP ECO/DEV WEALTH EQUILIB

B59
MAC MILLAN W.M.,THE ROAD TO SELF-RULE. SOUTH/AFR UK CULTURE SOCIETY AGRI LABOR NAT/G INT/TRADE CONTROL GP/REL...SOC 19/20. PAGE 92 A1884
AFR COLONIAL SOVEREIGN POLICY

B59
TUNSTALL W.C.B.,THE COMMONWEALTH AND REGIONAL DEFENCE (PAMPHLET). UK LAW VOL/ASSN PLAN AGREE REGION WAR ORD/FREE 20 CMN/WLTH NATO SEATO TREATY. PAGE 146 A2977
INT/ORG FORCES DIPLOM

S59
PADELFORD N.J.,"REGIONAL COOPERATION IN THE SOUTH PACIFIC: THE SOUTH PACIFIC COMMISSION." FUT NEW/ZEALND UK WOR+45 CULTURE ECO/UNDEV LOC/G VOL/ASSN...OBS CON/ANAL UNESCO VAL/FREE AUSTRAL 20. PAGE 112 A2308
INT/ORG ADMIN

N59
BRITISH COMMONWEALTH REL CONF,EXTRACTS FROM THE PROCEEDINGS OF THE SIXTH UNOFFICIAL CONFERENCE (PAMPHLET). GHANA INDIA RHODESIA UK FINAN FORCES DETER FEDERAL...LING 20 PARLIAMENT. PAGE 19 A0379
DIPLOM PARL/PROC INT/TRADE ORD/FREE

B60
ALBRECHT-CARRIE R.,FRANCE, EUROPE AND THE TWO WORLD WARS. EUR+WWI FRANCE GERMANY MOD/EUR UK ECO/DEV NAT/G FORCES BAL/PWR DOMIN ARMS/CONT PEACE PWR 20 TREATY EUROPE. PAGE 5 A0109
DIPLOM WAR

B60
ALLEN H.C.,THE ANGLO-AMERICAN PREDICAMENT: THE BRITISH COMMONWEALTH, THE UNITED STATES AND EUROPEAN UNITY. EUR+WWI FUT UK USA+45 WOR+45 ECO/DEV NAT/G PLAN DETER...CONCPT OBS TIME/SEQ TREND COLD/WAR VAL/FREE CMN/WLTH 20. PAGE 6 A0123
INT/ORG PWR BAL/PWR

B60
ENGELMAN F.L.,THE PEACE OF CHRISTMAS EVE. UK USA-45 NAT/G FORCES CONFER PERS/REL...AUD/VIS BIBLIOG 19 TREATY. PAGE 42 A0853
WAR PEACE DIPLOM PERSON

B60
FURNIA A.H.,THE DIPLOMACY OF APPEASEMENT: ANGLO-FRENCH RELATIONS AND THE PRELUDE TO WORLD WAR II 1931-1938. FRANCE GERMANY UK ELITES NAT/G DELIB/GP FORCES WAR PEACE RIGID/FLEX 20. PAGE 50 A1026
DIPLOM BAL/PWR COERCE

B60
GLUBB J.B.,WAR IN THE DESERT: AN R.A.F. FRONTIER CAMPAIGN. SAUDI/ARAB UK KIN SECT LEAD...GEOG 20 RAF. PAGE 53 A1083
COLONIAL WAR FORCES DIPLOM

B60
JEFFRIES C.,TRANSFER OF POWER: PROBLEMS OF THE PASSAGE TO SELFGOVERNMENT. CEYLON GHANA MALAYSIA NIGERIA UK INT/ORG CONSULT DELIB/GP LEGIS DIPLOM CONFER PARL/PROC 20. PAGE 73 A1502
SOVEREIGN COLONIAL ORD/FREE NAT/G

B60
KENEN P.B.,BRITISH MONETARY POLICY AND THE BALANCE OF PAYMENTS 1951-57. UK PLAN BUDGET ECO/TAC INT/TRADE PAY PRICE COST ATTIT 20. PAGE 77 A1585
BAL/PAY PROB/SOLV FINAN NAT/G

B60
KENNAN G.F.,RUSSIA AND THE WEST. ASIA COM EUR+WWI GERMANY UK USA+45 USA-45 USSR INT/ORG NAT/G VOL/ASSN DOMIN REV WAR PWR...TIME/SEQ 20. PAGE 78 A1590
EXEC DIPLOM

B60
KINGSTON-MCCLOUG E.,DEFENSE; POLICY AND STRATEGY. UK SEA AIR TEC/DEV DIPLOM ADMIN LEAD WAR ORD/FREE ...CHARTS 20. PAGE 79 A1627
FORCES PLAN POLICY DECISION

B60
LATIFI D.,INDIA AND UNITED STATES AID. ASIA INDIA UK USA+45 AGRI FINAN INDUS COLONIAL ORD/FREE SOVEREIGN WEALTH...METH/COMP 20. PAGE 85 A1743
FOR/AID DIPLOM ECO/UNDEV

B60
LEWIS P.R.,LITERATURE OF THE SOCIAL SCIENCES: AN INTRODUCTORY SURVEY AND GUIDE. UK LAW INDUS DIPLOM INT/TRADE ADMIN...MGT 19/20. PAGE 88 A1802
BIBLIOG/A SOC

B60
STRACHEY J.,THE END OF EMPIRE. UK WOR+45 WOR-45 DIPLOM INT/TRADE DOMIN ADJUST ORD/FREE WEALTH ...SOCIALIST GOV/COMP TIME COMMONWLTH. PAGE 139 A2841
COLONIAL ECO/DEV BAL/PWR LAISSEZ

B60
WHEARE K.C.,THE CONSTITUTIONAL STRUCTURE OF THE COMMONWEALTH. UK EX/STRUC DIPLOM DOMIN ADMIN COLONIAL CONTROL LEAD INGP/REL SUPEGO 20 CMN/WLTH. PAGE 163 A3325
CONSTN INT/ORG VOL/ASSN SOVEREIGN

L60
LAUTERPACHT E.,"THE SUEZ CANAL SETTLEMENT." FRANCE ISLAM ISRAEL UAR UK BAL/PWR DIPLOM LEGIT...JURID GEN/LAWS ANTHOL SUEZ VAL/FREE 20. PAGE 85 A1747
INT/ORG LAW

S60
CLARK W.,"NEW FORCES IN THE UN." FUT UK WOR+45 CONSTN BAL/PWR DIPLOM DRIVE PWR SKILL...CONCPT TREND UN TOT/POP 20. PAGE 27 A0543
INT/ORG ECO/UNDEV SOVEREIGN

S60
GRACIA-MORA M.R.,"INTERNATIONAL RESPONSIBILITY FOR SUBVERSIVE ACTIVITIES AND HOSTILE PROPAGANDA BY PRIVATE PERSONS AGAINST." COM EUR+WWI L/A+17C UK USA+45 USSR WOR-45 CONSTN NAT/G LEGIT ADJUD REV PEACE TOTALISM ORD/FREE...INT/LAW 20. PAGE 55 A1119
INT/ORG JURID SOVEREIGN

S60
KREININ M.E.,"THE 'OUTER-SEVEN' AND EUROPEAN INTEGRATION." EUR+WWI FRANCE GERMANY ITALY UK ECO/DEV DIST/IND INT/TRADE DRIVE WEALTH...MYTH CHARTS EEC OEEC 20. PAGE 82 A1682
ECO/TAC GEN/LAWS

C60
COX R.H.,"LOCKE ON WAR AND PEACE." UK DIPLOM DOMIN PWR...BIOG IDEA/COMP BIBLIOG 18. PAGE 32 A0646
CONCPT NAT/G PEACE WAR

B61
BELOFF M.,NEW DIMENSIONS IN FOREIGN POLICY: A STUDY IN BRITISH ADMINISTRATION. UK NAT/G ATTIT RIGID/FLEX ORD/FREE...GEN/LAWS EUR+WWI CMN/WLTH EEC 20. PAGE 13 A0260
INT/ORG DIPLOM

B61
BISHOP D.G.,THE ADMINISTRATION OF BRITISH FOREIGN RELATIONS. EUR+WWI MOD/EUR INT/ORG NAT/G POL/PAR DELIB/GP LEGIS TOP/EX ECO/TAC DOMIN EDU/PROP ADMIN COERCE 20. PAGE 14 A0292
ROUTINE PWR DIPLOM UK

B61
CAMERON J.,THE AFRICAN REVOLUTION. AFR UK ECO/UNDEV POL/PAR REGION RACE/REL DISCRIM PWR CONSERVE ...CONCPT SOC/INTEG 20 NEGRO. PAGE 23 A0472
REV COLONIAL ORD/FREE DIPLOM

B61
DALLIN D.J.,SOVIET FOREIGN POLICY AFTER STALIN. ASIA CHINA/COM EUR+WWI GERMANY IRAN UK YUGOSLAVIA INT/ORG NAT/G VOL/ASSN FORCES TOP/EX BAL/PWR DOMIN EDU/PROP COERCE ATTIT PWR 20. PAGE 33 A0679
COM DIPLOM USSR

B61
HAYTER W.,THE DIPLOMACY OF THE GREAT POWERS. FRANCE UK USSR WOR+45 EX/STRUC TOP/EX NUC/PWR PEACE...OBS 20. PAGE 63 A1296
DIPLOM POLICY NAT/G

B61
KERTESZ S.D.,AMERICAN DIPLOMACY IN A NEW ERA. COM
ANTHOL

S/ASIA UK USA+45 FORCES PROB/SOLV BAL/PWR ECO/TAC ADMIN COLONIAL WAR PEACE ORD/FREE 20 NATO CONGRESS UN COLD/WAR. PAGE 78 A1601
DIPLOM
TREND

B61
KITZINGER V.W.,THE CHALLENGE OF THE COMMON MARKET. EUR+WWI ECO/DEV DIST/IND PLAN ECO/TAC INT/TRADE LEGIT ATTIT PWR WEALTH...TIME/SEQ TREND CHARTS EEC 20. PAGE 80 A1647
MARKET
INT/ORG
UK

B61
LANDSKROY W.A.,OFFICIAL SERIAL PUBLICATIONS RELATING TO ECONOMIC DEVELOPMENT IN AFRICA SOUTH OF THE SAHARA (PAMPHLET). AFR UK R+D ACT/RES 20 UN. PAGE 84 A1720
BIBLIOG
ECO/UNDEV
COLONIAL
INT/ORG

B61
PANIKKAR K.M.,THE VOICE OF FREEDOM: SELECTED SPEECHES OF PANDIT MOTILAL NEHRU. INDIA UK CONSTN FINAN FORCES LEGIS DIPLOM TAX COLONIAL...POLICY MAJORIT ANTHOL 20 NEHRU/PM. PAGE 114 A2331
NAT/LISM
ORD/FREE
CHIEF
NAT/G

B61
SCHNAPPER B.,LA POLITIQUE ET LE COMMERCE FRANCAIS DANS LE GOLFE DE GUINEE DE 1838 A 1871. FRANCE GUINEA UK SEA EXTR/IND NAT/G DELIB/GP LEGIS ADMIN ORD/FREE...POLICY GEOG CENSUS CHARTS BIBLIOG 19. PAGE 129 A2636
COLONIAL
INT/TRADE
DOMIN
AFR

B61
WARD B.J.,INDIA AND THE WEST. INDIA UK USA+45 INT/TRADE GIVE COLONIAL ATTIT MARXISM 19/20. PAGE 161 A3279
PLAN
ECO/UNDEV
ECO/TAC
FOR/AID

B61
WRINCH P.,THE MILITARY STRATEGY OF WINSTON CHURCHILL. UK WOR-45 SEA VOL/ASSN TEC/DEV BAL/PWR LEAD WAR PEACE ATTIT...POLICY 20 CHURCHLL/W. PAGE 168 A3421
CIVMIL/REL
FORCES
PLAN
DIPLOM

S61
ANGLIN D.,"UNITED STATES OPPOSITION TO CANADIAN MEMBERSHIP IN THE PAN AMERICAN UNION: A CANADIAN VIEW." L/A+17C UK USA+45 VOL/ASSN DELIB/GP EX/STRUC PLAN DIPLOM DOMIN REGION ATTIT RIGID/FLEX PWR ...RELATIV CONCPT STERTYP CMN/WLTH OAS 20. PAGE 8 A0162
INT/ORG
CANADA

S61
BURNET A.,"TOO MANY ALLIES." COM EUR+WWI UK WOR+45 WOR-45 ACT/RES PLAN DISPL PWR SKILL...TIME/SEQ 20 CMN/WLTH SEATO NATO CENTO. PAGE 22 A0438
VOL/ASSN
INT/ORG
DIPLOM

S61
RAY J.,"THE EUROPEAN FREE-TRADE ASSOCIATION AND ITS IMPACT ON INDIA'S TRADE." EUR+WWI FRANCE GERMANY INDIA S/ASIA UK NAT/G VOL/ASSN PLAN INT/TRADE ROUTINE WEALTH...STAT CHARTS CMN/WLTH EEC OEEC 20 EFTA. PAGE 120 A2453
ECO/DEV
ECO/TAC

B62
BRYANT A.,A CHOICE FOR DESTINY: COMMONWEALTH AND THE COMMON MARKET. EUR+WWI FUT UK INT/TRADE COLONIAL ATTIT SOVEREIGN 20 CMN/WLTH EEC. PAGE 20 A0411
INT/ORG
VOL/ASSN
DIPLOM
CHOOSE

B62
FORD A.G.,THE GOLD STANDARD 1880-1914: BRITAIN AND ARGENTINA. UK ECO/UNDEV INT/TRADE ADMIN GOV/REL DEMAND EFFICIENCY...STAT CHARTS 19/20 ARGEN GOLD/STAND. PAGE 47 A0960
FINAN
ECO/TAC
BUDGET
BAL/PAY

B62
FRIEDMANN W.,METHODS AND POLICIES OF PRINCIPAL DONOR COUNTRIES IN PUBLIC INTERNATIONAL DEVELOPMENT FINANCING: PRELIMINARY APPRAISAL. FRANCE GERMANY/W UK USA+45 USSR WOR+45 FINAN TEC/DEV CAP/ISM DIPLOM ECO/TAC ATTIT 20 EEC. PAGE 49 A1002
INT/ORG
FOR/AID
NAT/COMP
ADMIN

B62
HETHERINGTON H.,SOME ASPECTS OF THE BRITISH EXPERIMENT IN DEMOCRACY. UK DIPLOM COLONIAL ...CONCPT 20 CMN/WLTH. PAGE 64 A1322
EDU/PROP
AFR
POPULISM
SOC/EXP

B62
HUTTENBACK R.A.,BRITISH RELATIONS WITH THE SIND, 1799-1843. FRANCE INDIA UK FORCES...POLICY CHARTS BIBLIOG 18/19 SIND. PAGE 69 A1425
COLONIAL
DIPLOM
DOMIN
S/ASIA

B62
KING-HALL S.,POWER POLITICS IN THE NUCLEAR AGE: A POLICY FOR BRITAIN. UK WOR+45 PLAN ECO/TAC CONTROL RISK ARMS/CONT MORAL PWR RESPECT...OLD/LIB 20. PAGE 79 A1625
BAL/PWR
NUC/PWR
POLICY
DIPLOM

B62
LIPPMANN W.,WESTERN UNITY AND THE COMMON MARKET. EUR+WWI FRANCE GERMANY/W UK USA+45 ECO/DEV AGRI FINAN MARKET INT/ORG NAT/G FOR/AID AGREE WEALTH 20 EEC. PAGE 89 A1831
DIPLOM
INT/TRADE
VOL/ASSN

B62
MONCRIEFF A.,THE STRATEGY OF SURVIVAL. UK FORCES BAL/PWR CONFER DETER WAR...ANTHOL 20 COLD/WAR. PAGE 102 A2104
PLAN
DECISION
DIPLOM
ARMS/CONT

B62
PAKISTAN MINISTRY OF FINANCE,FOREIGN ECONOMIC AID: A REVIEW OF FOREIGN ECONOMIC AID TO PAKISTAN. EUR+WWI PAKISTAN UK USA+45 USSR ECO/UNDEV INT/ORG DELIB/GP DIPLOM ECO/TAC...CHARTS CMN/WLTH CHINJAP. PAGE 113 A2318
FOR/AID
RECEIVE
WEALTH
FINAN

B62
ROBERTSON B.C.,REGIONAL DEVELOPMENT IN THE EUROPEAN ECONOMIC COMMUNITY. EUR+WWI FRANCE FUT ITALY UK ECO/UNDEV WORKER ACT/RES PROB/SOLV TEC/DEV ECO/TAC INT/TRADE EEC. PAGE 122 A2499
PLAN
ECO/DEV
INT/ORG
REGION

B62
STEEL R.,THE END OF THE ALLIANCE. FRANCE FUT GERMANY/E GERMANY/W UK USA+45 NAT/G FORCES FOR/AID 20 NATO. PAGE 137 A2809
EUR+WWI
POLICY
DIPLOM
INT/ORG

B62
TAYLOR D.,THE BRITISH IN AFRICA. UK CULTURE ECO/UNDEV INDUS DIPLOM INT/TRADE ADMIN WAR RACE/REL ORD/FREE SOVEREIGN...POLICY BIBLIOG 15/20 CMN/WLTH. PAGE 142 A2898
AFR
COLONIAL
DOMIN

B62
THOMSON G.P.,NUCLEAR ENERGY IN BRITAIN DURING THE LAST WAR: THE CHERWELL SIMON LECTURE (MONOGRAPH). UK R+D CONSULT FORCES PLAN DIPLOM TASK CIVMIL/REL ROLE...PHIL/SCI NEW/IDEA LAB/EXP 20 MAUD. PAGE 143 A2934
CREATE
TEC/DEV
WAR
NUC/PWR

S62
JOHNSON O.H.,"THE ENGLISH TRADITION IN INTERNATIONAL LAW." CHRIST-17C MOD/EUR EDU/PROP LEGIT CT/SYS ORD/FREE...JURID CONCPT TIME/SEQ. PAGE 75 A1526
LAW
INT/LAW
UK

S62
SCOTT J.B.,"ANGLO-SOVIET TRADE AND ITS EFFECTS ON THE COMMONWEALTH." COM FUT UK USSR WOR+45 ECO/DEV MARKET INT/ORG CONSULT WEALTH...POLICY TREND CMN/WLTH 20. PAGE 130 A2673
NAT/G
ECO/TAC

B63
BRITISH AID. UK AGRI DIST/IND INDUS SCHOOL TEC/DEV INT/TRADE COLONIAL DEMAND...TREND CHARTS 20. PAGE 3 A0064
FOR/AID
ECO/UNDEV
NAT/G
FINAN

B63
ADLER G.J.,BRITISH INDIA'S NORTHERN FRONTIER: 1865-95. AFGHANISTN RUSSIA UK PROVS COLONIAL COERCE PEACE...GEOG CHARTS BIBLIOG 19 TREATY. PAGE 4 A0091
S/ASIA
FORCES
DIPLOM
POLICY

B63
BELOFF M.,THE UNITED STATES AND THE UNITY OF EUROPE. EUR+WWI UK USA+45 WOR+45 VOL/ASSN DIPLOM REGION ATTIT PWR...CONCPT EEC OEEC 20 NATO. PAGE 13 A0261
ECO/DEV
INT/ORG

B63
CONF ON FUTURE OF COMMONWEALTH,THE FUTURE OF THE COMMONWEALTH. UK ECO/UNDEV AGRI EDU/PROP ADMIN SOC/INTEG 20 COMMONWLTH. PAGE 29 A0583
DIPLOM
RACE/REL
ORD/FREE
TEC/DEV

B63
GILBERT M.,THE APPEASERS. COM GERMANY UK PLAN ECO/TAC COLONIAL CONTROL EXEC ORD/FREE PWR FASCISM 20 PARLIAMENT. PAGE 52 A1068
DIPLOM
WAR
POLICY
DECISION

B63
HAILEY L.,THE REPUBLIC OF SOUTH AFRICA AND THE HIGH COMMISSION TERRITORIES. AFR SOUTH/AFR UK INT/ORG NAT/G PROVS RACE/REL SOVEREIGN...CHARTS 19/20 COMMONWLTH. PAGE 59 A1219
COLONIAL
DIPLOM
ATTIT

B63
HARTLEY A.,A STATE OF ENGLAND. UK ELITES SOCIETY ACADEM NAT/G SCHOOL INGP/REL CONSEN ORD/FREE NEW/LIB...POLICY 20. PAGE 62 A1275
DIPLOM
ATTIT
INTELL
ECO/DEV

B63
HUSSEY W.D.,THE BRITISH EMPIRE AND COMMONWEALTH 1500 TO 1961. UK USA-45 SOCIETY ECO/UNDEV NAT/G VOL/ASSN INT/TRADE DOMIN CONTROL WAR PWR ...DICTIONARY 16/20 COMMONWLTH TRUST/TERR. PAGE 69 A1422
COLONIAL
SOVEREIGN
INT/ORG

B63
JENNINGS W.I.,DEMOCRACY IN AFRICA. UK CULTURE STRUCT ECO/UNDEV DIPLOM COLONIAL GP/REL ADJUST NAT/LISM ORD/FREE...GOV/COMP 20 THIRD/WRLD. PAGE 74 A1512
PROB/SOLV
AFR
CONSTN
POPULISM

B63
JUDD P.,AFRICAN INDEPENDENCE: THE EXPLODING EMERGENCE OF THE NEW AFRICAN NATIONS. AFR UK LAW CONSTN CULTURE KIN DIPLOM ATTIT...CHARTS BIBLIOG 20 UN DEGAULLE/C NEGRO THIRD/WRLD. PAGE 75 A1542
ORD/FREE
POLICY
DOMIN
LOC/G

B63
LERCHE C.O. JR.,AMERICA IN WORLD AFFAIRS. COM UK USA+45 INT/ORG FORCES ECO/TAC INT/TRADE EDU/PROP WAR NAT/LISM PEACE...BIBLIOG 18/20 UN CONGRESS PRESIDENT COLD/WAR. PAGE 87 A1783
NAT/G
DIPLOM
PLAN

B63
LOOMIE A.J.,THE SPANISH ELIZABETHANS: THE ENGLISH EXILES AT THE COURT OF PHILIP II. SPAIN UK WAR INGP/REL DRIVE HABITAT CATHISM...BIOG 16/17 MIGRATION. PAGE 91 A1860
NAT/G
STRANGE
POLICY
DIPLOM

B63
MANSERGH N.,DOCUMENTS AND SPEECHES ON COMMONWEALTH
BIBLIOG/A

AFFAIRS 1952-1962. CANADA INDIA PAKISTAN UK CONSTN FORCES ECO/TAC EDU/PROP COLONIAL DETER WAR ORD/FREE SOVEREIGN...POLICY 20 AUSTRAL. PAGE 94 A1932 FEDERAL INT/TRADE DIPLOM B63

MAYNE R.,THE COMMUNITY OF EUROPE. UK CONSTN NAT/G CONSULT DELIB/GP CREATE PLAN ECO/TAC LEGIT ADMIN ROUTINE ORD/FREE PWR WEALTH...CONCPT TIME/SEQ EEC EURATOM 20. PAGE 97 A1985 EUR+WWI INT/ORG REGION B63

MONGER G.W.,THE END OF ISOLATION. FRANCE MOD/EUR RUSSIA UK NAT/G LEGIS TOP/EX GOV/REL PWR 20 TREATY CHINJAP. PAGE 103 A2106 DIPLOM POLICY WAR B63

PATRA A.C.,THE ADMINISTRATION OF JUSTICE UNDER THE EAST INDIA COMPANY IN BENGAL, BIHAR AND ORISSA. INDIA UK LG/CO CAP/ISM INT/TRADE ADJUD COLONIAL CONTROL CT/SYS...POLICY 20. PAGE 114 A2341 ADMIN JURID CONCPT B63

PERKINS B.,PROLOGUE TO THE WAR: ENGLAND AND THE UNITED STATES, 1805-1812. MOD/EUR UK USA-45 NAT/G ORD/FREE RESPECT SOVEREIGN...POLICY TREATY 19 WAR/1812. PAGE 115 A2358 WAR DIPLOM NEUTRAL B63

ROSNER G.,THE UNITED NATIONS EMERGENCY FORCE. FRANCE ISRAEL UAR UK WOR+45 CREATE WAR PEACE ORD/FREE PWR...INT/LAW JURID HIST/WRIT TIME/SEQ UN. PAGE 124 A2539 INT/ORG FORCES B63

SALENT W.S.,THE UNITED STATES BALANCE OF PAYMENTS IN 1968. EUR+WWI UK USA+45 AGRI R+D LABOR FORCES PRODUC...GEOG CONCPT CHARTS 20 CHINJAP EEC. PAGE 126 A2589 BAL/PAY DEMAND FINAN INT/TRADE B63

WALKER A.A.,OFFICIAL PUBLICATIONS OF SIERRA LEONE AND GAMBIA. GAMBIA SIER/LEONE UK LAW CONSTN LEGIS PLAN BUDGET DIPLOM...SOC SAMP CON/ANAL 20. PAGE 160 A3262 BIBLIOG NAT/G COLONIAL ADMIN B63

WATKINS K.W.,BRITAIN DIVIDED; THE EFFECT OF THE SPANISH CIVIL WAR ON BRITISH POLITICAL OPINION. SPAIN UK POL/PAR BAL/PWR LOBBY NEUTRAL 20. PAGE 162 A3293 EDU/PROP WAR POLICY DIPLOM S63

ALPHAND H.,"FRANCE AND HER ALLIES." EUR+WWI UK USA+45 ECO/DEV INT/ORG NAT/G VOL/ASSN FORCES TOP/EX DIPLOM ECO/TAC LEGIT ATTIT DRIVE ORD/FREE PWR WEALTH...STAT EEC TOT/POP 20. PAGE 6 A0130 ACT/RES FRANCE S63

BELOFF M.,"BRITAIN, EUROPE AND THE ATLANTIC COMMUNITY." EUR+WWI ELITES NAT/G VOL/ASSN TOP/EX ATTIT ORD/FREE PWR SOVEREIGN WEALTH EEC TOT/POP VAL/FREE CMN/WLTH 20. PAGE 13 A0262 INT/ORG ECO/DEV UK S63

DIEBOLD W. JR.,"THE NEW SITUATION OF INTERNATIONAL TRADE POLICY." EUR+WWI FRANCE FUT UK USA+45 WOR+45 DIST/IND PLAN INT/TRADE EDU/PROP PWR WEALTH ...RECORD TREND GEN/LAWS EEC VAL/FREE 20. PAGE 37 A0760 MARKET ECO/TAC S63

HALLSTEIN W.,"THE EUROPEAN COMMUNITY AND ATLANTIC PARTNERSHIP." EUR+WWI USA+45 MARKET NAT/G VOL/ASSN DELIB/GP ARMS/CONT NUC/PWR ATTIT PWR...CONCPT STAT TIME/SEQ TREND OEEC 20 EEC. PAGE 60 A1235 INT/ORG ECO/TAC UK S63

HAVILAND H.F.,"BUILDING A POLITICAL COMMUNITY." EUR+WWI FUT UK USA+45 ECO/DEV ECO/UNDEV INT/ORG NAT/G DELIB/GP BAL/PWR ECO/TAC NEUTRAL ROUTINE ATTIT PWR WEALTH...CONCPT COLD/WAR TOT/POP 20. PAGE 63 A1293 VOL/ASSN DIPLOM S63

MULLEY F.W.,"NUCLEAR WEAPONS: CHALLENGE TO NATIONAL SOVEREIGNTY." EUR+WWI FRANCE UK USA+45 VOL/ASSN EX/STRUC FORCES TOP/EX ACT/RES REGION DRIVE PWR 20 NATO DEGAULLE/C. PAGE 106 A2169 INT/ORG ATTIT DIPLOM NUC/PWR S63

SHONFIELD A.,"AFTER BRUSSELS." EUR+WWI FRANCE GERMANY UK ECO/DEV DIST/IND MARKET VOL/ASSN DELIB/GP CREATE INT/TRADE ATTIT RIGID/FLEX...RECORD TREND GEN/LAWS EEC CMN/WLTH 20. PAGE 132 A2705 PLAN ECO/TAC S63

WRIGHT Q.,"PROJECTED EUROPEAN UNION AND AMERICAN INTERNATIONAL PRESTIGE." EUR+WWI FRANCE GERMANY UK USA+45 INT/ORG NAT/G EDU/PROP ATTIT PERCEPT PWR ...CONCPT OBS EEC 20 UN. PAGE 168 A3417 FUT ORD/FREE REGION B64

THE SPECIAL COMMONWEALTH AFRICAN ASSISTANCE PLAN. AFR CANADA INDIA NIGERIA UK FINAN SCHOOL...CHARTS 20 COMMONWLTH. PAGE 3 A0065 ECO/UNDEV TREND FOR/AID ADMIN B64

ARNOLD G.,TOWARDS PEACE AND A MULTIRACIAL COMMONWEALTH. UK TEC/DEV BAL/PWR COLONIAL GP/REL NAT/LISM PEACE SOVEREIGN...POLICY SOC/INTEG 20 CMN/WLTH. PAGE 9 A0175 DIPLOM INT/TRADE FOR/AID ORD/FREE B64

BARKER A.J.,SUEZ: THE SEVEN DAY WAR. EUR+WWI ISLAM UAR INT/ORG NAT/G PLAN DIPLOM ECO/TAC DOMIN NAT/LISM DRIVE RIGID/FLEX PWR SOVEREIGN...POLICY JURID TREND CHARTS SUEZ UN 20. PAGE 11 A0221 FORCES COERCE UK B64

BELL C.,THE DEBATABLE ALLIANCE. COM UK USA+45 NAT/G FORCES PLAN BAL/PWR NUC/PWR WAR ATTIT...GOV/COMP 20. PAGE 13 A0256 DIPLOM PWR PEACE POLICY B64

BOYD J.P.,NUMBER 7: ALEXANDER HAMILTON'S SECRET ATTEMPTS TO CONTROL AMERICAN FOREIGN POLICY. AFR UK DIPLOM WAR RESPECT WEALTH...POLICY HIST/WRIT 18 HAMILTON/A. PAGE 18 A0364 USA-45 NAT/G TOP/EX PWR B64

CASEY R.G.,THE FUTURE OF THE COMMONWEALTH. INDIA PAKISTAN UK ECO/UNDEV INT/ORG TEC/DEV COLONIAL SUPEGO 20 EEC AUSTRAL. PAGE 25 A0505 DIPLOM SOVEREIGN NAT/LISM FOR/AID B64

COLUMBIA U SCHOOL OF LAW,PUBLIC INTERNATIONAL DEVELOPMENT FINANCING IN INDIA. GERMANY/W INDIA UK USA+45 INDUS PLAN TEC/DEV DIPLOM ECO/TAC GIVE ADMIN UTIL ATTIT 20. PAGE 28 A0572 ECO/UNDEV FINAN FOR/AID INT/ORG B64

DESHMUKH C.D.,THE COMMONWEALTH AS INDIA SEES IT. INDIA UK ECO/UNDEV TEC/DEV INT/TRADE GP/REL RACE/REL SOVEREIGN SOC/INTEG 19/20 COMMONWLTH. PAGE 36 A0733 DIPLOM COLONIAL NAT/LISM ATTIT B64

DONOUGHUE B.,BRITISH POLITICS AND THE AMERICAN REVOLUTION: THE PATH TO WAR 1773-75. UK USA-45 NAT/G LEGIS WAR 18 PRE/US/AM. PAGE 38 A0772 DIPLOM POLICY COLONIAL REV B64

DUROSELLE J.B.,POLITIQUES NATIONALES ENVERS LES JEUNES ETATS. FRANCE ISRAEL ITALY UK USA+45 USSR YUGOSLAVIA ECO/DEV FINAN ECO/TAC INT/TRADE ADMIN PWR 20. PAGE 40 A0809 DIPLOM ECO/UNDEV COLONIAL DOMIN B64

FINER H.,DULLES OVER SUEZ. FRANCE FUT UAR UK WOR+45 NAT/G PROB/SOLV CONTROL NUC/PWR WAR 20 DULLES/JF SUEZ. PAGE 46 A0932 DIPLOM POLICY REC/INT B64

GOWING M.,BRITAIN AND ATOMIC ENERGY 1939-1945. FRANCE UK USA+45 USA-45 NAT/G CREATE...PHIL/SCI 20 AEA. PAGE 54 A1118 NUC/PWR DIPLOM TEC/DEV B64

HINSHAW R.,THE EUROPEAN COMMUNITY AND AMERICAN TRADE: A STUDY IN ATLANTIC ECONOMICS AND POLICY. EUR+WWI UK USA+45 ECO/DEV ECO/UNDEV AGRI INDUS INT/ORG NAT/G ECO/TAC TARIFFS REGION...STAT CHARTS EEC 20. PAGE 65 A1337 MARKET TREND INT/TRADE B64

HORNE D.,THE LUCKY COUNTRY: AUSTRALIA TODAY. UK CULTURE STRATA ATTIT PWR PLURISM...GOV/COMP 20 AUSTRAL. PAGE 67 A1386 RACE/REL DIPLOM NAT/G STRUCT B64

IRISH M.D.,WORLD PRESSURES ON AMERICAN FOREIGN POLICY. ASIA COM L/A+17C SOUTH/AFR UK WOR+45 ECO/DEV ECO/UNDEV COLONIAL SANCTION COERCE REV TOTALISM...ANTHOL 20 COLD/WAR EUROPE/W INTERVENT. PAGE 72 A1467 DIPLOM POLICY B64

KOHNSTAMM M.,THE EUROPEAN COMMUNITY AND ITS ROLE IN THE WORLD. FUT MOD/EUR UK USA+45 ECO/DEV 20. PAGE 81 A1664 INT/ORG NAT/G REGION DIPLOM B64

KRAUSE L.B.,THE COMMON MARKET: PROGRESS AND CONTROVERSY. EUR+WWI UK ECO/DEV REGION...ANTHOL NATO EEC. PAGE 82 A1678 DIPLOM MARKET INT/TRADE INT/ORG B64

KRETZSCHMAR W.W.,AUSLANDSHILFE ALS MITTEL DER AUSSENWIRTSCHAFTS- UND AUSSENPOLITIK. ASIA GERMANY/W UK USA+45 SOCIETY STRUCT ECO/UNDEV LOBBY EFFICIENCY 20. PAGE 82 A1683 FOR/AID DIPLOM AGRI DIST/IND B64

LITTLE I.M.D.,AID TO AFRICA. AFR UK TEC/DEV DIPLOM ECO/TAC INCOME WEALTH 20. PAGE 90 A1844 FOR/AID ECO/UNDEV ADMIN POLICY B64

MACKESY P.,THE WAR FOR AMERICA, 1775-1783. UK FORCES DIPLOM...POLICY 18. PAGE 93 A1895 WAR COLONIAL LEAD REV B64

MAUD J.,AID FOR DEVELOPING COUNTRIES. COM EUR+WWI UK INT/TRADE ORD/FREE...GOV/COMP 20. PAGE 96 A1979 FOR/AID DIPLOM ECO/TAC ECO/UNDEV B64

QUIGG P.W.,AFRICA: A FOREIGN AFFAIRS READER. AFR FRANCE PORTUGAL UK DIPLOM LEAD PARL/PROC MARXISM COLONIAL SOVEREIGN

...MAJORIT METH/CNCPT GOV/COMP IDEA/COMP ANTHOL 19/20. PAGE 118 A2426 NAT/LISM RACE/REL

B64
SINGH N.,THE DEFENCE MECHANISM OF THE MODERN STATE. COM UK USA+45 CONSTN INT/ORG NUC/PWR WAR INGP/REL ROLE 20 DEPT/DEFEN COMMONWLTH. PAGE 134 A2735 FORCES TOP/EX NAT/G CIVMIL/REL

L64
SYMONDS R.,"REFLECTIONS IN LOCALISATION." AFR S/ASIA UK STRATA INT/ORG NAT/G SCHOOL EDU/PROP LEGIT KNOWL ORD/FREE PWR RESPECT CMN/WLTH 20. PAGE 140 A2874 ADMIN MGT COLONIAL

S64
KOJIMA K.,"THE PATTERN OF INTERNATIONAL TRADE AMONG ADVANCED COUNTRIES." EUR+WWI UK USA+45 WOR+45 MARKET NAT/G ECO/TAC WEALTH...MATH STAT CON/ANAL CHARTS EEC CHINJAP 20 CHINJAP. PAGE 81 A1665 ECO/DEV TREND INT/TRADE

B65
AMERICAN ECONOMIC ASSOCIATION,INDEX OF ECONOMIC JOURNALS 1886-1965 (7 VOLS.). UK USA+45 USA-45 AGRI FINAN PLAN ECO/TAC INT/TRADE ADMIN...STAT CENSUS 19/20. PAGE 7 A0145 BIBLIOG WRITING INDUS

B65
CALLEO D.P.,EUROPE'S FUTURE: THE GRAND ALTERNATIVES. UK INT/ORG DIPLOM PWR SOVEREIGN ...CONCPT IDEA/COMP NAT/COMP BIBLIOG 20 EEC EUROPE DEGAULLE/C NATO. PAGE 23 A0468 FUT EUR+WWI FEDERAL NAT/LISM

B65
COLLINS H.,KARL MARX AND THE BRITISH LABOUR MOVEMENT; YEARS OF THE FIRST INTERNATIONAL. FRANCE SWITZERLND UK CAP/ISM WAR...MARXIST IDEA/COMP BIBLIOG 19. PAGE 28 A0567 MARXISM LABOR INT/ORG REV

B65
COOPER S.,BEHIND THE GOLDEN CURTAIN: A VIEW OF THE USA. UK USA+45 SECT EDU/PROP COERCE LEISURE ORD/FREE WEALTH 20. PAGE 30 A0609 SOCIETY DIPLOM ATTIT ACT/RES

B65
COWEN Z.,THE BRITISH COMMONWEALTH OF NATIONS IN A CHANGING WORLD. UK ECO/UNDEV INT/ORG ECO/TAC INT/TRADE COLONIAL WAR GP/REL RACE/REL SOVEREIGN SOC/INTEG 20 TREATY EEC COMMONWLTH. PAGE 32 A0644 JURID DIPLOM PARL/PROC NAT/LISM

B65
FORGAC A.A.,NEW DIPLOMACY AND THE UNITED NATIONS. FRANCE GERMANY UK USSR INT/ORG DELIB/GP EX/STRUC PEACE...INT/LAW CONCPT UN. PAGE 47 A0965 DIPLOM ETIQUET NAT/G

B65
FRANKLAND N.,THE BOMBING OFFENSIVE AGAINST GERMANY. GERMANY UK TEC/DEV DIPLOM WAR...METH/COMP 20. PAGE 48 A0985 WEAPON PLAN DECISION FORCES

B65
GEORGE M.,THE WARPED VISION. EUR+WWI UK NAT/G POL/PAR LEGIS PARL/PROC SANCTION COERCE WAR GOV/REL PEACE RESPECT 20 CONSRV/PAR. PAGE 52 A1061 LEAD ATTIT DIPLOM POLICY

B65
GRAHAM G.S.,THE POLITICS OF NAVAL SUPREMACY; STUDIES IN BRITISH MARITIME ASCENDANCY. UK SEA NAT/G BAL/PWR LEAD WAR WEAPON PEACE...POLICY 18/19 COMMONWLTH. PAGE 55 A1126 FORCES PWR COLONIAL DIPLOM

B65
GRETTON P.,MARITIME STRATEGY - A STUDY OF DEFENSE PROBLEMS. ASIA UK USSR DIPLOM COERCE DETER NUC/PWR WEAPON...CONCPT NAT/COMP 20. PAGE 56 A1147 FORCES PLAN WAR SEA

B65
HART B.H.L.,THE MEMOIRS OF CAPTAIN LIDDELL HART (VOL. I). UK NAT/G PLAN TEC/DEV DIPLOM ADMIN WEAPON GOV/REL PERS/REL ATTIT PWR FASCISM...POLICY 20. PAGE 62 A1274 FORCES BIOG LEAD WAR

B65
HASSON J.A.,THE ECONOMICS OF NUCLEAR POWER. INDIA UK USA+45 WOR+45 INT/ORG TEC/DEV COST...SOC STAT CHARTS 20 EURATOM. PAGE 63 A1286 NUC/PWR INDUS ECO/DEV METH

B65
INGRAM D.,COMMONWEALTH FOR A COLOUR-BLIND WORLD. AFR INDIA UK STRATA ECO/UNDEV VOL/ASSN CREATE PLAN CONFER COLONIAL ORD/FREE SOC/INTEG 20 COMMONWLTH. PAGE 70 A1441 RACE/REL INT/ORG INGP/REL PROB/SOLV

B65
KIRKWOOD K.,BRITAIN AND AFRICA. AFR UK ECO/UNDEV ECO/TAC WAR NAT/LISM SOVEREIGN 19/20. PAGE 80 A1636 NAT/G DIPLOM POLICY COLONIAL

B65
LYONS G.M.,AMERICA: PURPOSE AND POWER. UK USA+45 FINAN INDUS MARKET WORKER TEC/DEV DIPLOM AUTOMAT NUC/PWR WAR RACE/REL ORD/FREE 20 EEC CONGRESS SUPREME/CT CIV/RIGHTS. PAGE 92 A1881 PWR PROB/SOLV ECO/DEV TASK

B65
MCCOLL G.D.,THE AUSTRALIAN BALANCE OF PAYMENTS. UK USA+45 AGRI WORKER DIPLOM EQUILIB PRODUC...STAT TREND CHARTS BIBLIOG/A 20 AUSTRAL. PAGE 97 A2001 ECO/DEV BAL/PAY INT/TRADE COST

B65
MEHROTRA S.R.,INDIA AND THE COMMONWEALTH 1885-1929. INDIA UK INT/ORG VOL/ASSN GP/REL ATTIT...POLICY BIBLIOG 19/20 CMN/WLTH. PAGE 99 A2034 DIPLOM NAT/G POL/PAR NAT/LISM

B65
NATIONAL CENTRAL LIBRARY,LATIN AMERICAN ECONOMIC AND SOCIAL SERIALS. UK SOCIETY NAT/G PLAN PROB/SOLV ...SOC 20. PAGE 107 A2202 BIBLIOG INT/TRADE ECO/UNDEV L/A+17C

B65
NEWBURY C.W.,BRITISH POLICY TOWARDS WEST AFRICA: SELECT DOCUMENTS 1786-1874. AFR UK INT/TRADE DOMIN ADMIN COLONIAL CT/SYS COERCE ORD/FREE...BIBLIOG/A 18/19. PAGE 108 A2224 DIPLOM POLICY NAT/G WRITING

B65
OGILVY-WEBB M.,THE GOVERNMENT EXPLAINS: A STUDY OF THE INFORMATION SERVICES. UK DELIB/GP LEGIS WORKER BUDGET DIPLOM 20. PAGE 111 A2284 EDU/PROP ATTIT NAT/G ADMIN

B65
QURESHI I.H.,THE STRUGGLE FOR PAKISTAN. INDIA PAKISTAN UK CULTURE LEGIS DIPLOM EDU/PROP COLONIAL ATTIT SOVEREIGN 19/20 MUSLIM. PAGE 118 A2429 GP/REL RACE/REL WAR SECT

B65
RODRIGUES J.H.,BRAZIL AND AFRICA. AFR BRAZIL PORTUGAL UK USA+45 USA-45 CULTURE ECO/UNDEV INT/ORG INT/TRADE RACE/REL ORD/FREE 15/20 UN MISCEGEN. PAGE 123 A2513 DIPLOM COLONIAL POLICY ATTIT

B65
ROLFE S.E.,GOLD AND WORLD POWER. UK USA+45 WOR-45 INDUS WORKER INT/TRADE DEMAND...MGT CHARTS 20 GOLD/STAND. PAGE 123 A2517 BAL/PAY EQUILIB ECO/TAC DIPLOM

B65
SANDERSON G.N.,ENGLAND, EUROPE, AND THE UPPER NILE 1882-1899. ISLAM MOD/EUR UAR UK CHIEF...POLICY CHARTS BIBLIOG/A 19 ARABS NEGRO. PAGE 127 A2600 AFR DIPLOM COLONIAL

B65
SOPER T.,EVOLVING COMMONWEALTH. AFR CANADA INDIA IRELAND UK LAW CONSTN POL/PAR DOMIN CONTROL WAR PWR ...AUD/VIS 18/20 COMMONWLTH OEEC. PAGE 135 A2769 INT/ORG COLONIAL VOL/ASSN

B65
WALKER A.A.,THE RHODESIAS AND NYASALAND: A GUIDE TO OFFICIAL PUBLICATIONS. RHODESIA UK OP/RES PLAN PROB/SOLV DIPLOM...POLICY SOC CON/ANAL 19/20 NYASALAND. PAGE 160 A3263 BIBLIOG NAT/G COLONIAL AFR

B65
WILLIAMSON J.A.,GREAT BRITAIN AND THE COMMONWEALTH. UK DOMIN COLONIAL INGP/REL...POLICY 18/20 CMN/WLTH. PAGE 165 A3355 NAT/G DIPLOM INT/ORG SOVEREIGN

B65
WITHERELL J.W.,MADAGASCAR AND ADJACENT ISLANDS; A GUIDE TO OFFICIAL PUBLICATIONS (PAMPHLET). FRANCE MADAGASCAR S/ASIA UK LAW OP/RES PLAN DIPLOM ...POLICY CON/ANAL 19/20. PAGE 165 A3371 BIBLIOG COLONIAL LOC/G ADMIN

S65
GANGAL S.C.,"SURVEY OF RECENT RESEARCH: INDIA AND THE COMMONWEALTH" INDIA UK NAT/G INT/TRADE PARTIC GOV/REL ROLE 20 CMN/WLTH. PAGE 51 A1039 BIBLIOG POLICY REGION DIPLOM

B66
CANNING HOUSE LIBRARY,AUTHOR AND SUBJECT CATALOGUES OF THE CANNING HOUSE LIBRARY (5 VOLS.). UK CULTURE LEAD...SOC 19/20. PAGE 24 A0478 BIBLIOG L/A+17C NAT/G DIPLOM

B66
CROWLEY D.W.,THE BACKGROUND TO CURRENT AFFAIRS. UK WOR+45 INT/ORG BAL/PWR NUC/PWR ATTIT ROLE 20 COLD/WAR. PAGE 33 A0665 DIPLOM PWR POLICY

B66
DYCK H.V.,WEIMAR GERMANY AND SOVIET RUSSIA 1926-1933. EUR+WWI GERMANY UK USSR ECO/TAC INT/TRADE NEUTRAL WAR ATTIT 20 WEIMAR/REP TREATY. PAGE 40 A0814 DIPLOM GOV/REL POLICY

B66
FABAR R.,THE VISION AND THE NEED: LATE VICTORIAN IMPERIALIST AIMS. MOD/EUR UK WOR-45 CULTURE NAT/G DIPLOM...TIME/SEQ METH/COMP 19 KIPLING/R COMMONWLTH. PAGE 43 A0880 COLONIAL CONCPT ADMIN ATTIT

B66
FRANK E.,LAWMAKERS IN A CHANGING WORLD. FRANCE UK USSR WOR+45 PARTIC EFFICIENCY ROLE ALL/IDEOS ...CHARTS ANTHOL PARLIAMENT 20 UN COLD/WAR. PAGE 48 A0979 GOV/COMP LEGIS NAT/G DIPLOM

B66
GILBERT M.,THE ROOTS OF APPEASEMENT. EUR+WWI GERMANY UK MUNIC BAL/PWR FASCISM...NEW/IDEA 20. PAGE 52 A1070 DIPLOM REPAR PROB/SOLV POLICY

B66
HAMILTON W.B.,A DECADE OF THE COMMONWEALTH, 1955-1964. UK LAW ELITES FINAN FOR/AID CONFER COLONIAL PWR...GEOG CHARTS ANTHOL 20 CMN/WLTH UN. INT/ORG INGP/REL DIPLOM

PAGE 61 A1247 NAT/G

B66
HUTTENBACK R.A.,BRITISH IMPERIAL EXPERIENCE. S/ASIA UK WOR-45 INT/ORG TEC/DEV...CHARTS 16/20 COMMONWLTH MERCANTLST. PAGE 69 A1424
COLONIAL TIME/SEQ INT/TRADE

B66
KEENLEYSIDE H.L.,INTERNATIONAL AID: A SUMMARY. AFR INDIA S/ASIA UK STRATA EXTR/IND TEC/DEV ADMIN RACE/REL DEMAND NAT/LISM WEALTH...TREND CHINJAP. PAGE 77 A1575
ECO/UNDEV FOR/AID DIPLOM TASK

B66
LUARD E.,THE EVOLUTION OF INTERNATIONAL ORGANIZATIONS. UK WOR+45 BUDGET INT/TRADE WAR BAL/PAY PEACE ORD/FREE...POLICY 19/20 EEC ILO LEAGUE/NAT UN. PAGE 91 A1871
INT/ORG EFFICIENCY CREATE TREND

B66
MCINTYRE W.D.,COLONIES INTO COMMONWEALTH. UK CONSTN VOL/ASSN DOMIN CONTROL...BIBLIOG 18/20 CMN/WLTH. PAGE 98 A2012
DIPLOM INT/ORG COLONIAL SOVEREIGN

B66
MCNAIR A.D.,THE LEGAL EFFECTS OF WAR. UK FINAN DIPLOM ORD/FREE 20 ENGLSH/LAW. PAGE 98 A2019
JURID WAR INT/TRADE LABOR

B66
MULLER C.F.J.,A SELECT BIBLIOGRAPHY OF SOUTH AFRICAN HISTORY; A GUIDE FOR HISTORICAL RESEARCH. SOUTH/AFR UK LAW CONSTN SOCIETY STRUCT AGRI SECT DIPLOM COLONIAL LEAD RACE/REL...POLICY 17/20 NEGRO. PAGE 106 A2167
BIBLIOG AFR NAT/G

B66
ROBERTSON D.J.,THE BRITISH BALANCE OF PAYMENTS. UK WOR+45 INDUS BUDGET TAX ADJUST...CHARTS ANTHOL 20. PAGE 122 A2500
FINAN BAL/PAY ECO/DEV INT/TRADE

B66
SINGER L.,ALLE LITTEN AN GROSSENWAHN: VON WOODROW WILSON BIS MAO TSE-TUNG. ASIA UK USSR INT/ORG DELIB/GP BAL/PWR DOMIN ATTIT PERSON 20 WILSON/W ROOSEVLT/F. PAGE 133 A2731
DIPLOM TOTALISM WAR CHIEF

B66
SMITH D.M.,AMERICAN INTERVENTION, 1917. GERMANY UK USA-45 SEA FORCES DIPLOM INT/TRADE EDU/PROP COERCE WEAPON PEACE 20 WILSON/W WWI. PAGE 134 A2746
WAR ATTIT POLICY NEUTRAL

B66
SPICER K.,A SAMARITAN STATE? AFR CANADA INDIA PAKISTAN UK USA+45 FINAN INDUS PRODUC...CHARTS 20 NATO. PAGE 136 A2787
DIPLOM FOR/AID ECO/DEV ADMIN

B66
THORNTON A.P.,THE IMPERIAL IDEA AND ITS ENEMIES. UK WOR+45 WOR-45 NAT/G PLAN DOMIN CONTROL WAR ATTIT PWR...TREND CHARTS 19/20 CMN/WLTH. PAGE 144 A2937
COLONIAL DIPLOM

B66
TINKER H.,SOUTH ASIA. UK LAW ECO/UNDEV AGRI ACADEM SECT DIPLOM EDU/PROP REV WEALTH ALL/IDEOS...CHARTS BIBLIOG GANDHI/M NEHRU/J. PAGE 144 A2945
S/ASIA COLONIAL TREND

B66
TYSON G.,NEHRU: THE YEARS OF POWER. INDIA UK STRATA ECO/UNDEV FINAN SECT TASK WAR ORD/FREE MARXISM ...POLICY BIBLIOG 20 NEHRU/J. PAGE 146 A2985
CHIEF PWR DIPLOM NAT/G

B66
US DEPARTMENT OF STATE,RESEARCH ON WESTERN EUROPE, GREAT BRITAIN, AND CANADA (EXTERNAL RESEARCH LIST NO 3-25). CANADA GERMANY/W UK LAW CULTURE NAT/G POL/PAR FORCES EDU/PROP REGION MARXISM...GEOG SOC WORSHIP 20 CMN/WLTH. PAGE 152 A3098
BIBLIOG/A EUR+WWI DIPLOM

B66
US LIBRARY OF CONGRESS,NIGERIA: A GUIDE TO OFFICIAL PUBLICATIONS. CAMEROON NIGERIA UK DIPLOM...POLICY 19/20 UN LEAGUE/NAT. PAGE 155 A3160
BIBLIOG ADMIN NAT/G COLONIAL

B66
WILLIAMS P.,AID IN UGANDA - EDUCATION. UGANDA UK FINAN ACADEM INT/ORG SCHOOL PROB/SOLV ECO/TAC UTIL ...STAT CHARTS 20. PAGE 165 A3352
PLAN EDU/PROP FOR/AID ECO/UNDEV

B66
WILSON H.A.,THE IMPERIAL POLICY OF SIR ROBERT BORDEN. CANADA UK ELITES INT/ORG VOL/ASSN CONTROL LEAD WAR ROLE 20 CMN/WLTH BORDEN/R. PAGE 165 A3360
INGP/REL COLONIAL CONSTN CHIEF

B66
ZEINE Z.N.,THE EMERGENCE OF ARAB NATIONALISM (REV. ED.). TURKEY UK NAT/G SECT TEC/DEV LEAD REV WAR AGE/Y ROLE ORD/FREE...TRADIT CHARTS BIBLIOG 20 ARABS OTTOMAN. PAGE 170 A3451
ISLAM NAT/LISM DIPLOM

S66
GREEN L.C.,"RHODESIAN OIL: BOOTLEGGERS OR PIRATES?" AFR RHODESIA UK WOR+45 INT/ORG NAT/G DIPLOM LEGIT COLONIAL SOVEREIGN 20 UN OAU. PAGE 55 A1139
INT/TRADE SANCTION INT/LAW POLICY

S66
MANSERGH N.,"THE PARTITION OF INDIA IN RETROSPECT." INDIA PAKISTAN S/ASIA UK DIPLOM COLONIAL GP/REL PWR 20. PAGE 94 A1933
NAT/G PARL/PROC POLICY POL/PAR

S66
PRATT R.C.,"AFRICAN REACTIONS TO THE RHODESIAN CRISIS." RHODESIA UK LAW DIPLOM...POLICY 20. PAGE 117 A2408
ATTIT AFR COLONIAL RACE/REL

N66
BRITISH DEVELOPMENT POLICIES: 1966 (PAMPHLET). UK AGRI TARIFFS BAL/PAY...TREND CHARTS 20 OVRSEA/DEV. PAGE 4 A0076
WEALTH DIPLOM INT/TRADE FOR/AID

B67
BLOM-COOPER L.,THE LITERATURE OF THE LAW AND THE LANGUAGE OF THE LAW (2 VOLS.). CANADA ISRAEL UK WOR+45 WOR-45 JUDGE CT/SYS ATTIT...CRIMLGY JURID ANTHOL CMN/WLTH. PAGE 15 A0312
BIBLIOG LAW INT/LAW ADJUD

B67
CECIL L.,ALBERT BALLIN; BUSINESS AND POLITICS IN IMPERIAL GERMANY 1888-1918. GERMANY UK INT/TRADE LEAD WAR PERS/REL ADJUST PWR WEALTH...MGT BIBLIOG 19/20. PAGE 25 A0510
DIPLOM CONSTN ECO/DEV TOP/EX

B67
LANDEN R.G.,OMAN SINCE 1856: DISRUPTIVE MODERNIZATION IN A TRADITIONAL ARAB SOCIETY. UK DIST/IND EXTR/IND SECT DIPLOM INT/TRADE...SOC LING CHARTS BIBLIOG 19/20. PAGE 84 A1714
ISLAM CULTURE ECO/UNDEV NAT/G

B67
MACDONALD D.F.,THE AGE OF TRANSITION: BRITAIN IN THE NINETEENTH & TWENTIETH CENTURIES. UK ECO/DEV LEGIS DIPLOM NEW/LIB...POLICY 19/20. PAGE 92 A1886
TREND INDUS SOCISM

B67
MAW B.,BREAKTHROUGH IN BURMA: MEMOIRS OF A REVOLUTION, 1939-1946. BURMA UK FORCES PROB/SOLV DIPLOM FOR/AID DOMIN LEAD...BIOG 20. PAGE 97 A1980
REV ORD/FREE NAT/LISM COLONIAL

S67
BUTT R.,"THE COMMON MARKET AND CONSERVATIVE POLITICS, 1961-2." UK CHIEF DIPLOM ECO/TAC INT/TRADE CONFER DEBATE REGION ATTIT...POLICY 20 EEC. PAGE 22 A0454
EUR+WWI INT/ORG POL/PAR

S67
FAWCETT J.E.S.,"GIBRALTAR* THE LEGAL ISSUES." SPAIN UK INT/ORG BAL/PWR LICENSE CONFER SANCTION PRIVIL ...JURID CHARTS 20. PAGE 44 A0905
INT/LAW DIPLOM COLONIAL ADJUD

S67
FELDMAN H.,"AID AS IMPERIALISM?" INDIA PAKISTAN UK USA+45 BAL/PWR CAP/ISM DIPLOM ECO/TAC DOMIN BAL/PAY WEALTH...POLICY 20. PAGE 45 A0914
COLONIAL FOR/AID S/ASIA ECO/UNDEV

S67
JACKSON W.G.F.,"NUCLEAR PROLIFERATION AND THE GREAT POWERS." FUT UK WOR+45 INT/ORG DOMIN ARMS/CONT DETER ORD/FREE PACIFIST. PAGE 72 A1480
NUC/PWR ATTIT BAL/PWR NAT/LISM

S67
KIERNAN V.G.,"INDIA AND THE LABOUR PARTY." INDIA UK CAP/ISM GP/REL EFFICIENCY NAT/LISM PWR SOCISM ...SOCIALIST TIME/SEQ 20. PAGE 79 A1616
COLONIAL DIPLOM POL/PAR ECO/UNDEV

S67
KYLE K.,"BACKGROUND TO THE CRISIS" ISLAM ISRAEL UAR UK USSR NAT/G PROB/SOLV LEGIT CONTROL REGION STRANGE MORAL 20 JEWS. PAGE 83 A1698
DIPLOM POLICY SOVEREIGN COERCE

S67
LEVI M.,"LES DIFFICULTES ECONOMIQUES DE LA GRANDE-BRETAGNE." UK INT/ORG TEC/DEV BARGAIN DIPLOM DOMIN REPRESENT DEMAND WEALTH...POLICY 20 EEC. PAGE 88 A1792
BAL/PAY INT/TRADE PRODUC

S67
MANN F.A.,"THE BRETTON WOODS AGREEMENT IN THE ENGLISH COURTS." UK JUDGE ADJUD CT/SYS...JURID PREDICT CON/ANAL 20. PAGE 94 A1923
LAW INT/LAW CONSTN

S67
PERLO V.,"NEW DIMENSIONS IN EAST-WEST TRADE." UK USA+45 USSR WOR+45 ECO/DEV NAT/G CAP/ISM PEACE WEALTH LAISSEZ...SOCIALIST MGT 20. PAGE 115 A2364
BAL/PWR ECO/TAC INT/TRADE

S67
SENCOURT R.,"FOREIGN POLICY* AN HISTORIC RECTIFICATION." EUR+WWI UK DIPLOM EDU/PROP LEAD WAR CHOOSE PERS/REL...METH/COMP PARLIAMENT. PAGE 131 A2685
POLICY POL/PAR NAT/G

C83
BURKE E.,"RESOLUTIONS FOR CONCILIATION WITH AMERICA" (1775), IN E. BURKE, COLLECTED WORKS, VOL. 2." UK USA-45 FORCES INT/TRADE TARIFFS TAX SANCTION PEACE...POLICY 18 PRE/US/AM. PAGE 21 A0436
COLONIAL WAR SOVEREIGN ECO/TAC

B90
HOSMAR J.K.,A SHORT HISTORY OF ANGLO-SAXON FREEDOM. UK USA-45 ROMAN/EMP NAT/G EX/STRUC LEGIS COLONIAL REV NAT/LISM POPULISM PARLIAMENT ANGLO/SAX
CONSTN ORD/FREE DIPLOM

MAGNA/CART. PAGE 68 A1394 — PARL/PROC

B96
SMITH A.,LECTURES ON JUSTICE, POLICE, REVENUE AND ARMS (1763). UK LAW FAM FORCES TARIFFS AGREE COERCE INCOME OWN WEALTH LAISSEZ...GEN/LAWS 17/18. PAGE 134 A2743 — DIPLOM JURID OLD/LIB TAX

B99
BROOKS S.,BRITAIN AND THE BOERS. AFR SOUTH/AFR UK CULTURE INSPECT LEGIT...INT/LAW 19/20 BOER/WAR. PAGE 19 A0396 — WAR DIPLOM NAT/G

UKRAINE

B39
WHEELER-BENNET J.W.,THE FORGOTTEN PEACE: BREST-LITOVSK. COM GERMANY USSR TOP/EX AGREE WAR PWR ...BIBLIOG 20 TREATY LENIN/VI UKRAINE. PAGE 163 A3326 — PEACE DIPLOM CONFER

ULAM A.B. A2992,A2993

ULYSSES A2994

UN A2995

UN....UNITED NATIONS; SEE ALSO INT/ORG, VOL/ASSN, INT/REL

N
CONOVER H.F.,WORLD GOVERNMENT: A LIST OF SELECTED REFERENCES (PAMPHLET). WOR+45 PROB/SOLV ARMS/CONT WAR PEACE 20 UN. PAGE 29 A0589 — BIBLIOG/A NUC/PWR INT/ORG DIPLOM

B
CURRENT THOUGHT ON PEACE AND WAR. WOR+45 INT/ORG FORCES PROB/SOLV DIPLOM NUC/PWR PERCEPT...POLICY SOC 20 UN NATO. PAGE 1 A0008 — BIBLIOG/A PEACE ATTIT WAR

B
UN DEPARTMENT SOCIAL AFFAIRS,SOCIAL WELFARE INFORMATION SERIES: CURRENT LITERATURE AND NATIONAL CONFERENCES. WOR+45 INDUS SERV/IND INT/ORG CONSULT ACT/RES WEALTH...HEAL UN. PAGE 147 A2997 — BIBLIOG/A SOC/WK DIPLOM ADMIN

N
AMERICAN POLITICAL SCIENCE REVIEW. USA+45 USA-45 WOR+45 WOR-45 INT/ORG ADMIN...INT/LAW PHIL/SCI CONCPT METH 20 UN. PAGE 1 A0003 — BIBLIOG/A DIPLOM NAT/G GOV/COMP

N
FOREIGN AFFAIRS. SPACE WOR+45 WOR-45 CULTURE ECO/UNDEV FINAN NAT/G TEC/DEV INT/TRADE ARMS/CONT NUC/PWR...POLICY 20 UN EURATOM ECSC EEC. PAGE 2 A0034 — BIBLIOG DIPLOM INT/ORG INT/LAW

N
ASIA FOUNDATION,LIBRARY NOTES. LAW CONSTN CULTURE SOCIETY ECO/UNDEV INT/ORG NAT/G COLONIAL LEAD REGION NAT/LISM ATTIT 20 UN. PAGE 9 A0189 — BIBLIOG/A ASIA S/ASIA DIPLOM

N
COUNCIL ON FOREIGN RELATIONS,DOCUMENTS ON AMERICAN FOREIGN RELATIONS. INT/ORG ECO/TAC NUC/PWR WAR WEAPON...POLICY CON/ANAL CHARTS 20 OAS UN. PAGE 31 A0639 — BIBLIOG USA+45 USA-45 DIPLOM

N
UNITED NATIONS,OFFICIAL RECORDS OF THE ECONOMIC AND SOCIAL COUNCIL OF THE UNITED NATIONS. WOR+45 DIPLOM INT/TRADE CONFER...SOC SOC/WK 20 UN UNESCO. PAGE 148 A3031 — INT/ORG DELIB/GP WRITING

N
UNITED NATIONS,OFFICIAL RECORDS OF THE UNITED NATIONS' ATOMIC ENERGY COMMISSION - DISARMAMENT COMMISSION. WOR+45 TEC/DEV DIPLOM WRITING NUC/PWR 20 UN. PAGE 148 A3032 — ARMS/CONT INT/ORG DELIB/GP CONFER

N
UNITED NATIONS,OFFICIAL RECORDS OF THE UNITED NATIONS' GENERAL ASSEMBLY. WOR+45 BUDGET DIPLOM ADMIN 20 UN. PAGE 148 A3033 — INT/ORG DELIB/GP INT/LAW WRITING

N
UNITED NATIONS,UNITED NATIONS PUBLICATIONS. WOR+45 ECO/UNDEV AGRI FINAN FORCES ADMIN LEAD WAR PEACE ...POLICY INT/LAW 20 UN. PAGE 148 A3034 — BIBLIOG INT/ORG DIPLOM

N
UNITED NATIONS,YEARBOOK OF THE INTERNATIONAL LAW COMMISSION....CON/ANAL 20 UN. PAGE 149 A3035 — BIBLIOG INT/ORG INT/LAW DELIB/GP

N
US SUPERINTENDENT OF DOCUMENTS,FOREIGN RELATIONS OF THE UNITED STATES; PUBLICATIONS RELATING TO FOREIGN COUNTRIES (PRICE LIST 65). UAR USA+45 VIETNAM ECO/UNDEV VOL/ASSN FOR/AID EDU/PROP ARMS/CONT HEALTH MARXISM...POLICY INT/LAW UN NATO. PAGE 157 A3201 — BIBLIOG/A DIPLOM INT/ORG NAT/G

N
WORLD PEACE FOUNDATION,DOCUMENTS OF INTERNATIONAL ORGANIZATIONS: A SELECTED BIBLIOGRAPHY. WOR+45 WOR-45 AGRI FINAN ACT/RES OP/RES INT/TRADE ADMIN ...CON/ANAL 20 UN UNESCO LEAGUE/NAT. PAGE 167 A3396 — BIBLIOG DIPLOM INT/ORG REGION

BLI
MOOR C.C.,HOW TO USE UNITED NATIONS DOCUMENTS (PAPER). WOR+45 ACADEM CONTROL 20 UN. PAGE 103 A2121 — BIBLIOG METH INT/ORG

N19
FANI-KAYODE R.,BLACKISM (PAMPHLET). AFR WOR+45 INT/ORG BAL/PWR CONTROL CENTRAL...DECISION 20 UN. PAGE 44 A0896 — RACE/REL ECO/UNDEV REGION DIPLOM

N19
FRANCK P.G.,AFGHANISTAN BETWEEN EAST AND WEST: THE ECONOMICS OF COMPETITIVE COEXISTENCE (PAMPHLET). AFGHANISTN USA+45 USA-45 USSR INDUS ECO/TAC INT/TRADE CONTROL NEUTRAL ORD/FREE MARXISM...GEOG 20 UN. PAGE 48 A0977 — FOR/AID PLAN DIPLOM ECO/UNDEV

N19
HIGGINS R.,THE ADMINISTRATION OF UNITED KINGDOM FOREIGN POLICY THROUGH THE UNITED NATIONS (PAMPHLET). UK NAT/G ADMIN GOV/REL...CHARTS 20 UN PARLIAMENT. PAGE 65 A1329 — DIPLOM POLICY INT/ORG

N19
MEZERIK A.G.,ATOM TESTS AND RADIATION HAZARDS (PAMPHLET). WOR+45 INT/ORG DIPLOM DETER 20 UN TREATY. PAGE 100 A2059 — NUC/PWR ARMS/CONT CONFER HEALTH

N19
MEZERIK A.G.,U-2 AND OPEN SKIES (PAMPHLET). USA+45 USSR INT/ORG CHIEF FORCES PLAN EDU/PROP CONTROL SANCTION ARMS/CONT 20 UN EISNHWR/DD. PAGE 100 A2060 — DIPLOM RISK DEBATE

N19
MEZERIK A.G.,COLONIALISM AND THE UNITED NATIONS (PAMPHLET). WOR+45 NAT/G ADMIN LEAD WAR CHOOSE EFFICIENCY PEACE ATTIT ORD/FREE...POLICY CHARTS UN COLD/WAR. PAGE 100 A2061 — COLONIAL DIPLOM BAL/PWR INT/ORG

N19
MEZERIK AG,OUTER SPACE: UN, US, USSR (PAMPHLET). USSR DELIB/GP FORCES DETER NUC/PWR SOVEREIGN ...POLICY 20 UN TREATY. PAGE 101 A2063 — SPACE CONTROL DIPLOM INT/ORG

N19
PROVISIONS SECTION OAU,ORGANIZATION OF AFRICAN UNITY: BASIC DOCUMENTS AND RESOLUTIONS (PAMPHLET). AFR CULTURE ECO/UNDEV DIPLOM ECO/TAC EDU/PROP COLONIAL ARMS/CONT NUC/PWR RACE/REL DISCRIM NAT/LISM 20 UN OAU. PAGE 118 A2415 — CONSTN EX/STRUC SOVEREIGN INT/ORG

N19
UNITED ARAB REPUBLIC,THE PROBLEM OF THE PALESTINIAN REFUGEES (PAMPHLET). ISRAEL UAR LAW PROB/SOLV EDU/PROP CONFER ADJUD CONTROL NAT/LISM HEALTH 20 JEWS UN MIGRATION. PAGE 148 A3029 — STRANGE GP/REL INGP/REL DIPLOM

B42
US LIBRARY OF CONGRESS,POSTWAR PLANNING AND RECONSTRUCTION: APRIL-DECEMBER 1942 (SUPPLEMENT 1). WOR+45 SOCIETY INT/ORG DIPLOM...SOC PREDICT 20 UN. PAGE 154 A3147 — BIBLIOG/A WAR PEACE PLAN

B43
FULLER G.F.,FOREIGN RELIEF AND REHABILITATION (PAMPHLET). FUT GERMANY UK USA-45 INT/ORG PROB/SOLV DIPLOM FOR/AID ADMIN ADJUST PEACE ALL/VALS...SOC/WK 20 UN JEWS. PAGE 50 A1018 — BIBLIOG/A PLAN GIVE WAR

B44
COMM. STUDY ORGAN. PEACE,UNITED NATIONS GUARDS AND TECHNICAL FIELD SERVICES. WOR+45 DELIB/GP EDU/PROP DRIVE PWR SKILL...CONCPT GEN/LAWS UN TOT/POP 20. PAGE 28 A0576 — INT/ORG FORCES PEACE

L44
CORWIN E.S.,"THE CONSTITUTION AND WORLD ORGANIZATION." FUT USA+45 USA-45 NAT/G EX/STRUC LEGIS PEACE KNOWL...CON/ANAL UN 20. PAGE 31 A0627 — INT/ORG CONSTN SOVEREIGN

B45
UNCIO CONFERENCE LIBRARY,SHORT TITLE CLASSIFIED CATALOG. WOR-45 DOMIN COLONIAL WAR...SOC/WK 20 LEAGUE/NAT UN. PAGE 147 A3006 — BIBLIOG DIPLOM INT/ORG INT/LAW

B46
BRODIE B.,THE OBSOLETE WEAPON: ATOMIC POWER AND WORLD ORDER. COM USA+45 USSR WOR+45 DELIB/GP PLAN ORD/FREE PWR...CONCPT TIME/SEQ TREND UN 20. PAGE 19 A0380 — INT/ORG TEC/DEV ARMS/CONT NUC/PWR

B46
STURZO D.L.,NATIONALISM AND INTERNATIONALISM. WOR-45 INT/ORG LABOR NAT/G POL/PAR TOTALISM MORAL ORD/FREE FASCISM...MAJORIT 19/20 UN LEAGUE/NAT MUSSOLIN/B. PAGE 140 A2857 — NAT/LISM DIPLOM WAR PEACE

C46
GOODRICH L.M.,"CHARTER OF THE UNITED NATIONS: COMMENTARY AND DOCUMENTS." EX/STRUC ADMIN...INT/LAW CON/ANAL BIBLIOG 20 UN. PAGE 54 A1106 — CONSTN INT/ORG DIPLOM

B47
CONOVER H.F.,NON-SELF-GOVERNING AREAS. BELGIUM FRANCE ITALY UK WOR+45 CULTURE ECO/UNDEV INT/ORG LOC/G NAT/G ECO/TAC INT/TRADE ADMIN HEALTH...SOC UN. PAGE 30 A0601 — BIBLIOG/A COLONIAL DIPLOM

B47
DE HUSZAR G.B.,PERSISTENT INTERNATIONAL ISSUES. WOR+45 WOR-45 AGRI INDUS INT/ORG PROB/SOLV EFFICIENCY WEALTH...CON/ANAL ANTHOL UN. PAGE 35 A0704
DIPLOM PEACE ECO/TAC FOR/AID

B47
HILL M.,IMMUNITIES AND PRIVILEGES OF INTERNATIONAL OFFICIALS. CANADA EUR+WWI NETHERLAND SWITZERLND LAW LEGIS DIPLOM LEGIT RESPECT...TIME/SEQ LEAGUE/NAT UN VAL/FREE 20. PAGE 65 A1330
INT/ORG ADMIN

B47
INTERNATIONAL COURT OF JUSTICE,CHARTER OF THE UNITED NATIONS, STATUTE AND RULES OF COURT AND OTHER CONSTITUTIONAL DOCUMENTS. SWITZERLND LAW ADJUD INGP/REL...JURID 20 ICJ UN. PAGE 71 A1453
INT/LAW INT/ORG CT/SYS DIPLOM

L47
COMM. STUDY ORGAN. PEACE,"SECURITY THROUGH THE UNITED NATIONS." COM FUT WOR+45 TOP/EX ACT/RES BAL/PWR ARMS/CONT NUC/PWR...CONCPT GEN/LAWS UN TOT/POP COLD/WAR 20. PAGE 28 A0577
INT/ORG ORD/FREE PEACE

L47
HISS D.,"UNITED STATES PARTICIPATION IN THE UNITED NATIONS." USA+45 EX/STRUC PLAN DIPLOM ROUTINE CHOOSE...PLURIST UN 20. PAGE 65 A1342
INT/ORG PWR

B48
FENWICK C.G.,INTERNATIONAL LAW. WOR+45 WOR-45 CONSTN NAT/G LEGIT CT/SYS REGION...CONCPT LEAGUE/NAT UN 20. PAGE 45 A0916
INT/ORG JURID INT/LAW

B48
JONES H.D.,UNESCO: A SELECTED LIST OF REFERENCES. CULTURE CREATE PEACE ATTIT DRIVE 20 UNESCO UN. PAGE 75 A1531
BIBLIOG/A INT/ORG DIPLOM EDU/PROP

B48
US DEPARTMENT OF STATE,FOREIGN AFFAIRS HIGHLIGHTS (NEWSLETTER). COM USA+45 INT/ORG PLAN BAL/PWR WAR PWR...BIBLIOG 20 COLD/WAR NATO UN DEPT/STATE. PAGE 151 A3083
DIPLOM NAT/G POLICY

L49
COMM. STUDY ORGAN. PEACE,"A TEN YEAR RECORD, 1939-1949." FUT WOR+45 LAW R+D CONSULT DELIB/GP CREATE LEGIT ROUTINE ORD/FREE...TIME/SEQ UN 20. PAGE 28 A0578
INT/ORG CONSTN PEACE

L49
HEINDEL R.H.,"THE NORTH ATLANTIC TREATY IN THE UNITED STATES SENATE." CONSTN POL/PAR CHIEF DEBATE LEAD ROUTINE WAR PEACE...CHARTS UN SENATE NATO. PAGE 64 A1309
DECISION PARL/PROC LEGIS INT/ORG

L49
UNESCO,"SOME SUGGESTIONS ON TEACHING ABOUT THE UN AND ITS SPECIALIZED AGENCIES." UNIV WOR+45 SOCIETY STRATA SCHOOL WAR ALL/VALS KNOWL...SOC CONCPT UNESCO 20 UN. PAGE 147 A3011
INT/ORG EDU/PROP

N49
UN DEPARTMENT PUBLIC INF,SELECTED BIBLIOGRAPHY OF THE SPECIALIZED AGENCIES RELATED TO THE UNITED NATIONS (PAMPHLET). USA+45 ROLE 20 UN. PAGE 146 A2996
BIBLIOG INT/ORG EX/STRUC ADMIN

B50
CHASE E.P.,THE UNITED NATIONS IN ACTION. WOR+45 CONSTN DELIB/GP LEGIT ROUTINE COERCE PEACE ORD/FREE PWR...CON/ANAL GEN/LAWS UN 20. PAGE 26 A0524
INT/ORG STRUCT ARMS/CONT

B50
DAVIS E.P.,PERIODICALS OF INTERNATIONAL ORGANIZATIONS; PART I, THE UN AND SPECIALIZED AGENCIES; PART II, INTER-AMERICAN ORGS. CULTURE AGRI FINAN INDUS LABOR INT/TRADE...GEOG HEAL STAT 20 UN OAS UNESCO. PAGE 34 A0689
BIBLIOG/A INT/ORG DIPLOM L/A+17C

B50
DE ARECHAGA E.J.,VOTING AND THE HANDLING OF DISPUTES IN THE SECURITY COUNCIL. WOR+45 CONSTN DIPLOM COERCE ORD/FREE...RECORD CON/ANAL GEN/METH COLD/WAR UN 20. PAGE 34 A0696
INT/ORG PWR

B50
DE RUSETT A.,STRENGTHENING THE FRAMEWORK OF PEACE. WOR+45 VOL/ASSN FORCES CREATE INSPECT ADJUD CONTROL WAR EQUILIB FEDERAL ORD/FREE 20 UN EUROPE. PAGE 35 A0711
INT/ORG DIPLOM PEACE METH/COMP

B50
DULLES J.F.,WAR OR PEACE. CHINA/COM USA+45 USSR INT/ORG SECT FORCES PLAN NUC/PWR WAR CENTRAL MARXISM...POLICY 20 UN ROOSEVLT/F STALIN/J. PAGE 39 A0797
PEACE DIPLOM TREND ORD/FREE

B50
JIMENEZ E.,VOTING AND HANDLING OF DISPUTES IN THE SECURITY COUNCIL. WOR+45 CONSTN INT/ORG DIPLOM LEGIT DETER CHOOSE MORAL ORD/FREE PWR...JURID TIME/SEQ COLD/WAR UN 20. PAGE 74 A1517
DELIB/GP ROUTINE

B50
LAUTERPACHT H.,INTERNATIONAL LAW AND HUMAN RIGHTS. USA+45 CONSTN STRUCT INT/ORG ACT/RES EDU/PROP PEACE PERSON ALL/VALS...CONCPT CON/ANAL GEN/LAWS UN 20. PAGE 86 A1750
DELIB/GP LAW INT/LAW

B50
LEVI W.,FUNDAMENTALS OF WORLD ORGANIZATION. WOR+45 WOR-45 CULTURE ECO/TAC GIVE RECEIVE PERSON WEALTH ...METH/COMP 19/20 UN LEAGUE/NAT. PAGE 88 A1793
INT/ORG PEACE ORD/FREE DIPLOM

B50
ROSS A.,CONSTITUTION OF THE UNITED NATIONS. CONSTN CONSULT DELIB/GP ECO/TAC...INT/LAW JURID 20 UN LEAGUE/NAT. PAGE 124 A2540
PEACE DIPLOM ORD/FREE INT/ORG

B50
SOHN L.B.,CASES AND OTHER MATERIALS ON WORLD LAW. FUT WOR+45 LAW INT/ORG...INT/LAW JURID METH/CNCPT 20 UN. PAGE 135 A2760
CT/SYS CONSTN

B50
US DEPARTMENT OF STATE,POINT FOUR: COOPERATIVE PROGRAM FOR AID IN THE DEVELOPMENT OF ECONOMICALLY UNDERDEVELOPED AREAS. WOR+45 AGRI INDUS INT/ORG PLAN TEC/DEV DIPLOM EDU/PROP ADMIN PEACE PRODUC WEALTH 20 CONGRESS UN. PAGE 151 A3085
ECO/UNDEV FOR/AID FINAN INT/TRADE

B50
US LIBRARY OF CONGRESS,THE UNITED STATES AND EUROPE: BIBLIOGRAPHY OF THOUGHT EXPRESSED IN AMERICAN PUBLICATIONS DURING 1950. EUR+WWI GERMANY USA+45 USSR INT/ORG DIPLOM COLONIAL SOVEREIGN ...POLICY 20 COLD/WAR UN BERLIN/BLO. PAGE 154 A3150
BIBLIOG/A SOC ATTIT

L50
US SENATE COMM. GOVT. OPER.,"REVISION OF THE UN CHARTER." FUT USA+45 WOR+45 CONSTN ECO/DEV ECO/UNDEV NAT/G DELIB/GP ACT/RES CREATE PLAN EXEC ROUTINE CHOOSE ALL/VALS...POLICY CONCPT CONGRESS UN TOT/POP 20 COLD/WAR. PAGE 157 A3196
INT/ORG LEGIS PEACE

B51
CORMACK M.,SELECTED PAMPHLETS ON THE UNITED NATIONS AND INTERNATIONAL RELATIONS (PAMPHLET). USA+45 R+D EX/STRUC PROB/SOLV ROUTINE...POLICY CON/ANAL 20 UN NATO. PAGE 31 A0624
BIBLIOG/A NAT/G INT/ORG DIPLOM

B51
HAVILAND H.F.,THE POLITICAL ROLE OF THE GENERAL ASSEMBLY. WOR+45 DELIB/GP EDU/PROP PEACE RIGID/FLEX PWR...CONCPT TIME/SEQ GEN/LAWS UN VAL/FREE 20. PAGE 63 A1290
INT/ORG ORD/FREE DIPLOM

B51
KELSEN H.,THE LAW OF THE UNITED NATIONS. WOR+45 STRUCT RIGID/FLEX ORD/FREE...INT/LAW JURID CONCPT CON/ANAL GEN/METH UN TOT/POP VAL/FREE 20. PAGE 77 A1581
INT/ORG ADJUD

B51
MACLAURIN J.,THE UNITED NATIONS AND POWER POLITICS. WOR+45 CONSULT EDU/PROP LEGIT ADJUD EXEC MORAL ORD/FREE...HUM JURID CONCPT RECORD TIME/SEQ UN COLD/WAR 20. PAGE 93 A1896
INT/ORG ROUTINE

B51
UNESCO,FREEDOM AND CULTURE. FUT WOR+45 CONSTN CULTURE PERF/ART VOL/ASSN EDU/PROP PEACE ATTIT ALL/VALS SOVEREIGN...POLICY MAJORIT CONCPT TREND STERTYP GEN/LAWS UN TOT/POP 20. PAGE 147 A3013
INT/ORG SOCIETY

B51
WELLES S.,SEVEN DECISIONS THAT SHAPED HISTORY. ASIA FRANCE FUT USA+45 WOR+45 WOR-45 CONSTN STRUCT INT/ORG NAT/G ACT/RES EDU/PROP DRIVE...POLICY CONCPT TIME/SEQ TREND TOT/POP UN 20 CHINJAP. PAGE 163 A3315
USA-45 DIPLOM WAR

L51
KELSEN H.,"RECENT TRENDS IN THE LAW OF THE UNITED NATIONS." KOREA WOR+45 CONSTN LEGIS DIPLOM LEGIT DETER WAR RIGID/FLEX HEALTH ORD/FREE RESPECT ...JURID CON/ANAL UN VAL/FREE 20 NATO. PAGE 77 A1582
INT/ORG LAW INT/LAW

C51
LEONARD L.L.,"INTERNATIONAL ORGANIZATION (1ST ED.)" WOR+45 FINAN DELIB/GP ECO/TAC GIVE DOMIN SANCTION PEACE BIO/SOC ORD/FREE...INT/LAW 20 UN LEAGUE/NAT. PAGE 87 A1779
BIBLIOG POLICY DIPLOM INT/ORG

B52
JACKSON E.,MEETING OF THE MINDS: A WAY TO PEACE THROUGH MEDIATION. WOR+45 INDUS INT/ORG NAT/G DELIB/GP DIPLOM EDU/PROP LEGIT ORD/FREE...NEW/IDEA SELF/OBS TIME/SEQ CHARTS GEN/LAWS TOT/POP 20 UN TREATY. PAGE 72 A1474
LABOR JUDGE

B52
UNESCO,CURRENT SOCIOLOGY (2 VOLS.). SOCIETY STRATA R+D GP/REL ATTIT PERSON 20 UN. PAGE 147 A3014
BIBLIOG SOC INT/ORG CULTURE

B52
VANDENBOSCH A.,THE UN: BACKGROUND, ORGANIZATION, FUNCTIONS, ACTIVITIES. WOR+45 LAW CONSTN STRUCT INT/ORG CONSULT BAL/PWR EDU/PROP EXEC ALL/VALS ...POLICY CONCPT UN 20. PAGE 158 A3218
DELIB/GP TIME/SEQ PEACE

L52
NIEBUHR R.,"THE MORAL IMPLICATIONS OF LOYALTY TO THE UNITED NATIONS." WOR+45 WOR-45 SOCIETY ECO/DEV INT/ORG VOL/ASSN PEACE ATTIT PERSON LOVE ORD/FREE PWR RESPECT...CONCPT UN TOT/POP COLD/WAR UNESCO 20. PAGE 109 A2236
SUPEGO GEN/LAWS

S52
MASTERS R.D.,"RUSSIA AND THE UNITED NATIONS." FUT USA+45 USSR WOR+45 CONSTN VOL/ASSN DELIB/GP TOP/EX
INT/ORG PWR

CREATE DIPLOM ADMIN...TREND STERTYP UN 20. PAGE 96 A1962

S52
SCHWEBEL S.M.,"THE SECRETARY-GENERAL OF THE UN." FUT INTELL CONSULT DELIB/GP ADMIN PEACE ATTIT ...JURID MGT CONCPT TREND UN CONGRESS 20. PAGE 130 A2663
INT/ORG TOP/EX

B53
MACK R.T.,RAISING THE WORLDS STANDARD OF LIVING. IRAN INT/ORG VOL/ASSN EX/STRUC ECO/TAC WEALTH...MGT METH/CNCPT STAT CONT/OBS INT TOT/POP VAL/FREE 20 UN. PAGE 92 A1893
WOR+45 FOR/AID INT/TRADE

B53
OPPENHEIM L.,INTERNATIONAL LAW: A TREATISE (7TH ED., 2 VOLS.). LAW CONSTN PROB/SOLV INT/TRADE ADJUD AGREE NEUTRAL WAR ORD/FREE SOVEREIGN...BIBLIOG 20 LEAGUE/NAT UN ILO. PAGE 112 A2294
INT/LAW INT/ORG DIPLOM

B53
ZIMMERN A.,THE AMERICAN ROAD TO PEACE. USA+45 LAW INT/ORG NAT/G EX/STRUC TOP/EX EDU/PROP LEGIT COERCE PEACE ATTIT ORD/FREE PWR...CONCPT TIME/SEQ LEAGUE/NAT TOT/POP VAL/FREE 20 UN. PAGE 170 A3455
USA-45 DIPLOM

S53
CORY R.H. JR.,"FORGING A PUBLIC INFORMATION POLICY FOR THE UNITED NATIONS." FUT WOR+45 SOCIETY ADMIN PEACE ATTIT PERSON SKILL...CONCPT 20 UN. PAGE 31 A0628
INT/ORG EDU/PROP BAL/PWR

B54
BECKEL G.,WORKSHOPS FOR THE WORLD; THE SPECIALIZED AGENCIES OF THE UN. WOR+45 AGRI DIST/IND CREATE TEC/DEV BUDGET CONTROL TASK WEALTH...CHARTS ORG/CHARTS 20 UN CASEBOOK. PAGE 12 A0246
INT/ORG DIPLOM PEACE CON/ANAL

B54
CHEEVER D.S.,ORGANIZING FOR PEACE. FUT WOR+45 WOR-45 STRATA STRUCT NAT/G CREATE DIPLOM LEGIT REGION COERCE DETER PEACE ATTIT DRIVE ALL/VALS ...TIME/SEQ TREND UN LEAGUE/NAT. PAGE 26 A0525
INT/ORG

B54
KENWORTHY L.S.,FREE AND INEXPENSIVE MATERIALS ON WORLD AFFAIRS (PAMPHLET). WOR+45 CULTURE ECO/UNDEV INT/TRADE ARMS/CONT NUC/PWR UN. PAGE 78 A1597
BIBLIOG/A NAT/G INT/ORG DIPLOM

B54
MANGONE G.,A SHORT HISTORY OF INTERNATIONAL ORGANIZATION. MOD/EUR USA+45 USA-45 WOR+45 WOR-45 LAW LEGIS CREATE LEGIT ROUTINE RIGID/FLEX PWR ...JURID CONCPT OBS TIME/SEQ STERTYP GEN/LAWS UN TOT/POP VAL/FREE 18/20. PAGE 94 A1921
INT/ORG INT/LAW

B54
SCHIFFER W.,THE LEGAL COMMUNITY OF MANKIND. UNIV WOR+45 WOR-45 SOCIETY NAT/G EDU/PROP LEGIT ATTIT PERSON ORD/FREE PWR...CONCPT HIST/WRIT TREND LEAGUE/NAT UN 20. PAGE 128 A2626
INT/ORG PHIL/SCI

B54
STRAUSZ-HUPE R.,INTERNATIONAL RELATIONS IN THE AGE OF THE CONFLICT BETWEEN DEMOCRACY AND DICTATORSHIP (2ND ED.). INT/ORG BAL/PWR EDU/PROP ADMIN WAR PEACE PWR...CONCPT CHARTS BIBLIOG 20 COLD/WAR UN LEAGUE/NAT. PAGE 139 A2846
DIPLOM POPULISM MARXISM

B54
STREIT C.K.,FREEDOM AGAINST ITSELF. LAW SOCIETY DIPLOM UTOPIA PWR SOVEREIGN ALL/IDEOS 17/20 NATO UN. PAGE 139 A2850
ORD/FREE CREATE INT/ORG CONCPT

B54
US DEPARTMENT OF STATE,PUBLICATIONS OF THE DEPARTMENT OF STATE, OCTOBER 1,1929 TO JANUARY 1, 1953. AGRI INT/ORG FORCES FOR/AID EDU/PROP ARMS/CONT NUC/PWR ATTIT 20 DEPT/STATE OAS UN NATO. PAGE 151 A3089
BIBLIOG DIPLOM

B54
US SENATE COMM ON FOREIGN REL,REVIEW OF THE UNITED NATIONS CHARTER: A COLLECTION OF DOCUMENTS. LEGIS DIPLOM ADMIN ARMS/CONT WAR REPRESENT SOVEREIGN ...INT/LAW 20 UN. PAGE 156 A3180
BIBLIOG CONSTN INT/ORG DEBATE

L54
OPLER M.E.,"SOCIAL ASPECTS OF TECHNICAL ASSISTANCE IN OPERATION." WOR+45 VOL/ASSN CREATE PLAN TEC/DEV EDU/PROP ALL/VALS...METH/CNCPT OBS RECORD TREND UN 20. PAGE 112 A2292
INT/ORG CONSULT FOR/AID

S54
DAWSON K.H.,"THE UNITED NATIONS IN A DISUNITED WORLD." WOR+45 WOR-45 LAW INTELL NAT/G PEACE ATTIT PERCEPT MORAL LEAGUE/NAT TOT/POP VAL/FREE 20 UN. PAGE 34 A0694
INT/ORG LEGIT

S54
DODD S.C.,"THE SCIENTIFIC MEASUREMENT OF FITNESS FOR SELF-GOVERNMENT." FUT CONSTN ECO/UNDEV INT/ORG PLAN PWR...CONCPT QUANT CON/ANAL SOC/EXP UN LEAGUE/NAT 20. PAGE 38 A0767
NAT/G STAT SOVEREIGN

S54
WOLFERS A.,"COLLECTIVE SECURITY AND THE WAR IN KOREA." ASIA KOREA USA+45 INT/ORG DIPLOM ROUTINE ...GEN/LAWS UN COLD/WAR 20. PAGE 166 A3381
ACT/RES LEGIT

B55
CHOWDHURI R.N.,INTERNATIONAL MANDATES AND TRUSTEESHIP SYSTEMS. WOR+45 STRUCT ECO/UNDEV INT/ORG LEGIS DOMIN EDU/PROP LEGIT ADJUD EXEC PWR ...CONCPT TIME/SEQ UN 20. PAGE 26 A0534
DELIB/GP PLAN SOVEREIGN

B55
COMM. STUDY ORGAN. PEACE,REPORTS. WOR-45 ECO/DEV ECO/UNDEV VOL/ASSN CONSULT FORCES PLAN TEC/DEV DOMIN EDU/PROP NUC/PWR ATTIT PWR WEALTH...JURID STERTYP FAO ILO 20 UN. PAGE 28 A0579
WOR+45 INT/ORG ARMS/CONT

B55
GOODRICH L.,THE UNITED NATIONS AND THE MAINTENANCE OF INTERNATIONAL PEACE AND SECURITY. WOR+45 CONSTN ACT/RES CREATE PLAN PERCEPT PWR...ORG/CHARTS GEN/LAWS UN 20. PAGE 54 A1102
INT/ORG ORD/FREE ARMS/CONT PEACE

B55
HOGAN W.N.,INTERNATIONAL CONFLICT AND COLLECTIVE SECURITY: THE PRINCIPLE OF CONCERN IN INTERNATIONAL ORGANIZATION. CONSTN EX/STRUC BAL/PWR DIPLOM ADJUD CONTROL CENTRAL CONSEN PEACE...INT/LAW CONCPT METH/COMP 20 UN LEAGUE/NAT. PAGE 66 A1361
INT/ORG WAR ORD/FREE FORCES

B55
THOMPSON V.,MINORITY PROBLEMS IN SOUTHEAST ASIA. CAMBODIA CHINA/COM LAOS S/ASIA KIN NAT/G SECT PROB/SOLV EDU/PROP REGION GP/REL RACE/REL MARXISM ...SOC 20 BUDDHISM UN. PAGE 143 A2933
INGP/REL GEOG DIPLOM STRUCT

B55
UN ECONOMIC AND SOCIAL COUNCIL,BIBLIOGRAPHY OF PUBLICATIONS OF THE UN AND SPECIALIZED AGENCIES IN THE SOCIAL WELFARE FIELD, 1946-1952. WOR+45 FAM INT/ORG MUNIC ACT/RES PLAN PROB/SOLV EDU/PROP AGE/C AGE/Y HABITAT...HEAL UN. PAGE 147 A3000
BIBLIOG/A SOC/WK ADMIN WEALTH

B55
UN HEADQUARTERS LIBRARY,BIBLIOQRAPHIE DE LA CHARTE DES NATIONS UNIES. CHINA/COM KOREA WOR+45 VOL/ASSN CONFER ADMIN COERCE PEACE ATTIT ORD/FREE SOVEREIGN ...INT/LAW 20 UNESCO UN. PAGE 147 A3001
BIBLIOG/A INT/ORG DIPLOM

B55
WILCOX F.O.,PROPOSALS FOR CHANGES IN THE UNITED NATIONS. WOR+45 CONSTN ACT/RES CREATE LEGIT ATTIT ORD/FREE...CONCPT ORG/CHARTS UN TOT/POP 20. PAGE 164 A3344
INT/ORG STRUCT

B56
BROOK D.,THE UNITED NATIONS AND CHINA DILEMMA. CHINA/COM FUT WOR+45 ECO/UNDEV NAT/G DELIB/GP ACT/RES DIPLOM ROUTINE NAT/LISM TOTALISM ATTIT DRIVE...CONCPT OBS TIME/SEQ UN TOT/POP TIME UN 20. PAGE 19 A0390
ASIA INT/ORG BAL/PWR

B56
BROOK D.,THE UNITED NATIONS AND CHINA DILEMMA. CHINA/COM FUT WOR+45 ECO/UNDEV NAT/G DELIB/GP ACT/RES DIPLOM ROUTINE NAT/LISM TOTALISM ATTIT DRIVE...CONCPT OBS TIME/SEQ UN TOT/POP TIME UN 20. PAGE 19 A0390
ASIA INT/ORG BAL/PWR

B56
GOODRICH L.,KOREA: A STUDY OF US POLICY IN THE UNITED NATIONS. ASIA USA+45 STRUCT CONSULT DELIB/GP ATTIT DRIVE PWR...JURID GEN/LAWS COLD/WAR 20 UN. PAGE 54 A1103
INT/ORG DIPLOM KOREA

B56
HOUSTON J.A.,LATIN AMERICA IN THE UNITED NATIONS. CONSULT DIPLOM LEGIT ROUTINE ATTIT ORD/FREE PWR ...JURID OBS RECORD TIME/SEQ CHARTS 20 UN. PAGE 68 A1395
L/A+17C INT/ORG INT/LAW REGION

B56
REITZEL W.,UNITED STATES FOREIGN POLICY, 1945-1955. USA+45 WOR+45 CONSTN INT/ORG EDU/PROP LEGIT EXEC COERCE NUC/PWR PEACE ATTIT ORD/FREE PWR...DECISION CONCPT OBS RECORD TIME/SEQ TREND COLD/WAR UN CONGRESS. PAGE 120 A2464
NAT/G POLICY DIPLOM

B56
ROBERTS H.L.,RUSSIA AND AMERICA. CHINA/COM S/ASIA USSR FORCES TEC/DEV FOR/AID NUC/PWR ALL/IDEOS ...MAJORIT TREND NAT/COMP 20 COLD/WAR UN NATO. PAGE 122 A2494
DIPLOM INT/ORG BAL/PWR TOTALISM

B56
SNELL J.L.,THE MEANING OF YALTA: BIG THREE DIPLOMACY AND THE NEW BALANCE OF POWER. EUR+WWI GERMANY USA-45 USSR FORCES PLAN BAL/PWR DIPLOM WAR CHOOSE PEACE...CHARTS BIBLIOG 20 UN CHINJAP ROOSEVLT/F. PAGE 134 A2749
CONFER CHIEF POLICY PROB/SOLV

B56
SOHN L.B.,BASIC DOCUMENTS OF THE UNITED NATIONS. WOR+45 LAW INT/ORG LEGIT EXEC ROUTINE CHOOSE PWR ...JURID CONCPT GEN/LAWS ANTHOL UN TOT/POP OAS FAO ILO 20. PAGE 135 A2761
DELIB/GP CONSTN

B56
UNITED NATIONS,BIBLIOGRAPHY ON INDUSTRIALIZATION IN UNDER-DEVELOPED COUNTRIES. WOR+45 R+D INT/ORG NAT/G FOR/AID ADMIN LEAD 20 UN. PAGE 149 A3036
BIBLIOG ECO/UNDEV INDUS TEC/DEV

B56
WATKINS J.T.,GENERAL INTERNATIONAL ORGANIZATION: A SOURCE BOOK. 19/20 LEAGUE/NAT UN. PAGE 162 A3292
BIBLIOG DIPLOM INT/ORG WRITING

S56
POTTER P.B.,"NEUTRALITY, 1955." WOR+45 WOR-45
NEUTRAL

INT/ORG NAT/G WAR ATTIT...POLICY IDEA/COMP 17/20 LEAGUE/NAT UN COLD/WAR. PAGE 117 A2399 — INT/LAW DIPLOM CONCPT

B57
ASHER R.E.,THE UNITED NATIONS AND THE PROMOTION OF THE GENERAL WELFARE. WOR+45 WOR-45 ECO/UNDEV EX/STRUC ACT/RES PLAN EDU/PROP ROUTINE HEALTH...HUM CONCPT CHARTS UNESCO UN ILO 20. PAGE 9 A0185 — INT/ORG CONSULT

B57
ASHER R.E.,THE UNITED NATIONS AND ECONOMIC AND SOCIAL COOPERATION. ECO/UNDEV COM/IND DIST/IND FINAN PLAN PROB/SOLV INT/TRADE TASK WEALTH...SOC 20 UN. PAGE 9 A0186 — INT/ORG DIPLOM FOR/AID

B57
BEAL J.R.,JOHN FOSTER DULLES, A BIOGRAPHY. USA+45 USSR WOR+45 CONSTN INT/ORG NAT/G EX/STRUC LEGIT ADMIN NUC/PWR DISPL PERSON ORD/FREE PWR SKILL ...POLICY PSY OBS RECORD COLD/WAR UN 20 DULLES/JF. PAGE 12 A0237 — BIOG DIPLOM

B57
BERLE A.A.,TIDES OF CRISIS: A PRIMER OF FOREIGN RELATIONS. USA+45 WOR+45 DOMIN NUC/PWR NAT/LISM PWR ...CONCPT STERTYP GEN/LAWS 20 UN. PAGE 14 A0276 — INT/ORG TREND PEACE

B57
BLOOMFIELD L.P.,EVOLUTION OR REVOLUTION: THE UNITED NATIONS AND THE PROBLEM OF PEACEFUL TERRITORIAL CHANGE. WOR+45 WOR-45 INT/ORG NAT/G DIPLOM ROUTINE REV ATTIT RIGID/FLEX PWR...CONCPT OBS HIST/WRIT UN LEAGUE/NAT 20. PAGE 15 A0315 — ORD/FREE LEGIT

B57
BRODY H.,UN DIARY: THE SEARCH FOR PEACE. HUNGARY WOR+45 DELIB/GP ROUTINE REV WAR ORD/FREE...AUD/VIS 20 UN SUEZ. PAGE 19 A0382 — INT/ORG PEACE DIPLOM POLICY

B57
COMM. STUDY ORGAN. PEACE,STRENGTHENING THE UNITED NATIONS. FUT USA+45 WOR+45 CONSTN NAT/G DELIB/GP FORCES LEGIS ECO/TAC LEGIT COERCE PEACE...JURID CONCPT UN COLD/WAR 20. PAGE 28 A0580 — INT/ORG ORD/FREE

B57
CONOVER H.F.,NORTH AND NORTHEAST AFRICA; A SELECTED ANNOTATED LIST OF WRITINGS. ALGERIA MOROCCO SUDAN UAR CULTURE INT/ORG PROB/SOLV ADJUD NAT/LISM PWR WEALTH...SOC 20 UN. PAGE 30 A0603 — BIBLIOG/A DIPLOM AFR ECO/UNDEV

B57
DUDDEN A.P.,WOODROW WILSON AND THE WORLD OF TODAY. USA-45 NAT/G PROVS CONTROL PARTIC WAR ISOLAT PWR SKILL...PERS/COMP ANTHOL 19/20 WILSON/W UN LEAGUE/NAT WWI. PAGE 39 A0794 — CHIEF DIPLOM POL/PAR LEAD

B57
HOLCOMBE A.N.,STRENGTHENING THE UNITED NATIONS. USA+45 ACT/RES CREATE PLAN EDU/PROP ATTIT PERCEPT PWR...METH/CNCPT CONT/OBS RECORD UN COLD/WAR 20. PAGE 66 A1365 — INT/ORG ROUTINE

B57
MURRAY J.N.,THE UNITED NATIONS TRUSTEESHIP SYSTEM. AFR WOR+45 CONSTN CONSULT LEGIS EDU/PROP LEGIT EXEC ROUTINE...INT TIME/SEQ SOMALI UN 20. PAGE 106 A2181 — INT/ORG DELIB/GP

B57
NEHRU J.,MILITARY ALLIANCE (PAMPHLET). INDIA WOR+45 NAT/G PLAN DETER NUC/PWR WAR...POLICY ANTHOL NEHRU/J SEATO UN. PAGE 108 A2212 — INT/ORG DIPLOM FORCES PEACE

B57
ROSENNE S.,THE INTERNATIONAL COURT OF JUSTICE. WOR+45 LAW DOMIN LEGIT PEACE PWR SOVEREIGN...JURID CONCPT RECORD TIME/SEQ CON/ANAL CHARTS UN TOT/POP VAL/FREE LEAGUE/NAT 20 ICJ. PAGE 124 A2537 — INT/ORG CT/SYS INT/LAW

B57
UNESCO,WORLD LIST OF SOCIAL SCIENCE PERIODICALS (2ND ED.). WOR+45 20 UN. PAGE 148 A3020 — BIBLIOG SOC INT/ORG

L57
HAAS E.B.,"REGIONAL INTEGRATION AND NATIONAL POLICY." WOR+45 VOL/ASSN DELIB/GP EX/STRUC ECO/TAC DOMIN EDU/PROP LEGIT COERCE ATTIT PERCEPT KNOWL ...TIME/SEQ COLD/WAR 20 UN. PAGE 59 A1203 — INT/ORG ORD/FREE REGION

S57
ALLEN R.L.,"UNITED NATIONS TECHNICAL ASSISTANCE: SOVIET AND EAST-EUROPEAN PARTICIPATION." COM WOR+45 AGRI INDUS INT/ORG NAT/G FOR/AID SKILL UN 20. PAGE 6 A0124 — ECO/UNDEV TEC/DEV USSR

B58
APPADORAI A.,THE USE OF FORCE IN INTERNATIONAL RELATIONS. WOR+45 CULTURE ECO/UNDEV CAP/ISM ARMS/CONT REV WAR ATTIT PERSON SOVEREIGN MARXISM ...INT/LAW PACIFIST 20 UN INTERVENT THIRD/WRLD COLD/WAR. PAGE 8 A0169 — PEACE FEDERAL INT/ORG

B58
BOWETT D.W.,SELF-DEFENSE IN INTERNATIONAL LAW. EUR+WWI MOD/EUR WOR+45 WOR-45 SOCIETY INT/ORG CONSULT DIPLOM LEGIT COERCE ATTIT ORD/FREE...JURID 20 UN. PAGE 17 A0353 — ADJUD CONCPT WAR INT/LAW

B58
BOWLES C.,IDEAS, PEOPLE AND PEACE. ASIA CHINA/COM FUT INDIA USA+45 USSR ECO/UNDEV INT/ORG LEAD TASK MARXISM 20 NATO UN COLD/WAR. PAGE 18 A0359 — PEACE POLICY NAT/G DIPLOM

B58
INSTITUTE MEDITERRANEAN AFF,THE PALESTINE REFUGEE PROBLEM. UAR WOR+45 INT/ORG PLAN PROB/SOLV PEACE ...POLICY GEOG STAT CHARTS 20 JEWS UN MIGRATION. PAGE 70 A1444 — STRANGE HABITAT GP/REL INGP/REL

B58
ISLAM R.,INTERNATIONAL ECONOMIC COOPERATION AND THE UNITED NATIONS. FINAN PLAN EXEC TASK WAR PEACE ...SOC METH/CNCPT 20 UN LEAGUE/NAT. PAGE 72 A1470 — INT/ORG DIPLOM ADMIN

B58
JAPANESE ASSOCIATION INT. LAW,JAPAN AND THE UNITED NATIONS. SOCIETY ROUTINE ATTIT DRIVE PERCEPT RIGID/FLEX ORD/FREE...METH/CNCPT CON/ANAL CHINJAP UN. PAGE 73 A1497 — ASIA INT/ORG

B58
MANSERGH N.,SURVEY OF BRITISH COMMONWEALTH AFFAIRS: PROBLEMS OF WARTIME CO-OPERATION AND POST-WAR CHANGE 1939-1952. INDIA IRELAND S/ASIA CONSTN INT/ORG BAL/PWR COLONIAL NEUTRAL WAR ADJUST PEACE ROLE ORD/FREE...CHARTS 20 CMN/WLTH NATO UN. PAGE 94 A1931 — VOL/ASSN CONSEN PROB/SOLV INGP/REL

B58
MUNKMAN C.A.,AMERICAN AID TO GREECE. GREECE USA+45 AGRI FINAN PROB/SOLV WAR PWR...CHARTS 20 UN. PAGE 106 A2171 — FOR/AID PLAN ECO/DEV INT/TRADE

B58
RIGGS R.,POLITICS IN THE UNITED NATIONS: A STUDY OF UNITED STATES INFLUENCE IN THE GENERAL ASSEMBLY. USA+45 WOR+45 LEGIS TOP/EX CREATE BAL/PWR DIPLOM DOMIN EDU/PROP COLONIAL ROUTINE ATTIT RIGID/FLEX PWR...CONCPT OBS HIST/WRIT CHARTS STERTYP GEN/LAWS UN COLD/WAR 20. PAGE 121 A2480 — INT/ORG

B58
RUSSELL R.B.,A HISTORY OF THE UNITED NATIONS CHARTER: THE ROLE OF THE UNITED STATES. SOCIETY NAT/G CONSULT DOMIN LEGIT ATTIT ORD/FREE PWR ...POLICY JURID CONCPT UN LEAGUE/NAT. PAGE 126 A2575 — USA-45 INT/ORG CONSTN

B58
SCOTT W.A.,THE UNITED STATES AND THE UNITED NATIONS: THE PUBLIC VIEW 1945-1955. USA+45 EDU/PROP ...INT QU KNO/TEST SAMP GP/COMP 20 UN. PAGE 130 A2674 — ATTIT DIPLOM INT/ORG

B58
SEYID MUHAMMAD V.A.,THE LEGAL FRAMEWORK OF WORLD TRADE. WOR+45 INT/ORG DIPLOM CONTROL...BIBLIOG 20 TREATY UN IMF GATT. PAGE 131 A2689 — INT/LAW VOL/ASSN INT/TRADE TARIFFS

B58
SOC OF COMP LEGIS AND INT LAW,THE LAW OF THE SEA... (PAMPHLET). WOR+45 NAT/G INT/TRADE ADJUD CONTROL NUC/PWR WAR PEACE ATTIT ORD/FREE...JURID CHARTS 20 UN TREATY RESOURCE/N. PAGE 135 A2756 — INT/LAW INT/ORG DIPLOM SEA

B58
STONE J.,AGGRESSION AND WORLD ORDER: A CRITIQUE OF UNITED NATIONS THEORIES OF AGGRESSION. LAW CONSTN DELIB/GP PROB/SOLV BAL/PWR DIPLOM DEBATE ADJUD CRIME PWR...POLICY IDEA/COMP 20 UN SUEZ LEAGUE/NAT. PAGE 138 A2835 — ORD/FREE INT/ORG WAR CONCPT

B58
UN INTL CONF ON PEACEFUL USE,PROGRESS IN ATOMIC ENERGY (VOL. I). WOR+45 R+D PLAN TEC/DEV CONFER CONTROL PEACE SKILL...CHARTS ANTHOL 20 UN BAGHDAD. PAGE 147 A3003 — NUC/PWR DIPLOM WORKER EDU/PROP

B58
US DEPARTMENT OF STATE,PUBLICATIONS OF THE DEPARTMENT OF STATE, JANUARY 1,1953 TO DECEMBER 31, 1957. AGRI INT/ORG FORCES FOR/AID EDU/PROP ARMS/CONT NUC/PWR ATTIT 20 DEPT/STATE OAS UN NATO. PAGE 151 A3092 — BIBLIOG DIPLOM

S58
MCDOUGAL M.S.,"PERSPECTIVES FOR A LAW OF OUTER SPACE." FUT WOR+45 AIR CONSULT DELIB/GP TEC/DEV CT/SYS ORD/FREE...POLICY JURID 20 UN. PAGE 98 A2004 — INT/ORG SPACE INT/LAW

C58
FIFIELD R.H.,"THE DIPLOMACY OF SOUTHEAST ASIA: 1945-1958." INT/ORG NAT/G COLONIAL REGION...CHARTS BIBLIOG 20 UN. PAGE 45 A0927 — S/ASIA DIPLOM NAT/LISM

C58
RAJAN M.S.,"UNITED NATIONS AND DOMESTIC JURISDICTION." WOR+45 WOR-45 PARL/PROC...IDEA/COMP BIBLIOG 20 UN. PAGE 119 A2434 — INT/LAW DIPLOM CONSTN INT/ORG

N58
US HOUSE COMM FOREIGN AFFAIRS,HEARINGS ON DRAFT LEGISLATION TO AMEND FURTHER THE MUTUAL SECURITY ACT OF 1954 (PAMPHLET). USA+45 CONSULT FORCES BUDGET DIPLOM DETER COST ORD/FREE...JURID 20 DEPT/DEFEN UN DEPT/STATE. PAGE 153 A3123 — LEGIS DELIB/GP CONFER WEAPON

B59
ALWAN M.,ALGERIA BEFORE THE UNITED NATIONS. AFR ASIA FRANCE ISLAM S/ASIA CONSTN SOCIETY STRUCT INT/ORG NAT/G ECO/TAC ADMIN COLONIAL NAT/LISM ATTIT — PLAN RIGID/FLEX DIPLOM

PWR...DECISION TREND 420 UN. PAGE 7 A0133 ALGERIA

B59
BLOOMFIELD L.P.,WESTERN EUROPE AND THE UN - TRENDS AND PROSPECTS. EUR+WWI BAL/PWR DIPLOM ECO/TAC COLONIAL ATTIT PWR...POLICY 20 UN EUROPE/W. PAGE 16 A0316 INT/ORG TREND FUT NAT/G

B59
CHINA INSTITUTE OF AMERICA.,CHINA AND THE UNITED NATIONS. CHINA/COM FUT STRUCT EDU/PROP LEGIT ADMIN ATTIT KNOWL ORD/FREE PWR...OBS RECORD STAND/INT TIME/SEQ UN LEAGUE/NAT UNESCO 20. PAGE 26 A0531 ASIA INT/ORG

B59
COMM. STUDY ORGAN. PEACE,ORGANIZING PEACE IN THE NUCLEAR AGE. FUT CONSULT DELIB/GP DOMIN ADJUD ROUTINE COERCE ORD/FREE...TECHNIC INT/LAW JURID NEW/IDEA UN COLD/WAR 20. PAGE 29 A0581 INT/ORG ACT/RES NUC/PWR

B59
COUDENHOVE-KALERGI,FROM WAR TO PEACE. USA+45 USSR WOR+45 WOR-45 LAW INT/ORG NAT/G LEGIT COERCE LOVE ...POLICY PLURIST METH/CNCPT STERTYP TOT/POP UN 20 NATO. PAGE 31 A0636 FUT ORD/FREE

B59
GOODRICH L.,THE UNITED NATIONS. WOR+45 CONSTN STRUCT ACT/RES LEGIT COERCE KNOWL ORD/FREE PWR ...GEN/LAWS UN 20. PAGE 54 A1104 INT/ORG ROUTINE

B59
GORDENKER L.,THE UNITED NATIONS AND THE PEACEFUL UNIFICATION OF KOREA. ASIA LAW LOC/G CONSULT ACT/RES DIPLOM DOMIN LEGIT ADJUD ADMIN ORD/FREE SOVEREIGN...INT GEN/METH UN COLD/WAR 20. PAGE 54 A1109 DELIB/GP KOREA INT/ORG

B59
KAPLAN D.,THE ARAB REFUGEES: AN ABNORMAL PROBLEM. UAR WOR+45 PROB/SOLV DIPLOM GOV/REL ADJUST EFFICIENCY...POLICY GEOG INT/LAW 20 UN JEWS MIGRATION. PAGE 76 A1557 STRANGE HABITAT GP/REL INGP/REL

B59
MACIVER R.M.,THE NATIONS AND THE UN. WOR+45 NAT/G CONSULT ADJUD ADMIN ALL/VALS...CONCPT DEEP/QU UN TOT/POP UNESCO 20. PAGE 92 A1892 INT/ORG ATTIT DIPLOM

B59
MEZERK A.G.,FINANCIAL ASSISTANCE FOR ECONOMIC DEVELOPMENT. WOR+45 INDUS DIPLOM INT/TRADE...CHARTS GOV/COMP UN. PAGE 101 A2064 FOR/AID FINAN ECO/TAC ECO/UNDEV

B59
PEARSON L.B.,DIPLOMACY IN THE NUCLEAR AGE. USA+45 USSR INT/ORG PWR...TREND 20 NATO UN. PAGE 114 A2343 NUC/PWR PEACE POLICY DIPLOM

B59
COLUMBIA U BUR APPL SOC RES,ATTITUDES OF PROMINENT AMERICANS TOWARD "WORLD PEACE THROUGH WORLD LAW" (SUPRA-NATL ORGANIZATION FOR WAR PREVENTION). USA+45 USSR ELITES FORCES PLAN PROB/SOLV CONTROL WAR PWR...POLICY SOC QU IDEA/COMP 20 UN. PAGE 117 A2403 ATTIT ACT/RES INT/LAW STAT

B59
TARDIFF G.,LA LIBERTAD; LA LIBERTAD DE EXPRESION, IDEALES Y REALIDADES AMERICANAS. ISLAM INT/ORG PROB/SOLV PRESS CONFER PARTIC CATHISM...INT/LAW SOC/INTEG UN MID/EAST. PAGE 141 A2889 ORD/FREE ATTIT DIPLOM CONCPT

B59
THOMAS N.,THE PREREQUISITES FOR PEACE. ASIA EUR+WWI FUT ISLAM S/ASIA WOR+45 FORCES PLAN BAL/PWR EDU/PROP LEGIT ATTIT PWR...SOCIALIST CONCPT COLD/WAR 20 UN. PAGE 143 A2924 INT/ORG ORD/FREE ARMS/CONT PEACE

B59
VAN WAGENEN R.W.,SOME VIEWS OF AMERICAN DEFENSE OFFICIALS ABOUT THE UNITED NATIONS (PAPER). FUT USA+45 NAT/G DIPLOM WAR EFFICIENCY PEACE...POLICY INT 20 UN DEPT/DEFEN. PAGE 158 A3216 INT/ORG LEAD ATTIT FORCES

B59
VORSPAN A.,JUSTICE AND JUDAISM. FAM DIPLOM ECO/TAC EDU/PROP CRIME RACE/REL MARRIAGE ANOMIE ATTIT ORD/FREE...POLICY 20 UN. PAGE 160 A3254 SECT CULTURE ACT/RES GP/REL

B59
WOLFERS A.,ALLIANCE POLICY IN THE COLD WAR. COM INT/ORG FORCES COLONIAL CONTROL NUC/PWR 20 NATO UN COLD/WAR. PAGE 166 A3384 DIPLOM DETER BAL/PWR

S59
BAILEY S.D.,"THE FUTURE COMPOSITION OF THE TRUSTEESHIP COUNCIL." FUT WOR+45 CONSTN VOL/ASSN ADMIN ATTIT PWR...OBS TREND CON/ANAL VAL/FREE UN 20. PAGE 10 A0203 INT/ORG NAT/LISM SOVEREIGN

S59
WARBURG J.P.,"THE CENTRAL EUROPEAN CRISIS: A PROPOSAL FOR WESTERN INITIATIVE." EUR+WWI INT/ORG NAT/G LEGIT DETER WAR...CONCPT BER/BLOC UN 20. PAGE 161 A3276 PLAN GERMANY

B60
ASPREMONT-LYNDEN H.,RAPPORT SUR L'ADMINISTRATION BELGE DU RUANDA-URUNDI PENDANT L'ANNEE 1959. BELGIUM RWANDA AGRI INDUS DIPLOM ECO/TAC INT/TRADE DOMIN ADMIN RACE/REL...GEOG CENSUS 20 UN. PAGE 9 A0192 AFR COLONIAL ECO/UNDEV INT/ORG

B60
BAILEY S.D.,THE GENERAL ASSEMBLY OF THE UNITED NATIONS. FUT WOR+45 STRUCT LEGIS ACT/RES PLAN EDU/PROP LEGIT ADMIN EXEC PEACE ATTIT HEALTH PWR ...CONCPT TREND CHARTS GEN/LAWS UN TOT/POP VAL/FREE COLD/WAR 20. PAGE 10 A0204 INT/ORG DELIB/GP DIPLOM

B60
ENGEL J.,THE SECURITY OF THE FREE WORLD. USSR WOR+45 STRATA STRUCT ECO/DEV ECO/UNDEV INT/ORG DELIB/GP FORCES DOMIN LEGIT ADJUD EXEC ARMS/CONT COERCE...POLICY CONCPT NEW/IDEA TIME/SEQ GEN/LAWS COLD/WAR WORK UN 20 NATO. PAGE 42 A0851 COM TREND DIPLOM

B60
HAAS E.B.,THE COMPARATIVE STUDY OF THE UNITED NATIONS. WOR+45 NAT/G DOMIN LEGIT ROUTINE PEACE ORD/FREE PWR UN VAL/FREE 20. PAGE 59 A1205 INT/ORG DIPLOM

B60
HOFFMANN P.G.,ONE HUNDRED COUNTRIES, ONE AND ONE QUARTER BILLION PEOPLE. MARKET INT/ORG TEC/DEV CAP/ISM...GEOG CHARTS METH/COMP 20 UN. PAGE 66 A1354 FOR/AID ECO/TAC ECO/UNDEV INT/TRADE

B60
HOVET T. JR.,BLOC POLITICS IN THE UNITED NATIONS. WOR+45...POLICY STAT CHARTS METH UN. PAGE 68 A1396 LOBBY INT/ORG DIPLOM CHOOSE

B60
HYDE L.K.G.,THE US AND THE UN. WOR+45 STRUCT ECO/DEV ECO/UNDEV NAT/G ACT/RES PLAN DIPLOM EDU/PROP ADMIN ALL/VALS...CONCPT TIME/SEQ GEN/LAWS UN VAL/FREE 20. PAGE 70 A1428 USA+45 INT/ORG FOR/AID

B60
KHRUSHCHEV N.S.,KHRUSHCHEV IN NEW YORK. USA+45 USSR ATTIT...ANTHOL 20 UN KHRUSH/N. PAGE 79 A1612 DIPLOM PEACE ARMS/CONT

B60
MUNRO L.,UNITED NATIONS, HOPE FOR A DIVIDED WORLD. FUT WOR+45 CONSTN DELIB/GP CREATE TEC/DEV DIPLOM EDU/PROP LEGIT PEACE ATTIT HEALTH ORD/FREE PWR ...CONCPT TREND UN VAL/FREE 20. PAGE 106 A2172 INT/ORG ROUTINE

B60
PENTONY D.E.,THE UNDERDEVELOPED LANDS. FUT WOR+45 CULTURE AGRI FINAN INDUS MARKET INT/ORG LABOR NAT/G VOL/ASSN CONSULT TEC/DEV ECO/TAC EDU/PROP COLONIAL ATTIT WEALTH...OBS RECORD SAMP TREND GEN/METH WORK UN 20. PAGE 115 A2351 ECO/UNDEV POLICY FOR/AID INT/TRADE

B60
RAO V.K.R.,INTERNATIONAL AID FOR ECONOMIC DEVELOPMENT - POSSIBILITIES AND LIMITATIONS. FINAN PLAN TEC/DEV ADMIN TASK EFFICIENCY...POLICY SOC METH/CNCPT CHARTS 20 UN. PAGE 119 A2444 FOR/AID DIPLOM INT/ORG ECO/UNDEV

B60
SPEER J.P.,FOR WHAT PURPOSE? CHINA/COM USSR CONSTN PROB/SOLV DIPLOM CONTROL TASK WAR NAT/LISM WORSHIP 20 UN. PAGE 136 A2778 PEACE SECT SUPEGO ALL/IDEOS

B60
TABORN P.,RECORDS OF THE HEADQUARTERS, UNITED NATIONS COMMAND (PRELIMINARY INVENTORIES; PAPER). WOR+45 DIPLOM CONFER PEACE ATTIT...POLICY UN. PAGE 141 A2881 BIBLIOG/A WAR ARMS/CONT INT/ORG

B60
TAYLOR M.D.,THE UNCERTAIN TRUMPET. USA+45 USSR WOR+45 INT/ORG NAT/G CONSULT DOMIN COERCE NUC/PWR WAR ATTIT ORD/FREE PWR...POLICY CONCPT TREND GEN/METH COLD/WAR UN NATO 20. PAGE 142 A2900 PLAN FORCES DIPLOM

B60
THE AFRICA 1960 COMMITTEE,MANDATE IN TRUST; THE PROBLEM OF SOUTH WEST AFRICA. GERMANY STRUCT REGION SANCTION CHOOSE DISCRIM...INT/LAW 20 AFRICA/SW UN LEAGUE/NAT TRUST/TERR. PAGE 142 A2910 NAT/G DIPLOM COLONIAL RACE/REL

B60
THEOBOLD R.,THE NEW NATIONS OF WEST AFRICA. GHANA NIGERIA CULTURE INT/ORG ECO/TAC FOR/AID COLONIAL RACE/REL POPULISM...ANTHOL BIBLIOG 20 UN. PAGE 143 A2916 AFR SOVEREIGN ECO/UNDEV DIPLOM

B60
UNITED WORLD FEDERALISTS,UNITED WORLD FEDERALISTS; PANORAMA OF RECENT BOOKS, FILMS, AND JOURNALS ON WORLD FEDERATION, THE UN, AND WORLD PEACE. CULTURE ECO/UNDEV PROB/SOLV FOR/AID ARMS/CONT NUC/PWR ...INT/LAW PHIL/SCI 20 UN. PAGE 149 A3039 BIBLIOG/A DIPLOM INT/ORG PEACE

B60
US DEPARTMENT OF THE ARMY,DISARMAMENT: A BIBLIOGRAPHIC RECORD: 1916-1960. DETER WAR WEAPON PEACE 20 UN LEAGUE/NAT COLD/WAR NATO. PAGE 152 A3103 BIBLIOG/A ARMS/CONT NUC/PWR DIPLOM

L60
LAUTERPACHT E.,"THE UNITED NATIONS EMERGENCY FORCE." R+D LEGIT ROUTINE COERCE KNOWL ORD/FREE SKILL...JURID UN 20. PAGE 85 A1746 INT/ORG FORCES

L60
RIGGS R.,"OVER-SELLING THE U.N. CHARTER, FACT AND MYTH." USA+45 SOCIETY NAT/G TOP/EX PLAN DIPLOM EDU/PROP PEACE ATTIT PERCEPT MORAL...POLICY SAMP UN INT/ORG MYTH

20. PAGE 121 A2481

S60
BOGARDUS E.S.,"THE SOCIOLOGY OF A STRUCTURED PEACE." FUT SOCIETY CREATE DIPLOM EDU/PROP ADJUD ROUTINE ATTIT RIGID/FLEX KNOWL ORD/FREE RESPECT ...POLICY INT/LAW JURID NEW/IDEA SELF/OBS TOT/POP 20 UN. PAGE 16 A0327
INT/ORG SOC NAT/LISM PEACE

S60
CLARK W.,"NEW FORCES IN THE UN." FUT UK WOR+45 CONSTN BAL/PWR DIPLOM DRIVE PWR SKILL...CONCPT TREND UN TOT/POP 20. PAGE 27 A0543
INT/ORG ECO/UNDEV SOVEREIGN

S60
COHEN A.,"THE NEW AFRICA AND THE UN." FUT ECO/UNDEV NAT/G ECO/TAC INT/TRADE CHOOSE ATTIT ORD/FREE PWR ...POLICY METH/CNCPT OBS TREND CON/ANAL GEN/LAWS TOT/POP VAL/FREE UN 20. PAGE 27 A0558
AFR INT/ORG BAL/PWR FOR/AID

S60
GOODMAN E.,"THE CRY OF NATIONAL LIBERATION: RECENT SOVIET ATTITUDES TOWARDS NATIONAL SELF-DETERMINATION." COM INT/ORG LEGIS ROUTINE PWR ...TIME/SEQ CON/ANAL STERTYP GEN/LAWS 20 UN. PAGE 54 A1101
ATTIT EDU/PROP SOVEREIGN USSR

S60
GOODRICH L.,"GEOGRAPHICAL DISTRIBUTION OF THE STAFF OF THE UN SECRETARIAT." FUT WOR+45 CONSTN BAL/PWR DIPLOM EDU/PROP LEGIT ROUTINE RIGID/FLEX...CHARTS UN 20. PAGE 54 A1105
INT/ORG EX/STRUC

S60
HAVILAND H.F.,"PROBLEMS OF AMERICAN FOREIGN POLICY." ASIA COM USA+45 WOR+45 INT/ORG NAT/G CONSULT ECO/TAC FOR/AID DOMIN COERCE NUC/PWR ATTIT DRIVE ORD/FREE PWR RESPECT SKILL...POLICY GEOG OBS SAMP TREND GEN/METH METH COLD/WAR UN 20. PAGE 63 A1292
ECO/UNDEV FORCES DIPLOM

S60
LYON P.,"NEUTRALITY AND THE EMERGENCE OF THE CONCEPT OF NEUTRALISM." WOR+45 WOR-45 INT/ORG NAT/G BAL/PWR NEUTRAL ATTIT PWR...POLICY TIME/SEQ TREND COLD/WAR TOT/POP VAL/FREE 20 UN. PAGE 92 A1878
CONCPT

S60
MUNRO L.,"CAN THE UNITED NATIONS ENFORCE PEACE." WOR+45 LAW INT/ORG VOL/ASSN BAL/PWR LEGIT ARMS/CONT COERCE DETER PEACE PWR...CONCPT REC/INT TREND UN 20 HAMMARSK/D. PAGE 106 A2173
FORCES ORD/FREE

S60
PADELFORD N.J.,"POLITICS AND CHANGE IN THE SECURITY COUNCIL." FUT WOR+45 CONSTN NAT/G EX/STRUC LEGIS ORD/FREE...CONCPT CHARTS UN 20. PAGE 113 A2309
INT/ORG DELIB/GP

S60
RIESELBACH Z.N.,"QUANTITATIVE TECHNIQUES FOR STUDYING VOTING BEHAVIOR IN THE UNITED NATIONS GENERAL ASSEMBLY." FUT S/ASIA USA+45 INT/ORG BAL/PWR DIPLOM ECO/TAC FOR/AID ADMIN PWR...POLICY METH/CNCPT METH UN 20. PAGE 121 A2478
QUANT CHOOSE

S60
SCHACHTER O.,"THE ENFORCEMENT OF INTERNATIONAL JUDICIAL AND ARBITRAL DECISIONS." WOR+45 NAT/G ECO/TAC DOMIN LEGIT ROUTINE COERCE ATTIT DRIVE ALL/VALS PWR...METH/CNCPT TREND TOT/POP 20 UN. PAGE 128 A2615
INT/ORG ADJUD INT/LAW

S60
SCHWELB E.,"INTERNATIONAL CONVENTIONS ON HUMAN RIGHTS." FUT WOR+45 LAW CONSTN CULTURE SOCIETY STRUCT VOL/ASSN DELIB/GP PLAN ADJUD SUPEGO LOVE MORAL...SOC CONCPT STAT RECORD HIST/WRIT TREND 20 UN. PAGE 130 A2664
INT/ORG HUM

S60
SWIFT R.,"THE UNITED NATIONS AND ITS PUBLIC." WOR+45 CONSTN FINAN CONSULT DELIB/GP ACT/RES ADMIN ROUTINE RIGID/FLEX SKILL UN 20. PAGE 140 A2870
INT/ORG EDU/PROP

B61
BAINS J.S.,STUDIES IN POLITICAL SCIENCE. INDIA WOR+45 WOR-45 CONSTN BAL/PWR ADJUD ADMIN PARL/PROC SOVEREIGN...SOC METH/COMP ANTHOL 17/20 UN. PAGE 10 A0209
DIPLOM INT/LAW NAT/G

B61
HANCOCK W.K.,FOUR STUDIES OF WAR AND PEACE IN THIS CENTURY. FUT WOR+45 WOR-45 ACT/RES LEGIT DETER HEALTH...TREND ANTHOL TOT/POP VAL/FREE UN 20. PAGE 61 A1250
INT/ORG POLICY ARMS/CONT

B61
HASAN H.S.,PAKISTAN AND THE UN. ISLAM WOR+45 ECO/DEV ECO/UNDEV NAT/G TOP/EX ECO/TAC FOR/AID EDU/PROP ADMIN DRIVE PERCEPT...OBS TIME/SEQ UN 20. PAGE 62 A1284
INT/ORG ATTIT PAKISTAN

B61
KERTESZ S.D.,AMERICAN DIPLOMACY IN A NEW ERA. COM S/ASIA UK USA+45 FORCES PROB/SOLV BAL/PWR ECO/TAC ADMIN COLONIAL WAR PEACE ORD/FREE 20 NATO CONGRESS UN COLD/WAR. PAGE 78 A1601
ANTHOL DIPLOM TREND

B61
KNORR K.E.,THE INTERNATIONAL SYSTEM. FUT SOCIETY INT/ORG NAT/G PLAN BAL/PWR DIPLOM WAR PWR ...DECISION METH/CNCPT CONT/OBS GAME METH UN 20. PAGE 81 A1655
ACT/RES SIMUL ECO/UNDEV

B61
LANDSKROY W.A.,OFFICIAL SERIAL PUBLICATIONS RELATING TO ECONOMIC DEVELOPMENT IN AFRICA SOUTH OF THE SAHARA (PAMPHLET). AFR UK R+D ACT/RES 20 UN. PAGE 84 A1720
BIBLIOG ECO/UNDEV COLONIAL INT/ORG

B61
MECHAM J.L.,THE UNITED STATES AND INTER-AMERICAN SECURITY, 1889-1960. L/A+17C USA+45 USA-45 CONSTN FORCES INT/TRADE PEACE TOTALISM ATTIT...JURID 19/20 UN OAS. PAGE 99 A2030
DIPLOM WAR ORD/FREE INT/ORG

B61
MEZERIK A.G.,ECONOMIC DEVELOPMENT AIDS FOR UNDERDEVELOPED COUNTRIES. WOR+45 FINAN LEGIS PROB/SOLV TEC/DEV DIPLOM FOR/AID GIVE TASK WAR 20 UN. PAGE 101 A2062
ECO/UNDEV INT/ORG WEALTH PLAN

B61
MILLER R.I.,DAG HAMMARSKJOLD AND CRISES DIPLOMACY. WOR+45 NAT/G PROB/SOLV LEAD ROLE...DECISION BIOG UN HAMMARSK/D. PAGE 101 A2079
DIPLOM INT/ORG CHIEF

B61
MORRAY J.P.,FROM YALTA TO DISARMAMENT: COLD WAR DEBATE. USA+45 CAP/ISM FOR/AID CONTROL NUC/PWR 20 UN COLD/WAR CHURCHLL/W. PAGE 104 A2145
MARXIST ARMS/CONT DIPLOM BAL/PWR

B61
PEASLEE A.J.,INTERNATIONAL GOVERNMENTAL ORGANIZATIONS (2 VOLS.). CONSTN VOL/ASSN DIPLOM ...GP/COMP 20 UN OAS EEC EFTA ECSC. PAGE 114 A2345
BIBLIOG INT/ORG INDEX LAW

B61
RICE G.W.,THE SOVIET POSITION ON DEPENDENT TERRITORIES IN THE UNITED NATIONS (THESIS, OHIO STATE UNIVERSITY). USSR PLAN SOVEREIGN...POLICY 20 UN. PAGE 121 A2473
INT/ORG COM DIPLOM COLONIAL

B61
RIENOW R.,CONTEMPORARY INTERNATIONAL POLITICS. WOR+45 INT/ORG BAL/PWR EDU/PROP COLONIAL NEUTRAL REGION WAR PEACE...INT/LAW 20 COLD/WAR UN. PAGE 121 A2476
DIPLOM PWR POLICY NAT/G

B61
ROBINS D.B.,EVOLVING UNITED STATES POLICIES TOWARD THE EMERGING NATIONS OF ASIA AND AFRICA (PAMPHLET). ISLAM ECO/UNDEV INT/ORG CONSULT CREATE PLAN TEC/DEV FOR/AID CONFER ALL/VALS 20 KENNEDY/JF EISNHWR/DD UN AID. PAGE 122 A2501
AFR S/ASIA DIPLOM BIBLIOG

B61
SCAMMEL W.M.,INTERNATIONAL MONETARY POLICY. WOR+45 WOR-45 ACT/RES ECO/TAC LEGIT WEALTH...GEN/METH UN 20. PAGE 127 A2611
INT/ORG FINAN BAL/PAY

B61
SHAPP W.R.,FIELD ADMINISTRATION IN THE UNITED NATIONS SYSTEM. FINAN PROB/SOLV INSPECT DIPLOM EXEC REGION ROUTINE EFFICIENCY ROLE...INT CHARTS 20 UN. PAGE 131 A2694
INT/ORG ADMIN GP/REL FOR/AID

B61
SHARP W.R.,FIELD ADMINISTRATION IN THE UNITED NATION SYSTEM: THE CONDUCT OF INTERNATIONAL ECONOMIC AND SOCIAL PROGRAMS. FUT WOR+45 CONSTN SOCIETY ECO/UNDEV R+D DELIB/GP ACT/RES PLAN TEC/DEV EDU/PROP EXEC ROUTINE HEALTH WEALTH...HUM CONCPT CHARTS METH ILO UNESCO VAL/FREE UN 20. PAGE 132 A2697
INT/ORG CONSULT

B61
SINGER J.D.,FINANCING INTERNATIONAL ORGANIZATION: THE UNITED NATIONS BUDGET PROCESS. WOR+45 FINAN ACT/RES CREATE PLAN BUDGET ECO/TAC ADMIN ROUTINE ATTIT KNOWL...DECISION METH/CNCPT TIME/SEQ UN 20. PAGE 133 A2726
INT/ORG MGT

B61
WINTER R.C.,BLUEPRINTS FOR INDEPENDENCE. WOR+45 INT/ORG DIPLOM COLONIAL CONTROL REV WAR PWR ...BIBLIOG 20 UN. PAGE 165 A3367
NAT/G ECO/UNDEV SOVEREIGN CONSTN

L61
CLAUDE I.,"THE UNITED NATIONS AND THE USE OF FORCE." FUT WOR+45 SOCIETY DIPLOM EDU/PROP LEGIT ADMIN ROUTINE COERCE WAR PEACE ORD/FREE...CONCPT TREND UN 20. PAGE 27 A0545
INT/ORG FORCES

L61
HOYT E.C.,"UNITED STATES REACTION TO THE KOREAN ATTACK." COM KOREA USA+45 CONSTN DELIB/GP FORCES PLAN ECO/TAC DOMIN EDU/PROP LEGIT ROUTINE COERCE WAR ATTIT DISPL RIGID/FLEX ORD/FREE PWR...POLICY INT/LAW TREND UN 20. PAGE 68 A1402
ASIA INT/ORG BAL/PWR DIPLOM

L61
TAUBENFELD H.J.,"A REGIME FOR OUTER SPACE." FUT UNIV R+D ACT/RES PLAN BAL/PWR LEGIT ARMS/CONT ORD/FREE...POLICY JURID TREND UN TOT/POP 20 COLD/WAR. PAGE 142 A2894
INT/ORG ADJUD SPACE

S61
"CRITERIA FOR ALLOCATING INVESTMENT RESOURCES AMONG VARIOUS FIELDS OF DEVELOPMENT IN UNDERDEVELOPED ECONOMIES." ASIA AGRI INT/ORG CAP/ISM BAL/PAY EFFICIENCY PROFIT WEALTH...STAT 20 UN. PAGE 3 A0061
BIBLIOG/A ECO/UNDEV PLAN TEC/DEV

S61
ALGER C.F.,"NON-RESOLUTION CONSEQUENCES OF THE
INT/ORG

UNITED NATIONS AND THEIR EFFECT ON INTERNATIONAL CONFLICT." WOR+45 CONSTN ECO/DEV NAT/G CONSULT DELIB/GP TOP/EX ACT/RES PLAN DIPLOM EDU/PROP ROUTINE ATTIT ALL/VALS...INT/LAW TOT/POP UN 20. PAGE 6 A0117
DRIVE BAL/PWR

S61
CASTANEDA J.,"THE UNDERDEVELOPED NATIONS AND THE DEVELOPMENT OF INTERNATIONAL LAW." FUT UNIV LAW ACT/RES FOR/AID LEGIT PERCEPT SKILL...JURID METH/CNCPT TIME/SEQ TOT/POP 20 UN. PAGE 25 A0507
INT/ORG ECO/UNDEV PEACE INT/LAW

S61
CLAUDE I.,"THE MANAGEMENT OF POWER IN THE CHANGING UNITED NATIONS." WOR+45 PERCEPT UN TOT/POP VAL/FREE 20. PAGE 27 A0544
INT/ORG DELIB/GP BAL/PWR

S61
GOODWIN G.L.,"THE EXPANDING UNITED NATIONS: 2-DIPLOMATIC PRESSURES AND TECHNIQUES." COM ECO/UNDEV TOP/EX BAL/PWR DIPLOM DOMIN...POLICY CONCPT UN COLD/WAR 20. PAGE 54 A1108
INT/ORG PWR

S61
JACKSON E.,"CONSTITUTIONAL DEVELOPMENTS OF THE UNITED NATIONS: THE GROWTH OF ITS EXECUTIVE CAPACITY." FUT WOR+45 CONSTN STRUCT ACT/RES PLAN ALL/VALS...NEW/IDEA OBS COLD/WAR UN 20. PAGE 72 A1475
INT/ORG EXEC

S61
JACKSON E.,"THE FUTURE DEVELOPMENT OF THE UNITED NATIONS: SOME SUGGESTIONS FOR RESEARCH." FUT LAW CONSTN ECO/DEV FINAN PEACE WEALTH...WELF/ST CONCPT UN 20. PAGE 72 A1476
INT/ORG PWR

S61
MILLER E.,"LEGAL ASPECTS OF UN ACTION IN THE CONGO." AFR CULTURE ADMIN PEACE DRIVE RIGID/FLEX ORD/FREE...WELF/ST JURID OBS UN CONGO 20. PAGE 101 A2076
INT/ORG LEGIT

S61
PADELFORD N.J.,"POLITICS AND THE FUTURE OF ECOSOC." AFR S/ASIA ECO/UNDEV INDUS NAT/G DELIB/GP ACT/RES ORD/FREE WEALTH...CONCPT CHARTS UN 20 ECOSOC. PAGE 113 A2310
INT/ORG TEC/DEV

S61
VIRALLY M.,"VERS UNE REFORME DU SECRETARIAT DES NATIONS UNIES." FUT WOR+45 CONSTN ECO/DEV TOP/EX BAL/PWR ADMIN ALL/VALS...CONCPT BIOG UN VAL/FREE 20. PAGE 159 A3243
INT/ORG INTELL DIPLOM

B62
ROUND TABLE ON EUROPE'S ROLE IN LATIN AMERICAN DEVELOPMENT. EUR+WWI L/A+17C PLAN BAL/PAY UTIL ROLE WEALTH...CHARTS ANTHOL 20 UN INT/AM/DEV. PAGE 3 A0063
ECO/UNDEV FINAN TEC/DEV FOR/AID

B62
AIR FORCE ACADEMY LIBRARY,INTERNATIONAL ORGANIZATIONS AND MILITARY SECURITY SYSTEMS (PAMPHLET) (SPECIAL BIBLIOGRAPHY SERIES, NUMBER 25). DIPLOM FOR/AID INT/TRADE NUC/PWR PEACE 20 UN NATO OAS SEATO LEAGUE/NAT. PAGE 5 A0104
BIBLIOG INT/ORG FORCES DETER

B62
ALEXANDROWICZ C.H.,WORLD ECONOMIC AGENCIES: LAW AND PRACTICE. WOR+45 DIST/IND FINAN LABOR CONSULT INT/TRADE TARIFFS REPRESENT HEALTH...JURID 20 UN GATT EEC OAS ECSC. PAGE 6 A0115
INT/LAW INT/ORG DIPLOM ADJUD

B62
BAILEY S.D.,THE SECRETARIAT OF THE UNITED NATIONS. FUT WOR+45 DELIB/GP PLAN BAL/PWR DOMIN EDU/PROP ADMIN PEACE ATTIT PWR...DECISION CONCPT TREND CON/ANAL CHARTS UN VAL/FREE COLD/WAR 20. PAGE 10 A0205
INT/ORG EXEC DIPLOM

B62
BOWLES C.,THE CONSCIENCE OF A LIBERAL. COM USA+45 WOR+45 STRUCT LOC/G NAT/G FORCES LEGIS GOV/REL DISCRIM 20 UN CIV/RIGHTS. PAGE 18 A0361
DIPLOM POLICY

B62
BRIMMER B.,A GUIDE TO THE USE OF UNITED NATIONS DOCUMENTS. WOR+45 ECO/UNDEV AGRI EX/STRUC FORCES PROB/SOLV ADMIN WAR PEACE WEALTH...POLICY UN. PAGE 19 A0378
BIBLIOG/A INT/ORG DIPLOM

B62
CALDER R.,COMMON SENSE ABOUT A STARVING WORLD. WOR+45 STRATA ECO/DEV PLAN GP/REL BIO/SOC HABITAT ...POLICY GEOG STAT RECORD 20 UN BIRTH/CON. PAGE 23 A0466
FOR/AID CENSUS ECO/UNDEV AGRI

B62
CALVOCORESSI P.,WORLD ORDER AND NEW STATES: PROBLEMS OF KEEPING THE PEACE. AFR EUR+WWI S/ASIA ELITES NAT/G ECO/TAC FOR/AID EDU/PROP COERCE ATTIT DRIVE ALL/VALS...GEN/LAWS COLD/WAR 20 UN. PAGE 23 A0471
INT/ORG PEACE

B62
DALLIN A.,THE SOVIET UNION AT THE UNITED NATIONS: AN INQUIRY INTO SOVIET MOTIVES AND OBJECTIVES. ACT/RES EDU/PROP LEGIT ATTIT KNOWL PWR...POLICY RECORD HIST/WRIT TIME/SEQ TREND ORG/CHARTS GEN/METH COLD/WAR FAO 20 UN. PAGE 33 A0675
COM INT/ORG USSR

B62
DUTOIT B.,LA NEUTRALITE SUISSE A L'HEURE EUROPEENNE. EUR+WWI MOD/EUR INT/ORG NAT/G VOL/ASSN PLAN BAL/PWR LEGIT NEUTRAL REGION PEACE ORD/FREE SOVEREIGN...CONCPT OBS TIME/SEQ TREND STERTYP VAL/FREE LEAGUE/NAT UN 20. PAGE 40 A0812
ATTIT DIPLOM SWITZERLND

B62
FAO,FOOD AND AGRICULTURE ORGANIZATION AFRICAN SURVEY. AFR CONGO/BRAZ GHANA STRATA AGRI INT/ORG TEC/DEV FOR/AID INT/TRADE RACE/REL DEMAND EFFICIENCY PRODUC...GEOG 20 UN CONGO/LEOP. PAGE 44 A0898
ECO/TAC WEALTH EXTR/IND ECO/UNDEV

B62
GYORGY A.,PROBLEMS IN INTERNATIONAL RELATIONS. COM CT/SYS NUC/PWR ALL/IDEOS 20 UN EEC ECSC. PAGE 58 A1199
DIPLOM NEUTRAL BAL/PWR REV

B62
HADWEN J.G.,HOW UNITED NATIONS DECISIONS ARE MADE. WOR+45 LAW EDU/PROP LEGIT ADMIN PWR...DECISION SELF/OBS GEN/LAWS UN 20. PAGE 59 A1212
INT/ORG ROUTINE

B62
HIGGANS B.,UNITED NATIONS AND U.S. FOREIGN ECONOMIC POLICY. FUT USA+45 WOR+45 ECO/DEV ECO/UNDEV NAT/G ECO/TAC WEALTH...TIME/SEQ TOT/POP UN 20. PAGE 65 A1328
INT/ORG ACT/RES FOR/AID DIPLOM

B62
KING G.,THE UNITED NATIONS IN THE CONGO: A QUEST FOR PEACE. WOR+45 NAT/G CONSULT FORCES LEGIT COERCE WAR ORD/FREE...JURID METH/CNCPT OBS INT HIST/WRIT TIME/SEQ CONGO UN 20 COLD/WAR. PAGE 79 A1624
AFR INT/ORG

B62
LAWSON R.,INTERNATIONAL REGIONAL ORGANIZATIONS. WOR+45 NAT/G VOL/ASSN CONSULT LEGIS EDU/PROP LEGIT ADMIN EXEC ROUTINE HEALTH PWR WEALTH...JURID EEC COLD/WAR 20 UN. PAGE 86 A1752
INT/ORG DELIB/GP REGION

B62
LEVY H.V.,LIBERDADE E JUSTICA SOCIAL (2ND ED.). BRAZIL COM L/A+17C USSR INT/ORG PARTIC GP/REL WEALTH 20 UN COM/PARTY. PAGE 88 A1798
ORD/FREE MARXISM CAP/ISM LAW

B62
LOWENSTEIN A.K.,BRUTAL MANDATE: A JOURNEY TO SOUTH WEST AFRICA. CULTURE INT/ORG NAT/G DIPLOM...GEOG 20 UN AFRICA/SW. PAGE 91 A1868
AFR POLICY RACE/REL PROB/SOLV

B62
MARTIN L.W.,NEUTRALISM AND NONALIGNMENT. WOR+45 ATTIT PWR...POLICY ANTHOL 20 UN. PAGE 95 A1952
DIPLOM NEUTRAL BAL/PWR INT/ORG

B62
NICHOLAS H.G.,THE UNITED NATIONS AS A POLITICAL INSTITUTION. WOR+45 CONSTN EX/STRUC ACT/RES LEGIT PERCEPT KNOWL PWR...CONCPT TIME/SEQ CON/ANAL ORG/CHARTS UN 20. PAGE 109 A2228
INT/ORG ROUTINE

B62
PERKINS D.,AMERICA'S QUEST FOR PEACE. USA+45 WOR+45 DIPLOM CONFER NAT/LISM ATTIT 20 UN TREATY. PAGE 115 A2361
INT/LAW INT/ORG ARMS/CONT PEACE

B62
RIVKIN A.,AFRICA AND THE WEST. AFR EUR+WWI FUT ISLAM ISRAEL USA+45 SOCIETY INT/ORG FORCES CREATE PLAN FOR/AID EDU/PROP ATTIT...CONCPT TREND EEC 20 CONGRESS UN. PAGE 121 A2488
ECO/UNDEV ECO/TAC

B62
ROSENNE S.,THE WORLD COURT: WHAT IT IS AND HOW IT WORKS. WOR+45 WOR-45 LAW CONSTN JUDGE EDU/PROP LEGIT ROUTINE CHOOSE PEACE ORD/FREE...JURID OBS TIME/SEQ CHARTS UN TOT/POP VAL/FREE 20. PAGE 124 A2538
INT/ORG ADJUD INT/LAW

B62
SCHWARTZ L.E.,INTERNATIONAL ORGANIZATIONS AND SPACE COOPERATION. VOL/ASSN CONSULT CREATE TEC/DEV SANCTION...POLICY INT/LAW PHIL/SCI 20 UN. PAGE 130 A2656
INT/ORG DIPLOM R+D SPACE

B62
SHAW C.,LEGAL PROBLEMS IN INTERNATIONAL TRADE AND INVESTMENT. WOR+45 ECO/DEV ECO/UNDEV MARKET DIPLOM TAX INCOME ROLE...ANTHOL BIBLIOG 20 TREATY UN IMF GATT. PAGE 132 A2698
INT/LAW INT/TRADE FINAN ECO/TAC

B62
STRACHEY J.,ON THE PREVENTION OF WAR. FUT WOR+45 INT/ORG NAT/G ACT/RES PLAN BAL/PWR DOMIN EDU/PROP PEACE ATTIT...POLICY TREND TOT/POP COLD/WAR 20 UN. PAGE 139 A2842
FORCES ORD/FREE ARMS/CONT NUC/PWR

B62
THANT U.,THE UNITED NATIONS' DEVELOPMENT DECADE: PROPOSALS FOR ACTION. WOR+45 SOCIETY ECO/UNDEV AGRI COM/IND FINAN R+D MUNIC SCHOOL VOL/ASSN CONSULT PLAN TEC/DEV ECO/TAC EDU/PROP ADMIN ROUTINE RIGID/FLEX...MGT SOC CONCPT UNESCO UN TOT/POP VAL/FREE. PAGE 142 A2906
INT/ORG ALL/VALS

B62
UNECA LIBRARY,BOOKS ON AFRICA IN THE UNECA LIBRARY. WOR+45 AGRI INT/ORG NAT/G PLAN WRITING REGION...SOC STAT UN. PAGE 147 A3008
BIBLIOG AFR ECO/UNDEV TEC/DEV

B62
UNECA LIBRARY,NEW ACQUISITIONS IN THE UNECA LIBRARY. LAW NAT/G PLAN PROB/SOLV TEC/DEV ADMIN REGION...GEOG SOC 20 UN. PAGE 147 A3009 — BIBLIOG AFR ECO/UNDEV INT/ORG

B62
UNESCO,GENERAL CATALOGUE OF UNESCO PUBLICATIONS AND UNESCO SPONSORED PUBLICATIONS, 1946-1959. WOR+45 ...POLICY ART/METH HUM PHIL/SCI UN. PAGE 148 A3022 — BIBLIOG INT/ORG ECO/UNDEV SOC

B62
UNIVERSITY OF TENNESSEE,GOVERNMENT AND WORLD CRISIS. USA+45 FOR/AID ORD/FREE...ANTHOL 20 UN. PAGE 149 A3048 — ECO/DEV DIPLOM NAT/G INT/ORG

L62
BAILEY S.D.,"THE TROIKA AND THE FUTURE OF THE UN." CONSTN CREATE LEGIT EXEC CHOOSE ORD/FREE PWR ...CONCPT NEW/IDEA UN COLD/WAR 20. PAGE 10 A0206 — FUT INT/ORG USSR

L62
CORET A.,"LES PROVINCES PORTUGALLES D'OUTREMER ET L'ONU." AFR PORTUGAL S/ASIA WOR+45 LOC/G NAT/G DOMIN...CONCPT TIME/SEQ UN 20 GOA. PAGE 31 A0620 — INT/ORG SOVEREIGN COLONIAL

L62
CORET A.,"L'INDEPENDANCE DU SAMOA OCCIDENTAL." S/ASIA LAW INT/ORG EXEC ALL/VALS SAMOA UN 20. PAGE 31 A0622 — NAT/G STRUCT SOVEREIGN

L62
GROSS L.,"IMMUNITIES AND PRIVILEGES OF DELIGATIONS TO THE UNITED NATIONS." USA+45 WOR+45 STRATA NAT/G VOL/ASSN CONSULT DIPLOM EDU/PROP ROUTINE RESPECT ...POLICY INT/LAW CONCPT UN 20. PAGE 57 A1176 — INT/ORG LAW ELITES

L62
MALINOWSKI W.R.,"CENTRALIZATION AND DE-CENTRALIZATION IN THE UNITED NATIONS' ECONOMIC AND SOCIAL ACTIVITIES." WOR+45 CONSTN ECO/UNDEV INT/ORG VOL/ASSN DELIB/GP ECO/TAC EDU/PROP ADMIN RIGID/FLEX ...OBS CHARTS UNESCO UN EEC OAS OEEC 20. PAGE 93 A1913 — CREATE GEN/LAWS

L62
NIZARD L.,"CUBAN QUESTION AND SECURITY COUNCIL." L/A+17C USA+45 ECO/UNDEV NAT/G POL/PAR DELIB/GP ECO/TAC PWR...RELATIV OBS TIME/SEQ TREND GEN/LAWS UN 20 UN. PAGE 109 A2242 — INT/ORG JURID DIPLOM CUBA

L62
NIZARD L.,"CUBAN QUESTION AND SECURITY COUNCIL." L/A+17C USA+45 ECO/UNDEV NAT/G POL/PAR DELIB/GP ECO/TAC PWR...RELATIV OBS TIME/SEQ TREND GEN/LAWS UN 20 UN. PAGE 109 A2242 — INT/ORG JURID DIPLOM CUBA

L62
STEIN E.,"MR HAMMARSKJOLD, THE CHARTER LAW AND THE FUTURE ROLE OF THE UNITED NATIONS SECRETARY-GENERAL." WOR+45 CONSTN INT/ORG DELIB/GP FORCES TOP/EX BAL/PWR LEGIT ROUTINE RIGID/FLEX PWR ...POLICY JURID OBS STERTYP UN COLD/WAR 20 HAMMARSK/D. PAGE 137 A2815 — CONCPT BIOG

L62
WILCOX F.O.,"THE UN AND THE NON-ALIGNED NATIONS." AFR S/ASIA USA+45 ECO/UNDEV INT/ORG TEC/DEV EDU/PROP RIGID/FLEX ORD/FREE PWR...POLICY HUM CONCPT STAT OBS TIME/SEQ STERTYP GEN/METH UN 20. PAGE 164 A3345 — ATTIT TREND

S62
BELSHAW C.,"TRAINING AND RECRUITMENT: SOME PRINCIPLES OF INTERNATIONAL AID." FUT WOR+45 SOCIETY INT/ORG NAT/G CREATE PLAN TEC/DEV ECO/TAC FOR/AID EDU/PROP ATTIT PERCEPT...HUM UN FAO ILO UNESCO 20. PAGE 13 A0263 — VOL/ASSN ECO/UNDEV

S62
BERKES R.N.B.,"THE NEW FRONTIER IN THE UN." FUT USA+45 WOR+45 INT/ORG DELIB/GP NAT/LISM PERCEPT RESPECT UN OAS 20. PAGE 13 A0272 — GEN/LAWS DIPLOM

S62
BLOOMFIELD L.P.,"THE UNITED NATIONS IN CRISIS: THE ROLE OF THE UN IN USA FOREIGN POLICY." FUT USA+45 WOR+45 ECO/UNDEV DIPLOM ATTIT ORD/FREE...CONCPT UN. PAGE 16 A0317 — INT/ORG TREND REV

S62
BROWN B.E.,"L'ONU ABANDONNE LA HONGRIE." COM USSR WOR+45 CONSTN NAT/G POL/PAR DELIB/GP ACT/RES TEC/DEV PWR...TIME/SEQ 20 UN. PAGE 20 A0400 — INT/ORG TOTALISM HUNGARY POLICY

S62
CLEVELAND H.,"THE FUTURE ROLE OF THE UNITED STATES IN THE UNITED NATIONS." USA+45 ECO/UNDEV INT/ORG EX/STRUC DIPLOM FOR/AID ROUTINE SKILL SOVEREIGN WEALTH UN 20. PAGE 27 A0550 — FUT ATTIT

S62
CORET A.,"LA DECLARATION DE L'ASSEMBLEE GENERAL DE L'ONU SUR L'OCTROI DE L'INDEPENDENCE AUX PAYS ET AUX PEUPLES." AFR ASIA ISLAM NIGERIA S/ASIA USSR WOR+45 ECO/UNDEV NAT/G DELIB/GP COLONIAL ALL/VALS ...CONCPT TIME/SEQ TREND UN TOT/POP 20 MEXIC/AMER. PAGE 31 A0621 — INT/ORG STRUCT SOVEREIGN

S62
DALLIN A.,"THE SOVIET VIEW OF THE UNITED NATIONS." WOR+45 VOL/ASSN TOP/EX DIPLOM DOMIN EDU/PROP LEGIT ATTIT RIGID/FLEX PWR...CONCPT OBS HIST/WRIT TIME/SEQ STERTYP GEN/LAWS COLD/WAR UN 20. PAGE 33 A0676 — COM INT/ORG USSR

S62
FOSTER W.C.,"ARMS CONTROL AND DISARMAMENT IN A DIVIDED WORLD." COM FUT USA+45 USSR WOR+45 INTELL INT/ORG NAT/G VOL/ASSN CONSULT CREATE PLAN TEC/DEV EDU/PROP LEGIT NUC/PWR ATTIT RIGID/FLEX...CONCPT TREND TOT/POP 20 UN. PAGE 47 A0971 — DELIB/GP POLICY ARMS/CONT DIPLOM

S62
GAREAU F.H.,"BLOC POLITICS IN WEST AFRICA." AFR CONGO/BRAZ GHANA GUINEA MALI WOR+45 STRUCT ECO/UNDEV INT/ORG VOL/ASSN CHOOSE ORD/FREE PWR UN 20. PAGE 51 A1048 — NAT/G NAT/LISM

S62
JACOBSON H.K.,"THE UNITED NATIONS AND COLONIALISM: A TENTATIVE APPRAISAL." AFR FUT S/ASIA USA+45 USSR WOR+45 NAT/G DELIB/GP PLAN DIPLOM ECO/TAC DOMIN ADMIN ROUTINE COERCE ATTIT RIGID/FLEX ORD/FREE PWR ...OBS STERTYP UN 20. PAGE 73 A1486 — INT/ORG CONCPT COLONIAL

S62
MILLAR T.B.,"THE COMMONWEALTH AND THE UNITED NATIONS." FUT WOR+45 STRUCT NAT/G VOL/ASSN CONSULT DELIB/GP EDU/PROP LEGIT ATTIT...POLICY CONCPT TREND CMN/WLTH UN 20. PAGE 101 A2072 — INT/ORG

S62
SPENSER J.H.,"AFRICA AT THE UNITED NATIONS: SOME OBSERVATIONS." FUT ECO/UNDEV NAT/G CONSULT DELIB/GP PLAN BAL/PWR ECO/TAC EDU/PROP ATTIT RIGID/FLEX HEALTH ORD/FREE PWR WEALTH...POLICY CONCPT OBS TREND STERTYP GEN/METH UN VAL/FREE. PAGE 136 A2786 — AFR INT/ORG REGION

B63
BAILEY S.D.,THE UNITED NATIONS: A SHORT POLITICAL GUIDE. FUT PROB/SOLV LEAD...INT/LAW 20 UN. PAGE 10 A0207 — INT/ORG PEACE DETER DIPLOM

B63
BOWETT D.W.,THE LAW OF INTERNATIONAL INSTITUTIONS. WOR+45 WOR-45 CONSTN DELIB/GP EX/STRUC JUDGE EDU/PROP LEGIT CT/SYS EXEC ROUTINE RIGID/FLEX ORD/FREE PWR...JURID CONCPT ORG/CHARTS GEN/METH LEAGUE/NAT OAS OEEC 20 UN. PAGE 17 A0354 — INT/ORG ADJUD DIPLOM

B63
BRECHER M.,THE NEW STATES OF ASIA. ASIA S/ASIA INT/ORG BAL/PWR COLONIAL NEUTRAL ORD/FREE PWR 20 UN. PAGE 18 A0369 — NAT/G ECO/UNDEV DIPLOM POLICY

B63
BURNS A.L.,PEACE-KEEPING BY U.N.FORCES - FROM SUEZ TO THE CONGO. AFR FUT ISLAM ISRAEL USSR WOR+45 NAT/G DELIB/GP BAL/PWR DOMIN LEGIT EXEC COERCE PEACE ATTIT PWR RESPECT SOVEREIGN...CONCPT UN 20. PAGE 22 A0441 — INT/ORG FORCES ORD/FREE

B63
FRANKEL J.,THE MAKING OF FOREIGN POLICY: AN ANALYSIS OF DECISION-MAKING. CHINA/COM EUR+WWI USA+45 ELITES INTELL FORCES LEGIS PLAN ATTIT ALL/VALS MORAL CONSERVE...GOV/COMP 20 PRESIDENT UN TREATY. PAGE 48 A0981 — POLICY DECISION PROB/SOLV DIPLOM

B63
GARDINIER D.E.,CAMEROON: UNITED NATIONS CHALLENGE TO FRENCH POLICY. AFR CAMEROON FRANCE NAT/G LEGIS CONTROL SOVEREIGN 20 UN. PAGE 51 A1042 — DIPLOM POLICY INT/ORG COLONIAL

B63
GOLDWIN R.A.,FOREIGN AND MILITARY POLICY. COM USSR WOR+45 ECO/DEV INT/ORG FORCES PLAN ECO/TAC REGION ARMS/CONT MARXISM 20 UN. PAGE 54 A1097 — DIPLOM POLICY PWR NAT/G

B63
HALASZ DE BEKY I.L.,A BIBLIOGRAPHY OF THE HUNGARIAN REVOLUTION 1956. COM HUNGARY USSR DIPLOM COERCE MARXISM...POLICY AUD/VIS 20 UN COLD/WAR. PAGE 59 A1221 — BIBLIOG REV FORCES ATTIT

B63
HOVET T. JR.,AFRICA IN THE UNITED NATIONS. AFR DELIB/GP EDU/PROP LOBBY CHOOSE ORD/FREE PWR RESPECT SKILL...STAT TIME/SEQ CON/ANAL CHARTS STERTYP VAL/FREE 20 UN. PAGE 68 A1397 — INT/ORG USSR

B63
JACOBSON H.K.,THE USSR AND THE UN'S ECONOMIC AND SOCIAL ACTIVITIES. COM WOR+45 DELIB/GP ACT/RES ECO/TAC EDU/PROP RIGID/FLEX SUPEGO HEALTH PWR SKILL ...POLICY CHARTS GEN/METH VAL/FREE UNESCO 20 UN. PAGE 73 A1487 — INT/ORG ATTIT USSR

B63
JUDD P.,AFRICAN INDEPENDENCE: THE EXPLODING EMERGENCE OF THE NEW AFRICAN NATIONS. AFR UK LAW CONSTN CULTURE KIN DIPLOM ATTIT...CHARTS BIBLIOG 20 UN DEGAULLE/C NEGRO THIRD/WRLD. PAGE 75 A1542 — ORD/FREE POLICY DOMIN LOC/G

B63
LERCHE C.O. JR.,AMERICA IN WORLD AFFAIRS. COM UK USA+45 INT/ORG FORCES ECO/TAC INT/TRADE EDU/PROP WAR NAT/LISM PEACE...BIBLIOG 18/20 UN CONGRESS PRESIDENT COLD/WAR. PAGE 87 A1783 — NAT/G DIPLOM PLAN

B63
LYON P.,NEUTRALISM. ECO/UNDEV EDU/PROP COLONIAL ALL/IDEOS...IDEA/COMP 20 COLD/WAR UN. PAGE 92 A1879
NAT/COMP NAT/LISM DIPLOM NEUTRAL

B63
MALIK C.,MAN IN THE STRUGGLE FOR PEACE. USSR WOR+45 CHIEF PLAN PROB/SOLV PARTIC NUC/PWR REV ORD/FREE ...IDEA/COMP METH/COMP 20 UN COLD/WAR. PAGE 93 A1912
PEACE MARXISM DIPLOM EDU/PROP

B63
NICOLSON H.,DIPLOMACY (3RD ED.). INT/ORG NAT/G CONSULT DELIB/GP CONFER 19/20 LEAGUE/NAT UN. PAGE 109 A2232
DIPLOM CONCPT NAT/COMP

B63
PADELFORD N.J.,AFRICA AND WORLD ORDER. AFR COLONIAL SOVEREIGN...ANTHOL BIBLIOG 20 UN UNIFICA COMMONWLTH. PAGE 113 A2312
DIPLOM NAT/G ORD/FREE

B63
QUAISON-SACKEY A.,AFRICA UNBOUND: REFLECTIONS OF AN AFRICAN STATESMAN. ISLAM CULTURE INTELL INT/ORG POL/PAR TOP/EX DOMIN EDU/PROP LEGIT ATTIT PERSON ...CONCPT OBS TIME/SEQ CHARTS STERTYP 20 UN. PAGE 118 A2423
AFR BIOG

B63
RIUKIN A.,THE AFRICAN PRESENCE IN WORLD AFFAIRS. AFR WOR+45 ECO/UNDEV AGRI INT/ORG BAL/PWR ECO/TAC COLONIAL NEUTRAL NAT/LISM PEACE SOVEREIGN 20 UN. PAGE 121 A2486
DIPLOM NAT/G POLICY PWR

B63
ROBERTSON A.H.,HUMAN RIGHTS IN EUROPE. CONSTN SOCIETY INT/ORG NAT/G VOL/ASSN DELIB/GP ACT/RES PLAN ADJUD REGION ROUTINE ATTIT LOVE ORD/FREE RESPECT...JURID SOC CONCPT SOC/EXP UN 20. PAGE 122 A2498
EUR+WWI PERSON

B63
ROSECRANCE R.N.,ACTION AND REACTION IN WORLD POLITICS. FUT WOR-45 SOCIETY DELIB/GP ACT/RES CREATE DIPLOM ECO/TAC DOMIN EDU/PROP COERCE ATTIT PERSON SUPEGO ORD/FREE PWR...CHARTS SIMUL LEAGUE/NAT VAL/FREE UN 19/20. PAGE 123 A2529
WOR+45 INT/ORG BAL/PWR

B63
ROSNER G.,THE UNITED NATIONS EMERGENCY FORCE. FRANCE ISRAEL UAR UK WOR+45 CREATE WAR PEACE ORD/FREE PWR...INT/LAW JURID HIST/WRIT TIME/SEQ UN. PAGE 124 A2539
INT/ORG FORCES

B63
ROSSI M.,THE THIRD WORLD. FUT WOR+45 INT/ORG NAT/G CAP/ISM COLONIAL PEACE PWR MARXISM 20 UN THIRD/WRLD. PAGE 124 A2542
ECO/UNDEV DIPLOM BAL/PWR NEUTRAL

B63
RUSK D.,THE WINDS OF FREEDOM. S/ASIA SOUTH/AFR INT/ORG FORCES NUC/PWR PEACE ORD/FREE 20 UN COLD/WAR. PAGE 125 A2569
DIPLOM FOR/AID INT/TRADE

B63
STEVENSON A.E.,LOOKING OUTWARD: YEARS OF CRISIS AT THE UNITED NATIONS. COM CUBA USA+45 WOR+45 SOCIETY NAT/G EX/STRUC ACT/RES LEGIT COLONIAL ATTIT PERSON SUPEGO ALL/VALS...POLICY HUM UN COLD/WAR CONGO 20. PAGE 138 A2823
INT/ORG CONCPT ARMS/CONT

B63
STROMBERG R.N.,COLLECTIVE SECURITY AND AMERICAN FOREIGN POLICY FROM THE LEAGUE OF NATIONS TO NATO. USA+45 USA-45 WOR-45 INT/ORG VOL/ASSN EX/STRUC FORCES LEGIT ROUTINE DRIVE...CONCPT TREND UN LEAGUE/NAT 20 NATO. PAGE 139 A2851
ORD/FREE TIME/SEQ DIPLOM

B63
THIEN T.T.,INDIA AND SOUTHEAST ASIA 1947-1960. COM INDIA S/ASIA SECT DELIB/GP FOR/AID RACE/REL NAT/LISM SOCISM...CHARTS BIBLIOG 20 UN NEHRU/J TREATY. PAGE 143 A2917
DRIVE DIPLOM POLICY

B63
UN SECRETARY GENERAL,PLANNING FOR ECONOMIC DEVELOPMENT. ECO/UNDEV FINAN BUDGET INT/TRADE TARIFFS TAX ADMIN 20 UN. PAGE 147 A3005
PLAN ECO/TAC MGT NAT/COMP

B63
US HOUSE COMM FOREIGN AFFAIRS,HEARINGS ON H.R. 5490 TO AMEND FURTHER THE FOREIGN ASSISTANCE ACT OF 1961. CUBA EUR+WWI INDIA INT/ORG DELIB/GP LEGIS DIPLOM CONFER ORD/FREE 20 DEPT/STATE DEPT/DEFEN UN. PAGE 153 A3129
FOR/AID INT/TRADE FORCES WEAPON

B63
US SENATE COMM ON FOREIGN REL,HEARINGS ON S 1276 A BILL TO AMEND FURTHER THE FOREIGN ASSISTANCE ACT OF 1961. USA+45 WOR+45 INDUS INT/ORG FORCES TAX WEAPON SUPEGO...NAT/COMP 20 UN CONGRESS PRESIDENT. PAGE 156 A3182
FOR/AID DIPLOM ECO/UNDEV ORD/FREE

B63
VAN SLYCK P.,PEACE: THE CONTROL OF NATIONAL POWER. CUBA WOR+45 FINAN NAT/G FORCES PROB/SOLV TEC/DEV BAL/PWR ADMIN CONTROL ORD/FREE...POLICY INT/LAW UN COLD/WAR TREATY. PAGE 158 A3214
ARMS/CONT PEACE INT/ORG DIPLOM

L63
PADELFORD N.J.,"FINANCIAL CRISIS AND THE UNITED NATIONS." FUT USSR WOR+45 LAW CONSTN FINAN INT/ORG DELIB/GP FORCES PLAN BUDGET DIPLOM COST WEALTH ...STAT CHARTS UN CONGO 20. PAGE 113 A2311
CREATE ECO/TAC

L63
RUSSETT B.M.,"TOWARD A MODEL OF COMPETITIVE INTERNATIONAL POLITICS." USA+45 WOR+45 INT/ORG NAT/G POL/PAR VOL/ASSN LEGIS BAL/PWR DIPLOM LEGIT PWR...CONCPT CONT/OBS STERTYP GEN/LAWS TOT/POP COLD/WAR 20 UN. PAGE 126 A2579
ATTIT EDU/PROP

S63
ALGER C.F.,"UNITED NATIONS PARTICIPATION AS A LEARNING EXPERIENCE." WOR+45 KNOWL ORD/FREE PWR ...INT VAL/FREE UN 20. PAGE 6 A0120
INT/ORG ATTIT

S63
BECHHOEFER B.G.,"UNITED NATIONS PROCEDURES IN CASE OF VIOLATIONS OF DISARMAMENT AGREEMENTS." COM USA+45 USSR LAW CONSTN NAT/G EX/STRUC FORCES LEGIS BAL/PWR EDU/PROP CT/SYS ARMS/CONT ORD/FREE PWR ...POLICY STERTYP UN VAL/FREE 20. PAGE 12 A0245
INT/ORG DELIB/GP

S63
BLOOMFIELD L.P.,"HEADQUARTERS-FIELD RELATIONS: SOME NOTES ON THE BEGINNING AND END OF ONUC." AFR INT/ORG ROUTINE COERCE WAR WEAPON UN CONGO 20. PAGE 16 A0319
FORCES ORD/FREE

S63
DAVEE R.,"POUR UN FONDS DE DEVELOPPEMENT SOCIAL." FUT WOR+45 INTELL SOCIETY ECO/DEV FINAN TEC/DEV ROUTINE WEALTH...TREND TOT/POP VAL/FREE UN 20. PAGE 34 A0684
INT/ORG SOC FOR/AID

S63
GANDILHON J.,"LA SCIENCE ET LA TECHNIQUE A L'AIDE DES REGIONS PEU DEVELOPPEES." FRANCE FUT WOR+45 ECO/DEV R+D PROF/ORG ACT/RES PLAN...MGT TOT/POP VAL/FREE 20 UN. PAGE 51 A1037
ECO/UNDEV TEC/DEV FOR/AID

S63
GIRAUD E.,"L'INTERDICTION DU RECOURS A LA FORCE, LA THEORIE ET LA PRATIQUE DES NATIONS UNIES." ALGERIA COM CUBA HUNGARY WOR+45 ADJUD TOTALISM ATTIT RIGID/FLEX PWR...POLICY JURID CONCPT UN 20 CONGO. PAGE 53 A1077
INT/ORG FORCES DIPLOM

S63
GROSS F.,"THE US NATIONAL INTEREST AND THE UN." FUT CONSTN NAT/G DELIB/GP CREATE DIPLOM RIGID/FLEX ORD/FREE...CONCPT GEN/LAWS 20 UN. PAGE 57 A1172
USA+45 INT/ORG PEACE

S63
LERNER D.,"FRENCH ELITE PERSPECTIVES ON THE UNITED NATIONS." EUR+WWI INT/ORG HEALTH ORD/FREE PWR RESPECT...STAT INT SAMP/SIZ VAL/FREE UN 20. PAGE 87 A1786
ATTIT STERTYP ELITES FRANCE

S63
LIPSHART A.,"THE ANALYSIS OF BLOC VOTING IN THE GENERAL ASSEMBLY." L/A+17C WOR+45 ACT/RES INGP/REL ...POLICY DECISION NEW/IDEA STAT IDEA/COMP UN. PAGE 90 A1832
CHOOSE INT/ORG DELIB/GP

S63
MANGONE G.,"THE UNITED NATIONS AND UNITED STATES FOREIGN POLICY." USA+45 WOR+45 ECO/UNDEV NAT/G DIPLOM LEGIT ROUTINE ATTIT DRIVE...TIME/SEQ UN COLD/WAR 20. PAGE 94 A1922
INT/ORG ECO/TAC FOR/AID

S63
MARTHELOT P.,"PROGRES DE LA REFORME AGRAIRE." INTELL ECO/DEV R+D FOR/AID ADMIN KNOWL...OBS VAL/FREE UN 20. PAGE 95 A1948
AGRI INT/ORG

S63
MURRAY J.N.,"UNITED NATIONS PEACE-KEEPING AND PROBLEMS OF POLITICAL CONTROL." FUT WOR+45 CONSTN DELIB/GP FORCES TOP/EX ACT/RES CREATE LEGIT PEACE PWR...METH/CNCPT CONGO UN 20. PAGE 106 A2182
INT/ORG ORD/FREE

S63
NICHOLAS H.G.,"UN PEACE FORCES AND THE CHANGING GLOBE: THE LESSONS OF SUEZ AND CONGO." FUT WOR+45 CONSTN INT/ORG CONSULT DELIB/GP TOP/EX CREATE DIPLOM DOMIN LEGIT COERCE WAR PERSON RIGID/FLEX PWR UN SUEZ CONGO UNEF 20. PAGE 109 A2229
ACT/RES FORCES

S63
SINGER M.R.,"ELECTIONS WITHIN THE UNITED NATIONS: AN EXPERIMENTAL STUDY UTILIZING STATISTICAL ANALYSIS." USA+45 WOR+45 DIPLOM ECO/TAC COERCE PWR WEALTH...STAT CHARTS SIMUL GEN/LAWS COLD/WAR VAL/FREE UN 20. PAGE 133 A2732
INT/ORG CHOOSE

S63
WRIGHT Q.,"PROJECTED EUROPEAN UNION AND AMERICAN INTERNATIONAL PRESTIGE." EUR+WWI FRANCE GERMANY UK USA+45 INT/ORG NAT/G EDU/PROP ATTIT PERCEPT PWR ...CONCPT OBS EEC 20 UN. PAGE 168 A3417
FUT ORD/FREE REGION

S63
WYZNER E.,"NIEKTORE ASPEKTY PRAWNE FINANSOWANIA OPERACJI ONZ W KONGO I NA BEIZKIM WSCHODZIE." S/ASIA CONSTN FINAN INT/ORG TOP/EX...TIME/SEQ UN 20 CONGRESS. PAGE 168 A3426
FORCES JURID DIPLOM

C63
ATTIA G.E.O.,"LES FORCES ARMEES DES NATIONS UNIES EN COREE ET AU MOYENORIENT." KOREA CONSTN DELIB/GP LEGIS PWR...IDEA/COMP NAT/COMP BIBLIOG UN SUEZ. PAGE 10 A0194
FORCES NAT/G INT/LAW

C63
CHARLETON W.G.,"THE REVOLUTION IN AMERICAN FOREIGN POLICY." COM PROB/SOLV FOR/AID DOMIN COLONIAL NEUTRAL DETER WAR ISOLAT NAT/LISM...BIBLIOG 19/20 UN COLD/WAR NATO. PAGE 26 A0523 — DIPLOM INT/ORG BAL/PWR

B64
BARKER A.J.,SUEZ: THE SEVEN DAY WAR. EUR+WWI ISLAM UAR INT/ORG NAT/G PLAN DIPLOM ECO/TAC DOMIN NAT/LISM DRIVE RIGID/FLEX PWR SOVEREIGN...POLICY JURID TREND CHARTS SUEZ UN 20. PAGE 11 A0221 — FORCES COERCE UK

B64
BLOOMFIELD L.P.,INTERNATIONAL MILITARY FORCES: THE QUESTION OF PEACE-KEEPING IN AN ARMED AND DISARMING WORLD. WOR+45 ACADEM ARMS/CONT REV PEACE 20 UN. PAGE 16 A0320 — INT/ORG FORCES FUT DIPLOM

B64
CLAUDE I.,SWORDS INTO PLOWSHARES. FUT WOR+45 WOR-45 DELIB/GP EX/STRUC LEGIT ATTIT ORD/FREE...CONCPT TIME/SEQ TREND UN TOT/POP 20. PAGE 27 A0547 — INT/ORG STRUCT

B64
DAVIES U.P. JR.,FOREIGN AND OTHER AFFAIRS. EUR+WWI L/A+17C S/ASIA USA+45 ECO/UNDEV CHIEF PLAN ECO/TAC PWR MARXISM 20 KENNEDY/JF UN. PAGE 34 A0688 — DIPLOM NAT/G POLICY FOR/AID

B64
DUROSELLE J.B.,LA COMMUNAUTE INTERNATIONALE FACE AUX JEUNES ETATS. CHINA/COM COM S/ASIA USSR INT/ORG ROLE...ANTHOL 20 UN SEATO THIRD/WRLD. PAGE 40 A0808 — DIPLOM COLONIAL ECO/UNDEV SOVEREIGN

B64
EAYRS J.,THE COMMONWEALTH AND SUEZ: A DOCUMENTARY SURVEY. FRANCE ISLAM VOL/ASSN FORCES CONFER COLONIAL WAR INGP/REL 20 CMN/WLTH SUEZ UN. PAGE 40 A0818 — DIPLOM NAT/LISM DIST/IND SOVEREIGN

B64
EPSTEIN H.M.,REVOLT IN THE CONGO. AFR CONGO/BRAZ WOR+45 NAT/G FORCES DOMIN WAR CIVMIL/REL INGP/REL MARXISM...RECORD GP/COMP 20 CONGO/LEOP UN. PAGE 42 A0856 — REV COLONIAL NAT/LISM DIPLOM

B64
FREYMOND J.,WESTERN EUROPE SINCE THE WAR. COM EUR+WWI USA+45 DIPLOM...BIBLIOG 20 NATO UN EEC. PAGE 49 A1001 — INT/ORG POLICY ECO/DEV ECO/TAC

B64
FRIEDMANN W.G.,THE CHANGING STRUCTURE OF INTERNATIONAL LAW. WOR+45 INT/ORG NAT/G PROVS LEGIT ORD/FREE PWR...JURID CONCPT GEN/LAWS TOT/POP UN 20. PAGE 49 A1006 — ADJUD TREND INT/LAW

B64
FRYDENSBERG P.,PEACE-KEEPING: EXPERIENCE AND EVALUATION: THE OSLO PAPERS. NORWAY FORCES PLAN CONTROL...INT/LAW 20 UN. PAGE 49 A1012 — INT/ORG DIPLOM PEACE COERCE

B64
HEKHUIS D.J.,INTERNATIONAL STABILITY: MILITARY, ECONOMIC AND POLITICAL DIMENSIONS. FUT WOR+45 LAW ECO/UNDEV INT/ORG NAT/G VOL/ASSN FORCES ACT/RES BAL/PWR PWR WEALTH...STAT UN 20. PAGE 64 A1310 — TEC/DEV DETER REGION

B64
KULSKI W.W.,INTERNATIONAL POLITICS IN A REVOLUTIONARY AGE. NEUTRAL NAT/LISM...POLICY DECISION INT/LAW CONCPT 20 UN. PAGE 83 A1693 — DIPLOM WAR NUC/PWR INT/ORG

B64
LUARD E.,THE COLD WAR: A RE-APPRAISAL. FUT USSR WOR+45 FORCES NUC/PWR NAT/LISM ORD/FREE SOVEREIGN ...INT 20 COLD/WAR STALIN/J TREATY UN. PAGE 91 A1870 — DIPLOM WAR PEACE TOTALISM

B64
NEWCOMER H.A.,INTERNATIONAL AIDS TO OVERSEAS INVESTMENTS AND TRADE. ECO/UNDEV TARIFFS PROFIT ...BIBLIOG 20 GATT UN. PAGE 108 A2225 — INT/TRADE FINAN DIPLOM FOR/AID

B64
PLISCHKE E.,SYSTEMS OF INTEGRATING THE INTERNATIONAL COMMUNITY. WOR+45 NAT/G VOL/ASSN ECO/TAC LEGIT PWR WEALTH...TIME/SEQ ANTHOL UN TOT/POP 20. PAGE 116 A2391 — INT/ORG EX/STRUC REGION

B64
REES D.,KOREA: THE LIMITED WAR. ASIA KOREA WOR+45 NAT/G CIVMIL/REL PERS/REL PERSON...POLICY CHARTS 20 UN TRUMAN/HS MACARTHR/D. PAGE 120 A2455 — DIPLOM WAR INT/ORG FORCES

B64
ROSENAU J.N.,INTERNATIONAL ASPECTS OF CIVIL STRIFE. CHINA/COM CUBA EUR+WWI USA+45 USSR BAL/PWR EDU/PROP NEUTRAL COERCE MORAL...NAT/COMP 20 COLD/WAR UN. PAGE 124 A2533 — POLICY DIPLOM REV WAR

B64
RUBINSTEIN A.Z.,THE SOVIETS IN INTERNATIONAL ORGANIZATIONS: CHANGING POLICY TOWARD DEVELOPING COUNTRIES, 1953-1963. COM DELIB/GP ACT/RES ECO/TAC EDU/PROP ADMIN ATTIT ORD/FREE PWR...INT VAL/FREE UN 20. PAGE 125 A2563 — ECO/UNDEV INT/ORG USSR

B64
RUSSELL R.B.,UNITED NATIONS EXPERIENCE WITH MILITARY FORCES: POLITICAL AND LEGAL ASPECTS. AFR KOREA WOR+45 LEGIS PROB/SOLV ADMIN CONTROL EFFICIENCY PEACE...POLICY INT/LAW BIBLIOG UN. PAGE 126 A2576 — FORCES DIPLOM SANCTION ORD/FREE

B64
SCHECHTER A.H.,INTERPRETATION OF AMBIGUOUS DOCUMENTS BY INTERNATIONAL ADMINISTRATIVE TRIBUNALS. WOR+45 EX/STRUC INT/TRADE CT/SYS SOVEREIGN 20 UN ILO EURCT/JUST. PAGE 128 A2620 — INT/LAW DIPLOM INT/ORG ADJUD

B64
SCHWELB E.,HUMAN RIGHTS AND THE INTERNATIONAL COMMUNITY. WOR+45 WOR-45 NAT/G SECT DELIB/GP DIPLOM PEACE RESPECT TREATY 20 UN. PAGE 130 A2666 — INT/ORG ORD/FREE INT/LAW

B64
SEGAL R.,SANCTIONS AGAINST SOUTH AFRICA. AFR SOUTH/AFR NAT/G INT/TRADE RACE/REL PEACE PWR ...INT/LAW ANTHOL 20 UN. PAGE 131 A2681 — SANCTION DISCRIM ECO/TAC POLICY

B64
STANGER R.J.,ESSAYS ON INTERVENTION. PLAN PROB/SOLV BAL/PWR ADJUD COERCE WAR ROLE PWR...INT/LAW CONCPT 20 UN INTERVENT. PAGE 137 A2803 — SOVEREIGN DIPLOM POLICY LEGIT

B64
THANT U.,TOWARD WORLD PEACE. DELIB/GP TEC/DEV EDU/PROP WAR SOVEREIGN...INT/LAW 20 UN MID/EAST. PAGE 142 A2907 — DIPLOM BIOG PEACE COERCE

B64
UN PUB. INFORM. ORGAN.,EVERY MAN'S UNITED NATIONS. UNIV WOR+45 CONSTN CULTURE SOCIETY ECO/DEV ECO/UNDEV NAT/G ACT/RES PLAN ECO/TAC INT/TRADE EDU/PROP LEGIT PEACE ATTIT ALL/VALS...POLICY HUM INT/LAW CONCPT CHARTS UN TOT/POP 20. PAGE 147 A3004 — INT/ORG ROUTINE

B64
US HOUSE COMM FOREIGN AFFAIRS,HEARINGS ON H.R. 10502 TO AMEND FURTHER THE FOREIGN ASSISTANCE ACT OF 1961. AFR ASIA L/A+17C INT/ORG CONSULT DELIB/GP TEC/DEV ECO/TAC EDU/PROP CONFER 20 UN NATO CONGRESS AID. PAGE 153 A3130 — FOR/AID DIPLOM ORD/FREE ECO/UNDEV

B64
VECCHIO G.D.,L'ETAT ET LE DROIT. ITALY CONSTN EX/STRUC LEGIS DIPLOM CT/SYS...JURID 20 UN. PAGE 158 A3225 — NAT/G SOVEREIGN CONCPT INT/LAW

B64
WAINHOUSE D.W.,REMNANTS OF EMPIRE: THE UNITED NATIONS AND THE END OF COLONIALISM. FUT PORTUGAL WOR+45 NAT/G CONSULT DOMIN LEGIT ADMIN ROUTINE ATTIT ORD/FREE...POLICY JURID RECORD INT TIME/SEQ UN CMN/WLTH 20. PAGE 160 A3260 — INT/ORG TREND COLONIAL

B64
WILLIAMS S.P.,TOWARD A GENUINE WORLD SECURITY SYSTEM (PAMPHLET). WOR+45 INT/ORG FORCES PLAN NUC/PWR ORD/FREE...INT/LAW CONCPT UN PRESIDENT. PAGE 165 A3353 — BIBLIOG/A ARMS/CONT DIPLOM PEACE

B64
WOODHOUSE C.M.,THE NEW CONCERT OF NATIONS. WOR+45 ECO/DEV ECO/UNDEV NAT/G BAL/PWR ECO/TAC NAT/LISM PWR SOVEREIGN ALL/IDEOS 20 UN COLD/WAR. PAGE 166 A3391 — DIPLOM MORAL FOR/AID COLONIAL

B64
WYTHE G.,THE UNITED STATES AND INTER-AMERICAN RELATIONS: A CONTEMPORARY APPRAISAL. L/A+17C USA+45 ECO/UNDEV INT/ORG NAT/G VOL/ASSN INT/TRADE EDU/PROP DRIVE...SOC TREND OAS UN 20. PAGE 168 A3425 — ATTIT ECO/TAC FOR/AID

L64
CARNEGIE ENDOWMENT INT. PEACE,"POLITICAL QUESTIONS (ISSUES BEFORE THE NINETEENTH GENERAL ASSEMBLY)." SPACE WOR+45 CONSTN FINAN NAT/G CONSULT DELIB/GP FORCES LEGIS TEC/DEV EDU/PROP LEGIT ARMS/CONT COERCE NUC/PWR ATTIT ALL/VALS...CONCPT OBS UN COLD/WAR 20. PAGE 24 A0490 — INT/ORG PEACE

L64
CARNEGIE ENDOWMENT INT. PEACE,"ECONOMIC AND SOCIAL QUESTION (ISSUES BEFORE THE NINETEENTH GENERAL ASSEMBLY)." WOR+45 ECO/DEV ECO/UNDEV INDUS R+D DELIB/GP CREATE PLAN TEC/DEV ECO/TAC FOR/AID BAL/PAY...RECORD UN 20. PAGE 24 A0493 — INT/ORG INT/TRADE

L64
CLAUDE I.,"THE OAS, THE UN, AND THE UNITED STATES." L/A+17C USA+45 CONSTN NAT/G DELIB/GP DOMIN EDU/PROP LEGIT REGION COERCE ORD/FREE PWR...TIME/SEQ TREND STERTYP OAS UN 20. PAGE 27 A0546 — INT/ORG POLICY

L64
CURTIS G.L.,"THE UNITED NATIONS OBSERVER GROUP IN LEBANON." ISLAM USA+45 NAT/G CONSULT ACT/RES PLAN BAL/PWR LEGIT ATTIT KNOWL...HIST/WRIT UN 20 UN. PAGE 33 A0669 — INT/ORG FORCES DIPLOM LEBANON

L64
CURTIS G.L.,"THE UNITED NATIONS OBSERVER GROUP IN LEBANON." ISLAM USA+45 NAT/G CONSULT ACT/RES PLAN BAL/PWR LEGIT ATTIT KNOWL...HIST/WRIT UN 20 UN. PAGE 33 A0669 — INT/ORG FORCES DIPLOM LEBANON

L64
MANZER R.A.,"THE UNITED NATIONS SPECIAL FUND." WOR+45 CONSTN ECO/UNDEV NAT/G TOP/EX LEGIT WEALTH ...CHARTS UN 20. PAGE 94 A1936
FINAN INT/ORG

L64
WORLD PEACE FOUNDATION,"INTERNATIONAL ORGANIZATIONS: SUMMARY OF ACTIVITIES." INDIA PAKISTAN TURKEY WOR+45 CONSTN CONSULT EX/STRUC ECO/TAC EDU/PROP LEGIT ORD/FREE...JURID SOC UN 20 CYPRESS. PAGE 167 A3397
INT/ORG ROUTINE

S64
CARNEGIE ENDOWMENT INT. PEACE,"COLONIAL COUNTRIES AND PEOPLES (ISSUES BEFORE THE NINETEENTH GENERAL ASSEMBLY)." AFR ISLAM L/A+17C WOR+45 DELIB/GP LEGIS ECO/TAC EDU/PROP NAT/LISM PEACE ALL/VALS...RECORD UN CMN/WLTH 20. PAGE 24 A0491
INT/ORG ECO/UNDEV COLONIAL

S64
CARNEGIE ENDOWMENT INT. PEACE,"HUMAN RIGHTS (ISSUES BEFORE THE NINETEENTH GENERAL ASSEMBLY)." AFR WOR+45 LAW CONSTN NAT/G EDU/PROP GP/REL DISCRIM PEACE ATTIT MORAL ORD/FREE...INT/LAW PSY CONCPT RECORD UN 20. PAGE 24 A0492
INT/ORG PERSON RACE/REL

S64
CARNEGIE ENDOWMENT INT. PEACE,"LEGAL QUESTIONS (ISSUES BEFORE THE NINETEENTH GENERAL ASSEMBLY)." WOR+45 CONSTN NAT/G DELIB/GP ADJUD PEACE MORAL ORD/FREE...RECORD UN 20 TREATY. PAGE 24 A0494
INT/ORG LAW INT/LAW

S64
CARNEGIE ENDOWMENT INT. PEACE,"ADMINISTRATION AND BUDGET (ISSUES BEFORE THE NINETEENTH GENERAL ASSEMBLY)." WOR+45 FINAN BUDGET ECO/TAC ROUTINE COST...STAT RECORD UN. PAGE 24 A0495
INT/ORG ADMIN

S64
COFFEY J.,"THE SOVIET VIEW OF A DISARMED WORLD." COM USA+45 INT/ORG NAT/G EX/STRUC EDU/PROP COERCE PERCEPT ORD/FREE PWR...TREND STERTYP VAL/FREE 20 UN. PAGE 27 A0556
FORCES ATTIT ARMS/CONT USSR

S64
GARDNER R.N.,"THE SOVIET UNION AND THE UNITED NATIONS." WOR+45 FINAN POL/PAR VOL/ASSN FORCES ECO/TAC DOMIN EDU/PROP LEGIT ADJUD ADMIN ARMS/CONT COERCE ATTIT ALL/VALS...POLICY MAJORIT CONCPT OBS TIME/SEQ TREND STERTYP UN. PAGE 51 A1046
COM INT/ORG USSR

S64
GARDNER R.N.,"GATT AND THE UNITED NATIONS CONFERENCE ON TRADE AND DEVELOPMENT." USA+45 WOR+45 SOCIETY ECO/UNDEV MARKET NAT/G DELIB/GP ACT/RES PLAN ECO/TAC TARIFFS EDU/PROP ROUTINE DRIVE RIGID/FLEX WEALTH...DECISION MGT TREND UN TOT/POP 20 GATT. PAGE 51 A1047
INT/ORG INT/TRADE

S64
GRZYBOWSKI K.,"INTERNATIONAL ORGANIZATIONS FROM THE SOVIET POINT OF VIEW." WOR+45 WOR-45 CULTURE ECO/DEV VOL/ASSN EDU/PROP ATTIT RIGID/FLEX KNOWL ...SOC OBS TIME/SEQ TREND GEN/LAWS VAL/FREE ILO UN 20. PAGE 58 A1184
COM INT/ORG DIPLOM USSR

S64
HOSCH L.G.,"PUBLIC ADMINISTRATION ON THE INTERNATIONAL FRONTIER." WOR+45 R+D NAT/G EDU/PROP EXEC KNOWL ORD/FREE VAL/FREE 20 UN. PAGE 68 A1390
INT/ORG MGT

S64
HOSKYNS C.,"THE AFRICAN STATES AND THE UNITED NATIONS: 1958-1964." SOUTH/AFR NAT/G VOL/ASSN CONSULT BAL/PWR EDU/PROP MORAL ORD/FREE PWR ...CONCPT TREND UN 20. PAGE 68 A1393
AFR INT/ORG DIPLOM

S64
HOVET T. JR.,"THE ROLE OF AFRICA IN THE UNITED NATIONS." FUT WOR+45 NAT/G DELIB/GP DOMIN EDU/PROP LEGIT ORD/FREE PWR RESPECT SKILL...OBS TIME/SEQ TREND VAL/FREE UN 20. PAGE 68 A1398
AFR INT/ORG DIPLOM

S64
JACK H.,"NONALIGNMENT AND A TEST BAN AGREEMENT: THE ROLE OF THE NON-ALIGNED STATES." WOR+45 INT/ORG CONSULT DOMIN EDU/PROP LEGIT CHOOSE PEACE ATTIT DRIVE KNOWL ORD/FREE...TREND CHARTS GEN/LAWS UN VAL/FREE 20. PAGE 72 A1471
PWR CONCPT NUC/PWR

S64
KHAN M.Z.,"THE PRESIDENT OF THE GENERAL ASSEMBLY." WOR+45 CONSTN DELIB/GP EDU/PROP LEGIT ROUTINE PWR RESPECT SKILL...DECISION SOC BIOG TREND UN 20. PAGE 78 A1609
INT/ORG TOP/EX

S64
KOTANI H.,"PEACE-KEEPING: PROBLEMS FOR SMALLER COUNTRIES." FUT WOR+45 NAT/G ACT/RES PLAN DOMIN EDU/PROP COERCE ALL/VALS...POLICY UN TOT/POP 20. PAGE 82 A1673
INT/ORG FORCES

S64
LEVI W.,"CHINA AND THE UNITED NATIONS." ASIA CHINA CHINA/COM WOR+45 WOR-45 CONSTN NAT/G DELIB/GP EX/STRUC FORCES ACT/RES EDU/PROP PWR...POLICY RECORD TIME/SEQ GEN/LAWS UN COLD/WAR 20. PAGE 88 A1794
INT/ORG ATTIT NAT/LISM

S64
MARTELLI G.,"PORTUGAL AND THE UNITED NATIONS." AFR EUR+WWI ELITES INT/ORG NAT/G PROVS PLAN DIPLOM ECO/TAC DOMIN COLONIAL RIGID/FLEX MORAL ORD/FREE PWR WEALTH...MYTH UN 20. PAGE 95 A1947
ATTIT PORTUGAL

S64
MAZRUI A.A.,"THE UNITED NATIONS AND SOME AFRICAN POLITICAL ATTITUDES." ECO/TAC FOR/AID DOMIN ROUTINE CHOOSE ATTIT DRIVE MORAL PWR RESPECT WEALTH...PSY CONCPT OBS TREND UN VAL/FREE 20. PAGE 97 A1987
AFR INT/ORG SOVEREIGN

S64
PRASAD B.,"SURVEY OF RECENT RESEARCH: STUDIES ON INDIA'S FOREIGN POLIC AND RELATIONS." ASIA INDIA PAKISTAN USA+45 NAT/G INT/TRADE GOV/REL 20 UN CMN/WLTH. PAGE 117 A2406
BIBLIOG DIPLOM ROLE POLICY

S64
RUBIN R.,"THE UN CORRESPONDENT." WOR+45 FACE/GP PROF/ORG EDU/PROP ROUTINE PERCEPT KNOWL...RECORD STAND/INT QU UN WORK TOT/POP VAL/FREE 20. PAGE 125 A2560
INT/ORG ATTIT DIPLOM

S64
SCHWELB E.,"OPERATION OF THE EUROPEAN CONVENTION ON HUMAN RIGHTS." EUR+WWI LAW SOCIETY CREATE EDU/PROP ADJUD ADMIN PEACE ATTIT ORD/FREE PWR...POLICY INT/LAW CONCPT OBS GEN/LAWS UN VAL/FREE ILO 20 ECHR. PAGE 130 A2665
INT/ORG MORAL

S64
TAUBENFELD R.K.,"INDEPENDENT REVENUE FOR THE UNITED NATIONS." WOR+45 SOCIETY STRUCT INDUS NAT/G CONSULT ACT/RES PLAN ECO/TAC LEGIT WEALTH...DECISION CON/ANAL GEN/METH UN 20. PAGE 142 A2896
INT/ORG FINAN

S64
VANDENBOSCH A.,"THE SMALL STATES IN INTERNATIONAL POLITICS AND ORGANIZATION." EUR+WWI MOD/EUR WOR+45 WOR-45 CONSTN DELIB/GP COERCE ORD/FREE PWR ...TIME/SEQ GEN/LAWS VAL/FREE LEAGUE/NAT UN 19/20. PAGE 158 A3219
NAT/G INT/ORG DIPLOM

B65
BRACKETT R.D.,PATHWAYS TO PEACE. SECT VOL/ASSN GP/REL PERS/REL DISCRIM...LING 20 UN PEACE/CORP. PAGE 18 A0366
PEACE INT/ORG EDU/PROP PARTIC

B65
CORDIER A.W.,THE QUEST FOR PEACE. WOR+45 NAT/G PLAN BAL/PWR ECO/TAC ARMS/CONT NUC/PWR PWR...ANTHOL UN COLD/WAR. PAGE 30 A0617
PEACE DIPLOM POLICY INT/ORG

B65
FLYNN A.H.,WORLD UNDERSTANDING: A SELECTED BIBLIOGRAPHY. WOR+45 PROB/SOLV BAL/PWR DIPLOM EFFICIENCY PEACE UN. PAGE 47 A0956
BIBLIOG/A INT/ORG EDU/PROP ROUTINE

B65
FORGAC A.A.,NEW DIPLOMACY AND THE UNITED NATIONS. FRANCE GERMANY UK USSR INT/ORG DELIB/GP EX/STRUC PEACE...INT/LAW CONCPT UN. PAGE 47 A0965
DIPLOM ETIQUET NAT/G

B65
FRASER S.,GOVERNMENTAL POLICY AND INTERNATIONAL EDUCATION. CHINA/COM COM USA+45 WOR+45 CONTROL MARXISM...ANTHOL BIBLIOG/A 20 UN. PAGE 48 A0989
EDU/PROP DIPLOM POLICY NAT/G

B65
FRIEDMANN W.,AN INTRODUCTION TO WORLD POLITICS (5TH ED.). WOR+45 ECO/UNDEV BAL/PWR FOR/AID INT/TRADE PEACE...STAT CENSUS CHARTS BIBLIOG T 20 COLD/WAR UN THIRD/WRLD. PAGE 49 A1003
DIPLOM INT/ORG PROB/SOLV

B65
HAGRAS K.M.,UNITED NATIONS CONFERENCE ON TRADE AND DEVELOPMENT: A CASE STUDY OF UN DIPLOMACY. CONSULT ACT/RES TEC/DEV FOR/AID INT/TRADE...BIBLIOG 20 UN LEAGUE/NAT UNCTAD. PAGE 59 A1213
INT/ORG ADMIN DELIB/GP DIPLOM

B65
HUSS P.J.,RED SPIES IN THE UN. CZECHOSLVK USA+45 USSR COM/IND FORCES EDU/PROP NUC/PWR MARXISM 20 UN COLD/WAR. PAGE 69 A1421
PEACE INT/ORG BAL/PWR DIPLOM

B65
LARUS J.,FROM COLLECTIVE SECURITY TO PREVENTIVE DIPLOMACY. FUT FORCES PROB/SOLV DEBATE AGREE COERCE WAR PWR...ANTHOL 20 LEAGUE/NAT UN. PAGE 85 A1736
INT/ORG PEACE DIPLOM ORD/FREE

B65
LEE M.,THE UNITED NATIONS AND WORLD REALITIES. ECO/UNDEV FORCES WAR PEACE ATTIT ROLE WEALTH 20 UN. PAGE 86 A1761
INT/ORG COLONIAL ARMS/CONT DIPLOM

B65
LEISS A.C.,APARTHEID AND UNITED NATIONS COLLECTIVE MEASURES. SOUTH/AFR ECO/UNDEV EXTR/IND FORCES WORKER ECO/TAC FOR/AID INT/TRADE WEALTH...TREND CHARTS 20 UN NEGRO. PAGE 86 A1770
DISCRIM RACE/REL STRATA DIPLOM

B65
MACDONALD R.W.,THE LEAGUE OF ARAB STATES: A STUDY IN THE DYNAMICS OF REGIONAL ORGANIZATION. ISRAEL UAR USSR FINAN INT/ORG DELIB/GP ECO/TAC AGREE NEUTRAL ORD/FREE PWR...DECISION BIBLIOG 20 TREATY UN. PAGE 92 A1888
ISLAM REGION DIPLOM ADMIN

B65
MOSKOWITZ H.,US SECURITY, ARMS CONTROL, AND DISARMAMENT 1961-1965. FORCES DIPLOM DETER WAR
BIBLIOG/A ARMS/CONT

WEAPON...CHARTS 20 UN COLD/WAR NATO. PAGE 105 A2154 NUC/PWR PEACE

B65
REQUA E.G.,THE DEVELOPING NATIONS: A GUIDE TO INFORMATION SOURCES CONCERNING THEIR ECON, POLIT, TECHNICAL, AND SOCIAL PROBLEMS. AFR ASIA ISLAM L/A+17C INDUS INT/ORG CONSULT PLAN PROB/SOLV...SOC 20 UN. PAGE 120 A2466
BIBLIOG/A ECO/UNDEV FOR/AID TEC/DEV

B65
RODRIGUES J.H.,BRAZIL AND AFRICA. AFR BRAZIL PORTUGAL UK USA+45 USA-45 CULTURE ECO/UNDEV INT/ORG INT/TRADE RACE/REL ORD/FREE 15/20 UN MISCEGEN. PAGE 123 A2513
DIPLOM COLONIAL POLICY ATTIT

B65
SHUKRI A.,THE CONCEPT OF SELF-DETERMINATION IN THE UNITED NATIONS. WOR+45 DIPLOM INT/TRADE SANCTION NAT/LISM...BIBLIOG 20 UN. PAGE 132 A2709
COLONIAL INT/ORG INT/LAW SOVEREIGN

B65
SPEECKAERT G.P.,SELECT BIBLIOGRAPHY ON INTERNATIONAL ORGANIZATION, 1885-1964. WOR+45 WOR-45 EX/STRUC DIPLOM ADMIN REGION 19/20 UN. PAGE 136 A2777
BIBLIOG INT/ORG GEN/LAWS STRATA

B65
THOMAS A.V.,NONINTERVENTION: THE LAW AND ITS IMPORT IN THE AMERICAS. L/A+17C USA+45 USA-45 WOR+45 DIPLOM ADJUD...JURID IDEA/COMP 20 UN INTERVENT. PAGE 143 A2920
INT/LAW PWR COERCE

B65
UN,SPACE ACTIVITIES AND RESOURCES: REVIEW OF UNITED NATION'S NATIONAL AND INTERNATIONAL PROGRAMS. INT/ORG LABOR PLAN TEC/DEV DIPLOM EFFICIENCY HEALTH ...GOV/COMP 20 UN. PAGE 146 A2995
SPACE NUC/PWR FOR/AID PEACE

B65
US SENATE COMM AERO SPACE SCI,INTERNATIONAL COOPERATION AND ORGANIZATION FOR OUTER SPACE. FUT USA+45 WOR+45 PROF/ORG VOL/ASSN CONSULT DELIB/GP PLAN TEC/DEV ARMS/CONT GP/REL PEACE 20 UN NASA. PAGE 155 A3167
DIPLOM SPACE R+D NAT/G

B65
US SENATE COMM ON FOREIGN REL,HEARINGS ON THE FOREIGN ASSISTANCE PROGRAM. AFR ASIA L/A+17C USA+45 WOR+45 FORCES TEC/DEV BUDGET CONTROL WEAPON ORD/FREE 20 UN CONGRESS SEC/STATE. PAGE 156 A3183
FOR/AID DIPLOM INT/ORG ECO/UNDEV

B65
VONGLAHN G.,LAW AMONG NATIONS: AN INTRODUCTION TO PUBLIC INTERNATIONAL LAW. UNIV WOR+45 LAW INT/ORG NAT/G LEGIT EXEC RIGID/FLEX...CONCPT TIME/SEQ GEN/LAWS UN TOT/POP 20. PAGE 160 A3253
CONSTN JURID INT/LAW

B65
WARBEY W.,VIETNAM: THE TRUTH. FRANCE S/ASIA USA+45 VIETNAM CULTURE INT/ORG NAT/G DIPLOM FOR/AID EDU/PROP ARMS/CONT PEACE 20 TREATY NLF UN. PAGE 161 A3274
WAR AGREE

B65
WASKOW A.I.,KEEPING THE WORLD DISARMED. AFR GERMANY/E DIPLOM CONTROL WAR 20 UN. PAGE 161 A3289
ARMS/CONT PEACE FORCES PROB/SOLV

B65
WEAVER J.N.,THE INTERNATIONAL DEVELOPMENT ASSOCIATION: A NEW APPROACH TO FOREIGN AID. USA+45 NAT/G OP/RES PLAN PROB/SOLV WEALTH...CHARTS BIBLIOG 20 UN. PAGE 162 A3295
FOR/AID INT/ORG ECO/UNDEV FINAN

C65
SEARA M.V.,"COSMIC INTERNATIONAL LAW." LAW ACADEM ACT/RES DIPLOM COLONIAL CONTROL NUC/PWR SOVEREIGN ...GEN/LAWS BIBLIOG UN. PAGE 131 A2678
SPACE INT/LAW IDEA/COMP INT/ORG

B66
ASAMOAH O.Y.,THE LEGAL SIGNIFICANCE OF THE DECLARATIONS OF THE GENERAL ASSEMBLY OF THE UNITED NATIONS. WOR+45 CREATE CONTROL...BIBLIOG 20 UN. PAGE 9 A0184
INT/LAW INT/ORG DIPLOM

B66
CLARK G.,WORLD PEACE THROUGH WORLD LAW; TWO ALTERNATIVE PLANS. WOR+45 DELIB/GP FORCES TAX CONFER ADJUD SANCTION ARMS/CONT WAR CHOOSE PRIVIL 20 UN COLD/WAR. PAGE 27 A0541
INT/LAW PEACE PLAN INT/ORG

B66
COYLE D.C.,THE UNITED NATIONS AND HOW IT WORKS. ECO/UNDEV DELIB/GP BAL/PWR EDU/PROP ARMS/CONT NUC/PWR WAR 20 UN. PAGE 32 A0648
INT/ORG PEACE DIPLOM INT/TRADE

B66
DOUMA J.,BIBLIOGRAPHY ON THE INTERNATIONAL COURT INCLUDING THE PERMANENT COURT, 1918-1964. WOR+45 WOR-45 DELIB/GP WAR PRIVIL...JURID NAT/COMP 20 UN LEAGUE/NAT. PAGE 38 A0780
BIBLIOG/A INT/ORG CT/SYS DIPLOM

B66
EPSTEIN F.T.,THE AMERICAN BIBLIOGRAPHY OF RUSSIAN AND EAST EUROPEAN STUDIES FOR 1964. USSR LOC/G NAT/G POL/PAR FORCES ADMIN ARMS/CONT...JURID CONCPT 20 UN. PAGE 42 A0855
BIBLIOG COM MARXISM DIPLOM

B66
FEHRENBACH T.R.,THIS KIND OF PEACE. WOR+45 LEAD PARTIC WAR EFFICIENCY ATTIT UN. PAGE 44 A0906
PEACE DIPLOM INT/ORG BAL/PWR

B66
FISHER S.N.,NEW HORIZONS FOR THE UNITED STATES IN WORLD AFFAIRS. USA+45 FOR/AID...ANTHOL 20 UN. PAGE 46 A0941
DIPLOM PLAN INT/ORG

B66
FRANK E.,LAWMAKERS IN A CHANGING WORLD. FRANCE UK USSR WOR+45 PARTIC EFFICIENCY ROLE ALL/IDEOS ...CHARTS ANTHOL PARLIAMENT 20 UN COLD/WAR. PAGE 48 A0979
GOV/COMP LEGIS NAT/G DIPLOM

B66
GERARD-LIBOIS J.,KATANGA SECESSION. INT/ORG FORCES DIPLOM ADMIN CONTROL WAR CHOOSE PWR...CHARTS 20 KATANGA TSHOMBE/M UN. PAGE 52 A1062
NAT/G REGION ORD/FREE REV

B66
GUPTA S.,KASHMIR - A STUDY IN INDIA-PAKISTAN RELATIONS. INDIA KASHMIR PAKISTAN CONSTN INT/ORG REV RACE/REL NAT/LISM 20 UN MUSLIM/LG. PAGE 58 A1194
DIPLOM GP/REL SOVEREIGN WAR

B66
HAMILTON W.B.,A DECADE OF THE COMMONWEALTH, 1955-1964. UK LAW ELITES FINAN FOR/AID CONFER COLONIAL PWR...GEOG CHARTS ANTHOL 20 CMN/WLTH UN. PAGE 61 A1247
INT/ORG INGP/REL DIPLOM NAT/G

B66
HERZ M.F.,BEGINNINGS OF THE COLD WAR. COM POLAND USA+45 USSR INT/ORG NAT/G CHIEF FOR/AID DOMIN CONFER AGREE WAR PEACE 20 STALIN/J COLD/WAR UN. PAGE 64 A1321
DIPLOM

B66
HOLLINS E.J.,PEACE IS POSSIBLE: A READER FOR LAYMEN. WOR+45 CULTURE PLAN RISK AGE/Y ALL/VALS SOVEREIGN...PSY CONCPT TREND 20 UN JOHN/XXIII KENNAN/G MYRDAL/G. PAGE 67 A1370
PEACE DIPLOM INT/ORG NUC/PWR

B66
KANET R.E.,THE SOVIET UNION AND SUB-SAHARAN AFRICA: COMMUNIST POLICY TOWARD AFRICA, 1917-1965. AFR USSR ECO/UNDEV TEC/DEV EDU/PROP TASK DISCRIM PEACE WEALTH ALL/IDEOS...CHARTS BIBLIOG SOC/INTEG 19/20 NEGRO UN INTERVENT. PAGE 76 A1555
DIPLOM ECO/TAC MARXISM

B66
KIRDAR U.,THE STRUCTURE OF UNITED NATIONS ECONOMIC AID TO UNDERDEVELOPED COUNTRIES. AGRI FINAN INDUS NAT/G EX/STRUC PLAN GIVE TASK...POLICY 20 UN. PAGE 79 A1631
INT/ORG FOR/AID ECO/UNDEV ADMIN

B66
LEAGUE OF WOMEN VOTERS OF US,FOREIGN AID AT THE CROSSROADS. USA+45 WOR+45 DELIB/GP PROB/SOLV DIPLOM INT/TRADE RECEIVE BAL/PAY...CHARTS 20 UN. PAGE 86 A1756
FOR/AID GIVE ECO/UNDEV PLAN

B66
LEWIS S.,TOWARDS INTERNATIONAL CO-OPERATION (1ST ED.). WOR+45 AGRI INDUS EDU/PROP RACE/REL ISOLAT NAT/LISM ATTIT HEALTH WEALTH...CHARTS WORSHIP 20 UN. PAGE 88 A1803
DIPLOM ANOMIE PROB/SOLV INT/ORG

B66
LUARD E.,THE EVOLUTION OF INTERNATIONAL ORGANIZATIONS. UK WOR+45 BUDGET INT/TRADE WAR BAL/PAY PEACE ORD/FREE...POLICY 19/20 EEC ILO LEAGUE/NAT UN. PAGE 91 A1871
INT/ORG EFFICIENCY CREATE TREND

B66
OBERMANN E.,VERTEIDIGUNG PER FREIHEIT. GERMANY/W WOR+45 INT/ORG COERCE NUC/PWR WEAPON MARXISM 20 UN NATO WARSAW/P TREATY. PAGE 111 A2273
FORCES ORD/FREE WAR PEACE

B66
POLLACK R.S.,THE INDIVIDUAL'S RIGHTS AND INTERNATIONAL ORGANIZATION. LAW INT/ORG DELIB/GP SUPEGO...JURID SOC/INTEG 20 TREATY UN. PAGE 117 A2394
INT/LAW ORD/FREE DIPLOM PERSON

B66
ROBOCK S.H.,INTERNATIONAL DEVELOPMENT 1965. AGRI INDUS VOL/ASSN PLAN TEC/DEV EDU/PROP HEALTH...JURID 20 UN PEACE/CORP. PAGE 122 A2508
FOR/AID INT/ORG GEOG ECO/UNDEV

B66
SANDERS R.E.,SPAIN AND THE UNITED NATIONS 1945-1950. SPAIN CHIEF DIPLOM CONFER SANCTION ATTIT ...POLICY 20 UN COLD/WAR. PAGE 127 A2599
INT/ORG FASCISM GP/REL STRANGE

B66
SINGH L.P.,THE POLITICS OF ECONOMIC COOPERATION IN ASIA; A STUDY OF ASIAN INTERNATIONAL ORGANIZATIONS. ASIA INT/ORG ACT/RES PLAN GP/REL...POLICY GP/COMP BIBLIOG 20 UN SEATO. PAGE 133 A2733
ECO/UNDEV ECO/TAC REGION DIPLOM

B66
UN ECAFE,ADMINISTRATIVE ASPECTS OF FAMILY PLANNING PROGRAMMES (PAMPHLET). ASIA THAILAND WOR+45 VOL/ASSN PROB/SOLV BUDGET FOR/AID EDU/PROP CONFER CONTROL GOV/REL TIME 20 UN BIRTH/CON. PAGE 147 A2999
PLAN CENSUS FAM ADMIN

B66
UNITED NATIONS,INTERNATIONAL SPACE BIBLIOGRAPHY.
BIBLIOG

FUT INT/ORG TEC/DEV DIPLOM ARMS/CONT NUC/PWR ...JURID SOC UN. PAGE 149 A3037 — SPACE PEACE R+D

B66
US HOUSE COMM FOREIGN AFFAIRS,HEARINGS ON HR 12449 A BILL TO AMEND FURTHER THE FOREIGN ASSISTANCE ACT OF 1961. AFR ASIA L/A+17C USA+45 VIETNAM INT/ORG TEC/DEV INT/TRADE ATTIT ORD/FREE 20 UN NATO CONGRESS AID. PAGE 154 A3132 — FOR/AID ECO/TAC ECO/UNDEV DIPLOM

B66
US LIBRARY OF CONGRESS,NIGERIA: A GUIDE TO OFFICIAL PUBLICATIONS. CAMEROON NIGERIA UK DIPLOM...POLICY 19/20 UN LEAGUE/NAT. PAGE 155 A3160 — BIBLIOG ADMIN NAT/G COLONIAL

B66
US SENATE COMM ON FOREIGN REL,HEARINGS ON S 2859 AND S 2861. USA+45 WOR+45 FORCES BUDGET CAP/ISM ADMIN DETER WEAPON TOTALISM...NAT/COMP 20 UN CONGRESS. PAGE 156 A3185 — FOR/AID DIPLOM ORD/FREE ECO/UNDEV

B66
VAN DYKE V.,INTERNATIONAL POLITICS. WOR+45 ECO/DEV ECO/UNDEV INT/ORG BAL/PWR AGREE ARMS/CONT NAT/LISM PEACE PWR...INT/LAW 20 TREATY UN. PAGE 158 A3212 — DIPLOM NAT/G WAR SOVEREIGN

B66
WAINHOUSE D.W.,INTERNATIONAL PEACE OBSERVATION: A HISTORY AND FORECAST. INT/ORG PROB/SOLV BAL/PWR AGREE ARMS/CONT COERCE NUC/PWR...PREDICT METH/COMP 20 UN LEAGUE/NAT OAS TREATY. PAGE 160 A3261 — PEACE DIPLOM

L66
MCDOUGAL M.S.,"CHINESE PARTICIPATION IN THE UNITED NATIONS: THE LEGAL IMPERATIVES OF A NEGOTIATED SOLUTION" CHINA/COM WOR+45 VOL/ASSN DIPLOM PARTIC ...DECISION IDEA/COMP 20 UN. PAGE 98 A2010 — INT/ORG REPRESENT POLICY PROB/SOLV

S66
AFRICAN BIBLIOGRAPHIC CENTER,"THE NEW AFRO-ASIAN STATES IN PERSPECTIVE, 1960-1963: A SELECT BIBLIOGRAPHY." AFR ASIA CULTURE SOCIETY INT/ORG LABOR TEC/DEV LITERACY 20 UN. PAGE 5 A0100 — BIBLIOG DIPLOM FOR/AID INT/TRADE

S66
ERB GF,"THE UNITED NATIONS CONFERENCE ON TRADE AND DEVELOPMENT (UNCTAD): A SELECTED CURRENT READING LIST." FINAN FOR/AID CONFER 20 UN. PAGE 42 A0858 — BIBLIOG/A INT/TRADE ECO/UNDEV INT/ORG

S66
GREEN L.C.,"RHODESIAN OIL: BOOTLEGGERS OR PIRATES?" AFR RHODESIA UK WOR+45 INT/ORG NAT/G DIPLOM LEGIT COLONIAL SOVEREIGN 20 UN OAU. PAGE 55 A1139 — INT/TRADE SANCTION INT/LAW POLICY

C66
BLAISDELL D.C.,"INTERNATIONAL ORGANIZATION." FUT WOR+45 ECO/DEV DELIB/GP FORCES EFFICIENCY PEACE ORD/FREE...INT/LAW 20 UN LEAGUE/NAT NATO. PAGE 15 A0304 — BIBLIOG INT/ORG DIPLOM ARMS/CONT

C66
DUROSELLE J.B.,"LE CONFLIT DE TRIESTE 1943-1954: ETUDES DE CAS DE CONFLITS INTERNATIONAUX III." ITALY USA+45 YUGOSLAVIA ELITES DELIB/GP PLAN ADJUST ...POLICY GEOG CHARTS IDEA/COMP TIME 20 TREATY UN COLD/WAR. PAGE 40 A0810 — BIBLIOG WAR DIPLOM GEN/LAWS

N66
US HOUSE COMM FOREIGN AFFAIRS,UNITED STATES POLICY TOWARD ASIA (PAMPHLET). CHINA/COM USA+45 USSR VIETNAM INT/ORG NAT/G PWR MARXISM 20 UN. PAGE 154 A3133 — POLICY ASIA DIPLOM PLAN

B67
BLOOMFIELD L.,THE UNITED NATIONS AND US FOREIGN POLICY. USA+45 DIPLOM LEAD ARMS/CONT DETER PWR 20 UN. PAGE 15 A0313 — INT/ORG PLAN CONFER IDEA/COMP

B67
LAWYERS COMM AMER POLICY VIET,VIETNAM AND INTERNATIONAL LAW: AN ANALYSIS OF THE LEGALITY OF THE US MILITARY INVOLVEMENT. VIETNAM LAW INT/ORG COERCE WEAPON PEACE ORD/FREE 20 UN SEATO TREATY. PAGE 86 A1753 — INT/LAW DIPLOM ADJUD WAR

B67
MILLER J.D.B.,THE POLITICS OF THE THIRD WORLD. AFR S/ASIA 20 UN. PAGE 101 A2078 — INT/ORG DIPLOM COLONIAL SOVEREIGN

B67
MURTY B.S.,PROPAGANDA AND WORLD PUBLIC ORDER. FUT WOR+45 COM/IND INT/ORG PROB/SOLV ATTIT KNOWL ORD/FREE...POLICY UN. PAGE 106 A2183 — EDU/PROP DIPLOM CONTROL JURID

B67
PADELFORD N.J.,THE DYNAMICS OF INTERNATIONAL POLITICS (2ND ED.). WOR+45 LAW INT/ORG FORCES TEC/DEV REGION NAT/LISM PEACE ATTIT PWR ALL/IDEOS UN COLD/WAR NATO TREATY. PAGE 113 A2314 — DIPLOM NAT/G POLICY DECISION

B67
SINGER D.,QUANTITATIVE INTERNATIONAL POLITICS* INSIGHTS AND EVIDENCE. WOR+45 WOR-45 PARTIC WAR INGP/REL ATTIT PERSON ROLE...PREDICT BIBLIOG 19/20 UN SENATE. PAGE 133 A2722 — DIPLOM NAT/G INT/ORG DECISION

B67
UNESCO,PRINCIPLES AND PROBLEMS OF NATIONAL SCIENCE POLICIES. WOR+45 ECO/DEV ECO/UNDEV R+D INT/ORG PROB/SOLV CONFER...PHIL/SCI CHARTS 20 UNESCO UN. PAGE 148 A3026 — NAT/COMP POLICY TEC/DEV CREATE

B67
US SENATE COMM AERO SPACE SCI,TREATY ON PRINCIPLES GOVERNING ACTIVITIES OF STATES IN EXPLORATION AND USE OF OUTER SPACE, INCLUDING...BODIES. DELIB/GP FORCES LEGIS DIPLOM...JURID 20 DEPT/STATE NASA DEPT/DEFEN UN. PAGE 155 A3169 — SPACE INT/LAW ORD/FREE PEACE

B67
US SENATE COMM ON FOREIGN REL,BACKGROUND INFORMATION RELATING TO SOUTHEAST ASIA AND VIETNAM (3RD REV. ED.). USA+45 VIETNAM/S VIETNAM/N...CHARTS 20 SENATE UN. PAGE 156 A3188 — DIPLOM WAR FOR/AID

B67
WATERS M.,THE UNITED NATIONS* INTERNATIONAL ORGANIZATION AND ADMINISTRATION. WOR+45 EX/STRUC FORCES DIPLOM LEAD REGION ARMS/CONT REPRESENT INGP/REL ROLE...METH/COMP ANTHOL 20 UN LEAGUE/NAT. PAGE 162 A3291 — CONSTN INT/ORG ADMIN ADJUD

L67
ANAND R.P.,"SOVEREIGN EQUALITY OF STATES IN INTERNATIONAL LAW." UNIV DIPLOM DOMIN CONFER DEBATE SANCTION ATTIT UN. PAGE 8 A0157 — INT/LAW INT/ORG CONCPT POLICY

L67
LANDIS E.S.,"THE SOUTH WEST AFRICA CASES* REMAND TO THE UNITED NATIONS." ETHIOPIA LIBERIA SOUTH/AFR BAL/PWR 20 UN. PAGE 84 A1719 — INT/LAW INT/ORG DIPLOM ADJUD

L67
MACDONALD R.S.J.,"THE RESORT TO ECONOMIC COERCION BY INTERNATIONAL POLITICAL ORGANIZATIONS." CUBA ETHIOPIA RHODESIA SOUTH/AFR NAT/G FOR/AID INT/TRADE DOMIN CONTROL SANCTION...DECISION LEAGUE/NAT UN OAS 20. PAGE 92 A1887 — INT/ORG COERCE ECO/TAC DIPLOM

L67
MOORE N.,"THE LAWFULNESS OF MILITARY ASSISTANCE TO THE REPUBLIC OF VIET NAM." USA+45 VIETNAM WOR+45 FOR/AID DOMIN DETER WAR WEAPON...DECISION INT/LAW 20 UN. PAGE 103 A2123 — PWR DIPLOM FORCES GOV/REL

S67
AFRICAN BIBLIOGRAPHIC CENTER,"THE SWORD AND GOVERNMENT: A PRELIMINARY AND SELECTED BIBLIOGRAPHICAL GUIDE TO AFRICAN MILITARY AFFAIRS; PART I." AFR USA+45 USSR INT/ORG POL/PAR FOR/AID COLONIAL ARMS/CONT PWR 20 UN. PAGE 5 A0101 — BIBLIOG/A FORCES CIVMIL/REL DIPLOM

S67
BLUM Y.Z.,"INDONESIA'S RETURN TO THE UNITED NATIONS." INDONESIA ADJUD SANCTION REPRESENT ...JURID 20 UN. PAGE 16 A0324 — CONSTN LAW DIPLOM INT/ORG

S67
COHN K.,"CRIMES AGAINST HUMANITY." GERMANY INT/ORG SANCTION ATTIT ORD/FREE...MARXIST CRIMLGY 20 UN. PAGE 28 A0564 — WAR INT/LAW CRIME ADJUD

S67
DOYLE S.E.,"COMMUNICATION SATELLITES* INTERNAL ORGANIZATION FOR DEVELOPMENT AND CONTROL." USA+45 R+D ACT/RES DIPLOM NAT/LISM...POLICY INT/LAW PREDICT UN. PAGE 38 A0781 — TEC/DEV SPACE COM/IND INT/ORG

S67
EISENDRATH C.,"THE OUTER SPACE TREATY." CHINA/COM COM USA+45 DIPLOM CONTROL NUC/PWR...INT/LAW 20 UN COLD/WAR TREATY. PAGE 41 A0831 — SPACE INT/ORG PEACE ARMS/CONT

S67
FOREIGN POLICY ASSOCIATION,"US CONCERN FOR WORLD LAW." USA+45 WOR+45 DELIB/GP JUDGE BAL/PWR CONFER PEACE ORD/FREE 20 UN. PAGE 47 A0962 — INT/LAW INT/ORG DIPLOM ARMS/CONT

S67
FRANK I.,"NEW PERSPECTIVES ON TRADE AND DEVELOPMENT." PROB/SOLV BARGAIN DIPLOM FOR/AID CONFER GP/REL WEALTH 20 UN GATT. PAGE 48 A0980 — ECO/UNDEV INT/ORG INT/TRADE ECO/TAC

S67
HAZARD J.N.,"POST-DISARMAMENT INTERNATIONAL LAW." FUT USSR WOR+45 INT/ORG DELIB/GP FORCES DETER EQUILIB SOVEREIGN MARXISM 20 UN. PAGE 63 A1301 — INT/LAW ARMS/CONT PWR PLAN

S67
HODGE G.,"THE RISE AND DEMISE OF THE UN TECHNICAL ASSISTANCE ADMINISTRATION." RISK TASK INGP/REL CONSEN EFFICIENCY 20 UN. PAGE 66 A1349 — ADMIN TEC/DEV EX/STRUC INT/ORG

S67
HUDSON R.,"WAS THIS WAR NECESSARY? THE UN AND THE MIDDLE EAST" WOR+45 STRUCT DIPLOM DOMIN CONTROL REPRESENT PWR...NEW/IDEA 20 UN MID/EAST. PAGE 69 A1410 — DELIB/GP INT/ORG PROB/SOLV PEACE

S67
HULL E.W.S.,"THE POLITICAL OCEAN." FUT UNIV WOR+45 — DIPLOM

EXTR/IND R+D VOL/ASSN PLAN BAL/PWR ECO/TAC PEACE WEALTH 20 UN. PAGE 69 A1414 — ECO/UNDEV INT/ORG INT/LAW

S67
KELLY F.K.,"A PROPOSAL FOR AN ANNUAL REPORT ON THE STATE OF MANKIND." FUT INTELL COM/IND INT/ORG CREATE PROB/SOLV PERS/REL...CONCPT 20 UN. PAGE 77 A1579 — SOCIETY UNIV ATTIT NEW/IDEA

S67
MUDGE G.A.,"DOMESTIC POLICIES AND UN ACTIVITIES* THE CASE OF RHODESIA AND THE REPUBLIC OF SOUTH AFRICA." RHODESIA SOUTH/AFR POL/PAR LEAD SANCTION CHOOSE RACE/REL CONSEN DISCRIM ATTIT...INT/LAW UN PARLIAMENT 20. PAGE 105 A2163 — AFR NAT/G POLICY

S67
REINTANZ G.,"THE SPACE TREATY." WOR+45 DIPLOM CONTROL ARMS/CONT NUC/PWR WAR...MARXIST 20 COLD/WAR UN TREATY. PAGE 120 A2461 — SPACE INT/LAW INT/ORG PEACE

S67
SCHACTER O.,"SCIENTIFIC ADVANCES AND INTERNATIONAL LAWMAKING." FUT R+D PLAN PROB/SOLV CONFER CONTROL ...POLICY PREDICT 20 UN. PAGE 128 A2617 — TEC/DEV INT/LAW INT/ORG ACT/RES

S67
STEEL R.,"WHAT CAN THE UN DO?" RHODESIA ECO/UNDEV DIPLOM ECO/TAC SANCTION...INT/LAW UN. PAGE 137 A2810 — INT/ORG BAL/PWR PEACE FOR/AID

S67
TACKABERRY R.B.,"ORGANIZING AND TRAINING PEACE-KEEPING FORCES* THE CANADIAN VIEW." CANADA PLAN DIPLOM CONFER ADJUD ADMIN CIVMIL/REL 20 UN. PAGE 141 A2882 — PEACE FORCES INT/ORG CONSULT

S67
VLASCIC I.A.,"THE SPACE TREATY* A PRELIMINARY EVALUATION." FUT USSR WOR+45 R+D ACT/RES TEC/DEV DIPLOM CONFER ARMS/CONT PEACE...PREDICT UN TREATY. PAGE 159 A3245 — SPACE INT/LAW INT/ORG NEUTRAL

C67
HUDSON G.F.,"THE HARD AND BITTER PEACE; WORLD POLITICS SINCE 1945." ASIA COM S/ASIA USSR WOR+45 COLONIAL WAR...TREND BIBLIOG/A 20 COLD/WAR UN. PAGE 68 A1405 — DIPLOM INT/ORG ARMS/CONT BAL/PWR

UN DEPARTMENT PUBLIC INF A2996

UN DEPARTMENT SOCIAL AFFAIRS A2997,A2998

UN ECAFE A2999

UN ECONOMIC AND SOCIAL COUNCIL A3000

UN HEADQUARTERS LIBRARY A3001,A3002

UN INTL CONF ON PEACEFUL USE A3003

UN PUB. INFORM. ORGAN. A3004

UN SECRETARY GENERAL A3005

UN/ILC....UNITED NATIONS INTERNATIONAL LAW COMMISSION

UN/SEC/GEN....UNITED NATIONS SECRETARY GENERAL

UNCIO CONFERENCE LIBRARY A3006

UNCSAT....UNITED NATIONS CONFERENCE ON THE APPLICATION OF SCIENCE AND TECHNOLOGY FOR THE BENEFIT OF THE LESS DEVELOPED AREAS

UNCTAD....UNITED NATIONS COMMISSION ON TRADE, AID, AND DEVELOPMENT

B65
HAGRAS K.M.,UNITED NATIONS CONFERENCE ON TRADE AND DEVELOPMENT: A CASE STUDY OF UN DIPLOMACY. CONSULT ACT/RES TEC/DEV FOR/AID INT/TRADE...BIBLIOG 20 UN LEAGUE/NAT UNCTAD. PAGE 59 A1213 — INT/ORG ADMIN DELIB/GP DIPLOM

UNDERDEVELOPED COUNTRIES....SEE ECO/UNDEV

UNDERHILL F.H. A3007

UNDP....UNITED NATIONS DEVELOPMENT PROGRAM

UNECA LIBRARY A3008,A3009

UNEF....UNITED NATIONS EMERGENCY FORCE

B60
US HOUSE COMM FOREIGN AFFAIRS,HEARINGS ON A BILL TO AMEND FURTHER THE MUTUAL SECURITY ACT OF 1954. USA+45 CONSULT FORCES BUDGET FOR/AID CONFER DETER ...CHARTS 20 DEPT/DEFEN DEPT/STATE UNEF. PAGE 153 A3127 — DIPLOM ORD/FREE DELIB/GP LEGIS

S63
NICHOLAS H.G.,"UN PEACE FORCES AND THE CHANGING GLOBE: THE LESSONS OF SUEZ AND CONGO." FUT WOR+45 CONSTN INT/ORG CONSULT DELIB/GP TOP/EX CREATE DIPLOM DOMIN LEGIT COERCE WAR PERSON RIGID/FLEX PWR UN SUEZ CONGO UNEF 20. PAGE 109 A2229 — ACT/RES FORCES

UNESCO A3010,A3011,A3012,A3013,A3014,A3015,A3016,A3017,A3018 , A3019,A3020,A3021,A3022,A3023,A3024,A3025,A3026

UNESCO....UNITED NATIONS EDUCATIONAL, SCIENTIFIC, AND CULTURAL ORGANIZATION; SEE ALSO UN, INT/ORG

N
THE WORLD OF LEARNING. INTELL ACT/RES EDU/PROP 20 UNESCO. PAGE 2 A0045 — BIBLIOG/A ACADEM R+D INT/ORG

N
UNESCO,INTERNATIONAL BIBLIOGRAPHY OF POLITICAL SCIENCE (VOLUMES 1-8). WOR+45 LAW NAT/G EX/STRUC LEGIS PROB/SOLV DIPLOM ADMIN GOV/REL 20 UNESCO. PAGE 147 A3010 — BIBLIOG CONCPT IDEA/COMP

N
UNITED NATIONS,OFFICIAL RECORDS OF THE ECONOMIC AND SOCIAL COUNCIL OF THE UNITED NATIONS. WOR+45 DIPLOM INT/TRADE CONFER...SOC SOC/WK 20 UN UNESCO. PAGE 148 A3031 — INT/ORG DELIB/GP WRITING

N
WORLD PEACE FOUNDATION,DOCUMENTS OF INTERNATIONAL ORGANIZATIONS: A SELECTED BIBLIOGRAPHY. WOR+45 WOR-45 AGRI FINAN ACT/RES OP/RES INT/TRADE ADMIN ...CON/ANAL 20 UN UNESCO LEAGUE/NAT. PAGE 167 A3396 — BIBLIOG DIPLOM INT/ORG REGION

B45
KANDELL I.L.,UNITED STATES ACTIVITIES IN INTERNATIONAL CULTURAL RELATIONS. INT/ORG NAT/G VOL/ASSN CREATE DIPLOM EDU/PROP ATTIT RIGID/FLEX KNOWL...PLURIST CONCPT OBS TREND GEN/LAWS TOT/POP UNESCO 20. PAGE 76 A1554 — USA-45 CULTURE

L47
BRUNER J.S.,"TOWARD A COMMON GROUND-INTERNATIONAL SOCIAL SCIENCE." FUT WOR+45 INTELL R+D NAT/G VOL/ASSN CONSULT DELIB/GP ACT/RES CREATE PLAN TEC/DEV ATTIT ORD/FREE...PSY SOC CONCPT ANTHOL UNESCO 20. PAGE 20 A0410 — INT/ORG KNOWL

B48
JONES H.D.,UNESCO: A SELECTED LIST OF REFERENCES. CULTURE CREATE PEACE ATTIT DRIVE 20 UNESCO UN. PAGE 75 A1531 — BIBLIOG/A INT/ORG DIPLOM EDU/PROP

B49
MARITAIN J.,HUMAN RIGHTS: COMMENTS AND INTERPRETATIONS. COM UNIV WOR+45 LAW CONSTN CULTURE SOCIETY ECO/DEV ECO/UNDEV SCHOOL DELIB/GP EDU/PROP ATTIT PERCEPT ALL/VALS...HUM SOC TREND UNESCO 20. PAGE 95 A1939 — INT/ORG CONCPT

L49
UNESCO,"SOME SUGGESTIONS ON TEACHING ABOUT THE UN AND ITS SPECIALIZED AGENCIES." UNIV WOR+45 SOCIETY STRATA SCHOOL WAR ALL/VALS KNOWL...SOC CONCPT UNESCO 20 UN. PAGE 147 A3011 — INT/ORG EDU/PROP

B50
DAVIS E.P.,PERIODICALS OF INTERNATIONAL ORGANIZATIONS; PART I, THE UN AND SPECIALIZED AGENCIES; PART II, INTER-AMERICAN ORGS. CULTURE AGRI FINAN INDUS LABOR INT/TRADE...GEOG HEAL STAT 20 UN OAS UNESCO. PAGE 34 A0689 — BIBLIOG/A INT/ORG DIPLOM L/A+17C

B51
MCKEON R.,DEMOCRACY IN A WORLD OF TENSION. UNIV LAW INTELL STRUCT R+D INT/ORG SCHOOL EDU/PROP LEGIT ATTIT DRIVE PERCEPT PERSON...POLICY JURID PSY SOC CONCPT METH/CNCPT OBS UNESCO TOT/POP VAL/FREE. PAGE 98 A2015 — SOCIETY ALL/VALS ORD/FREE

B52
ALEXANDROWICZ C.H.,INTERNATIONAL ECONOMIC ORGANIZATION. WOR+45 ECO/DEV ECO/UNDEV DIST/IND FINAN MARKET PLAN ECO/TAC LEGIT DRIVE WEALTH ...POLICY CONCPT QUANT OBS TIME/SEQ GEN/LAWS WORK EEC ILO OEEC UNESCO 20. PAGE 6 A0114 — INT/ORG INT/TRADE

B52
UN DEPT. SOC. AFF.,PRELIMINARY REPORT ON THE WORLD SOCIAL SITUATION. ISLAM L/A+17C WOR+45 STRATA AGRI EXTR/IND INDUS INT/ORG SCHOOL ADMIN...GEOG SOC TREND UNESCO WORK FAO 20. PAGE 147 A2998 — R+D HEALTH FOR/AID

L52
NIEBUHR R.,"THE MORAL IMPLICATIONS OF LOYALTY TO THE UNITED NATIONS." WOR+45 WOR-45 SOCIETY ECO/DEV INT/ORG VOL/ASSN PEACE ATTIT PERSON LOVE ORD/FREE PWR RESPECT...CONCPT UN TOT/POP COLD/WAR UNESCO 20. PAGE 109 A2236 — SUPEGO GEN/LAWS

B53
LARSEN K.,NATIONAL BIBLIOGRAPHIC SERVICES: THEIR CREATION AND OPERATION. WOR+45 COM/IND CREATE PLAN DIPLOM PRESS ADMIN ROUTINE...MGT UNESCO. PAGE 85 — BIBLIOG/A INT/ORG WRITING

A1733

B53
MURPHY G.,IN THE MINDS OF MEN: THE STUDY OF HUMAN BEHAVIOR AND SOCIAL TENSIONS IN INDIA. FUT S/ASIA FAM INT/ORG NAT/G DIPLOM EDU/PROP GP/REL ATTIT RIGID/FLEX ALL/VALS...SOC QU UNESCO 20. PAGE 106 A2176
SECT STRATA INDIA

B53
UNESCO,GUIDE DES CENTRES NATIONAUX D'INFORMATION BIBLIOGRAPHIQUE (VOL. III). WOR+45 INT/ORG NAT/G 20 UNESCO. PAGE 148 A3017
BIBLIOG/A COM/IND DIPLOM

L53
UNESCO,"THE TECHNIQUE OF INTERNATIONAL CONFERENCES." WOR+45 INT/ORG VOL/ASSN EDU/PROP ROUTINE ATTIT DRIVE KNOWL ORD/FREE...SOC UNESCO 20. PAGE 148 A3016
DELIB/GP ACT/RES

B54
MANNING C.A.W.,THE UNIVERSITY TEACHING OF SOCIAL SCIENCES: INTERNATIONAL RELATIONS. WOR+45 INTELL STRATA R+D ACADEM INT/ORG NAT/G CONSULT DELIB/GP ACT/RES EDU/PROP NAT/LISM ATTIT...POLICY CONT/OBS HYPO/EXP VAL/FREE LEAGUE/NAT UNESCO 20. PAGE 94 A1925
KNOWL PHIL/SCI DIPLOM

B55
MALCLES L.N.,BIBLIOGRAPHICAL SERVICES THROUGHOUT THE WORLD (VOL. 4). WOR+45 INT/ORG VOL/ASSN DIPLOM PRESS WRITING 20 UNESCO. PAGE 93 A1911
BIBLIOG ROUTINE COM/IND

B55
UN HEADQUARTERS LIBRARY,BIBLIOGRAPHIE DE LA CHARTE DES NATIONS UNIES. CHINA/COM KOREA WOR+45 VOL/ASSN CONFER ADMIN COERCE PEACE ATTIT ORD/FREE SOVEREIGN ...INT/LAW 20 UNESCO UN. PAGE 147 A3001
BIBLIOG/A INT/ORG DIPLOM

B55
UNESCO,BIBLIOGRAPHIC SERVICES THROUGHOUT THE WORLD (VOLS. I AND II). WOR+45 DIPLOM CONTROL 20 UNESCO. PAGE 148 A3018
BIBLIOG INT/ORG COM/IND

B57
ASHER R.E.,THE UNITED NATIONS AND THE PROMOTION OF THE GENERAL WELFARE. WOR+45 WOR-45 ECO/UNDEV EX/STRUC ACT/RES PLAN EDU/PROP ROUTINE HEALTH...HUM CONCPT CHARTS UNESCO UN ILO 20. PAGE 9 A0185
INT/ORG CONSULT

B57
LAVES W.H.C.,UNESCO. FUT WOR+45 NAT/G CONSULT DELIB/GP TEC/DEV ECO/TAC EDU/PROP PEACE ORD/FREE ...CONCPT TIME/SEQ TREND UNESCO VAL/FREE 20. PAGE 86 A1751
INT/ORG KNOWL

B58
MEYRIAT J.,ETUDES DES BIBLIOGRAPHIES COURANTES DES PUBLICATIONS OFFICIELLES NATIONALES. WOR+45 DIPLOM CONTROL 20 UNESCO. PAGE 100 A2056
BIBLIOG COM/IND NAT/G

B58
UNESCO,REPERTORIO DE PUBLICACIONES PERIODICAS ACTUALES LATINO AMERICANAS (VOL. VIII). LAW DIPLOM GP/REL...PHIL/SCI SOC 20 UNESCO. PAGE 148 A3021
BIBLIOG/A COM/IND L/A+17C

B59
CHINA INSTITUTE OF AMERICA.,CHINA AND THE UNITED NATIONS. CHINA/COM FUT STRUCT EDU/PROP LEGIT ADMIN ATTIT KNOWL ORD/FREE PWR...OBS RECORD STAND/INT TIME/SEQ UN LEAGUE/NAT UNESCO 20. PAGE 26 A0531
ASIA INT/ORG

B59
MACIVER R.M.,THE NATIONS AND THE UN. WOR+45 NAT/G CONSULT ADJUD ADMIN ALL/VALS...CONCPT DEEP/QU UN TOT/POP UNESCO 20. PAGE 92 A1892
INT/ORG ATTIT DIPLOM

B59
SCHNEIDER J.,TREATY-MAKING POWER OF INTERNATIONAL ORGANIZATIONS. FUT WOR+45 WOR-45 LAW NAT/G JUDGE DIPLOM LEGIT CT/SYS ORD/FREE PWR...INT/LAW JURID GEN/LAWS TOT/POP UNESCO 20 TREATY. PAGE 129 A2639
INT/ORG ROUTINE

B59
STANFORD RESEARCH INSTITUTE,POSSIBLE NONMILITARY SCIENTIFIC DEVELOPMENTS AND THEIR POTENTIAL IMPACT ON FOREIGN POLICY PROBLEMS OF THE UNITED. FUT USA+45 INT/ORG PROF/ORG CONSULT ACT/RES CREATE PLAN PEACE KNOWL SKILL...TECHNIC PHIL/SCI NEW/IDEA UNESCO 20. PAGE 137 A2802
R+D TEC/DEV

S59
PADELFORD N.J.,"REGIONAL COOPERATION IN THE SOUTH PACIFIC: THE SOUTH PACIFIC COMMISSION." FUT NEW/ZEALND UK WOR+45 CULTURE ECO/UNDEV LOC/G VOL/ASSN...OBS CON/ANAL UNESCO VAL/FREE AUSTRAL 20. PAGE 112 A2308
INT/ORG ADMIN

B60
CARNEGIE ENDOWMENT INT. PEACE,PERSPECTIVES ON PEACE - 1910-1960. WOR+45 WOR-45 INTELL INT/ORG CONSULT ACT/RES EDU/PROP ATTIT KNOWL ORD/FREE...TIME/SEQ TREND EEC OAS UNESCO NAZI 20. PAGE 24 A0489
FUT CONCPT ARMS/CONT PEACE

B60
SHONFIELD A.,THE ATTACK ON WORLD POVERTY. WOR+45 ECO/DEV ECO/UNDEV FINAN VOL/ASSN PLAN EDU/PROP DRIVE KNOWL WEALTH...CONT/OBS STAND/INT ORG/CHARTS TOT/POP UNESCO 20. PAGE 132 A2704
INT/ORG ECO/TAC FOR/AID INT/TRADE

B61
COLLISON R.L.,BIBLIOGRAPHICAL SERVICES THROUGHOUT THE WORLD: 1950-59 (VOL. 9). WOR+45 INT/ORG EDU/PROP PRESS WRITING ADMIN CENTRAL 20 UNESCO. PAGE 28 A0568
BIBLIOG COM/IND DIPLOM

B61
SHARP W.R.,FIELD ADMINISTRATION IN THE UNITED NATION SYSTEM: THE CONDUCT OF INTERNATIONAL ECONOMIC AND SOCIAL PROGRAMS. FUT WOR+45 CONSTN SOCIETY ECO/UNDEV R+D DELIB/GP ACT/RES PLAN TEC/DEV EDU/PROP EXEC ROUTINE HEALTH WEALTH...HUM CONCPT CHARTS METH ILO UNESCO VAL/FREE UN 20. PAGE 132 A2697
INT/ORG CONSULT

B62
THANT U.,THE UNITED NATIONS' DEVELOPMENT DECADE: PROPOSALS FOR ACTION. WOR+45 SOCIETY ECO/UNDEV AGRI COM/IND FINAN R+D MUNIC SCHOOL VOL/ASSN CONSULT PLAN TEC/DEV ECO/TAC EDU/PROP ADMIN ROUTINE RIGID/FLEX...MGT SOC CONCPT UNESCO UN TOT/POP VAL/FREE. PAGE 142 A2906
INT/ORG ALL/VALS

B62
VIET J.,INTERNATIONAL COOPERATION AND PROGRAMMES OF ECONOMIC AND SOCIAL DEVELOPMENT. TEC/DEV FOR/AID DOMIN COLONIAL PEACE WEALTH 20 UNESCO. PAGE 159 A3232
BIBLIOG/A INT/ORG DIPLOM ECO/UNDEV

L62
MALINOWSKI W.R.,"CENTRALIZATION AND DE-CENTRALIZATION IN THE UNITED NATIONS' ECONOMIC AND SOCIAL ACTIVITIES." WOR+45 CONSTN ECO/UNDEV INT/ORG VOL/ASSN DELIB/GP ECO/TAC EDU/PROP ADMIN RIGID/FLEX ...OBS CHARTS UNESCO UN EEC OAS OEEC 20. PAGE 93 A1913
CREATE GEN/LAWS

S62
BELSHAW C.,"TRAINING AND RECRUITMENT: SOME PRINCIPLES OF INTERNATIONAL AID." FUT WOR+45 SOCIETY INT/ORG NAT/G CREATE PLAN TEC/DEV ECO/TAC FOR/AID EDU/PROP ATTIT PERCEPT...HUM UN FAO ILO UNESCO 20. PAGE 13 A0263
VOL/ASSN ECO/UNDEV

B63
COMISION DE HISTORIO,GUIA DE LOS DOCUMENTOS MICROFOTOGRAFIADOS POR LA UNIDAD MOVIL DE LA UNESCO. SOCIETY ECO/UNDEV INT/ORG ADMIN...SOC 20 UNESCO. PAGE 28 A0573
BIBLIOG NAT/G L/A+17C DIPLOM

B63
JACOBSON H.K.,THE USSR AND THE UN'S ECONOMIC AND SOCIAL ACTIVITIES. COM WOR+45 DELIB/GP ACT/RES ECO/TAC EDU/PROP RIGID/FLEX SUPEGO HEALTH PWR SKILL ...POLICY CHARTS GEN/METH VAL/FREE UNESCO 20 UN. PAGE 73 A1487
INT/ORG ATTIT USSR

N63
LIBRARY HUNGARIAN ACADEMY SCI,HUNGARIAN PUBLICATIONS ON ASIA AND AFRICA, 1950-1962: A SELECTED BIBLIOGRAPHY (PAMPHLET). AFR ASIA HUNGARY S/ASIA ECO/UNDEV NAT/G EDU/PROP ATTIT 20 UNESCO. PAGE 88 A1807
BIBLIOG REGION DIPLOM WRITING

B65
UNESCO,INTERNATIONAL ORGANIZATIONS IN THE SOCIAL SCIENCES(REV. ED.). LAW ADMIN ATTIT...CRIMLGY GEOG INT/LAW PSY SOC STAT 20 UNESCO. PAGE 148 A3024
INT/ORG R+D PROF/ORG ACT/RES

B67
UNESCO,PRINCIPLES AND PROBLEMS OF NATIONAL SCIENCE POLICIES. WOR+45 ECO/DEV ECO/UNDEV R+D INT/ORG PROB/SOLV CONFER...PHIL/SCI CHARTS 20 UNESCO UN. PAGE 148 A3026
NAT/COMP POLICY TEC/DEV CREATE

UNIDO....UNITED NATIONS INDUSTRIAL DEVELOPMENT ORGANIZATION

UNIFICA....UNIFICATION AND REUNIFICATION OF GEOGRAPHIC-POLITICAL ENTITIES

B62
SCHMITT H.A.,THE PATH TO EUROPEAN UNITY. EUR+WWI USA+45 PLAN TEC/DEV DIPLOM FOR/AID CONFER...INT/LAW 20 EEC EURCOALSTL MARSHL/PLN UNIFICA. PAGE 128 A2634
INT/ORG INT/TRADE REGION ECO/DEV

B63
PADELFORD N.J.,AFRICA AND WORLD ORDER. AFR COLONIAL SOVEREIGN...ANTHOL BIBLIOG 20 UN UNIFICA COMMONWLTH. PAGE 113 A2312
DIPLOM NAT/G ORD/FREE

B66
WEINSTEIN F.B.,VIETNAM'S UNHELD ELECTIONS: THE FAILURE TO CARRY OUT THE 1956 REUNIFICATION ELECTIONS... (MONOGRAPH). VIETNAM/S VIETNAM/N LEGIT CONFER ADJUD WAR PEACE 20 TREATY GENEVA/CON UNIFICA. PAGE 162 A3306
AGREE NAT/G CHOOSE DIPLOM

S66
DINH TRANS V.A.N.,"VIETNAM: A THIRD WAY" S/ASIA USA+45 USSR VIETNAM VIETNAM/S NAT/G SECT FORCES CAP/ISM DIPLOM COLONIAL NEUTRAL MARXISM SOCISM 20 BUDDHISM UNIFICA. PAGE 38 A0766
WAR PLAN ORD/FREE SOCIALIST

UNIFORM NARCOTIC DRUG ACT....SEE NARCO/ACT

UNION AFRICAINE ET MALGACHE, ALSO OCAM....SEE UAM

UNION FOR THE NEW REPUBLIC....SEE UNR

UNION OF SOUTH AFRICA....SEE SOUTH/AFR

UNION OF SOVIET SOCIALIST REPUBLICS....SEE USSR

UNION POUR LA DEFENSE DE LA REPUBLIQUE (FRANCE)....SEE UDR

UNION OF INTERNATIONAL ASSNS A3027

UNION OF SOUTH AFRICA A3028

UNIONS....SEE LABOR

UNITED ARAB REPUBLIC....SEE UAR

UNITED KINGDOM....SEE UK, COMMONWLTH

UNITED NATIONS....SEE UN

UNITED NATIONS INTERNATIONAL LAW COMMISSION....SEE UN/ILC

UNITED NATIONS SECURITY COUNCIL....SEE SECUR/COUN

UNITED NATIONS SPECIAL FUND....SEE UNSF

UNITED STATES ARMS CONTROL AND DISARMAMENT AGENCY....SEE ACD

UNITED STATES FEDERAL POWER COMMISSION....SEE FPC

UNITED STATES HOUSING CORPORATION....SEE US/HOUSING

UNITED STATES MILITARY ACADEMY....SEE WEST/POINT

UNITED STATES SENATE COMMITTEE ON FOREIGN RELATIONS....SEE FOREIGNREL

UNITED ARAB REPUBLIC A3029,A3030

UNITED NATIONS A3031,A3032,A3033,A3034,A3035,A3036,A3037

UNITED STATES A3038, A3116

UNITED WORLD FEDERALISTS A3039

UNIV....UNIVERSAL TO MAN

UNIV KARACHI INST PUB BUS ADM A3040

UNIVERSAL REFERENCE SYSTEM A3041,A3042,A3043,A3044

UNIVERSES....SEE UNIVERSES AND SAMPLING INDEX, P. XIV

UNIVERSITIES....SEE ACADEM

UNIVERSITIES RESEARCH ASSOCIATION, INC.....SEE UNIVS/RES

UNIVERSITY MICROFILMS INC A3045

UNIVERSITY OF CALIFORNIA A3046

UNIVERSITY OF FLORIDA LIBRARY A3047

UNIVERSITY OF TENNESSEE A3048

UNIVS/RES....UNIVERSITIES RESEARCH ASSOCIATION, INC.

UNLABR/PAR....UNION LABOR PARTY

UNPLAN/INT....IMPROMPTU INTERVIEW

UNR....UNION FOR THE NEW REPUBLIC

UNRRA....UNITED NATIONS RELIEF AND REHABILITATION AGENCY

UNRWA....UNITED NATIONS RELIEF AND WORKS AGENCY

UNSF....UNITED NATIONS SPECIAL FUND

UPPER VOLTA....SEE UPPER/VOLT

UPPER/VOLT....UPPER VOLTA; SEE ALSO AFR

UPTON E. A3049

URBAN/LEAG....URBAN LEAGUE

URBAN/RNWL....URBAN RENEWAL

B57
DRUCKER P.F.,AMERICA'S NEXT TWENTY YEARS. USA+45 DIST/IND ACADEM MUNIC SCHOOL DIPLOM ECO/TAC AUTOMAT HABITAT HEALTH...SOC/WK TREND 20 URBAN/RNWL PUB/TRANS. PAGE 39 A0788 — WORKER FOR/AID CENSUS GEOG

B65
WHITE HOUSE CONFERENCE ON INTERNATIONAL COOPERATION(VOL.II). SPACE WOR+45 EXTR/IND INT/ORG LABOR WORKER NUC/PWR PEACE AGE/Y...CENSUS ANTHOL 20 RESOURCE/N URBAN/RNWL PUB/TRANS. PAGE 3 A0071 — R+D CONFER TEC/DEV DIPLOM

URUGUAY....URUGUAY

B33
AMERICAN FOREIGN LAW ASSN,BIOGRAPHICAL NOTES ON THE LAWS AND LEGAL LITERATURE OF URUGUAY AND CURACAO. URUGUAY CONSTN FINAN SECT FORCES JUDGE DIPLOM INT/TRADE ADJUD CT/SYS CRIME 20. PAGE 7 A0147 — BIBLIOG/A LAW JURID ADMIN

B64
MUSSO AMBROSI L.A.,BIBLIOGRAFIA DE BIBLIOGRAFIAS URUGUAYAS. URUGUAY DIPLOM ADMIN ATTIT...SOC 20. PAGE 106 A2185 — BIBLIOG NAT/G L/A+17C PRESS

B67
PIKE F.B.,FREEDOM AND REFORM IN LATIN AMERICA. BRAZIL URUGUAY CONSTN CULTURE SECT DIPLOM EDU/PROP PARTIC DRIVE ALL/VALS CATHISM...GEOG ANTHOL BIBLIOG REFORMERS BOLIV. PAGE 116 A2379 — L/A+17C ORD/FREE ECO/UNDEV REV

S67
FABREGA J.,"ANTECEDENTES EXTRANJEROS EN LA CONSTITUCION PANAMENA." CUBA L/A+17C PANAMA URUGUAY EX/STRUC LEGIS DIPLOM ORD/FREE 19/20 COLOMB MEXIC/AMER. PAGE 43 A0882 — CONSTN JURID NAT/G PARL/PROC

US AGENCY FOR INTERNATIONAL DEVELOPMENT....SEE US/AID

US ATOMIC ENERGY COMMISSION....SEE AEC

US ATTORNEY GENERAL....SEE ATTRNY/GEN

US BUREAU OF STANDARDS....SEE BUR/STNDRD

US BUREAU OF THE BUDGET....SEE BUR/BUDGET

US CENTRAL INTELLIGENCE AGENCY....SEE CIA

US CIVIL AERONAUTICS BOARD....SEE CAB

US CONGRESS RULES COMMITTEES....SEE RULES/COMM

US DEPARTMENT OF AGRICULTURE....SEE DEPT/AGRI

US DEPARTMENT OF COMMERCE....SEE DEPT/COM

US DEPARTMENT OF DEFENSE....SEE DEPT/DEFEN

US DEPARTMENT OF HEALTH, EDUCATION, AND WELFARE....SEE DEPT/HEW

US DEPARTMENT OF HOUSING AND URBAN DEVELOPMENT....SEE DEPT/HUD

US DEPARTMENT OF JUSTICE....SEE DEPT/JUST

US DEPARTMENT OF LABOR AND INDUSTRY....SEE DEPT/LABOR

US DEPARTMENT OF STATE....SEE DEPT/STATE

US DEPARTMENT OF THE INTERIOR....SEE DEPT/INTER

US DEPARTMENT OF THE TREASURY....SEE DEPT/TREAS

US FEDERAL AVIATION AGENCY....SEE FAA

US FEDERAL BUREAU OF INVESTIGATION....SEE FBI

US FEDERAL COMMUNICATIONS COMMISSION....SEE FCC

US FEDERAL COUNCIL FOR SCIENCE AND TECHNOLOGY....SEE FEDSCI/TEC

US FEDERAL HOUSING ADMINISTRATION....SEE FHA

US FEDERAL OPEN MARKET COMMITTEE....SEE FED/OPNMKT

US FEDERAL RESERVE SYSTEM....SEE FED/RESERV

US FEDERAL TRADE COMMISSION....SEE FTC

US HOUSE COMMITTEE ON SCIENCE AND ASTRONAUTICS....SE HS/SCIASTR

US HOUSE COMMITTEE ON UNAMERICAN ACTIVITIES....SEE HUAC

US HOUSE OF REPRESENTATIVES....SEE HOUSE/REP

US INFORMATION AGENCY....SEE USIA

US INTERNAL REVENUE SERVICE....SEE IRS

US INTERNATIONAL COOPERATION ADMINISTRATION....SEE ICA

US INTERSTATE COMMERCE COMMISSION....SEE ICC

US MILITARY ACADEMY....SEE WEST/POINT

US NATIONAL AERONAUTICS AND SPACE ADMINISTRATION....SEE NASA

N19
MEZERIK AG,OUTER SPACE: UN, US, USSR (PAMPHLET). USSR DELIB/GP FORCES DETER NUC/PWR SOVEREIGN ...POLICY 20 UN TREATY. PAGE 101 A2063
SPACE CONTROL DIPLOM INT/ORG

N19
MORGENSTERN O.,THE COMMAND AND CONTROL STRUCTURE (PAMPHLET). USSR COM/IND INT/ORG WEAPON PEACE UTIL ...TREND 20 NATO. PAGE 104 A2132
CONTROL FORCES EFFICIENCY PLAN

N19
SALKEVER L.R.,SUB-SAHARA AFRICA (PAMPHLET). AFR USSR EXTR/IND NAT/G SCHOOL DIPLOM COLONIAL WEALTH ...GEOG CHARTS 16/20. PAGE 127 A2594
ECO/UNDEV TEC/DEV TASK INT/TRADE

N19
TAYLOR T.G.,CANADA'S ROLE IN GEOPOLITICS (PAMPHLET). CANADA FUT USSR COLONIAL REGION WEALTH ...CHARTS 20. PAGE 142 A2901
GEOG DIPLOM SOCIETY ECO/DEV

B29
CONWELL-EVANS T.P.,THE LEAGUE COUNCIL IN ACTION. EUR+WWI TURKEY UK USSR WOR-45 INT/ORG FORCES JUDGE ECO/TAC EDU/PROP LEGIT ROUTINE ARMS/CONT COERCE ATTIT PWR...MAJORIT GEOG JURID CONCPT LEAGUE/NAT TOT/POP VAL/FREE TUNIS 20. PAGE 30 A0605
DELIB/GP INT/LAW

B29
DE REPARAZ G.,GEOGRAFIA Y POLITICA. CHILE SPAIN USSR NAT/G DIPLOM REV MARXISM...POLICY 19/20. PAGE 35 A0709
GEOG MOD/EUR

B29
LANGER W.L.,THE FRANCO-RUSSIAN ALLIANCE: 1890-1894. FRANCE MOD/EUR UK USSR NAT/G CHIEF FORCES BAL/PWR AGREE WAR PEACE PWR...TIME/SEQ TREATY 19 BISMARCK/O. PAGE 84 A1724
DIPLOM

B32
EAGLETON C.,INTERNATIONAL GOVERNMENT. BRAZIL FRANCE GERMANY ITALY UK USSR WOR-45 DELIB/GP TOP/EX PLAN ECO/TAC EDU/PROP LEGIT ADJUD REGION ARMS/CONT COERCE ATTIT PWR...GEOG MGT VAL/FREE LEAGUE/NAT 20. PAGE 40 A0816
INT/ORG JURID DIPLOM INT/LAW

B32
LENIN V.I.,THE WAR AND THE SECOND INTERNATIONAL. COM MOD/EUR USSR CAP/ISM DIPLOM NAT/LISM ATTIT MARXISM...CONCPT 20. PAGE 87 A1772
POL/PAR WAR SOCISM INT/ORG

B35
CONOVER H.F.,A SELECTED LIST OF REFERENCES ON THE DIPLOMATIC & TRADE RELATIONS OF THE US WITH THE USSR, 1919-1935 (PAMPHLET). USA-45 USSR DELIB/GP LEGIS OP/RES PROB/SOLV BAL/PWR BARGAIN 20. PAGE 29 A0590
BIBLIOG DIPLOM INT/TRADE

B38
HARPER S.N.,THE GOVERNMENT OF THE SOVIET UNION. COM USSR LAW CONSTN ECO/DEV PLAN TEC/DEV DIPLOM INT/TRADE ADMIN REV NAT/LISM...POLICY 20. PAGE 62 A1265
MARXISM NAT/G LEAD POL/PAR

B39
LENIN V.I.,IMPERIALISM: THE HIGHEST STAGE OF CAPITALISM. USSR WOR-45 DIST/IND INT/TRADE ATTIT MARXISM SOCISM...CHARTS 20. PAGE 87 A1773
MARXIST CAP/ISM COLONIAL DOMIN

B39
WHEELER-BENNET J.W.,THE FORGOTTEN PEACE: BREST-LITOVSK. COM GERMANY USSR TOP/EX AGREE WAR PWR ...BIBLIOG 20 TREATY LENIN/VI UKRAINE. PAGE 163 A3326
PEACE DIPLOM CONFER

S40
FLORIN J.,"BOLSHEVIST AND NATIONAL SOCIALIST DOCTRINES OF INTERNATIONAL LAW." EUR+WWI GERMANY USSR R+D INT/ORG NAT/G DIPLOM DOMIN EDU/PROP SOCISM ...CONCPT TIME/SEQ 20. PAGE 47 A0955
LAW ATTIT TOTALISM INT/LAW

B43
CONOVER H.F.,SOVIET RUSSIA: SELECTED LIST OF REFERENCES. USSR CULTURE INDUS NAT/G TOP/EX TEC/DEV BUDGET WAR CIVMIL/REL EFFICIENCY MARXISM 20. PAGE 29 A0597
BIBLIOG ECO/DEV COM DIPLOM

B43
GRIERSON P.,BOOKS ON SOVIET RUSSIA 1917-42: A BIBLIOGRAPHY AND A GUIDE TO READING. USSR CULTURE ELITES NAT/G PLAN DIPLOM REV...GEOG 20. PAGE 56 A1148
BIBLIOG/A COM MARXISM LEAD

B43
MICAUD C.A.,THE FRENCH RIGHT AND NAZI GERMANY 1933-1939: A STUDY OF PUBLIC OPINION. GERMANY UK USSR POL/PAR ARMS/CONT COERCE DETER PEACE RIGID/FLEX PWR MARXISM...FASCIST TREND 20 LEAGUE/NAT TREATY. PAGE 101 A2065
DIPLOM AGREE

B45
CONOVER H.F.,THE GOVERNMENTS OF THE MAJOR FOREIGN POWERS: A BIBLIOGRAPHY. FRANCE GERMANY ITALY UK USSR CONSTN LOC/G POL/PAR EX/STRUC FORCES ADMIN CT/SYS CIVMIL/REL TOTALISM...POLICY 19/20. PAGE 29 A0598
BIBLIOG NAT/G DIPLOM

B45
GALLOWAY E.,ABSTRACTS OF POSTWAR LITERATURE (VOL. IV) JAN.-JULY, 1945 NOS. 901-1074. POLAND USA+45 USSR WOR+45 INDUS LABOR PLAN ECO/TAC INT/TRADE TAX EDU/PROP ADMIN COLONIAL INT/LAW. PAGE 51 A1033
BIBLIOG/A NUC/PWR NAT/G DIPLOM

B46
BIBLIOGRAFIIA DISSERTATSII: DOKTORSKIE DISSERTATSII ZA 19411944 (2 VOLS.). COM USSR LAW POL/PAR DIPLOM ADMIN LEAD...PHIL/SCI SOC 20. PAGE 3 A0054
BIBLIOG ACADEM KNOWL MARXIST

B46
BLUM L.,FOR ALL MANKIND (TRANS. BY W. PICKLES). FRANCE GERMANY USSR LAW SOCIETY STRUCT POL/PAR WORKER DIPLOM DOMIN CHOOSE ORD/FREE FASCISM 20. PAGE 16 A0323
POPULISM SOCIALIST NAT/G WAR

B46
BRODIE B.,THE OBSOLETE WEAPON: ATOMIC POWER AND WORLD ORDER. COM USA+45 USSR WOR+45 DELIB/GP PLAN ORD/FREE PWR...CONCPT TIME/SEQ TREND UN 20. PAGE 19 A0380
INT/ORG TEC/DEV ARMS/CONT NUC/PWR

N47
FOX W.T.R.,UNITED STATES POLICY IN A TWO POWER WORLD. COM USA+45 USSR FORCES DOMIN AGREE NEUTRAL NUC/PWR ORD/FREE SOVEREIGN 20 COLD/WAR TREATY EUROPE/W INTERVENT. PAGE 48 A0972
DIPLOM FOR/AID POLICY

B48
KULISCHER E.M.,EUROPE ON THE MOVE: WAR AND POPULATION CHANGES, 1917-1947. COM EUR+WWI FUT GERMANY USSR DIST/IND PLAN INT/TRADE CONTROL WAR DRIVE...CENSUS TREND COLD/WAR 20. PAGE 82 A1690
ECO/TAC GEOG

B49
THE CURRENT DIGEST OF THE SOVIET PRESS. USSR WOR+45 LOC/G NAT/G DIPLOM EDU/PROP...MARXIST 20. PAGE 3 A0056
BIBLIOG/A COM ATTIT PRESS

B49
GORER G.,THE PEOPLE OF GREAT RUSSIA: A PSYCHOLOGICAL STUDY. RUSSIA USSR NAT/G DIPLOM LEAD AGE/C ANOMIE ATTIT DRIVE...POLICY 20. PAGE 54 A1116
ISOLAT PERSON PSY SOCIETY

B49
JACKSON R.H.,INTERNATIONAL CONFERENCE ON MILITARY TRIALS. FRANCE GERMANY UK USA+45 USSR VOL/ASSN DELIB/GP REPAR ADJUD CT/SYS CRIME WAR 20 WAR/TRIAL. PAGE 72 A1479
DIPLOM INT/ORG INT/LAW CIVMIL/REL

B49
STETTINIUS E.R.,ROOSEVELT AND THE RUSSIANS: THE YALTA CONFERENCE. UK USSR WOR+45 WOR-45 INT/ORG VOL/ASSN TOP/EX ACT/RES EDU/PROP PEACE ATTIT DRIVE PERSON SUPEGO PWR...POLICY CONCPT MYTH OBS TIME/SEQ AUD/VIS COLD/WAR 20 CHURCHLL/W YALTA ROOSEVLT/F. PAGE 138 A2819
DIPLOM DELIB/GP BIOG

B49
US DEPARTMENT OF STATE,SOVIET BIBLIOGRAPHY (PAMPHLET). CHINA/COM COM USSR LAW AGRI INT/ORG ECO/TAC EDU/PROP...POLICY GEOG 20. PAGE 151 A3084
BIBLIOG/A MARXISM CULTURE DIPLOM

B50
BARGHOORN F.C.,THE SOVIET IMAGE OF THE UNITED STATES: A STUDY IN DISTORTION. COM USSR DOMIN WAR NAT/LISM TOTALISM SOCISM...PSY 20. PAGE 11 A0220
PROB/SOLV EDU/PROP DIPLOM ATTIT

B50
BROOKINGS INSTITUTION,MAJOR PROBLEMS OF UNITED STATES FOREIGN POLICY. AFR ASIA INDIA UK USA+45 USSR BAL/PWR FOR/AID WAR PEACE TOTALISM MARXISM SOCISM 20 CHINJAP COLD/WAR. PAGE 19 A0393
DIPLOM POLICY ORD/FREE

B50
DULLES J.F.,WAR OR PEACE. CHINA/COM USA+45 USSR INT/ORG SECT FORCES PLAN NUC/PWR WAR CENTRAL MARXISM...POLICY 20 UN ROOSEVLT/F STALIN/J. PAGE 39 A0797
PEACE DIPLOM TREND ORD/FREE

B50
NORTHROP F.S.C.,THE TAMING OF THE NATIONS. KOREA USA+45 USSR WOR+45 STRUCT ECO/UNDEV INT/ORG NAT/G TOP/EX NUC/PWR ATTIT ALL/VALS...TIME/SEQ 20 HIROSHIMA. PAGE 110 A2255
CONCPT BAL/PWR

B50
US LIBRARY OF CONGRESS,THE UNITED STATES AND EUROPE: BIBLIOGRAPHY OF THOUGHT EXPRESSED IN AMERICAN PUBLICATIONS DURING 1950. EUR+WWI GERMANY USA+45 USSR INT/ORG DIPLOM COLONIAL SOVEREIGN ...POLICY 20 COLD/WAR UN BERLIN/BLO. PAGE 154 A3150
BIBLIOG/A SOC ATTIT

S50
WITTFOGEL K.A.,"RUSSIA AND ASIA: PROBLEMS OF CONTEMPORARY AREA STUDIES AND INTERNATIONAL RELATIONS." ASIA COM USA+45 SOCIETY NAT/G DIPLOM ECO/TAC FOR/AID EDU/PROP KNOWL...HIST/WRIT TOT/POP 20. PAGE 166 A3373
ECO/DEV ADMIN RUSSIA USSR

B51
BLANSHARD P.,COMMUNISM, DEMOCRACY AND CATHOLIC POWER. USSR VATICAN WOR+45 WOR-45 CULTURE ELITES INTELL SOCIETY STRUCT INT/ORG POL/PAR EDU/PROP COERCE ATTIT KNOWL PWR MARXISM...CONCPT COLD/WAR 20. PAGE 15 A0308
COM SECT TOTALISM

B51
BORKENAU F.,EUROPEAN COMMUNISM. COM EUR+WWI GERMANY SPAIN USSR INT/ORG PLAN REV WAR ATTIT 20 STALIN/J
MARXISM POLICY

HITLER/A. PAGE 17 A0342 — DIPLOM NAT/G

B51
BROGAN D.W.,THE PRICE OF REVOLUTION. FRANCE USA+45 USA-45 USSR CONSTN NAT/G DIPLOM COLONIAL NAT/LISM ORD/FREE POPULISM...CONCPT 18/20 PRE/US/AM. PAGE 19 A0386 — REV METH/COMP COST MARXISM

L51
ULAM A.B.,"THE COMIMFORM AND THE PEOPLE'S DEMOCRACIES." EUR+WWI WOR+45 STRUCT NAT/G POL/PAR TOP/EX ACT/RES PLAN ECO/TAC DOMIN ATTIT ALL/VALS ...HIST/WRIT TIME/SEQ 20 COMINFORM. PAGE 146 A2992 — COM INT/ORG USSR TOTALISM

C51
BEST H.,"THE SOVIET STATE AND ITS INCEPTION." USSR CULTURE INDUS DIPLOM WEALTH...GEOG SOC BIBLIOG 20. PAGE 14 A0281 — COM GEN/METH REV MARXISM

B52
U OF MICH SURVEY RESEARCH CTR,AMERICA'S ROLE IN WORLD AFFAIRS. ASIA COM EUR+WWI USA+45 USSR FOR/AID WAR AUTHORIT ORD/FREE...DEEP/QU 20. PAGE 146 A2986 — DIPLOM NAT/G ROLE POLICY

B52
ULAM A.B.,TITOISM AND THE COMINFORM. USSR WOR+45 STRUCT INT/ORG NAT/G ACT/RES PLAN EXEC ATTIT DRIVE ALL/VALS...CONCPT OBS VAL/FREE 20 COMINTERN TITO/MARSH. PAGE 146 A2993 — COM POL/PAR TOTALISM YUGOSLAVIA

S52
MASTERS R.D.,"RUSSIA AND THE UNITED NATIONS." FUT USA+45 USSR WOR+45 CONSTN VOL/ASSN DELIB/GP TOP/EX CREATE DIPLOM ADMIN...TREND STERTYP UN 20. PAGE 96 A1962 — INT/ORG PWR

B53
KALIJARVI T.V.,MODERN WORLD POLITICS (3RD ED.). AFR L/A+17C MOD/EUR S/ASIA UK USSR WOR+45 INT/ORG BAL/PWR WAR PWR 20. PAGE 76 A1552 — DIPLOM INT/LAW PEACE

B53
LANGER W.L.,THE UNDECLARED WAR, 1940-1941. EUR+WWI GERMANY USA-45 USSR AIR FORCES TEC/DEV CONFER CONTROL COERCE PERCEPT ORD/FREE PWR 20 CHINJAP EUROPE. PAGE 84 A1727 — WAR POLICY DIPLOM

B53
LENZ F.,DIE BEWEGUNGEN DER GROSSEN MACHTE. USA+45 USA-45 USSR SOCIETY STRATA STRUCT NAT/G PERSON MARXISM...CONCPT IDEA/COMP NAT/COMP 18/20. PAGE 87 A1777 — BAL/PWR TREND DIPLOM HIST/WRIT

B53
MCNEILL W.H.,AMERICA, BRITAIN, AND RUSSIA; THEIR COOPERATION AND CONFLICT. UK USA-45 USSR ECO/DEV ECO/UNDEV FORCES PLAN ADMIN AGREE PERS/REL ...DECISION 20 TREATY. PAGE 98 A2021 — WAR DIPLOM DOMIN

B53
MENDE T.,WORLD POWER IN THE BALANCE. FUT USA+45 USSR WOR-45 ECO/DEV ECO/TAC INT/TRADE EDU/PROP UTOPIA ATTIT...HUM CONCPT TREND COLD/WAR TOT/POP 20. PAGE 99 A2036 — WOR+45 PWR BAL/PWR

B53
SHIRATO I.,JAPANESE SOURCES ON THE HISTORY OF THE CHINESE COMMUNIST MOVEMENT (PAMPHLET). CHINA/COM USSR CONSTRUC NAT/G POL/PAR FORCES DIPLOM DOMIN EDU/PROP CONTROL WAR TOTALISM SOCISM 20. PAGE 132 A2702 — BIBLIOG/A MARXISM ECO/UNDEV

S53
LINCOLN G.,"FACTORS DETERMINING ARMS AID." COM FUT USA+45 USSR WOR+45 ECO/DEV NAT/G CONSULT PLAN TEC/DEV DIPLOM DOMIN EDU/PROP PERCEPT PWR ...DECISION CONCPT TREND MARX/KARL 20. PAGE 89 A1819 — FORCES POLICY BAL/PWR FOR/AID

B54
BUTOW R.J.C.,JAPAN'S DECISION TO SURRENDER. USA-45 USSR CHIEF FORCES DOMIN NUC/PWR...BIBLIOG 20 TREATY CHINJAP. PAGE 22 A0453 — ELITES DIPLOM WAR PEACE

B54
BUTZ O.,GERMANY: DILEMMA FOR AMERICAN POLICY. GERMANY USA+45 USA-45 USSR WOR+45 INT/ORG FORCES NUC/PWR EFFICIENCY PEACE PWR...GOV/COMP 20 COLD/WAR. PAGE 23 A0459 — DIPLOM NAT/G WAR POLICY

B55
TAN C.C.,THE BOXER CATASTROPHE. ASIA UK USSR ELITES POL/PAR VOL/ASSN FORCES PROB/SOLV DIPLOM ADMIN COLONIAL NAT/LISM PEACE TREATY 19/20 BOXER/REBL. PAGE 141 A2885 — REV NAT/G WAR

L55
ROSTOW W.W.,"RUSSIA AND CHINA UNDER COMMUNISM." CHINA/COM USSR INTELL STRUCT INT/ORG NAT/G POL/PAR TOP/EX ACT/RES PLAN ADMIN ATTIT ALL/VALS MARXISM ...CONCPT OBS TIME/SEQ TREND GOV/COMP VAL/FREE 20. PAGE 124 A2543 — COM ASIA

B56
BUREAU OF PUBLIC AFFAIRS,AMERICAN FOREIGN POLICY: CURRENT DOCUMENTS. COM USA+45 USSR WOR+45 DELIB/GP FOR/AID INT/TRADE ARMS/CONT NUC/PWR ALL/VALS ALL/IDEOS...DECISION 20 NATO. PAGE 21 A0434 — BIBLIOG/A DIPLOM POLICY

B56
KNORR K.E.,RUBLE DIPLOMACY: CHALLENGE TO AMERICAN FOREIGN AID(PAMPHLET). CHINA/COM USA+45 USSR PLAN TEC/DEV CAP/ISM INT/TRADE DOMIN EDU/PROP CONTROL LEAD 20 COLD/WAR. PAGE 81 A1654 — ECO/UNDEV COM DIPLOM FOR/AID

B56
ROBERTS H.L.,RUSSIA AND AMERICA. CHINA/COM S/ASIA USSR FORCES TEC/DEV FOR/AID NUC/PWR ALL/IDEOS ...MAJORIT TREND NAT/COMP 20 COLD/WAR UN NATO. PAGE 122 A2494 — DIPLOM INT/ORG BAL/PWR TOTALISM

B56
SNELL J.L.,THE MEANING OF YALTA: BIG THREE DIPLOMACY AND THE NEW BALANCE OF POWER. EUR+WWI GERMANY USA-45 USSR FORCES PLAN BAL/PWR DIPLOM WAR CHOOSE PEACE...CHARTS BIBLIOG 20 UN CHINJAP ROOSEVLT/F. PAGE 134 A2749 — CONFER CHIEF POLICY PROB/SOLV

B56
VON HARPE W.,DIE SOWJETUNION FINNLAND UND SKANDANAVIEN, 1945-1955. EUR+WWI FINLAND GERMANY USSR WAR INGP/REL ORD/FREE SOVEREIGN MARXISM ...POLICY GOV/COMP BIBLIOG 20 STALIN/J. PAGE 160 A3252 — DIPLOM COM NEUTRAL BAL/PWR

B56
WILBUR C.M.,DOCUMENTS ON COMMUNISM, NATIONALISM, AND SOVIET ADVISERS IN CHINA, 1918-1927. CHINA/COM USSR STRUCT DIPLOM LEAD NAT/LISM...BIBLIOG/A 20. PAGE 164 A3343 — REV POL/PAR MARXISM COM

B56
WOLFF R.L.,THE BALKANS IN OUR TIME. ALBANIA FUT MOD/EUR USSR YUGOSLAVIA CULTURE INT/ORG SECT DIPLOM EDU/PROP COERCE WAR ORD/FREE...CHARTS 4/20 BALKANS COMINFORM. PAGE 166 A3388 — GEOG COM

B57
BEAL J.R.,JOHN FOSTER DULLES, A BIOGRAPHY. USA+45 USSR WOR+45 CONSTN INT/ORG NAT/G EX/STRUC LEGIT ADMIN NUC/PWR DISPL PERSON ORD/FREE PWR SKILL ...POLICY PSY OBS RECORD COLD/WAR UN 20 DULLES/JF. PAGE 12 A0237 — BIOG DIPLOM

B57
BROMBERGER M.,LES SECRETS DE L'EXPEDITION D'EGYPTE. FRANCE ISLAM UAR UK USA+45 USSR WOR+45 INT/ORG NAT/G FORCES BAL/PWR ECO/TAC DOMIN WAR NAT/LISM ATTIT PWR SOVEREIGN...MAJORIT TIME/SEQ CHARTS SUEZ COLD/WAR 20. PAGE 19 A0387 — COERCE DIPLOM

B57
BUCK P.W.,CONTOL OF FOREIGN RELATIONS IN MODERN NATIONS. FRANCE L/A+17C NETHERLAND USSR WOR+45 INT/ORG TOP/EX BAL/PWR DOMIN EDU/PROP COERCE PEACE ATTIT...CONCPT TREND 20 CMN/WLTH. PAGE 21 A0427 — NAT/G PWR DIPLOM

B57
FRASER L.,PROPAGANDA. GERMANY USSR WOR+45 WOR-45 NAT/G POL/PAR CONTROL FEEDBACK LOBBY CROWD WAR CONSEN NAT/LISM 20. PAGE 48 A0988 — EDU/PROP FASCISM MARXISM DIPLOM

B57
FREUND G.,UNHOLY ALLIANCE. EUR+WWI GERMANY USSR FORCES ECO/TAC CONTROL WAR PWR...TREND TREATY. PAGE 49 A0999 — DIPLOM PLAN POLICY

B57
KENNAN G.F.,RUSSIA, THE ATOM AND THE WEST. COM EUR+WWI FUT WOR+45 SOCIETY ECO/DEV FORCES DIPLOM ECO/TAC DOMIN EDU/PROP COERCE NUC/PWR ATTIT DRIVE ORD/FREE PWR...POLICY OBS TIME/SEQ TREND COLD/WAR NATO 20. PAGE 77 A1574 — NAT/G INT/ORG USSR

B57
REISS J.,GEORGE KENNANS POLITIK DER EINDAMMUNG. USSR NAT/G FORCES TOTALISM ATTIT ORD/FREE...POLICY 20 NATO TRUMAN/HS MARSHL/PLN KENNAN/G. PAGE 120 A2463 — DIPLOM DETER PEACE

B57
TOMASIC D.A.,NATIONAL COMMUNISM AND SOVIET STRATEGY. UK USSR YUGOSLAVIA NAT/G POL/PAR CHIEF CREATE DOMIN REV WAR PWR...BIOG TREND 20 TITO/MARSH STALIN/J. PAGE 144 A2948 — COM NAT/LISM MARXISM DIPLOM

B57
US SENATE SPEC COMM FOR AID,HEARINGS BEFORE THE SPECIAL COMMITTEE TO STUDY THE FOREIGN AID PROGRAM. USA+45 USSR ECO/UNDEV INT/ORG FORCES WEAPON TOTALISM ATTIT SUPEGO...NAT/COMP CONGRESS. PAGE 157 A3198 — FOR/AID DIPLOM ORD/FREE TEC/DEV

S57
ALLEN R.L.,"UNITED NATIONS TECHNICAL ASSISTANCE: SOVIET AND EAST-EUROPEAN PARTICIPATION." COM WOR+45 AGRI INDUS INT/ORG NAT/G FOR/AID SKILL UN 20. PAGE 6 A0124 — ECO/UNDEV TEC/DEV USSR

S57
SPEIER H.,"SOVIET ATOMIC BLACKMAIL AND THE NORTH ATLANTIC ALLIANCE." EUR+WWI USA+45 USSR INT/ORG NAT/G FORCES DIPLOM DRIVE ORD/FREE PWR NATO VAL/FREE COLD/WAR 20. PAGE 136 A2781 — COM COERCE NUC/PWR

C57
TANG P.S.H.,"COMMUNIST CHINA TODAY: DOMESTIC AND FOREIGN POLICIES." CHINA/COM COM S/ASIA USSR STRATA FORCES DIPLOM EDU/PROP COERCE GOV/REL...POLICY MAJORIT BIBLIOG 20. PAGE 141 A2886 — POL/PAR LEAD ADMIN CONSTN

B58
ANGELL N.,DEFENCE AND THE ENGLISH-SPEAKING ROLE. CHINA/COM UK USSR INT/ORG FORCES EDU/PROP NEUTRAL — DIPLOM WAR

NUC/PWR NAT/LISM PEACE TOTALISM 20 COLD/WAR COEXIST. PAGE 8 A0161 — MARXISM ORD/FREE

B58
BERLINER J.S.,SOVIET ECONOMIC AID: THE AID AND TRADE POLICY IN UNDERDEVELOPED COUNTRIES. AFR COM ISLAM L/A+17C S/ASIA USSR ECO/DEV DIST/IND FINAN MARKET INT/ORG ACT/RES PLAN BAL/PWR WEAPON PWR WEALTH...CHARTS 20. PAGE 14 A0277 — ECO/UNDEV ECO/TAC FOR/AID

B58
BOWLES C.,IDEAS, PEOPLE AND PEACE. ASIA CHINA/COM FUT INDIA USA+45 USSR ECO/UNDEV INT/ORG LEAD TASK MARXISM 20 NATO UN COLD/WAR. PAGE 18 A0359 — PEACE POLICY NAT/G DIPLOM

B58
GARTHOFF R.L.,SOVIET STRATEGY IN THE NUCLEAR AGE. FUT USSR R+D INT/ORG NAT/G ACT/RES TEC/DEV DOMIN DETER WAR ATTIT PWR...RELATIV METH/CNCPT SELF/OBS TREND CON/ANAL STERTYP GEN/LAWS 20. PAGE 51 A1052 — COM FORCES BAL/PWR NUC/PWR

B58
GAVIN J.M.,WAR AND PEACE IN THE SPACE AGE. SPACE USA+45 USSR FORCES PLAN TEC/DEV BAL/PWR DIPLOM ARMS/CONT WEAPON CIVMIL/REL...CHARTS GP/COMP 20 NATO COLD/WAR. PAGE 52 A1055 — WAR DETER NUC/PWR PEACE

B58
KENNAN G.F.,RUSSIA, THE ATOM AND THE WEST. USA+45 USSR INT/ORG ARMS/CONT MARXISM 20 NATO. PAGE 77 A1587 — BAL/PWR NUC/PWR CONTROL DIPLOM

B58
KENNAN G.F.,THE DECISION TO INTERVENE: SOVIET-AMERICAN RELATIONS, 1917-1920 (VOL. II). CZECHOSLVK EUR+WWI USA-45 USSR ELITES NAT/G FORCES PROB/SOLV REV WAR TOTALISM PWR...CHARTS BIBLIOG 20 TREATY PRESIDENT CHINJAP. PAGE 78 A1588 — DIPLOM POLICY ATTIT

B58
MARTIN L.J.,INTERNATIONAL PROPAGANDA: ITS LEGAL AND DIPLOMATIC CONTROL. UK USA+45 USSR CONSULT DELIB/GP DOMIN CONTROL 20. PAGE 95 A1951 — EDU/PROP DIPLOM INT/LAW ATTIT

B58
MASON H.L.,TOYNBEE'S APPROACH TO WORLD POLITICS. AFR USA+45 USSR LAW WAR NAT/LISM ALL/IDEOS...HUM BIBLIOG. PAGE 95 A1957 — DIPLOM CONCPT PHIL/SCI SECT

S58
DAVENPORT J.,"ARMS AND THE WELFARE STATE." INTELL STRUCT FORCES CREATE ECO/TAC FOR/AID DOMIN LEGIT ADMIN WAR ORD/FREE PWR...POLICY SOC CONCPT MYTH OBS TREND COLD/WAR TOT/POP 20. PAGE 34 A0685 — USA+45 NAT/G USSR

B59
AIR FORCE ACADEMY ASSEMBLY '59,INTERNATIONAL STABILITY AND PROGRESS (PAMPHLET). USA+45 USSR ECO/UNDEV PROB/SOLV BUDGET DIPLOM ADMIN DETER COST ATTIT...TREND 20. PAGE 5 A0103 — FOR/AID FORCES WAR PLAN

B59
ALLEN R.L.,SOVIET INFLUENCE IN LATIN AMERICA. ECO/UNDEV FINAN PROC/MFG NAT/G TEC/DEV EDU/PROP EXEC ROUTINE ATTIT DRIVE PERSON ALL/VALS PWR...STAT CHARTS WORK 20. PAGE 6 A0125 — L/A+17C ECO/TAC INT/TRADE USSR

B59
CHALUPA V.,RISE AND DEVELOPMENT OF A TOTALITARIAN STATE. CZECHOSLVK USSR STRUCT INT/ORG WORKER DIPLOM ECO/TAC COERCE NAT/LISM ATTIT...POLICY 20 COM/PARTY. PAGE 25 A0516 — TOTALISM MARXISM REV POL/PAR

B59
CORBETT P.E.,LAW IN DIPLOMACY. UK USA+45 USSR CONSTN SOCIETY INT/ORG JUDGE LEGIT ATTIT ORD/FREE TOT/POP LEAGUE/NAT 20. PAGE 30 A0616 — NAT/G ADJUD JURID DIPLOM

B59
COUDENHOVE-KALERGI,FROM WAR TO PEACE. USA+45 USSR WOR+45 WOR-45 LAW INT/ORG NAT/G LEGIT COERCE LOVE ...POLICY PLURIST METH/CNCPT STERTYP TOT/POP UN 20 NATO. PAGE 31 A0636 — FUT ORD/FREE

B59
DAWSON R.H.,THE DECISION TO AID RUSSIA* FOREIGN POLICY AND DOMESTIC POLITICS. GERMANY USSR CHIEF EX/STRUC LEGIS TOP/EX PROB/SOLV WAR ATTIT...POLICY CONGRESS. PAGE 34 A0695 — DECISION DELIB/GP DIPLOM FOR/AID

B59
DEHIO L.,GERMANY AND WORLD POLITICS IN THE TWENTIETH CENTURY. EUR+WWI FRANCE GERMANY MOD/EUR UK USSR NAT/G CHIEF BAL/PWR DOMIN COLONIAL CONTROL LEAD...IDEA/COMP 20 VERSAILLES. PAGE 36 A0724 — DIPLOM WAR NAT/LISM SOVEREIGN

B59
EMME E.M.,THE IMPACT OF AIR POWER - NATIONAL SECURITY AND WORLD POLITICS. USA+45 USSR FORCES DIPLOM WEAPON PEACE TOTALISM...POLICY NAT/COMP 20 EUROPE. PAGE 42 A0850 — DETER AIR WAR ORD/FREE

B59
ETSCHMANN R.,DIE WAHRUNGS- UND DEVISENPOLITIK DES OSTBLOCKS UND IHRE AUSWIRKUNGEN AUF DIE WIRTSCHAFTSBEZIEHUNGEN ZWISCHEN OST U WEST. BULGARIA CZECHOSLVK HUNGARY POLAND USSR MARKET NAT/G PLAN DIPLOM...NAT/COMP 20. PAGE 42 A0867 — ECO/TAC FINAN POLICY INT/TRADE

B59
GOLDWIN R.A.,READINGS IN RUSSIAN FOREIGN POLICY. HUNGARY USSR YUGOSLAVIA ELITES INT/ORG NAT/G REV WAR NAT/LISM PERSON SOCISM...CHARTS 20 MAPS BOLSHEVISM. PAGE 53 A1095 — COM MARXISM DIPLOM POLICY

B59
HARRIMAN A.,PEACE WITH RUSSIA? USA+45 USSR SOCIETY ECO/TAC CONTROL TOTALISM ATTIT MARXISM...POLICY 20 STALIN/J KHRUSH/N. PAGE 62 A1266 — DIPLOM PEACE NAT/G TASK

B59
KULSKI W.W.,PEACEFUL CO-EXISTENCE: AN ANALYSIS OF SOVIET FOREIGN POLICY. WOR+45 INTELL SOCIETY ECO/UNDEV POL/PAR EDU/PROP COERCE DRIVE RIGID/FLEX PWR SKILL...PSY CONCPT HIST/WRIT CON/ANAL GEN/METH WORK VAL/FREE 20. PAGE 83 A1691 — PLAN DIPLOM USSR

B59
LAQUER W.Z.,THE SOVIET UNION AND THE MIDDLE EAST. COM UAR USSR ECO/UNDEV NAT/G VOL/ASSN ECO/TAC EDU/PROP COLONIAL EXEC PWR...TIME/SEQ TREND COLD/WAR 20. PAGE 85 A1730 — ISLAM DRIVE FOR/AID NAT/LISM

B59
MODELSKI G.,ATOMIC ENERGY IN THE COMMUNIST BLOC. FUT INT/ORG CONSULT FORCES ACT/RES PLAN KNOWL SKILL ...PHIL/SCI STAT CHARTS 20. PAGE 102 A2096 — TEC/DEV NUC/PWR USSR COM

B59
NOVE A.,COMMUNIST ECONOMIC STRATEGY: SOVIET GROWTH AND CAPABILITIES. USSR AGRI LABOR PLAN TEC/DEV CAP/ISM INT/TRADE EFFICIENCY MARXISM 20 THIRD/WRLD. PAGE 110 A2257 — FOR/AID ECO/TAC DIPLOM INDUS

B59
OKINSHEVICH L.A.,LATIN AMERICA IN SOVIET WRITINGS, 1945-1958: A BIBLIOGRAPHY. USSR LAW ECO/UNDEV LABOR DIPLOM EDU/PROP REV...GEOG SOC 20. PAGE 111 A2287 — BIBLIOG WRITING COM L/A+17C

B59
PEARSON L.B.,DIPLOMACY IN THE NUCLEAR AGE. USA+45 USSR INT/ORG PWR...TREND 20 NATO UN. PAGE 114 A2343 — NUC/PWR PEACE POLICY DIPLOM

B59
PO414COLUMBIA BUR OF APP SOC R,ATTITUDES OF PROMINENT AMERICANS TOWARD "WORLD PEACE THROUGH WORLD LAW" (SUPRA-NATL ORGANIZATION FOR WAR PREVENTION). USA+45 USSR ELITES FORCES PLAN PROB/SOLV CONTROL WAR PWR...POLICY SOC QU IDEA/COMP 20 UN. PAGE 117 A2403 — ATTIT ACT/RES INT/LAW STAT

B59
STERNBERG F.,THE MILITARY AND INDUSTRIAL REVOLUTION OF OUR TIME. USA+45 USSR WOR+45 WORKER COMPUTER PLAN TEC/DEV NUC/PWR GP/REL...POLICY NAT/COMP 20. PAGE 138 A2818 — DIPLOM FORCES INDUS CIVMIL/REL

B59
STRAUSZ-HUPE R.,PROTRACTED CONFLICT. CHINA/COM KOREA WOR+45 INT/ORG FORCES ACT/RES ECO/TAC LEGIT COERCE DRIVE PERCEPT KNOWL PWR...PSY CONCPT RECORD GEN/METH COLD/WAR VAL/FREE 20. PAGE 139 A2847 — COM PLAN USSR

B59
VINACKE H.M.,A HISTORY OF THE FAR EAST IN MODERN TIMES (6TH ED.). KOREA S/ASIA USSR CONSTN CULTURE STRATA ECO/UNDEV NAT/G CHIEF FOR/AID INT/TRADE GP/REL...SOC NAT/COMP 19/20 CHINJAP. PAGE 159 A3235 — STRUCT ASIA

B59
YRARRAZAVAL E.,AMERICA LATINE EN LA GUERRA FRIA. EUR+WWI L/A+17C USA+45 USSR WOR+45 INDUS INT/ORG NAT/LISM...POLICY COLD/WAR. PAGE 169 A3439 — REGION DIPLOM ECO/UNDEV INT/TRADE

S59
BROMKE A.,"DISENGAGEMENT IN EAST EUROPE." COM USSR INT/ORG DIPLOM EDU/PROP NEUTRAL NUC/PWR DRIVE RIGID/FLEX PWR...PSY CONCPT CON/ANAL GEN/METH VAL/FREE 20. PAGE 19 A0388 — BAL/PWR

S59
FISCHER L.,"THE SOVIET-AMERICAN ANTAGONISM: HOW WILL IT END." CONSTN CULTURE PLAN TEC/DEV RIGID/FLEX SUPEGO ORD/FREE...MARXIST DECISION PSY CONCPT CON/ANAL GEN/LAWS VAL/FREE 20 COLD/WAR. PAGE 46 A0936 — USA+45 PWR DIPLOM USSR

S59
HARTT J.,"ANTARCTICA: ITS IMMEDIATE PRACTICALITIES." FUT USA+45 USSR WOR+45 INT/ORG NAT/G CREATE TEC/DEV REGION KNOWL WEALTH...GEOG 20 ANTARTICA. PAGE 62 A1276 — VOL/ASSN ORD/FREE DIPLOM

S59
KISSINGER H.A.,"THE SEARCH FOR STABILITY." COM GERMANY MOD/EUR USA+45 USA-45 USSR INT/ORG ARMS/CONT NUC/PWR ORD/FREE PWR COLD/WAR 20 NATO. PAGE 80 A1641 — FUT ATTIT BAL/PWR

S59
REUBENS E.D.,"THE BASIS FOR REORIENATION OF AMERICAN FOREIGN AID POLICY." USA+45 USSR STRUCT INT/ORG CONSULT ECO/TAC ADMIN DRIVE MORAL ORD/FREE PWR WEALTH...RELATIV MATH STAT TREND GEN/LAWS VAL/FREE 20. PAGE 120 A2467 — ECO/UNDEV PLAN FOR/AID DIPLOM

S59
SAYEGH F.,"ARAB NATIONALISM AND SOVIET-AMERICAN RELATIONS." ISLAM USA+45 ECO/UNDEV PLAN ECO/TAC LEGIT NAT/LISM DRIVE PERCEPT KNOWL PWR...DECISION CONCPT STAT RECORD TREND CON/ANAL VAL/FREE 20 COLD/WAR. PAGE 127 A2610
DIPLOM USSR

S59
ZAUBERMAN A.,"SOVIET BLOC ECONOMIC INTEGRATION." COM CULTURE INTELL ECO/DEV INDUS TOP/EX ACT/RES PLAN ECO/TAC INT/TRADE ROUTINE CHOOSE ATTIT ...TIME/SEQ 20. PAGE 169 A3448
MARKET INT/ORG USSR TOTALISM

C59
KULSKI W.W.,"PEACEFUL COEXISTENCE." USSR ECO/UNDEV INT/ORG POL/PAR EDU/PROP COLONIAL CONTROL REV NAT/LISM PEACE PWR MARXISM...BIBLIOG 20. PAGE 83 A1692
COM DIPLOM DOMIN

N59
US HOUSE COMM FOREIGN AFFAIRS,HEARINGS ON DRAFT LEGISLATION TO AMEND FURTHER THE MUTUAL SECURITY ACT OF 1954 (PAMPHLET). USA+45 USSR CONSULT DELIB/GP FORCES ECO/TAC CONFER...POLICY 20 CONGRESS. PAGE 153 A3126
DIPLOM FOR/AID ORD/FREE LEGIS

B60
ALLEN R.L.,SOVIET ECONOMIC WARFARE. USSR FINAN INDUS NAT/G PLAN TEC/DEV FOR/AID DETER WEALTH ...TREND GEN/LAWS 20. PAGE 6 A0126
COM ECO/TAC

B60
BARNET R.,WHO WANTS DISARMAMENT. COM EUR+WWI USA+45 USSR INT/ORG NAT/G BAL/PWR DIPLOM EDU/PROP COERCE DETER NUC/PWR WAR WEAPON ATTIT PWR...TIME/SEQ COLD/WAR CONGRESS 20. PAGE 11 A0225
PLAN FORCES ARMS/CONT

B60
BILLERBECK K.,SOVIET BLOC FOREIGN AID TO UNDERDEVELOPED COUNTRIES. COM FUT USSR FINAN FORCES TEC/DEV DIPLOM INT/TRADE EDU/PROP NUC/PWR...TREND 20. PAGE 14 A0287
FOR/AID ECO/UNDEV ECO/TAC MARXISM

B60
CAMPAIGNE J.G.,AMERICAN MIGHT AND SOVIET MYTH. COM EUR+WWI ECO/DEV ECO/UNDEV INT/ORG NAT/G CAP/ISM ECO/TAC FOR/AID EDU/PROP ATTIT PWR WEALTH...POLICY CONCPT MYTH TREND STERTYP GEN/LAWS COLD/WAR. PAGE 23 A0473
USA+45 DOMIN DIPLOM USSR

B60
CENTRAL ASIAN RESEARCH CENTRE,RUSSIA LOOKS AT AFRICA (PAMPHLET). AFR USSR COLONIAL RACE/REL...HUM 19/20 STALIN/J. PAGE 25 A0511
BIBLIOG MARXISM TREND DIPLOM

B60
DEUTSCHER I.,THE GREAT CONTEST: RUSSIA AND THE WEST. USA+45 USSR SOCIETY INDUS ARMS/CONT ATTIT ...CONCPT IDEA/COMP 20 COLD/WAR. PAGE 37 A0749
PEACE DIPLOM PWR

B60
ENGEL J.,THE SECURITY OF THE FREE WORLD. USSR WOR+45 STRATA STRUCT ECO/DEV ECO/UNDEV INT/ORG DELIB/GP FORCES DOMIN LEGIT ADJUD EXEC ARMS/CONT COERCE...POLICY CONCPT NEW/IDEA TIME/SEQ GEN/LAWS COLD/WAR WORK UN 20 NATO. PAGE 42 A0851
COM TREND DIPLOM

B60
FISCHER L.,RUSSIA, AMERICA, AND THE WORLD. FUT USA+45 USSR WOR+45 FORCES PLAN BAL/PWR ECO/TAC FOR/AID NEUTRAL TASK NUC/PWR PWR 20 COLD/WAR. PAGE 46 A0937
DIPLOM POLICY MARXISM ECO/UNDEV

B60
FISCHER L.,THE SOVIETS IN WORLD AFFAIRS. CHINA/COM COM EUR+WWI USSR INT/ORG CONFER LEAD ARMS/CONT REV PWR...CHARTS 20 TREATY VERSAILLES. PAGE 46 A0938
DIPLOM NAT/G POLICY MARXISM

B60
FRANCK P.G.,AFGHANISTAN: BETWEEN EAST AND WEST. AFGHANISTN USA+45 USSR ECO/UNDEV PLAN ADMIN ROUTINE ATTIT PWR...STAT OBS CHARTS TOT/POP COLD/WAR 20. PAGE 48 A0978
ECO/TAC TREND FOR/AID

B60
KENNAN G.F.,RUSSIA AND THE WEST. ASIA COM EUR+WWI GERMANY UK USA+45 USA-45 USSR INT/ORG NAT/G VOL/ASSN DOMIN REV WAR PWR...TIME/SEQ 20. PAGE 78 A1590
EXEC DIPLOM

B60
KHRUSHCHEV N.,FOR VICTORY IN PEACEFUL COMPETITION WITH CAPITALISM. COM FUT USSR WOR+45 CONSTN SOCIETY INDUS INT/ORG DELIB/GP PLAN BAL/PWR DIPLOM PERSON MARXISM...MARXIST WORK 20 COLD/WAR. PAGE 79 A1611
TOP/EX PWR CAP/ISM SOCISM

B60
KHRUSHCHEV N.S.,KHRUSHCHEV IN NEW YORK. USA+45 USSR ATTIT...ANTHOL 20 UN KHRUSH/N. PAGE 79 A1612
DIPLOM PEACE ARMS/CONT

B60
KHRUSHCHEV N.S.,KHRUSHCHEV IN AMERICA. USA+45 USSR INT/TRADE EDU/PROP PRESS PEACE...MARXIST RECORD INT 20 COLD/WAR KHRUSH/N. PAGE 79 A1613
MARXISM CHIEF DIPLOM

B60
MOSELY P.E.,THE KREMLIN AND WORLD POLITICS. EUR+WWI GERMANY USA+45 USSR CHIEF TOP/EX BAL/PWR DOMIN PEACE PWR...METH 20 COLD/WAR STALIN/J EUROPE/E. PAGE 105 A2151
COM DIPLOM POLICY WAR

B60
MOUSKHELY M.,L'URSS ET LES PAYS DE L'EST. ASIA COM S/ASIA USSR PRESS...SOC 20. PAGE 105 A2156
BIBLIOG/A DIPLOM ATTIT

B60
SCHLESINGER J.R.,THE POLITICAL ECONOMY OF NATIONAL SECURITY. USA+45 USSR WOR+45 ECO/DEV ECO/UNDEV NAT/G DELIB/GP TOP/EX BAL/PWR DIPLOM INT/TRADE ATTIT PWR...STERTYP TOT/POP 20. PAGE 128 A2628
PLAN ECO/TAC

B60
SETON-WATSON H.,NEITHER WAR NOR PEACE. ASIA USSR WOR+45 ELITES INT/ORG NAT/G EX/STRUC FORCES BAL/PWR ECO/TAC EDU/PROP COERCE NAT/LISM ORD/FREE WEALTH TOT/POP 20. PAGE 131 A2688
ATTIT PWR DIPLOM TOTALISM

B60
SOBEL R.,THE ORIGINS OF INTERVENTIONISM: THE UNITED STATES AND THE RUSSO-FINNISH WAR. FINLAND USA-45 USSR LEGIS ATTIT RIGID/FLEX...BIBLIOG 20 INTERVENT. PAGE 135 A2755
DIPLOM WAR PROB/SOLV NEUTRAL

B60
SPEER J.P.,FOR WHAT PURPOSE? CHINA/COM USSR CONSTN PROB/SOLV DIPLOM CONTROL TASK WAR NAT/LISM WORSHIP 20 UN. PAGE 136 A2778
PEACE SECT SUPEGO ALL/IDEOS

B60
SPEIER H.,DIVIDED BERLIN: THE ANATOMY OF SOVIET POLITICAL BLACKMAIL. COM GERMANY USA+45 USSR WOR+45 NAT/G TOP/EX DOMIN EDU/PROP ALL/VALS...POLICY CONCPT COLD/WAR 20 U-2. PAGE 136 A2782
INT/ORG ACT/RES DIPLOM

B60
TAYLOR M.D.,THE UNCERTAIN TRUMPET. USA+45 USSR WOR+45 INT/ORG NAT/G CONSULT DOMIN COERCE NUC/PWR WAR ATTIT ORD/FREE PWR...POLICY CONCPT TREND GEN/METH COLD/WAR UN NATO 20. PAGE 142 A2900
PLAN FORCES DIPLOM

L60
BRENNAN D.G.,"SETTING AND GOALS OF ARMS CONTROL." FUT USA+45 USSR WOR+45 INTELL INT/ORG NAT/G VOL/ASSN CONSULT PLAN DIPLOM ECO/TAC ADMIN KNOWL PWR...POLICY CONCPT TREND COLD/WAR 20. PAGE 18 A0371
FORCES COERCE ARMS/CONT DETER

L60
DEAN A.W.,"SECOND GENEVA CONFERENCE OF THE LAW OF THE SEA: THE FIGHT FOR FREEDOM OF THE SEAS." FUT USA+45 USSR WOR+45 WOR-45 SEA CONSTN STRUCT PLAN INT/TRADE ADJUD ADMIN ORD/FREE...DECISION RECORD TREND GEN/LAWS 20 TREATY. PAGE 35 A0717
INT/ORG JURID INT/LAW

L60
FERNBACH A.P.,"SOVIET COEXISTENCE STRATEGY." WOR+45 PROF/ORG VOL/ASSN DIPLOM DOMIN EDU/PROP ATTIT DRIVE PERSON PWR SKILL WEALTH...POLICY OBS SAMP TREND STERTYP ILO WORK COLD/WAR 420. PAGE 45 A0919
LABOR INT/ORG USSR

L60
JACOB P.E.,"THE DISARMAMENT CONSENSUS." USA+45 USSR WOR+45 INT/ORG NAT/G ACT/RES TEC/DEV BAL/PWR EDU/PROP ADMIN COERCE DETER NUC/PWR CONSEN RIGID/FLEX PWR...CONCPT RECORD CHARTS COLD/WAR 20. PAGE 72 A1482
DELIB/GP ATTIT ARMS/CONT

S60
DOUGHERTY J.E.,"KEY TO SECURITY: DISARMAMENT OR ARMS STABILITY." COM USA+45 USSR INT/ORG NAT/G CREATE EDU/PROP COERCE DETER ATTIT PWR...DECISION CONCPT MYTH NEW/IDEA TREND 20 COLD/WAR. PAGE 38 A0777
FORCES ORD/FREE ARMS/CONT NUC/PWR

S60
GOODMAN E.,"THE CRY OF NATIONAL LIBERATION: RECENT SOVIET ATTITUDES TOWARDS NATIONAL SELF-DETERMINATION." COM INT/ORG LEGIS ROUTINE PWR ...TIME/SEQ CON/ANAL STERTYP GEN/LAWS 20 UN. PAGE 54 A1101
ATTIT EDU/PROP SOVEREIGN USSR

S60
GRACIA-MORA M.R.,"INTERNATIONAL RESPONSIBILITY FOR SUBVERSIVE ACTIVITIES AND HOSTILE PROPAGANDA BY PRIVATE PERSONS AGAINST." COM EUR+WWI L/A+17C UK USA+45 USSR WOR-45 CONSTN NAT/G LEGIT ADJUD REV PEACE TOTALISM ORD/FREE...INT/LAW 20. PAGE 55 A1119
INT/ORG JURID SOVEREIGN

S60
JACOBSON H.K.,"THE USSR AND ILO." COM STRUCT ECO/DEV ECO/UNDEV CONSULT DELIB/GP ECO/TAC ILO WORK COLD/WAR 20. PAGE 72 A1484
INT/ORG LABOR USSR

S60
KENNAN G.F.,"PEACEFUL CO-EXISTENCE: A WESTERN VIEW." COM EUR+WWI USA+45 USSR WOR+45 PLAN BAL/PWR DIPLOM INT/TRADE PWR...POLICY CONCPT OBS HIST/WRIT TREND GEN/LAWS COLD/WAR 20 KHRUSH/N. PAGE 78 A1589
ATTIT COERCE

S60
MIKESELL R.F.,"AMERICA'S ECONOMIC RESPONSIBILITY AS A GREAT POWER." COM FUT USA+45 USSR WOR+45 INT/ORG PLAN ECO/TAC FOR/AID EDU/PROP CHOOSE WEALTH ...POLICY 20. PAGE 101 A2069
ECO/UNDEV BAL/PWR CAP/ISM

S60
OWEN C.F.,"US AND SOVIET RELATIONS WITH UNDERDEVELOPED COUNTRIES: LATIN AMERICA-A CASE STUDY." AFR COM L/A+17C USA+45 USSR EXTR/IND MARKET TEC/DEV DIPLOM ECO/TAC NAT/LISM ORD/FREE PWR ...TREND WORK 20. PAGE 112 A2303
ECO/UNDEV DRIVE INT/TRADE

S60
PYE L.W.,"SOVIET AND AMERICAN STYLES IN FOREIGN AID." COM USA+45 USSR WOR+45 NAT/G PLAN ECO/TAC ROUTINE RIGID/FLEX...POLICY CONCPT TREND GEN/LAWS TOT/POP 20. PAGE 118 A2419
ECO/UNDEV ATTIT FOR/AID

S60
WRIGHT Q.,"LEGAL ASPECTS OF THE U-2 INCIDENT." COM USA+45 USSR STRUCT NAT/G FORCES PLAN TEC/DEV ADJUD RIGID/FLEX MORAL ORD/FREE...DECISION INT/LAW JURID PSY TREND GEN/LAWS COLD/WAR VAL/FREE 20 U-2. PAGE 168 A3413
PWR POLICY SPACE

C60
FITZSIMMONS T.,"USSR: ITS PEOPLE, ITS SOCIETY, ITS CULTURE." USSR FAM SECT DIPLOM EDU/PROP ADMIN RACE/REL ATTIT...POLICY CHARTS BIBLIOG 20. PAGE 46 A0944
CULTURE STRUCT SOCIETY COM

C60
HAZARD J.N.,"THE SOVIET SYSTEM OF GOVERNMENT." USSR SOCIETY INDUS NAT/G POL/PAR DIPLOM CT/SYS...JURID CHARTS BIBLIOG/A 20. PAGE 63 A1298
COM NAT/COMP STRUCT ADMIN

B61
AMORY J.F.,AROUND THE EDGE OF WAR: A NEW APPROACH TO THE PROBLEMS OF AMERICAN FOREIGN POLICY. COM L/A+17C USA+45 USSR FOR/AID EDU/PROP AGREE CONTROL ARMS/CONT NUC/PWR WAR PWR...IDEA/COMP 20 TREATY ESPIONAGE. PAGE 8 A0154
NAT/G DIPLOM POLICY

B61
AUBREY H.G.,COEXISTENCE: ECONOMIC CHALLENGE AND RESPONSE. USSR WOR+45 ACT/RES BAL/PWR CAP/ISM DIPLOM ECO/TAC FOR/AID INT/TRADE PEACE SOCISM ...METH/COMP NAT/COMP COLD/WAR. PAGE 10 A0196
POLICY ECO/UNDEV PLAN COM

B61
BECHHOEFER B.G.,POSTWAR NEGOTIATIONS FOR ARMS CONTROL. COM EUR+WWI USSR INT/ORG NAT/G ACT/RES BAL/PWR DIPLOM ECO/TAC EDU/PROP ADMIN REGION DETER NUC/PWR WAR WEAPON PEACE ATTIT PWR...POLICY TIME/SEQ COLD/WAR CONGRESS 20. PAGE 12 A0244
USA+45 ARMS/CONT

B61
DALLIN D.J.,SOVIET FOREIGN POLICY AFTER STALIN. ASIA CHINA/COM EUR+WWI GERMANY IRAN UK YUGOSLAVIA INT/ORG NAT/G VOL/ASSN FORCES TOP/EX BAL/PWR DOMIN EDU/PROP COERCE ATTIT PWR 20. PAGE 33 A0679
COM DIPLOM USSR

B61
EISENHOWER D.D.,PEACE WITH JUSTICE: SELECTED ADDRESSES. USSR PARTIC ARMS/CONT MORAL...TRADIT CONCPT GEN/LAWS ANTHOL 20 PRESIDENT COLD/WAR. PAGE 41 A0832
PEACE DIPLOM EDU/PROP POLICY

B61
FLEMING D.F.,THE COLD WAR AND ITS ORIGINS: 1917-1950 (VOL. I). ASIA USSR WOR+45 WOR-45 TEC/DEV FOR/AID NUC/PWR REV WAR PEACE FASCISM...T 20 COLD/WAR NATO BERLIN/BLO. PAGE 46 A0947
DIPLOM MARXISM BAL/PWR

B61
HARDT J.P.,THE COLD WAR ECONOMIC GAP. USA+45 USSR ECO/DEV FORCES INT/TRADE NUC/PWR PWR 20 COLD/WAR. PAGE 61 A1258
DIPLOM ECO/TAC NAT/COMP POLICY

B61
HAYTER W.,THE DIPLOMACY OF THE GREAT POWERS. FRANCE UK USSR WOR+45 EX/STRUC TOP/EX NUC/PWR PEACE...OBS 20. PAGE 63 A1296
DIPLOM POLICY NAT/G

B61
HENKIN L.,ARMS CONTROL: ISSUES FOR THE PUBLIC. EUR+WWI FUT USA+45 USSR INT/ORG NAT/G DIPLOM EDU/PROP DETER NUC/PWR ATTIT PWR...CONCPT RECORD HIST/WRIT TIME/SEQ TOT/POP COLD/WAR 20. PAGE 64 A1316
WOR+45 DELIB/GP ARMS/CONT

B61
HOLDSWORTH M.,SOVIET AFRICAN STUDIES 1918-1959. USSR ACADEM NAT/G DIPLOM REGION KNOWL 20. PAGE 66 A1366
BIBLIOG/A AFR HABITAT NAT/COMP

B61
HUDSON G.F.,THE SINO-SOVIET DISPUTE. CHINA/COM USSR INTELL INT/TRADE DEBATE REV...IDEA/COMP 20. PAGE 68 A1404
DIPLOM MARXISM PRESS ATTIT

B61
JAKOBSON M.,THE DIPLOMACY OF THE WINTER WAR. EUR+WWI FINLAND GERMANY USSR INT/ORG NAT/G PEACE TOTALISM PWR...POLICY CONCPT 20 TREATY. PAGE 73 A1492
WAR ORD/FREE DIPLOM

B61
LERCHE C.O. JR.,FOREIGN POLICY OF THE AMERICAN PEOPLE (REV. ED.). USA+45 USSR FORCES TEC/DEV EDU/PROP WAR PRODUC ORD/FREE MARXISM...POLICY TREND BIBLIOG 20 COLD/WAR. PAGE 87 A1781
DECISION PLAN PEACE DIPLOM

B61
LIPPMANN W.,THE COMING TESTS WITH RUSSIA. COM CUBA GERMANY USSR FORCES CONTROL NEUTRAL COERCE NUC/PWR REV WAR PWR...INT 20 KHRUSH/N BERLIN. PAGE 89 A1830
BAL/PWR DIPLOM MARXISM ARMS/CONT

B61
LUKACS J.,A HISTORY OF THE COLD WAR. ASIA COM EUR+WWI USA+45 USA-45 INT/ORG NAT/G DELIB/GP ACT/RES BAL/PWR DIPLOM DOMIN EDU/PROP LEGIT DRIVE ORD/FREE...TREND COLD/WAR 20. PAGE 91 A1872
PWR TIME/SEQ USSR

B61
MENDEL D.H. JR.,THE JAPANESE PEOPLE AND FOREIGN POLICY. CHINA/COM KOREA USA+45 USSR SOCIETY FORCES CHOOSE 20 CHINJAP. PAGE 99 A2037
NAT/G DIPLOM POLICY ATTIT

B61
NOLLAU G.,INTERNATIONAL COMMUNISM AND WORLD REVOLUTION: HISTORY AND METHODS. RUSSIA USSR INT/ORG NAT/G POL/PAR VOL/ASSN FORCES BAL/PWR DIPLOM EXEC REGION WAR ATTIT PWR MARXISM...CONCPT TIME/SEQ COLD/WAR 19/20. PAGE 102 A2100
COM REV

B61
MORLEY L.,THE PATCHWORK HISTORY OF FOREIGN AID. KOREA/S USA+45 USSR LAW FINAN INT/ORG TEC/DEV BAL/PWR GIVE 20 COLD/WAR NATO. PAGE 104 A2144
FOR/AID ECO/UNDEV FORCES DIPLOM

B61
NEAL F.W.,US FOREIGN POLICY AND THE SOVIET UNION. USA+45 USSR INT/ORG ECO/TAC ARMS/CONT MAJORITY NAT/LISM ATTIT RESPECT MARXISM 20. PAGE 108 A2207
DIPLOM POLICY PEACE

B61
NOGEE J.L.,SOVIET POLICY TOWARD INTERNATIONAL CONTROL OF ATOMIC ENERGY. COM USA+45 WOR+45 INTELL NAT/G ACT/RES DIPLOM EDU/PROP NUC/PWR TOTALISM PERCEPT KNOWL PWR...TIME/SEQ COLD/WAR 20. PAGE 109 A2247
INT/ORG ATTIT ARMS/CONT USSR

B61
OAKES J.B.,THE EDGE OF FREEDOM. EUR+WWI USA+45 USSR ECO/UNDEV BAL/PWR DIPLOM DOMIN COLONIAL PWR MARXISM POPULISM...IDEA/COMP 20 COLD/WAR. PAGE 111 A2271
AFR ORD/FREE SOVEREIGN NEUTRAL

B61
OVERSTREET H.,THE WAR CALLED PEACE. USSR WOR+45 COM/IND INT/ORG POL/PAR BAL/PWR EDU/PROP PEACE ATTIT...CONCPT 20 KHRUSH/N. PAGE 112 A2302
DIPLOM COM POLICY LEAD

B61
RICE G.W.,THE SOVIET POSITION ON DEPENDENT TERRITORIES IN THE UNITED NATIONS (THESIS, OHIO STATE UNIVERSITY). USSR PLAN SOVEREIGN...POLICY 20 UN. PAGE 121 A2473
INT/ORG COM DIPLOM COLONIAL

B61
SCHIEDER T.,DOCUMENTS ON THE EXPULSION OF THE GERMANS FROM EASTERN-CENTRAL-EUROPE (VOL. II/III). COM EUR+WWI GERMANY HUNGARY ROMANIA USSR DIPLOM RACE/REL 20 MIGRATION. PAGE 128 A2625
GEOG CULTURE

B61
SCHMIDT H.,VERTEIDIGUNG ODER VERGELTUNG. COM CUBA GERMANY/W USSR FORCES DIPLOM ARMS/CONT DETER NUC/PWR...POLICY CHARTS HYPO/EXP SIMUL BIBLIOG 20 NATO COLD/WAR. PAGE 128 A2630
PLAN WAR BAL/PWR ORD/FREE

B61
SCHONBRUNN G.,WELTKRIEGE UND REVOLUTIONEN 1914-1945. USSR DIPLOM TOTALISM ORD/FREE 20 TREATY WWI NAZI. PAGE 129 A2643
WAR REV FASCISM SOCISM

B61
SOKOL A.E.,SEAPOWER IN THE NUCLEAR AGE. USA+45 USSR DIST/IND FORCES INT/TRADE DETER WAR...POLICY NAT/COMP BIBLIOG COLD/WAR. PAGE 135 A2763
SEA PWR WEAPON NUC/PWR

B61
US LIBRARY OF CONGRESS,WORLD COMMUNIST MOVEMENT. USA+45 USSR WOR+45 INT/ORG DIPLOM REV ATTIT 19/20. PAGE 155 A3155
BIBLIOG/A EDU/PROP MARXISM POL/PAR

L61
HILSMAN R. JR.,"THE NEW COMMUNIST TACTIC: PRECIS-INTERNAL WAR." COM FUT USA+45 ECO/UNDEV POL/PAR FOR/AID RIGID/FLEX ALL/VALS...TREND COLD/WAR 20. PAGE 65 A1334
FORCES COERCE USSR GUERRILLA

S61
BARNET R.,"RUSSIA, CHINA, AND THE WORLD: THE SOVIET ATTITUDE ON DISARMAMENT (PART 3)." ASIA CHINA/COM FUT INT/ORG NAT/G POL/PAR VOL/ASSN ARMS/CONT ATTIT ...POLICY CONCPT TIME/SEQ TREND TOT/POP VAL/FREE 20. PAGE 11 A0226
COM PLAN TOTALISM USSR

S61
BRZEZINSKI Z.K.,"THE ORGANIZATION OF THE COMMUNIST CAMP." COM CZECHOSLVK COM/IND NAT/G DELIB/GP INT/TRADE DOMIN EDU/PROP EXEC ROUTINE COERCE ATTIT PWR...MGT CONCPT TIME/SEQ CHARTS VAL/FREE 20 TREATY. PAGE 20 A0416
VOL/ASSN DIPLOM USSR

S61
DANIELS R.V.,"THE CHINESE REVOLUTION IN RUSSIAN PERSPECTIVE." ASIA CHINA/COM COM USSR INTELL INT/ORG TOP/EX REV TOTALISM PWR...POLICY WORK VAL/FREE 20. PAGE 33 A0680
POL/PAR PLAN

S61
JUVILER P.H.,"INTERPARLIAMENTARY CONTACTS IN SOVIET FOREIGN POLICY." COM FUT WOR+45 WOR-45 SOCIETY CONSULT ACT/RES DIPLOM ADMIN PEACE ATTIT RIGID/FLEX WEALTH...WELF/ST SOC TOT/POP CONGRESS 19/20. PAGE 75 A1543
INT/ORG DELIB/GP USSR

S61
KRANNHALS H.V.,"COMMAND INTEGRATION WITHIN THE WARSAW PACT." COM USSR WOR+45 DELIB/GP EDU/PROP ...CONCPT AUD/VIS CHARTS COLD/WAR TOT/POP VAL/FREE 20 TREATY WARSAW/P. PAGE 82 A1675 — INT/ORG FORCES TOTALISM

S61
LIPSON L.,"AN ARGUMENT ON THE LEGALITY OF RECONNAISSANCE STATELLITES." COM USA+45 USSR WOR+45 AIR INTELL NAT/G CONSULT PLAN DIPLOM LEGIT ROUTINE ATTIT...INT/LAW JURID CONCPT METH/CNCPT TREND COLD/WAR 20. PAGE 90 A1833 — INT/ORG LAW SPACE

S61
NOVE A.,"THE SOVIET MODEL AND UNDERDEVELOPED COUNTRIES." COM FUT USSR WOR+45 CULTURE ECO/DEV POL/PAR FOR/AID EDU/PROP ADMIN MORAL WEALTH ...POLICY RECORD HIST/WRIT 20. PAGE 110 A2258 — ECO/UNDEV PLAN

S61
TUCKER R.C.,"TOWARDS A COMPARATIVE POLITICS OF MOVEMENT-REGIMES" (BMR)" USSR CONSTN NAT/G CREATE PROB/SOLV DIPLOM DOMIN REV...GP/COMP IDEA/COMP METH 20 STALIN/J BOLSHEVISM. PAGE 145 A2971 — MARXISM POLICY GEN/LAWS PWR

S61
WHELAN J.G.,"KHRUSHCHEV AND THE BALANCE OF WORLD POWER." FUT WOR+45 INT/ORG VOL/ASSN CAP/ISM DIPLOM SKILL...POLICY COLD/WAR 20 KHRUSH/N. PAGE 163 A3328 — COM PWR BAL/PWR USSR

S61
ZAGORIA D.S.,"SINO-SOVIET FRICTION IN UNDERDEVELOPED AREAS." ASIA CHINA/COM COM ACT/RES PLAN ATTIT ORD/FREE PWR COLD/WAR 20. PAGE 169 A3443 — ECO/UNDEV ECO/TAC INT/TRADE USSR

S61
ZAGORIA D.S.,"THE FUTURE OF SINO-SOVIET RELATIONS." CHINA/COM INT/ORG NAT/G POL/PAR VOL/ASSN ACT/RES PLAN PERSON...METH/CNCPT TIME/SEQ TOT/POP VAL/FREE 20 MAO KHRUSH/N. PAGE 169 A3444 — ASIA COM TOTALISM USSR

B62
ARNOLD H.J.P.,AID FOR DEVELOPING COUNTRIES. COM EUR+WWI USA+45 USSR WOR+45 EDU/PROP ATTIT DRIVE PWR WEALTH...TREND CHARTS STERTYP NAT/ 20. PAGE 9 A0177 — ECO/UNDEV ECO/TAC FOR/AID

B62
BOUSCAREN A.T.,SOVIET FOREIGN POLICY: A PATTERN OF PERSISTANCE. WOR+45 WOR-45 SOCIETY STRUCT INT/ORG POL/PAR CREATE PLAN EDU/PROP ROUTINE ATTIT RIGID/FLEX...POLICY CONCPT RECORD HIST/WRIT TIME/SEQ MARX/KARL 20. PAGE 17 A0352 — COM NAT/G DIPLOM USSR

B62
CADWELL R.,COMMUNISM IN THE MODERN WORLD. USSR WOR+45 SOCIETY AGRI INDUS INT/ORG SECT EDU/PROP COLONIAL PEACE...SOC 20. PAGE 23 A0463 — COM DIPLOM POLICY CONCPT

B62
CLUBB O.E. JR.,THE UNITED STATES AND THE SINO-SOVIET BLOC IN SOUTHEAST ASIA. ASIA CHINA/COM COM USA+45 USSR ECO/UNDEV INT/ORG NAT/G FORCES TOP/EX PLAN ECO/TAC DOMIN COERCE GUERRILLA ATTIT RIGID/FLEX...POLICY OBS TREND 20. PAGE 27 A0553 — S/ASIA PWR BAL/PWR DIPLOM

B62
DALLIN A.,THE SOVIET UNION AT THE UNITED NATIONS: AN INQUIRY INTO SOVIET MOTIVES AND OBJECTIVES. ACT/RES EDU/PROP LEGIT ATTIT KNOWL PWR...POLICY RECORD HIST/WRIT TIME/SEQ TREND ORG/CHARTS GEN/METH COLD/WAR FAO 20 UN. PAGE 33 A0675 — COM INT/ORG USSR

B62
DUROSELLE J.B.,LES NOUVEAUX ETATS DANS LES RELATIONS INTERNATIONALES. AFR CHINA/COM FRANCE MOROCCO S/ASIA USSR ECO/UNDEV INT/ORG PLAN ECO/TAC EDU/PROP ATTIT DRIVE...TREND TOT/POP TUNIS 20. PAGE 39 A0806 — NAT/G CONSTN DIPLOM

B62
ELLIOTT J.R.,THE APPEAL OF COMMUNISM IN THE UNDERDEVELOPED NATIONS. USSR WOR+45 INT/ORG NAT/G DIPLOM DOMIN EDU/PROP ROUTINE ATTIT RIGID/FLEX ORD/FREE PWR WEALTH MARXISM...POLICY SOC METH/CNCPT MYTH TOT/POP COLD/WAR 20. PAGE 41 A0842 — COM ECO/UNDEV

B62
EVANS M.S.,THE FRINGE ON TOP. USSR EX/STRUC FORCES DIPLOM ECO/TAC PEACE CONSERVE SOCISM...TREND 20 KENNEDY/JF. PAGE 43 A0877 — NAT/G PWR CENTRAL POLICY

B62
FRIEDMANN W.,METHODS AND POLICIES OF PRINCIPAL DONOR COUNTRIES IN PUBLIC INTERNATIONAL DEVELOPMENT FINANCING: PRELIMINARY APPRAISAL. FRANCE GERMANY/W UK USA+45 USSR WOR+45 FINAN TEC/DEV CAP/ISM DIPLOM ECO/TAC ATTIT 20 EEC. PAGE 49 A1002 — INT/ORG FOR/AID NAT/COMP ADMIN

B62
FRIEDRICH-EBERT-STIFTUNG,THE SOVIET BLOC AND DEVELOPING COUNTRIES. CHINA/COM COM GERMANY/E USSR WOR+45 ECO/UNDEV INT/ORG NAT/G TEC/DEV NEUTRAL PWR ...POLICY 20. PAGE 49 A1008 — MARXISM DIPLOM ECO/TAC FOR/AID

B62
HOOK S.,WORLD COMMUNISM: KEY DOCUMENTARY MATERIAL. CHINA/COM L/A+17C USA+45 USSR POL/PAR DIPLOM COLONIAL REV WAR...ANTHOL 20 MARX/KARL LENIN/VI COM/PARTY. PAGE 67 A1380 — MARXISM COM GEN/LAWS NAT/G

B62
KIRPICEVA I.K.,HANDBUCH DER RUSSISCHEN UND SOWJETISCHEN BIBLIOGRAPHIEN (5 VOLS.). USSR STRUCT ECO/DEV DIPLOM LEAD ATTIT 18/20. PAGE 80 A1637 — BIBLIOG/A NAT/G MARXISM COM

B62
KLUCKHOHN F.L.,THE NAKED RISE OF COMMUNISM. CHINA/COM COM USSR WOR+45 CONSTN POL/PAR PLAN CONTROL LEAD NEUTRAL CONSERVE 20 STALIN/J EUROPE/E COM/PARTY. PAGE 80 A1650 — MARXISM IDEA/COMP DIPLOM DOMIN

B62
LAQUEUR W.,THE FUTURE OF COMMUNIST SOCIETY. CHINA/COM USSR LAW ECO/DEV NAT/G POL/PAR PLAN PROB/SOLV DIPLOM LEAD...POLICY CONCPT IDEA/COMP ANTHOL 20. PAGE 85 A1731 — MARXISM COM FUT SOCIETY

B62
LAQUEUR W.,POLYCENTRISM. CHINA/COM COM USSR WOR+45 INT/ORG NAT/G ECO/TAC DOMIN LEAD ATTIT PWR SOVEREIGN...ANTHOL 20. PAGE 85 A1732 — MARXISM DIPLOM BAL/PWR POLICY

B62
LERNER M.,THE AGE OF OVERKILL: A PREFACE TO WORLD POLITICS. USA+45 USSR WOR+45 SOCIETY ECO/UNDEV BAL/PWR NEUTRAL PARTIC REV ALL/IDEOS MARXISM ...BIBLIOG/A 20. PAGE 87 A1787 — DIPLOM NUC/PWR PWR DEATH

B62
LESSING P.,AFRICA'S RED HARVEST. AFR CHINA/COM COM USSR ECO/UNDEV BAL/PWR DIPLOM CONTROL PWR 20 COLD/WAR INTERVENT. PAGE 87 A1789 — NAT/LISM MARXISM FOR/AID EDU/PROP

B62
LEVY H.V.,LIBERDADE E JUSTICA SOCIAL (2ND ED.). BRAZIL COM L/A+17C USSR INT/ORG PARTIC GP/REL WEALTH 20 UN COM/PARTY. PAGE 88 A1798 — ORD/FREE MARXISM CAP/ISM LAW

B62
MACKENTOSH J.M.,STRATEGY AND TACTICS OF SOVIET FOREIGN POLICY. CHINA/COM FUT USA+45 WOR+45 INT/ORG PLAN DOMIN LEGIT ROUTINE COERCE NUC/PWR WAR ATTIT DRIVE ORD/FREE PWR...CONCPT OBS TIME/SEQ TREND GEN/METH COLD/WAR 20. PAGE 92 A1894 — COM POLICY DIPLOM USSR

B62
MORGENSTERN O.,STRATEGIE - HEUTE (2ND ED.). USA+45 USSR ECO/DEV DELIB/GP WAR PEACE ORD/FREE...GOV/COMP NAT/COMP 20 COLD/WAR NATO. PAGE 104 A2134 — NUC/PWR DIPLOM FORCES TEC/DEV

B62
MORGENTHAU H.J.,POLITICS IN THE TWENTIETH CENTURY: IMPASSE OF AMERICAN FOREIGN POLICY. FUT GERMANY USA+45 USSR WOR+45 INT/ORG NAT/G ACT/RES PLAN FOR/AID EDU/PROP LEGIT COERCE WAR PWR...TIME/SEQ TREND COLD/WAR 20. PAGE 104 A2138 — SKILL DIPLOM

B62
MORGENTHAU H.J.,POLITICS IN THE 20TH CENTURY: RESTORATION OF AMERICAN POLITICS. ASIA GERMANY USA+45 USSR WOR+45 NAT/G PLAN EDU/PROP LEGIT NUC/PWR ATTIT PWR SKILL...CONCPT TREND COLD/WAR 20. PAGE 104 A2139 — INT/ORG DIPLOM

B62
NEAL F.W.,WAR AND PEACE AND GERMANY. EUR+WWI USSR STRUCT INT/ORG NAT/G FORCES DOMIN EDU/PROP LEGIT EXEC COERCE ORD/FREE...HUM SOC NEW/IDEA OBS TIME/SEQ TOT/POP COLD/WAR 20 BERLIN. PAGE 108 A2208 — USA+45 POLICY DIPLOM GERMANY

B62
PAKISTAN MINISTRY OF FINANCE,FOREIGN ECONOMIC AID: A REVIEW OF FOREIGN ECONOMIC AID TO PAKISTAN. EUR+WWI PAKISTAN UK USA+45 USSR ECO/UNDEV INT/ORG DELIB/GP DIPLOM ECO/TAC...CHARTS CMN/WLTH CHINJAP. PAGE 113 A2318 — FOR/AID RECEIVE WEALTH FINAN

B62
RIMALOV V.V.,ECONOMIC COOPERATION BETWEEN USSR AND UNDERDEVELOPED COUNTRIES. USSR FINAN TEC/DEV INT/TRADE DOMIN EDU/PROP COLONIAL NAT/LISM DRIVE SOVEREIGN...AUD/VIS 20. PAGE 121 A2482 — FOR/AID PLAN ECO/UNDEV DIPLOM

B62
SCHUMAN F.L.,THE COLD WAR: RETROSPECT AND PROSPECT. FUT USA+45 USSR WOR+45 BAL/PWR EDU/PROP ARMS/CONT ATTIT...MAJORIT IDEA/COMP ANTHOL BIBLIOG 20 COLD/WAR. PAGE 129 A2651 — MARXISM TEC/DEV DIPLOM NUC/PWR

B62
SCOTT W.E.,ALLIANCE AGAINST HITLER. EUR+WWI FRANCE GERMANY USSR BAL/PWR LEAD TOTALISM PWR FASCISM MARXISM...POLICY BIBLIOG 20 HITLER/A. PAGE 131 A2675 — WAR DIPLOM FORCES

B62
SHAPIRO D.,A SELECT BIBLIOGRAPHY OF WORKS IN ENGLISH ON RUSSIAN HISTORY, 1801-1917. COM USSR STRATA FORCES EDU/PROP ADMIN REV RACE/REL ATTIT 19/20. PAGE 131 A2693 — BIBLIOG DIPLOM COLONIAL

B62
SPANIER J.W.,THE POLITICS OF DISARMAMENT. COM USA+45 USSR EDU/PROP ATTIT ORD/FREE PWR RESPECT ...MYTH RECORD 20 COLD/WAR. PAGE 135 A2771 — INT/ORG DELIB/GP ARMS/CONT

B62
STARR R.E.,POLAND 1944-1962: THE SOVIETIZATION OF A CAPTIVE PEOPLE. COM POLAND USSR POL/PAR SECT LEGIS — MARXISM NAT/G

DIPLOM DOMIN EDU/PROP CHOOSE ORD/FREE...POLICY CHARTS BIBLIOG 20. PAGE 137 A2808
TOTALISM NAT/COMP

B62
STRAUSS L.L.,MEN AND DECISIONS. USA+45 USA-45 USSR CONSULT FORCES TOP/EX WAR PEACE 20. PAGE 139 A2844
DECISION PWR NUC/PWR DIPLOM

B62
TRISKA J.F.,THE THEORY, LAW, AND POLICY OF SOVIET TREATIES. WOR+45 WOR-45 CONSTN INT/ORG NAT/G VOL/ASSN DOMIN LEGIT COERCE ATTIT PWR RESPECT ...POLICY JURID CONCPT OBS SAMP TIME/SEQ TREND GEN/LAWS 20. PAGE 145 A2966
COM LAW INT/LAW USSR

B62
US DEPARTMENT OF THE ARMY,AFRICA: ITS PROBLEMS AND PROSPECTS. CHINA/COM USSR INT/ORG FOR/AID COLONIAL LEAD FEDERAL DRIVE SOVEREIGN MARXISM...GEOG 20 COLD/WAR. PAGE 152 A3104
BIBLIOG/A AFR NAT/LISM DIPLOM

L62
BAILEY S.D.,"THE TROIKA AND THE FUTURE OF THE UN." CONSTN CREATE LEGIT EXEC CHOOSE ORD/FREE PWR ...CONCPT NEW/IDEA UN COLD/WAR 20. PAGE 10 A0206
FUT INT/ORG USSR

L62
ULYSSES,"THE INTERNATIONAL AIMS AND POLICIES OF THE SOVIET UNION: THE NEW CONCEPTS AND STRATEGY OF KHRUSHCHEV." FUT USSR WOR+45 SOCIETY INT/ORG NAT/G POL/PAR FORCES TOP/EX PLAN DOMIN EDU/PROP COERCE ATTIT PERSON PWR...TREND COLD/WAR 20 KHRUSH/N. PAGE 146 A2994
COM POLICY BAL/PWR DIPLOM

S62
BROWN B.E.,"L'ONU ABANDONNE LA HONGRIE." COM USSR WOR+45 CONSTN NAT/G POL/PAR DELIB/GP ACT/RES TEC/DEV PWR...TIME/SEQ 20 UN. PAGE 20 A0400
INT/ORG TOTALISM HUNGARY POLICY

S62
BRZEZINSKI Z.K.,"PEACEFUL ENGAGEMENT IN COMMUNIST DISUNITY." ASIA CHINA/COM USA+45 USSR NAT/G TOP/EX CREATE ECO/TAC FOR/AID DOMIN ATTIT PERCEPT RIGID/FLEX PWR...PSY 20. PAGE 20 A0417
COM DIPLOM TOTALISM

S62
CORET A.,"LA DECLARATION DE L'ASSEMBLEE GENERAL DE L'ONU SUR L'OCTROI DE L'INDEPENDENCE AUX PAYS ET AUX PEUPLES." AFR ASIA ISLAM NIGERIA S/ASIA USSR WOR+45 ECO/UNDEV NAT/G DELIB/GP COLONIAL ALL/VALS ...CONCPT TIME/SEQ TREND UN TOT/POP 20 MEXIC/AMER. PAGE 31 A0621
INT/ORG STRUCT SOVEREIGN

S62
CRANE R.D.,"SOVIET ATTITUDE TOWARD INTERNATIONAL SPACE LAW." COM FUT USA+45 USSR AIR CONSTN DELIB/GP DOMIN PWR...JURID TREND TOT/POP 20. PAGE 32 A0657
LAW ATTIT INT/LAW SPACE

S62
DALLIN A.,"THE SOVIET VIEW OF THE UNITED NATIONS." WOR+45 VOL/ASSN TOP/EX DIPLOM DOMIN EDU/PROP LEGIT ATTIT RIGID/FLEX PWR...CONCPT OBS HIST/WRIT TIME/SEQ STERTYP GEN/LAWS COLD/WAR UN 20. PAGE 33 A0676
COM INT/ORG USSR

S62
DRACHKOVITCH M.M.,"THE EMERGING PATTERN OF YUGOSLAV-SOVIET RELATIONS." COM FUT USSR WOR+45 INT/ORG ECO/TAC FOR/AID DOMIN COERCE ATTIT PERSON ORD/FREE PWR...TIME/SEQ 20 TITO/MARSH KHRUSH/N STALIN/J. PAGE 38 A0783
TOP/EX DIPLOM YUGOSLAVIA

S62
FOCSANEANU L.,"LES GRANDS TRAITES DE LA REPUBLIQUE POPULAIRE DE CHINE." ASIA CHINA/COM COM USSR WOR+45 INT/ORG NAT/G POL/PAR ACT/RES PLAN DIPLOM EDU/PROP ...CONCPT TIME/SEQ 20 TREATY. PAGE 47 A0957
VOL/ASSN TOTALISM

S62
FOSTER W.C.,"ARMS CONTROL AND DISARMAMENT IN A DIVIDED WORLD." COM FUT USA+45 USSR WOR+45 INTELL INT/ORG NAT/G VOL/ASSN CONSULT CREATE PLAN TEC/DEV EDU/PROP LEGIT NUC/PWR ATTIT RIGID/FLEX...CONCPT TREND TOT/POP 20 UN. PAGE 47 A0971
DELIB/GP POLICY ARMS/CONT DIPLOM

S62
JACOBSON H.K.,"THE UNITED NATIONS AND COLONIALISM: A TENTATIVE APPRAISAL." AFR FUT S/ASIA USA+45 USSR WOR+45 NAT/G DELIB/GP PLAN DIPLOM ECO/TAC DOMIN ADMIN ROUTINE COERCE ATTIT RIGID/FLEX ORD/FREE PWR ...OBS STERTYP UN 20. PAGE 73 A1486
INT/ORG CONCPT COLONIAL

S62
LISSITZYN O.J.,"SOME LEGAL IMPLICATIONS OF THE U-2 AND RB-47 INCIDENTS." FUT USA+45 USSR WOR+45 AIR NAT/G DIPLOM LEGIT MORAL ORD/FREE SOVEREIGN...JURID GEN/LAWS GEN/METH COLD/WAR 20 U-2. PAGE 90 A1840
LAW CONCPT SPACE INT/LAW

S62
LONDON K.,"SINO-SOVIET RELATIONS IN THE CONTEXT OF THE 'WORLD SOCIALIST SYSTEM'." ASIA CHINA/COM COM USSR INT/ORG NAT/G TOP/EX BAL/PWR DIPLOM DOMIN ATTIT PERCEPT RIGID/FLEX PWR MARXISM...METH/CNCPT TREND 20. PAGE 91 A1854
DELIB/GP CONCPT SOCISM

S62
MCWHINNEY E.,"CO-EXISTENCE, THE CUBA CRISIS, AND COLD WAR-INTERNATIONAL WAR." CUBA USA+45 USSR WOR+45 NAT/G TOP/EX BAL/PWR DIPLOM DOMIN LEGIT PEACE RIGID/FLEX ORD/FREE...STERTYP COLD/WAR 20. PAGE 99 A2026
CONCPT INT/LAW

S62
NANES A.,"DISARMAMENT: THE LAST SEVEN YEARS." COM EUR+WWI USA+45 USSR INT/ORG FORCES TOP/EX CREATE LEGIT NUC/PWR DISPL ORD/FREE...CONCPT TIME/SEQ CON/ANAL 20. PAGE 107 A2195
DELIB/GP RIGID/FLEX ARMS/CONT

S62
RUBINSTEIN A.Z.,"RUSSIA AND THE UNCOMMITTED NATIONS." AFR INDIA ISLAM L/A+17C LAOS S/ASIA ELITES ECO/UNDEV INT/ORG KIN CREATE PLAN TEC/DEV NAT/LISM RIGID/FLEX PWR WEALTH...METH/CNCPT TIME/SEQ GEN/LAWS WORK. PAGE 125 A2562
ECO/TAC TREND COLONIAL USSR

S62
SCOTT J.B.,"ANGLO-SOVIET TRADE AND ITS EFFECTS ON THE COMMONWEALTH." COM FUT UK USSR WOR+45 ECO/DEV MARKET INT/ORG CONSULT WEALTH...POLICY TREND CMN/WLTH 20. PAGE 130 A2673
NAT/G ECO/TAC

S62
SPECTOR I.,"SOVIET POLICY IN ASIA: A REAPPRAISAL." ASIA CHINA/COM COM INDIA INDONESIA ECO/UNDEV INT/ORG DOMIN EDU/PROP REGION RESPECT...CONCPT TREND TOT/POP COLD/WAR 20 CHINJAP. PAGE 135 A2774
S/ASIA PWR FOR/AID USSR

S62
STRACHEY J.,"COMMUNIST INTENTIONS." ASIA USSR YUGOSLAVIA INT/ORG NAT/G FORCES DOMIN EDU/PROP COERCE NUC/PWR NAT/LISM PEACE RIGID/FLEX PWR MARXISM...CONCPT MYTH OBS TIME/SEQ TREND COLD/WAR TOT/POP 20. PAGE 139 A2843
COM ATTIT WAR

S62
THOMAS J.R.T.,"SOVIET BEHAVIOR IN THE QUEMOY CRISES OF 1958." CHINA/COM FUT USSR WOR+45 INT/ORG VOL/ASSN FORCES PLAN BAL/PWR DOMIN COERCE NUC/PWR REV WAR ATTIT DRIVE ORD/FREE...POLICY OBS RECORD COLD/WAR FOR/POL 20. PAGE 143 A2923
COM PWR

S62
TOWSTER J.,"THE USSR AND THE USA: CHALLENGE AND RESPONSE." COM GERMANY USA+45 USSR WOR+45 ECO/UNDEV INT/ORG VOL/ASSN EX/STRUC FORCES TOP/EX CREATE PLAN TEC/DEV DIPLOM ECO/TAC EDU/PROP COLONIAL COERCE PWR ...GEN/METH COLD/WAR 20 KENNEDY/JF. PAGE 145 A2956
ACT/RES GEN/LAWS

B63
BROEKMEIJER M.W.,DEVELOPING COUNTRIES AND NATO. USSR FORCES DIPLOM NUC/PWR WAR PEACE TOTALISM 20 NATO. PAGE 19 A0384
ECO/UNDEV FOR/AID ORD/FREE NAT/G

B63
BRZEZINSKI Z.K.,AFRICA AND THE COMMUNIST WORLD. AFR ASIA COM CULTURE SOCIETY INT/ORG DELIB/GP ACT/RES ECO/TAC COERCE ORD/FREE PWR WEALTH...STAT TOT/POP VAL/FREE 20. PAGE 21 A0418
ATTIT EDU/PROP DIPLOM USSR

B63
BURNS A.L.,PEACE-KEEPING BY U.N.FORCES - FROM SUEZ TO THE CONGO. AFR FUT ISLAM ISRAEL USSR WOR+45 NAT/G DELIB/GP BAL/PWR DOMIN LEGIT EXEC COERCE PEACE ATTIT PWR RESPECT SOVEREIGN...CONCPT UN 20. PAGE 22 A0441
INT/ORG FORCES ORD/FREE

B63
CERAMI C.A.,ALLIANCE BORN OF DANGER. EUR+WWI USA+45 USSR ECO/DEV INDUS VOL/ASSN ECO/TAC REGION ATTIT MARXISM ATLAN/ALL 20 NATO EEC. PAGE 25 A0514
DIPLOM INT/ORG NAT/G POLICY

B63
EL-NAGGAR S.,FOREIGN AID TO UNITED ARAB REPUBLIC. UAR USA+45 USSR AGRI FINAN INDUS FORCES EATING DEMAND...CHARTS METH/COMP 20 RESOURCE/N AID. PAGE 41 A0838
FOR/AID ECO/UNDEV RECEIVE PLAN

B63
FISCHER-GALATI S.,EASTERN EUROPE IN THE SIXTIES. ALBANIA USSR YUGOSLAVIA ECO/UNDEV AGRI MARKET LABOR WORKER DIPLOM INT/TRADE EDU/PROP GOV/REL PRODUC UTOPIA SOCISM 20. PAGE 46 A0939
MARXISM TEC/DEV BAL/PWR ECO/TAC

B63
FULBRIGHT J.W.,PROSPECTS FOR THE WEST. COM USA+45 USSR INT/ORG NAT/G SCHOOL PROB/SOLV NUC/PWR WAR PEACE ORD/FREE...PREDICT METH/COMP 20 DEGAULLE/C. PAGE 50 A1015
DIPLOM BAL/PWR CONCPT POLICY

B63
GALLAGHER M.P.,THE SOVIET HISTORY OF WORLD WAR II. EUR+WWI USSR DIPLOM DOMIN WRITING CONTROL WAR MARXISM...PSY TIME/SEQ 20 STALIN/J. PAGE 50 A1031
CIVMIL/REL EDU/PROP HIST/WRIT PRESS

B63
GOLDWIN R.A.,FOREIGN AND MILITARY POLICY. COM USSR WOR+45 ECO/DEV INT/ORG FORCES PLAN ECO/TAC REGION ARMS/CONT MARXISM 20 UN. PAGE 54 A1097
DIPLOM POLICY PWR NAT/G

B63
GORDON G.N.,THE IDEA INVADERS. USA+45 USSR CULTURE COM/IND DIPLOM PRESS TV TOTALISM MARXISM 20. PAGE 54 A1113
EDU/PROP ATTIT ORD/FREE CONTROL

B63
GRAEBNER N.A.,THE COLD WAR: IDEOLOGICAL CONFLICT OR POWER STRUGGLE? USSR WOR+45 WOR-45 PROB/SOLV EDU/PROP ARMS/CONT REV NAT/LISM PEACE ORD/FREE ...IDEA/COMP ANTHOL BIBLIOG/A 20 COLD/WAR. PAGE 55
DIPLOM BAL/PWR MARXISM

A1123

B63
GRIFFITH W.E.,ALBANIA AND THE SINO-SOVIET RIFT. ALBANIA CHINA/COM USSR POL/PAR CHIEF LEGIS DIPLOM DOMIN ATTIT PWR...POLICY 20 KHRUSH/N MAO. PAGE 57 A1161
EDU/PROP MARXISM NAT/LISM GOV/REL

B63
HALASZ DE BEKY I.L.,A BIBLIOGRAPHY OF THE HUNGARIAN REVOLUTION 1956. COM HUNGARY USSR DIPLOM COERCE MARXISM...POLICY AUD/VIS 20 UN COLD/WAR. PAGE 59 A1221
BIBLIOG REV FORCES ATTIT

B63
HALPERIN M.H.,LIMITED WAR IN A NUCLEAR AGE. CUBA KOREA USA+45 USSR INT/ORG FORCES PLAN DIPLOM DETER PWR...BIBLIOG/A 20. PAGE 60 A1238
WAR NUC/PWR CONTROL WEAPON

B63
HAMM H.,ALBANIA - CHINA'S BEACHHEAD IN EUROPE. ALBANIA CHINA/COM USSR YUGOSLAVIA ELITES SOCIETY POL/PAR DELIB/GP FORCES ECO/TAC COERCE ISOLAT PEACE MARXISM...IDEA/COMP 20 MAO. PAGE 61 A1248
DIPLOM REV NAT/G POLICY

B63
HONEY P.J.,COMMUNISM IN NORTH VIETNAM: ITS ROLE IN THE SINO-SOVIET DISPUTE. CHINA/COM INDIA USSR VIETNAM/N AGRI POL/PAR LEGIS ECO/TAC WAR PEACE ATTIT...GEOG IDEA/COMP 20. PAGE 67 A1378
POLICY MARXISM CHIEF DIPLOM

B63
HOVET T. JR.,AFRICA IN THE UNITED NATIONS. AFR DELIB/GP EDU/PROP LOBBY CHOOSE ORD/FREE PWR RESPECT SKILL...STAT TIME/SEQ CON/ANAL CHARTS STERTYP VAL/FREE 20 UN. PAGE 68 A1397
INT/ORG USSR

B63
HYDE D.,THE PEACEFUL ASSAULT. COM UAR USSR ECO/DEV ECO/UNDEV NAT/G POL/PAR CAP/ISM PWR 20. PAGE 69 A1427
MARXISM CONTROL ECO/TAC DIPLOM

B63
JACOBSON H.K.,THE USSR AND THE UN'S ECONOMIC AND SOCIAL ACTIVITIES. COM WOR+45 DELIB/GP ACT/RES ECO/TAC EDU/PROP RIGID/FLEX SUPEGO HEALTH PWR SKILL ...POLICY CHARTS GEN/METH VAL/FREE UNESCO 20 UN. PAGE 73 A1487
INT/ORG ATTIT USSR

B63
KORBEL J.,POLAND BETWEEN EAST AND WEST: SOVIET AND GERMAN DIPLOMACY TOWARD POLAND 1919-1933. EUR+WWI GERMANY POLAND USSR FORCES AGREE WAR SOVEREIGN ...BIBLIOG 20 TREATY. PAGE 81 A1670
BAL/PWR DIPLOM DOMIN NAT/LISM

B63
MALIK C.,MAN IN THE STRUGGLE FOR PEACE. USSR WOR+45 CHIEF PLAN PROB/SOLV PARTIC NUC/PWR REV ORD/FREE ...IDEA/COMP METH/COMP 20 UN COLD/WAR. PAGE 93 A1912
PEACE MARXISM DIPLOM EDU/PROP

B63
MILLER W.J.,THE MEANING OF COMMUNISM. USSR SOCIETY ECO/DEV EX/STRUC WORKER TEC/DEV ADMIN TOTALISM ...POLICY CONCPT CHARTS BIBLIOG T 20 COLD/WAR LENIN/VI STALIN/J. PAGE 101 A2080
MARXISM TRADIT DIPLOM NAT/G

B63
MOSELY P.E.,THE SOVIET UNION, 1922-1962: A FOREIGN AFFAIRS READER. ASIA POLAND USSR CULTURE INTELL AGRI POL/PAR WORKER INT/TRADE DOMIN WAR NAT/LISM MARXISM SOCISM 20 KHRUSH/N. PAGE 105 A2152
PWR POLICY DIPLOM

B63
NORTH R.C.,CONTENT ANALYSIS: A HANDBOOK WITH APPLICATIONS FOR THE STUDY OF INTERNATIONAL CRISIS. ASIA COM EUR+WWI MOD/EUR INT/ORG TEC/DEV DOMIN EDU/PROP ROUTINE COERCE PERCEPT RIGID/FLEX ALL/VALS ...QUANT TESTS CON/ANAL SIMUL GEN/LAWS VAL/FREE. PAGE 110 A2252
METH/CNCPT COMPUT/IR USSR

B63
NORTH R.C.,M. N. ROY'S MISSION TO CHINA: THE COMMUNIST-KUOMINTANG SPLIT OF 1927. ASIA USSR STRATA LEGIS WORKER LEAD REV ATTIT ROLE SOCISM 20 ROY/MN COM/PARTY. PAGE 110 A2253
POL/PAR MARXISM DIPLOM

B63
SWEARER H.R.,CONTEMPORARY COMMUNISM: THEORY AND PRACTICE. COM USSR SOCIETY ECO/DEV POL/PAR FORCES PLAN ADMIN LEAD NAT/LISM...POLICY ANTHOL 20 LENIN/VI COM/PARTY. PAGE 140 A2869
MARXISM CONCPT DIPLOM NAT/G

B63
TUCKER R.C.,THE SOVIET POLITICAL MIND. WOR+45 ELITES INT/ORG NAT/G POL/PAR PLAN DIPLOM ECO/TAC DOMIN ADMIN NUC/PWR REV DRIVE PERSON SUPEGO PWR WEALTH...POLICY MGT PSY CONCPT OBS BIOG TREND COLD/WAR MARX/KARL 20. PAGE 145 A2972
COM TOP/EX USSR

B63
US DEPARTMENT OF THE ARMY,SOVIET RUSSIA: STRATEGIC SURVEY (PAMPHLET). USSR POL/PAR PLAN DOMIN EDU/PROP ARMS/CONT GUERRILLA WAR WEAPON...TREND CHARTS ORG/CHARTS 20. PAGE 152 A3106
BIBLIOG/A MARXISM DIPLOM COERCE

B63
US SENATE,DOCUMENTS ON INTERNATIONAL AS"ECTS OF EXPLORATION AND USE OF OUTER SPACE, 1954-62: STAFF REPORT FOR COMM AERON SPACE SCI. USA+45 USSR LEGIS LEAD CIVMIL/REL PEACE...POLICY INT/LAW ANTHOL 20 CONGRESS NASA KHRUSH/N. PAGE 155 A3165
SPACE UTIL GOV/REL DIPLOM

B63
WHITNEY T.P.,KHRUSHCHEV SPEAKS. USSR AGRI LEAD ...BIOG ANTHOL 20 KHRUSH/N STALIN/J ESPIONAGE. PAGE 164 A3339
DIPLOM MARXISM CHIEF

B63
WHITTON J.B.,PROPAGANDA AND THE COLD WAR. USA+45 USSR INDUS NAT/G PLAN WRITING EFFICIENCY...POLICY 20 COLD/WAR. PAGE 164 A3341
ATTIT EDU/PROP COM/IND DIPLOM

L63
CRANE R.D.,"THE CUBAN CRISIS: A STRATEGIC ANALYSIS OF AMERICAN AND SOVIET POLICY." CUBA USA+45 USSR BAL/PWR RISK DETER NUC/PWR PERCEPT ORD/FREE 20. PAGE 32 A0658
DIPLOM POLICY FORCES

L63
MOUSKHELY M.,"LE BLOC COMMUNISTE ET LA COMMUNAUTE ECONOMIQUE EUROPEENNE." AFR COM EUR+WWI FUT USSR WOR+45 INTELL ECO/UNDEV LABOR POL/PAR NUC/PWR RIGID/FLEX...TIME/SEQ ORG/CHARTS EEC TOT/POP 20. PAGE 105 A2158
INT/ORG ECO/DEV

L63
PADELFORD N.J.,"FINANCIAL CRISIS AND THE UNITED NATIONS." FUT USSR WOR+45 LAW CONSTN FINAN INT/ORG DELIB/GP FORCES PLAN BUDGET DIPLOM COST WEALTH ...STAT CHARTS UN CONGO 20. PAGE 113 A2311
CREATE ECO/TAC

S63
ALEXANDER R.,"LATIN AMERICA AND THE COMMUNIST BLOC." ASIA COM CUBA L/A+17C USA+45 USSR NAT/G VOL/ASSN TEC/DEV FOR/AID LEGIT PWR WEALTH COLD/WAR 20. PAGE 6 A0112
ECO/UNDEV RECORD

S63
BECHHOEFER B.G.,"UNITED NATIONS PROCEDURES IN CASE OF VIOLATIONS OF DISARMAMENT AGREEMENTS." COM USA+45 USSR LAW CONSTN NAT/G EX/STRUC FORCES LEGIS BAL/PWR EDU/PROP CT/SYS ARMS/CONT ORD/FREE PWR ...POLICY STERTYP UN VAL/FREE 20. PAGE 12 A0245
INT/ORG DELIB/GP

S63
BRZEZINSKI Z.,"SOVIET QUIESCENCE." EUR+WWI USA+45 USSR FORCES CREATE PLAN COERCE DETER WAR ATTIT 20 TREATY EUROPE. PAGE 20 A0415
DIPLOM ARMS/CONT NUC/PWR AGREE

S63
DARLING F.C.,"THE GEOPOLITICS OF AMERICAN FOREIGN POLITICS IN ASIA." COM S/ASIA USA+45 USSR ECO/UNDEV NAT/G VOL/ASSN CONSULT PLAN GUERRILLA...STAT TOT/POP 20. PAGE 34 A0682
FORCES ECO/TAC FOR/AID DIPLOM

S63
ETIENNE G.,"'LOIS OBJECTIVES' ET PROBLEMES DE DEVELOPPEMENT DANS LE CONTEXTE CHINE-URSS." ASIA CHINA/COM COM FUT STRUCT INT/ORG VOL/ASSN TOP/EX TEC/DEV ECO/TAC ATTIT RIGID/FLEX...GEOG MGT TIME/SEQ TOT/POP 20. PAGE 42 A0866
TOTALISM USSR

S63
GARDNER R.N.,"COOPERATION IN OUTER SPACE." FUT USSR WOR+45 AIR LAW COM/IND CONSULT DELIB/GP CREATE KNOWL 20 TREATY. PAGE 51 A1045
INT/ORG ACT/RES PEACE SPACE

S63
GUPTA S.C.,"INDIA AND THE SOVIET UNION." CHINA/COM COM INDIA S/ASIA VOL/ASSN TOP/EX FOR/AID EDU/PROP PEACE PWR...RECORD COLD/WAR 20. PAGE 58 A1195
DISPL MYTH USSR

S63
HORVATH J.,"MOSCOW'S AID PROGRAM: THE PERFORMANCE SO FAR." COM FUT USSR WOR+45 ECO/DEV FINAN PLAN TEC/DEV FOR/AID EDU/PROP ATTIT ORD/FREE PWR WEALTH ...POLICY STAT CHARTS VAL/FREE 20. PAGE 68 A1389
ECO/UNDEV ECO/TAC

S63
KAWALKOWSKI A.,"POUR UNE EUROPE INDEPENDENTE ET REUNIFIEE." EUR+WWI FUT USA+45 USSR WOR+45 ECO/DEV PROC/MFG INT/ORG NAT/G ACT/RES TEC/DEV FEDERAL RIGID/FLEX...CONCPT METH/CNCPT OEEC TOT/POP 20 DEGAULLE/C. PAGE 77 A1573
R+D PLAN NUC/PWR

S63
MACWHINNEY E.,"LES CONCEPT SOVIETIQUE DE 'COEXISTENCE PACIFIQUE' ET LES RAPPORTS JURIDIQUES ENTRE L'URSS ET LES ETATS OCIDENTAUX." COM FUT WOR+45 LAW CULTURE INTELL POL/PAR ACT/RES BAL/PWR ...INT/LAW 20. PAGE 93 A1903
NAT/G CONCPT DIPLOM USSR

S63
MCDOUGAL M.S.,"THE SOVIET-CUBAN QUARANTINE AND SELF-DEFENSE." CUBA USA+45 USSR WOR+45 INT/ORG NAT/G BAL/PWR NUC/PWR ATTIT...JURID CONCPT. PAGE 98 A2008
ORD/FREE LEGIT SOVEREIGN

S63
NEIDLE A.F.,"PEACE KEEPING AND DISARMAMENT." COM USA+45 USSR WOR+45 INT/ORG NAT/G BAL/PWR EDU/PROP LEGIT ATTIT PWR 20. PAGE 108 A2214
DELIB/GP ACT/RES ARMS/CONT PEACE

S63
PHELPS J.,"INFORMATION AND ARMS CONTROL." COM SPACE USA+45 USSR WOR+45 R+D INT/ORG NAT/G DELIB/GP DIPLOM ORD/FREE...CONCPT 20. PAGE 116 A2374
KNOWL ARMS/CONT NUC/PWR

S63
RAMERIE L.,"TENSION AU SEIN DU COMECON: LE CAS ROUMAIN." COM EUR+WWI USSR WOR+45 ECO/DEV DIST/IND NAT/G POL/PAR VOL/ASSN EDU/PROP TOTALISM ATTIT
INT/ORG ECO/TAC INT/TRADE

WEALTH...TIME/SEQ 20 COMECON. PAGE 119 A2438 ROMANIA

S63
SHWADRAN B.,"MIDDLE EAST OIL, 1962." ISLAM USSR ECO/DEV DIST/IND INDUS PLAN BAL/PWR DISPL DRIVE ...POLICY STAT TREND GEN/LAWS EEC OEEC 20 OIL. PAGE 132 A2712 MARKET ECO/TAC INT/TRADE

S63
SONNENFELDT H.,"FOREIGN POLICY FROM MALENKOV TO KHRUSHCHEV." WOR+45 NAT/G FORCES BAL/PWR DIPLOM ECO/TAC COERCE ATTIT PWR...CONCPT HIST/WRIT COLD/WAR 20. PAGE 135 A2768 COM DOMIN FOR/AID USSR

S63
WOLF C.,"SOME ASPECTS OF THE 'VALUE' OF LESS-DEVELOPED COUNTRIES TO THE UNITED STATES." ASIA CHINA/COM COM USA+45 USSR ECO/UNDEV BAL/PWR ECO/TAC FOR/AID DOMIN EDU/PROP ATTIT PWR...POLICY METH/CNCPT CONT/OBS TREND CHARTS 20. PAGE 166 A3379 CONCPT GEN/LAWS DIPLOM

B64
CHENG C.,ECONOMIC RELATIONS BETWEEN PEKING AND MOSCOW: 1949-63. ASIA CHINA/COM COM USSR FINAN INDUS CONSULT TEC/DEV INT/TRADE...PREDICT CHARTS BIBLIOG 20. PAGE 26 A0527 DIPLOM FOR/AID MARXISM

B64
COHEN M.,LAW AND POLITICS IN SPACE: SPECIFIC AND URGENT PROBLEMS IN THE LAW OF OUTER SPACE. CHINA/COM COM USA+45 USSR WOR+45 COM/IND INT/ORG NAT/G LEGIT NUC/PWR ATTIT BIO/SOC...JURID CONCPT CONGRESS 20 STALIN/J. PAGE 28 A0561 DELIB/GP LAW INT/LAW SPACE

B64
DALLIN A.,THE SOVIET UNION, ARMS CONTROL AND DISARMAMENT. COM INT/ORG VOL/ASSN EX/STRUC DIPLOM NUC/PWR ATTIT PWR TOT/POP COLD/WAR 20. PAGE 33 A0678 ORD/FREE ARMS/CONT USSR

B64
DEUTSCHE GES AUSWARTIGE POL,STRATEGIE UND ABRUSTUNGSPOLITIK DER SOWJETUNION. USSR TEC/DEV DIPLOM COERCE DETER WEAPON...POLICY PSY 20 ABM/DEFSYS. PAGE 37 A0747 NUC/PWR WAR FORCES ARMS/CONT

B64
DUROSELLE J.B.,LA COMMUNAUTE INTERNATIONALE FACE AUX JEUNES ETATS. CHINA/COM COM S/ASIA USSR INT/ORG ROLE...ANTHOL 20 UN SEATO THIRD/WRLD. PAGE 40 A0808 DIPLOM COLONIAL ECO/UNDEV SOVEREIGN

B64
DUROSELLE J.B.,POLITIQUES NATIONALES ENVERS LES JEUNES ETATS. FRANCE ISRAEL ITALY UK USA+45 USSR YUGOSLAVIA ECO/DEV FINAN ECO/TAC INT/TRADE ADMIN PWR 20. PAGE 40 A0809 DIPLOM ECO/UNDEV COLONIAL DOMIN

B64
EHRENBURG I.,THE WAR: 1941-1945 (VOL. V OF "MEN, YEARS - LIFE," TRANS. BY TATIANA SHEBUNINA). GERMANY USSR PRESS WRITING PERS/REL PEACE ANOMIE ATTIT PERSON...CONCPT RECORD BIOG 20 STALIN/J HITLER/A. PAGE 40 A0827 WAR DIPLOM COM MARXIST

B64
ETZIONI A.,WINNING WITHOUT WAR. FUT MOD/EUR USA+45 WOR+45 ECO/DEV ECO/UNDEV INT/ORG NAT/G FORCES TOP/EX PLAN TEC/DEV ECO/TAC DOMIN EDU/PROP LEGIT COERCE CHOOSE ATTIT MORAL ORD/FREE RESPECT WEALTH MAJORIT. PAGE 43 A0871 PWR TREND DIPLOM USSR

B64
FULBRIGHT J.W.,OLD MYTHS AND NEW REALITIES. USA+45 USSR LEGIS INT/TRADE DETER ATTIT...POLICY 20 COLD/WAR TREATY. PAGE 50 A1016 DIPLOM INT/ORG ORD/FREE

B64
GRIFFITH W.E.,COMMUNISM IN EUROPE (2 VOLS.). CZECHOSLVK USSR WOR+45 WOR-45 YUGOSLAVIA INGP/REL MARXISM SOCISM...ANTHOL 20 EUROPE/E. PAGE 57 A1162 COM POL/PAR DIPLOM GOV/COMP

B64
HAMRELL S.,THE SOVIET BLOC, CHINA, AND AFRICA. AFR CHINA/COM COM USSR ECO/UNDEV EDU/PROP 20. PAGE 61 A1249 MARXISM DIPLOM CONTROL FOR/AID

B64
JOHNSON L.B.,MY HOPE FOR AMERICA. FUT USA+45 USSR LAW PLAN DIPLOM GIVE INCOME PEACE ATTIT ORD/FREE WEALTH 20 JOHNSON/LB PRESIDENT DEMOCRAT. PAGE 74 A1525 POLICY POL/PAR NAT/G GOV/REL

B64
KEEP J.,CONTEMPORARY HISTORY IN THE SOVIET MIRROR. COM USSR POL/PAR CREATE DIPLOM AGREE WAR ATTIT ...MYTH TREND ANTHOL 20 COLD/WAR STALIN/J MARX/KARL LENIN/VI. PAGE 77 A1576 HIST/WRIT METH MARXISM IDEA/COMP

B64
KIS T.I.,LES PAYS DE L'EUROPE DE L'EST: LEURS RAPPORTS MUTUELS ET LE PROBLEME DE LEUR INTEGRATION DANS L'ORBITE DE L'USSR. EUR+WWI RUSSIA USSR INT/ORG NAT/G REV ATTIT...JURID SOC BIBLIOG WARSAW/P COMECON EUROPE/E. PAGE 80 A1638 DIPLOM COM MARXISM REGION

B64
KOLARZ W.,BOOKS ON COMMUNISM. USSR WOR+45 CULTURE NAT/G POL/PAR DIPLOM LEAD...CONCPT GOV/COMP IDEA/COMP. PAGE 81 A1667 BIBLIOG/A SOCIETY COM MARXISM

B64
KOLARZ W.,COMMUNISM AND COLONIALISM. AFR ASIA USSR DISCRIM ATTIT ORD/FREE SOVEREIGN SOC/INTEG 20. PAGE 81 A1668 EDU/PROP DIPLOM TOTALISM COLONIAL

B64
LATOURETTE K.S.,CHINA. ASIA CHINA/COM FUT USSR ECO/UNDEV ECO/TAC WAR 19/20. PAGE 85 A1744 MARXISM NAT/G POLICY DIPLOM

B64
LENS S.,THE FUTILE CRUSADE. ASIA CHINA/COM L/A+17C USA+45 USSR WOR+45 ECO/DEV BAL/PWR DIPLOM NUC/PWR WAR NAT/LISM PEACE 20 COLD/WAR PRESIDENT CIA. PAGE 87 A1774 ORD/FREE ANOMIE COM MARXISM

B64
LUARD E.,THE COLD WAR: A RE-APPRAISAL. FUT USSR WOR+45 FORCES NUC/PWR NAT/LISM ORD/FREE SOVEREIGN ...INT 20 COLD/WAR STALIN/J TREATY UN. PAGE 91 A1870 DIPLOM WAR PEACE TOTALISM

B64
MCWHINNEY E.,"PEACEFUL COEXISTENCE" AND SOVIET-WESTERN INTERNATIONAL LAW. USSR DIPLOM LEAD...JURID 20 COLD/WAR. PAGE 99 A2027 PEACE IDEA/COMP INT/LAW ATTIT

B64
NOVE A.,COMMUNISM AT THE CROSSROADS. USSR INT/ORG POL/PAR TOTALISM...POLICY CONCPT 20. PAGE 110 A2259 DIPLOM BAL/PWR MARXISM ORD/FREE

B64
PERKINS D.,THE AMERICAN DEMOCRACY: ITS RISE TO POWER. ASIA USSR LAW CULTURE FINAN EDU/PROP COLONIAL CHOOSE...POLICY CHARTS BIBLIOG WORSHIP PRESIDENT 15/20 NEGRO. PAGE 115 A2362 LOC/G ECO/TAC WAR DIPLOM

B64
PITTMAN J.,PEACEFUL COEXISTENCE. USSR NAT/G NUC/PWR WAR ATTIT 20. PAGE 116 A2385 DIPLOM PEACE POLICY FORCES

B64
ROCK V.P.,A STRATEGY OF INTERDEPENDENCE. COM USSR WOR+45 NAT/G FORCES PROB/SOLV TEC/DEV DETER WAR ORD/FREE...CONCPT NEW/IDEA METH/COMP 20. PAGE 122 A2509 DIPLOM NUC/PWR PEACE POLICY

B64
ROSENAU J.N.,INTERNATIONAL ASPECTS OF CIVIL STRIFE. CHINA/COM CUBA EUR+WWI USA+45 USSR BAL/PWR EDU/PROP NEUTRAL COERCE MORAL...NAT/COMP 20 COLD/WAR UN. PAGE 124 A2533 POLICY DIPLOM REV WAR

B64
RUBIN J.A.,YOUR HUNDRED BILLION DOLLARS. USA+45 USSR INDUS INT/ORG TEC/DEV ECO/TAC...METH/COMP 20 PEACE/CORP. PAGE 125 A2559 FOR/AID DIPLOM ECO/UNDEV

B64
RUBINSTEIN A.Z.,THE SOVIETS IN INTERNATIONAL ORGANIZATIONS: CHANGING POLICY TOWARD DEVELOPING COUNTRIES, 1953-1963. COM DELIB/GP ACT/RES ECO/TAC EDU/PROP ADMIN ATTIT ORD/FREE PWR...INT VAL/FREE UN 20. PAGE 125 A2563 ECO/UNDEV INT/ORG USSR

B64
SAKAI R.K.,STUDIES ON ASIA, 1964. ASIA CHINA/COM ISRAEL MALAYSIA S/ASIA USA+45 USSR ECO/UNDEV FAM POL/PAR SECT CONSULT NAT/LISM...POLICY SOC 20 CHINJAP. PAGE 126 A2588 PWR DIPLOM

B64
SPECTOR S.D.,A CHECKLIST OF PAPERBOUND BOOKS ON RUSSIA. USSR SECT DIPLOM EDU/PROP HEALTH...PHIL/SCI PSY SOC SOC/WK WORSHIP 20. PAGE 135 A2775 BIBLIOG COM PERF/ART

B64
TEPASKE J.J.,EXPLOSIVE FORCES IN LATIN AMERICA. CULTURE INTELL ECO/UNDEV INT/ORG NAT/G SECT FORCES ECO/TAC EDU/PROP PWR WEALTH SOC. PAGE 142 A2903 L/A+17C RIGID/FLEX FOR/AID USSR

B64
TREADGOLD D.W.,THE DEVELOPMENT OF THE USSR. COM USSR ECO/DEV CREATE BAL/PWR DEBATE COLONIAL TOTALISM...HUM ANTHOL BIBLIOG 19/20. PAGE 145 A2960 MARXISM CONSERVE DIPLOM DOMIN

B64
TULLY A.,WHERE DID YOUR MONEY GO. USA+45 USSR ECO/UNDEV ADMIN EFFICIENCY WEALTH...METH/COMP 20. PAGE 146 A2976 FOR/AID DIPLOM CONTROL

B64
ZEBOT C.A.,THE ECONOMICS OF COMPETITIVE COEXISTENCE. CHINA/COM USSR WOR+45 FINAN MARKET FOR/AID PRICE DEMAND EQUILIB WEALTH ALL/IDEOS 20. PAGE 169 A3450 TEC/DEV DIPLOM METH/COMP

L64
CAMPBELL J.C.,"THE MIDDLE EAST IN THE MUTED COLD WAR." COM EUR+WWI UAR USA+45 USSR STRUCT ECO/UNDEV NAT/G VOL/ASSN EX/STRUC TOP/EX DIPLOM ECO/TAC EDU/PROP...TIME/SEQ COLD/WAR 20. PAGE 23 A0475 ISLAM FOR/AID NAT/LISM

L64
MILLIS W.,"THE DEMILITARIZED WORLD." COM USA+45 USSR WOR+45 CONSTN NAT/G EX/STRUC PLAN LEGIT ATTIT FUT INT/ORG

DRIVE...CONCPT TIME/SEQ STERTYP TOT/POP COLD/WAR 20. PAGE 102 A2085 — BAL/PWR PEACE

L64
WARD C.,"THE 'NEW MYTHS' AND 'OLD REALITIES' OF NUCLEAR WAR." COM FUT USA+45 USSR WOR+45 INT/ORG NAT/G DOMIN LEGIT EXEC ATTIT PERCEPT ALL/VALS ...POLICY RELATIV PSY MYTH TREND 20. PAGE 161 A3280 — FORCES COERCE ARMS/CONT NUC/PWR

S64
ARMSTRONG J.A.,"THE SOVIET-AMERICAN CONFRONTATION: A NEW STAGE?" CUBA USA+45 USSR PLAN PROB/SOLV INT/TRADE CONTROL ARMS/CONT NUC/PWR MARXISM 20 COLD/WAR INTERVENT. PAGE 9 A0174 — DIPLOM POLICY INSPECT

S64
COFFEY J.,"THE SOVIET VIEW OF A DISARMED WORLD." COM USA+45 INT/ORG NAT/G EX/STRUC EDU/PROP COERCE PERCEPT ORD/FREE PWR...TREND STERTYP VAL/FREE 20 UN. PAGE 27 A0556 — FORCES ATTIT ARMS/CONT USSR

S64
CRANE R.D.,"BASIC PRINCIPLES IN SOVIET SPACE LAW." FUT WOR+45 AIR INT/ORG DIPLOM DOMIN ARMS/CONT COERCE NUC/PWR PEACE ATTIT DRIVE PWR...INT/LAW METH/CNCPT NEW/IDEA OBS TREND GEN/LAWS VAL/FREE MARX/KARL 20. PAGE 32 A0659 — COM LAW USSR SPACE

S64
DELGADO J.,"EL MOMENTO POLITICO HISPANOAMERICA." CHINA/COM FUT PANAMA USA+45 USSR INT/ORG NAT/G POL/PAR FORCES DOMIN REGION COERCE ATTIT ALL/VALS ...TRADIT CONCPT COLD/WAR 20. PAGE 36 A0728 — L/A+17C EDU/PROP NAT/LISM

S64
DEVILLERS P.H.,"L'URSS, LA CHINE ET LES ORIGINES DE LA GUERRE DE COREE." ASIA CHINA/COM USSR INT/ORG ECO/TAC EDU/PROP ATTIT RIGID/FLEX PWR...STAND/INT HIST/WRIT COLD/WAR 20. PAGE 37 A0751 — WOR+45 KOREA

S64
GARDNER R.N.,"THE SOVIET UNION AND THE UNITED NATIONS." WOR+45 FINAN POL/PAR VOL/ASSN FORCES ECO/TAC DOMIN EDU/PROP LEGIT ADJUD ADMIN ARMS/CONT COERCE ATTIT ALL/VALS...POLICY MAJORIT CONCPT OBS TIME/SEQ TREND STERTYP UN. PAGE 51 A1046 — COM INT/ORG USSR

S64
GARMARNIKOW M.,"INFLUENCE-BUYING IN WEST AFRICA." COM FUT USSR INTELL NAT/G PLAN TEC/DEV ECO/TAC DOMIN EDU/PROP REGION NAT/LISM ATTIT DRIVE ALL/VALS SOVEREIGN...POLICY PSY SOC CONCPT TREND STERTYP WORK COLD/WAR 20. PAGE 51 A1049 — AFR ECO/UNDEV FOR/AID SOCISM

S64
GINSBURGS G.,"WARS OF NATIONAL LIBERATION - THE SOVIET THESIS." COM USSR WOR+45 WOR-45 LAW CULTURE INT/ORG DIPLOM LEGIT COLONIAL GUERRILLA WAR NAT/LISM ATTIT PERSON MORAL PWR...JURID OBS TREND MARX/KARL 20. PAGE 53 A1075 — COERCE CONCPT INT/LAW REV

S64
GRZYBOWSKI K.,"INTERNATIONAL ORGANIZATIONS FROM THE SOVIET POINT OF VIEW." WOR+45 WOR-45 CULTURE ECO/DEV VOL/ASSN EDU/PROP ATTIT RIGID/FLEX KNOWL ...SOC OBS TIME/SEQ TREND GEN/LAWS VAL/FREE ILO UN 20. PAGE 58 A1184 — COM INT/ORG DIPLOM USSR

S64
HORECKY P.L.,"LIBRARY OF CONGRESS PUBLICATIONS IN AID OF USSR AND EAST EUROPEAN RESEARCH." BULGARIA CZECHOSLVK POLAND USSR YUGOSLAVIA NAT/G POL/PAR DIPLOM ADMIN GOV/REL...CLASSIF 20. PAGE 67 A1382 — BIBLIOG/A COM MARXISM

S64
KARPOV P.V.,"PEACEFUL COEXISTENCE AND INTERNATIONAL LAW." WOR+45 LAW SOCIETY INT/ORG VOL/ASSN FORCES CREATE CAP/ISM DIPLOM ADJUD NUC/PWR PEACE MORAL ORD/FREE PWR MARXISM...MARXIST JURID CONCPT OBS TREND COLD/WAR MARX/KARL 20. PAGE 77 A1568 — COM ATTIT INT/LAW USSR

S64
LERNER W.,"THE HISTORICAL ORIGINS OF THE SOVIET DOCTRINE OF PEACEFUL COEXISTENCE." COM USSR INT/ORG NAT/G VOL/ASSN PLAN PEACE ATTIT RIGID/FLEX PWR MARXISM...TIME/SEQ COLD/WAR 20. PAGE 87 A1788 — EDU/PROP DIPLOM

S64
LIPSON L.,"PEACEFUL COEXISTENCE." COM USSR WOR+45 LAW INT/ORG DIPLOM LEGIT ADJUD ORD/FREE...CONCPT OBS TREND GEN/LAWS VAL/FREE COLD/WAR 20. PAGE 90 A1834 — ATTIT JURID INT/LAW PEACE

S64
MAGGS P.B.,"SOVIET VIEWPOINT ON NUCLEAR WEAPONS IN INTERNATIONAL LAW." USSR WOR+45 INT/ORG FORCES DIPLOM ARMS/CONT ATTIT ORD/FREE PWR...POLICY JURID CONCPT OBS TREND CON/ANAL GEN/LAWS VAL/FREE 20. PAGE 93 A1905 — COM LAW INT/LAW NUC/PWR

S64
PESELT B.M.,"COMMUNIST ECONOMIC OFFENSIVE." WOR+45 SOCIETY INT/ORG PLAN ECO/TAC DOMIN EDU/PROP ATTIT PERSON PWR WEALTH...TREND CHARTS 20. PAGE 115 A2366 — COM ECO/UNDEV FOR/AID USSR

S64
RUBINSTEIN A.Z.,"THE SOVIET IMAGE OF WESTERN EUROPE." COM EUR+WWI FRANCE GERMANY GERMANY/W USA+45 USSR INT/ORG NAT/G VOL/ASSN FORCES TOP/EX BAL/PWR EDU/PROP ORD/FREE PWR...MYTH RECORD NATO EEC 20. PAGE 125 A2564 — RIGID/FLEX ATTIT

S64
TRISKA J.F.,"SOVIET TREATY LAW: A QUANTITATIVE ANALYSIS." WOR+45 LAW ECO/UNDEV AGRI COM/IND INDUS CREATE TEC/DEV DIPLOM ATTIT PWR WEALTH...JURID SAMP TIME/SEQ TREND CHARTS VAL/FREE 20 TREATY. PAGE 145 A2967 — COM ECO/TAC INT/LAW USSR

B65
BROMKE A.,THE COMMUNIST STATES AT THE CROSSROADS BETWEEN MOSCOW AND PEKING. CHINA/COM USSR INGP/REL NAT/LISM TOTALISM 20. PAGE 19 A0389 — COM DIPLOM MARXISM REGION

B65
FORGAC A.A.,NEW DIPLOMACY AND THE UNITED NATIONS. FRANCE GERMANY UK USSR INT/ORG DELIB/GP EX/STRUC PEACE...INT/LAW CONCPT UN. PAGE 47 A0965 — DIPLOM ETIQUET NAT/G

B65
GILBERT M.,THE EUROPEAN POWERS 1900-45. EUR+WWI ITALY MOD/EUR USSR REV WAR PWR ALL/IDEOS FASCISM ...AUD/VIS CHARTS BIBLIOG 20. PAGE 52 A1069 — DIPLOM NAT/G POLICY BAL/PWR

B65
GRETTON P.,MARITIME STRATEGY - A STUDY OF DEFENSE PROBLEMS. ASIA UK USSR DIPLOM COERCE DETER NUC/PWR WEAPON...CONCPT NAT/COMP 20. PAGE 56 A1147 — FORCES PLAN WAR SEA

B65
HUSS P.J.,RED SPIES IN THE UN. CZECHOSLVK USA+45 USSR COM/IND FORCES EDU/PROP NUC/PWR MARXISM 20 UN COLD/WAR. PAGE 69 A1421 — PEACE INT/ORG BAL/PWR DIPLOM

B65
INTERNATIONAL SOCIAL SCI COUN,SOCIAL SCIENCES IN THE USSR. USSR ECO/DEV AGRI FINAN INDUS PLAN CAP/ISM...INT/LAW PHIL/SCI PSY SOC 20. PAGE 71 A1460 — BIBLIOG/A ACT/RES MARXISM JURID

B65
IRIYE A.,AFTER IMPERIALISM; THE SEARCH FOR A NEW ORDER IN THE FAR EAST 1921-1931. USA-45 USSR DOMIN AGREE COLONIAL REV PWR...BIBLIOG DICTIONARY 20 CHINJAP. PAGE 72 A1468 — DIPLOM ASIA SOVEREIGN

B65
JADOS S.S.,DOCUMENTS ON RUSSIAN-AMERICAN RELATIONS: WASHINGTON TO EISENHOWER. USA+45 USA-45 USSR INT/ORG LEGIS INT/TRADE WAR PEACE...ANTHOL BIBLIOG 18/20 PRESIDENT. PAGE 73 A1488 — DIPLOM CHIEF CONTROL

B65
LASKY V.,THE UGLY RUSSIAN. AFR ASIA USSR ECO/UNDEV NAT/LISM TOTALISM PERSON 20. PAGE 85 A1738 — FOR/AID ATTIT DIPLOM

B65
LERCHE C.O.,THE COLD WAR AND AFTER. AFR COM S/ASIA USA+45 USSR NUC/PWR SOVEREIGN MARXISM...TIME/SEQ TREND BIBLIOG 20 COLD/WAR. PAGE 87 A1784 — DIPLOM BAL/PWR IDEA/COMP

B65
MACDONALD R.W.,THE LEAGUE OF ARAB STATES: A STUDY IN THE DYNAMICS OF REGIONAL ORGANIZATION. ISRAEL UAR USSR FINAN INT/ORG DELIB/GP ECO/TAC AGREE NEUTRAL ORD/FREE PWR...DECISION BIBLIOG 20 TREATY UN. PAGE 92 A1888 — ISLAM REGION DIPLOM ADMIN

B65
MCSHERRY J.E.,RUSSIA AND THE UNITED STATES UNDER EISENHOWER, KHRUSHCHEV, AND KENNEDY. USSR EX/STRUC TOP/EX PRESS WAR...POLICY TREND 20. PAGE 99 A2024 — DIPLOM CHIEF NAT/G PEACE

B65
MEYERHOFF A.E.,THE STRATEGY OF PERSUASION: THE USE OF ADVERTISING SKILLS IN FIGHTING THE COLD WAR. USA+45 USSR PLAN ATTIT DRIVE...BIBLIOG 20 COLD/WAR. PAGE 100 A2054 — EDU/PROP SERV/IND METH/COMP DIPLOM

B65
MOSTECKY V.,SOVIET LEGAL BIBLIOGRAPHY. USSR LEGIS PRESS WRITING CONFER ADJUD CT/SYS REV MARXISM ...INT/LAW JURID DICTIONARY 20. PAGE 105 A2155 — BIBLIOG/A LAW COM CONSTN

B65
SCHREIBER H.,TEUTON AND SLAV - THE STRUGGLE FOR CENTRAL EUROPE (TRANS. BY J. CLEUGH). GERMANY POLAND PRUSSIA USSR SOCIETY STRUCT SECT DIPLOM BALTIC. PAGE 129 A2646 — GP/REL WAR RACE/REL NAT/LISM

B65
TREFOUSSE H.L.,THE COLD WAR: A BOOK OF DOCUMENTS. ASIA L/A+17C USSR WOR+45 WOR-45 ECO/TAC FOR/AID ARMS/CONT NUC/PWR PEACE ORD/FREE...ANTHOL 20 COLD/WAR KENNEDY/JF EISNHWR/DD. PAGE 145 A2961 — BAL/PWR DIPLOM MARXISM

B65
US DEPARTMENT OF DEFENSE,US SECURITY ARMS CONTROL, AND DISARMAMENT 1961-1965 (PAMPHLET). CHINA/COM COM GERMANY/W ISRAEL SPACE USA+45 USSR WOR+45 FORCES EDU/PROP DETER EQUILIB PEACE ALL/VALS...GOV/COMP 20 NATO. PAGE 151 A3077 — BIBLIOG/A ARMS/CONT NUC/PWR DIPLOM

B65
WINT G.,COMMUNIST CHINA'S CRUSADE: MAO'S ROAD TO POWER AND THE NEW CAMPAIGN FOR WORLD REVOLUTION. ASIA CHINA/COM USA+45 USSR NAT/G POL/PAR DOMIN COERCE WAR PWR...POLICY CHARTS IDEA/COMP BIBLIOG 20 MAO. PAGE 165 A3364 — DIPLOM MARXISM REV COLONIAL

B65
WINT G.,ASIA: A HANDBOOK. ASIA COM INDIA USSR CULTURE INTELL NAT/G...GEOG STAT CENSUS NAT/COMP WORSHIP 20 TREATY CHINJAP. PAGE 165 A3365
DIPLOM SOC

S65
"FURTHER READING." INDIA USSR FORCES ATTIT SOCISM 20. PAGE 3 A0068
BIBLIOG DIPLOM MARXISM

S65
DOSSICK J.J.,"DOCTORAL DISSERTATIONS ON RUSSIA, THE SOVIET UNION, AND EASTERN EUROPE." USSR ACADEM DIPLOM EDU/PROP MARXISM 19/20 COLD/WAR. PAGE 38 A0775
BIBLIOG HUM SOC

S65
FLEMING D.F.,"CAN PAX AMERICANA SUCCEED?" ASIA CHINA/COM EUR+WWI USSR VIETNAM BAL/PWR DIPLOM DOMIN COERCE GOV/REL 20. PAGE 46 A0948
DECISION ATTIT ECO/TAC

S65
HELMREICH E.C.,"KADAR'S HUNGARY." COM EUR+WWI HUNGARY USSR INTELL ECO/DEV AGRI INT/ORG TOP/EX DOMIN ALL/VALS WORK COLD/WAR 20. PAGE 64 A1311
NAT/G RIGID/FLEX TOTALISM

S65
HOLSTI O.R.,"EAST-WEST CONFLICT AND SINO-SOVIET RELATIONS" CHINA/COM USSR COMPUTER REGION DECISION. PAGE 67 A1373
VOL/ASSN DIPLOM CON/ANAL COM

S65
MAC CHESNEY B.,"SOME COMMENTS ON THE 'QUARANTINE' OF CUBA." USA+45 WOR+45 NAT/G BAL/PWR DIPLOM LEGIT ROUTINE ATTIT ORD/FREE...JURID METH/CNCPT 20. PAGE 92 A1883
INT/ORG LAW CUBA USSR

S65
RAY H.,"THE POLICY OF RUSSIA TOWARDS SINO-INDIAN CONFLICT." ASIA CHINA/COM INDIA USSR NAT/G TOP/EX FOR/AID EDU/PROP NEUTRAL COERCE PEACE RIGID/FLEX PWR...METH/CNCPT TIME/SEQ VAL/FREE 20. PAGE 120 A2452
S/ASIA ATTIT DIPLOM WAR

B66
BESSON W.,DIE GROSSEN MACHTE - STRUKTURFRAGEN DER GEGENWARTIGEN WELTPOLITIK. ASIA USSR WOR+45 ATTIT ...IDEA/COMP 20 KENNEDY/JF. PAGE 14 A0280
NAT/COMP DIPLOM STRUCT

B66
BLACKSTOCK P.W.,AGENTS OF DECEIT: FRAUDS, FORGERIES AND POLITICAL INTRIGUES AMONG NATIONS. USSR EDU/PROP WRITING KNOWL 18/20 COLD/WAR KENNAN/G. PAGE 15 A0302
CON/ANAL DIPLOM HIST/WRIT

B66
BLOOMFIELD L.P.,KHRUSHCHEV AND THE ARMS RACE. USA+45 USSR ECO/DEV BAL/PWR EDU/PROP CONFER NUC/PWR ATTIT...CHARTS 20 KHRUSH/N. PAGE 16 A0321
ARMS/CONT COM POLICY DIPLOM

B66
BRYNES A.,WE GIVE TO CONQUER. USA+45 USSR STRATA ECO/UNDEV INT/ORG NAT/G DIPLOM DRIVE...TREND IDEA/COMP 20. PAGE 20 A0414
FOR/AID CONTROL GIVE WAR

B66
DAVIDSON A.B.,RUSSIA AND AFRICA. USSR AGRI INT/TRADE...GEOG BIBLIOG/A 18/20. PAGE 34 A0687
MARXISM COLONIAL RACE/REL DIPLOM

B66
DRACHOVITCH M.M.,THE COMINTERN HISTORICAL HIGHLIGHTS. USSR INT/ORG EX/STRUC LEGIT LEAD GUERRILLA...ANTHOL 20 COMINTERN LENIN/VI. PAGE 38 A0784
DIPLOM REV MARXISM PERSON

B66
DYCK H.V.,WEIMAR GERMANY AND SOVIET RUSSIA 1926-1933. EUR+WWI GERMANY UK USSR ECO/TAC INT/TRADE NEUTRAL WAR ATTIT 20 WEIMAR/REP TREATY. PAGE 40 A0814
DIPLOM GOV/REL POLICY

B66
EPSTEIN F.T.,THE AMERICAN BIBLIOGRAPHY OF RUSSIAN AND EAST EUROPEAN STUDIES FOR 1964. USSR LOC/G NAT/G POL/PAR FORCES ADMIN ARMS/CONT...JURID CONCPT 20 UN. PAGE 42 A0855
BIBLIOG COM MARXISM DIPLOM

B66
EUDIN X.J.,SOVIET FOREIGN POLICY 1928-34: DOCUMENTS AND MATERIALS (VOL. I). ASIA USSR WOR-45 INT/ORG POL/PAR WORKER WAR PEACE...ANTHOL 20 TREATY LEAGUE/NAT INTERVENT. PAGE 43 A0873
DIPLOM POLICY GOV/REL MARXISM

B66
EWING B.G.,PEACE THROUGH NEGOTIATION: THE AUSTRIAN EXPERIENCE. AUSTRIA USSR VIETNAM CONFER CONTROL DETER WAR ATTIT HEALTH PWR...POLICY 20. PAGE 43 A0878
PEACE DIPLOM MARXISM

B66
FELKER J.L.,SOVIET ECONOMIC CONTROVERSIES. USSR INDUS PLAN INT/TRADE GP/REL MARXISM SOCISM...POLICY 20. PAGE 45 A0915
ECO/DEV MARKET PROFIT PRICE

B66
FRANK E.,LAWMAKERS IN A CHANGING WORLD. FRANCE UK USSR WOR+45 PARTIC EFFICIENCY ROLE ALL/IDEOS ...CHARTS ANTHOL PARLIAMENT 20 UN COLD/WAR. PAGE 48 A0979
GOV/COMP LEGIS NAT/G DIPLOM

B66
GRAHAM I.C.C.,PUBLICATIONS OF THE SOCIAL SCIENCE DEPARTMENT, THE RAND CORPORATION, 1948-1966. USSR WOR+45 NAT/G ARMS/CONT DETER WAR NAT/LISM...SOC GOV/COMP. PAGE 55 A1127
BIBLIOG DIPLOM NUC/PWR FORCES

B66
HALPERIN M.H.,CHINA AND NUCLEAR PROLIFERATION (PAMPHLET). CHINA/COM FUT INDIA USA+45 USSR ARMS/CONT WAR 20 CHINJAP. PAGE 60 A1239
NUC/PWR FORCES POLICY DIPLOM

B66
HERZ M.F.,BEGINNINGS OF THE COLD WAR. COM POLAND USA+45 USSR INT/ORG NAT/G CHIEF FOR/AID DOMIN CONFER AGREE WAR PEACE 20 STALIN/J COLD/WAR UN. PAGE 64 A1321
DIPLOM

B66
HORELICK A.L.,STRATEGIC POWER AND SOVIET FOREIGN POLICY. CUBA USSR FORCES PLAN CIVMIL/REL...POLICY DECISION 20 COLD/WAR. PAGE 67 A1383
DIPLOM BAL/PWR DETER NUC/PWR

B66
INTL CONF ON WORLD POLITICS-5,EASTERN EUROPE IN TRANSITION. EUR+WWI USSR ECO/TAC NAT/LISM ATTIT SOVEREIGN...CHARTS ANTHOL 20 TREATY WARSAW/P. PAGE 71 A1463
COM NAT/COMP MARXISM DIPLOM

B66
KANET R.E.,THE SOVIET UNION AND SUB-SAHARAN AFRICA: COMMUNIST POLICY TOWARD AFRICA, 1917-1965. AFR USSR ECO/UNDEV TEC/DEV EDU/PROP TASK DISCRIM PEACE WEALTH ALL/IDEOS...CHARTS BIBLIOG SOC/INTEG 19/20 NEGRO UN INTERVENT. PAGE 76 A1555
DIPLOM ECO/TAC MARXISM

B66
KIM Y.K.,PATTERNS OF COMPETITIVE COEXISTENCE: USA VS. USSR. USA+45 USSR ECO/DEV ECO/UNDEV INT/ORG FOR/AID INT/TRADE ARMS/CONT...BIBLIOG 20 COLD/WAR. PAGE 79 A1618
DIPLOM PEACE BAL/PWR DETER

B66
KUENNE R.E.,THE POLARIS MISSILE STRIKE* A GENERAL ECONOMIC SYSTEMS ANALYSIS. USA+45 USSR NAT/G BAL/PWR ARMS/CONT WAR...MATH PROBABIL COMPUT/IR CHARTS HYPO/EXP SIMUL. PAGE 82 A1689
NUC/PWR FORCES DETER DIPLOM

B66
LONDON K.,EASTERN EUROPE IN TRANSITION. CHINA/COM USSR DOMIN COLONIAL CENTRAL RIGID/FLEX PWR...SOC ANTHOL 20. PAGE 91 A1855
SOVEREIGN COM NAT/LISM DIPLOM

B66
MC LELLAN D.S.,THE COLD WAR IN TRANSITION. USSR WOR+45 CONTROL LEAD NUC/PWR NAT/LISM SOVEREIGN 20 COLD/WAR THIRD/WRLD. PAGE 97 A1994
BAL/PWR DETER DIPLOM POLICY

B66
MORRIS B.S.,INTERNATIONAL COMMUNISM AND AMERICAN POLICY. CHINA/COM USA+45 USSR INT/ORG POL/PAR GP/REL NAT/LISM ATTIT PERCEPT 20. PAGE 105 A2147
DIPLOM POLICY MARXISM

B66
MURPHY G.G.,SOVIET MONGOLIA: A STUDY OF THE OLDEST POLITICAL SATELLITE. USSR STRATA STRUCT COST INCOME ATTIT SOCISM 20. PAGE 106 A2177
DIPLOM ECO/TAC PLAN DOMIN

B66
O19VON BORCH H.,FRIEDETROTZ KRIEG. GERMANY USSR WOR+45 PEACE ANOMIE ATTIT 20. PAGE 112 A2305
DIPLOM NUC/PWR WAR COERCE

B66
SAGER P.,MOSKAUS HAND IN INDIEN. INDIA USSR DIPLOM DOMIN...PSY CONCPT 20 COM/PARTY. PAGE 126 A2586
PRESS EDU/PROP METH POL/PAR

B66
SINGER L.,ALLE LITTEN AN GROSSENWAHN: VON WOODROW WILSON BIS MAO TSE-TUNG. ASIA UK USSR INT/ORG DELIB/GP BAL/PWR DOMIN ATTIT PERSON 20 WILSON/W ROOSEVLT/F. PAGE 133 A2731
DIPLOM TOTALISM WAR CHIEF

B66
US DEPARTMENT OF STATE,RESEARCH ON THE USSR AND EASTERN EUROPE (EXTERNAL RESEARCH LIST NO 1-25). USSR LAW CULTURE SOCIETY NAT/G TEC/DEV DIPLOM EDU/PROP REGION...GEOG LING. PAGE 152 A3097
BIBLIOG/A EUR+WWI COM MARXISM

B66
US DEPARTMENT OF THE ARMY,COMMUNIST CHINA: A STRATEGIC SURVEY: A BIBLIOGRAPHY (PAMPHLET NO. 20-67). CHINA/COM COM INDIA USSR NAT/G POL/PAR EX/STRUC FORCES NUC/PWR REV ATTIT...POLICY GEOG CHARTS. PAGE 152 A3109
BIBLIOG/A MARXISM S/ASIA DIPLOM

B66
US SENATE COMM AERO SPACE SCI,SOVIET SPACE PROGRAMS, 1962-65; GOALS AND PURPOSES, ACHIEVEMENTS, PLANS, AND INTERNATIONAL IMPLICATIONS. USA+45 USSR R+D FORCES PLAN EDU/PROP PRESS ADJUD ARMS/CONT ATTIT MARXISM. PAGE 155 A3168
CONSULT SPACE FUT DIPLOM

B66
WESTIN A.F.,VIEWS OF AMERICA. COM USA+45 USSR SOCIETY ECO/UNDEV POL/PAR ECO/TAC GP/REL STRANGE MARXISM...MARXIST 20. PAGE 163 A3323
CONCPT ATTIT DIPLOM

IDEA/COMP

B66
WESTWOOD A.F.,FOREIGN AID IN A FOREIGN POLICY FRAMEWORK. AFR ASIA INDIA IRAN L/A+17C USA+45 USSR ECO/UNDEV AGRI FORCES LEGIS PLAN PROB/SOLV ...DECISION 20 COLD/WAR. PAGE 163 A3324
FOR/AID DIPLOM POLICY ECO/TAC

B66
WOHL R.,FRENCH COMMUNISM IN THE MAKING 1914-1924. FRANCE USSR LEAD REV...IDEA/COMP 20 COM/PARTY. PAGE 166 A3377
MARXISM WORKER DIPLOM

B66
ZABLOCKI C.J.,SINO-SOVIET RIVALRY. AFR ASIA CHINA/COM CUBA EUR+WWI L/A+17C USA+45 USSR WOR+45 POL/PAR FORCES COERCE NUC/PWR...GOV/COMP IDEA/COMP 20 MAO KHRUSH/N. PAGE 169 A3442
DIPLOM MARXISM COM

S66
CHIU H.,"COMMUNIST CHINA'S ATTITUDE TOWARD INTERNATIONAL LAW" CHINA/COM USSR LAW CONSTN DIPLOM GP/REL 20 LENIN/VI. PAGE 26 A0532
INT/LAW MARXISM CONCPT IDEA/COMP

S66
DINH TRANS V.A.N.,"VIETNAM: A THIRD WAY" S/ASIA USA+45 USSR VIETNAM VIETNAM/S NAT/G SECT FORCES CAP/ISM DIPLOM COLONIAL NEUTRAL MARXISM SOCISM 20 BUDDHISM UNIFICA. PAGE 38 A0766
WAR PLAN ORD/FREE SOCIALIST

S66
DUROSELLE J.B.,"THE FUTURE OF THE ATLANTIC COMMUNITY." EUR+WWI USA+45 USSR NAT/G CAP/ISM REGION DETER NUC/PWR ATTIT MARXISM...INT/LAW 20 NATO. PAGE 40 A0811
FUT DIPLOM MYTH POLICY

S66
FRIEND A.,"THE MIDDLE EAST CRISIS" COM ISLAM ISRAEL SYRIA UAR USA+45 USSR FORCES PLAN FOR/AID CONTROL ORD/FREE PWR...SOCIALIST TIME/SEQ 20 NASSER/G. PAGE 49 A1009
WAR INT/ORG DIPLOM PEACE

S66
MCNEAL R.H.,"THE LEGACY OF THE COMINTERN." USSR WOR+45 WOR-45 PROB/SOLV DIPLOM CONFER CONTROL LEAD WAR 20 STALIN/J COMINTERN. PAGE 98 A2020
MARXISM INT/ORG POL/PAR PWR

N66
US HOUSE COMM FOREIGN AFFAIRS,UNITED STATES POLICY TOWARD ASIA (PAMPHLET). CHINA/COM USA+45 USSR VIETNAM INT/ORG NAT/G PWR MARXISM 20 UN. PAGE 154 A3133
POLICY ASIA DIPLOM PLAN

B67
BRZEZINSKI Z.K.,IDEOLOGY AND POWER IN SOVIET POLITICS. USSR NAT/G POL/PAR PWR...GEN/LAWS 19/20. PAGE 21 A0419
DIPLOM EX/STRUC MARXISM

B67
BRZEZINSKI Z.K.,THE SOVIET BLOC: UNITY AND CONFLICT (2ND ED., REV., ENLARGED). COM POLAND USSR INTELL CHIEF EX/STRUC CONTROL EXEC GOV/REL PWR MARXISM ...TREND IDEA/COMP 20 LENIN/VI MARX/KARL STALIN/J. PAGE 21 A0420
NAT/G DIPLOM

B67
CHO S.S.,KOREA IN WORLD POLITICS 1940-1950; AN EVALUATION OF AMERICAN RESPONSIBILITY. KOREA USA+45 USSR CONSTN INT/ORG NAT/G FORCES FOR/AID ANOMIE SUPEGO MARXISM...DECISION BIBLIOG 20. PAGE 26 A0533
POLICY DIPLOM PROB/SOLV WAR

B67
FILENE P.G.,AMERICANS AND THE SOVIET EXPERIMENT, 1917-1933. USA-45 USSR INTELL NAT/G CAP/ISM DIPLOM EDU/PROP PRESS REV SOCISM...PSY 20. PAGE 45 A0930
ATTIT RIGID/FLEX MARXISM SOCIETY

B67
HALPERIN M.H.,CONTEMPORARY MILITARY STRATEGY. ASIA CHINA/COM USA+45 USSR INT/ORG FORCES ACT/RES PLAN TEC/DEV BAL/PWR COERCE WAR...METH/COMP BIBLIOG 20 NATO. PAGE 60 A1240
DIPLOM NUC/PWR DETER ARMS/CONT

B67
MCBRIDE J.H.,THE TEST BAN TREATY: MILITARY, TECHNOLOGICAL, AND POLITICAL IMPLICATIONS. USA+45 USSR DELIB/GP FORCES LEGIS TEC/DEV BAL/PWR TREATY. PAGE 97 A1995
ARMS/CONT DIPLOM NUC/PWR

B67
TROTSKY L.,PROBLEMS OF THE CHINESE REVOLUTION (3RD ED. TRANS. BY MAX SCHACTMAN). ASIA USSR DIPLOM MARXISM SOCISM...IDEA/COMP ANTHOL DICTIONARY 20 STALIN/J. PAGE 145 A2969
MARXIST REV

B67
US SUPERINTENDENT OF DOCUMENTS,LIBRARY OF CONGRESS (PRICE LIST 83). AFR ASIA EUR+WWI USA-45 USSR NAT/G DIPLOM CONFER CT/SYS WAR...DECISION PHIL/SCI CLASSIF 19/20 CONGRESS PRESIDENT. PAGE 157 A3205
BIBLIOG/A USA+45 AUTOMAT LAW

S67
"CHINESE STATEMENT ON NUCLEAR PROLIFERATION." CHINA/COM USA+45 USSR DOMIN COLONIAL PWR. PAGE 4 A0078
NUC/PWR BAL/PWR ARMS/CONT DIPLOM

S67
AFRICAN BIBLIOGRAPHIC CENTER,"THE SWORD AND GOVERNMENT: A PRELIMINARY AND SELECTED BIBLIOGRAPHICAL GUIDE TO AFRICAN MILITARY AFFAIRS; PART I." AFR USA+45 USSR INT/ORG POL/PAR FOR/AID COLONIAL ARMS/CONT PWR 20 UN. PAGE 5 A0101
BIBLIOG/A FORCES CIVMIL/REL DIPLOM

S67
DAVIS H.B.,"LENIN AND NATIONALISM: THE REDIRECTION OF THE MARXIST THEORY OF NATIONALISM." COM MOD/EUR USSR STRATA INT/ORG PLAN DOMIN COLONIAL FEDERAL ...TREND 20. PAGE 34 A0690
NAT/LISM MARXISM ATTIT CENTRAL

S67
EGBERT D.D.,"POLITICS AND ART IN COMMUNIST BULGARIA" BULGARIA COM USSR CULTURE DIPLOM INGP/REL TOTALISM...TREND 20. PAGE 40 A0825
CREATE ART/METH CONTROL MARXISM

S67
GOLDMAN M.I.,"SOVIET ECONOMIC GROWTH SINCE THE REVOLUTION." USSR WORKER INT/TRADE PRODUC MARXISM ...POLICY TIME/SEQ 20. PAGE 53 A1090
ECO/DEV AGRI ECO/TAC INDUS

S67
HAZARD J.N.,"POST-DISARMAMENT INTERNATIONAL LAW." FUT USSR WOR+45 INT/ORG DELIB/GP FORCES DETER EQUILIB SOVEREIGN MARXISM 20 UN. PAGE 63 A1301
INT/LAW ARMS/CONT PWR PLAN

S67
KYLE K.,"BACKGROUND TO THE CRISIS" ISLAM ISRAEL UAR UK USSR NAT/G PROB/SOLV LEGIT CONTROL REGION STRANGE MORAL 20 JEWS. PAGE 83 A1698
DIPLOM POLICY SOVEREIGN COERCE

S67
LACOUTRE J.,"HO CHI MINH." CHINA/COM USSR VIETNAM/N NAT/G CHIEF TOP/EX LEAD NEUTRAL...REALPOL PREDICT 20. PAGE 83 A1708
NAT/LISM MARXISM REV DIPLOM

S67
LIVNEH E.,"A NEW BEGINNING." ISRAEL USSR WOR+45 NAT/G DIPLOM INGP/REL FEDERAL HABITAT PWR...GEOG PSY JEWS. PAGE 90 A1847
WAR PERSON PEACE PLAN

S67
MEYER J.,"CUBA S'ENFERME DANS SA REVOLUTION." CHINA/COM CUBA USSR NAT/G TOP/EX DIPLOM LEAD ATTIT ...PREDICT 20. PAGE 100 A2053
MARXISM REV CHIEF NAT/LISM

S67
NIEBUHR R.,"THE SOCIAL MYTHS IN THE COLD WAR." USA+45 USSR VIETNAM PROB/SOLV BAL/PWR ARMS/CONT NAT/LISM PWR ALL/IDEOS CONCPT. PAGE 109 A2238
MYTH DIPLOM GOV/COMP

S67
PERLO V.,"NEW DIMENSIONS IN EAST-WEST TRADE." UK USA+45 USSR WOR+45 ECO/DEV NAT/G CAP/ISM PEACE WEALTH LAISSEZ...SOCIALIST MGT 20. PAGE 115 A2364
BAL/PWR ECO/TAC INT/TRADE

S67
SHULMAN M.D.,"'EUROPE' VERSUS 'DETENTE'." USA+45 USSR INT/ORG CONTROL ARMS/CONT DETER 20. PAGE 132 A2711
DIPLOM BAL/PWR NUC/PWR

S67
STEEL R.,"BEYOND THE POWER BLOCS." USA+45 USSR ECO/UNDEV NEUTRAL NUC/PWR NAT/LISM ATTIT...GEOG NATO WARSAW/P COLD/WAR. PAGE 137 A2811
DIPLOM TREND BAL/PWR PLAN

S67
TUCKER R.C.,"THE DERADICALIZATION OF MARXIST MOVEMENTS." USSR SOCIETY DIPLOM 20. PAGE 145 A2973
MARXISM ADJUST ATTIT REV

S67
VLASCIC I.A.,"THE SPACE TREATY* A PRELIMINARY EVALUATION." FUT USSR WOR+45 R+D ACT/RES TEC/DEV DIPLOM CONFER ARMS/CONT PEACE...PREDICT UN TREATY. PAGE 159 A3245
SPACE INT/LAW INT/ORG NEUTRAL

C67
GEHLEN M.P.,"THE POLITICS OF COEXISTENCE: SOVIET METHODS AND MOTIVES." COM USSR NAT/G INT/TRADE EDU/PROP ARMS/CONT DETER KNOWL...CHARTS IDEA/COMP 20 COLD/WAR. PAGE 52 A1056
BIBLIOG PEACE DIPLOM MARXISM

C67
HUDSON G.F.,"THE HARD AND BITTER PEACE; WORLD POLITICS SINCE 1945." ASIA COM S/ASIA USSR WOR+45 COLONIAL WAR...TREND BIBLIOG/A 20 COLD/WAR UN. PAGE 68 A1405
DIPLOM INT/ORG ARMS/CONT BAL/PWR

UTAH....UTAH

UTIL....UTILITY, USEFULNESS

B19
ROUSSEAU J.J.,A LASTING PEACE. INT/ORG NAT/G CHIEF DIPLOM DETER WAR POLICY. PAGE 124 A2550
PLAN PEACE UTIL

N19
MORGENSTERN O.,THE COMMAND AND CONTROL STRUCTURE (PAMPHLET). USSR COM/IND INT/ORG WEAPON PEACE UTIL ...TREND 20 NATO. PAGE 104 A2132
CONTROL FORCES EFFICIENCY PLAN

B38
FRANKEL S.H.,CAPITAL INVESTMENT IN AFRICA. AFR EUR+WWI RHODESIA SOUTH/AFR UK FINAN FOR/AID COLONIAL DEMAND UTIL WEALTH...METH/CNCPT CHARTS 20 CONGO/LEOP. PAGE 48 A0983
ECO/UNDEV EXTR/IND DIPLOM PRODUC

B56
UNDERHILL F.H.,THE BRITISH COMMONWEALTH: AN EXPERIMENT IN CO-OPERATION AMONG NATIONS. CANADA UK WOR+45 WOR-45 INT/ORG COLONIAL UTIL SOVEREIGN CONSERVE...OLD/LIB SOC/EXP BIBLIOG/A 19/20 CMN/WLTH. PAGE 147 A3007
VOL/ASSN NAT/LISM DIPLOM

B59
US GENERAL ACCOUNTING OFFICE,EXAM OF ECONOMIC AND TECHNICAL ASSISTANCE PROGRAM FOR INDIA INT'NAT'L COOP ADMIN REPORT TO CONGRESS 1955-1958. INDIA USA+45 ECO/UNDEV FINAN PLAN DIPLOM COST UTIL WEALTH ...CHARTS 20 CONGRESS AID. PAGE 153 A3114
FOR/AID EFFICIENCY ECO/TAC TEC/DEV

N60
ERDMAN P.E.,COMMON MARKETS AND FREE TRADE AREAS (PAMPHLET). USA+45 MARKET INT/ORG TEC/DEV DIPLOM UTIL...CON/ANAL CHARTS BIBLIOG 20 EEC OEEC. PAGE 42 A0859
TREND PROB/SOLV INT/TRADE ECO/DEV

B62
ROUND TABLE ON EUROPE'S ROLE IN LATIN AMERICAN DEVELOPMENT. EUR+WWI L/A+17C PLAN BAL/PAY UTIL ROLE WEALTH...CHARTS ANTHOL 20 UN INT/AM/DEV. PAGE 3 A0063
ECO/UNDEV FINAN TEC/DEV FOR/AID

B63
ROBOCK S.H.,OVERVIEW OF TOTAL BRAZILIAN SETTING, NEWER REGIONAL PATTERNS NING AND FOREIGN AID. BRAZIL ECO/UNDEV AGRI FINAN INDUS INT/ORG INCOME UTIL...CHARTS 20. PAGE 122 A2507
ECO/TAC REGION PLAN FOR/AID

B63
US SENATE,DOCUMENTS ON INTERNATIONAL AS"ECTS OF EXPLORATION AND USE OF OUTER SPACE, 1954-62: STAFF REPORT FOR COMM AERON SPACE SCI. USA+45 USSR LEGIS LEAD CIVMIL/REL PEACE...POLICY INT/LAW ANTHOL 20 CONGRESS NASA KHRUSH/N. PAGE 155 A3165
SPACE UTIL GOV/REL DIPLOM

B63
US SENATE COMM APPROPRIATIONS,PERSONNEL ADMINISTRATION AND OPERATIONS OF AGENCY FOR INTERNATIONAL DEVELOPMENT: SPECIAL HEARING. FINAN LEAD COST UTIL SKILL...CHARTS 20 CONGRESS AID CIVIL/SERV. PAGE 155 A3170
ADMIN FOR/AID EFFICIENCY DIPLOM

B64
COLUMBIA U SCHOOL OF LAW,PUBLIC INTERNATIONAL DEVELOPMENT FINANCING IN INDIA. GERMANY/W INDIA UK USA+45 INDUS PLAN TEC/DEV DIPLOM ECO/TAC GIVE ADMIN UTIL ATTIT 20. PAGE 28 A0572
ECO/UNDEV FINAN FOR/AID INT/ORG

B66
WILLIAMS P.,AID IN UGANDA - EDUCATION. UGANDA UK FINAN ACADEM INT/ORG SCHOOL PROB/SOLV ECO/TAC UTIL ...STAT CHARTS 20. PAGE 165 A3352
PLAN EDU/PROP FOR/AID ECO/UNDEV

S67
CHAND A.,"INDIA AND TANZANIA." INDIA TANZANIA TEC/DEV ECO/TAC FOR/AID COLONIAL PEACE UTIL WEALTH ...GOV/COMP 20. PAGE 25 A0518
ECO/UNDEV NEUTRAL DIPLOM PLAN

S67
PEUKERT W.,"WEST GERMANY'S 'RED TRADE'." COM GERMANY INDUS CAP/ISM DOMIN SANCTION DEMAND PEACE UTIL...MARXIST 20 COLD/WAR. PAGE 115 A2371
DIPLOM ECO/TAC INT/TRADE

S67
WINTHROP H.,"CONTEMPORARY ECONOMIC DEHUMANIZATION* SOME DIFFICULTIES SURROUNDING ITS REDUCTION." USA+45 WOR+45 ACT/RES PROB/SOLV DIPLOM ROUTINE DEMAND UTIL. PAGE 165 A3368
TEC/DEV SOCIETY WEALTH

UTILITAR....UTILITARIANISM

UTILITY....SEE UTIL

UTOPIA....ENVISIONED GENERAL SOCIAL CONDITIONS; SEE ALSO STERTYP

B41
SCHWARZENBERGER G.,POWER POLITICS: AN INTRODUCTION TO THE STUDY OF INTERNATIONAL RELATIONS AND POST-WAR PLANNING. INT/ORG FORCES COERCE WAR FEDERAL PEACE MORAL...POLICY CONCPT CON/ANAL BIBLIOG 20. PAGE 130 A2660
DIPLOM UTOPIA PWR

B42
TOLMAN E.C.,DRIVES TOWARD WAR. UNIV PLAN DIPLOM ECO/TAC COERCE PERS/REL ADJUST HAPPINESS BIO/SOC HEREDITY HEALTH KNOWL. PAGE 144 A2947
PSY WAR UTOPIA DRIVE

B53
MENDE T.,WORLD POWER IN THE BALANCE. FUT USA+45 USSR WOR-45 ECO/DEV ECO/TAC INT/TRADE EDU/PROP UTOPIA ATTIT...HUM CONCPT TREND COLD/WAR TOT/POP 20. PAGE 99 A2036
WOR+45 PWR BAL/PWR

B54
GIRAUD A.,CIVILISATION ET PRODUCTIVITE. UNIV INDUS WORKER DIPLOM REV INCOME UTOPIA...GEOG 20. PAGE 53 A1076
SOCIETY PRODUC ROLE

B54
STREIT C.K.,FREEDOM AGAINST ITSELF. LAW SOCIETY DIPLOM UTOPIA PWR SOVEREIGN ALL/IDEOS 17/20 NATO UN. PAGE 139 A2850
ORD/FREE CREATE INT/ORG CONCPT

B56
COMMONWEALTH OF WORLD CITIZENS,THE BIRTH OF A WORLD PEOPLE. WOR+45 CONSTN PROB/SOLV CONTROL TASK WAR GP/REL UTOPIA PWR...POLICY NEW/IDEA 20. PAGE 29 A0582
DIPLOM VOL/ASSN PEACE INT/ORG

B59
NIEBUHR R.,NATIONS AND EMPIRES. WOR+45 INT/ORG COLONIAL NUC/PWR TOTALISM UTOPIA ORD/FREE MARXISM WORSHIP 20 COLD/WAR PROTESTANT CHRISTIAN. PAGE 109 A2237
DIPLOM NAT/G POLICY PWR

B61
THEOBALD R.,THE CHALLENGE OF ABUNDANCE. USA+45 WOR+45 MARKET DIPLOM FOR/AID REV PRODUC UTOPIA SUPEGO...POLICY TREND BIBLIOG/A 20. PAGE 142 A2913
WELF/ST ECO/UNDEV PROB/SOLV ECO/TAC

B63
FISCHER-GALATI S.,EASTERN EUROPE IN THE SIXTIES. ALBANIA USSR YUGOSLAVIA ECO/UNDEV AGRI MARKET LABOR WORKER DIPLOM INT/TRADE EDU/PROP GOV/REL PRODUC UTOPIA SOCISM 20. PAGE 46 A0939
MARXISM TEC/DEV BAL/PWR ECO/TAC

S67
VAN DUSEN H.P.,"HAMMARSKOLD IN THE WORLD'S SERVICE." DIPLOM CONFER LEAD PEACE STRANGE UTOPIA MORAL SKILL OBJECTIVE...INT/LAW SELF/OBS 20. PAGE 158 A3211
INT/ORG CONSULT TOP/EX NEUTRAL

UTTAR/PRAD....UTTAR PRADESH, INDIA

UYEHARA C.H. A0566

V

VAGTS A. A3209

VALIDITY (AS CONCEPT)....SEE METH/CNCPT

VALUE ADDED TAX....SEE VALUE/ADD

VALUE/ADD....VALUE ADDED TAX

VALUE-FREE THOUGHT....SEE OBJECTIVE

VALUES....SEE VALUES INDEX, P. XIII

VAN DE VELDE R.W. A1375

VAN DEN BERGHE P.L. A3210

VAN DEUSEN G.G. A2362

VAN DUSEN H.P. A3211

VAN DYKE V. A3212

VAN ESSEN J.L.F. A1715,A1716

VAN HOOGSTRATE D.J. A3213

VAN JAARSVELD F.A. A2167

VAN SLYCK P. A3214

VAN VALKENBURG S. A3215

VAN WAGENEN R.W. A0425,A3216

VAN WIJK T. A2167

VANBUREN/M....PRESIDENT MARTIN VAN BUREN

VANCE H.L. A3217

VANDENBOSCH A. A3218,A3219

VANDERPOL A. A3220

VARG P.A. A3221

VARLEY D.H. A3222

VASAK K. A3223

VATICAN....VATICAN

B51
BLANSHARD P.,COMMUNISM, DEMOCRACY AND CATHOLIC POWER. USSR VATICAN WOR+45 WOR-45 CULTURE ELITES INTELL SOCIETY STRUCT INT/ORG POL/PAR EDU/PROP COERCE ATTIT KNOWL PWR MARXISM...CONCPT COLD/WAR 20. PAGE 15 A0308
COM SECT TOTALISM

B60
ENGEL-JANOSI F.,OSTERREICH UND DER VATIKAN (2 VOLS). AUSTRIA VATICAN NAT/LISM PEACE PERSON CATHISM 20. PAGE 42 A0852
DIPLOM ATTIT WAR

VEBLEN T.B. A3224

VEBLEN/T....THORSTEIN VEBLEN

VECCHIO G.D. A3225

VELIKONJA J. A3226

VELYAMINOV G. A3227

VENETIAN REPUBLIC....SEE VENICE

VENEZUELA....VENEZUELA; SEE ALSO L/A+17C

B48
NEUBURGER O.,GUIDE TO OFFICIAL PUBLICATIONS OF THE OTHER AMERICAN REPUBLICS: VENEZUELA (VOL. XIX). VENEZUELA FINAN LEGIS PLAN BUDGET DIPLOM CT/SYS PARL/PROC 19/20. PAGE 108 A2219
BIBLIOG/A NAT/G CONSTN LAW

B61
GRASES P.,ESTUDIOS BIBLIOGRAFICOS. VENEZUELA...SOC 20. PAGE 55 A1130
BIBLIOG NAT/G DIPLOM L/A+17C

B64
SEGUNDO-SANCHEZ M.,OBRAS (2 VOLS.). VENEZUELA EX/STRUC DIPLOM ADMIN 19/20. PAGE 131 A2682
BIBLIOG LEAD NAT/G L/A+17C

B66
GRENVILLE J.A.S.,POLITICS, STRATEGY, AND AMERICAN DEMOCRACY: STUDIES IN FOREIGN POLICY, 1873-1917. CUBA PHILIPPINE SPAIN USA-45 VENEZUELA ELITES NAT/G CREATE PARTIC WAR RIGID/FLEX ORD/FREE...DECISION TREND 19/20 HAWAII. PAGE 56 A1146
DIPLOM COLONIAL POLICY

B66
GROSS F.,WORLD POLITICS AND TENSION AREAS. CHINA/COM SOMALIA VENEZUELA COERCE GP/REL RACE/REL ATTIT HABITAT 19/20 CASEBOOK NEWYORK/C. PAGE 57 A1173
DIPLOM WAR PROB/SOLV

VENICE....VENETIAN REPUBLIC

VERBA S. A1655,A3228

VERMONT....VERMONT

VERNON R. A3229

VEROFF J. A3230

VERSAILLES....VERSAILLES, FRANCE

B40
WOLFERS A.,BRITAIN AND FRANCE BETWEEN TWO WORLD WARS. FRANCE UK INT/ORG NAT/G PLAN BARGAIN ECO/TAC AGREE ISOLAT ALL/IDEOS...DECISION GEOG 20 TREATY VERSAILLES INTERVENT. PAGE 166 A3380
DIPLOM WAR POLICY

B53
BRETTON H.L.,STRESEMANN AND THE REVISION OF VERSAILLES: A FIGHT FOR REASON. EUR+WWI GERMANY FORCES BUDGET ARMS/CONT WAR SUPEGO...BIBLIOG 20 TREATY VERSAILLES STRESEMN/G. PAGE 18 A0373
POLICY DIPLOM BIOG

B59
DEHIO L.,GERMANY AND WORLD POLITICS IN THE TWENTIETH CENTURY. EUR+WWI FRANCE GERMANY MOD/EUR UK USSR NAT/G CHIEF BAL/PWR DOMIN COLONIAL CONTROL LEAD...IDEA/COMP 20 VERSAILLES. PAGE 36 A0724
DIPLOM WAR NAT/LISM SOVEREIGN

B60
FISCHER L.,THE SOVIETS IN WORLD AFFAIRS. CHINA/COM COM EUR+WWI USSR INT/ORG CONFER LEAD ARMS/CONT REV PWR...CHARTS 20 TREATY VERSAILLES. PAGE 46 A0938
DIPLOM NAT/G POLICY MARXISM

B64
CZERNIN F.,VERSAILLES - 1919. EUR+WWI USA-45 FACE/GP POL/PAR VOL/ASSN DELIB/GP TOP/EX CREATE BAL/PWR DIPLOM LEGIT NAT/LISM PEACE ATTIT RIGID/FLEX ORD/FREE PWR...CON/ANAL LEAGUE/NAT 20 VERSAILLES. PAGE 33 A0671
INT/ORG STRUCT

VERTICAL TAKE-OFF AND LANDING AIRCRAFT....SEE VTOL

VERWOERD/H....HENDRIK VERWOERD

VETO....VETO AND VETOING

VICE/PRES....VICE-PRESIDENCY (ALL NATIONS)

VICEREGAL....VICEROYALTY; VICEROY SYSTEM

VICHY....VICHY, FRANCE

B62
NOBECOURT R.G.,LES SECRETS DE LA PROPAGANDE EN FRANCE OCCUPEE. FRANCE ELITES NAT/G DIPLOM GP/REL NAT/LISM TOTALISM ORD/FREE 20 VICHY VICHY. PAGE 109 A2244
METH/COMP EDU/PROP WAR CONTROL

B62
NOBECOURT R.G.,LES SECRETS DE LA PROPAGANDE EN FRANCE OCCUPEE. FRANCE ELITES NAT/G DIPLOM GP/REL NAT/LISM TOTALISM ORD/FREE 20 VICHY VICHY. PAGE 109 A2244
METH/COMP EDU/PROP WAR CONTROL

VICTORIA/Q....QUEEN VICTORIA

VIEN N.C. A3231

VIENNA/CNV....VIENNA CONVENTION ON CONSULAR RELATIONS

B66
LEE L.T.,VIENNA CONVENTION ON CONSULAR RELATIONS. WOR+45 LAW INT/ORG CONFER GP/REL PRIVIL...INT/LAW 20 TREATY VIENNA/CNV. PAGE 86 A1760
AGREE DIPLOM ADMIN

VIET J. A3232

VIET MINH....SEE VIETNAM, GUERRILLA, COLONIAL

VIET/CONG....VIET CONG

VIETNAM....VIETNAM IN GENERAL; SEE ALSO S/ASIA, VIETNAM/N, VIETNAM/S

N
WEINTAL E.,FACING THE BRINK* AN INTIMATE STUDY OF CRISIS DIPLOMACY. CYPRUS FRANCE USA+45 USSR VIETNAM YEMEN INT/ORG NAT/G...POLICY DECISION PREDICT COLD/WAR PRESIDENT NATO 20. PAGE 162 A3307
DIPLOM

N
US SUPERINTENDENT OF DOCUMENTS,FOREIGN RELATIONS OF THE UNITED STATES; PUBLICATIONS RELATING TO FOREIGN COUNTRIES (PRICE LIST 65). UAR USA+45 VIETNAM ECO/UNDEV VOL/ASSN FOR/AID EDU/PROP ARMS/CONT HEALTH MARXISM...POLICY INT/LAW UN NATO. PAGE 157 A3201
BIBLIOG/A DIPLOM INT/ORG NAT/G

N19
DEANE H.,THE WAR IN VIETNAM (PAMPHLET). CHINA/COM VIETNAM BAL/PWR DIPLOM ECO/TAC SOCISM INTERVENT COLD/WAR INTERVENT COLD/WAR. PAGE 35 A0720
WAR SOCIALIST MORAL CAP/ISM

B29
BOUDET P.,BIBLIOGRAPHIE DE L'INDOCHINE FRANCAISE. S/ASIA VIETNAM SECT...GEOG LING 20. PAGE 17 A0344
BIBLIOG ADMIN COLONIAL DIPLOM

B45
HARVARD WIDENER LIBRARY,INDOCHINA: A SELECTED LIST OF REFERENCES. CAMBODIA FRANCE S/ASIA VIETNAM COLONIAL...POLICY 19/20. PAGE 62 A1282
BIBLIOG/A ACADEM DIPLOM NAT/G

B50
CORNELL U DEPT ASIAN STUDIES,SOUTHEAST ASIA PROGRAM DATA PAPER. BURMA CAMBODIA INDONESIA MALAYSIA VIETNAM SOCIETY STRUCT NAT/G SECT DIPLOM FOR/AID PWR WEALTH...SOC 20. PAGE 31 A0625
BIBLIOG/A CULTURE S/ASIA ECO/UNDEV

C58
BUTTINGER J.,"THE SMALLER DRAGON; A POLITICAL HISTORY OF VIETNAM." VIETNAM SECT DIPLOM CIVMIL/REL ISOLAT NAT/LISM...BIBLIOG/A 3/20. PAGE 22 A0455
COLONIAL DOMIN SOVEREIGN REV

B59
AMERICAN FRIENDS OF VIETNAM,AID TO VIETNAM: AN AMERICAN SUCCESS STORY (PAMPHLET). ASIA FUT USA+45 VIETNAM ECO/UNDEV WAR CIVMIL/REL GOV/REL...ANTHOL 20. PAGE 7 A0148
DIPLOM NAT/G FOR/AID FORCES

B60
US SENATE COMM ON FOREIGN REL,SITUATION IN VIETNAM (2 VOLS.). USA+45 VIETNAM ECO/TAC COST SENATE DEPT/STATE. PAGE 156 A3181
FOR/AID PLAN EFFICIENCY INSPECT

S62
DIHN N.Q.,"L'INTERNATIONALISATION DU MEKONG." CAMBODIA LAOS VIETNAM WOR+45 INT/ORG NAT/G VOL/ASSN PEACE HEALTH...CONCPT TIME/SEQ CHARTS METH VAL/FREE 20. PAGE 37 A0761
S/ASIA DELIB/GP

B65
AUVADE R.,BIBLIOGRAPHIE CRITIQUE DES OEUVRES PARUES SUR L'INDOCHINE FRANCAISE: UN SIECLE D'HISTOIRE ET D'ENSEIGNEMENT. VIETNAM DIPLOM...SOC 20. PAGE 10 A0198
BIBLIOG/A R+D ACADEM COLONIAL

B65
LACOUTRE J.,VIETNAM: BETWEEN TWO TRUCES. USA+45 VIETNAM NAT/G REV 20. PAGE 83 A1707
WAR ECO/UNDEV DIPLOM POLICY

B65
WARBEY W.,VIETNAM: THE TRUTH. FRANCE S/ASIA USA+45 VIETNAM CULTURE INT/ORG NAT/G DIPLOM FOR/AID EDU/PROP ARMS/CONT PEACE 20 TREATY NLF UN. PAGE 161 A3274
WAR AGREE

S65
FLEMING D.F.,"CAN PAX AMERICANA SUCCEED?" ASIA CHINA/COM EUR+WWI USSR VIETNAM BAL/PWR DIPLOM DOMIN
DECISION ATTIT

COERCE GOV/REL 20. PAGE 46 A0948 ECO/TAC

B66
SUPPLEMENTAL FOREIGN ASSISTANCE FISCAL YEAR 1966: VIETNAM. CHINA/COM COM S/ASIA USA+45 VIETNAM EXTR/IND FINAN DIPLOM TAX GUERRILLA HABITAT ORD/FREE...STAT CHARTS 20 SENATE PRESIDENT. PAGE 4 A0077
CONFER LEGIS WAR FOR/AID

B66
AMERICAN FRIENDS SERVICE COMM,PEACE IN VIETNAM: A NEW APPROACH IN SOUTHEAST ASIA: A REPORT. ASIA S/ASIA USA+45 VIETNAM ORD/FREE 20 TREATY. PAGE 7 A0149
PEACE WAR NAT/LISM DIPLOM

B66
EWING B.G.,PEACE THROUGH NEGOTIATION: THE AUSTRIAN EXPERIENCE. AUSTRIA USSR VIETNAM CONFER CONTROL DETER WAR ATTIT HEALTH PWR...POLICY 20. PAGE 43 A0878
PEACE DIPLOM MARXISM

B66
FALL B.B.,VIET-NAM WITNESS, 1953-66. S/ASIA VIETNAM SECT PROB/SOLV COLONIAL GUERRILLA...CHARTS BIBLIOG 20. PAGE 44 A0895
MARXIST WAR DIPLOM

B66
JACK H.A.,RELIGION AND PEACE: PAPERS FROM THE NATIONAL INTER-RELIGIOUS CONFERENCE ON PEACE, WASHINGTON, 1966. CHINA/COM USA+45 VIETNAM WOR+45 FORCES FOR/AID LEAD PERS/REL. PAGE 72 A1472
PEACE SECT SUPEGO DIPLOM

B66
PAN S.,VIETNAM CRISIS. ASIA FRANCE USA+45 USA-45 VIETNAM CULTURE SOCIETY INT/ORG ECO/TAC AGREE CONTROL WAR MARXISM 20. PAGE 113 A2325
ECO/UNDEV POLICY DIPLOM NAT/COMP

B66
SOBEL L.A.,SOUTH VIETNAM: US-COMMUNIST CONFRONTATION IN SOUTHEAST ASIA 1961-65. VIETNAM FOR/AID CROWD DETER REV PEACE...GEOG 20 INTERVENT DIEM COLD/WAR. PAGE 134 A2754
WAR TIME/SEQ FORCES NAT/G

B66
US HOUSE COMM FOREIGN AFFAIRS,HEARINGS ON HR 12449 A BILL TO AMEND FURTHER THE FOREIGN ASSISTANCE ACT OF 1961. AFR ASIA L/A+17C USA+45 VIETNAM INT/ORG TEC/DEV INT/TRADE ATTIT ORD/FREE 20 UN NATO CONGRESS AID. PAGE 154 A3132
FOR/AID ECO/TAC ECO/UNDEV DIPLOM

B66
VIEN N.C.,SEEKING THE TRUTH. FRANCE VIETNAM AGRI ADMIN WAR...BIOG 20 BAO/DAI INTERVENT. PAGE 159 A3231
NAT/G CONSULT CONSTN

S66
DINH TRANS V.A.N.,"VIETNAM: A THIRD WAY" S/ASIA USA+45 USSR VIETNAM VIETNAM/S NAT/G SECT FORCES CAP/ISM DIPLOM COLONIAL NEUTRAL MARXISM SOCISM 20 BUDDHISM UNIFICA. PAGE 38 A0766
WAR PLAN ORD/FREE SOCIALIST

C66
TARLING N.,"A CONCISE HISTORY OF SOUTHEAST ASIA." BURMA CAMBODIA LAOS S/ASIA THAILAND VIETNAM ECO/UNDEV POL/PAR FORCES ADMIN REV WAR CIVMIL/REL ORD/FREE MARXISM SOCISM 13/20. PAGE 141 A2890
COLONIAL DOMIN INT/TRADE NAT/LISM

N66
US HOUSE COMM FOREIGN AFFAIRS,UNITED STATES POLICY TOWARD ASIA (PAMPHLET). CHINA/COM USA+45 USSR VIETNAM INT/ORG NAT/G PWR MARXISM 20 UN. PAGE 154 A3133
POLICY ASIA DIPLOM PLAN

B67
ANDREATTA L.,VIETNAM, A CHECKLIST. S/ASIA VIETNAM PRESS PEACE ATTIT...POLICY 20. PAGE 8 A0159
BIBLIOG DIPLOM WAR

B67
LAWYERS COMM AMER POLICY VIET,VIETNAM AND INTERNATIONAL LAW: AN ANALYSIS OF THE LEGALITY OF THE US MILITARY INVOLVEMENT. VIETNAM LAW INT/ORG COERCE WEAPON PEACE ORD/FREE 20 UN SEATO TREATY. PAGE 86 A1753
INT/LAW DIPLOM ADJUD WAR

B67
MCNELLY T.,SOURCES IN MODERN EAST ASIAN HISTORY AND POLITICS. KOREA VIETNAM CULTURE DIPLOM COLONIAL REV WAR PWR ALL/IDEOS MARXISM...ANTHOL 20 CHINJAP. PAGE 99 A2023
NAT/COMP ASIA S/ASIA SOCIETY

B67
RUSSELL B.,WAR CRIMES IN VIETNAM. USA+45 VIETNAM FORCES DIPLOM WEAPON RACE/REL DISCRIM ISOLAT BIO/SOC 20 COLD/WAR RUSSELL/B. PAGE 126 A2574
WAR CRIME ATTIT POLICY

L67
MOORE N.,"THE LAWFULNESS OF MILITARY ASSISTANCE TO THE REPUBLIC OF VIET NAM." USA+45 VIETNAM WOR+45 FOR/AID DOMIN DETER WAR WEAPON...DECISION INT/LAW 20 UN. PAGE 103 A2123
PWR DIPLOM FORCES GOV/REL

S67
ABT J.J.,"WORLD OF SENATOR FULBRIGHT." VIETNAM WOR+45 COERCE DETER REV ORD/FREE MARXISM...MARXIST 20. PAGE 4 A0084
DIPLOM PLAN PWR

S67
BATOR V.,"ONE WAR* TWO VIETNAMS." S/ASIA VIETNAM DIPLOM SUFF ATTIT ORD/FREE 20. PAGE 12 A0234
WAR BAL/PWR NAT/G STRUCT

S67
BENTLEY E.,"VIETNAM: THE STATE OF OUR FEELINGS." USA+45 VIETNAM PROB/SOLV DIPLOM GP/REL INGP/REL RACE/REL WEALTH. PAGE 13 A0271
WAR PARTIC ATTIT PEACE

S67
FRANKEL M.,"THE WAR IN VIETNAM." VIETNAM ECO/UNDEV DIPLOM CONFER INGP/REL PEACE PWR...POLICY PREDICT 20. PAGE 48 A0982
WAR COERCE PLAN GUERRILLA

S67
FRANKLIN W.O.,"CLAUSEWITZ ON LIMITED WAR." VIETNAM WOR+45 WOR-45 PROB/SOLV DIPLOM ECO/TAC DOMIN COLONIAL...METH/COMP 19/20. PAGE 48 A0986
COERCE WAR PLAN GUERRILLA

S67
NIEBUHR R.,"THE SOCIAL MYTHS IN THE COLD WAR." USA+45 USSR VIETNAM PROB/SOLV BAL/PWR ARMS/CONT NAT/LISM PWR ALL/IDEOS CONCPT. PAGE 109 A2238
MYTH DIPLOM GOV/COMP

S67
THIEN T.T.,"VIETNAM: A CASE OF SOCIAL ALIENATION." VIETNAM AGRI FORCES FOR/AID ADMIN REPRESENT INGP/REL PWR 19/20. PAGE 143 A2918
NAT/G ELITES WORKER STRANGE

S67
VERBA S.,"PUBLIC OPINION AND THE WAR IN VIETNAM." USA+45 VIETNAM DIPLOM WAR...CORREL STAT QU CHARTS 20. PAGE 158 A3228
ATTIT KNO/TEST NAT/G PLAN

S67
WILLIAMS B.H.,"FREEDOM AS A SLOGAN IN INTERNATIONAL CONFLICT." VIETNAM DIPLOM COLONIAL. PAGE 164 A3351
EDU/PROP ORD/FREE WAR PWR

VIETNAM/N....NORTH VIETNAM

N
KYRIAK T.E.,ASIAN DEVELOPMENTS: A BIBLIOGRAPHY. INDONESIA KOREA/N VIETNAM/N CULTURE SOCIETY ECO/UNDEV NAT/G DIPLOM...SOC TREND 20 MONGOLIA. PAGE 83 A1699
BIBLIOG/A ALL/IDEOS S/ASIA ASIA

B63
HONEY P.J.,COMMUNISM IN NORTH VIETNAM: ITS ROLE IN THE SINO-SOVIET DISPUTE. CHINA/COM INDIA USSR VIETNAM/N AGRI POL/PAR LEGIS ECO/TAC WAR PEACE ATTIT...GEOG IDEA/COMP 20. PAGE 67 A1378
POLICY MARXISM CHIEF DIPLOM

B66
KEYES J.G.,A BIBLIOGRAPHY OF WESTERN LANGUAGE PUBLICATIONS CONCERNING NORTH VIETNAM IN THE CORNELL LIBRARY. VIETNAM/N NAT/G FORCES TEC/DEV DIPLOM LEAD RACE/REL...GEOG SOC 20. PAGE 78 A1603
BIBLIOG/A CULTURE ECO/UNDEV S/ASIA

B66
LYND S.,THE OTHER SIDE. USA+45 VIETNAM/N NAT/G PEACE SOVEREIGN 20. PAGE 92 A1877
WAR POLICY MORAL DIPLOM

B66
WEINSTEIN F.B.,VIETNAM'S UNHELD ELECTIONS: THE FAILURE TO CARRY OUT THE 1956 REUNIFICATION ELECTIONS... (MONOGRAPH). VIETNAM/S VIETNAM/N LEGIT CONFER ADJUD WAR PEACE 20 TREATY GENEVA/CON UNIFICA. PAGE 162 A3306
AGREE NAT/G CHOOSE DIPLOM

B67
SALISBURY H.E.,BEHIND THE LINES - HANOI. VIETNAM/N NAT/G GUERRILLA CIVMIL/REL NAT/LISM KNOWL 20. PAGE 126 A2592
WAR PROB/SOLV DIPLOM OBS

B67
US SENATE COMM ON FOREIGN REL,BACKGROUND INFORMATION RELATING TO SOUTHEAST ASIA AND VIETNAM (3RD REV. ED.). USA+45 VIETNAM/S VIETNAM/N...CHARTS 20 SENATE UN. PAGE 156 A3188
DIPLOM WAR FOR/AID

S67
LACOUTRE J.,"HO CHI MINH." CHINA/COM USSR VIETNAM/N NAT/G CHIEF TOP/EX LEAD NEUTRAL...REALPOL PREDICT 20. PAGE 83 A1708
NAT/LISM MARXISM REV DIPLOM

VIETNAM/S....SOUTH VIETNAM

B58
US OPERATIONS MISSION TO VIET,BUILDING ECONOMIC STRENGTH (PAMPHLET). USA+45 VIETNAM/S INDUS TEC/DEV BUDGET ADMIN EATING HEALTH...STAT 20. PAGE 155 A3162
FOR/AID ECO/UNDEV AGRI EDU/PROP

B62
JORDAN A.A. JR.,FOREIGN AID AND THE DEFENSE OF SOUTHEAST ASIA. PAKISTAN VIETNAM/S FINAN PLAN BUDGET ECO/TAC DETER WAR ORD/FREE...POLICY DECISION CENSUS CHARTS BIBLIOG 20. PAGE 75 A1535
FOR/AID S/ASIA FORCES ECO/UNDEV

B65
US SENATE COMM ON JUDICIARY,REFUGEE PROBLEMS IN SOUTH VIETNAM AND LAOS: HEARINGS BEFORE SUBCOMMITTEE TO INVESTIGATE PROBLEMS OF REFUGEES, ESCAPEES. CHINA/COM LAOS USA+45 VIETNAM/S PROB/SOLV
STRANGE HABITAT FOR/AID CIVMIL/REL

DIPLOM GOV/REL GP/REL EFFICIENCY ORD/FREE...POLICY GEOG 20 CONGRESS MIGRATION. PAGE 157 A3194

B66
US HOUSE COMM GOVT OPERATIONS,AN INVESTIGATION OF THE US ECONOMIC AND MILITARY ASSISTANCE PROGRAMS IN VIETNAM. USA+45 VIETNAM/S SOCIETY CONSTRUC FINAN FORCES BUDGET INT/TRADE PEACE HEALTH...MGT HOUSE/REP AID. PAGE 154 A3139 FOR/AID ECO/UNDEV WAR INSPECT

B66
WEINSTEIN F.B.,VIETNAM'S UNHELD ELECTIONS: THE FAILURE TO CARRY OUT THE 1956 REUNIFICATION ELECTIONS... (MONOGRAPH). VIETNAM/S VIETNAM/N LEGIT CONFER ADJUD WAR PEACE 20 TREATY GENEVA/CON UNIFICA. PAGE 162 A3306 AGREE NAT/G CHOOSE DIPLOM

S66
DINH TRANS V.A.N.,"VIETNAM: A THIRD WAY" S/ASIA USA+45 USSR VIETNAM VIETNAM/S NAT/G SECT FORCES CAP/ISM DIPLOM COLONIAL NEUTRAL MARXISM SOCISM 20 BUDDHISM UNIFICA. PAGE 38 A0766 WAR PLAN ORD/FREE SOCIALIST

B67
US SENATE COMM ON FOREIGN REL,BACKGROUND INFORMATION RELATING TO SOUTHEAST ASIA AND VIETNAM (3RD REV. ED.). USA+45 VIETNAM/S VIETNAM/N...CHARTS 20 SENATE UN. PAGE 156 A3188 DIPLOM WAR FOR/AID

S67
BUTTINGER J.,"VIETNAM* FRAUD OF THE 'OTHER WAR'." VIETNAM/S ELITES STRUCT AGRI NAT/G FOR/AID RENT TREND. PAGE 22 A0456 PLAN WEALTH REV ECO/UNDEV

S67
YOUNG K.T.,"UNITED STATES POLICY AND VIETNAMESE POLITICAL VIABILITY 1954-1967." VIETNAM/S LOC/G MUNIC FOR/AID ORD/FREE...POLICY 20. PAGE 169 A3437 LEAD ADMIN GP/REL EFFICIENCY

VIGNES D. A3233

VIGON J. A3234

VILLA/P....PANCHO VILLA

B67
TEITELBAUM L.M.,WOODROW WILSON AND THE MEXICAN REVOLUTION 1913-1916: A HISTORY OF UNITED STATES-MEXICAN RELATIONS. USA-45 CHIEF TOP/EX WAR 20 MEXIC/AMER WILSON/W VILLA/P CARRANZA/V. PAGE 142 A2902 REV DIPLOM

VILLAGE....SEE MUNIC

VILLARD/OG....OSWALD GARRISON VILLARD

VINACKE H.M. A3235

VINER J. A3236,A3237,A3238,A3239,A3240

VINER/J....JACOB VINER

B59
STOVEL J.A.,CANADA IN THE WORLD ECONOMY. CANADA PRICE DEMAND...STAT CHARTS BIBLIOG 20 VINER/J. PAGE 139 A2838 INT/TRADE BAL/PAY FINAN ECO/TAC

VINOGRADOFF P. A3241

VINSON J.C. A3242

VIOLENCE....SEE COERCE, ALSO PROCESSES AND PRACTICES INDEX, PART G, PAGE XIII

VIRALLY M. A3243

VIRGIN/ISL....VIRGIN ISLANDS

VIRGINIA....VIRGINIA

B48
BELOFF M.,THOMAS JEFFERSON AND AMERICAN DEMOCRACY. USA-45 NAT/G DIPLOM GOV/REL PEACE 18/19 JEFFERSN/T PRESIDENT VIRGINIA. PAGE 13 A0258 BIOG CHIEF REV

B52
SHULIM J.I.,THE OLD DOMINION AND NAPOLEON BONAPARTE. POL/PAR DOMIN PRESS REV WAR 18/19 VIRGINIA. PAGE 132 A2710 ATTIT PROVS EDU/PROP DIPLOM

VISSON A. A3244

VISTA....VOLUNTEERS IN SERVICE TO AMERICA (VISTA)

VLASIC I.A. A2009,A3245

VOELKMANN K. A3246

VOGT W. A3247

VOL/ASSN....VOLUNTARY ASSOCIATION

N
US SUPERINTENDENT OF DOCUMENTS,FOREIGN RELATIONS OF THE UNITED STATES; PUBLICATIONS RELATING TO FOREIGN COUNTRIES (PRICE LIST 65). UAR USA+45 VIETNAM ECO/UNDEV VOL/ASSN FOR/AID EDU/PROP ARMS/CONT HEALTH MARXISM...POLICY INT/LAW UN NATO. PAGE 157 A3201 BIBLIOG/A DIPLOM INT/ORG NAT/G

N
US SUPERINTENDENT OF DOCUMENTS,MONTHLY CATALOG OF UNITED STATES GOVERNMENT PUBLICATIONS. USA+45 USA-45 AGRI LABOR FORCES INT/TRADE TARIFFS TAX EDU/PROP CT/SYS ARMS/CONT RACE/REL 19/20 CONGRESS PRESIDENT. PAGE 157 A3203 BIBLIOG NAT/G VOL/ASSN POLICY

B00
LORIMER J.,THE INSTITUTES OF THE LAW OF NATIONS. WOR-45 CULTURE SOCIETY NAT/G VOL/ASSN DIPLOM LEGIT WAR PEACE DRIVE ORD/FREE SOVEREIGN...CONCPT RECORD INT TREND HYPO/EXP GEN/METH TOT/POP VAL/FREE 20. PAGE 91 A1863 INT/ORG LAW INT/LAW

B08
ARON R.,WAR AND INDUSTRIAL SOCIETY. EUR+WWI MOD/EUR WOR+45 WOR-45 CONSTN SOCIETY INT/ORG POL/PAR VOL/ASSN DIPLOM INT/TRADE PEACE ATTIT...BIOG GEN/LAWS 19/20. PAGE 9 A0178 ECO/DEV WAR

B10
GRIFFIN A.P.C.,LIST OF REFERENCES ON RECIPROCITY (2ND REV. ED.). CANADA CUBA UK USA-45 WOR-45 NAT/G TARIFFS CONFER COLONIAL CONTROL SANCTION CONSEN ALL/VALS...DECISION 19/20. PAGE 56 A1157 BIBLIOG/A VOL/ASSN DIPLOM REPAR

B15
FARIES J.C.,THE RISE OF INTERNATIONALISM. ASIA MOD/EUR NAT/G VOL/ASSN DELIB/GP BAL/PWR EDU/PROP ARMS/CONT RIGID/FLEX TREND. PAGE 44 A0899 INT/ORG DIPLOM PEACE

B17
MEYER H.H.B.,THE UNITED STATES AT WAR, ORGANIZATIONS AND LITERATURE. USA-45 AGRI FINAN INDUS CHIEF FORCES DIPLOM FOR/AID INT/TRADE...SOC 20 PRESIDENT. PAGE 100 A2050 BIBLIOG/A WAR NAT/G VOL/ASSN

N19
STEUBER F.A.,THE CONTRIBUTION OF SWITZERLAND TO THE ECONOMIC AND SOCIAL DEVELOPMENT OF LOW-INCOME COUNTRIES (PAMPHLET). SWITZERLND FINAN NAT/G VOL/ASSN INT/TRADE DRIVE...CHARTS 20. PAGE 138 A2820 FOR/AID ECO/UNDEV PLAN DIPLOM

N19
VELYAMINOV G.,AFRICA AND THE COMMON MARKET (PAMPHLET). AFR MARKET VOL/ASSN ECO/TAC COLONIAL ORD/FREE...SOCIALIST 20 THIRD/WRLD. PAGE 158 A3227 INT/ORG INT/TRADE SOVEREIGN ECO/UNDEV

B20
BURNS C.D.,INTERNATIONAL POLITICS. WOR-45 CULTURE SOCIETY ECO/UNDEV NAT/G VOL/ASSN DELIB/GP ACT/RES CREATE DOMIN EDU/PROP LEGIT ATTIT DRIVE RIGID/FLEX ALL/VALS...PLURIST PSY CONCPT TREND. PAGE 22 A0442 INT/ORG PEACE SOVEREIGN

S23
DEWEY J.,"ETHICS AND INTERNATIONAL RELATIONS." FUT WOR-45 SOCIETY INT/ORG VOL/ASSN DIPLOM LEGIT ORD/FREE...JURID CONCPT GEN/METH 20. PAGE 37 A0752 LAW MORAL

B24
NAVILLE A.,LIBERTE, EGALITE, SOLIDARITE: ESSAIS D'ANALYSE. STRATA FAM VOL/ASSN INT/TRADE GP/REL MORAL MARXISM SOCISM...PSY TREATY. PAGE 107 A2205 ORD/FREE SOC IDEA/COMP DIPLOM

B26
INSTITUT INTERMEDIAIRE INTL,REPERTOIRE GENERAL DES TRAITES ET AUTRES ACTES DIPLOMATIQUES CONCLUS DEPUIS 1895 JUSQU'EN 1920. MOD/EUR WOR-45 INT/ORG VOL/ASSN DELIB/GP INT/TRADE WAR TREATY 19/20. PAGE 70 A1443 BIBLIOG DIPLOM

B28
HALL W.P.,EMPIRE TO COMMONWEALTH. FUT WOR-45 CONSTN ECO/DEV ECO/UNDEV INT/ORG PROVS PLAN DIPLOM EDU/PROP ADMIN COLONIAL PEACE PERSON ALL/VALS ...POLICY GEOG SOC OBS RECORD TREND CMN/WLTH PARLIAMENT 19/20. PAGE 60 A1229 VOL/ASSN NAT/G UK

B28
HURST C.,GREAT BRITAIN AND THE DOMINIONS. EUR+WWI CULTURE ECO/DEV INT/ORG NAT/G DIPLOM ECO/TAC COLONIAL ATTIT PWR SOVEREIGN...TIME/SEQ GEN/LAWS TOT/POP VAL/FREE 20 CMN/WLTH. PAGE 69 A1420 VOL/ASSN DOMIN UK

B31
BEALES A.C.,THE HISTORY OF PEACE. WOR-45 VOL/ASSN DELIB/GP CREATE PLAN EDU/PROP ATTIT MORAL ...TIME/SEQ VAL/FREE 19/20. PAGE 12 A0239 INT/ORG ARMS/CONT PEACE

B32
HANSEN A.H.,ECONOMIC STABILIZATION IN AN UNBALANCED WORLD. COM EUR+WWI USA-45 WOR-45 AGRI FINAN INDUS MARKET INT/ORG LABOR VOL/ASSN EDU/PROP ATTIT HEALTH KNOWL WEALTH...HIST/WRIT TREND VAL/FREE 20. PAGE 61 A1253 NAT/G ECO/DEV CAP/ISM SOCISM

B34
EINSTEIN A.,THE WORLD AS I SEE IT. WOR-45 INTELL SOCIETY

R+D INT/ORG NAT/G SECT VOL/ASSN FORCES CREATE EDU/PROP LEGIT ARMS/CONT WAR WEAPON NAT/LISM ALL/VALS...POLICY CONCPT 20. PAGE 41 A0828
PHIL/SCI DIPLOM PACIFISM

B34
GRAHAM F.D.,PROTECTIVE TARIFFS. FUT USA+45 WOR-45 INDUS MARKET VOL/ASSN PLAN CAP/ISM ECO/TAC PEACE ATTIT DRIVE HEALTH ORD/FREE...OBS TREND GEN/LAWS 20. PAGE 55 A1124
INT/ORG TARIFFS

B34
WOLFF C.,JUS GENTIUM METHODO SCIENTIFICA PERTRACTATUM. MOD/EUR INT/ORG VOL/ASSN LEGIT PEACE ATTIT...JURID 20. PAGE 166 A3387
NAT/G LAW INT/LAW WAR

S35
MCMAHON A.H.,"INTERNATIONAL BOUNDARIES." WOR-45 INT/ORG NAT/G LEGIT SKILL...CHARTS GEN/LAWS 20. PAGE 98 A2017
GEOG VOL/ASSN INT/LAW

B36
ROBINSON H.,DEVELOPMENT OF THE BRITISH EMPIRE. WOR-45 CULTURE SOCIETY STRUCT ECO/DEV ECO/UNDEV INT/ORG VOL/ASSN FORCES CREATE PLAN DOMIN EDU/PROP ADMIN COLONIAL PWR WEALTH...POLICY GEOG CHARTS CMN/WLTH 16/20. PAGE 122 A2503
NAT/G HIST/WRIT UK

B36
THWAITE D.,THE SEETHING AFRICAN POT: A STUDY OF BLACK NATIONALISM 1882-1935. ETHIOPIA SECT VOL/ASSN COERCE GUERRILLA MURDER DISCRIM MARXISM...PSY TIME/SEQ 18/20 NEGRO. PAGE 144 A2939
NAT/LISM AFR RACE/REL DIPLOM

B37
TUPPER E.,JAPAN IN AMERICAN PUBLIC OPINION. USA-45 POL/PAR VOL/ASSN INT/TRADE DISCRIM...BIBLIOG 20 CHINJAP TREATY. PAGE 146 A2979
ATTIT IDEA/COMP DIPLOM PRESS

C37
TUPPER E.,"JAPAN IN AMERICAN PUBLIC OPINION." USA+45 POL/PAR VOL/ASSN INT/TRADE DISCRIM ...IDEA/COMP 20 CHINJAP. PAGE 146 A2978
BIBLIOG ATTIT DIPLOM PRESS

B38
HOBSON J.A.,IMPERIALISM. MOD/EUR UK WOR-45 CULTURE ECO/UNDEV NAT/G VOL/ASSN PLAN EDU/PROP LEGIT REGION COERCE ATTIT PWR...POLICY PLURIST TIME/SEQ GEN/LAWS 19/20. PAGE 66 A1348
DOMIN ECO/TAC BAL/PWR COLONIAL

B39
DULLES J.,WAR, PEACE AND CHANGE. FRANCE ITALY UK USA-45 WOR-45 LAW INT/ORG NAT/G SECT VOL/ASSN FORCES TOP/EX DOMIN ARMS/CONT COERCE ATTIT PERSON RIGID/FLEX MORAL PWR...JURID STERTYP TOT/POP LEAGUE/NAT 20. PAGE 39 A0796
EDU/PROP TOTALISM WAR

L42
SHOTWELL J.,"LESSON OF THE LAST WORLD WAR." EUR+WWI MOD/EUR USA-45 SOCIETY ECO/UNDEV INDUS VOL/ASSN CONSULT ACT/RES CREATE CAP/ISM INT/TRADE DRIVE ALL/VALS...CONCPT NEW/IDEA SELF/OBS GEN/LAWS LEAGUE/NAT NAZI 20. PAGE 132 A2708
INT/ORG ORD/FREE

B43
MC DOWELL R.B.,IRISH PUBLIC OPINION, 1750-1800. IRELAND CONSTN VOL/ASSN WORKER ORD/FREE CATHISM CONSERVE...POLICY IDEA/COMP BIBLIOG 18/ PARLIAMENT. PAGE 97 A1992
ATTIT NAT/G DIPLOM REV

B44
BRIERLY J.L.,THE OUTLOOK FOR INTERNATIONAL LAW. FUT WOR-45 CONSTN NAT/G VOL/ASSN FORCES ECO/TAC DOMIN LEGIT ADJUD ROUTINE PEACE ORD/FREE...INT/LAW JURID METH LEAGUE/NAT 20. PAGE 18 A0376
INT/ORG LAW

B45
CARR E.H.,NATIONALISM AND AFTER. FUT WOR-45 NAT/G VOL/ASSN EX/STRUC PLAN ROUTINE TOTALISM ATTIT HEALTH ORD/FREE PWR...CONCPT 20. PAGE 25 A0499
INT/ORG TREND NAT/LISM REGION

B45
KANDELL I.L.,UNITED STATES ACTIVITIES IN INTERNATIONAL CULTURAL RELATIONS. INT/ORG NAT/G VOL/ASSN CREATE DIPLOM EDU/PROP ATTIT RIGID/FLEX KNOWL...PLURIST CONCPT OBS TREND GEN/LAWS TOT/POP UNESCO 20. PAGE 76 A1554
USA-45 CULTURE

B46
MITRANY D.,A WORKING PEACE SYSTEM. WOR+45 WOR-45 ECO/DEV INT/ORG NAT/G DELIB/GP ECO/TAC REGION ATTIT RIGID/FLEX...TREND GEN/LAWS LEAGUE/NAT 20. PAGE 102 A2091
VOL/ASSN PLAN PEACE SOVEREIGN

B47
BROOKINGS INST.,MAJOR PROBLEMS OF UNITED STATES FOREIGN POLICY. USA+45 WOR+45 STRUCT ECO/DEV ECO/UNDEV INT/ORG NAT/G POL/PAR VOL/ASSN DELIB/GP FORCES ECO/TAC LEGIT COERCE ORD/FREE PWR WEALTH ...POLICY STAT TREND CHARTS TOT/POP. PAGE 19 A0392
ACT/RES DIPLOM

L47
BRUNER J.S.,"TOWARD A COMMON GROUND-INTERNATIONAL SOCIAL SCIENCE." FUT WOR+45 INTELL R+D NAT/G VOL/ASSN CONSULT DELIB/GP ACT/RES CREATE PLAN TEC/DEV ATTIT ORD/FREE...PSY SOC CONCPT ANTHOL UNESCO 20. PAGE 20 A0410
INT/ORG KNOWL

B49
JACKSON R.H.,INTERNATIONAL CONFERENCE ON MILITARY TRIALS. FRANCE GERMANY UK USA+45 USSR VOL/ASSN DELIB/GP REPAR ADJUD CT/SYS CRIME WAR 20 WAR/TRIAL. PAGE 72 A1479
DIPLOM INT/ORG INT/LAW CIVMIL/REL

B49
MANSERGH N.,THE COMING OF THE FIRST WORLD WAR: A STUDY IN EUROPEAN BALANCE, 1878-1914. GERMANY MOD/EUR VOL/ASSN COLONIAL CONTROL PWR 19/20 TREATY. PAGE 94 A1928
DIPLOM WAR BAL/PWR

B49
PARMELEE M.,GEO-ECONOMIC REGIONAL AND WORLD FEDERATION. FUT WOR+45 WOR-45 SOCIETY VOL/ASSN PLAN ...METH/CNCPT SIMUL GEN/METH TOT/POP 20. PAGE 114 A2335
INT/ORG GEOG REGION

B49
STETTINIUS E.R.,ROOSEVELT AND THE RUSSIANS: THE YALTA CONFERENCE. UK USSR WOR+45 WOR-45 INT/ORG VOL/ASSN TOP/EX ACT/RES EDU/PROP PEACE ATTIT DRIVE PERSON SUPEGO PWR...POLICY CONCPT MYTH OBS TIME/SEQ AUD/VIS COLD/WAR 20 CHURCHLL/W YALTA ROOSEVLT/F. PAGE 138 A2819
DIPLOM DELIB/GP BIOG

S49
FOX W.T.R.,"INTERWAR INTERNATIONAL RELATIONS RESEARCH: THE AMERICAN EXPERIENCE." USA+45 USA-45 INTELL INT/ORG VOL/ASSN OP/RES ATTIT SKILL ...TIME/SEQ LEAGUE/NAT 20. PAGE 48 A0973
ACT/RES CON/ANAL

B50
DE RUSETT A.,STRENGTHENING THE FRAMEWORK OF PEACE. WOR+45 VOL/ASSN FORCES CREATE INSPECT ADJUD CONTROL WAR EQUILIB FEDERAL ORD/FREE 20 UN EUROPE. PAGE 35 A0711
INT/ORG DIPLOM PEACE METH/COMP

B50
LINCOLN G.,ECONOMICS OF NATIONAL SECURITY. USA+45 ELITES COM/IND DIST/IND INDUS NAT/G VOL/ASSN DELIB/GP EX/STRUC FOR/AID EDU/PROP COERCE NUC/PWR WAR ATTIT KNOWL ORD/FREE PWR COLD/WAR TOT/POP VAL/FREE 20. PAGE 89 A1818
FORCES ECO/TAC

S50
UNESCO,"MEETING ON UNIVERSITY TEACHING OF INTERNATIONAL RELATIONS." FUT WOR+45 R+D VOL/ASSN CONSULT PLAN EDU/PROP ATTIT...CONCPT TREND 20. PAGE 147 A3012
INT/ORG KNOWL DIPLOM

B51
PRICE D.K.,THE NEW DIMENSIONS OF DIPLOMACY: THE ORGANIZATION OF THE US GOVERNMENT FOR ITS NEW ROLE IN WORLD AFFAIRS (PAMPHLET). USA+45 WOR+45 INT/ORG VOL/ASSN CONSULT DELIB/GP PLAN PROB/SOLV 20 PRESIDENT. PAGE 117 A2411
DIPLOM GP/REL NAT/G

B51
UNESCO,FREEDOM AND CULTURE. FUT WOR+45 CONSTN CULTURE PERF/ART VOL/ASSN EDU/PROP PEACE ATTIT ALL/VALS SOVEREIGN...POLICY MAJORIT CONCPT TREND STERTYP GEN/LAWS UN TOT/POP 20. PAGE 147 A3013
INT/ORG SOCIETY

B51
WHITE L.C.,INTERNATIONAL NON-GOVERNMENTAL ORGANIZATIONS. AFR ASIA COM EUR+WWI USA+45 WOR+45 INT/ORG DIPLOM INT/TRADE ALL/VALS...HUM FAO ILO EEC 20. PAGE 164 A3337
VOL/ASSN CONSULT

L51
WHITAKER A.P.,"DEVELOPMENT OF AMERICAN REGIONALISM: THE ORGANIZATION OF AMERICAN STATES." L/A+17C USA+45 VOL/ASSN DELIB/GP FORCES TOP/EX ACT/RES ECO/TAC CT/SYS REGION PEACE ALL/VALS OAS 20. PAGE 163 A3330
INT/ORG TIME/SEQ DETER

S51
BELKNAP G.,"POLITICAL PARTY IDENTIFICATION AND ATTITUDES TOWARD FOREIGN POLICY" (BMR)" USA+45 VOL/ASSN CONTROL CHOOSE...STAT INT CHARTS 20. PAGE 12 A0254
POL/PAR ATTIT POLICY DIPLOM

S51
CONNERY R.H.,"THE MUTUAL DEFENSE ASSISTANCE PROGRAM." COM EUR+WWI KOREA USA+45 NAT/G VOL/ASSN CREATE PLAN BAL/PWR EDU/PROP PERCEPT...POLICY DECISION CONCPT NATO 20. PAGE 29 A0587
INT/ORG FORCES FOR/AID

S51
GYR J.,"ANALYSIS OF COMMITTEE MEMBER BEHAVIOUR IN FOUR CULTURES." ASIA ISLAM L/A+17C USA+45 INT/ORG VOL/ASSN LEGIT ATTIT...INT DEEP/QU SAMP CHARTS 20. PAGE 58 A1200
DELIB/GP CULTURE

B52
SCHUMAN F.,THE COMMONWEALTH OF MAN. WOR+45 WOR-45 LAW CULTURE ELITES SOCIETY FAM INT/ORG NAT/G VOL/ASSN TOP/EX PLAN BAL/PWR LEGIT ATTIT DISPL DRIVE...POLICY MYTH TREND TOT/POP ILO OEEC 20. PAGE 129 A2649
CONCPT GEN/LAWS

L52
NIEBUHR R.,"THE MORAL IMPLICATIONS OF LOYALTY TO THE UNITED NATIONS." WOR+45 WOR-45 SOCIETY ECO/DEV INT/ORG VOL/ASSN PEACE ATTIT PERSON LOVE ORD/FREE PWR RESPECT...CONCPT UN TOT/POP COLD/WAR UNESCO 20. PAGE 109 A2236
SUPEGO GEN/LAWS

S52
MASTERS R.D.,"RUSSIA AND THE UNITED NATIONS." FUT USA+45 USSR WOR+45 CONSTN VOL/ASSN DELIB/GP TOP/EX CREATE DIPLOM ADMIN...TREND STERTYP UN 20. PAGE 96 A1962
INT/ORG PWR

S52
SCHUMAN F.,"INTERNATIONAL IDEALS AND THE NATIONAL
ATTIT

INTEREST." WOR+45 WOR-45 INT/ORG VOL/ASSN DELIB/GP CREATE BAL/PWR DOMIN PEACE PERSON MORAL PWR SOVEREIGN...POLICY GEN/LAWS TOT/POP LEAGUE/NAT 20. PAGE 129 A2648
CONCPT

B53
COHEN B.C.,CITIZEN EDUCATION IN WORLD AFFAIRS. USA+45 INT/ORG VOL/ASSN CONSULT ATTIT PWR...INT TIME/SEQ 20. PAGE 27 A0559
KNOWL EDU/PROP DIPLOM

B53
GREENE K.R.C.,INSTITUTIONS AND INDIVIDUALS: AN ANNOTATED LIST OF DIRECTORIES USEFUL IN INTERNATIONAL ADMINISTRATION. USA+45 NAT/G VOL/ASSN ...INDEX 20. PAGE 56 A1141
BIBLIOG INT/ORG ADMIN DIPLOM

B53
MACK R.T.,RAISING THE WORLDS STANDARD OF LIVING. IRAN INT/ORG VOL/ASSN EX/STRUC ECO/TAC WEALTH...MGT METH/CNCPT STAT CONT/OBS INT TOT/POP VAL/FREE 20 UN. PAGE 92 A1893
WOR+45 FOR/AID INT/TRADE

L53
UNESCO,"THE TECHNIQUE OF INTERNATIONAL CONFERENCES." WOR+45 INT/ORG VOL/ASSN EDU/PROP ROUTINE ATTIT DRIVE KNOWL ORD/FREE...SOC UNESCO 20. PAGE 148 A3016
DELIB/GP ACT/RES

B54
COOK T.,POWER THROUGH PURPOSE. USA+45 WOR+45 WOR-45 INT/ORG VOL/ASSN BAL/PWR DIPLOM EDU/PROP LEGIT PERSON...GEN/LAWS LEAGUE/NAT 20. PAGE 30 A0606
ATTIT CONCPT

B54
MILLARD E.L.,FREEDOM IN A FEDERAL WORLD. FUT WOR+45 VOL/ASSN TOP/EX LEGIT ROUTINE FEDERAL PEACE ATTIT DISPL ORD/FREE PWR...MAJORIT INT/LAW JURID TREND COLD/WAR 20. PAGE 101 A2073
INT/ORG CREATE ADJUD BAL/PWR

B54
TAYLOR A.J.P.,THE STRUGGLE FOR MASTERY IN EUROPE 1848-1918. MOD/EUR VOL/ASSN FORCES BAL/PWR DOMIN CONTROL PEACE MORAL 19/20 TREATY EUROPE WWI. PAGE 142 A2897
DIPLOM WAR PWR

L54
OPLER M.E.,"SOCIAL ASPECTS OF TECHNICAL ASSISTANCE IN OPERATION." WOR+45 VOL/ASSN CREATE PLAN TEC/DEV EDU/PROP ALL/VALS...METH/CNCPT OBS RECORD TREND UN 20. PAGE 112 A2292
INT/ORG CONSULT FOR/AID

B55
COMM. STUDY ORGAN. PEACE,REPORTS. WOR-45 ECO/DEV ECO/UNDEV VOL/ASSN CONSULT FORCES PLAN TEC/DEV DOMIN EDU/PROP NUC/PWR ATTIT PWR WEALTH...JURID STERTYP FAO ILO 20 UN. PAGE 28 A0579
WOR+45 INT/ORG ARMS/CONT

B55
GULICK E.V.,EUROPE'S CLASSICAL BALANCE OF POWER: CASE HISTORY OF THEORY AND PRACTICE OF GREAT CONCEPTS OF EUROPEAN STATECRAFT. MOD/EUR INT/ORG VOL/ASSN FORCES ORD/FREE 18/19 TREATY. PAGE 58 A1192
IDEA/COMP BAL/PWR PWR DIPLOM

B55
MALCLES L.N.,BIBLIOGRAPHICAL SERVICES THROUGHOUT THE WORLD (VOL. 4). WOR+45 INT/ORG VOL/ASSN DIPLOM PRESS WRITING 20 UNESCO. PAGE 93 A1911
BIBLIOG ROUTINE COM/IND

B55
MYRDAL A.R.,AMERICA'S ROLE IN INTERNATIONATIONAL SOCIAL WELFARE. FUT WOR+45 SOCIETY R+D VOL/ASSN ECO/TAC EDU/PROP HEALTH KNOWL WEALTH...SOC CHARTS ORG/CHARTS TOT/POP 20. PAGE 107 A2188
PLAN SKILL FOR/AID

B55
SNYDER R.C.,AMERICAN FOREIGN POLICY. USA+45 USA-45 WOR+45 WOR-45 CONSTN INT/ORG POL/PAR VOL/ASSN DELIB/GP LEGIS CREATE DOMIN EDU/PROP EXEC COERCE ATTIT DRIVE ORD/FREE PWR...MGT OBS RECORD TIME/SEQ TREND. PAGE 134 A2752
NAT/G DIPLOM

B55
TAN C.C.,THE BOXER CATASTROPHE. ASIA UK USSR ELITES POL/PAR VOL/ASSN FORCES PROB/SOLV DIPLOM ADMIN COLONIAL NAT/LISM PEACE TREATY 19/20 BOXER/REBL. PAGE 141 A2885
REV NAT/G WAR

B55
TANNENBAUM F.,THE AMERICAN TRADITION IN FOREIGN POLICY. USA+45 USA-45 CONSTN INT/ORG NAT/G POL/PAR VOL/ASSN TOP/EX LEGIT DRIVE ORD/FREE PWR...CONCPT GEN/LAWS CONGRESS LEAGUE/NAT COLD/WAR OAS 18/20. PAGE 141 A2887
TIME/SEQ

B55
UN HEADQUARTERS LIBRARY,BIBLIOGRAPHIE DE LA CHARTE DES NATIONS UNIES. CHINA/COM KOREA WOR+45 VOL/ASSN CONFER ADMIN COERCE PEACE ATTIT ORD/FREE SOVEREIGN ...INT/LAW 20 UNESCO UN. PAGE 147 A3001
BIBLIOG/A INT/ORG DIPLOM

L55
KISER M.,"ORGANIZATION OF AMERICAN STATES." L/A+17C USA+45 ECO/UNDEV INT/ORG NAT/G PLAN TEC/DEV DIPLOM ECO/TAC INT/TRADE EDU/PROP ADMIN ALL/VALS...POLICY MGT RECORD ORG/CHARTS OAS 20. PAGE 80 A1639
VOL/ASSN ECO/DEV REGION

S55
HALLETT D.,"THE HISTORY AND STRUCTURE OF OEEC." EUR+WWI USA+45 CONSTN INDUS INT/ORG NAT/G DELIB/GP ACT/RES PLAN ORD/FREE WEALTH...CONCPT OEEC 20 CMN/WLTH. PAGE 60 A1234
VOL/ASSN ECO/DEV

S55
TORRE M.,"PSYCHIATRIC OBSERVATIONS OF INTERNATIONAL CONFERENCES." WOR+45 INT/ORG PROF/ORG VOL/ASSN CONSULT EDU/PROP ROUTINE ATTIT DRIVE KNOWL...PSY METH/CNCPT OBS/ENVIR STERTYP 20. PAGE 144 A2950
DELIB/GP OBS DIPLOM

B56
COMMONWEALTH OF WORLD CITIZENS,THE BIRTH OF A WORLD PEOPLE. WOR+45 CONSTN PROB/SOLV CONTROL TASK WAR GP/REL UTOPIA PWR...POLICY NEW/IDEA 20. PAGE 29 A0582
DIPLOM VOL/ASSN PEACE INT/ORG

B56
HAAS E.B.,DYNAMICS OF INTERNATIONAL RELATIONS. WOR-45 ELITES INT/ORG VOL/ASSN EX/STRUC FORCES ECO/TAC DOMIN LEGIT COERCE ATTIT PERSON PWR ...CONCPT TIME/SEQ CHARTS COLD/WAR 20. PAGE 58 A1202
WOR+45 NAT/G DIPLOM

B56
SPEECKAERT G.P.,INTERNATIONAL INSTITUTIONS AND INTERNATIONAL ORGANIZATIONS. PROF/ORG DELIB/GP KNOWL 19/20. PAGE 136 A2776
BIBLIOG INT/ORG DIPLOM VOL/ASSN

B56
UNDERHILL F.H.,THE BRITISH COMMONWEALTH: AN EXPERIMENT IN CO-OPERATION AMONG NATIONS. CANADA UK WOR+45 WOR-45 INT/ORG COLONIAL UTIL SOVEREIGN CONSERVE...OLD/LIB SOC/EXP BIBLIOG/A 19/20 CMN/WLTH. PAGE 147 A3007
VOL/ASSN NAT/LISM DIPLOM

S56
GORDON L.,"THE ORGANIZATION FOR EUROPEAN ECONOMIC COOPERATION." EUR+WWI INDUS INT/ORG NAT/G CONSULT DELIB/GP ACT/RES CREATE PLAN TEC/DEV EDU/PROP LEGIT WEALTH OEEC 20. PAGE 54 A1114
VOL/ASSN ECO/DEV

B57
ARON R.,L'UNIFICATION ECONOMIQUE DE L'EUROPE. EUR+WWI SWITZERLND UK INT/ORG NAT/G REGION NAT/LISM ORD/FREE PWR...CONCPT METH/CNCPT OBS TREND STERTYP GEN/LAWS EEC 20. PAGE 9 A0181
VOL/ASSN ECO/TAC

B57
JENKS C.W.,THE INTERNATIONAL PROTECTION OF TRADE UNION FREEDOM. FUT WOR+45 WOR-45 VOL/ASSN DELIB/GP CT/SYS REGION ROUTINE...JURID METH/CNCPT RECORD TIME/SEQ CHARTS ILO WORK OAS 20. PAGE 73 A1504
LABOR INT/ORG

B57
LEVONTIN A.V.,THE MYTH OF INTERNATIONAL SECURITY: A JURIDICAL AND CRITICAL ANALYSIS. FUT WOR+45 WOR-45 LAW NAT/G VOL/ASSN ACT/RES BAL/PWR ATTIT ORD/FREE ...JURID METH/CNCPT TIME/SEQ TREND STERTYP 20. PAGE 88 A1797
INT/ORG INT/LAW SOVEREIGN MYTH

L57
HAAS E.B.,"REGIONAL INTEGRATION AND NATIONAL POLICY." WOR+45 VOL/ASSN DELIB/GP EX/STRUC ECO/TAC DOMIN EDU/PROP LEGIT COERCE ATTIT PERCEPT KNOWL ...TIME/SEQ COLD/WAR 20 UN. PAGE 59 A1203
INT/ORG ORD/FREE REGION

S57
HOAG M.W.,"ECONOMIC PROBLEMS OF ALLIANCE." COM EUR+WWI WOR+45 ECO/DEV ECO/UNDEV NAT/G VOL/ASSN FORCES PLAN TEC/DEV DIPLOM COERCE ORD/FREE PWR WEALTH...DECISION GEN/LAWS NATO COLD/WAR. PAGE 65 A1345
INT/ORG ECO/TAC

B58
HAAS E.B.,THE UNITING OF EUROPE. EUR+WWI INT/ORG NAT/G POL/PAR TOP/EX ECO/TAC EDU/PROP LEGIT FEDERAL NAT/LISM DRIVE RIGID/FLEX ORD/FREE PWR PLURISM ...POLICY CONCPT INT GEN/LAWS ECSC EEC 20. PAGE 59 A1204
VOL/ASSN ECO/DEV

B58
JENNINGS W.I.,PROBLEMS OF THE NEW COMMONWEALTH. CEYLON INDIA MALAYSIA PAKISTAN ECO/UNDEV VOL/ASSN RACE/REL NAT/LISM ROLE 20 CMN/WLTH. PAGE 74 A1511
GP/REL INGP/REL COLONIAL INT/ORG

B58
KINDLEBERGER C.P.,INTERNATIONAL ECONOMICS. WOR+45 WOR-45 ECO/DEV ECO/UNDEV FINAN VOL/ASSN ACT/RES DIPLOM ECO/TAC LEGIT REGION ATTIT DRIVE ORD/FREE WEALTH...POLICY STAT TREND GEN/LAWS EEC ECSC OEEC 20. PAGE 79 A1620
INT/ORG BAL/PWR TARIFFS

B58
MANSERGH N.,COMMONWEALTH PERSPECTIVES. GHANA UK LAW VOL/ASSN CONFER HEALTH SOVEREIGN...GEOG CHARTS ANTHOL 20 CMN/WLTH AUSTRAL. PAGE 94 A1930
DIPLOM COLONIAL INT/ORG INGP/REL

B58
MANSERGH N.,SURVEY OF BRITISH COMMONWEALTH AFFAIRS: PROBLEMS OF WARTIME CO-OPERATION AND POST-WAR CHANGE 1939-1952. INDIA IRELAND S/ASIA CONSTN INT/ORG BAL/PWR COLONIAL NEUTRAL WAR ADJUST PEACE ROLE ORD/FREE...CHARTS 20 CMN/WLTH NATO UN. PAGE 94 A1931
VOL/ASSN CONSEN PROB/SOLV INGP/REL

B58
MOORE B.T.,NATO AND THE FUTURE OF EUROPE. EUR+WWI FUT USA+45 ECO/DEV INDUS MARKET NAT/G VOL/ASSN FORCES DIPLOM NUC/PWR ORD/FREE...CONCPT CHARTS ORG/CHARTS CMN/WLTH 20 NATO. PAGE 103 A2122
INT/ORG REGION

B58
REUTER P.,INTERNATIONAL INSTITUTIONS. WOR+45 WOR-45 CULTURE SOCIETY VOL/ASSN LEGIT ROUTINE GP/REL INGP/REL KNOWL...JURID METH/CNCPT TIME/SEQ 20. PAGE 120 A2469
INT/ORG PSY

B58
SEYID MUHAMMAD V.A.,THE LEGAL FRAMEWORK OF WORLD TRADE. WOR+45 INT/ORG DIPLOM CONTROL...BIBLIOG 20 TREATY UN IMF GATT. PAGE 131 A2689
INT/LAW VOL/ASSN INT/TRADE TARIFFS

L58
HAVILAND H.F.,"FOREIGN AID AND THE POLICY PROCESS: 1957." USA+45 FACE/GP POL/PAR VOL/ASSN CHIEF DELIB/GP ACT/RES LEGIT EXEC GOV/REL ATTIT DRIVE PWR ...POLICY TESTS CONGRESS 20. PAGE 63 A1291
LEGIS PLAN FOR/AID

L58
INT. SOC. SCI. BULL.,"TECHNIQUES OF MEDIATION AND CONCILIATION." EUR+WWI USA+45 SOCIETY INDUS INT/ORG LABOR NAT/G LEGIS DIPLOM EDU/PROP CHOOSE ATTIT RIGID/FLEX...JURID CONCPT GEN/LAWS 20. PAGE 70 A1447
VOL/ASSN DELIB/GP INT/LAW

S58
ELKIN A.B.,"OEEC-ITS STRUCTURE AND POWERS." EUR+WWI CONSTN INDUS INT/ORG NAT/G VOL/ASSN DELIB/GP ACT/RES PLAN ORD/FREE WEALTH...CHARTS ORG/CHARTS OEEC 20. PAGE 41 A0839
ECO/DEV EX/STRUC

S58
ROTHFELS H.,"THE GERMAN RESISTANCE IN ITS INTERNATIONAL ASPECTS" (BMR)" EUR+WWI GERMANY UNIV CHIEF DIPLOM WAR NAT/LISM ATTIT...POLICY 20 HITLER/A NAZI. PAGE 124 A2548
VOL/ASSN MORAL FASCISM CIVMIL/REL

B59
KNIERIEM A.,THE NUREMBERG TRIALS. EUR+WWI GERMANY VOL/ASSN LEAD COERCE WAR INGP/REL TOTALISM SUPEGO ORD/FREE...CONCPT METH/COMP. PAGE 80 A1651
INT/LAW CRIME PARTIC JURID

B59
LAQUER W.Z.,THE SOVIET UNION AND THE MIDDLE EAST. COM UAR USSR ECO/UNDEV NAT/G VOL/ASSN ECO/TAC EDU/PROP COLONIAL EXEC PWR...TIME/SEQ TREND COLD/WAR 20. PAGE 85 A1730
ISLAM DRIVE FOR/AID NAT/LISM

B59
SANNWALD R.E.,ECONOMIC INTEGRATION: THEORETICAL ASSUMPTIONS AND CONSEQUENCES OF EUROPEAN UNIFICATION. EUR+WWI FUT FINAN INDUS VOL/ASSN ACT/RES ECO/TAC...PLURIST EEC OEEC 20. PAGE 127 A2601
INT/ORG ECO/DEV INT/TRADE

B59
TUNSTALL W.C.B.,THE COMMONWEALTH AND REGIONAL DEFENCE (PAMPHLET). UK LAW VOL/ASSN PLAN AGREE REGION WAR ORD/FREE 20 CMN/WLTH NATO SEATO TREATY. PAGE 146 A2977
INT/ORG FORCES DIPLOM

B59
UNION OF INTERNATIONAL ASSNS,DIRECTORY OF PERIODICALS PUBLISHED BY INTERNATIONAL ORGANIZATIONS (2ND ED.)....INDEX 20. PAGE 148 A3027
BIBLIOG INT/ORG DIPLOM VOL/ASSN

L59
BEGUIN B.,"ILO AND THE TRIPARTITE SYSTEM." EUR+WWI WOR+45 WOR-45 CONSTN ECO/DEV ECO/UNDEV INDUS INT/ORG NAT/G VOL/ASSN DELIB/GP PLAN TEC/DEV LEGIT ORD/FREE WEALTH...CONCPT TIME/SEQ WORK ILO 20. PAGE 12 A0249
LABOR

S59
BAILEY S.D.,"THE FUTURE COMPOSITION OF THE TRUSTEESHIP COUNCIL." FUT WOR+45 CONSTN VOL/ASSN ADMIN ATTIT PWR...OBS TREND CON/ANAL VAL/FREE UN 20. PAGE 10 A0203
INT/ORG NAT/LISM SOVEREIGN

S59
HARTT J.,"ANTARCTICA: ITS IMMEDIATE PRACTICALITIES." FUT USA+45 USSR WOR+45 INT/ORG NAT/G CREATE TEC/DEV REGION KNOWL WEALTH...GEOG 20 ANTARTICA. PAGE 62 A1276
VOL/ASSN ORD/FREE DIPLOM

S59
HOFFMANN S.,"IMPLEMENTATION OF INTERNATIONAL INSTRUMENTS ON HUMAN RIGHTS." WOR+45 VOL/ASSN DELIB/GP JUDGE EDU/PROP LEGIT ROUTINE PEACE COLD/WAR 20. PAGE 66 A1355
INT/ORG MORAL

S59
KOHN L.Y.,"ISRAEL AND NEW NATION STATES OF ASIA AND AFRICA." AFR ASIA FUT S/ASIA VOL/ASSN TEC/DEV NAT/LISM RIGID/FLEX SKILL WEALTH...RELATIV OBS TREND CON/ANAL 20. PAGE 81 A1663
ECO/UNDEV ECO/TAC FOR/AID ISRAEL

S59
PADELFORD N.J.,"REGIONAL COOPERATION IN THE SOUTH PACIFIC: THE SOUTH PACIFIC COMMISSION." FUT NEW/ZEALND UK WOR+45 CULTURE ECO/UNDEV LOC/G VOL/ASSN...OBS CON/ANAL UNESCO VAL/FREE AUSTRAL 20. PAGE 112 A2308
INT/ORG ADMIN

S59
POTTER P.B.,"OBSTACLES AND ALTERNATIVES TO INTERNATIONAL LAW." WOR+45 NAT/G VOL/ASSN DELIB/GP BAL/PWR DOMIN ROUTINE...JURID VAL/FREE 20. PAGE 117 A2400
INT/ORG LAW DIPLOM INT/LAW

S59
STOESSINGER J.G.,"THE INTERNATIONAL ATOMIC ENERGY AGENCY: THE FIRST PHASE." FUT WOR+45 NAT/G VOL/ASSN DELIB/GP BAL/PWR LEGIT ADMIN ROUTINE PWR...OBS CON/ANAL GEN/LAWS VAL/FREE 20 IAEA. PAGE 138 A2829
INT/ORG ECO/DEV FOR/AID NUC/PWR

B60
ARMS CONTROL. FUT UNIV WOR+45 INTELL R+D INT/ORG NAT/G VOL/ASSN CONSULT CREATE EDU/PROP PEACE...HUM GEN/LAWS TOT/POP 20. PAGE 3 A0060
DELIB/GP ORD/FREE ARMS/CONT NUC/PWR

B60
BUCHAN A.,NATO IN THE 1960'S. EUR+WWI USA+45 WOR+45 INT/ORG ACT/RES PLAN LEGIT COERCE DETER ATTIT DRIVE RIGID/FLEX ORD/FREE...METH/CNCPT TIME/SEQ TREND GEN/LAWS COLD/WAR 20 NATO. PAGE 21 A0421
VOL/ASSN FORCES ARMS/CONT SOVEREIGN

B60
JENNINGS R.,PROGRESS OF INTERNATIONAL LAW. FUT WOR+45 WOR-45 SOCIETY NAT/G VOL/ASSN DELIB/GP DIPLOM EDU/PROP LEGIT COERCE ATTIT DRIVE MORAL ORD/FREE...JURID CONCPT OBS TIME/SEQ TREND GEN/LAWS. PAGE 74 A1509
INT/ORG LAW INT/LAW

B60
KENNAN G.F.,RUSSIA AND THE WEST. ASIA COM EUR+WWI GERMANY UK USA+45 USA-45 USSR INT/ORG NAT/G VOL/ASSN DOMIN REV WAR PWR...TIME/SEQ 20. PAGE 78 A1590
EXEC DIPLOM

B60
LINDSAY K.,EUROPEAN ASSEMBLIES: THE EXPERIMENTAL PERIOD 1949-1959. EUR+WWI ECO/DEV NAT/G POL/PAR LEGIS TOP/EX ACT/RES PLAN ECO/TAC DOMIN LEGIT ROUTINE ATTIT DRIVE ORD/FREE PWR SKILL...SOC CONCPT TREND CHARTS GEN/LAWS VAL/FREE. PAGE 89 A1823
VOL/ASSN INT/ORG REGION

B60
PENTONY D.E.,THE UNDERDEVELOPED LANDS. FUT WOR+45 CULTURE AGRI FINAN INDUS MARKET INT/ORG LABOR NAT/G VOL/ASSN CONSULT TEC/DEV ECO/TAC EDU/PROP COLONIAL ATTIT WEALTH...OBS RECORD SAMP TREND GEN/METH WORK UN 20. PAGE 115 A2351
ECO/UNDEV POLICY FOR/AID INT/TRADE

B60
SHONFIELD A.,THE ATTACK ON WORLD POVERTY. WOR+45 ECO/DEV ECO/UNDEV FINAN VOL/ASSN PLAN EDU/PROP DRIVE KNOWL WEALTH...CONT/OBS STAND/INT ORG/CHARTS TOT/POP UNESCO 20. PAGE 132 A2704
INT/ORG ECO/TAC FOR/AID INT/TRADE

B60
STEIN E.,AMERICAN ENTERPRISE IN THE EUROPEAN COMMON MARKET: A LEGAL PROFILE. EUR+WWI FUT USA+45 SOCIETY STRUCT ECO/DEV NAT/G VOL/ASSN CONSULT PLAN TEC/DEV ECO/TAC INT/TRADE ADMIN ATTIT RIGID/FLEX PWR...MGT NEW/IDEA STAT TREND COMPUT/IR SIMUL EEC 20. PAGE 137 A2814
MARKET ADJUD INT/LAW

B60
WHEARE K.C.,THE CONSTITUTIONAL STRUCTURE OF THE COMMONWEALTH. UK EX/STRUC DIPLOM DOMIN ADMIN COLONIAL CONTROL LEAD INGP/REL SUPEGO 20 CMN/WLTH. PAGE 163 A3325
CONSTN INT/ORG VOL/ASSN SOVEREIGN

L60
BRENNAN D.G.,"SETTING AND GOALS OF ARMS CONTROL." FUT USA+45 USSR WOR+45 INTELL INT/ORG NAT/G VOL/ASSN CONSULT PLAN DIPLOM ECO/TAC ADMIN KNOWL PWR...POLICY CONCPT TREND COLD/WAR 20. PAGE 18 A0371
FORCES COERCE ARMS/CONT DETER

L60
FERNBACH A.P.,"SOVIET COEXISTENCE STRATEGY." WOR+45 PROF/ORG VOL/ASSN DIPLOM DOMIN EDU/PROP ATTIT DRIVE PERSON PWR SKILL WEALTH...POLICY OBS SAMP TREND STERTYP ILO WORK COLD/WAR 420. PAGE 45 A0919
LABOR INT/ORG USSR

S60
MORA J.A.,"THE ORGANIZATION OF AMERICAN STATES." USA+45 LAW ECO/UNDEV VOL/ASSN DELIB/GP PLAN BAL/PWR EDU/PROP ADMIN DRIVE RIGID/FLEX ORD/FREE WEALTH ...TIME/SEQ GEN/LAWS OAS 20. PAGE 103 A2126
L/A+17C INT/ORG REGION

S60
MUNRO L.,"CAN THE UNITED NATIONS ENFORCE PEACE." WOR+45 LAW INT/ORG VOL/ASSN BAL/PWR LEGIT ARMS/CONT COERCE DETER PEACE PWR...CONCPT REC/INT TREND UN 20 HAMMARSK/D. PAGE 106 A2173
FORCES ORD/FREE

S60
SCHWELB E.,"INTERNATIONAL CONVENTIONS ON HUMAN RIGHTS." FUT WOR+45 LAW CONSTN CULTURE SOCIETY STRUCT VOL/ASSN DELIB/GP PLAN ADJUD SUPEGO LOVE MORAL...SOC CONCPT STAT RECORD HIST/WRIT TREND 20 UN. PAGE 130 A2664
INT/ORG HUM

B61
ASIA SOCIETY,AMERICAN INSTITUTIONS ANS ORGANIZATIONS INTERESTED IN ASIA; A REFERENCE DIRECTORY (2ND ED.). ASIA USA+45 CULTURE SECT DIPLOM EDU/PROP...INDEX 20. PAGE 9 A0190
VOL/ASSN ACADEM PROF/ORG

B61
BONNEFOUS M.,EUROPE ET TIERS MONDE. EUR+WWI SOCIETY INT/ORG NAT/G VOL/ASSN ACT/RES TEC/DEV CAP/ISM ECO/TAC ATTIT ORD/FREE SOVEREIGN...POLICY CONCPT TREND 20. PAGE 16 A0334
AFR ECO/UNDEV FOR/AID INT/TRADE

B61
DALLIN D.J.,SOVIET FOREIGN POLICY AFTER STALIN. ASIA CHINA/COM EUR+WWI GERMANY IRAN UK YUGOSLAVIA INT/ORG NAT/G VOL/ASSN FORCES TOP/EX BAL/PWR DOMIN EDU/PROP COERCE ATTIT PWR 20. PAGE 33 A0679
COM DIPLOM USSR

B61
FRIEDMANN W.G.,JOINT INTERNATIONAL BUSINESS VENTURES. ASIA ISLAM L/A+17C ECO/DEV DIST/IND FINAN PROC/MFG FACE/GP LG/CO NAT/G VOL/ASSN CONSULT EX/STRUC PLAN ADMIN ROUTINE WEALTH...OLD/LIB WORK 20. PAGE 49 A1004
ECO/UNDEV INT/TRADE

B61
NOLLAU G.,INTERNATIONAL COMMUNISM AND WORLD REVOLUTION: HISTORY AND METHODS. RUSSIA USSR INT/ORG NAT/G POL/PAR VOL/ASSN FORCES BAL/PWR DIPLOM EXEC REGION WAR ATTIT PWR MARXISM...CONCPT TIME/SEQ COLD/WAR 19/20. PAGE 102 A2100
COM REV

B61
PEASLEE A.J.,INTERNATIONAL GOVERNMENT ORGANIZATIONS, CONSTITUTIONAL DOCUMENTS. WOR+45 WOR-45 CONSTN VOL/ASSN DELIB/GP EX/STRUC ROUTINE KNOWL TOT/POP 20. PAGE 114 A2344
INT/ORG STRUCT

B61
PEASLEE A.J.,INTERNATIONAL GOVERNMENTAL ORGANIZATIONS (2 VOLS.). CONSTN VOL/ASSN DIPLOM ...GP/COMP 20 UN OAS EEC EFTA ECSC. PAGE 114 A2345
BIBLIOG INT/ORG INDEX LAW

B61
ROBERTSON A.H.,THE LAW OF INTERNATIONAL INSTITUTIONS IN EUROPE. EUR+WWI MOD/EUR INT/ORG NAT/G VOL/ASSN DELIB/GP...JURID TIME/SEQ TOT/POP 20 TREATY. PAGE 122 A2497
RIGID/FLEX ORD/FREE

B61
STONE J.,QUEST FOR SURVIVAL. WOR+45 NAT/G VOL/ASSN LEGIT ADMIN ARMS/CONT COERCE DISPL ORD/FREE PWR ...POLICY INT/LAW JURID COLD/WAR 20. PAGE 139 A2836
INT/ORG ADJUD SOVEREIGN

B61
WRINCH P.,THE MILITARY STRATEGY OF WINSTON CHURCHILL. UK WOR-45 SEA VOL/ASSN TEC/DEV BAL/PWR LEAD WAR PEACE ATTIT...POLICY 20 CHURCHLL/W. PAGE 168 A3421
CIVMIL/REL FORCES PLAN DIPLOM

B61
YDIT M.,INTERNATIONALISED TERRITORIES. FUT WOR+45 WOR-45 CONSTN VOL/ASSN CREATE PLAN LEGIT PEACE ORD/FREE...GEOG INT/LAW JURID SOC NEW/IDEA OBS RECORD SAMP TIME/SEQ TREND 19/20 BERLIN. PAGE 169 A3431
LOC/G INT/ORG DIPLOM SOVEREIGN

S61
ANGLIN D.,"UNITED STATES OPPOSITION TO CANADIAN MEMBERSHIP IN THE PAN AMERICAN UNION: A CANADIAN VIEW." L/A+17C UK USA+45 VOL/ASSN DELIB/GP EX/STRUC PLAN DIPLOM DOMIN REGION ATTIT RIGID/FLEX PWR ...RELATIV CONCPT STERTYP CMN/WLTH OAS 20. PAGE 8 A0162
INT/ORG CANADA

S61
BARNET R.,"RUSSIA, CHINA, AND THE WORLD: THE SOVIET ATTITUDE ON DISARMAMENT (PART 3)." ASIA CHINA/COM FUT INT/ORG NAT/G POL/PAR VOL/ASSN ARMS/CONT ATTIT ...POLICY CONCPT TIME/SEQ TREND TOT/POP VAL/FREE 20. PAGE 11 A0226
COM PLAN TOTALISM USSR

S61
BRZEZINSKI Z.K.,"THE ORGANIZATION OF THE COMMUNIST CAMP." COM CZECHOSLVK COM/IND NAT/G DELIB/GP INT/TRADE DOMIN EDU/PROP EXEC ROUTINE COERCE ATTIT PWR...MGT CONCPT TIME/SEQ CHARTS VAL/FREE 20 TREATY. PAGE 20 A0416
VOL/ASSN DIPLOM USSR

S61
BURNET A.,"TOO MANY ALLIES." COM EUR+WWI UK WOR+45 WOR-45 ACT/RES PLAN DISPL PWR SKILL...TIME/SEQ 20 CMN/WLTH SEATO NATO CENTO. PAGE 22 A0438
VOL/ASSN INT/ORG DIPLOM

S61
HAZARD J.N.,"CODIFYING PEACEFUL COEXISTANCE." FUT INTELL INT/ORG TEC/DEV PEACE HEALTH...INT/LAW CONT/OBS 20. PAGE 63 A1299
VOL/ASSN JURID

S61
MIKSCHE F.O.,"DEFENSE ORGANIZATION FOR WESTERN EUROPE." USA+45 INT/ORG NAT/G VOL/ASSN ACT/RES DOMIN LEGIT COERCE ORD/FREE PWR...RELATIV TREND 20 NATO. PAGE 101 A2071
EUR+WWI FORCES WEAPON NUC/PWR

S61
RAY J.,"THE EUROPEAN FREE-TRADE ASSOCIATION AND ITS IMPACT ON INDIA'S TRADE." EUR+WWI FRANCE GERMANY INDIA S/ASIA UK NAT/G VOL/ASSN PLAN INT/TRADE ROUTINE WEALTH...STAT CHARTS CMN/WLTH EEC OEEC 20 EFTA. PAGE 120 A2453
ECO/DEV ECO/TAC

S61
WEST F.J.,"THE NEW GUINEA QUESTION: AN AUSTRALIAN VIEW." WOR+45 INT/ORG VOL/ASSN LEGIT PERCEPT ...POLICY TIME/SEQ AUSTRAL VAL/FREE 20 CMN/WLTH. PAGE 163 A3320
S/ASIA ECO/UNDEV

S61
WHELAN J.G.,"KHRUSHCHEV AND THE BALANCE OF WORLD POWER." FUT WOR+45 INT/ORG VOL/ASSN CAP/ISM DIPLOM SKILL...POLICY COLD/WAR 20 KHRUSH/N. PAGE 163 A3328
COM PWR BAL/PWR USSR

S61
ZAGORIA D.S.,"THE FUTURE OF SINO-SOVIET RELATIONS." CHINA/COM INT/ORG NAT/G POL/PAR VOL/ASSN ACT/RES PLAN PERSON...METH/CNCPT TIME/SEQ TOT/POP VAL/FREE 20 MAO KHRUSH/N. PAGE 169 A3444
ASIA COM TOTALISM USSR

B62
BRYANT A.,A CHOICE FOR DESTINY: COMMONWEALTH AND THE COMMON MARKET. EUR+WWI FUT UK INT/TRADE COLONIAL ATTIT SOVEREIGN 20 CMN/WLTH EEC. PAGE 20 A0411
INT/ORG VOL/ASSN DIPLOM CHOOSE

B62
DREIER J.C.,THE ORGANIZATION OF AMERICAN STATES AND THE HEMISPHERE CRISIS. CUBA USA+45 CULTURE STRATA NAT/G VOL/ASSN CONSULT FORCES ACT/RES CREATE DIPLOM ECO/TAC FOR/AID ALL/VALS...POLICY OBS OAS 20. PAGE 38 A0786
L/A+17C CONCPT

B62
DUTOIT B.,LA NEUTRALITE SUISSE A L'HEURE EUROPEENNE. EUR+WWI MOD/EUR INT/ORG NAT/G VOL/ASSN PLAN BAL/PWR LEGIT NEUTRAL REGION PEACE ORD/FREE SOVEREIGN...CONCPT OBS TIME/SEQ TREND STERTYP VAL/FREE LEAGUE/NAT UN 20. PAGE 40 A0812
ATTIT DIPLOM SWITZERLND

B62
FORBES H.W.,THE STRATEGY OF DISARMAMENT. FUT WOR+45 INT/ORG VOL/ASSN CONSULT ARMS/CONT COERCE NUC/PWR WAR DRIVE RIGID/FLEX ORD/FREE PWR...POLICY CONCPT OBS TREND STERTYP 20. PAGE 47 A0959
PLAN FORCES DIPLOM

B62
GUENA Y.,HISTORIQUE DE LA COMMUNAUTE. FUT ECO/UNDEV NAT/G PLAN EDU/PROP COLONIAL REGION NAT/LISM ALL/VALS SOVEREIGN...CONCPT OBS CHARTS 20. PAGE 58 A1186
AFR VOL/ASSN FOR/AID FRANCE

B62
KRAFT J.,THE GRAND DESIGN. EUR+WWI USA+45 AGRI FINAN INDUS MARKET INT/ORG NAT/G PLAN ECO/TAC TARIFFS REGION DRIVE ORD/FREE WEALTH...POLICY OBS TREND EEC 20. PAGE 82 A1674
VOL/ASSN ECO/DEV INT/TRADE

B62
LAWSON R.,INTERNATIONAL REGIONAL ORGANIZATIONS. WOR+45 NAT/G VOL/ASSN CONSULT LEGIS EDU/PROP LEGIT ADMIN EXEC ROUTINE HEALTH PWR WEALTH...JURID EEC COLD/WAR 20 UN. PAGE 86 A1752
INT/ORG DELIB/GP REGION

B62
LIPPMANN W.,WESTERN UNITY AND THE COMMON MARKET. EUR+WWI FRANCE GERMANY/W UK USA+45 ECO/DEV AGRI FINAN MARKET INT/ORG NAT/G FOR/AID AGREE WEALTH 20 EEC. PAGE 89 A1831
DIPLOM INT/TRADE VOL/ASSN

B62
MULLEY F.W.,THE POLITICS OF WESTERN DEFENSE. EUR+WWI USA-45 WOR+45 VOL/ASSN EX/STRUC FORCES COERCE DETER PEACE ATTIT ORD/FREE PWR...RECORD TIME/SEQ CHARTS COLD/WAR 20 NATO. PAGE 106 A2168
INT/ORG DELIB/GP NUC/PWR

B62
OSGOOD R.E.,NATO: THE ENTANGLING ALLIANCE. USA+45 WOR+45 VOL/ASSN FORCES TOP/EX PLAN DETER WEAPON DRIVE RIGID/FLEX ORD/FREE PWR...TREND 20 NATO. PAGE 112 A2301
INT/ORG ARMS/CONT PEACE

B62
ROBINSON A.D.,DUTCH ORGANIZED AGRICULTURE IN INTERNATIONAL POLITICS, 1945-1960. EUR+WWI NETHERLAND STRUCT ECO/DEV NAT/G VOL/ASSN CONSULT DELIB/GP PLAN TEC/DEV INT/TRADE EDU/PROP ATTIT RIGID/FLEX ALL/VALS...NEW/IDEA TREND EEC 20. PAGE 122 A2502
AGRI INT/ORG

B62
SAVORD R.,AMERICAN AGENCIES INTERESTED IN INTERNATIONAL AFFAIRS. USA-45 R+D NAT/G VOL/ASSN ACT/RES EDU/PROP KNOWL...CONCPT 20. PAGE 127 A2608
INT/ORG CONSULT DIPLOM

B62
SCHRODER P.M.,METTERNICH'S DIPLOMACY AT ITS ZENITH, 1820-1823. MOD/EUR ELITES INT/ORG VOL/ASSN DELIB/GP ECO/TAC EDU/PROP DISPL PWR SOVEREIGN...POLICY CONCPT GEN/LAWS 19 METTRNCH/K. PAGE 129 A2647
ORD/FREE BIOG BAL/PWR DIPLOM

B62
SCHWARTZ L.E.,INTERNATIONAL ORGANIZATIONS AND SPACE COOPERATION. VOL/ASSN CONSULT CREATE TEC/DEV SANCTION...POLICY INT/LAW PHIL/SCI 20 UN. PAGE 130 A2656
INT/ORG DIPLOM R+D SPACE

B62
THANT U.,THE UNITED NATIONS' DEVELOPMENT DECADE: PROPOSALS FOR ACTION. WOR+45 SOCIETY ECO/UNDEV AGRI COM/IND FINAN R+D MUNIC SCHOOL VOL/ASSN CONSULT PLAN TEC/DEV ECO/TAC EDU/PROP ADMIN ROUTINE RIGID/FLEX...MGT SOC CONCPT UNESCO UN TOT/POP VAL/FREE. PAGE 142 A2906
INT/ORG ALL/VALS

B62
TOURE S.,THE INTERNATIONAL POLICY OF THE DEMOCRATIC PARTY OF GUINEA (VOL. VII). AFR ALGERIA GHANA GUINEA MALI CONSTN VOL/ASSN CHIEF WAR PEACE ATTIT ...WELF/ST 20 DEMOCRAT. PAGE 144 A2953
DIPLOM POLICY POL/PAR NEW/LIB

B62
TRISKA J.F.,THE THEORY, LAW, AND POLICY OF SOVIET TREATIES. WOR+45 WOR-45 CONSTN INT/ORG NAT/G VOL/ASSN DOMIN LEGIT COERCE ATTIT PWR RESPECT ...POLICY JURID CONCPT OBS SAMP TIME/SEQ TREND GEN/LAWS 20. PAGE 145 A2966
COM LAW INT/LAW USSR

B62
US CONGRESS,COMMUNICATIONS SATELLITE LEGISLATION: HEARINGS BEFORE COMM ON AERON AND SPACE SCIENCES ON BILLS S2550 AND 2814. WOR+45 LAW VOL/ASSN PLAN DIPLOM CONTROL OWN PEACE...NEW/IDEA CONGRESS NASA. PAGE 150 A3062
SPACE COM/IND ADJUD GOV/REL

B62
WILLIAMS W.A.,THE UNITED STATES, CUBA, AND CASTRO: AN ESSAY ON THE DYNAMICS OF REVOLUTION AND THE DISSOLUTION OF EMPIRE. CUBA USA+45 AGRI VOL/ASSN DIPLOM ECO/TAC DOMIN COERCE...POLICY 20 EISNHWR/DD CIA KENNEDY/JF CASTRO/F. PAGE 165 A3354
REV CONSTN COM LEAD

B62
YALEN R.,REGIONALISM AND WORLD ORDER. EUR+WWI WOR+45 WOR-45 INT/ORG VOL/ASSN DELIB/GP FORCES TOP/EX BAL/PWR DIPLOM DOMIN REGION ARMS/CONT PWR ...JURID HYPO/EXP COLD/WAR 20. PAGE 168 A3427 — ORD/FREE POLICY

L62
GROSS L.,"IMMUNITIES AND PRIVILEGES OF DELIGATIONS TO THE UNITED NATIONS." USA+45 WOR+45 STRATA NAT/G VOL/ASSN CONSULT DIPLOM EDU/PROP ROUTINE RESPECT ...POLICY INT/LAW CONCPT UN 20. PAGE 57 A1176 — INT/ORG LAW ELITES

L62
MALINOWSKI W.R.,"CENTRALIZATION AND DE-CENTRALIZATION IN THE UNITED NATIONS' ECONOMIC AND SOCIAL ACTIVITIES." WOR+45 CONSTN ECO/UNDEV INT/ORG VOL/ASSN DELIB/GP ECO/TAC EDU/PROP ADMIN RIGID/FLEX ...OBS CHARTS UNESCO UN EEC OAS OEEC 20. PAGE 93 A1913 — CREATE GEN/LAWS

S62
BELSHAW C.,"TRAINING AND RECRUITMENT: SOME PRINCIPLES OF INTERNATIONAL AID." FUT WOR+45 SOCIETY INT/ORG NAT/G CREATE PLAN TEC/DEV ECO/TAC FOR/AID EDU/PROP ATTIT PERCEPT...HUM UN FAO ILO UNESCO 20. PAGE 13 A0263 — VOL/ASSN ECO/UNDEV

S62
BOKOR-SZEGO H.,"LA CONVENTION DE BELGRADE ET LE REGIME DU DANUBE." COM EUR+WWI WOR+45 STRUCT POL/PAR VOL/ASSN PLAN EDU/PROP WEALTH...TIME/SEQ 20. PAGE 16 A0333 — INT/ORG TOTALISM YUGOSLAVIA

S62
BOULDING K.E.,"THE PREVENTION OF WORLD WAR THREE." FUT WOR+45 INT/ORG PLAN BAL/PWR PEACE ORD/FREE PWR ...NEW/IDEA TREND TOT/POP COLD/WAR 20. PAGE 17 A0348 — VOL/ASSN NAT/G ARMS/CONT DIPLOM

S62
CORET A.,"LE STATUT DE L'ILE CHRISTMAS DE L'OCEAN INDIEN." FUT S/ASIA ECO/DEV ECO/UNDEV VOL/ASSN DELIB/GP PLAN...RELATIV OBS TIME/SEQ TREND AUSTRAL 20. PAGE 30 A0619 — NAT/G INT/ORG NEW/ZEALND

S62
DALLIN A.,"THE SOVIET VIEW OF THE UNITED NATIONS." WOR+45 VOL/ASSN TOP/EX DIPLOM DOMIN EDU/PROP LEGIT ATTIT RIGID/FLEX PWR...CONCPT OBS HIST/WRIT TIME/SEQ STERTYP GEN/LAWS COLD/WAR UN 20. PAGE 33 A0676 — COM INT/ORG USSR

S62
DEUTSCH K.W.,"TOWARDS WESTERN EUROPEAN INTEGRATION: AN INTERIM ASSESSMENT." EUR+WWI STRUCT ECO/DEV INT/ORG ECO/TAC INT/TRADE EDU/PROP PEACE ATTIT DRIVE PWR SOVEREIGN...PSY SOC TIME/SEQ CHARTS STERTYP 20. PAGE 36 A0741 — VOL/ASSN RIGID/FLEX REGION

S62
DIHN N.Q.,"L'INTERNATIONALISATION DU MEKONG." CAMBODIA LAOS VIETNAM WOR+45 INT/ORG NAT/G VOL/ASSN PEACE HEALTH...CONCPT TIME/SEQ CHARTS METH VAL/FREE 20. PAGE 37 A0761 — S/ASIA DELIB/GP

S62
FENWICK C.G.,"ISSUES AT PUNTA DEL ESTE: NON-INTERVENTION VS COLLECTIVE SECURITY." L/A+17C USA+45 VOL/ASSN DELIB/GP ECO/TAC LEGIT ADJUD REGION ORD/FREE OAS COLD/WAR 20. PAGE 45 A0917 — INT/ORG CUBA

S62
FINKELSTEIN L.S.,"THE UNITED NATIONS AND ORGANIZATIONS FOR CONTROL OF ARMAMENT." FUT WOR+45 VOL/ASSN DELIB/GP TOP/EX CREATE EDU/PROP LEGIT ADJUD NUC/PWR ATTIT RIGID/FLEX ORD/FREE...POLICY DECISION CONCPT OBS TREND GEN/LAWS TOT/POP COLD/WAR. PAGE 46 A0933 — INT/ORG PWR ARMS/CONT

S62
FISCHER G.,"UNE NOUVELLE ORGANIZATION REGIONALE: L'ASA." S/ASIA WOR+45 ECO/UNDEV VOL/ASSN PERCEPT RIGID/FLEX...TIME/SEQ 20 ASA. PAGE 46 A0935 — INT/ORG DRIVE REGION

S62
FOCSANEANU L.,"LES GRANDS TRAITES DE LA REPUBLIQUE POPULAIRE DE CHINE." ASIA CHINA/COM COM USSR WOR+45 INT/ORG NAT/G POL/PAR ACT/RES PLAN DIPLOM EDU/PROP ...CONCPT TIME/SEQ 20 TREATY. PAGE 47 A0957 — VOL/ASSN TOTALISM

S62
FOSTER W.C.,"ARMS CONTROL AND DISARMAMENT IN A DIVIDED WORLD." COM FUT USA+45 USSR WOR+45 INTELL INT/ORG NAT/G VOL/ASSN CONSULT CREATE PLAN TEC/DEV EDU/PROP LEGIT NUC/PWR ATTIT RIGID/FLEX...CONCPT TREND TOT/POP 20 UN. PAGE 47 A0971 — DELIB/GP POLICY ARMS/CONT DIPLOM

S62
GAREAU F.H.,"BLOC POLITICS IN WEST AFRICA." AFR CONGO/BRAZ GHANA GUINEA MALI WOR+45 STRUCT ECO/UNDEV INT/ORG VOL/ASSN CHOOSE ORD/FREE PWR UN 20. PAGE 51 A1048 — NAT/G NAT/LISM

S62
MARIAS J.,"A PROGRAM FOR EUROPE." EUR+WWI INT/ORG NAT/G PLAN DIPLOM DOMIN PWR...STERTYP TOT/POP 20. PAGE 95 A1938 — VOL/ASSN CREATE REGION

S62
MILLAR T.B.,"THE COMMONWEALTH AND THE UNITED NATIONS." FUT WOR+45 STRUCT NAT/G VOL/ASSN CONSULT DELIB/GP EDU/PROP LEGIT ATTIT...POLICY CONCPT TREND CMN/WLTH UN 20. PAGE 101 A2072 — INT/ORG

S62
MOUSKHELY M.,"LA NAISSANCE DES ETATS EN DROIT INTERNATIONAL PUBLIC." UNIV SOCIETY INT/ORG VOL/ASSN LEGIT ATTIT RIGID/FLEX...JURID TIME/SEQ 20. PAGE 105 A2157 — NAT/G STRUCT INT/LAW

S62
SPRINGER H.W.,"FEDERATION IN THE CARIBBEAN: AN ATTEMPT THAT FAILED." L/A+17C ECO/UNDEV INT/ORG POL/PAR PROVS LEGIS CREATE PLAN LEGIT ADMIN FEDERAL ATTIT DRIVE PERSON ORD/FREE PWR...POLICY GEOG PSY CONCPT OBS CARIBBEAN CMN/WLTH 20. PAGE 136 A2791 — VOL/ASSN NAT/G REGION

S62
TATOMIR N.,"ORGANIZATIA INTERNATIONALA A MUNCII: ASPECTE NOI ALE PROBLEMEI IMBUNATATIRII MECANISMULUI EI." EUR+WWI ECO/DEV VOL/ASSN ADMIN ...METH/CNCPT WORK ILO 20. PAGE 141 A2891 — INT/ORG INT/TRADE

S62
THOMAS J.R.T.,"SOVIET BEHAVIOR IN THE QUEMOY CRISES OF 1958." CHINA/COM FUT USSR WOR+45 INT/ORG VOL/ASSN FORCES PLAN BAL/PWR DOMIN COERCE NUC/PWR REV WAR ATTIT DRIVE ORD/FREE...POLICY OBS RECORD COLD/WAR FOR/POL 20. PAGE 143 A2923 — COM PWR

S62
TOWSTER J.,"THE USSR AND THE USA: CHALLENGE AND RESPONSE." COM GERMANY USA+45 USSR WOR+45 ECO/UNDEV INT/ORG VOL/ASSN EX/STRUC FORCES TOP/EX CREATE PLAN TEC/DEV DIPLOM ECO/TAC EDU/PROP COLONIAL COERCE PWR ...GEN/METH COLD/WAR 20 KENNEDY/JF. PAGE 145 A2956 — ACT/RES GEN/LAWS

B63
BELOFF M.,THE UNITED STATES AND THE UNITY OF EUROPE. EUR+WWI UK USA+45 WOR+45 VOL/ASSN DIPLOM REGION ATTIT PWR...CONCPT EEC OEEC 20 NATO. PAGE 13 A0261 — ECO/DEV INT/ORG

B63
CERAMI C.A.,ALLIANCE BORN OF DANGER. EUR+WWI USA+45 USSR ECO/DEV INDUS VOL/ASSN ECO/TAC REGION ATTIT MARXISM ATLAN/ALL 20 NATO EEC. PAGE 25 A0514 — DIPLOM INT/ORG NAT/G POLICY

B63
GREAT BRITAIN CENTRAL OFF INF,CONSULTATION AND CO-OPERATION IN THE COMMONWEALTH. LAW R+D FORCES PLAN EDU/PROP CONFER INGP/REL...GEOG CENSUS 19/20 CMN/WLTH. PAGE 55 A1133 — DIPLOM DELIB/GP VOL/ASSN REGION

B63
HUSSEY W.D.,THE BRITISH EMPIRE AND COMMONWEALTH 1500 TO 1961. UK USA-45 SOCIETY ECO/UNDEV NAT/G VOL/ASSN INT/TRADE DOMIN CONTROL WAR PWR ...DICTIONARY 16/20 COMMONWLTH TRUST/TERR. PAGE 69 A1422 — COLONIAL SOVEREIGN INT/ORG

B63
LADOR-LEDERER J.J.,INTERNATIONAL NON-GOVERNMENTAL ORGANIZATIONS: A STUDY IN AUTONOMOUS ORGANIZATION AND IUS GENTIUM. LAW DELIB/GP LEGIS DIPLOM 20. PAGE 83 A1709 — INT/ORG INT/LAW INGP/REL VOL/ASSN

B63
LINDBERG L.,POLITICAL DYNAMICS OF EUROPEAN ECONOMIC INTEGRATION. EUR+WWI ECO/DEV INT/ORG VOL/ASSN DELIB/GP ADMIN WEALTH...DECISION EEC 20. PAGE 89 A1820 — MARKET ECO/TAC

B63
ROBERTSON A.H.,HUMAN RIGHTS IN EUROPE. CONSTN SOCIETY INT/ORG NAT/G VOL/ASSN DELIB/GP ACT/RES PLAN ADJUD REGION ROUTINE ATTIT LOVE ORD/FREE RESPECT...JURID SOC CONCPT SOC/EXP UN 20. PAGE 122 A2498 — EUR+WWI PERSON

B63
STROMBERG R.N.,COLLECTIVE SECURITY AND AMERICAN FOREIGN POLICY FROM THE LEAGUE OF NATIONS TO NATO. USA+45 USA-45 WOR-45 INT/ORG VOL/ASSN EX/STRUC FORCES LEGIT ROUTINE DRIVE...CONCPT TREND UN LEAGUE/NAT 20 NATO. PAGE 139 A2851 — ORD/FREE TIME/SEQ DIPLOM

B63
US GOVERNMENT,REPORT TO INTER-AMERICAN ECONOMIC AND SOCIAL COUNCIL AT SECOND ANNUAL MEETING. L/A+17C USA+45 VOL/ASSN TEC/DEV DIPLOM TAX EATING EFFICIENCY HEALTH...STAT CHARTS 20 AID. PAGE 153 A3116 — ECO/TAC FOR/AID FINAN PLAN

L63
RUSSETT B.M.,"TOWARD A MODEL OF COMPETITIVE INTERNATIONAL POLITICS." USA+45 WOR+45 INT/ORG NAT/G POL/PAR VOL/ASSN LEGIS BAL/PWR DIPLOM LEGIT PWR...CONCPT CONT/OBS STERTYP GEN/LAWS TOT/POP COLD/WAR 20 UN. PAGE 126 A2579 — ATTIT EDU/PROP

S63
ALEXANDER R.,"LATIN AMERICA AND THE COMMUNIST BLOC." ASIA COM CUBA L/A+17C USA+45 USSR NAT/G VOL/ASSN TEC/DEV FOR/AID LEGIT PWR WEALTH COLD/WAR 20. PAGE 6 A0112 — ECO/UNDEV RECORD

S63
ALPHAND H.,"FRANCE AND HER ALLIES." EUR+WWI UK USA+45 ECO/DEV INT/ORG NAT/G VOL/ASSN FORCES TOP/EX DIPLOM ECO/TAC LEGIT ATTIT DRIVE ORD/FREE PWR WEALTH...STAT EEC TOT/POP 20. PAGE 6 A0130 — ACT/RES FRANCE

S63
BANFIELD J.,"FEDERATION IN EAST-AFRICA." AFR UGANDA ELITES INT/ORG NAT/G VOL/ASSN LEGIS ECO/TAC FEDERAL — EX/STRUC PWR

ATTIT SOVEREIGN TOT/POP 20 TANGANYIKA. PAGE 11 A0216
REGION

S63
BELOFF M.,"BRITAIN, EUROPE AND THE ATLANTIC COMMUNITY." EUR+WWI ELITES NAT/G VOL/ASSN TOP/EX ATTIT ORD/FREE PWR SOVEREIGN WEALTH EEC TOT/POP VAL/FREE CMN/WLTH 20. PAGE 13 A0262
INT/ORG ECO/DEV UK

S63
BOHN L.,"WHOSE NUCLEAR TEST: NON-PHYSICAL INSPECTION AND TEST BAN." WOR+45 R+D INT/ORG VOL/ASSN ORD/FREE...GEN/LAWS GEN/METH COLD/WAR 20. PAGE 16 A0331
ADJUD ARMS/CONT TEC/DEV NUC/PWR

S63
CHAKRAVARTI P.C.,"INDIAN NON-ALIGNMENT AND UNITED STATES POLICY." ASIA INDIA S/ASIA USA+45 CULTURE ECO/UNDEV NAT/G VOL/ASSN DELIB/GP TOP/EX FOR/AID NEUTRAL...POLICY HUM CONCPT RECORD GEN/LAWS 20. PAGE 25 A0515
ATTIT ALL/VALS COLONIAL DIPLOM

S63
DARLING F.C.,"THE GEOPOLITICS OF AMERICAN FOREIGN POLITICS IN ASIA." COM S/ASIA USA+45 USSR ECO/UNDEV NAT/G VOL/ASSN CONSULT PLAN GUERRILLA...STAT TOT/POP 20. PAGE 34 A0682
FORCES ECO/TAC FOR/AID DIPLOM

S63
ETIENNE G.,"'LOIS OBJECTIVES' ET PROBLEMES DE DEVELOPPEMENT DANS LE CONTEXTE CHINE-URSS." ASIA CHINA/COM COM FUT STRUCT INT/ORG VOL/ASSN TOP/EX TEC/DEV ECO/TAC ATTIT RIGID/FLEX...GEOG MGT TIME/SEQ TOT/POP 20. PAGE 42 A0866
TOTALISM USSR

S63
GANDOLFI A.,"LES ACCORDS DE COOPERATION EN MATIERE DE POLITIQUE ETRANGERE ENTRE LA FRANCE ET LES NOUVEAUX ETATS AFRICAINS ET." AFR ISLAM MADAGASCAR WOR+45 ECO/DEV INT/ORG NAT/G DELIB/GP ECO/TAC ALL/VALS...CON/ANAL 20. PAGE 51 A1038
VOL/ASSN ECO/UNDEV DIPLOM FRANCE

S63
GORDON B.,"ECONOMIC IMPEDIMENTS TO REGIONALISM IN SOUTH EAST ASIA." BURMA FUT S/ASIA THAILAND USA+45 AGRI INDUS R+D NAT/G PLAN ECO/TAC WEALTH...STAT CONT/OBS 20. PAGE 54 A1110
VOL/ASSN ECO/UNDEV INT/TRADE REGION

S63
GROSSER A.,"FRANCE AND GERMANY IN THE ATLANTIC COMMUNITY." INT/ORG NAT/G TOP/EX DIPLOM REGION PEACE ATTIT ORD/FREE PWR...CONCPT RECORD TIME/SEQ GEN/LAWS VAL/FREE COLD/WAR 20. PAGE 57 A1178
EUR+WWI VOL/ASSN FRANCE GERMANY

S63
GUPTA S.C.,"INDIA AND THE SOVIET UNION." CHINA/COM COM INDIA S/ASIA VOL/ASSN TOP/EX FOR/AID EDU/PROP PEACE PWR...RECORD COLD/WAR 20. PAGE 58 A1195
DISPL MYTH USSR

S63
HALLSTEIN W.,"THE EUROPEAN COMMUNITY AND ATLANTIC PARTNERSHIP." EUR+WWI USA+45 MARKET NAT/G VOL/ASSN DELIB/GP ARMS/CONT NUC/PWR ATTIT PWR...CONCPT STAT TIME/SEQ TREND OEEC 20 EEC. PAGE 60 A1235
INT/ORG ECO/TAC UK

S63
HARNETTY P.,"CANADA, SOUTH AFRICA AND THE COMMONWEALTH." CANADA SOUTH/AFR LAW INT/ORG VOL/ASSN DELIB/GP LEGIS TOP/EX ECO/TAC LEGIT DRIVE MORAL...CONCPT CMN/WLTH 20. PAGE 62 A1263
AFR ATTIT

S63
HAVILAND H.F.,"BUILDING A POLITICAL COMMUNITY." EUR+WWI FUT UK USA+45 ECO/DEV ECO/UNDEV INT/ORG NAT/G DELIB/GP BAL/PWR ECO/TAC NEUTRAL ROUTINE ATTIT PWR WEALTH...CONCPT COLD/WAR TOT/POP 20. PAGE 63 A1293
VOL/ASSN DIPLOM

S63
HOLBO P.S.,"COLD WAR DRIFT IN LATIN AMERICA." CUBA L/A+17C USA+45 USA-45 INT/ORG NAT/G NEIGH VOL/ASSN ACT/RES PLAN ECO/TAC ATTIT RIGID/FLEX ALL/VALS ...RECORD TIME/SEQ OAS LAFTA 20 COLD/WAR. PAGE 66 A1363
DELIB/GP CREATE FOR/AID

S63
KISSINGER H.A.,"STRAINS ON THE ALLIANCE." EUR+WWI FRANCE GERMANY GERMANY/W USA+45 ECO/DEV INT/ORG NAT/G TOP/EX EDU/PROP NUC/PWR ATTIT PWR...PSY TREND 20. PAGE 80 A1643
VOL/ASSN DRIVE DIPLOM

S63
LIGOT M.,"LA COOPERATION MILITAIRE DANS LES ACCORDS, PASSES ENTRE LA FRANCE ET LES ETATS AFRICAINS ET MALGACHE D'EXPRESSION." ECO/UNDEV INT/ORG NAT/G VOL/ASSN...CONCPT TIME/SEQ 20. PAGE 89 A1814
AFR FORCES FOR/AID FRANCE

S63
MANOLIU F.,"PERSPECTIVES D'UNE INTEGRATION ECONOMIQUE LATINOAMERICAINE." FUT L/A+17C STRUCT MARKET LABOR POL/PAR VOL/ASSN PLAN RIGID/FLEX PWR ...METH/CNCPT OAS TOT/POP 20. PAGE 94 A1927
FINAN INT/ORG PEACE

S63
MODELSKI G.,"STUDY OF ALLIANCES." WOR+45 WOR-45 INT/ORG NAT/G FORCES LEGIT ADMIN CHOOSE ALL/VALS PWR SKILL...INT/LAW CONCPT GEN/LAWS 20 TREATY. PAGE 102 A2099
VOL/ASSN CON/ANAL DIPLOM

S63
MULLEY F.W.,"NUCLEAR WEAPONS: CHALLENGE TO NATIONAL SOVEREIGNTY." EUR+WWI FRANCE UK USA+45 VOL/ASSN EX/STRUC FORCES TOP/EX ACT/RES REGION DRIVE PWR 20 NATO DEGAULLE/C. PAGE 106 A2169
INT/ORG ATTIT DIPLOM NUC/PWR

S63
NOGEE J.L.,"PROPOGANDA AND NEGOTIATION: THE CASE OF THE TEN NATION DISARMAMENT COMMITTEE." COM EUR+WWI USA+45 VOL/ASSN DELIB/GP FORCES DIPLOM DOMIN LEGIT PWR...METH/CNCPT STERTYP COLD/WAR VAL/FREE 20. PAGE 110 A2248
INT/ORG EDU/PROP ARMS/CONT

S63
PINCUS J.,"THE COST OF FOREIGN AID." WOR+45 ECO/DEV FINAN NAT/G VOL/ASSN CREATE ECO/TAC EDU/PROP WEALTH ...METH/CNCPT STAT CHARTS HYPO/EXP TOT/POP VAL/FREE 20. PAGE 116 A2380
USA+45 ECO/UNDEV FOR/AID

S63
RAMERIE L.,"TENSION AU SEIN DU COMECON: LE CAS ROUMAIN." COM EUR+WWI USSR WOR+45 ECO/DEV DIST/IND NAT/G POL/PAR VOL/ASSN EDU/PROP TOTALISM ATTIT WEALTH...TIME/SEQ 20 COMECON. PAGE 119 A2438
INT/ORG ECO/TAC INT/TRADE ROMANIA

S63
SHONFIELD A.,"AFTER BRUSSELS." EUR+WWI FRANCE GERMANY UK ECO/DEV DIST/IND MARKET VOL/ASSN DELIB/GP CREATE INT/TRADE ATTIT RIGID/FLEX...RECORD TREND GEN/LAWS EEC CMN/WLTH 20. PAGE 132 A2705
PLAN ECO/TAC

S63
SPINELLI A.,"IL TRATTATO DI MOSCA E I PROBLEMI DELLA COESISTENZA PACIFICA." CHINA/COM COM FRANCE FUT WOR+45 INT/ORG VOL/ASSN PEACE...POLICY MYTH 20. PAGE 136 A2788
ATTIT ARMS/CONT TOTALISM

S63
TALLON D.,"L'ETUDE DU DROIT COMPARE COMME MOYEN DE RECHERCHER LES MATIERES SUSCEPTIBLES D'UNIFICATION INTERNATIONALE." WOR+45 LAW SOCIETY VOL/ASSN CONSULT LEGIT CT/SYS RIGID/FLEX KNOWL 20. PAGE 141 A2884
INT/ORG JURID INT/LAW

S63
WALKER H.,"THE INTERNATIONAL LAW OF COMMODITY AGREEMENTS." FUT WOR+45 ECO/DEV ECO/UNDEV FINAN INT/ORG NAT/G CONSULT CREATE PLAN ECO/TAC ATTIT PERCEPT...CONCPT GEN/LAWS TOT/POP GATT 20. PAGE 160 A3265
MARKET VOL/ASSN INT/LAW INT/TRADE

B64
ADAMS V.,THE PEACE CORPS IN ACTION. USA+45 VOL/ASSN EX/STRUC GOV/REL PERCEPT ORD/FREE...OBS 20 KENNEDY/JF PEACE/CORP. PAGE 4 A0087
DIPLOM FOR/AID PERSON DRIVE

B64
AMERICAN ASSEMBLY,THE UNITED STATES AND THE MIDDLE EAST. ISRAEL USA+45 STRUCT ECO/DEV ECO/UNDEV INT/ORG NAT/G SCHOOL SECT VOL/ASSN EX/STRUC TEC/DEV NAT/LISM...SOC 20. PAGE 7 A0135
ISLAM DRIVE REGION

B64
COTTRELL A.J.,THE POLITICS OF THE ATLANTIC ALLIANCE. EUR+WWI USA+45 INT/ORG NAT/G DELIB/GP EX/STRUC BAL/PWR DIPLOM REGION DETER ATTIT ORD/FREE ...CONCPT RECORD GEN/LAWS GEN/METH NATO 20. PAGE 31 A0632
VOL/ASSN FORCES

B64
CZERNIN F.,VERSAILLES - 1919. EUR+WWI USA-45 FACE/GP POL/PAR VOL/ASSN DELIB/GP TOP/EX CREATE BAL/PWR DIPLOM LEGIT NAT/LISM PEACE ATTIT RIGID/FLEX ORD/FREE PWR...CON/ANAL LEAGUE/NAT 20 VERSAILLES. PAGE 33 A0671
INT/ORG STRUCT

B64
DALLIN A.,THE SOVIET UNION, ARMS CONTROL AND DISARMAMENT. COM INT/ORG VOL/ASSN EX/STRUC DIPLOM NUC/PWR ATTIT PWR TOT/POP COLD/WAR 20. PAGE 33 A0678
ORD/FREE ARMS/CONT USSR

B64
DIAS R.W.M.,A BIBLIOGRAPHY OF JURISPRUDENCE (2ND ED.). VOL/ASSN LEGIS ADJUD CT/SYS OWN...INT/LAW 18/20. PAGE 37 A0754
BIBLIOG/A JURID LAW CONCPT

B64
EAYRS J.,THE COMMONWEALTH AND SUEZ: A DOCUMENTARY SURVEY. FRANCE ISLAM VOL/ASSN FORCES CONFER COLONIAL WAR INGP/REL 20 CMN/WLTH SUEZ UN. PAGE 40 A0818
DIPLOM NAT/LISM DIST/IND SOVEREIGN

B64
ESTHUS R.A.,FROM ENMITY TO ALLIANCE: US AUSTRALIAN RELATIONS. S/ASIA DIST/IND VOL/ASSN FORCES ATTIT 20 AUSTRAL TREATY CMN/WLTH. PAGE 42 A0863
DIPLOM WAR INT/TRADE FOR/AID

B64
FEIS H.,FOREIGN AID AND FOREIGN POLICY. USA+45 WOR+45 NAT/G VOL/ASSN ACT/RES TEC/DEV ATTIT HEALTH WEALTH...SOC GEN/LAWS 20. PAGE 45 A0912
ECO/UNDEV ECO/TAC FOR/AID DIPLOM

B64
GARDNER L.C.,ECONOMIC ASPECTS OF NEW DEAL DIPLOMACY. USA-45 WOR-45 LAW ECO/DEV INT/ORG NAT/G VOL/ASSN LEGIS TOP/EX EDU/PROP ORD/FREE PWR WEALTH ...POLICY TIME/SEQ VAL/FREE 20 ROOSEVLT/F. PAGE 51 A1043
ECO/TAC DIPLOM

B64
GREAT BRITAIN CENTRAL OFF INF,CONSTITUTIONAL DEVELOPMENT IN THE COMMONWEALTH. VOL/ASSN PLAN DIPLOM COLONIAL INGP/REL NAT/LISM ORD/FREE PWR
REGION CONSTN NAT/G

17/20 CMN/WLTH. PAGE 55 A1135 SOVEREIGN

B64
HEKHUIS D.J.,INTERNATIONAL STABILITY: MILITARY, ECONOMIC AND POLITICAL DIMENSIONS. FUT WOR+45 LAW ECO/UNDEV INT/ORG NAT/G VOL/ASSN FORCES ACT/RES BAL/PWR PWR WEALTH...STAT UN 20. PAGE 64 A1310 TEC/DEV DETER REGION

B64
IKLE F.C.,HOW NATIONS NEGOTIATE. COM EUR+WWI USA+45 INTELL INT/ORG VOL/ASSN DELIB/GP ACT/RES CREATE DOMIN EDU/PROP ADJUD ROUTINE ATTIT PERSON ORD/FREE RESPECT SKILL...PSY SOC OBS VAL/FREE. PAGE 70 A1433 NAT/G PWR POLICY

B64
MARKHAM J.W.,THE COMMON MARKET: FRIEND OR COMPETITOR. EUR+WWI FUT USA+45 INT/ORG LG/CO NAT/G VOL/ASSN DELIB/GP EX/STRUC PLAN TARIFFS ORD/FREE PWR WEALTH...POLICY STAT TREND EEC VAL/FREE 20. PAGE 95 A1943 ECO/DEV ECO/TAC

B64
NEWBURY C.W.,THE WEST AFRICAN COMMONWEALTH. CONSTN INTELL ECO/UNDEV VOL/ASSN CHIEF DELIB/GP LEGIS INT/TRADE COLONIAL FEDERAL ATTIT 20 COMMONWLTH AFRICA/W. PAGE 108 A2223 INT/ORG SOVEREIGN GOV/REL AFR

B64
PLISCHKE E.,SYSTEMS OF INTEGRATING THE INTERNATIONAL COMMUNITY. WOR+45 NAT/G VOL/ASSN ECO/TAC LEGIT PWR WEALTH...TIME/SEQ ANTHOL UN TOT/POP 20. PAGE 116 A2391 INT/ORG EX/STRUC REGION

B64
STOESSINGER J.G.,FINANCING THE UNITED NATIONS SYSTEM. FUT WOR+45 CONSTN NAT/G VOL/ASSN DELIB/GP EX/STRUC ECO/TAC LEGIT CT/SYS PWR WEALTH...STAT TIME/SEQ TREND CHARTS VAL/FREE. PAGE 138 A2830 FINAN INT/ORG

B64
SULLIVAN G.,THE STORY OF THE PEACE CORPS. USA+45 WOR+45 INTELL FACE/GP NAT/G SCHOOL VOL/ASSN CONSULT EX/STRUC PLAN EDU/PROP ADMIN ATTIT DRIVE ALL/VALS ...POLICY HEAL SOC CONCPT INT QU BIOG TREND SOC/EXP WORK. PAGE 140 A2861 INT/ORG ECO/UNDEV FOR/AID PEACE

B64
TAYLOR E.,RICHER BY ASIA. S/ASIA CULTURE VOL/ASSN ACT/RES ATTIT DISPL PERSON ALL/VALS...INT/LAW MYTH SELF/OBS 20. PAGE 142 A2899 SOCIETY RIGID/FLEX INDIA

B64
UNITED ARAB REPUBLIC,TOWARDS THE SECOND AFRICAN SUMMIT ASSEMBLY. AFR UAR CONSTN VOL/ASSN CHIEF PLAN DIPLOM AGREE 20 NASSER/G AFR/STATES. PAGE 148 A3030 CONFER DELIB/GP INT/ORG POLICY

B64
US AGENCY INTERNATIONAL DEV,REPORT TO CONGRESS ON THE FOREIGN ASSISTANCE PROGRAM. AFR ASIA L/A+17C USA+45 INT/ORG VOL/ASSN FORCES CAP/ISM ADMIN WEAPON. PAGE 149 A3052 FOR/AID ECO/UNDEV TEC/DEV BUDGET

B64
WARREN S.,THE PRESIDENT AS WORLD LEADER. USA+45 WOR+45 ELITES COM/IND INT/ORG NAT/G VOL/ASSN CHIEF EX/STRUC LEGIT COERCE ATTIT PERSON RIGID/FLEX...INT TIME/SEQ COLD/WAR 20 ROOSEVLT/F TRUMAN/HS EISNHWR/DD KENNEDY/JF. PAGE 161 A3286 TOP/EX PWR DIPLOM

B64
WYTHE G.,THE UNITED STATES AND INTER-AMERICAN RELATIONS: A CONTEMPORARY APPRAISAL. L/A+17C USA+45 ECO/UNDEV INT/ORG NAT/G VOL/ASSN INT/TRADE EDU/PROP DRIVE...SOC TREND OAS UN 20. PAGE 168 A3425 ATTIT ECO/TAC FOR/AID

L64
CAMPBELL J.C.,"THE MIDDLE EAST IN THE MUTED COLD WAR." COM EUR+WWI UAR USA+45 USSR STRUCT ECO/UNDEV NAT/G VOL/ASSN EX/STRUC TOP/EX DIPLOM ECO/TAC EDU/PROP...TIME/SEQ COLD/WAR 20. PAGE 23 A0475 ISLAM FOR/AID NAT/LISM

L64
LLOYD W.B.,"PEACE REQUIRES PEACEMAKERS." AFR INDIA S/ASIA SWITZERLND WOR+45 INT/ORG VOL/ASSN PLAN PERSON PWR 20. PAGE 90 A1848 CONSULT PEACE

S64
COCHRANE J.D.,"US ATTITUDES TOWARD CENTRAL-AMERICAN INTEGRATION." L/A+17C USA+45 ECO/UNDEV FACE/GP VOL/ASSN DELIB/GP ECO/TAC INT/TRADE EDU/PROP RIGID/FLEX ORD/FREE WEALTH...TIME/SEQ TOT/POP 20. PAGE 27 A0555 NAT/G ATTIT REGION

S64
DE GAULLE C.,"FRENCH WORLD VIEW." AFR ASIA CHINA/COM EUR+WWI ISLAM ECO/UNDEV INT/ORG NAT/G VOL/ASSN ACT/RES DIPLOM ECO/TAC EDU/PROP ATTIT DRIVE WEALTH 20. PAGE 35 A0702 TOP/EX PWR FOR/AID FRANCE

S64
DERWINSKI E.J.,"THE COST OF THE INTERNATIONAL COFFEE AGREEMENT." L/A+17C USA+45 WOR+45 ECO/UNDEV NAT/G VOL/ASSN LEGIS DIPLOM ECO/TAC FOR/AID LEGIT ATTIT...TIME/SEQ CONGRESS 20 TREATY. PAGE 36 A0732 MARKET DELIB/GP INT/TRADE

S64
GARDNER R.N.,"THE SOVIET UNION AND THE UNITED NATIONS." WOR+45 FINAN POL/PAR VOL/ASSN FORCES ECO/TAC DOMIN EDU/PROP LEGIT ADJUD ADMIN ARMS/CONT COERCE ATTIT ALL/VALS...POLICY MAJORIT CONCPT OBS TIME/SEQ TREND STERTYP UN. PAGE 51 A1046 COM INT/ORG USSR

S64
GROSSER A.,"Y A-T-IL UN CONFLIT FRANCO-AMERICAIN." EUR+WWI USA+45 INT/ORG NAT/G PLAN BAL/PWR DIPLOM EDU/PROP NUC/PWR ATTIT DRIVE ORD/FREE PWR...CONCPT OBS TIME/SEQ TREND STERTYP VAL/FREE COLD/WAR. PAGE 57 A1179 VOL/ASSN NAT/LISM FRANCE

S64
GRZYBOWSKI K.,"INTERNATIONAL ORGANIZATIONS FROM THE SOVIET POINT OF VIEW." WOR+45 WOR-45 CULTURE ECO/DEV VOL/ASSN EDU/PROP ATTIT RIGID/FLEX KNOWL ...SOC OBS TIME/SEQ TREND GEN/LAWS VAL/FREE ILO UN 20. PAGE 58 A1184 COM INT/ORG DIPLOM USSR

S64
HOFFMANN S.,"CE QU'EN PENSENT LES AMERICAINS." EUR+WWI INT/ORG VOL/ASSN PLAN BAL/PWR DIPLOM DOMIN EDU/PROP REGION ARMS/CONT DRIVE ORD/FREE PWR ...POLICY CONCPT OBS TREND STERTYP COLD/WAR VAL/FREE 20. PAGE 66 A1357 USA+45 ATTIT FRANCE

S64
HOSKYNS C.,"THE AFRICAN STATES AND THE UNITED NATIONS: 1958-1964." SOUTH/AFR NAT/G VOL/ASSN CONSULT BAL/PWR EDU/PROP MORAL ORD/FREE PWR ...CONCPT TREND UN 20. PAGE 68 A1393 AFR INT/ORG DIPLOM

S64
HUELIN D.,"ECONOMIC INTEGRATION IN LATIN AMERICAN: PROGRESS AND PROBLEMS." L/A+17C ECO/DEV AGRI DIST/IND FINAN INDUS NAT/G VOL/ASSN CONSULT DELIB/GP EX/STRUC ACT/RES PLAN TEC/DEV ECO/TAC ROUTINE BAL/PAY WEALTH WORK 20. PAGE 69 A1411 MARKET ECO/UNDEV INT/TRADE

S64
KARPOV P.V.,"PEACEFUL COEXISTENCE AND INTERNATIONAL LAW." WOR+45 LAW SOCIETY INT/ORG VOL/ASSN FORCES CREATE CAP/ISM DIPLOM ADJUD NUC/PWR PEACE MORAL ORD/FREE PWR MARXISM...MARXIST JURID CONCPT OBS TREND COLD/WAR MARX/KARL 20. PAGE 77 A1568 COM ATTIT INT/LAW USSR

S64
LERNER W.,"THE HISTORICAL ORIGINS OF THE SOVIET DOCTRINE OF PEACEFUL COEXISTENCE." COM USSR INT/ORG NAT/G VOL/ASSN PLAN PEACE ATTIT RIGID/FLEX PWR MARXISM...TIME/SEQ COLD/WAR 20. PAGE 87 A1788 EDU/PROP DIPLOM

S64
PADELFORD N.J.,"THE ORGANIZATION OF AFRICAN UNITY." ECO/UNDEV INT/ORG PLAN BAL/PWR DIPLOM ECO/TAC NAT/LISM ORD/FREE PWR WEALTH...CONCPT TREND STERTYP VAL/FREE COLD/WAR 20. PAGE 113 A2313 AFR VOL/ASSN REGION

S64
RUBINSTEIN A.Z.,"THE SOVIET IMAGE OF WESTERN EUROPE." COM EUR+WWI FRANCE GERMANY GERMANY/W USA+45 USSR INT/ORG NAT/G VOL/ASSN FORCES TOP/EX BAL/PWR EDU/PROP ORD/FREE PWR...MYTH RECORD NATO EEC 20. PAGE 125 A2564 RIGID/FLEX ATTIT

N64
GREAT BRITAIN CENTRAL OFF INF,THE COLOMBO PLAN (PAMPHLET). ASIA S/ASIA USA+45 VOL/ASSN...CHARTS 20 COMMONWLTH RESOURCE/N. PAGE 55 A1134 FOR/AID PLAN INT/ORG ECO/UNDEV

B65
BRACKETT R.D.,PATHWAYS TO PEACE. SECT VOL/ASSN GP/REL PERS/REL DISCRIM...LING 20 UN PEACE/CORP. PAGE 18 A0366 PEACE INT/ORG EDU/PROP PARTIC

B65
INGRAM D.,COMMONWEALTH FOR A COLOUR-BLIND WORLD. AFR INDIA UK STRATA ECO/UNDEV VOL/ASSN CREATE PLAN CONFER COLONIAL ORD/FREE SOC/INTEG 20 COMMONWLTH. PAGE 70 A1441 RACE/REL INT/ORG INGP/REL PROB/SOLV

B65
LEVENSTEIN A.,FREEDOM'S ADVOCATE - A TWENTY-FIVE YEAR CHRONICLE. USA+45 POL/PAR LEGIS DIPLOM WAR PEACE TOTALISM DRIVE MARXISM 20 FREEDOM/HS. PAGE 87 A1791 ORD/FREE VOL/ASSN POLICY ATTIT

B65
MEHROTRA S.R.,INDIA AND THE COMMONWEALTH 1885-1929. INDIA UK INT/ORG VOL/ASSN GP/REL ATTIT...POLICY BIBLIOG 19/20 CMN/WLTH. PAGE 99 A2034 DIPLOM NAT/G POL/PAR NAT/LISM

B65
MILLER J.D.B.,THE COMMONWEALTH IN THE WORLD (3RD ED.). CONSTN COLONIAL PWR SOVEREIGN 20 CMN/WLTH. PAGE 101 A2077 VOL/ASSN INT/ORG INGP/REL DIPLOM

B65
MONCRIEFF A.,SECOND THOUGHTS ON AID. WOR+45 ECO/UNDEV AGRI FINAN VOL/ASSN PLAN TEC/DEV GIVE EDU/PROP ROLE WEALTH 20. PAGE 102 A2105 FOR/AID ECO/TAC INT/ORG IDEA/COMP

B65
SABLE M.H.,MASTER DIRECTORY FOR LATIN AMERICA. AGRI COM/IND FINAN R+D ACADEM LABOR NAT/G POL/PAR VOL/ASSN INT/TRADE EDU/PROP 20. PAGE 126 A2582 INDEX L/A+17C INT/ORG DIPLOM

B65
SOPER T.,EVOLVING COMMONWEALTH. AFR CANADA INDIA IRELAND UK LAW CONSTN POL/PAR DOMIN CONTROL WAR PWR ...AUD/VIS 18/20 COMMONWLTH OEEC. PAGE 135 A2769 INT/ORG COLONIAL VOL/ASSN

B65
UNESCO,HANDBOOK OF INTERNATIONAL EXCHANGES. COM/IND R+D ACADEM PROF/ORG VOL/ASSN CREATE TEC/DEV INDEX INT/ORG

EDU/PROP AGREE 20 TREATY. PAGE 148 A3025 — DIPLOM PRESS

B65
US SENATE,US INTERNATIONAL SPACE PROGRAMS, 1959-65: STAFF REPORT FOR COMM ON AERONAUTICAL AND SPACE SCIENCES. WOR+45 VOL/ASSN CIVMIL/REL 20 CONGRESS NASA TREATY. PAGE 155 A3166 — SPACE DIPLOM PLAN GOV/REL

B65
US SENATE COMM AERO SPACE SCI,INTERNATIONAL COOPERATION AND ORGANIZATION FOR OUTER SPACE. FUT USA+45 WOR+45 PROF/ORG VOL/ASSN CONSULT DELIB/GP PLAN TEC/DEV ARMS/CONT GP/REL PEACE 20 UN NASA. PAGE 155 A3167 — DIPLOM SPACE R+D NAT/G

S65
AMRAM P.W.,"REPORT ON THE TENTH SESSION OF THE HAGUE CONFERENCE ON PRIVATE INTERNATIONAL LAW." USA+45 WOR+45 INT/ORG CREATE LEGIT ADJUD ALL/VALS ...JURID CONCPT METH/CNCPT OBS GEN/METH 20. PAGE 8 A0155 — VOL/ASSN DELIB/GP INT/LAW

S65
BROWN S.,"AN ALTERNATIVE TO THE GRAND DESIGN." EUR+WWI FUT USA+45 INT/ORG NAT/G EX/STRUC FORCES CREATE BAL/PWR DOMIN RIGID/FLEX ORD/FREE PWR ...NEW/IDEA RECORD EEC NATO 20. PAGE 20 A0407 — VOL/ASSN CONCPT DIPLOM

S65
HAZARD J.N.,"CO-EXISTENCE LAW BOWS OUT." WOR+45 R+D INT/ORG VOL/ASSN CONSULT DELIB/GP ACT/RES CREATE PEACE KNOWL...JURID CONCPT COLD/WAR VAL/FREE 20. PAGE 63 A1300 — PROF/ORG ADJUD

S65
HOLSTI O.R.,"EAST-WEST CONFLICT AND SINO-SOVIET RELATIONS" CHINA/COM USSR COMPUTER REGION DECISION. PAGE 67 A1373 — VOL/ASSN DIPLOM CON/ANAL COM

S65
SCHNEIDER R.M.,"THE US IN LATIN AMERICA." L/A+17C USA+45 NAT/G POL/PAR PLAN RIGID/FLEX ALL/VALS OAS 20. PAGE 129 A2640 — VOL/ASSN ECO/UNDEV FOR/AID

B66
GORDON B.K.,THE DIMENSIONS OF CONFLICT IN SOUTHEAST ASIA. S/ASIA FORCES ADJUD REGION...CHARTS 20. PAGE 54 A1111 — DIPLOM NAT/COMP INT/ORG VOL/ASSN

B66
HAY P.,FEDERALISM AND SUPRANATIONAL ORGANIZATIONS: PATTERNS FOR NEW LEGAL STRUCTURES. EUR+WWI LAW NAT/G VOL/ASSN DIPLOM PWR...NAT/COMP TREATY EEC. PAGE 63 A1294 — SOVEREIGN FEDERAL INT/ORG INT/LAW

B66
KAREFA-SMART J.,AFRICA: PROGRESS THROUGH COOPERATION. AFR FINAN TEC/DEV DIPLOM FOR/AID EDU/PROP CONFER REGION GP/REL WEALTH...HEAL SOC/INTEG 20. PAGE 76 A1566 — ORD/FREE ECO/UNDEV VOL/ASSN PLAN

B66
LENT H.B.,THE PEACE CORPS: AMBASSADORS OF GOOD WILL. USA+45 ECO/UNDEV...INT TESTS BIOG AUD/VIS SOC/INTEG 20 PEACE/CORP. PAGE 87 A1776 — VOL/ASSN FOR/AID DIPLOM CONSULT

B66
MCINTYRE W.D.,COLONIES INTO COMMONWEALTH. UK CONSTN VOL/ASSN DOMIN CONTROL...BIBLIOG 18/20 CMN/WLTH. PAGE 98 A2012 — DIPLOM INT/ORG COLONIAL SOVEREIGN

B66
OHLIN G.,FOREIGN AID POLICIES RECONSIDERED. ECO/DEV ECO/UNDEV VOL/ASSN CONSULT PLAN CONTROL ATTIT ...CONCPT CHARTS BIBLIOG 20. PAGE 111 A2286 — FOR/AID DIPLOM GIVE

B66
ROBOCK S.H.,INTERNATIONAL DEVELOPMENT 1965. AGRI INDUS VOL/ASSN PLAN TEC/DEV EDU/PROP HEALTH...JURID 20 UN PEACE/CORP. PAGE 122 A2508 — FOR/AID INT/ORG GEOG ECO/UNDEV

B66
UN ECAFE,ADMINISTRATIVE ASPECTS OF FAMILY PLANNING PROGRAMMES (PAMPHLET). ASIA THAILAND WOR+45 VOL/ASSN PROB/SOLV BUDGET FOR/AID EDU/PROP CONFER CONTROL GOV/REL TIME 20 UN BIRTH/CON. PAGE 147 A2999 — PLAN CENSUS FAM ADMIN

B66
US HOUSE COMM APPROPRIATIONS,HEARINGS ON FOREIGN OPERATIONS AND RELATED AGENCIES APPROPRIATIONS. CUBA USA+45 VOL/ASSN DELIB/GP DIPLOM CONFER ORD/FREE 20 CONGRESS MIGRATION INT/AM/DEV PEACE/CORP. PAGE 153 A3120 — FOR/AID BUDGET ECO/UNDEV FORCES

B66
WELCH R.H.W.,THE NEW AMERICANISM, AND OTHER SPEECHES AND ESSAYS. USA+45 ACADEM POL/PAR SCHOOL VOL/ASSN FORCES CAP/ISM TAX REV DISCRIM 20 CIV/RIGHTS COLD/WAR BIRCH/SOC. PAGE 163 A3313 — DIPLOM FASCISM MARXISM RACE/REL

B66
WILSON H.A.,THE IMPERIAL POLICY OF SIR ROBERT BORDEN. CANADA UK ELITES INT/ORG VOL/ASSN CONTROL LEAD WAR ROLE 20 CMN/WLTH BORDEN/R. PAGE 165 A3360 — INGP/REL COLONIAL CONSTN CHIEF

L66
MCDOUGAL M.S.,"CHINESE PARTICIPATION IN THE UNITED NATIONS: THE LEGAL IMPERATIVES OF A NEGOTIATED SOLUTION" CHINA/COM WOR+45 VOL/ASSN DIPLOM PARTIC ...DECISION IDEA/COMP 20 UN. PAGE 98 A2010 — INT/ORG REPRESENT POLICY PROB/SOLV

S66
"WORLD BANK CONVENTION ON INVESTMENT DISPUTES: A BIBLIOGRAPH ICAL NOTE." VOL/ASSN CONSULT CAP/ISM DIPLOM INT/TRADE 20 SENATE PRESIDENT. PAGE 4 A0074 — BIBLIOG ADJUD FINAN INT/ORG

S66
JAVITS J.K.,"POLITICAL ACTION VITAL FOR LATIN AMERICAN INTEGRATION." ECO/UNDEV INT/ORG POL/PAR VOL/ASSN PLAN PROB/SOLV INT/TRADE EFFICIENCY 20 OAS LAFTA. PAGE 73 A1500 — L/A+17C ECO/TAC REGION

B67
AUBREY H.G.,ATLANTIC ECONOMIC COOPERATION. ECO/DEV INDUS VOL/ASSN PROB/SOLV DIPLOM INT/TRADE TARIFFS CONFER 20. PAGE 10 A0197 — INT/ORG ECO/TAC TEC/DEV CAP/ISM

B67
US DEPARTMENT OF STATE,THE COUNTRY TEAM - AN ILLUSTRATED PROFILE OF OUR AMERICAN MISSIONS ABROAD. ECO/TAC FOR/AID EDU/PROP TASK PERS/REL ATTIT 20. PAGE 152 A3099 — DIPLOM NAT/G VOL/ASSN GOV/REL

B67
US SENATE COMM ON FOREIGN REL,HUMAN RIGHTS CONVENTIONS. USA+45 LABOR VOL/ASSN DELIB/GP DOMIN ADJUD REPRESENT...INT/LAW MGT CONGRESS. PAGE 156 A3189 — LEGIS ORD/FREE WORKER LOBBY

L67
SEGAL A.,"THE INTEGRATION OF DEVELOPING COUNTRIES: SOME THOUGHTS ON EAST AFRICA AND CENTRAL AMERICA." AFR L/A+17C INT/ORG NAT/G VOL/ASSN FOR/AID INT/TRADE EQUILIB NAT/LISM PWR 20. PAGE 131 A2680 — ECO/UNDEV DIPLOM REGION

S67
CARROLL K.J.,"SECOND STEP TOWARD ARMS CONTROL." WOR+45 INT/ORG VOL/ASSN FORCES PROB/SOLV RISK WEAPON 20 COLD/WAR. PAGE 25 A0503 — ARMS/CONT DIPLOM PLAN NUC/PWR

S67
COSGROVE C.A.,"AGRICULTURE, FINANCE AND POLITICS IN THE EUROPEAN COMMUNITY." EUR+WWI DIST/IND MARKET INT/ORG VOL/ASSN DELIB/GP TEC/DEV BAL/PWR BARGAIN ECO/TAC RATION CONFER 20 EEC. PAGE 31 A0630 — ECO/DEV DIPLOM AGRI INT/TRADE

S67
GODUNSKY Y.,"'APOSTLES OF PEACE' IN LATIN AMERICA." L/A+17C USA+45 BAL/PWR DIPLOM FOR/AID DOMIN COLONIAL CIVMIL/REL MARXIST. PAGE 53 A1086 — ECO/UNDEV REV VOL/ASSN EDU/PROP

S67
HULL E.W.S.,"THE POLITICAL OCEAN." FUT UNIV WOR+45 EXTR/IND R+D VOL/ASSN PLAN BAL/PWR ECO/TAC PEACE WEALTH 20 UN. PAGE 69 A1414 — DIPLOM ECO/UNDEV INT/ORG INT/LAW

S67
WEIL G.L.,"THE EUROPEAN COMMUNITY* WHAT LIES BEYOND THE POINT OF NO RETURN?" VOL/ASSN PROB/SOLV DIPLOM REGION INGP/REL CENTRAL PWR 20 EEC. PAGE 162 A3301 — INT/ORG ECO/DEV INT/TRADE PREDICT

B68
ANTWERP-INST UNIVERSITAIRE,BIBLIOGRAPHIC COMPENDIUM: DEVELOPING COUNTRIES (ANTWERP-INST UNIVERSITAIRE DES TERRITOIRES D'OUTRE-MER). AFR EUR+WWI SOCIETY AGRI FINAN NEIGH VOL/ASSN PROB/SOLV TEC/DEV FOR/AID INT/TRADE 20. PAGE 8 A0166 — BIBLIOG ECO/UNDEV DIPLOM PLAN

VOLPICELLI Z. A3248

VOLTAIRE....VOLTAIRE (FRANCOIS MARIE AROUET)

B55
ROWE C.,VOLTAIRE AND THE STATE. FRANCE MOD/EUR BAL/PWR CONTROL TASK SUPEGO ORD/FREE PWR...CONCPT 18 VOLTAIRE. PAGE 125 A2553 — NAT/G DIPLOM NAT/LISM ATTIT

VOLUNTARY ASSOCIATIONS....SEE VOL/ASSN

VON BECKERATH E. A3249
VON BORCH H. A2305
VON GLAHN G. A3250

VON HALLER A. A3251

VON HARPE W. A3252

VON/TRESCK....VON TRESCKOW

VONGLAHN G. A3253

VORSPAN A. A3254

VOSS E.H. A3255

VOTING....SEE CHOOSE, SUFF

VTOL....VERTICAL TAKE-OFF AND LANDING AIRCRAFT

VYAS R. A3256

W

WABEKE B.H. A3257

WADSWORTH J.J. A3258

WAELDER R. A3259

WAGES....SEE PRICE, WORKER, WEALTH

WAGNER/A....ADOLPH WAGNER

WAINHOUSE D.W. A3260,A3261

WALES....WALES

WALKER A.A. A3262,A3263

WALKER E.A. A3264

WALKER H. A3265

WALKER R.L. A3266

WALKER/E....EDWIN WALKER

WALLACE E. A2669

WALLACE R.J. A1190

WALLACE/G....GEORGE WALLACE

WALLACE/HA....HENRY A. WALLACE

WALLBANK T.W. A3267

WALLERSTEIN I.M. A3268,A3269

WALSH E. A3270

WALTERS F.P. A3271

WALTZ/KN....KENNETH N. WALTZ

WAMBAUCH S. A3272

WANDERSCHECK H. A3273

WAR....SEE ALSO COERCE

N
CONOVER H.F.,WORLD GOVERNMENT: A LIST OF SELECTED REFERENCES (PAMPHLET). WOR+45 PROB/SOLV ARMS/CONT WAR PEACE 20 UN. PAGE 29 A0589
BIBLIOG/A NUC/PWR INT/ORG DIPLOM

N
LONDON INSTITUTE WORLD AFFAIRS,THE YEAR BOOK OF WORLD AFFAIRS. FINAN BAL/PWR ARMS/CONT WAR ...INT/LAW BIBLIOG 20. PAGE 91 A1856
DIPLOM FOR/AID INT/ORG

N
TOSCANO M.,THE HISTORY OF TREATIES AND INTERNATIONAL POLITICS (REV. ED.). WOR-45 AGREE WAR ...BIOG 19/20 TREATY WWI. PAGE 144 A2951
DIPLOM INT/ORG

N
US DEPT OF STATE,FOREIGN RELATIONS OF THE UNITED STATES; DIPLOMATIC PAPERS. USA-45 NAT/G WAR PEACE ATTIT 19/20. PAGE 152 A3112
BIBLIOG DIPLOM POLICY

B
CURRENT THOUGHT ON PEACE AND WAR. WOR+45 INT/ORG FORCES PROB/SOLV DIPLOM NUC/PWR PERCEPT...POLICY SOC 20 UN NATO. PAGE 1 A0008
BIBLIOG/A PEACE ATTIT WAR

N
AMERICAN JOURNAL OF INTERNATIONAL LAW. WOR+45 WOR-45 CONSTN INT/ORG NAT/G CT/SYS ARMS/CONT WAR ...DECISION JURID NAT/COMP 20. PAGE 1 A0002
BIBLIOG/A INT/LAW DIPLOM ADJUD

N
INTERNATIONAL AFFAIRS. WOR+45 WOR-45 ECO/UNDEV INT/ORG NAT/G PROB/SOLV FOR/AID WAR...POLICY 20. PAGE 1 A0009
BIBLIOG/A DIPLOM INT/LAW INT/TRADE

N
JOURNAL OF ASIAN STUDIES. CULTURE ECO/DEV SECT DIPLOM EDU/PROP WAR NAT/LISM...PHIL/SCI SOC 20. PAGE 1 A0013
BIBLIOG ASIA S/ASIA NAT/G

N
JOURNAL OF CONFLICT RESOLUTION. FUT WOR+45 INT/ORG NAT/G FORCES CREATE PROB/SOLV ARMS/CONT NUC/PWR WEAPON SOC. PAGE 1 A0014
BIBLIOG/A DIPLOM WAR

N
JOURNAL OF INTERNATIONAL AFFAIRS. WOR+45 ECO/UNDEV POL/PAR ECO/TAC WAR PEACE PERSON ALL/IDEOS ...INT/LAW TREND. PAGE 1 A0015
BIBLIOG DIPLOM INT/ORG NAT/G

N
JOURNAL OF MODERN HISTORY. WOR+45 WOR-45 LEAD WAR ...TIME/SEQ TREND NAT/COMP 20. PAGE 1 A0016
BIBLIOG/A DIPLOM NAT/G

N
BIBLIOGRAPHIE DER SOZIALWISSENSCHAFTEN. WOR-45 CONSTN SOCIETY ECO/DEV ECO/UNDEV DIPLOM LEAD WAR PEACE...PHIL/SCI SOC 19/20. PAGE 2 A0030
BIBLIOG LAW CONCPT NAT/G

N
AIR UNIVERSITY LIBRARY,INDEX TO MILITARY PERIODICALS. FUT SPACE WOR+45 REGION ARMS/CONT NUC/PWR WAR PEACE INT/LAW. PAGE 5 A0105
BIBLIOG/A FORCES NAT/G DIPLOM

N
COUNCIL ON FOREIGN RELATIONS,DOCUMENTS ON AMERICAN FOREIGN RELATIONS. INT/ORG ECO/TAC NUC/PWR WAR WEAPON...POLICY CON/ANAL CHARTS 20 OAS UN. PAGE 31 A0639
BIBLIOG USA+45 USA-45 DIPLOM

N
TURNER R.K.,BIBLIOGRAPHY ON WORLD ORGANIZATION. INT/TRADE CT/SYS ARMS/CONT WEALTH...INT/LAW 20. PAGE 146 A2984
BIBLIOG/A INT/ORG PEACE WAR

N
UNITED NATIONS,UNITED NATIONS PUBLICATIONS. WOR+45 ECO/UNDEV AGRI FINAN FORCES ADMIN LEAD WAR PEACE ...POLICY INT/LAW 20 UN. PAGE 148 A3034
BIBLIOG INT/ORG DIPLOM

N
US DEPARTMENT OF STATE,BIBLIOGRAPHY (PAMPHLETS). AGRI INDUS INT/ORG FOR/AID EDU/PROP WAR MARXISM ...SOC GOV/COMP METH/COMP 20. PAGE 151 A3079
BIBLIOG DIPLOM ECO/DEV NAT/G

N
US LIBRARY OF CONGRESS,ACCESSIONS LIST -- ISRAEL. ISRAEL CULTURE ECO/UNDEV POL/PAR PLAN PROB/SOLV TEC/DEV DIPLOM EDU/PROP LEAD WAR ATTIT 20 JEWS. PAGE 154 A3143
BIBLIOG ISLAM NAT/G GP/REL

NLO
WHITE J.A.,THE DIPLOMACY OF THE RUSSO-JAPANESE WAR. ASIA KOREA RUSSIA FORCES CONFER CONTROL PEACE ...BIBLIOG 19 CHINJAP. PAGE 164 A3336
DIPLOM WAR BAL/PWR

B00
GROTIUS H.,DE JURE BELLI AC PACIS. CHRIST-17C UNIV LAW SOCIETY PROVS LEGIT PEACE PERCEPT MORAL PWR ...CONCPT CON/ANAL GEN/LAWS. PAGE 57 A1180
JURID INT/LAW WAR

B00
HOLLAND T.E.,STUDIES IN INTERNATIONAL LAW. TURKEY USSR WOR-45 CONSTN NAT/G DIPLOM DOMIN LEGIT COERCE WAR PEACE ORD/FREE PWR SOVEREIGN...JURID CHARTS 20 PARLIAMENT SUEZ TREATY. PAGE 66 A1367
INT/ORG LAW INT/LAW

B00
LORIMER J.,THE INSTITUTES OF THE LAW OF NATIONS. WOR-45 CULTURE SOCIETY NAT/G VOL/ASSN DIPLOM LEGIT WAR PEACE DRIVE ORD/FREE SOVEREIGN...CONCPT RECORD INT TREND HYPO/EXP GEN/METH TOT/POP VAL/FREE 20. PAGE 91 A1863
INT/ORG LAW INT/LAW

B00
MAINE H.S.,INTERNATIONAL LAW. MOD/EUR UNIV SOCIETY STRUCT ACT/RES EXEC WAR ATTIT PERSON ALL/VALS ...POLICY JURID CONCPT OBS TIME/SEQ TOT/POP. PAGE 93 A1908
INT/ORG LAW PEACE INT/LAW

B00
MOCKLER-FERRYMAN A.,BRITISH WEST AFRICA. FRANCE GERMANY NIGER SIER/LEONE UK CULTURE DIPLOM WAR RACE/REL PRODUC PROFIT WEALTH...POLICY PREDICT 19. PAGE 102 A2095
AFR COLONIAL INT/TRADE CAP/ISM

B00
OMAN C.,A HISTORY OF THE ART OF WAR: THE MIDDLE AGES FROM THE FOURTH TO THE FOURTEENTH CENTURY. CHRIST-17C MEDIT-7 CULTURE SOCIETY INT/ORG ROUTINE PERSON...CONT/OBS HIST/WRIT CHARTS VAL/FREE. PAGE 112 A2291
FORCES SKILL WAR

L00
HISTORICUS,"LETTERS AND SOME QUESTIONS OF INTERNATIONAL LAW." FRANCE NETHERLAND UK USA-45 WOR-45 LAW NAT/G COERCE...SOC CONCPT GEN/LAWS TOT/POP 19 CIVIL/WAR. PAGE 65 A1344
WEALTH JURID WAR INT/LAW

C05
DUNNING W.A.,"HISTORY OF POLITICAL THEORIES FROM LUTHER TO MONTESQUIEU." LAW NAT/G SECT DIPLOM REV WAR ORD/FREE SOVEREIGN CONSERVE...TRADIT BIBLIOG 16/18. PAGE 39 A0803
PHIL/SCI CONCPT GEN/LAWS

B07
GRIFFIN A.P.C.,LIST OF WORKS RELATING TO THE FRENCH ALLIANCE IN THE AMERICAN REVOLUTION. FRANCE FORCES DIPLOM 18 PRE/US/AM. PAGE 56 A1155
BIBLIOG/A REV WAR

B08
ARON R.,WAR AND INDUSTRIAL SOCIETY. EUR+WWI MOD/EUR WOR+45 WOR-45 CONSTN SOCIETY INT/ORG POL/PAR VOL/ASSN DIPLOM INT/TRADE PEACE ATTIT...BIOG
ECO/DEV WAR

GEN/LAWS 19/20. PAGE 9 A0178

B08
LABRIOLA A.,ESSAYS ON THE MATERIALISTIC CONCEPTION OF HISTORY. STRATA POL/PAR CAP/ISM DIPLOM INT/TRADE WAR 20. PAGE 83 A1706
MARXIST WORKER REV COLONIAL

B09
HOLLAND T.E.,LETTERS UPON WAR AND NEUTRALITY. WOR-45 NAT/G FORCES JUDGE ECO/TAC LEGIT CT/SYS NEUTRAL ROUTINE COERCE...JURID TIME/SEQ 20. PAGE 67 A1368
LAW INT/LAW INT/ORG WAR

B13
BORCHARD E.M.,BIBLIOGRAPHY OF INTERNATIONAL LAW AND CONTINENTAL LAW. EUR+WWI MOD/EUR UK LAW INT/TRADE WAR PEACE...GOV/COMP NAT/COMP 19/20. PAGE 17 A0338
BIBLIOG INT/LAW JURID DIPLOM

B14
BERNHARDI F.,ON THE WAR OF TODAY. MOD/EUR INT/ORG NAT/G TOP/EX PWR CHARTS. PAGE 14 A0278
FORCES SKILL WAR

B14
DE BLOCH J.,THE FUTURE OF WAR IN ITS TECHNICAL, ECONOMIC, AND POLITICAL RELATIONS (1899). MOD/EUR TEC/DEV BUDGET INT/TRADE DETER GUERRILLA WEAPON COST PEACE 20. PAGE 34 A0698
WAR BAL/PWR PREDICT FORCES

B16
PUFENDORF S.,LAW OF NATURE AND OF NATIONS (ABRIDGED). UNIV LAW NAT/G DIPLOM AGREE WAR PERSON ALL/VALS PWR...POLICY 18 DEITY NATURL/LAW. PAGE 118 A2416
CONCPT INT/LAW SECT MORAL

B16
ROOT E.,THE MILITARY AND COLONIAL POLICY OF THE US. L/A+17C USA-45 LAW SOCIETY STRATA STRUCT INT/ORG NAT/G SCHOOL FORCES EDU/PROP ALL/VALS...OBS VAL/FREE 19/20. PAGE 123 A2522
ACT/RES PLAN DIPLOM WAR

L16
WRIGHT Q.,"THE ENFORCEMENT OF INTERNATIONAL LAW THROUGH MUNICIPAL LAW IN THE US." USA-45 LOC/G NAT/G PUB/INST FORCES LEGIT CT/SYS PERCEPT ALL/VALS ...JURID 20. PAGE 167 A3401
INT/ORG LAW INT/LAW WAR

B17
DE VICTORIA F.,DE INDIS ET DE JURE BELLI (1557) IN F. DE VICTORIA, DE INDIS ET DE JURE BELLI REFLECTIONES. UNIV NAT/G SECT CHIEF PARTIC COERCE PEACE MORAL...POLICY 16 INDIAN/AM CHRISTIAN CONSCN/OBJ. PAGE 35 A0715
WAR INT/LAW OWN

B17
DILLA H.M.,CLASSIFIED LIST OF MAGAZINE ARTICLES ON THE EUROPEAN WAR. MOD/EUR USA-45 WOR-45 PEACE ATTIT 20. PAGE 37 A0762
BIBLIOG WAR DIPLOM POLICY

B17
MEYER H.H.B.,THE UNITED STATES AT WAR, ORGANIZATIONS AND LITERATURE. USA-45 AGRI FINAN INDUS CHIEF FORCES DIPLOM FOR/AID INT/TRADE...SOC 20 PRESIDENT. PAGE 100 A2050
BIBLIOG/A WAR NAT/G VOL/ASSN

B17
UPTON E.,THE MILITARY POLICY OF THE US. USA-45 STRUCT INT/ORG EXEC ATTIT PERCEPT...MGT CONCPT OBS HIST/WRIT CHARTS CONGRESS 18/20. PAGE 149 A3049
FORCES SKILL WAR

B17
VEBLEN T.B.,AN INQUIRY INTO THE NATURE OF PEACE AND THE TERMS OF ITS PERPETUATION. UNIV STRATA FINAN EDU/PROP PRICE COST DISCRIM NAT/LISM MORAL ORD/FREE PACIFIST 20 WORLDUNITY. PAGE 158 A3224
PEACE DIPLOM WAR NAT/G

B18
US LIBRARY OF CONGRESS,LIST OF REFERENCES ON A LEAGUE OF NATIONS. DIPLOM WAR PEACE 20 LEAGUE/NAT. PAGE 154 A3145
BIBLIOG INT/ORG ADMIN EX/STRUC

B19
KEYNES J.M.,THE ECONOMIC CONSEQUENCES OF THE PEACE. FUT GERMANY MOD/EUR RUSSIA UK USA-45 CULTURE ECO/DEV FINAN INDUS INT/ORG TOP/EX ECO/TAC ROUTINE WAR ATTIT PERCEPT ALL/VALS...OLD/LIB MYTH OBS TIME/SEQ TREND 20 TREATY. PAGE 78 A1605
EUR+WWI SOCIETY PEACE

B19
LONDON SCHOOL ECONOMICS-POL,ANNUAL DIGEST OF PUBLIC INTERNATIONAL LAW CASES. INT/ORG MUNIC NAT/G PROVS ADMIN NEUTRAL WAR GOV/REL PRIVIL 20. PAGE 91 A1858
BIBLIOG/A INT/LAW ADJUD DIPLOM

B19
MEYER H.H.B.,SELECT LIST OF REFERENCES ON ECONOMIC RECONSTRUCTION: INCLUDING REPORTS OF THE BRITISH MINISTRY OF RECONSTRUCTION. UK LABOR PLAN PROB/SOLV ECO/TAC INT/TRADE WAR DEMAND PRODUC 20. PAGE 100 A2051
BIBLIOG/A EUR+WWI ECO/DEV WORKER

B19
ROUSSEAU J.J.,A LASTING PEACE. INT/ORG NAT/G CHIEF DIPLOM DETER WAR POLICY. PAGE 124 A2550
PLAN PEACE UTIL

B19
US DEPARTMENT OF STATE,A TENTATIVE LIST OF TREATY COLLECTIONS. WOR-45 BAL/PWR INT/TRADE TARIFFS WAR PEACE ORD/FREE 20. PAGE 151 A3080
ANTHOL DIPLOM DELIB/GP

B19
VANDERPOL A.,LA DOCTRINE SCOLASTIQUE DU DROIT DE GUERRE. CHRIST-17C FORCES DIPLOM LEGIT SUPEGO MORAL ...BIOG AQUINAS/T SUAREZ/F CHRISTIAN. PAGE 158 A3220
WAR SECT INT/LAW

N19
DEANE H.,THE WAR IN VIETNAM (PAMPHLET). CHINA/COM VIETNAM BAL/PWR DIPLOM ECO/TAC SOCISM INTERVENT COLD/WAR INTERVENT COLD/WAR. PAGE 35 A0720
WAR SOCIALIST MORAL CAP/ISM

N19
FREEMAN H.A.,COERCION OF STATES IN FEDERAL UNIONS (PAMPHLET). WOR-45 DIPLOM CONTROL COERCE PEACE ORD/FREE...GOV/COMP METH/COMP NAT/COMP PACIFIST 20. PAGE 49 A0994
FEDERAL WAR INT/ORG PACIFISM

N19
GRANT N.,COMMUNIST PSYCHOLOGICAL OFFENSIVE: DISTORTION IN THE TRANSLATION OF OFFICIAL DOCUMENTS (PAMPHLET). USSR POL/PAR CHIEF FOR/AID PRESS WRITING COLONIAL LEAD WAR PEACE 20 KHRUSH/N. PAGE 55 A1129
MARXISM DIPLOM EDU/PROP

N19
MEZERIK A.G.,COLONIALISM AND THE UNITED NATIONS (PAMPHLET). WOR+45 NAT/G ADMIN LEAD WAR CHOOSE EFFICIENCY PEACE ATTIT ORD/FREE...POLICY CHARTS UN COLD/WAR. PAGE 100 A2061
COLONIAL DIPLOM BAL/PWR INT/ORG

N19
ZLOTNICK M.,WEAPONS IN SPACE (PAMPHLET). FUT WOR+45 TEC/DEV DIPLOM ARMS/CONT CIVMIL/REL PEACE HABITAT ...CONCPT NEW/IDEA CHARTS. PAGE 170 A3457
SPACE WEAPON NUC/PWR WAR

B21
BALFOUR A.J.,ESSAYS SPECULATIVE AND POLITICAL. SEA CULTURE CREATE WAR NAT/LISM PEACE LOVE...ART/METH INT/LAW CONCPT ANTHOL 20 JEWS. PAGE 10 A0211
PHIL/SCI SOCIETY DIPLOM

B22
REINSCH P.,SECRET DIPLOMACY: HOW FAR CAN IT BE ELIMINATED. FUT WOR-45 CULTURE INT/ORG NAT/G EDU/PROP WAR...MYTH HIST/WRIT CON/ANAL 20. PAGE 120 A2460
RIGID/FLEX PWR DIPLOM

B24
HALL W.E.,A TREATISE ON INTERNATIONAL LAW. WOR-45 CONSTN INT/ORG NAT/G DIPLOM ORD/FREE LEAGUE/NAT 20 TREATY. PAGE 60 A1228
PWR JURID WAR INT/LAW

C25
MOON P.T.,"SYLLABUS ON INTERNATIONAL RELATIONS." EUR+WWI MOD/EUR USA-45 FORCES COLONIAL WAR WEAPON NAT/LISM...POLICY BIBLIOG T 19/20. PAGE 103 A2120
INT/ORG DIPLOM NAT/G

B26
INSTITUT INTERMEDIAIRE INTL,REPERTOIRE GENERAL DES TRAITES ET AUTRES ACTES DIPLOMATIQUES CONCLUS DEPUIS 1895 JUSQU'EN 1920. MOD/EUR WOR-45 INT/ORG VOL/ASSN DELIB/GP INT/TRADE WAR TREATY 19/20. PAGE 70 A1443
BIBLIOG DIPLOM

B27
BRANDENBURG E.,FROM BISMARCK TO THE WORLD WAR; A HISTORY OF GERMAN FOREIGN POLICY, 1870-1914 (TRANS. BY ANNIE ELIZABETH ADAMS). GERMANY MOD/EUR FORCES AGREE PWR 19/20 TREATY CHAMBRLN/J WWI BISMARCK/O. PAGE 18 A0368
DIPLOM POLICY WAR

B28
HUBER G.,DIE FRANZOSISCHE PROPAGANDA IM WELTKRIEG GEGEN DEUTSCHLAND 1914 BIS 1918. FRANCE GERMANY MOD/EUR DIPLOM WAR...EXHIBIT 20 WWI. PAGE 68 A1403
EDU/PROP ATTIT DOMIN PRESS

B28
MILLER D.H.,THE DRAFTING OF THE COVENANT. UNIV WOR-45 INTELL NAT/G DELIB/GP PLAN ECO/TAC LEGIT WAR ATTIT PERCEPT...CONCPT TIME/SEQ LEAGUE/NAT TOT/POP 20. PAGE 101 A2074
INT/ORG STRUCT PEACE

B28
PLAYNE C.E.,THE PRE-WAR MIND IN BRITAIN. GERMANY MOD/EUR UK STRATA SECT DIPLOM EDU/PROP CROWD SUFF ...POLICY ANARCH PSY SOC IDEA/COMP 20 WWI. PAGE 116 A2388
PRESS WAR DOMIN ATTIT

C28
SCHNEIDER H.W.,"MAKING THE FASCIST STATE." ITALY CULTURE LABOR DIPLOM REV WAR NAT/LISM TOTALISM ATTIT DRIVE SOCISM...BIBLIOG PARLIAMENT 20. PAGE 129 A2638
FASCISM POLICY POL/PAR

B29
LANGER W.L.,THE FRANCO-RUSSIAN ALLIANCE: 1890-1894. FRANCE MOD/EUR UK USSR NAT/G CHIEF FORCES BAL/PWR AGREE WAR PEACE PWR...TIME/SEQ TREATY 19 BISMARCK/O. PAGE 84 A1724
DIPLOM

B29
STURZO L.,THE INTERNATIONAL COMMUNITY AND THE RIGHT OF WAR (TRANS. BY BARBARA BARCLAY CARTER). CULTURE CREATE PROB/SOLV DIPLOM ADJUD CONTROL PEACE PERSON ORD/FREE...INT/LAW IDEA/COMP PACIFIST 20 LEAGUE/NAT. PAGE 140 A2858
INT/ORG PLAN WAR CONCPT

B30
SCHMITT B.E.,THE COMING OF THE WAR, 1914 (2 VOLS.). AUSTRIA FRANCE GERMANY MOD/EUR RUSSIA UK PLAN ROUTINE ORD/FREE. PAGE 128 A2633
WAR DIPLOM

B31
HODGES C.,THE BACKGROUND OF INTERNATIONAL RELATIONS. WOR-45 SOCIETY ECO/DEV ECO/UNDEV INT/ORG DIPLOM DOMIN EDU/PROP LEGIT WAR ATTIT DRIVE PERSON ALL/VALS...CONCPT METH/CNCPT TIME/SEQ CHARTS WORK LEAGUE/NAT 19/20. PAGE 66 A1350
NAT/G BAL/PWR

B32
BLUM L.,PEACE AND DISARMAMENT (TRANS. BY A. WERTH). NAT/G FORCES WORKER DIPLOM AGREE WAR ATTIT AUTHORIT ORD/FREE. PAGE 16 A0322
SOCIALIST PEACE INT/ORG ARMS/CONT

B32
BRYCE J.,THE HOLY ROMAN EMPIRE. GERMANY ITALY MOD/EUR CULTURE SOCIETY STRUCT INT/ORG NAT/G SECT DIPLOM DOMIN WAR SUPEGO ALL/VALS SOVEREIGN...GEOG SOC TIME/SEQ CHARTS STERTYP. PAGE 20 A0413
CHRIST-17C NAT/LISM

B32
LENIN V.I.,THE WAR AND THE SECOND INTERNATIONAL. COM MOD/EUR USSR CAP/ISM DIPLOM NAT/LISM ATTIT MARXISM...CONCPT 20. PAGE 87 A1772
POL/PAR WAR SOCISM INT/ORG

B33
DAHLIN E.,FRENCH AND GERMAN PUBLIC OPINION ON DECLARED WAR AIMS 1914-1918. BELGIUM FRANCE GERMANY NAT/G POL/PAR DIPLOM COERCE REV WAR PEACE 20 WWI WILSON/W. PAGE 33 A0674
ATTIT EDU/PROP DOMIN NAT/COMP

B33
FERRERO G.,PEACE AND WAR (TRANS. BY BERTHA PRITCHARD). CULTURE FINAN SECT ATTIT SUPEGO MORAL ORD/FREE CONSERVE POPULISM SOCISM POLICY. PAGE 45 A0922
WAR PEACE DIPLOM PROB/SOLV

B33
GENTILI A.,DE JURE BELLI, LIBRI TRES (1612) (VOL. 2). FORCES DIPLOM AGREE PEACE SOVEREIGN. PAGE 52 A1059
WAR INT/LAW MORAL SUPEGO

B33
LAUTERPACHT H.,THE FUNCTION OF LAW IN THE INTERNATIONAL COMMUNITY. WOR-45 NAT/G FORCES CREATE DOMIN LEGIT COERCE WAR PEACE ATTIT ORD/FREE PWR SOVEREIGN...JURID CONCPT METH/CNCPT TIME/SEQ GEN/LAWS GEN/METH LEAGUE/NAT TOT/POP VAL/FREE 20. PAGE 85 A1749
INT/ORG LAW INT/LAW

B33
REID H.D.,RECUEIL DES COURS; TOME 45: LES SERVITUDES INTERNATIONALES III. FRANCE CONSTN DELIB/GP PRESS CONTROL REV WAR CHOOSE PEACE MORAL MARITIME TREATY. PAGE 120 A2457
ORD/FREE DIPLOM LAW

B34
EINSTEIN A.,THE WORLD AS I SEE IT. WOR-45 INTELL R+D INT/ORG NAT/G SECT VOL/ASSN FORCES CREATE EDU/PROP LEGIT ARMS/CONT WAR WEAPON NAT/LISM ALL/VALS...POLICY CONCPT 20. PAGE 41 A0828
SOCIETY PHIL/SCI DIPLOM PACIFISM

B34
LOVELL R.I.,THE STRUGGLE FOR SOUTH AFRICA, 1875-1899. GERMANY RHODESIA SOUTH/AFR UK NAT/G ECO/TAC HABITAT WEALTH...POLICY 19. PAGE 91 A1866
COLONIAL DIPLOM WAR GP/REL

B34
WOLFF C.,JUS GENTIUM METHODO SCIENTIFICA PERTRACTATUM. MOD/EUR INT/ORG VOL/ASSN LEGIT PEACE ATTIT...JURID 20. PAGE 166 A3387
NAT/G LAW INT/LAW WAR

B35
FOREIGN AFFAIRS BIBLIOGRAPHY: A SELECTED AND ANNOTATED LIST OF BOOKS ON INTERNATIONAL RELATIONS 1919-1962 (4 VOLS.). CONSTN FORCES COLONIAL ARMS/CONT WAR NAT/LISM PEACE ATTIT DRIVE...POLICY INT/LAW 20. PAGE 3 A0050
BIBLIOG/A DIPLOM INT/ORG

B35
LANGER W.L.,THE DIPLOMACY OF IMPERIALISM 1890-1902. FRANCE GERMANY ITALY UK WOR-45 BAL/PWR INT/TRADE LEGIT ADJUD CONTROL WAR PWR SOVEREIGN...CHARTS BIBLIOG/A 19/20. PAGE 84 A1726
DIPLOM COLONIAL DOMIN

B35
SIMONDS F.H.,THE GREAT POWERS IN WORLD POLITICS. FRANCE GERMANY UK WOR-45 INT/ORG NAT/G ARMS/CONT PEACE FASCISM...POLICY GEOG 20 DEPRESSION NAZI. PAGE 133 A2718
DIPLOM WEALTH WAR

B35
STALEY E.,WAR AND THE PRIVATE INVESTOR. UNIV WOR-45 INTELL SOCIETY INT/ORG NAT/G TOP/EX CAP/ISM ECO/TAC WAR ATTIT ALL/VALS...INT TIME/SEQ TREND CON/ANAL WORK TOT/POP 20. PAGE 137 A2799
FINAN INT/TRADE DIPLOM

B35
WEINBERG A.K.,MANIFEST DESTINY: A STUDY OF NATIONALIST EXPANSIONISM IN AMERICAN HISTORY. USA+45 USA-45 FORCES DIPLOM COLONIAL WAR ATTIT 18/20 INTERVENT. PAGE 162 A3305
NAT/LISM GEOG COERCE NAT/G

B36
BEARD C.A.,THE DEVIL THEORY OF WAR; AN INQUIRY INTO NATURE OF HISTORY AND THE POSSIBILITY OF KEEPING OUT OF WAR. USA-45 INT/ORG PROB/SOLV NEUTRAL ISOLAT ...CONCPT 20 LEAGUE/NAT WWI. PAGE 12 A0240
GEN/LAWS WAR POLICY DIPLOM

B36
BOYCE A.N.,EUROPE AND SOUTH AFRICA. FRANCE GERMANY ITALY SOUTH/AFR UK INDUS NAT/G CONTROL REV WAR NAT/LISM...CONCPT HIST/WRIT 20. PAGE 18 A0362
COLONIAL GOV/COMP NAT/COMP DIPLOM

B36
BRIERLY J.L.,THE LAW OF NATIONS (2ND ED.). WOR+45 WOR-45 INT/ORG AGREE CONTROL COERCE WAR NAT/LISM PEACE PWR 16/20 TREATY LEAGUE/NAT. PAGE 18 A0375
DIPLOM INT/LAW NAT/G

B36
HUDSON M.O.,INTERNATIONAL LEGISLATION: 1929-1931. WOR-45 SEA AIR AGRI FINAN LABOR DIPLOM ECO/TAC REPAR CT/SYS ARMS/CONT WAR WEAPON...JURID 20 TREATY LEAGUE/NAT. PAGE 69 A1409
INT/LAW PARL/PROC ADJUD LAW

B36
HUGENDUBEL P.,DIE KRIEGSMACHE DER FRANZOSISCHEN PRESSE. FRANCE GERMANY MOD/EUR COM/IND NAT/G DIPLOM DOMIN PWR 20. PAGE 69 A1412
PRESS EDU/PROP WAR ATTIT

B36
METZ I.,DIE DEUTSCHE FLOTTE IN DER ENGLISCHEN PRESSE, DER NAVY SCARE VOM WINTER 1904/05. GERMANY UK FORCES DIPLOM WAR 20 NAVY. PAGE 100 A2047
EDU/PROP ATTIT DOMIN PRESS

B37
BOURNE H.E.,THE WORLD WAR: A LIST OF THE MORE IMPORTANT BOOKS PUBLISHED BEFORE 1937 (PAMPHLET). EUR+WWI NAT/G DIPLOM ATTIT SOC. PAGE 17 A0351
BIBLIOG/A WAR FORCES PLAN

B37
DE KIEWIET C.W.,THE IMPERIAL FACTOR IN SOUTH AFRICA. AFR SOUTH/AFR UK WAR...POLICY SOC 19. PAGE 35 A0705
DIPLOM COLONIAL CULTURE

B37
KETCHAM E.H.,PRELIMINARY SELECT BIBLIOGRAPHY OF INTERNATIONAL LAW (PAMPHLET). WOR-45 LAW INT/ORG NAT/G PROB/SOLV CT/SYS NEUTRAL WAR 19/20. PAGE 78 A1602
BIBLIOG DIPLOM ADJUD INT/LAW

B37
KOHN H.,FORCE OR REASON; ISSUES OF THE TWENTIETH CENTURY. WOR+45 NAT/G DIPLOM WAR DRIVE ORD/FREE ALL/IDEOS FASCISM PLURISM...POLICY IDEA/COMP 20. PAGE 81 A1660
COERCE DOMIN RATIONAL COLONIAL

C37
ROWAN R.W.,"THE STORY OF THE SECRET SERVICE." WOR-45 REV...BIOG BIBLIOG. PAGE 124 A2552
WAR COERCE DIPLOM

B38
FLEMMING D.,THE UNITED STATES AND WORLD ORGANIZATION, 1920-1933. ASIA FUT WOR-45 NAT/G TOP/EX DIPLOM ECO/TAC EDU/PROP LEGIT COERCE WAR ...TIME/SEQ LEAGUE/NAT 20 CHINJAP. PAGE 47 A0951
USA-45 INT/ORG PEACE

B38
GRISWOLD A.W.,THE FAR EASTERN POLICY OF THE UNITED STATES. ASIA S/ASIA USA-45 INT/ORG INT/TRADE WAR NAT/LISM...BIBLIOG 19/20 LEAGUE/NAT ROOSEVLT/T ROOSEVLT/F WILSON/W TREATY. PAGE 57 A1166
DIPLOM POLICY CHIEF

B38
HAGUE PERMANENT CT INTL JUSTIC,WORLD COURT REPORTS: COLLECTION OF THE JUDGEMENTS ORDERS AND OPINIONS VOLUME 3 1932-35. WOR-45 LAW DELIB/GP CONFER WAR PEACE ATTIT...DECISION ANTHOL 20 WORLD/CT CASEBOOK. PAGE 59 A1214
INT/ORG CT/SYS DIPLOM ADJUD

B38
MCNAIR A.D.,THE LAW OF TREATIES: BRITISH PRACTICE AND OPINIONS. UK CREATE DIPLOM LEGIT WRITING ADJUD WAR...INT/LAW JURID TREATY. PAGE 98 A2018
AGREE LAW CT/SYS NAT/G

B38
SAINT-PIERRE C.I.,SCHEME FOR LASTING PEACE (TRANS. BY H. BELLOT). INDUS NAT/G CHIEF FORCES INT/TRADE CT/SYS WAR PWR SOVEREIGN WEALTH...POLICY 18. PAGE 126 A2587
INT/ORG PEACE AGREE INT/LAW

B39
BENES E.,INTERNATIONAL SECURITY. GERMANY UK NAT/G DELIB/GP PLAN BAL/PWR ATTIT ORD/FREE PWR LEAGUE/NAT 20 TREATY. PAGE 13 A0267
EUR+WWI INT/ORG WAR

B39
CARR E.H.,PROPAGANDA IN INTERNATIONAL POLITICS (PAMPHLET). EUR+WWI GERMANY MOD/EUR NAT/G AGREE WAR MORAL...POLICY 20 TREATY. PAGE 24 A0497
DIPLOM EDU/PROP CONTROL ATTIT

B39
DULLES J.,WAR, PEACE AND CHANGE. FRANCE ITALY UK USA-45 WOR-45 LAW INT/ORG NAT/G SECT VOL/ASSN FORCES TOP/EX DOMIN ARMS/CONT COERCE ATTIT PERSON RIGID/FLEX MORAL PWR...JURID STERTYP TOT/POP LEAGUE/NAT 20. PAGE 39 A0796
EDU/PROP TOTALISM WAR

B39
FULLER G.H.,A SELECTED LIST OF REFERENCES ON THE EXPANSION OF THE US NAVY, 1933-1939 (PAMPHLET). MOD/EUR USA-45 NAT/G PLAN DIPLOM DOMIN RISK ARMS/CONT EQUILIB PWR 20 NAVY. PAGE 50 A1019
BIBLIOG FORCES WEAPON WAR

B39
KOHN H.,REVOLUTIONS AND DICTATORSHIPS. COM EUR+WWI ISLAM MOD/EUR NAT/G CHIEF FORCES WAR CIVMIL/REL PWR MARXISM 18/20. PAGE 81 A1661
NAT/LISM TOTALISM REV FASCISM

B39
NICOLSON H.,CURZON: THE LAST PHASE, 1919-1925. UK NAT/G DELIB/GP TOP/EX ROUTINE WAR RIGID/FLEX ...METH/CNCPT 20 CURZON/GN. PAGE 109 A2231
POLICY DIPLOM BIOG

B39
ROBBINS L.,ECONOMIC CAUSES OF WAR. WOR-45 ECO/DEV ECO/UNDEV INT/ORG NAT/G TEC/DEV DIPLOM DOMIN COLONIAL ATTIT DRIVE PWR WEALTH...POLICY CONCPT OBS SAMP TREND CON/ANAL GEN/LAWS MARX/KARL 20. PAGE 122 A2493
COERCE ECO/TAC WAR

B39
SPEIER H.,WAR IN OUR TIME. WOR-45 AGRI FINAN FORCES TEC/DEV BAL/PWR EDU/PROP WEAPON PEACE PWR...ANTHOL 20. PAGE 136 A2779
FASCISM WAR DIPLOM NAT/G

B39
TAGGART F.J.,ROME AND CHINA. MEDIT-7 INT/ORG NAT/G FORCES LEGIS TOP/EX PLAN PWR SOVEREIGN...CHARTS TOT/POP ROM/EMP. PAGE 141 A2883
ASIA WAR

B39
WHEELER-BENNET J.W.,THE FORGOTTEN PEACE: BREST-LITOVSK. COM GERMANY USSR TOP/EX AGREE WAR PWR ...BIBLIOG 20 TREATY LENIN/VI UKRAINE. PAGE 163 A3326
PEACE DIPLOM CONFER

B39
WILSON G.G.,HANDBOOK OF INTERNATIONAL LAW. FUT UNIV USA-45 WOR-45 SOCIETY LEGIT ATTIT DISPL DRIVE ALL/VALS...INT/LAW TIME/SEQ TREND. PAGE 165 A3359
INT/ORG LAW CONCPT WAR

L39
NEARING S.,"A WARLESS WORLD." FUT WOR-45 SOCIETY INT/ORG NAT/G EX/STRUC PLAN DOMIN WAR ATTIT DRIVE PWR...POLICY PSY CONCPT OBS TREND HYPO/EXP MARX/KARL 20 MARX/KARL LENIN/VI. PAGE 108 A2210
COERCE PEACE

C39
SCOTT J.B.,"LAW, THESTATE, AND THE INTERNATIONAL COMMUNITY (2 VOLS.)" INTELL INT/ORG NAT/G SECT INT/TRADE WAR...INT/LAW GEN/LAWS BIBLIOG. PAGE 130 A2672
LAW PHIL/SCI DIPLOM CONCPT

B40
CONOVER H.F.,FOREIGN RELATIONS OF THE UNITED STATES: A LIST OF RECENT BOOKS (PAMPHLET). ASIA CANADA L/A+17C UK INT/ORG INT/TRADE TARIFFS NEUTRAL WAR PEACE...INT/LAW CON/ANAL 20 CHINJAP. PAGE 29 A0592
BIBLIOG/A USA-45 DIPLOM

B40
CONOVER H.F.,JAPAN-ECONOMIC DEVELOPMENT AND FOREIGN POLICY, A SELECTED LIST OF REFERENCES (PAMPHLET). CULTURE FINAN INDUS NAT/G FORCES INT/TRADE WAR ...SOC TREND 20 CHINJAP. PAGE 29 A0593
BIBLIOG ASIA ECO/DEV DIPLOM

B40
FULLER G.H.,A LIST OF BIBLIOGRAPHIES ON PROPAGANDA (PAMPHLET). MOD/EUR USA-45 CONSULT ACT/RES PRESS FEEDBACK TASK WAR ATTIT PWR...CON/ANAL METH/COMP 20. PAGE 50 A1020
BIBLIOG/A EDU/PROP DOMIN DIPLOM

B40
MIDDLEBUSH F.,ELEMENTS OF INTERNATIONAL RELATIONS. WOR-45 PROVS CONSULT EDU/PROP LEGIT WAR NAT/LISM ATTIT KNOWL MORAL ORD/FREE PWR...JURID LEAGUE/NAT TOT/POP VAL/FREE. PAGE 101 A2067
NAT/G INT/ORG PEACE DIPLOM

B40
MILLER E.,THE NEUROSES OF WAR. UNIV INTELL SOCIETY INT/ORG NAT/G EDU/PROP DISPL DRIVE PERCEPT PERSON RIGID/FLEX...SOC TIME/SEQ 20. PAGE 101 A2075
HEALTH PSY WAR

B40
NAFZIGER R.O.,INTERNATIONAL NEWS AND THE PRESS: COMMUNICATIONS, ORGANIZATION OF NEWS-GATHERING INTERNATIONAL AFFAIRS AND FOREIGN... COM/IND FORCES WAR ATTIT...POLICY 20. PAGE 107 A2191
BIBLIOG/A PRESS DIPLOM EDU/PROP

B40
RAPPARD W.E.,THE QUEST FOR PEACE. UNIV USA-45 WOR-45 SOCIETY INT/ORG NAT/G PLAN EXEC ROUTINE WAR ATTIT DRIVE ALL/VALS...POLICY CONCPT OBS TIME/SEQ LEAGUE/NAT TOT/POP 20. PAGE 119 A2450
EUR+WWI ACT/RES PEACE

B40
WANDERSCHECK H.,FRANKREICHS PROPAGANDA GEGEN DEUTSCHLAND. FRANCE GERMANY MOD/EUR UK NAT/G DIPLOM WAR 20 JEWS. PAGE 161 A3273
EDU/PROP ATTIT DOMIN PRESS

B40
WOLFERS A.,BRITAIN AND FRANCE BETWEEN TWO WORLD WARS. FRANCE UK INT/ORG NAT/G PLAN BARGAIN ECO/TAC AGREE ISOLAT ALL/IDEOS...DECISION GEOG 20 TREATY VERSAILLES INTERVENT. PAGE 166 A3380
DIPLOM WAR POLICY

B41
BIRDSALL P.,VERSAILLES TWENTY YEARS AFTER. MOD/EUR POL/PAR CHIEF CONSULT FORCES LEGIS REPAR PEACE ORD/FREE...BIBLIOG 20 PRESIDENT TREATY. PAGE 14 A0290
DIPLOM NAT/LISM WAR

B41
NIEMEYER G.,LAW WITHOUT FORCE: THE FUNCTION OF POLITICS IN INTERNATIONAL LAW. PLAN INSPECT DIPLOM REPAR LEGIT ADJUD WAR ORD/FREE...IDEA/COMP METH/COMP GEN/LAWS 20. PAGE 109 A2240
COERCE LAW PWR INT/LAW

B41
SCHWARZENBERGER G.,POWER POLITICS: AN INTRODUCTION TO THE STUDY OF INTERNATIONAL RELATIONS AND POST-WAR PLANNING. INT/ORG FORCES COERCE WAR FEDERAL PEACE MORAL...POLICY CONCPT CON/ANAL BIBLIOG 20. PAGE 130 A2660
DIPLOM UTOPIA PWR

B41
YOUNG G.,FEDERALISM AND FREEDOM. EUR+WWI MOD/EUR RUSSIA USA-45 WOR-45 SOCIETY STRUCT ECO/DEV INT/ORG EXEC FEDERAL ATTIT PERSON ALL/VALS...OLD/LIB CONCPT OBS TREND LEAGUE/NAT TOT/POP. PAGE 169 A3435
NAT/G WAR

L41
COMM. STUDY ORGAN. PEACE,"PRELIMINARY REPORT." WOR-45 SOCIETY DELIB/GP PLAN LEGIT WAR ORD/FREE ...CONCPT TOT/POP 20. PAGE 28 A0574
INT/ORG ACT/RES PEACE

B42
BORNSTEIN J.,ACTION AGAINST THE ENEMY'S MIND. EUR+WWI GERMANY USA-45 WOR-45 DIPLOM DOMIN PRESS LEAD GP/REL DISCRIM PERCEPT FASCISM MARXISM 20 JEWS NAZI ANTI/SEMIT. PAGE 17 A0343
EDU/PROP PSY WAR CONTROL

B42
CONOVER H.F.,NEW ZEALAND: A SELECTED LIST OF REFERENCES (PAMPHLET). NEW/ZEALND ECO/UNDEV AGRI INDUS LABOR NAT/G SCHOOL FORCES DIPLOM COLONIAL WAR ...HUM 20. PAGE 29 A0595
BIBLIOG/A S/ASIA CULTURE

B42
FEILCHENFELD E.H.,THE INTERNATIONAL ECONOMIC LAW OF BELLIGERENT OCCUPATION. EUR+WWI MOD/EUR USA-45 INT/ORG DIPLOM ADJUD ARMS/CONT LEAGUE/NAT 20. PAGE 44 A0907
ECO/TAC INT/LAW WAR

B42
FULLER G.H.,AUSTRALIA: A SELECT LIST OF REFERENCES. FORCES DIPLOM WAR 20 AUSTRAL. PAGE 50 A1022
BIBLIOG SOC

B42
JOSHI P.S.,THE TYRANNY OF COLOUR. INDIA SOUTH/AFR UK ECO/UNDEV NAT/G POL/PAR DIPLOM ECO/TAC WAR ...POLICY 19/20. PAGE 75 A1538
COLONIAL DISCRIM RACE/REL

B42
TOLMAN E.C.,DRIVES TOWARD WAR. UNIV PLAN DIPLOM ECO/TAC COERCE PERS/REL ADJUST HAPPINESS BIO/SOC HEREDITY HEALTH KNOWL. PAGE 144 A2947
PSY WAR UTOPIA DRIVE

B42
US LIBRARY OF CONGRESS,ECONOMICS OF WAR (APRIL 1941-MARCH 1942). WOR-45 FINAN INDUS LOC/G NAT/G PLAN BUDGET RATION COST DEMAND...POLICY 20. PAGE 154 A3146
BIBLIOG/A INT/TRADE ECO/TAC WAR

B42
US LIBRARY OF CONGRESS,POSTWAR PLANNING AND RECONSTRUCTION: APRIL-DECEMBER 1942 (SUPPLEMENT 1). WOR+45 SOCIETY INT/ORG DIPLOM...SOC PREDICT 20 UN. PAGE 154 A3147
BIBLIOG/A WAR PEACE PLAN

B43
BEMIS S.F.,THE LATIN AMERICAN POLICY OF THE UNITED STATES: AN HISTORICAL INTERPRETATION. INT/ORG AGREE COLONIAL WAR PEACE ATTIT ORD/FREE...POLICY INT/LAW CHARTS 18/20 MEXIC/AMER WILSON/W MONROE/DOC. PAGE 13 A0265
DIPLOM SOVEREIGN USA-45 L/A+17C

B43
BROWN A.D.,GREECE: SELECTED LIST OF REFERENCES. GREECE ECO/UNDEV AGRI FINAN INDUS LABOR SECT TEC/DEV INT/TRADE LEAD...SOC 20. PAGE 20 A0399
BIBLIOG/A WAR DIPLOM NAT/G

B43
CONOVER H.F.,THE BALKANS: A SELECTED LIST OF REFERENCES. ALBANIA BULGARIA ROMANIA YUGOSLAVIA INT/ORG PROB/SOLV DIPLOM LEGIT CONFER ADJUD WAR NAT/LISM PEACE PWR 20 LEAGUE/NAT. PAGE 29 A0596
BIBLIOG EUR+WWI

B43
CONOVER H.F.,SOVIET RUSSIA: SELECTED LIST OF REFERENCES. USSR CULTURE INDUS NAT/G TOP/EX TEC/DEV BUDGET WAR CIVMIL/REL EFFICIENCY MARXISM 20. PAGE 29 A0597
BIBLIOG ECO/DEV COM DIPLOM

B43
FULLER G.F.,FOREIGN RELIEF AND REHABILITATION (PAMPHLET). FUT GERMANY UK USA-45 INT/ORG PROB/SOLV DIPLOM FOR/AID ADMIN ADJUST PEACE ALL/VALS...SOC/WK 20 UN JEWS. PAGE 50 A1018
BIBLIOG/A PLAN GIVE WAR

B43
LIPPMANN W.,US FOREIGN POLICY: SHIELD OF THE REPUBLIC. USA-45 WOR-45 CULTURE INT/ORG POL/PAR CREATE BAL/PWR DOMIN EDU/PROP WAR ORD/FREE PWR ...PLURIST CONCPT TREND CON/ANAL 20. PAGE 89 A1827
NAT/G DIPLOM PEACE

B43
MAISEL A.Q.,AFRICA: FACTS AND FORECASTS. WOR+45 INT/ORG CONTROL RACE/REL SOVEREIGN...PREDICT CHARTS 20. PAGE 93 A1910
AFR WAR DIPLOM COLONIAL

B43
ST LEGER A.,SELECTION OF WORKS FOR AN UNDERSTANDING OF WORLD AFFAIRS SINCE 1914. WOR-45 INT/ORG CREATE BAL/PWR REV ADJUST 20. PAGE 137 A2796
BIBLIOG/A WAR SOCIETY DIPLOM

B43
SULZBACH W.,NATIONAL CONSCIOUSNESS. FUT WOR-45 INT/ORG PEACE MORAL FASCISM MARXISM...MAJORIT TREND WORSHIP 19/20 LEAGUE/NAT INTERVENT WWI. PAGE 140 A2862
NAT/LISM NAT/G DIPLOM WAR

B43
US LIBRARY OF CONGRESS,POLITICAL DEVELOPMENTS AND THE WAR: APRIL-DECEMBER 1942 (SUPPLEMENT 1). WOR-45 CONSTN NAT/G POL/PAR CREATE RECEIVE EDU/PROP ATTIT 20. PAGE 154 A3148
BIBLIOG/A WAR DIPLOM

B43
WALKER E.A.,BRITAIN AND SOUTH AFRICA. SOUTH/AFR POL/PAR GP/REL RACE/REL ATTIT ORD/FREE 17/20. PAGE 160 A3264
COLONIAL WAR DIPLOM SOVEREIGN

C43
BENTHAM J.,"PRINCIPLES OF INTERNATIONAL LAW" IN J. BOWRING, ED., THE WORKS OF JEREMY BENTHAM." UNIV NAT/G PLAN PROB/SOLV DIPLOM CONTROL SANCTION MORAL ORD/FREE PWR SOVEREIGN 19. PAGE 13 A0270
INT/LAW JURID WAR PEACE

B44
LIPPMANN W.,US WAR AIMS. USA-45 DIPLOM ATTIT MORAL ORD/FREE PWR...CONCPT TIME/SEQ GEN/LAWS TOT/POP 20. PAGE 89 A1828
FUT INT/ORG PEACE WAR

B44
MATTHEWS M.A.,INTERNATIONAL POLICE (PAMPHLET). WOR-45 DIPLOM ARMS/CONT WAR 20. PAGE 96 A1977
BIBLIOG INT/ORG FORCES PEACE

B44
PUTTKAMMER E.W.,WAR AND THE LAW. UNIV USA-45 CONSTN CULTURE SOCIETY NAT/G POL/PAR ROUTINE ALL/VALS ...JURID CONCPT OBS WORK VAL/FREE 20. PAGE 118 A2418
INT/ORG LAW WAR INT/LAW

B44
RUDIN H.R.,ARMISTICE 1918. FRANCE GERMANY MOD/EUR UK USA-45 NAT/G CHIEF DELIB/GP FORCES BAL/PWR REPAR ARMS/CONT 20 WILSON/W TREATY. PAGE 125 A2566
AGREE WAR PEACE DIPLOM

B44
WHITTON J.B.,THE SECOND CHANCE: AMERICA AND THE PEACE. EUR+WWI USA-45 SOCIETY STRUCT INT/ORG NAT/G LEGIT EXEC WAR ALL/VALS...SOC CONCPT TIME/SEQ TREND CONGRESS 20. PAGE 164 A3340
LEGIS PEACE

S44
WRIGHT Q.,"CONSTITUTIONAL PROCEDURES OF THE US FOR CARRYING OUT OBLIGATIONS FOR MILITARY SANCTIONS." EUR+WWI FUT USA-45 WOR-45 CONSTN INTELL NAT/G CONSULT EX/STRUC LEGIS ROUTINE DRIVE...POLICY JURID CONCPT OBS TREND TOT/POP 20. PAGE 167 A3406
TOP/EX FORCES INT/LAW WAR

C44
SUAREZ F.,"ON WAR" (1621) IN SELECTIONS FROM THREE WORKS, VOL. I." NAT/G SECT CHIEF DIPLOM LEGIT MORAL PWR...POLICY INT/LAW 17. PAGE 140 A2859
WAR REV ORD/FREE CATH

N45
INDIA QUARTERLY, A JOURNAL OF INTERNATIONAL AFFAIRS. INDIA LAW CONSTN ECO/UNDEV INT/ORG POL/PAR COLONIAL LEAD PARL/PROC WAR ATTIT...SOC 20 CMN/WLTH. PAGE 3 A0053
BIBLIOG/A S/ASIA DIPLOM NAT/G

B45
BEVERIDGE W.,THE PRICE OF PEACE. GERMANY UK WOR+45 WOR-45 NAT/G FORCES CREATE LEGIT REGION WAR ATTIT KNOWL ORD/FREE PWR...POLICY NEW/IDEA GEN/LAWS LEAGUE/NAT 20 TREATY. PAGE 14 A0284
INT/ORG TREND PEACE

B45
CONOVER H.F.,ITALY: ECONOMICS, POLITICS AND MILITARY AFFAIRS, 1940-1945. ITALY ELITES NAT/G POL/PAR EX/STRUC TOP/EX DIPLOM DOMIN CONTROL COERCE WAR CIVMIL/REL EFFICIENCY 20. PAGE 29 A0599
BIBLIOG TOTALISM FORCES

B45
CONOVER H.F.,THE NAZI STATE: WAR CRIMES AND WAR CRIMINALS. GERMANY CULTURE NAT/G SECT FORCES DIPLOM INT/TRADE EDU/PROP...INT/LAW BIOG HIST/WRIT TIME/SEQ 20. PAGE 30 A0600
BIBLIOG WAR CRIME

B45
ELTON G.E.,IMPERIAL COMMONWEALTH. INDIA UK DIPLOM DOMIN WAR NAT/LISM SOVEREIGN...TRADIT CHARTS T 15/20 CMN/WLTH AUSTRAL PRE/US/AM. PAGE 41 A0844
REGION CONCPT COLONIAL

B45
NELSON M.F.,KOREA AND THE OLD ORDERS IN EASTERN ASIA. ASIA FRANCE KOREA RUSSIA DELIB/GP INT/TRADE DOMIN CONTROL WAR ORD/FREE...POLICY BIBLIOG. PAGE 108 A2218
DIPLOM BAL/PWR ATTIT CONSERVE

B45
STRAUSZ-HUPE R.,THE BALANCE OF TOMORROW: POWER AND FOREIGN POLICY IN THE UNITED STATES. FUT USA+45 ECO/DEV EXTR/IND INT/ORG FORCES BAL/PWR REGION NUC/PWR...GEOG CHARTS 20 COLD/WAR EUROPE/W. PAGE 139 A2845
DIPLOM PWR POLICY WAR

B45
TINGSTERN H.,PEACE AND SECURITY AFTER WW II. WOR-45 DELIB/GP TOP/EX LEGIT CT/SYS COERCE PEACE ATTIT PERCEPT...CONCPT LEAGUE/NAT 20. PAGE 144 A2943
INT/ORG ORD/FREE WAR INT/LAW

B45
UNCIO CONFERENCE LIBRARY,SHORT TITLE CLASSIFIED CATALOG. WOR-45 DOMIN COLONIAL WAR...SOC/WK 20 LEAGUE/NAT UN. PAGE 147 A3006
BIBLIOG DIPLOM INT/ORG INT/LAW

B45
WEST R.,CONSCIENCE AND SOCIETY: A STUDY OF THE PSYCHOLOGICAL PREREQUISITES OF LAW AND ORDER. FUT UNIV LAW SOCIETY STRUCT DIPLOM WAR PERS/REL SUPEGO ...SOC 20. PAGE 163 A3321
COERCE INT/LAW ORD/FREE PERSON

B45
WOOLBERT R.G.,FOREIGN AFFAIRS BIBLIOGRAPHY, 1932-1942. INT/ORG SECT INT/TRADE COLONIAL RACE/REL NAT/LISM...GEOG INT/LAW GOV/COMP IDEA/COMP 20. PAGE 167 A3393
BIBLIOG/A DIPLOM WAR

C45
NELSON M.F.,"KOREA AND THE OLD ORDERS IN EASTERN ASIA." KOREA WOR-45 DELIB/GP INT/TRADE DOMIN CONTROL WAR ATTIT ORD/FREE CONSERVE...POLICY TREATY. PAGE 108 A2217
BIBLIOG DIPLOM BAL/PWR ASIA

B46
BLUM L.,FOR ALL MANKIND (TRANS. BY W. PICKLES). FRANCE GERMANY USSR LAW SOCIETY STRUCT POL/PAR WORKER DIPLOM DOMIN CHOOSE ORD/FREE FASCISM 20. PAGE 16 A0323
POPULISM SOCIALIST NAT/G WAR

B46
GRIFFIN G.G.,A GUIDE TO MANUSCRIPTS RELATING TO AMERICAN HISTORY IN BRITISH DEPOSITORIES. CANADA IRELAND MOD/EUR UK USA-45 LAW DIPLOM ADMIN COLONIAL WAR NAT/LISM SOVEREIGN...GEOG INT/LAW 15/19 CMN/WLTH. PAGE 56 A1159
BIBLIOG/A ALL/VALS NAT/G

B46
STURZO D.L.,NATIONALISM AND INTERNATIONALISM. WOR-45 INT/ORG LABOR NAT/G POL/PAR TOTALISM MORAL ORD/FREE FASCISM...MAJORIT 19/20 UN LEAGUE/NAT MUSSOLIN/B. PAGE 140 A2857
NAT/LISM DIPLOM WAR PEACE

S46
SILBERNER E.,"THE PROBLEM OF WAR IN NINETEENTH CENTURY ECONOMIC THOUGHT." EUR+WWI MOD/EUR UNIV LAW ECO/DEV ECO/UNDEV FINAN INDUS MARKET INT/ORG NAT/G CONSULT FORCES...CONCPT GEN/LAWS GEN/METH 19. PAGE 133 A2715
ATTIT ECO/TAC WAR

N46
HOBBS C.C.,SOUTHEAST ASIA, 1935-45: A SELECTED LIST OF REFERENCE BOOKS (PAMPHLET). S/ASIA AGRI INDUS NAT/G SECT DIPLOM WAR...ART/METH GEOG SOC LING 20. PAGE 65 A1346
BIBLIOG/A CULTURE HABITAT

B47
GORDON D.L.,THE HIDDEN WEAPON: THE STORY OF ECONOMIC WARFARE. EUR+WWI USA-45 LAW FINAN INDUS NAT/G CONSULT FORCES PLAN DOMIN PWR WEALTH ...INT/LAW CONCPT OBS TOT/POP NAZI 20. PAGE 54 A1112
INT/ORG ECO/TAC INT/TRADE WAR

B47
HYDE C.C.,INTERNATIONAL LAW, CHIEFLY AS INTERPRETED AND APPLIED BY THE UNITED STATES (3 VOLS., 2ND REV. ED.). USA-45 WOR+45 WOR-45 INT/ORG CT/SYS WAR NAT/LISM PEACE ORD/FREE...JURID 19/20 TREATY. PAGE 69 A1426
INT/LAW DIPLOM NAT/G POLICY

B47
SOCIAL SCIENCE RESEARCH COUN,PUBLIC REACTION TO THE ATOMIC BOMB AND WORLD AFFAIRS. SOCIETY CONFER ARMS/CONT...STAT QU SAMP CHARTS 20. PAGE 135 A2757
ATTIT NUC/PWR DIPLOM WAR

B47
US LIBRARY OF CONGRESS,POSTWAR PLANNING AND RECONSTRUCTION: JANUARY-MARCH 1943. WOR+45 SOCIETY INT/ORG DIPLOM...SOC PREDICT 20. PAGE 154 A3149
BIBLIOG/A WAR PEACE PLAN

B48
CLYDE P.H.,THE FAR EAST: A HISTORY OF THE IMPACT OF THE WEST ON EASTERN ASIA. CHINA/COM CULTURE INT/TRADE DOMIN COLONIAL WAR PWR...CHARTS BIBLIOG 19/20 CHINJAP. PAGE 27 A0554
DIPLOM ASIA

B48
GRIFFITH E.S.,RESEARCH IN POLITICAL SCIENCE: THE WORK OF PANELS OF RESEARCH COMMITTEE, APSA. WOR+45 WOR-45 COM/IND R+D FORCES ACT/RES WAR...GOV/COMP ANTHOL 20. PAGE 56 A1160
BIBLIOG PHIL/SCI DIPLOM JURID

B48
KULISCHER E.M.,EUROPE ON THE MOVE: WAR AND POPULATION CHANGES, 1917-1947. COM EUR+WWI FUT GERMANY USSR DIST/IND PLAN INT/TRADE CONTROL WAR DRIVE...CENSUS TREND COLD/WAR 20. PAGE 82 A1690
ECO/TAC GEOG

B48
LINEBARGER P.,PSYCHOLOGICAL WARFARE. NAT/G PLAN DIPLOM DOMIN ATTIT...POLICY CONCPT EXHIBIT 20 WWI. PAGE 89 A1824
EDU/PROP PSY WAR COM/IND

B48
LOGAN R.W.,THE AFRICAN MANDATES IN WORLD POLITICS. EUR+WWI GERMANY ISLAM INT/ORG BARGAIN...POLICY INT/LAW 20. PAGE 90 A1853
WAR COLONIAL AFR DIPLOM

B48
NAMIER L.B.,DIPLOMATIC PRELUDE 1938-1939. CZECHOSLVK EUR+WWI GERMANY POLAND UK FORCES DOMIN PWR 20 HITLER/A. PAGE 107 A2193
WAR TOTALISM DIPLOM

B48
US DEPARTMENT OF STATE,FOREIGN AFFAIRS HIGHLIGHTS (NEWSLETTER). COM USA+45 INT/ORG PLAN BAL/PWR WAR
DIPLOM NAT/G

PWR...BIBLIOG 20 COLD/WAR NATO UN DEPT/STATE. PAGE 151 A3083 — POLICY

B48
WHEELER-BENNETT J.W.,MUNICH: PROLOGUE TO TRAGEDY. EUR+WWI FRANCE GERMANY UK PLAN PROB/SOLV SOVEREIGN ...POLICY DECISION 20 HITLER/A. PAGE 163 A3327 — DIPLOM WAR PEACE

S48
MORGENTHAU H.J.,"THE TWILIGHT OF INTERNATIONAL MORALITY" (BMR)" WOR+45 WOR-45 BAL/PWR WAR NAT/LISM PEACE...POLICY INT/LAW IDEA/COMP 15/20 TREATY INTERVENT. PAGE 104 A2137 — MORAL DIPLOM NAT/G

B49
GROB F.,THE RELATIVITY OF WAR AND PEACE: A STUDY IN LAW, HISTORY, AND POLLTICS. WOR+45 WOR-45 LAW DIPLOM DEBATE...CONCPT LING IDEA/COMP BIBLIOG 18/20. PAGE 57 A1167 — WAR PEACE INT/LAW STYLE

B49
HINDEN R.,EMPIRE AND AFTER. UK POL/PAR BAL/PWR DIPLOM INT/TRADE WAR NAT/LISM PWR 17/20. PAGE 65 A1335 — NAT/G COLONIAL ATTIT POLICY

B49
JACKSON R.H.,INTERNATIONAL CONFERENCE ON MILITARY TRIALS. FRANCE GERMANY UK USA+45 USSR VOL/ASSN DELIB/GP REPAR ADJUD CT/SYS CRIME WAR 20 WAR/TRIAL. PAGE 72 A1479 — DIPLOM INT/ORG INT/LAW CIVMIL/REL

B49
KAFKA G.,FREIHEIT UND ANARCHIE. SECT COERCE DETER WAR ATTIT...IDEA/COMP 20 NATO. PAGE 75 A1545 — CONCPT ORD/FREE JURID INT/ORG

B49
MANSERGH N.,THE COMING OF THE FIRST WORLD WAR: A STUDY IN EUROPEAN BALANCE, 1878-1914. GERMANY MOD/EUR VOL/ASSN COLONIAL CONTROL PWR 19/20 TREATY. PAGE 94 A1928 — DIPLOM WAR BAL/PWR

B49
STREIT C.,UNION NOW. UNIV USA-45 WOR-45 INTELL STRUCT INT/ORG NAT/G PLAN DIPLOM EXEC ATTIT ...CONCPT TIME/SEQ. PAGE 139 A2849 — SOCIETY ACT/RES WAR

L49
HEINDEL R.H.,"THE NORTH ATLANTIC TREATY IN THE UNITED STATES SENATE." CONSTN POL/PAR CHIEF DEBATE LEAD ROUTINE WAR PEACE...CHARTS UN SENATE NATO. PAGE 64 A1309 — DECISION PARL/PROC LEGIS INT/ORG

L49
UNESCO,"SOME SUGGESTIONS ON TEACHING ABOUT THE UN AND ITS SPECIALIZED AGENCIES." UNIV WOR+45 SOCIETY STRATA SCHOOL WAR ALL/VALS KNOWL...SOC CONCPT UNESCO 20 UN. PAGE 147 A3011 — INT/ORG EDU/PROP

S49
DUNN F.,"THE PRESENT COURSE OF INTERNATIONAL RELATIONS RESEARCH." WOR+45 WOR-45 SOCIETY R+D INT/ORG WAR PERSON ORD/FREE...POLICY PSY SOC GEN/LAWS 20. PAGE 39 A0800 — CONCPT GEN/METH DIPLOM

C49
YANAGA C.,"JAPAN SINCE PERRY." S/ASIA CULTURE ECO/DEV FORCES WAR 19/20 CHINJAP. PAGE 168 A3430 — DIPLOM POL/PAR CIVMIL/REL NAT/LISM

B50
BARGHOORN F.C.,THE SOVIET IMAGE OF THE UNITED STATES: A STUDY IN DISTORTION. COM USSR DOMIN WAR NAT/LISM TOTALISM SOCISM...PSY 20. PAGE 11 A0220 — PROB/SOLV EDU/PROP DIPLOM ATTIT

B50
BROOKINGS INSTITUTION,MAJOR PROBLEMS OF UNITED STATES FOREIGN POLICY. AFR ASIA INDIA UK USA+45 USSR BAL/PWR FOR/AID WAR PEACE TOTALISM MARXISM SOCISM 20 CHINJAP COLD/WAR. PAGE 19 A0393 — DIPLOM POLICY ORD/FREE

B50
CHURCHILL W.,TRIUMPH AND TRAGEDY. UK WOR-45 INT/ORG NAT/G DELIB/GP FORCES TOP/EX DIPLOM COERCE CHOOSE ATTIT ORD/FREE PWR WEALTH...SELF/OBS CHARTS NAZI 20. PAGE 26 A0539 — BIOG PEACE WAR

B50
DE RUSETT A.,STRENGTHENING THE FRAMEWORK OF PEACE. WOR+45 VOL/ASSN FORCES CREATE INSPECT ADJUD CONTROL WAR EQUILIB FEDERAL ORD/FREE 20 UN EUROPE. PAGE 35 A0711 — INT/ORG DIPLOM PEACE METH/COMP

B50
DULLES J.F.,WAR OR PEACE. CHINA/COM USA+45 USSR INT/ORG SECT FORCES PLAN NUC/PWR WAR CENTRAL MARXISM...POLICY 20 UN ROOSEVLT/F STALIN/J. PAGE 39 A0797 — PEACE DIPLOM TREND ORD/FREE

B50
FEIS H.,THE ROAD TO PEARL HARBOR. USA-45 WOR-45 SOCIETY NAT/G FORCES WAR ORD/FREE 20 CHINJAP TREATY. PAGE 44 A0909 — DIPLOM POLICY ATTIT

B50
GATZKE H.W.,GERMANY'S DRIVE TO THE WEST. BELGIUM GERMANY MOD/EUR AGRI INDUS POL/PAR FORCES DOMIN AGREE CONTROL REGION COERCE 20 TREATY WWI. PAGE 51 A1053 — WAR POLICY NAT/G DIPLOM

B50
GLEASON J.H.,THE GENESIS OF RUSSOPHOBIA IN GREAT BRITAIN: A STUDY OF THE INTERACTION OF POLICY AND OPINION. ASIA RUSSIA UK NAT/G AGREE CONTROL REV WAR LOVE PWR TREATY 19. PAGE 53 A1080 — DIPLOM POLICY DOMIN COLONIAL

B50
LINCOLN G.,ECONOMICS OF NATIONAL SECURITY. USA+45 ELITES COM/IND DIST/IND INDUS NAT/G VOL/ASSN DELIB/GP EX/STRUC FOR/AID EDU/PROP COERCE NUC/PWR WAR ATTIT KNOWL ORD/FREE PWR COLD/WAR TOT/POP VAL/FREE 20. PAGE 89 A1818 — FORCES ECO/TAC

C50
NUMELIN R.,"THE BEGINNINGS OF DIPLOMACY." INT/TRADE WAR GP/REL PEACE STRANGE ATTIT...INT/LAW CONCPT BIBLIOG. PAGE 110 A2260 — DIPLOM KIN CULTURE LAW

N50
SCHAPIRO J.S.,THE WORLD IN CRISES: POLITICAL AND SOCIAL MOVEMENTS IN THE TWENTIETH CENTURY. USA+45 INT/ORG LABOR PLAN CAP/ISM DIPLOM COLONIAL PEACE TOTALISM ATTIT LAISSEZ...BIBLIOG 20 COLD/WAR. PAGE 128 A2618 — NAT/LISM TEC/DEV REV WAR

B51
BORKENAU F.,EUROPEAN COMMUNISM. COM EUR+WWI GERMANY SPAIN USSR INT/ORG PLAN REV WAR ATTIT 20 STALIN/J HITLER/A. PAGE 17 A0342 — MARXISM POLICY DIPLOM NAT/G

B51
CORBETT P.E.,LAW AND SOCIETY IN THE RELATIONS OF STATES. FUT WOR+45 WOR-45 CONTROL WAR PEACE PWR ...POLICY JURID 16/20 TREATY. PAGE 30 A0615 — INT/LAW DIPLOM INT/ORG

B51
HOLBORN H.,THE POLITICAL COLLAPSE OF EUROPE. EUR+WWI MOD/EUR USA-45 BAL/PWR PEACE POLICY. PAGE 66 A1364 — DIPLOM ORD/FREE WAR

B51
JENNINGS S.I.,THE COMMONWEALTH IN ASIA. CEYLON INDIA PAKISTAN S/ASIA UK CONSTN CULTURE SOCIETY STRATA STRUCT NAT/G POL/PAR EDU/PROP LEAD WAR 20 CMN/WLTH. PAGE 74 A1510 — NAT/LISM REGION COLONIAL DIPLOM

B51
RAPPAPORT A.,THE BRITISH PRESS AND WILSONIAN NEUTRALITY. UK WOR-45 SEA POL/PAR WAR CHOOSE PEACE ATTIT PERCEPT...GEOG 20 WILSON/W. PAGE 119 A2446 — PRESS DIPLOM NEUTRAL POLICY

B51
STANTON A.H.,PERSONALITY AND POLITICAL CRISIS. WOR+45 WOR-45 STRUCT DIPLOM INGP/REL TOTALISM MORAL ...ANTHOL 20 LASSWELL/H PARSONS/T RIESMAN/D. PAGE 137 A2806 — EDU/PROP WAR PERSON PSY

B51
SWISHER C.B.,THE THEORY AND PRACTICE OF AMERICAN NATIONAL GOVERNMENT. CULTURE LEGIS DIPLOM ADJUD ADMIN WAR PEACE ORD/FREE...MAJORIT 17/20. PAGE 140 A2872 — CONSTN NAT/G GOV/REL GEN/LAWS

B51
US HOUSE COMM APPROPRIATIONS,MUTUAL SECURITY PROGRAM APPROPRIATIONS FOR 1952: HEARINGS BEFORE A SUBCOMMITTEE OF THE COMMITTEE ON APPROPRIATIONS. KOREA L/A+17C ECO/DEV ECO/UNDEV INT/ORG INSPECT BAL/PWR DIPLOM DEBATE WAR...POLICY STAT ASIA/S 20 CONGRESS NATO COLD/WAR MID/EAST. PAGE 153 A3118 — LEGIS FORCES BUDGET FOR/AID

B51
VINER J.,INTERNATIONAL ECONOMICS. USA-45 WOR-45 ECO/DEV INDUS NAT/G ECO/TAC ALL/VALS...TIME/SEQ 20. PAGE 159 A3238 — FINAN INT/ORG WAR INT/TRADE

B51
WABEKE B.H.,A GUIDE TO DUTCH BIBLIOGRAPHIES. BELGIUM INDONESIA NETHERLAND DIPLOM INT/TRADE WAR NAT/LISM KNOWL...ART/METH HUM JURID CON/ANAL 14/20. PAGE 160 A3257 — BIBLIOG/A NAT/G CULTURE COLONIAL

B51
WELLES S.,SEVEN DECISIONS THAT SHAPED HISTORY. ASIA FRANCE FUT USA+45 WOR+45 WOR-45 CONSTN STRUCT INT/ORG NAT/G ACT/RES EDU/PROP DRIVE...POLICY CONCPT TIME/SEQ TREND TOT/POP UN 20 CHINJAP. PAGE 163 A3315 — USA-45 DIPLOM WAR

L51
KELSEN H.,"RECENT TRENDS IN THE LAW OF THE UNITED NATIONS." KOREA WOR+45 CONSTN LEGIS DIPLOM LEGIT DETER WAR RIGID/FLEX HEALTH ORD/FREE RESPECT ...JURID CON/ANAL UN VAL/FREE 20 NATO. PAGE 77 A1582 — INT/ORG LAW INT/LAW

B52
ALBERTINI L.,THE ORIGINS OF THE WAR OF 1914 (3 VOLS.). AUSTRIA FRANCE GERMANY MOD/EUR RUSSIA UK PROB/SOLV NEUTRAL PWR...BIBLIOG 19/20. PAGE 5 A0107 — WAR DIPLOM FORCES BAL/PWR

B52
BASSETT R.,DEMOCRACY AND FOREIGN POLICY: A CASE HISTORY, THE SINOJAPANESE DISPUTE, 1931-1933. ASIA UK 20 CHINJAP. PAGE 11 A0233 — DIPLOM WAR INT/ORG SANCTION

B52
FERRELL R.H.,PEACE IN THEIR TIME. FRANCE UK USA-45 INT/ORG NAT/G FORCES CREATE AGREE ARMS/CONT COERCE WAR TREATY 20 WILSON/W LEAGUE/NAT BRIAND/A. PAGE 45 — PEACE DIPLOM

A0920

B52
FIFIELD R.H.,WOODROW WILSON AND THE FAR EAST. ASIA CHIEF BAL/PWR CONFER COLONIAL ARMS/CONT WAR ...TIME/SEQ NAT/COMP BIBLIOG 19/20 WILSON/W LEAGUE/NAT PRESIDENT. PAGE 45 A0926
DIPLOM DELIB/GP INT/ORG

B52
LIPPMANN W.,ISOLATION AND ALLIANCES: AN AMERICAN SPEAKS TO THE BRITISH. USA+45 USA-45 INT/ORG AGREE COERCE DETER WAR PEACE MORAL 20 TREATY INTERVENT. PAGE 89 A1829
DIPLOM SOVEREIGN COLONIAL ATTIT

B52
MACARTHUR D.,REVITALIZING A NATION. ASIA COM FUT KOREA WOR+45 NAT/G FOR/AID TAX GIVE WAR ATTIT SOCISM 20 CHINJAP EUROPE. PAGE 92 A1885
LEAD FORCES TOP/EX POLICY

B52
MANTOUX E.,THE CARTHAGINIAN PEACE. GERMANY WOR-45 SOCIETY FINAN INT/ORG DELIB/GP FORCES PLAN LEGIT ...CONCPT TIME/SEQ 20 KEYNES/JM HITLER/A. PAGE 94 A1935
ECO/DEV INT/TRADE WAR

B52
SHULIM J.I.,THE OLD DOMINION AND NAPOLEON BONAPARTE. POL/PAR DOMIN PRESS REV WAR 18/19 VIRGINIA. PAGE 132 A2710
ATTIT PROVS EDU/PROP DIPLOM

B52
SKALWEIT S.,FRANKREICH UND FRIEDRICH DER GROSSE. FRANCE GERMANY PRUSSIA NAT/G DOMIN WAR 18 FREDERICK. PAGE 134 A2737
ATTIT EDU/PROP DIPLOM SOC

B52
SMITH C.M.,INTERNATIONAL COMMUNICATION AND POLITICAL WARFARE: AN ANNOTATED BIBLIOGRAPHY (A PAPER). WOR+45 INTELL R+D NAT/G FORCES ACT/RES DIPLOM COERCE ALL/IDEOS. PAGE 134 A2745
BIBLIOG/A EDU/PROP WAR COM/IND

B52
SPENCER F.A.,WAR AND POSTWAR GREECE: AN ANALYSIS BASED ON GREEK WRITINGS. GREECE SOCIETY NAT/G POL/PAR FORCES CREATE DIPLOM LEAD MARXISM...SOC 20. PAGE 136 A2784
BIBLIOG/A WAR REV

B52
U OF MICH SURVEY RESEARCH CTR,AMERICA'S ROLE IN WORLD AFFAIRS. ASIA COM EUR+WWI USA+45 USSR FOR/AID WAR AUTHORIT ORD/FREE...DEEP/QU 20. PAGE 146 A2986
DIPLOM NAT/G ROLE POLICY

L52
HILSMAN R. JR.,"INTELLIGENCE AND POLICY MAKING IN FOREIGN AFFAIRS." USA+45 CONSULT ACT/RES DIPLOM EDU/PROP ROUTINE PEACE PERCEPT PWR SKILL...POLICY MGT HYPO/EXP CONGRESS 20 CIA. PAGE 65 A1333
PROF/ORG SIMUL WAR

C52
FIFIELD R.H.,"WOODROW WILSON AND THE FAR EAST." ASIA CHIEF DELIB/GP BAL/PWR CONFER COLONIAL ARMS/CONT WAR...TIME/SEQ NAT/COMP 19/20 WILSON/W LEAGUE/NAT. PAGE 45 A0925
BIBLIOG DIPLOM INT/ORG

B53
BRETTON H.L.,STRESEMANN AND THE REVISION OF VERSAILLES: A FIGHT FOR REASON. EUR+WWI GERMANY FORCES BUDGET ARMS/CONT WAR SUPEGO...BIBLIOG 20 TREATY VERSAILLES STRESEMN/G. PAGE 18 A0373
POLICY DIPLOM BIOG

B53
COUSINS N.,WHO SPEAKS FOR MAN. GERMANY KOREA WOR+45 SOCIETY INT/ORG NAT/G CREATE EDU/PROP HEALTH KNOWL LOVE MORAL...OBS SELF/OBS BIOG HYPO/EXP TOT/POP 20 CHINJAP. PAGE 32 A0642
ATTIT WAR PEACE

B53
CRAIG G.A.,THE DIPLOMATS 1919-1939. WAR PEACE ATTIT ...POLICY BIOG 20. PAGE 32 A0651
DIPLOM ELITES FASCISM

B53
FEIS H.,THE CHINA TANGLE. ASIA COM USA+45 USA-45 FORCES ECO/TAC REV ATTIT 20 INTERVENT. PAGE 45 A0910
POLICY DIPLOM WAR FOR/AID

B53
KALIJARVI T.V.,MODERN WORLD POLITICS (3RD ED.). AFR L/A+17C MOD/EUR S/ASIA UK USSR WOR+45 INT/ORG BAL/PWR WAR PWR 20. PAGE 76 A1552
DIPLOM INT/LAW PEACE

B53
LANGER W.L.,THE UNDECLARED WAR, 1940-1941. EUR+WWI GERMANY USA-45 USSR AIR FORCES TEC/DEV CONFER CONTROL COERCE PERCEPT ORD/FREE PWR 20 CHINJAP EUROPE. PAGE 84 A1727
WAR POLICY DIPLOM

B53
MATLOFF M.,STRATEGIC PLANNING FOR COALITION WARFARE. UK USA-45 CHIEF DIPLOM EXEC GOV/REL ...METH/COMP 20. PAGE 96 A1967
WAR PLAN DECISION FORCES

B53
MCNEILL W.H.,AMERICA, BRITAIN, AND RUSSIA: THEIR COOPERATION AND CONFLICT. UK USA-45 USSR ECO/DEV ECO/UNDEV FORCES PLAN ADMIN AGREE PERS/REL ...DECISION 20 TREATY. PAGE 98 A2021
WAR DIPLOM DOMIN

B53
OPPENHEIM L.,INTERNATIONAL LAW: A TREATISE (7TH ED., 2 VOLS.). LAW CONSTN PROB/SOLV INT/TRADE ADJUD AGREE NEUTRAL WAR ORD/FREE SOVEREIGN...BIBLIOG 20 LEAGUE/NAT UN ILO. PAGE 112 A2294
INT/LAW INT/ORG DIPLOM

B53
ROSCIO J.G.,OBRAS. L/A+17C SPAIN DIPLOM REV WAR NAT/LISM TOTALISM PWR SOVEREIGN 19. PAGE 123 A2527
ORD/FREE COLONIAL NAT/G PHIL/SCI

B53
SHIRATO I.,JAPANESE SOURCES ON THE HISTORY OF THE CHINESE COMMUNIST MOVEMENT (PAMPHLET). CHINA/COM USSR CONSTRUC NAT/G POL/PAR FORCES DIPLOM DOMIN EDU/PROP CONTROL WAR TOTALISM SOCISM 20. PAGE 132 A2702
BIBLIOG/A MARXISM ECO/UNDEV

B53
SQUIRES J.D.,BRITISH PROPAGANDA AT HOME AND IN THE UNITED STATES FROM 1914 TO 1917. UK NAT/G PROB/SOLV DOMIN PRESS EFFICIENCY...PSY PREDICT 20 WWI INTERVENT PSY/WAR. PAGE 136 A2794
EDU/PROP CONTROL WAR DIPLOM

B54
ARON R.,CENTURY OF TOTAL WAR. FUT WOR+45 WOR-45 SOCIETY INT/ORG NAT/G FORCES TOP/EX CREATE BAL/PWR DOMIN EDU/PROP COERCE DETER PEACE TOTALISM PWR ...TIME/SEQ TREND COLD/WAR TOT/POP VAL/FREE LEAGUE/NAT 20. PAGE 9 A0179
ATTIT WAR

B54
BUTOW R.J.C.,JAPAN'S DECISION TO SURRENDER. USA-45 USSR CHIEF FORCES DOMIN NUC/PWR...BIBLIOG 20 TREATY CHINJAP. PAGE 22 A0453
ELITES DIPLOM WAR PEACE

B54
BUTZ O.,GERMANY: DILEMMA FOR AMERICAN POLICY. GERMANY USA+45 USA-45 USSR WOR+45 INT/ORG FORCES NUC/PWR EFFICIENCY PEACE PWR...GOV/COMP 20 COLD/WAR. PAGE 23 A0459
DIPLOM NAT/G WAR POLICY

B54
EPSTEIN L.D.,BRITAIN - UNEASY ALLY. KOREA UK USA+45 NAT/G POL/PAR ECO/TAC FOR/AID INT/TRADE WAR LABOR/PAR CONSRV/PAR. PAGE 42 A0857
DIPLOM ATTIT POLICY NAT/COMP

B54
MITCHELL P.,AFRICAN AFTERTHOUGHTS. UGANDA CONSTN NAT/G ADJUD COERCE WAR 20 WWI MAU/MAU. PAGE 102 A2090
BIOG CHIEF COLONIAL DOMIN

B54
NATION ASSOCIATES,SECURITY AND THE MIDDLE EAST - THE PROBLEM AND ITS SOLUTION. ISRAEL JORDAN LEBANON SYRIA UAR FORCES FOR/AID GP/REL NAT/LISM PEACE TOTALISM...POLICY 20. PAGE 107 A2198
DIPLOM ECO/UNDEV WAR PLAN

B54
REYNOLDS P.A.,BRITISH FOREIGN POLICY IN THE INTER-WAR YEARS. CZECHOSLVK GERMANY POLAND UK USA-45 POL/PAR FORCES ECO/TAC ARMS/CONT WAR ATTIT 20. PAGE 120 A2470
DIPLOM POLICY NAT/G

B54
SALVEMINI G.,PRELUDE TO WORLD WAR II. ITALY MOD/EUR INT/ORG BAL/PWR EDU/PROP CONTROL TOTALISM...TREND NAT/COMP BIBLIOG 19 HITLER/A LEAGUE/NAT MUSSOLIN/B. PAGE 127 A2597
WAR FASCISM LEAD PWR

B54
SHARMA J.S.,MAHATMA GANDHI: A DESCRIPTIVE BIBLIOGRAPHY. INDIA S/ASIA PROB/SOLV DIPLOM COLONIAL WAR NAT/LISM PEACE ATTIT PERSON SOVEREIGN ...CONCPT 20 GANDHI/M. PAGE 132 A2695
BIBLIOG/A BIOG CHIEF LEAD

B54
STONE J.,LEGAL CONTROLS OF INTERNATIONAL CONFLICT: A TREATISE ON THE DYNAMICS OF DISPUTES AND WAR LAW. WOR+45 WOR-45 NAT/G DIPLOM CT/SYS SOVEREIGN...JURID CONCPT METH/CNCPT GEN/LAWS TOT/POP VAL/FREE COLD/WAR LEAGUE/NAT 20. PAGE 138 A2834
INT/ORG LAW WAR INT/LAW

B54
STRAUSZ-HUPE R.,INTERNATIONAL RELATIONS IN THE AGE OF THE CONFLICT BETWEEN DEMOCRACY AND DICTATORSHIP (2ND ED.). INT/ORG BAL/PWR EDU/PROP ADMIN WAR PEACE PWR...CONCPT CHARTS BIBLIOG 20 COLD/WAR UN LEAGUE/NAT. PAGE 139 A2846
DIPLOM POPULISM MARXISM

B54
TAYLOR A.J.P.,THE STRUGGLE FOR MASTERY IN EUROPE 1848-1918. MOD/EUR VOL/ASSN FORCES BAL/PWR DOMIN CONTROL PEACE MORAL 19/20 TREATY EUROPE WWI. PAGE 142 A2897
DIPLOM WAR PWR

B54
US SENATE COMM ON FOREIGN REL,REVIEW OF THE UNITED NATIONS CHARTER: A COLLECTION OF DOCUMENTS. LEGIS DIPLOM ADMIN ARMS/CONT WAR REPRESENT SOVEREIGN ...INT/LAW 20 UN. PAGE 156 A3180
BIBLIOG CONSTN INT/ORG DEBATE

B54
WRIGHT Q.,PROBLEMS OF STABILITY AND PROGRESS IN INTERNATIONAL RELATIONSHIPS. FUT WOR+45 WOR-45 SOCIETY LEGIS CREATE TEC/DEV ECO/TAC EDU/PROP ADJUD WAR PEACE ORD/FREE PWR...KNO/TEST TREND GEN/LAWS 20. PAGE 167 A3409
INT/ORG CONCPT DIPLOM

B55
ALFIERI D.,DICTATORS FACE TO FACE. NAT/G TOP/EX DIPLOM EXEC COERCE ORD/FREE FASCISM...POLICY OBS 20
WAR CHIEF

HITLER/A MUSSOLIN/B. PAGE 6 A0116 TOTALISM PERS/REL

B55
CRAIG G.A.,THE POLITICS OF THE PRUSSIAN ARMY 1640-1945. CHRIST-17C EUR+WWI MOD/EUR PRUSSIA STRUCT DIPLOM ADMIN REV WAR...SOC BIBLIOG 17/20. PAGE 32 A0652
FORCES NAT/G ROLE CHIEF

B55
HOGAN W.N.,INTERNATIONAL CONFLICT AND COLLECTIVE SECURITY: THE PRINCIPLE OF CONCERN IN INTERNATIONAL ORGANIZATION. CONSTN EX/STRUC BAL/PWR DIPLOM ADJUD CONTROL CENTRAL CONSEN PEACE...INT/LAW CONCPT METH/COMP 20 UN LEAGUE/NAT. PAGE 66 A1361
INT/ORG WAR ORD/FREE FORCES

B55
INSTITUTE POLITISCHE WISSEN,POLITISCHE LITERATUR (3 VOLS.). INT/ORG LEAD WAR PEACE...CONCPT TREND NAT/COMP 20. PAGE 70 A1446
BIBLIOG/A NAT/G DIPLOM POLICY

B55
JOY C.T.,HOW COMMUNISTS NEGOTIATE. COM USA+45 CONSTN CULTURE ECO/UNDEV NAT/G CONSULT DELIB/GP FORCES PLAN ECO/TAC DOMIN EDU/PROP LEGIT EXEC ROUTINE COERCE WAR CHOOSE PEACE ATTIT RIGID/FLEX ORD/FREE PWR...POLICY 20. PAGE 75 A1539
ASIA INT/ORG DIPLOM

B55
PERKINS B.,THE FIRST RAPPROCHEMENTS: ENGLAND AND THE UNITED STATES, 1795-1805. UK USA-45 ATTIT ...HIST/WRIT BIBLIOG 18/19 MADISON/J WAR/1812. PAGE 115 A2357
DIPLOM COLONIAL WAR

B55
PYRAH G.B.,IMPERIAL POLICY AND SOUTH AFRICA 1902-1910. SOUTH/AFR UK NAT/G WAR DISCRIM...CONCPT CHARTS BIBLIOG/A 19/20 CMN/WLTH. PAGE 118 A2421
DIPLOM COLONIAL POLICY RACE/REL

B55
SEMJONOW J.M.,DIE FASCHISTISCHE GEOPOLITIK IM DIENSTE DES AMERIKANISCHEN IMPERIALISMUS. USA+45 USA-45 CAP/ISM PEACE ORD/FREE MARXISM SOCISM ...POLICY GEOG 20. PAGE 131 A2684
DIPLOM COERCE FASCISM WAR

B55
SVARLIEN O.,AN INTRODUCTION TO THE LAW OF NATIONS. SEA AIR INT/ORG NAT/G CHIEF ADMIN AGREE WAR PRIVIL ORD/FREE SOVEREIGN...BIBLIOG 16/20. PAGE 140 A2868
INT/LAW DIPLOM

B55
TAN C.C.,THE BOXER CATASTROPHE. ASIA UK USSR ELITES POL/PAR VOL/ASSN FORCES PROB/SOLV DIPLOM ADMIN COLONIAL NAT/LISM PEACE TREATY 19/20 BOXER/REBL. PAGE 141 A2885
REV NAT/G WAR

B55
VIGON J.,TEORIA DEL MILITARISMO. NAT/G DIPLOM COLONIAL COERCE GUERRILLA CIVMIL/REL NAT/LISM MORAL ALL/IDEOS PACIFISM 18/20. PAGE 159 A3234
FORCES PHIL/SCI WAR POLICY

B55
WOODWARD E.L.,DOCUMENTS ON BRITISH FOREIGN POLICY 1919-39 (9 VOLS.). EUR+WWI UK WOR-45 INT/ORG WAR 20. PAGE 167 A3392
BIBLIOG DIPLOM

B56
COMMONWEALTH OF WORLD CITIZENS,THE BIRTH OF A WORLD PEOPLE. WOR+45 CONSTN PROB/SOLV CONTROL TASK WAR GP/REL UTOPIA PWR...POLICY NEW/IDEA 20. PAGE 29 A0582
DIPLOM VOL/ASSN PEACE INT/ORG

B56
FORSTMANN A.,DIE GRUNDLAGEN DER AUSSENWIRTSCHAFTSTHEORIE. ECO/TAC TARIFFS PRICE WAR ...NAT/COMP 20. PAGE 47 A0967
INT/TRADE CONCPT DIPLOM ECO/DEV

B56
GILBERT R.,COMPETITIVE COEXISTENCE: THE NEW SOVIET CHALLENGE. WORKER DIPLOM WAR ORD/FREE 20 COLD/WAR. PAGE 52 A1071
NUC/PWR DOMIN MARXISM PEACE

B56
KOENIG L.W.,THE TRUMAN ADMINISTRATION: ITS PRINCIPLES AND PRACTICE. USA+45 POL/PAR CHIEF LEGIS DIPLOM DEATH NUC/PWR WAR CIVMIL/REL PEACE ...DECISION 20 TRUMAN/HS PRESIDENT TREATY. PAGE 81 A1658
ADMIN POLICY EX/STRUC GOV/REL

B56
KRAUS O.,THEORIE DER ZWISCHENSTAATLICHEN WIRTSCHAFTSBEZIEHUNGEN. TARIFFS WAR COST 20. PAGE 82 A1677
INT/TRADE DIPLOM BAL/PAY ECO/TAC

B56
SNELL J.L.,THE MEANING OF YALTA: BIG THREE DIPLOMACY AND THE NEW BALANCE OF POWER. EUR+WWI GERMANY USA-45 USSR FORCES PLAN BAL/PWR DIPLOM WAR CHOOSE PEACE...CHARTS BIBLIOG 20 UN CHINJAP ROOSEVLT/F. PAGE 134 A2749
CONFER CHIEF POLICY PROB/SOLV

B56
TOYNBEE A.,THE WAR AND THE NEUTRALS. L/A+17C PORTUGAL SPAIN SWEDEN SWITZERLND TURKEY WOR+45 WOR-45 ECO/TAC CONFER CONTROL REGION 20. PAGE 145 A2957
NEUTRAL WAR INT/TRADE DIPLOM

B56
VON HARPE W.,DIE SOWJETUNION FINNLAND UND SKANDANAVIEN, 1945-1955. EUR+WWI FINLAND GERMANY USSR WAR INGP/REL ORD/FREE SOVEREIGN MARXISM ...POLICY GOV/COMP BIBLIOG 20 STALIN/J. PAGE 160 A3252
DIPLOM COM NEUTRAL BAL/PWR

B56
WILSON P.,GOVERNMENT AND POLITICS OF INDIA AND PAKISTAN: 1885-1955; A BIBLIOGRAPHY OF WORKS IN WESTERN LANGUAGES. INDIA PAKISTAN CONSTN LOC/G POL/PAR FORCES DIPLOM ADMIN WAR CHOOSE...BIOG CON/ANAL 19/20. PAGE 165 A3361
BIBLIOG COLONIAL NAT/G S/ASIA

B56
WOLFF R.L.,THE BALKANS IN OUR TIME. ALBANIA FUT MOD/EUR USSR YUGOSLAVIA CULTURE INT/ORG SECT DIPLOM EDU/PROP COERCE WAR ORD/FREE...CHARTS 4/20 BALKANS COMINFORM. PAGE 166 A3388
GEOG COM

B56
WU E.,LEADERS OF TWENTIETH-CENTURY CHINA; AN ANNOTATED BIBLIOGRAPHY OF SELECTED CHINESE BIOGRAPHICAL WORKS IN HOOVER LIBRARY. ASIA INDUS POL/PAR DIPLOM ADMIN REV WAR...HUM MGT 20. PAGE 168 A3422
BIBLIOG/A BIOG INTELL CHIEF

S56
POTTER P.B.,"NEUTRALITY, 1955." WOR+45 WOR-45 INT/ORG NAT/G WAR ATTIT...POLICY IDEA/COMP 17/20 LEAGUE/NAT UN COLD/WAR. PAGE 117 A2399
NEUTRAL INT/LAW DIPLOM CONCPT

C56
DUPUY R.E.,"MILITARY HERITAGE OF AMERICA." USA+45 USA-45 TEC/DEV DIPLOM ROUTINE...POLICY TREND CHARTS IDEA/COMP BIBLIOG COLD/WAR. PAGE 39 A0804
FORCES WAR CONCPT

C56
VAGTS A.,"DEFENSE AND DIPLOMACY: THE SOLDIER AND THE CONDUCT OF FOREIGN RELATIONS." OP/RES CONFER DETER WAR PEACE RESPECT...POLICY DECISION CONCPT BIBLIOG 17/20. PAGE 158 A3209
DIPLOM FORCES HIST/WRIT

B57
ADLER S.,THE ISOLATIONIST IMPULSE: ITS TWENTIETH-CENTURY REACTION. USA+45 USA-45 POL/PAR WAR ISOLAT NAT/LISM 20. PAGE 5 A0093
DIPLOM POLICY ATTIT

B57
ALIGHIERI D.,ON WORLD GOVERNMENT. ROMAN/EMP LAW SOCIETY INT/ORG NAT/G POL/PAR ADJUD WAR GP/REL PEACE WORSHIP 15 WORLDUNITY DANTE. PAGE 6 A0121
POLICY CONCPT DIPLOM SECT

B57
BRODY H.,UN DIARY: THE SEARCH FOR PEACE. HUNGARY WOR+45 DELIB/GP ROUTINE REV WAR ORD/FREE...AUD/VIS 20 UN SUEZ. PAGE 19 A0382
INT/ORG PEACE DIPLOM POLICY

B57
BROMBERGER M.,LES SECRETS DE L'EXPEDITION D'EGYPTE. FRANCE ISLAM UAR UK USA+45 USSR WOR+45 INT/ORG NAT/G FORCES BAL/PWR ECO/TAC DOMIN WAR NAT/LISM ATTIT PWR SOVEREIGN...MAJORIT TIME/SEQ CHARTS SUEZ COLD/WAR 20. PAGE 19 A0387
COERCE DIPLOM

B57
DUDDEN A.P.,WOODROW WILSON AND THE WORLD OF TODAY. USA-45 NAT/G PROVS CONTROL PARTIC WAR ISOLAT PWR SKILL...PERS/COMP ANTHOL 19/20 WILSON/W UN LEAGUE/NAT WWI. PAGE 39 A0794
CHIEF DIPLOM POL/PAR LEAD

B57
FRASER L.,PROPAGANDA. GERMANY USSR WOR+45 WOR-45 NAT/G POL/PAR CONTROL FEEDBACK LOBBY CROWD WAR CONSEN NAT/LISM 20. PAGE 48 A0988
EDU/PROP FASCISM MARXISM DIPLOM

B57
FREUND G.,UNHOLY ALLIANCE. EUR+WWI GERMANY USSR FORCES ECO/TAC CONTROL WAR PWR...TREND TREATY. PAGE 49 A0999
DIPLOM PLAN POLICY

B57
INSTITUT DE DROIT INTL,TABLEAU GENERAL DES RESOLUTIONS (1873-1956). LAW NEUTRAL CRIME WAR MARRIAGE PEACE...JURID 19/20. PAGE 70 A1442
INT/LAW DIPLOM ORD/FREE ADJUD

B57
JASZI O.,AGAINST THE TYRANT. WOR+45 WOR-45 CONSTN DIPLOM CONTROL PARTIC REV WAR...CONCPT. PAGE 73 A1498
TOTALISM ORD/FREE CHIEF MURDER

B57
NEHRU J.,MILITARY ALLIANCE (PAMPHLET). INDIA WOR+45 NAT/G PLAN DETER NUC/PWR WAR...POLICY ANTHOL NEHRU/J SEATO UN. PAGE 108 A2212
INT/ORG DIPLOM FORCES PEACE

B57
PALMER N.D.,INTERNATIONAL RELATIONS. WOR+45 INT/ORG NAT/G ECO/TAC EDU/PROP COLONIAL WAR PWR SOVEREIGN ...POLICY T 20 TREATY. PAGE 113 A2321
DIPLOM BAL/PWR NAT/COMP

B57
PETERSON H.C.,OPPONENTS OF WAR 1917-1918. USA-45 POL/PAR DOMIN ORD/FREE PWR PACIFISM SOCISM 20 IWW CONSCN/OBJ. PAGE 115 A2368
WAR PEACE ATTIT EDU/PROP

B57
SINEY M.C.,THE ALLIED BLOCKADE OF GERMANY: 1914-1916. EUR+WWI GERMANY MOD/EUR USA-45 DIPLOM
DETER INT/TRADE

CONTROL NEUTRAL PWR 20. PAGE 133 A2721 INT/LAW WAR

B57
STRACHEY A.,THE UNCONSCIOUS MOTIVES OF WAR; A PSYCHO-ANALYTICAL CONTRIBUTION. UNIV SOCIETY DIPLOM DREAM GP/REL ADJUST ATTIT DISPL PERCEPT PERSON KNOWL MORAL. PAGE 139 A2840 WAR DRIVE LOVE PSY

B57
TOMASIC D.A.,NATIONAL COMMUNISM AND SOVIET STRATEGY. UK USSR YUGOSLAVIA NAT/G POL/PAR CHIEF CREATE DOMIN REV WAR PWR...BIOG TREND 20 TITO/MARSH STALIN/J. PAGE 144 A2948 COM NAT/LISM MARXISM DIPLOM

B57
WARBURG J.P.,AGENDA FOR ACTION. ISLAM ISRAEL USA+45 FOR/AID INT/TRADE WAR NAT/LISM 20 MID/EAST EUROPE ARABS. PAGE 161 A3275 DIPLOM POLICY INT/ORG BAL/PWR

S57
DEUTSCH K.W.,"MASS COMMUNICATIONS AND THE LOSS OF FREEDOM IN NATIONAL DECISION MAKING." FUT WOR+45 SOCIETY COM/IND INT/ORG NAT/G ACT/RES CREATE TEC/DEV EDU/PROP MAJORITY PERCEPT...METH/CNCPT 20. PAGE 36 A0737 COERCE DECISION WAR

S57
SCHELLING T.C.,"BARGAINING COMMUNICATION, AND LIMITED WAR." UNIV WOR+45 FACE/GP INT/ORG NAT/G FORCES ACT/RES WAR PERCEPT ALL/VALS...PSY OBS PROJ/TEST CHARTS HYPO/EXP GEN/LAWS TOT/POP 20. PAGE 128 A2622 ROUTINE DECISION

B58
ANGELL N.,DEFENCE AND THE ENGLISH-SPEAKING ROLE. CHINA/COM UK USSR INT/ORG FORCES EDU/PROP NEUTRAL NUC/PWR NAT/LISM PEACE TOTALISM 20 COLD/WAR COEXIST. PAGE 8 A0161 DIPLOM WAR MARXISM ORD/FREE

B58
APPADORAI A.,THE USE OF FORCE IN INTERNATIONAL RELATIONS. WOR+45 CULTURE ECO/UNDEV CAP/ISM ARMS/CONT REV WAR ATTIT PERSON SOVEREIGN MARXISM ...INT/LAW PACIFIST 20 UN INTERVENT THIRD/WRLD COLD/WAR. PAGE 8 A0169 PEACE FEDERAL INT/ORG

B58
ARON R.,ON WAR: ATOMIC WEAPONS AND GLOBAL DIPLOMACY (TRANS. BY TERENCE KILMARTIN). WOR+45 SOCIETY FORCES BAL/PWR WAR WEAPON PERSON...SOC 20. PAGE 9 A0182 ARMS/CONT NUC/PWR COERCE DIPLOM

B58
BOWETT D.W.,SELF-DEFENSE IN INTERNATIONAL LAW. EUR+WWI MOD/EUR WOR+45 WOR-45 SOCIETY INT/ORG CONSULT DIPLOM LEGIT COERCE ATTIT ORD/FREE...JURID 20 UN. PAGE 17 A0353 ADJUD CONCPT WAR INT/LAW

B58
CHANG H.,WITHIN THE FOUR SEAS. ASIA WAR MORAL MARXISM...IDEA/COMP NAT/COMP 20 CONFUCIUS. PAGE 26 A0521 PEACE DIPLOM KNOWL CULTURE

B58
CRAIG G.A.,FROM BISMARCK TO ADENAUER: ASPECTS OF GERMAN STATECRAFT. GERMANY INTELL FORCES ECO/TAC CONFER COERCE WAR GP/REL ORD/FREE PWR CONSERVE 19/20 BISMARCK/O ADENAUER/K. PAGE 32 A0653 DIPLOM LEAD NAT/G

B58
GARTHOFF R.L.,SOVIET STRATEGY IN THE NUCLEAR AGE. FUT USSR R+D INT/ORG NAT/G ACT/RES TEC/DEV DOMIN DETER WAR ATTIT PWR...RELATIV METH/CNCPT SELF/OBS TREND CON/ANAL STERTYP GEN/LAWS 20. PAGE 51 A1052 COM FORCES BAL/PWR NUC/PWR

B58
GAVIN J.M.,WAR AND PEACE IN THE SPACE AGE. SPACE USA+45 USSR FORCES PLAN TEC/DEV BAL/PWR DIPLOM ARMS/CONT WEAPON CIVMIL/REL...CHARTS GP/COMP 20 NATO COLD/WAR. PAGE 52 A1055 WAR DETER NUC/PWR PEACE

B58
ISLAM R.,INTERNATIONAL ECONOMIC COOPERATION AND THE UNITED NATIONS. FINAN PLAN EXEC TASK WAR PEACE ...SOC METH/CNCPT 20 UN LEAGUE/NAT. PAGE 72 A1470 INT/ORG DIPLOM ADMIN

B58
KENNAN G.F.,THE DECISION TO INTERVENE: SOVIET-AMERICAN RELATIONS, 1917-1920 (VOL. II). CZECHOSLVK EUR+WWI USA-45 USSR ELITES NAT/G FORCES PROB/SOLV REV WAR TOTALISM PWR...CHARTS BIBLIOG 20 TREATY PRESIDENT CHINJAP. PAGE 78 A1588 DIPLOM POLICY ATTIT

B58
MANSERGH N.,SURVEY OF BRITISH COMMONWEALTH AFFAIRS: PROBLEMS OF WARTIME CO-OPERATION AND POST-WAR CHANGE 1939-1952. INDIA IRELAND S/ASIA CONSTN INT/ORG BAL/PWR COLONIAL NEUTRAL WAR ADJUST PEACE ROLE ORD/FREE...CHARTS 20 CMN/WLTH NATO UN. PAGE 94 A1931 VOL/ASSN CONSEN PROB/SOLV INGP/REL

B58
MASON H.L.,TOYNBEE'S APPROACH TO WORLD POLITICS. AFR USA+45 USSR LAW WAR NAT/LISM ALL/IDEOS...HUM BIBLIOG. PAGE 95 A1957 DIPLOM CONCPT PHIL/SCI SECT

B58
MUNKMAN C.A.,AMERICAN AID TO GREECE. GREECE USA+45 AGRI FINAN PROB/SOLV WAR PWR...CHARTS 20 UN. PAGE 106 A2171 FOR/AID PLAN ECO/DEV

INT/TRADE

B58
NATIONAL PLANNING ASSOCIATION,1970 WITHOUT ARMS CONTROL (PAMPHLET). WOR+45 PROB/SOLV TEC/DEV DIPLOM CONFER DETER NUC/PWR WAR...CHARTS 20 COLD/WAR. PAGE 107 A2204 ARMS/CONT ORD/FREE WEAPON PREDICT

B58
ROCKEFELLER BROTH FUND INC,INTERNATIONAL SECURITY - THE MILITARY ASPECT. USA+45 INT/ORG NAT/G BUDGET ARMS/CONT WAR WEAPON PEACE ORD/FREE 20 NATO. PAGE 123 A2511 NUC/PWR DETER FORCES DIPLOM

B58
SCHOEDER P.W.,THE AXIS ALLIANCE AND JAPANESE-AMERICAN RELATIONS 1941. ASIA GERMANY UK USA-45 PEACE ATTIT...POLICY BIBLIOG 20 CHINJAP TREATY. PAGE 129 A2641 AGREE DIPLOM WAR

B58
SOC OF COMP LEGIS AND INT LAW,THE LAW OF THE SEA... (PAMPHLET). WOR+45 NAT/G INT/TRADE ADJUD CONTROL NUC/PWR WAR PEACE ATTIT ORD/FREE...JURID CHARTS 20 UN TREATY RESOURCE/N. PAGE 135 A2756 INT/LAW INT/ORG DIPLOM SEA

B58
STONE J.,AGGRESSION AND WORLD ORDER: A CRITIQUE OF UNITED NATIONS THEORIES OF AGGRESSION. LAW CONSTN DELIB/GP PROB/SOLV BAL/PWR DIPLOM DEBATE ADJUD CRIME PWR...POLICY IDEA/COMP 20 UN SUEZ LEAGUE/NAT. PAGE 138 A2835 ORD/FREE INT/ORG WAR CONCPT

S58
BOURBON-BUSSET J.,"HOW DECISIONS ARE MADE IN FOREIGN POLITICS: PSYCHOLOGY IN INTERNATIONAL POLITICS." WOR+45 NAT/G SECT REGION WAR MORAL ...CONCPT OBS STERTYP GEN/LAWS TOT/POP COLD/WAR 20. PAGE 17 A0350 INT/ORG DELIB/GP DIPLOM

S58
BURNS A.L.,"THE INTERNATIONAL CONSEQUENCES OF EXPECTING SURPRISE." WOR+45 INT/ORG NAT/G FORCES DIPLOM COERCE NUC/PWR WAR CHOOSE ORD/FREE ...METH/CNCPT STYLE OBS STERTYP TOT/POP VAL/FREE. PAGE 22 A0440 PLAN PWR DETER

S58
DAVENPORT J.,"ARMS AND THE WELFARE STATE." INTELL STRUCT FORCES CREATE ECO/TAC FOR/AID DOMIN LEGIT ADMIN WAR ORD/FREE PWR...POLICY SOC CONCPT MYTH OBS TREND COLD/WAR TOT/POP 20. PAGE 34 A0685 USA+45 NAT/G USSR

S58
ROTHFELS H.,"THE GERMAN RESISTANCE IN ITS INTERNATIONAL ASPECTS" (BMR)" EUR+WWI GERMANY UNIV CHIEF DIPLOM WAR NAT/LISM ATTIT...POLICY 20 HITLER/A NAZI. PAGE 124 A2548 VOL/ASSN MORAL FASCISM CIVMIL/REL

C58
WILDING N.,"AN ENCYCLOPEDIA OF PARLIAMENT." UK LAW CONSTN CHIEF PROB/SOLV DIPLOM DEBATE WAR INGP/REL PRIVIL...BIBLIOG DICTIONARY 13/20 CMN/WLTH PARLIAMENT. PAGE 164 A3349 PARL/PROC POL/PAR NAT/G ADMIN

B59
AIR FORCE ACADEMY ASSEMBLY '59,INTERNATIONAL STABILITY AND PROGRESS (PAMPHLET). USA+45 USSR ECO/UNDEV PROB/SOLV BUDGET DIPLOM ADMIN DETER COST ATTIT...TREND 20. PAGE 5 A0103 FOR/AID FORCES WAR PLAN

B59
AMERICAN FRIENDS OF VIETNAM,AID TO VIETNAM: AN AMERICAN SUCCESS STORY (PAMPHLET). ASIA FUT USA+45 VIETNAM ECO/UNDEV WAR CIVMIL/REL GOV/REL...ANTHOL 20. PAGE 7 A0148 DIPLOM NAT/G FOR/AID FORCES

B59
BEMIS S.F.,A SHORT HISTORY OF AMERICAN FOREIGN POLICY AND DIPLOMACY. USA+45 USA-45 INT/ORG NEUTRAL REV WAR ISOLAT ORD/FREE...CHARTS T 18/20. PAGE 13 A0266 DIPLOM ATTIT

B59
DAWSON R.H.,THE DECISION TO AID RUSSIA* FOREIGN POLICY AND DOMESTIC POLITICS. GERMANY USSR CHIEF EX/STRUC LEGIS TOP/EX PROB/SOLV WAR ATTIT...POLICY CONGRESS. PAGE 34 A0695 DECISION DELIB/GP DIPLOM FOR/AID

B59
DEHIO L.,GERMANY AND WORLD POLITICS IN THE TWENTIETH CENTURY. EUR+WWI FRANCE GERMANY MOD/EUR UK USSR NAT/G CHIEF BAL/PWR DOMIN COLONIAL CONTROL LEAD...IDEA/COMP 20 VERSAILLES. PAGE 36 A0724 DIPLOM WAR NAT/LISM SOVEREIGN

B59
EGYPTIAN SOCIETY OF INT LAW,THE MONROVIA CONFERENCE (PAMPHLET). AFR ALGERIA FRANCE UAR CONFER REGION NUC/PWR WAR DISCRIM 20 SAHARA AFR/STATES. PAGE 40 A0826 COLONIAL SOVEREIGN RACE/REL DIPLOM

B59
EMME E.M.,THE IMPACT OF AIR POWER - NATIONAL SECURITY AND WORLD POLITICS. USA+45 USSR FORCES DIPLOM WEAPON PEACE TOTALISM...POLICY NAT/COMP 20 EUROPE. PAGE 42 A0850 DETER AIR WAR ORD/FREE

B59
FERRELL R.H.,AMERICAN DIPLOMACY: A HISTORY. USA+45 USA-45 PLAN ROUTINE REV WAR PWR...T 18/20 EISNHWR/DD WWI. PAGE 45 A0921 DIPLOM NAT/G POLICY

B59
GILBERT R.,GENOCIDE IN TIBET. ASIA SECT CHIEF DIPLOM 20. PAGE 52 A1072 MARXISM MURDER

WAR GP/REL

B59
GOLDWIN R.A.,READINGS IN RUSSIAN FOREIGN POLICY. HUNGARY USSR YUGOSLAVIA ELITES INT/ORG NAT/G REV WAR NAT/LISM PERSON SOCISM...CHARTS 20 MAPS BOLSHEVISM. PAGE 53 A1095
COM MARXISM DIPLOM POLICY

B59
GOULD L.P.,THE PRICE OF SURVIVAL. EUR+WWI SPACE USA+45 FORCES ECO/TAC NUC/PWR WAR ORD/FREE MARXISM ...IDEA/COMP 20 COLD/WAR NATO. PAGE 54 A1117
POLICY PROB/SOLV DIPLOM PEACE

B59
GREENSPAN M.,THE MODERN LAW OF LAND WARFARE. WOR+45 INT/ORG NAT/G DELIB/GP FORCES ATTIT...POLICY HYPO/EXP STERTYP 20. PAGE 56 A1142
ADJUD PWR WAR

B59
HUGHES E.M.,AMERICA THE VINCIBLE. USA+45 FOR/AID ARMS/CONT NUC/PWR PERS/REL RATIONAL ATTIT ALL/VALS 20 COLD/WAR. PAGE 69 A1413
ORD/FREE DIPLOM WAR

B59
KARUNAKARAN K.P.,INDIA IN WORLD AFFAIRS, 1952-1958 (VOL. II). INDIA ECO/UNDEV SECT FOR/AID INT/TRADE ADJUD NEUTRAL REV WAR DISCRIM ORD/FREE MARXISM ...BIBLIOG 20. PAGE 77 A1569
DIPLOM INT/ORG S/ASIA COLONIAL

B59
KNIERIEM A.,THE NUREMBERG TRIALS. EUR+WWI GERMANY VOL/ASSN LEAD COERCE WAR INGP/REL TOTALISM SUPEGO ORD/FREE...CONCPT METH/COMP. PAGE 80 A1651
INT/LAW CRIME PARTIC JURID

B59
LINK R.G.,ENGLISH THEORIES OF ECONOMIC FLUCTUATIONS: 1815-1848. FRANCE UK AGRI WORKER DIPLOM PRICE TASK WAR DEMAND PRODUC...POLICY BIBLIOG 18 MALTHUS MILL/JS WILSON/J. PAGE 89 A1826
IDEA/COMP ECO/DEV WEALTH EQUILIB

B59
MATHISEN T.,METHODOLOGY IN THE STUDY OF INTERNATIONAL RELATIONS. FUT WOR+45 SOCIETY INT/ORG NAT/G POL/PAR WAR PEACE KNOWL PWR...RELATIV CONCPT METH/CNCPT TREND HYPO/EXP METH TOT/POP 20. PAGE 96 A1965
GEN/METH CON/ANAL DIPLOM CREATE

B59
MAYER A.J.,POLITICAL ORIGINS OF THE NEW DIPLOMACY, 1917-1918. EUR+WWI MOD/EUR USA-45 WAR PWR...POLICY INT/LAW BIBLIOG. PAGE 97 A1983
TREND DIPLOM

B59
NAHM A.C.,JAPANESE PENETRATION OF KOREA, 1894-1910. ASIA KOREA NAT/G...POLICY 20 CHINJAP. PAGE 107 A2192
BIBLIOG/A DIPLOM WAR COLONIAL

B59
PANHUYS H.F.,THE ROLE OF NATIONALITY IN INTERNATIONAL LAW. ADJUD CRIME WAR STRANGE...JURID TREND. PAGE 114 A2330
INT/LAW NAT/LISM INGP/REL

B59
COLUMBIA U BUR APPL SOC RES,ATTITUDES OF PROMINENT AMERICANS TOWARD "WORLD PEACE THROUGH WORLD LAW" (SUPRA-NATL ORGANIZATION FOR WAR PREVENTION). USA+45 USSR ELITES FORCES PLAN PROB/SOLV CONTROL WAR PWR...POLICY SOC QU IDEA/COMP 20 UN. PAGE 117 A2403
ATTIT ACT/RES INT/LAW STAT

B59
ROPKE W.,INTERNATIONAL ORDER AND ECONOMIC INTEGRATION. ECO/DEV ECO/UNDEV AGRI FINAN INDUS INT/ORG WAR PEACE ORD/FREE...SOC METH/COMP 20 EEC. PAGE 123 A2524
INT/TRADE DIPLOM BAL/PAY ALL/IDEOS

B59
TUNSTALL W.C.B.,THE COMMONWEALTH AND REGIONAL DEFENCE (PAMPHLET). UK LAW VOL/ASSN PLAN AGREE REGION WAR ORD/FREE 20 CMN/WLTH NATO SEATO TREATY. PAGE 146 A2977
INT/ORG FORCES DIPLOM

B59
VAN WAGENEN R.W.,SOME VIEWS OF AMERICAN DEFENSE OFFICIALS ABOUT THE UNITED NATIONS (PAPER). FUT USA+45 NAT/G DIPLOM WAR EFFICIENCY PEACE...POLICY INT 20 UN DEPT/DEFEN. PAGE 158 A3216
INT/ORG LEAD ATTIT FORCES

B59
YOUNG J.,CHECKLIST OF MICROFILM REPRODUCTIONS OF SELECTED ARCHIVES OF THE JAPANESE ARMY, NAVY, AND OTHER GOVT AGENCIES, 1868-1945. DELIB/GP LEGIS DIPLOM EDU/PROP CIVMIL/REL 19/20 CHINJAP. PAGE 169 A3436
BIBLIOG ASIA FORCES WAR

S59
PUGWASH CONFERENCE,"ON BIOLOGICAL AND CHEMICAL WARFARE." WOR+45 SOCIETY PROC/MFG INT/ORG FORCES EDU/PROP ADJUD RIGID/FLEX ORD/FREE PWR...DECISION PSY NEW/IDEA MATH VAL/FREE 20. PAGE 118 A2417
ACT/RES BIO/SOC WAR WEAPON

S59
WARBURG J.P.,"THE CENTRAL EUROPEAN CRISIS: A PROPOSAL FOR WESTERN INITIATIVE." EUR+WWI INT/ORG NAT/G LEGIT DETER WAR...CONCPT BER/BLOC UN 20. PAGE 161 A3276
PLAN GERMANY

B60
ALBRECHT-CARRIE R.,FRANCE, EUROPE AND THE TWO WORLD WARS. EUR+WWI FRANCE GERMANY MOD/EUR UK ECO/DEV NAT/G FORCES BAL/PWR DOMIN ARMS/CONT PEACE PWR 20 TREATY EUROPE. PAGE 5 A0109
DIPLOM WAR

B60
BARNET R.,WHO WANTS DISARMAMENT. COM EUR+WWI USA+45 USSR INT/ORG NAT/G BAL/PWR DIPLOM EDU/PROP COERCE DETER NUC/PWR WAR WEAPON ATTIT PWR...TIME/SEQ COLD/WAR CONGRESS 20. PAGE 11 A0225
PLAN FORCES ARMS/CONT

B60
BROWN H.,COMMUNITY OF FEAR. FORCES TEC/DEV ARMS/CONT COERCE PEACE 20. PAGE 20 A0402
NUC/PWR WAR DIPLOM DETER

B60
CONN S.,THE FRAMEWORK OF HEMISPHERE DEFENSE. CANADA L/A+17C USA-45 NAT/G FORCES BAL/PWR DOMIN WAR PEACE DISPL PWR RESPECT...PLURIST CONCPT HIST/WRIT HYPO/EXP MEXIC/AMER 20 ROOSEVLT/F. PAGE 29 A0585
USA+45 INT/ORG DIPLOM

B60
DAVIDS J.,AMERICA AND THE WORLD OF OUR TIME: UNITED STATES DIPLOMACY IN THE TWENTIETH CENTURY. USA-45 SOCIETY ECO/DEV INT/ORG NAT/G POL/PAR FORCES ECO/TAC DOMIN EDU/PROP EXEC COERCE WAR CHOOSE ATTIT PERSON ORD/FREE...CONCPT TIME/SEQ TOT/POP 20. PAGE 34 A0686
USA+45 PWR DIPLOM

B60
DE GAULLE C.,THE EDGE OF THE SWORD. EUR+WWI FRANCE ELITES CHIEF DIPLOM ROLE...REALPOL TRADIT. PAGE 34 A0701
FORCES SUPEGO LEAD WAR

B60
ENGEL-JANOSI F.,OSTERREICH UND DER VATIKAN (2 VOLS). AUSTRIA VATICAN NAT/LISM PEACE PERSON CATHISM 20. PAGE 42 A0852
DIPLOM ATTIT WAR

B60
ENGELMAN F.L.,THE PEACE OF CHRISTMAS EVE. UK USA-45 NAT/G FORCES CONFER PERS/REL...AUD/VIS BIBLIOG 19 TREATY. PAGE 42 A0853
WAR PEACE DIPLOM PERSON

B60
FEIS H.,BETWEEN WAR AND PEACE: THE POTSDAM CONFERENCE. EUR+WWI NAT/G DELIB/GP PROB/SOLV REPAR WAR CIVMIL/REL...BIBLIOG 20. PAGE 45 A0911
DIPLOM CONFER BAL/PWR

B60
FURNIA A.H.,THE DIPLOMACY OF APPEASEMENT: ANGLO-FRENCH RELATIONS AND THE PRELUDE TO WORLD WAR II 1931-1938. FRANCE GERMANY UK ELITES NAT/G DELIB/GP FORCES WAR PEACE RIGID/FLEX 20. PAGE 50 A1026
DIPLOM BAL/PWR COERCE

B60
GLUBB J.B.,WAR IN THE DESERT: AN R.A.F. FRONTIER CAMPAIGN. SAUDI/ARAB UK KIN SECT LEAD...GEOG 20 RAF. PAGE 53 A1083
COLONIAL WAR FORCES DIPLOM

B60
HANDLIN O.,AMERICAN PRINCIPLES AND ISSUES. USA+45 USA-45 DIPLOM WAR PERSON. PAGE 61 A1251
ORD/FREE NAT/LISM ATTIT

B60
HOLT R.T.,STRATEGIC PSYCHOLOGICAL OPERATIONS AND AMERICAN FOREIGN POLICY. ITALY USA+45 FOR/AID DOMIN RUMOR ADMIN TASK WAR CHOOSE ATTIT ALL/IDEOS...PSY COLD/WAR. PAGE 67 A1375
EDU/PROP ACT/RES DIPLOM POLICY

B60
JAECKH A.,WELTSAAT; ERLEBTES UND ERSTREBTES. GERMANY WOR+45 WOR-45 PLAN WAR...POLICY OBS/ENVIR NAT/COMP PERS/COMP 20. PAGE 73 A1489
BIOG NAT/G SELF/OBS DIPLOM

B60
KARDELJE,SOCIALISM AND WAR. CHINA/COM WOR+45 YUGOSLAVIA DIPLOM EDU/PROP ATTIT...POLICY CONCPT IDEA/COMP COLD/WAR. PAGE 76 A1565
MARXIST WAR MARXISM BAL/PWR

B60
KENNAN G.F.,RUSSIA AND THE WEST. ASIA COM EUR+WWI GERMANY UK USA+45 USA-45 USSR INT/ORG NAT/G VOL/ASSN DOMIN REV WAR PWR...TIME/SEQ 20. PAGE 78 A1590
EXEC DIPLOM

B60
KINGSTON-MCCLOUG E.,DEFENSE; POLICY AND STRATEGY. UK SEA AIR TEC/DEV DIPLOM ADMIN LEAD WAR ORD/FREE ...CHARTS 20. PAGE 79 A1627
FORCES PLAN POLICY DECISION

B60
MCCLELLAND C.A.,NUCLEAR WEAPONS, MISSILES, AND FUTURE WAR: PROBLEM FOR THE SIXTIES. WOR+45 FORCES ARMS/CONT DETER MARXISM...POLICY ANTHOL COLD/WAR. PAGE 97 A1998
DIPLOM NUC/PWR WAR WEAPON

B60
MINIFIE J.M.,PEACEMAKER OR POWDER-MONKEY. CANADA INT/ORG NAT/G FORCES LEAD WAR...PREDICT 20. PAGE 102 A2086
DIPLOM POLICY NEUTRAL PEACE

B60
MONTGOMERY B.L.,AN APPROACH TO SANITY; A STUDY OF EAST-WEST RELATIONS. CONFER WAR EFFICIENCY ATTIT ...POLICY 20 NATO COLD/WAR KHRUSH/N. PAGE 103 A2113
DIPLOM INT/ORG BAL/PWR DETER

B60
MORAES F.,THE REVOLT IN TIBET. ASIA CHINA/COM INDIA CULTURE CONTROL COERCE WAR TOTALISM...POLICY SOC WORSHIP 20 TIBET INTERVENT. PAGE 104 A2127
COLONIAL FORCES DIPLOM ORD/FREE

B60
MORISON E.E.,TURMOIL AND TRADITION: A STUDY OF THE LIFE AND TIMES OF HENRY L. STIMSON. USA+45 USA-45 POL/PAR CHIEF DELIB/GP FORCES BAL/PWR DIPLOM ARMS/CONT WAR PEACE 19/20 STIMSON/HL ROOSEVLT/F TAFT/WH HOOVER/H REPUBLICAN. PAGE 104 A2142
BIOG NAT/G EX/STRUC

B60
MOSELY P.E.,THE KREMLIN AND WORLD POLITICS. EUR+WWI GERMANY USA+45 USSR CHIEF TOP/EX BAL/PWR DOMIN PEACE PWR...METH 20 COLD/WAR STALIN/J EUROPE/E. PAGE 105 A2151
COM DIPLOM POLICY WAR

B60
PRINCETON U CONFERENCE,CURRENT PROBLEMS IN NORTH AFRICA. ALGERIA LIBYA MOROCCO USA+45 EXTR/IND POL/PAR PROB/SOLV DIPLOM ECO/TAC WAR...ANTHOL 20 TUNIS. PAGE 118 A2412
POLICY ECO/UNDEV NAT/G

B60
SETHE P.,SCHICKSALSSTUNDEN DER WELTGESCHICHTE (6TH ED.). NAT/G BAL/PWR DOMIN REV PWR...NAT/COMP 16/20. PAGE 131 A2687
DIPLOM WAR PEACE

B60
SOBEL R.,THE ORIGINS OF INTERVENTIONISM: THE UNITED STATES AND THE RUSSO-FINNISH WAR. FINLAND USA-45 USSR LEGIS ATTIT RIGID/FLEX...BIBLIOG 20 INTERVENT. PAGE 135 A2755
DIPLOM WAR PROB/SOLV NEUTRAL

B60
SPEER J.P.,FOR WHAT PURPOSE? CHINA/COM USSR CONSTN PROB/SOLV DIPLOM CONTROL TASK WAR NAT/LISM WORSHIP 20 UN. PAGE 136 A2778
PEACE SECT SUPEGO ALL/IDEOS

B60
TABORN P.,RECORDS OF THE HEADQUARTERS, UNITED NATIONS COMMAND (PRELIMINARY INVENTORIES; PAPER). WOR+45 DIPLOM CONFER PEACE ATTIT...POLICY UN. PAGE 141 A2881
BIBLIOG/A WAR ARMS/CONT INT/ORG

B60
TAYLOR M.D.,THE UNCERTAIN TRUMPET. USA+45 USSR WOR+45 INT/ORG NAT/G CONSULT DOMIN COERCE NUC/PWR WAR ATTIT ORD/FREE PWR...POLICY CONCPT TREND GEN/METH COLD/WAR UN NATO 20. PAGE 142 A2900
PLAN FORCES DIPLOM

B60
TURNER G.B.,NATIONAL SECURITY IN THE NUCLEAR AGE. KOREA USA+45 PLAN DIPLOM ARMS/CONT DETER WAR WEAPON ...BIBLIOG 20 COLD/WAR NATO. PAGE 146 A2982
NAT/G POLICY FORCES NUC/PWR

B60
US DEPARTMENT OF THE ARMY,DISARMAMENT: A BIBLIOGRAPHIC RECORD: 1916-1960. DETER WAR WEAPON PEACE 20 UN LEAGUE/NAT COLD/WAR NATO. PAGE 152 A3103
BIBLIOG/A ARMS/CONT NUC/PWR DIPLOM

B60
US HOUSE COMM. SCI. ASTRONAUT.,OCEAN SCIENCES AND NATIONAL SECURITY. FUT SEA ECO/DEV EXTR/IND INT/ORG NAT/G FORCES ACT/RES TEC/DEV ECO/TAC COERCE WAR BIO/SOC KNOWL PWR...CONCPT RECORD LAB/EXP 20. PAGE 154 A3141
R+D ORD/FREE

B60
WHITING A.S.,CHINA CROSSES THE YALU: THE DECISION TO ENTER THE KOREAN WAR. ASIA CHINA/COM KOREA ECO/UNDEV R+D INT/ORG TOP/EX ACT/RES BAL/PWR ATTIT PWR...GEN/METH 20. PAGE 164 A3338
PLAN COERCE WAR

B60
WODDIS J.,AFRICA: THE ROOTS OF REVOLT. SOUTH/AFR WORKER INT/TRADE RACE/REL DISCRIM ORD/FREE 20. PAGE 166 A3374
COLONIAL SOVEREIGN WAR ECO/UNDEV

S60
BRODY R.A.,"DETERRENCE STRATEGIES: AN ANNOTATED BIBLIOGRAPHY." WOR+45 PLAN ARMS/CONT NUC/PWR WAR WEAPON DECISION. PAGE 19 A0383
BIBLIOG/A FORCES DETER DIPLOM

S60
O'BRIEN W.,"THE ROLE OF FORCE IN THE INTERNATIONAL JURIDICAL ORDER." WOR+45 NAT/G FORCES DOMIN ADJUD ARMS/CONT DETER NUC/PWR WAR ATTIT PWR...CATH INT/LAW JURID CONCPT TREND STERTYP GEN/LAWS 20. PAGE 110 A2266
INT/ORG COERCE

C60
COX R.H.,"LOCKE ON WAR AND PEACE." UK DIPLOM DOMIN PWR...BIOG IDEA/COMP BIBLIOG 18. PAGE 32 A0646
CONCPT NAT/G PEACE WAR

B61
AMORY J.F.,AROUND THE EDGE OF WAR: A NEW APPROACH TO THE PROBLEMS OF AMERICAN FOREIGN POLICY. COM L/A+17C USA+45 USSR FOR/AID EDU/PROP AGREE CONTROL ARMS/CONT NUC/PWR WAR PWR...IDEA/COMP 20 TREATY ESPIONAGE. PAGE 8 A0154
NAT/G DIPLOM POLICY

B61
BAGU S.,ARGENTINA EN EL MUNDO. L/A+17C INDUS INT/TRADE WAR ATTIT ROLE...TREND 19/20 ARGEN OAS. PAGE 10 A0202
DIPLOM INT/ORG REGION ECO/UNDEV

B61
BECHHOEFER B.G.,POSTWAR NEGOTIATIONS FOR ARMS CONTROL. COM EUR+WWI USSR INT/ORG NAT/G ACT/RES BAL/PWR DIPLOM ECO/TAC EDU/PROP ADMIN REGION DETER NUC/PWR WAR WEAPON PEACE ATTIT PWR...POLICY TIME/SEQ COLD/WAR CONGRESS 20. PAGE 12 A0244
USA+45 ARMS/CONT

B61
BRENNAN D.G.,ARMS CONTROL, DISARMAMENT, AND NATIONAL SECURITY. WOR+45 NAT/G FORCES CREATE PROB/SOLV PARTIC WAR PEACE...DECISION INT/LAW ANTHOL BIBLIOG 20. PAGE 18 A0372
ARMS/CONT ORD/FREE DIPLOM POLICY

B61
CONFERENCE ATLANTIC COMMUNITY,AN INTRODUCTORY BIBLIOGRAPHY. COM WOR+45 FORCES DIPLOM ECO/TAC WAR ...INT/LAW HIST/WRIT COLD/WAR NATO. PAGE 29 A0584
BIBLIOG/A CON/ANAL INT/ORG

B61
DELZELL C.F.,MUSSOLINI'S ENEMIES - THE ITALIAN ANTI-FASCIST RESISTANCE. ITALY DIPLOM PRESS DETER WAR TOTALISM ORD/FREE MARXISM 20. PAGE 36 A0730
FASCISM GP/REL POL/PAR REV

B61
FLEMING D.F.,THE COLD WAR AND ITS ORIGINS: 1917-1950 (VOL. I). ASIA USSR WOR+45 WOR-45 TEC/DEV FOR/AID NUC/PWR REV WAR PEACE FASCISM...T 20 COLD/WAR NATO BERLIN/BLO. PAGE 46 A0947
DIPLOM MARXISM BAL/PWR

B61
FULLER J.F.C.,THE CONDUCT OF WAR, 1789-1961. FRANCE RUSSIA SOCIETY NAT/G FORCES PROB/SOLV AGREE NUC/PWR WEAPON PEACE...SOC 18/20 TREATY COLD/WAR. PAGE 50 A1025
WAR POLICY REV ROLE

B61
GALLOIS P.,THE BALANCE OF TERROR: STRATEGY FOR THE NUCLEAR AGE. FUT WOR+45 INT/ORG FORCES TOP/EX DETER WAR ATTIT RIGID/FLEX ORD/FREE PWR...HYPO/EXP 20. PAGE 50 A1032
PLAN DECISION DIPLOM NUC/PWR

B61
JAKOBSON M.,THE DIPLOMACY OF THE WINTER WAR. EUR+WWI FINLAND GERMANY USSR INT/ORG NAT/G PEACE TOTALISM PWR...POLICY CONCPT 20 TREATY. PAGE 73 A1492
WAR ORD/FREE DIPLOM

B61
KERTESZ S.D.,AMERICAN DIPLOMACY IN A NEW ERA. COM S/ASIA UK USA+45 FORCES PROB/SOLV BAL/PWR ECO/TAC ADMIN COLONIAL WAR PEACE ORD/FREE 20 NATO CONGRESS UN COLD/WAR. PAGE 78 A1601
ANTHOL DIPLOM TREND

B61
KHAN A.W.,INDIA WINS FREEDOM: THE OTHER SIDE. INDIA PAKISTAN CULTURE LEGIS DIPLOM PARL/PROC REV WAR NAT/LISM 20. PAGE 78 A1607
SOVEREIGN GP/REL RACE/REL ORD/FREE

B61
KNORR K.E.,THE INTERNATIONAL SYSTEM. FUT SOCIETY INT/ORG NAT/G PLAN BAL/PWR DIPLOM WAR PWR ...DECISION METH/CNCPT CONT/OBS GAME METH UN 20. PAGE 81 A1655
ACT/RES SIMUL ECO/UNDEV

B61
LARSON A.,WHEN NATIONS DISAGREE. USA+45 WOR+45 INT/ORG ADJUD COERCE CRIME OWN SOVEREIGN...POLICY JURID 20. PAGE 85 A1734
INT/LAW DIPLOM WAR

B61
LERCHE C.O. JR.,FOREIGN POLICY OF THE AMERICAN PEOPLE (REV. ED.). USA+45 USSR FORCES TEC/DEV EDU/PROP WAR PRODUC ORD/FREE MARXISM...POLICY TREND BIBLIOG 20 COLD/WAR. PAGE 87 A1781
DECISION PLAN PEACE DIPLOM

B61
LIPPMANN W.,THE COMING TESTS WITH RUSSIA. COM CUBA GERMANY USSR FORCES CONTROL NEUTRAL COERCE NUC/PWR REV WAR PWR...INT 20 KHRUSH/N BERLIN. PAGE 89 A1830
BAL/PWR DIPLOM MARXISM ARMS/CONT

B61
MATTHEWS T.,WAR IN ALGERIA. ALGERIA FRANCE CONTROL ATTIT SOVEREIGN 20. PAGE 96 A1978
REV COLONIAL DIPLOM WAR

B61
MECHAM J.L.,THE UNITED STATES AND INTER-AMERICAN SECURITY, 1889-1960. L/A+17C USA+45 USA-45 CONSTN FORCES INT/TRADE PEACE TOTALISM ATTIT...JURID 19/20 UN OAS. PAGE 99 A2030
DIPLOM WAR ORD/FREE INT/ORG

B61
MEZERIK A.G.,ECONOMIC DEVELOPMENT AIDS FOR UNDERDEVELOPED COUNTRIES. WOR+45 FINAN LEGIS PROB/SOLV TEC/DEV DIPLOM FOR/AID GIVE TASK WAR 20 UN. PAGE 101 A2062
ECO/UNDEV INT/ORG WEALTH PLAN

B61
NOLLAU G.,INTERNATIONAL COMMUNISM AND WORLD REVOLUTION: HISTORY AND METHODS. RUSSIA USSR INT/ORG NAT/G POL/PAR VOL/ASSN FORCES BAL/PWR DIPLOM EXEC REGION WAR ATTIT PWR MARXISM...CONCPT TIME/SEQ COLD/WAR 19/20. PAGE 102 A2100
COM REV

B61
PECKERT J.,DIE GROSSEN UND DIE KLEINEN MAECHTE. COM GERMANY/W ECO/DEV ECO/UNDEV NAT/G WAR RACE/REL PEACE...POLICY GP/COMP GOV/COMP 20 COLD/WAR.
DIPLOM ECO/TAC BAL/PWR

PAGE 114 A2346

B61

RIENOW R.,CONTEMPORARY INTERNATIONAL POLITICS. WOR+45 INT/ORG BAL/PWR EDU/PROP COLONIAL NEUTRAL REGION WAR PEACE...INT/LAW 20 COLD/WAR UN. PAGE 121 A2476

DIPLOM PWR POLICY NAT/G

B61

SCHMIDT H.,VERTEIDIGUNG ODER VERGELTUNG. COM CUBA GERMANY/W USSR FORCES DIPLOM ARMS/CONT DETER NUC/PWR...POLICY CHARTS HYPO/EXP SIMUL BIBLIOG 20 NATO COLD/WAR. PAGE 128 A2630

PLAN WAR BAL/PWR ORD/FREE

B61

SCHONBRUNN G.,WELTKRIEGE UND REVOLUTIONEN 1914-1945. USSR DIPLOM TOTALISM ORD/FREE 20 TREATY WWI NAZI. PAGE 129 A2643

WAR REV FASCISM SOCISM

B61

SLESSOR J.,WHAT PRICE COEXISTENCE? COM INT/ORG NAT/G FORCES COLONIAL ARMS/CONT WAR...POLICY TREND 20 NATO COLD/WAR. PAGE 134 A2741

DIPLOM PEACE WOR+45 NUC/PWR

B61

SOKOL A.E.,SEAPOWER IN THE NUCLEAR AGE. USA+45 USSR DIST/IND FORCES INT/TRADE DETER WAR...POLICY NAT/COMP BIBLIOG COLD/WAR. PAGE 135 A2763

SEA PWR WEAPON NUC/PWR

B61

SYATAUW J.J.G.,SOME NEWLY ESTABLISHED ASIAN STATES AND THE DEVELOPMENT OF INTERNATIONAL LAW. BURMA CEYLON INDIA INDONESIA ECO/UNDEV COLONIAL NEUTRAL WAR PEACE SOVEREIGN...CHARTS 19/20. PAGE 140 A2873

INT/LAW ADJUST SOCIETY S/ASIA

B61

UAR MINISTRY OF CULTURE,A BIBLIOGRAPHICAL LIST OF LIBYA. ISLAM LIBYA DIPLOM COLONIAL REV WAR 19/20. PAGE 146 A2988

BIBLIOG GEOG SECT NAT/LISM

B61

US SENATE COMM GOVT OPERATIONS,ORGANIZING FOR NATIONAL SECURITY. COM USA+45 BUDGET DIPLOM DETER NUC/PWR WAR WEAPON ORD/FREE...BIBLIOG 20 COLD/WAR. PAGE 156 A3172

POLICY PLAN FORCES COERCE

B61

WINTER R.C.,BLUEPRINTS FOR INDEPENDENCE. WOR+45 INT/ORG DIPLOM COLONIAL CONTROL REV WAR PWR ...BIBLIOG 20 UN. PAGE 165 A3367

NAT/G ECO/UNDEV SOVEREIGN CONSTN

B61

WRINCH P.,THE MILITARY STRATEGY OF WINSTON CHURCHILL. UK WOR-45 SEA VOL/ASSN TEC/DEV BAL/PWR LEAD WAR PEACE ATTIT...POLICY 20 CHURCHLL/W. PAGE 168 A3421

CIVMIL/REL FORCES PLAN DIPLOM

L61

CLAUDE I.,"THE UNITED NATIONS AND THE USE OF FORCE." FUT WOR+45 SOCIETY DIPLOM EDU/PROP LEGIT ADMIN ROUTINE COERCE WAR PEACE ORD/FREE...CONCPT TREND UN 20. PAGE 27 A0545

INT/ORG FORCES

L61

HALPERIN M.H.,"NUCLEAR WEAPONS AND LIMITED WARS." FUT UNIV WOR+45 INTELL SOCIETY ECO/DEV ACT/RES DRIVE PERCEPT RIGID/FLEX...CONCPT TIME/SEQ TREND TOT/POP 20. PAGE 60 A1237

PLAN COERCE NUC/PWR WAR

L61

HOYT E.C.,"UNITED STATES REACTION TO THE KOREAN ATTACK." COM KOREA USA+45 CONSTN DELIB/GP FORCES PLAN ECO/TAC DOMIN EDU/PROP LEGIT ROUTINE COERCE WAR ATTIT DISPL RIGID/FLEX ORD/FREE PWR...POLICY INT/LAW TREND UN 20. PAGE 68 A1402

ASIA INT/ORG BAL/PWR DIPLOM

L61

WRIGHT Q.,"STUDIES IN DETERRENCE: LIMITED WARS AND THE ROLE OF SEABORNE WEAPONS SYSTEMS." FUT USA+45 WOR+45 SEA INT/ORG NAT/G FORCES ACT/RES WAR WEAPON ORD/FREE TOT/POP 20. PAGE 168 A3415

TEC/DEV SKILL BAL/PWR DETER

S61

CARLETON W.G.,"AMERICAN FOREIGN POLICY: MYTHS AND REALITIES." FUT USA+45 WOR+45 ECO/UNDEV INT/ORG EX/STRUC ARMS/CONT NUC/PWR WAR ATTIT...POLICY CONCPT CONT/OBS GEN/METH COLD/WAR TOT/POP 20. PAGE 24 A0484

PLAN MYTH DIPLOM

S61

TRAMPE G.,"DIE FORM DER DIPLOMATIC ALS POLITSCHE WAFFE." WOR+45 WOR-45 SOCIETY STRATA INT/ORG NAT/G ACT/RES PLAN ECO/TAC EDU/PROP COERCE WAR ATTIT RIGID/FLEX...DECISION CONCPT TREND. PAGE 145 A2959

CONSULT PWR DIPLOM

B62

ABOSCH H.,THE MENACE OF THE MIRACLE: GERMANY FROM HITLER TO ADENAUER. EUR+WWI GERMANY/W CULTURE FORCES PRESS NUC/PWR WAR CHOOSE 20 HITLER/A ADENAUER/K. PAGE 4 A0082

DIPLOM PEACE POLICY

B62

APATHEKER H.,AMERICAN FOREIGN POLICY AND THE COLD WAR. USA+45 NAT/G POL/PAR COLONIAL NAT/LISM SOVEREIGN MARXISM SOCISM 20 COLD/WAR MARX/KARL LENIN/VI INTERVENT. PAGE 8 A0167

DIPLOM WAR PEACE

B62

BENNETT J.C.,NUCLEAR WEAPONS AND THE CONFLICT OF CONSCIENCE. WOR+45 PROB/SOLV DIPLOM WEAPON SUPEGO MORAL...ANTHOL WORSHIP 20. PAGE 13 A0268

POLICY NUC/PWR WAR

B62

BIBLIOTHEQUE PALAIS DE LA PAIX,CATALOGUE OF THE PEACE PALACE LIBRARY, SUPPLEMENT 1937-1952 (7 VOLS.). WOR+45 WOR-45 INT/ORG NAT/G ADJUD WAR PEACE ...JURID 20. PAGE 14 A0285

BIBLIOG INT/LAW DIPLOM

B62

BLACKETT P.M.S.,STUDIES OF WAR: NUCLEAR AND CONVENTIONAL. EUR+WWI USA+45 DELIB/GP ACT/RES CREATE PLAN TEC/DEV LEGIT COERCE WAR ORD/FREE PWR ...POLICY TECHNIC TIME/SEQ 20. PAGE 15 A0300

INT/ORG FORCES ARMS/CONT NUC/PWR

B62

BOULDING K.E.,CONFLICT AND DEFENSE: A GENERAL THEORY. FUT SOCIETY INT/ORG NAT/G CREATE BAL/PWR COERCE NAT/LISM DRIVE ALL/VALS...PLURIST DECISION CONCPT METH/CNCPT TREND HYPO/EXP TOT/POP 20. PAGE 17 A0347

MATH SIMUL PEACE WAR

B62

BRIMMER B.,A GUIDE TO THE USE OF UNITED NATIONS DOCUMENTS. WOR+45 ECO/UNDEV AGRI EX/STRUC FORCES PROB/SOLV ADMIN WAR PEACE WEALTH...POLICY UN. PAGE 19 A0378

BIBLIOG/A INT/ORG DIPLOM

B62

COLOMBOS C.J.,THE INTERNATIONAL LAW OF THE SEA. WOR+45 EXTR/IND DIPLOM INT/TRADE TARIFFS AGREE WAR ...TIME/SEQ 20 TREATY. PAGE 28 A0570

INT/LAW SEA JURID ADJUD

B62

DEHIO L.,THE PRECARIOUS BALANCE: FOUR CENTURIES OF THE EUROPEAN POWER STRUGGLE. FRANCE GERMANY SPAIN NAT/G DOMIN PWR...GOV/COMP 8/20. PAGE 36 A0725

BAL/PWR WAR DIPLOM COERCE

B62

DUROSELLE J.B.,HISTOIRE DIPLOMATIQUE DE 1919 A NOS JOURS (3RD ED.). FRANCE INT/ORG CHIEF FORCES CONFER ARMS/CONT WAR PEACE ORD/FREE...T TREATY 20 COLD/WAR. PAGE 39 A0807

DIPLOM WOR+45 WOR-45

B62

FORBES H.W.,THE STRATEGY OF DISARMAMENT. FUT WOR+45 INT/ORG VOL/ASSN CONSULT ARMS/CONT COERCE NUC/PWR WAR DRIVE RIGID/FLEX ORD/FREE PWR...POLICY CONCPT OBS TREND STERTYP 20. PAGE 47 A0959

PLAN FORCES DIPLOM

B62

GILPIN R.,AMERICAN SCIENTISTS AND NUCLEAR WEAPONS POLICY. COM FUT USA+45 WOR+45 INT/ORG NAT/G PROF/ORG CONSULT FORCES CREATE TEC/DEV BAL/PWR EDU/PROP ARMS/CONT WAR PERCEPT KNOWL MORAL PWR ...PHIL/SCI SOC CONCPT GEN/LAWS 20. PAGE 52 A1073

INTELL ATTIT DETER NUC/PWR

B62

GOLDWATER B.M.,WHY NOT VICTORY? A FRESH LOOK AT AMERICAN FOREIGN POLICY. USA+45 WOR+45 FOR/AID LEAD ARMS/CONT WAR PEACE ATTIT ORD/FREE PWR MARXISM ...INT/LAW 20 TREATY ECHR COUNCL/EUR. PAGE 53 A1092

DIPLOM POLICY CONSERVE NAT/LISM

B62

GUTTMAN A.,THE WOUND IN THE HEART: AMERICA AND THE SPANISH CIVIL WAR. SPAIN USA-45 POL/PAR LEGIS ECO/TAC CHOOSE ANOMIE ATTIT MARXISM...POLICY ANARCH BIBLIOG 20 ROOSEVLT/F. PAGE 58 A1198

ALL/IDEOS WAR DIPLOM CATHISM

B62

HENDRICKS D.,PAMPHLETS ON THE FIRST WORLD WAR: AN ANNOTATED BIBLIOGRAPHY (OCCASIONAL PAPER NO. 79). GERMANY WOR-45 EDU/PROP NAT/LISM ATTIT PWR ALL/IDEOS 20. PAGE 64 A1314

BIBLIOG/A WAR DIPLOM NAT/G

B62

HOOK S.,WORLD COMMUNISM: KEY DOCUMENTARY MATERIAL. CHINA/COM L/A+17C USA+45 USSR POL/PAR DIPLOM COLONIAL REV WAR...ANTHOL 20 MARX/KARL LENIN/VI COM/PARTY. PAGE 67 A1380

MARXISM COM GEN/LAWS NAT/G

B62

HUNTINGTON S.P.,CHANGING PATTERNS OF MILITARY POLITICS. EUR+WWI L/A+17C S/ASIA USA+45 WOR+45 CULTURE INT/ORG NAT/G CONSULT PLAN DOMIN EDU/PROP LEGIT DETER WAR ATTIT PERSON PWR...DECISION CONCPT SIMUL GEN/LAWS ANTHOL COLD/WAR 20. PAGE 69 A1419

FORCES RIGID/FLEX

B62

INGHAM K.,A HISTORY OF EAST AFRICA. NAT/G DIPLOM ADMIN WAR NAT/LISM...SOC BIOG BIBLIOG. PAGE 70 A1439

AFR CONSTN COLONIAL

B62

JELAVICH C.,TSARIST RUSSIA AND BALKAN NATIONALISM. BULGARIA MOD/EUR RUSSIA DOMIN GOV/REL...GEOG 19 SERBIA. PAGE 73 A1503

NAT/LISM DIPLOM WAR

B62

JORDAN A.A. JR.,FOREIGN AID AND THE DEFENSE OF SOUTHEAST ASIA. PAKISTAN VIETNAM/S FINAN PLAN BUDGET ECO/TAC DETER WAR ORD/FREE...POLICY DECISION CENSUS CHARTS BIBLIOG 20. PAGE 75 A1535

FOR/AID S/ASIA FORCES ECO/UNDEV

B62

KENT G.O.,A CATALOG OF FILES AND MICROFILMS OF THE GERMAN FOREIGN MINISTRY ARCHIVES, 1920-1945 (3 VOLS.). GERMANY WOR-45 WRITING WAR 20. PAGE 78 A1595

BIBLIOG NAT/G DIPLOM FASCISM

B62

KING G.,THE UNITED NATIONS IN THE CONGO: A QUEST FOR PEACE. WOR+45 NAT/G CONSULT FORCES LEGIT COERCE WAR ORD/FREE...JURID METH/CNCPT OBS INT HIST/WRIT

AFR INT/ORG

TIME/SEQ CONGO UN 20 COLD/WAR. PAGE 79 A1624

B62

LEOPOLD R.W.,THE GROWTH OF AMERICAN FOREIGN POLICY: A HISTORY. USA+45 USA-45 EX/STRUC LEGIS INT/TRADE WAR...CHARTS BIBLIOG/A T 18/20. PAGE 87 A1780
NAT/G DIPLOM POLICY

B62

MACKENTOSH J.M.,STRATEGY AND TACTICS OF SOVIET FOREIGN POLICY. CHINA/COM FUT USA+45 WOR+45 INT/ORG PLAN DOMIN LEGIT ROUTINE COERCE NUC/PWR WAR ATTIT DRIVE ORD/FREE PWR...CONCPT OBS TIME/SEQ TREND GEN/METH COLD/WAR 20. PAGE 92 A1894
COM POLICY DIPLOM USSR

B62

MONCRIEFF A.,THE STRATEGY OF SURVIVAL. UK FORCES BAL/PWR CONFER DETER WAR...ANTHOL 20 COLD/WAR. PAGE 102 A2104
PLAN DECISION DIPLOM ARMS/CONT

B62

MOON P.,DIVIDE AND QUIT. INDIA PAKISTAN STRATA DELIB/GP PLAN DIPLOM REPRESENT GP/REL INGP/REL CONSEN DISCRIM...OBS 20. PAGE 103 A2119
WAR REGION ISOLAT SECT

B62

MORGENSTERN O.,STRATEGIE - HEUTE (2ND ED.). USA+45 USSR ECO/DEV DELIB/GP WAR PEACE ORD/FREE...GOV/COMP NAT/COMP 20 COLD/WAR NATO. PAGE 104 A2134
NUC/PWR DIPLOM FORCES TEC/DEV

B62

MORGENTHAU H.J.,POLITICS IN THE TWENTIETH CENTURY: IMPASSE OF AMERICAN FOREIGN POLICY. FUT GERMANY USA+45 USSR WOR+45 INT/ORG NAT/G ACT/RES PLAN FOR/AID EDU/PROP LEGIT COERCE WAR PWR...TIME/SEQ TREND COLD/WAR 20. PAGE 104 A2138
SKILL DIPLOM

B62

MORTON L.,STRATEGY AND COMMAND: THE FIRST TWO YEARS. USA-45 NAT/G CONTROL EXEC LEAD WEAPON CIVMIL/REL PWR...POLICY AUD/VIS CHARTS 20 CHINJAP. PAGE 105 A2150
WAR FORCES PLAN DIPLOM

B62

NOBECOURT R.G.,LES SECRETS DE LA PROPAGANDE EN FRANCE OCCUPEE. FRANCE ELITES NAT/G DIPLOM GP/REL NAT/LISM TOTALISM ORD/FREE 20 VICHY VICHY. PAGE 109 A2244
METH/COMP EDU/PROP WAR CONTROL

B62

OSGOOD C.E.,AN ALTERNATIVE TO WAR OR SURRENDER. FUT UNIV CULTURE INTELL SOCIETY R+D INT/ORG CONSULT DELIB/GP ACT/RES PLAN CHOOSE ATTIT PERCEPT KNOWL ...PHIL/SCI PSY SOC TREND GEN/LAWS 20. PAGE 112 A2300
ORD/FREE EDU/PROP PEACE WAR

B62

PERRE J.,LES MUTATIONS DE LA GUERRE MODERNE: DE LA REVOLUTION FRANCAISE A LA REVOLUTION NUCLEAIRE. DIPLOM ARMS/CONT DEATH REV WEAPON GP/REL PEACE ATTIT...STAT PREDICT BIBLIOG 18/20 WWI. PAGE 115 A2365
WAR FORCES NUC/PWR

B62

SCOTT W.E.,ALLIANCE AGAINST HITLER. EUR+WWI FRANCE GERMANY USSR BAL/PWR LEAD TOTALISM PWR FASCISM MARXISM...POLICY BIBLIOG 20 HITLER/A. PAGE 131 A2675
WAR DIPLOM FORCES

B62

SOMMER T.,DEUTSCHLAND UND JAPAN ZWISCHEN DEN MACHTEN. GERMANY DELIB/GP BAL/PWR AGREE COERCE TOTALISM PWR 20 CHINJAP TREATY. PAGE 135 A2765
DIPLOM WAR ATTIT

B62

STRAUSS L.L.,MEN AND DECISIONS. USA+45 USA-45 USSR CONSULT FORCES TOP/EX WAR PEACE 20. PAGE 139 A2844
DECISION PWR NUC/PWR DIPLOM

B62

TAYLOR D.,THE BRITISH IN AFRICA. UK CULTURE ECO/UNDEV INDUS DIPLOM INT/TRADE ADMIN WAR RACE/REL ORD/FREE SOVEREIGN...POLICY BIBLIOG 15/20 CMN/WLTH. PAGE 142 A2898
AFR COLONIAL DOMIN

B62

THOMSON G.P.,NUCLEAR ENERGY IN BRITAIN DURING THE LAST WAR: THE CHERWELL SIMON LECTURE (MONOGRAPH). UK R+D CONSULT FORCES PLAN DIPLOM TASK CIVMIL/REL ROLE...PHIL/SCI NEW/IDEA LAB/EXP 20 MAUD. PAGE 143 A2934
CREATE TEC/DEV WAR NUC/PWR

B62

TOURE S.,THE INTERNATIONAL POLICY OF THE DEMOCRATIC PARTY OF GUINEA (VOL. VII). AFR ALGERIA GHANA GUINEA MALI CONSTN VOL/ASSN CHIEF WAR PEACE ATTIT ...WELF/ST 20 DEMOCRAT. PAGE 144 A2953
DIPLOM POLICY POL/PAR NEW/LIB

B62

US DEPARTMENT OF THE ARMY,GUIDE TO JAPANESE MONOGRAPHS AND JAPANESE STUDIES ON MANCHURIA: 1945-1960. CHINA/COM NAT/G DIPLOM LEAD COERCE WAR ...CHARTS 19/20 CHINJAP. PAGE 152 A3105
BIBLIOG/A FORCES ASIA S/ASIA

B62

US SENATE COMM ON JUDICIARY,CONSTITUTIONAL RIGHTS OF MILITARY PERSONNEL. USA+45 USA-45 FORCES DIPLOM WAR CONGRESS. PAGE 157 A3193
CONSTN ORD/FREE JURID CT/SYS

B62

WELLEQUET J.,LE CONGO BELGE ET LA WELTPOLITIK (1894-1914. GERMANY DOMIN EDU/PROP WAR ATTIT ...BIBLIOG T CONGO/LEOP. PAGE 163 A3314
ADMIN DIPLOM GP/REL COLONIAL

B62

WOETZEL R.K.,THE NURENBERG TRIALS IN INTERNATIONAL LAW. CHRIST-17C MOD/EUR WOR+45 SOCIETY NAT/G DELIB/GP DOMIN LEGIT ROUTINE ATTIT DRIVE PERSON SUPEGO MORAL ORD/FREE...POLICY MAJORIT JURID PSY SOC SELF/OBS RECORD NAZI TOT/POP. PAGE 166 A3376
INT/ORG ADJUD WAR

S62

FALK R.A.,"THE REALITY OF INTERNATIONAL LAW." WOR+45 NAT/G LEGIT COERCE DETER WAR MORAL ORD/FREE PWR SOVEREIGN...JURID CONCPT VAL/FREE COLD/WAR 20. PAGE 43 A0887
INT/ORG ADJUD NUC/PWR INT/LAW

S62

GREEN L.C.,"POLITICAL OFFENSES, WAR CRIMES AND EXTRADITION." WOR+45 YUGOSLAVIA INT/ORG LEGIT ROUTINE WAR ORD/FREE SOVEREIGN...JURID NAZI 20 INTERPOL. PAGE 55 A1138
LAW CONCPT INT/LAW

S62

GREENSPAN M.,"INTERNATIONAL LAW AND ITS PROTECTION FOR PARTICIPANTS IN UNCONVENTIONAL WARFARE." WOR+45 LAW INT/ORG NAT/G POL/PAR COERCE REV ORD/FREE ...INT/LAW TOT/POP 20. PAGE 56 A1143
FORCES JURID GUERRILLA WAR

S62

RUSSETT B.M.,"CAUSE, SURPRISE, AND NO ESCAPE." FUT WOR-45 CULTURE SOCIETY INT/ORG FORCES TEC/DEV BAL/PWR EDU/PROP ARMS/CONT NUC/PWR WAR WEAPON PEACE KNOWL ORD/FREE PWR...POLICY CONCPT RECORD TIME/SEQ TREND GEN/LAWS 20 WWI. PAGE 126 A2578
COERCE DIPLOM

S62

STRACHEY J.,"COMMUNIST INTENTIONS." ASIA USSR YUGOSLAVIA INT/ORG NAT/G FORCES DOMIN EDU/PROP COERCE NUC/PWR NAT/LISM PEACE RIGID/FLEX PWR MARXISM...CONCPT MYTH OBS TIME/SEQ TREND COLD/WAR TOT/POP 20. PAGE 139 A2843
COM ATTIT WAR

S62

THOMAS J.R.T.,"SOVIET BEHAVIOR IN THE QUEMOY CRISES OF 1958." CHINA/COM FUT USSR WOR+45 INT/ORG VOL/ASSN FORCES PLAN BAL/PWR DOMIN COERCE NUC/PWR REV WAR ATTIT DRIVE ORD/FREE...POLICY OBS RECORD COLD/WAR FOR/POL 20. PAGE 143 A2923
COM PWR

C62

BACON F.,"OF THE TRUE GREATNESS OF KINGDOMS AND ESTATES" (1612) IN F. BACON, ESSAYS." ELITES FORCES DOMIN EDU/PROP LEGIT...POLICY GEN/LAWS 16/17 TREATY. PAGE 10 A0200
WAR PWR DIPLOM CONSTN

C62

DUFFY J.,"PORTUGAL IN AFRICA." PORTUGAL SIER/LEONE INDUS WORKER INT/TRADE WAR CONSERVE...CATH GEOG TREND 16/20. PAGE 39 A0795
BIBLIOG RACE/REL ECO/UNDEV COLONIAL

B63

BLOCH-MORHANGE J.,VINGT ANNEES D'HISTOIRE CONTEMPORAINE. FORCES FOR/AID CONFER LEAD 20 COLD/WAR. PAGE 15 A0311
WAR DIPLOM INT/ORG CHIEF

B63

BOISSIER P.,HISTORIE DU COMITE INTERNATIONAL DE LA CROIX ROUGE. MOD/EUR WOR-45 CONSULT FORCES PLAN DIPLOM EDU/PROP ADMIN MORAL ORD/FREE...SOC CONCPT RECORD TIME/SEQ GEN/LAWS TOT/POP VAL/FREE 19/20. PAGE 16 A0332
INT/ORG HEALTH ARMS/CONT WAR

B63

BROEKMEIJER M.W.,DEVELOPING COUNTRIES AND NATO. USSR FORCES DIPLOM NUC/PWR WAR PEACE TOTALISM 20 NATO. PAGE 19 A0384
ECO/UNDEV FOR/AID ORD/FREE NAT/G

B63

DUNN F.S.,PEACE-MAKING AND THE SETTLEMENT WITH JAPAN. ASIA USA+45 USA-45 FORCES BAL/PWR ECO/TAC CONFER WAR PWR SOVEREIGN 20 CHINJAP COLD/WAR TREATY. PAGE 39 A0802
POLICY PEACE PLAN DIPLOM

B63

FRANZ G.,TEILUNG UND WIEDERVEREINIGUNG. GERMANY IRELAND ITALY NETHERLAND POLAND CULTURE BAL/PWR CHOOSE NAT/LISM ORD/FREE SOVEREIGN 19/20. PAGE 48 A0987
DIPLOM WAR NAT/COMP ATTIT

B63

FULBRIGHT J.W.,PROSPECTS FOR THE WEST. COM USA+45 USSR INT/ORG NAT/G SCHOOL PROB/SOLV NUC/PWR WAR PEACE ORD/FREE...PREDICT METH/COMP 20 DEGAULLE/C. PAGE 50 A1015
DIPLOM BAL/PWR CONCPT POLICY

B63

GALLAGHER M.P.,THE SOVIET HISTORY OF WORLD WAR II. EUR+WWI USSR DIPLOM DOMIN WRITING CONTROL WAR MARXISM...PSY TIME/SEQ 20 STALIN/J. PAGE 50 A1031
CIVMIL/REL EDU/PROP HIST/WRIT PRESS

B63

GILBERT M.,THE APPEASERS. COM GERMANY UK PLAN ECO/TAC COLONIAL CONTROL EXEC ORD/FREE PWR FASCISM 20 PARLIAMENT. PAGE 52 A1068
DIPLOM WAR POLICY DECISION

B63

HALPERIN M.H.,LIMITED WAR IN A NUCLEAR AGE. CUBA KOREA USA+45 USSR INT/ORG FORCES PLAN DIPLOM DETER
WAR NUC/PWR

PWR...BIBLIOG/A 20. PAGE 60 A1238 — CONTROL WEAPON

B63
HONEY P.J.,COMMUNISM IN NORTH VIETNAM: ITS ROLE IN THE SINO-SOVIET DISPUTE. CHINA/COM INDIA USSR VIETNAM/N AGRI POL/PAR LEGIS ECO/TAC WAR PEACE ATTIT...GEOG IDEA/COMP 20. PAGE 67 A1378 — POLICY MARXISM CHIEF DIPLOM

B63
HUSSEY W.D.,THE BRITISH EMPIRE AND COMMONWEALTH 1500 TO 1961. UK USA-45 SOCIETY ECO/UNDEV NAT/G VOL/ASSN INT/TRADE DOMIN CONTROL WAR PWR ...DICTIONARY 16/20 COMMONWLTH TRUST/TERR. PAGE 69 A1422 — COLONIAL SOVEREIGN INT/ORG

B63
KORBEL J.,POLAND BETWEEN EAST AND WEST: SOVIET AND GERMAN DIPLOMACY TOWARD POLAND 1919-1933. EUR+WWI GERMANY POLAND USSR FORCES AGREE WAR SOVEREIGN ...BIBLIOG 20 TREATY. PAGE 81 A1670 — BAL/PWR DIPLOM DOMIN NAT/LISM

B63
LEE C.,THE POLITICS OF KOREAN NATIONALISM. KOREA S/ASIA DIPLOM REV WAR 14/20 CHINJAP. PAGE 86 A1759 — NAT/LISM SOVEREIGN COLONIAL

B63
LERCHE C.O. JR.,CONCEPTS OF INTERNATIONAL POLITICS. WOR+45 WOR-45 LAW DELIB/GP EX/STRUC TEC/DEV ECO/TAC INT/TRADE LEGIT ROUTINE COERCE ATTIT ORD/FREE PWR RESPECT...STERTYP GEN/LAWS VAL/FREE. PAGE 87 A1782 — INT/ORG WAR

B63
LERCHE C.O. JR.,AMERICA IN WORLD AFFAIRS. COM UK USA+45 INT/ORG FORCES ECO/TAC INT/TRADE EDU/PROP WAR NAT/LISM PEACE...BIBLIOG 18/20 UN CONGRESS PRESIDENT COLD/WAR. PAGE 87 A1783 — NAT/G DIPLOM PLAN

B63
LOOMIE A.J.,THE SPANISH ELIZABETHANS: THE ENGLISH EXILES AT THE COURT OF PHILIP II. SPAIN UK WAR INGP/REL DRIVE HABITAT CATHISM...BIOG 16/17 MIGRATION. PAGE 91 A1860 — NAT/G STRANGE POLICY DIPLOM

B63
MANSERGH N.,DOCUMENTS AND SPEECHES ON COMMONWEALTH AFFAIRS 1952-1962. CANADA INDIA PAKISTAN UK CONSTN FORCES ECO/TAC EDU/PROP COLONIAL DETER WAR ORD/FREE SOVEREIGN...POLICY 20 AUSTRAL. PAGE 94 A1932 — BIBLIOG/A FEDERAL INT/TRADE DIPLOM

B63
MONGER G.W.,THE END OF ISOLATION. FRANCE MOD/EUR RUSSIA UK NAT/G LEGIS TOP/EX GOV/REL PWR 20 TREATY CHINJAP. PAGE 103 A2106 — DIPLOM POLICY WAR

B63
MOSELY P.E.,THE SOVIET UNION, 1922-1962: A FOREIGN AFFAIRS READER. ASIA POLAND USSR CULTURE INTELL AGRI POL/PAR WORKER INT/TRADE DOMIN WAR NAT/LISM MARXISM SOCISM 20 KHRUSH/N. PAGE 105 A2152 — PWR POLICY DIPLOM

B63
PACHTER H.M.,COLLISION COURSE; THE CUBAN MISSILE CRISIS AND COEXISTENCE. CUBA USA+45 DIPLOM ARMS/CONT PEACE MARXISM...DECISION INT/LAW 20 COLD/WAR KHRUSH/N KENNEDY/JF CASTRO/F. PAGE 112 A2307 — WAR BAL/PWR NUC/PWR DETER

B63
PECQUET P.,THE DIPLOMACY OF THE CONFEDERATE CABINET OF RICHMOND AND ITS AGENTS ABROAD (LIMITED ED.). MOD/EUR USA-45 LEAD...OBS 19 CIVIL/WAR SOUTH/US. PAGE 114 A2347 — DIPLOM WAR ORD/FREE

B63
PERKINS B.,PROLOGUE TO THE WAR: ENGLAND AND THE UNITED STATES, 1805-1812. MOD/EUR UK USA-45 NAT/G ORD/FREE RESPECT SOVEREIGN...POLICY TREATY 19 WAR/1812. PAGE 115 A2358 — WAR DIPLOM NEUTRAL

B63
ROSNER G.,THE UNITED NATIONS EMERGENCY FORCE. FRANCE ISRAEL UAR UK WOR+45 CREATE WAR PEACE ORD/FREE PWR...INT/LAW JURID HIST/WRIT TIME/SEQ UN. PAGE 124 A2539 — INT/ORG FORCES

B63
RUSSELL B.,UNARMED VICTORY. CHINA/COM CUBA INDIA USA+45 WAR MARXISM...POLICY IDEA/COMP 20 KHRUSH/N COLD/WAR. PAGE 125 A2573 — DIPLOM ATTIT SOCISM ORD/FREE

B63
THUCYDIDES,THE PELOPONESIAN WARS. MEDIT-7 CULTURE INT/ORG NAT/G FORCES TOP/EX PLAN ROUTINE PWR ...CONCPT. PAGE 144 A2938 — ATTIT COERCE WAR

B63
US DEPARTMENT OF THE ARMY,SOVIET RUSSIA: STRATEGIC SURVEY (PAMPHLET). USSR POL/PAR PLAN DOMIN EDU/PROP ARMS/CONT GUERRILLA WAR WEAPON...TREND CHARTS ORG/CHARTS 20. PAGE 152 A3106 — BIBLIOG/A MARXISM DIPLOM COERCE

B63
US DEPARTMENT OF THE ARMY,US OVERSEAS BASES: PRESENT STATUS AND FUTURE PROSPECTS (PAMPHLET). USA+45 DIPLOM NUC/PWR ATTIT ORD/FREE...POLICY CHARTS 20. PAGE 152 A3107 — BIBLIOG/A WAR BAL/PWR DETER

B63
WATKINS K.W.,BRITAIN DIVIDED; THE EFFECT OF THE SPANISH CIVIL WAR ON BRITISH POLITICAL OPINION. SPAIN UK POL/PAR BAL/PWR LOBBY NEUTRAL 20. PAGE 162 A3293 — EDU/PROP WAR POLICY DIPLOM

B63
WEINBERG A.,INSTEAD OF VIOLENCE: WRITINGS BY THE GREAT ADVOCATES OF PEACE AND NONVIOLENCE THROUGHOUT HISTORY. WOR+45 WOR-45 SOCIETY SECT PROB/SOLV DIPLOM GP/REL PERS/REL PEACE...ANTHOL PACIFIST. PAGE 162 A3304 — PACIFISM WAR IDEA/COMP

B63
YOUNG A.N.,CHINA AND THE HELPING HAND. ASIA USA+45 FINAN INDUS ECO/TAC GIVE WEALTH...METH/COMP 20 LEND/LEASE GOLD/STAND. PAGE 169 A3434 — FOR/AID DIPLOM WAR

L63
PHELPS J.,"STUDIES IN DETERRENCE VIII: MILITARY STABILITARY AND ARMS CONTROL: A CRITICAL SURVEY." FUT WOR+45 INT/ORG ACT/RES EDU/PROP COERCE NUC/PWR WAR HEALTH PWR...POLICY TECHNIC TREND SIMUL TOT/POP 20. PAGE 116 A2373 — FORCES ORD/FREE ARMS/CONT DETER

S63
BLOOMFIELD L.P.,"HEADQUARTERS-FIELD RELATIONS: SOME NOTES ON THE BEGINNING AND END OF ONUC." AFR INT/ORG ROUTINE COERCE WAR WEAPON UN CONGO 20. PAGE 16 A0319 — FORCES ORD/FREE

S63
BRZEZINSKI Z.,"SOVIET QUIESCENCE." EUR+WWI USA+45 USSR FORCES CREATE PLAN COERCE DETER WAR ATTIT 20 TREATY EUROPE. PAGE 20 A0415 — DIPLOM ARMS/CONT NUC/PWR AGREE

S63
MEYROWITZ H.,"LES JURISTES DEVANT L'ARME NUCLAIRE." FUT WOR+45 INTELL SOCIETY BAL/PWR DETER WAR...JURID CONCPT 20. PAGE 100 A2058 — ACT/RES ADJUD INT/LAW NUC/PWR

S63
NICHOLAS H.G.,"UN PEACE FORCES AND THE CHANGING GLOBE: THE LESSONS OF SUEZ AND CONGO." FUT WOR+45 CONSTN INT/ORG CONSULT DELIB/GP TOP/EX CREATE DIPLOM DOMIN LEGIT COERCE WAR PERSON RIGID/FLEX PWR UN SUEZ CONGO UNEF 20. PAGE 109 A2229 — ACT/RES FORCES

C63
CHARLETON W.G.,"THE REVOLUTION IN AMERICAN FOREIGN POLICY." COM PROB/SOLV FOR/AID DOMIN COLONIAL NEUTRAL DETER WAR ISOLAT NAT/LISM...BIBLIOG 19/20 UN COLD/WAR NATO. PAGE 26 A0523 — DIPLOM INT/ORG BAL/PWR

N63
PATEL H.M.,THE DEFENCE OF INDIA (PAMPHLET). CHINA/COM INDIA PAKISTAN WOR+45 TEC/DEV BAL/PWR DIPLOM CONTROL WAR. PAGE 114 A2340 — FORCES POLICY SOVEREIGN DETER

B64
ANDREWS D.H.,LATIN AMERICA: A BIBLIOGRAPHY OF PAPERBACK BOOKS. SECT INT/TRADE EDU/PROP WAR GOV/REL ADJUST NAT/LISM ATTIT...ART/METH LING BIOG 20. PAGE 8 A0160 — BIBLIOG L/A+17C CULTURE NAT/G

B64
BAILEY T.A.,A DIPLOMATIC HISTORY OF THE AMERICAN PEOPLE (7TH ED.). USA+45 USA-45 FOR/AID COLONIAL PARL/PROC WAR...CHARTS BIBLIOG/A T 18/20. PAGE 10 A0208 — DIPLOM NAT/G

B64
BELL C.,THE DEBATABLE ALLIANCE. COM UK USA+45 NAT/G FORCES PLAN BAL/PWR NUC/PWR WAR ATTIT...GOV/COMP 20. PAGE 13 A0256 — DIPLOM PWR PEACE POLICY

B64
BLANCHARD C.H.,KOREAN WAR BIBLIOGRAPHY. KOREA FAM BAL/PWR RATION MURDER WEAPON MARXISM...CHARTS 20. PAGE 15 A0306 — BIBLIOG/A WAR DIPLOM FORCES

B64
BOYD J.P.,NUMBER 7: ALEXANDER HAMILTON'S SECRET ATTEMPTS TO CONTROL AMERICAN FOREIGN POLICY. AFR UK DIPLOM WAR RESPECT WEALTH...POLICY HIST/WRIT 18 HAMILTON/A. PAGE 18 A0364 — USA-45 NAT/G TOP/EX PWR

B64
BUTWELL R.,SOUTHEAST ASIA TODAY - AND TOMORROW. NAT/G COLONIAL LEAD REGION WAR CHOOSE WEALTH MARXISM 20. PAGE 23 A0458 — S/ASIA DIPLOM ECO/UNDEV NAT/LISM

B64
CALDER R.,TWO-WAY PASSAGE. INT/ORG TEC/DEV WAR PERSON ORD/FREE 20. PAGE 23 A0467 — FOR/AID ECO/UNDEV ECO/TAC DIPLOM

B64
DEITCHMAN S.J.,LIMITED WAR AND AMERICAN DEFENSE POLICY. USA+45 WOR+45 INT/ORG NAT/G PLAN TEC/DEV COERCE NUC/PWR RIGID/FLEX PWR SKILL...DECISION METH/CNCPT TIME/SEQ TOT/POP COLD/WAR 20. PAGE 36 A0726 — FORCES WAR WEAPON

B64
DEUTSCHE GES AUSWARTIGE POL,STRATEGIE UND ABRUSTUNGSPOLITIK DER SOWJETUNION. USSR TEC/DEV DIPLOM COERCE DETER WEAPON...POLICY PSY 20 ABM/DEFSYS. PAGE 37 A0747 — NUC/PWR WAR FORCES ARMS/CONT

B64
DONOUGHUE B.,BRITISH POLITICS AND THE AMERICAN REVOLUTION: THE PATH TO WAR 1773-75. UK USA-45 — DIPLOM POLICY

NAT/G LEGIS WAR 18 PRE/US/AM. PAGE 38 A0772 COLONIAL REV

B64
DUTT R.P.,THE INTERNATIONALE. COM WOR+45 WOR-45 WORKER CAP/ISM WAR ATTIT...TREND GEN/LAWS 18/20 COM/PARTY. PAGE 40 A0813 ALL/IDEOS INT/ORG MARXIST ORD/FREE

B64
EAYRS J.,THE COMMONWEALTH AND SUEZ: A DOCUMENTARY SURVEY. FRANCE ISLAM VOL/ASSN FORCES CONFER COLONIAL WAR INGP/REL 20 CMN/WLTH SUEZ UN. PAGE 40 A0818 DIPLOM NAT/LISM DIST/IND SOVEREIGN

B64
EHRENBURG I.,THE WAR: 1941-1945 (VOL. V OF "MEN, YEARS - LIFE," TRANS. BY TATIANA SHEBUNINA). GERMANY USSR PRESS WRITING PERS/REL PEACE ANOMIE ATTIT PERSON...CONCPT RECORD BIOG 20 STALIN/J HITLER/A. PAGE 40 A0827 WAR DIPLOM COM MARXIST

B64
EPSTEIN H.M.,REVOLT IN THE CONGO. AFR CONGO/BRAZ WOR+45 NAT/G FORCES DOMIN WAR CIVMIL/REL INGP/REL MARXISM...RECORD GP/COMP 20 CONGO/LEOP UN. PAGE 42 A0856 REV COLONIAL NAT/LISM DIPLOM

B64
ESTHUS R.A.,FROM ENMITY TO ALLIANCE: US AUSTRALIAN RELATIONS. S/ASIA DIST/IND VOL/ASSN FORCES ATTIT 20 AUSTRAL TREATY CMN/WLTH. PAGE 42 A0863 DIPLOM WAR INT/TRADE FOR/AID

B64
FALL B.,STREET WITHOUT JOY. FRANCE USA+45 DIPLOM ECO/TAC FOR/AID GUERRILLA REV WEAPON...TREND 20. PAGE 44 A0894 WAR S/ASIA FORCES COERCE

B64
FINER H.,DULLES OVER SUEZ. FRANCE FUT UAR UK WOR+45 NAT/G PROB/SOLV CONTROL NUC/PWR WAR 20 DULLES/JF SUEZ. PAGE 46 A0932 DIPLOM POLICY REC/INT

B64
FREUD A.,OF HUMAN SOVEREIGNTY. WOR+45 INDUS SECT ECO/TAC CRIME CHOOSE ATTIT MORAL MARXISM...POLICY BIBLIOG 20. PAGE 49 A0998 NAT/LISM DIPLOM WAR PEACE

B64
GRZYBOWSKI K.,THE SOCIALIST COMMONWEALTH OF NATIONS: ORGANIZATIONS AND INSTITUTIONS. FORCES DIPLOM INT/TRADE ADJUD ADMIN LEAD WAR MARXISM SOCISM...BIBLIOG 20 COMECON WARSAW/P. PAGE 58 A1185 INT/LAW COM REGION INT/ORG

B64
JENSEN D.L.,DIPLOMACY AND DOGMATISM. FRANCE SPAIN REV WAR PERSON CATHISM...POLICY BIOG 16. PAGE 74 A1513 DIPLOM ATTIT SECT

B64
JOHNSON E.A.J.,THE DIMENSIONS OF DIPLOMACY. INT/ORG FORCES TEC/DEV WAR PEACE PWR...SOC ANTHOL 20. PAGE 74 A1522 DIPLOM POLICY METH

B64
KAUFMANN W.W.,THE MC NAMARA STRATEGY. TOP/EX INSPECT BAL/PWR DIPLOM CONTROL DETER GUERRILLA NUC/PWR WEAPON COST PWR...METH/COMP 20 MCNAMARA/R KENNEDY/JF JOHNSON/LB NATO DEPT/DEFEN. PAGE 77 A1572 FORCES WAR PLAN PROB/SOLV

B64
KEEP J.,CONTEMPORARY HISTORY IN THE SOVIET MIRROR. COM USSR POL/PAR CREATE DIPLOM AGREE WAR ATTIT ...MYTH TREND ANTHOL 20 COLD/WAR STALIN/J MARX/KARL LENIN/VI. PAGE 77 A1576 HIST/WRIT METH MARXISM IDEA/COMP

B64
KIMMINICH O.,RUSTUNG UND POLITISCHE SPANNUNG. INDUS ARMS/CONT COERCE NAT/LISM PEACE PERSON ORD/FREE ...POLICY GEOG 20. PAGE 79 A1619 DIPLOM FORCES WEAPON WAR

B64
KULSKI W.W.,INTERNATIONAL POLITICS IN A REVOLUTIONARY AGE. NEUTRAL NAT/LISM...POLICY DECISION INT/LAW CONCPT 20 UN. PAGE 83 A1693 DIPLOM WAR NUC/PWR INT/ORG

B64
LATOURETTE K.S.,CHINA. ASIA CHINA/COM FUT USSR ECO/UNDEV ECO/TAC WAR 19/20. PAGE 85 A1744 MARXISM NAT/G POLICY DIPLOM

B64
LENS S.,THE FUTILE CRUSADE. ASIA CHINA/COM L/A+17C USA+45 USSR WOR+45 ECO/DEV BAL/PWR DIPLOM NUC/PWR WAR NAT/LISM PEACE 20 COLD/WAR PRESIDENT CIA. PAGE 87 A1774 ORD/FREE ANOMIE COM MARXISM

B64
LENSEN G.A.,REVELATIONS OF A RUSSIAN DIPLOMAT: THE MEMOIRS OF DMITRII I. ABRIKOSSOV. ASIA MOD/EUR RUSSIA USA-45 ELITES ACADEM CHIEF FORCES REV WAR PWR CONSERVE MARXISM 19/20 ABRIKSSV/D CHINJAP BOLSHEVISM. PAGE 87 A1775 DIPLOM POLICY OBS

B64
LOCKHART W.B.,CASES AND MATERIALS ON CONSTITUTIONAL RIGHTS AND LIBERTIES. USA+45 FORCES LEGIS DIPLOM PRESS CONTROL CRIME WAR PWR...AUD/VIS T WORSHIP 20 NEGRO. PAGE 90 A1849 ORD/FREE CONSTN NAT/G

B64
LUARD E.,THE COLD WAR: A RE-APPRAISAL. FUT USSR WOR+45 FORCES NUC/PWR NAT/LISM ORD/FREE SOVEREIGN ...INT 20 COLD/WAR STALIN/J TREATY UN. PAGE 91 A1870 DIPLOM WAR PEACE TOTALISM

B64
MACKESY P.,THE WAR FOR AMERICA, 1775-1783. UK FORCES DIPLOM...POLICY 18. PAGE 93 A1895 WAR COLONIAL LEAD REV

B64
PERKINS D.,THE AMERICAN DEMOCRACY: ITS RISE TO POWER. ASIA USSR LAW CULTURE FINAN EDU/PROP COLONIAL CHOOSE...POLICY CHARTS BIBLIOG WORSHIP PRESIDENT 15/20 NEGRO. PAGE 115 A2362 LOC/G ECO/TAC WAR DIPLOM

B64
PITTMAN J.,PEACEFUL COEXISTENCE. USSR NAT/G NUC/PWR WAR ATTIT 20. PAGE 116 A2385 DIPLOM PEACE POLICY FORCES

B64
REES D.,KOREA: THE LIMITED WAR. ASIA KOREA WOR+45 NAT/G CIVMIL/REL PERS/REL PERSON...POLICY CHARTS 20 UN TRUMAN/HS MACARTHR/D. PAGE 120 A2455 DIPLOM WAR INT/ORG FORCES

B64
REGALA R.,WORLD PEACE THROUGH DIPLOMACY AND LAW. S/ASIA WOR+45 ECO/UNDEV INT/ORG FORCES PLAN PROB/SOLV FOR/AID NUC/PWR WAR...POLICY INT/LAW 20. PAGE 120 A2456 DIPLOM PEACE ADJUD

B64
ROBERTS HL,FOREIGN AFFAIRS BIBLIOGRAPHY, 1952-1962. ECO/DEV SECT PLAN FOR/AID INT/TRADE ARMS/CONT NAT/LISM ATTIT...INT/LAW GOV/COMP IDEA/COMP 20. PAGE 122 A2495 BIBLIOG/A DIPLOM INT/ORG WAR

B64
ROCK V.P.,A STRATEGY OF INTERDEPENDENCE. COM USSR WOR+45 NAT/G FORCES PROB/SOLV TEC/DEV DETER WAR ORD/FREE...CONCPT NEW/IDEA METH/COMP 20. PAGE 122 A2509 DIPLOM NUC/PWR PEACE POLICY

B64
ROSENAU J.N.,INTERNATIONAL ASPECTS OF CIVIL STRIFE. CHINA/COM CUBA EUR+WWI USA+45 USSR BAL/PWR EDU/PROP NEUTRAL COERCE MORAL...NAT/COMP 20 COLD/WAR UN. PAGE 124 A2533 POLICY DIPLOM REV WAR

B64
SINGH N.,THE DEFENCE MECHANISM OF THE MODERN STATE. COM UK USA+45 CONSTN INT/ORG NUC/PWR WAR INGP/REL ROLE 20 DEPT/DEFEN COMMONWLTH. PAGE 134 A2735 FORCES TOP/EX NAT/G CIVMIL/REL

B64
STANGER R.J.,ESSAYS ON INTERVENTION. PLAN PROB/SOLV BAL/PWR ADJUD COERCE WAR ROLE PWR...INT/LAW CONCPT 20 UN INTERVENT. PAGE 137 A2803 SOVEREIGN DIPLOM POLICY LEGIT

B64
STILLMAN E.O.,THE POLITICS OF HYSTERIA: THE SOURCES OF TWENTIETH-CENTURY CONFLICT. WOR+45 WOR-45 CULTURE ECO/UNDEV PLAN CAP/ISM WAR MARXISM ...PREDICT BIBLIOG 20 COLD/WAR. PAGE 138 A2828 DIPLOM IDEA/COMP COLONIAL CONTROL

B64
THANT U.,TOWARD WORLD PEACE. DELIB/GP TEC/DEV EDU/PROP WAR SOVEREIGN...INT/LAW 20 UN MID/EAST. PAGE 142 A2907 DIPLOM BIOG PEACE COERCE

B64
US AIR FORCE ACADEMY ASSEMBLY,OUTER SPACE: FINAL REPORT APRIL 1-4, 1964. FUT USA+45 WOR+45 LAW DELIB/GP CONFER ARMS/CONT WAR PEACE ATTIT MORAL ...ANTHOL 20 NASA. PAGE 150 A3055 SPACE CIVMIL/REL NUC/PWR DIPLOM

B64
WRIGHT Q.,A STUDY OF WAR. LAW NAT/G PROB/SOLV BAL/PWR NAT/LISM PEACE ATTIT SOVEREIGN...CENSUS SOC/INTEG. PAGE 168 A3419 WAR CONCPT DIPLOM CONTROL

L64
BARROS J.,"THE GREEK-BULGARIAN INCIDENT OF 1925: THE LEAGUE OF NATIONS AND THE GREAT POWERS." BULGARIA EUR+WWI NAT/G FORCES ECO/TAC EDU/PROP LEGIT ROUTINE COERCE WAR PEACE DRIVE PWR...JURID CONCPT METH/CNCPT GEN/LAWS GEN/METH LEAGUE/NAT TOT/POP 20. PAGE 11 A0228 INT/ORG ORD/FREE DIPLOM

S64
"FURTHER READING." INDIA PAKISTAN SECT WAR PEACE ATTIT...POLICY 20. PAGE 3 A0067 BIBLIOG GP/REL DIPLOM NAT/G

S64
COHEN M.,"BASIC PRINCIPLES OF INTERNATIONAL LAW." UNIV WOR+45 WOR-45 BAL/PWR LEGIT ADJUD WAR ATTIT MORAL ORD/FREE PWR...JURID CONCPT MYTH TOT/POP 20. PAGE 27 A0560 INT/ORG INT/LAW

S64
GINSBURGS G.,"WARS OF NATIONAL LIBERATION - THE SOVIET THESIS." COM USSR WOR+45 WOR-45 LAW CULTURE COERCE CONCPT

INT/ORG DIPLOM LEGIT COLONIAL GUERRILLA WAR NAT/LISM ATTIT PERSON MORAL PWR...JURID OBS TREND MARX/KARL 20. PAGE 53 A1075
INT/LAW REV

S64
HOWARD M.,"MILITARY POWER AND INTERNATIONAL ORDER." WOR+45 SOCIETY INT/ORG NAT/G BAL/PWR DOMIN COERCE NUC/PWR WEAPON PWR...NEW/IDEA 20. PAGE 68 A1400
FORCES ATTIT WAR

C64
EASTON S.C.,"THE RISE AND FALL OF WESTERN COLONIALISM." AFR ISLAM L/A+17C ECO/UNDEV REV NAT/LISM...CHARTS BIBLIOG 15/20. PAGE 40 A0817
COLONIAL DIPLOM ORD/FREE WAR

B65
PEACE RESEARCH ABSTRACTS. FUT WOR+45 R+D INT/ORG NAT/G PLAN TEC/DEV BAL/PWR DIPLOM FOR/AID NUC/PWR HEALTH. PAGE 4 A0072
BIBLIOG/A PEACE ARMS/CONT WAR

B65
ADENAUER K.,MEMOIRS 1945-53. EUR+WWI GERMANY/W ECO/DEV CHIEF FORCES ECO/TAC WAR GOV/REL PWR SOVEREIGN 20 NATO ADENAUER/K. PAGE 4 A0088
BIOG DIPLOM NAT/G PERS/REL

B65
ALBRECHT-CARRIE R.,THE MEANING OF THE FIRST WORLD WAR. MOD/EUR USA-45 INT/ORG BAL/PWR PEACE ATTIT LAISSEZ MARXISM...CONCPT BIBLIOG 19/20 LEAGUE/NAT WWI. PAGE 5 A0110
DIPLOM WAR

B65
BRIDGMAN J.,GERMAN AFRICA: A SELECT ANNOTATED BIBLIOGRAPHY. AFR AGRI DIPLOM REPAR WAR FASCISM 20. PAGE 18 A0374
BIBLIOG/A COLONIAL NAT/G EDU/PROP

B65
COLLINS H.,KARL MARX AND THE BRITISH LABOUR MOVEMENT; YEARS OF THE FIRST INTERNATIONAL. FRANCE SWITZERLND UK CAP/ISM WAR...MARXIST IDEA/COMP BIBLIOG 19. PAGE 28 A0567
MARXISM LABOR INT/ORG REV

B65
COWEN Z.,THE BRITISH COMMONWEALTH OF NATIONS IN A CHANGING WORLD. UK ECO/UNDEV INT/ORG ECO/TAC INT/TRADE COLONIAL WAR GP/REL RACE/REL SOVEREIGN SOC/INTEG 20 TREATY EEC COMMONWLTH. PAGE 32 A0644
JURID DIPLOM PARL/PROC NAT/LISM

B65
COX R.H.,THE STATE IN INTERNATIONAL RELATIONS. INT/ORG DIPLOM REV WAR PEACE MARXISM...CONCPT GOV/COMP. PAGE 32 A0647
SOVEREIGN NAT/G FASCISM ORD/FREE

B65
FANON F.,STUDIES IN A DYING COLONIALISM. ALGERIA FRANCE STRATA FAM DIPLOM DOMIN WAR RACE/REL DISCRIM HEALTH 20. PAGE 44 A0897
NAT/LISM COLONIAL REV SOVEREIGN

B65
FRANKLAND N.,THE BOMBING OFFENSIVE AGAINST GERMANY. GERMANY UK TEC/DEV DIPLOM WAR...METH/COMP 20. PAGE 48 A0985
WEAPON PLAN DECISION FORCES

B65
GEORGE M.,THE WARPED VISION. EUR+WWI UK NAT/G POL/PAR LEGIS PARL/PROC SANCTION COERCE WAR GOV/REL PEACE RESPECT 20 CONSRV/PAR. PAGE 52 A1061
LEAD ATTIT DIPLOM POLICY

B65
GILBERT M.,THE EUROPEAN POWERS 1900-45. EUR+WWI ITALY MOD/EUR USSR REV WAR PWR ALL/IDEOS FASCISM ...AUD/VIS CHARTS BIBLIOG 20. PAGE 52 A1069
DIPLOM NAT/G POLICY BAL/PWR

B65
GRAHAM G.S.,THE POLITICS OF NAVAL SUPREMACY; STUDIES IN BRITISH MARITIME ASCENDANCY. UK SEA NAT/G BAL/PWR LEAD WAR WEAPON PEACE...POLICY 18/19 COMMONWLTH. PAGE 55 A1126
FORCES PWR COLONIAL DIPLOM

B65
GRETTON P.,MARITIME STRATEGY - A STUDY OF DEFENSE PROBLEMS. ASIA UK USSR DIPLOM COERCE DETER NUC/PWR WEAPON...CONCPT NAT/COMP 20. PAGE 56 A1147
FORCES PLAN WAR SEA

B65
HART B.H.L.,THE MEMOIRS OF CAPTAIN LIDDELL HART (VOL. I). UK NAT/G PLAN TEC/DEV DIPLOM ADMIN WEAPON GOV/REL PERS/REL ATTIT PWR FASCISM...POLICY 20. PAGE 62 A1274
FORCES BIOG LEAD WAR

B65
JADOS S.S.,DOCUMENTS ON RUSSIAN-AMERICAN RELATIONS: WASHINGTON TO EISENHOWER. USA+45 USA-45 USSR INT/ORG LEGIS INT/TRADE WAR PEACE...ANTHOL BIBLIOG 18/20 PRESIDENT. PAGE 73 A1488
DIPLOM CHIEF CONTROL

B65
KAHN H.,ON ESCALATION; METAPHORS AND SCENARIOS. FORCES DIPLOM ARMS/CONT WAR CIVMIL/REL...INT/LAW 20. PAGE 76 A1548
NUC/PWR ACT/RES INT/ORG ORD/FREE

B65
KIRKWOOD K.,BRITAIN AND AFRICA. AFR UK ECO/UNDEV ECO/TAC WAR NAT/LISM SOVEREIGN 19/20. PAGE 80 A1636
NAT/G DIPLOM POLICY

COLONIAL

B65
LACOUTRE J.,VIETNAM: BETWEEN TWO TRUCES. USA+45 VIETNAM NAT/G REV 20. PAGE 83 A1707
WAR ECO/UNDEV DIPLOM POLICY

B65
LARUS J.,COMPARATIVE WORLD POLITICS. ASIA INDIA WOR+45 WOR-45 BAL/PWR WAR PEACE RATIONAL MORAL PWR ...REALPOL INT/LAW MUSLIM. PAGE 85 A1735
GOV/COMP IDEA/COMP DIPLOM NAT/COMP

B65
LARUS J.,FROM COLLECTIVE SECURITY TO PREVENTIVE DIPLOMACY. FUT FORCES PROB/SOLV DEBATE AGREE COERCE WAR PWR...ANTHOL 20 LEAGUE/NAT UN. PAGE 85 A1736
INT/ORG PEACE DIPLOM ORD/FREE

B65
LEE M.,THE UNITED NATIONS AND WORLD REALITIES. ECO/UNDEV FORCES WAR PEACE ATTIT ROLE WEALTH 20 UN. PAGE 86 A1761
INT/ORG COLONIAL ARMS/CONT DIPLOM

B65
LEVENSTEIN A.,FREEDOM'S ADVOCATE - A TWENTY-FIVE YEAR CHRONICLE. USA+45 POL/PAR LEGIS DIPLOM WAR PEACE TOTALISM DRIVE MARXISM 20 FREEDOM/HS. PAGE 87 A1791
ORD/FREE VOL/ASSN POLICY ATTIT

B65
LOEWENHEIM F.L.,PEACE OR APPEASEMENT? HITLER, CHAMBERLAIN AND THE MUNICH CRISIS. MUNIC DELIB/GP WAR TOTALISM ATTIT SOVEREIGN...TIME/SEQ ANTHOL BIBLIOG 20 HITLER/A CHAMBRLN/N. PAGE 90 A1851
DIPLOM LEAD PEACE

B65
LYONS G.M.,AMERICA: PURPOSE AND POWER. UK USA+45 FINAN INDUS MARKET WORKER TEC/DEV DIPLOM AUTOMAT NUC/PWR WAR RACE/REL ORD/FREE 20 EEC CONGRESS SUPREME/CT CIV/RIGHTS. PAGE 92 A1881
PWR PROB/SOLV ECO/DEV TASK

B65
MALLIN J.,FORTRESS CUBA; RUSSIA'S AMERICAN BASE. COM CUBA L/A+17C FORCES PLAN DIPLOM LEAD REV WAR ...POLICY 20 CASTRO/F GUEVARA/C INTERVENT. PAGE 93 A1914
MARXISM CHIEF GUERRILLA DOMIN

B65
MCSHERRY J.E.,RUSSIA AND THE UNITED STATES UNDER EISENHOWER, KHRUSHCHEV, AND KENNEDY. USSR EX/STRUC TOP/EX PRESS WAR...POLICY TREND 20. PAGE 99 A2024
DIPLOM CHIEF NAT/G PEACE

B65
MORGENTHAU H.,MORGENTHAU DIARY (CHINA) (2 VOLS.). ASIA USA+45 USA-45 LAW DELIB/GP EX/STRUC PLAN FOR/AID INT/TRADE CONFER WAR MARXISM 20 CHINJAP. PAGE 104 A2136
DIPLOM ADMIN

B65
MOSKOWITZ H.,US SECURITY, ARMS CONTROL, AND DISARMAMENT 1961-1965. FORCES DIPLOM DETER WAR WEAPON...CHARTS 20 UN COLD/WAR NATO. PAGE 105 A2154
BIBLIOG/A ARMS/CONT NUC/PWR PEACE

B65
O'CONNELL M.R.,IRISH POLITICS AND SOCIAL CONFLICT IN THE AGE OF THE AMERICAN REVOLUTION. FRANCE IRELAND MOD/EUR STRATA SECT LEGIS DIPLOM INT/TRADE DOMIN REV WAR...BIBLIOG 18 PARLIAMENT. PAGE 111 A2268
CATHISM ATTIT NAT/G DELIB/GP

B65
PANJAB U EXTENSION LIBRARY,INDIAN NEWS INDEX. INDIA ECO/UNDEV INDUS INT/ORG SCHOOL FORCES ADJUD WAR ATTIT WEALTH 20. PAGE 114 A2333
BIBLIOG PRESS WRITING DIPLOM

B65
QURESHI I.H.,THE STRUGGLE FOR PAKISTAN. INDIA PAKISTAN UK CULTURE LEGIS DIPLOM EDU/PROP COLONIAL ATTIT SOVEREIGN 19/20 MUSLIM. PAGE 118 A2429
GP/REL RACE/REL WAR SECT

B65
RANSOM H.H.,AN AMERICAN FOREIGN POLICY READER. USA+45 FORCES EDU/PROP COERCE NUC/PWR WAR PEACE ...DECISION 20. PAGE 119 A2443
NAT/G DIPLOM POLICY

B65
RAPPAPORT A.,ISSUES IN AMERICAN DIPLOMACY: WORLD POWER AND LEADERSHIP SINCE 1895 (VOL. II). CHINA/COM EUR+WWI L/A+17C USA+45 USA-45 NAT/G ECO/TAC DOMIN CONFER LEAD NUC/PWR WEAPON...DECISION 19/20 WILSON/W ROOSEVLT/F CHINJAP. PAGE 119 A2447
WAR POLICY DIPLOM

B65
RUBINSTEIN A.,THE CHALLENGE OF POLITICS: IDEAS AND ISSUES. BAL/PWR COLONIAL WAR TOTALISM ORD/FREE PWR MARXISM SOCISM...INT/LAW 20. PAGE 125 A2561
NAT/G SOVEREIGN DIPLOM NAT/LISM

B65
SCHREIBER H.,TEUTON AND SLAV - THE STRUGGLE FOR CENTRAL EUROPE (TRANS. BY J. CLEUGH). GERMANY POLAND PRUSSIA USSR SOCIETY STRUCT SECT DIPLOM BALTIC. PAGE 129 A2646
GP/REL WAR RACE/REL NAT/LISM

B65
SEABURY P.,BALANCE OF POWER. INT/ORG DETER PEACE ATTIT...INT/LAW. PAGE 131 A2677
BAL/PWR DIPLOM WAR

B65
SOPER T.,EVOLVING COMMONWEALTH. AFR CANADA INDIA IRELAND UK LAW CONSTN POL/PAR DOMIN CONTROL WAR PWR ...AUD/VIS 18/20 COMMONWLTH OEEC. PAGE 135 A2769
INT/ORG COLONIAL VOL/ASSN

B65
THAYER F.C. JR.,AIR TRANSPORT POLICY AND NATIONAL SECURITY: A POLITICAL, ECONOMIC, AND MILITARY ANALYSIS. DIST/IND OP/RES PLAN TEC/DEV DIPLOM DETER WAR COST EFFICIENCY...POLICY BIBLIOG 20 DEPT/DEFEN FAA CAB. PAGE 142 A2908
AIR FORCES CIVMIL/REL ORD/FREE

B65
US LIBRARY OF CONGRESS,RARE BOOKS DIVISION: GUIDE TO ITS COLLECTION AND SERVICES. LOC/G SECT WAR. PAGE 155 A3158
BIBLIOG/A NAT/G DIPLOM

B65
VON GLAHN G.,LAW AMONG NATIONS: AN INTRODUCTION TO PUBLIC INTERNATIONAL LAW. WOR+45 WOR-45 INT/ORG NAT/G CREATE ADJUD WAR...GEOG CLASSIF TREND BIBLIOG. PAGE 160 A3250
ACADEM INT/LAW GEN/LAWS LAW

B65
WARBEY W.,VIETNAM: THE TRUTH. FRANCE S/ASIA USA+45 VIETNAM CULTURE INT/ORG NAT/G DIPLOM FOR/AID EDU/PROP ARMS/CONT PEACE 20 TREATY NLF UN. PAGE 161 A3274
WAR AGREE

B65
WASKOW A.I.,KEEPING THE WORLD DISARMED. AFR GERMANY/E DIPLOM CONTROL WAR 20 UN. PAGE 161 A3289
ARMS/CONT PEACE FORCES PROB/SOLV

B65
WINT G.,COMMUNIST CHINA'S CRUSADE: MAO'S ROAD TO POWER AND THE NEW CAMPAIGN FOR WORLD REVOLUTION. ASIA CHINA/COM USA+45 USSR NAT/G POL/PAR DOMIN COERCE WAR PWR...POLICY CHARTS IDEA/COMP BIBLIOG 20 MAO. PAGE 165 A3364
DIPLOM MARXISM REV COLONIAL

L65
TUCKER R.W.,"PEACE AND WAR." UNIV CULTURE SOCIETY INT/ORG NAT/G ACT/RES DOMIN DETER WAR ATTIT DISPL ...POLICY CONCPT MYTH GEN/LAWS 20. PAGE 145 A2975
PWR COERCE ARMS/CONT PEACE

S65
"FURTHER READING." INDIA ADMIN COLONIAL WAR GOV/REL ATTIT 20. PAGE 3 A0069
BIBLIOG DIPLOM NAT/G POLICY

S65
PRABHAKAR P.,"SURVEY OF RESEARCH AND SOURCE MATERIALS; THE SINO-INDIAN BORDER DISPUTE." CHINA/COM INDIA LAW NAT/G PLAN BAL/PWR WAR...POLICY 20 COLD/WAR. PAGE 117 A2404
BIBLIOG ASIA S/ASIA DIPLOM

S65
RAY H.,"THE POLICY OF RUSSIA TOWARDS SINO-INDIAN CONFLICT." ASIA CHINA/COM COM INDIA USSR NAT/G TOP/EX FOR/AID EDU/PROP NEUTRAL COERCE PEACE RIGID/FLEX PWR...METH/CNCPT TIME/SEQ VAL/FREE 20. PAGE 120 A2452
S/ASIA ATTIT DIPLOM WAR

C65
MARK M.,"BEYOND SOVEREIGNTY." WOR+45 WOR-45 ECO/UNDEV BAL/PWR INT/TRADE NUC/PWR REV WAR MARXISM NEW/LIB BIBLIOG. PAGE 95 A1942
NAT/LISM NAT/G DIPLOM INTELL

C65
SCHWEBEL M.,"BEHAVIORAL SCIENCE AND HUMAN SURVIVAL." FORCES ARMS/CONT COERCE NUC/PWR WAR GP/REL NAT/LISM PERCEPT...POLICY PSY ANTHOL BIBLIOG/A 20 COLD/WAR. PAGE 130 A2662
PEACE ACT/RES DIPLOM HEAL

C65
US AIR FORCE ACADEMY,"AMERICAN DEFENSE POLICY." COM INT/ORG TEC/DEV FOR/AID ARMS/CONT DETER NUC/PWR ...POLICY DECISION CONCPT ANTHOL BIBLIOG/A 20 COLD/WAR NATO. PAGE 149 A3054
PLAN FORCES WAR COERCE

C65
WUORINEN J.H.,"SCANDINAVIA." DENMARK FINLAND ICELAND NORWAY SWEDEN SOCIETY AGRI POL/PAR DELIB/GP DIPLOM INT/TRADE NEUTRAL WAR...CHARTS TREATY 20. PAGE 168 A3423
BIBLIOG NAT/G POLICY

B66
SUPPLEMENTAL FOREIGN ASSISTANCE FISCAL YEAR 1966: VIETNAM. CHINA/COM COM S/ASIA USA+45 VIETNAM EXTR/IND FINAN DIPLOM TAX GUERRILLA HABITAT ORD/FREE...STAT CHARTS 20 SENATE PRESIDENT. PAGE 4 A0077
CONFER LEGIS WAR FOR/AID

B66
AMERICAN FRIENDS SERVICE COMM,PEACE IN VIETNAM: A NEW APPROACH IN SOUTHEAST ASIA: A REPORT. ASIA S/ASIA USA+45 VIETNAM ORD/FREE 20 TREATY. PAGE 7 A0149
PEACE WAR NAT/LISM DIPLOM

B66
BERNSTEIN B.J.,THE TRUMAN ADMINISTRATION. WOR+45 LABOR POL/PAR LEGIS DIPLOM NUC/PWR WAR ATTIT ...POLICY 20 TRUMAN/HS. PAGE 14 A0279
LEAD TOP/EX NAT/G

B66
BIRMINGHAM D.,TRADE AND CONFLICT IN ANGOLA. PORTUGAL CULTURE FORCES DIPLOM GP/REL PROFIT HABITAT NAT/COMP. PAGE 14 A0291
WAR INT/TRADE ECO/UNDEV COLONIAL

B66
BROWN J.F.,THE NEW EASTERN EUROPE. ALBANIA BULGARIA HUNGARY POLAND ROMANIA CULTURE AGRI POL/PAR WAR NAT/LISM MARXISM...CHARTS BIBLIOG 20. PAGE 20 A0404
DIPLOM COM NAT/G ECO/UNDEV

B66
BRYNES A.,WE GIVE TO CONQUER. USA+45 USSR STRATA ECO/UNDEV INT/ORG NAT/G DIPLOM DRIVE...TREND IDEA/COMP 20. PAGE 20 A0414
FOR/AID CONTROL GIVE WAR

B66
CANFIELD L.H.,THE PRESIDENCY OF WOODROW WILSON: PRELUDE TO A WORLD IN CRISIS. USA-45 ADJUD NEUTRAL WAR CHOOSE INGP/REL PEACE ORD/FREE 20 WILSON/W PRESIDENT TREATY LEAGUE/NAT. PAGE 24 A0477
PERSON POLICY DIPLOM GOV/REL

B66
CLARK G.,WORLD PEACE THROUGH WORLD LAW; TWO ALTERNATIVE PLANS. WOR+45 DELIB/GP FORCES TAX CONFER ADJUD SANCTION ARMS/CONT WAR CHOOSE PRIVIL 20 UN COLD/WAR. PAGE 27 A0541
INT/LAW PEACE PLAN INT/ORG

B66
CLAUSEWITZ C.V.,ON WAR (VOL. III). UNIV EDU/PROP ...POLICY DECISION METH 18/20. PAGE 27 A0548
WAR FORCES PLAN CIVMIL/REL

B66
COPLIN W.D.,THE FUNCTIONS OF INTERNATIONAL LAW. WOR+45 ECO/DEV ECO/UNDEV ADJUD COLONIAL WAR OWN SOVEREIGN...POLICY GEN/LAWS 20. PAGE 30 A0611
INT/LAW DIPLOM INT/ORG

B66
COYLE D.C.,THE UNITED NATIONS AND HOW IT WORKS. ECO/UNDEV DELIB/GP BAL/PWR EDU/PROP ARMS/CONT NUC/PWR WAR 20 UN. PAGE 32 A0648
INT/ORG PEACE DIPLOM INT/TRADE

B66
CRAIG G.A.,WAR, POLITICS, AND DIPLOMACY. PRUSSIA CONSTN FORCES CIVMIL/REL TOTALISM PWR 19/20 BISMARCK/O DULLES/JF NAPOLEON/B. PAGE 32 A0654
WAR DIPLOM BAL/PWR

B66
DAENIKER G.,STRATEGIE DES KLEIN STAATS. SWITZERLND ACT/RES CREATE DIPLOM NEUTRAL DETER WAR WEAPON PWR SOVEREIGN...IDEA/COMP 20 COLD/WAR. PAGE 33 A0673
NUC/PWR PLAN FORCES NAT/G

B66
DOUMA J.,BIBLIOGRAPHY ON THE INTERNATIONAL COURT INCLUDING THE PERMANENT COURT, 1918-1964. WOR+45 WOR-45 DELIB/GP WAR PRIVIL...JURID NAT/COMP 20 UN LEAGUE/NAT. PAGE 38 A0780
BIBLIOG/A INT/ORG CT/SYS DIPLOM

B66
DYCK H.V.,WEIMAR GERMANY AND SOVIET RUSSIA 1926-1933. EUR+WWI GERMANY UK USSR ECO/TAC INT/TRADE NEUTRAL WAR ATTIT 20 WEIMAR/REP TREATY. PAGE 40 A0814
DIPLOM GOV/REL POLICY

B66
ESTHUS R.A.,THEODORE ROOSEVELT AND JAPAN. ASIA USA-45 FORCES CONFER WAR SOVEREIGN...BIBLIOG 20 CHINJAP. PAGE 42 A0864
DIPLOM DELIB/GP

B66
EUBANK K.,THE SUMMIT CONFERENCES. EUR+WWI USA+45 USA-45 MUNIC BAL/PWR WAR PEACE PWR...POLICY AUD/VIS 20 GENEVA/CON TEHERAN YALTA POTSDAM. PAGE 43 A0872
CONFER NAT/G CHIEF DIPLOM

B66
EUDIN X.J.,SOVIET FOREIGN POLICY 1928-34: DOCUMENTS AND MATERIALS (VOL. I). ASIA USSR WOR-45 INT/ORG POL/PAR WORKER WAR PEACE...ANTHOL 20 TREATY LEAGUE/NAT INTERVENT. PAGE 43 A0873
DIPLOM POLICY GOV/REL MARXISM

B66
EWING B.G.,PEACE THROUGH NEGOTIATION: THE AUSTRIAN EXPERIENCE. AUSTRIA USSR VIETNAM CONFER CONTROL DETER WAR ATTIT HEALTH PWR...POLICY 20. PAGE 43 A0878
PEACE DIPLOM MARXISM

B66
EWING L.L.,THE REFERENCE HANDBOOK OF THE ARMED FORCES OF THE WORLD. WOR+45 ECO/TAC FOR/AID COERCE WAR PWR 20. PAGE 43 A0879
FORCES STAT DIPLOM PLAN

B66
FALL B.B.,VIET-NAM WITNESS, 1953-66. S/ASIA VIETNAM SECT PROB/SOLV COLONIAL GUERRILLA...CHARTS BIBLIOG 20. PAGE 44 A0895
MARXIST WAR DIPLOM

B66
FEHRENBACH T.R.,THIS KIND OF PEACE. WOR+45 LEAD PARTIC WAR EFFICIENCY ATTIT UN. PAGE 44 A0906
PEACE DIPLOM INT/ORG BAL/PWR

B66
FREIDEL F.,AMERICAN ISSUES IN THE TWENTIETH CENTURY. SOCIETY FINAN ECO/TAC FOR/AID CONTROL NUC/PWR WAR RACE/REL PEACE ATTIT...ANTHOL T 20 WILSON/W ROOSEVLT/F KENNEDY/JF TRUMAN/HS. PAGE 49 A0995
DIPLOM POLICY NAT/G ORD/FREE

B66
GARNER W.R.,THE CHACO DISPUTE; A STUDY OF PRESTIGE DIPLOMACY. L/A+17C PARAGUAY USA-45 INT/ORG AGREE PEACE...TIME/SEQ 20 BOLIV LEAGUE/NAT ARGEN
WAR DIPLOM CONCPT

CHACO/WAR. PAGE 51 A1050
PWR

B66
GERARD-LIBOIS J.,KATANGA SECESSION. INT/ORG FORCES DIPLOM ADMIN CONTROL WAR CHOOSE PWR...CHARTS 20 KATANGA TSHOMBE/M UN. PAGE 52 A1062
NAT/G REGION ORD/FREE REV

B66
GLAZER M.,THE FEDERAL GOVERNMENT AND THE UNIVERSITY. CHILE PROB/SOLV DIPLOM GIVE ADMIN WAR ...POLICY SOC 20. PAGE 53 A1079
BIBLIOG/A NAT/G PLAN ACADEM

B66
GRAHAM I.C.C.,PUBLICATIONS OF THE SOCIAL SCIENCE DEPARTMENT, THE RAND CORPORATION, 1948-1966. USSR WOR+45 NAT/G ARMS/CONT DETER WAR NAT/LISM...SOC GOV/COMP. PAGE 55 A1127
BIBLIOG DIPLOM NUC/PWR FORCES

B66
GRENVILLE J.A.S.,POLITICS, STRATEGY, AND AMERICAN DEMOCRACY: STUDIES IN FOREIGN POLICY, 1873-1917. CUBA PHILIPPINE SPAIN USA-45 VENEZUELA ELITES NAT/G CREATE PARTIC WAR RIGID/FLEX ORD/FREE...DECISION TREND 19/20 HAWAII. PAGE 56 A1146
DIPLOM COLONIAL POLICY

B66
GROSS F.,WORLD POLITICS AND TENSION AREAS. CHINA/COM SOMALIA VENEZUELA COERCE GP/REL RACE/REL ATTIT HABITAT 19/20 CASEBOOK NEWYORK/C. PAGE 57 A1173
DIPLOM WAR PROB/SOLV

B66
GUPTA S.,KASHMIR - A STUDY IN INDIA-PAKISTAN RELATIONS. INDIA KASHMIR PAKISTAN CONSTN INT/ORG REV RACE/REL NAT/LISM 20 UN MUSLIM/LG. PAGE 58 A1194
DIPLOM GP/REL SOVEREIGN WAR

B66
HALPERIN M.H.,CHINA AND NUCLEAR PROLIFERATION (PAMPHLET). CHINA/COM FUT INDIA USA+45 USSR ARMS/CONT WAR 20 CHINJAP. PAGE 60 A1239
NUC/PWR FORCES POLICY DIPLOM

B66
HAYER T.,FRENCH AID. AFR FRANCE AGRI FINAN BUDGET ADMIN WAR PRODUC...CHARTS 18/20 THIRD/WRLD OVRSEA/DEV. PAGE 63 A1295
TEC/DEV COLONIAL FOR/AID ECO/UNDEV

B66
HERZ M.F.,BEGINNINGS OF THE COLD WAR. COM POLAND USA+45 USSR INT/ORG NAT/G CHIEF FOR/AID DOMIN CONFER AGREE WAR PEACE 20 STALIN/J COLD/WAR UN. PAGE 64 A1321
DIPLOM

B66
HORMANN K.,PEACE AND MODERN WAR IN THE JUDGEMENT OF THE CHURCH. INT/ORG FORCES EDU/PROP ATTIT 20. PAGE 67 A1384
PEACE WAR CATH MORAL

B66
INTL ATOMIC ENERGY AGENCY,INTERNATIONAL CONVENTIONS ON CIVIL LIABILITY FOR NUCLEAR DAMAGE. FUT WOR+45 ADJUD WAR COST PEACE SOVEREIGN...JURID 20. PAGE 71 A1462
DIPLOM INT/ORG DELIB/GP NUC/PWR

B66
KNORR K.E.,ON THE USES OF MILITARY POWER IN THE NUCLEAR AGE. WOR+45 INT/ORG TEC/DEV ADMIN CONTROL WAR COST 20. PAGE 81 A1656
FORCES DIPLOM DETER NUC/PWR

B66
KUENNE R.E.,THE POLARIS MISSILE STRIKE* A GENERAL ECONOMIC SYSTEMS ANALYSIS. USA+45 USSR NAT/G BAL/PWR ARMS/CONT WAR...MATH PROBABIL COMPUT/IR CHARTS HYPO/EXP SIMUL. PAGE 82 A1689
NUC/PWR FORCES DETER DIPLOM

B66
LONG B.,THE WAR DIARY OF BRECKINRIDGE LONG: SELECTIONS FROM THE YEARS 1939-1944. USA-45 INT/ORG FORCES FOR/AID CHOOSE 20. PAGE 91 A1859
DIPLOM WAR DELIB/GP

B66
LUARD E.,THE EVOLUTION OF INTERNATIONAL ORGANIZATIONS. UK WOR+45 BUDGET INT/TRADE WAR BAL/PAY PEACE ORD/FREE...POLICY 19/20 EEC ILO LEAGUE/NAT UN. PAGE 91 A1871
INT/ORG EFFICIENCY CREATE TREND

B66
LYND S.,THE OTHER SIDE. USA+45 VIETNAM/N NAT/G PEACE SOVEREIGN 20. PAGE 92 A1877
WAR POLICY MORAL DIPLOM

B66
MARTIN L.W.,DIPLOMACY IN MODERN EUROPEAN HISTORY. EUR+WWI MOD/EUR INT/ORG NAT/G EX/STRUC ROUTINE WAR PEACE TOTALISM PWR 15/20 COLD/WAR EUROPE/W. PAGE 95 A1953
DIPLOM POLICY

B66
MAYER P.,THE PACIFIST CONSCIENCE. SECT CREATE ARMS/CONT WAR RACE/REL ATTIT LOVE...ANTHOL PACIFIST WORSHIP FREUD/S GANDHI/M LAO/TZU KING/MAR/L CONSCN/OBJ. PAGE 97 A1984
DIPLOM PACIFISM SUPEGO

B66
MCNAIR A.D.,THE LEGAL EFFECTS OF WAR. UK FINAN DIPLOM ORD/FREE 20 ENGLSH/LAW. PAGE 98 A2019
JURID WAR INT/TRADE LABOR

B66
OBERMANN E.,VERTEIDIGUNG PER FREIHEIT. GERMANY/W WOR+45 INT/ORG COERCE NUC/PWR WEAPON MARXISM 20 UN NATO WARSAW/P TREATY. PAGE 111 A2273
FORCES ORD/FREE WAR PEACE

B66
VON BORCH H.,FRIEDE TROTZ KRIEG. GERMANY USSR WOR+45 PEACE ANOMIE ATTIT 20. PAGE 112 A2305
DIPLOM NUC/PWR WAR COERCE

B66
PAN S.,VIETNAM CRISIS. ASIA FRANCE USA+45 USA-45 VIETNAM CULTURE SOCIETY INT/ORG ECO/TAC AGREE CONTROL WAR MARXISM 20. PAGE 113 A2325
ECO/UNDEV POLICY DIPLOM NAT/COMP

B66
RISTIC D.N.,YUGOSLAVIA'S REVOLUTION OF 1941. EUR+WWI YUGOSLAVIA NAT/G WAR ORD/FREE...RECORD BIBLIOG 20 HITLER/A TREATY. PAGE 121 A2484
REV ATTIT FASCISM DIPLOM

B66
SALTER L.M.,RESOLUTION OF INTERNATIONAL CONFLICT. USA+45 INT/ORG SECT DIPLOM ECO/TAC FOR/AID DETER NUC/PWR WAR 20. PAGE 127 A2595
PROB/SOLV PEACE INT/LAW POLICY

B66
SCHWARZ U.,AMERICAN STRATEGY: A NEW PERSPECTIVE. USA+45 USA-45 INT/ORG TEC/DEV BAL/PWR DIPLOM LEAD ARMS/CONT DETER NUC/PWR WAR 20 NATO. PAGE 130 A2659
NAT/G POLICY FORCES PWR

B66
SINGER L.,ALLE LITTEN AN GROSSENWAHN: VON WOODROW WILSON BIS MAO TSE-TUNG. ASIA UK USSR INT/ORG DELIB/GP BAL/PWR DOMIN ATTIT PERSON 20 WILSON/W ROOSEVLT/F. PAGE 133 A2731
DIPLOM TOTALISM WAR CHIEF

B66
SMITH D.M.,AMERICAN INTERVENTION, 1917. GERMANY UK USA-45 SEA FORCES DIPLOM INT/TRADE EDU/PROP COERCE WEAPON PEACE 20 WILSON/W WWI. PAGE 134 A2746
WAR ATTIT POLICY NEUTRAL

B66
SOBEL L.A.,SOUTH VIETNAM: US-COMMUNIST CONFRONTATION IN SOUTHEAST ASIA 1961-65. VIETNAM FOR/AID CROWD DETER REV PEACE...GEOG 20 INTERVENT DIEM COLD/WAR. PAGE 134 A2754
WAR TIME/SEQ FORCES NAT/G

B66
SPEARS E.L.,TWO MEN WHO SAVED FRANCE: PETAIN AND DE GAULLE. FRANCE CONSTN FORCES DIPLOM WAR PERSON 20 WWI PETAIN/HP DEGAULLE/C. PAGE 135 A2773
BIOG LEAD CHIEF NAT/G

B66
STADLER K.R.,THE BIRTH OF THE AUSTRIAN REPUBLIC, 1918-1921. AUSTRIA PLAN TASK PEACE...POLICY DECISION 20. PAGE 137 A2798
NAT/G DIPLOM WAR DELIB/GP

B66
THORNTON A.P.,THE IMPERIAL IDEA AND ITS ENEMIES. UK WOR+45 WOR-45 NAT/G PLAN DOMIN CONTROL WAR ATTIT PWR...TREND CHARTS 19/20 CMN/WLTH. PAGE 144 A2937
COLONIAL DIPLOM

B66
TYSON G.,NEHRU: THE YEARS OF POWER. INDIA UK STRATA ECO/UNDEV FINAN SECT TASK WAR ORD/FREE MARXISM ...POLICY BIBLIOG 20 NEHRU/J. PAGE 146 A2985
CHIEF PWR DIPLOM NAT/G

B66
US DEPARTMENT OF STATE,RESEARCH ON THE MIDDLE EAST (EXTERNAL RESEARCH LIST NO 4-25). GREECE ISRAEL SYRIA UAR YEMEN CULTURE SOCIETY POL/PAR SECT DIPLOM EDU/PROP WAR NAT/LISM...GEOG GOV/COMP 20. PAGE 152 A3096
BIBLIOG/A ISLAM NAT/G REGION

B66
US DEPARTMENT OF THE ARMY,SOUTH ASIA: A STRATEGIC SURVEY (PAMPHLET NO. 550-3). AFGHANISTN INDIA NEPAL PAKISTAN ECO/UNDEV INT/ORG POL/PAR FORCES FOR/AID INT/TRADE LEAD WAR...POLICY SOC TREND 20. PAGE 152 A3110
BIBLIOG/A S/ASIA DIPLOM NAT/G

B66
US HOUSE COMM GOVT OPERATIONS,AN INVESTIGATION OF THE US ECONOMIC AND MILITARY ASSISTANCE PROGRAMS IN VIETNAM. USA+45 VIETNAM/S SOCIETY CONSTRUC FINAN FORCES BUDGET INT/TRADE PEACE HEALTH...MGT HOUSE/REP AID. PAGE 154 A3139
FOR/AID ECO/UNDEV WAR INSPECT

B66
US SENATE COMM ON FOREIGN REL,UNITED STATES POLICY TOWARD EUROPE (AND RELATED MATTERS). COM EUR+WWI GERMANY PROB/SOLV REGION NUC/PWR WAR NAT/LISM PEACE PWR...NAT/COMP 20 NATO CONGRESS DEGAULLE/C. PAGE 156 A3184
DIPLOM INT/ORG POLICY WOR+45

B66
VAN DYKE V.,INTERNATIONAL POLITICS. WOR+45 ECO/DEV ECO/UNDEV INT/ORG BAL/PWR AGREE ARMS/CONT NAT/LISM PEACE PWR...INT/LAW 20 TREATY UN. PAGE 158 A3212
DIPLOM NAT/G WAR SOVEREIGN

B66
VIEN N.C.,SEEKING THE TRUTH. FRANCE VIETNAM AGRI ADMIN WAR...BIOG 20 BAO/DAI INTERVENT. PAGE 159
NAT/G CONSULT

A3231 CONSTN

B66
WEINSTEIN F.B.,VIETNAM'S UNHELD ELECTIONS: THE FAILURE TO CARRY OUT THE 1956 REUNIFICATION ELECTIONS... (MONOGRAPH). VIETNAM/S VIETNAM/N LEGIT CONFER ADJUD WAR PEACE 20 TREATY GENEVA/CON UNIFICA. PAGE 162 A3306
AGREE NAT/G CHOOSE DIPLOM

B66
WILSON H.A.,THE IMPERIAL POLICY OF SIR ROBERT BORDEN. CANADA UK ELITES INT/ORG VOL/ASSN CONTROL LEAD WAR ROLE 20 CMN/WLTH BORDEN/R. PAGE 165 A3360
INGP/REL COLONIAL CONSTN CHIEF

B66
ZEINE Z.N.,THE EMERGENCE OF ARAB NATIONALISM (REV. ED.). TURKEY UK NAT/G SECT TEC/DEV LEAD REV WAR AGE/Y ROLE ORD/FREE...TRADIT CHARTS BIBLIOG 20 ARABS OTTOMAN. PAGE 170 A3451
ISLAM NAT/LISM DIPLOM

B66
ZISCHKA A.,WAR ES EIN WUNDER? GERMANY/W ECO/DEV FINAN LG/CO BARGAIN CAP/ISM FOR/AID RATION 20 MARSHL/PLN. PAGE 170 A3456
ECO/TAC INT/TRADE INDUS WAR

S66
DINH TRANS V.A.N.,"VIETNAM: A THIRD WAY" S/ASIA USA+45 USSR VIETNAM VIETNAM/S NAT/G SECT FORCES CAP/ISM DIPLOM COLONIAL NEUTRAL MARXISM SOCISM 20 BUDDHISM UNIFICA. PAGE 38 A0766
WAR PLAN ORD/FREE SOCIALIST

S66
FRIEND A.,"THE MIDDLE EAST CRISIS" COM ISLAM ISRAEL SYRIA UAR USA+45 USSR FORCES PLAN FOR/AID CONTROL ORD/FREE PWR...SOCIALIST TIME/SEQ 20 NASSER/G. PAGE 49 A1009
WAR INT/ORG DIPLOM PEACE

S66
MCNEAL R.H.,"THE LEGACY OF THE COMINTERN." USSR WOR+45 WOR-45 PROB/SOLV DIPLOM CONFER CONTROL LEAD WAR 20 STALIN/J COMINTERN. PAGE 98 A2020
MARXISM INT/ORG POL/PAR PWR

S66
SHERMAN M.,"GUARANTEES AND NUCLEAR SPREAD." USA+45 WOR+45 INT/ORG PLAN DETER WAR ORD/FREE 20 NATO. PAGE 132 A2700
DIPLOM POLICY NAT/G NUC/PWR

C66
DUROSELLE J.B.,"LE CONFLIT DE TRIESTE 1943-1954: ETUDES DE CAS DE CONFLITS INTERNATIONAUX III." ITALY USA+45 YUGOSLAVIA ELITES DELIB/GP PLAN ADJUST ...POLICY GEOG CHARTS IDEA/COMP TIME 20 TREATY UN COLD/WAR. PAGE 40 A0810
BIBLIOG WAR DIPLOM GEN/LAWS

C66
TARLING N.,"A CONCISE HISTORY OF SOUTHEAST ASIA." BURMA CAMBODIA LAOS S/ASIA THAILAND VIETNAM ECO/UNDEV POL/PAR FORCES ADMIN REV WAR CIVMIL/REL ORD/FREE MARXISM SOCISM 13/20. PAGE 141 A2890
COLONIAL DOMIN INT/TRADE NAT/LISM

B67
ADAMS A.E.,AN ATLAS OF RUSSIAN AND EAST EUROPEAN HISTORY. CHRIST-17C COM MOD/EUR INDUS SECT FORCES DIPLOM COLONIAL REV WAR 4/20. PAGE 4 A0086
CHARTS REGION TREND

B67
ANDREATTA L.,VIETNAM, A CHECKLIST. S/ASIA VIETNAM PRESS PEACE ATTIT...POLICY 20. PAGE 8 A0159
BIBLIOG DIPLOM WAR

B67
BURNS E.L.M.,MEGAMURDER. WOR+45 LAW INT/ORG NAT/G BAL/PWR DIPLOM DETER MURDER WEAPON CIVMIL/REL PEACE ...INT/LAW TREND 20. PAGE 22 A0444
FORCES PLAN WAR NUC/PWR

B67
CECIL L.,ALBERT BALLIN; BUSINESS AND POLITICS IN IMPERIAL GERMANY 1888-1918. GERMANY UK INT/TRADE LEAD WAR PERS/REL ADJUST PWR WEALTH...MGT BIBLIOG 19/20. PAGE 25 A0510
DIPLOM CONSTN ECO/DEV TOP/EX

B67
CHO S.S.,KOREA IN WORLD POLITICS 1940-1950; AN EVALUATION OF AMERICAN RESPONSIBILITY. KOREA USA+45 USSR CONSTN INT/ORG NAT/G FORCES FOR/AID ANOMIE SUPEGO MARXISM...DECISION BIBLIOG 20. PAGE 26 A0533
POLICY DIPLOM PROB/SOLV WAR

B67
DILLARD D.,ECONOMIC DEVELOPMENT OF THE NORTH ATLANTIC COMMUNITY. EUR+WWI MOD/EUR USA+45 USA-45 ECO/UNDEV LABOR CAP/ISM WAR BAL/PAY...NAT/COMP 15/20. PAGE 37 A0763
ECO/DEV INT/TRADE INDUS DIPLOM

B67
FINE S.,RECENT AMERICA* CONFLICTING INTERPRETATIONS OF THE GREAT ISSUES (2ND ED.). USA+45 USA-45 POL/PAR SECT CONFER NUC/PWR WAR ATTIT...POLICY TREND ANTHOL PRESIDENT 20. PAGE 46 A0931
IDEA/COMP DIPLOM NAT/G

B67
HALPERIN M.H.,CONTEMPORARY MILITARY STRATEGY. ASIA CHINA/COM USA+45 USSR INT/ORG FORCES ACT/RES PLAN TEC/DEV BAL/PWR COERCE WAR...METH/COMP BIBLIOG 20 NATO. PAGE 60 A1240
DIPLOM NUC/PWR DETER ARMS/CONT

B67
HOLSTI K.J.,INTERNATIONAL POLITICS* A FRAMEWORK FOR ANALYSIS. WOR+45 WOR-45 NAT/G EDU/PROP DETER WAR WEAPON PWR BIBLIOG. PAGE 67 A1372
DIPLOM BARGAIN POLICY INT/LAW

B67
KATZ R.,DEATH IN ROME. EUR+WWI ITALY POL/PAR DIPLOM LEAD ATTIT PERSON ROLE CATHISM. PAGE 77 A1570
WAR MURDER FORCES DEATH

B67
KNOLES G.H.,THE RESPONSIBILITIES OF POWER, 1900-1929. USA-45 SOCIETY SECT JUDGE COLONIAL REPRESENT WEALTH POPULISM...IDEA/COMP ANTHOL PRESIDENT 20 LEAGUE/NAT. PAGE 81 A1653
PWR DIPLOM NAT/LISM WAR

B67
LAWYERS COMM AMER POLICY VIET,VIETNAM AND INTERNATIONAL LAW: AN ANALYSIS OF THE LEGALITY OF THE US MILITARY INVOLVEMENT. VIETNAM LAW INT/ORG COERCE WEAPON PEACE ORD/FREE 20 UN SEATO TREATY. PAGE 86 A1753
INT/LAW DIPLOM ADJUD WAR

B67
MAZRUI A.A.,TOWARDS A PAX AFRICANA. AFR STRUCT ECO/UNDEV NAT/G DIPLOM COLONIAL REGION WAR ATTIT 20. PAGE 97 A1988
PEACE FORCES PROB/SOLV SOVEREIGN

B67
MCCLINTOCK R.,THE MEANING OF LIMITED WAR. FUT WOR+45 NAT/G FORCES GUERRILLA REV...POLICY SAMP/SIZ TREND NAT/COMP 45 COLD/WAR. PAGE 97 A1999
WAR NUC/PWR BAL/PWR DIPLOM

B67
MCNELLY T.,SOURCES IN MODERN EAST ASIAN HISTORY AND POLITICS. KOREA VIETNAM CULTURE DIPLOM COLONIAL REV WAR PWR ALL/IDEOS MARXISM...ANTHOL 20 CHINJAP. PAGE 99 A2023
NAT/COMP ASIA S/ASIA SOCIETY

B67
RALSTON D.B.,THE ARMY OF THE REPUBLIC; THE PLACE OF THE MILITARY IN THE POLITICAL EVOLUTION OF FRANCE 1871-1914. FRANCE MOD/EUR EX/STRUC LEGIS TOP/EX DIPLOM ADMIN WAR GP/REL ROLE...BIBLIOG 19/20. PAGE 119 A2436
FORCES NAT/G CIVMIL/REL POLICY

B67
RUSSELL B.,WAR CRIMES IN VIETNAM. USA+45 VIETNAM FORCES DIPLOM WEAPON RACE/REL DISCRIM ISOLAT BIO/SOC 20 COLD/WAR RUSSELL/B. PAGE 126 A2574
WAR CRIME ATTIT POLICY

B67
SALISBURY H.E.,BEHIND THE LINES - HANOI. VIETNAM/N NAT/G GUERRILLA CIVMIL/REL NAT/LISM KNOWL 20. PAGE 126 A2592
WAR PROB/SOLV DIPLOM OBS

B67
SCOTT A.M.,THE FUNCTIONING OF THE INTERNATIONAL POLITICAL SYSTEM. INT/ORG OP/RES PROB/SOLV COERCE WAR EQUILIB...METH/CNCPT BIBLIOG. PAGE 130 A2671
DIPLOM DECISION BAL/PWR

B67
SINGER D.,QUANTITATIVE INTERNATIONAL POLITICS* INSIGHTS AND EVIDENCE. WOR+45 WOR-45 PARTIC WAR INGP/REL ATTIT PERSON ROLE...PREDICT BIBLIOG 19/20 UN SENATE. PAGE 133 A2722
DIPLOM NAT/G INT/ORG DECISION

B67
TEITELBAUM L.M.,WOODROW WILSON AND THE MEXICAN REVOLUTION 1913-1916: A HISTORY OF UNITED STATES-MEXICAN RELATIONS. USA-45 CHIEF TOP/EX WAR 20 MEXIC/AMER WILSON/W VILLA/P CARRANZA/V. PAGE 142 A2902
REV DIPLOM

B67
THORNE C.,THE APPROACH OF WAR, 1938-1939. EUR+WWI POL/PAR CHIEF FORCES LEAD DRIVE PWR FASCISM ...BIBLIOG/A 20 HITLER/A. PAGE 144 A2936
DIPLOM WAR ELITES

B67
US DEPARTMENT OF STATE,TREATIES IN FORCE. USA+45 WOR+45 AGREE WAR PEACE 20 TREATY. PAGE 152 A3101
BIBLIOG DIPLOM INT/ORG DETER

B67
US SENATE COMM ON FOREIGN REL,BACKGROUND INFORMATION RELATING TO SOUTHEAST ASIA AND VIETNAM (3RD REV. ED.). USA+45 VIETNAM/S VIETNAM/N...CHARTS 20 SENATE UN. PAGE 156 A3188
DIPLOM WAR FOR/AID

B67
US SUPERINTENDENT OF DOCUMENTS,LIBRARY OF CONGRESS (PRICE LIST 83). AFR ASIA EUR+WWI USA-45 USSR NAT/G DIPLOM CONFER CT/SYS WAR...DECISION PHIL/SCI CLASSIF 19/20 CONGRESS PRESIDENT. PAGE 157 A3205
BIBLIOG/A USA+45 AUTOMAT LAW

B67
WILLIS F.R.,DE GAULLE: ANACHRONISM, REALIST, OR PROPHET? FRANCE POL/PAR FORCES DIPLOM WAR PEACE ROLE ORD/FREE...POLICY IDEA/COMP ANTHOL 20 DEGAULLE/C. PAGE 165 A3356
BIOG PERSON CHIEF LEAD

L67
GENEVEY P.,"LE DESARMEMENT APRES LE TRAITE DE VERSAILLES." EUR+WWI GERMANY INT/ORG PROB/SOLV CONFER WAR...POLICY PREDICT 20. PAGE 52 A1057
ARMS/CONT PEACE DIPLOM FORCES

L67
MOORE N.,"THE LAWFULNESS OF MILITARY ASSISTANCE TO THE REPUBLIC OF VIET NAM." USA+45 VIETNAM WOR+45 FOR/AID DOMIN DETER WAR WEAPON...DECISION INT/LAW 20 UN. PAGE 103 A2123
PWR DIPLOM FORCES GOV/REL

S67
BATOR V.,"ONE WAR* TWO VIETNAMS." S/ASIA VIETNAM DIPLOM SUFF ATTIT ORD/FREE 20. PAGE 12 A0234
WAR BAL/PWR NAT/G STRUCT

S67
BELGION M.,"THE CASE FOR REHABILITATING MARSHAL PETAIN." EUR+WWI FRANCE NAT/G DIPLOM ATTIT PERSON MORAL PETAIN/HP. PAGE 12 A0253
WAR FORCES LEAD

S67
BENTLEY E.,"VIETNAM: THE STATE OF OUR FEELINGS." USA+45 VIETNAM PROB/SOLV DIPLOM GP/REL INGP/REL RACE/REL WEALTH. PAGE 13 A0271
WAR PARTIC ATTIT PEACE

S67
COHN K.,"CRIMES AGAINST HUMANITY." GERMANY INT/ORG SANCTION ATTIT ORD/FREE...MARXIST CRIMLGY 20 UN. PAGE 28 A0564
WAR INT/LAW CRIME ADJUD

S67
FRANKEL M.,"THE WAR IN VIETNAM." VIETNAM ECO/UNDEV DIPLOM CONFER INGP/REL PEACE PWR...POLICY PREDICT 20. PAGE 48 A0982
WAR COERCE PLAN GUERRILLA

S67
FRANKLIN W.O.,"CLAUSEWITZ ON LIMITED WAR." VIETNAM WOR+45 WOR-45 PROB/SOLV DIPLOM ECO/TAC DOMIN COLONIAL...METH/COMP 19/20. PAGE 48 A0986
COERCE WAR PLAN GUERRILLA

S67
KAHN H.,"CRITERIA FOR LONG-RANGE NUCLEAR CONTROL POLICIES." WOR+45 INT/ORG TEC/DEV DOMIN DETER WAR WEAPON ISOLAT ORD/FREE POLICY. PAGE 76 A1549
NUC/PWR ARMS/CONT BAL/PWR DIPLOM

S67
KIPP K.,"DIE POLITISCHE BEDEUTUNG DER 'GEGENKUSTE' DARGESTELLT AM BEISPIEL DER USA IM 20. JAHRHUNDERT" USA+45 USA-45 SEA NAT/G CONTROL COERCE WAR...POLICY GEOG 20. PAGE 79 A1629
FORCES ORD/FREE DIPLOM DETER

S67
LIVNEH E.,"A NEW BEGINNING." ISRAEL USSR WOR+45 NAT/G DIPLOM INGP/REL FEDERAL HABITAT PWR...GEOG PSY JEWS. PAGE 90 A1847
WAR PERSON PEACE PLAN

S67
NEUCHTERLEIN D.E.,"THAILAND* ANOTHER VIETNAM?" THAILAND ECO/UNDEV DIPLOM ADMIN REGION CENTRAL NAT/LISM...POLICY 20. PAGE 108 A2220
WAR GUERRILLA S/ASIA NAT/G

S67
REINTANZ G.,"THE SPACE TREATY." WOR+45 DIPLOM CONTROL ARMS/CONT NUC/PWR WAR...MARXIST 20 COLD/WAR UN TREATY. PAGE 120 A2461
SPACE INT/LAW INT/ORG PEACE

S67
SENCOURT R.,"FOREIGN POLICY* AN HISTORIC RECTIFICATION." EUR+WWI UK DIPLOM EDU/PROP LEAD WAR CHOOSE PERS/REL...METH/COMP PARLIAMENT. PAGE 131 A2685
POLICY POL/PAR NAT/G

S67
SHARP G.,"THE NEED OF A FUNCTIONAL SUBSTITUTE FOR WAR." FUT UNIV WOR+45 CULTURE SOCIETY INT/ORG CONSULT DELIB/GP ACT/RES CREATE BAL/PWR CONFER ARMS/CONT NUC/PWR 20. PAGE 132 A2696
PEACE WAR DIPLOM PROB/SOLV

S67
SHOEMAKER R.L.,"JAPANESE ARMY AND THE WEST." ASIA ELITES EX/STRUC DIPLOM DOMIN EDU/PROP COERCE ATTIT AUTHORIT PWR 1/20 CHINJAP. PAGE 132 A2703
FORCES TEC/DEV WAR TOTALISM

S67
STEELE R.,"A TASTE FOR INTERVENTION." USA+45 FOR/AID INT/TRADE EDU/PROP COLONIAL WAR PWR...TREND 20 COLD/WAR. PAGE 137 A2812
POLICY DIPLOM DOMIN ATTIT

S67
SUINN R.M.,"THE DISARMAMENT FANTASY* PSYCHOLOGICAL FACTORS THAT MAY PRODUCE WARFARE." DIPLOM RISK ARMS/CONT DETER ANOMIE PERSON GAME. PAGE 140 A2860
DECISION NUC/PWR WAR PSY

S67
SYRKIN M.,"I.F. STONE RECONSIDERS ISRAEL." ISRAEL WOR+45 DIPLOM NAT/LISM HABITAT...POLICY GEOG JEWS. PAGE 141 A2875
ISLAM WAR ATTIT MORAL

S67
TERRILL R.,"THE SIEGE MENTALITY." CHINA/COM NAT/G FORCES DIPLOM REV EFFICIENCY NAT/LISM MARXISM ...TREND 20. PAGE 142 A2904
EDU/PROP WAR DOMIN

S67
VERBA S.,"PUBLIC OPINION AND THE WAR IN VIETNAM." USA+45 VIETNAM DIPLOM WAR...CORREL STAT QU CHARTS 20. PAGE 158 A3228
ATTIT KNO/TEST NAT/G PLAN

S67
WILLIAMS B.H.,"FREEDOM AS A SLOGAN IN INTERNATIONAL CONFLICT." VIETNAM DIPLOM COLONIAL. PAGE 164 A3351
EDU/PROP ORD/FREE WAR PWR

S67
YEFROMEV A.,"THE TRUE FACE OF THE WEST GERMAN NATIONAL-DEMOCRATS." GERMANY/W NAT/G DOMIN LEAD SANCTION WAR ATTIT PERSON...MARXIST 20. PAGE 169 A3433
POL/PAR TOTALISM PARL/PROC DIPLOM

C67
HUDSON G.F.,"THE HARD AND BITTER PEACE; WORLD POLITICS SINCE 1945." ASIA COM S/ASIA USSR WOR+45 COLONIAL WAR...TREND BIBLIOG/A 20 COLD/WAR UN. PAGE 68 A1405
DIPLOM INT/ORG ARMS/CONT BAL/PWR

C67
LING D.L.,"TUNISIA: FROM PROTECTORATE TO REPUBLIC." CULTURE NAT/G POL/PAR CHIEF DIPLOM COERCE WAR PWR ...BIBLIOG 19/20 TUNIS. PAGE 89 A1825
AFR NAT/LISM COLONIAL PROB/SOLV

C67
SPANIER J.W.,"WORLD POLITICS IN AN AGE OF REVOLUTION." COM WOR+45 FORCES COERCE WAR NAT/LISM SOVEREIGN...POLICY BIBLIOG 20. PAGE 135 A2772
DIPLOM TEC/DEV REV ECO/UNDEV

C83
BURKE E.,"RESOLUTIONS FOR CONCILIATION WITH AMERICA" (1775), IN E. BURKE, COLLECTED WORKS, VOL. 2." UK USA-45 FORCES INT/TRADE TARIFFS TAX SANCTION PEACE...POLICY 18 PRE/US/AM. PAGE 21 A0436
COLONIAL WAR SOVEREIGN ECO/TAC

B86
MAS LATRIE L.,RELATIONS ET COMMERCE DE L'AFRIQUE SEPTENTRIONALE OU MAGREB AVEC LES NATIONS CHRETIENNES AU MOYEN AGE. CULTURE CHIEF FORCES WAR ...SOC CENSUS TREATY 10/16. PAGE 95 A1954
ISLAM SECT DIPLOM INT/TRADE

C93
PLAYFAIR R.L.,"A BIBLIOGRAPHY OF MOROCCO." MOROCCO CULTURE AGRI FORCES DIPLOM WAR HEALTH...GEOG JURID SOC CHARTS. PAGE 116 A2387
BIBLIOG ISLAM MEDIT-7

B98
GRIFFIN A.P.C.,LIST OF BOOKS RELATING TO CUBA (PAMPHLET). CUBA L/A+17C USA-45 INT/TRADE DOMIN WAR GP/REL ALL/VALS...GEOG SOC CHARTS 19/20. PAGE 56 A1158
BIBLIOG/A NAT/G COLONIAL

B99
BROOKS S.,BRITAIN AND THE BOERS. AFR SOUTH/AFR UK CULTURE INSPECT LEGIT...INT/LAW 19/20 BOER/WAR. PAGE 19 A0396
WAR DIPLOM NAT/G

WAR/TRIAL....WAR TRIAL; SEE ALSO NUREMBERG

B49
JACKSON R.H.,INTERNATIONAL CONFERENCE ON MILITARY TRIALS. FRANCE GERMANY UK USA+45 USSR VOL/ASSN DELIB/GP REPAR ADJUD CT/SYS CRIME WAR 20 WAR/TRIAL. PAGE 72 A1479
DIPLOM INT/ORG INT/LAW CIVMIL/REL

WAR/1812....WAR OF 1812

B55
PERKINS B.,THE FIRST RAPPROCHEMENTS: ENGLAND AND THE UNITED STATES, 1795-1805. UK USA-45 ATTIT ...HIST/WRIT BIBLIOG 18/19 MADISON/J WAR/1812. PAGE 115 A2357
DIPLOM COLONIAL WAR

B63
PERKINS B.,PROLOGUE TO THE WAR: ENGLAND AND THE UNITED STATES, 1805-1812. MOD/EUR UK USA-45 NAT/G ORD/FREE RESPECT SOVEREIGN...POLICY TREATY 19 WAR/1812. PAGE 115 A2358
WAR DIPLOM NEUTRAL

WARBEY W. A3274

WARBURG J.P. A3275,A3276,A3277

WARD B. A3278,A3279

WARD C. A3280

WARD P.W. A3281

WARD R.E. A3282

WARD....SEE LOC/G, POL/PAR

WARD/LEST....LESTER WARD

WARE E.E. A3283

WARNER D. A3284

WARREN S. A3285,A3286

WARRN/EARL....EARL WARREN

WARSAW PACT....SEE WARSAW/PCT

WARSAW....WARSAW, POLAND

WARSAW/PCT....WARSAW PACT TREATY ORGANIZATION

S61
KRANNHALS H.V.,"COMMAND INTEGRATION WITHIN THE WARSAW PACT." COM USSR WOR+45 DELIB/GP EDU/PROP ...CONCPT AUD/VIS CHARTS COLD/WAR TOT/POP VAL/FREE 20 TREATY WARSAW/P. PAGE 82 A1675
INT/ORG FORCES TOTALISM

B64
GRZYBOWSKI K.,THE SOCIALIST COMMONWEALTH OF NATIONS: ORGANIZATIONS AND INSTITUTIONS. FORCES DIPLOM INT/TRADE ADJUD ADMIN LEAD WAR MARXISM SOCISM...BIBLIOG 20 COMECON WARSAW/P. PAGE 58 A1185
INT/LAW COM REGION INT/ORG

B64
KIS T.I.,LES PAYS DE L'EUROPE DE L'EST: LEURS RAPPORTS MUTUELS ET LE PROBLEME DE LEUR INTEGRATION DANS L'ORBITE DE L'USSR. EUR+WWI RUSSIA USSR INT/ORG NAT/G REV ATTIT...JURID SOC BIBLIOG WARSAW/P COMECON EUROPE/E. PAGE 80 A1638
DIPLOM COM MARXISM REGION

B66
INTL CONF ON WORLD POLITICS-5,EASTERN EUROPE IN TRANSITION. EUR+WWI USSR ECO/TAC NAT/LISM ATTIT SOVEREIGN...CHARTS ANTHOL 20 TREATY WARSAW/P. PAGE 71 A1463
COM NAT/COMP MARXISM DIPLOM

B66
OBERMANN E.,VERTEIDIGUNG PER FREIHEIT. GERMANY/W WOR+45 INT/ORG COERCE NUC/PWR WEAPON MARXISM 20 UN NATO WARSAW/P TREATY. PAGE 111 A2273
FORCES ORD/FREE WAR PEACE

S67
STEEL R.,"BEYOND THE POWER BLOCS." USA+45 USSR ECO/UNDEV NEUTRAL NUC/PWR NAT/LISM ATTIT...GEOG NATO WARSAW/P COLD/WAR. PAGE 137 A2811
DIPLOM TREND BAL/PWR PLAN

WASHBURN A.M. A3287

WASHING/BT....BOOKER T. WASHINGTON

WASHING/DC....WASHINGTON, D.C.

B55
JONES J.M.,THE FIFTEEN WEEKS (FEBRUARY 21-JUNE 5, 1947). EUR+WWI USA+45 PROB/SOLV BAL/PWR...POLICY TIME/SEQ 20 COLD/WAR MARSHL/PLN TRUMAN/HS WASHING/DC. PAGE 75 A1532
DIPLOM ECO/TAC FOR/AID

WASHINGT/G....PRESIDENT GEORGE WASHINGTON

WASHINGTON....WASHINGTON, STATE OF

WASKOW A.I. A3288,A3289

WASP....WHITE-ANGLO-SAXON-PROTESTANT ESTABLISHMENT

WASSENBERGH H.A. A3290

WATANABE H. A3282

WATER POLLUTION....SEE POLLUTION

WATER....PERTAINING TO ALL NON-SALT WATER

WATERS M. A3291

WATKINS J.T. A3292

WATKINS K.W. A3293

WATT D.C. A3294

WATTS....WATTS, CALIFORNIA

WCC....WORLD COUNCIL CHURCHES

WCTU....WOMAN'S CHRISTIAN TEMPERANCE UNION

WEALTH....ACCESS TO GOODS AND SERVICES (ALSO POVERTY)

B
UN DEPARTMENT SOCIAL AFFAIRS,SOCIAL WELFARE INFORMATION SERIES: CURRENT LITERATURE AND NATIONAL CONFERENCES. WOR+45 INDUS SERV/IND INT/ORG CONSULT ACT/RES WEALTH...HEAL UN. PAGE 147 A2997
BIBLIOG/A SOC/WK DIPLOM ADMIN

N
INTERNATIONAL STUDIES. ASIA S/ASIA WOR+45 ECO/UNDEV INT/ORG NAT/G LEAD ATTIT WEALTH...SOC 20. PAGE 1 A0012
BIBLIOG/A DIPLOM INT/LAW INT/TRADE

N
TURNER R.K.,BIBLIOGRAPHY ON WORLD ORGANIZATION. INT/TRADE CT/SYS ARMS/CONT WEALTH...INT/LAW 20. PAGE 146 A2984
BIBLIOG/A INT/ORG PEACE WAR

B00
MOCKLER-FERRYMAN A.,BRITISH WEST AFRICA. FRANCE GERMANY NIGER SIER/LEONE UK CULTURE DIPLOM WAR RACE/REL PRODUC PROFIT WEALTH...POLICY PREDICT 19. PAGE 102 A2095
AFR COLONIAL INT/TRADE CAP/ISM

L00
HISTORICUS,"LETTERS AND SOME QUESTIONS OF INTERNATIONAL LAW." FRANCE NETHERLAND UK USA-45 WOR-45 LAW NAT/G COERCE...SOC CONCPT GEN/LAWS TOT/POP 19 CIVIL/WAR. PAGE 65 A1344
WEALTH JURID WAR INT/LAW

B03
MOREL E.D.,THE BRITISH CASE IN FRENCH CONGO. CONGO/BRAZ FRANCE UK COERCE MORAL WEALTH...POLICY INT/LAW 20 CONGO/LEOP. PAGE 104 A2130
DIPLOM INT/TRADE COLONIAL AFR

B09
FREMANTLE H.E.S.,THE NEW NATION, A SURVEY OF THE CONDITION AND PROSPECTS OF SOUTH AFRICA. SOUTH/AFR CONSTN POL/PAR DIPLOM DOMIN COLONIAL WEALTH...SOC TREND 19. PAGE 49 A0996
NAT/LISM SOVEREIGN RACE/REL REGION

N19
BENTHAM J.,A PLAN FOR AN UNIVERSAL AND PERPETUAL PEACE (1838) (PAMPHLET). NAT/G FORCES BAL/PWR INT/TRADE ADMIN AGREE CT/SYS ARMS/CONT SOVEREIGN WEALTH GEN/LAWS. PAGE 13 A0269
INT/ORG INT/LAW PEACE COLONIAL

N19
KUWAIT ARABIA,KUWAIT FUND FOR ARAB ECONOMIC DEVELOPMENT (PAMPHLET). ISLAM KUWAIT UAR ECO/UNDEV LEGIS ECO/TAC WEALTH 20. PAGE 83 A1697
FOR/AID DIPLOM FINAN ADMIN

N19
LANGE O.R.,"DISARMAMENT ECONOMIC GROWTH AND INTERNATIONAL CO-OPERATION" (PAMPHLET). WOR+45 DIST/IND PLAN INT/TRADE GIVE TASK DETER WEALTH SOCISM 18/19 BOLIVAR/S. PAGE 84 A1723
ARMS/CONT DIPLOM ECO/DEV ECO/UNDEV

N19
SALKEVER L.R.,SUB-SAHARA AFRICA (PAMPHLET). AFR USSR EXTR/IND NAT/G SCHOOL DIPLOM COLONIAL WEALTH ...GEOG CHARTS 16/20. PAGE 127 A2594
ECO/UNDEV TEC/DEV TASK INT/TRADE

N19
TAYLOR T.G.,CANADA'S ROLE IN GEOPOLITICS (PAMPHLET). CANADA FUT USSR COLONIAL REGION WEALTH ...CHARTS 20. PAGE 142 A2901
GEOG DIPLOM SOCIETY ECO/DEV

B20
WOOLF L.,EMPIRE AND COMMERCE IN AFRICA. EUR+WWI MOD/EUR FINAN INDUS MARKET INT/ORG PLAN COERCE ATTIT DRIVE PWR WEALTH...CONCPT TIME/SEQ TREND CHARTS 20. PAGE 167 A3394
AFR DOMIN COLONIAL SOVEREIGN

B32
HANSEN A.H.,ECONOMIC STABILIZATION IN AN UNBALANCED WORLD. COM EUR+WWI USA-45 WOR-45 AGRI FINAN INDUS MARKET INT/ORG LABOR VOL/ASSN EDU/PROP ATTIT HEALTH KNOWL WEALTH...HIST/WRIT TREND VAL/FREE 20. PAGE 61 A1253
NAT/G ECO/DEV CAP/ISM SOCISM

B32
WRIGHT Q.,GOLD AND MONETARY STABILIZATION. FUT USA-45 WOR-45 INTELL ECO/DEV INT/ORG NAT/G CONSULT PLAN ECO/TAC ADMIN ATTIT WEALTH...CONCPT TREND 20. PAGE 167 A3404
FINAN POLICY

B33
OHLIN B.,INTERREGIONAL AND INTERNATIONAL TRADE. USA-45 WOR-45 CULTURE FINAN MARKET CONSULT PLAN ECO/TAC ATTIT WEALTH...CONCPT MATH TOT/POP 20. PAGE 111 A2285
INT/ORG ECO/DEV INT/TRADE REGION

B34
LOVELL R.I.,THE STRUGGLE FOR SOUTH AFRICA, 1875-1899. GERMANY RHODESIA SOUTH/AFR UK NAT/G ECO/TAC HABITAT WEALTH...POLICY 19. PAGE 91 A1866
COLONIAL DIPLOM WAR GP/REL

B35
SIMONDS F.H.,THE GREAT POWERS IN WORLD POLITICS. FRANCE GERMANY UK WOR-45 INT/ORG NAT/G ARMS/CONT PEACE FASCISM...POLICY GEOG 20 DEPRESSION NAZI. PAGE 133 A2718
DIPLOM WEALTH WAR

B36
ROBINSON H.,DEVELOPMENT OF THE BRITISH EMPIRE. WOR-45 CULTURE SOCIETY STRUCT ECO/DEV ECO/UNDEV INT/ORG VOL/ASSN FORCES CREATE PLAN DOMIN EDU/PROP ADMIN COLONIAL PWR WEALTH...POLICY GEOG CHARTS CMN/WLTH 16/20. PAGE 122 A2503
NAT/G HIST/WRIT UK

B37
BLAKE J.W.,EUROPEAN BEGINNINGS IN WEST AFRICA 1454-1578. FRANCE GUINEA PORTUGAL UK PWR WEALTH 16/16 AFRICA/W. PAGE 15 A0305
DIPLOM COLONIAL INT/TRADE DOMIN

B37
ROBBINS L.,ECONOMIC PLANNING AND INTERNATIONAL ORDER. WOR-45 SOCIETY FINAN INDUS NAT/G ECO/TAC ROUTINE WEALTH...SOC TIME/SEQ GEN/METH WORK 20 KEYNES/JM. PAGE 122 A2492
INT/ORG PLAN INT/TRADE

B37
VINER J.,STUDIES IN THE THEORY OF INTERNATIONAL TRADE. WOR-45 CONSTN ECO/DEV AGRI INDUS MARKET INT/ORG LABOR NAT/G ECO/TAC TARIFFS COLONIAL ATTIT
CAP/ISM INT/TRADE

WEALTH...POLICY CONCPT MATH STAT OBS SAMP TREND GEN/LAWS MARX/KARL 20. PAGE 159 A3236

B38
COLBY C.C.,GEOGRAPHICAL ASPECTS OF INTERNATIONAL RELATIONS. WOR-45 ECO/DEV ECO/UNDEV AGRI EXTR/IND INDUS MARKET R+D INT/ORG NAT/G TEC/DEV ECO/TAC INT/TRADE NAT/LISM WEALTH...METH/CNCPT CHARTS GEN/LAWS 20. PAGE 28 A0565 — PLAN GEOG DIPLOM

B38
FRANKEL S.H.,CAPITAL INVESTMENT IN AFRICA. AFR EUR+WWI RHODESIA SOUTH/AFR UK FINAN FOR/AID COLONIAL DEMAND UTIL WEALTH...METH/CNCPT CHARTS 20 CONGO/LEOP. PAGE 48 A0983 — ECO/UNDEV EXTR/IND DIPLOM PRODUC

B38
SAINT-PIERRE C.I.,SCHEME FOR LASTING PEACE (TRANS. BY H. BELLOT). INDUS NAT/G CHIEF FORCES INT/TRADE CT/SYS WAR PWR SOVEREIGN WEALTH...POLICY 18. PAGE 126 A2587 — INT/ORG PEACE AGREE INT/LAW

B39
FURNIVALL J.S.,NETHERLANDS INDIA. INDIA NETHERLAND CULTURE INDUS NAT/G DIPLOM ADMIN WEALTH...POLICY CHARTS 17/20. PAGE 50 A1029 — COLONIAL ECO/UNDEV SOVEREIGN PLURISM

B39
ROBBINS L.,ECONOMIC CAUSES OF WAR. WOR-45 ECO/DEV ECO/UNDEV INT/ORG NAT/G TEC/DEV DIPLOM DOMIN COLONIAL ATTIT DRIVE PWR WEALTH...POLICY CONCPT OBS SAMP TREND CON/ANAL GEN/LAWS MARX/KARL 20. PAGE 122 A2493 — COERCE ECO/TAC WAR

B39
STALEY E.,WORLD ECONOMY IN TRANSITION. WOR-45 SOCIETY INT/ORG PROF/ORG ECO/TAC ATTIT WEALTH ...METH/CNCPT TREND GEN/LAWS 20. PAGE 137 A2800 — TEC/DEV INT/TRADE

B39
THOMAS J.A.,THE HOUSE OF COMMONS, 1832-1901; A STUDY OF ITS ECONOMIC AND FUNCTIONAL CHARACTER. UK LAW STRATA FINAN DIPLOM CONTROL LEAD LOBBY REPRESENT WEALTH...POLICY STAT BIBLIOG 19/20 PARLIAMENT. PAGE 143 A2922 — PARL/PROC LEGIS POL/PAR ECO/DEV

B39
ZIMMERN A.,MODERN POLITICAL DOCTRINE. WOR-45 CULTURE SOCIETY ECO/UNDEV DELIB/GP EX/STRUC CREATE DOMIN COERCE NAT/LISM ATTIT RIGID/FLEX ORD/FREE PWR WEALTH...POLICY CONCPT OBS TIME/SEQ TREND TOT/POP LEAGUE/NAT 20. PAGE 170 A3454 — NAT/G ECO/TAC BAL/PWR INT/TRADE

B41
KEESING F.M.,THE SOUTH SEAS IN THE MODERN WORLD. INDONESIA STRUCT FAM SECT EDU/PROP LEAD INCOME WEALTH...HEAL SOC 20. PAGE 77 A1577 — CULTURE ECO/UNDEV GOV/COMP DIPLOM

B44
MACIVER R.M.,TOWARDS AN ABIDING PEACE. USA-45 ECO/TAC EDU/PROP DRIVE ORD/FREE PWR WEALTH...CONCPT TIME/SEQ GEN/METH TOT/POP 20. PAGE 92 A1890 — INT/ORG PEACE INT/LAW

B44
RAGATZ L.J.,LITERATURE OF EUROPEAN IMPERIALISM. ECO/TAC INT/TRADE DOMIN GOV/REL DEMAND NAT/LISM PWR WEALTH 19/20. PAGE 119 A2432 — BIBLIOG COLONIAL INT/ORG ECO/UNDEV

B45
HILL N.,CLAIMS TO TERRITORY IN INTERNATIONAL LAW AND RELATIONS. WOR-45 NAT/G DOMIN EDU/PROP LEGIT REGION ROUTINE ORD/FREE PWR WEALTH...GEOG INT/LAW JURID 20. PAGE 65 A1332 — INT/ORG ADJUD SOVEREIGN

B47
BROOKINGS INST.,MAJOR PROBLEMS OF UNITED STATES FOREIGN POLICY. USA+45 WOR+45 STRUCT ECO/DEV ECO/UNDEV INT/ORG NAT/G POL/PAR VOL/ASSN DELIB/GP FORCES ECO/TAC LEGIT COERCE ORD/FREE PWR WEALTH ...POLICY STAT TREND CHARTS TOT/POP. PAGE 19 A0392 — ACT/RES DIPLOM

B47
DE HUSZAR G.B.,PERSISTENT INTERNATIONAL ISSUES. WOR+45 WOR-45 AGRI INDUS INT/ORG PROB/SOLV EFFICIENCY WEALTH...CON/ANAL ANTHOL UN. PAGE 35 A0704 — DIPLOM PEACE ECO/TAC FOR/AID

B47
GORDON D.L.,THE HIDDEN WEAPON: THE STORY OF ECONOMIC WARFARE. EUR+WWI USA-45 LAW FINAN INDUS NAT/G CONSULT FORCES PLAN DOMIN PWR WEALTH ...INT/LAW CONCPT OBS TOT/POP NAZI 20. PAGE 54 A1112 — INT/ORG ECO/TAC INT/TRADE WAR

B47
TOWLE L.W.,INTERNATIONAL TRADE AND COMMERCIAL POLICY. WOR+45 LAW ECO/DEV FINAN INDUS NAT/G ECO/TAC WEALTH...TIME/SEQ ILO 20. PAGE 144 A2955 — MARKET INT/ORG INT/TRADE

B48
CHURCHILL W.,THE GATHERING STORM. UK WOR-45 INT/ORG NAT/G FORCES TOP/EX DIPLOM ECO/TAC COERCE ATTIT ORD/FREE PWR WEALTH...POLICY SELF/OBS RECORD NAZI PARLIAMENT 20. PAGE 26 A0538 — BIOG

B48
GRAHAM F.D.,THE THEORY OF INTERNATIONAL VALUES. FUT WOR+45 WOR-45 ECO/DEV FINAN INT/ORG PLAN TEC/DEV CAP/ISM DIPLOM ECO/TAC TARIFFS ROUTINE BAL/PAY DRIVE PWR WEALTH SOCISM...POLICY STAT HYPO/EXP GEN/LAWS 20. PAGE 55 A1125 — NEW/IDEA INT/TRADE

B48
VISSON A.,AS OTHERS SEE US. EUR+WWI FRANCE UK USA+45 CULTURE INTELL SOCIETY STRATA NAT/G POL/PAR FOR/AID ATTIT DRIVE LOVE ORD/FREE RESPECT WEALTH ...PLURIST SOC OBS TOT/POP 20. PAGE 159 A3244 — USA-45 PERCEPT

B49
FORD FOUNDATION,REPORT OF THE STUDY FOR THE FORD FOUNDATION ON POLICY AND PROGRAM. SOCIETY R+D ACT/RES CAP/ISM FOR/AID EDU/PROP ADMIN KNOWL ...POLICY PSY SOC 20. PAGE 47 A0961 — WEALTH GEN/LAWS

B49
OGBURN W.,TECHNOLOGY AND INTERNATIONAL RELATIONS. WOR+45 WOR-45 ECO/DEV CREATE PLAN ECO/TAC EDU/PROP COERCE PWR SKILL WEALTH...TECHNIC PSY SOC NEW/IDEA CHARTS TOT/POP 20. PAGE 111 A2283 — TEC/DEV DIPLOM INT/ORG

B50
CHURCHILL W.,TRIUMPH AND TRAGEDY. UK WOR-45 INT/ORG NAT/G DELIB/GP FORCES TOP/EX DIPLOM COERCE CHOOSE ATTIT ORD/FREE PWR WEALTH...SELF/OBS CHARTS NAZI 20. PAGE 26 A0539 — BIOG PEACE WAR

B50
CORNELL U DEPT ASIAN STUDIES,SOUTHEAST ASIA PROGRAM DATA PAPER. BURMA CAMBODIA INDONESIA MALAYSIA VIETNAM SOCIETY STRUCT NAT/G SECT DIPLOM FOR/AID PWR WEALTH...SOC 20. PAGE 31 A0625 — BIBLIOG/A CULTURE S/ASIA ECO/UNDEV

B50
LEVI W.,FUNDAMENTALS OF WORLD ORGANIZATION. WOR+45 WOR-45 CULTURE ECO/TAC GIVE RECEIVE PERSON WEALTH ...METH/COMP 19/20 UN LEAGUE/NAT. PAGE 88 A1793 — INT/ORG PEACE ORD/FREE DIPLOM

B50
US DEPARTMENT OF STATE,POINT FOUR: COOPERATIVE PROGRAM FOR AID IN THE DEVELOPMENT OF ECONOMICALLY UNDERDEVELOPED AREAS. WOR+45 AGRI INDUS INT/ORG PLAN TEC/DEV DIPLOM EDU/PROP ADMIN PEACE PRODUC WEALTH 20 CONGRESS UN. PAGE 151 A3085 — ECO/UNDEV FOR/AID FINAN INT/TRADE

L51
MANGONE G.,"THE IDEA AND PRACTICE OF WORLD GOVERNMENT." FUT WOR+45 WOR-45 ECO/DEV LEGIS CREATE LEGIT ROUTINE ATTIT MORAL PWR WEALTH...CONCPT GEN/LAWS 20. PAGE 94 A1920 — INT/ORG SOCIETY INT/LAW

C51
BEST H.,"THE SOVIET STATE AND ITS INCEPTION." USSR CULTURE INDUS DIPLOM WEALTH...GEOG SOC BIBLIOG 20. PAGE 14 A0281 — COM GEN/METH REV MARXISM

B52
ALEXANDROWICZ C.H.,INTERNATIONAL ECONOMIC ORGANIZATION. WOR+45 ECO/DEV ECO/UNDEV DIST/IND FINAN MARKET PLAN ECO/TAC LEGIT DRIVE WEALTH ...POLICY CONCPT QUANT OBS TIME/SEQ GEN/LAWS WORK EEC ILO OEEC UNESCO 20. PAGE 6 A0114 — INT/ORG INT/TRADE

B52
HOSELITZ B.F.,THE PROGRESS OF UNDERDEVELOPED AREAS. FUT WOR+45 WOR-45 ECO/DEV ECO/TAC INT/TRADE WEALTH ...SOC TREND GEN/LAWS TOT/POP VAL/FREE COLD/WAR 20. PAGE 68 A1391 — ECO/UNDEV PLAN FOR/AID

B52
SURANYI-UNGER T.,COMPARATIVE ECONOMIC SYSTEMS. FINAN MARKET DIPLOM PRICE WEALTH...GEOG SOC BIBLIOG METH T 20. PAGE 140 A2865 — LAISSEZ PLAN ECO/DEV IDEA/COMP

B53
MACK R.T.,RAISING THE WORLDS STANDARD OF LIVING. IRAN INT/ORG VOL/ASSN EX/STRUC ECO/TAC WEALTH...MGT METH/CNCPT STAT CONT/OBS INT TOT/POP VAL/FREE 20 UN. PAGE 92 A1893 — WOR+45 FOR/AID INT/TRADE

B53
NEISSER H.,NATIONAL INCOMES AND INTERNATIONAL TRADE. FRANCE GERMANY SWEDEN UK USA-45 EXTR/IND FINAN INDUS TEC/DEV PRICE BAL/PAY EQUILIB INCOME WEALTH...CHARTS METH 19 CHINJAP. PAGE 108 A2215 — INT/TRADE PRODUC MARKET CON/ANAL

S53
BOULDING K.E.,"ECONOMIC ISSUES IN INTERNATIONAL CONFLICT." WOR+45 ECO/DEV NAT/G TOP/EX DIPLOM ECO/TAC DOMIN ATTIT WEALTH...MAJORIT OBS/ENVIR TREND GEN/LAWS COLD/WAR TOT/POP 20. PAGE 17 A0345 — PWR FOR/AID

B54
BECKEL G.,WORKSHOPS FOR THE WORLD; THE SPECIALIZED AGENCIES OF THE UN. WOR+45 AGRI DIST/IND CREATE TEC/DEV BUDGET CONTROL TASK WEALTH...CHARTS ORG/CHARTS 20 UN CASEBOOK. PAGE 12 A0246 — INT/ORG DIPLOM PEACE CON/ANAL

B54
NORTHROP F.S.C.,EUROPEAN UNION AND UNITED STATES FOREIGN POLICY: A STUDY IN SOCIOLOGICAL JURISPRUDENCE. EUR+WWI MOD/EUR USA+45 SOCIETY STRUCT NAT/G CREATE ECO/TAC DOMIN EDU/PROP REGION ATTIT RIGID/FLEX HEALTH ORD/FREE WEALTH ...METH/CNCPT TIME/SEQ TREND. PAGE 110 A2256 — INT/ORG SOC DIPLOM

B55
COMM. STUDY ORGAN. PEACE,REPORTS. WOR-45 ECO/DEV ECO/UNDEV VOL/ASSN CONSULT FORCES PLAN TEC/DEV DOMIN EDU/PROP NUC/PWR ATTIT PWR WEALTH...JURID STERTYP FAO ILO 20 UN. PAGE 28 A0579 — WOR+45 INT/ORG ARMS/CONT

B55
COTTRELL W.F.,ENERGY AND SOCIETY. FUT WOR+45 WOR-45 — TEC/DEV

ECO/DEV ECO/UNDEV INT/ORG NAT/G DETER ORD/FREE PWR BAL/PWR
SKILL WEALTH...SOC TIME/SEQ TOT/POP VAL/FREE 20. PEACE
PAGE 31 A0634

B55
MYRDAL A.R.,AMERICA'S ROLE IN INTERNATIONATIONAL PLAN
SOCIAL WELFARE. FUT WOR+45 SOCIETY R+D VOL/ASSN SKILL
ECO/TAC EDU/PROP HEALTH KNOWL WEALTH...SOC CHARTS FOR/AID
ORG/CHARTS TOT/POP 20. PAGE 107 A2188

B55
UN ECONOMIC AND SOCIAL COUNCIL,BIBLIOGRAPHY OF BIBLIOG/A
PUBLICATIONS OF THE UN AND SPECIALIZED AGENCIES IN SOC/WK
THE SOCIAL WELFARE FIELD, 1946-1952. WOR+45 FAM ADMIN
INT/ORG MUNIC ACT/RES PLAN PROB/SOLV EDU/PROP AGE/C WEALTH
AGE/Y HABITAT...HEAL UN. PAGE 147 A3000

S55
HALLETT D.,"THE HISTORY AND STRUCTURE OF OEEC." VOL/ASSN
EUR+WWI USA+45 CONSTN INDUS INT/ORG NAT/G DELIB/GP ECO/DEV
ACT/RES PLAN ORD/FREE WEALTH...CONCPT OEEC 20
CMN/WLTH. PAGE 60 A1234

B56
VON BECKERATH E.,HANDWORTERBUCH DER BIBLIOG
SOCIALWISSENSCHAFTEN (II VOLS.). EUR+WWI GERMANY INT/TRADE
POL/PAR WORKER DIPLOM LEAD CHOOSE SUFF WEALTH...SOC NAT/G
20. PAGE 159 A3249 ECO/DEV

S56
GORDON L.,"THE ORGANIZATION FOR EUROPEAN ECONOMIC VOL/ASSN
COOPERATION." EUR+WWI INDUS INT/ORG NAT/G CONSULT ECO/DEV
DELIB/GP ACT/RES CREATE PLAN TEC/DEV EDU/PROP LEGIT
WEALTH OEEC 20. PAGE 54 A1114

B57
ASHER R.E.,THE UNITED NATIONS AND ECONOMIC AND INT/ORG
SOCIAL COOPERATION. ECO/UNDEV COM/IND DIST/IND DIPLOM
FINAN PLAN PROB/SOLV INT/TRADE TASK WEALTH...SOC 20 FOR/AID
UN. PAGE 9 A0186

B57
BLOOMFIELD L.M.,EGYPT, ISRAEL AND THE GULF OF ISLAM
AQABA: IN INTERNATIONAL LAW. LAW NAT/G CONSULT INT/LAW
FORCES PLAN ECO/TAC ROUTINE COERCE ATTIT DRIVE UAR
PERCEPT PERSON RIGID/FLEX LOVE PWR WEALTH...GEOG
CONCPT MYTH TREND. PAGE 15 A0314

B57
CONOVER H.F.,NORTH AND NORTHEAST AFRICA; A SELECTED BIBLIOG/A
ANNOTATED LIST OF WRITINGS. ALGERIA MOROCCO SUDAN DIPLOM
UAR CULTURE INT/ORG PROB/SOLV ADJUD NAT/LISM PWR AFR
WEALTH...SOC 20 UN. PAGE 30 A0603 ECO/UNDEV

B57
MCNEILL W.H.,GREECE: AMERICAN AID IN ACTION. GREECE FOR/AID
UK USA+45 FINAN CAP/ISM INT/TRADE BAL/PAY PRODUC DIPLOM
WEALTH...POLICY METH/COMP 20. PAGE 99 A2022 ECO/UNDEV

B57
TRIFFIN R.,EUROPE AND THE MONEY MUDDLE. USA+45 EUR+WWI
INT/ORG NAT/G CONSULT PLAN ECO/TAC EXEC ROUTINE ECO/DEV
BAL/PAY WEALTH...METH/CNCPT OBS TREND CHARTS REGION
STERTYP GEN/METH EEC VAL/FREE ECSC. PAGE 145 A2962

S57
HOAG M.W.,"ECONOMIC PROBLEMS OF ALLIANCE." COM INT/ORG
EUR+WWI WOR+45 ECO/DEV ECO/UNDEV NAT/G VOL/ASSN ECO/TAC
FORCES PLAN TEC/DEV DIPLOM COERCE ORD/FREE PWR
WEALTH...DECISION GEN/LAWS NATO COLD/WAR. PAGE 65
A1345

B58
BERLINER J.S.,SOVIET ECONOMIC AID: THE AID AND ECO/UNDEV
TRADE POLICY IN UNDERDEVELOPED COUNTRIES. AFR COM ECO/TAC
ISLAM L/A+17C S/ASIA USSR ECO/DEV DIST/IND FINAN FOR/AID
MARKET INT/ORG ACT/RES PLAN BAL/PWR WEAPON PWR
WEALTH...CHARTS 20. PAGE 14 A0277

B58
IMLAH A.H.,ECONOMIC ELEMENTS IN THE PAX BRITANNICA. MARKET
MOD/EUR USA+45 USA-45 ECO/DEV INT/ORG NAT/G BAL/PWR UK
ECO/TAC PEACE ATTIT PWR WEALTH...STAT CHARTS
VAL/FREE 19. PAGE 70 A1436

B58
KINDLEBERGER C.P.,INTERNATIONAL ECONOMICS. WOR+45 INT/ORG
WOR-45 ECO/DEV ECO/UNDEV FINAN VOL/ASSN ACT/RES BAL/PWR
DIPLOM ECO/TAC LEGIT REGION ATTIT DRIVE ORD/FREE TARIFFS
WEALTH...POLICY STAT TREND GEN/LAWS EEC ECSC OEEC
20. PAGE 79 A1620

B58
PALMER E.E.,AMERICAN FOREIGN POLICY. USA+45 CULTURE DIPLOM
ECO/UNDEV NAT/G PLAN GIVE BAL/PAY ORD/FREE WEALTH ECO/TAC
POPULISM...DECISION ANTHOL 20. PAGE 113 A2319 POLICY

B58
PALYI M.,MANAGED MONEY AT THE CROSSROADS: THE FINAN
EUROPEAN EXPERIENCE. WOR+45 WOR-45 TEC/DEV DIPLOM ECO/TAC
INT/TRADE DEMAND WEALTH...CHARTS BIBLIOG 19/20 ECO/DEV
EUROPE GOLD/STAND SILVER. PAGE 113 A2324 PRODUC

B58
SCITOUSKY T.,ECONOMIC THEORY AND WESTERN EUROPEAN ECO/TAC
INTEGRATION. EUR+WWI INT/ORG ACT/RES INT/TRADE
REGION BAL/PAY WEALTH...METH/CNCPT STAT CHARTS
GEN/METH ECSC TOT/POP EEC OEEC 20. PAGE 130 A2668

B58
TILLION G.,ALGERIA: THE REALITIES. ALGERIA FRANCE ECO/UNDEV
ISLAM CULTURE STRATA PROB/SOLV DOMIN REV NAT/LISM SOC
WEALTH MARXISM...GEOG 20. PAGE 144 A2940 COLONIAL
DIPLOM

S58
ELKIN A.B.,"OEEC-ITS STRUCTURE AND POWERS." EUR+WWI ECO/DEV
CONSTN INDUS INT/ORG NAT/G VOL/ASSN DELIB/GP EX/STRUC
ACT/RES PLAN ORD/FREE WEALTH...CHARTS ORG/CHARTS
OEEC 20. PAGE 41 A0839

B59
CHANDLER E.H.S.,THE HIGH TOWER OF REFUGE: THE GIVE
INSPIRING STORY OF REFUGEE RELIEF THROUGHOUT THE WEALTH
WORLD. WOR+45 NEIGH SECT WORKER PROB/SOLV DIPLOM STRANGE
ECO/TAC EDU/PROP COST HABITAT. PAGE 25 A0519 INT/ORG

B59
DIEBOLD W. JR.,THE SCHUMAN PLAN: A STUDY IN INT/ORG
ECONOMIC COOPERATION, 1950-1959. EUR+WWI FRANCE REGION
GERMANY USA+45 EXTR/IND CONSULT DELIB/GP PLAN
DIPLOM ECO/TAC INT/TRADE ROUTINE ORD/FREE WEALTH
...METH/CNCPT STAT CONT/OBS INT TIME/SEQ ECSC 20.
PAGE 37 A0759

B59
FOX W.T.R.,THEORETICAL ASPECTS OF INTERNATIONAL DELIB/GP
RELATIONS. WOR+45 INT/ORG NAT/G POL/PAR CONSULT ANTHOL
PLAN ECO/TAC DOMIN EDU/PROP LEGIT EXEC COERCE PWR
WEALTH...RELATIV CONCPT 20. PAGE 48 A0975

B59
HEWES T.,EQUALITY OF OPPORTUNITY - THE AMERICAN POLICY
IDEAL AND KEY TO WORLD PEACE. USA+45 NAT/G OWN PEACE
WEALTH ALL/IDEOS SOCISM...CONCPT 20. PAGE 64 A1323 ECO/TAC
DIPLOM

B59
JOSEPH F.M.,AS OTHERS SEE US: THE UNITED STATES RESPECT
THROUGH FOREIGN EYES. AFR EUR+WWI ISLAM L/A+17C DOMIN
S/ASIA USA+45 CULTURE SOCIETY ECO/DEV ECO/UNDEV NAT/LISM
INT/ORG NAT/G DIPLOM ECO/TAC REV ATTIT RIGID/FLEX SOVEREIGN
HEALTH ORD/FREE WEALTH 20. PAGE 75 A1537

B59
LINK R.G.,ENGLISH THEORIES OF ECONOMIC IDEA/COMP
FLUCTUATIONS: 1815-1848. FRANCE UK AGRI WORKER ECO/DEV
DIPLOM PRICE TASK WAR DEMAND PRODUC...POLICY WEALTH
BIBLIOG 18 MALTHUS MILL/JS WILSON/J. PAGE 89 A1826 EQUILIB

B59
NUNEZ JIMENEZ A.,LA LIBERACION DE LAS ISLAS. CUBA AGRI
L/A+17C USA+45 LAW CHIEF PLAN DIPLOM FOR/AID OWN REV
WEALTH 20 CASTRO/F. PAGE 110 A2261 ECO/UNDEV
NAT/G

B59
REIFF H.,THE UNITED STATES AND THE TREATY LAW OF ADJUD
THE SEA. USA+45 USA-45 SEA SOCIETY INT/ORG CONSULT INT/LAW
DELIB/GP LEGIS DIPLOM LEGIT ATTIT ORD/FREE PWR
WEALTH...GEOG JURID TOT/POP 20 TREATY. PAGE 120
A2459

B59
US GENERAL ACCOUNTING OFFICE,EXAM OF ECONOMIC AND FOR/AID
TECHNICAL ASSISTANCE PROGRAM FOR INDIA INT'NAT'L EFFICIENCY
COOP ADMIN REPORT TO CONGRESS 1955-1958. INDIA ECO/TAC
USA+45 ECO/UNDEV FINAN PLAN DIPLOM COST UTIL WEALTH TEC/DEV
...CHARTS 20 CONGRESS AID. PAGE 153 A3114

L59
BEGUIN B.,"ILO AND THE TRIPARTITE SYSTEM." EUR+WWI LABOR
WOR+45 WOR-45 CONSTN ECO/DEV ECO/UNDEV INDUS
INT/ORG NAT/G VOL/ASSN DELIB/GP PLAN TEC/DEV LEGIT
ORD/FREE WEALTH...CONCPT TIME/SEQ WORK ILO 20.
PAGE 12 A0249

L59
MURPHY J.C.,"SOME IMPLICATIONS OF EUROPE'S COMMON MARKET
MARKET. IN (COOK P, ECONOMIC DEVELOPMENT AND INT/ORG
INTERNATIONAL TRADE,." EUR+WWI ECO/DEV DIST/IND REGION
INDUS NAT/G PLAN ECO/TAC INT/TRADE WEALTH...STAT
TREND OEEC TOT/POP 20 EEC. PAGE 106 A2178

S59
CARLSTON K.S.,"NATIONALIZATION: AN ANALYTIC INDUS
APPROACH." WOR+45 INT/ORG ECO/TAC DOMIN LEGIT ADJUD NAT/G
COERCE ORD/FREE PWR WEALTH SOCISM...JURID CONCPT NAT/LISM
TREND STERTYP TOT/POP VAL/FREE 20. PAGE 24 A0486 SOVEREIGN

S59
HARTT J.,"ANTARCTICA: ITS IMMEDIATE VOL/ASSN
PRACTICALITIES." FUT USA+45 USSR WOR+45 INT/ORG ORD/FREE
NAT/G CREATE TEC/DEV REGION KNOWL WEALTH...GEOG 20 DIPLOM
ANTARTICA. PAGE 62 A1276

S59
HARVEY M.F.,"THE PALESTINE REFUGEE PROBLEM: ACT/RES
ELEMENTS OF A SOLUTION." ISLAM LAW INT/ORG DELIB/GP LEGIT
TOP/EX ECO/TAC ROUTINE DRIVE HEALTH LOVE ORD/FREE PEACE
PWR WEALTH...MAJORIT FAO 20. PAGE 62 A1283 ISRAEL

S59
KINDLEBERGER C.P.,"UNITED STATES ECONOMIC FOREIGN FINAN
POLICY: RESEARCH REQUIREMENTS FOR 1965." FUT USA+45 ECO/DEV
WOR+45 DIST/IND MARKET INT/ORG ECO/TAC INT/TRADE FOR/AID
WEALTH...OBS TREND CON/ANAL GEN/LAWS VAL/FREE 20.
PAGE 79 A1621

S59
KOHN L.Y.,"ISRAEL AND NEW NATION STATES OF ASIA AND ECO/UNDEV
AFRICA." AFR ASIA FUT S/ASIA VOL/ASSN TEC/DEV ECO/TAC
NAT/LISM RIGID/FLEX SKILL WEALTH...RELATIV OBS FOR/AID
TREND CON/ANAL 20. PAGE 81 A1663 ISRAEL

S59
PLAZA G.,"FOR A REGIONAL MARKET IN LATIN AMERICA." MARKET
FUT L/A+17C CULTURE INDUS NAT/G ECO/TAC INT/TRADE INT/ORG

ATTIT WEALTH...NEW/IDEA TREND OAS 20. PAGE 116 REGION
A2389

S59
REUBENS E.D.,"THE BASIS FOR REORIENATION OF ECO/UNDEV
AMERICAN FOREIGN AID POLICY." USA+45 USSR STRUCT PLAN
INT/ORG CONSULT ECO/TAC ADMIN DRIVE MORAL ORD/FREE FOR/AID
PWR WEALTH...RELATIV MATH STAT TREND GEN/LAWS DIPLOM
VAL/FREE 20. PAGE 120 A2467

S59
SOLDATI A.,"EOCNOMIC DISINTEGRATION IN EUROPE." FINAN
EUR+WWI FUT WOR+45 INDUS INT/ORG NAT/G CAP/ISM ECO/TAC
WEALTH...NEW/IDEA OBS TREND CHARTS EEC 20. PAGE 135
A2764

B60
ALLEN R.L.,SOVIET ECONOMIC WARFARE. USSR FINAN COM
INDUS NAT/G PLAN TEC/DEV FOR/AID DETER WEALTH ECO/TAC
...TREND GEN/LAWS 20. PAGE 6 A0126

B60
APTHEKER H.,DISARMAMENT AND THE AMERICAN ECONOMY: A MARXIST
SYMPOSIUM. FUT USA+45 ECO/DEV DIST/IND FINAN INDUS ARMS/CONT
PROC/MFG LABOR NAT/G POL/PAR CONSULT PLAN CAP/ISM
INT/TRADE PEACE ATTIT MORAL WEALTH...TREND GEN/LAWS
TOT/POP 20. PAGE 9 A0172

B60
CAMPAIGNE J.G.,AMERICAN MIGHT AND SOVIET MYTH. COM USA+45
EUR+WWI ECO/DEV ECO/UNDEV INT/ORG NAT/G CAP/ISM DOMIN
ECO/TAC FOR/AID EDU/PROP ATTIT PWR WEALTH...POLICY DIPLOM
CONCPT MYTH TREND STERTYP GEN/LAWS COLD/WAR. USSR
PAGE 23 A0473

B60
KENEN P.B.,GIANT AMONG NATIONS: PROBLEMS IN UNITED FOR/AID
STATES FOREIGN ECONOMIC POLICY. USA+45 FINAN DIPLOM ECO/UNDEV
TARIFFS BAL/PAY WEALTH 20 COLD/WAR. PAGE 77 A1584 INT/TRADE
PLAN

B60
KRISTENSEN T.,THE ECONOMIC WORLD BALANCE. FUT ECO/UNDEV
WOR+45 CULTURE ECO/DEV BAL/PWR INT/TRADE REGION PWR ECO/TAC
WEALTH...STAT TREND CHARTS 20. PAGE 82 A1685 FOR/AID

B60
LATIFI D.,INDIA AND UNITED STATES AID. ASIA INDIA FOR/AID
UK USA+45 AGRI FINAN INDUS COLONIAL ORD/FREE DIPLOM
SOVEREIGN WEALTH...METH/COMP 20. PAGE 85 A1743 ECO/UNDEV

B60
LERNER A.P.,THE ECONOMICS OF CONTROL. USA+45 ECO/DEV
ECO/UNDEV INT/ORG ACT/RES PLAN CAP/ISM INT/TRADE ROUTINE
ATTIT WEALTH...SOC MATH STAT GEN/LAWS INDEX 20. ECO/TAC
PAGE 87 A1785 SOCISM

B60
LISKA G.,THE NEW STATECRAFT. WOR+45 WOR-45 LEGIS ECO/TAC
DIPLOM ADMIN ATTIT PWR WEALTH...HIST/WRIT TREND CONCPT
COLD/WAR 20. PAGE 90 A1837 FOR/AID

B60
LISTER L.,EUROPE'S COAL AND STEEL COMMUNITY. FRANCE EUR+WWI
GERMANY STRUCT ECO/DEV EXTR/IND INDUS MARKET NAT/G INT/ORG
DELIB/GP ECO/TAC INT/TRADE EDU/PROP ATTIT REGION
RIGID/FLEX ORD/FREE PWR WEALTH...CONCPT STAT
TIME/SEQ CHARTS ECSC 20. PAGE 90 A1843

B60
NEALE A.D.,THE FLOW OF RESOURCES FROM RICH TO POOR. FOR/AID
WOR+45 ECO/DEV ECO/UNDEV FINAN INDUS NAT/G PLAN DIPLOM
EFFICIENCY WEALTH...POLICY NAT/COMP 20 RESOURCE/N. METH/CNCPT
PAGE 108 A2209

B60
PENTONY D.E.,THE UNDERDEVELOPED LANDS. FUT WOR+45 ECO/UNDEV
CULTURE AGRI FINAN INDUS MARKET INT/ORG LABOR NAT/G POLICY
VOL/ASSN CONSULT TEC/DEV ECO/TAC EDU/PROP COLONIAL FOR/AID
ATTIT WEALTH...OBS RECORD SAMP TREND GEN/METH WORK INT/TRADE
UN 20. PAGE 115 A2351

B60
ROPKE W.,A HUMANE ECONOMY. CULTURE ECO/DEV FINAN ECO/TAC
INDUS GP/REL CENTRAL WEALTH...GEOG SOC IDEA/COMP 20 INT/ORG
EEC. PAGE 123 A2525 DIPLOM
ORD/FREE

B60
SETON-WATSON H.,NEITHER WAR NOR PEACE. ASIA USSR ATTIT
WOR+45 ELITES INT/ORG NAT/G EX/STRUC FORCES BAL/PWR PWR
ECO/TAC EDU/PROP COERCE NAT/LISM ORD/FREE WEALTH DIPLOM
TOT/POP 20. PAGE 131 A2688 TOTALISM

B60
SHONFIELD A.,THE ATTACK ON WORLD POVERTY. WOR+45 INT/ORG
ECO/DEV ECO/UNDEV FINAN VOL/ASSN PLAN EDU/PROP ECO/TAC
DRIVE KNOWL WEALTH...CONT/OBS STAND/INT ORG/CHARTS FOR/AID
TOT/POP UNESCO 20. PAGE 132 A2704 INT/TRADE

B60
STRACHEY J.,THE END OF EMPIRE. UK WOR+45 WOR-45 COLONIAL
DIPLOM INT/TRADE DOMIN ADJUST ORD/FREE WEALTH ECO/DEV
...SOCIALIST GOV/COMP TIME COMMONWLTH. PAGE 139 BAL/PWR
A2841 LAISSEZ

B60
THEOBALD R.,THE RICH AND THE POOR: A STUDY OF THE ECO/TAC
ECONOMICS OF RISING EXPECTATIONS. WOR+45 CONSTN INT/TRADE
ECO/DEV ECO/UNDEV INT/ORG NAT/G PLAN FOR/AID
ROUTINE BAL/PAY ORD/FREE PWR WEALTH...GEOG TREND
WORK 20. PAGE 142 A2912

L60
FERNBACH A.P.,"SOVIET COEXISTENCE STRATEGY." WOR+45 LABOR
PROF/ORG VOL/ASSN DIPLOM DOMIN EDU/PROP ATTIT DRIVE INT/ORG
PERSON PWR SKILL WEALTH...POLICY OBS SAMP TREND USSR
STERTYP ILO WORK COLD/WAR 420. PAGE 45 A0919

S60
FRANKEL S.H.,"ECONOMIC ASPECTS OF POLITICAL NAT/G
INDEPENDENCE IN AFRICA." AFR FUT SOCIETY ECO/UNDEV FOR/AID
COM/IND FINAN LEGIS PLAN TEC/DEV CAP/ISM ECO/TAC
INT/TRADE ADMIN ATTIT DRIVE RIGID/FLEX PWR WEALTH
...MGT NEW/IDEA MATH TIME/SEQ VAL/FREE 20. PAGE 48
A0984

S60
GULICK E.U.,"OUR BALANCE OF POWER SYSTEM IN INT/ORG
PERSPECTIVE." FUT WOR+45 WOR-45 ECO/DEV DOMIN TREND
ROUTINE NUC/PWR PEACE PWR WEALTH...PLURIST CONCPT ARMS/CONT
HIST/WRIT GEN/METH TOT/POP 20. PAGE 58 A1191 BAL/PWR

S60
KALUODA J.,"COMMUNIST STRATEGY IN LATIN AMERICA." COM
L/A+17C USA+45 INT/ORG NAT/G POL/PAR DIPLOM ECO/TAC PWR
EDU/PROP COERCE WEALTH...CONCPT OAS COLD/WAR 20. CUBA
PAGE 76 A1553

S60
KREININ M.E.,"THE 'OUTER-SEVEN' AND EUROPEAN ECO/TAC
INTEGRATION." EUR+WWI FRANCE GERMANY ITALY UK GEN/LAWS
ECO/DEV DIST/IND INT/TRADE DRIVE WEALTH...MYTH
CHARTS EEC OEEC 20. PAGE 82 A1682

S60
LINDHOLM R.W.,"ACCELERATED DEVELOPMENT WITH A ECO/DEV
MINIMUM OF FOREIGN AID AND ECONOMIC CONTROLS." FINAN
SOCIETY INDUS ECO/TAC WEALTH...CONCPT 20. PAGE 89 FOR/AID
A1822

S60
MIKESELL R.F.,"AMERICA'S ECONOMIC RESPONSIBILITY AS ECO/UNDEV
A GREAT POWER." COM FUT USA+45 USSR WOR+45 INT/ORG BAL/PWR
PLAN ECO/TAC FOR/AID EDU/PROP CHOOSE WEALTH CAP/ISM
...POLICY 20. PAGE 101 A2069

S60
MORA J.A.,"THE ORGANIZATION OF AMERICAN STATES." L/A+17C
USA+45 LAW ECO/UNDEV VOL/ASSN DELIB/GP PLAN BAL/PWR INT/ORG
EDU/PROP ADMIN DRIVE RIGID/FLEX ORD/FREE WEALTH REGION
...TIME/SEQ GEN/LAWS OAS 20. PAGE 103 A2126

S60
MORALES C.J.,"TRADE AND ECONOMIC INTEGRATION IN FINAN
LATIN AMERICA." FUT L/A+17C LAW STRATA ECO/UNDEV INT/TRADE
DIST/IND INDUS LABOR NAT/G LEGIS ECO/TAC ADMIN REGION
RIGID/FLEX WEALTH...CONCPT NEW/IDEA CONT/OBS
TIME/SEQ WORK 20. PAGE 104 A2128

S60
MURPHY J.C.,"INTERNATIONAL INVESTMENT AND THE FINAN
NATIONAL INTEREST." WOR+45 WOR-45 ECO/DEV ECO/UNDEV WEALTH
NAT/G ACT/RES...CHARTS TOT/POP COLD/WAR 20. FOR/AID
PAGE 106 A2179

S60
NANES A.,"THE EUROPEAN COMMUNITY AND THE UNITED INT/ORG
STATES: EVOLVING RELATIONS." EUR+WWI USA+45 WOR+45 REGION
ECO/UNDEV MARKET NAT/G DELIB/GP PLAN LEGIT ATTIT
PWR WEALTH...CONCPT STAT TIME/SEQ CON/ANAL EEC OEEC
20 EURATOM. PAGE 107 A2194

S60
RICHTER J.H.,"TOWARDS AN INTERNATIONAL POLICY ON AGRI
AGRICULTURAL TRADE." EUR+WWI USA+45 ECO/DEV NAT/G INT/ORG
PLAN ECO/TAC ATTIT PWR WEALTH...CONCPT GEN/LAWS 20.
PAGE 121 A2475

S60
RIVKIN A.,"AFRICAN ECONOMIC DEVELOPMENT: ADVANCED AFR
TECHNOLOGY AND THE STAGES OF GROWTH." CULTURE TEC/DEV
ECO/UNDEV AGRI COM/IND EXTR/IND PLAN ECO/TAC ATTIT FOR/AID
DRIVE RIGID/FLEX SKILL WEALTH...MGT SOC GEN/LAWS
WORK TOT/POP 20. PAGE 121 A2487

B61
BUSSCHAU W.J.,GOLD AND INTERNATIONAL LIQUIDITY. FINAN
WOR+45 PRICE EQUILIB WEALTH...CHARTS 20 GOLD/STAND. DIPLOM
PAGE 22 A0450 PROB/SOLV

B61
DIA M.,THE AFRICAN NATIONS AND WORLD SOLIDARITY. AFR
ISLAM CULTURE ELITES ECO/DEV ECO/UNDEV INT/ORG REGION
NAT/G PLAN ECO/TAC INT/TRADE EDU/PROP NAT/LISM SOCISM
ATTIT DRIVE ORD/FREE WEALTH...SOCIALIST CONCPT
CON/ANAL GEN/LAWS TOT/POP 20. PAGE 37 A0753

B61
EINZIG P.,A DYNAMIC THEORY OF FORWARD EXCHANGE. FUT FINAN
WOR+45 WOR-45 INT/TRADE BAL/PAY WEALTH...OLD/LIB ECO/TAC
NEW/IDEA OBS TREND 20. PAGE 41 A0830

B61
FRIEDMANN W.G.,JOINT INTERNATIONAL BUSINESS ECO/UNDEV
VENTURES. ASIA ISLAM L/A+17C ECO/DEV DIST/IND FINAN INT/TRADE
PROC/MFG FACE/GP LG/CO NAT/G VOL/ASSN CONSULT
EX/STRUC PLAN ADMIN ROUTINE WEALTH...OLD/LIB WORK
20. PAGE 49 A1004

B61
GANGULI B.N.,ECONOMIC INTEGRATION. FINAN LABOR ECO/TAC
CAP/ISM DIPLOM WEALTH...NAT/COMP 20. PAGE 51 A1041 METH/CNCPT
EQUILIB
ECO/UNDEV

B61
HARRIS S.E.,THE DOLLAR IN CRISIS. USA+45 MARKET BAL/PAY
INT/ORG ECO/TAC PRICE CONTROL WEALTH...METH/COMP DIPLOM

ANTHOL 20 GOLD/STAND. PAGE 62 A1269
FINAN INT/TRADE

B61
JAVITS B.A.,THE PEACE BY INVESTMENT CORPORATION. WOR+45 NAT/G LEGIS PROB/SOLV PERS/REL WEALTH ...POLICY 20. PAGE 73 A1499
ECO/UNDEV DIPLOM FOR/AID PEACE

B61
KITZINGER V.W.,THE CHALLENGE OF THE COMMON MARKET. EUR+WWI ECO/DEV DIST/IND PLAN ECO/TAC INT/TRADE LEGIT ATTIT PWR WEALTH...TIME/SEQ TREND CHARTS EEC 20. PAGE 80 A1647
MARKET INT/ORG UK

B61
MEZERIK A.G.,ECONOMIC DEVELOPMENT AIDS FOR UNDERDEVELOPED COUNTRIES. WOR+45 FINAN LEGIS PROB/SOLV TEC/DEV DIPLOM FOR/AID GIVE TASK WAR 20 UN. PAGE 101 A2062
ECO/UNDEV INT/ORG WEALTH PLAN

B61
OECD,STATISTICS OF BALANCE OF PAYMENTS 1950-61. WOR+45 FINAN ECO/TAC INT/TRADE DEMAND WEALTH...STAT NAT/COMP 20 OEEC OECD. PAGE 111 A2278
BAL/PAY ECO/DEV INT/ORG CHARTS

B61
SCAMMEL W.M.,INTERNATIONAL MONETARY POLICY. WOR+45 WOR-45 ACT/RES ECO/TAC LEGIT WEALTH...GEN/METH UN 20. PAGE 127 A2611
INT/ORG FINAN BAL/PAY

B61
SHARP W.R.,FIELD ADMINISTRATION IN THE UNITED NATION SYSTEM: THE CONDUCT OF INTERNATIONAL ECONOMIC AND SOCIAL PROGRAMS. FUT WOR+45 CONSTN SOCIETY ECO/UNDEV R+D DELIB/GP ACT/RES PLAN TEC/DEV EDU/PROP EXEC ROUTINE HEALTH WEALTH...HUM CONCPT CHARTS METH ILO UNESCO VAL/FREE UN 20. PAGE 132 A2697
INT/ORG CONSULT

B61
US HOUSE COMM APPROPRIATIONS,INTER-AMERICAN PROGRAMS FOR 1961: DENIAL OF 1962 BUDGET INFORMATION. CHILE L/A+17C USA+45 FINAN CONSULT BUDGET ADJUD COST EFFICIENCY WEALTH...POLICY CHARTS 20 CONGRESS. PAGE 153 A3119
LEGIS FOR/AID DELIB/GP ECO/UNDEV

B61
US SENATE COMM ON FOREIGN RELS,INTERNATIONAL DEVELOPMENT AND SECURITY: HEARINGS ON BILL (2 VOLS.). ECO/UNDEV FINAN FORCES REV COST WEALTH ...CHARTS 20 AID PRESIDENT. PAGE 157 A3191
FOR/AID CIVMIL/REL ORD/FREE ECO/TAC

S61
"CRITERIA FOR ALLOCATING INVESTMENT RESOURCES AMONG VARIOUS FIELDS OF DEVELOPMENT IN UNDERDEVELOPED ECONOMIES." ASIA AGRI INT/ORG CAP/ISM BAL/PAY EFFICIENCY PROFIT WEALTH...STAT 20 UN. PAGE 3 A0061
BIBLIOG/A ECO/UNDEV PLAN TEC/DEV

S61
BARALL M.,"THE UNITED STATES GOVERNMENT RESPONDS." L/A+17C USA+45 SOCIETY NAT/G CREATE PLAN DIPLOM ECO/TAC ATTIT DRIVE RIGID/FLEX KNOWL SKILL WEALTH ...METH/CNCPT TIME/SEQ GEN/METH 20. PAGE 11 A0217
ECO/UNDEV ACT/RES FOR/AID

S61
DELLA PORT G.,"PROBLEMI E PROSPETTIVE DI COESISTENZA FRA ORIENTE ED OCCIDENTE, (PART 3)." COM FUT WOR+45 NAT/G BAL/PWR FOR/AID BAL/PAY PWR WEALTH...SOC CONCPT GEN/LAWS COLD/WAR 20. PAGE 36 A0729
INT/TRADE

S61
DEUTSCH K.W.,"NATIONAL INDUSTRIALIZATION AND THE DECLINING SHARE OF THE INTERNATIONAL ECONOMIC SECTOR." EUR+WWI FUT WOR+45 WOR-45 MARKET PLAN EDU/PROP WEALTH...WELF/ST OBS TESTS 20. PAGE 36 A0740
DIST/IND ECO/DEV INT/TRADE

S61
GALBRAITH J.K.,"A POSITIVE APPROACH TO ECONOMIC AID." FUT USA+45 INTELL NAT/G CONSULT ACT/RES DIPLOM ECO/TAC EDU/PROP ATTIT KNOWL PWR WEALTH ...SOC STERTYP 20. PAGE 50 A1030
ECO/UNDEV ROUTINE FOR/AID

S61
HEILBRONER R.L.,"DYNAMICS OF FOREIGN AID: PROBLEMS OF UNDERDEVELOPED NATIONS PLAGUE ASSISTANCE PROGRAM." FUT USA+45 WOR+45 STRATA NAT/G PLAN TEC/DEV ATTIT DRIVE WEALTH WORK 20. PAGE 64 A1307
ECO/UNDEV ECO/TAC FOR/AID

S61
JACKSON E.,"THE FUTURE DEVELOPMENT OF THE UNITED NATIONS: SOME SUGGESTIONS FOR RESEARCH." FUT LAW CONSTN ECO/DEV FINAN PEACE WEALTH...WELF/ST CONCPT UN 20. PAGE 72 A1476
INT/ORG PWR

S61
JUVILER P.H.,"INTERPARLIAMENTARY CONTACTS IN SOVIET FOREIGN POLICY." COM FUT WOR+45 WOR-45 SOCIETY CONSULT ACT/RES DIPLOM ADMIN PEACE ATTIT RIGID/FLEX WEALTH...WELF/ST SOC TOT/POP CONGRESS 19/20. PAGE 75 A1543
INT/ORG DELIB/GP USSR

S61
LANFALUSSY A.,"EUROPE'S PROGRESS: DUE TO COMMON MARKET." EUR+WWI ECO/DEV DELIB/GP PLAN ECO/TAC ROUTINE WEALTH...GEOG TREND EEC 20. PAGE 84 A1721
INT/ORG MARKET

S61
NOVE A.,"THE SOVIET MODEL AND UNDERDEVELOPED COUNTRIES." COM FUT USSR WOR+45 CULTURE ECO/DEV POL/PAR FOR/AID EDU/PROP ADMIN MORAL WEALTH ...POLICY RECORD HIST/WRIT 20. PAGE 110 A2258
ECO/UNDEV PLAN

S61
OCHENG D.,"ECONOMIC FORCES AND UGANDA'S FOREIGN POLICY." AFR UGANDA INT/TRADE TARIFFS INCOME SOVEREIGN WEALTH 20 EACM EEC TANGANYIKA. PAGE 111 A2274
ECO/TAC DIPLOM ECO/UNDEV INT/ORG

S61
PADELFORD N.J.,"POLITICS AND THE FUTURE OF ECOSOC." AFR S/ASIA ECO/UNDEV INDUS NAT/G DELIB/GP ACT/RES ORD/FREE WEALTH...CONCPT CHARTS UN 20 ECOSOC. PAGE 113 A2310
INT/ORG TEC/DEV

S61
RAY J.,"THE EUROPEAN FREE-TRADE ASSOCIATION AND ITS IMPACT ON INDIA'S TRADE." EUR+WWI FRANCE GERMANY INDIA S/ASIA UK NAT/G VOL/ASSN PLAN INT/TRADE ROUTINE WEALTH...STAT CHARTS CMN/WLTH EEC OEEC 20 EFTA. PAGE 120 A2453
ECO/DEV ECO/TAC

B62
ROUND TABLE ON EUROPE'S ROLE IN LATIN AMERICAN DEVELOPMENT. EUR+WWI L/A+17C PLAN BAL/PAY UTIL ROLE WEALTH...CHARTS ANTHOL 20 UN INT/AM/DEV. PAGE 3 A0063
ECO/UNDEV FINAN TEC/DEV FOR/AID

B62
ARNOLD H.J.P.,AID FOR DEVELOPING COUNTRIES. COM EUR+WWI USA+45 USSR WOR+45 EDU/PROP ATTIT DRIVE PWR WEALTH...TREND CHARTS STERTYP NAT/ 20. PAGE 9 A0177
ECO/UNDEV ECO/TAC FOR/AID

B62
BRIMMER B.,A GUIDE TO THE USE OF UNITED NATIONS DOCUMENTS. WOR+45 ECO/UNDEV AGRI EX/STRUC FORCES PROB/SOLV ADMIN WAR PEACE WEALTH...POLICY UN. PAGE 19 A0378
BIBLIOG/A INT/ORG DIPLOM

B62
BUCHMANN J.,L'AFRIQUE NOIRE INDEPENDANTE. POL/PAR DIPLOM COLONIAL PARTIC CHOOSE GP/REL ATTIT ORD/FREE WEALTH NEGRO. PAGE 21 A0426
AFR NAT/LISM DECISION

B62
CARLSTON K.S.,LAW AND ORGANIZATION IN WORLD SOCIETY. WOR+45 FINAN ECO/TAC DOMIN LEGIT CT/SYS ROUTINE COERCE ORD/FREE PWR WEALTH...PLURIST DECISION JURID MGT METH/CNCPT GEN/LAWS 20. PAGE 24 A0487
INT/ORG LAW

B62
COUNCIL ON WORLD TENSIONS,A STUDY OF WORLD TENSIONS AND DEVELOPMENT. WOR+45 ECO/DEV ECO/UNDEV INT/ORG PLAN DIPLOM ECO/TAC EDU/PROP ATTIT KNOWL ORD/FREE PWR WEALTH...CONCPT TREND CHARTS STERTYP COLD/WAR TOT/POP 20. PAGE 31 A0640
TEC/DEV SOC

B62
ELLIOTT J.R.,THE APPEAL OF COMMUNISM IN THE UNDERDEVELOPED NATIONS. USSR WOR+45 INT/ORG NAT/G DIPLOM DOMIN EDU/PROP ROUTINE ATTIT RIGID/FLEX ORD/FREE PWR WEALTH MARXISM...POLICY SOC METH/CNCPT MYTH TOT/POP COLD/WAR 20. PAGE 41 A0842
COM ECO/UNDEV

B62
FAO,FOOD AND AGRICULTURE ORGANIZATION AFRICAN SURVEY. AFR CONGO/BRAZ GHANA STRATA AGRI INT/ORG TEC/DEV FOR/AID INT/TRADE RACE/REL DEMAND EFFICIENCY PRODUC...GEOG 20 UN CONGO/LEOP. PAGE 44 A0898
ECO/TAC WEALTH EXTR/IND ECO/UNDEV

B62
GRAEBNER N.,COLD WAR DIPLOMACY 1945-1960. WOR+45 INT/ORG ECO/TAC EDU/PROP COERCE ORD/FREE PWR WEALTH ...HIST/WRIT TOT/POP VAL/FREE COLD/WAR 20. PAGE 55 A1122
USA+45 DIPLOM

B62
HIGGANS B.,UNITED NATIONS AND U.S. FOREIGN ECONOMIC POLICY. FUT USA+45 WOR+45 ECO/DEV ECO/UNDEV NAT/G ECO/TAC WEALTH...TIME/SEQ TOT/POP UN 20. PAGE 65 A1328
INT/ORG ACT/RES FOR/AID DIPLOM

B62
HOLMAN A.G.,SOME MEASURES AND INTERPRETATIONS OF EFFECTS OF US FOREIGN ENTERPRISES ON US BALANCE OF PAYMENTS. USA+45 COST INCOME WEALTH...MATH CHARTS 20. PAGE 67 A1371
BAL/PAY INT/TRADE FINAN ECO/TAC

B62
HUMPHREY D.D.,THE UNITED STATES AND THE COMMON MARKET. USA+45 INDUS MARKET INT/ORG PLAN EDU/PROP BAL/PAY DRIVE PWR WEALTH...TREND STERTYP EEC 20. PAGE 69 A1415
ATTIT ECO/TAC

B62
KENNEDY J.F.,TO TURN THE TIDE. SPACE AGRI INT/ORG FORCES TEC/DEV ADMIN NUC/PWR PEACE WEALTH...ANTHOL 20 KENNEDY/JF CIV/RIGHTS. PAGE 78 A1592
DIPLOM CHIEF POLICY NAT/G

B62
KRAFT J.,THE GRAND DESIGN. EUR+WWI USA+45 AGRI FINAN INDUS MARKET INT/ORG NAT/G PLAN ECO/TAC TARIFFS REGION DRIVE ORD/FREE WEALTH...POLICY OBS TREND EEC 20. PAGE 82 A1674
VOL/ASSN ECO/DEV INT/TRADE

B62
LAWSON R.,INTERNATIONAL REGIONAL ORGANIZATIONS. WOR+45 NAT/G VOL/ASSN CONSULT LEGIS EDU/PROP LEGIT ADMIN EXEC ROUTINE HEALTH PWR WEALTH...JURID EEC COLD/WAR 20 UN. PAGE 86 A1752
INT/ORG DELIB/GP REGION

B62
LEVY H.V.,LIBERDADE E JUSTICA SOCIAL (2ND ED.).
ORD/FREE

BRAZIL COM L/A+17C USSR INT/ORG PARTIC GP/REL WEALTH 20 UN COM/PARTY. PAGE 88 A1798
MARXISM CAP/ISM LAW

B62
LEWIS J.P.,QUIET CRISIS IN INDIA. INDIA USA+45 CULTURE ECO/UNDEV AGRI INDUS PROC/MFG NAT/G PLAN TEC/DEV DRIVE PWR SKILL WEALTH...MYTH 20. PAGE 88 A1801
S/ASIA ECO/TAC FOR/AID

B62
LIPPMANN W.,WESTERN UNITY AND THE COMMON MARKET. EUR+WWI FRANCE GERMANY/W UK USA+45 ECO/DEV AGRI FINAN MARKET INT/ORG NAT/G FOR/AID AGREE WEALTH 20 EEC. PAGE 89 A1831
DIPLOM INT/TRADE VOL/ASSN

B62
LUTZ F.A.,THE PROBLEM OF INTERNATIONAL ECONOMIC EQUILIBRIUM. FINAN PRODUC WEALTH 20 MONEY. PAGE 92 A1876
DIPLOM EQUILIB BAL/PAY PROB/SOLV

B62
MEADE J.E.,CASE STUDIES IN EUROPEAN ECONOMIC UNION. BELGIUM EUR+WWI LUXEMBOURG NAT/G INT/TRADE REGION ROUTINE WEALTH...METH/CNCPT STAT CHARTS ECSC TOT/POP OEEC EEC 20. PAGE 99 A2028
INT/ORG ECO/TAC

B62
MOUSSA P.,THE UNDERPRIVILEGED NATIONS. FINAN INT/ORG PLAN PROB/SOLV CAP/ISM GIVE TASK WEALTH ...POLICY SOC 20. PAGE 105 A2159
ECO/UNDEV NAT/G DIPLOM FOR/AID

B62
PAKISTAN MINISTRY OF FINANCE,FOREIGN ECONOMIC AID: A REVIEW OF FOREIGN ECONOMIC AID TO PAKISTAN. EUR+WWI PAKISTAN UK USA+45 USSR ECO/UNDEV INT/ORG DELIB/GP DIPLOM ECO/TAC...CHARTS CMN/WLTH CHINJAP. PAGE 113 A2318
FOR/AID RECEIVE WEALTH FINAN

B62
SNOW J.H.,GOVERNMENT BY TREASON. USA+45 USA-45 LEGIS DIPLOM FOR/AID GIVE CONTROL WEALTH MARXISM ...MAJORIT 20 CONGRESS COLD/WAR. PAGE 134 A2750
FINAN TAX PWR POLICY

B62
THEOBALD R.,NATIONAL DEVELOPMENT EFFORTS (PAMPHLET). WOR+45 AGRI BUDGET FOR/AID INT/TRADE TAX 20. PAGE 142 A2914
ECO/UNDEV PLAN BAL/PAY WEALTH

B62
US CONGRESS,LEGISLATIVE HISTORY OF UNITED STATES TAX CONVENTIONS(VOL. 1). USA+45 USA-45 DELIB/GP WEALTH...CHARTS 20 CONGRESS. PAGE 150 A3061
TAX LEGIS LAW DIPLOM

B62
US CONGRESS JOINT ECO COMM,FACTORS AFFECTING THE UNITED STATES BALANCE OF PAYMENTS. USA+45 DELIB/GP PLAN DIPLOM FOR/AID PRODUC WEALTH...CHARTS 20 CONGRESS OEEC. PAGE 150 A3064
BAL/PAY INT/TRADE ECO/TAC FINAN

B62
VIET J.,INTERNATIONAL COOPERATION AND PROGRAMMES OF ECONOMIC AND SOCIAL DEVELOPMENT. TEC/DEV FOR/AID DOMIN COLONIAL PEACE WEALTH 20 UNESCO. PAGE 159 A3232
BIBLIOG/A INT/ORG DIPLOM ECO/UNDEV

S62
ALBONETTI A.,"IL SECONDO PROGRAMMA QUINQUENNALE 1963-67 ED IL BILANCIO RICERCHE ED INVESTIMENTI PER IL 1963 DELL'ERATOM." EUR+WWI FUT ITALY WOR+45 ECO/DEV SERV/IND INT/ORG TEC/DEV ECO/TAC ATTIT SKILL WEALTH...MGT TIME/SEQ OEEC 20. PAGE 5 A0108
R+D PLAN NUC/PWR

S62
BOKOR-SZEGO H.,"LA CONVENTION DE BELGRADE ET LE REGIME DU DANUBE." COM EUR+WWI WOR+45 STRUCT POL/PAR VOL/ASSN PLAN EDU/PROP WEALTH...TIME/SEQ 20. PAGE 16 A0333
INT/ORG TOTALISM YUGOSLAVIA

S62
CLEVELAND H.,"THE FUTURE ROLE OF THE UNITED STATES IN THE UNITED NATIONS." USA+45 ECO/UNDEV INT/ORG EX/STRUC DIPLOM FOR/AID ROUTINE SKILL SOVEREIGN WEALTH UN 20. PAGE 27 A0550
FUT ATTIT

S62
MORGENTHAU H.J.,"A POLITICAL THEORY OF FOREIGN AID." ECO/UNDEV NAT/G DELIB/GP PLAN ECO/TAC EDU/PROP EXEC ORD/FREE RESPECT WEALTH...METH/CNCPT TREND 20. PAGE 104 A2140
USA+45 PHIL/SCI FOR/AID

S62
ORBAN M.,"L'EUROPE EN FORMATION ET SES PROBLEMES." EUR+WWI FUT WOR+45 WOR-45 INTELL STRUCT DELIB/GP ACT/RES FEDERAL RIGID/FLEX WEALTH...CONCPT TIME/SEQ OEEC 20. PAGE 112 A2295
INT/ORG PLAN REGION

S62
RUBINSTEIN A.Z.,"RUSSIA AND THE UNCOMMITTED NATIONS." AFR INDIA ISLAM L/A+17C LAOS S/ASIA ELITES ECO/UNDEV INT/ORG KIN CREATE PLAN TEC/DEV NAT/LISM RIGID/FLEX PWR WEALTH...METH/CNCPT TIME/SEQ GEN/LAWS WORK. PAGE 125 A2562
ECO/TAC TREND COLONIAL USSR

S62
SCOTT J.B.,"ANGLO-SOVIET TRADE AND ITS EFFECTS ON THE COMMONWEALTH." COM FUT UK USSR WOR+45 ECO/DEV MARKET INT/ORG CONSULT WEALTH...POLICY TREND CMN/WLTH 20. PAGE 130 A2673
NAT/G ECO/TAC

S62
SPENSER J.H.,"AFRICA AT THE UNITED NATIONS: SOME OBSERVATIONS." FUT ECO/UNDEV NAT/G CONSULT DELIB/GP PLAN BAL/PWR ECO/TAC EDU/PROP ATTIT RIGID/FLEX HEALTH ORD/FREE PWR WEALTH...POLICY CONCPT OBS TREND STERTYP GEN/METH UN VAL/FREE. PAGE 136 A2786
AFR INT/ORG REGION

C62
BACON F.,"OF EMPIRE" (1612) IN F. BACON, ESSAYS." ELITES NAT/G PROB/SOLV DIPLOM ADMIN CONTROL WEALTH 16/17 KING. PAGE 10 A0201
PWR CHIEF DOMIN GEN/LAWS

B63
ABSHIRE D.M.,NATIONAL SECURITY: POLITICAL, MILITARY, AND ECONOMIC STRATEGIES IN THE DECADE AHEAD. ASIA COM USA+45 WOR+45 ECO/DEV ECO/UNDEV INT/ORG DELIB/GP FORCES ECO/TAC COERCE ATTIT RIGID/FLEX HEALTH ORD/FREE PWR WEALTH...POLICY STAT CHARTS ANTHOL COLD/WAR VAL/FREE. PAGE 4 A0083
FUT ACT/RES BAL/PWR

B63
BRZEZINSKI Z.K.,AFRICA AND THE COMMUNIST WORLD. AFR ASIA COM CULTURE SOCIETY INT/ORG DELIB/GP ACT/RES ECO/TAC COERCE ORD/FREE PWR WEALTH...STAT TOT/POP VAL/FREE 20. PAGE 21 A0418
ATTIT EDU/PROP DIPLOM USSR

B63
ELLENDER A.J.,A REPORT ON UNITED STATES FOREIGN OPERATIONS IN AFRICA. SOUTH/AFR USA+45 STRATA EXTR/IND FORCES RACE/REL ISOLAT SOVEREIGN...CHARTS 20 NEGRO. PAGE 41 A0840
FOR/AID DIPLOM WEALTH ECO/UNDEV

B63
INTERAMERICAN ECO AND SOC COUN,THE ALLIANCE FOR PROGRESS: ITS FIRST YEAR: 1961-1962. AGRI SCHOOL PLAN TEC/DEV INT/TRADE TAX GIVE ADMIN WEALTH...SOC 20 SOUTH/AMER. PAGE 71 A1449
INT/ORG PROB/SOLV ECO/TAC L/A+17C

B63
INTERNATIONAL MONETARY FUND,COMPENSATORY FINANCING OF EXPORT FLUCTUATIONS (PAMPHLET). WOR+45 ECO/DEV ECO/UNDEV INT/ORG WEALTH...TREND 20 IMF MONEY. PAGE 71 A1459
BAL/PAY FINAN BUDGET INT/TRADE

B63
LINDBERG L.,POLITICAL DYNAMICS OF EUROPEAN ECONOMIC INTEGRATION. EUR+WWI ECO/DEV INT/ORG VOL/ASSN DELIB/GP ADMIN WEALTH...DECISION EEC 20. PAGE 89 A1820
MARKET ECO/TAC

B63
MAYNE R.,THE COMMUNITY OF EUROPE. UK CONSTN NAT/G CONSULT DELIB/GP CREATE PLAN ECO/TAC LEGIT ADMIN ROUTINE ORD/FREE PWR WEALTH...CONCPT TIME/SEQ EEC EURATOM 20. PAGE 97 A1985
EUR+WWI INT/ORG REGION

B63
MYRDAL G.,CHALLENGE TO AFFLUENCE. USA+45 WOR+45 FINAN INT/ORG NAT/G PLAN ECO/TAC INT/TRADE BAL/PAY ORD/FREE 20 EUROPE/W. PAGE 107 A2189
ECO/DEV WEALTH DIPLOM PRODUC

B63
RAO V.K.R.,FOREIGN AID AND INDIA'S ECONOMIC DEVELOPMENT. INDIA INT/ORG PROB/SOLV TEC/DEV ECO/TAC CONTROL WEALTH...TREND 20. PAGE 119 A2445
FOR/AID ECO/UNDEV RECEIVE DIPLOM

B63
THEOBALD R.,FREE MEN AND FREE MARKETS. USA+45 USA-45 ECO/DEV NAT/G TEC/DEV DIPLOM INT/TRADE INCOME ORD/FREE WEALTH...TREND 19/20 KEYNES/JM. PAGE 143 A2915
CONCPT ECO/TAC CAP/ISM MARKET

B63
TUCKER R.C.,THE SOVIET POLITICAL MIND. WOR+45 ELITES INT/ORG NAT/G POL/PAR PLAN DIPLOM ECO/TAC DOMIN ADMIN NUC/PWR REV DRIVE PERSON SUPEGO PWR WEALTH...POLICY MGT PSY CONCPT OBS BIOG TREND COLD/WAR MARX/KARL 20. PAGE 145 A2972
COM TOP/EX USSR

B63
US SENATE COMM GOVT OPERATIONS,REPORT OF A STUDY OF US FOREIGN AID IN TEN MIDDLE EASTERN AND AFRICAN COUNTRIES. AFR ISLAM USA+45 FORCES PLAN BUDGET DIPLOM TAX DETER WEALTH...STAT CHARTS 20 CONGRESS AID MID/EAST. PAGE 156 A3174
FOR/AID EFFICIENCY ECO/TAC FINAN

B63
WESTERFIELD H.,THE INSTRUMENTS OF AMERICA'S FOREIGN POLICY. WOR+45 ECO/DEV NAT/G CONSULT EX/STRUC LEGIS BAL/PWR FOR/AID INT/TRADE DOMIN EDU/PROP LEGIT ATTIT KNOWL ORD/FREE PWR WEALTH...OBS COLD/WAR TOT/POP VAL/FREE. PAGE 163 A3322
USA+45 INT/ORG DIPLOM

B63
YOUNG A.N.,CHINA AND THE HELPING HAND. ASIA USA+45 FINAN INDUS ECO/TAC GIVE WEALTH...METH/COMP 20 LEND/LEASE GOLD/STAND. PAGE 169 A3434
FOR/AID DIPLOM WAR

L63
LISSITZYN O.J.,"INTERNATIONAL LAW IN A DIVIDED WORLD." FUT WOR+45 CONSTN CULTURE ECO/DEV ECO/UNDEV DIST/IND NAT/G FORCES ECO/TAC LEGIT ADJUD ADMIN COERCE ATTIT HEALTH MORAL ORD/FREE PWR RESPECT WEALTH VAL/FREE. PAGE 90 A1841
INT/ORG LAW

L63
PADELFORD N.J.,"FINANCIAL CRISIS AND THE UNITED NATIONS." FUT USSR WOR+45 LAW CONSTN FINAN INT/ORG DELIB/GP FORCES PLAN BUDGET DIPLOM COST WEALTH ...STAT CHARTS UN CONGO 20. PAGE 113 A2311
CREATE ECO/TAC

L63
PRINCETON UNIV. CONFERENCE,"ARAB DEVELOPMENT IN THE EMERGING INTERNATIONAL ECONOMY." FUT USA+45 DIST/IND FINAN DELIB/GP PLAN ECO/TAC WEALTH VAL/FREE 20. PAGE 118 A2413
ISLAM ECO/UNDEV FOR/AID INT/TRADE

S63
ALEXANDER R.,"LATIN AMERICA AND THE COMMUNIST BLOC." ASIA COM CUBA L/A+17C USA+45 USSR NAT/G VOL/ASSN TEC/DEV FOR/AID LEGIT PWR WEALTH COLD/WAR 20. PAGE 6 A0112
ECO/UNDEV RECORD

S63
ALPHAND H.,"FRANCE AND HER ALLIES." EUR+WWI UK USA+45 ECO/DEV INT/ORG NAT/G VOL/ASSN FORCES TOP/EX DIPLOM ECO/TAC LEGIT ATTIT DRIVE ORD/FREE PWR WEALTH...STAT EEC TOT/POP 20. PAGE 6 A0130
ACT/RES FRANCE

S63
ANGUILE G.,"CIVILISATION DU PLAN DANS L'EUROPE ET L'AFRIQUE DE DEMAIN." AFR EUR+WWI GABON ECO/DEV FINAN MARKET DELIB/GP ECO/TAC WEALTH...TREND 20. PAGE 8 A0163
ECO/UNDEV PLAN INT/TRADE

S63
BELOFF M.,"BRITAIN, EUROPE AND THE ATLANTIC COMMUNITY." EUR+WWI ELITES NAT/G VOL/ASSN TOP/EX ATTIT ORD/FREE PWR SOVEREIGN WEALTH EEC TOT/POP VAL/FREE CMN/WLTH 20. PAGE 13 A0262
INT/ORG ECO/DEV UK

S63
COUTY P.,"L'ASSISTANCE POUR LE DEVELOPPEMENT: POINT DE VUE SCANDINAVES." EUR+WWI FINLAND FUT SWEDEN WOR+45 ECO/DEV ECO/UNDEV COM/IND LABOR NAT/G PROF/ORG ACT/RES SKILL WEALTH TOT/POP 20. PAGE 32 A0643
FINAN ROUTINE FOR/AID

S63
DAVEE R.,"POUR UN FONDS DE DEVELOPPEMENT SOCIAL." FUT WOR+45 INTELL SOCIETY ECO/DEV FINAN TEC/DEV ROUTINE WEALTH...TREND TOT/POP VAL/FREE UN 20. PAGE 34 A0684
INT/ORG SOC FOR/AID

S63
DIEBOLD W. JR.,"THE NEW SITUATION OF INTERNATIONAL TRADE POLICY." EUR+WWI FRANCE FUT UK USA+45 WOR+45 DIST/IND PLAN INT/TRADE EDU/PROP PWR WEALTH ...RECORD TREND GEN/LAWS EEC VAL/FREE 20. PAGE 37 A0760
MARKET ECO/TAC

S63
EMERSON R.,"THE ATLANTIC COMMUNITY AND THE EMERGING COUNTRIES." FUT WOR+45 ECO/DEV ECO/UNDEV R+D NAT/G DELIB/GP BAL/PWR ECO/TAC EDU/PROP ROUTINE ORD/FREE PWR WEALTH...POLICY CONCPT TREND GEN/METH EEC 20 NATO. PAGE 42 A0848
ATTIT INT/TRADE

S63
ETZIONI A.,"EUROPEAN UNIFICATION: A STRATEGY OF CHANGE." EUR+WWI CULTURE ECO/DEV DELIB/GP ACT/RES ECO/TAC EDU/PROP ATTIT ORD/FREE PWR SKILL WEALTH ...STAT TIME/SEQ EEC TOT/POP VAL/FREE 20. PAGE 42 A0869
INT/ORG RIGID/FLEX

S63
ETZIONI A.,"EUROPEAN UNIFICATION AND PERSPECTIVES ON SOVEREIGNTY." EUR+WWI FUT DELIB/GP TEC/DEV ECO/TAC EDU/PROP DETER NUC/PWR ATTIT DRIVE ORD/FREE PWR WEALTH...CONCPT RECORD TIME/SEQ EEC VAL/FREE 20. PAGE 43 A0870
INT/ORG ECO/DEV SOVEREIGN

S63
GORDON B.,"ECONOMIC IMPEDIMENTS TO REGIONALISM IN SOUTH EAST ASIA." BURMA FUT S/ASIA THAILAND USA+45 AGRI INDUS R+D NAT/G PLAN ECO/TAC WEALTH...STAT CONT/OBS 20. PAGE 54 A1110
VOL/ASSN ECO/UNDEV INT/TRADE REGION

S63
HAVILAND H.F.,"BUILDING A POLITICAL COMMUNITY." EUR+WWI FUT UK USA+45 ECO/DEV ECO/UNDEV INT/ORG NAT/G DELIB/GP BAL/PWR ECO/TAC NEUTRAL ROUTINE ATTIT PWR WEALTH...CONCPT COLD/WAR TOT/POP 20. PAGE 63 A1293
VOL/ASSN DIPLOM

S63
HINDLEY D.,"FOREIGN AID TO INDONESIA AND ITS POLITICAL IMPLICATIONS." INDONESIA POL/PAR ATTIT SOVEREIGN...CHARTS 20. PAGE 65 A1336
FOR/AID NAT/G WEALTH ECO/TAC

S63
HORVATH J.,"MOSCOW'S AID PROGRAM: THE PERFORMANCE SO FAR." COM FUT USSR WOR+45 ECO/DEV FINAN PLAN TEC/DEV FOR/AID EDU/PROP ATTIT ORD/FREE PWR WEALTH ...POLICY STAT CHARTS VAL/FREE 20. PAGE 68 A1389
ECO/UNDEV ECO/TAC

S63
KRAVIS I.B.,"THE POLITICAL ARITHMETIC OF INTERNATIONAL BURDENSHARING." FUT USA+45 WOR+45 FINAN DELIB/GP ACT/RES CREATE TEC/DEV ATTIT PWR WEALTH...POLICY MATH STAT VAL/FREE 20. PAGE 82 A1681
INT/ORG ECO/TAC

S63
MATHUR P.N.,"GAINS IN ECONOMIC GROWTH FROM INTERNATIONAL TRADE." USA-45 ECO/DEV FINAN INDUS ATTIT WEALTH...MATH QUANT STAT BIOG TREND GEN/LAWS WORK 20. PAGE 96 A1966
MARKET ECO/TAC CAP/ISM INT/TRADE

S63
NADLER E.B.,"SOME ECONOMIC DISADVANTAGES OF THE ARMS RACE." USA+45 INDUS R+D FORCES PLAN TEC/DEV ECO/TAC FOR/AID EDU/PROP PWR WEALTH...TREND COLD/WAR 20. PAGE 107 A2190
ECO/DEV MGT BAL/PAY

S63
NYE J.S. JR.,"EAST AFRICAN ECONOMIC INTEGRATION." AFR UGANDA PROVS DELIB/GP PLAN ECO/TAC INT/TRADE ADMIN ROUTINE ORD/FREE PWR WEALTH...OBS TIME/SEQ VAL/FREE 20. PAGE 110 A2264
ECO/UNDEV INT/ORG

S63
PINCUS J.,"THE COST OF FOREIGN AID." WOR+45 ECO/DEV FINAN NAT/G VOL/ASSN CREATE ECO/TAC EDU/PROP WEALTH ...METH/CNCPT STAT CHARTS HYPO/EXP TOT/POP VAL/FREE 20. PAGE 116 A2380
USA+45 ECO/UNDEV FOR/AID

S63
RAMERIE L.,"TENSION AU SEIN DU COMECON: LE CAS ROUMAIN." COM EUR+WWI USSR WOR+45 ECO/DEV DIST/IND NAT/G POL/PAR VOL/ASSN EDU/PROP TOTALISM ATTIT WEALTH...TIME/SEQ 20 COMECON. PAGE 119 A2438
INT/ORG ECO/TAC INT/TRADE ROMANIA

S63
SCHMIDT W.E.,"THE CASE AGAINST COMMODITY AGREEMENTS." FUT L/A+17C STRATA CONSULT PLAN ECO/TAC EDU/PROP ATTIT DRIVE RIGID/FLEX WEALTH ...MYTH 20. PAGE 128 A2631
ECO/UNDEV ACT/RES INT/TRADE

S63
SCHOFLING J.A.,"EFTA: THE OTHER EUROPE." ECO/DEV MARKET CONSULT ECO/TAC WEALTH...TIME/SEQ EEC OEEC 20 EFTA. PAGE 129 A2642
EUR+WWI INT/ORG REGION

S63
SINGER M.R.,"ELECTIONS WITHIN THE UNITED NATIONS: AN EXPERIMENTAL STUDY UTILIZING STATISTICAL ANALYSIS." USA+45 WOR+45 DIPLOM ECO/TAC COERCE PWR WEALTH...STAT CHARTS SIMUL GEN/LAWS COLD/WAR VAL/FREE UN 20. PAGE 133 A2732
INT/ORG CHOOSE

S63
VINER J.,"REPORT OF THE CLAY COMMITTEE ON FOREIGN AID: A SYMPOSIUM." USA+45 WOR+45 NAT/G CONSULT PLAN BAL/PWR ATTIT WEALTH...MGT CONCPT TOT/POP 20. PAGE 159 A3240
ACT/RES ECO/TAC FOR/AID

B64
ALVIM J.C.,A REVOLUCAO SEM RUMO. BRAZIL NAT/G BAL/PWR DIPLOM INT/TRADE PARTIC WEALTH...POLICY SOC SOC/INTEG 20. PAGE 6 A0132
REV CIVMIL/REL ECO/UNDEV ORD/FREE

B64
BOYD J.P.,NUMBER 7: ALEXANDER HAMILTON'S SECRET ATTEMPTS TO CONTROL AMERICAN FOREIGN POLICY. AFR UK DIPLOM WAR RESPECT WEALTH...POLICY HIST/WRIT 18 HAMILTON/A. PAGE 18 A0364
USA-45 NAT/G TOP/EX PWR

B64
BUTWELL R.,SOUTHEAST ASIA TODAY - AND TOMORROW. NAT/G COLONIAL LEAD REGION WAR CHOOSE WEALTH MARXISM 20. PAGE 23 A0458
S/ASIA DIPLOM ECO/UNDEV NAT/LISM

B64
ETZIONI A.,WINNING WITHOUT WAR. FUT MOD/EUR USA+45 WOR+45 ECO/DEV ECO/UNDEV INT/ORG NAT/G FORCES TOP/EX PLAN TEC/DEV ECO/TAC DOMIN EDU/PROP LEGIT COERCE CHOOSE ATTIT MORAL ORD/FREE RESPECT WEALTH MAJORIT. PAGE 43 A0871
PWR TREND DIPLOM USSR

B64
FEIS H.,FOREIGN AID AND FOREIGN POLICY. USA+45 WOR+45 NAT/G VOL/ASSN ACT/RES TEC/DEV ATTIT HEALTH WEALTH...SOC GEN/LAWS 20. PAGE 45 A0912
ECO/UNDEV ECO/TAC FOR/AID DIPLOM

B64
GARDNER L.C.,ECONOMIC ASPECTS OF NEW DEAL DIPLOMACY. USA-45 WOR-45 LAW ECO/DEV INT/ORG NAT/G VOL/ASSN LEGIS TOP/EX EDU/PROP ORD/FREE PWR WEALTH ...POLICY TIME/SEQ VAL/FREE 20 ROOSEVLT/F. PAGE 51 A1043
ECO/TAC DIPLOM

B64
HANSEN B.,INTERNATIONAL LIQUIDITY. USA+45 INT/ORG ECO/TAC PRICE CONTROL WEALTH...POLICY 20. PAGE 61 A1254
BAL/PAY INT/TRADE DIPLOM FINAN

B64
HEKHUIS D.J.,INTERNATIONAL STABILITY: MILITARY, ECONOMIC AND POLITICAL DIMENSIONS. FUT WOR+45 LAW ECO/UNDEV INT/ORG NAT/G VOL/ASSN FORCES ACT/RES BAL/PWR PWR WEALTH...STAT UN 20. PAGE 64 A1310
TEC/DEV DETER REGION

B64
JOHNSON L.B.,MY HOPE FOR AMERICA. FUT USA+45 USSR LAW PLAN DIPLOM GIVE INCOME PEACE ATTIT ORD/FREE WEALTH 20 JOHNSON/LB PRESIDENT DEMOCRAT. PAGE 74 A1525
POLICY POL/PAR NAT/G GOV/REL

B64
KNIGHT R.,BIBLIOGRAPHY ON INCOME AND WEALTH, 1957-1960 (VOL VIII). WOR+45 ECO/DEV FINAN INT/TRADE...GOV/COMP METH/COMP. PAGE 80 A1652
BIBLIOG/A ECO/UNDEV WEALTH INCOME

B64
LITTLE I.M.D.,AID TO AFRICA. AFR UK TEC/DEV DIPLOM ECO/TAC INCOME WEALTH 20. PAGE 90 A1844
FOR/AID ECO/UNDEV ADMIN POLICY

B64
LUTHULI A.,AFRICA'S FREEDOM. KIN LABOR POL/PAR SCHOOL DIPLOM NEUTRAL REGION REV NAT/LISM PWR
AFR ECO/UNDEV

WEALTH SOCISM SOC/INTEG 20. PAGE 92 A1874 — COLONIAL

B64
MARKHAM J.W.,THE COMMON MARKET: FRIEND OR COMPETITOR. EUR+WWI FUT USA+45 INT/ORG LG/CO NAT/G VOL/ASSN DELIB/GP EX/STRUC PLAN TARIFFS ORD/FREE PWR WEALTH...POLICY STAT TREND EEC VAL/FREE 20. PAGE 95 A1943 — ECO/DEV ECO/TAC

B64
MORGAN T.,GOLDWATER EITHER/OR; A SELF-PORTRAIT BASED UPON HIS OWN WORDS. USA+45 CONSTN AGRI LABOR DIPLOM RACE/REL WEALTH POPULISM...POLICY MAJORIT 20 GOLDWATR/B REPUBLICAN. PAGE 104 A2131 — LEAD POL/PAR CHOOSE ATTIT

B64
OWEN W.,STRATEGY FOR MOBILITY. FUT WOR+45 WOR-45 DIST/IND INT/ORG NAT/G DELIB/GP PLAN TEC/DEV ECO/TAC ORD/FREE PWR WEALTH...STAT TIME/SEQ VAL/FREE 20. PAGE 112 A2304 — COM/IND ECO/UNDEV

B64
PLISCHKE E.,SYSTEMS OF INTEGRATING THE INTERNATIONAL COMMUNITY. WOR+45 NAT/G VOL/ASSN ECO/TAC LEGIT PWR WEALTH...TIME/SEQ ANTHOL UN TOT/POP 20. PAGE 116 A2391 — INT/ORG EX/STRUC REGION

B64
RAMAZANI R.K.,THE MIDDLE EAST AND THE EUROPEAN COMMON MARKET. EUR+WWI ISLAM ECO/DEV EXTR/IND MARKET PROC/MFG INT/ORG NAT/G TEC/DEV ECO/TAC REGION DRIVE WEALTH...STAT CHARTS EEC TOT/POP 20. PAGE 119 A2437 — ECO/UNDEV ATTIT INT/TRADE

B64
RUSSET B.M.,WORLD HANDBOOK OF POLITICAL AND SOCIAL INDICATORS. WOR+45 COM/IND ADMIN WEALTH...GEOG 20. PAGE 126 A2577 — DIPLOM STAT NAT/G NAT/COMP

B64
SINGER H.W.,INTERNATIONAL DEVELOPMENT: GROWTH AND CHANGE. AFR BRAZIL L/A+17C WOR+45 CULTURE AGRI INDUS NAT/G ACT/RES ECO/TAC EDU/PROP WEALTH...GEOG CONCPT METH/CNCPT STAT HYPO/EXP WORK TOT/POP 20. PAGE 133 A2723 — FINAN ECO/UNDEV FOR/AID INT/TRADE

B64
STOESSINGER J.G.,FINANCING THE UNITED NATIONS SYSTEM. FUT WOR+45 CONSTN NAT/G VOL/ASSN DELIB/GP EX/STRUC ECO/TAC LEGIT CT/SYS PWR WEALTH...STAT TIME/SEQ TREND CHARTS VAL/FREE. PAGE 138 A2830 — FINAN INT/ORG

B64
TEPASKE J.J.,EXPLOSIVE FORCES IN LATIN AMERICA. CULTURE INTELL ECO/UNDEV INT/ORG NAT/G SECT FORCES ECO/TAC EDU/PROP PWR WEALTH SOC. PAGE 142 A2903 — L/A+17C RIGID/FLEX FOR/AID USSR

B64
TULLY A.,WHERE DID YOUR MONEY GO. USA+45 USSR ECO/UNDEV ADMIN EFFICIENCY WEALTH...METH/COMP 20. PAGE 146 A2976 — FOR/AID DIPLOM CONTROL

B64
ZEBOT C.A.,THE ECONOMICS OF COMPETITIVE COEXISTENCE. CHINA/COM USSR WOR+45 FINAN MARKET FOR/AID PRICE DEMAND EQUILIB WEALTH ALL/IDEOS 20. PAGE 169 A3450 — TEC/DEV DIPLOM METH/COMP

L64
HAAS E.B.,"ECONOMICS AND DIFFERENTIAL PATTERNS OF POLITICAL INTEGRATION: PROJECTIONS ABOUT UNITY IN LATIN AMERICA." SOCIETY NAT/G DELIB/GP ACT/RES CREATE PLAN ECO/TAC REGION ROUTINE ATTIT DRIVE PWR WEALTH...CONCPT TREND CHARTS LAFTA 20. PAGE 59 A1208 — L/A+17C INT/ORG MARKET

L64
MANZER R.A.,"THE UNITED NATIONS SPECIAL FUND." WOR+45 CONSTN ECO/UNDEV NAT/G TOP/EX LEGIT WEALTH ...CHARTS UN 20. PAGE 94 A1936 — FINAN INT/ORG

L64
POUNDS N.J.G.,"THE POLITICS OF PARTITION." AFR ASIA COM EUR+WWI FUT ISLAM S/ASIA USA-45 LAW ECO/DEV ECO/UNDEV AGRI INDUS INT/ORG POL/PAR PROVS SECT FORCES TOP/EX EDU/PROP LEGIT ATTIT MORAL ORD/FREE PWR RESPECT WEALTH. PAGE 117 A2402 — NAT/G NAT/LISM

S64
ASHRAF S.,"INDIA AND WORLD AFFAIRS: AN ANNUAL BIBLIOGRAPHY, 1962." WOR+45 LAW ECO/UNDEV INT/ORG FORCES PLAN ECO/TAC COERCE ORD/FREE PWR WEALTH ...HIST/WRIT VAL/FREE. PAGE 9 A0188 — S/ASIA NAT/G

S64
COCHRANE J.D.,"US ATTITUDES TOWARD CENTRAL-AMERICAN INTEGRATION." L/A+17C USA+45 ECO/UNDEV FACE/GP VOL/ASSN DELIB/GP ECO/TAC INT/TRADE EDU/PROP RIGID/FLEX ORD/FREE WEALTH...TIME/SEQ TOT/POP 20. PAGE 27 A0555 — NAT/G ATTIT REGION

S64
DE GAULLE C.,"FRENCH WORLD VIEW." AFR ASIA CHINA/COM EUR+WWI ISLAM ECO/UNDEV INT/ORG NAT/G VOL/ASSN ACT/RES DIPLOM ECO/TAC EDU/PROP ATTIT DRIVE WEALTH 20. PAGE 35 A0702 — TOP/EX PWR FOR/AID FRANCE

S64
GARDNER R.N.,"GATT AND THE UNITED NATIONS CONFERENCE ON TRADE AND DEVELOPMENT." USA+45 WOR+45 SOCIETY ECO/UNDEV MARKET NAT/G DELIB/GP ACT/RES PLAN ECO/TAC TARIFFS EDU/PROP ROUTINE DRIVE RIGID/FLEX WEALTH...DECISION MGT TREND UN TOT/POP 20 GATT. PAGE 51 A1047 — INT/ORG INT/TRADE

S64
GERBET P.,"LA MISE EN OEUVRE DU MARCHE COMMUN AGRICOLE." ECO/DEV MARKET INT/ORG NAT/G PLAN EDU/PROP NAT/LISM WEALTH...OBS EEC VAL/FREE 20. PAGE 52 A1064 — EUR+WWI AGRI REGION

S64
HABERLER G.,"INTEGRATION AND GROWTH OF THE WORLD ECONOMY IN HISTORICAL PERSPECTIVE." FUT WOR+45 WOR-45 ECO/DEV ECO/UNDEV...TIME/SEQ TREND VAL/FREE 20. PAGE 59 A1209 — WEALTH INT/TRADE

S64
HUELIN D.,"ECONOMIC INTEGRATION IN LATIN AMERICAN: PROGRESS AND PROBLEMS." L/A+17C ECO/DEV AGRI DIST/IND FINAN INDUS NAT/G VOL/ASSN CONSULT DELIB/GP EX/STRUC ACT/RES PLAN TEC/DEV ECO/TAC ROUTINE BAL/PAY WEALTH WORK 20. PAGE 69 A1411 — MARKET ECO/UNDEV INT/TRADE

S64
KOJIMA K.,"THE PATTERN OF INTERNATIONAL TRADE AMONG ADVANCED COUNTRIES." EUR+WWI UK USA+45 WOR+45 MARKET NAT/G ECO/TAC WEALTH...MATH STAT CON/ANAL CHARTS EEC CHINJAP 20 CHINJAP. PAGE 81 A1665 — ECO/DEV TREND INT/TRADE

S64
MARTELLI G.,"PORTUGAL AND THE UNITED NATIONS." AFR EUR+WWI ELITES INT/ORG NAT/G PROVS PLAN DIPLOM ECO/TAC DOMIN COLONIAL RIGID/FLEX MORAL ORD/FREE PWR WEALTH...MYTH UN 20. PAGE 95 A1947 — ATTIT PORTUGAL

S64
MAZRUI A.A.,"THE UNITED NATIONS AND SOME AFRICAN POLITICAL ATTITUDES." ECO/TAC FOR/AID DOMIN ROUTINE CHOOSE ATTIT DRIVE MORAL PWR RESPECT WEALTH...PSY CONCPT OBS TREND UN VAL/FREE 20. PAGE 97 A1987 — AFR INT/ORG SOVEREIGN

S64
MOWER A.G.,"THE OFFICIAL PRESSURE GROUP OF THE COUNCIL OF EUROPE'S CONSULATIVE ASSEMBLY." EUR+WWI SOCIETY STRUCT FINAN CONSULT ECO/TAC ADMIN ROUTINE ATTIT PWR WEALTH...STAT CHARTS 20 COUNCL/EUR. PAGE 105 A2160 — INT/ORG EDU/PROP

S64
NEISSER H.,"THE EXTERNAL EQUILIBRIUM OF THE UNITED STATES ECONOMY." FUT USA+45 NAT/G ACT/RES PLAN ECO/TAC ATTIT WEALTH...METH/CNCPT GEN/METH VAL/FREE 20. PAGE 108 A2216 — FINAN ECO/DEV BAL/PAY INT/TRADE

S64
PADELFORD N.J.,"THE ORGANIZATION OF AFRICAN UNITY." ECO/UNDEV INT/ORG PLAN BAL/PWR DIPLOM ECO/TAC NAT/LISM ORD/FREE PWR WEALTH...CONCPT TREND STERTYP VAL/FREE COLD/WAR 20. PAGE 113 A2313 — AFR VOL/ASSN REGION

S64
PESELT B.M.,"COMMUNIST ECONOMIC OFFENSIVE." WOR+45 SOCIETY INT/ORG PLAN ECO/TAC DOMIN EDU/PROP ATTIT PERSON PWR WEALTH...TREND CHARTS 20. PAGE 115 A2366 — COM ECO/UNDEV FOR/AID USSR

S64
REIDY J.W.,"LATIN AMERICA AND THE ATLANTIC TRIANGLE." EUR+WWI FUT USA+45 INT/ORG NAT/G REGION COERCE ORD/FREE PWR...TIME/SEQ VAL/FREE 20. PAGE 120 A2458 — L/A+17C WEALTH POLICY

S64
SALVADORI M.,"EL CAPITALISMO EN LA EUROPA DE LA POSGUERRA." INT/ORG NAT/G POL/PAR PLAN ECO/TAC ATTIT ORD/FREE WEALTH...HIST/WRIT COLD/WAR EEC 20. PAGE 127 A2596 — EUR+WWI ECO/DEV CAP/ISM

S64
TAUBENFELD R.K.,"INDEPENDENT REVENUE FOR THE UNITED NATIONS." WOR+45 SOCIETY STRUCT INDUS NAT/G CONSULT ACT/RES PLAN ECO/TAC LEGIT WEALTH...DECISION CON/ANAL GEN/METH UN 20. PAGE 142 A2896 — INT/ORG FINAN

S64
TRISKA J.F.,"SOVIET TREATY LAW: A QUANTITATIVE ANALYSIS." WOR+45 LAW ECO/UNDEV AGRI COM/IND INDUS CREATE TEC/DEV DIPLOM ATTIT PWR WEALTH...JURID SAMP TIME/SEQ TREND CHARTS VAL/FREE 20 TREATY. PAGE 145 A2967 — COM ECO/TAC INT/LAW USSR

S64
WOOD H.B.,"STRETCHING YOUR FOREIGN-AID DOLLAR." USA+45 WOR+45 CONSULT EDU/PROP ATTIT WEALTH...OBS TOT/POP CONGRESS 20. PAGE 166 A3390 — ECO/UNDEV MGT FOR/AID

B65
CASSELL F.,GOLD OR CREDIT? THE ECONOMICS AND POLITICS OF INTERNATIONAL MONEY. WOR+45 PLAN PROB/SOLV BAL/PAY SOVEREIGN WEALTH 20 OEEC GOLD/STAND. PAGE 25 A0506 — FINAN INT/ORG DIPLOM ECO/TAC

B65
COOPER S.,BEHIND THE GOLDEN CURTAIN: A VIEW OF THE USA. UK USA+45 SECT EDU/PROP COERCE LEISURE ORD/FREE WEALTH 20. PAGE 30 A0609 — SOCIETY DIPLOM ATTIT ACT/RES

B65
DEMAS W.G.,THE ECONOMICS OF DEVELOPMENT IN SMALL COUNTRIES WITH SPECIAL REFERENCE TO THE CARIBBEAN. WOR+45 BAL/PAY DEMAND EFFICIENCY PRODUC...GEOG CARIBBEAN. PAGE 36 A0731 — ECO/UNDEV PLAN WEALTH INT/TRADE

B65
GERASSI J.,THE GREAT FEAR IN LATIN AMERICA. L/A+17C — SOCIETY

USA+45 ELITES STRUCT INT/ORG REV ORD/FREE WEALTH 20 LAFTA. PAGE 52 A1063 — FOR/AID DIPLOM

B65
HOSELITZ B.F.,ECONOMICS AND THE IDEA OF MANKIND. UNIV ECO/DEV ECO/UNDEV DIST/IND INDUS INT/ORG NAT/G ACT/RES ECO/TAC WEALTH...CONCPT STAT. PAGE 68 A1392 — CREATE INT/TRADE

B65
JALEE P.,THE PILLAGE OF THE THIRD WORLD (TRANS. BY MARY KLOPPER). WOR+45 AGRI INDUS ECO/TAC FOR/AID COLONIAL CONTROL PRODUC PWR WEALTH...STAT CHARTS 20 RESOURCE/N. PAGE 73 A1493 — ECO/UNDEV DOMIN INT/TRADE DIPLOM

B65
JOHNSTONE A.,UNITED STATES DIRECT INVESTMENT IN FRANCE: AN INVESTIGATION OF THE FRENCH CHARGES. FRANCE USA+45 ECO/DEV INDUS LG/CO NAT/G ECO/TAC CONTROL WEALTH...BIBLIOG 20 INTERVENT. PAGE 75 A1529 — FINAN DIPLOM POLICY SOVEREIGN

B65
LEE M.,THE UNITED NATIONS AND WORLD REALITIES. ECO/UNDEV FORCES WAR PEACE ATTIT ROLE WEALTH 20 UN. PAGE 86 A1761 — INT/ORG COLONIAL ARMS/CONT DIPLOM

B65
LEISS A.C.,APARTHEID AND UNITED NATIONS COLLECTIVE MEASURES. SOUTH/AFR ECO/UNDEV EXTR/IND FORCES WORKER ECO/TAC FOR/AID INT/TRADE WEALTH...TREND CHARTS 20 UN NEGRO. PAGE 86 A1770 — DISCRIM RACE/REL STRATA DIPLOM

B65
MONCRIEFF A.,SECOND THOUGHTS ON AID. WOR+45 ECO/UNDEV AGRI FINAN VOL/ASSN PLAN TEC/DEV GIVE EDU/PROP ROLE WEALTH 20. PAGE 102 A2105 — FOR/AID ECO/TAC INT/ORG IDEA/COMP

B65
PANJAB U EXTENSION LIBRARY,INDIAN NEWS INDEX. INDIA ECO/UNDEV INDUS INT/ORG SCHOOL FORCES ADJUD WAR ATTIT WEALTH 20. PAGE 114 A2333 — BIBLIOG PRESS WRITING DIPLOM

B65
US SENATE COMM BANKING CURR,BALANCE OF PAYMENTS - 1965. USA+45 ECO/TAC PRICE WEALTH...CHARTS 20 CONGRESS GOLD/STAND. PAGE 156 A3171 — BAL/PAY FINAN DIPLOM INT/TRADE

B65
US SENATE COMM ON JUDICIARY,ANTITRUST EXEMPTIONS FOR AGREEMENTS RELATING TO BALANCE OF PAYMENTS. FINAN ECO/TAC CONTROL WEALTH...POLICY 20 CONGRESS. PAGE 157 A3195 — BAL/PAY ADJUD MARKET INT/TRADE

B65
WEAVER J.N.,THE INTERNATIONAL DEVELOPMENT ASSOCIATION: A NEW APPROACH TO FOREIGN AID. USA+45 NAT/G OP/RES PLAN PROB/SOLV WEALTH...CHARTS BIBLIOG 20 UN. PAGE 162 A3295 — FOR/AID INT/ORG ECO/UNDEV FINAN

L65
LOFTUS M.L.,"INTERNATIONAL MONETARY FUND, 1962-1965: A SELECTED BIBLIOGRAPHY." WOR+45 PLAN BUDGET INCOME PROFIT WEALTH. PAGE 90 A1852 — BIBLIOG FINAN INT/TRADE INT/ORG

L65
MATTHEWS D.G.,"LE TIERS MONDE: A SELECT AND PRELIMINARY BIBLIOGRAPHIC SURVEY OF MANPOWER IN DEVELOPING COUNTRIES, 1960-1964." AFR ISLAM L/A+17C INDUS PLAN PROB/SOLV TEC/DEV INT/TRADE EFFICIENCY WEALTH...STAT 20. PAGE 96 A1971 — BIBLIOG/A ECO/UNDEV LABOR WORKER

L65
WIONCZEK M.,"LATIN AMERICA FREE TRADE ASSOCIATION." AGRI DIST/IND FINAN INDUS INT/ORG LABOR NAT/G TEC/DEV ECO/TAC HEALTH SKILL WEALTH...POLICY RELATIV MGT LAFTA 20. PAGE 165 A3369 — L/A+17C MARKET REGION

S65
KORBONSKI A.,"USA POLICY IN EAST EUROPE." COM EUR+WWI GERMANY USA+45 CULTURE ECO/UNDEV EDU/PROP RIGID/FLEX WEALTH 20. PAGE 82 A1672 — ACT/RES ECO/TAC FOR/AID

S65
QUADE Q.L.,"THE TRUMAN ADMINISTRATION AND THE SEPARATION OF POWERS: THE CASE OF THE MARSHALL PLAN." SOCIETY INT/ORG NAT/G CONSULT DELIB/GP LEGIS PLAN ECO/TAC ROUTINE DRIVE PERCEPT RIGID/FLEX ORD/FREE PWR WEALTH...DECISION GEOG NEW/IDEA TREND 20 TRUMAN/HS. PAGE 118 A2422 — USA+45 ECO/UNDEV DIPLOM

B66
CURRIE L.,ACCELERATING DEVELOPMENT: THE NECESSITY AND MEANS. COLOMBIA USA+45 INDUS DIPLOM EFFICIENCY WEALTH...METH/CNCPT NEW/IDEA 20. PAGE 33 A0668 — PLAN ECO/UNDEV FOR/AID TEC/DEV

B66
FITZGERALD C.P.,THE BIRTH OF COMMUNIST CHINA (2ND ED.). ASIA CHINA/COM STRUCT BAL/PWR DIPLOM ECO/TAC INT/TRADE WEALTH 20. PAGE 46 A0942 — REV MARXISM ECO/UNDEV

B66
HOROWITZ D.,HEMISPHERES NORTH AND SOUTH: ECONOMIC DISPARITY AMONG NATIONS. WOR+45 ECO/DEV ECO/UNDEV INT/ORG PLAN DIPLOM INT/TRADE GIVE PARTIC GP/REL ...WELF/ST 20. PAGE 67 A1387 — ECO/TAC FOR/AID STRATA WEALTH

B66
INTERNATIONAL ECO POLICY ASSN,THE UNITED STATES BALANCE OF PAYMENTS. INT/ORG NAT/G PROB/SOLV BUDGET DIPLOM INT/TRADE WEALTH 20. PAGE 71 A1454 — BAL/PAY ECO/TAC POLICY FINAN

B66
KANET R.E.,THE SOVIET UNION AND SUB-SAHARAN AFRICA: COMMUNIST POLICY TOWARD AFRICA, 1917-1965. AFR USSR ECO/UNDEV TEC/DEV EDU/PROP TASK DISCRIM PEACE WEALTH ALL/IDEOS...CHARTS BIBLIOG SOC/INTEG 19/20 NEGRO UN INTERVENT. PAGE 76 A1555 — DIPLOM ECO/TAC MARXISM

B66
KAREFA-SMART J.,AFRICA: PROGRESS THROUGH COOPERATION. AFR FINAN TEC/DEV DIPLOM FOR/AID EDU/PROP CONFER REGION GP/REL WEALTH...HEAL SOC/INTEG 20. PAGE 76 A1566 — ORD/FREE ECO/UNDEV VOL/ASSN PLAN

B66
KEENLEYSIDE H.L.,INTERNATIONAL AID: A SUMMARY. AFR INDIA S/ASIA UK STRATA EXTR/IND TEC/DEV ADMIN RACE/REL DEMAND NAT/LISM WEALTH...TREND CHINJAP. PAGE 77 A1575 — ECO/UNDEV FOR/AID DIPLOM TASK

B66
LEWIS S.,TOWARDS INTERNATIONAL CO-OPERATION (1ST ED.). WOR+45 AGRI INDUS EDU/PROP RACE/REL ISOLAT NAT/LISM ATTIT HEALTH WEALTH...CHARTS WORSHIP 20 UN. PAGE 88 A1803 — DIPLOM ANOMIE PROB/SOLV INT/ORG

B66
MAY E.R.,ANXIETY AND AFFLUENCE: 1945-1965. USA+45 DIPLOM FOR/AID ARMS/CONT RACE/REL CONSEN...ANTHOL 20 COLD/WAR KENNEDY/JF EISNHWR/DD TRUMAN/HS BERLIN/BLO. PAGE 97 A1982 — ANOMIE ECO/DEV NUC/PWR WEALTH

B66
TINKER H.,SOUTH ASIA. UK LAW ECO/UNDEV AGRI ACADEM SECT DIPLOM EDU/PROP REV WEALTH ALL/IDEOS...CHARTS BIBLIOG GANDHI/M NEHRU/J. PAGE 144 A2945 — S/ASIA COLONIAL TREND

B66
TRIFFIN R.,THE WORLD MONEY MAZE. INT/ORG ECO/TAC PRICE OPTIMAL WEALTH...METH/COMP 20 EEC OEEC GOLD/STAND SILVER. PAGE 145 A2964 — BAL/PAY FINAN INT/TRADE DIPLOM

B66
WHITAKER A.P.,NATIONALISM IN CONTEMPORARY LATIN AMERICA. AGRI NAT/G WEALTH...POLICY SOC CONCPT OBS TREND 20. PAGE 164 A3333 — NAT/LISM L/A+17C DIPLOM ECO/UNDEV

N66
BRITISH DEVELOPMENT POLICIES: 1966 (PAMPHLET). UK AGRI TARIFFS BAL/PAY...TREND CHARTS 20 OVRSEA/DEV. PAGE 4 A0076 — WEALTH DIPLOM INT/TRADE FOR/AID

B67
CECIL L.,ALBERT BALLIN; BUSINESS AND POLITICS IN IMPERIAL GERMANY 1888-1918. GERMANY UK INT/TRADE LEAD WAR PERS/REL ADJUST PWR WEALTH...MGT BIBLIOG 19/20. PAGE 25 A0510 — DIPLOM CONSTN ECO/DEV TOP/EX

B67
KNOLES G.H.,THE RESPONSIBILITIES OF POWER, 1900-1929. USA-45 SOCIETY SECT JUDGE COLONIAL REPRESENT WEALTH POPULISM...IDEA/COMP ANTHOL PRESIDENT 20 LEAGUE/NAT. PAGE 81 A1653 — PWR DIPLOM NAT/LISM WAR

B67
MACRIDIS R.C.,FOREIGN POLICY IN WORLD POLITICS (3RD ED.). EX/STRUC BAL/PWR COLONIAL NAT/LISM SKILL SOVEREIGN WEALTH...CONCPT TIME/SEQ ANTHOL 20 COLD/WAR. PAGE 93 A1902 — DIPLOM POLICY NAT/G IDEA/COMP

L67
DEVADHAR Y.C.,"THE ROLE OF FOREIGN PRIVATE CAPITAL IN INDIA'S ECONOMIC DEVELOPMENT* ASSESSMENT OF POLICY AND PERFORMANCE." INDIA INDUS PLAN TEC/DEV BUDGET DIPLOM ECO/TAC BAL/PAY PRODUC WEALTH ...CHARTS 20. PAGE 37 A0750 — CAP/ISM FOR/AID POLICY ACT/RES

S67
BENTLEY E.,"VIETNAM: THE STATE OF OUR FEELINGS." USA+45 VIETNAM PROB/SOLV DIPLOM GP/REL INGP/REL RACE/REL WEALTH. PAGE 13 A0271 — WAR PARTIC ATTIT PEACE

S67
BUTTINGER J.,"VIETNAM* FRAUD OF THE 'OTHER WAR'." VIETNAM/S ELITES STRUCT AGRI NAT/G FOR/AID RENT TREND. PAGE 22 A0456 — PLAN WEALTH REV ECO/UNDEV

S67
CHAND A.,"INDIA AND TANZANIA." INDIA TANZANIA TEC/DEV ECO/TAC FOR/AID COLONIAL PEACE UTIL WEALTH ...GOV/COMP 20. PAGE 25 A0518 — ECO/UNDEV NEUTRAL DIPLOM PLAN

S67
FALKOWSKI M.,"SOCIALIST ECONOMISTS AND THE DEVELOPING COUNTRIES." COM PLAN TEC/DEV ROUTINE DEMAND EFFICIENCY PRODUC WEALTH...MARXIST TREND GEN/METH. PAGE 44 A0893 — DIPLOM SOCISM ECO/UNDEV INDUS

S67
FELDMAN H.,"AID AS IMPERIALISM?" INDIA PAKISTAN UK USA+45 BAL/PWR CAP/ISM DIPLOM ECO/TAC DOMIN BAL/PAY WEALTH...POLICY 20. PAGE 45 A0914 — COLONIAL FOR/AID S/ASIA ECO/UNDEV

S67
FRANK I.,"NEW PERSPECTIVES ON TRADE AND DEVELOPMENT." PROB/SOLV BARGAIN DIPLOM FOR/AID — ECO/UNDEV INT/ORG

CONFER GP/REL WEALTH 20 UN GATT. PAGE 48 A0980
INT/TRADE ECO/TAC

S67
FRENCH D.S.,"DOES THE U.S. EXPLOIT THE DEVELOPING NATIONS?" INT/ORG NAT/G CAP/ISM BAL/PAY WEALTH POLICY. PAGE 49 A0997
ECO/UNDEV INT/TRADE ECO/TAC COLONIAL

S67
HULL E.W.S.,"THE POLITICAL OCEAN." FUT UNIV WOR+45 EXTR/IND R+D VOL/ASSN PLAN BAL/PWR ECO/TAC PEACE WEALTH 20 UN. PAGE 69 A1414
DIPLOM ECO/UNDEV INT/ORG INT/LAW

S67
LEFF N.H.,"EXPORT STAGNATION AND AUTARKIC DEVELOPMENT IN BRAZIL, 19471962." BRAZIL ECO/TAC TARIFFS 20. PAGE 86 A1764
BAL/PAY INT/TRADE WEALTH DIPLOM

S67
LEVI M.,"LES DIFFICULTES ECONOMIQUES DE LA GRANDE-BRETAGNE." UK INT/ORG TEC/DEV BARGAIN DIPLOM DOMIN REPRESENT DEMAND WEALTH...POLICY 20 EEC. PAGE 88 A1792
BAL/PAY INT/TRADE PRODUC

S67
PERLO V.,"NEW DIMENSIONS IN EAST-WEST TRADE." UK USA+45 USSR WOR+45 ECO/DEV NAT/G CAP/ISM PEACE WEALTH LAISSEZ...SOCIALIST MGT 20. PAGE 115 A2364
BAL/PWR ECO/TAC INT/TRADE

S67
SARBADHIKARI P.,"A NOTE ON THE DOMESTIC CRISIS OF NON-ALIGNMENT." ELITES INTELL ECO/UNDEV FOR/AID DOMIN. PAGE 127 A2605
NEUTRAL WEALTH TOTALISM BAL/PWR

S67
WINTHROP H.,"CONTEMPORARY ECONOMIC DEHUMANIZATION* SOME DIFFICULTIES SURROUNDING ITS REDUCTION." USA+45 WOR+45 ACT/RES PROB/SOLV DIPLOM ROUTINE DEMAND UTIL. PAGE 165 A3368
TEC/DEV SOCIETY WEALTH

B96
SMITH A.,LECTURES ON JUSTICE, POLICE, REVENUE AND ARMS (1763). UK LAW FAM FORCES TARIFFS AGREE COERCE INCOME OWN WEALTH LAISSEZ...GEN/LAWS 17/18. PAGE 134 A2743
DIPLOM JURID OLD/LIB TAX

WEAPON....NON-NUCLEAR WEAPONS

N
JOURNAL OF CONFLICT RESOLUTION. FUT WOR+45 INT/ORG NAT/G FORCES CREATE PROB/SOLV ARMS/CONT NUC/PWR WEAPON SOC. PAGE 1 A0014
BIBLIOG/A DIPLOM WAR

N
COUNCIL ON FOREIGN RELATIONS,DOCUMENTS ON AMERICAN FOREIGN RELATIONS. INT/ORG ECO/TAC NUC/PWR WAR WEAPON...POLICY CON/ANAL CHARTS 20 OAS UN. PAGE 31 A0639
BIBLIOG USA+45 USA-45 DIPLOM

N
KYRIAK T.E.,EAST EUROPE: BIBLIOGRAPHY--INDEX TO US JPRS RESEARCH TRANSLATIONS. ALBANIA BULGARIA COM CZECHOSLVK HUNGARY POLAND ROMANIA AGRI EXTR/IND FINAN SERV/IND INT/TRADE WEAPON...GEOG MGT SOC 20. PAGE 83 A1701
BIBLIOG/A PRESS MARXISM INDUS

B14
DE BLOCH J.,THE FUTURE OF WAR IN ITS TECHNICAL, ECONOMIC, AND POLITICAL RELATIONS (1899). MOD/EUR TEC/DEV BUDGET INT/TRADE DETER GUERRILLA WEAPON COST PEACE 20. PAGE 34 A0698
WAR BAL/PWR PREDICT FORCES

B17
MEYER H.H.B.,LIST OF REFERENCES ON EMBARGOES (PAMPHLET). USA-45 AGRI DIPLOM WRITING DEBATE WEAPON...INT/LAW 18/20 CONGRESS. PAGE 100 A2049
BIBLIOG DIST/IND ECO/TAC INT/TRADE

N19
MORGENSTERN O.,THE COMMAND AND CONTROL STRUCTURE (PAMPHLET). USSR COM/IND INT/ORG WEAPON PEACE UTIL ...TREND 20 NATO. PAGE 104 A2132
CONTROL FORCES EFFICIENCY PLAN

N19
ZLOTNICK M.,WEAPONS IN SPACE (PAMPHLET). FUT WOR+45 TEC/DEV DIPLOM ARMS/CONT CIVMIL/REL PEACE HABITAT ...CONCPT NEW/IDEA CHARTS. PAGE 170 A3457
SPACE WEAPON NUC/PWR WAR

C25
MOON P.T.,"SYLLABUS ON INTERNATIONAL RELATIONS." EUR+WWI MOD/EUR USA-45 FORCES COLONIAL WAR WEAPON NAT/LISM...POLICY BIBLIOG T 19/20. PAGE 103 A2120
INT/ORG DIPLOM NAT/G

B34
EINSTEIN A.,THE WORLD AS I SEE IT. WOR-45 INTELL R+D INT/ORG NAT/G SECT VOL/ASSN FORCES CREATE EDU/PROP LEGIT ARMS/CONT WAR WEAPON NAT/LISM ALL/VALS...POLICY CONCPT 20. PAGE 41 A0828
SOCIETY PHIL/SCI DIPLOM PACIFISM

B36
HUDSON M.O.,INTERNATIONAL LEGISLATION: 1929-193* WOR-45 SEA AIR AGRI FINAN LABOR DIPLOM ECO/TAC REPAR CT/SYS ARMS/CONT WAR WEAPON...JURID 20 TREATY LEAGUE/NAT. PAGE 69 A1409
INT/LAW PARL/PROC ADJUD LAW

B39
FULLER G.H.,A SELECTED LIST OF REFERENCES ON THE EXPANSION OF THE US NAVY, 1933-1939 (PAMPHLET). MOD/EUR USA-45 NAT/G PLAN DIPLOM DOMIN RISK ARMS/CONT EQUILIB PWR 20 NAVY. PAGE 50 A1019
BIBLIOG FORCES WEAPON WAR

B39
SPEIER H.,WAR IN OUR TIME. WOR-45 AGRI FINAN FORCES TEC/DEV BAL/PWR EDU/PROP WEAPON PEACE PWR...ANTHOL 20. PAGE 136 A2779
FASCISM WAR DIPLOM NAT/G

B42
FULLER G.H.,DEFENSE FINANCING: A SUPPLEMENTARY LIST OF REFERENCES (PAMPHLET). CANADA UK USA-45 ECO/DEV NAT/G DELIB/GP BUDGET ADJUD ARMS/CONT WEAPON COST PEACE PWR 20 AUSTRAL CHINJAP CONGRESS. PAGE 50 A1021
BIBLIOG/A FINAN FORCES DIPLOM

B56
ESTEP R.,AN AIR POWER BIBLIOGRAPHY. USA+45 TEC/DEV BUDGET DIPLOM EDU/PROP DETER CIVMIL/REL...DECISION INT/LAW 20. PAGE 42 A0862
BIBLIOG/A FORCES WEAPON PLAN

B56
FOSTER J.G.,BRITAIN IN WESTERN EUROPE: WEU AND THE ATLANTIC ALLIANCE. EUR+WWI FRANCE GERMANY GERMANY/W ITALY UK STRATA NAT/G DELIB/GP ECO/TAC ORD/FREE PWR ...TRADIT TIME/SEQ TREND OEEC PARLIAMENT 20 EUROPE/W. PAGE 47 A0969
INT/ORG FORCES WEAPON

B57
SPEIER H.,GERMAN REARMAMENT AND ATOMIC WAR: THE VIEWS OF GERMAN MILITARY AND POLITICAL LEADERS. FUT WOR+45 INT/ORG NAT/G WEAPON ATTIT PWR...INT QU TOT/POP VAL/FREE COLD/WAR 20. PAGE 136 A2780
TOP/EX FORCES NUC/PWR GERMANY

B57
US SENATE SPEC COMM FOR AID,HEARINGS BEFORE THE SPECIAL COMMITTEE TO STUDY THE FOREIGN AID PROGRAM. USA+45 USSR ECO/UNDEV INT/ORG FORCES WEAPON TOTALISM ATTIT SUPEGO...NAT/COMP CONGRESS. PAGE 157 A3198
FOR/AID DIPLOM ORD/FREE TEC/DEV

L57
FURNISS E.S.,"SOME PERSPECTIVES ON AMERICAN MILITARY ASSISTANCE." USA+45 WOR+45 ECO/UNDEV INT/ORG ECO/TAC ORD/FREE...GEOG TIME/SEQ TREND COLD/WAR 20. PAGE 50 A1028
FORCES FOR/AID WEAPON

B58
ARON R.,ON WAR: ATOMIC WEAPONS AND GLOBAL DIPLOMACY (TRANS. BY TERENCE KILMARTIN). WOR+45 SOCIETY FORCES BAL/PWR WAR WEAPON PERSON...SOC 20. PAGE 9 A0182
ARMS/CONT NUC/PWR COERCE DIPLOM

B58
BERLINER J.S.,SOVIET ECONOMIC AID: THE AID AND TRADE POLICY IN UNDERDEVELOPED COUNTRIES. AFR COM ISLAM L/A+17C S/ASIA USSR ECO/DEV DIST/IND FINAN MARKET INT/ORG ACT/RES PLAN BAL/PWR WEAPON PWR WEALTH...CHARTS 20. PAGE 14 A0277
ECO/UNDEV ECO/TAC FOR/AID

B58
GAVIN J.M.,WAR AND PEACE IN THE SPACE AGE. SPACE USA+45 USSR FORCES PLAN TEC/DEV BAL/PWR DIPLOM ARMS/CONT WEAPON CIVMIL/REL...CHARTS GP/COMP 20 NATO COLD/WAR. PAGE 52 A1055
WAR DETER NUC/PWR PEACE

B58
NATIONAL PLANNING ASSOCIATION,1970 WITHOUT ARMS CONTROL (PAMPHLET). WOR+45 PROB/SOLV TEC/DEV DIPLOM CONFER DETER NUC/PWR WAR...CHARTS 20 COLD/WAR. PAGE 107 A2204
ARMS/CONT ORD/FREE WEAPON PREDICT

B58
ROCKEFELLER BROTH FUND INC,INTERNATIONAL SECURITY - THE MILITARY ASPECT. USA+45 INT/ORG NAT/G BUDGET ARMS/CONT WAR WEAPON PEACE ORD/FREE 20 NATO. PAGE 123 A2511
NUC/PWR DETER FORCES DIPLOM

B58
US HOUSE COMM GOVT OPERATIONS,HEARINGS BEFORE A SUBCOMMITTEE OF THE COMMITTEE ON GOVERNMENT OPERATIONS. CAMBODIA PHILIPPINE USA+45 CONSTRUC TEC/DEV ADMIN CONTROL WEAPON EFFICIENCY HOUSE/REP. PAGE 154 A3135
FOR/AID DIPLOM ORD/FREE ECO/UNDEV

S58
JORDAN A.,"MILITARY ASSISTANCE AND NATIONAL POLICY." ASIA FUT USA+45 WOR+45 ECO/DEV ECO/UNDEV INT/ORG NAT/G PLAN ECO/TAC ROUTINE WEAPON ATTIT RIGID/FLEX PWR...CONCPT TREND 20. PAGE 75 A1533
FORCES POLICY FOR/AID DIPLOM

N58
US HOUSE COMM FOREIGN AFFAIRS,HEARINGS ON DRAFT LEGISLATION TO AMEND FURTHER THE MUTUAL SECURITY ACT OF 1954 (PAMPHLET). USA+45 CONSULT FORCES BUDGET DIPLOM DETER COST ORD/FREE...JURID 20 DEPT/DEFEN UN DEPT/STATE. PAGE 153 A3123
LEGIS DELIB/GP CONFER WEAPON

B59
EMME E.M.,THE IMPACT OF AIR POWER - NATIONAL SECURITY AND WORLD POLITICS. USA+45 USSR FORCES DIPLOM WEAPON PEACE TOTALISM...POLICY NAT/COMP 20 EUROPE. PAGE 42 A0850
DETER AIR WAR ORD/FREE

B59
US PRES COMM STUDY MIL ASSIST,COMPOSITE REPORT. USA+45 ECO/UNDEV PLAN BUDGET DIPLOM EFFICIENCY ...POLICY MGT 20. PAGE 155 A3164
FOR/AID FORCES WEAPON ORD/FREE

S59
PUGWASH CONFERENCE,"ON BIOLOGICAL AND CHEMICAL WARFARE." WOR+45 SOCIETY PROC/MFG INT/ORG FORCES
ACT/RES BIO/SOC

EDU/PROP ADJUD RIGID/FLEX ORD/FREE PWR...DECISION PSY NEW/IDEA MATH VAL/FREE 20. PAGE 118 A2417
WAR WEAPON

B60
BARNET R.,WHO WANTS DISARMAMENT. COM EUR+WWI USA+45 USSR INT/ORG NAT/G BAL/PWR DIPLOM EDU/PROP COERCE DETER NUC/PWR WAR WEAPON ATTIT PWR...TIME/SEQ COLD/WAR CONGRESS 20. PAGE 11 A0225
PLAN FORCES ARMS/CONT

B60
MCCLELLAND C.A.,NUCLEAR WEAPONS, MISSILES, AND FUTURE WAR: PROBLEM FOR THE SIXTIES. WOR+45 FORCES ARMS/CONT DETER MARXISM...POLICY ANTHOL COLD/WAR. PAGE 97 A1998
DIPLOM NUC/PWR WAR WEAPON

B60
TURNER G.B.,NATIONAL SECURITY IN THE NUCLEAR AGE. KOREA USA+45 PLAN DIPLOM ARMS/CONT DETER WAR WEAPON ...BIBLIOG 20 COLD/WAR NATO. PAGE 146 A2982
NAT/G POLICY FORCES NUC/PWR

B60
US DEPARTMENT OF THE ARMY,DISARMAMENT: A BIBLIOGRAPHIC RECORD: 1916-1960. DETER WAR WEAPON PEACE 20 UN LEAGUE/NAT COLD/WAR NATO. PAGE 152 A3103
BIBLIOG/A ARMS/CONT NUC/PWR DIPLOM

L60
NOGEE J.L.,"THE DIPLOMACY OF DISARMAMENT." WOR+45 INT/ORG NAT/G CONSULT DELIB/GP TOP/EX BAL/PWR DIPLOM EDU/PROP COERCE DETER WEAPON PEACE ATTIT ...RECORD TIME/SEQ TOT/POP VAL/FREE COLD/WAR 20. PAGE 109 A2246
PWR ORD/FREE ARMS/CONT NUC/PWR

S60
BRODY R.A.,"DETERRENCE STRATEGIES: AN ANNOTATED BIBLIOGRAPHY." WOR+45 PLAN ARMS/CONT NUC/PWR WAR WEAPON DECISION. PAGE 19 A0383
BIBLIOG/A FORCES DETER DIPLOM

S60
DYSON F.J.,"THE FUTURE DEVELOPMENT OF NUCLEAR WEAPONS." FUT WOR+45 DELIB/GP ACT/RES PLAN DETER WEAPON ATTIT PWR...POLICY 20. PAGE 40 A0815
INT/ORG ARMS/CONT NUC/PWR

B61
BECHHOEFER B.G.,POSTWAR NEGOTIATIONS FOR ARMS CONTROL. COM EUR+WWI USSR INT/ORG NAT/G ACT/RES BAL/PWR DIPLOM ECO/TAC EDU/PROP ADMIN REGION DETER NUC/PWR WAR WEAPON PEACE ATTIT PWR...POLICY TIME/SEQ COLD/WAR CONGRESS 20. PAGE 12 A0244
USA+45 ARMS/CONT

B61
FULLER J.F.C.,THE CONDUCT OF WAR, 1789-1961. FRANCE RUSSIA SOCIETY NAT/G FORCES PROB/SOLV AGREE NUC/PWR WEAPON PEACE...SOC 18/20 TREATY COLD/WAR. PAGE 50 A1025
WAR POLICY REV ROLE

B61
SOKOL A.E.,SEAPOWER IN THE NUCLEAR AGE. USA+45 USSR DIST/IND FORCES INT/TRADE DETER WAR...POLICY NAT/COMP BIBLIOG COLD/WAR. PAGE 135 A2763
SEA PWR WEAPON NUC/PWR

B61
US SENATE COMM GOVT OPERATIONS,ORGANIZING FOR NATIONAL SECURITY. COM USA+45 BUDGET DIPLOM DETER NUC/PWR WAR WEAPON ORD/FREE...BIBLIOG 20 COLD/WAR. PAGE 156 A3172
POLICY PLAN FORCES COERCE

L61
WRIGHT Q.,"STUDIES IN DETERRENCE: LIMITED WARS AND THE ROLE OF SEABORNE WEAPONS SYSTEMS." FUT USA+45 WOR+45 SEA INT/ORG NAT/G FORCES ACT/RES WAR WEAPON ORD/FREE TOT/POP 20. PAGE 168 A3415
TEC/DEV SKILL BAL/PWR DETER

S61
MIKSCHE F.O.,"DEFENSE ORGANIZATION FOR WESTERN EUROPE." USA+45 INT/ORG NAT/G VOL/ASSN ACT/RES DOMIN LEGIT COERCE ORD/FREE PWR...RELATIV TREND 20 NATO. PAGE 101 A2071
EUR+WWI FORCES WEAPON NUC/PWR

B62
BENNETT J.C.,NUCLEAR WEAPONS AND THE CONFLICT OF CONSCIENCE. WOR+45 PROB/SOLV DIPLOM WEAPON SUPEGO MORAL...ANTHOL WORSHIP 20. PAGE 13 A0268
POLICY NUC/PWR WAR

B62
MORTON L.,STRATEGY AND COMMAND: THE FIRST TWO YEARS. USA-45 NAT/G CONTROL EXEC LEAD WEAPON CIVMIL/REL PWR...POLICY AUD/VIS CHARTS 20 CHINJAP. PAGE 105 A2150
WAR FORCES PLAN DIPLOM

B62
OSGOOD R.E.,NATO: THE ENTANGLING ALLIANCE. USA+45 WOR+45 VOL/ASSN FORCES TOP/EX PLAN DETER WEAPON DRIVE RIGID/FLEX ORD/FREE PWR...TREND 20 NATO. PAGE 112 A2301
INT/ORG ARMS/CONT PEACE

B62
PERRE J.,LES MUTATIONS DE LA GUERRE MODERNE: DE LA REVOLUTION FRANCAISE A LA REVOLUTION NUCLEAIRE. DIPLOM ARMS/CONT DEATH REV WEAPON GP/REL PEACE ATTIT...STAT PREDICT BIBLIOG 18/20 WWI. PAGE 115 A2365
WAR FORCES NUC/PWR

S62
RUSSETT B.M.,"CAUSE, SURPRISE, AND NO ESCAPE." FUT WOR-45 CULTURE SOCIETY INT/ORG FORCES TEC/DEV BAL/PWR EDU/PROP ARMS/CONT NUC/PWR WAR WEAPON PEACE KNOWL ORD/FREE PWR...POLICY CONCPT RECORD TIME/SEQ TREND GEN/LAWS 20 WWI. PAGE 126 A2578
COERCE DIPLOM

B63
HALPERIN M.H.,LIMITED WAR IN A NUCLEAR AGE. CUBA KOREA USA+45 USSR INT/ORG FORCES PLAN DIPLOM DETER PWR...BIBLIOG/A 20. PAGE 60 A1238
WAR NUC/PWR CONTROL WEAPON

B63
US DEPARTMENT OF THE ARMY,SOVIET RUSSIA: STRATEGIC SURVEY (PAMPHLET). USSR POL/PAR PLAN DOMIN EDU/PROP ARMS/CONT GUERRILLA WAR WEAPON...TREND CHARTS ORG/CHARTS 20. PAGE 152 A3106
BIBLIOG/A MARXISM DIPLOM COERCE

B63
US HOUSE COMM FOREIGN AFFAIRS,HEARINGS ON H.R. 5490 TO AMEND FURTHER THE FOREIGN ASSISTANCE ACT OF 1961. CUBA EUR+WWI INDIA INT/ORG DELIB/GP LEGIS DIPLOM CONFER ORD/FREE 20 DEPT/STATE DEPT/DEFEN UN. PAGE 153 A3129
FOR/AID INT/TRADE FORCES WEAPON

B63
US SENATE COMM ON FOREIGN REL,HEARINGS ON S 1276 A BILL TO AMEND FURTHER THE FOREIGN ASSISTANCE ACT OF 1961. USA+45 WOR+45 INDUS INT/ORG FORCES TAX WEAPON SUPEGO...NAT/COMP 20 UN CONGRESS PRESIDENT. PAGE 156 A3182
FOR/AID DIPLOM ECO/UNDEV ORD/FREE

S63
BLOOMFIELD L.P.,"HEADQUARTERS-FIELD RELATIONS: SOME NOTES ON THE BEGINNING AND END OF ONUC." AFR INT/ORG ROUTINE COERCE WAR WEAPON UN CONGO 20. PAGE 16 A0319
FORCES ORD/FREE

B64
BLANCHARD C.H.,KOREAN WAR BIBLIOGRAPHY. KOREA FAM BAL/PWR RATION MURDER WEAPON MARXISM...CHARTS 20. PAGE 15 A0306
BIBLIOG/A WAR DIPLOM FORCES

B64
DEITCHMAN S.J.,LIMITED WAR AND AMERICAN DEFENSE POLICY. USA+45 WOR+45 INT/ORG NAT/G PLAN TEC/DEV COERCE NUC/PWR RIGID/FLEX PWR SKILL...DECISION METH/CNCPT TIME/SEQ TOT/POP COLD/WAR 20. PAGE 36 A0726
FORCES WAR WEAPON

B64
DEUTSCHE GES AUSWARTIGE POL,STRATEGIE UND ABRUSTUNGSPOLITIK DER SOWJETUNION. USSR TEC/DEV DIPLOM COERCE DETER WEAPON...POLICY PSY 20 ABM/DEFSYS. PAGE 37 A0747
NUC/PWR WAR FORCES ARMS/CONT

B64
FALL B.,STREET WITHOUT JOY. FRANCE USA+45 DIPLOM ECO/TAC FOR/AID GUERRILLA REV WEAPON...TREND 20. PAGE 44 A0894
WAR S/ASIA FORCES COERCE

B64
KAUFMANN W.W.,THE MC NAMARA STRATEGY. TOP/EX INSPECT BAL/PWR DIPLOM CONTROL DETER GUERRILLA NUC/PWR WEAPON COST PWR...METH/COMP 20 MCNAMARA/R KENNEDY/JF JOHNSON/LB NATO DEPT/DEFEN. PAGE 77 A1572
FORCES WAR PLAN PROB/SOLV

B64
KIMMINICH O.,RUSTUNG UND POLITISCHE SPANNUNG. INDUS ARMS/CONT COERCE NAT/LISM PEACE PERSON ORD/FREE ...POLICY GEOG 20. PAGE 79 A1619
DIPLOM FORCES WEAPON WAR

B64
SCHWARTZ M.D.,CONFERENCE ON SPACE SCIENCE AND SPACE LAW. FUT COM/IND NAT/G FORCES ACT/RES PLAN BUDGET DIPLOM NUC/PWR WEAPON...POLICY ANTHOL 20. PAGE 130 A2658
SPACE LAW PEACE TEC/DEV

B64
US AGENCY INTERNATIONAL DEV,REPORT TO CONGRESS ON THE FOREIGN ASSISTANCE PROGRAM. AFR ASIA L/A+17C USA+45 INT/ORG VOL/ASSN FORCES CAP/ISM ADMIN WEAPON. PAGE 149 A3052
FOR/AID ECO/UNDEV TEC/DEV BUDGET

S64
HOWARD M.,"MILITARY POWER AND INTERNATIONAL ORDER." WOR+45 SOCIETY INT/ORG NAT/G BAL/PWR DOMIN COERCE NUC/PWR WEAPON PWR...NEW/IDEA 20. PAGE 68 A1400
FORCES ATTIT WAR

B65
FRANKLAND N.,THE BOMBING OFFENSIVE AGAINST GERMANY. GERMANY UK TEC/DEV DIPLOM WAR...METH/COMP 20. PAGE 48 A0985
WEAPON PLAN DECISION FORCES

B65
GRAHAM G.S.,THE POLITICS OF NAVAL SUPREMACY; STUDIES IN BRITISH MARITIME ASCENDANCY. UK SEA NAT/G BAL/PWR LEAD WAR WEAPON PEACE...POLICY 18/19 COMMONWLTH. PAGE 55 A1126
FORCES PWR COLONIAL DIPLOM

B65
GRETTON P.,MARITIME STRATEGY - A STUDY OF DEFENSE PROBLEMS. ASIA UK USSR DIPLOM COERCE DETER NUC/PWR WEAPON...CONCPT NAT/COMP 20. PAGE 56 A1147
FORCES PLAN WAR SEA

B65
HART B.H.L.,THE MEMOIRS OF CAPTAIN LIDDELL HART (VOL. I). UK NAT/G PLAN TEC/DEV DIPLOM ADMIN WEAPON GOV/REL PERS/REL ATTIT PWR FASCISM...POLICY 20. PAGE 62 A1274
FORCES BIOG LEAD WAR

B65
MOSKOWITZ H.,US SECURITY, ARMS CONTROL, AND DISARMAMENT 1961-1965. FORCES DIPLOM DETER WAR WEAPON...CHARTS 20 UN COLD/WAR NATO. PAGE 105 A2154
BIBLIOG/A ARMS/CONT NUC/PWR PEACE

B65
RAPPAPORT A.,ISSUES IN AMERICAN DIPLOMACY: WORLD POWER AND LEADERSHIP SINCE 1895 (VOL. II). CHINA/COM EUR+WWI L/A+17C USA+45 USA-45 NAT/G ECO/TAC DOMIN CONFER LEAD NUC/PWR WEAPON...DECISION 19/20 WILSON/W ROOSEVLT/F CHINJAP. PAGE 119 A2447 — WAR POLICY DIPLOM

B65
US DEPARTMENT OF THE ARMY,NUCLEAR WEAPONS AND THE ATLANTIC ALLIANCE: A BIBLIOGRAPHIC SURVEY. ASIA COM EUR+WWI USA+45 FORCES DIPLOM WEAPON...STAT 20 NATO. PAGE 152 A3108 — BIBLIOG/A ARMS/CONT NUC/PWR BAL/PWR

B65
US SENATE COMM ON FOREIGN REL,HEARINGS ON THE FOREIGN ASSISTANCE PROGRAM. AFR ASIA L/A+17C USA+45 WOR+45 FORCES TEC/DEV BUDGET CONTROL WEAPON ORD/FREE 20 UN CONGRESS SEC/STATE. PAGE 156 A3183 — FOR/AID DIPLOM INT/ORG ECO/UNDEV

B66
DAENIKER G.,STRATEGIE DES KLEIN STAATS. SWITZERLND ACT/RES CREATE DIPLOM NEUTRAL DETER WAR WEAPON PWR SOVEREIGN...IDEA/COMP 20 COLD/WAR. PAGE 33 A0673 — NUC/PWR PLAN FORCES NAT/G

B66
OBERMANN E.,VERTEIDIGUNG PER FREIHEIT. GERMANY/W WOR+45 INT/ORG COERCE NUC/PWR WEAPON MARXISM 20 UN NATO WARSAW/P TREATY. PAGE 111 A2273 — FORCES ORD/FREE WAR PEACE

B66
SMITH D.M.,AMERICAN INTERVENTION, 1917. GERMANY UK USA-45 SEA FORCES DIPLOM INT/TRADE EDU/PROP COERCE WEAPON PEACE 20 WILSON/W WWI. PAGE 134 A2746 — WAR ATTIT POLICY NEUTRAL

B66
US SENATE COMM ON FOREIGN REL,HEARINGS ON S 2859 AND S 2861. USA+45 WOR+45 FORCES BUDGET CAP/ISM ADMIN DETER WEAPON TOTALISM...NAT/COMP 20 UN CONGRESS. PAGE 156 A3185 — FOR/AID DIPLOM ORD/FREE ECO/UNDEV

B67
BURNS E.L.M.,MEGAMURDER. WOR+45 LAW INT/ORG NAT/G BAL/PWR DIPLOM DETER MURDER WEAPON CIVMIL/REL PEACE ...INT/LAW TREND 20. PAGE 22 A0444 — FORCES PLAN WAR NUC/PWR

B67
HOLSTI K.J.,INTERNATIONAL POLITICS* A FRAMEWORK FOR ANALYSIS. WOR+45 WOR-45 NAT/G EDU/PROP DETER WAR WEAPON PWR BIBLIOG. PAGE 67 A1372 — DIPLOM BARGAIN POLICY INT/LAW

B67
LAWYERS COMM AMER POLICY VIET,VIETNAM AND INTERNATIONAL LAW: AN ANALYSIS OF THE LEGALITY OF THE US MILITARY INVOLVEMENT. VIETNAM LAW INT/ORG COERCE WEAPON PEACE ORD/FREE 20 UN SEATO TREATY. PAGE 86 A1753 — INT/LAW DIPLOM ADJUD WAR

B67
RUSSELL B.,WAR CRIMES IN VIETNAM. USA+45 VIETNAM FORCES DIPLOM WEAPON RACE/REL DISCRIM ISOLAT BIO/SOC 20 COLD/WAR RUSSELL/B. PAGE 126 A2574 — WAR CRIME ATTIT POLICY

B67
US SENATE COMM ON FOREIGN REL,UNITED STATES ARMAMENT AND DISARMAMENT PROBLEMS. USA+45 AIR BAL/PWR DIPLOM FOR/AID NUC/PWR ORD/FREE SENATE TREATY. PAGE 156 A3190 — ARMS/CONT WEAPON FORCES PROB/SOLV

L67
MOORE N.,"THE LAWFULNESS OF MILITARY ASSISTANCE TO THE REPUBLIC OF VIET NAM." USA+45 VIETNAM WOR+45 FOR/AID DOMIN DETER WAR WEAPON...DECISION INT/LAW 20 UN. PAGE 103 A2123 — PWR DIPLOM FORCES GOV/REL

S67
CARROLL K.J.,"SECOND STEP TOWARD ARMS CONTROL." WOR+45 INT/ORG VOL/ASSN FORCES PROB/SOLV RISK WEAPON 20 COLD/WAR. PAGE 25 A0503 — ARMS/CONT DIPLOM PLAN NUC/PWR

S67
HALL M.,"GERMANY, EAST AND WEST* DANGER AT THE CROSSROADS." GERMANY ELITES CHIEF FORCES DIPLOM ECO/TAC REPAR ARMS/CONT...SOCIALIST 20. PAGE 60 A1227 — NAT/LISM ATTIT FASCISM WEAPON

S67
KAHN H.,"CRITERIA FOR LONG-RANGE NUCLEAR CONTROL POLICIES." WOR+45 INT/ORG TEC/DEV DOMIN DETER WAR WEAPON ISOLAT ORD/FREE POLICY. PAGE 76 A1549 — NUC/PWR ARMS/CONT BAL/PWR DIPLOM

S67
KRUSCHE H.,"THE STRIVING OF THE KIESINGER-STRAUS GOVERNMENT FOR NUCLEAR WEAPONS IS A THREAT TO EUROPEAN SECURITY." EUR+WWI GERMANY BAL/PWR SANCTION WEAPON PEACE ORD/FREE...MARXIST 20 NATO COLD/WAR. PAGE 82 A1688 — ARMS/CONT INT/ORG NUC/PWR DIPLOM

WEATHER....WEATHER

WEATHERHEAD R.W. A1907

WEAVER J.H. A3295

WEBER/MAX....MAX WEBER

WECHSLER H. A3296

WEIDNER E.W. A3297

WEIGERT H.W. A3298

WEIL G.L. A3299,A3300,A3301

WEILLER J. A3302,A3303

WEIMAR/REP....WEIMAR REPUBLIC

B66
DYCK H.V.,WEIMAR GERMANY AND SOVIET RUSSIA 1926-1933. EUR+WWI GERMANY UK USSR ECO/TAC INT/TRADE NEUTRAL WAR ATTIT 20 WEIMAR/REP TREATY. PAGE 40 A0814 — DIPLOM GOV/REL POLICY

WEINBERG A. A3304

WEINBERG A.K. A3305

WEINBERG L. A3304

WEINSTEIN F.B. A3306

WEINTAL E. A3307

WEINTRAUB S. A3308

WEIS P. A3309

WEISNER J.B. A3310

WEISSBERG G. A3311

WEITZEL R. A2952

WELCH C.E. A3312

WELCH R.H.W. A3313

WELF/ST....WELFARE STATE ADVOCATE

B61
THEOBALD R.,THE CHALLENGE OF ABUNDANCE. USA+45 WOR+45 MARKET DIPLOM FOR/AID REV PRODUC UTOPIA SUPEGO...POLICY TREND BIBLIOG/A 20. PAGE 142 A2913 — WELF/ST ECO/UNDEV PROB/SOLV ECO/TAC

S61
DEUTSCH K.W.,"NATIONAL INDUSTRIALIZATION AND THE DECLINING SHARE OF THE INTERNATIONAL ECONOMIC SECTOR." EUR+WWI FUT WOR+45 WOR-45 MARKET PLAN EDU/PROP WEALTH...WELF/ST OBS TESTS 20. PAGE 36 A0740 — DIST/IND ECO/DEV INT/TRADE

S61
JACKSON E.,"THE FUTURE DEVELOPMENT OF THE UNITED NATIONS: SOME SUGGESTIONS FOR RESEARCH." FUT LAW CONSTN ECO/DEV FINAN PEACE WEALTH...WELF/ST CONCPT UN 20. PAGE 72 A1476 — INT/ORG PWR

S61
JUVILER P.H.,"INTERPARLIAMENTARY CONTACTS IN SOVIET FOREIGN POLICY." COM FUT WOR+45 WOR-45 SOCIETY CONSULT ACT/RES DIPLOM ADMIN PEACE ATTIT RIGID/FLEX WEALTH...WELF/ST SOC TOT/POP CONGRESS 19/20. PAGE 75 A1543 — INT/ORG DELIB/GP USSR

S61
MILLER E.,"LEGAL ASPECTS OF UN ACTION IN THE CONGO." AFR CULTURE ADMIN PEACE DRIVE RIGID/FLEX ORD/FREE...WELF/ST JURID OBS UN CONGO 20. PAGE 101 A2076 — INT/ORG LEGIT

S61
VERNON R.,"A TRADE POLICY FOR THE 1960'S." COM FUT USA+45 WOR+45 ECO/DEV ECO/UNDEV FINAN TOP/EX ACT/RES...WELF/ST METH/CNCPT CONT/OBS TOT/POP 20. PAGE 159 A3229 — PLAN INT/TRADE

B62
TOURE S.,THE INTERNATIONAL POLICY OF THE DEMOCRATIC PARTY OF GUINEA (VOL. VII). AFR ALGERIA GHANA GUINEA MALI CONSTN VOL/ASSN CHIEF WAR PEACE ATTIT ...WELF/ST 20 DEMOCRAT. PAGE 144 A2953 — DIPLOM POLICY POL/PAR NEW/LIB

B66
HOROWITZ D.,HEMISPHERES NORTH AND SOUTH: ECONOMIC DISPARITY AMONG NATIONS. WOR+45 ECO/DEV ECO/UNDEV INT/ORG PLAN DIPLOM INT/TRADE GIVE PARTIC GP/REL ...WELF/ST 20. PAGE 67 A1387 — ECO/TAC FOR/AID STRATA WEALTH

WELFARE....SEE RECEIVE, NEW/LIB, WELF/ST

WELFARE STATE....SEE NEW/LIB, WELF/ST

WELLEQUET J. A3314

WELLES S. A3315

UK USA-45 NAT/G CHIEF DELIB/GP FORCES BAL/PWR REPAR ARMS/CONT 20 WILSON/W TREATY. PAGE 125 A2566 — WAR PEACE DIPLOM

B51
RAPPAPORT A.,THE BRITISH PRESS AND WILSONIAN NEUTRALITY. UK WOR-45 SEA POL/PAR WAR CHOOSE PEACE ATTIT PERCEPT...GEOG 20 WILSON/W. PAGE 119 A2446 — PRESS DIPLOM NEUTRAL POLICY

B52
FERRELL R.H.,PEACE IN THEIR TIME. FRANCE UK USA-45 INT/ORG NAT/G FORCES CREATE AGREE ARMS/CONT COERCE WAR TREATY 20 WILSON/W LEAGUE/NAT BRIAND/A. PAGE 45 A0920 — PEACE DIPLOM

B52
FIFIELD R.H.,WOODROW WILSON AND THE FAR EAST. ASIA CHIEF BAL/PWR CONFER COLONIAL ARMS/CONT WAR ...TIME/SEQ NAT/COMP BIBLIOG 19/20 WILSON/W LEAGUE/NAT PRESIDENT. PAGE 45 A0926 — DIPLOM DELIB/GP INT/ORG

C52
FIFIELD R.H.,"WOODROW WILSON AND THE FAR EAST." ASIA CHIEF DELIB/GP BAL/PWR CONFER COLONIAL ARMS/CONT WAR...TIME/SEQ NAT/COMP 19/20 WILSON/W LEAGUE/NAT. PAGE 45 A0925 — BIBLIOG DIPLOM INT/ORG

B57
DUDDEN A.P.,WOODROW WILSON AND THE WORLD OF TODAY. USA-45 NAT/G PROVS CONTROL PARTIC WAR ISOLAT PWR SKILL...PERS/COMP ANTHOL 19/20 WILSON/W UN LEAGUE/NAT WWI. PAGE 39 A0794 — CHIEF DIPLOM POL/PAR LEAD

B62
QUIRK R.E.,AN AFFAIR OF HONOR: WOODROW WILSON AND THE OCCUPATION OF VERACRUZ. L/A+17C USA-45 COLONIAL SUPEGO PWR 20 WILSON/W MEXIC/AMER. PAGE 118 A2428 — DOMIN DIPLOM COERCE PROB/SOLV

B65
RAPPAPORT A.,ISSUES IN AMERICAN DIPLOMACY: WORLD POWER AND LEADERSHIP SINCE 1895 (VOL. II). CHINA/COM EUR+WWI L/A+17C USA+45 USA-45 NAT/G ECO/TAC DOMIN CONFER LEAD NUC/PWR WEAPON...DECISION 19/20 WILSON/W ROOSEVLT/F CHINJAP. PAGE 119 A2447 — WAR POLICY DIPLOM

B66
CANFIELD L.H.,THE PRESIDENCY OF WOODROW WILSON: PRELUDE TO A WORLD IN CRISIS. USA-45 ADJUD NEUTRAL WAR CHOOSE INGP/REL PEACE ORD/FREE 20 WILSON/W PRESIDENT TREATY LEAGUE/NAT. PAGE 24 A0477 — PERSON POLICY DIPLOM GOV/REL

B66
FREIDEL F.,AMERICAN ISSUES IN THE TWENTIETH CENTURY. SOCIETY FINAN ECO/TAC FOR/AID CONTROL NUC/PWR WAR RACE/REL PEACE ATTIT...ANTHOL T 20 WILSON/W ROOSEVLT/F KENNEDY/JF TRUMAN/HS. PAGE 49 A0995 — DIPLOM POLICY NAT/G ORD/FREE

B66
SINGER L.,ALLE LITTEN AN GROSSENWAHN: VON WOODROW WILSON BIS MAO TSE-TUNG. ASIA UK USSR INT/ORG DELIB/GP BAL/PWR DOMIN ATTIT PERSON 20 WILSON/W ROOSEVLT/F. PAGE 133 A2731 — DIPLOM TOTALISM WAR CHIEF

B66
SMITH D.M.,AMERICAN INTERVENTION, 1917. GERMANY UK USA-45 SEA FORCES DIPLOM INT/TRADE EDU/PROP COERCE WEAPON PEACE 20 WILSON/W WWI. PAGE 134 A2746 — WAR ATTIT POLICY NEUTRAL

B67
TEITELBAUM L.M.,WOODROW WILSON AND THE MEXICAN REVOLUTION 1913-1916: A HISTORY OF UNITED STATES-MEXICAN RELATIONS. USA-45 CHIEF TOP/EX WAR 20 MEXIC/AMER WILSON/W VILLA/P CARRANZA/V. PAGE 142 A2902 — REV DIPLOM

WING D. A3363

WINOGRAD B. A2745

WINT G. A3364,A3365,A3366

WINTER R.C. A3367

WINTHROP H. A3368

WIONCZEK M. A3369

WIRETAPPING....SEE PRIVACY

WISCONSIN....WISCONSIN

WISCONSN/U....WISCONSIN STATE UNIVERSITY

B65
EDUCATION AND WORLD AFFAIRS,THE UNIVERSITY LOOKS ABROAD: APPROACHES TO WORLD AFFAIRS AT SIX AMERICAN UNIVERSITIES. USA+45 CREATE EDU/PROP CONFER LEAD KNOWL 20 CORNELL/U MICH/STA/U STANFORD/U TULANE/U WISCONSN/U. PAGE 40 A0822 — ACADEM DIPLOM ATTIT GP/COMP

WITHERELL J.W. A3370,A3371

WITHERS W. A3372

WITHERSPOON J.V. A0432

WITHEY S.B. A2674

WITTFOGEL K.A. A3373

WITTGEN/L....LUDWIG WITTGENSTEIN

WODDIS J. A3374

WOETZEL R.K. A3375,A3376

WOHL R. A3377

WOLF C. A3378,A3379

WOLFERS A. A3380,A3381,A3382,A3383,A3384,A3385,A3386

WOLFF C. A3387

WOLFF R.L. A3388

WOLFF/C....CHRISTIAN WOLFF

B96
DE VATTEL E.,THE LAW OF NATIONS. AGRI FINAN CHIEF DIPLOM INT/TRADE AGREE OWN ALL/VALS MORAL ORD/FREE SOVEREIGN...GEN/LAWS 18 NATURL/LAW WOLFF/C. PAGE 35 A0714 — LAW CONCPT NAT/G INT/LAW

WOLFF/RP....ROBERT PAUL WOLFF

WOMAN....SEE FEMALE/SEX

WOMEN....SEE FEMALE/SEX

WOMEN'S CHRISTIAN TEMPERANCE UNION....SEE WCTU

WOOD B. A3389

WOOD H.B. A3390

WOOD/CHAS....SIR CHARLES WOOD

B66
MOORE R.J.,SIR CHARLES WOOD'S INDIAN POLICY: 1853-66. INDIA POL/PAR CHIEF DELIB/GP DIPLOM CONTROL LEAD WOOD/CHAS. PAGE 103 A2124 — COLONIAL ADMIN CONSULT DECISION

WOODHOUSE C.M. A3391

WOODWARD E.L. A3392

WOOLBERT R.G. A3393

WOOLF L. A3394

WOOLLEY H.B. A3395

WOR+45....WORLDWIDE, 1945 TO PRESENT

WOR-45....WORLDWIDE, TO 1945

WORK....SEE WORKER

WORK PROJECTS ADMINISTRATION....SEE WPA

B31
HODGES C.,THE BACKGROUND OF INTERNATIONAL RELATIONS. WOR-45 SOCIETY ECO/DEV ECO/UNDEV INT/ORG DIPLOM DOMIN EDU/PROP LEGIT WAR ATTIT DRIVE PERSON ALL/VALS...CONCPT METH/CNCPT TIME/SEQ CHARTS WORK LEAGUE/NAT 19/20. PAGE 66 A1350 — NAT/G BAL/PWR

B35
STALEY E.,WAR AND THE PRIVATE INVESTOR. UNIV WOR-45 INTELL SOCIETY INT/ORG NAT/G TOP/EX CAP/ISM ECO/TAC WAR ATTIT ALL/VALS...INT TIME/SEQ TREND CON/ANAL WORK TOT/POP 20. PAGE 137 A2799 — FINAN INT/TRADE DIPLOM

B37
ROBBINS L.,ECONOMIC PLANNING AND INTERNATIONAL ORDER. WOR-45 SOCIETY FINAN INDUS NAT/G ECO/TAC ROUTINE WEALTH...SOC TIME/SEQ GEN/METH WORK 20 KEYNES/JM. PAGE 122 A2492 — INT/ORG PLAN INT/TRADE

B44
PUTTKAMMER E.W.,WAR AND THE LAW. UNIV USA-45 CONSTN CULTURE SOCIETY NAT/G POL/PAR ROUTINE ALL/VALS ...JURID CONCPT OBS WORK VAL/FREE 20. PAGE 118 A2418 — INT/ORG LAW WAR INT/LAW

B45
RANSHOFFEN-WERTHEIMER EF,THE INTERNATIONAL SECRETARIAT: A GREAT EXPERIMENT IN INTERNATIONAL ADMINISTRATION. EUR+WWI FUT CONSTN FACE/GP CONSULT DELIB/GP ACT/RES ADMIN ROUTINE PEACE ORD/FREE...MGT RECORD ORG/CHARTS LEAGUE/NAT WORK 20. PAGE 119 A2442 — INT/ORG EXEC

B52
ALEXANDROWICZ C.H.,INTERNATIONAL ECONOMIC ORGANIZATION. WOR+45 ECO/DEV ECO/UNDEV DIST/IND FINAN MARKET PLAN ECO/TAC LEGIT DRIVE WEALTH ...POLICY CONCPT QUANT OBS TIME/SEQ GEN/LAWS WORK EEC ILO OEEC UNESCO 20. PAGE 6 A0114 INT/ORG INT/TRADE

B52
RIGGS F.W.,FORMOSA UNDER CHINESE NATIONALIST RULE. CHINA/COM USA+45 CONSTN AGRI FINAN LABOR LOC/G NAT/G POL/PAR FORCES HEALTH KNOWL...STAT WORK VAL/FREE 20. PAGE 121 A2479 ASIA FOR/AID DIPLOM

B52
UN DEPT. SOC. AFF.,PRELIMINARY REPORT ON THE WORLD SOCIAL SITUATION. ISLAM L/A+17C WOR+45 STRATA AGRI EXTR/IND INDUS INT/ORG SCHOOL ADMIN...GEOG SOC TREND UNESCO WORK FAO 20. PAGE 147 A2998 R+D HEALTH FOR/AID

B57
FRAZIER E.F.,RACE AND CULTURE CONTACTS IN THE MODERN WORLD. WOR+45 SOCIETY ECO/DEV AGRI INDUS INT/ORG LABOR NAT/G PERSON RIGID/FLEX ALL/VALS...SOC TIME/SEQ WORK 19/20. PAGE 48 A0991 CULTURE RACE/REL

B57
JENKS C.W.,THE INTERNATIONAL PROTECTION OF TRADE UNION FREEDOM. FUT WOR+45 WOR-45 VOL/ASSN DELIB/GP CT/SYS REGION ROUTINE...JURID METH/CNCPT RECORD TIME/SEQ CHARTS ILO WORK OAS 20. PAGE 73 A1504 LABOR INT/ORG

L57
WARREN S.,"FOREIGN AID AND FOREIGN POLICY." USA+45 WOR+45 WOR-45 DIST/IND INDUS MARKET CONSULT CREATE DIPLOM EDU/PROP LEGIT ATTIT RIGID/FLEX...TIME/SEQ GEN/LAWS WORK 20. PAGE 161 A3285 ECO/UNDEV ALL/VALS ECO/TAC FOR/AID

B58
HOLT R.T.,RADIO FREE EUROPE. FUT USA+45 CULTURE ECO/DEV INT/ORG KIN POL/PAR SECT FORCES ACT/RES DIPLOM COERCE REV CHOOSE PEACE ATTIT PWR...MAJORIT CONCPT COLD/WAR WORK 20 RFE. PAGE 67 A1374 COM EDU/PROP COM/IND

B59
ALLEN R.L.,SOVIET INFLUENCE IN LATIN AMERICA. ECO/UNDEV FINAN PROC/MFG NAT/G TEC/DEV EDU/PROP EXEC ROUTINE ATTIT DRIVE PERSON ALL/VALS PWR...STAT CHARTS WORK 20. PAGE 6 A0125 L/A+17C ECO/TAC INT/TRADE USSR

B59
KULSKI W.W.,PEACEFUL CO-EXISTENCE: AN ANALYSIS OF SOVIET FOREIGN POLICY. WOR+45 INTELL SOCIETY ECO/UNDEV POL/PAR EDU/PROP COERCE DRIVE RIGID/FLEX PWR SKILL...PSY CONCPT HIST/WRIT CON/ANAL GEN/METH WORK VAL/FREE 20. PAGE 83 A1691 PLAN DIPLOM USSR

L59
BEGUIN B.,"ILO AND THE TRIPARTITE SYSTEM." EUR+WWI WOR+45 WOR-45 CONSTN ECO/DEV ECO/UNDEV INDUS INT/ORG NAT/G VOL/ASSN DELIB/GP PLAN TEC/DEV LEGIT ORD/FREE WEALTH...CONCPT TIME/SEQ WORK ILO 20. PAGE 12 A0249 LABOR

S59
TIPTON J.B.,"PARTICIPATION OF THE UNITED STATES IN THE INTERNATIONAL LABOR ORGANIZATION." USA+45 LAW STRUCT ECO/DEV ECO/UNDEV INDUS TEC/DEV ECO/TAC ADMIN PERCEPT ORD/FREE SKILL...STAT HIST/WRIT GEN/METH ILO WORK 20. PAGE 144 A2946 LABOR INT/ORG

B60
ENGEL J.,THE SECURITY OF THE FREE WORLD. USSR WOR+45 STRATA STRUCT ECO/DEV ECO/UNDEV INT/ORG DELIB/GP FORCES DOMIN LEGIT ADJUD EXEC ARMS/CONT COERCE...POLICY CONCPT NEW/IDEA TIME/SEQ GEN/LAWS COLD/WAR WORK UN 20 NATO. PAGE 42 A0851 COM TREND DIPLOM

B60
FOOTMAN D.,INTERNATIONAL COMMUNISM. ASIA EUR+WWI FRANCE FUT GERMANY MOD/EUR S/ASIA USA-45 WOR+45 WOR-45 INTELL LABOR TOTALISM MARXISM WORK 20. PAGE 47 A0958 COM INT/ORG STRUCT REV

B60
KHRUSHCHEV N.,FOR VICTORY IN PEACEFUL COMPETITION WITH CAPITALISM. COM FUT USSR WOR+45 CONSTN SOCIETY INDUS INT/ORG DELIB/GP PLAN BAL/PWR DIPLOM PERSON MARXISM...MARXIST WORK 20 COLD/WAR. PAGE 79 A1611 TOP/EX PWR CAP/ISM SOCISM

B60
PENTONY D.E.,THE UNDERDEVELOPED LANDS. FUT WOR+45 CULTURE AGRI FINAN INDUS MARKET INT/ORG LABOR NAT/G VOL/ASSN CONSULT TEC/DEV ECO/TAC EDU/PROP COLONIAL ATTIT WEALTH...OBS RECORD SAMP TREND GEN/METH WORK UN 20. PAGE 115 A2351 ECO/UNDEV POLICY FOR/AID INT/TRADE

B60
THEOBALD R.,THE RICH AND THE POOR: A STUDY OF THE ECONOMICS OF RISING EXPECTATIONS. WOR+45 CONSTN ECO/DEV ECO/UNDEV INT/ORG NAT/G PLAN FOR/AID ROUTINE BAL/PAY ORD/FREE PWR WEALTH...GEOG TREND WORK 20. PAGE 142 A2912 ECO/TAC INT/TRADE

L60
FERNBACH A.P.,"SOVIET COEXISTENCE STRATEGY." WOR+45 PROF/ORG VOL/ASSN DIPLOM DOMIN EDU/PROP ATTIT DRIVE PERSON PWR SKILL WEALTH...POLICY OBS SAMP TREND STERTYP ILO WORK COLD/WAR 420. PAGE 45 A0919 LABOR INT/ORG USSR

S60
JACOBSON H.K.,"THE USSR AND ILO." COM STRUCT ECO/DEV ECO/UNDEV CONSULT DELIB/GP ECO/TAC ILO WORK COLD/WAR 20. PAGE 72 A1484 INT/ORG LABOR USSR

S60
KEYFITZ N.,"WESTERN PERSPECTIVES AND ASIAN PROBLEMS." ASIA EUR+WWI S/ASIA SOCIETY FOR/AID ...POLICY SOC CONCPT STERTYP WORK TOT/POP 20. PAGE 78 A1604 CULTURE ATTIT

S60
MORALES C.J.,"TRADE AND ECONOMIC INTEGRATION IN LATIN AMERICA." FUT L/A+17C LAW STRATA ECO/UNDEV DIST/IND INDUS LABOR NAT/G LEGIS ECO/TAC ADMIN RIGID/FLEX WEALTH...CONCPT NEW/IDEA CONT/OBS TIME/SEQ WORK 20. PAGE 104 A2128 FINAN INT/TRADE REGION

S60
OWEN C.F.,"US AND SOVIET RELATIONS WITH UNDERDEVELOPED COUNTRIES: LATIN AMERICA-A CASE STUDY." AFR COM L/A+17C USA+45 USSR EXTR/IND MARKET TEC/DEV DIPLOM ECO/TAC NAT/LISM ORD/FREE PWR ...TREND WORK 20. PAGE 112 A2303 ECO/UNDEV DRIVE INT/TRADE

S60
RIVKIN A.,"AFRICAN ECONOMIC DEVELOPMENT: ADVANCED TECHNOLOGY AND THE STAGES OF GROWTH." CULTURE ECO/UNDEV AGRI COM/IND EXTR/IND PLAN ECO/TAC ATTIT DRIVE RIGID/FLEX SKILL WEALTH...MGT SOC GEN/LAWS WORK TOT/POP 20. PAGE 121 A2487 AFR TEC/DEV FOR/AID

B61
FRIEDMANN W.G.,JOINT INTERNATIONAL BUSINESS VENTURES. ASIA ISLAM L/A+17C ECO/DEV DIST/IND FINAN PROC/MFG FACE/GP LG/CO NAT/G VOL/ASSN CONSULT EX/STRUC PLAN ADMIN ROUTINE WEALTH...OLD/LIB WORK 20. PAGE 49 A1004 ECO/UNDEV INT/TRADE

B61
WARNER D.,HURRICANE FROM CHINA. ASIA CHINA/COM FUT L/A+17C USA+45 CULTURE NAT/G FORCES TOP/EX FOR/AID DRIVE PWR...CONCPT TIME/SEQ SEATO WORK 20. PAGE 161 A3284 ATTIT TREND REV

S61
DANIELS R.V.,"THE CHINESE REVOLUTION IN RUSSIAN PERSPECTIVE." ASIA CHINA/COM COM USSR INTELL INT/ORG TOP/EX REV TOTALISM PWR...POLICY WORK VAL/FREE 20. PAGE 33 A0680 POL/PAR PLAN

S61
HEILBRONER R.L.,"DYNAMICS OF FOREIGN AID: PROBLEMS OF UNDERDEVELOPED NATIONS PLAGUE ASSISTANCE PROGRAM." FUT USA+45 WOR+45 STRATA NAT/G PLAN TEC/DEV ATTIT DRIVE WEALTH WORK 20. PAGE 64 A1307 ECO/UNDEV ECO/TAC FOR/AID

S62
RUBINSTEIN A.Z.,"RUSSIA AND THE UNCOMMITTED NATIONS." AFR INDIA ISLAM L/A+17C LAOS S/ASIA ELITES ECO/UNDEV INT/ORG KIN CREATE PLAN TEC/DEV NAT/LISM RIGID/FLEX PWR WEALTH...METH/CNCPT TIME/SEQ GEN/LAWS WORK. PAGE 125 A2562 ECO/TAC TREND COLONIAL USSR

S62
TATOMIR N.,"ORGANIZATIA INTERNATIONALA A MUNCII: ASPECTE NOI ALE PROBLEMEI IMBUNATATIRII MECANISMULUI EI." EUR+WWI ECO/DEV VOL/ASSN ADMIN ...METH/CNCPT WORK ILO 20. PAGE 141 A2891 INT/ORG INT/TRADE

L63
SZASZY E.,"L'EVOLUTION DES PRINCIPES GENERAUX DU DROIT INTERNATIONAL PRIVE DANS LES PAYS DE DEMOCRATIE POPULAIRE." COM FUT WOR+45 LAW ECO/DEV PERF/ART POL/PAR PROF/ORG ECO/TAC INT/TRADE EDU/PROP ATTIT RIGID/FLEX ALL/VALS SOCISM...JURID TREND GEN/LAWS WORK 20. PAGE 141 A2876 DIPLOM TOTALISM INT/LAW INT/ORG

S63
MATHUR P.N.,"GAINS IN ECONOMIC GROWTH FROM INTERNATIONAL TRADE." USA-45 ECO/DEV FINAN INDUS ATTIT WEALTH...MATH QUANT STAT BIOG TREND GEN/LAWS WORK 20. PAGE 96 A1966 MARKET ECO/TAC CAP/ISM INT/TRADE

B64
SINGER H.W.,INTERNATIONAL DEVELOPMENT: GROWTH AND CHANGE. AFR BRAZIL L/A+17C WOR+45 CULTURE AGRI INDUS NAT/G ACT/RES ECO/TAC EDU/PROP WEALTH...GEOG CONCPT METH/CNCPT STAT HYPO/EXP WORK TOT/POP 20. PAGE 133 A2723 FINAN ECO/UNDEV FOR/AID INT/TRADE

B64
SULLIVAN G.,THE STORY OF THE PEACE CORPS. USA+45 WOR+45 INTELL FACE/GP NAT/G SCHOOL VOL/ASSN CONSULT EX/STRUC PLAN EDU/PROP ADMIN ATTIT DRIVE ALL/VALS ...POLICY HEAL SOC CONCPT INT QU BIOG TREND SOC/EXP WORK. PAGE 140 A2861 INT/ORG ECO/UNDEV FOR/AID PEACE

L64
ARMENGALD A.,"ECONOMIE ET COEXISTENCE." COM EUR+WWI FUT USA+45 WOR+45 ECO/DEV ECO/UNDEV FINAN INT/ORG NAT/G EXEC CHOOSE ATTIT ALL/VALS...POLICY RELATIV DECISION TREND SOC/EXP COLD/WAR WORK 20. PAGE 9 A0173 MARKET ECO/TAC CAP/ISM

S64
GARMARNIKOW M.,"INFLUENCE-BUYING IN WEST AFRICA." COM FUT USSR INTELL NAT/G PLAN TEC/DEV ECO/TAC DOMIN EDU/PROP REGION NAT/LISM ATTIT DRIVE ALL/VALS SOVEREIGN...POLICY PSY SOC CONCPT TREND STERTYP WORK COLD/WAR 20. PAGE 51 A1049 AFR ECO/UNDEV FOR/AID SOCISM

S64
HUELIN D.,"ECONOMIC INTEGRATION IN LATIN AMERICAN: PROGRESS AND PROBLEMS." L/A+17C ECO/DEV AGRI DIST/IND FINAN INDUS NAT/G VOL/ASSN CONSULT DELIB/GP EX/STRUC ACT/RES PLAN TEC/DEV ECO/TAC MARKET ECO/UNDEV INT/TRADE

ROUTINE BAL/PAY WEALTH WORK 20. PAGE 69 A1411

S64
RUBIN R.,"THE UN CORRESPONDENT." WOR+45 FACE/GP PROF/ORG EDU/PROP ROUTINE PERCEPT KNOWL...RECORD STAND/INT QU UN WORK TOT/POP VAL/FREE 20. PAGE 125 A2560
INT/ORG ATTIT DIPLOM

S65
HELMREICH E.C.,"KADAR'S HUNGARY." COM EUR+WWI HUNGARY USSR INTELL ECO/DEV AGRI INT/ORG TOP/EX DOMIN ALL/VALS WORK COLD/WAR 20. PAGE 64 A1311
NAT/G RIGID/FLEX TOTALISM

S65
KHOURI F.J.,"THE JORDON RIVER CONTROVERSY." LAW SOCIETY ECO/UNDEV AGRI FINAN INDUS SECT FORCES ACT/RES PLAN TEC/DEV ECO/TAC EDU/PROP COERCE ATTIT DRIVE PERCEPT RIGID/FLEX ALL/VALS...GEOG SOC MYTH WORK. PAGE 78 A1610
ISLAM INT/ORG ISRAEL JORDAN

S65
SPAAK P.H.,"THE SEARCH FOR CONSENSUS: A NEW EFFORT TO BUILD EUROPE." FRANCE GERMANY ECO/DEV NAT/G CONSULT FORCES PLAN EDU/PROP REGION CONSEN ATTIT ...SOC METH/CNCPT OBS TREND EEC NATO WORK 20. PAGE 135 A2770
EUR+WWI INT/ORG

WORKER....WORKER, LABORER

N
MURRA R.O.,POST-WAR PROBLEMS: A CURRENT LIST OF UNITED STATES GOVERNMENT PUBLICATIONS (PAMPHLET). WOR+45 SOCIETY FINAN INT/ORG SCHOOL WORKER TEC/DEV ECO/TAC...SOC 20. PAGE 106 A2180
BIBLIOG/A ADJUST AGRI INDUS

N
US SUPERINTENDENT OF DOCUMENTS,GOVERNMENT PERIODICALS AND SUBSCRIPTION SERVICES (PRICE LIST 36). LAW WORKER CT/SYS HEALTH. PAGE 157 A3202
BIBLIOG/A USA+45 NAT/G DIPLOM

B02
MOREL E.D.,AFFAIRS OF WEST AFRICA. UK FINAN INDUS FAM KIN SECT CHIEF WORKER DIPLOM RACE/REL LITERACY HEALTH...CHARTS 18/20 AFRICA/W NEGRO. PAGE 104 A2129
COLONIAL ADMIN AFR

B08
LABRIOLA A.,ESSAYS ON THE MATERIALISTIC CONCEPTION OF HISTORY. STRATA POL/PAR CAP/ISM DIPLOM INT/TRADE WAR 20. PAGE 83 A1706
MARXIST WORKER REV COLONIAL

B19
MEYER H.H.B.,SELECT LIST OF REFERENCES ON ECONOMIC RECONSTRUCTION: INCLUDING REPORTS OF THE BRITISH MINISTRY OF RECONSTRUCTION. UK LABOR PLAN PROB/SOLV ECO/TAC INT/TRADE WAR DEMAND PRODUC 20. PAGE 100 A2051
BIBLIOG/A EUR+WWI ECO/DEV WORKER

B27
SIEGFRIED A.,AMERICA COMES OF AGE: A FRENCH ANALYSIS (TRANS. BY H.H. HEMMING AND DORIS HEMMING). FRANCE UK POL/PAR WORKER TEC/DEV DIPLOM REGION RACE/REL ADJUST PRODUC HEREDITY...TIME/SEQ GP/COMP SOC/INTEG 20 DEMOCRAT REPUBLICAN KKK. PAGE 132 A2714
USA-45 CULTURE ECO/DEV SOC

B32
BLUM L.,PEACE AND DISARMAMENT (TRANS. BY A. WERTH). NAT/G FORCES WORKER DIPLOM AGREE WAR ATTIT AUTHORIT ORD/FREE. PAGE 16 A0322
SOCIALIST PEACE INT/ORG ARMS/CONT

B35
BUREAU ECONOMIC RES LAT AM,THE ECONOMIC LITERATURE OF LATIN AMERICA (2 VOLS.). CHRIST-17C AGRI DIST/IND EXTR/IND INDUS WORKER INT/TRADE...GEOG 16/20. PAGE 21 A0433
BIBLIOG L/A+17C ECO/UNDEV FINAN

B43
MC DOWELL R.B.,IRISH PUBLIC OPINION, 1750-1800. IRELAND CONSTN VOL/ASSN WORKER ORD/FREE CATHISM CONSERVE...POLICY IDEA/COMP BIBLIOG 18/ PARLIAMENT. PAGE 97 A1992
ATTIT NAT/G DIPLOM REV

B46
BLUM L.,FOR ALL MANKIND (TRANS. BY W. PICKLES). FRANCE GERMANY USSR LAW SOCIETY STRUCT POL/PAR WORKER DIPLOM DOMIN CHOOSE ORD/FREE FASCISM 20. PAGE 16 A0323
POPULISM SOCIALIST NAT/G WAR

B54
GIRAUD A.,CIVILISATION ET PRODUCTIVITE. UNIV INDUS WORKER DIPLOM REV INCOME UTOPIA...GEOG 20. PAGE 53 A1076
SOCIETY PRODUC ROLE

B55
GLLICK C.A.,HISTORY AND THEORIES OF WORKING-CLASS MOVEMENTS: A SELECT BIBLIOGRAPHY. EUR+WWI MOD/EUR UK USA-45 INT/ORG. PAGE 58 A1190
BIBLIOG WORKER LABOR ADMIN

B56
GILBERT R.,COMPETITIVE COEXISTENCE: THE NEW SOVIET CHALLENGE. WORKER DIPLOM WAR ORD/FREE 20 COLD/WAR. PAGE 52 A1071
NUC/PWR DOMIN MARXISM PEACE

B56
VON BECKERATH E.,HANDWORTERBUCH DER SOCIALWISSENSCHAFTEN (II VOLS.). EUR+WWI GERMANY POL/PAR WORKER DIPLOM LEAD CHOOSE SUFF WEALTH...SOC 20. PAGE 159 A3249
BIBLIOG INT/TRADE NAT/G ECO/DEV

B57
DRUCKER P.F.,AMERICA'S NEXT TWENTY YEARS. USA+45 DIST/IND ACADEM MUNIC SCHOOL DIPLOM ECO/TAC AUTOMAT HABITAT HEALTH...SOC/WK TREND 20 URBAN/RNWL PUB/TRANS. PAGE 39 A0788
WORKER FOR/AID CENSUS GEOG

B57
US COMMISSION GOVT SECURITY,RECOMMENDATIONS; AREA: IMMIGRANT PROGRAM. USA+45 LAW WORKER DIPLOM EDU/PROP WRITING ADMIN PEACE ATTIT...CONCPT ANTHOL 20 MIGRATION SUBVERT. PAGE 150 A3060
POLICY CONTROL PLAN NAT/G

B58
UN INTL CONF ON PEACEFUL USE,PROGRESS IN ATOMIC ENERGY (VOL. I). WOR+45 R+D PLAN TEC/DEV CONFER CONTROL PEACE SKILL...CHARTS ANTHOL 20 UN BAGHDAD. PAGE 147 A3003
NUC/PWR DIPLOM WORKER EDU/PROP

L58
TRAGER F.N.,"A SELECTED AND ANNOTATED BIBLIOGRAPHY ON ECONOMIC DEVELOPMENT, 1953-1957." WOR+45 AGRI FINAN INDUS MARKET LABOR MUNIC WORKER PLAN INT/TRADE PRODUC CENSUS. PAGE 145 A2958
BIBLIOG/A ECO/UNDEV ECO/DEV

B59
CHALUPA V.,RISE AND DEVELOPMENT OF A TOTALITARIAN STATE. CZECHOSLVK USSR STRUCT INT/ORG WORKER DIPLOM ECO/TAC COERCE NAT/LISM ATTIT...POLICY 20 COM/PARTY. PAGE 25 A0516
TOTALISM MARXISM REV POL/PAR

B59
CHANDLER E.H.S.,THE HIGH TOWER OF REFUGE: THE INSPIRING STORY OF REFUGEE RELIEF THROUGHOUT THE WORLD. WOR+45 NEIGH SECT WORKER PROB/SOLV DIPLOM ECO/TAC EDU/PROP COST HABITAT. PAGE 25 A0519
GIVE WEALTH STRANGE INT/ORG

B59
LINK R.G.,ENGLISH THEORIES OF ECONOMIC FLUCTUATIONS: 1815-1848. FRANCE UK AGRI WORKER DIPLOM PRICE TASK WAR DEMAND PRODUC...POLICY BIBLIOG 18 MALTHUS MILL/JS WILSON/J. PAGE 89 A1826
IDEA/COMP ECO/DEV WEALTH EQUILIB

B59
SHANNON D.A.,THE DECLINE OF AMERICAN COMMUNISM; A HISTORY OF THE COMMUNIST PARTY OF THE UNITED STATES SINCE 1945. USA+45 LAW SOCIETY LABOR NAT/G WORKER DIPLOM EDU/PROP LEAD...POLICY BIBLIOG 20 KHRUSH/N NEGRO AFL/CIO COLD/WAR COM/PARTY. PAGE 131 A2692
MARXISM POL/PAR ATTIT POPULISM

B59
STERNBERG F.,THE MILITARY AND INDUSTRIAL REVOLUTION OF OUR TIME. USA+45 USSR WOR+45 WORKER COMPUTER PLAN TEC/DEV NUC/PWR GP/REL...POLICY NAT/COMP 20. PAGE 138 A2818
DIPLOM FORCES INDUS CIVMIL/REL

B60
LEVIN J.V.,THE EXPORT ECONOMIES: THEIR PATTERN OF DEVELOPMENT IN HISTORICAL PERSPECTIVE. BURMA PERU AGRI WORKER COLONIAL COST DEMAND INCOME 20. PAGE 88 A1795
INT/TRADE ECO/UNDEV BAL/PAY EXTR/IND

B60
WODDIS J.,AFRICA: THE ROOTS OF REVOLT. SOUTH/AFR WORKER INT/TRADE RACE/REL DISCRIM ORD/FREE 20. PAGE 166 A3374
COLONIAL SOVEREIGN WAR ECO/UNDEV

B61
FUCHS G.,GEGEN HITLER UND HENLEIN. CZECHOSLVK GERMANY DIPLOM CHOOSE GP/REL TOTALISM SOVEREIGN 20 HITLER/A. PAGE 50 A1013
FASCISM WORKER POL/PAR NAT/LISM

B61
HADDAD J.A.,REVOLUCAO CUBANA E REVOLUCAO BRASILEIRA. BRAZIL CUBA L/A+17C STRATA AGRI WORKER EDU/PROP REGION...POLICY NAT/COMP 20. PAGE 59 A1210
REV ORD/FREE DIPLOM ECO/UNDEV

B61
LIEFMANN-KEIL E.,OKONOMISCHE THEORIE DER SOZIALPOLITIK. INT/ORG LABOR WORKER COST INCOME NEW/LIB...CONCPT SOC/INTEG 20. PAGE 88 A1810
ECO/DEV INDUS NAT/G SOC/WK

B61
NOLLAU G.,INTERNATIONAL COMMUNISM AND WORLD REVOLUTION; HISTORY AND METHODS (TRANS. BY VICTOR ANDERSEN). COM WORKER DIPLOM CONFER INGP/REL ...CONCPT BIBLIOG 20 STALIN/J LENIN/VI COMINTERN COMINFORM WORLD/CONG. PAGE 110 A2249
MARXISM POL/PAR INT/ORG REV

B62
FATOUROS A.A.,GOVERNMENT GUARANTEES TO FOREIGN INVESTORS. WOR+45 ECO/UNDEV INDUS WORKER ADJUD ...NAT/COMP BIBLIOG TREATY. PAGE 44 A0903
NAT/G FINAN INT/TRADE ECO/DEV

B62
KYRIAK T.E.,INTERNATIONAL COMMUNIST DEVELOPMENTS 1957-1961: INDEX TO TRANSLATIONS FROM AFRICA, ASIA, LATIN AMERICA, WEST EUROPE. COM WOR+45 NAT/G WORKER DIPLOM NAT/LISM. PAGE 83 A1704
BIBLIOG/A MARXISM LABOR POL/PAR

B62
LAUERHAUSS L.,COMMUNISM IN LATIN AMERICA: THE POST-WAR YEARS (1945 -1960) (PAPER). INTELL STRATA ECO/UNDEV AGRI WORKER FOR/AID INT/TRADE COLONIAL GUERRILLA 20. PAGE 85 A1745
BIBLIOG L/A+17C MARXISM REV

B62
ROBERTSON B.C.,REGIONAL DEVELOPMENT IN THE EUROPEAN ECONOMIC COMMUNITY. EUR+WWI FRANCE FUT ITALY UK
PLAN ECO/DEV

ECO/UNDEV WORKER ACT/RES PROB/SOLV TEC/DEV ECO/TAC INT/TRADE EEC. PAGE 122 A2499 — INT/ORG REGION

C62
DUFFY J.,"PORTUGAL IN AFRICA." PORTUGAL SIER/LEONE INDUS WORKER INT/TRADE WAR CONSERVE...CATH GEOG TREND 16/20. PAGE 39 A0795 — BIBLIOG RACE/REL ECO/UNDEV COLONIAL

B63
FISCHER-GALATI S.,EASTERN EUROPE IN THE SIXTIES. ALBANIA USSR YUGOSLAVIA ECO/UNDEV AGRI MARKET LABOR WORKER DIPLOM INT/TRADE EDU/PROP GOV/REL PRODUC UTOPIA SOCISM 20. PAGE 46 A0939 — MARXISM TEC/DEV BAL/PWR ECO/TAC

B63
FLORES E.,LAND REFORM AND THE ALLIANCE FOR PROGRESS (PAMPHLET). L/A+17C USA+45 STRUCT ECO/UNDEV NAT/G WORKER CREATE PLAN ECO/TAC COERCE REV 20. PAGE 47 A0953 — AGRI INT/ORG DIPLOM POLICY

B63
KHRUSHCHEV N.S.,THE NEW CONTENT OF PEACEFUL COEXISTENCE IN THE NUCLEAR AGE. GERMANY/E WORKER NUC/PWR REV SOCISM 20 COLD/WAR. PAGE 79 A1614 — MARXISM POL/PAR PEACE DIPLOM

B63
MILLER W.J.,THE MEANING OF COMMUNISM. USSR SOCIETY ECO/DEV EX/STRUC WORKER TEC/DEV ADMIN TOTALISM ...POLICY CONCPT CHARTS BIBLIOG T 20 COLD/WAR LENIN/VI STALIN/J. PAGE 101 A2080 — MARXISM TRADIT DIPLOM NAT/G

B63
MOSELY P.E.,THE SOVIET UNION, 1922-1962: A FOREIGN AFFAIRS READER. ASIA POLAND USSR CULTURE INTELL AGRI POL/PAR WORKER INT/TRADE DOMIN WAR NAT/LISM MARXISM SOCISM 20 KHRUSH/N. PAGE 105 A2152 — PWR POLICY DIPLOM

B63
NORTH R.C.,M. N. ROY'S MISSION TO CHINA: THE COMMUNIST-KUOMINTANG SPLIT OF 1927. ASIA USSR STRATA LEGIS WORKER LEAD REV ATTIT ROLE SOCISM 20 ROY/MN COM/PARTY. PAGE 110 A2253 — POL/PAR MARXISM DIPLOM

B64
DUTT R.P.,THE INTERNATIONALE. COM WOR+45 WOR-45 WORKER CAP/ISM WAR ATTIT...TREND GEN/LAWS 18/20 COM/PARTY. PAGE 40 A0813 — ALL/IDEOS INT/ORG MARXIST ORD/FREE

B64
REMAK J.,THE GENTLE CRITIC: THEODOR FONTANE AND GERMAN POLITICS, 1848-1898. GERMANY PRUSSIA CULTURE ELITES BAL/PWR DIPLOM WRITING GOV/REL...HUM BIOG 19 BISMARCK/O JUNKER FONTANE/T. PAGE 120 A2465 — PERSON SOCIETY WORKER CHIEF

B64
REUSS H.S.,THE CRITICAL DECADE - AN ECONOMIC POLICY FOR AMERICA AND THE FREE WORLD. USA+45 FINAN POL/PAR WORKER PLAN DIPLOM ECO/TAC TARIFFS BAL/PAY ...POLICY 20 CONGRESS GOLD/STAND. PAGE 120 A2468 — FOR/AID INT/TRADE LABOR LEGIS

S64
RUSK D.,"THE MAKING OF FOREIGN POLICY" USA+45 CHIEF DELIB/GP WORKER PROB/SOLV ADMIN ATTIT PWR ...DECISION 20 DEPT/STATE RUSK/D GOLDMAN/E. PAGE 125 A2570 — DIPLOM INT POLICY

B65
WHITE HOUSE CONFERENCE ON INTERNATIONAL COOPERATION(VOL.II). SPACE WOR+45 EXTR/IND INT/ORG LABOR WORKER NUC/PWR PEACE AGE/Y...CENSUS ANTHOL 20 RESOURCE/N URBAN/RNWL PUB/TRANS. PAGE 3 A0071 — R+D CONFER TEC/DEV DIPLOM

B65
LEISS A.C.,APARTHEID AND UNITED NATIONS COLLECTIVE MEASURES. SOUTH/AFR ECO/UNDEV EXTR/IND FORCES WORKER ECO/TAC FOR/AID INT/TRADE WEALTH...TREND CHARTS 20 UN NEGRO. PAGE 86 A1770 — DISCRIM RACE/REL STRATA DIPLOM

B65
LYONS G.M.,AMERICA: PURPOSE AND POWER. UK USA+45 FINAN INDUS MARKET WORKER TEC/DEV DIPLOM AUTOMAT NUC/PWR WAR RACE/REL ORD/FREE 20 EEC CONGRESS SUPREME/CT CIV/RIGHTS. PAGE 92 A1881 — PWR PROB/SOLV ECO/DEV TASK

B65
MCCOLL G.D.,THE AUSTRALIAN BALANCE OF PAYMENTS. UK USA+45 AGRI WORKER DIPLOM EQUILIB PRODUC...STAT TREND CHARTS BIBLIOG/A 20 AUSTRAL. PAGE 97 A2001 — ECO/DEV BAL/PAY INT/TRADE COST

B65
MURUMBI J.,PROBLEMS OF ECONOMIC DEVELOPMENT IN EAST AFRICA. FINAN INDUS WORKER TEC/DEV INT/TRADE TAX DEMAND EFFICIENCY PRODUC SOCISM...TREND CHARTS 20 AFRICA/E. PAGE 106 A2184 — AGRI ECO/TAC ECO/UNDEV PROC/MFG

B65
NKRUMAH K.,NEO-COLONIALISM: THE LAST STAGE OF IMPERIALISM. AFR INT/ORG WORKER FOR/AID INT/TRADE EDU/PROP GOV/REL NAT/LISM SOVEREIGN POPULISM SOCISM ...SOCIALIST 20 THIRD/WRLD INTRVN/ECO. PAGE 109 A2243 — COLONIAL DIPLOM ECO/UNDEV ECO/TAC

B65
OGILVY-WEBB M.,THE GOVERNMENT EXPLAINS: A STUDY OF THE INFORMATION SERVICES. UK DELIB/GP LEGIS WORKER BUDGET DIPLOM 20. PAGE 111 A2284 — EDU/PROP ATTIT NAT/G ADMIN

B65
ROLFE S.E.,GOLD AND WORLD POWER. UK USA+45 WOR-45 INDUS WORKER INT/TRADE DEMAND...MGT CHARTS 20 GOLD/STAND. PAGE 123 A2517 — BAL/PAY EQUILIB ECO/TAC DIPLOM

L65
MATTHEWS D.G.,"LE TIERS MONDE: A SELECT AND PRELIMINARY BIBLIOGRAPHIC SURVEY OF MANPOWER IN DEVELOPING COUNTRIES, 1960-1964." AFR ISLAM L/A+17C INDUS PLAN PROB/SOLV TEC/DEV INT/TRADE EFFICIENCY WEALTH...STAT 20. PAGE 96 A1971 — BIBLIOG/A ECO/UNDEV LABOR WORKER

B66
EUDIN X.J.,SOVIET FOREIGN POLICY 1928-34: DOCUMENTS AND MATERIALS (VOL. I). ASIA USSR WOR-45 INT/ORG POL/PAR WORKER WAR PEACE...ANTHOL 20 TREATY LEAGUE/NAT INTERVENT. PAGE 43 A0873 — DIPLOM POLICY GOV/REL MARXISM

B66
O'CONNER A.M.,AN ECONOMIC GEOGRAPHY OF EAST AFRICA. AFR TANZANIA UGANDA AGRI WORKER INT/TRADE COLONIAL GOV/REL...CHARTS METH/COMP 20 AFRICA/E. PAGE 111 A2269 — ECO/UNDEV EXTR/IND GEOG HABITAT

B66
WOHL R.,FRENCH COMMUNISM IN THE MAKING 1914-1924. FRANCE USSR LEAD REV...IDEA/COMP 20 COM/PARTY. PAGE 166 A3377 — MARXISM WORKER DIPLOM

L66
AMERICAN ECONOMIC REVIEW,"SIXTY-THIRD LIST OF DOCTORAL DISSERTATIONS IN POLITICAL ECONOMY IN AMERICAN UNIVERSITIES AND COLLEGES." ECO/DEV AGRI FINAN LABOR WORKER PLAN BUDGET INT/TRADE ADMIN DEMAND...MGT STAT 20. PAGE 7 A0146 — BIBLIOG/A CONCPT ACADEM

B67
INTERNATIONAL LABOUR OFFICE,SUBJECT GUIDE TO PUBLICATIONS OF THE INTERNATIONAL LABOUR OFFICE, 1919-1964. DIPLOM 20. PAGE 71 A1457 — BIBLIOG LABOR INT/ORG WORKER

B67
US SENATE COMM ON FOREIGN REL,HUMAN RIGHTS CONVENTIONS. USA+45 LABOR VOL/ASSN DELIB/GP DOMIN ADJUD REPRESENT...INT/LAW MGT CONGRESS. PAGE 156 A3189 — LEGIS ORD/FREE WORKER LOBBY

S67
ADIE W.A.C.,"CHINA'S 'SECOND LIBERATION'." CHINA/COM SOCIETY WORKER DIPLOM TASK 20 MAO. PAGE 4 A0090 — MARXISM REV INGP/REL ANOMIE

S67
GOLDMAN M.I.,"SOVIET ECONOMIC GROWTH SINCE THE REVOLUTION." USSR WORKER INT/TRADE PRODUC MARXISM ...POLICY TIME/SEQ 20. PAGE 53 A1090 — ECO/DEV AGRI ECO/TAC INDUS

S67
JOHNSON J.,"THE UNITED STATES AND THE LATIN AMERICAN LEFT WINGS." L/A+17C STRATA POL/PAR INT/TRADE 20. PAGE 74 A1524 — ECO/UNDEV WORKER ECO/TAC REGION

S67
THIEN T.T.,"VIETNAM: A CASE OF SOCIAL ALIENATION." VIETNAM AGRI FORCES FOR/AID ADMIN REPRESENT INGP/REL PWR 19/20. PAGE 143 A2918 — NAT/G ELITES WORKER STRANGE

S67
VELIKONJA J.,"ITALIAN IMMIGRANTS IN THE UNITED STATES IN THE MID-SIXTIES" ITALY USA+45 KIN MUNIC NAT/G WORKER DIPLOM REGION GP/REL ADJUST...GEOG CHARTS SOC/INTEG 20. PAGE 158 A3226 — HABITAT ORD/FREE TREND STAT

WORKING....SEE ROUTINE

WORLD COUNCIL OF CHURCHES....SEE WCC

WORLD HEALTH ORGANIZATION....SEE WHO

WORLD WAR I....SEE WWI

WORLD WAR II....SEE WWII

WORLD PEACE FOUNDATION A3396,A3397

WORLD/BANK....WORLD BANK

B59
ROBINSON J.A.,THE MONRONEY RESOULUTION: CONGRESSIONAL INITIATIVE IN FOREIGN POLICY MAKING. USA+45 POL/PAR TOP/EX DIPLOM INT/TRADE 20 CONGRESS WORLD/BANK INTL/DEV. PAGE 122 A2504 — LEGIS FINAN ECO/UNDEV CHIEF

B63
INTERNATIONAL BANK RECONST DEV,THE WORLD BANK GROUP IN ASIA. ASIA S/ASIA INDUS TEC/DEV ECO/TAC...RECORD 20 IBRD WORLD/BANK. PAGE 71 A1451 — INT/ORG DIPLOM ECO/UNDEV FINAN

B67
HIRSCHMAN A.O.,DEVELOPMENT PROJECTS OBSERVED. INDUS INT/ORG CONSULT EX/STRUC CREATE OP/RES ECO/TAC DEMAND...POLICY MGT METH/COMP 20 WORLD/BANK. PAGE 65 A1339 — ECO/UNDEV R+D FINAN PLAN

WORLD/CONG....WORLD CONGRESS

B61
NOLLAU G.,INTERNATIONAL COMMUNISM AND WORLD REVOLUTION; HISTORY AND METHODS (TRANS. BY VICTOR ANDERSEN). COM WORKER DIPLOM CONFER INGP/REL ...CONCPT BIBLIOG 20 STALIN/J LENIN/VI COMINTERN COMINFORM WORLD/CONG. PAGE 110 A2249
MARXISM POL/PAR INT/ORG REV

WORLD/CT....WORLD COURT; SEE ALSO ICJ

B38
HAGUE PERMANENT CT INTL JUSTIC,WORLD COURT REPORTS: COLLECTION OF THE JUDGEMENTS ORDERS AND OPINIONS VOLUME 3 1932-35. WOR-45 LAW DELIB/GP CONFER WAR PEACE ATTIT...DECISION ANTHOL 20 WORLD/CT CASEBOOK. PAGE 59 A1214
INT/ORG CT/SYS DIPLOM ADJUD

B43
HAGUE PERMANENT CT INTL JUSTIC,WORLD COURT REPORTS: COLLECTION OF THE JUDGEMENTS ORDERS AND OPINIONS VOLUME 4 1936-42. WOR-45 CONFER PEACE ATTIT ...DECISION JURID ANTHOL 20 WORLD/CT CASEBOOK. PAGE 59 A1215
INT/ORG CT/SYS DIPLOM ADJUD

WORLDUNITY....WORLD UNITY, WORLD FEDERATION (EXCLUDING UN AND LEAGUE OF NATIONS)

B17
VEBLEN T.B.,AN INQUIRY INTO THE NATURE OF PEACE AND THE TERMS OF ITS PERPETUATION. UNIV STRATA FINAN EDU/PROP PRICE COST DISCRIM NAT/LISM MORAL ORD/FREE PACIFIST 20 WORLDUNITY. PAGE 158 A3224
PEACE DIPLOM WAR NAT/G

B57
ALIGHIERI D.,ON WORLD GOVERNMENT. ROMAN/EMP LAW SOCIETY INT/ORG NAT/G POL/PAR ADJUD WAR GP/REL PEACE WORSHIP 15 WORLDUNITY DANTE. PAGE 6 A0121
POLICY CONCPT DIPLOM SECT

WORSHIP....SEE ALSO SECT

N
EUROPA PUBLICATIONS LIMITED,THE EUROPA YEAR BOOK. CONSTN FINAN INDUS POL/PAR DIPLOM TV CT/SYS...STAT BIOG CHARTS WORSHIP 20. PAGE 43 A0874
BIBLIOG NAT/G PRESS INT/ORG

N19
BARROS J.F.P.,THE INTERNATIONAL POLICE: THE USE OF FORCE IN THE STRUCTURE OF PEACE (PAMPHLET). BRAZIL WOR+45 WOR-45 FORCES DISCRIM NAT/LISM ORD/FREE SOVEREIGN...POLICY NEW/IDEA WORSHIP 20. PAGE 11 A0229
PEACE INT/ORG COERCE BAL/PWR

B40
NIEBUHR R.,CHRISTIANITY AND POWER POLITICS. WOR-45 SECT DIPLOM GP/REL SUPEGO ALL/IDEOS WORSHIP 20 CHRISTIAN. PAGE 109 A2234
PARTIC PEACE MORAL

B43
SULZBACH W.,NATIONAL CONSCIOUSNESS. FUT WOR-45 INT/ORG PEACE MORAL FASCISM MARXISM...MAJORIT TREND WORSHIP 19/20 LEAGUE/NAT INTERVENT WWI. PAGE 140 A2862
NAT/LISM NAT/G DIPLOM WAR

B47
HEIMANN E.,FREEDOM AND ORDER: LESSONS FROM THE WAR. WOR-45 CONSTN FORCES CHOOSE CIVMIL/REL PERSON ALL/IDEOS SOCISM...SOC IDEA/COMP WORSHIP 20. PAGE 64 A1308
NAT/G SOCIETY ORD/FREE DIPLOM

B57
ALIGHIERI D.,ON WORLD GOVERNMENT. ROMAN/EMP LAW SOCIETY INT/ORG NAT/G POL/PAR ADJUD WAR GP/REL PEACE WORSHIP 15 WORLDUNITY DANTE. PAGE 6 A0121
POLICY CONCPT DIPLOM SECT

B59
NIEBUHR R.,NATIONS AND EMPIRES. WOR+45 INT/ORG COLONIAL NUC/PWR TOTALISM UTOPIA ORD/FREE MARXISM WORSHIP 20 COLD/WAR PROTESTANT CHRISTIAN. PAGE 109 A2237
DIPLOM NAT/G POLICY PWR

B60
MORAES F.,THE REVOLT IN TIBET. ASIA CHINA/COM INDIA CULTURE CONTROL COERCE WAR TOTALISM...POLICY SOC WORSHIP 20 TIBET INTERVENT. PAGE 104 A2127
COLONIAL FORCES DIPLOM ORD/FREE

B60
SPEER J.P.,FOR WHAT PURPOSE? CHINA/COM USSR CONSTN PROB/SOLV DIPLOM CONTROL TASK WAR NAT/LISM WORSHIP 20 UN. PAGE 136 A2778
PEACE SECT SUPEGO ALL/IDEOS

B62
BENNETT J.C.,NUCLEAR WEAPONS AND THE CONFLICT OF CONSCIENCE. WOR+45 PROB/SOLV DIPLOM WEAPON SUPEGO MORAL...ANTHOL WORSHIP 20. PAGE 13 A0268
POLICY NUC/PWR WAR

B63
JAIRAZBHOY R.A.,FOREIGN INFLUENCE IN ANCIENT INDIA. INDIA ELITES SECT DIPLOM EDU/PROP COLONIAL REGION GP/REL...ART/METH LING WORSHIP +/14 GRECO/ROMN MESOPOTAM PERSIA PARTH/SASS. PAGE 73 A1491
CULTURE SOCIETY COERCE DOMIN

B64
HALPERN J.M.,GOVERNMENT, POLITICS, AND SOCIAL STRUCTURE IN LAOS. LAOS CULTURE SOCIETY STRATA STRUCT FAM DIPLOM DOMIN MARXISM...INT GOV/COMP WORSHIP SOC/INTEG 20. PAGE 60 A1242
NAT/G SOC LOC/G

B64
LOCKHART W.B.,CASES AND MATERIALS ON CONSTITUTIONAL RIGHTS AND LIBERTIES. USA+45 FORCES LEGIS DIPLOM PRESS CONTROL CRIME WAR PWR...AUD/VIS T WORSHIP 20 NEGRO. PAGE 90 A1849
ORD/FREE CONSTN NAT/G

B64
PERKINS D.,THE AMERICAN DEMOCRACY: ITS RISE TO POWER. ASIA USSR LAW CULTURE FINAN EDU/PROP COLONIAL CHOOSE...POLICY CHARTS BIBLIOG WORSHIP PRESIDENT 15/20 NEGRO. PAGE 115 A2362
LOC/G ECO/TAC WAR DIPLOM

B64
SPECTOR S.D.,A CHECKLIST OF PAPERBOUND BOOKS ON RUSSIA. USSR SECT DIPLOM EDU/PROP HEALTH...PHIL/SCI PSY SOC SOC/WK WORSHIP 20. PAGE 135 A2775
BIBLIOG COM PERF/ART

B65
WINT G.,ASIA: A HANDBOOK. ASIA COM INDIA USSR CULTURE INTELL NAT/G...GEOG STAT CENSUS NAT/COMP WORSHIP 20 TREATY CHINJAP. PAGE 165 A3365
DIPLOM SOC

B66
BOULDING K.E.,THE IMPACT OF THE SOCIAL SCIENCES. UNIV LAW SOCIETY CREATE PROB/SOLV...TREND WORSHIP. PAGE 17 A0349
SOC DIPLOM

B66
LEWIS S.,TOWARDS INTERNATIONAL CO-OPERATION (1ST ED.). WOR+45 AGRI INDUS EDU/PROP RACE/REL ISOLAT NAT/LISM ATTIT HEALTH WEALTH...CHARTS WORSHIP 20 UN. PAGE 88 A1803
DIPLOM ANOMIE PROB/SOLV INT/ORG

B66
MAYER P.,THE PACIFIST CONSCIENCE. SECT CREATE ARMS/CONT WAR RACE/REL ATTIT LOVE...ANTHOL PACIFIST WORSHIP FREUD/S GANDHI/M LAO/TZU KING/MAR/L CONSCN/OBJ. PAGE 97 A1984
DIPLOM PACIFISM SUPEGO

B66
US DEPARTMENT OF STATE,RESEARCH ON AFRICA (EXTERNAL RESEARCH LIST NO 5-25). LAW CULTURE ECO/UNDEV POL/PAR DIPLOM EDU/PROP LEAD REGION MARXISM...GEOG LING WORSHIP 20. PAGE 152 A3094
BIBLIOG/A ASIA S/ASIA NAT/G

B66
US DEPARTMENT OF STATE,RESEARCH ON THE AMERICAN REPUBLICS (EXTERNAL RESEARCH LIST NO 6-25). CULTURE SOCIETY POL/PAR DIPLOM EDU/PROP MARXISM WORSHIP 20 OAS. PAGE 152 A3095
BIBLIOG/A L/A+17C REGION NAT/G

B66
US DEPARTMENT OF STATE,RESEARCH ON WESTERN EUROPE, GREAT BRITAIN, AND CANADA (EXTERNAL RESEARCH LIST NO 3-25). CANADA GERMANY/W UK LAW CULTURE NAT/G POL/PAR FORCES EDU/PROP REGION MARXISM...GEOG SOC WORSHIP 20 CMN/WLTH. PAGE 152 A3098
BIBLIOG/A EUR+WWI DIPLOM

WPA....WORK PROJECTS ADMINISTRATION

WRESZIN M. A3398

WRIGGINS W.H. A3399

WRIGHT Q. A3401,A3402,A3403,A3404,A3405,A3406,A3407,A3408,A3409 A3410,A3411,A3412,A3413,A3414,A3415,A3416,A3417,A3418 , A3419

WRIGHT T.P. A3420

WRINCH P. A3421

WRITING....SEE ALSO HIST/WRIT

N
LONDON TIMES OFFICIAL INDEX. UK LAW ECO/DEV NAT/G DIPLOM LEAD ATTIT 20. PAGE 2 A0038
BIBLIOG INDEX PRESS WRITING

N
PUBLISHERS' CIRCULAR, THE OFFICIAL ORGAN OF THE PUBLISHERS' ASSOCIATION OF GREAT BRITAIN AND IRELAND. EUR+WWI MOD/EUR UK LAW PROB/SOLV DIPLOM COLONIAL ATTIT...HUM 19/20 CMN/WLTH. PAGE 2 A0039
BIBLIOG NAT/G WRITING LEAD

N
DEUTSCHE BUCHEREI,JAHRESVERZEICHNIS DES DEUTSCHEN SCHRIFTUMS. AUSTRIA EUR+WWI GERMANY SWITZERLND LAW LOC/G DIPLOM ADMIN...MGT SOC 19/20. PAGE 37 A0745
BIBLIOG WRITING NAT/G

N
UNITED NATIONS,OFFICIAL RECORDS OF THE ECONOMIC AND SOCIAL COUNCIL OF THE UNITED NATIONS. WOR+45 DIPLOM INT/TRADE CONFER...SOC SOC/WK 20 UN UNESCO. PAGE 148 A3031
INT/ORG DELIB/GP WRITING

N
UNITED NATIONS,OFFICIAL RECORDS OF THE UNITED NATIONS' ATOMIC ENERGY COMMISSION - DISARMAMENT COMMISSION. WOR+45 TEC/DEV DIPLOM WRITING NUC/PWR 20 UN. PAGE 148 A3032
ARMS/CONT INT/ORG DELIB/GP CONFER

N
UNITED NATIONS,OFFICIAL RECORDS OF THE UNITED NATIONS' GENERAL ASSEMBLY. WOR+45 BUDGET DIPLOM ADMIN 20 UN. PAGE 148 A3033
INT/ORG DELIB/GP INT/LAW WRITING

N
UNIVERSITY MICROFILMS INC,DISSERTATION ABSTRACTS: ABSTRACTS OF DISSERTATIONS AND MONOGRAPHS IN MICROFILM. CANADA DIPLOM ADMIN...INDEX 20. PAGE 149 A3045
BIBLIOG/A ACADEM PRESS WRITING

N
US SUPERINTENDENT OF DOCUMENTS,CATALOGUE OF PUBLIC DOCUMENTS OF CONGRESS AND OF ALL DEPARTMENTS OF THE GOVERNMENT OF THE UNITED STATES. DIPLOM ATTIT ...POLICY DICTIONARY 20 CONGRESS. PAGE 157 A3200
BIBLIOG NAT/G WRITING USA-45

B03
FORTESCUE G.K.,SUBJECT INDEX OF THE MODERN WORKS ADDED TO THE LIBRARY OF THE BRITISH MUSEUM IN THE YEARS 1881-1900 (3 VOLS.). UK LAW CONSTN FINAN NAT/G FORCES INT/TRADE COLONIAL 19. PAGE 47 A0968
BIBLIOG INDEX WRITING

B17
MEYER H.H.B.,LIST OF REFERENCES ON EMBARGOES (PAMPHLET). USA-45 AGRI DIPLOM WRITING DEBATE WEAPON...INT/LAW 18/20 CONGRESS. PAGE 100 A2049
BIBLIOG DIST/IND ECO/TAC INT/TRADE

N19
GRANT N.,COMMUNIST PSYCHOLOGICAL OFFENSIVE: DISTORTION IN THE TRANSLATION OF OFFICIAL DOCUMENTS (PAMPHLET). USSR POL/PAR CHIEF FOR/AID PRESS WRITING COLONIAL LEAD WAR PEACE 20 KHRUSH/N. PAGE 55 A1129
MARXISM DIPLOM EDU/PROP

B22
MYERS D.P.,MANUAL OF COLLECTIONS OF TREATIES AND OF COLLECTIONS RELATING TO TREATIES. MOD/EUR INT/ORG LEGIS WRITING ADMIN SOVEREIGN...INT/LAW 19/20. PAGE 106 A2186
BIBLIOG/A DIPLOM CONFER

B37
THOMPSON J.W.,SECRET DIPLOMACY: A RECORD OF ESPIONAGE AND DOUBLE-DEALING: 1500-1815. CHRIST-17C MOD/EUR NAT/G WRITING RISK MORAL...ANTHOL BIBLIOG 16/19 ESPIONAGE. PAGE 143 A2927
DIPLOM CRIME

B38
MCNAIR A.D.,THE LAW OF TREATIES: BRITISH PRACTICE AND OPINIONS. UK CREATE DIPLOM LEGIT WRITING ADJUD WAR...INT/LAW JURID TREATY. PAGE 98 A2018
AGREE LAW CT/SYS NAT/G

B49
BOZZA T.,SCRITTORI POLITICI ITALIANI DAL 1550 AL 1650. CHRIST-17C ITALY DIPLOM DOMIN 16/17. PAGE 18 A0365
BIBLIOG/A NAT/G CONCPT WRITING

B50
BOHATTA H.,INTERNATIONALE BIBLIOGRAPHIE. WOR+45 LAW CULTURE PRESS. PAGE 16 A0330
BIBLIOG DIPLOM NAT/G WRITING

B51
BISSAINTHE M.,DICTIONNAIRE DE BIBLIOGRAPHIE HAITIENNE. HAITI ELITES AGRI LEGIS DIPLOM INT/TRADE WRITING ORD/FREE CATHISM...ART/METH GEOG 19/20 NEGRO TREATY. PAGE 15 A0295
BIBLIOG L/A+17C SOCIETY NAT/G

B51
YOUNG T.C.,NEAR EASTERN CULTURE AND SOCIETY. ISLAM ECO/UNDEV SECT WRITING ATTIT HABITAT ORD/FREE 20. PAGE 169 A3438
CULTURE STRUCT REGION DIPLOM

B52
UNESCO,THESES DE SCIENCES SOCIALES: CATALOGUE ANALYTIQUE INTERNATIONAL DE THESES INEDITES DE DOCTORAT, 1940-1950. INT/ORG DIPLOM EDU/PROP...GEOG INT/LAW MGT PSY SOC 20. PAGE 147 A3015
BIBLIOG ACADEM WRITING

N52
COORDINATING COMM DOC SOC SCI,INTERNATIONAL REPERTORY OF SOCIAL SCIENCE DOCUMENTATION CENTERS (PAMPHLET). ACT/RES OP/RES WRITING KNOWL...CON/ANAL METH. PAGE 30 A0610
BIBLIOG/A R+D NAT/G INT/ORG

B53
LARSEN K.,NATIONAL BIBLIOGRAPHIC SERVICES: THEIR CREATION AND OPERATION. WOR+45 COM/IND CREATE PLAN DIPLOM PRESS ADMIN ROUTINE...MGT UNESCO. PAGE 85 A1733
BIBLIOG/A INT/ORG WRITING

B55
MALCLES L.N.,BIBLIOGRAPHICAL SERVICES THROUGHOUT THE WORLD (VOL. 4). WOR+45 INT/ORG VOL/ASSN DIPLOM PRESS WRITING 20 UNESCO. PAGE 93 A1911
BIBLIOG ROUTINE COM/IND

B55
PLISCHKE E.,AMERICAN FOREIGN RELATIONS: A BIBLIOGRAPHY OF OFFICIAL SOURCES. USA+45 USA-45 INT/ORG FORCES PRESS WRITING DEBATE EXEC...POLICY INT/LAW 18/20 CONGRESS. PAGE 116 A2390
BIBLIOG/A DIPLOM NAT/G

B55
TROTIER A.H.,DOCTORAL DISSERTATIONS ACCEPTED BY AMERICAN UNIVERSITIES 1954-55. SECT DIPLOM HEALTH ...ART/METH GEOG INT/LAW SOC LING CHARTS 20. PAGE 145 A2968
BIBLIOG ACADEM USA+45 WRITING

B56
SIPKOV I.,LEGAL SOURCES AND BIBLIOGRAPHY OF BULGARIA. BULGARIA COM LEGIS WRITING ADJUD CT/SYS ...INT/LAW TREATY 20. PAGE 134 A2736
BIBLIOG LAW TOTALISM MARXISM

B56
WATKINS J.T.,GENERAL INTERNATIONAL ORGANIZATION: A SOURCE BOOK. 19/20 LEAGUE/NAT UN. PAGE 162 A3292
BIBLIOG DIPLOM INT/ORG WRITING

B57
BEERS H.P.,THE FRENCH IN NORTH AMERICA. FRANCE USA-45...TIME/SEQ BIBLIOG. PAGE 12 A0247
HIST/WRIT DIPLOM BIOG WRITING

B57
US COMMISSION GOVT SECURITY,RECOMMENDATIONS; AREA: IMMIGRANT PROGRAM. USA+45 LAW WORKER DIPLOM EDU/PROP WRITING ADMIN PEACE ATTIT...CONCPT ANTHOL 20 MIGRATION SUBVERT. PAGE 150 A3060
POLICY CONTROL PLAN NAT/G

B59
OKINSHEVICH L.A.,LATIN AMERICA IN SOVIET WRITINGS, 1945-1958: A BIBLIOGRAPHY. USSR LAW ECO/UNDEV LABOR DIPLOM EDU/PROP REV...GEOG SOC 20. PAGE 111 A2287
BIBLIOG WRITING COM L/A+17C

B61
COLLISON R.L.,BIBLIOGRAPHICAL SERVICES THROUGHOUT THE WORLD: 1950-59 (VOL. 9). WOR+45 INT/ORG EDU/PROP PRESS WRITING ADMIN CENTRAL 20 UNESCO. PAGE 28 A0568
BIBLIOG COM/IND DIPLOM

B61
SOCIAL SCIENCE SERIALS IN SPECIAL LIBRARIES IN THE NEW YORK AREA; A SELECTED LIST. R+D ACADEM EDU/PROP WRITING...PSY 20. PAGE 119 A2448
BIBLIOG DIPLOM SOC

B62
KENT G.O.,A CATALOG OF FILES AND MICROFILMS OF THE GERMAN FOREIGN MINISTRY ARCHIVES, 1920-1945 (3 VOLS.). GERMANY WOR-45 WRITING WAR 20. PAGE 78 A1595
BIBLIOG NAT/G DIPLOM FASCISM

B62
UNECA LIBRARY,BOOKS ON AFRICA IN THE UNECA LIBRARY. WOR+45 AGRI INT/ORG NAT/G PLAN WRITING REGION...SOC STAT UN. PAGE 147 A3008
BIBLIOG AFR ECO/UNDEV TEC/DEV

B63
DALLIN A.,DIVERSITY IN INTERNATIONAL COMMUNISM: A DOCUMENTARY RECORD, 1961-1963. CHINA/COM CHIEF PRESS WRITING DEBATE LEAD...POLICY ANTHOL 20. PAGE 33 A0677
COM DIPLOM POL/PAR CONFER

B63
GALLAGHER M.P.,THE SOVIET HISTORY OF WORLD WAR II. EUR+WWI USSR DIPLOM DOMIN WRITING CONTROL WAR MARXISM...PSY TIME/SEQ 20 STALIN/J. PAGE 50 A1031
CIVMIL/REL EDU/PROP HIST/WRIT PRESS

B63
WHITTON J.B.,PROPAGANDA AND THE COLD WAR. USA+45 USSR INDUS NAT/G PLAN WRITING EFFICIENCY...POLICY 20 COLD/WAR. PAGE 164 A3341
ATTIT EDU/PROP COM/IND DIPLOM

N63
LIBRARY HUNGARIAN ACADEMY SCI,HUNGARIAN PUBLICATIONS ON ASIA AND AFRICA, 1950-1962: A SELECTED BIBLIOGRAPHY (PAMPHLET). AFR ASIA HUNGARY S/ASIA ECO/UNDEV NAT/G EDU/PROP ATTIT 20 UNESCO. PAGE 88 A1807
BIBLIOG REGION DIPLOM WRITING

B64
EHRENBURG I.,THE WAR: 1941-1945 (VOL. V OF "MEN, YEARS - LIFE," TRANS. BY TATIANA SHEBUNINA). GERMANY USSR PRESS WRITING PERS/REL PEACE ANOMIE ATTIT PERSON...CONCPT RECORD BIOG 20 STALIN/J HITLER/A. PAGE 40 A0827
WAR DIPLOM COM MARXIST

B64
NICE R.W.,TREASURY OF LAW. WOR+45 WOR-45 SECT ADJUD MORAL ORD/FREE...INT/LAW JURID PHIL/SCI ANTHOL. PAGE 108 A2227
LAW WRITING PERS/REL DIPLOM

B64
REMAK J.,THE GENTLE CRITIC: THEODOR FONTANE AND GERMAN POLITICS, 1848-1898. GERMANY PRUSSIA CULTURE ELITES BAL/PWR DIPLOM WRITING GOV/REL...HUM BIOG 19 BISMARCK/O JUNKER FONTANE/T. PAGE 120 A2465
PERSON SOCIETY WORKER CHIEF

B65
AMERICAN ECONOMIC ASSOCIATION,INDEX OF ECONOMIC JOURNALS 1886-1965 (7 VOLS.). UK USA+45 USA-45 AGRI FINAN PLAN ECO/TAC INT/TRADE ADMIN...STAT CENSUS 19/20. PAGE 7 A0145
BIBLIOG WRITING INDUS

B65
MEDIVA J.T.,LA IMPRENTA EN MEXICO, 1539-1821 (8 VOLS.). SOCIETY ECO/UNDEV DIPLOM COLONIAL GP/REL 16/19 MEXIC/AMER. PAGE 99 A2031
BIBLIOG WRITING NAT/G L/A+17C

B65
MOSTECKY V.,SOVIET LEGAL BIBLIOGRAPHY. USSR LEGIS PRESS WRITING CONFER ADJUD CT/SYS REV MARXISM ...INT/LAW JURID DICTIONARY 20. PAGE 105 A2155
BIBLIOG/A LAW COM CONSTN

B65
NEWBURY C.W.,BRITISH POLICY TOWARDS WEST AFRICA: SELECT DOCUMENTS 1786-1874. AFR UK INT/TRADE DOMIN ADMIN COLONIAL CT/SYS COERCE ORD/FREE...BIBLIOG/A 18/19. PAGE 108 A2224
DIPLOM POLICY NAT/G WRITING

B65
PANJAB U EXTENSION LIBRARY,INDIAN NEWS INDEX. INDIA ECO/UNDEV INDUS INT/ORG SCHOOL FORCES ADJUD WAR ATTIT WEALTH 20. PAGE 114 A2333
BIBLIOG PRESS WRITING DIPLOM

B66
BLACKSTOCK P.W.,AGENTS OF DECEIT: FRAUDS, FORGERIES AND POLITICAL INTRIGUES AMONG NATIONS. USSR EDU/PROP WRITING KNOWL 18/20 COLD/WAR KENNAN/G. PAGE 15 A0302
CON/ANAL DIPLOM HIST/WRIT

WU E. A3422

WUORINEN J.H. A3423

WURFEL D. A3424

WWI....WORLD WAR I

N
TOSCANO M.,THE HISTORY OF TREATIES AND INTERNATIONAL POLITICS (REV. ED.). WOR-45 AGREE WAR ...BIOG 19/20 TREATY WWI. PAGE 144 A2951
DIPLOM INT/ORG

B27
BRANDENBURG E.,FROM BISMARCK TO THE WORLD WAR; A HISTORY OF GERMAN FOREIGN POLICY, 1870-1914 (TRANS. BY ANNIE ELIZABETH ADAMS). GERMANY MOD/EUR FORCES AGREE PWR 19/20 TREATY CHAMBRLN/J WWI BISMARCK/O. PAGE 18 A0368
DIPLOM POLICY WAR

B28
HUBER G.,DIE FRANZOSISCHE PROPAGANDA IM WELTKRIEG GEGEN DEUTSCHLAND 1914 BIS 1918. FRANCE GERMANY MOD/EUR DIPLOM WAR...EXHIBIT 20 WWI. PAGE 68 A1403
EDU/PROP ATTIT DOMIN PRESS

B28
PLAYNE C.E.,THE PRE-WAR MIND IN BRITAIN. GERMANY MOD/EUR UK STRATA SECT DIPLOM EDU/PROP CROWD SUFF ...POLICY ANARCH PSY SOC IDEA/COMP 20 WWI. PAGE 116 A2388
PRESS WAR DOMIN ATTIT

B33
DAHLIN E.,FRENCH AND GERMAN PUBLIC OPINION ON DECLARED WAR AIMS 1914-1918. BELGIUM FRANCE GERMANY NAT/G POL/PAR DIPLOM COERCE REV WAR PEACE 20 WWI WILSON/W. PAGE 33 A0674
ATTIT EDU/PROP DOMIN NAT/COMP

B33
WAMBAUCH S.,PLEBISCITES SINCE THE WORLD WAR: WITH A COLLECTION OF OFFICIAL DOCUMENTS. WOR-45 COLONIAL SANCTION...MAJORIT DECISION CHARTS BIBLIOG 19/20 WWI. PAGE 161 A3272
DIPLOM CONSTN NAT/G CHOOSE

B36
BEARD C.A.,THE DEVIL THEORY OF WAR; AN INQUIRY INTO NATURE OF HISTORY AND THE POSSIBILITY OF KEEPING OUT OF WAR. USA-45 INT/ORG PROB/SOLV NEUTRAL ISOLAT ...CONCPT 20 LEAGUE/NAT WWI. PAGE 12 A0240
GEN/LAWS WAR POLICY DIPLOM

B43
SULZBACH W.,NATIONAL CONSCIOUSNESS. FUT WOR-45 INT/ORG PEACE MORAL FASCISM MARXISM...MAJORIT TREND WORSHIP 19/20 LEAGUE/NAT INTERVENT WWI. PAGE 140 A2862
NAT/LISM NAT/G DIPLOM WAR

B48
LINEBARGER P.,PSYCHOLOGICAL WARFARE. NAT/G PLAN DIPLOM DOMIN ATTIT...POLICY CONCPT EXHIBIT 20 WWI. PAGE 89 A1824
EDU/PROP PSY WAR COM/IND

B50
GATZKE H.W.,GERMANY'S DRIVE TO THE WEST. BELGIUM GERMANY MOD/EUR AGRI INDUS POL/PAR FORCES DOMIN AGREE CONTROL REGION COERCE 20 TREATY WWI. PAGE 51 A1053
WAR POLICY NAT/G DIPLOM

B53
SQUIRES J.D.,BRITISH PROPAGANDA AT HOME AND IN THE UNITED STATES FROM 1914 TO 1917. UK NAT/G PROB/SOLV DOMIN PRESS EFFICIENCY...PSY PREDICT 20 WWI INTERVENT PSY/WAR. PAGE 136 A2794
EDU/PROP CONTROL WAR DIPLOM

B54
MITCHELL P.,AFRICAN AFTERTHOUGHTS. UGANDA CONSTN NAT/G ADJUD COERCE WAR 20 WWI MAU/MAU. PAGE 102 A2090
BIOG CHIEF COLONIAL DOMIN

B54
TAYLOR A.J.P.,THE STRUGGLE FOR MASTERY IN EUROPE 1848-1918. MOD/EUR VOL/ASSN FORCES BAL/PWR DOMIN CONTROL PEACE MORAL 19/20 TREATY EUROPE WWI. PAGE 142 A2897
DIPLOM WAR PWR

B57
DUDDEN A.P.,WOODROW WILSON AND THE WORLD OF TODAY. USA-45 NAT/G PROVS CONTROL PARTIC WAR ISOLAT PWR SKILL...PERS/COMP ANTHOL 19/20 WILSON/W UN LEAGUE/NAT WWI. PAGE 39 A0794
CHIEF DIPLOM POL/PAR LEAD

B59
FERRELL R.H.,AMERICAN DIPLOMACY: A HISTORY. USA+45 USA-45 PLAN ROUTINE REV WAR PWR...T 18/20 EISNHWR/DD WWI. PAGE 45 A0921
DIPLOM NAT/G POLICY

B61
SCHONBRUNN G.,WELTKRIEGE UND REVOLUTIONEN 1914-1945. USSR DIPLOM TOTALISM ORD/FREE 20 TREATY WWI NAZI. PAGE 129 A2643
WAR REV FASCISM SOCISM

B62
PERRE J.,LES MUTATIONS DE LA GUERRE MODERNE: DE LA REVOLUTION FRANCAISE A LA REVOLUTION NUCLEAIRE. DIPLOM ARMS/CONT DEATH REV WEAPON GP/REL PEACE ATTIT...STAT PREDICT BIBLIOG 18/20 WWI. PAGE 115 A2365
WAR FORCES NUC/PWR

S62
RUSSETT B.M.,"CAUSE, SURPRISE, AND NO ESCAPE." FUT WOR-45 CULTURE SOCIETY INT/ORG FORCES TEC/DEV BAL/PWR EDU/PROP ARMS/CONT NUC/PWR WAR WEAPON PEACE KNOWL ORD/FREE PWR...POLICY CONCPT RECORD TIME/SEQ TREND GEN/LAWS 20 WWI. PAGE 126 A2578
COERCE DIPLOM

B65
ALBRECHT-CARRIE R.,THE MEANING OF THE FIRST WORLD WAR. MOD/EUR USA-45 INT/ORG BAL/PWR PEACE ATTIT LAISSEZ MARXISM...CONCPT BIBLIOG 19/20 LEAGUE/NAT WWI. PAGE 5 A0110
DIPLOM WAR

B66
SMITH D.M.,AMERICAN INTERVENTION, 1917. GERMANY UK USA-45 SEA FORCES DIPLOM INT/TRADE EDU/PROP COERCE WEAPON PEACE 20 WILSON/W WWI. PAGE 134 A2746
WAR ATTIT POLICY NEUTRAL

B66
SPEARS E.L.,TWO MEN WHO SAVED FRANCE: PETAIN AND DE GAULLE. FRANCE CONSTN FORCES DIPLOM WAR PERSON 20 WWI PETAIN/HP DEGAULLE/C. PAGE 135 A2773
BIOG LEAD CHIEF NAT/G

WWII....WORLD WAR II

WYOMING....WYOMING

WYTHE G. A3425

WYZNER E. A3426

X

XENOPHOBIA....SEE NAT/LISM

XENOPHON....XENOPHON

XHOSA....XHOSA TRIBE (SOUTH AFRICA)

Y

YALE/U....YALE UNIVERSITY

YALEN R. A3427

YALTA....YALTA CONFERENCE

B49
STETTINIUS E.R.,ROOSEVELT AND THE RUSSIANS: THE YALTA CONFERENCE. UK USSR WOR+45 WOR-45 INT/ORG VOL/ASSN TOP/EX ACT/RES EDU/PROP PEACE ATTIT DRIVE PERSON SUPEGO PWR...POLICY CONCPT MYTH OBS TIME/SEQ AUD/VIS COLD/WAR 20 CHURCHLL/W YALTA ROOSEVLT/F. PAGE 138 A2819
DIPLOM DELIB/GP BIOG

B66
EUBANK K.,THE SUMMIT CONFERENCES. EUR+WWI USA+45 USA-45 MUNIC BAL/PWR WAR PEACE PWR...POLICY AUD/VIS 20 GENEVA/CON TEHERAN YALTA POTSDAM. PAGE 43 A0872
CONFER NAT/G CHIEF DIPLOM

YAMADA H. A3428

YAMAMURA K. A3429

YANAGA C. A3430

YANKEE/C....YANKEE CITY - LOCATION OF W.L. WARNEROS STUDY OF SAME NAME

YARBROGH/R....RALPH YARBOROUGH

YAZOO....YAZOO LAND SCANDAL

YDIT M. A3431

YEAGER L.B. A3432

YEFROMEV A. A3433

YEMEN....SEE ALSO ISLAM

N
WEINTAL E.,FACING THE BRINK* AN INTIMATE STUDY OF CRISIS DIPLOMACY. CYPRUS FRANCE USA+45 USSR VIETNAM YEMEN INT/ORG NAT/G...POLICY DECISION PREDICT COLD/WAR PRESIDENT NATO 20. PAGE 162 A3307
DIPLOM

B63
UAR MINISTRY OF CULTURE,A BIBLIOGRAPHICAL LIST OF ARABIAN PENINSULA. ISLAM SAUDI/ARAB YEMEN FINAN NAT/G DIPLOM 19/20. PAGE 146 A2990
BIBLIOG GEOG INDUS SECT

B66
US DEPARTMENT OF STATE,RESEARCH ON THE MIDDLE EAST
BIBLIOG/A

(EXTERNAL RESEARCH LIST NO 4-25). GREECE ISRAEL SYRIA UAR YEMEN CULTURE SOCIETY POL/PAR SECT DIPLOM EDU/PROP WAR NAT/LISM...GEOG GOV/COMP 20. PAGE 152 A3096
ISLAM NAT/G REGION

YORUBA....YORUBA TRIBE

YOUNG A.N. A3434

YOUNG G. A3435

YOUNG G.B. A1146

YOUNG J. A3436

YOUNG K.T. A3437

YOUNG T.C. A3438

YOUNG/TURK....YOUNG TURK POLITICAL PARTY

YOUTH....SEE AGE/Y

YRARRAZAVAL E. A3439

YUAN TUNG-LI A3440,A3441

YUDELMAN/M....MONTEGU YUDELMAN

YUGOSLAVIA....YUGOSLAVIA; SEE ALSO COM

B18
KERNER R.J.,SLAVIC EUROPE: A SELECTED BIBLIOGRAPHY IN THE WESTERN EUROPEAN LANGUAGES. BULGARIA CZECHOSLVK GERMANY/E POLAND RUSSIA YUGOSLAVIA NAT/G DIPLOM MARXISM...LING 19/20. PAGE 78 A1598
BIBLIOG SOCIETY CULTURE COM

B43
CONOVER H.F.,THE BALKANS: A SELECTED LIST OF REFERENCES. ALBANIA BULGARIA ROMANIA YUGOSLAVIA INT/ORG PROB/SOLV DIPLOM LEGIT CONFER ADJUD WAR NAT/LISM PEACE PWR 20 LEAGUE/NAT. PAGE 29 A0596
BIBLIOG EUR+WWI

B52
ULAM A.B.,TITOISM AND THE COMINFORM. USSR WOR+45 STRUCT INT/ORG NAT/G ACT/RES PLAN EXEC ATTIT DRIVE ALL/VALS...CONCPT OBS VAL/FREE 20 COMINTERN TITO/MARSH. PAGE 146 A2993
COM POL/PAR TOTALISM YUGOSLAVIA

B56
WOLFF R.L.,THE BALKANS IN OUR TIME. ALBANIA FUT MOD/EUR USSR YUGOSLAVIA CULTURE INT/ORG SECT DIPLOM EDU/PROP COERCE WAR ORD/FREE...CHARTS 4/20 BALKANS COMINFORM. PAGE 166 A3388
GEOG COM

B57
TOMASIC D.A.,NATIONAL COMMUNISM AND SOVIET STRATEGY. UK USSR YUGOSLAVIA NAT/G POL/PAR CHIEF CREATE DOMIN REV WAR PWR...BIOG TREND 20 TITO/MARSH STALIN/J. PAGE 144 A2948
COM NAT/LISM MARXISM DIPLOM

B58
NEAL F.W.,TITOISM IN ACTION. COM YUGOSLAVIA AGRI LOC/G DIPLOM TOTALISM...BIBLIOG 20 TITO/MARSH. PAGE 107 A2206
MARXISM POL/PAR CHIEF ADMIN

B59
GOLDWIN R.A.,READINGS IN RUSSIAN FOREIGN POLICY. HUNGARY USSR YUGOSLAVIA ELITES INT/ORG NAT/G REV WAR NAT/LISM PERSON SOCISM...CHARTS 20 MAPS BOLSHEVISM. PAGE 53 A1095
COM MARXISM DIPLOM POLICY

B60
KARDELJE,SOCIALISM AND WAR. CHINA/COM WOR+45 YUGOSLAVIA DIPLOM EDU/PROP ATTIT...POLICY CONCPT IDEA/COMP COLD/WAR. PAGE 76 A1565
MARXIST WAR MARXISM BAL/PWR

B61
DALLIN D.J.,SOVIET FOREIGN POLICY AFTER STALIN. ASIA CHINA/COM EUR+WWI GERMANY IRAN UK YUGOSLAVIA INT/ORG NAT/G VOL/ASSN FORCES TOP/EX BAL/PWR DOMIN EDU/PROP COERCE ATTIT PWR 20. PAGE 33 A0679
COM DIPLOM USSR

S62
BOKOR-SZEGO H.,"LA CONVENTION DE BELGRADE ET LE REGIME DU DANUBE." COM EUR+WWI WOR+45 STRUCT POL/PAR VOL/ASSN PLAN EDU/PROP WEALTH...TIME/SEQ 20. PAGE 16 A0333
INT/ORG TOTALISM YUGOSLAVIA

S62
DRACHKOVITCH M.M.,"THE EMERGING PATTERN OF YUGOSLAV-SOVIET RELATIONS." COM FUT USSR WOR+45 INT/ORG ECO/TAC FOR/AID DOMIN COERCE ATTIT PERSON ORD/FREE PWR...TIME/SEQ 20 TITO/MARSH KHRUSH/N STALIN/J. PAGE 38 A0783
TOP/EX DIPLOM YUGOSLAVIA

S62
GREEN L.C.,"POLITICAL OFFENSES, WAR CRIMES AND EXTRADITION." WOR+45 YUGOSLAVIA INT/ORG LEGIT ROUTINE WAR ORD/FREE SOVEREIGN...JURID NAZI 20 INTERPOL. PAGE 55 A1138
LAW CONCPT INT/LAW

S62
STRACHEY J.,"COMMUNIST INTENTIONS." ASIA USSR YUGOSLAVIA INT/ORG NAT/G FORCES DOMIN EDU/PROP COERCE NUC/PWR NAT/LISM PEACE RIGID/FLEX PWR MARXISM...CONCPT MYTH OBS TIME/SEQ TREND COLD/WAR TOT/POP 20. PAGE 139 A2843
COM ATTIT WAR

B63
DRACHKOVITCH,UNITED STATES AID TO YUGOSLAVIA AND POLAND. POLAND USA+45 YUGOSLAVIA LEGIS EXEC TOTALISM MARXISM 20 CONGRESS. PAGE 38 A0782
FOR/AID POLICY DIPLOM ATTIT

B63
FISCHER-GALATI S.,EASTERN EUROPE IN THE SIXTIES. ALBANIA USSR YUGOSLAVIA ECO/UNDEV AGRI MARKET LABOR WORKER DIPLOM INT/TRADE EDU/PROP GOV/REL PRODUC UTOPIA SOCISM 20. PAGE 46 A0939
MARXISM TEC/DEV BAL/PWR ECO/TAC

B63
HAMM H.,ALBANIA - CHINA'S BEACHHEAD IN EUROPE. ALBANIA CHINA/COM USSR YUGOSLAVIA ELITES SOCIETY POL/PAR DELIB/GP FORCES ECO/TAC COERCE ISOLAT PEACE MARXISM...IDEA/COMP 20 MAO. PAGE 61 A1248
DIPLOM REV NAT/G POLICY

B64
DUROSELLE J.B.,POLITIQUES NATIONALES ENVERS LES JEUNES ETATS. FRANCE ISRAEL ITALY UK USA+45 USSR YUGOSLAVIA ECO/DEV FINAN ECO/TAC INT/TRADE ADMIN PWR 20. PAGE 40 A0809
DIPLOM ECO/UNDEV COLONIAL DOMIN

B64
GJUPANOVIC H.,LEGAL SOURCES AND BIBLIOGRAPHY OF YUGOSLAVIA. COM YUGOSLAVIA LAW LEGIS DIPLOM ADMIN PARL/PROC REGION CRIME CENTRAL 20. PAGE 53 A1078
BIBLIOG/A JURID CONSTN ADJUD

B64
GRIFFITH W.E.,COMMUNISM IN EUROPE (2 VOLS.). CZECHOSLVK USSR WOR+45 WOR-45 YUGOSLAVIA INGP/REL MARXISM SOCISM...ANTHOL 20 EUROPE/E. PAGE 57 A1162
COM POL/PAR DIPLOM GOV/COMP

S64
HORECKY P.L.,"LIBRARY OF CONGRESS PUBLICATIONS IN AID OF USSR AND EAST EUROPEAN RESEARCH." BULGARIA CZECHOSLVK POLAND USSR YUGOSLAVIA NAT/G POL/PAR DIPLOM ADMIN GOV/REL...CLASSIF 20. PAGE 67 A1382
BIBLIOG/A COM MARXISM

B66
RISTIC D.N.,YUGOSLAVIA'S REVOLUTION OF 1941. EUR+WWI YUGOSLAVIA NAT/G WAR ORD/FREE...RECORD BIBLIOG 20 HITLER/A TREATY. PAGE 121 A2484
REV ATTIT FASCISM DIPLOM

B66
SPULBER N.,THE STATE AND ECONOMIC DEVELOPMENT IN EASTERN EUROPE. BULGARIA COM CZECHOSLVK HUNGARY POLAND YUGOSLAVIA CULTURE PLAN CAP/ISM INT/TRADE CONTROL...POLICY CHARTS METH/COMP BIBLIOG/A 19/20. PAGE 136 A2793
ECO/DEV ECO/UNDEV NAT/G TOTALISM

C66
DUROSELLE J.B.,"LE CONFLIT DE TRIESTE 1943-1954: ETUDES DE CAS DE CONFLITS INTERNATIONAUX III." ITALY USA+45 YUGOSLAVIA ELITES DELIB/GP PLAN ADJUST ...POLICY GEOG CHARTS IDEA/COMP TIME 20 TREATY UN COLD/WAR. PAGE 40 A0810
BIBLIOG WAR DIPLOM GEN/LAWS

YUKON....YUKON, CANADA

Z

ZABLOCKI C.J. A3442

ZAGORIA D.S. A3443,A3444

ZALESKI E. A2108,A2109,A2110

ZAMBIA....SEE ALSO AFR

ZANDE....ZANDE, AFRICA

ZANZIBAR....SEE TANZANIA

ZARTMAN I.W. A3445,A3446,A3447

ZAUBERMAN A. A3448

ZAWODNY J.K. A3449

ZEBOT C.A. A3450

ZEINE Z.N. A3451

ZIMMERMAN I. A3452

ZIMMERN A. A3453,A3454,A3455

ZIONISM....SEE ISRAEL, NAT/LISM

ZISCHKA A. A3456

ZLATOVRT/N....NIKOLAI ZLATOVRATSKII

ZLOTNICK M. A3457

ZONING....ZONING REGULATIONS

ZOOK P.D. A3458

ZUCKERMAN S. A3459

ZULU....ZULU - MEMBER OF BANTU NATION (SOUTHEAST AFRICA)

ZUNI....ZUNI - NEW MEXICAN INDIAN TRIBE

ZWINGLI/U....ULRICH ZWINGLI

ZYZNIEWSKI S. A3460

Directory of Publishers

Abelard-Schuman Ltd., New York
Abeledo-Perrot, Buenos Aires
Abingdon Press, Nashville, Tenn.; New York
Academic Press, London; New York
Academy of the Rumanian People's Republic Scientific Documentation Center, Bucharest
Academy Publishers, New York
Accra Government Printer, Accra, Ghana
Acharya Book Depot, Baroda, India
Acorn Press, Phoenix, Ariz.
Action Housing, Inc., Pittsburgh, Pa.
Adams & Charles Black, London
Addison-Wesley Publishing Co., Inc., Reading, Mass.
Adelphi, Greenberg, New York
Adelphi Terrace, London
Advertising Research Foundation, New York
Advisory Committee on Intergovernmental Relations, Washington
Africa Bureau, London
Africa 1960 Committee, London
African Bibliographical Center, Inc., Washington
African Research Ltd., Exeter, England
Agarwal Press, Allahabad, India
Agathon Press, New York
Agency for International Development, Washington
Agrupacion Bibliotecalogica, Montevideo
Aguilar, S. A. de Ediciones, Madrid
Air University, Montgomery, Ala.
Akademiai Kiado, Budapest
Akademische Druck-und Verlagsanstalt, Graz, Austria
Akhil Bharat Sarva Seva Sangh, Rajghat, Varanasi, India; Rajghat, Kashi, India
Al Jadidah Press, Cairo
Alba House, New York
Eberhard Albert Verlag, Freiburg, Germany
Alcan, Paris
Aldine Publishing Co., Chicago
Aligarh Muslim University, Department of History, Aligarh, India
All-India Congress Committee, New Delhi
Allen and Unwin, Ltd., London
Howard Allen, Inc., Cleveland, Ohio
W. H. Allen & Co., Ltd., London
Alliance Inc., New York
Allied Publishers, Private, Ltd., Bombay; New Delhi
Allyn and Bacon, Inc., Boston
Almquist-Wiksell, Stockholm; Upsala
Ambassador Books, Ltd., Toronto, Ontario
American Academy of Arts and Sciences, Harvard University, Cambridge, Mass.
American Academy of Political and Social Science, Philadelphia
American Anthropological Association, Washington, D. C.
American Arbitration Association, New York
American-Asian Educational Exchange, New York
American Assembly, New York
American Association for the Advancement of Science, Washington, D. C.
American Association for the United Nations, New York
American Association of University Women, Washington, D. C.
American Bankers Association, New York
American Bar Association, Chicago
American Bar Foundation, Chicago
American Bibliographical Center-Clio Press, Santa Barbara, Calif.
American Bibliographic Service, Darien, Conn.
American Book Company, New York
American Civil Liberties Union, New York
American Council of Learned Societies, New York
American Council on Education, Washington
American Council on Public Affairs, Washington
American Data Processing, Inc., Detroit, Mich.
American Documentation Institute, Washington
American Economic Association, Evanston, Ill.
American Elsevier Publishing Co., Inc., New York
American Enterprise Institute for Public Policy Research, Washington, D. C.
American Features, New York
American Federation of Labor & Congress of Industrial Organizations, Washington, D. C.
American Foreign Law Association, Chicago
American Forest Products Industries, Washington, D. C.
American Friends of Vietnam, New York
American Friends Service Committee, New York
American Historical Association, Washington, D. C.
American Historical Society, New York
American Institute for Economic Research, Great Barrington, Mass.
American Institute of Consulting Engineers, New York
American Institute of Pacific Relations, New York
American International College, Springfield, Mass.
American Jewish Archives, Hebrew Union College—Jewish Institute of Religion, Cincinnati, Ohio
American Jewish Committee Institute of Human Relations, New York
American Judicature Society, Chicago
American Law Institute, Philadelphia
American Library Association, Chicago
American Management Association, New York
American Marketing Association, Inc., Chicago
American Municipal Association, Washington
American Museum of Natural History Press, New York
American Nepal Education Foundation, Eugene, Oregon
American Newspaper Publishers' Association, New York
American Opinion, Belmont, Mass.
American Philosophical Society, Philadelphia
American Political Science Association, Washington
American Psychiatric Association, New York
American Public Welfare Association, Chicago
American Research Council, Larchmont, N. Y.
American Society of African Culture, New York
American Society of International Law, Chicago
American Society for Public Administration, Chicago; Washington
American Textbook Publishers Council, New York
American Universities Field Staff, New York
American University, Washington, D. C.
American University of Beirut, Beirut
American University of Cairo, Cairo
American University Press, Washington
American University Press Services, Inc., New York
Ampersand Press, Inc., London, New York
Amsterdam Stock Exchange, Amsterdam
Anchor Books, New York
Anderson Kramer Association, Washington, D. C.
Anglo-Israel Association, London
Angus and Robertson, Sydney, Australia
Ann Arbor Publications, Ann Arbor, Mich.
Anthropological Publications, Oosterhout, Netherlands
Anti-Defamation League of B'nai B'rith, New York
Antioch Press, Yellow Springs, Ohio
Antwerp Institut Universitaire des Territoires d'Outre-Mer, Antwerp, Belgium
APEC Editora, Rio de Janeiro
Apollo Editions, New York
Ludwig Appel Verlag, Hamburg
Appleton-Century-Crofts, New York
Aqueduct Books, Rochester, N. Y.
Arbeitsgemeinschaft fur Forschung des Landes Nordrhein-Westfalen, Dusseldorf, Germany
Arcadia, New York
Architectural Press, London
Archon Books, Hamden, Conn.
Arco Publishing Company, New York
Arizona Department of Library and Archives, Tucson
Arizona State University, Bureau of Government Research, Tucson
Arlington House, New Rochelle, N. Y.
Arnold Foundation, Southern Methodist University, Dallas
Edward Arnold Publishers, Ltd., London
J. W. Arrowsmith, Ltd., London
Artes Graficas, Buenos Aires
Artes Graficas Industrias Reunidas SA, Rio de Janeiro
Asia Foundation, San Francisco
Asia Publishing House, Bombay; Calcutta; London; New York
Asia Society, New York
Asian Studies Center, Michigan State University, East Lansing, Mich.
Asian Studies Press, Bombay
Associated College Presses, New York

Associated Lawyers Publishing Co., Newark, N. J.
Association for Asian Studies, Ann Arbor
Association of National Advertisers, New York
Association of the Bar of the City of New York, New York
Association Press, New York
Associated University Bureaus of Business and Economic Research, Eugene, Ore.
M. L. Atallah, Rotterdam
Atheneum Publishers, New York
Atherton Press, New York
Athlone Press, London
Atlanta University Press, Atlanta, Ga.
The Atlantic Institute, Boulogne-sur-Seine
Atlantic Provinces Research Board, Fredericton, Newfoundland
Atma Ram & Sons, New Delhi
Atomic Industrial Forum, New York
Augustan Reprint Society, Los Angeles, Calif.
Augustana College Library, Rock Island, Ill.
Augustana Press, Rock Island, Ill.
J. J. Augustin, New York
Augustinus Verlag, Wurzburg
Australian National Research Council, Melbourne
Australian National University, Canberra
Australian Public Affairs Information Service, Sydney
Australian War Memorial, Canberra
Avi Publishing Co., Westport, Conn.
Avtoreferaty Dissertatsii, Moscow
N. W. Ayer and Sons, Inc., Philadelphia, Pa.
Aymon, Paris

La Baconniere, Neuchatel; Paris
Richard G. Badger, Boston
Baker Book House, Grand Rapids, Mich.
Baker, Vorhis, and Co., Boston
John Baker, London
A. A. Balkema, Capetown
Ballantine Books, Inc., New York
James Ballantine and Co., London
Baltimore Sun, Baltimore, Md.
Banco Central de Venezuela, Caracas
Bank for International Settlements, Basel
Bank of Finland Institute for Economic Research, Helsinki
Bank of Italy, Rome
Bankers Publishing Co., Boston
George Banta Publishing Co., Menasha, Wis.
Bantam Books, Inc., New York
A. S. Barnes and Co., Inc., Cranbury, N. J.
Barnes and Noble, Inc., New York
Barre Publishers, Barre, Mass.
Basic Books, Inc., New York
Batchworth Press Ltd., London
Bayerische Akademie der Wissenschaften, Munich
Bayerischer Schulbuch Verlag, Munich
Ebenezer Baylis and Son, Ltd., Worcester, England
Baylor University Press, Waco, Texas
Beacon Press, Boston
Bechte Verlag, Esslingen, Germany
H. Beck, Dresden
Bedminster Press, Inc., Totowa, N. J.
Beechhurst Press, New York
Behavioral Research Council, Great Barrington, Mass.
Belknap Press, Cambridge, Mass.
G. Bell & Sons, London
Bellman Publishing Co., Inc., Cambridge, Mass.
Matthew Bender and Co., Albany, New York
Bengal Publishers, Ltd., Calcutta
Marshall Benick, New York
Ernest Benn, Ltd., London
J. Bensheimer, Berlin; Leipzig; Mannheim
Benziger Brothers, New York
Berkley Publishing Corporation, New York
Bernard und Graefe Verlag fur Wehrwesen, Frankfurt
C. Bertelsmann Verlag, Gutersloh
Bharati Bhawan, Bankipore, India
Bharatiyi Vidya Bhavan, Bombay
G. R. Bhatkal for Popular Prakashan, Bombay
Bibliographical Society, London
Bibliographical Society of America, New York
Bibliographie des Staats, Dresden
Biblioteca de la II feria del libro exposicion nacional del periodismo, Panuco, Mexico
Biblioteca Nacional, Bogota
Biblioteka Imeni V. I. Lenina, Moscow
Bibliotheque des Temps Nouveaux, Paris
Bibliotheque Nationale, Paris
Adams & Charles Black, London
Basil Blackwell, Oxford
William Blackwood, Edinburgh
Blaisdell Publishing Co., Inc., Waltham, Mass.
Blanford Press, London
Blass, S. A., Madrid
Geoffrey Bles, London
BNA, Inc. (Bureau of National Affairs), Washington, D. C.
Board of Trade and Industry Estates Management Corp., London
T. V. Boardman and Co., London
Bobbs-Merrill Company, Inc., Indianapolis, Ind.
The Bodley Head, London
Bogen-Verlag, Munich
Bohlau-Verlag, Cologne; Graz; Tubingen
H. G. Bohn, London
Boni and Gaer, New York
Bonn University, Bonn
The Book of the Month Club, Johannesburg
Bookcraft, Inc., Salt Lake City, Utah
Bookfield House, New York
Bookland Private, Ltd., Calcutta; London
Bookmailer, New York
Bookman Associates, Record Press, New York
Books for Libraries, Inc., Freeport, N. Y.
Books International, Jullundur City, India
Borsenverein der deutschen Buchhandler, Leipzig
Bossange, Paris
Boston Book Co., Boston
Boston College Library, Chestnut Hill, Boston
Boston University, African Research Program, Boston
Boston University Press, Boston
H. Bouvier Verlag, Bonn
Bowes and Bowes, Ltd., Cambridge, England
R. R. Bowker Co., New York
John Bradburn, New York
George Braziller, Inc., New York
Brentano's, New York
Brigham Young University, Provo, Utah
E. J. Brill, Leyden
British Borneo Research Project, London
British Broadcasting Corp., London
British Council, London
British Liberal Party Organization, London
British Museum, London
Broadman Press, Nashville, Tenn.
The Brookings Institution, Washington
Brown University Press, Providence, R. I.
A. Brown and Sons, Ltd., London
William C. Brown Co., Dubuque, Iowa
Brown-White-Lowell Press, Kansas City
Bruce Publishing Co., Milwaukee, Wis.
Buchdruckerei Meier, Bulach, Germany
Buchhandler-Vereinigung, Frankfurt
Buijten & Schipperheijn, Amsterdam
Building Contractors Council, Chicago
Bureau of Public Printing, Manila
Bureau of Social Science Research, Washington, D. C.
Business Economists Group, Oxford
Business Publications, Inc., Chicago
Business Service Corp., Detroit, Mich.
Buttenheim Publishing Corp., New York
Butterworth's, London; Washington, D. C.; Toronto

Anne Cabbott, Manchester, England
California, Assembly of the State of, Sacramento, Calif.
California State Library, Sacramento
Calman Levy, Paris
Camara Oficial del Libro, Madrid
Cambridge Book Co., Inc., Bronxville, N. Y.
Cambridge University Press, Cambridge; London; New York
Camelot Press Ltd., London
Campion Press, London
M. Campos, Rio de Janeiro
Canada, Civil Service Commission, Ottawa
Canada, Civil Service Commission, Organization Division, Ottawa
Canada, Ministry of National Health and Welfare, Ottawa
Canada, National Joint Council of the Public Service, Ottawa

Canadian Dept. of Mines and Technical Surveys, Ottawa
Canadian Institute of International Affairs, Toronto
Canadian Peace Research Institute, Clarkson, Ont.
Canadian Trade Committee, Montreal
Candour Publishing Co., London
Jonathan Cape, London
Cape and Smith, New York
Capricorn Books, New York
Caribbean Commission, Port-of-Spain, Trinidad
Carleton University Library, Ottawa
Erich Carlsohn, Leipzig
Carnegie Endowment for International Peace, New York
Carnegie Endowment for International Peace, Washington, D. C.
Carnegie Foundation for the Advancement of Teaching, New York
Carnegie Press, Pittsburgh, Pa.
Carswell Co., Ltd., Toronto, Canada
Casa de las Americas, Havana
Case Institute of Technology, Cleveland, Ohio
Frank Cass & Co., Ltd., London
Cassell & Co., Ltd., London
Castle Press, Pasadena, Calif.
Catholic Historical Society of Philadelphia, Philadelphia
Catholic Press, Beirut
Catholic Students Mission Crusade Press, Cincinnati, Ohio
Catholic University Press, Washington
The Caxton Printers, Ltd., Caldwell, Idaho
Cedesa, Brussels
Cellar Book Shop, Detroit, Mich.
Center for Applied Research in Education, New York
Center for Applied Research in Education, Washington, D. C.
Center for Research on Economic Development, Ann Arbor, Mich.
Center for the Study of Democratic Institutions, Santa Barbara, Calif.
Center of Foreign Policy Research, Washington, D. C.
Center of International Studies, Princeton
Center of Planning and Economic Research, Athens, Greece; Washington, D. C.
Central Asian Research Centre, London
Central Bank of Egypt, Cairo
Central Book Co., Inc., Brooklyn, N. Y.
Central Book Department, Allahabad, India
Central Law Book Supply, Inc., Manila
Central News Agency, Ltd., Capetown, S. Afr.
Central Publicity Commission, Indian National Congress, New Delhi
Centre de Documentation CNRS, Paris
Centre de Documentation Economique et Sociale Africaine, Brussels
Centre d'Etudes de Politique Etrangere, Paris
Centre de Recherches sur l'URSS et les pays de l'est, Strasbourg
Centro de Estudios Monetarios Latino-Americanos, Mexico City
Centro Editorial, Guatemala City
Centro Mexicano de Escritores, Mexico City
Centro Para el "Desarrollo Economico y Social de America Latina", Santiago, Chile
The Century Co., New York
Century House, Inc., Watkins Glen, N. Y.
Cercle de la Librairie, Paris
Leon Chaillez Editeur, Paris
Chaitanya Publishing House, Allahabad, India
Chamber of Commerce of the United States, Washington, D. C.
S. Chand and Co., New Delhi
Chandler Publishing Co., San Francisco
Chandler-Davis, Lexington, Mass.
Chandler-Davis Publishing Co., West Trenton, N. J.
Channel Press, Inc., Great Neck, N. Y.
Chapman and Hall, London
Geoffrey Chapman, London
Chatham College, Pittsburgh, Pa.
Chatto and Windus, Ltd., London
F. W. Cheshire, London
Chestnut Hill, Boston College Library, Boston
Chicago Joint Reference Library, Chicago
Chilean Development Corp., New York
Chilmark Press, New York
Chilton Books, New York
China Viewpoints, Hong Kong
Chinese-American Publishing Co., Shanghai
Chiswick Press, London
Christian Crusade, Tulsa, Okla.
Georg Christiansen, Itzehoe, Germany
Christopher Publishing House, Boston
Chulalongkorn University, Bangkok
Church League of America, Wheaton, Ill.
C. I. Associates, New York
Cincinnati Civil Service, Cincinnati, Ohio
Citadel Press, New York
City of Johannesburg Public Library, Johannesburg
Citizens Research Foundation, Paris
Citizens Research Foundation, Princeton, N. J.
Ciudad Universitaria, San Jose, Calif.
Ciudad y Espiritu, Buenos Aires
Claremont Colleges, Claremont, Calif.
Clarendon Press, London
Clark, Irwin and Co., Ltd., Toronto
Clark University Press, Worcester, Mass.
Classics Press, New York
Clay and Sons, London
Cleveland Civil Service Commission, Cleveland
Clio Press, Santa Barbara, Calif.
William Clowes and Sons, Ltd., London
Colin (Librairie Armand) Paris
College and University Press, New Haven
Collet's Holdings, Ltd., London
Colliers, New York
F. Collin, Brussels
Collins, London
Colloquium Verlag, Berlin
Colombo Plan Bureau, Colombo, Ceylon
Colonial Press Inc., Northport, Ala.; New York
Colorado Bibliographic Institute, Denver
Colorado Legislature Council, Denver
Colorado State Board of Library Commissioners, Denver
Columbia University, New York
Columbia University, Bureau of Applied Social Research, New York
Columbia University, Center for Urban Education, New York
Columbia University, East Asian Institute, New York
Columbia University, Graduate School of Business, New York
Columbia University, Institute of French Studies, New York
Columbia University, Institute of Public Administration, New York
Columbia University, Institute of Russian Studies, New York
Columbia University, Institute of War-Peace Studies, New York
Columbia University, Law Library, New York
Columbia University, Parker School, New York
Columbia University, School of International Affairs, New York
Columbia University, School of Library Service, New York
Columbia University Press, New York
Columbia University Teachers College, New York
Combat Forces Press, Washington, D. C.
Comet Press, New York
Comision Nacional Ejecutiva, Buenos Aires
Commerce Clearing House, Chicago; Washington; New York
Commercial Credit Co., Baltimore, Md.
Commissao do iv Centenario de Ciudade, Sao Paulo
Commission for Technical Cooperation, Lahore
Commission to Study the Organization of Peace, New York
Committee for Economic Development, New York
Committee on Africa, New York
Committee on Federal Tax Policy, New York
Committee on Near East Studies, Washington
Committee on Public Administration, Washington, D. C.
Committee to Frame World Constitution, New York
Common Council for American Unity, New York
Commonwealth Agricultural Bureau, London
Commonwealth Economic Commission, London
Community Publications, Manila
Community Renewal Program, San Francisco
Community Studies, Inc., Kansas City
Companhia Editora Forense, Rio de Janeiro
Companhia Editora Nacional, Sao Paulo
Compass Books, New York
Concordia Publishing House, St. Louis, Mo.
Confederate Publishing Co., Tuscaloosa, Ala.
Conference on Economic Progress, Washington, D. C.
Conference on State and Economic Enterprise in Modern Japan, Estes Park, Colo.
Congress for Cultural Freedom, Prabhakar

Congressional Quarterly Service, Washington
Connecticut Personnel Department, Hartford
Connecticut State Civil Service Commission, Hartford
Conseil d'Etat, Paris
Conservative Political Centre, London
Constable and Co., London
Archibald Constable and Co., Edinburgh
Cooper Square Publishers, New York
U. Cooper and Partners, Ltd., London
Corinth Books, New York
Cornell University, Dept. of Asian Studies, Ithaca
Cornell University, Graduate School of Business and Public Administration, Ithaca
Cornell University Press, Ithaca
Cornell University, School of Industry and Labor Planning, Ithaca
Council for Economic Education, Bombay
Council of Education, Johannesburg
Council of Europe, Strasbourg
Council of State Governments, Chicago, Ill.
Council of the British National Bibliography, Ltd., London
Council on Foreign Relations, New York
Council on Public Affairs, Washington, D. C.
Council on Religion and International Affairs, New York
Council on Social Work Education, Washington, D. C.
Covici, Friede, Inc., New York
Coward-McCann, Inc., New York
Cresset Press, London
Crestwood Books, Springfield, Va.
Criterion Books, Inc., New York
S. Crofts and Co., New York
Crosby, Lockwood, and Sons, Ltd., London
Crosscurrents Press, New York
Thomas Y. Crowell Co., New York
Crowell-Collier and MacMillan, New York
Crown Publishers, Inc., New York
C.S.I.C., Madrid
Cuadernos de la Facultad de Derecho Universidad Veracruzana, Mexico City
Cuerpo Facultativo de Archiveros, Bibliotecarios y Argueologos, Madrid
Cultural Center of the French Embassy, New York
Current Scene, Hong Kong
Current Thought, Inc., Durham, N. C.
Czechoslovak Foreign Institute in Exile, Chicago

Da Capo Press, New York
Daguin Freres, Editeurs, Paris
Daily Telegraph, London
Daily Worker Publishing Co., Chicago
Dalloz, Paris
Damascus Bar Association, Damascus
Dangary Publishing Co., Baltimore
David Davies Memorial Institute of Political Studies, London
David-Stewart, New York
John Day Co., Inc., New York
John de Graff, Inc., Tuckahoe, N. Y.
La Decima Conferencia Interamericana, Caracas
Delacorte Press, New York
Dell Publishing Co., New York
T. S. Denison & Co., Inc., Minneapolis, Minn.
J. M. Dent, London
Departamento de Imprensa Nacional, Rio de Janeiro
Deseret Book Co., Salt Lake City, Utah
Desert Research Institute Publications' Office, Reno, Nev.
Deus Books, Paulist Press, Glen Rock, N. J.
Andre Deutsch, Ltd., London
Deutsche Afrika Gesellschaft, Bonn
Deutsche Bibliographie, Frankfurt am Main
Deutsche Bucherei, Leipzig
Deutsche Gesellschaft fur Volkerrecht, Karlsruhe
Deutsche Gesellschaft fur Auswartige Politik, Bonn
Deutsche Verlagsanstalt, Stuttgart
Deutscher Taschenbuch Verlag, Munich
Deva Datta Shastri, Hoshiarpur
Development Loan Fund, Washington, D. C.
Devin-Adair, Co., New York
Diablo Press, Inc., Berkeley, Calif.
Dial Press, Inc., New York
Dibco Press, San Jose, Cal.
Dickenson Publishing Co., Inc., Belmont, Calif.
Didier Publishers, New York

Firmin Didot Freres, Paris
Dietz Verlag, Berlin
Difusao Europeia do Livro, Sao Paulo
Diplomatic Press, London
Direccion General de Accion Social, Lisbon
District of Columbia, Office of Urban Renewal, Washington, D. C.
Djambatan, Amsterdam
Dennis Dobson, London
Dobunken Co., Ltd., Tokyo
La Documentation Francaise, Paris
Documents Index, Arlington, Virginia
Dodd, Mead and Co., New York
Octave Doin et Fils, Paris
Dolphin Books, Inc., New York
Dominion Press, Chicago
Walter Doon Verlag, Bremen
George H. Doran Co., New York
Dorrance and Co., Inc., Philadelphia, Pa.
Dorsey Press, Homewood, Illinois
Doubleday and Co., Inc., Garden City, N. Y.
Dover Publications, New York
Dow Jones and Co., Inc., New York
Dragonfly Books, Hong Kong
Drei Masken Verlag, Munich
Droemersche Verlagsanstalt, Zurich
Droste Verlag, Dusseldorf
Druck und Verlag von Carl Gerolds Sohn, Vienna
Guy Drummond, Montreal
The Dryden Press, New York
Dryfus Conference on Public Affairs, Hanover, N. H.
Duckworth, London
Duell, Sloan & Pearce, New York
Dufour Editions, Inc., Chester Springs, Pa.
Carl Duisburg-Gesellschaft fur Nachwuchsforderung, Cologne
Duke University, School of Law, Durham, N. C.
Duke University Press, Durham, N. C.
Dulau and Co., London
Duncker und Humblot, Berlin
Duquesne University Press, Pittsburgh, Pa.
R. Dutt, London
E. P. Dutton and Co., Inc., Garden City, N. Y.

E. P. & Commercial Printing Co., Durban, S. Africa
East Africa Publishing House, Nairobi
East European Fund, Inc., New York
East-West Center Press, Honolulu
Eastern Kentucky Regional Development Commission, Frankfort, Ky.
Eastern World, Ltd., London
Emil Ebering, Berlin
Echter-Verlag, Wurzburg
Ecole Francaise d'Extreme Orient, Paris
Ecole Nationale d'Administration, Paris
Econ Verlag, Dusseldorf; Vienna
Economic Research Corp., Ltd., Montreal
Economic Society of South Africa, Johannesburg
The Economist, London
Edicao Saraiva, Sao Paulo
Ediciones Ariel, Barcelona
Ediciones Cultura Hispanica, Madrid
Ediciones del Movimiento, Borgos, Spain
Ediciones Nuestro Tiempo, Montevideo
Ediciones Rialp, Madrid
Ediciones Riaz, Lima
Ediciones Siglo Veinte, Buenos Aires
Ediciones Tercer Mundo, Bogota
Edicoes de Revista de Estudes Politos, Rio de Janeiro
Edicoes Do Val, Rio de Janeiro
Edicoes GRD, Rio de Janeiro
Edicoes o Cruzeiro, Rio de Janeiro
Edicoes Tempo Brasileiro, Ltda., Rio de Janeiro
Edinburgh House Press, Edinburgh
Editions Albin Michel, Paris
Editions Alsatia, Paris
Editions Berger-Levrault, Paris
Editions Cujas, Paris
Editions de l'Epargne, Paris
Editions de l'Institut de Sociologie de l'Universite Libre de Bruxelles, Brussels
Editions d'Organisation, Paris
Editions Denoel, Paris
Editions John Didier, Paris

Editions du Carrefour, Paris
Editions du Cerf, Paris
Editions du Livre, Monte Carlo
Editions du Monde, Paris
Editions du Rocher, Monaco
Editions du Seuil, Paris
Editions du Tiers-Monde, Algiers
Editions du Vieux Colombier, Paris
Editions Eyrolles, Paris
Editions Internationales, Paris
Editions Mont Chrestien, Paris
Editions Nauwelaerts, Louvain
Editions Ouvrieres, Paris
Editions A. Pedone, Paris
Editions Presence Africaine, Paris
Editions Rouff, Paris
Editions Sedif, Paris
Editions Sirey, Paris
Editions Sociales, Paris
Editions Techniques Nord Africaines, Rabat
Editions Universitaires, Paris
Editora Brasiliense, Sao Paulo
Editora Civilizacao Brasileira S. A., Rio de Janeiro
Editora Fulgor, Sao Paulo
Editora Saga, Rio de Janerio
Editores letras e artes, Rio de Janeiro
Editores Mexicanos, Mexico City
Editores Mexicanos Unidos, Mexico City
Editorial AIP, Miami
Editorial Amerinda, Buenos Aires
Editorial Columbia, Buenos Aires
Editorial Freeland, Buenos Aires
Editorial Gustavo Gili, Barcelona
Editorial Jus, Mexico City, Mexico
Editorial Lex, Havana
Editorial Losa da Buenos Aires, Buenos Aires
Editorial Marymar, Buenos Aires
Editorial Mentora, Barcelona
Editorial Nascimento, Santiago
Editorial Palestra, Buenos Aires
Editorial Patria, Mexico City
Editorial Pax, Bogota
Editorial Pax-Mexico, Mexico City
Editorial Platina, Buenos Aires
Editorial Porrua, Mexico City
Editorial Stylo Durangozgo, Mexico City
Editorial Universitaria de Buenos Aires, Buenos Aires
Editorial Universitaria de Puerto Rico, San Jose
Editorial Universitaria Santiago, Santiago
Le Edizioni de Favoro, Rome
Edizioni di Storia e Letteratura, Rome
Edizioni Scientifiche Italiane, Naples
Education and World Affairs, New York
Educational Heritage, Yonkers, N. Y.
Edwards Brothers, Ann Arbor
Effingham Wilson Publishers, London
Egyptian Library Press, Cairo
Egyptian Society of International Law, Cairo
Elex Books, London
Elsevier Publishing Co., Ltd., London
EMECE Editores, Buenos Aires
Emerson Books, New York
Empresa Editora Austral, Ltd., Santiago
Encyclopedia Britannica, Inc., Chicago
English Universities Press, London
Ferdinand Enke Verlag, Bonn; Erlangen; Stuttgart
Horst Erdmann Verlag, Schwarzwald
Paul Eriksson, Inc., New York
Escorpion, Buenos Aires
Escuela de Historia Moderna, Madrid
Escuela Nacional de Ciencias Politicas y Sociales, Mexico City
Escuela Superior de Administracion Publica America Central, San Jose, Costa Rica
Essener Verlagsanstalt, Essen
Essential Books, Ltd., London
Ethiopia, Ministry of Information, Addis Ababa
Etudes, Paris
Euroamerica, Madrid
Europa-Archiv, Frankfurt am Main
Europa Publications Ltd., London
Europa Verlag, Zurich; Vienna
Europaische Verlagsanstalt, Frankfurt
European Committee for Economic and Social Progress, Milan
European Free Trade Association, Geneva
Evangelischer Verlag, Zurich
Edward Evans and Sons, Shanghai
Everline Press, Princeton
Excerpta Criminologica Foundation, Leyden, Netherlands
Exchange Bibliographies, Eugene, Ore.
Export Press, Belgrade
Exposition Press, Inc., New York
Eyre and Spottiswoode, Ltd., London
Extending Horizon Books, Boston

F. and T. Publishers, Seattle, Washington
Faber and Faber, Ltd., London
Fabian Society, London
Facing Reality Publishing Corporation, Detroit, Mich.
Facts on File, Inc., New York
Fairchild Publishing, Inc., New York
Fairleigh Dickinson Press, Rutherford, N. J.
Falcon Press, London
Family Service Association of America, New York
Farrar and Rinehart, New York
Farrar, Strauss & Giroux, Inc., New York
Fawcett World Library, New York
F. W. Faxon Co., Inc., Boston
Fayard, Paris
Federal Legal Publications, Inc., New York
Federal Reserve Bank of New York, New York
Federal Trust for Education and Research, London
Fellowship Publications, New York
Feltrinelli Giangiacomo (Editore), Milan
Au Fil d'Ariadne, Paris
Filipiniana Book Guild, Manila
Financial Index Co., New York
Finnish Political Science Association, Helsinki
Fischer Bucherei, Frankfurt
Fischer Verlag, Stuttgart
Gustav Fischer Verlag, Jena
Flammarion, Paris
Fleet Publishing Co., New York
Fletcher School of Law and Diplomacy, Boston
R. Flint and Co., London
Florida State University, Tallahassee
Follett Publishing Co., Chicago
Fondation Nationale des Sciences Politiques, Paris
Fondo Historico y Bibliografico Jose Foribio, Medina, Santiago
Fondo de Cultura Economica, Mexico
B. C. Forbes and Sons, New York
Ford Foundation, New York
Fordham University Press, New York
Foreign Affairs Association of Japan, Tokyo
Foreign Affairs Bibliography, New York
Foreign Language Press, Peking
Foreign Language Publishing House, Moscow
Foreign Policy Association, New York
Foreign Policy Clearing House, Washington, D. C.
Foreign Policy Research Institute, University of Pennsylvania, Philadelphia, Pa.
Foreign Trade Library, Philadelphia
Arnold Forni Editore, Bologna
Forschungs-Berichte des Landes Nordrhein-Westfalen, Dusseldorf, Germany
Fortress Press, Philadelphia, Pa.
Foundation for Economic Education, Irvington-on-Hudson, N. Y.
Foundation for Social Research, Los Angeles, Calif.
Foundation Press, Inc., Brooklyn, N. Y.; Mineola, N. Y.
Foundation Press, Inc., Chicago
Foundation for Research on Human Behavior, New York
France Editions Nouvelles, Paris
France, Ministere de l'Education Nationale, Paris
France, Ministere d'Etat aux Affaires Culturelles, Paris
France, Ministere des Finances et des Affaires Economiques, Paris
Francois Maspera, Paris
Francke Verlag, Munich
Ben Franklin Press, Pittsfield, Mass.
Burt Franklin, New York
Free Europe Committee, New York
Free Press, New York
Free Press of Glencoe, Glencoe, Ill.; New York

Free Speech League, New York
Freedom Books, New York
Freedom Press, London
Ira J. Friedman, Inc., Port Washington, N. Y.
Friends General Conference, Philadelphia, Pa.
Friendship Press, New York
M. L. Fuert, Los Angeles
Fund for the Republic, New York
Fundacao Getulio Vargas, Rio de Janeiro
Funk and Wagnalls Co., Inc., New York
Orell Fuessli Verlag, Zurich

Galaxy Books, Oxford
Gale Research Co., Detroit
Galton Publishing Co., New York
A. R. Geoghegan, Buenos Aires
George Washington University, Population Research Project, Washington, D. C.
Georgetown University Press, Washington, D. C.
Georgia State College, Atlanta, Ga.
Georgia State Library, Atlanta, Ga.
Germany (Territory under Allied Occupation, 1945—U. S. Zone) Office of Public Information, Information Control Division, Bonn
Germany, Bundesministerium fur Vertriebene, Fluechtlinge, und Kriegsbeschadigte (Federal Ministry for Expellees, Refugees, and War Victims), Bonn
Gerold & Co. Verlag, Vienna, Austria
Ghana University Press, Accra, Ghana
Gideon Press, Beirut
Gustavo Gili, Barcelona
Ginn and Co., Boston
Glanville Publishing Co., New York
Glasgow University Press, Glasgow
Gleditsch Brockhaus, Leipzig
Glencoe Free Press, London
Golden Bell Press, Denver, Colo.
Victor Gollancz, Ltd., London
Gordon and Breach Science Publications, New York
Gothic Printing Co., Capetown, S. Afr.
Gould Publications, Jamaica, N. Y.
Government Affairs Foundation, Albany, N. Y.
Government Data Publications, New York
Government of India National Library, Calcutta
Government Printing Office, Washington
Government Publications of Political Literature, Moscow
Government Research Institute, Cleveland
Grafica Americana, Caracas
Grafica Editorial Souza, Rio de Janeiro
Graficas Gonzales, Madrid
Graficas Uguina, Madrid
Graphic, New York
H. W. Gray, Inc., New York
Great Britain, Administrative Staff College, London
Great Britain, Committee on Ministers' Powers, London
Great Britain, Department of Technical Cooperation, London
Great Britain, Foreign Office, London
Great Britain, Ministry of Overseas Development, London
Great Britain, Treasury, London
Greater Bridgeport Region, Planning Agency, Trumbull
W. Green and Son, Edinburgh
Green Pagoda Press, Hong Kong
Greenwich Book Publications, New York
Greenwood Periodicals, New York
Griffin Press, Adelaide, Australia
Grolier, Inc., New York
J. Groning, Hamburg
Grosset and Dunlap, Inc., New York
Grossman Publishers, New York
G. Grote'sche Verlagsbuchhandlung, Rastalt, Germany
Group for the Advancement of Psychiatry, New York
Grove Press, Inc., New York
Grune and Stratton, New York
Gruyter and Co., Walter de, Berlin
E. Guilmato, Paris
Democratic Party of Guinea, Guinea
Gulf Publishing Co., Houston, Texas
J. Chr. Gunderson Boktrykkeri og Bokbinderi, Oslo
Hans E. Gunther Verlag, Stuttgart
Gutersloher Verlagshaus, Gutersloh

Hadar Publishing Co., Tel-Aviv
Hafner Publishing Co., Inc., New York
G. K. Hall, Boston
Robert Hall, London
Charles Hallberg and Co., Chicago
Hamburgisches Wirtschafts Archiv, Hamburg
Hamilton & Co., London
Hamilton County Research Foundation, Cincinnati
Hamish Hamilton, London
Hanover House, New York
Hansard Society, London
Harcourt, Brace and World, New York
Harlo Press, Detroit, Mich.
Harper and Row Publishers, New York; London
George Harrap and Co., London
Otto Harrassowitz, Wiesbaden
Harrison Co., Atlanta, Ga.
Rupert Hart-Davis, London
Hartford Printing Co., Hartford, Conn.
Harvard Center for International Affairs, Cambridge, Mass.
Harvard Law School, Cambridge, Mass.
Harvard Law Review Association, Cambridge, Mass.
Harvard University Center for East Asian Studies, Cambridge, Mass.
Harvard University, Center for Russian Research and Studies, Cambridge, Mass.
Harvard University, Graduate School of Business Administration, Cambridge, Mass.
Harvard University, Peabody Museum, Cambridge, Mass.
Harvard University, Widener Library, Cambridge
Harvard University Press, Cambridge
V. Hase und Kohler Verlag, Mainz
Hastings House, New York
Hauser Press, New Orleans, La.
Hawthorne Books, Inc., New York
Hayden Book Company, New York
The John Randolph Haynes and Dora Haynes Foundation, Los Angeles
The Edward D. Hazen Foundation, New Haven, Conn.
D. C. Heath and Co., Boston
Hebrew University Press, Jerusalem
Heffer and Sons Ltd., Cambridge, England
William S. Hein and Co., Buffalo
James H. Heineman, Inc., New York
Heinemann Ltd., London
Heirsemann, Leipzig
A. Hepple, Johannesburg
Helicon Press, Inc., Baltimore, Md.
Herald Press, Scottdale, Penna.
Herder and Herder, New York
Herder Book Co., New York, St. Louis
Johann Gottfried Herder, Marburg, Germany
Heritage Foundation, Chicago
The Heritage Press, New York
Hermitage Press, Inc., New York
Heron House Winslow, Washington, D. C.
Herzl Press, New York
Carl Heymanns Verlag, Berlin
Hill and Wang, Inc., New York
Hillary House Publishers, Ltd., New York
Hind Kitabs, Ltd., Bombay
Hinds, Noble, and Eldridge, New York
Ferdinand Hirt, Kiel, Germany
Historical Society of New Mexico, Albuquerque, N. M.
H. M. Stationery Office, London
Hobart and William Smith Colleges, Geneva, N. Y.
Hobbs, Dorman and Co., New York
Hodden and Staughton, London
William Hodge and Co., Ltd., London
Hodges Figgis and Co., Ltd., Dublin
J. G. Hodgson, Fort Collins, Colo.
Hogarth Press, London
The Hokuseido Press, Tokyo
Holborn Publishing House, London
Hollis and Carter, London
Hollywood A.S.P. Council, Hollywood, Calif.
Holt and Williams, New York
Holt, Rinehart and Winston, New York
Henry Holt and Co., New York
Holzner Verlag, Wurzburg
Home and Van Thal, London
Hong Kong Government Press, Hong Kong
Hong Kong University Press, Hong Kong
Hoover Institute on War, Revolution and Peace, Stanford, Calif.

Hope College, Holland, Mich.
Horizon Press, Inc., New York
Houghton, Mifflin Co., Boston
Houlgate House, Los Angeles
Howard University Press, Washington
Howell, Sosbin and Co., New York
Hudson Institute, Inc., Harmon-on-Hudson, New York
B. W. Huebsch, Inc., New York
H. Hugendubel Verlag, Munich
Human Relations Area Files Press (HRAF), New Haven
Human Rights Publications, Caulfield, Victoria, Australia
Human Sciences Research, Inc., Arlington, Va.
Humanities Press, New York
Humon and Rousseau, Capetown
Hungarian Academy of Science, Publishing House of, Budapest
Hunter College Library, New York
R. Hunter, London
Huntington Library, San Marino, Calif.
Hutchinson and Co., London
Hutchinson University Library, London

Ibadan University Press, Ibadan, Nigeria
Iberia Publishing Company, New York
Ibero-American Institute, Stockholm
Illini Union Bookstore, Champaign, Ill.
Illinois State Publications, Springfield
Ilmgau Verlag, Pfaffenhofen
Imago Publishing Co., Ltd., London
Imprenta Calderon, Honduras
Imprenta Mossen Alcover, Mallorca
Imprenta Nacional, Caracas
Imprimerie d'Extreme Orient, Hanoi
Imprimerie Nationale, Paris
Imprimerie Sefan, Tunis
Imprimerie Fr. Van Muysewinkel, Brussels
Incentivist Publications, Greenwich, Conn.
Index Society, New York
India and Pakistan: Combined Interservice Historical Section, New Delhi
India, Government of, Press, New Delhi
India, Ministry of Community Development, New Delhi
India, Ministry of Finance, New Delhi
India, Ministry of Health, New Delhi
India, Ministry of Home Affairs, New Delhi
India, Ministry of Information and Broadcasting, Faridabad; New Delhi
India, Ministry of Law, New Delhi
Indian Council on World Affairs, New Delhi
Indian Institute of Public Administration, New Delhi
Indian Ministry of Information and Broadcasting, New Delhi
Indian Press, Ltd., Allahabad
Indian School of International Studies, New Delhi
Indiana University, Bureau of Government Research, Bloomington
Indiana University, Institute of Training for Public Service, Department of Government, Bloomington
Indiana University Press, Bloomington
Indraprastha Estate, New Delhi
Industrial Areas Foundations, Chicago
Industrial Council for Social and Economic Studies, Upsala
Industrial Press, New York
Infantry Journal Press, Washington, D. C.
Information Bulletin Ltd., London
Insel Verlag, Frankfurt
Institut Afro-Asiatique d'Etudes Syndicales, Tel Aviv
Institut de Droit International, Paris
Institut des Hautes Etudes de l'Amerique Latine, Rio de Janeiro
Institut des Relations Internationales, Brussels
Institut fur Kulturwissenschaftliche Forschung, Freiburg
Institut fur Politische Wissenschaft, Frankfurt
Institut International de Collaboration Philosophique, Paris
Institute for Comparative Study of Political Systems, Washington, D. C.
Institute for Defense Analyses, Washington, D. C.
Institute for International Politics and Economics, Prague
Institute for International Social Research, Princeton, N. J.
Institute for Mediterranean Affairs, New York
Institute for Monetary Research, Washington, D. C.
Institute for Social Science Research, Washington, D. C.
Institute of Brazilian Studies, Rio de Janeiro
Institute of Early American History and Culture, Williamsburg, Va.
Institute of Economic Affairs, London
Institute of Ethiopian Studies, Addis Ababa
Institute of Human Relations Press, New York
Institute of Islamic Culture, Lahore
Institute of Labor and Industrial Relations, Urbana, Ill.
Institute of Judicial Administration, New York
Institute of National Planning, Cairo
Institute of Pacific Relations, New York
Institute of Professional Civil Servants, London
Institute of Public Administration, Dublin
Instituto de Antropologia e Etnologia de Para, Belem, Para, Brazil
Instituto Brasileiro de Estudos Afro-Asiaticos, Rio de Janeiro
Instituto Caro y Cuervo, Bogota
Instituto de Derecho Comparedo, Barcelona
Instituto de Estudios Africanos, Madrid
Instituto de Estudios Politicos, Madrid
Instituto de Investigaciones Historicas, Mexico City
Instituto Guatemalteco-Americano, Guatemala City
Instituto Internacional de Ciencias Administrativas, Rio de Janeiro
Instituto Nacional do Livro, Rio de Janeiro
Instituto Nazionale di Cultura Fascista, Firenze
Instituto Pan Americano de Geografia e Historia, Mexico City
Integrated Education Associates, Chicago
Inter-American Bibliographical and Library Association, Gainesville, Fla.
Inter-American Development Bank, Buenos Aires
Inter-American Statistical Institute, Washington
Intercollegiate Case Clearing House, Boston
International African Institute, London
International Association for Research in Income and Wealth, New Haven, Conn.
International Atomic Energy Commission, Vienna
International Bank for Reconstruction and Development, Washington, D. C.
International Center for African Economic and Social Documentation, Brussels
International Chamber of Commerce, New York
International City Managers' Association, Chicago
International Commission of Jurists, Geneva
International Committee for Peaceful Investment, Washington, D. C.
International Congress of History of Discoveries, Lisbon
International Congress of Jurists, Rio de Janeiro
International Cotton Advisory Committee, Washington, D. C.
International Court of Justice, The Hague
International Development Association, Washington, D. C.
International Economic Policy Association, Washington, D. C.
International Editions, New York
International Federation for Documentation, The Hague
International Federation for Housing and Planning, The Hague
International Finance, Princeton, N. J.
International Institute of Administrative Science, Brussels
International Institute of Differing Civilizations, Brussels
International Labour Office, Geneva
International Managers' Association, Chicago
International Monetary Fund, Washington
International Press Institute, Zurich
International Publications Service, New York
International Publishers Co., New York
International Publishing House, Meerat, India
International Review Service, New York
International Textbook Co., Scranton, Penna.
International Union for Scientific Study of Population, New York
International Universities Press, Inc., New York
Interstate Printers and Publishers, Danville, Ill.
Iowa State University, Center for Agricultural and Economic Development, Ames
Iowa State University Press, Ames
Irish Manuscripts Commission, Dublin
Richard D. Irwin, Inc., Homewood, Ill.
Isar Verlag, Munich
Isbister and Co., London
Italian Library of Information, New York; Rome
Italy, Council of Ministers, Rome

Jacaranda Press, Melbourne
Mouriel Jacobs, Inc., Philadelphia
Al Jadidah Press, Cairo
Jain General House, Jullundur, India
Japan, Ministry of Education, Tokyo

Japan, Ministry of Justice, Tokyo
Japanese National Commission for UNESCO, Tokyo
Jarrolds Publishers, Ltd., London
Jewish Publication Society of America, Philadelphia, Pa.
Johns Hopkins Press, Baltimore
Johns Hopkins School of Advanced International Studies, Baltimore
Johns Hopkins School of Hygiene, Baltimore
Johnson Publishing Co., Chicago
Christopher Johnson Publishers, Ltd., London
Johnstone and Hunter, London
Joint Center for Urban Studies, Cambridge, Mass.
Joint Committee on Slavic Studies, New York
Joint Council on Economic Education, New York
Joint Library of IMF and IBRD, Washington
Joint Reference Library, Chicago
Jonathan Cape, London
Jones and Evans Book Shop, Ltd., London
Marshall Jones, Boston
Jornal do Commercio, Rio de Janeiro
Michael Joseph, Ltd., London
Jowett, Leeds, England
Juilliard Publishers, Paris
Junker und Dunnhaupt Verlag, Berlin
Juta and Co., Ltd., Capetown, South Africa

Kallman Publishing Co., Gainesville, Fla.
Karl Karusa, Washington, D. C.
Katzman Verlag, Tubingen
Kay Publishing Co., Salt Lake City
Nicholas Kaye, London
Calvin K. Kazanjian Economics Foundation, Westport, Conn.
Kegan, Paul and Co., Ltd., London
P. G. Keller, Winterthur, Switz.
Augustus M. Kelley, Publishers, New York
Kelly and Walsh, Ltd., Baltimore, Md.
P. J. Kenedy, New York
Kennikat Press, Port Washington, N. Y.
Kent House, Port-of-Spain
Kent State University Bureau of Economic and Business Research, Kent, Ohio
Kentucky State Archives and Records Service, Frankfort
Kentucky State Planning Commission, Frankfort
Kenya Ministry of Economic Planning and Development, Nairobi
Charles H. Kerr and Co., Chicago
Khadiand Village Industries Commission, Bombay
Khayat's, Beirut
Khun Aroon, Bangkok
P. S. King and Son, Ltd., London
King's College, Cambridge
King's Crown Press, New York
Kino Kuniva Bookstore Co., Ltd., Tokyo
Kitab Mahal, Allahabad, India
Kitabistan, Allahabad
B. Klein and Co., New York
Ernst Klett Verlag, Stuttgart
V. Klostermann, Frankfurt
Fritz Knapp Verlag, Frankfurt
Alfred Knopf, New York
John Knox Press, Richmond, Va.
Kodansha International, Ltd., Tokyo
W. Kohlhammer Verlag, Stuttgart; Berlin; Cologne; Mainz
Korea Researcher and Publisher, Inc., Seoul
Korea, Ministry of Reconstruction, Seoul
Korea, Republic of, Seoul
Korea University, Asiatic Research Center, Seoul
Korean Conflict Research Foundation, Albany, N. Y.
Kosel Verlag, Munich
Kossuth Foundation, New York
Guillermo Kraft, Ltd., Buenos Aires
John F. Kraft, Inc., New York
Krasnzi Proletarii, Moscow
Kraus, Ltd., Dresden
Kraus Reprint Co., Vaduz, Liechtenstein
Kreuz-Verlag, Stuttgart
Kumasi College of Technology, The Library, Kumasi, Ghana
Kuwait, Arabia, Government Printing Press, Kuwait

Labor News Co., New York
Robert Laffont, Paris
Lambarde Press, Sidcup, Kent, England
Albert D. and Mary Lasker Foundation, Washington, D. C.
Harold Laski Institute of Political Science, Ahmedabad
Guiseppe Laterza e Figli, Bari, Italy
T. Werner Laurie, Ltd., London
Lawrence Brothers, Ltd., London
Lawrence and Wishart, London
Lawyers Co-operative Publishing Co., Rochester, N. Y.
League for Industrial Democracy, New York
League of Independent Voters, New Haven
League of Nations, Geneva
League of Women Voters, Cambridge
League of Women Voters of U. S., Washington, D. C.
Leeds University Press, Leeds, Engand
J. F. Lehmanns Verlag, Munich
Leicester University Press, London
F. Leitz, Frankfurt
Lemcke, Lemcke and Beuchner, New York
Michel Levy Freres, Paris
Lexington Publishing Co., New York
Liberal Arts Press, Inc., New York
Liberia Altiplano, La Paz
Liberia Anticuaria, Barcelona
Liberia Campos, San Juan
Liberia Panamericana, Buenos Aires
Liberty Bell Press, Jefferson City, Mo.
Librairie Academique Perrin, Paris
Librairie Artheme Fayard, Paris
Librairie Beauchemin, Montreal
Librairie Armand Colin, Paris
Librairie Firmin Didot et Cie., Paris
Librairie Droz, Geneva
Librairie de Medicis, Paris
Librairie de la Societe du Recueil Sirey, Paris
Librairie des Sciences Politiques et Sociales, Paris
Librairie Felix Alcan, Paris
Librairie Gallimard, Paris
Librairie Hachette et Cie., Paris
Librairie Julius Abel, Greiswald
Librairie La Rose, Paris
Librairie Letouzey, Paris
Librairie Payot, Paris
Librairie Philosophique J. Vrin, Paris
Librairie Plon, Paris
Librairie Marcel Riviere et Cie., Paris
Librairie Stock Delamain et Boutelleau, Paris
Library, Kumasi College of Technology, Kumasi
Library Association, London
Library of Congress, Washington
Library House, London
Library of International Relations, Chicago
Libyan Publishing, Tripoli
Light and Life Press, Winona Lake, Ind.
Lincoln University, Lincoln, Pa.
J. B. Lippincott Co., New York, Philadelphia
Little, Brown and Co., Boston
Liverpool University Press, Liverpool
Horace Liveright, New York
Living Books, New York
Livraria Agir Editora, Rio de Janeiro
Livraria Editora da Casa di Estudante do Brazil, Sao Paulo
Livraria Jose Olympio Editora, Rio de Janeiro
Livraria Martins Editora, Sao Paulo
Lok Sabha Secretariat, New Delhi
London Conservative Political Centre, London
London Historical Association, London
London Institute of World Affairs, London
London Library Association, London
London School of Economics, London
London Times, Inc., London
London University, School of Oriental and African Studies, London
Roy Long and Richard R. Smith, Inc., New York
Long House, New Canaan, Conn.
Longmans, Green and Co., New York, London
Los Angeles Board of Civil Service Commissioners, Los Angeles
Louisiana State Legislature, Baton Rouge
Louisiana State University Press, Baton Rouge
Loyola University Press, Chicago
Lucas Brothers, Columbia
Herman Luchterhand Verlag, Neuwied am Rhein
Lyle Stuart, Inc., New York

MIT Center of International Studies, Cambridge

MIT Press, Cambridge
MIT School of Industrial Management, Cambridge
Macfadden-Bartwell Corp., New York
MacGibbon and Kee, Ltd., London
Macmillan Co., New York; London
Macmillan Co., of Canada, Ltd., Toronto
Macrae Smith Co., Philadelphia, Pa.
Magistrats Druckerei, Berlin
Magnes Press, Jerusalem
S. P. Maisonneuve et La Rose, Paris
Malaysia Publications, Ltd., Singapore
Malhorta Brothers, New Delhi
Manager Government of India Press, Kosib
Manaktalas, Bombay
Manchester University Press, Manchester, England
Manhattan Publishing Co., New York
Manzsche Verlag, Vienna
Marathon Oil Co., Findlay, Ohio
Marisal, Madrid
Marquette University Press, Milwaukee
Marshall Benick, New York
Marzani and Munsell, New York
Marzun Kabushiki Kaisha, Tokyo
Mascat Publications, Ltd., Calcutta
Francois Maspera, Paris
Massachusetts Mass Transportation Commission, Boston
Masses and McInstream, New York
Maurice Falk Institute for Economic Research, Jerusalem
Maxwell Air Force Base, Montgomery, Ala.
Robert Maxwell and Co., Ltd., London
McBride, Nast and Co., New York
McClelland and Stewart, Ltd., London
McClure and Co., Chicago
McClure, Phillips and Co., New York
McCutchan Publishing Corp., Berkeley
McDonald and Evans, Ltd., London
McDowell, Obolensky, New York
McFadden Bartwell Corp., New York
McGill University Industrial Relations Section, Montreal
McGill University, Institute of Islamic Studies, Montreal
McGill University Press, Montreal
McGraw Hill Book Co., New York
David McKay Co., Inc., New York
McKinley Publishing Co., Philadelphia
George J. McLeod, Ltd., Toronto
McMullen Books, Inc., New York
Meador Publishing Co., Boston
Mediaeval Academy of Americana, Cambridge
Felix Meiner Verlag, Hamburg
Melbourne University Press, Melbourne, Victoria, Australia
Mendonca, Lisbon
Mental Health Materials Center, New York
Mentor Books, New York
Meredith Press, Des Moines
Meridian Books, New York
Merit Publishers, New York
The Merlin Press, Ltd., London
Charles E. Merrill Publishing Co., Inc., Columbus
Methuen and Co., Ltd., London
Metropolitan Book Co., Ltd., New Delhi
Metropolitan Housing and Planning Council, Chicago
Metropolitan Police District, Scotland Yard, London
Alfred Metzner Verlag, Frankfurt
Meyer London Memorial Library, London
Miami University Press, Oxford, Ohio
Michie Co., Charlottesville, Va.
Michigan Municipal League, Ann Arbor
Michigan State University, Agricultural Experiment Station, East Lansing
Michigan State University, Bureau of Business and Economic Research, East Lansing
Michigan State University, Bureau of Social and Political Research, East Lansing
Michigan State University, Governmental Research Bureau, East Lansing
Michigan State University, Institute for Community Development and Services, East Lansing
Michigan State University, Institute for Social Research, East Lansing
Michigan State University, Labor and Industrial Relations Center, East Lansing
Michigan State University Press, East Lansing
Michigan State University School of Business Administration, East Lansing
Michigan State University, Vietnam Advisory Group, East Lansing
Mid-European Studies Center, Free European Committee, New York
Middle East Institute, Washington
Middle East Research Associates, Arlington, Va.
Middlebury College, Middlebury, Vt.
Midwest Administration Center, Chicago
Midwest Beach Co., Sioux Falls
Milbank Memorial Fund, New York
M. S. Mill and Co., Inc., Division of William Morrow and Co., Inc., New York
Ministere de l'Education Nationale, Paris
Ministere d'Etat aux Affaires Culturelles, Paris
Ministerio de Educacao e Cultura, Rio de Janeiro
Ministerio de Relaciones Exteriores, Havana
Minnesota Efficiency in Government Commission, St. Paul
Minton, Balch and Co., New York
Missionary Research Library, New York
Ernst Siegfried Mittler und Sohn, Berlin
Modern Humanities Research Association, Chicago
T. C. B. Mohr, Tubingen
Moira Books, Detroit
Monarch Books, Inc., Derby, Conn.
Monthly Review, New York
Mont Pelerin Society, University of Chicago, Chicago
Hugh Moore Fund, New York
T. G. Moran's Sons, Inc., Baton Rouge
William Morrow and Co., Inc., New York
Morus Verlag, Berlin
Mosaik Verlag, Hamburg
Motilal Banarsidass, New Delhi
Mouton and Co., The Hague; Paris
C. F. Mueller Verlag, Karlsruhe, Germany
Muhammad Mosque of Islam #2, Chicago
Firma K. L. Mukhopadhyaz, Calcutta
F. A. W. Muldener, Gottingen, Germany
Frederick Muller, Ltd., London
Municipal Finance Officers Association of the United States and Canada, Chicago
Munksgaard International Booksellers and Publishers, Copenhagen
John Murray, London
Museum fur Volkerkunde, Vienna
Museum of Honolulu, Honolulu
Musterschmidt Verlag, Gottingen

NA Tipographia do Panorama, Lisbon
Nassau County Planning Committee, Long Island
Natal Witness, Ltd., Pietermaritzburg
The Nation Associates, New York
National Academy of Sciences-National Research Council, Washington, D. C.
National Archives of Rhodesia and Nyasaland, Salisbury
National Assembly on Teaching The Principles of the Bill of Rights, Washington
National Association of Counties Research Foundation, Washington, D. C.
National Association of County Officials, Chicago
National Association of Home Builders, Washington, D. C.
National Association of Local Government Officers, London
National Association of State Libraries, Boston
National Bank of Egypt, Cairo
National Bank of Libya, Tripoli
National Board of YMCA, New York
National Book League, London
National Bureau of Economic Research, New York
National Capitol Publishers, Manassas, Va.
National Central Library, London
National Citizens' Commission on International Cooperation, Washington, D. C.
National Council for the Social Sciences, New York
National Council for the Social Studies, New York
National Council of Applied Economic Research, New Delhi
National Council of Churches of Christ in USA, New York
National Council of National Front of Democratic Germany, Berlin
National Council on Aging, New York
National Council on Crime and Delinquency, New York
National Economic and Social Planning Agency, Washington

National Education Association, Washington
National Home Library Foundation, Washington, D. C.
National Industrial Conference Board, New York
National Institute for Personnel Research, Johannesburg
National Institute of Administration, Saigon
National Institute of Economic Research, Stockholm
National Labor Relations Board Library, Washington
National Labour Press, London
National Library of Canada, Ottawa
National Library Press, Ottawa
National Municipal League, New York
National Observer, Silver Springs, Md.
National Opinion Research Center, Chicago
National Peace Council, London
National Planning Association, Washington, D. C.
National Press, Palo Alto, Calif.
National Review, New York
National Science Foundation Scientific Information, Washington, D. C.
Natural History Press, Garden City, N. Y.
Nauka Publishing House, Moscow
Navahind, Hyderabad
Navajiran Publishing House, Ahmedabad
Thomas Nelson and Sons, London; New York
Neukirchener Verlag des Erziehungsvereins, Neukirchen
New American Library, New York
New Century Publishers, New York
New Jersey Department of Agriculture, Rural Advisory Council, Trenton
New Jersey Department of Civil Service, Trenton
New Jersey Department of Conservation and Economic Development, Trenton
New Jersey Division of State and Regional Planning, Trenton
New Jersey Housing and Renewal, Trenton
New Jersey State Department of Education, Trenton
New Jersey State Legislature, Trenton
New Republic, Washington, D. C.
New School of Social Research, New York
New World Press, New York
New York City College Institute for Pacific Relations, New York
New York City Department of Correction, New York
New York City Temporary Committee on City Finance, New York
New York Public Library, New York
New York State College of Agriculture, Ithaca
New York State Library, Albany
New York State School of Industrial and Labor Relations, Cornell University, Ithaca
New York, State University of, at Albany, Albany
New York, State University of, State Education Department, Albany
New York, State University of, State Education Department, Office of Foreign Area Studies, Albany
New York Times, New York
New York University School of Commerce, Accounts and Finance, New York
New York University, School of Law, New York
New York University Press, New York
Newark Public Library, Newark
Newman Press, Westminster, Md.
Martinus Nijhoff, The Hague; Geneva
James Nisbet and Co., Ltd., Welwyn, Herts, England
Noonday Press, New York
North American Review Publishing Co., New York
North Atlantic Treaty Organization, Brussels
North Holland Publishing Co., Amsterdam, Holland
Northern California Friends Committee on Legislation, San Francisco
Northern Michigan University Press, Marquette
Northwestern University, Evanston
Northwestern University, African Department, Evanston, Ill.
Northwestern University, International Relations Conference, Chicago
Northwestern University Press, Evanston, Ill.
W. W. Norton and Co., Inc., New York
Norwegian Institute of International Affairs, Oslo
Norwegian University Press, Oslo
Nouvelle Librairie Nationale, Paris
John Nuveen and Co., Chicago
Novelty and Co., Patna, India
Novostii Press Agency Publishing House, Moscow
Nymphenburger Verlagsbuchhandlung, Munich

Oak Publications, New York
Oak Ridge Associated Universities, Oak Ridge, Tenn.
Oceana Publishing Co., Dobbs Ferry, N. Y.
Octagon Publishing Co., New York
Odyssey Press, New York
Oesterreichische Ethnologische Gesellschaft, Vienna
Oficina Internacional de Investigaciones Sociales de Freres, Madrid
W.E.R. O'Gorman, Glendale, Calif.
O'Hare, Flanders, N. J.
Ohio State University, Columbus
Ohio State University, College of Commerce and Administration, Bureau of Business Research, Columbus
Ohio State University Press, Columbus
Ohio University Press, Athens
Old Lyme Press, Old Lyme, Conn.
R. Oldenbourg, Munich
Oliver and Boyd, London, Edinburgh
Guenter Olzog Verlag, Munich
Open Court Publishing Co., La Salle, Ill.
Operation America, Inc., Los Angeles
Operations and Policy Research, Inc., Washington, D. C.
Oregon Historical Society, Portland
Organization for European Economic Cooperation and Development (OEEC), Paris
Organization of African Unity, Addis Ababa
Organization of American States, Rio de Janeiro
Organization of Economic Aid, Washington, D. C.
Orient Longman's, Bombay
Oriole Press, Berkeley Heights, N. J.
P. O'Shey, New York
Osaka University of Commerce, Tokyo
James R. Osgood and Co., Boston
Oslo University Press, Oslo
Oswald-Wolff, London
John Ousley, Ltd., London
George Outram Co., Ltd., Glasgow
Overseas Development Institute, Ltd., London
R. E. Owen, Wellington, N. Z.
Oxford Book Co., New York
Oxford University Press, Capetown; London; Madras; Melbourne; New York

Pacific Books, Palo Alto, Calif.
Pacific Coast Publishing Co., Menlo Park, Calif.
Pacific Philosophy Institute, Stockton, Calif.
Pacific Press Publishing Association, Mountain View, Calif.
Pacifist Research Bureau, Philadelphia
Padma Publications, Ltd., Bombay
Hermann Paetel Verlag, Berlin
Pageant Press, New York
Paine-Whitman, New York
Pakistan Academy for Rural Development, Peshawar
Pakistan Association for Advancement of Science, Lahore
Pakistan Bibliographical Working Group, Karachi
Pakistan Educational Publishers, Ltd., Karachi
Pakistan Ministry of Finance, Rawalpindi
Pall Mall Press, London
Pan American Union, Washington
Pantheon Books, Inc., New York
John W. Parker, London
Patna University Press, Madras
B. G. Paul and Co., Madras
Paulist Press, Glen Rock, N. J.
Payne Fund, New York
Peabody Museum, Cambridge
Peace Publications, New York
Peace Society, London
P. Pearlman, Washington
Pegasus, New York
Peking Review, Peking
Pelican Books, Ltd., Hammonsworth, England
Pemberton Press, Austin
Penguin Books, Baltimore
Penn.-N.J.-Del. Metropolitan Project, Philadelphia, Pa.
Pennsylvania German Society, Lancaster, Pa.
Pennsylvania Historical and Museum Commission, Harrisburg
Pennsylvania State University, Department of Religious Studies, University Park, Pa.

Pennsylvania State University, Institute of Public Administration, University Park, Pa.
Pennsylvania State University Press, University Park, Pa.
People's Publishing House, Ltd., New Delhi
Pergamon Press, Inc., New York
Permanent Secretariat, AAPS Conference, Cairo
Perrine Book Co., Minneapolis
Personnel Administration, Washington
Personnel Research Association, New York
George A. Pflaum Publishers, Inc., Dayton, Ohio
Phelps-Stokes Fund, Capetown; New York
Philadelphia Bibliographical Center, Philadelphia
George Philip & Son, London
Philippine Historical Society, Manila
Philippine Islands Bureau of Science, Manila
Philosophical Library Inc., New York
Phoenix House, Ltd., London
Pichon et Durand-Auzias, Paris
B. M. Pickering, London
Oskar Piest, New York
Pilot Press, London
Pioneer Publishers, New York
R. Piper and Co. Verlag, Munich
Pitman Publishing Corp., New York
Plimpton Press, Norwood, Mass.
PLJ Publications, Manila
Pocket Books, Inc., New York
Polish Scientific Publishers, Warsaw
Polygraphischer Verlag, Zurich
The Polynesian Society, Inc., Wellington, N. Z.
Popular Book Depot, Bombay
Popular Prakashan, Bombay
Population Association of America, Washington
Population Council, New York
Post Printing Co., New York
Post Publishing Co., Bangkok
Potomac Books, Washington, D. C.
Clarkson N. Potter, Inc., New York
Prabhakar Sahityalok, Lucknow, India
Practicing Law Institute, New York
Frederick A. Praeger, Inc., New York
Prager, Berlin
Prensa Latino Americana, Santiago
Prentice Hall, Inc., Englewood Cliffs, N. J.
Prentice-Hall International, London
Presence Afrique, Paris
President's Press, New Delhi
Press & Information Division of the French Embassy, New York
The Press of Case Western Reserve University, Cleveland
Presses de l'Ecole des Hautes Etudes Commerciales, Montreal
Presses Universitaires de Bruxelles, Brussels
Presses Universitaires de France, Paris
Presseverband der Evangelischen Kirche im Rheinland, Dusseldorf
Princeton Research Publishing Co., Princeton
Princeton University, Princeton, N. J.
Princeton University, Center of International Studies, Woodrow Wilson School of Public and International Affairs, Princeton, N. J.
Princeton University, Department of Economics, Princeton, N. J.
Princeton University, Department of History, Princeton, N. J.
Princeton University, Department of Oriental Studies, Princeton, N. J.
Princeton University, Department of Philosophy, Princeton, N. J.
Princeton University, Department of Politics, Princeton, N. J.
Princeton University, Department of Psychology, Princeton
Princeton University, Department of Sociology, Princeton, N. J.
Princeton University, Econometric Research Program, Princeton, N. J.
Princeton University, Firestone Library, Princeton, N. J.
Princeton University, Industrial Relations Center, Princeton
Princeton University, International Finance Section, Princeton, N. J.
Princeton University, Princeton Public Opinion Research Project, Princeton, N. J.
Princeton University Press, Princeton
Edouard Privat, Toulouse
Arthur Probsthain, London
Professional Library Press, West Haven, Conn.
Programa Interamericano de Informacion Popular, San Jose
Progress Publishing Co., Indianapolis
Progressive Education Association, New York
Prolog Research and Publishing Association, New York
Prometheus Press, New York
Psycho-Sociological Press, New York
Public Administration Clearing House, Chicago
Public Administration Institute, Ankara
Public Administration Service, Chicago
Public Affairs Forum, Bombay
Public Affairs Press, Washington
Public Enterprises, Tequcigalpa
Public Personnel Association, Chicago
Publications Centre, University of British Columbia, Vancouver
Publications de l'Institut Pedagogique National, Paris
Publications de l'Institut Universitaire des Hautes Etudes Internationales, Paris
Publications du CNRS, Paris
Publisher's Circular, Ltd., London, England
Publisher's Weekly, Inc., New York
Publishing House Jugoslavia, Belgrade
Punjab University, Pakistan
Punjab University Extension Library, Ludhiana, Punjab
Purdue University Press, Lafayette, Ind.
Purnell and Sons, Capetown
G. P. Putnam and Sons, New York

Quadrangle Books, Inc., Chicago
Bernard Quaritch, London
Queen's Printer, Ottawa
Queen's University, Belfast
Quell Verlag, Stuttgart, Germany
Quelle und Meyer, Heidelberg
Queromon Editores, Mexico City

Atma Ram and Sons, New Delhi
Ramsey-Wallace Corporation, Ramsey, New Jersey
Rand Corporation, Publications of the Social Science Department, New York
Rand McNally and Co., Skokie, Ill.
Random House, Inc., New York
Regents Publishing House, Inc., New York
Regional Planning Association, New York
Regional Science Research Institute, Philadelphia
Henry Regnery Co., Chicago
D. Reidel Publishing Co., Dordrecht, Holland
E. Reinhardt Verlag, Munich
Reinhold Publishing Corp., New York; London
Remsen Press, New York
La Renaissance de Loire, Paris
Eugen Rentsch Verlag, Stuttgart
Republican National Committee, Washington, D. C.
Research Institute on Sino-Soviet Bloc, Washington, D. C.
Research Microfilm Publications, Inc., Annapolis
Resources for the Future, Inc., Washington, D. C.
Revista de Occidente, Madrid
Revue Administrative, Paris
Renyal and Co., Inc., New York
Reynal & Hitchcock, New York
Rheinische Friedrich Wilhelms Universitat, Bonn
Rice University, Fondren Library, Houston
Richards Rosen Press, New York
The Ridge Press, Inc., New York
Rinehart, New York
Ring-Verlag, Stuttgart
Riverside Editions, Cambridge
Robinson and Co., Durban, South Africa
J. A. Rogers, New York
Roques Roman, Trujillo
Rudolf M. Rohrer, Leipzig
Ludwig Rohrscheid Verlag, Bonn
Walter Roming and Co., Detroit
Ronald Press Co., New York
Roper Public Opinion Poll Research Center, New York
Ross and Haine, Inc., Minneapolis, Minn.
Fred B. Rothman and Co., S. Hackensack, N. J.
Rotterdam University Press, Rotterdam
Routledge and Kegan Paul, London
George Routledge and Sons, Ltd., London
Row-Peterson Publishing Co., Evanston, Ill.

Rowohlt, Hamburg
Roy Publishers, Inc., New York
Royal African Society, London
Royal Anthropological Institute, London
Royal Colonial Institute, London
Royal Commission of Canada's Economic Prospects, Ottawa
Royal Commonwealth Society, London
Royal Geographical Society, London
Royal Greek Embassy Information Service, Washington, D. C.
Royal Institute of International Affairs, London; New York
Royal Institute of Public Administration, London
Royal Netherlands Printing Office, Schiedam
Royal Statistical Society, London
Rubin Mass, Jerusalem
Rule of Law Press, Durham
Rupert Hart-Davis, London
Russell and Russell, Inc., New York
Russell Sage College, Institute for Advanced Study in Crisis, NDEA Institute, Troy, N. Y.
Russell Sage Foundation, New York
Rutgers University, New Brunswick, N. J.
Rutgers University Bureau of Government Research, New Brunswick, N. J.
Rutgers University, Institute of Management and Labor Relations, New Brunswick, N. J.
Rutgers University, Urban Studies Conference, New Brunswick, N. J.
Rutgers University Press, New Brunswick, N. J.
Rutten und Loening Verlag, Munich
Ryerson Press, Toronto

Sage Publications, Beverly Hills, Calif.
Sahitya Akademi, Bombay
St. Andrews College, Drygrange, Scotland
St. Clement's Press, London
St. George Press, Los Angeles
St. John's University Bookstore, Annapolis
St. John's University Press, Jamaica, N. Y.
St. Louis Post-Dispatch, St. Louis
St. Martin's Press, New York
St. Michael's College, Toronto
San Diego State College Library, San Diego
San Francisco State College, San Francisco
The Sapir Memorial Publication Fund, Menasha, Wis.
Sarah Lawrence College, New York
Sarah Lawrence College, Institute for Community Studies, New York
Porter Sargent, Publishers, Boston, Mass.
Sauerlaender and Co., Aarau, Switz.
Saunders and Ottey, London
W. B. Saunders Co., Philadelphia, Pa.
Scandinavian University Books, Copenhagen
Scarecrow Press, Metuchen, N. J.
L. N. Schaffrath, Geldern, Germany
Robert Schalkenbach Foundation, New York
Schenkman Publishing Co., Cambridge
P. Schippers, N. V., Amsterdam
Schocken Books, Inc., New York
Henry Schuman, Inc., New York
Carl Schunemann Verlag, Bremen
Curt E. Schwab, Stuttgart
Otto Schwartz und Co., Gottingen
Science and Behavior Books, Palo Alto, Calif.
Science Council of Japan, Tokyo
Science of Society Foundation, Baltimore, Md.
Science Press, New York
Science Research Associates, Inc., Chicago
Scientia Verlag, **Aalen**, Germany
SCM Press, London
Scott, Foresman and Co., Chicago
Scottish League for European Freedom, Edinburgh
Chas. Scribner's Sons, New York
Seabury Press, New York
Sears Publishing Co., Inc., New York
Secker and Warburg, Ltd., London
Secretaria del Consejo Nacional Economia, Tegucigalpa
Securities Study Project, Vancouver, Wash.
Seewald Verlag, Munich; Stuttgart
Selbstverlag Jakob Rosner, Vienna
Seldon Society, London
Robert C. Sellers and Associates, Washington, D. C.
Thomas Seltzer Inc., New York
Seminar, New Delhi
C. Serbinis Press, Athens
Service Bibliographique des Messageries Hachette, Paris
Service Center for Teaching of History, Washington, D. C.
Servicos de Imprensa e Informacao da Exbaixada, Lisbon
Sheed and Ward, New York
Shoestring Press, Hamden, Conn.
Shuter and Shooter, Pietermaritzburg
Siam Society, Bangkok
Sidgewick and Jackson, London
K. G. Siegler & Co., Bonn
Signet Books, New York
A. W. Sijthoff, Leyden, Netherlands
Silver Burdett, Morristown, N. J.
Simmons Boardman Publishing Co., New York
Simon and Schuster, Inc., New York
Simpkin, Marshall, et al., London
Sino-American Cultural Society, Washington
William Sloane Associates, New York
Small, Maynard and Co., Boston
Smith-Brook Printing Co., Denver
Smith College, Northampton, Mass.
Smith, Elder and Co., London
Smith, Keynes and Marshall, Buffalo, N. Y.
Allen Smith Co., Indianapolis, Ind.
Peter Smith, Gloucester, Mass.
Richard R. Smith Co. Inc., Peterborough, N. H.
Smithsonian Institute, Washington, D. C.
Social Science Research Center, Rio Piedras, Puerto Rico
Social Science Research Council, New York
Social Science Research Council, Committee on the Economy of China, Berkeley, Calif.
Social Science Research Council of Australia, Sydney
The Social Sciences, Mexico City
Societa Editrice del "Foro Italiano", Rome
Societas Bibliographica, Lausanne, Switzerland
Societe d'Edition d'Enseignement Superieur, Paris
Societe Francaise d'Imprimerie et Librairie, Paris
Society for Advancement of Management, New York
Society for Promoting Christian Knowledge, London
Society for the Study of Social Problems, Kalamazoo, Mich.
Society of Comparative Legislative and International Law, London
Sociological Abstracts, New York
Solidaridad Publishing House, Manila
Somerset Press, Inc., Somerville, N. J.
Soney and Sage Co., Newark, N. J.
South Africa Commission on Future Government, Capetown
South Africa State Library, Pretoria
South African Congress of Democrats, Johannesburg
South African Council for Scientific and Industrial Research, Pretoria
South African Institute of International Affairs, Johannesburg
South African Institute of Race Relations, Johannesburg
South African Public Library, Johannesburg
South Carolina Archives, State Library, Columbia
South Pacific Commission, Noumea, New Caledonia
South Western Publishing Co., Cincinnati, Ohio
Southern Illinois University Press, Carbondale, Ill.
Southern Methodist University Press, Dallas, Tex.
Southern Political Science Association, New York
Southworth Anthoensen Press, Portland, Maine
Sovetskaia Rossiia, Moscow
Soviet and East European Research and Translation Service, New York
Spartan Books, Washington, D. C.
Special Libraries Association, New York
Specialty Press of South Africa, Johannesburg
Robert Speller and Sons, New York
Lorenz Spindler Verlag, Nuremberg
Julius Springer, Berlin
Springer-Verlag, New York; Stuttgart; Gottingen; Vienna
Stackpole Co., New York
Gerhard Stalling, Oldenburg, Germany
Stanford Bookstore, Stanford
Stanford University Comparative Education Center, Stanford, Calif.
Stanford University Institute for Communications Research, Stanford
Stanford University, Institute of Hispanic-American and Luso-Brazilian Studies, Stanford, Calif.
Stanford University, Project on Engineering-Economic Planning, Stanford, Calif.

Stanford University Research Institute, Menlo Park, Calif.
Stanford University, School of Business Administration, Stanford, Calif.
Stanford University, School of Education, Stanford, Calif.
Stanford University Press, Stanford, Cal.
Staples Press, New York
State University of New York at Albany, Albany
Stein & Day Publishers, New York
Franz Steiner Verlag, Wiesbaden
Ulrich Steiner Verlag, Wurttemburg
H. E. Stenfert Kroese, Leyden
Sterling Printing and Publishing Co., Ltd., Karachi
Sterling Publishers, Ltd., London
Stevens and Hayes, London
Stevens and Sons, Ltd., London
George W. Stewart, Inc., New York
George Stilke Berlin
Frederick A. Stokes Publishing Co., New York
C. Struik, Capetown
Stuttgarter Verlags Kantor, Stuttgart
Summy-Birchard Co., Evanston, Ill.
Swann Sonnenschein and Co., London
Philip Swartzwelder, Pittsburgh, Pa.
Sweet and Maxwell, Ltd., London
Swiss Eastern Institute, Berne
Sydney University Press, Sydney, Australia
Syracuse University, Maxwell School of Citizenship and Public Affairs, Syracuse, N. Y.
Syracuse University Press, Syracuse
Szczesnez Verlag, Munich

Talleres Graficos de Manuel Casas, Mexico City
Talleres de Impresion de Estampillas y Valores, Mexico City
Taplinger Publishing Co., New York
Tavistock, London
Tax Foundation, New York
Teachers' College, Bureau of Publications, Columbia University, New York
Technical Assistance Information Clearing House, New York
Technology Press, Cambridge
de Tempel, Bruges, Belgium
B. G. Teubner, Berlin; Leipzig
Texas College of Arts and Industries, Kingsville
Texas Western Press, Dallas
Texian Press, Waco, Texas
Thacker's Press and Directories, Ltd., Calcutta
Thailand, National Office of Statistics, Bangkok
Thailand National Economic Development Board, Bangkok
Thames and Hudson, Ltd., London
Thammasat University Institute of Public Administration, Bangkok, Thailand
E. J. Theisen, East Orange, N. J.
Charles C. Thomas, Publisher, Springfield, Ill.
Tilden Press, New York
Time, Inc., New York
Time-Life Books, New York
Times Mirror Printing and Binding, New York
Tipografia de Archivos, Madrid
Tipografia Mendonca, Lisbon
Tipografia Nacional, Guatemala, Guatemala City
Tipographia Nacional Guatemala, Guatemala City
H. D. Tjeenk Willink, Haarlem, Netherlands
J. C. Topping, Cambridge, Mass.
Transatlantic Arts, Inc., New York
Trejos Hermanos, San Jose
Trenton State College, Trenton
Tri-Ocean Books, San Francisco
Trident Press, New York
Trowitzsch and Son, Berlin
Truebner and Co., London
Tufts University Press, Medford, Mass.
Tulane University, School of Business Administration, New Orleans, La.
Tulane University Press, New Orleans
Turnstile Press, London
Tuskegee Institute, Tuskegee, Ala.
Charles E. Tuttle Co., Tokyo
Twayne Publishers Inc., New York
The Twentieth Century Fund, New York
Twin Circle Publishing Co., New York
Typographische Anstalt, Vienna
Tyrolia Verlag, Innsbruck

UNESCO, Paris
N. V. Uitgeverij W. Van Hoeve, The Hague
Frederick Ungar Publishing Co., Inc., New York
Union Federaliste Inter-Universitaire, Paris
Union of American Hebrew Congregations, New York
Union of International Associations, Brussels
Union of Japanese Societies of Law and Politics, Tokyo
Union of South Africa, Capetown
Union of South Africa, Government Information Office, New York
Union Press, Hong Kong
Union Research Institute, Hong Kong
United Arab Republic, Information Department, Cairo
United Nations Economic Commission for Asia and the Far East, Secretariat of Bangkok, Bangkok
United Nations Educational, Scientific and Cultural Organization, Paris
United Nations Food and Agriculture Organization, Rome
United Nations International Conference on Peaceful Uses of Atomic Energy, Geneva
United Nations Publishing Service, New York
United States Air Force Academy, Colorado Springs, Colo.
United States Bureau of the Census, Washington, D. C.
United States Business and Defense Services Administration, Washington D.C.
United States Civil Rights Commission, Washington, D. C.
United States Civil Service Commission, Washington, D. C.
United States Consulate General, Hong Kong
United States Department of Agriculture, Washington, D. C.
United States Department of the Army, Washington
United States Department of the Army, Office of Chief of Military History, Washington, D. C.
United States Department of Correction, New York
United States Department of State, Washington
United States Department of State, Government Printing Office, Washington, D. C.
United States Government Printing Office, Washington
United States Housing and Home Financing Agency, Washington, D. C.
United States Mutual Security Agency, Washington, D. C.
United States National Archives General Services, Washington, D. C.
United States National Referral Center for Science and Technology, Washington, D. C.
United States National Resources Committee, Washington, D. C.
United States Naval Academy, Annapolis, Md.
United States Naval Institute, Annapolis, Md.
United States Naval Officers Training School, China Lake, Cal.
United States Operations Mission to Vietnam, Washington, D. C.
United States President's Committee to Study Military Assistance, Washington, D. C.
United States Small Business Administration, Washington, D. C.
United World Federalists, Boston
Universal Reference System; see Princeton Research Publishing Co., Princeton, N.J.
Universidad Central de Venezuela, Caracas
Universidad de Buenos Aires, Instituto Sociologia, Buenos Aires
Universidad de Chile, Santiago
Universidad de el Salvador, El Salvador
Universidad Nacional Autonomo de Mexico, Direccion General de Publicaciones, Mexico
Universidad Nacional de la Plata, Argentina
Universidad Nacional Instituto de Historia Antonoma de Mexico, Mexico City
Universidad Nacional Mayor de San Marcos, Lima
Universidad de Antioquia, Medellin, Colombia
Universite de Rabat, Rabat, Morocco
Universite Fouad I, Cairo
Universite Libre de Bruxelles, Brussels
Universite Mohammed V, Rabat, Morocco
University Books, Inc., Hyde Park, New York
University Bookstore, Hong Kong
University Microfilms, Inc., Ann Arbor
University of Alabama, Bureau of Public Administration, University, Ala.
University of Alabama Press, University, Ala.
University of Ankara, Ankara
University of Arizona Press, Tucson
University of Bombay, Bombay

University of Bonn, Bonn
University of British Columbia Press, Vancouver
University of California, Berkeley, Calif.
University of California at Los Angeles, Bureau of Government Research, Los Angeles
University of California at Los Angeles, Near Eastern Center, Los Angeles
University of California, Bureau of Business and Economic Research, Berkeley, Calif.
University of California, Bureau of Government Research, Los Angeles
University of California, Bureau of Public Administration, Berkeley
University of California, Department of Psychology, Los Angeles
University of California, Institute for International Studies, Berkeley, Calif.
University of California, Institute of East Asiatic Studies, Berkeley, Calif.
University of California, Institute of Governmental Affairs, Davis
University of California, Institute of Governmental Studies, Berkeley
University of California, Institute of Urban and Regional Development, Berkeley, Calif.
University of California, Latin American Center, Los Angeles
University of California Library, Berkeley, Calif.
University of California Press, Berkeley
University of California Survey Research Center, Berkeley, Calif.
University of Canterbury, Christchurch, New Zealand
University of Capetown, Capetown
University of Chicago, Chicago
University of Chicago, Center for Policy Study, Chicago
University of Chicago, Center for Program in Government Administration, Chicago
University of Chicago, Center of Race Relations, Chicago
University of Chicago, Graduate School of Business, Chicago
University of Chicago Law School, Chicago
University of Chicago, Politics Department, Chicago
University of Chicago Press, Chicago
University of Cincinnati, Cincinnati
University of Cincinnati, Center for Study of United States Foreign Policy, Cincinnati
University of Colorado Press, Boulder
University of Connecticut, Institute of Public Service, Storrs, Conn.
University of Dar es Salaam, Institute of Public Administration, Dar es Salaam
University of Denver, Denver
University of Detroit Press, Detroit
University of Edinburgh, Edinburgh, Scotland
University of Florida, Public Administration Clearing Service, Gainesville, Fla.
University of Florida, School of Inter-American Studies, Gainesville, Fla.
University of Florida Libraries, Gainesville
University of Florida Press, Gainesville
University of Georgia, Institute of Community and Area Development, Athens, Georgia
University of Georgia Press, Athens
University of Glasgow Press, Glasgow, Scotland
University of Glasgow Press, Fredericton, New Brunswick, Canada
University of Hawaii Press, Honolulu
University of Hong Kong Press, Hong Kong
University of Houston, Houston
University of Illinois, Champaign
University of Illinois, Graduate School of Library Science, Urbana
University of Illinois, Institute for Labor and Industrial Relations, Urbana
University of Illinois, Institute of Government and Public Affairs, Urbana, Ill.
University of Illinois Press, Urbana
University of Iowa, Center for Labor and Management, Iowa City
University of Iowa, School of Journalism, Iowa City
University of Iowa Press, Iowa City
University of Kansas, Bureau of Government Research, Lawrence, Kans.
University of Kansas Press, Lawrence
University of Karachi, Institute of Business and Public Administration, Karachi
University of Karachi Press, Karachi
University of Kentucky, Bureau of Governmental Research, Lexington
University of Kentucky Press, Lexington
University of London, Institute of Advanced Legal Studies, London
University of London, Institute of Commonwealth Studies, London
University of London, Institute of Education, London
University of London, School of Oriental and African Studies, London
University of London Press, London
University of Lund, Lund, Sweden
University of Maine Studies, Augusta, Me.
University of Malaya, Kualalumpur
University of Manchester Press, Manchester, England
University of Maryland, Bureau of Governmental Research, College of Business and Public Administration, College Park, Md.
University of Maryland, Department of Agriculture and Extension Education, College Park, Md.
University of Massachusetts, Bureau of Government Research, Amherst, Mass.
University of Massachusetts Press, Amherst
University of Melbourne Press, Melbourne, Australia
University of Miami Law Library, Coral Gables
University of Miami Press, Coral Gables
University of Michigan, Center for Research on Conflict Resolution, Ann Arbor
University of Michigan, Department of History and Political Science, Ann Arbor
University of Michigan, Graduate School of Business Administration, Ann Arbor
University of Michigan, Institute for Social Research, Ann Arbor
University of Michigan, Institute of Public Administration, Ann Arbor
University of Michigan Law School, Ann Arbor
University of Michigan, Survey Research Center, Ann Arbor
University of Michigan Press, Ann Arbor
University of Minnesota, St. Paul; Duluth
University of Minnesota, Industrial Relations Center, Minneapolis
University of Minnesota Press, Minneapolis
University of Mississippi, Bureau of Public Administration, University, Miss.
University of Missouri, Research Center, School of Business and Public Administration, Columbia
University of Missouri Press, Columbia
University of Natal Press, Pietermaritzburg
University of Nebraska Press, Lincoln
University of New England, Grafton, Australia
University of New Mexico, Department of Government, Albuquerque, N. Mex.
University of New Mexico, School of Law, Albuquerque
University of New Mexico Press, Albuquerque
University of North Carolina, Department of City and Regional Planning, Chapel Hill
University of North Carolina, Institute for International Studies, Chapel Hill
University of North Carolina, Institute for Research in the Social Sciences, Center for Urban and Regional Studies, Chapel Hill
University of North Carolina, Institute of Government, Chapel Hill
University of North Carolina Library, Chapel Hill
University of North Carolina Press, Chapel Hill
University of Notre Dame, Notre Dame, Ind.
University of Notre Dame Press, Notre Dame, Ind.
University of Oklahoma Press, Norman
University of Oregon Press, Eugene
University of Panama, Panama City
University of Paris (Conferences du Palais de la Decouverte), Paris
University of Pennsylvania, Philadelphia, Pa.
University of Pennsylvania, Department of Translations, Philadelphia
University of Pennsylvania Law School, Philadelphia, Pa.
University of Pennsylvania Press, Philadelphia
University of Pittsburgh, Institute of Local Government, Pittsburgh, Pa.
University of Pittsburgh Book Centers, Pittsburgh
University of Pittsburgh Press, Pittsburgh

University of Puerto Rico, San Juan
University of Rochester, Rochester, N. Y.
University of Santo Tomas, Manila
University of South Africa, Pretoria
University of South Carolina Press, Columbia
University of Southern California, Middle East and North Africa Program, Los Angeles
University of Southern California, School of International Relations, Los Angeles
University of Southern California Press, Los Angeles
University of Southern California, School of Public Administration, Los Angeles
University of State of New York, State Education Department, Albany
University of Sussex, Sussex, England
University of Sydney, Department of Government and Public Administration, Sydney
University of Tennessee, Knoxville
University of Tennessee, Bureau of Public Administration, Knoxville
University of Tennessee, Municipal Technical Advisory Service, Division of University Extension, Knoxville
University of Tennessee Press, Knoxville
University of Texas, Austin
University of Texas, Bureau of Business Research, Austin
University of Texas Press, Austin
University of the Philippines, Quezon City
University of the Punjab, Department of Public Administration, Lahore, Pakistan
University of the Witwatersrand, Johannesburg
University of Toronto, Toronto
University of Toronto Press, Toronto; Buffalo, N. Y.
University of Utah Press, Salt Lake City
University of Vermont, Burlington
University of Virginia, Bureau of Public Administration, Charlottesville
University of Wales Press, Cardiff
University of Washington, Bureau of Governmental Research and Services, Seattle
University of Washington Press, Seattle
University of Wisconsin, Madison
University of Wisconsin Press, Madison
University Press, University of the South, Sewanee, Tenn.
University Press of Virginia, Charlottesville
University Publishers, Inc., New York
University Publishing Co., Lincoln, Nebr.
University Society, Inc., Ridgewood, N. J.
Unwin University Books, London
T. Fisher Unwin, Ltd., London
Upjohn Institute for Employment Research, Kalamazoo, Mich; Los Angeles; Washington, D. C.
Urban America, New York
Urban Studies Center, New Brunswick, N. J.

VEB Verlag fur Buch-und Bibliothekwesen, Leipzig
Franz Vahlen, Berlin
Vallentine, Mitchell and Co., London
Van Nostrand Co., Inc., Princeton
Van Rees Press, New York
Vandenhoeck und Ruprecht, Gottingen
Vanderbilt University Press, Nashville, Tenn.
Vanguard Press, Inc., New York
E. C. Vann, Richmond, Va.
Vantage Press, New York
G. Velgaminov, New York
Verein fur Sozial Politik, Berlin
Vergara Editorial, Barcelona
Verlag Karl Alber, Freiburg
Verlag Georg D. W. Callwey, Munich
Verlag der Wiener Volksbuchhandlung, Vienna
Verlag der Wirtschaft, Berlin
Verlag Deutsche Polizei, Hamburg
Verlag Felix Dietrich, Osnabrueck
Verlag Kurt Dosch, Vienna
Verlag Gustav Fischer, Jena
Verlag Huber Frauenfeld, Stuttgart
Verlag fur Buch- und Bibliothekwesen, Leipzig
Verlag fur Literatur und Zeitgeschehen, Hannover, Germany
Verlag fur Recht und Gesellschaft, Basel
Verein fuer Sozialpolitik, Wirtschaft und Statistik, Berlin
Verlag Anton Hain, Meisenheim
Verlag Hans Krach, Mainz
Verlag Edward Krug, Wurttemburg
Verlag Helmut Kupper, Godesberg
Verlag August Lutzeyer, Baden-Baden
Verlag Mensch und Arbeit, Bruckmann, Munich
Verlag C. F. Muller, Karlsruhe
Verlag Anton Pustet, Munich
Verlag Rombach und Co., Freiburg
Verlag Heinrich Scheffler, Frankfurt
Verlag Hans Schellenberg, Winterthur, Switz.
Verlag P. Schippers, Amsterdam
Verlag Lambert Schneider, Heidelberg
Verlag K. W. Schutz, Gottingen
Verlag Styria, Graz, Austria
Lawrence Verry, Publishers, Mystic, Conn.
Viking Press, New York
Villanova Law School, Philadelphia
J. Villanueva, Buenos Aires
Vintage Books, New York
Virginia Commission on Constitutional Government, Richmond
Virginia State Library, Richmond
Vishveshvaranand Vedic Research Institute, Hoshiarpur
Vista Books, London
F. & J. Voglrieder, Munich
Voigt und Gleibner, Frankfurt
Voltaire Verlag, Berlin
Von Engelhorn, Stuttgart
Vora and Co. Publishers, Bombay
J. Vrin, Paris

Karl Wachholtz Verlag, Neumunster
Wadsworth Publishing Co., Belmont, Cal.
Walker and Co., New York
Ives Washburn, Inc., New York
Washington State University Press, Pullman
Washington University Libraries, Washington
Franklin Watts, Inc., New York
Waverly Press, Inc., Baltimore, Md.
Wayne State University Press, Detroit, Mich.
Christian Wegner Verlag, Hamburg
Weidenfield and Nicolson, London
R. Welch, Belmont, Mass.
Wellesley College, Wellesley, Mass.
Herbert Wendler & Co., Berlin
Wenner-Gren Foundation for Anthropological Research, New York
Wesleyan University Press, Middletown, Conn.
West Publishing Co., St. Paul, Minn.
Westdeutscher Verlag, Cologne
Western Islands Publishing Co., Belmont, Mass.
Western Publishing Co., Inc., Racine, Wis.
Western Reserve University Press, Cleveland
Westminster Press, Philadelphia, Pa.
J. Whitaker and Sons, Ltd., London
Whitcombe and Tombs, Ltd., Christchurch
Whiteside, Inc., New York
Thomas Wilcox, Los Angeles
John Wiley and Sons, Inc., New York
William-Frederick Press, New York
Williams and Vorgate, Ltd., London
Williams and Wilkins Co., Baltimore, Md.
Wilshire Book Co., Hollywood, Calif.
H. W. Wilson Co., New York
Winburn Press, Lexington, Ky.
Allan Wingate, Ltd., London
Carl Winters Universitats-Buchhandlung, Heidelberg
Wisconsin State University Press, River Falls
Wisconsin State Historical Society, Madison
Witwatersrand University Press, Capetown
Woking Muslim Mission and Literary Trust, Surrey
Wolters, Groningen, Netherlands
Woodrow Wilson Foundation, New York
Woodrow Wilson Memorial Library, New York
World Law Fund, New York
World Peace Foundation, Boston
World Press, Ltd., Calcutta
World Publishing Co., Cleveland
World Trade Academy Press, New York
World University Library, New York

Yale University, New Haven, Conn.
Yale University, Department of Industrial Administration, New Haven, Conn.

Yale University, Harvard Foundation, New Haven, Conn.
Yale University, Institute of Advanced Studies, New Haven, Conn.
Yale University Press, New Haven
Yale University, Southeast Asia Studies, New Haven
Yeshiva University Press, New York
Thomas Yoseloff, New York

T. L. Yuan, Tokyo

Zambia, Government Printer, Lusaka
Otto Zeller, Osnabruck, Germany
Zentral Verlag der NSDAP, Munich
Zwingli Verlag, Zurich

List of Periodicals Cited in this Volume

Academy of Political Science (Columbia University), Proceedings
Administrative Science Quarterly
African Forum
American Behavioral Scientist
American Economic Review
American Historical Review
American Journal of International Law
American Journal of Sociology
American Philosophical Society, Proceedings
American Political Science Review
American Psychologist
American Slavic and East European Review
American Society of International Law, Proceedings
American Sociological Review
Annals of the American Academy of Political and Social Science
Annuaire Europeen
Annuaire Francais de Droit International
Asian Survey
Assembly of Captive European Nations News
Behavioral Science
Board of Trade Journal
Boston University Law Review
Bulletin of the Atomic Scientists
Business Topics
Cahiers du Droit Europeen
California Law Review
Canadian Bar Review
Canadian Public Administration
Catholic Lawyer
Center Magazine
Centro
China Mainland Review
China Quarterly
Co-Existence
Colorado Quarterly
Columbia University Forum
Commentary
Commonweal
Comparative Studies in Society and History
Comunita Internazionale
Contemporary Review
Cooperation and Conflict
Cornell Law Quarterly
Current History
Daedalus
Department of State Bulletin
Dissent
Duquesne Review
East Europe
Economic Development and Cultural Change
Etudes de Droit Compare
Esprit
Ethics
Foreign Affairs
Foreign Service Journal
Fortune
German Foreign Policy
Government and Opposition
Historical Studies of Australia and New Zealand
Hitotsubashi Journal of Economy
Human Organization
Human Relations
Illinois University Studies in Social Science
India Quarterly
Indian and Foreign Review
Indiana Law Journal
Institute of World Affairs, Proceedings
Instituto de Ciencias Sociales, Revista (Barcelona)
Inter-American Economic Affairs
Intercom
International Affairs (U.K.)
International Affairs (U.S.S.R.)
International and Comparative Law Quarterly
International Conciliation
International Journal
International Journal of Opinion and Attitude Research
International Journal of Social Psychiatry
International Migration Review
International Monetary Fund Staff Papers
International Organization
International Relations
International Social Science Bulletin
International Studies
Journal of Applied Behavioral Science
Journal of Arms Control
Journal of Asian Studies
Journal of Common Market Studies
Journal of Commonwealth Political Studies
Journal of Conflict Resolution
Journal of Human Relations
Journal of Inter-American Studies
Journal of International Affairs
Journal of Modern African Studies
Journal of Philosophy
Journal of Political Economy
Journal of Politics
Journal of the Royal Society of Arts
Journal of Social Issues
Kyklos
Latin American Research Review
Law and Contemporary Problems
Lex et Scientia
Lloyd Bank Review
McGill Law Journal
Memoirs Publics de Social Sciences, Arts et Letters de Hainaut
Michigan Law Review
Middle East Journal
Middle Eastern Affairs
Midstream
Midwestern Journal of Political Science
Military Review
Modern Age
Monthly Review

Mulino
Neue Politische Literatur
New Leader
New Left Review
New Politics
New World Review
Northwestern University Law Review
Orbis
Pacific Affairs
Panstwo I Pravo
Partisan Review
Political Quarterly
Political Science Quarterly
Political Studies
Politique Etrangere
Politische Studien
Problems of Communism
Public Administration Review
Public and International Affairs
Public Opinion Quarterly
Public Personnel Review
Quarterly Journal of Economics
Quarterly Review
Review of Economics and Statistics
Review of Politics
Revue Critical de Droit International Prive
Revue d'Economie Politique
Revue de Droit International
Revue Economique
Revue Francaise de Science Politique
Revue Generale de Droit International Public
Revue Juridique et Politique d'Outre-mer
Royal Central Asian Society Journal
Russian Review
Saturday Review
Science and Society
Scientific Monthly
Seminar
Slavic Review
Social and Economic Studies
Social Research
Social Science
Societas Scientiarum Fennica
Sociology and Social Research
Southern Economic Journal
Survey
Survival
Table Ronde
Texas Quarterly
Tiers-Monde
Trans-Action
Travaux de Recherche de l'Institut de Droit Compare de l'Universite de Paris
Tri-Quarterly Review
United Asia
University of Chicago Law Review
University of Toronto Law Journal
Virginia Law Review
Virginia Quarterly Review
War/Peace Report
Wehrkunde
Western Political Quarterly
World Affairs
World Justice
World Politics
World Today
Yale Law Journal
Yale Review
Yearbook of World Affairs

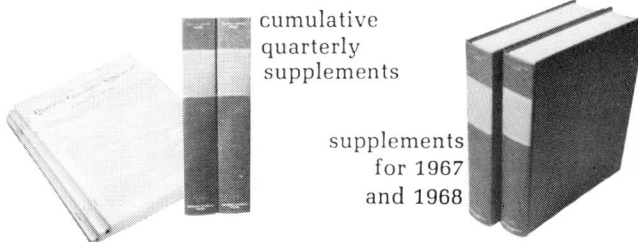